CRUDEN'S

COMPLETE CONCORDANCE TO THE BIBLE

With Notes and Biblical Proper Names under one Alphabetical Arrangement

Alexander Cruden

Edited by
C. H. Irwin M.A., D.D.
A. D. Adams, M.A.
S. A. Waters

Lutterworth Press
Cambridge

The Lutterworth Press
P.O. Box 60
Cambridge
CB1 2NT

British Library Cataloguing in Publication Data:
A catalogue record is available from the British Library.

ISBN 0 7188 2956 5 paperback edition
ISBN 0 7188 2957 3 cased edition

First published 1839 by The Lutterworth Press

First paperback edition published 1977 by The Lutterworth Press
Reprinted 1979, 1980 (revised), 1982, 1984, 1987 (revised),
1990, 1992

This edition first published in hardback 1930 by The Lutterworth Press
Reprinted 1941 (revised), 1954 (revised), 1979 (revised),
1982, 1985, 1990

Printed in Great Britain by Biddles Ltd
Guildford & King's Lynn

CONTENTS

ALEXANDER CRUDEN'S
PREFACE TO THE FIRST EDITION

A Concordance is a Dictionary, or an Index, to the Bible, wherein all the words used throughout the inspired writings are arranged alphabetically, and the various places where they occur are referred to, to assist us in finding our passages, and comparing the several significations of the same word. A work of this kind, which tends so much to render the study of the holy Scriptures more easy to all Christians, must be acknowledged to be very useful; for if a good Index to any other book is to be valued, much more ought one to the Bible, which is a revelation from God, given as the only rule of our faith and practice, and to discover to us the way to eternal life only through our Lord Jesus Christ.

I do not here propose to treat of the incomparable excellences of that divine book, which is above all commendation, and will be in the highest esteem by all the true members of the church of God, whose faith, hope and comfort are built upon these divine Oracles.

What I shall further do in this Preface, shall be to present the Reader with a short historical account of Concordances, which will tend to display their great usefulness; and then acquaint him with the method I have followed in this.

Hugo de S. Charo, a preaching Friar of the Dominican order, who was afterwards a Cardinal, was the first who compiled a Concordance to the holy Scriptures; he died in the year 1262. He had studied the Bible very closely, and for carrying on this great and laborious work the more successfully, we are told he employed five hundred Monks of his order to assist him. He framed an Index of all the declinable words, and referred to the places where they were to be found.

This Latin Concordance has been frequently printed with improvements; and since that time works of this sort have been brought to much greater perfection than formerly. At first it was thought sufficient to specify the chapter wherein the word occurred, with these letters a, b, c, d, as marks to point our the beginning, the middle, or the end of the chapter. But after Robert Stephens, in the year 1545, had divided the chapters of the Bible into verses, the verses likewise began to be numbered, and the letters in the editions of the Concordances to be suppressed. And in 1555 this eminent Printer published his fine Concordance, wherein the chapters and verses are exactly distinguished.

It could not be thought that when so useful a work as Cardinal Hugo's came to be known, men, who carefully studied the Scriptures, would be satisfied that such assistance should be confined only to those who understood Latin: accordingly several have been published in various languages, particularly Rabbi Mordecai Nathan, otherwise called Isaac Nathan, composed an Hebrew Concordance in imitation of Cardinal Hugo's. He began it in the year 1438, and completed it in 1448, being no less than 10 years in finishing it; and besides, as he himself says, he was obliged to employ a great many writers in this work. After printing was invented, it was printed several times: first in Venice by Daniel Bomberg, in the year 1523, under the title of *Meir Netib*, that is to say, *Which giveth light in the way*; at Basil by Frobenius in 1581, and at Rome in 1621. This was the foundation of that noble work published by John Buxtorf, the son, being assisted by his father's papers at Basil, in 1632.

As to the Greek text of the New Testament, a Concordance was published by Henry Stephens at Geneva in 1599, and republished in 1624: but a more accurate one was compiled by Erasmus Schmidius, and published at Wittemberg in 1638, which was republished more correctly at Leipsic in 1716, and is reckoned a very complete performance.

A Greek Concordance to the Septuagint Version of the Old Testament must be owned to be very useful to such as are for comparing the expressions used in it with those of the New Testament, and to those who read the Fathers. Conrad Kircher of Augsbourg is celebrated for his Greek Concordance of the Old Testament printed at Francfort in 1602. This author has inserted the Hebrew words in an alphabetical order, and placed under them the Greek words to which they answer. But since that time an excellent Concordance has been published at Amsterdam in 1718, by the aged and worthy Minister of Groningen, M. Abraham Trommius, who instead of following the Hebrew alphabet with Kircher, has chosen rather to observe the order of the Greek alphabet.

There have been Concordances likewise published in various modern languages; in French by M. Gravelin; in High Dutch and Low Dutch by several; the most complete one in Low Dutch is that begun by M. Martinitz, and finished by M. Trommius before mentioned. In English we have had many. The first was published by Mr. Marbeck in 1550, which is dedicated to the pious King Edward VI, but is referred only to chapters, not verses. Then Mr. Cotton published a pretty large Concordance, which has been often printed. Afterwards Mr. Newman published one more complete; and lastly, we have one published under the title of the Cambridge Concordance. There have been several abstracts of small Concordances published: First by Mr. Downame, the next by Mr. Vavasor Powell, then by Mr. John Jackson, and afterwards by Mr. Samuel Clarke. As also other works of this nature have been written by way of a Dictionary or Concordance, but in a different method, as Mr. Wilson's *Christian Dictionary*, Mr. Knight's *Axiomatical Concordance*, Mr. Bernard's *Thesaurus Biblicus*, and Mr. Wicken's *Concordance*, &c.

Thus it appears that we have had Concordances to the Bible some centuries ago; and the world has been so sensible of their usefulness, that many of them have been composed and published in different languages. But as there are several in our language, it may be inquired, What occasioned my undertaking this great laborious work, or what advantages it has above any other hitherto published?

When I began this work, I designed to compose a useful Concordance in Octavo; but after I had printed several specimens, I found it necessary to alter my scheme, and to compile one to be printed in this large volume, in order to make those improvements which now render it preferable to any other.

The method is easy and regular, and each text of Scripture is generally contained in one line, whereby the reader may readily find the place he wants, if he remember any material word. When there are two or more texts of Scripture that are parallel, I have generally mentioned the first that occurs in order in the Bible, and have added the parallel texts. It is printed with a good letter, though pretty small, which was necessary in order to bring it into this volume, and make it contain *multum in parvo*, much in a little compass; and great care has been taken that the figures referring to the chapters and verses of the Bible be exact and correct.

This Concordance is divided into three Alphabets.

The first Alphabet contains the appellative or common words, which is the principal part. It is very full and large, and any text may be found by looking for any material word, whether it be substantive, adjective, verb, &c.

In this part, I have given the various significations of the principal words, which, I hope, will be esteemed a useful improvement, there not being any thing of this kind in the other large Concordances. By this improvement the Reader will have many texts explained, and difficulties removed; and the meaning of the Scripture may be here known by that which is accounted the best rule of interpreting Scripture, namely, by comparing one Scripture with another. There is so large a collection of the various Significations of many words in Scripture, as may, perhaps, be not only useful to private Christians, but also those who preach the Gospel; for hereby many important things may be observed at one view, without the trouble of turning over several volumes; and occasion is sometimes taken to give an account of the Jewish customs and ceremonies, by which the Reader is led into the meaning of many passages of Scripture, as may be seen in the words, Elder, Ephod, Synagogue, &c.

The second Alphabet contains the proper Names* in the holy Scriptures, which the Reader will receive with improvements, as in Abraham, David, &c. The texts referred to where those names are mentioned, give a short historical account of the remarkable things recorded in Scripture concerning them. To this part is prefixed a Table, containing the Significations of the words in the original languages from which they are derived.

The third and last alphabet is a concordance for those books that are called Apocryphal*, which is only added that this work might not be deficient in anything that is treated of in any other Concordance; those books not being of divine Inspiration, nor any part of the Canon of Scripture, and therefore are of no authority in the church of God.

I conclude this preface, with praying that God, who hath graciously enabled me to bring this large Work to a conclusion, would render it useful to those who seriously and carefully search the Scriptures; and grant that the sacred writings, which are so important and highly worthy of esteem, may meet with all that affection and regard which they deserve. May those who profess to believe the Scriptures to be a Revelation from God, apply themselves to the reading and study of them; and may they by the Holy Spirit of God, who indited the Scriptures, be made wise to salvation through faith which is in Christ Jesus.

Alexander Cruden
London
October 1737

* In the present edition, the Proper Names have been incorporated into the main part of the Concordance, and the section on the Apocrypha has been omitted.

PUBLISHER'S PREFACE

For over two hundred years 'Cruden's Concordance' has been a household word wherever the English language is spoken and the English Bible read.

'Cruden's Concordance' was first issued by the Religious Tract Society of London in 1839, and reached its forty-second edition in 1879. Successive editions were published up to 1920 when a major revision was undertaken by William Youngman, and later in 1927-30 by C. H. Irwin, D.D., A. D. Adams, M.A., and S. A. Waters. The successors to the Religious Tract Society – The Lutterworth Press – have continued to issue 'Cruden', and the present edition may justly claim to be an accurate and complete Concordance to the Old and New Testaments, with upwards of 225,000 references, and further corrections ahve been made.

The text quoted throughout is that of the Authorised Version of 1611, known in America as the 'King James's Version', and its spelling and punctuation have generally been followed. Where the Revised Version of 1881 has altered the sense or made the meaning clearer, this is indicated by an asterisk [*]. Where such alteration has been made by the American Revision, this is indicated by a dagger [†]. At these points reference should also be made to the American Revised Standard Version for its renderings. Every quotation and reference in the Concordance has received careful scrutiny.

The grouping of Proper Names and the general Concordance under one Alphabetical arrangement will be found greatly to facilitate the use of the volume. In the Appendix is given a list of Proper Names seldom mentioned in Scripture and not included in the body of the Concordance. Every endeavour has been made, in the necessarily shortened quotations, to include the most essential words, and to preserve the true meaning of the text.

The quotation occupies the first position in the column, followed by the main reference, and then by reference to other passages where the principal word is used. The principal word quoted is indicated by its *initial letter in italics*. A colon between the figures (1:6) divides chapter and verse, a semicolon (*Isa* 9:6; *John* 3:16, 17) divides the main reference from succeeding references; while a comma divides verses in the same chapter.

Thus, under the heading *Aaron*:

A. shall bear their.	Ex 28:12; 29:30
A. shall burn sweet incense.	30:7
A. lighteth the lamps at even.	8
A. shall make an atonement once.	10

In the first line there are two passages quoted with chapter and verse; in the second line one chapter and verse, while the third and fourth lines have the verse only, being in each case a verse of chapter 30 quoted in the second line.

In a work of this kind, however carefully revised, mistakes are almost inevitable. The Publishers will be glad to hear of any which may be found, so that they may be corrected in future editions.

ALEXANDER CRUDEN

His Life and Work

It has sometimes been said that Alexander Cruden died insane, presumably because of the labours of compiling his Concordance. It would probably be more accurate to say that he was always an eccentric, but that his Concordance provided a healthy outlet for his eccentricity and so enabled what might so easily have been a human tragedy to become a means of service to millions of biblical students all over the world.

It is not always appreciated that the division of Scripture into chapters and verses does not go back to the original script , but was a later addition. Whether an understanding of Scripture has been helped or hindered by such a division is debatable and certainly there are instances where the actual divisions have been unwisely made, but the system has certainly come to stay and has proved a great help to scholars, preachers and students in their public speaking and writing. Alexander Cruden, however, was one of the first to see that what was really needed was a reference book or index of quotations, and he set himself to the task of producing it. Many who have proved its usefulness will like to have some brief details as to his life and character.

He was born in 1699, the second son of a public figure in Aberdeen, where he attended the local Grammar School. He took his M.A. at Marischal College, at the age of nineteen, attended lectures in Divinity, and might well have entered the Ministry were it not for an unhappy love affair which so distressed him that it was probably this more than anything else which was the cause of his distracted mind.

The lady in question was the daughter of an Aberdeen Minister. Cruden fell in love with her whilst he was a student at the University but his love was not returned. Nor in this case was manly persistence to be rewarded. All it did was to increase the lady's resistance, until Alexander was so depressed that he had to be confined in a asylum. Since it was subsequently discovered that she had been the victim of a guilty attachment to one of her brothers, it was thought by some that confinement in the asylum had saved him from a worse fate, but he never saw it that way and his grief stayed with him to the end of his life.

His period of confinement was not long and on his release in 1722 he left Aberdeen for London, where he held a number of engagements acting as a private tutor to young men preparing for university, but by 1732 he was working as a proofreader in a printing firm, for which his knowledge, industry and attention to detail admirably fitted him. He was thought well of by his employers as well as by a number of other distinguished people, including Sir Robert Walpole, who used his influence to have Cruden appointed bookseller to Queen Caroline, Consort of George II, in 1735.

It was at this point that he began to apply himself to the composition of his Concordance and we can only marvel that the first edition appeared as early as 1737. He presented a copy to the Queen, to whom it was dedicated, but since she died within sixteen days of saying that 'she would not fail to remember the author', she was never able to fulfil her good intentions.

Since Cruden had put what little he had into this enterprise his disappointment was sufficient to bring on a further bout of illness and he spent nine weeks and six days in a private asylum in Bethnal Green, from which he tried to escape, even though he was chained to the bedstead, and after which he published the story of his sufferings.

He also continued to work as a proofreader and for the next fifteen years he presided over the publication of several editions of the Greek and Roman Classics, but after a dispute with his sister he suffered a further seventeen days' confinement, this time at Chelsea in 1753, followed by the publication of a further account of his sufferings. At this point he also entered into correspondence with his friends and his sister, suggesting ways in which they might recompense him for the harm they had inflicted. He would have liked his friends to have submitted to a period of imprisonment in Newgate. For his sister he proposed what to him were very mild terms – a fine of £10 of £15, followed by 48 hours in either Newgate, Reading, Aylesbury Prison or Windsor Castle.

It has been said that the remainder of his life was passed in 'a kind of happy and harmless lunacy' though he was in sufficient command of his faculties to pursue a steady job.

Sometimes the acknowledged state of his mind led people to forgive his aberrations, which in other circumstances might have brought him more hurt. He tried, for example, to set himself up as a 'Corrector of the people', writing and publishing tracts in which he was severely critical of the way of life of many of his contemporaries, and actually applying for a knighthood, not for reasons of personal vanity, but because he thought it would help his cause. He was a true Calvanistic dissenter, and for him religion and morality went hand in hand.

At other times his eccentricity led him to works of unusual benevolence to his fellow-men. In 1762, for example, a poor and ignorant sailor called Richard Potter was found guilty at the Old Bailey of forging a woman's Will. Alexander Cruden was in Court and was convinced that Potter was the victim of somebody else's villainy. He visited him often in Newgate, as a result of which the man was converted to faith in God. Cruden's persistence again came to his aid. He made representation to many senior officials, including Lord Halifax, Secretary of State, and finally succeeded in having the sentence changed from death to transportation.

It is no criticism of Cruden that he was unable to change conditions in Newgate; that had to wait for Elizabeth Fry. But he was extremely sensitive to conditions there and did all he could to relieve hardship in individual cases. One Sunday evening he met a miserable man on the point of committing suicide and gave him hope and, on another occasion, he was so concerned about a poor girl who accosted him for help that he made her an assistant to his own servant, and she continued in his pay until he died.

He never married. In his fifties he did pay attention to the daughter of Sir Thomas Absey of Newington, but she resisted all his approaches.

It was also about this time that hc corrected his Concordance and prepared a new edition which appeared in 1761. He did the work whilst he was in full-time employment, often working until after midnight and then rising at six so as to give himself to his Bible and his Concordance. This time he was slightly more successful financially in that when he presented a copy to the King he received a donation of £100. He also had the honour of presenting a copy to Queen Charlotte and to the Princess Dowager of Wales. Altogether he received £500 for this edition and a further £300 for the third, which appeared in 1769 and contained the author's last corrections.

He died on 1 November, 1770 and, except for a small sum of money which he gave to his native City of Aberdeen to be expended in religious books for the poor, most of his meagre resources were distributed among his relations.

His death was as simple as his life had been eccentric. He retired to bed as usual, suffering from nothing more than a slight attack of asthma. When he did not come down to breakfast his maid went to look for him. She found him dead in the bathroom, kneeling by a chair as if at prayer.

So ended the life of a man who discovered that what would have been to others intolerable drudgery was to him a sedative to his agitated mind. And labour which would have wasted the energies of a happier man was the balm of his wounded spirit.

CRUDEN'S COMPLETE CONCORDANCE

NOTE.—*A list of Proper Names, seldom mentioned in Scripture, and not included in the Concordance, will be found in an Appendix.*

An asterisk [*] *following a reference means that the Revised Versions have altered the sense of the verse or have made the meaning clearer.*

A dagger [†] *following a reference means that the American Revision alone has made this change.*

No mark is found where the Revisions are not materially different.

A

Aaron

is not *A.* the Levite thy? *Ex* 4:14
they met Moses and *A.* who. 5:20
A. took Elisheba . . . to wife. 6:23
and *A.* thy brother shall be thy. 7:1
but *A.* rod swallowed up their. 12
A. laid up the pot of manna. 16:34
and *A.* and Hur stayed up. 17:12
shalt come up, thou and *A.* 19:24
and behold *A.* and Hur are. 24:14
A. shall bear their. 28:12; 29:30
A. shall burn sweet incense. 30:7
A. lighteth the lamps at even. 8
A. shall make an atonement once. 10
they made the calf, which *A.* 32:35
Moses and *A.* and his sons. 40:31
he poured oil on *A.* head. *Lev* 8:12
he sprinkled blood on *A.* and. 30
A. blessed them. 9:22
A. held his peace. 10:3
thus shall *A.* come into the holy. 16:3
A. shall cast lots. 8
A. shall lay his hands on the. 21
A. shall order it. 24:3
A. shall number them by. *Num* 1:3
A. shall offer the Levites. 8:11
what is *A.* that ye murmur? 16:11
they, and *A.* to-morrow. 16
Moses and *A.* came before the. 43
write *A.* name upon the rod. 17:3
A. rod again before the testimony. 10
thou and *A.* thy brother speak. 20:8
A. died there in the top of the mount. 28; 33:38; *Deut* 32:50
A. was 123 years old. *Num* 33:39
was very angry with *A.* *Deut* 9:20
I sent Moses and *A.* *Josh* 24:5
1 Sam 12:8; *Mi* 6:4
advanced Moses and *A.* *1 Sam* 12:6
A. and Moses. *1 Chr* 6:3; 23:13
people by Moses and *A.* *Ps* 77:20
Moses and *A.* among his. 99:6
they envied *A.* the saint. 106:16
O house of *A.* trust in the. 115:10
Lord will bless the house of *A.* 12
house of *A.* say, his mercy. 118:3
ran down upon *A.* beard. 133:2
the Lord, O house of *A.* 135:19
was of the daughters of *A.* *Luke* 1:5
saying to *A.* make us gods to. *Acts* 7:40
called of God, as was *A.* *Heb* 5:4
called after the order of *A.* 7:11
A. rod that budded and tables. 9:4
Sons of **Aaron**, *see* **Abihu** *and* **Nadab**

Aaronites

was leader of the *A.* *1 Chr* 12:27
Zadok was the ruler of the *A.* 27:17

Abaddon

the bottomless pit is *A.* *Rev* 9:11

Abagtha

A. was chamberlain to. *Esth* 1:10

Abana

(*Revised Version,* Abanah)
are not rivers *A.* and. *2 Ki* 5:12

Abarim

get thee up into this mount *A.* *Num* 27:12; *Deut* 32:49
in the mountains of *A.* *Num* 33:47

abase

(*To bring low, usually in spirit; to humble*)
proud, and *a.* him. *Job* 40:11
lion will not *a.* himself. *Isa* 31:4
and *a.* him that is high. *Ezek* 21:26
in pride, is able to *a.* *Dan* 4:37

abased

shall exalt himself shall be *a.* *Mat* 23:12; *Luke* 14:11; 18:14
I know how to be *a.* *Phil* 4:12

abasing

an offence in *a.* myself. *2 Cor* 11:7

abated

(*Decreased*)
the waters were *a.* *Gen* 8:3, 11
a. from thy estimation. *Lev* 27:18
Moses' natural force *a.* *Deut* 34:7
anger was *a.* toward him. *Judg* 8:3

abba

a. Father, all things are. *Mark* 14:36
whereby we cry, *a.* Father. *Rom* 8:15
into your hearts crying *a.* *Gal* 4:6

Abda

Adoniram son of A. was. *1 Ki* 4:6
A. was for thanksgiving. *Neh* 11:17

Abdi

Kish the son of *A.* *2 Chr* 29:12
A. of them that married. *Ezra* 10:26

Abdon

A. judged Israel. *Judg* 12:13
A. died. 15
commanded *A.* to inquire. *2 Chr* 34:20

Abed-nego

Azariah the name of *A.* *Dan* 1:7
the king set *A.* over. 2:49; 3:30
A. fell down bound into the. 3:23

Abel, *person, place.*

Lord had respect to A. *Gen* 4:4
stone of *A.* whereon. *1 Sam* 6:18*
ask counsel at *A.* *2 Sam* 20:18
blood of *A.* *Mat* 23:35; *Luke* 11:51
A. offered more excellent. *Heb.* 11:4
things than the blood of *A.* 12:24

Abel-beth-maachah

captains smote *A.* *1 Ki* 15:20
came and took *A.* *2 Ki* 15:29

Abel-maim

Ijon, and Dan, and *A.* *2 Chr* 16:4

Abel-meholah

fled to the border of *A.* *Judg* 7:22
son of Shaphat of *A.* *1 Ki* 19:16

Abel-mizraim

name of it was called *A.* *Gen* 50:11

abhor

[1] *To loath or detest,* Job 42:6. [2] *To despise or neglect,* Ps. 22:24; Amos 6:8. [3] *To reject or cast off,* Ps. 89:38.
my soul shall not *a.* you. *Lev* 26:11
or if your soul *a.* my judgments. 15
destroy, and my soul shall *a.* 30
nor will I *a.* them, to destroy. 44
utterly *a.* it, a cursed. *Deut* 7:26
a. an Edomite, an Egyptian. 23:7
his people to *a.* him. *1 Sam* 27:12
own clothes shall *a.* me. *Job* 9:31
they *a.* me, they flee far. 30:10
I *a.* myself, and repent. 42:6
Lord will *a.* the bloody man. *Ps.* 5:6
I hate and *a.* lying. 119:163
nations shall *a.* him. *Pr* 24:24
do not *a.* us. *Jer* 14:21
a. him that speaketh. *Amos* 5:10
I *a.* the excellency of Jacob. 6:8
hear, ye that *a.* judgment. *Mi* 3:9
a. that which is evil. *Rom* 12:9

abhorred

made our savour to be *a.* *Ex* 5:21
therefore I *a.* them. *Lev.* 20:23
their soul *a.* my statutes. 26:43
Lord saw it, he *a.* *Deut.* 32:19
for men *a.* the offering. *1 Sam* 2:17
art *a.* of thy father. *2 Sam* 16:21
Hadad *a.* Israel. *1 Ki* 11:25
inward friends *a.* me. *Job* 19:19
nor *a.* the affliction of. *Ps* 22:24
and greatly *a.* Israel. 78:59
thou hast cast off and *a.* 89:38*
he *a.* his own inheritance. 106:40
a. of the Lord shall fall. *Pr* 22:14
Lord hath *a.* his sanctuary. *Lam* 2:7
thy beauty to be *a.* *Ezek* 16:25*
and their soul also *a.* me. *Zech* 11:8

abhorrest

the land that thou *a.* *Isa* 7:16
thou that *a.* idols, dost. *Rom* 2:22

abhorreth

life *a.* bread, and his soul. *Job* 33:20
covetous, whom the Lord *a.* *Ps* 10:3*
mischief on his bed, he *a.* not evil. 36:4
soul *a.* all manner of meat. 107:18
nation *a.* to a servant. *Isa* 49:7

abhorring

be an *a.* to all flesh. *Isa* 66:24

Abia, Abiah
Samuel's second son was *A.* *1 Sam* 8:2
A. Hezron's wife. *1 Chr* 2:24
Rehoboam was *A.* 3:10; *Mat* 1:7
sons of Becher, *A.* *1 Chr* 7:8

Abi-albon
A. was one of David's. *2 Sam* 23:31

Abiathar
A. escaped and fled. *1 Sam* 22:20
A. son of Ahimelech fled. 23:6
David said to. *A* bring. 9; 30:7
Zadok and *A.* were priests. *2 Sam.* 8:17; 17:15; 20:25; *1 Ki* 4; 4
Adonijah conferred with *A.* *1 Ki* 1:7
kingdom for him and *A.* *1 Ki* 2; 22
so Solomon thrust out *A.* 26. 27. 35
house of G. in days of *A.* *Mark* 2:26

Abib
in the month *A.* *Ex* 13:4; 34:18
the feast of unleavened bread in the month *A.* 23:15; 34:18; *Deut* 16:1

Abidan
A. son of Gideoni. *Num* 1:11; 2:22
A. of Benjamin offered. 7:60, 65

abide
[1] *To stay,* Gen 22:5. [2] *To dwell or live in a place,* Gen 29:19; Ps 15:1. [3] *To bear or endure,* Jer 10:10; Joel 2:11. [4] *To continue,* Eccl 8:15; John 14:16. [5] *To wait for,* Acts 20:23. [6] *To rest,* Pr 19:23. [7] *To stand firm,* Ps 119:90; 125:1.

a. in the street all night. *Gen* 19:2
a. you here with the ass, and I. 22:5
damsel *a.* with us a few days. 24:55
I give her to thee, *a.* with me. 29:19
a. instead of the lad. 44:33
a. ye every man. *Ex* 16:29
therefore *a.* at the door. *Lev* 8:35
wages of him hired shall not *a.* 19:13
shall *a.* to the death. *Num* 35:25
a. here fast by my maidens. *Ruth* 2:8
before the Lord, and *a.* *1 Sam* 1:22
ark of God shall not *a.* 5:7
a. thou with me, fear not. 22:23
made to *a.* at brook Besor. 30:21
and with him will I *a.* *2 Sam* 16:18
nor *a.* in the paths of. *Job* 24:13
and *a.* in the covert to lie. 38:40
unicorn be willing to *a.* by. 39:9
shall *a.* in thy tabernacle? *Ps* 15:1
I will *a.* in thy tabernacle. 61:4
he shall *a.* before God for ever. 7
shall *a.* under the shadow of. 91:1
feet *a.* not in her house. *Pr* 7:11
he that hath it shall *a.* 19:23
a. with him of his labour. *Eccl* 8:15
nations not able to *a.* his. *Jer* 10:10
if ye *a.* in this land I. 42:10
no man shall *a.* 49:18, 33; 50:40
shalt *a.* for me many days. *Hos* 3:3
sword shall *a.* on his cities. 11:6*
is terrible, who can *a.* it? *Joel* 2:11
they shall *a.* for now shall. *Mi* 5:4
who can *a.* in the fierceness. *Nah* 1:6
a. the day of his coming? *Mal* 3:2
there *a.* *Mat* 10:11; *Mark* 6:10 *Luke* 9:4
I must *a.* at thy house. *Luke* 19:5
a. with us, for it is towards. 24:29
not *a.* in darkness. *John* 12:46
Comforter that he may *a.* 14:16
a. in me and I in you, except ye *a.* in me. 15:4, 7
if a man *a.* not in me, he is cast. 6
ye shall *a.* in my love, and *a.* 10
it pleased Silas to *a.* *Acts* 15:34
come into my house and *a.* 16:15
bonds and afflictions *a.* me. 20:23
except these *a.* in ship. 27:31
if any man's work *a.* he. *1 Cor* 3:14
it is good for them if they *a.* 7:8
man *a.* in the same calling. 20
she is happier if she *a.* after. 40
to *a.* in the flesh is more *Phil* 1:24
I know that I shall *a.* with. 25
I besought thee to *a.* *1 Tim* 1:3
let that *a.* in you which. *1 John* 2:24
ye shall *a.* in him. 27
children *a.* in him. 28

abideth
Ziba said, behold he *a.* *2 Sam* 16:3
man being in honour *a.* *Ps* 49:12
hear, even he that *a.* of. 55:19
the earth, and it *a.* 119:90
mount Zion, which *a.* for ever. 125:1
heareth reproof, *a.* *Pr* 15:31
but the earth *a.* for ever. *Eccl.* 1:4
he that *a.* in this city. *Jer* 21:9
but the wrath of God *a.* *John* 3:36
servant *a.* not, but the son *a.* 8:35
corn of wheat die, it *a.* 12:24
we have heard that Christ *a.* 34
he that *a.* in me bringeth. 15:5
a. faith, hope, charity. *1 Cor* 13:13
yet he *a.* faithful. *2 Tim* 2:13
Melchizedec *a.* a priest. *Heb* 7:3
word of God which *a.* *1 Pet* 1:23
that saith he *a.* in him. *1 John* 2:6
he that loveth his brother *a.* in. 10
and the word of God *a.* in you. 14
he that doeth the will of God *a.* 17
anointing *a.* in you and teacheth. 27
whosoever *a.* in him sinneth not. 3:6
loveth not his brother *a.* in death. 14
we know that he *a.* in us. 24
whoso *a.* not in the doctrine of Christ hath not God, he that *a.* hath the. *2 John* 9

abiding
Balaam saw Israel *a.* *Num* 24:2
a. in the inheritance. *1 Sam* 26:19*
shadow, there is none *a.* *1 Chr* 29:15
shepherds *a.* in the field. *Luke* 2:8
not his word *a.* in you. *John* 5:38
no murderer hath eternal life *a.* in him. *1 John* 3:15

Abiezer
lot for the children of *A.* *Josh* 17:2
A. was gathered after. *Judg* 6:34
better than the vintage of *A.* 8:2
A was one of David's. *2 Sam* 23:27

Abi-ezrite
pertained to Joash the *A.* *Judg.* 6:11

Abigail
of Nabal's wife was *A.* *1 Sam* 25:3
with his two wives, Ahinoam and *A.* 27:3; 30:5; *2 Sam* 2:2
sisters were Zeruiah and *A.* *1 Chr.* 2:16

Abihail
Rehoboam took *A.* *2 Chr* 11:18
Esther the daughter of *A.* *Esth* 2:15 9:29

Abihu
Aaron's sons Nadab and A. Ex 6:23; 28:1; Lev 10:1; Num 3:2; 26:60; 1 Chr 6:3; 24:1.

come up, *A.* *Ex* 24:1
then *A.* went up. 9
A. died before. *Num* 3:4; 26:61

Abijah, Abijam
A. the son of Jeroboam. *1 Ki* 14:1
A. the son of Rehoboam. 31; 15:1, 7
eighth lot came forth to *A.* *1 Chr* 24:10
mother's name was *A.* *2 Chr* 29:1
those that sealed were *A.* *Neh* 10:7
went up with Zerubbabel *A.* 12:4
of *A.* Zichri. 17

ability
his *a.* that vowed, priest. *Lev* 27:8
they gave after their *a.* *Ezra* 2:69
we after our *a.* redeemed. *Neh* 5:8
a. to stand in the king's. *Dan* 1:4
each according to his *a.* *Mat* 25:15
a. determined to send. *Acts* 11:29
as of the *a.* God giveth. *1 Pet* 4:11*

Abimelech
A. king of Gerar sent. *Gen* 20:2
A. and Phichol spake to. 21:22
Isaac went unto *A.* 26:1
A. said, go from us. 16
concubine bare him *A.* *Judg* 8:31
A. the son of Jerubbaal went. 9:1
A. son of Jerubbesheth. *2 Sam* 11:21
Zadok and *A.* were. *1 Chr* 18:16

Abinadab
ark into the house of *A.* *1 Sam* 7:1
Jesse called *A.* made him. 16:8
A. followed Saul to the. 17:13
A. son of Saul. 31:2; *1 Chr* 10:2
ark on new cart, it out of the house of *A.* *2 Sam* 6:3; *1 Chr* 13:7
A. had Solomon's daughter. *1 Ki* 4:11

Abinoam, *see* **Barak**

Abiram
Dathan and *A.* the sons. *Num* 16:1 26:9
sent to call Dathan and *A.* 12
he did to Dathan and *A.* *Deut* 11:6
laid the foundation in *A.* *1 Ki* 16:34
the company of *A.* *Ps* 106:17

Abishag
and *A.* ministered to. *1 Ki* 1:15
and why dost thou ask *A.* 2:22

Abishai
A. said, I will go. *1 Sam* 26:6
sons of Zeruiah there, Joab, *A.* and Asahel. *2 Sam* 2:18; *1 Chr* 2:16
fled also before *A.* *2 Sam* 10:14
king charged thee, and *A.* 18:12
A. succoured him and smote. 21:17
A. was chief. 23:18; *1 Chr* 11:20
A. slew of the Edomites. *1 Chr* 18:12

Abiud
Zerobabel begat *A.* and *A.* *Mat* 1:13

abjects
the *a.* gathered together. *Ps* 35:15

able
provide out of all the people *a.* men. *Ex* 18:21, 25
pigeons, such as he is *a.* *Lev* 14:22 31
a. to go to war *Num* 1:3, 20, 22, 24, 26, 28, 30, 32, 34, 36, 38, 40, 42, 45; 26:2.
are well *a.* to overcome it. 13:30
shall give as he is *a.* *Deut* 16:17
no man hath been *a.* to. *Josh* 23:9
a. to stand before this. *1 Sam* 6:20
a. to judge so great a. *1 Ki* 3:9
is *a.* to build him. *2 Chr* 2:6
none is *a.* to withstand thee. 20:6
is *a.* to give thee much more. 25:9
who then is *a.* to stand. *Job* 41:10
a. to stand before envy. *Pr* 27:4
offering shall be as he is *a.* *Ezek* 46:11
God whom we serve is *a.* *Dan* 3:17
thy God is *a.* to deliver. 6:20
God is *a.* of these stones to raise up children. *Mat* 3:9; *Luke* 3:8
believe ye that I am *a.* to. *Mat* 9:28
a. to destroy soul and body. 10:28
he that is *a.* to receive it, let. 19:12
are ye *a.* to drink of the cup. 20:22
no man was *a.* to answer. 22:46
spake he, as they were *a.* *Mark* 4:33
no man is *a.* to pluck. *John* 10:29
yoke our fathers nor we *a.* *Acts* 15:10
his grace, *a.* to build you. 20:32
among you are *a.* go down. 25:5*
he was *a.* to perform. *Rom* 4:21
for God is *a.* to graff them in. 11:23
God is *a.* to make him stand. 14:4
ye are *a.* also to admonish. 15:14
a. nor yet now are ye *a.* *1 Cor* 3:2
tempted above that ye are *a.* 10:13
made us *a.* ministers. *2 Cor* 3:6*
God is *a.* to make all grace. 9:8
a. to do abundantly above. *Eph.* 3:20
he is *a.* to subdue all. *Phil* 3:21
he is *a.* to keep that I. *2 Tim* 1:12
a. to come to the knowledge. 3:7
holy scriptures *a.* to make wise. 15
he is *a.* to succour them. *Heb* 2:18
to him that was *a.* to save him. 5:7
a. to save to the uttermost. 7:25
God was *a.* to raise him up. 11:19
the word which is *a.* to. *Jas* 1:21
a. also to bridle the whole. 3:2
one lawgiver *a.* to save. 4:12
to him that is *a.* to keep. *Jude* 24
a. to open the book nor. *Rev* 5:3
a. to make war with the. 13:4
a. to enter into the temple. 15:8

***be* able**
himself *be a.* to redeem. *Lev* 25:26
man *be a.* to stand. *Deut* 7:24 11:25
be a. to stand before. *Josh* 1:5

I shall *be a.* to drive. Josh 14:12
if he *be a.* to fight with. 1 Sam 17:9
be a. to offer willingly. 1 Chr 29:14
God should *be a.* to. 2 Chr 32:14
thou shalt *be a.* to. Isa 47:12
righteous *be a.* to live. Ezek 33:12
be a. with 10,000 to. Luke 14:31
be a. to separate us from. Rom 8:39
ye may *be a.* to bear. 1 Cor 10:13
be a. to comprehend. Eph 3:18*
be a. to stand against the. 6:11
ye shall *be a.* to quench. 16
be a. to teach others. 2 Tim 2:2
be a. by sound doctrine. Tit 1:9
be a. after my decease. 2 Pet 1:15
who shall *be a.* to stand? Rev 6:17

***not be* able**

not be a. to deliver. 2 Ki 18:29
Isa 36:14
shall *not be a.* to rise. Ps 36:12
shall he *not be a.* to find. Eccl 8:17
not be a. to put it off. Isa 47:11
not be a. to escape. Jer 11:11
not be a. to hide. 49:10
not be a. to deliver. Ezek 7:19
seek, *not be a.* Luke 13:24
not be a. to gainsay. 21:15

***not* able**

not a. to bring a lamb. Lev 5:7
I am *not a.* to bear all. Num 11:14
not a. to go up against. 13:31
Lord was *not a.* 14:16; Deut 9:28
not a. to go to Tarshish. 2 Chr 20:37
not a. to stand without. Ezra 10:13
not a. to build the wall. Neh 4:10
they were *not a.* to rise. Ps 18:38
they are *not a.* to perform. 21:11
hold on me, so that I am *not a.* 40:12
land is *not a.* to bear. Amos 7:10
not a. to do the thing. Luke 12:26
foundation, and is *not a.* to. 14:29
not a. to draw it for the fishes.
John 21:6
not a. to resist the wisdom. Acts 6:10

Abner

Ner father of *A.* was. 1 Sam 14:51
Saul said to *A.* whose son? 17:55
A. and the people lay round. 26:7
cried, answerest thou not, *A.*? 14
A. said, let young men. 2 Sam 2:14
Jacob said, thou knowest *A.* 3:25
Joab and Abishai his brother slew *A.* 30
buried *A.* in Hebron, king wept. 32
king said, died *A.* as a fool? 33
was not of the king to slay *A.* 37
when Saul's son heard that *A.* 4:1
buried Ish-bosheth's head in *A.* 12
what Joab did to *A.* 1 Ki 2:5
that *A.* had dedicated. 1 Chr 26:28
Jaasiel son of *A.* ruler of. 27:21

aboard

ship sailing, we went *a.* Acts 21:2

abode, *substantive*

but I know thy *a.* 2 Ki 19:27*
Isa 37:28*
make our *a.* with him. John 14:23

abode, *verb*

Jacob *a.* with him the. Gen 29:14
but his bow *a.* in strength. 49:24
glory of the Lord *a.* on Sinai.
Ex 24:16
cloud *a.* Israel. Num 9:17, 18, 21
a. in their tents. 20, 22
and *a.* at Hazeroth. 11:35
a. in Kadesh. 20:1; Judg 11:17
princes *a.* with Balaam. Num 22:8
a. in Kadesh many. Deut 1:46
we *a.* in the valley. 3:29
I *a.* in the mount. 9:9
they *a.* in their places. Josh 5:8
they *a.* between Bethel and Ai. 8:9
Gilead *a.* beyond Jordan, Asher continued on the sea-shore, and *a.*
Judg 5:17
Levite *a.* with him three. 19:4
a. in the rock Rimmon. 20:47
woman *a.* and gave. 1 Sam 1:23
ark *a.* in Kirjath-jearim. 7:2
Saul and Jonathan *a.* 13:16
Saul *a.* 22:6*
David *a.* 23:14, 25; 26:3
David *a.* in wood. 1 Sam 23:18
a. at Ziklag. 2 Sam 1:1
Uriah *a.* in Jerusalem. 11:12
while I *a.* at Geshur. 15:8
to a loft where he *a.* 1 Ki 17:19
Jeremiah *a.* in the court. Jer 38:28
while they *a.* in Galilee. Mat 17:22
Mary *a.* with her. Luke 1:56
nor *a.* in any house, but in. 8:27
Spirit, and it *a.* upon. John 1:32
they came and *a.* with him. 39
words he *a.* in Galilee. 7:9
murderer, and *a.* 8:44*
a. two days still in the place. 11:6
upper room where *a.* Acts 1:13
long time *a.* they speaking. 14:3
Paul *a.* with them and. 18:3
a. with the brethren one day. 21:7
house of Philip and *a.* with him. 8
I went and *a.* with Peter. Gal. 1:18

abode *there* **or** *there* **abode**

days that ye *a. there.* Deut 1:46
and *a. there* 3 days. Josh 2:22
the people *a. there* till. Judg 21:2
there a. we in tents. Ezra 8:15
Jerusalem and *a. there* three. 32
Jesus *a. there* two days. John 4:40
first baptized, and *there a.* 10:40
Cesarea, and *there a.* Acts 12:19*
there they *a.* long time. 14:28
Silas and Timotheus *a. there.* 17:14

abodest

why *a.* thou among the. Judg 5:16*

abolish

idols he shall utterly *a.* Isa. 2:18*

abolished

righteousness shall not be *a.* Isa 51:6
your works may be *a.* Ezek 6:6
end of that which is *a.* 2 Cor 3:13*
a. in his flesh the enmity. Eph 2:15
Christ, who hath *a.* death.
2 Tim 1:10

abominable

touch any *a.* unclean. Lev 7:21
shall not make yourselves *a.* 11:43
any of these *a.* customs. 18:30
on the third day, it is *a.* 19:7
shall not make your souls *a.* 20:25
not eat any *a.* thing. Deut 14:3
king's word was *a.* 1 Chr 21:6
Asa put away the *a.* idols. 2 Chr 15:8
much more *a.* and filthy. Job 15:16
they have done *a.* works. Ps 14:1
and have done *a.* iniquity. 53:1
out like an *a.* branch. Isa 14:19
broth of *a.* things is in. 65:4
carcases of their *a.* Jer 16:18
O, do not this *a.* thing that. 44:4
nor came *a.* flesh into. Ezek 4:14
saw and behold *a.* beasts. 8:10
thy sins committed more *a.* 16:52
scant measure that is *a.* Mi 6:10
and I will cast *a.* filth. Nah 3:6
works deny him, being *a.* Tit 1:16
walked in *a.* idolatries. 1 Pet 4:3
unbelieving, and the *a.* Rev 21:8

abominably

Ahab did very *a.* in. 1 Ki 21:26

abomination

[1] *A thing hateful and detestable,* Gen 43:32; Pr 29:27. [2] *An idol,* 2 Ki 23:13; Isa 44:19.

an *a.* to the Egyptians. Gen 43:32
every shepherd is an *a.* to. 46:34
sacrifice the *a.* of Egyptians. Ex 8:26
shall be an *a.* Lev 7:18; 11:41, 42
shall be an *a.* to. 11:10, 12, 20, 23
womankind it is *a.* 18:22; 20:13
a. to the Lord. Deut 7:25; 17:1
bring an *a.* into thy house. 7:26
every *a.* they have done to. 12:31
such *a.* is wrought. 13:14; 17:4
these things are an *a.* 18:12; 22:5
are an *a.* to the Lord. 23:18
an *a.* before the Lord. 24:4
unrighteously are an *a.* to. 25:16
the man that maketh *a.* 27:15
in *a.* with Philistines. 1 Sam 13:4
Milcom the *a.* 1 Ki 11:5, 7
Chemosh the *a.* of Moab. 7
Ashtaroth the *a.* of the. 2 Ki 23:13
thou hast made me an *a.* Ps 88:8
the froward is an *a.* to. Pr 3:32
seven things are an *a.* to him. 6:16
wickedness is an *a.* to my lips. 8:7
a false balance is an *a.* to. 11:1
they of a froward heart are an *a.* 20
lying lips are *a.* to. 12:22
a. to fools to depart. 13:19
of the wicked is an *a.* 15:8; 21:27
way of the wicked is an *a.* to. 15:9
thoughts of the wicked are an *a.* 26
is proud in heart is an *a.* 16:5
it is an *a.* to kings to commit. 12
both are an *a.* to the Lord. 17:15
both of them are alike *a.* to. 20:10
divers weights are an *a.* to the. 23
the scorner is an *a.* to men. 24:9
his prayer shall be *a.* 28:9
is an *a.* to the just, and he that is upright in the way, is *a.* 29:27
incense is an *a.* to me. Isa 1:13
an *a.* is he that chooseth you. 41:24
the residue thereof an *a*? 44:19
eating swine's flesh, and the *a.* 66:17
ye made my heritage an *a.* Jer 2:7
they committed *a.* 6:15; 8:12
do this *a.* to cause Judah. 32:35
and committed *a.* Ezek 16:50
eyes to idols and committed *a.* 18:12
a. with his neighbour's wife. 22:11
your sword and ye work *a.* 33:26
a. that maketh desolate. Dan. 11:31
a. that maketh desolate set. 12:11
a. is committed in Israel. Mal 2:11
ye see *a.* of desolation. Mat 24:15
Mark 13:14
men is *a.* with God. Luke 16:15
enter that worketh *a.* Rev 21:27

abominations

not learn to do after the *a.*
Deut 18:9
with *a.* provoked they him to. 32:16
according to all *a.* 1 Ki 14:24
through fire according to *a.*
2 Ki 16:3; 2 Chr 28:3
Manasseh did evil after the *a.* of the heathen. 2 Ki 21:2; 2 Chr 33:2
a. spied did Josiah put. 2 Ki 23:24
2 Chr 34:33
Jehoiakim and his *a.* 2 Chr 36:8
people transgressed after all *a.* 14
for there are seven *a.* in. Pr 26:25
could not bear for the *a.* Jer 44:22
for all the evil *a.* of. Ezek 6:11
seest thou the great *a.* of Israel, but thou shalt see greater *a.* 8:6
13, 15
behold the wicked *a.* that they do. 9
light thing to commit *a.* here? 17
sigh and cry for all the *a.* 9:4
take away all the *a.* thereof. 11:18
your faces from all your *a.* 14:6
cause Jerusalem to know her *a.* 16:2
righteous doth according to all *a.*
18:24
cause them to know the *a.* 20:4
cast ye away every man the *a.* 7
they did not cast away the *a.* 8
shalt shew her all her *a.* 22:2
loathe yourselves for all your *a.*
36:31
it suffice you of all your *a.* 44:6
broken my covenant for all your *a.* 7
the overspreading of *a.* Dan 9:27
a. from between his teeth. Zech 9:7
cup in her hand full of *a.* Rev 17:4
mother of harlots and *a.* of. 5

***their* abominations**

not to do after all *their a.*
Deut 20:18
seen *their a.* and *their.* 29:17
doing according to *their a.* Ezra 9:1
their a. which have filled. 11
soul delighteth in *their a.* Isa 66:3
their a. in the house.
Jer 7:30; 32:34
committed in all *their a.* Ezek 6:9
made the images of *their a.* 7:20
heart walketh after *their a.* 11:21
may declare all *their a.* 12:16
thou not done after *their a.* 16:47
ye whoredom after *their a.* 20:30
yea, declare to them *their a.* 23:36
desolate because of all *their a.* 33:29

defiled my holy name by ***their a.*** *Ezek* 43:8
bear their shame and *their a.* 44:13
their a. were according. *Hos* 9:10

***these* abominations**
commit any of *these a.* *Lev* 18:26
all *these a.* have the men of. 27
shall commit any of *these a.* 29
because of *these a.* the. *Deut* 18:12
Manasseh . . . *these a.* *2 Ki* 21:11
affinity with people of *these a.* *Ezra* 9:14
delivered to do all *these a.* *Jer* 7:10
these a. shall surely die. *Ezek* 18:13

***thine* or *thy* abominations**
wilt put away *thine a.* *Jer* 4:1
seen *thine a.* on the hills. 13:27
I have not, because of *thine a.* *Ezek* 5:9
defiled my sanctuary with *thy a.* 11
on thee all *thine a.* 7:3, 4, 8, 9
all *thine a.* thou has not. 16:22
with all the idols of *thine a.* 36
lewdness above all *thine a.* 43
multiplied *thine a.* 51
hast borne *thine a.* saith. 58

abound
the faithful man shall *a.* *Pr* 28:20
because inquity shall *a.* *Mat* 24:12*
that the offence might *a.* *Rom* 5:20
in sin, that grace may *a.* ? 6:1
that ye may *a.* in hope through. 15:13
sufferings *a.* so consolation. *2 Cor* 1:5
a. in every thing, see that ye *a.* 8:7
God is able to make all grace *a.* 9:8
your love may *a.* more. *Phil* 1:9
I know how to *a.* both to *a.* 4:12
but I desire fruit that may *a.* 17*
but I have all and *a.* I am full. 18
Lord make you to *a.* *1 Thes* 3:12
so ye would *a.* more and more. 4:1
things be in you and *a.* *2 Pet* 1:8

abounded, -eth, -ing
fountains *a.* with water. *Pr* 8:24
man *a.* in transgression. 29:22
truth of God hath more *a.* *Rom* 3:7
grace by Jesus Christ hath *a.* 5:15
sin *a.* grace did much more *a.* 20
always *a.* in the work. *1 Cor* 15:58
poverty *a.* to the riches. *2 Cor* 8:2
wherein he hath *a.* toward. *Eph* 1:8
therein with thanksgiving. *Col* 2:7
towards each other *a.* *2 Thes* 1:3

about
a. three months after. *Gen* 38:24
shewed Pharaoh what he is *a.* 41:25
turned himself *a.* from them. 42:24
trade hath been *a.* cattle. 46:34*
a. midnight will I go out. *Ex* 11:4
God led the people *a.* through. 13:18
set bounds *a.* the mount. 19:23
fell that day *a.* 3000 men. 32:28
that *a.* which he hath. *Lev* 6:5
a. the tabernacle of. *Num* 16:24
a. and instructed him. *Deut* 32:10
to go down *a.* a day. *Josh* 10:13
a. which thou cursedst. *Judg* 17:2
and it was *a.* an ephah of. *Ruth* 2:17
was come *a.* Hannah. *1 Sam* 1:20
the ark of God be carried *a.* 5:8
came to pass, *a.* the spring. 9:26
women have been kept from us *a.* 21:5
to fetch *a.* this form. *2 Sam* 14:20*
kingdom is turned *a.* *1 Ki* 2:15
a. going down of sun. 22:36
2 Chr 18:34
a. this season according. *2 Ki* 4:16
which I am *a.* to build *2 Chr* 2:9
employed *a.* this matter. *Ezra* 10:15*
is *a.* to fill his belly. *Job* 20:23
bind them *a.* thy. *Pr* 3:3; 6:21
that goeth *a.* as a tale-bearer. 20:19
heap of wheat set *a.* *S of S* 7:2
compass yourselves *a.* *Isa* 50:11
why gaddest thou *a.* so. *Jer* 2:36
how long wilt thou go *a.* 31:22*
people cast *a.* and returned. 41:14
doings have beset them *a.* *Hos* 7:2
went out *a.* the third. *Mat* 20:3
not so much as *a.* the. *Mark* 2:2
set an hedge *a.* it, and. *Mark* 12:1
a. my Father's business. *Luke* 2:49*
Jesus began to be *a.* thirty. 3:23
loins be girded *a.* and. 12:35
a question *a.* purifying. *John* 3:25
why go ye *a.* to kill me ? 7:19*
of the men was *a.* 5000. *Acts* 4:4
when Paul was *a.* to open. 18:14
a. to flee out of the ship. 27:30*
he was *a.* 100 years old. *Rom* 4:19
going *a.* to establish their own. 10:3*
power to lead *a.* a. *1 Cor* 9:5
bearing *a.* in the body. *2 Cor* 4:10
loins girt *a.* with truth. *Eph* 6:14
wandering *a.* from house. *1 Tim* 5:13
when he was *a.* to make. *Heb* 8:5
silence *a.* the space of half. *Rev.* 8:1
I was *a.* to write, and I. 10:4
see **gone, him, me, thee, them, round, stood, this, time, went.**

above
[1] *Aloft, high,* Gen 6:16; *Pr* 8:28.
[2] *More than,* Gen 3:14; 48:22;
2 Cor 1:8. [3] *Upwards,* Ex 30:14;
Lev 27:7. [4] *A higher state or*
rank, Num 16:3; Deut 28:13. [5]
Heaven, or the highest place, Job
3:4; Rom 10:6. [6] *Things that*
relate to heaven, Gal 4:26; Col 3:1.
[7] *God,* Jas 1:17.

waters *a.* the firmament. *Gen* 1:7
fowl that may fly *a.* the earth. 20
cursed *a.* all cattle, *a.* beast. 3:14
shalt thou finish the ark *a.* 6:16
and the ark was lifted up *a.* 7:17
one portion *a.* thy brethren. 48:22
prevailed *a.* the blessings of. 49:26
I will commune from *a.* *Ex* 25:22
a. the curious girdle of. 28:27, 28
from twenty years old and *a.* 30:14
1 Chr 23:27
which have legs *a.* their. *Lev* 11:21
from sixty years old and *a.* 27:7
a. the congregation. *Num* 16:3
heart be not lifted up *a.* *Deut* 17:20
lest if he should beat him *a.* 25:3
be *a.* only, and not beneath. 28:13
multiply thee *a.* thy fathers. 30:5
come down from *a.* *Josh* 3:13, 16
blessed shall she be *a.* women. *Judg* 5:24
sent from *a.* *2 Sam* 22:17; *Ps* 18:16
covered ark *a.* *1 Ki* 8:7; *2 Chr* 5:8
a. the throne of kings. *2 Ki* 25:28
Jer 52:32
Judah prevailed *a.* his. *1 Chr* 5:2
Benaiah was mighty and *a.* 27:6
Hananiah feared God *a.* *Neh* 7:2
up *a.* the house of David. 12:37
not God regard it from *a.* *Job* 3:4
a. shall his branch be cut. 18:16
price of wisdom is *a.* rubies. 28:18
portion of God is there from *a.* ? 31:2
have denied the God that is *a.* 28
thy judgments are *a.* out. *Ps* 10:5
liftest me *a.* those that rise. 18:48
head be lifted up *a.* enemies. 27:6
oil of gladness *a.* 45:7; *Heb* 1:9
the clouds from *a.* *Ps* 78:23
commandments *a.* gold. 119:127
that stretched out the earth *a.* 136:6
if I prefer not Jerusalem *a.* 137:6
send thine hand from *a.* rid. 144:7
his glory is *a.* the earth. 148:13
established the clouds *a.* *Pr* 8:28
way of life is *a.* to the wise. 15:24
for her price is far *a.* rubies. 31:10
man hath no pre-eminence *a.* *Eccl* 3:19
mountain shall be exalted *a.* *Isa* 2:2
a. it stood the seraphims, each. 6:2
the depth or in the height *a.* 7:11
widows increased *a.* sand. *Jer* 15:8
from *a.* hath he sent fire. *Lam* 1:13
appearance of a man *a.* *Ezek* 1:26
God was over them *a.* 10:19; 11:22
exalt itself any more *a.* the. 29:15
Daniel was preferred *a.* *Dan* 6:3
king magnify himself *a.* 11:36
destroyed his fruit from *a.* *Amos* 2:9
multiplied thy merchants *a.* *Nah* 3:16
disciple not *a.* *Mat* 10:24; *Luke* 6:40
remained over and *a.* *John* 6:13
from *a.* ye are of this world. 8:23
it were given him from *a.* 19:11
man was *a.* forty years. *Acts* 4:22
I saw a light *a.* the brightness. 26:13
bring Christ down from *a.* *Rom* 10:6
esteemeth one day *a.* another. 14:5
not to think of men *a.* *1 Cor* 4:6
you to be tempted *a.* that ye. 10:13
was seen of *a.* 500 brethren. 15:6
out of measure *a.* strength. *2 Cor* 1:8
more, in stripes *a.* measure. 11:23
a. fourteen years ago, whether. 12:2
lest any man should think of me *a.* 6
Jerusalem which is *a.* *Gal* 4:26
given him a name *a.* *Phil* 2:9
seek those things which are *a.* *Col* 3:1
set your affection on things *a.* not. 2
servant, but *a.* a servant. *Philem* 16
a. when he said, sacrifice. *Heb* 10:8
perfect gift is from *a.* *Jas* 1:17
wisdom descendeth not from *a.* 3:15

above *all*
is cursed *a. all* cattle. *Gen* 3:14
very meek *a. all* the men. *Num* 12:3
blessed *a. all* people. *Deut* 7:14
he chose you *a. all* people, as. 10:15
a. all the nations. 14:2; 26:19; 28:1
done evil *a. all* that were. *1 Ki* 14:9
provoked *a. all* that their. 22
Ahab did evil *a. all* that. 16:30
done wickedly *a. all* the. *2 Ki* 21:11
over and *a. all* I have. *1 Chr* 29:3
art exalted as head *a. all.* 11
Maachah *a. all* his. *2 Chr* 11:21
for Ezra was *a. all.* *Neh* 8:5
king loved Esther *a. all.* *Esth* 2:17
Lord art high *a. all* the. *Ps* 97:9
is high *a. all* people. 99:2; 113:4
magnified thy word *a. all* thy. 138:2
a. all that were in Jerusalem. *Eccl* 2:7
heart is deceitful *a. all.* *Jer* 17:9
this lewdness *a. all.* *Ezek* 16:43
his height was exalted *a. all.* 31:5
magnify himself *a. all.* *Dan* 11:37
added yet this *a. all.* *Luke* 3:20
sinners *a. all* the Galileans. 13:2, 4
from heaven is *a. all.* *John* 3:31
far *a. all* principality and. *Eph* 1:21
a. all that we ask. 3:20
one God *a. all.* 4:6
a. all taking the shield of faith. 6:16
a. all these things put on. *Col* 3:14
a. all that is called God. *2 Thes* 2:4
a. all things, my brethren. *Jas* 5:12
a. all things have fervent. *1 Pet* 4:8
I wish *a. all* things that. 3 *John* 2:1
above ***all* gods,** *see* **gods ; above** *heaven, see* **heaven** ; *stood* **above,** *see* **stood ; above** *me, him, them, see* **him, me, them.**

Abram, Abraham
Lord said to *A.* get out. *Gen* 12:1
A. went down into Egypt to. 10
A. went up out of Egypt, he. 13:1
A. dwelt in land of Canaan, and. 12
A. came and dwelt in the plain. 18
A. armed his trained servants. 14:14
fear not, *A.* I am thy. 15:1
Lord made a covenant with *A.* 18
thy name shall be *A.* 17:5
1 Chr 1:27; *Neh* 9:7
A. hastened into the tent. *Gen* 18:6
shall I hide from *A.* that thing. 17
but *A.* stood yet before the Lord. 22
A. said of Sarah his wife, she. 20:2
and *A.* planted a grove in. 21:33
God did tempt *A.* and said. 22:1
out of heaven, and said, *A. A.* 11
Sarah died, and *A.* came to. 23:2
A. bought the field of. 17; 49:30
50:13
the Lord had blessed *A.* in all. 24:1
A. said, put thy hand under my. 2
Eliezer said, I am *A.* servant. 34
God of my master *A.* prosper. 42
they sent away Rebekah and *A.* 59
and *A.* gave all that he had. 25:5
the days of the years of *A.* life. 7
Hagar the Egyptian bare to. 12
that was in the days of *A.* 26:1
because *A.* obeyed my voice, kept. 5

multiply thy seed for *A*. *Gen* 26:24
give thee the blessing of *A*. 28:4
except the God of *A*. had. 31:42
which he sware to *A*. 50:24
Ex 33:1; *Num* 32:11; *Deut* 1:8
6:10; 30:20
I am the God of *A*. *Ex* 3:6, 15, 16
4:5; *Mat* 22:32; *Mark* 12:26
Luke 20:37; *Acts* 3:13; 7:32
remember *A*. Isaac. *Ex* 32:13
Deut 9:27
people of the God of *A*. *Ps* 47:9
covenant he made with *A*. 105:9
remembered his promise, and *A*. 42
Lord, who redeemed *A*. *Isa* 29:22
art our father, though *A*. be. 63:16
A. was one, and he. *Ezek* 33:24
perform the mercy to *A*. *Mi* 7:20
son of David, the son of *A*. *Mat* 1:1
raise up children unto *A*. 3:9
Luke 3:8
sit down with *A*. *Mat* 8:11
was the son of *A*. son. *Luke* 3:34
shall see *A*. in the kingdom. 13:28
his eyes, and seeth *A*. 16:23
as he also is the son of *A*. 19:9
this did not *A*. *John* 8:40
A. is dead. 52
hast thou seen *A* ? 57
before *A*. was, I am. 58
of the stock of *A*. *Acts* 13:26
A. were justified by works. *Rom* 4:2
A. believed God, and it was counted.
3, 9; *Gal* 3:6; *Jas* 2:23
faith are the children of *A*. *Gal* 3:7
preached before the gospel to *A*. 8
faith are blessed with faithful *A*. 9
God gave the inheritance to *A*. 18
A. had two sons, the one by a. 4:22
God made promise to *A*. *Heb* 6:13
who met *A*. returning from. 7:1
say, Levi payed tithes in *A*. 9
A. obeyed. 11:8
by faith *A*. offered up Isaac. 17

Abraham with *father*

oath to *A*. thy *father*. *Gen* 26:3
God of *A*. thy *father*. 24; 28:13
O God of my *father A*. and. 32:9
I took your *father A*. *Josh* 24:3
look to *A*. your *father*. *Isa* 51:2
A. to our *father*. *Mat* 3:9; *Luke* 3:8
he sware to our *father A*. *Luke* 1:73
he said, *father A*. have mercy. 16:24
nay, *father A*. but if one went. 30
to him *A*. is our *father*. *John* 8:39
greater than our *father A*. ? 53
your *father A*. rejoiced to see. 56
appeared to our *father A*. *Acts* 7:2
say that *A*. our *father*. *Rom* 4:1
of that faith of our *father A*. 12
faith of *A*. who is the *father*. 16
was not *A*. our *father* justified ?
Jas 2:21

Abraham with *seed*

gavest it to *seed* of *A*. *2 Chr* 20:7
O ye *seed* of *A*. his. *Ps* 105:6
Israel, the *seed* of *A*. *Isa* 41:8
rulers over the *seed* of *A*. *Jer* 33:26
spake to *A*. and his *seed*. *Luke* 1:55
we be *A*. *seed* and were. *John* 8:33
I know ye are *A*. *seed* but ye. 37
was not to *A*. or his *seed*. *Rom* 4:13
they are *seed* of *A*. 9:7
of the *seed* of *A*. 11:1; *2 Cor* 11:22
to *A*. and his *seed* were *Gal* 3:16
be Christ's, then are ye *A*. *seed* 29
took on him the *seed* of *A*. *Heb* 2:16

abroad

ought of the flesh *a*. *Ex* 12:46
a leprosy break out *a*. *Lev* 13:12
be born at home or *a*. 18:9
shall he go *a*. out of. *Deut* 23:10
wilt ease thyself *a*. shalt dig. 13
took daughters from *a*. *Judg* 12:9
borrow thee vessels *a*. *2 Ki* 4:3
it to carry it out *a*. *2 Chr* 29:16
the commandment came *a*. 31:5
queen shall come *a*. *Esth* 1:17
wandereth *a*. for bread. *Job* 15:23
he goeth *a*. he telleth it. *Ps* 41:6
fountains be dispersed *a*. *Pr* 5:16
spreadeth *a*. the earth. *Isa* 44:24
it out on the children *a*. *Jer* 6:11*
a. the sword bereaveth. *Lam* 1:20
began to blaze *a*. the. *Mark* 1:45
but that it should come *a*. 4:22*
sayings were noised *a*. *Luke* 1:65
made known *a*. the saying. 2:17
this was noised *a*. the. *Acts* 2:6*
love of God is shed *a*. in. *Rom* 5:5
for your obedience is come *a*. 16:19
see **cast, spread, stand, scatter, went.**

Absalom

A. the son of. *2 Sam* 3:3; *1 Chr* 3:2
A. spake to Amnon neither.
2 Sam 13:22
A. had sheep-shearers in. 23
saying, *A*. hath slain all the. 30
longed to go forth to *A*. 39
Joab arose and brought *A*. 14:23
to be so much praised as *A*. 25
A. said, O that I were made a. 15:4
A. stole the hearts of the men of. 6
among the conspirators with *A*. 31
A. went in unto his father's 16:22
Ahithophel's counsel pleased *A*. 17:4
Lord might bring evil upon *A*. 14
and when *A*. servants came to. 20
A. passed over Jordan. 24
A. pitched in Gilead. 26
deal gently for my sake with *A*. 18:5
I saw *A*. hanged in an oak. 10
darts through the heart of *A*. 14
it is called unto this day *A*. 18
is young man *A*. safe ? 29, 32
O my son *A*. 33
if *A*. had lived, and all we had. 19:6
I fled because of *A*. *1 Ki* 2:7
Adonijah, though not after *A*. 28
Maacah daughter of *A*. *2 Chr* 11:20

absence

to betray him in *a*. of. *Luke* 22:6
more in my *a*. work. *Phil* 2:12

absent

when we are *a*. one. *Gen* 31:49
I verily as *a*. in body. *1 Cor* 5:3
at home in body are *a*. *2 Cor* 5:6
to be *a*. from the body, present. 8
whether present or *a*. 9
being *a*. am bold toward you. 10:1
are by letters when we are *a*. 11
being *a*. now I write to. 13:2, 10
I come, or else be *a*. *Phil* 1:27
though I be *a*. in the flesh. *Col* 2:5

abstain

a. from pollutions of. *Acts* 15:20
that ye *a*. from meats offered. 29
that ye should *a*. from. *1 Thes* 4:3
a. from all appearance of evil. 5:22
commanding to *a*. from. *1 Tim* 4:3
a. from fleshly lusts. *1 Pet* 2:11

abstinence

after long *a*. Paul. *Acts* 27:21*

abundance

God for the *a*. of all. *Deut* 28:47
they shall suck of the *a*. of. 33:19
out of the *a*. of my. *1 Sam* 1:16
no more such *a*. of spices. *1 Ki* 10:10
sycamore-trees for *a*. 27; *2 Chr* 1:15
sound of *a*. of rain. *1 Ki* 18:41
of spices great *a*. *2 Chr* 9:9
a. of waters. *Job* 22:11; 38:34
shall be *a*. of peace. *Ps* 72:7
nor he that loveth *a*. *Eccl* 5:10
the *a* of the rich will not suffer. 12*
a. of milk he shall eat. *Isa* 7:22
the *a*. they have gotten. 15:7
great *a*. of thy enchantments. 47:9
a. of the sea shall be. 60:5
delighted with the *a*. of her. 66:11
I will reveal to them *a*. *Jer* 33:6
a. of idleness was in. *Ezek* 16:49*
of the *a*. of his horses. 26:10
silver, and apparel in great *a*.
Zech 14:14
a. of the heart. *Mat* 12:34
Luke 6:45
shall have more *a*. *Mat* 13:12; 25:29
cast in of their *a*. *Mark* 12:44*
Luke 21:4*
receive *a*. of grace. *Rom* 5:17
a. of their joy abounded. *2 Cor* 8:2
your *a*. a supply, their *a*. a. 14
exalted through the *a*. of the. 12:7*
waxed rich thro' the *a*. of. *Rev* 18:3*

in **abundance**

spoil of the city *in a*. *2 Sam* 12:30
slain oxen *in a*. *1 Ki* 1:19, 25
prepared brass *in a*. *1 Chr* 22:3, 14
trees *in a*. marble *in a*. 4; 29:2
workmen with thee *in a*. *1 Chr* 22:15
they offered sacrifices *in a*. 29:21
me timber *in a*. *2 Chr* 2:9
all these vessels *in* great *a*. 4:18
Sheba brought gold *in a*. 9:1
gave his sons victuals *in a*. 11:23
sheep and camels *in a*. 14:15
fell to Asa out of Israel *in a*. 15:9
to Jehoshaphat, and he had riches
and honour *in a*. 17:5; 18:1
sheep for Jehoshaphat *in a*. 18:2
Jehoshaphat found spoil *in a*. 20:25
they gathered money *in a*. 24:11
the burnt-offerings were *in a*. 29:35
Israel brought *in a*. first-fruits. 31:5
made darts and shields *in a*. 32:5
cities and possessions *in a*. 29
and fruit-trees *in a*. *Neh* 9:25
them royal wine *in a*. *Esth* 1:7
he giveth meat *in a*. *Job* 36:31
delight themselves *in a*. *Ps* 37:11
trusted *in* the *a*. of his riches. 52:7
brought forth frogs *in a*. 105:30
life consisteth not *in a*. *Luke* 12:15
man blame us *in* this *a*. *2 Cor* 8:20*

abundant

Lord God *a*. in goodness. *Ex* 34:6
day, and much more *a*. *Isa* 56:12*
Babylon, *a*. in treasures. *Jer* 51:13
bestow more *a*. honour. *1 Cor* 12:23
having given more *a*. honour to. 24
a. grace might redound. *2 Cor* 4:15*
his inward affection is more *a*. 7:15
for the administration is *a*. 9:12*
in labours more *a*. in stripes. 11:23
rejoicing may be more *a*. *Phil* 1:26
Lord was exceeding *a*. *1 Tim* 1:14
according to his *a*. mercy. *1 Pet* 1:3*

abundantly

waters bring forth *a*. *Gen* 1:20, 21
breed *a*. in the earth. 8:17
bring forth *a*. in the earth. 9:7
Israel increased *a*. *Ex* 1:7
river shall bring forth frogs *a*. 8:3*
the water came out *a*. *Num* 20:11
oil, oxen, and sheep *a*. *1 Chr* 12:40
so David prepared *a*. before. 22:5
thou hast shed blood *a*. and made. 8
brought they in *a*. *2 Chr* 31:5
hand God bringeth *a*. *Job* 12:6
drop, and distil upon man *a*. 36:28
they shall be *a*. satisfied. *Ps* 36:8
waterest the ridges thereof *a*. 65:10
I will *a*. bless her provision. 132:15
shall *a*. utter the memory. 145:7*
drink *a*. O beloved. *S of S* 5:1
shall howl, weeping *a*. *Isa* 15:3
it shall blossom *a*. and rejoice. 35:2
our God, for he will *a*. pardon. 55:7
have life more *a*. *John* 10:10
I laboured more *a*. *1 Cor* 15:10
conversation, and more *a*. to.
2 Cor 1:12
love I have more *a*. to you. 2:4
according to our rule *a*. 10:15
though the more *a*. I love you. 12:15
that is able to do exceeding *a*.
Eph 3:20
endeavoured more *a*. to see.
1 Thes 2:17*
he shed on us *a*. through Jesus.
Tit 3:6*
God willing more *a*. to. *Heb* 6:17
be ministered to you *a*. *2 Pet* 1:11*

abuse, -ed

a. her all the night. *Judg* 19:25
lest uncircumcised *a*. me.
1 Sam 31:4; *1 Chr* 10:4
I *a*. not my power in. *1 Cor* 9:18*

abusers, -ing

nor *a*. of themselves. *1 Cor* 6:9
use this world as not *a*. it. 7:31*

accept

[1] *To receive favourably*, Gen 4:7; Job 42:9; Mal 1:10, 13; Acts 10:35. [2] *To show partiality*, Job 13:10; 32:21; Pr 18:5

[3] *To regard or value*, 2 Cor 8:12.
[4] *To highly esteem*, Luke 4:24.
peradventure he will *a.* Gen 32:20
and the owner shall *a.* Ex 22:11
a. of the punishment. Lev 26:41, 43
bless and *a.* the work. Deut 33:11
let him *a.* an offering. 1 Sam 26:19
the L., thy God *a.* thee. 2 Sam 24:23
will ye *a.* his person ? Job 13:8
if ye do secretly *a.* persons. 10
not *a.* any man's person. 32:21
pray for you, for him will I *a.* 42:8
and *a.* thy burnt-sacrifice. Ps 20:3
a. the persons of the wicked. 82:2
a. I beseech thee the free-. 119:108
not good to *a.* the person. Pr 18:5
the Lord doth not *a.* them. Jer 14:10
I will not *a.* them. 12; Amos 5:22
there will I *a.* them. Ezek 20:40
a. you with your sweet savour. 41
and I will *a.* you, saith the. 43:27
will he be pleased, or *a.* ? Mal 1:8
nor will I *a.* an offering at your. 10
should I *a.* this of your hands ? 13
a. it always, and in all. Acts 24:3

acceptable
Often has the stronger meaning of well-pleasing, Rom 14:18; Eph 5:10.
shall not be *a.* for you. Lev 22:20
Asher be *a.* to his. Deut 33:24
meditation of my heart be *a.* Ps 19:14
thee, O Lord, in an *a.* time. 69:13
righteous know what is *a.* Pr 10:32
justice and judgment is more *a.* 21:3
preacher sought out *a.* Eccl 12:10
in an *a.* time have I heard. Isa 49:8
call this an *a.* day to the ? 58:5
to proclaim the *a.* year of. 61:2†
burnt-offerings are not *a.* Jer 6:20
O king, let my counsel be *a.* Dan 4:27
to preach the *a.* year of. Luke 4:19
living sacrifice, holy, *a.* Rom 12:1
is that good and *a.* will of God. 2
a. to God and approved of. 14:18
of the Gentiles might be *a.* 15:16
proving what is *a.* unto. Eph 5:10
sacrifice *a.* well-pleasing. Phil 4:18
this is *a.* in the sight. 1 Tim 2:3
is good and *a.* before God. 5:4
sacrifices *a.* to God. 1 Pet 2:5
this is *a.* with God. 20

acceptably
we may serve God *a.* Heb 12:28

acceptance
with *a.* on mine altar. Isa 60:7

acceptation
saying worthy of all *a.* 1 Tim 1:15 4:9

accepted
well, shalt thou not be *a.* Gen 4:7
have *a.* thee concerning this. 19:21
they may be *a.* before. Ex 28:38
offering shall be *a.* Lev 1:4; 22:27
it shall not be *a.* 7:18; 19:7 22:23, 25
should it have been *a.* in. 10:19*
shall be perfect, to be *a.* 22:21
shall wave the sheaf to be *a.* 23:11
he was *a.* in the sight. 1 Sam 18:5*
David said, see I have *a.* 25:35
a. of the multitude of. Esth 10:3
the Lord also *a.* Job. Job 42:9
sacrifice shall be *a.* on. Isa 56:7
let my supplication be *a.* Jer 37:20
out supplication be *a.* before. 42:2
no prophet is *a.* in his. Luke 4:24
worketh righteousness is *a.* Acts 10:35
my service may be *a.* of. Rom 15:31
present, we may be *a.* 2 Cor 5:9
time *a.* now is the *a.* time. 6:2
is *a.* according to that a man. 8:12
for indeed he *a.* the exhortation. 17
gospel which ye have not *a.* 11:4
made us *a.* in the beloved. Eph 1:6*

acceptest
neither *a.* thou the person. Luke 20:21

accepteth
him that *a.* not persons. Job 34:19
eat with joy, for God now *a.* Eccl 9:7
sacrifice, but the Lord *a.* Hos 8:13
God *a.* no man's person. Gal 2:6

accepting, *see* **deliverance.**

access
also we *a.* by faith. Rom 5:2
through him we both have *a.* to. Eph 2:18
have boldness and *a.* by faith. 3:12

Accho
drive out inhabitants of *A.* Judg 1:31

accompanied
brethren from Joppa *a.* Acts 10:23
these six brethren *a.* me. 11:12
Sopater of Berea *a.* Paul. 20:4
and they *a.* him unto the ship. 38

accompany, *see* **salvation.**

accomplish
(*To perform, finish, or fulfil.*)
sacrifice to *a.* his vow. Lev 22:21
a. my desire in giving. 1 Ki 5:9
a. as an hireling his day. Job 14:6
they *a.* a diligent search. Ps 64:6
shall *a.* that which I. Isa 55:11
surely *a.* your vows. Jer 44:25
thus will I *a.* my fury. Ezek 6:12
now will I *a.* mine anger upon. 7:8
I *a.* my wrath upon the wall. 13:15
my fury to *a.* my anger. 20:8, 21
would *a.* seventy years. Dan 9:2
a. at Jerusalem. Luke 9:31

accomplished
by Jeremiah might be *a.* 2 Chr 36:22
of purification were *a.* Esth 2:12 Luke 2:22
shall be *a.* before his. Job 15:32
the desire *a.* is sweet. Pr 13:19
that her warfare is *a.* Isa 40:2
when seventy years are *a.* Jer 25:12 29:10
your dispersions are *a.* 25:34*
my words shall be *a.* before. 39:16
the Lord hath *a.* his fury. Lam 4:11
punishment of thine iniquity is *a.* 22
when hast *a.* them, lie on. Ezek 4:6
thus shall mine anger be *a.* 5:13
till the indignation be *a.* Dan 11:36
a. to scatter the power of the. 12:7*
his ministration were *a.* Luke 1:23
days were *a.* that she should. 2:6
days were *a.* for circumcising. 21
am I straitened till it be *a.* 12:50
the Son of man, shall be *a.* 18:31
must yet be *a.* in me. 22:37*
all things were now *a.* John 19:28*
we had *a.* those days. Acts 21:5
same afflictions are *a.* in. 1 Pet 5:9

accomplishing, *see* **service.**

accomplishment
signify the *a.* of days of. Acts 21:26

accord
groweth of its own *a.* Lev 25:5
with Israel with one *a.* Josh 9:2
all continued with one *a.* Acts 1:14
all with one *a.* in one place. 2:1*
daily with one *a.* in temple. 46
their voice to God with one *a.* 4:24
one *a.* in Solomon's porch. 5:12
ran upon Stephen with one *a.* 7:57
people with one *a.* gave heed. 8:6
opened to them of his own *a.* 12:10
they came with one *a.* to him. 20
being assembled with one *a.* 15:25
with one *a.* made insurrection. 18:12
with one *a.* into the theatre. 19:29
forward of his own *a.* 2 Cor 8:17
being of one *a.* of one. Phil 2:2

according
done *a.* as thou badest. Gen 27:19
a. as Joseph had said. 41:54
the Lord will give *a.* Ex 12:25
be great, *a.* as thou. Num 14:17
inheritance *a.* as God. Deut 10:9
a. as the Lord thy God. 16:10
a. as he walked before. 1 Ki 3:6
to find *a.* to his ways. Job 34:11
Jer 17:10; 21:14; 32:19
went and did *a.* as the Lord. Job 42:9
judge me, O God, *a.* to my. Ps 7:8
the Lord *a.* to his righteousness. 17
a. to thy mercy remember thou me.
25:7; 51:1; 106:45; 109:26 119:124
a. to their deeds, and *a.* 28:4
mercy be on us *a.* as we. 33:22
judge me, O God, *a.* to thy. 35:24
a. to thy name, so is thy. 48:10*
renderest to every man *a.* 62:12 Pr 24:12, 29
a. to the greatness of thy. Ps 79:11
a. to thy fear, so is thy wrath. 90:11
rewarded us *a.* to our. 103:10
a. to thy word. 119:25, 28, 41, 58
65, 76, 107, 116, 154, 169, 170
quicken me *a.* to. 119:159; Isa 63:7
praise him *a.* to his excellent. Ps 150:2
speak not *a.* to this word. Isa 8:20
joy *a.* to the joy in harvest. 9:3
a. to all that the Lord has. 63:7
recompense her *a.* to her. Jer 50:29
shall rule, and do *a.* Dan 11:3
a. to the love of the Lord. Hos 3:1
the Lord will punish Jacob *a.* 12:2
a. to the days of thy coming. Mi 7:15*
a. to your faith be it. Mat 9:29
he will reward every man *a.* to.
16:27; Rom 2:6; 2 Tim 4:14 Rev 2:23
nor did *a.* to his will. Luke 12:47
judge not *a.* to the. John 7:24
made to every man *a.* as. Acts 4:35
seed of David *a.* to the flesh. Rom 1:3
called *a.* to his purpose. 8:28
gifts differing *a.* to the grace. 12:6
to be like-minded *a.* 15:5
Christ died *a.* to the. 1 Cor 15:3
man *a.* as he purposeth. 2 Cor 9:7
end shall be *a.* to their works. 11:15
who gave himself *a.* to. Gal 1:4
Abraham's seed, and heirs *a.* 3:29
a. as he hath chosen us in him. Eph 1:4
a. to good pleasure. 5
a. to riches of his grace. 7
predestinated *a.* to the purpose. 11
a. to the power that worketh. 3:20
a. to the working. Phil 3:21
God shall supply our need *a.* 4:19
not *a.* to our works. 2 Tim 1:9
a. to his mercy he saved us. Tit 3:5
not *a.* to the covenant. Heb 8:9
a. to his mercy hath. 1 Pet 1:3
live *a.* to God in the Spirit. 4:6
a. as his divine power. 2 Pet 1:3*
we *a.* to his promise look. 3:13
judged *a.* to their works. Rev 20:12 13
I come to give *a.* as his work. 22:12

according *to all, see* **all.**

according *to that*
obey my voice *a. to that.* Gen 27:8
do to me *a. to that.* Judg 11:36
slew not *a. to that* which. 2 Ki 14:6
a. to that which was. 2 Chr 35:26
Tatnai did *a. to that* Darius. Ezra 6:13
a. to that which was spoken. Rom 4:18
a. to that he hath done. 2 Cor 5:10
a. to that a man hath, not *a. to that.* 8:12

accordingly, *see* **repay.**

account
your *a.* for the lamb. Ex 12:4
that passeth the *a.* 2 Ki 12:4*
number put in the *a.* 1 Chr 27:24
number of their *a.* 2 Chr 26:11*
for he giveth not *a.* Job 33:13
man that thou makest *a.* Ps 144:3
one to find out the *a.* Eccl 7:27
the princes might give *a.* Dan 6:2
give *a.* thereof in the day. Mat 12:36
take *a.* of his servants. 18:23*
a. of thy stewardship. Luke 16:2
we may give an *a.* of. Acts 19:40
every one shall give *a.* Rom 14:12
may abound to your *a.* Phil 4:17
put that on mine *a.* Philem 18

they watch as they that must give *a.* *Heb* 13:17
who shall give *a.* to him. *1 Pet* 4:5

account, -ed

which also were *a.* giants. *Deut* 2:11
that also was *a.* a land of giants. 20
Solomon shall be *a.* *1 Ki* 1:21
silver was nothing *a.* of. 10:21
2 Chr 9:20
be *a.* to the Lord for a. *Ps* 22:30*
wherein is he to be *a.* of? *Isa* 2:22
a. to rule over Gentiles. *Mark* 10:42
a. worthy to obtain. *Luke* 20:35
should be *a.* the greatest. 22:24
we are *a.* as sheep for. *Rom* 8:36
let a man so *a.* of us as. *1 Cor* 4:1
a. to him for righteousness. *Gal* 3:6*
a. that the long-suffering *2 Pet* 3:15

accounting

a. that God was able to. *Heb* 11:19

accursed

[1] *Devoted to destruction,* Josh 6:17, *etc.* [2] *Separated from the church,* Rom 9:3; Gal 1:8, 9. (*Anathema*)

is hanged, is *a.* of God. *Deut* 21:23
city shall be *a.* it and. *Josh* 6:17
any wise keep from the *a.* thing. 18
a. thing; Achan took of *a.* 7:1
even taken of the *a.* thing. 11
because they were *a.* except ye destroy the *a.* 12
there is an *a.* thing in the midst. 13
that is taken with the *a.* thing. 15
commit trespass in *a.* thing. 22:20
in the thing *a.* *1 Chr* 2:7
100 years old shall be *a.* *Isa* 65:20
I could wish myself *a.* *Rom* 9:3
Spirit, calleth Jesus *a.* *1 Cor* 12:3
gospel, let him be *a.* *Gal* 1:8, 9

accusation

wrote they to him an *a.* *Ezra* 4:6
set over his head his *a.* *Mat* 27:37
Mark 15:26
they might find an *a.* *Luke* 6:7
taken any thing by false *a.* 19:8*
what *a.* bring ye against? *John* 18:29
they brought no *a.* as. *Acts* 25:18
elder receive not an *a.* *1 Tim* 5:19
bring not a railing *a.* *2 Pet* 2:11*
durst not bring a railing *a.* *Jude* 9*

accuse

a. not a servant to his. *Pr* 30:10*
a. him. *Mat* 12:10; *Mark* 3:2
nor *a.* any falsely, and be. *Luke* 3:14
they began to *a.* him, saying. 23:2
those things whereof ye *a.* him. 14
will *a.* you to the Father. *John* 5:45
that they might have to *a.* him. 8:6
Tertullus began to *a.* him. *Acts* 24:2
of all things whereof we *a.* 8
prove things whereof they *a.* me. 13
go down with me, and *a.* 25:5
none of those whereof these *a.* 11
ought to *a.* my nation of. 28:19
falsely *a.* your good. *1 Pet* 3:16*

accused

near, and *a.* the Jews. *Dan* 3:8
them which had *a.* Daniel. 6:24
a. he answered nothing. *Mat* 27:12
priests *a.* him. *Mark* 15:3
Luke 23:10
a. that he had wasted. *Luke* 16:1
certainty wherefore he was *a.*
Acts 22:30
cause whereof they *a.* him. 23:28
be *a.* of questions of their law. 29
is *a.* have the accusers. 25:16
things whereof I am *a.* 26:2
for which hope's sake I am *a.* of 7
faithful children, not *a.* of. *Tit.* 1:6
who *a.* them before our. *Rev* 12:10

accuser, *see* **cast** *down*

accusers

where are those thine *a.*? *John* 8:10*
commandment to his *a.* *Acts* 23:30
hear thee when thine *a.* are. 35
commanding his *a.* to come. 24:8*
before he have the *a.* face. 25:16
against whom, when the *a.* 18
natural affection, false *a.* *2 Tim* 3:3*
a. not given to much wine. *Tit* 2:3*

accuseth, -ing

that *a.* you, even Moses. *John* 5:45
thoughts *a.* or excusing. *Rom* 2:15

accustomed, *see* **do evil.**

aceldama, *see* **field**

Achaia

was the deputy of *A.* *Acts* 18:12
disposed to pass into *A.* 27; 19:21
it pleased them of *A.* to. *Rom* 15:26
Epenetus, the first-fruits of *A.* 16:5
Stephanas, first-fruits of *A.*
1 Cor 16:15
that *A.* was ready a year. *2 Cor* 9:2
stop me in the regions of *A.* 11:10
ensamples to all in *A.* *1 Thes* 1:7
the word sounded not only in *A.* 8

Achaicus

glad of the coming of *A.* *1 Cor* 16:17

Achan, *or* **Achar**

A. of the tribe of Judah. *Josh* 7:18
did not *A.* son of Zerah commit
22:20
A. the troubler of Israel. *1 Chr* 2:7

Achim

Sadoc begat *A.* and *A.* *Mat* 1:14

Achish

fled and went to *A.* *1 Sam* 21:10
27:2
was afraid of *A.* 21:12
A. gave him Ziklag. 27:6
on in the rereward with *A.* 29:2
A. said, I know thou art good in. 9
Shimei went to Gath to *A.* *1 Ki* 2:40

Achmetha

was found at *A.* a roll. *Ezra* 6:2

Achor

called the valley of *A.* *Josh* 7:26
valley of *A.* a place. *Isa* 65:10
give the valley of *A.* for. *Hos* 2:15

Achsah

will give *A.* to wife. *Josh* 15:16
Judg 1:12

Achshaph

Jabin sent to king of *A.* *Josh* 11:1
king of *A.* one. 12:20
their border *A.* 19:25

Achzib

lot from the coast to *A.* *Josh* 19:29
the houses of *A.* shall be. *Mi* 1:14

acknowledge

[1] *To own, or confess,* Gen 38:26; Ps 32:5. [2] *To esteem and respect,* Isa 61:9; 1 Cor 16:18. [3] *To approve of,* 2 Cor 1:13; Philem 6. [4] *To worship,* Dan 11:39.

a. the son of the hated. *Deut* 21:17
nor did he *a.* his brethren. 33:9
I *a.* my sin. *Ps* 32:5
I *a.* my transgression. 51:3
in all thy ways *a.* him, he. *Pr* 3:6
are near, *a.* my might. *Isa* 33:13
that see them, shall *a.* them. 61:9
father, though Israel *a.* us not. 63:16
only *a.* thine iniquity. *Jer* 3:13
a. O Lord, our wickedness. 14:20
a. them that are carried. 24:5*
god whom he shall *a.* *Dan* 11:39
I will go, till they *a.* *Hos* 5:15
let him *a.* the things. *1 Cor* 14:37*
therefore *a.* ye them that are. 16:18
a. and I trust shall *a.* *2 Cor* 1:13

acknowledged

Judah *a.* them, and said. *Gen* 38:26
also you have *a.* us in. *2 Cor* 1:14

acknowledgeth

a. the Son hath the Father.
1 John 2:23

acknowledging

(*Revised Version,* knowledge)

the *a.* of the truth. *2 Tim* 2:25
a. the truth which is after. *Tit* 1:1
by the *a.* every good thing. *Philem* 6

acknowledgment

a. of the mystery of God. *Col* 2:2*

acquaint, -ed, -ing

a. thyself with him and. *Job* 22:21
thou art *a.* with all my. *Ps* 139:3
a. my heart with wisdom. *Eccl* 2:3
of sorrows, and *a.* with. *Isa* 53:3

acquaintance

let priests take it, every man of his *a.*
2 Ki 12:5
no more money of your *a.* 7
a. are estranged from me. *Job* 19:13
all that had been of his *a.* 42:11
and a fear to mine *a.* *Ps* 31:11
mine equal, and mine *a.* 55:13*
put away mine *a.* far from me. 88:8
lover put from me, and my *a.* 18
sought him among their *a.* *Luke* 2:44
a. stood afar off, beholding. 23:49
forbid none of his *a.* to. *Acts* 24:23*

acquit

not *a.* me from mine iniquity.
Job 10:14
the Lord will not at all *a.* the *Nah.* 1:3

acre, -s

half an *a.* of land. *1 Sam* 14:14
ten *a.* of vineyard shall. *Isa* 5:10

act

pass his *a.* his strange *a.* *Isa* 28:21
the *a.* of violence is in their. 59:6
in adultery, in the very *a.* *John* 8:4

actions

the Lord *a.* are weighed. *1 Sam* 2:3

activity

if knowest any man of *a.* *Gen* 47:6

acts

a. which he did in Egypt. *Deut* 11:3
eyes have seen the great *a.* of. 7
rehearse the righteous *a.* *Judg* 5:11
reason of all righteous *a.* *1 Sam* 12:7
Benaiah the son . . . who had done many *a.* *2 Sam* 23:20; *1 Chr* 11:22
report I heard of thy *a.* *1 Ki* 10:6
a. of Solomon, are they not written in the book of the *a.* 11:41; *2 Chr* 9:5
the *a.* of Jehu, and all. *2 Ki* 10:34
according to all the *a.* he had. 23:19
the *a.* of Josiah and all that he. 28
the *a.* of David, first. *1 Chr* 29:29
behold the *a.* of Asa. *2 Chr* 16:11
the *a.* of Jehoshaphat, first. 20:34
a. of Hezekiah. 32:32; *2 Ki* 20:20
all the *a.* of his power. *Esth* 10:2
a. to the children of Israel. *Ps* 103:7
who can utter the mighty *a.* 106:2
declare thy mighty *a.* 145:4, 6, 12
praise him for his mighty *a.* 150:2

Adam

A. gave names to all cattle. *Gen* 2:20
and called their name *A.* 5:2
separated the sons of *A.* *Deut* 32:8
my transgressions as *A.* *Job* 31:33
death reigned from *A.* to. *Rom* 5:14
for as in *A.* all die. *1 Cor* 15:22
first man *A.* the last *A.* a. 45
for *A.* was first formed. *1 Tim* 2:13
and *A.* was not deceived, but. 14
Enoch the seventh from *A.* *Jude* 14

Adam

the city *A.* that is beside. *Josh* 3:16

adamant

a. have I made thy forehead.
Ezek 3:9
their hearts as an *a.* stone. *Zech* 7:12

Adar

finished on third day of *A.* *Ezra* 6:15
lot till the twelfth month *A.* *Esth* 3:7
13th day of month *A.* 13; 8:12
9:1, 17
gathered on the 14th day of *A.* 9:15
Jews made 14th day of *A.* a day. 19
14th and 15th days of *A.* yearly. 21

add

[1] *To join or put to,* Deut 4:2; Acts 2:41; 2 Pet 1:5. [2] *To increase,* Pr 16:23. [3] *To give, or bestow,* Gen 30:24; Mat 6:33.

a. to me another son. *Gen* 30:24
he shall *a.* a fifth part. *Lev* 5:16
6:5; 27:13, 15, 19, 27, 31; *Num* 5:7
to cities of refuge *a.* forty-two.
Num 35:6
not *a.* to the word. *Deut* 4:2; 12:32
thou shalt *a.* three cities. 19:9
to *a.* drunkenness to thirst. 29:19*
the Lord thy God *a.* to. *2 Sam* 24:3
I will *a.* to your yoke. *1 Ki* 12:11
14; *2 Chr* 10:14

I *a.* to thy days. *2 Ki* 20:6; *Isa* 38:5
mayest *a.* thereto. *1 Chr* 22:14
ye intend to *a.* more to. *2 Chr* 28:13
a. iniquity to their iniquity. *Ps* 69:27
peace shall they *a.* to thee. *Pr* 3:2
a. thou not to his words, lest. 30:6
a. ye year to year, let. *Isa* 29:1
that they may *a.* sin to sin. 30:1
a. one cubit to his. *Mat* 6:27
Luke 12:25
supposing to *a.* affliction. *Phil* 1:16*
this *a.* to your faith. *2 Pet* 1:5
any *a.* God shall *a.* to him. *Rev.* 22:18

added

voice, and he *a.* no more. *Deut* 5:22
a. to all our sins this. *1 Sam* 12:19
were *a.* besides many like words.
Jer 36:32
the Lord hath *a.* grief to my. 45:3
majesty was *a.* to me. *Dan* 4:36
a. to you. *Mat* 6:33; *Luke* 12:31
Herod *a.* yet this above. *Luke* 3:20
they heard, he *a.* and. 19:11
day there were *a.* 3000. *Acts* 2:41
the Lord *a.* to the church daily. 47
believers were the more *a.* to. 5:14
much people were *a.* to the. 11:24
somewhat, *a.* nothing to. *Gal* 2:6
a. because of transgressions. 3:19

adder

Dan shall be an *a.* in. *Gen* 49:17
they are like the deaf *a.* *Ps* 58:4
tread on the lion and *a.* 91:13
a. poison is under their lips. 140:3
last stingeth like an *a.* *Pr* 23:32

addeth

a. rebellion to his sin. *Job* 34:37
and he *a.* no sorrow. *Pr* 10:22
heart of the wise *a.* learning. 16:23
disannulleth or *a.* thereto. *Gal* 3:15

Addi

was the son of *A.* son. *Luke* 3:28

addicted

a. themselves to the. *1 Cor* 16:15*

additions

(*Revised Version,* wreaths)
certain *a.* were made. *1 Ki* 7:29
molten at the side of every *a.* 30
he graved cherubims, and *a.* 36

adjure

[1] *To bind under the penalty of a fearful curse,* Josh 6:26. [2] *To charge earnestly by word or oath,* 1 Ki 22:16; Mat 26:63.

how many times shall I *a.* thee to tell. *1 Ki* 22:16; *2 Chr* 18:15
I *a.* thee by the living. *Mat* 26:63
I *a.* thee by God, thou. *Mark* 5:7
we *a.* you by Jesus. *Acts* 19:13

adjured

Joshua *a.* them at that. *Josh* 6:26
for Saul had *a.* the. *1 Sam* 14:24

Admah

Shinab king of *A.* *Gen* 14:2
like the overthrow of *A.* *Deut* 29:23
shall I make thee as *A*? *Hos* 11:8

administered

(*Revised Version,* ministered)
a. by us to the glory of. *2 Cor* 8:19
in this abundance which is *a.* 20

administration, -s

(*Revised Version,* ministration)
are differences of *a.* *1 Cor* 12:5
for the *a.* of this service. *2 Cor* 9:12

admiration

having men's persons in *a.* *Jude* 16*
I wondered with great *a.* *Rev* 17:6*

admired

to be *a.* in all them. *2 Thes* 1:10*

admonish, -ed

who will no more be *a.* *Eccl* 4:13
by these, my son, be *a.* 12:12
that I have *a.* you. *Jer* 42:19
now past, Paul *a.* them. *Acts* 27:9
also to *a.* one another. *Rom* 15:14
a. one another in psalms. *Col* 3:16
you in Lord, and *a.* you. *1 Thes* 5:12
a. him as a brother. *2 Thes* 3:15
as Moses was *a.* of God. *Heb* 8:5

admonition

are written for our *a.* *1 Cor* 10:11
bring them up in the *a.* of. *Eph* 6:4
the first and second *a.* *Tit* 3:10

ado

why make ye this *a.*? *Mark* 5:39*

Adoni-Bezek

they found *A.* in Bezek. *Judg* 1:5

Adonijah

A. the son of. *2 Sam* 3:4; *1 Chr* 3:2
then *A.* exalted himself. *1 Ki* 1:5
hast thou not heard that *A.*? 11
God save the king *A.* 25
A. feared. 50, 51
let Abishag be given to *A.* 2:21
A. shall be put to death this day. 25
Joab had turned after *A.* though. 28
sent Levites to teach *A.* *2 Chr* 17:8
sealed, *A.* and Adin. *Neh* 10:16

Adonikam

the children of *A.*, 666. *Ezra* 2:13
Neh 7:18

adoption

[1] *A legal action by which a person takes into his family a child not his own, and usually of no kin to him, with the purpose of treating him as, and giving him all the privileges of, an own son. So Moses was adopted by Pharaoh's daughter,* Ex 2:10, *and Esther by Mordecai,* Esth 2:7, 15. *The custom was not common among the Jews, but was so among the Romans, with whom, as with us, an adopted child is legally entitled to all rights and privileges of a natural-born child.*

[2] *The custom, being well-known where Rome held sway, is used in the New Testament to refer:* (a) *to the choice by Jehovah of Israel to be his special people,* Rom 9:4; (b) *the special sense in which all true Christians are the sons of God,* Gal 4:5; Eph 1:4, 5; *and* (c) *the final redemption of the body,* Rom 8:23.

received the spirit of *a.* *Rom* 8:15
for the *a.* the redemption of 23
to whom pertaineth the *a.* 9:4
might receive the *a.* of sons. *Gal* 4:5
us to the *a.* of children. *Eph* 1:5

adorn, -ed, -eth, -ing

as a bride *a.* herself with. *Isa* 61:10
be again *a.* with tabrets. *Jer* 31:4
the temple was *a.* with. *Luke* 21:5
women *a.* in modest. *1 Tim* 2:9
a. the doctrine of God. *Tit* 2:10
whose *a.* let it not be that outward *a.*
1 Pet 3:3
women who trusted in God *a.* 5
a bride *a.* for her husband. *Rev* 21:2

Adrammelech

burnt children to *A.* *2 Ki* 17:31
A. and Sharezer. 19:37; *Isa* 37:38

Adramyttium

entering into a ship of *A.* *Acts* 27:2

Adria

driven up and down in *A.* *Acts* 27:27

Adriel

given unto *A.* to wife. *1 Sam* 18:19
she brought up for *A.* *2 Sam* 21:8

Adullam

the cave *A.* *1 Sam* 22:1; *1 Chr* 11:15
came to David to *A.* *2 Sam* 23:13
come to *A.* the glory of. *Mi* 1:15

adulterer, -s

a. shall surely be put. *Lev* 20:10
the eye of the *a.* waiteth. *Job* 24:15
been partaker with *a.* *Ps* 50:18
seed of *a.* and the whore. *Isa* 57:3
they be all *a.* an assembly. *Jer* 9:2
for the land is full of *a.* for. 23:10
they are all *a.* as an oven. *Hos* 7:4
swift witness against the *a.* *Mal* 3:5
others, extortioners, *a.* *Luke* 18:11
neither *a.* shall inherit. *1 Cor* 6:9
whoremongers and *a.* *Heb* 13:4
ye *a.* know ye not that the. *Jas* 4:4

adulteress, -es

a. shall surely be put. *Lev* 20:10
the *a.* will hunt for the. *Pr* 6:26
shall judge them as *a.* *Ezek* 23:45
love a woman, yet an *a.* *Hos* 3:1
she is no *a.* though she be. *Rom* 7:3

adulterous

way of an *a.* woman. *Pr* 30:20
an *a.* generation. *Mat* 12:39; 16:4
be ashamed in this *a.* *Mark* 8:38

adultery, -ies

[1] *Natural,* Mat 5:28; Mark 10: 11. [2] *Spiritual, which is idolatry,* Jer 3:9; Ezek 23:37.

thou shalt not commit *a.* *Ex* 20:14
Deut 5:18; Mat 5:27; 19:18
Rom 13:9
committeth *a.*, even he that committeth *a.* shall surely be. *Lev* 20:10
commits *a.* lacketh. *Pr* 6:32
Israel committed *a.* *Jer* 3:8
committed *a.* with stones and. 9
then they committed *a.* 5:7
steal, murder, and commit *a.* 7:9
I have seen thine *a.* and. 13:27
they commit *a.* and walk in. 23:14
they have committed *a.* 29:23
wife that committeth *a.* *Ezek* 16:32
have they committed *a.* 23:37
said I to her that was old in *a.* 43
put away her *a.* between. *Hos* 2:2
by lying and committing *a.* 4:2
your spouses shall commit *a.* 13
them when they commit *a.* 14
hath committed *a.* in. *Mat* 5:28
her that is divorced committeth *a.*
32; 19:9; *Luke* 16:18
heart proceed *a.* *Mat* 15:19
Mark 7:21
marry another, committeth *a.*
Mark 10:11; *Luke* 16:18
do not commit *a.* *Mark* 10:19
Luke 18:20; *Jas* 2:11
a woman taken in *a.* *John* 8:3, 4
should not commit *a.* *Rom* 2:22
the flesh are manifest, *a.* *Gal* 5:19
having eyes full of *a.* *2 Pet* 2:14
cast them that commit *a.* *Rev* 2:22

advanced

Lord that *a.* Moses. *1 Sam* 12:6*
Ahasuerus *a.* Haman the. *Esth* 3:1
told him how he had *a.* him. 5:11
whereto the king *a.* 10:2

advantage, -ed, -eth

what *a.* will it be to thee. *Job* 35:3
is a man *a.* if he gain. *Luke* 9:25
what *a.* then hath the Jew. *Rom* 3:1
a. it me if the dead? *1 Cor* 15:32
Satan should get an *a.* *2 Cor* 2:11
in admiration, because of *a.* *Jude* 16

adventure, -ed

not *a.* to set the sole. *Deut* 28:56
father sought and *a.* his. *Judg* 9:17
that he would not *a.* *Acts* 19:31

adversaries

lest their *a.* should. *Deut* 32:27
render vengeance to his *a.* 43
for us, or for our *a.*? *Josh* 5:13
the *a.* of the Lord. *1 Sam* 2:10
this day be *a.* to me. *2 Sam* 19:22
when *a.* of Judah and. *Ezra* 4:1
our *a.* said, they shall not. *Neh* 4:11
evil for good, are my *a.* *Ps* 38:20
mine *a.* are all before thee. 69:19
confounded that are *a.* to. 71:13
my hand against their *a.* 81:14
the right hand of his *a.* 89:42
for my love they are my *a.* 109:4
let this be the reward of my *a.* 20
let my *a.* be clothed with shame. 29
I will ease me of my *a.* *Isa* 1:24
shall set up the *a.* of Rezin. 9:11
the *a.* of Judah shall be. 11:13*
he will repay fury to his *a.* 59:18
our *a.* have trodden down. 63:18
thy name known to thine *a.* 64:2
all thine *a.* shall go into. *Jer* 30:16
he may avenge him of his *a.* 46:10
their *a.* said, we offend not. 50:7
her *a.* are the chief. *Lam* 1:5
the *a.* saw her, and did mock. 7
his *a.* should be round about him. 17
hath set up the horn of thine *a.* 2:17
shall be lifted up upon thy *a.* *Mi* 5:9
take vengeance on his *a.* *Nah* 1:2

all his *a.* were ashamed. *Luke* 13:17
your *a.* shall not be able. 21:15
and there are many *a.* *1 Cor* 16:9
terrified by your *a.* *Phil* 1:28
which shall devour the *a.* *Heb* 10:27

adversary

an *a.* to thine adversaries. *Ex* 23:22
an *a.* against Balaam. *Num* 22:22
her *a.* also provoked her. *1 Sam* 1:6*
in the battle he be an *a.* to us. 29:4
is neither *a.* nor evil. *1 Ki* 5:4
Lord stirred up an *a.* to 11:14, 23
was an *a.* to Israel all the days. 25
the *a.* and enemy is this. *Esth* 7:6
a. had written a book. *Job* 31:35
shall the *a.* reproach? *Ps* 74:10
who is mine *a.* let him. *Isa* 50:8
the *a.* hath spread out. *Lam* 1:10
with his right hand as an *a.* 2:4
the *a.* should have entered. 4:12
an *a.* shall be round. *Amos* 3:11
agree with thine *a.* quickly, lest at any time the *a.* deliver. *Mat* 5:25
goest with thine *a.* *Luke* 12:58
saying, avenge me of mine *a.* 18:3
no occasion to the *a.* *1 Tim* 5:14
a. the devil as a roaring. *1 Pet* 5:8

adversity, -ies

saved you out of all *a.* *1 Sam* 10:19
my soul out of all *a.* *2 Sam* 4:9
did vex them with all *a.* *2 Chr* 15:6
I shall never be in *a.* *Ps* 10:6
thou hast known my soul in *a.* 31:7
but in my *a.* they rejoiced. 35:15
rest from the days of *a.* 94:13
brother is born for *a.* *Pr* 17:17
if thou faint in day of *a.* 24:10
but in the day of *a.* *Eccl* 7:14
give you the bread of *a.* *Isa* 30:20
them which suffer *a.* *Heb* 13:3*

advertise (*To notify, or warn*)

I will *a.* thee, what. *Num* 24:14
I thought to *a.* thee. *Ruth* 4:4*

advice

take *a.* and speak your. *Judg* 19:30
give here your *a.* and counsel. 20:7
blessed be thy *a.* *1 Sam* 25:33*
that our *a.* should. *2 Sam* 19:43
what *a.* give ye, that. *2 Chr* 10:9
after the *a.* of young men. 14
king Amaziah took *a.* and. 25:17
with good *a.* make war. *Pr* 20:18
and herein I give my *a.* *2 Cor* 8:10

advise, -ed

a. and see. *2 Sam* 24:13; *1 Chr* 21:12
how do ye *a.* that. *1 Ki* 12:6
with the well-*a.* is wisdom. *Pr* 13:10
a. to depart thence also. *Acts* 27:12

advisement

the lords upon *a.* sent. *1 Chr* 12:19

advocate

we have an *a.* with. *1 John* 2:1

Æ.—(*For proper names beginning with Æ, see* E)

afar, *usually joined with* **off**

[1] *The distance between place and place,* Gen 37:18. [2] *Estrangement from another,* Ps 38:11.

saw the place *a. off.* *Gen* 22:4
brethren saw Joseph *a. off.* 37:18
and worship ye *a. off.* *Ex* 24:1
pitch the tabernacle *a. off.* 33:7
be in a journey *a. off.* *Num* 9:10
man of God saw her *a. off.* *2 Ki* 4:25
noise was heard *a. off.* *Ezra* 3:13
Jerusalem was heard *a. off.* *Neh* 12:43
my knowledge from *a.* *Job* 36:3
a man may behold it *a. off.* 25
and her eyes behold *a. off.* 39:29
them that are *a. off.* *Ps* 65:5
proud he knoweth *a. off.* 138:6
my thoughts *a. off.* 139:2
her food from *a.* *Pr* 31:14
shall carry her *a. off.* *Isa* 23:7
escape to the isles *a. off.* 66:19
and not a God *a. off*? *Jer* 23:23
save thee from *a.* 30:10; 46:27
declare it in the isles *a off.* 31:10
get you *a. off,* dwell. 49:30
remember the Lord *a. off.* 51:50
rebuke strong nations *a. off.* *Mi* 4:3
Peter followed him *a. off.* *Mat* 26:58
Mark 14:54; *Luke* 22:54
beholding *a. off.* *Mat* 27:55
Mark 15:40
saw Jesus *a. off,* he. *Mark* 5:6
and seeing a fig-tree *a. off.* 11:13
seeth Abraham *a. off.* *Luke* 16:23
to all that are *a. off.* *Acts* 2:39
preached peace to you which were *a. off,* and to them that. *Eph* 2:17
seen the promises *a. off.* *Heb* 11:13
and cannot see *a. off.* *2 Pet* 1:9

see **far, stand, stood**

affairs

to God, and *a.* of the. *1 Chr* 26:32
he will guide his *a.* *Ps* 112:5*
Shadrach over *a.* of the. *Dan* 2:49
Jews whom thou set over *a.* 3:12
ye also may know my *a.* *Eph* 6:21
that ye might know our *a.* 22*
I may hear of your *a.* *Phil* 1:27
himself with the *a.* of life. *2 Tim* 2:4

affect, -ed, -eth

mine eye *a.* my heart. *Lam* 3:51
minds evil *a.* against. *Acts* 14:2
a. you, that ye might *a.* *Gal* 4:17*
good to be zealously *a.* in a. 18*

affection

a. to the house of God. *1 Chr* 29:3
natural *a.* *Rom* 1:31; *2 Tim* 3:3
a. is more abundant. *2 Cor* 7:15
set your *a.* on things. *Col* 3:2*
fornication, inordinate *a.* 5

affectionately

so being *a.* desirous of. *1 Thes* 2:8

affectioned

kindly *a.* one to another. *Rom* 12:10

affections

gave them up to vile *a.* *Rom* 1:26
the flesh with the *a.* *Gal* 5:24

affinity

Solomon made *a.* with. *1 Ki* 3:1
Jehoshaphat joined in *a.* *2 Chr* 18:1
should we join in *a.* *Ezra* 9:14

affirm

To maintain the truth of a thing, Acts 25:19; Tit 3:8.

as some *a.* that we say. *Rom* 3:8
nor whereof they *a.* *1 Tim* 1:7
things I will that thou *a.* *Tit* 3:8

affirmed

an hour after another *a.* *Luke* 22:59
Rhoda constantly *a.* that. *Acts* 12:15
and of Jesus, whom Paul *a.* 25:19

afflict, -est

shall *a.* them 400 years. *Gen* 15:13
if thou shalt *a.* my daughters. 31:50
task-masters to *a.* them. *Ex* 1:11
ye shall not *a.* any widow. 22:22
if thou *a.* them in any wise, and. 23
ye shall *a.* your souls. *Lev* 16:29
31; 23:27, 32; *Num* 29:7
Chittim shall *a.* Ashur. *Num* 24:24
binding oath to *a.* the soul. 30:13
we bind him to *a.* him. *Judg* 16:5
mightest be bound to *a.* thee. 6
to *a.* him, and his strength went. 19
of wickedness *a.* them. *2 Sam* 7:10
will for this *a.* the seed. *1 Ki* 11:39
thou dost *a.* *2 Chr* 6:26; *1 Ki* 8:35
we might *a.* ourselves. *Ezra* 8:21*
Almighty, he will not *a.* *Job* 37:23
how thou didst *a.* the. *Ps* 44:2
God shall hear and *a.* them. 55:19*
son of wickedness *a.* him. 89:22
O Lord, they *a.* thine heritage. 94:5
all them that *a.* my soul. 143:12
did more grievously *a.* her. *Isa* 9:1*
the hand of them that *a.* thee. 51:23
day for a man to *a.* his soul? 58:5
O Lord, wilt thou *a.* us? 64:12
to destroy and to *a.* *Jer* 31:28
the Lord doth not *a.* *Lam* 3:33
they *a.* the just, they. *Amos* 5:12
shall *a.* you from Hemath. 6:14
have afflicted, I will *a.* *Nah* 1:12
will undo all that *a.* thee. *Zeph* 3:19

afflicted

more they *a.* the more. *Ex* 1:12
shall not be *a.* that day. *Lev* 23:29
hast thou *a.* thy? *Num* 11:11*
the Egyptians *a.* us. *Deut* 26:6
the Almighty hath *a.* me. *Ruth* 1:21
and the *a.* people thou. *2 Sam* 22:28
a. in all . . . my father was *a.* *1 Ki* 2:26
rejected Israel and *a.* *2 Ki* 17:20
to him that is *a.* pity. *Job* 6:14*
loosed my cord, and *a.* me. 30:11
heareth the cry of the *a.* 34:28
wilt save the *a.* people. *Ps* 18:27
affliction of the *a.* 22:24
me, for I am desolate and *a.* 25:16
do justice to the *a.* and needy. 82:3
hast *a.* me with all thy waves. 88:7
am *a.* and ready to die from my. 15
days wherein thou hast *a.* us. 90:15
of their iniquities, are *a.* 107:17
I was greatly *a.* 116:10
before I was *a.* 119:67
for me that I have been *a.* 71
thou in faithfulness hast *a.* me. 75
I am *a.* very much, quicken me. 107
they *a.* me from youth. 129:1, 2
maintain the cause of the *a.* 140:12
all the days of the *a.* are. *Pr* 15:15
oppress the *a.* in the gate. 22:22
hateth those that are *a.* 26:28*
pervert the judgment of the *a.* 31:5
when at first he lightly *a.* *Isa* 9:1*
Lord will have mercy on his *a.* 49:13
hear now this, thou *a.* and. 51:21
him smitten of God and *a.* 53:4
he was oppressed, and was *a.* 7
O thou *a.* tossed with. 54:11
have we *a.* our souls? 58:3
if thou satisfy the *a.* soul. 10
sons of them that *a.* thee. 60:14
in all their affliction he was *a.* 63:9
sigh, her virgins are *a.* *Lam* 1:4
prosper, for the Lord hath *a.* her. 5
wherewith the Lord hath *a.* me. 12
gather her that I have *a.* *Mi* 4:6
I have *a.* I will afflict. *Nah* 1:12
leave in thee an *a.* people. *Zeph* 3:12
deliver you up to be *a.* *Mat* 24:9*
whether we be *a.* it is for. *2 Cor* 1:6
she have relieved the *a.* *1 Tim* 5:10
being destitute, *a.* and. *Heb* 11:37
be *a.* and mourn, and. *Jas* 4:9
is any among you *a.*? let. 5:13*

affliction

[1] *Adversity, trouble, or distress,* Job 5:6; Jonah 2:2. [2] *Outward oppression,* Ex 3:7; 14:31; Mark 4:17; Heb 10:32. [3] *Correction from God.*

Lord hath heard thy *a.* *Gen* 16:11
hath looked upon my *a.* 29:32
God hath seen mine *a.* and. 31:42
fruitful in the land of *a.* 41:52
a. of my people. *Ex* 3:7; *Acts* 7:34
bring you out of the *a.* of. *Ex* 3:17
he had looked on their *a.* 4:31
eat even the bread of *a.* *Deut* 16:3
1 Ki 22:27; *2 Chr* 18:26
looked on our *a.* *Deut* 26:7
indeed look on my *a.* *1 Sam* 1:11
Lord will look on my *a.* *2 Sam* 16:12*
the Lord saw the *a.* *2 Ki* 14:26
cry to thee in our *a.* *2 Chr* 20:9
Manasseh was in *a.* and. 33:12*
remnant are in great *a.* *Neh* 1:3
didst see the *a.* of our fathers. 9:9
though *a.* cometh not forth. *Job* 5:6
confusion, see thou mine *a.* 10:15
the days of *a.* have taken. 30:16
the days of *a.* prevented me. 27
they be holden in cords of *a.* 36:8
he delivereth the poor in his *a.* 15
hast thou chosen rather than *a.* 21
my *a.* and pain, forgive. *Ps* 25:18
and forgettest our *a.* and. 44:24
thou laidst *a.* upon our loins. 66:11*
mourneth by reason of *a.* 88:9
he regarded their *a.* 106:44*
being bound in *a.* and iron. 107:10
they are brought low through *a.* 39*
he the poor on high from *a.* 41
this is my comfort in my *a.* 119:50
then have perished in mine *a.* 92
consider mine *a.* and deliver me. 153
give you water of *a.* *Isa* 30:20

thee in the furnace of a. Isa 48:10
in all their a. he was afflicted. 63:9
publisheth a. from mount. Jer 4:15*
thee well in the time of a. 15:11
my refuge in the day of a. 16:19
why criest thou for thine a.? 30:15*
Moab's calamity is near, and a. 48:16
captivity because of a. Lam 1:3
remembered in the days of her a. 7
O Lord, behold mine a. 9
I am the man that hath seen a. 3:1
remembering my a. and my. 19
in their a. they will seek. Hos 5:15
grieved for the a. of. Amos 6:6
have looked on their a. Ob 13
cried by reason of my a. Jonah 2:2
a. shall not rise up the. Nah 1:9
tents of Cushan in a. Hab 3:7
helped forward the a. Zech 1:15
or came in, because of a. 8:10*
pass through the sea with a. 10:11
when a. ariseth for the. Mark 4:17*
for in those days shall be a. 13:19*
a dearth, and great a. Acts 7:11
out of much a. I wrote. 2 Cor 2:4
our light a. which is but for. 4:17
how that in a great trial of a. 8:2
supposing to add a. to. Phil 1:16
with me in my a. 4:14
the word in much a. 1 Thes 1:6
over you in all our a. 3:7
to suffer a. with people. Heb 11:25
the fatherless in their a. Jas 1:27
for an example of suffering a. 5:10*

afflictions

many are the a. of. Ps. 34:19
David, and all his a. 132:1
him out of all his a. Acts 7:10
saying, that bonds and a. 20:23
in much patience, in a. 2 Cor 6:4
behind of the a. of Christ. Col 1:24
be moved by these a. 1 Thes 3:3
be partakers of the a. 2 Tim 1:8*
known the a. which came to. 3:11*
watch in all things, endure a. 4:5*
a great fight of a. Heb 10:32*
were made a gazing-stock by a. 33
same a. accomplished 1 Pet 5:9*

affording

garners full, a. all. Ps 144:13

affright, -ed

shalt not be a. at them. Deut 7:21
with a loud voice to a. 2 Chr 32:18
that went before were a. Job 18:20
at fear, and is not a. 39:22*
panted, fearfulness a. me. Isa 21:4
burnt, and men of war a. Jer 51:32
they were a. Mark 16:5*; Luke 24:37
be not a. ye seek Jesus. Mark 16:6*
the remnant were a. Rev 11:13

afoot

many ran a. thither out. Mark 6:33
minding himself to go a. Acts 20:13*

afore

a. Isaiah was gone out. 2 Ki 20:4
which withereth a. it. Ps 129:6
a. the harvest when the. Isa 18:5
a. he that was escaped. Ezek 33:22
which he had promised a. Rom 1:2
he had a. prepared unto glory. 9:23
mystery, as I wrote a. in. Eph 3:3

aforehand

come a. to anoint my. Mark 14:8

aforetime

and a. I was as a tabret. Job 17:6*
my people went down a. Isa 52:4
also shall be as a. Jer 30:20
his God, as he did a. Dan 6:10
brought him that a. John 9:13
things were written a. Rom 15:4

afraid

money, they were a. Gen 42:35
they were a. to come. Ex 34:30
make you a. Lev 26:6; Job 11:19
why not a. to speak? Num 12:8
people of whom thou art a.
Deut 7:19
whosoever is fearful and a. Judg 7:3
the Philistines were a. 1 Sam 4:7
Saul was yet the more a. of. 18:29
now wast thou not a. to 2 Sam 1:14
people have made me a. 2 Sam 14:15
come on him, and make him a. 17:2
men made me a. 22:5; Ps 18:4
they all made us a. saying. Neh 6:9
I am a. of all my sorrows. Job 9:28
none shall make thee a. 11:19
his excellency make you a.? 13:11
let not thy dread make me a. 21
anguish shall make him a. 15:24
terrors shall make him a. on. 18:11
when I remember, I am a. 21:6*
when I consider, I am a. 23:15
terror shall not make thee a. 33:7
a. as a grasshopper. 39:20*
himself, the mighty are a. 41:25
what time I am a. I will. Ps 56:3
that dwell are a. at thy tokens. 65:8
saw thee, and they were a. 77:16
make them a. with thy storm. 83:15
I am a. of thy judgments. 119:120
none shall make them a. Isa 17:2
Ezek 34:28; Mi 4:4; Zeph 3:13
the sinners in Zion are a. Isa 33:14
ends of the earth were a. 41:5*
of whom hast thou been a. 57:11
none shall make him a. Jer 30:10
yet they were not a. nor. 36:24
Zedekiah said, I am a. of 38:19
men, of whom thou art a. 39:17
made them a. Ezek 39:26; Nah 2:11
dream, which made me a. Dan 4:5
mariners were a. Jonah 1:5, 10
made them a. because of. Hab 2:17
mind, were a. Mark 5:15; Luke 8:35
understood not, and were a.
Mark 9:32
followed, they were a. 10:32
any thing, for they were a. 16:8
they being a. wondered. Luke 8:25
they were all a. of Saul. Acts 9:26
me saw the light, and were a. 22:9*
I am a. of you, lest I. Gal 4:11
not a. of the king's. Heb 11:23
are not a. with any. 1 Pet 3:6
are not a. to speak evil. 2 Pet 2:10*

be afraid

neither be a. of. Deut 1:29; 31:6
behold we be a. here in. 1 Sam 23:3
be a. out of close. 2 Sam 22:46*
Ps 18:45*
hired that I should be a. Neh 6:13
thou be a. of destruction. Job 5:21
be ye a. of the sword, for. 19:29
of whom shall I be a.? Ps 27:1
their fear, nor be a. Isa 8:12; 44:8
maketh mention, shall be a. 19:17
that thou shouldest be a. 51:12
which is evil, be a. Rom 13:4

not be afraid

not be a. of the face of. Deut 1:17
thou shalt not be a. 7:18; 18:22
I will not be a. of ten. Ps 3:6
I will not be a. what man can. 56:11
thou shalt not be a. for the. 91:5
he shall not be a. of evil. 112:7
is established, he shall not be a. 8
liest down, shalt not be a. Pr 3:24
will trust and not be a. Isa 12:2
will not be a. of their voice. 31:4
and people not be a. Amos 3:6
wilt thou then not be a.? Rom 13:3

be not afraid

be not a. of them. Deut 20:1
Josh 11:6; Neh 4:14; Jer 10:5
Ezek 2:6; Luke 12:4
Saul said, be not a. 1 Sam 28:13
go down, be not a. 2 Ki 1:15
be not a. when one is. Ps 49:16
be not a. of sudden fear. Pr 3:25
voice, lift it up, be not a. Isa 40:9
be not a. of their faces. Jer 1:8
son of man be not a. Ezek 2:6
it is I, be not a. Mat 14:27
Mark 6:50; John 6:20
arise, be not a. Mat 17:7
be not a. go tell my brethren. 28:10
saith to the ruler, be not a.
Mark 5:36
be not a. but speak, and. Acts 18:9
be not a. of their terror. 1 Pet 3:14

sore afraid

and men were sore a. Gen 20:8
marched, they were sore a. Ex 14:10
Moab was sore a. of. Num 22:3
therefore we were sore a. Josh 9:24
Goliath, and were sore a.
1 Sam 17:24
on the earth, and was sore a. 28:20
was sore a. 31:4; 1 Chr 10:4
sorrow, and was very sore a. Neh 2:2
say, for they were sore a. Mark 9:6
and they were sore a. Luke 2:9

was afraid

thy voice, and I was a. Gen 3:10
I laughed not, for she was a. 18:15
then Jacob was greatly a. and 32:7
Moses hid his face, was a. Ex 3:6
I was a. of the anger. Deut 9:19
midnight the man was a. Ruth 3:8
Saul was a. 1 Sam 18:12, 15*
Ahimelech was a. at the. 21:1*
host of Philistines, he was a. 28:5
David was a. 2 Sam 6:9; 1 Chr 13:12
not go, for he was a. 1 Chr 21:30
which I was a. of, is come. Job 3:25
I was a. and durst not shew. 32:6*
Urijah heard it, he was a. Jer 26:21
when he came, was a. Dan 8:17
thy speech, and was a. Hab 3:2
was a. before my name. Mal 2:5*
Joseph was a. to go. Mat 2:22
the wind boisterous, was a. 14:30
I was a. and hid thy talent. 25:25
heard, he was the more a. John 19:8
Cornelius looked, he was a. Acts 10:4

afresh

crucify the Son of God a. Heb 6:6

after

a. I am waxed old. Gen 18:12
three months a. it was told. 38:24
ye seek not a. your. Num 15:39
not go a. other gods. Deut 6:14
that before it, or a. Josh 10:14
turned again a. Saul. 1 Sam 15:31
a. whom is the king come out? a. a
dog. 24:14
and a. make for thee. 1 Ki 17:13
opened till a. the sabbath. Neh 13:19
thou inquirest a. mine. Job 10:6
cried a. them, as a. a thief. 30:5
give them a. the work of. Ps 28:4
that shall come a. Eccl 1:11
judge a. the sight of eyes. Isa 11:3
a. it shall return to the. Ezek 46:17*
shall walk a. the Lord. Hos 11:10
a. I am risen again, I. Mat 26:32
which had seen him a. Mark 16:14
so then a. the Lord had spoken. 19
on the second sabbath a. Luke 6:1*
a. a little while another. 22:58
space of an hour a. another. 59
he might bear it a. Jesus. 23:26
a. the sop Satan entered. John 13:27
space of three hours a. Acts 5:7
which was 430 years a. Gal 3:17
to those that a. should. 2 Pet 2:6*

after that

and a. that he will let. Ex 3:20
her a. that she is defiled. Deut 24:4
avenged, and a. that I. Judg 15:7
a. that God was intreated for.
2 Sam 21:14
a. that I have spoken, Job 21:3
and a. that they go to the. Eccl 9:3
a. that I was turned. Jer 31:19
a. that have no more. Luke 12:4
a. that thou shalt cut it. 13:9*
a. that which is lost, until he. 15:4
a. that shall they come. Acts 7:7
a. that he was seen of. 1 Cor 15:6
and a. that he must be. Rev 20:3

after this

a. this Abraham buried. Gen 23:19
a. this David enquired. 2 Sam 2:1
a. this I will return. Acts 15:16

afternoon

they tarried till a. and. Judg 19:8*

afterward, -s

a. he will let you go. Ex 11:1
a. shalt thou be gathered. Num 31:2
a. shall thy hands be. Judg 7:11
the sacrifice, a. they eat. 1 Sam 9:13
a. David's heart smote him. 24:5
and a. we will speak. Job 18:2
guide me, and a. receive. Ps 73:24

deceit is sweet, but a. Pr 20:17
prepare thy work, and a. 24:27
a. shall find more favour. 28:23
wise man keepeth it in till a. 29:11*
a. shall the children of. Hos 3:5
a. I will pour out my Spirit. Joel 2:28
a. an hungered. Mat 4:2; Luke 4:2
seen it, repented not a. Mat 21:32
a. Jesus findeth him in. John 5:14
but thou shalt follow me a. 13:36
a. they that are Christ's. 1 Cor 15:23
the faith that should a. Gal 3:23
would not a. have spoken. Heb 4:8
a. it yieldeth the peaceable. 12:11
a. when he would have inherited. 17
a. destroyed them that. Jude 5

Agabus
one of them, named A. Acts 11:28
a prophet named A. 21:10

Agag
shall be higher than A. Num 24:7
the people spared A. 1 Sam 15:9
Samuel hewed A. in pieces. 33

Agagite, *see* **Haman**

again
I will not a. curse, nor a. Gen 8:21
but they shall come hither a. 15:16
a. feed and keep thy flock. 30:31
Judah knew her a. no more. 38:26
I will see a. thy face no. Ex 10:29
ye shall see them a. no more. 14:13
surely bring it back to him a. 23:4
will yet a. leave them in. Num 32:15
circumcise a. the children. Josh 5:2
and a. whom should. 2 Sam 16:19
child came into him a. 1 Ki 17:22
shall yet a. take root. 2 Ki 19:30
a. break thy commandments. Ezra 9:14
if ye do so a. I will lay. Neh 13:21
man die, shall he live a.? Job 14:14
revive us a. that thy. Ps 85:6
a. they minished and. 107:39
that they rise not up a. 140:10
that go to her return a. Pr 2:19
deliver him, thou must do it a. 19:19
a. there be wicked men. Eccl. 8:14
thou never be found a. Ezek 26:21
will not a. pass by. Amos 7:8; 8:2
shall fall, and never rise up a. 8:14
choose Jerusalem a. Zech 2:12
this water shall thirst a. John 4:13
spirit of bondage a. to. Rom 8:15
rejoice in the Lord, a. I. Phil 4:4
a. I will be to him a. Heb 1:5
and a. I will put my trust in. 2:13
begotten us a. to a lively. 1 Pet 1:3
see **born, bring, brought, come, turn, turned.**

against
hand will be a. every. Gen 16:12
river's brink a. he come. Ex 7:15*
set my face a. Lev 20:3; Deut 29:20
Urijah made it a. king. 2 Ki 16:11
a. whom hast thou exalted. 19:22
have pronounced a. it. Jer 25:13
I am a. your pillows. Ezek 13:20
a. his father. Mat 10:35; Luke 12:53
not with me, is a. me. Mat 12:30
which shall be spoken a. Luke 2:34
a. him with 20,000 to. 14:31
cannot be spoken a. Acts 19:36*
sect is every where spoken a. 28:22
see **another, God, him, Jerusalem, Israel, Lord, me, over, thee, them, us, you.**

Agar
bondage, which is A. Gal 4:24
A. is mount Sinai in Arabia. 25

agate, -s
an a. an amethyst. Ex 28:19; 39:12
make thy windows of a. Isa 54:12
in thy fairs with a. Ezek 27:16*

age
[1] *The whole continuance of a man's life,* Gen 47:28. [2] *Times past, present, or to come,* Eph 2:7; 3:5.
the whole a. of Jacob. Gen 47:28
eyes of Israel were dim for a. 48:10
from the a. of 50 years. Num 8:25
die in the flower of their a. 1 Sam 2:33
were set by reason of a. 1 Ki 14:4
from the a. of 30. 1 Chr 23:3
from the a. of twenty years and. 24
that stooped for a. 2 Chr 36:17*
thy grave in a full a. Job 5:26
I pray thee, of the former a. 8:8
thy a. shall be clearer than. 11:17*
my a. is as nothing before. Ps 39:5
my a. is departed and. Isa 38:12†
man with his staff for a. Zech 8:4
a. of 12 years. Mark 5:42; Luke 8:42
was of a great a. Luke 2:36
to be about 30 years of a. 3:23
he is of a. ask him. John 9:21, 23
pass the flower of her a. 1 Cor 7:36
belongs to them of full a. Heb 5:14*
delivered when she was past a. 11:11
see **old, stricken**

aged
was a very a. man. 2 Sam 19:32
the understanding of a. Job 12:20
grey-headed and very a. men. 15:10
and the a. arose and stood up. 29:8
neither do the a. understand. 32:9
a. with him that is full. Jer 6:11
the a. men be sober, grave. Tit 2:2
the a. women, that they be. 3
such an one as Paul the a. Philem 9

ages
in the a. to come he might. Eph 2:7
in other a. was not made. 3:5*
in the church through all a. 21*
which hath been hid from a. Col 1:26

ago
were lost three days a. 1 Sam 9:20
heard long a. 2 Ki 19:25; Isa 37:26
builded many years a. Ezra 5:11
that fashioned it long a. Isa 22:11
repented long a. Mat 11:21
Luke 10:13
long a. since this came. Mark 9:21
4 days a. I was fasting. Acts 10:30
how that a good while a. 15:17
be forward a year a. 2 Cor 8:10
Achaia was ready a year a. 9:2
a man above fourteen years a. 12:2

agone
(Revised Version, ago)
three days a. I fell sick. 1 Sam 30:13

agony
being in an a. he prayed. Luke 22:44

agree, -ed, -eth
[1] *To bargain with,* Mat 20:2, 13. [2] *To approve, or give consent to,* Acts 5:40. [3] *To be like,* Mark 14:70. [4] *To conspire, or resolve,* John 9:22.
together except they be a. Amos 3:3
a. with thine adversary. Mat 5:25
if two of you shall a. on. 18:19
when he had a. with labourers. 20:2
not a. with me for a penny? 13
a. not together. Mark 14:56, 59
art a Galilean, and thy speech a. 70*
out of the new, a. not. Luke 5:36
Jews had a. already. John 9:22
is it that ye have a. to. Acts 5:9
to him they a. and when they. 40
to this a. the words of the. 15:15
Jews have a. to desire. 23:20
when they a. not among. 28:25
blood, these a. in one. 1 John 5:8
a. to give their kingdom. Rev 17:17

agreement
make an a. by a. 2 Ki 18:31
Isa 36:16*
said, with hell are we at a. Isa 28:15
your a. with hell shall not stand. 18
of the north, to make an a. Dan 11:6
what a. hath the temple. 2 Cor 6:16

Agrippa
A. and Bernice came to. Acts 25:13
A. said, I would also hear the. 22
specially before thee, O king A. 26
for which hope's sake, king A. 26:7
A. believest thou the prophets? 27
A. said, almost thou persuadest. 28

aground
met, they ran the ship a. Acts 27:41

ague
(Revised Version, fever)
terror and the burning a. Lev 26:16

Agur
the words of A. the son of. Pr 30:1

ah
nor say, a. so would. Ps 35:25*
a. sinful nation, a people. Isa. 1:4
a. I will ease me of mine. 24
said I, a. Lord God, I. Jer 1:6
a. Lord God, thou hast. 4:10
a. Lord God, the prophets. 14:13
a. brother, a. sister, a. Lord, a. 22:18
a. Lord, thou hast made the. 32:17
lament thee, saying, a. Lord. 34:5
a. Lord, my soul hath not. Ezek 4:14
a. Lord, wilt thou destroy the. 9:8
a. Lord, wilt thou make a full. 11:13
a. Lord, they say of me, doth. 20:49
a. the sword is made bright, it. 21:15
a. thou that destroyest. Mark 15:29*

aha
they said, a. our eye. Ps 35:21
desolate, that say unto me a. 40:15
turned back that say a. a. 70:3
a. I am warm, I have. Isa 44:16
a. against my sanctuary. Ezek. 25:3
because Tyrus hath said, a. 26:2
a. the ancient places are ours. 36:2

Ahab
A. did evil above all. 1 Ki 16:30
A. did more to provoke Lord. 33
Elijah, go shew thyself to A. 18:1
A. went one way, and Obadiah. 6
deliver me into the hand of A. 9
so A. went up to eat and to drink. 42
Elijah ran before A. to the. 46
there came a prophet to A. 20:13
A. came to his house heavy. 21:4
I will cut off from A. him that. 21
there was none like A. who did. 25
seest thou how A. humbleth. 29
persuade A. that he may go up and fall at? 22:20; 2 Chr 18:19
so A. slept with his fathers. 1 Ki 22:40
after death of A. 2 Ki 1:1; 3:5
Jeroboam walked as did the house of A. for the daughter of A. 8:18, 27
thou shalt smite the house of A. 9:7
for the whole house of A. shall. 8
when I and thou rode after A. 25
slew all that remained of A. 10:11
Manasseh did as A. king of. 21:3
the plummet of house of A. 13
of the house of A. 2 Chr. 21:13
saith the Lord of A. son. Jer 29:21
the Lord make thee like A. 22
works of the house of A. Mi 6:16

Ahasuerus
in the reign of A. wrote. Ezra 4:6
this is A. which reigned. Esth 1:1
Esther was taken unto king A. 2:16
to lay hand on the king A. 21; 6:2
in the name of A. was it. 3:12; 8:10
A. gave to Esther the house. 8:1
the Jew was next to king A. 10:3
first year of Darius son of A. Dan 9:1

Ahava
the river that runneth to A. Ezra 8:15
a fast at A. 21
then we departed from A. 31

Ahaz
A. was twenty years old when he began to. 2 Ki 16:2; 2 Chr 28:1
made an altar against A. 2 Ki 16:11
in the dial of A. 20:11; Isa 38:8
the altars of A. did Josiah. 2 Ki 23:12
Micah, Pithon, A. 1 Chr 8:35; 9:41
Judah low, because of A. 2 Chr 28:19
this is that king, A. 22
A. gathered vessels. 24
the vision in days of A. Isa 1:1
Hos 1:1; Mi 1:1
go forth to meet A. Isa 7:3
the Lord spake to A. 10

Ahaziah
A. reigned in. 1 Ki 22:40; 2 Ki 8:24
A. fell through a lattice. 2 Ki 1:2
A. king of Judah went down. 8:29
A. there is treachery, O A. 9:23

A. fled, and Jehu followed. *2 Ki* 9:27
we are the brethren of *A.* 10:13
did join with *A.* *2 Chr* 20:35
destruction of *A.* was of God. 22:7
house of *A.* had no power to keep. 9

Ahiah

A. son of Ahitub, the. *1 Sam* 14:3
Saul said to *A.* bring hither the. 18
Elihoreph and *A.* were. *1 Ki* 4:3

Ahijah

the prophet *A.* found. *1 Ki* 11:29
his saying, which the Lord spake by *A.* 12:15; *2 Chr* 10:15
there is *A.* which told me I. *1 Ki* 14:2
wife came to the house of *A.* 4
it was so, when *A.* heard the. 6
Baasha son of *A.* conspired 15:27
Jerahmeel, Hezron, *A.* *1 Chr* 2:25
David's valiant men, *A.* the. 11:36
over treasury of Levites *A.* 26:20
Solomon in prophecy of *A.* *2 Chr* 9:29
sealed the covenant, *A.* *Neh* 10:26

Ahikam

commanded *A.* the son of Shaphan. *2 Ki* 22:12; *2 Chr* 34:20
Gedaliah the son of *A.* *2 Ki* 25:22
the hand of *A.* was with. *Jer* 26:24
to Gedaliah the son of *A.* 40:6
***see* Gedaliah**

Ahimaaz

was the daughter of *A.* *1 Sam* 14:50
Jonathan and *A.* staid. *2 Sam* 17:17
is like the running of *A.* son. 18:27
A. was in Naphtali, he. *1 Ki* 4:15
begat Zadok, and Zadok *A.* *1 Chr* 6:8

Ahiman

A. was of the children. *Num* 13:22
Judah slew *A.* *Judg* 1:10
porters, *A.* *1 Chr* 9:17

Ahimelech

A. was afraid at the. *1 Sam* 21:1
the son of Jesse coming to *A.* 22:9
thou shalt surely die, *A.* 16
David said to *A.* who will go? 26:6
Zadok and *A.* priests. *2 Sam* 8:17
1 Chr 18:16
A. of the sons of Ithamar. *1 Chr* 24:3
scribe wrote them before *A.* 6
in the presence of David and *A.* 31

Ahinoam

Saul's wife was *A.* *1 Sam* 14:50
David also took *A.* of Jezreel. 25:43
***see* Abigail**

Ahio

A. drave the cart. *2 Sam* 6:3
1 Chr 13:7

Ahisamach

both he and the son of *A.* *Ex* 35:34

Ahithophel

Absalom sent for *A.* *2 Sam* 15:12
Lord, turn the counsel of *A.* into. 31
thou defeat the counsel of *A.* 34
to Jerusal, and *A.* with him. 16:15
counsel of *A.* was as if a man. 23
the counsel of *A.* is not good. 17:7
thus did *A.* counsel Absalom. 15
A. saw that his counsel was not. 23
A. was the king's. 1 *Chr* 27:33

Ahitub

hear now, thou son of *A.* *1 Sam* 22:12
son of *A.* *2 Sam* 8:17; *1 Chr* 18:16

Aholah, Aholibah

is *A.* Jerusalem Aholibah. *Ezek* 23:4
judge *A.* and Aholibah? 36

Aholiab

wrought Bezaleel and *A.* *Exod* 36:1

Aholibamah

Esau took to wife *A.* *Gen* 36:2
A. bare Jeush. 5

Ai, *or* Hai

between Beth-el and *A.* *Gen* 13:3
fled before the men of *A.* *Josh* 7:4
go up to *A.* 8:1
Gibeon was greater than *A.* 10:2
men of Beth-el and *A.* *Ezra* 2:28
Neh 7:32
howl, O Heshbon, for *A.* *Jer* 49:3

Aiath

he is come to *A.* he is. *Isa* 10:28

aided

a. him in the killing of. *Judg* 9:24

ailed, -eth

what *a.* thee, Hagar? *Gen* 21:17
to Micah, what *a.* thee? *Judg* 18:23
a. the people to weep? *1 Sam* 11:5
said, what *a.* *2 Sam* 14:5; *2 Ki* 6:28
what *a.* thee, O sea, that? *Ps* 114:5
what *a.* thee now, that. *Isa* 22:1

air

nor birds of the *a.* to. *2 Sam* 21:10
no *a.* can come between. *Job* 41:16
way of an eagle in the *a.* *Pr* 30:19
bird of the *a.* shall carry. *Eccl* 10:20
the birds of the *a.* have. *Mat.* 8:20*
the birds of the *a.* come and lodge in. 13:32*; *Mark* 4:32*; *Luke* 9:58*
they threw dust into the *a.* *Acts* 22:23
I, not as one that beateth the *a.* *1 Cor* 9:26
for ye shall speak into the *a.* 14:9
prince of the power of the *a.* *Eph* 2:2
meet the Lord in the *a.* *1 Thes* 4:17
the sun and the *a.* were. *Rev* 9:2
poured out his vial into the *a.* 16:17
***see* fowls**

Ajalon

moon, in the valley of *A.* *Josh* 10:12

alabaster

having an *a.* box. *Mat* 26:7
Mark 14:3

alarm

blow an *a.* then the. *Num* 10:5, 6
blow, but shall not sound an *a.* 7
go to war, then ye shall blow an *a.* 9
trumpets to cry an *a.* *2 Chr* 13:12
O my soul, the *a.* of war. *Jer* 4:19
day is come, I will cause an *a.* 49:2
sound an *a.* in my holy. *Joel* 2:1
a day of *a.* against the. *Zeph* 1:16

alas

Aaron said to Moses, *a.* *Num* 12:11
a. who shall live when God? 24:23
Joshua said, *a.* O Lord, *Josh* 7:7
a. because I have seen an. *Judg* 6:22
a. daughter, thou hast brought. 11:35
mourned over him, *a.* *1 Ki* 13:30
a. that the Lord hath. *2 Ki* 3:10
he cried *a.* master, for it was. 6:5
servant said, *a.* my master, how. 15
a. for that day is great. *Jer* 30:7
with thy foot, and say *a.* *Ezek* 6:11
a. for the day, for the. *Joel* 1:15
say in the highways, *a.* *Amos* 5:16
a. a. that great city, Babylon *Rev.* 18:10*, 16, 19*

albeit

the Lord saith, *a.* I have. *Ezek* 13:7
a. I say not, how thou. *Philem* 19

Alexander

Simon the father of *A.* *Mark* 15:21
Annas, Caiaphas, *A.* were. *Acts* 4:6
they drew *A.* out of the. 19:33
is Hymeneus and *A.* *1 Tim* 1:20
A. the copper smith did. *2 Tim* 4:14

Alexandria, -ans

of the Libertines and *A.* *Acts* 6:9
named Apollos, born at *A.* 18:24
centurion found a ship of *A.* 27:6

alien, -s

an *a.* in a strange land. *Ex* 18:3
mayest sell it to an *a.* *Deut* 14:21
I am an *a.* in their sight. *Job* 19:15
a. to my mother's children. *Ps* 69:8
sons of the *a.* shall be. *Isa* 61:5
houses are turned to *a.* *Lam* 5:2
a. from the commonwealth. *Eph* 2:12
flight the armies of *a.* *Heb* 11:34

alienate, -ed

her mind was *a.* from. *Ezek* 23:17
mind was *a.* from her as from. 18
from whom thy mind is *a.* 22, 28
they shall not *a.* the first fruits. 48:14
a. from the life of God. *Eph* 4:18
sometimes *a.* enemies. *Col* 1:21

alike

and clean eat *a.* *Deut* 12:22; 15:22
they shall part *a.* *1 Sam* 30:24
they shall lie down *a.* in. *Job* 21:26
fashioneth their hearts *a.* *Ps.* 33:15*
and light are both *a.* *Ps* 139:12
both are *a.* abomination to. *Pr* 20:10
a contentious woman are *a.* 27:15
all things come *a.* to all. *Eccl* 9:2
they both shall be *a.* good. 11:6
esteemeth every day *a.* *Rom* 14:5

alive

[1] *Naturally,* Gen 43:27. [2] *Supernaturally, being raised from the dead,* Luke 24:23. [3] *Spiritually,* Rom 6:11.

Noah only remained *a.* *Gen* 7:23
kill me, and save thee *a.* 12:12
day, to save much people *a.* 50:20
the men children *a.* *Ex* 1:17, 18
every daughter ye shall save *a.* 22
theft be found in his hand *a.* 22:4
Aaron's sons left *a.* *Lev* 10:16
command to take two birds *a.* 14:4
scapegoat shall be presented *a.* 16:10
are left *a.* of you, I will send. 26:36
they went down *a.* into. *Num* 16:33
Og, till there was none left *a.* 21:35
slain thee, and saved her *a.* 22:33
ye saved all the women *a.*? 31:15
are *a.* every one of you. *Deut* 4:4
who are all of us *a.* here this. 5:3
he might preserve us *a.* at. 6:24
a. nothing that breatheth. 20:16
and I make *a.* 32:39; *1 Sam* 2:6
will save *a.* my father. *Josh* 2:13
saved Rahab the harlot *a.* 6:25
the king of Ai they took *a.* 8:23
Lord hath kept me *a.* as he. 14:10
if ye had saved them *a.* I. *Judg* 8:19
which they had saved *a.* 21:14
Agag the king of Amalek *a.* *1 Sam* 15:8
left neither man nor woman *a.* 27:9
horses and mules *a.* *1 Ki* 18:5
peace or war take them *a.* 20:18
Naboth is not *a.* but dead. 21:15
God, to kill and make *a.*? *2 Ki* 5:7
if they save us *a.* we shall live. 7:4
out we shall catch them *a.* 12
a. and they took them *a.* 10:14
ten thousand left *a.* *2 Chr* 25:12
thou hast kept me *a.* *Ps* 30:3
let us swallow them up *a.* *Pr* 1:12
fatherless I will preserve *a.* *Jer* 49:11
will ye save the souls *a.*? *Ezek* 13:18
save the souls *a.* that should. 19
right, he shall save his soul *a.* 18:27
whom he would, he kept *a.* *Dan* 5:19
heard that he was *a.* *Mark* 16:11
was dead and is *a.* *Luke* 15:24, 32
angels who said he was *a.* 24:23
shewed himself *a.* after his. *Acts* 1:3
the widows, presented her *a.* 9:41
they brought the young man *a.* 20:12
whom Paul affirmed to be *a.* 25:19
a. to God through Christ. *Rom* 6:11
God, as those that are *a.* from. 13
for I was *a.* without the law. 7:9
so in Christ shall all be made *a.* *1 Cor* 15:22
are *a.* and remain. *1 Thes* 4:15, 17
and behold I am *a.* for. *Rev* 1:18
last, which was dead, and is *a.* 2:8
both cast *a.* into a lake of fire. 19:20

***keep* alive, *see* keep**

***yet* alive**

is your father *yet a.*? *Gen* 43:7
is he *yet a.*? 27
he is well, he is *yet a.* 28
saying, Joseph is *yet a.* 45:26, 28
die, because thou art *yet a.* 46:30
see whether they be *yet a.* *Ex* 4:18
I am *yet a.* with you. *Deut* 31:27
child was *yet a.* *2 Sam* 12:18; 21, 22
while he was *yet a.* in the. 18:14
is he *yet a.*? he is my. *1 Ki* 20:32
living which are *yet a.* *Eccl* 4:2
although they were *yet a.* *Ezek* 7:13
said, while he was yet *a.* *Mat* 27:63

all

surely die, thou and *a.* *Gen* 20:7
to him hath he given *a.* that. 24:36
Laban said, *a.* that thou. 31:43
Jacob loved Joseph more than *a.* 37:3

Lord made a. he did to. Gen 39:3
we are a. one man's sons, we. 42:11
lest thou and a. thou hast. 45:11
the God which fed me a. my. 48:15
earth, sea, and a. in them. Ex 20:11
I will make a. my goodness. 33:19
a. that come into the tent. Num 19:14
and shalt not see them a. 23:13
are a. of us here alive. Deut 5:3
days shalt thou labour and do a. 13
ye stand a. of you before the? 29:10
a. came to pass. Josh 21:45; 23:14
plague was on you a. 1 Sam 6:4
I will tell thee a. that is in. 9:19
Samuel said, are here a. thy? 16:11
and without fail recover a. 30:8
are a. that pertained to. 2 Sam 16:4
away dung till it be a. 1 Ki 14:10
Omri did worse than a. before. 16:25
lord, I am thine, and a. that. 20:4
the son of Uzzi, a. of. 1 Chr 7:3
is against a. that forsake. Ezra 8:22
thou preservest them a. and. Neh 9:6
comforters are ye a. Job 16:2
for they a. are the work of. 34:19
a. gone aside, a. become. Ps 14:3
a. my bones, they stare upon. 22:17
delivereth him out of them a. 34:19
Lord, a. my desire is before. 38:9
a. this is come upon us, yet. 44:17
mine adversaries are a. 69:19
these wait a. on thee, that. 104:27
they continue, for a. are thy. 119:91
cast in thy lot, let us a have. Pr 1:14
Lord is the maker of them a. 22:2
a. are of dust, a. turn to. Eccl 3:20
behold, see, we are a. thy. Isa 64:9
a. adulterers. Jer 9:2; Hos 7:4
a. of them mourning. Ezek 7:16
a. of them in the land shall. 20:40
king shall be king to them a. 37:22
son of man, declare a. that. 40:4
shew them a. the forms, a. the. 43:11
among them a. none. Dan 1:19
been a rebuker of them a. Hos 5:2
cut them in the head a. Amos 9:1
city, it is a. full of lies. Nah 3:1
have we not a. one Father. Mal 2:10
bring a. the tithes into the. 3:10*
pass from the law till a. Mat 5:18
sisters, are they not a. 13:56
she be, for they a. had her. 22:28
than a. burnt-offerings. Mark 12:33
cast in a. even a. 44; Luke 21:4
thou worship me, a. shall. Luke 4:7
looking round about on them a. 6:10
they were a. waiting for him. 8:40
except ye repent, ye shall a. 13:3
he said, son a. that I have is. 15:31
ye, when ye have done a. say. 17:10
sell a. that thou hast, and. 18:22
of his fulness have a. we. John 1:16
woman said, he told me a. 4:39
saith, ye are clean, but not a. 13:10
that they a. may be one, as. 17:21
grace was upon them a. Acts 4:33
we are a. here present before 10:33
he exhorted them a. to cleave. 11:23
do thyself no harm, we are a. 16:28
zealous towards God, as ye a. 22:3
but also a. that hear me this. 26:29
thanks in presence of them a. 27:35
through Jesus Christ for you a. Rom 1:8
delivered him up for us a. 8:32
a. are yours, and ye. 1 Cor 3:22
more abundantly than they a. 15:10
concluded a. under sin. Gal 3:22
but I have a. and abound. Phil 4:18
that they a. might be. 2 Thes 2:12
out of them a. the Lord. 2 Tim 3:11
they not a. ministering. Heb 1:14
chastisement, whereof a. are. 12:8
be ye a. of one mind. 1 Pet 3:8
that a. should come to. 2 Pet 3:9
that they were not a. of. 1 John 2:19

above **all**, *see* **above**

according to **all**

Noah did ac. to a. Gen 6:22; 7:5
according to a. the Lord. Ex 31:11
36:1; 39:32, 42; 40:16; Num 2:34
8:20; 9:5; 29:40; Deut 1:3, 41
took the land ac. to a. Josh 11:23
given rest ac. to a. that. 1 Ki 8:56
shalt reign ac. to a. that thy. 11:37
ac. to a. his father had done. 22:53
2 Ki 23:32, 37; 24:9, 19
2 Chr 26:4; 27:2
done ac. to a. that was. 2 Ki 10:30
ac. to a. David. 18:3; 2 Chr 29:2
ac. to a. these words, ac. to a. this. 1 Chr 17:15
think ... for good, ac. to a. Neh 5:19
ac. to a. his wondrous. Jer 21:2
ac. to a. that the Lord shall. 42:20
ac. to a. that Babylon hath. 50:29
ac. to a. that he hath. Ezek 24:24
ac. to a. thy righteousness. Dan 9:16

after **all**

not to do after a. their. Deut. 20:18
the word to do after a. 2 Chr 34:21
after a. that is come on. Ezra 9:13
after a. thy wickedness. Ezek 16:23
after a. these things do. Mat 6:32
for he longed after you a. Phil 2:26

at **all**

delivered thy people at a. Ex 5:23
afflict, and they cry at a. to. 22:23
if he will at a. redeem. Lev 27:13*
I now any power at a. Num 22:38
if thou do at a. forget. Deut 8:19*
if thy father at a. miss. 1 Sam 20:6
if ye shall at a. turn. 1 Ki 9:6*
not save them at a. Jer 11:12
mind shall not be at a. Ezek 20:32
most High, none at a. Hos 11:7
weep ye not at a. roll. Mi 1:10
Lord will not at a. acquit. Nah 1:3
have no power at a. John 19:11
his will was not at a. 1 Cor 16:12
him is no darkness at a. 1 John 1:5
be found no more at a. Rev 18:21
shall be heard no more at a. 22

before **all**

before a. that went in at. Gen 23:18
before a. the people I will. Lev 10:3
I have chosen before a. 2 Chr 33:7
an honour before a. Jer 33:9
denied before them a. Mat 26:70
to Peter before them a. Gal 2:14
sin rebuke before a. that. 1 Tim 5:20

for **all**

Levites for a. first-born. Num 8:18
for a. that do so. Deut 22:5; 25:16
hide my face in that day for a. 31:18
for a. his enemies, he. Ps 10:5
for a. this they sinned still. 78:32
what render to the Lord for a. 116:12
profit of the earth is for a. Eccl 5:9
for a. these God will bring thee. 11:9
hath received double for a. Isa 40:2
alas for a. the evil. Ezek 6:11
loathe yourselves for a. 20:43
and in it was meat for a. Dan 4:21
for a. the evils Herod. Luke 3:19
God of the living, for a. live. 20:38
for a. have sinned and. Rom 3:23
if one died for a. then. 2 Cor 5:14
for a. seek their own, not. Phil 2:21
himself a ransom for a. 1 Tim 2:6
for a. shall know me. Heb 8:11
the body of Christ once for a. 10:10

from **all**

redeemed me from a. Gen 48:16
be clean from a. your. Lev 16:30
and delivered me from a. Ps 34:4
from a. lands whither he. Jer 16:15
diverse from a. the beasts. Dan 7:7
seventh day from a. works. Heb 4:4

in **all**

in a. that Sarah hath said. Gen 21:12
God is with thee in a. that thou. 22
ye may prosper in a. Deut 29:9
obeyed my voice in a. Josh 22:2
thirty and seven in a. 2 Sam 23:39
thou mayest prosper in a. 1 Ki 2:3
afflicted in a. my father was. 26
Zerah, five of them in a. 1 Chr 2:6
just in a. that is brought. Neh 9:33
God is not in a. his. Ps 10:4
in a. thy ways acknowledge. Pr 3:6
nothing in a. his dominion. Isa 39:2
in a. their afflictions he was. 63:9
have done evil in a. they. Jer 38:9
in a. your doings your. Ezek 21:24
in a. my labours shall find. Hos 12:8
in a. in the ship 276 souls. Acts 27:37
in a. these more than. Rom 8:37
God worketh all in a. 1 Cor 12:6
that God may be all in a. 15:28
him that filleth all in a. Eph 1:23
but Christ is all and in a. Col 3:11
to be admired in a. 2 Thes 1:10
is honourable in a. Heb 13:4
as also in a. his epistles. 2 Pet 3:16

all *night*, *see* **night**

of **all**

took them wives of a. Gen 6:2
him tithes of a. 14:20; Heb 7:2
of a. that thou shalt give. Gen 28:22
nothing die of a. that is. Ex 9:4
not a word of a. which Josh 8:35
of a. I said to the. Judg 13:13
shall hands of a. with. 2 Sam 16:21
Jehu said, to which of a. 2 Ki 9:5
let nothing fail of a. thou. Esth 6:10
so are the paths of a. that. Job 8:13
he wanteth nothing of a. Eccl. 6:2
if they be ashamed of a. Ezek 43:11
you only have I known of a. Amos 3:2
be servant of a. Mark 9:35; 10:44
of a. which hath given. John 6:39
Christ, he is Lord of a. Acts 10:36
of a. judged of a. 1 Cor 14:24
heir, though he be lord of a. Gal 4:1
God who is Father of a. Eph. 4:6
to God the Judge of a. Heb 12:23
one point, he is guilty of a. Jas 2:10

on or *upon* **all**

of the Lord was upon a. Gen 39:5
for upon a. the glory shall. Isa 4:5
set thy heart upon a. that. Ezek 40:4
unto all, and upon a. them. Rom 3:22
might have mercy upon a. 11:32
execute judgment upon a. Jude 15
temptation shall come upon a. Rev 3:10

over **all**

mayest reign over a. 2 Sam 3:21
and thou reignest over a. 1 Chr 29:12
kingdom ruleth over a. Ps 103:19
ruler over a. Mat 24:47; Luke 12:44
given him power over a. John 17:2
who is over a. God blessed. Rom 9:5
the same Lord over a. is rich. 10:12

all, *that he had*

him and a. that he had. Gen 12:20
of Egypt, and a. that he had. 13:1
Abraham gave a. that he had. 25:5
Jacob fled with a. that he had. 31:21
a. that he had he put into. 39:4
Lord was on a. that he had. 5
sold, a. that he had. Mat 18:25
spent a. that she had. Mark 5:26
cast in a. that she had. 12:44
Luke 21:4

all *these*

he took to him a. these. Gen 15:10
Jacob said, a. these things. 42:36
a. these are the twelve tribes. 49:28
God spake a. these words. Ex. 20:1
not that in a. these. Job 12:9
for a. these nations are. Jer 9:26
shall not a. these take. Hab 2:6
a. these shall. Mat 6:33; Luke 12:31
a. these are the beginning. Mat 24:8
a. these evil things. Mark 7:23
are not a. these which. Acts 2:7
a. these worketh that. 1 Cor 12:11
now you put off a. these. Col 3:8
a. these died in faith, not. Heb 11:13

all *the while*

a. the while David. 1 Sam 22:4
nothing missing a. the while. 25:7
manner a the while he. 27:11
a. the while my breath is. Job 27:3*

all *this*

hath shewed thee a. this. Gen 41:39
Lord hath not done a. this. Deut 32:27
is a. this befallen us? Judg 6:13
knew nothing of a. this. 1 Sam 22:15
hand of Joab in a. this? 2 Sam 14:19
a. this the Lord made. 1 Chr 28:19
after a. this the Lord. 2 Chr 21:18
a. this continued till the. 29:28
a. this was a burnt-. Ezra 8:35

because of a. this we. Neh 9:38
yet a. this availeth me. Esth 5:13
a. this Job sinned. Job 1:22; 2:10
lo, mine eye hath seen a. this. 13:1
a. this is come upon us, yet. Ps 44:17
for a. this they sinned still. 78:32
a. this have I proved by. Eccl 7:23
a. this have I seen, and applied. 8:9
a. this I considered in my heart, to declare a. this. 9:1
for a. this his anger is not. Isa 5:25
9:12, 17, 21; 10:4
thou hast heard, see a. this. 48:6
a. this came upon. Dan 4:28
though thou knewest a. this. 5:22
asked him the truth of a. this. 7:16
nor seek him for a. this. Hos 7:10
of Jacob is a. this. Mi 1:5
a. this was done that the prophets might be. Mat 1:22; 21:4; 26:56
a. this there is a gulf. Luke 16:26
besides a. this to-day is. 24:21

to or unto all

the Lord is good to a. and. Ps 145:9
event happeneth to a. Eccl 2:14
9:3, 11
things come alike to a. one. 9:2
so is Pharaoh to a. that. Isa 36:6
I say unto a. watch. Mark 13:37
to us, or even to a.? Luke 12:41
the promise is to a. that. Acts 2:39
manifest to a. that dwell in. 4:16
Lord is rich unto a. that. Rom 10:12
render therefore to a. their. 13:7
myself a servant unto a. 1 Cor 9:19
profiting may appear to a. 1 Tim 4:15

with all

with a. that appertain. Num 16:30
Lord with a. thy heart, with a. thy.
Deut 6:5; 11:13; Mat 22:37
with a. the children of. 2 Chr 25:7
with a. thy getting, get. Pr 4:7
feared God with a. Acts 10:2; 16:34
with a. that in every place. 1 Cor 1:2
and continue with you a. Phil 1:25
I joy and rejoice with you a. 2:17

all ye

a. ye assemble yourselves. Isa 48:14
behold a. ye that kindle a. 50:11
be glad with her, a. ye that. 66:10
hear the word, a. ye of. Jer 29:20
it nothing to you, a. ye? Lam 1:12
come to me, a. ye that. Mat 11:28
one is your master; and a. ye. 23:8
a. ye shall be. 26:31; Mark 14:27
a. ye that dwell at. Acts 2:14
see further other usual substantives: **congregation, day, earth, Israel, men, people, things**, etc.

alleging

a. Christ must needs. Acts 17:3

allegory

which things are an a. for. Gal 4:24

alleluiah

(Revised Version, hallelujah)
I heard a great voice, saying, a.
Rev 19:1, 3, 4, 6

allied

Eliashib the priest was a. Neh 13:4

allow

that ye a. the deeds. Luke 11:48*
they themselves also a. Acts 24:15*
that which I do, I a. not. Rom 7:15*

allowance

his a. was a continual a. 2 Ki 25:30

allowed, -eth

(Revised Version, approved, -eth)
that thing which he a. Rom 14:22
but as we were a. of. 1 Thes 2:4

allure

I will a. and bring her into. Hos 2:14
they a. through the lusts. 2 Pet 2:18

almighty

I am the a. God, walk. Gen 17:1
God a. bless thee, and make. 28:3
I am God a. be fruitful and. 35:11
God a give you mercy before. 43:14
God a. appeared to me at Luz. 48:3
by the a. who shall bless thee. 49:25
Abram by the name God a. Ex 6:3
the vision of the a. Num 24:4, 16
for the a. hath dealt. Ruth 1:20
seeing the a. hath afflicted me. 21
the chastening of the a. Job 5:17
for the arrows of the a. are. 6:4
he forsaketh the fear of the a. 14
or doth the a. pervert justice? 8:3
make thy supplication to the a. 5
canst thou find out the a.? 11:7
surely I would speak to the a. 13:3
himself against the a. 15:25
what is the a. that we? 21:15
drink of the wrath of the a. 20
is it any pleasure to the a.? 22:3
which said, what can the a. do? 17
if thou return to the a. thou shalt. 23
yea, the a. shall be thy defence. 25
thou have thy delight in the a. 26
my heart soft, and the a. 23:16
times are not hid from the a. 24:1
and the a. who hath vexed my. 27:2
will he delight himself in the a.? 10
with the a. will I not conceal. 11
which they shall receive of the a. 13
when the a. was yet with me. 29:5
what inheritance of the a.? 31:2
my desire is, that the a. would. 35
inspiration of the a. giveth. 32:8
and the breath of the a. hath. 33:4
far be it from the a. to. 34:10
neither will the a. pervert. 12
the a. will not regard vanity. 35:13
touching the a. we cannot. 37:23
contendeth with the a. instruct. 40:2
when the a. scattered. Ps 68:14
under the shadow of the a. 91:1
as destruction from the a. Isa 13:6
the voice of the a. Ezek 1:24; 10:5
as destruction from the a. Joel 1:15
sons, saith the Lord a. 2 Cor 6:18
was, and is to come, the a. Rev 1:8
Lord God a. which was. 4:8; 11:17
Lord a. just and true are. 15:3; 16:7
of that great day of God a. 16:14
wine-press of wrath of the a. 19:15
God a. and the Lamb are. 21:22

almond, -s

spices, myrrh, nuts, and a. Gen 43:11
made like to a. Ex 25:33*, 34*
37:19, 20*
Aaron for Levi yielded a. Num 17:8
when the a. tree shall. Eccl 12:5
I see a rod of an a. tree. Jer 1:11

almost

they be a. ready to stone. Ex 17:4
me, my feet were a. gone. Ps 73:2
soul had a. dwelt in silence. 94:17*
they had a. consumed me. 119:87
I was a. in all evil in the. Pr 5:14*
came a. the whole city. Acts 13:44
only at Ephesus, but a. 19:26
seven days were a. ended. 21:27
a. thou persuadest me to. 26:28*
were both a. and altogether. 29*
a. all things by the law. Heb 9:22

alms

that ye do not your a. Mat 6:1*
therefore when thou doest thine a. 2*
that thine a. may be in secret, and. 4
give a. of such things. Luke 11:41
sell that ye have, and give a. 12:33
they laid, to ask a. of. Acts 3:2
seeing Peter and John, asked an a. 3
that it was he which sat for a. 10
Cornelius gave much a. to the. 10:2
a. are come up for a memorial. 4, 31
I came to bring a. to my. 24:17

almsdeeds

Dorcas full of a. which. Acts 9:36

almug-trees

Ophir plenty of a.-trees. 1 Ki 10:11
a.-tree pillars, there came no such a.-trees. 12

aloes

thy garments smell of a. Ps 45:8
perfumed my bed with a. Pr 7:17
myrrh, a. with all the. S of S 4:14
brought a mixture of a. John 19:39

alone

that man should be a. Gen 2:18
perform it thyself a. Ex 18:18
Moses a. shall come near. Ex 24:2
leper dwell a. without. Lev 13:46
to bear all this people a. Num 11:14
Deut 1:9, 12
thou bear it not thyself a. Num 11:17
the people shall dwell a. not. 23:9
so the Lord a. did lead. Deut 32:12
then shall dwell in safety a. 33:28*
Achan perished not a. Josh 22:20
a man running a. 2 Sam 18:24, 26
if he be a. there is tidings in his. 25
they two were a. in. 1 Ki 11:29
art the God a. 2 Ki 19:15; Isa 37:16
Ps 86:10
Solomon, whom a. God. 1 Chr 29:1
lay hands on Mordecai a. Esth 3:6
escaped a. to tell. Job 1:15, 16, 17, 19
God who a. spreadeth out the. 9:8
to whom a. the earth was. 15:19
eaten my morsel myself a.? 31:17
thou whose name a. is. Ps 83:18
watch and am as a sparrow a. 102:7
who a. doth great wonders. 136:4
for his name a. is excellent. 148:13
is one a. and there is not. Eccl 4:8
but woe to him that is a. when he. 10
Lord a. shall be exalted. Isa 2:11, 17
none shall be a. in his. 14:31*
I called him a. and blessed. 51:2*
have trodden the wine-press a. 63:3
he sitteth a. and keepeth. Lam 3:28
I Daniel a. saw the vision. Dan 10:7
to Assyria, a wild ass a. Hos 8:9
live by bread a. Mat 4:4; Luke 4:4
come, he was a. Mat 14:23
Luke 9:18
between thee and him a. Mat 18:15
when they were a. he. Mark 4:34
was in midst of sea, and he a. 6:47
forgive sins but God a.? Luke 5:21
to eat, but for the priests a. 6:4
came to pass, as Jesus was a. 9:18
voice was past, Jesus was found a. 36
sister hath left me to serve a. 10:40
into a mountain a. John 6:15
disciples were gone away a. 22
for I am not a. but I. 8:16; 16:32
neither pray I for these a. 17:20
and hear that not a. Acts 19:26
written for his sake a. Rom 4:23
have rejoicing in himself a. Gal 6:4
went the high-priest a. Heb 9:7
not works is dead, being a. Jas 2:17*

left alone

Jacob left a. and there. Gen 32:24
dead, and he is left a. 42:38*; 44:20
I was left a. these where. Isa 49:21
I was left a. and saw this. Dan 10:8
and Jesus was left a. John 8:9
the Father hath not left me a. for. 29
I am left a. and they. Rom 11:3

let alone

let us a. that we may serve. Ex 14:12
let me a. that my wrath may. 32:10
let me a. that I may. Deut 9:14
let me a. two months. Judg 11:37
let him a. let him curse. 2 Sam 16:11
let her a. her soul is. 2 Ki 4:27
let the work of this . . . a. Ezra 6:7
let me a. that I may. Job 10:20
hold your peace let me a. that. 13:13
joined to idols, let him a. Hos 4:17
let them a. they be blind. Mat 15:14
let us a. what have we to do with thee? Mark 1:24*; Luke 4:34*
Jesus said, let her a. why? Mark 14:6
let a. let us see whether. 15:36*
Lord, let it a. this year. Luke 13:8
if we let him a. all men. John 11:48
let her a. against the day of my. 12:7*
from these men, let them a. Acts 5:38

along

will go a. by the king's. Num 21:22
kine went a. the highway. 1 Sam 6:12
then Saul fell all a. on the. 28:20*
went with her a. 2 Sam 3:16*
Shimei went a. cursing, and. 16:13
went, weeping all a. Jer 41:6

aloof

my friends stand a. from. Ps 38:11

aloud, see **cry, cried, sing**

Alpha
A. and Omega. Rev 1:8; 21:6; 22:13

Alpheus
James the son of A. Mat 10:3
Mark 3:18; Luke 6:15; Acts 1:13
he saw Levi the son of A. Mark 2:14

already
Joseph was in Egypt a. Ex 1:5
it hath been a. of old. Eccl 1:10
I have cursed them a. Mal 2:2
unto you, Elias is come a. Mat 17:12
not is condemned a. John 3:18
in spirit, have judged a. 1 Cor 5:3
whereto we have a. Phil 3:16
are a. turned aside. 1 Tim 5:15
but that which ye have a. Rev 2:25

also
man, for that he a. is flesh. Gen 6:3
ye the priesthood a.? Num 16:10
Saul answered, God do so and more
a. 1 Sam 14:44; 2 Sam 3:35; 19:13
if we sit still here, we die a. 2 Ki 7:4
yea, for the rebellious a. Ps 68:18
ye weary my God a.? Isa 7:13
of hosts I will go a. Zech 8:21
heart be a. Mat 6:21; Luke 12:34
surely thou art a. one of. Mat 26:73
I may preach there a. Mark 1:38
Son of man is Lord a. 2:28*
Luke 6:5*
thou reproachest us a. Luke 11:45
what he doth, these a. John 5:19
where I am, there shall a. 12:26
where I am, there ye may be a. 14:3
proceeded to take Peter a. Acts 12:3
many, and of myself a. Rom 16:2*
not the law the same a. 1 Cor 9:8
last of all, he was seen of me a. 15:8
persuaded that in thee a. 2 Tim 1:5
without works is dead, a. Jas 2:26
God, love his brother a. 1 John 4:21

altar
Literally, any structure on which sacrifices were offered. In speaking of spiritual worship the word is used figuratively as a symbol easily understood by both Jew and Gentile, 2 Ki 18:22.
Noah builded an a. to. Gen 8:20
Abraham built an a. to. 12:7; 22:9
Beth-el, and make there an a. 35:1
Beth-el, I will make there an a. 3
built an a. Jehovah-nissi. Ex 17:15
an a. of earth shalt thou make. 20:24
shalt take him from mine a. 21:14
sanctify it, it shall be an a. 29:37
sanctify the tabernacle and a. 44
a. of incense. 30:27
a. of burnt-offering. 40:10
the fire of the a. shall. Lev 6:9
the dedication of the a. Num 7:84
they shall not come nigh the a. 18:3
of Gad called the a. Ed. Josh 22:34
throw down the a. of Baal. Judg 6:25
because one hath cast down his a. 31
not cut off mine a. 1 Sam 2:33
go up, rear an a. to the. 2 Sam 24:18
against the a. O. a. a. 1 Ki 13:2
Elijah repaired the a. of the. 18:30
and the water ran about the a. 35
before this a. 2 Ki 18:22; Isa 36:7
so will I compass thine a. Ps 26:6
will I go to the a. of God, to. 43:4
a. to the Lord in the. Isa 19:19
stones of the a. as chalk-stones. 27:9
sacrifices be accepted on mine a. 56:7
Lord hath cast off his a. Lam 2:7
the porch and a. 25 men. Ezek 8:16
howl, ye ministers of the a. Joel 1:13
weep between the porch and a. 2:17
to pledge by every a. Amos 2:8
polluted bread on mine a. Mal 1:7
nor do kindle fire on mine a. 10
covering the a. of the Lord. 2:13
thou bring thy gift to the a. Mat 5:23
whoso shall swear by the a. 23:18
the temple and a. 35; Luke 11:51
I found an a. with this. Acts 17:23
the a. partakers with a. 1 Cor 9:13
10:18
gave attendance at the a. Heb 7:13
we have an a. whereof they. 13:10

I saw under the a. the. Rev 6:9
it with prayers on the golden a. 8:3
voice from horns of the golden a. 9:13
see **built**

altars
shall destroy their a. Ex 34:13
Deut 7:5; 12:3
build here seven a. Num 23:1
thrown down thine a. 1 Ki 19:10, 14
bones of priests on the a. 2 Chr 34:5
thine a. O Lord of hosts. Ps 84:3
he shall not look to the a. Isa 17:8
graven on horns of the a. Jer 17:1
their children remember their a. 2
your a. shall be desolate. Ezek 6:4
made a. to sin, a. shall be. Hos 8:11
thistle shall come on their a. 10:8
a. are as heaps in the furrows. 12:11
I will also visit the a. of. Amos 3:14
digged down thine a. Rom 11:3

alter
he shall not a. it, a good. Lev 27:10
that whosoever shall a. Ezra 6:11
all that put their hand to a. this. 12
nor a. the thing gone out. Ps 89:34

altered
be not a. that Vashti. Esth 1:19
his countenance was a. Luke 9:29

altereth
the law which a. not. Dan 6:8, 12

although
a. that was near, for God. Ex 13:17
a. my house be not so. 2 Sam 23:5*
a. thou movedst me. Job 2:3
a. I was an husband unto. Jer 31:32
a. I have cast them far. Ezek 11:16*
a. the fig-tree shall not. Hab 3:17
a. all shall be offended. Mark 14:29

altogether
make thyself a. a. Num 16:13*
which is a. just shalt. Deut 16:20
are a. become filthy. Ps 14:3; 53:3
of the Lord are righteous a. 19:9
man at his best state is a. 39:5
that I was a. such a one as. 50:21
O Lord, thou knowest it a. 139:4
sweet, yea, he is a. S of S 5:16
thou wast a. born in. John 9:34
almost and a. such as. Acts 26:29*
a. with the fornicators. 1 Cor 5:10†
or saith he it a. for our sakes? 9:10

alway, always
keep my commands a. Deut 5:29
keep his commandments a. 11:1
learn to fear the Lord a. 14:23
it, I would not live a. Job 7:16
will he a. call upon God? 27:10*
I have set the Lord a. Ps 16:8
he will not a. chide, nor keep. 103:9
to perform thy statutes a. 119:112*
I was by him, rejoicing a. Pr 8:30
neither will I be a. wroth. Isa 57:16
I am with you a. to the. Mat 28:20
ye have not a. Mark 14:7; John 12:8
I do a. those things. John 8:29
I know that thou hearest me a. 11:42
Cornelius prayed to God a. Acts 10:2
God, who a. causeth us. 2 Cor 2:14
a. in every prayer of. Phil 1:4
as a. so now also, Christ shall. 20
as ye have a. obeyed, not. 2:12
rejoice in the Lord a. and. 4:4
to fill up their sins a. 1 Thes 2:16
a. in remembrance. 2 Pet 1:15*

am I
am I my brother's keeper? Gen 4:9
am I in God's stead, who? 30:2
am I God, to kill and? 2 Ki 5:7
am I come up. 18:25; Isa 36:10
am I a God at hand. Jer 23:23
there am I in the midst. Mat 18:20
yet a little while am I. John 7:33
am I not an apostle? am I not free?
1 Cor 9:1
weak, then am I strong. 2 Cor 12:10

I am
amongst whom I am. Num 11:21
there that being as I am. Neh 6:11
he is not a man as I am. Job 9:32
say to my soul, I am thy. Ps 35:3
I may know how frail I am. 39:4

O Israel, I am God, even. Ps 50:7
destroy them, for I am thy. 143:12
I am the first, I am the. Isa 44:6
48:12
I am, and none. 47:8; Zeph 2:15
and he shall say, here I am. Isa 58:9
men say that I the Son of man am?
Mat 16:13; Mark 8:27; Luke 9:18
God, ye say that I am. Luke 22:70
Jesus said, I am the bread. John 6:35
I am the light of the world. 8:12
before Abraham was, I am. 58
where I am there shall my. 12:26
may be with me where I am. 17:24
altogether such as I am. Acts 26:29
angel of God, whose I am, and. 27:23
I am what I am. 1 Cor 15:10
as I am, for I am. Gal 4:12
learned in what state I am. Phil 4:11
I am he that liveth, I am. Rev 1:18
see thou do it not, I am thy. 19:10

I am that I am
I am that I am hath sent. Ex 3:14

here am I, or here I am, see here

Amalek
to Eliphas Esau's son A. Gen 36:12
then came A. and fought. Ex 17:8
out the remembrance of A. 14
sworn he will have war with A. 16
when he looked on A. . . . parable and
said, A. was. Num 24:20
what A. did. Deut 25:17; 1 Sam 15:2
the remembrance of A. Deut 25:19
was a root against A. Judg 5:14
smite A. 1 Sam 15:3
Saul came to the city of A. 5
not execute his wrath on A. 28:18
Gebal, Ammon, A. are. Ps 83:7

Amalekite, -s
the A. came down and. Num 14:45
Israel had sown the A. Judg 6:3
Midianites and A. lay like. 7:12
the A. did oppress you, and. 10:12
Saul smote the A. 1 Sam 14:48; 15:7
get you from among A. 15:6
I have utterly destroyed the A. 20
and his men invaded the A. 27:8
the A. had invaded the south. 30:1
from the slaughter of A. 2 Sam 1:1
answered him, I am an A. 8, 13
smote the rest of the A. 1 Chr 4:43

Amana
look from the top of A. S of S 4:8

Amasa
Absalom made A. captain of the host,
which A. was the. 2 Sam 17:25
Joab took A. by the beard to. 20:9
A. wallowed in blood in the. 12
what Joab did to A. 1 Ki 2:5, 32
Abigail bare A. the. 1 Chr 2:17
A. son of Hadlai stood. 2 Chr 28:12

amazed
of Benjamin were a. Judg 20:41*
were a. they answered. Job 32:15
be a. one at another. Isa 13:8
many people a. at thee. Ezek 32:10
were exceedingly a. Mat 19:25
all a. and glorified God. Mark 2:12
Luke 5:26
began to be sore a. and. Mark 14:33
all a. and spake among. Luke 4:36
were all a. at the mighty. 9:43
that heard Saul were a. Acts 9:21

amazement
filled with a. at what had. Acts 3:10
are not afraid with any a. 1 Pet 3:6*

Amaziah
A. his son reigned. 2 Ki 12:21
2 Chr 24:27
fought against A. 2 Ki 13:12; 14:15
A. would not hear, therefore. 14:11
father A. had done. 15:3; 2 Chr 26:4
of Merari, A. the son. 1 Chr 6:45
after A. did turn from. 2 Chr 25:27
A. priest of Beth-el sent. Amos 7:10

ambassador
but a faithful a. is health. Pr 13:17
an a. sent to the heathen. Jer 49:14
Ob 1
which I am an a. in bonds. Eph 6:20

ambassadors
as if they had been *a*. *Josh* 9:4
the business of the *a*. *2 Chr* 32:31
he sent *a*. what have I to. 35:21
that sendeth *a*. by the sea. *Isa* 18:2
princes at Zoan, his *a*. came. 30:4
a. of peace shall weep bitterly. 33:7
rebelled in sending *a*. *Ezek* 17:15
then we are *a*. for Christ. *2 Cor* 5:20

ambassage
sendeth an *a*. and. *Luke* 14:32

amber, *see* **colour**

ambush, -es
lay thee an *a*. for the. *Josh* 8:2
watchmen, prepare the *a*. *Jer* 51:12

ambushment, -s
caused an *a*. the *a*. was. *2 Chr* 13:13
Lord set *a*. against Ammon. 20:22

amen
The Hebrew means true, faithful, certain. It is used in the end of prayer as an earnest wish to be heard; amen, so be it, so shall it be. *The word* amen *is used in many languages*.
woman shall say *a*. *a*. *Num* 5:22
the people shall say *a*. *Deut* 27:15
Benaiah answered *a*. the. *1 Ki* 1:36
people said *a*. and. *1 Chr* 16:36
to everlasting; *a*. and *a*. *Ps* 41:13
with his glory; *a*. and *a*. 72:19
Lord for evermore *a*. and *a*. 89:52
and let all the people say *a*. 106:48
prophet Jeremiah said *a*. *Jer* 28:6
the glory for ever, *a*. *Mat* 6:13
of the unlearned, say *a*. *1 Cor* 14:16
in him are yea and *a*. *2 Cor* 1:20
am alive for evermore, *a*. *Rev* 1:18
write these things, saith the *a*. 3:14
four beasts said *a*. 5:14; 19:4
come quickly, *a*. even so. 22:20

amend
a. ways, and doings. *Jer* 7:3, 5
26:13; 35:15
hour when he began to *a*. *John* 4:52

amends
(*Revised Version*, restitution)
make *a*. for the harm. *Lev* 5:16

amerce
(*Punish by fine*)
a. him in an 100 shekels. *Deut* 22:19

amethyst, *see* **agate** *and* **jacinth**

amiable
how *a*. are thy tabernacles. *Ps* 84:1

amiss
sinned, we have done *a*. *2 Chr* 6:37*
speak any thing *a*. against. *Dan* 3:29
man hath done nothing *a*. *Luke* 23:41
not, because ye ask *a*. *Jas* 4:3

Ammah
were come to the hill *A*. *2 Sam* 2:24

Ammi
unto your brethren, *A*. *Hos* 2:1

Amminadab
Elisheba daughter of *A*. *Ex* 6:23
A begat. *Ruth* 4:20; *Mat* 1:4

Ammi-nadib
me like the chariots of *A*. *S of S* 6:12

Ammon
father of children of *A*. *Gen* 19:38
I deliver you from *A*.? *Judg* 10:11
the children of *A*. made war. 11:4
the land of the children of *A*. 15
thus the children of *A*. were. 33
if the children of *A*. be too strong for thee. *2 Sam* 10:11; *1 Chr* 19:12
children of *A*. saw that. *2 Sam* 10:14
with sword of children of *A*. 12:9
all children of *A*. 31; *1 Chr* 20:3
the abomination of the children of *A*. *1 Ki* 11:7; *2 Ki* 23:13
god of the children of *A*. *1 Ki* 11:33
had married wives of *A*. *Neh* 13:23
Gebal and *A*. confederate. *Ps* 83:7
the children of *A*. shall. *Isa* 11:14
punish the children of *A*. *Jer* 9:26
made children of *A*. to drink. 25:21
bring again the captivity of *A*. 49:6
escape, the chief of *A*. *Dan* 11:41
children of *A*. shall be as. *Zeph* 2:9

Ammonite, -s
A. not enter. *Deut* 23:3; *Neh* 13:1
slew the *A*. till the. *1 Sam* 11:11
loved women of the *A*. *1 Ki* 11:1
and the *A*. gave gifts. *2 Chr* 26:8
to the abomination of *A*. *Ezra* 9:1
send to the king of *A*. *Jer* 27:3
to be heard in Rabbah of *A*. 49:2
make *A*. a couchingplace. *Ezek* 25:5
A. may not be remembered. 10

Amnon
David's first-born was *A*.
2 Sam 3:2; *1 Chr* 3:12
A. vexed, fell sick for. *2 Sam* 13:2
I pray thee, let my brother *A*. 26
when I say, smite *A*. then kill. 28
Shimon, *A*. Rinnah. *1 Chr* 4:20

Amon
back to *A*. *1 Ki* 22:26; *2 Chr* 18:25
A. reigned. *2 Ki* 21:18
his servants slew *A*. 23
A. sacrificed to carved. *2 Chr* 33:22
captivity children of *A*. *Neh* 7:59
Manasses begat *A*. and *A*. *Mat* 1:10

among
thou, Lord, art *a*. them. *Num* 14:14
a. the sons of the priests. *Ezra* 10:18
yet *a*. many nations. *Neh* 13:26
an interpreter, one *a*. *Job* 33:23
their life is *a*. the unclean. 36:14
evil common *a*. men. *Eccl* 6:1
one *a*. 1,000, but a woman *a*. 7:28
chiefest *a*. ten thousand. *S of S* 5:10
a. my people are found. *Jer* 5:26
there is none upright *a*. *Mi* 7:2
blessed art thou *a*. *Luke* 1:28*
I send you forth as lambs *a*. 10:3
what are they *a*. so many? *John* 6:9

Amorite, -s
iniquity of the *A*. is not. *Gen* 15:16
which I took from *A*. with. 48:22
utterly destroy the *A*. *Deut* 20:17
fail drive out the *A*. *Josh* 3:10
the Lord delivered up *A*. 10:12
or gods of *A*. in whose land. 24:15
not the gods of the *A*. *Judg* 6:10
God hath dispossessed the *A*. 11:23
between Israel and the *A*. *1 Sam* 7:14
Gibeonites were of the *A*. *2 Sam* 21:2
abominably as did the *A*. *1 Ki* 21:26
above all the *A*. did. *2 Ki* 21:11
father an *A*. mother. *Ezek* 16:3, 45
yet destroyed I the *A*. *Amos* 2:9

Amos, or, Amoz
Isaiah the son of *A*. *2 Ki* 19:2, 20
20:1; *2 Chr* 26:22; 32:20, 32
Isa. 1:1; 2:1; 13:1; 20:2; 37:2
21; 38:1
then *A*. said, I was no. *Amos* 7:14
which was the son of *A*. *Luke* 3:25

Amphipolis
had passed through *A*. *Acts* 17:1

Amplias
greet *A*. my beloved in. *Rom* 16:8

Amram
of Kohath, *A*. *Ex* 6:18; *Num* 3:19
Dishon, *A*. and Eshban. *1 Chr* 1:41
the children of *A*. Aaron. 6:3
sons of Bani, Maadai, *A*. *Ezra* 10:34

Anah
this was that *A*. that. *Gen* 36:24

Anak
saw the children of *A*. *Num* 13:28, 33
before the children of *A*. *Deut* 9:2
Caleb drove thence the three sons of *A*. *Josh* 15:14; *Judg* 1:20

Anakims
and tall as the *A*. *Deut* 2:10; 9:2
none of the *A*. were left. *Josh* 11:22
was a great man among the *A*. 14:15

Anammelech
Adrammelech, *A*. gods. *2 Ki* 17:31

Ananias
A. hearing these words. *Acts* 5:5
seen in a vision *A*. 9:12; 22:12
high-priest *A*. commanded. 23:2
A. the priest descended with. 24:1

Anathema
him be *a*. maran-atha. *1 Cor* 16:22

Anathoth
of Benjamin, *A*. with her suburbs, Almon. *Josh* 21:18; *1 Chr* 6:60
get thee to *A*. to. *1 Ki* 2:26
the sons of Becher *A*. *1 Chr* 7:8
A. and Nebai sealed. *Neh* 10:19
up thy voice, O poor *A*. *Isa* 10:30
evil on the men of *A*. *Jer* 11:23
not reproved Jeremiah of *A*. 29:27
my field that is in *A*. 32:7, 8

ancestors
the covenant of their *a*. *Lev* 26:45

anchor
they would have cast *a*. *Acts* 27:30
hope we have as an *a*. *Heb* 6:19

ancient
[1] *Old, of former time*. 1 Chr 4:22. [2] *Very old men*, Job 12:12. [3] *Men of former times*, 1 Sam 24:13 [4] *Elders of the people* Jer 19:1.
the chief things of the *a*. *Deut* 33:15
a. river, the river Kishon. *Judg* 5:21
of *a*. times. *2 Ki* 19:25; *Isa* 37:26
and these are *a*. things. *1 Chr* 4:22
were *a*. men, and had. *Ezra* 3:12*
with the *a*. is wisdom. *Job* 12:12*
remove not the *a*. land-. *Pr* 22:28
prudent and *a*. the Lord. *Isa* 3:2*
the *a*. and honourable, he. 9:15*
say ye, I am the son of *a*.? 19:11
whose antiquity is of *a*. days. 23:7
since I appointed the *a*. people. 44:7
upon the *a*. hast thou laid thy. 47:6*
of the Lord, as in the *a*. days. 51:9*
to stumble from *a*. paths. *Jer* 18:15
then they began at the *a*. *Ezek* 9:6
the *a*. of days did sit. *Dan* 7:9
the Son of man came to *a*. of. 13
till the *a*. of days came, and. 22

ancients
(*Revised Version, usually*, elders)
the proverb of the *a*. *1 Sam* 24:13
more than the *a*. *Ps* 119:100
into judgment with the *a*. *Isa* 3:14
Lord shall reign before his *a*. 24:23
a. of the people and *a*. of. *Jer* 19:1
shall perish from the *a*. *Ezek* 7:26
hast thou seen what the *a*. do? 8:12
the *a*. of Gebal were in thee. 27:9

ancle bones
a. *bones* received strength. *Acts* 3:7

ancles
the waters were to the *a*. *Ezek* 47:3

Andrew
into the house of *A*. *Mark* 1:29
James, John, and *A*. asked. 13:3
which heard was *A*. *John* 1:40
of Bethsaida the city of *A*. 44
Philip telleth *A*. and *A*. told. 12:22
Peter, John, James, and *A*. *Acts* 1:13

Andronicus
salute *A*. and Junia my. *Rom* 16:7

Aner
A. Eshcol, let them take. *Gen* 14:24
half tribe of Manasseh, *A*. *1 Chr* 6:70

angel
Literally 'messenger': [1] *A celestial being, a messenger of God*, Gen 24:7; Dan 3:28; Acts 12:8. [2] *A minister or pastor of a church*, Rev 2:1. [3] *An evil, or fallen angel*, Mat 25:41.
a. of the Lord said. *Gen* 22:11
send his *a*. before thee. 24:7, 40
the *a*. who redeemed me. 48:16
send *a*. before thee. *Ex* 23:20, 23
32:34; 33:2
sent an *a*. and brought. *Num* 20:16
the *a*. did wondrously. *Judg* 13:19
the *a*. stretched out his hand, the *a*. that. *2 Sam* 24:16; *1 Chr* 21:15
spake . . . saw the *a*. *2 Sam* 24:17
a. spake to me by the. *1 Ki* 13:18
an *a*. touched Elijah and said. 19:5
God sent an *a*. to. *1 Chr* 21:15
turned back, and saw the *a*. 20
the Lord commanded the *a*. and. 27
the Lord sent an *a*. *2 Chr* 32:21
nor say before the *a*. *Eccl* 5:6
the *a*. of his presence. *Isa* 63:9
God who hath sent *a*. and. *Dan* 3:28

God hath sent his a. and. Dan 6:22
he had power over the a. Hos 12:4
a. talked with me said. Zech 1:9; 4:5
Lord answered the a. that. 1:13
a. that communed with me said. 14
a. that talked. 19; 4:4; 5:10; 6:4
a. that talked . . . and another a. 2:3
and stood before the a. 3:3
a. that talked with me, went. 5:5
a. answered, these are the four. 6:5
a. answered the woman. Mat 28:5
the a. said, fear not. Luke 1:13
the a. answered and said, I am. 19
in the sixth month the a. Gabriel. 26
a. said to her, fear not, Mary. 30
a. answered, Holy Ghost shall. 35
a. said to the shepherds, fear. 2:10
suddenly there was with the a. a. 13
so named of the a. before he was. 21
an a. strengthening him. 22:43
an a. went down at a. John 5:4*
others said, an a. spake to. 12:29
been the face of an a. Acts 6:15
hands of the a. that appeared. 7:35
in the wilderness with the a. 38
a. which spake to Cornelius. 10:7
from God by an holy a. to send. 22
how he had seen an a. in his. 11:13
the a. said to Peter, bind on. 12:8
true which was done by the a. 9
forthwith the a. departed from. 10
the Lord hath sent his a. and. 11
then said they, it is his a. 15
Sadducees say, neither a. 23:8
if a spirit or an a. hath spoken to. 9
into an a. of light. 2 Cor 11:14
an a. from heaven preach. Gal 1:8
he signified it by his a. Rev 1:1
a. of the church. 2:1, 8, 12, 18
3:1, 7, 14
I saw a strong a. proclaiming. 5:2
I saw another a. ascending. 7:2
another a. came and stood. 8:3
ascended before God out of the a. 4
the a. took the censer, and filled. 5
the first a. sounded. 7
second a. sounded. 8
third a. sounded. 10
fourth a. sounded. 12
I heard an a. flying through 13*
fifth a. sounded. 9:1
the a. of the bottomless pit. 11
sixth a. sounded. 13
to the sixth a. loose the four a. 14
I saw another a. 10:1; 18:1; 20:1
the a. which I saw stand on. 10:5
days of the voice of the seventh a. 7
the book in the hand of the a. 8
I took the book. 10
and the a. stood, saying. 11:1*
seventh a. sounded, and there. 15
I saw another a. fly in. 14:6
another a. followed saying. 8
third a. followed. 9
another a. came. 15, 17, 18
and the a. thrust in his sickle in. 19
a. poured out. 16:2, 3, 4, 8, 10, 12, 17
and I heard the a. of the waters. 5
a. said, wherefore didst thou. 17:7
mighty a. took up a stone. 18:21
and I saw an a. standing in. 19:17
of a man, that is of the a. 21:17
to worship before the feet of a. 22:8
I Jesus have sent mine a. to. 16

angel *of God*

a. of God who went. Ex 14:19
countenance of an a. of God.
Judg 13:6
sight, as an a. of God. 1 Sam 29:9
as an a. of God. 2 Sam 14:17; 19:27
the wisdom of an a. of God. 14:20
this night the a. of God. Acts 27:23
me as an a. of God. Gal 4:14

angel *of the Lord*

a. of the L. found Hagar. Gen 16:7
the a. of the L. said. 9, 10, 11; 22:11
Num 22:32, 35; Judg 13:18
2 Ki 1:3, 15
a. of the L. called. Gen 22:11, 15
ass saw the a. of the L. Num 22:23
25:27
a. of the L. stood in a path. 22:24, 26
Balaam saw a. of the L. standing. 31
Balaam said to a. of the L. Num 22:34
a. of the L. said to Balaam, go. 35
a. of the L. came up. Judg 2:1
1 Ki 19:7; Acts 12:7
when a. of the L. spake. Judg 2:4
Meroz, said the a. of the L. 5:23
came an a. of the L. and sat. 6:11
a. of the L. appeared to Gideon. 12
the a. of the L. put forth the. 21
perceived he was an a. of the L. 22
a. of the L. appeared to the. 13:3
knew not he was an a. of the L. 16
a. of the L. ascended in the flame. 20
a. of the L. was by threshing.
2 Sam 24:16; 1 Chr 21:15
a. of the L. smote. 2 Ki 19:35
Isa 37:36
a. of the L. destroying. 1 Chr 21:12
a. of the L. commanded Gad to. 18
the sword of a. of the L. 30
a. of the L. encampeth. Ps 34:7
let a. of the L. chase them. 35:5
let a. of the L. persecute them. 6
answered the a. of the L. Zech 1:11
a. of the L. answered, wilt thou. 12
a. of the L. stood by Joshua. 3:5
a. of the L. protested. 6
of David as the a. of the L. 12:8
a. of the L. Mat 1:20; 2:13, 19
Joseph did as the a. of the L. 1:24
for the a. of the L. descended. 28:2
Zacharias an a. of the L. Luke 1:11
a. of the L. came upon them. 2:9
a. of the L. by night. Acts 5:19
a. of the L. spake to Philip. 8:26
a. of the L. smote Herod. 12:23

angels

there came two a. to. Gen 19:1
when the morning arose, the a. 15
lower than the a. Ps 8:5*; Heb 2:7, 9
of God are thousands of a. Ps 68:17*
man did eat a. food, he sent. 78:25*
and trouble, by sending evil a. 49
a. came and. Mat 4:11; Mark 1:13
the reapers are the a. Mat 13:39
the a. shall come forth and sever. 49
their a. always behold the. 18:10
a. in heaven. 24:36; Mark 13:32
Son of man, and all the holy a. with.
Mat 25:31
more than twelve legions of a. 26:53
Son of man . . . of his Father with
the holy a. Mark 8:38; Luke 9:26
marry, but are as the a. Mark 12:25
as the a. were gone. Luke 2:15
and was carried by the a. 16:22
they are equal unto the a. 20:36
had also seen a vision of a. 24:23
seeth two a. in white. John 20:12
law by disposition of a. Acts 7:53
a. able to separate us. Rom 8:38
to the world, to a. and. 1 Cor 4:9
not that we shall judge a.? 6:3
on her head, because of the a. 11:10
with tongues of men and a. 13:1
it was ordained by a. in. Gal 3:19
you in worshipping of a. Col 2:18
heaven with mighty a. 2 Thes 1:7
seen of a. preached to. 1 Tim 3:16
before God and the elect a. 5:21
so much better than the a. Heb 1:4
the a. said he at any time. 5, 13
a. he saith, who maketh his a. 1:7
if the word spoken by a. was. 2:2
a. hath he not put in subjection. 5
him the nature of a. but seed. 16
innumerable company of a. 12:22
for some have entertained a. 13:2
which things the a. 1 Pet 1:12
a. and powers being made. 3:22
if God spared not the a. 2 Pet 2:4
whereas a. greater in power and. 11
a. who kept not their first. Jude 6
seven stars, a. of the. Rev 1:20
the voice of many a. about. 5:11
I saw four a. standing on the. 7:1
with a loud voice to the four a. 2
all the a. stood round about the. 11
trumpet of the three a. which. 8:13
loose the four a. which are. 9:14
the a. were loosed, which were. 15
in presence of the holy a. 14:10
and at the gates twelve a. 21:12

angels *of God*

a. of God ascend and descend.
Gen 28:12; John 1:51
and a. of God met him. Gen 32:1
as a. of God. Mat 22:30; Mark 12:25
confess before a. of God. Luke 12:8
be denied before the a. of God. 9
the presence of the a. of God. 15:10
all the a. of God worship. Heb 1:6

his **angels**

and his a. he charged with. Job 4:18
give his a. charge. Ps 91:11
Mat 4:6; Luke 4:10
ye his a. which excel in. Ps 103:20
his a. spirits. 104:4*; Heb 1:7
all his a. praise. Ps 148:2
man shall send forth his a. Mat 13:41
glory of his Father with his a. 16:27
send his a. with a great sound. 24:31
Mark 13:27
for the devil and his a. Mat 25:41
before my Father and his a. Rev 3:5
his a. the dragon, and his a. 12:7
dragon was cast out, and his a. 9

anger, *verb*

foolish nation I will a. Rom 10:19

anger

till thy brother's a. turn. Gen 27:45
and let not thine a. burn. 44:18
cursed be their a. for it was. 49:7
dancing, Moses' a. waxed. Ex 32:19
Aaron said, let not the a. of my. 22
I was afraid of the a. and. Deut 9:19
from the fierceness of his a. 13:17
Josh 7:26
heat of this great a.? Deut 29:24
then their a. was abated. Judg 8:3
Ahasuerus his a. burned. Esth 1:12
will not withdraw his a. Job 9:13
oven in the time of thine a. Ps 21:9
a. endureth but a moment. 30:5
cease from a. and forsake. 37:8
my flesh because of thine a. 38:3
let thy wrathful a. take hold. 69:24
why doth thy a. smoke. 74:1
and a. also came up against. 78:21
many a time turned he his a. 38
on them the fierceness of his a. 49
he made a way to his a. he. 50
the fierceness of thine a. 85:3
and cause thine a. towards us to. 4
wilt thou draw out thine a. to? 5
we are consumed by thine a. 90:7
knoweth the power of thine a. 11
nor will he keep his a. for. 103:9
Jer 3:5
grievous words stir up a. Pr 15:1
of a man deferreth his a. 19:11
a gift in secret pacifieth a. 21:14
the rod of his a. shall fail. 22:8
wrath is cruel, and a. is. 27:4
a. resteth in the bosom of. Eccl 7:9
for all this his a. is not turned away.
Isa 5:25; 9:12, 17, 21; 10:4
fear not, for the a. of Rezin. 7:4
O Assyrian, the rod of mine a. 10:5
shall cease, and my a. in their. 25
thou wast angry, thine a. 12:1
the Lord cometh with fierce a. 13:9
day of his fierce a. 13; Lam 1:12
Lord cometh burning with a. Isa 30:27
shew the indignation of his a. 30
poured on him the fury of a. 42:25
sake will I defer mine a. 48:9
will come to render his a. 66:15
surely his a. shall turn. Jer 2:35
mine a. to fall on you, I am merciful,
and I will not keep mine a. 3:12
were broken down by his a. 4:26
mine a. shall be poured on. 7:20
them in the time of thine a. 18:23
desolate because of his a. 25:38
as a provocation of mine a. 32:31
great is the a. the Lord hath. 36:7
as mine a. hath been poured. 42:18
wherefore mine a. was poured. 44:6
on them, my fierce a. 49:37
his footstool in the day a. Lam 2:1
in the indignation of his a. 6
them in the day of thine a. 21
in the day of the Lord's a. none. 22
thou hast covered with a. and. 3:43
he hath poured out his fierce a. 4:11

mine a. be accomplished. Ezek 5:13
I will send mine a. upon thee. 7:3
accomplish mine a. on. 8; 20:8, 21
Edom, according to mine a. 25:14
even do according to thine a. 35:11
thine a. be turned away. Dan 9:16
the fierceness of mine a. Hos 11:9
for mine a. is turned away. 14:4
a. did tear perpetually. Amos 1:11
turn from his fierce a. Jonah 3:9
he retained not his a. for. Mi 7:18
abide . . . fierceness of his a.? Nah 1:6
a. against the rivers? Hab 3:8
them all my fierce a. Zeph 3:8
looked on them with a. Mark 3:5
all a. be put. Eph 4:31; Col 3:8

anger *of the Lord*

fierce a. of the Lord may. Num 25:4
augment the a. of the Lord. 32:14
a. of the Lord shall. Deut 29:20
a. of the Lord against Israel. Judg 2:14, 20; 3:8; 10:7
through the a. of the Lord it came to pass. 2 Ki 24:20; Jer 52:3
fierce a. of the Lord is not. Jer 4:8
fierce a. of the Lord. 12:13; 25:37
a. of the Lord shall not. 23:20; 30:24
from the fierce a. of the Lord. 51:45
a. of the Lord hath. Lam 4:16
before the fierce a. of the Lord. Zeph 2:2
be hid in the day of a. of the Lord. 3

in **anger**

for in their a. they slew. Gen 49:6
out from Pharaoh in a. Ex 11:8
Lord overthrew in a. Deut 29:23
them out of the land in a. 28
rose from the table in a. 1 Sam 20:34
home in great a. 2 Chr 25:10
overturneth them in his a. Job 9:5
he teareth himself in his a. 18:4
distributeth sorrows in his a. 21:17
not so, he hath visited in his a. 35:15
me not in thy a. Ps 6:1; Jer 10:24
arise, O Lord, in thine a. lift. Ps 7:6
put not thy servant away in a. 27:9
in thine a. cast down the. 56:7
hath he in a. shut up his? 77:9
called my mighty ones in a. Isa 13:3
he that ruled the nations in a. 14:6
tread them in mine a. 63:3, 6
against you, even in a. Jer 21:5
have driven them in mine a. 32:37
whom I have slain in mine a. 33:5
Zion with a cloud in his a. Lam 2:1
he hath cut off in a. all the horn. 3
and destroy them in a. 3:66
judgments in thee in a. Ezek 5:15
overflowing shower in mine a. 13:13
gather you in mine a. and. 22:20
have consumed them in mine a. 43:8
destroyed, neither in a. Dan 11:20
thee a king in mine a. Hos 13:11
execute vengeance in a. Mi 5:15
thresh the heathen in a. Hab 3:12

anger *kindled*

a. of Jacob was k. against. Gen 30:2
a. of the Lord was k. against Moses. Ex 4:14
a. of the Lord was k. Num 11:1, 10
12:9; 22:22
Balaam's a. was k. and he. 22:27
Balak's a. was k. against. 24:10
the a. of the Lord was k. against Israel. 25:3; 32:13; Josh 7:1
2 Sam 24:1; 2 Ki 13:3
Lord's a. was k. the same. Num 32:10
lest the a. of the Lord be k. against thee. Deut 6:15
so will the a. of the Lord be k. 7:4
the a. of the Lord was k. against this land. 29:27
mine a. shall be k. 31:17; Josh 23:16
fire is k. in a. Deut 32:22; Jer 15:14
Zebul's a. was k. Judg 9:30
Samson's a. k. and he went. 14:19
Saul heard, his a. was k. 1 Sam 11:6
Eliab's a. was k. against. 17:28
Saul's a. was k. against. 20:30
a. of Lord k. against Uzzah. 2 Sam 6:7; 1 Chr 13:10
David's a. was k. against the. 2 Sam 12:5
wherewith his a. was k. 2 Ki 23:26
their a. was k. against. 2 Chr 25:10
a. of the Lord was k. against Amaziah. 15
the a. of the Lord k. against his people. Isa 5:25
have k. a fire in mine a. Jer 17:4
mine a. is k. against them. Hos 8:5
mine a. was k. against the shepherds. Zech 10:3

provoke or *provoked to* **anger**

to pr. him to a. Deut 4:25; 9:18
31:29; 2 Ki 17:17; 21:6; 23:19
2 Chr 33:6
abominations pr. to a. Deut 32:16
pr. me to a. I will pr. them to a. 21
and pr. the Lord to a. Judg 2:12
images to pr. to a. 1 Ki 14:9; 15:30
groves pr. Lord to a. 14:15; 16: 7, 13
to pr. me to a. with their sins. 16:2
2 Ki 17:11; Jer 11:17; 32:29, 32
Ezek 16:26
Ahab did pr. the Lord to a. 1 Ki 16:33
thou hast pr. me to a. 21:22
Ahaz pr. to a. the Lord God. 22:53
pr. me to a. since the day. 2 Ki 21:15
that they might pr. me to a. 22:17
2 Chr 34:25; Jer 25:7
pr. to a. the Lord God. 2 Chr 28:25
have pr. thee to a. before. Neh 4:5
pr. him to a. with. Ps 78:58; 106:29
whoso pr. him to a. sinneth. Pr 20:2
pr. the Holy One . . . to a. Isa 1:4*
a people that pr. me to a. 65:3*
may pr. me to a. Jer 7:18
do they pr. me to a. 19
why have they pr. to a. 8:19
pr. me not to a. 25:6
Israel have pr. me to a. 32:30
their wickedness to pr. me to a. 44:3
Ezek 8:17
Ephraim pr. him to a. Hos 12:14
pr. not your children to a. Col 3:21*

slow to **anger**

ready to pardon, slow to a. Neh 9:17
slow to a. plenteous. Ps 103:8; 145:8
he that is slow to a. Pr 15:18
he that is slow to a. better. 16:32
slow to a. of great. Joel 2:13
Jonah 4:2
the Lord is slow to a. great. Nah 1:3

angered

they a. him at the waters. Ps 106:32

angle

they that cast a. shall. Isa 19:8
up all of them with the a. Hab 1:15

angry

let not the Lord be a. Gen 18:30, 32
be not a. with yourselves that. 45:5
and Moses was a. with. Lev 10:16
a. with me for you. Deut 1:37; 4:21
Lord was a. with you to have. 9:8
the Lord was very a. with Aaron. 20
lest a. fellows run upon. Judg 18:25
wherefore be ye a. for. 2 Sam 19:42
be a. with them. 1 Ki 8:46; 2 Ch 6:36
Lord was a. with Solomon. 1 Ki 11:9
therefore the Lord was a. 2 Ki 17:18
wouldst thou not be a. Ezra 9:14
I was very a. when I. Neh 5:6
kiss the Son, lest he be a. Ps 2:12
God is a. with the wicked. 7:11
stand when once thou art a.? 76:7
wilt thou be a.? 79:5; 80:4; 85:5
he that is soon a. dealeth. Pr 14:17
wilderness, than with an a. 21:19*
friendship with an a. man. 22:24
a. countenance, a backbiting. 25:23
a. man stirreth up strife, and. 29:22
wherefore should God be a.? Eccl 5:6
be not hasty in thy spirit to be a. 7:9
mother's children were a. S of S 1:6
though thou wast a. with. Isa 12:1
and will be no more a. Ezek 16:42
this cause the king was a. Dan 2:12
and he was very a. Jonah 4:1
Doest thou well to be a.? 4:4, 9
he said, I do well to be a. even. 9
whosoever is a. with his. Mat 5:22
of the house being a. Luke 14:21
he was a. and would not. 15:28
are ye a. at me because. John 7:23
be a. and sin not, let not. Eph 4:26
be blameless, not soon a. Tit 1:7
the nations were a. thy. Rev 11:18

anguish

in that we saw the a. Gen 42:21*
hearkened not to Moses for a. Ex 6:9
tremble, and be in a. Deut 2:25
slay me, for a. is come. 2 Sam 1:9
I will speak in the a. of my. Job 7:11
trouble and a. shall make him. 15:24
trouble and a. have. Ps 119:143
when distress and a. come. Pr 1:27
and behold dimness of a. Isa 8:22
into the land of trouble and a. 30:6
a. as of her that bringeth. Jer 4:31
a. hath taken. 6:24; 49:24; 50:43
no more her a. for joy. John 16:21
tribulation and a. upon. Rom 2:9
for out of much a. of heart. 2 Cor 2:4

anise

ye pay tithe of mint, a. Mat 23:23

Anna

A. a prophetess daughter. Luke 2:36

Annas

A. and Caiaphas being. Luke 3:2
A. was father in law to. John 18:13
A. had sent Jesus bound to. 24

anoint

[1] *To pour oil upon with the idea of consecrating the person or thing to God, or to set him apart for an office,* Gen 31:13; Ex 28:41. *Since kings and priests were the persons most frequently anointed on taking office, they were frequently spoken of as God's anointed,* 2 Sam 23:1; Isa 45:1. *In like manner Jesus Christ as King and Priest, was so termed,* Acts 10:38. [2] *Anointing with various preparations was one of the principal methods of healing in the small knowledge of medicine in Palestine in Bible times,* Jas 5:14. *The word is so used of Jesus in healing the eyes of the blind,* John 9:6, 11.

a. and consecrate. Ex 28:41; 30:30
40:15
oil and a. him. 29:7; 40:13
thou shalt a. the altar. 29:36; 40:10
a. the tabernacle. 30:26; 40:9
thou shalt a. the laver and. 40:11
priest whom he shall a. Lev 16:32
but thou shalt not a. Deut 28:40
the trees went to a. a king. Judg 9:8
if in truth ye a. me king over. 15
thyself therefore and a. Ruth 3:3
a. him to be captain. 1 Sam 9:16
Lord sent me to a. thee king. 15:1
thou shalt a. him whom I name. 16:3
the Lord said, arise, a. him, this. 12
a. not thyself with oil. 2 Sam 14:2
let Zadok a. him king. 1 Ki 1:34
a. Hazael king. 19:15
a. Jehu, a. Elisha. 16
arise ye princes, and a. Isa 21:5
seal up the vision, and a. Dan 9:24
neither did I a. myself at all. 10:3
a. themselves with the. Amos 6:6
the olives, but not a. Mi 6:15
when thou fastest a. thine. Mat 6:17
is come to a. my body. Mark 14:8
spices that they might a. him. 16:1
with oil thou didst not a. Luke 7:46
a. thine eyes with eye-. Rev 3:18

anointed

sons after him, to be a. Ex 29:29
if the priest that is a. do sin. Lev 4:3
of Aaron, when he is a. 6:20
in the day that he a. them. 7:36
a. the tabernacle. 8:10
a. the altar. 11; Num 7:1
oil on Aaron's head, and a. Lev 8:12
sons of Aaron a. Num 3:3
offered after it was a. 7:10, 84, 88
Lord a. thee captain. 1 Sam 10:1
a. Saul. 15:17
a. David. 16:13; 2 Sam 2:4, 7
5:3, 17; 12:7; 2 Ki 9:3, 6, 12
1 Chr 11:3; 14:8
house of Judah have a. 2 Sam 2:7
day weak, though a. king. 3:39

from the earth, and *a.* *2 Sam* 12:20
David the *a.* of the God of. 23:1
the Lord hath *a.* *Isa* 61:1; *Luke* 4:18
thou art the *a.* cherub. *Ezek* 28:14
kissed his feet and *a.* *Luke* 7:38
but this woman hath *a.* my feet. 46
he *a.* the eyes of the blind. *John* 9:6
Jesus made clay, and *a.* mine. 11
it was that Mary which *a.* the. 11:2
took Mary ointment and *a.* 12:3
Jesus, whom thou hast *a.* *Acts* 4:27
how God *a.* Jesus of Nazareth. 10:38
which hath *a.* us is God. *2 Cor* 1:21

anointed *ones*

are the two *a. ones.* *Zech* 4:14

his **anointed**

and exalt horn of *his a.* *1 Sam* 2:10
me before the Lord and *his a.* 12:3
the Lord and *his a.* is witness. 5
sheweth mercy to his *a.* *2 Sam* 22:51
Ps 18:50
the Lord, and against *his a.* *Ps* 2:2
that the Lord saveth *his a.* 20:6
the saving strength of *his a.* 28:8
thus saith the Lord to *his a.* *Isa* 45:1

Lord's **anointed**

surely the *Lord's a.* is. *1 Sam* 16:6
to my master, the *Lord's a.* 24:6
my lord, for he is the *Lord's a.* 10
his hand against the *Lord's a.* 26:9
ye have not kept the *Lord's a.* 16
not afraid to destroy the *Lord's a.*?
2 Sam 1:14
because he cursed the *Lord's a.* 19:21
the *a. of Lord* was taken. *Lam* 4:20

mine **anointed**

walk before *mine a.* *1 Sam* 2:35
not *mine a.* *1 Chr* 16:22; *Ps* 105:15
a lamp for *mine a.* *Ps* 132:17

anointed *with oil*

priest *a.* with holy *oil.* *Num* 35:25
had not been *a. with oil.* *2 Sam* 1:21
God *a.* thee *with oil* of. *Ps* 45:7
Heb 1:9
with my holy *oil* have I *a.* *Ps* 89:20
I shall be *a. with* fresh *oil.* 92:10

thine **anointed**

O Lord God, turn not away the face
of *thine a.* *2 Chr* 6:42; *Ps* 132:10
look on face of *thine a.* *Ps* 84:9
been wroth with *thine a.* 89:38
the footsteps of *thine a.* 51
for salvation with *thine a.* *Hab* 3:13

anointedst

of Beth-el where thou *a.* *Gen* 31:13
a. my head with oil, my. *Ps* 23:5

anointing

their *a.* be an everlasting. *Ex* 40:15
destroyed because of the *a.* *Isa* 10:27
but the *a.* which ye have received of
him as the same *a.* *1 John* 2:27

anointing *oil*

he made the holy *a. oil.* *Ex* 37:29
he poured of the *a. oil.* *Lev* 8:12
for the *a. oil* of the Lord is. 10:7
on whose head the *a. oil* was 21:10
Eleazar pertaineth *a. oil.* *Num* 4:16
a. him with *oil* in the. *Jas* 5:14

anon

(*Revised Version,* straightway)
neareth, and *a.* with joy. *Mat* 13:20
mother lay sick, and *a.* *Mark* 1:30

another

appointed me *a.* seed. *Gen* 4:25
Lord shall add to me *a.* son. 30:24
asked us, have ye *a.* brother? 43:7
thing, which *a.* challengeth. *Ex* 22:9*
Caleb, because he had *a.* *Num* 14:24
a. generation that knew. *Judg* 2:10
be weak, and be as *a.* man. 16:7
shalt be turned into *a.* *1 Sam* 10:6
was so, that God gave him *a.* 9
give her royal estate to *a.* *Esth* 1:19
shall behold and not *a.* *Job* 19:27†
let *a.* take his. *Ps* 109:8; *Acts* 1:20
not a secret to *a.* *Pr* 25:9
let *a.* praise thee, and not thy. 27:2
will I not give to *a.* *Isa* 42:8; 48:11
a. shall call himself by the. 44:5
hast discovered thyself to *a.* 57:8
call his servants by *a.* name. 65:15
shalt not be for *a.* man. *Hos* 3:3*
man strive nor reprove *a.* *Hos* 4:4*
or do we look for *a.*? *Mat* 11:3
is it I? *a.* said, is it I? *Mark* 14:19
said he to *a.* how much. *Luke* 16:7
faithful in that which is *a.* man's. 12
a. Jesus, *a.* Spirit, or *a.* *2 Cor* 11:4*
which is not *a.* but there be. *Gal* 1:7
rejoicing in himself and not in *a.* 6:4*
exhort one *a.* while. *Heb* 3:13; 10:25
not have spoken of *a.* day. 4:8

one **another**, *see* **love**

one against **another**

one man sin *against a.* *1 Sam* 2:25
dash them *one against a.* *Jer* 13:14
puffed up *one against a.* *1 Cor* 4:6
grudge not *one against a.* *Jas* 5:9

one for **another**

to eat, tarry *one for a.* *1 Cor* 11:33
have same care *one for a.* 12:25
pray *one for a.* that ye may. *Jas* 5:16

answer

[1] *To reply,* Pr 26:4. [2] *To begin to speak, when no question is asked,* Dan 2:26; Acts 5:8. [3] *To witness,* Gen 30:33. [4] *To grant what one desires in prayer,* Ps 27:7; 86:7; Isa 65:24.

Pharaoh an *a.* of peace. *Gen* 41:16
the city make thee an *a.* *Deut* 20:11
see what *a.* I shall. *2 Sam* 24:13
return Mordecai this *a.* *Esth* 4:15
and he gave me no *a.* *Job* 19:16
because they found no *a.* 32:3
cry, but none giveth *a.* 35:12
a soft *a.* turneth away. *Pr* 15:1
a man hath joy by the *a.* of his. 23
the *a.* of the tongue is from. 16:1
his lips that giveth a right *a.* 24:26
him, but he gave me no *a.* *S of S* 5:6
the lips, for there is no *a.* *Mi* 3:7
they marvelled at his *a.* *Luke* 20:26
that we may give *a.* to. *John* 1:22
thou? Jesus gave him no *a.* 19:9
what saith the *a.* of God? *Rom* 11:4
mine *a.* to them that do. *1 Cor* 9:3
my first *a.* none stood. *2 Tim* 4:16*
be ready to give an *a.* *1 Pet* 3:15
a. of a good conscience towards. 21

answers

in your *a.* remaineth. *Job* 21:34
because of his *a.* for wicked. 34:36
were astonished at his *a.* *Luke* 2:47

answer, *verb*

my righteousness *a.* for. *Gen* 30:33
all the people shall *a.* *Deut* 27:15
voice, nor any to *a.* *1 Ki* 18:29
thou, and I will *a.* and *a.* *Job* 13:22
the words that he would *a.* me. 23:5
visiteth, what shall I *a.* him? 31:14
a. thee, God is greater. 33:12; 35:4
that reproveth God, let him *a.* 40:2
mercy also on me, and *a.* *Ps* 27:7
things in right, wilt thou *a.* us. 65:5
thee, for thou wilt *a.* me. 86:7
the day when I call, *a.* me. 102:2
thy right hand, and *a.* me. 108:6
O Lord, in thy faithfulness *a.* 143:1
the righteous studieth to *a.* *Pr* 15:28
thou mightest *a.* the words. 22:21*
a. a fool according to his folly. 26:5
what shall one then *a.* *Isa* 14:32
was there none to *a.*? 50:2; 66:4
thou call, and the Lord will *a.* 58:9
are not careful to *a.* thee. *Dan* 3:16
yea the Lord will *a.* and. *Joel* 2:19
what I shall *a.* when I. *Hab* 2:1
no man was able to *a.* *Mat* 22:46
heaven or of men? *a.* *Mark* 11:30
wist they what to *a.* him. 14:40
he from within shall *a.* *Luke* 11:7
how or what thing ye shall *a.* 12:11
he shall *a.* I know you not. 13:25
before what ye shall *a.* 21:14
more cheerfully *a.* for myself.
Acts 24:10*; 25:16*; 26:2*
have somewhat to *a.* *2 Cor* 5:12
know how ye ought to *a.* *Col* 4:6

I will **answer**

call, *I will a.* *Job* 13:22; 14:15
Ps 91:15; *Jer* 33:3
before they call *I will a.* *Isa* 65:24
I the Lord *will a.* him. *Ezek* 14:4

not **answer**

brethren could *not a.* him. *Gen* 45:3
he could *not a.* Abner. *2 Sam* 3:11
was, *a. not.* *2 Ki* 18:36; *Isa* 36:21
a. him one of a thousand. *Job* 9:3
but I will *not a.* *Pr* 1:28
a. not a fool according to his. 26:4
understand, he will *not a.* 29:19*
I called, ye did *not a.* *Isa* 65:12
but they will *not a.* thee. *Jer* 7:27
they could *not a.* him. *Luke* 14:6
if I ask, you will *not a.* nor. 22:68

answerable

a. to the hangings of the. *Ex* 38:18

answered

(*Revised Version, frequently,* said)
Penuel *a.* as ... of Succoth *a.* *Judg* 8:8
and he *a.* here am I. *1 Sam* 3:4, 16
the women *a.* one another as. 18:7*
men of Judah *a.* the. *2 Sam* 19:42
and thus he *a.* me. *1 Ki* 2:30
king *a.* people. 12:13; *2 Chr* 10:13
no voice, nor any that *a.* *1 Ki* 18:26
the man of God *a.* the. *2 Chr* 25:9
multitude of words be *a.*? *Job* 11:2
I *a.* O Lord God, thou. *Ezek* 37:3
Daniel *a.* with counsel. *Dan* 2:14
Balaam the son of Beor *a.* *Mi* 6:5
accused he *a.* nothing. *Mat* 27:12
14; *Mark* 14:61; 15:5; *Luke* 23:9
perceiving that he had *a.* *Mark* 12:28
when Jesus saw that he *a.* 34
held their peace, James *a.* *Acts* 15:13
I *a.* who art thou, Lord? and. 22:8
he *a.* for himself. 25:8*; 26:1*

answered, *referring to God*

who *a.* me in the day of. *Gen* 35:3
Moses spake, and God *a.* *Ex* 19:19
and the Lord *a.* it is. *2 Sam* 21:1
he *a.* him from heaven. *1 Chr* 21:26
that the Lord had *a.* him. 28
a. thee in the secret place. *Ps* 81:7
the Lord, and he *a.* them. 99:6
the Lord *a.* me, and set me. 118:5
a. till the cities be wasted. *Isa* 6:11
what hath the Lord *a.* *Jer* 23:35, 37
the Lord *a.* me, write the. *Hab* 2:2
the Lord *a.* the angel. *Zech* 1:13
he *a.* one of them and. *Mat* 20:13
his lord *a.* and said, thou. 25:26

answered *not*

she *a.* not, nor did she. *1 Sam* 4:20
he *a.* him *not* that day. 14:37; 28:6
a. them *not.* *2 Sam* 22:42; *Ps* 18:41
people *a.* him *not* a word. *1 Ki* 18:21
2 Ki 18:36; *Isa* 36:21
you, but ye *a. not.* *Jer* 7:13; 35:17
but he *a.* her *not* a word. *Mat* 15:23

answered *and said*

Moses *a. and said,* will not. *Ex* 4:1
servants *a. and said,* let. *2 Ki* 7:13
then *a.* I them *and said.* *Neh* 2:20
Job *a. and said.* *Job* 6:1; 9:1
12:1; 16:1; 19:1
a. and said, Babylon is. *Isa* 21:9
then *a.* I *and said,* so be it. *Jer* 11:5

answeredst

thou *a.* them, O Lord our. *Ps* 99:8
day when I cried thou *a.* me. 138:3

answerest

David cried, *a.* thou? *1 Sam* 26:14
thee, that thou *a.*? *Job* 16:3
a. thou nothing? *Mat* 26:62
Mark 14:60; 15:4
a. thou the high-priest? *John* 18:22

answereth

God is departed and *a.* *1 Sam* 28:15
let the God that *a.* by. *1 Ki* 18:24
on God, and he *a.* him. *Job* 12:4
that *a.* a matter before. *Pr* 18:13
the poor intreat, but the rich *a.* 23
as face *a.* to face, so the. 27:19
God *a.* him in the joy of. *Eccl* 5:20
maketh merry, but money *a.* 10:19
and *a.* to Jerusalem that. *Gal* 4:25

answering

the other *a.* rebuked. *Luke* 23:40
be obedient, not *a.* again. *Tit* 2:9

ant, -s

go to the *a.* thou sluggard. *Pr* 6:6
the *a.* are a people not strong. 30:25

Antichrist, -s
A. will come, now there are many A. 1 John 2:18
he is A. that denieth the Father. 22
this is that spirit of A. whereof. 4:3
this is a deceiver and an A. 2 John 7

Antioch
travelled as far as A. Acts 11:19, 22
when they were come to A. spake. 20
were called Christians first in A. 26
they came to A. in Pisidia. 13:14
from Attalia they sailed to A. 14:26
of their own company to A. 15:22
Barnabas continued in A. 35
when Peter was come to A. Gal 2:11
which came to me at A. 2 Tim 3:11

Antipas, *see* **Martyr**

Antipatris
Paul by night to A. Acts 23:31

antiquity
joyous city, whose a. is of. Isa 23:7

anvil
him that smote the a. Isa 41:7

any
against a. of the children. Ex 11:7
sin against a. of the commandments. Lev 4:2, 13, 22, 27; 5:17
lieth, in a. of all these that a. 6:3
nor a. that can deliver. Deut 32:39
word with a. 2 Sam 7:7; 1 Chr 17:6
yet a. left of the house? 2 Sam 9:1
was no voice, nor a. 1 Ki 18:26
he looketh, and if a. say. Job 33:27*
who will shew us a. good? Ps 4:6
turneth not away for a. Pr 30:30
no God, I know not a. Isa 44:8
shall say, is there yet a. Amos 6:10
nor go nor tell it to a. in. Mark 8:26*
if ye have ought against a. 11:25
nor could be healed of a. Luke 8:43
if he found a. of this way. Acts 9:2
brought under power of a. 1 Cor 6:12
if a. lack wisdom, let him. Jas 1:5
not willing that a. should. 2 Pet 3:9
if there come a. and bring. 2 John 10
see **further, God, man, more, thing, time, while, wise.**

apace, *see* **flee, fled**

apart
shalt set a. all that open. Ex 13:12
shall be put a. seven. Lev 15:19*
approach, as long as she is a. 18:19*
the Lord hath set a. him. Ps 4:3
a. their wives a. Zech 12:12, 14
into a desert place a. Mat 14:13
into a mountain a. 23; 17:1
the disciples to Jesus a. 17:19
come ye yourselves a. Mark 6:31
lay a. all filthiness. Jas 1:21

Apelles
salute A. approved in. Rom 16:10

Aphek
pitched in A. 1 Sam 4:1; 29:1
the rest fled to A. there. 1 Ki 20:30
smite the Syrians in A. 2 Ki 13:17

apes, *see* **peacocks**

apiece
five shekels a. by poll. Num 3:47
spoons weighing ten shekels a. 7:86
their princes gave him a rod a. 17:6
eighteen cubits high a. 1 Ki 7:15
nor have two coats a. Luke 9:3
two or three firkins a. John 2:6

Apollonia
had passed through A. Acts 17:1

Apollos
certain Jew named A. Acts 18:24
I am of A. 1 Cor 1:12; 3:4
who is A.? 3:5
I have planted, A. watered, God. 3:6
in a figure transferred to A. 4:6
bring Zenas and A. on. Tit 3:13

Apollyon
tongue, his name is A. Rev 9:11

apostle
Literally, one sent forth. Used as referring [1] *chiefly to one of the 12 disciples of Christ,* Matt. 10:2; or [2] *to any of various other followers of Christ who did evangelistic work,* Rom 1:1.
called to be an a. Rom 1:1; 1 Cor 1:1
inasmuch as I am the a. Rom 11:13
am I not an a.? 1 Cor 9:1, 2
meet to be called an a. 15:9
an a. of Jesus. 2 Cor 1:1; Eph 1:1
Col 1:1; 1 Tim 1:1; 2 Tim 1:1
Gal 1:1
signs of an a. were. 2 Cor 12:12
ordained an a. 1 Tim 2:7; 2 Tim 1:11
Paul a servant of God, and a. Tit 1:1
the a. and high-priest. Heb 3:1

apostles
names of the 12 a. Mat 10:2
a. gathered themselves. Mark 6:30
whom he named a. Luke 6:13
a. when they were returned. 9:10
send them prophets and a. 11:49
a. said to the Lord, increase. 17:5
and the twelve a. with him. 22:14
told these things to the a. 24:10
with the eleven a. Acts 1:26
were done by the a. 2:43; 5:12
down at the a. feet. 4:35, 37; 5:2
laid their hands on the a. and. 5:18
scattered abroad, except the a. 8:1
of note among the a. Rom 16:7
set forth us the a. last. 1 Cor 4:9
God hath set first a. 12:28
are all a.? 29
for I am the least of the a. 15:9
behind the chiefest a. 2 Cor 11:5
12:11
false a. deceitful workers. 11:13
them that were a. before. Gal 1:17
but other of the a. saw I none. 19
now revealed to his holy a. Eph 3:5
some a and some prophets. 4:11
burdensome as the a. 1 Thes 2:6
commandment of us the a. 2 Pet 3:2
words spoken before of the a. Jude 17
them which say they are a. Rev 2:2
rejoice over her, ye holy a. 18:20

apostleship
(*The office of the apostles*)
he may take part of this a. Acts 1:25
have received grace and a. Rom 1:5
the seal of mine a. are ye. 1 Cor 9:2
effectually in Peter to the a. Gal 2:8

apothecary
(*Revised Version,* perfumer)
compounded after art of a. Ex 30:25
after the art of the a. 35; 37:29
the ointment of the a. Eccl 10:1

apparel
arose and changed his a. 2 Sam 12:20
the attendance of his ministers, and their a. 1 Ki 10:5; 2 Chr 9:4
the changeable suits of a. Isa 3:22*
and wear our own a. 4:1
that is glorious in his a. 63:1
are clothed in strange a. Zeph 1:8
stood by them in white a. Acts 1:10
coveted no man's silver or a. 20:33
themselves in modest a. 1 Tim 2:9
if a man come in goodly a. Jas 2:2
gold, or putting on a. 1 Pet 3:3
see **royal**

apparelled
virgins, were a. 2 Sam 13:18
which are gorgeously a. Luke 7:25

apparently
(*Revised Version,* manifestly)
I speak even a. and not. Num 12:8

appeal, -ed
I a. unto Caesar. Acts 25:11, 21
liberty, if he had not a. to. 26:32
I was constrained to a. to. 28:19

appear
God said, let the dry land a. Gen 1:9
and none shall a. before me empty. Ex 23:15; 34:20; Deut 16:16
the year all males shall a. Ex 23:17
when thou shalt go to a. 34:24
Israel is come to a. Deut 31:11
when shall I come and a.? Ps 42:2
thy work a. to thy servants. 90:16
flowers a. on the earth. S of S 2:12*
a flock of goats that a. 4:1*; 6:5
when ye come to a. Isa 1:12
that thy shame may a. Jer 13:26
doings your sins do a. Ezek 21:24
that they may a. to men. Mat 6:16
so ye outwardly a. righteous. 23:28
then shall a. the sign of the. 24:30
as graves which a. not. Luke 11:44
kingdom of God should a. 19:11
in which I will a. to thee. Acts 26:16
but sin, that it might a. Rom 7:13
we must all a. before. 2 Cor 5:10*
who is our life shall a. then. Col 3:4
that thy profiting may a. 1 Tim 4:15
now to a. in the presence. Heb 9:24
to them shall he a. the second. 28
not made of things which do a. 11:3
ungodly and sinner a.? 1 Pet 4:18
when the chief Shepherd shall a. 5:4
when he shall a. we may. 1 John 2:28
it doth not yet a. what we shall . . . know that when he shall a. we. 3:2
thy nakedness do not a. Rev 3:18

appear, *referred to God*
to-day the Lord will a. to. Lev 9:4, 6
I will a. in the cloud on the. 16:2
did I plainly a. to the. 1 Sam 2:27
that night did God a. 2 Chr 1:7
build up Zion, he shall a. Ps 102:16
he shall a. to your joy. Isa 66:5*
in the which I will a. Acts 26:16

appearance
as the a. of fire. Num 9:15, 16
looketh on the outward a. 1 Sam 16:7
as the a. of a man. Dan 8:15; 10:18
his face as the a. of lightning. 10:6
not according to the a. John 7:24
which glory in a. and. 2 Cor 5:12
things after the outward a.? 10:7*
abstain from all a. of. 1 Thes 5:22*

appeared
a. to Abram. Gen 12:7; 17:1; 18:1
Lord a. to Isaac, and said. 26:2, 24
Jacob said, God Almighty a. to. 48:3
angel of the Lord a. in. Ex 3:2
the Lord hath not a. to thee. 4:1
I a. to Abraham by name of. 6:3
returned when the morning a. 14:27
channels of the sea a. 2 Sam 22:16
which had a. to Solomon. 1 Ki 11:9
there a. a chariot of fire. 2 Ki 2:11
the work till the stars a. Neh 4:21
the Lord hath a. of old to. Jer 31:3
what time the star a. Mat 2:7
the blade sprung, then a. the. 13:26
a. to them Moses. 17:3; Mark 9:4
holy city, and a. to many. Mat 27:53
Jesus a. first to Mary. Mark 16:9
after that he a. in another form to. 12
after he a. to the eleven as they. 14
there a. to him an angel. Luke 1:11
who a. in glory, and spake. 9:31
there a. an angel to him. 22:43
Lord is risen indeed, and a. 24:34
there a. to them cloven. Acts 2:3
the God of glory a. to our. 7:2
even Jesus, that a. to thee. 9:17
I have a. to thee for this. 26:16
neither sun nor stars a. 27:20
the grace of God hath a. Tit 2:11
love of God toward man a. 3:4
in the end hath he a. to. Heb 9:26
there a. a great wonder. Rev 12:1, 3

appeareth
as the leprosy a. in the. Lev 13:43
deliver him, as a. this. Deut 2:30*
every one of them in Zion a. Ps 84:7
the hay a. and the tender. Pr 27:25*
for evil a. out of the north. Jer 6:1
shall stand when he a.? Mal 3:2
is even as a vapour that a. Jas 4:14

appearing
commandment till a. 1 Tim 6:14
made manifest by the a. 2 Tim 1:10
the quick and dead at his a. 4:1
all them also that love his a. 8
looking for glorious a. of. Tit 2:13
found to praise at the a. 1 Pet 1:7

appease
I will a. him with the. Gen 32:20

appeased, -eth
Ahasuerus a. he. Esth 2:1
slow to anger a. strife. Pr 15:18
town-clerk had a. the. Acts 19:35

appertain
them, with all that *a.* *Num* 16:30
fear, for to thee doth it a. *Jer* 10:7
see **pertain**

appertained
men that *a.* to Korah. *Num* 16:32, 33

appertaineth, -ing
give it to him to whom it *a.* *Lev* 6:5
Abraham, our father, as *a.* *Rom* 4:1

appetite
wilt thou fill the *a.* of the. *Job* 38:39
if thou be a man given to *a.* *Pr* 23:2
all labour for mouth, yet *a.* *Eccl* 6:7
awaketh, and his soul hath *a.* *Isa* 29:8

Appii-forum
meet us as far as *A.* *Acts* 28:15

apple *of the eye*
(*The eyeball*)
as the *a. of his eye.* *Deut* 32:10
keep me as the *a. of the eye.* *Ps* 17:8
law as the *a. of thine eye.* *Pr* 7:2
let not the *a. of thine eye.* *Lam* 2:18
toucheth the *a. of his eye.* *Zech* 2:8

apples
like *a.* of gold in pictures. *Pr* 25:11
comfort me with *a.* for I. *S of S* 2:5
and smell of thy nose like *a.* 7:8

apple-tree
as the *a.-tree* among. *S of S* 2:3
raised thee up under the *a.-tree.* 8:5
palm-tree and *a.-tree.* *Joel* 1:12

applied
I *a.* my heart to know. *Eccl* 7:25*
I *a.* my heart to every work. 8:9
when I *a.* mine heart to know. 16

apply
we may *a.* our hearts. *Ps* 90:12*
and *a.* thine heart to. *Pr* 2:2
hear words, *a.* thine heart to. 22:17
a. thine heart to instruction. 23:12

appoint
(*To establish, to set apart for an office, or to decree*)
a. me thy wages, and I. *Gen* 30:28
let Pharaoh *a.* officers over. 41:34
I will *a.* over you terror. *Lev* 26:16
Aaron and his sons *a.* *Num* 4:19
to *a.* me ruler over the. *2 Sam* 6:21
I will *a.* a place for my people. 7:10
that thou wouldest *a.* me. *Job* 14:13
salvation will God *a.* for. *Isa* 26:1
a. them that mourn in Zion. 61:3
a. over them four kinds. *Jer* 15:3
chosen man that I may *a.* over her? who will *a.* me? 49:19; 50:44
the kingdoms *a.* a captain. 51:27
a. these two ways. *Ezek* 21:19
a. a way that. 20
they shall *a.* themselves. *Hos* 1:11
a. him his portion with the. *Mat* 24:51
a. him his portion with. *Luke* 12:46
I *a.* you a kingdom, as my. 22:29
seven men whom we *a.* *Acts* 6:3

appointed
God hath *a.* me another seed *Gen* 4:25
She *that* thou hast *a.* for thy 24:14
passover in *a.* season *Num* 9:2, 3, 7
brought not offering in *a.* season. 13
these were the cities *a.* *Josh* 20:9
was an *a.* sign between. *Judg* 20:38
not within the days *a.* *1 Sam* 13:11
Samuel standing as *a.* over. 19:20*
Lord had *a.* to defeat. *2 Sam* 17:14
I have *a.* him to be ruler. *1 Ki* 1:35
let go a man whom I had *a.* 20:42*
thou hast *a.* prophets to. *Neh* 6:7
their rebellion *a.* a captain to. 9:17
wearisome nights are *a.* to. *Job* 7:3
thou hast *a.* his bounds, that. 14:5
and the heritage *a.* to him. 20:29
to death, and to the house *a.* 30:23
hast given us like sheep *a.* *Ps* 44:11
a. a law in Israel, which he. 78:5
those that are *a.* to die. 79:11
to loose those that are *a.* to. 102:20
come home at the day *a.* *Pr* 7:20*
when he *a.* the foundations of. 8:29
cause of all such as are *a.* to. 31:8*
new-moons and your *a.* *Isa* 1:14
who, since I *a.* the ancient. *Isa* 44:7†
he reserveth the *a.* weeks. *Jer* 5:24
sea-shore, there hath he *a.* 47:7
I have *a.* thee each day. *Ezek* 4:6
the rod, and who hath *a.* it. *Mi* 6:9
field, as the Lord *a.* *Mat* 27:10
more than what is *a.* you. *Luke* 3:13
after these the Lord *a.* other. 10:1
kingdom, as my Father hath *a.* 22:29
they *a.* two, Joseph and. *Acts* 1:23*
he hath *a.* a day in which. 17:31
apostles last, *a.* to death. *1 Cor* 4:9*
you know that we are *a.* *1 Thes* 3:3
God hath not *a.* us to wrath. 5:9
whereunto I am *a.* a. *2 Tim* 1:11
elders in every city, as I *a.* *Tit* 1:5
faithful to him that *a.* *Heb* 3:2
as it is *a.* to men once to die. 9:27
also they were *a.* *1 Pet* 2:8

appointed *time* **and** *times*
at the *time a.* will I. *Gen* 18:14
Lord *a.* a set *time,* saying. *Ex* 9:5
unleavened bread in *time a.* 23:15
the set *time* Samuel *a.* *1 Sam* 13:8
into the field at the *time a.* 20:35
the set *time a.* him. *2 Sam* 20:5
to their *a. time* every. *Esth* 9:27
is there not an *a. time* to? *Job* 7:1*
the days of my *a. time* will. 14:14*
trumpet in the *time a.* *Ps* 81:3*
be alone in his *a. times.* *Isa* 14:31
heaven knoweth her *a. times.* *Jer* 8:7
he hath passed the *time a.* 46:17
for at the *time a.* the end. *Dan* 8:19
thing was true, but the *time a.* 10:1*
end shall be at the *time a.* 11:27
time a. shall return, and come. 29
because it is yet for a *time a.* 35
vision is yet for an *a. time.* *Hab* 2:3
times before *a.* *Acts* 17:26
under tutors, until the *time a.* *Gal* 4:2

appointeth
he *a.* over it whomsoever. *Dan* 5:21*

appointment
at the *a.* of Aaron and. *Num* 4:27*
by the *a.* of Absalom. *2 Sam* 13:32
wheat, salt according to *a.* *Ezra* 6:9*
had made an *a.* together. *Job* 2:11

apprehend
(*To seize or take prisoner*)
garrison desirous to *a.* *2 Cor* 11:32*
I may *a.* that for which. *Phil* 3:12

apprehended
when he *a.* Peter, he put. *Acts* 12:4
I am *a.* of Christ Jesus. *Phil* 3:12
not myself to have *a.* but. 13

approach
[1] *To draw nigh, or come near,* 2 Sam 11:20; Ps 65:4; Isa 58:2. [2] *To contract marriage with,* Lev 18:6.
none of you shall *a.* to. *Lev* 18:6
not *a.* to offer the bread. 21:17, 18
ye *a.* this day to battle. *Deut* 20:3
behold, thy days *a.* that thou. 31:14
make his sword to *a.* *Job* 40:19†
man whom thou causeth to *a.* *Ps* 65:4
a. to me, for who is this that engaged his heart to *a.* to me? *Jer* 30:21
light no man can *a.* unto. *1 Tim* 6:16

approached
wherefore *a.* ye so? *2 Sam* 11:20
the king *a.* to the altar. *2 Ki* 16:12

approacheth, -ing
they take delight in *a.* to. *Isa* 58:2
where no thief *a.* nor. *Luke* 12:33
more as ye see the day *a.* *Heb* 10:25

approve
(*To like or commend*)
yet their posterity *a.* *Ps* 49:13
whom you shall *a.* by. *1 Cor* 16:3
that ye may *a.* things. *Phil* 1:10

approved
Jesus, a man *a.* of God. *Acts* 2:22
acceptable to God, and *a.* *Rom* 14:18
salute Apelles *a.* in Christ. 16:10
are *a.* may be made. *1 Cor* 11:19
in all things you have *a.* *2 Cor* 7:11
commendeth himself is *a.* 10:18
not that we should appear *a.* but. 13:7
study to shew thyself *a.* *2 Tim* 2:15

approvest, -eth
a man, the Lord *a.* not. *Lam* 3:36
a. the things that are. *Rom* 2:18

approving
but in all things *a.* *2 Cor* 6:4

apron, -s
fig-leaves together, and made *a.* *Gen* 3:7
brought to the sick *a.* *Acts* 19:12

apt
a. for war, king of. *2 Ki* 24:16
be *a.* to teach. *1 Tim* 3:2; *2 Tim* 2:24

Aquila
a certain Jew named *A.* *Acts* 18:2, 18
when *A.* and Priscilla heard. 26
greet *A.* and Priscilla. *Rom* 16:3
2 Tim 4:19
A. and Priscilla salute. *1 Cor* 16:19

Ar
consumed *A.* of Moab. *Num* 21:28
I have given *A.* to the. *Deut* 2:9
in the night *A.* of Moab is. *Isa* 15:1

Arabia
kings of *A.* *1 Ki* 10:15; *2 Chr* 9:14
A. shall lodge in *A.* *Isa* 21:13
all the kings of *A.* *Jer* 25:24
I went into *A.* and. *Gal* 1:17
Agar is mount Sinai in *A.* 4:25

Arabian, -s
the *A.* brought. *2 Chr* 17:11
helped Uzziah against the *A.* 26:7
nor shall the *A.* pitch tent. *Isa* 13:20
thou sattest for them as *A.* *Jer* 3:2
Cretes and *A.* we do hear. *Acts* 2:11

Aram
sons of Shem, Lud, *A.* *Gen* 10:22
1 Chr 1:17
Moab brought me from *A.* *Num* 23:7
Esrom begat *A.* *Mat* 1:3
A. begat Aminadab. 1:4
which was the son of *A.* *Luke* 3:33
see **Padan**

Ararat
on the mountains of *A.* *Gen* 8:4
her the kingdoms of *A.* *Jer* 51:27

Araunah
the threshing-place of *A.* *2 Sam* 24:16
all these did *A.* as a king give. 23

Arba
A. was a great man. *Josh* 14:15

Arba
gave them *A.* which city. *Josh* 21:11

archangel
with the voice of the *a.* *1 Thes* 4:16
Michael the *a.* when. *Jude* 9

archer, -s
grew and became an *a.* *Gen* 21:20
the *a.* have sorely grieved. 49:23
a. hit him. *1 Sam* 31:3; *1 Chr* 10:3
his *a.* compass me round. *Job* 16:13
they are bound by the *a.* *Isa* 22:3
bendeth let *a.* bend bow. *Jer* 51:3

arches
narrow windows to the *a.* *Ezek* 40:16

Archelaus
heard that *A.* did reign. *Mat* 2:22

Archippus
say to *A.* take heed to. *Col* 4:17
Paul to *A.* fellow-soldier. *Philem* 2

Arcturus
which maketh *A.* Orion and. *Job* 9:9
or canst thou guide *A.* with? 38:32

Areopagite
was Dionysius the *A.* *Acts* 17:34

Areopagus
and brought him to *A.* *Acts* 17:19

Aretas
the governor under *A.* *2 Cor* 11:32

Argob
region of *A.* *Deut* 3:4; 13:14
1 Ki 4:13

arguing
doth your *a.* reprove? *Job* 6:25*

arguments
would fill my mouth with *a.* *Job* 23:4

Ariel
sent for Eliezer and A. Ezra 8:16
woe to A. the city where. Isa 29:1
A. it shall be to me as A. 2
nations that fight against A. 7

aright
his conversation a. Ps 50:23
that set not their heart a. 78:8
the wise useth knowledge a. Pr 15:2
wine, when it moveth itself a. 23:31
but they spake not a. Jer 8:6

Arimathea
Joseph of A. who was. Mat 27:57
Mark 15:43; Luke 23:51
John 19:38

Arioch
in the days of A. king of. Gen 14:1
then A. brought in Daniel. Dan 2:25

arise
[1] *To proceed from,* Acts 20:30. [2] *To be raised and comforted,* Amos 7:2.
now a. get thee out of. Gen 31:13
a. go up to Beth-el, and. 35:1
if there a. among you a. Deut 13:1
then shalt thou a. and get. 17:8
now therefore a. go over. Josh 1:2
a. Barak, lead thy. Judg 5:12
let the young men a. 2 Sam 2:14
I will a and gather all Israel. 3:21
so be that the king's wrath a. 11:20
after thee shall any a. 1 Ki 3:12
make Jehu a. from. 2 Ki 9:2
a. be doing, the Lord. 1 Chr 22:16
we his servants will a. Neh 2:20
a. too much contempt. Esth 1:18
then shall enlargement a. to. 4:14
when shall I a. and night? Job 7:4
whom doth not his light a.? 25:3
a. O Lord, save me, O my. Ps 3:7
a. O Lord, in thine anger lift. 7:6
now will I a. saith the Lord, I. 12:5
a. for our help, and redeem. 44:26
let God a. let his enemies be. 68:1
shall the dead a. and praise? 88:10
when the waves of sea a. thou. 89:9
thou shalt a. and have mercy. 102:13
when wilt thou a. out of. Pr 6:9
a. my love, my fair one. S of S 2:13
a. ye princes, and anoint. Isa 21:5
my dead body shall they a. 26:19
kings shall a. princes shall. 49:7
a. shine, for thy light is come. 60:1
but the Lord shall a. upon thee. 2
in trouble they will say. a. Jer 2:27
shall they fall and not a.? 8:4
a. ye, let us go up to Zion to. 31:6
a. cry out in the night. Lam 2:19
after thee shall a. Dan 2:39
whom shall Jacob a. Amos 7:2*, 5
a. ye and depart. Mi 2:10
a. and thresh, O daughter of. 4:13
enemy, when I fall I shall a. 7:8
saith to the dumb stone a. Hab 2:19
Sun of righteousness a. Mal 4:2
say a. and walk? Mat 9:5; Mark 2:9
there shall a. false Christs. Mat 24:24
say to thee a. Mark 5:41; Luke 8:54
man, I say to thee a. Luke 7:14
I will a. and go to my father. 15:18
and why do thoughts a. in? 24:38
even so I do, a. let us. John 14:31
body said, Tabitha, a. Acts 9:40
selves shall men a. speaking. 20:30
why tarriest thou? a. and be. 22:16
a. from the dead, and. Eph 5:14
till the day-star a. in. 2 Pet 1:19
see **rise**

ariseth
behold, there a. a little. 1 Ki 18:44
to the upright a. light in. Ps 112:4
a. to shake terribly the. Isa 2:19, 21
when persecution a. Mat 13:21
Mark 4:17
for out of Galilee a. John 7:52
the similitude of Melchizedec a. Heb 7:15
see **sun**

Aristarchus
caught Gaius and A. Acts 19:29
A. accompanied Paul into. 20:4
one A. a Macedonian being. 27:2
A. fellow-prisoner. Col 4:10
Philem 24

Aristobulus
that are of A. household. Rom 16:10

ark
[1] *A chest or coffer to keep things sure or secret,* Ex 2:3. [2] *The great vessel in which Noah and his family were preserved during the flood,* Gen 6:14, 15; Heb 11:7. [3] *That chest wherein the two tables of the law, Aaron's rod, and the pot of manna were kept,* Ex 37:1; Heb 9:4.
an a. of gopher-wood. Gen 6:14
and the a. went on the face of. 7:18
she took for him an a. of. Ex 2:3
put into the a. the testimony which I shall give thee. 25:16, 21; 40:3, 20
made the a. of shittim-wood. 37:1
charge shall be the a. Num 3:31
a. of the Lord. Josh 4:11; 6:12
1 Sam 4:6; 6:1; 2 Sam 6:9
they looked into a. 1 Sam 6:19
the a. and Israel abide. 2 Sam 11:11
thou barest the a. of. 1 Ki 2:26
was nothing in the a. save the. 8:9
after that the a. had. 1 Chr 6:31
let us bring again the a. of. 13:3
put forth his hand to hold the a. 9
prepared a place for the a. 15:1
and a. of thy strength. 2 Chr 6:41
Ps 132:8
whereunto the a. hath. 2 Chr 8:11
Noah entered the a. Mat 24:38
Luke 17:27
of God prepared an a. Heb 11:7
waited while the a was. 1 Pet 3:20
seen in his temple the a. Rev 11:19

before the **ark**
altar of gold *before the a.* Ex 40:5
were cut off *before the a.* Josh 4:7
earth on his face *before the a.* 7:6
his face *before the a.* 1 Sam 5:3
left *before the a.* Asaph. 1 Chr 16:37
assembled *before the a.* 2 Chr 5:6

ark *of the covenant*
a. *of covenant* of Lord. Num 10:33
inside of a. *of covenant.* Deut. 31:26
off before a. *of covenant.* Josh 4:7
a. *of covenant* of God. Judg 20:27
the a. *of the covenant* of. 1 Sam 4:3
bearing a. *of covenant.* 2 Sam 15:24
a. *of covenant* remained. 1 Chr 17:1
more, the a. *of covenant.* Jer 3:16
had the a. *of the covenant.* Heb 9:4

ark *of God*
where the a. *of God* was. 1 Sam 3:3
the a. *of God* was taken. 4:11; 17:22
if ye send away the a. *of God.* 6:3
died before the a. *of God.* 2 Sam 6:7
but the a. *of God* dwelleth. 7:2
carry back the a. *of God* into. 15:25
I bring the a. *of God.* 1 Chr 13:12
ought to carry the a. *of God.* 15:2

arm
Literally, for the part of the body so called, 2 Sam 1:10. [2] *Figuratively for power or strength,* Ps 10:15; Jer 27:5; Isa 53:1; John 12:38.
by greatness of thine a. Ex 15:16
he teareth the a. with. Deut 33:20
I will cut off thine a. 1 Sam 2:31
that was on his a. 2 Sam 1:10
with him is an a. of. 2 Chr 32:8
savest thou the a. that. Job 26:2
a. fall from my shoulder. 31:22*
cry out by reason of the a. of. 35:9
the high a. shall be broken. 38:15
hast thou an a. like God? 40:9
break thou the a. of the. Ps 10:15
own a. save them, but thy a. 44:3
hast with thy a. redeemed. 77:15
thou hast a mighty a. strong. 89:13
mine a. also shall strengthen him. 21
his holy a. hath gotten him. 98:1
set me as a seal on thine a. S of S 8:6
man the flesh of his a. Isa 9:20
thou their a. every morning. 33:2
God will come, and his a. shall. 40:10
gather the lambs with his a. 11
a. shall judge the people, the isles ... me, and on my a. Isa 51:5
put on strength, O a. of the Lord. 9
hath made bare his holy a. 52:10
believed our report? and to whom is the a. of the? 53:1; John 12:38
a. brought salvation. Isa 59:16; 63:5
Lord hath sworn by the a. of. 62:8
led them with his glorious a. 63:12
that maketh flesh his a. Jer 17:5
fight against you with a strong a. 21:5
and thine a. shall be. Ezek 4:7
I have broken a. of Pharaoh. 30:21
into hell that where his a. 31:17
retain the power of the a. Dan 11:6
sword be on his a. his a. Zech 11:17
strength with his a. Luke 1:51
with an high a. brought. Acts 13:17

arm, *verb*
a. some of yourselves to. Num 31:3
a. yourselves with the. 1 Pet 4:1

stretched-out **arm**
you with a *stretched-out a.* Ex 6:6
nation with *stretched-out a.* Deut 4:34
thee out thence with a *stretched-out a.* 5:15; 7:19; 26:8; Jer 32:21
not seen *stretched-out a.* Deut 11:2
come for thy *stretched-out a.* 2 Chr 6:32
with a *stretched-out a.* Ps 136:12
my *stretched-out a.* Jer 27:5; 32:17
with a *stretched-out a.* Ezek 20:33
with a *stretched-out a.* and fury. 34

Armageddon
them together to A. Rev 16:16

armed
Abram a. his trained. Gen 14:14
tribe, twelve thousand a. Num 31:5
ourselves will go ready a. 32:17, 32
pass over a. Deut 3:18; Josh 1:14
let him that is a. pass on. Josh 6:7
so the a. men left the. 2 Chr 28:14
he goeth on to meet the a. Job 39:21
of Ephraim being a. Ps 78:9
want as an a. man. Pr 6:11; 24:34
when a strong man a. Luke 11:21

Armenia
into land of A. 2 Ki 19:37; Isa 37:38

arm-holes
rags under thy *a.-holes.* Jer 38:12
sew pillows to *a.-holes.* Ezek 13:18

armies
(*Used frequently in the sense of hosts, great numbers*)
and bring forth my a. Ex 7:4
same day I brought your a. 12:17
went forth with their a. Num 33:1
captains of the a. to lead. Deut 20:9
I defy the a. of Israel. 1 Sam 17:10
that he should defy the a. of the. 26
name of the God of the a. of. 45
there any number of his a.? Job 25:3
not forth with our a. Ps 44:9
kings of a. did flee apace, she. 68:12
the company of two a. S of S 6:13
his fury upon all their a. Isa 34:2
he sent forth his a. and. Mat 22:7
compassed with a. Luke 21:20
who turned to flight the a. Heb 11:34
and the a. in heaven. Rev 19:14
kings of the earth and their a. 19

armour
[1] *Weapons or instruments of war,* 1 Sam 17:54. [2] *Those things in which one trusts for protection,* Luke 11:22; Rom 13:12; Eph 6:11.
David put Goliath's a. 1 Sam 17:54
and take thee his a. 2 Sam 2:21
they washed his a. 1 Ki 22:38*
all able to put on a. 2 Ki 3:21
have a fenced city also and a. 10:2
silver and gold, the house of his a. 20:13; Isa 39:2
look in that day to a. of. Isa 22:8
taketh his a. wherein he. Luke 11:22
and let us put on the a. Rom 13:12
approving by the a. of. 2 Cor 6:7
put on the a. of God to. Eph 6:11
take to you the whole a. of God. 13

armour-bearer
called his a.-b., saying. Judg 9:54
a.-b. said, do all that is. 1 Sam 14:7
David, and he became his a.-b. 16:21
his three sons, and his a.-b. 31:6

armoury
of David builded for an a. S of S 4:4
the Lord hath opened his a. Jer 50:25

arms
the a. of his hands were. Gen 49:24
are the everlasting a. Deut 33:27
brake them from his a. Judg 16:12
steel is broken by mine a.
2 Sam 22:35; Ps 18:34
Jehoram between his a. 2 Ki 9:24
the a. of the fatherless. Job 22:9
the a. of the wicked shall. Ps 37:17
strengtheneth her a. Pr 31:17
with strength of his a. Isa 44:12
bring thy sons in their a. 49:22
and my a. shall judge the. 51:5
tear them from your a. Ezek 13:20
will break Pharaoh's a. 30:22, 24
will strengthen the a. of king. 24, 25
breast and his a. of silver. Dan 2:32
a. and feet like to polished. 10:6
the a. of the south shall not. 11:15
with the a. of a flood shall they. 22
and a. shall stand on this part. 31
and strengthened their a. Hos 7:15
to go, taking them by their a. 11:3
taken him in his a. he. Mark 9:36
them up in his a. put his hands. 10:16
took Christ in his a. Luke 2:28

army
what he did to the a. of. Deut 11:4
give bread to thine a. Judg 8:6
he said, increase thine a. 9:29
of Benjamin out of a. 1 Sam 4:12
Philistines had put a. against a. 17:21
thee an a. like the a. 1 Ki 20:25
praise before the a. 2 Chr 20:21
O king, let not the a. of Israel. 25:7
his brethren, and the a. Neh 4:2
I dwelt as a king in the a. Job 29:25
as an a. with banners. S of S 6:4, 10
up for fear of Pharaoh's a. Jer 37:11
caused his a. to serve. Ezek 29:18
up an exceeding great a. 37:10
to his will in the a. of. Dan 4:35
his voice before his a. Joel 2:11
locust, my great a. which I sent. 25
house, because of the a. Zech 9:8
then came I with an a. Acts 23:27
the number of the a. of. Rev 9:16
that sat on horse and his a. 19:19
see **Chaldeans**

Arnon
he did in the brooks of A. Num 21:14
met Balaam in the border of A. 22:36
and pass over the river A. Deut 2:24
dwelt by the coasts of A. Judg 11:26
Moab shall be at fords of A. Isa 16:2
tell ye it in A. that Moab is. Jer 48:20

Aroer
children of Gad built A. Num 32:34
a present to them in A. 1 Sam 30:28
Jordan and pitched in A. 2 Sam 24:5
Bela, who dwelt in A. 1 Chr 5:8
cities of A. are forsaken. Isa 17:2
O inhabitant of A. stand. Jer 48:19

arose
perceived not when she a. Gen 19:33
lo my sheaf a. and. 37:7
a. up a new king. Ex 1:8; Acts 7:18
a. a generation that knew. Judg 2:10
till I Deborah a. till I a. a. 5:7
all the people a. as one man. 20:8
they a. early. 1 Sam 9:26; Isa 37:36
when he a. against me. 1 Sam 17:35
neither after him a. 2 Ki 23:25
the wrath of the Lord a. 2 Chr 36:16
young men hid, aged a. Job 29:8
when God a. to judgement. Ps 76:9
to his place where he a. Eccl 1:5
king a. early and went. Dan 6:19
a. and took the young. Mat 2:14, 21
a. and ministered. 8:15; Luke 4:39
he a. and rebuked the winds and the
Mat 8:26; Mark 4:39; Luke 8:24
a. and followed. Mat 9:9, 19
Mark 2:14
the hand, and the maid a. Mat 9:25
bodies of saints which slept a. 27:52
lifted him up, and he a. Mark 9:27
flood a. the stream beat. Luke 6:48
he a. and came to his father. 15:20
persecution which a. Acts 11:19
there a. no small stir about. 19:23
said there a. dissension. 23:7, 10
see **rose**

arose *and went*
Samuel a. and went to. 1 Sam 3:6
Jonathan a. and went to David. 23:16
David a. and went to the. 25:1
Elisha a. and went after. 1 Ki 19:21
Jonah a. and went to. Jonah 3:3
then Peter a. and went. Acts 9:39

Arpad, Arphad
gods of A. 2 Ki 18:34; Isa 36:19
where is the king of A.? 2 Ki 19:13
Isa 37:13
is not Hamath as A.? Isa 10:9
is confounded and A. Jer 49:23

Arphaxad
the son of Shem A. Gen 10:22
11:10; 1 Chr 1:17
who was the son of A. Luke 3:36

array
[1] *To put on apparel*, Esth 6:9; Rev. 7:13. [2] *To put an army in a fit posture to fight*, 2 Sam 10:9.
that they may a. the man. Esth 6:9
a. thyself with glory. Job 40:10
shall a. himself with the. Jer 43:12
adorn, not with costly a. 1 Tim 2:9

array
Joab put the choice in a. 2 Sam 10:9
God set themselves in a. Job 6:4
yourselves in a. against. Jer 50:14
see **battle**

arrayed
Pharaoh a. Joseph in fine. Gen 41:42
captives, with spoil a. 2 Chr 28:15
not a. like. Mat 6:29; Luke 12:27
his men of war a. Christ. Luke 23:11
Herod a. in royal apparel. Acts 12:21
are these that are a. in? Rev 7:13
the woman was a. in purple. 17:4
her was granted to be a. in fine. 19:8

arrived
they a. at the country of. Luke 8:26
and the next day we a. Acts 20:15

arrogancy
not a. come out of your. 1 Sam 2:3
pride and a. and the evil. Pr 8:13
cause the a. of the proud. Isa 13:11
Moab, his loftiness, his a. Jer 48:29

arrow
[1] *Literally, a dart used for pleasure or in war*, 1 Sam 20:20; Jer 51:11. [2] *Figuratively, any word or judgement which pierces the mind or the soul as does an arrow the flesh*, Job 6:4; Ps 64:3; 2 Sam 22:15.
Jonathan shot an a. 1 Sam 20:36
and the a. went out at. 2 Ki 9:24
a. of Lord's deliverance from. 13:17
shoot an a. there. 19:32; Isa 37:33
a. cannot make him flee. Job 41:28
they make ready their a. Ps 11:2
with an a. suddenly shall. 64:7
afraid for the a. that flieth. 91:5
false witness is a sharp a. Pr 25:18
their tongue is as an a. shot. Jer 9:8
set me as a mark for the a. Lam 3:12
his a. shall go forth as. Zech 9:4

arrows
them through with his a. Num 24:8
I will spend mine a. Deut 32:23
I will make mine a. drunk with. 42
I will shoot three a. on. 1 Sam 20:20
he sent out a. and scattered them.
2 Sam 22:15; Ps 18:14
a. took to him bow and a. 2 Ki 13:15
take the a. and smite upon the. 18
the a. of the Almighty are. Job 6:4
he ordaineth a. against the. Ps 7:13
shalt make ready thine a. 21:12
for thine a. stick fast in me. 38:2
thine a. are sharp in the heart. 45:5
whose teeth are spears and a. 57:4
bendeth his bow to shoot his a. Ps 58:7
bows to shoot their a. even. 64:3
brake he the a. of the bow, the. 76:3
clouds poured, thine a. also. 77:17
sharp a. of the mighty, with. 120:4
as a. are in the hand of a. 127:4
shoot out thine a. and destroy. 144:6
mad man who casteth a. Pr 26:18
whose a. are sharp and. Isa 5:28
with a. and bows shall men. 7:24
their a. shall be as of an. Jer 50:9
shoot at Babylon, spare no a. 14
make bright the a. gather the. 51:11
hath caused the a. of his. Lam 3:13
I shall send the evil a. Ezek 5:16
he made his a. bright, he. 21:21
I will cause thy a. to fall out. 39:3
go forth, and burn bows and a. 9
at the light of thine a. Hab 3:11

art, *verb*
to Adam, where a. thou? Gen 3:9
from the place where thou a. 13:14
whose daughter a. thou? 24:23, 47
and he said a. thou my very? 27:24
whose a. thou? whither goest? 32:17
thee, because thou a. his wife. 39:9
discreet and wise as thou a. 41:39
die because thou a. yet alive. 46:30
a bloody husband thou a. Ex 4:26
a. thou for us, or our? Josh 5:13
they answered, as thou a. Judg 8:18
the men said to him, a. thou? 12:5
a. thou the man that spakest? 13:11
stand by where thou a. 1 Sam 19:3
a prophet also as thou a. 1 Ki 13:18
said, I am as thou a. 22:4; 2 Ki 3:7
a. not thou our God. 2 Chr 20:7
hurt a man as thou a. Job 35:8
a. thou also become . . . ? a. Isa 14:10
a. not thou he, O Lord our? Jer 14:22
a. thou he that should? Luke 7:19
Rabbi, thou a. the Son of. John 1:49
a. not thou that Egyptian? Acts 21:38
the captain said, tell me, a? 22:27
a. and wast, and a. Rev 11:17; 16:5

art, -s, *substantive*
ointment after the a. of. Ex 30:25
spices prepared by a. 2 Chr 16:14
like stones graven by a. Acts 17:29
of them which used curious a. 19:19

Artaxerxes
in the days of A. wrote. Ezra 4:7
to the commandment of A. 6:14
in the reign of A. Ezra. 7:1; 8:1
the copy of a letter that A. gave. 7:11
I, even I A. the king do make a. 21
in 20th year of A. wine was. Neh 2:1
from 20th to 32nd year of A. 5:14

Artemas
when I shall send A. to. Tit 3:12

artificer
an instructor of every a. Gen 4:22
captain and the cunning a. Isa 3:3

artificers
of works made by a. 1 Chr 29:5
to a. and builders gave. 2 Chr 34:11

artillery
Jonathan gave his a. 1 Sam 20:40

as
ye shall be a. gods. Gen 3:5
behold the man is become a. 22
the Lord seeth not a. 1 Sam 16:7
he did evil a. did the. 2 Ki 8:27
had made in the temple, a. 24:13
a. thou hast said, so. Ezra 10:12
a. for such a. turn aside. Ps 125:5
say not, I will do to him a. Pr 24:29
a. with the people, a. Isa 24:2
a. his master, servant a. Mat 10:25
love thy neighbour a. thyself. 19:19
Rom 13:9
the glory a. of the only-. John 1:14
ye resist Holy Ghost, a. Acts 7:51
but a. of sincerity, but a. 2 Cor 2:17
be a. I am, for I am a. ye. Gal 4:12
a. ye have received Christ. Col 2:6

even as
even as the Lord gave to. 1 Cor 3:5
so love his wife even a. Eph 5:33
even a. Christ forgave you. Col 3:13
even a. I received of my. Rev 2:27

Asa
A. did what. 1 Ki 15:11; 2 Chr 14:2
A. heart. 1 Ki 15:14; 2 Chr 15:17
A. took the silver. 1 Ki 15:18
2 Chr 16:2
Berechiah the son of A. 1 Chr 9:16
A. cried to the Lord. 2 Chr 14:11
Azariah went out to meet A. 15:2
no war to the 35th year of A. 19
A. was wroth . . . A. oppressed. 16:10
the pit was it which A. had. Jer 41:9
Abia begat A. Mat 1:7
A. begat Josaphat. 8

Asahel
sons of Zeruiah, Joab, A. 2 Sam 2:18
1 Chr 2:16
A. would not turn aside. 2 Sam 2:21
they took up A. and buried him. 32
Abner died for the blood of A. 3:27
A. was one of the thirty. 23:24
1 Chr 11:26
Levites, Zebadiah, A. 2 Chr 17:8
Jehiel, Nahath and A. were. 31:13
son of A. was employed. Ezra 10:15

Asaiah
Jeshohaiah and A. 1 Chr 4:36
sons of Merari, Haggiah, A. 6:30
Shilonites, A. the first-born. 9:5
king Josiah sent A. to. 2 Chr 34:20

Asaph
Joah the son of A. the recorder.
2 Ki 18:18, 37; Isa 36:3, 22
A. son of Berechiah. 1 Chr 6:39
9:15; 15:17
delivered first this psalm to A. 16:7
of the sons of A. 25:1, 2; 26:1
2 Chr 5:12; 20:14; 29:13; 35:15
Ezra 2:41; 3:10; Neh 7:44; 11:17
22, 12:35.
first lot came forth for A. 1 Chr 25:9
to sing with words of A. 2 Chr 29:30
to the commandment of A. 35:15
a letter to A. keeper of the. Neh 2:8
in the days of A. were songs. 12:46

ascend
[1] *To climb up*, Josh 6:5. [2] *To go up to heaven*, Eph 4:9, 10.
the people shall a. up. Josh 6:5
a. into the hill of the Lord, and shall stand in? Ps 24:3; Rom 10:6
he causeth vapours to a. Ps 135:7
Jer 10:13; 51:16
if I a. up into heaven, thou. Ps 139:8
hast said, I will a. Isa 14:13, 14
thou shalt a. and come. Ezek 38:9
see the Son of man a. up. John 6:62
a. to my Father, and your. 20:17
beast shall a. out of the. Rev 17:8

ascended
the angel of the Lord a. Judg 13:20
thou hast a. up on high. Ps 68:18
who hath a. up into heaven. Pr 30:4
no man hath a. to heaven. John 3:13
touch me not, I am not yet a. 20:17
David is not yet a. into. Acts 2:34
when he a. up on high, he. Eph 4:8
now that he a. 9
is the same also that a. 10
the smoke of the incense a. Rev 8:4
they a. up to heaven in a cloud. 11:12

ascendeth
the beast that a. out of. Rev 11:7
the smoke of their torment a. 14:11

ascending
the angels of God a. and. Gen 28:12
said, I saw gods a. out. 1 Sam 28:13
he went before, a. up to. Luke 19:28
of God a. and descending. John 1:51
I saw another angel a. from. Rev 7:2

ascent
up by the a. of Olivet. 2 Sam 15:30
and his a. by. 1 Ki 10:5; 2 Chr 9:4

ascribe
a. ye greatness to our. Deut 32:3
I will a. righteousness to. Job 36:3
a. ye strength to God, his. Ps 68:34

ascribed
a. to David 10,000, to me a. but. 1 Sam 18:8

Asenath
A. daughter of. Gen 41:45, 50; 46:20

ash
he planteth an a. the rain. Isa 44:14*

ashamed
(*The American Revision frequently changes this word to* confounded *or* put to shame)
and his wife were not a. Gen 2:25
tarried till they were a. Judg 3:25
the men were greatly a. 2 Sam 10:5
1 Chr 19:5
being a. steal away. 2 Sam 19:3
urged him till he was a. 2 Ki 2:17
his countenance till he was a. 8:11
the Levites were a. 2 Chr 30:15
a. to require of the king. Ezra 8:22
a. and blush to lift up my face. 9:6
came thither, and were a. Job 6:20
shall no man make a.? 11:3
are not a. to make yourselves. 19:3
their faces were not a. Ps 34:5
not the oppressed return a. 74:21
she that maketh a. is as. Pr 12:4
shall be a. of Ethiopia. Isa 20:5
the sun shall be a. when the. 24:23
all a. of a people that could. 30:5
earth mourneth, Lebanon is a. 33:9
as the thief is a. when he. Jer 2:26
a.? they were not at all a. 6:15; 8:12
the wise men are a. they are. 8:9
plowmen were a. they covered. 14:4
a. of Chemosh, as Israel was a. 48:13
of the Philistines are a. Ezek 16:27
with terror they are a. of. 32:30
his adversaries were a. Luke 13:17
I cannot dig, to beg I am a. 16:3
I am not a. of the gospel. Rom 1:16
hope maketh not a. because the. 5:5
things whereof ye are now a. 6:21
anything, I am not a. 2 Cor 7:14
nevertheless I am not a. 2 Tim 1:12
Onesiphorus was not a. of my. 16
he is not a. to call them. Heb 2:11
God is not a. to be called. 11:16
ashamed *and confounded*, **see confounded**

***be* ashamed**
it to her, lest we be a. Gen 38:23
let all my enemies be a. and. Ps 6:10
wait on thee be a. let them be a. who transgress without cause. 25:3
put my trust, let me never be a. 31:1
be a. let the wicked be a. 17; 35:26
let not them that wait be a. 69:6
hate me, may see it and be a. 86:17
they arise, let them be a. 109:28
let proud be a. for they. 119:78
for they shall be a. of the. Isa 1:29
be thou a. O Zidon, the sea. 23:4
they shall see and be a. for. 26:11
they shall be greatly a. that. 42:17
know, that they may be a. 44:9
fellows shall be a. shall be a. 11
incensed against him shall be a. 45:24
rejoice, but ye shall be a. 65:13
your joy, and they shall be a. 66:5
shalt be a. of Egypt, as a. Jer 2:36
forehead, refusedst to be a. 3:3
they shall be a. of your. 12:13
all that forsake thee shall be a. 17:13
shall stumble and be a. 20:11
Moab shall be a. of Chemosh. 48:13
that bare you shall be a. 50:12
thy ways, and be a. Ezek 16:61
shew Israel, they may be a. 43:10
and if they be a. of all that. 11
they shall be a. because. Hos 4:19
and Israel shall be a. of his. 10:6
be ye a. O ye husbandmen. Joel 1:11
people shall never be a. 2:26, 27
her expectation shall be a. Zech 9:5
the prophets every one be a. 13:4
shall be a. of me and. Mark 8:38
Luke 9:26
should be a. in this same. 2 Cor 9:4
in nothing I shall be a. Phil 1:20
him, that he may be a. 2 Thes 3:14
on the contrary part may be a. Tit 2:8
be a. that falsely accuse. 1 Pet 3:16

***not be, or be not,* ashamed**
should she not be a.? Num 12:14
in thee, let me not be a. Ps 25:2
me not be a. O Lord. 31:17; 119:116
shall not be a. in the evil time. 37:19
then shall I not be a. when. Ps 119:6
of thy testimonies, and not be a. 46
heart be sound, that I be not a. 80
they shall not be a. but shall. 127:5
Lord, Jacob shall not be a. Isa 29:22
ye shall not be a. world. 45:17
they shall not be a. that wait. 49:23
flint, I know I shall not be a. 50:7
fear not, for thou shalt not be a. 54:4
shalt thou not be a. Zeph 3:11
him shall not be a. Rom 9:33; 10:11
boast, I should not be a. 2 Cor 10:8
be not therefore a. of. 2 Tim 1:8
workman that needeth not be a. 2:15
Christian, let him not be a. 1 Pet 4:16
not be a. before him. 1 John 2:28

Ashdod
brought the ark to A. 1 Sam 5:1
Lord was heavy on them of A. 6
wall of A. and built cities about A.
2 Chr 26:6
had married wives of A. Neh 13:23
spake half in the speech of A. 24
came and fought against A. Isa 20:1
I made remnant of A. Jer 25:20
the inhabitant from A. Amos 1:8
publish in the palaces at A. and 3:9
they shall drive out A. Zeph 2:4
a bastard shall dwell in A. Zech 9:6

Asher
Leah called his name A. Gen 30:13
Zilpah, Leah's maid, Gad, A. 35:26
the children of A. 46:17; Num 1:40
26:44; 1 Chr 7:30, 40; 12:36
out of A. his bread shall. Gen 49:20
A. was Pagiel. Num 1:13; 2:27; 7:72
the name of the daughter of A. 26:46
to curse; Gad and A. Deut 27:13
A. he said, let A. be blessed. 33:24
A. continued on the sea. Judg 5:17
Gideon sent messengers to A. 6:35
men out of A. pursued the. 7:23
son of Hushai was in A. 1 Ki 4:16
A. expert in war 40,000. 1 Chr 12:36
divers of A. humbled. 2 Chr 30:11
a portion for A. Ezek 48:2
one gate of A. 34

***tribe of* Asher**
the tribe of A. 41,500. Num 1:41
the tribe of A. shall encamp. 2:27
over the host of tribe of A. 10:26
of the tribe of A. to spy the. 13:13
prince of the tribe of A. to. 34:27
lot for the tribe of A. Josh 19:24
inheritance of the tribe of A. 31
had cities out of the tribe of A. 21:6
30; 1 Chr 6:62, 74
of Phanuel of tribe of A. Luke 2:36
the tribe of A. were sealed. Rev 7:6

ashes
The remains of fuel after it has been burned, 2 Pet 2:6. *They were used in mourning to show that joy had perished*, Esth 4:1; Isa 61:3.
which am but dust and a. Gen 18:27
priest shall take up the a. Lev 6:10
and carry forth the a. without. 11
clean shall gather the a. Num 19:9
Tamar put a. on her. 2 Sam 13:19
altar shall be rent, and a. 1 Ki 13:3
disguised himself with a. 20:38*
put on sackcloth with a. Esth 4:1
and many lay in sackcloth and a. 3
Job sat down among the a. Job 2:8
remembrances are like to a. 13:12
I am become like dust and a. 30:19
and repent in dust and a. 42:6
have eaten a. like bread. Ps 102:9
the hoar-frost like a. 147:16
he feedeth on a. a. Isa 44:20
to spread sackcloth and a. 58:5
to give them beauty for a. the. 61:3
wallow thyself in a. Jer 6:26
hath covered me with a. Lam 3:16
I will bring thee to a. on. Ezek 28:18
to seek in sackcloth and a. Dan 9:3
sackcloth, and sat in a. Jonah 3:6
wicked shall be a. under. Mal 4:3
have repented long ago in sackcloth and a. Mat 11:21; Luke 10:13
a. of an heifer sanctifieth. Heb 9:13
cities of Sodom into a. 2 Pet 2:6

Ashtaroth

Og, who dwelt at *A*. *Deut* 1:4
Josh 9:10; 12:4
Israel served *A*. *Judg* 2:13; 10:6
strange gods and *A*. *1 Sam* 7:3, 4
because we have served *A*. 12:10
armour in the house of *A*. 31:10
have worshipped *A*. *1 Ki* 11:33
Gershom was given *A*. *1 Chr* 6:71

Ashur, or Assur

A. went forth and built. *Gen* 10:11
Shem, Elam and *A*. 22; *1 Chr* 1:17
till *A*. shall carry thee. *Num* 24:22
from Chittim and afflict *A*. 24
Hezron's wife bare him *A*. *1 Chr* 2:24
A. had two wives, Helah and. 4:5
Esar-haddon king of *A*. *Ezra* 4:2
A. also is joined with them. *Ps* 83:8
A. and Chilmad were. *Ezek* 27:23
A. is there, and all her. 32:22
A. shall not save us, we. *Hos* 14:3

Asia

A. disputing with Stephen. *Acts* 6:9
to preach the word in *A*. 16:6
all they that dwelt in *A*. heard. 19:10
A. and the world worshippeth. 27
certain of the chief of *A*. sent. 31
he would not spend time in *A*. 20:16
first day that I came into *A*. 18
meaning to sail by coasts of *A*. 27:2
churches of *A*. salute. *1 Cor* 16:19
which came to us in *A*. *2 Cor* 1:8
they which are in *A*. *2 Tim* 1:15
strangers scattered in *A*. *1 Pet* 1:1

***see* churches**

aside

said, thou shalt set *a*. *2 Ki* 4:4
he took him *a*. from the. *Mark* 7:33
he riseth and laid *a*. his. *John* 13:4
let us lay *a*. every weight. *Heb* 12:1

***see* go, gone, turn, went, lay**

ask

[1] *To enquire*, Gen 32:29; Mark 9:32. [2] *To require, or demand*, Gen 34:12; Dan 2:10. [3] *To seek counsel*, Isa 30:2; Hag 2:11. [4] *To pray*, John 15:7; *Jas* 1:6. [5] *To expect*, Luke 12:48.

wherefore dost thou *a*.? *Gen* 32:29
a. me never so much dowry. 34:12
for *a*. now of the days. *Deut* 4:32
shall *a*. diligently, and if it be. 13:14
a. thy father, and he will shew. 32:7
children *a*. their fathers. *Josh* 4:6, 21
a. counsel, we pray thee. *Judg* 18:5
added this evil to *a*. *1 Sam* 12:19
why dost thou *a*. of me? 28:16
from me the thing I *a*. *2 Sam* 14:18
a. what I shall. *1 Ki* 3:5; *2 Chr* 1:7
Jeroboam cometh to *a*. *1 Ki* 14:5
Elijah said *a*. what I shall. *2 Ki* 2:9
Judah gathered to *a*. *2 Chr* 20:4
a the beasts, and they. *Job* 12:7
a. of me, and I will give. *Ps* 2:8
a. thee a sign of Lord, *a*. it. *Isa* 7:11
I will not *a*. nor will I tempt. 12
the Lord, *a*. me of things. 45:11
they *a*. of me the ordinances of. 58:2
a. for the old paths, and. *Jer* 6:16
who shall go aside, to *a*. what. 15:5
a. ye now among the heathen. 18:13
a. and see whether a man doth. 30:6
I will *a*. thee a thing, hide. 38:14
a. him that fleeth, and her. 48:19
they shall *a*. the way to Zion. 50:5
the young children *a*. bread. *Lam* 4:4
a. a petition of any. *Dan* 6:7, 12
my people *a*. counsel at. *Hos* 4:12
a. now the priests. *Hag* 2:11
a. ye of the Lord rain. *Zech* 10:1
need of, before ye *a*. him. *Mat* 6:8
a. and it shall be. 7:7; *Luke* 11:9
his son *a*. bread. *Mat* 7:9; *Luke* 11:11
good things to them that *a*. *Mat* 7:11
her whatsoever she would *a*. 14:7
touching any thing they shall *a*. 18:19
what ye *a*. 20:22; *Mark* 10:38
whatsoever ye *a*. in prayer. *Mat* 21:22
nor durst any man *a*. him more.
22:46; *Mark* 12:34; *Luke* 20:40
a. what thou wilt. *Mark* 6:22, 23
afraid to *a*. him. 9:32; *Luke* 9:45
taketh thy goods, *a*. them. *Luke* 6:30
Holy Spirit to them that *a*. 11:13
of him they will *a*. more. 12:48
Jews sent priests to *a*. *John* 1:19
he is of age, *a*. him. 9:21, 23
thou wilt *a*. of God, he will. 11:22
to him that he should *a*. 13:24*
whatsoever ye *a*. in. 14:13; 15:16
if ye *a*. any thing in my name I. 14:14
if ye abide in me, *a*. what ye. 15:7
that they were desirous to *a*. 16:19
and in that day ye shall *a*. me. 23
a. and ye shall receive, that your. 24
that any man should *a*. thee. 30
a. them which heard me what. 18:21
I *a*. therefore for what. *Acts* 10:29
them *a*. their husbands. *1 Cor* 14:35
above all that we can *a*. *Eph* 3:20
lack wisdom, let him *a*. *Jas* 1:5
but let him *a*. in faith, nothing. 6
yet ye have not, because ye *a*. 4:2
a. and receive not, because ye *a*. 3
whatsoever we *a*. we. *1 John* 3:22
if we *a*. any thing according to. 5:14
he heareth us, whatsoever we *a*. 15
is not unto death, he shall *a*. 16

***see* counsel**

asked

Jacob *a*. him and said. *Gen* 32:29
the man *a*. us straitly of our. 43:7
him the city which he *a*. *Josh* 19:50
he *a*. water, she gave. *Judg* 5:25
I *a*. him not whence he was. 13:6
petition thou hast *a*. *1 Sam* 1:17
hath given me my petition I *a*. 27
a. this thing and not *a*. *1 Ki* 3:11
thou hast *a*. a hard thing. *2 Ki* 2:10
a. their names to certify. *Ezra* 5:10
have ye not *a*. them that. *Job* 21:29
he *a*. life of thee, thou. *Ps* 21:4
the people *a*. and he. 105:40
and have not *a*. at my. *Isa* 30:2
when I *a*. of them, could. 41:28
I am sought of them that *a*. 65:1
there is no king that *a*. *Dan* 2:10
I came and *a*. him the truth of. 7:16
he *a*. his disciples. *Mat* 16:13
Mark 8:27; *Luke* 9:18
Sadducees *a*. him. *Mat* 22:23, 35
Mark 9:11; 10:2; 12:18
when come near he *a*. *Luke* 18:40
thou wouldest have *a*. *John* 4:10
hitherto have ye *a*. nothing. 16:24
to them that *a*. not. *Rom* 10:20

Askelon, or Ashkelon

Judah took Gaza and *A*. *Judg* 1:18
Samson went down to *A*. and. 14:19
for *A*. one, for Gath one. *1 Sam* 6:17
not in the streets of *A*. *2 Sam* 1:20
I made *A*. and Azzah to. *Jer* 25:20
A. is cut off with remnant of. 47:5
hath given it a charge against *A*. 7
that holds sceptre from *A*. *Amos* 1:8
Gaza shall be forsaken, *A*. *Zeph* 2:4
in the houses of *A*. shall they lie. 7
A. shall see it, and fear; king shall perish from Gaza, and *A*. *Zech* 9:5

askest

why *a*. thou thus after. *Judg* 13:18
a. drink of me, a woman. *John* 4:9
why *a*. thou me, ask them. 18:21

asketh

thy son *a*. thee. *Ex* 13:14; *Deut* 6:20
prince *a*. and the judge *a*. *Mi* 7:3
give to him that *a*. thee. *Mat* 5:42
Luke 6:30
that *a*. receiveth. *Mat* 7:8; *Luke* 11:10
of you *a*. me, whither? *John* 16:5
to every one that *a*. you. *1 Pet* 3:15

asking

wickedness in *a*. a king. *1 Sam* 12:17
Saul died for *a*. counsel. *1 Chr* 10:13
tempted God by *a*. meat. *Ps* 78:18
hearing them, and *a*. *Luke* 2:46
they continued *a*. he lifted. *John* 8:7
a. no question for. *1 Cor* 10:25, 27

asleep

[1] *To take rest in sleep*, Jonah 1:5; Mat 26:40. [2] *To die*, Acts 7:60; 2 Pet 3:4.

for Sisera was fast *a*. *Judg* 4:21
lips of those that are *a*. *S of S* 7:9
Jonah lay, and was fast *a*. *Jonah* 1:5
but he was *a*. *Mat* 8:24; *Mark* 4:38
disciples *a*. *Mat* 26:40; *Mark* 14:40
had said this, he fell *a*. *Acts* 7:60
but some are fallen *a*. *1 Cor* 15:6
which are fallen *a*. in Christ. 18
them that are *a*. *1 Thes* 4:13
shall not prevent them that are *a*. 15
since the fathers fell *a*. *2 Pet* 3:4

Asnappar

whom the noble *A*. brought. *Ezra* 4:10

asp, -s

is the cruel venom of *a*. *Deut* 32:33
his meat is the gall of *a*. *Job* 20:14
suck the poison of *a*. the viper's. 16
play on the hole of the *a*. *Isa* 11:8
the poison of *a*. is under. *Rom* 3:13

ass

up early, and saddled his *a*. *Gen* 22:3
abide you here with the *a*. and I. 5
Issachar is a strong *a*. 49:14
every firstling of an *a*. *Ex* 13:13
if thou meet thine enemy's *a*. 23:4
that thine ox and thine *a*. may. 12
taken one *a*. from them. *Num* 16:15
the *a*. saw the angel. 22:23; 25:27
opened the mouth of the *a*. 22:28
a. said to Balaam, am not I thine *a*.? 30
plow with an ox and *a*. *Deut* 22:10
lighted off her *a*. Caleb. *Josh* 15:18
Judg 1:14; *1 Sam* 25:23
the jaw-bone of an *a*. *Judg* 15:16
had not torn the *a*. *1 Ki* 13:28
until an *a*. head sold for. *2 Ki* 6:25
they drive away the *a*. of. *Job* 24:3
a bridle for the *a*. and a. *Pr* 26:3
ox his owner, and the *a*. his. *Isa* 1:3
forth the feet of the ox and *a*. 32:20
with the burial of an *a*. *Jer* 22:19
riding on an *a*. and on a colt the foal of an *a*. *Zech* 9:9; *Mat* 21:5
be the plague of the *a*. *Zech* 14:15
ye shall find an *a*. tied. *Mat* 21:2
not each loose his *a*. on. *Luke* 13:15
which of you shall have an *a*. 14:5
he found a young *a*. sat. *John* 12:14
the dumb *a*. speaking. *2 Pet* 2:16

***see* saddle**

***wild* ass**

doth the *wild a*. bray when? *Job* 6:5
sent out the *wild a*. free? 39:5
a *wild a*. used to the. *Jer* 2:24
they are gone, a *wild a*. alone. *Hos* 8:9

assault, -ed

perish all that would *a*. *Esth* 8:11
when there was an *a*. *Acts* 14:5
they *a*. the house of Jason, and. 17:5

assay, -ed, -ing

hath God *a*. to go and. *Deut* 4:34
David *a*. to go, for he. *1 Sam* 17:39
if we *a*. to commune with. *Job* 4:2
Saul *a*. to join himself to. *Acts* 9:26
they *a*. to go to Bithynia, but. 16:7
the Egyptians *a*. to do. *Heb* 11:29

assemble

the assembly shall *a*. *Num* 10:3
a. me the men of Judah. *2 Sam* 20:4
he shall *a*. the outcasts. *Isa* 11:12
a. yourselves, and come, draw. 45:20
all ye *a*. yourselves and hear. 48:14
a. yourselves, and let us go. *Jer* 4:5
why do we sit still? *a*. 8:14
I will *a*. you out of the. *Ezek* 11:17
a. yourselves, gather to my. 39:17
they *a*. themselves for corn. *Hos* 7:14
a. the elders, gather the. *Joel* 2:16
a. yourselves and come, all. 3:11
a. yourselves on the. *Amos* 3:9
I will surely *a*. O Jacob. *Mi* 2:12
saith the Lord I will *a*. her. 4:6
I will *a*. the kingdoms to. *Zeph* 3:8

assembled

women which *a*. at the. *Ex* 38:8*
with the women that *a*. *1 Sam* 2:22*
David *a*. the children of. *1 Chr* 15:4
a. much people to keep. *2 Chr* 30:13
then *a*. to me every one. *Ezra* 9:4
had prayed, there *a*. to him. 10:1
the children of Israel *a*. *Neh* 9:1
lo the kings were *a*. they. *Ps* 48:4

let the people be *a.* who. *Isa* 43:9
a. themselves by troops in. *Jer* 5:7
these men *a.* and found. *Dan* 6:11
when they *a.* they gave. *Mat* 28:12
the disciples *a.* for fear. *John* 20:19
being *a.* commanded them. *Acts* 1:4
shaken where they were *a.* 4:31
a whole year they *a.* with. 11:26
it seemed good to us *a.* with. 15:25

assemblies
the *a.* of violent men. *Ps* 86:14*
by the masters of *a.* *Eccl* 12:11
the calling of *a.* I cannot. *Isa* 1:13
God will create on her *a.* a. 4:5
my laws in all mine *a.* *Ezek* 44:24*
smell in your solemn *a.* *Amos* 5:21

assembling
forsake not the *a.* *Heb* 10:25

assembly
to their *a.* mine honour be. *Gen* 49:6
the whole *a.* shall kill it. *Ex* 12:6
to kill this whole *a.* with. 16:3
hid from the eyes of the *a.* *Lev* 4:13
trumpets for calling the *a.* *Num* 10:2
Aaron went from presence of *a.* 20:6
of the midst of the fire, in the day of your *a.* *Deut* 9:10; 10:4; 18:16
Jabesh-Gilead to the *a.* *Judg* 21:8
all this *a.* shall know. *1 Sam* 17:47
whole *a.* took counsel. *2 Chr* 30:23
I set a great *a.* against. *Neh* 5:7
the *a.* of the wicked have. *Ps* 22:16
God is to be feared in the *a.* 89:7*
praise him in the *a.* of the. 107:32
I will praise him in the *a.* of. 111:1
evil in the midst of the *a.* *Pr* 5:14
I will pour it on the *a.* of. *Jer* 6:11
for they be an *a.* of treacherous. 9:2
in the *a.* of the mockers. 15:17
the places of the *a.* *Lam* 2:6
shall not be in the *a.* of. *Ezek* 13:9*
against Aholibah with an *a.* 23:24
the *a.* was confused, and. *Acts* 19:32
determined in a lawful *a.* 39
thus spoken, he dismissed the *a.* 41
to the general *a.* of the. *Heb* 12:23
if there come to your *a.* *Jas* 2:2

solemn **assembly**
on the eighth day it is a *solemn a.* *Lev* 23:36; *Num* 29:35; *Neh* 8:18
seventh day a *solemn a.* *Deut* 16:8
proclaim a *solemn a.* *2 Ki* 10:20
eighth day . . . a *solemn a.* *2 Chr* 7:9
call a *solemn a.* *Joel* 1:14; 2:15
are sorrowful for the *solemn a.* *Zeph* 3:18

assent, -ed
to the king with one *a.* *2 Chr* 18:12
Jews also *a.* that these. *Acts* 24:9

asses
had he-*a.* and she-*a.* *Gen* 12:16
much cattle, camels, and *a.* 30:43
as he fed the *a.* of Zibeon. 36:24
bread in exchange for *a.* 47:17
ye that ride on white *a.* *Judg* 5:10
he will take your *a.* to. *1 Sam* 8:16
the *a.* of Kish, Saul's. 9:3
thy *a.* that were lost, they. 20; 10:2
the *a.* be for the king's. *2 Sam* 16:2
and over the *a.* was. *1 Chr* 27:30
feeble of them upon *a.* *2 Chr* 28:15
a. that went up. *Ezra* 2:67; *Neh* 7:69
and a thousand she-*a.* *Job* 42:12
he saw a chariot of *a.* and. *Isa* 21:7
flesh is as the flesh of *a.* *Ezek* 23:20

wild **asses**
as *wild a.* in the desert. *Job* 24:5
the *wild a.* quench their. *Ps* 104:11
shall be a joy of *wild a.* *Isa* 32:14
wild a. snuffed up the wind. *Jer* 14:6
dwelling, was with *w. a.* *Dan* 5:21

young **asses**
their riches on *young a.* *Isa* 30:6
young a. that ear the ground shall. 24

assigned
priests had a portion *a.* *Gen* 47:22
they *a.* Bezer a city of. *Josh* 20:8
he *a.* Uriah to a place. *2 Sam* 11:16

assist
that ye *a.* her in. *Rom* 16:2

associate
a. yourselves and ye shall. *Isa* 8:9*

as soon
a. as I am gone out of the. *Ex* 9:29
a. as the commandment. *2 Chr* 31:5
a. as they hear of me. *Ps* 18:44
a. as Zion travailed, she. *Isa* 66:8
a. as the voice of thy. *Luke* 1:44
a. as it was sprung up, it. 8:6
a. as he said, I am he. *John* 18:6
came I *a.* as I was. *Acts* 10:29
a. as it was day there was no. 12:18
a. as I had eaten it, my. *Rev* 10:10
for to devour the child *a.* as it. 12:4

ass's colt
binding his *a. colt* to the. *Gen* 49:11
born like a wild *a. colt.* *Job* 11:12
sitting on an *a. colt.* *John* 12:15

assurance
have none *a.* of thy life. *Deut* 28:66
effect of righteousness, *a.* *Isa* 32:17*
whereof he hath given *a.* *Acts* 17:31
to all riches of the full *a.* of. *Col* 2:2
gospel came in much *a.* *1 Thes* 1:5
to the full *a.* of hope to. *Heb* 6:11*
let us draw near in full *a.* 10:22*

assure
shall *a.* our hearts. *1 John* 3:19

assured
fifth, and it shall be *a.* *Lev* 27:19
I will give you *a.* peace in. *Jer* 14:13
things thou hast been *a.* *2 Tim* 3:14

assuredly
know *a.* thou shalt go. *1 Sam* 28:1
a. Solomon thy son. *1 Ki* 1:13, 17, 30
plant them in this land *a.* *Jer* 32:41
if thou *a.* go forth to the. 38:17
they have *a.* drunken, and. 49:12
house of Israel know *a.* *Acts* 2:36
a. gathering that the Lord. 16:10

asswage, -ed
(*Old spelling of* assuage)
and the waters were *a.* *Gen* 8:1
of my lips should *a.* your. *Job* 16:5
I speak, yet my grief is not *a.* 6

Assyria
goeth toward the east of *A.* *Gen* 2:14
sons dwelt as thou goest to *A.* 25:18
carried captive to *A.* *2 Ki* 15:29; 17:6; 18:11
bee that is in the land of *A.* *Isa* 7:18
remnant of his people from *A.* 11:11
for his people left from *A.* 16
an highway out of Egypt to *A.* 19:23
be the third with Egypt and *A.* 24
blessed be *A.* the work of my. 25
who were ready to perish in *A.* 27:13
to do in the way of *A.* ? *Jer* 2:18
Egypt, as wast ashamed of *A.* 36
whoredoms with men of *A.* *Ezek* 23:7
they go to *A.* *Hos* 7:11
they are gone up to *A.* 8:9
shall eat unclean things in *A.* 9:3
it shall be carried to *A.* for a. 10:6
as a dove out of land of *A.* 11:11
shall waste the land of *A.* *Mi* 5:6
he shall come to thee from *A.* 7:12
and he will destroy *A.* *Zeph* 2:13
gather them out of *A.* *Zech* 10:10
the pride of *A.* shall be brought. 11

***see* king, kings**

Assyrian
O *A.* the rod of mine anger. *Isa* 10:5
people, be not afraid of the *A.* 24
that I will break the *A.* in my. 14:25
this people was not till the *A.* 23:13
the *A.* shall be beaten down. 30:31
then shall the *A.* fall with the. 31:8
the *A.* oppressed them without. 52:4
the *A.* was a cedar in. *Ezek* 31:3
went Ephraim to the *A.* *Hos* 5:13
but the *A.* shall be his king. 11:5
be the peace when *A.* come. *Mi* 5:5
shall he deliver us from the *A.* 6

Assyrians
smote in the camp of *A.* 185,000 men. *2 Ki* 19:35; *Isa* 37:36
given the hand to the *A.* *Lam* 5:6
the whore with the *A.* *Ezek* 16:28
she doted on the *A.* her. 23:5, 12
delivered her into the hand of the *A.* 9
I will bring all the *A.* against. 23
a covenant with the *A.* *Hos* 12:1

astonied
(*Old form of* astonished)
the hair, and sat down *a.* *Ezra* 9:3
upright men shall be *a.* at. *Job* 17:8
come after him shall be *a.* 18:20
that they may be *a.* one. *Ezek* 4:17
Nebuchadnezzar was *a.* *Dan* 3:24
Daniel was *a.* for one hour. 4:19
was changed, his lords *a.* 5:9*

astonished
your enemies shall be *a.* *Lev* 26:32
passeth by shall be *a.* *1 Ki* 9:8
Jer 18:16; 19:8; 49:17; 50:13
heaven tremble and are *a.* *Job* 26:11
as many were *a.* at thee. *Isa* 52:14
be *a.* O ye heavens, at this. *Jer* 2:12
heart of the priests shall be *a.* 4:9
shouldest thou be as a man *a.* 14:9
I remained *a.* among them. *Ezek* 3:15
at every moment, and be *a.* 26:16
know thee shall be *a.* at thee. 28:19
Daniel was *a.* at the vision. *Dan* 8:27
the people were *a.* *Mat* 7:28; 22:33
Mark 1:22; 6:2; 11:18; *Luke* 4:32
they were *a.* with great. *Mark* 5:42
beyond measure *a.* 7:37; 10:26
the disciples were *a.* at his. 10:24
a. at his understanding. *Luke* 2:47
a. at the draught of fishes. 5:9
her parents were *a.* but he. 8:56
certain women also made us *a.* 24:22
Saul trembling and *a.* said. *Acts* 9:6*
which believed, were *a.* 10:45
and saw Peter, they were *a.* 12:16
he saw, believed, being *a.* 13:12

astonishment
shall smite thee with *a.* *Deut* 28:28
thou shalt become an *a.* and a. 37
this house shall be an *a.* *2 Chr* 7:21
he hath delivered them to *a.* 29:8
to drink the wine of *a.* *Ps* 60:3*
I am black, *a.* hath taken. *Jer* 8:21
I will make them an *a.* 25:9, 18
land shall be a desolation and *a.* 11
them to be a curse and an *a.* 29:18
an execration and an *a.* 42:18; 44:12
therefore is your land an *a.* 44:22
shall become heaps and an *a.* 51:37
they shall drink water by measure, and with *a.* *Ezek* 4:16; 12:19
it shall be an *a.* to the nations. 5:15
filled with the cup of *a.* 23:33
smite every horse with *a.* *Zech* 12:4

astray, *see* went, go, gone

astrologers
[1] *Those we now call astrologers.*
[2] *Enchanters of any sort.*
a. the star-gazers, stand. *Isa* 47:13
ten times better than *a.* *Dan* 1:20
secret cannot the *a.* shew to. 2:27
in the magicians and the *a.* 4:7
cried aloud, to bring in the *a.* 5:7

asunder, *see* cleave, cut, divide, put

as well
as well the stranger, as. *Lev* 24:16
one law, *as well* for the stranger. 22
heart faint, *as well* as. *Deut* 20:8
devours one *as well* as. *2 Sam* 11:25
they cast lots, *as well.* *1 Chr* 25:8
to give *as well* to the. *2 Chr* 31:15
understanding *as well* as. *Job* 12:3
as well the singers as the. *Ps* 87:7
the Holy Ghost *as well.* *Acts* 10:47
about a sister *as well* as. *1 Cor* 9:5
gospel preached *as well* as. *Heb* 4:2

Asyncritus
salute *A.* Phlegon. *Rom* 16:14

Atad
to the threshing-floor of *A.* *Gen* 50:10
saw mourning in floor of *A.* 11

ate
a. the sacrifices of the. *Ps* 106:28
I *a.* no pleasant bread. *Dan* 10:3
took the little book, and *a.* *Rev* 10:10

Athaliah
mother was *A.* *2 Ki* 8:26; *2 Chr* 22:2
A. arose. *2 Ki* 11:1; *2 Chr* 22:10
hid from *A.* *2 Ki* 11:2; *2 Chr* 22:11
they slew *A.* *2 Ki* 11:20; *2 Chr* 23:21
Shehariah and *A.* *1 Chr* 8:26

sons of *A.* that wicked. *2 Chr* 24:7
Jeshaiah son of *A.* with. *Ezra* 8:7

Athenians

A. spent their time in. *Acts* 17:21

Athens

and brought Paul to *A.* *Acts* 17:15
while Paul waited for them at *A.* 16
ye men of *A.* I perceive ye are. 22
Paul departed from *A.* and. 18:1
good to be left at *A.* *1 Thes* 3:1

athirst

Samson was sore *a.* and. *Judg* 15:18
when *a.* go to the vessels. *Ruth* 2:9
when saw we thee *a.*? *Mat* 25:44
give to him that is *a.* of. *Rev* 21:6
bride say, let him that is *a.* 22:17

atonement

Reconciliation, at-one-ment; chiefly used of Christ's atoning death, Rom 5:11.

eat things wherewith *a.* *Ex* 29:33
offer a bullock every day for *a.* 36
seven days thou shalt make *a.* for. 37
once in year shall make *a.* 30:10
to make an *a.* for your. 15; *Lev* 17:11
thou shalt take the *a.* money. *Ex* 30:16
I shall make an *a.* for sin. 32:30
accepted for him to make *a.* *Lev* 1:4
priest shall make an *a.* for them. 4:20
26, 31, 35; 5:6; 6:7; 12:8; 14:18
Num 15:25
hath commanded to make *a.* *Lev* 8:34
make *a.* for thyself and. 9:7; 16:24
given it you to make *a.* for. 10:17
make an *a.* for her, and she. 12:7
make an *a.* for the house. it. 14:53
shall be presented to make *a.* 16:10
Aaron shall make an *a.* for. 11
he shall make an *a.* for the holy. 16
no man there, when he maketh *a.* 17
he shall go and make *a.* for the. 18
was brought in to make *a.* 27
he shall make *a.* for the holy. 33
everlasting statute to make *a.* 34
there shall be a day of *a.* 23:27
it is a day of *a.* to make *a.* 28
in the day of *a.* make the. 25:9
given Levites to make *a.* *Num* 8:19
made *a.* for the Levites. 21
go quickly, make *a.* for wrath. 16:46
because he made an *a.* 25:13
sin-offering to make *a.* 28:22, 30
goats to make an *a.* for you. 29:5
ear-rings to make an *a.* for. 31:50
shall I make the *a.*? *2 Sam* 21:3
sons appointed to make *a.* *1 Chr* 6:49
killed them to make *a.* *2 Chr* 29:24
for offering to make an *a.* *Neh* 10:33
we have now received *a.* *Rom* 5:11

attain

(*To reach by growth, or by continued effort*)

it is high, I cannot *a.* unto. *Ps* 139:6
of understanding shall *a.* *Pr* 1:5
as his hand shall *a.* to it. *Ezek* 46:7*
ere they *a.* to innocency? *Hos* 8:5
they might *a.* to Phenice. *Acts* 27:12
a. to the resurrection. *Phil* 3:11

attained

have not *a.* to the days of. *Gen* 47:9
he *a.* not to the first. *2 Sam* 23:19
23; *1 Chr* 11:21, 25
the Gentiles have *a.* to. *Rom* 9:30
Israel hath not *a.* to the law of. 31
though I had already *a.* *Phil* 3:12
whereto we have already *a.* let. 16
whereto thou hast *a.* *1 Tim* 4:6

Attalia

they went down into *A.* *Acts* 14:25

attend

he appointed to *a.* her. *Esth* 4:5
a. to my cry. *Ps* 17:1; 61:1; 142:6
a. to me, hear me, I mourn. 55:2
and *a.* to the voice of. 86:6
hear and *a.* to know. *Pr* 4:1
my son, *a.* to my words. 20; 7:24
my son, *a.* to my wisdom, and. 5:1
may *a.* on the Lord. *1 Cor* 7:35

attendance

the *a.* of his ministers. *1 Ki* 10:5
2 Chr 9:4
till I come, give *a.* to. *1 Tim* 4:13*
which no man gave *a.* at. *Heb* 7:13

attended

I *a.* to you, none of you. *Job* 32:12
he hath *a.* to the voice of. *Ps* 66:19
she *a.* to the things. *Acts* 16:14*

attending

ministers *a.* continually. *Rom* 13:6

attent

(*Old form of* attentive)

let thine ears be *a.* to. *2 Chr* 6:40
mine ears shall be *a.* at the. 7:15

attentive

ear now be *a.* *Neh* 1:6, 11; *Ps* 130:2
the people were *a.* 8:3; *Luke* 19:48

attentively

hear *a.* the noise of his. *Job* 37:2*

attire, -ed

mitre shall Aaron be *a.* *Lev* 16:4
him a woman with *a.* of an. *Pr* 7:10
can a bride forget her *a.*? *Jer* 2:32
exceeding in dyed *a.* on. *Ezek* 23:15

audience

(*Used as* hearing, *not* a company of hearers)

spake to Ephron in *a.* of. *Gen* 23:13
covenant, and read in *a.* *Ex* 24:7
maid speak in thy *a.* *1 Sam* 25:24
in the *a.* of our God. *1 Chr* 28:8
the book of Moses in the *a.* *Neh* 13:1
all his sayings in the *a.* *Luke* 7:1
in *a.* of the people he said to. 20:45
ye that fear God, give *a.* *Acts* 13:16
then all the multitude gave *a.* 15:12
they gave him *a.* to this. 22:22

augment

ye are risen to *a.* the. *Num* 32:14

Augustus

a decree from Caesar *A.* *Luke* 2:1
had appealed to *A.* *Acts* 25:21, 25
Julius, a centurion of *A.* band. 27:1

aunt

to his wife, she is thy *a.* *Lev* 18:14

austere

because thou art an *a.* *Luke* 19:21

author

God is not the *a.* of. *1 Cor* 14:33*
became the *a.* of eternal. *Heb* 5:9
Jesus, the *a.* and finisher of. 12:2

authority

[1] *Power, rule, or dignity,* Mat 7:29; 20:25; Luke 19:17. [2] *A warrant or order,* Mat 21:23; Acts 9:14.

Mordecai wrote with *a.* *Esth* 9:29
when righteous are in *a.* *Pr* 29:2*
taught them as one having *a.*
Mat 7:29; *Mark* 1:22
a man under *a.* *Mat* 8:9; *Luke* 7:8
exercise *a.* *Mat* 20:25; *Mark* 10:42
by what *a.* doest thou these things?
Mat 21:23; *Mark* 11:28
with *a.* commandeth he even the unclean. *Mark* 1:27; *Luke* 4:36
his house, and gave *a.* to. *Mark* 13:34
gave them power and *a.* *Luke* 9:1
been faithful, have thou *a.* 19:17
might deliver him to *a.* of. 20:20
that exercise *a.* are called. 22:25
hath given him *a.* to. *John* 5:27
eunuch of great *a.* under. *Acts* 8:27
hath *a.* to bind. 9:14; 26:10, 12
have put down all *a.* *1 Cor* 15:24
somewhat more of our *a.* *2 Cor* 10:8
for kings and all in *a.* *1 Tim* 2:2
I suffer not a woman to usurp *a.* 12
and rebuke with all *a.* *Tit* 2:15
angels and *a.* made. *1 Pet* 3:22
him power and great *a.* *Rev* 13:2

availeth

yet all this *a.* me nothing. *Esth* 5:13
circumcision *a.* not. *Gal* 5:6*; 6:15
a righteous man *a.* much. *Jas* 5:16

Aven

the young men of *A.* *Ezek* 30:17
the high places of *A.* the. *Hos* 10:8
cut off the inhabitant of *A.* *Amos* 1:5

avenge

thou shalt not *a.* nor. *Lev* 19:18*
that shall *a.* the quarrel of. 26:25*
a. Israel of the Midianites. *Num* 31:2
he will *a.* the blood of. *Deut* 32:43
the Lord judge and *a.* *1 Sam* 24:12
of Ahab, that I may *a.* *2 Ki* 9:7
Jews *a.* themselves on. *Esth* 8:13
a. me of mine enemies. *Isa* 1:24
vengeance that he may *a.* *Jer* 46:10
a. the blood of Jezreel. *Hos* 1:4
saying, *a.* me of mine. *Luke* 18:3
shall not God *a.* his own elect. 7
I tell you that he will *a.* them. 8
a. not yourselves, but. *Rom* 12:19
how long dost thou not *a.*? *Rev* 6:10

avenged

should be *a.* seven-fold. *Gen* 4:24
stayed till people had *a.* *Josh* 10:13
done this, yet I will be *a.* *Judg* 15:7
may be *a.* on Philistines for. 16:28
food, that I may be *a.* *1 Sam* 14:24
hundred foreskins, to be *a.* 18:25
or that my Lord hath *a.* 25:31
the Lord hath *a.* my. *2 Sam* 4:8
how the Lord hath *a.* him of. 18:19
the Lord hath *a.* thee this day. 31
my soul be *a.* on such a nation.
Jer 5:9, 29; 9:9
Moses *a.* him that was. *Acts* 7:24
rejoice, for God hath *a.* *Rev* 18:20*
hath *a.* blood of his servants. 19:2

avenger

cities for refuge from the *a.*
Num 35:12; *Josh* 20:3
lest the *a.* of blood pursue. *Deut* 19:6
him into the hand of the *a.* 12
if the *a.* of blood pursue. *Josh* 20:5
not die by the hand of the *a.* till. 9
still the enemy and *a.* *Ps* 8:2
by reason of the enemy and *a.* 44:16
the Lord is the *a.* *1 Thes* 4:6

avengeth

God that *a.* *2 Sam* 22:48; *Ps* 18:47

avenging

praise the Lord for the *a.* *Judg* 5:2*
withholden thee from *a.* *1 Sam* 25:26
thou who kept me from *a.* 33

averse

by securely, as men *a.* *Mi* 2:8

avoid

(*To shun, turn away from, escape from*)

a. it, pass not by it. *Pr* 4:15
cause divisions, and *a.* *Rom* 16:17
to *a.* fornication, let. *1 Cor* 7:2
unlearned questions *a.* *2 Tim* 2:23
a. foolish questions and. *Tit* 3:9

avoided, -ing

David *a.* out of his. *1 Sam* 18:11
a. this, that no man. *2 Cor* 8:20
a. profane and vain. *1 Tim* 6:20

avouched

(*Acknowledged deliberately and openly*)

this day *a.* the Lord to. *Deut* 26:17
the Lord hath *a.* thee to be his. 18

awake

[1] *To come out of natural sleep,* Luke 9:32. [2] *To rouse out of spiritual sleep,* Rom 13:11; Eph 5:14. [3] *To raise from the dead,* Job 14:12; John 11:11.

a. Deborah *a. a.* utter. *Judg* 5:12
surely now he would *a.* *Job* 8:6
no more, they shall not *a.* 14:12
a. for me to the. *Ps* 7:6; 35:23
be satisfied when I *a.* with. 17:15
a. why sleepest thou, O Lord? 44:23
a. my glory, I myself will *a.* 57:8
108:2
they prepare, *a.* to help me. 59:4
O Lord God, *a.* to visit all the. 5
when shall I *a.* I will seek. *Pr* 23:35
a. my love. *S of S* 2:7; 3:5; 8:4
a. O north wind, and come. 4:16
a. and sing ye that dwell. *Isa* 26:19
a a. put on strength, O arm of the Lord, *a.* as in the. 51:9; 52:1
a. a. stand up, O Jerusalem. 51:17
perpetual sleep, and not *a.* *Jer* 51:57
sleep in the dust shall *a.* *Dan* 12:2
a. ye drunkards, weep. *Joel* 1:5
shall they not *a.* that. *Hab* 2:7

him that saith to the wood *a*. *Hab* 2:19
a. O sword, against my. *Zech* 13:7
asleep, and they *a*. him. *Mark* 4:38
when they were *a*. they. *Luke* 9:32
I go that I may *a*. him. *John* 11:11
it is high time to *a*. out. *Rom* 13:11
a. to righteousness, and. *1 Cor* 15:34
a. thou that sleepest, and. *Eph* 5:14

awaked

Jacob *a*. out of his sleep. *Gen* 28:16
Samson *a*. and went. *Judg* 16:14
nor knew it, neither *a*. *1 Sam* 26:12
and must be *a*. *1 Ki* 18:27
him, the child is not *a*. *2 Ki* 4:31
I *a*. for the Lord sustained. *Ps* 3:5
then the Lord *a*. as one out. 78:65
upon this I *a*. and beheld. *Jer* 31:26

awakest

when thou *a*. shalt despise. *Ps* 73:20
when thou *a*. it shall talk. *Pr* 6:22

awaketh, -ing

as a dream when one *a*. so. *Ps* 73:20
a. and his soul is empty, *a*. *Isa* 29:8
keeper of the prison *a*. *Acts* 16:27

aware

I was *a*. my soul made. *S of S* 6:12
Babylon, and thou art not *a*. *Jer* 50:24
over them, are not *a*. *Luke* 11:44

away

Abraham drove them *a*. *Gen* 15:11
not go very far *a*. *Ex* 8:28
the Lord said to him, *a*. get. 19:24*
have me *a*. for I am. *2 Chr* 35:23
assemblies I cannot, *a*. *Isa* 1:13
a. with this man, release. *Luke* 23:18
a. with him, *a*. with him. *John* 19:15
Acts 21:36
a. with such a fellow. *Acts* 22:22

awe

stand in *a*. and sin not. *Ps* 4:4
of the world stand in *a*. of him. 33:8
my heart standeth in *a*. of. 119:161

awl

bore his ear with an *a*. *Ex* 21:6
thou shalt take an *a*. *Deut* 15:17

awoke

Noah *a*. from his wine. *Gen* 9:24
fat kine, so Pharaoh *a*. 41:4, 7, 21
Samson *a*. out of his. *Judg* 16:20
Solomon *a*. and behold it. *1 Ki* 3:15
disciples came and *a*. him. *Mat* 8:25
Luke 8:24

axe

[1] *Literally, the axe similar to that in modern use.* [2] *Figuratively, any instrument used in inflicting judgement,* Isa 10:15; Mat 3:10.

a stroke with the *axe*. *Deut* 19:5
the trees by forcing an *axe*. 20:19
Abimelech took an *axe* in. *Judg* 9:48
down to sharpen his *axe*. *1 Sam* 13:20
neither hammer nor *axe*. *1 Ki* 6:7
the *axe*-head fell into. *2 Ki* 6:5
shall the *axe* boast itself. *Isa* 10:15
cutteth a tree with the *axe*. *Jer* 10:3
thou art my battle-*axe* and. 51:20
now also the *axe* is laid unto the root of the trees. *Mat* 3:10; *Luke* 3:9

axes

had a file for the *a*. *1 Sam* 13:21
under saws and *a*. of iron, and made them. *2 Sam* 12:31; *1 Chr* 20:3
famous as he lifted up *a*. *Ps* 74:5
down the carved work with *a*. 6
come against her with *a*. *Jer* 46:22
with *a*. he shall break. *Ezek* 26:9

axle-trees

the *a*.-*t*. of the wheel join. *1 Ki* 7:32
a.-*t*. naves, and felloes, were. 33

Azariah

A. was one of Solomon's. *1 Ki* 4:2
A. the son of Nathan was over. 5
Judah made *A*. king. *2 Ki* 14:21
A. son of Ethan. *1 Chr* 2:8
Jehu begat *A*. 38
Amaziah his son, *A*. his son. 3:12
Ahimaaz begat *A*. 6:9
Johanan begat *A*. 10
Hilkiah begat *A*. 13
Zephaniah begat *A*. 36
of God came on *A*. *2 Chr* 15:1
A. son of Jehoshaphat. *2 Chr* 21:2
A. son of Jehoram. 22:6
A. son of Jehoram, and *A*. 23:1
A. the priest went in. 26:17, 20
the son of *A*. the son. *Ezra* 7:1, 3
A. the son of Maaseiah. *Neh* 3:23
Nehemiah *A*. came up with. 7:7
A. caused the people to. 8:7
those that sealed were *A*. 10:2
A. and all the proud men. *Jer* 43:2
of Judah was Daniel, *A*. *Dan* 1:6
A. the name of Abed-nego. 7
made the thing known to *A*. 2:17

Azekah

stones on them to *A*. *Josh* 10:11
Babylon fought against *A*. *Jer* 34:7

B

Baal

to high places of *B*. *Num* 22:41
Israel served *B*. and. *Judg* 2:13
throw down the altar of *B*. 6:25
will ye plead for *B*.? will ye? 31
Ahab served *B*. and. *1 Ki* 16:31
but if *B*. be God, then follow. 18:21
name of *B*. saying, O *B*. hear. 26
take the prophets of *B*. let none. 40
seven thousand in Israel . . . not bowed to *B*. 19:18; *Rom* 11:4
sacrifice to do to *B*. *2 Ki* 10:19
a solemn assembly for *B*. 20
thus Jehu destroyed *B*. out of. 28
brake down the house of *B*. 11:18
host of heaven, served *B*. 17:16
reared up altars for *B*. 21:3
all the vessels made for *B*. 23:4
them that burnt incense to *B*. 5
prophets prophesied by *B*. *Jer* 2:8
burn incense to *B*.? 7:9; 11:13, 17
32:29
my people to swear by *B*. 12:16
built the high places of *B*. . . . fire for burnt-offerings to *B*. 19:5
they prophesied in *B*. and. 23:13
have forgotten my name for *B*. 27
which they prepared for *B*. *Hos* 2:8
when Ephraim offended in *B*. 13:1
cut off the remnant of *B*. *Zeph* 1:4

Baal-berith

of Israel made *B*. *Judg* 8:33

Baal-hamon

had a vineyard at *B*. *S of S* 8:11

Baali

shalt call me no more *B*. *Hos* 2:16

Baalim

Israel served *B*. *Judg* 2:11; 3:7
10:6, 10
Israel went a whoring after *B*. 8:33
of Israel put away *B*. *1 Sam* 7:4
thou hast followed *B*. *1 Ki* 18:18
sought not unto *B*. *2 Chr* 17:3
things did they bestow on *B*. 24:7
also molten images for *B*. 28:2
reared up altars for *B*. 33:3
brake down the altars of *B*. 34:4
I have not gone after *B*. *Jer* 2:23
have walked after *B*. which. 9:14
visit on her the days of *B*. *Hos* 2:13
take away the names of *B*. 17

Baalis

B. king of Ammonites hath. *Jer* 40:14

Baal-meon

Beth-jeshimoth, *B*. *Ezek* 25:9

Baal-peor

Israel joined himself to *B*. and the. *Num* 25:3; *Ps* 106:28; *Hos* 9:10
men that were joined unto *B*.
Num 25:5
Lord did because of *B*. *Deut* 4:3

Baal-perazim

that place *B*. *2 Sam* 5:20; *1 Chr* 14:11

Baal-shalisha

came a man from *B*. *2 Ki* 4:42

Baal-tamar

themselves in array at *B*. *Judg* 20:33

Baal-zebub

enquire of *B*. the God. *2 Ki* 1:2, 16

Baal-zephon

over against *B*. *Ex* 14:2; *Num* 33:7

Baanah

Rechab and *B*. his. *2 Sam* 4:6
Heleb the son of *B*. one of. 23:29
B. the son of Hushai. *1 Ki* 4:16
B. came to. *Ezra* 2:2; *Neh* 7:7
Harim, *B*. sealed the. *Neh* 10:27

Baasha

war between Asa and *B*. *1 Ki* 15:16, 32
thy league with *B*. 19; *2 Chr* 16:3
B. son of Ahijah conspired. *1 Ki* 15:27
Lord came to Jehu against *B*. 16:1
B. slept with his fathers and was. 6
slew all the house of *B*. 11, 12
like the house of *B*. 21:22; *2 Ki* 9:9
Asa made for fear of *B*. *Jer* 41:9

babbler

will bite, and a *b*. is. *Eccl* 10:11*
what will this *b*. say? *Acts* 17:18

babbling, -s

contentions? who hath *b*.? *Pr* 23:29*
profane and vain *b*. *1 Tim* 6:20
shun profane and vain *b*. *2 Tim* 2:16

babe

[1] *An infant or child,* Ex 2:6; Luke 2:12. [2] *Such as are weak in faith and knowledge,* 1 Cor 3:1; Heb 5:13.

child, and behold the *b*. *Ex* 2:6
heard Mary, the *b*. *Luke* 1:41
the *b*. leaped in my womb for joy. 44
find *b*. wrapped in swaddling. 2:12
came and found the *b*. lying in. 16
the word, for he is a *b*. *Heb* 5:13

Babel

of his kingdom was *B*. *Gen* 10:10
is the name of it called *B*. 11:9

babes

the mouth of *b*. *Ps* 8:2; *Mat* 21:16
of their substance to their *b*. *Ps* 17:14
their princes and *b*. shall. *Isa* 3:4
hast revealed them to *b*. *Mat* 11:25
Luke 10:21
foolish, a teacher of *b*. *Rom* 2:20
carnal, even as unto *b*. *1 Cor* 3:1
as new-born *b*. desire the. *1 Pet* 2:2

Babylon

the men of *B*. made. *2 Ki* 17:30
that were in *B*. 25:28; *Jer* 52:32
of the princes of *B*. *2 Chr* 32:31
vessels in his temple at *B*. 36:7
take out of temple of *B*. *Ezra* 5:14
treasures were laid up in *B*. 6:1
mention of Rahab and *B*. *Ps* 87:4
by the rivers of *B*. there we. 137:1
burden of *B*. which Isaiah. *Isa* 13:1
B. shall be as when God. 19
B. is fallen. 21:9; *Jer* 51:8
Rev 14:8; 18:2
will do his pleasure on *B*. *Isa* 48:14
go ye forth of *B*. flee from the. 20
carry them captive into *B*. *Jer* 20:4
of Judah that went into *B*. 28:4
be accomplished at *B*. 29:10
raised us up prophets in *B*. 15
to come with me into *B*. 40:4
the Lord spake against *B*. 50:1
remove out of the midst of *B*. 8
one that goeth by *B*. shall hiss. 13
how is *B*. become a desolation? 23
together the archers against *B*. 29
disquiet the inhabitants of *B*. 34
counsel of the Lord against *B*. 45
flee out of the midst of *B*. 51:6
violence done to me be upon *B*. 35
the sea is come up upon *B*. she is. 42
and earth shall sing for *B*. 48
at *B*. shall fall the slain of all. 49
though *B*. should mount up. 53
because the Lord hath spoiled *B*. 55
broad walls of *B*. shall be. 58
the evil that shall come on *B*. 60
thus shall *B*. sink, and shall not. 64
him in the midst of *B*. *Ezek* 17:16
is not this great *B*. that I? *Dan* 4:30
till the carrying into *B*. *Mat* 1:17
carry you away beyond *B*. *Acts* 7:43
the church at *B*. saluteth. *1 Pet* 5:13
great *B*. came in. *Rev* 16:19
B. the great, the mother of. 17:5
alas, alas, that great city *B*. 18:10
thus shall that great city *B*. be. 21
see **daughter, province,** *wise* **men**

from **Babylon**
country *from B.* 2 Ki 20:14; Isa 39:3
began he to go up *from B.* Ezra 7:9
went up with me *from B.* 8:1
I will cut off *from B.* the. Isa 14:22
off the sower *from B.* Jer 50:16
sound of a cry cometh *from B.* 51:54
which are come *from B.* Zech 6:10

king of **Babylon**
serve the *king of B.* 2 Ki 25:24
Jer 27:17; 40:9
the hand of the *king of B.* the.
Ezra 5:12; Jer 21:7; 22:25
proverb against *king of B.* Isa 14:4
fight against the *king of B.* Jer 21:4
serve the *king of B.* 70 years. 25:11
I will punish the *king of B.* 12
will not serve *king of B.* 27:8, 13
the yoke of the *king of B.* 28:11
whom the *king of B.* roasted. 29:22
behold the eyes of *king of B.* 34:3
king of B. shall certainly come. 36:29
king of B. gave charge. 39:11
be not afraid of the *king of B.* 42:11
king of B. hath taken counsel. 49:30
the *king of B.* hath broken. 50:17
sword of the *king of B.* Ezek 21:19
king of B. caused his army. 29:18
give Egypt unto the *king of B.* 19
the arms of *king of B.* 30:24, 25
sword of the *king of B.* shall. 32:11

to or *unto* **Babylon**
shall be carried *to B.* 2 Ki 20:17
24:15; 25:7, 13; 1 Chr 9:1
2 Chr 36:6, 7, 20; Ezra 5:12; Isa
39:6; Jer 27:20; 28:3; 29:1, 4
40:1, 7
and carried him *to B.* 2 Chr 33:11
all these he brought *to B.* 36:18
sake I have sent *to B.* Isa 43:14
thou shalt come *to B.* Jer 20:6
thou shalt go *to B.* 34:3
I will render *unto B.* 51:24
when comest *to B.* 61
I will bring him *to B.* Ezek 17:20
of Zion shall go *to B.* Mi 4:10
they were carried *to B.* Mat 1:11

Babylonians
manner of the *B.* of. Ezek 23:15
the *B.* came to her into the bed. 17

Babylonish
saw a goodly *B.* garment. Josh 7:21

Baca
through the valley of *B.* Ps 84:6

back
after he had sent her *b.* Ex 18:2
astray, thou shalt bring it *b.* 23:4
I will get me *b.* Num 22:34
Lord hath kept thee *b.* 24:11
drew not his hand *b.* till. Josh 8:26
damsel that came *b.* Ruth 2:6
return, and take *b.* thy. 2 Sam 15:20
not of bringing the king *b.*? 19:10
but camest *b.* and hast. 1 Ki 13:22
and carry him *b.* to Amon. 22:26
when Judah looked *b.* 2 Chr 13:14
soldiers that Amaziah sent *b.* 25:13
he holdeth *b.* the face of. Job 26:9
fled apace, and look not *b.* Jer 46:5
slideth *b.* as a backsliding. Hos 4:16
they cry, none shall look *b.* Nah 2:8
that is in field return *b.* Mat 24:18
angel rolled *b.* the stone from. 28:2
the ship, and returned *b.* Luke 8:37
to plough, and looking *b.* 9:62
let him likewise not return *b.* 17:31
see **draw, go, bring, keep, kept, turn, went**

back, *substantive*
he turned his *b.* to go. 1 Sam 10:9
behind thy *b.* 1 Ki 14:9; Ezek 23:35
make them turn their *b.* Ps 21:12
the plowers plowed on my *b.* 129:3
b. of him. Pr 10:13; 19:29; 26:3
cast my sins behind thy *b.* Isa 38:17
I gave my *b.* to the smiters. 50:6
they have turned their *b.* Jer 2:27
I will shew them the *b.* and. 18:17
have turned to me the *b.* 32:33
how hath Moab turned the *b.* 48:39
which had on the *b.* of it. Dan 7:6
bow down their *b.* alway. Rom 11:10

backbiters
b. haters of God. Rom 1:30

backbiteth
he that *b.* not with his. Ps 15:3*

backbiting
countenance, a *b.* tongue. Pr 25:23
be debates, strifes, *b.* 2 Cor 12:20

back-bone
take off hard by the *b.-b.* Lev 3:9

back-parts
thou shalt see my *b.-p.* Ex 33:23

backs
thy law behind their *b.* Neh 9:26
with their *b.* towards. Ezek 8:16
their whole body and *b.* full. 10:12
see **turned**

backside
Moses led the flock to the *b.* Ex 3:1
shall hang over the *b.* 26:12
on the *b.* sealed with seven. Rev 5:1

backslider
b. in heart be filled. Pr 14:14

backsliding, -s
and thy *b.* shall reprove. Jer 2:19
hast thou seen what *b.* Israel? 3:6
whereby *b.* Israel committed. 8
the *b.* Israel hath justified. 11
return thou *b.* Israel, saith the. 12
b. children, saith the Lord. 14, 22
their transgressions and *b.* 5:6
slidden back by a perpetual *b.* 8:5
for our *b.* are many, we sinned. 14:7
about, O *b.* daughter. 31:22; 49:4
slideth back, as a *b.* Hos 4:16*
my people are bent to *b.* 11:7
I will heal their *b.* I will love. 14:4

backward
b. and their faces were *b.* Gen 9:23
that his rider shall fall *b.* 49:17
fell from off the seat *b.* 1 Sam 4:18
let the shadow return *b.* 2 Ki 20:10
Isa 38:8
b. but I cannot perceive. Job 23:8
let them be driven *b.* that. Ps 40:14
them be turned *b.* that desire. 70:2
and are gone away *b.* Isa 1:4
that they might go and fall *b.* 28:13
that turneth wise men *b.* and. 44:25
judgement is turned away *b.* 59:14
but they went *b.* and not. Jer 7:24
thou art gone *b.* therefore I. 15:6
sigheth and turneth *b.* Lam 1:8
they went *b.* and fell to. John 18:6

bad
speak to thee *b.* or good. Gen 24:50
to Jacob good or *b.* 31:24, 29
good for a *b.* or a *b.* for. Lev 27:10
value it, whether it be good or *b.* 12
house, whether it be good or *b.* 14
search whether it be good or *b.* 33
dwell in, if good or *b.* Num 13:19
to do either good or *b.* of my. 24:13
neither good nor *b.* 2 Sam 13:22
lord the king to discern good or *b.*
14:17
may discern good and *b.* 1 Ki 3:9*
the rebellious and *b.* city. Ezra 4:12
be eaten, they were so *b.* Jer 24:2
good but cast the *b.* away. Mat 13:48
good and *b.* and the wedding was.
22:10
done, whether good or *b.* 2 Cor 5:10

bade, -est
according as thou *b.* me. Gen 27:19
the man did as Joseph *b.* 43:17
till morning, as Moses *b.* Ex 16:24
all the congregation *b.* Num 14:10
to them as the Lord *b.* Josh 11:9
that her mother-in-law *b.* Ruth 3:6
some *b.* me kill thee. 1 Sam 24:10
David *b.* them teach. 2 Sam 1:18
for thy servant Joab he *b.* me. 14:19
third day as the king *b.* 2 Chr 10:12
Esther *b.* them return. Esth 4:15
how he *b.* them not. Mat 16:12
b. thee and him. Luke 14:9, 10
man made a supper and *b.* 16
and the Spirit *b.* me go. Acts 11:12
but *b.* them farewell, saying. 18:21
b. that he should be 22:24

badgers'-skins
(*Revised Version,* seal-skins)
take of them. *b.-skins.* Ex 25:5
for the tent above of *b.-skins.* 26:14
rams' skins dyed red, *b.-skins.* 35:7
found skins of rams, and *b.-skins.* 23
made a covering of *b.-skins.* 36:19
a covering of *b.-skins.* Num 4:10
shod thee with *b.-skins.* Ezek 16:10

badness
the land of Egypt for *b.* Gen 41:19

bag
thy *b.* divers weights. Deut 25:13
and put them in a *b.* 1 Sam 17:40
is sealed up in a *b.* Job 14:17
he hath taken a *b.* of. Pr 7:20
all the weights of the *b.* 16:11
lavish gold out of the *b.* Isa 46:6
the *b.* of deceitful weights. Mi 6:11
to put in a *b.* with holes. Hag 1:6
a thief, and had the *b.* John 12:6
because Judas had the *b.* 13:29

bags
two talents in two *b.* 2 Ki 5:23
they put up in *b.* and told. 12:10
provide yourselves *b.* Luke 12:33*

Bahurim
weeping behind her to *B.* 2 Sam 3:16
when David came to *B.* Shimei. 16:5
came to a man's house in *B.* 17:18
a Benjamite of *B.* 19:16; 1 Ki 2:8

Bajith
up to *B.* and to Dibon to. Isa 15:2

bake
Lot did *b.* unleavened. Gen 19:3
b. that which you will *b.* Ex 16:23
take flour and *b.* twelve. Lev 24:5
ten women shall *b.* your. 26:26
woman at Endor did *b.* 1 Sam 28:24
took flour and did *b.* 2 Sam 13:8
shalt *b.* it with man's. Ezek 4:12
the place where they shall *b.* 46:20

baked
they *b.* unleavened cakes. Ex 12:39
and *b.* it in pans, and. Num 11:8*
and for that which is *b.* 1 Chr 23:29

bake-meats
manner of *b.-meats* for. Gen 40:17

baken
meat-offering *b.* in. Lev 2:4; 7:9
it shall not be *b.* with leaven. 6:17
two wave-loaves shall be *b.* 23:17
behold, a cake was *b.* 1 Ki 19:6

baker
the butler and *b.* had. Gen 40:1
head of the chief butler and *b.* 20
he hanged the *b.* as Joseph. 22
ward both me and the chief *b.* 41:10
as an oven heated by the *b.* Hos 7:4
their *b.* sleepeth all the night. 6

bakers
against the chief of the *b.* Gen 40:2
your daughters to be *b.* 1 Sam 8:13
Jeremiah bread out of *b.* Jer 37:21

baketh
he *b.* bread, yea, he. Isa 44:15

Balaam
sent messengers to *B.* Num 22:5
God came to *B.* and said, what. 9
they said, *B.* refuseth to come. 14
the ass crushed *B.* foot against. 25
Lord opened the eyes of *B.* 31
B. went with the princes of Balak. 35
God met *B.* and said. 23:4, 16
Balak did as *B.* had said, and. 30
B. lifted up his eyes and saw. 24:2
B. the son of Beor hath said. 3, 15
B. rose up and returned to his. 25
B. the son of Beor. 31:8; Josh 13:22
the counsel of *B.* to. Num 31:16
they hired *B.* Deut 23:4; Neh 13:2
would not hearken to *B.* Deut 23:5
Balak sent and called *B.* Josh 24:9
remember what *B.* Mi 6:5
way of B. the son of Bosor. 2 Pet 2:15
after the error of *B.* Jude 11
hold the doctrine of *B.* Rev 2:14

Balak
B. was king of the. Num 22:4
saith *B.* let nothing hinder thee. 16

B. did as Balaam had. *Num* 23:2. 30
B. king of Moab hath brought me. 7
rise up B. and hear. 18
B. anger kindled. 24:10
if B. would give me his house. 13
then B. arose and warred. *Josh* 24:9
any thing better than B.? *Judg* 11:25
remember what B. king of. *Mi* 6:5
B. to cast a stumbling. *Rev* 2:14

balance
be weighed in an even b. *Job* 31:6
laid in the b. are altogether. *Ps* 62:9
a false b. is. *Pr* 11:1; 20:23
a just weight and b. are the. 16:11
weighed the hills in a b.? *Isa* 40:12
as the small dust of the b. 15
gold, and weigh silver in the b. 46:6

balances
just b. a just. *Lev* 19:36; *Ezek* 45:10
calamity laid in the b. *Job* 6:2
him the money in the b. *Jer* 32:10
b. to weigh, and divide. *Ezek* 5:1
thou art weighed in the b. *Dan* 5:27
the b. of deceit are in. *Hos* 12:7
and falsifying the b. by. *Amos* 8:5
them pure with wicked b.? *Mi* 6:11
on him had a pair of b. *Rev* 6:5

balancings
dost thou know the b.? *Job* 37:16

bald
is b. yet is he clean. *Lev* 13:40, 41
b. head, go up thou b. *2 Ki* 2:23
nor make themselves b. *Jer* 16:6
every head shall be b. and. 48:37
themselves utterly b. *Ezek* 27:31
every head was made b. and. 29:18
make thee b. and poll thee. *Mi* 1:16

bald-locust
ye may eat the b.-locust. *Lev* 11:22

baldness
Frequently a sign of mourning, Isa. 15:2; Jer 47:5.
they shall not make b. *Lev* 21:5
nor make any b. between. *Deut* 14:1
of well set hair, b. *Isa* 3:24
on all their heads shall be b. 15:2
did call to mourning and to b. 22:12
b. is come upon Gaza. *Jer* 47:5
and b. upon all. *Ezek* 7:18; *Amos* 8:10
enlarge thy b. as the eagle. *Mi* 1:16

ball
turn and toss thee like a b. *Isa* 22:18

balm
Ishmaelites bearing b. *Gen* 37:25
take in your vessels a little b. 43:11
is there no b. in Gilead? *Jer* 8:22
go up to Gilead, and take b. 46:11
howl for her, take b. for her. 51:8
honey, and oil, and b. *Ezek* 27:17

Bamah
thereof is called B. *Ezek* 20:29

band, -s
[1] *Material chains,* Luke 8:29; Acts 16:26. [2] *Moral or spiritual bonds, as government and laws,* Ps 2:3; *or faith and love,* Col 2:19.
a b. round that it should. *Ex* 39:23
I have broken the b. of. *Lev* 26:13
his b. loosed from off. *Judg* 15:14
put Jehoahaz in b. *2 Ki* 23:33
darkness a swaddling b. *Job* 38:9
Pleiades, or loose the b. of? 31
or who hath loosed the b. of? 39:5
bind the unicorn with his b.? 10
let us break their b. asunder. *Ps* 2:3
for there are no b. in their. 73:4
he brake their b. in sunder. 107:14
heart snares, hands as b. *Eccl* 7:26
be not mockers, lest b. *Isa* 28:22
loose thyself from the b. of thy. 52:2
this the fast, to loose the b. 58:6
thy yoke, burst thy b. *Jer* 2:20
they shall put b. on thee. *Ezek* 3:25
and behold I will lay b. upon. 4:8
when I have broken the b. 34:27
a b. of iron and brass. *Dan* 4:15, 23
drew them with b. of love. *Hos* 11:4
two staves, beauty and b. *Zech* 11:7
asunder mine other staff, even b. 14
he brake b. and was. *Luke* 8:29
and every one's b. were. *Acts* 16:26
loosed Paul from his b. 22:30
which all the body by b. *Col* 2:19
see **bonds**

band, -s
(*Company of soldiers*)
the camels into two b. *Gen* 32:7
and now I am become two b. 10
went with him a b. *1 Sam* 10:26*
two men, captains of b. *2 Sam* 4:2
so the b. of Syria came. *2 Ki* 6:23
b. of the Moabites invaded. 13:20
burying a man, they spied a b. 21
against him b. of Chaldeans, b. 24:2
them were b. of soldiers. *1 Chr* 7:4
made them captains of the b. 12:18
helped David against the b. of. 21
require of the king a b. *Ezra* 8:22
made out three b. and fell. *Job* 1:17
the b. of the wicked. *Ps* 119:61
go forth all of them by b. *Pr* 30:27
I will scatter all his b. *Ezek* 12:14
all his b. Togarmah his b. 38:6
rain upon him and upon his b. 22
of Israel thou and thy b. 39:4
him whole b. *Mat* 27:27; *Mark* 15:16
having received a b. *John* 18:3
the b. and captain and officers. 12
the b. called the Italian b. *Acts* 10:1
to the chief captain of the b. 21:31
a centurion of Augustus' b. 27:1

banded
certain of the Jews b. *Acts* 23:12

banished
not fetch home his b. *2 Sam* 14:13
doth devise means that his b. 14

banishment
it be to death or to b. *Ezra* 7:26
burdens and causes of b. *Lam* 2:14

bank
[1] *The side, or brink of a river,* Gen 41:17. [2] *A mound, or heap of earth raised to cover besiegers, while they batter the walls of a city, or shoot at those who defend them,* 2 Sam 20:15. [3] *A place where there is a great sum of money taken in, and let out to use,* Luke 19:23.
behold I stood on the b. *Gen* 41:17
by the b. of the river Arnon.
Deut 4:48; *Josh* 12:2*; 13:9, 16*
cast up a b. against. *2 Sam* 20:15
Elisha stood by the b. *2 Ki* 2:13
shall not cast a b. 19:32; *Isa* 37:33
at the b. of the river. *Ezek* 47:7
the b. of the river, the other on that side of the b. *Dan* 12:5
my money into the b.? *Luke* 19:23

banks
overfloweth all his b. *Josh* 3:15; 4:18
had overflowed his b. *1 Chr* 12:15
shall go over all his b. *Isa* 8:7
man's voice between the b. *Dan* 8:16

banner
hast given a b. to them. *Ps* 60:4
to banquet, and his b. *S of S* 2:4
lift ye up a b. on the high. *Isa* 13:2

banners
our God we set up our b. *Ps* 20:5
terrible as an army with b. *S of S* 6:4

banquet
Haman come to the b. *Esth* 5:4, 5, 8
to Esther at the b. of wine. 6; 7:2
companions make a b of? *Job* 41:6*
the b. of them that. *Amos* 6:7

banquet-house
came into the b.-house. *Dan* 5:10

banqueting, -s
me into the b.-house. *S of S* 2:4
in lusts, revellings, b. *1 Pet* 4:3

baptism
[1] *The outward ordinance, or sacrament, wherein the washing with water represents the cleansing of the souls,* Luke 7:29; Acts 18:25; 1 Pet 3:21. [2] *Inward spiritual washing, signified by the outward sign,* Mat 3:11. [3] *The sufferings of Christ,* Mat 20:22; Luke 12:50.
Pharisees come to his b. *Mat* 3:7
be baptized with the b. 20:22*
Mark 10:38
the b. of John, whence was it, from?
Mat 21:25; *Mark* 11:30; *Luke* 20:4
and preach the b. *Mark* 1:4; *Luke* 3:3
baptized with the b. of. *Luke* 7:29
I have a b. to be baptized. 12:50
beginning from the b. of. *Acts* 1:22
word, after the b. which John. 10:37
preached the b. of repentance. 13:24
Apollos knowing only the b. 18:25
they said unto John's b. 19:3
John baptized with the b. of. 4
buried with him by b. *Rom* 6:4
one Lord, one faith, one b. *Eph* 4:5
buried with him in b. ye. *Col* 2:12
of doctrine of b. and laying. *Heb* 6:2
figure whereunto, even b. *1 Pet* 3:21

Baptist
in those days came John B. *Mat* 3:1
there hath not risen a greater than John the B. 11:11; *Luke* 7:28
the days of John the B. *Mat* 11:12
this is John the B. he is risen. 14:2
said, give me John the B. head in. 8
art John the B. 16:14; *Mark* 8:28
he spake of John the B. *Mat* 17:13
John the B. was risen. *Mark* 6:14
charger the head of John the B. 25
John the B. hath sent us. *Luke* 7:20
John the B. came neither eating. 33
answering said, John the B. 9:19

baptize
I b. you with water, he shall b.
Mat 3:11; *Mark* 1:8; *Luke* 3:16
John 1:26
John did b. in the. *Mark* 1:4
that sent me to b. said. *John* 1:33
Christ sent me not to b. *1 Cor* 1:17

baptized
b. of him in. *Mat* 3:6; *Mark* 1:5
cometh Jesus to John to be b.
Mat 3:13
I have need to be b. of thee. 14
Jesus, when he was b. went up. 16
Jesus was b. of John. *Mark* 1:9
I am b. withal, shall ye be b. 10:39
he that believeth and is b. 16:16
that came to be b. *Luke* 3:7
publicans to be b. 12; 7:29
Jesus being b. and praying. 3:21
lawyers, being not b. of him. 7:30
tarried with them and b. *John* 3:22
and they came and were b. 23
Jesus made and b. more. 4:1
though Jesus himself b. not, but. 2
place where John at first b. 10:40
b. with water, but ye shall be b. with.
Acts 1:5; 11:16
repent, be b. every one of you. 2:38
gladly received his word were b. 41
they were b. both men and. 8:12
believed also, and when he was b. 13
only they were b. in the name of. 16
what doth hinder me to be b.? 36
Philip and eunuch, and he b. him. 38
sight, and arose and was b. 9:18
that these should not be b. 10:47
Peter commanded them to be b. 48
Lydia when she was b. and. 16:15
jailer was b. and all his. 33
Corinth. believed, and were b. 18:8
to what then were ye b.? 19:3
when they heard this they were b. 5
arise, and be b. and wash. 22:16
b. into Jesus, were b. *Rom* 6:3
were ye b. in the name? *1 Cor* 1:13
thank God that I b. none of you. 14
b. household of Stephanas, not b. 16
and were all b. to Moses in. 10:2
by one Spirit are we all b. 12:13
what shall they do who are b. for the dead, why are they b.? 15:29
have been b. into Christ. *Gal* 3:27

baptizest
why b. thou, if thou be? *John* 1:25

baptizeth
the same is he who b. *John* 1:33
behold, the same b. all men. 3:26

baptizing
teach all nations, b. them. *Mat* 28:19

Jordan, where John was b. John 1:28
am I come b. with water. 31
and John was also b. in Enon. 3:23

bar
them shut the doors, and b. Neh 7:3

bar, *substantive*
the middle b. in midst of. Ex 26:28
made the middle b. to shoot. 36:33
shall put it upon a b. Num 4:10*, 12*
of the city, posts, b. Judg 16:3
I will break also the b. Amos 1:5

Barabbas
release B. Mat 27:17, 21
Mark 15:11; Luke 23:18
not this man but B. now B. was a.
John 18:40

Barachias
of Zacharias, son of B. Mat 23:35

Barak
Deborah called B. the son. Judg 4:6
Deborah went with B. 9
B. pursued after. 16
then sang Deborah and B. son. 5:1
arise B. and lead thy captivity. 12
would fail me to tell of B. Heb 11:32

barbarian
a b. and he a b. to me. 1 Cor 14:11
neither Greek nor Jew, b. Col 3:11

barbarians
the b. saw the venomous. Acts 28:4
both to the Greeks and b. Rom 1:14

barbarous
b. people shewed no. Acts 28:2

barbed
fill his skin with b. irons ? Job 41:7

barber
son of man, take thee a b. Ezek 5:1

bare
b. the ark. Gen 7:17; Deut 31:9, 25
Josh 3:15; 4:10; 8:33; 2 Sam 6:13
1 Chr 15:15, 26, 27
torn of beasts, I b. the. Gen 31:39
how I b. you on eagles'. Ex 19:4
thy God b. thee as a. Deut 1:31
sent the people that b. Judg 3:18
the young man that b. his armour.
1 Sam 14:1, 6; 2 Sam 18:15
that b. burdens. 1 Ki 5:15; Neh 4:17
of Judah that b. shield. 1 Chr 12:24
2 Chr 14:8
he b. the sin of many. Isa 53:12
he b. them all the days of old. 63:9
the stuff I b. upon my. Ezek 12:7
saying, himself b. our. Mat 8:17
and they that b. him. Luke 7:14
made wine, and they b. it. John 2:8
had the bag, and b. what was. 12:6
his own self b. our sins. 1 Pet 2:24

bare
was 60 years, when she b. Gen 25:26
then all the cattle b. speckled. 31:8
at Chezib, when she b. him. 38:5
ye know that my wife b. me. 44:27
Jochebed b. to Amram. Ex 6:20
wife was barren, and b. Judg 13:2
child Uriah's wife b. 2 Sam 12:15
his mother b. him after. 1 Ki 1:6
Jabez, because I b. him. 1 Chr 4:9
bitterness to her that b. Pr 17:25
she that b. thee shall rejoice. 23:25
choice one of her that b. S of S 6:9
brought thee forth that b. thee. 8:5
look unto Sarah that b. you. Isa 51:2
their mother that b. them. Jer 16:3
wherein my mother b. me. 20:14
and thy mother that b. thee. 22:26
b. you shall be ashamed. 50:12
the womb that b. thee. Luke 11:27
are the wombs that never b. 23:29

bare *fruit*
sprang up, and b. *fruit*. an Luke 8:8
b. twelve manner of *fruits*. Rev 22:2

bare *rule*
officers that b. *rule* over the people.
1 Ki 9:23; 2 Chr 8:10
their servants b. *rule*. Neh 5:15

bare *witness, and record*
b. false *witness*. Mark 14:56, 57
all b. him *witness*, and. Luke 4:22
b. *witness* of him. John 1:15, 32, 34
John b. *witness* to truth. John 5:33
that was with him b. *record*. 12:17
he that saw it b. *record*, and. 19:35
hearts, b. them *witness*. Acts 15:8
who b. *record* of the word. Rev 1:2

bare, *adjective*
be rent and his head b. Lev 13:45*
whether it be b. within or without. 55
strip ye, make ye b. and. Isa 32:11
b. the leg, uncover the thigh. 47:2
the Lord hath made b. his. 52:10
are thy heels made b. Jer 13:22
I have made Esau b. I have. 49:10
thou wast naked and b. Ezek 16:7
when thou wast naked, and b. 22
leave thee naked and b. 39; 23:29
hath made it clean and b. Joel 1:7
shall be, but b. grain. 1 Cor 15:37

barefoot
he went b. and the. 2 Sam 15:30
so, walking naked and b. Isa 20:2, 3
Egyptians prisoners, naked and b. 4

barest
because thou b. the ark. 1 Ki 2:26
never b. rule over them. Isa 63:19
he to whom thou b. John 3:26

Bar-jesus
whose name was B. Acts 13:6

Bar-jona
blessed art thou, Simon B. Mat 16:17

bark
dumb dogs, they cannot b. Isa 56:10

barked
laid my vine waste, and b. Joel 1:7

barley
b. was smitten, for b. Ex 9:31
an homer of b. seed. Lev 27:16
part of an ephah of b. Num 5:15
a land of wheat, and b. Deut 8:8
cake of b. bread tumbled. Judg 7:13
beginning of b. harvest. Ruth 1:22
gleaned about an ephah of b. 2:17
she kept fast to the end of b. 23
Boaz winnoweth b. to-night. 3:2
he measured six measures of b. 15
is near, he hath b. 2 Sam 14:30
Barzillai brought beds, b. and. 17:28
Saul's sons were hanged in b. 21:9
b. also and straw for the. 1 Ki 4:28
of God 20 loaves of b. 2 Ki 4:42
of b. for a shekel. 7:1, 16, 18
of ground full of b. 1 Chr 11:13
20,000 measures of b. 2 Chr 2:10
wheat, and b. the oil, and wine. 15
gave 10,000 measures of b. 27:5
cockle grow instead of b. Job 31:40
wheat, and appointed b. Isa 28:25
treasures of wheat and b. Jer 41:8
take to thee wheat, and b. Ezek 4:9
thou shalt eat it as b. cakes, and. 12
pollute me for handfuls of b. 13:19
an ephah of an homer of b. 45:13
an homer of b. and half. Hos 3:2
howl for wheat and b. Joel 1:11
which hath five b. loaves. John 6:9
fragments of the five b. loaves. 13
voice say, 3 measures of b. Rev 6:6

barn
(*A storehouse for grain*)
thee out of the b. floor ? 2 Ki 6:27
thy seed into the b. Job 39:12*
is seed yet in b. vine. Hag 2:19
the wheat into my b. Mat 13:30
no store-house nor b. Luke 12:24

Barnabas
apostles was surnamed B. Acts 4:36
B. should go as far as. 11:22
departed B. to Tarsus to seek. 25
by the hands of B. and Saul. 30
B. and Saul returned from. 12:25
at Antioch were teachers, as B. 13:1
Holy Ghost said, separate me B. 2
persecution, against Paul and B. 50
they called B. Jupiter; Paul. 14:12
Paul and B. had no small. 15:2
the multitude gave audience to B. 12
B. determined to take with. 37
or I only and B. have. 1 Cor 9:6
again to Jerusalem with B. Gal 2:1
gave to me and B. the right hands. 9
B. carried away with their. Gal 2:13
Marcus, sister's son to B. Col 4:10
see **Saul, Paul**

barns
so shall thy b. be filled. Pr 3:10
the b. are broken down. Joel 1:17
not, nor gather into b. Mat 6:26
I will pull down my b. Luke 12:18

barrel, -s
(*American Revision,* jar, jars)
handful of meal in a b. 1 Ki 17:12
the b. of meal shall not waste. 14
fill four b. with water, and. 18:33

barren
but Sarai was b. she had. Gen 11:30
Rebekah was b. 25:21
Rachel was b. 29:31
cast young nor be b. Ex 23:26
not be male or female b. Deut 7:14
was b. and bare not. Judg 13:2, 3
so that the b. hath born. 1 Sam 2:5
naught, and the ground b. 2 Ki 2:19
from thence death, or b. land. 21
he evil entreateth the b. Job 24:21
I have made the b. land his. 39:6
he maketh the b. woman. Ps 113:9
the grave and b. womb. Pr 30:16
b. among them. S of S 4:2*; 6:6*
sing, O b. thou that didst. Isa 54:1
drive him into a land b. Joel 2:20
because Elisabeth was b. Luke 1:7
with her, who was called b. 36
shall say, blessed are the b. 23:29
is written, rejoice thou b. Gal 4:27
that ye be neither b. nor. 2 Pet 1:8*

barrenness
a fruitful land into b. Ps 107:34*

bars
b. of shittim-wood for the boards.
Ex 26:26; 36:31
of the sons of Merari, shall be the
boards and b. Num 3:36; 4:31
fenced with gates and b. Deut 3:5
1 Ki 4:13; 2 Chr 8:5; 14:7
a town that hath b. 1 Sam 23:7
set up locks thereof and b. Neh 3:3
6, 13, 14, 15
shall go down to the b. Job 17:16
set b. and doors for the sea. 38:10
his bones are like b. of iron. 40:18
cut b. of iron. Ps 107:16; Isa 45:2
hath strengthened the b. Ps 147:13
contentions are like the b. Pr 18:19
have neither gates nor b. Jer 49:31
they have Babylon, her b. 51:30
and broken her b. Lam 2:9
neither gates nor b. Ezek 38:11
the earth with her b. was. Jonah 2:6
fire shall devour thy b. Nah 3:13

Barsabas
Joseph called B. Acts 1:23
Judas B. 15:22

Bartholomew
Mat 10:3; Mark 3:18; Luke 6:14
Acts 1:13

Bartimaeus
B. sat by the way-side. Mark 10:46

Baruch
B. son of Zabbai earnestly. Neh 3:20
B. sealed the covenant. 10:6
Maaseiah son of B. dwelt at. 11:5
the evidence to B. Jer 32:12, 16
Jeremiah called B. and B. 36:4
read B. in the book in the house. 10
B. took the roll in his hand and. 14
king commanded to take B. the. 26
B. setteth thee on against us. 43:3
Johanan took Jeremiah and B 6
word that Jeremiah spake to B. 45:1

Barzillai
B. of Rogelim brought. 2 Sam 17:27
B. was a very aged man. 19:32
the king kissed B. and blessed. 39
brought up for Adriel son of B. 21:8
kindness to the sons of B. 1 Ki 2:7
of B. which took a wife of the daughters of B. Ezra 2:61; Neh 7:63

base, -s
b. four cubits the length of one b.
1 Ki 7:27
the b. Solomon made. 2 Ki 25:13, 16

set the altar upon his *b.* *Ezra* 3:3
set there upon her own *b.* *Zech* 5:11

base, *adjective*

(Used mainly in the obsolete sense of humble, lowly)

and will be *b.* in mine. *2 Sam* 6:22
they were children of *b.* *Job* 30:8
and the *b.* against the. *Isa* 3:5
kingdom might be *b.* *Ezek* 17:14
and they shall be there a *b.* 29:14
I have made you *b.* *Mal* 2:9
b. things of this world. *1 Cor* 1:28
who in presence am *b.* *2 Cor* 10:1

baser

lewd fellows of the *b.* *Acts* 17:5*

basest

Pathros shall be the *b.* *Ezek* 29:15
up over it the *b.* of men. *Dan* 4:17*

Bashan

up by the way of *B.* *Num* 21:33
Deut 3:1
Og king of *B.* *Num* 32:33; *Deut* 1:4
3:1, 3, 11; 4:47; 29:7; *Josh* 9:10
12:4; 13:30; *1 Ki* 4:19; *Neh* 9:22
Ps 135:11; 136:20
kingdom of Og in *B.* *Deut* 3:4, 10
Josh 13:12, 30, 31
Golan in *B.* *Deut* 4:43; *Josh* 20:8
21:27
rams of the breed of *B.* *Deut* 32:14
Dan shall leap from *B.* 33:22
he had Gilead and *B.* *Josh* 17:1
even Gilead and *B.* *2 Ki* 10:33
of Gershon, Golan in *B.* *1 Chr* 6:71
strong bulls of *B.* have. *Ps* 22:12
hill of God is as the hill of *B.* 68:15
I will bring again from *B.* 22
B. and Carmel shake off. *Isa* 33:9
lift up thy voice in *B.* *Jer* 22:20
shall feed on Carmel and *B.* 50:19
all of them fatlings of *B.* *Ezek* 39:18
this word, ye kine of *B.* *Amos* 4:1
let them feed in *B.* as in. *Mi* 7:14
B. languished, Carmel. *Nah* 1:4

see **oaks**

Bashemath

Esau took to wife *B.* the. *Gen* 26:34
B. Ishmael's daughter, sister of. 36:3

basket

These were of different sizes, shapes, and construction, and had different names. [1] Sal, *made of twigs, specially for bread,* Gen 40:17. [2] Salsillōth, *a similar basket used for gathering grapes,* Jer 6:9. [3] Tene, *in which the first-fruits were offered,* Deut 26:4. [4] Dud, *to carry fruit,* Jer 24:1; *and clay to the brickyard,* Ps 81:6 (pote, *in Authorized Version*), *or for holding bulky articles,* 2 Ki 10:6. *In the New Testament there were three names used. One meant the small wallet carried by travellers and another the large sort in which Saul escaped from Damascus,* Acts 9:25.

in the *b.* all manner of. *Gen* 40:17
b. of the unleavened. *Ex* 29:23
Lev 8:2, 26; *Num* 6:15, 17
the bread in the *b.* of. *Lev* 8:31
priest shall take the *b.* *Deut* 26:4
blessed shall be thy *b.* and thy. 28:5
cursed shall be thy *b.* and thy. 17
put the flesh in a *b.* *Judg* 6:19
b. had very good figs, the other *b.*
Jer 24:2
a *b.* of summer fruit. *Amos* 8:1, 2
wall in a *b.* *Acts* 9:25; *2 Cor* 11:33

baskets

I had three white *b.* *Gen* 40:16
Joseph said, the three *b.* are. 18
put their heads in *b.* *2 Ki* 10:7
grape-gatherer into the *b.* *Jer* 6:9
behold, two *b.* of figs were set. 24:1
took up twelve *b.* full. *Mat* 14:20
Mark 6:43; *Luke* 9:17; *John* 6:13
seven *b.* full. *Mat* 15:37; *Mark* 8:8
five loaves, and how many *b.* ye took up? *Mat* 16:9, 10; *Mark* 8:19, 20

bason

(*Revised Version,* basin)

blood that is in the *b.* *Ex* 12:22
by weight for every *b.* *1 Chr* 28:17
he poureth water into a *b.* *John* 13:5

basons

(*Revised Version,* basins)

put half of the blood in *b.* *Ex* 24:6
brought beds and *b.* *2 Sam* 17:28
lavers and the shovels and the *b.*
1 Ki 7:40, 45; *2 Chr* 4:8, 11
b. and fire-pans the. *Jer* 52:19

bastard, -s

a *b.* shall not enter into. *Deut* 23:2
b. shall dwell in Ashdod. *Zech* 9:6
chastisement, then are *b.* *Heb* 12:8

bat, -s

lapwing and *b.* are. *Lev* 11:19
Deut 14:18
his idols to the moles and *b.* *Isa* 2:20

bath

(A measure used among the Hebrews which contained about nine gallons. It was equal to the Ephah)

vineyard shall yield one *b.* *Isa* 5:10
just ephah, a just *b.* *Ezek* 45:10
the ephah and *b.* shall be of one. 11
offer the tenth part of a *b.* 14

bathe

shall *b.* himself in water. *Lev* 15:5
8, 11, 13, 21, 22, 27; 16:26, 28
17:15; *Num* 19:7, 8, 19
them not, nor *b.* his flesh. *Lev* 17:16

bathed

my sword shall be *b.* in. *Isa* 34:5*

baths

sea contained 2000 *b.* *1 Ki* 7:26
one laver containing 40 *b.* every. 38
servants 20,000 *b.* of. *2 Chr* 2:10
sea received and held 3000 *b.* 4:5
b. of wine, 100 *b.* of oil. *Ezra* 7:22
homer of ten *b.* for ten *b.* *Ezek* 45:14

Bath-sheba

is not this *B.* daughter. *2 Sam* 11:3
David comforted *B.* his wife. 12:24
B. went to the king into. *1 Ki* 1:15
then the king said, call me *B.* 28
B. bowed. 31
Adonijah came to *B.* the. 2:13

battered

people with Joab *b.* *2 Sam* 20:15

battering

set *b.* rams against it. *Ezek* 4:2
to appoint *b.* rams against. 21:22

battle

[1] *A general fight,* Deut 20:3. [2] *Victory,* Eccl 9:11.

they joined *b.* *Gen* 14:8; *1 Sam* 4:2
1 Ki 20:29
before the Lord to *b.* *Num* 32:27
contend with Sihon in *b.* *Deut* 2:24
approach this day to *b.* 20:3
return, lest he die in the *b.* 5, 6, 7
all other they took in *b.* *Josh* 11:19
yet again go out to *b.*? *Judg* 20:28
they turned, but the *b.* overtook. 42
after Philistines in *b.* *1 Sam* 14:22
the host shouted for the *b.* 17:20
art come down to see the *b.* 28
b. is the Lord's. 47; *2 Chr* 20:15
shall descend into the *b.* *1 Sam* 26:10
thou shalt go out with me to *b.* 28:1
in the *b.* he be an adversary. 29:4
go forth to *b.* *2 Sam* 11:1; *1 Chr* 20:1
front of the hottest *b.* *2 Sam* 11:15
we anointed is dead in *b.* 19:10
if thy people go out to *b.* *1 Ki* 8:44
went out into midst of the *b.* 20:39
go with me to *b.*? 22:4; *2 Ki* 3:7
they cried to God in the *b.* *1 Chr* 5:20
men of war fit for the *b.* 12:8
David came upon them, and set *b.* in.
19:17; *2 Chr* 13:3; 14:10
do it, be strong for *b.* *2 Chr* 25:8
as a king ready to the *b.* *Job* 15:24
he smelleth the *b.* afar off. 39:25
remember the *b.* do no more. 41:8
me with strength to *b.* *Ps* 18:39
glory, the Lord mighty in *b.* 24:8
delivered my soul from the *b.* 55:18
shield, the sword, and the *b.* 76:3
made him to stand in the *b.* *Ps* 89:43
not to the swift, nor *b.* *Eccl* 9:11
every *b.* of the warrior. *Isa* 9:5*
mustereth the host of the *b.* 13:4
thy slain men are not dead in *b.* 22:2
and thorns against me in *b.* 27:4
that turn the *b.* to the gate. 28:6
on him the strength of the *b.* 42:25
horse rusheth into the *b.* *Jer* 8:6
men be slain by sword in *b.* 18:21
and shield, draw near to *b.* 46:3
her, and rise up to the *b.* 49:14
a sound of *b.* is in the land. 50:22
in array, like a man to *b.* against. 42
but none goeth to the *b.* *Ezek* 7:14
to stand in the *b.* in the day. 13:5
save them by bow nor by *b.* *Hos* 1:7
I will break the bow and *b.* 2:18
b. in Gibeah; did not overtake. 10:9
a strong people set in *b.* *Joel* 2:5
rise up against Edom in *b.* *Ob* 1
his goodly horse in the *b.* *Zech* 10:3
down their enemies in the *b.* 5
nations against Jerusalem to *b.* 14:2
prepare himself to the *b.*? *1 Cor* 14:8
like horses prepared to *b.* *Rev* 9:7
of many horses running to *b.* 9
the *b.* of the great day. 16:14; 20:8

day of **battle**

pass in the *day of b.* *1 Sam* 13:22
against the *day of b.* *Job* 38:23
back in the *day of b.* *Ps* 78:9
my head in the *day of b.* 140:7
prepared against the *day of b.*
Pr 21:31
Beth-arbel in *day of b.* *Hos* 10:14
shouting in the *day of b.* *Amos* 1:14
fought in the *day of b.* *Zech* 14:3

battle-ax, *see* **ax**

battle-bow

and the *b.-bow* shall be. *Zech* 9:10
of him came forth the *b.-bow.* 10:4

battlement, -s

thou shalt make a *b.* for. *Deut* 22:8
take away her *b.* they. *Jer* 5:10*

battles

before us and fight our *b.* *1 Sam* 8:20
valiant, and fight the Lord's *b.* 18:17
my lord fighteth the *b.* of the. 25:28
spoils won in *b.* dedicate. *1 Chr* 26:27
God, to fight our *b.* *2 Chr* 32:8
and in *b.* of shakings. *Isa* 30:32

bay

grizzled and *b.* horses. *Zech* 6:3
and the *b.* went forth and sought. 7

bay-tree

like a green *b.-tree.* *Ps* 37:35*

bdellium

in Havilah there is *b.* *Gen* 2:12
manna as the colour of *b.* *Num* 11:7

be

that man should *be* alone. *Gen* 2:18
whether thou *be* my very son. 27:21
there they *be* as the. *Deut* 10:5
if the Lord *be* with us. *Judg* 6:13
thine enemies *be* as. *2 Sam* 18:32
they that *be* with us are more than they that *be.* *2 Ki* 6:16
God *be* with. *2 Chr* 36:23; *Ezra* 1:3
be ye far from thence. *Ezra* 6:6
if I *be* wicked, woe to me; if I *be.*
Job 10:15
and *be* it indeed that I have. 19:4
see if there *be* any. *Ps* 139:24
be a wall, if she *be* a. *S of S* 8:9
be your fear, let him *be.* *Isa* 8:13
former things what they *be.* 41:22
none know where you *be.* *Jer* 36:19
it *be* ere thou *be* quiet? 47:6
thy way till the end *be.* *Dan* 12:13
how long will it *be* ere? *Hos* 8:5
if thou *be* the Son of God. *Mat* 4:3, 6
27:40
and many there *be* that go. 7:13
the things that *be* of God, but those that *be.* 16:23; *Mark* 8:33
be to thee as an heathen. *Mat* 18:17
put away, except it *be.* 19:9
if the son of peace *be.* *Luke* 10:6
how can these things *be*? *John* 3:9
there *be* any Holy Ghost. *Acts* 19:2

bay—from the *b.* *Josh* 15:2, 5; north *b* of the Salt Sea. 18:19

except it *be* for this one Acts 24:21
those things which *be* not. Rom 4:17
if God *be* for us, who can *be* ? 8:31
that he might *be* Lord of the. 14:9
that God may *be* all in. 1 Cor 15:28
him *be* anathema maran-atha. 16:22
if there *be* first a willing. 2 Cor 8:12
they which *be* of faith are. Gal 3:9
I beseech you, *be* as I am, for. 4:12
judgement, whosoever he *be*. 5:10
let this mind *be* in you. Phil 2:5
but if ye *be* without. Heb 12:8
if so *be* ye have tasted. 1 Pet 2:3
if the will of God *be* so. 3:17
whatsoever craft he *be*. Rev 18:22
let him *be* unjust still; he which is
filthy, let him *be* filthy. 22:11

if it be

if it be your mind that I. Gen 23:8
she said, *if it be* so, why ? 25:22
if it be a son kill him, *if it be* a.
Ex 1:16
if it be, give me thy. 2 Ki 10:15
if it be marvellous in the. Zech 8:6
if it be thou, bid me. Mat 14:28
if it be of God, ye. Acts 5:39
but *if it be* a question of. 18:15
in vain ? *if it be* in vain. Gal 3:4

may **be**, *see* **may**; *peace* **be**, *see* **peace**

not be. be not

let it *not be* grievous in. Gen 21:12
if the woman will *not be*. 24:5
the seed should *not be* his. 38:9
my father, and the lad *be not*. 44:30
ye should *not be* their. Lev 26:13
let her *not be* as one. Num 12:12
that he *be not* as Korah and. 16:40
neither will I *be* with. Josh 7:12
man will *not be* in rest. Ruth 3:18
be not like your fathers. 2 Chr 30:7
Zech 1:4
be not thou far away. Ps 22:19
35:22; 38:21; 71:12
be ye *not* mockers, lest. Isa 28:22
I will *not be* to the. Zech 8:11
for it *cannot be* that a. Luke 13:33
he *cannot be* my disciple. 14:26, 33
if thou *be not* that Christ. John 1:25
be not wise in your own. Rom 12:16
if I *be not* an apostle. 1 Cor 9:2
be not children in. 14:20
be not unequally yoked. 2 Cor 6:14
should *not be* the servant. Gal 1:10
be not therefore partakers. Eph 5:7
be ye *not* unwise, but. 17
works, that they *be not*. Tit 3:14
thy benefit should *not be*. Philem 14
on earth, should *not be* a. Heb 8:4
not be that outward. 1 Pet 3:3

let there be

let there be light. Gen 1:3
let there be a firmament. 6
let there be no strife between. 13:8
let there be now an oath. 26:28
let there be more work laid. Ex 5:9
let there be search made. Ezra 5:17

shall be, or shalt be

they *shall be* one flesh. Gen 2:24
to thee *shall be* his desire. 4:7
a servant *shall* he *be* to his. 9:25
Shem, and Canaan *shall be*. 26
and thou *shalt be* a blessing. 12:2
so *shall* thy seed *be*. 15:5; Rom 4:18
Sarah *shall be* a mother. Gen 17:16
and he *shall be* blessed. 27:33
then *shall* Lord *be* my God. 28:21
Israel *shall be*. 35:10; 1 Ki 18:31
God *shall be* with you. Gen 48:21
shall the gathering of the people *be*.
49:10
shalt be to him instead. Ex 4:16
ye *shall be* a peculiar. 19:5
the dead *shall be* his own. 21:36
shall his habitation *be*. Lev 13:46
shall be holy to me, ye *shall be*.
20:26
shall be head, and thou *shalt be*.
Deut 28:44
I see what their end *shall be*. 32:20
Philistine *shall be* as. 1 Sam 17:36
shall thy judgement *be*. 1 Ki 20:40
the Lord *shall be*. 2 Chr 19:11

in fulness he *shall be* in. Job 20:22
yea, the Almighty *shall be*. 22:25
happy *shalt* thou *be*, it *shall be*.
Ps 128:2
my prayer also *shall be* in. 141:5
is that which *shall be*. Eccl 1:9
man cannot tell what *shall be*. 10:14
falleth, there it *shall be*. 11:3
the holy seed *shall be*. Isa 6:13
the glory of the Lord *shall be*. 58:8
when *shall* it once *be*. Jer 13:27
thou *shalt be* as my mouth. 15:19
and there *shall* he *be* till I. 32:5
it *shall be* to me a name of. 33:9
neither *shall be* so. Ezek 16:16
wicked *shall be* on him. 18:20
shalt be a terror, and never *shalt be*.
27:36
what *shall be* in the latter. Dan 2:28
the end *shall be*. 8:19; 11:27
known that which *shall be*. Hos 5:9
God of hosts *shall be*. Amos 5:14
save you, and *shall be* a. Zech 8:13
shall be as David, house of David
shall be as. 12:8
shall be a delightsome. Mal 3:12
no, nor ever *shall be*. Mat 24:21
Mark 13:19
shall I *be* with you. Mark 9:19
Luke 9:41
with you, and *shall be* in. John 14:17
lots for it, whose it *shall be*. 19:24
that it *shall be* even as. Acts 27:25
that body that *shall be*. 1 Cor 15:37
appear what we *shall be*. 1 John 3:2
and wast, and *shall be*. Rev 16:5
man as his work *shall be*. 22:12

shall not, or shalt not be

saying, this *shall not be*. Gen 15:4
thou *shalt not be* to him. Ex 22:25
shalt not be beneath. Deut 28:13
see me not, it *shall not be* so.
2 Ki 2:10
morning, but I *shall not be*. Job 7:21
it *shall not be*. Ps 37:10; Jer 48:30
Dan 11:29; Amos 7:3, 6
thou *shalt not be* for. Hos 3:3
this *shall not be* to thee. Mat 16:22
shall not be so among you. 20:26
Mark 10:43; Luke 22:26

to be

to be a God to thee and. Gen 17:7
hearkened not to her *to be*. 39:10
out *to be* your God. Lev 22:33; 25:38
desire *to be* with them. Pr 24:1
that which is *to be* hath. Eccl 3:15
spent all, he began *to be*. Luke 15:14
good for a man so *to be*. 1 Cor 7:26
which he seeth me *to be*. 2 Cor 12:6
having a desire *to be*. Phil 1:23
things ought not so *to be*. Jas 3:10
persons ought ye *to be*. 2 Pet 3:11

will be

will be a wild man, his hand *will be*
against every man. Gen 16:12
I *will be* their God. 17:8; Ex 29:45
Jer 24:7; 32:38; 2 Cor 6:16
I *will be* with thee. Gen 26:3; 31:3
Ex 3:12; Judg 6:16; 1 Ki 11:38
if God *will be* with me. Gen 28:20
if ye *will be* as we be. 34:15
all places they *will be*. Neh 4:12
he *will be* our guide. Ps 48:14
I *will be* your God. Jer 7:23; 30:22
I *will be* to them as a. Ezek 11:16
that ye say, we *will be* as. 20:32
O death, I *will be* thy plagues, O
grave, I *will be* thy. Hos 13:14
I *will be* as the dew unto Israel. 14:5
the Lord *will be* the hope. Joel 3:16
will be to her a wall of fire round
about, I *will be* the. Zech 2:5
there *will* your heart *be*. Mat 6:21
I *will be* a Father to you. 2 Cor 6:18
such *will* we *be* also indeed. 10:11
they that *will be* rich fall. 1 Tim 6:9
I *will be* to him a Father. Heb 1:5
I *will be* to them a God, they. 8:10
whosoever *will be* a friend. Jas 4:4
I *will be* his God, and. Rev 21:7

beacon

be left as a *b*. on the. Isa 30:17

beam

with the pin of the *b*. Judg 16:14
his spear was like a weaver's *b*.
1 Sam 17:7; 1 Chr 11:23; 20:5
and take thence a *b*. 2 Ki 6:2
as one was felling a *b*. ax-head. 5
the *b*. out of the timber. Hab 2:11
not the *b*. Mat 7:3; Luke 6:41, 42
behold, a *b*. is in thine own. Mat 7:4
first cast out the *b*. 5; Luke 6:42

beams

overlaid the *b*. the posts. 2 Chr 3:7
give timber to make *b*. Neh 2:8
who layeth the *b*. in the. Ps 104:3
b. of our house are cedar. S of S 1:17

beans

Barzillai brought *b*. 2 Sam 17:28
take unto thee wheat, *b*. Ezek 4:9

bear

[1] *To carry*, Jer 17:21; Mat 27:32.
[2] *To bring forth, produce, or yield*, Gen 18:13; Jas 3:12. [3]
To uphold, or support, Ps 91:12.

is greater than I can *b*. Gen 4:13
land not able to *b*. them. 13:6; 36:7
let me *b*. the blame. 43:9; 44:32
Issachar bowed to *b*. 49:15
they shall *b*. the burden. Ex 18:22
b. the ark. 25:27; 27:7; 30:4; 37:5
Deut 10:8; Josh 3:8, 13, 14 ; 4:16
2 Sam 15:24
Aaron shall *b*. their names. Ex 28:12
shalt not *b*. any grudge. Lev 19:18
not able to *b*. all this people.
Num 11:14; Deut 1:9
how long shall I *b*. with ? Num 14:27
children shall *b*. 33; Ezek 23:35
God bare as a man *b*. Deut 1:31
let me *b*. the king. 2 Sam 18:19
puttest on me, I will *b*. 2 Ki 18:14
b. up pillars of the earth. Ps 75:3*
how I do *b*. in my bosom the. 89:50
they shall *b*. thee up. 91:12
Mat 4:6; Luke 4:11
scornest, thou shalt *b*. it. Pr 9:12
a wounded spirit who can *b*. ? 18:14
for four which it cannot *b*. 30:21
feasts, I am weary to *b*. Isa 1:14
I have made and I will *b*. you. 46:4
b. him upon the shoulder. 7
be clean that *b*. vessels of. 52:11
truly this grief, I must *b*. Jer 10:19
b. no burden sabbath-day. 17:21, 27
I did *b*. the reproach of my. 31:19
so the Lord could no longer *b*. 44:22
good to *b*. yoke in youth. Lam 3:27
their sight shalt thou *b*. Ezek 12:6
the prince shall *b*. upon his. 12
b. punishment of iniquity. 14:10
b. thine own shame for. 16:52, 54
b. shame with. 32:30; 36:7; 44:13
nor *b*. shame of the heathen.
Ezek 34:29; 36:15
land is not able to *b*. Amos 7:10
b. reproach of my people. Mi 6:16
I will *b*. indignation of the. 7:9
one *b*. holy flesh in skirt. Hag 2:12
do these *b*. ephah ? Zech 5:10
he shall *b*. glory. 6:13
shoes I am not worthy to *b*. Mat 3:11
found Simon, compelled him to *b*.
27:32; Mark 15:21; Luke 23:26
doth not *b*. his cross. Luke 14:27
avenge elect, though he *b*. 18:7
ye cannot *b*. them now. John 16:12
is chosen to *b*. my name. Acts 9:15
a yoke, we were able to *b*. 15:10
reason I should *b*. with you. 18:14
b. infirmities of the weak. Rom 15:1
were not able to *b*. it. 1 Cor 3:2
to escape, that ye may *b*. 10:13
shall *b*. the image of heavenly. 15:49
ye could *b*. with me. 2 Cor 11:1
ye might well *b*. with him. 4
b. one another's burdens. Gal 6:2
for every man shall *b*. his own. 5
b. in my body marks of Lord. 17
fig-tree *b*. olive-berries ? Jas 3:12
not *b*. them that are evil. Rev 2:2

bear *fruit, see* **fruit**

bear *iniquity*

Aaron may *b*. *iniq*. Ex 28:38
and his sons *b* not *iniq*. 43

he shall b. his iniq. Lev 5:1, 17
7:18; 17:16; 19:8; 20:17
hath given to you to b. iniq. 10:17
the goat b. upon him all iniq. 16:22
they shall b. their iniq. 20:19
Num 18:23; Ezek 44:10, 12
or suffer them to b. iniq. Lev 22:16
this woman b. her iniq. Num 5:31
ye shall b. your iniq. 14:34
Aaron and his sons b. iniq. 18:1
he heard, he shall b. her iniq. 30:15
my servant shall b. iniq. Isa 53:11
number of days, thou shalt b. iniq.
Ezek 4:4; 5:6
not son b. iniq. of father ? 18:19
the son not b. the iniq. of. 20

bear *judgement*
Aaron shall b. judg. of. Ex 28:30
that troubleth b. his judg. Gal 5:10

bear *record, see* **record**

bear *rule*
man b. rule in his house. Esth 1:22
hand of diligent b. rule. Pr 12:24
the priests b. rule by. Jer 5:31
strong rods for them that b. rule.
Ezek 19:11
of brass shall b. rule. Dan 2:39

bear *sin*
they shall b. their sin. Lev 20:20
lest they b. sin for it, and die. 22:9
curseth his God, shall b. sin. 24:15
that man shall b. his sin. Num 9:13
come nigh, lest they b. sin. 18:22
shall b. no sin when ye heaved. 32
ye b. sin of your idols. Ezek 23:49
Christ was once offered to b. sin.
Heb 9:28

bear *witness*
shalt not b. false wit. Ex 20:16
Deut 5:20; Mat 19:18; Rom 13:9
set two men to b. wit. 1 Ki 21:10
do not b. false wit. Mark 10:19
Luke 18:20
ye b. wit. that ye allow. Luke 11:48*
same came to b. wit. John 1:7
was sent to b. wit. of that light. 8
yourselves b. me wit. that. 3:28
if I b. wit. of myself. 5:31
works I do b. wit. of me. 36; 10:25
b. wit. of myself, and the. 8:18
ye shall also b. wit. 15:27
if I have spoken evil, b. wit. 18:23
that I should b. wit. 37
priest doth b. me wit. Acts 22:5
thou must b. wit. at Rome. 23:11
have seen and b. wit. 1 John 1:2
three that b. wit. in earth. 5:8

bear
Sarah that is old b ? Gen 17:17
shall I of a surety b. a child. 18:13
but if she b. a maid child. Lev 12:5
her children she shall b. Deut 28:57
conceive and b. a son. Judg 13:3
not my son that I did b. 1 Ki 3:21
every one b. twins. S of S 4:2, 6:6
a virgin shall b. a son, and. Isa 7:14
sing, O barren, that didst not b. 54:1
b. sons and daughters. Jer 29:6
Elisabeth shall b. a son. Luke 1:13
women marry, b. children. 1 Tim 5:14

bear, -s
came a lion and a b. 1 Sam 17:34
servant slew the lion and the b. 36
chafed, as a b. robbed. 2 Sam 17:8
came forth two she-b. 2 Ki 2:24
b. robbed of her whelps. Pr 17:12
a roaring lion, and ranging b. 28:15
cow and b. feed their. Isa 11:7
we roar like b. mourn like. 59:11
to me as a b. in wait. Lam 3:10
beast, a second like to a b. Dan 7:5
them as a b. bereaved. Hos 13:8
as a man did flee from b. Amos 5:19
his feet as the feet of a b. Rev 13:2

beard, -s
a man hath plague on b. Lev 13:29
shall shave hair off head and b. 14:9
mar the corners of b. 19:27; 21:5
I caught him by his b. 1 Sam 17:35
David let spittle fall on his b. 21:13
tarry at Jericho till b. grow, then.
2 Sam 10:5; 1 Chr 19:5

Mephibosheth trimmed not b.
2 Sam 19:24
Joab took Amasa by the b. 20:9
plucked off hair of my b. Ezra 9:3
down on b, Aaron's b. Ps 133:2
shall also consume the b. Isa 7:20
on heads baldness, every b. cut. 15:2
fourscore men their b. Jer 41:5
head bald, every b. clipt. 48:37
a razor to pass on b. Ezek 5:1

bearers
set 70,000 to be b. of. 2 Chr 2:18
also they were over the b. 34:13
strength of the b. is. Neh 4:10

bearest
art barren, and b. not. Judg 13:3
favour thou b. thy people. Ps 106:4
b. record of thyself, thy. John 8:13
b. not the root. Rom 11:18
rejoice thou that b. not. Gal 4:27

beareth
he that b. the carcase. Lev 11:28
and he that b. these things. 15:10
as a father b. child. Num 11:12
first-born she b. succeed. Deut 25:6
there be a root that b. gall. 29:18
it is not sown, nor b. 23
as an eagle b. her young. 32:11
evil entreateth that b. not. Job 24:21
every one b. twins. S of S 6:6
not afraid, the tree b. fruit. Joel 2:22
which also b. fruit. Mat 13:23
every branch that b. not. John 15:2
b. not the sword in vain. Rom 13:4
charity b. all things. 1 Cor 13:7
which b. thorns is rejected. Heb 6:8

beareth *rule*
when the wicked b. rule. Pr 29:2

beareth *witness*
b. wit. to my face. Job 16:8
b. false wit. is a maul. Pr 25:18
another that b. wit. of me. John 5:32
and the Father b. wit. of me. 8:18
the Spirit b. wit. with. Rom 8:16
the Spirit that b. wit. 1 John 5:6

bearing
every herb b. seed. Gen 1:29
the Lord restrained me from b. 16:2
called his name Judah, left b. 29:35
Ishmaelites b. spicery. 37:25
forward, b. tabernacle. Num 10:17
Kohathites set forward, b. 21
the priest b. the ark. Josh 3:3, 14
2 Sam 15:24
one b. a shield went. 1 Sam 17:7
goeth b. precious seed. Ps 126:6
meet you a man b. a pitcher of water.
Mark 14:13; Luke 22:10
he b. his cross, went. John 19:17
conscience b. witness. Rom 2:15
my conscience b. me witness. 9:1
b. in the body dying of. 2 Cor 4:10
God also b. them witness. Heb 2:4
let us go forth b. his reproach. 13:13
be saved in child-b. 1 Tim 2:15

beast
(Used for cattle, wild beasts or any living thing apart from man)
let earth bring forth b. Gen 1:24
God made b. of the earth. 25
serpent more subtil than any b. 3:1
evil b. hath devoured him. 37:20, 33
every firstling of a b. Ex 13:12
put his b. in another's field. 22:5
deliver to his neighbour any b. 10
whoso lieth with b. be put to. 19
Lev 18:23; 20:15, 16; Deut 27:21
the b. of the field multiply. Ex 23:29
b. that may be eaten, and b. that
may not. Lev 11:47
if it be b. men bring offering. 27:9
the likeness of any b. Deut 4:17
smote as well men as b. Judg 20:48
nor any b. save b. I rode. Neh 2:12
so ignorant, I was as a b. Ps 73:22
he giveth to the b. his food. 147:9
man regards life of b. Pr 12:10
no pre-eminence above b. Eccl 3:19
the b. shall honour me. Isa 43:20
as a b. that goeth into valley. 63:14
dead or torn, fowl or b. Ezek 44:31
let a b. heart be given. Dan 4:16

I beheld till the b. was. Dan 7:11
the truth of the fourth b. 19
set him on his own b. Luke 10:34
Paul shook off the b. Acts 28:5
a b. touch the mountain. Heb 12:20
first b. like a lion, second b. Rev 4:7
I heard the second b. say. 6:3
b. that ascendeth out of the pit. 11:7
I saw a b. rise up out of. 13:1
I beheld a b. out of earth. 11
got the victory over the b. 15:2
spirits out of mouth of b. 16:13
thou sawest the b. that. 17:8, 11
I saw b. and kings of the. 19:19
where b. and false prophet. 20:10

every **beast**
to every b. green herb. Gen 1:30
God formed every b. 2:19
gave names to every b. 20
art cursed above every b. 3:14
of every clean b. take to. 7:2, 8
and every b. after his kind. 14
every b. went out of the ark. 8:19
of every clean b. he offered. 20
of you shall be on every b. 9:2
your blood I require of every b. 5
to every b. of the earth. 10
shall not every b. be ours ? 34:23
the carcases of every b. which
divideth. Lev 11:26; Deut 14:6
every b. of the forest is. Ps 50:10
they give drink to every b. 104:11
my flock meat to every b. Ezek 34:8
son of man, speak to every b. 39:17

beast, joined with *man*
will destroy both man and b. Gen 6:7
became lice in man and b. Ex 8:17
with blains on man and b. 9:9, 10
hail on man and b. 19, 22, 25
a dog move against man or b. 11:7
smite first-born in Egypt, man and b.
12:12; 13:15; Ps 135:8
first-born of man and b. is mine.
Ex 13:2; Num 8:17
man or b. it shall not live. Ex 19:13
thing of man or b. Lev 27:28
first-born of man and b. Num 3:13
prey taken, both of man and b. 31:26
thou preservest man and b. Ps. 36:6
fury on man and b. Jer 7:20; 21:6
36:29; Ezek 14:13, 17, 19, 21
25:13; 29:8; Zeph 1:3
I have made man and b. Jer 27:5
sow with seed of man and b. 31:27
it is desolate without man or b.
32:43, 33:10, 12 ; 36:29; 51:62
they shall depart man and b. 50:3
will multiply man and b. Ezek 36:11
let not man nor b. taste. Jonah 3:7

unclean **beast**
soul touch unclean b. Lev 5:2; 7:21
if it be unclean b. 27:11, 27

wild **beast**
there passed by a wild b. and trod
down. 2 Ki 14:9; 2 Chr 25:18
wild b. may break them. Job 39:15
the wild b. of the field. Ps 80:13
wild b. shall tear them. Hos 13:8

beasts
that which was torn of b. Gen 31:39
Ex. 22:31; Lev 7:24; 17:15; 22:8
Esau took all his b. Gen 36:6
lade your b. and go. 45:17
the first-born of b. shall die. Ex 11:5
b. ye shall eat. Lev 11:2; Deut 14:4
chew cud among b. Lev 11:3
Deut 14:6
for b. increase be meat. Lev 25:7
I will rid evil b. out of land. 26:6
congregation and b. drink. Num 20:8
of all b. give to the Levites. 31:30
I will send b. on them. Deut 32:24
Solomon spake of b. 1 Ki 4:33
find grass, that we lose not b. 18:5
drink ye, cattle and b. 2 Ki 3:17
help him with b. Ezra 1:4
ask the b. and they shall. Job 12:7
wherefore are we counted as b. 18:3
then the b. go into dens. 37:8
man is like the b. that. Ps 49:12, 20
wherein the b. of forest. 104:20
the sea, both small and great b. 25

b. and all cattle, praise. Ps 148:10
wisdom hath killed her b. Pr 9:2
a lion strongest among b. 30:30
themselves are b. Eccl 3:18
befalleth men, befalleth b. 19
burden of b. of the south. Isa 30:6
b. thereof for a burnt-offering. 40:16
their idols were on b. and. 46:1
swift b. to my holy mountain. 66:20
the b. are fled. Jer 9:10
the b. are consumed. 12:4
I send famine and evil b. pestilence. Ezek. 5:17; 14:15
I will fill the b. of whole. 32:4
I will destroy all the b. 13; 34:25, 28
let the b. get away. Dan 4:14
let his portion be with the b. 15
four great b. are four kings. 7:17
that no b. might stand before. 8:4
how do the b. groan ! Joel 1:18
peace-offerings of fat b. Amos 5:22
spoil of b. Hab 2:17
place for b. to lie down. Zeph 2:15
the plague of all the b. Zech 14:15
have ye offered slain b. ? Acts 7:42
provide b. to set Paul on. 23:24
an image made like to b. Rom 1:23
if I have fought with b. 1 Cor 15:32
for every kind of b. is tamed. Jas 3:7
these as natural brute b. 2 Pet 2:12
what they know as brute b. Jude 10
four b. full of eyes. Rev 4:6
the four b. had each six wings. 8
when b. give glory and honour. 9
midst of throne and four b. a. 5:6
the four b. said Amen. 14
one of four b. saying. 6:1; 15:7
angels about throne and four b. 7:11
song before throne and four b. 14:3
the elders and b. fell down to. 19:4

beasts *of the earth*

meat to all b. of earth. Deut 28:26
of Philistines to b. of earth. 1 Sam 17:46
afraid of the b. of earth. Job 5:22
teacheth more than b. of earth. 35:11
saints to the b. of earth. Ps 79:2
be left to the b. of earth. Isa 18:6
the people meat for b. of the earth. Jer 7:33; 16:4; 19:7; 34:20
appoint b. of earth to devour. 15:3
all four-footed b. of the earth. Acts 10:12; 11:6
kill with the b. of earth. Rev 6:8

beasts *of the field*

poor leave, b. of field eat. Ex 23:11
lest b. of field increase. Deut 7:22
thy flesh to b. of field. 1 Sam 17:44
b. of the field by night. 2 Sam 21:10
b. of the field at peace. Job 5:23
where b. of the field play. 40:20
b. of field under his feet. Ps 8:7
b. of field come to devour. Isa 56:9
assemble all b. of field. Jer 12:9
b. of the field have I given him 27:6; 28:14; Dan 2:38
I have given thee for meat to b. of the field. Ezek 29:5; 34:5; 39:4
his branches b of the field. 31:6
b. of field on his branches. 13
b. of the field shall shake. 38:20
b. of field had shadow. Dan 4:12
dwelling with b. of field. 25, 32
covenant for with b. of field. Hos 2:18
land shall mourn with b. of field. 4:3
b. of field cry also to. Joel 1:20
be not afraid, ye b. of field. 2:22

wild **beasts**

I will also send wild b. Lev 26:22
Philistines to wild b. 1 Sam 17:46
wild b. of the field are. Ps 50:11
wild b. of the desert lie. Isa 13:21
wild b. of the islands cry. 22
wild b. of desert shall meet with wild b. of the island. 34:14; Jer 50:39
Christ was with wild b. Mark 1:13
sheet, with wild b. Acts 10:12; 11:6

beat

[1] *To strike, pound, or bruise,* Num 11:8; 2 Ki 3:25; Mat 21:35. [2] *To get the better of, or overcome,* 2 Ki 13:25.

shalt b. spices very small. Ex 30:36
they b. the gold into thin. 39:3
people b. manna in a. Num 11:8
lest he exceed and b. him. Deut 25:3
b. down tower of Penuel. Judg 8:17
Abimelech b. down the city. 9:45
sons of Belial b. at the door. 19:22
b. that she had gleaned. Ruth 2:17
I b. them small. 2 Sam 22:43 Ps 18:42
Israelites b. down the. 2 Ki 3:25
Joash did b. Ben-hadad. 13:25
altars did the king b. down. 23:12
I will b. down his foes. Ps 89:23
b. him with the rod. Pr 23:14
b. their swords. Isa 2:4; Mi 4:3
what mean ye, to b. my people ? Isa 3:15*
Lord shall b. off from channel. 27:12
thresh mountains, b. small. 41:15
b. plowshares into swords. Joel 3:10
sun b. on head of Jonah. Jonah 4:8
b. in pieces many people. Mi 4:13
and b. on that house. Mat 7:25, 27 Luke 6:48, 49
his servants, and b. one. Mat 21:35 Mark 12:3; Luke 20:10, 11
waves b. into the ship. Mark 4:37
b. the men-servants. Luke 12:45
commanded to beat them. Acts 16:22
Greeks took Sosthenes and b. 18:17
imprisoned and b. in every. 22:19

beaten

officers of Israel were b. Ex 5:14, 16
cherubims of b. work. 25:18; 37:17 22; Num 8:4
two cherubims b. out of one. Ex 37:7
offer corn b. out of full. Lev 2:14
man be worthy to be b. Deut 25:2
made as if were b. Josh 8:15
Abner was b. and men. 2 Sam 2:17
b. images to powder. 2 Chr 34:7
they have b. me. Pr 23:35
fitches are b. with staff. Isa 28:27
the Assyrian shall be b. 30:31*
their mighty ones are b. Jer 46:5
graven images b. to pieces. Mi 1:7
synagogue ye shall be b. Mark 13:9
and did not shall be b. Luke 12:47
called the apostles and b. Acts 5:40
b. us openly uncondemned. 16:37
thrice, was I b. with. 2 Cor 11:25

beaten *gold*

candlestick was b. gold. Num 8:4
targets of b. gold. 1 Ki 10:16
shields of b. gold. 17; 2 Chr 9:16
shekels of b. gold. 2 Chr 9:15

beaten *oil*

pure oil b. for the light. Ex 27:20 Lev 24:2
an hin of b. oil. Ex 29:40; Num 28:5

beatest

when thou b. olive tree. Deut 24:20
b. him with rod, shall not. Pr 23:13

beateth

as one that b. the air. 1 Cor 9:26

beating

b. down one another. 1 Sam 14:16*
b. some, and killing. Mark 12:5

beauties

in b. of holiness, from. Ps 110:3*

beautiful

Rachel was b. Gen 29:17
the captives a b. woman. Deut 21:11
of a b. countenance. 1 Sam 16:12
Abigail of a b. countenance. 25:3
Bath-sheba was very b. 2 Sam 11:2
Esther was fair and b. Esth 2:7
b. for situation is mount. Ps 48:2
hath made every thing b. Eccl 3:11
thou art b. O my love. S of S 6:4
how b. thy feet, O princess. 7:1
the branch of Lord be b. Isa 4:2
Zion, put on thy b. garments. 52:1
b. feet of them that. 7; Rom 10:15
our holy and b. house is. Isa 64:11
where is thy b. flock ? Jer 13:20
how is staff broken, and b. 48:17
a b. crown upon thine. Ezek 16:12
thou wast exceeding b. 13
the Sabeans put on b. crowns. 23:42
sepulchres, appear b. Mat 23:27
at the gate called b. Acts 3:2, 10

beautify

king's heart to b. Lord's. Ezra 7:27
he will b. the meek with. Ps 149:4
b. place of my sanctuary. Isa 60:13

beauty

[1] *Literally, outward comeliness, or handsomeness,* 2 Sam 14:25. [2] *Figuratively, for* (a) *a chief person, or city,* 2 Sam 1:19; Isa 13:19; Lam 2:1; (b) *Splendour, glory, or dignity,* Lam 1:6; (c) *Joy and gladness,* Isa 61:3.

for Aaron, for glory and b. Ex 28:2
the b. of Israel is slain. 2 Sam 1:19*
so praised as Absalom for b. 14:25
worship the Lord in b. of holiness. 1 Chr 16:29; Ps 29:2; 96:9
praise b. of holiness. 2 Chr 20:21
to shew her b. Esth 1:11
array with glory and b. Job 40:10*
to behold the b. of the. Ps 27:4
makest his b. to consume. 39:11
shall greatly desire thy b. 45:11
their b. shall consume in. 49:14
perfection of b. God shined. 50:2
let the b. of the Lord be on. 90:17*
strength and b. in his sanctuary. 96:6
lust not after b. in thy. Pr 6:25
b. of old men is grey head. 20:29
favour is deceitful, b. is vain. 31:30
burning instead of b. Isa 3:24
Babylon the b. of the. 13:19
glorious b. is a fading. 28:1, 4
Lord will be for a diadem of b. 5
shalt see the King in his b. 33:17
according to the b. of a man. 44:13
no b. that we should desire. 53:2
them that mourn b. for ashes. 61:3*
Zion all b. is departed. Lam 1:6*
cast down from heaven b. of. 2:1
city men call the perfection of b. 15
the b. of his ornament. Ezek 7:20
went among heathen for b. 16:14
thou didst trust in thine own b. 15
thou hast made thy b. abhorred. 25
said, I am of perfect b. 27:3; 28:12
builders have perfected thy b. 27:4, 11
swords against b. of thy. 28:7
heart lifted up because of thy b. 17
no tree was like Assyrian in b. 31:8
whom dost thou pass in b ? 32:19
b. shall be as the olive-. Hos 14:6
great his goodness and b. Zech 9:17
two staves, one I called b. 11:7, 10

became

man b. a living soul. Gen 2:7
Lot's wife b. a pillar of salt. 19:26
Issachar b. a servant. 49:15
it b. a serpent. Ex 4:3
b. a rod in his hand. 4
coupled it, it b. one tabernacle. 36:13
Nabal's heart b. as a. 1 Sam 25:37
thing b. a sin. 1 Ki 12:30; 13:34
the stone b. a great. Dan 2:35
to the Jews I b. a Jew. 1 Cor 9:20
such an High Priest b. us. Heb 7:26
whilst ye b. companions of. 10:33
the sea b. as blood of. Rev 16:3

becamest

thou, Lord, b. their God. 1 Chr 17:22
thou b. mine. Ezek 16:8

because

b. thou hast done this. Gen 3:14
b. even b. they despised. Lev 26:43
b. he did this, b. he had. 2 Sam 12:6
b. I called, and ye refused. Pr 1:24
b. even b. they seduced. Ezek 13:10
shall be offended b. of. Mat 26:31*
water, b. ye belong to. Mark 9:41
ye seek me, not b. ye saw, but b. ye did eat and were filled. John 6:26
even b. ye cannot hear my. 8:43
fleeth, b. he is an hireling. 10:13
b. I live, ye shall live also. 14:19
life b. of righteousness. Rom 8:10
b. of these cometh wrath. Eph 5:6
b. he could swear by no. Heb 6:13
b. we love brethren. 1 John 3:14
we love him b. he first loved. 4:19

beckoned
Zacharias *b.* speechless. *Luke* 1:22*
b. to their partners in other. 5:7
Peter *b.* that he should. *John* 13:24
Alexander *b.* with his. *Acts* 19:33
Paul stood on stairs, and *b.* 21:40
Paul, after the governor had *b.* 24:10

beckoning
Peter *b.* unto them. *Acts* 12:17
Paul stood up, *b.* with his. 13:16

become
man is *b.* as one of us. *Gen* 3:22
what will *b.* of his dreams. 37:20
the Lord my strength, is *b.* my.
Ex 15:2; *Ps* 118:14; *Isa* 12:2
this Moses that brought us up, what
is *b.* *Ex* 32:1, 23; *Acts* 7:40
thou art *b.* the people. *Deut* 27:9
Lord is *b.* thine enemy. *1 Sam* 28:16
what would *b.* of the city. *Jonah* 4:5
is *b.* head of corner. *Mat* 21:42*
Mark 12:10*; *Luke* 20:17*
Acts 4:11*
power to *b.* the sons of. *John* 1:12
all things are *b.* new. *2 Cor* 5:17
b. the kingdoms of Lord. *Rev* 11:15

becometh
(*Sometimes used as meaning* worthy of, *or* worthily)
holiness *b.* thy house. *Ps* 93:5
he *b.* poor that dealeth. *Pr* 10:4
excellent speech *b.* not a fool. 17:7
man void of understanding *b.* 18
born in his kingdom *b.* *Eccl* 4:14*
thus it *b.* us to fulfil all. *Mat* 3:15
deceitfulness of riches choketh word,
he *b.* 13:22; *Mark* 4:19
b. a tree. *Mat* 13:32; *Mark* 4:32
our sister as *b.* saints. *Rom* 16:2
not be named, as *b.* saints. *Eph* 5:3
be as *b.* the gospel. *Phil* 1:27
b. women professing. *1 Tim* 2:10
behaviour as *b.* holiness. *Tit* 2:3*

bed
(*Usually only a thick quilt or thin mattrass. Sometimes the rich had couches made of valuable materials. Bedsteads such as we use were rare*)
bowed on *b.* *Gen* 47:31; *1 Ki* 1:47
thy father's *b.* *Gen* 49:4; *1 Chr* 5:1
he die not, keepeth his *b.* *Ex* 21:18
b. whereon he lieth. *Lev* 15:4, 24
took image laid it in *b.* *1 Sam* 19:13
who lay on a *b.* at noon. *2 Sam* 4:5
David arose from his *b.* 11:2
not come from that *b.* *2 Ki* 1:4; 6:16
let us set there for him a *b.* 4:10
my *b.* shall comfort me. *Job* 7:13
made my *b.* in the darkness. 17:13
in slumberings upon the *b.* 33:15
your heart on your *b.* *Ps* 4:4
he deviseth mischief on his *b.* 36:4
all his *b.* in his sickness. 41:3
I remember thee upon my *b.* 63:6
nor go up into my *b.* till. 132:3
if I make my *b.* in hell, thou. 139:8
my *b.* with tapestry. *Pr* 7:16, 17
why should he take thy *b.*? 22:27
the slothful on his *b.* 26:14
also our *b.* is green. *S of S* 1:16
by night on my *b.* I sought. 3:1
behold, his *b.* which is Solomon's. 7*
the *b.* is shorter than. *Isa* 28:20
mountain hast thou set thy *b.* 57:7
out in the corner of a *b.* *Amos* 3:12
take up thy *b.* and walk. *Mat* 9:6
Mark 2:9, 11; *John* 5:11, 12
a candle under a *b.* *Mark* 4:21
Luke 8:16
children with me in *b.* *Luke* 11:7
two men in one *b.* one taken. 17:34
I will cast her into a *b.* *Rev* 2:22

bed *of love*
Babylonians in *b. of love.* *Ezek* 23:17

bed *of spices*
are as a *b. of spices.* *S of S* 5:13
is gone to the *b. of spices.* 6:2

bed *undefiled*
honourable and *b. unde.* *Heb* 13:4

Bedan
the Lord sent *B.* and. *1 Sam* 12:11
the sons of Ulam, *B.* *1 Chr* 7:17

bed-chamber
frogs came into thy *b.-c.* *Ex* 8:3
lay in his *b.-c.* they. *2 Sam* 4:7
telleth the words in *b.-c.* *2 Ki* 6:12
hid him in *b.-c.* 11:2; *2 Chr* 22:11
curse not . . . in thy *b.-c.* *Eccl* 10:20

beds
sing aloud on their *b.* *Ps* 149:5
they shall rest in their *b.* *Isa* 57:2
they howled upon their *b.* *Hos* 7:14
lie on *b.* of ivory. *Amos* 6:4
them that work evil on *b.* *Mi* 2:1

bedstead
(*Rarely used, and only here named in the Bible*)
his *b.* was a *b.* of iron. *Deut* 3:11

bee, bees
chased you as *b.* in Seir. *Deut* 1:44
a swarm of *b.* in carcase. *Judg* 14:8
compassed me like *b.* *Ps* 118:12
hiss for the *b.* in Assyria. *Isa* 7:18

Beelzebub
have called the master *B.* *Mat* 10:25
cast out devils, but by *B.* prince of.
12:24; *Mark* 3:22; *Luke* 11:15
if I by *B.* cast. *Mat* 12:27
Luke 11:18, 19

been
pleasant hast thou *b.* *2 Sam* 1:26
if that had *b.* too little. 12:8
then had I *b.* at rest. *Job* 3:13
thou hast *b.* my help. *Ps* 27:9; 63:7
unless the Lord had *b.* my. 94:17
thy peace *b.* as a river. *Isa* 48:18
these, where had they *b.*? 49:21
we had *b.* in days of our. *Mat* 23:30
we trusted it had *b.* he. *Luke* 24:21
they had *b.* with Jesus. *Acts* 4:13
we had *b.* as Sodom. *Rom* 9:29
widow, having *b.* wife of. *1 Tim* 5:9
it had *b.* better not to. *2 Pet* 2:21
if they hath *b.* of us. *1 John* 2:19

hath **been**
God of my father *hath b.* *Gen* 31:5
thy God *hath b.* with. *Deut* 2:7
wherein this sin *hath b.* *1 Sam* 14:38
Israel *hath b.* without. *2 Chr* 15:3
which *hath b.* is now, that which is to
be *hath* already *b.* *Eccl* 3:15
this *hath b.* thy manner. *Jer* 22:21
hath this *b.* in your days? *Joel* 1:2
hath b. dead four days. *John* 11:39
hath b. his counsellor? *Rom* 11:34

have **been**
servants as they *have b.* *1 Sam* 4:9
have b. with thee. *1 Chr* 17:8
our fathers *have* we *b.* *Ezra* 9:7
have b. as if I had not *b.* *Job* 10:19
thy tender mercies *have b.* *Ps* 25:6
have b. young, and now old. 37:25
my tears *have b.* my meat. 42:3
have b. as Sodom, *have b.* *Isa* 1:9
so *have* we *b.* in thy sight, O. 26:17
have b. with child, *have b.* in. 18
all those things *have b.* saith. 66:2*
have I *b.* a wilderness? *Jer* 2:31
the prophets that *have b.* 28:8
I *have b.* a rebuker of. *Hos* 5:2*
have b. partial in the law. *Mal* 2:9*
they *have b.* with me. *Mark* 8:2
have b. since the world. *Luke* 1:70
have I *b.* so long time? *John* 14:9
because ye *have b.* with me. 15:27
what manner I *have b.* *Acts* 20:18
have I *b.* in the deep. *2 Cor* 11:25
righteousness should *have b.* by.
Gal 3:21

not **been**
as hath *not b.* in Egypt. *Ex* 9:18
hast *not b.* as my servant. *1 Ki* 14:8
untimely birth I had *not b.* *Job* 3:16
b. as though I had *not b.* 10:19
if it had *not b.* the Lord. *Ps* 124:1, 2
better is he that hath *not b.* *Eccl* 4:3
as though they had *not b.* *Ob* 16
good he had *not b.* born. *Mat* 26:24
have *not b.* faithful. *Luke* 16:11, 12

Beer-sheba
in wilderness of *B.* *Gen* 21:14
Abraham planted a grove in *B.* 33
to *B.* Abraham dwelt at *B.* 22:19
the name of the city is *B.* *Gen* 26:33
Jacob went out from *B.* 28:10
his journey and came to *B.* 46:1
in their inheritance *B.* *Josh* 19:2
for his life and came to *B.* *1 Ki* 19:3
Beth-el, and pass not to *B.* *Amos* 5:5
the manner of *B.* liveth. 8:14

beetle
(*Revised Version,* cricket)
ye may eat, the *b.* *Lev* 11:22

beeves
(*The plural of* beef, *used as a generic term for bulls, cows, or oxen*)
offer of the *b.* *Lev* 22:19
offers a freewill offering in *b.* 21
tribute to the Lord of *b.* *Num* 31:28
Lord's tribute of *b.* threescore and. 38

befall
(*To happen or occur to, to come upon*)
lest mischief *b.* him. *Gen* 42:4
if mischief *b.* him then. 38; 44:29
that I may tell you what shall *b.*
49:1; *Deut* 31:29; *Dan* 10:14
troubles shall *b.* them. *Deut* 31:17
shall no evil *b.* thee. *Ps* 91:10
things that shall *b.* me. *Acts* 20:22

befallen
such things have *b.* me. *Lev* 10:19
travail that hath *b.* us. *Num* 20:14
many troubles are *b.* *Deut* 31:21
why is all this *b.* us? *Judg* 6:13
something had *b.* him. *1 Sam* 20:26
every thing that had *b.* *Esth* 6:13
was *b.* to the possessed. *Mat* 8:33

befalleth
which *b.* sons of men, *b.* beasts, even
one thing *b.* them. *Eccl* 3:19

befell
worse than all that *b.* *2 Sam* 19:7
told how it *b.* to him. *Mark* 5:16
b. me by the lying in. *Acts* 20:19

before
[1] *In sight of,* Gen. 43:14. [2] *Rather than,* 2 Sam 6:21. [3] *Free to one's view and choice,* Gen 20:15. [4] *First,* (a) *In order of time,* Isa 43:13 (*Revised Version frequently changes to* beforehand); (b) *In order of place,* Josh 8:10; Luke 22:47.
behold my land is *b.* *Gen* 20:15
b. I had done speaking. 24:45
countenance was not as *b.* 31:2
Lord give you mercy *b.* the. 43:14
he set Ephraim *b.* Manasseh. 48:20
Aaron laid it up *b.* the. *Ex* 16:34
days that were *b.* shall be. *Num* 6:12
flowed over banks as *b.* *Josh* 4:18
was no day like that *b.* it. 10:14
such as *b.* knew nothing. *Judg* 3:2
said, I will go as *b.* 16:20
chose me *b.* thy father, and *b.* his.
2 Sam 6:21
saw battle was against him *b.* 10:9
1 Chr 19:10
hand became as it was *b.* *1 Ki* 13:6
the battle was *b.* and. *2 Chr* 13:14
Manasseh his trespass *b.* 33:19
my sighing cometh *b.* I eat. *Job* 3:24
b. I go, whence I shall not. 10:21
Job twice as much as he had *b.* 42:10
I am cut off from *b.* *Ps* 31:22
spare me *b.* I go hence. 39:13
thou preparedst room *b.* it. 80:9
b. I was afflicted I went. 119:67
hast beset me behind and *b.* 139:5
thou die *b.* thy time? *Eccl* 7:17
Syrians *b.* and Philistines. *Isa* 9:12
and behold, *b.* the morning. 17:14
b. the day was, I am he. 43:13*
that *b.* they call I will. 65:24
b. I formed thee I knew. *Jer* 1:5
ministered *b.* their idols. *Ezek* 44:12
a widow that had a priest *b.* 22*
doings, are *b.* my face. *Hos* 7:2
every cow at that *b.* her *Amos* 4:3
me, and was afraid *b.* *Mal* 2:5*
send Elijah *b.* the coming. 4:5
b. they came together. *Mat* 1:18
knoweth what things ye need *b.* 6:8

come to torment us b.? Mat 8:29
behold, I have told you b. 24:25
not see death b. he had. Luke 2:26
for b. they were at enmity. 23:12
of man where he was b. John 6:62
law judge man b. it hear? 7:51
I tell you b. it come. 13:19; 14:29
he seeing this b. spake. Acts 2:31
do thy counsel determined b. 4:28
to witnesses chosen b. of God. 10:41
who have begun b. to. 2 Cor 8:10*
of which I tell you b. Gal 5:21*
to things that are b. Phil 3:13
whereof ye heard b. in. Col 1:5
that we had suffered b. 1 Thes 2:2
with you, we told you b. 3:4
was b. a blasphemer. 1 Tim 1:13
the command going b. Heb 7:18*
after that he had said b. 10:15*
of words spoken b. 2 Pet 3:2
seeing ye know these things b. 17
to worship b. thy feet. Rev 3:9
full of eyes b. and behind. 4:6

come **before**

shall come b. the judges. Ex 22:9
come b. his presence. Ps 100:2
shall I come b. the Lord? Mi 6:6
come b. winter. 2 Tim 4:21

before *the people*

bowed b. the people. Gen 23:12
of fire from b. the people. Ex 13:22
said, go on b. the people. 17:5
b. thy people I will do marvels. 34:10
went b. the people to Ai. Josh 8:10
came in b. the people. 1 Sam 18:13
set them b. the people. Mark 8:6
his words, b. the people. Luke 20:26
b. many peoples. Rev 10:11*

before *whom*

Lord b. whom I walk. Gen 24:40
God b. whom my fathers. 48:15
As the Lord liveth, b. whom I stand.
1 Ki 17:1; 18:15; 2 Ki 3:14; 5:16
b. whom thou hast begun. Esth 6:13
b. whom were three horns. Dan 7:8
and b. whom three fell. 20
the king b. whom I. Acts 26:26
see further, **all, ark, God, him, Lord, me, mount, stand, stood, thee, them, as, went, you.**

beforehand

take no thought b. Mark 13:11
make up b. your bounty. 2 Cor 9:5
some men's sins open b. 1 Tim 5:24*
works of some are manifest b. 25*
testified b. sufferings of. 1 Pet 1:11

beforetime

he hated him not b. Josh 20:5
b. in Israel, when a man went to enquire; he now called a prophet was b. called a seer. 1 Sam 9:9
nor afflict them as b. 2 Sam 7:10*
Israel dwelt in tents as b. 2 Ki 13:5
I had not been b. sad. Neh 2:1
who hath declared b. Isa 41:26
Simon which b. used. Acts 8:9

beg

be vagabonds and b. Ps 109:10
shall the sluggard b. Pr 20:4
I cannot dig, to b. I am. Luke 16:3

began

b. men to call on the. Gen 4:26
b. to commit whoredom. Num 25:1
they b. to smite Israel. Judg 20:31
Lord b. to cut Israel. 2 Ki 10:32
when they b. to sing. 2 Chr 20:22
in the third month they b. 31:7
young Josiah b. to seek God. 34:3
then they b. at the ancient. Ezek 9:6
then Jesus b. to preach. Mat 4:17
been since the world b. Luke 1:70
this man b. to build. 14:30
the hour when he b. to. John 4:52
since the world b. 9:32; Acts 3:21
Rom 16:25*
In Christ before the world b.
2 Tim 1:9*; Tit 1:2*
salvation at first b. to be. Heb 2:3*

begat

hearken to him that b. Pr 23:22
concerning fathers that b. Jer 16:3
and he that b. her. Dan 11:6
and mother that b. him. Zech 13:3
of his own will b. he us. Jas 1:18
that loveth him that b. 1 John 5:1

beget

twelve princes shall he b. Gen 17:20
thou shalt b. children. Deut 4:25
thou shalt b. sons, but shalt. 28:41
sons which thou shalt b. shall they.
2 Ki 20:18; Isa 39:7
if a man b. 100 children. Eccl 6:3
take wives, and b. sons. Jer 29:6
if he b. a son that is. Ezek 18:10
he b. a son that seeth all. 14

begettest

issue which thou b. thine. Gen 48:6
his father, what b. thou? Isa 45:10

begetteth

he that b. a fool, doeth it. Pr 17:21
that b. a wise child shall. 23:24
he b. a son, and nothing. Eccl 5:14

beggar

he lifteth the b. from. 1 Sam 2:8*
a b. named Lazarus. Luke 16:20
b. died, and was carried by. 22

beggarly

turn ye again to b. elements. Gal 4:9

begged

b. the body of Jesus. Mat 27:58
Luke 23:52
is not this he that b.? John 9:8

begging

have not seen his seed b. Ps 37:25
Bartimaeus sat b. Mark 10:46
Luke 18:35

begin

this they b. to do, and. Gen 11:6
day I b. to put dread. Deut 2:25
day will I b. to magnify. Josh 3:7
when I b. I will also. 1 Sam 3:12
did I then b. to inquire of? 22:15
Mattaniah to b. Neh 11:17
I b. to bring evil on the. Jer 25:29
and b. at my sanctuary. Ezek 9:6
and b. not to say. Luke 3:8
then shall he b. to say. 13:26
all that behold it, b. to mock. 14:29
these things b. to come to. 21:28
do we b. again to? 2 Cor 3:1
that judgement b. at the house of God, and if it first b. at us. 1 Pet 4:17

beginnest

thou b. to put sickle. Deut 16:9

beginning, *noun*

[1] *That which is the first,* Ex 12:2.
[2] *The creation,* Gen 1:1.

Reuben, thou art the b. of. Gen 49:3
this month shall be the b. Ex 12:2
is the b. of his strength. Deut 21:17
though thy b. was small. Job 8:7
the latter more than b. 42:12
fear of Lord b. Ps 111:10; Pr 9:10
fear of the Lord is the b. of. Pr 1:7
b. of strife, as when one. 17:14
is the end than the b. Eccl 7:8
b. of words of his mouth is. 10:13
since b. of the world. Isa 64:4*
is the b. of sin to the. Mi 1:13
these are b. of sorrows. Mat 24:8
Mark 13:8
tribulation, not since the b.
Mat 24:21
the b. of the gospel. Mark 1:1
this b. of miracles did. John 2:11
who is the b. the first born. Col 1:18
if we hold the b. of our. Heb 3:14
having neither b. of days. nor. 7:3
end is worse than the b. 2 Pet 2:20
I am the b. Rev 1:8*; 21:6; 22:13
these things saith the b. of. 3:14

at the **beginning**

kindness than at the b. Ruth 3:10
waste as at b. 1 Chr 17:9*
an inheritance at the b. Pr 20:21
counsellors as at the b. Isa 1:26
at the b. of supplications. Dan 9:23
made them, at b. made. Mat 19:4
things I said not at the b. John 16:4
them as on us at the b Acts 11:15

from the **beginning**

from the b. of year. Deut 11:12
from the b. of revenges. 32:42
is true from the b. Ps 119:160*
I was set up from the b. Pr 8:23
work God maketh from b. Eccl 3:11
a people terrible from b. Isa 18:2, 7
not been told from the b.? 40:21
who hath declared from b.? 41:26
declaring the end from the b. 46:10
not spoken in secret from b. 48:16
high throne from the b. Jer 17:12
from the b. it was not so. Mat 19:8
us, which from b. were. Luke 1:2
Jesus knew from the b. John 6:64
saith, I said to you from b. 8:25
was a murderer from b. and. 44
been with me from the b. 15:27
which from b. of the world. Eph 3:9*
hath from b. chosen. 2 Thes 2:13
continue as from the b. 2 Pet 3:4
which ye have heard from b.
1 John 2:7; 3:11
have known him that is from b. 2:13
for the devil sinneth from the b. 3:8
which we had from the b. 2 John 5

in the **beginning**

in the b. God created. Gen 1:1
possessed me in the b. of. Pr 8:22
in b. was the Word. John 1:1
the same was in the b. with God. 2
ye know that in the b. Phil 4:15
thou Lord in the b. hast. Heb 1:10

beginning, *verb*

b. to sink he cried, Lord. Mat 14:30
give their hire, b. from the. 20:8
among all nations, b. at. Luke 24:47
went out, b. at the eldest. John 8:9
b. from baptism of John. Acts 1:22

beginnings

in b. of months. Num 10:10; 28:11
I will do better than at b. Ezek 36:11

begotten

have I b. them? Num 11:12
children b. of them. Deut 23:8
Gideon had 70 sons, b. Judg 8:30
or who hath b. drops of? Job 38:28
Son, this day have I b. thee. Ps 2:7
Acts 13:33; Heb 1:5; 5:5
say, who hath b. these? Isa 49:21
have b. strange children. Hos 5:7
glory as of the only b. of. John 1:14
only b. Son, he hath declared. 18
loved, that he gave his only b. 3:16
not believed in the only b. Son. 18
I have b. you through. 1 Cor 4:15
Onesimus, I have b. Philem 10
bringeth in first b. Heb 1:6
by faith offered up only b. 11:17
who hath b. us again to. 1 Pet 1:3
sent his only b. Son. 1 John 4:9
that begat, loveth him that is b. 5:1
he that is b. of God keepeth. 18
Jesus who is the first b. Rev 1:5

beguile

lest any b. you with words. Col 2:4*
let no man b. you of your. 18*

beguiled, -ing

said, serpent b. me. Gen 3:13
wherefore hast thou b. me? 29:25
b. you in the matter. Num 25:18
wherefore have ye b. us? Josh 9:22
fear lest as the serpent b. 2 Cor 11:3
cease from sin, b. 2 Pet 2:14*

begun

the plague is b. Num 16:46
the plague was b. 47
b. to shew greatness. Deut 3:24
thou hast b. to fall. Esth 6:13
undertook to do as they had b. 9:23
he had b. to reckon. Mat 18:24
as he had b. so he would. 2 Cor 8:6
expedient for you who have b. 10
are ye so foolish, having b.? Gal 3:3
which hath b. a good work. Phil 1:6
have b. to wax wanton. 1 Tim 5:11

behalf

a statute on b. of Israel. Ex 27:21
Abner sent David on b. 2 Sam 3:12
strong in b. of them. 2 Chr 16:9

yet to speak on God's *b.* *Job* 36:2
a prince for his own *b.* *Dan* 11:18*
glad on your *b.* *Rom* 16:19*
thank my God on your *b.* *1 Cor* 1:4*
thanks given on your *b.* *2 Cor* 1:11
occasion to glory on our *b.* 5:12
it is given in *b.* of Christ. *Phil* 1:29
glorify God on this *b.* *1 Pet* 4:16

behave

lest adversaries *b.* *Deut* 32:27*
let us *b.* ourselves. *1 Chr* 19:13*
I will *b.* wisely in perfect. *Ps* 101:2
the child shall *b.* himself. *Isa* 3:5
charity doth not *b.* itself. *1 Cor* 13:5
now thou oughtest to *b.* *1 Tim* 3:15

behaved

David *b.* wisely. *1 Sam* 18:5
14, 15, 30
b. as though he had been. *Ps* 35:14
I have *b.* myself as a child. 131:2*
b. themselves ill in doings. *Mi* 3:4*
how unblameably we *b.* *1 Thes* 2:10
b. not ourselves disorderly.
2 Thes 3:7

behaveth

think he *b.* uncomely to. *1 Cor* 7:36

behaviour

David changed his *b.* *1 Sam* 21:13
bishop must be of good *b.* *1 Tim* 3:2*
women in *b.* becometh. *Tit* 2:3*

beheaded

hands over the heifer *b.* *Deut* 21:6*
smote Ish-bosheth, and *b.* him.
2 Sam 4:7
b. John. *Mat* 14:10; *Mark* 6:16, 27
Luke 9:9
souls of them that were *b.* *Rev* 20:4

beheld

he *b.* serpent of brass. *Num* 21:9
hath not *b.* iniquity in Jacob. 23:21
destroying, the Lord *b.* *1 Chr* 21:15
if I *b.* the sun when it. *Job* 31:26
I *b.* transgressors. *Ps* 119:158
I *b.* but there was no man. 142:4*
b. among the simple ones. *Pr* 7:7
then I *b.* the work of God. *Eccl* 8:17
I *b.* and there was no man. *Isa* 41:28
Jer 4:25
I *b.* the earth without form. *Jer* 4:23
Mary Magdalene and Mary *b.*
Mark 15:47; *Luke* 23:55
I *b.* Satan as lightning. *Luke* 10:18
he *b.* the city, and wept over. 19:41
and we *b.* his glory. *John* 1:14
while they *b.* Jesus was. *Acts* 1:9*
I passed by and *b.* your. 17:23
I *b.* and in midst of the. *Rev* 5:6
and their enemies *b.* them. 11:12

behemoth

(*Probably the hippopotamus*)
behold now *b.* which I. *Job* 40:15

behind

[1] *Backwards,* Judg 20:40. [2] *After,* 2 Sam 3:16. [3] *Remaining,* Lev 25:51. [4] *Past,* Phil. 3:13.

shall not an hoof be left *b.* *Ex* 10:26
be yet many years *b.* *Lev* 25:51*
Benjamites looked *b.* *Judg* 20:40
those left *b.* stayed. *1 Sam* 30:9
husband went weeping *b.* *2 Sam* 3:16
cast me *b.* thy back. *1 Ki* 14:9
Ezek 23:35
rulers were *b.* Judah. *Neh* 4:16
cast thy law *b.* their backs. 9:26
he standeth *b.* our wall. *S of S* 2:9
cast all my sins *b.* thy. *Isa* 38:17
she came in the press *b.* *Mark* 5:27
the child Jesus tarried *b.* *Luke* 2:43
so that ye come *b.* in. *1 Cor* 1:7
I was not *b.* *2 Cor* 11:5; 12:11
forgetting those things *b.* *Phil* 3:13
what is *b.* of afflictions. *Col* 1:24*

see further, **before, him, we, thee, them, us**

behold

(*An interjection, calling attention to what is to follow. Literally,* lo, look)

b. I am with thee, and. *Gen* 28:15
looked, and *b.* they were sad. 40:6
b. thy father is sick 48:1
Israel said, *b.* I die. *Gen* 48:21
b. the bush burned with. *Ex* 3:2
b. I will rain bread from. 16:4
b. I send an angel before. 23:20
b. we are in Kadesh. *Num* 20:16
b. king ye have chosen. *1 Sam* 12:13
answered, *b.* thy servant. *2 Sam* 9:6
b. child shall be born to. *1 Ki* 13:2
b. they spied band of. *2 Ki* 13:21
b. I will bring evil upon this. 22:16
2 Chr 34:24
b. I say, how they. *2 Chr* 20:11
b. all that he hath is in. *Job* 1:12
b. the fear of the Lord. 28:28
b. in this thou art not just. 33:12
b. God is mighty, despiseth. 36:5, 26
b. I am vile, what shall I? 40:4
b. eye of the Lord is on. *Ps* 33:18
b. I was shapen in iniquity. 51:5
b. these are the ungodly. 73:12
b. he smote the rock, waters. 78:20
if I make my bed in hell, *b.* 139:8
b. thou art fair, my love *b.*
S of S 1:15, 16; 4:1
b. a virgin. *Isa* 7:14; *Mat* 1:23
b. I and the children. *Isa* 8:18
Heb 2:13
look to the earth, and *b.* *Isa* 8:22
b. God is my salvation, I will. 12:2
hungry man dreameth, and *b.* 29:8
say to Judah, *b.* your God. 40:9
first shall say to Zion, *b. b.* 41:27
b. my servant whom I uphold. 42:1
b. I will do a new thing. 43:19
lest thou shouldest say *b.* I. 48:7
looked for peace *b.* *Jer* 8:15; 14:19
b. I am in your hands. 26:14
b. I am for you, and. *Ezek* 36:9
b. I will bring my servant. *Zech* 3:8
b. the man whose name is. 6:12
b. thy King cometh. 9:9; *Mat* 21:5
John 12:15
b. I will send my messenger. *Mal* 3:1
4:5; *Mat* 11:10; *Mark* 1:2
and *b.* beam in thine own. *Mat* 7:4
b. he is in the desert, *b.* he. 24:26
is risen *b.* the place. *Mark* 16:6
b. I send the promise. *Luke* 24:49
b. the Lamb of God. *John* 1:29, 36
b. an Israelite indeed. 47
Pilate saith *b.* the man. 19:5
Saul of Tarsus, for *b.* he. *Acts* 9:11
as dying, and *b.* we live. *2 Cor* 6:9
b. what manner of love. *1 John* 3:1
b. I stand at the door. *Rev* 3:20
b. I come as a thief, blessed. 16:15
b. I come quickly. 22:7, 12

behold *it is*

b. it is between Kadesh. *Gen* 16:14
the land, *b. it is* large enough. 34:21
b. it is a stiff-necked. *Ex* 32:9
but now *b. it is* dry. *Josh* 9:12
seen the land, *b. it is.* *Judg* 18:9
that doth speak, *b. it is* I. *Isa* 52:6
b. the day, *b. it is* come. *Ezek* 7:10
b. it is come, and it is done. 39:8

now **behold,** or **behold** *now*

now b. the king walketh. *1 Sam* 12:2
now b. thou trustest on. *2 Ki* 18:21
also *now b.* my witness. *Job* 16:19
now b. I loose thee this. *Jer* 40:4
now b. ye have heard. *Mat* 26:65
now b. the hand of the. *Acts* 13:11
now b. I go bound in the. 20:22
b. now is the time, *b. now.* *2 Cor* 6:2

behold *it was,* **behold** *there was, see* **was**

behold, *verb*

[1] *To look on a thing with our eyes,* Num 24:17. [2] *To think over a thing in our minds,* Lam 1:12; Rom 11:22.

b. this heap, *b.* this. *Gen* 31:51
Moses said, *b.* the blood. *Ex* 24:8
of the Lord shall he *b.* *Num* 12:8
see him, from the hills I *b.* 23:9
but not now, shall *b.* him. 24:17
b. it with thine eyes. *Deut* 3:27
b. the king whom ye. *1 Sam* 12:13
mine eyes shall *b.* and. *Job* 19:27
nor shall his place any more *b.* 20:9
but I cannot *b.* him. 23:9
hideth his face, who can *b.*? 34:29
his work, which men *b.* *Job* 36:24*
his eyes *b.* his eye-lids. *Ps* 11:4
countenance doth *b.* the upright. 7
let thine eyes *b.* the things. 17:2
will *b.* thy face in righteousness. 15
b. the beauty of the Lord. 27:4
mark the perfect man, *b.* 37:37
come, *b.* the works of the Lord. 46:8
awake to help me, and *b.* 59:4
ruleth for ever, his eyes *b.* 66:7
look down from heaven, *b.* 80:14
with thine eyes shalt thou *b.* 91:8
from heaven did the Lord *b.* 102:19
he humbleth himself to *b.* 113:6
open mine eyes, that I may *b.* 119:18
thine eyes shall *b.* *Pr* 23:33
pleasant thing it is to *b.* *Eccl* 11:7
he will not *b.* majesty of. *Isa* 26:10
I said, I shall *b.* man no more. 38:11
or evil, that we may *b.* it. 41:23
b. from thy habitation. 63:15
I said, *b.* me, *b.* me, to a. 65:1
thine eyes shall *b.* thy. *Jer* 20:4
neither *b.* the good I will do. 29:32
his eyes shall *b.* his. 32:4; 34:3
but a few, as thine eyes do *b.* 42:2
b. and see if any sorrow. *Lam* 1:12
hear all people, and *b.* my. 18
the Lord look down and *b.* 3:50
O Lord, consider and *b.* 5:1
b. the wicked. *Ezek* 8:9
kings that they may *b.* 28:17
ashes in sight of all that *b.* 18
man, *b.* with thine eyes. 40:4; 44:5
open thine eyes, and *b.* *Dan* 9:18
light, and I shall *b.* *Mi* 7:9
enemy, mine eyes shall *b.* her. 10
cause me to *b.* grievances? *Hab* 1:3
art of purer eyes than to *b.* evil. 13
their angels alway *b.* *Mat* 18:10
all that *b.* it mock him. *Luke* 14:29
for these things which ye *b.* 21:6
b. my hands and my feet. 24:39
with me, to *b.* my glory. *John* 17:24
as he drew near to *b.* it. *Acts* 7:31
Moses trembled, and durst not *b.* 32
Israel could not *b.* face. *2 Cor* 3:7
your good works they *b.* *1 Pet* 2:12
they *b.* your chaste conversation. 3:2
they *b.* the beast that. *Rev* 17:8

beholdest

thou *b.* all mischief to. *Ps* 10:14
why *b.* thou the mote? *Mat* 7:3
Luke 6:41
b. not the beam that is. *Luke* 6:42

beholdeth

b. not way of vineyards. *Job* 24:18*
the Lord *b.* all the sons. *Ps* 33:13
he *b.* himself and goeth. *Jas* 1:24

beholding

turn mine eyes from *b.* *Ps* 119:37
Lord in every place, *b.* evil. *Pr* 15:3*
saving the *b.* of them. *Eccl* 5:11
women *b.* *Mat* 27:55; *Luke* 23:49
Jesus *b.* him, loved him. *Mark* 10:21
people stood *b.* and. *Luke* 23:35
b. things done, smote their. 48
b. man which was healed. *Acts* 4:14
Paul earnestly *b.* the council. 23:1*
with open face *b.* as in. *2 Cor* 3:18
in spirit, joying, and *b.* *Col* 2:5
a man *b.* his natural face. *Jas* 1:23

behoved

(*Was necessary or proper for*)
it *b.* Christ to suffer. *Luke* 24:46
b. him to be made like. *Heb* 2:17

being

I *b.* in the way, the. *Gen* 24:27*
the owner thereof not *b.* *Ex* 22:14
shall not defile himself, *b.* *Lev* 21:4
vow *b.* in her father's. *Num* 30:3, 16
our enemies *b.* judges. *Deut* 32:31
freed from *b.* bondmen. *Josh* 9:23
rejected thee from *b.* king.
1 Sam 15:23, 26
Maachah his mother, he removed from *b.* *1 Ki* 15:13; *2 Chr* 15:16
in *b.* like the house. *1 Ki* 16:7
who is there that *b.* as? *Neh* 6:11
man *b.* in honour, abideth. *Ps* 49:12
cut them off from *b.* a nation. 83:4
b. an Hebrew or. *Jer* 34:9
her husband *b.* a just. *Mat* 1:19

woman *b.* a daughter. *Luke* 13:16
in hell he lift up his eyes *b.* 16:23
b. children of the resurrection. 20:36
b. in agony, he prayed. 22:44
conveyed—multitude *b.* *John* 5:13
that thou, *b.* a man, makest. 10:33
all the members *b.* *1 Cor* 12:12
Jesus Christ *b.* the chief. *Eph* 2:20
who *b.* in the form of God. *Phil* 2:6
as *b.* yourselves also. *Heb* 13:3
she *b.* with child, cried. *Rev* 12:2

being

praise my God while I have my *b.*
Ps 104:33; 146:2
in him move, and have *b.* *Acts* 17:28

bekah

a *b.* for each, that is half a. *Ex* 38:26

Bel

B. boweth down, Nebo. *Isa* 46:1
Babylon is taken, *B.* is. *Jer* 50:2
I will punish *B.* in Babylon. 51:44

belch

behold, they *b.* out. *Ps* 59:7

Belial

certain children of *B.* *Deut* 13:13
certain sons of *B.* beset. *Judg* 19:22
the man, the children of *B.* 20:13
a daughter of *B.* *1 Sam* 1:16
sons of Eli were sons of *B.* 2:12
children of *B.* said, how shall? 10:27
he is such a son of *B.* 25:17
lord regard this man of *B.* 25
then answered the men of *B.* 30:22
out, thou man of *B.* *2 Sam* 16:7
to be there a man of *B.* Sheba. 20:1
the sons of *B.* shall be as. 23:6
set two sons of *B.* *1 Ki* 21:10, 13
Jeroboam children of *B.* *2 Chr* 13:7
hath Christ with *B.*? *2 Cor* 6:15

belied

they have *b.* the Lord. *Jer* 5:12

belief

sanctification of Spirit, and *b.* of.
2 Thes 2:13

believe

[1] *To give credit to any thing,* Gen 45:26, Acts 8:13. [2] *To be fully* persuaded, John 1:12; 3:15, 16; 6:69; Rom 9:33; 10:4. [3] *To put confidence in,* 2 Chr 20:20.

that they may *b.* Lord hath. *Ex* 4:5
that they may hear and *b.* 19:9
how long ere they *b.*? *Num* 14:11
b. in the Lord God, *b.* *2 Chr* 20:20
ye may know and *b.* me. *Isa* 43:10
b. ye that I am able? *Mat* 9:28
whoso offend one of these little ones
which *b.* in me. 18:6; *Mark* 9:42
repented not that ye might *b.*
Mat 21:32
let him come down, we will *b.* 27:42
repent and *b.* the gospel. *Mark* 1:15
be not afraid, *b.* 5:36; *Luke* 8:50
thou canst *b.* all things. *Mark* 9:23*
Lord, I *b.* help mine. 24; *John* 9:38
shall *b.* those things. *Mark* 11:23
b. ye receive, and ye shall. 24
descend, that we may *b.* 15:32
shall follow them which *b.* 16:17
taketh word, lest they *b.* *Luke* 8:12
no root, which for a while *b.* 13
slow of heart to *b.* 24:25
men through him might *b.* *John* 1:7
of God, even to them that *b.* 12
how shall ye *b.* if I tell you? 3:12
woman, *b.* me, hour cometh. 4:21
now we *b.* not because of. 42
ye *b.* which receive honour? 5:44
if not writings, how shall ye *b.*? 47
work of God, that ye *b.* on. 6:29
we *b.* and are sure that thou art. 69
neither did his brethren *b.* in. 7:5
Spirit, which they that *b.* 39
dost thou *b.* on Son of God? 9:35
who is he, Lord, that I might *b.*? 36
b. works, that ye may *b.* 10:38*
not there, to intent ye may *b.* 11:15
I *b.* that thou art the Christ. 27
said I not, if thou wouldst *b.* 40
they may *b.* that thou hast sent. 42
let him alone, all men will *b.* 48
while ye have light, *b.* in. *John* 12:36
it come to pass, ye may *b.* 13:19
not troubled, ye *b.* in God, *b.* 14:1
b. I am in the Father, or *b.* 11
when it come to pass ye might *b.* 29
by this we *b.* thou camest. 16:30
Jesus answered, do ye now *b.*? 31
I pray for them which shall *b.* 17:20
that world may *b.* thou hast. 21
he saith true, that ye might *b.* 19:35
written that ye might *b.* 20:31
b. Jesus Christ is Son. *Acts* 8:37*
by him all that *b.* are. 13:39
a work you shall in no wise *b.* 41
by me should hear and *b.* 15:7
b. through grace we shall be. 11
b. on the Lord Jesus, and. 16:31
b. on him that should come. 19:4
many Jews there are which *b.* 21:20
touching the Gentiles which *b.* 25
I *b.* God that it shall be as. 27:25
righteousness on all that *b.*
Rom 3:22
father of all them that *b.* 4:11
it shall be imputed, if we *b.* 24
if dead, we *b.* that we shall live. 6:8
b. in thy heart that God raised. 10:9
how shall they *b.* in him? 14
save them that *b.* *1 Cor* 1:21
be divisions, and I partly *b.* it. 11:18
that *b.* but prophesying serveth them
which *b.* 14:22
we also *b.* and therefore. *2 Cor* 4:13
promise given to them that *b.*
Gal 3:22
of power to us who *b.* *Eph* 1:19
it is given not only to *b.* *Phil* 1:29
ensamples to all that *b.* *1 Thes* 1:7
we behaved among you that *b.* 2:10
which worketh in you that *b.* 13
if we *b.* that Jesus died and. 4:14
admired in all those that *b.*
2 Thes 1:10
delusion that they should *b.* 2:11
pattern to them that *b.* *1 Tim* 1:16
thanksgiving of them that *b.* 4:3
Saviour, especially those that *b.* 10
them that *b.* to saving. *Heb* 10:39*
that cometh to God must *b.* 11:6
the devils also *b.* and. *Jas* 2:19
who by him do *b.* in. *1 Pet* 1:21
to you which *b.* he is precious. 2:7
commandment that we should *b.*
1 John 3:23
to you that *b.* that ye may *b.* 5:13*

believe *not,* or *not* **believe**

behold, they will *not b.* me. *Ex* 4:1
come to pass, if they will *not b.* 8, 9
yet in this ye did *not b.* *Deut* 1:32
their fathers did *not b.* *2 Ki* 17:14
yet would I *not b.* that he. *Job* 9:16
speaketh fair, *b.* him *not.* *Pr* 26:25
if ye will *not b.* ye shall not. *Isa* 7:9
b. not them. *Jer* 12:6
which ye will *not b.* *Hab* 1:5
why did ye *not b.* him? *Mat* 21:25
Mark 11:31
b. it *not.* *Mat* 24:23, 26; *Mark* 13:21
if I tell you will *not b.* *Luke* 22:67
earthly things, ye *b. not.* *John* 3:12
except ye see ye will *not b.* 4:48
whom he hath sent, ye *b. not.* 5:38
b. not his writings how shall ye *b.*
my words? 47
also have seen me and *b. not.* 6:36
there some of you which *b. not.* 64
ye *b. not* I am he, ye shall die. 8:24
I tell you truth, ye *b.* me *not.* 45
why do ye *not b.* me? 46
ye *b. not,* because ye are not. 10:26
do not the works, *b.* me *not.* 37
though ye *b. not* me, believe. 38
they could *not b.* because. 12:39
if any hear words, and *b. not.* 47
reprove of sin, they *b. not.* 16:9
into his side, I will *not b.* 20:25
what if some did *not b.*? *Rom* 3:3*
from them that do *not b.* 15:31*
if any that *b. not* bid. *1 Cor* 10:27
a sign to them that *b. not.* 14:22
blinded minds that *b. not.* *2 Cor* 4:4
if we *b. not,* he abideth. *2 Tim* 2:13*
b. not every spirit. *1 John* 4:1

believed

b. in the Lord. *Gen* 15:6; *Rom* 4:3
Gal 3:6; *Jas* 2:23
Aaron spake, people *b.* *Ex* 4:31
b. the Lord and Moses. 14:31
and Achish *b.* David. *1 Sam* 27:12
had fainted, unless I had *b.* *Ps* 27:13
then *b.* they his words, they. 106:12
I *b.*, therefore have I spoken. 116:10
2 Cor 4:13
teach me, for I have *b.* *Ps* 119:66
who hath *b.* our report? *Isa* 53:1
John 12:38; *Rom* 10:16
hurt on him, because he *b.* *Dan* 6:23*
people of Nineveh *b.* God. *Jonah* 3:5
as thou hast *b.* so be it. *Mat* 8:13
publicans and harlots *b.* him. 21:32
and told it, neither *b.* *Mark* 16:13
which are most surely *b.* *Luke* 1:1
blessed is she that *b.* for there. 45
his glory, and disciples *b.* *John* 2:11
they *b.* the scripture. 22
the man *b.* the word. 4:50
the father himself *b.* and. 53
ye *b.* Moses, ye would have *b.* 5:46
have any rulers or Pharisees *b.*? 7:48
said Jesus to Jews that *b.* 8:31
had seen things Jesus did, *b.* 11:45
the Jews went away and *b.* 12:11
loveth you, because you *b.* 16:27
they have *b.* thou didst send. 17:8
that other disciple saw and *b.* 20:8
hast *b.* have not seen and *b.* 29
all that *b.* were together. *Acts* 2:44
many of them which heard *b.* 4:4
multitude of them that *b.* were. 32
but when they *b.* Philip. 8:12
then Simon himself *b.* also. 13
they of circumcision who *b.* 10:45
gave them gift as us who *b.* 11:17
great number *b.* and turned. 21
deputy *b.* being astonished. 13:12
were ordained to eternal life *b.* 48
of both Jews and Greeks *b.* 14:1
commended them to Lord they *b.* 23
some of them *b.* and. 17:4*
certain men clave to him and *b.* 34
Crispus chief ruler *b.* on Lord. 18:8
helped them which had *b.* 27
the Holy Ghost since ye *b.*? 19:2
beat in synagogue them that *b.* 22:19
the centurion *b.* the master. 27:11*
some *b.*, and some *b.* not. 28:24
against hope *b.* in hope. *Rom* 4:18
salvation nearer than when we *b.*
13:11
ministers by whom ye *b.* *1 Cor* 3:5
unless ye have *b.* in vain. 15:2
so we preach, and so ye *b.* 11
even we have *b.* in Jesus. *Gal* 2:16
in whom after ye *b.* *Eph* 1:13
our testimony was *b.* *2 Thes* 1:10
b. on in the world. *1 Tim* 3:16
I know whom I have *b.* *2 Tim* 1:12
they which have *b.* in God. *Tit* 3:8
which have *b.* do enter. *Heb* 4:3
have *b.* the love of God. *1 John* 4:16

many **believed**

at the passover *many b.* *John* 2:23
many of the Samaritans *b.* on. 4:39
many of the Jews *b.* 11:45
the chief rulers also *many b.* 12:42
many of Corinthians *b.* *Acts* 18:8
many that *b.* came and. 19:18

believed *not,* or *not* **believed**

heart fainted, he *b. not.* *Gen* 45:26
because he *b.* me *not.* *Num* 20:12
rebelled, and *b.* him *not.* *Deut* 9:23
I *b. not* words. *1 Ki* 10:7; *2 Chr* 9:6
I laughed, they *b.* it *not.* *Job* 29:24
because they *b. not* in God. *Ps* 78:22
sinned, and *b. not* for his. 32
despised the land, *b. not.* 106:24
but Gedaliah *b.* them *not.* *Jer* 40:14
world would *not* have *b.* *Lam* 4:12
came, and ye *b.* him *not.* *Mat* 21:32
they heard he was alive *b. not.*
Mark 16:11
because they *b. not.* 14
why then *b.* him *not*? *Luke* 20:5
while they *b. not* for joy. 24:41
because he hath *not b.* *John* 3:18
Jesus knew who *b. not.* 6:64

I told you and ye *b. not. John* 10:25
many miracles, yet they *b. not.* 12:37
afraid, and *b. not* that. *Acts* 9:26
Jews which *b. not* moved. 17:5
were hardened and *b. not.* 19:9*
in whom they have *not b. Rom* 10:14
times past have *not b.* God. 11:30*
even so have these *not b.* 31
damned who *b.* not. *2 Thes* 2:12
into rest, that *b. not.* *Heb* 3:18*
not with them that *b. not.* 11:31*
destroyed them that *b. not.* *Jude* 5

believers

b. were the more added. *Acts* 5:14
be thou an example of *b. 1 Tim* 4:12

believest

dumb because thou *b.* not. *Luke* 1:20
I saw thee, *b.* thou ? *John* 1:50
in me shall never die, *b.* ? 11:26
b. thou not ? 14:10
thou *b.* with thine heart. *Acts* 8:37*
b. thou ? I know thou *b.* 26:27
b. that there is one God. *Jas* 2:19

believeth

he *b.* not that he shall. *Job* 15:22
simple *b.* every word. *Pr* 14:15
that *b.* not make haste. *Isa* 28:16
possible to him that *b.* *Mark* 9:23
he that *b.* and is baptized . . he that *b.* not shall be damned. 16:16
b. in him not perish. *John* 3:15, 16
he that *b.* on him is not condemned, that *b.* not is condemned. 18
that *b.* hath everlasting. 36; 6:47
b. on him that sent me hath. 5:24
he that *b.* shall never thirst. 6:35
he that seeth the Son and *b.* 40
he that *b.* on me, out of his. 7:38
he that *b.* though he were. 11:25
whosoever liveth and *b.* in me. 26
he that *b.* on me, *b.* not on. 12:44
whoso *b.* on me, should not. 46
he that *b.* on me, the works. 14:12
whoso *b.* in him receive. *Acts* 10:43
God to every one that *b. Rom* 1:16
the justifier of him that *b.* 3:26*
him that worketh not, but *b.* 4:5
whoso *b.* shall not be. 9:33; 10:11
end of law to every one that *b.* 10:4
for with the heart man *b.* 10
for one *b.* that he may eat. 14:2*
hath a wife that *b.* not. *1 Cor* 7:12
love *b.* all things, hopeth all. 13:7
come in one that *b.* not. 14:24
part hath he that *b.*? *2 Cor* 6:15
if any man that *b.* have. *1 Tim* 5:16
he that *b.* shall not be. *1 Pet* 2:6
whoso *b.* Jesus is Christ. *1 John* 5:1
overcometh, but he that *b.* 5
that *b.* on the Son; he that *b.* not God, because he *b.* not the record. 10

believing

ask in prayer, *b.* receive. *Mat* 21:22
be not faithless but *b.* *John* 20:27
that *b.* ye might have life. 31
rejoiced, *b.* in God. *Acts* 16:34
b. all things which are written. 24:14
all joy and peace in *b.* *Rom* 15:13
they that have *b.* masters. *1 Tim* 6:2
yet *b.* ye rejoice with. *1 Pet* 1:8

bell, -s

b. of gold. *Ex* 28:33; 39:25
a golden *b.* and pomegranate. 28:34
39, 26
upon *b.* of horses. *Zech* 14:20

bellow, *see* **bulls**

bellies

are alway liars, slow *b.* *Tit* 1:12

bellows

b. are burnt, lead. *Jer* 6:29

belly

[1] *The part of the body which contains the bowels,* Mat 15:17. [2] *The womb,* Jer 1:5.

b. shalt thou go, and. *Gen* 3:14
goeth upon the *b.* *Lev* 11:42
thigh to rot, thy *b.* *Num* 5:21†
and woman through the *b.* 25:8†
and thrust it in his *b.* *Judg* 3:21†
over against the *b.* *1 Ki* 7:20
give up ghost out of the *b. Job* 3:11†
fill his *b.* with the east wind. *Job* 15:2
vanity, and their *b.* prepareth. 35
shall cast out of his *b.* 20:15
not feel quietness in his *b.* 20*
about to fill his *b.* God shall. 23
behold my *b.* is as wine. 32:19†
whose *b.* thou fillest. *Ps* 17:14
my God from my mother's *b.* 22:10
soul bowed down, *b.* 44:25†
the *b.* of the wicked. *Pr* 13:25
innermost parts of the *b.* 18:8†
26:22†
a man's *b.* shall be satisfied. 18:20
inward parts of the *b.* 20:27†
stripes inward parts of *b.* 30†
his *b.* is as bright ivory. *S of S* 5:14*
b. is like an heap of wheat. 7:2†
borne by me from the *b.* *Isa* 46:3
I formed thee in the *b.* I. *Jer* 1:5
he hath filled his *b.* with. 51:34*
man, cause thy *b.* to eat. *Ezek* 3:3
this image's *b.* of brass. *Dan* 2:32
Jonah was in *b.* of the fish.
Jonah 1:17; *Mat* 12:40
out of the *b.* of hell cried. *Jonah* 2:2
I heard, my *b.* trembled. *Hab* 3:16†
entereth mouth goeth into the *b.*
Mat 15:17; *Mark* 7:19
fain have filled his *b.* *Luke* 15:16
out of his *b.* shall flow. *John* 7:38†
our Lord but their own *b. Rom* 16:18
meats for the *b.* and *b.* *1 Cor* 6:13
whose God is their *b.* *Phil* 3:19
shall make thy *b.* bitter. *Rev* 10:9
as soon as I had eaten it, my *b.* 10

belong

interpretations *b.* to God. *Gen* 40:8
return to whom it did *b.* *Lev* 27:24
secret things *b.* to God, revealed *b.*
Deut 29:29
shields of earth *b.* to God. *Ps* 47:9
to our God *b.* the issues. 68:20
these things *b.* to wise. *Pr* 24:23
to the Lord *b.* mercies. *Dan* 9:9
my name, because ye *b. Mark* 9:41
the things which *b.* to. *Luke* 19:42
careth for things that *b.* *1 Cor* 7:32

belonged, -est

to whom *b.* thou ? *1 Sam* 30:13
mighty men, which *b.* to. *1 Ki* 1:8
as he knew he *b.* to. *Luke* 23:7

belongeth

to me *b.* vengeance. *Deut* 32:35
Ps 94:1; *Heb* 10:30
b. to Benjamin *Judg* 19:14; 20:4
arise, for this matter *b.* *Ezra* 10:4
salvation *b.* unto the Lord. *Ps* 3:8
have I heard, power *b.* 62:11
also unto thee, *b.* mercy. 12
righteousness *b.* to thee. *Dan* 9:7
to us *b.* confusion of face. 8
strong meat *b.* to them. *Heb* 5:14

belonging

of sanctuary *b.* to them. *Num* 7:9
part of a field *b.* to Boaz. *Ruth* 2:3
meddleth with strife *b.* *Pr* 26:17
he went into a desert *b.* *Luke* 9:10

beloved

two wives, the one *b.* *Deut* 21:15
b. of the Lord shall dwell. 33:12
Solomon, *b.* of his God. *Neh* 13:26
that thy *b.* may. *Ps* 60:5; 108:6
for so he giveth his *b.* sleep. 127:2
and only *b.* in the sight of. *Pr* 4:3
drink abundantly, O *b.* *S of S* 5:1
is thy *b.* more than another *b.* ? 9
whither is thy *b.* gone ? 6:1
who cometh leaning on her *b.* ? 8:5
art greatly *b.* *Dan* 9:23; 10:11, 19
go yet, love a woman *b.* *Hos* 3:1
I will slay the *b.* 9:16
men with *b.* Barnabas. *Acts* 15:25
to all that are in Rome, *b. Rom* 1:7
I will call *b.* which was not *b.* 9:25
they are *b.* for Father's sake. 11:28
salute *b.* Persis who. 16:12
accepted in the *b.* *Eph* 1:6
a *b.* brother and. 6:21; *Col* 4:7
elect of God, holy and *b.* *Col* 3:12
Onesimus, a faithful and *b.* 4:9
Luke the *b.* physician and. 14
knowing *b.* your election. *1 Thes* 1:4
because they are *b.* *1 Tim* 6:2
a servant, a brother *b.* *Philem* 16
b. we are persuaded. *Heb* 6:9
b. be not ignorant of this. *2 Pet* 3:8
even as our *b.* brother Paul. 15
b. now are we sons of. *1 John* 3:2
b. condemn us not. 21
b. believe not every spirit, but. 4:1
b. let us love one another. 7
b. if God so loved us, we. 11
b. follow not evil, but. *3 John* 11
but ye *b.* building up. *Jude* 20
compassed the *b.* city. *Rev* 20:9

dearly **beloved,** *see* **dearly**

my **beloved**

my b. is a cluster of. *S of S* 1:14
behold thou art fair, *my b.* 16
as the apple-tree, so is *my b.* 2:3
it is the voice of *my b.* 2:8; 5:2
my b. is like a roe or a. 2:9
my b. is mine, I am his. 16; 6:3
turn *my b.* and be thou like. 2:17
let *my b.* come into his garden. 4:16
I rose up to open to *my b.* 5:5
I opened to *my b.* 6
my b. is white and ruddy. 10
this is *my b.* 16
my b. is gone. 6:2
I am *my b.* and *my b.* mine. 3; 7:10
I have laid up for thee, *my b.* 7:13
a song of *my b.* touching. *Isa* 5:1
what hath *my b.* to do? *Jer* 11:15
my b. Son. *Mat* 3:17; 17:5
Mark 1:11; 9:7; *Luke* 3:22
9:35*; *2 Pet* 1:17
behold *my b.* in whom my. *Mat* 12:18
I will send *my b.* son. *Luke* 20:13
greet Amplias *my b.* *Rom* 16:8
as *my b.* sons I warn. *1 Cor* 4:14
Timothy *my b.* son. 17; *2 Tim* 1:2
do not err, *my b.* brethren. *Jas* 1:16

Belshazzar

O *B.* hast not humbled. *Dan* 5:22
in the first year of *B.* 7:1
in third year of *B.* 8:1

Belteshazzar

to Daniel the name of *B.* *Dan* 1:7
name was *B.* 2:26; 4:8, 9, 19
5:12; 10:1

bemoan, -ed, -ing

they *b.* Job, comforted. *Job* 42:11
who shall *b.* thee ? *Jer* 15:5
neither go to lament, nor *b.* 16:5
weep not for the dead, nor *b.* 22:10
I have heard Ephraim *b.* 31:18
all ye that are about him *b.* 48:17
is laid waste, who will *b.* ? *Nah* 3:7

Benaiah

did *B.* *2 Sam* 23:22; *1 Chr* 11:24
call me Zadok and *B.* *1 Ki* 1:32
the king put *B.* in Joab's room. 2:35
B. the son of Jehoiada was. 4:4
Jesimiel and *B.* sons. *1 Chr* 4:36
B. the Pirathonite, a mighty. 11:31
second degree *B.* 15:18,20; 16:5, 6
captain for third month, *B.* 27:5
for the eleventh month, *B.* 14
Mahath and *B.* were. *2 Chr* 31:13
B. son of Parosh. *Ezra* 10:25
B. son of Pahath-moab. 30
B. the son of Bani. 35
B. son of Nebo. 43
I saw Pelatiah son of *B. Ezek* 11:1
when I prophesied, the son of *B.* 13

Ben-ammi

called his name *B.* *Gen* 19:38

benches

thy *b.* of ivory. *Ezek* 27:6

bend

the wicked *b.* their bow. *Ps* 11:2
who *b.* their bows to shoot. 64:3*
b. their tongue like a bow. *Jer* 9:3
Lydians, handle and *b.* bow. 46:9
all ye that *b.* the bow. 50:14, 29
against him, let the archer *b.* 51:3
this vine did *b.* roots. *Ezek* 17:7

bendeth, -ing

when he *b.* his bow. *Ps* 58:7*
that afflicted thee shall *b. Isa* 60:14
against him that *b.* let. *Jer* 51:3*

beneath
in the earth *b.* *Ex* 20:4; *Deut* 5:8
he brake the tables *b.* mount. *Ex* 32:19
on the earth *b.* there. *Deut* 4:39
be above only, and not be *b.* 28:13
the deep that coucheth *b.* 33:13
roots shall be dried up *b.* *Job* 18:16
that ye depart from hell *b.* *Pr* 15:24
hell from *b.* is moved. *Isa* 14:9
your eyes, look on the earth *b.* 51:6
foundations can be searched *b.* *Jer* 31:37
ye are from *b.* I am. *John* 8:23

benefactors
that exercise authority are called *b.* *Luke* 22:25

benefit
good wherewith I *b.* them. *Jer* 18:10

benefit, -s
[1] *The gifts and favours of God to men,* 2 Chr 32:25; Ps 68:19; 103:2
not according to *b.* *2 Chr* 32:25
Lord loadeth us with *b.* *Ps* 68:19*
the Lord, forget not all his *b.* 103:2
shall I render for his *b.*? 116:12
might have second *b.* *2 Cor* 1:15
partakers of the *b.* *1 Tim* 6:2
b. should not be of. *Philem* 14*

benevolence
husband render due *b.* *1 Cor* 7:3*

Ben-hadad
to *B.* *1 Ki* 15:18; *2 Chr* 16:2
thus saith *B.* thy silver. *1 Ki* 20:2
B. was drinking himself drunk. 16
B. escaped on an horse, with. 20
thy servant *B.* saith, I pray thee. 32
B. went up and besieged. *2 Ki* 6:24
B. was sick. 8:7
thy son *B.* hath sent me. 9
Israel into the hand of *B.* 13:3
took again out of the hand of *B.* 25
palaces of *B.* *Jer* 49:27; *Amos* 1:4

Benjamin
his father called him *B.* *Gen* 35:18
Rachel, Joseph and *B.* 24; 46:19
not, and ye will take *B.* 42:36
away your brother and *B.* 43:14
and when Joseph saw *B.* 16, 29
B. mess was five times so. 34
cup was found in *B.* sack. 44:12
he fell on his brother *B.* neck. 45:14
sons of *B.* 46:21; *Num* 26:38, 41
1 Chr 7:6; 8:1, 40; 9:7; *Neh* 11:7
B. shall ravin as a wolf. *Gen* 49:27
prince of *B.* was Abidan. *Num* 1:11
stand to bless, Joseph, *B.* *Deut* 27:12
of *B.* Moses said, the. 33:12
after thee, *B.* among thy. *Judg* 5:14
Gibeah, which belongs to *B.* 19:14
out to battle against *B.* 20:20
the Lord smote *B.* before Israel. 35
all day of *B.* were 25,000 men. 46
give his daughter to *B.* 21:1, 18
women are destroyed out of *B.* 16
there ran a man of *B.* *1 Sam* 4:12
there was a man of *B.* whose. 9:1
sepulchre, in the border of *B.* 10:2
in Gibeah of *B.* 13:2; 14:16; 15:16
by number twelve of *B.* *2 Sam* 2:15
also spake in the ears of *B.* 3:19
were a thousand men of B. 19:17
Saul buried they in *B.* 21:14
son of Elah officer in *B.* *1 Ki* 4:18
Bilhan, Jeush and *B.* *1 Chr* 7:10
Levi and *B.* counted he not. 21:6
over *B.* was Jaasiel the son. 27:21
of *B.* Eliada a mighty. *2 Chr* 17:17
all in Jerusalem and *B.* 34:32
after him repaired *B.* and. *Neh* 3:23
there is little *B.* with. *Ps* 68:27
before *B.* and Manasseh, stir. 80:2
was in the gate of *B.* *Jer* 37:13
sitting in the gate of *B.* 38:7
B. shall have a portion. *Ezek* 48:23
one gate of *B.* 32
Beth-aven, after thee, O *B.* *Hos* 5:8
possess Ephraim, *B.* shall. *Ob* 19
inhabited from *B.* gate. *Zech* 14:10
see **children**

Benjamin with *Judah*
to fight *Judah* and *B.* *Judg* 10:9
speak to house of *Judah* and *B.* *1 Ki* 12:23; *2 Chr* 11:3
came of *B.* and *Judah.* *1 Chr* 12:16
having *Judah* and *B.* *2 Chr* 11:12
Asa, and all *Judah* and *B.* 15:2
idols out of *Judah* and *B.* 8
captains through *Judah* and *B.* 25:5
altars out of *Judah* and *B.* 31:1
was gathered of *Judah* and *B.* 34:9
fathers of *Judah* and *B.* *Ezra* 1:5
the adversaries of *Judah* and *B.* 4:1
children of *Judah* and *B.* *Neh* 11:4
after them went *Judah, B.* 12:34
border of *Judah* and *B.* *Ezek* 48:22

land of **Benjamin**
go into the *land of B.* *Judg* 21:21
man out of the land *of B.* *1 Sam* 9:16
idols out of *land of* B. *2 Chr* 15:8
from *land of B.* bringing. *Jer* 17:26
witnesses in the *land of B.* 32:44
in the *land of B.* shall flocks. 33:13
went to go into the *land of B.* 37:12

tribe of **Benjamin**
tribe of B. numbered. *Num* 1:37
captain of the *tribe of B.* 2:22; 10:24
of the *tribe of B.* to spy the. 13:9
of the *tribe of B.* to divide. 34:21
the lot of the *tribe of B.* *Josh* 18:11
the cities of the *tribe of B.* 21
of the tribe of Judah and the *tribe of B.* 21:4, 17; *1 Chr* 6:60, 65
men through all the *tribe of B.* *Judg* 20:12
families of the *tribe of B.* *1 Sam* 9:21
come near, the *tribe of B.* 10:20
man of the *tribe of B.* *Acts* 13:21
the *tribe of B.* *Rom* 11:1; *Phil* 3:5
of the *tribe of B.* were. *Rev* 7:8

Benjamite
Ehud a *B.* *Judg* 3:15
Kish a *B.* *1 Sam* 9:1
and said, am not I a *B.*? 21
Shimei a *B.* *2 Sam* 16:11; 19:16; *1 Ki* 2:8
Sheba a *B.* *2 Sam* 20:1
Mordecai a *B.* *Esth* 2:5

Benjamites
men of the place were *B.* *Judg* 19:16
destroyed of the *B.* 25,100. 20:35
thus they inclosed the *B.* round. 43
Saul, hear now, ye *B.* *1 Sam* 22:7
was Abiezer of *B.* *1 Chr* 27:12

Benoni
she called his name *B.* *Gen* 35:18

bent
b. his bow. *Ps* 7:12; *Lam* 2:4; 3:12
have *b.* their bow to cast. *Ps* 37:14
sharp, and their bows *b.* *Isa* 5:28
fled from the swords and *b.* 21:15
people *b.* to backsliding. *Hos* 11:7
when I have *b.* Judah. *Zech* 9:13

Beor
son of *B.* reigned. *Gen* 36:32; *1 Chr* 1:43
Balaam the son of *B.* *Num* 22:5
24:3, 15; 31:8; *Deut* 23:4
Josh 13:22; 24:9; *Mi* 6:5

Berachah
B. came to David. *1 Chr* 12:3
called the valley of *B.* *2 Chr* 20:26

Berea
and Silas by night to *B.* *Acts* 17:10
heard that Paul preached at *B.* 13
Sopater of *B.* accompanied. 20:4

bereave
I labour and *b.* my soul. *Eccl* 4:8*
I will *b.* them. *Jer* 15:7; 18:21
evil beasts shall *b.* thee. *Ezek* 5:17
no more *b.* them of men. 36:12, 14
bring up children, will I *b.* *Hos* 9:12

bereaved
have *b.* of my children. *Gen* 42:36
b. of my children, I am *b.* 43:14
land hast *b.* thy nations. *Ezek* 36:13
meet them as a bear *b.* *Hos* 13:8

bereaveth
abroad the sword *b.* *Lam* 1:20

Berith
the house of their God *B.* *Judg* 9:46

Bernice
B. came unto. *Acts* 25:13, 23
the governor and *B.* 26:30

berries
two or three *b.* in bough. *Isa* 17:6
fig-tree bear olive *b.*? *Jas* 3:12*

beryl
his body was like the *b.* *Dan* 10:6
eighth foundation was *b.* *Rev* 21:20

beseech
(*Beg, pray, intreat*)
I *b.* thee shew me thy. *Ex* 33:18
heal, O Lord, I *b.* thee. *Num* 12:13
return, we *b.* thee. *Ps* 80:14
Lord, I *b.* thee deliver me. 116:4
save I *b.* O Lord, I *b.* thee. 118:25
accept, I *b.* thee, offerings. 119:108
obey, I *b.* thee, voice of. *Jer* 38:20
O Lord God, forgive I *b.* *Amos* 7:2
we *b.* thee, O Lord, we *b.* *Jonah* 1:14
O Lord, take, I *b.* thee my. 4:3
b. God, that he will be. *Mal* 1:9
I *b.* thee, torment me. *Luke* 8:28
saying, master, I *b.* thee look. 9:38
wherefore I *b.* thee to hear. *Acts* 26:3
I *b.* you by the mercies. *Rom* 12:1
I *b.* you, be followers. *1 Cor* 4:16
I *b.* you, confirm your. *2 Cor* 2:8
as though God did *b.* you by. 5:20
we *b.* you receive not. 6:1
I Paul *b.* you by the meekness. 10:1
I *b.* you, be as I am. *Gal* 4:12
prisoner of the Lord *b.* *Eph* 4:1
yet for love's sake I *b.* *Philem* 9
I *b.* thee for my son Onesimus. 10
but I *b.* you the rather. *Heb* 13:19
I *b.* you as strangers. *1 Pet* 2:11
now I *b.* thee, lady, not. *2 John* 5
see **brethren**

beseeching
came a centurion *b.* him. *Mat* 8:5; *Luke* 7:3
there came a leper *b.* *Mark* 1:40

beset
sons of Belial *b.* *Judg* 19:22; 20:5
bulls of Bashan have *b.* *Ps* 22:12
thou hast *b.* me behind and. 139:5
their own doings have *b.* *Hos* 7:2
sin which doth so easily *b.* *Heb* 12:1

beside, besides
hast thou here any *b.* *Gen* 19:12
a famine *b.* the first famine. 26:1
b. the other in her life. *Lev* 18:18
b. the sabbaths, *b.* gifts, *b.* vows *b.* your offerings, which ye give. 23:38
man has lain with thee *b.* *Num* 5:20
law of Nazarite, *b.* that his. 6:21
there is nothing *b.* manna. 11:6
offer *b.* burnt-offering. 28:23; 29:6
b. the covenant he made. *Deut* 29:1
in building an altar, *b.* *Josh* 22:19, 29
if it be dry on earth *b.* *Judg* 6:37
b. her Jephthah had no. 11:34
I will go out and stand *b.* *1 Sam* 19:3
b. that which Solomon. *1 Ki* 10:13
not a prophet *b.* 22:7; *2 Chr* 18:6
b. his sin, wherewith he. *2 Ki* 21:16
he leadeth me *b.* still. *Ps* 23:2
feed thy kids *b.* the tents. *S of S* 1:8
blessed ye that sow *b.* all. *Isa* 32:20
I will gather others to him *b.* 56:8
b. this, between us and. *Luke* 16:26
b. all this, to-day is the third. 24:21
to me thine ownself *b.* *Philem* 19

beside
friends said, he is *b.* *Mark* 3:21
Paul, thou art *b.* thyself. *Acts* 26:24
we be *b.* ourselves. *2 Cor* 5:13

besiege
he shall *b.* thee in gates. *Deut* 28:52
if enemies *b.* *1 Ki* 8:37; *2 Chr* 6:28
go, O Elam, *b.* O Media. *Isa* 21:2

besieged
dried up all rivers of *b.* places. *2 Ki* 19:24*; *Isa* 37:25*
great king and *b.* it. *Eccl* 9:14
daughter of Zion is as a *b.* *Isa* 1:8
he that is *b.* shall die by. *Ezek* 6:12

besom
(*A broom*)
it with *b.* of destruction. *Isa* 14:23

Besor
men came to the brook *B.* *1 Sam* 30:9

besought
(*Begged, prayed, intreated*)
when he *b.* we would not. *Gen* 42:21
b. the Lord. *Ex* 32:11; *Deut* 3:23
David *b.* God for. *2 Sam* 12:16
and the man of God *b.* *1 Ki* 13:6
fell on his knees and *b.* *2 Ki* 1:13
Jehoahaz *b.* the Lord. 13:4
Manasseh *b.* the Lord. *2 Chr* 33:12
we fasted and *b.* our God. *Ezra* 8:23
b. him with tears to put. *Esth* 8:3
not Hezekiah fear, and *b. Jer* 26:19
so the devils *b.* him. *Mat* 8:31
Mark 5:10, 12; *Luke* 8:31, 32
b. him to depart. *Mat* 8:34
Luke 8:37
Jairus *b.* him greatly. *Mark* 5:23
Luke 8:41
Samaritans *b.* that he. *John* 4:40
nobleman of Capernaum *b.* 47
b. Pilate that he might take. 19:38
Gentiles *b.* that these. *Acts* 13:42
Lydia *b.* us, saying, if ye. 16:15
magistrates *b.* them, and. 39
b. him not to go to Jerusalem. 21:12
for this thing I *b.* Lord. *2 Cor* 12:8

best
take of the *b.* fruits in. *Gen* 43:11
in *b.* of land make father. 47:6, 11
of *b.* of his own field. *Ex* 22:5
heave-offering of the *b. Num* 18:29
marry to whom they think *b.* 36:6
dwell where it likes him *b.* *Deut* 23:16
he will take the *b.* of. *1 Sam* 8:14
Saul spared the *b.* of sheep. 15:9, 15
seemeth you *b.* I will. *2 Sam* 18:4
look out the *b.* of your. *2 Ki* 10:3
every man at *b.* state is. *Ps* 39:5
of thy mouth like *b.* wine. *S of S* 7:9
b. of them is as a brier. *Mi* 7:4
bring forth the *b.* robe. *Luke* 15:22
covet earnestly the *b.* *1 Cor* 12:31

bestead
pass through it hardly *b.* *Isa* 8:21†

bestir
hearest the sound *b.* *2 Sam* 5:24

bestow
that he may *b.* a blessing. *Ex* 32:29
b. money for what. *Deut* 14:26
they did *b.* on Baalim. *2 Chr* 24:7
thou shalt have occasion to *b.* out of the king's treasure-. *Ezra* 7:20
no room where to *b.* my. *Luke* 12:17
and there will I *b.* all my fruits. 18
on these we *b.* more. *1 Cor* 12:23
though I *b.* all my goods to. 13:3

bestowed
Gehazi *b.* them in house. *2 Ki* 5:24
Lord *b.* on Solomon. *1 Chr* 29:25
all the Lord hath *b.* on us. *Isa* 63:7
reap that whereon ye *b.* *John* 4:38
greet Mary, who *b.* much. *Rom* 16:6
his grace *b.* on me not. *1 Cor* 15:10
for the gift *b.* on us. *2 Cor* 1:11
do you to wit of the grace *b.* 8:1
lest I have *b.* on you. *Gal* 4:11
love Father *b.* on us. *1 John* 3:1

Bethabara
these things done in *B.* *John* 1:28

Bethany
Jesus went into *B. Mat* 21:17; 26:6
Mark 11:1, 11; 14:3; *Luke* 19:29
John 12:1
when come from *B.* *Mark* 11:12
out as far as to *B.* *Luke* 24:50
sick, named Lazarus of *B. John* 11:1

Beth-aven
Ai, which is beside *B.* *Josh* 7:2
battle passed over to *B. 1 Sam* 14:23
Gilgal, nor go ye up to *B.* *Hos* 4:15
cry aloud at *B.* after thee. 5:8
because of the calves of *B.* 10:5

Beth-diblathaim
judgement is come upon *B. Jer* 48:22

Beth-el
the place *B.* *Gen* 28:19; 35:15
I am God of *B.* where thou. 31:13
go up to *B.* 35:1, 3
so Jacob came to *B.* 6
Joseph goeth from *B.* *Josh* 16:2
Joseph went up against *B. Judg* 1:22
between Ramah and *B.* 4:5
is on the north side of *B.* 21:19
from year to year to *B. 1 Sam* 7:16
men going up to God to *B.* 10:3
were with Saul in mount *B.* 13:2
them which were in *B.* 30:27
the one calf in *B.* *1 Ki* 12:29, 33
a man of God to *B.* 13:1
against the altar in *B.* 4, 32
dwelt an old prophet in *B.* 13:11
Lord hath sent me to *B.* *2 Ki* 2:2
went up from thence unto *B.* 23
not from the calves in *B.* 10:29
priests came and dwelt in *B.* 17:28
and carried the ashes to *B.* 23:4
the altar at *B.* Josiah brake. 15
against the altar of *B.* 17
all that he had done in *B.* 19
men of *B.* *Ezra* 2:28; *Neh* 7:32
Israel was ashamed of *B. Jer* 48:13
so shall *B.* do to you. *Hos* 10:15
he found him in *B.* there he. 12:4
visit the altars of *B.* *Amos* 3:14
come to *B.* and transgress. 4:4
seek not *B.* for *B.* shall come. 5:5
be none to quench it in *B.* 6
not again any more at *B.* 7:13

Beth-elite
Hiel the *B.* did build. *1 Ki* 16:34

Bether
on the mountains of *B.* *S of S* 2:17

Bethesda
pool called in Hebrew *B.* *John* 5:2

Beth-ezel
in the mourning of *B.* *Mi* 1:11

Beth-gamul
judgement is come upon *B. Jer* 48:23

Beth-haccerem
set up a sign of fire in *B.* *Jer* 6:1

Beth-horon
going down to *B.* the. *Josh* 10:11
gave Levites *B.* 21:22; *1 Chr* 6:68
company turned to *B.* *1 Sam* 13:18
Solomon built *B.* *1 Ki* 9:17
2 Chr 8:5
daughter Sherah built *B. 1 Chr* 7:24

bethink
if they shall *b.* in the land whither were. *1 Ki* 8:47; *2 Chr* 6:37

Bethlehem
Rachel died in way to *B.* *Gen* 35:19; 48:7
Idalah and *B.* cities of. *Josh* 19:15
after him Ibzan of *B.* *Judg* 12:8
went till they came to *B. Ruth* 1:19
Boaz came from *B.* 2:4
be famous in *B.* 4:11
Samuel came to *B.* *1 Sam* 16:4
asked leave to run to *B.* 20:6, 28
would give me water of the well of *B.* *2 Sam* 23:15; *1 Chr* 11:17
Salma father of *B.* *1 Chr* 2:51, 54
first-born of Ephratah, of *B.* 4:4
Rehoboam built *B.* *2 Chr* 11:6
children of *B. Ezra* 2:21; *Neh* 7:26
dwelt in habitation by *B.* *Jer* 41:17
Jesus was born in *B.* *Mat* 2:1, 5
B. in land of Judah, art not. 6
slew children in *B.* 16
went up from Galilee to *B. Luke* 2:4
let us now go to *B.* and see. 15
Christ cometh out of *B.* *John* 7:42

Beth-lehem-ephratah
thou *B.-Ephratah*, though. *Mi* 5:2

Beth-lehemite
Jesse the *B. 1 Sam* 16:1, 18; 17:58
Elhanan the *B.* slew. *2 Sam* 21:19

Beth-lehem-judah
a Levite of *B.* went. *Judg* 17:7, 8, 9
Levite took concubine out of *B.* 19:1
passing from *B.* I went to *B.* 18
Elimelech of *B.* went. *Ruth* 1:1
son of Ephrathite of *B. 1 Sam* 17:12

Beth-peor
in valley over-against *B.* *Deut* 3:29
Moses spake over-against *B.* 4:46
buried Moses over-against *B.* 34:6

Bethphage
come to *B.* *Mat* 21:1; *Mark* 11:1
Luke 19:29

Bethsaida
woe unto *B.* *Mat* 11:21; *Luke* 10:13
disciples to go to *B.* *Mark* 6:45
cometh to *B.* they bring blind. 8:22
he went into a desert place belonging to *B.* *Luke* 9:10
Philip was of *B.* *John* 1:44; 12:21

Beth-shan
fastened body to wall of *B.* *1 Sam* 31:10

Beth-shemesh
border of Judah went to *B.* *Josh* 15:10
Issachar's coast reacheth *B.* 19:22
Beth-anath and *B.* cities of. 38
Judah gave to Levites *B.* 21:16
inhabitants of *B.* *Judg* 1:33
goeth up by way of *B.* *1 Sam* 6:9
kine took straight way to *B.* 12
he smote the men of *B.* 19
son of Dekar was in *B.* *1 Ki* 4:9
looked one another in the face at *B.* *2 Ki* 14:11; *2 Chr* 25:21
Philistines had taken *B. 2 Chr* 28:18
break the images of *B.* *Jer* 43:13

Bethuel
Milcah bare to Nahor, *B. Gen* 22:22
B. begat Rebekah. 23; 24:15; 25:20
I am the daughter of *B.* 24:24, 47
go to the house of *B.* 28:2

betimes
[1] *Early*, Gen 26:31. [2] *Seasonably, in due and proper time*, Pr 13:24. [3] *Diligently*, Job 8:5.
rose up *b.* and. *Gen* 26:31
God sent by messengers rising *b.* *2 Chr* 36:15
thou wouldest seek God *b. Job* 8:5
as wild asses go they, rising *b.* 24:5
loveth, chasteneth him *b.* *Pr* 13:24

betray
if ye be come to *b.* me. *1 Chr* 12:17
and shall *b.* one another. *Mat* 24:10
he sought opportunity to *b.* him.
26:16; *Mark* 14:11; *Luke* 22:6
one of you shall *b.* me. *Mat* 26:21
Mark 14:18; *John* 13:21
he is at hand and doth *b. Mat* 26:46
brother shall *b.* brother. *Mark* 13:12
Jesus knew who should *b.* him.
John 6:64; 13:11
put into heart of Judas to *b.* 13:2

betrayed
Judas who *b.* him. *Mat* 10:4
Mark 3:19
Son of man *b.* into hands of men.
Mat 17:22; 20:18; 26:2, 45
Mark 14:41
woe to man by whom Son of man is *b.* *Mat* 26:24; *Mark* 14:21
Luke 22:22
he that *b.* *Mat* 26:48; *Mark* 14:44
I have sinned, in that I *b. Mat* 27:4
and ye shall be *b.* *Luke* 21:16
Judas which *b.* him. *John* 18:2
night he was *b.* he took. *1 Cor* 11:23

betrayers
of whom ye have been *b. Acts* 7:52

betrayest, -eth
let us go, lo, he that *b.* *Mark* 14:42
the hand of him that *b.* *Luke* 22:21
b. thou the Son of man with ? 48
which is he that *b.* ? *John* 21:20

betroth
(*In Bible times a betrothal was considered as binding as a marriage, and there were formal ceremonies to celebrate it*)
shall *b.* a wife, another. *Deut* 28:30
I will *b.* thee to me for. *Hos* 2:19
b. thee to me in faithfulness. 20

betrothed

please not master who b. Ex 21:8*
man entice a maid not b. 22:16
Deut 22:28
lieth with a woman b. Lev 19:20
who hath b. a wife, and. Deut 20:7
if a man find a virgin b. and. 22:23
b. damsel cried there was none. 27

better

[1] More valuable, or preferable, Eccl. 9:4, 16, 18. [2] More acceptable, 1 Sam 15:22. [3] More able, Dan 1:20. [4] More advantageous, Phil 1:23. [5] More holy, 1 Cor 8:8. [6] More safe, Ps 118:8. [7] More comfortable, Pr 15:16, 17. [8] More precious, Pr 8:11.

b. I give her to thee. Gen 29:19
b. for us to have served. Ex 14:12
were it not b. for us to ? Num 14:3
gleanings of Ephraim b. Judg 8:2
nor art thou any thing b. 11:25
am not I b. to thee ? 1 Sam 1:8
nothing b. than to go to. 27:1
name of king Solomon b. 1 Ki 1:47
fell upon two men b. than he. 2:32
Elijah said, I am not b. than. 19:4
I will give thee for it a b. 21:2
rivers of Damascus b. 2 Ki 5:12
hast slain brethren b. 2 Chr 21:13
shall please the Lord b. Ps 69:31
nothing b. for a man than. Eccl 2:24
nothing b. than to rejoice in. 3:22
b. is he than both they, which. 4:3
two are b. than one. 9
what is man the b. ? 6:11
that the former days were b. 7:10
bite, and a babbler is no b. 10:11*
give a name b. than of. Isa 56:5
they that be slain are b. Lam 4:9
will settle you, and do b. Ezek 36:11
in all matters he found b. Dan 1:20
then was it b. than now. Hos 2:7
be they b. than these ? Amos 6:2
art thou b. than populous ? Nah 3:8
the fowls of the air, are you not much b. ? Mat 6:26; Luke 12:24
how much is a man b. ? Mat 12:12
were b. that a millstone were about. Mat 18:6; Mark 9:42; Luke 17:2
are we b. than they ? no. Rom 3:9
giveth her not, doth b. 1 Cor 7:38
for neither if we eat are we b. 8:8
b. for me to die, than to. 9:15
you come together not for b. 11:17
let each esteem other b. Phil 2:3
being made so much b. Heb 1:4
beloved, we are persuaded b. 6:9
contradiction less is blessed of b. 7:7
bringing in of a b. hope did. 19
Jesus was made a surety of a b. 22
he is the Mediator of a b. covenant, established on b. promises. 8:6
heavenly things with b. 9:23
in heaven a b. and enduring. 10:34
they desire a b. country, an. 11:16
they might obtain a b. 35
God having provided b. thing. 40
speaketh b. things than Abel. 12:24
b. for them not to have. 2 Pet 2:21

better *is*

b. is little with fear of. Pr 15:16
b. is a dinner of herbs where. 17
b. is a little with righteousness. 16:8
how much b. is it to get wisdom. 16
b. is a dry morsel and. 17:1
b. is the poor. 19:1; 28:6
b. is a neighbour that is near. 27:10
b. is an handful with. Eccl 4:6
b. is a poor wise child than. 13
b. is the sight of the eyes than. 6:9
b. is the end of a thing than. 7:8
b. is thy love than wine. S of S 4:10

is **better**, or *is it* **better**

whether is b. for you. Judg 9:2
is it b. to be a priest to one ? 18:19
thy daughter is b. to. Ruth 4:15
obey is b. than sacrifice. 1 Sam 15:22
given to a neighbour that is b. 28
counsel of Hushai is b. 2 Sam 17:14
estate to another that is b. Esth 1:19
righteous man hath is b. Ps 37:16
loving-kindness is b. than. Ps 63:3
a day in thy courts is b. than. 84:10
the law of thy mouth is b. 119:72
merchandise of wisdom is b. Pr 3:14
wisdom is b. than rubies. 8:11
my fruit is b. than gold. 19
is b. than he that honoureth. 12:9
slow to anger is b. than. 16:32
and a poor man is b. than a. 19:22
open rebuke is b. than secret. 27:5
untimely birth is b. than. Eccl 6:3
a good name is b. than precious. 7:1
sorrow is b. than laughter, by sadness of countenance heart is b. 3
patient in spirit is b. than proud. 8
living dog is b. than a dead lion. 9:4
wisdom is b. than strength. 16
wisdom is b. than weapons. 18
thy love is b. than wine. S of S 1:2
he saith, the old is b. Luke 5:39
to be with Christ, is far b. Phil 1:23

it is **better**, or **better** *it is*

it is b. I give her to thee. Gen 29:19
it is b. thou succour us. 2 Sam 18:3
it is b. to trust in the Lord than. Ps 118:8, 9
b. it is to be of humble. Pr 16:19
it is b. to dwell in a. 21:9; 25:24
it is b. to dwell in wilderness. 21:19
b. it is that it be said to thee. 25:7
b. it is that thou shouldest. Eccl 5:5
it is b. to go to house of. 7:2
it is b. to hear rebuke of wise. 5
it is b. for me to die. Jonah 4:3, 8
it is b. to enter into life halt or. Mat 18:8, 9; Mark 9:43, 45, 47
for it is b. to marry than. 1 Cor 7:9
it is b. that ye suffer for. 1 Pet 3:17

bettered

was nothing b. but. Mark 5:26

between

I will put enmity b. thy. Gen 3:15
the covenant b. God and. 9:16
a burning lamp passeth b. 15:17
nor a lawgiver from b. his. 49:10
a division b. my people. Ex 8:23
and a memorial b. thine eyes. 13:9, 16; Deut 6:8; 11:18
they come, and I judge b. Ex 18:16
vail shall divide b. holy. 26:33
while flesh was b. Num 11:33
b. blood and blood, b. plea, b. Deut 17:8
he shall dwell b. his shoulders. 33:12
Deborah dwelt b. Ramah. Judg 4:5
there was peace b. 1 Sam 7:14
b. good and evil. 2 Sam 19:35
1 Ki 3:9
how long halt ye b. two ? 1 Ki 18:21
the lot parteth b. Pr 18:18
passed b. parts of. Jer 34:18, 19
b. cattle and cattle, b. rams. Ezek 34:17
her adulteries from b. Hos 2:2
the priests weep b. Joel 2:17
break brotherhood b. Zech 11:14
slew b. the temple and. Mat 23:35
b. John's disciples and. John 3:25
no difference b. Jew and. Rom 10:12
difference b. wife and a. 1 Cor 7:34
one Mediator b. God. 1 Tim 2:5

betwixt

the cloud that cometh b. Job 36:32*
lie all night b. my. S of S 1:13
I am in a strait b. two. Phil 1:23

Beulah

call thy land B. for Lord. Isa 62:4

bewail

b. the burning the Lord. Lev 10:6
and b. her father and. Deut 21:13
I may go and b. Judg 11:37, 38
I will b. with weeping of. Isa 16:9
that I shall b. many. 2 Cor 12:21
shall b. her. Rev 18:9

bewailed, -eth

daughter of Zion that b. Jer 4:31*
and all wept and b. her. Luke 8:52
of women also who b. 23:27

beware

(To take care; to be on one's guard)
b. that thou bring not my. Gen 24:6
b. of him and obey. Ex 23:21
b. lest thou forget. Deut 6:12; 8:11
b. there be not a wicked. 15:9
b. I pray thee. Judg 13:4, 13
b. that none touch. 2 Sam 18:12
b. that thou pass not. 2 Ki 6:9
b. lest he take thee away. Job 36:18
scorner, and simple b. Pr 19:25*
b. lest Hezekiah persuade. Isa 36:18
b. of false prophets. Mat 7:15
b. of men. 10:17
b. of the leaven of the. 16:6, 11
Mark 8:15; Luke 12:1
b. of the scribes. Mark 12:38
Luke 20:46
take heed and b. Luke 12:15*
b. lest that come which. Acts 13:40
b. of dogs, b. of evil workers, b. of. Phil 3:2
b. lest any man spoil. Col 2:8
b. lest ye also. 2 Pet 3:17

bewitched

Simon b. the people. Acts 8:9*, 11
Galatians, who hath b. ? Gal 3:1

bewray

(American Revision, betray)
hide the outcasts, b. not. Isa 16:3

bewrayeth

of his right hand b. Pr 27:16*
heareth cursing, and b. it. 29:24*
of them, speech b. thee. Mat 26:73*

beyond

Balaam said, I cannot go b. word. Num 22:18; 24:13
nor is it b. the sea. Deut 30:13
arrows b. thee. 1 Sam 20:22; 36:37
b. the river. 2 Sam 10:16; 1 Ki 14:15
1 Chr 19:16; Ezra 4:17, 20
6:6, 8; 7:21, 25; Neh 2:7, 9
Isa 7:20; 18:1; Zeph 3:10
b. the sea. 2 Chr 20:2; Jer 25:22
amazed b. measure. Mark 6:51
7:37
and b. their power. 2 Cor 8:3
for we stretch not b. 10:14
b. measure I persecuted. Gal 1:13
that no man go b. and. 1 Thes 4:6

beyond *Jordan, see* **Jordan**

Bezaleel

I have called by name B. of tribe of. Ex 31:2; 35:30; 1 Chr 2:20
then wrought B. Ex 36:1
B. made the ark. 37:1
B. made all Lord commanded. 38:22
the brazen altar B. had. 2 Chr 1:5
sons of Pahath-moab, B. Ezra 10:30

Bezek

slew in B. 10,000 men. Judg 1:4, 5
numbered Israel in B. 1 Sam 11:8

Bichri

Sheba the son of B. 2 Sam 20:1
man followed Sheba son of B. 2
now shall the son of B. do. 6
cut off head of Sheba son of B. 22

bid

[1] To invite, Mat 22:9; Luke 14:12. [2] To command, Mat 14:28 [3] To wish, 2 John 10.

the day I b. you shout. Josh 6:10
b. the servant pass on. 1 Sam 9:27
how long ere b. people. 2 Sam 2:26
not riding except I b. 2 Ki 4:24
if the prophet had b. thee do. 5:13
all that thou shalt b. us. 10:5
the preaching that I b. Jonah 3:2
for the Lord hath b. Zeph 1:7
b. me come to thee. Mat 14:28
as many as ye shall find b. 22:9
what they b. you observe. 23:3
let me first b. them. Luke 9:61
b. her therefore that she. 10:40
lest they also b. thee again. 14:12
if any that believe not b. 1 Cor 10:27
receive him not, nor b. 2 John 10*

bidden

they eat that be b. 1 Sam 9:13
curse, for Lord hath b. 2 Sam 16:11
Joseph did as angel had b. Mat 1:24
sent to call them that were b. 22:3
tell them b. I have prepared my. 4
they who were b. were not. 8

the Pharisee who had *b.* *Luke* 7:39
a parable to those who were *b.* 14:7
when thou art *b.* lest a more honourable man be *b.* 8
when thou art *b.* go and sit in. 10
none of those *b.* shall taste. 24

biddeth, bidding

goeth at thy *b.* *1 Sam* 22:14
he that *b.* him God. *2 John* 11*

bide

if they *b.* not in unbelief. *Rom* 11:23

Bidkar

Jehu said to *B.* his. *2 Ki* 9:25

bier

David followed the *b.* *2 Sam* 3:31
came and touched the *b.* *Luke* 7:14

Bigthan

B. sought to lay hand on. *Esth* 2:21
that Mordecai had told *B.* 6:2

Bildad

B. the Shuhite. *Job* 2:11; 8:1
18:1; 25:1; 42:9

Bilhah

Laban gave to Rachel *B.* *Gen* 29:29
behold my maid *B.* go in. 30:3, 4
B. conceived. 5, 7
Reuben lay with *B.* 35:22
sons of *B.* 35:25; 37:2; 46:25
1 Chr 7:13
his sons dwelt at *B.* *1 Chr* 4:29

bill

take thy *b.* and write 50. *Luke* 16:6*
take thy *b.* 7*
see **divorce**

billows

thy *b.* gone over me. *Ps* 42:7
Jonah 2:3

bind

[1] *To tie up, or fasten together,* Gen 37:7; Deut 14:25. [2] *To keep fast, or sure,* Pr 3:3; 6:21. [3] *To engage by vow, or promise,* Num 30:2. [4] *To restrain,* Job 28:11.

they shall *b.* the breast-. *Ex* 28:28
swear an oath to *b.* his. *Num.* 30:2
shalt *b.* them for a sign. *Deut* 6:8
shalt *b.* up the money. 14:25
thou shalt *b.* this line. *Josh* 2:18
to *b.* Samson are we. *Judg* 15:10
we are come down to *b.* thee. 12
no, but we will *b.* thee fast. 13
that we may *b.* Samson. 16:5
I will *b.* it as a crown. *Job* 31:36
canst *b.* sweet influences? 38:31
canst thou *b.* the unicorn? 39:10
hide them, and *b.* their. 40:13
wilt thou *b.* Leviathan? 41:5
to *b.* his princes at his. *Ps* 105:22
b. the sacrifice with cords. 118:27
to *b.* their kings with. 149:8
b. them about thy neck. *Pr* 3:3
b. them continually. 6:21
b. them on thy fingers, write. 7:3
b. up the testimony. *Isa* 8:16
and *b.* them on thee as a. 49:18
he hath sent me to *b.* up the. 61:1
I will *b.* up what was. *Ezek* 34:16
commanded most mighty men to *b.*
Dan 3:20
smitten us, and will *b.* us. *Hos* 6:1
when they *b.* themselves. 10:10
b. the chariot to the swift. *Mi* 1:13
first *b.* the strong man, then will.
Mat 12:29; *Mark* 3:27
b. the tares in bundles. *Mat* 13:30
whatsoever thou shalt *b.* 16:19; 18:18
b. him hand and foot. 22:13
b. heavy burdens. 23:4
no man could *b.* him. *Mark* 5:3
authority to *b.* all that. *Acts* 9:14
gird thyself, *b.* on thy sandals. 12:8
so shall the Jews *b.* 21:11

bindeth

maketh sore and *b.* up. *Job* 5:18
b. up the waters in his. 26:8
he *b.* the floods. 28:11
it *b.* me about as the collar. 30:18
they cry not when he *b.* them. 36:13
nor he that *b.* sheaves. *Ps* 129:7
the broken in heart, *b.* up. *Ps* 147:3
as he that *b.* a stone. *Pr* 26:8
the Lord *b.* up the breach. *Isa* 30:26

binding

we were *b.* sheaves in. *Gen* 37:7
b. his foal to the vine. 49:11
every *b.* oath. *Num* 30:13
b. and delivering into. *Acts* 22:4

bird

(*A fowl, small or large*)

every *b.* of every sort. *Gen* 7:14
cleanse the house with living *b.*
Lev 14:52
play with him as with a *b.*? *Job* 41:5
flee as a *b.* to your. *Ps* 11:1
our soul is escaped as a *b.* 124:7
net spread in sight of *b.* *Pr* 1:17
and as a *b.* from the hand. 6:5
as a *b.* hasteth to the snare. 7:23
as the *b.* by wandering. 26:2*
as a *b.* that wandereth from. 27:8
b. of the air shall tell. *Eccl* 10:20
rise up at the voice of the *b.* 12:4
as a wandering *b.* *Isa* 16:2
calling a ravenous *b.* 46:11
heritage is as speckled *b.* *Jer* 12:9
chased me like a *b.* *Lam* 3:52
shall fly away like a *b.* *Hos* 9:11
they shall tremble as a *b.* 11:11
can a *b.* fall where no gin? *Amos* 3:5
of unclean and hateful *b.* *Rev* 18:2

birds

the *b.* divided he not. *Gen* 15:10
the *b.* did eat them. 40:17
the *b.* shall eat thy flesh. 19
command to take two *b.* *Lev* 14:4
of all clean *b.* eat. *Deut* 14:11
suffered not *b.* to rest. *2 Sam* 21:10
where *b.* make their nests. *Ps* 104:17
as *b.* that are caught. *Eccl* 9:12
time of singing of *b.* is. *S of S* 2:12
as *b.* flying, so will Lord. *Isa* 31:5
all the *b.* of the heaven. *Jer* 4:25
as a cage full of *b.* so are. 5:27
beasts are consumed and *b.* 12:4
the *b.* round about are against. 9
give thee to ravenous *b.* *Ezek* 39:4
nails were grown like *b.* *Dan* 4:33
b. of the air. *Mat* 8:20; *Luke* 9:58
b. lodge in the branches. *Mat* 13:32
into an image like to *b.* *Rom* 1:23
of fishes, another of *b.* *1 Cor* 15:39
every kind of beasts and *b.* *Jas* 3:7

birth

Is [1] *Natural,* Ex 28:10. [2] *Supernatural, as was the birth of Christ,* Mat 1:18; Luke 1:14. [3] *Figurative,* 2 Ki 19:3; Tit 3:5; Gal 4:19.

children come to *b.* *2 Ki* 19:3
Isa 37:3
as an hidden untimely *b.* *Job* 3:16
pass like the untimely *b.* *Ps* 58:8
an untimely *b.* is better. *Eccl* 6:3
day of death better than day of *b.* 7:1
shall I bring to the *b.*? *Isa* 66:9
thy *b.* and nativity. *Ezek* 16:3
glory of Ephraim fly from *b.* *Hos* 9:11
the *b.* of Jesus Christ. *Mat* 1:18
shall rejoice at his *b.* *Luke* 1:14
a man blind from his *b.* *John* 9:1
of whom I travail in *b.* *Gal* 4:19
cried, travailing in *b.* *Rev* 12:2

birthday

third day, Pharaoh's *b.* *Gen* 40:20
Herod's *b.* *Mat* 14:6; *Mark* 6:21

birthright

sell me this day thy *b.* *Gen* 25:31
he sware, and sold his *b.* 33
thus Esau despised *b.* 34
took my *b.*, now my blessing. 27:36
first-born according to *b.* 43:33
Reuben's *b.* given to sons. *1 Chr* 5:1
for one morsel sold *b.* *Heb* 12:16

bishop, -s

saints at Philippi, with *b.* *Phil.* 1:1
if man desire office of *b.* *1 Tim* 3:1
a *b.* must be blameless. 2; *Tit* 1:7
returned to *b.* of your souls.
1 Pet 2:25

bishopric

his *b.* let another take. *Acts* 1:20*

bit, -s

mouth must be held in with *b.*
Ps 32:9
put *b.* in horses' mouths. *Jas* 3:3

bit

fiery serpents, *b.* people. *Num* 21:6
and a serpent *b.* him. *Amos* 5:19

bite

serpent shall *b.* him. *Eccl* 10:8
the serpent will *b.* without. 11
serpents, they shall *b.* you. *Jer* 8:17
command serpent, and he shall *b.*
Amos 9:3
prophets that *b.* with teeth. *Mi* 3:5
they rise up that shall *b.*? *Hab* 2:7
if ye *b.* and devour one. *Gal* 5:15

biteth

Dan an adder, that *b.* *Gen* 49:17
at the last it *b.* like. *Pr* 23:32

Bithynia

assayed to go into *B.* *Acts* 16:7
scattered throughout *B.* *1 Pet* 1:1

bitten

every one that is *b.* *Num* 21:8
if a serpent had *b.* any man. 9

bitter

Esau cried with a *b.* cry. *Gen* 27:34
made their lives *b.* *Ex* 1:14
with *b.* herbs eat it. 12:8; *Num* 9:11
waters of Marah were *b.* *Ex* 15:23
devoured with *b.* destruction.
Deut 32:24
grapes of gall, their clusters are *b.* 32
saw affliction of Israel it was *b.*
2 Ki 14:26
cried with a *b.* cry. *Esth* 4:1
is life given to *b.* in soul? *Job* 3:20
thou writest *b.* things against. 13:26
even to-day is my complaint *b.* 23:2*
their arrows, *b.* words. *Ps* 64:3
end is *b.* as wormwood. *Pr* 5:4
hungry soul *b.* thing is sweet. 27:7
I find more *b.* than death. *Eccl* 7:26
that put *b.* for sweet, sweet for *b.*
Isa 5:20
strong drink shall be *b.* to. 24:9
it is an evil thing and *b.* *Jer* 2:19
thy wickedness, because it is *b.* 4:18
most *b.* lamentation as for a. 6:26
voice heard in Ramah, *b.* 31:15
weep with *b.* wailing. *Ezek* 27:31
end thereof, as a *b.* day. *Amos* 8:10
Chaldeans, that *b.* and. *Hab* 1:6
love your wives, be not *b.* *Col* 3:19
if ye have *b.* envying. *Jas* 3:14
of waters because made *b.* *Rev* 8:11
eat it, it shall make thy belly *b.* 10:9
soon as I had eaten, belly was *b.* 10

bitter *water*

the *b.* *water* that causeth. *Num* 5:18
send sweet *water* and *b.*? *Jas* 3:11

bitterly

curse *b.* the inhabitants. *Judg* 5:23
Almighty hath dealt *b.* *Ruth* 1:20
look from me, I will weep *b.* *Isa* 22:4
of peace shall weep *b.* 33:7
pilots of Tyre shall cry *b.* *Ezek* 27:30
Ephraim provoked him *b.* *Hos* 12:14
mighty man shall cry *b.* *Zeph* 1:14
Peter wept *b.* *Mat* 26:75
Luke 22:62

bittern

(*Revised Version,* porcupine)

a possession for the *b.* *Isa* 14:23
34:11
the *b.* shall lodge in the. *Zeph* 2:14

bitterness

Hannah was in *b.* of. *1 Sam* 1:10
surely the *b.* of death is past. 15:32
the sword will be *b.* *2 Sam* 2:26
I will complain in *b.* *Job* 7:11
but filleth me with *b.* 9:18
I will speak in *b.* of my soul. 10:1
another dieth in the *b.* of. 21:25
heart knoweth his own *b.* *Pr* 14:10
a foolish son is *b.* 17:25
go softly all my years in *b.* *Isa* 38:15
behold, for peace I had great *b.* 17
are afflicted, she is in *b.* *Lam* 1:4

he hath filled me with *b*. *Lam* 3:15
took me, I went in *b*. *Ezek* 3:14
with *b*. sigh before their eyes. 21:6
shall weep for thee with *b*. 27:31
be in *b*. as one that is in *b*. *Zech* 12:10
thou art in the gall of *b*. *Acts* 8:23
whose mouth is full of *b*. *Rom* 3:14
let all *b*. be put away. *Eph* 4:31
any root of *b*. springing. *Heb* 12:15

black

there is no *b*. hair in it. *Lev* 13:31
and there is *b*. hair grown. 37
the heaven was *b*. *1 Ki* 18:45
my skin is *b*. upon me. *Job* 30:30
in the evening, in the *b*. *Pr* 7:9*
I am *b*. but comely, O. *S of S* 1:5*
look not upon me, I am *b*. 6*
his locks are bushy and *b*. 5:11
the heavens shall be *b*. *Jer* 4:28
my people am I hurt, I am *b*. 8:21
gates thereof languish, are *b*. 14:2
skin was *b*. like an oven. *Lam* 5:10
in second chariot *b*. *Zech* 6:2
b. horses go forth into north. 6
make one hair white or *b*. *Mat* 5:36
I beheld, lo a *b*. horse. *Rev* 6:5
sun became *b*. as sackcloth. 12

blacker

visage is *b*. than a coal. *Lam* 4:8

blackish

b. by reason of the ice. *Job* 6:16

blackness

let *b*. of the day terrify it. *Job* 3:5
I clothe heavens with *b*. *Isa* 50:3
all faces gather *b*. *Joel* 2:6* *Nah* 2:10
are not come to *b*. *Heb* 12:18
to whom is reserved *b*. of. *Jude* 13

blade

also went in after the *b*. *Judg* 3:22
arm fall from shoulder-*b*. *Job* 31:22
b. was sprung up. *Mat* 13:26 *Mark* 4:28

blains

a boil breaking forth with *b*. *Ex* 9:9, 10

blame

let me bear *b*. *Gen* 43:9; 44:32
no man should *b*. us. *2 Cor* 8:20
holy and without *b*. *Eph* 1:4*

blamed

the ministry be not *b*. *2 Cor* 6:3
because he was to be *b*. *Gal* 2:11*

blameless

ye shall be *b*. *Gen* 44:10
we will be *b*. of this. *Josh* 2:17
now shall I be more *b*. *Judg* 15:3
profane sabbath, are *b*. *Mat* 12:5
ordinances of the Lord *b*. *Luke* 1:6
ye may be *b*. in the day. *1 Cor* 1:8
b. and harmless. *Phil* 2:15
touching righteousness of law *b*. 3:6
spirit, soul, and body, *b*. *1 Thes* 5:23
bishop must be *b*. *1 Tim* 3:2 *Tit* 1:7
office of a deacon, found *b*. *1 Tim* 3:10
in charge, that they may be *b*. 5:7
if any be *b*. the husband of. *Tit* 1:6
without spot and *b*. *2 Pet* 3:14

blaspheme

(*In old Jewish law, to revile or curse God, or the king, who was God's representative. It means intentional indignity offered to God or sacred things*)

enemies of Lord to *b*. *2 Sam* 12:14
b. God and the king. *1 Ki* 21:10, 13
shall the enemy *b*. thy ? *Ps* 74:10
wherewith they shall *b*. *Mark* 3:28
that shall *b*. against Holy Ghost. 29
I compelled them to *b*. *Acts* 26:11
may learn not to *b*. *1 Tim* 1:20
do not they *b*. that worthy ? *Jas* 2:7
to *b*. his name and. *Rev* 13:6

blasphemed

Israelitish woman's son *b*. *Lev* 24:11
servants of king of Assyria have *b*. me. *2 Ki* 19:6, 22; *Isa* 37:6, 23
foolish have *b*. thy name. *Ps* 74:18
my name continually is *b*. *Isa* 52:5
have burnt incense, and *b*. 65:7
your fathers have *b*. me. *Ezek* 20:27
opposed themselves and *b*. *Acts* 18:6
the name of God is *b*. *Rom* 2:24
God and doctrine be not *b*. *1 Tim* 6:1
that word of God be not *b*. *Tit* 2:5
scorched with heat, and *b*. *Rev* 16:9
b. the God of heaven because. 11
men *b*. God because of plague. 21

blasphemer, -s

nor *b*. of your goddess. *Acts* 19:37
who was before a *b*. *1 Tim* 1:13
last days men shall be *b*. *2 Tim* 3:2

blasphemest, -eth

whoso *b*. the Lord, be. *Lev* 24:16
the voice of him that *b*. *Ps* 44:16
scribes said, this man *b*. *Mat* 9:3
Father sanctified, thou *b*. *John* 10:36

blasphemies

I have heard all thy *b*. *Ezek* 35:12
out of heart proceed *b*. *Mat* 15:19
doth this man speak *b*.? *Mark* 2:7
and *b*. wherewith they shall. 3:28
who speaketh *b*.? *Luke* 5:21
given him speaking *b*. *Rev* 13:5

blaspheming

contradicting and *b*. *Acts* 13:45

blasphemous

heard him speak *b*. words. *Acts* 6:11
ceaseth not to speak *b*. words. 13

blasphemously

many things *b*. spake. *Luke* 22:65

blasphemy

this day of *b*. *2 Ki* 19:3; *Isa* 37:3
all manner of *b*. forgiven, *b*. against Holy Ghost not be. *Mat* 12:31
he hath spoken *b*., now ye have heard his *b*. 26:65; *Mark* 14:64
out of heart proceed *b*. *Mark* 7:22
stone thee not, but for *b*. *John* 10:33
ye also put off malice, *b*. *Col* 3:8
I know the *b*. of them that. *Rev* 2:9
upon his heads the name of *b*. 13:1
and he opened his mouth in *b*. 6

blast

[1] *A violent gust of wind*, Job 4:9. [2] *To wither or blight*, Gen 41:6.

with *b*. of thy nostrils. *Ex* 15:8
when they make a long *b*. *Josh* 6:5
at rebuke of Lord, at *b*. of breath of. *2 Sam* 22:16; *Ps* 18:15
a *b*. on Sennacherib. *2 Ki* 19:7* *Isa* 37:7*
by *b*. of God they perish. *Job* 4:9*
when the *b*. of the terrible. *Isa* 25:4

blasted

seven thin ears *b*. with the east wind. *Gen* 41:6, 23, 27
as corn *b*. *2 Ki* 19:26; *Isa* 37:27

blasting

Lord shall smite with *b*. *Deut* 28:22
if there be *b*. *1 Ki* 8:37; *2 Chr* 6:28
have smitten you with *b*. *Amos* 4:9
smote you with *b*. *Hag* 2:17

Blastus

having made *B*. friend. *Acts* 12:20

blaze

he began to *b*. abroad. *Mark* 1:45*

bleating, -s

abodest to hear *b*. of. *Judg* 5:16
what meaneth this *b*.? *1 Sam* 15:14

blemish

lamb without *b*. *Ex* 12:5; *Lev* 9:3 14:10; 23:12; *Num* 6:14
two rams without *b*. *Ex* 29:1; *Lev* 5:15, 18 6:6; 9:2; *Ezek* 46:4
male without *b*. *Lev* 1:3, 10; 4:23 22:19
male or female without *b*. 3:1, 6
bullock without *b*. 4:3; *Deut* 17:1 *Ezek* 45:18
bring kid, a female without *b*. *Lev* 4:28
hath *b*. not approach. 21:17, 18, 21, 23
but whatsoever hath a *b*. shall not be acceptable. 22:20; *Deut* 15:21
in offering no *b*. *Lev* 22:21
if a man cause *b*. in neighbour 24:19
as he hath caused a *b*. in a man. 20
a red heifer without *b*. *Num* 19:2
bullock, ram, lambs without *b*. 29:2
no *b*. in Absalom. *2 Sam* 14:25
in whom was no *b*. *Dan* 1:4
holy and without *b*. *Eph* 5:27
as of a lamb without *b*. *1 Pet* 1:19

blemishes

b. in them, they shall. *Lev* 22:25
spots they are and *b*. *2 Pet* 2:13

bless

I. *God blesses*. [1] *By giving riches and prosperity*, Gen 30:27; 39:5. [2] *By giving spiritual and temporal good things*, Ps 29:11; Eph 1:3. [3] *By consecrating or hallowing*, Gen 2:3; Ex 20:11. II. *Men bless God*. [1] *When they praise him for his goodness*, Ps 104:1. [2] *When they thank him for his benefits to them*, Ps 103:1. III. *Men bless other men*. [1] *When they utter a solemn benediction, as a father praying for his son, and naming him heir and successor*, Gen 27:23. [2] *When they pray to God for his blessing on other men*, Num 6:23, 24; 2 Sam 6:18.

bless, *God being agent*

I will *b*. thee. *Gen* 12:2; 26:3, 24
I will *b*. them that bless thee. 12:3
I will *b*. her and give. 17:16
blessing I will *b*. thee. 22:17 *Heb* 6:14
God Almighty *b*. thee, and. *Gen* 28:3
let thee go, except thou *b*. 32:26
b. the lads, and let my name. 48:16
the Almighty who shall *b*. 49:25
come to thee, and *b*. thee. *Ex* 20:24
he shall *b*. thy bread and. 23:25
the Lord *b*. thee. *Num* 6:24
name on Israel, I will *b*. them. 27
saw it pleased the Lord to *b*. 24:1
b. you as he hath. *Deut* 1:11
he will *b*. thee, *b*. the fruit. 7:13
the Lord *b*. thee. 14:29; 23:20 24:19
no poor, for Lord shall *b*. thee. 15:4
the Lord thy God shall *b*. 10
Lord thy God shall *b*. thee. 18; 30:16
the Lord shall *b*. thee. 16:15
look down and *b*. thy people. 26:15
he shall *b*. thee in the land. 28:8
b. all the work of thine hand. 12
b. Lord, his substance. 33:11
the Lord *b*. thee. *Ruth* 2:4 *Jer* 31:23
let it please thee to *b*. the house of thy. *2 Sam* 7:29; *1 Chr* 17:27
O that thou wouldest *b*. *1 Chr* 4:10
thou, Lord, wilt *b*. righteous. *Ps* 5:12
save thy people, *b*. thine. 28:9
the Lord will *b*. his people. 29:11
God, our God, shall *b*. us. 67:1, 6, 7
the Lord will *b*. us, *b*. the house of Israel, *b*. the house of. 115:12
b. them that fear the Lord. 13
Lord shall *b*. thee out of Zion. 128:5
abundantly *b*. her provision. 132:15
Lord *b*. thee out of Zion. 134:3
the Lord of hosts shall *b*. *Isa* 19:25
this day will I *b*. you. *Hag* 2:19
sent him to *b*. you. *Acts* 3:26

bless, *God being the object*

then thou shalt *b*. the. *Deut* 8:10
b. ye the Lord. *Judg* 5:9; *Ps* 103:21 134:1
David said, now *b*. Lord. *1 Chr* 29:20
stand up and *b*. the Lord. *Neh* 9:5
I will *b*. the Lord. *Ps* 16:7
in congregations will I *b*. Lord. 26:12
I will *b*. the Lord at all times. 34:1
thus will I *b*. thee while I live. 63:4
O *b*. our God. 66:8
b. ye God in congregations. 68:26
sing to the Lord, *b*. his name. 96:2
be thankful, *b*. his name. 100:4 103:1
b. the Lord. 103:1, 2, 22; 104:1, 35
b. the Lord, ye his angels. 103:20

b. the Lord, ye his hosts. *Ps* 103:21
b. the Lord all his works. 22
we will *b.* the Lord. 115:18
lift your hands, *b.* the Lord. 134:2
b. the Lord, O Israel, *b.* the Lord, O house of Aaron. 135:19
O, ye that fear the Lord, *b.* the. 20
I will *b.* thy name for ever. 145:1
every day will I *b.* thee. 2
O Lord, thy saints shall *b.* thee. 10
let all flesh *b.* his holy name. 21
therewith *b.* we God. *Jas* 3:9

bless, *man agent* and *object*

my soul may *b.* thee. *Gen* 27:4, 25
b. me, even me my father, 34, 38
them to me, and I will *b.* 48:9
in thee shall Israel *b.* saying. 20
take flocks and begone, *b.* *Ex* 12:32
on this wise *b.* Israel. *Num* 6:23
received commandment to *b.* 23:20
neither curse them, nor *b.* 25
Lord separated Levi to *b.* *Deut* 10:8; 21:5
in his own raiment, and *b.* 24:13
shall stand on Gerizim to *b.* 27:12
heareth words of curse, he *b.* 29:19
commanded they should *b.* *Josh* 8:33
he doth *b.* the sacrifice. *1 Sam* 9:13
David returned to *b.* his household. *2 Sam* 6:20; *1 Chr* 16:43
sent Joram to *b.* David. *2 Sam* 8:10
that ye may *b.* the inheritance. 21:3
came to *b.* David. *1 Ki* 1:47
and to *b.* in his name. *1 Chr* 23:13
they *b.* with their mouths. *Ps* 62:4
let them curse, but *b.* thou. 109:28
we *b.* you in name of the. 129:8
generation that curseth father, and doth not *b.* mother. *Pr* 30:11
shall *b.* himself in God. *Isa* 65:16
nations shall *b.* themselves. *Jer* 4:2
b. them that curse you. *Mat* 5:44 *Luke* 6:28
b. them which persecute you, *b.* and curse not. *Rom* 12:14
being reviled we *b.* *1 Cor* 4:12
else when shalt thou *b.* 14:16

bless

cup of blessing we *b.* *1 Cor* 10:16

blessed, *man agent* and *object*

Melchisedek *b.* Abram, and said *b.* *Gen* 14:19
they *b.* Rebekah, and said. 24:60
Isaac *b.* Jacob and said. 27:23, 27
and *b.* be he that blesseth thee. 29
I have *b.* him, and he shall be *b.* 33
blessing wherewith his father *b.* 41
Isaac called Jacob, *b.* him. 28:1
as he *b.* him he gave. 6; *Heb* 11:20
daughters will call me *b.* *Gen* 30:13*
sons and daughters, and *b.* 31:55
Jacob *b.* Pharaoh. 47:7, 10
he *b.* Joseph. 48:15
Jacob *b.* Manasseh and. 48:20 *Heb* 11:21
Jacob *b.* his sons, every one he *b.* *Gen* 49:28
Moses *b.* them. *Ex* 39:43 *Deut* 33:1
Aaron lifted up hand and *b.* *Lev* 9:22
Moses and Aaron *b.* people. 23
whom thou blessest is *b.* *Num* 22:6
thou hast *b.* them. 23:11; 24:10
b. he that enlargeth Gad. *Deut* 33:20
let Asher be *b.* with children. 24
Joshua *b.* Caleb, and. *Josh* 14:13
Joshua *b.* them. 22:6, 7
therefore Balaam *b.* you still. 24:10
b. above women Jael. *Judg* 5:24
b. be he that did take. *Ruth* 2:19
Eli *b.* Elkanah and. *1 Sam* 2:20
b. be thy advice, and *b.* be. 25:33
Saul said, *b.* be thou my son. 26:25
David *b.* the people. *2 Sam* 6:18 *1 Chr* 16:2
he would not go, but *b.* him. *2 Sam* 13:25
king kissed Barzillai, and *b.* 19:39
king Solomon shall be *b.* *1 Ki* 2:45
Solomon *b.* congregation. 8:14, 55
congregation *b.* Solomon. 66 *2 Chr* 6:3
and Levites *b.* people. *2 Chr* 30:27
people *b.* all that offered. *Neh* 11:2
the ear heard me, it *b.* *Job* 29:11
if his loins have not *b.* me. 31:20
while he lived *b.* his soul. *Ps* 49:18
men *b.* in him, nations call him *b.* 72:17*
b. he that cometh in name of the Lord, we have *b.* you. 118:26
her children call her *b.* *Pr* 31:28
b., O land, when thy king. *Eccl* 10:17*
daughters saw her, and *b.* *S of S* 6:9
incense, as if he *b.* idol. *Isa* 66:3
my mother bare me be *b.* *Jer* 20:14
all nations shall call you *b.* *Mal* 3:12*
b. be the kingdom of. *Mark* 11:10
all generations call me *b.* *Luke* 1:48
Simeon *b.* them, and said. 2:34
more *b.* to give than to. *Acts* 20:35
looking for that *b.* hope. *Tit* 2:13
met Abraham and *b.* him. *Heb* 7:1, 6
the less is *b.* of the better. 7

blessed, *God the agent*

God *b.* them. *Gen* 1:22, 28; 5:2
b. the seventh day. 2:3; *Ex* 20:11
b. Noah and his sons. *Gen* 9:1
in thee all families be *b.* 12:3; 18:18 22:18; 26:4; 28:14; *Acts* 3:25 *Gal* 3:8
I have *b.* Ishmael. *Gen* 17:20
Lord *b.* Abraham. 24:1
he said, come in, *b.* of the. 31
God *b.* Isaac. 25:11; 26:12
thou art the *b.* of the Lord. 26:29
smell of a field Lord hath *b.* 27:27
that the Lord hath *b.* me. 30:27
the Lord hath *b.* thee since. 30
b. Jacob there. 32:29; 35:9; 48:3
that the Lord *b.* Egyptian's. 39:5
for the people are *b.* *Num* 22:12
he hath *b.* and I cannot. 23:20
thy God hath *b.* thee. *Deut* 2:7 12:7; 15:14; 16:10
shalt be *b.* above all people. 7:14
when the Lord hath *b.* 14:24
b. shalt thou be in the city, *b.* 28:3
b. shall be fruit of thy body. 4
b. thy basket. 5
of Joseph he said, *b.* of Lord. 33:13
as the Lord hath *b.* me. *Josh* 17:14
Samson grew, the Lord *b.* *Judg* 13:24
b. be thou of Lord. 17:2; *Ruth* 3:10 *1 Sam* 15:13
b. be he of the Lord. *Ruth* 2:20
b. be thou of the Lord. 3:10
b. be ye. *1 Sam* 23:21; *2 Sam* 2:5
the Lord *b.* Obed-edom. *2 Sam* 6:11 12; *1 Chr* 13:14; 26:5
house of thy servant be *b.* *2 Sam* 7:29
O Lord, and it shall be *b.* *1 Chr* 17:27
the Lord hath *b.* *2 Chr* 31:10
thou hast *b.* the work. *Job* 1:10
Lord *b.* latter end of Job. 42:12
hast made him most *b.* *Ps* 21:6
b. is the nation whose God is. 33:12
such as be *b.* of him. 37:22
lendeth, and his seed is *b.* 26
and he shall be *b.* 41:2
therefore God hath *b.* thee. 45:2
b. is the people that know. 89:15
the upright shall be *b.* 112:2
you are *b.* of the Lord. 115:15
b. are the undefiled. 119:1
b. is every one that feareth. 128:1
thus the man be *b.* that feareth. 4
he hath *b.* thy children. 147:13
let thy fountain be *b.* *Pr* 5:18
the memory of the just is *b.* 10:7
just man's children are *b.* 20:7
end thereof shall not be *b.* 21
he that hath bountiful eye be *b.* 22:9
b. be Egypt my people. *Isa* 19:25
for I called him and *b.* him. 51:2
seed the Lord hath *b.* 61:9; 65:23
b. are the poor in spirit. *Mat* 5:3
b. are the meek. 5
b. are the merciful. 7
b. are the pure in heart. 8
b. are the peace-makers. 9
b. are they which are persecuted. 10
b. are your eyes. 13:16; *Luke* 10:23
he *b.* and brake. *Mat* 14:19; 26:26 *Mark* 6:41; 14:22; *Luke* 9:16 24:30
Jesus said, *b.* art thou. *Mat* 16:17
b. that servant. 24:46; *Luke* 12:43
come ye *b.* of my Father. *Mat* 25:34
them up in his arms, *b.* *Mark* 10:16
art thou Christ, Son of the *b.*? 14:61
b. among women. *Luke* 1:28, 42
b. is she that believed. 45
b. be ye poor. 6:20
b. is the womb that bare. 11:27
b. are those servants whom Lord shall find watching. 12:37, 38
thou shalt be *b.* 14:14
b. be the King that cometh. 19:38
b. are the barren that never. 23:29
he *b.* them. 24:50
while he *b.* them. 51
b. with faithful Abraham. *Gal* 3:9
b. us with spiritual. *Eph* 1:3
this man shall be *b.* *Jas* 1:25
b. are the dead. *Rev* 14:13

blessed, *God the object*

he said, *b.* be the Lord. *Gen* 9:26 24:27; *Ex* 18:10; *Ruth* 4:14 *1 Sam* 25:32, 39; *2 Sam* 18:28 *1 Ki* 1:48; 5:7; 8:15, 56; 10:9 *1 Chr* 16:36; *2 Chr* 2:12; 6:4; 9:8 *Ezra* 7:27; *Ps* 28:6; 31:21; 41:13 68:19; 72:18; 89:52; 106:48; 124:6; 135:21; 144:1; *Zech* 11:5 *Luke* 1:68
b. be most high God. *Gen* 14:20
children of Israel *b.* God. *Josh* 22:33
and *b.* be my rock. *2 Sam* 22:47 *Ps* 18:46
David *b.* the Lord, *b.* *1 Chr* 29:10
all the congregation *b.* Lord. 20
there they *b.* Lord. *2 Chr* 20:26
they saw the heaps, they *b.* 31:8
and Ezra *b.* the Lord. *Neh* 8:6
b. be thy glorious. 9:5; *Ps* 72:19
b. be the name of Lord. *Job* 1:21 *Ps* 113:2
b. be God. *Ps* 66:20; 68:35 *2 Cor* 1:3
b. art thou, O Lord, teach. *Ps* 119:12
b. be the glory of. *Ezek* 3:12
Daniel *b.* God of. *Dan* 2:19, 20
Nebuchadnezzar *b.* most High. 4:34
him in his arms and *b.* *Luke* 2:28
b. is the King of Israel. *John* 12:13
than Creator, who is *b.* *Rom* 1:25
Christ, who is over all, God *b.* 9:5
is *b.* for evermore. *2 Cor* 11:31
b. be the Father. *Eph* 1:3; *1 Pet* 1:3
Gospel of the *b.* God. *1 Tim* 1:11
the *b.* and only Potentate. 6:15

blessed *are they*

b. are they that put trust. *Ps* 2:12
b. are they that dwell. 84:4
b. are they that keep judgement. 106:3
b. are they that keep. 119:2
for *b. are they* that keep. *Pr* 8:32
b. are they that wait. *Isa* 30:18
b. are they that mourn. *Mat* 5:4
b. are they who hunger. 6
b. are they who are persecuted. 10
b. are they that hear. *Luke* 11:28
b. are they that believed. *John* 20:29
b. are they whose iniquities. *Rom* 4:7
b. are they who are called. *Rev* 19:9
b. are they that do his. 22:14

blessed *are ye*

b. are ye that sow. *Isa* 32:20
b. are ye when men. *Mat* 5:11
b. are ye that hunger, be filled; *b. are ye* that weep. *Luke* 6:21
b. are ye when men hate you. 22

blessed *is he*

b. is he that blesseth. *Num* 24:9
b. is he whose sin is. *Ps* 32:1
b. is he that considereth poor. 41:1
b. is he that waiteth. *Dan* 12:12
and *b. is he* whosoever shall not be. *Mat* 11:6; *Luke* 7:23
b. is he that cometh in name. *Mat* 21:9; 23:39; *Mark* 11:9 *Luke* 13:35
b. is he that shall eat. *Luke* 14:15
b. is he that readeth. *Rev* 1:3
b. is he that watcheth. 16:15
b. is he that hath part in. 20:6
b. is he that keepeth savings. 22:7

blessed *is the man*
b. *is the man* that walketh not in. Ps 1:1
b. *is the man* to whom Lord imputeth not iniquity. 32:2; Rom 4:8
b. *is the man* that trusteth in him. Ps 34:8; 84:12; Jer 17:7
b. *is the man* that maketh the Lord. Ps 40:4
b. *is the man* whom thou choosest. 65:4
b. *is the man* whose strength. 84:5
b. *is the man* thou chastenest. 94:12
b. *is the man* that feareth Lord. 112:1
b. *is the man* that heareth. Pr 8:34
b. *is the man* that doth this. Isa 56:2
b. *is the man* that endureth. Jas 1:12

blessedness
as David describeth b. Rom 4:6
cometh this b. on the ? 9
where is then the b.? Gal 4:15*

blessest
I wot that he thou b. Num 22:6
thou b. O Lord, and it. 1 Chr 17:27
thou b. the springing. Ps. 65:10

blesseth
blessed is he that b. thee. Gen 27:29 Num 24:9
thy God b. thee as he. Deut 15:6
b. covetous whom the. Ps 10:3*
he b. them so that they are. 107:38
but he b. the habitation. Pr 3:33
he that b. his friend. 27:14
he b. himself in the earth. Isa 65:16

blessing
[1] *The favour, kindness, and goodness of God, making what his people do succeed and prosper,* Ps 3:8. [2] *All good things which God bestows upon his people, whether spiritual or temporal,* Deut 28:2; Ps 24:5; Isa 44:3; Eph 1:3. [3] *The means of conveying a blessing to others,* Isa 19:24. [4] *Wishing, praying for, and endeavouring the good of our enemies,* 1 Pet 3:9. [5] *A gift, or present,* Gen 33:11; 1 Ki 5:15.

bless thee, thou shalt be a b. Gen 12:2
in b. I will bless. 22:17; Heb 6:14
a curse on me, not a b. Gen 27:12
brother hath taken thy b. 35
hast thou but one b.? 38
God give thee b. of Abraham. 28:4
take, I pray thee, my b. 33:11*
the b. of the Lord was on all. 39:5
every one according to his b. 49:28
bestow on you a b. Ex 32:29
command my b. on you. Lev 25:21
set before you b. Deut 11:26; 30:19
a b. if ye obey the. 11:27
put the b. on Gerizim. 29
to the b. of the Lord. 12:15; 16:17
Lord turned curse into b. 23:5
command a b. on store-houses. 28:8
is the b. wherewith Moses. 33:1, 7
let the b. come upon. 33:16
Naphtali full with the b. 23
give me a b. Josh 15:19; Judg 1:15
b. thy handmaid hath. 1 Sam 25:27*
with thy b. let my house. 2 Sam 7:29
I pray thee take a b. 2 Ki 5:15*
exalted above all b. and. Neh 9:5
God turned the curse into a b. 13:2
b. of him that was ready. Job 29:13
thy b. is upon thy people. Ps 3:8
he shall receive the b. 24:5
as he delighted not in b. 109:17
b. of the Lord be upon you. 129:8
Lord commanded the b. 133:3
b. of Lord maketh rich. Pr 10:22
by the b. of the upright the. 11:11
a b. on the head of him. 26
a good b. shall come on. 24:25
a b. in midst of land. Isa 19:24
and I will pour my b. on thy. 44:3
destroy it not, a b. is in it. 65:8
I will make them a b. there shall be showers of b. Ezek 34:26
may cause the b to rest. 44:30
if he will leave a b. Joel 2:14
I will save, ye shall be a b. Zech 8:13
and pour you out a b. Mal 3:10
in the temple b. God. Luke 24:53
in the fulness of the b. Rom 15:29
the cup of b. which. 1 Cor 10:16
the b. of Abraham. Gal 3:14
for the earth receiveth b. Heb 6:7
he would have inherited the b. 12:17
of same mouth proceed b. Jas 3:10
but contrariwise b., that ye should inherit a b. 1 Pet 3:9
to receive honour glory, b. Rev 5:12
b. to him that sitteth on the. 13
b. and glory to our God. 7:12

blessings
Almighty bless thee with b. of heaven, b. of deep, b. Gen 49:25
b. of father prevailed above b. of. 26
all these b. shall come. Deut 28:2
afterwards he read the b. Josh 8:34
thou preventest him with b. Ps 21:3
b. are upon head of just. Pr 10:6
faithful man abound with b. 28:20
and will curse your b. Mal 2:2
blessed us with spiritual b. Eph 1:3

blew, *verb*
priests passed on and b. Josh 6:8
Ehud b. a trumpet. Judg 3:27
Spirit come on Gideon, he b. 6:34
they b. the trumpets. 7:19, 20, 22
Saul b. saying, let. 1 Sam 13:3
Joab b. a trumpet. 2 Sam 2:28 18:16; 20:22
Sheba b. a trumpet and said. 20:1
b. the trumpet, people said, God. 1 Ki 1:39; 2 Ki 9:13; 11:14
winds b., beat on house. Mat 7:25, 27
a great wind that b. John 6:18
when the south-wind b. Acts 27:13 28:13*

blind
[1] *Those deprived of natural sight,* John 9:1; Acts 13:11. [2] *The morally blind, whose judgement is so corrupted by taking of bribes that they cannot, or will not discern between right and wrong,* Ex 23:8; Deut. 16:19. [3] *The spiritually blind, whether through ignorance or self-will,* Mat 15:14; Deut 27:18.

who maketh the seeing b. Ex 4:11
stumbling-block before b. Lev 19:14
a b. or lame man not offer. 21:18
not offer the b. to the Lord. 22:22 Deut 15:21
that maketh the b. to. Deut 27:18
grope at noon-day, as b. 28:29
take away the b. and. 2 Sam 5:6
the lame and b., the b. and the lame shall not come into house. 8
I was eyes to the b. Job 29:15
Lord openeth eyes of b. Ps 146:8
eyes of b. shall see. Isa 29:18; 35:5
a light to open the b. eyes. 42:7
bring b. by a way they knew not. 16
hear ye deaf, look, ye b. 18
who is b. but my servant? b. as he that is perfect, and b.? 19
bring forth the b. people. 43:8
his watchmen are b. 56:10
grope for the wall like the b. 59:10
gather with them the b. Jer 31:8
they wandered as b. Lam 4:14
shall walk like b. men. Zeph 1:17
offer the b. for sacrifice. Mal 1:8
two b. men followed him. Mat 9:27 20:30
b. receive their sight. 11:5; 12:22 Luke 7:22
b. leaders of the b. if the b. lead the b. both. Mat 15:14; Luke 6:39
woe to you, ye b. guides. Mat 23:16
ye fools and b. 17, 19
b. Pharisee, cleanse first within. 26
he took the b. by hand. Mark 8:23
b. Bartimaeus sat by the way. 10:46
recovery of sight to b. Luke 4:18
to many that were b. he gave. 7:21
thou makest a feast, call b. 14:13
lay a great mulitude of b. John 5:3
he saw a man b. from his birth. 9:1
they which see might be made b. 39
are we b. also? John 9:40
if ye were b. 41
can a devil open eyes of b.? 10:21
thou shalt be b. not. Acts 13:11
thou art a guide to the b. Rom 2:19
he that lacketh these is b. 2 Pet 1:9
not that thou art b. Rev 3:17

blind, *verb*
a gift doth b. the eyes. Deut 16:19
received I a bribe to b. 1 Sam 12:3

blinded, -eth
take no gift, a gift b. Ex 23:8
he hath b. their eyes. John 12:40
obtained, the rest are b. Rom 11:7
their minds were b. 2 Cor 3:14
god of this world hath b. the. 4:4
because darkness hath b. his eyes. 1 John 2:11

blindfolded
when they had b. him. Luke 22:64

blindness
smote the men with b. Gen 19:11
shall smite thee with b. Deut 28:28
Elisha prayed, smite this people with b., smote them with b. 2 Ki 6:18
smite every horse with b. Zech 12:4
b. in part has happened. Rom 11:25
because of b. of heart. Eph 4:18

block, *see* **stumbling**

blood
The word is used [1] *literally as in* Ex 29:12; Acts 17:26. [2] *Figuratively, for murder,* Hab 2:12; Mat 27:24; *and for the blood of Christ, the blood of the covenant, where the idea is the death of Christ on the cross,* Rom 3:25; 5:9; Eph 1:7.

thy brother's b. crieth. Gen 4:10
the life which is the b. 9:4
your b. of your lives, I will require. 5
killed kid and dipped coat in b. 37:31
water shall become b. on. Ex 4:9
waters shall be turned into b. 7:17
b. shall be for a token, when I see b. 12:13
shalt not offer the b. with leaven. 23:18; 34:25
thou shalt take of the b. 29:21
b. of it was not brought. Lev 10:18
and if issue in flesh shall be b. 15:19
b. imputed unto that man. 17:4
for it is the b. that maketh. 11
not stand against the b. of thy. 19:16
and drink the b. of. Num 23:24
not cleansed but by the b. 35:33
matter between b. and b. Deut 17:8; 2 Chr 19:10
the b. shall be forgiven. Deut 21:8
battlement, that bring not b. 22:8
avenge the b. of his servants. 32:43
and their b. be laid upon. Judg 9:24
let not my b. fall. 1 Sam 26:20
David said, thy b. be. 2 Sam 1:16
from the b. of the slain, from. 22
I and kingdom guiltless the b. 3:28
hath returned upon thee the b. 16:8
Amasa wallowed in b. 20:12
b. of the men? 23:17; 1 Chr 11:19
the b. of war on his girdle. 1 Ki 2:5
b. on thy head. 37; Ezek 33:4
the b. gushed out upon. 1 Ki 18:28
saw the waters red as b. 2 Ki 3:22
said, this is b. the kings are. 23
I have seen b. of Naboth, b. of. 9:26
O earth, cover not my b. Job 16:18
the eagles' young suck up b. 39:30
what profit is in my b.? Ps 30:9
or will I drink b. of goats? 50:13
righteous wash his feet in b. 58:10
foot may be dipped in the b. 68:23
precious shall their b. be in. 72:14
doth violence to b. of any. Pr 28:17
hands are full of b. Isa 1:15
the Lord shall purge the b. of. 4:4
noise, and garments rolled in b. 9:5
the waters of Dimon full of b. 15:9
his ear from hearing of b. 33:15
shall be melted with their b. 34:3
is found the b. of the poor. Jer 2:34
pour out their b. by the. 18:21*
he that keepeth sword from b. 48:10

b. be on the inhabitants. *Jer* 51:35
polluted themselves with *b.*
Lam 4:14
pestilence and *b.* pass. *Ezek* 5:17
the land is full of *b.* 9:9
pour out my fury upon it in *b.* 14:19
to thee when thou wast in thy *b.* 16:6
I will give thee *b.* in fury and. 38
beget son that is shedder of *b.* 18:10
he shall die, his *b.* shall be upon. 13
mother is like a vine in thy *b.* 19:10
thy *b.* in midst of land. 21:32; 22:12
the city sheddeth *b.* in the. 22:3
and *b.* is in their hands. 23:37, 45
I have set her *b.* on the rock. 24:8
I will send *b.* into her streets. 28:23
I water with thy *b.* the land. 32:6
I will prepare thee to *b.* thou hast not hated *b.* even *b.* shall. 35:6
offer my bread, fat and *b.* 44:7, 15
I will avenge the *b.* *Hos* 1:4
b. fire, and pillars of smoke.
Joel 2:30; *Acts* 2:19
moon turned into *b.* *Joel* 2:31
Acts 2:20
I will cleanse their *b.* *Joel* 3:21
their *b.* shall be poured. *Zeph* 1:17
issue of *b.* twelve years. *Mat* 9:20
Mark 5:25; *Luke* 8:43
b. hath not revealed. *Mat* 16:17
not partakers in the *b.* of. 23:30
b. of righteous Abel. 35; *Luke* 11:51
b. of the new testament. *Mat* 26:28
Mark 14:24
because it is price of *b.* *Mat* 27:6
called the field of *b.* 8; *Acts* 1:19
innocent of the *b.* of this. *Mat* 27:24
whose *b.* Pilate had. *Luke* 13:1
the new testament in my *b.* 22:20
1 Cor 11:25
sweat was as great drops of *b.*
Luke 22:44
which were born not of *b.* *John* 1:13
my flesh drinketh my *b.* 6:54, 56
my flesh is meat, my *b.* is drink. 55
forthwith came thereout *b.* 19:34
ye bring this man's *b.* *Acts* 5:28
they abstain from *b.* 15:20, 29; 21:25
and hath made of one *b.* all. 17:26
your *b.* be on your own heads. 18:6
I am pure from the *b.* of all. 20:26
guilty of body and *b.* of. *1 Cor* 11:27
flesh and *b.* cannot inherit. 15:50
not against flesh and *b.* *Eph* 6:12
peace through *b.* of cross. *Col* 1:20
partakers of flesh and *b.* *Heb* 2:14
not without *b.* which he offered. 9:7
by *b.* of goats, but by his own *b.* 12
b. of bulls and goats sanctifieth. 13
this is the *b.* of the testament. 20
without shedding of *b.* there is. 22
into holiest by *b.* of Jesus. 10:19
passover, and sprinkling of *b.* 11:28
ye have not yet resisted unto *b.* 12:4
b. of sprinkling that speaketh. 24
whose *b.* is brought into. 13:11
sprinkling of *b.* of Jesus. *1 Pet* 1:2
b. of Jesus Christ cleanseth us.
1 John 1:7
he that came by water and *b.* 5:6
three in earth, Spirit, water, *b.* 8
hast redeemed us by thy *b.* *Rev* 5:9
dost thou not avenge our *b.*? 6:10
and the moon became as *b.* 12
white in the *b.* of the Lamb. 7:14
third part of sea became *b.* 8:8; 16:3
power to turn the waters into *b.* 11:6
overcame him by *b.* of Lamb. 12:11
b. came out of the wine-press. 14:20
thou hast given them *b.* to drink. 16:6
in her was found the *b.* of. 18:24
avenged the *b.* of his servants. 19:2
clothed with vesture dipped in *b.* 13

see **avenger, revenger**

blood *be upon*
curseth his father, his *b.* *be upon.*
Lev 20:9
sodomy, their *b.* *be upon* them. 13
wizard, their *b.* *be upon* them. 27
b. shed, and *be upon.* *Deut* 19:10
abominations, his *b.* *be upon.*
Ezek 18:13
warning, his *b.* shall *be upon.* 33:5*

blood with *bullock*
take *b.* of *bullock.* *Ex* 29:12
Lev 4:5; 16:14, 18
pour *b.* of *bullock* at. *Lev* 4:7
he did with *b.* of the *bullock.* 16:15
delight not in *b.* of *bullocks.* *Isa* 1:11

blood *of Christ*
communion of the *b.* *of Christ*?
1 Cor 10:16
made nigh by *b.* of *Christ.* *Eph* 2:13
shall *b.* *of Christ* purge? *Heb* 9:14
b. *of Christ* as of a lamb. *1 Pet* 1:19
b. *of Christ* cleanseth us. *1 John* 1:7

blood *of the covenant*
behold the *b.* *of the covenant.*
Ex 24:8
by the *b.* *of* thy *covenant.* *Zech* 9:11
hath counted *b.* *of covenant* unholy.
Heb 10:29
b. *of the* everlasting *covenant.* 13:20

blood, with *eat*
eat neither fat nor *b.* *Lev* 3:17
ye shall *eat* no manner of *b.* 7:26
27; 17:14; *Deut* 12:16, 23; 15:23
eateth *b.* that soul be cut off.
Lev 7:27, 17:10
people did *eat* with *b.* *1 Sam* 14:32
ye eat with *b.* and. *Ezek* 33:25

for **blood**
not pollute land, *for b.* *Num* 35:33
died *for* the *b.* of Asahel. *2 Sam* 3:27
for the *b.* of the sons. *2 Chr* 24:25
he maketh inquisition *for b.* *Ps* 9:12
let us lay wait *for b.* *Pr* 1:11, 18
wicked are to lie in wait *for b.* 12:6
they all lie in wait *for b.* *Mi* 7:2

his **blood**
if we conceal *his b.* *Gen* 37:26
behold *his b.* is required. 42:22
his b. shall be upon his. *Josh* 2:19
I not require *his b.*? *2 Sam* 4:11
Lord shall return *his b.* *1 Ki* 2:32
die in his iniquity, but *his b.* will I require. *Ezek* 3:18, 20; 33:4, 6, 8
shall he leave *his b.* on. *Hos* 12:14
take away *his b.* *Zech* 9:7
his b. be on us. *Mat* 27:25
purchased with *his b.* *Acts* 20:28
through faith in *his b.* *Rom* 3:25
being now justified by *his b.* 5:9
redemption through *his b.* *Eph* 1:7
Col 1:14
by *his* own *b.* he entered. *Heb* 9:12
he might sanctify with *his b.* 13:12
from our sins in *his b.* *Rev* 1:5

innocent **blood**
innoc. b. be not shed. *Deut* 19:10
put away guilt of *innoc. b.* 13; 21:9
lay not *innoc. b.* to people's 21:8
sin against *innocent b.* *1 Sam* 19:5
take away *innoc. b.* *1 Ki* 2:31
shed *innoc. b.* *2 Ki* 21:16; 24:4
they condemn *innoc. b.* *Ps* 94:21
shed *innoc b.*, *b.* of sons and. 106:38
hands that shed *innoc. b.* *Pr* 6:17
haste to shed *innoc. b.* *Isa* 59:7
shed not *innoc. b.* *Jer* 7:6; 22:3
eyes and heart shed *innoc. b.* 22:17
ye shall surely bring *innoc. b.* 26:15
they have shed *innoc. b.* *Joel* 3:19
lay not on us *innoc. b.* *Jonah* 1:14
I have betrayed *innoc. b.* *Mat* 27:4

shed **blood**
sheddeth man's *b.* his *b.* be *shed.*
Gen 9:6
Reuben said, *shed* no *b.* 37:22
there shall no *b.* be *shed.* *Ex.* 22:2
be risen upon him, *b.* be *shed.* 3*
hath *shed b.* that man. *Lev* 17:4
cleansed of *b.* *shed* but by *b.*
Num 35:33
have not *shed* this *b.* *Deut* 21:7
coming to *shed b.* *1 Sam* 25:26*
slew and *shed b.* of war. *1 Ki* 2:5
thou hast *shed b.* much *b.*
1 Chr 22:8; 28:3
their *b.* *shed* like water. *Ps* 79:3
revenging *b.* of thy servants *shed.* 10
make haste to *shed b.* *Pr* 1:16
Rom 3:15
prophets have *shed* the *b.* *Lam* 4:13

as women that *shed b.* *Ezek* 16:38
23:45
guilty in thy *b.* thou hast *shed.* 22:4
to their power to *shed b.* 6
women that *shed b.* 23:45
ye *shed b.* shall ye possess? 33:25
thou hast *shed b.* of children. 35:5*
fury on them for *b.* they *shed.* 36:18
all the righteous *b.* *shed.* *Mat* 23:25
my *b.* which is *shed.* *Mark* 14:24
Luke 22:20
b. of the prophets *shed.* *Luke* 11:50
b. of Stephen was *shed.* *Acts* 22:20
they have *shed* the *b.* *Rev* 16:6

sprinkle **blood**
ram's *b.* and *sprinkle* it. *Ex* 29:16
sprinkle b. on altar. 20; *Lev* 1:5
11; 3:2, 8, 13; 7:2; 17:6
Num 18:17
sprinkle b. seven times. *Lev* 4:6, 17
16:14, 19
sprinkle b. of sin-offering on. 5:9
the priests that *sprinkle* the *b.* 7:14
sprinkle of the *b.* before. *Num* 19:4
sprinkle on it the *b.* *2 Ki* 16:15
an altar to *sprinkle b.* *Ezek* 43:18

blood *sprinkled*
half of *b.* Moses *sprinkled* on.
Ex 24:6; *Lev* 8:19, 24
Moses took *b.* and *sprinkled* on.
Ex 24:8
when there is *sprinkled b.* *Lev* 6:27
took *b.* and *sprinkled* on Aaron. 8:30
Aaron's sons *b.* *he sprinkled.* 9:12, 18
Athaliah's *b.* *sprinkled* on. *2 Ki* 9:33
Ahaz *sprinkled* the *b.* of his. 16:13
sprinkled b. of bullocks. *2 Chr* 29:22
30:16
the priests *sprinkled* the *b.* 35:11
their *b.* shall be *sprinkled.* *Isa* 63:3
he *sprinkled* with *b.* the. *Heb* 9:21

with **blood**
make atonement *with b.* *Ex* 30:10
cleanse the house *with b.* *Lev* 14:52
ye not eat any thing *with b.* 19:26
head bring down *with b.* *1 Ki* 2:9
land was polluted *with b.* *Ps* 106:38
filled *with b.* made fat *with b.*
Isa 34:6
their land shall be soaked *with b.* 7
be drunken *with* their own *b.* 49:26
your hands are defiled *with b.* 59:3
filled this place *with b.* *Jer* 19:4
be made drunk *with* their *b.* 46:10
polluted themselves *with b.*
Lam 4:14
plead against him *with b.* *Ezek* 38:22
a city polluted *with b.* *Hos* 6:8
they build up Zion *with b.* *Mi* 3:10
buildeth a town *with b.* *Hab* 2:12
I conferred not *with b.* *Gal* 1:16
all things purged *with b.* *Heb* 9:22
and fire, mingled *with b.* *Rev* 8:7
saw woman drunken *with b.* 17:6

bloodguiltiness
deliver me from *b.* *Ps* 51:14

bloodthirsty
the *b.* hate the upright. *Pr* 29:10

bloody
a *b.* husband art thou. *Ex* 4:25, 26
come out, thou *b.* man. *2 Sam* 16:7
famine is for Saul, and his *b.* 21:1
Lord will abhor *b.* man. *Ps* 5:6
gather not my life with *b.* men. 26:9
b. men not live out half their. 55:23
deliver me, save me from *b.* 59:2
depart from me ye *b.* men. 139:19
land is full of *b.* crimes. *Ezek* 7:23
wilt thou judge the *b.* city? 22:2
woe to the *b.* city. 24:6, 9; *Nah* 3:1
lay sick of a *b.* flux. *Acts* 28:8*

bloomed
Aaron's rod *b.* blossoms. *Num* 17:8

blossom
her *b.* shot forth. *Gen* 40:10
their *b.* shall go as dust. *Isa* 5:24

blossom, -ed
[1] *To put forth flowers,* Num 17:5; Hab 3:17. [2] *To increase and prosper,* Isa 27:6.
the man's rod shall *b.* *Num* 17:5*

Israel shall *b.* and bud. *Isa* 27:6
desert shall rejoice and *b.* 35:1
b. abundantly and rejoice. 2
the rod hath *b.* pride. *Ezek* 7:10
fig-tree shall not *b.* nor. *Hab* 3:17

blot
(*Spot, stain, disgrace*)
if any *b.* hath cleaved. *Job* 31:7
the wicked, getteth a *b.* *Pr* 9:7

blot *out*
(*Cancel, expunge, efface*)
not, *b.* me *out* of thy book. *Ex* 32:32
whosoever sinned, will I *b. out.* 33
shall *b.* them *out* with. *Num* 5:23
me alone that I *b. out.* *Deut* 9:14
b. out the remembrance of. 25:19
Lord shall *b. out* his name. 29:20
he would *b. out* Israel. *2 Ki* 14:27
have mercy, O God, *b. out.* *Ps* 51:1
hide my sins and *b. out* all. 9
nor *b. out* their sin from. *Jer* 18:23
I will not *b.* his name *out.* *Rev* 3:5

blotted
let not their sin be *b.* out. *Neh* 4:5
let them be *b.* out of. *Ps* 69:28
let their name be *b.* out. 109:13
not the sin of his mother be *b.* 14
b. out as a thick cloud. *Isa* 44:22
your sins may be *b.* out. *Acts* 3:19

blotteth, -ing
I am he that *b.* out thy. *Isa* 43:25
b. out the hand-writing. *Col* 2:14

blow
consumed by the *b.* of thy. *Ps* 39:10
broken with grievous *b.* *Jer* 14:17*

blow, *verb*
didst *b.* with thy wind. *Ex* 15:10
when ye *b.* an alarm. *Num* 10:5, 6
then ye shall *b.* an alarm. 9*
when I *b.*, then *b.* ye. *Judg* 7:18
caused an east-wind to *b.* *Ps* 78:26
caused his wind to *b.* 147:18
come, thou south, *b.* *S of S* 4:16
he shall also *b.* upon them. *Isa* 40:24
I *b.* against thee. *Ezek* 21:31; 22:21
b. ye the cornet in Gibeah. *Hos* 5:8
b. the trumpet in Zion. *Joel* 2:15
ye brought it, I did *b.* *Hag* 1:9
ye see south-wind *b.* *Luke* 12:55
that wind should not *b.* *Rev* 7:1
see **trumpet**

bloweth
Spirit of the Lord *b.* on it. *Isa* 40:7
I have created smith that *b.* 54:16
wind *b.* where it listeth. *John* 3:8

blown
fire not *b.* shall consume. *Job* 20:26

blue
b. purple. *Ex* 25:4; 26:1, 31, 36
27:16
robe of the ephod of *b.* 28:31; 39:22
cut gold to work it in the *b.* 39:3
the fringes ribband of *b.* *Num* 15:38
cunning to work in *b.* *2 Chr* 2:7, 14
b. hangings, pavement of *b.* *Esth* 1:6*
Mordecai went in apparel of *b.* 8:15
b. and purple is their. *Jer* 10:9
Assyrians clothed with *b.* *Ezek* 23:6
b. and purple from the isles. 27:7
in *b.* clothes and broidered. 24
see **purple, cloth, lace, loops**

blueness
b. of a wound cleanseth. *Pr* 20:30*

blunt
if iron be *b.* and he do. *Eccl* 10:10

blush
I *b.* to lift my face to thee. *Ezra* 9:6
neither could they *b.* *Jer* 6:15; 8:12

Boanerges
surnamed them *B.* *Mark* 3:17

boar
b. out of the wood. *Ps* 80:13

board, -s
overlay *b.* with gold. *Ex* 26:29; 36:34
hollow with *b.* make. 27:8
under every *b.* were two. 36:30
under Merari shall be *b.* *Num* 3:36
will enclose her with *b.* *S of S* 8:9
the rest, some on *b.* *Acts* 27:44*

boast, *substantive*
my soul shall make her *b.* *Ps* 34:2
Jew, and makest thy *b.* *Rom* 2:17*
thou that makest thy *b.* 23*

boast, *verb*
not *b.* as he that putteth. *1 Ki* 20:11
heart lifteth thee to *b.* *2 Chr* 25:19
in God we *b.* all the day. *Ps* 44:8
b. themselves in their riches. 49:6
the workers of inquity *b.* 94:4
confounded be they that *b.* of. 97:7
b. not thyself of. *Pr* 27:1
shall the axe *b.* itself. *Isa* 10:15
in their glory shall you *b.* 61:6
b. not against branches, if thou *b.*
Rom 11:18*
for which I *b.* to them. *2 Cor* 9:2*
for though I should *b.* 10:8*
we will not *b.* of things. 13*
to *b.* in another man's line. 16*
receive me that I may *b.* 11:16*
not of works lest any *b.* *Eph* 2:9*

boasted
with mouth ye have *b.* *Ezek* 35:13*
if I have *b.* any thing. *2 Cor* 7:14*

boasters
proud, *b.* inventors of. *Rom* 1:30
covetous, *b.* proud. *2 Tim* 3:2

boastest, -eth
the wicked *b.* of his. *Ps* 10:3
why *b.* thou in mischief ? 52:1
gone his way, then he *b.* *Pr* 20:14
whoso *b.* of a false gift. 25:14
a little member, and *b.* *Jas* 3:5

boasting, *participle*
rose Theudas, *b.* himself. *Acts* 5:36*
not *b.* of things without. *2 Cor* 10:15*

boasting, *substantive*
where is *b.* then ? *Rom* 3:27*
b. before Titus is. *2 Cor* 7:14*
shew ye the proof of our *b.* 8:24*
lest our *b.* of you should be. 9:3*
should be ashamed in confident *b.* 4*
shall stop me of this *b.* 11:10*
were foolishly in confidence of *b.* 17*
but now ye rejoice in *b.* *Jas* 4:16

boat, -s
people saw there was no *b.*, and that
Jesus went not into *b.* *John* 6:22
came other *b.* from Tiberias. 23
work to come by the *b.* *Acts* 27:16
when they had let down the *b.* 30
soldiers cut off the ropes of *b.* 32

Boaz
left pillar called *B.* *1 Ki* 7:21
2 Chr 3:17

Boaz
kinsman, his name was *B.* *Ruth* 2:1
with whom I wrought, is *B.* 19
is not *B.* of our kindred ? 3:2
when *B.* had eaten. 7
then went *B.* up to the gate. 4:1
so *B.* took Ruth. 13
B. begat Obed. 21; *1 Chr* 2:12
Mat 1:5
Obed the son of *B.* *Luke* 3:32

Bochim
came from Gilgal to *B.* *Judg* 2:1
called the name of place *B.* 5

bodies
ought left, but our *b.* *Gen* 47:18
took *b.* of Saul's sons. *1 Sam* 31:12
1 Chr 10:12
dominion over our *b.* *Neh* 9:37
b. are like unto *b.* of. *Job* 13:12*
two wings covered *b.* *Ezek* 1:11 23
on whose *b.* fire had. *Dan* 3:27
yielded their *b.* that they might. 28
many *b.* of saints which. *Mat* 27:52
b. should not remain on. *John* 19:31
to dishonour their own *b.* *Rom* 1:24
shall quicken your mortal *b.* 8:11
that ye present your *b.* a. 12:1
b. are members of. *1 Cor* 6:15
are celestial *b.* and *b.* 15:40
their wives as their own *b.* *Eph* 5:28
b. washed with pure. *Heb* 10:22
the *b.* of beasts, whose. 13:11

dead **bodies**
were *dead b.* fallen. *2 Chr* 20:24
they found with *dead* 25
dead b. of thy servants. *Ps* 79:2
fill the places with the *dead b.* 110:6
valley of *dead b.* shall be. *Jer* 31:40
fill them with *dead b.* of men. 33:5
dead b. shall be for meat. 34:20
wherein Ishmael cast *dead b.* 41:9
shall be many *dead b.* *Amos* 8:3
dead b. shall lie in. *Rev* 11:8
nations see their *dead b.*, nor suffer
their *dead b.* to be put in. 9

bodily
descended in *b.* shape. *Luke* 3:22
his *b.* presence is weak. *2 Cor* 10:10
fulness of the Godhead *b.* *Col* 2:9
b. exercise profiteth little. *1 Tim* 4:8

body
[1] *The physical part of man as distinct from the spiritual,* 1 Sam 31:4; Mat 6:22. [2] *Used figuratively for the Church,* 1 Cor 12:27; Eph 3:6.

as the *b.* of heaven in. *Ex* 24:10*
took the *b.* of Saul. *1 Sam* 31:12
1 Chr 10:12
sake of my own *b.* *Job* 19:17†
my skin worms destroy this *b.* 26
drawn and cometh out of *b.* 20:25
when thy flesh and *b.* *Pr* 5:11
consume both soul and *b.* *Isa* 10:18
and thou hast laid thy *b.* 51:23*
their whole *b.* full. *Ezek* 10:12
in spirit in midst of *b.* *Dan* 7:15
whole *b.* be cast into. *Mat* 5:29, 30
light of *b.* is eye. 6:22; *Luke* 11:34
b. full of light. *Mat* 6:22
Luke 11:34, 36
b. shall be full of darkness. *Mat* 6:23
no thought for *b.* 25; *Luke* 12:22
b. more than raiment. *Mat* 6:25
Luke 12:23
them which kill *b.* *Mat* 10:28
Luke 12:4
disciples came and took *b.* *Mat* 14:12
poured this ointment on my *b.* 26:12
Jesus said, take, eat, this is my *b.*
26:26; *Mark* 14:22; *Luke* 22:19
1 Cor 11:24
Joseph begged the *b.* of Jesus. *Mat*
27:58; *Mark* 15:43; *Luke* 23:52
in *b.* that she was healed. *Mark* 5:29
is come to anoint my *b.* 14:8
a linen cloth cast about his *b.* 51
gave *b.* to Joseph. 15:45; *Mat* 27:58
where the *b.* is, thither. *Luke* 17:37
found not *b.* of Lord Jesus. 24:3
the *b.* of Jesus had lain. *John* 20:12
the *b.* of sin destroyed. *Rom* 6:6
dead to the law by *b.* of Christ. 7:4
deliver me from *b.* of this ? 24
Christ in you, the *b.* is dead. 8:10
the Spirit mortify deeds of *b.* 13
adoption, redemption of *b.* 23
b. is not for fornication, but the Lord,
and the Lord for *b.* *1 Cor* 6:13
every sin is without the *b.* 18
b. is the temple of Holy Ghost. 19
hath no power of her own *b.* 7:4
I keep under my *b.* 9:27
communion of the *b.* of Christ. 10:16
guilty of the *b.* and blood of. 11:27
not discerning the Lord's *b.* 29
for the *b.* is not one member. 12:14
is it therefore not of *b.* ? 15, 16
whole *b.* were an eye where. 12:17
where were the *b.* ? 19
yet but one *b.* 20
now ye are the *b.* of Christ. 27
though I give my *b.* to be. 13:3
with what *b.* do dead come ? 15:35
thou sowest not that *b.* that. 37
but God giveth it a *b.* as. 38
natural *b.* raised spiritual *b.* 44
to be absent from *b.* *2 Cor* 5:8
fellow-heirs of the same *b.* *Eph* 3:6
for edifying of *b.* of Christ. 4:12
from whom whole *b.* fitly joined. 16
he is the Saviour of the *b.* 5:23
shall change our vile *b.* *Phil* 3:21
he is the head of the *b.* *Col* 1:18
in putting off the *b.* of the sins. 2:11
a shadow, but the *b.* is of Christ. 17
from which the *b.* by joints. 19
shew of wisdom in neglecting *b.* 23

pray your soul and *b.* *1 Thes* 5:23
b. hast thou prepared me. *Heb* 10:5
through offering of the *b.* of Jesus. 10
not things needful to *b.* *Jas* 2:16
as *b.* without the Spirit is dead. 26
and is able to bridle the whole *b.* 3:2
we turn about their whole *b.* 3
the tongue defileth the whole *b.* 6
disputed about *b.* of Moses *Jude* 9

dead **body**

not go into any *dead b.* *Lev* 21:11
Num 6:6
defiled by a *dead b.* *Num* 9:6, 7
unclean by *dead b.* 10; *Hag* 2:13
toucheth *dead b.* *Num* 19:11, 16
restored a *dead b.* to life. *2 Ki* 8:5*
with my *dead b.* shall. *Isa* 26:19*
cast his *dead b.* into. *Jer* 26:23
his *dead b.* shall be cast out. 36:30

fruit of the **body**

blessed the *fruit of thy b.* *Deut* 28:4
plenteous in *fruit of thy b.* 11; 30:9
cursed shall be *fruit of thy b.* 28:18
shalt eat the *fruit of thy b.* 53
fruit of thy b. will I set. *Ps* 132:11
fruit of my b. for sin of my. *Mi* 6:7

his **body**

his b. not remain. *Deut* 21:23
had 70 sons of *his b.* *Judg* 8:30
fastened *his b.* to wall. *1 Sam* 31:10
his b. wet with dew. *Dan* 4:33; 5:21
till beast was slain, and *his b.* 7:11
his b. also was like the beryl. 10:6
how *his b.* was laid. *Luke* 23:55
when they found not *his b.* 24:23
the temple of *his b.* *John* 2:21
his b. were brought. *Acts* 19:12
he considered not *his b.* *Rom* 4:19
sinneth against *his b.* *1 Cor* 6:18
the power of *his* own *b.* 7:4
the things done in *his b.* *2 Cor* 5:10
which is *his b.* fulness. *Eph* 1:23
like to *his* glorious *b.* *Phil* 3:21
for *his b.* sake. *Col* 1:24
bare our sins in *his b.* *1 Pet* 2:24

in **body**

ruddy *in b.* than rubies. *Lam* 4:7
let not sin reign *in b.* *Rom* 6:12
I verily as absent *in b.* *1 Cor* 5:3
glorify God *in* your *b.* 6:20
that she may be holy *in b.* 7:34
members every one *in* the *b.* 12:18
be no schism *in* the *b.* 25
bearing *in* the *b.* the dying of our
Lord that life *in* our *b.* *2 Cor* 4:10
whilst we are at home *in b.* 5:6
in b. or out of the *b.* 12:2
I bear *in b.* marks of Lord. *Gal* 6:17
Christ magnified *in* my *b.* *Phil* 1:20
reconciled *in b.* of his. *Col* 1:22
yourselves also *in* the *b.* *Heb* 13:3

one **body**

many members in *one b.* *Rom* 12:4
are *one b.* in Christ. 5; *1 Cor* 10:17
joined to harlot, is *one b.* *1 Cor* 6:16
as the *b.* is *one.* 12:12
baptized into *one b.* whether. 13
many members, yet but *one b.* 20
both to God in *one b* *Eph* 2:16
there is *one b.* and one Spirit. 4:4
ye are called in *one b.* *Col* 3:15

boil

it shall be a *b.* with blains. *Ex* 9:9
it became a *b.* breaking forth. 10
could not stand because of the *b.* 11
b. the flesh at the door. *Lev* 8:31
flesh also in which was a *b.* 13:18
took figs and laid on the *b.* *2 Ki* 20:7
Isa 38:21
smote Job with sore *b.* *Job* 2:7
he maketh the deep to *b.* 41:31
fire causeth waters to *b.* *Isa* 64:2
and make it *b.* well. *Ezek* 24:5
place where priests shall *b.* 46:20, 24

boiled

yoke of oxen and *b.* them. *1 Ki* 19:21
so we *b.* my son. *2 Ki* 6:29
my bowels *b.*, rested not. *Job* 30:27

boiling

made with *b.* places. *Ezek* 46:23

boisterous

when he saw wind *b.* *Mat* 14:30*

bold

righteous are *b.* as a lion. *Pr* 28:1
and Barnabas waxed *b.* *Acts* 13:46
Esaias is very *b.* and. *Rom* 10:20
being absent, am *b.* *2 Cor* 10:1*
b. wherewith I think to be *b.* 2*
wherein any is *b.* I am *b.* 11:21
much more *b.* to speak. *Phil* 1:14
we were *b.* in our God. *1 Thes* 2:2
though I might be much *b.* *Philem* 8

boldly

Levi came on the city *b.* *Gen* 34:25*
came, and went in *b.* *Mark* 15:43
he speaketh *b.* and. *John* 7:26*
how he preached *b.* *Acts* 9:27
he spake *b.* in name of the Lord. 29
time abode they, speaking *b.* 14:3
Apollos began to speak *b.* 18:26
spake *b.* for the space of. 19:8
have written the more *b.* *Rom* 15:15
I may open my mouth *b.* *Eph* 6:19
that I may speak *b.* as I ought. 20
let us come *b.* to. *Heb* 4:16
that we may *b.* say. 13:6*

boldness

the *b.* of his face shall. *Eccl* 8:1*
when they saw the *b.* of. *Acts* 4:13
that with all *b.* they may speak. 29
spake the word of God with *b.* 31
great is my *b.* of speech. *2 Cor* 7:4
in whom we have *b.* *Eph* 3:12
but that with all *b.* *Phil* 1:20
they purchase great *b.* *1 Tim* 3:13
having *b.* to enter. *Heb* 10:19
that we may have *b.* *1 John* 4:17

bolled

(*Gone to seed*)

barley in the ear, and flax *b.* *Ex* 9:31

bolster

goats' hair for his *b.* *1 Sam* 19:13, 16
spear at *b.* 26:7, 11, 12
water at *b.* 16

bolt, -ed

b. the door. *2 Sam* 13:17
he *b.* the door. 18

bond

bind his soul with a *b.* *Num* 30:2
vow and bind herself by a *b.* 3
father hear her vow and her *b.* 4
I will bring you into *b.* *Ezek* 20:37
be loosed from his *b.* *Luke* 13:16
in the *b.* of inquity. *Acts* 8:23
baptized into one body, *b.* or free.
1 Cor 12:13
unity of the Spirit, in *b.* *Eph* 4:3
put on charity, the *b.* of. *Col* 3:14

see **free**

bondage

[1] *Slavery*, Ex 2:23; Ezra 9:8, 9. [2] *Subjection to sin*, Gal 4:3. [3] *Subjection to the ceremonial law*, Gal 2:4.

lives bitter with hard *b.* *Ex* 1:14
Israel sighed by reason of the *b.*
cried to God by reason of *b.* 2:23
I will rid you out of their *b.* 6:6
not to Moses for cruel *b.* 9
ye came out of the house of *b.* 13:3
Lord brought us out of *b.* 14; 20:2
Deut 5:6; 6:12; 8:14; 13:5, 10
Josh 24:17; *Judg* 6:8
laid upon us hard *b.* *Deut* 26:6
bring into *b.* our sons and daughters,
some are brought into *b.* *Neh* 5:5
because the *b.* was heavy. 18
a captain to return to *b.* 9:17
rest from thy hard *b.* *Isa* 14:3
not received spirit of *b.* *Rom* 8:15
delivered from *b.* of. 21
Sinai, which gendereth to *b.* *Gal* 4:24
be not entangled with yoke of *b.* 5:1
all their life subject to *b.* *Heb* 2:15

in, into, or *under* **bondage**

the Egyptians keep *in b.* *Ex* 6:5
a little reviving *in* our *b.* *Ezra* 9:8
God hath not forsaken us *in b.* 9
we were never *in b.* to. *John* 8:33
should bring them *into b.* *Acts* 7:6
nation to whom they be *in b.* 7
or sister not *under b.* *1 Cor* 7:15
a man bring you *into b.* *2 Cor* 11:20
bring us *into b.* *Gal* 2:4
were *in b.* under the elements. 4:3
ye desire again to be *in b.* 9
to Jerusalem, which is *in b.* 25
is he brought *into b.* *2 Pet* 2:19

bondmaid, -s

whoso lieth with a *b.* *Lev* 19:20
b. shall be heathen, buy ye *b.* 25:44
one by a *b.* the other by. *Gal* 4:22*

bondman

abide instead of lad a *b.* *Gen* 44:33
thou wast a *b.* the Lord redeemed.
Deut 15:15; 16:12; 24:18, 22
every *b.* hid themselves. *Rev* 6:15

bondmen

he may take us for *b.* *Gen* 43:18
we will be my lord's *b.* 44:9
shall not be sold as *b.* *Lev* 25:42
b. of the heathen, of them buy *b.* 44
they shall be your *b.* for ever. 46
that ye should not be their *b.* 26:13
we were Pharaoh's *b.* *Deut* 6:21
you out of house of *b.* 7:8*
there ye shall be sold for *b.* 28:68
of you freed from *b.* *Josh* 9:23
Solomon made no *b.* *1 Ki* 9:22
to take my two sons to be *b.* *2 Ki* 4:1
children of Judah for *b.* *2 Chr* 28:10
we were *b.* yet God hath. *Ezra* 9:9
if we had been sold for *b.* *Esth* 7:4
out of the house of *b.* *Jer* 34:13*

bonds

not any of her vows or *b.* *Num* 30:5
b. wherewith she bound her. 7
he established all her *b.* 14
he looseth *b.* of kings. *Job* 12:18
thou hast loosed my *b.* *Ps* 116:16
the yoke, and burst the *b.* *Jer* 5:5*
make thee *b.* and yokes. 27:2*
his yoke, and burst thy *b.* 30:8*
I will burst *b.* in sunder. *Nah* 1:13
b. with afflictions abide. *Acts* 20:23
worthy of death or *b.* 23:29; 26:31
a certain man left in *b.* by. 25:14*
such as I am, except these *b.* 26:29
I am an ambassador in *b.* *Eph* 6:20*
in *b.* ye are partakers of. *Phil* 1:7
b. in Christ are manifest. 13
waxing confident by my *b.* 14
supposing to add affliction to *b.* 16
for which I am in *b.* *Col* 4:3
remember my *b.* 18
I suffer trouble, even to *b.* *2 Tim* 2:9
I have begotten in my *b.* *Philem* 10
ministered to me in the *b.* 13
had compassion in my *b.* *Heb* 10:34
of *b.* and imprisonment. 11:36
remember them that are in *b.* 13:3

bondservant

him to serve as a *b.* *Lev* 25:39

bondservice

levy a tribute of *b.* *1 Ki* 9:21

bondwoman

cast out this *b.* and her son, son of
b. shall not. *Gen* 21:10; *Gal* 4:30
not grievous because of *b.* *Gen* 21:12
son of the *b.* will I make. 13
son of the *b.* was born. *Gal* 4:23*
we are not children of the *b.* 31*

bondwomen, *see* **bondmen**

bone

this is *b.* of my bones. *Gen* 2:23
surely thou art my *b.* 29:14
break a *b.* *Ex* 12:46; *Num* 9:12
toucheth a *b.* of a man. *Num* 19:16
that I am your *b.* *Judg* 9:2
are thy *b.* *2 Sam* 5:1; *1 Chr* 11:1
art thou not of my *b.*? *2 Sam* 19:13
touch his *b.* and flesh. *Job* 2:5
my *b.* cleaveth to my skin. 19:20
arm be broken from the *b.* 31:22
soft tongue breaketh *b.* *Pr* 25:15
bones came together, *b.* to his *b.*
Ezek 37:7
when any seeth a man's *b.* 39:15
a *b.* shall not be broken. *John* 19:36

bones

(*Sometimes used as meaning the whole body*)

Moses took the *b.* of. *Ex* 13:19
the *b.* of Joseph. *Josh* 24:32

divided his concubine with her *b.* *Judg* 19:29*
took the *b.* of Saul, *b.* *2 Sam* 21:12
b. of Saul and Jonathan buried. 14
men's *b.* shall be burnt. *1 Ki* 13:2
touched the *b.* of Elisha. *2 Ki* 13:21
filled the places with *b.* of. 23:14
and took the *b.* out of the. 16
he burnt men's *b.* upon altars. 20
he burnt the *b.* of the. *2 Chr* 34:5
hast fenced me with *b.* *Job* 10:11
b. thou hast broken may. *Ps* 51:8
God scattereth the *b.* of him. 53:5
our *b.* are scattered at grave's. 141:7
it shall be marrow to thy *b.* *Pr* 3:8
envy the rottenness of *b.* 14:30
a good report maketh the *b.* 15:30
pleasant words health to *b.* 16:24
a broken spirit drieth the *b.* 17:22
nor how the *b.* do grow. *Eccl* 11:5
Lord shall make fat thy *b.* *Isa* 58:11
your *b.* shall flourish. 66:14
bring the *b.* of the kings, *b.* of priests, *b.* of prophets, and *b.* *Jer* 8:1
I will scatter your *b.* *Ezek* 6:5
fill it with the choice *b.* 24:4
burn *b.* 5, 10
valley full of *b.* 37:1
can these *b.* live? 3
prophesy upon these *b*, O ye dry *b.* 4
these *b.* are house of Israel, our *b.* 11
because he burnt *b.* of. *Amos* 2:1
burneth him, to bring out *b.* 6:10
they gnaw not the *b.* till. *Zeph* 3:3*
full of dead men's *b.* *Mat* 23:27
spirit hath not flesh and *b.* *Luke* 24:39

his **bones**

lay my *b.* beside *his b.* *1 Ki* 13:31
man move *his b.* so they let *his b.* *2 Ki* 23:18
his b. are full of sin of. *Job* 20:11
his b. are moistened with. 21:24
the multitude of *his b.* 33:19
and *his b.* that were not seen. 21
his b. as brass, *his b.* as iron. 40:18*
he keepeth all *his b.* *Ps* 34:20
let it come like oil into *his b.* 109:18
as rottenness in *his b.* *Pr* 12:4
hath broken *his b.* *Jer* 50:17
of his flesh and of *his b.* *Eph* 5:30
gave command concerning *his b.* *Heb* 11:22

my **bones**

carry up *my b.* *Gen* 50:25; *Ex* 13:19
ye are *my b.* and my. *2 Sam* 19:12
my b. beside his *b.* *1 Ki* 13:31
made all *my b.* to shake. *Job* 4:14
my b. are pierced in me. 30:17
my skin is black, *my b.* burnt. 30
O Lord, heal me, *my b.* are. *Ps* 6:2
all *my b.* are out of joint. 22:14
I may tell *my b.* 17
my b. are consumed. 31:10
my b. waxed old. 32:3
my b. shall say, Lord who? 35:10
neither there rest in *my b.* 38:3
as with a sword in *my b.* 42:10
days consumed, *my b.* are. 102:3
by reason of groaning *my b.* 5
so will he break all *my b.* *Isa* 38:13
as a fire shut up in *my b.* *Jer* 20:9
is broken, all *my b.* shake. 23:9
he sent fire into *my b.* *Lam* 1:13
he hath broken *my b.* 3:4
rottenness entered *my b.* *Hab* 3:16

their **bones**

Israel shall break *their b.* *Num* 24:8
their b. and buried. *1 Sam* 31:13
buried *their b.* under. *1 Chr* 10:12
skin cleaveth to *their b.* *Lam* 4:8
shall be on *their b.* *Ezek* 32:27
lions brake all *their b.* *Dan* 6:24
skin and flesh from *their b.* *Mi* 3:2
they break *their b.* and chop. 3

bonnets

(*Revised Version,* headtires)
thou shalt make *b.* *Ex* 28:40
put the *b.* on them. 29:9; *Lev* 8:13
they made goodly *b.* *Ex* 39:28
Lord will take away *b.* *Isa* 3:20
they shall have linen *b.* *Ezek* 44:18

book

(*A record written in some permanent form. Ancient books were written on clay tablets, as in Assyria; on sheets of papyrus fastened together and (usually) rolled on one or two sticks; or of parchment in like form. Rarely sheets were fastened together somewhat like our books. The word book is sometimes used merely meaning record of any sort*)
a memorial in a *b.* *Ex* 17:14
blot me out of thy *b.* 32:32
sinned, will I blot out of my *b.* 33
write these curses in a *b.* *Num* 5:23
it is said in the *b.* of the wars. 21:14
a copy of his law in a *b.* *Deut* 17:18
made end of writing law in *b.* 31:24
in the book of Jasher. *Josh* 10:13 *2 Sam* 1:18
seven parts in a *b.* *Josh* 18:9
Samuel wrote it in a *b.* *1 Sam* 10:25
written in the *b.* of acts. *1 Ki* 11:41
Hilkiah gave the *b.* to. *2 Ki* 22:8
Hilkiah delivered me a *b.* 10 *2 Chr* 34:15, 18
all the words of the *b.* *2 Ki* 22:16
the words written in *b.* 23:24
written in *b.* of kings. *1 Chr* 9:1
written in the *b.* of Samuel. 29:29*
acts of Solomon in *b.* *2 Chr* 9:29*
acts of Rehoboam in *b.* 12:15*
acts of Jehoshaphat in *b.* 20:34*
Shaphan carried *b.* to king. 34:16
words of the *b.* that is found. 21
curses that are written in the b. 24
search may be made in *b.* *Ezra* 4:15
Ezra opened the *b.* *Neh* 8:5
commanded to bring the *b.* *Esth* 6:1
Purim, and it was written in *b.* 9:32
they were printed in *b.* *Job* 19:23
adversary had written a *b.* 31:35*
in thy *b.* *Ps* 40:7; *Heb* 10:7
tears, are they not in thy *b.*? *Ps* 56:8
let them be blotted out of *b.* 69:28
in thy *b.* all my members. 139:16
as the words of a *b.* *Isa* 29:11
b. is delivered to him that. 12
deaf shall hear words of the *b.* 18
now go and note it in a *b.* 30:8
seek ye out of *b.* of the Lord. 34:16
write the words in a *b.* *Jer* 30:2
that subscribed the *b.* of. 32:12*
take a roll of a *b.* 36:2
read in the *b.* 10
written the words in a *b.* 45:1
so Jeremiah wrote in a *b.* all. 51:60
and lo, a roll of a *b.* *Ezek* 2:9
one found written in *b.* *Dan* 12:1
O Daniel, seal the *b.* 4
b. of the vision of Nahum. *Nah* 1:1
a *b.* of remembrance. *Mal* 3:16
the *b.* of the generation. *Mat* 1:1
as it is written in the *b.* *Luke* 3:4
delivered to Jesus the *b.* of prophet Esaias, and he opened the *b.* 4:17
he closed the *b.* and gave it to. 20
in *b.* of Psalms. 20:42; *Acts* 1:20
it is written in the *b.* *Acts* 7:42
he sprinkled the *b.* *Heb* 9:19
what thou seest, write in *b.* *Rev* 1:11
a *b.* written within. 5:1
who is worthy to open the *b.*? 2
no man was able to open the *b.* 3
he had in his hand a little *b.* 10:2
go and take the little *b.* 8
give me the little *b.* 9
I took the little *b.* 10
another *b.* was opened, the *b.* 20:12
if any take away from words of *b.* 22:19*

see **covenant**

book *of the law*

plague not in *b. of law.* *Deut* 28:61
curses in this *b. of the law.* 29:21
statutes in this *b. of the law.* 30:10
take this *b. of the law.* 31:26
this *b. of the law.* *Josh* 1:8
in *b. of the law.* 8:31; *2 Ki* 14:6
have found *b. of the law.* *2 Ki* 22:8
read in the *b. of the law.* *Neh* 8:8
are written in *b. of the law.* *Gal* 3:10

book *of life*

are written in *b. of life.* *Phil* 4:3
his name out of *b. of life.* *Rev* 3:5
not written in *b. of life.* 13:8; 17:8
b. opened, which is *b. of life.* 20:12
was not found in the *b. of life.* 15
written in Lamb's *b. of life.* 21:27
his part out of the *b. of life.* 22:19

book *of Moses*

is written in *b. of Moses.* *2 Chr* 25:4
as it is written in *b. of Moses.* 35:12
priests, as written in *b. of Moses.* *Ezra* 6:18
day they read in the *b. of Moses.* *Neh* 13:1
ye not read in the *b. of Moses*? *Mark* 12:26

this **book**

this is the *b.* of generation. *Gen* 5:1
do all written in *this b.* *Deut* 28:58 *2 Chr* 34:21
curses written in *this b.* *Deut* 29:20, 27
words of *this b.*, not hearkened to the words of *this b.* *2 Ki* 22:13
perform words written in *this b.* 23:3
all that is written in *this b.* *Jer* 25:13
an end of reading *this b.* 51:63
are not written in *this b.* *John* 20:30
the prophecy of *this b.* *Rev* 22:7
keep the sayings of *this b.* 9
seal not prophecy of *this b.* 10
prophecy of *this b.* if any add, add to him plagues written in *this b.* 18
his part from things in *this b.* 19

books

of making many *b.* *Eccl* 12:12
the *b.* were opened. *Dan* 7:10 *Rev* 20:12
I understood by *b.* the. *Dan* 9:2
could not contain the *b.* *John* 21:25
many brought their *b.* *Acts* 19:19
bring the *b.* especially. *2 Tim* 4:13
dead judged out of *b.* *Rev* 20:12

booth

as *b.* the keeper maketh. *Job* 27:18
Jonah made him a *b.* *Jonah* 4:5

booths

and Jacob made *b.* for. *Gen* 33:17
ye shall dwell in *b.* *Lev* 23:42
children of Israel dwell in *b.* 43
Israel should dwell in *b.* *Neh* 8:14
made *b.* 16

booty, -ies

b. the rest of the prey. *Num* 31:32
their camels shall be a *b.* *Jer* 49:32
thou shalt be for *b.* *Hab* 2:7
goods shall become a *b.* *Zeph* 1:13

border

Zebulun his *b.* shall. *Gen* 49:13
or touch the *b.* of the. *Ex* 19:12
it a *b.* of a handbreath, make a golden crown to the *b.* 25:25
Israel through his *b.* *Num* 21:23
ye shall point out your *b.* 34:8
slayer shall come without *b.* 35:26
Lord shall enlarge thy *b.* *Deut* 12:20
Lord made Jordan a *b.* *Josh* 22:25
buried Joshua in the *b.* of his inheritance in. 24:30; *Judg* 2:9
he went to recover his *b.* *2 Sam* 8:3*
Solomon reigned over kingdoms unto *b.* of. *1 Ki* 4:21; *2 Chr* 9:26
were able stood in *b.* *2 Ki* 3:21
brought them to the *b.* of. *Ps* 78:54
he will establish the *b.* *Pr* 15:25
into the height of his *b.* *Isa* 37:24
children come again to *b.* *Jer* 31:17
judge you in *b.* of. *Ezek* 11:10, 11
this shall be the *b.* whereby. 47:13
remove them from their *b.* *Joel* 3:6
might enlarge their *b.* *Amos* 1:13
their *b.* greater than your *b.* 6:2
have brought thee even to *b.* *Ob* 7
themselves against their *b.* *Zeph* 2:8
shall call them the *b.* of. *Mal* 1:4
Lord will be magnified from *b.* of. 5
if it were but the *b.* *Mark* 6:56
behind, and touched *b.* *Luke* 8:44

see **east, south**

border, *verb*

Hamath shall *b.* thereby. *Zech* 9:2

borders
the trees in all the *b.* *Gen* 23:17
till they come to the *b.* *Ex* 16:35
out nations, and enlarge *b.* 34:24
fringes in *b.* on fringe of *b.* a ribband.
Num 15:38
until we passed *b.* 20:17; 21:22
they had *b.* and *b.* were. *1 Ki* 7:28†
Ahaz cut off the *b.* of. *2 Ki* 16:17
I will enter lodgings of his *b.* 19:23*
thou hast set the *b.* of the. *Ps* 74:17
he maketh peace in thy *b.* 147:14
we will make the *b.* of. *S of S* 1:11*
I will make thy *b.* of. *Isa* 54:12
for all thy sins, in thy *b.* *Jer* 15:13
shall be holy in the *b.* *Ezek* 45:1
he treadeth within our *b.* *Mi* 5:6
in the *b.* of Zabulon. *Mat* 4:13
enlarge the *b.* of their garments. 23:5

bore, -ed
master shall *b.* his ear. *Ex* 21:6
Jehoiada took chest *b.* *2 Ki* 12:9
canst thou *b.* his jaw? *Job* 41:2*

born *again*
except a man be *b. a.* *John* 3:3, 5
ye must be *b. a.* 7
being *b. a.* not of. *1 Pet* 1:23

***see* first-born**

born, for *brought forth*
a child *b.* to him. *Gen* 17:17; 21:5
I have *b.* him a son. 21:7
Rebekah came, who was *b.* 24:15
because I have *b.* him three. 29:34
because I have *b.* him six. 30:20
children which they have *b.*? 31:43
every son *b.* ye shall cast. *Ex* 1:22
law of her that hath *b.* *Lev* 12:7
stranger shall be as one *b.* 19:34*
Israelites *b.* shall dwell in. 23:42
law for him that is *b.* *Num* 15:29
b. in the wilderness. *Josh* 5:5
as well stranger, as he *b.* 8:33*
the child that shall be *b.* *Judg* 13:8
city after name of Dan *b.* to. 18:29
daughter-in-law hath *b.* *Ruth* 4:15
so that the barren hath *b.* *1 Sam* 2:5
fear not, thou hast *b.* a son. 4:20
child *b.* to thee shall. *2 Sam* 12:14
a child shall be *b.* to. *1 Ki* 13:2
the men of Gath *b.* in. *1 Chr* 7:21
behold a son shall be *b.* 22:9
day perish wherein I was *b.* *Job* 3:3
yet man is *b.* to trouble as. 5:7
though man be *b.* like a wild. 11:12
thou the first man *b.*? 15:7
because thou wast then *b.*? 38:21
to people that shall be *b.* *Ps* 22:31
go astray as soon as they be *b.* 58:3
even children that should be *b.* 78:6
this man was *b.* there. 87:4, 6
that man *b.* 5
a brother is *b.* for. *Pr* 17:17
a time to be *b.* *Eccl* 3:2
b. in his kingdom. 4:14
for unto us a child is *b.* *Isa* 9:6
shall a nation be *b.* at once? 66:8
she that hath *b.* seven. *Jer* 15:9
woe is me, that thou hast *b.* 10
sons and daughters *b.* in this. 16:3
cursed be day wherein I was *b.* 20:14
where ye were not *b.* there. 22:26
in day thou wast *b.* *Ezek* 16:4
thy person in day thou wast *b.* 5
sons whom thou hast *b.* to me. 20
in the day that she was *b.* *Hos* 2:3
where is he that is *b.* king? *Mat* 2:2
where Christ should be *b.* 4
eunuchs which were so *b.* 19:12
had not been *b.* 26:24; *Mark* 14:21
holy thing that shall be *b.* *Luke* 1:35
to you is *b.* this day in city. 2:11
can a man be *b.* when? *John* 3:4
except a man be *b.* of water. 5
that *b.* of flesh is flesh, that *b.* of. 6
so is every one that is *b.* of. 8
they said to him, we be not *b.* 8:41
did sin, that he was *b.* blind? 9:2
wast altogether *b.* in sins, and? 34
for joy that a man is *b.* 16:21
to this end was I *b.* 18:37
tongue wherein we were *b.* *Acts* 2:8
in which time Moses was *b.* 7:20
Jew named Aquila *b.* in. *Acts* 18:2*
a Jew named Apollos *b.* at. 24*
I am a Jew *b.* in Tarsus. 22:3
I was free *b.* 28
children being not yet *b.* *Rom* 9:11
seen of me, as of one *b.* *1 Cor* 15:8
of bond-woman, *b.* *Gal* 4:23, 29
by faith Moses when *b.* *Heb* 11:23
as new *b.* babes desire. *1 Pet* 2:2
righteousness, is *b.* of. *1 John* 2:29*
the child as soon as *b.* *Rev* 12:4

born *of God*
b. not of blood, but *of God.*
John 1:13
b. of God doth not commit sin, because *b. of God.* *1 John* 3:9
one that loveth is *b. of God.* 4:7
Jesus is Christ is *b. of God.* 5:1
is *b. of God* overcometh. 4
is *b. of God* sinneth not. 18

born *in the house*
servants *b. in* his *house.* *Gen* 14:14
one *b. in* my *house* is my heir. 15:3
b. in the house circumcised. 17:12
13, 23, 27
b. in the priest's *house.* *Lev* 22:11
servants *b. in* my *house.* *Eccl* 2:7

born *in the land*
stranger or *b. in the land.* *Ex* 12:19
the stranger as *b. in the land.* 48
b. in the land that blasphemeth.
Lev 24:16*
stranger and *b. in land.* *Num* 9:14
whether *b. in land.* 15:30*

born *of a woman,* or *women*
man that is *b. of a woman.* *Job* 14:1
that is *b. of a woman* that he? 15:14
he be clean *b. of a woman*? 25:4
them that are *b. of a woman.*
Mat 11:11; *Luke* 7:28

borne
ark may be *b.* with them. *Ex* 25:14
that the table may be *b.* with. 28
which the house was *b.* *Judg* 16:29
I have *b.* chastisement. *Job* 34:31
enemy, then I could have *b.* *Ps* 55:12
for thy sake I have *b.* 69:7
surely he hath *b.* griefs. *Isa* 53:4
ye shall be *b.* upon her sides. 66:12
they must be *b.* because. *Jer* 10:5
because he hath *b.* it. *Lam* 3:28*
fathers sinned, and we have *b.* 5:7
hast *b.* thy lewdness. *Ezek* 16:58
b. their shame. 32:24; 36:6; 39:26
have *b.* the tabernacle of. *Amos* 5:26
which have *b.* burden. *Mat* 20:12
burdens, grievous to be *b.* 23:4
Luke 11:46
sick of palsy, was *b.* of. *Mark* 2:3
hast *b.* him hence tell. *John* 20:15
he was *b.* of the soldiers. *Acts* 21:35
as we have *b.* image of. *1 Cor* 15:49
has *b.* and hast patience. *Rev* 2:3

***see* witness**

borrow
every woman shall *b.* of. *Ex* 3:22*
11:2*
if a man *b.* ought. 22:14
thou shalt not *b.* *Deut* 15:6; 28:12
go *b.* vessels abroad, *b.* *2 Ki* 4:3
him that would *b.* of thee. *Mat* 5:42

borrowed
they *b.* of Egyptians. *Ex* 12:35*
alas, master, for it was *b.* *2 Ki* 6:5
we have *b.* money for. *Neh* 5:4

borrower
and the *b.* is servant to. *Pr* 22:7
with the lender, so with *b.* *Isa* 24:2

borroweth
wicked *b.* and payeth not. *Ps* 37:21

bosom
given my maid into thy *b.* *Gen* 16:5
put now thy hand into thy *b.* *Ex* 4:6
carry them in thy *b.* *Num* 11:12
the wife of thy *b.* entice. *Deut* 13:6
evil toward the wife of his *b.* 28:54
evil toward husband of her *b.* 56
child and laid it in her *b.* *Ruth* 4:16
lay in his *b.* *2 Sam* 12:3
thy master's wives into thy *b.* 8
let her lie in thy *b.* *1 Ki* 1:2
took my son, and laid it in her *b.* and laid dead child in my *b.* *1 Ki* 3:20
Elijah took him out of her *b.* 17:19
hiding iniquity in my *b.* *Job* 31:33
prayer returned into my *b.* *Ps* 35:13
right hand out of thy *b.* 74:11
render seven-fold into their *b.* 79:12
bear in my *b.* the reproach. 89:50
he that bindeth sheaves, his *b.* 129:7
wilt thou embrace the *b.*? *Pr* 5:20
can a man take fire in his *b.*? 6:27
man taketh gift out of the *b.* 17:23
hideth his hand in *b.* 19:24*; 26:15*
a reward in the *b.* pacifieth. 21:14
anger resteth in the *b.* of. *Eccl* 7:9
carry the lambs in his *b.* *Isa* 40:11
even recompense into their *b.* 65:6
measure former work into their *b.* 7
iniquity of fathers into *b.* *Jer* 32:18
poured into mother's *b.* *Lam* 2:12
from her that lieth in thy *b.* *Mi* 7:5
good measure into your *b.* *Luke* 6:38
angels into Abraham's *b.* 16:22
Abraham, and Lazarus in his *b.* 23
in the *b.* of the Father. *John* 1:18
leaning on Jesus' *b.* a disciple. 13:23

Bosor, *see* **Balaam**

bosses
thick *b.* of his bucklers. *Job* 15:26

botch
(*Revised Version,* boil)
the Lord will smite thee with the *b.*
Deut 28:27, 35

both
were *b.* naked. *Gen* 2:25
the eyes of *b.* opened. 3:7
b. the daughters of Lot with. 19:36
b. of them made a covenant. 21:27
so they went *b.* of them. 22:8
deprived of you *b.* in one day? 27:45
they may judge betwixt us *b.* 31:37
cause of *b.* shall come. *Ex* 22:9
oath of the Lord be between *b.* 11
b. of them surely be put to death.
Lev 20:11, 12; *Deut* 22:22
and Miriam, *b.* came. *Num* 12:5
Phinehas thrust *b.* through. 25:8
shall stand before Lord. *Deut* 19:17
they shall die *b.* of them. *1 Sam* 2:34
went out *b.* of them. 9:26
as we have sworn *b.* of us. 20:42
that might lay hand on *b.* *Job* 9:33
b. are abomination. *Pr* 17:15; 20:10
the Lord hath made even *b.* 20:12
knoweth the ruin of them *b.*? 24:22
better than *b.* is he that. *Eccl* 4:3
they shall *b.* burn together. *Isa* 1:31
land shall be forsaken of *b.* 7:16
and they are fallen *b.* *Jer* 46:12
b. twain shall come forth. *Ezek* 21:19
then I saw that they *b.* 23:13
do evil with *b.* hands. *Mi* 7:3
of peace between *b.* *Zech* 6:13
b. shall fall. *Mat* 15:14; *Luke* 6:39
frankly forgave them *b.* *Luke* 7:42
but Pharisees confess *b.* *Acts* 23:8
peace, who hath made *b.* *Eph* 2:14
he might reconcile *b.* unto God. 16
in *b.* I stir up your *2 Pet* 3:1
b. were cast alive into. *Rev* 19:20

bottle
(*Ancient Eastern bottles were generally the skins of the smaller animals. Clay bottles made by the potters were less common, but are meant in some verses, as* Jer 19:1. *Glass bottles were known in Egypt and so probably to the Hebrews, but were largely* tear-bottles, *in which mourners collected their tears, afterwards putting them into the tombs. This custom is referred to in* Ps 56:8)
took a *b.* of water. *Gen* 21:14
water was spent in the *b.* 15
she filled the *b.* 19
she opened a *b.* of milk. *Judg* 4:19
Hannah took a *b.* of. *1 Sam* 1:24
meet another carrying a *b.* 10:3
Jesse took a *b.* of wine. 16:20
fruits, a *b.* of wine. *2 Sam* 16:1
thou my tears into thy *b.* *Ps* 56:8

I am become like a b. Ps 119:83
every b. shall be filled. Jer 13:12
get a potter's earthen b. 19:1
break the b. 10
puttest thy b. to him. Hab 2:15*

bottles
(*Revised Version*, wine-skins, *except where marked* *)
Gibeonites took wine b. Josh 9:4
b. of wine which we filled. 13
Abigail took two b. of. 1 Sam 25:18
ready to burst like new b. Job 32:19
or who can stay the b. of ? 38:37
empty his vessels, break b. Jer 48:12
sick with b. of wine. Hos 7:5*
into old b. else b. break. Mat 9:17
Mark 2:22; Luke 5:37, 38

bottom
they sank into the b. as. Ex 15:5
pour blood beside b. of altar. 29:12
Lev 4:7, 18, 25, 30; 5:9; 8:15; 9:9
covereth the b. of the sea. Job 36:30
the b. thereof of gold. S of S 3:10
they came at the b. of. Dan 6:24
hid from my sight in b. Amos 9:3
I went down to the b. of. Jonah 2:6
myrtle-trees in the b. Zech 1:8
top to b. Mat 27:51; Mark 15:38

bottomless *pit*
(*Revised Version*, abyss)
given the key of the b. pit. Rev 9:1
he opened the b. pit. 2
a king, the angel of the b. pit. 11
that ascendeth out of b. pit. 11:7
beast shall ascend out of b. pit. 17:8
angel having key of the b. pit. 20:1
and cast him into the b. pit. 3

bough
Joseph is a fruitful b. even a b. by a well. Gen 49:22
Abimelech cut down a b. Judg 9:48
cut down every man his b. 49
the Lord shall lop the b. Isa 10:33
berries in top of uttermost b. 17:6
strong cities be as a forsaken b. 9*

boughs
b. of goodly trees, b. Lev 23:40*
shalt not go over b. Deut 24:20
mule went under the b. 2 Sam 18:9
and brought forth b. like. Job 14:9
b. were like cedar-trees. Ps 80:10
she sent out her b. 11
I will take hold of the b. S of S 7:8
when the b. thereof are. Isa 27:11
it shall bring forth b. Ezek 17:23
was among the thick b. 31:3, 14
made their nests in b. 6; Dan 4:12

bought
man-child born in house b. with his.
Gen 17:12, 13, 23, 27; Ex 12:24
Jacob b. a field. Gen 33:19
Josh 24:32
Potiphar b. Joseph of the. Gen 39:1
money for the corn they b. 47:14
Joseph b. all land of Egypt. 20, 23
Abraham b. 49:30; 50:13; Acts 7:16
in hand of him that b. it. Lev 25:28
established for ever to him that b. 30
reckon with him that b. him. 50
the money that he was b. for. 51
sanctify a field which he b. 27:22
return to him of whom it was b. 24
father that b. thee? Deut 32:6
I have b. all that was. Ruth 4:9
little ewe-lamb he had b. 2 Sam 12:3
David b. threshing-floor and. 24:24
Omri b. the hill Samaria. 1 Ki 16:24
continued in work, nor b. Neh 5:16
I b. the field of Hanameel. Jer 32:9
fields shall be b. in this land. 43
I b. her to me for 15 pieces. Hos 3:2
all that he had, and b. Mat 13:46
cast out them that sold and b. in.
21:12; Mark 11:15; Luke 19:45
took counsel, and b. field. Mat 27:7
Joseph b. fine linen. Mark 15:46
had b. sweet spices to come. 16:1
I have b. a piece of. Luke 14:18
I have b. five yoke of oxen. 19
did eat, they drank, they b. 17:28
are b. with a price. 1 Cor 6:20; 7:23
denying the Lord that b. 2 Pet 2:1

bound, *actively*
b. Isaac his son, and laid. Gen 22:9
the midwife b. on his hand. 38:28
took Simeon and b. him. 42:24
he b. the ephod with. Lev 8:7
she had b. her soul. Num 30:4, 5
6, 7, 8, 9, 10, 11
she b. a scarlet line in. Josh 2:21
they b. Samson with. Judg 15:13
b. with withs. 16:8
b. with ropes. 12
b. with fetters. 21
he b. two talents of silver. 2 Ki 5:23
he shut up Hoshea and b. 17:4
they b. Zedekiah with. 25:7
b. Manasseh. 2 Chr 33:11
b. Jehoiakim. 36:6
who hath b. the waters in. Pr 30:4
have b. and strengthened. Hos 7:15
Herod b. John. Mat 14:3
Mark 6:17
b. Jesus. Mat 27:2; Mark 15:1
John 18:12
daughter whom Satan b. Luke 13:16
Agabus b. his own. Acts 21:11
as they b. Paul he said. 22:25*, 29
b. themselves under curse. 23:12
14, 21
b. Satan a thousand years. Rev 20:2

bound, *passively*
king's prisoners are b. Gen 39:20
prison where Joseph was b. 40:3
butler and baker which were b. 5
one of your brethren be b. 42:19
no cover b. on it. Num 19:15
mightest be b. Judg 16:6, 10, 13
soul of my lord b. 1 Sam 25:29
thy hands were not b. 2 Sam 3:34
if they be b. in fetters. Job 36:8
being b. in affliction. Ps 107:10
foolishness is b. in heart. Pr 22:15
b. by the archers, all are b. Isa 22:3
of prison to them that are b. 61:1
of my transgressions is b. Lam 1:14
b. in their coats. Dan 3:21
fell down b. 23
did not we cast three men b.? 24
be b. in heaven. Mat 16:19; 18:18
lay b. with them that. Mark 15:7
b. hand and foot, face b. John 11:44
b. to Caiaphas. 18:24
bring them b. Acts 9:2, 21; 22:5
Peter b. with chains. 12:6
behold I go b. in the Spirit. 20:22
I am ready not to be b. only. 21:13
left Paul b. 24:27
b. by law of husband. Rom 7:2
1 Cor 7:39
art thou b. unto a wife? 1 Cor 7:27
b. to thank God. 2 Thes 1:3; 2:13
the word of God is not b. 2 Tim 2:9
that are in bonds, as b. Heb 13:3
loose the angels b. Rev 9:14

bound *with chains*
which are b. with chains. Ps 68:6*
Zedekiah b. with chains.
Jer 39:7; 52:11
Jeremiah b. with chains. 40:1
great men b. with chains. Nah 3:10
been often b. with chains. Mark 5:4
was kept b. with chains. Luke 8:29
Paul to be b. with two chains.
Acts 21:33
I am b. with this chain. 28:20

bound *up*
his life is b. up in the. Gen 44:30
not been closed neither b. up. Isa 1:6
plead, that thou be b. up. Jer 30:13
it shall not be b. up. Ezek 30:21
nor have ye b. up that. 34:4
the wind hath b. her up. Hos 4:19*
iniquity of Ephraim is b. up. 13:12
he b. up his wounds. Luke 10:34

bound, *substantive*
to utmost b. of the. Gen 49:26
take it to the b. thereof. Job 38:20
to waters set a b. Ps 104:9
sand for the b. of the sea. Jer 5:22
them that remove the b. Hos 5:10*

bounds
thou shalt set b. to the. Ex 19:12
set b. about the mount. 23
I will set thy b. from the. 23:31
he set the b. of the. Deut 32:8
hast appointed his b. Job 14:5
compassed the waters with b. 26:10*
I have removed the b. Isa 10:13
hast determined the b. Acts 17:26

bountiful
he that hath a b. eye. Pr 22:9
churl be said to be b. Isa 32:5

bountifully
he hath dealt b. with me. Ps 13:6
the Lord hath dealt b. 116:7
deal b. with thy servant. 119:17
thou shalt deal b. with me. 142:7
soweth b. shall reap b. 2 Cor 9:6

bountifulness
enriched to all b. 2 Cor 9:11*

bounty
gave of his royal b. 1 Ki 10:13
and make up your b. that the same might be ready as b. 2 Cor. 9:5

bow, *noun*
[1] *An instrument for shooting arrows*, Gen 27:3; 2 Ki 9:24. [2] *The rainbow*, Gen 9:13, 14. [3] *Faith and patience*, Gen 49:24.
set my b. in the cloud. Gen 9:13
the b. shall be seen. 14, 16
take, thy quiver and thy b. 27:3
I took of the Amorite with b. 48:22
his b. abode in strength. 49:24
with thy sword nor b. Josh 24:12
gave David his sword, b. 1 Sam 18:4
Judah use of the b. 2 Sam 1:18
the b. of Jonathan turned not. 22
a certain man drew a b. and smote the king. 1 Ki 22:34; 2 Chr 18:33
smite those taken with b. 2 Ki 6:22
Jehu drew a b. with his full. 9:24
take b. and arrows, he took b. 13:15
put thy hand upon the b. 16
able to shoot with b. 1 Chr 5:18
armed with b. and shooting b. 12:2
my b. was renewed. Job 29:20
I will not trust in my b. Ps 44:6
he breaketh the b. and. 46:9
there brake arrows of the b. 76:3
aside like a deceitful b. 78:57
gave them as stubble to b. Isa 41:2
escape to nations that draw b. 66:19
they shall lay hold on b. Jer 6:23
behold, I will break the b. 49:35
they shall hold the b. 50:42
he hath bent his b. Lam 2:4
as appearance of the b. Ezek 1:28
I will smite thy b. 39:3
I will break b. of Israel. Hos 1:5
I will not save them by b. 7
I will break the b. 2:18
they are like a deceitful b. 7:16
he that handleth b. Amos 2:15
thy b. was made naked. Hab 3:9
when I filled the b. Zech 9:13
sat on the horse had a b. Rev 6:2
see **bend, bent, battle-bow**

bow, *verb*
nor serve, nor b. yourselves to their gods. Josh 23:7; 2 Ki 17:35
I b. myself in house of. 2 Ki 5:18
they b. themselves. Job 39:3
go down to dust, shall b. Ps 22:29
dwell in wilderness shall b. 72:9
b. thy heavens, O Lord. 144:5
and b. thine ear, to my. Pr 5:1*
evil b. before the good. 14:19
the strong men shall b. Eccl 12:3
and b. myself before? Mi 6:6
the perpetual hills did b. Hab 3:6

bow *down*
b. down, mother's sons b. down.
Gen 27:29
shall thy brethren b. down? 37:10
father's children shall b. down. 49:8
servants shall b. down to. Ex 11:8
shalt not b. down. 20:5; Deut 5:9
thou shalt not b. down to. Ex 23:24
up image to b. down to it. Lev 26:1
other gods to b. down. Judg 2:19
I b. down in house of. 2 Ki 5:18
b. down thine ear. 19:16*; Ps 86:1
and let others b. down. Job 31:10
b. down thine ear. Ps 31:2; Pr 22:17

let us worship and b. down. Ps 95:6
without me they b. down. Isa 10:4
they stoop, they b. down. 46:2
and queens shall b. down. 49:23
have said, b. down. 51:23
is it to b. down his head ? 58:5
despised thee shall b. down. 60:14
ye shall all b. down to. 65:12
eyes darkened, b. down. Rom 11:10

bow knee

before him b. the knee. Gen 41:43
every knee shall b. Isa 45:23
Rom 14:11
I b. my knees unto Father. Eph 3:14
every knee shall b. Phil 2:10

bowed

and their children b. Gen 33:6
Leah with children b., Rachel b. 7
Joseph's brethren b. 43:26
Issachar b. his shoulder. 49:15
served other gods, and b. to them.
Josh 23:16; Judg 2:12, 17
he b. where he b. he fell. Judg 5:27
fell on her face and b. Ruth 2:10
Phinehas' wife b. 1 Sam 4:19
David b. himself. 20:41
Abigail b. 25:23, 41
David b. the heart of. 2 Sam 19:14
he b. heavens. 22:10; Ps 18:9
Bath-sheba b. 1 Ki 1:16, 31
not b. to Baal. 19:18; Rom 11:4
sons of the prophets b. 2 Ki 2:15
b. herself to ground. 4:37
b. themselves upon the. 2 Chr 7:3
the king and all present b. 29:29
b. to Haman. Esth 3:2
Mordecai b. not. 5
b. the knee before him. Mat 27:29*
spirit of infirmity, was b. Luke 13:11

bowed down

Abraham b. down. Gen 23:12
Joseph's brethren b. down. 42:6
43:28
did eat, and b. down to. Num 25:2
of the people b. down on. Judg 7:6
be his gods, and b. down. 2 Chr 25:14
I b. down heavily. Ps 35:14
I am b. down greatly. 38:6
our soul is b. down. 44:25
my soul is b. down. 57:6
raiseth those b. down. 145:14
146:8
haughtiness of men shall be b. down.
Isa 2:11
loftiness of man be b. down. 17
I was b. down at the hearing. 21:3*
were afraid and b. down. Luke 24:5

bowed head

man b. his head. Gen 24:26, 48
they b. their heads. 43:28
then they b. their heads and.
Ex 4:31; 12:27; Neh 8:6
Moses b. his head to earth. Ex 34:8
Balaam b. his head. Num 22:31
b. down their heads. 1 Chr 29:20
Jehoshaphat b. his head. 2 Chr 20:18
sang praises and b. heads. 29:30
Jesus b. his head and. John 19:30

bowed himself

Abraham b. himself. Gen 18:2; 23:7, 12
Lot b. himself. 19:1
Jacob b. himself. 33:3; 47:31
Joseph b. himself. 48:12
Samson b. himself. Judg 16:30
David stooped and b. himself.
1 Sam 24:8*
Saul b. himself. 28:14*
Mephibosheth b. himself.
2 Sam 9:8*
Joab b. himself. 14:22*
Absalom b. himself. 33
Cushi b. himself to Joab. 18:21
Araunah b. himself before king.
24:20; 1 Chr 21:21
Nathan b. himself. 1 Ki 1:23
the king b. himself on bed. 47
Adonijah came and b. himself. 53*
Solomon rose and b. himself. 2:19

bowels

(Used often in Scripture for the seat of pity or kindness)

out of thine own b. shall. Gen 15:4
people shall be from thy b. 25:23
for his b. did yearn. 43:30
water shall go into thy b. Num 5:22
which proceed of thy b. 2 Sam 7:12
son which came forth of my b. 16:11
Joab shed out Amasa's b. 20:10
for her b. yearned. 1 Ki 3:26
by disease of thy b. 2 Chr 21:15
the Lord smote him in his b. 18
his b. fell out. 19
that came of his own b. slew. 32:21
meat in his b. is turned. Job 20:14
my b. boiled, and rested not. 30:27
in the midst of my b. Ps 22:14
took me out of my mother's b. 71:6
let it come into his b. 109:18*
my b. were moved. S of S 5:4
my b. shall sound. Isa 16:11
the offspring of thy b. 48:19
from the b. of my mother. 49:1
is the sounding of thy b. ? 63:15
my b. my b. I am pained. Jer 4:19
therefore my b. are troubled. 31:20
O Lord, my b. are. Lam 1:20; 2:11
fill thy b. with this roll. Ezek 3:3
satisfy their souls, nor fill b. 7:19
Judas burst, and all his b. Acts 1:18
straitened in your b. 2 Cor 6:12*
long after you in b. of. Phil 1:8*
in Christ if there be any b. 2:1*
put on b. of mercies. Col 3:12*
the b. of the saints are. Philem 7*
receive him that is my own b. 12
yea, brother, refresh my b. 20*
and shutteth up his b. 1 John 3:17*

boweth

b. on his knees to drink. Judg 7:5
the mean man b. Isa 2:9

bowing

Eliezer b. himself to. Gen 24:52
set their eyes, b. down. Ps 17:11*
as a b. wall shall ye be. 62:3*
did spit upon him, b. Mark 15:19

bowl

each b. weighing seventy. Num 7:85
wringed the dew, a b. Judg 6:38
the golden b. be broken. Eccl 12:6
candlestick of gold with b. Zech 4:2
olive trees one on right side of b. 3

bowls

make b. to cover. Ex 25:29; 37:16
dishes and b. Num 4:7
b. and snuffers of pure. 1 Ki 7:50
1 Chr 28:17
that drink wine in b. Amos 6:6
shall be filled like b. Zech 9:15
pots in Lord's house like b. 14:20

bowmen

from the noise of the b. Jer 4:29

bows

b. are broken. 1 Sam 2:4
were armed with b. 1 Chr 12:2
army that drew b. 2 Chr 14:8
Uzziah prepared for them b. 26:14
I set the people with b. Neh 4:13
the other half held spears and b. 16
their b. shall be broken. Ps 37:15
with arrows and b. Isa 7:24
their b. shall dash young men. 13:18
every one of their b. Jer 51:56
they shall burn the b. Ezek 39:9

bowshot

him as it were a b. Gen 21:16

box

(Revised Version, vial or cruse)
take this b. of oil. 2 Ki 9:1, 3
alabaster b. Mat 26:7; Mark 14:3
brake b. and poured. Mark 14:3
Luke 7:37

box-tree

the desert the pine and b. Isa 41:19
of Lebanon shall come, the b. 60:13

boy, -s

the b. grew, and Esau. Gen 25:27
they have given a b. Joel 3:3
streets shall be full of b. Zech 8:5

Bozrah

Jobab of B. reigned. Gen 36:33
Lord hath a sacrifice in B. Isa 34:6
with dyed garments from B. Isa 63:1
judgement is come from B. Jer 48:24
B. shall become desolation. 49:13
shall spread his wings over B. 22
shall devour palaces of B. Amos 1:12
together as sheep of B. Mi 2:12

bracelet, -s

when he saw b. Gen 24:30
thy signet, thy b. 38:18*, 25
were willing, brought b. Ex 35:22*
Num 31:50
the b. on his arm. 2 Sam 1:10
take away the chains, b. Isa 3:19
and I put b. Ezek 16:11

brake

the hail b. every tree. Ex 9:25
the people b. off the ear-rings. 32:3
cast tables and b. 19; Deut 9:17
they b. pitchers. Judg 7:19, 20
a piece of a millstone to b. 9:53
b. the withs as a thread. 16:9
b. new ropes. 12
Eli fell and his neck b. 1 Sam 4:18
mighty men b. through. 2 Sam 23:16
1 Chr 11:18
strong wind b. in pieces. 1 Ki 19:11
Baal's images b. they. 2 Ki 11:18
b. images, b. brazen serpent. 18:4
Josiah b. the images. 23:14
2 Chr 34:4
Arabians came and b. 2 Chr 21:17
shut up the sea when it b. ? 38:8
and b. up for it my decreed. 10*
there b. he the arrows. Ps 76:3
moreover, he b. the whole. 105:16
smote their vines, b. trees. 33
and the plague b. in. 106:29
out of darkness he b. their. 107:14
took the yoke and b. it. Jer 28:10
my covenant they b. through. 31:32
whose covenant he b. Ezek 17:16
spirit troubled and sleep b. Dan 2:1
smote the image and b. feet. 34, 45
the lions b. all their bones. 6:24
fourth beast devoured and b. 7:7
goat smote ram, and b. his. 8:7
blessed and b. Mat 14:19; 15:36
26:26; Mark 6:41; 8:6; 14:22
Luke 9:16; 22:19; 24:30
1 Cor 11:24
I b. the five loaves. Mark 8:19
she b. the box and poured. 14:3
their net b. Luke 5:6
he b. the bands. 8:29
soldiers b. the legs. of. John 19:32
saw that he was dead, b. not legs. 33

brake down

b. down image of Baal. 2 Ki 10:27
2 Chr 23:17
people went and b. down. 2 Ki 11:18
king of Israel b. down wall. 14:13
2 Chr 25:23; 36:19; Jer 39:8
52:14
he b. down the houses of. 2 Ki 23:7
he b. down high places. 8
b. down altars. 12, 15
Asa b. down images. 2 Chr 14:3
Uzziah b. down the wall of. 26:6
they b. down the altars. 34:4

brakest

the first table thou b. Ex 34:1
Deut 10:2
thou b. heads of. Ps 74:13, 14
leaned on thee, thou b. Ezek 29:7

bramble, -s

said all the trees to b. Judg 9:14
b. said, let fire come out of b. 15
nettles and b. shall come. Isa 34:13*
nor of a b.-bush gather. Luke 6:44

branch

knop and flower in one b. Ex 25:33
37:19
cut down a b. with. Num 13:23
his b. shooteth forth. Job 8:16*
and the tender b. thereof. 14:7
and his b. shall not be green. 15:32
above shall his b. be cut off. 18:16
dew lay all night upon my b. 29:19
the b. thou madest strong. Ps 80:15
righteous flourish as a b. Pr 11:28*
in that day shall b. of the. Isa 4:2
the Lord will cut off b. and. 9:14*

and a *b.* shall grow out. *Isa* 11:1
cast out like an abominable *b.* 14:19
cities be as an uppermost *b.* 17:9*
nor any work which *b.* or. 19:15*
the *b.* of terrible ones shall. 25:5*
the *b.* of my planting. 60:21
to David a righteous *b.* *Jer* 23:5
b. of righteousness grow. 33:15
they put the *b.* to their. *Ezek* 8:17
the vine tree more than *b.*? 15:2
eagle took the highest *b.* 17:3*, 22*
out of a *b.* of her roots. *Dan* 11:7*
forth my servant the *b.* *Zech* 3:8
the man whose name is the *b.* 6:12
them neither root nor *b.* *Mal* 4:1
when *b.* is yet tender. *Mat* 24:32
Mark 13:28
every *b.* that beareth not, and every *b.* that beareth. *John* 15:2
as the *b.* cannot bear fruit itself. 4
he is cast forth as a *b.* 6

branches

in vine were three *b.* *Gen* 40:10
the three *b.* are three days. 12
a bough, whose *b.* run over. 49:22
six *b.* come out of candlestick, three *b.* *Ex* 25:32; 37:18, 21
take *b.* of palm trees. *Lev* 23:40
Neh 8:15
flame shall dry up his *b.* *Job* 15:30
she sent out her *b.* to. *Ps* 80:11*
fowls which sing among *b.* 104:12
Moab's *b.* are stretched. *Isa* 16:8
in the utmost fruitful *b.* 17:6
take away and cut down *b.* 18:5*
there shall he consume the *b.* 27:10
and the *b.* are broken. *Jer* 11:16
spreading vine whose *b.* *Ezek* 17:6
she was fruitful and full of *b.* 19:10
fire is gone out of a rod of her *b.* 14
not like the Assyrian's *b.* 31:8
of Israel, ye shall shoot *b.* 36:8
hew down tree, cut off *b.* *Dan* 4:14
consume Ephraim's *b.* *Hos* 11:6*
his *b.* shall spread. 14:6
my vine waste, *b.* *Joel* 1:7
have marred their vine *b.* *Nah* 2:2
be these two olive *b.*? *Zech* 4:12
birds lodge in the *b.* *Mat* 13:32
Luke 13:19
others cut down *b.* *Mat* 21:8
Mark 11:8; *John* 12:13
shooteth out *b.* *Mark* 4:32
I am the vine, ye are *b.* *John* 15:5
root be holy, so the *b.* *Rom* 11:16
if the *b.* be broken off. 17, 19
boast not against the *b.* 18
God spared not the natural *b.* 21

brand, -s

he had set *b.* on fire. *Judg* 15:5
is not this a *b.* plucked.? *Zech* 3:2

brandish

shall I *b.* my sword? *Ezek* 32:10

brasen

(*American Revision,* brazen)
make *b.* rings. *Ex* 27:4
b. grate. 35:16; 38:4
their *b.* sockets twenty. 38:10
sodden in a *b.* pot. *Lev* 6:28
b. censers. *Num* 16:39
b. bars. *1 Ki* 4:13
b. wheels. 7:30
made *b.* shields. 14:27
b. oxen. *2 Ki* 16:17
brake the *b.* serpent. 18:4
b. sea Chaldees. 25:13; *Jer* 52:17
made a *b.* scaffold. *2 Chr* 6:13
made thee this day *b.* *Jer* 1:18
make thee a fenced *b.* wall. 15:20
the *b.* bulls. 52:20
b. vessels. *Mark* 7:4

brass

(*Modern brass, the alloy of copper and zinc, is not meant by the name in the Bible, as zinc was not then known. The word is generally used of a simple metal, and means copper. In other places it is properly bronze, the alloy of copper and tin. The word is very often used figuratively to represent great strength, or great hardness*)
take gold, silver, *b.* *Ex* 25:3; 35:5
taches of *b.* 26:11; 36:18
cast five sockets of *b.* 26:37; 27:10
17, 18; 36:38; 38:11, 17, 19
overlay altar with *b.* 27:2, 6; 38:2
net work of *b.* 27:4
pins of the court of *b.* 19
laver of *b.*, foot of *b.* 30:18
work in gold, silver, *b.* 31:4; 35:32
rings of *b.* 38:5
overlaid the staves with *b.* 6
the *b.* of the offering was. 29
brasen altar, and grate of *b.* 39:39
made a serpent of *b.*... a pole, when he beheld serpent of *b.* *Num* 21:9
hills thou mayest dig *b.* *Deut* 8:9
heaven over thy head be *b.* 28:23
bound with fetters of *b.* *Judg* 16:21
Goliath had an helmet of *b.*
1 Sam 17:5, 38
and he had greaves of *b.* 6
David took much *b.* *2 Sam* 8:8
1 Chr 18:8
Hiram was worker in *b.* *1 Ki* 7:14
cast pillars of *b.* 7:15; *2 Ki* 25:13
chapiters of *b.* *1 Ki* 7:16; *2 Ki* 25:17
Jer 52:22
bases of *b.* *1 Ki* 7:27
plates of *b.* 30
lavers of *b.* 38; *2 Chr* 4:16
pots and shovels of bright *b.*
1 Ki 7:45
weight of the *b.* was not found.
47; *2 Chr* 4:18
Zedekiah with fetters of *b.* *2 Ki* 25:7
carried *b.* to Babylon. 13; *Jer* 52:17
sound with cymbals of *b.* *1 Chr* 15:19.
b. in abundance. 22:3; 29:7
prepared the *b.* for things of *b.* 29:2
Rehoboam made shields of *b.*
2 Chr 12:10
is my flesh *b.*? *Job* 6:12
bones are as strong pieces of *b.* 40:18
Leviathan esteemeth *b.* as. 41:27
hath broken gates of *b.* *Ps* 107:16
in pieces the gates of *b.* *Isa* 45:2
for wood I bring *b.* for *b.* 60:17
that the *b.* of it may. *Ezek* 24:11
belly and thighs were of *b.* *Dan* 2:32
another third kingdom of *b.* 39
whose nails were of *b.* 7:19
his feet in colour polished *b.* 10:6
horn iron, and hoofs *b.* *Mi* 4:13
were mountains of *b.* *Zech* 6:1
provide neither gold nor *b.* *Mat* 10:9
sounding *b.* or cymbal. *1 Cor* 13:1
feet like to fine *b.* *Rev* 1:15; 2:18
should not worship idols of *b.* 9:20

iron and **brass**

instructor in *b. and iron.* *Gen* 4:22
your heaven *iron,* your earth *b.*
Lev 26:19
b. and iron which may. *Num* 31:22
shoes be *iron and b.* as. *Deut* 33:25
return with *b. and iron.* *Josh* 22:8
prepared *b. and iron.* *1 Chr* 22:14, 16
to work in *b. and iron.* *2 Chr* 2:7, 14
wrought in *iron and b.* to. 24:12
iron out of the earth, *and b.* *Job* 28:2
an *iron* sinew, *and* brow *b.* *Isa* 48:4
for *b.* gold, for *iron* silver. 60:17
they are *b. and iron.* *Jer* 6:28
Ezek 22:18
they gather *iron and b.* *Ezek* 22:20
was *iron,* clay, *b.* *Dan* 2:35, 45
a band of *iron and b.* in. 4:15, 23
gods of silver, *b. and iron.* 5:4

vessels of **brass**

make all *vessels of b.* *Ex* 27:3
made *vessels of b.* 38:3
all *vessels of b.* *Josh* 6:19
vessels of b. and iron they put. 24
brought *vessels of b.* *2 Sam* 8:10
1 Chr 18:10
vessels of b. took they. *2 Ki* 25:14
Jer 52:18
the *b. of* all these *vessels* was without weight. *2 Ki* 25:16; *Jer* 52:20
traded in *vessels of b.* *Ezek* 27:13
Rev 18:12

bravery

will take away their *b.* *Isa* 3:18†

brawler, -s

(*Revised Version,* contentious)
a bishop must be no *b.* *1 Tim* 3:3
to be no *b.* *Tit* 3:2

brawling

with *b.* woman in. *Pr* 25:24

bray, -ed

doth the wild ass *b.* *Job* 6:5
among the bushes they *b.* 30:7
though thou shouldest *b.* *Prov.* 27:22

breach

(*A gap; a rupture; a breaking. Used literally and figuratively*)
the midwife said, this *b.* *Gen* 38:29
b. for *b.* eye for eye. *Lev* 24:20
ye shall know my *b.* *Num* 14:34*
the Lord hath made a *b.* *Judg* 21:15
broken forth as the *b.* *2 Sam* 5:20
Lord made a *b.* on Uzzah. 6:8*
1 Chr 13:11*
any *b.* shall be found. *2 Ki* 12:5
Lord our God made a *b.* *1 Chr* 15:13
and there was no *b.* *Neh* 6:1
he breaketh me with *b.* upon *b.*
Job 16:14
Moses stood in the *b.* *Ps* 106:23
but perverseness is a *b.* *Pr* 15:4
us make a *b.* therein. *Isa* 7:6
iniquity shall be to you as *b.* 30:13
the day the Lord bindeth up *b.* 26*
called repairer of the *b.* 58:12
people broken with a *b.* *Jer* 14:17
thy *b.* is great like sea. *Lam* 2:13
a city wherein is a *b.* *Ezek* 26:10

breaches

Asher abode in his *b.* *Judg* 5:17*
repaired *b.* of the city. *1 Ki* 11:27
let them repair the *b.* *2 Ki* 12:5
priests had not repaired the *b.* 6
masons to repair *b.* of. 12; 22:5
b. began to be stopped. *Neh* 4:7
heal the *b.* thereof. *Ps* 60:2
ye have seen the *b.* *Isa* 22:9
shall go out at the *b.* *Amos* 4:3
smite the great house with *b.* 6:11
I will close up the *b.* thereof. 9:11

bread

[1] *The eatable made of grain,* Gen 3:19; 49:20. [2] *All things necessary for this life,* Mat 6:11. [3] *Manna wherewith God fed the children of Israel in the wilderness,* Neh 9:15; John 6:31.

(*The word is used figuratively in many ways. The best known is its use for Christ in the term* bread of life)
king of Salem brought *b.* *Gen* 14:18
I will fetch a morsel of *b.* 18:5
Abraham took *b.* and gave to. 21:14
then Jacob gave Esau *b.* 25:34
savoury meat and *b.* to. 27:17
in land of Egypt was *b.* 41:54
people cried to Pharaoh for *b.* 55
set on *b.* 43:31
b. for his father. 45:23
his father's house with *b.* 47:12
give us *b.* 15
gave them *b.* for horses. 17
buy us and our land for *b.* 19
out of Asher his *b.* shall. 49:20
I will rain *b.* from heaven. *Ex* 16:4
in the morning *b.* to the full. 8, 12
giveth on the sixth day the *b.* 29
they may see the *b.* 32
he shall bless thy *b.* and. 23:25
and the *b.* in the basket. 29:32
if ought of the *b.* remain unto. 34
he set the *b.* in order. 40:23
he took a cake of oiled *b.* *Lev* 8:26
what remaineth of *b.* ye shall. 32
b. of their God. 21:6, 8, 17, 21, 22
nor from stranger offer *b.* 22:25
ye shall offer with the *b.* 23:18
women shall bake your *b.* 26:26
the continual *b.* shall be. *Num* 4:7
the people of the land are *b.* 14:9
b. nor water, our soul ... *b.* 21:5
my *b.* for my sacrifices. 28:2
man doth not live by *b.* only.
Deut 8:3; *Mat* 4:4; *Luke* 4:4
met you not with *b.* and. *Deut* 23:4

ye have not eaten *b.* nor. *Deut* 29:6
all *b.* of their provision. *Josh* 9:5
this our *b.* we took hot for. 12
a cake of barley *b.* *Judg* 7:13
give *b.* to thy army. 8:6, 15
comfort thy heart with *b.* 19:5
and there is *b.* and wine. 19
visited his people giving *b. Ruth* 1:6
hired themselves for *b.* *1 Sam* 2:5
crouch to him for a morsel of *b.* 36
for the *b.* is spent in our. 9:7
took an ass laden with *b.* 16:20
but there is hallowed *b.* 21:4
b. is common. 5*
hallowed *b.* to put hot *b.* in day. 6
thou hast given him *b.* 22:13
shall I take my *b.* and my. 25:11
let me set a morsel of *b.* 28:22
Egyptian and gave him *b.* 30:11
fail one that lacketh *b.* *2 Sam* 3:29
if I taste *b.* or ought else till. 35
to every one a cake of *b.* 6:19
back and hast eaten *b.* *1 Ki* 13:22
after he had eaten *b.* and. 23
ravens brought *b.* and. 17:6
bring me, a morsel of *b.* 11
fed them with *b.* and. 18:4, 13
brought the man of God *b. 2 Ki* 4:42
take you to a land of *b.* 18:32
Isa 36:17
Zabulon brought *b.* *1 Chr* 12:40
have not eaten the *b.* *Neh* 5:14
and gavest them *b.* from. 9:15
they met not Israel with *b.* 13:2
wandereth abroad for *b.* *Job* 15:23
thou hast withholden *b.* from. 22:7
offspring shall not be satisfied with *b.* 27:14
the earth, out of it cometh *b.* 28:5
his life abhorreth *b.* and. 33:20
nor his seed begging *b.* *Ps* 37:25
can he give *b.*? 78:20
feedest them with *b.* of tears. 80:5
eaten ashes like *b.* 102:9
and *b.* which strengtheneth. 104:15
satisfied them with the *b.* 105:40
let them seek their *b.* 109:10
will satisfy her poor with *b.* 132:15
b. eaten secret is pleasant. *Pr* 9:17
better than he that honoureth himself and lacketh *b.* 12:9
land be satisfied with *b.* 11; 28:19
thou shalt be satisfied with *b.* 20:13
b. of deceit is sweet to a man. 17
he giveth of his *b.* to the poor. 22:9
eateth not the *b.* of idleness. 31:27
is not to swift, nor *b.* to. *Eccl* 9:11
cast thy *b.* upon the waters. 11:1
away the whole stay of *b.* *Isa* 3:1
for in my house is neither *b.* nor. 7
they prevented with their *b.* 21:14
the *b.* of adversity. 30:20
his *b.* shall be given him. 33:16
he baketh *b.* on coals. 44:15, 19
should not die, nor his *b.* fail. 51:14
money for that which is not *b.*? 55:2
seed to the sower, *b.* to eater. 10
is it not to deal thy *b.* to? 58:7
nor have hunger of *b.* *Jer* 42:14
people sigh, they seek *b.* *Lam* 1:11
young children ask *b.* no man. 4:4
to be satisfied with *b.* 5:6
we gat our *b.* with peril of our. 9
thou shalt prepare thy *b. Ezek* 4:15
that they may want *b.* and water. 17
pride, fulness of *b.* 16:49
given his *b.* to the hungry. 18:7, 16
strangers when ye offer my *b.* 44:7
lovers that give me *b.* *Hos* 2:5
sacrifices shall be as the *b.* of. 9:4
given you want of *b.* *Amos* 4:6
not a famine of *b.* but of. 8:11
if one do touch *b.* or. *Hag* 2:12
ye offer polluted *b.* *Mal* 1:7
these stones be made *b.* *Mat* 4:3
Luke 4:3
our daily *b. Mat* 6:11; *Luke* 11:11
if son ask *b.* will he give? *Mat* 7:9
take children's *b.* 15:26; *Mark* 7:27
whence have so much *b.*? *Mat* 15:33
Mark 8:4
had forgotten to take *b.* *Mat* 16:5
Mark 8:14
I spake not concerning *b. Mat* 16:11
not beware of leaven of *b. Mat* 16:12
Jesus took *b.* and blessed it. 26:26
Mark 14:22
came neither eating *b.* *Luke* 7:33
nothing for journey, neither *b.* 9:3
servants of my father's have *b.* 15:17
took *b.* gave thanks. 22:19; 24:30
known of them in breaking *b.* 24:35
two hundred penny-worth of *b.*
John 6:5
Moses gave you not that *b.*... Father giveth you the true *b.* *John* 6:32
the *b.* of God is he. 33
Lord, give us this *b.* 34
I am the *b.* of life. 35, 48
I am *b.* which came down. 41, 50, 58
he that eateth of this *b.* shall. 58
he that eateth *b.* with me. 13:18
fire and fish laid thereon and *b.* 21:9
Jesus then taketh *b.* and giveth. 13
continued in breaking of *b. Acts* 2:42
and breaking *b.* from house. 46
the disciples came to break *b.* 20:7
when he had broken *b.* and eaten. 11
he took *b.* and gave thanks. 27:35
b. we break, is it not? *1 Cor* 10:16
we being many are one *b.* 17
Lord Jesus, the same night in which he was betrayed, took *b.* 11:23
minister *b.* to your food. *2 Cor* 9:10

see **affliction**

bread corn

b. corn is bruised. *Isa* 28:28

bread, with *eat*

sweat of thy face *eat b.* *Gen* 3:19
Lord will give me *b.* to *eat.* 28:20
called his brethren to *eat b.* 31:54
brethren sat down to *eat b.* 37:25
he had, save *b.* he did *eat.* 39:6
heard they should *eat b.* there. 43:25
Egyptians might not *eat b.* with. 32
him that he may *eat b.* *Ex* 2:20
and when we did *eat b.* 16:3
b. Lord hath given you to *eat.* 15
came to *eat b.* with. 18:12
did not *eat b.* forty days. 34:28
Deut 9:9, 18
there *eat* it, with the *b.* *Lev* 8:31
he shall *eat* the *b.* of his God. 21:22
ye shall neither *eat b.* nor. 23:14
ye shall *eat* your *b.* to the full. 26:5
when ye *eat* the *b.* of. *Num* 15:19
thou shalt *eat b.* without. *Deut* 8:9
I will not *eat* thy *b.* *Judg* 13:16
come thou, and *eat b.* *Ruth* 2:14
eat b. at my table. *2 Sam* 9:7, 10
neither did he *eat b.* with. 12:17
set *b.* and he did *eat.* 20
didst rise and *eat b.* 21
b. and summer fruit to *eat.* 16:2
nor will I *eat b.* *1 Ki* 13:8, 16
charged me, saying, *eat* no *b.* 9
come home with me and *eat b.* 15
arise, *eat b.* let thy heart. 21:7
constrained Elisha to *eat b. 2 Ki* 4:8
b. and water, they may *eat.* 6:22
did *eat* of the unleavened *b.* 23:9
did *eat b.* before. 25:29; *Jer* 52:33
and did *eat b.* with Job. *Job* 42:11
eat up my people, as they eat *b.*
Ps 14:4; 53:4
who did *eat* of my *b.* hath. 41:9
that I forget to *eat* my *b.* 102:4
vain to sit up late, to *eat* the *b.* 127:2
they *eat b.* of wickedness. *Pr* 4:17
come, *eat* of my *b.* and drink of. 9:5
eat not the *b.* of him that hath. 23:6
if enemy hunger, give *b.* to *eat.* 25:21
go thy way, *eat* thy *b.* with. *Eccl* 9:7
we will *eat* our *b.* and wear. *Isa* 4:1
eat up thy harvest and thy *b.*
Jer 5:17
there they did *eat b.* together. 41:1
they *eat* their defiled *b.* *Ezek* 4:13
they shall *eat b.* by weight and. 16
eat b. with quaking. 12:18
eat b. with care. 19
and *eat* not *b.* of men. 24:17, 22
prince sit in it to *eat b.* before. 44:3
into Judah, there *eat b.* *Amos* 7:12
they that *eat* thy *b.* have. *Ob* 7
wash not when they *eat b. Mat* 15:2
not so much as *eat b.* *Mark* 3:20
b. they have nothing to *eat. Mark* 6:36
saw disciples *eat b.* with. 7:2, 5
Pharisee's house to *eat b. Luke* 14:1
is he that shall *eat b.* 15
b. that these may *eat*? *John* 6:5
place where they did *eat b.* 23
gave them *b.* from heaven to *eat.* 31
if any man *eat* of this *b.* he shall. 51
as often as ye *eat* this *b. 1 Cor* 11:26
whosoever shall *eat* this *b.* and. 27
we *eat* any man's *b.*? *2 Thes* 3:8
quietness they work and *eat b.* 12

leavened **bread**

(Bread leavened with yeast)

who eateth *leav. b.* that. *Ex* 12:15
no *leav. b.* be eaten. 13:3
no *leav. b.* be seen. 7; *Deut* 16:3, 4
not offer blood with *leav. b. Ex* 23:18
shall offer *leav. b.* *Lev* 7:13

loaf, or *loaves of* **bread**

(In the East, flat cakes like the large, thin, American pilot bread)

one *loaf of b.* with ram. *Ex* 29:23
give *loaf of b.* to people. *Judg* 8:5
three *loaves of b.* *1 Sam* 10:3
and give thee two *loaves of b.* 4
give me five *loaves of b.* 21:3
two hundred *loaves of b. 2 Sam* 16:1
one of Israel a *loaf of b. 1 Chr* 16:3

no **bread**

there was *no b.* in the. *Gen* 47:13
there is *no b.* and our. *Num* 21:5
there is *no* common *b.* *1 Sam* 21:4
for there was *no b.* there, but. 6
Saul had eaten *no b.* all the. 28:20
the Egyptian had eaten *no b.* 30:12
eat *no b.* nor. *1 Ki* 13:9; 17:22
away, and would eat *no b.* 21:4
that thou eatest *no b.*? 5
there was *no b.* for the. *2 Ki* 25:3
Jer 52:6
came, he did eat *no b.* *Ezra* 10:6
there is *no* more *b.* in. *Jer* 38:9
I ate *no* pleasant *b.* nor. *Dan* 10:3
it is because we have taken *no b.*
Mat 16:7, 8; *Mark* 8:16, 17
take no scrip, *no b.* no. *Mark* 6:8

piece, or *pieces of* **bread**

I may eat a *piece of b.* *1 Sam* 2:36
brought to a *piece of b.* *Pr* 6:26
for a *piece of b.* that man. 28:21
Jeremiah daily *piece of b. Jer* 37:21
ye pollute me for *pieces of b.*?
Ezek 13:19

shewbread, *see* **shew**

staff of **bread**

broken *staff of* your *b.* *Lev* 26:26
brake whole *staff of b.* *Ps* 105:16
I will break *staff of b.* *Ezek* 4:16
5:16; 14:13

unleavened **bread**

(Bread without yeast, used figuratively for purity)

Lot did bake *unleav. b.* *Gen* 19:3
eat passover with *unleav. b.*
Ex 12:18; *Num* 9:11
seven days eat *unleav. b.* *Ex* 12:15
13:6, 7; 23:15; 34:18; *Lev* 23:6
Num 28:17; *Deut* 16:3
on fourteenth day eat *unleav. b.*
Ex 12:18
your habitations eat *unleav. b.* 20
take *unleav. b.* to hallow. 29:2
shall eat with *unleav. b.* *Lev* 6:16
wafers of *unleav. b.* *Num* 6:15
six days eat *unleav. b.* *Deut* 16:8
did bake *unleav. b.* *1 Sam* 28:24
did eat *unleav. b.* *2 Ki* 23:9
passover of *unleav. b.* *Ezek* 45:21
first day of *unleav. b.* *Mark* 14:12
came days of *unleav. b.* *Luke* 22:7
Acts 12:3
after days of *unleav. b.* *Acts* 20:6
with the *unleav. b.* *1 Cor* 5:8

see **basket, feast**

breadth

ark, and *b.* fifty cubits. *Gen* 6:15
through the land in the *b.* of. 13:17
b. of the court fifty cubits. *Ex* 27:18
a span the *b.* thereof. 28:6; 39:9
five cubits the *b.* thereof. 38:1

so much as a foot b. Deut 2:5*
stones at an hair's b. Judg 20:16
the b. of the Lord's house. 1 Ki 6:2
2 Chr 3:3
b. of the porch was thirty. 1 Ki 7:6
the b. of the altar was. 2 Chr 4:1
b. of the Lord's house. Ezra 6:3
and the b. of the waters. Job 37:10
hast thou perceived the b.? 38:18
wings shall fill the b. Isa 8:8
the b. of the building. Ezek 40:5
b. of the entry. 11
the b. of the gate. 13, 20, 48
b. of the porch. 49
the b. of the tabernacle. 41:1
b. of the door. 2, 3
b. of side chambers. 5
b. of house was upward. 7
the b. of place left. 11
b. of face of the house. 14
the b. of the holy portion. 45:1
the b. of the image. Dan 3:1
march through b. of land. Hab 1:6
Jerusalem, to see the b. Zech 2:2
I see a flying roll, the b. 5:2
what is the b. and length. Eph 3:18
they went up on the b. Rev 20:9
length is as large as the b. 21:16

break

to Hebron at b. of day. 2 Sam 2:32
he talked till b. of day. Acts 20:11

break

they came near to b. Gen 19:9
thou shalt b. his yoke from. 27:40*
nor b. a bone. Ex 12:46; Num 9:12
shalt b. his neck. Ex 13:13; 34:20
but ye shall b. their images. 34:13
vessel unclean ye shall b. Lev 11:33
I will b. the pride of your. 26:19
shall b. their bones. Num 24:8
if a man vow, he shall not b. 30:2
ye shall b. their pillars. Deut 12:3
b. away every man. 1 Sam 25:10
b. thy league with. 1 Ki 15:19
2 Chr 16:3
should we again b. thy. Ezra 9:14
wilt thou b. a leaf? Job 13:25*
forgetteth wild beast may b. 39:15*
let us b. their bands. Ps 2:3
shalt b. them with a rod of iron. 9
b. thou the arm of wicked. 10:15
b. their teeth, O God. 58:6
if they b. my statutes. 89:31
an oil which shall not b. 141:5*
day b. and shadows flee away.
S of S 2:17*; 4:6*
I will b. the Assyrians. Isa 14:25
b. the clods. 28:24
not b. it with a wheel. 28
b. it as a potter's vessel. 30:14
as a lion so will he b. all. 38:13
reed will he not b. 42:3; Mat 12:20
is not this the fast, ye b.? Isa 58:6
shall iron b. the northern? Jer 15:12
b. bottle, so will I b. 19:10, 11
will b. yoke of king. 28:4, 11; 30:8
he shall b. the images. 43:13
I will send wanderers and b. 48:12
saith Lord, I will b. bow of. 49:35
b. the staff of bread. Ezek 4:16
5:16; 14:13
as women that b. wedlock. 16:38
thou shalt b. sherds thereof. 23:34*
they took hold thou didst b. 29:7
I shall b. the yokes of Egypt. 30:18
I will b. Pharaoh's arms. 22, 24
I will b. the bow of Israel. Hos 1:5
I will b. the bow. 2:18
shall plow, Jacob shall b. 10:11
march and not b. Joel 2:7
b. the bar of Damascus. Amos 1:5
flay their skin, and b. Mi 3:3
now will I b. his yoke. Nah 1:13
that I might b. the. Zech 11:14
b. one of these least. Mat 5:19
else the bottles b. and the. 9:17*
came together to b. Acts 20:7
mean ye to weep and to b.? 21:13
bread we b. is it? 1 Cor 10:16

break *covenant*

but that ye b. my cov. Lev 26:15
I will not b. my cov. 44
people will b. cov. Deut 31:16, 20
I will never b. my cov. Judg 2:1
my cov. will I not b. Ps 89:34
remember, b. not thy cov. Jer 14:21
if you can b. my cov. 33:20
shall he b. cov.? Ezek 17:15
that I might b. my cov. Zech 11:10

break *down*

b. down their images. Ex 23:24
Deut 7:5
shall b. down house. Lev 14:45
I will b. down tower. Judg 8:9
if a fox go up, b. down. Neh 4:3
now they b. down the. Ps 74:6
a time to b. down and. Eccl 3:3
I will b. down the wall. Isa 5:5
over them to b. down. Jer 31:28
I have built will I b. down. 45:4
so will I b. down wall. Ezek 13:14
b. down thy high places. 16:39
b. down the towers of Tyrus. 26:4
they shall b. down thy walls. 12
he shall b. down their. Hos 10:2

break *forth*

lest Lord b. forth. Ex 19:22, 24
they b. forth into singing. Isa 14:7
44:23; 49:13; 54:1
b. forth into joy. 52:9
for thou shalt b. forth on the. 54:3
hills shall b. forth before. 55:12
then shall thy light b. forth. 58:8
north an evil shall b. forth. Jer 1:14
b. forth and cry. Gal 4:27

break *off*

thou shalt b. his yoke off. Gen 27:40
b. off golden ear-rings. Ex 32:2, 24
O king, b. off thy sins by. Dan 4:27

break *out*

if fire b. out. Ex 22:6
if leprosy b. out. Lev 13:12
if the plague again b. out. 14:43
b. out the great teeth of. Ps 58:6
wilderness waters b. out. Isa 35:6
b. out, and blood. Hos 4:2
lest he b. out like fire. Amos 5:6

break *in pieces*

Chaldeans b. in pieces. 2 Ki 25:13
will ye b. me in pieces? Job 19:2
shall b. in pieces mighty. 34:24
he shall b. in pieces the. Ps 72:4
they b. in pieces thy people. 94:5
I will b. in pieces the gates. Isa 45:2
thee will I b. in pieces. Jer 51:20
b. in pieces horse and rider. 21
with thee b. in pieces man. 22
b. in pieces and bruise. Dan 2:40, 44
fourth beast shall b. in pieces. 7:23

break *through*

lest they b. through to. Ex 19:21
not priests and people b. through. 24
to b. through to the king. 2 Ki 3:26
thieves b. through. Mat 6:19
thieves b. not through. 20

break *up*

b. up fallow ground. Jer 4:3
Hos 10:12

breaker

b. is come up. Mi 2:13
if a b. of law. Rom 2:25

breakers

covenant b. Rom 1:31

breakest

thou b. ships of Tarshish. Ps 48:7

breaketh

let me go, for the day b. Gen 32:26
for he b. me with tempest. Job 9:17
he b. down, and it cannot. 12:14
he b. me with breach upon. 16:14
the blood b. out from. 28:4
b. the cedars. Ps 29:5
he b. the bow. 46:9
my soul b. for the longing. 119:20
a soft tongue b. the bone. Pr 25:15
whoso b. an hedge, a. Eccl 10:8
which is crushed b. out. Isa 59:5
as one b. a potter's vessel. Jer 19:11
my word like hammer that b.? 23:29
ask bread, no man b. Lam 4:4
forasmuch as iron b. in. Dan 2:40*

breaking

wrestled a man till b. of. Gen 32:24
shall be a boil b. forth. Ex. 9:9, 10
if a thief be found b. up. Ex 22:2
on enemies, like b. 1 Chr 14:11
upon me as a wide b. Job 30:14
by reason of b. they. 41:25
that there be no b. Ps 144:14
b. down walls, and of. Isa 22:5
whose b. cometh suddenly. 30:13
shall break it as the b. of. 14
despised the oath in b. Ezek 16:59
17:18
sigh, son of man, with b. 21:6
long in place of b. Hos 13:13
known of them in b. of. Luke 24:35
continued in b. of bread. Acts 2:42
in the temple, b. bread from. 46
through b. the law. Rom 2:23*

breast

take the b. of the ram. Ex 29:26
shall sanctify b. of wave. 27
fat with b., b. be waved. Lev 7:30
but the b. shall be Aaron's. 31
the wave-b. and heave-shoulder. 34
Moses took the b. and waved. 8:29
the wave-b. shall ye eat. 10:14
to the priest, with wave-b. Num 6:20
as wave-b. and right. 18:18
pluck fatherless from b. Job 24:9
thou shall suck the b. of. Isa 60:16
sea monsters draw out b. Lam 4:3
head of gold, his b. Dan 2:32
publican smote upon b. Luke 18:13
on Jesus' b. saith. John 13:25; 21:20

breastplate

[1] *A piece of embroidery about ten inches square, of very rich work, which the high-priest wore upon his breast, and which was set with four rows of precious stones, upon every one of which was engraven the name of one of the tribes of Israel. It was double, or made of two pieces folded one upon the other, like a kind of bag, in which were put the* Urim *and* Thummim, Lev 8:8. [2] *A piece of defensive armour,* Rev 9:9. *In which sense, faith and love are called* breastplates, 1 Thes 5:8.

stones to be set in b. Ex 25:7; 35:9
make a b. and. 28:4, 15; 39:8
make upon the b. chains. 28:22
rings on ends of b. 28:23, 26; 39:16
bind b. by the rings. 28:28; 39:21
bear the names of Israel in b. 28:29
b. of judgement Urim. 30; Lev 8:8
put on righteousness as b. Isa 59:17
having on the b. of. Eph 6:14
putting on the b. of. 1 Thes 5:8
b. as it were b. of iron. Rev. 9:9
having b. of fire, of jacinth. 17

breasts

bless with blessings of b. Gen 49:25
put fat on the b. Lev 9:20
b. Aaron waved. 21
the b. that I should suck. Job 3:12
his b. full of milk, and. 21:24
I was on mother's b. Ps 22:9
let her b. satisfy thee. Pr 5:19
all night betwixt my b. S of S 1:13
two b. like two young roes. 4:5; 7:3
thy b. are like two clusters. 7:7
thy b. shall be as clusters. 8
my brother that sucked the b. 8:1
a little sister, and she hath no b. 8
I am a wall and my b. like towers. 10
weaned from the b. Isa 28:9
be satisfied with the b. of her. 66:11
thy b. are fashioned. Ezek 16:7
there were their b. pressed. 23:3
and they bruised the b. 8
thou shalt pluck off thine own b. 34
away adulteries from her b. Hos 2:2
miscarrying womb and dry b. 9:14
those that suck the b. Joel 2:16
doves tabering on their b. Nah 2:7
the people smote their b. Luke 23:48
having their b. girded. Rev 15:6

breath

(Used figuratively many times for the life of man, or the anger of God)

his nostrils the b. of life. Gen 2:7
flesh wherein is the b. of life. 6:17

and two wherein is b. of. Gen 7:15
all in whose nostrils was b. of. 22
foundations discovered, at blast of b. of his. 2 Sam 22:16; Ps 18:15
and there was no b. 1 Ki 17:17
by the b. of his nostrils. Job 4:9*
not suffer to take my b. 9:18
in whose hand is the b. of. 12:10
by the b. of his mouth. 15:30
my b. is corrupt, my days. 17:1*
my b. is strange to my wife. 19:17
all the while my b. is in me. 27:3
the b. of the Almighty hath. 33:4
gather to himself Spirit and b. 34:14
by b. of God frost is given. 37:10
his b. kindleth coals. 41:21
all of them made by b. of. Ps 33:6
takest away their b. they. 104:29
nor is there any b. in their. 135:17
his b. goeth forth. 146:4
every thing that hath b. praise. 150:6
they have all one b. Eccl 3:19
cease from man, whose b. Isa 2:22
with b. of his lips will he slay. 11:4
his b. as an overflowing. 30:28
b. of the Lord like a stream. 33
your b. as fire shall devour. 33:11
giveth b. to the people upon it. 42:5
no b. in them. Jer 10:14; 51:17
the b. of our nostrils. Lam 4:20
I will cause b. to enter. Ezek 37:5
cover you with skin and put b. 6
there was no b. in them. 8
and say, come, O b. 9
and the b. came into them. 10
God in whose hand b. is. Dan 5:23
no strength, neither is there b. 10:17
there is no b. at all in. Hab 2:19
giveth to all life and b. Acts 17:25

breathe

was not any left to b. Josh 11:11, 14
such as b. out cruelty. Ps 27:12
come, O breath, and b. Ezek 37:9

breathed

b. into man's nostrils the breath of life. Gen 2:7
destroyed all that b. Josh 10:40
to Jeroboam any that b. 1 Ki 15:29
he b. on them and saith. John 20:22

breatheth, -ing

save alive nothing that b. Deut 20:16
not thine ear at my b. Lam 3:56
Saul yet b. out. Acts 9:1

bred

some left, and it b. Ex 16:20

breeches

make them linen b. Ex 28:42; 39:28
priest shall put on linen b. Lev 6:10
he shall have the linen b. 16:4
they shall have linen b. Ezek 44:18

breed

they may b. abundantly. Gen 8:17
rams of b. of Bashan. Deut 32:14

breeding

as Sodom, even b. of. Zeph 2:9*

brethren

[1] *The sons of one father and mother, or of either of them,* Gen 42:13. [2] *Those neighbours or kinsmen who are closely banded together,* Gen 13:8; 19:7. [3] *Those who have made profession of the same faith and religion,* Acts 6:3, *etc.*

be no strife, we be b. Gen 13:8
Lot said, I pray you b. do not. 19:7
led me to my master's b. 24:27
said to her father and to her b. 34:11
Dinah's b. took each man his. 25
Joseph's ten b. went down. 42:3
b. came and bowed. 6
we are twelve b. 13, 32
Joseph's b. are come. 45:16
are b. of cruelty. 49:5
Joseph's b. saw their father. 50:15
possession among the b. Num 27:4
possession among our father's b. 7
no b. give it to his father's b. 10
if his father have no b. ye shall. 11
if b. dwell together. Deut 25:5
brought out father and b. Josh 6:23
an inheritance among the b. Josh 17:4
went to his mother's b. Judg 9:1
his mother's b. spake of him to. 3
answered, we are b. 2 Ki 10:13
there came of Saul's b. 1 Chr 12:2
sons of Shemaiah, whose b. 26:7
Elihu, one of the b. of David. 27:18
he had b. the sons. 2 Chr 21:2
when Jehu found the b. 22:8
pleasant for b. to dwell. Ps 133:1
soweth discord among b. Pr 6:19
part of the inheritance among b. 17:2
all the b. of the poor do hate. 19:7
Jesus saw two b. Mat 4:18
saw other two b. 21
hath forsaken houses, b. 19:29
indignation against two b. 20:24
with us seven b. 22:25; Mark 12:20
your Master, all ye are b. Mat 23:8
no man hath left b. for my sake. Mark 10:29; Luke 18:29
receive hundred-fold, b. Mark 10:30
and hate not children, b. Luke 14:26
for I have five b. that he. 16:28
betrayed by parents and b. 21:16
went abroad among b. John 21:23
b. I wot that through. Acts 3:17
wherefore b. look among. 6:3
sirs, ye are b. 7:26
which when the b. knew. 9:30
certain b. from Joppa. 10:23
moreover these six b. 11:12
determined to send relief to b. 29
these things to James and to b. 12:17
minds evil-affected against b. 14:2
men from Judea taught the b. 15:1
caused great joy to all the b. 3
and Silas chief among the b. 22
apostles and elders and b. send greeting to b. of the Gentiles. 23
exhorted the b. 15:32; 1 Thes 5:14
let go in peace from the b. Acts 15:33
being recommended by the b. 40
well reported of by the b. 16:2
when they had seen the b. 40
drew Jason and certain b. 17:6
b. immediately sent Paul. 10, 14
Paul took his leave of the b. 18:18
the b. wrote exhorting to. 27
now b. I commend you to. 20:32
to Ptolemais and saluted b. 21:7
come to Jerusalem, b. received. 17
also I received letters to the b. 22:5
I wist not b. that he was. 23:5
where we found b. and were. 28:14
when the b. heard of us. 15
nor any of the b. that came. 21
you ignorant b. Rom 1:13; 11:25
1 Cor 10:1; 12:1; 1 Thes 4:13
know ye not b. that the law. Rom 7:1
b. we are debtors, not to. 8:12
first-born among many b. 29
b. my prayer to God for Israel. 10:1
I beseech you therefore b. 12:1
15:30; 16:17; 1 Cor 1:10; 16:15
Gal 4:12; Heb 13:22
salute the b. Rom 16:14; Col 4:15
ye see your calling b. 1 Cor 1:26
and I b. when I came to you. 2:1
I b. could not speak to you. 3:1
these things b. I have in a. 4:6
but this I say b. 7:29; 15:50
when ye sin so against the b. 8:12
and as the b. of the Lord. 9:5
now I praise you b. 11:2
how is it b. when ye? 14:26
seen of above 500 b. at once. 15:6
beloved b. be steadfast. 58; Jas 2:5
I look for him with the b. 1 Cor 16:11
I desired him to come with b. 12
the b. greet you. 20; Phil 4:21
yet have I sent the b. 2 Cor 9:3
I thought it necessary to exhort b. 5
the b. which came from. 11:9
in perils among false b. 26
finally b. farewell. 13:11
all b. that are with me. Gal 1:2
because of false b. 2:4
peace to the b. Eph. 6:23
many of the b. Phil 1:14
to saints and faithful b. Col 1:2
we beseech you b. 1 Thes 4:1, 10
5:12; 2 Thes 2:1
ye do it toward all b. 1 Thes 4:10
b. pray for us. 1 Thes 5:25; 2 Thes 3:1
greet b. with holy kiss. 1 Thes 5:26
this epistle be read to the holy b. 27
put b. in remembrance. 1 Tim 4:6
intreat younger men as b. 5:1
despise them because they are b. 6:2
ashamed to call them b. Heb 2:11
holy b. partakers, consider. 3:1
unfeigned love of b. 1 Pet 1:22
be of one mind, love as b. 3:8
because we love b. 1 John 3:14
lay down our lives for the b. 16
rejoiced greatly when b. 3 John 3
whatsoever thou dost to the b. 5
neither doth he receive the b. 10

his brethren

Ham told his two b. Gen 9:22
a servant of servants to his b. 25
in presence of his b. 16:12; 25:18
his b. have I given to him. 27:37
feeding the flock with his b. 37:2
dreamed a dream and told his b. 5
his b. envied him. 11
Reuben returned to his b. 30
lest he die also as his b. did. 38:11
let the lad go up with his b. 44:33
nourished his father and his b. 47:12
separate from his b. 49:26
Deut 33:16
Joseph died, his b. and. Ex 1:6
Moses went out to his b. ... spied an Egyptian smiting one of his b. 2:11
high-priest among his b. Lev 21:10
one of his b. may redeem. 25:48
brought to his b. Num 25:6
give his inheritance to his b. 27:9
no part with his b. Deut 10:9
be not lifted up above his b. 17:20
he shall minister as all his b. 18:7
lest his b. heart faint as. 20:8
stealing any of his b. 24:7
nor did he acknowledge his b. 33:9
blessed and acceptable to his b. 24
Abimelech slew his b. Judg 9:5
Gaal came with his b. 26
which he did in slaying his 70 b. 56
Jephthah fled from his b. 11:3
be not cut off from his b. Ruth 4:10
anointed him in midst of his b. 1 Sam 16:13
when his b. and father's. 22:1
rise up from among his b. 2 Ki 9:2
honourable than his b. 1 Chr 4:9
Judah prevailed above his b. 5:2
Ephraim mourned, his b. came. 7:22
with his b. and sons were. 25:9
Jehoram slew all his b. 2 Chr 21:4
was accepted of his b. Esth 10:3
fruitful among his b. Hos 13:15
remnant of his b. shall. Mi 5:3
his mother and his b. Mat 12:46
Mark 3:31; Luke 8:19
neither did his b. believe. John 7:5
was known to his b. Acts 7:13
into Moses' heart to visit his b. 23
for he supposed his b. would. 25
to judge between his b. 1 Cor 6:5
made like to his b. Heb 2:17

men and brethren

men and b. this scripture. Acts 1:16
men and b. let me freely. 2:29
to Peter and rest, men and b. 37
he said, men, b. and fathers. 7:2
men and b. if ye have any. 13:15
men and b. children of stock of. 26
be it known to you, men and b. 38
men and b. ye know God. 15:7
answered, men and b. hearken. 13
men, b. and fathers, hear my. 22:1
men and b. I have lived in all. 23:1
men and b. I am a Pharisee. 6
men and b. I have committed. 28:17

my brethren

my b. whence be ye? Gen 29:4
set it here before my b. and. 31:37
I seek my b. tell me where. 37:16
my b. and father's. 46:31; 47:1
return to my b. in Egypt. Ex 4:18
alive father and my b. Josh 2:13
my b. made the heart of. 14:8
they were my b. Judg 8:19
my b. I pray you, do not. 19:23
away, and see my b. 1 Sam 20:29

ye shall not do so, *my b.* *1 Sam* 30:23
ye are *my b.* my bones. *2 Sam* 19:12
said, hear me, *my b.* *1 Chr* 28:2
Hanani, one of *my b.* *Neh* 1:2
I nor *my b.* nor guard put off. 4:23
I and *my b.* might exact. 5:10
and *my b.* have not eaten bread. 14
my b. dealt deceitfully. *Job* 6:15
he hath put *my b.* far from. 19:13
thy name unto *my b.* *Ps* 22:22
Heb 2:12
I am a stranger unto *my b.* *Ps* 69:8
for *my b.* and companions. 122:8
who are *my b.*? *Mat* 12:48
Mark 3:33
mother and *my b.* *Mat* 12:49
Mark 3:34
the least of these *my b.* *Mat* 25:40
go tell *my b.* that they go. 28:10
my b. are these which. *Luke* 8:21
go to *my b.* and say. *John* 20:17
from Christ for *my b.* *Rom* 9:3
take *my b.* the prophets. *Jas* 5:10
above all things, *my b.* swear not. 12

our brethren

before *our b.* discern. *Gen* 31:32
when *our b.* died before. *Num* 20:3
our b. have discouraged. *Deut* 1:28
have *our b.* stolen? *2 Sam* 19:41
send abroad to our *b.* *1 Chr.* 13:2
flesh is as flesh of *our b.* *Neh* 5:5
ability have redeemed *our b.* 8
us go again visit *our b.* *Acts* 15:36
or *our b.* be inquired of. *2 Cor* 8:23
the accuser of *our b.* *Rev* 12:10

their brethren

minister with *their b.* *Num* 8:26
no inheritance among *their b.*
Deut 18:2
a prophet from among *their b.* 18
to the voice of *their b.* *Judg* 20:13
when *their b.* come to us. 21:22
from following *their b.* *2 Sam* 2:26
bread among *their b.* *2 Ki* 23:9
dwelt with *their b.* *1 Chr* 8:32; 9:38
all *their b.* were at their. 12:32
drinking, for *their b.* had. 39
brought them to *their b.* *2 Chr.* 28:15
cry against *their b.* the. *Neh* 5:1
to distribute to *their b.* 13:13
inheritance among *their b.* *Job* 42:15
slew them not among *their b.*
Jer 41:8
tithes of people, of *their b.* *Heb* 7:5
their b. should be killed. *Rev* 6:11

thy brethren

be lord over *thy b.* *Gen* 27:29
set it before *thy b.* 31:37
I and *thy b.* come to bow? 37:10
do not *thy b.* feed the flock? 13
whether it be well with *thy b.* 14
one portion above *thy b.* 48:22
he whom *thy b.* shall. 49:8
if a poor man of *thy b.* *Deut* 15:7
from among *thy b.* shalt thou. 17:15
will raise a prophet of *thy b.* 18:15
not oppress the poor of *thy b.* 24:14
thou shalt bring *thy b.* *Josh* 2:18
among daughters of *thy b.* *Judg* 14:3
thy b. run to camp to *thy b.*
1 Sam 17:17
look how *thy b.* fare. 18
return, take *thy b.* *2 Sam* 15:20
hast slain *thy b.* *2 Chr* 21:13
thy b. dealt treacherously. *Jer* 12:6
thy b. even *thy b.* *Ezek* 11:15
mother and *thy b.* stand. *Mat* 12:47
Mark 3:32; *Luke* 8:20
call not *thy b.* *Luke* 14:12
strengthen *thy b.* 22:32
not, I am of *thy b.* *Rev* 19:10; 22:9

your brethren

one of *your b.* be. *Gen* 42:19
leave one of *your b.* here. 33
carry *your b.* from before. *Lev* 10:4
let *your b.* bewail the burning. 6
over *your b.* ye shall not. 25:46
I have taken *your b.* the. *Num* 18:6
shall *your b.* go to war and? 32:6
causes between *your b.* *Deut* 1:16
over armed before *your b.* 3:18
Josh 1:14
rest to *your b.* *Deut* 3:20; *Josh* 1:15
ye have not left *your b.* *Josh* 22:3
hath given rest to *your b.* 4
divide the spoil with *your b.* 8
fight against *your b.* *1 Ki* 12:24
2 Chr 11:4
come to you of *your b.* and wrath
come upon *your b.* *2 Chr* 19:10
captives of *your b.* 28:11
be ye not like *your b.* which. 30:7
if ye turn, *your b.* shall. 9
and fight for *your b.* *Neh* 4:14
will you even sell *your b.*? 5:8
your b. that hated you. *Isa* 66:5
bring *your b.* for an. 20
I have cast out all *your b.* *Jer* 7:15
say to *your b.* Ammi. *Hos* 2:1
if ye salute *your b.* only. *Mat* 5:47
a prophet of *your b.* *Acts* 3:22; 7:37
defraud and that *your b.* *1 Cor* 6:8
accomplished in *your b.* *1 Pet* 5:9

bribe, -s

Samuel's sons took *b.* *1 Sam* 8:3
whose hand received any *b.*? 12:3*
right hand is full of *b.* *Ps* 26:10
shaketh his hands from *b.* *Isa* 33:15
they take a *b.* and turn. *Amos* 5:12

bribery

consume tabernacles of *b.* *Job* 15:34

brick

us make *b.* they had *b.* *Gen* 11:3
made their lives bitter in *b.* *Ex* 1:14
more give straw to make *b.* 5:7, 16
incense on altars of *b.* *Isa* 65:3

brickkiln

them pass through *b.* *2 Sam* 12:31
stones in the clay in *b.* *Jer* 43:9*
make strong the *b.* *Nah* 3:14

bricks

the tale of *b.* you shall lay. *Ex* 5:8
yet shall ye deliver tale of *b.* 18, 19
the *b.* are fallen down. *Isa* 9:10

bride

them on thee, as *b.* doth. *Isa* 49:18
as a *b.* adorneth herself. 61:10
as bridegroom rejoiceth over *b.* 62:5
a *b.* forget her attire? *Jer* 2:32
cease the voice of *b.* 7:34; 16:9
25:10
in this place voice of the *b.* 33:11
and let the *b.* go out. *Joel* 2:16
he that hath the *b.* is the. *John* 3:29
voice of the *b.* heard. *Rev* 18:23
prepared as a *b.* adorned. 21:2
I will shew thee the *b.* the. 9
the Spirit and the *b.* say. 22:17

bridechamber

children of the *b.* mourn? *Mat* 9:15
children of *b.* fast? *Mark* 2:19
Luke 5:34

bridegroom

as a *b.* coming out of. *Ps* 19:5
as a *b.* decketh himself. *Isa* 61:10
as *b.* rejoiceth over bride. 62:5
children mourn while *b.*? *Mat* 9:15
Mark 2:19; *Luke* 5:34
went forth to meet *b.* *Mat* 25:1
while the *b.* tarried. 5
cry made, *b.* cometh. 6, 10
governor of feast called *b.* *John* 2:9
hath the bride is the *b.* but friend of
b. rejoiceth because of *b.* 3:29

see **bride**

bridle

(*Used both literally; and figuratively for restraint*)
put my *b.* in thy lips. *2 Ki* 19:28
Isa 37:29
have let loose the *b.* *Job* 30:11
to him with his double *b.*? 41:13
mouth must be held with a *b.* *Ps* 32:9
keep my mouth with a *b.* 39:1
a *b.* for the ass, a rod. *Pr* 26:3
there shall be a *b.* *Isa* 30:28
any seem religious and *b.* *Jas* 1:26
able also to *b.* the whole body. 3:2
blood came out of wine-press even
unto horse *b.* *Rev* 14:20

briefly

it is *b.* comprehended. *Rom* 13:9*
Sylvanus I have written *b.* *1 Pet* 5:12

brier

instead of the *b.* come up. *Isa* 55:13
no more a pricking *b.* *Ezek* 28:24
best of them is as a *b.* *Mi* 7:4

briers

will tear your flesh with *b.* *Judg* 8:7
took the elders of the city and *b.* 16
there shall come up *b.* and. *Isa* 5:6
it shall even be for *b.* 7:23
land shall become *b.* and thorns. 24
not come thither the fear of *b.* 25
wickedness shall devour *b.* 9:18
devour his *b.* and thorns. 10:17
would set *b.* and thorns. 27:4
on the land shall come up *b.* 32:13
though *b.* and thorns be. *Ezek* 2:6
that which beareth *b.* and. *Heb* 6:8*

brigandine

(*Revised Version*, coat of mail)
put on the *b.* *Jer* 46:4
that lifteth up himself in his *b.* 51:3

bright

have a *b.* spot. *Lev* 13:2, 24, 38
if the *b.* spot be white in the skin. 4
if *b.* spot stay in his place. 23, 28*
law for a scab and for a *b.* spot. 14:56
vessels Hiram made were of *b.*
1 Ki 7:45*; *2 Chr* 4:16
scattered his *b.* cloud. *Job* 37:11*
now men see not the *b.* light. 21
belly is as *b.* ivory. *S of S* 5:14*
make *b.* the arrows. *Jer* 51:11*
the fire was *b.* *Ezek* 1:13
the sword is made *b.* 21:15*
king of Babylon made arrows *b.* 21*
b. iron and cassia were in. 27:19
b. lights I will make dark. 32:8
horseman lifteth up *b.* *Nah* 3:3*
Lord make *b.* clouds. *Zech* 10:1*
behold a *b.* cloud. *Mat* 17:5
as when the *b.* shining. *Luke* 11:36
man stood before me in *b.* *Acts* 10:30
the *b.* and morning star. *Rev* 22:16

brightness

through *b.* before him were coals of
fire. *2 Sam* 22:13; *Ps* 18:12
the moon walking in *b.* *Job* 31:26
we wait for *b.* but walk. *Isa* 59:9
kings shall come to the *b.* 60:3
nor for *b.* shall the moon give. 19
righteousness go forth as *b.* 62:1
a fire and a *b.* about it. *Ezek* 1:4, 27
so was the appearance of *b.* 28
as the appearance of *b.* as. 8:2
the court was full of *b.* 10:4
strangers shall defile thy *b.* 28:7
corrupted by reason of thy *b.* 17
great image, whose *b.* *Dan* 2:31
my honour and *b.* returned. 4:36
wise shall shine as the *b.* 12:3
be very dark and no *b.* *Amos* 5:20
his *b.* was as the light. *Hab* 3:4
from heaven above *b.* *Acts* 26:13
destroy with the *b.* *2 Thes* 2:8*
being the brightness of his. *Heb* 1:3

brim

feet of priest dipped in *b.* *Josh* 3:15*
b. like *b.* of a cup. *1 Ki* 7:26
2 Chr 4:5
a molten sea from *b.* to *b.* *2 Chr* 4:2
filled them up to the *b.* *John* 2:7

brimstone

(*Sulphur*)
rained *b.* *Gen* 19:24; *Luke* 17:29
the whole land is *b.* *Deut* 29:23
b. shall be scattered on. *Job* 18:15
upon wicked he shall rain fire and *b.*
Ps 11:6; *Ezek* 38:22
like a stream of *b.* *Isa* 30:33
and the dust turned into *b.* 34:9
issued fire and *b.* *Rev* 9:17
third part of men killed by *b.* 18
tormented with fire and *b.* 14:10
of fire, burning with *b.* 19:20; 20:10
shall have their part in lake which
burneth with fire and *b.* 21:8

bring

I do *b.* a flood of waters. *Gen* 6:17
two of every sort shalt thou *b.* 19
when I *b.* a cloud over earth. 9:14
Abraham did *b.* them. 18:16
the Lord may *b.* on Abraham. 19

b. to me that I may eat. Gen 27:4, 25
b. me venison. 5
I shall b. a curse on me. 12
b. your youngest brother. 42:20, 34
if I b. him not. 37; 43:9; 44:32
b. these men home. 43:16
take wagons and b. your. 45:19
b. them I pray to me. 48:9
else to-morrow I will b. Ex 10:4
yet will I b. one plague more. 11:1
the Lord shall b. thee. 13:5, 11
that thou mayest b. causes. 18:19
his master shall b. him to. 21:6
if it be torn in pieces, b. it. 22:13
thou shalt surely b. it back. 23:4
first of first-fruits shalt b. 19; 34:26
I will send an Angel to b. thee. 23:20
of a willing heart, let him b. 35:5
the people b. much more. 36:5
not able to b. a lamb. Lev 5:7, 11
12:8
he shall b. them to the priest. 5:8, 12
shall b. fire and incense. 16:12
that Israel may b. their. 17:5
shalt b. the Levites. Num 8:9, 10
Lord delight in us, he will b. 14:8
Lord was not able to b. 16
Deut 9:28
Caleb, him will I b. Num 14:24
b. before the Lord every man. 16:17
shall not b. this congregation. 20:12
give this land, and b. us not. 32:5
too hard for you, b. it to. Deut 1:17
when the Lord shall b. thee. 7:1
then thou shalt b. her home. 21:12
then thou shalt b. it unto. 22:2
b. it to us. 30:12, 13
hear, Lord, and b. Judah. 33:7
child be weaned, then I will b. him.
1 Sam 1:22
Saul, what shall we b. the man ? 9:7
b. the portion I gave thee. 23
b. the men, that we may. 11:12
why shouldest thou b. me ? 20:8
hand with thee, to b. 2 Sam 3:12
except thou b. Michal. 13
saith aught to thee, b. him. 14:10
are ye last to b. the king ? 19:11
and the king said, b. me. 1 Ki 3:24
the wicked, to b. his way. 8:32
b. him back with thee. 13:18
b. me a morsel of bread. 17:11
he said, go ye b. him. 20:33
b. me a new cruse. 2 Ki 2:20
b. yet a vessel. 4:6
b. meal and cast it. 41
I will b. you to the man. 6:19
b. an offering and come. 1 Chr 16:29
of them to me, that I may b. 21:2
since people began to b. 2 Chr 31:10
did not our God b. ? Neh 13:18
did I say b. unto me. Job 6:22
wilt thou b. me into ? 10:9
who can b. a clean thing ? 14:4
b. him to the king of terrors. 18:14
I know thou wilt b. me to. 30:23
to b. back his soul. 33:30
b. me to thy holy hill. Ps 43:3
b. me into strong city ? 60:9; 108:10
the mountains shall b. peace. 72:3
he shall b. on them. 94:23
scornful men b. Pr 29:8
who shall b. him ? Eccl 3:22
know that God will b. 11:9
God shall b. every work. 12:14
I would b. thee into my. S of S 8:2
Lord shall b. on thee. Isa 7:17
the people shall b. them. 14:2
for I will b. more upon Dimon. 15:9
shall he b. to the ground. 25:12
tell ye and b. them near. 45:21
I b. near my righteousness. 46:13
them will I b. to my holy. 56:7
that thou b. the poor to thy. 58:7
for brass b. gold, for iron b. 60:17
b. their fear upon them. 66:4
I will take you and b. Jer 3:14
not in anger, lest thou b. 10:24
I will b. on them all the. 11:8
b. upon them, day of evil. 17:18
I will b. them from north. 31:8
I will b. on them all the good. 32:42
I will b. it health and. 33:6
them that shall b. sacrifice of. 11
behold, I will b. a fear upon. Jer 49:5
I, even I, will b. a sword. Ezek 6:3
I will b. you out of. 11:9
that I would not b. them. 20:15
I will b. on the necks of. 21:29
I will b. them against thee. 23:22
b. them to land. 34:13; 36:24; 37:21
that I would b. thee against. 38:17
I will allure and b. her. Hos 2:14
b. and let us drink. Amos 4:1
b. your sacrifices. 4
yet will I b. an heir to. Mi 1:15
I will b. them, and. Zech 8:8
b. all the tithes into the. Mal 3:10
be thou there till I b. Mat 2:13
therefore if thou b. thy. 5:23
b. him hither to. 17:17; Mark 9:19
ass and a colt, loose them and b.
Mat 21:2; Mark 11:2; Luke 19:30
and they b. to him. Mark 7:32
for I b. you good tidings. Luke 2:10
choked with tares, b. no fruit. 8:14
when they b. you into the. 12:11
them also I must b. John 10:16
and b. all things to your. 14:26
what accusation b. you ? 18:29
b. of the fish which ye have. 21:10
ye intend to b. this. Acts 5:28
that they should b. them. 7:6
b. them bound to Jerusalem. 9:2, 21
went to Damascus to b. them. 22:5
commanded to b. Paul into. 23:10
b. this young man to the chief. 17
I will b. to nothing. 1 Cor 1:19
b. to nought things that are. 28
shall b. you into remembrance. 4:17
keep under my body, b. it. 9:27
that ye may b. me on my. 16:6
ye suffer, if a man b. 2 Cor 11:20
schoolmaster to b. us. Gal 3:24
will God b. with him. 1 Thes 4:14
take Mark and b. him. 2 Tim 4:11
he might b. us to God. 1 Pet 3:18
if any come and b. not. 2 John 10
whom if thou b. forward. 3 John 6
kings do b. their glory. Rev 21:24
b. the glory of nations into it. 26

see **home, hither**

bring *again*

I b. thy son again ? Gen 24:5
thou b. not my son again. 6, 8
I will b. thee again. 28:15; 48:21
and b. word again. 37:14
I will b. him to thee again. 42:37
b. it back to him again. Ex 23:4
b. Aaron's rod again. Num 17:10
lodge this night, b. word again. 22:8
b. us word again what. Deut 1:22
in any case b. them again. 22:1
b. thee into Egypt again. 28:68
if ye b. me home again. Judg 11:9
and went to b. her again. 19:3
can I b. him again ? 2 Sam 12:23
b. young man Absalom again. 14:21
the Lord shall b. me again. 15:8
he will b. me again and shew me. 25
forgive and b. again. 1 Ki 8:34
2 Chr 6:25
b. kingdom again to Rehoboam.
1 Ki 12:21; 2 Chr 11:1
let us b. again the ark. 1 Chr 13:3
what word I shall b. again. 21:2
sent prophets to b. them again.
2 Chr 24:19
mightest b. them again. Neh 9:29
Lord said, I will b. again, I will b.
again my people. Ps 68:22
not b. it to his mouth again. Pr 19:24
grieveth him to b. it again. 26:15
I will b. again the shadow. Isa 38:8
b. it again to mind. 46:8
to b. Jacob again to him. 49:5
when the Lord shall b. again. 52:8
will b. them again. Jer 12:15; 50:19
then will I b. thee again. Jer 15:19
I will b. them again to their land.
16:15; 24:6; 32:37
I will b. them again into their. 23:3
in two years I will b. again the. 28:3
b. again to this place Jeconiah. 4, 6
I will b. again captivity. 30:3, 18
31:23; Ezek 39:25; Amos 9:14
b. again captivity of Moab. Jer 48:47
b. again captivity of Ammon. Jer 49:6
when I b. again their captivity, I will
b. again. Ezek 16:53
b. again the captivity of Egypt. 29:14
I will b. again that. Ezek 34:16
that time I b. you again. Zeph 3:20
I will b. them again. Zech. 10:6
I will b. them again out of. 10
b. me word again. Mat 2:8

see **captivity**

bring *down*

b. down my grey hairs. Gen 42:38
44:29, 31
b. your brother down. 43:7; 44:21
haste and b. down my father. 45:13
he shall b. them down. Deut 9:3
b. them down to the water. Judg 7:4
b. me down, I will b. thee down.
1 Sam 30:15
haughty, to b. down. 2 Sam 22:28
Solomon b. him down. 1 Ki 1:33
his hoary head b. thou down. 2:9
b. down high looks. Ps 18:27
shalt b. them down to pit. 55:23
b. down noise of strangers. Isa 25:5
he shall b. down their pride. 11
the high fort shall he b. down. 12
I will b. down their strength. 63:6
I b. down from thence. Jer 49:16
Ob 4
I will b. them down like. Jer 51:40
I shall b. thee down. Ezek 26:20
they shall b. thee down to pit. 28:8
I will b. them down. Hos 7:12
b. them down to valley. Joel 3:2
b. down thy strength. Amos 3:11
thence will b. them down. 9:2
who shall b. me down ? Ob 3
that he b. him down. Acts 23:15
desire thou wouldst b. down. 20
that is to b. Christ down. Rom 10:6

see **evil**

bring *forth*

let earth b. forth. Gen 1:11, 24
waters b. forth. 20
in sorrow thou shalt b. forth. 3:16
and thistles shall it b. forth. 18
b. forth every living thing. 8:17
b. forth abundantly in the. 9:7
Judah said b. her forth. 38:24
thou mayest b. forth. Ex 3:10
that I should b. forth Israel ? 11
may b. forth my armies. 7:4
the river shall b. forth frogs. 8:3
magicians did so to b. forth lice. 18
b. forth him that hath cursed.
Lev 24:14, 23
it shall b. forth fruit for. 25:21
ye shall eat and b. forth. 26:10
shalt b. forth water. Num 20:8
b. forth all tithe of. Deut 14:28
b. forth that man or woman. 17:5
b. forth the tokens of. 22:15
b. forth the men. Josh 2:3
till I come and b. forth. Judg 6:18
b. forth the man that came. 19:22
b. forth vestments for. 2 Ki 10:22
is no strength to b. forth. 19:3
Isa 37:3
b. forth all the vessels. 2 Ki 23:4
those did Cyrus b. forth. Ezra 1:8
it will bud and b. forth. Job 14:9
mischief, and b. forth vanity. 15:35
thou b. forth Mazzaroth ? 38:32
wild goats b. forth ? 39:1, 2, 3
surely the mountains b. forth. 40:20
b. forth thy righteousness. Ps 37:6
they shall still b. forth fruit. 92:14
that he may b. forth food. 104:14
that our sheep may b. forth. 144:13
what a day may b. forth ? Pr 27:1
that it b. forth grapes. Isa 5:2, 4
I travail not, nor b. forth. 23:4
conceive chaff, and b. forth. 33:11
b. forth your strong reasons. 41:21
let them b. forth and shew. 22
he shall b. forth judgement. 42:1
b. forth judgement unto truth. 3
b. forth blind people. 43:8
let them b. forth witnesses. 9
open, and b. forth salvation. 45:8
earth, and maketh it b. forth. 55:10
mischief, and b. forth iniquity. 59:4

and I will b. forth a seed. Isa 65:9
not labour in vain, nor b. forth. 23
earth be made to b. forth in ? 66:8
and not cause to b. forth ? 9
grow, they b. forth fruit. Jer 12:2
b. forth out of mouth what. 51:44
b. forth thy stuff. Ezek 12:4
and it shall b. forth boughs. 17:23
to b. them forth of the land. 20:6
I will b. them forth out of. 38
therefore will I b. forth a fire. 28:18
I will b. thee forth thine army. 38:4
shall b. forth new fruit. 47:12
Ephraim shall b. forth. Hos 9:13
though they b. forth, yet will I. 16
labour to b. forth, O Zion. Mi 4:10
he will b. me forth to the light. 7:9
before the decree b. forth. Zeph 2:2
I will b. forth my servant. Zech 3:8
shall b. forth the head-stone. 4:7
b. forth a curse, and it shall. 5:4
virgin shall b. forth a son. Mat 1:21, 23
b. forth fruit meet. 3:8; Luke 3:8
cannot b. forth evil fruit. Mat 7:18
Luke 6:43
b. forth fruit, some 30. Mark 4:20
b. forth a son, and shalt. Luke 1:31
word, keep it, and b. forth fruit. 8:15
b. forth the best robe. 15:22
may b. forth more fruit. John 15:2
that you should b. forth fruit. 16
I b. him forth to you. 19:4
Easter to b. him forth. Acts 12:4
that we should b. forth. Rom 7:4
the motions of sin to b. forth. 5

bring in

I will b. you into the land. Ex 6:8
shall b. in and plant them. 15:17
prepare that they b. in. 16:5
Angel shall b. thee in. 23:23
them will I b. in. Num 14:31
proclamation to b. in to the Lord the collection Moses laid. 2 Chr 24:9
ye shall not b. in the captives. 28:13
b. in no burden on the. Jer 17:24
b. me in before the king. Dan 2:24
king cried to b. in astrologers. 5:7
b. in everlasting righteousness. 9:24
sown much and b. in little. Hag 1:6
means to b. him in. Luke 5:18
b. in hither the poor, the. 14:21
b. in damnable heresies. 2 Pet 2:1

bring out

b. them out to us. Gen 19:5, 8, 12
make mention, and b. me out. 40:14
God will visit and b. you out. 50:24
I will b. you out from. Ex 6:6
charge to b. Israel out of. 13, 26, 27
7:5; 12:51; Jer 31:32
mishief did he b. them out. Ex 32:12
lay hold and b. him out. Deut 21:19
b. out the damsel. 22:21
b. both out to the gate. 24
shall b. out the pledge. 24:11
b. out thence Rahab. Josh 6:22
b. out those five kings. 10:22
b. out thy son that. Judg 6:30
them I will b. out. 19:24
O b. thou me out of. Ps 25:17
b. my soul out of prison. 142:7
O Lord, b. my soul out. 143:11
to b. out the prisoners. Isa 42:7
shall b. out the bones. Jer 8:1
b. out all thy wives and. 38:23
I will b. you forth out. Ezek 11:7
b. you out from people. 20:34; 34:13
accept you, when I b. you out. 20:41
b. it out piece by piece. 24:6
burneth him to b. out. Amos 6:10
sought to b. them out. Acts 17:5

bring to pass

will shortly b. it to pass. Gen 41:32
to b. to pass as at this day. 50:20
he shall b. it to pass. Ps 37:5
and b. to pass his act. Isa 28:21
I will also b. it to pass. 46:11

bring up

will also b. thee up again. Gen 46:4
and to b. them up out. Ex 3:8
I have said, I will b. you up out. 17
see, thou sayest to me, b. up. 33:12
men that b. up evil. Num 14:37
b. up Aaron and his son. 20:25
b. up an evil name. Deut 22:14
did not the Lord b. us up ? Judg 6:13
b. him up in the bed. 1 Sam 19:15
whom shall I b. up, b. up ? 28:11
men did David b. up. 2 Sam 2:3
to b. up from thence the ark. 6:2
1 Ki 8:1, 4; 1 Chr 13:6; 15:3, 12
14, 25; 2 Chr 5:2, 5
since I did b. up Israel. 1 Chr 17:5
did Sheshbazzar b. up. Ezra 1:11
shall b. up tithes. Neh 10:38
b. not forth children, nor nourish up young men, nor b. up. Isa 23:4
then will I b. them up. Jer 27:22
shall b. up a company. Ezek 16:40
I will b. up a company. 23:46
when I shall b. up the. 26:19
will b. thee up out of the midst. 29:4
a company shall b. thee up. 32:3
I will b. up flesh on you. 37:6
though they b. up children. Hos 9:12
I will b. up sackcloth. Amos 8:10
to b. up Christ. Rom 10:7
b. them up in nurture of. Eph 6:4

bringers

the b. up of children. 2 Ki 10:5

bringest

and b. me into judgement. Job 14:3
O Jerusalem that b. good. Isa 40:9
thou b. strange things. Acts 17:20

bringeth

who b. you out from. Ex 6:7
I am the Lord that b. you Lev 11:45
b. it not to door of tabernacle. 17:4, 9
the Lord b. thee into. Deut 8:7
b. down to the grave, and b. up. 1 Sam 2:6
Lord maketh poor, he b. low. 7
that b. down the people. 2 Sam 22:48
and that b. me forth from. 49
into whose hand God b. Job 12:6
he b to light the shadow. 22
wrath b. the punishments. 19:29
the thing that is hid b. he. 28:11
that b. forth his fruit. Ps 1:3
b. back the captivity. 14:7; 53:6
Lord b. the counsel of the. 33:10
the man who b. wicked. 37:7
he b. out them that are bound. 68:6
and b. them out. 107:28
he b. them to their desired. 30
b. wind out of treasuries. 135:7
Jer 10:13; 51:16
the mouth of the just b. Pr 10:31
moving his lips he b. evil. 16:30
a man's gift b. him. 18:16
son that causeth shame, and b. 19:26
a wise king b. the wheel. 20:26
much more when he b. it. 21:27
a child left, b. his mother. 29:15
ho that delicately b. up servant. 21
the fear of man b. a snare. 25
b. forth butter, b. blood, b. 30:33
like ships, she b. her food. 31:14
water the wood that b. Eccl 2:6*
Lord b. on them waters. Isa 8:7
b. down them that dwell on high, b. to dust. 26:5
b. the princes to nothing. 40:23
that b. out their host. 26
which b. forth the chariot. 43:17
the smith that b. forth. 54:16
for as the earth b. forth. 61:11
anguish of her that b. Jer 4:31
which b. iniquity. Ezek 29:16
Israel b. forth fruit. Hos 10:1
which ground b. forth. Hag 1:11
that b. not forth good fruit is hewn down. Mat 3:10; 7:19; Luke 3:9
every good tree, b. forth. Mat 7:17
good man b. forth good things, evil man b. forth. 12:35; Luke 6:45
b. forth some an hundred. Mat 13:23
who b. out of his treasures. 52
Jesus b. them up into. 17:1
the earth b. forth fruit. Mark 4:28
good tree b. not forth. Luke 6:43
if it die, b. forth. John 12:24; 15:5
gospel b. forth fruit. Col 1:6
grace of God b. salvation. Tit 2:11
b. in the first-begotten. Heb 1:6
the earth b. forth herbs. Heb 6:7
lust b. forth sin, sin b. Jas 1:15

see **tidings**

bringing

much observed for b. Ex 12:42
people were restrained from b. 36:6
an offering b. iniquity. Num 5:15
by b. up a slander upon. 14:36
of b. the king back. 2 Sam 19:10, 43
navy b. gold and silver. 1 Ki 10:22
2 Chr 9:21
I am b. such evil on. 2 Ki 21:12
on the sabbath b. in. Neh 13:15
rejoicing, b. his sheaves. Ps 126:6
b. burnt-offerings, b. Jer 17:26
made myself known in b. Ezek 20:9
his word by b. upon us. Dan 9:12
to a nation b. forth. Mat 21:43
b. one sick of the palsy. Mark 2:3
b. the spices which. Luke 24:1
multitude b. sick folks. Acts 5:16
b. me into captivity to. Rom 7:23
and b. into captivity. 2 Cor 10:5
b. many sons unto glory. Heb 2:10
the b. in of a better hope. 7:19
b. in the flood on the. 2 Pet 2:5

brink

by the kine on the b. Gen 41:3
ark in flags by river's b. Ex 2:3
shalt stand by the river's b. 7:15
from Aroer by the b. of. Deut 2:36
when ye are come to b. of. Josh 3:8
caused me return to the b. Ezek 47:6

broad

make censers, b. plates. Num 16:38
make b. plates for the. 39*
repaired, and they fortified Jerusalem to the b. wall. Neh 3:8; 12:38
out of strait into b. place. Job 36:16
thy commandment is exceeding b. Ps 119:96
in the b. ways I will seek. S of S 3:2
Lord will be place of b. Isa 33:21
know and seek in the b. Jer 5:1
the b. walls of Babylon. 51:58
chariots shall justle in b. Nah 2:4
b. is the way that leadeth. Mat 7:13
make b. their phylacteries. 23:5

broader

the measure is b. than. Job 11:9

broidered

make a robe, a b. coat. Ex 28:4*
clothed thee with b. Ezek 16:10
raiment was of silk and b. 13
tookest thy b. garments and. 18
princes put off b. garments. 26:16
linen with b. work from. 27:7
occupied in thy fairs with b. 16
merchants in blue clothes and b. 24
women adorn, not with b. 1 Tim 2:9

broiled

gave him a piece of b. Luke 24:42

broken

b. my covenant. Gen 17:14; Ps 55:20
Isa 24:5; 33:8; Jer 11:10
vessel wherein sodden, shall be b. Lev 6:28
vessel that he touched be b. 15:12
man that is b. footed, or b. 21:19
that hath his stones b. let. 20
blind, b. or maimed. 22:22, 24
and I have b. the bands. 26:13
when I have b. the staff of. 26
because he hath b. Num 15:31
were the horse-hoofs b. Judg 5:22
the withs, as a thread is b. 16:9
bows of the mighty are b. 1 Sam 2:4
a bow of steel is b. 2 Sam 22:35
Ps 18:34
the ships were b. 1 Ki 22:48
God hath b. in upon. 1 Chr 14:11
b. thy works, ships b. 2 Chr 20:37
also he built wall that was b. 32:5
teeth of young lions are b. Job 4:10
my skin is b. and become. 7:5
I was at ease, but he hath b. 16:12
arms of fatherless have been b. 22:9
and wickedness shall be b. 24:20
and let mine arm be b. from. 31:22
the high arm shall be b. 38:15

thou hast b. the teeth of. Ps 3:7
forgotten, I am like b. vessel. 31:12
Lord is nigh them of b. 34:18; 51:17
keepeth his bones, not one is b. 34:20
their bows shall be b. 37:15
arms shall be b. 17
I am feeble and sore b. 38:8
though thou hast b. us in the. 44:19
that the bones thou hast b. 51:8
sacrifices of God are a b. spirit. 17
the earth to tremble, hast b. 60:2
reproach hath b. my heart. 69:20
he hath b. the gates of brass. 107:16
he might even slay the b. 109:16
the snare is b. and we are. 124:7
he healeth the b. in heart. 147:3
suddenly shall he be b. Pr 6:15
sorrow of heart spirit is b. 15:13
a b. spirit drieth the bones. 17:22
is like a b. tooth and a foot. 25:19
cord is not quickly b. Eccl 4:12
golden bowl be b. or pitcher b. 12:6
nor latchet of shoes be b. Isa 5:27
sixty-five years Ephraim be b. 7:8
many shall fall and be b. 8:15
for thou hast b. the yoke. 9:4
the Lord hath b. the staff. 14:5
rod of him that smote thee is b. 29
shall be b. in the purposes. 19:10
all graven images he hath b. 21:9
might fall backward and be b. 28:13
he hath b. the covenant. 33:8
nor the cords thereof be b. 20
trustest in staff of this b. reed. 36:6
hewed out b. cisterns that. Jer 2:13
the children have b. crown. 16
of old I have b. thy yoke. 20
these have b. thy yoke. 5:5
all my cords are b. 10:20
the branches of it are b. 11:16
daughter of my people is b. 14:17
Coniah a despised b. idol? 22:28
mine heart is b. because. 23:9
I have b. the yoke of the. 28:2
Hananiah, thou hast b. 13
may also my covenant be b. 33:21
how is the strong staff b.? 48:17
the arm of Moab is b. 25
I have b. Moab like a vessel. 38
this Nebuchadnezzar hath b. 50:17
hammer of whole earth cut and b. 23
every one of their bows is b. 51:56
walls of Babylon be utterly b. 58
he hath destroyed and b. Lam 2:9
he hath b. my bones. 3:4
he hath b. my teeth. 16
altars, and images be b. Ezek 6:4, 6
because I am b. with their. 9
my covenant that he hath b. 17:19
her strong rods were b. 19:12
aha, she is b. that was the. 26:2
the east-wind hath b. 27:26
time when thou shalt be b. 34
I have b. the arm of Pharaoh. 30:21
strong and that which was b. 22
his boughs are b. by all. 31:12
be b. in the midst of the. 32:28
nor bound up that which was b. 34:4
bind up that which was b. 16
when I have b. the bands. 27
and they have b. my covenant. 44:7
kingdom partly strong, and partly b. Dan 2:42
the great horn was b. 8:8
now that being b. whereas four. 22
shall be b. without hand. 25
his kingdom shall be b. 11:4
with flood be overthrown and b. 22
Ephraim is oppressed and b. Hos 5:11
ship was like to be b. Jonah 1:4
and it was b. in that day. Zech 11:11
shall not heal that which is b. 16
took up of the b. meat. Mat 15:37; Mark 8:8
on this stone, shall be b. Mat 21:44; Luke 20:18
suffered house to be b. Luke 12:39
not only b. the sabbath. John 5:18
that law of Moses not be b. 7:23
and scripture cannot be b. 10:35
besought Pilate their legs be b. 19:31
a bone of him shall not be b. 36
so many, yet was not net b. 21:11
had b. bread and talked. Acts 20:11
gave thanks, when he had b. 27:35
but the hinder part was b. 41*
my body b. for you. 1 Cor 11:24
as vessels shall they be b. Rev 2:27

broken *down*

oven or ranges b. d. Lev 11:35
altar that was b. d. 1 Ki 18:30
watch, that it be not b. d. 2 Ki 11:6*
Hezekiah had b. d. 2 Chr 33:3
Josiah had b. d. the altars. 34:7
wall of Jerusalem is b. d. Neh 1:3
viewed walls which were b. d. 2:13
why hast thou b. d.? Ps 80:12
thou hast b. d. all his hedges. 89:40
the stone wall was b. d. Pr 24:31
like a city b. d. 25:28
b. d. the principal plants. Isa 16:8
the houses have ye b. d. 22:10
city of confusion is b. d. 24:10
the earth is utterly b. d. 19
cities were b. d. Jer 4:26
Moab b. d. 48:20, 39
foundations shall be b. d. Ezek 30:4
the barns are b. d. Joel 1:17
Christ hath b. d. middle. Eph 2:14

broken *forth*

how hast thou b. forth? Gen 38:29
the Lord hath b. forth. 2 Sam 5:20

broken *in*

God hath b. in. 1 Chr 14:11

broken *off*

my purposes are b. off. Job 17:11
boughs are withered, they shall be b. off. Isa 27:11
branches be b. off. Rom 11:17, 19
unbelief they were b. off. 20

broken *out*

leprosy b. out of the. Lev 13:20, 25

broken *in*, or *to pieces*

adversaries b. in pieces. 2 Sam 2:10
rock, were b. in pieces. 2 Chr 25:12
hast b. Rahab in pieces. Ps 89:10
ye shall be b. in pieces. Isa 8:9
potter's vessel b. in pieces. 30:14
Merodach is b. in pieces. Jer 50:2*
silver, gold, b. to pieces. Dan 2:35
of Samaria b. in pieces. Hos 8:6
and fetters been b. in p. Mark 5:4

broken *up*

the great deep b. up. Gen 7:11
city Jerusalem was b. up. 2 Ki 25:4; Jer 39:2; 52:7
sons of Athaliah b. up. 2 Chr. 24:7
the depths are b. up. Pr 3:20
of Chaldeans was b. up. Jer 37:11
they have b. up and. Mi 2:13
suffered house be b. up. Mat 24:43
they had b. roof up. Mark 2:4
congregation was b. up. Acts 13:43

brokenhearted

to bind up the b. Isa 61:1
to heal b., to preach. Luke 4:18

brood

as a hen gathers her b. Luke 13:34

brook

sent them over the b. Gen 32:23*
take willows of the b. Lev 23:40
came to b. Eshcol and. Num 13:23*
called, b. Eshcol because of. 24*
b. Zered, went over b. Deut 2:13, 14
and cast the dust thereof into b. 9:21
smooth stones out of b. 1 Sam 17:40
David came to the b. Besor. 30:9
king passed over the b. 2 Sam 15:23
they be gone over the b. 17:20
day thou passest over b. 1 Ki 2:37
idol burnt by the b. Kidron. 15:13; 2 Chr 15:16
hide thyself by b. Cherith. 1 Ki 17:3, 5
he drank of the b. 6
brought them to the b. Kishon. 18:40
burnt the grove at the b. 2 Ki 23:6
dust into b. Kidron. 12; 2 Chr 30:14
find them at end of the b. 2 Chr 20:16
Levites carried it to the b. 29:16
people stopped the b. 32:4
went up by the b. and. Neh 2:15
dealt deceitfully as a b. Job 6:15
the willows of the b. compass. 40:22
as to Jabin at b. Kison. Ps 83:9*
he shall drink of the b. in. 110:7
wisdom as a flowing b. Pr 18:4
carry away to the b. Isa 15:7
fields to b. Kidron be holy. Jer 31:40
with his disciples over b. John 18:1

brooks

in Red sea and b. of. Num 21:14
at the stream of the b. that. 15*
to a land of b. of water. Deut 8:7
of the b. of Gaash. 2 Sam 23:30; 1 Chr 11:32
go unto all b. of water. 1 Ki 18:5
and as the stream of b. Job 6:15
he shall not see the b. of. 20:17*
gold as stones of the b. 22:24
hart panteth after water b. Ps 42:1
b. of defence shall be. Isa 19:6*
paper reeds by the b., by the b., every thing sown by the b. 7*
they that cast angle into the b. 8

broth

Gideon put the b. in a. Judg 6:19
angel said, pour out the b. 20
b. of abominable things. Isa 65:4

brother

(*For uses see* **brethren**)

hand of every man's b. Gen 9:5
Rebekah had a b. 24:29
gave also to her b. and mother. 53
told Rachel he was father's b. 29:12
to tell ye had yet a b., have ye another b.? 43:6, 7; 44:19
her husband's b. shall. Deut 25:5
blood laid on their b. Judg 9:24
repented them for their b. 21:6
eating in their elder b. Job 1:13, 18
I am a b. to dragons. 30:29
and a b. is born for. Pr 17:17
he that is slothful is b. to him. 18:9
a b. offended is harder to be. 19
friend that sticketh closer than b. 24
better neighbour near than b. 27:10
he hath neither child nor b. Eccl 4:8
trust not in any b. for b. will. Jer 9:4
for b. they may. Ezek 44:25
not Esau Jacob's b.? Mal 1:2
b. shall deliver up the b. Mat 10:21; Mark 13:12
if a man's b. die and. Mark 12:19; Luke 20:28
Mary, whose b. Lazarus. John 11:2
comfort them concerning their b. 19
b. Saul, receive. Acts 9:17; 22:13
he killed James the b. of. 12:2
thou seest, b. how many. 21:20
and Quartus a b. Rom 16:23
if any man called a b. 1 Cor 5:11
b. goeth to law with b. 6:6
if any b. hath a wife. 7:12
a b. or sister is not under. 15
thy knowledge shall weak b. 8:11
have sent with him the b. 2 Cor 8:18
withdraw from every b. 2 Thes 3:6
but admonish him as a b. 15
are refreshed by thee, b. Philem 7
but above a servant, a b. 16

his **brother**

and after that came his b. Gen 25:26
should give seed to his b. 38:9
his b. is dead. 42:38; 44:20
slay every man his b. Ex 32:27
for his father or his b. Lev 21:2
not make unclean for his b. Num 6:7
not exact of neighbour or his b. Deut 15:2
thought to have done to his b. 19:19
succeed in name of his b. 25:6
shall be evil towards his b. 28:54
fear of Abimelech his b. Judg 9:21
for blood of Asahel his b. 2 Sam 3:27
but Solomon his b. 1 Ki 1:10
usury every one of his b. Neh 5:7
none can redeem his b. Ps 49:7
shall take hold of his b. Isa 3:6
no man shall spare his b. 9:19
fight every one against his b. 19:2
every one said to his b. 41:6
no more every man his b. Jer 31:34; Heb 8:11
none serve of a Jew his b. Jer 34:9
let ye go every man his b. 14
liberty every one to his b. 17

because he spoiled his b. Ezek 18:18
speak every one to his b. 33:30
Jacob took his b. Hos 12:3
he did pursue his b. Amos 1:11
hunt every man his b. Mi 7:2
by the sword of his b. Hag 2:22
mercy every man to his b. Zech 7:9
none imagine evil against his b. 10
treacherously against his b.? Mal 2:10
shall say to his b., Raca! Mat 5:22
also to you, if ye from your hearts forgive not every one his b. 18:35
raise seed to his b. 22:24
Mark 12:19; Luke 20:28
left his wife unto his b. Mat 22:25
he findeth his b. John 1:41
occasion to fall in his b. way. Rom 14:13
no man defraud his b. 1 Thes 4:6
evil of his b. and judgeth his b. Jas 4:11
and hateth his b. 1 John 2:9, 11
he that loveth his b. 10
he that loveth not his b. 3:10, 14
who was of that wicked one, and slew his b. because his b. 3:12
hatheth his b. is a. 3:15; 4:20
loveth God, love his b. 4:21
if any see his b. sin a. 5:16

my brother

am I my b. keeper? Gen 4:9
said, he is my b. 20:5, 13; 1 Ki 20:32
then I slay my b. Jacob. Gen 27:41
because thou art my b. 29:15
battle against Benjamin my b. Judg 20:23, 28
for thee, my b. 2 Sam 1:26
nay my b. do not force me. 13:12
saying, alas my b. 1 Ki 13:30
as he had been my b. Ps 35:14
thou wert as my b. S of S 8:1
lament, saying, ah my b. Jer 22:18
is my b. and sister. Mat 12:50
Mark 3:35
how oft shall my b. sin? Mat 18:21
speak to my b. Luke 12:13
if hadst been here, my b. John 11:21
if meat make my b. to. 1 Cor 8:13
I found not Titus my b. 2 Cor 2:13

our brother

profit if we slay our b.? Gen 37:26
for he is our b. 27; Judg 9:3
guilty concerning our b. Gen 42:21
if thou wilt send our b. 43:4
sent with them our b. 2 Cor 8:22
and Timothy our b. Philem 1

thy brother

where is Abel thy b.? Gen 4:9
voice of thy b. blood. 10
and shalt serve thy b. 27:40
thy b. wife raise up seed to thy b. 38:8
is not Aaron thy b.? Ex 4:14
take to thee Aaron thy b. 28:1
shalt not hate thy b. Lev 19:17
fear thy God that thy b. 25:36
Aaron thy b. Num 27:13; Deut 32:50
if thy b. entice thee. Deut 13:6
open thy hand wide to thy b. 15:11
if thy b. an Hebrew be sold. 12
bring them again to thy b. 22:1
with all lost things of thy b. 3
not abhor Edomite, he is thy b. 23:7
not lend upon usury to thy b. 19
up my face to thy b. 2 Sam 2:22
hold thy peace, he is thy b. 13:20
said, thy b. Benhadad. 1 Ki 20:33
a pledge from thy b. Job 22:6
speakest against thy b. Ps 50:20
nor go into thy b. house. Pr 27:10
thy violence against thy b. Ob 10
looked on the day of thy b. 12
rememberest that thy b. Mat 5:23
first be reconciled to thy b. 24
mote in thy b. eye. 7:3, 5
Luke 6:41, 42
if thy b. trespass, hast gained thy b. Mat 18:15; Luke 17:3
thy b. shall rise again. John 11:23
judge thy b.? why dost thou set at nought thy b.? Rom 14:10

your brother

bring your b. so will I deliver you your b. Gen 42:34
not see my face, except your b. 43:3
take your b. arise, and go. 13
I am Joseph your b. 45:4
king, because he is your b. Judg 9:18
John, who also am your b. Rev 1:9

brotherhood

might break b. between. Zech 11:14
love the b. fear God. 1 Pet 2:17

brotherly

remembered not the b. Amos 1:9
affectioned, with b. love. Rom 12:10
as touching b. love. 1 Thes 4:9
let b. love continue. Heb 13:1
to godliness b. kindness, and to b. kindness charity. 2 Pet 1:7

brought

hast b. on me and my. Gen 20:9
the Lord thy God b. it to. 27:20
that torn of beasts I b. not. 31:39
they b. him the present. 43:26
beast in field not b. Ex 9:19
b. east-wind, east-wind b. 10:13
hard causes they b. to Moses. 18:26
how I bare you and b. you. 19:4
man that b. us out of Egypt. 32:1, 23
that thou hast b. so great a sin. 21
had purple and scarlet b. 35:23
b. to Aaron the priest. Lev 13:2, 9
till he have b. an offering. 23:14
they b. the blasphemer. 24:11
he shall be b. to door. Num 6:13
because b. not the offering. 9:13
wherefore hath the Lord b.? 14:3
and he hath b. thee near. 16:10
Moses b. their cause. 27:5
have therefore b. an oblation. 31:50
till we have b. them. 32:17
the Lord thy God b. Deut 5:15
I have b. the first-fruits. 26:10
I have b. away the hallowed. 13
in morning ye shall be b. Josh 7:14
they took and b. them. 23
they b. them to the valley. 24
Lord b. the sea upon them. 24:7
I have b. you unto land. Judg 2:1
the Philistines b. money. 16:18
who b. thee hither? 18:3
she b. Samuel to the. 1 Sam 1:24
they slew a bullock and b. 25
despised him, and b. him no. 10:27
wherefore then have ye b.? 21:14
what Abigail had b. him. 25:35
found and b. an Egyptian to. 30:11
crown and bracelet, b. 2 Sam 1:10
who am I? what is my house, that thou hast b.? 7:18; 1 Chr 17:16
Lord b. evil. 1 Ki 9:9; 2 Chr 7:22
they b. every man his present. 1 Ki 10:25; 2 Chr 9:24
hast thou also b. evil? 1 Ki 17:20
the king died, and was b. to. 22:37
not receiving what he b. 2 Ki 5:20
Hoshea b. no presents to. 17:4
carry thither the priest ye b. 27
he b. the shadow ten degrees. 20:11
craftsmen the king b. captive. 24:16
with jeopardy of lives b. 1 Chr 11:19
the Lord b. fear of him. 14:17
children of Israel b. 2 Chr 13:18
b. to Jehoshaphat presents. 17:5
b. Ahaziah to Jehu, and. 22:9
the king of Syria b. Israel. 28:5
b. captives to Jericho to. 15
many b. gifts to the Lord. 32:23
they b. us a man of. Ezra 8:18
God had b. counsel. Neh 4:15
people b. them and made. 8:16
thou art just in all that is b. 9:33
Judah b. tithe of corn and. 13:12
the royal apparel be b. Esth 6:8
of slain in Shushan b. 9:11
a thing was secretly b. Job 4:12
yet shall he be b. to the. 21:32
be b. to confusion. Ps 35:4, 26
with joy shall they be b. 45:15
they are b. to shame. 71:24
a man is b. to a piece. Pr 6:26
b. me to banqueting-. S of S 2:4
Ar is b. to silence, Kir of Moab b. to silence. Isa 15:1
b. Chaldeans to ruin. Isa 23:13
terrible one is b. to nought. 29:20
hast not b. small cattle. 43:23, 24
have called him, I have b. 48:15
b. as a lamb to the slaughter. 53:7
arm b. salvation. 59:16; 63:5
that their kings may be b. 60:11
they that b. it shall drink. 62:9
as an ox that is b. Jer 11:19
I have b. on them a spoiler. 15:8
as I have b. all this evil. 32:42
now Lord hath b. it and done. 40:3
concerning the evil I b. Ezek 14:22
left she her whoredoms b. 23:8
thou shalt not be b. together. 29:5
might shew them, art thou b. 40:4
b. me through the waters to. 47:3, 4
nor instruments of music b. Dan 6:18
b. him near before ancient of. 7:13
Lord watched evil, and b. it. 9:14
given up, and they that b. her. 11:6
when ye b. it home. Hag 1:9
ye b. what was torn. Mal 1:13
shall be b. before kings. Mat 10:18
Mark 13:9; Luke 21:12
kingdom b. to desolation. Mat 12:25
Luke 11:17
b. John Baptist's head. Mat 14:11
I b. him to thy disciples. 17:16
one was b. that owed him. 18:24
b. to him little children. 19:13
Mark 10:13
a candle b. to be put. Mark 4:21
king commanded head to be b. 6:27
disciples rebuked those that b. 10:13
b. him to Jerusalem. Luke 2:22
a woman b. an alabaster box. 7:37
b. him to an inn and. 10:34
why have ye not b. him? John 7:45
prison to have them b. Acts 5:21
Barnabas b. him to the. 9:27
and being b. on their way. 15:3
who b. her masters gain. 16:16
b. them to the magistrates. 20
from his body were b. 19:12
b. their books, and burned them. 19
Demetrius b. no small gain. 24
ye b. hither these men, no robbers. 37
and they b. the young man. 20:12
they all b. us on our way. 21:5
commanded Paul to be b. 25:6
thou must be b. before Caesar. 27:24
to be b. on my way. Rom 15:24
I will not be b. under. 1 Cor 6:12
of you to be b. on. 2 Cor 1:16
b. life and immortality. 2 Tim 1:10
grace that is to be b. to. 1 Pet 1:13
of the same is he b. in. 2 Pet 2:19

brought *again*

Abram b. again his. Gen 14:16
the money that was b. again. 43:12
Moses and Aaron b. again. Ex 10:8
the Lord b. again the waters. 15:19
b. us word again and. Deut 1:25
b. him word again. Josh 14:7
hath b. me home again. Ruth 1:21
Philistines b. again ark. 1 Sam 6:21
b. again Abner. 2 Sam 3:26
came and b. the king word again. 2 Ki 22:9, 20; 1 Ki 20:9; 2 Chr 34:28
b. Manasseh again. 2 Chr 33:13
b. I again the vessels of. Neh 13:9
vessels shall be b. again. Jer 27:16
ye have not b. again. Ezek 34:4
when I have b. again. 39:27
repented and b. again. Mat 27:3
of peace that b. again. Heb 13:20

brought *back*

Abram b. back all. Gen 14:16
b. back word to them. Num 13:26
prophet whom he had b. back. 1 Ki 13:23
Jehoshaphat b. them back. 2 Chr 19:4
hast b. back captivity of. Ps 85:1
come into land b. back. Ezek 38:8

brought *down*

Joseph was b. down into. Gen 39:1
he b. down the people. Judg 7:5
Philistines b. down Samson. 16:21
he had b. him down. 1 Sam 30:16
they b. Adonijah down. 1 Ki 1:53
Elijah b. the child down 17:23

b. them down to brook. 1 Ki 18:40
are b. down and fallen. Ps 20:8
he b. down their heart. 107:12
mean man shall be b. down. Isa 5:15
thy pomp is b. down to. 14:11
thou shalt be b. down to hell. 15
shalt be b. down and speak. 29:4
your sake I have b. down. 43:14
he hath b. them down. Lam 2:2
the Lord have b. down. Ezek 17:24
shall be b. down with. 31:18
of Assyria be b. down. Zech 10:11
Capernaum be b. down. Mat 11:23
brethren b. him down. Acts 9:30

brought forth

earth b. forth grass and. Gen 1:12
waters b. forth abundantly. 21
king of Salem b. forth. 14:18
Lord b. forth Abram abroad. 15:5
angels b. Lot forth, and. 19:16
the servant b. forth jewels. 24:53
when b. forth, she sent to. 38:25
earth b. forth by handfuls. 41:47
when thou hast b. forth. Ex 3:12
for ye have b. us forth. 16:3
Lord who b. them forth out of Egypt.
29:46; Lev 25:38; 26:13, 45
Aaron's rod b. forth. Num 17:8
sent an angel, and b. us forth. 20:16
God b. him forth out of. 24:8
who b. thee forth. Deut 6:12; 8:14
who b. forth water out of. 8:15
people b. forth have corrupted. 9:12
the Lord b. us forth with a. 26:8
made when he b. them forth. 29:25
for precious fruits b. forth. 33:14
b. forth those five kings. Josh 10:23
she b. forth butter in. Judg 5:25
b. you forth out of house of. 6:8
Moses, who b. forth. 1 Sam 12:8
b. me forth into large. 2 Sam 22:20
Ps 18:19
forsook the Lord who b. forth their
fathers. 1 Ki 9:9; 2 Chr 7:22
b. forth vestments. 2 Ki 10:22
b. forth the king's son. 11:12
hast b. me forth out. Job 10:18
wicked shall be b. forth. 21:30
mischief, and b. forth. Ps 7:14
before mountains were b. forth. 90:2
their land b. forth frogs. 105:30
he b. forth his people with. 43
I was b. forth. Pr 8:24
before the hills was I b. forth. 25
mother b. thee forth, she b. forth.
S of S 8:5
for grapes, and it b. forth. Isa 5:2
b. forth wind. 26:18
what hast thou b. forth. 45:10
among sons, she hath b. forth. 51:18
she travailed, she b. forth. 66:7
as Zion travailed, she b. forth. 8
thou hast b. me forth. Jer 2:27
commanded in day I b. forth. 11:4
34:13
Pashur b. forth Jeremiah. 20:3
hast b. forth thy people. 32:21
Lord b. forth the weapons. 50:25
the Lord hath b. forth our. 51:10
I b. forth my stuff by. Ezek 12:7
a remnant shall be b. forth. 14:22
in whose sight b. them forth. 20:22
travaileth hath b. forth. Mi 5:3
olive-tree hath not b. forth. Hag 2:19
till she had b. forth her. Mat 1:25
good ground, and b. forth fruit.
13:8; Mark 4:8
Elisabeth's time came, she b. forth.
Luke 1:57
she b. forth her first-born son. 2:7
ground of a rich man b. forth. 12:16
that, he b. forth Jesus. John 19:13
prison doors, b. them forth. Acts 5:19
Herod would have b. him forth. 12:6
the man to be b. forth. 25:17
and the earth b. forth. Jas 5:18
she b. forth a man-child. Rev 12:5
persecuted woman which b. forth. 13

brought in

hath b. in an Hebrew. Gen 39:14
Joseph b. in Jacob his father. 47:7
blood was not b. in. Lev 10:18
goat, whose blood was b. in. 16:27
not till Miriam was b. in. Num 12:15
for righteousness Lord b. me in.
Deut 9:4
when the Lord hath b. thee in. 11:29
Joab b. in a great spoil. 2 Sam 3:22
b. in the ark of the Lord. 6:17
1 Ki 8:6
no burden b. in on the. Neh 13:19
by his power he b. in. Ps 78:26
then was Daniel b. in. Dan 5:13
John's head was b. in. Mat 14:11
b. in with Jesus into. Acts 7:45
false brethren b. in to. Gal 2:4

brought into

not b. us into a land. Num 16:14
Lord hath b. thee into. Deut 6:10
31:20
b. ark into Dagon's. 1 Sam 5:2
b. them into the parlour. 9:22
b. thy servant into a. 20:8
sin-money not b. into. 2 Ki 12:16
hast b. me into. Ps 22:15
king hath b. me into his. S of S 1:4
I b. you into a plentiful. Jer 2:7
hath b. me into darkness. Lam 3:2
have b. thee into waters. Ezek 27:26
b. into my sanctuary. 44:7
led him and b. him into. Acts 9:8
b. Greeks into the temple. 21:28
we b. nothing into. 1 Tim 6:7
whose blood is b. into. Heb 13:11

brought low

hast b. me very low. Judg 11:35
Lord b. Judah low. 2 Chr 28:19
they are b. low. Job 14:21
wicked are gone and b. low. 24:24
prevent us, we are b. low. Ps 79:8
and were b. low for. 106:43
are b. low, through. 107:39
I was b. low, and he helped. 116:6
for I am b. very low. 142:6
of music shall be b. low. Eccl 12:4
lifted up, shall be b. low. Isa 2:12
of terrible ones be b. low. 25:5
mountain and hill b. low. Luke 3:5
Isa 40:4

brought out

that b. thee out of Ur. Gen 15:7
they b. him hastily out. 41:14
and he b. Simeon out. 43:23
by strength of hand Lord b. you out.
Ex 13:3, 9, 14, 16; Deut 6:21
which b. out. Ex 20:2; Lev 19:36
Num 15:41; Deut 5:6; Ps 81:10
b. them out of Egypt. Lev 23:43
1 Ki 8:21
Lord b. thee out thence. Deut 5:15
b. them out to slay them. 9:28
young men b. out Rahab. Josh 6:23
afterward I b. you out. 24:5
servant b. her out. 2 Sam 13:18
he b. out the grove. 2 Ki 23:6
he b. out the people. 1 Chr 20:3
b. out the king's son. 2 Chr 23:11
priests b. out all uncleanness. 29:16
he b. streams also out. Ps 78:16
b. a vine out of Egypt. 80:8
he b. them out of darkness. 107:14
and b. out Israel from. 136:11
in the day I b. them out. Jer 7:22
father b. out of Jewry. Dan 5:13
the Lord b. Israel out. Hos 12:13
Moses, which b. us out. Acts 7:40
how the Lord b. him out. 12:17
with an high arm b. them out. 13:17
b. out, and said, what must? 16:30
besought them, and b. them out. 39

brought to pass

I have b. it to pass. 2 Ki 19:25
Isa 37:26
and shall be b. to pass. Ezek 21:7
shall be b. to pass. 1 Cor 15:54

brought up

hast thou b. us up? Ex 17:3
Num 21:5
Moses that b. us up. Ex 32:1, 23
gods which b. thee up. 4, 8
1 Ki 12:28
and people thou hast b. up. Ex 33:1
b. up an evil report. Num 13:32
thing that thou hast b. us up? 16:13
have ye b. up congregation of? 20:4
with thee, which b. up. Deut 20:1
because he b. up an evil. 22:19
he it is that b. us up. Josh 24:17
bones of Joseph b. up. 32
I b. you up from Egypt. Judg 6:8
1 Sam 10:18
b. Samson up. Judg 15:13
the lords b. up to her. 16:8
b. him up and buried. 31
all flesh-hook b. up the. 1 Sam 2:14
day I b. them up. 8:8; 2 Sam 7:6
1 Chr 17:5
that b. your fathers up. 1 Sam 12:6
David went and b. up. 2 Sam 6:12
15; 1 Ki 8:4; 1 Chr 15:28; 2 Chr 1:4
b. up for Adriel. 2 Sam 21:8
b. up the bones of Saul. 13
that b. up Ahab's. 2 Ki 10:1, 6
against Lord who b. them up. 17:7
the Lord who b. you up. 36
b. up Zedekiah to king. 25:6
Jer 39:5
Solomon b. up daughter. 2 Chr 8:11
with young men b. up. 10:8, 10
all these vessels b. up. Ezra 1:11
king of Assur b. us up hither. 4:2
God that b. thee up. Neh 9:18
Mordecai b. up Esther. Esth 2:7
like as when she was b. up. 20
from youth he was b. up. Job 31:18
thou hast b. up my soul. Ps 30:3
b. me up out of an horrible pit. 40:2
as one b. up with him. Pr 8:30
I nourished and b. up. Isa 1:2
who hath b. up these? 49:21
to guide of sons she b. up. 51:18
he that b. them up? 63:11; Jer 2:6
in the day I b. them up. Jer 11:7
Lord that b. up Israel. 16:14; 23:7
b. up Israel from the north. 15; 23:8
those I b. up hath my. Lam 2:22
that were b. up in scarlet. 4:5
b. up one of her whelps. Ezek 19:3
when I have b. you up out. 37:13
I b. you up. Amos 2:10; 3:1; 9:7
Mi 6:4
yet hast b. up my. Jonah 2:6
she shall be b. up. Nah 2:7
where he had been b. up. Luke 4:16
been b. up with Herod. Acts 13:1
yet b. up in this city at feet. 22:3
widow, if she have b. up. 1 Tim 5:10

broughtest

thy people thou b. out. Ex 32:7
thou b. up this people. Num 14:13
lest land whence thou b. Deut 9:28
thine inheritance thou b. out. 29
1 Ki 8:51
he that b. in Israel. 2 Sam 5:2
1 Chr 11:2
b. our fathers out of. 1 Ki 8:53
b. him forth out of Ur. Neh 9:7
thou b. forth water for them. 15
b. them into the land. 23
thou b. us into the net. Ps 66:11
but thou b. us out into a. 12

brow

iron sinew, thy b. brass. Isa 48:4
led him to the b. of hill. Luke 4:29

brown

(Revised Version, black)
b. cattle among the sheep. Gen 30:32
35:40
every one that is not b. shall be. 30:33

bruise, noun

saith the Lord, thy b. is. Jer 30:12*
is no healing of thy b. Nah 3:19*

bruise

b. thy head, thou shalt b. Gen 3:15
nor will he b. it with. Isa 28:28*
it pleased the Lord to b. him. 53:10
iron shall it break and b. Dan 2:40*
of peace shall b. Satan. Rom 16:20

bruised

not offer to Lord what is b. Lev 22:24
trusteth on staff of this b. 2 Ki 18:21
b. reed shall he not break. Isa 42:3
Mat 12:20
he was b. for our iniquities. Isa 53:5
there they b. the teats. Ezek 23:3
b. the breasts of her virginity. 8
liberty them that are b. Luke 4:18

bruises

soundness, but wounds, *b.* *Isa* 1:6

bruising

b. thy teats by Egyptians. *Ezek* 23:21

the spirit *b.* him, hardly. *Luke* 9:39

bruit

behold, the noise of the *b.* *Jer* 10:22*

all that hear *b.* of thee. *Nah* 3:19†

brute, *see* **beasts**

brutish

fool and the *b.* person. *Ps* 49:10

a *b.* man knoweth not. 92:6

understand, ye *b.* among. 94:8

he that hateth reproof is *b.* *Pr* 12:1

I am more *b.* than any man. 30:2

counsel of the wise counsellors of Pharaoh is become *b.* *Isa* 19:11

they are altogether *b.* *Jer* 10:8

every man is *b.* 14; 51:17

pastors are become *b.* 10:21

deliver into hand of *b.* *Ezek* 21:31

bucket, -s

pour water out of his *b.* *Num* 24:7

nations are as a drop of a *b.* *Isa* 40:15

buckler

A shield, 1 Chr 5:18. *God is often called the buckler, or shield of his people,* Ps 18:2; Pr 2:7. *Faith is called the Christian's shield,* Eph 6:16.

b. to all that trust in. *2 Sam* 22:31 *Ps* 18:30

men able to bear *b.* *1 Chr* 5:18

Gadites that could handle *b.* 12:8*

Lord is my God, my *b.* *Ps* 18:2

take hold of shield and *b.* 35:2

truth shall be thy shield and *b.* 91:4

he is a *b.* to them that. *Pr* 2:7

order ye the *b.* and shield. *Jer* 46:3

set against the *b.* shield. *Ezek* 23:24

shall lift up the *b.* against. 26:8

bucklers

Jehoiada delivered spears, *b.* *2 Chr* 23:9

upon thick bosses of *b.* *Job* 15:26

hang a thousand *b.* *S of S* 4:4

great company with *b.* *Ezek* 38:4

set on fire shields, *b.* and. 39:9

bud, *noun*

cause *b.* of the tender. *Job* 38:27

afore harvest, when *b.* is. *Isa* 18:5*

as earth bringeth forth her *b.* 61:11

thee to multiply as *b.* *Ezek* 16:7

b. shall yield no meal. *Hos* 8:7*

bud, *verb*

scent of water it will *b.* *Job* 14:9

horn of David to *b.* *Ps* 132:17

if pomegranates *b.* forth. *S of S* 7:12

Israel shall blossom and *b.* *Isa* 27:6

earth to bring forth and *b.* 55:10

cause horn of Israel to *b.* *Ezek* 29:21

budded

vine was as though it *b.* *Gen* 40:10

the house of Levi *b.* *Num* 17:8

whether pomegranates *b.* *S of S* 6:11

blossomed, pride hath *b.* *Ezek* 7:10

was Aaron's rod that *b.* *Heb* 9:4

buds

rod brought forth *b.* *Num* 17:8

buffet

messenger of Satan to *b.* *2 Cor* 12:7

buffeted

and *b.* him. *Mat* 26:67; *Mark* 14:65

to present hour we are *b.* *1 Cor* 4:11

if when ye be *b.* for. *1 Pet* 2:20

build referred to *God*

up a priest, and will *b.* *1 Sam* 2:35 *2 Sam* 7:27; *1 Ki* 11:38

that the Lord will *b.* *1 Chr* 17:10

hast told that thou wilt *b.* him. 25

shall destroy, and not *b.* *Ps* 28:5

do good to Zion, *b.* the walls. 51:18

for God will *b.* the cities. 69:35

and *b.* up thy throne to. 89:4

when Lord shall *b.* up Zion. 102:16

except Lord *b.* house. 127:1

Lord doth *b.* up Jerusalem. 147:2

concerning a nation to *b.* *Jer* 18:9

b. and not pull down. 24:6; 31:28

again I will *b.* thee. *Jer* 31:4

I will *b.* Judah and Israel. 33:7

abide in this land I will *b.* 42:10

I the Lord *b.* ruined. *Ezek* 36:36

I *b.* it as in days of old. *Amos* 9:11

on this rock will I *b.* *Mat* 16:18

able to *b.* it in three days. 26:61 *Mark* 14:58

I will *b.* again tabernacle. *Acts* 15:16

build *altars*

shalt not *b.* an *altar* of. *Ex* 20:25

b. me here seven *altars.* *Num* 23:1 29

thou shalt *b.* an *altar.* *Deut* 27:5

thou shalt *b.* *altar* of Lord of. 6

we rebel and *b.* an *altar.* *Josh* 22:29

see **began**

build joined with *house*

not *b.* his brother's *house.* *Deut* 25:9

shalt *b.* an *house,* not dwell. 28:30 *Zeph* 1:13

two did *b.* the *house* of. *Ruth* 4:11

shalt *b.* me an *house* ? *2 Sam* 7:5

spake I, why *b.* ye not me an *h.* ? 7

he shall *b.* an *house.* 7:13; *1 Ki* 5:5 8:19; *1 Chr* 17:12; 22:10

b. thee an *h.* in Jerusalem. *1 Ki* 2:36

David could not *b.* an *house.* 5:3

I purpose to *b.* an *house* to Lord. 5 *2 Chr* 2:1

no city to *b.* an *house.* *1 Ki* 8:16 *2 Chr* 6:5

heart of David my father to *b.* *house.* *1 Ki* 8:17; *1 Chr* 28:2; *2 Chr* 6:7

shall *b.* me an *house.* *1 Chr* 17:12 *2 Chr* 6:9

shalt not *b.* an *house* because. *1 Chr* 22:8

my son, *b.* the *house* of Lord. 11

Solomon shall *b.* my *house.* 28:6

behold, I *b.* an *house.* *2 Chr* 2:4

the *house* I *b.* is great. 5

who is able to *b.* him an *house* ? that I should *b.* an *house.* 6

charged me to *b.* an *house.* 36:23 *Ezra* 1:2

go to *b.* the *house of* Lord. *Ezra* 1:3

commanded you to *b.* *house* ? 5:3, 9

let the governor *b.* this *house.* 6:7

except the Lord *b.* *house.* *Ps* 127:1

afterwards *b.* thy *house.* *Pr* 24:27

they shall *b.* *houses* and. *Isa* 65:21

where is the *house* that ye *b.* ? 66:1

I will *b.* me a wide *house.* *Jer* 22:14

b. *houses* and dwell in. 29:5, 28

neither shall ye *b.* *house* nor. 35:7

not near, let us *b.* *houses.* *Ezek* 11:3

safely, and shall *b.* *houses.* 28:26

bring wood, *b.* house. *Hag* 1:8

to *b.* it an *house* in the. *Zech* 5:11

what *house* will ye *b.* ? *Acts* 7:49

build

let us *b.* us a city and a. *Gen* 11:4

and they left off to *b.* the city. 8

we will *b.* sheep-folds. *Num* 32:16

b. cities for your little ones. 24

thou shalt *b.* bulwarks. *Deut* 20:20

Solomon desired to *b.* in Jerusalem. *1 Ki* 9:19; *2 Chr* 8:6

then did *b.* Millo. *1 Ki* 9:24

Solomon did *b.* an high place. 11:7

Hiel the Bethelite *b.* Jericho. 16:34

b. ye the sanctuary. *1 Chr* 22:19

an heart to *b.* the palace. 29:19

let us *b.* these cities. *2 Chr* 14:7

let us *b.* with you. *Ezra* 4:2

let us *b.* the wall. *Neh* 2:17

let us rise and *b.* 18

we his servants will rise and *b.* 20

which they *b.* if a fox go up. 4:3

so that we are not able to *b.* 10

and a time to *b.* up. *Eccl* 3:3

we will *b.* upon her. *S of S* 8:9

are fallen, but we will *b.* *Isa* 9:10

he shall *b.* my city. 45:13

b. the old waste places. 58:12; 61:4

sons of strangers shall *b.* up. 60:10

they shall not *b.* and another. 65:22

set thee over nations to *b.* *Jer* 1:10

b. a fort against it. *Ezek* 4:2; 21:22

restore and *b.* Jerusalem. *Dan* 9:25

b. it as in the days of old. *Amos* 9:11

Israel shall *b.* the waste cities. 14

they *b.* up Zion with blood. *Mi* 3:10

he shall *b.* the temple. *Zech* 6:12, 13

that are far off shall *b.* 15

Tyrus did *b.* herself a strong. 9:3

they shall *b.* but I. *Mal* 1:4

ye *b.* tombs of prophets. *Mat* 23:29 *Luke* 11:47, 48

down my barns and *b.* *Luke* 12:18

which of you intending to *b.* ? 14:28

this man began to *b.* and not. 30

able to *b.* you up. *Acts* 20:32

I *b.* on another man's *Rom* 15:20

b. on this foundation. *1 Cor* 3:12

if I *b.* again the things. *Gal* 2:18

builded

Cain *b.* a city. *Gen* 4:17

Noah *b.* an altar to the Lord. 8:20

Asher *b.* Nineveh, Rehoboth. 10:11

the tower children of men *b.* 11:5

Abram *b.* an altar. 12:7; 13:18

Isaac *b.* an altar. 26:25

Moses *b.* an altar under. *Ex* 24:4

ye have *b.* an altar. *Josh* 22:16

less this house I have *b.* *1 Ki* 8:27,43

wherewith Baasha had *b.* 15:22

Solomon had *b.* for. *2 Ki* 23:13

house to be *b.* must be. *1 Chr* 22:5

adversaries heard that they *b.* *Ezra* 4:1

that if this city be *b.* 13, 16

that this city be not *b.* 4:21

house of great God which is *b.* 5:8

we build the house that was *b.* 11

let the house of God be *b.* 15; 6:3

elders of the Jews *b.* 6:14

his sword girded, and so *b.* *Neh* 4:18

away an house he *b.* not. *Job* 20:19

Jerusalem is *b.* a city. *Ps* 122:3

Wisdom hath *b.* her house. *Pr* 9:1

through wisdom is house *b.* 24:3

I *b.* me houses, I. *Eccl* 2:4

like tower of David *b.* *S of S* 4:4

the city shall be *b.* *Jer* 30:18

he hath *b.* against me. *Lam* 3:5

waste shall be *b.* *Ezek* 36:10, 33

sold, they plant, they *b.* *Luke* 17:28

in whom ye are *b.* together. *Eph* 2:22

he who *b.* the house hath. *Heb* 3:3

for every house is *b.* by some. 4

builder, -s

Solomon's and Hiram's *b.* *1 Ki* 5:18

laid money out to the *b.* *2 Ki* 12:11

carpenters and *b.* 22:6; *2 Chr* 34:11

when *b.* laid foundation. *Ezra* 3:10

to anger before the *b.* *Neh* 4:5

stone which *b.* refused. *Ps* 118:22 *Mat* 21:42; *Mark* 12:10 *Luke* 20:17; *Acts* 4:11

thy *b.* have perfected. *Ezek* 27:4

as a wise master-*b.* I. *1 Cor* 3:10

city whose *b.* and maker. *Heb* 11:10

the stone which the *b.* *1 Pet* 2:7

buildest

goodly cities thou *b.* not. *Deut* 6:10

thou *b.* a new house. 22:8

for which cause thou *b.* *Neh* 6:6

in that thou *b.* thine. *Ezek* 16:31

thou that destroyest the temple and *b.* it in. *Mat* 27:40; *Mark* 15:29

buildeth

cursed be the man that *b.* *Josh* 6:26

b. his house as a moth. *Job* 27:18

every wise woman *b.* her. *Pr* 14:1

woe to him that *b.* by. *Jer* 22:13

Israel *b.* temples. *Hos* 8:14

it is he that *b.* his stories. *Amos* 9:6

woe to him that *b.* a. *Hab* 2:12

foundation, another *b.* *1 Cor* 3:10

building

not against Lord in *b.* *Josh* 22:19

till he made an end of *b.* *1 Ki* 3:1

no tool of iron heard while *b.* 6:7

so was Solomon seven years in *b.* 38

Solomon was *b.* his own house. 7:1

wherewith Baasha was *b.* *2 Chr* 16:6

b. rebellious and bad city. *Ezra* 4:12

by *b.* forts to cut off. *Ezek* 17:17

temple was forty-six years in *b.* *John* 2:20

b. up yourselves on holy. *Jude* 20

building, *substantive*

Solomon finished *b.* house. *1 Ki* 9:1

he left off b. of Ramah. 1 Ki 15:21
2 Chr 16:5
made ready for the b. 1 Chr 28:2
instructed for the b. 2 Chr 3:3
of men that made this b. Ezra 5:4
what ye shall do for the b. of. 6:8
by slothfulness the b. Eccl 10:18*
measured the breadth of the b.
Ezek 40:5; 41:15
there was a row of b. round. 46:23
God's husbandry, God's b. 1 Cor 3:9
we have a b. of God. 2 Cor 5:1
in whom all the b. Eph 2:21
tabernacle not of this b. Heb 9:11*
b. of wall was of jasper. Rev 21:18

buildings

to shew him b. of temple. Mat 24:1
see what b. are here. Mark 13:1, 2

built

it shall not be b. again. Deut 13:16
the cities that Ahab b. 1 Ki 22:39
every side, so they b. 2 Chr 14:7
have b. thee a sanctuary. 20:8
Uzziah b. towers in. 26:9, 10
Jotham b. in the forests. 27:4
who b. desolate places. Job 3:14
breaketh down, cannot be b. 12:14
to Almighty, shalt be b. up. 22:23
he b. his sanctuary. Ps 78:69
I have said, mercy shall be b. 89:2
b. a tower in the midst. Isa 5:2
saith to Judah, ye shall be b. 44:26
Jerusalem, thou shalt be b. 28
shall they be b. in midst. Jer 12:16
be b. O virgin of Israel. 31:4
provocation from day they b. 32:31
which I have b. will I break. 45:4
thou hast b. to thee. Ezek 16:24
hast b. thy high place at. 25
thou shalt be b. no more. 26:14
great Babylon I have b.? Dan 4:30
the street shall be b. again. 9:25
that temple be b. Zech 8:9
b. a tower. Mat 21:33; Mark 12:1
the centurion hath b. us. Luke 7:5
abide which he hath b. 1 Cor 3:14
b. on the foundation of. Eph 2:20
rooted and b. up in him. Col 2:7
he that b. all things is God. Heb 3:4

built *altar*

Moses b. an altar. Ex 17:15; 24:4
Aaron b. an altar. 32:5
Joshua b. an altar. Josh 8:30
half tribe b. an altar. 22:10
Gideon b. an altar. Judg 6:24
people b. an altar. 21:4
Samuel b. an altar. 1 Sam 7:17
Saul b. an altar. 14:35
David b. an altar. 2 Sam 24:25
offered on the altar he b. 1 Ki 9:25
with stones Elisha b. altar in. 18:32
Urijah b. an altar. 2 Ki 16:11

built *altars*

Balak b. seven altars. Num 23:14
he b. altars in house of. 2 Ki 21:4
b. altars for all the host. 5; 2 Chr 33:5
away altars he had b. 2 Chr 33:15

built *city*

let city of Sihon be b. Num 21:27
Joshua b. the city. Josh 19:50
Danites b. city. Judg 18:28
Omri b. city. 1 Ki 16:24
David b. city round. 1 Chr 11:8
no city it shall never be b. Isa 25:2
city shall be b. to Lord. Jer 31:38
hill whereon city was b. Luke 4:29

built *cities*

b. for Pharaoh treasure-cities.
Ex 1:11
cities which ye b. not. Josh 24:13
cities which Asa b. 1 Ki 15:23
cities Huram restored, Solomon b.
2 Chr 8:2
Rehoboam b. cities for defence. 11:5
Asa b. fenced cities in Judah. 14:6
Jehoshaphat b. castles and c. 17:12
Uzziah b. cities about. 26:6
Jotham b. cities in mountains. 27:4
saith to cities of Judah, ye shall be b.
Isa 44:26

built *high places*

Judah b. high p. images. 1 Ki 14:23
Israel b. high p. in cities. 2 Ki 17:9
Manasseh b. up again high p. 21:3
2 Chr 33:3
b. high p. of Tophet. Jer 7:31
b. high p. of Baal. 19:5; 32:35

built *house*, or *houses*

hast b. goodly houses. Deut 8:12
man hath b. a new house? 20:5
there was no house b. to. 1 Ki 3:2
Solomon b. houses. 6:9, 14
I have b. thee an house. 8:13
and have b. an house for the. 20
toward house I have b. 8:44, 48
2 Chr 6:34, 38
sure house, as I b. for David.
1 Ki 11:38
ye not b. me an house? 1 Chr 17:6
less this house I have b.? 2 Chr 6:18
ye have b. houses of. Amos 5:11
Lord's house should be b. Hag 1:2
my house shall he b. in. Zech 1:16
b. his house on a rock. Mat 7:24
Luke 6:48
b. his house on sand. Mat 7:26
Luke 6:49
Solomon b. him an house. Acts 7:47
are b. up a spiritual h. 1 Pet 2:5

built *wall*, or *walls*

Solomon b. walls of. 1 Ki 6:15
on walls of Ophel he b. 2 Chr 27:3
Hezekiah b. up the wall. 32:5
Manasseh b. a wall without. 33:14
so b. we the wall. Neh 4:6
when wall was b. 7:1
one b. up the wall. Ezek 13:10
street be b. again and wall. Dan 9:25
day thy walls are to be b. Mi 7:11

Bul

in month B. house was. 1 Ki 6:38

bull

[1] *The beast so called, or representations of it*, Job 21:10; Jer 52:20. [2] *Wicked, violent, and furious enemies*, Ps 22:12.

their b. gendereth and. Job 21:10
thy sons lie as wild b. Isa 51:20*

bullock

(*Generally used for a young bull*)

in the basket with b. Ex 29:3
kill b. before Lord. 11; Lev 1:5
9:18*
bring the b. to the door. Lev 4:4
b. a meat-offering. Num 15:9; 29:37
sacrifice to Lord any b. Deut 17:1*
glory is like firstling of a b. 33:17
young b. the second b. Judg 6:25, 26
choose one b. 1 Ki 18:23, 25
Elijah cut b. in pieces. 33
I will take no b. out. Ps 50:9
better than a b. that hath. 69:31
lion eat straw like b. Isa 65:25*
as b. unaccustomed to. Jer 31:18*

bullock with *sin-offering*

a b. for a sin-offering. Ex 29:36
offer b. of the sin-offering. Lev 16:6
prepare a b. for a sin-offering.
Ezek 45:22

see **blood**

young **bullock**

bring a young b. Lev 4:3
Ezek 43:19
shall offer a young b. Lev 4:14
Num 15:24
holy place with a young b. Lev 16:3
one young b. one. Num 7:15, 21, 27
33, 39, 45, 51, 57, 63, 69, 75, 81
himself with young b. 2 Chr 13:9
take a young b. and. Ezek 45:18
day of new moon a young b. 46:6

bullocks

fourth day ten b. two. Num 29:23
offered thousand b. for. 1 Chr 29:21
the dedication 100 b. Ezra 6:17
shall they offer b. on thy. Ps 51:19
I will offer unto thee b. 66:15
delight not in the blood of b. Isa 1:11
the b. with the bulls shall. 34:7
hired men like fatted b. Jer 46:21*
slay all her b. let them go. 50:27
the blood of goats, of b. Ezek 39:18
they sacrifice b. in Gilgal. Hos 12:11

see **seven**

bulls

Jacob took ten b. as. Gen 32:15
b. have compassed me, strong b.
Ps 22:12
will I eat flesh of b. or drink. 50:13
rebuke multitude of the b. 68:30
bullocks with the b. Isa 34:7
ye bellow as b. Jer 50:11*
twelve brasen b. under the. 52:20
if the blood of b. and. Heb 9:13
not possible blood of b. take. 10:4

bulrush, -es

took for him an ark of b. Ex 2:3
ambassadors in vessels of b.
Isa 18:2*
bow down his head like a b.? 58:5*

bulwarks

thou shalt build b. Deut 20:20
engines on the b. 2 Chr 26:15
mark well her b. consider. Ps 48:13
king came and built b. Eccl 9:14
appoint for walls and b. Isa 26:1

bunch, -es

take a b. of hyssop and. Ex 12:22
with 100 b. of raisins. 2 Sam 16:1
Zebulun brought b. of. 1 Chr 12:40
treasures upon b. of. Isa 30:6†

bundle, -s

every man's b. of money. Gen 42:35
bound in b. of life. 1 Sam 25:29
a b. of myrrh my well-. S of S 1:13
bind the tares in b. Mat 13:30
Paul had gathered a b. of. Acts 28:3

burden

A weight or load of the capacity of the bearer to carry, 2 Ki 5:17; Jer 17:27. *This may be used literally or figuratively of taxes, grief or illness*, Ps 55:22; Hos 8:10; Gal 6:2.

bear the b. with thee. Ex 18:22
Num 11:17
the ass lying under b. Ex 23:5
appoint each to his b. Num 4:19
layest the b. of all this people. 11:11
I myself bear your b.? Deut 1:12
then thou shalt be a b. 2 Sam 15:33
should thy servant be a b.? 19:35
servant two mules' b. of. 2 Ki 5:17
forty camels' b. to Elisha. 8:9
it shall not be a b. 2 Chr 35:3
no b. be brought in. Neh 13:19
I am a b. to myself. Job 7:20
iniquities as a b. they are. Ps 38:4
cast thy b. on the Lord. 55:22
removed his shoulder from b. 81:6
grasshopper shall be a b. Eccl 12:5
broken the yoke of his b. Isa 9:4
his b. shall be taken from. 10:27
b. depart from off their. 14:25
name of the Lord, the b. 30:27*
your carriages are a b. to. 46:1
no b. on sabbath. Jer 17:21, 22, 27
reproach of it was a b. Zeph 3:18
and my b. is light. Mat 11:30
which have borne the b. and. 20:12
lay on you no greater b. Acts 15:28
the ship was to unlade b. 21:3
put upon you none other b. Rev 2:24

burden

(*Meaning here a prophecy of doom*)

Lord laid this b. upon. 2 Ki 9:25
the b. of Babylon. Isa 13:1
king Ahaz died, was this b. 14:28
the b. of Moab. 15:1
the b. of Damascus. 17:1
the b. of Egypt. 19:1
the b. of the desert of the sea. 21:1
the b. of Dumah. 11
the b. upon Arabia. 13
the b. of the valley of vision. 22:1
the b. that was upon it shall. 25
the b. of Tyre. 23:1
b. of the beasts of south. 30:6
what is b. of the Lord? what b.?
Jer 23:33
the b. of the Lord shall ye. 36
but since ye say, the b. of. 38
this b. concerneth the. Ezek 12:10
sorrow a little for the b. Hos 8:10

the *b.* of Nineveh. *Nah* 1:1
b. which Habakkuk the. *Hab* 1:1
b. of the word of the Lord. *Zech* 9:1
b. of the word of the Lord for. 12:1
b. of the word of the Lord to. *Mal* 1:1
every man bear his own *b.* *Gal* 6:5

burden, -ed

all that *b.* themselves. *Zech* 12:3
we groan being *b.* *2 Cor* 5:4
not that others be eased, you *b.* 8:13
but be it so, I did not *b.* you. 12:16

burdens

couching between two *b.* *Gen* 49:14
to afflict them with their *b.* *Ex* 1:11
Moses looked on their *b.* 2:11
get you to your *b.* 5:4
you make them rest from *b.* 5
bring you from the *b.* of. 6:6, 7
appoint to them all their *b.* *Num* 4:27
strength of bearers of *b.* *Neh* 4:10
they that bare *b.* with other. 17
all manner of *b.* brought in. 13:15
the fast, to undo heavy *b.* *Isa* 58:6*
prophets have seen for thee false *b.* *Lam* 2:14
ye take from the poor *b.* *Amos* 5:11*
bind heavy *b.* *Mat* 23:4; *Luke* 11:46
bear ye one another's *b.* *Gal* 6:2

burdensome

Jerusalem a *b.* stone. *Zech* 12:3
kept myself from being *b.* *2 Cor* 11:9
it be that I was not *b.* 12:13
third time I come, I will not be *b.* 14
we might have been *b.* *1 Thes* 2:6†

burial

also that he have no *b.* *Eccl* 6:3
joined with them in *b.* *Isa* 14:20
buried with the *b.* of an. *Jer* 22:19
she did it for my *b.* *Mat* 26:12
carried Stephen to his *b.* *Acts* 8:2

buried

there was Abraham *b.* *Gen* 25:10
b. Abraham and Sarah, Isaac and Rebekah, there I *b.* Leah. 49:31
there they *b.* people. *Num* 11:34
Miriam died, and was *b.* there. 20:1
Egyptians *b.* all first-born. 33:4
died, and there he was *b.* *Deut* 10:6
the bones of Joseph *b.* *Josh* 24:32
die, and there will be *b.* *Ruth* 1:17
took head and *b.* it. *2 Sam* 4:12
Saul and Jonathan they *b.* 21:14
where man of God is *b.* *1 Ki* 13:31
and so I saw the wicked *b.* *Eccl* 8:10
not be gathered nor *b.* *Jer* 8:2
16:6; 20:6; 25:33
shall not be lamented nor *b.* 16:4
be *b.* with the burial of an ass. 22:19
sign, till buriers have *b.* *Ezek* 39:15
took the body and *b.* it. *Mat* 14:12
rich man died and was *b.* *Luke* 16:22
David is dead and *b.* *Acts* 2:29
feet of them which *b.* thy. 5:9
carrying her forth, *b.* her by. 10
b. with him by baptism. *Rom* 6:4
that he was *b.* and rose. *1 Cor* 15:4
b. with him in baptism. *Col* 2:12

buried *him*

he *b.* *him* in a valley. *Deut* 34:6
blessed be ye that *b.* Saul. *2 Sam* 2:5
they *b.* *him*, all Israel. *1 Ki* 14:18
they *b.* Jehoram in. *2 Chr* 21:20
b. Jehoiada in city of David. 24:16
they *b.* *him* not in the sepulchres. 25
men carried and *b.* *him*. *Acts* 5:6

buried *in*

and thou shalt be *b.* *in* a. *Gen* 15:15
David was *b.* *in* the city. *1 Ki* 2:10
Joab *b.* *in* his own house. 34
Manasseh was *b.* *in*. *2 Ki* 21:18
Amon was *b.* *in* sepulchre, in. 26
that remain be *b.* *in*. *Job* 27:15

buried *with his fathers*

Rehoboam *b.* *with his f.* *1 Ki* 14:31
Asa *b.* *with his f.* 15:24
Jehoshaphat *b.* *with his f.* 22:50
Joram *b.* *with his f.* *2 Ki* 8:24
Joash *b.* *with his f.* 12:21
Amaziah *b.* *with his f.* 14:20
Azariah *b.* *with his f.* 15:7
Jotham *b.* *with his f.* 38
Ahaz *b.* *with his f.* 16:20

buriers

set up a sign till *b.* have. *Ezek* 39:15

burn

(*To consume, or destroy with fire,* Josh 11:13. *Used also figuratively for intense indignation, passion, or zeal*)

let not thine anger *b.* *Gen* 44:18
bring pure olive-oil to cause the lamp to *b.* alway. *Ex* 27:20; *Lev* 24:2
take caul, kidneys and fat and *b.* *Ex* 29:13, 18, 25; *Lev* 1:9, 15
2:2, 9, 16; 3:5, 11, 16; 5:12; 6:15
9:17; *Num* 5:26
fat and *b.* upon. *Lev* 4:19, 26, 31
7:31; 16:25; 17:6; *Num* 18:17
one shall *b.* the heifer. *Num* 19:5
Hazor did, Joshua *b.* *Josh* 11:13
let them not fail to *b.* *1 Sam* 2:16
save only to *b.* sacrifice. *2 Chr* 2:6
and they *b.* to the Lord. 13:11
they shall both *b.* together. *Isa* 1:31
it shall *b.* and devour. 10:17
go through them, and *b.* 27:4
Lebanon is not sufficient to *b.* 40:16
shall it be for a man to *b.* 44:15
my fury shall *b.* and not. *Jer* 7:20
so shall they *b.* odours for. 34:5
that the king would not *b.* 36:25
b. also the bones under it. *Ezek* 24:5
of it may be hot and may *b.* 11
they shall set on fire and *b.* 39:9
he shall *b.* bullock in the. 43:21
I will *b.* her chariots. *Nah* 2:13
day cometh that shall *b.* *Mal* 4:1
tares in bundles to *b.* *Mat* 13:30
but chaff he will *b.* with. *Luke* 3:17
did not heart *b.* within us? 24:32
better to marry than to *b.* *1 Cor* 7:9
offended, and I *b.* not? *2 Cor* 11:29

burn, joined with *fire*

remaineth till morning *b.* with *fire*. *Ex* 12:10; 29:34; *Lev* 8:32
b. that wherein the plague is with *fire*. *Lev* 13:57
b. with *fire* their skins, flesh. 16:27
mountain did *b.* with *fire*. *Deut* 5:23
b. their images with *fire*. 7:5, 25
b. groves with *fire*. 12:3
fire shall *b.* to lowest hell. 32:22
Jer 17:4
b. their chariots with *fire*. *Josh* 11:6
tower to *b.* it with *fire*. *Judg* 9:52
we will *b.* thine house with *fire*. 12:1
b. thee with *fire*. 14:15
thy jealousy *b.* like *fire*? *Ps* 79:5
thy wrath *b.* like *fire*? 89:46
the *fire* shall *b.* them. *Isa* 47:14
forth like *fire* and *b.* *Jer* 4:4; 21:12
b. sons and daughters in *fire*. 7:31
19:5
shall *b.* city with *fire*. 21:10; 32:29
34:2, 22; 37:8, 10; 38:18
b. with *fire* a third part. *Ezek* 5:2
they *b.* thine houses with *fire*. 16:41
23:47
b. up the chaff with unquenchable *fire*. *Mat* 3:12; *Luke* 3:17
flesh and *b.* her with *fire*. *Rev* 17:16

burn *incense*

an altar to *b.* *inc.* on. *Ex* 30:1
b. thereon sweet *inc.* 7, 8
by the altar to *b.* *inc.* *1 Ki* 13:1
Israel did *b.* *inc.* to it. *2 Ki* 18:4
and his sons to *b.* *inc.* *1 Chr* 23:13
house to *b.* sweet *inc.* *2 Chr* 2:4
b. every morning sweet *inc.* 13:11
into temple to *b.* *inc.* 26:16, 19
made high places to *b.* *inc.* 28:25
Lord hath chosen you to *b.* *inc.* 29:11
and *b.* *inc.* on it. 32:12
steal and *b.* *inc.* to Baal? *Jer* 7:9
11:13
b. *inc.* to the queen of heaven. 44:17
they *b.* *inc.* upon the hills. *Hos* 4:13
therefore they *b.* *inc.* *Hab* 1:16
his lot was to *b.* *inc.* *Luke* 1:9

burned

bush *b.* with fire. *Ex* 3:2
the mountain *b.* with fire. *Deut* 4:11
I came down, and mount *b.* 9:15
b. them with fire. *Josh* 7:25
b. Ziklag with fire. *1 Sam* 30:1
men *b.* their images. *2 Sam* 5:21*
shall be utterly *b.* with fire. 23:7
b. the grove at the brook. *2 Ki* 23:6
b. the chariots with fire. 11
she *b.* the high place. 15
bones out of sepulchres and *b.* 16
gods were *b.* with fire. *1 Chr* 14:12
Amaziah *b.* incense to. *2 Chr* 25:14
forsaken me, and *b.* incense. 34:25
gates thereof *b.* with. *Neh* 1:3; 2:17
wroth, anger *b.* in him. *Esth* 1:12
God hath *b.* up the sheep. *Job* 1:16
and my bones are *b.* with heat. 30:30
I was musing, fire *b.* *Ps* 39:3*
b. up all the synagogues. 74:8
it is *b.* with fire, it is cut. 80:16
my skin black, bones are *b.* 102:3
flame *b.* up the wicked. 106:18
his clothes not be *b.* *Pr* 6:27
on coals and his feet not be *b.*? 28*
your cities are *b.* with fire. *Isa* 1:7
inhabitants of the earth are *b.* 24:6
it *b.* him, yet he laid it not. 42:25
walkest through fire not be *b.* 43:2
and beautiful house *b.* with. 64:11
which have *b.* incense on the. 65:7
his cities are *b.* *Jer* 2:15
the bellows are *b.* 6:29
b. up that none can pass. 9:10, 12
my people have *b.* incense to. 18:15
in roll Jehoiakim hath *b.* 36:28
city shall not be *b.* with fire. 38:17
cause this city to be *b.* with fire. 23
that their wives had *b.* incense. 44:15
daughters be *b.* with fire. 49:2
reeds they have *b.* with fire. 51:32
high gates shall be *b.* with fire. 58
he *b.* against Jacob like. *Lam* 2:3
and all faces shall be *b.* *Ezek* 20:47
and let the bones be *b.* 24:10
wherein she *b.* incense. *Hos* 2:13
they sacrificed and *b.* incense. 11:2
the flame hath *b.* all the. *Joel* 1:19
because he *b.* the bones. *Amos* 2:1
hires thereof be *b.* with. *Mi* 1:7
and the earth is *b.* at. *Nah* 1:5
king sent and *b.* up their. *Mat* 22:7
are gathered and *b.* *John* 15:6
their books and *b.* *Acts* 19:19
b. in their lust one. *Rom* 1:27
if any man's work be *b.* *1 Cor* 3:15
I give my body to be *b.* 13:3
whose end is to be *b.* *Heb* 6:8
not come to the mount that *b.* 12:18
those beasts are *b.* 13:11
works therein be *b.* up. *2 Pet* 3:10
his feet like brass, as if *b.* *Rev* 1:15
she be utterly *b.* with fire. 18:8

burneth

he that *b.* them shall wash clothes. *Lev* 16:28; *Num* 19:8
breaketh the bow and *b.* *Ps* 46:9
as the fire *b.* wood, and as. 83:14
a fire *b.* up his enemies. 97:3
for wickedness *b.* as fire. *Isa* 9:18
he *b.* part thereof in fire. 44:16
thereof as a lamp that *b.* 62:1
as when the melting fire *b.* 64:2
are a smoke and fire that *b.* 65:5
he that *b.* incense, as if he. 66:3
cause to cease that *b.* *Jer* 48:35
behind them a flame *b.* *Joel* 2:3
part in lake which *b.* with. *Rev* 21:8

burning

b. lamp passed between. *Gen* 15:17
fire of altar shall be *b.* in it. *Lev* 6:9*
12, 13
appoint over you the *b.* ague. 26:16*
be devoured with *b.* heat. 32:24
of his mouth go *b.* lamps. *Job* 41:19
let *b.* coals fall upon. *Ps* 140:10
there is as a *b.* fire. *Pr* 16:27
as coals are to *b.* coals. 26:21*
b. lips and a wicked heart are. 23
of Lord cometh far, *b.* *Isa* 30:27
land shall become *b.* pitch. 34:9
was in my heart as *b.* fire. *Jer* 20:9
was like *b.* coals. *Ezek* 1:13
into midst of *b.* furnace. *Dan* 3:6, 11
able to deliver us from *b.* furnace. 17
and to cast them into the *b.* fiery furnace. 3:20; 21, 23

Nebuchadnezzar came near the b. Dan 3:26
his wheels were as b. fire. 7:9
and b. coals went forth at. Hab 3:5*
be girded, and lights b. Luke 12:35
he was a b. and shining. John 5:35
were seven lamps b. before. Rev 4:5
as it were a great mountain b. 8:8
there fell a great star b. 10
were cast alive into a lake b. 19:20

burning, *substantive*

b. for b. wound for. Ex 21:25
bewail the b. which Lord. Lev 10:6
if spot stay, it is rising of b. 13:28
the Lord shall smite thee with an extreme b. Deut 28:22*
is brimstone, salt, and b. 29:23
made a very great b. 2 Chr 16:14
people made no b. like the b. 21:19
there shall be b. instead. Isa 3:24*
purged Jerusalem by spirit of b. 4:4
but this shall be with b. and. 9:5
kindle b. like b. of fire. 10:16
people shall be as the b. of. 33:12
plucked out of the b. Amos 4:11
they see the smoke of b. Rev 18:9

burnings

dwell with everlasting b.? Isa 33:14
with b. of thy fathers. Jer 34:5

burnished

they sparkled like b. brass. Ezek 1:7

burnt

her forth, let her be b. Gen 38:24
see why bush is not b. Ex 3:3
for they shall not be b. Lev 2:12
meat-offering be wholly b. 6:22, 23
8:21
sought goat, and it was b. 10:16
took the brazen censers, wherewith they that were b. Num 16:39
shall be b. with hunger. Deut 32:24
before they b. fat. 1 Sam 2:15
men's bones shall be b. 1 Ki 13:2
Asa b. her idol. 15:13; 2 Chr 15:16
b. the house of Lord. 2 Ki 25:9
2 Chr 36:19
I will make thee a b. Jer 51:25

burnt, joined with *fire*

he b. the calf in the fire. Ex 32:20
Deut 9:21
sin-offering be b. in the fire. Lev 6:30
of flesh of sacrifice on third day be b. with fire. 7:17; 19:6
man take a wife and her mother they shall be b. with fire. 20:14
daughter of priest profane by playing whore ... be burnt with fire. 21:9
fire of the Lord b. Num 11:1, 3
daughters b. in the fire. Deut 12:31
b. Jericho with fire. Josh 6:24
he that is taken with the accursed thing shall be b. with fire. 7:15
b. their chariots with fire. 11:9
took Hazor and b. it with fire. 11
b. her and father with fire. Judg 15:6
as flax that was b. with fire. 14
Laish and b. it with fire. 18:27
had b. Gezer with fire. 1 Ki 9:16
Zimri b. king's house with fire. 16:18
fire from heaven b. 2 Ki 1:14
b. their children with fire. 17:31
man's house b. he with fire. 25:9
b. his children in the fire. 2 Chr 28:3

burnt *incense*

b. sweet inc. thereon. Ex 40:27
only Solomon b. inc. 1 Ki 3:3
Solomon b. inc. upon the. 9:25
Jeroboam offered and b. inc. 12:33
people b. inc. 22:43; 2 Ki 12:3
14:4; 15:4, 35
Ahaz b. inc. in high. 2 Ki 16:4
2 Chr 28:3, 4
and have not b. inc. 2 Chr 29:7

burnt-offering

is lamb for a b.-off.? Gen 22:7
God will provide a lamb for b.-off. 8
he offered him for a b.-off. 13
Jethro took a b.-off. Ex 18:12
the ram is a b.-off. 29:18
hand on head of b.-off. Lev 1:4
slay sin-offering in place of b.-off. Lev 4:29, 33; 6:25; 7:2; 14:13
this is law of the b.-off. 6:9; 7:37
priest have skin of b.-off. 7:8
ram for a b.-off. 9:2; 16:3, 5; 23:18
calf and a lamb for a b.-off. 9:3; 12:6
23:12
one lamb of first year for a b.-off. Num 7:15, 21, 27, 33, 39, 51, 57
63, 69, 75, 81; Ezek 45:15
stand by thy b.-off. Num 23:3, 15
this is the b.-off. 28:10
for a b.-off. of a sweet savour. 13
this is the b.-off. of every month. 14
meat-offering and daily b.-off. 29:6
altar not for a b.-off. Josh 22:26
a b.-off. at our hands. Judg 13:23
was offering up a b.-off. 1 Sam 7:10
offered a b.-off. 13:12
offered him for a b.-off. 2 Ki 3:27
fire consumed the b.-off. 2 Chr 7:1
the b.-off. should be made. 29:24
b.-off. hast thou not. Ps 40:6
delightest not in b.-off. 51:16
with b.-off. and whole b.-off. 19
nor beasts for a b.-off. Isa 40:16
for I hate robbery for b.-off. 61:8*
shall slay the b.-off. Ezek 44:11
prepare the b.-off. for Israel. 45:17
priest prepare prince's b.-off. 46:2
thou shalt daily prepare a b.-off. 13

continual **burnt-offering**

a continual b.-off. Ex 29:42
Num 28:3, 6, 10, 15, 24, 31; 29:11
16, 19, 22; Ezra 3:5; Neh 10:33
Ezek 46:15

offer **burnt-offering**

offer him there for a b.-off. Gen 22:2
and offer thy b.-off. Lev 9:7
of months offer b.-off. Num 28:11
offer these besides b.-off. 23
offer it up for a b.-off. Judg 11:31
if thou offer a b.-off. offer. 13:16
offered kine for b.-off. 1 Sam 6:14
Samuel offered a sucking lamb for a b.-off. 7:9
offer neither b.-off. 2 Ki 5:17
commanded to offer b.-off. 2 Chr 29:27
offer up a b.-off. Job 42:8
b.-off. prince shall offer. Ezek 46:4

burnt-offerings

Noah offered b.-off. Gen 8:20
give sacrifices and b.-off. Ex 10:25
sacrifice thereon thy b.-off. 20:24
trumpets over b.-off. Num 10:10
bring your b.-off. Deut 12:6, 11
14, 27
of the Lord with b.-off. Josh 22:27
great delight in b.-off. 1 Sam 15:22
Solomon offered b.-off. 1 Ki 3:15
of the court, he offered b.-off. 8:64
they offered b.-off. to. 1 Chr 29:21
I build house for b.-off. 2 Chr 2:4
altar not able to receive b.-off. 7:7
have not offered b.-off. in. 29:7
could not slay all the b.-off. 34
Levites brought b.-off. 30:15
busied in offering b.-off. 35:14
offered daily b.-off. Ezra 3:4
they have need for b.-off. 6:9
offered b.-off. according. Job 1:5
not reprove thee for b.-off. Ps 50:8
into thy house with b.-off. 66:13
full of the b.-off. of. Isa 1:11
small cattle of thy b.-off. 43:23
their b.-off. shall be accepted. 56:7
your b.-off. are not. Jer 6:20
put your b.-off. to your. 7:21
spake not concerning b.-off. 22
from south, bringing b.-off. 17:26
burn their sons for b.-off. 19:5
part to give b.-off. Ezek 45:17
knowledge more than b.-off. Hos 6:6
before him with b.-off.? Mi 6:6
is more than b.-off. Mark 12:33
in b.-off. for sin thou. Heb 10:6

offer **burnt-offerings**

down to offer b.-off. 1 Sam 10:8
nor offer b.-off. of that which cost me. 2 Sam 24:24; 1 Chr 21:24
b.-off. did Solomon offer. 1 Ki 3:4
year did Solomon offer b.-off. 1 Ki 9:25
builded altar to offer b.-off. Ezra 3:2
want man to offer b.-off. Jer 33:18
make it to offer b.-off. Ezek 43:18
ye offer me b.-off. Amos 5:22

burnt-sacrifice

strange incense, nor b.-s. Ex 30:9
burn all to be a b.-s. Lev 1:9; 3:5
lo, he stood by his b.-s. Num 23:6
put whole b.-s. on. Deut 33:10
here be oxen for b.-s. 2 Sam 24:22
fire consumed the b.-s. 1 Ki 18:38
altar burn king's b.-s. 2 Ki 16:15
accept thy b.-s. Ps. 20:3

burnt-sacrifices

b.-s. in the sabbaths. 1 Chr 23:31
and evening b.-s. 2 Chr 13:11
I will offer to thee b.-s. Ps 66:15

burnt *up*

the foxes b. up shocks. Judg 15:5
fire came down, and b. up. 2 Ki 1:14
third part of trees was b. up, and all green grass was b. up. Rev 8:7

burst

to b. like new bottles. Job 32:19
presses shall b. with new. Pr 3:10
I have b. thy bands. Jer 2:20; 5:5
30:8; Nah 1:13
new wine b. bottles. Mark 2:22
Luke 5:37
he b. asunder in midst. Acts 1:18

bursting

not be found in the b. Isa 30:14*

bury

that I may b. my dead. Gen 23:4
choice of our sepulchres b. 6, 11, 15
b. me not in Egypt. 47:29; 49:29
let me go and b. my father. 50:5
go up and b. thy father. 6
shalt in any wise b. Deut 21:23
fall upon Joab and b. 1 Ki 2:31
Joab was gone up to b. the. 11:15
came to mourn and b. 13:29
when I am dead, b. me in the. 31
Israel shall mourn and b. him. 14:13
be none to b. Jezebel. 2 Ki 9:10
see now this cursed woman, b. 34
they went to b. her, but. 35
there was none to b. them. Ps 79:3
shall b. in Tophet. Jer 7:32; 19:11
they shall have none to b. 14:16
there shall they b. Gog. Ezek 39:11
people of the land shall b. them. 13
Memphis shall b. them. Hos 9:6
me to go b. my father. Mat 8:21
Luke 9:59
let dead b. their dead. Mat 8:22
Luke 9:60
potter's field to b. Mat 27:7
manner of Jews is to b. John 19:40

burying

a possession of a b. place. Gen 23:4
9; 49:30; 50:13
buried Samson in b. Judg 16:31
as they were b. a man. 2 Ki 13:21
months shall Israel be b. Ezek 39:12
anoint my body to b. Mark 14:8
against day of my b. John 12:7

bush, -es

in fire in the b. Ex 3:2; Acts 7:30
out of the midst of the b. Ex 3:4
of him that dwelt in b. Deut 33:16
cut up mallows by the b. Job 30:4
among the b. they brayed. 7
come and rest upon all b. Isa 7:19*
how in b. God spake. Mark 12:26*
nor of a bramble b. Luke 6:44
dead are raised, Moses shewed at the b. 20:37
angel which appeared in b. Acts 7:35

bushel

put it under a b. but on. Mat 5:15
Mark 4:21; Luke 11:33

bushy

his locks are b. and. S of S 5:11

business

into house to do his b. Gen 39:11
nor charged with any b. Deut 24:5
if ye utter not our b. Josh 2:14
if thou utter this our b. we will. 20

no b. with any man. *Judg* 18:7*, 28*
hide thyself when b. *1 Sam* 20:19
let no man know of the b. 21:2
because king's b. required haste. 8
Levites wait on their b. *2 Chr* 13:10*
in the b. of the ambassadors. 32:31
every man in his b. *Neh* 13:30*
that have charge of b. *Esth* 3:9*
do b. in great waters. *Ps* 107:23
man diligent in his b.? *Pr* 22:29
through multitude of b. *Eccl* 5:3
and did the king's b. *Dan* 8:27
about my Father's b.? *Luke* 2:49*
we may appoint over b. *Acts* 6:3
not slothful in b. *Rom* 12:11*
assist her in what b. 16:2*
study to do your own b. *1 Thes* 4:11

busy, -ied
servant was b. here and. *1 Ki* 20:40
the sons of Aaron b. in. *2 Chr* 35:14

busybody, -ies
but some of you are b. *2 Thes* 3:11
1 Tim 5:13
none of you suffer as a b. *1 Pet* 4:15

but
b. a step between me. *1 Sam* 20:3
kill us, we shall b. die. *2 Ki* 7:4
b. speak not; eyes b. *Ps* 115:5
ears b. hear not; noses b. 6
have hands b. handle not; feet b. 7
b. of that day and hour. *Mat* 24:36
b. as the days of Noe were. 37
said, if I may touch b. *Mark* 5:28
know not the speech, b. *1 Cor* 4:19
b. ye are washed. 6:11
yet not I, b. the Lord. 7:10
b. the same Spirit. 12:4
b. the same Lord. 5
b. it is the same God which. 6
hath not grieved me b. *2 Cor* 2:5
our light affliction, which is b. 4:17

butler
b. of the king of Egypt. *Gen* 40:1
chief b. told dream to Joseph. 9
he restored his chief b. to his. 21
the chief b. said, I remember. 41:9

butter
(*While butter was not unknown the word usually means curdled milk*)
Abraham took b. and. *Gen* 18:8
b. of kine, milk of. *Deut* 32:14
she brought forth b. *Judg* 5:25
Barzillai brought b. *2 Sam* 17:29
brooks of honey and b. *Job* 20:17
I washed my steps with b. 29:6
words smoother than b. *Ps* 55:21
of milk bringeth forth b. *Pr* 30:33
b. and honey shall he. *Isa* 7:15, 22

buttocks
cut to b. *2 Sam* 10:4; *1 Chr* 19:4
with b. uncovered to the. *Isa* 20:4

buy
you down to Egypt and b. *Gen* 42:2
land of Canaan to b. food. 7; 43:20
b. us and our land for bread. 47:19
if thou b. an Hebrew. *Ex* 21:2
if priests b. any soul. *Lev* 22:11
after the jubilee b. of thy. 25:15
of them shall ye b. bondmen. 44, 45
ye shall b. meat of them. *Deut* 2:6
be sold, and no man shall b. 28:68
b. it before inhabitants. *Ruth* 4:4
thou must b. it also of Ruth. 5
b. the threshing-floor. *2 Sam* 24:21
24; *1 Chr* 21:24
masons b. timber. *2 Ki* 12:12; 22:6
we would not b. it on. *Neh* 10:31
come, b. and eat, b. wine. *Isa* 55:1
b. thee my field that is in. *Jer* 32:7
men shall b. fields for money. 44
b. victuals. *Mat* 14:15; *Mark* 6:36
go to them that sell, and b. *Mat* 25:9
while they went to b. the. 10
shall we go and b.? *Mark* 6:37
except we b. meat for. *Luke* 9:13
sell his garment and b. one. 22:36
disciples were gone to b. *John* 4:8
whence shall we b. bread? 6:5
b. those things that we have. 13:29
they that b. as though. *1 Cor* 7:30
and we will b. and sell. *Jas* 4:13
I counsel thee to b. of me. *Rev* 3:18
no man b. or sell, save he. 13:17

buy *corn*
came to Joseph to b. *corn*. *Gen* 41:57
brethren went to b. *corn*. 42:3
our lands to b. *corn*. *Neh* 5:3

buy *poor*
that we may b. the *poor*. *Amos* 8:6

buy *truth*
b. the *truth* and sell it not. *Pr* 23:23

buyer
it is naught, saith the b. *Pr* 20:14
as with the b. so with. *Isa* 24:2
let not the b. rejoice. *Ezek* 7:12

buyest
if thou sell ought, or b. *Lev* 25:14
day thou b. field of. *Ruth* 4:5

buyeth
considereth a field, b. it. *Pr* 31:16
selleth all he hath, and b. *Mat* 13:44
man b. her merchandise. *Rev* 18:11

Buz
Milcah bare to Nahor B. *Gen* 22:21
Jahdo, the son of B. *1 Chr* 5:14
made Dedan and B. to. *Jer* 25:23

Buzi
Ezekiel the priest, son of B. *Ezek* 1:3

Buzite
Elihu son of the B. *Job* 32:2, 6

by *and* **by**
b. *and* b. he is offended. *Mat* 13:21
give me b. *and* b. in a. *Mark* 6:25
say to him b. *and* b. *Luke* 17:7
but the end is not b. *and* b. 21:9

by-ways
walked through b. *Judg* 5:6

by-word
thou shalt become a b. *Deut* 28:37
Israel shall be a b. *1 Ki* 9:7
house a proverb and a b. *2 Chr* 7:20
he hath made me a b. *Job* 17:6
I their song, yea, their b. 30:9
thou makest us a b. *Ps* 44:14

C

cab
(*A measure of about 2 quarts*)
fourth part of a c. of. *2 Ki* 6:25

cabins
(*Revised Version*, cells)
Jeremiah entered the c. *Jer* 37:16

Cabul
called them land of C. *1 Ki* 9:13

Caesar (Cesar)
to give tribute to C.? *Mat* 22:17
Mark 12:14; *Luke* 20:22
to C. the things that are *Cesar's*, to.
Mat 22:21; *Mark* 12:17
decree from C. Augustus. *Luke* 2:1
the fifteenth year of Tiberius C. 3:1
forbidding to give tribute to C. 23:2
thou art not *Cesar's* friend speaketh against C. *John* 19:12
we have no king but C. 15
in days of Claudius C. *Acts* 11:28
do contrary to decrees of C. 17:7
nor against C. have I offended. 25:8
I appeal unto C. 11
till I send him to C. 21
if he had not appealed to C. 26:32
must be brought before C. 27:24
constrained to appeal to C. 28:19
they that are of *C.'s* *Phil* 4:22

cage
as a c. is full of birds. *Jer* 5:27
Babylon is c. of unclean. *Rev* 18:2*

Caiaphas
high-priest who was C. *Mat* 26:3
they led Jesus away to C. 57
C. said, ye know nothing. *John* 11:49
C. was he that gave counsel. 18:14
led Jesus from C. to the hall. 28
see **Annas**

Cain
C. and Gibeah cities. *Josh* 15:57

Cain
but C. was a tiller of. *Gen* 4:2
to C. and his offering he. 5
the Lord set a mark on C. *Gen* 4:15
seed instead of Abel whom C. 25
excellent sacrifice than C. *Heb* 11:4
not as C. who was of. *1 John* 3:12
gone in the way of C. *Jude* 11

Cainan
was the son of C. *Luke* 3:36, 37

cake, -s
they baked unleavened c. *Ex* 12:39
thanksgiving, unleavened c. *Lev* 7:12
take fine flour, bake twelve c. 24:5
offer up a c. of the first. *Num* 15:20
and lo, a c. tumbled. *Judg* 7:13
dealt to every one c. *2 Sam* 6:19
make me a couple of c. 13:6
I have not a c. *1 Ki* 17:12
make me a little c. first. 13
there was a c. baken on coals. 19:6
to make c. to the. *Jer* 7:18; 44:19
shalt eat it as barley c. *Ezek* 4:12
Ephraim is a c. not turned. *Hos* 7:8
see **figs, unleavened**

calamity, -ies
the day of their c. *Deut* 32:35
in day of c. *2 Sam* 22:19; *Ps* 18:18
and my c. laid in. *Job* 6:2
they set forward my c. 30:13
my refuge until these c. *Ps* 57:1
prayer also be in their c. 141:5*
I will laugh at your c. *Pr* 1:26
therefore his c. shall come. 6:15
he that is glad at c. shall. 17:5
a foolish son is the c. 19:13
their c. shall rise suddenly. 24:22
brother's house in day of c. 27:10
shew the back in day of c. *Jer* 18:17
the day of their c. was come. 46:21
the c. of Moab is near to. 48:16
for I will bring the c. 49:8
I will bring their c. from all. 32
blood of Israel in their c. *Ezek* 35:5
in the day of their c. *Ob* 13

calamus
of sweet c. 250 shekels. *Ex* 30:23
spikenard, saffron, c. *S of S* 4:14
c. was in the market of. *Ezek* 27:19

caldron
struck it into the pan, c. *1 Sam* 2:14
as out of a seething c. *Job* 41:20*
this city is the c. *Ezek* 11:3, 7
this city shall not be your c. 11
chop them as flesh within c. *Mi* 3:3

caldrons
sold they in pots and c. *2 Chr* 35:13
c. also and spoons. *Jer* 52:18, 19

Caleb
the tribe of Judah, C. *Num* 13:6
and C. stilled the people. 30
my servant C. having another spirit.
14:24, 30; 32:12; *Deut* 1:36
and C. lived. *Num* 14:38; 26:65
of the tribe of Judah, C. 34:19
Joshua gave C. Hebron. *Josh* 14:13
C. drove thence three sons of. 15:14
C. said, he that smiteth. 16
C. gave her the springs. *Judg* 1:15
Nabal was of house of C. *1 Sam* 25:3
C. begat children. *1 Chr* 2:18, 42, 50
4:15

Caleb
on the south of C. we. *1 Sam* 30:14

Caleb-ephratah
Hezron was dead in C. *1 Chr* 2:24

calf
Abraham fetched a c. *Gen* 18:7
he made it a molten c. *Ex* 32:4
Moses burnt c. and strawed. 20
take thee a young c. *Lev* 9:2
take a c. and a lamb for. 3
and made a molten c. *Deut* 9:16
Neh 9:18; *Ps* 106:19
and casteth not her c. *Job* 21:10
them to skip like a c. *Ps* 29:6
the c. and the young lion. *Isa* 11:6
there shall the c. feed. 27:10
when they cut the c. *Jer* 34:18
were like the sole of a c. *Ezek* 1:7
thy c. O Samaria, hath. *Hos* 8:5
c. of Samaria shall be broken. 6
hither the fatted c. *Luke* 15:23

hath killed fatted c. *Luke* 15:27, 30
and they made a c. in. *Acts* 7:41
second beast was like a c. *Rev* 4:7

calkers

of Gebal were thy c. *Ezek* 27:9
c. shall fall into midst. 27

call

to see what he would c. *Gen* 2:19
c. to thee a nurse of the. *Ex* 2:7
where is he ? c. him that he. 20
Moses sent to c. Dathan. *Num* 16:12
if the men c. thee, rise up. 22:20
God is in all things we c. *Deut* 4:7
I c. to witness. 26; 30:19; 31:28
c. for Samson that he. *Judg* 16:25
they sent to c. peaceably. 21:13
thou didst c. me. *1 Sam* 3:6, 8
c. Jesse to the sacrifice, and. 16:3
king sent to c. Ahimelech. 22:11
then said Absalom, c. *2 Sam* 17:5
c. Bath-sheba. *1 Ki* 1:28
c. Zadok and Nathan. 32
hearken to them in all they c. 8:52
art come to me to c. my sin? 17:18
c. ye on name of your. 18:24, 25
Elisha said, c. this. *2 Ki* 4:12
c. unto me all the prophets. 10:19
c. now if there be any. *Job* 5:1
c. thou, I will answer. 13:22; 14:15
hear when I c. O God of. *Ps* 4:1
the Lord will hear when I c. 3
who eat up my people, and c. 14:4
let king hear us when we c. 20:9
they c. their lands after their. 49:11
I c. to remembrance my song. 77:6
plenteous in mercy to all that c. 86:5
Samuel among them that c. 99:6
in the day when I c. answer. 102:2
Lord is nigh all them that c. 145:18
unto you, O men, I c. *Pr* 8:4
to c. passengers who go right. 9:15
children arise, c. her blessed. 31:28
to them that c. evil good. *Isa* 5:20
in that day did the Lord c. 22:12
I the Lord which c. thee. 45:3
they c. themselves of holy. 48:2
when I c. to them they stand. 13
c. ye upon him while he is. 55:6
wilt thou c. this a fast ? 58:5
c. the sabbath a delight, holy. 13
c. his servants by another. 65:15
it shall come, that before they c. 24
consider and c. for the. *Jer* 9:17
c. unto me, and I will. 33:3
is this city that men c. ? *Lam* 2:15
the Lord said, c. his. *Hos* 1:4
God said unto him, c. her name. 6
c. his name Lo-ammi, for ye are. 9
they c. to Egypt, they go. 7:11
sanctify a fast, c. *Joel* 1:14; 2:15
O sleeper, arise, c. *Jonah* 1:6
ye shall c. every man. *Zech* 3:10
now we c. proud happy. *Mal* 3:15
not come to c. righteous. *Mat* 9:13
Mark 2:17; *Luke* 5:32
c. the labourers and give. *Mat* 20:8
sent his servants to c. them. 22:3
how then doth David in spirit c. ? 43
c. no man your father upon. 23:9
why c. ye me Lord and ? *Luke* 6:46
when thou makest a feast c. 14:13
go c. thy husband and. *John* 4:16
ye c. me Master and Lord. 13:13
to bind all that c. on. *Acts* 9:14
to c. over them which had. 19:13
after the way they c. heresy. 24:14
Lord is rich to all that c. *Rom* 10:12
I c. God for a record. *2 Cor* 1:23
when I c. to remembrance. *2 Tim* 1:5
follow peace with them that c. 2:22
not ashamed to c. them. *Heb* 2:11
but c. to remembrance. 10:32
let him c. the elders of. *Jas* 5:14
if ye c. on the Father. *1 Pet* 1:17

call *on the name of the Lord*

c. upon *name of the L.* *Gen* 4:26
I will c. *on the name of the L.*
1 Ki 18:24; *Ps* 116:17
he will c. *on name of L.* *2 Ki* 5:11
c. upon his *name.* *1 Chr* 16:8
Ps 105:1; *Isa* 12:4
whosoever shall c. *on name of L.*
Joel 2:32; *Acts* 2:21; *Rom* 10:13
all c. upon *name of L.* *Zeph* 3:9
c. on the name of the L. *1 Cor* 1:2

not **call**

not c. her name Sarai. *Gen* 17:15
didst *not* c. us to go. *Judg* 12:1
c. me *not* Naomi, c. me. *Ruth* 1:20
and they c. *not* upon. *Ps* 14:4
yet he will *not* c. back. *Isa* 31:2
upon families that c. *not.* *Jer* 10:25
c. *not* thy friends. *Luke* 14:12
I c. you *not* servants. *John* 15:15
c. *not* thou common. *Acts* 10:15; 11:9
God hath shewed me *not* to c. 10:28

shall or *shalt* **call**

and thou *shalt* c. his. *Gen* 17:19
elders of this city *shall* c. *Deut* 25:8
thou *shalt* c. them to mind. 30:1
they *shall* c. the people. 33:19
thou *shalt* c. and I will. *Job* 14:15
he *shall* c. to the heavens. *Ps* 50:4
all nations *shall* c. him. 72:17
shall c. his name Immanuel (or Emmanuel). *Isa* 7:14; *Mat* 1:23
they *shall* c. the nobles to. *Isa* 34:12
from rising of sun *shall* he c. 41:25
another *shall* c. himself by. 44:5
and who, as I, *shall* c. and. 7
thou *shalt* c. a nation that. 55:5
then *shalt* thou c. and Lord. 58:9
they *shall* c. thee the city of. 60:14
shalt c. thy walls salvation. 18
men *shall* c. you ministers of. 61:6
shalt c. them the holy people. 62:12
they *shall* c. Jerusalem. *Jer* 3:17
shalt c. me, my father. 19
reprobate silver *shall* men c. 6:30
shalt c. to them, but they will. 7:27
thou *shalt* c. me no more. *Hos* 2:16
whom the Lord *shall* c. *Joel* 2:32
shall c. the husbandmen. *Amos* 5:16
shall c. on my name. *Zech* 13:9
they *shall* c. them the. *Mal* 1:4
all nations *shall* c. you blessed. 3:12
shalt c. his name Jesus. *Mat* 1:21
how much more *shall* c. them ? 10:25
shalt c. his name John. *Luke* 1:13
all generations *shall* c. me. 48
many as the Lord *shall* c. *Acts* 2:39
how then *shall* they c. on. *Rom* 10:14

will **call**

we *will* c. the damsel. *Gen* 24:57
daughters *will* c. me blessed. 30:13
I *will* c. unto Lord. *1 Sam* 12:17
will c. on the. *2 Sam* 22:4; *Ps* 18:3
will hypocrite c. on God ? *Job* 27:10
I will c. upon God. *Ps* 55:16; 86:7
quicken us, and we *will* c. 80:18
therefore *will* I c. on him. 116:2
that I *will* c. my servant. *Isa* 22:20
I *will* c. all families of. *Jer* 1:15
I will c. for sword. 25:29; *Ezek* 38:21
will c. to remembrance. *Ezek* 21:23
I *will* c. for the corn. 36:29
season I *will* c. for. *Acts* 24:25
I *will* c. them my people. *Rom* 9:25

call *upon me*

c. *upon me* in day of. *Ps* 50:15
he shall c. *upon me*, and. 91:15
shall c. *upon me*, but. *Pr* 1:28
shall ye c. *upon me* and. *Jer* 29:12

called

the name of it c. Babel. *Gen* 11:9
angel of God c. to Hagar. 21:17
angel c. to Abraham out. 22:11
name shall not be c. Jacob. 35:10
c. him Ben-oni, but his father c. 18
she c. to the men of her. 39:14
King of Egypt c. for the. *Ex* 1:18
Pharaoh c. for Moses. 8:8, 25
9:27; 10:16, 24; 12:31
Moses c. Oshea son of. *Num* 13:16
Moses c. all Israel. *Deut* 5:1; 29:2
not exact it, because it is c. 15:2
shall see thou art c. by. 28:10
have ye c. us to take ? *Judg* 14:15
cast away the jaw-bone, and c. 15:17
Samson was sore athirst, and c. 18
Samson c. to the Lord. 16:28
c. a prophet, c. a seer. *1 Sam* 9:9
whose name is c. by. *2 Sam* 6:2
take the city, and it be c. 12:28
watchman c. to porter. *2 Sam* 18:26
the king c. the Gibeonites. 21:2
Adonijah c. all. *1 Ki* 1:9; 19:25
Ahab c. Obadiah. 18:3
c. on the name of Baal. 26
c. to her husband and. *2 Ki* 4:22
they came and c. to porter. 7:10
and Jabez c. on the. *1 Chr* 4:10
ark of God, whose name is c. 13:6
David c. on the Lord. 21:26
except she were c. *Esth* 2:14
who is not c. I have not been c. 4:11
people have not c. upon G. *Ps* 53:4
the kingdoms that have not c. 79:6
of shepherds is c. forth. *Isa* 31:4
but thou hast not c. on me. 43:22
O Jacob, ye that are c. by. 48:1
hearken, O Jacob, and Israel my c. 12
that they might be c. trees of. 61:3
shall no more be c. *Jer* 7:32
wilt bring day thou hast c. *Lam* 1:21
thou hast c. as a solemn day. 2:22
thereof is c. Bamah. *Ezek* 20:29
now let Daniel be c. and. *Dan* 5:12
Jesus, who is c. Christ. *Mat* 1:16
first Simon, who is c. Peter. 10:2
is not his mother c. Mary ? 13:55
Jesus c. a little child unto. 18:2
many be c. few chosen. 20:16; 22:14
and Jesus stood still, and c. 20:32
be not ye c. Rabbi. 23:8, 10
one of the twelve c. Judas. 26:14
release Jesus, c. Christ ? 27:17, 22
commanded him to be c. *Mark* 10:49
Peter c. to mind the word. 14:72
of thy kindred is c. *Luke* 1:61
signs how he would have him c. 62
no more worthy to be c. thy. 15:19, 21
commanded servants to be c. 19:15
to the place that is c. Calvary. 23:33
before that Philip c. thee. *John* 1:48
Messiah cometh, who is c. 4:25
a man c. Jesus made clay. 9:11
into the street c. Straight. *Acts* 9:11
disciples were c. Christians. 11:26
who c. for Barnabas and Saul. 13:7
then Saul, c. Paul, filled with. 9
on whom my name is c. 15:17
to be c. in question for. 19:40
I am c. in question. 23:6; 24:21
Paul the prisoner c. and. 23:18
Paul c. to be an. *Rom* 1:1; *1 Cor* 1:1
among whom are ye also c. *Rom* 1:6
c. to be saints. 7; *1 Cor* 1:2
thou art c. a Jew. *Rom* 2:17
who are the c. 8:28
by whom ye were c. *1 Cor* 1:9
to them which are c. 24
not many mighty are c. 26
if any man c. a brother be. 5:11
is any man c. being circumcised ? is any c. in uncircumcision ? 7:18
art thou c. being a servant ? 21
let every man wherein he is c. 24
removed from him that c. *Gal* 1:6
brethren, ye have been c. 5:13
c. uncircumcision by that c. *Eph* 2:11
vocation wherewith ye are c. 4:1
even as ye are c. in one hope. 4
to the which ye are c. *Col* 3:15
Jesus, which is c. Justus. 4:11
above all that is c. God. *2 Thes* 2:4
whereto thou art c. *1 Tim* 6:12
of science, falsely so c. 20
exhort daily while it is c. *Heb* 3:13
the tabernacle which is c. the. 9:2
they that are c. might receive. 15
God is not ashamed to be c. 11:16
Moses refused to be c. son of. 24
name by which ye are c. *Jas* 2:7
of him who hath c. you. *1 Pet* 2:9
for hereunto were ye c. 21
knowing ye are thereunto c. 3:9
that hath c. us to glory. *2 Pet* 1:3
that we should be c. the. *1 John* 3:1
in Jesus Christ, and c. *Jude* 1
name of the star is c. *Rev* 8:11
spiritually is c. Sodom and. 11:8
that old serpent c. the Devil. 12:9
that are with him, are c. 17:14
blessed that are c. to the. 19:9

called, joined with *God* or *Lord*

c. light day, darkness he c. *Gen* 1:5

God c. firmament, Heaven. Gen 1:8
c. dry-land Earth, waters c. Seas. 10
and c. their name Adam. 5:2
God c. to him out of the. Ex 3:4
the Lord c. to him out of the. 19:3
the Lord c. Moses up to the top. 20
see, the Lord hath c. my. 35:30
Lord c. Aaron and. Num 12:5
Lord c. Samuel. 1 Sam 3:4, 6, 8, 10
c. these three kings. 2 Ki 3:10, 13
the Lord hath c. for a famine. 8:1
Lord hath c. the earth. Ps 50:1
Lord raised, and c. him. Isa 41:2
the Lord have c. thee. 42:6
the Lord hath c. me. 49:1
the Lord hath c. thee as a. 54:6
Lord c. thy name a green. Jer 11:16
hath not c. thy name Pashur. 20:3
Lord God c. to contend. Amos 7:4
that the Lord had c. us. Acts 16:10
but God hath c. us. 1 Cor 7:15
as the Lord hath c. every one. 17
it pleased God, who c. Gal 1:15
c. you to his kingdom. 1 Thes 2:12
for God hath not c. us to. 4:7
whereunto God c. you. 2 Thes 2:14
who hath c. us. 2 Tim 1:9
but he that is c. of God. Heb 5:4
c. of God an high-priest after. 10
God of all grace, who c. 1 Pet 5:10

he **called**

he c. that place Beer-sheba. Gen 21:31
he c. their names as his. 26:18
thy name is Jacob, *he* c. his. 35:10
the Lord c. to Moses. Ex 24:16
he c. him Jerubbaal. Judg 6:32
he saw me and c. to me. 2 Sam 1:7
then *he* c. his servant that. 13:17
Solomon his brother *he* c. not. 1 Ki 1:10; 19:26
he c. them land of Cabul. 9:13
he c. to Gehazi, so *he* c. 2 Ki 4:36
brake brazen serpent, *he* c. 18:4
he c. for a famine. Ps 105:16
then c. *he* Johanan and. Jer 42:8
he hath c. an assembly. Lam 1:15
he c. to the man. Ezek 9:3
he c. the twelve. Mat 10:1
he c. the multitude. 15:10
straightway *he* c. them. Mark 1:20
Jesus saw her, *he* c. Luke 13:12
if *he* c. them gods. John 10:35
he had c. the saints. Acts 9:41
then c. *he* them in. 10:23
then *he* c. for a light. 16:29
whom *he* c. together. 19:25
he c. unto him two centurions. 23:23
he also c. whom *he* c. Rom 8:30
even us whom *he* hath c. not. 9:24
as *he* which hath c. you. 1 Pet 1:15

see **called** *the name*

I **called**, or, *I have* **called**

I c. thee to curse. Num 24:10
when *I* c. you, ye. Judg 12:2
Eli said, *I* c. not. 1 Sam 3:5, 6
I have c. thee. 28:15
in my distress *I* c. 2 Sam 22:7
Ps 18:6; 118:5
I c. the priests. Neh 5:12
if *I* had c. and he had. Job 9:16
I c. my servant, and he gave. 19:16
I have c. on thee, for. Ps 17:6
not be ashamed, for *I have* c. 31:17
Lord, *I have* c. daily upon. 88:9
then c. *I* upon the Lord. 116:4
because *I have* c. Pr 1:24
I c. him, but he gave. S of S 5:6
I have c. my mighty ones. Isa 13:3
I have c. thee from the. 41:9
I c. thee by thy name. 43:1; 45:4
yea, *I have* c. him. 48:15
when *I* c. was there none ? 50:2
for *I* c. him alone. 51:2
I c. ye did not answer. 65:12
Jer 7:13
because when *I* c. none did. Isa 66:4
because *I have* c. to them. Jer 35:17
I c. for my lovers. Lam 1:19
I c. on thy name out of. 3:55
drewest near in the day *I* c. 57
I c. my Son out of Egypt. Hos 11:1
Mat 2:15
I c. for a drought upon. Hag 1:11
one *I* c. Beauty, the other *I* c. Zech 11:7
not servants, *I have* c. John 15:15
work whereto *I have* c. Acts 13:2
for this cause *have I* c. for. 28:20

called *by my name*

people who are c. *by my n.* 2 Chr 7:14
one that is c. *by my n.* Isa 43:7
nation that was not c. *by my n.* 65:1
house c. *by my n.* Jer 7:10, 11, 14
30; 32:34; 34:15
evil on the city c. *by my n.* 25:29
heathen which are c. *by my n.* Amos 9:12

called *by thy name*

house is c. *by thy n.* 1 Ki 8:43
2 Chr 6:33
let us be c. *by thy n.* to. Isa 4:1
c. thee *by thy n.* 43:1; 45:4
they were not c. *by thy n.* 63:19
Lord, we are c. *by thy n.* Jer 14:9
for I am c. *by thy n.* 15:16
city which is c. *by thy n.* Dan 9:18
city and people are c. *by thy n.* 19

called *his name*

he c. *his n.* Israel. Gen 35:10
she c. *his n.* Benoni. 18
mother c. his *n.* Jabez. 1 Chr 4:9
she c. *his n.* Peresh. 7:16
and he c. *his n.* Beriah. 23
and he c. *his n.* Jesus. Mat 1:25
and *his name is* c. the. Rev 19:13

called *the name*

c. *the n.* of place. Gen 28:19; 35:15
Israel c. *the n.* manna. Ex 16:31
c. *the n.* of the place Massah. 17:7
Moses c. *the n.* of the altar. 15
Samson c. *the n.* Judg 15:19
c. *the n.* of that place. 2 Sam 5:20
c. *the n.* thereof Jachin. 1 Ki 7:21
2 Chr 3:17
he c. *the n.* of the first. Job 42:12

sent and **called**

she *sent and* c. Jacob. Gen 27:42
Jacob *sent and* c. Rachel. 31:4
then Pharaoh *sent and* c. 41:14
Balak *sent and* c. Balaam. Josh 24:9
she *sent and* c. Barak. Judg 4:6
she *sent and* c. the lords. 16:18
he *sent and* c. his name. 2 Sam 12:25
king *sent and* c. for. 1 Ki 2:36, 42
sent and c. Jeroboam. 12:3
2 Chr 10:3
Haman *sent and* c. for. Esth 5:10
sent to Ephesus, *and* c. Acts 20:17

shall be **called**

shall be c. woman. Gen 2:23
thy name *shall be* c. Abraham. 17:5
in Isaac *shall* thy seed *be* c. 21:12
Rom 9:7; Heb 11:18
shall be c. no more Jacob. Gen 32:28
thy issue *shall be* c. after. 48:6
his name *shall be* c. in. Deut 25:10
wise in heart *shall be* c. Pr 16:21
deviseth evil, *shall be* c. a. 24:8
Jerusalem *shall be* c. Isa 4:3
name *shall be* c. Wonderful. 9:6
one *shall be* c. the city of. 19:18
vile person *shall* no more *be* c. 32:5
shall be c. way of holiness. 35:8
the whole earth *shall* he *be* c. 54:5
shall be c. house of prayer. 56:7
Mat 21:13
shall no more *be* c. Tophet. Jer 7:32; 19:6
shall be c. Lord our. 23:6; 33:16
Jerusalem *shall be* c. a. Zech 8:3
be fulfilled, *shall be* c. a. Mat 2:23
peace-makers *shall be* c. 5:9
he *shall be* c. the least in. 19
and he *shall be* c. the. Luke 1:32
that holy thing *shall be* c. the. 35
mother said he *shall be* c. John. 60
every male *shall be* c. holy. 2:23
she be married, *shall be* c. Rom 7:3
they *shall be* c. the children. 9:26

shalt be **called**

thou *shalt be* c. the city of. Isa 1:26
thou *shalt be* c. no more tender. 47:1
thou *shalt* no more *be* c. lady of. 5
thou *shalt be* c. the repairer. 58:12
shalt be c. by a new name. Isa 62:2
thou *shalt be* c. Hephzi-bah. 4
thou *shalt be* c. sought for. 12
thou *shalt be* c. Prophet. Luke 1:76
thou *shalt be* c. Cephas. John 1:42

they **called**

they c. Lot, and said. Gen 19:5
they c. the people to. Num 25:2
they c. for Samson. Judg 16:25
they c. these days Purim. Esth 9:26
they c. upon the Lord. Ps 99:6
they have c. a multitude. Jer 12:6
because *they* c. thee an. 30:17
as *they* c. to them, so. Hos 11:2
they c. them to the most High. 7
if *they* have c. master. Mat 10:25
they c. him Zacharias. Luke 1:59
they c. parents of him. John 9:18
then again *they* c. the man. 24
they c. them, and. Acts 4:18
when *they* had c. the apostles. 5:40
they c. Barnabas, Jupiter. 14:12

was **called**

which *was* c. the land of. Deut 3:13
place *was* c. the valley. 2 Chr 20:26
was c. after their name. Ezra 2:61
Neh 7:63
wast c. a transgressor. Isa 48:8
whose name *was* c. Dan 10:1
priest, who *was* c. Caiaphas. Mat 26:3
was c. the field of blood. 27:8
her who *was* c. barren. Luke 1:36
his name *was* c. Jesus. 2:21
Jesus *was* c. and his. John 2:2
Simeon, that *was* c. Niger. Acts 13:1
and when he *was* c. forth. 24:2
knew the island *was* c. Melita. 28:1
calling wherein he *was* c. 1 Cor 7:20
Abraham when he *was* c. Heb 11:8
was c. the friend of God. Jas 2:23
that set on him *was* c. Rev 19:11

calledst, callest

that thou c. us not when. Judg 8:1
here am I, for thou c. 1 Sam 3:5
thou c. in trouble, and I. Ps 81:7
c. to remembrance. Ezek 23:21
why c. thou me good ? Mat 19:17
Mark 10:18; Luke 18:19

calleth

do according to all that the stranger c. to. 1 Ki 8:43; 2 Chr 6:33
who c. on God, and he. Job 12:4
deep c. unto deep at. Ps 42:7
c. them all by their names. 147:4
Isa 40:26
fool's mouth c. for strokes. Pr 18:6
he c. to me out of Seir. Isa 21:11
none c. for justice. 59:4
there is none that c. on thy. 64:7
there is none that c. to. Hos 7:7
c. for waters of the sea. Amos 5:8
9:6
c. for Elias. Mat 27:47; Mark 15:35
c. to him whom he would. Mark 3:13
c. to him the twelve. 6:7
Jesus c. his disciples. 8:1
arise, he c. thee. 10:49
if David therefore c. him Lord. 12:37
Luke 20:44
he c. together his friends. Luke 15:6
she c. her friends and her. 9
when he c. the Lord. 20:37
and he c. his own sheep. John 10:3
master is come and c. for. 11:28
c. things which be not, as. Rom 4:17
might stand, of him that c. 9:11
no man by the Spirit c. 1 Cor 12:3
cometh not of him that c. Gal 5:8
faithful is he that c. 1 Thes 5:24
Jezebel, that c. herself a. Rev 2:20

calling

[1] *Any lawful employment, or way of living,* 1 Cor 7:20. [2] *The calling of the gospel of Christ,* Phil 3:14; Heb 3:1.

use trumpets for c. of. Num 10:2
the c. of assemblies. Isa 1:13
in c. to remembrance. Ezek 23:19
the c. of God without. Rom 11:29
see your c. brethren. 1 Cor 1:26
let every man abide in same c. 7:20
what is the hope of his c. Eph 1:18

called in one hope of your *c*. *Eph* 4:4
for the prize of the high *c*. *Phil* 3:14
you worthy of this *c*. *2 Thes* 1:11
called us with an holy *c*. *2 Tim* 1:9
partakers of the heavenly *c*. *Heb* 3:1
your *c*. and election sure. *2 Pet* 1:10

calling, *participle*

c. the generations from. *Isa* 41:4
c. a ravenous bird from the. 46:11
c. to their fellows. *Mat* 11:16
Luke 7:32
Peter, *c*. to remembrance. *Mark* 11:21
stoned Stephen *c*. upon. *Acts* 7:59
wash away thy sins, *c*. on. 22:16
obeyed Abraham, *c*. *1 Pet* 3:6

calm

maketh the storm a *c*. *Ps* 107:29
that the sea may be *c*. *Jonah* 1:11
so shall the sea be *c*. to you. 12
there was a great *c*. *Mat* 8:26
Mark 4:39; *Luke* 8:24

Calneh

Babel and *C*. in land of. *Gen* 10:10
pass ye unto *C*. from. *Amos* 6:2

Calno

not *C*. as Carchemish? *Isa* 10:9

Calvary

come to place called *C*. *Luke* 23:33

calve, -ed, -eth

their cow *c*. and casteth. *Job* 21:10
mark when the hinds do *c*.? 39:1
Lord maketh hinds to *c*. *Ps* 29:9
the hind *c*. in the field. *Jer* 14:5

calves

and bring their *c*. home. *1 Sam* 6:7
king made two *c*. of gold. *1 Ki* 12:28
sacrificing to the *c*. that he. 32
not from the golden *c*. *2 Ki* 10:29
ordained priests, for *c*. *2 Chr* 11:15
there are with you golden *c*. 13:8
rebuke bulls with the *c*. *Ps* 68:30
fear, because of the *c*. of. *Hos* 10:5
men that sacrifice kiss the *c*. 13:2
so will we render the *c*. of. 14:2
and eat *c*. out of the midst. *Amos* 6:4
shall I come with *c*.? *Mi* 6:6
grow up as *c*. of the stall. *Mal* 4:2
by blood of goats and *c*. *Heb* 9:12
took blood of *c*. and sprinkled. 19

came

of whom *c*. *Gen* 10:14; *1 Chr* 1:12
c. two angels to Sodom. *Gen* 19:1
God *c*. to Abimelech. 20:3
brother *c*. with subtilty. 27:35
God *c*. to Laban the Syrian. 31:24
c. to thy brother Esau, he. 32:6
laid up garment until his lord *c*. 39:16
c. to the land whither. *Num* 13:27
red heifer, upon which never *c*. 19:2
God *c*. to Balaam at. 22:9, 20
Spirit of God *c*. on him. 24:2
Judg 3:10; *1 Sam* 10:10
we *c*. to Kadesh-barnea. *Deut* 1:19
the Lord *c*. from Sinai. 33:2
as she *c*. to him she moved.
Josh 15:18; *Judg* 1:14
kings *c*. and fought. *Judg* 5:19
cake of bread *c*. to a tent. 7:13
they robbed all that *c*. along. 9:25
upon them *c*. curse of Jotham. 57
c. not within border of Moab. 11:18
the man that *c*. to me. 13:10
Manoah arose and *c*. to the. 11
bring forth the man that *c*. 19:22
all that *c*. to hand. 20:48
Moabitish damsel that *c*. *Ruth* 2:6
priest's servant, *c*. *1 Sam*. 2:13, 15
to all Israelites that *c*. thither. 14
there *c*. a man of God to Eli. 27
and the word of Samuel *c*. 4:1
they *c*. no more into coast. 7:13
told Samuel before Saul *c*. 9:15
saw asses no where, *c*. to. 10:14
but Samuel *c*. not to Gilgal. 13:8
there *c*. a lion and a bear. 17:34
men of Judah *c*. and. *2 Sam* 2:4
thou knowest Abner, that *c*. 3:25
the way tidings *c*. to David. 13:30
behold, king's sons *c*. and wept. 36
when any *c*. to king. 15:2
Absalom and Ahithophel *c*.
2 Sam 16:15
saw every one that *c*. by him. 20:12
Jonathan son of Abiathar *c*. *1 Ki* 1:42
c. of all people to hear wisdom. 4:34
there *c*. no more such spices. 10:10
there *c*. no such almug-trees. 12
Jeroboam and all the people *c*.
12:12; *2 Chr* 10:12
not by way he *c*. to. *1 Ki* 13:10
he *c*. thither to a cave. 19:9
king of Israel *c*. heavy to. 20:43
it fell on a day that he *c*. *2 Ki* 4:11
when she *c*. to the man of God. 27
Naaman *c*. and stood before. 5:15
the bands of Syria *c*. 6:23
but ere messenger *c*. to him. 32
Hazael departed from Elisha, *c*. 8:14
wherefore *c*. this mad fellow? 9:11
Jehu arose, departed, and *c*. 10:12
all worshippers of Baal *c*. 21
of the priests *c*. and dwelt. 17:28
by the way that he *c*. shall. 19:33
command of the Lord *c*. this. 24:3
these *c*. in the days of. *1 Chr* 4:41
Judah prevailed, of him *c*. 5:2
Ephraim's brethren *c*. to. 7:22
are they that *c*. to David. 12:1
there *c*. to David to help him. 22
Levites left all and *c*. *2 Chr* 11:14
guard *c*. and fetched the. 12:11
fear of Lord *c*. upon them. 14:14
the band of men that *c*. with. 22:1
wrath *c*. on Judah and. 24:18
not hear, for it *c*. of God. 25:20
humbled themselves and *c*. 30:11
as soon as commandment *c*. 31:5
which *c*. with Zerubbabel. *Ezra* 2:2
cease till matter *c*. to Darius. 5:5
when seventh month *c*. *Neh* 7:73
Vashti brought in, she *c*. *Esth* 1:17
then thus *c*. every maiden to. 2:13
Mordecai *c*. even before. 4:2
whither the king's decree *c*. 8:17
rest, yet trouble *c*. *Job* 3:26
of him ready to perish *c*. 29:13
evil *c*. darkness *c*. 30:26
my cry *c*. before me. *Ps* 18:6
when my foes *c*. upon me. 27:2
wrath of God *c*. upon them. 78:31
until time that his word *c*. 105:19
spake, and there *c*. divers sorts. 31
he spake, and locusts *c*. and. 34
to go as he *c*. *Eccl* 5:15, 16
year that Tartan *c*. *Isa* 20:1
and his ambassadors *c*. to. 30:4
ends of earth, drew near and *c*. 41:5
nor *c*. it into my mind. *Jer* 7:31
19:5; 32:35
looked for peace, no good *c*. 8:15
incense you burnt, *c*. it not? 44:21
nor *c*. abominable flesh. *Ezek* 4:14
c. to Lebanon, and took the. 17:3
afore he that escaped *c*. 33:22
the bones *c*. together. 37:7
breath *c*. into them, they lived. 10
glory of God of Israel *c*. 43:2
all this *c*. on the king. *Dan* 4:28
one like Son of Man *c*. 7:13
till the ancient of days *c*. 22
to whom house of Israel *c*. *Amos* 6:1
for word *c*. to the king. *Jonah* 3:6
God *c*. from Teman, and. *Hab* 3:3
and lo it *c*. to little. *Hag* 1:9
when one *c*. to the press-fat. 2:16
c. a great wrath from. *Zech* 7:12
of all the nations that *c*. 14:16
c. wise men from the east. *Mat* 2:1
till it *c*. and stood over where. 9
those days *c*. John the Baptist. 3:1
descended, and floods *c*. 7:25, 27
he passed over and *c*. into. 9:1
a woman *c*. behind, touched. 20
the blind men *c*. to Jesus. 28
Son of Man *c*. not to be. 20:28
c. to the first and said. 21:28
he *c*. to the second, and said. 30
John *c*. to you in the way of. 32
went to buy, bridegroom *c*. 25:10
in prison, and ye *c*. to me. 36
forthwith he *c*. to Jesus. 26:49
though false witnesses *c*. yet. 60
his disciples *c*. by night. 28:13
what he did, *c*. to him. *Mark* 3:8
how long is it since this *c*.? *Mark* 9:21
one of the scribes *c*. 12:28
c. a certain poor widow. 42
there *c*. a cloud and. *Luke* 9:34
there *c*. a voice out of the cloud. 35
when he *c*. to himself. 15:17
he arose and *c*. to his father. 20
same *c*. to bear witness. *John* 1:7
he *c*. to his own, and his own. 11
but grace and truth *c*. by Jesus. 17
same *c*. to Jesus by night. 3:2
7:50; 19:39
and they *c*. and were baptized. 3:23
upon this *c*. his disciples. 4:27
gods to whom word of God *c*. 10:35
the voice *c*. not because. 12:30
at even *c*. Jesus, and stood. 20:19
preached, till he *c*. to. *Acts* 8:40
c. hither for that intent. 9:21
as many as *c*. with Peter. 10:45
the vessel descended, and it *c*. 11:5
when he *c*. and had seen. 23
and many that believed *c*. 19:18
nor brethren that *c*. spake. 28:21
judgement *c*. free gift *c*. *Rom* 5:18
when the commandment *c*. sin. 7:9
concerning the flesh, Christ *c*. 9:5
man *c*. death, by man *c*. *1 Cor* 15:21
for before that certain *c*. *Gal* 2:12
before faith *c*. we were kept. 3:23
and *c*. and preached peace. *Eph* 2:17
our gospel *c*. not in word. *1 Thes* 1:5
that Christ *c*. to save. *1 Tim* 1:15
persecutions which *c*. *2 Tim* 3:11
there *c*. such a voice. *2 Pet* 1:17
this voice which *c*. from heaven. 18
prophecy *c*. not in old time. 21
this is he that *c*. by. *1 John* 5:6
when brethren *c*. and. *3 John* 3
and great Babylon *c*. *Rev* 16:19

see *Spirit of the* **Lord**

came *again*

angel *c*. *again* to the. *Judg* 13:9
spirit *c*. *again*. 15:19; *1 Sam* 30:12
and Benjamin *c*. *again*. *Judg* 21:14
soul of the child *c*. *again*. *1 Ki* 17:22
angel of the Lord *c*. *again*. 19:7
his flesh *c*. *again* like. *2 Ki* 5:14
lepers *c*. *again*, and entered. 7:8
these *c*. *again* to. *Ezra* 2:1; *Neh* 7:6
Mordecai *c*. *again*. *Esth* 6:12
c. *again* and touched. *Dan* 10:18
the angel *c*. *again*. *Zech* 4:1
her spirit *c*. *again*. *Luke* 8:55
and early he *c*. *again*. *John* 8:2

came *down*

Lord *c*. *down* to see. *Gen* 11:5
when the fowls *c*. *down*. 15:11
O sir, we *c*. *down* at first. 43:20
the Lord *c*. *down* upon. *Ex* 19:20
when Moses *c*. *down*. 34:29
and Aaron *c*. *down*. *Lev* 9:22
Lord *c*. *down* in a cloud. *Num* 11:25
12:5
then Amalekites *c*. *down*. 14:45
out of Machir *c*. *down*. *Judg*. 5:14
and *c*. *down*. *2 Sam* 22:10; *Ps* 18:9
c. *down* fire from heaven. *2 Ki* 1:10
12, 14
men of Gath *c*. *down*. *1 Chr* 7:21
of praying, fire *c*. *down*. *2 Chr* 7:1, 3
therefore she *c*. *down*. *Lam* 1:9
an holy one *c*. *down*. *Dan* 4:13
evil *c*. *down* from Lord. *Mi* 1:12
c. *down* from mountain. *Mat* 17:9
Mark 9:9
c. *down* a certain priest. *Luke* 10:31
he made haste and *c*. *down*. 19:6
he that *c*. *down* from. *John* 3:13
I *c*. *down* from heaven, not. 6:38
bread which *c*. *down*. 41, 51, 58
men which *c*. *down*. *Acts* 15:1
c. *down* from Judea a. 21:10
fire *c*. *down* from God. *Rev* 20:9

came *forth*

to me when I *c*. *forth*. *Ex* 13:8
why *c*. we *forth* out of Egypt?
Num 11:20
Aaron and Miriam, *c*. *forth*. 12:5
water when ye *c*. *forth*. *Deut* 23:4
hot on day we *c*. *forth*. *Josh* 9:12
out of eater *c*. *forth* meat, and out of strong *c*. *forth*. *Judg* 14:14

Shimei c. forth and. 2 Sam 16:5
son which c. forth of my bowels. 11
c. forth a spirit, and. 1 Ki 22:21
c. forth little children. 2 Ki 2:23
c. forth two she-bears and tare. 24
fathers c. forth, 21:15; Jer 7:25
c. forth of his bowels. 2 Chr 32:21
therefore c. I forth to. Pr 7:15
as he c. forth naked. Eccl 5:15
wherefore c. I forth. Jer 20:18
they c. forth of the. Dan 3:26
c. forth fingers and wrote. 5:5
a fiery stream c. forth. 7:10
out of one of them c. forth. 8:9
the command c. forth and I. 9:23
out of him c. forth corner. Zech 10:4
for therefore c. I forth. Mark 1:38
that was dead c. forth. John 11:44
I c. forth from the Father. 16:28
Jesus c. forth wearing the. 19:5

I came

I c. this day to the well. Gen 24:42
little thou hadst before I c. 30:30
which were born before I c. 48:5
when I c. from Padan. Rachel. 7
I c. to speak to Pharaoh. Ex 5:23
when I c. to her found. Deut 22:14
I c. into Gibeah. Judg 20:4
believed not till I c. 1 Ki 10:7
2 Chr 9:6
afterwards I c. to the. Neh 6:10
I c. to the king and. 13:6
I c. to Jerusalem and understood. 7
wherefore, when I c. Isa 50:2
then I c. to them of the. Ezek 3:15
when I c. to destroy the city. 43:3
I c. not to send peace. Mat 10:34
I c. not to call the righteous.
Mark 2:17; Luke 5:32
I know whence I c. John 8:14
I c. from God, nor c. I of. 42
but for this cause I c. 12:27
for I c. not to judge the world. 47
for this cause c. I into the. 18:37
therefore c. I as soon as. Acts 10:29
the first day I c. into Asia. 20:18
being led by the hand, I c. 22:11
then c. I with an army. 23:27
I c. to bring alms to my. 24:17
when I c. to you I c. not. 1 Cor 2:1
to spare you I c. not. 2 Cor 1:23
lest when I c. I should have. 2:3
when I c. to Troas to preach. 12
afterwards I c. into. Gal 1:21

came in

sons of God, c. in to. Gen 6:4
where are the men that c. in. 19:5
Judah c. in unto her. 38:18
he c. in to lie with me. 39:14
if he c. in by himself. Ex 21:3
went out, and none c. in. Josh 6:1
went out and c. in. 1 Sam 18:13, 16
she c. in to him. 2 Sam 11:4
as she c. in at the door. 1 Ki 14:6
no peace to him that c. in. 2 Chr 15:5
Zech 8:10
c. in unto the king no more. Esth 2:14
and they c. in and. Jer 32:23
now Jeremiah c. in and went. 37:4
way of the gate he c. in. Ezek 46:9
c. in the magicians. Dan 4:7; 5:8
but at the last Daniel c. in. 4:8
my prayer c. in. Jonah 2:7
when the king c. in to. Mat 22:11
the angel c. in to Mary. Luke 1:28
this woman since I c. in. 7:45
wife not knowing c. in. Acts 5:7
the young men c. in and found. 10
who c. in privily to spy. Gal 2:4

came near

they pressed, and c. near. Gen 19:9
the one c. not near the. Ex 14:20
when they c. near to the altar. 40:32
captains c. near to Moses.
Num 31:48
the chief of Joseph c. near. 36:1
ye c. near to me. Deut 1:22; 5:23
c. near and put feet on. Josh 10:24
c. near before Eleazar. 17:4; 21:1
Elijah c. near and said. 1 Ki 18:36
Gehazi c. near to thrust. 2 Ki 4:27
Zedekiah c. near and. 2 Chr 18:23

even to greatest c. near. Jer 42:1
Chaldeans c. near and. Dan 3:8
Nebuchadnezzar c. near to. 26
he c. near to Damascus. Acts 9:3

came nigh

as soon as he c. nigh. Ex 32:19
the children of Israel c. nigh. 34:32
when any c. nigh to do. 2 Sam 15:5
Jesus c. nigh to the sea. Mat 15:29
when they c. nigh to. Mark 11:1
when he c. nigh to gate. Luke 7:12

came over

Israel c. over this Jordan. Josh 4:22
the Levite c. over. Judg 19:10
they c. over to the other. Mark 5:1

came out

behold Rebekah c. out. Gen 24:15
first c. out red, all over like. 25:25
midwife said, this c. out first. 38:28
all the souls which c. out of. 46:26
day in which ye c. out. Ex 13:3, 4
a fire c. out. Lev 9:24; Num 16:35
they three c. out. Num 12:4
Dathan and Abiram c. out. 16:27
smote rock, and water c. out. 20:11
Egypt whence ye c. out. Deut 11:10
all that c. out were. Josh 5:4, 5
all that c. out of Egypt. 6
Jael c. out to meet him. Judg 4:22
I am he that c. out. 1 Sam 4:16
three days since I c. out. 21:5
spear c. out behind. 2 Sam 2:23
Michal c. out to meet David. 6:20
men prevailed and c. out. 11:23
and all the people c. out. 18:4
covenant with Israel when they c.
out of. 1 Ki 8:9; 2 Chr 5:10
princes of provinces c. out. 1 Ki 20:19
when they c. out. 2 Chr 20:10
naked c. I out of my. Job 1:21
why did I not give up the ghost,
when I c. out of the belly? 3:11
that which c. out of my. Jer 17:16
whirlwind c. out of the. Ezek 1:4
c. out as a whirlwind. Hab 3:14
c. out two women. Zech 5:9
the whole city c. out to. Mat 8:34
return to house whence I c. out.
12:44; Luke 11:24
as they c. out they found. Mat 27:32
and c. out of the graves after. 53
unclean spirit c. out. Mark 1:26
9:26
c. out he saw much people. 6:34
a voice c. out of the cloud. 9:7
when he c. out he could. Luke 1:22
and he c. out of him. 4:35
therefore c. out his father. 15:28
believed I c. out from. John 16:27
have known that I c. out. 17:8
forthwith c. out blood and. 19:34
unclean spirits c. out. Acts 8:7
and the spirit c. out. 16:18
c. word of God out. 1 Cor 14:36
not all that c. out of. Heb 3:16
c. out of great tribulation. Rev 7:14
angel c. out of the temple. 14:15, 17
angel c. out from the altar. 18
seven angels c. out of temple. 15:6
a voice c. out of the throne. 19:5

came to pass

it c. to pass, even the self-same day
it c. to pass. Ex 12:41, 51
it c. to pass. Deut 2:16; 1 Sam 13:22
2 Ki 15:12; Esth 2:8; Acts 27:44
it c. to pass when Israel. Josh 17:13
all c. to pass. 21:45
for it c. to pass. Judg 13:20
1 Ki 11:4, 15
but it c. to pass. Judg 15:1; 2 Ki 3:5
Neh 2:1; 4:1, 7; 6:1; 7:1
Jer 35:11
it c. to pass when the. 1 Sam 1:20
and all those signs c. to pass. 10:9
it c. to pass when the evil. 16:23
it c. to pass after. 2 Sam 2:1; 8:1
10:1; 2 Ki 6:24; 2 Chr 20:1
it c. to pass on morrow. 2 Ki 8:15
1 Chr 10:8; Jer 20:3; Acts 4:5
and they c. to pass. Isa 48:3
before it c. to pass I shewed. 5
even as it c. to pass. 1 Thes 3:4

then came

then c. Amalek and. Ex 17:8
then c. the daughters. Num 27:1
then c. David to. 1 Sam 21:1
then c. all the tribes. 2 Sam 5:1
then they c. to Gilead. 24:6
then c. Eliakim. 2 Ki 18:37
Isa 36:22
then c. Solomon. 2 Chr 1:13
then c. Shemaiah the prophet. 12:5
then c. Sheshbazzar. Ezra 5:16
then Hanani c. Neh 1:2
then I c. to the governors. 2:9
for good, then evil c. Job 30:26
then c. Jeremiah from. Jer 19:14
then c. all the princes. 38:27
then c. certain of elders. Ezek 14:1
then they c. the same day. 23:39
then c. to him the. Mat 9:14
then c. to Jesus scribes and. 15:1
then c. his disciples. 12; 17:19
then c. she, and worshipped. 15:25
Mark 7:25
then c. Peter to him. Mat 18:21
then c. mother of Zebedee's. 20:20
then c. they, and laid hands. 26:50
then c. also publicans. Luke 3:12
then c. day of unleavened. 22:7
then c. the officers to. John 7:45
then c. a voice from heaven. 12:28
then c. Jesus, the doors. 20:26

they came, or came they

they c. to Haran and. Gen 11:31
into the land of Canaan, they c. 12:5
they c. to the place which God. 22:9
till they c. to a land. Ex 16:35
same day c. they into the 19:1
they c. he lay on bed. 2 Sam 4:7
and Nathan, they c. 1 Ki 1:32
so they c. to me, when I fled. 2:7
they c. and told it in city. 13:25
I will not leave, so they c. 2 Ki 2:4
when they c. to Jordan. 6:4
whence c. they? 20:14; Isa 39:3
out of all Judah they c. 2 Chr 20:4
on eighth day c. they to. 29:17
some when they c. offered. Ezra 2:68
from that time c. they. Neh 13:21
they c. thither and were. Job 6:20
they c. upon me as a wide. 30:14
they c. round about me. Ps 88:17
they c. to the pits. Jer 14:3
c. they even to Tahpanhes. 43:7
messenger was sent, lo they c.
Ezek 23:40
they c. and stood before. Dan 2:2
or ever they c. at the bottom. 6:24
before they c. together. Mat 1:18
they c. into the land of. 14:34
they c. and told their Lord all.
18:31; Luke 14:21
after a while c. they. Mat 26:73
they c. to him from. Mark 1:45
whom he would, and they c. 3:13
they c. with haste. Luke 2:16
they c. saying, that they. 24:23
and they c. not for Jesus'. John 12:9
they c. unto a certain. Acts 8:36
they c. to the iron gate. 12:10
they c. with one accord and. 20
they c. thither also and stirred. 17:13
they c. to the chief priests. 23:14
who when they c. to Caesarea. 33
and whence c. they? Rev 7:13

word of the Lord came

word of Lord c. to Abram.
Gen 15:1, 4
word of Lord c. to Samuel.
1 Sam 15:10
c. the word of Lord to Gad.
2 Sam 24:11
word of Lord c. to Solomon. 1 Ki 6:11
word of Lord c. to Jehu. 16:1, 7
the word of Lord c. unto Elijah.
17:2, 8; 18:1; 19:9; 21:17, 28
whom word of Lord c. saying. 18:31
word of Lord c. to Isaiah.
2 Ki 20:4; Isa 38:4
word of Lord c. to Nathan.
1 Chr 17:3
word of Lord c. to David. 22:8
word of Lord c. to Shemaiah.
2 Chr 11:2; 12:7; 1 Ki 12:22

word of Lord c. to Jeremiah. Jer 1:2 4; 2:1; 14:1; 29:30; 33:1, 19 Dan 9:2
word of Lord c. expressly to Ezekiel. Ezek 1:3; 3:16
word of Lord c. to Hosea. Hos 1:1
word of Lord c. to Joel. Joel 1:1
word of Lord c. to Jonah. Jonah 1:1 3:1
word of Lord c. to Micah. Mi 1:1
word of Lord c. to Zephaniah. Zeph 1:1
word of Lord c. by Haggai. Hag 1:1
word of Lord c. to Zechariah. Zech 1:1
c. word of Lord of hosts. 7:4; 8:1

camel

(*Camels were the usual riding animals in the East, as they were stronger than horses, and had much more endurance. As so much of the Bible world was either desert, or dry at certain seasons of the year, the peculiar adaptation of the camel to deserts was of unusual importance. Very frequently a man's wealth was estimated in camels. They were bred for work or for swift riding, and their hair was used for clothing*)

saw Isaac, lighted off c. Gen 24:64
shall not eat, the c. Lev 11:14 Deut 14:7
slay infant, ox, and c. 1 Sam 15:3
the plague of the c. and. Zech 14:15
easier for a c. to go. Mat 19:24 Mark 10:25; Luke 18:25
at a gnat and swallow a c. Mat 23:24

camels

Abram had sheep, oxen, c. Gen 12:16
will draw water for thy c. 24:19, 44
had much cattle, asses, c. 30:43
Rachel put them in the c. 31:34
Ishmaelites came with their c. 37:25
hand of Lord on c. and. Ex 9:3
they and their c. Judg 6:5; 7:12
ornaments on c. necks. 8:21, 26
David took away c. and. 1 Sam 27:9
men who rode on c. and fled. 30:17
to Jerusalem with c. 1 Ki 10:2 2 Chr 9:1
Hazael took forty c. 2 Ki 8:9
took away of c. 50,000. 1 Chr 5:21
Zebulun brought bread on c. 11:40
over the c. also was Obil. 27:30
c. were 435. Ezra 2:67; Neh 7:69
by post on mules, c. Esth 8:10*, 14*
also was three thousand c. Job 1:3
the Chaldeans fell on the c. 17
chariot of asses and of c. Isa 21:7
carry treasures on bunches of c. 30:6
multitude of c. cover thee. 60:6
take to themselves their c. Jer 49:29
their c. shall be a booty. 32
Rabbah a stable for c. Ezek 25:5
raiment of c. hair. Mat 3:4 Mark 1:6

camest

Hagar, whence c. thou? Gen 16:8
the land from whence thou c. 24:5
eaten of all before thou c. 27:33
in it thou c. from Egypt. Ex 23:15 34:18
wherefore c. thou not? Num 22:37
to land of Ammon c. not. Deut 2:37
day thou c. thou c. in haste. 16:3
thou c. not within the. 1 Sam 13:11
why c. thou down hither? 17:28
c. thou not from thy? 2 Sam 11:10
whereas thou c. but yesterday. 15:20
by the way thou c. 1 Ki 13:9, 17
art thou the man of God that c.? 14
turn thee back by the way by which thou c. 2 Ki 19:28; Isa 37:29
thou c. down also on. Neh 9:13
c. down the mountains. Isa 64:3
before thou c. forth, I. Jer 1:5
and thou c. forth with. Ezek 32:2*
friend, how c. thou in? Mat 22:12
said, Rabbi, when c.? John 6:25
we believe that thou c. forth. 16:30
to thee in way, as thou c. Acts 9:17

Camon

Jair died, was buried in C. Judg 10:5

camp

of Lord went before c. Ex 14:19
quails came up and covered c. 16:13
there is a noise of war in c. 32:17
go through c. and slay every. 27
proclaimed through the c. 36:6
man killeth goat in c.? Lev 17:3
strove together in the c. 24:10
every one by his own c. Num 1:52
on the east-side shall the c. of. 2:3
when c. setteth forward. 4:5
as the c. is to set forward. 15
them in utmost parts of the c. 11:1
and Medad prophesied in the c. 26
shall not come within c. Deut 23:10
Lord walked in midst of thy c. 14
make c. of Israel a curse. Josh 6:18
to the outside of the c. Judg 7:17
began to move him in the c. 13:25
there came none to the c. 21:8
they brought them to the c. 12
this great shout in the c.? 1 Sam 4:6
and run to the c. to thy. 17:17
made Omri king in c. 1 Ki 16:16
such a place shall be my c. 2 Ki 6:8
they left the c. as it was. 7:7
when these lepers came to c. 8
angel of Lord smote c. of Assyrians. 19:35; Isa 37:36
came with Arabians to c. 2 Chr 22:1
fall in the midst of their c. Ps 78:28
envied Moses also in the c. 106:16
lay siege, set the c. also. Ezek 4:2
for his c. is very great. Joel 2:11
compassed c. of saints. Rev 20:9

into the **camp**

he shall come into c. Lev 14:8 16:26, 28
Moses gat him into c. Num 11:30
he shall come into c. Deut 23:11
God is come into c. 1 Sam 4:7

out of the **camp**

forth people out of the c. Ex 19:17
your brethren out of c. Lev 10:4
priest shall go forth out of the c. 14:3
killeth a goat out of the c. 17:3
him that had cursed out of c. 24:23
put every leper out of c. Num 5:2
Miriam be shut out of the c. 12:14
Moses departed not out of c. 14:44
shall go abroad out of c. Deut 23:10
spoilers came out of c. 1 Sam 13:17
out of c. from Saul. 2 Sam 1:2
out of c. of Israel am I escaped. 3

round about the **camp**

quails fell, spread them round about c. Num 11:31, 32
stood every man in place round about c. Judg 7:21

without the **camp**

burn without the c. Ex 29:14 Lev 8:17; 9:11; 16:27
sought Lord, went without c. Ex 33:7
ashes without the c. Lev 6:11
plague shall dwell without c. 13:46
leper be without the c. Num 5:3
stoned without the c. 15:35
bring red heifer without c. 19:3
do ye abide without the c. 31:19
place also without c. Deut 23:12
left kindred without the c. Josh 6:23
beasts burnt without c. Heb 13:11
let us go forth to him without c. 13

camp

I will c. against thee. Isa 29:3
bend the bow c. against. Jer 50:29
which c. in the hedges in. Nah 3:17

camped

there Israel c. before the. Ex 19:2

camphire

beloved is as cluster of c. S of S 1:14
plants are an orchard of c. 4:13

camps

that they defile not their c Num 5:3
trumpets for journeying of c. 10:2
made stink of your c. Amos 4:10

can

c. we find such a one as? Gen 41:38
I c. no more go out. Deut 31:2
he is dead, c. I bring? 2 Sam 12:23
c. I discern, c. I hear voice? 19:35
c. that which is unsavoury? Job 6:6
c. rush grow without mire? c. 8:11
c. a man be profitable to God? 22:2
c. he judge through dark cloud? 13
c. any understand spreading? 36:29
c. God furnish a table? Ps 78:19
c. he give bread also? c. he? 20
who c. be compared? c. be? 89:6
c. a man take fire in his? Pr 6:27
c. one go on hot coals and? 28
yet c. he not answer. Isa 46:7
c. a woman forget her? 49:15
c. a maid forget her? Jer 2:32
c. any hide himself in secret? 23:24
c. two walk together? Amos 3:3
c. a bird fall in a snare where? 5
who c. but prophesy? 8
who c. be saved? Mat 19:25 Mark 10:26; Luke 18:26
make it as sure as you c. Mat 27:65
c. children of bridechamber fast? Mark 2:19
this kind c. come forth but. 9:29
c. ye drink of the cup? 10:38
c. the blind lead blind? Luke 6:39
c. any good come out? John 1:46
hard saying, who c. hear it? 6:60
c. a devil open the eyes of? 10:21
no more c. ye except ye. 15:4
c. any man forbid water? Acts 10:47
to law, ncr indeed c. Rom 8:7
not works, c. faith save? Jas 2:14
c. the fig-tree bear olive-? 3:12

how **can**

how c. I alone bear? Deut 1:12
how c. I go, if Saul? 1 Sam 16:2
how c. I endure to see? Esth 8:6
how c. a man be justified? Job 25:4
how c. man understand? Pr 20:24
how c. one be warm? Eccl 4:11
how c. it be quiet seeing? Jer 47:7
how c. ye being evil? Mat 12:34
how c. a man be born? John 3:4
how c. these things be? 9
how c. this man give us? 6:52
how c. we know the way? 14:5
how c. I except some? Acts 8:31

Cana

was a marriage in C. John 2:1
beginning of miracles in C. 11
so Jesus came again into C. 4:46
Thomas and Nathanael of C. 21:2

Canaan

Ham is the father of C. Gen 9:18
Ham the father of C. saw the. 22
cursed be C. 25
C. shall be his servant. 26, 27
C. begat Sidon. 10:15; 1 Chr 1:13
wife of daughters of C. Gen 28:1

Canaan

the inhabitants of C. Ex 15:15
not known all wars of C. Judg 3:1
sold them to Jabin king of C. 4:2
God subdued Jabin king of C. 23, 24
then fought the kings of C. 5:19
sacrificed to the idols of C. Ps 106:38
smote the kingdoms of C. 135:11
Egypt speak language of C. Isa 19:18
O C. I will even destroy. Zeph 2:5
a woman of C. cried. Mat 15:22

land of **Canaan**

go into the land of C. Gen 12:5
dwelt ten years in land of C. 16:3
give thee land of C. 17:8; Lev 25:38 Num 34:2; Deut 32:49 1 Chr 16:18; Ps 105:11
Jacob dwelt in land of C. Gen 37:1
famine was in the land of C. 42:5
they said, from land of C. 7
sons of one man in land of C. 13
get ye up unto land of C. 45:17
carried him into land of C. 50:13
come into the land of C. Lev 14:34 Num 34:2
after doings of land of C. Lev 18:3
sent to spy land of C. Num 13:17
over armed into land of C. 32:32
fruit of land of C. Josh 5:12
altar over against land of C. 22:11
led him through the land of C. 24:3

nativity is of land of C. Ezek 16:3
dearth over all land of C. Acts 7:11
seven nations in land of C. 13:19

Canaanite, -s

C. was then in land. Gen 12:6; 13:7
the Amorites, C., Girgashites. 15:21
Ex. 3:8, 17; 23:23; Deut 7:1
20:17; Josh 3:10; 12:8; Judg 3:5
Neh 9:8
shalt not take a wife of C. Gen 24:3
make me to stink amongst C. 34:30
daughter of a certain C. 38:2
drive out the C. Ex 23:28; 33:2
34:11
Lord delivered up the C. Num 21:3
Neh 9:24
C. would dwell in land. Josh 17:12
Judg 1:27
shalt drive out the C. Josh 17:18
up against the C. first? Judg 1:1
to fight against the C. 9, 10
did Ephraim drive out C. 29
Naphtali dwelt among the C. 33
Pharaoh had slain the C. 1 Ki 9:16
to abominations of C. Ezra 9:1
shall possess that of C. Ob 20
no more C. in house of. Zech 14:21
Simon the C. Mat 10:4; Mark 3:18

Canaanitess

to Judah of Shua the C. 1 Chr 2:3

Candace

eunuch of great authority under C.
Acts 8:27

candle

(*Revised Version,* lamp *in every case. The candle, as we know it, was not used in the East, the reference being to small earthen lamps in which a wick floating in the oil gave a feeble light. They were of different sizes and shapes. The word* candlestick, *however, remains in the Revisions in nearly every instance, a few being translated* lampstand, Mat 5:15)

his c. shall be put out. Job 18:6
how oft is c. of wicked put? 21:17
his c. shined upon my head. 29:3
thou wilt light my c. God. Ps 18:28
spirit of man is c. of. Pr 20:27
c. of wicked shall be put out. 24:20
her c. goeth not out by night. 31:18
from them light of c. Jer 25:10
light a c. and put it under. Mat 5:15
Mark 4:21; Luke 8:16; 11:33
bright shining of a c. Luke 11:36
doth not she light a c. and. 15:8
light of a c. shine no. Rev 18:23
and they need no c. nor light. 22:5

candles

search Jerusalem with c. Zeph 1:12

candlestick

c. of pure gold. Ex 25:31; 37:17
Num 8:4
six branches out of the c. Ex 25:33
37:19
in c. four bowls. 25:34; 37:20
thou shalt set the c. over. 26:35
put the c. in the tent. 40:24
order the lamps on the c. Lev 24:4
charge shall be ark and c. Num 3:31
take a cloth and cover the c. 4:9
light over against the c. 8:2
a bed, a table, a c. 2 Ki 4:10
by weight for every c. 1 Chr 28:15
set they in order the c. 2 Chr 13:11
wrote over against the c. Dan 5:5
I looked, and behold a c. Zech 4:2
two olive-trees on right side of c. 11
a c. and it giveth light. Mat 5:15*
Luke 8:16; 11:33
is a candle brought not to be set on a
c.? Mark 4:21*
first, wherein was the c. Heb 9:2
I come and remove thy c. Rev 2:5

candlesticks

made c. of pure gold. 1 Ki 7:49
2 Chr 4:7
weight for the c. of gold. 1 Chr 28:15
he took away the c. Jer 52:19
two c. standing before the. Rev 11:4
see **seven**

cane

brought me no sweet c. Isa 43:24
sweet c. from a far. Jer 6:20

canker, -ed

will eat as doth a c. 2 Tim 2:17*
your gold and silver is c. Jas 5:3*

cankerworm

c. eaten, and what c. left. Joel 1:4
2:25
like c. make thyself as c. Nah 3:15
the c. spoileth, and fleeth away. 16

cannot

calling of assemblies I c. Isa 1:13
read this, he saith, I c. for. 29:11
waves c. prevail, c. pass. Jer 5:22
c. I do with you as this potter? 18:6
secret king demanded, c. Dan 2:27
c. ye discern the signs? Mat 16:3
c. be that a prophet. Luke 13:33
pass from hence to you c. 16:26
of which we c. now speak. Heb 9:5

canst

c. not see my face and. Ex 33:20
itch, whereof thou c. Deut 28:27
if thou c. answer me, set. Job 33:5
Lord, if thou wilt, thou c. Mat 8:2
if thou c. do any thing. Mark 9:22
chief captain said, c.? Acts 21:37

Capernaum

Nazareth, dwelt in C. Mat 4:13
Jesus was entered into C. 8:5
thou C. which art exalted. 11:23
Luke 10:15
they were come to C. Mat 17:24
they went into C. Mark 1:21; 2:1
have heard done in C. Luke 4:23
not many days in C. John 2:12
whose son was sick at C. 4:46
over the sea towards C. 6:17
people came to C. seeking. 24
things said he, as he taught in C. 59

Caphtor

country of C. Jer 47:4; Amos 9:7
which came forth out of C. Deut 2:23

Cappadocia

the dwellers in C. we hear. Acts 2:9
strangers scattered throughout C.
1 Pet 1:1

captain

A name applied, [1] *To the king, or prince of a people,* 1 Sam 9:16. [2] *To a general, or commander in an army,* Gen 26:26; 2 Sam 5:8. [3] *To the head of a family, or tribe,* Num 2:3. [4] *To such as have the command of a company,* Deut 1:15. [5] *Christ Jesus is called the Captain of salvation,* Heb 2:10.

Joseph to Potiphar, c. Gen 37:36
c. of the guard charged Joseph. 40:4
Nahshon, c. of children of. Num 2:3
Nethaneel, c. of the children of. 5
make a c. and return. 14:4
Neh 9:17
as c. of the host of the. Josh 5:14
the c. of the Lord's host. 15
c. of Jabin's host. Judg 4:2, 7
1 Sam 12:9
come and be our c. Judg 11:6
him head and c. over them. 11
anoint him c. over. 1 Sam 9:16; 10:1
commanded him to be c. 13:14
these ten cheeses to the c. 17:18
and David became a c. 22:2
shalt feed, and be a c. 2 Sam 5:2
be chief and c. 8; 1 Chr 11:6
if thou be not c. of host. 2 Sam 19:13
Abishai was therefore their c. 23:19
Israel made Omri, c. 1 Ki 16:16
the king sent a c. with. 2 Ki 1:9
sent to him another c. 11, 13
thou be spoken for to c.? 4:13
Naaman, c. of the host of. 5:1
I have an errand to thee, O c. 9:5
Pekah, a c. of his, conspired. 15:25
turn away face of one c. 18:24
Isa 36:9
tell Hezekiah c. of my. 2 Ki 20:5
Nebuzar-adan, c. of guard. 25:8
Jer 52:12

for he was their c. 1 Chr 11:21
killed Shophach c. of. 19:18
2 Sam 10:18
the third c. Benaiah. 1 Chr 27:5
fourth c. Asahel. 7
the fifth c. Shamhuth. 8
the sixth c. Ira. 9
God himself is our c. 2 Chr 13:12
Lord doth take away c. Isa 3:3
a c. of the ward Irijah. Jer 37:13
c. of the guard took Jeremiah. 40:2
c. gave victuals and a reward. 5
call together, appoint a c. 51:27
band and the c. took. John 18:12
the c. with officers went. Acts 5:26
c. of their salvation. Heb 2:10

captains

chosen c. also are drowned. Ex 15:4
Moses was wroth with c. Num 31:14
I made wise men c. over. Deut 1:15
shall make c. of the army. 20:9
he will appoint him c. 1 Sam 8:12
son of Jesse make you all c. 22:7
king gave all c. charge. 2 Sam 18:5
sat in the seat chief among c. 23:8
what Joab did to the c. 1 Ki 2:5
they were his princes, and c. 9:22
take kings away, and put c. 20:24
when c. perceived that he was not
king of Israel. 22:23; 2 Chr 18:32
Jehoiada commanded c. 2 Ki 11:15
having for c. Pelatiah. 1 Chr 4:42
now three of the 30 c. went. 11:15
of Naphtali a thousand c. 12:34
smote Edomites and c. 2 Chr 21:9
Lord brought on them the c. 33:11
the king had sent c. of. Neh 2:9
the thunder of the c. Job 39:25
hast taught them to be c. Jer 13:21*
will I break in pieces c. 51:23
I will make drunk her c. 57
c. to open the mouth in. Ezek 21:22
c. and rulers all. 23:6, 12, 23
the c. saw these men. Dan 3:27
the c. have consulted to. 6:7
thy c. as the great. Nah 3:17
made supper to his c. Mark 6:21
communed with the c. Luke 22:4
may eat the flesh of c. Rev 19:18

captive

his brother was taken c. Gen 14:14
their wives took they c. 34:29
unto first-born of the c. Ex 12:29
hast taken them c. Deut 21:10
away c. a little maid. 2 Ki 5:2
smite those thou hast taken c. 6:22
I am desolate, a c. and. Isa 49:21
or shall the lawful c. be? 24
the c. exile hasteneth, that. 51:14
loose thyself, O c. daughter. 52:2
go c. with first that go c. Amos 6:7
who are taken c. by will. 2 Tim 2:26

carry or *carried* **captive,** or **captives**

carried away daughters as c.
Gen 31:26
shall *carry* thee away c. Num 24:22
they *carry* them away c. 1 Ki 8:46
2 Chr 6:36
if bethink in land whither they were
carried c. 1 Ki 8:47; 2 Chr 6:37
carried them c. to. 2 Ki 15:29
carried people of Damascus c. 16:9
king of Assyria *carried* c. 1 Chr 5:6
other 10,000 did Judah *carry* c.
2 Chr 25:12
carried a great multitude c. 28:5
carried c. of their brethren. 8
that *carried* them c. Ps 106:46
that *carried* us c. required. 137:3
Lord's flock is *carried* c. Jer 13:17
Judah shall be *carried* away c. 19
carry them c. to Babylon. 20:4
them that are *carried* c. 24:5
took not when he *carried* c. 27:20
to all that are *carried* c. 29:4
bring you into place whence I caused
you to be *carried* away c. 14
which were *carried* c. 40:1; 52:27
that were not *carried* c. 40:7
Ishmael *carried* away c. 41:10
shall *carry* the Egyptians c. 43:12
Nebuchadnezzar *carried* c. 52:29

carried away c. of the Jews. Jer 52:30
whither they be carried c. Ezek 6:9
and shall also carry c. Dan 11:8
because they carried c. Amos 1:6
that strangers carried c. Ob 11

carrying **captive**

carrying away of Jerusalem c. Jer 1:3

lead, or *led* **captive**

lead thy captivity c. thou. Judg 5:12
enemies who led them c. 1 Ki 8:48
before them that lead c. 2 Chr 30:9
hast led captivity c. Ps 68:18
Eph 4:8
whither they led him c. Jer 22:12
Israel shall be led c. out. Amos 7:11
led c. her maids shall lead. Nah 2:7
shall be led away c. Luke 21:24
lead c. silly women. 2 Tim 3:6

captives

all women of Midian c. Num 31:9
they brought the c. 12
purify your c. 19
seest among the c. a. Deut 21:11
arrows drunk with blood of c. 32:42
two wives were taken c. 1 Sam 30:5
from Jerusalem 10,000 c. 2 Ki 24:14
me, and deliver the c. 2 Chr 28:11
ye shall not bring in the c. hither. 13
take them c. whose c. Isa 14:2
lead away the Ethiopians c. 20:4
he shall let go my c. not for. 45:13
c. of the mighty shall be. 49:25
proclaim liberty to the c. 61:1
Luke 4:18
daughters are taken c. Jer 48:46
all that took them c. held. 50:33
I was among the c. by. Ezek 1:1
bring again captivity of thy c. 16:53
found a man of the c. Dan 2:25

captivity

(The servitudes spoken of in Judges, and those under the Greeks and the Romans, are sometimes spoken of as Captivities. *More exactly, however, the word is used of the carrying away of the people of Israel and of Judah into Babylonia and Assyria, when the kingdom of Israel was finally destroyed, and the kingdom of Judah lost its independence, Jerusalem and the Temple being destroyed.*
The word is also frequently used in the Bible in its ordinary sense of bondage or servitude without reference to any historical event)

his daughters into c. Num 21:29
put raiment of c. from. Deut 21:13
Lord will turn thy c. and have. 30:3
till the day of the c. Judg 18:30
carried into c. to Babylon. 2 Ki 24:15
thirty-seventh year of the c. 25:27
Jer 52:31
in their steads until c. 1 Chr 5:22
Jehozadak went into c. when. 6:15
pray to thee in land of c. 2 Chr 6:37
return to thee in land of their c. 38
sons and our wives are in c. 29:9
have been delivered to c. Ezra 9:7
Jews which were left of c. Neh 1:2
them for a prey in land of c. 4:4
carried away with the c. Esth 2:6
Lord turned the c. of Job. Job 42:10
bringeth back the c. Ps 14:7; 85:1
delivereth his strength into c. 78:61
when Lord turned again c. 126:1
turn again our c. O Lord. 4
my people are gone into c. Isa 5:13
thee away with a mighty c. 22:17
themselves are gone into c. 46:2
for the c. to the c. Jer 15:2; 43:11
I will turn away your c. 29:14
30:3; 32:44; 33:7, 11, 26
hear ye, all ye of c. 29:20
a curse by all the c. of Judah. 22
this c. is long. 28
send to all them of the c. saying. 31
from the land of c. 30:10; 46:27
nor hath he gone into c. 48:11
Judah is gone into c. Lam 1:3
her children are gone into c. 5
to turn away thy c. Lam 2:14
no more carry thee into c. 4:22
fifth year of Jehoiachin's c. Ezek 1:2
get to them of the c. 3:11
I came to them of the c. 15; 11:24
I spake to them of the c. 11:25
as stuff for c. 12:7
bring again their c. the c. of Sodom, c. of Samaria. 16:53
when thou went into c. 25:3
in the twelfth year of the c. 33:21
house of Israel went into c. 39:23
five and twentieth year of c. 40:1
Daniel which is of the c. Dan 6:13
shall fall by c. and by spoil. 11:33
when I return the c. of. Hos 6:11
the c. of this host, the c. Ob 20
they are gone into c. Mi 1:16
she [No] went into c. Nah 3:10
shall gather c. as sand. Hab 1:9
shall turn away c. Zeph 2:7; 3:20
take of them of the c. Zech 6:10
and bringing me into c. Rom 7:23
bringing into c. every. 2 Cor 10:5

see **captive**

bring **captivity**

bring up with them of c. Ezra 1:11
God bringeth back c. Ps 53:6
I will bring again the c. Jer 30:18
I shall bring again their c. 31:23
yet will I bring again the c. 48:47
I will bring again the c. of Ammon. 49:6
I will bring again the c. of Elam. 39
I will bring again the c. of Egypt. Ezek 29:14
now will I bring again the c. 39:25
when I bring again the c. Joel 3:1
I will bring again the c. of my people. Amos 9:14

children of **captivity**

heard that children of c. Ezra 4:1
the rest of children of c. 6:16
the children of c. kept passover. 19
killed passover for children of c. 20
proclamation to children of c. 10:7
the children of c. did so. 16
of children of c. of Judah. Dan 5:13

go into **captivity**

daughters shall go into c. Deut 28:41
thine house shall go into c. Jer 20:6
thy lovers shall go into c. 22:22
one of them shall go into c. 30:16
furnish thyself to go into c. 46:19
Chemosh shall go into c. 48:7
their kings go into c. 49:3
as they that go into c. Ezek 12:4
these cities shall go into c. 30:17
her daughters shall go into c. 18
Syria shall go into c. unto. Amos 1:5
their king shall go into c. 15
Gilgal shall surely go into c. 5:5
will I cause you to go into c. 27
Israel shall surely go into c. 7:17
and though they go into c. 9:4
half of city shall go into c. Zech 14:2
leadeth into c. go into c. Rev 13:10

out of **captivity**

these went up out of c. Ezra 2:1
Neh 7:6
up out of c. Ezra 3:8; Neh 8:17
children of Israel which were come again out of c. did eat. Ezra 6:21
were come out of c. offered. 8:35

carbuncle, -s

(A precious stone of a red colour. Probably the red garnet)

first row shall be a c. Ex 28:17
39:10
I will make thy gates of c. Isa 54:12
topaz and c. were thy. Ezek 28:13

carcase

touch c. of unclean thing. Lev 5:2
c. ye shall not touch. 11:8
Deut 14:8
c. shall be meat unto. Deut 28:26
should take his c. down. Josh 8:29
see the c. of the lion, honey in c. Judg 14:8
thy c. shall not come to. 1 Ki 13:22
c. cast in way, a lion stood by c. 24
the c. of Jezebel. 2 Ki 9:37
cast out as a c. trodden. Isa 14:19
where the c. is, there. Mat 24:28

carcases

fowls came down on c. Gen 15:11
c. in abomination. Lev 11:11, 26
cast your c. on c. of your idols. 26:30
your c. shall fall in. Num 14:29
I will give the c. of. 1 Sam 17:46
their c. were torn in midst. Isa 5:25
stink shall come up out of c. 34:3
look on c. of them that have. 66:24
c. of this people shall be meat for the. Jer 7:33; 16:4; 19:7
filled mine inheritance with c. 16:18
I will lay the c. of Israel. Ezek 6:5
my name no more defile by c. 43:7
put c. of their kings far from me. 9
there is a great number of c. Nah 3:3
grieved with them whose c. Heb 3:17

Carchemish

up to fight against C. 2 Chr 35:20
is not Calno as C.? Isa 10:9
river Euphrates in C. Jer 46:2

care

(Formerly used in the sense of anxiety, especially the wearing, painful sense of anxiety. This is a common meaning of the word in the Bible, and in almost all such cases the Revised Version replaces it by a more modern term)

father hath left the c. 1 Sam 10:2
careful for us with all this c. 2 Ki 4:13
nation that dwelleth without c. Jer 49:31
bread by weight with c. Ezek 4:16*
c. of this world chokes. Mat 13:22
he took c. of him. Luke 10:34
take c. of him. 35
doth God c. for oxen? 1 Cor 9:9*
should have the same c. one. 12:25
but that our c. for you. 2 Cor 7:12
put the same earnest c. in. 8:16
besides c. of all churches. 11:28*
shall he take c. of church. 1 Tim 3:5
casting your c. on him. 1 Pet 5:7*

care, -ed

we flee, they will not c. 2 Sam 18:3
no man c. for my soul. Ps 142:4
dost thou not c. that my? Luke 10:40
he said, not that he c. John 12:6
and Gallio c. for none. Acts 18:17
being a servant, c. not. 1 Cor 7:21
who will naturally c. for. Phil 2:20

careful

behold thou hast been c. 2 Ki 4:13
shall not be c. in year. Jer 17:8
O Nebuchadnezzar, we are not c. Dan 3:16*
Martha, thou art c. Luke 10:41
c. for nothing, but by. Phil 4:6
wherein ye were c. but lacked. 10*
c. to maintain good works. Tit 3:8

carefully

(Revised Version, diligently*)*

thou c. hearken unto. Deut 15:5
of Maroth waiteth c. Mi 1:12
I sent him the more c. Phil 2:28
though he sought it c. Heb 12:17

carefulness

drink water with trembling and c. Ezek 12:18
they shall eat their bread with c. 19
have you without c. 1 Cor 7:32*
c. it wrought in you. 2 Cor 7:11*

careless

saw how they dwelt c. Judg 18:7*
hear my voice, ye c. Isa 32:9
shall be troubled ye c. women. 10
ye c. ones: strip you, and. 11
make c. Ethiopians afraid. Ezek 30:9

carelessly

now thou that dwellest c. Isa 47:8
among them that dwell c. Ezek 39:6*
rejoicing city that dwelt c. Zeph 2:15

cares

c. of this world choke. Mark 4:19
they are choked with c. Luke 8:14
be overcharged with the c. 21:34

carest, -eth, -ing
which the Lord c. for. Deut 11:12
lest thy father leave c. 1 Sam 9:5
thou art true, nor c. Mat 22:16
c. thou not that we perish? Mark 4:38
art true, and c. for no man. 12:14
because an hireling c. John 10:13
unmarried c. for things. 1 Cor 7:32
married c. for things of. 33, 34
on him, for he c. for you. 1 Pet 5:7

Carmel
C. and Ziph in the. Josh 15:55
Saul came to C. 1 Sam 15:12
Nabal's possessions were in C. 25:2
all the while they were in C. 7
were come to Abigail to C. 40
all Israel to mount C. 1 Ki 18:19
Elijah went up to top of C. 42
Elisha went to mount C. 2 Ki 2:25
of Shunem came to mount C. 4:25
into forest of his C. 19:23; Isa 37:24
vine-dressers in C. 2 Chr 26:10
thine head is like C. S of S 7:5
the excellency of C. Isa 35:2
and as C. by the sea. Jer 46:18
the top of C. shall wither. Amos 1:2
they hide in the top of C. 9:3
solitarily in the midst of C. Mi 7:14
see **Bashan**

Carmelite
wife of Nabal the C. 1 Sam 30:5
2 Sam 2:2; 3:3
Hezrai the C. 2 Sam 23:35

Carmi
C. son of Reuben. Gen 46:9
Achan the son of C. Josh 7:1, 18
1 Chr 2:7
sons of Judah, Hezron, C. 1 Chr 4:1

carnal
(Belonging to the flesh in distinction from the spirit. It does not necessarily infer sin, although when definitely contrasted with spirit it sometimes is so intended. It comes from the Latin carnis, *flesh)*
spiritual, but I am c. Rom 7:14
the c. mind is enmity against. 8:7*
duty to minister to them in c. 15:27
as unto c. even to babes. 1 Cor 3:1
for ye are yet c. 3
are ye not c.? 4*
thing if we reap c. things? 9:11
of our warfare not c. 2 Cor 10:4*
not after the law of a c. Heb 7:16
which stood in c. ordinances. 9:10

carnally
shalt not lie c. with thy. Lev 18:20
lieth c. with a bond-maid. 19:20
a man lie with her c. Num 5:13
for to be c. minded is. Rom 8:6*

carpenter, -s
sent c. to David. 2 Sam 5:11
1 Chr 14:1
they laid it out to c. 2 Ki 12:11
hired c. to repair. 2 Chr 24:12
Ezra 3:7
c. encouraged goldsmith. Isa 41:7
c. stretcheth out his rule. 44:13
c. and smiths he carried away. Jer 24:1*; 29:2*
Lord shewed me four c. Zech 1:20*
is not this the c. son? Mat 13:55
is not this the c. the son? Mark 6:3

Carpus
cloke that I left with C. 2 Tim 4:13

carriage, -s
(This word means things carried, or burdens, not vehicles, and is so put in Revisions)
the Danites, and the c. Judg 18:21*
left c. with keeper of c. 1 Sam 17:22
he hath laid up his c. at. Isa 10:28
your c. were heavy laden. 46:1
we took up our c. went. Acts 21:15

carried
sons of Israel c. Jacob. Gen 46:5
50:13
c. them in their coats. Lev 10:5
they c. the stones over. Josh 4:8
he c. them up to top of. Judg 16:3
let ark of God be c. 1 Sam 5:8
David c. the ark aside. 2 Sam 6:10
1 Chr 13:13
Abiathar c. ark of God. 2 Sam 15:29
he c. him into a loft. 1 Ki 17:19
they c. Naboth forth and. 21:13
and c. thence silver and. 2 Ki 7:8
c. him in a chariot. 9:28; 23:30
laid up in store shall be c. to Babylon. 20:17; Isa 39:6
c. the ashes of the vessels. 2 Ki 23:4
he c. out thence all the. 24:13
bound Zedekiah and c. him. 25:7
c. the chest to his. 2 Chr 24:11
and c. all the feeble of them. 28:15
who took and c. Manasseh. 33:11
Shaphan c. the book to. 34:16
Necho took and c. Jehoahaz. 36:4
of the froward is c. Job 5:13
I should have been c. from. 10:19
the mountains be c. into. Ps 46:2
remnant which are c. from. Isa 46:3
thy daughters shall be c. on. 49:22
borne our griefs, c. our. 53:4
he bare and c. them all. 63:9
c. into Babylon. Jer 27:22; 28:3
52:11, 17
he c. twigs into a. Ezek 17:4
and c. me out in the Spirit. 37:1
which he c. into land. Dan 1:2
be also c. into Assyria. Hos 10:6
make a covenant, and oil is c. 12:1
and ye have c. into your. Joel 3:5
was a dead man c. out. Luke 7:12
and beggar was c. by angels. 16:22
parted from them, and c. up. 24:51
lame from his mother's womb was c. Acts 3:2
young men c. Ananias out. 5:6
our fathers were c. over into. 7:16
devout men c. Stephen to. 8:2
commanded him to be c. 21:34
c. about with every wind. Eph 4:14
be not c. about with. Heb 13:9
clouds that are c. with. 2 Pet 2:17
clouds without water, c. Jude 12
see **captive**

carried *away*
Jacob c. away all his. Gen 31:18
hath c. away my daughters. 26
but c. them away. 1 Sam 30:2, 18
c. Israel away. 2 Ki 17:6, 23
heathen whom Lord c. away. 11
one whom they had c. away. 28
c. away all Jerusalem. 24:14
c. away Jehoiachin to Babylon. 15
so Judah was c. away. 25:21
Tilgath-pilneser c. away. 1 Chr 5:26
when the Lord c. away Judah. 6:15
who were c. away for their. 9:1
Shishak c. away the. 2 Chr 12:9
c. away much spoil. 14:13
21:17
they c. away sheep and camels. 14:15
these that had been c. away. Ezra 2:1
Neh 7:6
that had been c. away. Ezra 9:4; 10:6
congregation of those c. away. 10:8
upon camels, c. them away. Job 1:17
to be c. away captive. Jer 29:4
and winds c. them away. Dan 2:35
No was c. away into. Nah 3:10
time they were c. away. Mat 1:11
c. Jesus away and. Mark 15:1
were Gentiles c. away. 1 Cor 12:2
Barnabas was c. away. Gal 2:13
cause her to be c. away. Rev 12:15
c. me away in Spirit. 17:3; 21:10

carriest, -eth, -ing
one c. three kids, c. 1 Sam 10:3
chaff that storm c. away. Job 21:18
east-wind c. rich man away. 27:21
Ephraim c. bows. Ps 78:9
thou c. them away as with. 90:5
c. into Babylon, from the c. Mat 1:17
they c. her and buried. Acts 5:10
mystery of beast that c. Rev 17:7

carry
Ishmaelites going to c. Gen 37:25
go ye, c. corn for the famine. 42:19
c. the man a present. 43:11
the money brought, c. 12
as much as they can c. 44:1
wagons Joseph sent to c. him. 45:27
46:5
c. up my bones. 50:25; Ex 13:19
presence go not, c. us not. Ex 33:15
c. your brethren out of. Lev 10:4
c. them in thy bosom. Num 11:12
thou art not able to c. it. Deut 14:24
c. the twelve stones over. Josh 4:3
c. these ten cheeses. 1 Sam 17:18
Jonathan said, go c. them. 20:40
a ferry-boat to c. over. 2 Sam 19:18
Spirit of the Lord shall c. 1 Ki 18:12
his father said, c. him. 2 Ki 4:19
c. Jehu to an inner chamber. 9:2
c. thither one of the priests. 17:27
sent to Philistines to c. 1 Chr 10:9
none ought to c. the ark but. 15:2
the Levites shall no more c. 23:26
thou shalt c. the wood. 2 Chr 2:16
c. him to Babylon. 36:6; Jer 39:7
c. vessels into temple. Ezra 5:15
c. the silver and gold freely. 7:15
bird of the air shall c. Eccl 10:20
her own feet shall c. her. Isa 23:7
they will c. their riches on. 30:6
c. the lambs in his bosom. 40:11
even to hoary hairs will I c. you. 46:4
they c. him and set him in. 7
will I take them and c. Jer 20:5
should c. Jeremiah home. 39:14
in thee are men c. tales. Ezek 22:9
and began to c. about. Mark 6:55
not suffer any to c. a vessel. 11:16
c. neither purse, nor. Luke 10:4
not lawful for thee to c. John 5:10
and c. thee whither thou. 21:18

carry *away*
Assyria did c. away. 2 Ki 18:11
did Nebuzar-adan c. away. 25:11
than they could c. away. 2 Chr 20:25
heart c. thee away? Job 15:12
dieth he shall c. nothing away. Ps 49:17
which he may c. away. Eccl 5:15
c. the prey away safe. Isa 5:29
laid up, shall they c. away. 15:7
the Lord will c. thee away. 22:17
wind c. them away. 41:16; 57:13
no more c. thee away. Lam 4:22
come to c. away silver? Ezek 38:13
and I will c. you away. Acts 7:43
see **captive**

carry *back*
c. back the ark of God. 2 Sam 15:25
c. Micaiah back. 1 Ki 22:26
2 Chr 18:25

carry *forth*
shalt not c. forth aught. Ex 12:46
thus with us to c. us forth. 14:11
bullock shall he c. forth. Lev 4:12, 21
c. forth ashes without camp. 6:11
14:45; 16:27
c. forth filthiness out. 2 Chr 29:5
nor c. forth a burden on. Jer 17:22
c. it forth in twilight. Ezek 12:6

carry *out*
shalt c. me out of Egypt. Gen 47:30
shall c. much seed out. Deut 28:38
then c. him out and. 1 Ki 21:10
c. me out of the host. 22:34
2 Chr 18:33
c. it out abroad into. 2 Chr 29:16
and c. out thereby. Ezek 12:5
and shall c. thee out. Acts 5:9
we can c. nothing out. 1 Tim 6:7

cart
new c. and tie kine to c. 1 Sam 6:7
set ark on a new c. 2 Sam 6:3
and Ahio drave the c. 1 Chr 13:7
corn with wheel of c. Isa 28:28
as a c. is pressed that is. Amos 2:13

cart rope
draw sin as with a c. rope. Isa 5:18

cart wheel
nor is c. wheel turned. Isa 28:27

carved, -ing, -ings
c. of timber. Ex 31:5; 35:33
fetched the c. image. Judg 18:18*
of house within was c. 1 Ki 6:18
he c. all the walls of house. 29, 32
he set a c. image in. 2 Chr 33:7*
Amon sacrificed to c. images. 22*
purged Judah from c. images. 34:3*
he cut down the c. images. 4
they break down the c. Ps 74:6
decked bed with c. work. Pr 7:16*

case, -s
that they were in evil c. Ex 5:19
is the c. of the slayer. Deut 19:4
thou shalt in any c. bring. 22:1
in any c. thou shalt deliver. 24:13
happy people in such a c. Ps 144:15
ye shall in no c. enter. Mat 5:20*
if the c. of the man be so. 19:10
been long time in that c. John 5:6
under bondage in such c. 1 Cor 7:15

casement
I looked through my c. Pr 7:6*

Casiphia
chief at the place C. Ezra 8:17

cassia
(*A sweet spice, called in Hebrew* Kiddah, Ex 30:21. *This aromatic is said to be the bark of a tree very like cinnamon, and grows in the* Indies *without cultivation*)
take of c. 500 shekels. Ex 30:24
smell of aloes and c. Ps 45:8
c. and calamus were. Ezek 27:19

cast
about a stone's c. Luke 22:41

cast
[1] *To fling, or throw,* Dan 3:6. [2] *To miscarry,* Gen 31:38, Ex 23:26. [3] *To melt, make, or frame,* Ex 25:12.
c. the child under a. Gen 21:15
she-goats have not c. their. 31:38
let us slay him, and c. him. 37:20
his master's wife c. her eyes. 39:7
every son ye shall c. Ex 1:22
said, c. it, and he c. the rod. 4:3
Zipporah c. the foreskin at. 25
took locusts and c. them. 10:19
Pharaoh's chariots he c. 15:4
c. the tree into the waters. 25
not eat flesh torn of beasts, c. 22:31
shall nothing c. their young. 23:26
c. four rings of. 25:12; 37:3, 13; 38:5
Moses c. tables out of his. 32:19
I c. into the fire, there came. 24
talents of the silver were c. 38:27
priest c. cedar wood. Num 19:6
c. any thing on him without. 35:22
seeing him not, and c. it. 23
the Lord c. them into. Deut 29:28
c. king of Ai at the gate. Josh 8:29
c. them into the cave wherein. 10:27
c. every one ear-rings. Judg 8:25
c. piece of millstone. 9:53; 2 Sam 11:21
c. the javelin. 1 Sam 18:11; 20:33
Shimei c. stones at. 2 Sam 16:6
threw stones and c. dust. 13
c. Absalom into a great pit. 18:17
Joab's man c. a cloth upon. 20:12
in plain of Jordan c. 1 Ki 7:46; 2 Chr 4:17
thou hast c. me behind. 1 Ki 14:9
Elijah c. mantle upon Elisha. 19:19
lest the Spirit c. him. 2 Ki 2:16
went to spring and c. salt in. 21
every good piece of land c. 3:25
then bring meal, and he c. it. 4:41
he c. in the stick. 6:6
c. him in portion of field. 9:25, 26
c. the man into the. 13:21
neither c. he them from. 23
c. their gods into. 19:18; Isa 37:19
nor c. a bank. 2 Ki 19:32; Isa 37:33
c. thy law behind their. Neh 9:26
they c. Pur, that is. Esth 3:7
Haman had c. Pur, that is. 9:24
for he is c. into a net. Job 18:8
God shall c. the fury of his. 20:23
God shall c. upon him, and. 27:22
hath c. me into the mire. Job 30:19
c. abroad the rage of thy. 40:11
I was c. upon thee from. Ps 22:10
they c. iniquity on me. 55:3
c. thy burden on the Lord. 22
they have c. fire into sanctuary. 74:7
chariot and horse are c. into. 76:6
he c. on them the fierceness. 78:49
let him be c. into the fire. 140:10
c. in thy lot among us. Pr 1:14
the lot is c. into the lap. 16:33
c. thy bread on the. Eccl 11:1
a man shall c. his idols. Isa 2:20
the face of the covering c. 25:7
thou hast c. all my sins. 38:17
are c. into a land which. Jer 22:28
c. Urijah's body into the. 26:23
c. it into the fire that was. 36:23
c. Jeremiah into dungeon. 38:6, 9
took thence old c. clouts and. 11
put now these old c. clouts under. 12
Ishmael slew, and c. them. 41:7
cut off my life, and c. Lam 3:53
they shall c. their silver. Ezek 7:19
although I have c. them far. 11:16
the vine-tree is c. into the. 15:4
because thou hast c. me. 23:35
I will c. thee to the ground. 28:17
be c. into the midst of a. Dan 3:6
to c. them into the fiery furnace. 20
these were c. into the midst of. 21
did not we c. three men bound? 24
be c. into the den of lions. 6:7, 16
c. them into the den of lions. 24
for thou hadst c. me. Jonah 2:3
then I said, I am c. out of. 4
I will make her c. off. Mi 4:7
wilt c. all their sins into. 7:19
will c. abominable filth on. Nah 3:6
c. it into the ephah, c. the. Zech 5:8
c. it to the potter, c. them. 11:13
nor vine c. her fruit. Mal 3:11
down, c. into the fire. Mat 3:10; 7:19; Luke 3:9
John was c. into prison. Mat 4:12
deliver thee to judge, be c. 5:25
and c. it from thee. 29, 30; 18:8, 9
to-morrow is c. into oven. 6:30; Luke 12:28
nor c. your pearls before. Mat 7:6
children's bread, and c. it to. 15:26; Mark 7:27
c. an hook, and take up. Mat 17:27
c. him into prison, till he pay. 18:30
be thou c. into the sea. 21:21
c. him into outer. 22:13; 25:30
the thieves c. the same in. 27:44
oft-times it hath c. him. Mark 9:22
he were c. into sea. 42; Luke 17:2
two eyes, feet, c. Mark 9:45, 47
c. their garments on him. 11:7; Luke 19:35
at him they c. stones. Mark 12:4
c. money into the. 41; Luke 21:4
widow hath c. more. Mark 12:43, 44
power to c. into hell. Luke 12:5
thy enemies shall c. a trench. 19:43
for murder c. into prison. 23:19, 25
for John was not yet c. John 3:24
let him first c. a stone at her. 8:7
Peter did c. himself into sea. 21:7
c. thy garment about. Acts 12:8
c. Paul and Silas into prison. 16:23
we must be c. on a certain. 27:26
who could swim c. themselves. 43
not that I may c. snare. 1 Cor 7:35
devil should c. some of. Rev 2:10
who taught Balak to c. 14
I will c. her into a bed, and. 22
the elders c. their crowns. 4:10
hail and fire were c. on the. 8:7
a mountain burning was c. into. 8
dragon saw that he was c. 12:13
like a mill-stone and c. it. 18:21
these both were c. alive into. 19:20
the devil was c. into lake. 20:10
death and hell were c. into. 14
not found in the book of life, c. 15

cast *away*
I will not c. them away. Lev 26:44*
c. away the jaw-bone. Judg 15:17
of the mighty is c. away. 2 Sam 1:21
Syrians had c. away in. 2 Ki 7:15
Ahaz did c. away. 2 Chr 29:19
have c. them away for. Job 8:4*
behold God will not c. away a. 20
let us c. away their cords. Ps 2:3
c. me not away from thy. 51:11
time to c. away stones. Eccl 3:5, 6
have c. away the law. Isa 5:24*
shall c. them away as a. 30:22
every man shall c. away his. 31:7
thee, and not c. thee away. 41:9
cut off hair, and c. it away. Jer 7:29
I c. away the seed of Jacob. 33:26
c. away from you all. Ezek 18:31
c. away abominations of his. 20:7
they did not c. away the. 8
my God will c. them away. Hos 9:17
but c. the bad away. Mat 13:48
or be c. away. Luke 9:25
hath God c. away his. Rom 11:1
God hath not c. away his people. 2
c. not away your confidence. Heb 10:35

cast *down*
Aaron c. down his rod. Ex 7:10
they c. down. 12
c. down great stones. Josh 10:11
altar of Baal was c. down. Judg 6:28
Elijah c. himself down. 1 Ki 18:42
to help and c. down. 2 Chr 25:8
and c. them down from the top. 12
they were c. down in. Neh 6:16
own counsel c. him down. Job 18:7
when men are c. down. 22:29
countenance c. not down. 29:24
shall not one be c. down? 41:9
disappoint him, c. him down. Ps 17:13
they are c. down and shall. 36:12
bent their bow to c. down. 37:14
shall not be utterly c. down. 24
art thou c. down? 42:5, 11; 43:5
O my God, my soul is c. down. 42:6
in anger c. down the people. 56:7
consult to c. him down from. 62:4
thou hast c. his throne down. 89:44
me up, and c. me down. 102:10
for she hath c. down. Pr 7:26
the Lord shall c. down. Isa 28:2
they shall be c. down. Jer 6:15; 8:12
c. down to the earth the. Lam 2:1
I will c. down your slain. Ezek 6:4
thy mother was c. down to. 19:12
c. the Assyrian down to hell. 31:16
for Egypt, and c. her down. 32:18
the thrones were c. down. Dan 7:9*
the he-goat c. down the ram. 8:7
c. down some of the host. 10
sanctuary was c. down. 11
c. down truth to the ground. 12
he shall c. down many. 11:12
c. thyself down. Mat 4:6; Luke 4:9
c. them down at Jesus' feet. Mat 15:30
he c. down the pieces of silver. 27:5
might c. Jesus down. Luke 4:29
we are c. down. 2 Cor 4:9
comforteth those are c. down. 7:6
but c. the angels down. 2 Pet 2:4
of brethren is c. down. Rev 12:10

cast *forth*
c. forth household stuff. Neh 13:8
c. forth lightning. Ps 144:6
Jehoiakim c. forth. Jer 22:19
I will c. thee forth. Ezek 32:4
shall c. forth his roots. Hos 14:5
mariners c. forth the. Jonah 1:5
c. me forth into the sea. 12
took Jonah and c. him forth. 15
would c. forth devil. Mark 7:26
c. forth as a branch. John 15:6

cast *lots*
Aaron shall c. lots. Lev 16:8
Joshua c. lots. Josh 18:10
c. lots between me. 1 Sam 14:42
c. lots as well small as. 1 Chr 26:13
they c. lots upon my vesture. Ps 22:18; Mat 27:35; John 19:24
hath c. the lot for them. Isa 34:17
c. lots for my people. Joel 3:3
c. lots upon Jerusalem. Ob 11
come and let us c. lots. Jonah 1:7
and they c. lots for her. Nah 3:10

cast off
I will c. off this city. 2 Ki 23:27
he will c. thee off for. 1 Chr 28:9
Jeroboam had c. them off. 2 Chr 11:14
shall c. off his flower. Job 15:33
dost thou c. me off? Ps 43:2
thou hast c. off. 44:9; 60:1, 10 89:38; 108:11
O Lord, c. us not off for ever. 44:23
c. me not off in the time of. 71:9
hast thou c. us off for ever? 74:1
will the Lord c. off for ever? 77:7
not c. off his people. 94:14 Lam 3:31
I will c. Hananiah off. Jer 28:16
c. off seed of Israel. 31:37; 33:24
hath c. off his altar. Lam 2:7
Israel hath c. off the thing. Hos 8:3
calf, O Samaria, hath c. thee off. 5
Edom did c. off all pity. Amos 1:11
I had not c. them off. Zech 10:6
they cried and c. off. Acts 22:23
let us c. off works of. Rom 13:12
c. off their first faith. 1 Tim 5:12*

cast out
c. out this bondwoman. Gen 21:10
I will c. out the nations. Ex 34:24
nations are defiled which I c. out. Lev 18:24; 20:23; Deut 7:1
I c. the two tables out. Deut 9:17
Moses smite, and c. out. Josh 13:12
c. out Sheba's head to. 2 Sam 20:22
house will I c. out. 1 Ki 9:7 2 Chr 7:20
Amorites, whom the Lord c. out. 1 Ki 21:26; 2 Ki 16:3
the captains c. them out. 2 Ki 10:25
till he had c. them out. 17:20; 24:20
have ye not c. out priests? 2 Chr 13:9
to come to c. us out of. 20:11
they were of you c. out. Neh 1:9
God shall c. them out of. Job 20:15
bow themselves, they c. out. 39:3
c. them out in their. Ps 5:10
I did c. them out as dirt. 18:42
afflict people and c. them out. 44:2
over Edom will I c. out. 60:8; 108:9
c. out the heathen. 78:55; 80:8
c. out scorner, contention go out. Pr 22:10
art c. out of thy grave. Isa 14:19
as a wandering bird c. out of. 16:2
earth shall c. out the dead. 26:19
their slain also be c. out. 34:3
bring poor that are c. out. 58:7
brethren that c. you out for. 66:5
c. you out of my sight, as I have c. out. Jer 7:15
our dwellings have c. us out. 9:19
c. them out of my sight. 15:1 23:39; 52:3
will I c. you out of this land. 16:13
I will c. thee out, and thy. 22:26
his dead body shall be c. out. 36:30
Nebuchadnezzar hath c. me out. 51:34
but thou wast c. out in. Ezek 16:5
will c. thee as profane out. 28:16
land shall be c. out. Amos 8:8
my people have ye c. out. Mi 2:9
Lord hath c. out thine. Zeph 3:15
to c. out the horns of. Zech 1:21
the Lord will c. her out. 9:4
unsavoury to be c. out. Mat 5:13 Luke 14:35
first c. out the beam. Mat 7:5 Luke 6:42
in thy name c. out devils? Mat 7:22
of the kingdom be c. out. 8:12
and he c. out the spirits with. 16
if thou c. us out, suffer us to. 31
when the devil was c. out. 9:33
against spirits to c. them out. 10:1
raise the dead, c. out devils. 8
not c. out devils. 12:24; Luke 11:18
if Satan c. out Satan. Mat 12:26
the Spirit of God c. out devils. 28
into belly, and is c. out. 15:17
could not we c. him out? 17:19 Mark 9:28
c. out all that sold. Mat 21:12 Mark 11:15; Luke 19:45
c. him out of vineyard. Mat 21:39 Mark 12:8; Luke 20:15
and c. out many devils. Mark 1:34 39; 6:13
power to heal and c. out devils. 3:15
how can Satan c. out Satan? 23
out of whom he had c. seven. 16:9
in my name shall they c. out. 17
c. out your name as evil. Luke 6:22
if I with finger of God c. out. 11:20
I c. out devils, and do cures. 13:32
wounded him also and c. him out. 20:12
I will in no wise c. out. John 6:37
and they c. him out. 9:34
prince of this world be c. out. 12:31
c. out their young. Acts 7:19
Moses was c. out Pharaoh's. 21
they c. Stephen out of the city. 58
third day we c. out the. 27:19
c. four anchors out. 29
c. out wheat into the sea. 38
c. out the bondwoman. Gal 4:30
great dragon was c. out. Rev 12:9
serpent c. out of his mouth. 15, 16

Lord **cast out**
which the Lord c. out. 1 Ki 14:24 2 Ki 16:3; 2 Chr 28:3; 33:2
Lord c. out before. 2 Ki 17:8; 21:2
the Lord will c. her out. Zech 9:4

cast up
they c. up a bank. 2 Sam 20:15
c. ye up, prepare. Isa 57:14; 62:10
sea, whose waters c. up. 57:20
in a way not c. up. Jer 18:15
c. her up as heaps. 50:26
c. up dust. Lam 2:10; Ezek 27:30
king of north shall c. up. Dan 11:15

castaway
I myself should be a c. 1 Cor 9:27*

castest, -eth
yea, thou c. off fear and. Job 15:14
thy cow calveth and c. not. 21:10
seeing thou c. my words. Ps 50:17
thou c. them down into. 73:18
why c. thou off my soul? 88:14
the Lord c. the wicked down. 147:6
he c. forth his ice like morsels. 17
he c. away the substance. Pr 10:3
slothfulness c. into a deep. 19:15
c. down the strength of the. 21:22
as a madman c. fire-brands. 26:18
as a fountain so she c. Jer 6:7
c. out devils. Mat 9:34; Mark 3:22 Luke 11:15
but perfect love c. fear. 1 John 4:18
c. them out of church. 3 John 10
fig-tree c. untimely figs. Rev 6:13

casting
he smote Moab, c. 2 Sam 8:2
all of them had one c. 1 Ki 7:37
weeping and c. himself. Ezra 10:1
ye see my c. down and. Job 6:21
by c. down dwelling place. Ps 74:7
profaned his crown by c. it. 89:39
thy c. down shall be in. Mi 6:14
c. a net into the sea. Mat 4:18
parted his garments, c. lots. 27:35 Mark 15:24
saw one c. out devils. Mark 9:38 Luke 9:49
he saw the rich men c. Luke 21:1
also a poor widow c. in two mites. 2
if c. away of them be. Rom 11:15
c. down imaginations. 2 Cor 10:5
c. all your care upon him. 1 Pet 5:7

castle
David took c. of Zion. 1 Chr 11:5*
David dwelt in c. the city of. 7*
are like bars of a c. Pr 18:19
Paul to be carried into c. Acts 21:34 37; 22:24; 23:10
into the c. and told Paul. 23:16

castles
of Ishmael's sons by their c. Gen 25:16*
burnt their goodly c. Num 31:10
these the priests' c. in. 1 Chr 6:54*
over treasures, and in c. 27:25
Jehoshaphat built c. in. 2 Chr 17:12
Jotham in the forest built c. 27:4

castor, *see* **sign**

catch
fire break out and c. Ex 22:6
c. you every man his. Judg 21:21
men did hastily c. it. 1 Ki 20:33
we shall c. them alive. 2 Ki 7:12
wait to c. poor, he doth c. Ps 10:9
let his net that he hath hid c. 35:8
let the extortioner c. all. 109:11
set a trap, they c. men. Jer 5:26
learned to c. the prey. Ezek 19:3, 6
c. them in their net and. Hab 1:15
send Herodians to c. Mark 12:13
thou shalt c. men. Luke 5:10
seeking to c. something. 11:54

catcheth, -ing
who c. any beast or. Lev 17:13
the devil c. away. Mat 13:19
wolf c. and scattereth. John 10:12

caterpiller, -s
if there be any c. 1 Ki 8:37 2 Chr 6:28
gave their increase to c. Ps 78:46
he spake, and c. came. 105:34
spoil like gathering of c. Isa 33:4
thee with men as with c. Jer 51:14
horses come up as the rough c. 27
worm left, hath c. eaten. Joel 1:4
restore the years the c. hath. 2:25

cattle
(*This word is sometimes used for sheep, etc., and is then translated in the Revised Version by* flock *or* flocks)
God made the c. after. Gen 1:25
thou art cursed above all c. 3:14
died, both of fowl and c. 7:21
God remembered Noah, and c. 8:1
establish covenant with fowls, c. 9:10
Abram was very rich in c. 13:2
put them not to Laban's c. 30:40
God hath taken away the c. 31:9
these c. are my c. all. 43
his sons were with the c. 34:5
trade hath been to feed c. 46:32
make them rulers over my c. 47:6
gave bread in exchange for c. 17
sever between c. of Israel and c. Ex 9:4
made his servants and c. flee. 20
smote all first-born of c. 12:29
bring your offering of c. Lev 1:2
take c. of the Levites. Num 3:41
if I and my c. drink, I will. 20:19
land for c. thy servants have c. 32:4
c. we took for a. Deut 2:35; 3:7
c. shall ye take for a prey. Josh 8:2
only c. Israel took. 27; 11:14
slew oxen and c. 1 Ki 1:9, 19, 25
the c. also concerning the. Job 36:33
c. upon a thousand hills. Ps 50:10
causeth grass to grow for c. 104:14
beasts and all c. praise. 148:10
of great and small c. Eccl 2:7
for treading of lesser c. Isa 7:25
hast not brought small c. 43:23
idols were upon beasts and c. 46:1
hear the voice of the c. Jer 9:10
between c. and c. Ezek 34:17, 20, 22
drought upon land and c. Hag 1:11
multitude of men and c. Zech 2:4
men taught me to keep c. 13:5
servant feeding c. will. Luke 17:7
children drank, and his c. John 4:12

much **cattle**
and had much c. Gen 30:43
of Egypt with much c. Ex 12:38
I know ye have much c. Deut 3:19
return with very much c. Josh 22:8
Uzziah had much c. 2 Chr 26:10
wherein is much c. Jonah 4:11

our **cattle**
our c. also shall go. Ex 10:26
our children, and our c. 17:3
that we and our c. Num 20:4
build sheepfolds for our c. 32:16
all our c. shall be there. 26
with suburbs for our c. Josh 21:2
over our bodies and our c. Neh 9:37
first-born of our sons and our c. 10:36

their **cattle**
shall not their c. and. Gen 34:23

took spoil of *their c.* Num 31:9
for *their c.* 35:3; Josh 14:4
Midianites came up with *their c.*
Judg 6:5
brought away *their c.* 1 Sam 23:5
because *their c.* were. 1 Chr 5:9
down to take away *their c.* 7:21
he gave up *their c.* also. Ps 78:48
he suffered not *their c.* to. 107:38
camels a booty, *their c.* Jer 49:32

***thy* cattle**

knowest how *thy c.* was. Gen 30:29
thee six years for *thy c.* 31:41
of the Lord is on *thy c.* Ex 9:3
send now and gather *thy c.* 19
servant nor *thy c.* do any. 20:10
Deut 5:14
firstling among *thy c.* is. Ex 34:19
let not *thy c.* gender. Lev 19:19
the land meat for *thy c.* 25:7
grass in fields for *thy c.* Deut 11:15
be the fruit of *thy c.* 28:4, 11; 30:9
shall eat the fruit of *thy c.* 28:51
day shall *thy c.* feed. Isa 30:23

***your* cattle**

give *your c.*; and I will give you for
your c. Gen 47:16
will destroy *your c.* Lev 26:22
your c. shall abide in. Deut 3:19
Josh 1:14
be barren among *your c.* Deut 7:14
drink, both ye and *your c.* 2 Ki 3:17

caught

behind him a ram c. by. Gen 22:13
she c. him by garment. 39:12
put forth his hand, and c. Ex 4:4
the men of war had c. Num 31:32
c. Adoni-bezek, and cut. Judg 1:6
c. a young man of the men. 8:14
Samson went and c. 300. 15:4
took wives whom they c. 21:23
I c. him by his beard. 1 Sam 17:35
and they c. every one. 2 Sam 2:16
Absalom's head c. hold of. 18:9
and Adonijah c. hold. 1 Ki 1:50
Joab c. hold on the horns of. 2:28
Ahijah c. the new garment. 11:30
the Shunammite c. Elisha. 2 Ki 4:27
they c. Ahaziah and. 2 Chr 22:9
so she c. him, and kissed. Pr 7:13
thou art found and also c. Jer 50:24
Jesus c. Peter, and said. Mat 14:31
the husbandmen c. him. 21:39
they c. the servant and. Mark 12:3
oftentimes it c. him. Luke 8:29
that night c. nothing. John 21:3
came upon Stephen and c. Acts 6:12
Spirit of the Lord c. away. 8:39
they c. Paul and Silas. 16:19
for these causes the Jews c. 26:21
when the ship was c. we let. 27:15
I know a man c. up to. 2 Cor 12:2
how he was c. up into paradise. 4
being crafty, I c. you with guile. 16
we shall be c. up. 1 Thes 4:17
her child was c. up to God. Rev 12:5

caul, -s

the c. above liver. Ex 29:13, 22
Lev 3:4, 10, 15; 4:9; 7:4; 8:16,
25; 9:10, 19
will take away their c. Isa 3:18
will rend the c. of their. Hos 13:8

cause

[1] *A ground, reason, or motive,* 1 Sam 17:29. **[2]** *A suit, action, or controversy,* Ex 22:9; Isa 1:23. **[3]** *Sake, or account,* 2 Cor 7:12.

c. of both shall come. Ex 22:9
nor speak in a c. to decline. 23:2
countenance a poor man in his c. 3
wrest judgement of poor in his c. 6
for which c. thou and all. Num 16:11
Moses brought their c. before. 27:5
the c. that is too hard. Deut 1:17
manslayer shall declare his c.
Josh 20:4
said, is there not a c.? 1 Sam 17:29
Lord hath pleaded the c. of. 25:39
there is no c. this evil. 2 Sam 13:16
that hath any suit or c. 15:4
maintain their c. 1 Ki 8:45, 49, 59
2 Chr 6:35, 39
was the c. that he lift. 1 Ki 11:27
for the c. was from the Lord. 12:15
2 Chr 10:15
he be a c. of trespass. 1 Chr 21:3
what c. shall come. 2 Chr 19:10
for which c. this city. Ezra 4:15
for which c. thou buildest. Neh 6:6
God will I commit my c. Job 5:8
I have ordered my c. 13:18
I would order my c. before. 23:4
the c. which I knew not. 29:16
if I did despise the c. of my. 31:13
hast maintained my c. Ps 9:4
awake to my c. my God. 35:23
that favour my righteous c. 27
Lord will maintain the c. 140:12
first in his own c. Pr 18:17
debate thy c. with thy. 25:9
righteous considereth the c. 29:7
for the dumb in the c. 31:8
what is the c. that. Eccl 7:10
nor doth c. of the widow. Isa 1:23
produce your c. saith the. 41:21
God that pleadeth the c. of. 51:22
judge not the c. of the. Jer 5:28
thee have I revealed my c. 11:20
unto thee have I opened my c. 20:12
he judged the c. of the. 22:16
to subvert in a c. the. Lam 3:36
Lord, judge my c. 59
know for whose c. Jonah 1:7, 8
wife, saving for the c. Mat 5:32
put away his wife for every c. 19:3
declared for what c. Luke 8:47
found no c. of death in him. 23:22
what the c. wherefore? Acts 10:21
though they found no c. of. 13:28
Festus declared Paul's c. to. 25:14
was no c. of death in me. 28:18
which c. we faint not. 2 Cor 4:16
it is for your c. 5:13
I did it not for his c. that had. 7:12
for the same c. also do. Phil 2:18
for which c. I suffer. 2 Tim 1:12
for which c. he is not. Heb 2:11

***plead* cause**

the Lord *plead* my c. 1 Sam 24:15
Ps 35:1; 43:1; 119:154
plead thine own c. Ps 74:22
Lord will *plead* their c. Pr 22:23
he shall *plead* their c. 23:11
open thy mouth, *plead* the c. 31:9
none to *plead* thy c. Jer 30:13
thoroughly *plead* their c. 50:34
behold, I will *plead* thy c. 51:36
until he *plead* my c. Mi 7:9

***for this* cause**

for this c. have I raised. Ex 9:16
for this c. Hezekiah. 2 Chr 32:20
for this c. the king. Dan 2:12
for this c. shall a man. Mat 19:5
Mark 10:7; Eph 5:31
but *for this c.* came I. John 12:27
and *for this c.* came I. 18:37
for this c. God gave. Rom 1:26
for this c. pay ye tribute. 13:6
for this c. I will confess to. 15:9
for this c. many are. 1 Cor 11:30
for this c. I bow my knees. Eph 3:14
for this c. thank God. 1 Thes 2:13
for this c. God shall. 2 Thes 2:11
howbeit, *for this c.* I. 1 Tim 1:16
for this c. he is the. Heb 9:15
for this c. was the gospel. 1 Pet 4:6

***without* cause**

slay David *without* a c.? 1 Sam 19:5
destroy him *without* a c. Job 2:3
my wounds *without* c. 9:17
I delivered him that *without* c. is.
Ps 7:4
that transgress *without* c. 25:3
without c. they hid for me a net,
digged a pit *without* c. 35:7
that hate me *without* c. 19; 69:4
John 15:25
against me *without* c. Ps 109:3
perversely with me *without* c. 119:78
persecuted me *without* c. 161
for the innocent *without* c. Pr 1:11
strive not with a man *without* c. 3:30
who hath wounds *without* c.? 23:29
against neighbour *without* c. 24:28
oppressed them *without* c. Isa 52:4
me sore *without* c. Lam 3:52
have not done *without* c. Ezek 14:23
with his brother *without* c. Mat 5:22

cause

I will c. it to rain upon the. Gen 7:4
he cried, c. every man to go. 45:1
c. frogs to come up on land. Ex 8:5
and shall c. him to be. 21:19
thy daughter, to c. her. Lev 19:29
and c. sorrow of heart. 26:16
is holy, the Lord will c. Num 16:5
he shall c. Israel to inherit it.
Deut 1:38; 3:28; 31:7
choose to c. his name to. 12:11
thou shalt not c. the land. 24:4
whither shall I c. my? 2 Sam 13:13
oath laid on him to c. 1 Ki 8:31
c. him to fall by sword. 2 Ki 19:7
Isa 37:7
outlandish women c. to. Neh 13:26
c. to perish all the Jews. Esth 3:13
8:11
c. Haman make haste to do. 5:5
c. me to understand. Job 6:24
c. every man to find. 34:11
wilt c. thine ear to hear. Ps 10:17
c. his face to shine. 67:1; 80:3
7, 19
thou didst c. judgement to. 76:8
c. me to hear, c. me to. 143:8
unless they c. some to fall. Pr 4:16
suffer not thy mouth to c. Eccl 5:6
hearken to thy voice, c. S of S 8:13
who lead thee c. Isa 3:12; 9:16
he shall c. them of Jacob. 27:6
this is the rest ye may c. 28:12
the Lord c. his glorious voice. 30:30
nor c. his voice to be heard. 42:2
I will c. thee to ride upon. 58:14
Lord will c. righteousness. 61:11
bring to birth, and not c.? 66:9
not c. mine anger to fall. Jer 3:12
I will c. you to dwell in this. 7:3, 7
Lord before he c. darkness. 13:16
I will c. the enemy to. 15:11
think to c. my people. 23:27
Israel, when I went to c. 31:2
I will c. them to walk by rivers. 9
c. their captivity to. 32:44; 33:26
though he c. grief. Lam 3:32
I will c. you to pass. Ezek 20:37
that it might c. fury to come. 24:8
I will c. them to lie down. 34:15
I will c. men to walk on you. 36:12
he shall c. craft to prosper. Dan 8:25
c. thy face to shine on. 9:17
thither c. thy mighty. Joel 3:11
c. the seat of violence to. Amos 6:3
I will c. sun to go down at. 8:9
c. me to behold grievance? Hab 1:3
c. them to be put to death. Mat 10:21
Mark 13:12; Luke 21:16
mark them who c. Rom 16:17
c. that it be read in. Col 4:16

cause *to cease, see* **cease**

caused

God c. a deep sleep to. Gen 2:21
God c. me to wander from. 20:13
Lord c. the sea to go. Ex 14:21
c. Israel to commit. Num 31:16
is the land, I have c. Deut 34:4
c. thee to rest from. 2 Sam 7:11
c. a seat to be set for. 1 Ki 2:19
he c. all present in. 2 Chr 34:32
God hath c. his name. Ezra 6:12
Levites c. people to. Neh 8:7, 8
Haman c. gallows to be. Esth 5:14
if I have c. eyes of. Job 31:16
hast c. men to ride. Ps 66:12
and c. them to pass through. 78:13
he c. an east-wind to blow in. 26
word on which thou hast c. 119:49
with fair speech she c. Pr 7:21
they have c. Egypt to err. Isa 19:14
I have not c. thee to serve. 43:23
Spirit of the Lord c. him. 63:14
I have c. my people Israel. Jer 12:14
I have c. to cleave to me. 13:11
Shemaiah c. you to trust in. 29:31
therefore thou hast c. all this. 32:23
c. the servants to return. 34:11, 16
her little ones have c. a cry. 48:4
I have c. thee to multiply. Ezek 16:7

till I have *c.* my fury to. *Ezek* 24:13
Nebuchadnezzar *c.* his army. 29:18
c. terror in land. 32:23, 24, 25, 26
Gabriel being *c.* to fly. *Dan* 9:21
spirit of whoredoms *c.* *Hos* 4:12
their lies *c.* them to err. *Amos* 2:4
I *c.* rain on one city, I *c.* not. 4:7
I have *c.* thine iniquity. *Zech* 3:4
ye have *c.* many to. *Mal* 2:8
have *c.* this man should. *John* 11:37
they *c.* great joy to all. *Acts* 15:3
but if any have *c.* grief. *2 Cor* 2:5
c. all to receive a mark. *Rev* 13:16

causeless

thou hast shed blood *c.* *1 Sam* 25:31
curse *c.* shall not come. *Pr* 26:2

causes

that thou mayest bring *c.* *Ex* 18:19
hard *c.* they brought to Moses. 26
hear the *c.* between. *Deut* 1:16
c. whereby backsliding. *Jer* 3:8
but have seen for thee *c.* *Lam* 2:14
thou hast pleaded the *c.* of. 3:58
for these *c.* the Jews. *Acts* 26:21

causest

thou *c.* me to ride. *Job* 30:22
blessed is man thou *c.* *Ps* 65:4

causeth

water that *c.* curse. *Num* 5:18, 19
22, 24, 27
c. them to wander in. *Job* 12:24
Ps 107:40
spirit of understanding *c.* *Job* 20:3
he *c.* it to come hither. 37:13
c. the grass to grow. *Ps* 104:14
c. vapours to ascend. 135:7
Jer 10:13; 51:16
c. his wind to blow. *Ps* 147:18
son that *c.* shame. *Pr* 10:5; 17:2
19:26
servant shall rule over a son *c.* 17:2
instruction that *c.* to err. 19:27
whoso *c.* righteous to go. 28:10
fire *c.* the waters to boil. *Isa* 64:2
any thing that *c.* sweat. *Ezek* 44:18
put away wife *c.* her to. *Mat* 5:32
thanks be to God, who *c.* *2 Cor* 2:14*
c. through us thanksgiving. 9:11
c. the earth to worship. *Rev* 13:12

causeway

lot came forth by *c.* of. *1 Chr* 26:16
at Parbar westward, four at *c.* 18

causing

c. the lips of those. *S of S* 7:9*
a bridle in the jaws *c.* *Isa* 30:28
in *c.* you to return to. *Jer* 29:10
shepherds *c.* their flocks. 33:12

cave, -s

Lot dwelt in a *c.* he and. *Gen* 19:30
field and *c.* made sure. 23:17, 20
buried Sarah in the *c.* 19
me with my father in *c.* 49:29
kings fled and hid in *c.* *Josh* 10:16
17
Midianites Israel made *c.* *Judg* 6:2
hide in *c.* in rocks. *1 Sam* 13:6
David escaped to the *c.* of. 22:1
into my hand in the *c.* 24:10
came to David to *c.* *2 Sam* 23:13
hid by fifty in a *c.* *1 Ki* 18:4, 13
Elijah came to a *c.* and. 19:9
they shall go into *c.* *Isa* 2:19
die that be in the *c.* *Ezek* 33:27
grave, it was a *c.* a. *John* 11:38
wandered in dens and *c.* *Heb* 11:38*

cease

day and night shall not *c.* *Gen* 8:22
the thunder shall *c.* *Ex* 9:29
from age of fifty shall *c.* *Num* 8:25
elders prophesied, did not *c.* 11:25
I will make to *c.* murmurings. 17:5
the poor shall never *c.* *Deut* 15:11
remembrance of them to *c.* 32:26
so make our children *c.* *Josh* 22:25
be avenged, after I will *c.* *Judg* 15:7
go to battle, or shall I *c.*? 20:28
c. not to cry to Lord. *1 Sam* 7:8
Baasha heard it, let his work *c.*
2 Chr 16:5
made them to *c.* by force. *Ezra* 4:23
why should the work *c.*? *Neh* 6:3
there the wicked *c.* from. *Job* 3:17
my days few, *c.* then. 10:20
branch thereof will not *c.* 14:7
c. from anger, forsake. *Ps* 37:8
he maketh wars to *c.* to the. 46:9
hast made his glory to *c.* 89:44
c. to hear instruction. *Pr* 19:27
honour for a man to *c.* from. 20:3*
yea strife and reproach shall *c.* 22:10
labour to be rich, *c.* from. 23:4
the grinders *c.* because. *Eccl* 12:3
c. to do evil. *Isa* 1:16
c. ye from man. 2:22
and indignation shall *c.* 10:25*
their vintage shouting to *c.* 16:10
the fortress also shall *c.* from. 17:3
thereof have I made to *c.* 21:2
when thou shalt *c.* to spoil. 33:1
and let them not *c.* *Jer* 14:17
leaf green, nor shall *c.* from. 17:8
then seed of Israel shall *c.* 31:36
not apple of thine eye *c.* *Lam* 2:18
idols may be broken and *c.* *Ezek* 6:6
pomp of the strong to *c.* 7:24
I will make this proverb *c.* 12:23
I make thy lewdness to *c.* 23:27
the multitude of Egypt to *c.* 30:10
of her strength shall *c.* 18; 33:28
c. by whom shall Jacob. *Amos* 7:5
will not *c.* to pervert. *Acts* 13:10
be tongues, they shall *c.* *1 Cor* 13:8
I *c.* not to give thanks. *Eph* 1:16
we do not *c.* to pray for. *Col* 1:9
eyes that cannot *c.* from. *2 Pet* 2:14

***cause to* cease**

cause these men *to c.* *Ezra* 4:21
they could not *cause* them *to c.* 5:5
slay and *cause* work *to c.* *Neh* 4:11
cause thine anger *to c.* *Ps* 85:4
lot *causeth* contentions *to c.* *Pr* 18:18
cause arrogancy of proud *to c.*
Isa 13:11
cause holy One of Israel *to c.* 30:11
cause mirth *to c.* from. *Jer* 7:34
cause to c. man. 36:29; *Hos* 2:11
I will *cause to c.* in. *Jer* 48:35
cause thee *to c.* from. *Ezek* 16:41
will I *cause* lewdness *to c.* 23:48
cause noise of thy songs *to c.* 26:13
I will *cause* their images *to c.* 30:13
cause them *to c.* from. 34:10
I will *cause to c.* evil beasts. 25
cause the oblation *to c.* *Dan* 9:27
cause reproach offered by him *to c.*
11:18
will *cause to c.* kingdom. *Hos* 1:4

ceased

it *c.* to be with Sarai. *Gen* 18:11
thunders and hail *c.* *Ex* 9:33
saw that the thunders *c.* 34
the manna *c.* on the. *Josh* 5:12
they *c.* not from their. *Judg* 2:19
inhabitants of villages *c.* they *c.* 5:7
they that were hungry *c.* *1 Sam* 2:5
in the name of David and *c.* 25:9
then *c.* the work of. *Ezra* 4:24
so these three men *c.* to. *Job* 32:1
did tear me and *c.* not. *Ps* 35:15
sore ran in the night and *c.* 77:2*
oppressor *c.* golden city *c.* *Isa* 14:4
the elders have *c.* from. *Lam* 5:14
the joy of our heart is *c.* 15
took up Jonah, sea *c.* *Jonah* 1:15
the wind *c.* *Mat* 14:32; *Mark* 4:39
6:51
woman hath not *c.* to. *Luke* 7:45
praying in a place, when he *c.* 11:1
they *c.* not to teach and. *Acts* 5:42
after the uproar was *c.* Paul. 20:1
by space of three years I *c.* not. 31
would not be persuaded we *c.* 21:14
then is offence of cross *c.* *Gal* 5:11*
he also hath *c.* from his. *Heb* 4:10*
then they would not have *c.* 10:2
suffered in flesh, hath *c.* *1 Pet* 4:1

ceaseth

help, Lord, for godly man *c.* *Ps* 12:1
precious, and it *c.* for ever. 49:8*
is no tale-bearer strife *c.* *Pr* 26:20
the spoiler *c.* *Isa* 16:4
of tabrets *c.* joy of harp *c.* 24:8
the way-faring man *c.* 33:8
eye trickleth down *c.* not. *Lam* 3:49
c. from raising after he. *Hos* 7:4
this man *c.* not to speak. *Acts* 6:13

ceasing

I should sin in *c.* to. *1 Sam* 12:23
was made without *c.* *Acts* 12:5*
without *c.* I make. *Rom* 1:9
1 Thes 1:3
we thank God without *c.* *1 Thes* 2:13
pray without *c.* in every. 5:17
without *c.* I have. *2 Tim* 1:3

cedar

(*An evergreen tree of great value to building in Bible times. It was much used in building the Temple. The cedars of Lebanon are the most famous; of them only a few remain*)

I dwell in an house of *c.* *2 Sam* 7:2
build ye not me an house of *c.*? 7
he spake from the *c.* to. *1 Ki* 4:33
all thy desire concerning *c.* 5:8
thistle sent to the *c.* *2 Ki* 14:9
2 Chr 25:18
moveth his tail like a *c.* *Job* 40:17
shall grow like a *c.* *Ps* 92:12
beams of house are *c.* *S of S* 1:17
inclose her with boards of *c.* 8:9
in the wilderness the *c.* *Isa* 41:19
it is cieled with *c.* *Jer* 22:14
thou closest thyself in *c.* 15
eagle took highest branch of *c.*
Ezek 17:3
of the highest branch of the *c.* 22
bear fruit and be a goodly *c.* 23
chests made of *c.* among. 27:24
the Assyrian was a *c.* in. 31:3
he shall uncover the *c.* *Zeph* 2:14
howl, fir-tree, for the *c.* *Zech* 11:2

cedar trees

Israel's tabernacles are *c.* *Num* 24:6
Hiram sent *c.* to David. *2 Sam* 5:11
they hew me *c.* cut of. *1 Ki* 5:6
so Hiram gave Solomon *c.* 10; 9:11
cut down the tall *c.* *2 Ki* 19:23
David prepared *c.* in. *1 Chr* 22:4
c. made he as sycomore. *2 Chr* 1:15
9:27
send me *c.* and fir-trees. 2:8
gave money to bring *c.* *Ezra* 3:7

cedar wood

c. and hyssop. *Lev* 14:4, 6, 49, 51, 52
priest shall take *c.* and. *Num* 19:6
they brought much *c.* *1 Chr* 22:4

cedars

c. made he to be as. *1 Ki* 10:27
I dwell in an house of *c.* *1 Chr* 17:1
didst send David *c.* to. *2 Chr* 2:3
voice of Lord breaketh *c.* *Ps* 29:5
boughs were like goodly *c.* 80:10
praise him also *c.* and. 148:9
excellent as the *c.* *S of S* 5:15
the sycomores into *c.* *Isa* 9:10
I will cut down the tall *c.* 37:24
he heweth him down *c.* 44:14
cut down thy choice *c.* *Jer* 22:7
Lebanon, that makest nest in *c.* 23
c. in garden of God. *Ezek* 31:8
height as height of *c.* *Amos* 2:9
fire may devour thy *c.* *Zech* 11:1

cedars ***of Lebanon***

fire devour *c. of Leb.* *Judg* 9:15
the *c. of Leb.* which. *Ps* 104:16
upon all the *c. of Leb.* *Isa* 2:13
c. of Leb. rejoice at thee. 14:8
c. from *Leb.* to make. *Ezek* 27:5

Cedron

disciples over brook *C.* *John* 18:1*

celebrate

from even to even shall *c.* *Lev* 23:32
a statute, ye shall *c.* it in. 41
death cannot *c.* the. *Isa* 38:18

celestial

c. bodies, glory of *c.* is. *1 Cor* 15:40

cellars

over the *c.* of oil was. *1 Chr* 27:28

Cenchrea

shorn his head in *C.* *Acts* 18:18
a servant of church at *C.* *Rom* 16:1

censer, -s
took either of them c. Lev 10:1
he shall take a c. full of. 16:12
upon it vessels, even c. Num 4:14*
this do, take ye c. 16:6
every man his c. 17
Eleazar took the brasen c. 39
made c. of pure gold. 1 Ki 7:50*
2 Chr 4:22*
Uzziah had a c. in his. 2 Chr 26:19
with every man his c. Ezek 8:11
had the golden c. and the ark of the covenant. Heb 9:4
came, having a golden c. Rev 8:3
the angel took the c. and filled. 5

centurion, -s
(Officer in the Roman army over a century, or 100 men)
there came unto him a c. Mat 8:5
c. said, Lord, I am not worthy. 8
when the c. saw earthquake. 27:54
certain c.'s servant, who was dear unto him. Luke 7:2
now when the c. saw what. 23:47
Cornelius was a c. of. Acts 10:1
Cornelius the c. a just man. 22
who immediately took soldiers and c. and ran down. 21:32
when the c. heard that. 22:26
Paul called one of the c. to. 23:17
called to him two c. saying. 23
and he commanded a c. to. 24:23
delivered Paul to Julius a c. 27:1
c. believed the master more. 11
c. willing to save Paul, kept. 43
c. delivered the prisoners to. 28:16

Cephas
thou shalt be called C. John 1:42
I am of C. 1 Cor 1:12
whether Paul, or Apollos, or C. 3:22
brethren of the Lord, and C. 9:5
that he was seen of C. 15:5
James, C. and John, who seemed to be pillars. Gal 2:9

ceremonies
passover according to all the c. thereof. Num 9:3*

certain
gather a c. rate every day. Ex 16:4
Korah rose with c. of. Num 16:2
c. men the children of Belial. Deut 13:13
wicked man be beaten by a c. 25:2
after a c. rate every day, offering according. 2 Chr 8:13
Hanani came, he and c. Neh 1:2
I mourned c. days, and fasted. 4
a c. portion should be for the singers. 11:23
I smote c. of them, and. 13:25
came c. from Shechem. Jer 41:5
captain carried away c. of. 52:15
fainted and was sick c. Dan 8:27
king of north shall come after c. years. 11:13
likened to c. king. Mat 18:28; 22:2
and her sons desiring a c. 20:20
came a c. poor widow. Mark 12:42
Luke 21:2
arose c. and bare false witness against him. Mark 14:57
when he was in a c. Luke 5:12
told him by c. thy mother. 8:20
went into a c. village. 10:38; 17:12
a c. woman lifted up voice. 11:27
a c. Pharisee besought him to. 37
this parable to c. who trusted. 18:9
who for a c. sedition and. 23:19
c. women also made us. 24:22
c. of them with us went to the. 24
angel went down at a c. John 5:4
Saul was c. days with. Acts 9:19
prayed Peter to tarry c. days. 10:48
Herod the king to vex c. 12:1
c. which went from us have. 15:24
as c. of your own poets. 17:28
contribution for c. saints. Rom 15:26
for before that c. came. Gal 2:12
one in a c. place testified. Heb 2:6
he spake in a c. place of the seventh day. 4:4
he limiteth a c. day, saying. 7
a c. fearful looking for. Heb 10:27
there are c. men crept in. Jude 4

certain
it be truth and thing c. Deut 13:14
17:4
for c. thou shalt die. 1 Ki 2:37, 42
know for c. if ye put. Jer 26:15
the dream is c. and. Dan 2:45
I have no c. thing to write unto my lord. Acts 25:26
no c. dwelling-place. 1 Cor 4:11
c. we can carry nothing. 1 Tim 6:7

certainly
I will c. return to thee. Gen 18:10
we saw c. that the Lord was with thee. 26:28
could we c. know he would. 43:7*
such a man as I can c.? 44:15
will c. requite us all the. 50:15*
c. I will be with thee. Ex 3:12
if theft be c. found in his. 22:4
he hath c. trespassed. Lev 5:19
congregation shall c. stone. 24:16
because it was c. told. Josh 9:24
if ye can c. declare the. Judg 14:12
thy father c. knoweth. 1 Sam 20:3
if I knew c. evil were. 9*
c. heard that Saul will. 23:10
Lord will c. make my lord. 25:28
even so will I c. do. 1 Ki 1:30
thou mayest c. recover. 2 Ki 8:10
thou c. return in peace. 2 Chr 18:27
for riches c. make. Pr 23:5
lo, c. in vain made he it. Jer 8:8
do we not c. know every. 13:12
ye shall c. drink. 25:28
king of Babylon shall c. 36:29
dost thou c. know that Baal? 40:14
know c. I have admonished. 42:19
c. ye shall die by sword and. 22
c. do what thing goeth out. 44:17
c. this is the day that. Lam 2:16
one shall c. come. Dan 11:10*, 13*
saying, c. this was a righteous man. Luke 23:47

certainty
know for c. Lord will. Josh 23:13
come ye again with c. 1 Sam 23:23
make known the c. of. Pr 22:21
I know of c. ye would. Dan 2:8
thou mightest know the c. Luke 1:4
could not know the c. Acts 21:34
would have known the c. 22:30

certify, -ied
word from you to c. 2 Sam 15:28
we sent and c. the king. Ezra 4:14
we c. the king, that if this city. 16
their names also to c. thee. 5:10
we c. you not to impose toll. 7:24
Esther c. king thereof. Esth 2:22*
I c. you gospel I preached. Gal 1:11*

Cesar, *see* **Caesar**

Cesarea (Caesarea)
came into coasts of C. Mat 16:13
into the towns of C. Mark 8:27
till he came to C. Acts 8:40
brought Paul down to C. 9:30
morrow after entered into C. 10:24
sent three men from C. 11:11
Herod went from Judea to C. 12:19
when he had landed at C. 18:22
with us also certain of the disciples of C. 21:16
200 soldiers to go to C. 23:23
3 days he ascended from C. 25:1
Paul should be kept at C. 4

chafed
they be c. in their minds. 2 Sam 17:8

chaff
(The refuse of winnowed grain)
as c. that the storm carrieth away. Job 21:18
like the c. which the wind. Ps 1:4
let them be as c. before wind. 35:5
as flame consumeth the c. Isa 5:24*
nations shall be chased as c. 17:13
terrible ones shall be as c. 29:5
ye shall conceive c. and. 33:11
and make the hills as c. 41:15
is the c. to the wheat? Jer 23:28*
became like the c. of. Dan 2:35
as the c. which is driven. Hos 13:3
before day pass as c. Zeph 2:2
burn up the c. with fire. Mat 3:12
Luke 3:17

chain
gold c. about his neck. Gen 41:42
Dan 5:7, 16, 29
them about as a c. Ps 73:6
ravished my heart with one c. of thy neck. S of S 4:9
hath made my c. heavy. Lam 3:7
make a c. for land is full of crimes. Ezek 7:23
bracelets, and a c. on thy. 16:11
I am bound with this c. Acts 28:20
not ashamed of my c. 2 Tim 1:16
an angel and a great c. Rev 20:1

chains
fasten the wreathen c. Ex 28:14, 24
made on breast-plate c. 39:15
for atonement, c. and. Num 31:50*
besides the c. about. Judg 8:26
by the c. of gold before. 1 Ki 6:21
bind their kings with c. Ps 149:8
instruction shall be c. Pr 1:9
thy neck comely with c. S of S 1:10*
Lord will take away c. Isa 3:19*
and casteth silver c. 40:19
shall come after thee in c. 45:14
loose thee this day from c. Jer 40:4
brought him with c. into. Ezek 19:4*
they put in ward in c. 9
bind him, no not with c. Mark 5:3
the c. had been oft plucked by him. 4
Peter's c. fell off. Acts 12:7
delivered them into c. of. 2 Pet 2:4
reserved in everlasting c. Jude 6*
see **bound**

chainwork
wreaths of c. for. 1 Ki 7:17

chalcedony
third foundation was a c. Rev 21:19

Chalcol
Solomon was wiser than C. 1 Ki 4:31
of Zerah, Heman, C. 1 Chr 2:6

Chaldea
C. shall be a spoil. Jer 50:10
render to inhabitants of C. 51:24
blood be upon inhabitants of C. 35
thy fornication to C. Ezek 16:29
messengers to them into C. 23:16

Chaldean
hand of Nebuchadnezzar the C. Ezra 5:12
asked such things at any C. Dan 2:10

Chaldeans
C. made out three bands. Job 1:17
land of C. the Assyrian. Isa 23:13
I have brought down the C. 43:14
throne, O daughter of the C. 47:1
darkness, O daughter of the C. 5
his arm shall be on the C. 48:14
flee from the C. 20
ye fight against the C. Jer 21:4
he that falleth to the C. 9; 38:2
punish land of C. 25:12; 50:1, 45
though ye fight with the C. 32:5
is given into hand of the C. 24, 43
the C. shall come and set fire. 29
come to fight with the C. 33:5
the C. shall come again and. 37:8
surely the C. shall depart. 9
though ye had smitten army of C. 10
I fall not away to the C. 14
of Jews that are fallen to C. 38:19
bring out thy children to the C. 23
C. burnt king's house, and. 39:8
fear not to serve the C. 40:9
at Mizpah, to serve the C. 10
Ishmael slew the C. that were. 41:3
thee on to deliver us to C. 43:3
a sword is upon the C. 50:35
Lord hath purposed against C. 45
shall fall in the land of C. 51:4
army of C. pursued Zedekiah. 52:8
to the land of the C. Ezek 12:13
she saw the images of the C. 23:14
teach tongue of the C. Dan 1:4
king commanded to call the C. 2:2
at that time certain C. accused. 3:8

then came in the *C.* and the. *Dan* 4:7
king cried aloud to bring in *C.* 5:7
thy father made master of *C.* 11
Darius made king over the *C.* 9:1
lo, I raise up the *C.* that. *Hab* 1:6
came out of land of *C.* *Acts* 7:4

Chaldees

him bands of the *C.* *2 Ki* 24:2
the *C.* were against the city. 25:4
the army of the *C.* brake. 10
for they were afraid of the *C.* 26
brought king of *C.* *2 Chr* 36:17
Babylon the beauty of *C.* *Isa* 13:19

see **Ur**

chalk-stones

stones of the altar *c.* *Isa* 27:9

challengeth

any lost thing another *c.* *Ex* 22:9

chamber

(*An apartment, or room in a house, not confined, as now generally understood, to bed-chamber,* 2 Sam 13:10; Ps 104:3; Ezek 42:13)

Joseph entered into his *c.* *Gen* 43:30
in to my wife into the *c.* *Judg* 15:1
in wait abiding in the *c.* 16:9, 12
bring meat into the *c.* *2 Sam* 13:10
Elisha turned into the *c.* *2 Ki* 4:11
for Tobiah a great *c.* *Neh* 13:5
cast household stuff out of the *c.* 8
bridegroom cometh out of his *c.* *Ps* 19:5
into the *c.* of her that. *S of S* 3:4
read the book in the *c.* *Jer* 36:10
laid up the roll in *c.* of. 20
c. whose prospect. *Ezek* 40:45, 46
being open in his *c.* to. *Dan* 6:10
bridegroom go forth of *c.* *Joel* 2:16

bed-chamber, *see* **bed**; **guard-chamber,** *see* **guard**

guest-**chamber**

where is the *guest-c.*? *Mark* 14:14
Luke 22:11

inner **chamber**

and came into *inner c.* *1 Ki* 20:30
into *inner c.* to hide. 22:25
2 Chr 18:24
carry Jehu into *inner c.* *2 Ki* 9:2

little **chamber**

let us make a *little c.* *2 Ki* 4:10
little c. was one reed. *Ezek* 40:7*
gate from roof of one *little c.* 13*

side **chamber, -s**

breadth of every *side-c.* *Ezek* 41:5
the *side-c.* were three, one. 6
thickness of wall for *side-c.* 9

upper **chamber**

lattice in his *upper-c.* *2 Ki* 1:2
altars in top of the *upper-c.* 23:12
laid Dorcas in an *upper-c.* *Acts* 9:37
Peter, when come into *upper-c.* 39
many lights in *upper-c.* where. 20:8

chambering

walk not in *c.* and. *Rom* 13:13

chamberlain, -s

chamber of the *c.* *2 Ki* 23:11
seven *c.* that served. *Esth* 1:10
but what Hegai the king's *c.* 2:15
two of king's *c.* were wroth. 21
Blastus the king's *c.* *Acts* 12:20
Erastus, *c.* of the city. *Rom* 16:23

chambers

wall of house he built *c.* *1 Ki* 6:5
chief porters over the *c.* *1 Chr* 9:26
23:28
to prepare *c.* *2 Chr* 31:11
ye weigh them in the *c.* *Ezra* 8:29
and they cleansed the *c.* *Neh* 13:9
which maketh the *c.* of. *Job* 9:9
layeth beams of his *c.* *Ps* 104:3
watereth the hills from his *c.* 13
brought forth frogs in *c.* 105:30
to hell going down to *c.* *Pr* 7:27
by knowledge *c.* shall be. 24:4
hath brought me into *c.* *S of S* 1:4
enter thou into thy *c.* *Isa* 26:20
woe to him that buildeth *c.* *Jer* 22:13
a wide house, and large *c.* 14
Rechabites into one of *c.* 35:2
every man in the *c.* *Ezek* 8:12
entereth into their privy *c.* *Ezek* 21:14
they be holy *c.* where priests. 42:13
he is in the secret *c.* *Mat* 24:26

upper-**chambers**

overlaid the *upper-c.* *2 Chr* 3:9
the *upper-c.* were shorter. *Ezek* 42:5

chameleon

ferret, and the *c.* and. *Lev* 11:30

chamois

eat, wild ox and the *c.* *Deut* 14:5

champaign

who dwell in the *c.* *Deut* 11:30*

champion

there went out a *c.* *1 Sam* 17:4
when Philistines saw *c.* was dead. 51

chance

if a bird's nest *c.* to. *Deut* 22:6
it may *c.* of wheat. *1 Cor* 15:37

chance

it was a *c.* that. *1 Sam* 6:9
as I happened by *c.* *2 Sam* 1:6
time and *c.* happeneth. *Eccl* 9:11
by *c.* a priest came. *Luke* 10:31

chancellor

Rehum *c.* wrote letter. *Ezra* 4:8, 9
king sent answer to Rehum the *c.* 17

chanceth

uncleanness that *c.* him. *Deut* 23:10

change, -s

both it and the *c.* *Lev* 27:33
will give you thirty *c.* *Judg* 14:12
shall give me thirty *c.* of. 13
days will I wait till my *c.* *Job* 14:14
with them given to *c.* *Pr* 24:21
clothe thee with *c.* of. *Zech* 3:4*
necessity a *c.* of the law. *Heb* 7:12

change, *verb*

be clean and *c.* your. *Gen* 35:2
he shall not *c.* it. *Lev* 27:10
nor *c.* it, if he *c.* 33
they *c.* the night into day. *Job* 17:12
as a vesture shalt thou *c.* *Ps* 102:26
but we will *c.* them. *Isa* 9:10
gaddest thou to *c.* thy way ? *Jer* 2:36
can Ethiopian *c.* his skin ? 13:23
think to *c.* times and laws. *Dan* 7:25
I will *c.* their glory into. *Hos* 4:7
then shall his mind *c.* *Hab* 1:11
I am the Lord, I *c.* not. *Mal* 3:6
shall *c.* the customs. *Acts* 6:14
their women did *c.* the. *Rom* 1:26
present, and *c.* my voice. *Gal* 4:20
who shall *c.* our vile body. *Phil* 3:21

changeable

Lord take away the *c.* *Isa* 3:22*

changed, -eth

father *c.* my wages. *Gen* 31:7, 41
Joseph *c.* his raiment, and. 41:14
raw flesh turn and be *c.* *Lev* 13:16
if plague have not *c.* his colour. 55
he *c.* his behaviour. *1 Sam* 21:13
David *c.* his apparel. *2 Sam* 12:20
king of Babylon *c.* his. *2 Ki* 24:17
c. prison-garments. 25:29; *Jer* 52:33
disease is my garment *c.* *Job* 30:18*
sweareth to his hurt, *c.* not. *Ps* 15:4
as vesture shall be *c.* 102:26
Heb 1:12
thus they *c.* their glory. *Ps* 106:20
boldness of face shall be *c.* *Eccl* 8:1
c. the ordinance, broken. *Isa* 24:5
c. their gods, people have *c.* *Jer* 2:11
and his scent is not *c.* 48:11
is the most fine gold *c.*! *Lam* 4:1
hath *c.* my judgements. *Ezek* 5:6*
till the time be *c.* *Dan* 2:9
he *c.* the times and seasons. 21
form of his visage was *c.* 3:19
nor were their coats *c.* nor 27
let his heart be *c.* from man's. 4:16
sign writing that it be not *c.* 6:8
no decree may be *c.* 15
purpose might not be *c.* 17
he hath *c.* the portion of. *Mi* 2:4
the barbarians *c.* their. *Acts* 28:6
c. the glory of the. *Rom* 1:23
c. the truth of God into a lie. 25
we shall all be *c.* *1 Cor* 15:51, 52
c. into same image from. *2 Cor* 3:18
for priesthood being *c.* a. *Heb* 7:12

changers

tables of money-*c.* *Mat* 21:12
Mark 11:15; *John* 2:14, 15

changes

he gave *c.* to Benjamin five *c.* *Gen* 45:22
took with him ten *c.* *2 Ki* 5:5
give them, I pray thee, two *c.* 22
bound two *c.* of garments. 23
c. and war are against. *Job* 10:17
because they have no *c.* *Ps* 55:19

changest, -ed, *countenance*

thou *c.* his *countenance.* *Job* 14:20
king's *countenance* was *c.* *Dan* 5:6, 9
nor let thy *countenance* be *c.* 10
my *countenance c.* in me. 7:28

changing

in Israel concerning *c.* *Ruth* 4:7

channel, -s

c. of the sea appeared. *2 Sam* 22:16
Ps 18:15
come up over all his *c.* *Isa* 8:7
Lord shall beat off from *c.* 27:12*

chant

they *c.* to the sound of. *Amos* 6:5*

chapel

it is the king's *c.* *Amos* 7:13*

chapiter, -s

(*American Revision,* capital)

overlaid their *c.* with gold. *Ex* 36:38; 38:28
overlaying of their *c.* 38:17, 19
made two *c.* of brass. *1 Ki* 7:16
2 Chr 4:12, 13
c. upon it was brass. *2 Ki* 25:17
Jer 52:22

chapmen

besides what *c.* and. *2 Chr* 9:14*

chapt

because ground is *c.* *Jer* 14:4

Charashim

father of the valley of *C.* *1 Chr* 4:14

charge

[1] *To command,* Ex 1:22. [2] *To adjure, or bind by a solemn oath,* 1 Sam 14:27. [3] *To load, or burden,* Deut 24:5; *1 Tim* 5:16. [4] *An office, or duty,* Num 8:26.

Abraham kept my *c.* *Gen* 26:5
Isaac gave Jacob a *c.* saying. 28:6
Moses and Aaron a *c.* *Ex* 6:13
this is the *c.* of their. *Num* 4:31
the Levites, touching their *c.* 8:26
Israel kept *c.* of the Lord. 9:19, 23
gave Joshua a *c.* 27:23; *Deut* 31:23
blood to people's *c.* *Deut* 21:8
Reubenites have kept *c.* *Josh* 22:3
the king gave *c.* *2 Sam* 18:5
ruler over all the *c.* *1 Ki* 11:28
the lord to have the *c.* *2 Ki* 7:17
because the *c.* was. *1 Chr* 9:27
Levites had the *c.* of. *2 Chr* 30:17
I gave Hanani *c.* over. *Neh* 7:2
of those that had *c.* of. *Esth* 3:9
who hath given him a *c.* *Job* 34:13
laid to my *c.* things I. *Ps* 35:11
king of Babylon gave *c.* *Jer* 39:11
Lord hath given it a *c.* 47:7
cause them that have *c.* *Ezek* 9:1
ye have not kept the *c.* of. 44:8
priests that kept the *c.* of. 15
priests kept my *c.* who. 48:11
lay not this sin to their *c.* *Acts* 7:60
an eunuch, who had *c.* of. 8:27
received such a *c.* thrust. 16:24
nothing laid to his *c.* worthy. 23:29
shall lay any thing to *c.* *Rom* 8:33
gospel of Christ without *c.* *1 Cor* 9:18
c. I commit to thee. *1 Tim* 1:18
not be laid to their *c.* *2 Tim* 4:16

see **keep**

give **charge**

and *give* Joshua a *c.* *Num* 27:19
I may *give* him a *c.* *Deut* 31:14
go, and I will *give c.* *2 Sam* 14:8
give thee wisdom and *c.* *1 Chr* 22:12
give his angels *c.* *Ps* 91:11
Mat 4:6; *Luke* 4:10

will I *give* him a c. *Isa* 10:6
these things *give* in c. *1 Tim* 5:7
I *give* thee c. in sight of God. 6:13

charge
go down, c. the people. *Ex* 19:21
priest shall c. her. *Num* 5:19
but c. Joshua and. *Deut* 3:28
to c. ourselves yearly. *Neh* 10:32
c. Esther that she go in. *Esth* 4:8
I c. you, O ye daughters. *S of S* 2:7
3:5; 5:8; 8:4
that thou dost so c. us? 5:9
I c. thee come out and. *Mark* 9:25
I c. you that this. *1 Thes* 5:27
c. that they teach no. *1 Tim* 1:3
I c. thee before God and. 5:21
2 Tim 4:1
c. them that are rich in. *1 Tim* 6:17

chargeable
lest we be c. to thee. *2 Sam* 13:25*
governors were c. to. *Neh* 5:15
with you, I was c. *2 Cor* 11:9*
we would not be c. *1 Thes* 2:9*
we might not be c. to. *2 Thes* 3:8*

charged
Abimelech c. his people. *Gen* 26:11
Isaac called Jacob, and c. 28:1
captain of the guard c. 40:4
Jacob c. his sons, and. 49:29
Pharaoh c. all his people. *Ex* 1:22
I c. your judges. *Deut* 1:16
nor shall he be c. with. 24:5
Moses c. the people the. 27:11
when Saul c. people. *1 Sam* 14:27
the king c. thee. *2 Sam* 18:12
David c. Solomon his son. *1 Ki* 2:1
the commandment that I have c. 43
so was it c. me by. 13:9
Lord c. me to build. *2 Chr* 36:23
Ezra 1:2
c. they not be opened. *Neh* 13:19
as Mordecai c. her. *Esth* 2:10, 20
Job sinned not, nor c. *Job* 1:22
and his angels he c. with folly. 4:18
c. Baruch before them. *Jer* 32:13
Jonadab in all that he c. us. 35:8
Jesus straitly c. them. *Mat* 9:30
Mark 5:43; *Luke* 9:21
Jesus c. them not make him known.
Mat 12:16 *Mark* 3:12
c. not to tell. *Mark* 7:36; 8:30
9:9; *Luke* 5:14; 8:56
many c. him that he. *Mark* 10:48
we c. every one of. *1 Thes* 2:11
let not church be c. *1 Tim* 5:16

chargedst
thou c. us, saying. *Ex* 19:23

charger, -s
(*A sort of dish or platter*)
offering was one silver c. *Num* 7:13
19, 25, 31, 37, 43, 49, 61, 67, 73, 79
dedication of altar, twelve c. 7:84
each c. of silver weighing 130. 85
number one thousand c. *Ezra* 1:9
John Baptist's head in a c. *Mat* 14:8
Mark 6:25

charges
the Levites to their c. *2 Chr* 8:14
from 20 years old in their c. 31:17
he set priests in their c. 35:2
them take, and be at c. *Acts* 21:24
warfare at his own c.? *1 Cor* 9:7

chargest
thou c. me to day. *2 Sam* 3:8

charging
c. the jailor to keep. *Acts* 16:23
c. that they strive. *2 Tim* 2:14

chariot
(*Among the ancients a two-wheeled vehicle for war, racing, or pleasure*)
to ride in the second c. *Gen* 41:43
Lord took off c. wheels. *Ex* 14:25
like work of a c. wheel. *1 Ki* 7:33
prepare thy c. and get. 18:44
number thee c. for c. and. 20:25
caused him to come into the c. 33
blood ran into the midst of c. 22:35
washed the c. in pool of. 38
appeared a c. of fire and. *2 Ki* 2:11
father, the c. of Israel. 12; 13:14
lighted from the c. to meet. 5:21
Jehu rode in a c. *2 Ki* 9:16
smite him in the c. 27
carried him in a c. to. 28; 23:30
gold for pattern of c. *1 Chr* 28:18
took him out of the c. *2 Chr* 35:24
he burneth the c. in. *Ps* 46:9
c. and horse are cast into. 76:6
made a c. of the wood. *S of S* 3:9*
a c. with horsemen, a c. *Isa* 21:7*
here cometh a c. of men. 9*
who bringeth forth the c. 43:17
break in pieces the c. *Jer* 51:21
bind the c. to the swift. *Mi* 1:13
first c. red horses, second c.
Zech 6:2
I will cut off the c. from. 9:10
go join thyself to his c. *Acts* 8:29
commanded c. to stand still. 38

***his* chariot**
Joseph made ready *his* c. *Gen* 46:29
Pharaoh made ready *his* c. *Ex* 14:6
Sisera lighted off *his* c. *Judg* 4:15
why is *his* c. so long in? 5:28
made speed to *his* c. *1 Ki* 12:18
2 Chr 10:18
said to the driver of *his* c. *1 Ki* 22:34
Ahab was stayed up in *his* c. 35
Naaman came with *his* c. *2 Ki* 5:9
turned again from *his* c. 26
his c. was made ready, went out each
in *his* c. 9:21
and he sunk down in *his* c. 24
made him to ride in *his* c. 10:16
who maketh clouds *his* c. *Ps* 104:3
his c. shall be as a. *Jer* 4:13
sitting in *his* c. read. *Acts* 8:28

chariot-cities
horsemen placed in c.-*cities*.
2 Chr 1:14
all the c.-*cities*. 8:6
bestowed in the c.-*cities* and. 9:25

chariot-horses
houghed all c.-*horses*. *2 Sam* 8:4
1 Chr 18:4
therefore two c.-*horses*. *2 Ki* 7:14

chariot-man
he said to the c.-*man*. *2 Chr* 18:33

chariots
went up with Joseph c. *Gen* 50:9
took 600 c. and all the c. *Ex* 14:7
I will get honour upon his c. 17
the waters covered all the c. 28
Pharaoh's c. and host. 15:4
horse of Pharaoh went in with c. 19
have c. of iron. *Josh* 17:16, 18
Judg 1:19; 4:3
Sisera and all his c. *Judg* 4:15
why tarry the wheels of his c.? 5:28
appoint them for his c. *1 Sam* 8:11
fight against Israel, 30,000 c. 13:5
c. and horsemen followed. *2 Sam* 1:6
David slew the men of 700 c. 10:18
Solomon had 1400 c. *1 Ki* 10:26
Zimri captain of half his c. 16:9
when the captains of the c. 22:32
left but ten c. and. *2 Ki* 13:7
thy trust on Egypt for c. 18:24
Isa 36:9
the c. of God are 20,000. *Ps* 68:17
my soul like the c. of. *S of S* 6:12
nor is any end of their c. *Isa* 2:7
c. of thy glory be the shame. 22:18
woe to them that trust in c. 31:1
by the multitude of my c. 37:24
Lord will come with fire and c. 66:15
Jer 4:13; *Dan* 11:40
at rushing of his c. *Jer* 47:3
come against thee with c. *Ezek* 23:24
shake at the noise of the c. 26:10
like the noise of the c. *Joel* 2:5
off horses, and destroy c. *Mi* 5:10
c. shall be with flaming. *Nah* 2:3
c. shall rage in streets and. 4
I am against, and will burn her c. 13
I will overthrow the c. *Hag* 2:22
as the sound of c. *Rev* 9:9

chariots with *horses*
the *horses* and c. of. *Ex* 14:9, 23
did to their *horses* and c. *Deut* 11:4
when thou seest *horses* and c. 20:1
hough their *horses*, burn c. *Josh* 11:6
houghed *horses*, burnt their c. 9
prepared *horses* and c. *2 Sam* 15:1
Samaria with c. and *horses*.
1 Ki 20:1
was full of c. and *horses*. *2 Ki* 6:17
to hear a noise of *horses* and c. 7:6
are with you c. and *horses*. 10:2
in c. and some in *horses*. *Ps* 20:7
to *horses* in Pharaoh's c. *S of S* 1:9
on *horses* and in c. *Isa* 66:20
enter princes riding in c. and on
horses. *Jer* 17:25; 22:4
ye *horses*, and rage, ye c. 46:9
upon their *horses* and their c. 50:37
with *horses* and with c. *Ezek* 26:7
my table with *horses* and c. 39:20
prancing *horses* and jumping c.
Nah 3:2
ride on thy *horses* and c. *Hab* 3:8
buys their *horses* and c. *Rev* 18:13

charitably
now walkest not c. *Rom* 14:15*

charity
[1] *Christian love or benevolence.* [2] *More generally, love, good will.* [3] *Good will to the poor, hence almsgiving. The word is used in the New Testament only, and in the Revised Version is always translated* love, *since the word* charity *has now come to have to most readers only the third meaning given above.*
but c. edifieth. *1 Cor* 8:1
and have not c. 13:1, 2, 3
c. suffereth long, and is kind, c. 4
c., but the greatest of these is c. 13
follow after c. and desire. 14:1
all things be done with c. 16:14
above all put on c. *Col* 3:14
of your faith and c. *1 Thes* 3:6
c. towards each other. *2 Thes* 1:3
end of commandment is c. *1 Tim* 1:5
continue in faith and c. 2:15
be an example in c. in spirit. 4:12
follow faith, c. peace. *2 Tim* 2:22
my doctrine, life, faith, c. 3:10
sound in faith, in c. *Tit* 2:2
fervent c. for c. shall. *1 Pet* 4:8
one another with a kiss of c. 5:14
to brotherly-kindness, c. *2 Pet* 1:7
borne witness of thy c. *3 John* 6
spots in your feasts of c. *Jude* 12
I know thy works, and c. *Rev* 2:19

charmed
serpents which will not be c. *Jer* 8:17

charmer, -s
found among you a c. *Deut* 18:11
not hearken to voice of c. *Ps* 58:5

Charran
Abraham dwelt in C. *Acts* 7:2, 4

chase
shall c. your enemies. *Lev* 26:7
five of you shall c. an. 8
sound of a shaking leaf shall c. 36
should one c. 1000. *Deut* 32:30
Josh 23:10
let angel of Lord c. *Ps* 35:5*

chased, -eth, -ing
the Amorites c. you as. *Deut* 1:44
Abimelech c. him. *Judg* 9:40
inclosed Benjamites and c. 20:43
Israel returned from c. *1 Sam* 17:53
therefore I c. him. *Neh* 13:28
he shall be c. out of. *Job* 18:18
he shall be c. away as a vision. 20:8
and he that c. away. *Pr* 19:26
it shall be as the c. roe. *Isa* 13:14
they shall be c. as the chaff. 17:13
mine enemies c. me sore. *Lam* 3:52

chaste
you as a c. virgin. *2 Cor* 11:2
young women be c. obedient. *Tit* 2:5
your c. conversation. *1 Pet* 3:2

chasten
(*To correct or punish*)
I will c. him with rod. *2 Sam* 7:14
nor c. me in displeasure. *Ps* 6:1
38:1
c. thy son while there is. *Pr* 19:18
thou didst c. thyself. *Dan* 10:12*
as I love I rebuke and c. *Rev* 3:19

chastened
they have *c.* him. *Deut* 21:18
he is *c.* also with pain. *Job* 33:19
I wept, and *c.* my soul. *Ps* 69:10
all day been plagued, and *c.* 73:14
Lord hath *c.* me sore. 118:18
we are *c.* that we be. *1 Cor* 11:32
dying, yet live, as *c.* and. *2 Cor* 6:9
they for a few days *c.* *Heb* 12:10

chastenest, -eth, -ing
c. his son, so Lord *c.* *Deut* 8:5
despise not thou the *c.* of Almighty. *Job* 5:17; *Pr* 3:11; *Heb* 12:5
is the man whom thou *c.* *Ps* 94:12
he that loveth him *c.* *Pr* 13:24
a prayer when thy *c.* *Isa* 26:16
whom Lord loveth he *c.* *Heb* 12:6
endure *c.* what son father *c.* not? 7
no *c.* for present seems to be. 11

chastise
I will *c.* you seven. *Lev* 26:28
take the man and *c.* *Deut* 22:18
I will *c.* you with. *1 Ki* 12:11, 14; *2 Chr* 10:11, 14
I will *c.* them as their. *Hos* 7:12
my desire that I should *c.* 10:10
I will *c.* him, and. *Luke* 23:16, 22

chastised, -eth
c. you with whips. *1 Ki* 12:11, 14; *2 Chr* 10:11, 14
he that *c.* heathen. *Ps* 94:10
hast *c.* me, and I was *c.* *Jer* 31:18

chastisement
who have not seen the *c.* *Deut* 11:2
I have borne *c.* I will not. *Job* 34:31
c. of our peace was. *Isa* 53:5
have wounded with the *c.* *Jer* 30:14
if without *c.* then are. *Heb* 12:8

chatter
so did I *c.* *Isa* 38:14

Chebar
by river of *C.* *Ezek* 1:1, 3; 3:15, 23; 10:15, 20

check
I have heard the *c.* of. *Job* 20:3*

checker work
Hiram made nets of *c.-w* *1 Ki* 7:17

cheek
smote Micaiah on the *c.* *1 Ki* 22:24; *2 Chr* 18:23
smitten me on the *c.* *Job* 16:10
he giveth his *c.* to him. *Lam* 3:30
Judge with a rod on the *c.* *Mi* 5:1
smiteth one *c.* offer also. *Luke* 6:29

right **cheek**
smite thee on thy *right c.* *Mat* 5:39

cheek-bone
all mine enemies on *c.-bone.* *Ps* 3:7

cheeks
to priest the two *c.* *Deut* 18:3
thy *c.* are comely with. *S of S* 1:10
his *c.* are as a bed of spices. 5:13
I gave my *c.* to them. *Isa* 50:6
and her tears are on her *c.* *Lam* 1:2

cheek-teeth
come up, hath *c.-teeth.* *Joel* 1:6

cheer
shall *c.* up his wife he. *Deut* 24:5
let thy heart *c.* thee in. *Eccl* 11:9
on, be of good *c.* thy. *Mat* 9:2
be of good *c.* it is I. 14:27; *Mark* 6:50
be of good *c.* *John* 16:33
be of good *c.* Paul. *Acts* 23:11
I exhort you to be of good *c.* 27:22
wherefore, sirs, be of good *c.* 25
then were they all of good *c.* 36

cheereth
leave my wine, which *c.* *Judg* 9:13

cheerful
merry heart maketh a *c.* *Pr* 15:13
house of Judah joy and *c.* *Zech* 8:19
corn shall make young men *c.* 9:17*
for God loveth a *c.* *2 Cor* 9:7

cheerfully
I do the more *c.* answer. *Acts* 24:10

cheerfulness
sheweth mercy with *c.* *Rom* 12:8

cheese, -s
carry these ten *c.* to. *1 Sam* 17:18
sheep and *c.* to David. *2 Sam* 17:29
curdled me like *c.*? *Job* 10:10

Chemarims
cut off the name of *C.* *Zeph* 1:4

Chemosh
undone, O people of *C.* *Num* 21:29
possess what *C.* giveth? *Judg* 11:24
an high place for *C.* *1 Ki* 11:7, 33
and *C.* shall go forth. *Jer* 48:7
Moab shall be ashamed of *C.* 13
woe to thee, O Moab, people of *C.* 46

Chenaniah
C. chief of Levites. *1 Chr* 15:22, 27

Cherethims
behold, I will cut off *C.* *Ezek* 25:16

Cherethites
invasion on south of *C.* *1 Sam* 30:14
Benaiah was over *C.* *2 Sam* 8:18; 20:23; *1 Chr* 18:17
unto the nation of the *C.* *Zeph* 2:5

cherish
let her *c.* him, and lie. *1 Ki* 1:2

cherished
damsel was fair, and *c.* *1 Ki* 1:4

cherisheth
c. his own flesh, as the. *Eph* 5:29
gentle, even as a nurse *c.* *1 Thes* 2:7

Cherith
hide thyself by brook *C.* *1 Ki* 17:3

cherub
[1] *One of an order of angels, usually below the seraphim. Plural properly* cherubim, *in Authorized Version* cherubims. [2] *A winged figure used in connection with the mercy seat of the Jewish ark of the covenant,* Ex 25:18–22; 37:7–9. [3] *A mysterious composite figure described in* Ezek 1 and 10.
one *c.* on one end, and the other *c.* *Ex* 25:19; 37:8
he rode upon a *c.* *2 Sam* 22:11; *Ps* 18:10
other *c.* was ten cubits. *1 Ki* 6:25
the height of one *c.* ten cubits. 26
glory of God was gone from the *c.* to. *Ezek* 9:3; 10:4
and one *c.* stretched forth his. 10:7
first face was the face of a *c.* 14
thou art the anointed *c.* 28:14
will destroy thee, O covering *c.* 16
between a *c.* and a *c.* every *c.* 41:18

cherubims
at the east of the garden *c.* *Gen* 3:24
thou shalt make two *c.* *Ex* 25:18
tabernacle of *c.* of cunning. 26:1, 31
he made two *c.* of beaten. 37:7
within oracle two *c.* *1 Ki* 6:23
both the *c.* were of one measure. 25
overlaid the *c.* with gold. 28
c. covered the ark. 8:7; *2 Chr* 5:8; *Heb* 9:5
most holy place two *c.* *2 Chr* 3:10
sound of the *c.* wings. *Ezek* 10:5
when *c.* went, the wheels went. 16
c. lift up their wings and. 19; 11:22

between the **cherubims**
thee from *between the c.* *Ex* 25:22
from *between the* two *c.* *Num* 7:89
dwelleth *between the c.* *1 Sam* 4:4; *2 Sam* 6:2; *2 Ki* 19:15; *Isa* 37:16
dwelleth *between the c.* shine. *Ps* 80:1
he sitteth *between the c.* 99:1
of fire from *between c.* *Ezek* 10:2
between c. to fire was *between c.* 7

chesnut-tree, -s
took him rods of *c.-tree.* *Gen* 30:37*
the *c.-trees* were not. *Ezek* 31:8*

chest, -s
Jehoiada took *c.* and. *2 Ki* 12:9
they made *c.* *2 Chr* 24:8
and emptied the *c.* 11
in *c.* of rich apparel. *Ezek* 27:24

chew
of them that *c.* cud. *Lev* 11:4; *Deut* 14:7

chewed
ere the flesh was *c.* *Num* 11:33

cheweth
because he *c.* cud. *Lev* 11:4, 5, 6; *Deut* 14:6
swine *c.* not cud. *Lev* 11:7; *Deut* 14:8

chickens
a hen gathereth her *c.* *Mat* 23:37

chide
people did *c.*, why *c.* ye? *Ex* 17:2*
men of Ephraim did *c.* *Judg* 8:1
he will not always *c.* *Ps* 103:9

chiding
Meribah, because of *c.* *Ex* 17:7*

chief
[1] *The head of a family, tribe, army, etc.,* Num 3:30; Deut 1:15; 1 Sam 14:38; 2 Sam 5:8. *In such cases the Revised Version commonly changes the word to* princes, *or* captains, *or* heads. [2] *The best, or most valuable,* 1 Sam 15:21. [3] *The dearest, or most familiar,* Pr 16:28.
the *c.* butler told his. *Gen* 40:9
he restored the *c.* butler to. 21
but hanged the *c.* baker as. 22
c. over *c.* of Levites. *Num* 3:32
the *c.* of your tribes. *Deut* 1:15
the people took the *c.* *1 Sam* 15:21
brother of Joab *c.* *2 Sam* 23:18
these were the *c.* of. *1 Ki* 9:23
of Judah came the *c.* *1 Chr* 5:2
first shall be *c.* and captain, Joab went first and was *c.* 11:6
sons of David were *c.* about. 18:17
his father made him *c.* 26:10
the rulers have been *c.* *Ezra* 9:2
c. of the province that. *Neh* 11:3
taketh away heart of *c.* *Job* 12:24
chose out their way, and sat *c.* 29:25
behemoth is the *c.* of the. 40:19
smote *c.* of their strength. *Ps* 78:51; 105:36
Jerusalem above my *c.* joy. 137:6
Wisdom crieth in *c.* place. *Pr* 1:21
a whisperer separateth *c.* friends. 16:28
orchard with all the *c.* *S of S* 4:14
stirreth up the *c.* ones. *Isa* 14:9
hast taught them as *c.* *Jer* 13:21
sing and shout among the *c.* 31:7
her adversaries are the *c.* *Lam* 1:5
c. of children of Ammon. *Dan* 11:41
which are named *c.* *Amos* 6:1
anoint themselves with *c.* 6
whosoever will be *c.* *Mat* 20:27
c. seats in the synagogues. 23:6; *Mark* 12:39
supper to his *c.* estates. *Mark* 6:21
out devils through *c.* *Luke* 11:15
house of one of *c.* Pharisees. 14:1
they chose *c.* rooms. 7; 20:46
and he that is *c.* as he that. 22:26
among *c.* rulers many. *John* 12:42
Paul was the *c.* speaker. *Acts* 14:12
and of *c.* women not a few. 17:4
c. of Asia. 19:31*
the *c.* corner-stone. *Eph* 2:20; *1 Pet* 2:6
sinners, of whom I *c.* *1 Tim* 1:15
when *c.* Shepherd shall. *1 Pet* 5:4

chief *captain*
shall be *c.* and *captain.* *2 Sam* 5:8
came to the *c. captain.* *Acts* 21:31
when they saw the *c. captain.* 32
this young man to *c. captain.* 23:17
c. captain Lysias came upon. 24:7
c. captain shall come. 22

chief *captains*
Tachmonite sat *c.* among *captains.* *2 Sam* 23:8
c. of all the *captains.* *1 Chr* 27:3
c. of Solomon's *captains.* *2 Chr* 8:9
Agrippa entered with *c. captains.* *Acts* 25:23
rich men and *c. captains.* *Rev* 6:15

chief *fathers*
thou and *c. fathers* of. *Num* 31:26
c. fathers of Levites. *1 Chr* 9:34
the *c. fathers* of priests and. 24:31
2700 *c. fathers* made rulers. 26:32

of c. *fathers* of mighty. *2 Chr* 26:12
c. of the *fathers* of Judah. *Ezra* 1:5
c. of the *fathers* gave. *Neh* 7:70, 71

chief *house*

c. of *house* of Gershonites. *Num* 3:24
c. of *house* of Kohathites. 30
c. of the *house* of the Merarites. 35
Zimri was of a c. *house*. 25:14
Cozbi, of a c. *house* in Midian. 15
out of each c. *house* a. *Josh* 22:14

chief *man*, or *men*

being a c. *man* *Lev* 21:4
all of them c. *men*. *1 Chr* 7:3
more c. *men* of Eleazar than. 24:4
names of *men* that were c. *Ezra* 5:10
I gathered together c. *men*. 7:28
thee from the c. *men*. *Isa* 41:9
Jews stirred up c. *men*. *Acts* 13:50
Judas and Silas, c. *men*. 15:22
possessions of the c. *man*. 28:7

chief *priest*

Seraiah the c. *priest*. *2 Ki* 25:18
Benaiah a c. *priest*. *1 Chr* 27:5
anointed Zadok to be c. *priest*. 29:22
Amariah c. *priest* is. *2 Chr* 19:11
and Azariah the c. *priest*. 26:20

chief *priests*

twelve of c. of *priests*. *Ezra* 8:24
made the c. *priests* and all. 10:5
these were c. *priests* in. *Neh* 12:7
many things of c. *priests*. *Mat* 16:21
multitude from the c. *priests*. 26:47
c. *priests* sought to. 59
Mark 14:1, 55; *Luke* 9:22; 22:2
was accused of c. *priests*. *Mat* 27:12
Mark 15:3
c. *priests* mocking. *Mat* 27:41
Mark 15:31
voices of them and c. *priests*. *Luke* 23:23
c. *priests* sent officers to. *John* 7:32
18:3
c. *priests* answered, we have. 19:15
authority from c. *priests*. *Acts* 9:14
26:10
commanded the c. *priests*. 22:30

chief *prince*, or *princes*

of Asher, c. of *princes*. *1 Chr* 7:40
Gog c. *prince* of. *Ezek* 38:2, 3; 39:1
Michael one of c. *princes*. *Dan* 10:13

chief *singer*, or *singers*

were c. of the *singers*. *Neh* 12:46
to the c. *singer* on my. *Hab* 3:19

chiefest

fat with c. offerings. *1 Sam* 2:29
made them sit in c. place. 9:22
Doeg an Edomite, c. of herd-. 21:7
Hezekiah buried in c. *2 Chr* 32:33
my beloved is the c. *S of S* 5:10
who will be c. shall. *Mark* 10:44
not a whit behind c. *2 Cor* 11:5
12:11

chiefly

c. because to them were. *Rom* 3:2
c. of they that are of. *Phil* 4:22
c. them that walk after. *2 Pet* 2:10

child

[1] *One young in years*, 1 Sam 1:22. [2] *One weak in knowledge*, Isa 10:19; 1 Cor 13:11. [3] *Such as are humble and docile*, Mat 18:3, 4.

(*The words child, children are frequently used for any descendant or descendants however remote, as the children of Israel. Such expressions as children of light, children of darkness, mean those who follow the light, or try to hide in the darkness. "Children of God" in the Old Testament is used sometimes for angels, sometimes for good men. In the New Testament the term is more often used of those who have believed and accepted Christ*)

see **son, sons**

Hagar cast the c. under. *Gen* 21:15
let me not see the death of c. 16
the c. is not, and I, whither? 37:30
do not sin against the c.? *Gen* 42:22
called the c. mother. *Ex* 2:8
not afflict any fatherless c. 22:22
was his only c. *Judg* 11:34
teach us what we shall do to c. 13:8
brought the c. to Eli. *1 Sam* 1:25
the Lord had called the c. 3:8
c. that is born to thee. *2 Sam* 12:14
Lord struck the c. that Uriah's. 15
David besought God for the c. 16
David perceived that c. was dead. 19
divide the living c. in. *1 Ki* 3:25
what shall become of the c. 14:3
the soul of the c. came into. 17:22
he told him, the c. is. *2 Ki* 4:31
the c. sneezed, and c. opened. 35
correction from the c. *Pr* 23:13
he hath neither c. nor. *Eccl* 4:8
with second c. that shall stand. 15
c. shall behave himself. *Isa* 3:5
for before the c. shall know. 7:16
the c. shall know to cry, my. 8:4
weaned c. shall put his hand. 11:8
the c. shall die an hundred. 65:20
bringeth forth her first c. *Jer* 4:31
is he a pleasant c.? 31:20
cut off man, woman, and c. 44:7
father shall deliver c. to. *Mat* 10:21
the c. was cured from. 17:18
twofold more the c. of hell. 23:15
came to circumcise c. *Luke* 1:59
what manner of c. shall this? 66
thou c. shalt be called Prophet. 76
the c. grew, and waxed. 80; 2:40
parents brought in c. Jesus. 2:27
my son, he is my only c. 9:38
Jesus healed c. and delivered. 42
come down ere my c. die. *John* 4:49
as she is delivered of c. 16:21
against thy holy c. Jesus. *Acts* 4:27*
signs may be done by name of c. 30*
Saul said, thou c. of the devil. 13:10
to devour her c. as soon. *Rev* 12:4
her c. was caught up to God. 5

a **child**

bear *a* c. who am old? *Gen* 18:13
father, and *a* c. of his old age. 44:20
saw he was *a* goodly c. *Ex* 2:2
Heb 11:23
Samuel, *a* c. girded. *1 Sam* 2:18
wast delivered of *a* c. *1 Ki* 3:17
a c. shall be born to house of. 13:2
shall be fresher than *a* c. *Job* 33:25
as *a* c. as *a* weaned c. *Ps* 131:2
even *a* c. is known. *Pr* 20:11
train up *a* c. in the way he. 22:6
bound in the heart of *a* c. 15
a c. left to himself bringeth. 29:15
bringeth up his servant from *a* c. 21
better is *a* wise c. than. *Eccl* 4:13
to thee, when thy king is *a* c. 10:16
for unto us *a* c. is born. *Isa* 9:6
trees shall be few, that *a* c. 10:19
cannot speak, I am *a* c. *Jer* 1:6, 7
tidings, saying, *a* man c. is. 20:15
when Israel was *a* c. *Hos* 11:1
he said of *a* c. *Mark* 9:21
took *a* c. and set. 36; *Luke* 9:47
a c. I spake as *a* c. understood as *a* c. I thought as *a* c. *1 Cor* 13:11
heir as long as he is *a* c. *Gal* 4:1
from *a* c. hast known. *2 Tim* 3:15
Sarah delivered of *a* c. *Heb* 11:11
brought forth *a* man c. *Rev* 12:5

little **child**

am a *little* c. I know not. *1 Ki* 3:7
fled into Egypt, being a *little* c. 11:17
the flesh of a *little* c. *2 Ki* 5:14
a *little* c. shall lead them. *Isa* 11:6
Jesus called a *little* c. to. *Mat* 18:2
shall receive one such *little* c. 5
not receive the kingdom of God as a *little* c. *Mark* 10:15; *Luke* 18:17

no **child**

but Sarai had *no* c. *Gen* 11:30
priest's daughter have *no* c. *Lev* 22:13
die, and have *no* c. *Deut* 25:5
Michal had *no* c. unto. *2 Sam* 6:23
verily she hath *no* c. *2 Ki* 4:14
they had *no* c. because. *Luke* 1:7
promised when he had *no* c. *Acts* 7:5

sucking **child**

father beareth *sucking* c. *Num* 11:12
sucking c. shall play on. *Isa* 11:8
woman forget her *sucking* c.? 49:15
tongue of *sucking* c. *Lam* 4:4

this **child**

take *this* c. and nurse. *Ex* 2:9
told concerning *this* c. *Luke* 2:17
this c. is set for fall and rising. 34
whoso shall receive *this* c. 9:48

with **child**

Hagar, thou art *with* c. *Gen* 16:11
daughters of Lot were *with* c. 19:36
Tamar thy daughter is *with* c. 38:24
whose these are, am I *with* c. 25
hurt a woman *with* c. *Ex* 21:22
Phinehas' wife was *with* c. *1 Sam* 4:19
Bath-sheba said, I am *with* c. *2 Sam* 11:5
rip up women *with* c. *2 Ki* 8:12
15:16
of her that is *with* c. *Eccl* 11:5
like a woman *with* c. *Isa* 26:17
we have been *with* c. we have. 18
that didst not travail *with* c. 54:1
man doth travail *with* c. *Jer* 30:6
from north woman *with* c. 31:8
their women *with* c. *Hos* 13:16
ripped up the women *with* c. *Amos* 1:13
she was found *with* c. of. *Mat* 1:18
a virgin shall be *with* c. 23
woe to them that are *with* c. 24:19
Mark 13:17; *Luke* 21:23
Mary, being great *with* c. *Luke* 2:5
upon a woman *with* c. *1 Thes* 5:3
she being *with* c. cried. *Rev* 12:2

young **child**

and the c. was *young*. *1 Sam* 1:24
search diligently for the *young* c. *Mat* 2:8
take *young* c. and his mother. 13
took the *young* c. and his mother. 14

childbearing

she shall be saved in c. *1 Tim* 2:15

childhood

before you from my c. *1 Sam* 12:2
c. and youth are vanity. *Eccl* 11:10

childish

I put away c. things. *1 Cor* 13:11

childless

give me, seeing I go c.? *Gen* 15:2
their sin, shall die c. *Lev* 20:20
thy sword hath made women c. so shall thy mother be c. *1 Sam* 15:33
write you this man c. *Jer* 22:30
her to wife, and died c. *Luke* 20:30

children

(*Revised Version frequently changes this word to sons*)

in sorrow bring forth c. *Gen* 3:16
it may be I may obtain c. 16:2
the c. struggled together. 25:22
give me c. or I die. 30:1
the c. which God hath given. 33:5
thy father's c. shall bow down. 49:8
600,000 men, besides c. *Ex* 12:37
iniquity of the fathers upon c. 20:5
34:7; *Num* 14:18; *Deut* 5:9
the wife and her c. shall. *Ex* 21:4
saw the c. of Anak. *Num* 13:28
the c. of Korah died not. 26:11
Ar to the c. of Lot. *Deut* 2:9, 19
can stand before the c. of Anak? 9:2
the c. of Belial are gone. 13:13*
ye are the c. of the Lord. 14:1
have born him c. both beloved. 21:15
the c. begotten of them shall. 23:8
fathers shall not be put to death for c. nor c. for. 24:16; *2 Chr* 25:4
c. in whom there is no faith. *Deut* 32:20
let Asher be blessed with c. 33:24
c. of Reuben, Gad and Manasseh, built there an. *Josh* 22:9, 10, 11
take 10,000 men of c. of. *Judg* 4:6
each one resembled the c. of. 8:18
a riddle to c. of people. 14:16
deliver us the c. of Belial. 20:13*

she that hath many c. *1 Sam* 2:5
c. of Belial said, how shall? 10:27†
neither shall c. of wickedness afflict
them. *2 Sam* 7:10; *1 Chr* 17:9
two men, c of Belial. *1 Ki* 21:13*
bears came and tare 42 c. *2 Ki* 2:24
Elisha called one of the c. 9:1
salute the c. of the king, c. 10:13
but the c. of murderers he slew not.
14:6; *2 Chr* 25:4
do as Lord commanded c. *2 Ki* 17:34
c. are come to birth. 19:3; *Isa* 37:3
Seled died without c. *1 Chr* 2:30
and Jether died without c. 32
Shimei's brethren had not many c.
4:27
c. of Jacob his. 16:13; *Ps* 105:6
gathered to Jeroboam c. *2 Chr* 13:7*
Lord is not with the c. of. 25:7
smote of c. of Seir 10,000. 11
are c. of the province. *Ezra* 2:1
Neh 7:6
by whom they had c. *Ezra* 10:44
c. multipliedst thou as. *Neh* 9:23
I intreated for the c. sake. *Job* 19:17
were c. of fools, yea c. 30:8
he is a king over all the c. 41:34
they are full of c. and. *Ps* 17:14
come, ye c. hearken to me. 34:11
an alien to my mother's c. 69:8
he shall save the c. of needy. 72:4
the c. which should be born. 78:6
and all of you are c. of the 82:6
have holpen the c. of Lot. 83:8
the c. of thy servants shall. 102:28
to be a joyful mother of c. 113:9
lo c. are an heritage of Lord. 127:3
as arrows in the hand, so are c. 4
remember, O Lord, c. of. 137:7
let old men and c. praise. 148:12
let the c. of Zion be joyful. 149:2
hear, ye c. instruction. *Pr* 4:1
5:7; 7:24; 8:32
and the glory of c. are. 17:6
her c. arise up and call her. 31:28
if a man beget 100 c. *Eccl* 6:3
mother's c. were angry. *S of S* 1:6
I have brought up c. *Isa* 1:2
ah sinful nation, c. that are. 4
they please themselves in c. 2:6
I will give c. to be their princes. 3:4
as for my people, c. are their. 12
c. whom Lord hath. 8:18; *Heb* 2:13
their eye not spare c. *Isa* 13:18
mighty men of c. of Kedar. 21:17
I travail not, nor bring forth c. 23:4
woe to the rebellious c. saith. 30:1
lying c. c. that will not hear Lord. 9
father to the c. make known. 38:19
neither know the loss of c. 47:8
come in one day the loss of c. 9
the c. which thou shalt have. 49:20
for more are c. of the desolate than c.
54:1; *Gal* 4:27
are ye not c. of transgression?
Isa 57:4
slaying the c. in the valleys. 5
they are my people, c. that. 63:8
she brought forth c. 66:8
turn, O backsliding c. *Jer* 3:14, 22
how shall I put thee among c.? 19
they are sottish c. 4:22
I will pour it out upon the c. 6:11
the c. gather wood. 7:18
for death entered to cut off c. 9:21
I will bereave them of c. 15:7
weeping for her c. 31:15; *Mat* 2:18
c. teeth are set on edge. *Jer* 31:29
Ezek 18:2
shall the women eat c.? *Lam* 2:20
young men to grind, c. fell. 5:13
for they are impudent c. *Ezek* 2:4
the c. rebelled against me. 20:21
the c. still are talking. 33:30
strangers shall beget c. 47:22
c. in whom was no blemish. *Dan* 1:4
fairer and fatter than all c. 15
as for these four c. God gave. 17
Michael shall stand for the c. 12:1
take unto thee c. of. *Hos* 1:2
not have mercy on her c. they be c.
2:4
the battle against the c. of. 10:9
dashed in pieces upon her c. 14
then the c. shall tremble. *Hos* 11:10
in place of breaking forth of c. 13:13
gather c. and those that. *Joel* 2:16
be glad then ye c. of Zion. 23
are ye not as c. of the? *Amos* 9:7
poll thee for delicate c. *Mi* 1:16
I will punish the king's c. *Zeph* 1:8
turn the heart of fathers to the c. and
heart of c. *Mal* 4:6; *Luke* 1:17
Herod slew all the c. in. *Mat* 2:16
of these stones to raise up c. 3:9
Luke 3:8
that ye may be c. of your. *Mat* 5:45
but the c. of the kingdom. 8:12
can c. of bride-chamber mourn?
9:15; *Mark* 2:19; *Luke* 5:34
c. shall rise against. *Mat* 10:21
Mark 13:12
wisdom justified of her c. *Mat* 11:19*
Luke 7:35
good seed are the c. of kingdom,
tares are the c. of. *Mat* 13:38
not meet to take c. bread. 15:26
Mark 7:27
then are the c. free. *Mat* 17:26
forsaken wife or c. for my. 19:29
Mark 10:29
mother of Zebedee's c. *Mat* 20:20
priests and scribes saw c. 21:15
c. of them that killed. 23:31
let the c. first be filled. *Mark* 7:27
dogs eat of the c. crumbs. 28
receive one of such c. 9:37, 41
be the c. of the Highest. *Luke* 6:35
c. of this world wiser than c. 16:8
a wife, and died without c. 20:29
the c. of this world marry. 34
if ye were Abraham's c. *John* 8:39
c. have ye any meat? 21:5
ye are c. of the prophets. *Acts* 3:25
if c. then heirs, heirs of. *Rom* 8:17
seed of Abraham are they all c. 9:7
for c. being not yet born, nor. 11
be not c. in understanding; howbeit
in malice be ye c. *1 Cor* 14:20
c. ought not to lay up for the parents,
but parents for c. *2 Cor* 12:14
of faith, the same are c. *Gal* 3:7
so we, when we were c. were. 4:3
in bondage with her c. 25
are not c. of bond-woman. 31
us to adoption of c. *Eph* 1:5
the spirit that worketh in c. 2:2
were by nature c. of wrath. 3
no more c., tossed to and fro. 4:14
followers of God as dear c. 5:1
wrath cometh on c. of. 6; *Col* 3:6
c. obey your parents. *Eph* 6:1
Col 3:20
if any widow have c. *1 Tim* 5:4
if she hath brought up c. 10
younger women marry, bear c. 14
the c. are partakers of. *Heb* 2:14
speaketh to you as to c. 12:5
as obedient c. not. *1 Pet* 1:14
of adultery, cursed c. *2 Pet* 2:14
c. of God manifest, c. of. *1 John* 3:10
to the elect lady and her c. *2 John* 1
c. of thy elect sister greet thee. 13
I will kill her c. with. *Rev* 2:23

see **Ammon, captivity**

children *of Benjamin*
of the c. of B. by their. *Num* 1:36
c. of B. did not drive. *Judg* 1:21
c. of B. would not hearken. 20:13
c. of B. gathered. *2 Sam* 2:25
dwelt of c. of B. *1 Chr* 9:3
Neh 11:4
there came of c. of B. *1 Chr* 12:16
O ye c. of Benjamin. *Jer* 6:1

children's **children**
thou and thy ch. c. *Gen* 45:10
iniquity of fathers on ch. c. *Ex* 34:7
beget c. and ch. c. *Deut* 4:25
both their c. and ch. c. *2 Ki* 17:41
righteousness unto ch. c. *Ps* 103:17
shalt see thy ch. c. and. 128:6
inheritance to his ch. c. *Pr* 13:22
ch. c. are crown of old men, glory of
c. 17:6
with your ch. c. will I plead. *Jer* 2:9
their ch. c. for ever. *Ezek* 37:25

fatherless **children**
any to favour father. c. *Ps* 109:12
leave thy father. c. I. *Jer* 49:11

children *of God*
be called the c. of G. *Mat* 5:9
the c. of G. being c. of. *Luke* 20:36
together in one c. of G. *John* 11:52
that we are the c. of G. *Rom* 8:16
glorious liberty of c. of G. 21
c. of the flesh, not c. of G. 9:8
be called c. of living G. 26
ye are all c. of G. by. *Gal* 3:26
c. of G. manifest, c. of. *1 John* 3:10
know that we love c. of G. 5:2

his **children**
Abraham will command his c.
Gen 18:19
loved Joseph more than his c. 37:3
his days, he and his c. *Deut* 17:20
their spot is not spot of his c. 32:5
nor knew his own c. 33:9
his wife and his c. *1 Sam* 30:22
it grew up with his c. *2 Sam* 12:3
give him a light, and his c. *2 Ki* 8:19
burnt his c. in fire after. *2 Chr* 28:3
caused his c. to pass through. 33:6
his c. are far from safety. *Job* 5:4
even the eyes of his c. 17:5
his c. shall seek to please. 20:10
layeth up his iniquity for his c. 21:19
if his c. be multiplied, it is. 27:14
if his c. forsake my law. *Ps* 89:30
as a father pitieth his c. 103:13
let his c. be fatherless. 109:9
let his c. be vagabonds. 10
his c. shall have a place. *Pr* 14:26
the just man, his c. are. 20:7
slaughter for his c. for. *Isa* 14:21
when he seeth his c. in. 29:23
Ephraim bring forth his c. *Hos* 9:13
his c. and cattle drank. *John* 4:12
charged you as father doth his c.
1 Thes 2:11
having his c. in subjection. *1 Tim* 3:4

children *of Israel*
an oath of the c. of Isr. *Gen* 50:25
c. of Isr. were fruitful. *Ex* 1:7
grieved because of c. of Isr. 12
c. of Isr. sighed. 2:23
God looked on c. of Isr. 25
Lord had visited c. of Isr. 4:31
heard groaning of the c. of Isr. 6:5
bring c. of Isr. out. 13, 26, 27; 12:51
nothing die of all that is c. of Isr. 9:4
c. of Isr. journeyed about. 12:37
there I will meet with c. of Isr. 29:43
sign between me and c. of Isr. 31:17
whosoever he be, c. of Isr. *Lev* 17:13
for to me the c. of Isr. 25:55
Lord appeared before c. of Isr.
Num 14:10
c. of Isr. could not stand. *Josh* 7:12
numbered c. of Isr. *1 Sam* 11:8
were not of c. of Isr. *2 Sam* 21:2
them instead of c. of Isr. *2 Ki* 17:24
had not the c. of Isr. done. *Neh* 8:17
his acts to c. of Isr. *Ps* 103:7
even of the c. of Isr., a. 148:14
one by one, O ye c. of Isr. *Isa* 27:12
when c. of Isr. went. *Ezek* 44:15
48:11
thus, O ye c. of Isr.? *Amos* 2:11
liketh you, O ye c. of Isr. 4:5
many of the c. of Isr. *Luke* 1:16
visit brethren c. of Isr. *Acts* 7:23
Moses which said to the c. of Isr. 37
bear my name before c. of Isr. 9:15
word God sent to c. of Isr. 10:36
number of c. of Isr. be. *Rom* 9:27
c. of Isr. could not behold face of.
2 Cor 3:7
of departing of c. of Isr. *Heb* 11:22
block before c. of Isr. *Rev* 2:14
of all tribes of the c. of Isr. 7:4
of twelve tribes of c. of Isr. 21:12

children *of Judah*
of the c. of Judah by. *Num* 1:26
c. of Judah came to. *Josh* 14:6
bade teach c. of Judah. *2 Sam* 1:18
c. of Judah prevailed. *2 Chr* 13:18
other 10,000 did c. of Judah. 25:12
to keep under c. of Judah. 28:10

the evil of c. of Judah. Jer 32:32
they and the c. of Judah going. 50:4
Israel and c. of Judah were. 33
against the c. of Judah. Joel 3:19

children *of light*

c. of this world wiser than c. of light. Luke 16:8
may be the c. of light. John 12:36
walk as c. of light. Eph 5:8
ye are all c. of light. 1 Thes 5:5

little **children**

little c. stood in door. Num 16:27
came forth little c. and. 2 Ki 2:23
one day to destroy little c. Esth 3:13
slay utterly maids, little c. Ezek 9:6
and become as little c. Mat 18:3
were brought to him little c. 19:13
suffer little c. to come. 14
Mark 10:14; Luke 18:16
little c. yet a little while. John 13:33
my little c. of whom. Gal 4:19
my little c. I write. 1 John 2:1, 12, 13
are of God, little c. and have. 4:4
little c. keep from idols. 5:21

children *of men*

tower which c. of men. Gen 11:5
if they be c. of men. 1 Sam 26:19
with stripes of c. of men. 2 Sam 7:14
hearts of c. of men. 1 Ki 8:39
2 Chr 6:30
eye-lids try the c. of men. Ps 11:4
fail from among c. of men. 12:1
down upon c. of men. 14:2; 53:2
c. of men put their trust. 36:7
thou art fairer than c. of men. 45:2
sayest, return ye c. of men. 90:3
works to c. of men. 107:8, 15, 21, 31
earth given to c. of men. 115:16
then hearts of c. of men. Pr 15:11
nor grieve c. of men. Lam 3:33
wherever c. of men dwell. Dan 2:38

men-**children**

saved men-c. alive. Ex 1:17, 18
all the men-c. shall appear. 34:23
the male c. of Manasseh. Josh 17:2

men, women, and **children**

destroyed m. w. and c. Deut 3:6
gather m. w. and c. to hear. 31:12
smote Nob, m. w. and c. and.
1 Sam 22:19
congregation of m. w. and c.
Ezra 10:1
to Gedaliah m. w. and c. Jer 40:7
about 5000 m. beside w. and c.
Mat 14:21; 15:38

my **children**

my wives and my c. for. Gen 30:26
these c. are my c. these cattle. 31:43
me ye have bereaved of my c. 42:36
if I be bereaved of my c. I. 43:14
the first-born of my c. Ex 13:15
love my master, wife, and my c. 21:5
for my wives and my c. 1 Ki 20:7
that I were as when my c. Job 29:5
seeing I have lost my c. Isa 49:21
my c. are gone forth of. Jer 10:20
my c. are desolate. Lam 1:16
thou hast slain my c.? Ezek 16:21
trouble me not, my c. Luke 11:7
I speak as to my c. 2 Cor 6:13
joy to hear that my c. walk. 3 John 4

no **children**

Abram's wife bare him no c.
Gen 16:1
Rachel saw that she bare no c. 30:1
died, and had no c. Num 3:4
but Hannah had no c. 1 Sam 1:2
man die having no c. Mat 22:24
Mark 12:19
seven left no c. Luke 20:31

our **children**

riches are ours and our c. Gen 31:16
to kill us, and our c. Ex 17:3
our wives and our c. be. Num 14:3
belong to us and to our c.
Deut 29:29
your c. speak to our c. Josh 22:24
your c. make our c. cease from. 25
brethren, our c. as their c. Neh 5:5
blood be on us and our c. Mat 27:25

children *of promise*

c. of prom. are counted. Rom 9:8
Isaac was, are c. of prom. Gal 4:28

strange **children**

deliver me from strange c. Ps 144:7†
11†
have begotten strange c. Hos 5:7

their **children**

to daughters or their c. Gen 31:43
they may teach their c. Deut 4:10
might be well with their c. 5:29
that their c. may learn to. 31:13
and their c. them Joshua. Josh 5:7
of their c. did Solomon. 1 Ki 9:21
wilt dash their c. and. 2 Ki 8:12
burnt their c. in the fire to. 17:31
their c. served images as did. 41
with wives and their c. 2 Chr 20:13
he slew not their c. but did. 25:4
their c. thou multipliedst. Neh 9:23
their c. spake half in the. 13:24
their c. dance. Job 21:11
yieldeth food for their c. 24:5
not hide them from their c. Ps 78:4
and declare them to their c. 6
let thy glory appear to their c. 90:16
their c. shall sit on thy. 132:12
their c. shall be dashed. Isa 13:16
whilst their c. remember. Jer 17:2
therefore deliver up their c. 18:21
their c. also shall be as. 30:20
iniquity into bosom of their c. 32:18
for good of them and of their c. 39
shall not look back to their c. 47:3
have sodden their c. Lam 4:10
I said to their c. in. Ezek 20:18
when they had slain their c. 23:39
they and their c. shall. 37:25
cast them and their c. Dan 6:24
though bring up their c. Hos 9:12
c. tell their c. and their c. Joel 1:3
from their c. have ye taken. Mi 2:9
yea, their c. shall see it. Zech 10:7
they shall live with their c. 9
fulfilled to us their c. Acts 13:33
deacons rule their c. 1 Tim 3:12
to love husbands and their c. Tit 2:4

thy **children**

first-born among thy c. Ex 13:13
well with thy c. Deut 4:40; 12:25, 28
teach them diligently to thy c. 6:7
thou and thy c. shall obey. 30:2
be thine and thy c. for. Josh 14:9
are here all thy c.? 1 Sam 16:11
if thy c. take heed to. 1 Ki 2:4
that thy c. heed. 8:25; 2 Chr 6:16
wives also and thy c. 1 Ki 20:3
live thou and thy c. 2 Ki 4:7
thy c. of fourth generation. 10:30
smite thy people and c. 2 Chr 21:14
if thy c. have sinned. Job 8:4
instead of fathers shall be thy c.
Ps 45:16
against generation of thy c. 73:15
thy c. like olive-plants. 128:3
if thy c. will keep my. 132:12
he hath blessed thy c. 147:13
thy c. shall make haste. Isa 49:17
and I will save thy c. 25
thy c. shall be taught of Lord, great shall be peace of thy c. 54:13
thy c. have forsaken me. Jer 5:7
there is hope that thy c. shall. 31:17
they shall bring out thy c. to. 38:23
by blood of thy c. thou. Ezek 16:36
I will also forget thy c. Hos 4:6
would I have gathered thy c.
Mat 23:37; Luke 13:34
shall lay thy c. within. Luke 19:44
found of thy c. walking. 2 John 4

your **children**

when your c. shall say. Ex 12:26
wives be widows, and your c. 22:24
as inheritance for your c. Lev 25:46
beasts shall rob you of your c. 26:22
your c. shall wander. Num 14:33
your c. shall go in thither. Deut 1:39
I speak not with your c. who. 11:2
ye shall teach them your c. 19
days of your c. be multiplied. 21
generation to come of your c. 29:22
ye shall command your c. 32:46
when your c. ask. Josh 4:6, 21
then ye shall let your c. know. 22
if your c. turn from. 1 Ki 9:6
an inheritance to your c. 1 Chr 28:8
Ezra 9:12
your c. shall find. 2 Chr 30:9
increase you and your c. Ps 115:14
have I smitten your c. Jer 2:20
good gifts to your c. Mat 7:11
Luke 11:13
by whom do your c. cast? Mat 12:27
weep for yourselves and your c.
Luke 23:28
for the promise is unto you and to your c. Acts 2:39
else were your c. unclean. 1 Cor 7:14
provoke not your c. to. Eph 6:4
Col 3:21

young **children**

young c. despised me. Job 19:18
the young c. ask bread. Lam 4:4
her young c. were dashed. Nah 3:10
brought young c. to him. Mark 10:13
cast out their young c. Acts 7:19

Chilion, *see* **Mahlon**

Chilmad

Ashur and C. were. Ezek 27:23

Chimham

thy servant C. 2 Sam 19:37, 38, 40
dwelt in habitation of C. Jer 41:17

chimney

be as smoke out of the c. Hos 13:3

Chios

next day over-against C. Acts 20:15

Chisleu

in the month C. Neh 1:1
ninth month C. Zech 7:1

Chittim

ships shall come from C. Num 24:24
from the land of C. Isa 23:1
pass over to C. 12
pass over the isles of C. Jer 2:10
ivory brought out of isles C.
Ezek 27:6
ships of C. shall come. Dan 11:30

Chiun

have born Moloch and C. Amos 5:26

Chloe

which are of house of C. 1 Cor 1:11

chode

Jacob was wroth, and c. Gen 31:36
people c. with Moses. Num 20:3*

choice

in c. of our sepulchres. Gen 23:6
ass's colt to the c. vine. 49:11
bring all your c. vows. Deut 12:11
Saul a c. young man. 1 Sam 9:2
c. of Israel. 2 Sam 10:9; 1 Chr 19:10
cut down c. fir-trees. 2 Ki 19:23
Isa 37:24
found 300,000 c. men. 2 Chr 25:5
for me daily six c. sheep. Neh 5:18
knowledge rather than c. gold.
Pr 8:10
revenue is better than c. silver. 19
tongue of just is as c. silver. 10:20
she is the c. one of her. S of S 6:9
they shall cut down thy c. Jer 22:7
set on a pot, fill it with c. Ezek 24:4
take the c. of the flock and burn. 5
God made c. among us. Acts 15:7

choicest

vineyard with the c. vine. Isa 5:2
thy c. valley shall be full of. 22:7

choke

deceitfulness of riches c. the word.
Mat 13:22; Mark 4:19

choked

thorns c. them. Mat 13:7
Mark 4:7; Luke 8:7
were c. in the sea. Mark 5:13
Luke 8:33†
go forth and are c. with. Luke 8:14

choler

an he-goat moved with c. Dan 8:7
south shall be moved with c. 11:11

choose, *as an act of God*

Lord doth c. shall be holy. Num 16:7
man's rod whom I shall c. 17:5

Lord did not c. you. *Deut* 7:7
place Lord shall c. 12:5, 11, 14, 18
26; 14:23, 24, 25; 15:20; 16:2, 6
7, 15, 16; 17:8, 10; 18:6; 26:2
31:11; *Josh* 9:27
king, whom Lord shall c. *Deut* 17:15
did I c. him out of. *1 Sam* 2:28
Lord and his people c. *2 Sam* 16:18
in Gibeah whom Lord did c. 21:6
city which Lord did c. *1 Ki* 14:21
God who didst c. Abram. *Neh* 9:7
teach in way he shall c. *Ps* 25:12
he shall c. our inheritance. 47:4
the Lord will yet c. Israel. *Isa* 14:1
he shall c. thee. 49:7
I also will c. their delusions. 66:4
yet c. Jerusalem. *Zech* 1:17; 2:12

choose

c. us out men, and go. *Ex* 17:9
dwell in place he shall c. *Deut* 23:16
therefore c. life, that thou. 30:19
c. this day whom you. *Josh* 24:15
c. you a man for you. *1 Sam* 17:8
let me c. 12,000 men. *2 Sam* 17:1
c. one of them. 24:12; *1 Chr* 21:10
c. one bullock. *1 Ki* 18:23, 25
c. out my words to reason. *Job* 9:14
let us c. to us judgement. 34:4
thou refuse, or whether thou c. 33
and did not c. the fear. *Pr* 1:29
the oppressor, and c. none. 3:31
refuse evil, and c. good. *Isa* 7:15, 16
to the eunuchs that c. things. 56:4
and did c. that wherein I. 65:12
c. a place, c. it at the. *Ezek* 21:19*
yet what I shall c. *Phil* 1:22

choosest, -eth, -ing

so that my soul c. *Job* 7:15
and thou c. the tongue of. 15:5
blessed is the man whom thou c. *Ps* 65:4
he c. a tree that will not. *Isa* 40:20
abomination is he that c. you. 41:24
c. rather to suffer. *Heb* 11:25

chop

break bones and c. them. *Mi* 3:3

Chorazin

woe unto thee, C. *Mat* 11:21 *Luke* 10:13

chose

wives of all which they c. *Gen* 6:2
then Lot c. him all the plain. 13:11
Moses c. able men, and. *Ex* 18:25
he c. their seed. *Deut* 4:37; 10:15
c. 30,000 mighty men. *Josh* 8:3
they c. new gods. *Judg* 5:8
the Lord who c. me. *2 Sam* 6:21
I c. no city out of all Israel to build. *1 Ki* 8:16; *2 Chr* 6:5
the Lord c. me before. *1 Chr* 28:4
I c. out their way. *Job* 29:25
and c. not the tribe of. *Ps* 78:67
but c. the tribe of Judah. 68
he c. David also his servant. 70
and c. that in which I. *Isa* 66:4
day when I c. Israel. *Ezek* 20:5
of his disciples he c. *Luke* 6:13
when he marked how they c. 14:7
c. Stephen a man full of. *Acts* 6:5
God of this people Israel c. 13:17
Paul c. Silas and departed. 15:40

chosen

his c. captains are drowned. *Ex* 15:4
him whom he hath c. *Num* 16:5
ye have c. you the Lord. *Josh* 24:22
cry to gods ye have c. *Judg* 10:14
king ye have c. *1 Sam* 8:18; 12:13
I know that thou hast c. the. 20:30
hast c. a great people. *1 Ki* 3:8
the city thou hast c. 8:44, 48
2 Chr 6:34, 38
children of Jacob his c. *1 Chr* 16:13
this hast thou c. *Job* 36:21
people he hath c. for. *Ps* 33:12
made a covenant with my c. 89:3
I have exalted one c. 19
ye children of Jacob his c. 105:6
forth his c. with gladness. 43
see the good of thy c. 106:5
had not Moses his c. stood. 23
understanding to be c. *Pr* 16:16
good name rather to be c. 22:1
drink to my people, my c. *Isa* 43:20
your name a curse to my c. 65:15
they have c. their own ways. 66:3
death shall be c. rather. *Jer* 8:3
who is a c. man. 49:19; 50:44
called, but few c. *Mat* 20:16; 22:14
elect whom he hath c. *Mark* 13:20
and Mary hath c. the. *Luke* 10:42
Have not I c. twelve? *John* 6:70
of these two thou hast c. *Acts* 1:24
for he is a c. vessel to me. 9:15
salute Rufus, c. in the. *Rom* 16:13
c. of the churches to. *2 Cor* 8:19
please him who hath c. *2 Tim* 2:4
ye are a c. generation. *1 Pet* 2:9
they are called, c. *Rev* 17:14

chosen *of God*

Christ, the c. *of God*. *Luke* 23:35
witnesses c. before *of God*. *Acts* 10:41
living stone, c. *of God*. *1 Pet* 2:4

God hath **chosen**

God hath c. to put. *Deut* 12:21
16:11
God hath c. to minister unto. 21:5
Solomon whom *God hath* c. *1 Chr* 29:1
God of our fathers *hath* c. *Acts* 22:14
God hath c. foolish things, *God hath* c. weak things. *1 Cor* 1:27
things despised *God hath* c. and. 28
God from the beginning *hath* c. *2 Thes* 2:13
hath not *God* c. the poor? *Jas* 2:5

I have **chosen**

David's sake and Jerusalem's sake *I have* c. *1 Ki* 11:13; *2 Ki* 21:7
23:27; *2 Chr* 6:6
the city which *I have* c. *1 Ki* 11:32
them to place *I have* c. *Neh* 1:9
I have c. way of. *Ps* 119:30, 173
Jacob whom *I have* c. *Isa* 41:8
I have c. thee, and not cast. 9
servant whom *I have* c. 43:10
Mat 12:18
Israel whom *I have* c. *Isa* 44:1
Jesurun whom *I have* c. 2
I have c. thee in the furnace. 48:10
this the fast *I have* c.? 58:5, 6
I have c. thee, saith. *Hag* 2:23
I know whom *I have* c. *John* 13:18
not c. me, but *I have* c. 15:16
I have c. you out of the world. 19

Lord hath **chosen**

Lord hath c. thee. *Deut* 7:6; 14:2
the *Lord hath* c. him out of. 18:5
whom *Lord hath* c. like. *1 Sam* 10:24
neither *hath* the *Lord* c. this. 16:8
the *Lord hath* not c. these. 10
them the *Lord hath* c. *1 Chr* 15:2
Lord hath c. Judah ruler. 28:4
Lord hath c. Solomon to sit. 5, 10
Lord hath c. you to. *2 Chr* 29:11
Aaron whom *he had* c. *Ps* 105:26
Lord hath c. Zion. 132:13
Lord hath c. Jacob. 135:4
families *Lord hath* c. *Jer* 33:24
Lord that *hath* c. Jerusalem. *Zech* 3:2
according as *he hath* c. *Eph* 1:4

chosen *men*

seven hundred c. *men*. *Judg* 20:16
Judah 180,000 c. *men*. *1 Ki* 12:21
2 Chr 11:1
array with 400,000 c. *men*, Jeroboam with 800,000 c. *men*. *2 Chr* 13:3
smote down the c. *men* of Israel. *Ps* 78:31*
to send c. men of. *Acts* 15:22*, 25

Christ

The anointed one. The Greek name Christos *from the word anointed. The Hebrew word was* Messiah. *The expected king and deliverer of the Jews, who expected a strong and glorious earthly king, to deliver them from oppressors and form again a great independent kingdom of the Jews. He was to be a descendant of David, and bring the whole world under his sway.*

There are many passages in the Old Testament which refer to this great deliverer under various names. Among these references are verses in Ps 22, 45, 55; Isa 9, 11, 53; Dan 2, 9; etc.

The Jews were looking for this deliverer down the ages from the time of the Captivity, and more definitely at about the time of the coming of Jesus. When he was announced as being the Christ, *or* the Messiah, *the rulers among the Jews refused to accept him largely because he and the method of his coming were so utterly different from their ideas of what the Messiah was to be. There are, however, very many verses in the Old Testament which were believed by the Jews themselves to refer to the Messiah and his coming which speak of his suffering and lowliness, etc. But their minds were shut against such ideas as these.*

In modern usage the name is used as a synonym for Jesus, *or added to that name to refer to* Jesus, *the* Christ *of the* Jews, *and the Saviour of mankind.*

see **Messiah, Jesus**

demanded where C. *Mat* 2:4
thou art C. the Son of the. 16:16
is your Master, even C. 23:8, 10
I am C. and shall deceive. 24:5
Mark 13:6; *Luke* 21:8
thou C. who smote thee. *Mat* 26:68
because ye belong to C. *Mark* 9:41
let C. descend now from. 15:32
not die, before he had seen C. *Luke* 2:26
they knew that he was C. 4:41
if he be C. the chosen of God. 23:35
saying, if thou be C. save. 39
ought not C. have suffered? 24:26
thus it behoved C. to suffer. 46
which is called C. *John* 4:25
when C. cometh no man. 7:27, 28
when C. cometh, will he do? 31
shall C. come out of Galilee? 41
C. cometh of seed of David. 42
any did confess that he was C. 9:22
we have heard that C. abideth. 12:34
he would raise up C. to. *Acts* 2:30*
made that Jesus both Lord and C. 36
God had before shewed that C. 3:18
Philip went and preached C. to. 8:5
straightway he preached C. 9:20*
alleging that C. must needs. 17:3
that C. should suffer. 26:23
in due time C. died for. *Rom* 5:6
we were yet sinners C. died. 8
like as C. was raised up from. 6:4
knowing that C. being raised. 9
dead to law by the body of C. 7:4
if any have not the Spirit of C. 8:9
if C. be in you, the body is dead. 10
he that raised up C. from dead. 11
wish myself accursed from C. 9:3
of whom C. came, who is over. 5
C. is the end of the law for. 10:4
that is, to bring C. down. 6
that is, to bring up C. 7
for to this end C. died. 14:9
destroy not him for whom C. died. 15
that in these things serveth C. 18
for even C. pleased not himself. 15:3
as C. also received us. 7
of things which C. hath not. 18
I strived to preach, not where C. 20
the first-fruits of Achaia to C. 16:5
we preach C. crucified. *1 Cor* 1:23
C. the power of God. 24
ye are C. and C. is God's. 3:23
C. our passover is sacrificed. 5:7
brother perish, for whom C. 8:11
but under the law to C. 9:21
and that rock was C. 10:4
nor let us tempt C. as some. 9*
how C. died for our sins. 15:3
if C. be preached that he rose. 12
dead rise not, then is not C. 16

and if C. be not raised. 1 Cor 15:17
every man in his own order, C. 23
trust have we through C. 2 Cor 3:4
though we have known C. 5:16
what concord hath C. with? 6:15
you as a chaste virgin to C. 11:2
I live, yet not I, but C. Gal 2:20
then C. died in vain. 21
C. hath redeemed us from. 3:13
our schoolmaster, to bring us to C. 24
if ye be C. then are Abraham's. 29
heir of God through C. 4:7*
of whom I travail, till C. be. 19
the liberty wherewith C. hath. 5:1
if ye be circumcised, C. shall. 2
C. is become of no effect unto. 4
that are C. have crucified flesh. 24
ye were without C. Eph 2:12
C. may dwell in your hearts. 3:17
which is the head, even C. 4:15
ye have not so learned C. 20
as C. also loved us, and hath. 5:2
arise from the dead, and C. shall. 14
head of the wife, as C. is the head. 23
as the church is subject to C. 24
love your wives, as C. also. 25
but I speak concerning C. and. 32
in singleness of heart as to C. 6:5
some indeed preach C. Phil 1:15
the one preach C. of contention. 16
C. is preached, and I therein. 18
so now C. shall be magnified in. 20
but dung, that I may win C. 3:8
I can do all through C. who. 4:13*
world, and not after C. Col 2:8
where C. sitteth on the right. 3:1
when C. who is our life shall. 4
bond nor free, but C. is all. 11
even as C. forgave you. 13*
for ye serve the Lord C. 24
but C. as a son. Heb 3:6
so also C. glorified not himself. 5:5
C. being come an high-priest. 9:11
C. not entered into holy place. 24
C. was once offered to bear the. 28
because C. also suffered. 1 Pet 2:21
C. hath once suffered for sins. 3:18
C. suffered for us in the flesh. 4:1
of our Lord and his C. Rev 11:15
now is come power of his C. 12:10

against **Christ**

gathered *against* his C. Acts 4:26*
sin against brethren ye sin *against* C. 1 Cor 8:12
wax wanton *against* C. 1 Tim 5:11

by **Christ**

consolation aboundeth *by* C. 2 Cor 1:5
seek to be justified *by* C. Gal 2:17
glory in church *by* C. Jesus. Eph 3:21

for **Christ**

for C. sent me not to. 1 Cor 1:17
fools *for* C. sake, ye are wise in C. 4:10
are ambassadors *for* C. 2 Cor 5:20
pleasure in distresses *for* C. 12:10
as God *for* C. sake hath. Eph 4:32
those I counted loss *for* C. Phil 3:7
patient waiting *for* C. 2 Thes 3:5

Jesus with **Christ**

Jesus, who is called C. Mat 1:16
27:17, 22
truth came by *Jesus* C. John 1:17
know thee, and *Jesus* C. 17:3
baptized in name of *Jesus* C. Acts 2:38
in the name of *Jesus* C. rise up. 3:6
shall send *Jesus* C. who was. 20
by the name of *Jesus* C. doth. 4:10
ceased not to preach *Jesus* C. 5:42
Philip preaching things concerning *Jesus* C. they were baptized. 8:12
I believe that *Jesus* C. is the. 37*
Jesus C. maketh thee whole. 9:34
preaching peace by *Jesus* C. 10:36
in name of *Jesus* C. come out. 16:18
Jesus I preach to you is C. 17:3
to the Jews that *Jesus* was C. 18:5
the scriptures that *Jesus* was C. 28
should believe on C. *Jesus*. 19:4*
Paul a servant of *Jesus* C. Rom 1:1
Phil 1:1
concerning Son *Jesus* C. Rom 1:3*
the called of *Jesus* C. 6
through *Jesus* C. for you all. 8
secrets of men by *Jesus* C. 2:16
which is by faith of *Jesus* C. 3:22
through redemption in *Jesus* C. 24
which is by one man *Jesus* C. 5:15
reign in life by one *Jesus* C. 17
were baptized into *Jesus* C. 6:3
to them that are in C. *Jesus*. 8:1
Spirit of life in C. *Jesus* hath. 2
my helpers in C. *Jesus*. 16:3
Paul apostle of *Jesus* C. 1 Cor 1:1
2 Cor 1:1; Eph 1:1
call on the name of *Jesus* C. 1 Cor 1:2
grace given you by *Jesus* C. 4
but of him are ye in C. *Jesus*. 30
save *Jesus* C. crucified. 2:2
for in C. *Jesus* have I begotten. 4:15
knowledge of God in *Jesus* C. 2 Cor 4:6
us to himself by *Jesus* C. 5:18
how that *Jesus* C. is in you. 13:5
by the faith of *Jesus* C. Gal 2:16
the Gentiles through *Jesus* C. 3:14
for ye are all one in C. *Jesus*. 28
an angel, even as C. *Jesus*. 4:14
heavenly places in C. *Jesus*. Eph 2:6
Jesus C. the chief corner stone. 20
I long after you in *Jesus* C. Phil 1:8
which was also in C. *Jesus*. 2:5
Jesus C. is Lord, to glory of. 2:11
all the things which are *Jesus* C. 21
loss for excellency of C. *Jesus*. 3:8
I am apprehended of C. *Jesus*. 12
riches in glory by C. *Jesus*. 4:19
have received C. *Jesus* so. Col 2:6
C. *Jesus* came to save. 1 Tim 1:15
one mediator, man C. *Jesus*. 2:5
before C. *Jesus* who witnessed. 6:13
grace given us in C. *Jesus*. 2 Tim 1:9
love, which is in C. *Jesus*. 13
prisoner of *Jesus* C. Philem 1, 9, 23
Jesus C. same yesterday. Heb 13:8
blood of *Jesus* C. 1 John 1:7*
an advocate, *Jesus* C. the. 2:1
by water and blood, *Jesus* C. 5:6
even in his Son *Jesus* C. 20

Lord Jesus **Christ**

believed on the L. J. C. Acts 11:17
through the grace of L. J. C. 15:11
believe on the L. J. C. 16:31*
faith toward our L. J. C. 20:21
peace with God through L. J. C. Rom 5:1
joy in God, through our L. J. C. 11
eternal life through our L. J. C. 6:23
love of God in C. J. our L. 8:39
put ye on L. J. C. and make. 13:14
grace of L. J. C. be with. 16:20, 24*
2 Cor 13:14; Gal 6:18
2 Thes 3:18; Rev 22:21
for coming of L. J. C. 1 Cor 1:7
but to us one L. J. C. by whom. 8:6
victory through our L. J. C. 15:57
any man love not the L. J. C. 16:22
and peace from L. J. C. 2 Cor 1:2
Gal 1:3; Eph 1:2; Col 1:2*
know grace of our L. J. C. 2 Cor 8:9
in cross of our L. J. C. Gal 6:14
Father of our L. J. C. Eph 1:3
God of our L. J. C. give you. 17
of hope in our L. J. C. 1 Thes 1:3
joy in presence of our L. J. C. 2:19
at coming of our L. J. C. 3:13
unto coming of our L. J. C. 5:23
by coming of L. J. C. 2 Thes 2:1
now our L. J. C. hath given us. 16
charge before L. J. C. 1 Tim 5:21
2 Tim 4:1
the L. J. C. be with thy. 2 Tim 4:22
into kingdom of L. J. C. 2 Pet 1:11
in knowledge of L. J. C. 3:18

in **Christ**

concerning the faith *in* C. Acts 24:24
I say the truth *in* C. Rom 9:1
many are one body *in* C. 12:5
of note, who also were *in* C. 16:7
salute Urbane, our helper *in* C. 9
salute Apelles approved *in* C. 10
even as unto babes *in* C. 1 Cor 3:1
fools, but ye are wise *in* C. 4:10
10,000 instructors *in* C. not. 15
fallen asleep *in* C. 1 Cor 15:18
in this life only hope *in* C. 19
even so *in* C. shall all be made. 22
stablisheth us *in* C. 2 Cor 1:21
causeth us to triumph *in* C. 2:14
speak we *in* C. 17
vail is done away *in* C. 3:14
if any man be *in* C. he is. 5:17
that God was *in* C. reconciling. 19
we pray you *in* C. stead. 20
I knew a man *in* C. above. 12:2
we speak before God, *in* C. 19
to churches of Judea *in* C. Gal 1:22
confirmed before of God *in* C. 3:17*
as have been baptized *into* C. 27
spiritual blessings *in* C. Eph 1:3
gather in one all things *in* C. 10
his glory, who first trusted *in* C. 12
which he wrought *in* C. 20
partakers of his promise *in* C. 3:6
bonds *in* C. are manifest. Phil 1:13
if there be any consolation *in* C. 2:1
stedfastness of faith *in* C. Col 2:5
dead *in* C. shall rise. 1 Thes 4:16
I speak the truth *in* C. 1 Tim 2:7
good conversation *in* C. 1 Pet 3:16

is **Christ**

say, lo, here *is* C. Mat 24:23
Mark 13:21
C. *is* the son of David. Mark 12:35
Luke 20:41
Saviour who *is* C. the. Luke 2:11
he himself *is* C. a king. 23:2
others said, this *is* the C. John 7:41
proving this *is* very C. Acts 9:22
Jesus whom I preach you *is* C. 17:3
it *is* C. that died, yea. Rom 8:34
is C. divided? 1 Cor 1:13
being free, *is* C.'s servant. 7:22
the head of every man *is* C. 11:3
many are one body, so *is* C. 12:12
dead rise not, then *is* C. 15:13, 16
but now is C. risen from dead. 20
trust that he *is* C. 2 Cor 10:7
is therefore C. the? Gal 2:17
to thy seed, which *is* C. 3:16
for me to live *is* C. Phil 1:21
which *is* C. in you the hope. Col 1:27

of **Christ**

in prison works *of* C. Mat 11:2
what think you *of* C.? 22:42
have not the Spirit *of* C. Rom 8:9
separate us from love *of* C.? 35
before judgement seat *of* C. 14:10*
lest cross *of* C. be made. 1 Cor 1:17
we have the mind *of* C. 2:16
bodies are members *of* C. 6:15
cup, communion of blood *of* C. bread, communion of body *of* C. 10:16
followers of me, as I am *of* C. 11:1
the head *of* C. is God. 3
now ye are the body *of* C. 12:27
as the sufferings *of* C. 2 Cor 1:5
forgave it in the person *of* C. 2:10
a sweet savour *of* C. 15
ye are the epistles *of* C. 3:3
light of glorious gospel *of* C. 4:4
love *of* C. constraineth us. 5:14
they are the glory *of* C. 8:23
meekness and gentleness *of* C. 10:1
thought to the obedience *of* C. 5
as the truth *of* C. is in me. 11:10
power of C. may rest on me. 12:9
Rev 12:10
ye seek a proof *of* C. 2 Cor 13:3
not be servant *of* C. Gal 1:10
be justified by the faith *of* C. 2:16
persecution for the cross *of* C. 6:12
nigh by the blood *of* C. Eph 2:13
knowledge in mystery *of* C. 3:4
preach unsearchable riches *of* C. 8
know the love *of* C. which. 19
the measure of the gift *of* C. 4:7
inheritance in the kingdom *of* C. 5:5
as servants *of* C. doing. 6:6
offence till day *of* C. Phil 1:10
it is given in behalf *of* C. 29
rejoice in the day *of* C. 2:16
for work *of* C. he was nigh to. 30
enemies of the cross *of* C. 3:18
fill up afflictions *of* C. Col 1:24
mystery of Father, and *of* C. 2:2
shadow, but the body is *of* C. 17

let the word *of C.* dwell in. *Col* 3:16
to speak the mystery *of C.* 4:3
nameth the name *of C.* *2 Tim* 2:19*
we are partakers *of C.* if. *Heb* 3:14
how much more blood *of C* 9:14
reproach *of C.* greater. 11:26
what time Spirit *of C.* *1 Pet* 1:11
redeemed with blood *of C.* 19
partakers *of C.* sufferings. 4:13
reproached for name *of C.* 14
priests of God and *of C.* *Rev* 20:6

that **Christ**

if be not *that* C. nor Elias. *John* 1:25
we are sure thou art *that C.* 6:69*

the **Christ**

tell no man he was *the C.* *Mat* 16:20
tell whether thou be *the C.* 26:63
thou art *the C.* *Mark* 8:29
art thou *the C.* the Son of ? 14:61
whether he were *the C.* *Luke* 3:15
thou art *the C.* of God. 9:20
art thou *the C.*? tell us. 22:67
confessed, I am not *the C.* *John* 1:20
the Messias, which is *the C.* 41
I said, I am not *the C.* but. 3:28
is not this *the C.*? 4:29
this is indeed *the C.* 42; 7:26
others said, this is *the C.* but. 7:41
if thou be the *C.* tell us. 10:24
I believe thou art *the C.* 11:27
believe that Jesus is *the C.* 20:31
denieth that Jesus is *the C.*
1 John 2:22
whoso believeth Jesus is *the C.* 5:1

with **Christ**

if we be dead *with C.* *Rom* 6:8
then joint-heirs *with C.* 8:17
crucified *with C.* I live, C. *Gal* 2:20
quickened us together *with C.*
Eph 2:5
to depart and be *with C.* *Phil* 1:23
if ye be dead *with C.* *Col* 2:20
if ye be risen *with C.* seek. 3:1
and your life is hid *with C.* 3
and they reigned *with C.* *Rev* 20:4

christian, -s

disciples first called *c.* *Acts* 11:26
almost persuadest me to be *c.* 26:28
any man suffer as a *c.* not. *1 Pet* 4:16

christs

there shall arise false *c.* *Mat* 24:24
Mark 13:22

chronicles

acts of Jeroboam are in *c.* *1 Ki* 14:19
put in the account of *c.* *1 Chr* 27:24
book of the records of *c.* *Esth* 6:1

see **book**

chrysolite

(*A semi-precious stone of a yellow or green colour*)
seventh foundation *c.* *Rev* 21:20

chrysoprasus

(*A light green chalcedony*)
tenth foundation of city was a *c.*
Rev 21:20

church

[1] *The body of Christians in general.* [2] *A body of Christians with the same general creed and under the same ecclesiastical authority.* [3] *Any body of worshippers of God, as the* Jewish church, Acts 7:38.

rock I will build my *c.* *Mat* 16:18
tell it to *c.* if he neglect to hear *c.*
18:17
Lord added to *c.* daily. *Acts* 2:47
fear came on all the *c.* and as. 5:11
great persecution against *c.* 8:1
assembled themselves with *c.* 11:26
ordained elders in every *c.* 14:23
gathered the *c.* together. 27
brought on way by the *c.* 15:3
it pleased elders with whole *c.* 22
gone up and saluted the *c.* 18:22
greet the *c.* that is in. *Rom* 16:5
every where, in every *c.* *1 Cor* 4:17
prophesieth edifieth the *c.* 14:4
except interpret that the *c.* may. 5
if the *c.* be come together. 23
salute you, with *c.* that is. 16:19
head over all to the *c.* *Eph* 1:22
might be known by the *c.* the. 3:10
as the *c.* is subject to Christ. 5:24
Christ loved the *c.* and gave. 25
present to himself a glorious *c.* 27
even as the Lord the *c.* 29
speak concerning Christ and *c.* 32
persecuting the *c.* *Phil* 3:6
no *c.* communicated with me. 4:15
head of the body the *c.* *Col* 1:18
body's sake, which is the *c.* 24
salute the *c.* which is in. 4:15
let not the *c.* be charged. *1 Tim* 5:16
Paul a prisoner, to *c.* in. *Philem* 2
to *c.* of the first-born in. *Heb* 12:23
the *c.* at Babylon. *1 Pet* 5:13
witness of thy charity before *c.*
3 John 6
I wrote unto *c.* but Diotrephes. 9

in the **church**

is he that was *in the c.* *Acts* 7:38
prophets *in the c.* at Antioch. 13:1
least esteemed *in the c.* *1 Cor* 6:4
ye come together *in the c.* 11:18
God hath set some *in the c.* 12:28
yet *in the c.* I had rather. 14:19
let him keep silence *in the c.* 28
for women to speak *in the c.* 35
to him be glory *in the c.* *Eph* 3:21
it to be read *in the c.* *Col* 4:16

of the **church**

made havock *of the c.* *Acts* 8:3
tidings came to ears *of the c.* 11:22
Herod vexed certain *of the c.* 12:1
prayer was made *of the c.* unto. 5
they were received *of the c.* 15:4
called the elders *of the c.* 20:17
a servant *of the c.* *Rom* 16:1
mine host and *of the* whole *c.* 23
excel to edifying *of the c.* *1 Cor* 14:12
Christ is head *of the c.* *Eph* 5:23
In midst *of the c.* I will. *Heb* 2:12
call for elders *of the c.* *Jas* 5:14
casteth them out *of the c.* *3 John* 10
angel *of the c.* of Ephesus. *Rev* 2:1
of the c. in Smyrna. 8
of the c. in Pergamos. 12
of the c. in Thyatira. 18
of the c. of Sardis. 3:1
of the c. in Philadelphia. 7
of the c. of the Laodiceans. 14

church *of God*

feed the *c. of God.* *Acts* 20:28
to the *c. of God* which. *1 Cor* 1:2
none offence to *c. of God.* 10:32
or despise ye the *c. of God.* 11:22
I persecuted *c. of God.* 15:9
Gal 1:13
care of the *c. of God*? *1 Tim* 3:5

churches

then had the *c.* rest. *Acts* 9:31
through Syria confirming the *c.* 15:41
so were the *c.* established. 16:5
who are neither robbers of *c.* 19:37*
to whom all *c.* of. *Rom* 16:4
salute one another, the *c.* of. 16
so ordain I in all *c.* *1 Cor* 7:17
neither *c.* of Christ. 11:16
author of peace as in all *c.* 14:33
women keep silence in the *c.* 34
as I have given order to *c.* 16:1
c. of Asia salute you. 19
the grace bestowed on *c.* *2 Cor* 8:1
who was chosen of the *c.* to. 19
are the messengers of the *c.* 23
I robbed other *c.* taking. 11:8
upon me daily care of all *c.* 28
wherein ye were inferior to *c.*? 12:13
unknown by face to *c.* of. *Gal* 1:22
followers of *c.* of God. *1 Thes* 2:14
glory in you in the *c.* *2 Thes* 1:4
John to the seven *c.* in. *Rev* 1:4
send it to the seven *c.* which. 11
angels of the seven *c.* and seven candlesticks are the seven *c.* 20
hear what Spirit saith unto *c.* 2:7
11, 17, 29; 3:6, 13, 22
c. know I am he which. 2:23
testify these things in the *c.* 22:16

churl

nor shall the *c.* be said. *Isa* 32:5
instruments also of the *c.* are. 7

churlish

man Nabal was *c.* and. *1 Sam* 25:3

churning

surely the *c.* of milk. *Pr* 30:33

Chushan-rishathaim

Israel into the hand of *C.* *Judg* 3:8

Chuza

Joanna wife of *C.* *Luke* 8:3

cieled (ceiled)

he *c* the greater house. *2 Chr* 3:5
it is *c.* with cedar and. *Jer* 22:14
to dwell in your *c.* houses. *Hag* 1:4

cieling (ceiling)

built walls of house with *c.* *1 Ki* 6:15

Cilicia

they of *C.* disputed with. *Acts* 6:9
which are of Gentiles in *C.* 15:23
through *C.* confirming the. 41
of Tarsus, a city in *C.* 21:39; 22:3
23:34
sailed over the sea of *C.* 27:5
into the regions of *C.* *Gal* 1:21

cinnamon

take of sweet *c.* half so. *Ex* 30:23
my bed with aloes and *c.* *Pr* 7:17
an orchard of calamus and *c.*
S of S 4:14
her merchandise of *c.* *Rev* 18:13

circle

he that sitteth on the *c.* *Isa* 40:22

circuit, -s

from year to year in *c.* *1 Sam* 7:16
he walked in the *c.* of. *Job* 22:14†
c. and his *c.* from ends. *Ps* 19:6
again according to his *c.* *Eccl* 1:6

circumcise

ye shall *c.* the flesh of. *Gen* 17:11
c. therefore fore-skin. *Deut* 10:16
the Lord thy God will *c.* 30:6
c. again children of Israel. *Josh* 5:2
this is cause why Joshua did *c.* 4
c. yourselves to the Lord. *Jer* 4:4
day they came to *c.* *Luke* 1:59
ye on the sabbath-day *c.* *John* 7:22
it was needful to *c.* them. *Acts* 15:5
that they ought not to *c.* 21:21

circumcised

every man-child be *c.* *Gen* 17:10
whose flesh is not *c.* that soul. 14
and Abraham *c.* the flesh of their. 23
in that day Abraham was *c.* 26
that every male of you be *c.* 34:15
every male was *c.* 24; *Ex* 12:48
Joshua *c.* children of. *Josh* 5:3
because they had not *c.* them. 7
will punish all *c.* with. *Jer* 9:25
except ye be *c.* ye. *Acts* 15:1, 24
Paul *c.* Timothy because. 16:3
that believe, though not *c.* *Rom* 4:11
c. let him not become uncircumcised, in uncircumcision not be *c.*
1 Cor 7:18
neither Titus be *c.* *Gal* 2:3
if *c.* Christ profit you nothing. 5:2
constrain you to be *c.* lest. 6:12
they that are *c.* kept not the law. 13
c. the eighth day. *Phil* 3:5
in whom also ye are *c.* *Col* 2:11

circumcising

when they had done *c.* *Josh* 5:8
accomplished for *c.* child. *Luke* 2:21

circumcision

(*Literally, the cutting off of the prepuce, a religious rite of the Jews. Metaphorically, the purifying spiritually. Since all male Jews must by law be circumcised, the word is often used to mean the Jews in distinction from Gentiles. In this case also it is used metaphorically*)

Moses gave unto you *c.* *John* 7:22
if man on sabbath-day receive *c.* 23
c. profiteth, if thou keep law; if break law, *c.* is made. *Rom* 2:25
nor is that *c.* which is outward. 28
and *c.* is that of the heart. 29
who shall justify the *c.* 3:30
blessedness then on *c.* only? 4:9
when he was in *c.*? not in *c.* 10

c is the keeping of the. 1 Cor 7:19
they should go unto the c. Gal 2:9
in Jesus Christ neither c. 5:6; 6:15
brethren, if I yet preach c. 5:11
that which is called c. Eph 2:11
we are the c. which. Phil 3:3
c. without hands, by c. of. Col 2:11
neither c. nor uncircumcision. 3:11

of circumcision

bloody husband, because of c. Ex 4:26
Abraham covenant of c. Acts 7:8
they of c. which believed. 10:45
they of the c. contended with. 11:2
what profit is there of c.? Rom 3:1
he received the sign of c. a. 4:11
father of c. to them not of c. 12
Jesus Christ a minister of c. 15:8
as the gospel of c. was. Gal 2:7
Peter to apostleship of the c. 8
who are of c. salute you. Col 4:11
especially they of the c. Tit 1:10

circumspect

I have said to you, be c. Ex 23:13*

circumspectly

see that ye walk c. not as. Eph 5:15*

cistern

(An artificial reservoir, built of rock or brick, excavated in the rock to hold rain water. Many of the houses had their own private cisterns, provided with a bucket and windlass (Eccl. 12:6) and filled as are ours by water conducted to them from the roof)

drink ye waters of his c. 2 Ki 18:31
waters out of thine own c. Pr 5:15
wheel broken at the c. Eccl 12:6
drink waters of own c. Isa 36:16

cisterns

hewed out c. broken c. Jer 2:13

cities

destroyed the c. of the. Gen 19:29
terror of God upon the c. 35:5
laid up food in the c. 41:48
people removed to the c. 47:21
the c. of the Levites. Lev 25:32
what c. they be that. Num 13:19
every one shall give of his c. 35:8
nor camest thou to c. Deut 2:37
c. thereof gave I to Reubenites. 3:12
abide in your c. which I have. 19
to give thee great and goodly c. 6:10
flee to one of these c. 19:5
Israel came to their c. Josh 9:17
not to enter into their c. 10:19
as for the c. that stood still in. 11:13
described it by c. into seven. 18:9
buried in one of the c. Judg 12:7
set fire on all the c. they. 20:48
they repaired the c. 21:23
Israelites forsook the c. 1 Sam 31:7
for the c. of our God. 2 Sam 10:12
1 Chr 19:13
from Tyre to see the c. 1 Ki 9:12
what c. are these that thou? 13
the c. my father took I will. 20:34
Jair had 23 c. in the. 1 Chr 2:22
these were their c. to the. 4:31
so did he in the c. of. 2 Chr 34:6
Israelites were in their c. Ezra 3:1
Neh 7:73
nine parts dwell in other c. Neh 11:1
dwelleth in desolate c. Job 15:28
thou hast destroyed c. Ps 9:6
answered, till c. be wasted. Isa 6:11
nor fill face of world with c. 14:21
in that day shall five c. in. 19:18
he hath despised the c. he. 33:8
thy holy c. are a wilderness. 64:10
his c. are burnt. Jer 2:15
according to thy c. 28; 11:13
c. of south be shut up. 13:19
that man be as the c. which. 20:16
turn again to these thy c. 31:21
all the c. thereof shall be. 49:13
I will kindle fire in his c. 50:32
like the c. that are not. Ezek 26:19
and these c. shall go into. 30:17
thy c. shall not return. 35:9
I will send fire upon his c. Hos 8:14
sword shall abide on his c. 11:6
two or three c. wandered. Amos 4:8
I will cut off the c. of. Mi 5:11
so will I destroy thy c. 14
their c. are destroyed. Zeph 3:6
my c. by prosperity shall. Zech 1:17
not have gone over c. Mat 10:23
teach and preach in their c. 11:1
persecuted them even to strange c. Acts 26:11
turning c. of Sodom and. 2 Pet 2:6
and c. about them in like. Jude 7
the c. of the nations. Rev 16:19

all cities

took all these c. and dwelt in c. Num 21:25; Deut 2:34; 3:4
Josh 10:39
they burnt all their c. Num 31:10
Judg 20:48
all c. of Levites 48 c. Num 35:7
thus do to all c. Deut 20:15
all the c. of the kings. Josh 11:12
all c. of Aaron were 13 c. 21:19
all c. of Gershonites were 13 c. 33
all c. of Merari by lot 12 c. 40
all c. of Levites were 48 c. 41
women came out of all c. 1 Sam 18:6
thus did he to all c. 2 Sam 12:31
they came to all the c. of. 24:7
all c. Ahab built are. 1 Ki 22:39
Asa smote all the c. 2 Chr 14:14
tithes in all the c. of. Neh 10:37
all the c. thereof were. Jer 4:26
in all c. thereof an habitation. 33:12
save thee in all thy c. Hos 13:10
preached in all c. till he. Acts 8:40

defenced cities

against the defenced c. Isa 36:1
lay waste the defenced c. 37:26
let us go into defenced c. Jer 4:5
8:14
these defenced c. remained. 34:7

fenced cities

dwell in the fenced c. Num 32:17
all these c. were fenced. Deut 3:5
c. fenced to heaven. 9:1; Josh 14:12
entered into fenced c. Josh 10:20
lest he get him fenced c. 2 Sam 20:6
Shishak took fenced c. 2 Chr 12:4
Asa built fenced c. in Judah. 14:6
forces in the fenced c. 17:2
through all fenced c. of. 19:5
gave his sons fenced c. in. 21:3
impoverish thy fenced c. Jer 5:17
take the most fenced c. Dan 11:15
Judah multiplied fenced c. Hos 8:14
alarm against fenced c. Zeph 1:16

cities of Judah

to any of c. of Judah. 2 Sam 2:1
incense in c. of Judah. 2 Ki 23:5
gave the c. of Judah. 1 Chr 6:57
to teach in c. of Judah. 2 Chr 17:7
business in c. of Judah. 13
set judges in c. of Judah. 19:5
Levites out of all c. of Judah. 23:2
Israel in the c. of Judah. 31:6
of war in c. of Judah. 33:14
in c. of Judah each dwelt. Neh 11:3
Zion, build c. of Judah. Ps 69:35
say to the c. of Judah. Isa 40:9
and that saith to c. of Judah. 44:26
north against c. of Judah. Jer 1:15
against the c. of Judah. 4:16
do in the c. of Judah. 7:17
c. of Judah desolate. 9:11; 10:22
34:22
shall c. of Judah go and cry. 11:12
witness in the c. of Judah. 32:44
even in the c. of Judah. 33:10
in c. of Judah shall flocks pass. 13
anger kindled in c. of Judah. 44:6
incense burnt in c. of Judah. 21
maids in the c. of Judah. Lam 5:11
mercy on the c. of Judah. Zech 1:12

cities of refuge

six c. for refuge. Num 35:6, 13, 14
appoint c. of refuge. 11; Josh 20:2
of Kohath of c. of refuge. 1 Chr 6:67

six cities

six c. for refuge. Num 35:6, 13, 15
mountains of Judah six c. Josh 15:59

cities with suburbs

the suburbs of their c. Lev 25:34
to Levites suburbs for c. Num 35:2
Levites c. and suburbs. Josh 21:3
c. of Levites 48 with suburbs. 41

cities with villages

c. and country villages. 1 Sam 6:18
houses in c. and villages. 1 Chr 27:25
all the c. and villages teaching and preaching. Mat 9:35; Luke 13:22
entered into villages or c. Mark 6:56

cities with waste

make your c. waste. Lev 26:31, 33
waste c. desolations. Isa 61:4
c. shall be laid waste. Jer 4:7
dwellings your c. shall be waste. Ezek 6:6
laid waste their c. 19:7
I will lay thy c. waste. 35:4
waste c. are become fenced. 36:35
so shall waste c. be filled. 38
shall build thy waste c. Amos 9:14

your cities

your c. are burnt with fire. Isa 1:7
and dwell in your c. Jer 40:10
cleanness of teeth in your c. Amos 4:6

citizen, -s

joined himself to a c. Luke 15:15
his c. hated him, and sent. 19:14
I am of Tarsus, a c. of. Acts 21:39
but fellow-c. with saints. Eph 2:19

city

(In Hebrew usage, a collection of permanent human habitations, whether many or few, especially if surrounded by a wall. The word was also used, as now, metaphorically for the people of the city)

Cain builded a c. and. Gen 4:17
let us build us a c. and a. 11:4
Lord came down to see c. and. 5
and they left off to build c. 8
fifty righteous within the c. 18:26
destroy all c. for lack of five? 28
daughters of the c. come to. 24:13
all that went out of gate of c. 34:24
came upon the c. boldly. 25
flame is gone out from c. Num 21:28
there was not one c. Deut 2:36
not one c. we took not from. 3:4
smite inhabitants of that c. 13:15
c. next to slain man take. 21:3, 6
very far from c. Adam. Josh 3:16
ye shall compass c. and go. 6:3, 7
burnt the c. with fire. 24; Deut 13:16
Josh 8:8, 19; Judg 1:8; 18:27
an ambush for c. behind it. Josh 8:2
they left the c. open, and. 17
smoke of the c. ascended up. 20
was not a c. made peace. 11:19
c. of Arba, which c. is. 15:13
they gave Joshua the c. which. 19:50
at the entry of the gate of c. 20:4
feared men of the c. Judg 6:27
Gideon slew men of the c. 8:17
and beat down the c. and. 9:45
all they of the c. fled, and. 51
flame of the c. ascended. 20:40
all the c. was moved. Ruth 1:19
for all the c. of my people. 3:11
this man went out of c. 1 Sam 1:3
when man told it, all c. cried. 4:13
deadly destruction through c. 5:11
go ye every man to his c. 8:22
1 Ki 22:36; Ezra 2:1; Neh 7:6
buried him in Ramah, his c. 1 Sam 28:3
two men in one c. one. 2 Sam 12:1
of what c. art thou? 15:2
I may die in mine own c. 19:37
seekest to destroy a c. and. 20:19
so that the c. rang again. 1 Ki 1:45
for Jerusalem's sake, c. 11:32, 36
neither is this the c. 2 Ki 6:19
and the c. was in quiet. 11:20
c. Jerusalem was. 24:10; 25:2
was destroyed of c. for. 2 Chr 15:6
judges in the land c. by c. 19:5
posts passed from c. to c. 30:10
that they might take the c. 32:18
building the rebellious c. Ezra 4:12
sad, when c. lieth waste. Neh 2:3, 5

Judah was second over *c.* *Neh* 11:9
but the *c.* Shushan. *Esth* 3:15
c. of Shushan rejoiced. 8:15
c. of the great King. *Ps* 48:2
Mat 5:35
go round about the *c.* *Ps* 59:6, 14
they of *c.* shall flourish. 72:16
they found no *c.* to dwell in. 107:4
Jerusalem is builded as a *c.* 122:3
except Lord keep the *c.* 127:1
Wisdom crieth at entry of *c.* *Pr* 8:3
wealth is his strong *c.* 10:15; 18:11
c. rejoiceth, shouting when. 11:10
by blessing of upright the *c.* 11
than he that taketh a *c.* 16:32
is like a *c.* broken down. 25:28
scornful men bring a *c.* into. 29:8
there was a little *c.* *Eccl* 9:14
poor wise man delivered the *c.* 15
c. of righteousness, faithful *c.*
Isa 1:26, 21
cry, O *c.* whole Palestina. 14:31
taken away from being a *c.* 17:1
shall fight, *c.* against *c.* 19:2
the *c.* of confusion is. 24:10
of a *c.* an heap, to be no *c.* 25:2
Zion, *c.* of our solemnities. 33:20
they shall call thee the *c.* of. 60:14
thou shalt be called a *c.* 62:12
I will take you one of a *c.* *Jer* 3:14
whole *c.* shall flee from noise. 4:29
even make this *c.* as Tophet. 19:12
to bring evil on the *c.* called. 25:29
come to the *c.* and the *c.* is. 32:24
the *c.* was broken up. 39:2; 52:7
I will destroy the *c.* and the. 46:8
c. of praise not left, *c.* of joy. 49:25
how doth *c.* sit solitary! *Lam* 1:1
c. that men called perfection? 2:15
pourtray on it the *c.* even. *Ezek* 4:1
make a chain, for the *c.* is. 7:23
them that have charge over *c.* 9:1
go through midst of *c.* Jerusalem. 4
land full of blood, the *c.* is full. 9
scatter coals of fire over *c.* 10:2
what *c.* is like Tyrus? 27:32
the *c.* is smitten. 33:21
name of the *c.* shall be. 48:35
the *c.* called by thy. *Dan* 9:18, 19
Gilead a *c.* of them. *Hos* 6:8
I caused to rain on one *c.* *Amos* 4:7
c. that went out by thousand. 5:3
Lord's voice crieth to *c.* *Mi* 6:9
him that stablisheth *c.* by. *Hab* 2:12
to polluted, oppressing *c.* *Zeph* 3:1
Jerusalem called a *c.* of. *Zech* 8:3
streets of the *c.* shall be full. 5
c. shall be taken, residue of people
shall not be cut off from *c.* 14:2
a *c.* that is set on a hill. *Mat* 5:14
Jerusalem, is *c.* of great King. 35
the whole *c.* came out to. 8:34
into whatsoever *c.* ye shall. 10:11
than for that *c.* 15; *Mark* 6:11
Luke 10:12
all the *c.* was moved. *Mat* 21:10
sent and burnt up their *c.* 22:7
persecute them from *c.* to *c.* 23:34
all *c.* was gathered. *Mark* 1:33
told it in *c.* 5:14; *Luke* 8:34
every one to his own *c.* *Luke* 2:3
much people of the *c.* was. 7:12
he beheld the *c.* and wept. 19:41
of Arimathaea, a *c.* of the. 23:51
many of that *c.* believed. *John* 4:39
great joy in that *c.* *Acts* 8:8
almost the whole *c.* to hear. 13:44
we were abiding in that *c.* 16:12
set all the *c.* in an uproar. 17:5
the whole *c.* was filled. 19:29
all the *c.* was moved, and. 21:30
he looked for a *c.* that. *Heb* 11:10
hath prepared for them a *c.* 16
ye are come to the *c.* of the. 12:22
we have no continuing *c.* 13:14
go into such a *c.* buy and. *Jas* 4:13
compassed the beloved *c.* *Rev* 20:9
wall of the *c.* had twelve. 21:14
c. was pure gold, like to. 18
c. had no need of the sun nor. 23

bloody **city**

thou judge the *bloody c.*? *Ezek* 22:2
woe to *bloody c.* 24:6, 9; *Nah* 3:1

defenced **city**

of a *defenced c.* a ruin. *Isa* 25:2
the *defenced c.* shall be. 27:10
thee this day a *defenced c.* *Jer* 1:18

city *of David*

the *c. of D.* *2 Sam* 5:9; *1 Chr* 11:7
the ark into the *c. of D.* *2 Sam* 6:10
ark into the *c. of D.* 12, 16
David buried in *c. of D.* *1 Ki* 2:10
brought her into the *c. of D.* 3:1
ark out of *c. of D.* 8:1; *2 Chr* 5:2
Solomon buried in *c. of D.*
1 Ki 11:43; *2 Chr* 9:31
Rehoboam buried in *c. of D.*
1 Ki 14:31; *2 Chr* 12:16
buried Abijam in *c. of D.* *1 Ki* 15:8
2 Chr 14:1
Jehoshaphat buried in *c. of D.*
1 Ki 22:50; *2 Chr* 21:1
Joram buried in *c. of D.* *2 Ki* 8:24
2 Chr 21:20
Ahaziah buried in *c. of D.* *2 Ki* 9:28
Jehoash buried in *c. of D.* 12:21
2 Chr 24:25
Amaziah buried in *c. of D.* *2 Ki* 14:20
Azariah buried in *c. of D.* 15:7
Jothan buried in *c. of D.* 38
2 Chr 27:9
Ahaz buried in *c. of D.* *2 Ki* 16:20
buried Jehoiada in *c. of D.* *2 Chr* 24:16
breaches of the *c. of D.* *Isa* 22:9
the *c.* where *D.* dwelt. 29:1
Joseph went into *c. of D.* *Luke* 2:4
to you is born in *c. of D.* a. 11

elders with **city**

elders of his *c.* shall. *Deut* 19:12
the *elders* of that *c.* next to. 21:6
say to the *elders* of his *c.* our. 20
spread cloth before *elders* of *c.* 22:17
elders of his *c.* shall call him. 25:8
cause to *elders* of *c.* *Josh* 20:4
Gideon took *elders* of *c.* *Judg* 8:16
ten men of *elders* of *c.* *Ruth* 4:2
them *elders* of every *c.* *Ezra* 10:14

every **city**

smote men of *every c.* *Judg* 20:48
smite *every* fenced *c.* *2 Ki* 3:19
in *every c.* Rehoboam. *2 Chr* 11:12
in *every c.* of Judah he. 28:25
of sons of Aaron in *every c.* 31:19
every c. shall be forsaken. *Jer* 4:29
spoiler come upon *every c.* 48:8
every c. divided against. *Mat* 12:25
two and two into *every c.* *Luke* 10:1
hath in *every c.* them. *Acts* 15:21
visit our brethren in *every c.* 36
witnesseth in *every c.* that. 20:23
ordain elders in *every c.* *Tit* 1:5

fenced **city**

with you a *fenced c.* *2 Ki* 10:2
watchmen to the *fenced c.* 17:9
dispersed of all his children unto
every *fenced c.* *2 Chr* 11:23

city *of God*

make glad the *c. of G.* *Ps* 46:4
to be praised in *c. of* our *G.* 48:1
c. of G. God will establish it. 8
spoken of thee, O *c. of G.* 87:3
to the *c. of* the living *G.* *Heb* 12:22
the name of *c. of* my *G.* *Rev* 3:12

great **city**

Resen, same is a *great c.* *Gen* 10:12
Gibeon was a *great c.* *Josh* 10:2
c. was large and *great.* *Neh* 7:4
done thus to this *great c.*? *Jer* 22:8
Nineveh, that *great c.* *Jonah* 1:2; 3:2
was an exceeding *great c.* 3:3
spare Nineveh that *great c.*? 4:11
bodies in streets of *great c.* *Rev* 11:8
that *great c.* 14:8; 18:10, 16, 19, 21
the *great c.* was divided. 16:19
the woman is that *great c.* 17:18
he shewed me that *great c.* 21:10

holy **city**

in Jerusalem the *holy c.* *Neh* 11:1
the Levites of the *holy c.* were. 18
themselves of the *holy c.* *Isa* 48:2
beautiful garments, O *holy c.* 52:1
determined on thy *holy c.* *Dan* 9:24
taketh him up into *holy c.* *Mat* 4:5
went into the *holy c.* and. 27:53
holy c. shall they tread. *Rev* 11:2
I John saw the *holy c.* coming. 21:2
his part out of the *holy c.* 22:19

in, or *into the* **city**

hast *in the c.* bring. *Gen* 19:12
all that is *in the c.* *Deut* 20:14
blessed shalt thou be *in the c.* 28:3
cursed shalt thou be *in the c.* 16
people went *into the c.* *Josh* 6:20
destroyed all that was *in the c.* 21
they entered *into the c.* and. 8:19
the entrance *into the c.* *Judg* 1:24
Gideon put the ephod *in* his *c.* 8:27
man came *into the c.* *1 Sam* 4:13
carry ark *into the c.* *2 Sam* 15:25
return *into the c.* and your. 27
and told it *in the c.* *1 Ki* 13:25
dieth of Jeroboam *in the c.* 14:11
when thy feet enter *into the c.* 12
that dieth of Baasha *in the c.* 16:4
came *into the c.* into an. 20:30
in the c. dogs eat. 21:24
we will enter *into the c.* *2 Ki* 7:4
catch them, get *into the c.* 12
brought water *into the c.* 20:20
famine prevailed *in the c.* 25:3
he hath shewed me marvellous
kindness *in* a strong *c.* *Ps* 31:21
violence and strife *in the c.* 55:9
in the c. Wisdom. *Pr* 1:21
mighty men *in the c.* *Eccl* 7:19
wicked were forgotten *in c.* 8:10
in the c. is left desolation. *Isa* 24:12
if I enter *into the c.* *Jer* 14:18
is no more bread *in the c.* 38:9
famine was sore *in the c.* 52:6
gave up the ghost *in the c.* *Lam* 1:19
in the c. famine shall. *Ezek* 7:15
went forth and slew *in the c.* 9:7
I will not enter *into the c.* *Hos* 11:9
run to and fro *in the c.* *Joel* 2:9
trumpet be blown *in the c.* shall
there be evil *in* a *c.* *Amos* 3:6
an harlot *in the c.* thy sons. 7:17
began to enter *into the c.* *Jonah* 3:4
and came *into* his own *c.* *Mat* 9:1
into any *c.* of the Samaritans. 10:5
and *into* whatsoever *c.* ye. 11
go *into the c.* to such a man. 26:18
some of watch came *into the c.* 28:11
saith, go *into the c.* *Mark* 14:13
Acts 9:6
taxed, every one *into* his *c.* *Luke* 2:3
a woman *in the c.* which. 7:37
there was *in* a *c.* a judge. 18:2
there was a widow *in* that *c.* 3
when ye are entered *into the c.* 22:10
tarry ye *in the c.* of. 24:49
were gone *into the c.* *John* 4:8
I was *in the c.* of Joppa. *Acts* 11:5
rose up and came *into the c.* 14:20
Trophimus with him *in the c.* 21:29
in synagogues nor *in the c.* 24:12
perils *in the c.* in sea. *2 Cor* 11:26
through gates *into the c.* *Rev* 22:14

city *of the Lord*

wicked doers from *c. of L.* *Ps* 101:8
call thee *c. of the L.* *Isa* 60:14

out of the **city**

were gone *out of the c.* *Gen* 44:4
as I am gone *out of the c.* *Ex* 9:29
Moses went *out of the c.* 33
them forth *out of the c.* *Lev* 14:45
side issued *out of the c.* *Josh* 8:22
man come *out of the c.* *Judg* 1:24
succour us *out of the c.* *2 Sam* 18:3
a wise woman *out of the c.* 20:16
Naboth *out of the c.* *1 Ki* 21:13
come *out of the c.* *2 Ki* 7:12
let none escape *out of the c.* 9:15
much spoil *out of the c.* *1 Chr* 20:2
cast idols *out of the c.* *2 Chr* 33:15
groan from *out of the c.* *Job* 24:12
went *out of the c.* *Jer* 39:4; 52:7
the goings *out of the c.* *Ezek* 48:30
go forth *out of the c.* *Mi* 4:10
left them, and went *out of the c.*
Mat 21:17
even was come, went *out of the c.*
Mark 11:19
thrust him *out of the c.* *Luke* 4:29
when ye go *out of* that *c.* 9:5

went out of c. and came. John 4:30
cast Stephen out of the c. Acts 7:58
Paul, drew him out of the c. 14:19
sabbath we went out of the c. 16:13
till we were out of the c. 21:5

city of refuge

restore him to c. of refuge. Num 35:25
without border of c. of refuge. 26, 27
remained in the c. of refuge. 28
fled to the c. of refuge. 32
Hebron to be a c. of refuge. Josh 21:13, 21, 27, 32, 38
of Aaron, Hebron a c. of refuge. 1 Chr 6:57

this city

Lord will destroy this c. Gen 19:14
behold now, this c. is near to. 20
I will not overthrow this c. 21
he that buildeth this c. Josh 6:26
us turn in unto this c. Judg 19:11
there is in this c. a. 1 Sam 9:6
the situation of this c. 2 Ki 2:19
this c. shall not. 18:30; Isa 36:15
not come into this c. 2 Ki 19:32, 33
Isa 37:34
I will defend this c. 2 Ki 19:34
20:6; Isa 37:35; 38:6
cast off this c. Jerusalem. 2 Ki 23:27
pray to thee toward this c. 2 Chr 6:34
if this c. be builded. Ezra 4:13, 16
this c. is a rebellious city. 15
bring evil up on this c.? Neh 13:18
this is the c. to be visited. Jer 6:6
Jerusalem, and this c. shall. 17:25
I will make this c. desolate. 19:8
break this people and this c. 11
I will bring upon this c. and. 15
the strength of this c. 20:5
he that abideth in this c. shall. 21:9
I set my face against this c. 10
Lord done thus unto this c.? 22:8
I will make this c. a curse. 26:6
innocent blood on this c. 15
should this c. be laid waste? 27:17
this c. to Chaldeans. 32:3, 28; 34:2
this c. hath been to me as a. 32:31
have hid my face from this c. 33:5
cause them to return to this c. 34:22
this c. shall not be burnt. 38:17
thou shalt cause this c. to be. 23
my words on this c. for evil. 39:16
wicked counsel in this c. Ezek 11:2
this c. is the caldron, and we. 3, 7
this c. shall not be your caldron. 11
persecute you in this c. Mat 10:23
much people in this c. Acts 18:10
I was brought up in this c. 22:3

without the city

men set him without the c. Gen 19:16
unclean place without the c. Lev 14:40, 41
measure from without c. Num 35:5
fountains without the c. 2 Chr 32:3
trodden without the c. Rev 14:20

clad

Jeroboam c. himself with. 1 Ki 11:29
for clothing was c. with. Isa 59:17

clamorous

a foolish woman is c. Pr 9:13

clamour

all anger and c. be put. Eph 4:31

clap

men shall c. hands at. Job 27:23
c. your hands, all ye. Ps 47:1
let floods c. their hands, let. 98:8
trees of the field shall c. Isa 55:12
all that pass by c. their. Lam 2:15
fruit of thee shall c. Nah 3:19

clapped

c. their hands, and said. 2 Ki 11:12
thou hast c. thine hands. Ezek 25:6

clappeth

he c. his hands among us. Job 34:37

clave
(Cut, split)

Abraham c. the wood. Gen 22:3
the ground c. asunder. Num 16:31
God c. an hollow place. Judg 15:19
they c. wood of cart. 1 Sam 6:14
c. the rocks in. Ps 78:15; Isa 48:21

clave
(Held to, clung to)

his soul c. to Dinah. Gen 34:3
but Ruth c. to her. Ruth 1:14
men of Judah c. to. 2 Sam 20:2
he smote till his hand c. to. 23:10
Solomon c. to these in. 1 Ki 11:2
for Hezekiah c. to Lord. 2 Ki 18:6
they c. to their brethren. Neh 10:29
certain men c. to Paul. Acts 17:34

claws

cleaveth cleft in two c. Deut 14:6*
nails grown like birds' c. Dan 4:33
he shall tear their c. Zech 11:16*

clay

dwell in houses of c. Job 4:19
thou hast made me as the c. 10:9
bodies are like to bodies of c. 13:12
prepare raiment as the c. 27:16
am formed out of the c. 33:6
it is turned as c. to the seal. 38:14
brought me out of miry c. Ps 40:2
esteemed as potter's c. Isa 29:16
as the potter treadeth the c. 41:25
shall the c. say to him? 45:9
we are c. thou our potter 64:8
vessel that he made of c. Jer 18:4
as c. is in the potter's hand. 6
stones, hide them in the c. 43:9*
part of iron, part c. Dan 2:33, 34, 42
c. broken in pieces. 35, 45
feet and toes part of potter's c. 41
go into c. and tread the. Nah 3:14
ladeth himself with c. Hab 2:6*
made c. of spittle, anointed eyes of blind man with c. John 9:6
he put c. on mine eyes, I see. 15
potter power over the c.? Rom 9:21

clean

not make c. riddance in. Lev 23:22
passed c. over Jordan. Josh 3:17
4:1, 11
is his mercy c. gone for? Ps 77:8
earth is c. dissolved, is. Isa 24:19
he hath made it c. bare. Joel 1:7
arm shall be c. dried up. Zech 11:17
c. escaped from them. 2 Pet 2:18

clean, *adjective*

[1] *Free from filth or dirt.* [2] *Ceremonially pure,* Lev 10:10; Acts 10:15. [3] *Metaphorically, innocent, delivered from the power of sin,* Acts 18:6; Ps 51:10; 1 John 1:9.

of every c. beast thou. Gen 7:2
of every c. beast and c. fowl. 8:20
Jacob said, be c. and change. 35:2
bullock unto c. place. Lev 4:12; 6:11
the flesh, all that be c. shall. 7:19
put difference between c. 10:10
11:47; 20:25; Ezek 22:26; 44:23
eat in c. place. Lev 10:14; Num 19:9
that ye may be c. from. Lev 16:30
not eat of holy things till he be c. 22:4
on seventh day be c. Num 19:12
a c. person shall take hyssop. 18
unclean and c. may eat. Deut 12:15
15:22
not c. surely he is not c. 1 Sam 20:26
again, and thou be c. 2 Ki 5:10, 14
I wash in them and be c.? 12
wash and be c. 13
I am c. in thine eyes. Job 11:4
who can bring a c. thing out? 14:4
man that he should be c.? 15:14
heavens are not c. in his sight. 15
how can he be c. that is? 25:4
I am c. without transgression. 33:9
the ways of a man are c. Pr 16:2
things come alike to the c. Eccl 9:2
wash ye, make you c. Isa 1:16
so that there is no place c. 28:8
and young asses shall eat c. 30:24*
be ye c. that bear the vessels. 52:11
bring an offering in a c. vessel. 66:20
wilt thou not be made c.? Jer 13:27
then will I sprinkle c. Ezek 36:25
thou canst make me c. Mat 8:2
Mark 1:40; Luke 5:12
I will, be thou c. Mat 8:3
Mark 1:41; Luke 5:13
make c. the outside. Mat 23:25
Luke 11:39
all things are c. unto you. Luke 11:41
ye are not all c. John 13:11
now ye are c. through word I. 15:3
own heads, I am c. Acts 18:6
in fine linen, c. Rev 19:8*, 14*

clean hands

make my hands ever so c. Job 9:30
he that hath c. hands shall. 17:9
he that hath c. hands and a pure heart. Ps 24:4

clean heart

create in me a c. heart. Ps 51:10
and such as are of a c. heart. 73:1*
I have made my heart c.? Pr 20:9

is clean

he is c. Lev 13:13, 17, 37, 39
yet is he c. 40, 41
spit on him that is c. 15:8
man that is c. Num 9:13; 19:9
fear of the Lord is c. Ps 19:9
no oxen are, the crib is c. Pr 14:4
wash his feet, but is c. John 13:10

pronounce clean

pronounce him c. Lev 13:6; 14:7

shall be clean

is water shall be c. Lev 11:36
she shall be c. 12:8; 15:28
it shall be c. 13:58; 14:53
Num 31:23
in water, he shall be c. Lev 14:9, 20
15:13; 17:15; 22:7; Num 19:12, 19
and ye shall be c. Num 31:24
Ezek 36:25
hyssop, and I shall be c. Ps 51:7

cleanness

to c. of my hands hath Lord.
2 Sam 22:21; Ps 18:20
to my c. in his sight. 2 Sam 22:25
Ps 18:24
I have also given you c. Amos 4:6

cleanse

shalt c. altar. Ex 29:36; Lev 16:19
to c. house, two birds. Lev 14:49, 52
take the Levites and c. Num 8:6
c. house of Lord. 2 Chr 29:15, 16
Levites should c. themselves.
Neh 13:22
c. thou me from secret. Ps 19:12*
wash me throughly, and c. 51:2
a young man c. his way? 119:9
wind not to fan nor to c. Jer 4:11
c. them from iniquity. 33:8
Ezek 37:23
from idols will I c. you. Ezek 36:25
they may c. the land. 39:12, 16
thus shalt thou c. and purge it. 43:20
a young bullock, and c. the. 45:18
I will c. their blood. Joel 3:21
heal the sick, c. lepers. Mat 10:8
c. first that which is within. 23:26
let us c. ourselves from. 2 Cor 7:1
might c. it with washing. Eph 5:26
c. your hands, ye sinners. Jas 4:8
to c. us from all. 1 John 1:9

cleansed

so shall it be c. Lev 11:32
she shall be c. from the issue. 12:7
him that is to be c. 14:4, 7, 8, 14
17, 18, 19, 25, 28, 29, 31
the land cannot be c. Num 35:33
from which we are not c. Josh 22:17
we have c. all house of. 2 Chr 29:18
many had not c. themselves. 30:18
though he be not c. 19
Josiah c. Judah and Jerusalem. 34:5
they c. the chambers. Neh 13:9
thus I c. them from strangers. 30
what profit, if I be c.? Job 35:3*
I have c. my heart in vain. Ps 73:13
the land that is not c. Ezek 22:24
after he is c. reckon to him. 44:26
then shall sanctuary be c. Dan 8:14
c. their blood I have not c. Joel 3:21
his leprosy was c. Mat 8:3
the lepers are c. 11:5; Luke 7:22
leprosy departed, and he was c.
Mark 1:42
was c. save Naaman. Luke 4:27
the lepers c., the deaf hear. 7:22
as lepers went they were c. 17:14

were there not ten c.? Luke 17:17
what God hath c. Acts 10:15; 11:9

cleanseth
wind passeth and c. them. Job 37:21
blueness of a wound c. Pr 20:30
blood of Jesus Christ c. 1 John 1:7

cleansing
of the priest for his c. Lev 13:7
shave head in day of his c. Num 6:9
go and offer for thy c. Mark 1:44
Luke 5:14

clear
thou shalt be c. from. Gen 24:8, 41
how shall we c. ourselves? 44:16
no means c. the guilty. Ex 34:7
as tender grass, by c. 2 Sam 23:4
mightest be c. when. Ps 51:4
c. as the sun, terrible as. S of S 6:10
dwelling-place like a c. Isa 18:4
darken earth in a c. day. Amos 8:9
light shall not be c. nor. Zech 14:6*
approved yourselves to be c.
2 Cor 7:11*
c. as crystal. Rev 21:11; 22:1*
city was pure gold, like to c. 21:18*

clearer
thine age shall be c. Job 11:17

clearing
and by no means c. Num 14:18
what c. of yourselves. 2 Cor 7:11

clearly
my lips shall utter knowledge c.
Job 33:3
see c. to pull out the. Mat 7:5
Luke 6:42
and saw every man c. Mark 8:25
things from creation c. Rom 1:20

clearness
body of heaven in his c. Ex 24:10

cleave
man shall c. to his wife. Gen 2:24
Mat 19:5; Mark 10:7
he shall c. it with the. Lev 1:17
ye that did c. to Lord. Deut 4:4
to him shalt thou c. 10:20; 11:22
13:4; 30:20; Josh 22:5
shall c. nought of cursed. Deut 13:17
but c. to Lord your God. Josh 23:8
leprosy of Naaman shall c. 2 Ki 5:27
and the clods c. fast. Job 38:38
thou didst c. the fountain. Ps 74:15
hate the work, it shall not c. 101:3
my bones c. to my skin. 102:5
let my tongue c. to roof of. 137:6
they shall c. to house of. Isa 14:1
so have I caused to c. Jer 13:11
I make thy tongue c. to. Ezek 3:26
but they shall not c. one. Dan 2:43
many shall c. to them with. 11:34
thou didst c. the earth. Hab 3:9
the mount shall c. in. Zech 14:4
with purpose of heart c. Acts 11:23
abhor evil, c. to that. Rom 12:9

cleaved
Jehoram c. to Jeroboam's. 2 Ki 3:3
their tongue c. to roof of. Job 29:10
and if any blot have c. to my. 31:7

cleaveth
my bone c. to my skin. Job 19:20
my tongue c. to jaws. Ps 22:15
an evil disease, say they, c. 41:8
our belly c. to earth. 44:25
my soul c. to the dust. 119:25
as the girdle c. to loins of. Jer 13:11
tongue of sucking child c. Lam 4:4
their skin c. to their bones. 8
dust of your city which c. Luke 10:11

cleaveth
beast that c. the cleft. Deut 14:6*
he c. my reins asunder. Job 16:13
when one cutteth and c. Ps 141:7
that c. wood shall be. Eccl 10:9

cleft
that cleaveth the c. Deut 14:6*
the valleys shall be c. as. Mi 1:4

clefts
thou art in c. of the. S of S 2:14
into the c. of the rocks. Isa 2:21*
thou that dwellest in c. Jer 49:16
Ob 3
smite little house with c. Amos 6:11

clemency
hear us of thy c. a few. Acts 24:4

Cleopas
whose name was C. Luke 24:18
Mary the wife of C. John 19:25

clerk
when town c. had. Acts 19:35

cliff, -s
come up by the c. of. 2 Chr 20:16*
to dwell in the c. of the. Job 30:6*

clift, -s
will put thee in the c. Ex 33:22*
in valleys under c. of. Isa 57:5*

climb, -ed, -eth
Jonathan c. up upon. 1 Sam 14:13
they shall c. up upon. Jer 4:29
they shall c. the wall. Joel 2:7
they shall c. up upon the houses. 9
they c. up to heaven. Amos 9:2
Zaccheus c. up into a. Luke 19:4
c. up some other way. John 10:1

clipped
head be bald, beard be c. Jer 48:37

clods
flesh is clothed with c. Job 7:5
the c. of the valley shall. 21:33
and the c. cleave fast. 38:38
doth plowman break c.? Isa 28:24
Jacob shall break his c. Hos 10:11
seed is rotten under c. Joel 1:17

cloke
clad with zeal as a c. Isa 59:17†
let him have thy c. also. Mat 5:40
him that taketh thy c. Luke 6:29
now they have no c. John 15:22*
nor used we a c. of. 1 Thes 2:5
the c. I left at Troas. 2 Tim 4:13
not using liberty for a c. 1 Pet 2:16

close
and it be kept c. from. Num 5:13
afraid out of c. places. 2 Sam 22:46
Ps 18:45
David yet kept himself c. 1 Chr 12:1
and kept c. from fowls. Job 28:21
shut up together as with a c. 41:15
famine follow c. after you. Jer 42:16
and I saw him come c. Dan 8:7
and c. up the breaches. Amos 9:11
kept it c. and told no man. Luke 9:36
they sailed c. by Crete. Acts 27:13

closed
Lord c. up the flesh. Gen 2:21
the Lord had fast c. up all. 20:18
earth c. upon them. Num 16:33
fat c. upon the blade. Judg 3:22
they have not been c. Isa 1:6
Lord hath c. your eyes. 29:10
for the words are c. up. Dan 12:9
the depth c. me round. Jonah 2:5
eyes have c. Mat 13:15; Acts 28:27
he c. book, and gave it. Luke 4:20

closer
friend that sticketh c. Pr 18:24

closest
thou reign, because c. Jer 22:15*

closet, -s
bride go out of her c. Joel 2:16
enter into thy c. Mat 6:6*
ye have spoken in c. Luke 12:3*

cloth
spread on them a c. Num 4:8
put them in a c. of blue. 12
shall spread the c. Deut 22:17*
covered image with a c. 1 Sam 19:13
sword of Goliath, wrapt in a c. 21:9
and cast a c. on him. 2 Sam 20:12*
Hazael took a thick c. 2 Ki 8:15*
away as a menstruous c. Isa 30:22*
putteth a piece of new c. Mat 9:16
Mark 2:21
he wrapped it in a linen c. Mat 27:59
having a linen c. Mark 14:51

clothe
bring his sons and c. Ex 40:14
raiment to c. Mordecai. Esth 4:4
I will c. her priests. Ps 132:16
his enemies will I c. with. 18
drowsiness shall c. a. Pr 23:21
I will c. him with thy robe. Isa 22:21
thou shalt surely c. thee. Isa 49:18
I c. the heavens with blackness. 50:3
shall c. themselves with. Ezek 26:16
ye eat the fat, and c. you. 34:3
ye c. you, but there is. Hag 1:6
I will c. thee with. Zech 3:4
if God so c. grass of field, much more
c. you? Mat 6:30; Luke 12:28

clothed
coats of skins and c. Gen 3:21
Moses c. Aaron with robe. Lev 8:7
weep over Saul who c. 2 Sam 1:24
David and Israel c. with. 1 Chr 21:16
priests be c. with. 2 Chr 6:41
king of Israel and Judah c. 18:9
spoil c. all that were naked. 28:15
none enter king's gate c. Esth 4:2
flesh is c. with worms. Job 7:5
c. me with skin and flesh. 10:11
put on righteousness and it c. 29:14
hast thou c. his neck. 39:19
be c. with shame. Ps 35:26; 109:29
the pastures are c. with. 65:13
c. with majesty, Lord is c. 93:1
thou art c. with honour and. 104:1
as he c. himself with cursing. 109:18
let thy priests be c. with. 132:9
her household are c. with. Pr 31:21
c. me with garments of. Isa 61:10
I c. thee also with. Ezek 16:10
c. Daniel with scarlet. Dan 5:29
all such as are c. with. Zeph 1:8
Joshua was c. with filthy. Zech 3:3
man c. in soft raiment. Mat 11:8
Luke 7:25
naked and ye c. me. Mat 25:36
naked and ye c. me not. 43
John was c. with camel's. Mark 1:6
sitting and c. 5:15; Luke 8:35
c. Jesus with purple. Mark 15:17
certain rich man c. in. Luke 16:19
desiring to be c. upon. 2 Cor 5:2
if so be that being c. we shall not. 3
and be c. with humility. 1 Pet 5:5*
that thou mayest be c. Rev 3:18
I saw another mighty angel c. 10:1
two witnesses shall prophesy c. 11:3
appeared a woman c. with. 12:1
he was c. with a vesture 19:13

clothed with *linen*
one man c. with *linen*. Ezek 9:2
be c. with *linen* garments. 44:17
certain man c. with *linen*. Dan 10:5
said to man c. in *linen*. 12:6
c. in pure and white *linen*. Rev 15:6
18:16; 19:14

shall be **clothed**
that hate thee *shall be* c. Job 8:22
the prince *shall be* c. Ezek 7:27
read this writing, *shall be* c. Dan 5:7
wherewithal *shall* we *be* c.?
Mat 6:31
overcometh *shall be* c. Rev 3:5; 4:4

clothes
he washed his c. in the. Gen 49:11
troughs bound up in their c. Ex 12:34
the c. of service. 35:19; 39:1, 41
nor rend your c. Lev 10:6; 21:10
c. are not waxen old. Deut 29:5
Neh 9:21
Saul stript off his c. 1 Sam 19:24
covered David with c. 1 Ki 1:1
took hold of his own c. 2 Ki 2:12
thou didst rend thy c. 2 Chr 34:27
none of us put off our c. Neh 4:23
and my own c. shall abhor. Job 9:31
take fire, and his c. not? Pr 6:27
strip thee also of c. Ezek 16:39
23:26
return back to take his c. Mat 24:18
if I touch but his c. Mark 5:28
put his own c. on him. 15:20
him in swaddling c. Luke 2:7, 12
a man that ware no c. neither. 8:27
went they spread their c. 19:36
the linen c. laid. 24:12; John 20:5
bound with grave c. John 11:44
and wound it in linen c. 19:40
napkin not lying with linen c. 20:7*
laid down their c. Acts 7:58
cried out and cast off their c. 22:23

rent **clothes**
Reuben *rent* his *c.* *Gen* 37:29
Jacob *rent* his *c.* 34
Joseph's brethren *rent* their *c.* 44:13
and Caleb *rent* their *c.* *Num* 14:6
Joshua *rent* his *c.* *Josh* 7:6
Jephthah *rent* his *c.* *Judg* 11:35
rend your *c.* gird you. *2 Sam* 3:31
Ahab *rent* his *c.* *1 Ki* 21:27
king of Israel *rent c.* *2 Ki* 5:8; 6:30
Athaliah *rent* her *c.* 11:14
2 Chr 23:13
Hezekiah heard he *rent* his *c.*
2 Ki 19:1; *Isa* 37:1
Mordecai perceived, he *rent* his *c.*
Esth 4:1
high priest *rent* his *c.* *Mat* 26:65
Mark 14:63
and Paul *rent* their *c.* *Acts* 14:14
magistrates *rent* off their *c.* 16:22

clothes *rent*
leper's *c.* shall be *rent.* *Lev* 13:45
to Shiloh with *c. rent.* *1 Sam* 4:12
from Saul with *c. rent.* *2 Sam* 1:2
servants stood with *c. rent.* 13:31
to Hezekiah with *c. rent.* *2 Ki* 18:37
Isa 36:22
men having their *c. rent.* *Jer* 41:5

wash **clothes**
wash their *c.* *Ex* 19:10; *Num* 8:7
wash his *c.* *Lev* 11:25, 40; 13:6
14:8, 9, 47; 15:5, 8, 11, 22; 16:26
28; *Num* 19:10, 19
priest shall *wash c.* *Num* 19:7, 8, 19
ye shall *wash* your *c.* on. 31:24

washed **clothes**
people *washed* their *c.* *Ex* 19:14
Levites *washed* their *c.* *Num* 8:21
washed not his *c.* *2 Sam* 19:24

clothest
though thou *c.* thyself. *Jer* 4:30

clothing
stripped naked of their *c.* *Job* 22:6
naked to lodge without *c.* 24:7
to go naked without *c.* 10
any perish for want of *c.* 31:19
as for me, my *c.* was. *Ps* 35:13
king's daughter, her *c.* is. 45:13
lambs are for thy *c.* *Pr* 27:26
virtuous woman's *c.* is silk. 31:22
strength and honour are her *c.* 25
thou hast *c.* be thou our. *Isa* 3:6
house is neither bread nor *c.* 7
shall be for durable *c.* 23:18
garments of vengeance for *c.* 59:17
and purple is their *c.* *Jer* 10:9
in sheep's *c.* *Mat* 7:15
that wear soft *c.* 11:8
scribes that go in long *c.* *Mark* 12:38
man stood before me in bright *c.*
Acts 10:30
him that weareth gay *c.* *Jas* 2:3

cloud
In addition to the common meaning this word is used frequently of, [1] *A great number,* Heb 12:1. [2] *A fog, or mist,* Hos 6:4. [3] *The sky,* Ps 36:5; 68:34; Pr 8:28.
(*At the Exodus God gave the Israelites a pillar of cloud to direct them in their march. This attended them through the wilderness. It was clear and bright during the night, in order to give them light when it grew dark; and in the day time it was thick and gloomy, the better to defend them from the excessive heats of the Arabian deserts. It also gave the signal for marching and for halting*)
set my bow in the *c.* for. *Gen* 9:13
bow shall be seen in *c.* 14, 16
it was *c.* and darkness. *Ex* 14:20
glory of Lord appeared in *c.* 16:10
I come unto thee in a thick *c.* 19:9
Moses went up, and a *c.* 24:15
c. covered it six days, seventh day
God called out of *c.* 16
Moses went into midst of *c.* 18
Lord descended in the *c.* 34:5
Num 11:25
c. covered the tent of the. *Ex* 40:34
the *c.* of Lord was on the. 38
I will appear in the *c.* *Lev* 16:2
when the *c.* tarried long. *Num* 9:19
the *c.* of the Lord was upon. 10:34
the *c.* filled house of Lord. *1 Ki* 8:10
2 Chr 5:13; *Ezek* 10:4
ariseth a little *c.* like. *1 Ki* 18:44
day be darkness, let a *c.* *Job* 3:5
he judge through dark *c.*? 22:13
welfare passeth away as a *c.* 30:15
when I made the *c* the. 38:9
day-time led them with *c.* *Ps* 78:14
spread a *c.* for a covering. 105:39
his favour is as a *c.* *Pr* 16:15
create on her assemblies *c.* *Isa* 4:5
like a *c.* of dew in heat of. 18:4
Lord rideth upon a swift *c.* 19:1
blotted out as a thick *c.* transgressions, and as *c.* thy sins. 44:22
are these that flee as a *c.*? 60:8
daughter of Zion with *c.* *Lam* 2:1
covered thyself with a *c.* 3:44
a great *c.* and a fire. *Ezek* 1:4
appearance of bow in the *c.* 28
a thick *c.* of incense. 8:11
the house was filled with the *c.* 10:4
as for her, a *c.* shall cover. 30:18
I will cover sun with a *c.* 32:7
shalt be like a *c.* to. 38:9, 16
a bright *c.* overshadowed them and a voice out of *c.* said. *Mat.* 17:5
Mark 9:7; *Luke* 9:34, 35
when ye see a *c.* rise. *Luke* 12:54
Son of Man coming in a *c.* 21:27
a *c.* received him out of. *Acts* 1:9
fathers were under the *c.* *1 Cor* 10:1
all baptized to Moses in the *c.* 2
angel clothed with a *c.* *Rev* 10:1
ascended to heaven in a *c.* 11:12
c. and upon *c.* one sat. 14:14, 15, 16

cloud *abode*
because the *c. abode.* *Ex* 40:35
where *c. abode* there. *Num* 9:17
as long as *c. abode* they. 18

morning **cloud**
is as a *morning c.* *Hos* 6:4
shall be as the *morning c.* 13:3

pillar of **cloud**
by day in a *p. of c.* *Ex* 13:21
took not away the *p. of c.* 22
on Egyptians through *p. of c.* 14:24
down in *p. of c.* and. *Num* 12:5
in *p. of c.* and *p. of c.* *Deut* 31:15
p. of c. departed not. *Neh* 9:19

cloud *taken up*
the *c.* was *taken up.* *Ex* 40:36
Num 9:17
if the *c.* were not *taken up.* *Ex* 40:37
c. was *taken up* from tabernacle.
Num 9:17; 10:11

white **cloud**
a *white c.* and on *c.* one. *Rev* 14:14

cloud *of witnesses*
with so great a *c.* of *w.* *Heb* 12:1

clouds
with darkness, *c.* and. *Deut* 4:11
heavens dropped, *c.* also. *Judg* 5:4
about him thick *c.* of. *2 Sam* 22:12
as a morning without *c.* 23:4
heaven was black with *c.* *1 Ki* 18:45
though head reach to *c.* *Job* 20:6
thick *c.* are a covering that. 22:14
bindeth up waters in thick *c.* 26:8
understand spreadings of *c.*? 36:29
the balancings of the *c.*? 37:16
who can number the *c.* in ? 38:37
faithfulness reacheth to *c.* *Ps* 36:5
thy truth reacheth to the *c.* 57:10
108:4
and his strength is in the *c.* 68:34
c. poured out water. 77:17
commanded the *c.* from. 78:23
c. and darkness are round. 97:2
maketh the *c.* his chariot. 104:3
covers heaven with *c.* 147:8
c. dropped down the dew. *Pr* 3:20
when he established the *c.* 8:28
is like *c.* and wind without. 25:14
regardeth the *c.* shall not. *Eccl* 11:4
nor *c.* return after the rain. 12:2
I will command the *c.* *Isa* 5:6
ascend above height of the *c.* 14:14
shall come up as *c.* and. *Jer* 4:13
with the *c.* of heaven. *Dan* 7:13
c. and darkness. *Joel* 2:2; *Zeph* 1:15
c. are the dust of his feet. *Nah* 1:3
Lord shall make bright *c.* *Zech* 10:1
Son of Man coming in *c.* *Mat* 24:30
26:64; *Mark* 13:26; 14:62
up with them in *c.* *1 Thes* 4:17
they are *c.* carried. *2 Pet* 2:17
c. they are without water. *Jude* 12
behold he cometh with *c.* *Rev* 1:7

cloudy
the *c.* pillar descended. *Ex* 33:9
people saw the *c.* pillar. 10
in day by *c.* pillar. *Neh* 9:12
spake in the *c.* pillar. *Ps* 99:7
day of the Lord, a *c.* day. *Ezek* 30:3
been scattered in the *c.* day. 34:12

clouted
old shoes and *c.* on. *Josh* 9:5†

clouts
took old cast *c.* and rags. *Jer* 38:11
put these old cast *c.* under. 12

cloven
whatsoever is *c.*-footed. *Lev* 11:3
though the swine be *c.*-footed. 7
not *c.*-footed are unclean to you. 26
Deut 14:7
to them *c.* tongues. *Acts* 2:3*

cluster
a branch with one *c.* *Num* 13:23
my beloved is as a *c.* *S of S* 1:14
wine found in the *c.* so. *Isa* 65:8
woe is me, there is no *c.* *Mi* 7:1

clusters
the *c.* thereof brought. *Gen* 40:10
grapes their *c.* bitter. *Deut* 32:32
Abigail brought 100 *c.* *1 Sam* 25:18
gave the Egyptian two *c.* 30:12
breasts like two *c.* of. *S of S* 7:7, 8
gather the *c.* of the vine. *Rev* 14:18

coal
so shall quench my *c.* *2 Sam* 14:7
seraphim having a live *c.* *Isa* 6:6
there shall not be a *c.* to. 47:14
visage is blacker than *c.* *Lam* 4:8

coals
censer full of burning *c.* *Lev* 16:12
a cake baken on the *c.* *1 Ki* 19:6
his breath kindleth *c.* *Job* 41:21
there went fire, *c.* were. *Ps* 18:8
hail-stones and *c.* of fire. 12
arrows of mighty with *c.* 120:4
let burning *c.* fall on them. 140:10
can one go on hot *c.*? *Pr* 6:28
heap *c.* of fire. 25:22; *Rom* 12:20
as *c.* are to burning *c.* and. *Pr* 26:21
c. thereof are *c.* of fire. *S of S* 8:6
the smith worketh in *c.* *Isa* 44:12
have baked bread upon the *c.* 19
smith that bloweth the *c.* 54:16
appearance like burning *c.* *Ezek* 1:13
fill thine hand with *c.* of fire. 10:2
set it empty on the *c.* 24:11
burning *c.* went forth at. *Hab* 3:5
had made a fire of *c.* *John* 18:18
they saw a fire of *c.* and fish. 21:9

coast
(*Not as now* sea-coast *but* border, *whether by the sea or not. It is usually rendered in the Revisions by* border, *or* side)
the locusts into thy *c.* *Ex* 10:4
ships shall come from *c.* *Num* 24:24
uttermost sea shall *c.* be. *Deut* 11:24
if the Lord enlarge thy *c.* 19:8
going down of sun your *c.* *Josh* 1:4
Judah shall abide in their *c.* 18:5
not Israel to pass his *c.* *Judg* 11:20
up by way of his own *c.* *1 Sam* 6:9
no more into the *c.* of Israel. 7:13
to seek any more in any *c.* 27:1
made an invasion on the *c.* 30:14
Jeroboam restored *c.* of. *2 Ki* 14:25
me, and enlarge my *c.* *1 Chr* 4:10
the *c.* shall be for the. *Zeph* 2:7

***sea* coast**

remnant of the *sea c.* *Ezek* 25:16
woe to inhabitants of *sea c.* *Zeph* 2:5
the *sea c.* shall be dwellings for. 6
in Capernaum upon *sea c.* *Mat* 4:13
multitude from *sea c.* *Luke* 6:17

***south* coast**

uttermost part of *south c.* *Josh* 15:1
this shall be your *south c.* 4
this was the *south c.* 18:19

coasts

locusts rested in all the *c.* *Ex* 10:14
not one locust in all the *c.* of. 19
to pass through *c.* of. *Deut* 2:4
no leavened bread seen in thy *c.* 16:4
thou shalt divide the *c.* 19:3
shall abide in their *c.* on. *Josh* 18:5
five men from their *c.* *Judg* 18:2*
sent concubine into all the *c.* 19:29
the *c.* thereof did Israel. *1 Sam* 7:14
send messengers into all *c.* 11:3, 7
destroyed from *c.* of. *2 Sam* 21:5
destroyed through all *c.* *1 Chr* 21:12
to him out of all *c.* *2 Chr* 11:13
lice in all their *c.* *Ps* 105:31
and brake trees of their *c.* 33
whirlwind raised from *c.* *Jer* 25:32
take a man of their *c.* *Ezek* 33:2
to do with me, all *c.* *Joel* 3:4*
slew children in all *c.* *Mat* 2:16
depart out of their *c.* 8:34; *Mark* 5:17
Jesus departed into *c.* of Tyre. *Mat* 15:21*
departing from *c.* of. *Mark* 7:31
and Barnabas out of *c.* *Acts* 13:50

coat

Jacob made Joseph a *c.* *Gen* 37:3
sent *c.* of many colours, and said, know whether it be thy son's *c.* 32
Aaron a robe and a broidered *c.* *Ex* 28:4
shalt put upon Aaron the *c.* 29:5
he put upon him the *c.* *Lev* 8:7
put on the holy linen *c.* 16:4
made Samuel a little *c.* *1 Sam* 2:19*
armed with a *c.* of mail. 17:5, 38
met David with *c.* rent. *2 Sam* 15:32
as collar of my *c.* *Job* 30:18
I have put off my *c.* *S of S* 5:3
and take away thy *c.* *Mat* 5:40
forbid not to take thy *c.* *Luke* 6:29
c. was without seam. *John* 19:23
Peter girt his fisher's *c.* unto. 21:7

coats

God made *c.* of skins. *Gen* 3:21
for Aaron's sons make *c.* *Ex* 28:40
and put *c.* on them. 29:8; 40:14
Moses put *c.* upon. *Lev* 8:13
they carried them in their *c.* 10:5
were bound in their *c.* *Dan* 3:21*
nor were their *c.* changed, nor. 27*
neither provide two *c.* *Mat* 10:10
and put not on two *c.* *Mark* 6:9
he that hath two *c.* *Luke* 3:11
shewing the *c.* which. *Acts* 9:39

cock

night before *c.* crow. *Mat* 26:34, 75
Mark 14:30, 72; *Luke* 22:34, 61
c. crew. *Mat* 26:74; *Luke* 22:60
John 18:27
master cometh at *c.* crow. *Mark* 13:35
porch, and the *c.* crew. 14:68, 72
the *c.* shall not crow till thou hast denied me thrice. *John* 13:38

cockatrice, -s

(*A basilisk, or adder*)

his hand on the *c.* den. *Isa* 11:8
root shall come forth a *c.* 14:29
they hatch *c.* eggs. 59:5
I will send serpents, *c.* *Jer* 8:17

cockle

and let *c.* grow instead. *Job* 31:40

coffer

jewels of gold in a *c.* *1 Sam* 6:8
they laid ark and *c.* with mice. 11
Levites took down the *c.* with. 15

coffin

Joseph was put in *c.* in. *Gen* 50:26

cogitations

my *c.* much troubled me. *Dan* 7:28*

cold

c. and heat, day and. *Gen* 8:22
no covering in the *c.* *Job* 24:7
and *c.* cometh out of north. 37:9
stand before his *c.*? *Ps* 147:17
not plow by reason of *c.* *Pr* 20:4*
as the *c.* of snow in time. 25:13
taketh away a garment in *c.* 20
as *c.* waters to a thirsty soul. 25
shall *c.* flowing waters ? *Jer* 18:14
camp in hedges in *c.* day. *Nah* 3:17
a cup of *c.* water. *Mat* 10:42
love of many shall wax *c.* 24:12
a fire, for it was *c.* *John* 18:18
received us, because of *c.* *Acts* 28:2
in fastings often, in *c.* *2 Cor* 11:27
neither *c.* nor hot. *Rev* 3:15, 16

collar, -s

from Midian, beside *c.* *Judg* 8:26*
disease bindeth me as *c.* *Job* 30:18

collection

bring out of Judah *c.* *2 Chr* 24:6*, 9*
concerning the *c.* for. *1 Cor* 16:1

college

dwelt in *c.* *2 Ki* 22:14*; *2 Chr* 34:22*

collops

because he maketh *c.* of. *Job* 15:27†

colony

city of Macedonia, and *c.* *Acts* 16:12

Colosse

saints and brethren at *C.* *Col* 1:2

colour

have not changed his *c.* *Lev* 13:55
the *c.* as the *c.* of. *Num* 11:7*
when wine giveth his *c.* *Pr* 23:31
as the *c.* of amber. *Ezek* 1:4†
sparkled like *c.* of. 7† ; *Dan* 10:6
wheels like unto *c.* of a. *Ezek* 1:16†
10:9
firmament was as the *c.* of. 1:22†
under *c.* as though they. *Acts* 27:30
in purple and scarlet *c.* *Rev* 17:4*

coloured

woman sit on scarlet *c.* *Rev* 17:3

colours

coat of many *c.* for. *Gen* 37:3
Sisera a prey of divers *c.* *Judg* 5:30
a garment of divers *c.* *2 Sam* 13:18
stones of divers *c.* *1 Chr* 29:2
lay thy stones with fair *c.* *Isa* 54:11
deckedst high places with *c.* *Ezek* 16:16
an eagle with divers *c.* came. 17:3

colt, -s

camels with their *c.* forty. *Gen* 32:15
binding his ass' *c.* to the. 49:11
sons that rode on 30 ass *c.* *Judg* 10:4
nephews rode on 70 ass *c.* 12:14
born like a wild ass's *c.* *Job* 11:12
riding upon a *c.* *Zech* 9:9; *Mat* 21:5
John 12:15
find ass tied, *c.* with her. *Mat* 21:2
Mark 11:2; *Luke* 19:30
brought ass and *c.* and. *Mat* 21:7
Mark 11:7
what do ye, loosing the *c.*? *Mark* 11:5; *Luke* 19:33
cast garments on *c.* *Luke* 19:35

come

[1] *To draw nigh, or approach,* Ex 34:3. [2] *To proceed from,* 1 Chr 29:14. [3] *To attain to,* Acts 26:7. [4] *To touch,* Ezek 44:25. [5] *To arise,* Num 24:7.

two of every sort shall *c.* *Gen* 6:20
c. thou, and all thy house. 7:1
c. let us make our father. 19:32
wherefore *c.* ye to me ? 26:27
c. let us make a covenant. 31:44
c. let us slay him, and cast. 37:10
whence *c.* ye ? 42:7; *Josh* 9:8
bring your father and *c.* *Gen* 45:19
from Judah till Shiloh *c.* 49:10
lo, I *c.* to thee in a. *Ex* 19:9
I record name I will *c.* and. 20:24
people to whom thou shalt *c.* 23:27
c. thou with us, we will. *Num* 10:29
c. I pray thee, curse this. 22:6, 11
out of Jacob shall *c.* he. 24:19
if a Levite *c.* and *c.* *Deut* 18:6
all these blessings shall *c.* *Deut* 28:2
all these curses *c.* on thee. 15, 45
no razor *c.* on his head. *Judg* 13:5
1 Sam 1:11
shall *c.* on thy two sons. *1 Sam* 2:34
people will not eat till he *c.* 9:13
tarry, till I *c.* to thee. 10:8
but I *c.* to thee in the name. 17:45
then *c.* thou, for there is. 20:21
shall ark of Lord *c.* to ? *2 Sam* 6:9
I will *c.* on him while he is. 17:2
c. thou over with me and I. 19:33
and the oath *c.* before. *1 Ki* 8:31
if any thing would *c.* from. 20:33
feed this fellow until I *c.* in. 22:27
let him *c.* now to me. *2 Ki* 5:8
till I *c.* and take. 18:32; *Isa* 36:17
riches and honour *c.* *1 Chr* 29:12
all things *c.* of thee, and of. 14
ark of Lord hath *c.* *2 Chr* 8:11
Vashti refused to *c.* at. *Esth* 1:12
how endure to see evil *c.* to ? 8:6
let no joyful voice *c.* *Job* 3:7
that I may speak, let *c.* on. 13:13
will I wait till my change *c.* 14:14
his sons *c.* to honour, and he. 21
caused it to *c.* for correction. 37:13
hitherto shalt thou *c.* but. 38:11
lo, I *c.* *Ps* 40:7; *Heb* 10:7, 9
when shall I *c.* and appear? *Ps* 42:2
our God shall *c.* and not. 50:3
unto thee shall all flesh *c.* 65:2
stir up thy strength, and *c.* 80:2
all nations shall *c.* and. 86:9
when wilt thou *c.* unto me ? 101:2
loved cursing, so let it *c.* 109:17
mercies *c.* unto me. 119:41, 77
shall thy poverty *c.* *Pr* 6:11; 24:34
fear of the wicked shall *c.* 10:24
curse causeless shall not *c.* 26:2
all things *c.* alike to all. *Eccl* 9:2
up, my love, and *c.* *S of S* 2:10, 13
c. with me from Lebanon. 4:8
and *c.* thou south, blow upon. 16
of Holy One of Israel *c.* *Isa* 5:19
c. from a far country. 13:5
the day of the Lord, it shall *c.* 6
inquire ye ; return, *c.* 21:12
c. my people, enter into. 26:20
cause them that *c.* of Jacob. 27:6
c. with vengeance, he will *c.* 35:4
the Lord will *c.* with a. 40:10
raised up one, and he shall *c.* 41:25
things coming, and shall *c.* 44:7
assemble yourselves, and *c.* 45:20
even to him shall men *c.* 24
the redeemed shall *c.* with. 51:11
c. ye to the waters, *c.* ye, buy, *c.* 55:1
c. unto me, hear, and your. 3
and the Redeemer shall *c.* 59:20
Gentiles shall *c.* to thy light. 60:3, 5
behold, Lord will *c.* with fire. 66:15
say they, we will *c.* *Jer* 2:31
behold, we *c.* to thee, for thou. 3:22
mourning women, that they *c.* 9:17
wherefore *c.* these things ? 13:22
word of the Lord ? let it *c.* 17:15
him till time of his land *c.* 27:7
they shall *c.* with weeping. 31:9
princes hear, and *c.* to thee. 38:25
good to *c.* if ill to *c.* forbear. 40:4
as Carmel, so shall he *c.* 46:18
trusted, saying, who shall *c.*? 49:4
none *c.* to solemn feasts. *Lam* 1:4
let all their wickedness *c.* 22
abominations whither they *c.* *Ezek* 12:16
save souls alive that *c.*? 13:18
that sword may *c.* 21:19, 20 ; 32:11
shall be no more, till he *c.* 21:27
he seeth the sword *c.* on. 33:3, 6
they *c.* to thee as the people. 31
lo it will *c.* then shall know. 33
they are at hand to *c.* 36:8
c. let us return to Lord. *Hos* 6:1
and he shall *c.* to us, as the. 3
to seek the Lord till he *c.* 10:12
as a destruction shall it *c.* *Joel* 1:15
before terrible day of Lord *c.* 2:31
c. let us cast lots. *Jonah* 1:7
to thee shall it *c.* kingdom *c.* *Mi* 4:8
because it will surely *c.* *Hab* 2:3
anger of Lord *c.* on you. *Zeph* 2:2
what *c.* these to do ? *Zech* 1:21

God shall c. and all the. Zech 14:5
Lord ye seek shall c. Mal 3:1
lest I c. and smite the earth. 4:6
for out of thee shall c. Mat 2:6
first be reconciled, then c. 5:24
thy kingdom c. thy. 6:10; Luke 11:2
false prophets c. to you in. Mat 7:15
Jesus saith to him, I will c. 8:7
not worthy thou shouldest c. 8
and to another, c. and. 9; Luke 7:8
many shall c. from east. Mat 8:11
he that should c.? 11:3; Luke 7:19, 20
c. all ye that labour and. Mat 11:28
if any man will c. after me. 16:24
Elias must first c.? 17:10, 11
sell, and c. 19:21; Luke 18:22
all things are ready, c. Mat 22:4
preached, then shall end c. 24:14
what hour your Lord doth c. 42
c. ye blessed of my Father. 25:34
art thou c. to destroy us? Mark 1:24 Luke 4:34
whosoever will c. after me let him deny. Mark 8:34; Luke 9:23; 14:27
suffer the little children to c. unto me. Mark 10:14; Luke 18:16
c. take up the cross. Mark 10:21
this is the heir, c. let us kill. 12:7
Luke 20:14
he himself would c. Luke 10:1
three years I c. seeking fruit. 13:7
there are six days, in them c. 14
kingdom of God should c. 17:20
occupy till I c. 19:13
he shall c. and destroy. 20:16
till kingdom of God shall c. 22:18
c. and see. John 1:39
baptizeth, and all men c. to him. 3:26
lest a worse thing c. to thee. 5:14
ye will not c. to me, that ye. 40
Father giveth me shall c. 6:37
c. to me, except Father. 44, 65
thither ye cannot c. 7:34
let him c. to me and drink. 37
ye cannot tell whence I c. and. 8:14
you before it c. that when it c. 13:19
comfortless, I will c. 14:18
and we will c. unto him. 23
these are in the world, I c. 17:11, 13
if I will he tarry till I c.? 21:22, 23
this Jesus shall so c. Acts 1:11
and notable day of Lord c. 2:20
when times of refreshing c. 3:19
c. down and now c. I will send. 7:34
pray that none of these c. 8:24
that he would not delay to c. 9:38
lest that c. on you that is. 13:40
c. over into Macedonia. 16:9
believe on him that should c. 19:4
forbid no acquaintance to c. 24:23
our twelve tribes hope to c. 26:7*
and Moses did say should c. 22
let us do evil, that good c. Rom 3:8
at this time, will I c. 9:9
judge nothing till Lord c. 1 Cor 4:5
the Lord's death till he c. 11:26
rest will I set in order when I c. 34
with what body do they c.? 15:35
no gatherings when I c. 16:2
if Timothy c. see he be with you. 10
I desired him to c. to you. 12
I was minded to c. to. 2 Cor 1:15
for I fear, lest when I c. I. 12:20
if righteousness c. by law. Gal 2:21
blessing of Abraham c. on. 3:14
till the seed should c. to whom. 19
when he shall c. to be. 2 Thes 1:10
day shall not c. except there c. 2:3*
and of that to c. 1 Tim 4:8
till I c. give attendance to. 13
perilous times shall c. 2 Tim 3:1
time will c. they will not endure. 4:3
be diligent to c. to me. Tit 3:12
let us c. boldly to the. Heb 4:16
he is able to save them that c. 7:25
he that shall c. will c. and. 10:37
whence c. wars, c. they? Jas 4:1
weep for miseries that shall c. 5:1
but that all should c. 2 Pet 3:9
day of Lord will c. as a thief in the night. 10; Rev 3:3; 16:15
antichrist shall c. 1 John 2:18
if I c. I will remember. 3 John 10
repent, or else I will c. Rev 2:5
hold fast till I c. 25
I c. quickly, hold. 3:11; 22:7, 20
four beasts, saying, c. 6:1, 3, 5, 7
in one hour is judgement c. 18:10
and let him that is athirst c. 22:17

come *again*

so that I c. again to my. Gen 28:21
that waters may c. again. Ex 14:26
if the plague c. again. Lev 14:43
when I c. again in peace. Judg 8:9
let man of God c. again to us. 13:8
to Gath, and was c. again. 1 Ki 2:41
and then c. again. 12:5; 2 Chr 10:5
this child's soul c. again. 1 Ki 17:21
Israel c. again. Ezra 6:21; Neh 8:17
he shall c. again. Ps 126:6
say not go and c. again. Pr 3:28
Chaldeans shall c. again. Jer 37:8
when I c. again I will. Luke 10:35
I will c. again and. John 14:3
I go away and c. again. 28
that I would not c. again. 2 Cor 2:1
lest, when I c. again, God. 12:21
I write, that if I c. again. I. 13:2

come *down*

c. down to me, tarry not. Gen 45:9
I am c. down to deliver. Ex 3:8
the Lord will c. down on. 19:11
I will c. down and talk. Num 11:17
from heaven it c. down. Deut 28:24
saying, c. down against. Judg 7:24
they said, we are c. down. 15:12
c. down and fetch ark. 1 Sam 6:21
will Saul c. down? he will c. down. 23:11
c. down, according to the. 20
thou shalt not c. down. 2 Ki 1:4
6:16
thou man of God, c. down. 1:9
let fire c. down. 10, 11, 12
work, I cannot c. down. Neh 6:3
his dealing shall c. down. Ps 7:16
he shall c. down like rain. 72:6
the heavens, and c. down. 144:5
my sword, it shall c. down. Isa 34:5
c. down, sit in the dust. 47
that thou wouldest c. down. 64:1
your principalities shall c. down. Jer 13:18
who shall c. down against us? 21:13
c. down from thy glory. 48:18
of the sea shall c. down. Ezek 26:16
all pilots shall c. down from. 27:29
of her power shall c. down. 30:6
cause mighty to c. down. Joel 3:11
not c. down to take. Mat 24:17
c. down from cross. 27:40, 42
Mark 15:30
fire to c. down? Luke 9:54
Zacchaeus, haste and c. down. 19:5
Sir, c. down ere child. John 4:49
the gods are c. down. Acts 14:11
devil is c. down to you. Rev 12:12
maketh fire c. down from. 13:13
angel c. down having key. 20:1

come *forth*

he that shall c. forth out. Gen 15:4
Hebrews c. forth out. 1 Sam 14:11
thus saith king, c. forth. 1 Ki 2:30
slay them, let none c. forth. 2 Ki 10:25
I shall c. forth as gold. Job 23:10
let my sentence c. forth. Ps 17:2
and I cannot c. forth. 88:8
feareth God shall c. forth. Eccl 7:18
shall c. forth a rod out of. Isa 11:1
art c. forth out of waters. 48:1
my fury c. forth like fire. Jer 4:4*
Pharaoh's army was c. forth. 37:5, 7
let mighty men c. forth. 46:9*
a fire shall c. forth out of. 48:45
twain shall c. forth out. Ezek 21:19
servants of most high God, c. forth. Dan 3:26
O Daniel, I am c. forth to. 9:22
a fountain shall c. forth. Joel 3:18
out of thee shall c. forth. Mi 5:2
c. forth and flee from land. Zech 2:6
angels shall c. forth. Mat 13:49
c. forth from the heart. 15:18
this kind c. forth by. Mark 9:29
and will c. forth and. Luke 12:37
shall c. forth, they that. John 5:29
cried, Lazarus, c. forth. 11:43
shall c. forth and serve. Acts 7:7

come *hither*

fourth generation c. hither. Gen 15:16
Samson is c. hither. Judg 16:2
c. thou hither and eat. Ruth 2:14
inquired if the man should c. hither. 1 Sam 10:22
not sit down till he c. hither. 16:11
c. hither that I may. 2 Sam 14:32
say to Joab, c. hither that I. 20:16
man of God is c. hither. 2 Ki 8:7
said to thee, c. up hither. Pr 25:7
c. forth and c. hither. Dan 3:26
thou c. hither to torment? Mat 8:29
neither c. hither to draw. John 4:15
call thy husband and c. hither. 16
turned world are c. hither. Acts 17:6
c. up h. Rev 4:1; 11:12; 17:1; 21:9

I am **come**, or *am I* **come**

I thy father-in-law am c. Ex 18:6
lo I am c. to thee. Num 22:38
I am c. into country. Deut 26:3
I am c. to sacrifice. 1 Sam 16:2, 5
now that I am c. to. 2 Sam 14:15
wherefore am I c. from? 32
I am c. first to meet my. 19:20
I am c. into deep waters. Ps 69:2
I communed, lo, I am c. Eccl 1:16
I am c. into my garden. S of S 5:1
I am c. to shew. Dan 9:23; 10:14
I am c. for thy words. 10:12
think not I am c. to. Mat 5:17
I am not c. to call righteous. 9:13
think not that I am c. to. 10:34
I am c. to set a man at. 35
suppose ye that I am c. Luke 12:51
am I c. baptizing with. John 1:31
I am c. in my Father's name. 5:43
I am not c. of myself. 7:28
for judgement I am c. into. 9:39
I am c. that they might have. 10:10
I am c. a light into world. 12:46
I am c. into the world. 16:28

come *in*, or *into*

shalt c. into the ark, and. Gen 6:18
not a man in earth to c. in. 19:31
said, c. in thou blessed of. 24:31
destroyer to c. in. Ex 12:23
when they c. in unto the. 28:43*
afterward shall c. into the camp. Lev 16:26, 28; Num 19:7; 31:24
at his word shall c. in. Num 27:21
no more go out and c. in. Deut 31:2
to go out and c. in. Josh 14:11
I will c. in after thee. 1 Ki 1:14
not how to go out or c. in. 3:7
he said, c. in thou wife of. 14:6
suffer any to go out or c. in. 15:17
when c. in shut door. 2 Ki 4:4
took each his men to c. in. 11:9
go out and c. in before. 2 Chr 1:10
let none go out or c. in to Asa. 16:1
none c. into the house of Lord. 23:6
till I c. into Judah. Neh 2:7
Esther let no man c. in. Esth 5:12
king said, let Haman c. in. 6:5
King of glory shall c. in. Ps 24:7, 9
for the waters are c. in. 69:1
offering and c. into his courts. 96:8
so let it c. into his bowels. 109:18
let my beloved c. into. S of S 4:16
Lord shall c. into Egypt. Isa 19:1
the Assyrian shall c. into. 23
shut up, that no man c. in. 24:10
when the enemy shall c. in. 59:19
the kings of Judah c. in. Jer 17:19
and let Jerusalem c. into. 51:50
strangers are c. into the. 51
things that c. into mind. Ezek 11:5
shall things c. into thy mind. 38:10
Assyrian shall c. into land. Mi 5:5
ye c. into an house. Mat 10:12*
Son of man shall c. in glory. 16:27
many shall c. in my name. 24:5
Mark 13:6; Luke 21:8
Son of man c. in his glory. Mat 25:31
which c. in may see. Luke 11:33*
c. in second watch, or c. in. 12:38

will c. in a day when he. Luke 12:46
and compel them to c. in. 14:23
lest they c. into this place. 16:28
c. in my Father's name, if another c.
in his own name. John 5:43
should c. into world. 6:14; 11:27
Lydia, saying, c. into. Acts 16:15
of Gentiles be c. in. Rom 11:25
there c. in those that. 1 Cor 14:23
if there c. in one that. 24
there c. in also a poor man. Jas 2:2
I will c. in to him, and. Rev 3:20

come, *passive*

the end of all flesh is c. Gen 6:13
for therefore are ye c. to. 18:5
the cry which is c. to me. 21
therefore is this distress c. 42:21
cry of children of Israel is c. Ex 3:9
fear not, for God is c. to. 20:20
there is a people c. out. Num 22:11
when all Israel is c. to. Deut 31:11
host of Lord am I c. Josh 5:14
Samson is c. hither. Judg 16:2
said, God is c. into. 1 Sam 4:7
because their cry is c. to me. 9:16
anguish is c. upon me. 2 Sam 1:9
speech of all Israel is c. to. 19:11
the creditor is c. to. 2 Ki 4:1
when this letter is c. to thee. 5:6
man of God is c. hither. 8:7
and after all that is c. Ezra 9:13
thing I feared is c. Job 3:25; 4:5
all this is c. upon us. Ps 44:17
salvation of Israel were c. 53:6
and trembling are c. 55:5
I am c. into deep waters. 69:2
yea the set time is c. 102:13
he is c. to Aiath. Isa 10:28
my salvation is near to c. 56:1
light is c. and glory of Lord. 60:1
year of my redeemed is c. 63:4
sinned, therefore this is c. Jer 40:3
baldness is c. on Gaza. 47:5
woe to them, their day is c. 50:27
thy day is c. the time that. 31
on many waters, thy end is c. 51:13
our end is c. Lam 4:18
remember, O Lord, what is c. 5:1
end, the end is c. Ezek 7:2, 6
an only evil, behold, is c. 5
the morning is c. upon thee. 7
the day, behold, it is c. 10; 39:8
king of Babylon is c. to. 17:12
prince whose day is c. 21:25, 29
all this evil is c. on us. Dan 9:13
the end is c. on my. Amos 8:2
he is c. to gate of my. Mi 1:9
to flee from wrath to c.? Mat 3:7
the kingdom of God is c. 12:28
when he is c. he findeth it. 44
Son of man is c. to save lost. 18:11
because the harvest is c. Mark 4:29
she is c. aforehand to anoint. 14:8
it is enough, the hour is c. 41
the Son of man is c. Luke 7:34
thy brother is c. father hath. 15:27
this day is salvation c. to this. 19:9
the Son of man is c. to seek. 10
that light is c. into the. John 3:19
when he is c. he will tell. 4:25
the Master is c. and calleth. 11:28
hour is c. Son of man. 12:23; 17:1
when the Comforter is c. 15:26
when he is c. he will reprove. 16:8
when the Spirit of truth is c. 13
sorrow because hour is c. 21
salvation is c. unto the. Rom 11:11
for your obedience is c. 16:19
is perfect is c. then. 1 Cor 13:10
but after that faith is c. Gal 3:25
which gospel is c. to you. Col 1:6
Jesus Christ is c. in. 1 John 4:2
confesseth not that Jesus Christ is c.
in flesh is not of God. 3; 2 John 7
know Son of God is c. 1 John 5:20
great day of wrath is c. Rev 6:17
and thy wrath is c. and. 11:18
is c. salvation and strength. 12:10
hour of his judgement is c. 14:7
great riches is c. to nought. 18:17
for marriage of Lamb is c. 19:7

come *near*

Abram was c. near to. Gen 12:11
Abimelech had not c. near. Gen 20:4
let him c. near and keep. Ex 12:48
c. near before the Lord. 16:9
c. near to the altar. 28:43; 30:20
cause him to c. near. Num 16:5
that no stranger c. near to. 40
c. near, put feet on. Josh 10:24
caused tribes to c. near. 1 Sam 10:20
lest they c. near unto thee. Ps 32:9*
let my cry c. near before. 119:169
let us c. near together. Isa 41:1
c. ye near unto me, hear ye. 48:16
adversary ? let him c. near me. 50:8
nor hath c. near to a. Ezek 18:6
which c. near to the Lord to. 40:46
they shall c. near to me. 44:15
they shall c. near to my table. 16
of violence to c. near. Amos 6:3
and I will c. near to you. Mal 3:5
when he was c. near. Luke 19:41
we, or he c. near, are. Acts 23:15

come *nigh*

afraid to c. nigh him. Ex 34:30
sanctified in all that c. nigh me.
Lev 10:3
hath blemish c. nigh. 21:21, 23
a stranger not c. nigh. Num 18:4
you are c. nigh to battle. Deut 20:2
kingdom of God c. nigh unto you.
Luke 10:9, 11

come *not*

be ready, c. not at your. Ex 19:15
but they shall not c. nigh. 24:2
ye shall not c. into land. Num 14:30
we will not c. up. 16:12, 14
unclean shall not c. Deut 23:10
c. not near unto the ark. Josh 3:4
that ye c. not among. 23:7
hath not c. a razor on. Judg 16:17
would not c. he sent the second time,
he would not c. 2 Sam 14:29
carcase not c. to. 1 Ki 13:22
king of Assyria shall not c. into.
2 Ki 19:32, 33; Isa 37:33, 34
I c. not against thee. 2 Chr 35:21
whosoever would not c. Ezra 10:8
Moabite not c. into. Neh 13:1*
not c. into the number. Job 3:6
an hypocrite shall not c. 13:16
floods they shall not c. Ps 32:6
let them not c. into thy. 69:27
it shall not c. nigh thee. 91:7
I will not c. into tabernacle. 132:3
c. not nigh the door. Pr 5:8
days that have not c. Isa 7:17
there shall not c. the fear of. 25
scourge shall not c. to me. 28:15
the gathering shall not c. 32:10
terror, it shall not c. near thee. 54:14
by thyself, c. not near me. 65:5
king of Babylon shall not c. Jer 37:19
like things shall not c. Ezek 16:16
they shall not c. near to me. 44:13
c. not ye unto Gilgal. Hos 4:15
their soul shall not c. into. 9:4
family of Egypt c. not. Zech 14:18*
and they would not c. Mat 22:3
could not c. nigh for. Mark 2:4
Luke 8:19
married a wife, I cannot c.
Luke 14:20
and shall not c. into. John 5:24
ye will not c. to me that ye. 40
thither ye cannot c. 7:34, 36
think ye that he will not c.? 11:56
if I had not c. they had. 15:22
not away, Comforter will not c. 16:7
as though I would not c. 1 Cor 4:18

come *out*

afterwards shall c. out. Gen 15:14
kings c. out of thee. 17:6; 35:11
daughters of city c. out. 24:13
till he c. out and have. Lev 16:17
shall eat till it c. out. Num 11:20
c. out ye three unto. 12:4
lest I c. out against thee. 20:18
people c. out of Egypt. 22:5, 11
year after Israel were c. out. 33:38
c. out one way, and. Deut 28:7
let fire c. out of the. Judg 9:15
increase army and c. out. 29
let not arrogancy c. out. 1 Sam 2:3
to-morrow we will c. out. 11:3, 10
king of Israel c. out ? 1 Sam 24:14
c. out, c. out, thou. 2 Sam 16:7*
480th year after Israel were c. out.
1 Ki 6:1
there are men c. out. 20:17
he will c. out to me. 2 Ki 5:11
agreement and c. out. 18:31
Isa 36:16
behold, he is c. out to fight. 2 Ki 19:9
salvation were c. out. Ps 14:7
princes shall c. out of. 68:31
the just shall c. out. Pr 12:13
their stink shall c. out. Isa 34:3
there is one c. out. Nah 1:11*
by no means c. out till. Mat 5:26
are ye c. out as against a thief? 26:55
Mark 14:48; Luke 22:52
hold thy peace, and c. out of him.
Mark 1:25; Luke 4:35
c. out, unclean spirit. Mark 5:8
Luke 8:29
any good thing c. out of? John 1:46
Christ c. out of Galilee ? 7:41
name of Jesus to c. out. Acts 16:18
there shall c. out of. Rom 11:26
wherefore c. out from. 2 Cor 6:17
though they c. out of loins. Heb 7:5
saw spirits c. out of. Rev 16:13
c. out of her, my people. 18:4

come *to pass*

it shall c. to pass if they. Ex 4:8, 9
word shall c. to pass or. Num 11:23
c. to pass the man's rod I. 17:5
c. to pass if ye hearken. Deut 7:12
11:13; 28:1
sign or wonder c. to pass. 13:2
all are c. to pass, no. Josh 23:14
let thy words c. to pass. Judg 13:12
when thy sayings c. to pass. 17
why is this c. to pass in? 21:3
shall surely c. to pass. 1 Ki 13:32
nor shall it c. to pass. Isa 7:7
so shall it c. to pass. 14:24
former things are c. to pass. 42:9
it shall c. to pass if ye. Jer 17:24
hast spoken is c. to pass. 32:24
I speak shall c. to pass. Ezek 12:25
it shall c. to pass, I will do it. 24:14
to thee what shall c. to p. Dan 2:29
c. to pass that I will break. Hos 1:5
c. to pass that whosoever. Joel 2:32
c. to pass I will cause sun. Amos 8:9
this shall c. to pass. Zech 6:15
therefore it is c. to pass, that. 7:13
things must c. to pass. Mat 24:6
saith shall c. to pass. Mark 11:23
ye shall see these c. to pass. 13:29
Luke 21:31
thing which is c. to pass. Luke 2:15
sign when things shall c. to pass.
21:7, 28
wondering at what was c. to pass.
24:12
not known things which c. to pass. 18
when it is c. to pass. John 13:19
14:29
c. to pass that every. Acts 3:23
must shortly c. to pass. Rev 1:1
22:6

come *short*

sinned and c. short of. Rom 3:23
seem to c. short of it. Heb 4:1

come joined with *time*

answer in time to c. Gen 30:33
son asketh thee in time to c.
Ex 13:14; Deut 6:20; Josh 4:6, 21
in time to c. your. Josh 22:24, 28
time was c. after. 1 Sam 1:20
time to favour Zion, set time is c.
Ps 102:13
rejoice in time to c. Pr 31:25
time of singing of birds is c.
S of S 2:12
her time is near to c. Isa 13:22
that it may be for time to c. 30:8
hearken and hear for time to c. 42:23
time is c. the day of. Ezek 7:7
time is not c. the Lord's. Hag 1:2
time was c. he should. Luke 9:51
fulness of time was c. Gal 4:4
foundation against time to c.
1 Tim 6:19
time is c. that judgement. 1 Pet 4:17

come *together*
we should *c. together*. *Job* 9:32
his troops *c. together* against. 19:12
shall *c. together* out of. *Jer* 3:18
and Judah shall *c. together*. 50:4
were *c. together*. *Acts* 1:6; 28:17
many that were *c. together*. 10:27
wherefore they were *c. together*. 19:32
multitude must *c. together*. 21:22
c. together again, that. *1 Cor* 7:5*
c. together, not for better. 11:17
c. together in church. 18, 20, 33
14:26
c. not *together* to condemnation. 11:34
if church be *c. together*. 14:23

come *up*
trumpet sound shall *c. up*. *Ex* 19:13
thou shalt *c. up*, thou and. 24
c. up to me into the mount. 24:12
I will *c. up* into midst of. 33:5
and *c. up* in the morning to. 34:2
no man shall *c. up* with thee. 3
us *c. up* out of Egypt? *Num* 20:5
c. up out of Jordan. *Josh* 4:16, 17, 18
c. up to me, and help me to. 10:4
c. up to us quickly, save us. 6
c. up with me into my lot. *Judg* 1:3
why are ye *c. up* against? 15:10
saying, *c. up* this once. 16:18
if they say, *c. up* to us. *1 Sam* 14:10
this man that is *c. up*? 17:25
then ye shall *c. up*. *1 Ki* 1:35
king of Syria will *c. up*. 20:22
c. up and save me. *2 Ki* 16:7
am I now *c. up* without Lord. 18:25
Isa 36:10
they *c. up* by the cliff. *2 Chr* 20:16
shall *c.* up no more. *Job* 7:9
be said, *c. up* hither. *Pr* 25:7
there shall *c. up* briers. *Isa* 5:6
and he shall *c. up* over all his. 8:7
laid down no fellow is *c. up*. 14:8
they shall *c. up* with. 60:7
death is *c. up* into our. *Jer* 9:21
c. up like a lion. 49:19; 50:44
behold, he shall *c. up* and fly. 49:22
cause the horses to *c. up* as. 51:27
sea is *c. up* upon Babylon. 42
and *c. up* upon my neck. *Lam* 1:14
cause fury to *c. up* to. *Ezek* 24:8
and cause you to *c. up* out. 37:12
thou shalt *c. up* against my. 38:16
c. up out of the land. *Hos* 1:11*
the thistle shall *c. up* on. 10:8
wind of Lord shall *c. up*. 13:15
and ill savour shall *c. up*. *Joel* 2:20
draw near, let them *c. up*. 3:9
let heathen *c. up* to valley of. 12
of your camps to *c. up*. *Amos* 4:10
saviours shall *c. up* on. *Obad* 21
wickedness is *c. up* before me.
Jonah 1:2
made a gourd to *c. up* over. 4:6
the breaker *c. up* before. *Mi* 2:13
dasheth in pieces is *c. up*. *Nah* 2:1
whoso will not *c. up*. *Zech* 14:17
desired Philip to *c. up*. *Acts* 8:31
were *c. up* out of the water. 39
Cornelius, thy alms are *c. up*. 10:4*
c. up hither, and I. *Rev* 4:1; 11:12

yet **come**
ye are not as *yet c*. *Deut* 12:9
my hour is not *yet c*. *John* 2:4
my time is not *yet c*. 7:6, 8
his hour was not *yet c*. 30; 8:20
Jesus was not *yet c*. 11:30
the other is not *yet c*. *Rev* 17:10

comeliness
he hath no form nor *c.* nor. *Isa* 53:2
perfect through my *c*. *Ezek* 16:14*
Persia and Lud set forth thy *c.* 27:10
my *c.* was turned in me. *Dan* 10:8
have more abundant *c.* *1 Cor* 12:23

comely
David, a *c.* person. *1 Sam* 16:18
not conceal *c.* proportion. *Job* 41:12†
praise is *c.* for the. *Ps* 33:1; 147:1
yea, four are *c.* in going. *Pr* 30:29*
it is *c.* for one to eat. *Eccl.* 5:18
I am black but *c*. *S of S* 1:5
thy cheeks are *c.* with rows. 10
and thy countenance is *c*. *S of S* 2:14
thy speech is *c*. 4:3
thou art *c*. O my love, as. 6:4
shall be excellent and *c*. *Isa* 4:2
daughter of Zion to a *c*. *Jer* 6:2
speak for that which is *c*. *1 Cor* 7:35*
is it *c.* that a woman pray? 11:13*
our *c.* parts have no need. 12:24

comers
can never make the *c*. *Heb* 10:1*

comest
from Sidon as thou *c*. *Gen* 10:19*
Egypt, as thou *c.* unto Zoar. 13:10*
when thou *c.* to my kindred. 24:41
thou *c.* nigh children of. *Deut* 2:19
when thou *c.* nigh to city. 20:10*
blessed when thou *c.* in. 28:6
cursed when thou *c.* in. 19
Micah ... whence *c.* thou? *Judg* 17:9
old man ... whence *c.* thou? 19:17
c. thou peaceably? *1 Sam* 16:4
1 Ki 2:13
I a dog, that thou *c.* to. *1 Sam* 17:43
thou *c.* to me with a sword. 45
bring Michal when *c*. *2 Sam* 3:13
when thou *c.* anoint. *1 Ki* 19:15
whence *c.* thou, Gehazi? *2 Ki* 5:25
whence *c.* thou? Satan. *Job* 1:7; 2:2
when thou *c.* to Babylon. *Jer* 51:61
occupation? whence *c.*? *Jonah* 1:8
and *c.* thou to me? *Mat* 3:14
remember me when *c*. *Luke* 23:42

cometh
behold this dreamer *c*. *Gen* 37:19
on which such water *c.* is. *Lev* 11:34
beside what *c.* of sale. *Deut* 18:8
cover that which *c.* from. 23:13
when ark *c.* among us. *1 Sam* 4:3
all that man of God saith *c*. 9:6
wherefore *c.* not the son of? 20:27
he *c.* not to the king's table. 29
for when she *c.* in will. *1 Ki* 14:5
but he *c.* not again. *2 Ki* 9:18, 20
king as he *c.* in. 11:8; *2 Chr* 23:7
for death, and it *c.* not. *Job* 3:21
whence *c.* wisdom? 28:20
but joy *c.* in the morning. *Ps* 30:5
from him cometh my salvation. 62:1
promotion *c.* not from the east. 75:6
before Lord, for he *c.* to. 96:13
blessed is he that *c.* in name. 118:26
from whence *c.* my help. 121:1
my help *c.* from the Lord. 2
will mock when your fear *c*. *Pr* 1:26
when your destruction *c*. 27
when pride *c.* then *c.* shame. 11:2
when the wicked *c.* then *c*. 18:3
he *c.* in with vanity. *Eccl* 6:4
all that *c.* is vanity. 11:8
he *c.* leaping upon. *S of S* 2:8
the day of the Lord *c*. *Isa* 13:9
whose breaking *c.* suddenly. 30:13
the name of the Lord *c.* from. 27
behold, thy salvation *c*. 62:11
is this that *c.* from Edom? 63:1
shall not see when good *c*. *Jer* 17:6
and shall not see when heat *c*. 8
when he *c.* he shall smite. 43:11
saith, and it *c.* to pass. *Lam* 3:37
c. to a prophet to. *Ezek* 14:4, 7
that which *c.* in your mind. 20:32
because it *c.* behold it *c*. 21:7
when this *c.* ye shall know I. 24:24
come to thee as people *c*. 33:31
when this *c.* to pass, then shall. 33
thing live whither rivers *c*. 47:9
that *c.* against him. *Dan* 11:16
blessed is he that *c.* to. 12:12
the thief *c.* in, and the. *Hos* 7:1*
day of the Lord *c*. *Joel* 2:1
Zech 14:1; *1 Thes* 5:2
from Assyrians when he *c*. *Mi* 5:6
the day *c.* that shall burn as an oven;
the day that *c*. *Mal* 4:1
he that *c.* after me is. *Mat* 3:11
Mark 1:7; *Luke* 3:16
more than these *c.* of evil. *Mat* 5:37
come, and he *c*. 8:9; *Luke* 7:8
then *c.* the wicked one. *Mat* 13:19
king *c.* unto thee. 21:5; *John* 12:15
he that *c.* in name of Lord. *Mat* 21:9
Mark 11:9; *Luke* 13:35; 19:38
lord of those servants *c*. *Mat* 25:19
he *c.* to them walking. *Mark* 6:48
be ashamed when he *c.* in. 8:38
Elias *c.* first, and restoreth. 9:12
while he yet spake, *c.* Judas. 14:43
whoso *c.* to me. *Luke* 6:47
the Lord when he *c*. 12:37
Son of man *c.* at an hour. 40
his lord, when he *c.* shall find. 43
there will be heat, and it *c*. 55
kingdom of God *c.* not. 17:20
Son of man *c.* shall he find? 18:8
canst not tell whence it *c*. *John* 3:8
nor *c.* to the light. 20
he that doth the truth, *c.* to the. 21
the hour *c*. 4:21, 23; 16:32
he that *c.* to me shall. 6:35, 37
learned of the Father *c.* to me. 45
when Christ *c.* no man. 7:27, 31
Christ *c.* of the seed of. 42
the night *c.* when no man can. 9:4
c. unto the Father but by me. 14:6
the time *c.* that whosoever. 16:2
time *c.* I shall no more speak. 25
the hour *c.* that ye shall be. 32
who when he *c.* shall. *Acts* 10:32
c. this blessedness upon? *Rom* 4:9*
so then, faith *c.* by hearing. 10:17
then *c.* the end, when. *1 Cor* 15:24
besides that which *c*. *2 Cor* 11:28*
c. wrath of God. *Eph* 5:6; *Col* 3:6
day of Lord so *c.* as a *1 Thes* 5:2
he that *c.* to God must. *Heb* 11:6
the Lord *c.* with 10,000 of. *Jude* 14
he *c.* with clouds. *Rev* 1:7
when he *c.* he must continue a. 17:10

cometh *down*
as the rain *c. down*. *Isa* 55:10
is he which *c. down*. *John* 6:33, 50
and perfect gift *c. down*. *Jas* 1:17
Jerusalem which *c. down*. *Rev* 3:12

cometh *forth*
when virgin *c. forth*. *Gen* 24:43
also behold he *c. forth*. *Ex* 4:14
Pharaoh, lo, he *c. forth* to. 8:20
c. forth of the doors. *Judg* 11:31
whosoever *c.* not *forth*. *1 Sam* 11:7
affliction *c.* not *forth*. *Job* 5:6
he *c. forth* like a flower. 14:2
this also *c. forth* from. *Isa* 28:29
words *c. forth* from. *Ezek* 33:30
behold, the Lord *c. forth*. *Mi* 1:3

cometh *nigh*
the stranger that *c. nigh* shall be.
Num 1:51; 3:10, 38; 18:7

cometh *out*
be heard when he *c. out*. *Ex* 28:35
when he *c. out*. *Num* 12:12
toward young that *c. out*. *Deut* 28:57
a stranger that *c. out* of. *1 Ki* 8:41
drawn, and *c. out* of. *Job* 20:25
fair weather *c. out* of the. 37:22
who is this that *c. out*? *S of S* 3:6
the Lord *c. out* of his. *Isa* 26:21
and that which *c. out* of it. 42:5
it *c. out* of the north. *Jer* 46:20
it with dung that *c. out*. *Ezek* 4:12
that which *c. out* of the mouth.
Mat 15:11*; *Mark* 7:20
for as lightning *c. out* of. 24:27

cometh *up*
old man *c. up* covered. *1 Sam* 28:14
who is this that *c. up*? *S of S* 8:5
and he that *c. up* out. *Isa* 24:18
who is this that *c. up*? *Jer* 46:7*
out of north there *c. up* a. 50:3
when he *c. up* to people. *Hab* 3:16
up the fish first *c. up*. *Mat* 17:27

comfort, *substantive*
then should I yet have *c*. *Job* 6:10†
that I may take *c.* a little. 10:20
this is my *c.* in my. *Ps* 119:50
kindness be for my *c*. 76
should I receive *c.*? *Isa* 57:6*
thou art a *c.* to them. *Ezek* 16:54
daughter, be of good *c*. *Mat* 9:22*
Luke 8:48
be of good *c.* rise. *Mark* 10:49*
walking in the *c.* of the. *Acts* 9:31
through patience and *c*. *Rom* 15:4
to exhortation and *c*. *1 Cor* 14:3*
even the God of all *c*. *2 Cor* 1:3
by the *c.* wherewith we are. 4

I am filled with *c*. *2 Cor* 7:4
comforted in your *c*. 13
be perfect, be of good *c*. 13:11
if there be any *c*. of love. *Phil* 2:1*
that I may also be of good *c*. 19
have been a *c*. to me. *Col* 4:11

comfort, *verb*

this same shall *c*. us. *Gen* 5:29
c. ye your hearts. 18:5
as touching thee doth *c*. 27:42
and daughters rose up to *c*. 37:35
c. thy heart with a. *Judg* 19:5, 8
David sent to *c*. him. *2 Sam* 10:2
1 Chr 19:2
brethren came to *c*. him. *1 Chr* 7:22
came to Hanun to *c*. him. 19:2
to mourn with and *c*. *Job* 2:11
I say, my bed shall *c*. me. 7:13
I will forget, I will *c*. myself. 9:27*
how then *c*. ye me in vain. 21:34
rod and thy staff, they *c*. *Ps* 23:4
thou shalt increase and *c*. 71:21
when wilt thou *c*. me ? 119:82
c. me with apples. *S of S* 2:5
labour not to *c*. me. *Isa* 22:4
c. ye, *c*. ye my people. 40:1
Lord shall *c*. Zion, he will *c*. 51:3
by whom shall I *c*. thee ? 19
he hath sent me to *c*. 61:2
so will I *c*. you. 66:13
when I would *c*. myself. *Jer* 8:18
neither shall men tear to *c*. 16:7
for I will *c*. them. 31:13
hath none to *c*. her. *Lam* 1:2, 17
there is none to *c*. me. 21
that I may *c*. thee ? 2:13
they shall *c*. you when. *Ezek* 14:23
Lord shall yet *c*. Zion. *Zech* 1:17
told false dreams, they *c*. in. 10:2
to *c*. them concerning. *John* 11:19*
we may be able to *c*. *2 Cor* 1:4
rather to forgive and *c*. him. 2:7
and that he might *c*. *Eph* 6:22
know your estate, *c*. *Col* 4:8
to *c*. you concerning. *1 Thes* 3:2
wherefore *c*. one another. 4:18
wherefore *c*. yourselves. 5:11*
c. the feeble-minded. 14*
our Lord Jesus *c*. *2 Thes* 2:17

comfortable

word of my Lord be *c*. *2 Sam* 14:17
the angel with *c*. words. *Zech* 1:13

comfortably

go forth and speak *c*. *2 Sam* 19:7
he spake *c*. to all. *2 Chr* 30:22
over people, and spake *c*. 32:6
speak *c*. to Jerusalem. *Isa* 40:2
allure her, and speak *c*. *Hos* 2:14

comforted

Isaac was *c*. after his. *Gen* 24:67
Jacob refused to be *c*. 37:35
Judah was *c*. and went. 38:12
Joseph *c*. his brethren. 50:21
that thou hast *c*. me. *Ruth* 2:13
David *c*. Bath-sheba. *2 Sam* 12:24
c. concerning Ammon. 13:39
all his brethren *c*. him. *Job* 42:11
my soul refused to be *c*. *Ps* 77:2
Lord, hast holpen and *c*. 86:17
judgements, have *c*. myself. 119:52
hath *c*. his people. *Isa* 49:13; 52:9
afflicted, tossed, and not *c*. 54:11
ye shall be *c*. in Jerusalem. 66:13
refused to be *c*. for child. *Jer* 31:15
to rest, I will be *c*. *Ezek* 5:13
ye shall be *c*. concerning. 14:22
all that drink water be *c*. 31:16
see them, and shall be *c*. 32:31
would not be *c*. because. *Mat* 2:18
for they shall be *c*. 5:4
now he is *c*. and thou. *Luke* 16:25
the Jews which *c*. her. *John* 11:31
seen brethren, *c*. them. *Acts* 16:40
were not a little *c*. 20:12
that I may be *c*. with. *Rom* 1:12
and all may be *c*. *1 Cor* 14:31
wherewith we are *c*. of. *2 Cor* 1:4
God *c*. us by coming of Titus. 7:6
wherewith he was *c*. in you. 7
therefore we were *c*. in your. 13
their hearts might be *c*. *Col* 2:2
how he exhorted and *c*. *1 Thes* 2:11*
we were *c*. over you in all. 3:7

comfortedst

is turned away, thou *c*. *Isa* 12:1*

comforter, -s

hath sent *c*. *2 Sam* 10:3; *1 Chr* 19:3
miserable *c*. are ye all. *Job* 16:2
I looked for *c*. but. *Ps* 69:20
and they had no *c*. *Eccl* 4:1
she had no *c*. *Lam* 1:9
c. that should relieve is far. 16
whence shall I seek *c*.? *Nah* 3:7
another *C*. to abide. *John* 14:16
the *C*. which is Holy Ghost. 26
when the *C*. is come. 15:26
if I go not *C*. will not come. 16:7

comforteth

I dwelt, as one that *c*. *Job* 29:25
I, even I, am he that *c*. *Isa* 51:12
as one whom his mother *c*. 66:13
who *c*. us in all our. *2 Cor* 1:4
God that *c*. those that are cast. 7:6

comfortless

I will not leave you *c*. *John* 14:18*

comforts

thy *c*. delight my soul. *Ps* 94:19
and restore *c*. to him. *Isa* 57:18

coming

blessed thee since my *c*. *Gen* 30:30*
nothing hinder from *c*. *Num* 22:16
chariot so long in *c*.? *Judg* 5:28
tremble at his *c*. *1 Sam* 16:4*
c. in with me, since day of *c*. 29:6
going out and thy *c*. in. *2 Sam* 3:25
invaded the land at *c*. *2 Ki* 13:20
going out and *c*. in. 19:27; *Isa* 37:28
he seeth that his day is *c*. *Ps* 37:13
preserve going out and *c*. in. 121:8
to meet thee at *c*. *Isa* 14:9
the things that are *c*. let. 44:7
observe time of their *c*. *Jer* 8:7
saw an holy one *c*. down. *Dan* 4:23
days of *c*. out of Egypt. *Mi* 7:15
may abide day of his *c*.? *Mal* 3:2
before the *c*. of the great day. 4:5
they see Son of man *c*. *Mat* 16:28
shall be the sign of thy *c*.? 24:3
so shall the *c*. of the Son. 27, 37, 39
see the Son of man *c*. 30; 26:64
Mark 13:26; 14:62; *Luke* 21:27
my Lord delayeth *c*. *Mat* 24:48
Luke 12:45
at my *c*. received own. *Mat* 25:27
Luke 19:23
for there were many *c*. *Mark* 6:31
as he was yet *c*. the. *Luke* 9:42
lest by her continual *c*. she. 18:5
while I am *c*. another *John* 5:7
the hour is *c*. 25, 28
seeth the wolf *c*. 10:12
shewed before of the *c*. *Acts* 7:52
with them *c*. in and going. 9:28*
as Peter was *c*. in Cornelius. 10:25
had preached before his *c*. 13:24
waiting for the *c*. of. *1 Cor* 1:7*
they that are Christ's at his *c*. 15:23
glad of *c*. of Stephanas and. 16:17
comforted us by the *c*. *2 Cor* 7:6
not by his *c*. only, but by. 7
more abundant by my *c*. *Phil* 1:26*
rejoicing at our Lord's *c*. *1 Thes* 2:19
hearts unblameable at the *c*. 3:13
we who remain to the *c*. 4:15
preserved blameless to the *c*. 5:23
beseech you by *c*. of. *2 Thes* 2:1
destroy with brightness of his *c*. 8
even him whose *c*. is after the. 9
patient, brethren, to the *c*. *Jas* 5:7
for the *c*. of the Lord. 8
to whom *c*. as unto a. *1 Pet* 2:4
make known power and *c*. *2 Pet* 1:16
where is promise of his *c*.? 3:4
looking and hasting to the *c*. of. 12
not be ashamed before him at his *c*.
1 John 2:28
beheld another beast *c*. *Rev* 13:11
Jerusalem *c*. down from God. 21:2

comings

goings out and *c*. in. *Ezek* 43:11

command

Abraham will *c*. his. *Gen* 18:19
sacrifice as God shall *c*. *Ex* 8:27
and God *c*. thee so. 18:23
hear what Lord will *c*. *Num* 9:8
thing which the Lord doth *c*. 36:6
the Lord shall *c*. the. *Deut* 28:8
ye shall *c*. your children. 32:46
so did Moses *c*. Joshua. *Josh* 11:15
eagle mount up at thy *c*.? *Job* 39:27
the Lord will *c*. his. *Ps* 42:8
art my king, O God, *c*. 44:4
work of my hands, *c*. me. *Isa* 45:11
c. them to say to their. *Jer* 27:4
heathen didst *c*. they. *Lam* 1:10
c. these stones be made. *Mat* 4:3
Luke 4:3
why did Moses *c*. to ? *Mat* 19:7
c. therefore that sepulchre. 27:64
what did Moses *c*. you ? *Mark* 10:3
he would not *c*. them. *Luke* 8:31
wilt thou we *c*. fire to come ? 9:54
did not we straitly *c*. you ? *Acts* 5:28
and to *c*. them to keep. 15:5
and will do things we *c*. *2 Thes* 3:4
we *c*. you, brethren, in name. 6
that are such we *c*. and exhort. 12
these *c*. and teach. *1 Tim* 4:11

***I* command**

speak all that *I c*. thee. *Ex* 7:2
Jer 1:7, 17
observe what *I c*. thee. *Ex* 34:11
Deut 12:28
I will *c*. my blessing. *Lev* 25:21
not add to the word *I c*. *Deut* 4:2
I c. thee this day. 7:11; 8:11; 10:13
11:8, 27; 13:18; 30:8
I c. thee to do this. 24:18, 22
I c. thee this day to love. 30:16
I will *c*. the clouds. *Isa* 5:6
do all which *I c*. you. *Jer* 11:4
I will *c*. saith the Lord. 34:22
thence will *I c*. serpent. *Amos* 9:3
thence *I c*. the sword. 4
I will *c*. and I will sift the. 9
friends, if ye do what *I c*. *John* 15:14
these things *I c*. you, that ye. 17
I c. thee in the name. *Acts* 16:18
I c. yet not I, but Lord. *1 Cor* 7:10

commanded

now thou art *c*. this do. *Gen* 45:19
to him as he *c*. them. 50:12
not as king of Egypt *c*. *Ex* 1:17
for so I am *c*. *Lev* 10:13
I c. you all things. *Deut* 1:18
3:18, 21
Israel did as Joshua *c*. *Josh* 4:8
see I have *c*. you. 8:8
obeyed my voice in all I *c*. 22:2
all that I *c*. her. *Judg* 13:14
hath *c*. me to be there. *1 Sam* 20:29
the king *c*. me a business. 21:2
have not I *c*. you ? *2 Sam* 13:28
performed all the king *c*. 21:14
that Jehoiada priest *c*. *2 Ki* 11:9
to all that king Ahaz *c*. 16:16
is it not I *c*. people to ? *1 Chr* 21:17
David man of God *c*. *2 Chr* 8:14
Asa *c*. Judah to seek Lord. 14:4
Manasseh *c*. Judah. 33:16
I *c*. that the gates. *Neh* 13:19
I *c*. Levites to cleanse. 22
for the king had so *c*. *Esth* 3:2
according to all that Haman *c*. 12
according as Esther *c*. him. 4:17
according to all Mordecai *c* 8:9
hast thou *c*. morning ? *Job* 38:12
my molten image hath *c*. *Isa* 48:5
our father *c*. us. *Jer* 35:6, 10, 14, 16
18
so as I was *c*. *Ezek* 12:7; 37:7
to you it is *c*. O people. *Dan* 3:4
he *c*. that they should heat. 19
king *c*. and they brought Daniel. 6:16
king *c*. and they brought those. 24
c. the prophets, saying. *Amos* 2:12
c. it to be given her. *Mat* 14:9
Mark 6:27
c. multitude to sit down. *Mat* 14:19
15:35; *Mark* 6:39
his lord *c*. him to be sold. *Mat* 18:25
and did as Jesus *c*. them. 21:6*
observe all things I have *c*. 28:20
he *c*. them to tell no. *Luke* 9:21
c. them to be baptized. *Acts* 10:48
Festus *c*. Paul to be brought. 25:6
c. to be under. *1 Cor* 14:34*

with hands as we *c.* *1 Thes* 4:11
we *c.* you that if any. *2 Thes* 3:10
endure that which was *c.* *Heb* 12:20
it was *c.* them not to. *Rev* 9:4

God **commanded**

God c. man to eat. *Gen* 2:16
according to all that *God c.* 6:22
into ark as *God* had *c.* 7:9, 16
21:4; *Deut* 20:17; *Josh* 10:40
God c. thee to keep. *Deut* 5:15
do as the Lord your *God c.* 32
in ways the Lord your *God c.* 33
God c. to teach you. 6:1, 20; 13:5
this day Lord thy *God c.* 26:16
hath not Lord *God c.* to go? *Judg* 4:6
did as *God c.* him. *1 Chr* 14:16
God c. me, make haste. *2 Chr* 35:21
c. by the *God* of heaven. *Ezra* 7:23
God hath *c.* thy strength. *Ps* 68:28
for *God c.* saying. *Mat* 15:4
things that are *c.* of *God.* *Acts* 10:33
God who *c.* light to. *2 Cor* 4:6

Lord or *God* **commanded**

tree I *c.* not to eat. *Gen* 3:11, 17
according to all *Lord c.* 7:5
did as the *Lord c.* them. *Ex* 7:6
10:20; 12:28, 50; *Num* 17:11
this is the thing *Lord c.* *Ex* 16:16
32; 35:4; *Num* 30:1
Lord c. Moses. *Ex* 16:34; 34:4
39:1, 5, 7, etc.; 40:19, etc.
Lev 8:9; 9:10
as I *c.* in the time. *Ex* 23:15
in the day he *c.* the. *Lev* 7:38
did as *Lord c.* him. 8:4
Num 20:27; 27:11
strange fire which he *c.* not.
Lev 10:1
Lord c. my lord to. *Num* 36:2
the *Lord c.* us to do all. *Deut* 6:24
aside out of the way *Lord c.* 9:16
there they be as *Lord c.* 10:5
gods, which I have not *c.* 17:3
18:20; *Jer* 19:5; 23:32; 29:23
have not I *c.* thee? *Josh* 1:9
my covenant I *c.* 7:11; *Judg* 2:20
lot, as I have *c.* thee. *Josh* 13:6
Lord c. him to be. *1 Sam* 13:14
c. to feed my people. *2 Sam* 7:7
1 Chr 17:6
since I *c.* judges. *2 Sam* 7:11
1 Chr 17:10
went up, as *Lord c.* *2 Sam* 24:19
c. him concerning this. *1 Ki* 11:10
I have *c.* the ravens to feed. 17:4
I have *c.* a widow woman. 9
the word which he *c.* to. *1 Chr* 16:15
Ps 105:8
in the law, which he *c.* *1 Chr* 16:40
Lord c. the angel. 21:27
Lord God of Israel *c.* him. 24:19
to judgement thou has *c.* *Ps* 7:6
he *c.* and it stood fast. 33:9
whom the *Lord c.* them. 106:34
c. his covenant for ever. 111:9
thou hast *c.* us to keep thy. 119:4
testimonies thou hast *c.* are. 138
there the *Lord c.* the blessing. 133:3
for the Lord *c.* and they. 148:5
I have *c.* my sanctified. *Isa* 13:3
for my mouth it hath *c.* 34:16
heavens and their host I *c.* 45:12
but this thing *c.* I them. *Jer* 7:23
c. them not. 31; 19:5; 32:35
words of covenant which I *c.* 11:8
by Euphrates, as *Lord c.* 13:5
hallow the sabbath, as I *c.* 17:22
all that I have *c.* thee. 50:21
Lord hath *c.* concerning. *Lam* 1:17
his word he had *c.* in days. 2:17
I have done as thou hast *c.* me.
Ezek 9:11
in morning as I was *c.* 24:18; 37:10
my words which I *c.* *Zech* 1:6
law which I *c.* in Horeb. *Mal* 4:4
is done as thou hast *c.* *Luke* 14:22
he *c.* us to preach to. *Acts* 10:42
so hath the *Lord c.* 13:46, 47

Moses **commanded**

took as *Moses* had *c.* *Num* 16:47
aside from way I *c.* *Deut* 31:29
Moses c. us a law. 33:4
according to all *Moses c.* *Josh* 1:7
kept all that *Moses c.* you. 22:2
Moses c. according to. *1 Chr* 15:15
offer the gift that *Moses c.* *Mat* 8:4
offer those things which *Moses c.*
Mark 1:44; *Luke* 5:14
Moses in law *c.* that. *John* 8:5

commandedst

which thou *c.* thy. *Neh* 1:7, 8
thou *c.* them precepts. 9:14
done nothing that thou *c.* *Jer* 32:23

commander

him for a leader and *c.* *Isa* 55:4

commandest

all that thou *c.* us we. *Josh* 1:16
hearken in all that thou *c.* 18
nothing of all thou *c.* *Jer* 32:23
c. me to be smitten? *Acts* 23:3

commandeth

will do as my lord *c.* *Num* 32:25
God, who *c.* the sun. *Job* 9:7
he *c.* that they return from. 36:10
and *c.* it not to shine. 32
they may do whatever he *c.* 37:12
he *c.* and raiseth the. *Ps* 107:25
when Lord *c.* it not? *Lam* 3:37
Lord *c.* and he will. *Amos* 6:11
he *c.* the unclean spirits. *Mark* 1:27
Luke 4:36
he *c.* the winds. *Luke* 8:25
c. all men to repent. *Acts* 17:30

commanding

Jacob made an end of *c.* *Gen* 49:33
Jesus made an end of *c.* *Mat* 11:1
c. his accusers to come. *Acts* 24:8
c. to abstain from meats. *1 Tim* 4:3

commandment

he gave them in *c.* all. *Ex* 34:32
broken his *c.* that soul. *Num* 15:31
I have received *c.* to bless. 23:20
ye rebelled against my *c.* 27:14
this *c.* I command. *Deut* 30:11
thou not kept the *c.* I? *1 Ki* 2:43
king's *c.* was, answer him not.
2 Ki 18:36; *Isa* 36:21
brethren were at their *c.* *1 Chr* 12:32
people will be wholly at thy *c.* 28:31
according to the *c.* of. *2 Chr* 8:13
shall come between law and *c.* 19:10
one heart to do the *c.* of. 30:12
and as soon as the *c.* came. 31:5
I sent them with *c.* to. *Ezra* 8:17
those that tremble at the *c.* 10:3
it was the king's *c.* *Neh* 11:23
to come at king's *c.* *Esth* 1:12
Esther did the *c.* of Mordecai. 2:20
transgressest thou king's *c.*? 3:3
when king's *c.* drew nigh to be. 9:1
nor gone back from *c.* *Job* 23:12
thy *c.* is exceeding broad. *Ps* 119:96
he sendeth forth his *c.* 147:15
the *c.* is a lamp. *Pr* 6:23
waters should not pass his *c.* 8:29
he that feareth the *c.* shall. 13:13
he that keepeth the *c.* 19:16
whoso keepeth *c.* shall. *Eccl* 8:5
their father Jonadab's *c.* *Jer* 35:14
because the king's *c.* *Dan* 3:22
the *c.* came forth, and I am. 9:23
willingly walked after *c.* *Hos* 5:11
O ye priests, this *c.* is for. *Mal* 2:1
that I have sent this *c.* to. 4
why transgress the *c.* of? *Mat* 15:3
thus have ye made the *c.* of. 6
which is the great *c.* in law? 22:36
first and great *c.* 38; *Mark* 12:30
aside the *c.* of God. *Mark* 7:8
full well ye reject the *c.* of. 9
is no other *c.* greater than. 12:31
transgressed I thy *c.* *Luke* 15:29
rested according to the *c.* 23:56
this *c.* have I received. *John* 10:18
he gave me a *c.* what. 12:49
I know that his *c.* is life. 50
as the Father gave me *c.* 14:31
my *c.* that ye love one. 15:12
1 John 3:23
we gave no such *c.* *Acts* 15:24
receiving a *c.* to Silas. 17:15
and gave *c.* to his accusers. 23:30
at Festus' *c.* Paul was. 25:23
sin taking occasion by *c.* *Rom* 7:8, 11
when the *c.* came, sin revived. 9
c. which was ordained to life. 10
and the *c.* is holy, and just. 12
that sin by *c.* might become. 13
if there be any other *c.* it is. 13:9
according to the *c.* of the. 16:26
by permission, not of *c.* *1 Cor* 7:6
I speak not by *c.* but by. *2 Cor* 8:8
the first *c.* with promise. *Eph* 6:2
by the *c.* of God our. *1 Tim* 1:1
Tit 1:3
the end of the *c.* is charity. *1 Tim* 1:5
not after law of a carnal *c.* *Heb* 7:16
there is a disannulling of *c.* 18
Joseph gave *c.* concerning. 11:22
not afraid of the king's *c.* 23
to turn from holy *c.* *2 Pet* 2:21
mindful of *c.* of us the apostles. 3:2
but an old *c.* *1 John* 2:7
this is his *c.* that we should. 3:23
this *c.* have we from him. 4:21
we have received a *c.* *2 John* 4
this is the *c.* that as ye have. 6

give or *given* **commandment**

which I will *give* thee in *c.* *Ex* 25:22
Lord had *given* him in *c.* *Deut* 1:3
give c. to cease till *c.* *Ezra* 4:21
hast *given c.* to save me. *Ps* 71:3
hath *given c.* against. *Isa* 23:11
hath *given c.* concerning. *Nah* 1:14
given c. if any knew. *John* 11:57

keep **commandment,** *see* **keep**

commandment *of the Lord*

journeyed according to the *c. of Lord.*
Ex 17:1; *Num* 9:18, 20; 10:13
numbered at *c. of Lord.* *Num* 3:39
go beyond *c. of Lord* to. 24:13
went up to Hor at *c. of Lord.* 33:38
charge of *c. of Lord* your. *Josh* 22:3
not rebel against the *c. of Lord.*
1 Sam 12:14
but rebel against *c. of Lord.* 15
hast not kept the *c. of Lord.* 13:13
I have performed the *c of Lord.* 15:13
have transgressed the *c. of Lord.* 24
despised *c. of Lord.* *2 Sam* 12:9
at the *c. of Lord* came. *2 Ki* 24:3
for so was *c. of Lord.* *2 Chr* 29:25
the *c. of Lord* is pure. *Ps* 19:8
I have no *c. of Lord.* *1 Cor* 7:25

new **commandment**

a *new c.* I give unto. *John* 13:34
I write no *new c.* unto. *1 John* 2:7
a *new c.* I write unto you. 8
though I wrote a *new c.* *2 John* 5

rebelled against the **commandment**

ye *rebelled ag.* my *c.* *Num* 27:14
ye *rebelled ag. c.* of the Lord your God. *Deut* 1:26, 43
rebelled ag. c. of Lord and. 9:23
I have *rebelled ag.* his *c.* *Lam* 1:18

commandments

Abraham kept my *c.* *Gen* 26:5
thou wilt give ear to his *c.* *Ex* 15:26
wrote on tables the ten *c.* 34:28
Deut 4:13; 10:4
somewhat against any of the *c.*
Lev 4:13, 27
commit sin forbidden by *c.* 5:17
these are the *c.* the Lord. 27:34
remember all the *c.* of. *Num* 15:39
in not keeping *c.* *Deut* 8:11
shall hearken to *c.* 11:13; 28:13
Judg 3:4
if ye obey the *c.* of. *Deut* 11:27
if ye will not obey the *c.* of. 28
hath not performed *c.* *1 Sam* 15:11
because he kept my *c.* *1 Ki* 11:34
David who kept my *c.* 14:8
in that ye have forsaken *c.* 18:18
and they left all *c.* of. *2 Ki* 17:16
Judah kept not the *c.* of. 19
but kept his *c.* which he. 18:6
if ye forsake my *c.* *2 Chr* 7:19
why transgress ye the *c.* of? 24:20
we have forsaken thy *c.* *Ezra* 9:10
should we again break thy *c.* 14
if they keep not my *c.* *Ps* 89:31
all his *c.* are sure. 111:7*
delighteth greatly in his *c.* 112:1

me not wander from thy c. Ps 119:10
I am a stranger, hide not thy c. 19
make me to go in path of thy c. 35
I will delight in thy c. 47
I have believed thy c. 66
that I may learn thy c. 73
all thy c. are faithful. 86
thou through thy c. hast made. 98
I love thy c. 127
I longed for thy c. 131
thy c. are my delights. 143
all thy c. are truth. 151
I have done thy c. 166
all thy c. are righteousness. 172
not forget thy c. 176
if thou wilt hide my c. Pr 2:1
keep my words and lay up c. 7:1
wise in heart will receive c. 10:8
hadst hearkened to my c. Isa 48:18
break one of these least c. Mat 5:19
for doctrines the c. of men. 15:9*
Mark 7:7*
on these two c. hang all. Mat 22:40
thou knowest the c. Mark 10:19
Luke 18:20
the first of all the c. is. Mark 12:29
walking in all the c. of. Luke 1:6
he that hath my c. and. John 14:21
c. as I have kept Father's c. 15:10
keeping the c. of God. 1 Cor 7:19
things I write you, are the c. 14:37
after the c. and. Col 2:22*
for ye know what c. 1 Thes 4:2*
that keepeth not his c. 1 John 2:4
he that keepeth his c. dwelleth. 3:24
that we walk after his c. 2 John 6

do commandments

do all my c. and be. Num 15:40
observe to do all c. Deut 6:25
15:5; 28:1, 15; 30:8
constant to do my c. 1 Chr 28:7
remember his c. to do. Ps 103:18*
they that do his c. 111:10†
blessed that do his c. Rev 22:14*

not do commandments

ye will not do these c. Lev 26:14
so that ye will not do all my c. 15

keep commandments, see keep

commend

[1] *To praise,* 2 Cor 3:1; 5:12. [2] *To commit, or give in charge,* Luke 23:46. [3] *To make one more acceptable,* 1 Cor 8:8.

into thy hands I c. my. Luke 23:46
brethren, I c. you to God. Acts 20:32
our unrighteousness c. Rom 3:5
I c. unto you Phebe our sister. 16:1
do we begin again to c.? 2 Cor 3:1
for we c. not ourselves. 5:12
ourselves with some that c. 10:12

commendation

need we, epistles of c.? 2 Cor 3:1

commended

the princes c. Sarai. Gen 12:15*
a man shall be c. Pr 12:8
then I c. mirth. Eccl 8:15
Lord c. the unjust. Luke 16:8
c. them to the Lord. Acts 14:23
I ought to have been c. 2 Cor 12:11

commendeth

but God c. his love. Rom 5:8
but meat c. us not to. 1 Cor 8:8
not he that c. himself is approved.
2 Cor 10:18

commending

c. ourselves to every. 2 Cor 4:2

commission, -s

delivered the king's c. Ezra 8:36
as I went with c. from. Acts 26:12

commit

thou shalt not c. adultery. Ex 20:14
Deut 5:18; Mat 5:27; 19:18
Rom 13:9
if sin, and c. any of. Lev 5:17
not c. any of these. 18:26, 30
who shall c. any of these. 29
if man or woman c. any. Num 5:6
c. no more any such. Deut 19:20
caused Jerusalem to c. 2 Chr 21:11
unto God would I c. my. Job 5:8
into thine hand I c. my. Ps 31:5
c. thy way unto the Lord. Ps 37:5
c. thy works unto the. Pr 16:3
an abomination to kings to c. 12
I will c. thy government. Isa 22:21
c. Jeremiah to court of. Jer 37:21
why c. ye this great evil? 44:7
c. abominations they c. Ezek 8:17
and thou shalt not c. this. 16:43
in the midst of thee they c. 22:9
priests murder, they c. Hos 6:9
for they c. falsehood, and. 7:1
and did c. things worthy. Luke 12:48
who will c. to your trust? 16:11
Jesus did not c. himself. John 2:24
they which c. such things. Rom 1:32
against them which c. such. 2:2
abhorrest idols, dost thou c.? 22
neither c. fornication. 1 Cor 10:8
this charge I c. to thee. 1 Tim 1:18
the same c. thou to. 2 Tim 2:2
respect to persons ye c. Jas 2:9
c. the keeping of souls. 1 Pet 4:19
born of God doth not c. 1 John 3:9
Israel to c. fornication. Rev 2:14
my servants to c. fornication. 20

see adultery

commit iniquity

if he c. iniquity I will. 2 Sam 7:14
he should c. iniquity. Job 34:10
themselves to c. iniquity. Jer 9:5
and c. iniquity. Ezek 3:20; 33:13

commit trespass

if a soul c. a trespass. Lev 5:15
go aside and c. trespass. Num 5:12
caused Israel to c. trespass. 31:16
Achan c. a trespass. Josh 22:20

commit whoredom or whoredoms

will cut off that c. whor. Lev 20:5
to c. whor. with the. Num 25:1
and thou didst c. whor. Ezek 16:17
none followeth to c. whor. 34
c. ye whor. after their? 20:30
will they c. whor. with her. 23:43
they shall c. whor. and. Hos 4:10
daughters shall c. whor. 13, 14

committed

c. all that he hath to. Gen 39:8
the keeper c. to Joseph all. 22
for sin he hath c. Lev 4:35
customs which were c. 18:30
they c. these things, and. 20:23
if aught be c. by. Num 15:24*
man or woman that c. Deut 17:5
if a man have c. a sin worthy. 21:22
they have c. folly and. Judg 20:6
sinned, we have c. 1 Ki 8:47
provoked him with sins, they c. 14:22
brasen shields c. he. 27; 2 Chr 12:10
died for his transgression he c.
1 Chr 10:13
people have c. two evils. Jer 2:13
and horrible thing is c. in. 5:30
our sin that we have c. 16:10
which they have c. to 44:3, 9
hast c. fornication with. Ezek 16:26
nor hath Samaria c. half. 51
from all sins he hath c. 18:21, 22, 28
for evils ye have c. 20:43
they c. whoredoms in Egypt. 23:3
thus she c. whoredoms with. 7
none of the sins he c. shall. 33:16
for the land hath c. great. Hos 1:2
they have c. whoredom. 4:18
who had c. murder in. Mark 15:7
to whom men have c. Luke 12:48
Father hath c. judgement. John 5:22
c. them to prison. Acts 8:3
if I have c. any thing. 25:11
had found he had c. nothing. 25
they c. themselves to sea. 27:40*
though I have c. nothing. 28:17
to them were c. oracles. Rom 3:2
gospel is c. to me. 1 Cor 9:17
Tit 1:3
fornication as some of them c. 10:8
hath c. to us the word. 2 Cor 5:19
lasciviousness which they c. 12:21
gospel of uncircumcision c. Gal 2:7
1 Tim 1:11
keep what is c. to thee. 1 Tim 6:20
to keep that which I c. 2 Tim 1:12
if he have c. sins, they. Jas 5:15
c. himself to him that. 1 Pet 2:23
deeds which they have c. Jude 15
kings c. fornication. Rev 17:2
18:3, 9

see abominations

committed iniquity

we have c. iniq. we. Ps 106:6
for iniq. he hath c. Ezek 33:13, 18
we have c. iniq. and. Dan 9:5

committed trespass

for his tres. he c. two. Lev 5:7
Israel c. a tres. in the. Josh 7:1
what tres. is this ye have c.? 22:16
not c. this tres. against Lord. 31
they have c. tres., I will. Ezek 15:8
in that they c. a tres. 20:27

committest, -eth, -ing

poor c. himself to thee. Ps 10:14
abomination that Israel c. Ezek 8:6
in statutes of life without c. 33:15
killing, stealing, and c. Hos 4:2
O Ephraim, thou c. whoredom. 5:3
whosoever c. sin is the. John 8:34
he that c. fornication. 1 Cor 6:18
c. sin transgresseth. 1 John 3:4
he that c. sin is of the devil. 8

commodious

the haven was not c. to. Acts 27:12

common

[1] *That which is ordinary, or usual;* as a common death, Num 16:29. [2] *That which is ceremonially unclean,* Acts 11:9. [3] *Had in common; to use together as belonging to all,* Acts 2:44.

if these men die the c. Num 16:29
there is no c. bread. 1 Sam 21:4
bread is in a manner c. 5
an evil, and it is c. Eccl 6:1*
shall eat them as c. things. Jer 31:5*
men of c. sort were. Ezek 23:42
took Jesus into the c. Mat 27:27*
had all things c. Acts 2:44; 4:32
put apostles in the c. prison. 5:18*
never eaten anything c. 10:14; 11:8
God cleansed call not c. 10:15; 11:9
should not call any thing c. 10:28
no temptation but c. 1 Cor 10:13*
my own son, after c. faith. Tit 1:4
to write to you of the c. Jude 3

common people

if any of c. people sin. Lev 4:27
body into graves of c. people.
Jer 26:23
and the c. people heard. Mark 12:37

commonwealth

being aliens from c. of. Eph 2:12

commonly, see reported

commotion, -s

a great c. out of north. Jer 10:22
when ye hear of c. be. Luke 21:9*

commune

I will meet and c. with. Ex 25:22
c. with David secretly. 1 Sam 18:22
and I will c. with my father. 19:3
if we essay to c. with thee? Job 4:2
c. with your own heart on. Ps 4:4
they c. of laying snares. 64:5
in the night I c. with mine. 77:6

communed

Abraham c. with them. Gen 23:8
Hamor c. with Jacob. 34:6, 8
Joseph c. with them. 42:24
Abimelech c. with them. Judg 9:1
Samuel c. with Saul. 1 Sam 9:25
David c. with Abigail. 25:39
queen of Sheba c. with Solomon of.
1 Ki 10:2; 2 Chr 9:1
they c. with Huldah. 2 Ki 22:14
I c. with mine own heart. Eccl 1:16
and king c. with them. Dan 1:19
the angel that c. with. Zech 1:14
they c. what they might. Luke 6:11
Judas c. to betray Jesus. 22:4
while they c. Jesus himself. 24:15
Felix sent and c. Acts 24:26

communicate

let him that is taught c. to. Gal 6:6
that ye did c. with my. Phil 4:14*

do good, be willing to *c.* *1 Tim* 6:18
to do good and to *c.* *Heb* 13:16

communicated

I *c.* to them that gospel. *Gal* 2:2*
no church *c.* with me. *Phil* 4:15

communication, -s

Abner had *c.* with. *2 Sam* 3:17
the man and his *c.* *2 Ki* 9:11*
let your *c.* be yea. *Mat* 5:37
what manner of *c.* are? *Luke* 24:17
evil *c.* corrupt good. *1 Cor* 15:33*
no corrupt *c.* proceed. *Eph* 4:29
Col 3:8
that *c.* of thy faith may. *Philem* 6*

communing

Lord left *c.* with. *Gen* 18:33
had made an end of *c.* on. *Ex* 31:18

communion

This word signifies fellowship, concord, or agreement, 2 Cor 6:14. *Communion is likewise taken for a sacrament, or sacred sign of our spiritual fellowship with Christ,* 1 Cor 10:16.

blood of Christ, *c.* of body of Christ. *1 Cor* 10:16
what *c.* hath light with? *2 Cor* 6:14
c. of the Holy Ghost be. 13:14

compact

Jerusalem is a city *c.* *Ps* 122:3

compacted

body fitly joined and *c.* *Eph* 4:16*

companied

these men which have *c.* *Acts* 1:21

companies

men into three *c.* *Judg* 7:16
three *c.* blew the trumpets. 20
against Shechem in four *c.* 9:34
divided them into three *c.* 43
put people in three *c.* *1 Sam* 11:11
spoilers came out in three *c.* 13:17
Syrians had gone out by *c.* *2 Ki* 5:2*
two great *c.* of them. *Neh* 12:31, 40
the *c.* of Sheba waited. *Job* 6:19
O ye travelling *c.* of. *Isa* 21:13†
when thou criest, let thy *c.* 57:13*
make all sit down by *c.* *Mark* 6:39

companion

slay every man his *c.* *Ex* 32:27
wife given to *c.* *Judg* 14:20; 15:6
Hushai was king's *c.* *1 Chr* 27:33*
brother to dragons, a *c.* *Job* 30:29
I am a *c.* to all them. *Ps* 119:63
but a *c.* of fools shall. *Pr* 13:20
but a *c.* of riotous men. 28:7
the same is the *c.* of a destroyer. 24
yet she is thy *c.* wife. *Mal* 2:14
and *c.* in labour. *Phil* 2:25*
I John, your brother and *c.* *Rev* 1:9*

companions

with her *c.* and bewailed. *Judg* 11:38
they brought thirty *c.* to. 14:11
answer thee and thy *c.* *Job* 35:4
shall the *c.* make a banquet. 41:6*
her *c.* shall be brought. *Ps* 45:14
for my *c.* sake, I will say. 122:8
aside by flocks of thy *c.* *S of S* 1:7
c. hearken to thy voice. 8:13
princes are rebellious and *c.* *Isa* 1:23
Judah and Israel his *c.* *Ezek* 37:16
the thing known to his *c.* *Dan* 2:17
having caught Paul's *c.* *Acts* 19:29
ye became *c.* of them. *Heb* 10:33*

company

if Esau come to the one *c.* *Gen* 32:8
lodged that night in the *c.* 21
a *c.* of nations shall be of. 35:11
Korah and his *c.* *Num* 16:6
be thou and all thy *c.* 16*
he be not as Korah and *c.* 40
now shall this *c.* lick up. 22:4*
strove in *c.* of Korah. 26:9; 27:3
another *c.* come along. *Judg* 9:37
thou comest with such a *c.*? 18:23
thou shalt meet a *c.* of. *1 Sam* 10:5*
they saw the *c.* of prophets. 19:20
bring me down to this *c.*? 30:15*
he and all his *c.* came. *2 Ki* 5:15
c. of Jehu, said, I see a *c.* 9:17
came with a small *c.* *2 Chr* 24:24
made desolate all my *c.* *Job* 16:7
goeth in *c.* with workers of. 34:8
to house of God in *c.* *Ps* 55:14*
rebuke the *c.* of spearmen. 68:30*
earth covered *c.* of Abiram. 106:17
fire was kindled in their *c.* 18
that keepeth *c.* with. *Pr* 29:3
to a *c.* of horses in. *S of S* 1:9*
as it were the *c.* of two. 6:13*
bring up a *c.* against. *Ezek* 16:40*
I will bring up a *c.* on them. 23:46*
Ashur is there and all her *c.* 32:22
thou and all thy *c.* 38:7
c. of priests murder in. *Hos* 6:9
supposing him in the *c.* *Luke* 2:44
he came down the *c.* of. 6:17
separate you from their *c.* 22
sit down by fifties in a *c.* 9:14*
a man of the *c.* cried out. 38
a woman of our *c.* made. 24:22
they went to their own *c.* *Acts* 4:23
unlawful for Jew to keep *c.* 10:28*
to send chosen men of their *c.* 15:22
Jews gathered a *c.* and set. 17:5*
we of Paul's *c.* departed. 21:8
filled with your *c.* *Rom* 15:24
not to keep *c.* with a. *1 Cor* 5:11
and have no *c.* with. *2 Thes* 3:14
to an innumerable *c.* of. *Heb* 12:22*
c. in ships and sailors. *Rev* 18:17*

great **company**

with Joseph a *great c.* *Gen* 50:9
Sheba came with *great c.* *2 Chr* 9:1*
no might against this great *c.* 20:12
great was the *c.* of those. *Ps* 68:11*
a *great c.* shall return. *Jer* 31:8
Pharaoh with *great c.* *Ezek* 17:17
saw a *great c.* come to. *John* 6:5
great c. of priests. *Acts* 6:7

comparable

precious sons of Zion *c.* to. *Lam* 4:2

compare, -ed, -ing

who in heaven can be *c.*? *Ps* 89:6
all the things thou canst desire are not to be *c.* unto her. *Pr* 3:15; 8:11
I have *c.* thee, O my. *S of S* 1:9
what likeness will ye *c.*? *Isa* 40:18
to whom will ye *c.* me? 46:5
are not worthy to be *c.* *Rom* 8:18
c. spiritual things. *1 Cor* 2:13†
c. ourselves with some, *c.* themselves amongst. *2 Cor* 10:12

comparison

have I done in *c.* of? *Judg* 8:2, 3
it not in your eyes in *c.*? *Hag* 2:3
or with what *c.* shall it? *Mark* 4:30*

compass, *substantive*

put the net under the *c.* *Ex* 27:5*
a grate of net-work under *c.* 38:4*
but fetch a *c.* behind. *2 Sam* 5:23*
they fetched a *c.* of. *2 Ki* 3:9*
when he set a *c.* on the. *Pr* 8:27*
marketh image out with *c.* *Isa* 44:13
thence we fetched a *c.* *Acts* 28:13*

compass, *verb*

they journeyed to *c.* the. *Num* 21:4
ye shall *c.* the city. *Josh* 6:3
the seventh day *c.* the city. 4
c. the king round about. *2 Ki* 11:8
2 Chr 23:7
his archers *c.* me round. *Job* 16:13
willows of the brook *c.* 40:22
with favour wilt thou *c.* *Ps* 5:12
congregation of the people *c.* 7:7
deadly enemies who *c.* me. 17:9
so will I *c.* thine altar, O Lord. 26:6
shalt *c.* me about with songs. 32:7
trusteth in Lord, mercy shall *c.* 10
iniquity of my heels shall *c.* 49:5
the head of those that *c.* 140:9
the righteous shall *c.* me. 142:7
that *c.* yourselves about. *Isa* 50:11*
a woman shall *c.* a man. *Jer* 31:22
the wicked doth *c.* about. *Hab* 1:4
woe to you, ye *c.* sea. *Mat* 23:15
thine enemies shall *c.* *Luke* 19:43

compassed

the men of Sodom *c.* *Gen* 19:4
and we *c.* mount Seir. *Deut* 2:1
ark of the Lord *c.* city. *Josh* 6:11
then they *c.* land of. *Judg* 11:18
they *c.* Samson, and laid. 16:2
Saul and his men *c.* *1 Sam* 23:26
waves of death *c.* me. *2 Sam* 22:5
Ps 18:4; 116:3
host *c.* city with horses. *2 Ki* 6:15*
smote Edomites which *c.* *2 Chr* 21:9
God hath *c.* me with his. *Job* 19:6
he hath *c.* the waters. 26:10*
they have now *c.* us in. *Ps* 17:11
many bulls *c.* me. 22:12
for dogs have *c.* me. 16
he hath *c.* me with. *Lam* 3:5
ye see Jerusalem *c.* *Luke* 21:20
that he himself also is *c.* *Heb* 5:2

compassed *about*

men *c.* Absalom *about.* *2 Sam* 18:15
sorrows of hell *c.* me *about.* 22:6
Ps 18:5
night and *c.* city *about.* *2 Ki* 6:14
Edomites which *c.* him *about.* 8:21
c. about Jehoshaphat. *2 Chr* 18:31
evils have *c.* me *about.* *Ps* 40:12
they *c.* me *about* together. 88:17
109:3; 118:11, 12
all nations *c.* me *about.* 118:10
floods *c.* me *about* thy. *Jonah* 2:3
Jericho fell, *c. about* 7. *Heb* 11:30
c. about with such a cloud of. 12:1
c. camp of saints *about.* *Rev* 20:9

compassest, -eth

c. Havilah. *Gen* 2:11
c. the land of Ethiopia. 13
c. them about as a chain. *Ps* 73:6
thou *c.* my path and my. 139:3*
Ephraim *c.* me about. *Hos* 11:12

compassion

(*Literally, suffering with another; hence having pity or sympathy for another*)

give them *c.* before. *1 Ki* 8:50
children shall find *c.* *2 Chr* 30:9
Jesus moved with *c.* *Mat* 9:36
14:14; *Mark* 6:34
lord of servant moved with *c.* *Mat* 18:27
Jesus moved with *c.* *Mark* 1:41
be of one mind, having *c.* *1 Pet* 3:8
shutteth up bowels of *c.* *1 John* 3:17

full of **compassion**

(*Revised Version,* merciful)

being *full of c.* forgave. *Ps* 78:38
thou art a God *full of c.* 86:15
111:4; 112:4; 145:8

have or *had* **compassion**

and she *had c.* on him. *Ex* 2:6
Lord may *have c.* on. *Deut* 13:17
Lord thy God will *have c.* on. 30:3
be ye, for ye *have c.* *1 Sam* 23:21
that they may *have c.* *1 Ki* 8:50
was gracious and *had c.* *2 Ki* 13:23
because he *had c.* on. *2 Chr* 36:15
Chaldees *had* no *c.* on young. 17
she should not *have c.* *Isa* 49:15
return and *have c.* on. *Jer* 12:15
will he *have c.* *Lam* 3:32; *Mi* 7:19
I *have c.* *Mat* 15:32; *Mark* 8:2
also have *had c.* on thy. *Mat* 18:33*
so Jesus *had c.* on them. 20:34
Lord hath *had c.* on. *Mark* 5:19*
if thou canst, *have c.* on us. 9:22
saw her, he *had c.* on. *Luke* 7:13
Samaritan saw him, *had c.* 10:33
father *had c.* and ran and. 15:20
have c. on whom I *have c.* *Rom* 9:15
can *have c.* on ignorant. *Heb* 5:2*
had c. of me in my bonds. 10:34
of some *have c.* making. *Jude* 22*

compassions

not consumed, because his *c.* *Lam* 3:22
shew mercy and *c.* every. *Zech* 7:9

compel

not *c.* him to serve as a. *Lev* 25:39
c. thee to go a mile. *Mat* 5:41
they *c.* one Simon to. *Mark* 15:21
go into highways, *c.* *Luke* 14:23

compelled, -est

servants with woman *c.* *1 Sam* 28:23
Jehoram *c.* Judah. *2 Chr* 21:11
Simon, him they *c.* to. *Mat* 27:32
I *c.* them to blaspheme. *Acts* 26:11*
glorying, ye have *c.* me. *2 Cor* 12:11

nor Titus a Greek was *c*. *Gal* 2:3
why *c*. thou the Gentiles to ? 14

complain, -ed, -ing

people *c*. it displeased. *Num* 11:1
brethren came to us to *c*. *Judg* 21:22
I will *c*. in bitterness of. *Job* 7:11
furrows likewise thereof *c*. 31:38*
I *c*. and my spirit was. *Ps* 77:3
that there be no *c*. in. 144:14
doth a living man *c*.? *Lam* 3:39

complainers

these are murmurers, *c*. *Jude* 16

complaint, -s

of abundance of my *c*. *1 Sam* 1:16
couch shall ease my *c*. *Job* 7:13
if I say, I will forget my *c*. 9:27
I will leave my *c*. on myself. 10:1
as for me, is my *c*. to man ? 21:4
even to-day is my *c*. bitter. 23:2
I mourn in my *c*. *Ps* 55:2
I poured out my *c*. before. 142:2
laid *c*. against Paul. *Acts* 25:7

complete

seven sabbaths shall be *c*. *Lev* 23:15
ye are *c*. in him who is. *Col* 2:10
that ye may stand *c*. in all. 4:12

composition

nor make any after *c*. *Ex* 30:32, 37

compound, -eth

an ointment *c*. after art. *Ex* 30:25
whosoever *c*. any thing like it. 33

comprehend

things which we cannot *c*. *Job* 37:5
able to *c*. with saints. *Eph* 3:18*

comprehended

hath *c*. the dust of the. *Isa* 40:12
the darkness *c*. it not. *John* 1:5*
is briefly *c*. in this saying. *Rom* 13:9*

conceal, -ed, -eth

If we slay brother and *c*. *Gen* 37:26
neither shalt thou *c*. him. *Deut* 13:8
I have not *c*. the words. *Job* 6:10*
the Almighty will I not *c*. 27:11
I will not *c*. his parts nor. 41:12*
not *c*. thy loving-kindness. *Ps* 40:10
of a faithful spirit *c*. the. *Pr* 11:13
a prudent man *c*. knowledge. 12:23
it is the glory of God to *c*. 25:2
publish and *c*. not. *Jer* 50:2

conceit, -s

as an high wall in *c*. *Pr* 18:11*
lest he be wise in his own *c*. 26:5
seest a man wise in his own *c*.? 12
sluggard is wiser in his own *c*. 16
rich man is wise in his own *c*. 28:11
ye be wise in own *c*. *Rom* 11:25
be not wise in your own *c*. 12:16

conceive, -ing

they should *c*. when. *Gen* 30:38
shall be free, and *c*. seed. *Num* 5:28
c. and bear a son. *Judg* 13:3, 5, 7
Luke 1:31
they *c*. mischief. *Job* 15:35; *Isa* 59:4
in sin did my mother *c*. me. *Ps* 51:5
a virgin shall *c*. and bear. *Isa* 7:14
shall *c*. chaff. 33:11
c. words of falsehood. 59:13
received strength to *c*. *Heb* 11:11

conceived

Eve *c*. and bare Cain. *Gen* 4:1
Cain's wife *c*. and bare Enoch. 17
Hagar *c*. 16:4
Sarah *c*. and bare Isaac. 21:2
Rebekah his wife *c*. 25:21
Leah *c*. 29:32, 33
Bilhah *c*. 30:5
Rachel *c*. and bare a son. 23
the flocks *c*. 39; 31:10
Shuah *c*. 38:3, 4, 5
Tamar *c*. 18
Jochebed *c*. and bare. *Ex* 2:2
have *c*. seed, and born. *Lev* 12:2
have I *c*. all this people ? *Num* 11:12
c. and bare son, Samuel. *1 Sam* 1:20
2:21
Bath-sheba *c*. and sent. *2 Sam* 11:5
Shunammite *c*. *2 Ki* 4:17
prophetess *c*. *Isa* 8:3
there is a man child *c*. *Job* 3:3
c. mischief, brought forth. *Ps* 7:14
chamber of her that *c*. *S of S* 3:4
and hath *c*. a purpose. *Jer* 49:30
Gomer which *c*. and. *Hos* 1:3
she that *c*. them hath done. 2:5
that which is *c*. in her is of the Holy Ghost. *Mat* 1:20
Elisabeth hath *c*. a son. *Luke* 1:36
named before he was *c*. 2:21
hast thou *c*. this thing ? *Acts* 5:4
when Rebekah had *c*. *Rom* 9:10
when lust hath *c*. it. *Jas* 1:15

conception

multiply sorrow and *c*. *Gen* 3:16
the Lord gave her *c*. *Ruth* 4:13
shall flee from birth and *c*. *Hos* 9:11

concern, -eth

this burden *c*. the prince. *Ezek* 12:10
things which *c*. Lord Jesus Christ. *Acts* 28:31
glory in things which *c*. *2 Cor* 11:30

concerning

accepted thee *c*. this. *Gen* 19:21
c. which I did swear to. *Ex* 6:8
Num 14:30
atonement for him *c*. *Lev* 4:26; 5:6
found what was lost, lieth *c*. it. 6:3
hath spoken good *c*. *Num* 10:29
commanded him *c*. this. *1 Ki* 11:10
I asked them *c*. the Jews. *Neh* 1:2
repent thee *c*. servants. *Ps* 90:13
135:14
dost not inquire wisely *c*. *Eccl* 7:10
therefore have I cried *c*. this. 30:7
ask me *c*. my sons, and *c*. 45:11
saith Lord *c*. sons, *c*. daughters, *c*. mothers, *c*. fathers. *Jer* 16:3
c. pillars, *c*. sea, *c*. bases, *c*. vessels. 27:19
comforted *c*. the evil, even *c*. all that I have brought. *Ezek* 14:22
the Lord *c*. Ammonites. 21:28
c. which I have lifted up. 47:14
desire mercies of God *c*. *Dan* 2:18
might not be changed *c*. Daniel. 6:17
I speak it not to you *c*. *Mat* 16:11
saw, told also *c*. swine. *Mark* 5:16
expounded the things *c*. *Luke* 24:27
as *c*. that he raised. *Acts* 13:34
as *c*. this sect, we know. 28:22
as *c*. flesh Christ came. *Rom* 9:5
as *c*. the gospel, are enemies. 11:28
and simple *c*. evil. 16:19
I speak as *c*. reproach. *2 Cor* 11:21
but I speak *c*. Christ. *Eph* 5:32
c. giving and receiving. *Phil* 4:15
professing have erred *c*. *1 Tim* 6:21
who *c*. the truth have. *2 Tim* 2:18
reprobates *c*. the faith. 3:8
think it not strange *c*. *1 Pet* 4:12
see **him, me, thee, them, us, you**

concision

(*A cutting off, hence,* a faction)
beware of the *c*. *Phil* 3:2

conclude

we *c*. a man is justified. *Rom* 3:28*

concluded

the Gentiles, we have *c*. *Acts* 21:25*
for God hath *c*. them. *Rom* 11:32*
the scripture hath *c*. *Gal* 3:22*

conclusion

let us hear the *c*. of. *Eccl* 12:13

concord

what *c*. hath Christ ? *2 Cor* 6:15

concourse

crieth in chief place of *c*. *Pr* 1:21
give account of this *c*. *Acts* 19:40

concubine

(*A secondary wife under the system of polygamy practised by the Jews and named in the Bible. Concubines were frequently purchased slaves. They were more easily put away than a wife, but their rights were carefully guarded under Jewish law*)
his *c*. played the whore. *Judg* 19:2
he laid hold on his *c*. and. 29
Gibeah, I and my *c*. to. 20:4
in to my father's *c*.? *2 Sam* 3:7
Rizpah the *c*. of Saul had. 21:11

concubines

to sons of *c*. Abraham. *Gen* 25:6
David took more *c*. *2 Sam* 5:13
Absalom went in to father's *c*. 16:22
thy life, and lives of thy *c*. 19:5
king put his *c*. in ward and. 20:3
had three hundred *c*. *1 Ki* 11:3
Rehoboam took threescore *c*. *2 Chr* 11:21
Shaashgaz who kept *c*. *Esth* 2:14
60 queens and 80 *c*. and. *S of S* 6:8
yea, the queens and the *c*. 9
king and his *c*. drank. *Dan* 5:3, 23

concupiscence

wrought all manner of *c*. *Rom* 7:8*
mortify members, evil *c*. *Col* 3:5*
not in the lust of *c*. *1 Thes* 4:5*

condemn

whom the judges shall *c*. *Ex* 22:9
judge them, and *c*. the. *Deut* 25:1
my mouth shall *c*. me. *Job* 9:20
I will say to God do not *c*. 10:2
and wilt thou *c*. him ? 34:17
wilt thou *c*. me, that thou ? 40:8
not leave him, nor *c*. *Ps* 37:33
they *c*. the innocent blood. 94:21
save him from those that *c*. 109:31
wicked devices will he *c*. *Pr* 12:2
is he that shall *c*. me ? *Isa* 50:9
shall rise against thee shall *c*. 54:17
shall *c*. it. *Mat* 12:41; *Luke* 11:32
rise up in judgement and *c*. it. *Mat* 12:42; *Luke* 11:31
c. him to death. *Mat* 20:18
Mark 10:33
c. not, and ye shall not. *Luke* 6:37
God sent not Son to *c*. *John* 3:17
neither do I *c*. thee, go and. 8:11
I speak not this to *c*. *2 Cor* 7:3
if our heart *c*. us, God. *1 John* 3:20
if our heart *c*. us not, then. 21

condemnation

[1] *Declaring guilty, or pronouncing the sentence,* John 8:10. [2] *Censuring other men's persons, purposes, words, or actions, either rashly, unjustly, or uncharitably,* Luke 6:37.
thou art in the same *c*. *Luke* 23:40
this is the *c*. that light. *John* 3:19*
believeth not come into *c*. 5:24*
judgement was by one to *c*. *Rom* 5:16
judgement came on all men to *c*. 18
there is no *c*. to them who are. 8:1
come not together to *c*. *1 Cor* 11:34*
if the ministration of *c*. *2 Cor* 3:9
lest he fall into the *c*. *1 Tim* 3:6
shall receive greater *c*. *Jas* 3:1*
lest ye fall into *c*. 5:12
of old ordained to this *c*. *Jude* 4

condemned

and *c*. the land in. *2 Chr* 36:3*
answer, yet had *c*. Job. *Job* 32:3
judged, let him be *c*. *Ps* 109:7
drink the wine of *c*. in. *Amos* 2:8*
would not have *c*. the. *Mat* 12:7
by thy words thou shalt be *c*. 37
when he saw that he was *c*. 27:3
they all *c*. him to be. *Mark* 14:64
delivered him to be *c*. *Luke* 24:20
believeth on him is not *c*. but he that believeth not is *c*. *John* 3:18*
hath no man *c*. thee ? 8:10
c. sin in the flesh. *Rom* 8:3
we should not be *c*. *1 Cor* 11:32
speech that cannot be *c*. *Tit* 2:8
sinneth, being *c*. of himself. 3:11
by which he *c*. the world. *Heb* 11:7
ye have *c*. and killed just. *Jas* 5:6
not one another, lest ye be *c*. 9*
God *c*. them with. *2 Pet* 2:6

condemnest, eth, -ing

judge thy servants *c*. *1 Ki* 8:32
thine own mouth *c*. thee. *Job* 15:6
he that *c*. the just, is. *Pr* 17:15
fulfilled them in *c*. him. *Acts* 13:27
judgest another thou *c*. *Rom* 2:1
who is he that *c*.? 8:34
that *c*. not himself in that. 14:22

condescend

not high things, but *c*. *Rom* 12:16

condition, -s
on this *c.* I will make. *1 Sam* 11:2
sendeth and desireth *c.* *Luke* 14:32

conduct, -ed
came to *c.* king. *2 Sam* 19:15, 31
all the people of Judah *c.* 40*
they that *c.* Paul. *Acts* 17:15
c. him forth in peace. *1 Cor* 16:11*

conduit
came and stood by *c.* *2 Ki* 18:17
Isa 36:2
he made a pool and a *c.* *2 Ki* 20:20
meet Ahaz at end of the *c.* *Isa* 7:3

coney, -ies
(*A variety of rabbit*)
and the *c.* because he is unclean to.
Lev 11:5; *Deut* 14:7
rocks are a refuge for *c.* *Ps* 104:18
c. are but a feeble folk. *Pr* 30:26

confection
shalt make a *c.* after. *Ex* 30:35*

confectionaries
your daughters to be *c.* *1 Sam* 8:13†

confederacy
a *c.* to whom people say a *c.*
Isa 8:12*
all men of thy *c.* brought. *Ob* 7

confederate
and these were *c.* *Gen* 14:13
they are *c.* against thee. *Ps* 83:5*
it was told, Syria is *c.* *Isa* 7:2

conference
for they in *c.* added. *Gal* 2:6*

conferred
Adonijah *c.* with Joab. *1 Ki* 1:7
they *c.* among themselves. *Acts* 4:15
Festus, when he had *c.* 25:12
immediately I *c.* not with. *Gal* 1:16

confess
[1] *Publicly to own and acknowledge as his own*, Luke 12:8. [2] *To profess Christ, and to obey his commandments*, Mat 10:32. [3] *To own our sins and offences, either in private or public*, Josh 7:19; Ps 32:5; Mat 3:6; Jas 5:16; 1 John 1:9.

he shall *c.* that he hath. *Lev* 5:5
Aaron shall *c.* over live goat. 16:21
if they shall *c.* their iniquity. 26:40
they shall *c.* their sins. *Num* 5:7
Israel *c.* thy name and. *1 Ki* 8:33
2 Chr 6:24
c. thy name and turn. *1 Ki* 8:35
2 Chr 6:26
and *c.* the sins of the. *Neh* 1:6
I will *c.* that thy hand. *Job* 40:14
I will *c.* my transgressions. *Ps* 32:5
shall *c.* me before men, him will I *c.*
before. *Mat* 10:32; *Luke* 12:8
if any man did *c.* that. *John* 9:22
rulers did not *c.* him. 12:42
but Pharisees *c.* both. *Acts* 23:8
this I *c.* that after the way. 24:14
shalt *c.* with thy mouth. *Rom* 10:9
every tongue shall *c.* to God. 14:11
I will *c.* to thee among the. 15:9*
every tongue shall *c.* *Phil* 2:11
c. your faults one to. *Jas* 5:16
if we *c.* our sins. *1 John* 1:9
whoso shall *c.* that Jesus. 4:15
who *c.* not that Jesus. *2 John* 7
but I will *c.* his name. *Rev* 3:5

confessed, -eth, -ing
when Ezra had *c.* *Ezra* 10:1
c. their sins, a fourth part *c.* *Neh* 9:2
but whoso *c.* and forsaketh. *Pr* 28:13
while *c.* my sin and the. *Dan* 9:20
baptized *c.* their sins. *Mat* 3:6
John *c.* I am not Christ. *John* 1:20
many came and *c.* and. *Acts* 19:18
these *c.* that they were. *Heb* 11:13
every spirit that *c.* Christ. *1 John* 4:2
every spirit that *c.* not that. 3

confession
and make *c.* to him. *Josh* 7:19
offerings and making *c.* *2 Chr* 30:22
now therefore make *c.* *Ezra* 10:11
to my God and made *c.* *Dan* 9:4
with the mouth *c.* is. *Rom* 10:10
Pilate witnessed good *c.* *1 Tim* 6:13

confidence
[1] *Boldness*, Acts 28:31. [2] *Trust*, Job 4:6. [3] *That wherein one trusts*, Jer 48:13.

put their *c.* in Gaal. *Judg* 9:26
great king of Assyria, what *c.* is this
wherein? *2 Ki* 18:19; *Isa* 36:4
is not this thy fear, thy *c.*? *Job* 4:6
his *c.* shall be rooted out. 18:14
thou art my *c.* 31:24
who art the *c.* of all. *Ps* 65:5
trust in Lord than to put *c.* 118:8
to trust in Lord than to put *c.* in. 9
for Lord shall be thy *c.* *Pr* 3:26
in fear of Lord is strong *c.* 14:26
the strength of the *c.* thereof. 21:22
c. in an unfaithful man is. 25:19
in quietness and *c.* shall. *Isa* 30:15
ashamed of Beth-el their *c.* *Jer* 48:13
they shall dwell with *c.* *Ezek* 28:26
no more the *c.* of house of. 29:16
put ye not *c.* in a guide. *Mi* 7:5
of God with all *c.* *Acts* 28:31
in this *c.* I was minded. *2 Cor* 1:15
having *c.* in you all. 2:3
I rejoice that I have *c.* 7:16
the great *c.* I have in you. 8:22
that *c.* wherewith I think to. 10:2
foolishly in this *c.* of boast. 11:17
I have *c.* in you through. *Gal* 5:10
in whom access with *c.* *Eph* 3:12
having this *c.* I shall. *Phil* 1:25
and have no *c.* in flesh. 3:3
though I might have *c.* in flesh. 4
we have *c.* in Lord. *2 Thes* 3:4
c. in thy obedience. *Philem* 21
if we hold fast the *c.* *Heb* 3:6
hold beginning of our *c.* stedfast. 14
cast not away your *c.* 10:35
appear, we may have *c.* *1 John* 2:28
then have *c.* toward God. 3:21
and this is the *c.* that we. 5:14

confidences
Lord hath rejected thy *c.* *Jer* 2:37

confident
in this will I be *c.* *Ps* 27:3
the fool rageth and is *c.* *Pr* 14:16
art *c.* thou thyself art a. *Rom* 2:19
we are always *c.* *2 Cor* 5:6
we are *c.* willing rather to be. 8
ashamed in this same *c.* 9:4
c. of this very thing. *Phil* 1:6
many of the brethren waxing *c.* 14

confidently
another *c.* affirmed. *Luke* 22:59

confirm
[1] *To strengthen, settle, or establish*, 1 Chr 14:2; Acts 14:22. [2] *To give new assurance of the truth and certainty of any thing*, 1 Ki 1:14; 2 Cor 2:8. [3] *To ratify, or make sure*, Ruth 4:7.

the manner for to *c.* all. *Ruth* 4:7
come in after and *c.* thy. *1 Ki* 1:14
to *c.* the kingdom. *2 Ki* 15:19
wrote to *c.* second letter. *Esth* 9:29
to *c.* these days of Purim in. 31
didst *c.* thine inheritance. *Ps* 68:9
weak hands and *c.* feeble. *Isa* 35:3
hope that they would *c.* *Ezek* 13:6
he shall *c.* the covenant. *Dan* 9:27
even I stood to *c.* and to. 11:1
to *c.* the promises made. *Rom* 15:8
who shall also *c.* you. *1 Cor* 1:8
ye would *c.* your love. *2 Cor* 2:8

confirmation
in defence and *c.* of the. *Phil* 1:7
an oath of *c.* is to them. *Heb* 6:16

confirmed
c. to thyself thy people. *2 Sam* 7:24
soon as kingdom was *c.* *2 Ki* 14:5
Lord had *c.* him king. *1 Chr* 14:2
hath *c.* the same. 16:17; *Ps* 105:10
Esther *c.* these matters. *Esth* 9:32
hath *c.* his words which. *Dan* 9:12
exhorted brethren and *c.* *Acts* 15:32
testimony of Christ was *c.* *1 Cor* 1:6
yet if it be *c.* no man. *Gal* 3:15
the covenant that was *c.* 17
was *c.* to us by them. *Heb* 2:3
immutability of counsel, he *c.* 6:17

confirmeth, -ing
bonds on her, he *c.* *Num* 30:14
cursed be he that *c.* not. *Deut* 27:26
that *c.* the word of. *Isa* 44:26
preached, *c.* word with. *Mark* 16:20
c. souls of the disciples. *Acts* 14:22
through Syria and Cilicia *c.* 15:41

confiscation
let judgement be executed to *c.*
Ezra 7:26

conflict
having the same *c.* *Phil* 1:30
ye knew what great *c.* *Col* 2:1*

conformable
him, being made *c.* *Phil* 3:10*

conformed
predestinate to be *c.* *Rom* 8:29
be not *c.* to this world. 12:2*

confound
[1] *To throw into confusion*, Gen 11:7. [2] *To confute*, Acts 9:22. [3] *To discomfit*, Job 6:20. [4] *To be amazed, astonished*, Acts 2:6.

let us go down and *c.* *Gen* 11:7, 9
be not dismayed, lest I *c.* *Jer* 1:17*
c. the wise, to *c.* things. *1 Cor* 1:27*

confounded
the inhabitants were *c.* *2 Ki* 19:26
Isa 37:27
they were *c.* because. *Job* 6:20
let them be *c.* that seek. *Ps* 35:4*
not those that seek thee be *c.* 69:6*
let them be *c.* that are. 71:13*
for they are *c.* that seek. 24
let them be *c.* and troubled. 83:17*
c. be all they that serve. 97:7*
let them all be *c.* turned. 129:5*
shall be *c.* for gardens. *Isa* 1:29
weave net-works shall be *c.* 19:9*
were dismayed and *c.* 37:27
greatly *c.* because we have. *Jer* 9:19
is *c.* by graven image. 10:14*; 51:17
let them be *c.* that persecute. 17:18*
daughter of Egypt *c.* 46:24*
Moab is *c.* 48:20*
Hamath is *c.* 49:23
Babylon taken, Bel *c.* 50:2*
mother shall be sore *c.* 12*
her whole land shall be *c.* 51:47*
we are *c.* because we have. 51*
be thou *c.* and. *Ezek* 16:52*, 54, 63
nations shall see and be *c.* *Mi* 7:16*
riders on horses be *c.* *Zech* 10:5
came together and were *c.* *Acts* 2:6
Saul *c.* the Jews who dwelt. 9:22

ashamed and **confounded**
asha. and c. that seek. *Ps* 40:14
70:2
moon be *c. and* sun *asha.* *Isa* 24:23
thee shall be *asha. and c.* 41:11
idol-makers be *asha. and c.* 45:16
not be *asha.*, neither be thou *c.* 54:4
little ones *asha. and c.* *Jer* 14:3
hath been *asha. and c.* 15:9
shalt thou be *asha. and c.* 22:22
I was *asha.* yea, even *c.* 31:19
be *asha. and c.* for your. *Ezek* 36:32
seers be *asha. and* diviners *c.* *Mi* 3:7

not **confounded**
trusted, and were *not c.* *Ps* 22:5*
not ashamed nor *c.* *Isa* 45:17
therefore shall I *not* be *c.* 50:7
believeth on him *not* be *c.* *1 Pet* 2:6*

confused
battle of warrior with *c.* *Isa* 9:5
for the assembly was *c.* *Acts* 19:32

confusion
lie down thereto, it is *c.* *Lev* 18:23
put to death, have wrought *c.* 20:12
chosen David to thine own *c.* and
unto the *c.* *1 Sam* 20:30*
been delivered to *c.* of. *Ezra* 9:7
I am full of *c.* therefore. *Job* 10:15*
let them be brought to *c.* *Ps* 35:4*
c. is continually before me. 44:15*
let them be put to *c.* that. 70:2*
let me never be put to *c.* 71:1*
cover themselves with own *c.* 109:29*

the city of c. is broken. *Isa* 24:10
in the shadow of Egypt your c. 30:3
stretch out upon it line of c. 34:11
images are wind and c. 41:29
makers of idols go to c. 45:16
for c. they shall rejoice in. 61:7*
lie in shame and our c. *Jer* 3:25
provoke themselves to c. 7:19
their everlasting c. shall. 20:11*
us belongeth c. of face. *Dan* 9:7, 8
city was filled with c. *Acts* 19:29
God is not author of c. *1 Cor* 14:33
and strife is, there is c. *Jas* 3:16

congealed

the depths were c. in. *Ex* 15:8

congratulate

of his welfare and c. *1 Chr* 18:10*

congregation

(*Generally this means assembly or meeting*)

a sin-offering for the c. *Lev* 4:21
you to bear iniquity of c. 10:17
make an atonement for the c. 16:33
the renowned of the c. *Num* 1:16
but when c. is to be gathered. 10:7
shall I bear with this evil c.? 14:27
one ordinance shall be for c. 15:15
separate yourselves from c. 16:21
get you from among this c. 45
Aaron ran into the midst of c. 47
that soul cut off from the c. 19:20
Lord set a man over the c. 27:16
manslayer die not, till he stand before c. 35:12; *Josh* 20:6
drawers of water for c. *Josh* 9:27
the c. was gathered as. *Judg* 20:1
came not up with the c. 21:5
called Jeroboam to c. *1 Ki* 12:20
Hezekiah did give to c. *2 Chr* 30:24
separated from the c. *Ezra* 10:8
should not come into the c. *Neh* 13:1
for the c. of hypocrites. *Job* 15:34
I stood up and cried in the c. 30:28
nor sinners in the c. of. *Ps* 1:5
in the midst of the c. will I. 22:22
I have hated the c. of evil. 26:5
speak righteousness, O c.? 58:1
remember thy c. thou hast. 74:2
forget not the c. of thy poor. 19*
when I receive the c. I will. 75:2*
God standeth in the c. of the. 82:1
thy faithfulness also in c. 89:5
let them exalt him also in c. 107:32
Lord in the assembly and c. 111:1
in all evil in midst of c. *Pr* 5:14
men shall remain in the c. 21:16
sit upon the mount of c. *Isa* 14:13
and know, O c. what is. *Jer* 6:18
their c. shall be established. 30:20
not enter into thy c. *Lam* 1:10
chastise them as their c. *Hos* 7:12
sanctify the c. *Joel* 2:16
now when the c. was. *Acts* 13:43*

all the **congregation**

gather *all the c.* together. *Lev* 8:3
atonement for *all the c.* 16:17
all the c. stone him. 24:14, 16 *Num* 15:35
all the c. bade stone. *Num* 14:10
seeing *all the c.* are holy. 16:3
wilt thou be wroth with *all c.*? 22
in sight of *all the c.* 20:27; 25:6
Eleazar and *all the c.* 27:19, 22
read not before *all the c.* *Josh* 8:35
all the c. murmured. 9:18
wrath fell on *all the c.* 22:20
king blessed *all the c.* *1 Ki* 8:14, 55
all the c. blessed. *1 Chr* 29:20
all the c. made a. *2 Chr* 23:3
all the c. worshipped and. 29:28
all the c. said, amen. *Neh* 5:13
all the c. that were come. 8:17

elders of the **congregation**

elders of the c. shall. *Lev* 4:15
elders of c. said, how? *Judg* 21:16

great **congregation**

a feast, all Israel with him, a *great c.* *1 Ki* 8:65; *2 Chr* 7:8; 30:13
out of Israel a *great c.* *Ezra* 10:1
be of thee in the *great c.* *Ps* 22:25
thanks in the great c. 35:18
righteousness in the *great c.* *Ps* 40:9
not concealed truth from *great c.* 10

congregation *of Israel*

c. of Israel shall kill it. *Ex* 12:6
cut off from the *c. of Israel.* 19
all the *c. of Israel* shall keep. 47
if whole *c. of Israel* sin. *Lev* 4:13
separated you from *c. of Israel.* *Num* 16:9
Solomon and *c. of Israel.* *2 Chr* 5:6
commandment of *c. of Israel.* 24:6

congregation *of the Lord*

why lift yourselves above the *c. of the Lord?* *Num* 16:3
c. of Lord not as sheep that. 27:17
plague among *c. of the Lord.* 31:16 *Josh* 22:17
not enter into the *c. of the Lord.* *Deut* 23:1, 2, 3
in sight of *c. of Lord.* *1 Chr* 28:8
a cord by lot in *c. of Lord.* *Mi* 2:5

tabernacle of the **congregation**

brought before *tab. of c.* *Ex* 29:10
I will sanctify *tab. of c.* 44
anoint *tab. of c.* 30:26
called it the *tab. of c.* went out to the *tab. of c.* 33:7
kill it before *tab. of c.* *Lev* 3:8, 13
bring it to *tab. of c.* 4:5
not go out from door of *tab. of c.* 10:7
no wine when ye go into *tab. of c.* 9
so do for *tab. of c.* 16:16
atonement for *tab. of c.* 33
work of *tab. of c.* *Num* 4:3, 23, 25 30, 35, 39, 43
bring Levites before *tab. of c.* 8:9
come out ye three to *tab. of c.* 12:4
appeared in the *tab. of c.* 14:10
lay up in *tab. of c.* 17:4
keep charge of *tab. of c.* 18:4
weeping before door of *tab. of c.* 25:6
yourselves in *tab. of c.* *Deut* 31:14
set up *tab of c.* there. *Josh* 18:1
brought up *tab. of c.* *1 Ki* 8:4 *2 Chr* 5:5
was *tab. of c.* of God. *2 Chr* 1:3

see **door**

tent of the **congregation**

tent of the c. finished. *Ex* 39:32
set up *tent of the c.* 40:2
table in *tent of the c.* 22
candlestick in *tent of the c.* 24
golden altar in the *tent of the c.* 26
cloud covered the *tent of the c.* 34
not able to enter into *tent of the c.* 35

whole **congregation**

the *whole c.* of Israel. *Ex* 16:2
the charge of *whole c.* *Num* 3:7
be wroth with *whole c.* *Josh* 22:18
whole c. sent to speak. *Judg* 21:13
king blessed the *whole c.* *2 Chr* 6:3
the *whole c.* *Ezra* 2:64; *Neh* 7:66
shewed before *whole c.* *Pr* 26:26

congregations

in the c. will I bless. *Ps* 26:12
bless ye God in the c. even. 68:26
enemies roar in midst of thy c. 74:4

Coniah

though C. were the signet. *Jer* 22:24
man C. despised, broken idol? 28
Zedekiah reigned instead of C. 37:1

conquer

conquering and to c. *Rev* 6:2

conquerors

we are more than c. *Rom* 8:37

conscience

(*That faculty within us which decides as to the moral quality of our thoughts, words, and acts. It gives consciousness of the good of one's conduct or motives, or causes feelings of remorse at evil-doing. A conscience can be educated, or trained to recognize good and evil, but its action is involuntary. A good conscience is one which has no feeling of reproach against oneself, does not accuse oneself of wilful wrong,* Acts 24:16)

convicted by their own c. *John* 8:9
I have lived in all good c. *Acts* 23:1
to have a c. void of offence. 24:16
their c. also bearing. *Rom* 2:15
my c. bearing me witness in. 9:1
subject also for c. sake. 13:5
with c. of the idol to this hour eat it, and their c. being weak. *1 Cor* 8:7
shall not c. of him which is weak? 10
when ye wound their weak c. 12
no question for c. sake. 10:25, 27
eat not, for c. sake. 28
c. I say, not thine own, but. 29
testimony of our c. *2 Cor* 1:12
commending to every man's c. 4:2
pure heart, and a good c. *1 Tim* 1:5
holding faith and a good c. 19
mystery of faith in a pure c. 3:9
having their c. seared. 4:2
God, whom I serve with c. *2 Tim* 1:3
even their mind and c. is. *Tit* 1:15
as pertaining to the c. *Heb* 9:9
purge c. from dead works to. 14
should have had no more c. of. 10:2
hearts sprinkled from an evil c. 22
we trust we have a good c. 13:18
if a man for c. toward. *1 Pet* 2:19
having a good c. as they. 3:16
but the answer of a good c. 21

consciences

made manifest in your c. *2 Cor* 5:11

consecrate

To devote any thing to God's worship and service; to hallow, or sanctify whether persons, Ex 13:2, 12, 15; 19:6; Num 1:49; 3:12 1 Sam 1:11, 22; *or things,* Lev 27:28.

c. Aaron. *Ex* 28:3*
anoint and c. Aaron's sons. 41
c. Aaron and sons. 29:9; 30:30*
seven days shalt thou c. 35; *Lev* 8:33
Moses said, c. yourselves. *Ex* 32:29
shall c. to Lord the days. *Num* 6:12*
to c. his service this. *1 Chr* 29:5
to c. himself with a. *2 Chr* 13:9
they shall c. themselves. *Ezek* 43:26*
I will c. their gain to. *Mi* 4:13*

consecrated

sons of Aaron, whom he c. *Num* 3:3
vessels are c. to the. *Josh* 6:19
Micah c. one of sons. *Judg* 17:5, 12
Jeroboam c. him. *1 Ki* 13:33
ye have c. yourselves. *2 Chr* 29:31
c. things were 600 oxen. 33
holy things which were c. 31:6
feasts of Lord that were c. *Ezra* 3:5
the Son, c. for evermore. *Heb* 7:28*
living way which he hath c. 10:20*

consecration, -s

of ram, for it is ram of c. *Ex* 29:22
if aught of the flesh of the c. 34
this is the law of the c. *Lev* 7:37
c. for a sweet savour to the. 8:28
with bread that is in basket of c. 31
till the days of your c. be. 33
because the c. of his God. *Num* 6:7*
hath defiled the head of his c. 9

consent, -ed, -ing

but in this will we c. *Gen* 34:15
only let us c. to them. 23
shalt not c. to him. *Deut* 13:8
but would not c. *Judg* 11:17
hearken not to him, nor c. *1 Ki* 20:8
the priests c. to receive. *2 Ki* 12:8
sawest a thief, thou c. *Ps* 50:18
if sinners entice thee, c. not. *Pr* 1:10
so he c. to them, and. *Dan* 1:14*
the same had not c. *Luke* 23:51
and Saul was c. to. *Acts* 8:1; 22:20
tarry longer with them, c. not. 18:20
if I do that which I would not, I c. unto the law. *Rom* 7:16
if any man c. not to. *1 Tim* 6:3

consent, *substantive*

came out with one c. *1 Sam* 11:7*
together with one c. *Ps* 83:5
of the priests murder by c. *Hos* 6:9
to serve him with one c. *Zeph* 3:9
all with one c. began to. *Luke* 14:18
except it be with c. for. *1 Cor* 7:5

consider

[1] *To meditate upon,* 2 Tim 2:7.
[2] *To view, or observe,* Lev 13:13.

[3] *To determine,* Judg 18:14. [4] *To pity, comfort, or relieve,* Ps 41:1. [5] *To remember,* 1 Sam 12:24.
then the priest shall *c.* *Lev* 13:13
know this day and *c.* *Deut* 4:39
that they were wise to *c.* 32:29
now therefore *c.* what. *Judg* 18:14
c. how great things. *1 Sam* 12:24
therefore know and *c.* what. 25:17
will he not then *c.* it? *Job* 11:11
when I *c.* I am afraid of him. 23:15
and would not *c.* of his ways. 34:27
stand still and *c.* the works. 37:14
c. my meditation. *Ps.* 5:1
when I *c.* the heavens. 8:3
c. my trouble. 9:13
c. and hear. 13:3; 45:10
c. my enemies. 25:19
shalt diligently *c.* his place. 37:10
c. her palaces, that ye may. 48:13
now *c.* this, ye that forget. 50:22
for they shall wisely *c.* 64:9
I will *c.* thy testimonies. 119:95
c. mine affliction, and deliver. 153
c. how I love thy precepts. 159
go to the ant, *c.* her ways. *Pr* 6:6
with a ruler, *c.* diligently. 23:1
pondereth the heart *c.* it? 24:12
for they *c.* not that they. *Eccl* 5:1
c. the work of God, who. 7:13
but in day of adversity *c.* 14
my people doth not *c.* *Isa* 1:3
neither *c.* the operation of. 5:12
narrowly look upon thee and *c.* 14:16
and I will *c.* in my dwelling-. 18:4
may see, and know, and *c.* 41:20
remember ye not, nor *c.* 43:18
had not heard shall they *c.* 52:15
c. and see if there be. *Jer* 2:10
latter days ye shall *c.* 23:20; 30:24
O Lord, *c.* to whom. *Lam* 2:20
O Lord, *c.* and behold our. 5:1
it may be they will *c.* *Ezek* 12:3
understand, and *c.* the vision. *Dan* 9:23
they *c.* not in their hearts. *Hos* 7:2
c. your ways. *Hag* 1:5, 7
pray you, *c.* from this day. 2:15, 18
c. the lilies. *Mat* 6:28; *Luke* 12:27
c. the ravens, for they. *Luke* 12:24
nor *c.* it is expedient. *John* 11:50
the elders came to *c.* *Acts* 15:6
c. and the Lord give. *2 Tim* 2:7
brethren, *c.* the Apostle. *Heb* 3:1
now *c.* how great this man. 7:4
c. one another to provoke. 10:24
c. him that endured. 12:3

considered, -est

when I *c.* in morning. *1 Ki* 3:21
I have *c.* things which thou. 5:8
c. my servant Job? *Job* 1:8; 2:3
glad, for thou hast *c.* my. *Ps* 31:7
then I saw and *c.* it well. *Pr* 24:32
I *c.* all the oppressions. *Eccl* 4:1
again I *c.* all travail. 4
for all this I *c.* in my heart. 9:1
c. not what this people. *Jer* 33:24
c. the horns, and behold. *Dan* 7:8
c. not the beam that is. *Mat* 7:3
they *c.* not the miracle. *Mark* 6:52
when Peter had *c.* the. *Acts* 12:12
he *c.* not his own body. *Rom* 4:19

considereth, -ing

hearts alike, he *c.* all. *Ps* 33:15
blessed is he that *c.* the poor. 41:1
righteous man *c.* house. *Pr* 21:12
and *c.* not that poverty shall. 28:22
the righteous *c.* the cause of. 29:7
c. a field, and buyeth it. 31:16
none *c.* in his heart to say. *Isa* 44:19
none *c.* that the righteous is. 57:1
c. and doth not. *Ezek* 18:14, 28
as I was *c.* behold. *Dan* 8:5
c. thyself, lest thou. *Gal* 6:1
c. the end of their. *Heb* 13:7

consist, -eth

a man's life *c.* not in. *Luke* 12:15
by him all things *c.* *Col* 1:17

consolation

(*Comfort or relief in distress or depression*)
men give them cup of *c.* *Jer* 16:7
waiting for the *c.* of. *Luke* 2:25
for ye have received your *c.* 6:24
interpreted, the son of *c.* *Acts* 4:36*
they rejoiced for the *c.* 15:31
God of *c.* grant you to. *Rom* 15:5
so our *c.* also aboundeth. *2 Cor* 1:5
we be afflicted, it is for your *c.* 6
so shall ye be partakers of the *c.* 7
but by the *c.* wherewith he was. 7:7
if there be any *c.* in Christ. *Phil* 2:1*
given us everlasting *c.* *2 Thes* 2:16
have great joy and *c.* *Philem* 7
might have a strong *c.* *Heb* 6:18*

consolations

are the *c.* of God small? *Job* 15:11
and let this be your *c.* 21:2
with the breasts of her *c.* *Isa* 66:11

consorted

(*Companied with*)
some of them *c.* with. *Acts* 17:4

conspiracy

and Absalom's *c.* was. *2 Sam* 15:12
his servants made a *c.* *2 Ki* 12:20
made a *c.* against Amaziah. 14:19
2 Chr 25:27
Shallum and his *c.* *2 Ki* 15:15
Hoshea made a *c.* against. 30
the king of Assyria found *c.* 17:4
a *c.* is found among the. *Jer* 11:9
is a *c.* of her prophets. *Ezek* 22:25
forty who had made this *c.* *Acts* 23:13

conspirators

Ahithophel is among *c.* *2 Sam* 15:31

conspired

they *c.* against Joseph. *Gen* 37:18
that all of you have *c.* *1 Sam* 22:8
why have ye *c.* against me? 13
Baasha son of Ahijah *c.* *1 Ki* 15:27
Zimri *c.* against Elah. 16:9, 16
Jehu son of Nimshi *c.* *2 Ki* 9:14
I *c.* against my master. 10:9
Shallum *c.* against Zachariah. 15:10
Pekah *c.* against Pekahiah. 25
servants of Amon *c.* 21:23
slew all that *c.* 24; *2 Chr* 33:25
they *c.* against Jehoiada. *2 Chr* 24:21
the servants of Joash *c.* 25, 26
c. all of them together. *Neh* 4:8
Amos hath *c.* against. *Amos* 7:10

constant, -ly

if he be *c.* to do my. *1 Chr* 28:7
that heareth, speaketh *c.* *Pr* 21:28*
Rhoda *c.* affirmed that. *Acts* 12:15*
these things thou affirm *c.* *Tit* 3:8*

constellations

the *c.* thereof shall not. *Isa* 13:10

constrain

c. you to be circumcised. *Gal* 6:12*

constrained, -eth

woman of Shunem *c.* *2 Ki* 4:8
spirit within me *c.* me. *Job* 32:18
Jesus *c.* his disciples. *Mat* 14:22
Mark 6:45
they *c.* him, saying. *Luke* 24:29
Lydia *c.* us to come. *Acts* 16:15
I was *c.* to appeal to Caesar. 28:19
for love of Christ *c.* us. *2 Cor* 5:14

constraint

oversight, not by *c.* but. *1 Pet* 5:2

consult

only *c.* to cast him down. *Ps* 62:4

consultation

chief priests held a *c.* *Mark* 15:1

consulted

Rehoboam *c.* with. *1 Ki* 12:6, 8
David *c.* with captains. *1 Chr* 13:1
Jehoshaphat *c.* with. *2 Chr* 20:21
I *c.* with myself, and. *Neh* 5:7
they have *c.* against thy. *Ps* 83:3
for they have *c.* together with. 5
king of Babylon *c.* with. *Ezek* 21:21
presidents and captains *c.* *Dan* 6:7
Balak king of Moab *c.* *Mi* 6:5
hast *c.* shame to thy. *Hab* 2:10
c. that they might take. *Mat* 26:4
chief priests *c.* to put. *John* 12:10

consulter

not found among you a *c.* *Deut* 18:11

consulteth

c. whether he be able. *Luke* 14:31

consume

[1] *To destroy,* Ex 32:10. [2] *To spend, or squander away,* Jas 4:3. [3] *To burn up,* Luke 9:54.
famine shall *c.* the land. *Gen* 41:30
lest I *c.* thee in the way. *Ex* 33:3, 5
that shall *c.* the eyes. *Lev* 26:16
this great fire will *c.* us. *Deut* 5:25
thou shalt *c.* all people. 7:16
for locust shall *c.* it. 28:38, 42*
kindled in mine anger shall *c.* 32:22*
will *c.* you after he hath. *Josh* 24:20
shall be to *c.* thine eyes. *1 Sam* 2:33
let fire *c.* thee and. *2 Ki* 1:10, 12
fire shall *c.* the tabernacles. *Job* 15:34
a fire not blown shall *c.* him. 20:26*
drought and heat *c.* the. 24:19
c. into smoke shall they *c.* *Ps* 37:20
makest his beauty to *c.* 39:11
their beauty shall *c.* in. 49:14
their days did he *c.* in. 78:33
it shall also *c.* the beard. *Isa* 7:20
and shall *c.* the glory of his. 10:18
there shall the calf *c.* the. 27:10
fire shall *c.* the palaces. *Jer* 49:27*
and *c.* away for their. *Ezek* 4:17*
hail-stones in my fury to *c.* it. 13:13
is drawn, it is furbished to *c.* 21:28*
I will *c.* thy filthiness out. 22:15
kindle the fire, *c.* the flesh. 24:10*
desolate, are given us to *c.* 35:12*
c. all these kingdoms. *Dan* 2:44
and the sword shall *c.* *Hos* 11:6
I will *c.* all things from. *Zeph* 1:2
c. man and beast, I will *c.* fowls. 3
remain in his house and *c.* *Zech* 5:4
their flesh, eyes, shall *c.* away. 14:12
whom the Lord shall *c.* *2 Thes* 2:8*
ye ask that ye may *c.* *Jas* 4:3*

consume *them*

that I may *c. them.* *Ex* 32:10, 12
c. them in moment. *Num* 16:21, 45
thou mayest not *c. them.* *Deut* 7:22
didst not utterly *c. them.* *Neh* 9:31
c. them in wrath, *c. them.* *Ps* 59:13
I will surely *c. them.* *Jer* 8:13
but I will *c. them* by the. 14:12
fury on them to *c. them.* *Ezek* 20:13
and *c. them,* as Elias did. *Luke* 9:54

consumed

lest thou be *c.* in the. *Gen* 19:15
mountain, lest thou be *c.* 17
in day the drought *c.* me. 31:40
bush burned, was not *c.* *Ex* 3:2
sentest thy wrath, which *c.* 15:7
if the corn or the field be *c.* 22:6
and *c.* upon the altar. *Lev* 9:24
c. them in uttermost. *Num* 11:1*
one of whom flesh is half *c.* 12:12
depart lest ye be *c.* in all. 16:26
there came out fire and *c.* the. 35*
a fire is gone out, it hath *c.* 21:28*
I *c.* not the children of Israel. 25:11
generation . . . done evil was *c.* 32:13
men of war were *c.* *Deut* 2:16
rose fire out of rock and *c.* *Judg* 6:21
the man that *c.* us. *2 Sam* 21:5
fire of Lord fell and *c.* *1 Ki* 18:38
2 Chr 7:1
fire *c.* him and fifty. *2 Ki* 1:10, 12
children of Israel *c.* not. *2 Chr* 8:8
gates are *c.* with fire. *Neh* 2:3, 13
fire of God hath *c.* sheep. *Job* 1:16
by breath of his nostrils *c.* 4:9
snow and ice are *c.* out. 6:17
as the cloud is *c.* and. 7:9
though my reins be *c.* 19:27
his flesh is *c.* away. 33:21
mine eyes *c.* *Ps* 6:7; 31:9
my bones *c.* 31:10*; 102:3
I am *c.* by the blow of. 39:10
be confou ded and *c.* that. 71:13
are utterly *c.* with terrors. 73:19
fire *c.* their young men. 78:63*
for we are *c.* by thine anger. 90:7
let the sinners be *c.* out of. 104:35
they had almost *c.* me upon. 119:87
my zeal hath *c.* me. 139
flesh and thy body are *c.* *Pr* 5:11
the oppressors are *c.* *Isa* 16:4
scorner is *c.* and all that. 29:20
thou hast *c.* us. 64:7
hast *c.* them, but they. *Jer* 5:3

the lead is c. Jer 6:29
the beasts are c. 12:4
that my days should be c. 20:18
till all the roll was c. 36:23
we have been c. by sword. 44:18
hath mine enemy c. Lam 2:22
Lord's mercies we are not c. 3:22
her rods broken, fire c. Ezek 19:12
22:31
that the scum of it may be c. 24:11
wherefore I have c. them. 43:8
sons of Jacob are not c. Mal 3:6
take heed ye be not c. Gal 5:15

shall be **consumed**

in wilderness *shall be c.* Num 14:35
shall die, *shall* we *be c.*? 17:13*
ye *shall be c.* both you. 1 Sam 12:25
forsake Lord *shall be c.* Isa 1:28
shall be c. together: they that eat swine's flesh *shall be c.* 66:17
famine *shall* prophets *be c.* Jer 14:15
shall be c. by sword. 16:4; 44:12, 27
famine *shall* they *be c.* Ezek 5:12
it shall fall, ye *shall be c.* in. 13:14
they *shall be* no more c. 34:29
nor *shall* the fruit *be c.* 47:12*
by his hand *shall be c.* Dan 11:16*

consumed with *till*, or *until*

to destroy, *until* they were c. Deut 2:15; Josh 5:6
until he have c. thee. Deut 28:21
slaying them *till* they were c. Josh 10:20
fight *until* they be c. 1 Sam 15:18
I turned not again *until* I had c. them. 2 Sam 22:38; Ps 18:37
Syrians *until* thou have c. 1 Ki 22:11
2 Ki 13:17, 19; 2 Chr 18:10
angry *till* thou hadst c. us. Ezra 9:14
a sword after them *till* I have c. Jer 9:16; 24:10; 27:8; 49:37

consumeth, -ing

thy God is a c. fire. Deut 4:24*
Heb 12:29
before thee as a c. fire. Deut 9:3*
he c. as a garment. Job 13:28
remnant of them the fire c. 22:20
for it is a fire that c. to. 31:12
as the flame c. chaff. Isa 5:24*

consummation

desolate, even until c. Dan 9:27

consumption

(*Wasting*)

appoint over you terror, c. Lev 26:16
Lord smite thee with a c. Deut 28:22
the c. decreed shall. Isa 10:22
Lord God of hosts make a c. 23*
I have heard from Lord God of hosts a c. 28:22*

contain

of heavens cannot c. thee. 1 Ki 8:27
2 Chr 2:6; 6:18
bath may c. tenth part. Ezek 45:11
the world could not c. John 21:25
but if they cannot c. 1 Cor 7:9*

contained, -eth, -ing

drink of sister's cup, it c. Ezek 23:32
six water-pots c. 2 or 3. John 2:6
do by nature things c. Rom 2:14
having abolished law c. Eph 2:15
it is c. in scripture. 1 Pet 2:6

contemn, -ed, -eth

(*To scorn or despise*)

do the wicked c. God? Ps 10:13
a vile person is c. 15:4
they c. the counsel of the. 107:11
for love, it would be c. S of S 8:7
glory of Moab shall be c. Isa 16:14
it c. the rod of my son. Ezek 21:10
and what if the sword c. even? 13

contempt

thus shall arise much c. Esth 1:18
he poureth c. on princes. Job 12:21
Ps 107:40
did c. of families terrify? Job 31:34
remove reproach and c. Ps 119:22
are exceedingly filled with c. 123:3
our soul is filled with the c. 4
then cometh c. Pr 18:3
to bring into c. all the. Isa 23:9
awake to everlasting c. Dan 12:2

contemptible

ye say, table of Lord is c. Mal 1:7
even his meat is c. 12
I also made you c. 2:9
is weak, his speech c. 2 Cor 10:10

contemptuously

which speak c. against. Ps 31:18

contend

To strive, either bodily or in debate or discussion, to dispute, Job 9:3; 40:2; Jer 18:19; Acts 11:2.

c. with Moabites. Deut 2:9, 24
if c. he cannot answer. Job 9:3
accept his person, and c. 13:8
such as keep the law c. Pr 28:4
nor may he c. with him. Eccl 6:10
c. with them that c. with. Isa 49:25
that justifieth me, who will c.? 50:8
I will not c. for ever. 57:16
then how canst thou c.? Jer 12:5
to voice of them that c. with. 18:19
Lord God called to c. Amos 7:4
hear ye, arise, c. thou. Mi 6:1
should earnestly c. for faith. Jude 3

contended

then c. I with rulers. Neh 13:11, 17
I c. with them, and cursed. 25
servants when they c. Job 31:13
not find them that c. Isa 41:12
they of circumcision c. Acts 11:2

contendest

shew me wherefore thou c. Job 10:2

contendeth

shall he that c. with? Job 40:2
if a wise man c. with. Pr 29:9

contending

c. with devil, he disputed. Jude 9

content

his brethren were c. Gen 37:27
Moses was c. to dwell. Ex 2:21
heard that, he was c. Lev 10:20
to God we had been c. Josh 7:7
Levite was c. to dwell. Judg 17:11
be c. I pray thee, and. 19:6
Naaman said, be c. 2 Ki 5:23
one said, be c. and go with. 6:3
now therefore be c. Job 6:28
nor will he rest c. though. Pr 6:35
Pilate willing to c. Mark 15:15
nor accuse falsely, be c. Luke 3:14
in every state to be c. Phil 4:11
and raiment, let us be c. 1 Tim 6:8
be c. with such things. Heb 13:5
and not c. with prating. 3 John 10

contention

only by pride cometh c. Pr 13:10
leave off c. before it be. 17:14
a fool's lips enter into c. 18:6
cast out the scorner, and c. 22:10
hast borne me a man of c. Jer 15:10
that raise up strife and c. Hab 1:3
the c. was so sharp. Acts 15:39
preach Christ of c. Phil 1:16*
gospel of God with much c. 1 Thes 2:2

contentions

lot causeth c. to cease. Pr 18:18
and their c. are like the bars. 19
c. of a wife are a. 19:13; 27:15
who hath woe? who hath c.? 23:29
that there are c. among. 1 Cor 1:11
avoid c. and strivings. Tit 3:9

contentious

than with a c. and angry. Pr 21:19
as wood to fire, so is a c. 26:21
a continual dropping and a c. 27:15
but to them that are c. Rom 2:8*
if any man seem to be c. 1 Cor 11:16

contentment

but godliness with c. 1 Tim 6:6

continual

this shall be a c. burnt-. Ex 29:42
and the c. bread shall. Num 4:7
house for c. shew-bread. 2 Chr 2:4
merry heart hath a c. feast. Pr 15:15
smote the people with c. Isa 14:6
for in going up c. weeping. Jer 48:5
there was a c. diet given him. 52:34
2 Ki 25:30
sever out men of c. Ezek 39:14

lest by her c. coming she. Luke 18:5
that I have c. sorrow. Rom 9:2*

continually

imagination of heart evil c. Gen 6:5
before the Lord c. Ex 28:30
lambs of first year, day by day c. 29:38
to cause lamps to burn c. Lev 24:2
David's enemy c. 1 Sam 18:29
eat bread at my table c. 2 Sam 9:7
Jehoiakim eat bread c. 2 Ki 25:29
Jer 52:33
seek his face c. 1 Chr 16:11
between Jeroboam and Rehoboam c. 2 Chr 12:15
his sons, thus did Job c. Job 1:5
his praise shall be c. Ps 34:1; 71:6
say c. the Lord be magnified. 35:27
40:16; 70:4
and my sorrow is c. before. 38:17
loving-kindness and truth c. 40:11
they c. say, Where is thy God? 42:3
my confusion is c. before me. 44:15
burnt-offerings to have been c. 50:8
goodness of God endureth c. 52:1
whereunto I c. resort. 71:3
my praise shall be c. 6
I will hope c. and praise thee. 14
I am c. with thee. 73:23
tumult increaseth c. 74:23
be before the Lord c. 109:15
so shall I keep thy law c. 119:44
my soul is c. in my hand. 109
have respect to thy statutes c. 117
c. are they gathered for war. 140:2
he deviseth mischief c. Pr 6:14
bind them c. on thy heart. 21
I stand c. upon watch-. Isa 21:8
walls are c. before me. 49:16
and hast feared c. every day. 51:13
my name c. every day is. 52:5
Lord shall guide thee c. 58:11
thy gates shall be open c. 60:11
provoketh me to anger c. 65:3
before me c. is grief and. Jer 6:7
a meat-offering c. to. Ezek 46:14
God whom thou servest c. Dan 6:16, 20
committed whoredom c. Hos 4:18
and wait on thy God c. 12:6
so shall the heathen drink c. Ob 16
thy wickedness passed c.? Nah 3:19
shall they not spare c.? Hab 1:17
were c. in the temple. Luke 24:53
we will give ourselves c. Acts 6:4*
that waited on Cornelius c. 10:7
attending c. upon this. Rom 13:6
abideth a priest c. Heb 7:3
sacrifices offered year by year c. 10:1
offer the sacrifice of praise c. 13:15

continuance

great plagues of long c. Deut 28:59
my members which in c. Ps 139:16*
in those is c. and we. Isa 64:5*
by patient c. in well doing. Rom 2:7*

continue

if he c. a day or two. Ex 21:21
c. in blood of purifying. Lev 12:4, 5
c. following the Lord. 1 Sam 12:14
thy kingdom shall not c. 13:14
that it may c. for ever. 2 Sam 7:29
Lord may c. his word. 1 Ki 2:4*
nor shall his substance c. Job 15:29
doth not mine eye c. in their? 17:2
O c. thy loving-kindness. Ps 36:10
that their houses shall c. 49:11
children of thy servants c. 102:28
they c. according to thine. 119:91
that c. till night, till wine. Isa 5:11
that the evidences may c. Jer 32:14
c. more years than the. Dan 11:8*
because they c. with me. Mat 15:32
if ye c. in my word. John 8:31
so have I loved you, c. 15:9
persuaded to c. in. Acts 13:43
and exhorting them to c. 14:22
obtained help of God, I c. 26:22
shall we c. in sin that? Rom 6:1
goodness, if thou c. in. 11:22
truth of gospel might c. Gal 2:5
I know that I shall c. Phil 1:25

if ye *c.* in the faith. *Col* 1:23
c. in prayer, and watch. 4:2
if they *c.* in faith. *1 Tim* 2:15
take heed to thy doctrine, *c.* 4:16
c. in the things which. *2 Tim* 3:14
priests not suffered to *c.* *Heb* 7:23
let brotherly love *c.* 13:1
and *c.* there a year. *Jas* 4:13
the fathers, all things *c.* *2 Pet* 3:4
ye shall *c.* in the Son. *1 John* 2:24
power was given him to *c.* *Rev* 13:5
when he cometh, he must *c.* 17:10

continued

served them, and *c.* a. *Gen* 40:4
as she *c.* praying. *1 Sam* 1:12
c. till burnt-offering was. *2 Chr* 29:28
also I *c.* in the work of. *Neh* 5:16
his name shall be *c.* as. *Ps* 72:17
Daniel *c.* to first year. *Dan* 1:21
c. all night in prayer. *Luke* 6:12
ye are they that *c.* with me. 22:28
all *c.* with one accord. *Acts* 1:14
they *c.* stedfastly in the. 2:42
Simon himself *c.* with Philip. 8:13
but Peter *c.* knocking. 12:16
Paul preached and *c.* his. 20:7
because they *c.* not in. *Heb* 8:9
would no doubt have *c.* *1 John* 2:19

continueth, -ing

as a shadow, and *c.* *Job* 14:2
a *c.* whirlwind, it shall. *Jer* 30:23
c. daily with one accord. *Acts* 2:46
rejoicing in hope, *c.* *Rom* 12:12
cursed that *c.* not in all. *Gal* 3:10
she that is a widow *c.* *1 Tim* 5:5
this man, because he *c.* *Heb* 7:24*
here we have no *c.* city. 13:14*
into perfect law, and *c.* *Jas* 1:25

contradicting

filled with envy, *c.* and. *Acts* 13:45

contradiction

without *c.* the less is. *Heb* 7:7
him that endured such *c.* 12:3*

contrariwise

c. ye ought rather to. *2 Cor* 2:7
c. when they saw the gospel. *Gal* 2:7
not rendering railing, *c.* *1 Pet* 3:9

contrary

if ye walk *c.* *Lev* 26:21, 23, 27, 40
then will I walk *c.* to you. 24, 28, 41
it was turned to the *c.* *Esth* 9:1
the *c.* is in thee, therefore thou art *c.* *Ezek* 16:34
for the wind was *c.* *Mat* 14:24
these all do *c.* to the. *Acts* 17:7
men to worship *c.* to the law. 18:13
me to be smitten *c.* to the law. 23:3
to do many things *c.* to the. 26:9
grafted *c.* to nature into. *Rom* 11:24
c. to the doctrine ye have. 16:17
and these are *c.* the one. *Gal* 5:17
hand-writing which was *c.* *Col* 2:14
not God, and are *c.* to. *1 Thes* 2:15
if any thing that is *c.* *1 Tim* 1:10
that he of the *c.* part. *Tit* 2:8

contribution

to make *c.* for the poor. *Rom* 15:26

contrite

saveth such as be of *c.* *Ps* 34:18
a *c.* heart, O God, thou. 51:17
c. and humble spirit, to revive heart of *c.* ones. *Isa* 57:15
that is of a *c.* spirit and. 66:2

controversy

being matters of *c.* *Deut* 17:8
men between whom the *c.* 19:17
shall every *c.* be tried. 21:5
if there be a *c.* between men. 25:1
any that had a *c.* came. *2 Sam* 15:2
set the Levites for *c.* *2 Chr* 19:8
recompences for the *c.* of. *Isa* 34:8
the Lord hath a *c.* *Jer* 25:31
in *c.* they shall stand. *Ezek* 44:24
the Lord hath a *c.* with. *Hos* 4:1
Lord hath a *c.* with Judah. 12:2
Lord hath *c.* with his people. *Mi* 6:2
without *c.* great is the. *1 Tim* 3:16

convenient

[1] *Needful*, Pr 30:8. [2] *Fitting*, Rom 1:28. [3] *Befitting*, Eph 5:4; *Philem* 8.

feed me with food *c.* *Pr* 30:8*
seemeth good and *c.* *Jer* 40:4, 5
when a *c.* day was. *Mark* 6:21
when I have a *c.* season. *Acts* 24:25
things which are not *c.* *Rom* 1:28*
he shall have *c.* time. *1 Cor* 16:12*
jesting, which are not *c.* *Eph* 5:4*
to enjoin that which is *c.* *Philem* 8*

conveniently

how he might *c.* betray. *Mark* 14:11

conversant

and strangers were *c.* *Josh* 8:35
as long as we were *c.* *1 Sam* 25:15

conversation

(*Behaviour, or manner of life. It does not in the Bible mean discourse with another. The Revised Versions change the word in all cases*)

slay such as be of upright *c.* *Ps* 37:14
to him that ordereth his *c.* 50:23
we have had our *c.* *2 Cor* 1:12
ye have heard of my *c.* *Gal* 1:13
whom also we all had our *c.* *Eph* 2:3
put off concerning former *c.* 4:22
only let your *c.* be as. *Phil* 1:27
for our *c.* is in heaven. 3:20
example of believers in *c.* *1 Tim* 4:12
let your *c.* be without. *Heb* 13:5
considering the end of their *c.* 7
shew out of a good *c.* *Jas* 3:13
holy in all manner of *c.* *1 Pet* 1:15
corruptible things from vain *c.* 18
having your *c.* honest among. 2:12
they also may be won by the *c.* 3:1
behold your chaste *c.* 2
falsely accuse your good *c.* 16
Lot vexed with filthy *c.* *2 Pet* 2:7
ought ye to be, in all holy *c.* 3:11

conversion

(*Literally, a turning, the word is used to mean, theologically, the spiritual or moral change which accompanies the turning of a sinner from his sins to God*, Ps 51:13)

the *c.* of the Gentiles. *Acts* 15:3

convert, -ed

(*The Revised Versions usually use the literal form*, turn again)

and sinners shall be *c.* *Ps* 51:13
they understand, and *c.* *Isa* 6:10
abundance of sea shall be *c.* 60:5*
should be *c.* and I should heal them. *Mat* 13:15; *Mark* 4:12
ye be *c.* and become as. *Mat* 18:3
when *c.* strengthen thy. *Luke* 22:32
be *c.* and I heal them. *John* 12:40; *Acts* 28:27
repent and be *c.* that sins. *Acts* 3:19
err from truth, and one *c.* *Jas* 5:19

converteth, -ing

law of Lord is perfect, *c.* *Ps* 19:7*
that he who *c.* a sinner. *Jas* 5:20

converts

her *c.* shall be redeemed. *Isa* 1:27

convey, -ed

I will *c.* them by sea. *1 Ki* 5:9*
that they may *c.* me over. *Neh* 2:7
Jesus had *c.* himself. *John* 5:13

convicted

c. by their own conscience. *John* 8:9

convince, -ed, -eth

none of you *c.* Job. *Job* 32:12
which of you *c.* me of? *John* 8:46*
for he mightily *c.* the. *Acts* 18:28*
he is *c.* of all, he is. *1 Cor* 14:24*
that he may be able to *c.* *Tit* 1:9*
and are *c.* of the law. *Jas* 2:9*
to *c.* all that are ungodly. *Jude* 15*

convocation, -s

(*An assembly of persons called together for a purpose*)

shall be an holy *c.* *Ex* 12:16
Lev 23:7, 24, 35; *Num* 28:18; 29:1
proclaim to be holy *c.* *Lev* 23:2
4, 21, 37
seventh day as an holy *c.* 23:3, 8
Num 28:25
tenth day an holy *c.* *Lev* 23:27
Num 29:7

eighth day shall be holy *c.* *Lev* 23:36
first-fruits have holy *c.* *Num* 28:26
day seventh month holy *c.* 29:12

cook, -s

take daughters to be *c.* *1 Sam* 8:13
Samuel said to *c.* bring portion. 9:23
c. took up the shoulder and set. 24

cool

walking in garden in the *c.* *Gen* 3:8
dip tip of finger and *c.* *Luke* 16:24

copied

men of Hezekiah *c.* out. *Pr* 25:1

coping

stones from foundation to *c.* *1 Ki* 7:9

copper

two vessels of fine *c.* *Ezra* 8:27

coppersmith

Alexander the *c.* did. *2 Tim* 4:14

copulation

if any man's seed of *c.* *Lev* 15:16
skin whereon is seed of *c.* shall. 17
shall lie with seed of *c.* 18

copy

write him a *c.* of law. *Deut* 17:18
he wrote on stones a *c.* *Josh* 8:32
c. of a letter sent. *Ezra* 4:11; 5:6
c. of Artaxerxes' letter was. 4:23
c. of the letter Artaxerxes gave. 7:11
c. of a writing for. *Esth* 3:14; 8:13
Mordecai gave Hatach a *c.* 4:8

cor

(*A measure, either dry or liquid. About* 11 *bushels or* 90 *gallons*)

part of a bath out of *c.* *Ezek* 45:14

coral

no mention made of *c.* *Job* 28:18
was thy merchant in *c.* *Ezek* 27:16

corban

it is *c.* that is to say. *Mark* 7:11

cord

let spies down by a *c.* *Josh* 2:15
he hath loosed my *c.* *Job* 30:11
out leviathan's tongue with *c.*? 41:1
a threefold *c.* is not. *Eccl* 4:12
or ever the silver *c.* be loosed. 12:6
spare not, lengthen *c.* *Isa* 54:2
a *c.* by lot in congregation. *Mi* 2:5

cords

of the court and their *c.* *Ex* 35:18
Samson with new *c.* *Judg* 15:13*
if they be holden in *c.* *Job* 36:8
cast away their *c.* from us. *Ps* 2:3
bind the sacrifice with *c.* 118:27
he hath cut asunder the *c.* 129:4
have hid a snare and *c.* 140:5
shall be holden with *c.* *Pr* 5:22
that draw iniquity with *c.* *Isa* 5:18
nor shall any of the *c.* thereof. 33:20
all my *c.* broken. *Jer* 10:20
let down Jeremiah with *c.* 38:6
drew up Jeremiah with *c.* 13
in chests bound with *c.* *Ezek* 27:24
I drew them with the *c.* *Hos* 11:4
a scourge of small *c.* *John* 2:15

coriander

manna was like *c.* seed. *Ex* 16:31
Num 11:7

Corinth

things, Paul came to *C.* *Acts* 18:1
while Apollos was at *C.* 19:1
unto church of God at *C.* to them. *1 Cor* 1:2; *2 Cor* 1:1
I came not as yet to *C.* *2 Cor* 1:23
Erastus abode at *C.* *2 Tim* 4:20

Corinthians

many of the *C.* hearing. *Acts* 18:8
O ye *C.* our mouth is. *2 Cor* 6:11

cormorant

have in abomination *c.* and great. *Lev* 11:7; *Deut* 14:17
but the *c.* shall possess. *Isa* 34:11*
Zeph 2:14*

corn

(*Always, in the Bible, grain of various sorts, not Indian corn as would be understood in the United States by the term. The American Revision changes the word in the Old Testament to* grain)

came to Joseph to buy *c. Gen* 41:57
there was *c.* in Egypt. 42:2
Acts 7:12
carry *c.* for the famine. *Gen* 42:19
so that the stacks of *c.* *Ex* 22:6
burn part of beaten *c.* *Lev* 2:16
neither bread nor parched *c.* 23:14
as though it were the *c. Num* 18:27
to put the sickle to *c.* *Deut* 16:9
not muzzle ox when he treadeth out *c.* 25:4; *1 Cor* 9:9; *1 Tim* 5:18
did eat of the old *c.* *Josh* 5:11, 12
he reached her parched *c. Ruth* 2:14
lie down at end of heap of *c.* 3:7
an ephah of parched *c.* *1 Sam* 17:17
five measures of parched *c.* 25:18
brought parched *c.* *2 Sam* 17:28
as blasted *c.* *2 Ki* 19:26; *Isa* 37:27
we take up *c.* for them. *Neh* 5:2
as a shock of *c.* cometh. *Job* 5:26
they reap every one his *c.* 24:6
young ones grow up with *c.* 39:4
preparest them *c.* *Ps* 65:9
valleys are covered with *c.* 13
there shall be a handful of *c.* 72:16
had given them of the *c.* 78:24
that withholdeth *c.* *Pr* 11:26
harvest-man gathereth *c.* *Isa* 17:5
I will no more give thy *c.* 62:8
I will call for the *c.* *Ezek* 36:29
I will take away my *c.* *Hos* 2:9
loveth to tread out the *c.* 10:11
they shall revive as the *c.* 14:7
for the *c.* is wasted. *Joel* 1:10
barns are broken down, for *c.* 17
that we may sell *c.* *Amos* 8:5
I will sift Israel like as *c.* 9:9
after that the full *c.* *Mark* 4:28
except a *c.* of wheat. *John* 12:24*

ears of **corn**

seven *ears of c.* came up. *Gen* 41:5
offer green *ears of c.* *Lev* 2:14
let me glean *ears of c.* *Ruth* 2:2
brought full *ears of c.* *2 Ki* 4:42
off as tops of the *ears of c. Job* 24:24
to pluck *ears of c.* *Mat* 12:1
Mark 2:23; *Luke* 6:1

corn *fields*

c. fields on the sabbath. *Mark* 2:23
Mat 12:1; *Luke* 6:1

corn *floor*

and the *c.* of my *floor.* *Isa* 21:10
reward on every *c. floor.* *Hos* 9:1

standing **corn**

that the *standing c.* be. *Ex* 22:6
come into *standing c.* *Deut* 23:25
foxes go into *standing c.* burn up *standing c.* *Judg* 15:5

corn *and wine*

plenty of *c. and wine.* *Gen* 27:28
with *c. and wine* have I. 37
bless thy *c. and wine.* *Deut* 7:13
gather in thy *c. and wine.* 11:14
not eat tithe of *c. and wine.* 12:17
14:23
hast gathered in *c. and wine.* 16:13
first-fruit of *c. and wine* and. 18:4
not leave thee *c. and wine* or. 28:51
upon a land of *c. and wine.* 33:28
to a land of *c. and wine. 2 Ki* 18:32
Isa 36:17
brought first-fruits of *c. and wine.*
2 Chr 31:5
for increase of *c. and wine.* 32:28
restore part of *c. wine.* *Neh* 5:11
of *c.* of new *wine.* 10:39; 13:5, 12
in time their *c. and wine.* *Ps* 4:7
where is *c. and wine* ? *Lam* 2:12
I gave her *c. wine,* and oil. *Hos* 2:8
earth shall hear *c. and wine.* 22
assemble for *c. and wine.* 7:14
will send you *c. and wine.* *Joel* 2:19
drought on *c. and* new *wine.*
Hag 1:11
c. shall make young men cheerful, *and* new *wine* maids. *Zech* 9:17

Cornelius

man in Cesarea, called *C. Acts* 10:1
the angel which spake to *C.* 7
C. met Peter, and fell down. 25
C. thy prayer is heard. 31

corner

shave off the *c.* of their. *Lev* 21:5
altars in every *c.* of. *2 Chr* 28:24
through street near *c.* *Pr* 7:8
lieth in wait at every *c.* 12
better to dwell in *c.* of. 21:9; 25:24
not be removed into a *c.* *Isa* 30:20
flame shall devour the *c.* *Jer* 48:45
take of thee a stone for a *c.* 51:26
in every *c.* of court. *Ezek* 46:21
in Samaria in the *c.* of. *Amos* 3:12
came forth the *c.* and. *Zech* 10:4*
stone builders rejected is become head of *c. Mat* 21:42; *Ps* 118:22
Mark 12:10; *Luke* 20:17
Acts 4:11; *1 Pet* 2:7
was not done in a *c.* *Acts* 26:26

corner-gate

Ephraim to the *c.-gate.* *2 Ki* 14:13
towers at *c.-gate.* *2 Chr* 26:9
built from tower to *gate* of *c.*
Jer 31:38
inhabited to the *c.-gate.* *Zech* 14:10

corner-stone

or who laid the *c.-stone* ? *Job* 38:6
head-*stone* of the *c.* *Ps* 118:22
daughters be as *c.-stones.* 144:12
a precious *c.-stone.* *Isa* 28:16
1 Pet 2:6
Christ chief *c.-stone.* *Eph* 2:20

corners

rings in four *c.* of ark. *Ex* 25:12*
26; 27:4; 37:13
horns upon the four *c.* 27:2; 38:2
not reap the *c.* of field. *Lev* 19:9
23:22
ye shall not round *c.* of heads. 27
shall smite *c.* of Moab. *Num* 24:17
will scatter them into *c. Deut* 32:26*
thou didst divide into *c.* *Neh* 9:22*
wind smote the four *c.* *Job* 1:19
dispersed of Judah from *c. Isa* 11:12
punish circumcised with ... in uttermost *c. Jer* 9:25, 26; 25:23; 49:32
end is come upon four *c.* *Ezek* 7:2
put blood upon four *c.* 45:19
pray in *c.* of the streets. *Mat* 6:5
sheet knit at *c.* *Acts* 10:11; 11:5
angels standing on four *c.* *Rev* 7:1

cornet

ark with sound of *c.* *1 Chr* 15:28
with sound of the *c.* make. *Ps* 98:6
hear the sound of *c.* *Dan* 3:5, 15
every man shall hear sound of *c.* 10
blow ye the *c.* in Gibeah. *Hos* 5:8

cornets

played before Lord on *c. 2 Sam* 6:5*
shouting with *c.* *2 Chr* 15:14

corpse, -s

they were all dead *c.* *2 Ki* 19:35
Isa 37:36
no end of *c.* stumble on *c.* *Nah* 3:3
disciples took John's *c.* *Mark* 6:29

correct

when thou dost *c.* man. *Ps* 39:11
heathen, shall not he *c.*? 94:10
c. thy son, and he shall. *Pr* 29:17
own wickedness shall *c.* *Jer* 2:19
c. me, but with judgement. 10:24
c. thee in measure. 30:11; 46:28

corrected, -eth

is man whom God *c.* *Job* 5:17
whom Lord loveth, he *c.* *Pr* 3:12*
a servant will not be *c.* 29:19
of our flesh which *c.* *Heb* 12:9*

correction

whether for *c.* or mercy. *Job* 37:13
neither be weary of his *c.* *Pr* 3:11*
he goeth as a fool to the *c.* 7:22
c. is grievous to him that. 15:10
but the rod of *c.* shall. 22:15
withhold not *c.* from child. 23:13
children received no *c.* *Jer* 2:30
have refused to receive *c.* 5:3
a nation that receiveth not *c.* 7:28*
hast established them for *c. Hab* 1:12
obeyed not, received not *c. Zeph* 3:2
scripture is profitable for *c.*
2 Tim 3:16

corrupt

[1] *To consume,* Mat 6:19. [2] *To defile, or pollute,* Ex 32:7. [3] *To mar, or spoil,* 1 Cor 15:33. [4] *To pervert or lead astray,* 2 Cor 11:3. [5] *To break, or make void,* Mal 2:8. [6] *Vicious and unsound,* 1 Tim 6:5; 2 Tim 3:8.

earth also was *c.* *Gen* 6:11, 12
my breath is *c.* my days. *Job* 17:1*
they are *c.* *Ps* 14:1; 53:1; 73:8
my wounds stink and are *c.* 38:5
troubled fountain and *c.* *Pr* 25:26
not according to your *c. Ezek* 20:44
she was more *c.* in her. 23:11
lying and *c.* words. *Dan* 2:9
that sacrificeth a *c.* thing. *Mal* 1:14*
a *c.* tree bringeth forth. *Mat* 7:17
nor can a *c.* tree. 18; *Luke* 6:43
tree *c.* and his fruit *c.* *Mat* 12:33
the old man which is *c.* *Eph* 4:22
let no *c.* communication proceed. 29
disputings of men of *c.* *1 Tim* 6:5
men of *c.* minds. *2 Tim* 3:8

corrupt, *verb*

lest ye *c.* yourselves. *Deut* 4:16, 25
after my death ye will *c.* 31:29
do wickedly shall he *c.* *Dan* 11:32*
behold I will *c.* your. *Mal* 2:3*
moth and rust doth *c.* *Mat* 6:19*
neither moth nor rust doth *c.* 20*
evil communications *c. 1 Cor* 15:33
which *c.* the word of God. *2 Cor* 2:17
in those things they *c.* *Jude* 10*
great whore did *c.* earth. *Rev* 19:2

corrupted, -eth

for all flesh had *c.* his way. *Gen* 6:12
the land was *c.* by. *Ex* 8:24
for thy people have *c.* themselves.
32:7; *Deut* 9:12; 32:5
c. themselves more. *Judg* 2:19
thou wast *c.* more. *Ezek* 16:47
thou hast *c.* thy wisdom. 28:17
have deeply *c.* themselves. *Hos* 9:9
rose early and *c.* all. *Zeph* 3:7
ye have *c.* covenant of. *Mal* 2:8
nor moth *c.* *Luke* 12:33
have *c.* no man. *2 Cor* 7:2
lest your minds be *c.* from. 11:3
your riches are *c.* *Jas* 5:1, 2

corrupters

children that are *c.* *Isa* 1:4
brass and iron, all *c.* *Jer* 6:28

corruptible

image made like to *c.* *Rom* 1:23
they do it to obtain *c.* *1 Cor* 9:25
for this *c.* must put on. 15:53
not redeemed with *c.* *1 Pet* 1:18
born again, not of *c.* seed. 23
let it be in that which is not *c.* 3:4

corrupting

daughter of women *c.* *Dan* 11:17

corruption

(*Frequently used as a synonym of death; laying stress on the decay of the body after it is in the grave*)

their *c.* is in them. *Lev* 22:25
right hand of mount of *c. 2 Ki* 23:13
I have said to *c.* thou. *Job* 17:14
nor wilt thou suffer thine holy One to see *c. Ps* 16:10; *Acts* 2:27; 13:35
live for ever, and not see *c. Ps* 49:9
delivered it from pit of *c. Isa* 38:17
was turned in me to *c.* *Dan* 10:8
up my life from *c.* *Jonah* 2:6*
nor his flesh did see *c.* *Acts* 2:31
no more to return to *c.* 13:34
laid to his fathers and saw *c.* 36
raised again saw no *c.* 37
from the bondage of *c.* *Rom* 8:21
it is sown in *c.*; raised. *1 Cor* 15:42
neither doth *c.* inherit. 50
shall of flesh reap *c.* *Gal* 6:8
escaped the *c.* that. *2 Pet* 1:4
utterly perish in own *c.* 2:12*
themselves are servants of *c.* 19

corruptly

people did yet *c.* *2 Chr* 27:2
we have dealt very *c.* *Neh* 1:7

cost

eaten at all of king's *c.*? *2 Sam* 19:42

of that which *c.* nothing. *2 Sam* 24:24
offerings without *c.* *1 Chr* 21:24
and counteth *c.* *Luke* 14:28

costliness

ships made rich by her *c. Rev* 18:19

costly

they brought *c.* stones. *1 Ki* 5:17
all these were of *c.* stones. 7:9
foundation was of *c.* stones. 10
and above were *c.* stones. 11
of spikenard, very *c.* *John* 12:3*
not with *c.* array. *1 Tim* 2:9

cotes

Hezekiah made *c.* *2 Chr* 32:28*

cottage, -s

of Zion is left as a *c.* *Isa* 1:8*
earth shall be removed like *c.* 24:20*
sea-coast shall be *c.* *Zeph* 2:6

couch, -es

and went up to my *c.* *Gen* 49:4
I say, my *c.* shall ease. *Job* 7:13
all night I water my *c.* *Ps* 6:6
in Damascus in a *c.* *Amos* 3:12
stretch themselves upon *c.* 6:4
through tiling with his *c. Luke* 5:19
arise, take up thy *c.* 24
laid sick folk on *c.* *Acts* 5;15

couch

when they *c.* in dens. *Job* 38:40

couched

Judah *c.* as a lion. *Gen* 49:9
he *c.* he lay down as. *Num* 24:9

coucheth

and for deep that *c.* *Deut* 33:13

couching

Issachar *c.* down. *Gen* 49:14
make Ammonites a *c.* *Ezek* 25:5

could

old, so that he *c.* not see. *Gen* 27:1
forth lice, but *c.* not. *Ex* 8:18
he *c.* not see. *1 Sam* 3:2
Ahijah *c.* not see. *1 Ki* 14:4
to king of Edom, *c.* not. *2 Ki* 3:26
but David *c.* not go. *1 Chr* 21:30
c. not withstand them. *2 Chr* 13:7
but he *c.* not be found. *Ps* 37:36
what *c.* have been done? *Isa* 5:4
my mind *c.* not be. *Jer* 15:1
bring it to land, *c.* not. *Jonah* 1:13
Herodias would have killed him, but she *c.* not. *Mark* 6:19
cast him out, *c.* not. 9:18; *Luke* 9:40
she hath done what she *c. Mark* 14:8
the world *c.* not contain. *John* 21:25
from which ye *c.* not be. *Acts* 13:39

couldest

evil things as thou *c.* *Jer* 3:5*
yet *c.* not be satisfied. *Ezek* 16:28

coulter -s

to sharpen each his *c.* *1 Sam* 13:20
they had a file for their *c.* 21

council, -s

shall be in danger of *c.* *Mat* 5:22
deliver you to *c.* 10:17; *Mark* 13:9
sought false witness. *Mat* 26:59
Mark 14:55
elders, scribes and whole *c.*
Mark 15:1
elders led Jesus into *c. Luke* 22:66
chief priests gathered *c. John* 11:47
Acts 5:21
them to go out of the *c.* *Acts* 4:15
and set them before the *c.* 5:27
then stood up one in the *c.* 34
departed from the *c.* rejoicing. 41
and brought him to the *c.* 6:12
all in the *c.* looking on him. 15
commanded all their *c.* to. 22:30
ye with the *c.* signify to the. 23:15
while I stood before the *c.* 24:20

counsel

[1] *Advice,* Pr 20:18; Dan 4:27. [2] *God's purpose,* Acts 4:28. [3] *The most secret resolutions,* 1 Cor 4:5.

I will give thee *c.* *Ex* 18:19
Eleazar, who shall ask *c.* for.
Num 27:21*
caused Israel through *c.* of Balaam, to commit trespass. 31:16
are a nation void of *c.* *Deut* 32:28
asked not *c.* at mouth. *Josh* 9:14
give here advice and *c.* *Judg* 20:7
turn *c.* of Ahithophel. *2 Sam* 15:31
all the *c.* of Ahithophel. 16:23
Lord defeated the good *c.* of. 17:14
shall surely ask *c.* at Abel. 20:18
let me give thee *c.* *1 Ki* 1:12
forsook *c.* of old men. 12:8, 13
2 Chr 10:8, 13
king of Syria took *c.* *2 Ki* 6:8
c. and strength for war. 18:20
Isa 36:5
Saul died for asking *c. 1 Chr* 10:13
Ahaziah walked after *c. 2 Chr* 22:5
art thou made of king's *c.*? 25:16
the king had taken *c.* to. 30:2
the assembly took *c.* to keep. 23
according to *c.* of my. *Ezra* 10:3
according to the *c.* of the princes. 8
God brought their *c.* to. *Neh* 4:15
the *c.* of the froward. *Job* 5:13
should shine upon the *c.* of. 10:3
and strength he hath *c.* and. 12:13
the *c.* of the wicked is. 21:16; 22:18
who is this that darkeneth *c.*? 38:2
who is he that hideth *c.*? 42:3
walketh not in the *c.* *Ps* 1:1
you have shamed the *c.* of. 14:6
who hath given me *c.* 16:7
and fulfil all thy *c.* 20:4
while they took *c.* together. 31:13
Lord brings the *c.* of the. 33:10
we took sweet *c.* together. 55:14
hide me from the secret *c.* 64:2
princes of Judah and their *c.* 68:27
shalt guide me with thy *c.* 73:24
they have taken crafty *c.* 83:3
they waited not for his *c.* 106:13
provoked him with their *c.* 43
the *c.* of the Most High. 107:11
c. is mine, sound wisdom. *Pr* 8:14
where no *c.* is, the people. 11:14*
he that hearkeneth unto *c.* 12:15
without *c.* purposes are. 15:22
hear *c.* and receive. 19:20
c. in the heart of man is. 20:5
every purpose established by *c.* 18
there is no wisdom nor *c.* 21:30
for by wise *c.* thou shalt. 24:6*
of a friend by hearty *c.* 27:9
let *c.* of the Holy One. *Isa* 5:19
they have taken evil *c.* 7:5
spirit of *c.* and might shall. 11:2
I will destroy the *c.* of Egypt. 19:3
c. of counsellors of Pharaoh. 11
taken this *c.* against Tyre? 23:8*
Lord, who is wonderful in *c.* 28:29
that seek deep to hide *c.* 29:15
with whom took he *c.*? 40:14
and performeth the *c.* 44:26
nor shall *c.* perish. *Jer* 18:18
thou knowest all their *c.* 23
I will make void *c.* of Judah. 19:7
mighty God, great in *c.* 32:19
if I give thee *c.* wilt not. 38:15
is *c.* perished from prudent? 49:7
king of Babylon hath taken *c.* 30
and *c.* shall perish. *Ezek* 7:26
and that give wicked *c.* 11:2
Daniel answered with *c.* *Dan* 2:14
my people ask *c.* at their. *Hos* 4:12
neither understand his *c.* *Mi* 4:12
the *c.* of peace shall be. *Zech* 6:13
the Pharisees held a *c.* *Mat* 12:14
they took *c.* and bought. 27:7
when they had taken *c.* 28:12
took *c.* against Jesus. *Mark* 3:6
John 11:53
not consented to the *c. Luke* 23:51
Caiaphas gave *c.* *John* 18:14
what thy *c.* determined. *Acts* 4:28
when they heard, they took *c.* 5:33*
if this *c.* be of men, it will. 38
the Jews took *c.* to kill him. 9:23*
soldiers' *c.* was to kill the. 27:42
worketh after the *c.* of. *Eph* 1:11
the immutability of his *c. Heb* 6:17

counsel *of God or Lord*

ask *c.* we pray *of God.* *Judg* 18:5
Israel asked *c. of God.* 20:18
Saul asked *c. of God. 1 Sam* 14:37
c. of the *Lord* standeth. *Ps* 33:11
c. of the *Lord* of hosts. *Isa* 19:17*
stood in *c. of the Lord*? *Jer* 23:18*
hear *c. of the Lord.* 49:20; 50:45
rejected the *c. of God.* *Luke* 7:30
by determinate *c. of God. Acts* 2:23
declare to you all *c. of God.* 20:27

my **counsel**

not hearkened to *my c. 2 Chr* 25:16
kept silence at *my c.* *Job* 29:21
set at nought all *my c.* *Pr* 1:25
they would none of *my c.* 30
my c. shall stand and. *Isa* 46:10
man that executeth *my c.* 11
they had stood in *my c.* *Jer* 23:22
my c. be acceptable to. *Dan* 4:27

own **counsel**

his *own c.* shall cast him. *Job* 18:7
ashamed of his *own c.* *Hos* 10:6

take **counsel**

let us *take c.* together. *Neh* 6:7
rulers *take c.* against. *Ps* 2:2
how long shall I *take c.*? 13:2
take c. together. 71:10
take c. and it shall. *Isa* 8:10
take c. execute judgement. 16:3
woe to children that *take c.* 30:1
let them *take c.* together. 45:21

counsel, -ed

which Ahithophel *c.* *2 Sam* 16:23
c. that all Israel be gathered. 17:11
thus Ahithophel *c.* thus I *c.* 15, 21
how hast thou *c.* him? *Job* 26:3
c. thee to keep the king's. *Eccl* 8:2
I *c.* thee to buy of me. *Rev* 3:18

counsellor

David's *c. 2 Sam* 15:12; *1 Chr* 27:33
Zechariah his son, a wise *c.*
1 Chr 26:14
David's uncle, was a *c.* 27:32
Athaliah was his *c.* *2 Chr* 22:3
Lord taketh away the *c.* *Isa* 3:3
shall be called Wonderful, *C.* 9:6
or being his *c.* hath taught? 40:13
there was no man, no *c.* 41:28
is thy *c.* perished? *Mi* 4:9
out of thee a wicked *c.* *Nah* 1:11
Joseph an honourable *c. Mark* 15:43
Luke 23:50
who hath been his *c.*? *Rom* 11:34

counsellors

they were his *c.* after. *2 Chr* 22:4
they hired *c.* against them. *Ezra* 4:5
sent of king, and his seven *c.* 7:14
mercy to me before king and *c.* 28
gold, which king and *c.* had. 8:25
rest with kings and *c.* *Job* 3:14
leadeth *c.* away spoiled. 12:17
thy testimonies my *c.* *Ps* 119:24
in multitude of *c.* *Pr* 11:14; 24:6
deceit in heart, but to the *c.* 12:20
in the multitude of *c.* they. 15:22
I will restore thy *c.* *Isa* 1:26
counsel of wise *c.* of Pharaoh. 19:11
said to his *c.* did not we? *Dan* 3:24
king's *c.* being gathered, saw. 27
my *c.* and my lords sought. 4:36
all the *c.* and the captains. 6:7

counsels

turned round by his *c.* *Job* 37:12*
them fall by their own *c.* *Ps* 5:10
walked in their own *c.* 81:12
shall attain to wise *c.* *Pr* 1:5
c. of the wicked are deceit. 12:5
written excellent things in *c.*? 22:20
thy *c.* of old are. *Isa* 25:1
wearied in multitude of *c.* 47:13
walked in the *c.* of their. *Jer* 7:24
because of their own *c.* *Hos* 11:6
walk in *c.* of house of. *Mi* 6:16
will make manifest *c.* of. *1 Cor* 4:5

count

shall make your *c.* *Ex* 12:4
c. from the morrow after. *Lev* 23:15
let him *c.* the years. 25:27, 52
who can *c.* the dust? *Num* 23:10
c. not me daughter of. *1 Sam* 1:16
and my maids *c.* me. *Job* 19:15
doth not he see my ways, *c.*? 31:4*
the Lord shall *c.* when. *Ps* 87:6
if I *c.* them, they are more. 139:18
I *c.* them mine enemies. 22

shall I *c.* them pure. *Mi* 6:11*
neither *c.* I my life dear. *Acts* 20:24*
I *c.* all things loss, and do *c.* them. *Phil* 3:8
I *c.* not myself to have. 13
God would *c.* you. *2 Thes* 1:11
c. him not as an enemy. 3:15
c. their masters worthy. *1 Tim* 6:1
if thou *c.* me a partner. *Philem* 17
c. it joy when ye fall. *Jas* 1:2
behold, we *c.* them happy. 5:11*
as they that *c.* it pleasure. *2 Pet* 2:13
as some men *c.* slackness. 3:9
let him *c.* the number. *Rev* 13:18

counted

believed, and he *c.* it for. *Gen* 15:6
Ps 106:31; *Rom* 4:3; *Gal* 3:6
the sheep that shall be *c.* *Gen* 30:33
are we not *c.* strangers? 31:15
cannot be numbered or *c.* *1 Ki* 3:8
Levi and Benjamin *c.* *1 Chr* 21:6
for they were *c.* faithful. *Neh* 13:13
wherefore we are *c.* as. *Job* 18:3
darts are *c.* as stubble. 41:29
we are *c.* as sheep for. *Ps* 44:22
I am *c.* with them that go. 88:4
a fool, when he holdeth his peace is *c.* wise. *Pr* 17:28
rising early, it shall be *c.* 27:14
horses' hoofs shall be *c.* *Isa* 5:28
and the fruitful field be *c.* 32:15
where is he that *c.* towers? 33:18*
the nations are *c.* as. 40:15
all nations are *c.* to him. 17
but they were *c.* as a. *Hos* 8:12
c. him as a prophet. *Mat* 14:5
Mark 11:32
be *c.* worthy to escape. *Luke* 21:36
that they were *c.* worthy. *Acts* 5:41
burned their books, and *c.* 19:19
uncircumcision be *c.* for. *Rom* 2:26
him that believeth, his faith is *c.* 4:5
children of promise are *c.* 9:8
gain, those I *c.* loss for. *Phil* 3:7
c. worthy of kingdom of. *2 Thes* 1:5
for that he *c.* me faithful. *1 Tim* 1:12
let elders be *c.* worthy of. 5:17
this man was *c.* worthy. *Heb* 3:3
he whose descent is not *c.* 7:6
hath *c.* blood of the covenant. 10:29

***see* accounted**

countenance

wroth, and his *c.* fell. *Gen* 4:5
Jacob beheld the *c.* of Laban. 31:2
I see your father's *c.* that it. 5
nor shalt thou *c.* a poor. *Ex* 23:3*
the Lord lift up his *c.* *Num* 6:26
bring a nation of fierce *c.* *Deut* 28:50
c. was like *c.* of an angel. *Judg* 13:6
Hannah, her *c.* was no. *1 Sam* 1:18
look not on his *c.* or the. 16:7
David was of beautiful *c.* 12; 17:42
Abigail of beautiful *c.* 25:3
Tamar of a fair *c.* *2 Sam* 14:27
settled his *c.* stedfastly. *2 Ki* 8:11
why is thy *c.* sad? *Neh* 2:2
why should not my *c.* be sad? 3
thou changest his *c.* and. *Job* 14:20
and the light of my *c.* 29:24
lift thou up the light of thy *c.* *Ps* 4:6
wicked, through pride of *c.* 10:4
his *c.* doth behold upright. 11:7
made him glad with thy *c.* 21:6*
praise him for help of his *c.* 42:5
who is the health of my *c.* 11; 43:5
light of thy *c.* did save them. 44:3
perish at rebuke of thy *c.* 80:16
in the light of thy *c.* 89:15
our secret sins in light of thy *c.* 90:8
heart maketh cheerful *c.* *Pr* 15:13
in the light of the king's *c.* 16:15
so doth the angry *c.* a. 25:23
so a man sharpeneth the *c.* 27:17
by sadness of *c.* the. *Eccl* 7:3
see thy *c.* thy *c.* is. *S of S* 2:14
his *c.* is as Lebanon. 5:15*
the shew of their *c.* doth. *Isa* 3:9
troubled in their *c.* *Ezek* 27:35
king's *c.* was changed. *Dan* 5:6
king of fierce *c.* shall stand. 8:23
hypocrites, of a sad *c.* *Mat* 6:16
c. like lightning. 28:3*; *Luke* 9:29
full of joy with thy *c.* *Acts* 2:28
Moses for glory of his *c.* *2 Cor* 3:7
and his *c.* was as. *Rev* 1:16

***see* changed**

countenances

let our *c.* be looked. *Dan* 1:13
their *c.* appeared fairer and. 15

countervail

enemy could not *c.* king's. *Esth* 7:4*

counteth, -ing

c. me as one of his enemies. *Job* 19:11; 33:10
c. one by one, to find. *Eccl* 7:27*
down first, *c.* the cost. *Luke* 14:28

countries

will I give these *c.* *Gen* 26:3, 4
all *c.* came into Egypt to. 41:57
who among all *c.* *2 Ki* 18:35
and glory throughout *c.* *1 Chr* 22:5
fear of God on all those *c.* *2 Chr* 20:29
because of people of *c.* *Ezra* 3:3
who have ruled over all *c.* 4:20
wound heads over many *c.* *Ps* 110:6
give ear all ye of far *c.* *Isa* 8:9
gather remnant of my flock out of all *c.* and. *Jer* 23:3, 8; 32:37
prophesied against many *c.* 28:8
Jerusalem in midst of *c.* *Ezek* 5:5
changed my statutes more than *c.* 6
be scattered through the *c.* 6:8
scattered among the *c.* yet I will be as a little sanctuary in *c.* 11:16
assemble you out of *c.* 17; 20:34, 41
thee a mocking to all *c.* 22:4
cause thee to perish out of *c.* 25:7
disperse them through *c.* 29:12
36:19
these two *c.* shall be mine. 35:10
he shall enter into *c.* *Dan* 11:40
many *c.* shall be overthrown. 41
stretch forth his hand upon *c.* 42
remember me in far *c.* *Zech* 10:9
not them that are in *c.* *Luke* 21:21

country

smoke of the *c.* went up. *Gen* 19:28
but thou shalt go to my *c.* 24:4
must not be so done in our *c.* 29:26
that I may go to my *c.* 30:25
Shechem the prince of the *c.* 34:2
the lord of the *c.* said unto us. 42:33
all born in the *c.* shall. *Num* 15:13*
the *c.* which the Lord smote. 32:4
I am come into the *c.* *Deut* 26:3
men to search out the *c.* *Josh* 2:2, 3
go up and view the *c.* 7:2
possessed that *c.* *Judg* 11:21
and the destroyer of our *c.* 16:24
came into the *c.* of Moab. *Ruth* 1:2
returned out of *c.* of Moab. 22
cities and *c.* villages. *1 Sam* 6:18
all thy *c.* wept with. *2 Sam* 15:23
bones of Saul buried they in *c.* 21:14
Syrians filled the *c.* *1 Ki* 20:27
and the *c.* was filled. *2 Ki* 3:20
your *c.* is desolate, your. *Isa* 1:7
toss thee like a ball in large *c.* 22:18
nor see his native *c.* *Jer* 22:10
bring them from the north *c.* 31:8
is come upon the plain *c.* 48:21
to come from the north *c.* 50:9
them forth out of the *c.* *Ezek* 20:38
glory of *c.* Beth-jeshimoth. 25:9
be to you as born in the *c.* 47:22*
when I was yet in my *c.* *Jonah* 4:2
abroad his fame in *c.* *Mat* 9:31
not send them out of *c.* *Mark* 5:10
told it in city, and *c.* 14; *Luke* 8:34
to a citizen of that *c.* *Luke* 15:15
c. was nourished by king's *c.* *Acts* 12:20
they drew near to some *c.* 27:27
promise as in strange *c.* *Heb* 11:9*
that they seek a *c.* 14
had been mindful of that *c.* 15
now they desire a better *c.* 16

***far* country**

be come from *far c.* *Josh* 9:6, 9
out of *far c.* *1 Ki* 8:41; *2 Chr* 6:32
they are come from a *far c.* *2 Ki* 20:14; *Isa* 39:3
good news from a *far c.* *Pr* 25:25
from a *far c.* to destroy. *Isa* 13:5
my counsel from *far c.* *Isa* 46:11
watchers come from *far c.* *Jer* 4:16
them that dwell in a *far c.* 8:19*
went into a *far c.* *Mat* 21:33
Mark 12:1
man travelling into *far c.* *Mat* 25:14
his journey into *far c.* *Luke* 15:13

***own* country**

one of your *own c.* *Lev* 16:29*
17:15*; 24:22*
went to her *own c.* *1 Ki* 10:13
that I may go to my *own c.* 11:21
every man to his *own c.* 22:36
go every one to his *own c.* *Jer* 51:9
departed into their *own c.* *Mat* 2:12
save in his *own c.* 13:57
Mark 6:4; *Luke* 4:24
and came into his *own c.* *Mark* 6:1
prophet hath no honour in *own c.* *John* 4:44

***thy* country**

get thee out of *thy c.* *Gen* 12:1
Acts 7:3
return unto *thy c.* and. *Gen* 32:9
us pass through *thy c.* *Num* 20:17
what is *thy c.*? *Jonah* 1:8
do here in *thy c.* *Luke* 4:23

countrymen

in perils by mine own *c.* *2 Cor* 11:26
like things of your *c.* *1 Thes* 2:14

couple

make me a *c.* of cakes. *2 Sam* 13:6
Ziba met David with a *c.* 16:1
chariot with a *c.* of. *Isa* 21:7, 9

couple, *verb*

c. curtains with taches. *Ex* 26:6, 9
make taches to *c.* tent. 11; 36:18
made shoulder-pieces to *c.* 39:4*

coupled, -eth

curtains be *c.* *Ex* 26:3; 36:10, 13, 16
in edge of the curtain which *c.* 26:10
two boards shall be *c.* 24; 36:29
by the two edges was it *c.* 39:4*
chaste conversation *c.* *1 Pet* 3:2

coupling, -s

loops from selvedge in *c.* *Ex* 26:4
36:11
in *c.* of second. 26:4; 36:11, 12
that is outmost in *c.* 26:10; 36:17
over-against other *c.* 28:27; 39:20
stone and timber for *c.* *2 Chr* 34:11

courage

remain any more *c.* *Josh* 2:11*
he took *c.* and put. *2 Chr* 15:8
shall stir up his *c.* *Dan* 11:25
Paul thanked God, took *c.* *Acts* 28:15

***good* courage**

be ye of *good c.* and. *Num* 13:20
strong, and of *good c.* *Deut* 31:6
7, 23; *Josh* 1:6, 9, 18; 10:25
1 Chr 22:13; 28:20
be of *good c.* let us. *2 Sam* 10:12
1 Chr 19:13; *Ezra* 10:4; *Isa* 41:6
be of *good c.* and he shall strengthen thine heart. *Ps* 27:14; 31:24

courageous

be thou strong and very *c.* *Josh* 1:7
23:6; *2 Chr* 32:7
fear not, be *c.* and be. *2 Sam* 13:28
that is *c.* among mighty. *Amos* 2:16

courageously

deal *c.* and Lord shall. *2 Chr* 19:11

course

[1] *A prescribed track for a race. Used figuratively for the work given one to do in life,* Acts 13:25; 2 Tim 4:7. [2] *Order or turn,* 2 Chr 5:11. [3] *Progress and success,* 2 Thes 3:1. [4] *A voyage,* Acts 21:7.

chief fathers of every *c.* *1 Chr* 27:1
priests did not wait by *c.* *2 Chr* 5:11
they sung together by *c.* *Ezra* 3:11
of earth are out of *c.* *Ps* 82:5*
every one turned to his *c.* *Jer* 8:6
their *c.* is evil, and their. 23:10
Zacharias was of the *c.* *Luke* 1:5
executed in the order of his *c.* 8
as John fulfilled his *c.* *Acts* 13:25
came with straight *c.* 16:11; 21:1

might finish my *c.* with joy. *Acts* 20:24
we had finished our *c.* 21:7*
three, and that by *c.* *1 Cor* 14:27
the Lord have free *c.* *2 Thes* 3:1*
I have finished my *c.* *2 Tim* 4:7
tongue setteth on fire *c.* of. *Jas* 3:6*

water-course, *see* **water**

courses

stars in their *c.* fought. *Judg* 5:20
divided Levites into *c.* *1 Chr* 23:6
Solomon appointed *c.* *2 Chr* 8:14
Jehoiada dismissed not the *c.* 23:8
Hezekiah appointed the *c.* 31:2
Levites stood in their *c.* 35:10
set the Levites in their *c.* *Ezra* 6:18

court

In the Bible, [1] *Usually the uncovered area enclosed within the walls of the tabernacle or temple; or* [2] *a similar area surrounded by the rooms of the house, that being the general way of building in the East,* 2 Sam 17:18; Esth 6:4, 5. (*The great* courts *belonging to the temple were three; the first called the* court *of the Gentiles, because the Gentiles were allowed to enter so far, and no farther. The second called the* court *of Israel, because all the Israelites, if purified, had the right of admission. The third* court *was that of the Priests, where the altar of burnt-offerings stood, and where the Priests and Levites exercised their ministry*)

c. of tabernacle: shall be hangings for *c.* *Ex* 27:9; 35:17; 38:9; 39:40
breadth of the *c.* 27:12, 13
length of the *c.* 18
pins of the *c.* 19; 35:18; 38:20, 31
thou shalt set up the *c.* 40:8
in *c.* of tabernacle eat. *Lev* 6:16, 26
had a well in his *c.* *2 Sam* 17:18
Isaiah gone into middle *c.* *2 Ki* 20:4*
stood before the new *c.* *2 Chr* 20:5
stoned Zechariah in *c.* of. 24:21
out the uncleanness into *c.* 29:16
Esther stood in inner *c.* *Esth* 5:1
king said, who is in the *c.*? 6:4
behold Haman standeth in *c.* 5
and a *c.* for owls. *Isa* 34:13
Jeremiah stood in the *c.* *Jer* 19:14
stand in the *c.* of the Lord's. 26:2
prophet was shut in *c.* of. 32:2
33:1; 39:15
into the dungeon in the *c.* 38:6
me to the door of *c.* *Ezek* 8:7, 16
the cloud filled the inner *c.* 10:3
into outward *c.* 40:17; 42:1; 46:21
he brought me to the inner *c.* 40:28
Spirit brought me into inner *c.* 43:5
blood upon gate of inner *c.* 45:19
in every corner of *c.* was a *c.* 46:21
and it is the king's *c.* *Amos* 7:13*
c. without the temple. *Rev* 11:2

courteous

love, be pitiful, be *c.* *1 Pet* 3:8*

courteously

Julius *c.* entreated Paul. *Acts* 27:3*
and lodged us 3 days *c.* 28:7

courts

altars for all host of heaven in two *c.* *2 Ki* 21:5; *2 Chr* 33:5
altars in the two *c.* *2 Ki* 23:12
office was to wait in *c.* *1 Chr* 23:28
Solomon shall build my *c.* 28:6
David gave Solomon pattern of *c.* 12
people shall be in the *c.* *2 Chr* 23:5
that he dwell in thy *c.* *Ps* 65:4
my soul fainteth for the *c.* 84:2
shall flourish in the *c.* of. 92:13
offering and come into *c.* 96:8
enter into his *c.* with praise. 100:4
pay my vows in the *c.* 116:19
ye that stand in the *c.* of. 135:2
this to tread my *c.*? *Isa* 1:12
they shall drink in the *c.* 62:9
fill the *c.* with slain. *Ezek* 9:7
my house, and keep my *c.* *Zech* 3:7
live delicately in king's *c.* *Luke* 7:25

cousin

thy *c.* Elisabeth hath. *Luke* 1:36*

cousins

her neighbours and *c.* *Luke* 1:58*

covenant

The most common uses of the word in the Bible are for the covenant between God and his people. [1] *The covenant between God and man, of continued life and favour on condition of obedience,* Gen 2:16. [2] *That between God and Noah, that there should not be another flood,* Gen 9:12-16. [3] *With Abraham and his descendants as individuals and as a nation, frequently mentioned throughout the history. This was the Old Covenant, the Old Dispensation. The New Covenant is the spiritual covenant of God in Christ with his followers, frequently mentioned in the New Testament.*

token of *c.* *Gen* 9:12; 13:17; 17:11
behold, my *c.* is with thee. 17:4
c. be in your flesh for everlasting *c.* 13
he hath broken my *c.* 14
sabbath for a perpetual *c.* *Ex* 31:16
he wrote the words of the *c.* 34:28
but ye break my *c.* *Lev* 26:15
I give to him my *c.* *Num* 25:12
c. of everlasting priesthood. 13
declared unto you his *c.* *Deut* 4:13
lest ye forget the *c.* of the. 23
Lord will not forget the *c.* 31
gone to receive tables of *c.* 9:9
Lord gave me tables of the *c.* 11
the two tables of the *c.* were. 15
these are the words of the *c.* 29:1
thou shouldest enter into *c.* 12
according to curses of the *c.* 21
because ye have forsaken the *c.* 25
provoke me, and break *c.* 31:20
I will never break my *c.* *Judg* 2:1
thy servant into *c.* of. *1 Sam* 20:8
Israel have forsaken *c.* *1 Ki* 19:10
14
I will send thee away with *c.* 20:34
because of his *c.* with. *2 Ki* 13:23
to perform words of *c.* and people stood to *c.* 23:3; *2 Chr* 34:31
be always of *c.* *1 Chr* 16:15
they entered into *c.* *2 Chr* 15:12
they have defiled the *c.* *Neh* 13:29
he will shew them his *c.* *Ps* 25:14
neither dealt falsely in *c.* 44:17
that thou shouldest take my *c.* 50:16
he hath broken *c.* 55:20
have respect to the *c.* 74:20
nor were they stedfast in *c.* 78:37
mercy keep and *c.* shall. 89:28
my *c.* will I not break. 34
thou hast made void the *c.* 39
will ever be mindful of his *c.* 111:5
commanded his *c.* for ever. 9
and forgetteth the *c.* of. *Pr* 2:17
your *c.* with death shall. *Isa* 28:18
he hath broken the *c.* he. 33:8
and give thee for a *c.* 42:6; 49:8
nor the *c.* of my peace be. 54:10
eunuchs that take hold of *c.* 56:4, 6
as for me, this is my *c.* 59:21
hear words of this *c.* *Jer* 11:2, 6
man that obeyeth not words of *c.* 3
break not thy *c.* with us. 14:21
they have forsaken the *c.* of. 22:9
which my *c.* they brake. 31:32
break my *c.* of day and *c.* 33:20
then may *c.* be broken with. 21
if my *c.* be not with day. 25
had entered into *c.* heard. 34:10
not performed words of this *c.* 18
join to Lord in perpetual *c.* 50:5
and entered into a *c.* with. *Ezek* 16:8
in breaking the *c.* 59; 17:18
for daughters, not by thy *c.* 16:61
or shall he break the *c.*? 17:15
oath he despised, whose *c.* 16
my *c.* he hath broken, it. 19
bring you into bond of *c.* 20:37
they have broken my *c.* 44:7
confirm *c.* with many. *Dan* 9:27
yea also the prince of the *c.* 11:22
shall be against the holy *c.* 28
indignation against holy *c.* *Dan* 11:30
such as do wickedly against *c.* 32
falsely in making *c.* *Hos* 10:4
I might break my *c.* *Zech* 11:10
my *c.* might be with. *Mal* 2:4, 5
ye have corrupted *c.* of Levi. 8
by profaning the *c.* of our. 10
and the wife of thy *c.* 14
even messenger of the *c.* 3:1
ye are children of *c.* *Acts* 3:25
and he gave him the *c.* of. 7:8
c. breakers. *Rom* 1:31
this is my *c.* when I take. 11:27
though it be a man's *c.* *Gal* 3:15
that the *c.* was confirmed. 17
Mediator of a better *c.* *Heb* 8:6
if first *c.* had been faultless. 7
they continued in my *c.* 9
then verily the first *c.* 9:1
and tables of the *c.* 4

see **ark, blood, break**

book of the **covenant**

took the *book of the c.* *Ex* 24:7
Josiah read all the words of the *book of the c.* *2 Ki* 23:2; *2 Chr* 34:30
it is written in *book of c.* *2 Ki* 23:21

establish **covenant**

will I *establish* my *c.* *Gen* 6:18; 9:9
I will *establish* my *c.* between. 17:7
establish c. with Isaac and. 19, 21
I have *established* my *c.* *Ex* 6:4
establish my *c.* with you. *Lev* 26:9
he may *establish* his *c.* *Deut* 8:18
establish to thee an everlasting *c.* *Ezek* 16:60
I will *establish* my *c.* with thee. 62

everlasting **covenant**

remember *everlast. c.* *Gen* 9:16
in your flesh for an *everlast. c.* 17:13
c. with Isaac for an *everlast. c.* 19
Israel by an *everlast. c.* *Lev* 24:8
with me an *everlast. c.* *2 Sam* 23:5
confirmed the same to Israel for *everlast. c.* *1 Chr* 16:17; *Ps* 105:10
broken the *everlast. c.* *Isa* 24:5
make *everlast. c.* with you. 55:3
61:8; *Jer* 32:40
an *everlast. c.* with them. *Ezek* 37:26
blood of the *everlast. c.* *Heb* 13:20

keep, keeping, keepeth, or *kept* **covenant**

thou shalt *keep* my *c.* *Gen* 17:9
my *c.* which ye shall *keep.* 10
my voice and *keep* my *c.* *Ex* 19:5
who *keepeth c.* *Deut* 7:9, 12
1 Ki 8:23; *2 Chr* 6:14; *Neh* 1:5
9:32
keep the words of this *c.* *Deut* 29:9
observed thy word, *kept c.* 33:9
not *kept* my *c.* *1 Ki* 11:11; *Ps* 78:10
to such as *keep c.* *Ps* 25:10; 103:18
children will *keep* my *c.* and. 132:12
by *keeping* of his *c.* *Ezek* 17:14
keeping c. and mercy to. *Dan* 9:4

made **covenant**

day the Lord *made a c.* *Gen* 15:18
and Abimelech *made* a *c.* 21:27, 32
I have *made* a *c.* with. *Ex* 34:27
Lord our God *made* a *c.* *Deut* 5:2
made not this *c.* with. 3; *Heb* 8:9
besides the *c.* he *made.* *Deut* 29:1
break my *c.* I have *made.* 31:16
Joshua *made* a *c.* with. *Josh* 24:25
David *made c.* *1 Sam* 18:3; 23:18
Jonathan *made* a *c.* with. 20:16
Lord *made* a *c.* with. *1 Ki* 8:9
2 Chr 6:11
c. of Lord which he *made.* *1 Ki* 8:21
made a *c.* with Ben-hadad. 20:34
Jehoiada *made* a *c.* *2 Ki* 11:4
made c. between the Lord and. 17
Israel rejected his *c.* he *made.* 17:15
whom the Lord had *made* a *c.* 35
the *c. made* with you ye shall. 38
Josiah *made* a *c.* 23:3; *2 Chr* 34:31
David *made* a *c.* with. *1 Chr* 11:3
mindful even of the *c. made* with. 16:16; *Neh* 9:8; *Ps* 105:9
of *c.* he had *made* with David. *2 Chr* 21:7
all congregation *made* a *c.* 23:3
I *made* a *c.* with mine. *Job* 31:1

that have *made* a c. with. *Ps* 50:5
have *made* a c. with my. 89:3
ye have *made* a c. with. *Isa* 28:15
enlarged thy bed, and *made* c. 57:8
broke the c. I *made*. *Jer* 11:10
not according to c. I *made*. 31:32
Zedekiah had *made* a c. 34:8, 15
saith the Lord, I *made* a c. 13
ye had *made* a c. before me. 15
words of the c. ye had *made*. 18
and *made* a c. with him. *Ezek* 17:13

make **covenant**

I will *make* my c. *Gen* 17:2
let us *make* a c. 26:28; 31:44
Ezra 10:3
shalt *make* no c. *Ex* 23:32; *Deut* 7:2
I *make* a c. before all thy. *Ex* 34:10
lest thou *make* a c. with. 12, 15
do I *make* this c. *Deut* 29:14
make a c. with us. *1 Sam* 11:1
on this condition will I *make* c. 2
my heart to *make* a c. *2 Chr* 29:10
and we *make* a sure c. *Neh* 9:38
will he *make* a c.? *Job* 41:4
this shall be the c. that I will *make*. *Jer* 31:33; *Heb* 8:10; 10:16
make with them a c. of peace. *Ezek* 34:25; 37:26
I will *make* a c. for them. *Hos* 2:18
and they do *make* a c. with. 12:1

new **covenant**

new c. with Israel. *Jer* 31:31
Heb 8:8
a *new* c. he hath made. *Heb* 8:13
Jesus the Mediator of *new* c. 12:24

remember **covenant**

I will *remember* my c. *Gen* 9:15
Lev 26:42; *Ezek* 16:60
I have *rem.* my c. *Ex* 6:5, 6
for their sakes *rem.* c. *Lev* 26:45
hath *rem.* c. for ever. *Ps* 105:8
106:45
rem. not brotherly c. *Amos* 1:9
and to *rem.* his holy c. *Luke* 1:72

covenant *of salt*

the *salt of* c. of thy God. *Lev* 2:13
it is a c. *of salt* for. *Num* 18:19
to David and sons by c. *of salt*. *2 Chr* 13:5

transgressed **covenant**

hath wrought wickedness in *trans.* his c. *Deut* 17:2
have also *trans.* my c. *Josh* 7:11
he *trans.* c. of Lord. 15; *Judg* 2:20
2 Ki 18:12
ye *trans.* c. of the Lord. *Josh* 23:16
men that *trans.* my c. *Jer* 34:18
men have *trans.* the c. *Hos* 6:7
because they have *trans.* my c. 8:1

covenanted

according as I have c. *2 Chr* 7:18
the word that I c. with. *Hag* 2:5
they c. with him for. *Mat* 26:15*
were glad, and c. to. *Luke* 22:5

covenants

pertaineth the glory and c. *Rom* 9:4
these are the two c. *Gal* 4:24
strangers from the c. of. *Eph* 2:12

cover

[1] *To hide*, Pr 12:16. [2] *To clothe*, 1 Sam 28:14. [3] *To protect and defend*, Ps 91:4. [4] *To pardon, or forgive*, Ps. 32:1; Rom 4:7. [5] *To vail*, 1 Cor 11:6.

the locusts shall c. the. *Ex* 10:5
shall dig a pit and not c. it. 21:33
linen breeches to c. 28:42
I will c. thee with my hand. 33:22
thou shalt c. the ark with. 40:3*
cloud of incense may c. *Lev* 16:13
pour out the blood, and c. 17:13
behold they c. the face. *Num* 22:5
and c. that which. *Deut* 23:13
the Lord shall c. him all day. 33:12
Saul went in to c. his. *1 Sam* 24:3
c. not their iniquity. *Neh* 4:5
c. not thou my blood. *Job* 16:18
down in dust, worms shall c. 21:26
abundance of waters c. thee. 22:11
38:34
the shady trees c. him with. 40:22
he shall c. thee with his. *Ps* 91:4
they turn not again to c. 104:9
c. themselves with their. 109:29
surely darkness shall c. me. 139:11*
mischief of their lips c. them. 140:9
as the waters c. the sea. *Isa* 11:9
Hab 2:14
the worms c. thee. *Isa* 14:11
the Lord will surely c. thee. 22:17*
the earth shall no more c. 26:21
that c. with a covering. 30:1†
that thou c. him. 58:7
neither c. themselves. 59:6
darkness shall c. the earth. 60:2
multitude of camels shall c. 6
and will c. the earth. *Jer* 46:8
horror shall c. them. *Ezek* 7:18
thou shalt c. thy face. 12:6
he shall c. his face that. 12
poured it not on ground to c. 24:7
c. not thy lips, and eat not. 17
ye shall not c. your lips. 22
their dust shall c. thee. 26:10
great waters shall c. thee. 19
a cloud shall c. her and. 30:18
I will c. the heaven, I will c. 32:7
I will c. you with skin. 37:6
like a cloud to c. land. 38:9, 16
recover my flax given to c. *Hos* 2:9
say to the mountains, c. us. 10:8
Luke 23:30
shame shall c. thee. *Ob* 10
yea, they shall all c. their. *Mi* 3:7
and shame shall c. her that. 7:10
violence of Lebanon c. *Hab* 2:17
to spit on him and c. *Mark* 14:65
a man ought not to c. *1 Cor* 11:7*
for charity shall c. the. *1 Pet* 4:8

covered

mountains were c. *Gen* 7:19, 20
they c. the nakedness of. 9:23
took a vail and c. herself. 24:65
Tamar c. her with a vail. 38:14
frogs came up and c. land. *Ex* 8:6
the waters c. the chariots. 14:28
the depths c. them, they. 15:5
the sea c. them. 10; *Josh* 24:7
came and c. the camp. *Ex* 16:13
a cloud c. the mount. 24:15, 16
c. with their wings over. 37:9
the vail c. the ark of the. 40:21*
a cloud c. the tent of the. 34
if the leprosy have c. *Lev* 13:13
when holy things are c. *Num* 4:20*
cloud c. the tabernacle. 9:15, 16
16:42
waxen fat, thou art c. *Deut* 32:15*
Jael c. him with a. *Judg* 4:18, 19
Michal c. the pillow. *1 Sam* 19:13
an old man cometh up c. 28:14
c. king David with clothes. *1 Ki* 1:1
cherubims c. ark. 8:7; *1 Chr* 28:18
2 Chr 5:8
rent his clothes and c. *2 Ki* 19:1
Isa 37:1
nor c. he the darkness. *Job* 23:17
if I c. my transgressions. 31:33
shame of face hath c. me. *Ps* 44:15
though thou hast c. us with. 19
the valleys also are c. over. 65:13
as the wings of a dove c. 68:13
let them be c. with reproach. 71:13
glory to cease, thou hast c. 89:45
the earth c. the company of. 106:17
thou hast c. me in my. 139:13
like a potsherd c. with. *Pr* 26:23*
whose hatred is c. by deceit. 26
his name shall be c. with. *Eccl* 6:4
he c. his face, he c. his feet. *Isa* 6:2
and the seers hath he c. 29:10
I have c. thee in the shadow. 51:16
he c. me with the robe of. 61:10
she is c. with multitude. *Jer* 51:42
c. the daughter of Zion. *Lam* 2:1
he hath me with ashes. 3:16
thou hast c. with anger. 43
thou hast c. thyself with a cloud. 44
two wings c. bodies. *Ezek* 1:11, 23
I spread my skirt, and c. thy. 16:8
girded thee with linen, I c. thee. 10
and hath c. the naked. 18:7, 16
that her blood should not be c. 24:8
blue and purple c. thee. 27:7*
I c. the deep for him. *Ezek* 31:15
flesh came up, and skin c. 37:8
the king of Nineveh c. *Jonah* 3:6
let man and beast be c. 8
God came, his glory c. *Hab* 3:3
the ship was c. with. *Mat* 8:24
there is nothing c. that shall not be revealed. 10:26; *Luke* 12:2
if the woman be not c. *1 Cor* 11:6

covered *face*

Tamar had c. her *face*. *Gen* 38:15
the locusts c. the *face* of. *Ex* 10:15
David c. his *face* and. *2 Sam* 19:4
they c. Haman's *face*. *Esth* 7:8
shame hath c. my *face*. *Ps* 69:7
nettles had c. the *face*. *Pr* 24:31
with twain he c. his *face*. *Isa* 6:2
shame hath c. our *face*. *Jer* 51:51

head **covered**

man had his *head* c. *2 Sam* 15:30
mourning, his *head* c. *Esth* 6:12
hast c. my *head* in the. *Ps* 140:7
confounded, and c. their *heads*. *Jer* 14:3, 4
praying, having his *head* c. *1 Cor* 11:4

covered *sin*, or *sins*

whose *sin* is c. *Ps* 32:1; *Rom* 4:7
thou hast c. all their *sins*. *Ps* 85:2

coveredst

thou c. it with the deep. *Ps* 104:6
garments and c. them. *Ezek* 16:18

coverest

wherewith thou c. thyself. *Deut* 22:12
who c. thyself with light. *Ps* 104:2

covereth

take all the fat that c. *Ex* 29:13, 22
Lev 3:3, 9, 14; 4:8; 7:3; 9:19
a people which c. the. *Num* 22:11
surely he c. his feet in. *Judg* 3:24
c. the faces of the judges. *Job* 9:24
because he c. his face. 15:27
he c. the bottom of the sea. 36:30
with clouds he c. light. 32
violence c. them as a. *Ps* 73:6
as the garment which c. him. 109:19
c. the heavens with clouds. 147:8
violence c. the mouth. *Pr* 10:6, 11
love c. all sins. 12
a prudent man c. shame. 12:16
he that c. a transgression. 17:9
he that c. his sins shall not. 28:13
our confusion c. us. *Jer* 3:25
anointed cherub that c. *Ezek* 28:14
one c. violence with his. *Mal* 2:16
he lighted candle c. it. *Luke* 8:16

covering

Noah removed the c. *Gen* 8:13
behold, he is to thee a c. 20:16
that is his c. raiment. *Ex* 22:27
leper shall put a c. on. *Lev* 13:45
vessel which hath no c. *Num* 19:15
woman spread a c. *2 Sam* 17:19
thick clouds are a c. *Job* 22:14
that the naked have no c. 24:7
destruction hath no c. 26:6
seen any poor without c. 31:19
a cloud for c. and fire. *Ps* 105:39
the c. of it of purple. *S of S* 3:10
he discovered c. of Judah. *Isa* 22:8
destroy the face of the c. 25:7
the c. narrower than he can. 28:20
that cover with a c. but not. 30:1
ye shall defile the c. of thy. 22
and make sackcloth their c. 50:3
stones was thy c. *Ezek* 28:13
hair is given her for a c. *1 Cor* 11:15
see **badgers'** *skins*

covering

c. the mercy seat with. *Ex* 25:20
take down the c. vail. *Num* 4:5*
thee, O c. cherub. *Ezek* 28:16
c. the altar with tears. *Mal* 2:13

coverings

decked my bed with c. *Pr* 7:16*
she maketh herself c. of. 31:22*

covers

and make c. thereof. *Ex* 25:29*
he made his c. 37:16
put thereon c. to cover. *Num* 4:7*

covert

[1] *A covered, protected place,* 1 Sam 25:20. [2] *A thicket for wild beasts,* Job 38:40.

Abigail came down by c. 1 Sam 25:20
the c. for the sabbath. 2 Ki 16:18*
lions abide in the c. Job 38:40
behemoth lieth in the c. 40:21
will trust in the c. of. Ps 61:4
a tabernacle for a c. Isa 4:6
be thou a c. to them from. 16:4
a man shall be a c. from. 32:2
he hath forsaken his c. Jer 25:38

covet

(*To wish for with eagerness; usually used in the sense of a fault, though not always*)

thou shalt not c. thy. Ex 20:17
Deut 5:21; Rom 7:7; 13:9
they c. fields and take. Mi 2:2
but c. earnestly the. 1 Cor 12:31*
c. to prophesy, and forbid. 14:39*

coveted

then I c. them, took. Josh 7:21
c. no man's silver or. Acts 20:33
which while some c. 1 Tim 6:10*

coveteth

he c. greedily all the. Pr 21:26
woe to him that c. an. Hab 2:9*

covetous

the wicked blesseth c. Ps 10:3
Pharisees who were c. Luke 16:14*
not altogether with c. 1 Cor 5:10
if any brother be c. with such. 11
nor c. shall inherit. 6:10; Eph 5:5
a bishop must not be c. 1 Tim 3:3*
men shall be c. boasters. 2 Tim 3:2*
with c. practices. 2 Pet 2:14*

covetousness

able men, men hating c. Ex 18:21*
incline not my heart to c. Ps 119:36
he that hateth c. shall. Pr 28:16
for the iniquity of his c. Isa 57:17
is given to c. Jer 6:13; 8:10
but for thy c. 22:17
and the measure of thy c. 51:13
their heart goeth after their c.
Ezek 33:31*
him that coveteth an evil c. Hab 2:9*
of heart proceedeth c. Mark 7:22
heed, and beware of c. Luke 12:15
being filled with all c. Rom 1:29
of bounty, and not of c. 2 Cor 9:5*
but c. let it not be named. Eph 5:3
mortify your members and c. Col 3:5
nor used we a cloke of c. 1 Thes 2:5
let your conversation be without c.
Heb 13:5*
through c. shall they make. 2 Pet 2:3

cow

whether c. or ewe. Lev 22:28
firstling of a c. thou. Num 18:17*
their c. calveth, and. Job 21:10
nourisheth a young c. Isa 7:21
and the c. and the bear shall. 11:7
I have given thee c. Ezek 4:15
every c. at that which. Amos 4:3*

Cozbi

name of woman was C. Num 25:15
beguiled you in matter of C. 18

crackling

as c. of thorns under a pot. Eccl 7:6

cracknels

thee ten loaves and c. 1 Ki 14:3†

craft

policy shall cause c. to. Dan 8:25
take him by c. and put. Mark 14:1
he was of the same c. Acts 18:3*
ye know that by this c. 19:25*
so that not only this our c. 27*
of whatsoever c. he be. Rev 18:22

craftiness

the wise in their c. Job 5:13
1 Cor 3:19
he perceived their c. Luke 20:23
not walking in c. nor. 2 Cor 4:2
no more carried by c. Eph 4:14

craftsman

the work of the c. Deut 27:15
no c. shall be found any. Rev 18:22

craftsmen

carried away all c. 2 Ki 24:14, 16
for they were c. 1 Chr 4:14
the valley of c. Neh 11:35
all of it the work of c. Hos 13:2
no small gain to c. Acts 19:24
if the c. have a matter. 38

crafty

disappointed devices of c. Job 5:12
choosest the tongue of the c. 15:5
have taken c. counsel. Ps 83:3
being c. I caught. 2 Cor 12:16

crag

the eagle abideth on c. Job 39:28†

crane

like a c. or swallow. Isa 38:14
c. and swallow observe time. Jer 8:7

crashing

there shall be a great c. Zeph 1:10

craved

Joseph went, and c. Mark 15:43*

craveth

his mouth c. it. Pr 16:26

create

To bring into being, usually understood as meaning to make out of nothing, Gen 1:1.

c. in me a clean heart. Ps 51:10
c. on every dwelling-place. Isa 4:5
and c. darkness, I c. evil. 45:7
I c. the fruit of the lips. 57:19
behold, I c. new heavens. 65:17
rejoice for ever in that which I c. 18

created

in the beginning God c. Gen 1:1
God c. great whales and. 21
c. man in his own image, male and female c. he them. 27; 5:2
he had rested from all he c. 2:3
I will destroy man whom I c. 6:7
since day God c. man. Deut 4:32
and south thou hast c. Ps 89:12
people which shall be c. 102:18
forth thy Spirit, they are c. 104:30
commanded, and they were c. 148:5
behold who hath c. Isa 40:26
holy One of Israel hath c. it. 41:20
he that c. the heavens. 42:5
Lord that c. thee, O Jacob. 43:1
have c. him for my glory. 7
I the Lord have c. it. 45:8
I have made the earth, and c. 12
he hath established it, c. it. 18
they are c. now, and not. 48:7
I have c. the smith, I have c. 54:16
for the Lord hath c. a. Jer 31:22
judge thee where thou wast c.
Ezek 21:30
in the day that thou wast c. 28:13
perfect from day that thou wast c. 15
hath not one God c. us? Mal 2:10
creation which God c. Mark 13:19
neither was the man c. 1 Cor 11:9
we are his workmanship, c. Eph 2:10
hid in God, who c. all things. 3:9
the new man, after God is c. 4:24
by him were all things c., all things were c. by him. Col 1:16
after image of him that c. him. 3:10
from meats which God c. 1 Tim 4:3
thou hast c. all things, and for thy pleasure they were c. Rev 4:11
who c. heaven and the things. 10:6

createth

he that c. the wind. Amos 4:13

creation

from the c. God made. Mark 10:6
was not from beginning of c. 13:19
things of him from c. Rom 1:20
we know that the whole c. 8:22
continue as from the c. 2 Pet 3:4
beginning of the c. of God. Rev 3:14

creator

remember thy c. in the. Eccl 12:1
the Lord, the c. of the. Isa 40:28
Lord, the c. of Israel. 43:15
creature more than the c. Rom 1:25
in well-doing as to a faithful c.
1 Pet 4:19

creature

bring forth moving c. Gen 1:20
is the law of every c. Lev 11:46
the gospel to every c. Mark 16:15*
Col 1:23
expectation of c. waiteth. Rom 8:19
for c. was made subject to. 20*
the c. shall be delivered. 21*
nor any c. shall be able to. 39
in Christ, he is a new c. 2 Cor 5:17
but a new c. Gal 6:15
first-born of every c. Col 1:15*
for every c. of God. 1 Tim 4:4
nor is there any c. that. Heb 4:13
every c. in heaven heard. Rev 5:13*

***living* creature**

created every *living* c. Gen 1:21
earth bring forth the *living* c. 24
Adam called every *living* c. 2:19
covenant with every *living* c. 9:10
between me and *living* c. 12, 15
law of every *living* c. Lev 11:46
spirit of *living* c. Ezek 1:20, 21
10:17
the *living* c. that I saw. 10:15, 20

creatures

houses full of doleful c. Isa 13:21
a kind of first-fruits of c. Jas 1:18
a third part of the c. in. Rev 8:9

***living* creatures**

likeness of four *living* c. Ezek 1:5
up and down among the *living* c. 13
living c. ran, and returned. 14
living c., one wheel by *living* c. 15
when the *living* c. went, the. 19
noise of wings of *living* c. 3:13

creditor

every c. that lendeth. Deut 15:2
c. is come to take my. 2 Ki 4:1
there was a certain c. Luke 7:41*

creditors

which of my c. is it? Isa 50:1

creek

discovered a certain c. Acts 27:39*

creep

unclean among all that c. Lev 11:31
beasts of the forest do c. Ps 104:20
this sort are they who c. 2 Tim 3:6

creepeth

every thing that c. Gen 1:25, 26
to every thing that c. upon. 30
every thing that c. went. 7:8, 14
died of every thing that c. 21
bring forth every thing that c. 8:17
whatsoever c. on the earth. 19*
c. on the earth shall be an abomination. Lev 11:41*, 43, 44; 20:25*
likeness of any thing that c. on.
Deut 4:18

creeping

dominion over every c. Gen 1:26
every c. thing after his kind. 7:14
touch carcase of c. things. Lev 5:2
these may ye eat, of c. thing. 11:21
whosoever toucheth c. thing. 22:5
every c. thing that. Deut 14:19
spake of beasts, c. things. 1 Ki 4:33
in the sea are c. things. Ps 104:25
all cattle, c. things praise. 148:10
form of c. things. Ezek 8:10
all c. things shall shake. 38:20
a covenant with the c. Hos 2:18
maketh men as c. things. Hab 1:14
Peter saw c. things. Acts 10:12
11:6
an image like c. things. Rom 1:23

crept

for there are certain men c. Jude 4

Crescens

C. is departed to Galatia. 2 Tim 4:10

Crete

we sailed under C. Acts 27:7
Phenice, an haven of C. 12
close by C. 13
and not have loosed from C. 21
cause left I thee in C. Tit 1:5

Cretes

C., we do hear them speak. Acts 2:11

Cretians

the C. are always liars. Tit 1:12

crew

immediately the cock *c.* *Mat* 26:74 *Mark* 14:68; *Luke* 22:60
second time cock *c.* *Mark* 14:72 *John* 18:27

crib

will unicorn abide by *c.*? *Job* 39:9
where no oxen are, the *c.* is. *Pr* 14:4
ass knoweth his master's *c.* *Isa* 1:3

cried

Esau *c.* with a great. *Gen* 27:34
lifted up my voice and *c.* 39:15
and they *c.* before him. 41:43
people *c.* to Pharaoh for. 55
he *c.* cause every man to go. 45:1
the officers came and *c.* *Ex* 5:15
the people *c.* to Moses. *Num* 11:2
damsel, because she *c.* *Deut* 22:24
the damsel *c.* and there was. 27
Sisera's mother *c.* *Judg* 5:28
and all the host ran and *c.* 7:21
and ye *c.* to me, and I. 10:12
he stood and *c.* unto the. *1 Sam* 17:8
Jonathan *c.* after the lad. 20:37, 38
then *c.* a wise woman. *2 Sam* 20:16
I *c.* to my God, and he did. 22:7
he *c.* against the altar. *1 Ki* 13:2, 4
and they *c.* aloud. 18:28
Elisha saw it, and *c.* *2 Ki* 2:12
he *c.* alas, master, for it was. 6:5
the woman *c.* to the king. 8:5
and Athaliah *c.*, Treason. 11:14
they *c.* to God in battle. *1 Chr* 5:20
Isaiah prayed and *c.* *2 Chr* 32:20
when they *c.* to thee. *Neh* 9:27, 28
delivered the poor that *c.* *Job* 29:12
they *c.* after them. 30:5
in my distress I *c.* unto. *Ps* 18:6
they *c.* but there was none. 41
they *c.* to thee and. 22:5
but when he *c.* unto him. 24
O Lord my God, I *c.* to thee. 30:2
I *c.* to thee, O Lord, and. 8
my supplications when I *c.* 31:22
this poor man *c.* and the. 34:6
I *c.* unto him with. 66:17; 77:1
O Lord, I have *c.* day and. 88:1
unto thee have I *c.* O Lord. 13
I *c.* with my whole heart. 119:145
out of the depths have I *c.* 130:1
in the day when I *c.* thou. 138:3
moved at voice of him that *c.* *Isa* 6:4
therefore I *c.* concerning this. 30:7
upon destruction is *c.* *Jer* 4:20
fell on my face and *c.* *Ezek* 9:8
it was *c.* to them in my. 10:13
c. with a lamentable voice. *Dan* 6:20
they have not *c.* to me. *Hos* 7:14
the mariners *c.* every. *Jonah* 1:5
c. by reason of mine affliction; out of the belly of hell *c.* I. 2:2
as he *c.* and they would not hear, so they *c.* and I would. *Zech* 7:13
Peter *c.* saying, Lord. *Mat* 14:30
they *c.* the more, saying. 20:31 *Mark* 10:48; *Luke* 18:39
the spirit *c.* and rent. *Mark* 9:26
Jesus *c.* if any man thirst. *John* 7:37
some *c.* one thing. *Acts* 19:32; 21:34
might know wherefore they *c.* 22:24
when he *c.* seven thunders. *Rev* 10:3
and she being with child, *c.* 12:2
c. with a loud cry to him. 14:18
he *c.* mightily with a strong. 18:2
c. when they saw the smoke. 18
they *c.* weeping and wailing. 19

cried *to the Lord*

Moses *c. to Lord.* *Ex* 8:12; 15:25 17:4; *Num* 12:13
Israel *c. to the Lord.* *Ex* 14:10 *Judg* 3:9, 15; 4:3; 6:7; 10:10
when we *c. to the Lord.* *Num* 20:16 *Deut* 26:7
when they *c. to the Lord.* *Josh* 24:7
Samuel *c. to Lord.* *1 Sam* 7:9; 15:11
Elijah *c. to the Lord.* *1 Ki* 17:20, 21
Isaiah *c. to the Lord.* *2 Ki* 20:11
they *c. to the Lord.* *2 Chr* 13:14 *Ps* 107:6, 13; *Jonah* 1:14
Asa *c. to the Lord.* *2 Chr* 14:11
I *c. to Lord.* *Ps* 3:4; 120:1; 142:1
their heart *c. to the Lord.* *Lam* 2:18

cried *with a loud voice*

woman *c. with a loud voice.* *1 Sam* 28:12
David *c. with loud voice.* *2 Sam* 19:4
Rabshakeh *c. with a loud voice.* *2 Ki* 18:28; *Isa* 36:13
Levites *c. with loud voice.* *Neh* 9:4
Ezekiel *c. with a loud voice.* *Ezek* 11:13
Jesus *c. with loud voice.* *Mat* 27:46 50; *Mark* 15:34, 37; *Luke* 23:46 *John* 11:43
evil spirit *c. with a loud voice.* *Mark* 1:26
Stephen's enemies *c. with a loud voice.* *Acts* 7:57
Stephen *c. with a loud voice.* 60
Paul *c. with a loud voice.* 16:28
they *c. with loud voice.* *Rev* 6:10
angel *c. with a loud voice.* 7:2; 10:3 19:17
before Lamb *c. with a loud voice.* 7:10

cried *out*

all the city *c. out.* *1 Sam* 4:13
Ekronites *c. out.* 5:10
Jehoshaphat *c. out.* *1 Ki* 22:32 *2 Chr* 18:31
c. out, there is death. *2 Ki* 4:40
I *c. out,* I cried violence. *Jer* 20:8
the spirits *c. out.* *Mat* 8:29 *Luke* 4:33
disciples *c. out* for fear. *Mat* 14:26 *Mark* 6:49
blind men *c. out,* have. *Mat* 20:30
they *c.* out the more. 27:23 *Mark* 15:13; *Luke* 23:18 *John* 19:6
with unclean spirit *c. out.* *Mark* 1:23
father of the child *c. out.* 9:24 *Luke* 9:38
they *c. out,* saying. *Acts* 19:28, 34
as they *c. out,* and threw. 22:23
Paul *c. out* in the council. 23:6

cries

the *c.* of them that reaped. *Jas* 5:4

criest, -eth

of thy brother's blood *c.* *Gen* 4:10
wherefore *c.* thou to me? *Ex* 14:15
when he *c.* unto me. 22:27
who art thou that *c.* to? *1 Sam* 26:14
soul of wounded *c.* out. *Job* 24:12
deliver needy when he *c.* *Ps* 72:12
my heart and flesh *c.* out for. 84:2
wisdom *c.* *Pr* 1:20; 8:3; 9:3
yea, if thou *c.* after. 2:3
like as a woman that *c.* *Isa* 26:17
the voice of him that *c.* in. 40:3
when thou *c.* let companies. 57:13
my heritage *c.* out. *Jer* 12:8
c. thou for thine affliction? 30:15
Lord's voice *c.* to city. *Mi* 6:9
send her away, she *c.* *Mat* 15:23
he suddenly *c.* out. *Luke* 9:39
Esaias also *c.* concerning. *Rom* 9:27
hire of the labourers *c.* *Jas* 5:4

crime, -s

this is an heinous *c.* *Job* 31:11
land is full of bloody *c.* *Ezek* 7:23
to answer concerning *c.* *Acts* 25:16*
and not to signify the *c.* 27

crimson

(*A deep red colour tinged with blue, derived from* kermes, *the dried bodies of certain insects allied to the cochineal insects. Three Hebrew words are used, the most frequent being* cochineal)

a man cunning to work in *c.* *2 Chr* 2:7, 14
the vail of blue, *c.* and. 3:14
your sins be red like *c.* *Isa* 1:18
clothest thyself with *c.* *Jer* 4:30*

cripple

being a *c.* from his. *Acts* 14:8

crisping-pins

take away mantles and *c.* *Isa* 3:22*

Crispus

C. chief ruler of the. *Acts* 18:8
that I baptized none of you, but *C.* *1 Cor* 1:14

crookbackt

a man that is *c.* shall. *Lev* 21:20

crooked

and *c.* generation. *Deut* 32:5
hand formed *c.* serpent. *Job* 26:13*
turn aside to their *c.* ways. *Ps* 125:5
whose ways are *c.* and. *Pr* 2:15
what is *c.* cannot. *Eccl* 1:15; 7:13
punish Leviathan, that *c.* *Isa* 27:1
c. be made straight. 40:4; 42:16 *Luke* 3:5
make *c.* places straight. *Isa* 45:2*
they have made them *c.* paths. 59:8
he hath made my paths *c.* *Lam* 3:9
in midst of a *c.* nation. *Phil* 2:15

crop

shall pluck away his *c.* *Lev* 1:16
I will *c.* off from top. *Ezek* 17:22

cropped

he *c.* off the top of his. *Ezek* 17:4

cross

[1] *An instrument of punishment used by the Romans generally for the punishment of slaves. Specifically, the cross on which our Lord died, as recorded in the Gospels.* [2] *Trials or misfortunes, especially when considered as tests of Christian patience or virtue,* Mat 16:24.

he that taketh not his *c.* *Mat* 10:38 *Luke* 14:27
take up his *c.* and follow. *Mat* 16:24 *Mark* 8:34; 10:21; *Luke* 9:23
compelled to bear his *c.* *Mat* 27:32 *Mark* 15:21; *Luke* 23:26
be Son of God, come down from *c.* *Mat* 27:40, 42; *Mark* 15:30, 32
he bearing his *c.* went. *John* 19:17
a title, and put it on the *c.* 19
there stood by the *c.* of Jesus. 25
should not remain on the *c.* on. 31
lest *c.* of Christ be. *1 Cor* 1:17
preaching of the *c.* is to them. 18
then is offence of the *c.* *Gal* 5:11
persecution for the *c.* of Christ. 6:12
glory, save in the *c.* 14
reconcile both by the *c.* *Eph* 2:16
obedient unto death of the *c.* *Phil* 2:8
enemies of the *c.* of Christ. 3:18
peace through blood of *c.* *Col* 1:20
nailing it to his *c.* 2:14
before him, endured the *c.* *Heb* 12:2

crossway

thou have stood in *c.* *Ob* 14

crouch

shall come and *c.* to. *1 Sam* 2:36*

croucheth

he *c.* humbleth himself. *Ps* 10:10

crow, crowing, *see* **cock**

crown

A garland or fillet for the head, used as a mark of distinction. Hence [1] *the special head-dress of a sovereign,* 2 Ki 11:12. [2] *The wreath given to a victor in a Greek game,* 1 Cor 9:25. [3] *Any honour or dignity,* Lam 5:16; Phil 4:1; Rev 4:4.

shalt make a golden *c.* *Ex* 25:25
put the holy *c.* upon the mitre. 29:6
rings to it under the *c.* 30:4; 37:27
the plate of the *c.* of gold. 39:30
he put the holy *c.* *Lev* 8:9
c. of the anointing oil is. 21:12
put the *c.* upon Joash. *2 Ki* 11:12 *2 Chr* 23:11
bring Vashti with the *c.* *Esth* 1:11
I would bind it as a *c.* *Job* 31:36
thou hast profaned his *c.* *Ps* 89:39
upon himself shall his *c.* 132:18
a *c.* of glory shall she. *Pr* 4:9
a virtuous woman is a *c.* 12:4
the *c.* of the wise is their. 14:24
hoary head is a *c.* of glory. 16:31
children's children are *c.* of. 17:6
doth the *c.* endure to every? 27:24
king Solomon with *c.* *S of S* 3:11
woe to the *c.* of pride. *Isa* 28:1

Lord of hosts shall be for a c. Isa 28:5
thou shalt also be a c. of glory. 62:3
the c. of your glory shall. Jer 13:18
take off the c. Ezek 21:26
as stones of a c. lifted. Zech 9:16
Jesus wearing a c. of. John 19:5
to obtain a corruptible c. 1 Cor 9:25
my joy and c. Phil 4:1
what is our hope, or c. 1 Thes 2:19
is laid up for me a c. 2 Tim 4:8
shall receive the c. of life. Jas 1:12
receive a c. of glory. 1 Pet 5:4
I will give a c. of life. Rev 2:10
that no man take thy c. 3:11
a c. given to him, went forth. 6:2

crown *of gold*

make upon it a c. of gold. Ex 25:11
24; 30:3; 37:2, 11, 12, 26
out with great c. of gold. Esth 8:15
c. of pure gold on his head. Ps 21:3

crown *with head*

on c. of Joseph's head. Gen 49:26
arm with c. of head. Deut 33:20
took c. upon his head. 2 Sam 1:10
took king's c. from his head. 12:30
1 Chr 20:2
even to c. of his head. 2 Sam 14:25
Job 2:7
set royal c. on her head. Esth 2:17
the c. royal upon his head. 6:8
taken c. from my head. Job 19:9
smite with scab c. of head. Isa 3:17
broken the c. of thy head. Jer 2:16
the c. of the head of the. 48:45
c. is fallen from our head. Lam 5:16
c. on thine head. Ezek 16:12
c. of thorns, and put it on his head.
Mat 27:29; Mark 15:17; John 19:2
upon her head a c. of. Rev 12:1
having on his head a golden c. 14:14

crowned

thou hast c. him with glory. Ps 8:5
the prudent are c. with. Pr 14:18
wherewith his mother c. S of S 3:11
thy c. are as the locusts. Nah 3:17
he is not c. except he. 2 Tim 2:5
we see Jesus c. with. Heb 2:9

crownedst

thou c. him with glory. Heb 2:7

crownest

c. year with thy goodness. Ps 65:11

crowneth

who c. thee with loving-. Ps 103:4

crowning

against Tyre the c. city. Isa 23:8

crowns

c. on their heads. Ezek 23:42
take gold, and make c. Zech 6:11
the c. shall be to Helem. 14
elders had c. of gold. Rev 4:4
and they cast their c. before. 10
on locusts' heads were c. 9:7
red dragon having seven c. 12:3*
upon his horns ten c. 13:1*
on his head were many c. 19:12*

crucified

is betrayed to be c. Mat 26:2
Luke 24:7
said, let him be c. Mat 27:22, 23
delivered him to be c. 26; John 19:16
c. him and parted his garments.
Mat 27:35; John 19:23
two thieves c. with. Mat 27:38, 44
Mark 15:32; Luke 23:33
John 19:18
I know ye seek Jesus which was c.
Mat 28:5; Mark 16:6
where Jesus was c. John 19:20, 41
by wicked hands have c. Acts 2:23
Jesus, whom ye c. Lord. 36; 4:10
our old man is c. with. Rom 6:6
was Paul c. for you? 1 Cor 1:13
we preach Christ c. unto the. 23
save Jesus Christ and him c. 2:2
would not have c. Lord of glory. 8
for though he was c. 2 Cor 13:4
I am c. with Christ. Gal 2:20
Christ hath been set forth, c. 3:1
they that are Christ's have c. 5:24
by whom the world is c. to me. 6:14
also our Lord was c. Rev 11:8

crucify

To put to death on a cross (Latin crux, gen. crucis, a cross)

him to Gentiles to c. Mat 20:19
of them ye shall kill, and c. 23:34
led him away to c. him. 27:31
Mark 15:20
cried out again, c. Mark 15:13, 14
with him they c. two thieves. 27
cried, c. him, c. him. Luke 23:21
John 19:6, 15
they c. to themselves. Heb 6:6

cruel

their wrath, for it was c. Gen 49:7
hearkened not for c bondage. Ex 6:9
wine as the c. venom. Deut 32:33
thou art become c. to me. Job 30:21
hate me with c. hatred. Ps 25:19
deliver me out of hand of c. 71:4
thou give thy years to c. Pr 5:9
but he that is c. troubleth. 11:17
mercies of wicked are c. 12:10
a c. messenger shall be sent. 17:11
wrath is c. 27:4
jealousy is c. S of S 8:6
day of Lord cometh, c. Isa 13:9
Egyptians will I give over to c. 19:4
they are c. and. Jer 6:23; 50:42
with chastisement of a c. 30:14
of my people is become c. Lam 4:3
trial of c. mockings. Heb 11:36

cruelly

because he c. oppressed. Ezek 18:18

cruelty

instruments of c. are. Gen 49:5*
c. done to the sons of. Judg 9:24*
such as breathe out c. Ps 27:12
full of habitations of c. 74:20*
force and c. have ye. Ezek 34:4*

crumbs

dogs eat of the c. which fall from.
Mat 15:27; Mark 7:28
to be fed with c. which. Luke 16:21

cruse

take spear and c. of. 1 Sam 26:11
took the spear and c. 12, 16
take with thee a c. 1 Ki 14:3
I have but a little oil in a c. 17:12
nor c. of oil fail, till the Lord. 14, 16
Elijah had a c. of water. 19:6
bring me a new c. 2 Ki 2:20

crush

forgetteth her foot may c. Job 39:15
assembly against me to c. Lam 1:15
to c. under his feet the. 3:34
kine of Bashan which c. Amos 4:1

crushed

not offer that which is c. Lev 22:24
the ass c. Balaam's. Num 22:25
oppressed and c. alway. Deut 28:33
in dust, which are c. Job 4:19
children far from safety, are c. 5:4
that which is c. breaketh. Isa 59:5
Nebuchadnezzar hath c. Jer 51:34

cry

according to the c. Gen 18:21
their c. came up. Ex 2:23; 3:9
I have heard their c. 3:7
Israel fled at the c. of. Num 16:34
c. of the city went up. 1 Sam 5:12
because their c. is come up. 9:16
and my c. did enter. 2 Sam 22:7
hearken unto the c. and to the
prayer. 1 Ki 8:28; 2 Chr 6:19
angry when I heard their c. Neh 5:6
thou heardest their c. by the. 9:9
with loud and bitter c. Esth 4:1
of their fastings and their c. 9:31
O earth, let my c. have. Job 16:18
cause the c. of the poor to come, he
heareth the c. of the. 34:28
hearken to voice of my c. Ps 5:2
forgetteth not the c. of. 9:12
O Lord, attend unto my c. 17:1
my c. came before him. 18:6
his ears are open to their c. 34:15
O Lord, give ear to my c. 39:12
unto me, and heard my c. 40:1
incline thine ear unto my c. 88:2
O Lord, and let my c. come. 102:1
when he heard their c. 106:44
let my c. come near. Ps 119:169
attend to my c. 142:6
stoppeth his ears at c. of. Pr 21:13
more than the c. of him. Eccl 9:17
righteousness, behold a c. Isa 5:7
they shall raise up a c. of. 15:5
the c. is gone round about the. 8
gracious at voice of thy c. 30:19
Chaldeans, whose c. is in. 43:14
nor lift up c. nor. Jer 7:16; 11:14
voice of the c. of my people. 8:19
the c. of Jerusalem is gone up. 14:2
let a c. be heard from. 18:22
c. of the shepherds shall be. 25:36
thy c. hath filled the land. 46:12
her little ones have caused a c. 48:4
the enemies have heard a c. of. 5
the earth is moved at the c. 49:21
the c. is heard at taking of. 50:46
a sound of a c. cometh. 51:54
not thine ear at my c. Lam 3:56
suburbs shake at c. of. Ezek 27:28
there shall be a c. from. Zeph 1:10
at midnight a c. made. Mat 25:6

great **cry**

c. of Sodom is great. Gen 18:20
19:13
with a great and bitter c. 27:34
a great c. through Egypt. Ex 11:6
was a great c. in Egypt. 12:30
was great c. of the people. Neh 5:1
there arose a great c. Acts 23:9

hear **cry**

will surely hear their c. Ex 22:23
will God hear his c.? Job 27:9
hear my c. O God. Ps 61:1
he also will hear their c. 145:19
let them hear the c. Jer 20:16

not hear **cry**

I will not hear their c. Jer 14:12

cry, *verb*

idle, therefore they c. Ex 5:8
and they c. unto me. 22:23
is it voice of them that c. 32:18
cover his upper lip, and c. Lev 13:45
go c. to the gods ye. Judg 10:14
right have I yet to c. 2 Sam 19:28
she went to c. for her. 2 Ki 8:3
and c. in our affliction. 2 Chr 20:9
I c. unto thee. Job 30:20
c. in his destruction. 24
make oppressed to c. they c. 35:9
they c. but none giveth answer. 12
they c. not when he. 36:13
when his young ones c. to. 38:41
I c. in the day time. Ps 22:2
hear, O Lord, when I c. 27:7; 28:2
to thee will I c. O Lord. 28:1, 2
the righteous c. and the. 34:17
when I c. then shall mine. 56:9
I will c. to God most high. 57:2
from end of earth will I c. 61:2
O Lord, for I c. to thee. 86:3
he shall c. unto me. 89:26
Lord, I c. unto thee. 141:1
food to young ravens which c. 147:9
doth not wisdom c. and. Pr 8:1
he also shall c. but shall. 21:13
child have knowledge to c. Isa 8:4
wild beasts of island shall c. 13:22
c. O city, thou Palestina. 14:31
Heshbon shall c. and Elealeh. 15:4
their valiant ones shall c. 33:7
and the satyr shall c. to. 34:14
c. to Jerusalem, her warfare. 40:2
c. and he said, what shall I c.? 6
he shall not c. nor cause. 42:2
he shall c. yea, prevail. 13
now will I c. like a travailing. 14
one shall c. to him, yet can. 46:7
thou shalt c. and he shall say. 58:9
ye shall c. for sorrow of. 65:14
c. in ears of Jerusalem. Jer 2:2
wilt thou not from this time c.? 3:4
blow trumpet in land, c. gather. 4:5
though they c. to me. 11:11
c. to the gods to whom they. 12
not hear when they c. 14; Ezek 8:18
go up to Lebanon, and c. Jer 22:20
howl, ye shepherds, and c. 25:34
48:20; Ezek 21:12

watchmen on Ephraim shall *c.* *Jer* 31:6
when I *c.* and shout he. *Lam* 3:8
c. for all abominations. *Ezek* 9:4
forbear to *c.* make no. 24:17*
shake, when the wounded *c.* 26:15
they shall *c.* bitterly for. 27:30
Israel shall *c.* unto me. *Hos* 8:2
O Lord, to thee will I *c.* *Joel* 1:19
the beasts of the field *c.* 20
let man and beast *c.* *Jonah* 3:8
bite with their teeth, and *c.* *Mi* 3:5
stand, stand, shall they *c.* *Nah* 2:8
mighty men shall *c.* *Zeph* 1:14
angel said unto me, *c.* *Zech* 1:14
shall not strive, nor *c.* *Mat* 12:19
God avenge elect, who *c.* *Luke* 18:7
the Spirit, whereby we *c.* *Rom* 8:15
break forth and *c.* thou. *Gal* 4:27

cry *against*

c. to the Lord *against.* *Deut* 15:9
24:15
to *c.* alarm *against* you. *2 Chr* 13:12
if my land *c. against* me. *Job* 31:38
to Nineveh, *c. against* it. *Jonah* 1:2

cry *aloud*

Elijah said, *c. aloud.* *1 Ki* 18:27
I *c. aloud*, but there is no. *Job* 19:7
will I pray and *c. aloud.* *Ps* 55:17
they shall *c. aloud* from. *Isa* 24:14
into singing, and *c. aloud.* 54:1
c. aloud, spare not. 58:1
in Ramah, *c. aloud* at. *Hos* 5:8
why dost thou *c. aloud* ? *Mi* 4:9

cry *to the Lord*

c. unto *the Lord* for us. *1 Sam* 7:8
they *c. to the Lord* in. *Ps* 107:19, 28
they shall *c. to the Lord.* *Isa* 19:20
fast, and *c. to the Lord.* *Joel* 1:14
shall *c. to the Lord*, but. *Mi* 3:4

cry *out*

ye shall *c. out* that day. *1 Sam* 8:18
I *c. out* of wrong, but. *Job* 19:7
they *c. out* by reason of. 35:9
c. out and shout. *Isa* 12:6
soldiers of Moab shall *c. out.* 15:4
my heart shall *c. out* for Moab. 5
wonder, *c. out* and cry. 29:9*
I will howl, and *c. out* for. *Jer* 48:31
arise, *c. out* in the night. *Lam* 2:19
will a young lion *c. out* ? *Amos* 3:4
I *c. out* to thee, but. *Hab* 1:2
for the stone shall *c. out* of. 2:11
he began to *c. out* and. *Mark* 10:47
stones would *c. out.* *Luke* 19:40

crying

Eli heard noise of the *c.* *1 Sam* 4:14
ashes, and went on *c.* *2 Sam* 13:19
nor regardeth he the *c.* *Job* 39:7
thy soul spare for his *c.* *Pr* 19:18
leech hath two daughters *c.* 30:15
it is day of trouble and *c.* *Isa* 22:5
there is a *c.* for wine. 24:11
voice of *c.* shall be no more. 65:19
a voice of *c.* shall be. *Jer* 48:3
forth head-stone with *c.* *Zech* 4:7
altar of the Lord with *c.* *Mal* 2:13
voice of one *c.* in wilderness. *Mat* 3:3
Mark 1:3; *Luke* 3:4; *John* 1:23
and saw children *c.* in. *Mat* 21:15
devils *c.* thou art Christ. *Luke* 4:41
for unclean spirits *c.* *Acts* 8:7
ran in among the people, *c.* 14:14
laid hands on him, *c.* out. 21:28
the multitude followed, *c.* away. 36
Spirit into your hearts, *c.* *Gal* 4:6
prayers with strong *c.* *Heb* 5:7
no more death nor *c.* *Rev* 21:4

crystal

the gold and the *c.* *Job* 28:17*
as colour of terrible *c.* *Ezek* 1:22
a sea of glass like unto *c.* *Rev* 4:6
light of city was clear as *c.* 21:11
river of water of life, clear as *c.* 22:1

cubit

(*The distance from the elbow bending inwards to the extremity of the middle finger, or about 18 inches. Standards varied, however, in different places, and no measures can be defined with exactness. Different periods also had different standards*)

in a *c.* shalt thou finish. *Gen* 6:16
breadth of it, after *c.* *Deut* 3:11
compassing it, ten in a *c.* *1 Ki* 7:24
ten in a *c.* compassing. *2 Chr* 4:3
the *c.* is a *c.* and an. *Ezek* 43:13
add one *c.* to stature. *Mat* 6:27
Luke 12:25

cubits

of ark 300 *c.* breadth 50 *c.* *Gen* 6:15
fifteen *c.* upward did the. 7:20
two *c.* and a half the. *Ex* 25:10
Goliath's height six *c.* *1 Sam* 17:4
length of the house 60 *c.* *1 Ki* 6:2
each of cherubims ten *c.* 23
and every laver was four *c.* 7:38
brake down the walls of Jerusalem, 400 *c.* *2 Ki* 14:13; *2 Chr* 25:23
height 60 *c.* breadth 60 *c.* *Ezra* 6:3
gallows be fifty *c.* high. *Esth* 5:14
7:9
from gate to gate 100 *c.* *Ezek* 40:23
the court 100 *c.* 47
breadth of the door was ten *c.* 41:2
thickness of the wall five *c.* 9
and the altar twelve *c.* long. 43:16
the settle 14 *c.* 17
height of image 60 *c.* *Dan* 3:1
length of flying roll 20 *c.* *Zech* 5:2
land as it were 200 *c.* *John* 21:8
the wall of the city 144 *c.* *Rev* 21:17

cuckow

c. have in abomination. *Lev* 11:16*
Deut 14:15*

cucumbers

we remember the *c.* and. *Num* 11:5
a lodge in a garden of *c.* *Isa* 1:8

cud, *see* **chew** and **cheweth**

cumbered

Martha was *c.* about. *Luke* 10:40

cumbereth

cut it down, why *c.* it ? *Luke* 13:7

cumbrance

can I alone bear your *c.*? *Deut* 1:12

cummin

doth he not scatter *c.* *Isa* 28:25
cart-wheel turned upon the *c.* but the *c.* is beaten out with a. 27
ye pay tithes of *c.* *Mat* 23:23

cunning

(*American Revision changes to* skilful *or* expert)

Esau was a *c.* hunter. *Gen* 25:27
cherubims of *c.* work. *Ex* 26:1; 36:8
make breast-plate of *c.* work. 28:15
to devise *c.* works in gold. 31:4
Aholiab a *c.* workman and. 38:23
made breast-plate of *c.* work. 39:8
man who is a *c.* player. *1 Sam* 16:16
seen a son of Jesse that is *c.* 18
all that were *c.* in songs. *1 Chr* 25:7
man *c.* to work in gold. *2 Chr* 2:7
I have sent a *c.* man of Huram. 13
let right hand forget her *c.* *Ps* 137:5
work of a *c.* workman. *S of S* 7:1
take away the *c.* artificer. *Isa* 3:3
seeketh to him a *c.* workman. 40:20
send for *c.* women that. *Jer* 9:17
they are all the work of *c.* 10:9
well favoured, *c.* in. *Dan* 1:4
about by *c.* craftiness. *Eph* 4:14

cunningly

not followed *c.* devised. *2 Pet* 1:16

cup

This word is used, [1] *literally, for a material cup from which one drinks; and* [2] *figuratively, for the contents of a cup,* 1 Cor 11:27; *or* [3] *for sufferings which one undergoes as one drinks a cup of nauseous medicine to the dregs,* Isa 51:17; Mat 26:39; *or* [4] *for the blessings which God gives to us, as a pleasant and refreshing drink,* Ps 23:5.

and Pharaoh's *c.* was in. *Gen* 40:11
put my *c.* my silver *c.* in the. 44:2
it drank of its own *c.* *2 Sam* 12:3
wrought like brim of a *c.* *1 Ki* 7:26
2 Chr 4:5
be the portion of their *c.* *Ps* 11:6
Lord is the portion of my *c.* 16:5
my *c.* runneth over. 23:5
waters of a full *c.* are wrung. 73:10
in the hand of Lord there is a *c.* 75:8
I will take the *c.* of salvation. 116:13
giveth his colour in the *c.* *Pr* 23:31
drunk at the hand of the Lord the *c.* the dregs of the *c.* of. *Isa* 51:17
taken out of thy hand *c.* of. 22
nor shall men give them *c.* *Jer* 16:7
take the wine-*c.* of his fury. 25:15
then took I the *c.* at the Lord's. 17
if they refuse to take the *c.* 28
judgement was not to drink *c.* 49:12
Babylon hath been a golden *c.* 51:7
c. also shall pass through. *Lam* 4:21
I will give her *c.* into. *Ezek* 23:31
thou shalt drink of thy sister's *c.* 32
c. of Lord's right hand. *Hab* 2:16
Jerusalem *c.* of trembling. *Zech* 12:2
c. of cold water only. *Mat* 10:42
Mark 9:41
are ye able to drink of the *c.*?
Mat 20:22; *Mark* 10:38
ye shall drink indeed of my *c.*
Mat 20:23; *Mark* 10:39
make clean outside of *c.* *Mat* 23:25
cleanse first what is within *c.* 26
took the *c.* and gave thanks. 26:27
Mark 14:23; *Luke* 22:17, 20
1 Cor 11:25
let this *c.* pass from. *Mat* 26:39
Mark 14:36; *Luke* 22:42
this *c.* may not pass away. *Mat* 26:42
c. is the new testament. *Luke* 22:20
1 Cor 11:25
c. which my Father hath. *John* 18:11
the *c.* of blessing we. *1 Cor* 10:16
the *c.* of Lord and *c.* of devils. 21
as often as ye drink of this *c.* 11:26
and drink this *c.* of the Lord. 27
without mixture into *c.* *Rev* 14:10
to give unto her the *c.* 16:19
the woman having a golden *c.* 17:4
in the *c.* she filled, fill to her. 18:6

cup-bearer, -s

queen of Sheba saw *cup-bearers.*
1 Ki 10:5; *2 Chr* 9:4
was the king's *cup-bearer.* *Neh* 1:11

cups

pure gold for the *c.* *1 Chr* 28:17
on Eliakim vessels of *c.* *Isa* 22:24
sets pots full of wine and *c.* *Jer* 35:5
took away spoons and *c.* 52:19
washing of *c.* and pots. *Mark* 7:4, 8

curdled

hast not thou *c.* me ? *Job* 10:10

cure, -ed

I will *c.* them, and will. *Jer* 33:6
of Egypt, shalt not be *c.* 46:11
yet could he not *c.* you. *Hos* 5:13
they could not *c.* him. *Mat* 17:16
the child was *c.* from that. 18
in that hour he *c.* many. *Luke* 7:21
gave them power to *c.* diseases. 9:1
said to him that was *c.* *John* 5:10

cures

cast out devils, do *c.* *Luke* 13:32

curious

c. girdle. *Ex* 28:8*, 27*, 28*; 29:5*
39:5*; *Lev* 8:7*
and to devise *c.* works. *Ex* 35:32*
used *c.* arts brought. *Acts* 19:19

curiously

and *c.* wrought in the. *Ps* 139:15

current

c. money with the. *Gen* 23:16

curse

[1] *To call on divine power to send some injury upon the one cursed. This was often pronounced as by a mouthpiece of God to man, and sometimes as a statement of what would happen, uttered without ill-feeling,* Gen 9:25; 49:7; Josh 6:26. [2] *Profanity or blasphemy,* Ex 22:28; Ps 11:26; Mat 26:74.

I shall bring a *c.* on me. *Gen* 27:12
upon me be thy *c.* my son. 13

the bitter water that causeth the *c.*
Num 5:18, 19, 22, 24, 27
the woman shall be a *c.* 27
I set before you a blessing and *c.*
Deut 11:26; 30:1
a *c.* if you will not obey the. 11:28
and shalt put the *c.* upon. 29
c. into a blessing. 23:5; *Neh* 13:2
heareth words of this *c. Deut* 29:19
make camp of Israel a *c. Josh* 6:18
on them came the *c.* of. *Judg* 9:57
me with a grievous *c.* *1 Ki* 2:8
they should become a *c. 2 Ki* 22:19
they entered into a *c.* *Neh* 10:29
to sin by wishing a *c.* *Job* 31:30
the *c.* of Lord is in the. *Pr* 3:33
so the *c.* causeless shall not. 26:2
it shall be counted a *c.* to. 27:14
eyes shall have many a *c.* 28:27
hath the *c.* devoured. *Isa* 24:6
come down on people of my *c.* 34:5
I have given Jacob to the *c.* 43:28
shall leave your name for a *c.* 65:15
them to be a taunt and *c.* *Jer* 24:9
25:18; 29:18*; 42:18; 44:8, 12
I will make this city a *c.* 26:6
therefore is your land a *c.* 44:22
that Bozrah shall become a *c.* 49:13
give them sorrow, thy *c.* *Lam* 3:65
therefore the *c.* is poured. *Dan* 9:11
this is the *c.* that goeth. *Zech* 5:3
that as we were a *c.* among. 8:13
I will send a *c.* upon you. *Mal* 2:2
ye are cursed with a *c.* 3:9
and smite the earth with a *c.* 4:6
themselves under *c.* *Acts* 23:12, 14
of law, are under the *c.* *Gal* 3:10
from the *c.* being made a *c.* 13
shall be no more *c.* but. *Rev* 22:3

curse, *verb*

Lord said, I will not *c.* *Gen* 8:21
and I will *c.* him that curseth. 12:3
thou shalt not *c.* ruler. *Ex* 22:28
thou shalt not *c.* the deaf. *Lev* 19:14
I pray thee, *c.* me this. *Num* 22:6, 17
now, *c.* me them. 11; 23:7, 13
thou shalt not *c.* the people. 22:12
how shall I *c.* whom God ? 23:8
to *c.* mine enemies. 11; 24:10
neither *c.* them at all. 23:25
hired Balaam to *c.* thee. *Deut* 23:4
Neh 13:2
stand on mount Ebal to *c. Deut* 27:13
called Balaam to *c.* *Josh* 24:9
c. ye Meroz, said the angel, *c.* ye bitterly. *Judg* 5:23
should this dead dog *c.*? *2 Sam* 16:9
let him *c.* because Lord hath said unto him, *c.* David. 10, 11
and he will *c.* thee. *Job* 1:11*; 2:5*
said his wife to him, *c.* God. 2:9*
let them *c.* it that *c.* the day. 3:8
bless with mouth but *c.* *Ps* 62:4
let them *c.* but bless thou. 109:28
people shall *c.* him. *Pr* 11:26
him shall the people *c.* 24:24
servant to master, lest he *c.* 30:10
hear thy servant *c.* thee. *Eccl* 7:21
c. not the king in thought, *c.* 10:20
c. their king and God. *Isa* 8:21
every one of them doth *c.* *Jer* 15:10
I will *c.* your blessings, I. *Mal* 2:2
bless them that *c.* you. *Mat* 5:44
Luke 6:28
he began to *c.* and to. *Mat* 26:74
Mark 14:71
bless and *c.* not. *Rom* 12:14
therewith *c.* we men. *Jas* 3:9

cursed

the serpent *c.* *Gen* 3:14
c. is the ground. 17
now art thou [Cain] *c.* 4:11
ground which Lord hath *c.* 5:29
Noah said, *c.* be Canaan. 9:25
c. be every one. 27:29; *Num* 24:9
c. be their anger, for it. *Gen* 49:7
he hath *c.* his father or. *Lev* 20:9
name of the Lord and *c.* 24:11
bring forth him that *c.* 14, 23
whom thou cursest is *c.* *Num* 22:6
c. be he. *Deut* 27:15, 16, 17, 18
19, 20, 21, 22, 23, 24, 25, 26
c. shalt thou be in the city, *c.* 28:16
c. shall be thy basket. *Deut* 28:17
c. shall be the fruit of thy body. 18
c. when thou comest in, when. 19
c. be man that buildeth. *Josh* 6:26
ye Gibeonites are *c.* none of. 9:23
eat and drink, and *c.* *Judg* 9:27
c. be he that giveth a wife to. 21:18
c. that eateth food. *1 Sam* 14:24, 28
and the Philistine *c.* David. 17:43
but if men, *c.* be they before. 26:19
came forth, and *c.* still. *2 Sam* 16:5
7, 13
for this, because he *c.* the. 19:21
Shimei who *c.* me with. *1 Ki* 2:8
and *c.* them in the name. *2 Ki* 2:24
go see now this *c.* woman. 9:34
I contended with them, and *c.*
Neh 13:25
my sons have sinned and *c. Job* 1:5
Job opened his mouth and *c.* 3:1
taking root, suddenly I *c.* 5:3
their portion is *c.* in earth. 24:18
they that be *c.* of him. *Ps* 37:22
rebuked the proud that are *c.* 119:21
likewise hast *c.* others. *Eccl* 7:22
c. be the man obeyeth not. *Jer* 11:3
c. be the man that trusteth. 17:5
c. be the day wherein I was. 20:14
c. be the man who brought. 15
c. be he that doeth Lord's work deceitfully *c.* that keepeth. 48:10
but *c.* be the deceiver. *Mal* 1:14
yea, I have *c.* your blessings. 2:2
ye are *c.* with a curse, for. 3:9
depart from me, ye *c.* *Mat* 25:41
knoweth not law, are *c.* *John* 7:49
c. is every one that. *Gal* 3:10
c. is every one that hangeth. 13
c. children, who have. *2 Pet* 2:14*

cursed *thing*

be a *c. thing*, for it is a *c. thing.*
Deut 7:26*
cleave nought of the *c. thing.* 13:17*

cursedst

from thee, which thou *c.* *Judg* 17:2
the fig-tree thou *c.* is. *Mark* 11:21

curses

shall write these *c.* in. *Num* 5:23
all these *c.* shall. *Deut* 28:15, 45
all the *c.* that are written. 29:20, 27
2 Chr 34:24
all *c.* of the covenant in. *Deut* 29:21
thy God will put these *c.* on. 30:7

curseth

c. his father or mother shall be put.
Ex 21:17; *Lev* 20:9; *Pr* 20:20
whosoever *c.* his God. *Lev* 24:15
generation that *c.* father. *Pr* 30:11
he that *c.* father or mother, let.
Mat 15:4*; *Mark* 7:10*

cursing

woman with oath of *c.* *Num* 5:21
shall send upon thee *c.* *Deut* 28:20
set before you blessing and *c.* 30:19
me good for his *c.* *2 Sam* 16:12
his mouth is full of *c.* *Ps* 10:7
Rom 3:14
and for *c.* and lying. 59:12
as he loved *c.* so let it. 109:17
as he clothed himself with *c.* 18
he heareth *c.* and. *Pr* 29:24*
beareth thorns is nigh to *c. Heb* 6:8
same mouth blessing and *c. Jas* 3:10

cursings

read the blessings and *c.* *Josh* 8:34

curtain, -s

tabernacle with ten *c.* *Ex* 26:1, 2
36:9
bear the *c.* of tabernacle. *Num* 4:25
ark dwelleth within *c.* *2 Sam* 7:2
1 Chr 17:1
stretchest out the heavens like a *c.*
Ps 104:2; *Isa* 40:22
but I am comely as the *c.* *S of S* 1:5
let them stretch forth *c.* *Isa* 54:2
tents spoiled, and my *c.* *Jer* 4:20
and set up my *c.* 10:20
take to themselves their *c.* 49:29
c. of the land of Midian. *Hab* 3:7

Cush

sons of Ham, *C. Gen* 10:6; *1 Chr* 1:8
the sons of *C.* Seba, and. *Gen* 10:7
1 Chr 1:9
remnant left from *C.* *Isa* 11:11

Cushan

I saw the tents of *C.* in. *Hab* 3:7

Cushi

C. tell the king what. *2 Sam* 18:21
Ahimaaz ran, and overran *C.* 23
all princes sent son of *C.* *Jer* 36:14
to Zephaniah son of *C.* *Zeph* 1:1

custody

c. of sons of Merari. *Num* 3:36*
fair virgins to the *c.* *Esth* 2:3, 8
to the *c.* of Shaashgaz the king's. 14

custom

[1] *Manner, or way,* Luke 4:16. [2] *A duty paid to the king or prince upon the importation or exportation of goods,* Rom 13:7.

for the *c.* of women is. *Gen* 31:35
and it was a *c.* in Israel. *Judg* 11:39
the priests' *c.* with. *1 Sam* 2:13
according to the *c.* *Ezra* 3:4*
Jer 32:11
not pay toll, tribute, and *c. Ezra* 4:13
been mighty kings, and *c.* was. 20
not be lawful to impose *c.* on. 7:24
sitting at the receipt of *c. Mat* 9:9*
Mark 2:14*; *Luke* 5:27*
kings of earth take *c.*? *Mat* 17:25*
according to the *c.* of. *Luke* 1:9
to do for him after *c.* of law. 2:27
went to Jerusalem after the *c.* 42
as Jesus' *c.* was, he went. 4:16
ye have a *c.* that I should. *John* 18:39
render *c.* to whom *c.* is. *Rom* 13:7
we have no such *c.* nor. *1 Cor* 11:16

customs

commit none of these *c.* *Lev* 18:30
c. of the people are vain. *Jer* 10:3
shall change the *c.* Moses. *Acts* 6:14
teach *c.* which are not lawful. 16:21
ought not to walk after *c.* 21:21
thee to be expert in all *c.* 26:3
committed nothing against *c.* 28:17

cut

and *c.* it in wires to work. *Ex* 39:3
shall *c.* the burnt-. *Lev* 1:6, 12
c. ram into pieces. 8:20; *Ex* 29:17
not offer to Lord what is *c. Lev* 22:24
ye shall not *c.* yourselves. *Deut* 14:1
my concubine and *c.* *Judg* 20:6
c. bullock in pieces. *1 Ki* 18:23, 33
c. themselves after their manner. 28
he *c.* in pieces all the vessels of.
2 Ki 24:13; *2 Chr* 28:24
people, he *c.* them with. *1 Chr* 20:3
servants can skill to *c. 2 Chr* 2:8, 10
let them be as *c.* in pieces. *Ps* 58:7
c. bars of iron. 107:16; *Isa* 25:4
art thou not it that hath *c.*? *Isa* 51:9
nor lament, nor *c.* *Jer* 16:6
when they *c.* the calf in. 34:18
he *c.* the roll with the. 36:23
clothes rent, and having *c.* 41:5
how long wilt thou *c.* thyself ? 47:5
born thy navel was not *c. Ezek* 16:4
ye will not, ye shall be *c.* *Dan* 2:5
speak against God shall be *c.* 3:29
and *c.* them in the head. *Amos* 9:1*
all that burden themselves with it shall be *c.* *Zech* 12:3*
when they heard that, they were *c.* to the heart. *Acts* 5:33; 7:54

cut *asunder*

he hath *c. asunder* cords. *Ps* 129:4
hammer of earth *c. asunder.*
Jer 50:23
staff Beauty, and *c.* it *asunder.*
Zech 11:10
then I *c. asunder* my other staff. 14
shall *c.* him *asunder.* *Mat* 24:51
Luke 12:46

cut *down*

but ye shall *c. down.* *Ex* 34:13
will *c. down* your images. *Lev* 26:30
c. down from thence. *Num* 13:23, 24
and *c. down* groves. *Deut* 7:5*
2 Ki 18:4; 23:14
thou shalt not *c.* them *down.*
Deut 20:19

not for meat c. down. Deut 20:20
and c. down the grove. Judg 6:25
I will c. down cedars. 2 Ki 19:23
Isa 37:24
Asa c. down her idol. 2 Chr 15:16
Josiah c. down all the idols. 34:7*
greenness, not c. down. Job 8:12
cometh like a flower, is c. down. 14:2
hope of a tree if it be c. down. 7
the wicked were c. down. 22:16*
our substance is not c. down. 20
shall soon be c. down. Ps 37:2
is burnt, and is c. down. 80:16
in the evening it is c. down. 90:6
sycamores are c. down. Isa 9:10
how art thou c. down! 14:12
nail be removed and c. down. 22:25*
shall c. down thy choice. Jer 22:7
peaceable habitation c. down. 25:37*
also thou shalt be c. down. 48:2*
your images be c. down. Ezek 6:6*
yet shall they be c. down. Nah 1:12
merchant-people are c. down.
Zeph 1:11*
others c. down branches. Mat 21:8
Mark 11:8
c. it down; why cumbereth it the ground? Luke 13:7
after that thou shalt c. it down. 9

cut off

neither all flesh be c. off. Gen 9:11
uncircumcised child be c. off. 17:14
and c. off fore-skin of son. Ex 4:25
soul shall be c. off from. 12:15, 19
31:14; Num 15:30, 31; 19:13
and I will c. them off. Ex 23:23
be c. off from people. 30:33, 38
Lev 7:20, 21, 25, 27; 17:4, 9
19:8; 23:29; Num 9:13
will c. him off from his people.
Lev 17:10; 18:29; 20:3, 6, 18
Num 19:20
whosoever eateth blood be c. off.
Lev 17:14
shall be c. off in sight of. 20:17
that soul shall be c. off from. 22:3
c. ye not off the tribe. Num 4:18
that soul shall utterly be c. off. 15:31
when God shall c. off. Deut 12:29
hath c. off nations. 19:1; Josh 23:4
hath privy member c. off. Deut 23:1
thou shalt c. off her hand. 25:12
waters of Jordan shall be c. off.
Josh 3:13, 16; 4:7
and shall c. off our name. 7:9
at that time Joshua c. off. 11:21
and c. off his thumbs. Judg 1:6
there is one tribe c. off from. 21:6
name of dead be not c. off. Ruth 4:10
days come that I will c. off.
1 Sam 2:31
man whom I shall not c. off. 33
palms of Dagon's hands c. off. 5:4
David ran and c. off. 17:51
not c. off kindness from my. 20:15
David c. off the skirt of. 24:4, 5
for in that I c. off the. 11
thou wilt not c. off my seed. 21
knowest how Saul hath c. off. 28:9
and they c. off Saul's head. 31:9
slew them and c. off. 2 Sam 4:12
and c. off their garments in the.
10:4; 1 Chr 19:4
c. off head of Sheba. 2 Sam 20:22
then will I c. off Israel. 1 Ki 9:7
till he had c. off every male. 11:16
to c. off Jeroboam's. 13:34; 14:14
I will c. off from Jeroboam. 14:10
when Jezebel c. off prophets. 18:4
I will c. off from Ahab him. 21:21
2 Ki 9:8
Ahaz c. off borders. 2 Ki 16:17
Hezekiah c. off the gold from. 18:16
have c. off all thine. 1 Chr 17:8
Lord anointed to c. off. 2 Chr 22:7
angel to c. off all mighty men. 32:21
were the righteous c. off? Job 4:7
loose his hand, and c. me off. 6:9
whose hope shall be c. off. 8:14*
if he c. off, then who can? 11:10*
shall his branch be c. off. 18:16
of his months is c. off. 21:21
because I was not c. off. 23:17
they are c. off as tops of. Job 24:24
when people are c. off in their. 36:20
the Lord shall c. off all. Ps 12:3
I am c. off from before. 31:22
to c. off remembrance of. 34:16
for evil doers shall be c. off. 37:9
cursed of him, shall be c. off. 22
seed of wicked shall be c. off. 28
when the wicked are c. off. 34
end of wicked shall be c. off. 38
he shall reward, c. them off. 54:5
horns of wicked will I c. off. 75:10
he shall c. off the spirit. 76:12
come, and let us c. them off. 83:4
and they are c. off from thy. 88:5
terrors have c. me off. 16
he shall c. them off in their. 94:23
neighbour will I c. off. 101:5*
that I may c. off all wicked doers. 8
let his posterity be c. off. 109:13
that the Lord may c. off the. 15
and of thy mercy c. off. 143:12
wicked shall be c. off from. Pr 2:22
expectation not be c. off. 23:18
24:14
Lord will c. off from Israel. Isa 9:14
to destroy and c. off nations. 10:7
adversaries of Judah be c. off. 11:13
I will c. off from Babylon. 14:22
and every beard c. off. 15:2
burden upon it shall be c. off. 22:25
watch for iniquity are c. off. 29:20*
he will c. me off with. 38:12*
refrain, that I c. thee not off. 48:9
name should not have been c. off. 19
he was c. off out of the land. 53:8
a sign that shall not be c. off. 55:13
as if he c. off a dog's neck. 66:3*
truth is perished and c. off. Jer 7:28
c. off thine hair, O Jerusalem. 29
to c. off the children without. 9:21
let us c. him off from land. 11:19
to c. off from you man and. 44:7
that ye might c. yourselves off. 8
and to c. off all Judah. 11
to c. off from Tyrus. 47:4
Ashkelon is c. off. 5*
come, let us c. it off from. 48:2
horn of Moab is c. off, his arm. 25
men of war be c. off. 49:26*; 50:30*
c. off the sower from. 50:16
flee out, and be not c. off. 51:6
against this place to c. it off. 62
c. off in his anger the. Lam 2:3
they have c. off my life in. 3:53
and I will c. him off. Ezek 14:8
c. off man and beast. 13, 17, 19, 21
25:13; 29:8
shall he not c. off fruit? 17:9
building forts to c. off many. 17
c. off the righteous and. 21:3, 4
behold, I will c. thee off. 25:7
I will c. off the Cherethims. 16
and I will c. off the multitude. 30:15
terrible nations c. him off. 31:12
I will c. off from Seir him. 35:7
hope is lost, we are c. off. 37:11
hew down the tree, c. off. Dan 4:14
Messiah shall be c. off. 9:26
made idols, that they be c. off.
Hos 8:4
her king is c. off as the. 10:7, 15
the new wine is c. off. Joel 1:5, 9
is not the meat c. off? 16
I will c. off the inhabitant. Amos 1:5
I will c. off the inhabitant from Ashdod. 8
I will c. off the judge from. 2:3
horns of altar shall be c. off. 3:14
by night, art thou c. off. Ob 5
every one of Esau may be c. off. 9
and thou shalt be c. off for ever. 10
nor stand to c. off those of his. 14
thine enemies shall be c. off. Mi 5:9
witchcrafts be c. off. 12
graven images I c. off. 13; Nah 1:14
wicked is utterly c. off. Nah 1:15
and I will c. off thy prey. 2:13
the sword shall c. thee off. 3:15
the flock shall be c. off. Hab 3:17
I will c. off man from. Zeph 1:3
c. off remnant of Baal. 4
that bear silver c. off. 11
I have c. off the nations. 3:6
should not be c. off. Zeph 3:7
stealeth, and every one that sweareth, shall be c. off. Zech 5:3
I will c. off pride of Philistines. 9:6
I will c. off chariot from. 10
three shepherds also I c. off. 11:8
is to be c. off, let it be c. off. 9
I will c. off the names of. 13:2
two parts in land shall be c. off. 8
of people shall not be c. of. 14:2
Lord will c. off the. Mal 2:12
right hand offend thee, c. it off.
Mat 5:30; 18:8; Mark 9:43, 45
and c. off his ear. Mark 14:47*
Luke 22:50*; John 18:10, 26
soldiers c. off the ropes. Acts 27:32
thou shalt also be c. off. Rom 11:22
I may c. off occasion. 2 Cor 11:12
I would they were c. off. Gal 5:12

cut out

froward tongue be c. out. Pr 10:31
stone c. out without. Dan 2:34, 45
for if thou wert c. out. Rom 11:24

cut short

began to c. Israel short. 2 Ki 10:32
will finish and c. it short. Rom 9:28

cut up

who c. up mallows by. Job 30:4*
as thorns c. up shall. Isa 33:12

cuttest, -eth

when thou c. down. Deut 24:19*
he c. out rivers among. Job 28:10
he breaketh bow, and c. Ps 46:9
as when one c. and cleaveth. 141:7
message by fool, c. off. Pr 26:6
one c. a tree out of the. Jer 10:3
build chambers and c. him. 22:14

cutting

c. of stones to set. Ex 31:5; 35:33
I said in the c. off of my. Isa 38:10*
consulted shame by c. Hab 2:10
crying and c. himself. Mark 5:5

cuttings

not any c. for dead. Lev 19:28; 21:5
all hands shall be c. and. Jer 48:37

cymbal

brass, or a tinkling c. 1 Cor 13:1

cymbals

played on cornets and c. 2 Sam 6:5
1 Chr 13:8
harps and c. 1 Chr 15:16; 16:42
Asaph made a sound with c. 16:5
in the house of Lord with c. 25:6
lift up their voice with c. 2 Chr 5:13
Levites in house of Lord with c. 29:25
sons of Asaph with c. Ezra 3:10
Neh 12:27
upon loud-sounding c. Ps 150:5

cypress

he taketh the c. and oak. Isa 44:14*

Cyprus

Joses was of country of C. Acts 4:36
as far as Phenice and C. 11:19
some of them were men of C. 20
from Seleucia they sailed to C. 13:4
Barnabas sailed to C. 15:39
when we had discovered C. 21:3
with him Mnason of C. 16
launched, sailed under C. 27:4

Cyrene

found a man of C. Mat 27:32
parts of Lybia about C. Acts 2:10
were men of Cyprus and C. 11:20
Lucius of C. was in church. 13:1

Cyrenian

compel Simon a C. to. Mark 15:21

Cyrenians

the synagogue of the C. Acts 6:9

Cyrenius

made when C. was. Luke 2:2

Cyrus

first year of C. the Lord stirred up spirit of C. 2 Chr 36:22; Ezra 1:1
saith C. king of Persia. 2 Chr 36:23
Ezra 1:2
C. brought forth. Ezra 1:7, 8; 5:14
grant they had of C. 3:7
will build as C. the king hath. 4:3
C. made a decree to build. 5:13, 17
that saith of C. he is. Isa 44:28

saith Lord to anointed, to *C.* *Isa* 45:1
to the first year of *C.* *Dan* 1:21
Daniel prospered in reign of *C.* 6:28
third year of *C.* a thing was. 10:1

D

Dabbasheth
toward sea reached to *D.* *Josh* 19:11

Daberath
and then goeth out to *D.* *Josh* 19:12
out of Issachar, *D.* *1 Chr* 6:72

dagger
Ehud made him a *d.* *Judg* 3:16*
took the *d.* from right thigh. 21*
that he could not draw the *d.* 22*

Dagon
to offer a sacrifice to *D.* *Judg* 16:23
ark into the house of *D.* *1 Sam* 5:2
D. was fallen. 3
the head of *D.* was cut off. 4
is sore on us, and on *D.* our. 7
head in temple of *D.* *1 Chr* 10:10

daily
as much as gathered *d.* *Ex* 16:5
d. meat-offering. *Num* 4:16*
Ezek 46:13
after this manner offer *d.* *Num* 28:24
beside the *d.* burnt-offering. 29:6*
Ezra 3:4
when she pressed him *d.* *Judg* 16:16
allowance was a *d.* rate. *2 Ki* 25:30
was prepared for me *d.* *Neh* 5:18*
spake *d.* hearkened not. *Esth* 3:4
sorrow in my heart *d.* *Ps* 13:2*
while they say *d.* to me. 42:10*
be merciful, he fighting *d.* 56:1*
mine enemies would *d.* swallow. 2*
I will sing, that I may *d.* 61:8
the Lord who *d.* loadeth us. 68:19
he shall live and *d.* shall be. 72:15*
man reproacheth thee *d.* 74:22*
I cry to thee *d.* 86:3*
I called *d.* upon thee. 88:9
came round about me *d.* 17*
I was *d.* his delight. *Pr* 8:30
that heareth me, watching *d.* 34
yet they seek me *d.* and. *Isa* 58:2
d. rising up early and. *Jer* 7:25
I am in derision *d.* 20:7*, 8*
Noph have distresses *d.* *Ezek* 30:16*
king appointed them a *d.* *Dan* 1:5
and by him the *d.* sacrifice was.
8:11*; 11:31*; 12:11*
Ephraim *d.* increaseth. *Hos* 12:1*
give us this day our *d.* bread.
Mat 6:11; *Luke* 11:3
sat *d.* with you teaching. *Mat* 26:55
Mark 14:49; *Luke* 19:47; 22:53
take up his cross *d.* *Luke* 9:23
continuing *d.* with one. *Acts* 2:46
Lord added to the church *d.* 47
widows were neglected in *d.* 6:1
churches increased in number *d.*
16:5
searched the scriptures *d.* 17:11
I die *d.* *1 Cor* 15:31
but exhort *d.* *Heb* 3:13
who needeth not *d.* to. 7:27
and destitute of *d.* food. *Jas* 2:15

dainty, -ies
shall yield royal *d.* *Gen* 49:20
soul abhorreth *d.* meat. *Job* 33:20
let me not eat of their *d.* *Ps* 141:4
be not desirous of his *d.* *Pr* 23:3
neither desire thou his *d.* meats. 6
all things which were *d.* *Rev* 18:14

dale
which is the king's *d.* *Gen* 14:17*
a pillar in the king's *d.* *2 Sam* 18:18

Dalmatia
Titus is departed to *D.* *2 Tim* 4:10

dam
seven days with his *d.* on eighth give
it me. *Ex* 22:30; *Lev* 22:27
shalt not take the *d.* *Deut* 22:6
in any wise let the *d.* go. 7

damage
d. grow to the hurt of. *Ezra* 4:22
not countervail king's *d.* *Esth* 7:4

and drinketh *d.* *Pr* 26:6
king should have no *d.* *Dan* 6:2
with hurt and much *d.* *Acts* 27:10*
that ye might receive *d.* *2 Cor* 7:9*

Damaris
and a woman named *D.* *Acts* 17:34

Damascus
steward is Eliezer of *D.* *Gen* 15:2
David put garrisons in Syria of *D.*
2 Sam 8:6; *1 Chr* 18:6
Rezon went to *D.* reigned in *D.*
1 Ki 11:24
on way to wilderness of *D.* 19:15
make streets for thee in *D.* 20:34
Pharpar, rivers of *D.*? *2 Ki* 5:12
Elisha came to *D.* 8:7
Jeroboam recovered *D.* 14:28
king of Assyria went against *D.* 16:9
Ahaz saw an altar at *D.* 10
Syrians of *D.* came to. *1 Chr* 18:5
the spoil to king of *D.* *2 Chr* 24:23
multitude of captives to *D.* 28:5
Ahaz sacrified to gods of *D.* 23
Lebanon, looketh toward *D.*
S of S 7:4
of Syria is *D.* head of *D.* *Isa* 7:8
riches of *D.* shall be taken. 8:4
is not Samaria as *D.*? 10:9
the burden of *D.* 17:1; *Jer* 49:23
kingdom cease from *D.* *Isa* 17:3
D. is waxed feeble. *Jer* 49:24
I will kindle a fire in wall of *D.* 27
D. thy merchant in. *Ezek* 27:18
three transgressions of *D.* *Amos* 1:3
I will break also the bar of *D.* 5
that dwell in *D.* in a couch. 3:12
go into captivity beyond *D.* 5:27
and *D.* shall be the rest. *Zech* 9:1
desired letters to *D.* *Acts* 9:2
there was a disciple at *D.* 10
was Saul with the disciples at *D.* 19
confounded Jews who dwelt at *D.* 22
how he preached boldly at *D.* 27
come nigh to *D.* 22:6; 26:12
arise, and go into *D.* 22:10
in *D.* governor desirous. *2 Cor* 11:32
I returned again unto *D.* *Gal* 1:17

damnable
shall bring in *d.* heresies. *2 Pet* 2:1*

damnation
(In Revised Versions this word is rendered judgement *or* condemnation *in every case except those starred. A similar change also in the other forms of the word)*
receive the greater *d.* *Mat* 23:14*
Mark 12:40; *Luke* 20:47
can ye escape *d.* of hell? *Mat* 23:33
is in danger of eternal *d.* *Mark* 3:29*
to the resurrection of *d.* *John* 5:29
good may come, whose *d.* *Rom* 3:8
shall receive to themselves *d.* 13:2
eateth and drinketh *d.* *1 Cor* 11:29
having *d.* because they. *1 Tim* 5:12
not, and their *d.* *2 Pet* 2:3*

damned
believeth not shall be *d.* *Mark* 16:16
he that doubteth is *d.* *Rom* 14:23
all might be *d.* who. *2 Thes* 2:12

damsel
the *d.* abide few days. *Gen* 24:55
loved *d.* and spake kindly to *d.* 34:3
but give me the *d.* to wife. 12
forth tokens of the *d.* *Deut* 22:15
tokens be not found for the *d.* 20
they shall bring out the *d.* and. 21
the *d.* because she cried not. 24
there is in the *d.* no sin worthy. 26
shall give the *d.*'s father fifty. 29
to every man a *d.* *Judg* 5:30
the *d.*'s father retained him. 19:4
Boaz said, whose *d.* is? *Ruth* 2:5
it is Moabitish *d.* that came back. 6
and the *d.* was very fair. *1 Ki* 1:4
brought in a charger, and given to *d.*
Mat 14:11; *Mark* 6:28
a *d.* came to Peter. *Mat* 26:69*
John 18:17*
the *d.* is not dead. *Mark* 5:39
father and mother of the *d.* and entereth in where *d.* was lying. 40

a *d.* came to hearken. *Acts* 12:13*
a certain *d.* possessed with. 16:16*

damsels
Rebekah arose and her *d.* *Gen* 24:61
Abigail rode with five *d.* *1 Sam* 25:42
amongst them were the *d.* *Ps* 68:25

Dan, *a person*
called she his name *D.* *Gen* 30:6
son of Bilhah, *D.* 35:25
sons of *D.* 46:23; *Num* 26:42
D. shall judge his people. *Gen* 49:16
D. shall be a serpent by. 17
of *D.* Ahiezer the son. *Num* 1:12
standard of the camp of *D.* 2:25
all numbered in the camp of *D.* 31
of *D.* he said, *D.* is. *Deut* 33:22
after the name of *D.* *Josh* 19:47
Judg 18:29
and why did *D.* remain? *Judg* 5:17
moved him in camp of *D.* 13:25
a portion for *D.* *Ezek* 48:1
one gate of *D.* 32

***see* children**

tribe of **Dan**
Aholiab of the *tribe of D.* *Ex* 31:6
35:34; 38:23
Dibri, of *tribe of D.* *Lev* 24:11
of *tribe of D.* 62,700. *Num* 1:39
of *tribe of D.* to spy the land. 13:12
of *tribe of D.* to divide the. 34:22
for the *tribe of D.* *Josh* 19:40, 48
out of the *tribe of D.* 21:5, 23
priests to *tribe of D.* *Judg* 18:30

Dan, *a place*
pursued them unto *D.* *Gen* 14:14
Moses all Gilead unto *D.* *Deut* 34:1
they called Leshem, *D.* *Josh* 19:47
Judg 18:29
from *D.* to Beer-sheba. *Judg* 20:1
1 Sam 3:20; *2 Sam* 3:10; 17:11
24:2, 15; *1 Ki* 4:25; *1 Chr* 21:2
2 Chr 30:5
other calf put he in *D.* *1 Ki* 12:29
2 Ki 10:29
smote *D.* *1 Ki* 15:20; *2 Chr* 16:4
voice declareth from *D.* *Jer* 4:15
of horses heard from *D.* 8:16
D. and Javan occupied. *Ezek* 27:19
thy God, O *D.* liveth. *Amos* 8:14

dance
praise in the *d.* *Ps* 149:3; 150:4
virgins shall rejoice in *d.* *Jer* 31:13
d. is turned into mourning. *Lam* 5:15

dance, *verb*
of Shiloh come to *d.* *Judg* 21:21
their children *d.* *Job* 21:11
mourn, a time to *d.* *Eccl* 3:4
satyrs shall *d.* there. *Isa* 13:21

danced
to their number that *d.* *Judg* 21:23
and David *d.* before. *2 Sam* 6:14
and ye have not *d.* *Mat* 11:17
Luke 7:32
daughter of Herodias *d.* *Mat* 14:6
Mark 6:22

dances
went after her with *d.* *Ex* 15:20
to meet him with *d.* *Judg* 11:34
not sing of him in *d.* *1 Sam* 21:11
29:5
shalt go forth in the *d.* *Jer* 31:4

dancing
he saw the calf and *d.* *Ex* 32:19
came out singing and *d.* *1 Sam* 18:6
on all earth, eating and *d.* 30:16*
she saw king David *d.* *2 Sam* 6:16
1 Chr 15:29
my mourning into *d.* *Ps* 30:11
he heard music and *d.* *Luke* 15:25

dandled
and ye shall be *d.* upon. *Isa* 66:12

danger
shall be in *d.* of. *Mat* 5:21, 22
be in *d.* of the council, in *d.* 22
but is in *d.* of eternal. *Mark* 3:29*
this our craft is in *d.* *Acts* 19:27
in *d.* to be called in question. 40

dangerous
when sailing was now *d.* *Acts* 27:9

Daniel
David had *D.* of. *1 Chr* 3:1

of Ithamar, D. Ezra 8:2
D. sealed. Neh 10:6
though Noah, D. Ezek 14:14, 20
thou art wiser than D. 28:3
D. of Judah. Dan 1:6
to D. the name of Belteshazzar. 7
D. had understanding in. 17
none was found like D. 19
sought D. to be slain. 2:13
then D. went in. 16
the secret was revealed to D. 19
Nebuchadnezzar worshipped D. 46
then king made D. a great man. 48
D. sat in the gate. 49
at last D. came in. 4:8
then D. was astonied for. 19
of doubts found in D. 5:12
they clothed D. with scarlet and. 29
of whom D. was first. 6:2
not find occasion against D. 5
these men found D. praying. 11
D. regardeth not thee, O king, 13
king set his heart on D. 14
that they should take up D. 23
men tremble before God of D. 26
who hath delivered D. from. 27
so this D. prospered in reign. 28
D. had a dream, and visions. 7:1
as for me D. 28
a vision, even unto me D. 8:1
he said, fear not, D. 10:12
he said, go thy way, D. 12:9
of desolation, spoken of by D. Mat 24:15; Mark 13:14

I Daniel

I D. was grieved. Dan 7:15
when I, even I D. had seen. 8:15
I D. fainted. 27
I D. understood by books. 9:2
I D. was mourning three. 10:2
I D. alone saw the vision. 7
I D. looked. 12:5

O Daniel

O D. servant of the. Dan 6:20
O D. I am now come to. 9:22
O D. a man greatly beloved. 10:11
O D. shut up the words and. 12:4

dare

none is so fierce that d. Job 41:10
good man some would d. Rom 5:7
for I will not d. to speak of. 15:18
d. any of you go to law? 1 Cor 6:1
d. not make ourselves. 2 Cor 10:12*

Darius

till the reign of D. Ezra 4:5, 24
till the matter came to D. 5:5
D. the king made a decree. 6:1, 12
finished in sixth year of D. 15
priests to the reign of D. Neh 12:22
D. the Median took. Dan 5:31
king D. signed the writing. 6:9
king D. wrote to all people. 25
in the first year of D. 9:1; 11:1
in second year of D. Hag 1:1, 15
2:10; Zech 1:7
in fourth year of D. Zech 7:1

dark

went down, and it was d. Gen 15:17
if plague be d. Lev 13:6, 21, 26, 28, 56
and not in d. speeches. Num 12:8
when it was d. the men. Josh 2:5
d. waters. 2 Sam 22:12; Ps 18:11
Jerusalem began to be d. Neh 13:19
stars of the twilight be d. Job 3:9
they grope in the d. 12:25
the light shall be d. in his. 18:6
judge through the d. cloud? 22:13
in the d. they dig through. 24:16
let their way be d. and. Ps 35:6
I will open my d. saying. 49:4
d. places of the earth are. 74:20
I will utter d. sayings of old. 78:2
thy wonders be known in d.? 88:12
sent darkness and made it d. 105:28
words of wise and their d. Pr 1:6
in the black and d. night. 7:9
their works are in the d. Isa 29:15
not spoken in a d. place. 45:19
feet stumble upon the d. Jer 13:16
he hath set me in d. places. Lam 3:6
house of Israel do in the d. Ezek 8:12
make the stars thereof d. Ezek 32:7
bright lights of heaven I make d. 8
in the cloudy and d. day. 34:12
king understanding d. Dan 8:23
sun and moon shall be d. Joel 2:10
that maketh day d. Amos 5:8, 20
it shall be d. unto you, the day shall be d. Mi 3:6*
light not be clear, nor d. Zech 14:6*
light, having no part d. Luke 11:36
and it was now d. John 6:17
early, when it was yet d. 20:1
light that shineth in a d. 2 Pet 1:19

darken

I will d. the earth. Amos 8:9

darkened

so that the land was d. Ex 10:15
let eyes be d. Ps 69:23; Rom 11:10
or the stars be not d. Eccl 12:2
look out of the windows be d. 3
the light is d. in the. Isa 5:30
the land is d. 9:19*
the sun d. 13:10; Joel 3:15
all joy is d. the mirth of. Isa 24:11
Tehaphnehes day be d. Ezek 30:18*
eye shall be utterly d. Zech 11:17
then shall the sun be d. Mat 24:29
Mark 13:24
and the sun was d. Luke 23:45*
their foolish heart was d. Rom 1:21
the understanding d. Eph 4:18
third part of them was d. Rev 8:12
the sun and the air were d. 9:2

darkeneth

who is this that d.? Job 38:2

darkish

bright spots in skin be d. Lev 13:39

darkly

see through a glass d. 1 Cor 13:12

darkness

Literally, the absence of natural light, Mat 27:45.
Figuratively, [1] *The place of misery,* Mat 22:13. [2] *Ignorance,* John 3:19. [3] *Secret,* Mat 10:27. [4] *The land of darkness is the grave,* Job 10:21, 22. [5] *The children of darkness are the wicked, in opposition to the good who are called children of light,* 2 Cor 6:14.

d. was upon face of deep. Gen 1:2
the light day, and the d. night. 5
to divide the light from the d. 18
an horror of great d. fell upon. 15:12
there be d. over Egypt. Ex 10:21
there was a thick d. in all. 22
it was a cloud and d. to. 14:20
Moses drew near to thick d. 20:21
burnt with thick d. Deut 4:11
Lord spake out of thick d. 5:22
d. between you and the. Josh 24:7
d. was under his feet. 2 Sam 22:10
Ps 18:9
made d. pavilions. 2 Sam 22:12
will enlighten my d. 29; Ps 18:28
d. and the shadow of. Job 3:5
as for that night, let d. seize. 6
meet with d. in the day time. 5:14
a land of d. as d. itself. 10:22†
and he hath set d. in my. 19:8
all d. shall be hid in his. 20:26
or d. that thou canst not see. 22:11
not cut off before d. neither hath he covered the d. 23:17
an end to d. the stones of d. 28:3
no d. where workers of. 34:22
our speech by reason of d. 37:19
when I made thick d. a. 38:9
and as for d. where is the? 19
d. his secret place. Ps 18:11
mine acquaintance into d. 88:18
clouds and d. round about. 97:2
makest d. and it is night. 104:20
he sent d. and made it dark. 105:28
if I say, surely the d. shall. 139:11
yea, d. hideth not from thee. 12
to walk in ways of d. Pr 2:13
the way of wicked is as d. 4:19
name be covered with d. Eccl 6:4
look to the land, behold d. Isa 5:30
and behold trouble and d. 8:22
give thee treasures of d. Isa 45:3
get thee into d. O daughter of. 47:5
d. shall cover the earth, and gross d. the people, but. 60:2
d. and make gross d. Jer 13:16
I will set d. upon thy. Ezek 32:8
d. of clouds and of thick d. Joel 2:2
sun shall be turned into d. 31
Acts 2:20
maketh the morning d. Amos 4:13
d. shall pursue his enemies. Nah 1:8
whole body full of d. Mat 6:23
Luke 11:34
cast out into outer d. Mat 8:12
22:13; 25:30
from sixth hour was d. 27:45
Mark 15:33
hour and power of d. Luke 22:53
there was d. over all earth. 23:44
on him a mist and a d. Acts 13:11
fellowship with works of d. Eph 5:11
against the rulers of the d. 6:12
us from power of d. Col 1:13
not of night nor of d. 1 Thes 5:5
to blackness and d. Heb 12:18
delivered them into d. 2 Pet 2:4
to whom the mist of d. is. 17
because that d. hath. 1 John 2:11
in chains under d. Jude 6
is reserved blackness of d. 13
kingdom was full of d. Rev 16:10

darkness with *day*

let that *day* be d. let not. Job 3:4
he knoweth that *day* of d. 15:23
remember the *days* of d. Eccl 11:8
thy d. be as noon-*day*. Isa 58:10
a *day* of d. and gloominess. Joel 2:2; Zeph 1:15
day of the Lord be d.? Amos 5:20

in **darkness**

grope as the blind *in* d. Deut 28:29
wicked be silent *in* d. 1 Sam 2:9
Lord said that he would dwell *in* thick d. 1 Ki 8:12; 2 Chr 6:1
made my bed *in* the d. Job 17:13
they walk on *in* d. Ps 82:5
thou hast laid me *in* d. 88:6
pestilence that walketh *in* d. 91:6
such as sit *in* d. and shadow. 107:10
made me to dwell *in* d. 143:3
lamp be put out *in* d. Pr 20:20
the fool walketh *in* d. Eccl 2:14
he eateth *in* d. 5:17
he departeth *in* d. 6:4
bring them that sit *in* d. Isa 42:7
to them that are *in* d. 49:9
wait for light, we walk *in* d. 59:9
as slippery ways *in* d. Jer 23:12
knoweth what is *in* the d. Dan 2:22
me shall not walk *in* d. John 8:12
that walketh *in* d. knoweth not. 12:35
should not abide *in* d. 46
brethren, are not *in* d. 1 Thes 5:4
and walk *in* d. we lie. 1 John 1:6
hateth his brother, is *in* d. 2:9
he that hateth his brother, is *in* d. and walketh *in* d. 11

land of **darkness**

even to the *land of* d. Job 10:21
a *land of* d. as d. itself. 22
have I been a *land of* d.? Jer 2:31

darkness with *light*

divided *light* from the d. Gen 1:4
lights to divide *light* from d. 18
a land where *light* is as d. Job 10:22
light is short because of d. 17:12
driven from *light* into d. 18:18
his *light* I walked through d. 29:3
for *light*, there came d. 30:26
there ariseth *light* in d. Ps 112:4
d. and *light* are both alike. 139:12
far as *light* excelleth d. Eccl 2:13
d. *for light*, and *light* for d. Isa 5:20
walked in d. have seen great *light*, upon them *light*. 9:2; Mat 4:16
make d. *light* before. Isa 42:16
I form *light* and create d. 45:7
walketh in d. and hath no *light*. 50:10
light, he make gross d. Jer 13:16
d. but not into *light*. Lam 3:2
Lord is d. and not *light*. Amos 5:18
in d. Lord shall be a *light*. Mi 7:8

light in thee be *d.* how great is that *d.*! *Mat* 6:23
tell in *d.* speak in *light.* 10:27
Luke 12:3
light to them that sit in *d.*
Luke 1:79; *Rom* 2:19
light which is in thee be not *d.*
Luke 11:35
light shineth in *d. d.* *John* 1:5
men loved *d.* rather than *light.* 3:19
while ye have *light,* lest *d.* 12:35
them from *d.* to *light.* *Acts* 26:18
works of *d.* put on *light.* *Rom* 13:12
to *light* hidden things of *d. 1 Cor* 4:5
light to shine out of *d.* *2 Cor* 4:6
communion hath *light* with *d.*? 6:14
d. into marvellous *light.* *1 Pet* 2:9
God is *light,* and in him is no *d.*
1 John 1:5
d. is past, and true *light* now. 2:8

out of **darkness**

the voice *out of* the *d.* *Deut* 5:22
deep things *out of d.* *Job* 12:22
he shall return *out of d.* 15:22
he shall not depart *out of d.* 30
brought them *out of d.* *Ps* 107:14
of blind shall see *out of d. Isa* 29:18

darling

deliver my *d.* from power. *Ps* 22:20
rescue my *d.* from the lions. 35:17

dart, -s

Joab took three *d.* in. *2 Sam* 18:14
Hezekiah made *d.* and. *2 Chr* 32:5*
the spear nor the *d.* *Job* 41:26
d. are counted as stubble. 29*
till a *d.* strike through. *Pr* 7:23*
to quench the fiery *d.* *Eph* 6:16
thrust through with a *d.* *Heb* 12:20*

dash

thou wilt *d.* their children. *2 Ki* 8:12
lest *d.* them in pieces like. *Ps* 2:9
bear thee up, lest thou *d.* thy foot.
91:12; *Mat* 4:6; *Luke* 4:11
their bows shall *d.* the. *Isa* 13:18
I will *d.* them one. *Jer* 13:14

dashed

hand, hath *d.* in pieces. *Ex* 15:6
children also shall be *d.* *Isa* 13:16
Hos 13:16; *Nah* 3:10
the mother was *d.* upon. *Hos* 10:14

dasheth

that *d.* thy little ones. *Ps* 137:9

Dathan, *see* **Abiram**

daub, -ed, -ing

she *d.* the ark with slime. *Ex* 2:3
others *d.* it with. *Ezek* 13:10
say to them which *d.* it. 11
where is *d.* wherewith ye *d.* it ? 12
break down wall ye have *d.* 14
her prophets have *d.* them. 22:28

daughter

[1] *A female child, without particular meaning as to exact relationship,* Gen 34:1; Ex 2:21; Ruth 3:18.
[2] *The inhabitants of a city or country,* Isa 16:2; Mat 21:5.
[3] *In a figurative use, as daughters of music, or singing birds, which may mean the power of making music,* Eccl 12:4.

d. of my father, not *d.* *Gen* 20:12
whose *d.* art thou ? 24:23, 47
take my master's brother's *d.* 48
Dinah, the *d.* of Leah. 34:1
folly in lying with Jacob's *d.* 7
Shechem longeth for your *d.* 8
then will we take our *d.* and. 17
he had delight in Jacob's *d.* 19
but if it be a *d.* then. *Ex* 1:16
whether he gored a son or a *d.* 21:31
days are fulfilled for a *d.* *Lev* 12:6
nor take her daughter's *d.* 18:17
the *d.* of any priest, if she. 21:9
if the priest's *d.* be married. 22:12
if the priest's *d.* be a widow. 13
if he have no *d.* give. *Num* 27:9
every *d.* that possesseth an. 36:8
lieth with sister, *d.* of his father or *d.* of his mother. *Deut* 27:22
eye be evil towards her *d.* 28:56
Jephthah's *d.* came out. *Judg* 11:34
to lament Jephthah's *d.* *Judg* 11:40
not thine handmaid a *d. 1 Sam* 1:16†
when Saul's *d.* should have. 18:19
lamb was unto him as *d. 2 Sam* 12:3
Solomon took Pharaoh's *d. 1 Ki* 3:1
with the *d.* of Pharaoh. 11:1
the *d.* of Ahab was. *2 Ki* 8:18
Jezebel, for she is a king's *d.* 9:34
and the *d.* of Caleb. *1 Chr* 2:49
uncle's *d.* for his own *d.* *Esth* 2:7
O *d.* and consider, and. *Ps* 45:10
king's *d.* is all glorious within. 13
with shoes, O prince's *d. S of S* 7:1
about, backsliding *d. Jer* 31:22; 49:4
O *d.* dwelling in Egypt. 46:19
d. that dost inhabit Dibon. 48:18
deliver son nor *d. Ezek* 14:16; 18:20
is the mother, so is her *d.* 16:44
thou art thy mother's *d.* that. 45
for son or *d.* they may defile. 44:25
king's *d.* of the south. *Dan* 11:6
shall give him the *d.* of women. 17
again, and bare a *d.* *Hos* 1:6
O *d.* of troops. *Mi* 5:1
d. riseth up against her mother. 7:6
Mat 10:35; *Luke* 12:53
d. of my dispersed shall. *Zeph* 3:10
hath married the *d.* of. *Mal* 2:11
d. be of good comfort. *Mat* 9:22
Mark 5:34; *Luke* 8:48
he that loveth son or *d.* *Mat* 10:37
the *d.* of Herodias danced. 14:6
her *d.* was made whole from. 15:28
forth devil out of her *d.* *Mark* 7:26
he had one only *d.* *Luke* 8:42
not this woman, being *d.* 13:16
Pharaoh's *d.* took him. *Acts* 7:21
to be son of Pharaoh's *d. Heb* 11:24

daughter *of Babylon*

O *d. of Babylon,* who art. *Ps* 137:8
O *d. of Babylon,* sit on. *Isa* 47:1
against thee *d. of Babylon. Jer* 50:42
d. of Babylon is like a. 51:33
O Zion, that dwellest with the *d. of Babylon.* *Zech* 2:7

daughter *of the Chaldeans*

throne, O *d. of Chaldeans. Isa* 47:1
darkness, O *d. of Chaldeans.* 5

daughter *of Edom*

be glad, O *d. of Edom.* *Lam* 4:21
visit thine iniquity, O *d. of Edom.* 22

daughter *of Egypt*

O virgin, *d. of Egypt.* *Jer* 46:11
d. of Egypt shall be confounded. 24

daughter *of Gallim*

voice, O *d. of Gallim.* *Isa* 10:30

his **daughter**

Rachel *his d.* cometh. *Gen* 29:6
if a man sell *his d.* *Ex* 21:7
for his son or *his d.* *Lev* 21:2
to pass to *his d.* *Num* 27:8
between the father and *his d.* 30:16
nor *his d.* shalt thou. *Deut* 7:3
that maketh *his d.* to pass through fire. 18:10; *2 Ki* 23:10
not any of us give *his d.* *Judg* 21:1
and give him his *d.* *1 Sam* 17:25

daughter *of Jerusalem*

the *d.* of *Jerusalem* hath shaken.
2 Ki 19:21; *Isa* 37:22
I liken to thee, O *d. of Jerusalem.*
Lam 2:13
wag head at *d. of Jerusalem.* 15
come to *d. of Jerusalem.* *Mi* 4:8
rejoice, O *d. of Jerusalem.*
Zeph 3:14
shout, O *d. of Jerusalem. Zech* 9:9

daughter *of Judah*

trodden *d. of Judah.* *Lam* 1:15
strong holds of *d. of Judah.* 2:2
increased in *d. of Judah* mourning. 5

daughter-in-law

she was his *d.-in-law.* *Gen* 38:16
Tamar thy *d.-in-law* hath. 24
uncover thy *d.-in-law.* *Lev* 18:15
a man lie with his *d.-in-law.* 20:12
and Ruth her *d.-in-law.* *Ruth* 1:22
d.-in-law which loveth thee. 4:15
d.-in-law Phinehas' wife. *1 Sam* 4:19
defileth his *d.-in-law.* *Ezek* 22:11
d.-in-law riseth up against the.
Mi 7:6; *Mat* 10:35; *Luke* 12:53

my **daughter**

gave *my d.* to this man. *Deut* 22:16
the tokens of *my d.'s* virginity. 17
him will I give *my d.* *Josh* 15:16
Judg 1:12
alas, *my d.* thou hast. *Judg* 11:35
behold, here is *my d.* a. 19:24
said unto her, go, *my d.* *Ruth* 2:2
blessed be thou of Lord, *my d.* 3:10
who art thou, *my d.*? 16
sit still, *my d.* till thou know. 18
a ruler, saying, *my d.* *Mat* 9:18
my d. is grievously vexed. 15:22
my little *d.* lieth at death. *Mark* 5:23

daughter *of my people*

spoiling of *d. of my p.* *Isa* 22:4
wind toward *d. of my p.* *Jer* 4:11
healed hurt of *d. of my p.* 6:14; 8:11
O, *d. of my people,* gird thee. 6:26
voice of cry of *d. of my p.* 8:19
for hurt of *d. of my p.* am I. 21
why is not health of *d. of my p.*? 22
weep for slain of *d. of my p.* 9:1
how shall I do for *d. of my p.*? 7
virgin *d. of my p.* is broken. 14:17
destruction of *d. of my p. Lam* 2:11
3:48
d. of my p. is become cruel. 4:3
the iniquity of the *d. of my p.* 6
meat in destruction of *d. of my p.* 10

daughter *of Tarshish*

a river, O *d. of Tarshish. Isa* 23:10

thy **daughter**

7 years for *thy* younger *d. Gen* 29:18
nor thy son, nor *thy d.* *Ex* 20:10
Deut 5:14
nakedness of *thy* daughter's *d.*
Lev 18:10
do not prostitute *thy d.* to. 19:29
thy d. shalt thou not. *Deut* 7:3
rejoice and *thy d.* 12:18; 16:11, 14
if thy son or thy *d.* entice. 13:6
I found not *thy d.* a maid. 22:17
give *thy d.* to my son. *2 Ki* 14:9
2 Chr 25:18
said, *thy d.* is dead. *Mark* 5:35
Luke 8:49
devil is gone out of *thy d. Mark* 7:29

daughter *of Tyre*

d. of Tyre shall be there. *Ps* 45:12

daughter *of Zidon*

virgin, *d. of Zidon.* *Isa* 23:12

daughter *of Zion*

d. of Z. hath despised thee.
2 Ki 19:21; *Isa* 37:22
the gates of the *d. of Z.* *Ps* 9:14
d. of Z. left as a cottage. *Isa* 1:8
washed away filth of *d. of Z.* 4:4
against mount of *d. of Z.* 10:32; 16:1
loose thyself, *d. of Z.* 52:2
say to the *d. of Z.* thy. 62:11
voice of the *d. of Z.* *Jer* 4:31
I have likened *d. of Z.* to a. 6:2
of war against thee, O *d. of Z.* 23
from the *d. of Z.* beauty. *Lam* 1:6
Lord covereth the *d. of Z.* 2:1
slew in tabernacle of *d. of Z.* 4
to destroy wall of *d. of Z.* 8
the elders of *d. of Z.* sit on the. 10
shall I equal to thee, *d. of Z.*? 13
O wall of the *d. of Z.* let tears. 18
accomplished, O *d. of Z.* 4:22
beginning of sin to *d. of Z.* *Mi* 1:13
strong hold of the *d. of Z.* 4:8
labour to bring forth, O *d. of Z.* 10
arise and thresh, O *d. of Z.* 13
sing, O *d. of Z.* shout. *Zeph* 3:14
rejoice, O *d. of Z.* *Zech* 2:10; 9:9
tell ye the *d. of Z.* thy. *Mat* 21:5
fear not, *d. of Z.* thy. *John* 12:15

daughter *of Zur*

Cozbi the *d. of Zur.* *Num* 25:15

daughters

and when *d.* were born. *Gen* 6:1
sons of God saw the *d.* of men. 2
sons of God came in unto *d.* 4
to them which married his *d.* 19:14
both *d.* of Lot with child by. 36

a wife of d. of Canaan. Gen 24:3, 37
28:1, 6
the d. of the city came. 24:13
because of the d. of Heth. 27:46
happy am I, for the d. will. 30:13
thou hast carried away my d. 31:26
these d. are my d. 43
if thou afflict my d. 50
Dinah went out to see d. 34:1
give your d. to us, and take our d. 9
we give our d. to you, take d. 16
priest of Midian had seven d. Ex 2:16
deal with her after manner of d. 21:9
their d. go a whoring after. 34:16
the flesh of your d. shall. Lev 26:29
d. of Zelophehad. Num 26:33; 27:1
Josh 17:3
d. of Zelophehad speak. Num 27:7
so did the d. of Zelophehad. 36:10
no whore of the d. of. Deut 23:17
they took their d. to be. Judg 3:6
we will not give them of our d. 21:7
not give them wives of our d. 18
turn again, my d. Ruth 1:11, 12
nay, my d. it grieveth me. 13
take your d. to be. 1 Sam 8:13
were king's d. virgins. 2 Sam 13:18
Shallum, he and his d. Neh 3:12
d. are brought into bondage. 5:5
one of d. of Barzillai to wife. 7:63
Ezra 2:61
not give our d. to people. Neh 10:30
women so fair as d. of. Job 42:15
king's d. among thy. Ps 45:9
that our d. may be as. 144:12
d. have done virtuously. Pr 31:29
so is my love among d. S of S 2:2
the d. saw her and blessed. 6:9
ye careless d. give ear. Isa 32:9
thy d. shall be nursed at. 60:4
teach your d. wailing. Jer 9:20
give your d. to husbands, that. 29:6
her d. shall be burnt with. 49:2
cry, ye d. of Rabbah, gird ye. 3
because of all the d. of. Lam 3:51
set thy face against d. Ezek 13:17
and her d. Sodom, and her d. 16:46
idleness was in her and in her d. 49
bring back the captivity of her d. 53
when thy sister Sodom and d. 55
I will give them unto thee for d. 61
two women, the d. of one. 23:2
her d. shall be slain. 26:6, 8
d. shall go into captivity. 30:18
the d. of the nations shall. 32:16
your d. shall commit. Hos 4:13
I will not punish your d. when. 14
his wife was of the d. of. Luke 1:5
the same man had four d. Acts 21:9
whose d. ye are as long. 1 Pet 3:6*

daughters *of Israel*
be no whore of d. of Isr. Deut 23:17
d. of Isr. went yearly. Judg 11:40
ye d. of Isr. weep. 2 Sam 1:24

daughters *of Jerusalem*
comely, O d. of Jerus. S of S 1:5
charge you, O d. of Jerus. 2:7
3:5; 5:8; 8:4
love for the d. of Jerus. 3:10
my beloved, O d. of Jerus. 5:16
d. of Jerus. weep not. Luke 23:28

daughters *of Judah*
let d. of Judah be glad. Ps 48:11
the d. of Judah rejoiced. 97:8

daughters-in-law
arose with her d.-in-law. Ruth 1:6, 7
Naomi said to her two d.-in-law. 8

daughters *of Moab*
whoredom with d. of M. Num 25:1
so the d. of M. shall be at. Isa 16:2

daughters *of music*
the d. of music shall be. Eccl 12:4

daughters *of the Philistines*
woman of d. of Phil. Judg 14:1
seen a woman of d. of Phil. 2
lest d. of Phil. rejoice. 2 Sam 1:20
delivered thee to d. of Phil.
Ezek 16:27
the d. of Phil. which despise. 57

daughters *of Shiloh*
d. of Shiloh come out, catch a wife of d. of Shiloh. Judg 21:21

daughters joined with *sons*
he begat sons and d. Gen 5:4
7:10, 13, 16; 11:11
thy sons and d. bring out. 19:12
to kiss my sons and d. 31:28
he kissed his sons and d. and. 55
all his sons and d. rose to. 37:35
them on your sons and d. Ex 3:22
with our sons and with our d. 10:9
she have born him sons or d. 21:4
ear-rings of your sons and d. 32:2
take of their d. to thy sons. 34:16
thou, thy sons and d. shall eat in the.
Lev 10:14; Num 18:11, 19
given his sons and d. Num 21:29
Zelophehad had no sons, but d.
26:33; Josh 17:3
ye and your sons and d. rejoice.
Deut 12:12
sons and d. they have burnt in fire.
31; 2 Ki 17:17; Jer 7:31; 32:35
thy sons and d. given to. Deut 28:32
beget sons and d. but shalt not. 41
the flesh of thy sons and d. 53
provoking of his sons and d. 32:19
Achan, his sons and d. Josh 7:24
d. of Manasseh had inheritance among sons. 17:6
gave their d. to their sons. Judg 3:6
took in thirty d. for his sons. 12:9
Peninnah, her sons and d. portions.
1 Sam 1:4
Hannah bare three sons and two d.
2:21
their sons and d. were taken. 30:3
grieved, every man for sons and d. 6
lacking, neither sons nor d. 19
were yet sons and d. born to David.
2 Sam 5:13; 1 Chr 14:3
saved lives of thy sons and d.
2 Sam 19:5
Sheshan had no sons but d.
1 Chr 2:34
Shimei had sixteen sons six d. 4:27
died, and had no sons but d. 23:22
Heman fourteen sons and three d.
25:5
had 28 sons and 60 d. 2 Chr 11:21
Abijah begat 22 sons and d. 13:21
wives and begat sons and d. 24:3
200,000 women, sons and d. 28:8
our sons, d. and wives are in. 29:9
genealogy of their sons and d. 31:18
of their d. for their sons. Ezra 9:2
give not your d. to their sons. 12
Neh 13:25
fight for your sons and d. Neh 4:14
our sons and our d. are many 5:2
bondage our sons and our d. 5
their sons and d. clave to. 10:28
born to Job 7 sons and 3 d. Job 1:2
42:13
a day when sons and d. 1:13, 18
their sons and d. to devils. Ps 106:37
shed blood of their sons and d. 38
my sons from far, and my d. from.
Isa 43:6
sons in their arms, and thy d. 49:22
a name better than of s. and d. 56:5
devoured sons and d. Jer 3:24
eat that which thy sons and d. 5:17
sons and their d. shall die. 11:22
none to bury their sons and d. 14:16
have sons and d. in this place. 16:2
concerning the sons and d. 3
eat the flesh of sons and d. 19:9
wives and beget sons and d. 29:6
we, our sons and our d. drink. 35:8
sons and thy d. taken captives. 48:46
deliver neither sons nor d.
Ezek 14:16, 18
brought forth, sons and d. 22
sons and d. and sacrificed. 16:20
mine, and bare sons and d. 23:4
her sons and d. and slew her. 10, 25
they shall slay their sons and d. 47
your sons and d. fall by sword.
24:21; Amos 7:17
take from them their sons and d.
Ezek 24:25
sons and d. prophesy. Joel 2:28
Acts 2:17
will sell your sons and d. Joel 3:8
shall be my sons and d. 2 Cor 6:18

daughters *of Syria*
reproach of d. of Syria. Ezek 16:57

two **daughters**
I have two d. let me. Gen 19:8
take thy wife and thy two d. 15
in a cave, he and his two d. 30
Laban had two d. Leah and. 29:16
fourteen years for thy two d. 31:41
went out with her two d. Ruth 1:7
Hannah conceived and bare two d.
1 Sam 2:21
two d. were Merab and Michal. 14:49
the horseleech hath two d. Pr 30:15

daughters *of the uncircumcised*
lest d. of the uncirc. 2 Sam 1:20

daughters *of Zion*
go forth, O ye d. of Z. S of S 3:11
because the d. of Z. Isa 3:16
smite head of the d. of Z. 17
washed away filth of d. of Z. 4:4

David
Jesse begat D. Ruth 4:22; Mat 1:6
Luke 3:31
Spirit of Lord came upon D.
1 Sam 16:13
send me D. thy son. 19
D. came to Saul. 21
D. played. 23; 18:10; 19:9
D. was youngest. 17:14
D. returned from Saul. 15
D. heard the words of Goliath. 23
Eliab's anger kindled against D. 28
Saul armed D. 38
when Goliath saw D. 42
the Philistines cursed D. 43
D. prevailed over Philistine. 50
as D. returned from slaughter. 57
soul of Jonathan knit to D. 18:1
Jonathan and D. made a covenant. 3
D. went out whithersoever Saul. 5
D. hath slain ten thousands. 7; 29:5
Saul eyed D. from that day. 18:9
D. behaved himself wisely in all. 14
all Israel and Judah loved D. 16
on this manner spake D. 24
knew the Lord was with D. 28
and Saul became D.'s enemy. 29
spake to his servants to kill D. 19:1
against innocent blood to slay D.? 5
sought to smite D. but D. 10, 18
D. is at Naioth. 19
where are Samuel and D.? 22
D. asked leave of me to. 20:6, 28
and Jonathan caused D. to. 17
D. hid himself. 24
D.'s place was empty. 25, 27
for he was grieved for D. 34
wept one with another till D. 41
afraid at the meeting of D. 21:1
D. arose, and fled to Achish. 10
is not this D. the king? 11; 29:3
D. departed and escaped to. 22:1
and D. went thence to Mizpeh. 3
D. departed and came into forest. 5
who is so faithful as D.? 14
their hand also is with D. 17
D. inquired of the Lord. 23:2, 4
30:8; 2 Sam 2:1; 3:19, 22; 21:1
D. and his men went to. 1 Sam 23:5
D. knew that Saul practised. 9
D. was in the wilderness of Ziph. 15
D. and his men were in. 24
Saul returned from pursuing D. 28
D. is in wilderness of En-gedi. 24:1
D.'s heart smote him. 5
D. stayed his servants. 7
this thy voice, my son D.? 16; 26:17
D. sware unto Saul. 24:22
D. went to Paran. 25:1
D. sent out ten young men. 5
do God to the enemies of D. 22
doth not D. hide himself in? 26:1
and D. beheld the place where. 5
D. took the spear and the cruse. 12
Saul knew D.'s voice. 17
return, my son D. 21
D. said, I shall perish by the. 27:1
D. was fled to Gath. 4
D. invaded Geshurites. 8
so did D. and so will be. 11
it to thy neighbour, to D. 28:17
is not this D.? 29:3

then Achish called D. 1 Sam 29:6
when D. and his men were. 30:1
and D.'s two wives were taken. 5
D. pursued. 10
D. smote them from the twilight. 17
D. recovered all. 18, 19
D. took the flocks. 20
D. took hold on clothes. 2 Sam 1:11
D. called one of the young men. 15
D. lamented over Saul. 17
D. sent messengers to men. 2:5
house of Judah followed D. 10
house of D. waxed stronger. 3:1
unto D. were sons born in Hebron. 2
except as Lord hath sworn to D. 9
ye sought for D. in times past. 17
D. said, I and my kingdom are. 28
came all tribes of Israel to D. 5:1
thinking, D. cannot come in. 6
D. took the strong-hold of Zion. 7
D. grew great. 10
D. perceived the Lord had. 12
D. heard of it, and went down. 17
D. burnt their images. 21
D. went to bring up the ark. 6:2
D. all Israel played before the. 5
and D. was afraid of the Lord. 9
D. danced. 14
so D. brought up the ark. 15
what can D. say more to thee ?
7:20; 1 Chr 17:18
D. smote the Philistines. 2 Sam 8:1
D. smote Hadadezer. 3
Lord preserved D. 6, 14
D. took shields of gold. 7; 1 Chr 18:7
D. gat him a name. 2 Sam 8:13
D. reigned over. 15; 1 Chr 18:14
D. reigned; executed. 2 Sam 8:15
D. sent to comfort. 10:2; 1 Chr 19:2
thinkest thou D. doth honour thy ?
2 Sam 10:3; 1 Chr 19:3
D. slew men of 700. 2 Sam 10:18
D. sent and enquired after. 11:3
D. sent for Uriah. 6
D. wrote a letter to Joab. 14
the thing D. had done displeased. 27
D.'s anger was kindled. 12:5
D. said, I have sinned against. 13
D. besought God for child, D. 16
D. perceived child was dead. 19
and D. comforted Bath-sheba. 24
D. fought against Rabbah and. 29
king's crown was set on D. 30
D. sent to Tamar. 13:7
tidings came to D. 30
D. went up by the ascent of. 15:30
Shimei cast stones at D. 16:6
said unto him, curse D. 10
I will arise and pursue after D. 17:1
send quickly and tell D. 16
then D. arose. 22
D. was come to Mahanaim. 27
honey for D. 29
D. numbered the people that. 18:1
D. sat between the two gates. 24
we have also more right in D. 19:43
we have no part in D. 20:1
and D. came to his house. 3
he that is for D. let him go. 11
Ishbi-benob thought to have slain D.
21:16
mercy unto D. 22:51; Ps 18:50
the last words of D. 2 Sam 23:1
mighty men D. had. 8; 1 Chr 11:10
D. longed and said. 2 Sam 23:15
D.'s heart smote him. 24:10
D. built there an altar unto. 25
and D. our Lord. 1 Ki 1:11
D. slept with his fathers. 2:10
slew them, my father D. not. 32
knowest what thou didst to D. 44
thou wilt walk as thy father D. 3:14
who hath given D. a wise son. 5:7
D. to be over my people. 8:16
I am risen up in the room of D. 20
as I promised to D. 9:5
as I built for D. 11:38
for this afflict the seed of D. 39
portion have we in D.? see to thine
own house, D. 12:16; 2 Chr 10:16
turned kingdom to D. 1 Chr 10:14
D. made a covenant with them. 11:3
thine are we, D. then D. 12:18
they helped D. against the. 21
the fame of D. went out. 1 Chr 14:17
D. was clothed with a robe. 15:27
set the ark in tent D. had. 16:1
and D. returned to bless his. 43
Ornan saw D. bowed to D. 21:21
so when D. was old and full. 23:1
D. blessed Lord before the. 29:10
great mercy unto D. 2 Chr 1:8
began to seek after God of D. 34:3
of sons of D. Hattush. Ezra 8:2
against sepulchres of D. Neh 3:16
with musical instruments of D. 12:36
prayers of D. the son of. Ps 72:20
I will not lie unto D. 89:35
swarest to D. 49
Lord, remember D. 132:1
hath sworn to D. 11
there will I make horn of D. to 17
is like the tower of D. S of S 4:4
on the throne of D. and. Isa 9:7
woe to Ariel, city where D. 29:1
the sure mercies of D. 55:3
Acts 13:34
sitting on throne of D. Jer 17:25
I will raise to D. a righteous. 23:5
branch to grow up unto D. 33:15
D. shall never want a man to. 17
none to sit on throne of D. 36:30
of music like D. Amos 6:5
will I raise up the tabernacle of D.
9:11; Acts 15:16
feeble be as D. and D. Zech 12:8
son of D. have mercy. Mat 9:27
15:22; 20:30, 31; Mark 10:47, 48
Luke 18:38, 39
D. did when he was an hungered ?
Mat 12:3; Mark 2:25; Luke 6:3
is not this the son of D.? Mat 12:23
Hosanna to the son of D. 21:9, 15
Christ is the son of D. 22:42
Mark 12:35
if D. then call him Lord. Mat 22:45
Mark 12:37; Luke 20:41, 44
the kingdom of our father D.
Mark 11:10
Christ cometh of the seed of D.
John 7:42
speak of patriarch D. Acts 2:29
for D. is not ascended into the. 34
he raised up to them D. to. 13:22
for D. fell on sleep. 36
made of the seed of D. Rom 1:3
2 Tim 2:8
even as D. also describeth. Rom 4:6
certain day, saying, in D. Heb 4:7
time would fail me to tell of D. 11:32
hath the key of D. Rev 3:7
root of D. 5:5; 22:16

see **city, father**

days of **David**

famine in the days of D. 2 Sam 21:1
days of D. drew nigh. 1 Ki 2:1
number was in days of D. 1 Chr 7:2
in the days of D. were. Neh 12:46
drave out unto days of D. Acts 7:45

hand of **David**

require it at h. of D. 1 Sam 20:16
thee into h. of D. 2 Sam 3:8
by h. of my servant D. I will. 18
fell by h. of D. 21:22; 1 Chr 20:8

house of **David**

covenant with h. of D. 1 Sam 20:16
the h. of Saul and D. 2 Sam 3:1, 6
let h. of thy servant D. 7:26
Israel rebelled against the h. of D.
1 Ki 12:19; 2 Chr 10:19
none followed h. of D. 1 Ki 12:20
shall kingdom return to h. of D. 26
a child be born to the h. of D. 13:2
rent kingdom from h. of D. 14:8
2 Ki 17:21
not destroy the h. of D. 2 Chr 21:7
thrones of the h. of D. Ps 122:5
it was told the h. of D. Isa 7:2
hear, O h. of D. 13; Jer 21:12
key of h. of D. I will lay. Isa 22:22
that the glory of h. of D. Zech 12:7
feeble as D. and the h. of D. 8
I will pour on h. of D. the spirit. 10
the family of the h. of D. shall. 12
a fountain opened to h. of D. 13:1
was Joseph, of h. of D. Luke 1:27
horn of salvation in h. of D. Luke 1:69
was of h. and lineage of D. 2:4

David *joined with* *king*

is not this D. the king ? 1 Sam 21:11
they anointed D. king. 2 Sam 2:4
time that D. was king in Hebron. 11
and king D. himself followed. 3:31
king D. made a league ... anointed
D. king. 5:3; 1 Chr 11:3; 12:31, 38
which king D. did dedicate to Lord.
2 Sam 8:11; 1 Chr 26:26
against king, even D. 2 Sam 20:21
than throne of king D. 1 Ki 1:37
servants came to bless king D. 47
D. the king rejoiced. 1 Chr 29:9
to D. the king a wise son. 2 Chr 2:12
ordained by D. king of. 29:27
Ezra 3:10
serve Lord and D. their king. Jer 30:9
seek Lord and D. their king. Hos 3:5
D. the king and D. the king. Mat 1:6
raised up D. to be king. Acts 13:22

servant **David**

by hand of my servant D. 2 Sam 3:18
go and tell my servant D. 7:5, 8
let the house of thy servant D. be
established. 26; 1 Chr 17:24
shewed thy servant D. 1 Ki 3:6
kept with thy servant D. that. 8:24
keep with thy servant D. 25, 26
2 Chr 6:16
done for D. his servant. 1 Ki 8:66
D. my servant's sake, and for Jerusalem's. 11:13, 32, 34; Ps 132:10
Isa 37:35
D. my servant may have a light.
1 Ki 11:36
keep my statutes, as my servant D.
38; 14:8
mercies of D. thy servant. 2 Chr 6:42
chose D. also his servant. Ps 78:70
sworn unto D. my servant. 89:3
I have found D. my servant. 20
who delivered D. his servant. 144:10
broken with D. my servant. Jer 33:21
multiply seed of D. my servant. 22
away the seed of D. my servant. 26
my servant D. shall feed them.
Ezek 34:23
my servant D. shall be a prince. 24
D. my servant shall be king. 37:24
servant D. shall be their prince. 25
house of his servant D. Luke 1:69
mouth of thy servant D. Acts 4:25

dawn, -ing

they rose about the d. Josh 6:15
woman in the d. of day. Judg 19:26
neither let it see the d. of. Job 3:9
full of tossings to the d. of. 7:4
I prevented the d. of. Ps 119:147
as it began to d. towards. Mat 28:1
till day d. and day-star. 2 Pet 1:19

day

The word day is used of [1] *one period of the earth's revolution, or twenty-four hours,* Gen 7:24; Job 3:6. *This period the Hebrews reckoned as beginning at sunset,* Lev 23:32. [2] *The period between dawn and dark, variable in different latitudes and at different seasons,* Gen 8:22, Ps 19:2; 2 Pet 1:19. [3] *Any period of action or state of being, without definite reference to time,* Job 19:25; Zech 4:10; Hos 1:11; Eccl. 7:14; Ezek 30:9. In the day that *usually has merely the meaning of* when, *and is sometimes so translated,* 1 Ki 2:8; Isa 30:26. "*In thy days*" *means* "*in thy lifetime,*" 1 Ki 11:12.

God called the light d. Gen 1:5
let me go, for d. breaketh. 32:26
if he continue a d. or two. Ex 21:21
journeyed not, till the d. it. 40:37
every thing upon his d. Lev 23:37
the d. I smote first-born. Num 3:13
offer his offering on his d. 7:11
each d. for a year shall bear. 14:34
husband disallow her on d. 30:8, 12
d. thou stoodest before. Deut 4:10
no manner of similitude on d. 15

from d. thou didst depart. Deut 9:7
have been rebellious from d. 24
at his d. thou shalt give him. 24:15
till d. I bid you shout. Josh 6:10
on d. we came forth to go to. 9:12
sun hasted not down about a d. 10:13
was no d. like that before or. 14
when it is d. we shall kill. Judg 16:2*
from the d. that Israel came out. 30
what d. thou buyest the. Ruth 4:5
Lord told Samuel a d. 1 Sam 9:15
behold the d. of which the. 24:4
smite him, or his d. shall. 26:10
while it was yet d. 2 Sam 3:35
Jer 15:9
d. he forced his sister. 2 Sam 13:32
from d. king departed, till d. 19:24
on d. thou goest out. 1 Ki 2:37, 42
till d. the Lord sendeth rain. 17:14
it fell on a d. that Elisha passed.
2 Ki 4:8, 11, 18
they make an end in a d.? Neh 4:2
and labour in the d. 22
d. of feasting. Esth 9:17, 18, 19
feasted, every one his d. Job 1:4
a d. when sons of God. 6, 13; 2:1
let d. perish wherein I was. 3:3
till he accomplish his d. 14:6
be astonied at his d. 18:20
he shall stand at latter d. 19:25
the wicked is reserved to d. 21:30
d. unto d. uttereth speech. Ps 19:2
seeth that his d. is coming. 37:13
nor remembered d. when he. 78:42
a d. in thy courts is better. 84:10
seven times a d. do I. 119:164
and more to perfect d. Pr 4:18
he will come home at the d. 7:20*
knowest not what a d. may. 27:1
till d. break, and. S of S 2:17; 4:6
from d. that Ephraim. Isa 7:17
before the d. was, I am he. 43:13
a d. for a man to afflict his soul ? this
a fast, an acceptable d. to ? 58:5
d. of vengeance of God. 61:2; 63:4
prepare them for the d. Jer 12:3
there shall they be till d. 27:22
d. they built it, even to this d. 32:31
d. I spake, even to this d. 36:2
till d. Jerusalem was taken. 38:28
because of the d. that cometh. 47:4
woe, for their d. is come. 50:27
appointed thee each d. Ezek 4:6
behold the d. behold it is. 7:10
wicked prince, whose d. 21:25, 29
from d. thou wast created. 28:15
howl ye, woe worth the d.! 30:2
for the d. is near. 3
at Tehaphnehes the d. shall. 18
petition three times a d. Dan 6:10
13
will ye do in solemn d.? Hos 9:5
a d. of darkness and. Joel 2:2
him that maketh d. dark. Amos 5:8
the end thereof as a bitter d. 8:10
and d. shall be dark. Mi 3:6
the d. of thy watchmen. 7:4
before decree, the d. pass. Zeph 2:2
till the d. that I rise up to. 3:8
who hath despised d.? Zech 4:10
who may abide the d.? Mal 3:2
d. cometh that shall burn. 4:1
till the d. Noe entered. Mat 24:38
Luke 17:27
come in a d. when he looketh not.
Mat 24:50; Luke 12:46
neither know the d. nor. Mat 25:13
great while before d. Mark 1:35
dumb till d. these things. Luke 1:20
child grew till d. of his shewing. 80
trespass seven times in a d. 17:4
Son of man be in his d. 24
raise it again at last d. John 6:39
raise him up at last d. 40, 44, 54
Abraham rejoiced to see my d. 8:56
work of him while it is d. 9:4
until the d. in which he. Acts 1:2
on a set d. Herod sat upon. 12:21
when it was d. 16:35; 23:12; 27:39
he hath appointed a d. 17:31
anchors, and wished for d. 27:29
wrath against the d. of. Rom 2:5
d. is at hand, let us therefore. 13:12
regardeth a d. regardeth it. 14:6
for the d. shall declare it. 1 Cor 3:13
behold, now is the d. of. 2 Cor 6:2
ye are sealed to the d. Eph 4:30
will perform it until d. Phil 1:6
ye are all children of d. 1 Thes 5:5
let us who are of d. be sober. 8
he limiteth a certain d. Heb 4:7
afterward spoken of another d.? 8
the more as ye see the d. 10:25
till the d. dawn, and the. 2 Pet 1:19
hasting to coming of the d. 3:12
in the Spirit on the Lord's d. Rev. 1:10
for an hour and a d. 9:15

see atonement, battle, calamity, darkness, evil, holy, last

all the **day**

on thee do I wait all the d. Ps 25:5
forth thy salvation all the d. 71:15
shall they rejoice all the d. 89:16
reproach me all the d. 102:8
law is my meditation all the d. 119:97
plowman plow all d. Isa 28:24*
spread out hands all the d. 65:2
a fire that burneth all the d. 5
and faint all the d. Lam 1:13
turneth hand against me all d. 3:3
derision to my people all the d. 14
their device against me all the d. 62
here all the d. idle ? Mat 20:6

all the **day** *long*

longing for them all the d. long.
Deut 28:32
shall cover him all the d. long. 33:12
roaring all the d. long. Ps 32:3
thy praise all the d. long. 35:28
I go mourning all the d. long. 38:6
imagine deceits all the d. long. 12
God we boast all the d. long. 44:8
thy sake are killed all the d. long. 22
righteousness all the d. long. 71:24
for all the d. long have I. 73:14
greedily all the d. long. Pr 21:26
in fear of Lord all the d. long. 23:17
all d. long I stretched. Rom 10:21

by **day**, *and* **day** *by* **day**

spake to Joseph d. by d. Gen 39:10
went before them by d. Ex 13:21
not away pillar of cloud by d. 22
two lambs of the first year d. by d.
29:38; Num 28:3
cloud was upon the tabernacle by d.
fire by. Ex 40:38; Num 9:16*
cloud was on them by d. Num 10:34
14:14; Deut 1:23; Neh 9:19
he could not do it by d. Judg 6:27
nor birds rest by d. 2 Sam 21:10
d. by d. there came to. 1 Chr 12:22
of the sickness d. by d. 2 Chr 21:15
thus they did d. by d. and. 24:11
priests praised Lord d. by d. 30:21
let it be given d. by d. Ezra 6:9
d. by d. he read in law. Neh 8:18
nor arrow that flieth by d. Ps 91:5
sun shall not smite thee by d. 121:6
sun to rule by d. for his. 136:8
no more thy light by d. Isa 60:19
the sun for a light by d. Jer 31:35
and remove by d. in. Ezek 12:3
I brought forth my stuff by d. 7
give us d. by d. our. Luke 11:3
man renewed d. by d. 2 Cor 4:16
gates not be shut by d. Rev 21:25

day *of death*

I know not d. of my death. Gen 27:2
be a Nazarite to d. of his death.
Judg 13:7
see Saul till d. of death. 1 Sam 15:35
no child till d. of death. 2 Sam 6:23
shut up to d. of their death. 20:3
Uzziah was a leper to the d. of his
death. 2 Ki 15:5; 2 Chr 26:21
d. of death better than d. Eccl 7:1
power in the d. of death. 8:8
prison till d. of his death. Jer 52:11
portion, till d. of his death. 34

every **day**

a certain rate every d. Ex 16:4
offer a bullock every d. 29:36
sought David every d. 1 Sam 23:14
David mourned for his son every d.
2 Sam 13:37
daily rate for every d. 2 Ki 25:30
minister, as every d. 1 Chr 16:37
a certain rate every d. 2 Chr 8:13
duty every d. required. 14; Ezra 3:4
singers, due for every d. Neh 11:23
and the porters every d. his. 12:47
Mordecai walked every d. Esth 2:11
angry with wicked every d. Ps 7:11
every d. they wrest my words. 56:5
every d. will I bless thee. 145:2
feared continually every d. Isa 51:13
and my name every d. is. 52:5
prepare every d. a goat. Ezek 43:25
sumptuously every d. Luke 16:19
esteemeth every d. alike. Rom 14:5

feast **day**

trumpet on solemn feast-d. Ps 81:3
they said, not on the feast-d.
Mat 26:5*; Mark 14:2*
feast-d. many believed. John 2:23*

first **day**

and morning were first d. Gen 1:5
on first d. of the month mountains.
8:5, 13; Ex 40:2, 17; Lev 23:24
the first d. put away leaven, whoso
eateth from first d. Ex 12:15
in the first d. an holy convocation. 16
Lev 23:7, 35; Num 28:18; 29:1
first d. shall be sabbath. Lev 23:39
shall take on first d. boughs of. 40
spake to Moses on first d. Num 1:1
assembled congregation on first d. 18
on the first d. Aaron went. 33:38
flesh sacrificed first d. not. Deut 16:4
on first d. to sanctify. 2 Chr 29:17
from the first d. began. Ezra 3:6
on the first d. began he to go up . . . on
first d. came he to Jerusalem. 7:9
sat down on first d. of the. 10:16
by first d. of first month they. 17
brought law on first d. of. Neh 8:2
from first unto last d. he read. 18
in first d. word of Lord. Ezek 26:1
29:17; 31:1; 32:1; Hag 1:1
in first d. of the month. Ezek 45:18
from first d. thou didst. Dan 10:12
first d. of unleavened bread.
Mat 26:17; Mark 14:12
first d. I came into Asia. Acts 20:18
fellowship from first d. Phil 1:5

see week

second **day**

and morning second d. Gen 1:8
went out the second d. Ex 2:13
on second d. Nethaneel. Num 7:18
on second d. offer twelve. 29:17
second d. they compassed. Josh 6:14
took Lachish on second d. 10:32
Benjamin second d. Judg 20:24
eat no meat second d. 1 Sam 20:34
began to build second d. 2 Chr 3:2
on the second d. were. Neh 8:13
to Esther the second d. Esth 7:2
second d. after he had. Jer 41:4
second d. thou shalt offer a kid.
Ezek 43:22

third **day**

and morning third d. Gen 1:13
on third d. Abraham saw. 22:4
it was told Laban on third d. 31:22
on third d. when they were. 34:25
ready against the third d. for the
third d. Lord will. Ex 19:11, 15
remainder of flesh of sacrifice on
third d. shall be. Lev 7:17; 19:6
purify himself on third d.
Num 19:12; 31:19
sprinkle unclean on third d. 19:19
on third d. eleven bullocks. 29:20
to cities on third d. Josh 9:17
Benjamin the third d. Judg 20:30
to Rehoboam third d. 1 Ki 12:12
2 Chr 10:12
on the third d. go up. 2 Ki 20:5, 8
house finished on third d. Ezra 6:15
on third d. Esther put on. Esth 5:1
in third d. he will raise. Hos 6:2
and be raised again the third d.
Mat 16:21; 17:23; Luke 9:22
the third d. rise again. Mat 20:19
Mark 9:31; 10:34; Luke 18:33
24:7, 46
sepulchre be made sure till the third
d. Mat 27:64

the *third d.* I shall be. *Luke* 13:32
to-day is the *third d.* since. 24:21
on *third d.* there was a. *John* 2:1
the *third d.* we cast out. *Acts* 27:19
he rose again the *third d.* *1 Cor* 15:4

fourth **day**

and morning *fourth d.* *Gen* 1:19
fourth d. ten bullocks. *Num* 29:23
on the *fourth d.* they assembled. *2 Chr* 20:26
on *fourth d.* was silver. *Ezra* 8:33
Zechariah on *fourth d.* *Zech* 7:1

fifth **day**

and morning *fifth d.* *Gen* 1:23
fifth d. nine bullocks. *Num* 29:26
in the *fifth d.* of. *Ezek* 1:1, 2; 8:1
in the *fifth d.* one came. 33:21

sixth **day**

and morning *sixth d.* *Gen* 1:31
on *sixth d.* gather twice. *Ex* 16:5, 22
giveth you on the *sixth d.* bread. 29
on the *sixth d.* Eliasaph. *Num* 7:42
on *sixth d.* eight bullocks. 29:29

seventh **day**

seventh d. God ended his. *Gen* 2:2
God blessed *seventh d.* 3; *Ex* 20:11
leaven from first *d.* to *seventh d.* *Ex* 12:15
on *seventh d.* an holy convocation. 16; *Lev* 23:8; *Num* 28:25
in the *seventh d.* shall be. *Ex* 13:6
but the *seventh d.* is the sabbath. 16:26; 20:10; *Lev* 23:3; *Deut* 5:14
went some on *seventh d.* *Ex* 16:27
out of his place on *seventh d.* 29
seventh d. he called Moses. 24:16
seventh d. God rested. 31:17 *Heb* 4:4
seventh d. thou shalt rest. *Ex* 34:21
seventh d. there shall be holy *d.* 35:2
priest shall look on him *seventh d.* *Lev* 13:5, 6, 27, 32, 34, 51; 14:39
the *seventh d.* he shall shave. 14:9 *Num* 6:9
seventh d. he shall be clean. *Num* 19:12
on the *seventh d.* purify. 19; 31:19
wash your clothes on *seventh d.* 31:24
on *seventh d.* a solemn. *Deut* 16:8
seventh d. compass. *Josh* 6:4, 15
seventh d. they said to. *Judg* 14:15
on the *seventh d.* he told her. 17
seventh d. child died. *2 Sam* 12:18
in *seventh d.* battle was. *1 Ki* 20:29
seventh d. came Nebuzar-adan. *2 Ki* 25:8
seventh d. when Ahasuerus was. *Esth* 1:10
seventh d. word came. *Ezek* 30:20
and so do the *seventh d.* 45:20
spake of *seventh d.* on this wise, God did rest *seventh d.* *Heb* 4:4

eighth **day**

on the *eighth d.* thou. *Ex* 22:30
on the *eighth d.* Moses. *Lev* 9:1
on *eighth d.* flesh of fore-skin. 12:3
eighth d. take two he-lambs. 14:10
two turtles *on eighth d.* 23; 15:14 *Num* 6:10
the *eighth d.* it shall be. *Lev* 22:27
on the *eighth d.* shall be an. 23:36
on the *eighth d.* a sabbath. 39
eighth d. a solemn assembly. *Num* 29:35; *2 Chr* 7:9; *Neh* 8:18
on *eighth d.* priests. *Ezek* 43:27
eighth d. came to circumcise child. *Luke* 1:59; *Acts* 7:8; *Phil* 3:5

ninth **day**

your souls in *ninth d.* *Lev* 23:32
on *ninth d.* famine was. *2 Ki* 25:3 *Jer* 52:6
the *ninth d.* the city. *Jer* 39:2

tenth **day**

tenth d. of this month. *Ex* 12:3
tenth d. of month ye shall afflict. *Lev* 16:29; 23:27; *Num* 29:7
on *tenth d.* the trumpet of. *Lev* 25:9
of Jordan on *tenth d.* *Josh* 4:19
tenth d. Nebuchadnezzar came. *2 Ki* 25:1; *Jer* 52:4; *Ezek* 24:1
tenth d. burnt house of. *Jer* 52:12
on *tenth d.* elders came. *Ezek* 20:1
on *tenth d.* hand of Lord was. 40:1

eleventh **day**

eleventh d. Pagiel offered. *Num* 7:72

twelfth **day**

on *twelfth d.* Ahira. *Num* 7:78
departed on *twelfth d.* to. *Ezra* 8:31
on *twelfth d.* word came. *Ezek* 29:1

thirteenth **day**

scribes were called on *thirteenth d.* *Esth* 3:12
destroy all Jews on *thirteenth d.* 13; 8:12; 9:1
thirteenth d. of Adar they. 9:17
Jews assembled on *thirteenth d.* 18

fourteenth **day**

lamb till *fourteenth d.* *Ex* 12:6
on *fourteenth d.* ye shall eat. 18
fourteenth d. is the Lord's. *Lev* 23:5 *Num* 9:3, 5; 28:16; *Josh* 5:10 *2 Chr* 30:15; 35:1; *Ezra* 6:19 *Ezek* 45:21
on *fourteenth d.* at even. *Num* 9:11
gathered on *fourteenth d.* *Esth* 9:15
fourteenth d. of same rested. 17
this is *fourteenth d.* ye. *Acts* 27:33

fifteenth **day**

of Sinai on *fifteenth d.* *Ex* 16:1
on *fifteenth d.* is feast. *Lev* 23:6 *Num* 28:17
fifteenth d. of seventh month. *Lev* 23:34, 39; *Num* 29:12 *Ezek* 45:25
Ramases on *fifteenth d.* *Num* 33:3
feast on *fifteenth d.* *1 Ki* 12:32, 33
fifteenth d. rested. *Esth* 9:18, 21
on *fifteenth d.* word. *Ezek* 32:17

sixteenth **day**

in *sixteenth d.* they. *2 Chr* 29:17

seventeenth **day**

on *seventeenth d.* were. *Gen* 7:11
ark rested on *seventeenth d.* 8:4

twentieth **day**

on *twentieth d.* cloud. *Num* 10:11
on *twentieth d.* people. *Ezra* 10:9

twenty-first **day**

bread till *twenty-first d.* *Ex* 12:18
twenty-first d. came word. *Hag* 2:1

twenty-third **day**

twenty-third day Solomon sent. *2 Chr* 7:10
on *twenty-third d.* written. *Esth* 8:9

twenty-fourth **day**

twenty-fourth d. Israel. *Neh* 9:1
twenty-fourth d. I was by. *Dan* 10:4
in *twenty-fourth d.* Lord. *Hag* 1:15
in *twenty-fourth d.* word. 2:10, 20
consider from *twenty-fourth d.* 18
on *twenty-fourth d.* came word to Zechariah. *Zech* 1:7

twenty-fifth **day**

finished in *twenty-fifth d.* *Neh* 6:15
on *twenty-fifth d.* Evil-merodach. *Jer* 52:31

twenty-seventh **day**

on *twenty-seventh d.* was. *Gen* 8:14
on *twenty-seventh d.* Evil-merodach. *2 Ki* 25:27

good **day**

we come in a *good d.* *1 Sam* 25:8
gladness and a *good d.* *Esth* 8:17 9:19
from mourning into a *good d.* 9:22

great **day**

alas, that *d.* is *great.* *Jer* 30:7
for *great* shall be the *d.* *Hos* 1:11
d. of the Lord is *great.* *Joel* 2:11
before the *great* and terrible *d.* of the Lord come. 31; *Acts* 2:20
the *great d.* of the Lord. *Zeph* 1:14
before coming of *great d.* *Mal* 4:5
that *great d.* of the feast. *John* 7:37
the judgement of *great d.* *Jude* 6
great d. of his wrath is. *Rev* 6:17
gather to battle of the *great d.* 16:14

in the **day**

in the d. the Lord made. *Gen* 2:4
in the d. thou eatest thereof. 17
in the d. ye eat, your eyes. 3:5
in the d. drought consumed. 31:40
answered me *in the d.* of. 35:3
in the d. when I visit. *Ex* 32:34
in the d. of his trespass. *Lev* 6:5
offer *in the d.* when he is. 20; 7:36
in the d. he presented. 7:35
law of leper *in the d.* 14:2; *Num* 6:9
in the d. of first-fruits. *Num* 28:26
if her father disallow *in the d.* 30:5
husband held his peace *in the d.* 7
in the d. Lord delivered. *Josh* 10:12
as strong as I was *in the d.* 14:11
put hot bread *in the d.* *1 Sam* 21:6
in the d. the Lord had. *2 Sam* 22:1
cursed me *in the d.* that. *1 Ki* 2:8
in the day wherein they. *Neh* 13:15
in the d. the enemies. *Esth* 9:1
goods flow away *in the d.* *Job* 20:28
as *in the d.* of temptation. *Ps* 95:8 *Heb* 3:8
hide not thy face *in the d.* of trouble, *in the d.* when I call. *Ps* 102:2
people be willing *in the d.* 110:3
strike through kings *in the d.* 5
remember Edom *in the d.* of. 137:7
in the d. when I cried, thou. 138:3
not spare *in the d.* of. *Pr* 6:34
riches profit not *in the d.* of. 11:4
faint *in the d.* of adversity. 24:10
in the d. of prosperity be joyful, *in the d.* of adversity. *Eccl* 7:14
power *in the d.* of death. 8:8
in the d. when the keepers. 12:3
crowned him *in the d.* of his espousals, and *in the d.* *S of S* 3:11
in the d. when she shall be. 8:8
broken yoke as *in the d.* *Isa* 9:4
what will ye do *in the d.* of? 10:3
in the d. he came out of Egypt. 11:16 *Hos* 2:15
remove *in the d.* of his. *Isa* 13:13
in the d. shalt thou make thy plant grow, *in the d.* of grief. 17:11
in the d. of great slaughter. 30:25
in the d. that the Lord bindeth. 26
in the d. of your fast you. 58:3
my refuge *in the d.* of. *Jer* 16:19
my hope *in the d.* of evil. 17:17
back and not face *in the d.* 18:17
dead body be cast out *in the d.* 36:30
afflicted me *in the d.* of. *Lam* 1:12
not his footstool *in the d.* of. 2:1
thou drewest near *in the d.* 3:57
not deliver them *in the d.* *Ezek* 7:19
thy nativity *in the d.* thou. 16:4, 5
Sodom not mentioned *in the d.* 56
fall *in the d.* of thy ruin. 27:27
great pain came as *in the d.* of. 30:9
every man for life *in the d.* 32:10
in the d. he turneth from wickedness, not able to live *in the d.* 33:12
lest I set her as *in the d.* *Hos* 2:3
shalt thou fall *in the d.* 4:5
with a tempest *in the d.* *Amos* 1:14
darken earth *in the* clear *d.* 8:9
in the d. thou stoodest. *Ob* 11
nor rejoiced *in the d.* of their. 12
did remain *in the d.* of distress. 14
in the d. that I shall do. *Mal* 4:3
in the d. when Son is. *Luke* 17:30
if any walk *in the d.* he. *John* 11:9
in d. when God shall. *Rom* 2:16
walk honestly as *in the d.* 13:13
be blameless *in the d.* *1 Cor* 1:8
in the d. of salvation I. *2 Cor* 6:2
rejoice *in the d.* of Christ. *Phil* 2:16
in the d. when I took them. *Heb* 8:9
glorify God *in the d.* of. *1 Pet* 2:12

day *of judgement*

tolerable for Sodom in *d. of judg.* *Mat* 10:15; 11:24; *Mark* 6:11*
and Sidon in *d. of judg.* *Mat* 11:22
give account in *d. of judg.* 12:36
the unjust to *d. of judg.* *2 Pet* 2:9
reserved against *d. of judg.* 3:7
boldness in *d. of judg.* *1 John* 4:17

day *of the Lord*

d. of the L. shall be on. *Isa* 2:12
d. of the L. is at hand. 13:6 *Joel* 1:15; *Zeph* 1:7
d. of the L. cometh. *Isa* 13:9 *Joel* 2:1; *Zech* 14:1
d. of the L.'s vengeance. *Isa* 34:8
this is the *d. of the L.* *Jer* 46:10
in *d. of the L.*'s anger. *Lam* 2:22

in battle in d. of the L. Ezek 13:5
the d. of the L. is near. 30:3
Joel 3:14; Ob 15
desire the d. of the L. Amos 5:18
in d. of the L.'s sacrifice. Zeph 1:8
deliver them in d. of L.'s wrath. 18
before the d. of the L.'s anger. 2:2
hid in d. of the L.'s anger. 3
coming of the d. of the L. Mal 4:5
saved in d. of the L. 1 Cor 5:5
ours in the d. of the L. 2 Cor 1:14
d. of the L. cometh as a thief.
1 Thes 5:2; 2 Pet 3:10

one day

of you both in one d.? Gen 27:45
not kill it and her young both in one d. Lev 22:28
ye shall not eat one d. Num 11:19
in one d. they shall die. 1 Sam 2:34
I shall one d. perish by the. 27:1
provision for one d. was. 1 Ki 4:22
of Syrians 100,000 in one d. 20:29
in Judah 120,000 in one d. 2 Chr 28:6
is this work of one d. Ezra 10:13
kill in one d. Esth 3:13; 8:12
branch and rush in one d. Isa 9:14
his thorns and briers in one d. 10:17
two things shall come in one d. 47:9
earth bring forth in one d.? 66:8
iniquity of land in one d. Zech 3:9
it shall be one d. which. 14:7
abode with brethren one d. Acts 21:7
after one d. the south wind. 28:13
one esteemeth one d. Rom 14:5
fell in one d. 23,000. 1 Cor 10:8
one d. is with the Lord as. 2 Pet 3:8
her plagues come in one d. Rev 18:8

day joined with night

to divide d. from night. Gen 1:14
rule over d. and over the night. 18
cold and heat, d. and night. 8:22
whether stolen by d. or night. 31:39
east-wind d. and night. Ex 10:13
light to go by d. and night. 13:21
abide at door d. and night. Lev 8:35
that d. and all night. Num 11:32
shalt fear d. and night. Deut 28:66
thou shalt meditate therein d. and night. Josh 1:8; Ps 1:2
that d. and that night. 1 Sam 19:24
toward this house night and d.
1 Ki 8:29; 2 Chr 6:20
I pray before thee d. and night.
Neh 1:6
watch against them d. and night. 4:9
eat nor drink night or d. Esth 4:16
they change night into d. Job 17:12
till the d. and night come. 26:10*
d. and night thy hand was. Ps 32:4
tears my meat d. and night. 42:3
d. and night they go about it. 55:10
the d. is thine, the night also. 74:16
I have cried d. and night. 88:1
the night shineth as the d. 139:12
neither d. nor night seeth. Eccl 8:16
smoke by d., fire by night. Isa 4:5
Lord will keep it d. and night. 27:3
not be quenched d. nor night. 34:10
sickness from d. to night. 38:12
from d. to night wilt thou make. 13
not be shut d. nor night. 60:11
hold their peace d. nor night. 62:6
might weep d. and night. Jer 9:1
eyes run down tears d. and night.
14:17; Lam 2:18
other gods d. and night. Jer 16:13
should not be d. nor night. 33:20
not d. nor night. Zech 14:7
and rise night and d. Mark 4:27
d. and night he was in. 5:5
this d. even this night, before. 14:30
and prayers night and d. Luke 2:37
elect, which cry d. and night. 18:7
watched gates night and d. Acts 9:24
warn every one night and d. 20:31
serving God d. and night. 26:7
suffered shipwreck, a night and a d. I have been. 2 Cor 11:25
labouring d. and night. 1 Thes 2:9
night and d. praying. 3:10; 1 Tim 5:5
with labour night and d. 2 Thes 3:8
remembrance of thee in my prayers night and d. 2 Tim 1:3

rest not d. and night. Rev 4:8
and serve him d. and night. 7:15
d. shone not for a third part of it and the night. 8:12
accused them d. and night. 12:10
have no rest d. nor night. 14:11
tormented d. and night for ever.
20:10

sabbath-day

seventh d. is the sabbath. Ex 16:26
20:10
remember the sabbath-d. to. 20:8
Deut 5:12
Lord blessed the sabbath-d. Ex 20:11
doth any work on sabbath-d. 31:15
kindle no fire on sabbath-d. 35:3
sticks on sabbath-d. Num 15:32
offer on sabbath-d. two lambs. 28:9
to keep the sabbath-d. Deut 5:15
sell victuals on sabbath-d. Neh 10:31
burdens brought on sabbath-d. 13:15
and profane the sabbath-d. 17
no burden brought in sabbath-d. 19
keep gates to sanctify sabbath-d. 22
no burden on sabbath-d. Jer 17:21
nor carry burden on sabbath-d. 22
shall offer in sabbath-d. Ezek 46:4
the sabbath-d. through the corn.
Mat 12:1; Mark 2:23
Son of man is Lord of sabbath-d.
Mat 12:8
a pit on sabbath-d. 11; Luke 14:5
flight be not on sabbath-d. Mat 24:20
why do they on sabbath-d. that?
Mark 2:24
would heal on sabbath-d. 3:2
Luke 6:7
into synagogue on the sabbath-d.
Mark 6:2; Luke 4:16; Acts 13:14
from bond on sabbath-d. Luke 13:16
to eat bread on sabbath-d. 14:1
and rested the sabbath-d. 23:56
it is sabbath-d. it is not. John 5:10
done these things on sabbath-d. 16
ye on sabbath-d. circumcise. 7:22
it was the sabbath-d. when. 9:14
remain on cross on sabbath-d. 19:31
read every sabbath-d. Acts 13:27
15:21
next sabbath-d. came almost. 13:44

same day

the same d. were the. Gen 7:11
the self-same d. entered Noah. 13
in that same d. the Lord. 15:18
same d. I brought. Ex 12:17, 51
flesh eaten same d. Lev 7:15, 16
19:6; 22:30
no parched corn till same d. 23:14
do no work in that same d. 28
not be afflicted in that same d. 29
his head that same d. Num 6:11
to Moses that same d. Deut 32:48
same d. king hallowed. 1 Ki 8:64
a sign the same d. saying. 13:3
defiled my sanctuary, same d.
Ezek 23:38, 39
same d. king of Babylon set himself against Jerusalem same d. 24:2
same d. will I punish. Zeph 1:9
and come the same d. Zech 6:10
the same d. Lot went. Luke 17:29
same d. Pilate and Herod. 23:12
and on the same d. was. John 5:9
same d. at evening, Jesus. 20:19
unto the same d. that he. Acts 1:22
same d. were added to church. 2:41

since the day

since the d. they were. Ex 10:6
since the d. that God. Deut 4:32
since the d. that I brought them.
1 Sam 8:8; 1 Ki 8:16; 1 Chr 17:5
since the day that she left. 2 Ki 8:6
since the d. your fathers. Jer 7:25
as in you, since the d. Col 1:6
since the d. we heard it, do not. 9

that day

I will sever in that d. land. Ex 8:22
east-wind on land all that d. 10:13
that d. thou seest my face, thou. 28
shalt shew thy son in that d. 13:8
Lord saved Israel that d. 14:30
fell of the people that d. 32:28
that d. shall the priest. Lev 16:30

not keep passover that d. Num 9:6
held his peace in that d. 30:14
your children in that d. Deut 1:39
in any wise bury him that d. 21:23
hide my face in that d. 31:18
that d. they compassed. Josh 6:15
heardest in that d. how. 14:12
fasted that d. Judg 20:26; 1 Sam 7:6
cry out in that d. and Lord will not hear you in that d. 1 Sam 8:18
did eat with Samuel that d. 9:24
signs came to pass that d. 10:9
sent thunder and rain that d. 12:18
Lord saved Israel that d. 14:23
he answered him not that d. 37
of Lord on David from that d. 16:13
Saul eyed David from that d. 18:9
afraid of Lord that d. 2 Sam 6:9
abode in Jerusalem that d. 11:12
cut off Jeroboam that d. 1 Ki 14:14
thou shalt see on that d. 2 Chr 18:24
to that d. Israel had not. Neh 8:17
ready against that d. Esth 3:14; 8:13
let that d. be darkness. Job 3:4
in that very d. his. Ps 146:4
shall be exalted that d. Isa 2:11, 17
he remain at Nob that d. 10:32
Egyptians know Lord that d. 19:21
in that d. the Lord shall. 24:21
in that d. shall this song be. 26:1
in that d. shall the deaf hear. 29:18
they shall know in that d. 52:6
accomplished in that d. Jer 39:16
I will deliver thee in that d. 17
in that d. Israel shall be. Ezek 29:21
in that d. there shall be a. 38:19
know I am Lord from that d. 39:22
name of city from that d. 48:35
in that d. will I make. Hos 2:18
in that d. mountains shall. Joel 3:18
flee away naked in that d. Amos 2:16
songs be howlings in that d. 8:3
shall I not in that d. destroy? Ob 8
that d. is a day of wrath. Zeph 1:15
joined to Lord in that d. Zech 2:11
God shall save them in that d. 9:16
my covenant broken in that d. 11:11
the feeble at that d. shall be. 12:8
that d. shall be great mourning. 11
that d. shall there be a fountain. 13:1
his feet shall stand that d. 14:4
in that d. shall there be one Lord. 9
that d. when I make up. Mal 3:17
many will say in that d. Mat 7:22
of that d. knoweth no man. 24:36
Mark 13:32
that d. I drink it new. Mat 26:29
Mark 14:25
rejoice ye in that d. Luke 6:23
more tolerable in that d. 10:12
and so that d. come on you. 21:34
that d. was the preparation. 23:54
abode with him that d. John 1:39
from that d. they took. 11:53
at that d. ye shall know I. 14:20
in that d. ye shall ask me. 16:23
that d. ye shall ask in my name. 26
that d. should overtake. 1 Thes 5:4
testimony was believed in that d.
2 Thes 1:10
that d. shall not come, except. 2:3
to him against that d. 2 Tim 1:12
find mercy of Lord in that d. 18
Lord shall give me at that d. 4:8

this day

driven me out this d. Gen 4:14
send me good speed this d. 24:12
sell me this d. thy birthright. 25:31
swear this d. and he sware. 33
I remember my faults this d. 41:9
fed me all my life to this d. 48:15
this d. shall be for a. Ex 12:14
therefore observe this d. in. 17
remember this d. in which. 13:3, 4
this d. as the stars of. Deut 1:10
this d. will I begin to put dread. 2:25
alive every one this d. 4:4; 5:3
I command thee this d. 4:40; 6:6
7:11; 8:1, 11; 10:13; 30:2, 8
this d. that God doth talk. 5:24
it is at this d. 6:24; 8:18; Ezra 9:7
testify against you this d. Deut 8:19
I command you this d. 11:8, 13, 27
28; 13:18; 15:5; 19:9; 27:1, 4

set before you *this d.* *Deut* 11:32
all things ye do here *this d.* 12:8
avouched *this d.* the Lord. 26:17
this d. thou art become people. 27:9
you ears to hear to *this d.* 29:4
ye stand *this d.* all of you. 10
whose heart turneth away *this d.* 18
before thee *this d.* life. 30:15, 19
I commanded thee *this d.* to. 16
yet alive with you *this d.* 31:27
knoweth his sepulchre to *this d.* 34:6
this d. will I begin to. *Josh* 3:7
twelve stones there unto *this d.* 4:9
Lord shall trouble thee *this d.* 7:25
now I am *this d.* eighty-five. 14:10
I am as strong *this d.* as when. 11
to turn away *this d.* from. 22:16
not cleansed till *this d.* 17
save us not *this d.* 22
cleave to Lord as unto *this d.* 23:8
choose you *this d.* whom ye. 24:15
Luz is name unto *this d.* *Judg* 1:26
us only, we pray thee, *this d.* 10:15
Israel came up out of Egypt to *this d.* 19:30; *1 Sam* 8:8; *2 Sam* 7:6
2 Ki 21:15; *1 Chr* 17:5; *Jer* 7:25
are witnesses *this d.* *Ruth* 4:9, 10
have *this d.* rejected. *1 Sam* 10:19
man be put to death *this d.* 11:13
hath wrought with God *this d.* 14:45
rent kingdom from thee *this d.* 15:28
I defy armies of Israel *this d.* 17:10
thou shalt *this d.* be my. 18:21
it were sanctified *this d.* in. 21:5
lie in wait as at *this d.* 22:8, 13
Lord which sent thee *this d.* 25:32
who kept me *this d.* from. 33
precious in thine eyes *this d.* 26:21
thy life was much set by *this d.* 24
ordinance for Israel to *this d.* 30:25
I am *this d.* weak. *2 Sam* 3:39
sojourners unto *this d.* 4:3
his commands as at *this d.* *1 Ki* 8:61
this d. is a day of good. *2 Ki* 7:9
this d. do after former. 17:34, 41
there it is unto *this d.* *2 Chr* 5:9
come not against thee *this d.* 35:21
we are servants *this d.* *Neh* 9:36
thou art my Son, *this d.* have I.
Ps 2:7; *Acts* 13:33; *Heb* 1:5
this is the *d.* which the Lord. 118:24
they continue *this d.* 119:91
this d. have I paid vows. *Pr* 7:14
made known to thee *this d.* 22:19
praise thee, as I do *this d.* *Isa* 38:19
to-morrow shall be as *this d.* 56:12
a curse, as at *this d.* *Jer* 25:18
44:22
for to *this d.* they drink none. 35:14
days of Josiah even to this *d.* 36:2
not humbled even unto *this d.* 44:10
certainly *this* is the *d.* *Lam* 2:16
this is the *d.* whereof. *Ezek* 39:8
of faces, as at *this d.* *Dan* 9:7
consider from *this d.* *Hag* 2:15, 18
from *this d.* will I bless you. 19
this d. our daily bread. *Mat* 6:11
have remained to *this d.* 11:23
field of blood to *this d.* 27:8
suffered many things *this d.* 19
reported among Jews to *this d.* 28:15
to you is born *this d.* *Luke* 2:11
this d. is this scripture. 4:21
this d. is salvation come to. 19:9
hadst known, in *this* thy *d.* 42
cock not crow *this d.* before. 22:34
his sepulchre is with us to *this d.*
Acts 2:29
as ye are all *this d.* 22:3
before God till *this d.* 23:1
in question by you *this d.* 24:21
unto *this d.* witnessing to. 26:22
I would all that hear me *this d.* 29
not hear unto *this d.* *Rom* 11:8
till *this d.* remaineth. *2 Cor* 3:14, 15

to-day

heard I of it but *to-d.* *Gen* 21:26
pass through all thy flock *to-d.* 30:32
look ye so sadly *to-d.*? 40:7
are come so soon *to-d.*? *Ex* 2:18
salvation he will shew *to-d.* 14:13
bake that which you will *to-d.* 16:23*
consecrate yourselves *to-d.* 32:29
for *to-d.* the Lord will. *Lev* 9:4
command thee this *to-d.* *Deut* 15:15
he may establish thee *to-d.* 29:13
Lord smitten us *to-d.*? *1 Sam* 4:3
to-d. Lord wrought salvation. 11:13
the Lord had delivered thee *to-d.* into mine hand. 24:10; 26:23
glorious was king *to-d.*! *2 Sam* 6:20
to-d. shall house of Israel. 16:3
shew myself to him to-*d.* *1 Ki* 18:15
enquire at word of Lord *to-d.* 22:5
2 Chr 18:4
thou go to him *to-d.*? *2 Ki* 4:23
son that we may eat him *to-d.* 6:28
to-d. is my complaint. *Job* 23:2
to-d. if ye will hear his voice.
Ps 95:7; *Heb* 3:7, 15; 4:7
to-d. do I declare. *Zech* 9:12
grass of field, which *to-d.* is, and.
Mat 6:30; *Luke* 12:28
son, go work *to-d.* in. *Mat* 21:28
seen strange things *to-d.* *Luke* 5:26
behold, I do cures *to-d.* and. 13:32
I must walk *to-d.* and the day. 33
for *to-d.* I must abide at thy. 19:5
to-d. shalt thou be with me. 23:43
besides all this, *to-d.* is the. 24:21
while it is called *to-d.* *Heb* 3:13
thou art my Son, *to-d.* have I. 5:5
Christ, same yesterday, *to-d.* 13:8
ye that say, *to-d.* or. *Jas* 4:13

day ***to*** **day**

why art thou lean from *day to d.*?
2 Sam 13:4
shew from *day to d.* his salvation.
1 Chr 16:23; *Ps* 96:2
cast the lot from *day to d.* *Esth* 3:7
vexed righteous soul from *day to d.*
2 Pet 2:8

day ***of trouble***

is a *d. of trouble.* *2 Ki* 19:3
Isa 37:3
hear thee in *d. of trouble.* *Ps* 20:1
call upon me in *d. of trouble.* 50:15
my refuge in *d. of trouble.* 59:16
in the *d. of trouble* I sought. 77:2
in *d. of trouble* I will call on. 86:7
it is a *d. of trouble,* and. *Isa* 22:5
in the *d. of trouble* they. *Jer* 51:2
time is come, *d. of trouble.* *Ezek* 7:7
strong hold in *d. of trouble.* *Nah* 1:7
might rest in *d. of trouble.* *Hab* 3:16
that day is a *d. of trouble.* *Zeph* 1:15

days

after 150 *d.* waters were. *Gen* 8:3
d. of mourning for my father. 27:41
the *d.* of my pilgrimage are. 47:9
when the *d.* of his mourning. 50:4
after the number of *d.* ye. *Num* 14:34
ask now of the *d.* past. *Deut* 4:32
I stayed in the mount forty *d.* 10:10
camest not within *d.* *1 Sam* 13:11
and the *d.* were not expired. 18:26
been with me these *d.* 29:3
the *d.* David reigned. *1 Ki* 2:11
house built to Lord till those *d.* 3:2
d. that Jeroboam reigned. 14:20
war all their *d.* 30
between Asa and Baasha all their *d.*
15:16, 32
into the hand of Ben-hadad all their *d.* *2 Ki* 13:3
to those *d.* Israel did burn. 18:4
from *d.* of the judges. 23:22
David old and full of *d.* *1 Chr* 23:1
d. are on earth as. 29:15; *Job* 8:9
died full of *d.* riches. *1 Chr* 29:28
Jehoiada was old and full of *d.*
2 Chr 24:15
d. Esar-haddon brought us. *Ezra* 4:2
since *d.* of our fathers have we. 9:7
and mourned certain *d.* *Neh* 1:4
since *d.* of Jeshua, son of. 8:17
as the *d.* whereon the. *Esth* 9:22
they called these *d.* Purim. 26
these *d.* should be remembered. 28
let it not be joined to the *d.* *Job* 3:6
are not his *d.* also like the *d.*? 7:1
in length of *d.* understanding. 12:12
they spend their *d.* in wealth. 21:13
the *d.* of affliction have taken. 30:16
the *d.* of affliction prevented me. 27
I said, *d.* should speak, and. 32:7
he shall return to the *d.* of. *Job* 33:25
they shall spend their *d.* in. 36:11
Job died, old and full of *d.* 42:17
gavest him length of *d.* *Ps* 21:4
the Lord knoweth the *d.* of. 37:18
work thou didst in their *d.* 44:1
not live out half their *d.* 55:23
I have considered the *d.* of old. 77:5
d. did he consume in vanity. 78:33
his throne as *d.* of heaven. 89:29
the *d.* of his youth hast thou. 45
all our *d.* are passed away in. 90:9
d. of our years threescore and. 10
so teach us to number our *d.* 12
and be glad all our *d.* 14
give him rest from the *d.* 94:13
how many are the *d.* of thy? 119:84
I remember the *d.* of old. 143:5
length of *d.* shall they add. *Pr* 3:2
length of *d.* is in her right hand. 16
not much remember *d.* of. *Eccl* 5:20
the cause that the former *d.* 7:10
shall abide with him the *d.* 8:15
him remember *d.* of darkness. 11:8
while the evil *d.* come not. 12:1
antiquity is of ancient *d.* *Isa* 23:7
according to *d.* of one king. 15
the *d.* of thy mourning shall. 60:20
no more thence an infant of *d.* 65:20
as the *d.* of a tree are the *d.* 22
forgotten me *d.* without. *Jer* 2:32
with him that is full of *d.* 6:11
after those *d.* I will put my. 31:33
from the *d.* of Josiah even to. 36:2
our *d.* are fulfilled, our. *Lam* 4:18
to number of the *d.* *Ezek* 4:4; 5:9
d. are at hand, and effect. 12:23
not remembered *d.* of youth. 16:22
43
unto 2300 *d.* sanctuary. *Dan* 8:14*
abomination set up, 1290 *d.* 12:11
blessed that waiteth to 1335 *d.* 12
I will visit on her the *d.* *Hos* 2:13
d. of visitation, *d.* of recompence. 9:7
sinned from *d.* of Gibeah. 10:9
according to *d.* of thy coming. 7:15
since those *d.* were. *Hag* 2:16*
ye that hear in these *d.* *Zech* 8:9
before these *d.* there was no. 10
I will not be as in former *d.* 11
so have I thought in these *d.* 15
from *d.* of our fathers ye. *Mal* 3:7
from *d.* of John the. *Mat* 11:12
except those *d.* should be shortened.
24:22; *Mark* 13:20
as *d.* of Noe, so shall the coming.
Mat 24:37
after those *d.* Elisabeth. *Luke* 1:24
these be the *d.* of vengeance. 21:22
likewise foretold of these *d.*
Acts 3:24
for before these *d.* rose up. 5:36
in these *d.* came prophets. 11:27
the *d.* of unleavened bread. 12:3
sailed after *d.* of unleavened. 20:6
which before these *d.* madest. 21:38
ye observed *d.* and. *Gal* 4:10
because the *d.* are evil. *Eph* 5:16
neither beginning of *d.* nor. *Heb* 7:3
to remembrance former *d.* 10:32
would see good *d.* let. *1 Pet* 3:10
shall prophesy 1260 *d.* in. *Rev* 11:3
should feed her there 1260 *d.* 12:6

see **David, last, old, journey**

all the **days**

dust shalt thou eat *all the d.*
Gen 3:14
all the d. Adam lived 930 years. 5:5
all the d. of Seth 912 years. 8
all the d. of Enos 905 years. 11
all the d. of Cainan 910 years. 14
all the d. of Enoch 365 years. 23
all the d. of Methuselah 969. 27
all the d. of Noah 950 years. 9:29
all the d. wherein plague. *Lev* 13:46
all the d. of her issue. 15:25, 26
all the d. of his separation. *Num* 6:4
5, 6, 8
from thy heart *all the d.* *Deut* 4:9
to fear me *all the d.* 10; *1 Ki* 8:40
to possess it *all the d.* ye. 12:1
served Lord *all the d.* of Joshua and *all the d.* *Josh* 24:31; *Judg* 2:7

delivered them *all the d.* *Judg* 2:18
him to Lord *all d.* of. *1 Sam* 1:11
against Philistines *all* the *d.* 7:13
Samuel judged Israel *all the d.* 15
dwelt safely *all the d.* *1 Ki* 4:25
Rezon was adversary *all the d.* 11:25
oppressed Israel *all the d.* *2 Ki* 13:22
nor in *all the d.* of kings of. 23:22
all the d. of Jehoiada. *2 Chr* 24:2, 14
their purposes *all the d.* *Ezra* 4:5
all the d. of my appointed. *Job* 14:14
mercy shall follow me *all the d.*
Ps 23:6
in the house of Lord *all the d.* 27:4
all the d. of afflicted are. *Pr* 15:15
not evil, *all the d.* of her life. 31:12
in holiness *all the d.* *Luke* 1:75

see his **life**, *thy* **life**

days *come*

bring *d.* that have not *come.* *Isa* 7:17
behold the *d. come.* *Jer* 23:5, 7
30:3; 31:27, 31, 38
d. come that he will. *Amos* 4:2
d. shall *come* when bridegroom.
Mat 9:15; *Mark* 2:20; *Luke* 5:35
d. come when ye shall. *Luke* 17:22
d. come thy enemies shall. 19:43
d. come in which there shall. 21:6
d. come when I will make. *Heb* 8:8

few **days**

abide with us a *few d.* *Gen* 24:55
tarry a *few d.* till thy. 27:44
seemed to him but a *few d.* 29:20
few and evil are the *d.* of. 47:9
cloud was a *few d.* on. *Num* 9:20
born of woman is of *few d.* *Job* 14:1
let his *d.* be *few.* *Ps* 109:8
within *few d.* he shall be. *Dan* 11:20
for a *few d.* chastened. *Heb* 12:10

his **days**

his d. shall be 120 years. *Gen* 6:3
in *his d.* was earth divided. 10:25
1 Chr 1:19
her away all *his d.* *Deut* 22:19, 29
Asa was perfect all *his d.*
1 Ki 15:14; *2 Chr* 15:17
in *his d.* did Hiel build. *1 Ki* 16:34
not bring the evil in *his d.* 21:29
in *his d.* Edom revolted. *2 Ki* 8:20
2 Chr 21:8
Jehoash did right all *his d.* *2 Ki* 12:2
he departed not all *his d.* 15:18
quietness to Israel in *his d.*
1 Chr 22:9
all *his d.* departed. *2 Chr* 34:33
his d. are determined. *Job* 14:5
travaileth with pain all *his d.* 15:20
know him not see *his d.*? 24:1
in *his d.* shall righteous. *Ps* 72:7
as for man, *his d.* are as. 103:15
his d. are as a shadow. 144:4
covetousness prolong *his d.* *Pr* 28:16
all *his d.* are sorrows. *Eccl* 2:23
all *his d.* also he eateth in. 5:17
though *his d.* be prolonged. 8:12
wicked shall not prolong *his d.* 13
that hath not filled *his d.* *Isa* 65:20
leave them in midst of *his d.*
Jer 17:11
that shall not prosper in *his d.* 22:30
in *his d.* Judah shall be saved. 23:6

in the **days**

Reuben went *in the d.* *Gen* 30:14
in the d. of Shamgar, *in the d.*
Judg 5:6
quietness 40 years *in the d.* 8:28
old man *in the d.* of. *1 Sam* 17:12
famine *in the d.* of. *2 Sam* 21:1
put to death *in the d.* of harvest, *in the* first *d.* in beginning of. 9
silver was nothing accounted of *in the d.* of. *1 Ki* 10:21; *2 Chr* 9:20
remained *in the d.* of Asa.
1 Ki 22:46
in the d. of Hezekiah. *1 Chr* 4:41
enquired not at it *in the d.* of. 13:3
sought God *in the d.* of. *2 Chr* 26:5
came not on them *in the d.* 32:26
in the d. when God. *Job* 29:2
as I was *in the d.* of my youth. 4
in the d. of famine. *Ps* 37:19
should I fear *in the d.* of evil? 49:5
in the d. to come shall. *Eccl* 2:16
thy heart cheer thee *in the d.* 11:9
remember thy Creator *in the d.* 12:1
Micah prophesied *in the d.* *Jer* 26:18
Jerusalem remembered *in the d.*
Lam 1:7
my covenant *in the d.* *Ezek* 16:60
or hands be strong *in the d.* 22:14
in the d. of these kings. *Dan* 2:44
in the d. of thy father, light. 5:11
shall sing as *in the d.* *Hos* 2:15
deeply corrupted as *in the d.* 9:9
to dwell, as *in the d.* of the. 12:9
hath this been *in the d.*? *Joel* 1:2
Jesus was born *in the d.* *Mat* 2:1
if we had been *in the d.* of. 23:30
for as *in the d.* that were. 24:38
the house of God *in d.* *Mark* 2:26*
dealt with me *in the d.* *Luke* 1:25
many widows were *in the d.* 4:25
as *in the d.* of Noe. 17:26
in the d. of Lot. 28
rose up Judas *in the d.* *Acts* 5:37
came to pass *in the d.* of. 11:28
who *in the d.* of his flesh. *Heb* 5:7
waited *in the d.* of Noah. *1 Pet* 3:20
in the d. of the voice. *Rev* 10:7
that it rain not *in the d.* of. 11:6

in those **days**

giants in earth *in those d.* *Gen* 6:4
judge *in those d.* *Deut* 17:9; 19:17
priest that shall be *in those d.* 26:3
in those d. there was no king in.
Judg 17:6; 18:1; 21:25
ark of God there *in those d.* 20:27
word precious *in those d.* *1 Sam* 3:1
counselled *in those d.* *2 Sam* 16:23
in those d. was Hezekiah sick unto.
2 Ki 20:1; *2 Chr* 32:24; *Isa* 38:1
in those d. shall *Judah.* *Jer* 33:16
in those d. Israel shall go up. 50:4
in those d. iniquity shall be. 20
in those d. will I pour out my Spirit.
Joel 2:29; *Acts* 2:18
give suck *in those d.* *Mat* 24:19
Mark 13:17; *Luke* 21:23
Mary arose *in those d.* *Luke* 1:39
one of *those d.* as he taught. 20:1
made a calf *in those d.* *Acts* 7:41
not denied faith *in those d.* *Rev* 2:13
in those d. shall men seek. 9:6

latter **days**

to thy people in *latter d.* *Num* 24:14
latter d. if thou turn. *Deut* 4:30
evil befall you in *latter d.* 31:29
latter d. consider. *Jer* 23:20; 30:24
captivity of Moab in *latter d.* 48:47
captivity of Elam in *latter d.* 49:39
people in the *latter d.* *Ezek* 38:16
what shall be in *latter d.* *Dan* 2:28
befall thy people in *latter d.* 10:14
fear Lord in *latter d.* *Hos* 3:5

many **days**

mourned for son *many d.* *Gen* 37:34
brethren these *many d.* *Josh* 22:3
at Jerusalem *many d.* *1 Ki* 2:38
her house, did eat *many d.* 17:15
Ephraim mourned *many d.* *1 Chr* 7:22
what man loveth *many d.*? *Ps* 34:12
how *many* are the *d.* of? 119:84
d. of his years be *many.* *Eccl* 6:3
shalt find it after *many d.* 11:1
after *many d.* shall they be visited.
Isa 24:22; *Ezek* 38:8
many d. and years shall ye. *Isa* 32:10
continue *many d.* *Jer* 32:14; 35:7
remained there *many d.* 37:16
the vision is for *many d.* *Ezek* 12:27
Dan 8:26; 10:14
captivity spoil *many d.* *Dan* 11:33
abide for me *many d.* *Hos* 3:3
Israel shall abide *many d.* 4
not *many d.* after. *Luke* 15:13
continued not *many d.* *John* 2:12
Holy Ghost, not *many d.* *Acts* 1:5
he was seen *many d.* of. 13:31
this did she *many d.* 16:18
nor sun nor stars in *many d.* 27:20

my **days**

me my wife, for *my d.* *Gen* 29:21
and truth be in *my d.* *2 Ki* 20:19
my d. are swifter than a. *Job* 7:6
for *my d.* are vanity. 16
now *my d.* are swifter than. *Job* 9:25
are not *my d.* few? cease then. 10:20
my d. are extinct, graves are. 17:1
my d. are past, my purposes. 11
shall multiply *my d.* as sand. 29:18
and measure of *my d.* *Ps* 39:4
hast made *my d.* as an hand-breadth.
5
for *my d.* are consumed like. 102:3
my d. are like a shadow that. 11
he shortened *my d.* 23
take not away in midst of *my d.* 24
in cutting off of *my d.* *Isa* 38:10
peace and truth in *my d.* 39:8
my d. shall be consumed. *Jer* 20:18

*now-a-***days**

many servants *now-a-d.* break.
1 Sam 25:10

prolong, -ed, -eth, **days**

ye shall not *prolong* your *d.*
Deut 4:26; 30:18
thou mayest *prolong d.* 4:40; 22:7
that thy *d.* be *prolonged.* 5:16; 6:2
prolong your *d.* in land. 5:33; 11:9
end that he may *prolong d.* 17:20
ye shall *prolong* your *d.* in. 32:47
fear of Lord *prolongeth d.* *Pr* 10:27
covetousness, *prolong* his *d.* 28:16
sinner's *d.* be *prolonged.* *Eccl* 8:12
neither wicked *prolong* his *d.* 13
d. shall not be *prolonged.* *Isa* 13:22
seed, he shall *prolong* his *d.* 53:10
d. are *prolonged,* vision. *Ezek* 12:22

*sabbath-***days**

how on the *sabbath-d.* *Mat* 12:5
is it lawful to heal on *sabbath-d.*? 10
to do well on the *sabbath-d.* 12
do good on *sabbath-d.* *Mark* 3:4
Luke 6:9
taught them on *sabbath-d.* *Luke* 4:31
not lawful to do on *sabbath-d.* 6:2
three *sabbath-d.* reasoned. *Acts* 17:2
in respect of *sabbath-d.* *Col* 2:16

thy **days**

honour thy father and thy mother, that *thy d.* may be. *Ex* 20:12
the number of *thy d.* I will. 23:26
prosperity all *thy d.* *Deut* 23:6
thy d. may be lengthened. 25:15
and the length of thy *d.* 30:20
thy d. approach that thou. 31:14
and as *thy d.* so shall thy. 33:25
evil not found all *thy d.* *1 Sam* 25:28
and when *thy d.* be. *2 Sam* 7:12
any like thee all *thy d.* *1 Ki* 3:13
then I will lengthen *thy d.* 14
in *thy d.* I will not do it. 11:12
I will add to *thy d.* 15 years.
2 Ki 20:6; *Isa* 38:5
when *thy d.* be expired. *1 Chr* 17:11
thy d. as the days of man. *Job* 10:5
morning since *thy d.*? 38:12
the number of *thy d.* is great. 21
for by me *thy d.* shall be. *Pr* 9:11
thou hast caused *thy d.* *Ezek* 22:4

two **days**

sixth day bread of *two d.* *Ex* 16:29
whether it were *two d.* *Num* 9:22
not eat one, nor *two d.* nor. 11:19
David had abode *two d.* *2 Sam* 1:1
work of one day or *two d.* *Ezra* 10:13
would keep these *two d.* *Esth* 9:27
after *two d.* will he revive. *Hos* 6:2
after *two d.* is the feast. *Mat* 26:2
Mark 14:1
he abode there *two d.* *John* 4:40
now after *two d.* he departed. 43
he abode *two d.* still in the. 11:6

three **days**

branches are *three d.* *Gen* 40:12
within *three d.* shall Pharaoh. 13, 19
three baskets are *three d.* 18
into ward *three d.* 42:17
let us go *three d.* journey to sacrifice. *Ex* 3:18; 5:3; 8:27; 15:22
darkness in Egypt *three d.* 10:22
rose any from place for *three d.* 23
three d. ye shall pass. *Josh* 1:11
hide yourselves *three d.* 2:16, 22
abode with him *three d.* *Judg* 19:4
asses lost *three d.* ago. *1 Sam* 9:20
kept from us these *three d.* 21:5

had eaten **no bread** *three d.* *1 Sam* 30:12
master left me, because *three d.* 13
assembled men of Judah in *three d.* *2 Sam* 20:4
there be *three d.*' pestilence. 24:13 *1 Chr* 21:12
depart for *three d.* *1 Ki* 12:5 *2 Chr* 10:5
sought him *three d.* *2 Ki* 2:17
were *three d.* gathering. *2 Chr* 20:25
abode in tents *three d.* *Ezra* 8:15
would not come in *three d.* 10:8, 9
eat nor drink *three d.* *Esth* 4:16
Jonah was in belly of fish *three d.* *Jonah* 1:17; *Mat* 12:40
they continue with me now *three d.* *Mat* 15:32; *Mark* 8:2
build it in *three d.* *Mat* 26:61; 27:40 *Mark* 14:58; 15:29; *John* 2:19
after *three d.* I will rise again. *Mat* 27:63; *Mark* 8:31
after *three d.* found him. *Luke* 2:46
three d. without sight. *Acts* 9:9
Publius lodged us *three d.* 28:7
their dead bodies *three d.* *Rev* 11:9
after *three d.* and an half. 11

four **days**
lament *four d.* *Judg* 11:40
lain in grave *four d.* *John* 11:17
he hath been dead *four d.* 39
four d. ago I was fasting. *Acts* 10:30

five **days**
nor *five d.* nor ten *d.* *Num* 11:19
came to Troas *in five d.* *Acts* 20:6
after *five d.* Ananias the high. 24:1

six **days**
six d. ye shall gather it. *Ex* 16:26
six d. shalt thou labour and do all. 20:9; 23:12; 34:21; *Deut* 5:13
six d. Lord made heaven. *Ex* 20:11; 31:17
cloud covered Sinai *six d.* 24:16
six d. may work be done. 31:15 35:2; *Lev* 23:3
six d. shalt thou eat. *Deut* 16:8
thus shalt thou do *six d.* *Josh* 6:3
so they did *six d.* 14
gate shut *six* working *d.* *Ezek* 46:1
six d. in which men. *Luke* 13:14
Jesus *six d.* before. *John* 12:1

seven **days**
yet *seven d.* I will cause. *Gen* 7:4
stayed yet other *seven d.* 8:10, 12
Joseph mourned *seven d.* 50:10
seven d. eat unleavened. *Ex* 12:15 13:6, 7; 23:15; 34:18; *Lev* 23:6 *Num* 28:17; *Deut* 16:3
seven d. no leaven be found. *Ex* 12:19; *Deut* 16:4
seven d. with the dam. *Ex* 22:30 *Lev* 22:27
priest shall put them on *seven d.* *Ex* 29:30
seven d. shalt thou consecrate. 35 *Lev* 8:33
seven d. shalt make an atonement. *Ex* 29:37
shall be unclean *seven d.* *Lev* 12:2
then priest shall shut him up *seven d.* 13:5, 21, 26, 33, 50, 54
abroad out of tent *seven d.* 14:8
shall be put apart *seven d.* 15:19
offering by fire to Lord *seven d.* 23:8
keep a feast to the Lord *seven d.* 23:39, 40, 41; *Num* 29:12
be ashamed *seven d.*? *Num* 12:14
shall be unclean *seven d.* 19:14
of tabernacles *seven d.* *Deut* 16:13
it to me within *seven d.* *Judg* 14:12
wept before him *seven d.* 17
seven d. shalt thou tarry till I come. *1 Sam* 10:8
give us *seven d.*' respite. 11:3
he tarried *seven d.* according. 13:8
fasted *seven d.* 31:13; *1 Chr* 10:12
feast before Lord *seven d.* *1 Ki* 8:65
Zimri did reign *seven d.* in. 16:15
of altar *seven d.* *2 Chr* 7:9
kept the feast of unleavened bread *seven d.* 30:21; 35:17; *Ezra* 6:22
to keep other *seven d.* *2 Chr* 30:23
a feast *seven d.* *Esth* 1:5
as the light of *seven d.* *Isa* 30:26
astonished *seven d.* *Ezek* 3:15
seven d. shall they purge. 43:26
were compassed *seven d.* *Heb* 11:30

eight **days**
he that is *eight d.* old shall be circumcised. *Gen* 17:12; 21:4
sanctify house in *eight d.* *2 Chr* 29:17
when *eight d.* were accomplished. *Luke* 2:21
after *eight d.* Jesus. *John* 20:26

ten **days**
not eat *ten d.* nor. *Num* 11:19
ten d. after Lord smote. *1 Sam* 25:38
once in *ten d.* store of. *Neh* 5:18
after *ten d.* word of Lord. *Jer* 42:7
prove thy servants *ten d.* *Dan* 1:12
at the end of *ten d.* their. 15
tarried more than *ten d.* *Acts* 25:6
have tribulation *ten d.* *Rev* 2:10

eleven **days**
eleven d.' journey. *Deut* 1:2

twelve **days**
there are but *twelve d.* *Acts* 24:11

fourteen **days**
held a feast *fourteen d.* *1 Ki* 8:65

fifteen **days**
abode with Peter *fifteen d.* *Gal* 1:18

twenty **days**
not eat flesh *twenty d.* *Num* 11:19

twenty-one **days**
withstood me *twenty-one d.* *Dan* 10:13

thirty **days**
for Aaron *thirty d.* *Num* 20:29
wept for Moses *thirty d.* *Deut* 34:8
to king these *thirty d.* *Esth* 4:11
petition for *thirty d.* *Dan* 6:7, 12

thirty-three **days**
purifying *thirty-three d.* *Lev* 12:4

forty **days**
to rain on earth *forty d.* *Gen* 7:4
forty d. were fulfilled for. 50:3
in mount *forty d.* and *forty* nights. *Ex* 24:18; 34:28; *Deut* 9:9; 10:10
returned after *forty d.* *Num* 13:25 14:34
before the Lord *forty d.* *Deut* 9:25
strength of meat *forty d.* *1 Ki* 19:8
iniquity of Judah *forty d.* *Ezek* 4:6
forty d. and Nineveh be. *Jonah* 3:4
fasted *forty d.* and forty. *Mat* 4:2
Jesus was *forty d.* in the wilderness. *Mark* 1:13; *Luke* 4:2
seen of them *forty d.* *Acts* 1:3

fifty-two **days**
wall was finished in *fifty-two d.* *Neh* 6:15

your **days**
that *your d.* may be. *Deut* 11:21
to cease in *your d.* mirth. *Jer* 16:9
all *your d.* ye shall dwell in. 35:7
your d. will I say word. *Ezek* 12:25
hath this been in *your d.*? *Joel* 1:2
work a work in *your d.* *Hab* 1:5 *Acts* 13:41

daysman
neither is there any *d.* *Job* 9:33

dayspring
caused the *d.* to know. *Job* 38:12
d. from on high visited. *Luke* 1:78

daystar
and the *d.* arise in. *2 Pet* 1:19

daytime
meet with darkness in *d.* *Job* 5:14
through houses marked in *d.* 24:16
I cry in the *d.* but thou. *Ps* 22:2
command loving-kindness in *d.* 42:8
in *d.* also he led them. 78:14
tabernacle for shadow in *d.* *Isa* 4:6
I stand on watch-tower in *d.* 21:8
in *d.* he was teaching in. *Luke* 21:37
it pleasure to riot in *d.* *2 Pet* 2:13

deacon, -s
saints with bishops and *d.* *Phil* 1:1
the *d.* must be grave. *1 Tim* 3:8
let them use the office of a *d.* 10, 13
d. be the husband of one wife. 12

dead
[1] *Deprived of natural life,* Ruth 1:8; Job 1:19. [2] *Without warmth or fervour, or energy in the spiritual life,* Eph 2:1; 1 Tim 5:6. [3] *Entirely without life,* Isa 8:19; Mat 22:32.

thou art but a *d.* man. *Gen* 20:3
Abraham stood up from his *d.* 23:3
the men are *d.* which. *Ex* 4:19
not one of Israelites' cattle *d.* 9:7
house where was not one *d.* 12:30
Egyptians said, we be all *d.* men. 33
Israel saw Egyptians *d.* on. 14:30
the *d.* beast shall be his. 21:34, 36
and the *d.* ox also they shall. 35
thing unclean by the *d.* *Lev* 22:4
whosoever is defiled by *d.* *Num* 5:2
let her not be as one *d.* 12:12
he stood between the *d.* and. 16:48
wife of the *d.* not marry. *Deut* 25:5
lord was fallen down *d.* *Judg* 3:25
he came in, Sisera lay *d.* 4:22
the *d.* which Samson slew. 16:30
as ye have dealt with *d.* *Ruth* 1:8
to raise up name of the *d.* 4:5
and Phinehas are *d.* *1 Sam* 4:17
father-in-law and husband were *d.* 19
thou pursue? after a *d.* dog. 24:14
Saul and his sons were *d.* 31:7 *1 Chr* 10:7
on such a *d.* dog as I. *2 Sam* 9:8
all the king's sons are *d.* 13:33
why should this *d.* dog curse. 16:9
my father's house were but *d.* 19:28
the living is my son, and the *d.* is thy son. *1 Ki* 3:22, 23
when I am *d.* bury me in. 13:31
Naboth is not alive but *d.* 21:15
on young men, they are *d.* *Job* 1:19
d. things are formed from. 26:5
forgotten as a *d.* man. *Ps* 31:12
and horse are cast into *d.* 76:6
free among the *d.* like slain. 88:5
wilt thou shew wonders to *d.*? 10
ate the sacrifices of the *d.* 106:28
the *d.* praise not the Lord. 115:17
those that have been long *d.* 143:3
and her paths unto the *d.* *Pr* 2:18
he knoweth not that the *d.* 9:18
remain in congregation of *d.* 21:16
the *d.* which are already *d.* *Eccl* 4:2
and after that they go to the *d.* 9:3
living dog is better than *d.* lion. 4
the *d.* know not any thing. 5
d. flies cause the ointment. 10:1
for the living to the *d.* *Isa* 8:19
it stirreth up the *d.* for thee. 14:9
not slain with sword, nor *d.* 22:2
they are *d.*, they shall not live. 26:14
d. men shall live, with my *d.* 19
desolate places as *d.* men. 59:10
they that be *d.* of old. *Lam* 3:6
come at no *d.* person. *Ezek* 44:25
are *d.* that sought the. *Mat* 2:20
and let the *d.* bury their *d.* 8:22
give place, for the maid is not *d.* 9:24; *Mark* 5:39; *Luke* 8:52
heal sick, raise the *d.* *Mat* 10:8
deaf hear, *d.* are raised. 11:5 *Luke* 7:22
touching resurrection of the *d.* *Mat* 22:31; *Mark* 12:26
not the God of the *d.* but. *Mat* 22:32 *Mark* 12:27; *Luke* 20:38
full of *d.* men's bones. *Mat* 23:27
the keepers became as *d.* 28:4
one *d.* many said, he is *d.* *Mark* 9:26
if he were already *d.* 15:44
a *d.* man carried out. *Luke* 7:12
departed, leaving him half *d.* 10:30
why seek ye living among *d.*? 24:5
the Father raiseth up *d.* *John* 5:21
when the *d.* shall hear voice of. 25
did eat manna, and are *d.* 6:49, 58
believeth, though he were *d.* 11:25
patriarch David is both *d.* *Acts* 2:29
came in and found her *d.* 5:10
ordained of God to be the Judge of quick and *d.* 10:42; *2 Tim* 4:1
supposing he had been *d.* *Acts* 14:19
down, and was taken up *d.* 20:9
that God should raise the *d.* 26:8

swollen, or fallen down d. Acts 28:6
God who quickeneth d. Rom 4:17
considered not his body now d. 19
thro' offence of one many be d. 5:15
we that are d. to sin, live. 6:2
if we be d. with Christ. 8
reckon ye yourselves to be d. to. 11
if husband be d. 7:2, 3; 1 Cor 7:39
are become d. to the law. Rom 7:4
Gal 2:19
lord both of d. and living. Rom 14:9
if so be that d. rise not. 1 Cor 15:15
how are the d. raised? 35
and the d. shall be raised. 52
trust in God who raiseth d. 2 Cor 1:9
one died for all, then all d. 5:14
were d. in trespasses and sins.
Eph 2:1, 5; Col 2:13
if ye be d. with Christ. Col 2:20
2 Tim 2:11
ye are d. and your life hid. Col 3:3
and the d. in Christ. 1 Thes 4:16
repentance from d. works. Heb 6:1
conscience from d. works. 9:14
is of force after men are d. 17
and by it he being d. yet. 11:4
of one, and him as good as d. 12
women received their d. raised. 35
we being d. to sin should. 1 Pet 2:24
ready to judge the quick and d. 4:5
gospel preached to them that are d. 6
twice d. plucked up by the. Jude 12
first-begotten of the d. Rev 1:5
saw him, fell at his feet as d. 17
name that thou livest, and art d. 3:1
blessed are the d. who die. 14:13
sea became as blood of a d. 16:3
rest of the d. lived not again. 20:5
saw the d. stand before God. 12
sea gave up d. which were in it. 13

see **body, bury, carcase, resurrection**

***for the* dead**

not make cuttings for d. Lev 19:28
none be defiled for the d. 21:1
not make baldness for d. Deut 14:1
not given ought thereof for d. 26:14
that mourned for the d. 2 Sam 14:2
to comfort them for the d. Jer 16:7
weep ye not for the d. nor. 22:10
no mourning for the d. Ezek 24:17
baptized for the d. why baptized for the d.? 1 Cor 15:29

***from the* dead**

he is risen from the d. Mat 14:2
rising from the d. mean? Mark 9:10
if one went from the d. Luke 16:30
though one rose from the d. 31
rise from the d. third day. 24:46
John 20:9
after he rose from d. Acts 10:41
first that should rise from d. 26:23
that are alive from the d. Rom 6:13
bring Christ again from the d. 10:7
be, but life from the d.? 11:15
be preached that rose from the d.
1 Cor 15:12
arise from the d. Christ. Eph 5:14
first-born from the d. Col 1:18
able to raise him from d. Heb 11:19
brought again from the d. 13:20

see **raised, risen**

***is* dead**

his brother is d. Gen 42:38; 44:20
name of brother that is d. Deut 25:6
Moses my servant is d. Josh 1:2
they forced, that she is d. Judg 20:5
Saul is d. 2 Sam 2:7; 4:10
Uriah is d. 11:21, 24
the child is d. 12:18, 19
Amnon only is d. 13:32
a widow, my husband is d. 14:5
2 Ki 4:1
because king's son is d. 2 Sam 18:20
Absalom is d. 19:10
Naboth is d. 1 Ki 21:14
priests not eat that is d. Ezek 44:31
my daughter is d. Mat 9:18
Mark 5:35; Luke 8:49
that many said, he is d. Mark 9:26
Abraham is d. and. John 8:52, 53
Lazarus is d. 11:14
he that is d. is freed. Rom 6:7
if Christ be in you, body is d. 8:10
law, Christ is d. in vain. Gal 2:21
liveth in pleasure, is d. 1 Tim 5:6
hath not works is d. Jas 2:17, 20*
body without spirit is d. so. 26

***was* dead**

when the judge was d. Judg 2:19
men saw Abimelech was d. 9:55
their champion was d. 1 Sam 17:51
David heard Nabal was d. 25:39
saw Saul was d. 31:5; 1 Chr 10:5
son heard Abner was d. 2 Sam 4:1
Bath-sheba heard husband was d.
11:26
David perceived child was d. 12:19
Amnon, seeing he was d. 13:39
my child suck, it was d. 1 Ki 3:21
Hadad heard that Joab was d. 11:21
Jezebel heard Naboth was d. 21:15
when Ahab was d. Moab. 2 Ki 3:5
child was d. and laid on his. 4:32
Athaliah saw her son was d. 11:1
2 Chr 22:10
but when Herod was d. Mat 2:19
he that was d. sat up. Luke 7:15
to scorn, knowing she was d. 8:53
my son was d. and is alive. 15:24
for this thy brother was d. and is. 32
sister of him that was d. John 11:39
and he that was d. came forth. 44
saw that Jesus was d. brake. 19:33
Jesus which was d. Acts 25:19
without the law sin was d. Rom 7:8
he that liveth, and was d. Rev 1:18

deadly

was a d. destruction. 1 Sam 5:11
deliver me from d. enemies. Ps 17:9
groanings of a d. wounded man.
Ezek 30:24
drink d. thing, it shall. Mark 16:18
unruly evil, full of d. Jas 3:8
d. wound was healed. Rev 13:3, 12

deadness

neither yet the d. of. Rom 4:19

deaf

or who maketh the d.? Ex 4:11
shalt not curse the d. Lev 19:14
but I as a d. man heard. Ps 38:13
they are like the d. adder. 58:4
in that day shall d. hear. Isa 29:18
the ears of the d. shall be. 35:5
hear, ye d. look, ye blind. 42:18
who is d. as my messenger? 19
bring forth blind, and the d. 43:8
their ears shall be d. Mi 7:16
the d. hear. Mat 11:5; Luke 7:22
brought one that was d. Mark 7:32
he maketh the d. to hear. 37
thou dumb and d. spirit. 9:25

deal, *verb*

now will we d. worse. Gen 19:9
now if you will d. truly. 24:49
return, and I will d. well with. 32:9
should he d. with our sister? 34:31
come on, let us d. wisely. Ex 1:10
d. with her after the manner. 21:9
in like manner d. with thy. 23:11
not steal, nor d. falsely. Lev 19:11
if thou d. thus with me. Num 11:15
thus shall ye d. with. Deut 7:5
as thou didst d. with David my father, even so d. 2 Chr 2:3
lest I d. with you after. Job 42:8
I said to fools, d. not. Ps 75:4
d. subtilly with his. 105:25
d. bountifully with. 119:17; 142:7
d. with thy servant. 119:124
but they that d. truly. Pr 12:22
he will d. unjustly. Isa 26:10
my servant shall d. prudently. 52:13
is it not to d. thy bread to? 58:7
d. thus with them in. Jer 18:23
if so be that the Lord d. with. 21:2
will I also d. in fury. Ezek 8:18
I will d. with thee as thou. 16:59
hands be strong in days I d. 22:14
and they shall d. furiously. 23:25
he shall surely d. with him. 31:11
and as thou seest d. Dan 1:13
and shall d. against them and. 11:7

see **treacherously**

deal

a tenth d. of flour. Ex 29:40*
Lev 14:21*; Num 15:4*; 29:4*
a several tenth d. Num 28:13*
29:15*
so much more a great d. Mark 7:36
cried a great d. Son of David. 10:48

dealer

the treacherous d. dealeth. Isa 21:2

dealers

treacherous d. have dealt. Isa 24:16

dealest

wherefore d. thou thus? Ex 5:15
thee that spoilest and d. Isa 33:1

dealeth

thus and thus d. Micah. Judg 18:4
told me he d. subtilly. 1 Sam 23:22
he becometh poor that d. Pr 10:4
every prudent man d. 13:16*
that is soon angry d. foolishly. 14:17
scorner is his name, who d. 21:24*
treacherous dealer d. Isa 21:2
from the prophet even to the priest every one d. Jer 6:13; 8:10
God d. with you as sons. Heb 12:7

dealing, -s

I hear of your evil d. 1 Sam 2:23
his violent d. shall come. Ps 7:16
the Jews have no d. with. John 4:9

deals

(*Revised Version*, parts of an ephah)
take three tenth d. of fine flour.
Lev 14:10; Num 15:9
two tenth d. for a meat. Lev 23:13
Num 28:9
two wave-loaves of two tenth d.
Lev 23:17
two tenth d. in one cake. 24:5
for a ram two tenth d. of flour.
Num 15:6; 28:20, 28; 29:3, 9, 14
three tenth d. 28:20, 28; 29:3, 9, 14

dealt

when Sarai d. hardly. Gen 16:6
God hath d. graciously with. 33:11
wherefore d. ye so ill with me? 43:6
therefore God d. well. Ex 1:20
wherefore hast thou d. thus? 14:11
wherein they d. proudly. 18:11
seeing he hath d. deceitfully. 21:8
if ye have d. well with Jerubbaal.
Judg 9:16
if ye have d. truly, rejoice in. 19
have d. with the dead. Ruth 1:8
the Almighty hath d. bitterly. 20
hast d. well with me. 1 Sam 24:18
Lord shall have d. well. 25:31
d. among the people. 2 Sam 6:19
1 Chr 16:3
they d. faithfully. 2 Ki 12:15; 22:7
Manasseh d. with familiar. 21:6
2 Chr 33:6
so d. David with cities. 1 Chr 20:3
amiss, and d. wickedly. 2 Chr 6:37
Rehoboam d. wisely. 11:23
have d. very corruptly. Neh 1:7
knewest they d. proudly. 9:10; 16:29
have d. deceitfully. Job 6:15
Lord hath d. bountifully. Ps 13:6
116:7
nor have we d. falsely in. 44:17
and d. unfaithfully like. 78:57
he hath not d. with us. 103:10
hast d. well with servant. 119:65
they d. perversely with me. 78*
he hath not d. so with. 147:20
dealers have d. very. Isa 24:16
Jer 3:20; 5:11; 12:6; Lam 1:2
they d. by oppression. Ezek 22:7
Edom hath d. against Judah. 25:12
because Philistines have d. 15
have d. treacherously. Hos 5:7
d. treacherously against me. 6:7
of your God that hath d. Joel 2:26
Lord thought, so hath he d. Zech 1:6
Judah hath d. treacherously and.
Mal 2:11
thou hast d. treacherously. 14
thus hath Lord d. with. Luke 1:25*
hast thou thus d. with us? 2:48
the same d. subtilly with. Acts 7:19
multitude of Jews have d. 25:24*
according as God hath d. Rom 12:3

dear

Ephraim my *d.* son, is he ? *Jer* 31:20
servant, who was *d.* to. *Luke* 7:2
neither count I my life *d. Acts* 20:24
followers of God as *d.* *Eph* 5:1*
of Epaphras our *d.* fellow. *Col* 1:7*
into kingdom of his *d.* Son. 13*
because ye were *d.* unto. *1 Thes* 2:8*

dearly *beloved*

(*In the Revised Versions the word* dearly *is omitted in all but the first of these references*)

given *d. beloved* of my soul to. *Jer* 12:7
d. beloved, avenge not. *Rom* 12:19
my *d. beloved.* *1 Cor* 10:14
Phil 4:1; *2 Tim* 1:2
d. beloved. *2 Cor* 7:1; 12:19
1 Pet 2:11
Philemon our *d. beloved. Philem* 1

dearth

d. began to come, *d.* *Gen* 41:54*
there was a *d.* in land. *2 Ki* 4:38
if there be a *d.* in land. *2 Chr* 6:28*
buy corn because of the *d. Neh* 5:3
to Jeremiah concerning *d. Jer* 14:1*
there came a *d.* over. *Acts* 7:11*
there should be a great *d.* 11:28*

death

[1] *Total and final cessation of all vital functions,* Gen 25:11. [2] *Cessation of spiritual life, spoken of as spiritual death,* Rom 7:24; 1 John 3:14. [3] *Used figuratively for what would cause death,* 2 Ki 4:40. [4] *Gates of death, the brink of the grave,* Ps 9:13.

let me not see the *d.* of. *Gen* 21:16
comforted after mother's *d.* 24:67
after the *d.* of Abraham, God. 25:11
and bless thee before my *d.* 27:7
bless thee before his *d.* 10
take from me this *d.* only. *Ex* 10:17
men die common *d.* of. *Num* 16:29
let me die *d.* of righteous. 23:10
slayer shall abide in it unto *d.* of. 35:25, 28, 32; *Josh* 20:6
life of murderer guilty *d. Num* 35:31
set before you life and good, *d.* and evil. *Deut* 30:15; *Jer* 21:8
rebel after my *d.*! *Deut* 31:27
I know after my *d.* ye will. 29
blessed Israel before his *d.* 33:1
jeoparded lives to the *d. Judg* 5:18
that his soul was vexed unto *d.* 16:16
dead which he slew at his *d.* 30
if ought but *d.* part thee. *Ruth* 1:17
all thou hast done since *d.* of. 2:11
about time of her *d.* *1 Sam* 4:20
surely the bitterness of *d.* 15:32
but a step between me and *d.* 20:3
I have occasioned *d.* of thy. 22:22
in their *d.* were not. *2 Sam* 1:23
in *d.* or life, there will thy. 15:21
when waves of *d.* compassed me. 22:5; *Ps* 18:4; 116:3
the snares of *d.* prevented me. *2 Sam* 22:6; *Ps* 18:5
Egypt till *d.* of Solomon. *1 Ki* 11:40
shall not be any more *d.* *2 Ki* 2:21
man of God, there is *d.* in pot. 4:40
so David prepared before his *d.* *1 Chr* 22:5
counsellors after *d.* of. *2 Chr* 22:4
did Hezekiah honour at his *d.* 32:33
whether it be unto *d.* or to. *Ezra* 7:26
which long for *d.* but it. *Job* 3:21
so that my soul chooseth *d.* 7:15
first-born of *d.* shall devour. 18:13
remain of him be buried in *d.* 27:15
destruction and *d.* say, we. 28:22
thou wilt bring me to *d.* 30:23
in *d.* is no remembrance. *Ps* 6:5
prepared instruments of *d.* 7:13
lest I sleep the sleep of *d.* 13:3
brought me into dust of *d.* 22:15
be our guide, even unto *d.* 48:14
grave, *d.* shall feed on them. 49:14
terrors of *d.* are fallen upon me. 55:4
let *d.* seize on them, and let. 15
there are no bands in their *d.* 73:4
man liveth, shall not see *d.*? 89:48
loose those appointed to *d. Ps* 102:20
precious in sight of Lord is *d.* 116:15
not given me over unto *d.* 118:18
her house inclineth to *d.* *Pr* 2:18
her feet go down to *d.*; her steps. 5:5
going down to chambers of *d.* 7:27
all they that hate me love *d.* 8:36
evil, pursueth it to his own *d.* 11:19
ways thereof there is no *d.* 12:28
to depart from the snares of *d.* 13:14; 14:27
righteous hath hope in his *d.* 14:32
as messengers of *d.* 16:14
d. and life are in the power. 18:21
of them that seek *d.* 21:6
them that are drawn to *d.* 24:11
who casteth arrows and *d.* 26:18
I find more bitter than *d. Eccl* 7:26
for love is strong as *d.* *S of S* 8:6
he will swallow up *d.* in. *Isa* 25:8
for *d.* cannot celebrate thee. 38:18
and with the rich in his *d.* 53:9
he poured out his soul unto *d.* 12
d. shall be chosen rather. *Jer* 8:3
d. is come up to our windows. 9:21
such as are for *d.* to *d.* 15:2; 43:11
at home there is as *d.* *Lam* 1:20
no pleasure in the *d.* of the wicked. *Ezek* 18:32; 33:11
are all delivered unto *d.* 31:14
O *d.* I will be thy plagues. *Hos* 13:14
to be angry even unto *d. Jonah* 4:9
who is as *d.* and cannot. *Hab* 2:5
there till *d.* of Herod. *Mat* 2:15
brother deliver brother to *d.* 10:21
Mark 13:12
curseth father or mother, let him die the *d.* *Mat* 15:4; *Mark* 7:10
shall not taste of *d.* till. *Mat* 16:28
Mark 9:1; *Luke* 9:27
shall condemn him to *d. Mat* 20:18
Mark 10:33
soul is sorrowful to *d.* *Mat* 26:38
Mark 14:34
said, he is guilty of *d.* *Mat* 26:66
Mark 14:64
lieth at the point of *d.* *Mark* 5:23
should not see *d.* before. *Luke* 2:26
with thee both to prison and *d.* 22:33
I have found no cause of *d.* 23:22
heal his son, at point of *d. John* 4:47
if a man keep my saying, he shall never see *d.* 8:51, 52
this sickness is not unto *d.* 11:4
howbeit, Jesus spake of his *d.* 13
signifying what *d.* 12:33; 18:32
by what *d.* he should glorify. 21:19
having loosed pains of *d. Acts* 2:24
Saul consenting to his *d.* 8:1; 22:20
found no cause of *d.* in him. 13:28
persecuted this way unto *d.* 22:4
was no cause of *d.* in me. 28:18
we were reconciled to God by the *d.* of his Son. *Rom* 5:10; *Col* 1:22
and *d.* by sin, and so *d.* *Rom* 5:12
d. reigned from Adam to. 14, 17
as sin hath reigned to *d.* even. 21
so many of us as were baptized into Christ, baptized into his *d.*? 6:3
buried with him by baptism into *d.* 4
planted in likeness of his *d.* 5
dieth no more, *d.* hath no more. 9
servants, whether of sin unto *d.* 16
for end of those things is *d.* 21
for the wages of sin is *d.* but. 23
sins did work to bring *d.* 7:5
commandment of life to be to *d.* 10
which is good made *d.* to me ? 13
me from the body of this *d.*? 24
free from law of sin and *d.* 8:2
to be carnally minded is *d.* but. 6
nor *d.* nor life shall separate us. 38
world, life, or *d.* all are. *1 Cor* 3:22
as it were appointed to *d.* 4:9
ye do shew the Lord's *d.* 11:26
for since by man came *d.* by. 15:21
last enemy be destroyed is *d.* 26
d. is swallowed up in victory. 54
O *d.*, where is thy sting ? 55
sting of *d.* is sin. 56
we had the sentence of *d.* *2 Cor* 1:9
delivered us from so great a *d.* 10
we are the savour of *d.* unto *d.* 2:16
if the ministration of *d.* was. 3:7
always delivered to *d.* *2 Cor* 4:11
so then *d.* worketh in us. 12
sorrow of world worketh *d.* 7:10
whether by life or by *d.* *Phil* 1:20
obedient unto *d.* even *d.* of. 2:8
Epaphroditus was nigh to *d.* 27
work of Christ was nigh to *d.* 30
made conformable unto his *d.* 3:10
who hath abolished *d.* *2 Tim* 1:10
Jesus, for suffering of *d.* crowned, that he should taste *d.* *Heb* 2:9
through *d.* might destroy him that had power of *d.* 14
them who through fear of *d.* 15
to continue, by reason of *d.* 7:23
that by means of *d.* for the. 9:15
there must of necessity be *d.* 16
that he should not see *d.* 11:5
finished bringeth forth *d.* *Jas* 1:15
his brother abideth in *d. 1 John* 3:14
there is a sin unto *d.* 5:16
a sin not unto *d.* 17
keys of hell and of *d.* *Rev* 1:18
be faithful unto *d.* I will give. 2:10
shall not be hurt of second *d.* 11
name that sat on him was *d.* 6:8
men shall seek *d.* and *d.* shall. 9:6
loved not their lives to *d.* 12:11
as it were wounded to *d.* 13:3
plagues come in one day, *d.* 18:8
on such the second *d.* hath no. 20:6
and *d.* and hell delivered up. 13
d. and hell cast into lake, this is the second *d.* 14
and there shall be no more *d.* 21:4

see **day**

from **death**

deliver our lives *from d.* *Josh* 2:13
shall redeem thee *from d.* *Job* 5:20
deliver their soul from *d.* *Ps* 33:19
delivered my soul *from d.* 56:13
116:8
to God belong issues *from d.* 68:20
spared not their soul *from d.* 78:50
delivereth *from d.* *Pr* 10:2; 11:4
will redeem thee *from d.* *Hos* 13:14
is passed *from d.* to life. *John* 5:24
1 John 3:14
able to save him *from d.* *Heb* 5:7
shall save a soul *from d.* *Jas* 5:20

gates of **death**

have *gates of d.* been ? *Job* 38:17
me up from *gates of d.*? *Ps* 9:13
draw near to the *gates of d.* 107:18

put to **death**

man, shall be *put to d.* *Gen* 26:11
his owner also be *put to d. Ex* 21:29
on sabbath, shall be *put to d.* 35:2
shall not be *put to d.* *Lev* 19:20
both of them shall be *put to d.* 20:11
killeth *put to d.* 24:21; *Num* 35:30
stranger that cometh nigh be *put to d.* *Num* 1:51; 3:10, 38; 18:7
dreamer be *put to d.* *Deut* 13:5
first upon him to *put to d.* 9; 17:7
of one witness not be *put to d.* 17:6
be *put to d.* and thou hang. 21:22
not be *put to d.* for children, nor children *put to d.* 24:16; *2 Ki* 14:6
rebel be *put to d.* *Josh* 1:18
for Baal be *put to d.* *Judg* 6:31
we may *put* them *to d.* 20:13
1 Sam 11:12
not a man be *put to d.* *1 Sam* 11:13
2 Sam 19:22
measured he to *put to d.* *2 Sam* 8:2
shall not Shimei be *put to d.*? 19:21
were *put to d.* in the days. 21:9
I will not *put* thee *to d.* *1 Ki* 2:8
Adonijah shall be *put to d.* 24
not at this time *put* thee *to d.* 26
seek Lord be *put to d.* *2 Chr* 15:13
into house, shall be *put to d.* 23:7
law of his to *put* him *to d. Esth* 4:11
their men be *put to d.* *Jer* 18:21
that if ye *put* me *to d.* 26:15
all Judah *put* him at all *to d.*? 19
sought to *put* Urijah *to d.* 21
let this man be *put to d.* 38:4
thou not surely *put* me *to d.*? 15
I will not *put* thee *to d.* 16, 25
that they might *put* us *to d.* 43:3
and *put* them *to d.* in Riblah 52:27

cause them to be *put to d.* *Mat* 10:21
Mark 13:12; *Luke* 21:16
would *put* him *to d.* he. *Mat* 14:5
sought false witness to *put* him *to d.*
26:59; 27:1; *Mark* 14:55
by craft and *put to d.* *Mark* 14:1
scourge and *put to d.* *Luke* 18:33
malefactors led to be *put to d.* 23:32
counsel to *put* him *to d.* *John* 11:53
put Lazarus also *to d.* 12:10
for us to *put* any man *to d.* 18:31
keepers to be *put to d.* *Acts* 12:19
when they were *put to d.* I. 26:10
put to d. in flesh, but. *1 Pet* 3:18

see **surely**

shadow of **death**

let the *shad. of d.* stain it. *Job* 3:5
darkness and *shad. of d.* 10:21, 22
bringeth to light *shad. of d.* 12:22
on eyelids is *shad. of d.* 16:16
morning is even as *shad. of d.* 24:17
out darkness and *shad. of d.* 28:3
is no *shad. of d.* where. 34:22
seen doors of the *shad. of d.*? 38:17
valley of *shad. of d.* *Ps* 23:4
covered us with *shad. of d.* 44:19
in darkness, and *shad. of d.* 107:10
of darkness and *shad. of d.* 14
in land of the *shad. of d.* *Isa* 9:2
land of *shad. of d.* *Jer* 2:6
light, he turn it into *shad. of d.* 13:16
turneth *shad. of d.* into. *Amos* 5:8
in region and *shad. of d.* *Mat* 4:16
light to them in *shad. of d.* *Luke* 1:79

ways of **death**

the end *ways of d.* *Pr* 14:12; 16:25

with **death**

made a covenant *with d.* *Isa* 28:15
your covenant *with d.* shall. 18
kill her children *with d.* *Rev* 2:23
power was given to kill *with d.* 6:8

worthy of **death**

that is *worthy of d.* *Deut* 17:6*
he was not *worthy of d.* 19:6
committed a sin *worthy of d.* 21:22
in damsel no sin *worthy of d.* 22:26
thou art *worthy of d.* *1 Ki* 2:26
lo, nothing *worthy of d.* *Luke* 23:15
his charge *worthy of d.* *Acts* 23:29
any thing *worthy of d.* 25:11
committed nothing *worthy of d.* 25
doth nothing *worthy of d.* 26:31
such things *worthy of d.* *Rom* 1:32

deaths

shall die of grevious *d.* *Jer* 16:4
shalt die *d.* of them that. *Ezek* 28:8
thou shalt die the *d.* of the. 10
in prisons frequent, in *d.* *2 Cor* 11:23

debase

and didst *d.* thyself. *Isa* 57:9

debate, *verb*

d. thy cause with thy. *Pr* 25:9
in measure, thou wilt *d.* *Isa* 27:8*

debate, -s

ye fast for strife and *d.* *Isa* 58:4*
full of envy, murder, *d.* *Rom* 1:29*
I fear lest there be *d.* wrath.
2 Cor 12:20*

Deborah

but *D.* Rebekah's nurse. *Gen* 35:8
D. a prophetess judged. *Judg* 4:4
D. arose a mother in Israel. 5:7
awake *D.* 12
the princes were with *D.* 15

debt

That which is due by one man to another, Neh 10:31. *Sins are by resemblance called* debts, Mat 6:12.

every one that was in *d.* *1 Sam* 22:2
sell the oil, pay thy *d.* *2 Ki* 4:7
the exaction of every *d.* *Neh* 10:31
and forgave him the *d.* *Mat* 18:27
cast into prison till he pay *d.* 30
I forgave thee all that *d.* 32
reckoned of grace but *d.* *Rom* 4:4

debtor

restored to the *d.* his. *Ezek* 18:7
by gold of temple is a *d.* *Mat* 23:16
I am *d.* to the Greeks. *Rom* 1:14
he is a *d.* to do the whole. *Gal* 5:3

debtors

as we forgive our *d.* *Mat* 6:12
creditor had two *d.* *Luke* 7:41
called every one of his lord's *d.* 16:5
we are *d.* not to flesh. *Rom* 8:12
and their *d.* they are 15:27

debts

that are sureties for *d.* *Pr* 22:26
forgive us our *d.* as we. *Mat* 6:12

Decapolis

followed him from *D.* *Mat* 4:25
he began to publish in *D.* *Mark* 5:20
through midst of coasts of *D.* 7:31

decay

be poor and fallen in *d.* *Lev* 25:35*

decayed

of bearers of burdens *d.* *Neh* 4:10
I will raise up the *d.* *Isa* 44:26*

decayeth

and as the flood *d.* and. *Jer* 14:11†
slothfulness building *d.* *Eccl* 10:18*
that which *d.* is ready to. *Heb* 8:13*

decease

and spake of his *d.* at. *Luke* 9:31
after my *d.* to have in. *2 Pet* 1:15

deceased

they are *d.* they shall. *Isa* 26:14
when he had married, *d.* *Mat* 22:25

deceit

their belly prepareth *d.* *Job* 15:35
nor my tongue utter *d.* 27:4
if my foot hath hasted to *d.* 31:5
full of cursing, *d.* and. *Ps* 10:7
words are iniquity and *d.* 36:3
thy tongue frameth *d.* 50:19
d. and guile depart not. 55:11*
redeem their soul from *d.* 72:14*
he that worketh *d.* shall not. 101:7
them that err, their *d.* is. 119:118
counsels of the wicked are *d.* *Pr* 12:5
a false witness sheweth forth *d.* 17
d. is in the heart of them that. 20
but the folly of fools is *d.* 14:8
bread of *d.* is sweet to a. 20:17
he that hateth, layeth up *d.* 26:24
whose hatred is covered by *d.* 26
neither was any *d.* in his. *Isa* 53:9
so are houses full of *d.* *Jer* 5:27
hold fast *d.* they refuse to. 8:5
through *d.* they refuse to know. 9:6
tongue, it speaketh *d.* 8
they prophesy the *d.* of their. 14:14
they are prophets of *d.* 23:26
compasseth me with *d.* *Hos* 11:12
the balances of *d.* are in. 12:7
falsifying balances by *d.* *Amos* 8:5
fill masters' houses with *d.* *Zeph* 1:9
heart of men proceed *d.* *Mark* 7:22
of murder, debate, *d.* *Rom* 1:29
tongues they have used *d.* 3:13
through philosophy and vain *d.*
Col 2:8
exhortation was not of *d.* *1 Thes* 2:3*

deceitful

abhor bloody and *d.* man. *Ps* 5:6
they devise *d.* matters. 35:20
deliver me from the *d.* and. 43:1
O thou *d.* tongue. 52:4
bloody and *d.* men shall not. 55:23
turned aside like a *d.* bow. 78:57
the mouth of the *d.* are. 109:2
deliver my soul from a *d.* 120:2
wicked worketh a *d.* work. *Pr* 11:18
but a *d.* witness speaketh. 14:25
for they are *d.* meat. 23:3
kisses of an enemy are *d.* 27:6*
the poor and the *d.* man. 29:13*
favour is *d.* and beauty is. 31:30
heart is *d.* above all. *Jer* 17:9
are like a *d.* bow. *Hos* 7:16
and with bag of *d.* weights. *Mi* 6:11
and their tongue is *d.* in. 12
nor shall a *d.* tongue be. *Zeph* 3:13
apostles, *d.* workers. *2 Cor* 11:13
corrupt according to *d.* *Eph* 4:22

deceitfully

Hamor and Shechem *d.* *Gen* 34:13
let not Pharaoh deal *d.* *Ex* 8:29
seeing he hath dealt *d.* with. 21:8
which he hath *d.* gotten. *Lev* 6:4
brethren have dealt *d.* *Job* 6:15
will ye talk *d.* for him? *Job* 13:7
up his soul nor sworn *d.* *Ps* 24:4
a sharp razor, working *d.* 52:2
doeth the work of Lord *d.* *Jer* 48:10
made, he shall work *d.* *Dan* 11:23
handling word of God *d.* *2 Cor* 4:2

deceitfulness

and the *d.* of riches choke the word.
Mat 13:22; *Mark* 4:19
hardened through *d.* of sin. *Heb* 3:13

deceits

and imagine *d.* all day. *Ps* 38:12
smooth things, prophesy *d.* *Isa* 30:10

deceive

Abner came to *d.* thee. *2 Sam* 3:25
I say, do not *d.* me? *2 Ki* 4:28
let not Hezekiah *d.* you. 18:29
2 Chr 32:15; *Isa* 36:14
let not thy God *d.* thee. *2 Ki* 19:10
Isa 37:10
be not a witness, and *d.* *Pr* 24:28
they will *d.* every one. *Jer* 9:5
that be in midst of you *d.* 29:8
saith the Lord *d.* not yourselves. 37:9
neither wear garment to *d.* *Zech* 13:4
take heed that no man *d.* you.
Mat 24:4; *Mark* 13:5
I am Christ; and shall *d.* many.
Mat 24:5, 11; *Mark* 13:6
if possible they shall *d.* *Mat* 24:24
by fair speech *d.* the. *Rom* 16:18
let no man *d.* himself. *1 Cor* 3:18
they lie in wait to *d.* *Eph* 4:14
let no man *d.* you. 5:6; *2 Thes* 2:3
1 John 3:7
we have no sin, we *d.* *1 John* 1:8
that he should *d.* the. *Rev* 20:3
go to *d.* nations in four quarters. 8

deceivableness

and with all *d.* of. *2 Thes* 2:10

deceived

father hath *d.* me and. *Gen* 31:7
or if a soul sin, or hath *d.* *Lev* 6:2*
your heart be not *d.* *Deut* 11:16
why hast thou *d.* me? *1 Sam* 19:17
28:12
O king, my servant *d.* *2 Sam* 19:26
the *d.* and the deceiver. *Job* 12:16
let not him that is *d.* trust. 15:31
if mine heart have been *d.* 31:9
princes of Noph are *d.* *Isa* 19:13
a *d.* heart hath turned him. 44:20
thou hast greatly *d.* *Jer* 4:10
thou hast *d.* me, and I was *d.* 20:7
thy terribleness hath *d.* thee. 49:16
my lovers, but they *d.* *Lam* 1:19
if prophet be *d.* I have *d.* *Ezek* 14:9
of thine heart hath *d.* *Ob* 3
men at peace with thee have *d.* 7
heed that ye be not *d.* *Luke* 21:8
answered, are ye also *d.*? *John* 7:47
by commandment *d.* me. *Rom* 7:11
be not *d.* *1 Cor* 6:9; 15:33; *Gal* 6:7
d. but woman being *d.* *1 Tim* 2:14
deceiving and being *d.* *2 Tim* 3:13
we were foolish, *d.* *Tit* 3:3
all nations were *d.* *Rev* 18:23
he *d.* them that had received. 19:20
devil that *d.* them was cast. 20:10

deceiver

seem to my father as a *d.* *Gen* 27:12
the deceived and the *d.* *Job* 12:16
cursed be *d.* who hath. *Mal* 1:14
remember that that *d.* *Mat* 27:63
not Jesus this is a *d.* *2 John* 7

deceivers

and good report, as *d.* *2 Cor* 6:8
many *d.* especially of. *Tit* 1:10
for many *d.* are entered. *2 John* 7

deceiveth

so is the man that *d.* his. *Pr* 26:19
nay, but he *d.* the people. *John* 7:12
when nothing, *d.* himself. *Gal* 6:3
d. his own heart. *Jas* 1:26
called the devil, which *d.* *Rev* 12:9
and *d.* them that dwell on. 13:14

deceiving

men wax worse, *d.* *2 Tim* 3:13
not hearers only, *d.* your. *Jas* 1:22

deceivings
sporting with their own *d.* *2 Pet* 2:13

decently
let all things be done *d.* *1 Cor* 14:40

decided
thyself hast *d.* it. *1 Ki* 20:40

decision
in valley of *d.* for day. *Joel* 3:14

deck
d. thyself now with. *Job* 40:10
they *d.* it with silver. *Jer* 10:4

decked
d. my bed with covering. *Pr* 7:16*
I *d.* thee also with. *Ezek* 16:11
thou wast thus *d.* with gold. 13
and she *d.* herself with. *Hos* 2:13
was arrayed and *d.* with. *Rev* 17:4
that great city that was *d.* 18:16

deckedst
didst take garments and *d.*
Ezek 16:16*
didst wash and *d.* thyself. 23:40

deckest, -eth
as a bridegroom *d.* *Isa* 61:10
though thou *d.* thee with. *Jer* 4:30

declaration
d. of the greatness of. *Esth* 10:2*
and hear my *d.* with. *Job* 13:17
to set forth in order a *d.* *Luke* 1:1*
and to the *d.* of your. *2 Cor* 8:19*

declare
none that could *d.* it. *Gen* 41:24
Moab began Moses to *d.* *Deut* 1:5
d. his cause in ears of. *Josh* 20:4
if ye can *d.* it me within. *Judg* 14:12
words of the prophets *d.* good.
1 Ki 22:13; *2 Chr* 18:12
d. his glory among the heathen.
1 Chr 16:24; *Ps* 96:3
to shew copy and *d.* it. *Esth* 4:8
fishes of the sea shall *d.* *Job* 12:8
d. his way to his face ? 21:31
then did he see it, and *d.* it. 28:27
I would *d.* to him the. 31:37
foundations of earth, *d.* if thou. 38:4
breadth of earth, *d.* if thou. 18
will demand of thee, *d.* 40:7; 42:4
d. among the people his. *Ps* 9:11
the heavens *d.* the glory. 19:1
come and *d.* righteousness. 22:31
50:6; 97:6
shall it *d.* thy truth ? 30:9
if I would *d.* and speak of. 40:5
what hast thou to do to *d.*? 50:16
all men shall fear and *d.* 64:9
trust in Lord that I may *d.* 73:28*
is near, wondrous works *d.* 75:1*
should arise and *d.* them. 78:6*
to *d.* the name of the Lord. 102:21
and *d.* his works with. 107:22
but live and *d.* the works. 118:17
one generation shall *d.* thy. 145:4
in my heart even to *d.* *Eccl* 9:1*
d. their sin as Sodom. *Isa* 3:9
d. his doings among people. 12:4
set a watchman, let him *d.* 21:6
or let them *d.* to us things. 41:22
and new things do I *d.* 42:9
and let them *d.* his praise. 12
who among them can *d.* this ? 43:9
d. thou that thou mayest be. 26*
I shall call, and shall *d.* it ? 44:7
I the Lord *d.* things that are. 45:19
all this, and will not ye *d.* 48:6
who shall *d.* his generation ? 53:8*
Acts 8:33
they shall *d.* my glory. *Isa* 66:19
d. this in house of Jacob. *Jer* 5:20
hath spoken, that he may *d.* 9:12
d. it in isles afar off, and say. 31:10
if I *d.* it to thee, wilt thou ? 38:15
d. unto us what thou hast said. 25
what God shall say, *d.* to us. 42:20
d. in Zion the vengeance of. 50:28
let us *d.* in Zion work of. 51:10
may *d.* all their. *Ezek* 12:16; 23:36
d. all that thou seest to the. 40:4
O Belteshazzar, *d.* the. *Dan* 4:18
to *d.* to Jacob his. *Mi* 3:8
even to-day do I *d.* that. *Zech* 9:12
d. unto us this parable. *Mat* 13:36*
d. unto us this parable. 15:15
d. unto you glad. *Acts* 13:32*
though a man *d.* it to you. 41
ignorantly worship, him *d.* 17:23*
not shunned to *d.* to you the. 20:27
set forth to *d.* his righteousness.
Rom 3:25*, 26*
the day shall *d.* it. *1 Cor* 3:13
in this that I *d.* to you. 11:17*
I *d.* unto you the gospel. 15:1*
state shall Tychicus *d.* *Col* 4:7*
that say such things *d.* *Heb* 11:14*
which we have seen *d.* *1 John* 1:3
then is message which we *d.* 5*

***I will* declare**
I have seen *I will d.* *Job* 15:17
I will d. the decree. *Ps* 2:7*
I will d. thy name to brethren.
22:22; *Heb* 2:12
I will d. mine iniquity. *Ps* 38:18
I will d. what he hath done. 66:16
but *I will d.* for ever, I will. 75:9
I will d. thy greatness. 145:6
I will d. thy righteousness. *Isa* 57:12
I will d. it, I will keep. *Jer* 42:4
thy name, *will d.* it. *John* 17:26*

declare *ye*
a voice of singing *d. ye.* *Isa* 48:20
d. ye in Judah, and. *Jer* 4:5
d. ye in Egypt, and publish. 46:14
d. ye among the nations. 50:2
d. ye it not at Gath. *Mi* 1:10*

declared
that my name may be *d.* *Ex* 9:16
Moses *d.* to children of. *Lev* 23:44
they *d.* their pedigrees. *Num* 1:18
because it was not *d.* 15:34
and he *d.* to you his. *Deut* 4:13
for thou hast *d.* this. *2 Sam* 19:6
words that were *d.* to. *Neh* 8:12
plentifully *d.* thing as it. *Job* 26:3
I have *d.* thy faithfulness. *Ps* 40:10
hitherto have I *d.* thy works. 71:17
hast *d.* thy strength among. 77:14*
loving-kindness be *d.* in the. 88:11
with my lips have I *d.* all. 119:13
I have *d.* my ways, and thou. 26
a grievous vision is *d.* *Isa* 21:2
heard of God have I *d.* unto you. 10
who hath *d.* from. 41:26; 45:21*
I have *d.* and have saved. 43:12
44:8; 48:5
I have *d.* former things from. 48:3
them hath *d.* these things ? 14
Micaiah *d.* all the words. *Jer* 36:13
I have this day *d.* it to you. 42:21
she *d.* to him before all. *Luke* 8:47
he hath *d.* him. *John* 1:18
I have *d.* to them thy name. 17:26*
he *d.* to them how he had. *Acts* 9:27
when he had *d.* all these. 10:8*
d. how Lord had brought him. 12:17
d. all things that God had. 15:4*
Simeon had *d.* how God at. 14*
Festus *d.* Paul's cause to. 25:14
d. to be the Son of God. *Rom* 1:4
that my name might be *d.* 9:17*
for it hath been *d.* to. *1 Cor* 1:11*
d. to be the epistle of. *2 Cor* 3:3*
who also *d.* to us your. *Col* 1:8
of God be finished as he *d.* *Rev* 10:7

declareth, -ing
there is none that *d.* *Isa* 41:26
d. the end from beginning. 46:10
a voice *d.* from Dan. *Jer* 4:15
my people, their staff *d.* *Hos* 4:12
he that *d.* to man what. *Amos* 4:13
d. the conversion of the. *Acts* 15:3
d. what miracles God hath. 12*
d. to you the testimony. *1 Cor* 2:1*

decline
(*To turn aside, deviate, or stray*)
speak in a cause, to *d.* *Ex* 23:2
not *d.* from sentence. *Deut* 17:11
d. from thy testimonies. *Ps* 119:157
neither *d.* from words of. *Pr* 4:5
heart *d.* to her ways, go not. 7:25

declined, -eth
d. neither to right hand. *2 Chr* 34:2
way have I kept and not *d.* *Job* 23:11
nor have our steps *d.* *Ps* 44:18
days are like shadow that *d.* 102:11
like the shadow when it *d.* *Ps* 109:23
yet have I not *d.* from thy. 119:51

decrease
and suffer not cattle to *d.* *Ps* 107:38
increase, but I must *d.* *John* 3:30

decreased
waters *d.* continually until. *Gen* 8:5

decree, *substantive*
[1] *An authoritative order,* 2 Chr 30:5; Ezra 6:1. [2] *An eternal purpose of God,* Ps 2:7; Dan 4:24.
so they established a *d.* *2 Chr* 30:5
king Cyrus made a *d.* *Ezra* 5:13, 17
Darius made a *d.* 6:1, 12
Artaxerxes do make a *d.* 7:21
the *d.* was given to Shushan.
Esth 3:15; 9:14
d. of Esther confirmed. 9:32
made a *d.* for the rain. *Job* 28:26
I will declare the *d.* the. *Ps* 2:7
he hath made a *d.* which. 148:6
he gave to sea his *d.* *Pr* 8:29
sea by a perpetual *d.* *Jer* 5:22
there is but one *d.* for. *Dan* 2:9
this matter is by the *d.* of the. 4:17
this is the *d.* of the most High. 24
now, O king, establish the *d.* 6:8
regardeth not thee, nor *d.* 13
I make a *d.* that in every. 26
proclaimed by the *d.* of. *Jonah* 3:7
in that day shall the *d.* be. *Mi* 7:11
before the *d.* bring forth. *Zeph* 2:2
there went out a *d.* *Luke* 2:1

decree, *verb*
thou shalt also *d.* a. *Job* 22:28
kings reign, and princes *d.* *Pr* 8:15
woe to them that *d.* *Isa* 10:1

decreed
remembered what was *d.* *Esth* 2:1
as they had *d.* for themselves. 9:31
brake up for it my *d.* *Job* 38:10
consumption *d.* overflow. *Isa* 10:22
hath so *d.* in his heart. *1 Cor* 7:37

decrees
that decree unrighteous *d.* *Isa* 10:1
they delivered them the *d.* *Acts* 16:4
do contrary to the *d.* of Caesar. 17:7

Dedan
Sheba, *D.* *Gen* 10:7; *1 Chr* 1:9
Jokshan, Sheba, and *D.* *1 Chr* 1:32
made *D.* and Tema, and. *Jer* 25:23
deep, O inhabitants of *D.* 49:8
they of *D.* shall fall by. *Ezek* 25:13
D. was thy merchant in. 27:20

Dedanim
travelling companies of *D.* *Isa* 21:13

dedicate
die and another man *d.* *Deut* 20:5
which also David did *d.* *2 Sam* 8:11
out of spoils did they *d.* to. 27
I build an house to *d.* *2 Chr* 2:4

dedicated
a new house and not *d.* *Deut* 20:5
I had wholly *d.* the silver. *Judg* 17:3
things which David had *d.* *1 Ki* 7:51
1 Chr 18:11; *2 Chr* 5:1
the king and Israel *d.* *1 Ki* 8:63
2 Chr 7:5
had *d.* and things himself had *d.*
1 Ki 15:15; *2 Chr* 15:18
all the money of the *d.* *2 Ki* 12:4*
hallowed things that kings of Judah had *d.* 12:18
over treasures of *d.* *1 Chr* 26:20, 26
captains of hosts had *d.* 26
that Samuel, Saul, and Joab *d.* 28
pattern of the treasuries of the *d.* things 28:12
the *d.* things did they bestow.
2 Chr 24:7
and brought in the *d.* things. 31:12
every *d.* thing in Israel. *Ezek* 44:29*
nor first testament *d.* *Heb* 9:18

dedicating
princes offered for *d.* *Num* 7:10
each prince on his day for *d.* 11

dedication
this was the *d.* of. *Num* 7:84, 88
for they kept the *d.* of. *2 Chr* 7:9

kept the *d.* with joy. *Ezra* 6:16
offered at *d.* of house of God. 17
at the *d.* of the wall. *Neh* 12:27
come to *d.* of image. *Dan* 3:2, 3
at Jerusalem feast of *d.* *John* 10:22

deed

what *d.* is this ye have? *Gen* 44:15
in very *d.* for this cause. *Ex* 9:16
was no such *d.* done. *Judg* 19:30
in very *d.* except thou. *1 Sam* 25:34
Saul was come in very *d.* 26:4*
by this *d.* given great. *2 Sam* 12:14
for this *d.* of queen shall. *Esth* 1:17
had not consented to *d.* *Luke* 23:51
a prophet mighty in *d.* 24:19
be examined of the good *d.* *Acts* 4:9
obedient by word and *d.* *Rom* 15:18
that hath done this *d.* *1 Cor* 5:2
him that hath done this *d.* 3
ye do in word or *d.* do. *Col* 3:17
shall be blessed in his *d.* *Jas* 1:25
love in *d.* and in truth. *1 John* 3:18

deeds

hast done *d.* that ought not. *Gen* 20:9
make known his *d.* *1 Chr* 16:8
Ps 105:1
his *d.* first and last. *2 Chr* 35:27
come upon us for evil *d.* *Ezra* 9:13
also reported his good *d.* *Neh* 6:19
wipe not out my good *d.* 13:14
them according to their *d.* *Ps* 28:4
according to their *d.* *Isa* 59:18
they overpass the *d.* of. *Jer* 5:28
them according to their *d.* 25:14
that ye allow the *d.* of. *Luke* 11:48
the due reward of our *d.* 23:41
because their *d.* were. *John* 3:19
to the light, lest his *d.* should. 20
that his *d.* may be made. 21
ye do the *d.* of your father. 8:41
mighty in word and in *d.* *Acts* 7:22
Dorcas was full of alms-*d.* 9:36
confessed, and shewed their *d.* 19:18
very worthy *d.* are done. 24:2*
man according to his *d.* *Rom* 2:6
by the *d.* of the law shall no. 3:20
is justified by faith without *d.* 28*
if ye mortify the *d.* of the. 8:13
in signs and mighty *d.* *2 Cor* 12:12
put off old man with his *d.* *Col* 3:9
soul with their unlawful *d.* *2 Pet* 2:8
is partaker of his evil *d.* *2 John* 11
I will remember his *d.* *3 John* 10
them of their ungodly *d.* *Jude* 15
thou hatest the *d.* of the. *Rev* 2:6
except they repent of their *d.* 22
repented not of their *d.* 16:11

deemed

the shipmen *d.* that. *Acts* 27:27

deep

[1] *Extending a great way below the surface,* Ezek 32:24. [2] *The sea,* Job 41:31. [3] *Used for any great danger or profound or incomprehensible matter,* Ps 69:15; Isa 33:19; Dan 2:22.

darkness was upon the face of the *d.* *Gen* 1:2
the fountains of the *d.* were. 7:11
fountains also of the *d.* were. 8:2
thee with blessings of the *d.* 49:25
the *d.* that coucheth. *Deut* 33:13
face of the *d.* is frozen. *Job* 38:30
the *d.* to boil like a pot. 41:31
would think the *d.* to be hoary. 32
judgements are a great *d.* *Ps* 36:6
d. calleth unto *d.* at noise of. 42:7
neither let the *d.* swallow. 69:15
coveredst it with the *d.* as. 104:6
these see wonders in the *d.* 107:24
strengthens fountains of *d.* *Pr* 8:28
saith to the *d.* be dry. *Isa* 44:27
dried waters of great *d.*? 51:10
led them through the *d.* 63:13
when I bring up the *d.* *Ezek* 26:19
the *d.* set him on high with. 31:4
I covered the *d.* for him. 15
devoured great *d.* and. *Amos* 7:4
hast cast me into the *d.* *Jonah* 2:3
the *d.* uttered his voice. *Hab* 3:10
launch out into the *d.* and. *Luke* 5:4
command them to go into *d.* 8:31*
shall descend into *d.*? *Rom* 10:7*
night and day in the *d.* *2 Cor* 11:25

deep, *adjective*

he discovereth *d.* things. *Job* 12:22
thought and heart is *d.* *Ps* 64:6
I sink in *d.* mire, I am come into *d.* waters. 69:2
delivered out of the *d.* waters. 14
didst cause it to take *d.* root. 80:9
thy thoughts are very *d.* 92:5
in his hand are the *d.* places. 95:4
in the seas and all *d.* places. 135:6
them be cast into *d.* pits. 140:10
mouth are as *d.* waters. *Pr* 18:4
counsel is like *d.* waters. 20:5
of strange women is a *d.* pit. 22:14
for a whore is a *d.* ditch. 23:27
exceeding *d.* who can? *Eccl* 7:24
woe to them that seek *d.* *Isa* 29:15
made Tophet *d.* and large. 30:33
turn back, dwell *d.* *Jer* 49:8
drink thy sister's cup *d.* *Ezek* 23:32
will I make their waters *d.* 32:14*
and to have drunk *d.* waters. 34:18*
he revealeth the *d.* and. *Dan* 2:22
digged *d.* laid foundation. *Luke* 6:48
to draw, and well is *d.* *John* 4:11
Spirit searcheth *d.* *1 Cor* 2:10
d. poverty abounded to. *2 Cor* 8:2

deep ***sleep***

God caused a *d. sleep.* *Gen* 2:21
a *d. sleep* fell on Abram. 15:12
a *d. sleep* was fallen. *1 Sam* 26:12
d. sleep falleth. *Job* 4:13; 33:15
casteth into *d. sleep.* *Pr* 19:15
on you spirit of *d. sleep.* *Isa* 29:10
I was in a *d. sleep.* *Dan* 8:18; 10:9
fallen into *d. sleep.* *Acts* 20:9

deeper

plague in sight be *d.* than skin. *Lev* 13:3; 25:30
bright spot in sight be not *d.* 13:4
31, 32, 34
it is *d.* than hell. *Job* 11:8
a people of *d.* speech. *Isa* 33:19

deeply

of Israel *d.* revolted. *Isa* 31:6
they have *d.* corrupted. *Hos* 9:9
Jesus sighed *d.* in his. *Mark* 8:12

deepness

they had no *d.* of earth. *Mat* 13:5

deeps

thou threwest into *d.* *Neh* 9:11
hast laid me in the *d.* *Ps* 88:6
praise Lord, dragons and all *d.* 148:7
all the *d.* of the river. *Zech* 10:11

deer

shall eat the fallow *d.* *Deut* 14:5*
Solomon had fallow *d.* *1 Ki* 4:23

defamed

being *d.* we intreat. *1 Cor* 4:13

defaming

for I heard *d.* of many. *Jer* 20:10

defeat

d. the counsel of Ahithophel. *2 Sam* 15:34; 17:14

defence

their *d.* is departed. *Num* 14:9
Rehoboam built cities for *d.* *2 Chr* 11:5
Almighty shall be thy *d.* *Job* 22:25*
my *d.* is of God who. *Ps* 7:10*
be thou an house of *d.* to. 31:2
for God is my *d.* 59:9*, 17*
thou hast been my *d.* and. 16*
God is my *d.* I shall not. 62:2*, 6*
for the Lord is our *d.* 89:18*
Lord is my *d.* and God. 94:22*
is a *d.* money is a *d.* *Eccl* 7:12
all glory shall be a *d.* *Isa* 4:5*
the brooks of *d.* shall be. 19:6*
his place of *d.* shall be the. 33:16
the *d.* shall be prepared. *Nah* 2:5*
would have made his *d.* *Acts* 19:33
hear my *d.* which I make. 22:1
in my bonds and in *d.* *Phil* 1:7
I am set for the *d.* of the gospel. 17

defenced

(Fortified by a wall)

of a *d.* city a ruin. *Isa* 25:2
against all *d.* cities of Judah. *Isa* 36:1
to lay waste *d.* cities into. 37:26
let us go into the *d.* cities. *Jer* 4:5
for these *d.* cities remained. 34:7

see **city, cities**

defend

Tolah arose to *d.* Israel. *Judg* 10:1*
I will *d.* city. *2 Ki* 19:34; 20:6
Isa 37:35; 38:6
name of God of Jacob *d.* *Ps* 20:1*
d. me from them that rise up. 59:1*
d. the poor and fatherless. 82:3*
so will Lord of hosts *d.* *Isa* 31:5*
Lord of hosts shall *d.* *Zech* 9:15
d. inhabitants of Jerusalem. 12:8

defended

Shammah stood and *d.* *2 Sam* 23:12
he *d.* them and. *Acts* 7:24

defendest

for joy, because thou *d.* *Ps* 5:11

defending

d. Jerusalem he will. *Isa* 31:5

defer

thou vowest a vow, *d.* *Eccl* 5:4
name's sake will I *d.* *Isa* 48:9
d. not for thine own sake. *Dan* 9:19

deferred

the young man *d.* not. *Gen* 34:19
hope *d.* maketh heart sick. *Pr* 13:12
when Felix heard he *d.* *Acts* 24:22

deferreth

discretion of a man *d.* *Pr* 19:11*

defied

whom Lord hath not *d.*? *Num* 23:8
he hath *d.* the armies. *1 Sam* 17:36
the God whom thou hast *d.* 45
when he *d.* Israel, Jonathan slew him. *2 Sam* 21:21; *1 Chr* 20:7
d. the Philistines. *2 Sam* 23:9

defile

[1] *To make foul,* 1 Cor 8:7; Tit 1:15. [2] *To make ceremonially unclean,* Lev 11:44; Mark 7:2.

nor *d.* yourselves. *Lev* 11:44; 18:24
when they *d.* my tabernacle. 15:31
to *d.* thyself with thy. 18:20
neither lie with any beast to *d.* 23
spue not you out when ye *d.* 28
to *d.* my sanctuary. 20:3
he shall not *d.* himself. 21:4
nor *d.* himself for his father or. 11
he shall not eat to *d.* himself. 22:8
they *d.* not their camps. *Num* 5:3
d. not the land which ye. 35:34
high places did king *d.* *2 Ki* 23:13
how shall I *d.* them? *S of S* 5:3
shall *d.* the covering of. *Isa* 30:22
called by my name to *d.* *Jer* 32:34
robbers enter into it and *d.* it. *Ezek* 7:22*
d. the house, fill courts with. 9:7
d. not yourselves with idols. 20:7, 18
idols against herself to *d.* 22:3
they shall *d.* thy brightness. 28:7
ye *d.* every one his. 33:26
nor shall they *d.* themselves. 37:23
name shall Israel no more *d.* 43:7
at no dead person to *d.* 44:25
would not *d.* himself. *Dan* 1:8
and they *d.* the man. *Mat* 15:18
Mark 7:15, 23
if any man *d.* temple. *1 Cor* 3:17*
law is for them that *d.* *1 Tim* 1:10*
these filthy dreamers *d.* *Jude* 8

defiled

with Dinah, and *d.* her. *Gen* 34:2*
Jacob heard that he had *d.* Dinah. 5
because he had *d.* Dinah. 13, 27
a man shall be *d.* with. *Lev* 5:3
that he should be *d.* thereby. 11:43
plague is in him be *d.* 13:46*
the law of him that is *d.* 15:32*
all these things nations are *d.* 18:24
the land is *d.* I visit. 25, 27
seek after wizards to be *d.* 19:31
shall none be *d.* for the dead. 21:1
a virgin, for her may he be *d.* 3
put out whosoever is *d.* *Num* 5:2*
and if she be *d.* 13, 27
if she be not *d.* 14, 28

and he hath d. the head of. Num 6:9
because his separation was d. 12
men who were d. by dead. 9:6*, 7*
d. the sanctuary of Lord. 19:20
that thy land be not d. Deut 21:23
fruit of thy vineyard be d. 22:9*
may not take her after d. 24:4
Josiah d. high places. 2 Ki 23:8
d. Topheth. 10
forasmuch as he d. his. 1 Chr 5:1
because they have d. Neh 13:29
I have d. my horn. Job 16:15*
d. dwelling-place of. Ps 74:7*; 79:1
thus were they d. with. 106:39
the earth is d. under. Isa 24:5*
your hands are d. with blood. 59:3
but when ye entered, ye d. Jer 2:7
lightness of whoredom she d. 3:9*
because they have d. land. 16:18*
of the kings of Judah be d. 19:13
Israel eat d. bread. Ezek 4:13*
surely because thou hast d. 5:11
their holy places shall be d. 7:24*
neither d. neighbour's wife. 18:6, 15
hath even d. his neighbour's. 11
wherein ye have been d. 20:43*
and hast d. thyself. 22:4; 23:7
another hath lewdly d. his. 22:11
I saw that she was d. 23:13
the Babylonians d. her. 17
they have d. my sanctuary. 38
thou hast d. thy sanctuaries. 28:18*
they d. it by their own way. 36:17
they have d. my holy name. 43:8
and Israel is d. Hos 5:3; 6:10
nations say, let her be d. Mi 4:11
disciples eat bread with d. Mark 7:2
not in, lest they be d. John 18:28
conscience being weak is d. 1 Cor 8:7
to d. is nothing pure, mind and conscience d. Tit 1:15
and therefore many be d. Heb 12:15
a few who have not d. Rev 3:4
these are they who are not d. 14:4

defiledst

to father's bed, then d. it. Gen 49:4

defileth

that d. sabbath. Ex 31:14*
d. the tabernacle. Num 19:13
not pollute land, blood d. 35:33
goeth into the mouth d. Mat 15:11
eat with unwashen hands d. not. 20
out of man that d. Mark 7:20
so is tongue, that it d. the. Jas 3:6
enter any thing that d. Rev 21:27*

defraud

not d. thy neighbour. Lev 19:13*
do not bear false witness, d. not. Mark 10:19
nay you do wrong, and d. 1 Cor 6:8
d. not, except it be with. 7:5
no man d. his brother. 1 Thes 4:6*

defrauded

whom have I d.? 1 Sam 12:3
thou hast not d. nor oppressed. 4
rather suffer yourselves to be d. 1 Cor 6:7
wronged no man, have d. 2 Cor 7:2*

defy

curse me Jacob, d. Num 23:7
how shall I d. whom Lord hath? 8
I d. the armies of. 1 Sam 17:10
is come up, surely to d. Israel. 25
that he should d. the armies. 26

degenerate

turned into the d. plant. Jer 2:21

degree, -s

Songs of degrees: *This title is given to fifteen Psalms, from 120 to 134, inclusive. The* Hebrew *text calls each, A song of ascents. There is a great diversity of views as to the meaning of this title, but the most probable is that they were pilgrim songs, sung by the people as they went up to Jerusalem.*

or backward ten d. 2 Ki 20:9*, 10* 11*; Isa 38:8*
brethren of second d. 1 Chr 15:18
state of a man of high d. 17:17
low d. vanity, high d. a lie. Ps 62:9
exalted them of low d. Luke 1:52
to themselves a good d. 1 Tim 3:13*
let brother of low d. Jas 1:9

delay, -ed, -eth

thou shalt not d. to offer. Ex 22:29
the people saw that Moses d. 32:1
d. not to keep thy. Ps 119:60
my lord d. his coming. Mat 24:48* Luke 12:45
that he would not d. Acts 9:38
without any d. I sat on. 25:17

delectable

their d. things not profit. Isa 44:9

delicacies

merchants rich through d. Rev 18:3*

delicate

the d. man or. Deut 28:54, 56
more called tender and d. Isa 47:1
Zion to comely d. woman. Jer 6:2
bald for thy d. children. Mi 1:16*

delicately

Agag came to him d. 1 Sam 15:32†
he that d. bringeth up his. Pr 29:21
they that did feed d. are. Lam 4:5
they that live d. are in. Luke 7:25

delicateness

foot on ground for d. Deut 28:56

delicates

filled his belly with d. Jer 51:34†

deliciously

glorified herself and lived d. Rev 18:7*, 9*

delight, *substantive*

Shechem had d. in. Gen 34:19
Lord had a d. in thy. Deut 10:15
if thou have no d. in her. 21:14
great d. in offerings? 1 Sam 15:22
behold, the king hath d. in. 18:22
I have no d. in thee. 2 Sam 15:26
shalt thou have d. in. Job 22:26
but his d. is in the law. Ps 1:2
excellent, in whom is my d. 16:3
testimonies also are my d. 119:24
for thy law is my d. 77, 174
I was daily his d. Pr 8:30
a just weight is the Lord's d. 11:1
upright in their way are his d. 20
they that deal truly are his d. 12:22
prayer of the upright is his d. 15:8
righteous lips are d. of kings. 16:13
fool hath no d. in understanding. 18:2
d. is not seemly for a fool. 19:10*
that rebuke him shall be d. 24:25
he shall give d. unto thy soul. 29:17
under his shadow with d. S of S 2:3
take d. in approaching to. Isa 58:2
if thou call the sabbath a d. 13
they have no d. in word. Jer 6:10

delight, *verb*

if the Lord d. in us, then. Num 14:8
why should the king d.? 2 Sam 24:3
will he d. himself in? Job 27:10
that he d. himself with God. 34:9
d. thyself also in the Lord. Ps 37:4
meek shall d. in abundance of. 11
I d. to do thy will, O my God. 40:8
they d. in lies. 62:4
the people that d. in war. 68:30
thy comforts d. my soul. 94:19
d. myself in thy statutes. 119:16, 35
d. in thy commandments. 47
I d. in thy law 70
how long will scorners d.? Pr 1:22
and d. in frowardness of. 2:14
I d. not in the blood of. Isa 1:11
they shall not d. in it. 13:17
and let your soul d. itself 55:2
they seek me, and d. to know. 58:2
then shalt thou d. thyself in. 14
in these things I d. Jer 9:24
covenant whom ye d. in. Mal 3:1
I d. in the law of God. Rom 7:22

delighted

Jonathan d. much in. 1 Sam 19:2
because he d. in me. 2 Sam 22:20 Ps 18:19
the Lord who d. in thee. 1 Ki 10:9 2 Chr 9:8
and d. themselves in thy. Neh 9:25
no more, except king d. Esth 2:14
deliver him, seeing he d. Ps 22:8
as he d. not in blessing. 109:17
choose that wherein I d. not. Isa 65:12; 66:4
be d. with the abundance of. 66:11

delightest

not sacrifice, thou d. not. Ps 51:16

delighteth

king d. to honour. Esth 6:6, 7, 9, 11
ordered by Lord, and he d. Ps 37:23
that d. greatly in his. 112:1
he d. not in the strength. 147:10
as father son in whom he d. Pr 3:12
in whom my soul d. Isa 42:1
Hephzi-bah, for the Lord d. 62:4
and their soul d. in their. 66:3
not anger, d. in mercy. Mi 7:18
when ye say, God d. in. Mal 2:17

delights

in scarlet with other d. 2 Sam 1:24*
unless law had been my d. Ps 119:92
thy commandments are my d. 143
my d. with the sons of. Pr 8:31
men-singers, and d. of. Eccl 2:8
art thou, O love, for d. S of S 7:6

delightsome

ye shall be a d. land. Mal 3:12

Delilah

in valley of Sorek, D. Judg 16:4
D. therefore took new ropes. 12

deliver

[1] *Restore, or give,* Gen 37:22; 40:13. [2] *Save, rescue,* Ps 7:2; 2 Cor 1:10.

thou shalt d. Pharaoh's. Gen 40:13*
yet shall ye d. the tale. Ex 5:18
if a man shall d. unto. 22:7, 10
d. it by that the sun goes down. 26*
I will d. the inhabitants of. 23:31
if thou wilt indeed d. Num 21:2
the congregation shall d. the. 35:25
he shall d. their kings. Deut 7:24
thou shalt not d. to his. 23:15
to d. her husband out of the. 25:11
any that can d. out. 32:39; Isa 43:13
that ye will d. our lives. Josh 2:13
for your God will d. it into. 8:7
they shall not d. the slayer. 20:5
and d. the Midianites. Judg 7:7
if thou shalt without fail d. 11:30
Samson shall begin to d. 13:5*
the coasts did Israel d. 1 Sam 7:14
which cannot profit nor d. 12:21
I will d. the Philistines. 23:4 2 Sam 5:19
I will d. thine enemy. 1 Sam 24:4
the Lord will d. Israel to. 28:19
king will hear to d. his. 2 Sam 14:16
d. thy servant to Ahab. 1 Ki 18:9
I will d. this multitude. 20:13, 28
go up, for the Lord shall d. it. 22:6, 12, 15; 2 Chr 18:5, 11
he will d. the Moabites. 2 Ki 3:18
d. it for breaches of house. 12:7
Lord d. Jerusalem. 18:35; Isa 36:20
let them d. it into hand. 2 Ki 22:5
who could not d. their. 2 Chr 25:15
now hear me and d. the. 28:11*
gods of nations able to d.? 32:13
that your God be able to d. 14, 17
those d. thou before the. Ezra 7:19
there is none can d. out. Job 10:7
he shall d. the island of. 22:30
he will d. his soul from. 33:28*
d. my soul. Ps 6:4; 17:13; 22:20 116:4; 120:2
while there is none to d. 7:2; 50:22
nor shall he d. any by his. 33:17
to d. their soul from death. 19
not d. my feet from falling? 56:13
for he shall d. the needy. 72:12
d. not soul of thy turtle-dove. 74:19
d. poor and needy out of. 82:4
shall he d. his soul from? 89:48
crown of glory shall she d. to. Pr 4:9
do this now, and d. thyself. 6:3
thou shalt d. his soul from. 23:14
wickedness d. those. Eccl 8:8
safe, and none shall d. it. Isa 5:29
which men d. to one. 29:11
defending also he will d. it. 31:5
he cannot d. his soul. 44:20
they stoop, they could not d. 46:2
they shall not d. themselves. 47:14

have I no power to d.? Isa 50:2
residue of them will I d. Jer 15:9
therefore d. up their children. 18:21
I will d. all strength of city. 20:5*
afterwards I will d. Zedekiah. 21:7
d. the spoiled out of the hand. 22:3
d. such as are for death. 43:11
d. every man his soul. 51:6*, 45*
I will d. my people. Ezek 13:21, 23
should d. but own souls. 14:14, 20
shall d. neither sons nor. 16, 18, 20
taketh warning shall d. soul. 33:5
I will d. my flock from. 34:10
no other god can d. Dan 3:29
nor was there any that could d. 8:4
none that could d. the ram. 7
none shall d. her out of. Hos 2:10
neither shall mighty d. Amos 2:14
swift of foot shall not d. himself. 15
I will d. the city. 6:8
in pieces and none d. Mi 5:8
take hold, but shalt not d. 6:14*
d. thyself, O Zion, that. Zech 2:7*
I will d. every one into his. 11:6
brother shall d. brother. Mat 10:21
manner of Romans to d. Acts 25:16*
d. such one to Satan. 1 Cor 5:5
from death, and doth d. 2 Cor 1:10
Lord knoweth how to d. 2 Pet 2:9

deliver *him*

rid him, to d. him to. Gen 37:22*
d. him into my hand. 42:37
but God will d. him. Ex 21:13
that he might d. him. Deut 2:30
I will d. him and his people. 3:2
d. him into the hand of. 19:12
in any case shalt d. him. 24:13*
draw Sisera and d. him. Judg 4:7
our part be to d. him. 1 Sam 23:20
d. him that smote his. 2 Sam 14:7
d. him and I will depart. 20:21
d him from going down. Job 33:24
d. him, let him d. him. Ps 22:8*
Lord will d. him in time of. 41:1
thou wilt not d. him to will of. 2
for there is none to d. him. 71:11
therefore will I d. him. 91:14
I will be with him, will d. him. 15
if thou d. him, thou must. Pr 19:19
d. him that is spoiled. Jer 21:12
righteousness of righteous shall not d. him. Ezek 33:12
on Daniel to d. him. Dan 6:14*
a shadow to d. him from. Jonah 4:6
d. him to Gentiles to crucify. Mat 20:19; Mark 10:33
Luke 20:20; Acts 21:11
give, and I will d. him. Mat 26:15
let him d. him now. 27:43

deliver *me*

d. me, I pray thee, from. Gen 32:11
he will d. me out of. 1 Sam 17:37
will men of Keilah d. me? 23:11, 12
and d. me out of thy hand. 24:15
let him d. me out of all. 26:24
nor d. me into the hands. 30:15
d. me my wife Michal. 2 Sam 3:14
d. me silver and gold. 1 Ki 20:5
d. me from enemies. Job 6:23
Ps 31:15; 59:1
me from them and d. me. Ps 7:1
keep my soul, and d. me. 25:20
d. me not over to the will. 27:12
d. me in thy righteousness. 31:1
71:2
d. me speedily. 31:2
d. me from my transgressions. 39:8
be pleased to d. me. 40:13
d. me from the deceitful and. 43:1
d. me from blood-guiltiness. 51:14
d. me from workers of. 59:2
d. me out of the mire. 69:14
and redeem it, d. me. 18*
make haste to d. me. 70:1
d. me, O my God, out of. 71:4*
mercy is good d. thou me. 109:21
d. me from oppression. 119:134*
mine affliction, and d. me. 153
plead my cause, and d. me. 154*
d. me according to thy word. 170
d. me, O Lord, from the evil. 140:1
d. me from my persecutors. 142:6
d. me from mine enemies. 143:9

d. me out of great waters. Ps 144:7
d. me from the hand of strange. 11
d. me, for thou art my. Isa 44:17
the Jews, lest they d. me. Jer 38:19
no man may d. me. Acts 25:11*
who shall d. me from? Rom 7:24
the Lord shall d. me. 2 Tim 4:18

deliver *thee*

people which Lord d. thee. Deut 7:16
midst of thy camp to d. thee. 23:14
that we may d. thee. Judg 15:12, 13
the Lord will d. thee. 1 Sam 17:46
they will d. thee up. 23:12
I will d. thee two. 2 Ki 18:23*
will d. thee and city. 20:6; Isa 38:6
d. thee in six troubles. Job 5:19
great ransom cannot d. thee. 36:18*
I will d. thee, and thou. Ps 50:15
he shall d. thee from snare. 91:3
to d. thee from the way. Pr 2:12
to d. thee from the strange. 16
let thy companies d. thee. Isa 57:13
to d. thee. Jer 1:8, 19; 15:20, 21
they shall not d. thee. 38:20
I will d. thee in that day. 39:17
I will surely d. thee. 18
d. thee into the hand. Ezek 21:31
I will d. thee to them. 23:28
I will d. thee to men of east. 25:4
I will d. thee for a spoil. 7
thou servest will d. thee. Dan 6:16
is thy God able to d. thee? 20
how shall I d. thee, Israel? Hos 11:8
judge d. thee to the. Mat 5:25
Luke 12:58

deliver *them*

come down to d. them. Ex 3:8
Acts 7:34
thy God shall d. them. Deut 7:2, 23
to-morrow will I d. them. Josh 11:6
and if the Lord d. them. Judg 11:9
to-morrow I will d. them. 20:28
wilt thou d. them. 1 Sam 14:37
2 Sam 5:19; 1 Chr 14:10
d. them to the enemy. 1 Ki 8:46
2 Ki 21:14
d. them into hand of. 2 Ki 3:10, 13
will d. them into thy. 1 Chr 14:10
and d. them over. 2 Chr 6:36
that he might d. them. 25:20
times didst d. them. Neh 9:28
neither any to d. them. Job 5:4
trusted, thou didst d. them. Ps 22:4
the Lord shall d. them. 37:40*
many times did he d. them. 106:43
of upright shall d. them. Pr 11:6
mouth of upright shall d. them. 12:6
forbear to d. them that. 24:11
a Saviour and d. them. Isa 19:20
I will d. them to. Jer 24:9*; 29:18
d. them into hand of. 29:21; 46:26
gold shall not d. them. Ezek 7:19
Zeph 1:18
will I seek and d. them. Ezek 34:12
carried away to d. them. Amos 1:6
I will not d. them. Zech 11:6
God would d. them. Acts 7:25
d. them who through fear. Heb 2:15

deliver *us*

to d. us into hand of. Deut 1:27
Josh 7:7
d. us only, we pray. Judg 10:15
d. us the men, the children. 20:13
who shall d. us out of? 1 Sam 4:8
d. us out of hand of enemies. 12:10
the Lord will d. us. 2 Ki 18:30, 32
Isa 36:15, 18
d. us from the heathen. 1 Chr 16:35
our God shall d. us. 2 Chr 32:11
d. us, and purge away. Ps 79:9
to d. us into the hand. Jer 43:3
none that doth d. us out. Lam 5:8
to d. us, and will d. us. Dan 3:17
thus shall he d. us from. Mi 5:6
but d. us from evil. Mat 6:13
Luke 11:4
that he will yet d. us. 2 Cor 1:10
that he might d. us from. Gal 1:4

deliver *you*

I d. you your brother. Gen 42:34
they shall d. you your. Lev 26:26

did not I d. you from? Judg 10:11*
forsaken me, I will d. you no. 13*
let them d. you in the time of. 14*
he will d. you from. 1 Sam 7:3
he shall d. you from. 2 Ki 17:39
shall not be able to d. you. 18:29
Isa 36:14
be able to d. you out. 2 Chr 32:14
I will carry, and will d. you. Isa 46:4
I will d. you into hands. Ezek 11:9
God that shall d. you? Dan 3:15
for they will d. you up. Mat 10:17
Mark 13:9
but when they d. you up. Mat 10:19
24:9; Mark 13:11

deliverance

your lives by a great d. Gen 45:7
hast given this great d. Judg 15:18
Lord had given d. to. 2 Ki 5:1*
arrow of the Lord's d. of d. 13:17*
saved them by great d. 1 Chr 11:14*
grant them some d. 2 Chr 12:7
given us such a d. as. Ezra 9:13*
d. arise to the Jews. Esth 4:14
great d. giveth he to. Ps 18:50
with songs of d. 32:7
wrought any d. in earth. Isa 26:18
in Jerusalem shall be d. Joel 2:32*
upon mount Zion shall be d. Ob 17*
sent me to preach d. to. Luke 4:18*
tortured, not accepting d. Heb 11:35

deliverances

my King, command d. Ps 44:4

delivered

into your hand are they d. Gen 9:2
God who d. thine enemies. 14:20
when her days to be d. 25:24
d. ere the midwives come. Ex 1:19
neither hast thou d. thy. 5:23
smote the Egyptians, and d. 12:27
who hath d. people from. 18:10
the Lord our God d. all. Deut 2:36
God d. into our hands the. 3:3
Lord d. unto me two tables. 9:10
and Moses d. the law unto. 31:9
Lord d. their enemies. Josh 21:44
he d. the Canaanites into. Judg 1:4
after him Shamgar d. Israel. 3:31*
they that are d. from the. 5:11*
when Lord hath d. Zebah and. 8:7
Lord d. Sihon into hand. 11:21
our god hath d. Samson. 16:23, 24
was near to be d. 1 Sam 4:19
I smote him and d. it. 17:35
who d. the company that. 30:23
of Saul's sons be d. 2 Sam 21:6
and I was d. of child. 1 Ki 3:17
I was d. this woman was d. 18
and shalt thou be d.? 2 Ki 19:11
Isa 37:11
d. that parcel and slew. 1 Chr 11:14*
on that day David d. 16:7*
Jehoiada d. to the. 2 Chr 23:9
d money that was brought. 34:9
Hilkiah d. book to Shaphan. 15
the vessels were d. to. Ezra 5:14
d. the king's commissions. 8:36
it is d. by the pureness. Job 22:30
so should I be d. for ever. 23:7
I d. the poor that cried. 29:12
cried to thee, and were d. Ps 22:5
a mighty man is not d. by. 33:16
he hath d. my soul in peace. 55:18*
d. my soul from death. 56:13; 86:13
116:8
beloved may be d. 60:5; 108:6
let me be d. from them. 69:14
and d. his strength into. 78:61
the righteous is d. out of. Pr 11:8
knowledge shall the just be d. 9
seed of righteous shall be d. 21
whoso walketh wisely be d. 28:26
by wisdom he d. city. Eccl 9:15
to be d. from the king. Isa 20:6
the book is d. to him that is. 29:12
and have they d. Samaria? 36:19
thou hast d. it from the pit of. 38:17
shall the lawful captive be d.? 49:24
prey of the terrible shall be d. 25
before pain came, she was d. 66:7
we are d. to do all. Jer 7:10
d. the soul of the poor. 20:13
when I had d. the evidence. 32:16

but thou hast d. thy soul.
Ezek 3:19, 21; 33:9
they only shall be d. 14:16, 18
break covenant and be d.? 17:15*
for they are all d. unto. 31:14
she is d. to the sword. 32:20
and d. his servants. Dan 3:28
who d. Daniel from the power. 6:27
thy people shall be d. 12:1
name of Lord shall be d. Joel 2:32
that escapeth not be d. Amos 9:1*
there shalt thou be d. Mi 4:10*
that he may be d. from. Hab 2:9
they that tempt God d. Mal 3:15†
all things are d. unto me of my.
Mat 11:27; Luke 10:22
commanded body be d. Mat 27:58*
tradition which ye have d. Mark 7:13
Son of man shall be d. to. 10:33
Barabbas, and d. Jesus. 15:15
Luke 23:25
time that she be d. Luke 1:57; 2:6
that is d. unto me, and to. 4:6
there was d. unto him the book. 17
Son of man shall be d. into. 9:44
diligence that thou be d. 12:58*
for he shall be d. unto. 18:32
as soon as she is d. of. John 16:21
that I should not be d. 18:36
being d. by the counsel. Acts 2:23
came to Antioch and d. 15:30
and they d. the epistle to. 23:33
they d. Paul to one Julius. 27:1
yet was I d. prisoner. 28:17
was d. for our offences. Rom 4:25
now we are d. from the law. 7:6*
creature itself shall be d. 8:21
I may be d. from them. 15:31
are alway d. to death. 2 Cor 4:11
we may be d. from. 2 Thes 3:2
I have d. to Satan. 1 Tim 1:20
d. out of mouth of lion. 2 Tim 4:17
by faith Sarah was d. Heb 11:11
and d. just Lot. 2 Pet 2:7
from the commandment d. 21
the faith which was once d. Jude 3
and pained to be d. Rev 12:2
before woman ready to be d. 4

see **hand, hands**

delivered *him*
Reuben d. him. Gen 37:21
was d. him to keep. Lev 6:2*, 4
Lord our God d. him. Deut 2:33
Lord d. him to the lion. 1 Ki 13:26
Elijah d. him unto his mother. 17:23
d. him that is mine. Ps 7:4
the Lord d. him to the. Mat 18:34
d. him to Pilate. 27:2; Mark 15:1
for envy they had d. him. Mat 27:18
Mark 15:10
d. him to be crucified. Mat 27:26
John 19:16
and Jesus d. him to. Luke 7:15*
healed child and d. him. 9:42
d. him to be condemned. 24:20
not have d. him to thee. John 18:30
God d. him out of his. Acts 7:10
d. him to four quaternions. 12:4

delivered *me*
God d. me from sword. Ex 18:4
I saw ye d. me not. Judg 12:3*
the Lord that d. me. 1 Sam 17:37
d. me from strong. 2 Sam 22:18
he d. me because. 20; Ps 18:19
hast d. me from violent man.
2 Sam 22:49; Ps 18:48
Hilkiah d. me a book. 2 Ki 22:10
God hath d. me to the. Job 16:11
d. me from strong enemies. Ps 18:17
hast d. me from the strivings. 43
the Lord heard and d. me. 34:4
d. me out of all trouble. 54:7
he that d. me to thee. John 19:11
of them all Lord d. me. 2 Tim 3:11

delivered *thee*
Lord d. thee to-day. 1 Sam 24:10
I d. thee out of hand of. 2 Sam 12:7
in trouble, and I d. thee. Ps 81:7
I d. thee to will of them. Ezek 16:27
chief priests d. thee. John 18:35

delivered *them*
how the Lord d. them. Ex 18:8
tables of stone, d. them. Deut 5:22*
deliverer, who d. them. Judg 3:9*
gods of nations d. them. 2 Ki 19:12
Isa 37:12
hath d. them to trouble. 2 Chr 29:8
when he d. them. Ps 78:42*
d. them out of their. 107:6
d. them from destructions. 20
d. them to the slaughter. Isa 34:2
d. them to cause them. Ezek 16:21
and d. to them his goods. Mat 25:14
even as they d. them to. Luke 1:2
he d. them ten pounds, and. 19:13*
they d. them the decrees. Acts 16:4
as I d. them to you. 1 Cor 11:2
and d. them into chains. 2 Pet 2:4*

delivered *up*
Lord d. up Canaanites. Num 21:3
Lord d. up Amorites. Josh 10:12
d. up the men that. 2 Sam 18:28
because they d. up the. Amos 1:9
nor shouldest have d. up. Ob 14
his Son whom ye d. up. Acts 3:13
but d. him up for us. Rom 8:32
have d. up kingdom. 1 Cor 15:24
death and hell d. up. Rev 20:13*

delivered *us*
an Egyptian d. us from. Ex 2:19
customs Moses d. us. Acts 6:14
d. us from so great a. 2 Cor 1:10
hath d. us from power of. Col 1:13
Jesus, who d. us from. 1 Thes 1:10

delivered *you*
doctrine which was d. you. Rom 6:17
I received of the Lord that which also
I d. unto you. 1 Cor 11:23; 15:3

deliveredst, -est
thou d. them to enemies. Neh 9:27
who d. poor from him. Ps 35:10
what thou d. will I give. Mi 6:14*
Lord, thou d. unto me. Mat 25:20
thou d. unto me two talents. 22

deliverer
a d. to Israel. Judg 3:9*, 15*
there was no d. 18:28
Lord is my rock and d. 2 Sam 22:2
Ps 18:2
my help and my d. Ps 40:17; 70:5
my high tower, and my d. 144:2
did God send to be a d. Acts 7:35
out of Sion the d. Rom 11:26

delivereth
he d. the poor in his. Job 36:15
he d. me from mine. Ps 18:48*
and d. them. 34:7
the Lord d. them out of. 17*, 19
he d. them out of the hand. 97:10
who d. David from. 144:10*
righteousness d. Pr 10:2; 11:4
a true witness d. souls. 14:25
and she d. girdles. 31:24
for a prey, and none d. Isa 42:22
God d. and rescueth. Dan 6:27

delivering
d. you up to synagogues. Luke 21:12
d. into prisons both. Acts 22:4
d. thee from the people. 26:17

delivery
near the time of her d. Isa 26:17

delusion
send them strong d. 2 Thes 2:11*

delusions
I also will choose their d. Isa 66:4

demand
the d. by the word of. Dan 4:17

demand, -ed, *verb*
d. why have ye not? Ex 5:14
David d. of Uriah. 2 Sam 11:7*
I will d. of thee, answer. Job 38:3
40:7; 42:4
secret which the king d. Dan 2:27
d. where Christ should. Mat 2:4*
the soldiers d. of him. Luke 3:14*
and when he was d. of the. 17:20*
the chief captain d. Acts 21:33*

Demas
Luke and D. greet you. Col 4:14
Philem 24
D. hath forsaken me. 2 Tim 4:10

Demetrius
D. a silversmith, who. Acts 19:24
if D. have a matter against. 38
D. hath good report of. 3 John 12

demonstration
but in d. of the Spirit. 1 Cor 2:4

den, -s
of Israel made them d. Judg 6:2
then beasts go into d. Job 37:8*
they couch in their d. 38:40
in wait as a lion in his d. Ps 10:9
lay themselves down in d. 104:22
from the lion's d. S of S 4:8
hand on cockatrice' d. Isa 11:8*
the towers shall be for d. 32:14
house become a d. of? Jer 7:11
Jerusalem a d. of dragons. 9:11*
cities of Judah a d. of. 10:22*
cast into d. of lions. Dan 6:7, 12
they cast him into the d. 16
king arose went in haste to the d. 19
take Daniel up out of the d. 23
cast them into the d. of lions. 24
lion cry out of his d.? Amos 3:4
the lion filled his d. with. Nah 2:12
house of prayer, but ye have made
it a d. Mat 21:13; Mark 11:17
in deserts and in d. Heb 11:38*
and freeman hid in d. Rev 6:15*

denied
Sarah d. saying, I. Gen 18:15
and I d. him not. 1 Ki 20:7
I should have d. God. Job 31:28*
Peter d. before them all, saying, I.
Mat 26:70, 72; Mark 14:70
Luke 22:57; John 18:25, 27
when all d. that they. Luke 8:45
who denies shall be d. before. 12:9
and d. not, I am not. John 1:20
till thou hast d. me thrice. 13:38
d. in presence of Pilate. Acts 3:13
but ye d. the holy One and the. 14
he hath d. the faith. 1 Tim 5:8
and not d. my faith. Rev 2:13
and hast not d. my name. 3:8

denieth, -ing
he that d. me before. Luke 12:9
form of godliness, but d. 2 Tim 3:5
that d. ungodliness and. Tit 2:12
even d. the Lord that. 2 Pet 2:1
is a liar, that d. Jesus. 1 John 2:22
who d. the Son. 23
d. the only Lord God. Jude 4

denounce
I d. this day. Deut 30:18

deny
lest ye d. your God. Josh 24:27
d. me not. 1 Ki 2:16; Pr 30:7
then it shall d. him. Job 8:18
lest I be full and d. thee. Pr 30:9
d. me, him will I d. Mat 10:33
let him d. himself. 16:24
Mark 8:34; Luke 9:23
cock crow thou shalt d. me thrice.
Mat 26:34, 75; Mark 14:30, 72
yet will I not d. thee. Mat 26:35
Mark 14:31
d. there is any resurrection.
Luke 20:27
d. him, he will d. us. 2 Tim 2:12
abideth faithful, cannot d. 13
but in works they d. him. Tit 1:16

depart
if thou d. to the right. Gen 13:9
Moses let father-in-law d. Ex 18:27
d. thou and the people thou. 33:1
I will d. to mine own. Num 10:30
from day thou didst d. Deut 9:7
Joshua let people d. to. Josh 24:28
Levite rose up to d. Judg 19:5, 7, 8, 9
abide not in hold, d. 1 Sam 22:5
be up and have light, d. 29:10
and his men rose up to d. 11
lead them away and d. 30:22
I will let thee d. 2 Sam 11:12
make speed to d. lest. 15:14
d. for three days. 1 Ki 12:5
increase of house shall d. Job 20:28
envy of Ephraim shall d. Isa 11:13
d. ye, d. ye, out. 52:11; Lam 4:15
for the mountains shall d. Isa 54:10
they shall d. man and. Jer 50:3

arise ye, and d. this is. Mi 2:10
sceptre of Egypt shall d. Zech 10:11
besought him that he d. out of their coasts. Mat 8:34; Mark 5:17
when ye d. out of that house or city. Mat 10:14; Mark 6:11; Luke 9:4
thy servant d. in peace. Luke 2:29
d. hence, Herod will kill thee. 13:31
which are in midst d. out. 21:21
they said, d. hence and. John 7:3
when Jesus knew he should d. 13:1
but if I d. I will send him. 16:7
d. and go in peace. Acts 16:36
desired them to d. out of city. 39
them ready to d. on morrow. 20:7
d. for I will send thee to the. 22:21
that he himself would d. 25:4
more part advised to d. 27:12
if she d. let her remain. 1 Cor 7:11
if the unbelieving d. let him d. 15
a desire to d. and to be. Phil 1:23
say to them, d. in peace. Jas 2:16

depart *from*

frogs shall d. from thee. Ex 8:11
swarms of flies may d. from. 29
so that her fruit d. from. 21:22
then shall he d. from. Lev 25:41
d. from the tents of. Num 16:26
lest they d. from thy. Deut 4:9
fearful, let him d. from. Judg 7:3
d. from the Amalekites. 1 Sam 15:6
sword never d. from. 2 Sam 12:10
and I will d. from the city. 20:21
d. from me. 1 Ki 15:19; 2 Chr 16:3
moved them to d. from. 2 Chr 18:31
to God, d. from us. Job 21:14; 22:17
and to d. from evil is. 28:28
d. from me, ye workers. Ps 6:8
Mat 7:23; Luke 13:27
d. from evil, and do good. Ps 34:14
37:27
froward heart shall d. from. 101:4
d. from me, ye evil doers. 119:115
d. from me therefore. 139:19
and d. from evil. Pr 3:7
to d. from the snares. 13:14; 14:27
to fools to d. from evil. 13:19
that he may d. from hell. 15:24
fear of Lord men d. from evil. 16:6
of upright is to d. from evil. 17
his burden d. from off. Isa 14:25
lest my soul d. from thee. Jer 6:8*
that d. from me shall be. 17:13
if those ordinances d. from. 31:36
Chaldeans shall surely d. from. 37:9
jealousy shall d. from. Ezek 16:42
to them when I d. from. Hos 9:12
d. from me, ye cursed. Mat 25:41
abide, till ye d. from. Mark 6:10
d. from me, I am a sinful. Luke 5:8
besought him to d. from. 8:37
not d. from Jerusalem. Acts 1:4
all the Jews to d. from Rome. 18:2
let not wife d. from her. 1 Cor 7:10
that it might d. from. 2 Cor 12:8
shall d. from the faith. 1 Tim 4:1*
d. from iniquity. 2 Tim 2:19

not **depart**

sceptre shall not d. Gen 49:10
book of law shall not d. Josh 1:8
d. not hence, till I come. Judg 6:18
my mercy shall not d. 2 Sam 7:15
his statutes, I did not d. from. 22:23
they might not d. 2 Chr 35:15
how long wilt thou not d.? Job 7:19*
shall not d. out of darkness. 15:30
deceit and guile d. not. Ps 55:11
let them not d. Pr 3:21; 4:21
hear me, and d. not from. 5:7
evil shall not d. from his. 17:13
when old he will not d. from it. 22:6
will not his foolishness d. 27:22
kindness shall not d. Isa 54:10
Spirit, and words, shall not d. 59:21
they shall not d. from. Jer 32:40
for they shall not d. 37:9
they need not d. give. Mat 14:16
that should not d. from. Luke 4:42
thou shalt not d. thence, till. 12:59

departed

so Abraham d. as. Gen 12:4
they took Lot and d. 14:12
Hagar d. 21:14
Eliezer d. Gen 24:10
Isaac d. 26:17
Laban d. 31:55
they are d. hence, to Dothan. 37:17
laded their asses and d. 42:26
brethren away, and they d. 45:24
was kindled, and he d. Num 12:9
elders of Moab and Midian d. 22:7
spies away, and they d. Josh 2:21
d. every man to his. Judg 9:55
2 Sam 6:19
then the five men d. Judg 18:7, 21
the Levite d. 19:10
Israel d. thence. 21:24
Israel go, and they d.? 1 Sam 6:6
David d. 20:42; 22:1, 5
so Nathan d. 2 Sam 12:15
from day the king d. 19:24
and the people d. 1 Ki 12:5
2 Chr 10:5
wife arose and d. to. 1 Ki 14:17
Elijah d. and. 19:19; 2 Ki 1:4
the messengers d. and. 1 Ki 20:9
prophet d. and waited for. 38
Naaman d. 2 Ki 5:5
Jehu arose and d. 10:12, 15
so Sennacherib d. 19:36; Isa 37:37
all people d. every. 1 Chr 16:43
wherefore Joab d. and. 21:4
Jehoram d. without. 2 Chr 21:20
Egypt glad when they d. Ps 105:38
mine age is d. and. Isa 38:12
Ishmael d. to go over. Jer 41:10
all her beauty is d. Lam 1:6
king, wise men d. Mat 2:9, 12
arose, and d. into Egypt. 14
Jesus d. 4:12; 9:27; 11:1; 12:9
13:53; 14:13; 15:21, 29; 16:4
19:15; Mark 1:35; 6:46
8:13; Luke 4:42; John 4:3, 43
6:15; 12:36
Judas d. Mat 27:5
Zacharias d. to his house. Luke 1:23
he d. to his own house. 5:25
messengers of John were d. 7:24
out of whom the devils were d. 8:35
thieves wounded him and d. 10:30
when the Samaritan d. 35
the man d. and told. John 5:15
when the angel d. Acts 10:7
Barnabas d. 11:25
Peter d. 12:17
they d. to Seleucia. 13:4
Paul d. 14:20; 18:7, 23
20:1, 11
Paul and Barnabas d. asunder. 15:39
Paul and Silas d. 16:40
d. and went. 21:5, 8; 28:10, 11
these words, the Jews d. 28:29
forsaken me, is d. to. 2 Tim 4:10
perhaps he therefore d. Philem 15*
and the heaven d. as. Rev 6:14

departed *from*

arose and d. from. Gen 26:31
my sleep d. from mine. 31:40*
were d. from. Ex 19:2; Num 33:15
all Israel d. from presence. Ex 35:20
plague be d. from them. Lev 13:58
they d. from the mount. Num 10:33*
the cloud d. from off. 12:10
defence is d. from them. 14:9
they d. from Rameses. 33:3
d. from Succoth. 6
d. from Pi-hahiroth. 8
d. from Dophkah. 13
All their departures set down to verse 49
we d. from Horeb. Deut 1:19
not that Lord d. from. Judg 16:20
glory is d. from. 1 Sam 4:21, 22
when thou art d. from me. 10:2
Kenites d. from among the. 15:6
Spirit d. from Saul. 16:14; 18:12
the evil spirit d. from him. 23
God is d. from me. 28:15
seeing the Lord is d. from thee. 16
as thou art d. from me. 1 Ki 20:36
they d. from him to. 2 Ki 3:27
so he d. from Elisha. 5:19; 8:14
Sennacherib d. from. 19:8; Isa 37:8
they were d. from him. 2 Chr 24:25
then we d. from the river. Ezra 8:31
wickedly d. from my God. Ps 18:21
Ephraim d. from Judah. Isa 7:17
smiths were d. from. Jer 29:2
Chaldeans heard they d. from. 37:5*
which hath d. from us. Ezek 6:9
glory of the Lord d. from. 10:18
the kingdom is d. from. Dan 4:31
glory of Samaria d. from. Hos 10:5
Jesus d. from thence. Mat 15:29
he d. from Galilee. 19:1
as they d. from Jericho. 20:29
Jesus d. from the temple. 24:1
they d. quickly from the. 28:8
leprosy d. from him. Mark 1:42
Luke 5:13
angel d. from Mary. Luke 1:38
the devil d. from him for. 4:13
as they d. from him. 9:33
d. from the presence. Acts 5:41
forthwith angel d. from him. 12:10
they had d. from Perga. 13:14*
John d. from them from. 15:38
Paul d. from them. 17:33; 18:1
19:9; Phil 4:15
diseases d. from them. Acts 19:12
after are d. from thee, and all things dainty are d. from. Rev 18:14*

departed *not from*

not d. from my God. 2 Sam 22:22
Ps 18:21
he d. not therefrom. 2 Ki 3:3; 13:2
Jehu d. not from sins of. 10:29, 31
13:6, 11; 14:24; 15:9, 18; 17:22
Hezekiah d. not from. 18:6
d. not from commandment of.
2 Chr 8:15
Jehoshaphat d. not from the. 20:32*
d. not from following Lord. 34:33
cloud d. not from them. Neh 9:19
I have not d. from thy. Ps 119:102
Anna d. not from temple. Luke 2:37

departed *out*

old when he d. out of. Gen 12:4
when she is d. out of. Deut 24:2
angel of the Lord d. out. Judg 6:21
Levite d. out of Beth-lehem. 17:8
David and men d. out. 1 Sam 23:13
Uriah d. out of king's. 2 Sam 11:8
ye are d. out of the way. Mal 2:8*
devil, and he d. out of. Mat 17:18

departed *not out*

Joshua d. not out of. Ex 33:11
and Moses d. not out. Num 14:44

departeth

him away, and he d. Job 27:21
a wise man feareth, and d. Pr 14:16
in with vanity, and d. Eccl 6:4
he that d. from evil. Isa 59:15
wife treacherously d. Jer 3:20
cursed be man whose heart d. 17:5
bloody city, prey d. not. Nah 3:1
hardly d. from him. Luke 9:39

departing

as her soul was in d. Gen 35:18
after their d. out of land. Ex 16:1
in lying and d. away. Isa 59:13
we have sinned, by d. Dan 9:5*, 11
committed whoredom d. Hos 1:2
the people saw them d. Mark 6:33
d. from coast of Tyre and. 7:31
John d. from them. Acts 13:13
after my d. shall wolves. 20:29
an evil heart, in d. Heb 3:12
Joseph made mention of d. 11:22

departure

isles shall be troubled at thy d.
Ezek 26:18
time of my d. is at hand. 2 Tim 4:6

deposed

was d. from kingly. Dan 5:20

deprived

why should I be d.? Gen 27:45*
because God hath d. her. Job 39:17
I am d. of the residue of. Isa 38:10

depth

d. saith it is not in me. Job 28:14*
walked in search of the d.? 38:16*
he layeth up the d. Ps 33:7*
compass on face of the d. Pr 8:27*
and the earth for d. 25:3
ask it either in the d. Isa 7:11

the *d.* closed me round. *Jonah* 2:5
drowned in the *d.* of the. *Mat* 18:6
because it had no *d.* of. *Mark* 4:5
nor *d.* separate us from. *Rom* 8:39
O the *d.* of the riches both. 11:33
what is breadth and *d.* *Eph* 3:18

depths

the *d.* have covered them. *Ex* 15:5
the *d.* were congealed in the. 8*
the *d.* that spring out of. *Deut* 8:7
my people from the *d.* *Ps* 68:22
shall bring me up from the *d.* 71:20
waters were afraid, the *d.* 77:16
drink as out of great *d.* 78:15
he led them through *d.* as. 106:9
they go down again to *d.* 107:26
out of the *d.* have I cried. 130:1
by his knowledge the *d.* *Pr* 3:20
when there no *d.* I was. 8:24
guests are in *d.* of hell. 9:18
that hath made the *d.* of. *Isa* 51:10
broken in *d.* of waters. *Ezek* 27:34
cast their sins into *d.* of. *Mi* 7:19
have not known the *d.* *Rev* 2:24

deputed

there is no man *d.* of. *2 Sam* 15:3

deputies

written to *d.* and rulers. *Esth* 8:9*
and the *d.* and officers. 9:3*
there are *d.* let them. *Acts* 19:38*

deputy

no king in Edom, a *d.* *1 Ki* 22:47
Bar-jesus which was with the *d.* *Acts* 13:7*
seeking to turn away the *d.* 8*
and when Gallio was the *d.* 18:12*

deride

shall *d.* every strong hold. *Hab* 1:10

derided

these things, and *d.* *Luke* 16:14
rulers also with people *d.* 23:35

derision

than I, have me in *d.* *Job* 30:1
Lord shall have them in *d.* *Ps* 2:4
a *d.* to them that are. 44:13; 79:4
all the heathen in *d.* 59:8
proud had me greatly in *d.* 119:51
I am in *d.* daily. *Jer* 20:7
was made a *d.* daily. 8
Moab also shall be in *d.* 48:26, 39
for was not Israel a *d.*? 27
I was a *d.* to my people. *Lam* 3:14
drink and be glad in *d.* *Ezek* 23:32
to cities which became a *d.* 36:4
this shall be their *d.* *Hos* 7:16

descend

the border shall *d.* *Num* 34:11
he shall *d.* into battle. *1 Sam* 26:10
his glory shall not *d.* *Ps* 49:17
with them that *d.* *Ezek* 26:20; 31:16
let Christ *d.* now. *Mark* 15:32
vessel *d.* as a great sheet. *Acts* 11:5
or who shall *d.* into ? *Rom* 10:7
Lord shall *d.* from. *1 Thes* 4:16

descended

because the Lord *d.* on. *Ex* 19:18
the cloudy pillar *d.* 33:9
d. in a cloud. 34:5
brook that *d.* out of. *Deut* 9:21
so the two men *d.* *Josh* 2:23
as dew that *d.* on. *Ps* 133:3
up to heaven, or *d.*? *Pr* 30:4
the rain *d.* and. *Mat* 7:25, 27
for angel of the Lord *d.* 28:2
the Holy Ghost *d.* in a. *Luke* 3:22
Ananias high-priest *d.* *Acts* 24:1
he that *d.* is the same. *Eph* 4:10

descendeth

this wisdom *d.* not from. *Jas* 3:15

descending

and angels ascending and *d.* *Gen* 28:12; *John* 1:51
saw the Spirit of God *d.* *Mat* 3:16; *Mark* 1:10
I saw the Spirit *d.* from. *John* 1:32
whom thou shalt see the Spirit *d.* 33
a vessel *d.* as it had. *Acts* 10:11
that great city *d.* out of. *Rev* 21:10

descent

when come nigh at *d.* *Luke* 19:37
father, mother, and *d.* *Heb* 7:3*
but he whose *d.* is not counted. 6*

describe, -ed, -eth

go through land *d.* it. *Josh* 18:4, 6, 8
charged them that went to *d.* 8
and they *d.* it by cities into seven. 9
he *d.* to him the princes. *Judg* 8:14
even as David also *d.* *Rom* 4:6
for Moses *d.* righteousness. 10:5*

description

and ye shall bring the *d.* *Josh* 18:6

descry

of Joseph sent to *d.* *Judg* 1:23*

desert

(*In the Bible this word means a deserted place, wilderness, not desert in the modern usage of the term. Revised Versions frequently translate by* wilderness)

flock to backside of the *d.* *Ex* 3:1
three days' journey into *d.* 5:3
they were come to the *d.* 19:2
I will set thy bounds from *d.* 23:31
Israel came into *d.* of Zin. *Num* 20:1
against me in the *d.* of Zin. 27:14
removed from the *d.* of Sinai. 33:16
built towers in the *d.* *2 Chr* 26:10
as wild asses in the *d.* go. *Job* 24:5
grieve him in the *d.*? *Ps* 78:40
like pelican, an owl of *d.* 102:6
and tempted God in the *d.* 106:14
wild beasts of *d.* shall lie. *Isa* 13:21; 34:14; *Jer* 50:39
so it cometh from the *d.* *Isa* 21:1
the *d.* shall rejoice. 35:1
streams in the *d.* 6
make straight in *d.* a high. 40:3
I will set in *d.* the fir-tree. 41:19
make rivers in the *d.* 43:19, 20
will make her *d.* like garden. 51:3
be like heath in the *d.* *Jer* 17:6
people that dwell in *d.* shall. 25:24
be a dry land and a *d.* 50:12
waters go down into *d.* *Ezek* 47:8*
behold, he is in the *d.* *Mat* 24:26
did eat manna in the *d.* *John* 6:31
to Gaza, which is *d.* *Acts* 8:26

desert

render them their *d.* *Ps* 28:4

desert *land*

found him in a *d. land.* *Deut* 32:10

desert *place*

departed into a *d. place.* *Mat* 14:13; *Mark* 6:32; *Luke* 4:42
this is a *d. place.* *Mat* 14:15; *Mark* 6:35; *Luke* 9:12
come ye into a *d. place.* *Mark* 6:31
aside into a *d. place.* *Luke* 9:10

deserts

he led them through *d.* *Isa* 48:21
that led us through *d.* *Jer* 2:6
prophets like foxes in *d.* *Ezek* 13:4
John was in the *d.* till. *Luke* 1:80
they wandered in *d.* *Heb* 11:38

deserts

according to their *d.* *Ezek* 7:27

deserve

less than our iniquities *d.* *Ezra* 9:13

deserveth

less than thy iniquity *d.* *Job* 11:6

deserving

done according to *d.* of. *Judg* 9:16

desirable

all of them *d.* young men. *Ezek* 23:6, 12, 23

desire

[1] *Longing, coveting,* 2 Sam 23:5; Pr 11:23; 2 Cor 7:7. [2] *An expressed wish, or petition,* Ps 10:17; 1 Ki 2:20.

thy *d.* shall be to thy. *Gen* 3:16
to thee shall be his *d.* 4:7
and come with all the *d.* *Deut* 18:6
and hast a *d.* to her. 21:11
on whom is the *d.* of Israel ? *1 Sam* 9:20*
according to all the *d.* of. 23:20
my salvation, all my *d.* *2 Sam* 23:5
I will do all thy *d.* *1 Ki* 5:8
thou shalt accomplish my *d.* 9
to all Solomon's *d.* *1 Ki* 5:10; 9:11
and all his *d.* 9:1
gave to the queen of Sheba all her *d.* 10:13; *2 Chr* 9:12
sought him with their whole *d.* *2 Chr* 15:15
thou wilt have a *d.* to work. *Job* 14:15
withheld poor from their *d.* 31:16
my *d.* is that Almighty would. 35*
d. is that Job may be tried. 34:36*
boasteth of his heart's *d.* *Ps* 10:3
thou hast heard the *d.* of. 17
hast given his heart's *d.* 21:2
Lord, all my *d.* is before. 38:9
eye hath seen his *d.* 54:7; 92:11
God shall let me see my *d.* 59:10
he gave them their own *d.* 78:29*
mine ears shall hear my *d.* of. 92:11
till he see his *d.* on his. 112:8
d. of the wicked shall perish. 10
therefore shall I see my *d.* 118:7
thou satisfiest the *d.* of. 145:16
he will fulfil the *d.* of them. 19
the *d.* of righteous shall. *Pr* 10:24
the *d.* of the righteous is. 11:23
but when *d.* cometh. 13:12
the *d.* accomplished is sweet. 19
d. of a man is his kindness. 19:22*
the *d.* of the slothful. 21:25
than wandering of *d.* *Eccl* 6:9
d. shall fail, because man. 12:5*
my beloved's, his *d.* is. *S of S* 7:10
d. of our soul is to thy. *Isa* 26:8
snuffeth up wind at *d.* *Jer* 2:24
land to which you have a *d.* 44:14
I will take from thee *d.* *Ezek* 24:16
profane *d.* of your eyes. 21, 25
neither shall he regard *d.* *Dan* 11:37
it is my *d.* I should. *Hos* 10:10
uttereth his mischievous *d.* *Mi* 7:3
enlargeth his *d.* as hell. *Hab* 2:5
the *d.* of all nations. *Hag* 2:7*
with *d.* have I desired. *Luke* 22:15
my heart's *d.* to God. *Rom* 10:1
having a great *d.* to come. 15:23
told us your earnest *d.* *2 Cor* 7:7
what fear, what vehement *d.* 11
in a strait, having a *d.* to. *Phil* 1:23
your face with great *d.* *1 Thes* 2:17

desire, *verb*

for that ye did *d.* *Ex* 10:11
neither shall any man *d.* 34:24
nor shalt thou *d.* thy. *Deut* 5:21
thou shalt not *d.* the silver. 7:25*
I would *d.* a request of. *Judg* 8:24
I *d.* one small petition. *1 Ki* 2:20
did I *d.* a son of my lord ? *2 Ki* 4:28
thy servants who *d.* to. *Neh* 1:11*
surely I *d.* to reason. *Job* 13:3
for we *d.* not knowledge of. 21:14
speak, for I *d.* to justify thee. 33:32
d. not the night when. 36:20
offering thou didst not *d.* *Ps* 40:6
so shall the king greatly *d.* 45:11
put to confusion that *d.* my. 70:2
there is none on earth I *d.* 73:25
all thou canst *d.* are not. *Pr* 3:15
neither *d.* thou his dainty. 23:6
against evil men, nor *d.* to be. 24:1
no beauty that we should *d.* *Isa* 53:2
land whereunto they *d.* *Jer* 22:27
die in the place whither ye *d.* 42:22
I would *d.* mercies of the. *Dan* 2:18
woe to you that *d.* day. *Amos* 5:18
if any man *d.* to be first. *Mark* 9:35
for us whatsoever we shall *d.* 10:35
what things soever ye *d.* 11:24
began to *d.* him to do as. 15:8
when ye shall *d.* to see. *Luke* 17:22
the scribes which *d.* to walk. 20:46
Jews have agreed to *d.* *Acts* 23:20
we *d.* to hear of thee. 28:22
follow after charity, *d.* *1 Cor* 14:1
from them which *d.* *2 Cor* 11:12
though I would *d.* to glory. 12:6
whereunto ye *d.* again to. *Gal* 4:9
I *d.* to be present with you now. 20
tell me, ye that *d.* to be under ? 21
as many as *d.* to make fair. 6:12
but *d.* to have you circumcised. 13
wherefore I *d.* that ye. *Eph* 3:13
d. a gift, but I *d.* fruit. *Phil* 4:17
to *d.* that ye might be filled. *Col* 1:9

if a man d. the office of a. 1 Tim 3:1
we d. every one of you. Heb 6:11
they d. a better country. 11:16
ye kill, ye d. to have. Jas 4:2*
which things angels d. to. 1 Pet 1:12
as new-born babes d. sincere. 2:2
men shall d. to die, and. Rev 9:6

desired

and a tree to be d. to. Gen 3:6
the king whom ye d. 1 Sam 12:13
desire which Solomon d. 1 Ki 9:19
2 Chr 8:6
and Rehoboam d. many. 2 Chr 11:23
whatsoever she d. was. Esth 2:13
save of that which he d. Job 20:20*
more to be d. are they. Ps 19:10
one thing I d. of the Lord. 27:4
bringeth them to d. haven. 107:30
he hath d. Zion for his. 132:13
will I dwell, for I have d. 14
all that may be d. not. Pr 8:11
there is a treasure to be d. 21:20*
what my eyes d. I kept. Eccl 2:10
of the oaks ye have d. Isa 1:29
with my soul have I d. 26:9
nor have I d. woeful day. Jer 17:16
Daniel went and d. of. Dan 2:16
known unto me what we d. 23
for I d. mercy and not. Hos 6:6
no cluster, my soul d. fruit. Mi 7:1
O nation not d. Zeph 2:1*
righteous men have d. to. Mat 13:17
the Pharisees d. he would. 16:1
prisoner whom they d. Mark 15:6
Luke 23:25
one of the Pharisees d. Luke 7:36
Herod d. to see him. 9:9*
many kings have d. to. 10:24
I have d. to eat passover. 22:15
Satan hath d. to have you to. 31
released him whom they d. 23:25
d. a murderer to be. Acts 3:14
and d. to find a tabernacle. 7:46
the eunuch d. Philip to come. 8:31
Paul d. of the high priest. 9:2
Tyre and Sidon d. peace. 12:20
Sergius Paulus d. to hear. 13:7*
afterward they d. a king. 21
yet d. they Pilate that he. 28
and d. them to depart out of. 16:39
d. favour against Paul that. 25:3
I greatly d. him to. 1 Cor 16:12
we d. Titus to finish in. 2 Cor 8:6*
I d. Titus, and with him. 12:18*
we have petitions we d. 1 John 5:15

desiredst

according to all thou d. Deut 18:16
thee, because thou d. Mat 18:32

desires

he shall give thee the d. Ps 37:4
grant not, O Lord, the d. 140:8
fulfilling the d. of the. Eph 2:3

desirest

thou d. truth in the. Ps 51:6
thou d. not sacrifice. 16*

desireth

whatsoever thy soul d. Deut 14:26
take as much as soul d. 1 Sam 2:16
king d. not any dowry. 18:25
what thy soul d. 20:4; 1 Ki 11:37
over all that thy heart d. 2 Sam 3:21
as a servant earnestly d. Job 7:2
what his soul d. even that. 23:13
what man is he that d. life. Ps 34:12
the hill which God d. to. 68:16
the wicked d. the net. Pr 12:12
the soul of the sluggard d. 13:4
soul of the wicked d. evil. 21:10
nothing of all that he d. Eccl 6:2
old wine straightway d. Luke 5:39
he sendeth and d. conditions. 14:32
office of a bishop, he d. 1 Tim 3:1

desiring

his brethren d. to. Mat 12:46*, 47*
worshipping and d. a. 20:20
brethren stand without d. Luke 8:20
d. to be fed with the crumbs. 16:21
d. to have judgement. Acts 25:15*
d. to be clothed upon. 2 Cor 5:2
d. greatly to see us. 1 Thes 3:6
d. to be teachers. 1 Tim 1:7
greatly d. to see thee. 2 Tim 1:4

desirous

be not d. of his dainties. Pr 23:3
Herod was d. to see him. Luke 23:8
Jesus knew they were d. John 16:19
with a garrison d. to. 2 Cor 11:32*
let us not be d. of vain. Gal 5:26*
so being affectionately d. 1 Thes 2:8

desolate

[1] *Deserted, hence gloomy,* Jer 6:8; 12:10. [2] *Laid waste,* Isa 1:7. [3] *Left alone; forsaken,* Ps 34:22.

Tamar remained d. 2 Sam 13:20
he dwelleth in d. cities. Job 15:28
made d. all my company. 16:7
wilderness in former time d. 30:3
to satisfy the d. and waste. 38:27
mercy on me, for I am d. Ps 25:16
let them be d. for a reward. 40:15
let their habitation be d. 69:25
my heart within me is d. 143:4
your country is d. your. Isa 1:7
she being d. shall sit upon. 3:26
shall rest all of them in d. 7:19
beast shall cry in their d. 13:22*
they that dwell therein are d. 24:6*
to inherit the d. heritages. 49:8
have lost my children, am d. 21*
more are the children of the d. 54:1
Gal 4:27
make the d. cities to be. Isa 54:3
be ye very d. saith. Jer 2:12
lest I make thee d. a land not. 6:8
make cities of Judah d. 9:11; 10:22
33:10; 44:6
have made his habitation d. 10:25
made it d. and being d. it. 12:11
I will make this city d. 19:8*
it is d. without. 32:43; 33:12
their habitations d. 49:20; 50:45
all her gates are d. Lam 1:4
he hath made me d. 13; 3:11
my children are d. the. 1:16
did feed delicately are d. 4:5
mountain of Zion which is d. 5:18
altars may be made d. Ezek 6:6
he knew their d. palaces. 19:7
that I might make them d. 20:26
I will make Edom d. from. 25:13
when I make thee a d. city. 26:19
midst of countries that are d. 29:12
I will make Pathros d. and. 30:14
I will make thee most d. 35:3, 7
they are d. they are given us. 12
I will make thee d. 14
rejoice, because it was d. 15
because they have made you d. 36:3
saith Lord to hills and d. wastes. 4
the d. cities are become fenced. 35
I plant that that was d. 36
on sanctuary that is d. Dan 9:17
for abominations shall make it d. 27
that maketh d. 11:31; 12:11
Samaria shall become d. Hos 13:16*
the garners are laid d. Joel 1:17
flocks of sheep are made d. 18
the idols thereof will I lay d. Mi 1:7
in making thee d. because of. 6:13
their towers are d. Zeph 3:6
house is left to you d. Mat 23:38
Luke 13:35
let his habitation be d. Acts 1:20
a widow indeed and d. 1 Tim 5:5
hate whore, and make d. Rev 17:16
in one hour is she made d. 18:19

land **desolate**

seed that *land* be not d. Gen 47:19
lest *land* become d. Ex 23:29
land enjoy her sabbaths lieth d.
Lev 26:34, 35, 43; 2 Chr 36:21
until the *land* be utterly d. Isa 6:11
cometh to lay the *land* d. 13:9
land any more be termed d. 62:4
gone forth to make *land* d. Jer 4:7
the whole *land* shall be d. 27
for the *land* shall be d. 7:34
d. the whole *land* is made d. 12:11
to make their *land* d. and. 18:16*
for their *land* is d. because. 25:38
land whereof ye say it is d. 32:43
nation which shall make *land* d. 50:3
the *land* d. yea more d. Ezek 6:14
her *land* may be d. from. 12:19
cities laid waste, *land* be d. 20
land shall be d. Ezek 14:16; Mi 7:13
I will make the *land* d. Ezek 15:8
land was d. and the fulness. 19:7
the *land* of Egypt shall be d. 29:9
10, 12; 30:7; 32:15
I will lay the *land* most d. 33:28
when I have laid the *land* most d. 29
d. *land* tilled, whereas it lay d. 36:34
the *land* that was d. is like. 35
to a *land* barren and d. Joel 2:20
land was d. for they laid pleasant
land d. Zech 7:14

desolate *places*

which built d. *places* for. Job 3:14*
bread out of d. *places.* Ps 109:10
thy waste and d. *places.* Isa 49:19
we are in d. *places* as dead. 59:10*
high *places* shall be d. Ezek 6:6
set thee in *places* d. of old. 26:20
thine hand upon the d. *places.* 38:12
high *places* of Isaac be d. Amos 7:9
return, and build d. *places.* Mal 1:4

shall be, or *shalt be* **desolate**

your highways *shall be* d. Lev 26:22
your land *shall be* d. 33
hypocrites *shall be* d. Job 15:34*
hate righteous *shall be* d. Ps 34:21*
none that trust in him *shall be* d. 22*
many houses *shall be* d. Isa 5:9
waters of Nimrim *shall be* d. 15:6
Jer 48:34
defenced city *shall be* d. Isa 27:10*
this city *shall be* d. Jer 26:9
place which ye say *shall be* d. 33:10
Noph *shall be* d. without. 46:19*
cities thereof *shall be* d. 48:9
Rabbah *shall be* a d. heap. 49:2
Babylon *shall be* wholly d. 50:13
thou *shalt be* d. for ever. 51:26
your altars *shall be* d. Ezek 6:4
cities of Egypt *shall be* d. 29:12
mountains of Israel *shall be* d. 33:28
mount Seir, thou *shalt be* d. 35:4, 15
Ephraim *shall be* d. in day. Hos 5:9

desolate *wilderness*

portion a d. *wilderness.* Jer 12:10
behind it is a d. *wilderness.* Joel 2:3
and Edom a d. *wilderness.* 3:19

desolation

your sanctuaries to d. Lev 26:31
and I will bring the land into d. 32
made Ai a d. unto this day. Josh 8:28
that they become a d. 2 Ki 22:19
who gave them to d. 2 Chr 30:7
in d. they rolled. Job 30:14*
to d. in a moment. Ps 73:19
your fear cometh as d. Pr 1:27*
be not afraid of d. of wicked. 3:25
in that day shall be d. Isa 17:9
in the city is left d. the gate. 24:12
and d. shall come upon thee. 47:11
two things come unto thee, d. 51:19
a wilderness, Jerusalem a d. 64:10
house shall become a d. Jer 22:5
this whole land shall be a d. 25:11
make Jerusalem and Judah a d. 18
I will make cities of Judah a d. 34:22
this day they are a d. 44:2
is your land a d. and a curse. 22
Bozrah a d. 49:13*
Edom a d. 17*
Hazor a d. 33
how is Babylon become a d.! 50:23
to make Babylon a d. 51:29
her cities are a d. a dry land. 43*
snare is come on us, d. Lam 3:47*
prince be clothed with d. Ezek 7:27
filled with the cup of d. 23:33
the transgression of d. Dan 8:13
increaseth lies and d. Hos 12:1
and Edom shall be a d. Joel 3:19
I should make thee a d. Mi 6:16
houses shall become a d. Zeph 1:13
day of wrath, wasteness, and d. 15
Ashkelon shall be a d. 2:4
Moab a perpetual d. 9
he will make Nineveh a d. 13
d. shall be in thresholds. 14
how is Nineveh become a d.! 15
every kingdom divided against itself
is brought to d. Mat 12:25
Luke 11:17

see abomination of d. Mat 24:15
Mark 13:14
then know that the d. Luke 21:20

desolations

and to repair d. thereof. Ezra 9:9*
what d. he hath made. Ps 46:8
lift up thy feet to perpetual d. 74:3*
shall raise up the former d. the d. of many generations. Isa 61:4
these nations perpetual d. Jer 25:9
land of Chaldeans perpetual d. 12
mount Seir perpetual d. Ezek 35:9
seventy years in d. of. Dan 9:2
thine eyes, and behold our d. 18
to the end of the war d. 26

despair

and Saul shall d. of me. 1 Sam 27:1
cause my heart to d. Eccl 2:20
perplexed, but not in d. 2 Cor 4:8

despaired

insomuch that we d. 2 Cor 1:8

desperate

reprove speeches of one d. Job 6:26
of grief and of d. sorrow. Isa 17:11

desperately

deceitful, and d. wicked. Jer 17:9

despise

if ye shall d. my statutes. Lev 26:15*
that d. me shall be. 1 Sam 2:30
why then did ye d. us? 2 Sam 19:43
they d. their husbands. Esth 1:17*
d. not thou the chastening of the. Job 5:17; Pr 3:11; Heb 12:5
I were perfect, I would d. Job 9:21
thou shouldest d. the work of. 10:3
if I did d. the cause of my. 31:13
heart, thou wilt not d. Ps 51:17
thou shalt d. their image. 73:20
he will not d. their prayer. 102:17
but fools d. wisdom. Pr 1:7
d. not chastening of Lord. 3:11
Heb 12:5
men do not d. a thief, if. Pr 6:30
a fool will d. the wisdom of. 23:9
and d. not thy mother when. 22
because ye d. this word. Isa 30:12
thy lovers will d. thee. Jer 4:30
say still to them that d. me. 23:17
all that honoured her, d. Lam 1:8
Philistines which d. thee. Ezek 16:57*
judgement on all that d. 28:26*
I hate, I d. your feast. Amos 5:21
O priests, that d. my. Mal 1:6
one, and d. the other. Mat 6:24
Luke 16:13
that ye d. not one of these. Mat 18:10
not him that eateth, d. Rom 14:3*
or d. ye the church of. 1 Cor 11:22
let no man therefore d. him. 16:11
d. not prophesyings. 1 Thes 5:20
let none d. thy youth. 1 Tim 4:12
let them not d. them. 6:2
let no man d. thee. Tit 2:15
them that d. government. 2 Pet 2:10
d. dominion, and speak evil. Jude 8*

despised

Hagar's mistress was d. Gen 16:4
she had conceived, I was d. 5
thus Esau d. his birthright. 25:34
they d. my judgements. Lev 26:43*
ye have d. the Lord. Num 11:20*
know the land ye have d. 14:31*
because ye d. word of Lord. 15:31
the people thou hast d.? Judg 9:38
d. him and brought. 1 Sam 10:27
she d. him in her heart. 2 Sam 6:16
1 Chr 15:29
why hast thou d. commandment? 2 Sam 12:9
because thou hast d. me. 10
daughter of Zion hath d. thee. 2 Ki 19:21; Isa 37:22
but they mocked and d. 2 Chr 36:16
laughed us to scorn and d. Neh 2:19
hear, for we are d. and turn. 4:4
he is a lamp d. of him. Job 12:5*
yea, young children d. me. 19:18
I am d. of the people. Ps 22:6
Isa 53:3
he hath not d. the affliction. Ps 22:24
because God hath d. them. 53:5*
yea, they d. the pleasant. 106:24
I am small and d. yet do. Ps 119:141
they d. all my reproof. Pr 1:30
hath my heart d. reproof? 5:12
of a perverse heart shall be d. 12:8
he that is d. and hath a servant. 9*
poor man's wisdom is d. Eccl 9:16
yea I should not be d. S of S 8:1
d. the word of holy One. Isa 5:24
he hath d. the cities, he. 33:8
he is d. and rejected of men, he was d. and we esteemed him not. 53:3
all they that d. thee shall bow. 60:14
Coniah a d. broken idol. Jer 22:28
thus they have d. my people. 33:24
I will make thee small and d. 49:15
he hath d. in indignation. Lam 2:6
hast d. oath. Ezek 16:59; 17:16
18, 19
they d. my judgements. 20:13*
because they d. my judgements. 16*
but had d. my statutes. 24*
thou hast d. mine holy things. 22:8
because they d. the law. Amos 2:4*
thou art greatly d. Ob 2
who hath d. day of? Zech 4:10
have we d. thy name? Mal 1:6
righteous, and d. others. Luke 18:9*
of Diana should be d. Acts 19:27*
things which are d. hath. 1 Cor 1:28
ye are honourable, we are d. 4:10*
my temptation ye d. not. Gal 4:14
d. Moses' law, died. Heb 10:28*
but ye have d. the poor. Jas 2:6*

despisers

behold, ye d. and. Acts 13:41
incontinent, fierce, d. of. 2 Tim 3:3*

despisest

or d. thou the riches of? Rom 2:4

despiseth

God is mighty, and d. not. Job 36:5
for the Lord d. not. Ps 69:33
void of wisdom d. Pr 11:12
whoso d. the word shall be. 13:13
perverse in his ways d. him. 14:2
that d. his neighbour sinneth. 21
fool d. his father's instruction. 15:5
but a foolish man d. his mother. 20
he that refuseth instruction d. 32
he that d. his ways shall. 19:16*
eye that d. to obey his mother. 30:17
he that d. the gain of. Isa 33:15
saith Lord to him whom man d. 49:7
d. you, d. me; d. me, d. him that. Luke 10:16*
d. d. not man but God. 1 Thes 4:8*

despising

the cross, d. the shame. Heb 12:2

despite

thy d. against the land. Ezek 25:6
hath done d. to the Spirit. Heb 10:29

despiteful

vengeance with a d. Ezek 25:15
with d. minds to cast it out. 36:5
haters of God, d. proud. Rom 1:30*

despitefully

pray for them that d. Mat 5:44
Luke 6:28
assault was made to use them d. Acts 14:5*

destitute

who hath not left d. my. Gen 24:27
regard prayer of the d. Ps 102:17
leave not my soul d. 141:8
folly is joy to him that is d. Pr 15:21*
be d. of that whereof. Ezek 32:15
of corrupt minds, d. of. 1 Tim 6:5*
being d. afflicted. Heb 11:37
or sister be naked and d. Jas 2:15*

destroy

This is used [1] *of demolishing buildings or cities,* Gen 18:28; Jer 6:5; [2] *of putting an end to anything,* 1 Ki 16:12; Jer 51:20; [3] *of killing a person or persons,* Deut 9:14, 25; [4] *of nullifying,* Isa 19:3.

wilt thou d. righteous? Gen 18:23
wilt thou d. and not spare? 24
wilt thou d. all city for? 28
we will d. this place. 19:13
d. this city. 14
my hand shall d. them. Ex 15:9
ye shall d. their altars. 34:13
Deut 7:5
I will send beasts to d. Lev 26:22
d. the children of Sheth. Num 24:17
and ye shall d. all this people. 32:15
shall d. their pictures and. 33:52
lest anger of Lord d. thee. Deut 6:15
Lord shall d. them with a. 7:23*
thou shalt d. their name. 24
he shall d. them, and. 9:3
let me alone, that I may d. 14
Lord had said he would d. 25
trees that are not for meat d. 20:20
the Lord thy God he will d. 31:3
d. the young man and virgin. 32:25
thrust out enemy, and say, d. 33:27
except ye d. accursed. Josh 7:12
depart, lest I d. you. 1 Sam 15:6
we will d. the heir also. 2 Sam 14:7
not suffer revengers to d. any more, lest they d. my son. 11
that would d. me and my son. 16
I should swallow or d. 20:20
I might d. them that hate me. 22:41
Ps 18:40
thus did Zimri d. the. 1 Ki 16:12
he might d. worshippers. 2 Ki 10:19
against this land, and d. it. 18:25
Isa 36:10
d. kings that shall put to. Ezra 6:12
if he d. him from his place. Job 8:18
yet thou dost d. me. 10:8
after my skin worms d. this. 19:26
thou shalt d. them. Ps 5:6
d. them, O God, let them fall. 10*
their fruit shalt thou d. 21:10
he shall d. them, and not. 28:5
God shall likewise d. thee. 52:5
d. O Lord, and divide their. 55:9
that would d. me are mighty. 69:4
let us d. them together. 74:8
and d. all them that afflict. 143:12
shoot out thine arrows and d. 144:6*
all the wicked will he d. 145:20
prosperity of fools shall d. Pr 1:32
of transgressors shall d. 11:3
Lord will d. house of proud. 15:25
robberies of wicked shall d. 21:7
why should God d. work? Eccl 5:6
why shouldest thou d. thyself? 7:16
and they d. the way of. Isa 3:12
nor d. in holy mountain. 11:9; 65:25
he shall d. the sinners thereof. 13:9
he will d. in this mountain. 25:7
go ye upon her walls and d. Jer 5:10
let us go by night and d. her. 6:5
let us d. the tree with the. 11:19
I will pluck up and d. that. 12:17
spare nor have mercy, but d. 13:14
my hand against thee and d. 15:6
and d. them with double. 17:18
woe to pastors that d. sheep. 23:1
king of Babylon shall d. 36:29
he shall d. thy strong holds. 48:18
thieves by night will d. 49:9
spare ye not, d. ye utterly all. 51:3
persecute and d. them. Lam 3:66
thou d. all the residue? Ezek 9:8
d. the remnant of sea-coast. 25:16
and they shall d. the walls. 26:4
shall d. thy pleasant houses. 12
hew tree down and d. it. Dan 4:23
d. wonderfully, and d. mighty. 8:24
by peace shall he d. many. 25
people shall d. the city and. 9:26
that feed on his meat shall d. 11:26
shall I not d. the wise men? Ob 8
it is polluted, it shall d. Mi 2:10
north, and d. Assyria. Zeph 2:13
they might d. him. Mat 12:14
Mark 3:6; 11:18
d. those wicked men. Mat 21:41
should ask Barabbas, and d. 27:20
will d. the husbandmen. Mark 12:9
Luke 20:16
d. this temple. John 2:19
Jesus of Nazareth shall d. Acts 6:14
God shall d. both it and. 1 Cor 6:13
shall d. with brightness. 2 Thes 2:8
d. him that had power of. Heb 2:14
that he might d. works. 1 John 3:8
d. them which d. earth. Rev 11:18

I will, or will I destroy

I will d. man whom I. Gen 6:7
I will d. them with the earth. 13
every living substance will I d. 7:4
and I will d. all people. Ex 23:27*
the same soul will I d. Lev 23:30
I will d. your high places. 26:30
Ezek 6:3
I will early d. all wicked. Ps 101:8
name of Lord will I d. 118:10, 11, 12
and I will d. the counsel. Isa 19:3
I will cry, I will d. and. 42:14*
I will d. my people. Jer 15:7
I will d. the city, and the. 46:8
I will d. from thence the king. 49:38
battle-ax, with thee will I d. 51:20
I the Lord will d. that. Ezek 14:9
I will d. thee, and thou shalt know.
25:7; 28:16; Zeph 2:5
I will d. the idols. Ezek 30:13
I will d. also all the beasts. 32:13
but I will d. the fat and. 34:16
I will d. her vines and. Hos 2:12
and I will d. thy mother. 4:5
I will d. sinful kingdom. Amos 9:8
I will d. thy chariots. Mi 5:10
so will I d. thy cities. 14
I will d. the strength of. Hag 2:22
I will d. this temple. Mark 14:58
I will d. the wisdom of. 1 Cor 1:19

not destroy

find forty-five I will not d. Gen 18:28
will not d. it for twenty's sake. 31
not d. Sodom for ten's sake. 32
not forsake thee, nor d. Deut 4:31
d. not thy people and. 9:26
the Lord would not d. thee. 10:10
thou shalt not d. the trees. 20:19
wilt not d. my name. 1 Sam 24:21
David said to Abishai, d. not. 26:9
would not d. Judah for. 2 Ki 8:19
would not d. them, nor cast. 13:23
therefore I will not d. 2 Chr 12:7
that the Lord would not d. him. 12
Lord would not d. the house. 21:7
forbear that he d. thee not. 35:21
they did not d. nations. Ps 106:34
d. it not, for a blessing is in it: that I
may not d. them all. Isa 65:8
that I should not d. it. Ezek 22:30
d. not the wise men of. Dan 2:24
he shall not d. fruits of. Mal 3:11
d. not him with thy meat. Rom 14:15
for meat d. not the work of God. 20

to destroy

flood of waters to d. all. Gen 6:17
any more a flood to d. 9:11, 15
the Lord hath sent us to d. it. 19:13
intreat for thee to d. frogs. Ex 8:9
plague shall not be on you to d. 12:13
to deliver us into hand of Amorites
to d. us. Deut 1:27; Josh 7:7
hand of Lord to d. them. Deut 2:15
them that hate him to d. them. 7:10
was wroth against you to d. 9:19
Lord will rejoice over you to d. 28:63
to d. all the inhabitants. Josh 9:24
to d. land where Reubenites. 22:33
Midianites entered to d. Judg. 6:5
Saul seeketh to d. city. 1 Sam 23:10
came in one of people to d. 26:15
not afraid to d. Lord's. 2 Sam 1:14
suffer revengers of blood to d. 14:11
thou seekest to d. a. 20:19
his hand on Jerusalem to d. 24:16
house of Jeroboam to d. 1 Ki 13:34
them against Judah to d. 2 Ki 24:2
angel to Jerusalem to d. 1 Chr 21:15
determined to d. thee. 2 Chr 25:16
Haman sought to d. Jews. Esth 3:6
13; 4:7, 8; 9:24
thou movedst me to d. Job 2:3
it would please God to d. me. 6:9
seek after my soul to d. it.
Ps 40:14; 63:9
wicked have waited to d. me. 119:95
it is in his heart to d. and. Isa 10:7
they come from far to d. 13:5
hath given commandment to d. 23:11
deviseth wicked devices to d. 32:7
oppressor were ready to d. 51:13
I have created waster to d. 54:16
I have set thee to d. Jer 1:10
18:7; 31:28
appoint beasts of earth to d. 15:3
device against Babylon to d. it. 51:11
Lord hath purposed to d. Lam 2:8
I will send to d. you. Ezek 5:16
and to d. souls, to get gain. 22:27
a despiteful heart to d. it. 25:15
nations shall be brought to d. 30:11
vision I saw when I came to d. 43:3
to d. all wise men of. Dan 2:12, 24
and to d. his dominion. 7:26
go forth with great fury to d. 11:44
not return to d. Ephraim. Hos 11:9
that I will seek to d. all. Zech 12:9
seek young child to d. Mat 2:13
think not that I am come to d. law, I
am not come to d. but to. 5:17
fear him who is able to d. 10:28
I am able to d. the temple. 26:61
art thou come to d. us? Mark 1:24
Luke 4:34
sabbath to save life or to d. Luke 6:9
Son of man is not come to d. 9:56
chief of people sought to d. 19:47
thief cometh not but to d. John 10:10
able to save and to d. Jas 4:12

destroyed

before Lord d. Sodom. Gen 13:10
when God d. the cities of. 19:29
knowest not Egypt is d.? Ex 10:7
the Lord d. them. Deut 2:21; 4:3
11:4; 2 Ki 21:9; 2 Chr 33:9
destruction, till they be d. Deut 7:23
able to stand till thou have d. 24
was angry with you to have d. 9:8
after that they be d. from. 12:30
until thou be d. 28:20, 24, 45, 51, 61
yoke on thy neck till he have d. 48
and I d. them from. Josh 24:8
Benjamin d. of Israel. Judg 20:21, 25
children of Israel d. 35, 42
that we should be d. 2 Sam 21:5
the angel that d. 24:16; 1 Chr 21:15
Asa d. her idol and. 1 Ki 15:13
thus Jehu d. Baal. 2 Ki 10:28
Athaliah arose and d. all the. 11:1
they have d. them. 19:18; Isa 37:19
people whom God d. 1 Chr 5:25
were d. before Lord. 2 Chr 14:13
nation was d. of nation. 15:6
which kings of Judah had d. 34:11
for which cause was city d. Ezra 4:15
written, that they may be d. Esth 3:9
he hath d. me on every. Job 19:10
thou hast d. the wicked. Ps 9:5
thou hast d. cities. 6
d. all them that go a whoring. 73:27
frogs among them, which d. 78:45
he d. their vines with hail, and. 47
Babylon, who art to be d. 137:8
there is that is d. for. Pr 13:23
because thou hast d. land. Isa 14:20
hast thou visited and d. 26:14
many pastors have d. Jer 12:10
Moab is d. 48:4
Babylon is suddenly d. 51:8
hath d. out of Babylon. 55
Lord hath d. his strong. Lam 2:5
he hath d. his places of the. 6
he hath d. and broken her bars. 9
Tyrus, like the d. in the. Ezek 27:32
beast was slain, his body d. Dan 7:11
O Israel, thou hast d. Hos 13:9
yet d. I the Amorite, I d. Amos 2:9
sent his armies and d. Mat 22:7
the flood came, and d. Luke 17:27
it rained fire from heaven and d. 29
is not this he that d.? Acts 9:21
when he had d. seven nations. 13:19
magnificence should be d. 19:27*
body of sin might be d. Rom 6:6
d. of serpents. 1 Cor 10:9
d. of the destroyer. 10
preacheth faith which he d. Gal 1:23
build again things which I d. 2:18
lest he that d. first-born. Heb 11:28
as brute beasts made to be d.
2 Pet 2:12
the Lord afterward d. them. Jude 5
third part of ships were d. Rev 8:9

are destroyed

the women are d. out. Judg 21:16
they are d. from morning. Job 4:20
overturneth them so they are d. 34:25
are led of them are d. Isa 9:16
for all thy lovers are d. Jer 22:20
my people are d. for lack. Hos 4:6
their cities are d. Zeph 3:6

not destroyed

but they d. them not. 2 Chr 20:10
Ps 78:38
kingdom which shall not be d.
Dan 7:14
cast down, but not d. 2 Cor 4:9

shall be destroyed

and I shall be d. I and. Gen 34:30
father's house shall be d. Esth 4:14
transgressors shall be d. Ps 37:38
it is that they shall be d. 92:7
despiseth word shall be d. Pr 13:13
companion of fools shall be d. 20*
hardeneth his neck shall be d. 29:1
the yoke shall be d. Isa 10:27
the plain shall be d. Jer 48:8
all her helpers shall be d. Ezek 30:8
a kingdom which shall never be d.
Dan 2:44; 6:26
within few days he shall be d. 11:20
sin of Israel shall be d. Hos 10:8
will not hear shall be d. Acts 3:23
last enemy that shall be d. is death.
1 Cor 15:26

utterly destroyed

sacrificeth to any god, save unto the
Lord, shall be utterly d. Ex 22:20
utterly d. the Canaanites. Num 21:3
we utterly d. Sihon. Deut 2:34
we utterly d. cities of Og. 3:6
Josh 2:10
if ye corrupt yourselves ye shall be
utterly d. Deut 4:26
Jericho utterly d. Josh 6:21
Ai utterly d. 8:26; 10:1
Hebron utterly d. 10:37
he utterly d. all that breathed. 40
Joshua utterly d. them. 11:12, 21
and Simeon utterly d. Judg 1:17
Saul utterly d. people. 1 Sam 15:8
he would not utterly d. the best. 9
and rest we have utterly d. 15
I have utterly d. Amalekites. 20
should have been utterly d. 21*
[of Gedor] utterly d. 1 Chr 4:41
Hezekiah utterly d. the images.
2 Chr 31:1
nations my father utterly d. 32:14
hath utterly d. all nations. Isa 34:2

destroyer

will not suffer d. to come. Ex 12:23
hath delivered the d. of. Judg 16:24
in prosperity d. shall. Job 15:21
kept me from paths of d. Ps 17:4
is the companion of a d. Pr 28:24
the d. of the Gentiles. Jer 4:7
were destroyed of the d. 1 Cor 10:10

destroyers

life draweth near to d. Job 33:22
thy d. shall go forth. Isa 49:17
and I will prepare d. Jer 22:7
ye rejoiced, O d. of my. 50:11*

destroyest, -eth

as nations the Lord d. Deut 8:20
he d. the perfect and the. Job 9:22
increaseth the nations, and d. 12:23
and thou d. the hope of man. 14:19
he that doth it, d. his. Pr 6:32
hypocrite with his mouth d. 11:9
thy ways to that which d. kings. 31:3
and a gift d. heart. Eccl 7:7
sinner d. much good. 9:18
which d. all the earth. Jer 51:25
thou that d. the temple. Mat 27:40
Mark 15:29

destroying

angel of the Lord d. 1 Chr 21:12
as he was d. the Lord repented. 15
a strong one, as a d. Isa 28:2
sword devoured like a d. Jer 2:30
against Babylon a d. wind. 51:1
against thee, O d. mountain. 25
withdrawn his hand from d. Lam 2:8
every man with d. weapon. Ezek 9:1
mine eye spared them from d. 20:17

see **utterly**

destruction
destroy them with a mighty d. Deut 7:23*
devoured with bitter d. 32:24
Lord was against the city with a great d. 1 Sam 5:9*
for there was a deadly d. 11*
I appointed to utter d. 1 Ki 20:42
his counsellors to his d. 2 Chr 22:4
d. of Ahaziah was of God, by. 7
heart was lifted up to his d. 26:16*
how endure to see the d.? Esth 8:6
smote their enemies with d. 9:5
neither be afraid of d. Job 5:21
at d. and famine thou shalt laugh. 22
and d. shall be ready. 18:12*
how oft cometh their d.? 21:17*
his eyes shall see his d. and. 20
wicked is reserved to day of d. 30*
hell is naked before him, d. 26:6*
d. and death say, we have. 28:22
against me ways of their d. 30:12
though they cry in his d. 24*
is not d. to the wicked ? 31:3
a fire that consumeth to d. 12
for d. from God was a terror. 23*
if I rejoiced at the d. of him. 29
let d. come upon him, his net catch himself, into that very d. Ps 35:8
them down to the pit of d. 55:23
castedst them down into d. 73:18
faithfulness be declared in d.? 88:11
thou turnest man to d. and. 90:3
nor for the d. that wasteth. 91:6
redeemeth thy life from d. 103:4
when your d. cometh. Pr 1:27*
mouth of foolish is near d. 10:14
the d. of poor is their poverty. 15
d. shall be to workers of. 29; 21:15
openeth his lips shall have d. 13:3
want of people is the d. of. 14:28
hell and d. are before Lord. 15:11*
pride goeth before d. 16:18
that exalteth gate seeketh d. 17:19
a fool's mouth is his d. 18:7
before d. the heart of man is. 12
for their heart studieth d. 24:2*
hell and d. are never full. 27:20*
as are appointed to d. 31:8
d. of transgressors and. Isa 1:28
anger shall cease in their d. 10:25
it shall come as a d. from. 13:6
Babylon with the besom of d. 14:23
shall raise up a cry of d. 15:5
shall be called city of d. 19:18
the gate is smitten with d. 24:12
the land of thy d. shall be. 49:19
desolation and d. are come. 51:19
wasting and d. are in their. 59:7
d. shall no more be heard. 60:18
from north a great d. Jer 4:6; 6:1
d. upon d. is cried, for the land. 4:20
destroy them with double d. 17:18
d. cometh, it cometh out. 46:20
Horonaim, spoiling and d. 48:3
enemies have heard a cry of d. 5
a sound of great d. is in. 50:22
great d. from land of. 51:54
d. of the daughter. Lam 2:11; 3:48
desolation and d. is come. 3:47
in the d. of the daughter of. 4:10
send famine for their d. Ezek 5:16
d. cometh, and they shall. 7:25
when I bring thy d. among. 32:9
d. to them, because they. Hos 7:13
they are gone, because of d. 9:6
I will be thy d. repentance hid. 13:14
as a d. from Almighty. Joel 1:15
rejoiced in day of their d. Ob 12
destroy you with a sore d. Mi 2:10
be no more utter d. Zech 14:11*
is way that leadeth to d. Mat 7:13
d. and misery are in. Rom 3:16
vessels of wrath fitted to d. 9:22
deliver to Satan for d. 1 Cor 5:5
given us not for your d. 2 Cor 10:8
13:10
walk whose end is d. Phil 3:19*
then sudden d. cometh. 1 Thes 5:3
punished with everlasting d. 2 Thes 1:9
which drown men in d. 1 Tim 6:9
upon themselves swift d. 2 Pet 2:1
unstable wrest to their own d. 3:16

destructions
O enemy, d. are come. Ps 9:6*
rescue my soul from their d. 35:17
delivereth them from their d. 107:20

detain, -ed
let us d. thee till we. Judg 13:15
though thou d. me, I will not. 16
Doeg was that day d. 1 Sam 21:7

determinate
delivered by d. counsel. Acts 2:23

determination
d. is to gather nations. Zeph 3:8

determine
shall pay as the judges d. Ex 21:22

determined
sure that evil is d. by. 1 Sam 20:7
if I knew that evil were d. 9
Jonathan knew that it was d. 33
for evil is d. against our. 25:17
Absalom hath been d. 2 Sam 13:32
Solomon d. to build a. 2 Chr 2:1
I know that God hath d. 25:16
that there was evil d. Esth 7:7
seeing his days are d. Job 14:5
a consumption d. Isa 10:23; 28:22
of Lord which hath d. 19:17*
seventy weeks are d. Dan 9:24*
to end of war desolations are d. 26
and that d. shall be poured upon. 27
that is d. shall be done. 11:36
of man goeth as was d. Luke 22:22
when Pilate was d. to. Acts 3:13
to do what thy counsel d. 4:28*
the disciples d. to send. 11:29
d. that Paul and Barnabas. 15:2*
and Barnabas d. to take with. 37*
and hath d. the times before. 17:26
be d. in a lawful assembly. 19:39
for Paul had d. to sail by. 20:16
I have d. to send Paul. 25:25
it was d. that we should sail. 27:1
I d. not to know any thing. 1 Cor 2:2
but I d. this with myself. 2 Cor 2:1
Nicopolis, for I have d. Tit 3:12

detest
but thou shalt utterly d. Deut 7:26

detestable
defiled my land with d. Jer 16:18
defiled sanctuary with d. Ezek 5:11
made images of their d. things. 7:20
shall take away all d. things. 11:18
heart walketh after their d. things. 21
any more defile with their d. 37:23

device
to find out every d. 2 Chr 2:14
to put away his d. that. Esth 8:3
his wicked d. should return. 9:25
imagined a mischievous d. Ps 21:11
further not his wicked d. 140:8
there is no work nor d. Eccl 9:10
I devise a d. against you. Jer 18:11
for his d. is against Babylon. 51:11
and their d. against me. Lam 3:62*
stone graven by man's d. Acts 17:29

devices
he disappointeth the d. Job 5:12
d. which ye wrongfully. 21:27
let them be taken in d. Ps 10:2
he maketh the d. of people. 33:10*
man who bringeth wicked d. 37:7
filled with their own d. Pr 1:31
but a man of wicked d. will. 12:2
there are many d. in a man's. 19:21
he deviseth wicked d. to. Isa 32:7
they had devised d. Jer 11:19
we will walk after our own d. 18:12
come and let us devise d. 18
he shall forecast his d. Dan 11:24
for they shall forecast d. 25
are not ignorant of his d. 2 Cor 2:11

devil
[1] *Satan, (i.e. adversary), the supreme evil spirit, referred to in the N.T. under the name of devil,* Mat 4:1; Luke 8:12; John 8:44; Rev 12:9. *The word devil is not used of Satan in the Old Testament. Abaddon in Hebrew, Apollyon in Greek, that is, destroyer,* Rev 9:11.—*Angel of the bottomless pit,* Rev. 9:11.—*Prince of this world,* John 12:31.—*Prince of darkness,* Eph 6:12.—*A roaring Lion, and an Adversary,* 1 Pet 5:8.—*Beelzebub,* Mat 12:24.—*Accuser,* Rev 12:10.—*Dragon,* Rev 12:7.—*Lucifer,* Isa 14:12.—*Serpent,* Rev 20:2.—*Satan,* Job 2:6.—*The god of this world,* 2 Cor 4:4.
[2] *Inferior evil spirits. In this sense the American Revision translates the word* demon.
led to be tempted of the d. Mat 4:1
d. taketh him up to holy city. 5
the d. taketh him up to an high. 8
d. leaveth him. 11
man possessed with d. 9:32; 12:22
say he hath a d. 11:18; Luke 7:33
that sowed them is d. Mat 13:39
daughter is vexed with a d. 15:22
Jesus rebuked the d. 17:18
fire, prepared for the d. 25:41
possessed with the d. Mark 5:15
16, 18
the d. is gone out of. 7:29, 30
forty days tempted of d. Luke 4:2
the d. said to him, all this power. 3, 6
the d. taking him up. 5
when the d. had ended all the. 13
had a spirit of an unclean d. 33
and when the d. had thrown him. 35
then cometh the d. and taketh. 8:12
was driven of the d. into the. 29
as he was coming the d. 9:42
casting out a d. when the d. 11:14
and one of you is a d. John 6:70
said, thou hast a d. 7:20; 8:48
ye are of your father the d. 8:44
I have not a d. 49
we know that thou hast a d. 52
many said, he hath a d. 10:20
not words of him that hath a d. 21
the d. having put into heart. 13:2
that were oppressed of d. Acts 10:38
thou child of the d. 13:10
neither give place to d. Eph 4:27
to stand against wiles of d. 6:11
into condemnation of d. 1 Tim 3:6
into reproach, and snare of d. 7
out of the snare of the d. 2 Tim 2:26
power of death, that is d. Heb 2:14
resist the d. and he will. Jas 4:7
your adversary the d. 1 Pet 5:8
sin is of the d. that he might destroy the works of the d. 1 John 3:8
in this the children of the d. are 10
when contending with the d. Jude 9
the d. shall cast some. Rev 2:10
the old serpent called the d. 12:9
for the d. is come down to you. 12
that old serpent, which is d. 20:2
d. that deceived them was cast. 10

devilish
this wisdom is earthy, d. Jas 3:15

devils
more offer sacrifices to d. Lev 17:7*
they sacrificed to d. Deut 32:17*
he ordained him priests for the d. 2 Chr 11:15*
sons and daughters to d. Ps 106:37*
those possessed with d. Mat 4:24
8:16, 28, 33; Mark 1:32; Luke 8:36
the d. besought him. Mat 8:31
Mark 5:12
saw one casting out d. in thy name. Mark 9:38; Luke 9:49
my name shall cast out d. Mark 16:17
and d. also came out of. Luke 4:41
out of whom went seven d. 8:2
he that was possessed of d. 36
and authority over all d. 9:1
even the d. are subject to us. 10:17
that fox, behold, I cast out d. 13:32
sacrifice to d. . . . ye should have fellowship with d. 1 Cor 10:20
cup of Lord and cup of d; of Lord's table and of table of d. 21
heed to doctrines of d. 1 Tim 4:1
the d. also believe and. Jas 2:19
should not worship d. Rev 9:20
spirits of d. working miracles. 16:14
is become habitation of d. 18:2
see cast

devise

d. cunning works in gold. Ex 31:4
35:35
to d. curious works in gold. 35:32
yet doth he d. means. 2 Sam 14:14
to confusion, that d. my. Ps 35:4
but they d. deceitful matters. 20
against me do they d. my hurt. 41:7
d. not evil against. Pr 3:29
they not err that d. evil ? mercy and
truth to them that d. good. 14:22
shutteth his eyes to d. 16:30
behold, I d. a device. Jer 18:11
come and let us d. devices. 18
men that d. mischief. Ezek 11:2
woe to them that d. Mi 2:1
against this family do I d. an evil. 3

devised

that consumed us d. 2 Sam 21:5
month which he had d. of. 1 Ki 12:33
devise that he had d. Esth 8:3
be written to reverse letters d. 5
d. to take away my life. Ps 31:13
not that they had d. Jer 11:19
in Heshbon they have d. evil. 48:2
Lord hath both d. and done. 51:12
Lam 2:17
not followed cunningly d. 2 Pet 1:16

deviseth

he d. mischief on his bed. Ps 36:4
thy tongue d. mischief like. 52:2
d. mischief continually. Pr 6:14
an heart that d. wicked. 18
man's heart d. his way. 16:9
d. to do evil shall be called. 24:8
he d. wicked devices to. Isa 32:7
but the liberal d. liberal things. 8

devote

thing that a man shall d. Lev 27:28

devoted

to Lord, as a field d. Lev 27:21
no d. thing sold, every d. thing. 28
every thing d. in Israel. Num 18:14
thy servant, who is d. Ps 119:38*

devotions

by and beheld your d. Acts 17:23*

devour

[1] *To eat up, or swallow greedily, either literally or figuratively,* Gen 37:20; Mat 23:14. [2] *To waste, or spend riotously,* Luke 15:30.

in morning he shall d. Gen 49:27
and sword d. flesh. Deut 32:42
shall sword d. for ever ? 2 Sam 2:26
command locusts to d. 2 Chr 7:13
firstborn of death shall d. Job 18:13
wild beasts of field doth d. Ps 80:13
jaw-teeth as knives to d. Pr 30:14
your land strangers d. it. Isa 1:7
they shall d. Israel with. 9:12
for wickedness shall d. briers. 18
not of a mean man, shall d. 31:8
I will destroy and d. at. 42:14*
all ye beasts of the field come to d.
56:9; Jer 12:9; 15:3
that d. Israel shall offend. Jer 2:3
sword of the Lord shall d. 12:12
46:10, 14
and all that d. thee shall. 30:16
flame shall d. corner of Moab. 48:45
and pestilence shall d. Ezek 7:15
neither shall beasts of land d. 34:28
therefore shalt thou d. men. 36:14
arise, d. much flesh. Dan 7:5
d. whole earth. 23
now shall a month d. them. Hos 5:7
sword shall d. his branches. 11:6
there will I d. them like a lion. 13:8
fire shall d. the palaces. Amos 1:4
7, 10, 12
kindle in them, and d. them. Ob 18
sword shall d. young. Nah 2:13
rejoicing was as to d. Hab 3:14
they shall d. and subdue. Zech 9:15
they shall d. all the people. 12:6
you, hypocrites, for ye d. Mat 23:14
Mark 12:40; Luke 20:47
suffer, if a man d. you. 2 Cor 11:20
but if ye bite and d. one. Gal 5:15
shall d. adversaries. Heb 10:27
seeking whom he may d. 1 Pet 5:8
to d. her child as soon. Rev 12:4

***fire* devour**

let fire d. the cedars. Judg 9:15
let fire d. the men of Shechem. 20
and fire shall d. them. Ps 21:9
shall come, a fire shall d. 50:3
fire of thine enemies shall d.
Isa 26:11
your breath as fire shall d. 33:11
another fire shall d. Ezek 15:7
for them through fire to d. 23:37
break out like fire and d. Amos 5:6
the fire shall d. thy bars. Nah 3:13
there shall the fire d. thee. 15
fire may d. thy cedars. Zech 11:1

***it shall* devour**

it shall d. the strength. Job 18:13
it shall burn and d. his. Isa 10:17
my words fire, it shall d. Jer 5:14
a fire and it shall d. the palaces of
Jerusalem. 17:27; Amos 2:5
it shall d. all things. Jer 21:14
50:32
it shall d. every tree. Ezek 20:47
it shall d. and I will bring. 28:18
it shall d. palaces of Judah. Hos 8:14
it shall d. palaces of Rabbah.
Amos 1:14
it shall d. palaces of Kirioth. 2:2

devoured

and quite d. our money. Gen 31:15
some evil beast hath d. 37:20, 33
seven thin ears d. seven. 41:7, 24
fire from Lord and d. Lev 10:2
time the fire d. 250 men. Num 26:10
my face, they shall be d. Deut 31:17
they shall be d. with burning. 32:24
d. more than sword d. 2 Sam 18:8
and fire out of his mouth d. 22:9
Ps 18:8
sorts of flies which d. Ps 78:45
for they have d. Jacob. 79:7
the locusts d. the fruit of. 105:35
if ye rebel, ye shall be d. Isa 1:20
therefore hath the curse d. 24:6
sword hath d. prophets. Jer 2:30
for shame hath d. the labour. 3:24
they are come, and have d. 8:16
have eaten up Jacob, and d. 10:25
that devour thee shall be d. 30:16
all that found them have d. 50:7
king of Assyria hath d. him. 17
Nebuchadrezzar hath d. me. 51:34
it hath d. foundations. Lam 4:11
when the fire hath d. it. Ezek 15:5
sacrificed thy sons to be d. 16:20
to catch prey, d. men. 19:3, 6
fire is gone out, which hath d. 14
a roaring lion, they have d. 22:25
and thy residue shall be d. 23:25
give to the beasts to be d. 33:27
39:4
d. and brake in pieces. Dan 7:7, 19
and have d. their judges. Hos 7:7
strangers have d. his strength. 9
fire hath d. pastures. Joel 1:19, 20
palmer-worm d. them. Amos 4:9
and it d. the great deep. 7:4
they shall be d. as stubble. Nah 1:10
land shall be d. by fire. Zeph 1:18
all the earth shall be d. with. 3:8
Tyrus shall be d. with fire. Zech 9:4
fowls came and d. them. Mat 13:4
Mark 4:4; Luke 8:5
thy son who hath d. Luke 15:30
fire came down and d. Rev 20:9

devourer

I will rebuke the d. for. Mal 3:11

devourest

thou land d up men. Ezek 36:13

devoureth

sword d. one as well. 2 Sam 11:25
mouth of the wicked d. Pr 19:28
a snare to the man who d. 20:25
as fire d. stubble, and. Isa 5:24
Joel 2:5
a flaming fire which d. Lam 2:3
the fire d. both the ends. Ezek 15:4
a fire d. before them. Joel 2:3
wicked d. man that is. Hab 1:13
fire d. their enemies. Rev 11:5

devouring

appearance like d. fire. Ex 24:17
thou lovest all d. words. Ps 52:4
visited with d. fire. Isa 29:6; 30:30
his tongue is as a d. fire. 30:27
shall dwell with the d. fire ? 33:14

devout

Simeon was just and d. Luke 2:25
at Jerusalem Jews, d. Acts 2:5
d. men carried Stephen to his. 8:2
Cornelius was a d. man. 10:2
a d. soldier. 7
Jews stirred up d. women. 13:50
of the d. Greeks a multitude. 17:4
Paul disputed with Jews and d. 17
Ananias a d. man. 22:12

dew

This was formerly thought to fall like a light rain during the night, and the references to it in the Bible are usually worded according to this idea, as are many of our customary phrases with reference to it as the falling of the dew. In warm countries, and in places where it rains but seldom, the night-dews supply in some sort the want of rain. And therefore the bestowing of it is a blessing from God, Deut 33:13; *and the withholding of it a curse,* 2 Sam 1:21.

God give thee of d. of. Gen 27:28, 39
in the morning d. lay. Ex 16:13
and when the d. that lay was. 14
when d. fell on camp. Num 11:9
speech shall distil as d. Deut 32:2
blessed is Joseph's land for d. 33:13
his heaven shall drop down d. 28
if d. be on fleece only. Judg 6:37
on ground let there be d. 39
there was d. 40
let there be no d. nor. 2 Sam 1:21
we will light on him as d. 17:12
there shall not be d. nor. 1 Ki 17:1
the d. lay all night on. Job 29:19
hath begotten drops of d.? 38:28
hast the d. of thy youth. Ps 110:3
as d. of Hermon, and as d. 133:3
clouds drop down the d. Pr 3:20
but his favour is as d. 19:12
my head is filled with d. S of S 5:2
like a cloud of d. in heat. Isa 18:4
for thy d. is as the d. of. 26:19
wet with d. of heaven. Dan 4:15, 23
shall wet thee with d. of heaven. 25
his body was wet with d. 33; 5:21
goodness is as early d. Hos 6:4
13:3
I will be as d. to Israel. 14:5
Jacob shall be as the d. Mi 5:7
over you stayed from d. Hag 1:10
heavens shall give their d. Zech 8:12

diadem

was as a robe and a d. Job 29:14
and for a d. of beauty. Isa 28:5
and a royal d. in the hand. 62:3
remove the d. take off. Ezek 21:26*

dial

gone down in d. of Ahaz. 2 Ki 20:11
Isa 38:8

diamond

second row a d. Ex 28:18; 39:11
is written with point of d. Jer 17:1
the d. the beryl. Ezek 28:13

Diana

silver shrines for D. Acts 19:24
temple of great goddess D. 27
great is D. of Ephesians. 28, 34
worshipper of the goddess D. 35

Dibon

perished even to D. Num 21:30
children of Gad built D. 32:34
Moses gave D. to Reuben. Josh 13:17
Judah dwelt at D. Neh 11:25
gone up to D. the high. Isa 15:2
that dost inhabit D. Jer 48:18
judgement is come upon D. 22

Dibon-gad

pitched in D. Num 33:45
removed from D. 46

did

mischief that Hadad d. 1 Ki 11:25
d. right according to all David d. 2 Ki 18:3
I knew not what I d. Neh 2:16
to know how Esther d. Esth 2:11
not read what David d.? Mat 12:3
saw wonderful things he d. 21:15
what great things he d. Mark 3:8
saw miracles which he d. John 2:23
6:2, 14
me all things that ever I d. 4:29, 39
what d. he to thee ? 9:26
works which none other man d. 15:24
through ignorance ye d. it, as d. Acts 3:17
I also d. in Jerusalem. 26:10
and this they d. not as. 2 Cor 8:5
who d. no sin, nor was. 1 Pet 2:22

did joined with *as*

Lord d. to Sarah as he. Gen 21:1
the man d. as Joseph bade. 43:17
his sons d. to him as he. 50:12
d. as Lord commanded. Ex 7:6
10, 20; 12:28, 50; 39:32; Lev 8:4
16:34; 24:23; Num 1:54; 2:34
20:7; 27:22; 31:31
as he d. with the bullock. Lev 4:20
16:15
Balak d. as Balaam. Num 23:2, 30
as Israel d. to the land. Deut 2:12
as he d. to children of Esau. 22
as we d. unto Sihon. 3:6
flowed, as they d. before. Josh 4:18
as the Lord your God d. to. 23
d. to king of Makkedah, as he d. 10:28
Joshua d. to them as Lord. 11:9
Gideon d. as Lord had. Judg 6:27
as they d. to me, so I have. 15:11
as what the king d. 2 Sam 3:36
and David d. so as the Lord. 5:25
elders d. as Jezebel had. 1 Ki 21:11
Ahab d. according as d. the. 26
Jehoram, as d. the. 2 Ki 8:18
as d. the heathen which. 17:11
as d. their fathers, so do they. 41
David d. as God. 1 Chr 14:16
d. as it is written in law. 2 Chr 25:4
seek me as a nation that d. Isa 58:2
gave thanks as he d. Dan 6:10
Joseph d. as the angel. Mat 1:24
d. as Jesus commanded. 21:6; 26:19
so watch d. as they were. 28:15
them, even as Elias d. Luke 9:54
ignorance ye did it, as d. Acts 3:17
Holy Ghost, as your fathers d. 7:51
gave them like gift, as he d. 11:17
from works, as God d. Heb 4:10

did joined with *evil*

requite us the evil we d. Gen 50:15
for they d. to thee evil. 17
d. evil in sight of Lord. Judg 2:11
3:7, 12; 4:1; 6:1; 10:6; 13:1
1 Ki 14:22; 15:26, 34; 16:7, 30
2 Ki 8:27; 13:2, 11; 14:24; 15:9
18, 24, 28; 17:2; 2 Chr 22:4
Solomon d. evil in sight. 1 Ki 11:6
Manasseh d. evil. 2 Ki 21:2
2 Chr 33:2
Jehoahaz d. evil. 2 Ki 23:32
Jehoiakim d. evil. 37
Jehoiachim d. evil. 24:9
Zedekiah d. evil. 19
Rehoboam d. evil. 2 Chr 12:14
Amon d. evil. 33:22
they had rest, they d. evil. Neh 9:28
the evil that Eliashib d. 13:7
but d. evil before mine eyes. Isa 65:12; 66:4
Alexander d. me much evil. 2 Tim 4:14

did *not*

midwives d. not as king. Ex 1:17
Ahaz d. not what was right. 2 Ki 16:2; 2 Chr 28:1
d. not your fathers thus, and d. not our God bring this ? Neh 13:18
but they d. them not. Jer 11:8
of the evil, and d. it not. Jonah 3:10
d. not many mighty. Mat 13:58
d. it not to these, d. it not to. 25:45
me, this d. not Abraham. John 8:40
I d. it not for his cause. 2 Cor 7:12*

did *so*

as God commanded so d. he. Gen 6:22
Jacob d. so and fulfilled. 29:28
youngest brother, they d. so. 42:20
Lord commanded so d. Ex 7:6, 10
12:28, 50; 39:32; 40:16; Num 1:54
magicians d. so. Ex 7:22; 8:7, 18
Lord d. so. 8:24
Moses d. so. 17:6
Joshua d. so. 10
Aaron d. so. Num 8:3
so d. the daughters of. 36:10
city, so they d. six days. Josh 6:14
so d. Moses command, and so d. 11:15
they d. not so. Judg 2:17
God d. so that night. 6:40
as he d. so year by year. 1 Sam 1:7
so they d. in Shiloh to all. 2:14
so d. David, and so will be. 27:11
so d. he in Beth-el. 1 Ki 12:32
Jeroboam's wife d. so, and. 14:4
so they d. Ezra 6:13
but so d. not I. Neh 5:15
Isaiah d. so, walking naked. Isa 20:2
Jeremiah d. so. Jer 38:12
and I d. so. Ezek 12:7
Jesus arose, and so d. Mat 9:19
his hand, and he d. so. Luke 6:10
so d. their fathers to false. 26
followed Jesus and so d. John 18:15
sons of Sceva who d. so. Acts 19:14

thus **did**

fill their sacks, thus d. Gen 42:25
thus d. he to both of. Ex 36:29
thus d. Moses, according as. 40:16
thus d. your fathers. Num 32:8
thus d. he to all cities. 2 Sam 12:31
thus d. Urijah the priest. 2 Ki 16:16
thus they d. day by day. 2 Chr 24:11
thus d. Hezekiah throughout. 31:20
d. not your fathers thus. Neh 13:18
sanctified them, thus d. Job 1:5

didst

d. this in integrity of. Gen 20:6
do as thou d. to Sihon. Num 21:34
Deut 3:2
as thou d. to Jericho. Josh 8:2
thou d. it secretly. 2 Sam 12:12
than other that thou d. to. 13:16
that thou d. to David. 1 Ki 2:44
d. well that it was in thy. 8:18
2 Chr 6:8
thy wonders that thou d. Neh 9:17
dumb, because thou d. it. Ps 39:9
told us what work thou d. 44:1
when d. terrible things. Isa 64:3
thou kill me as thou d.? Acts 7:28*

Didymus

Thomas, who is called D. John 11:16
20:24; 21:2

die

see **dead** and **death**

every thing in earth shall d. Gen 6:17
overdrive them, flock will d. 33:13
let him d. 44:9
his father would d. 22
now let me d. 46:30
that Israel must d. 47:29
fish in the river shall d. Ex 7:18
nothing shall d. that is the. 9:4
thou seest my face shalt d. 10:28
firstborn in land of Egypt shall d. 11:5
that they bear not iniquity and d. 28:43; Lev 22:9
beast which ye may eat d. Lev 11:39
sin, they shall d. childless. 20:20
holy thing, lest they d. Num 4:15
things covered, lest they d. 20
if any man d. very suddenly. 6:9
and there they shall d. 14:35
if these d. the common death. 16:29
near tabernacle d. 17:13; 18:22
neither they, nor you also d. 18:3*
Aaron, shall d. on mount Hor. 20:26
let me d. death of righteous. 23:10
speak, saying, if a man d. 27:8
shalt stone them that they d. Deut 17:5; 22:21, 24
that men shall d. 17:12
prophet shall d. 18:20
both shall d. 22:22
the man only shall d. 25
if the latter husband d. 24:3
that thief shall d. 7
one d. and have no children. 25:5
Mark 12:19
to Moses, thy days approach that thou d. Deut 31:14
land of Canaan, and d. 32:50
me d. with Philistines. Judg 16:30
increase of house shall d. 1 Sam 2:33
in one day they shall d. both. 34
said, shall Jonathan d.? 14:45
nor if half of us d. 2 Sam 18:3
enter city, child shall d. 1 Ki 14:12
shalt d. and not live. 2 Ki 20:1
Isa 38:1
fathers **not** d. for children, man shall d. 2 Chr 25:4; Jer 31:30
wife said, curse God and d. Job 2:9
excellency goeth away, they d. 4:21
wisdom shall d. with you. 12:2
though the stock thereof d. 14:8
if a man d. shall he live again ? 14
in a moment shall they d. 34:20
if obey not, they shall d. 36:12
they d. in youth, their life is. 14
seeth that wise men d. Ps 49:10
away their breath, they d. 104:29
fools d. for want of. Pr 10:21
shouldest thou d. before ? Eccl 7:17
living know they shall d. but. 9:5
country, there thou shalt d. Isa 22:18
that dwell therein shall d. 51:6
be afraid of a man that shall d. 12
for child shall d. a hundred. 65:20
young men shall d. by sword, their sons and daughters d. Jer 11:22
shall d. of grievous deaths. 16:4
both great and small shall d. 6
this year thou shalt d. 28:16
but thou shalt d. in peace. 34:5
the soul that sinneth, it shall d. Ezek 18:4, 20
thou shalt d. deaths of them. 28:8
thou shalt d. the deaths of the. 10
that wicked man shall d. in. 33:8
they in the caves shall d. 27
Moab shall d. with. Amos 2:2
men in one house they shall d. 6:9
Jeroboam shall d. by sword. 7:11
shalt d. in a polluted land. 17
sinners of my people shall d. 9:10
that that dieth, let it d. Zech 11:9
two parts shall be cut off and d. 13:8
he that curseth father or mother, let him d. Mat 15:4; Mark 7:10
man d. having no seed. Mat 22:24
Luke 20:28
nor can they d. any. Luke 20:36
down ere my child d. John 4:49
one man d. for people. 11:50; 18:14
prophesied that Jesus should d. 11:51
corn of wheat d. but if it d. it. 12:24
righteous man will one d. Rom 5:7
for as in Adam all d. 1 Cor 15:22
sowest not quickened except it d. 36
here men that d. receive. Heb 7:8
blessed are dead that d. Rev 14:13

he **die**

for he said, lest he d. as. Gen 38:11
lad is not with us, he will d. 44:31
a man, so that he d. Ex 21:12
take him from altar, that he d. 14
smite his servant, and he d. 20
found and smitten that he d. 22:2
smite him so that he d. Num 35:16
20, 21, 23; Deut 13:10; 19:5, 11
21:21
wherewith he may d. Num 35:17
18:23; Deut 19:12
return, lest he d. in battle. Deut 20:5, 6, 7
bring thy son that he d. Judg 6:30
from him that he d. 2 Sam 11:15
if wickedness be in him, he shall d. 1 Ki 1:52
of David drew nigh that he d. 2:1
Elijah requested that he might d. 19:4

stone him that he may d. 1 Ki 21:10
when shall he d. and ? Ps 41:5
he shall d. without instruction. Pr 5:23
he that hateth reproof d. 15:10
he that despiseth ways shall d. 19:16
he shall d. whither they. Jer 22:12
out of dungeon before he d. 38:10
wicked, he shall d. in his. Ezek 3:19
20; 18:18, 24, 26; 33:9, 13, 18
not see it, though he shall d. 12:13
in Babylon he shall d. 17:16
what death he should d. John 12:33
18:32

I die

evil take me, and I d. Gen 19:19
I said, lest I d. for her. 26:9
soul may bless thee before I d. 27:4
give me children, or else I d. 30:1
go and see him before I d. 45:28
said to Joseph, behold, I d. 48:21
lo, I d. there bury me. 50:5
Joseph said to his brethren, I d. 24
I must d. in this land. Deut 4:22
now shall I d. for thirst. Judg 15:18
where thou diest will I d. Ruth 1:17
but taste, and I must d. 1 Sam 14:43
that I may d. in mine. 2 Sam 19:37
nay, but I will d. here. 1 Ki 2:30
till I d. I will not remove. Job 27:5
then I said, I shall d. in my. 29:18
deny me them not before I d. Pr 30:7
to return, lest I d. there. Jer 37:20
though I should d. with. Mat 26:35
Mark 14:31
by your rejoicing, I d. 1 Cor 15:31

not die

may live and not d. Gen 42:2; 43:8
47:19
be verified, ye shall not d. 42:20
and he d. not, but. Ex 21:18
sound heard, that he d. not. 28:35
that they d. not. 30:20, 21
charge of the Lord that ye d. not. Lev 8:35
they d. not. 15:31; Num 4:19; 17:10
at all times, that he d. not. Lev 16:2
cloud cover mercy-seat, he d. not. 13
the manslayer d. not. Num 35:12
Josh 20:9
this fire, that I d. not. Deut 18:16
let Reuben live and not d. 33:6
fear not, thou shalt not d. Judg 6:23
1 Sam 20:2; 2 Sam 12:13; 19:23
Jer 38:24
for us, that we d. not. 1 Sam 12:19
kindness of Lord that I d. not. 20:14
ye may live and not d. 2 Ki 18:32
fathers shall not d. for. 2 Chr 25:4
I shall not d. but live. Ps 118:17
with rod, he shall not d. Pr 23:13
Ezek 18:17, 21, 28; 33:15
John 21:23
that he should not d. Isa 51:14
their worm shall not d. nor. 66:24
d. not by our hand. Jer 11:21
Zedekiah, thou shalt not d. by. 34:4
souls that should not d. Ezek 13:19
we shall not d. Lord. Hab 1:12
eat thereof, and not d. John 6:50
that disciple should not d. 21:23

surely die

shalt surely d. Gen 2:17; 20:7
1 Sam 14:44; 22:16; 1 Ki 2:37, 42
Jer 26:8; Ezek 3:18; 33:8, 14
ye shall not surely d. Gen 3:4
they shall surely d. Num 26:65
we shall surely d. Judg 13:22
my son, he shall surely d.
1 Sam 14:39; 20:31; 2 Sam 12:5
2 Ki 8:10; Ezek 18:13
child born to thee shall surely d.
2 Sam 12:14
shalt not come down, but shalt surely d. 2 Ki 1:4, 6, 16

to die

I am at the point to d. Gen 25:32
to d. in the wilderness. Ex 14:11
Num 21:5
any, to cause him to d. Num 35:30
his day shall come to d. 1 Sam 26:10
ye are worthy to d. because. 16
my life, to cause me to d. 28:9
to give yourselves to d. 2 Chr 32:11
that are appointed to d. Ps 79:11
afflicted and ready to d. 88:15
to be born, a time to d. Eccl 3:2
is worthy to d. Jer 26:11
not worthy to d. 16
he is like to d. for hunger. 38:9
return to Jonathan's house to d. 26
better for me to d. Jonah 4:3, 8
wished in himself to d. 8
servant ready to d. Luke 7:2
by our law he ought to d. John 19:7
I am ready also to d. Acts 21:13
I refuse not to d.: but if. 25:11
Romans to deliver any to d. 16
would even dare to d. Rom 5:7
better for me to d. than. 1 Cor 9:15
are in our hearts to d. 2 Cor 7:3
live is Christ, and to d. is. Phil 1:21
to men once to d. Heb 9:27
that are ready to d. Rev 3:2
desire to d. and death shall. 9:6

we die

why should we d.? Gen 47:15
than that we should d. Ex 14:12
let not God speak, lest we d. 20:19
Deut 5:25
we d. we perish, we all. Num 17:12
we and out cattle should d. 20:4
pray, that we d. not. 1 Sam 12:19
for we must needs d. 2 Sam 14:14
we may eat it and d. 1 Ki 17:12
sit we here till we d.? 2 Ki 7:3, 4
if they kill us, we shall but d. 4
to-morrow we shall d. Isa 22:13
1 Cor 15:32
let us go that we may d. John 11:16
whether we d. we d. Rom 14:8

ye die

neither touch it, lest ye d. Gen 3:3
rend clothes, lest ye d. Lev 10:6*
go out from door, lest ye d. 7
nor pollute, lest ye d. Num 18:32
but ye shall d. like men. Ps 82:7
not be purged till ye d. Isa 22:14
there shall ye d. Jer 22:26; 42:16
for why will ye d.? 27:13
Ezek 18:31; 33:11
know that ye shall d. Jer 42:22
ye shall d. in sins. John 8:21, 24
after the flesh ye shall d. Rom 8:13

died

all flesh d. Gen 7:21, 22
and Haran d. 11:28
Terah d. 32
Sarah d. 23:2
Abraham d. 25:8
Ishmael d. 17
Deborah the nurse d. 35:8
Rachel d. 18, 19; 48:7
Isaac d. 35:29
Belah d. 36:33
Jobab d. 34
Husham d. 35
Hadad d. 36; 1 Chr 1:51
Samlah d. Gen 36:37
Saul d. 38
Baal-hanan son of Achbor d. 39
Judah's wife d. 38:12
Er and Onan d. in Canaan. 46:12
Jacob d. 50:16
Joseph d. 26; Ex 1:6
the king of Egypt d. Ex 2:23
the fish d. 7:21
the frogs d. 8:13
the cattle of Egypt d. 9:6
would to God we had d. in Egypt. 16:3
Num 14:2; 20:3; 26:10
Nadab and Abihu d. Lev 10:2; 16:1
Num 3:4; 26:61; 1 Chr 24:2
searchers of the land d. Num 14:37
Aaron d. 20:28; 33:38, 39
Deut 10:6; 32:50
they that d. beside them that d. about matter of Korah. Num 16:49
Miriam d. 20:1
much people of Israel d. 21:6
those that d. in plague were. 25:9
the children of Korah d. not. 26:11
Zelophehad our father, d. in the wilderness, but d. in his own sin. 27:3
Moses d. Deut 34:5
he was 120 years when he d. 7
even all men of war d. Josh 5:4
which d. with hailstones. 10:11
Joshua the son of Nun d. 24:29
Judg 2:8
Eleazar the son of Aaron d.
Josh 24:33; 1 Chr 23:22
Adonibezek d. Judg 1:7
Othniel d. 3:11
Gibeon d. 8:32
men of tower of Shechem d. 9:49
Tola d. 10:2
Jair d. 5
judged Israel six years, then d. 12:7
Ibzan d. 10
Elon d. 12
Abdon d. 15
Elimelech d. Ruth 1:3
Mahlon, Chilion d. 5
that d. not were smitten. 1 Sam 5:12
Samuel d. 25:1
Nabal's heart d. within him. 37
Saul was dead, armour-bearer . . . and d. 31:5, 6; 1 Chr 10:5, 13
Asahel d. 2 Sam 2:23
d. Abner as a fool. 3:33
he d. before Lord. 6:7; 1 Chr 13:10
king of Ammon d. 2 Sam 10:1
1 Chr 19:1
Shobach d. 2 Sam 10:18
Uriah the Hittite d. 11:17
on seventh day child d. 12:18
Ahithophel hanged himself d. 17:23
would God I had d. for thee. 18:33
and all we had d. this day. 19:6
d. of people, even from Dan. 24:15
this woman's child d. 1 Ki 3:19
came to threshold child d. 14:17
Zimri d. 16:18
Tibni d. 22
Ahab d. 22:35, 37
till noon and then d. 2 Ki 4:20
fled to Megiddo and d. there. 9:27
Elisha d. 13:14, 20
Hazael king of Syria d. 24
came to Egypt and d. there. 23:34
but Seled d. without. 1 Chr 2:30
and Jether d. 32
Asa d. 2 Chr 16:13
Jehoiada full of days d. 24:15
when he d. he said. 22
why d. I not from womb ? Job 3:11
so Job d. being old and. 42:17
year that king Uzziah d. Isa 6:1
year that king Ahaz d. 14:28
Hananiah d. Jer 28:17
Pelatiah d. Ezek 11:13
at even my wife d. 24:18
he offended in Baal, he d. Hos 13:1
last of all the woman d. Mat 22:27
Mark 12:22; Luke 20:32
d. rich man also d. Luke 16:22
my brother not d. John 11:21, 32
this man should not have d. 37
Dorcas was sick and d. Acts 9:37
in due time Christ d. Rom 5:6, 8
sin revived and I d. 7:9
it is Christ that d. 8:34
to this end Christ both d. rose. 14:9
destroy not him with thy meat for whom Christ d. 15; 1 Cor 8:11
how that Christ d. 1 Cor 15:3
if one d. for all, then. 2 Cor 5:14
should live to him who d. for. 15
we believe that Jesus d. 1 Thes 4:14
who d. for us that we should. 5:10
despised Moses' law d. Heb 10:28
these d. in faith, not having. 11:13
by faith Joseph when he d. 22
third part of creatures d. Rev 8:9
many men d. of waters that. 11
every living soul d. in the sea. 16:3

and he, so he, that he died

Adam 930 years and he d. Gen 5:5
Noah's days 950 years, and he d.
9:29
into his temple, so he d. Judg 4:21
Eli's neck brake and he d. for he.
1 Sam 4:18
Jonathan that he d. not. 14:45
Lord smote Nabal that he d. 25:38
Abimelech that he d. 2 Sam 11:21
stoned Adoram that he d.
1 Ki 12:18; 2 Chr 10:18

so he d. according to the. 2 Ki 1:17
him in the gate and he d. 7:17, 20
cloth on his face, so that he d. 8:15
Jeroboam and he d. 2 Chr 13:20
bowels fell out, so he d. 21:19
and he d. without. Luke 20:29, 30
Jacob d. in Egypt, he and. Acts 7:15
in that he d. he d. unto. Rom 6:10
that he d. for all. 2 Cor 5:15

diest

where thou d. will I die. Ruth 1:17

diet

for his d. there was a continual d. given him. Jer 52:34*

dieth

fat of beast that d. of. Lev 7:24
d. of itself not eat. 22:8; Deut 14:21
when a man d. in a tent. Num 19:14
died Abner as a fool d.? 2 Sam 3:33
him that d. in the city. 1 Ki 14:11
d. in field fowls of air. 16:4; 21:24
man d. and wasteth. Job 14:10
one d. in his full strength. 21:23
another d. in the bitterness. 25
when he d. he shall carry. Ps 49:17
when a wicked man d. Pr 11:7
how d. the wise man? Eccl 2:16
as the one d. so d. the other. 3:19
their fish stinketh and d. Isa 50:2
he that eateth of their eggs d. 59:5
nor eaten that which d. Ezek 4:14
committeth iniquity, and d. 18:26
in the death of him that d. 32
that that d. let it die. Zech 11:9
worm d. not. Mark 9:44, 46, 48
raised from dead d. no. Rom 6:9
and no man d. to himself. 14:7

differ

who maketh thee to d.? 1 Cor 4:7

difference

Lord put a d. between. Ex 11:7
put a d. between holy. Lev 10:10
to make a d. between unclean. 11:47
d. between clean beasts and. 20:25*
no d. they shewed no d. Ezek 22:26*
shall teach my people the d. 44:23
and put no d. between. Acts 15:9*
for there is no d. Rom 3:22*
is no d. between Jew and. 10:12*
is d. between a wife and. 1 Cor 7:34
compassion making a d. Jude 22*

differences

d. of administration. 1 Cor 12:5*

differeth

star d. from another in. 1 Cor 15:41
heir when a child d. Gal 4:1

differing

gifts d. according to the grace. Rom 12:6

dig

if a man d. a pit, and not. Ex 21:33
of whose hills mayest d. Deut 8:9
shalt have a paddle, and d. 23:13
d. for it more than for. Job 3:21
ye d. a pit for your friend. 6:27*
thou shalt d. about thee. 11:18*
in the dark they d. 24:16
son of man, d. now in. Ezek 8:8
d. thou through the wall. 12:5, 12
though they d. in hell. Amos 9:2
let it alone, till I shall d. Luke 13:8
cannot d. to beg I am ashamed. 16:3

digged

a witness that I have d. Gen 21:30
wells his father's servants had d. 26:15, 18
Isaac's servants d. in. 19, 21, 22, 25
told Isaac of well they had d. 32
in their self-will they d. 49:6*
my grave which I had d. 50:5
Egyptians d. for water to. Ex 7:24
princes d. the well, nobles d. it. Num 21:18*
wells d. thou. Deut 6:11*; Neh 9:25*
I have d. and drunk strange waters, and dried. 2 Ki 19:24; Isa 37:25
Uzziah d. many wells. 2 Chr 26:10*
made a pit and d. it. Ps 7:15; 57:6
without cause they d. a pit. 35:7
till pit be d. for the wicked. 94:13
proud have d. pits for me. 119:85
shall not be pruned nor d. Isa 5:6*
all hills be d. with the mattock. 7:25
to the pit whence ye are d. 51:1
I went to Euphrates and d. Jer 13:7
have d. a pit for my soul. 18:20, 22
when I had d. in the wall. Ezek 8:8
hedged it, and d. a. Mat 21:33
d. in the earth, and hid. 25:18
who d. and laid the. Luke 6:48
Lord, they have d. down. Rom 11:3

diggedst

wells digged which thou d. not. Deut 6:11*

diggeth

an ungodly man d. up. Pr 16:27*
whoso d. pit fall. 26:27; Eccl 10:8

dignity

thou art excellency of d. Gen 49:3
what d. hath been done? Esth 6:3
folly is set in great d. Eccl 10:6
d. shall proceed of. Hab 1:7

dignities

speak evil of d. 2 Pet 2:10; Jude 8

diligence

keep thy heart with all d. Pr 4:23
give d. that thou mayest. Luke 12:58
that ruleth with d. Rom 12:8
abound in faith and d. 2 Cor 8:7*
do thy d. to come. 2 Tim 4:9, 21
one of you shew same d. Heb 6:11
giving all d. to add to. 2 Pet 1:5
brethren, give d. to make your. 10
when I gave all d. to write. Jude 3

diligent

judges shall make d. Deut 19:18
take d. heed to do the. Josh 22:5
accomplish a d. search. Ps 64:6
and spirit made d. search. 77:6
but the hand of the d. Pr 10:4
the hand of the d. bear rule. 12:24
but the substance of a d. man. 27
but the soul of the d. shall. 13:4
the thoughts of d. tend. 21:5
seest thou a man d. in his? 22:29
be thou d. to know state of. 27:23
proved d. but now much more d. 2 Cor 8:22*
be d. to come unto me. Tit 3:12
be d. that ye be found. 2 Pet 3:14

diligently

if thou wilt d. hearken to. Ex 15:26
Deut 11:13; 28:1; Jer 17:24
Moses d. sought the goat. Lev 10:16
heed and keep soul d. Deut 4:9
thou shalt teach them d. to. 6:7
d. keep commandments. 17; 11:22
make search, and ask d. 13:14
heed that thou observe d. 24:8
now the men did d. 1 Ki 20:33
let it be d. done for. Ezra 7:23*
hear d. my speech. Job 13:17; 21:2
shalt d. consider his place. Ps 37:10
us to keep thy precepts d. 119:4
I came forth d. to. Pr 7:15
he that d. seeketh good. 11:27
consider d. what is before thee. 23:1
he hearkened d. with. Isa 21:7
hearken d. to me, and eat. 55:2
consider d. see if there. Jer 2:10
if they will d. learn the ways. 12:16
if ye will d. obey the. Zech 6:15
he inquired d. when. Mat 2:7*
Herod said, go and search d. 8
which he had d. inquired. 16*
sweep house and seek d. Luke 15:8
taught d. the things of. Acts 18:25
if she have d. followed. 1 Tim 5:10
in Rome he sought me d. 2 Tim 1:17
bring Zenas and Apollos on their journey d. Tit 3:13
rewarder of them that d. Heb 11:6
looking d. lest any man fail. 12:15*
the prophets searched d. 1 Pet 1:10

dim

Isaac was old, his eyes d. Gen 27:1
the eyes of Israel were d. 48:10
Moses' eye was not d. Deut 34:7
Eli's eyes began to wax d. 1 Sam 3:2; 4:15*
mine eye also is d. by. Job 17:7
eyes of them that see not be d. Isa 32:3
how is gold become d.! Lam 4:1
for these things our eyes are d. 5:17

diminish, -ed

you shall not d. ought. Ex 5:8
not ought of your work be d. 11, 19
duty of marriage not d. 21:10
to the years thou d. Lev 25:16
nor shall you d. Deut 4:2; 12:32
gotten by vanity be d. Pr 13:11
men of Kedar shall be d. Isa 21:17*
speak, d. not a word. Jer 26:2
may be increased and not d. 29:6
will I also d. thee. Ezek 5:11
behold, I have d. thine. 16:27
I will d. them, they shall. 29:15

diminishing

d. of them be riches. Rom 11:12*

dimness

behold trouble darkness d. Isa 8:22*
d. shall not be such as was. 9:1*

Dimon

waters of D. shall be full of blood, for I will bring more upon D. Isa 15:9

Dinah

bare daughter called D. Gen 30:21
Jacob heard he had defiled D. 34:5

dine, -d

these men shall d. Gen 43:16
Pharisee besought him to d. Luke 11:37
come and d. John 21:12*
so when they had d. Jesus. 15*

dinner

better is a d. of herbs. Pr 15:7
I have prepared my d. Mat 22:4
first washed before d. Luke 11:38
when makest a d. or supper. 14:12

Dionysius

among which was D. Acts 17:34

Diotrephes

D. who loveth to have pre-eminence. 3 John 9

dip

d. it in the blood that is. Ex 12:22
priest shall d. finger. Lev 4:6; 17:14
16
d. the cedar wood and. 14:6, 51
clean person should d. Num 19:18
let Asher d. his foot in. Deut 33:24
Boaz said to Ruth, d. Ruth 2:14
Lazarus that he may d. Luke 16:24

dipped, -eth

d. the coat in blood. Gen 37:31
Aaron d. his finger in the. Lev 9:9
the priests' feet were d. Josh 3:15
he d. end of rod in an. 1 Sam 14:27
Naaman d. in Jordan. 2 Ki 5:14
Hazael took a cloth and d. it. 8:15
that thy foot be d. in. Ps 68:23
he that d. his hand with me in the. Mat 26:23; Mark 14:20
I give a sop, when I have d.; d. the sop, gave it to Judas. John 13:26
with a vesture d. in blood. Rev 19:13

direct

he sent Judah to d. his. Gen 46:28*
in the morning will I d. Ps 5:3*
he shall d. thy paths. Pr 3:6
righteousness of perfect shall d. 11:5
wisdom is profitable to d. Eccl 10:10
raised him up, I will d. Isa 45:13*
I will d. their way in truth. 61:8*
man that walketh to d. Jer 10:23
Lord Jesus Christ d. 1 Thes 3:11
Lord d. your hearts into. 2 Thes 3:5

directed

he hath not d. his words. Job 32:14
that my ways were d. to. Ps 119:5*
who hath d. the Spirit? Isa 40:13

directeth

he d. it under the heaven. Job 37:3*
ways, but the Lord d. his. Pr 16:9
as for upright he d. his way. 21:29*

direction

princes judged it by d. Num 21:18*

directly

sprinkle blood d. before. Num 19:4*
even the way d. before. Ezek 42:12

dirt
fat closed, and *d.* came. *Judg* 3:22
cast them out as *d.* in. *Ps* 18:42*
waters cast up mire and *d. Isa* 57:20

disallow, -ed
because her father *d.* *Num* 30:5
but if her husband *d.* her. 8
he *d.* her not. 11
d. indeed of men, but. *1 Pet* 2:4*
stone which the builders *d.* is. 7*

disannul
wilt thou also *d.* my ? *Job* 40:8†
purposed who shall *d.* it ? *Isa* 14:27†
covenant law cannot *d.* *Gal* 3:17

disannulled
with death shall be *d.* *Isa* 28:18†

disannulleth
covenant no man *d.* or. *Gal* 3:15*

disannulling
there is a *d.* of the. *Heb* 7:18

disappoint
arise, O Lord, *d.* him. *Ps* 17:13*

disappointed
without counsel purposes *d. Pr* 15:22

disappointeth
he *d.* devices of crafty. *Job* 5:12*

discern
[1] *To see and identify by noting differences,* Gen 31:32. [2] *To see by the eye or the understanding,* 2 Sam 14:17; Heb 5:14.

d. thou what is thine. *Gen* 31:32
d. I pray thee, whose are. 38:25
so is my lord to *d.* *2 Sam* 14:17
can I *d.* between good and ? 19:35
I may *d.* between good. *1 Ki* 3:9
hast asked understanding to *d.* 11
people could not *d.* the. *Ezra* 3:13
but I could not *d.* the. *Job* 4:16
my taste *d.* perverse things ? 6:30
d. between unclean and. *Ezek* 44:23
d. between right hand. *Jonah* 4:11
d. between the righteous. *Mal* 3:18
d. the face of the sky. *Mat* 16:3
Luke 12:56
senses exercised to *d.* *Heb* 5:14

discerned, -eth
d. him not, his hands. *Gen* 27:23
king of Israel *d.* him. *1 Ki* 20:41
I *d.* among the youth a. *Pr* 7:7
a wise man *d.* time and. *Eccl* 8:5
they are spiritually *d.* *1 Cor* 2:14

discerner
word is a *d.* of thoughts. *Heb* 4:12

discerning
unworthily, not *d.* *1 Cor* 11:29
another is given *d.* of spirits. 12:10

discharge, -d
will cause them to be *d.* *1 Ki* 5:9*
there is no *d.* in that war. *Eccl* 8:8

disciple
Literally, a scholar, a learner ; especially one who believes in the doctrine of his teacher and follows him. In the New Testament the followers of John the Baptist were called his disciples, Mark 2:18; John 3:25. *Also the followers of Moses, in distinction from the followers of John or Jesus,* Mark 2:18; John 9:28. *But most often the word is used with reference to the believers in Christ, both those who believed during his life, and those who later joined the early Church,* Matt 27:57; John 19:38; Acts 9:36. *The twelve Apostles, also, are frequently called by this name,* Mat. 10:1; John 20:2.

d. not above master. *Mat* 10:24
Luke 6:40
it is enough for the *d.* *Mat* 10:25
give a cup of cold water to a *d.* 42
of Arimathaea was Jesus' *d.* 27:57
thou art his *d.* we are. *John* 9:28
so did another *d.* that *d.* was. 18:15
then went out that other *d.* that. 16
the *d.* standing by, whom. 19:26
to that *d.* behold thy mother, and from that hour that *d.* took. *John* 19:27
being a *d.* but secretly, for fear. 38
other *d.* Jesus loved. 20:2; 21:7, 20
went forth, and that other *d.* 20:3
the other *d.* did outrun Peter. 4
went in also that other *d.* and. 8
saying, that that *d.* should. 21:23
this is the *d.* that testifieth these. 24
there was a certain *d.* at. *Acts* 9:10
believed not that he was a *d.* 26
at Joppa a *d.* named Tabitha. 36
a certain *d.* was there. 16:1
an old *d.* with whom we. 21:16

my **disciple**
not life, cannot be *my d. Luke* 14:26
bear his cross, cannot be *my d.* 27
forsaketh not all, cannot be my *d.* 33

disciples
then came the *d.* of John. *Mat* 9:14
unto him his twelve *d.* 10:1
an end of commanding his *d.* 11:1
when the *d.* saw him walking. 14:26
when the *d.* heard it they. 17:6
the *d.* rebuked them. 19:13
Mark 10:13
Jesus took the twelve *d. Mat* 20:17
Jesus sent two *d.* saying, go. 21:1
sent unto him their *d.* 22:16
bread, and gave it to the *d.* 26:26
not deny thee, likewise said the *d.* 35
then all the *d.* forsook him. 56
do *d.* of John and of Pharisees fast, thy *d.*? *Mark* 2:18; *Luke* 5:33
now *d.* had forgotten to. *Mark* 8:14
the *d.* began to rejoice. *Luke* 19:37
between John's *d.* and. *John* 3:25
that Jesus baptized more *d.* 4:1
but we are Moses' *d.* 9:28
he began to wash the *d'.* feet. 13:5
also one of this man's *d.*? 18:17
Mary told *d.* that she had. 20:18
out slaughter against *d.* *Acts* 9:1
Saul essayed to join himself to *d.* 26
the *d.* were called Christians. 11:26
and finding certain *d.* 19:1
Paul would have entered, *d.* 30
first day of week *d.* came. 20:7
to draw away *d.* after them. 30

his **disciples**
his d. came and awoke. *Mat* 8:25
and followed, and so did *his d.* 9:19
and tell *his d.* he is risen. 28:7
say ye, *his d.* came by night and. 13
in house *his d.* asked. *Mark* 10:10
murmured against *his d. Luke* 5:30
he lifted up his eyes on *his d.* 6:20
teach us, as John taught *his d.* 11:1
his glory, and *his d.* *John* 2:11
Jesus baptized not, but *his d.* 4:2
upon this came *his d.* and. 27
and there he sat with *his d.* 6:3
but *his d.* were gone away alone. 22
will ye be *his d.* 9:27
said *his d.* Lord if he sleep. 11:12
he went with *his d.* over brook. 18:1
often resorted thither with *his d.* 2
again, *his d.* were within. 20:26

of his **disciples**
John sent two *of his d.* *Mat* 11:2
Mark 11:1; 14:13; *Luke* 19:29
some *of his d.* eat with. *Mark* 7:2
time many *of his d.* *John* 6:66
priest asked Jesus *of his d.* 18:19
art not thou also one *of his d.*? 25
none *of his d.* durst ask him. 21:12

to his **disciples**
gave the loaves *to his d. Mat* 14:19
all things *to his d.* *Mark* 4:34
turned *to his d.* and. *Luke* 10:23
shewed himself *to his d. John* 21:14

my **disciples**
seal law among *my d.* *Isa* 8:16
keep the passover at thy house with *my d.* *Mat* 26:18
Mark 14:14; *Luke* 22:11
then are ye *my d. John* 8:31; 13:35
so shall ye be *my d.* 15:8

thy **disciples**
we fast, *thy d.* fast not. *Mat* 9:14
Mark 2:18
thy d. do that which is not. *Mat* 12:2
why do *thy d.* trangress the ? 15:2
I brought him to *thy d.* they. 17:16
why walk not *thy d.*? *Mark* 7:5
to *thy d.* to cast him out. 9:18
Luke 9:40
Master, rebuke *thy d.* *Luke* 19:39
thy d. may see works. *John* 7:3

discipline
also their ears to *d.* *Job* 36:10*

disclose
earth also shall *d.* her. *Isa* 26:21

discomfited
Joshua *d.* Amalek and. *Ex* 17:13
smote and *d.* them. *Num* 14:45
d. them before Israel. *Josh* 10:10
the Lord *d.* Sisera and. *Judg* 4:15
Gideon pursued them, and *d.* 8:12
Philistines, and *d.* them. *1 Sam* 7:10
and *d.* them. *2 Sam* 22:15; *Ps* 18:14
young men shall be *d.* *Isa* 31:8*

discomfiture
was a very great *d.* *1 Sam* 14:20

discontented
every one that was *d.* *1 Sam* 22:2

discontinue
and thou shalt *d.* from. *Jer* 17:4

discord
mischief, he soweth *d.* *Pr* 6:14
and him that soweth *d.* 19

discover
[1] *An old meaning, reveal, uncover.* [2] *To manifest, especially unintentionally,* Pr 18:2. [3] *To detect for the first time,* Acts 27:39.

a man shall not *d.* his. *Deut* 22:30
we will *d.* ourselves. *1 Sam* 14:8
who can *d.* the face ? *Job* 41:13
that his heart may *d.* *Pr* 18:2
and *d.* not a secret to another. 25:9
the Lord will *d.* their. *Isa* 3:17
I will *d.* thy skirts. *Jer* 13:26
Nah 3:5
of Edom, he will *d.* thy. *Lam* 4:22
I will *d.* thy nakedness. *Ezek* 16:37
I will *d.* her lewdness. *Hos* 2:10
I will *d.* the foundations. *Mi* 1:6

discovered
thy nakedness be not *d.* *Ex* 20:26
he hath *d.* her fountain. *Lev* 20:18
both *d.* themselves. *1 Sam* 14:11
Saul heard David was *d.* 22:6
foundations of world were *d.* at the rebuking. *2 Sam* 22:16; *Ps* 18:15
he *d.* covering of Judah. *Isa* 22:8
for thou hast *d.* thyself to. 57:8
iniquity are thy skirts *d.* *Jer* 13:22
have not *d.* thine iniquity. *Lam* 2:14
foundation thereof be *d. Ezek* 13:14
thy nakedness *d.* through. 16:36
before thy wickedness was *d.* 57
your transgressions are *d.* 21:24
in thee have they *d.* their. 22:10
these *d.* nakedness, they. 23:10
she *d.* her whoredoms, *d.* her. 18
of whoredoms shall be *d.* 29
iniquity of Ephraim was *d. Hos* 7:1
when we had *d.* Cyprus. *Acts* 21:3*
but they *d.* a certain creek. 27:39*

discovereth
he *d.* deep things out of. *Job* 12:22
voice of Lord *d.* forest. *Ps* 29:9

discovering
by *d.* the foundation to. *Hab* 3:13

discourage
why *d.* ye hearts of people ?
Num 32:7

discouraged
soul of people much *d.* *Num* 21:4
they *d.* the heart of children. 32:9
it, fear not, nor be *d.* *Deut* 1:21
our brethren have *d.* our heart. 28
shall not fail nor be *d.* *Isa* 42:4
children, lest they be *d.* *Col* 3:21

discreet
look out a man *d.* and. *Gen* 41:33
there is none so *d.* and wise as. 39
teach young women to be *d* *Tit* 2:5*

discreetly
saw that he answered *d. Mark* 12:34

discretion
guide his affairs with *d.* *Ps* 112:5*
young man knowledge and *d.* *Pr* 1:4
d. shall preserve thee. 2:11
keep sound wisdom and *d.* 3:21
thou mayest regard *d.* and keep. 5:2
fair woman who is without *d.* 11:22
d. of a man deferreth his. 19:11
doth instruct him to *d.* *Isa* 28:26*
out heavens by his *d.* *Jer* 10:12*

disdained
Goliath saw David, he *d.* him. *1 Sam* 17:42
would *d.* to set with dogs. *Job* 30:1

disease
The ancient Hebrews, who were very little versed in the study of natural philosophy, and not much accustomed to consult physicians when they were sick, imputed their diseases generally to evil spirits, or to the hand of God, generally in punishment for some sin; and king Asa is blamed for placing his confidence in physicians, when he had a very painful fit of the gout in his feet, instead of to God, 2 Chr. 16:12.

In the New Testament, the cause of many diseases is attributed to the devil, Luke 13:16. *And the various forms of insanity and allied troubles were spoken of as being possessed of a devil. There seems to have been also something beyond ordinary insanity included among these, but there is no means of telling either what it was, or what proportion of the cases might be considered as coming under it.*

The diseases of *Egypt, from which God promised to defend his people,* Ex 15:26; *and which he threatens, in case of their disobedience, to inflict upon them,* Deut 28:60; *are either the plagues with which God afflicted Egypt before the departure of the Israelites, or the diseases which were most common in the country, such as blindness, ulcers in the legs, consumptions, and the leprosy, called* Elephantiasis, *which was peculiar to this country* (Pliny).

if I shall recover of *d.* *2 Ki* 1:2
shall I recover of this *d.*? 8:8, 9
Asa diseased till his *d.* was exceeding great, yet in his *d.* *2 Chr* 16:12
great sickness by *d.* of thy. 21:15
smote him with an incurable *d.* 18
my *d.* is my garment. *Job* 30:18
filled with a loathsome *d.* *Ps* 38:7*
an evil *d.* say they, cleaveth. 41:8
vanity, and it is an evil *d.* *Eccl.* 6:2
healing all manner of *d.* *Mat* 4:23; 9:35; 10:1
whole of whatsoever *d.* *John* 5:4

diseased
Asa was *d.* in his feet. *1 Ki* 15:23; *2 Chr* 16:12
d. have not strengthened. *Ezek* 34:4
pushed the *d.* with your horns. 21
d. with an issue of blood. *Mat* 9:20
they brought all that were *d.* 14:35; *Mark* 1:32
did on them that were *d.* *John* 6:2

diseases
put none of these *d.* on you. *Ex* 15:26; *Deut* 7:15
thee all the *d.* of Egypt. *Deut* 28:60
out, he died of sore *d.* *2 Chr* 21:19
him in great *d.* his servants. 24:25
Lord, who healeth all thy *d.* *Ps* 103:3
people that were taken with divers *d.* *Mat* 4:24; *Mark* 1:34; *Luke* 4:40
over devils, and cure *d.* *Luke* 9:1
d. departed from them. *Acts* 19:12
others which had *d.* in island. 28:9

disfigure
hypocrites, for they *d.* *Mat* 6:16

disgrace
do not *d.* the throne. *Jer* 14:21

disguise, -d
and Saul *d.* himself. *1 Sam* 28:8
Jeroboam said, arise, and *d.* *1 Ki* 14:2
sons of the prophets *d.* 20:38
Ahab king of Israel said, I will *d.* myself, and he *d.* 22:30; *2 Chr* 18:29
Josiah *d.* himself to. *2 Chr* 35:22

disguiseth
waiteth and *d.* his face. *Job* 24:15

dish, -es
make *d.* thereof. *Ex* 25:29; 37:16
thereon *d.* and spoons. *Num* 4:7
forth butter in a lordly *d.* *Judg* 5:25
as a man wipeth a *d.* *2 Ki* 21:13
dippeth with me in the *d.* *Mat* 26:23; *Mark* 14:20

dishonest, *see* **gain**

dishonesty
hidden things of *d.* *2 Cor* 4:2

dishonour
for us to see king's *d.* *Ezra* 4:14
clothed with shame and *d.* *Ps* 35:26; 71:13
known my shame and my *d.* 69:19
wound and *d.* shall he get. *Pr* 6:33
to honour, another to *d.* *Rom* 9:21
sown in *d.* it is raised. *1 Cor* 15:43
by honour and *d.* by. *2 Cor* 6:8
to honour, some to *d.* *2 Tim* 2:20

dishonour, -est, -eth, *verb*
for the son *d.* father. *Mi* 7:6
my Father, and ye *d.* me. *John* 8:49
to *d.* their own bodies. *Rom* 1:24
of the law, *d.* thou God? 2:23
man *d.* his head. *1 Cor* 11:4
woman *d.* her head. 5

disinherit
will *d.* them, and make. *Num* 14:12

dismayed
nor forsake thee, fear not, nor be *d.* *Deut* 31:8; *Josh* 1:9; 8:1; 10:25; *1 Chr* 22:13; 28:20; *2 Chr* 20:15, 17; 32:7
they were *d.* *1 Sam* 17:11; *2 Ki* 19:26; *Isa* 37:27
I was bowed down, *d.* at. *Isa* 21:3
fear not, be not *d.* 41:10; *Jer* 1:17; 10:2; 23:4; 30:10; 46:27; *Ezek* 2:6; 3:9
may be *d.* and behold it. *Isa* 41:23
wise men are *d.* *Jer* 8:9; 10:2
be *d.* but let not me be *d.* 17:18
seen them *d.* turned back? 46:5
Misgab is *d.* 48:1*
cause Elam to be *d.* 49:37
men of Babylon shall be *d.* 50:36
O Teman, shall be *d.* *Ob* 9

dismaying
Moab shall be a *d.* to. *Jer* 48:39†

dismissed
Jehoiada the priest *d.* not. *2 Chr* 23:8
d. they came to Antioch. *Acts* 15:30
spoken, he *d.* assembly. 19:41

disobedience
by one man's *d.* many. *Rom* 5:19
to revenge all *d.* *2 Cor* 10:6
worketh in children of *d.* *Eph* 2:2
wrath of God on children of *d.* 5:6; *Col* 3:6
d. received a just. *Heb* 2:2

disobedient
who was *d.* to the word. *1 Ki* 13:26
were *d.* and rebelled. *Neh* 9:26
turn *d.* to the wisdom of. *Luke* 1:17
not *d.* to the heavenly. *Acts* 26:19
boasters *d.* to parents. *Rom* 1:30; *2 Tim* 3:2
forth my hands to a *d.* *Rom* 10:21
made for lawless and *d.* *1 Tim* 1:9*
being abominable and *d.* *Tit* 1:16
we also were sometimes *d.* 3:3
which be *d.* stone which. *1 Pet* 2:7*
who stumble at word, being *d.* 8
spirits in prison, which sometime were *d.* 3:20

disobeyed
hast *d.* mouth of Lord. *1 Ki* 13:21

disorderly
warn them that are *d.* *1 Thes* 5:14
brother who walks *d.* *2 Thes* 3:6
we behaved not ourselves *d.* 7
some who walk among you *d.* 11

dispatch
d. them with swords. *Ezek* 23:47

dispensation
a *d.* of the gospel is. *1 Cor* 9:17*
in *d.* of fulness of times. *Eph* 1:10
ye have heard of the *d.* of grace. 3:2
a minister according to *d.* *Col* 1:25

disperse
Saul said, *d.* *1 Sam* 14:34
lips of wise *d.* knowledge. *Pr* 15:7
scatter them and *d.* *Ezek* 12:15; 20:23; 29:12; 30:23, 26
and I will *d.* thee in countries. 22:15

dispersed
Rehoboam *d.* of all his. *2 Chr* 11:23
certain people *d.* among. *Esth* 3:8
he hath *d.* he hath given. *Ps* 112:9; *2 Cor* 9:9
let thy fountains be *d.* *Pr* 5:16
together *d.* of Judah. *Isa* 11:12
d. through countries. *Ezek* 36:19
daughter of my *d.* shall. *Zeph* 3:10
to *d.* among Gentiles? *John* 7:35*
as obeyed him were *d.* *Acts* 5:37*

dispersions
days of your *d.* are. *Jer* 25:34*

displayed
banner that it may be *d.* *Ps* 60:4

displease
let it not *d.* my lord. *Gen* 31:35*
if it *d.* thee, I will get. *Num* 22:34
that thou *d.* not lords. *1 Sam* 29:7
to Joab, let not this *d.* *2 Sam* 11:25
Lord see it, and it *d.* him. *Pr* 24:18

displeased
he did *d.* the Lord. *Gen* 38:10*
on head of Ephraim, it *d.* 48:17
complained, it *d.* Lord. *Num* 11:1*
was kindled, Moses also was *d.* 10
but the thing *d.* Samuel. *1 Sam* 8:6
very wroth, and the saying *d.* 18:8
David was *d.* because the Lord had. *2 Sam* 6:8; *1 Chr* 13:11
David had done *d.* Lord. *2 Sam* 11:27
his father had not *d.* him. *1 Ki* 1:6
king of Israel went to his house *d.* 20:43; 21:4
God was *d.* with this. *1 Chr* 21:7
been *d.* O turn thyself to. *Ps* 60:1
d. him that there was. *Isa* 59:15
the king was sore *d.* *Dan* 6:14
it *d.* Jonah exceedingly. *Jonah* 4:1
was the Lord *d.* against? *Hab* 3:8
Lord hath been sore *d.* *Zech* 1:2
I am very sore *d.* with heathen; for I was but a little *d.* they helped. 15
scribes saw, were *d.* *Mat* 21:15*
Jesus saw it, he was much *d.* *Mark* 10:14*
began to be much *d.* with James. 41*
d. was highly *d.* with. *Acts* 12:20

displeasure
afraid of the hot *d.* of. *Deut* 9:19
though I do them a *d.* *Judg* 15:3*
vex them in his sore *d.* *Ps* 2:5
neither chasten me in hot *d.* 6:1; 38:1

disposed
who hath *d.* whole world? *Job* 34:13
thou know when God *d.*? 37:15*
when he was *d.* to pass. *Acts* 18:27*
and ye be *d.* to go. *1 Cor* 10:27

disposing
the whole *d.* thereof is. *Pr* 16:33

disposition
received law by *d.* of. *Acts* 7:53*

dispossess, -ed
children of Machir *d.* *Num* 32:39
ye shall *d.* the inhabitants of. 33:53
how can I *d.* them? *Deut* 7:17
Lord God hath *d.* the. *Judg* 11:23

disputation
had no small *d.* *Acts* 15:2*

disputations
but not to doubtful *d.* *Rom* 14:1

dispute
there righteous might *d.* *Job* 23:7*

disputed
was it that ye d.? Mark 9:33*
for they had d. who should be. 34
Saul d. against Grecians. Acts 9:29
Paul d. in synagogue with. 17:17*
Michael d. about body of. Jude 9

disputer
where is d. of world? 1 Cor 1:20

disputing
them of Asia d. with. Acts 6:9
had been much d. Peter rose. 15:7
d. and persuading things. 19:8*, 9*
they neither found me d. 24:12

disputings
things without murmurings and d. Phil 2:14†
perverse d. of men of. 1 Tim 6:5*

disquiet
and d. inhabitants of. Jer 50:34

disquieted
why hast thou d. me? 1 Sam 28:15
surely they are d. in vain. Ps 39:6
O my soul, why art thou d. within? 42:5, 11; 43:5
three things earth is d. Pr 30:21*

disquietness
roared by reason of d. Ps 38:8

dissembled
also stolen and d. also. Josh 7:11
for ye d. in your hearts. Jer 42:20*
other Jews d. likewise. Gal 2:13

dissemblers
nor will I go in with d. Ps 26:4

dissembleth
he that hateth d. with. Pr 26:24

dissension
Barnabas had no small d. Acts 15:2
arose a d. between Pharisees. 23:7
when there arose a great d. 10

dissimulation
let love be without d. Rom 12:9*
Barnabas carried away with their d. Gal 2:13

dissolve
that thou canst d. doubts. Dan 5:16

dissolved
and all inhabitants are d. Ps 75:3
whole Palestina are d. Isa 14:31*
earth is clean d. the earth. 24:19
the host of heaven be d. 34:4
and the palace shall be d. Nah 2:6
this tabernacle were d. 2 Cor 5:1
all these things shall be d. 2 Pet 3:11
heavens being on fire shall be d. 12

dissolvest
and thou d. my substance. Job 30:22

dissolving
d. of doubts found in. Dan 5:12

distaff
her hands hold the d. Pr 31:19

distant
had two tenons equally d. Ex 36:22*

distil
speech shall d. as dew. Deut 32:2
the clouds d. on man. Job 36:28*

distinction
except they give a d. 1 Cor 14:7

distinctly
in book of the law of God d. Neh 8:8

distracted
suffer thy terrors, I am d. Ps 88:15

distraction
attend on Lord without d. 1 Cor 7:35

distress
me in day of my d. Gen 35:3
therefore is this d. come. 42:21
me now, when in d. Judg 11:7
one in d. came to David. 1 Sam 22:2
in my d. I called on the. 2 Sam 22:7
Ps 18:6; 118:5; 120:1
my soul out of all d. 1 Ki 1:29*
his d. Ahaz trespassed. 2 Chr 28:22
I said, ye see the d. Neh 2:17*
and we are in great d. 9:37
enlarged me when I was in d. Ps 4:1
I will mock when d. Pr 1:27
strength to the needy in d. Isa 25:4
O Lord, for I am in d. Lam 1:20
proudly in day of d. Ob 12
delivered up those in day of d. 14
a day of trouble and d. Zeph 1:15
I will bring d. upon men. 17
there shall be great d. Luke 21:23
on the earth d. of nations. 25
d. separate us from love. Rom 8:35*
good for the present d. 1 Cor 7:26
over you in your d. 1 Thes 3:7

distress, -ed, verb
was greatly afraid and d. Gen 32:7
Moab was d. Num 22:3
d. not the Moabites. Deut 2:9*
Ammonites, d. them not. 19*
enemies shall d. 28:53†, 55†, 57†
Israel d. Judg 2:15; 10:9
for people were d. did. 1 Sam 13:6
men of Israel were d. 14:24
Saul was d. 28:15
David was greatly d. for. 30:6
I am d. for thee. 2 Sam 1:26
king of Assyria d. Ahaz. 2 Chr 28:20
yet I will d. Ariel. Isa 29:2
that d. her shall be as a dream. 7
I will d. the inhabitants. Jer 10:18
on every side, yet not d. 2 Cor 4:8*

distresses
bring thou me out of my d. Ps 25:17
delivered them out of their d. 107:6
saved them out of their d. 13, 19
bringeth them out of their d. 28
Noph shall have d. Ezek 30:16*
approving ourselves in d. 2 Cor 6:4
I take pleasure in d. for. 12:10

distribute
which Moses did d. for. Josh 13:32
Kore to d. oblations. 2 Chr 31:14
office was to d. to. Neh 13:13
sell all thou hast, and d. Luke 18:22
rich to be ready to d. 1 Tim 6:18

distributed
Eleazar and Joshua d. for. Josh 14:1
David d. them, according to their. 1 Chr 24:3*; 2 Chr 23:18
Jesus gave thanks and d. John 6:11
but as God hath d. 1 Cor 7:17
the rule God hath d. to. 2 Cor 10:13

distributeth, -ing
God d. sorrows in his. Job 21:17
d. to the necessities of. Rom 12:13*

distribution
d. was made to every one. Acts 4:35
for your liberal d. to. 2 Cor 9:13

ditch
shalt thou plunge me in d. Job 9:31
he is fallen into the d. Ps 7:15
a whore is a deep d. Pr 23:27
ye made a d. between. Isa 22:11*
both shall fall into d. Mat 15:14*
Luke 6:39*

ditches
this valley full of d. 2 Ki 3:16*

divers, diverse
cattle gender with d. Lev 19:19
not sow vineyard with d. Deut 22:9*
not wear garment of d. sorts. 11*
not have in thy bag d. 25:13
in thy house d. measures. 14
of d. colours, a prey of d. Judg 5:30
Tamar had a garment of d. colours. 2 Sam 13:18, 19
glistering stones of d. 1 Chr 29:2
they laid Asa in the bed filled with odours and d. kinds. 2 Chr 16:14
Jehoram slew d. of the princes. 21:4
d. of Asher humbled. 30:11
the vessels being d. one. Esth 1:7
their laws are d. from all. 3:8
he sent d. sorts of flies. Ps 78:45*
there came d. sorts of flies. 105:31*
d. weights and d. measures. Pr 20:10
d. weights are an abomination to. 23
there are also d. vanities. Eccl 5:7
deckest high places with d. colours. Ezek 16:16
great eagle had d. colours. 17:3
beasts came up, d. one. Dan 7:3
a fourth beast d. from all. 7, 19
d. from all kingdoms. 23
d. from the first. 24
brought to Jesus sick people with d. Mat 4:24; Mark 1:34; Luke 4:40
pestilences, and earthquakes in d. Mat 24:7; Mark 13:8; Luke 21:11
for d. of them came. Mark 8:3*
when d. were hardened. Acts 19:9*
to another d. kinds. 1 Cor 12:10
women led away with d. 2 Tim 3:6
deceived, serving d. lusts. Tit 3:3
who in d. manners spake. Heb 1:1
witness with signs and d. 2:4*
stood in d. washings. 9:10
d. and strange doctrines. 13:9
fall into d. temptations. Jas 1:2*

diversities
d. of gifts. 1 Cor 12:4
d. of operations. 6
God hath set in church d. 28*

divide
and let the firmament d. Gen 1:6
be lights, to d. day from. 14, 18
and at night he shall d. 49:27
hand over sea and d. it. Ex 14:16
d. the money, d. the dead ox. 21:35
veil shall d. between holy. 26:33
but not d. it asunder. Lev 1:17; 5:8
not eat of them that d. hoof. 11:4, 7
Deut 14:7
and d. the prey into. Num 31:27
d. land by lot. 33:54*; 34:17, 18, 29
d. the coasts of thy land. Deut 19:3
d. for an inheritance. Josh 1:6*
13:6*, 7; 18:5
d. the spoil of your enemies. 22:8
thou and Ziba d. land. 2 Sam 19:29
d. living child in two. 1 Ki 3:25, 26
thou didst d. the sea. Neh 9:11
Ps 74:13
and thou didst d. them into. Neh 9:22*
innocent shall d. silver. Job 27:17
and d. their tongues. Ps 55:9
than to d. the spoil. Pr 16:19
as men rejoice when they d. Isa 9:3
he shall d. the spoil with. 53:12
take the balances and d. Ezek 5:1
d. land by lot. 45:1; 47:21, 22
the land which ye shall d. 48:29
he shall d. the land. Dan 11:39
that he d. inheritance. Luke 12:13
take this, and d. it among. 22:17

I will divide
I will d. them in Jacob. Gen 49:7
enemy said, I will d. Ex 15:9
I will d. Shechem. Ps 60:6; 108:7
will I d. him a portion. Isa 53:12

divided
God d. the light. Gen 1:4
God d. the waters. 7
these the isles of Gentiles d. 10:5
in his days was the earth d. 25
1 Chr 1:19
by these were nations d. Gen 10:32
Abram d. himself against. 14:15
Abram d. them, the birds d. 15:10
Jacob d. the people that was. 32:7
d. children to Leah and. 33:1
and waters were d. Ex 14:21
to these land shall be d. Num 26:53
lot shall possession of land be d. 56
which Moses d. from men. 31:42
which Lord hath d. Deut 4:19
when the most High d. to. 32:8*
they d. the land. Josh 14:5; 18:10
19:51*; 23:4
have they not d. the prey. Judg 5:30
d. the 300 men into three. 7:16
Abimelech d. them into three. 9:43
Levite d. her with her bones. 19:29
death they were not d. 2 Sam 1:23
were people of Israel d. 1 Ki 16:21
Ahab and Obadiah d. the land. 18:6
waters were d. hither. 2 Ki 2:8
David d. them into. 1 Chr 23:6
chief men, thus were they d. 24:4, 5
they d. other offerings. 2 Chr 35:13*
hath d. a water-course? Job 38:25*
that tarried at home d. Ps 68:12
he d. the sea and caused. 78:13*
d. them an inheritance by line. 55*
Acts 13:19
which d. the Red Sea. Ps 136:13
is prey of great spoil d. Isa 33:23
his hand hath d. it to them. 34:17

the Lord that *d.* the sea. *Isa* 51:15*
anger of the Lord hath *d.* *Lam* 4:16
nor shall they be *d.* into. *Ezek* 37:22
kingdom shall be *d.* but. *Dan* 2:41
thy kingdom is *d.* and given. 5:28
his kingdom shall be *d.* toward. 11:4
their heart is *d.* now. *Hos* 10:2
thy land shall be *d.* by line. *Amos* 7:17
he hath *d.* our fields. *Mi* 2:4
thy spoil shall be *d.* in. *Zech* 14:1
kingdom or house *d.* *Mat* 12:25
Mark 3:24, 25; *Luke* 11:17
he is *d.* against himself. *Mat* 12:26
Mark 3:26; *Luke* 11:18
the two fishes *d.* he. *Mark* 6:41
five in one house *d.* *Luke* 12:52
the father shall be *d.* against. 53
he *d.* unto them his living. 15:12
multitude of the city was *d.*
Acts 14:4; 23:7
is Christ *d.*? *1 Cor* 1:13
the great city was *d.* *Rev* 16:19

divider

who made me a *d.* over? *Luke* 12:14

divideth

cheweth cud, but *d.* *Lev* 11:4, 5, 6
carcases of every beast which *d.* 26
swine, because it *d.* *Deut* 14:8
d. the sea with his. *Job* 26:12*
voice of the Lord *d.* *Ps* 29:7
which *d.* the sea when. *Jer* 31:35*
as a shepherd *d.* his. *Mat* 25:32
his armour, and *d.* *Luke* 11:22

dividing

an end of *d.* the land. *Josh* 19:49*
so they made an end of *d.* the. 51
led them, *d.* the water. *Isa* 63:12
times, and a *d.* of time. *Dan* 7:25
d. to every man. *1 Cor* 12:11
a workman rightly *d.* *2 Tim* 2:15
piercing to *d.* asunder. *Heb* 4:12

divination

A foreseeing or foretelling of future events or discovery of hidden knowledge. In eastern nations, and especially in Bible times, this was done by interpreting dreams or other signs, or by some peculiarities in the sacrifices, whether offered to God or to an idol. There were several sorts of divinations, *namely, by water, fire, earth, air; by the flight of birds, and their singing; by lots, by dreams, by the staff, or wand, by the entrails of victims, and by cups. The custom has been universal in all ages and all nations, civilized or savage. In the Bible the word is used of false systems of ascertaining the Divine will.*

with the rewards of *d.* *Num* 22:7
neither is there any *d.* 23:23
or that useth *d.* *Deut* 18:10
2 Ki 17:17
prophesy visions and *d.* *Jer* 14:14
nor flattering *d.* in. *Ezek* 12:24
seen vanity, and lying *d.* 13:6
have ye not spoken a lying *d.*? 7
of Babylon stood to use *d.* 21:21
at his right hand was the *d.* of. 22
as a false *d.* in their sight. 23
possessed with spirit of *d.* *Acts* 16:16

divinations

see no more divine *d.* *Ezek* 13:23

divine

such a man as I can *d.* *Gen* 44:15
d. to me by familiar. *1 Sam* 28:8
on prophets that *d.* lies. *Ezek* 13:9
no more vanity, or *d.* divinations. 23
whiles they *d.* a lie unto thee. 21:29
you, that ye shall not *d.* *Mi* 3:6
and the prophets thereof *d.* 11

divine, *adjective*

a *d.* sentence is in the. *Pr* 16:10
had ordinances of *d.* *Heb* 9:1
as his *d.* power hath. *2 Pet* 1:3
be partakers of the *d.* nature. 4

diviner, -s

nations hearkened to *d.* *Deut* 18:14
Philistines called for *d.* *1 Sam* 6:2
turneth, that maketh *d.* *Isa* 44:25
hearken not to your *d.* *Jer* 27:9
let not your prophets and *d.* 29:8
and the *d.* confounded. *Mi* 3:7
the *d.* have seen a lie. *Zech* 10:2

divineth

it whereby indeed he *d.*? *Gen* 44:5

divining

and *d.* lies unto them *Ezek* 22:28

division

will put a *d.* between. *Ex* 8:23
according to the *d.* of. *2 Chr* 35:5*
nay, but rather *d.* *Luke* 12:51
a *d.* among the people, because of.
John 7:43; 9:16; 10:19

divisions

gave the land to Israel, according to their *d.* *Josh* 11:23; 12:7; 18:10
2 Chr 35:5, 12
for *d.* of Reuben, there were great thoughts of heart. *Judg* 5:15*, 16*
these are *d.* of the sons of. 24:1*
the *d.* of porters. 26:1*, 12*, 19*
the priests in their *d.* *Ezra* 6:18
Neh 11:36*
them which cause *d.* *Rom* 16:17
that there be no *d.* *1 Cor* 1:10
is among you strife and *d.* 3:3
I hear there be *d.* among you 11:18

divorce

The legal dissolution of marriage. Moses tolerated divorces, Deut 24:1-4.

The school of Shammah, who lived a little before our Saviour, taught, that a man could not lawfully be divorced from his wife, unless he had found her guilty of some action which was really infamous, and contrary to the rules of virtue. But the school of Hillel, who was Shammah's disciple, taught, on the contrary, that the least reasons were sufficient to authorize a man to put away his wife; for example, if she did not cook his food well, or if he found any woman whom he liked better.

The Pharisees attempted to trap our Lord into some statement with which they could take issue, but he declined to interpret Moses' words, though he declared that he regarded all lesser causes than fornication as standing on too weak ground.

and given a bill of *d.* *Jer* 3:8

divorced

high priest not take a *d.* woman.
Lev 21:14
daughter be a widow or *d.* 22:13
vow of her that is *d.* *Num* 30:9
marry her that is *d.* *Mat* 5:32

divorcement

write her a bill of *d.* *Deut* 24:1, 3
is bill of your mother's *d.*? *Isa* 50:1
suffered to write bill of *d.* *Mark* 10:4
see **writing**

do

do to her as it pleaseth. *Gen* 16:6
Judge of all earth *do* right? 18:25
God hath said to thee, *do.* 31:16
I will surely *do* thee good. 32:12
what he is about to *do.* 41:25, 28
teach you what ye shall *do.* *Ex* 4:15
if thou wilt *do* that which is. 15:26
Deut 6:18; 12:25; 13:18; 21:9
the work that they must *do.*
Ex 18:20
Lord hath spoken we will *do.* 19:8
six days *do* all thy work. 20:9; 23:12
Deut 5:13
shalt thou *do* to Aaron. *Ex* 29:35
ye shall *do* my judgements. *Lev* 18:4
19:37; 20:22; *Ezek* 36:27
which if a man *do.* *Lev* 18:5
Neh 9:29; *Ezek* 20:11, 13, 21
ye shall *do* my statutes. *Lev* 25:18
20:8; 22:31; *Deut* 17:19; 26:16
that shalt thou *do.* *Num* 22:20
what this people shall *do* to. 24:14
servants will *do* as my lord. 32:25
keep commandments to *do* them.
Deut 7:11; 11:22
do according to sentence. 17:10, 11
do to him as he thought to *do.* 19:19
shalt thou *do* to all the cities. 20:15
all the words of this law to *do.* 27:26
may hear it and *do* it. 30:12, 13
the Lord shall *do* to them as. 31:4
do ye thus requite the Lord. 32:6
thus shalt thou *do* six days. *Josh* 6:3
what wilt thou *do* to thy? 7:9
thus shall the Lord *do* to. 10:25
what have ye to *do* with God? 22:24
d. all that is written in book of law of.
23:6; *1 Chr* 16:40; *2 Chr* 34:21
as I *do* so shall ye *do.* *Judg* 7:17
what was I able to *do* in? 8:3
do to us whatsoever seemeth. 10:15
what ye have to *do.* 18:14
then said the priest, what *do* ye? 18
tell thee what thou shalt *do.* *Ruth* 3:4
shew thee what thou shalt *do.*
1 Sam 16:3
till I know what God will *do.* 22:3
thou shalt *do* great things. 26:25
now then *do* it. *2 Sam* 3:18
I were judge, I would *do.* 15:4
here I am, let him *do* to me. 26
do it to thee. 24:12; *1 Chr* 21:10
do therefore according. *1 Ki* 2:6
do as he hath said. 31
then hear, and *do,* and judge. 8:32
forgive, and *do.* 39; *2 Chr* 6:23
do that is right. *1 Ki* 11:33, 38; 14:8
do it the second time, *do* it. 18:34
what hast thou to *do*? *2 Ki* 9:18, 19
to this day they *do* after the. 17:34
the Lord will *do* as he. 20:9
Nathan said, *do* all that. *1 Chr* 17:2
and *do* as thou hast said. 23
do away the iniquity of. 21:8
king, to *do* judgement. *2 Chr* 9:8
take heed what ye *do.* 19:6
now take heed and *do* it. 7
thus shall ye *do* in the fear of. 9
nor know we what to *do.* 20:12
if thou wilt go, *do* it, be strong. 25:8
seek your God, as ye *do.* *Ezra* 4:2
to seek law of Lord, and *do.* 7:10
that *do* after the will of your. 18
hath put in my heart to *do.* *Neh* 2:12
they should *do* according to. 5:12
that they might *do* with them. 9:24
what shall I *do* to thee? *Job* 7:20
as heaven, what canst thou *do*? 11:8
only *do* not two things unto. 13:20
I delight to *do* thy will. *Ps* 40:8
what hast thou to *do* to? 50:16
do unto them as unto the. 83:9
but *do* thou for me. 109:21*
as thou usest to *do* to those. 119:132
teach me to *do* thy will. 143:10
power of thy hand to *do.* *Pr* 3:27
do it with thy might. *Eccl* 9:10
what will ye *do* in day of? *Isa* 10:3
that he may *do* his work. 28:21
I the Lord *do* all these things. 45:7
hast thou to *do* in way of Egypt?
what hast thou to *do* in? *Jer* 2:18
what wilt thou *do*? 4:30
and what will ye *do* in the end? 5:31
seest thou not what they *do*? 7:17
obey my voice, and *do* them. 11:4
what hath my beloved to *do* in? 15
how wilt thou *do* in swelling? 12:5
do thou it for thy name's sake. 14:7
do to him, even as he shall. 39:12
shew thing that we may *do.* 42:3
as she hath done, *do.* 50:15, 29
do unto them as thou. *Lam* 1:22
seest thou what they *do*? *Ezek* 8:6
no eye pitied thee, to *do* any. 16:5
man be just, and *do* that which is.
18:5, 21; 33:14, 19
shall *do* as I have done. 24:22, 24
I will be enquired of to *do* it. 36:37
hearken and *do,* defer. *Dan* 9:19
do according to will. 11:3, 16, 36
thus shall he *do* in the most. 39
what will ye *do* in solemn? *Hos* 9:5
what then should a king *do*? 10:3
what have ye to *do* with? *Joel* 3:4
the Lord will *do* nothing. *Amos* 3:7
I *do* well to be angry. *Jonah* 4:9

can or *canst* **do**

do with *evil*

do joined with *good*

have I to **do**

I shall, or *I will* **do**; or *will I*, *shall I* **do**

without thy mind would I do nothing. Philem 14
see judgement
must do
work that they must do. Ex 18:20
all the Lord speaketh, that I must do. Num 23:26
thou must do it again. Pr 19:19
must I do to be saved? Acts 16:30
do joined with no, or not
not do it for forty's sake. Gen 18:29
I will not do it if I find thirty. 30
I cannot do any thing till. 19:22
deferred not to do the thing. 34:19
shalt not do any work. Ex 20:10
Lev 23:31
if he do not these three. Ex 21:11
shalt not do after their works. 23:24
afflict your souls and do no work.
Lev 16:29; 23:3, 28; Deut 15:19
Jer 17:24
doings ye shall not do. Lev 18:3
do no unrighteousness. 19:15, 35
do no servile work. 23:7, 8, 21
25, 35, 36; Num 28:18, 25, 26
will not do my commandments. Lev 26:14, 15
fifty years shall do no. Num 8:26
said, and shall he not do it? 23:19
ye shall not do any work. 29:7
Deut 5:14; 16:8
shall not do after all the. Deut 12:8
do no more such wickedness. 13:11
fear and do no more. 17:13
could not do it by day. Judg 6:27
I pray you, do not this folly. 19:23
to this man do not so vile a. 24
will not do the part of a. Ruth 3:13
no more do thee harm. 1 Sam 26:21
days I will not do it. 1 Ki 11:12
lepers said we do not. 2 Ki 7:9
charged they should not do. 17:15
not hear them, nor do them. 18:12
whoso will not do law. Ezra 7:26
only do not two things. Job 13:20
God will not do wickedly. 34:12
remember the battle, do no. 41:8
they do no iniquity. Ps 119:3
cannot I do with you as this potter? Jer 18:6
do no wrong, do no violence. 22:3
be a true witness, if we do not. 42:5
I will not do any more. Ezek 5:9
may be taught not to do after. 23:48
but they will not do them. 33:31
but they do them not. 32
Lord, will not do iniquity. Zeph 3:5
remnant of Israel shall not do. 13
do not even publicans? Mat 5:46, 47
take heed ye do not your. 6:1
doest alms do not sound a trumpet. 2
which is not lawful to do on. 12:2
thou shalt do no murder. 19:18
friend, I do thee no wrong. 20:13
do not after their works, they say and do not. 23:3
could there do no mighty. Mark 6:5
and do not the things. Luke 6:46
I came down not to do. John 6:38
if I do not the works of. 10:37
would, that do I not. Rom 7:15, 19
for what law could not do. 8:3
ye cannot do the things. Gal 5:17
lie, and do not the truth. 1 John 1:6
see thou do it not. Rev 19:10; 22:9
observe with do
ye shall observe to do as. Deut 5:32
8:1; 11:32; 12:1; 24:8; 2 Ki 17:37
observe to do. Deut 6:3; 12:32
28:13, 15, 58; 31:12; 32:46
if we observe to do these. 6:25
to observe to do all these. 15:5
thou shalt observe and do. 16:12
shalt observe to do as they. 17:10
mayest observe to do. Josh 1:7
if they will observe to do. 2 Ki 21:8
oath to observe and do. Neh 10:29
observe and do them. Ezek 37:24
bid, that observe and do. Mat 23:3
will we do, we will do
said we will do. Ex 19:8; 24:3, 7
goodness will we do to. Num 10:32
we will hear it and do it. Deut 5:27
thou commandest us we will do. Josh 1:16
thing which we will do. Judg 20:9
we will do all that thou. 2 Ki 10:5
we will every one do. Jer 18:12
declare unto us, we will do it. 42:20
we will certainly do. 44:17
shall we do, we shall do
teach us what we shall do. Judg 13:8
how shall we do unto him? 12
how shall we do for wives? 21:7, 16
shall we do with ark? 1 Sam 5:8
what shall we do to the ark? 6:2
counsel what shall do. 2 Sam 16:20
shall we do after this saying? 17:6
master, how shall we do? 2 Ki 6:15
shall we do for the 100? 2 Chr 25:9
shall we do to the queen? Esth 1:15
through God we shall do. Ps 60:12
108:13
what shall we do for our? S of S 8:8
what shall we do to thee? Jonah 1:11
what shall we do? Luke 3:10, 12, 14
shall we do that we? John 6:28
brethren, what shall we do? Acts 2:37
shall we do to these men? 4:16
do joined with so
so do as thou hast said. Gen 18:5
do not so wickedly. 19:7; Judg 19:23
forbid that I should do so. Gen 44:17
it is not meet so to do. Ex 8:26
so shall he do. Lev 4:20; 16:16
Num 9:14; 15:14
so Lord hath commanded to do. Lev 8:34
so will I do. Num 14:28; 32:31
Isa 65:8; Ezek 35:15
so shall he do to every one. Num 15:12
was I ever wont to do so? 22:30
if ye will not do so ye have. 32:23
so shall the Lord do to. Deut 3:21
shall not do so to the Lord. 12:4, 31
nations serve gods? so I do. 30
hath not suffered thee so to do. 18:14
and so shalt thou do with. 22:3
all that do so are abomination. 5
as I do, so shall ye do. Judg 7:17
if we do not so according. 11:10
so used the young men to do. 14:10
this man do not so vile a. 19:24
Lord do so to me. Ruth 1:17
1 Sam 14:44
God do so to thee. 1 Sam 3:17
so do they also to thee. 8:8
Lord do so and much more. 20:13
so and more also do God. 25:22
shall not do so, my brethren. 30:23
so do God to Abner, even so I do to. 2 Sam 3:9
do so to me, and more. 3:35; 19:13
1 Ki 2:23; 20:10; 2 Ki 6:31
so shall thy servant do. 2 Sam 9:11
so will I certainly do. 1 Ki 1:30
so will thy servant do. 2:38
so let the gods do to me. 19:2
forth and do so. 22:22; 2 Chr 18:21
did their fathers, so do. 2 Ki 17:41
said they would do so. 1 Chr 13:4
hast said, so must we do. Ezra 10:12
said, so will we do as. Neh 5:12
I should be afraid, and do so. 6:13
if ye do so again I will. 13:21
do even so to Mordecai. Esth 6:10
is he durst presume to do so? 7:5
man mocketh, do ye so? Job 13:9
so do stripes the inward. Pr 20:30*
say not, I will do so to him as. 24:29
I so do to Jerusalem. Isa 10:11
the Lord do so, the Lord. Jer 28:6
so thou shalt do seventh. Ezek 45:20
so shall he do, he shall. Dan 11:30
so shall Beth-el do to. Hos 10:15
do not even publicans so? Mat 5:47
do to you, do ye even so to. 7:12
so shall my heavenly Father do. 18:35
commandment, so I do. John 14:31
as fathers did, so do ye. Acts 7:51
order, even so do ye. 1 Cor 16:1
Christ forgave you, so do. Col 3:13
which is in faith, so do. 1 Tim 1:4
so do ye, as they that. Jas 2:12
do joined with this
and this they begin to do. Gen 11:6
I do this great wickedness. 39:9
let Pharaoh do this, let him. 41:34
Joseph said, this do and. 42:18
it must be, do this. 43:11; 45:17, 19
I will do this to you. Lev 26:16
this do, take you censers. Num 16:6
this we will do to the. Josh 9:20
I pray, do not this folly. Judg 19:23
do not thou this folly. 2 Sam 13:12
far from me that I do this. 23:17
zeal of Lord shall do this. 2 Ki 19:31
Isa 37:32
this do and ye shall. 2 Chr 19:10
fail not to do this. Ezra 4:22
do this now, my son. Pr 6:3
praise thee, as I do this. Isa 38:19
they should do this. Jer 32:35
I would do this evil. Ezek 6:10
I do not this for your. 36:22, 32
because I will do this. Amos 4:12
in day that I shall do this. Mal 4:3
to my servant, do this, and he doeth it. Mat 8:9; Luke 7:8
I am able to do this? Mat 9:28
ye shall not only do this. 21:21
why do ye this? Mark 11:3
whom he should do this. Luke 7:4
he said to him, this do, and. 10:28
he said, this will I do. 12:18
this do in remembrance. 22:19
1 Cor 11:24, 25
do therefore this. Acts 21:23
if I do this thing. 1 Cor 9:17
and this I do for the gospel's. 23
and this will we do. Heb 6:3
I beseech you rather to do this. 13:19
we will do this or that. Jas 4:15
see this, thing
do well
learn to do well. Isa 1:17
I do well to be angry. Jonah 4:9
do well to Jerusalem. Zech 8:15
is lawful to do well on. Mat 12:12
sleep, he shall do well. John 11:12
yourselves, ye do well. Acts 15:29
royal law, ye do well. Jas 2:8
praise of them that do well. 1 Pet 2:14
but if when ye do well and. 20
daughters as long as ye do well. 3:6
whereto ye do well. 2 Pet 1:19
thou bring, shalt do well. 3 John 6
doctor
(Used in its old meaning of teacher, or learned man. Latin, doctor from docere, to teach)
stood up Gamaliel, a d. Acts 5:34
doctors
Jesus sitting in midst of the d. Luke 2:46
there were Pharisees and d. 5:17
doctrine
(Used in old meaning of teaching, instruction (see **doctor**). In the New Testament the Revised Version almost universally translates it teaching)
make to understand d. Isa 28:9*
murmured shall learn d. 29:24†
the stock is a d. of vanities. Jer 10:8
people astonished at his d. Mat 7:28
22:33; Mark 1:22; 11:18
Luke 4:32
beware of the d. of the. Mat 16:12
saying, what new d.? Mark 1:27
and said to them in d. 4:2; 12:38
he shall know of the d. John 7:17
priest then asked Jesus of d. 18:19
continued in apostles' d. Acts 2:42
filled Jerusalem with your d. 5:28
astonished at d. of Lord. 13:12
know what this new d. is? 17:19
obeyed that form of d. Rom 6:17
contrary to the d. which ye. 16:17
except I speak by d. 1 Cor 14:6
every one of you hath a d. 26
with every wind of d. Eph 4:14
they teach no other d. 1 Tim 1:3
attendance to reading, to d. 4:13

heed to thyself, and to thy *d*. *1 Tim* **4:16**
labour in the word and *d*. 5:17
the name of God and his *d*. be. 6:1
and to *d*. which is according to. 3
is profitable for *d*. *2 Tim* 3:16
with all long suffering and *d*. 4:2
in *d*. shewing incorruptness. *Tit* 2:7
that they may adorn the *d*. of. 10
leaving principles of *d*. *Heb* 6:1*
of the *d*. of baptisms, and of. 2
whoso abideth not in the *d*.; he that abideth in *d*. of Christ. *2 John* 9
hast them that hold *d*. of. *Rev* 2:14
that hold *d*. of the Nicolaitans. 15

***good* doctrine**

I give you *good d*. *Pr* 4:2
in the words of *good d*. *1 Tim* 4:6

***my* doctrine**

my d. shall drop as rain. *Deut* 32:2
my d. is pure, and I am. *Job* 11:4
my d. is not mine. *John* 7:16
hast fully known *my d*. *2 Tim* 3:10

***sound* doctrine**

is contrary to *sound d*. *1 Tim* 1:10
will not endure *sound d*. *2 Tim* 4:3
by *sound d*. to exhort. *Tit* 1:9
things which become *sound d*. 2:1

***this* doctrine**

and bring not *this d*. *2 John* 10
many as have not *this d*. *Rev* 2:24

doctrines

for *d*. the commandments of men. *Mat* 15:9; *Mark* 7:7
after commandments and *d*. *Col* 2:22
heed to *d*. of devils. *1 Tim* 4:1
about with strange *d*. *Heb* 13:9

Doeg

and his name was *D*. *1 Sam* 21:7
D. turned and slew priests. 22:18
I knew it that day *D*. was there. 22

doer

he was the *d*. of it. *Gen* 39:22
Lord reward *d*. of evil. *2 Sam* 3:39
rewardeth the proud *d*. *Ps* 31:23
a wicked *d*. giveth heed. *Pr* 17:4
an hypocrite and evil *d*. *Isa* 9:17
suffer trouble as an evil *d*. *2 Tim* 2:9
a hearer, not a *d*. of word. *Jas* 1:23
not a forgetful hearer, but a *d*. 25
thou art not a *d*. of the law. 4:11
none suffer as an evil *d*. *1 Pet* 4:15

doers

let them give it to the *d*. *2 Ki* 22:5*
cut off all wicked *d*. *Ps* 101:8*
but the *d*. of the law. *Rom* 2:13
be ye *d*. of the word. *Jas* 1:22
see **evil**

doest

if *d*. well, and if thou *d*. not. *Gen* 4:7
with thee in all that thou *d*. 21:22
that thou *d*. is not good. *Ex* 18:17
when thou *d*. that which. *Deut* 12:28
bless thee in all that thou *d*. 15:18
to know all that thou *d*. *2 Sam* 3:25
prosper in all thou *d*. *1 Ki* 2:3
what *d*. thou here, Elijah? 19:9, 13
and see what thou *d*. 20:22
say, what *d*. thou? *Job* 9:12
Eccl 8:4; *Dan* 4:35
if thou sinnest, what *d*.? *Job* 35:6
when thou *d*. well to. *Ps* 49:18
the God that *d*. wonders. 77:14
thou art great, and *d*. 86:10
thou art good, and *d*. good. 119:68
when thou *d*. evil. *Jer* 11:15
aside to ask how thou *d*.? 15:5*
house said, what *d*. thou? *Ezek* 12:9
weak heart, seeing thou *d*. 16:30
these are to us, that thou *d*. 24:19
d. thou well to be angry? *Jonah* 4:4, 9
thou *d*. thine alms. *Mat* 6:2, 3
what authority *d*. thou these things? 21:23; *Mark* 11:28; *Luke* 20:2
sign seeing that thou *d*.? *John* 2:18
these miracles that thou *d*. 3:2
disciples may see works thou *d*. 7:3
that thou *d*. do quickly. 13:27
take heed what thou *d*. *Acts* 22:26

thou that judgest, *d*. *Rom* **2:1, 3**
believest on God, thou *d*. *Jas* 2:19
d. faithfully what thou *d*. *3 John* 5

doeth

seen all that Laban *d*. to. *Gen* 31:12
whosoever *d*. work therein shall be cut off. *Ex* 31:14, 15; *Lev* 23:30
these that a man *d*. *Lev* 6:3
shall live when God *d*.! *Num* 24:23
to God who *d*. great. *Job* 5:9
9:10; 37:5; *Ps* 72:18; 136:4
soul desireth, that he *d*. *Job* 23:13
whatsoever he *d*. prosper. *Ps* 1:3
there is none that *d*. good. 14:1, 3
53:1, 3; *Rom* 3:12
he that *d*. these things shall. *Ps* 15:5
blessed is he that *d*. 106:3
right hand of Lord *d*. 118:15, 16
he that *d*. it, destroyeth. *Pr* 6:32
merciful man *d*. good to. 11:17
a merry heart *d*. good like. 17:22
I said of mirth, what *d*. it? *Eccl* 2:2
God *d*. shall be for ever, and God *d*. it that men should fear. 3:14
there is not a man *d*. good. 7:20
he *d*. whatsoever pleaseth him. 8:3
blessed is the man that *d*. *Isa* 56:2
shall he escape that *d*.? *Ezek* 17:15
that *d*. the like to any one of. 18:10
that *d*. not any of those duties. 11
d. that which is lawful and. 27
d. according to will in. *Dan* 4:35
God is righteous in all he *d*. 9:14
saith Lord that *d*. this. *Amos* 9:12
cut off man that *d*. this. *Mal* 2:12
know what thy right *d*. *Mat* 6:3
he that *d*. will of my Father. 7:21
whoso heareth sayings, and *d*. 24
heareth and *d*. not. 26; *Luke* 6:49
and he *d*. it. *Mat* 8:9; *Luke* 7:8
every one that *d*. evil. *John* 3:20
but he that *d*. truth cometh. 21
things soever he *d*. these *d*. 5:19
hear him and know what he *d*. 7:51
but if any man *d*. his will. 9:31
knoweth not what his lord *d*. 15:15
will think he *d*. God service. 16:2
every soul that *d*. evil. *Rom* 2:9
the man that *d*. these things shall live by them. 10:5; *Gal* 3:12
wrath upon him that *d*. *Rom* 13:4
every sin a man *d*. is. *1 Cor* 6:18
that he keep his virgin, *d*. well. 7:37
giveth her in marriage *d*. well. 38
d. he it by works of law? *Gal* 3:5
good thing any man *d*. *Eph* 6:8
forth fruit, as it *d*. also. *Col* 1:6
but he that *d*. wrong, shall. 3:25
exhorted as a father *d*. *1 Thes* 2:11
to do good, and *d*. it not. *Jas* 4:17
he that *d*. will of God. *1 John* 2:17
that *d*. righteousness is born. 29; 3:7
remember his deeds which he *d*. *3 John* 10
but he that *d*. evil hath not. 11
and he *d*. great wonders. *Rev* 13:13

dog

Frequently mentioned in the Scripture. It was used by the Hebrews as a watch for their houses, Isa 56:10, *and for guarding their flocks,* Job 30:1. *There were numerous troops of wild, masterless dogs which devoured dead bodies and other offal,* 1 Ki 14:11, *and became so fierce and such objects of dislike that fierce and cruel enemies were poetically called dogs,* Ps 22:16, etc. *The dog being an unclean animal the name was used as a term of reproach, or of humility of speaking of oneself,* 1 Sam 24:14; 2 Sam 16:9.

against Israel shall not a *d*. *Ex* 11:7
not bring price of a *d*. *Deut* 23:18
that lappeth as a *d*. *Judg* 7:5
Philistine said to David, am I a *d*.? *1 Sam* 17:43
thou pursue? after a *d*.? 24:14
Abner said, am I a *dog's*? *2 Sam* 3:8
look upon such dead *d*. as I am. 9:8
this dead *d*. curse my lord? 16:9
is thy servant a *d*.? *2 Ki* 8:13

darling from power of *d*. *Ps* 22:20
they make a noise like a *d*. 59:6, 14
as *d*. returneth to his vomit, so a fool. *Pr* 26:11; *2 Pet* 2:22
like one that taketh a *d*. *Pr* 26:17
a living *d*. is better than. *Eccl* 9:4
as if he cut off a *dog's*. *Isa* 66:3

dogs

torn of beasts, ye shall cast it to *d*. *Ex* 22:31; *Mat* 15:26; *Mark* 7:27
shall the *d*. eat. *1 Ki* 14:11; 16:4
21:24
place where *d*. licked the blood of Naboth, shall *d*. lick thy. 21:19
d. eat Jezebel. 23; *2 Ki* 9:10, 36
d. licked up Ahab's. *1 Ki* 22:38
to have set with *d*. of. *Job* 30:1
for *d*. have compassed me. *Ps* 22:16
and the tongue of thy *d*. in. 68:23
they are all dumb *d*. *Isa* 56:10
greedy *d*. 11
to slay, the *d*. to tear. *Jer* 15:3
give not holy unto *d*. *Mat* 7:6
d. eat of crumbs. 15:27; *Mark* 7:28
d. came and licked. *Luke* 16:21
beware of *d*. beware of. *Phil* 3:2
for without are *d*. and. *Rev* 22:15

doing

done foolishly in so *d*. *Gen* 31:28
ye have done evil in so *d*. 44:5
in praises, *d*. wonders. *Ex* 15:11
without *d*. any thing. *Num* 20:19
ye sinned in *d*. wickedly. *Deut* 9:18
he sinned in *d*. evil. *1 Ki* 16:19
2 Ki 21:16
d. that which was right. *1 Ki* 22:43
2 Chr 20:32
arise, and be *d*. *1 Chr* 22:16
I am *d*. a great work. *Neh* 6:3
in so *d*. my Maker. *Job* 32:22
wisely consider of his *d*. *Ps* 64:9
he is terrible in *d*. toward. 66:5
the Lord's *d*. marvellous in our. 118:23; *Mat* 21:42; *Mark* 12:11
keepeth his hand from *d*. *Isa* 56:2
from *d*. thy pleasure on my. 58:13
his Lord shall find so *d*. *Mat* 24:46
Luke 12:43
who went about *d*. good. *Acts* 10:38
they have found any evil *d*. in. 24:20
for in so *d*. thou shalt. *Rom* 12:20
therefore perform the *d*. *2 Cor* 8:11
servants of Christ, *d*. will. *Eph* 6:6
in *d*. this shalt save. *1 Tim* 4:16
d. nothing by partiality. 5:21

***well*-doing**

patient continuance in *well-d*. *Rom* 2:7
not be weary in *well-d*. *Gal* 6:9
2 Thes 3:13
with *well-d*. ye may. *1 Pet* 2:15
better that ye suffer for *well-d*. 3:17
their souls to him in *well-d*. 4:19

doings

after *d*. of Egypt, and after *d*. of Canaan, shall ye not. *Lev* 18:3
of wickedness of thy *d*. *Deut* 28:20
not from their own *d*. *Judg* 2:19
and evil in his *d*. *1 Sam* 25:3
walked not after the *d*. *2 Chr* 17:4
among the people his *d*. *Ps* 9:11
Isa 12:4
I will talk of thy *d*. *Ps* 77:12
child is known by his *d*. *Pr* 20:11
put away evil of your *d*. *Isa* 1:16
because their tongue and *d*. 3:8
shall eat the fruit of their *d*. 10
because of the evil of your *d*. *Jer* 4:4; 21:12; 26:3; 44:22
thy *d*. have procured these. 4:18
amend your *d*. 7:3, 5; 26:13; 35:15
thou shewedst me their *d*. 11:18
according to fruit of *d*. 17:10; 21:14
make your ways and *d*. good. 18:11
upon you evil of your *d*. 23:2
from evil of their *d*. 22; 25:5
Zech 1:4
according to fruit of his *d*. *Jer* 32:19
see their way and *d*. *Ezek* 14:22
shall ye remember your *d*. 20:43
nor according to your corrupt *d*. 44
in all your *d*. your sins do. 21:24
according to thy *d*. shall. 24:14

defiled it by their own way and d. Ezek 36:17
and according to their d. I. 19
remember your d. that were. 31
and reward their d. Hos 4:9
they will not frame their d. to. 5:4
now their own d. have set. 7:2
for the wickedness of their d. 9:15
according to his d. will he. 12:2
Jacob, are these his d.? Mi 2:7
themselves ill in their d. 3:4
desolate for fruit of their d. 7:13
corrupted all their d. Zeph 3:7
not be ashamed for all thy d.? 11
according to our d. so. Zech 1:6

doleful

houses full of d. creatures. Isa 13:21
day shall lament with a d. Mi 2:4

dominion

[1] *Supreme power or sovereignty*, Neh 9:28; Rom 6:9. [2] *Persons or territory ruled over*, Ps 114:2.

have d. over fish. Gen 1:26, 28
when thou shalt have d. 27:40*
shalt thou indeed have d.? 37:8
he that shall have d. Num 24:19
he made him have d. Judg 5:13*
time Philistines had d. over. 14:4*
Solomon had d. over all. 1 Ki 4:24
build in land of his d. 9:19; 2 Chr 8:6
nothing in his house or in all his d. 2 Ki 20:13; Isa 39:2
men of Chozeba had d. 1 Chr 4:22
as he went to stablish his d. 18:3
Edomites from under Judah's d. 2 Chr 21:8*
so that they had the d. Neh 9:28
also they have d. over our. 37*
d. and fear are with him. Job 25:2
canst thou set d. thereof? 38:33
to have d. over the works. Ps 8:6
let them not have d. over. 19:13
the upright shall have d. 49:14
he shall have d. also from. 72:8
bless Lord in places of his d. 103:22
his sanctuary, Israel his d. 114:2
let not iniquity have d. 119:133
thy d. endureth through. 145:13
other lords had d. over. Isa 26:13
his d. is from generation. Dan 4:3
thy d. reacheth to the end. 22
whose d. is an everlasting d. 34; 7:14
d. of my kingdom men tremble before God of Daniel, his d. 6:26
beast had four heads, and d. 7:6
the rest of the beasts had their d. 12
there was given him d. and. 14
they shall take away his d. 26
d. shall be given to saints of. 27
mighty king rule with great d. 11:3, 5
not according to his d. which he. 4
shall come even first d. Mi 4:8
d. shall be from sea to. Zech 9:10
of Gentiles exercise d. Mat 20:25*
death hath no more d. Rom 6:9
sin shall not have d. over you. 14
law hath d. over a man as long. 7:1
not that we have d. 2 Cor 1:24*
all power, might, and d. Eph 1:21
to whom be praise and d. 1 Pet 4:11
5:11; Rev 1:6
to the only wise God be d. Jude 25

dominions

and all d. shall serve. Dan 7:27
they be thrones, or d. or. Col 1:16

done

what younger son had d. Gen 9:24
they have d. according to the. 18:21
told Isaac all that he had d. 24:66
have d. to thee nothing but. 26:29
not be d. in our country. 29:26
folly, which ought not to be d. 34:7
ye have d. evil in so doing. 44:5
what deed is this ye have d.? 15
have ye d. this thing? Ex 1:18
stood to wit what would be d. 2:4
no manner of work shall be d., save that which man must eat. 12:16
this is d. because of that the. 13:8
Jethro heard all that God had d. 18:1
goodness which Lord had d. 9
this judgement shall it be d. 21:31
six days work be d. Ex 31:15; 35:2
Lev 23:3
they had d. it as Lord commanded, even so had they d. it. Ex 39:43
things forbidden to be d. Lev 5:17
commanded to be d. 8:5; Deut 26:14
wherein any work is d. Lev 11:32
have the men of land d. 18:27
eye for eye, so shall it be d. 24:20
confess sin they have d. Num 5:7
wherein we have d. foolishly. 12:11
not declared what should be d. 15:34
Balak saw all that Israel had d. 22:2
name of father be d. away? 27:4*
all that had d. evil in sight. 32:13
is thy God that hath d. Deut 10:21
so shall it be d. to that man. 25:9
wherefore hath the Lord d. thus to? 29:24; 1 Ki 9:8; 2 Chr 7:21
as he had d. also to. Josh 10:32, 39
he had d. to Lachish. 35
he had d. to Eglon. 37
if we had not rather d. it. 22:24
had known all that he had d. 24:31
not works he had d. Judg 2:10
because they had d. evil in. 3:12
d. truly and sincerely, and have d. to Jerubbaal according to. 9:16
cruelty d. to the seventy sons of. 24
there was no such deed d. 19:30
her all the man had d. Ruth 3:16
what is there d. my son? 1 Sam 4:16*
so shall it be d. to his oxen. 11:7
what shall be d. to the man? 17:26
so shall it be d. to the man that. 27
when Lord shall have d. 25:30
Lord hath d. as he spake. 28:17
Ezek 12:28
thing David had d. 2 Sam 11:27
no such thing ought to be d. in. 13:12
have they d.? 24:17; 1 Chr 21:17
goodness Lord hath d. 1 Ki 8:66
above all their fathers had d. 14:22
told Jezebel all Elijah had d. 19:1
according to all his father had d. 22:53; 2 Ki 15:3, 9, 34; 23:32
what is to be d. for thee? 2 Ki 4:13
great things Elisha hath d. 8:4
d. that which he spake by servant. 10:10; Isa 38:15; Jer 40:3
heard what kings of Assyria have d. 2 Ki 19:11; 2 Chr 32:13; Isa 37:11
they have d. evil. 2 Ki 21:15
2 Chr 29:6
all acts that he had d. in. 2 Ki 23:19
because he had d. good. 2 Chr 24:16
rejoiced, for the thing was d. 29:36
not according to benefit d. to. 32:25
to inquire of wonder that was d. 31
a decree, let it be d. Ezra 6:12
when these things were d. the. 9:1
are no such things d. Neh 6:8
we have d. wickedly. 9:33; Ps 106:6
Dan 9:5, 15
Vashti, and what she had d. Esth 2:1
Mordecai perceived all was d. 4:1
what shall be d. to the man? 6:6
thus shall it be d. to the man. 9
him what he hath d.? Job 21:31
whether it be d. against a. 34:29
he spake and it was d. Ps 33:9
he hath d. great things. 71:19
106:21; 126:2, 3
what shall be d. to thee? 120:3
strive not if he have d. Pr 3:30
sleep not, except they have d. 4:16
d. is that which shall be d. Eccl 1:9
have seen the works are d. 14; 4:1, 3
that which hath been already d. 2:12
who hath wrought and d. it? Isa 41:4
sing, for the Lord hath d. 44:23
lest my idol hath d. them. 48:5
backsliding Israel hath d. Jer 3:6
thus shall it be d. unto them. 5:13
ye have d. all these works. 7:13
children of Judah have d. evil. 30
had d. right in my sight. 34:15
have d. all that Jonadab. 35:10, 18
these men have d. evil to. 38:9
have d. we and our fathers. 44:17
and say, what is d. 48:19
vengeance as she hath d. 50:15, 29
the violence d. to me. 51:35
Lord hath d. that which. Lam 2:17
thus have they d. in. Ezek 23:39
it is come, it is d. saith. 39:8
of all that they have d. 43:11
and for all that shall be d. 44:14
is determined shall be d. Dan 11:36
priests have d. violence. Zeph 3:4
thy will be d. Mat 6:10; 26:42
Luke 11:2; 22:42
believed, so be it d. Mat 8:13
mighty works d. in you had been d. 11:21; Luke 10:13
they ask, it shall be d. for. Mat 18:19
fellow-servants saw what was d. 31
cast into sea, it shall be d. 21:21
these ought ye to have d. 23:23
Luke 11:42
well d. good and. Mat 25:21, 23
as ye have d. it to one of least of these my brethren, ye have d. 40
things that were d. 27:54; 28:11
out to see what was d. Mark 5:14
Luke 8:35
tell what great things the Lord hath d. for. Mark 5:19, 20; Luke 8:39
what was d. in her. Mark 5:33
told him what they had d. 6:30
have d. to him whatsoever. 9:13
not pass till these things be d. 13:30
him to do, as he had ever d. 15:8
he that is mighty hath d. Luke 1:49
for the evils Herod had d. 3:19
to tell no man what was d. 8:56
told him all that they had d. 9:10
Lord, it is d. as thou. 14:22
ye, when ye shall have d. all, we have d. that which was our duty. 17:10
what shall be d. in the dry? 23:31
centurion saw what was d. 47
third day since these were d. 24:21
d. good to resurrection of life; have d. evil, to damnation. John 5:29
what ye will, and it shall be d. 15:7
these things were d. that the. 19:36
many signs were d. by. Acts 2:43
of the good deed d. to the. 4:9
a notable miracle hath been d. 16
God for that which was d. 21
determined before to be d. 28
wife, not knowing what was d. 5:7
not it was true which was d. 12:9
all that God had d. 14:27; 15:4
the will of the Lord be d. 21:14
captain demanded what he had d. 33
neither having d. good. Rom 9:11
nor that it should be d. 1 Cor 9:15
in part shall be d. away. 13:10
all things be d. to edifying. 14:26
be d. decently. 40
be d. with charity. 16:14
glory was to be d. away. 2 Cor 3:7
which veil is d. away in Christ. 14
receive the things d. in his body, according to that he hath d. 5:10
things which are d. of. Eph 5:12
and having d. all to stand. 6:13
nothing be d. through. Phil 2:3
ye have well d. that ye did. 4:14
known all things that are d. Col 4:9
righteousness we have d. Tit 3:5
d. despite to the Spirit. Heb 10:29
saying, it is d. Rev 16:17; 21:6
which must shortly be d. 22:6

***have I* done**

in innocency *have I* d. Gen 20:5
and here also *have I* d. 40:15
what *have I* d.? Num 22:28
1 Ki 19:20; Mi 6:3
thus and thus *have I* d. Josh 7:20
what *have I* now d.? Judg 8:2
1 Sam 17:29
what *have I* d.? 1 Sam 20:1; 26:18
29:8; Jer 8:6
transgressions *have I* d. Ezek 39:24
Jews *have I* d. no wrong. Acts 25:10

***he hath* done, or, *hath he* done**

he hath d. evil to this. Ex 5:23
for harm *he hath* d. Lev 5:16
as *he hath* d. so Lord. 8:34
atonement for sin *he hath* d. 19:21
as *he hath* d. so shall it be. 24:19
you, after *he hath* d. Josh 24:20
to him as *he hath* d. to. Judg 15:10
then *he hath* d. us this. 1 Sam 6:9

how great things he hath d. 1 Sam 12:24
what hath he d.? 20:32
marvellous works that he hath d. 1 Chr 16:12; Ps 78:4; 98:1; 105:5
declare what he hath d. Ps 66:16
God hath d. whatsoever he. 115:3
to him as he hath d. to me. Pr 24:29
to Lord for he hath d. Isa 12:5
righteousness he hath d. Ezek 3:20
18:24
he hath d. these things. 17:18
he hath d. all these abominations. 18:13
father's sins which he hath d. 14
righteousness that he hath d. 22
to all that he hath d. 24:24
he hath d. that which is. 33:16
because he hath d. great. Joel 2:20
what evil hath he d.? Mat 27:23
Mark 15:14; Luke 23:22
he hath d. all things. Mark 7:37
much evil hath he d. to. Acts 9:13
receive according to that he hath d. 2 Cor 5:10
for wrong he hath d. Col 3:25

I have done

nor smite every thing as I have d. Gen 8:21
kindness I have d. thee. 21:23
I have d. as thou badest me. 27:19
till I have d. that which I. 28:15
my service I have d. thee. 30:26
signs which I have d. Ex 10:2
have seen what I have d. Josh 24:7
as I have d. so God hath. Judg 1:7
they did to me, so have I d. 15:11
behold now I have d. 2 Sam 14:21
I have sinned in that I have d., I have d. very. 24:10; 1 Chr 21:8
and I have d. wickedly. 2 Sam 24:17
I have d. according to. 1 Ki 3:12
heard, how I have d. it? 2 Ki 19:25
that I have d. for house. Neh 13:14
if I have d. iniquity. Job 34:32
O Lord, if I have d. this. Ps 7:3
I have d. judgement and. 119:121
I have d. no wickedness. Pr 30:20
as I have d. to Samaria. Isa 10:11
strength of my hand I have d. 13
ye far off what I have d. 33:13
not heard how I have d. it? 37:26
repent of evil I have d. to. Jer 42:10
I have d. as thou hast. Ezek 9:11
as I have d. so shall it be. 12:11
know that I have not d. without cause, all that I have d. in. 14:23
ye shall do as I have d. 24:22
thee, have I d. no hurt. Dan 6:22
weep, as I have d. these. Zech 7:3
I have d. one work. John 7:21
he had washed their feet, he said, know ye what I have d. to? 13:12
should do as I have d. to you. 15

hast thou done

said, what hast thou d.? Gen 4:10
31:26; Num 23:11; 1 Sam 13:11
2 Sam 3:24; John 18:35
what hast thou d. to us? Gen 20:9
Judg 15:11
to heart hast thou d. 2 Sam 7:21
wherefore hast thou d. so? 16:10
why hast thou d. so? 1 Ki 1:6
O Lord, hast thou d. 1 Chr 17:19
these things hast thou d. Ps 50:21
why hast thou d. this? Jonah 1:10

thou hast done

is this that thou hast d.? Gen 3:13
12:18; 26:10; 29:25; Judg 15:11
2 Sam 12:21
because thou hast d. this. Gen 3:14
22:16; 2 Chr 25:16
thou hast d. deeds which. Gen 20:9
that which thou hast d. to. 27:45
thou hast now d. foolishly. 31:28
1 Sam 13:13; 2 Chr 16:9
tell me what thou hast d. Josh 7:19
1 Sam 14:43
me all thou hast d. Ruth 2:11
thou hast d. to me this. 1 Sam 24:19
not good that thou hast d. 26:16
but thou hast d. evil. 1 Ki 14:9
thou hast d. well in. 2 Ki 10:30
thou hast d. against altar. 2 Ki 23:17
for thou hast d. right. Neh 9:33
works which thou hast d. Ps 40:5
thee, because thou hast d. it. 52:9
know that thou hast d. it. 109:27
if thou hast d. foolishly. Pr 30:32
exalt thee, for thou hast d. Isa 25:1
know what thou hast d. Jer 2:23
thou hast spoken and d. evil. 3:5
glad that thou hast d. it. Lam 1:21
do unto them as thou hast d. 22
consider to whom thou hast d. 2:20
Sodom hath not done as thou hast d. Ezek 16:48
abominations which thou hast d. 51
deal with thee as thou hast d. 59
pacified for all that thou hast d. 63
as thou hast d. it shall be. Ob 15
O Lord, thou hast d. as. Jonah 1:14
thou hast d. well that. Acts 10:33

not done

that ought not to be d. Gen 20:9
which thing ought not to be d. 34:7
such as have not been d. Ex 34:10
things which ought not to be d. Lev 4:2, 13
I have not d. them of. Num 16:28
Lord hath not d. all. Deut 32:27
wouldest thou not have d.? 2 Ki 5:13
they had not d. it of. 2 Chr 30:5
from work, that it be not d. Neh 6:9
Israel had not d. so. 8:17
Vashti had not d. wrong. Esth 1:16
that I have not d. Isa 5:4
things that are not yet d. 46:10
neither shall that be d. Jer 3:16
in thee that I have not d. Ezek 5:9
for under heaven hath not been d. as hath been done upon. Dan 9:12
that which fathers have not d. 11:24
and Lord hath not d. it. Amos 3:6
if I had not d. among. John 15:24
scarce restrained they had not d. Acts 14:18
this thing not d. in a corner. 26:26

done with this

wot not who hath d. this. Gen 21:26
what is this that God hath d.? 42:28
deed is this that ye have d.? 44:15
have ye d. this thing. Ex 1:18
this is d. because of that which. 13:8
why have we d. this? 14:5
afraid, and have d. this? Josh 9:24
as ye have d. to this day. 23:8
why have ye d. this? Judg 2:2
who hath d. this thing? 6:29; 15:6
she said, let this thing be d. 11:37
ye have d. this, yet will. 15:7
wickedness is this that is d. 20:12
d. all this wickedness. 1 Sam 12:20
hath the Lord d. this thing. 28:18
ye have d. this thing. 2 Sam 2:6
man that hath d. this thing. 12:5
hath Joab d. this thing? 14:20
now, I have d. this thing. 21
is this d. by my lord? 1 Ki 1:27
forasmuch as this is d. of. 11:11
return, for this thing is d. 2 Chr 11:4
O Lord, if I have d. this. Ps 7:3
declare that he hath d. this. 22:31
I have sinned, and d. this evil. 51:4
hand of Lord hath d. this. Isa 41:20
this they have d. unto. Ezek 23:38
this have ye d. again. Mal 2:13
now all this was d. Mat 1:22; 21:4
26:56
an enemy hath d. this. 13:28
this which is d. to fig-tree. 21:21
this that this woman hath d. 26:13
Mark 14:9
that had d. this thing. Mark 5:32
when they had d. this. Luke 5:6
but this man hath d. nothing. 23:41
miracles than these this man hath d.? John 7:31
heard he had d. this miracle. 12:18
what power have ye d. this? Acts 4:7
this was d. thrice. 10:16; 11:10
so when this was d. others. 28:9
not mourned that he hath d. this. 1 Cor 5:2

door

Besides its common uses as the entrance to a house or building, this word is used metaphorically as the entrance to any thing: as our Saviour says, I am the door, *the entrance into the kingdom,* John 10:1. *The* door of faith *is the opportunity of belief offered to the Gentiles,* Acts 14:27. *Elsewhere also it means opportunity,* 2 Cor 2:12; Rev 3:8.

sin lieth at the d. Gen 4:7
came near to break the d. 19:9
Lord will pass over d. Ex 12:23
master shall bring him to d. 21:6
it through his ear to d. Deut 15:17
put her from me, bolt d. 2 Sam 13:17
and he bolted the d. after her. 18
called, she stood in d. 2 Ki 4:15
then open the d. and flee. 9:3
those who kept d. Esth 2:21* 6:2*
laid wait at neighbour's d. Job 31:9
that I went not out of the d.? 34
keep d. of my lips. Ps 141:3
as d. turneth upon. Pr 26:14
hand by hole of d. S of S 5:4
if she be a d. we will inclose. 8:9
brought me to the d. Ezek 8:3, 7
digged in the wall, behold a d. 8
every one stood at the d. 10:19
behold, at the d. of the gate. 11:1
the breadth of the d. was. 41:2*
people shall worship at the d. 46:3
valley of Achor for a d. of. Hos 2:15
smite the lintel of the d. Amos 9:1*
he rolled a great stone to the d. of. Mat 27:60; Mark 15:46
angel rolled stone from d. Mat 28:2*
city was gathered at d. Mark 1:33
not so much as about the d. 2:2
shall roll the stone from d.? 16:3
entereth not by the d. John 10:1
that entereth in by the d. 2
I am the d. 10:9
but Peter stood at the d. 18:16
damsel that kept the d. to Peter. 17
feet of them are at the d. Acts 5:9
as Peter knocked at the d. 12:13
when they had opened the d. 16
opened the d. of faith to. 14:27
a great d. and effectual. 1 Cor 16:9
a d. was opened to me. 2 Cor 2:12
God would open a d. of. Col 4:3
judge standeth before d. Jas 5:9
set before thee an open d. Rev 3:8
at d. and knock, if any open d. 20
I looked, and a d. was open. 4:1

door with house

smote them at d. of the house. Gen 19:11
communed at d. of the house. 43:19
out at d. of his house. Ex 12:22
shall go to d. of house. Lev 14:38
d. of her father's house. Deut 22:21
fell down at d. of the man's house. Judg 19:26, 27
slept at d. of king's house. 2 Sam 11:9
Naaman stood at d. of house. 2 Ki 5:9
unto the d. of the house. Neh 3:20
repaired from d. of the house. 21
not nigh d. of her house. Pr 5:8
sitteth at the d. of her house. 9:14
to d. of Lord's h. Ezek 8:14; 47:1

door with shut

Lot shut the d. Gen 19:6
angels shut the d. 10
when come in shalt shut d. 2 Ki 4:4
she shut d. upon her. 5
she shut d. on him. 21
he went in and shut the d. 33
shut the d. and hold him at d. 6:32
when thou hast shut thy d. Mat 6:6
the d. was shut. 25:10
the d. is now shut. Luke 11:7
and hath shut to the d. 13:25
open d. no man can shut. Rev 3:8

door with tabernacle

bring to d. of tabernacle. Ex 29:4
40:12; Lev 4:4; 8:3, 4; 12:6
Num 6:10

kill bullock by *d.* of *tabernacle.*
Ex 29:11, 32; 40:29; *Lev* 1:5
Num 27:2
burnt offering at *d.* of *tabernacle.*
Ex 29:42; 33:9, 10; 38:8; 40:28
Lev 1:3; 3:2; 4:7, 18
before the *d.* of the *tabernacle.*
Ex 40:6; *Num* 25:6
at the *d.* of the *tabernacle. Lev* 8:31
35; 14:11; 16:7; 17:6; *Num* 6:18
10:3; *Josh* 19:51
not go out of *d.* of the *tabernacle.*
Lev 8:33
go out from *d.* of *tabernacle.* 10:7
unto *d.* of *tabernacle.* 14:23; 15:14
29; 19:21; *Num* 16:18, 19, 50; 20:6
not to *d.* of *tabernacle. Lev* 17:4, 9
stood in the *d.* of the *tabernacle.*
Num 12:5; 16:18
pillar of cloud over *d.* of *tabernacle.*
Deut 31:15
porter of *d.* of *tabernacle. 1 Chr* 9:21

door joined with *tent*
Abraham sat in *tent d.* *Gen* 18:1
he ran to meet them from *tent d.* 2
Sarah heard it in the *tent d.* 10
every man at *tent d.* *Ex* 33:8
worshipped, every man in *tent d.* 10
weeping, every man in the *d.* of his *tent.* *Num* 11:10
Abiram in *d.* of their *tents.* 16:27
stand in *d.* of the *tent.* *Judg* 4:20

doorkeeper
be a *d.* in house of God. *Ps* 84:10
of Maaseiah *keeper* of *d.* *Jer* 35:4

doorkeepers
which *keepers* of the *d.* *2 Ki* 22:4
the *keepers* of the *d.* to bring. 23:4
of guard took chief priest and three *keepers* of *d.* 25:18; *Jer* 52:24
Berechiah, Elkanah, *d.* *1 Chr* 15:23
Obed-edom and Jehiah *d.* 24
keepers of the *d.* sought. *Esth* 6:2*

door-post
bring him to the *d.-post.* *Ex* 21:6
measured *post* of the *d.* *Ezek* 41:3*

door-posts
blood on upper *d.-posts.* *Ex* 12:7*
write them on *d.-posts. Deut* 11:20
the *posts* of the *d.* moved. *Isa* 6:4
he measured the *d.-posts.*
Ezek 41:16*

doors
shall go out of the *d.* *Josh* 2:19
the *d.* of the parlour. *Judg* 3:24
opened not *d.* of the parlour. 25
what cometh forth of the *d.* 11:31
Samson took the *d.* of the gate. 16:3
her lord rose up, opened the *d.* 19:27
Samuel opened the *d.* *1 Sam* 3:15
David scrabbled on the *d.* of. 21:13
cut off gold from the *d.* *2 Ki* 18:16
Levites be porters of *d.* *2 Chr* 23:4
Hezekiah opened the *d.* of. 29:3
set up the *d.* of it. *Neh* 3:1, 3; 7:1
but I opened my *d.* to. *Job* 31:32
when I set bars and *d.* 38:10
hast thou seen the *d.* of the ? 17*
who can open the *d.* of his ? 41:14
up, ye everlasting *d.* *Ps* 24:7, 9
though he had opened *d.* of. 78:23
crieth at coming in at *d.* *Pr* 8:3
waiting at the posts of my *d.* 34
behind *d.* hast thou set up. *Isa* 57:8
still talking in the *d.* *Ezek* 33:30
keep the *d.* of thy mouth. *Mi* 7:5
open thy *d.* O Lebanon. *Zech* 11:1
know it is near, at the *d. Mat* 24:33
Mark 13:29
angel opened prison *d.* *Acts* 5:19
keepers standing before the *d.* 23
immediately all the *d.* were. 16:26
awaking and seeing prison *d.* 27

shut **doors**
Ehud *shut* the *d.* of. *Judg* 3:23
Ahaz *shut* up the *d.* of. *2 Chr* 28:24
our fathers have *shut* the *d.* 29:7
and let us *shut* the *d.* of. *Neh* 6:10
shut the *d.* and bar them. 7:3
because *shut* not up *d.* of. *Job* 3:10
or who *shut* up sea with *d.*? 38:8
the *d.* shall be *shut* in. *Eccl* 12:4

enter, and *shut* thy *d.* *Isa* 26:20
that would *shut* the *d.*? *Mal* 1:10
when *d.* were *shut.* *John* 20:19, 26
forthwith *d.* were shut. *Acts* 21:30

Dor
drive out inhabitants of *D. Judg* 1:27
Abinadab in region of *D.* *1 Ki* 4:11

Dorcas
by interpretation is *D.* *Acts* 9:36
shewing coats and garments *D.* 39

dote
and they shall *d.* *Jer* 50:36

doted
Aholah *d.* on her lovers. *Ezek* 23:5
whoredoms with all on whom she *d.* 7
Assyrians, on whom she *d.* 9, 12
as soon as she saw them, she *d.* 16
for she *d.* upon their paramours. 20

Dothan
to *D.* he found them in *D. Gen* 37:17
behold Elisha is in *D.* *2 Ki* 6:13

doting
d. about questions and. *1 Tim* 6:4

double
and take *d.* money in. *Gen* 43:12
and they took *d.* money. 15
theft be found, restore *d.* *Ex* 22:4
if found, let him pay *d.* 7
he shall pay *d.* 9
made breast-plate *d.* a span. 39:9
been worth a *d.* hired. *Deut* 15:18
by giving him a *d.* portion. 21:17
let a *d.* portion of thy. *2 Ki* 2:9
they were not of a *d.* *1 Chr* 12:33
that they are *d.* to that. *Job* 11:6*
to him with his *d.* bridle ? 41:13
with a *d.* heart do speak. *Ps* 12:2
she hath received *d.* for. *Isa* 40:2
for shame ye shall have *d.* in their land they shall possess the *d.* 61:7
recompense their sin *d.* *Jer* 16:18
destroy them with *d.* 17:18
I will render *d.* to thee. *Zech* 9:12
deacons grave, not *d.* *1 Tim* 3:8
counted worthy of *d.* honour. 5:17
d. unto her, *d.* according to works, cup fill to her *d.* *Rev* 18:6

double, *verb*
shalt *d.* sixth curtain. *Ex* 26:9
and *d.* unto her *d.* *Rev* 18:6

double-minded
d.-minded man is unstable. *Jas* 1:8
your hearts, ye *d.-minded.* 4:8

doubled
the dream was *d.* to. *Gen* 41:32
four-square, being *d.* *Ex* 28:16
was breadth thereof, being *d.* 39:9
let the sword be *d.* the. *Ezek* 21:14

doubt
Joseph is without *d.* *Gen* 37:33
life shall hang in *d.* *Deut* 28:66
no *d.* but ye are the people. *Job* 12:2
no *d.* kingdom of God. *Luke* 11:20
were in *d.* saying. *Acts* 2:12*
no *d.* this man is a murderer. 28:4
for our sakes, no *d.* *1 Cor* 9:10
voice I stand in *d.* of you. *Gal* 4:20*
no *d.* have continued. *1 John* 2:19

doubt, *verb*
wherefore didst thou *d.*? *Mat* 14:31
if ye have faith, and *d.* not. 21:21
not *d.* in his heart, but. *Mark* 11:23
thou make us to *d.*? *John* 10:24

doubted
worshipped him, some *d. Mat* 28:17
they *d.* whereunto. *Acts* 5:24*
now while Peter *d.* in. 10:17*
because I *d.* of such manner. 25:20*

doubteth
d. is damned if he eat. *Rom* 14:23

doubtful
neither be of *d.* mind. *Luke* 12:29
not to *d.* disputations. *Rom* 14:1

doubting
looked, *d.* of whom he. *John* 13:22
with them, nothing *d.* *Acts* 10:20
11:12*
pray without wrath and *d. 1 Tim* 2:8*

doubtless
d. ye shall not come. *Num* 14:30
I will *d.* deliver the. *2 Sam* 5:19
he shall *d.* come again. *Ps* 126:6
d. thou art our Father. *Isa* 63:16
if not to others, yet *d.* *1 Cor* 9:2
is not expedient for me *d. 2 Cor* 12:1
yea *d.* I count all things. *Phil* 3:8

doubts
dissolving of *d.* was. *Dan* 5:12
heard that thou canst dissolve *d.* 16

dough
people took their *d.* before it was leavened. *Ex* 12:34
unleavened cakes of the *d.* 39
offer a cake of the first of your *d.*
Num 15:20, 21
bring firstfruits of our *d.* *Neh* 10:37
women knead their *d.* to. *Jer* 7:18
priests first of your *d.* *Ezek* 44:30
he hath kneaded the *d.* *Hos* 7:4

dove
[1] *Any one of numerous birds of the pigeon family, although commonly the name is applied to the smaller varieties. This bird is very common in Palestine. It was considered clean and was used in sacrifices. Because of this they were sold in the temple courts,* Lev 12:6, 8; Luke 2:24; Mark 11:15. [2] *The dove is the symbol of gentleness and innocence,* Mat 10:16. *It is defenceless, faithful to its mate and home-loving. This last is the secret of the success of the training of carrier-pigeons.* [3] *The dove is used as a symbol of the Holy Spirit,* Mat 3:16.
The expression dove's dung, in 2 Ki 6:25, *may mean what it apparently does ; or it may mean a common plant which had some nutritive quality, and which rose to famine prices at the siege of Jerusalem.*

Noah sent forth a *d. Gen* 8:8, 10, 12
the *d.* found no rest for the. 8:9
the *d.* came in to him in the. 11
take a turtle-*d.* 15:9; *Lev* 12:6
oh that I had wings like a *d. Ps* 55:6
ye shall be as wings of a *d.* 68:13
not the soul of thy turtle-*d.* 74:19
thou hast *d.* eyes. *S of S* 1:15; 4:1
O my *d.* let me see thy. 2:14
open to me, my sister, my *d.* 5:2
my *d.* my undefiled is but one. 6:9
I did mourn as a *d.* *Isa* 38:14
dwell in rock, be like *d.* *Jer* 48:28
Ephraim is like a silly *d.* *Hos* 7:11
shall tremble as a *d.* out. 11:11
God descending like a *d.* *Mat* 3:16
Mark 1:10; *Luke* 3:22; *John* 1:32

doves
fourth part of a cab of *d.* *2 Ki* 6:25
eyes are as eyes of *d.* *S of S* 5:12
we mourn sore like *d.* *Isa* 59:11
that flee as the *d.* to their. 60:8
shall be like the *d.* of. *Ezek* 7:16
lead her as with voice of *d. Nah* 2:7
serpents, harmless as *d.* *Mat* 10:16
of them that sold *d.* 21:12
Mark 11:15
temple those that sold *d.* *John* 2:14
said unto them that sold *d.* 16

turtle-**doves**
shall take two *turtle-d.* *Lev* 14:22
sacrifice of two *turtle-d.* *Luke* 2:24

down
when the sun is *d.* *Lev* 22:7
Deut 23:11
sun was *d.* commanded to take king of Ai's carcase *d.* *Josh* 8:29
taste aught till sun be *d. 2 Sam* 3:35
walking up and *d.* *Job* 1:7; 2:2
let them wander up and *d. Ps* 59:15
I am tossed up and *d.* as. 109:23
hast walked up and *d.* *Ezek* 28:14
shall walk up and *d.* *Zech* 10:12
we were driven up and *d. Acts* 27:27
clothed with a garment *d.* *Rev* 1:13

down-sitting
thou knowest my *d.-s.* *Ps* 139:2
downward
again take root *d.* *2 Ki* 19:30
Isa 37:31
of beast that goeth *d.* *Eccl* 3:21
appearance of his loins *d.* *Ezek* 1:27
8:2
dowry
(*The money or estate a woman brings to her husband on marriage*)
endued me with good *d.* *Gen* 30:20
ask me never so much *d.* and. 34:12
pay according to the *d.* *Ex* 22:17
king desireth not any *d.* *1 Sam* 18:25
drag
gather them in their *d.* *Hab* 1:15
they burn incense to their *d.* 16
dragging
in little ship, *d.* the net. *John* 21:8
dragon
[1] *The Hebrew word* tan, *translated in Authorized Version* dragon, *is always used in the plural, and is applied to some creatures inhabiting the desert. It probably refers to wild beasts and not to any of the serpent family to which a dragon belongs. The Revised Version translates it in every case by the word* jackals. [2] *The Hebrew word* tannin *seems to refer to any great monster of land or sea, usually some kind of serpent or reptile, but not invariably. In the New Testament it is found only in the Revelation, applied metaphorically to* Satan, Rev 12:3, etc. *Either word is frequently used metaphorically.*
d. shalt thou trample. *Ps* 91:13*
he shall slay the *d.* that. *Isa* 27:1†
Rahab, and wounded the *d.* 51:9†
hath swallowed me up like a *d.*
Jer 51:34†
Pharaoh, the great *d.* *Ezek* 29:3
behold, a great red *d.* *Rev* 12:3
the *d.* stood. 4
d. fought. 7
d. was cast out. 9, 13
flood which the *d.* cast out. 16
the *d.* was wroth with the woman. 17
the *d.* gave him his power. 13:2
they worshipped the *d.* 4
he spake as a *d.* 11
frogs came out of mouth of *d.* 16:13
he laid hold on the *d.* 20:2
dragons
wine is the poison of *d.* *Deut* 32:33
I am a brother to *d.* *Job* 30:29*
broken us in place of *d.* *Ps* 44:19*
thou breakest the heads of *d.* 74:13
praise Lord from earth, ye *d.* 148:7
d. in pleasant palaces. *Isa* 13:22*
an habitation for *d.* 34:13*; 35:7*
the *d.* and owls shall honour. 43:20*
Jerusalem a den of *d.* *Jer* 9:11*
cities of Judah a den of *d.* 10:22*
snuffed up the wind like *d.* 14:6*
Hazor a dwelling for *d.* 49:33*
Babylon a dwelling for *d.* 51:37*
make a wailing like the *d.* *Mi* 1:8*
his heritage waste for *d.* *Mal* 1:3*
dragon well
even before the *d.-well.* *Neh* 2:13
drams
(*The Persian* daric *worth about five dollars, or a little more than an English pound.* Daric *always in Revisions*)
gold ten thousand *d.* *1 Chr* 29:7
gave 61,000 *d.* of gold. *Ezra* 2:69
of gold, of a thousand *d.* 8:27
a thousand *d.* of gold. *Neh* 7:70
twenty thousand *d.* of gold. 71, 72
drank
Noah *d.* of the wine. *Gen* 9:21
I *d.* and she made camels drink.
24:46
brought him wine, and he *d.* 27:25
the congregation *d.* *Num* 20:11
and *d.* wine of their. *Deut* 32:28
nor *d.* water three days. *1 Sam* 30:12
his own meat, and *d.* *2 Sam* 12:3
his house, and *d.* water. *1 Ki* 13:19
flesh, and he *d.* of the brook. 17:6
of the wine which he *d.* *Dan* 1:5
not defile himself with wine he *d.* 8
Belshazzar *d.* wine before the. 5:1
wives and his concubines *d.* in. 3
d. wine, and praised the gods. 4
and they all *d.* of it. *Mark* 14:23
they eat, they *d.* *Luke* 17:27, 28
our father Jacob who *d.* *John* 4:12
d. of that spiritual rock. *1 Cor* 10:4
draught
is cast out in the *d.* *Mat* 15:17
Mark 7:19
let down your nets for a *d.* *Luke* 5:4
for he was astonished at the *d.* 9
draught house
made Baal's house a *d.-h.* *2 Ki* 10:27
drave
(*The old form of* drove. *The American Revision replaces it with the modern form*)
chariot wheels, they *d.* *Ex* 14:25
they *d.* not out the. *Josh* 16:10
and *d.* them out. 24:12; *Judg* 6:9
Lord *d.* out before us all. *Josh* 24:18
Judah *d.* out inhabitants. *Judg* 1:19
which they *d.* before. *1 Sam* 30:20
Uzzah and Ahio *d.* the new cart.
2 Sam 6:3; *1 Chr* 13:7
that time Rezin *d.* Jews. *2 Ki* 16:6
Jeroboam *d.* Israel from. 18:21
whom God *d.* out. *Acts* 7:45*
Gallio *d.* them from. 18:16
see **drove**
draw
and I will also *d.* for. *Gen* 24:44
said, I will *d.* my sword. *Ex* 15:9
d. toward mount Tabor. *Judg* 4:6
will *d.* to thee Sisera. 7
Abimelech said, *d.* thy sword. 9:54
1 Sam 31:4; *1 Chr* 10:4
d. them from the city. *Judg* 20:32
d. that city into river. *2 Sam* 17:13
every man shall *d.* after. *Job* 21:33
d. me not away with the. *Ps* 28:3
d. me, we will run after. *S of S* 1:4
woe to those who *d.* iniquity. *Isa* 5:18
to the nations that *d.* the bow. 66:19
I will *d.* my sword out. *Ezek* 21:3
strangers shall *d.* their swords. 28:7
they shall *d.* their swords. 30:11
d. her, and all her multitudes. 32:20
hast nothing to *d.* with. *John* 4:11
thirst not, nor come hither to *d.* 15
except Father which sent me *d.* 6:44
I be lifted up from earth, *d.* all. 12:32
now they were not able to *d.* 21:6
to *d.* away disciples. *Acts* 20:30
d. you before judgement seats.
Jas 2:6*
draw *back*
faith, but if any *d. back.* *Heb* 10:38*
are not of them who *d. back* to. 39*
draw *near*
let us *d. near* to one. *Judg* 19:13
let us *d. near* to God. *1 Sam* 14:36
Saul said, *d.* ye *near* hither. 38
good for me to *d. near.* *Ps* 73:28
they *d. near* to the gates. 107:18
this people *d. near* with their lips.
Isa 29:13
d. near, ye that are escaped. 45:20
d. near hither, ye sons of. 57:3
will cause him to *d. near.* *Jer* 30:21
order buckler, and *d. near* to. 46:3
charge over city to *d. near.* *Ezek* 9:1
hast caused thy days to *d. near.* 22:4
let all men of war *d. near.* *Joel* 3:9
d. near with a true heart. *Heb* 10:22
draw *nigh*
d. not *nigh* hither, put off. *Ex* 3:5
d. nigh to my soul. *Ps* 69:18
d. nigh that follow mischief. 119:150
nor years *d. nigh.* *Eccl* 12:1
counsel of Holy One *d. nigh.* *Isa* 5:19
by the which we *d. nigh.* *Heb* 7:19
d. nigh to God, will *d. nigh.* *Jas* 4:8
draw *out*
d. out and take you a. *Ex* 12:21
I will *d. out* a sword. *Lev* 26:33
could not *d.* dagger *out.* *Judg* 3:22
thou *d. out* leviathan ? *Job* 41:1
d. out also the spear. *Ps* 35:3
wilt thou *d. out* thine anger ? 85:5
of understanding will *d. out.* *Pr* 20:5
against whom do ye *d. out* ? *Isa* 57:4
if thou *d. out* thy soul to the. 58:10
least of the flock *d.* them *out.*
Jer 49:20*; 50:45*
even sea monsters *d. out.* *Lam* 4:3
I will *d. out* a sword after them.
Ezek 5:2, 12; 12:14
one came to *d. out* fifty. *Hag* 2:16
d. out now, and bear to. *John* 2:8
draw *up*
trusteth that he can *d. up.* *Job* 40:23*
draw joined with *water.*
women go out to *d. water.*
Gen 24:11, 43
daughters come out to *d. water.* 13
ran again to well to *d. water.* 20
maidens going to *d. water.*
1 Sam 9:11
with joy shall ye *d. water.* *Isa* 12:3
d. thee *waters* for siege. *Nah* 3:14
of Samaria to *d. water.* *John* 4:7
drawer
from hewer of wood to *d.* *Deut* 29:11
drawers
be *d.* of water to. *Josh* 9:21, 27
d. of water for house of my God. 23
draweth
wife of the one *d.* near. *Deut* 25:11
now the day *d.* towards. *Judg* 19:9
he *d.* also the mighty. *Job* 24:22
yea his soul *d.* near to grave. 33:22
catch the poor when he *d.* *Ps* 10:9
my life *d.* nigh unto the grave. 88:3
that *d.* near the time of. *Isa* 26:17
time is come, day *d.* *Ezek* 7:12
this people *d.* nigh with. *Mat* 15:8
I am Christ, the time *d.* *Luke* 21:8
for your redemption *d.* nigh. 28
the coming of Lord *d.* nigh. *Jas* 5:8
drawing
delivered in places of *d.* *Judg* 5:11
they see Jesus *d.* nigh. *John* 6:19
drawn
angel, and his sword *d.* *Num* 22:23
31; *Josh* 5:13; *1 Chr* 21:16
heifer, which hath not *d.* *Deut* 21:3
but shalt be *d.* away, and. 30:17
till we have *d.* them. *Josh* 8:6
they were *d.* away. 16; *Judg* 20:31
which young men have *d.* *Ruth* 2:9
it is *d.* and cometh out. *Job* 20:25
wicked have *d.* out sword. *Ps* 37:14
softer than oil, yet *d.* swords. 55:21
deliver them that are *d.* *Pr* 24:11*
fled from the *d.* swords. *Isa* 21:15
that are *d.* from the breasts. 28:9
d. and cast forth beyond. *Jer* 22:19
with lovingkindness have I *d.* 31:3
d. back his right hand. *Lam* 2:3
I Lord have *d.* sword. *Ezek* 21:5, 28
all were *d.* up again to. *Acts* 11:10
when he is *d.* away of. *Jas* 1:14
dread
the *d.* of you shall be on. *Gen* 9:2
fear and *d.* shall fall upon. *Ex* 15:16
this day will I begin to put the *d.*
Deut 2:25; 11:25
shall not his *d.* fall ? *Job* 13:11
let not thy *d.* make me afraid. 21*
let him be your *d.* *Isa* 8:13
dread, *verb*
I said to you, *d.* not. *Deut* 1:29
be strong, *d.* not. *1 Chr* 22:13*
dreadful
how *d.* is this place ! *Gen* 28:17
a *d.* sound in his ears. *Job* 15:21
their rings, they were *d.* *Ezek* 1:18
fourth beast, *d.* and. *Dan* 7:7*, 19*
O Lord, the great and *d.* God. 9:4
the Chaldeans are terrible and *d.*
Hab 1:7
my name is *d.* among. *Mal* 1:14*
coming of great and *d.* day. 4:5*

dream

The Eastern people, and in particular the Jews, had a very great regard for dreams; they observed them, and applied to those who professed to explain them. We see the antiquity of this custom among the Egyptians, in the history of Pharaoh's butler and baker, and in Pharaoh himself, Gen 40:5, 8; 41:15. *Nebuchadnezzar is an instance of the same among the Chaldeans,* Dan 2:1, 2, 3, etc.

As the belief in dreams was generally connected with consultation of idol-priests, or those pretending to deal in magic, the Israelites were warned against dealing with these. But God revealed his will frequently in dreams, and there were those who could explain them, Gen 20:3; 28:12; 37:4; Num 12:6; Deut 13:1.

to Abimelech in a *d.* *Gen* 20:3, 6
Jacob saw in a *d.* the rams. 31:10
angel of God spake to Jacob in *d.* 11
God came to Laban in a *d.* 24
Joseph dreamed a *d.* 37:5, 9, 10
butler and baker dreamed a *d.* 40:5
and behold, it was a *d.* 41:7
1 Ki 3:15
to each according to *d.* *Gen* 41:12
the *d.* of Pharaoh is one. 25, 26
for that the *d.* was doubled. 32
will speak to him in a *d.* *Num* 12:6
a man that told a *d.* to. *Judg* 7:13
Gideon heard telling of the *d.* 15
Lord appeared in a *d.* *1 Ki* 3:5
shall fly away as a *d.* *Job* 20:8
in a *d.* he openeth the ears. 33:15
as a *d.* when one awaketh. *Ps* 73:20
for a *d.* cometh through. *Eccl* 5:3
against Ariel be as a *d.* *Isa* 29:7
hath a *d.* let him tell a *d.* *Jer* 23:28
was troubled to know *d.* *Dan* 2:3
tell thy servants the *d.* 4
if ye shew the *d.* 6
this is the *d.* and we will tell. 36
my lord, the *d.* be to them. 4:19
Daniel had a *d.* he wrote the *d.* 7:1
the angel appeared to Joseph in a *d.* *Mat* 1:20; 2:13, 19
being warned of God in a *d.* 2:12, 22
suffered many things in a *d.* 27:19

dream, *verb*

we were like them that *d.* *Ps* 126:1
your old men *d.* dreams. *Joel* 2:28
Acts 2:17

dreamed

Jacob *d.* *Gen* 28:12
Joseph *d.* a dream. 37:5
the officers *d.* 40:5
Pharaoh *d.* 41:1, 15
Joseph remembered the dreams which he *d.* 42:9
I have *d.* I have *d.* *Jer* 23:25
dreams which you cause to be *d.* 29:8
Nebuchadnezzar *d.* dreams. *Dan* 2:1
the king said, I have *d.* a dream. 5

dreamer

behold, this *d.* cometh. *Gen* 37:19
if a *d.* of dreams arise. *Deut* 13:1
thou shalt not hearken to that *d.* 3
that prophet or *d.* of dreams. 5

dreamers

not to diviners nor *d.* *Jer* 27:9
those filthy *d.* defile flesh. *Jude* 8

dreameth

man *d.* a thirsty man *d.* *Isa* 29:8

dreams

hated Joseph for his *d.* *Gen* 37:8
see what will become of his *d.* 20
and he interpreted our *d.* 41:12
Joseph remembered the *d.* he. 42:9
Lord answered him not by *d.* *1 Sam* 28:6, 15
thou scarest me with *d.* *Job* 7:14
in multitude of *d.* are. *Eccl* 5:7
forget my name with *d.* *Jer* 23:27
them that prophesy false *d.* 32
Daniel had understanding in *d.* *Dan* 1:17; 5:12
diviners have told false *d.* *Zech* 10:2

dregs

d. thereof the wicked. *Ps* 75:8
hast drunken the *d.* *Isa* 51:17*, 22*

dress

[1] *To till or prune, as land, trees, etc.,* Gen 2:15. [2] *To prepare for food,* Gen 18:7.

man into the garden to *d.* *Gen* 2:15
a young man, he hasted to *d.* 18:7
plant vineyards, and *d.* *Deut* 28:39
to *d.* of his own for the. *2 Sam* 12:4
let Tamar *d.* the meat in. 13:5
go to Amnon's house, *d.* him meat. 7
that I may *d.* it for me. *1 Ki* 17:12
I will *d.* the other bullock. 18:23
d. it first, for ye are many. 25

dressed

took calf which he had *d.* *Gen* 18:8
d. in the fryingpan be. *Lev* 7:9
took five sheep ready *d.* *1 Sam* 25:18
poor man's lamb and *d.* *2 Sam* 12:4
Mephibosheth had not *d.* his. 19:24
they *d.* it, and called on. *1 Ki* 18:26
herbs for them by whom it is *d.* *Heb* 6:7*

dresser

then said he to the *d.* *Luke* 13:7

dresseth

when he *d.* the lamps. *Ex* 30:7

drew

Rebekah *d.* water. *Gen* 24:20, 45
they *d.* and lifted up Joseph. 37:28
Zarah *d.* back his hand. 38:29
because I *d.* him out of. *Ex* 2:10
Jethro's daughters came and *d.* 16
an Egyptian *d.* water enough. 19
for Joshua *d.* not his hand. *Josh* 8:26
fell 120,000 men that *d.* *Judg* 8:10
but the youth *d.* not his sword. 20
chief of Israel 400,000 that *d.* 20:2
numbered 26,000 that *d.* sword. 15
all these *d.* the sword. 25, 35
liers in wait *d.* themselves along. 37
of Benjamin 25,000 that *d.* sword. 46
buy it for thee, so he *d.* *Ruth* 4:8
to Mizpeh, and *d.* water. *1 Sam* 7:6
David *d.* Goliath's sword. 17:51
he took me, he *d.* me out of many waters. *2 Sam* 22:17; *Ps* 18:16
three mighty men *d.* water out of well of. *2 Sam* 23:16; *1 Chr* 11:18
in Israel 800,000 that *d.* *2 Sam* 24:9
certain man *d.* a bow. *1 Ki* 22:34
2 Chr 18:33
Moab took 700 that *d.* *2 Ki* 3:26
Jehu *d.* a bow with his full. 9:24
they sent and *d.* forth. *1 Chr* 19:16
eleven hundred thousand men that *d.* sword, Judah 470,000 that *d.* 21:5
d. out staves of the ark. *2 Chr* 5:9
1 Ki 8:8
of Benjamin that *d.* bows. *2 Chr* 14:8
they *d.* up Jeremiah. *Jer* 38:13
I *d.* them with cords. *Hos* 11:4
full, they *d.* to shore. *Mat* 13:48
Mark 6:53*
Peter *d.* his sword. *Mat* 26:51
Mark 14:47; *John* 18:10
and the sabbath *d.* on. *Luke* 23:54
servants which *d.* water. *John* 2:9
and *d.* the net to land full. 21:11
and *d.* away much people. *Acts* 5:37
stoned Paul and *d.* him out. 14:19
and *d.* Paul and Silas into. 16:19
the jailor *d.* his sword, and. 27
they *d.* Jason and certain. 17:6
d. Alexander out of the. 19:33
they took Paul and *d.* him out. 21:30
his tail *d.* the third part. *Rev* 12:4

drew *near*, or *nigh*

Abraham *d. near* and. *Gen* 18:23
time *d. nigh* that Israel. 47:29
when Pharaoh *d. nigh.* *Ex* 14:10
Moses *d. near* to thick. 20:21
the congregation *d. near.* *Lev* 9:5
people *d. nigh* before Ai. *Josh* 8:11
the Philistines *d. near.* *1 Sam* 7:10
Saul *d. near* to Samuel. 9:18
Goliath *d. near* morning and. 17:16
41, 48
David *d. near* to Goliath the. 40
Joab *d. nigh* against. *2 Sam* 10:13
Ahimaaz came and *d. near.* 18:25
Esther *d. near* and. *Esth* 5:2
the king's decree *d. near* to be. 9:1
she *d.* not *near* to God. *Zeph* 3:2
and when they *d. nigh.* *Mat* 21:1
when the time of fruit *d. near.* 34
d. near the publicans. *Luke* 15:1
elder son came, as he *d. nigh.* 25
feast of unleavened bread *d.* nigh. 22:1
and Judas *d. near* to Jesus. 47
Jesus himself *d. near.* 24:15
they *d. nigh* to the village where. 28
time of promise *d. nigh.* *Acts* 7:17
as he *d. near* to behold it. 31
as they *d. nigh* to the city. 10:9
deemed that they *d. near.* 27:27

drewest

thou *d.* near in the day. *Lam* 3:57

dried

until waters were *d.* up. *Gen* 8:7, 13
twenty-seventh day was earth *d.* 14
green ears of corn *d.* by. *Lev* 2:14
nor eat moist grapes or *d.* *Num* 6:3
our soul is *d.* away. 11:6
heard how Lord *d.* up. *Josh* 2:10
your God *d.* up Jordan, as Lord did Red sea, which he *d.* up. 4:23
heard Lord had *d.* up Jordan. 5:1
bind with withs never *d.* *Judg* 16:7
Jeroboam's hand *d.* up. *1 Ki* 13:4
brook *d.* because there had. 17:7
with the sole of my feet have I *d.* all the rivers. *2 Ki* 19:24; *Isa* 37:25
his roots shall be *d.* up. *Job* 18:16
they are *d.* up, they are. 28:4
my strength is *d.* up. *Ps* 22:15
my throat is *d.* mine eyes. 69:3
the Red sea, and it was *d.* 106:9
and their multitude *d.* up. *Isa* 5:13
river shall be wasted and *d.* up. 19:5
of defence be emptied and *d.* up. 6
art thou not it which hath *d.*? 51:10
places of wilderness *d.* up. *Jer* 23:10
and they shall be *d.* up. 50:38
know that I have *d.* up. *Ezek* 17:24
the east wind *d.* up her fruit. 19:12
our bones are *d.* and hope is. 37:11
their root is *d.* up. *Hos* 9:16
his fountain shall be *d.* up. 13:15
the new wine is *d.* up. *Joel* 1:10
the vine is *d.* up. 12
rivers of water are *d.* up. 20
arm shall be clean *d.* up. *Zech* 11:17
fountain of blood was *d.* *Mark* 5:29
they saw the fig tree *d.* up. 11:20
water of Euphrates was *d.* up. *Rev* 16:12

driedst

the flood, thou *d.* up. *Ps* 74:15

drieth

flood decayeth and *d.* up. *Job* 14:11
but a broken spirit *d.* *Pr* 17:22
makes sea dry, and *d.* *Nah* 1:4

drink, *noun*

bottle, and gave lad *d.* *Gen* 21:19
I will give thy camels *d.* 24:14, 46
all *d.* that may be drunk. *Lev* 11:34
give the congregation *d.* *Num* 20:8
she gave Sisera *d.* and. *Judg* 4:19
gave meat and *d.* to. *Ezra* 3:7
them *d.* in vessels of gold. *Esth* 1:7
he gave them *d.* as out. *Ps* 78:15
I have mingled my *d.* with. 102:9
gave *d.* to every beast of. 104:11
he will cause the *d.* of. *Isa* 32:6
to give *d.* to my people. 43:20
my lovers that give me *d.* *Hos* 2:5
their *d.* is sour, they have. 4:18
giveth his neighbour *d.* *Hab* 2:15
ye are not filled with *d.* *Hag* 1:6
I was thirsty, and ye gave me *d.* *Mat* 25:35
when gave thee *d.*? 37
thirsty, and ye gave me no *d.* 42
a Jew, askest *d.* of me. *John* 4:9
my blood is *d.* indeed. 6:55
enemy thirst, give him *d.* *Rom* 12:20
of God not meat and *d.* 14:17
drink same spiritual *d.* *1 Cor* 10:4
man judge in meat or in *d.* *Col* 2:16

drink, *verb*

The word drink is frequently used of taking in through the senses, or through the mind, the pleasures or the sorrows sent upon man. To eat and drink meant to enjoy themselves in any manner, Eccl 5:18. To drink blood *was to be satiated with slaughter,* Ezek 39:18. *As cup is used figuratively for the blessings and punishments of God, so to drink of the cup was to receive these,* Ps 75:8.

let me d. Gen 24:14, 17, 45
d. my lord. 18, 46
rods when flocks came to d. 30:38
what shall we d.? Ex 15:24
Moses made Israel d. of it. 32:20
not d. wine nor strong d. Lev 10:9
neither shall he d. Num 6:3
down on knees to d. Judg 7:5
go to the vessels and d. Ruth 2:9
drew water, but David would not d. 2 Sam 23:16, 17; 1 Chr 11:18, 19
that thou shalt d. of. 1 Ki 17:4
and Haman sat down to d. Esth 3:15
he shall d. the wrath of. Job 21:20
make them d. of the river. Ps 36:8
made us to d. the wine of. 60:3
they gave me vinegar to d. 69:21
wicked of earth shall d. 75:8
they could not d. 78:44
thou gavest them tears to d. 80:5
he shall d. of the brook. 110:7
for they d. the wine of. Pr 4:17
lest they d. and forget law. 31:5
let him d. and forget his poverty. 7
d. yea d. abundantly. S of S 5:1
bitter to them that d. it. Isa 24:9
thou shalt no more d. it. 51:22
shall d. it in the courts. 62:9
my servants shall d. but ye. 65:13
cup of consolation to d. Jer 16:7
make them d. water of gall. 23:15
nations, to whom I send thee, to d. 25:15
and they shall d. and be moved. 16
cup and made all nations to d. 17
d. ye, and be drunken, and spue. 27
saith Lord, ye shall certainly d. 28
to this day they d. none. 35:14
they whose judgement was not to d. cup, shalt surely d. of it. 49:12
d. by measure, from time to time shalt thou d. Ezek 4:11
shalt d. of sister's cup deep. 23:32
they d. that which ye have. 34:19
that concubines might d. Dan 5:2
bring, and let us d. Amos 4:1
so shall all the heathen d., yea, they shall d. and shall. Ob 16
d. thou, let thy foreskin. Hab 2:16
ye d. but ye are not filled. Hag 1:6
and they shall d. and. Zech 9:15
whoso shall give to d. Mat 10:42
able to d. of cup that I shall d. of and be baptized? 20:22; Mark 10:38
d. indeed of my cup. Mat 20:23
Mark 10:39
gave the cup, saying d. Mat 26:27
not d. henceforth till that day when I d. 29; Mark 14:25; Luke 22:18
if cup may not pass except I d. Mat 26:42
gave him vinegar to d. 27:34
filled a sponge with vinegar, and gave him to d. 48; Mark 15:36
d. any deadly thing. Mark 16:18
to thee, give me to d. John 4:10
let him come to me and d. 7:37
cup given me, shall I not d.? 18:11
all d. same spiritual drink. 1 Cor 10:4
cannot d. the cup of the Lord. 21
oft as ye d. in remembrance. 11:25
have been all made to d. into. 12:13

strong **drink**

do not drink strong d. Lev 10:9
himself from strong d. Num 6:3
money for strong d. Deut 14:26
nor have ye drunk strong d. 29:6
not drink strong d. Judg 13:4, 7, 14
wine nor strong d. 1 Sam 1:15
wine is a mocker, strong d. Pr 20:1
for princes to drink strong d. Pr 31:4
give strong d. to him that is. 6
may follow strong d. woe. Isa 5:11
of strength to mingle strong d. 22
strong d. shall be bitter to. 24:9
erred through strong d. and are out of way through strong d. 28:7
stagger, but not with strong d. 29:9
fill ourselves with strong d. 56:12
of wine and strong d. Mi 2:11
drink wine nor strong d. Luke 1:15

drink *water,* or *waters*

water of thy pitcher to d. Gen 24:43
shall lothe to d. water. Ex 7:18, 21
digged about river for water to d. 24
could not d. of the waters. 15:23
no water for the people to d. 17:1
water out of it, that they may d. 6
cause to d. bitter water. Num 5:24
26:27
neither any water to d. 20:5; 33:14
nor will we d. of water. 20:17; 21:22
buy water for money, that ye may d. Deut 2:6, 28
give me a little water to d. Judg 4:19
bowed upon knees to d. water. 7:6
the Egyptian d. water. 1 Sam 30:11
to d. of the water of well of Bethlehem. 2 Sam 23:15; 1 Chr 11:17
eat bread, nor d. water. 1 Ki 13:8, 9
water in a vessel that I may d. 17:10
filled with water that ye may d. 2 Ki 3:17
d. every one waters of his. 18:31
Isa 36:16
given water to weary to d. Job 22:7
d. waters out of thine own. Pr 5:15
if enemy be thirsty, give water to d. 25:21
to d. the waters of Sihor. Jer 2:18
water of gall to d. 8:14; 9:15
d. water by measure. Ezek 4:11, 16
d. thy water with trembling. 12:18
they shall d. their water with. 19
all trees that d. water. 31:14, 16
pulse to eat, water to d. Dan 1:12
wandered to d. water but. Amos 4:8
not feed nor d. water. Jonah 3:7
a cup of water to d. Mark 9:41
give me water to d. John 4:7
d. no longer water, but. 1 Tim 5:23

drink with *wine*

our father d. wine. Gen 19:32, 34
made their father d. wine. 33, 35
nor d. wine when ye go. Lev 10:9
Nazarite d. no vinegar of wine. Num 6:3
after that Nazarite may d. wine. 20
plant vineyards, but shalt not d. of wine. Deut 28:39; Amos 5:11
Manoah's wife might d. no wine. Judg 13:4, 7, 14
wine, that such as be faint may d. 2 Sam 16:2
hast made us d. wine of. Ps 60:3
for they d. the wine of. Pr 4:17
and d. of the wine which I. 9:5
not for kings, to d. wine. 31:4
go and d. thy wine Eccl 9:7
thee to d. spiced wine. S of S 8:2
are mighty to d. wine. Isa 5:22
shall not d. wine with a song. 24:9
of stranger not d. thy wine. 62:8
give Rechabites wine to d. Jer 35:2
will d. no wine, ye shall d. no wine. 6
shall any priest d. wine. Ezek 44:21
took away wine that they should d. Dan 1:16
sold a girl for wine to d. Joel 3:3
they d. the wine of the. Amos 2:8
gave the Nazarites wine to d. 12
that d. wine in bowls. 6:6
plant vineyards, and d. wine. 9:14
but shall not d. wine. Mi 6:15
Zeph 1:13
gave him to d. wine. Mark 15:23
John shall d. neither wine. Luke 1:15
to eat flesh or d. wine. Rom 14:21
all nations d. of the wine. Rev 14:8
same shall d. of the wine of the. 10

drinkers

and howl, all ye d. of wine. Joel 1:5

drinketh

in which my lord d.? Gen 44:5
land d. water of rain. Deut 11:11
the poison whereof d. up. Job 6:4
who d. iniquity like water! 15:16
like Job who d. up scorning. 34:7
behold, he d. up a river. 40:23*
sendeth by a fool, d. Pr 26:6
he d. but he awaketh. Isa 29:8
the smith, he d. no water. 44:12
he d. with publicans? Mark 2:16
whosoever d. of this water shall. John 4:13
whosoever d. of water that I. 14
whoso d. of my blood. 6:54
that d. my blood dwelleth in me. 56
he that d. unworthily d. 1 Cor 11:29
earth which d. in rain. Heb 6:7

drinking

camels till they have done d. Gen 24:19
as camels had done d. man took. 22
till Boaz have done eating and d. Ruth 3:3
eating and d. and. 1 Sam 30:16
multitude, eating and d. 1 Ki 4:20
d. vessels of gold. 10:21; 2 Chr 9:20
Elah was d. 1 Ki 16:9
Ben-hadad was d. 20:12, 16
three days eating and d. 1 Chr 12:39
d. was according to the law. Esth 1:8
and daughters were d. Job 1:13, 18
eating flesh, and d. wine. Isa 22:13
John came neither eating nor d. Mat 11:18; Luke 7:33
Son of man came eating and d. Mat 11:19; Luke 7:34
were eating and d. till. Mat 24:38
eating and d. such things. Luke 10:7

drink offering

Jacob poured a d.-off. Gen 35:14
and fourth part of an hin of wine for d.-off. Ex 29:40; Num 15:5
do according to the d.-off. Ex 29:41
nor shall ye pour d.-off. 30:9
d.-off. shall be of wine. Lev 23:13
priest shall offer also his d.-off. Num 6:17
for a d.-off. a third part. 15:7
bring for a d.-off. half an hin. 10
his d.-off. according to the. 24
besides the continual d.-off. 28:10
15, 24; 29:16
hast thou poured a d.-off. Isa 57:6
that furnish the d.-off. 65:11*
the d.-off. is cut off from. Joel 1:9
the d.-off. is withholden. 13
return and leave a d.-off. 2:14

drink offerings

for a burnt-offering with d.-off. Lev 23:18, 37; Num 6:15; 28:31
29:11, 18, 19, 21, 24, 30, 33, 37, 39
their d.-off. shall be. Num 28:14
drank the wine of their d.-off. Deut 32:38
offered with their d.-off. 1 Chr 29:21
2 Chr 29:35
buy meat-offerings and d.-off. Ezra 7:17
their d.-off. of blood. Ps 16:4
pour out d.-off. to other gods. Jer 7:18; 19:13; 32:29
pour out d.-off. 44:17, 18, 19, 25
poured out their d.-off. Ezek 20:28
princes part to give d.-off. 45:17

drinks

only in meats, and d. Heb 9:10

drive

strong hand shall he d. Ex 6:1
send hornets, which shall d. 23:28
I will not d. them out before thee. 29
by little and little I will d. them. 30
and thou shalt d. them out. 31
I will d. out the Canaanite. 33:2
behold I d. out before thee. 34:11
I may d. them out of the. Num 22:6
I may be able to overcome and d. 11
then shall ye d. out all. 33:52
but if ye will not d. out the. 55
to d. out nations greater and. Deut 4:38; 9:4, 5; Josh 3:10
so shalt thou d. them out. Deut 9:3

then will the Lord *d.* out. *Deut* 11:23
Lord thy God doth *d.* them. 18:12
them will I *d.* out from. *Josh* 13:6
then I shall be able to *d.* them. 14:12
children of Judah could not *d.* 15:63
of Manasseh could not *d.* out. 17:12
did not utterly *d.* them out. 13
Judg 1:28
shalt *d.* out Canaanites. *Josh* 17:18
Lord shall *d.* them out of. 23:5
the Lord will no more *d.* out. 13
Judg 2:3, 21
not *d.* inhabitants of. *Judg* 1:19
did not *d.* out Jebusites. 21
other tribes, 27, 29, 30, 31, 33
whom Lord our God shall *d.* 11:24*
d. go forward, slack not. *2 Ki* 4:24
who didst *d.* out the. *2 Chr* 20:7
make afraid, and *d.* *Job* 18:11*
they *d.* away the ass of. 24:3
how thou didst *d.* out. *Ps* 44:2
smoke is driven away, so *d.* 68:2
rod of correction shall *d.* it. *Pr* 22:15
and I will *d.* thee from. *Isa* 22:19*
be a curse, whither I shall *d. Jer* 24:9
that I should *d.* you out. 27:10, 15
because Lord did *d.* them. 46:15
Gentiles, whither I will *d. Ezek* 4:13
and they shall *d.* thee. *Dan* 4:25, 32
I will *d.* them out of my. *Hos* 9:15
I will *d.* the northern. *Joel* 2:20
shall *d.* out Ashdod. *Zeph* 2:4
ship was caught, we let her *d.*
Acts 27:15

driven
thou hast *d.* me out this. *Gen* 4:14
were *d.* from Pharaoh's. *Ex* 10:11
the beast be *d.* away. 22:10
have *d.* out enemies. *Num* 32:21
thou shouldest be *d.* to. *Deut* 4:19*
whither Lord hath *d.* thee. 30:1
if any of them be *d.* out to. 4*
the Lord hath *d.* out. *Josh* 23:9
they have *d.* me out. *1 Sam* 26:19
wisdom *d.* quite from me? *Job* 6:13
wilt thou break a leaf *d.* to? 13:25
he shall be *d.* from light into. 18:18
d. forth from among men. 30:5
let them be *d.* backward. *Ps* 40:14
as smoke is *d.* away, so drive. 68:2
Jordan was *d.* back. 114:3, 5*
wicked is *d.* away in his. *Pr* 14:32*
shall be *d.* to darkness. *Isa* 8:22
sown by brooks be *d.* away. 19:7
he gave them as *d.* stubble. 41:2
places whither I have *d.* *Jer* 8:3
23:3, 8; 29:14, 18; 32:37
from lands whither he had *d.* 16:15
ye have *d.* them away. 23:2
shall be *d.* on and fall therein. 12
out of all places whither they were *d.*
40:12; 43:5
of nations whither I have *d.* 46:28
ye shall be *d.* out every man. 49:5
the lions have *d.* him away. 50:17
I have *d.* him out for his. *Ezek* 31:11
again which was *d.* away. 34:4, 16
and he was *d.* from men. *Dan* 4:33
5:21
countries whither thou hast *d.* 9:7
as the chaff that is *d.* *Hos* 13:3
I will gather her that was *d. Mi* 4:6
Zeph 3:19
he was *d.* of the devil. *Luke* 8:29
strake sail, and were *d.* *Acts* 27:17
we were *d.* up and down in. 27
is like a wave of the sea *d.* *Jas* 1:6
ships though great are *d.* of. 3:4

driver
Ahab said to *d.* of his. *1 Ki* 22:34
nor regardeth crying of *d.* *Job* 39:7

driveth
is like Jehu, for he *d.* *2 Ki* 9:20
like chaff which wind *d.* *Ps* 1:4
the north wind *d.* away. *Pr* 25:23*
the spirit *d.* him into. *Mark* 1:12

driving
those nations without *d.* *Judg* 2:23
d. is like the *d.* of Jehu. *2 Ki* 9:20
by *d.* out nations before. *1 Chr* 17:21

dromedaries
(*Originally this word was applied to any fleet camel bred especially for riding. See* **camel**)
barley and straw for *d.* *1 Ki* 4:28*
letters by riders on *d.* *Esth* 8:10*
d. of Midian and Ephah. *Isa* 60:6

dromedary
thou art a swift *d.* *Jer* 2:23

drop
nations are as the *d.* of. *Isa* 40:15

drop, *verb*
my doctrine shall *d.* as. *Deut* 32:2
heavens shall *d.* down dew. 33:28
Pr 3:20
which clouds do *d.* and. *Job* 36:28*
and thy paths *d.* fatness. *Ps* 65:11
they *d.* on the pastures of the. 12
lips of a strange woman *d.* *Pr* 5:3
thy lips, my spouse, *d.* *S of S* 4:11
d. down, ye heavens. *Isa* 45:8
d. thy word toward. *Ezek* 20:46
d. thy word toward holy places. 21:2
mountains shall *d.* down new wine.
Joel 3:18; *Amos* 9:13
d. not thy word against. *Amos* 7:16

dropped
d. the clouds also *d.* water. *Judg* 5:4
into wood, honey *d.* *1 Sam* 14:26
till water *d.* on them. *2 Sam* 21:10
and my speech *d.* upon. *Job* 29:22
the heavens also *d.* at. *Ps* 68:8
my hands *d.* with myrrh. *S of S* 5:5

droppeth
idleness the house *d.* *Eccl* 10:18*

dropping
contentions of a wife are a continual *d.* *Pr* 19:13; 27:15
d. sweet smelling myrrh. *S of S* 5:13

drops
he maketh small the *d.* *Job* 36:27
who hath begotten the *d.*? 38:28
my locks with the *d.* *S of S* 5:2
sweat was as great *d.* *Luke* 22:44

dropsy
a man before him, who had *d.*
Luke 14:2

dross
take away the *d.* from. *Pr* 25:4
potsherd covered with silver *d.* 26:23
silver is become *d.* wine. *Isa* 1:22
I will purely purge away thy *d.* 25
house of Israel is to me become *d.*
Ezek 22:18, 19

drought
in the day *d.* consumed. *Gen* 31:40
fiery serpents and *d.* *Deut* 8:15*
d. and heat consume. *Job* 24:19
moisture is turned into *d.* *Ps* 32:4
Lord satisfy thy soul in *d. Isa* 58:11*
us through a land of *d.* *Jer* 2:6
not be careful in year of *d.* 17:8
a *d.* is upon her waters. 50:38
thee in land of great *d.* *Hos* 13:5
and I called for a *d.* *Hag* 1:11

drove, -s
every *d.* by themselves, and put a space betwixt *d.* and *d. Gen* 32:16
commanded all that followed *d.* 19
meanest thou by all this *d.*? 33:8*

drove, *verb*
so God *d.* out the man. *Gen* 3:24
fowls came, Abram *d.* them. 15:11
shepherds came and *d.* *Ex* 2:17
they *d.* out the Amorites. *Num* 21:32
Caleb *d.* thence the. *Josh* 15:14
who *d.* away the. *1 Chr* 8:13*
and *d.* asunder the nations. *Hab* 3:6
he *d.* them all out of. *John* 2:15*

drown
love, nor can floods *d.* it. *S of S* 8:7
foolish lusts, that *d.* *1 Tim* 6:9

drowned
chosen captains are *d.* *Ex* 15:4*
it shall be *d.* as by flood. *Amos* 8:8*
9:5*
better he were *d.* in. *Mat* 18:6*
Egyptians assaying to do, were *d.*
Heb 11:29*

drowsiness
d. shall clothe a man. *Pr* 23:21

drunk
all drink that may be *d.* *Lev* 11:34
not eaten bread, nor *d.* *Deut* 29:6
I will make mine arrows *d.* 32:42
when Samson had *d.* *Judg* 15:19
Boaz had eaten and *d.* *Ruth* 3:7
Hannah rose up after they *d.*
1 Sam 1:9
I have *d.* neither wine nor. 15
David made Uriah *d.* *2 Sam* 11:13
hast eaten bread and *d.* *1 Ki* 13:22
Elah was in Tirzah, drinking himself *d.* 16:9
Ben-hadad drinking himself *d.* 20:16
they had eaten and *d.* *2 Ki* 6:23
digged and *d.* strange waters. 19:24
Isa 37:25
I have *d.* my wine with. *S of S* 5:1
which hast *d.* the cup of. *Isa* 51:17
will make them *d.* in my fury. 63:6
sword shall be made *d.* *Jer* 46:10
I will make *d.* her princes. 51:57
and to have *d.* of the. *Ezek* 34:18
they *d.* wine, and praised. *Dan* 5:4
and thy concubines have *d.* 23
as ye have *d.* upon my. *Ob* 16
man having *d.* old wine. *Luke* 5:39
we have eaten and *d.* in. 13:26
when men have well *d.* *John* 2:10
be not *d.* with wine. *Eph* 5:18
made *d.* with the wine of. *Rev* 17:2
for all nations have *d.* of wine. 18:3

drunkard
son is a glutton and *d.* *Deut* 21:20
for *d.* and glutton shall. *Pr* 23:21
thorn goeth up into hand of *d.* 26:9
reel to and fro like a *d.* *Isa* 24:20
with a fornicator or *d.* eat. *1 Cor* 5:11

drunkards
I was the song of the *d.* *Ps* 69:12
woe to pride, to the *d.* *Isa* 28:1, 3
awake, ye *d.* and weep. *Joel* 1:5
they are drunken as *d.* *Nah* 1:10
nor *d.* shall inherit the. *1 Cor* 6:10

drunken
Noah was *d.* and he. *Gen* 9:21
Hannah had been *d.* *1 Sam* 1:13
how long wilt thou be *d.*? 14
merry, for he was very *d.* 25:36
to stagger like a *d.* man. *Job* 12:25
Ps 107:27
as a *d.* man staggereth. *Isa* 19:14
they are *d.* but not. 29:9; 51:21
be *d.* with their own blood. 49:26
thou hast *d.* the dregs of cup. 51:17
I am like a *d.* man. *Jer* 23:9
be *d.* and spue, and fall. 25:27
make ye him *d.* for he. 48:26
they have assuredly *d.* and. 49:12
cup that made all earth *d.* 51:7
I will make them *d.* that they. 39
he hath made me *d.* *Lam* 3:15*
O Edom, thou shalt be *d.* 4:21
Nah 3:11
have *d.* water for money. *Lam* 5:4
drink blood till ye be *d.* *Ezek* 39:19
and while they are *d.* *Nah* 1:10
and makest him *d.* also. *Hab* 2:15
fellow-servants, to eat and drink with *d.* *Mat* 24:49; *Luke* 12:45
till I have eaten and *d.* *Luke* 17:8
for these are not *d.* as. *Acts* 2:15
and another is *d.* *1 Cor* 11:21
they that be *d.* are *d.* *1 Thes* 5:7
I saw the woman *d.* with. *Rev* 17:6

drunkenness
to add *d.* to thirst. *Deut* 29:19*
strength, and not for *d.* *Eccl* 10:17
of Jerusalem with *d.* *Jer* 13:13
shalt be filled with *d.* *Ezek* 23:33
be overcharged with *d.* *Luke* 21:34
not in rioting and *d.* *Rom* 13:13
of flesh are murders, *d.* *Gal* 5:21

Drusilla
came with his wife *D.* *Acts* 24:24

dry
mingled with oil and *d.* *Lev* 7:10
it is a *d.* scald, a leprosy. 13:30
was *d.* and mouldy. *Josh* 9:5, 12
it be *d.* on all earth. *Judg* 6:37
it now be *d.* only on the fleece. 39

wilt thou pursue the d.? Job 13:25
they ran in d. places. Ps 105:41
better is a d. morsel and. Pr 17:1
as the heat in a d. place. Isa 25:5
as rivers of water in a d. 32:2
that saith to the deep, be d. 44:27
neither let eunuch say, I am a d. 56:3
a d. wind, not to fan, nor. Jer 4:11*
dry up, and make springs d. 51:36
made the d. tree flourish. Ezek 17:24
it shall devour every d. tree. 20:47
I will make the rivers d. 30:12
the bones were very d. 37:2
O ye d. bones. 4
Lord give them d. breasts. Hos 9:14
spring shall become d. 13:15
the sea, and maketh it d. Nah 1:4
devoured as stubble fully d. 10
will make Nineveh d. Zeph 2:13
he walketh through d. places. Mat 12:43; Luke 11:24
green tree what shall be done in d.? Luke 23:31

dry *ground*
face of the ground was d. Gen 8:13
shall go on d. ground. Ex 14:16, 22
ark stood on d. ground, Israel passed on d. ground. Josh 3:17
Elijah and Elisha went on d. ground. 2 Ki 2:8
springs into d. ground. Ps 107:33*
turneth d. ground into water. 35
floods upon the d. ground. Isa 44:3
root out of a d. ground. 53:2
a d. and thirsty ground. Ezek 19:13
see **land**

dry, *verb*
waters and they d. up. Job 12:15
the flame shall d. up his. 15:30
d. up herbs, I will d. up. Isa 42:15
I will d. up thy rivers. 44:27
I d. up the sea. 50:2
Lord, I will d. up her sea. Jer 51:36
deeps of river shall d. up. Zech 10:11

dryshod
river, and men go d.-shod. Isa 11:15

due
thy d. and thy son's d. Lev 10:13, 14
this shall be priest's d. Deut 18:3
sought him not after d. 1 Chr 15:13*
the glory d. to his name. 16:29 Ps 29:2; 96:8
portion for singers, d. for. Neh 11:23
withhold not to whom it is d. Pr 3:27
he pay all that was d. Mat 18:34
receive the d. reward. Luke 23:41
to whom tribute is d. Rom 13:7

due *benevolence*
render to wife d. ben. 1 Cor 7:3

due *season*
you rain in d. season. Lev 26:4 Deut 11:14
to me in their d. season. Num 28:2
give them their meat in d. season. Ps 104:27; 145:15
word spoken in d. season. Pr 15:23
princes eat in d. season. Eccl 10:17
to give them meat in d. season. Mat 24:45; Luke 12:42
in d. season we shall reap. Gal 6:9

due *time*
foot shall slide in d. time. Deut 32:35
in d. time Christ died. Rom 5:6
one born out of d. time. 1 Cor 15:8
ransom, testified in d. time. 1 Tim 2:6
in d. time manifested. Tit 1:3
exalt you in d. time. 1 Pet 5:6

dues
to all their d. tribute. Rom 13:7

duke
d. Alvah, d. Jetheth. Gen 36:40† 1 Chr 1:51†

dukes
d. of sons of Esau. Gen 36:15†, 19†
the d. of the Horites. 21†, 29†
then the d. of Edom. Ex 15:15†
which were d. of Sihon. Josh 13:21*

dulcimer
flute, d. all kinds. Dan 3:5, 10, 15

dull
heart is waxed gross, and ears are d. Mat 13:15; Acts 28:27
utter, seeing ye are d. Heb 5:11

Dumah
sons of Ishmael, D. Massa. Gen 25:14; 1 Chr 1:30

Dumah
D. was in Judah's. Josh 15:52
the burden of D. he. Isa 21:11

dumb
[1] *Unable to speak for want of physical power,* Ex 4:11. [2] *Unable to speak to, and teach others, for lack of grace and knowledge,* Isa 56:10. [3] *Unable to speak for oneself, either through ignorance or fear of those in whose presence one is,* Ps 39:9; Pr 31:8; Dan 10:15.
who maketh the d. or deaf? Ex 4:11
I was as a d. man. Ps 38:13
I was d. with silence. 39:2, 9
open thy mouth for d. Pr 31:8
and the tongue of the d. Isa 35:6
a sheep before shearers is d. 53:7
are blind, all d. dogs. 56:10
be d. and shalt not be. Ezek 3:26
speak, and be no more d. 24:27
and I was no more d. 33:22
face to ground, became d. Dan 10:15
to make him d. idols. Hab 2:18
woe to him that saith to d. stone. 19
brought to him a d. man. Mat 9:32
devil was cast out, the d. spake. 33 Luke 11:14
one blind and d. and he. Mat 12:22
those that were blind, d. 15:30
wondered, when they saw the d. speak, the blind. 31; Mark 7:37
son who hath a d. spirit. Mark 9:17
thou d. spirit, I charge thee. 25
be d. until the day that. Luke 1:20
like a lamb d. before. Acts 8:32
carried away to d. idols. 1 Cor 12:2
the d. ass speaking with. 2 Pet 2:16

dung
By dung is represented any thing that is nauseous or loathsome, Jer 8:2; 9:22; Job 20:7; Phil 3:8.
flesh, skin, and d. burn. Ex 29:14 Lev 4:11; 8:17; 16:27; Num 19:5
a man taketh away d. 1 Ki 14:10
of a cab of doves' d. 2 Ki 6:25
of Jezebel shall be as d. 9:37
eat their own d. 18:27; Isa 36:12
for ever like his own d. Job 20:7
they became as d. Ps 83:10
they shall be for d. on. Jer 8:2
they shall be as d. 16:4
they shall be d. 25:33
bake it with d. that. Ezek 4:12
given thee cow's d. for man's d. 15
flesh shall be as the d. Zeph 1:17
spread d. on your faces, even the d. of your solemn feasts. Mal 2:3
count all things but d. Phil 3:8†

dove's dung, see on **dove**

dung, *verb*
I dig about it, and d. it. Luke 13:8

dungeon
should put me into d. Gen 40:15
Joseph hastily out of d. 41:14
firstborn of captive in d. Ex 12:29
was entered into the d. Jer 37:16
cast him into d. no water in d. 38:6, 9
take up Jeremiah out of the d. 10
down by cords into the d. to. 11
drew up Jeremiah out of d. 13
cut off my life in the d. Lam 3:53
I called on thy name, out of d. 55

dung gate
valley gate to d.-gate. Neh 3:13
the d.-gate repaired Malchiah. 14
company went toward d.-gate. 12:31

dunghill
lifteth up beggar from d. 1 Sam 2:8 Ps 113:7
his house be made a d. Ezra 6:11
straw is trodden for d. Isa 25:10
your houses be made a d. Dan 2:5
their houses shall be made a d. 3:29
unsavoury salt not fit for land or d. Luke 14:35

dunghills
up in scarlet, embrace d. Lam 4:5

Dura
set image up in plain of D. Dan 3:1

durable
yea, d. riches and. Pr 8:18
merchandise shall be for d. Isa 23:18

dureth
not root in himself, d. Mat 13:21

durst
he that d. presume in. Esth 7:5
afraid, I d. not shew. Job 32:6
nor d. ask any more. Mat 22:46 Mark 12:34; Luke 20:40
none of disciples d. ask. John 21:12
and of the rest d. no man. Acts 5:13
Moses trembled and d. not. 7:32
he d. not bring a railing. Jude 9

dust
The Hebrews, when they mourned, put dust or ashes upon their heads, Josh 7:6; Isa 47:1; Lam 3:29. *The dust denotes likewise the grave and death,* Gen 3:19; Job 7:21; Ps 22:15. *The dust represents also a multitude,* Gen 13:16; Num 23:10; Ps 78:27.
d. shalt thou eat all days. Gen 3:14
thou art, and unto d. shalt. 19
if a man can number the d. 13:16
speak to Lord, who am but d. 18:27
say to Aaron, smite the d. Ex 8:16
Aaron smote d. of the earth. 17
become small d. in all the land. 9:9
shall pour out the d. Lev 14:41*
pour out blood, cover it with d. 17:13
can count the d. of Jacob? 23:10
I cast the d. into brook. Deut 9:21 2 Ki 23:12
make rain of thy land d. Deut 28:24
and the elders put d. on. Josh 7:6
Shimei cursed David, and cast d. 2 Sam 16:13
fire of Lord consumed d. 1 Ki 18:38
if the d. of Samaria shall. 20:10
Josiah made d. of the. 2 Chr 34:4
they sprinkled d. upon. Job 2:12
with worms and clods of d. 7:5
wilt bring me into d. again? 10:9
as for the earth, it hath d. of. 28:6
man shall turn again to d. 34:15
d. groweth into hardness. 38:38
repent in d. and ashes. 42:6
brought me into the d. Ps 22:15
shall d. praise thee, shall it? 30:9
his enemies shall lick the d. 72:9
flesh also upon them as d. 78:27
thy servants favour the d. 102:14
remembereth that we are d. 103:14
then shall d. return. Eccl 12:7
their d. shall be made fat. Isa 34:7
the d. thereof shall be turned. 9
who hath comprehended d.? 40:12
lick up the d. of thy feet. 49:23
shake thyself from the d. 52:2
d. shall be the serpent's meat. 65:25
cast d. on their heads. Lam 2:10 Ezek 27:30
to cover it with d. Ezek 24:7
I will also scrape her d. from. 26:4
their d. shall cover thee. 10
that pant after the d. of. Amos 2:7
shall lick the d. like. Mi 7:17
and the clouds are the d. Nah 1:3
for they shall heap d. Hab 1:10
shake off the d. of your. Mat 10:14 Mark 6:11; Luke 9:5
d. of your city we do. Luke 10:11
they shook off the d. Acts 13:51
as they threw d. into the air. 22:23
cast d. on their heads. Rev 18:19

as the **dust**
and make thy seed as the d. of the. Gen 13:16; 28:14; 2 Chr 1:9
calf small as the d. Deut 9:21
I beat them as small as d. 2 Sam 22:43; Ps 18:42
lay up gold as the d. Job 22:24
heap up silver as the d. 27:16
blossom shall go up as d. Isa 5:24

nations *as the* small *d.* of. *Isa* 40:15
he gave them *as the d.* to his. 41:2
blood be poured out *as d. Zeph* 1:17
Tyrus heaped up silver *as the d.* *Zech* 9:3

in the **dust**

foundation is *in the d.* *Job* 4:19
now shall I sleep *in the d.* 7:21
defiled my horn *in the d.* 16:15
rest together is *in the d.* 17:16
lie down with him *in the d.* 20:11
shall lie down alike *in the d.* 21:16
warmeth them *in the d.* 39:14
hide them *in the d.* together. 40:13
lay mine honour *in the d.* *Ps* 7:5
hide thee *in the d.* for fear. *Isa* 2:10
sing, ye that dwell *in the d.* 26:19
come down and sit *in the d.* 47:1
putteth his mouth *in the d. Lam* 3:29
many that sleep *in the d. Dan* 12:2
roll thyself *in the d.* *Mi* 1:10
nobles shall dwell *in the d. Nah* 3:18

like the **dust**

make them *like the d.* *2 Ki* 13:7
thy strangers be *like d.* *Isa* 29:5

of the **dust**

Lord formed man *of the d.* *Gen* 2:7
priest take *of the d.* *Num* 5:17
of serpents *of the d.* *Deut* 32:24
raiseth poor out *of the d. 1 Sam* 2:8 *Ps* 113:7
exalted thee out *of the d. 1 Ki* 16:2
affliction cometh not *of the d. Job* 5:6
things that grow out *of the d.* 14:19
nor highest part *of the d.* *Pr* 8:26
all are *of the d.* *Eccl* 3:20
speech shall be out *of the d. Isa* 29:4

to the **dust**

all that go down *to the d.* *Ps* 22:29
soul is bowed down *to the d.* 44:25
die and return *to* their *d.* 104:29
my soul cleaveth *to the d.* 119:25
d. and all turn *to d.* again. *Eccl* 3:20
bring fortress *to the d.* *Isa* 25:12
the lofty city *to the d.* 26:5

duties

son that doth not those *d. Ezek* 18:11

duty

her *d.* of marriage shall. *Ex* 21:10
perform *d.* of husband's. *Deut* 25:5
will not perform the *d.* of my. 7
d. of every day required. *2 Chr* 8:14 *Ezra* 3:4
this is whole *d.* of man. *Eccl* 12:13
which was our *d.* to do. *Luke* 17:10
their *d.* is to minister. *Rom* 15:27*

dwarf

a *d.* shall not come nigh. *Lev* 21:20

dwell

(*To abide as a resident ; live ; reside. To continue a long time*)
Japhet shall *d.* in tents. *Gen* 9:27
he shall *d.* in the presence 16:12
for he feared to *d.* in Zoar. 19:30
d. where it pleaseth thee. 20:15
Canaanites, amongst whom I *d.* 24:3
land before you, *d.* and trade. 34:10
we will *d.* with you, and. 16
go up to Beth-el, and *d.* there. 35:1
Moses was content to *d.* *Ex* 2:21
d. amongst them. 25:8; 29:46
I will *d.* amongst children of. 29:45
unclean shall *d.* alone. *Lev* 13:46
d. in booths. 23:42, 43; *Neh* 8:14
camps, in the midst whereof I *d.* *Num* 5:3
lo, the people shall *d.* alone. 23:9
our little ones shall *d.* in. 32:17
give to the Levites, cities to *d.* in. 35:2, 3; *Josh* 14:4; 21:2
Lord *d.* among children. *Num* 35:34
to cause his name to *d.* there. *Deut* 12:11; *Ezra* 6:12
servant escaped shall *d. Deut* 23:16
he shall *d.* between his. 33:12
ye *d.* among us. *Josh* 9:7, 22
he shall *d.* in that city. 20:6
cities ye built not, and ye *d.* 24:13
Gaal should not *d.* in. *Judg* 9:41
Micah said to Levite, *d.* with. 17:10
that I may *d.* there, why should thy servant *d.* in the ? *1 Sam* 27:5
d. among children of. *1 Ki* 6:13
would *d.* in thick darkness. 8:12 *2 Chr* 6:1
to Zarephath, and *d.* there. *1 Ki* 17:9
I *d.* among own people. *2 Ki* 4:13
let them go and *d.* there. 17:27
let a cloud *d.* upon it. *Job* 3:5
let not wickedness *d.* in thy. 11:14
shall *d.* in his tabernacle. 18:15
to *d.* in the clifts of the. 30:6
neither evil *d.* with thee. *Ps* 5:4*
who shall *d.* in thy holy hill ? 15:1
his soul shall *d.* at ease. 25:13
depart from evil, and *d.* 37:27
that he may *d.* in thy courts. 65:4
they that *d.* in uttermost parts. 8
hill which God desireth to *d.* in, yea the Lord will *d.* in it. 68:16
Lord might *d.* among them. 18
build Judah that they may *d.* 69:35
they that *d.* in the wilderness. 72:9
and made Israel to *d.* in. 78:55
d. in tents of wickedness. 84:10
faithful, that they may *d.* with. 101:6
they found no city to *d.* in. 107:4
he maketh the hungry to *d.* 36
that I *d.* in tents of Kedar. 120:5
will I *d.* for I have desired it. 132:14
if I *d.* in uttermost parts of. 139:9
upright shall *d.* in thy. 140:13
made me to *d.* in darkness. 143:3
hearkeneth to me shall *d.* *Pr* 1:33
I wisdom *d.* with prudence. 8:12
it is better to *d.* in wilderness. 21:19
I *d.* in midst of a people. *Isa* 6:5
the wolf shall *d.* with the. 11:6
owls shall *d.* there, satyrs. 13:21
let mine outcasts *d.* with thee. 16:4
merchandise for them that *d.* 23:18
that *d.* therein are desolate. 24:6
bringeth down them that *d.* on. 26:5
awake and sing, ye that *d.* 19
people *d.* in Zion at Jerusalem. 30:19
then judgement shall *d.* in. 32:16
people *d.* in peaceful habitation. 18
who shall *d.* with devouring fire ? who *d.* with everlasting ? 33:14
he shall *d.* on high. 16
the people that *d.* therein. 24
owl and the raven shall *d.* 34:11
them out as a tent to *d.* in. 40:22
give place that I may *d.* 49:20
restorer of paths to *d.* in. 58:12
and my servants shall *d.* there. 65:9
Shemaiah shall not have a man to *d.* *Jer* 29:32
shall *d.* in Judah husbandmen. 31:24
all your days ye shall *d.* in. 35:7
and *d.* with him among. 40:5
d. at Mizpah to serve Chaldeans. 10
into Egypt, and there *d.* 42:14
a desire to return to *d.* there. 44:14
flee ye, *d.* deep, O inhabitants. 49:8
nor a son of man *d.* 18*, 33*; 50:40*
which *d.* alone. 49:31
that *d.* in midst of them. 51:1
dost *d.* among scorpions. *Ezek* 2:6
and her daughters *d.* at left. 16:46
where I will *d.* in midst of Israel for. 43:7, 9; *Zech* 2:10, 11
I will make thee to *d.* in. *Hos* 12:9
they that *d.* under his shadow. 14:7
but Judah shall *d.* for ever. *Joel* 3:20
be taken out that *d.* in. *Amos* 3:12*
thou shalt *d.* in the field. *Mi* 4:10
the flock which *d.* solitarily. 7:14
thy nobles *d.* in dust. *Nah* 3:18*
to *d.* in cieled houses ? *Hag* 1:4
old men and women shall *d.* in. *Zech* 8:4
a bastard shall *d.* in Ashdod. 9:6
and men shall *d.* in it. 14:11
enter in and *d.* there. *Mat* 12:45 *Luke* 11:26
as a snare shall it come on all that *d.* *Luke* 21:35; *Acts* 17:26
into land wherein ye *d.* *Acts* 7:4
Paul was suffered to *d.* by. 28:16
Spirit of God *d.* in you. *Rom* 8:9, 11
and she be pleased to *d. 1 Cor* 7:12
God hath said, I will *d.* *2 Cor* 6:16
Christ may *d.* in your. *Eph* 3:17
in him should all fulness *d. Col* 1:19
word of Christ *d.* in you richly. 3:16
likewise, ye husbands, *d.* *1 Pet* 3:7
know we that we *d.* in. *1 John* 4:13
on the throne shall *d.* *Rev* 7:15*
heavens, and ye that *d.* in. 12:12
against them that *d.* in heaven. 13:6
men, and he will *d.* with them. 21:3

dwell with *earth*

will God *d.* on *earth* ? *1 Ki* 8:27 *2 Chr* 6:18
languages, that *d.* in all the *earth.* *Dan* 4:1; 6:25
try them that *d.* on *earth. Rev* 3:10
avenge on them that *d.* on *earth.* 6:10
they that *d.* on the *earth.* 11:10
all that *d.* on the *earth* shall. 13:8
deceiveth them that *d.* on *earth.* 14
preach to them that *d.* on *earth.* 14:6
they that *d.* on the *earth.* 17:8

dwell with *house*

build an *house,* and not *d.* therein. *Deut* 28:30; *Amos* 5:11
I *d.* in a *house* of cedar. *2 Sam* 7:2 *1 Chr* 17:1
shall build me an *house* to *d.* in. *2 Sam* 7:5; *1 Chr* 17:1
build *house* in Jerusalem and *d.* *1 Ki* 2:36
this woman *d.* in one *house.* 3:17
surely built thee *house* to *d.* in. 8:13
not *d.* in *house* of David. *2 Chr* 8:11
that *d.* in *houses* of clay. *Job* 4:19
they that *d.* in my *house.* 19:15
will *d.* in the *house* of the. *Ps* 23:6
that I may *d.* in the *house* of. 27:4
blessed that *d.* in thy *house.* 84:4
worketh deceit, shall not *d.* in my *house.* 101:7
better *d.* in the corner of a *house.* *Pr* 21:9; 25:24
d. in thy *house* go to. *Jer* 20:6
build ye *houses, d.* in them. 29:5, 28
not to build *houses* for us to *d.* 35:9

dwell with *Jerusalem*

d. in *Jerusalem* for ever. *1 Chr* 23:25
of ten to *d.* in *Jerusalem. Neh* 11:1
offered to *d.* at *Jerusalem.* 2
Jerusalem shall *d.* safely. *Jer* 33:16
for fear we *d.* at *Jerusalem.* 35:11
d. in midst of *Jerusalem.* *Zech* 8:3
d. in the midst of *Jerusalem.* 8
all ye that *d.* at *Jerusalem. Acts* 2:14
all them that *d.* in *Jerusalem.* 4:16
they that *d.* at *Jerusalem.* 13:27

dwell with *land*

Canaanites in whose *land* I *d.* *Gen* 24:37
d. in the *land* which I shall. 26:2
let them *d.* in the *land.* 34:21
and thou shalt *d.* in *land.* 45:10
may *d.* in the *land* of Goshen. 46:34
in *land* of Goshen let them *d.* 47:6
land of Goshen, in which my people *d.* *Ex* 8:22
they shall not *d.* in thy *land.* 23:33
ye shall *d.* in the *land.* *Lev* 25:18
shall eat and *d.* in your *land.* 26:5
what the *land* is they *d. Num* 13:19
defile not *land* wherein I *d.* 35:34
d. in the *land* which the Lord giveth. *Deut* 12:10
d. in the *land* Lord sware. 30:20
but the Canaanites would *d.* in that *land.* *Josh* 17:12; *Judg* 1:27
the gods in whose *land* ye *d.* *Josh* 24:15; *Judg* 6:10
fear not, *d.* in *land.* *2 Ki* 25:24 *Jer* 25:5; 40:9
so shalt thou *d.* in the *land. Ps* 37:3
rebellious *d.* in a dry *land.* 68:6
glory may *d.* in our *land.* 85:9
upright shall *d.* in *land.* *Pr* 2:21
d. in *land* of shadow. *Isa* 9:2
d. in their own *land. Jer* 23:8; 27:11
that *d.* in the *land* of Egypt. 24:8 44:1, 8, 13, 26
ye shall *d.* in the *land.* 35:15 *Ezek* 36:28; 37:25
we will not *d.* in this *land. Jer* 42:13
to *d.* in the *land* of Judah. 43:4, 5*
land desolate, none shall *d.* 50:3
then *d.* in their *land.* *Ezek* 28:25
people that *d.* in midst of *land.* 38:12
not *d.* in Lord's *land.* *Hos* 9:3

violence of *land*, and all that *d*. *Hab* 2:8, 17
riddance of all that *d*. in the *land*. *Zeph* 1:18

dwell with *place*

place thou hast made to *d*. *Ex* 15:17
made them to *d*. in this *place*. *1 Sam* 12:8
may *d*. in a *place* of. *2 Sam* 7:10
place where we *d*. is. *2 Ki* 6:1
make us a *place* where we may *d*. 2
shall *d*. in their *place*. *1 Chr* 17:9
d. in high and holy *place*. *Isa* 57:15
I will cause you to *d*. in this *place*. *Jer* 7:3, 7

dwell *safely*

hearkeneth to me shall *d*. *safely*. *Pr* 1:33
Israel shall *d*. *safely*. *Jer* 23:6
Ezek 28:26; 34:25, 28; 38:8
cause them to *d*. *safely*. *Jer* 32:37
at rest that *d*. *safely*. *Ezek* 38:11

dwell *in safety*

and ye shall *d*. in the land *in safety*. *Lev* 25:18, 19; *Deut* 12:10
of Lord *d*. *in safety*. *Deut* 33:12
Israel shall *d*. *in safety* alone. 28
makest me to *d*. *in safety*. *Ps* 4:8

dwell *therein*

enemies which *d*. *therein*. *Lev* 27:32
land I sware to make you *d*. *therein*. *Num* 14:30
shall *d*. *therein*. 33:53; *Deut* 11:31
world and they that *d*. *therein*. *Ps* 24:1
righteous shall *d*. *therein*. 37:29
love his name shall *d*. *therein*. 69:36
for wickedness of them that *d*. *therein*. 107:34; *Jer* 12:4
that *d*. *therein* are desolate. *Isa* 24:6; *Amos* 9:5
people that *d*. *therein* are. *Isa* 33:24
to generation shall *d*. *therein*. 34:17
they that *d*. *therein* shall die. 51:6
not a man *d*. *therein*. *Jer* 4:29
the city, all that *d*. *therein*. 8:16
wickedness of them that *d*. *therein*. 12:4
land and them that *d*. *therein*. 47:2
desolate without any to *d*. *therein*. 48:9
and the owls shall *d*. *therein*. 50:39
violence of them that *d*. *therein*. *Ezek* 12:19
smite them that *d*. *therein*. 32:15
they and children *d*. *therein*. 37:25
desolate, because of them that *d*. *therein*. *Mi* 7:13
world is burnt, and all that *d*. *therein*. *Nah* 1:5
his habitation, let no man *d*. *therein*. *Acts* 1:20

dwell *together*

d. *together*, their substance . . . they could not *d*. *together*. *Gen* 13:6
more than might *d*. *together*. 36:7
if brethren *d*. *together*. *Deut* 25:5
for brethren to *d*. *together*. *Ps* 133:1

dwelled

the Perizzite *d*. then in. *Gen* 13:7
Abram *d*. in the land of Canaan, Lot *d*. in the cities of the plain. 12
Abraham *d*. between Kadesh. 20:1
d. there about ten years. *Ruth* 1:4
delivered you, ye *d*. *1 Sam* 12:11

dwellers

ye *d*. on earth, see ye. *Isa* 18:3
it was known to the *d*. *Acts* 1:19
the *d*. in Mesopotamia. 2:9

dwellest

succeedest them and *d*. *Deut* 12:29
God of Israel, which *d*. between. *2 Ki* 19:15*; *Ps* 80:1*; *Isa* 37:16*
O thou that *d*. in the. *Ps* 123:1*
thou that *d*. in gardens. *S of S* 8:13
O my people that *d*. in. *Isa* 10:24
hear now this, thou that *d*. 47:8
thou that *d*. in the clefts. *Jer* 49:16 *Ob* 3
that *d*. upon many waters. *Jer* 51:13
of Edom, that *d*. in land. *Lam* 4:21
thou that *d*. in the land. *Ezek* 7:7
d. in the midst of rebellious. 12:2
that *d*. with the daughter. *Zech* 2:7
Master, where *d*. thou? *John* 1:38
works, and where thou *d*. *Rev* 2:13

dwelleth

stranger that *d*. with you. *Lev* 19:34*
brother that *d*. by thee be. 25:39, 47
God *d*. as a lion. *Deut* 33:20
Rahab *d*. in Israel. *Josh* 6:25
wherein Lord's tabernacle *d*. 22:19
covenant of Lord, who *d*. *1 Sam* 4:4* *2 Sam* 6:2*; *1 Chr* 13:6*
ark *d*. within curtains. *2 Sam* 7:2
he *d*. in desolate cities. *Job* 15:28
where is way where light *d*.? 38:19
she *d*. and abideth on rock. 39:28
to the Lord who *d*. in Zion. *Ps* 9:11
place where thine honour *d*. 26:8
d. in secret place of most High. 91:1
Lord our God who *d*. on high? 113:5
blessed be the Lord who *d*. 135:21
seeing he *d*. securely. *Pr* 3:29
Lord, who *d*. in mount. *Isa* 8:18
Lord is exalted, for he *d*. on. 33:5
desolation, and no man *d*. *Jer* 44:2
wealthy nation that *d*. without. 49:31
she *d*. among the heathen. *Lam* 1:3
younger sister *d*. at right. *Ezek* 16:46
where king *d*. that made him. 17:16
and the light *d*. with him. *Dan* 2:22
land shall mourn, every one that *d*. therein. *Hos* 4:3; *Amos* 8:8
the Lord *d*. in Zion. *Joel* 3:21
sweareth by it and him that *d*. *Mat* 23:21
drinketh my blood, *d*. in. *John* 6:56
the Father that *d*. in me. 14:10
the Spirit, for he *d*. in you. 17
d. not in temples made with hands. *Acts* 7:48; 17:24
more I, but sin that *d*. *Rom* 7:17, 20
I know that in my flesh *d*. no. 18
by his Spirit that *d*. in you. 8:11
that Spirit of God *d*. in. *1 Cor* 3:16
d. fulness of Godhead. *Col* 2:9
Holy Ghost which *d*. in. *2 Tim* 1:14
spirit that *d*. in us lusteth. *Jas* 4:5
a new earth wherein *d*. *2 Pet* 3:13
how *d*. the love of God? *1 John* 3:17
keepeth his commandments, *d*. 24
love one another, God *d*. in. 4:12
Jesus is Son of God, God *d*. in. 15
he that *d*. in love, *d*. in God. 16
truth's sake which *d*. in us. *2 John* 2
among you, where Satan *d*. *Rev* 2:13

dwelling, *substantive*

d. shall be the fatness. *Gen* 27:39
at beginning of their *d*. *2 Ki* 17:25
built a place for thy *d*. *2 Chr* 6:2
in grave from their *d*. *Ps* 49:14
any plague come nigh thy *d*. 91:10
there is oil in the *d*. of. *Pr* 21:20
lay not wait against the *d*. 24:15
Hazor shall be a *d*. for. *Jer* 49:33
gods, whose *d*. is not. *Dan* 2:11
thy *d*. be with beasts. 4:25, 32; 5:21
where is the *d*. of lions? *Nah* 2:11
his *d*. among the tombs. *Mark* 5:3

dwelling

Jacob a plain man, *d*. in. *Gen* 25:27
any man sell a *d*. house. *Lev* 25:29
strong is thy *d*. place. *Num* 24:21
hear in heaven thy *d*. place. *1 Ki* 8:30
39, 43, 49; *2 Chr* 6:21, 30, 39
their prayer came up to his holy *d*. *2 Chr* 30:27
Lord hath compassion on *d*. 36:15
the *d*. place of the wicked. *Job* 8:22
are *d*. places of wicked? 21:28
d. places to all generations. *Ps* 49:11
pluck thee out of thy *d*. 52:5
by casting down the *d*. place. 74:7
Salem his tabernacle, his *d*. 76:2
have laid waste his *d*. place. 79:7
Lord, thou hast been our *d*. 90:1
Lord will create on every *d*. *Isa* 4:5
I will consider in my *d*. place. 18:4
I will have mercy on his *d*. *Jer* 30:18
O thou daughter *d*. in Egypt. 46:19
have burnt their *d*. places. 51:30
Babylon shall become a *d*. place. 37
all your *d*. places the cities. *Ezek* 6:6
save them out of all *d*. *Ezek* 37:23
all of them *d*. without walls. 38:11
Lord your God *d*. in Zion. *Joel* 3:17
to possess the *d*. places. *Hab* 1:6
their *d*. should not be cut. *Zeph* 3:7
were *d*. at Jerusalem. *Acts* 2:5
known to the Greeks, *d*. at. 19:17
have no certain *d*. place. *1 Cor* 4:11
d. in the light no man. *1 Tim* 6:16
d. in tabernacles with. *Heb* 11:9
Lot, that righteous man, *d*. *2 Pet* 2:8

dwellings

of Israel had light in *d*. *Ex* 10:23
perpetual statute throughout your *d*. *Lev* 3:17; 23:14; *Num* 35:29
no blood in any of your *d*. *Lev* 7:26
do no work in all your *d*. 23:3, 31
have any remaining in *d*. *Job* 18:19*
surely such are the *d*. of the. 21
made the barren land his *d*. 39:6
wickedness is in their *d*. *Ps* 55:15
more than all the *d*. of Jacob. 87:2
people dwell in sure *d*. *Isa* 32:18
our *d*. have cast us out. *Jer* 9:19
men of east make their *d*. *Ezek* 25:4
sea coast shall be *d*. *Zeph* 2:6*

dwelt

and they *d*. there. *Gen* 11:2, 31
26:17; *2 Ki* 16:6; *1 Chr* 4:43 *2 Chr* 28:18
d. among children of. *Gen* 23:10*
of Egypt wherein ye *d*. *Lev* 18:3
wherein they *d*. *Num* 31:10 *2 Ki* 17:29
d. an old prophet. *1 Ki* 13:11, 25
and I *d*. as a king in. *Job* 29:25
Zion wherein thou hast *d*. *Ps* 74:2
Ariel, city where David *d*. *Isa* 29:1*
a land where no man *d*. *Jer* 2:6
Jeremiah *d*. among people. 39:14
d. by the river of Chebar. *Ezek* 3:15
under shadow *d*. great. 31:6, 17
lands wherein your fathers *d*. 37:25
which beasts of field *d*. *Dan* 4:21
rejoicing city that *d*. *Zeph* 2:15
fear came on all that *d*. *Luke* 1:65
Word was made flesh and *d*. *John* 1:14
came and saw where he *d*. 39
they *d*. as strangers. *Acts* 13:17*
good report of all that *d*. 22:12
Paul *d*. two years in his own. 28:30
tormented them that *d*. *Rev* 11:10

dwelt *at*

and Abraham *d*. *at* Beer-sheba. *Gen* 22:19
Amorites which *d*. *at* Heshbon. *Num* 21:34; *Deut* 3:2
Abimelech *d*. *at* Arumah. *Judg* 9:41
Ben-hadad *d*. *at* Damascus. *1 Ki* 15:18; *2 Chr* 16:2
Sennacherib *d*. *at* Nineveh. *2 Ki* 19:36; *Isa* 37:37
of the scribes which *d*. *at*. *1 Chr* 2:55
of Levites *d*. *at* Jerusalem. 9:34
Saul confounded Jews that *d*. *at*. *Acts* 9:22
Peter came to saints who *d*. *at*. 32

dwelt *in*

we have *d*. *in* Egypt. *Num* 20:15
Israel *d*. *in* the land of the. 21:31
d. *in* their stead. *Deut* 2:12, 21, 22 23; *1 Chr* 5:22
good will of him that *d*. *in*. *Deut* 33:16
way of them that *d*. *in*. *Judg* 8:11
Jerubbaal went and *d*. *in* his. 29
and Samuel *d*. *in*. *1 Sam* 19:18
Philistines came and *d*. *in* them. 31:7; *1 Chr* 10:7
I have not *d*. *in* any house since I brought. *2 Sam* 7:6; *1 Chr* 17:5
that *d*. *in* house of Ziba. *2 Sam* 9:12
Absalom *d*. two full years *in*. 14:28
Shimei *d*. *in* Jerusalem. *1 Ki* 2:28
Jeroboam fled from Solomon, *d*. *in* Egypt. 12:2
Israel *d*. *in* their tents. *2 Ki* 13:5
Ahaziah *d*. *in* a. 15:5; *2 Chr* 26:21
Huldah the prophetess *d*. *in* Jerusalem. *2 Ki* 22:14; *2 Chr* 34:22
and *d*. *in* their rooms. *1 Chr* 4:41
Hagarites fell, and they *d*. *in*. 5:10
chief men *d*. *in* Jerusalem. 8:28

and David d. in the castle. 1 Chr 11:7
2 Sam 5:9
priests, Levites, and Nethinims, d. in. Ezra 2:70; Neh 3:26; 11:21
Nethinims and all Israel d. in their. Neh 7:73
honourable men d. in it. Job 22:8
my soul had almost d. in. Ps 94:17
nor shall it be d. in from generation. Isa 13:20; Jer 50:39
but we have d. in tents. Jer 35:10
they d. in the habitation. 41:17
Israel d. in their own. Ezek 36:17
when d. safely in their land. 39:26
fowls of the heaven d. in. Dan 4:12
Joseph d. in a city called. Mat 2:23
Jesus d. in Capernaum. 4:13
sinners above all d. in. Luke 13:4
Abraham d. in Charran. Acts 7:2, 4
all they who d. in Asia heard. 19:10
faith which d. first in thy grandmother Lois. 2 Tim 1:5

dwelt *therein*

gave Gilead to Machir, he d. therein. Num 32:40
Enims d. therein. Deut 2:10
giants d. therein in old time. 20
Damascus and d. therein. 1 Ki 11:24
built Shechem, and d. therein. 12:25
there d. men of Tyre also therein. Neh 13:16
thy congregation hath d. therein. Ps 68:10

dwelt *with*

and Ruth d. with her. Ruth 2:23
and mother d. with. 1 Sam 22:4
there they d. with king. 1 Chr 4:23
d. with their brethren. 8:32; 9:38
my soul hath long d. with. Ps 120:6
Jeremiah d. with him. Jer 40:6

dyed

rams' skins d. red. Ex 25:5; 26:14
35:7; 36:19; 39:34
cometh with d. garments. Isa 63:1
exceeding in d. attire. Ezek 23:15

dying

be consumed with d.? Num 17:13*
the first, d. left no seed. Mark 12:20
Jairus' daughter lay a d. Luke 8:42
bearing in body the d. of. 2 Cor 4:10
as d. and behold we live. 6:9
by faith, Jacob when d. Heb 11:21

E

each

Abram laid e. piece. Gen 15:10
Simeon and Levi took e. 34:25
e. man his dream. 40:5
e. changes of raiment. 45:22
asked e. other of their. Ex 18:7
of e. there be a like weight. 30:34
e. one was for house of. Num 1:44
they brought for e. one an ox. 7:3
thou also and Aaron e. of you. 16:17
of e. chief house a prince, e. one. Josh 22:14
e. one resembled children. Judg 8:18
we reserved not to e. man. 21:22
they may find rest e. of you. Ruth 1:9
e. man his month in year. 1 Ki 4:7
and the kings e. sat on. 22:10
exacted of e. man fifty. 2 Ki 15:20
and peace kissed e. other. Ps 85:10
they made e. one for. Isa 2:20
stood the seraphims, e. one. 6:2
where e. lay, shall be grass. 35:7
e. one walking in uprightness. 57:2
appointed thee e. day for. Ezek 4:6
doth not e. on sabbath. Luke 13:15
cloven tongues sat upon e. Acts 2:3
let e. esteem other better. Phil 2:3
charity toward e. other. 2 Thes 1:3
four beasts had e. of them. Rev 4:8

eagle

At least eight distinct kinds of eagles and vultures have been observed in Palestine. The Hebrew word nesher *is used almost entirely in the Bible for eagle, and it is impossible to determine exactly which is intended. Most probably it is the general term for any eagle, as it merely means a tearer with the beak.*

Most frequently in the Bible the reference is to some characteristic of the eagle, and is made as a vivid expression of some quality in that which is compared to it. Among these are its swiftness of flight, Deut 28:49; Pr 23:5; *its strength of wing,* Pr 30:19; Ezek 17:3; *its eating of carrion,* Mat 24:28 *(this is true only of the vultures); the building of its nest high on the mountain cliff,* Jer 49:16; *the baldness of one variety,* Mi 1:16. *There is also reference to the ancient belief that at the end of a certain period the eagle moults and by some unknown means renews its youth,* Ps 103:5; *probably derived from the extreme length of the eagle's vigorous life. The custom of carrying its young from the inaccessible cliffs on its broad wings is also made a symbol for the deliverance of the Israelites,* Ex 19:4.

have e. in abomination. Lev 11:13
Deut 14:12
a nation as swift as e. Deut 28:49
as an e. stirreth up her nest. 32:11
as the e. that hasteth. Job 9:26
doth the e. mount up at thy? 39:27
riches fly away as an e. Pr 23:5
the way of an e. in the air. 30:19
fly as an e. over Moab. Jer 48:40
make thy nest high as e. 49:16
four also had the face of an e. Ezek 1:10; 10:14
a great e. with great wings. 17:3, 7
grown like e. feathers. Dan 4:33
like a lion, and had e. wings. 7:4
as an e. against the house. Hos 8:1
though thou exalt thyself as e. Ob 4
enlarge thy baldness as e. Mi 1:16
Chaldeans shall fly as e. Hab 1:8
beast was like a flying e. Rev 4:7
were given wings of great e. 12:14

eagles

I bare you on e'. wings. Ex 19:4
were swifter than e. 2 Sam 1:23
thy youth is renewed like e. Ps 103:5
and the young e. shall. Pr 30:17
mount up with wings as e. Isa 40:31
horses are swifter than e. Jer 4:13
persecutors swifter than e. Lam 4:19
there will e. be gathered. Mat 24:28
Luke 17:37

ear

(The use of the word ear *in the Bible is used most often as attention, hearing, etc., rather than of the actual physical ear. To have the ears heavy is to pay no attention; to open the ear is to pay attention; uncircumcised ears are those which are deaf to the word of God. To tell something in the ear, is to speak in secret)*

master shall bore his e. Ex 21:6
Deut 15:17
hath told Samuel in e. 1 Sam 9:15*
bow down thine e. 2 Ki 19:16
Ps 31:2; 86:1
let thine e. be attentive. Neh 1:6, 11
mine e. received a little. Job 4:12
doth not the e. try? 12:11; 34:3
mine e. hath heard and. 13:1
when the e. heard me. 29:11
to me men gave e. waited. 21
behold, I gave e. to. 32:11*
he openeth also their e. 36:10
of thee by hearing of the e. 42:5
wilt cause thine e. to hear. Ps 10:17
bow down thine e. to me. 31:2
deaf adder, that stoppeth her e. 58:4
unto God, and he gave e. 77:1
he that planted the e. 94:9
because he hath inclined e. 116:2
and bow thine e. to my. Pr 5:1
nor inclined my e. to them. 13
the e. that heareth the. 15:31
and a liar giveth e. to a. 17:4
e. of the wise seeketh. 18:15
hearing e. the seeing eye. Pr 20:12
bow thine e. hear the words. 22:17
a wise reprover on obedient e. 25:12
that turneth away his e. from. 28:9
nor is the e. filled. Eccl 1:8
thine e. was not opened. Isa 48:8
he wakeneth my e. to hear. 50:4
Lord hath opened mine e. 5
nor is his e. heavy that it. 59:1
not heard, nor perceived by e. 64:4
behold, their e. is. Jer 6:10
not, nor inclined e. 7:24, 26; 11:8
17:23; 25:4; 34:14; 44:5
let your e. receive the word. 9:20
ye have not inclined your e. 35:15
hide not thine e. at my. Lam 3:56
from lion a piece of an e. Amos 3:12
what ye hear in the e. Mat 10:27
smote off his e. 26:51; Mark 14:47
ye have spoken in e. Luke 12:3
and he touched his e. 22:51
servant, whose e. Peter. John 18:26
not seen, nor e. heard. 1 Cor 2:9
if e. shall say, because I am. 12:16
he that hath an e. let. Rev 2:7, 11
17, 29; 3:6, 13, 22; 13:9

give **ear**

if wilt give e. to his. Ex 15:26
Lord would not hearken nor give e. Deut 1:45; 2 Chr 24:19; Neh 9:30
give e. O heavens. Deut 32:1
O ye kings, give e. O. Judg 5:3
give e. to me, ye that. Job 34:2
give e. to my words. Ps 5:1; 54:2
give e. unto my prayer. 17:1; 55:1
86:6
give e. to my cry. 39:12; 141:1
give e. all ye inhabitants. 49:1
give e. O my people. 78:1
give e. shepherd. 80:1
hear my prayer, give e. 84:8
give e. to my supplications. 143:1
give e. O earth, for the. Isa 1:2
give e. to law of our God. 10
give e. all ye of far countries. 8:9
give ye e. and hear my voice. 28:23
careless daughters, give e. to. 32:9
who among you will give e.? 42:23
hearken and give e. to me. 51:4
give e. be not proud. Jer 13:15
and give ye e. O house of. Hos 5:1
give e. all ye inhabitants. Joel 1:2

incline **ear**

incline thine e. to me. Ps 17:6
71:2; 88:2; Isa 37:17; Dan 9:18
consider, and incline thine e. Ps 45:10
I will incline mine e. to a. 49:4
thou incline thine e. to. Pr 2:2
my son, incline thine e. 4:20
incline your e. and come. Isa 55:3

right **ear**

upon tip of right e. of. Ex 29:20
Lev 8:23, 24; 14:14, 17, 25, 28
one cut off his right e. Luke 22:50
John 18:10

ear, *grain*

for barley was in the e. Ex 9:31
e. the full corn in the e. Mark 4:28

ear, *verb*

(An old word for plow *or* till)
king will set them to e. 1 Sam 8:12*
oxen that e. the ground. Isa 30:24*

eared

rough valley neither e. Deut 21:4*

earing

neither e. nor harvest. Gen 45:6*
in e. time and harvest. Ex 34:21*

early

ye shall rise e. and go. Gen 19:2
fearful, let him depart e. Judg 7:3
to-morrow get you e. on your. 19:9
man of God was risen e. 2 Ki 6:15
help her, and that right e. Ps 46:5
myself will awake e. 57:8; 108:2
my God, e. will I seek thee. 63:1†
and enquired e. after God. 78:34
O satisfy us e. with thy. 90:14
I will e. destroy all the. 101:8
they shall seek me e. Pr 1:28*
those that seek me e. shall. 8:17*
let us get up e. to the. S of S 7:12
will I seek thee e. Isa 26:9†

in affliction seek me e. *Hos* 5:15*
and as the e. dew it. 6:4; 13:3
women who were e. at. *Luke* 24:22
Jesus to hall, it was e. *John* 18:28
cometh Mary Magdalene e. 20:1
receive the e. and latter. *Jas* 5:7
see **arose, rise, risen, rising, rose, morning**

earnest

(*The word used as a noun means a pledge; as an adjective or adverb, eager, sincere, serious, etc.*)

e. expectation of the. *Rom* 8:19
hath given the e. of the Spirit. *2 Cor* 1:22; 5:5
he told us your e. desire. 7:7*
put same e. care into Titus. 8:16
the e. of our inheritance. *Eph* 1:14
e. expectation and hope. *Phil* 1:20
ought to give the more e. *Heb* 2:1

earnestly

did I not e. send to? *Num* 22:37
David e. asked leave of me. *1 Sam* 20:6, 28
Baruch e. repaired the. *Neh* 3:20
as a servant e. desireth. *Job* 7:2
for I e. protested to. *Jer* 11:7
I do e. remember him still. 31:20
do evil with both hands e. *Mi* 7:3*
agony prayed more e. *Luke* 22:44
but a certain maid e. looked. 56*
why look ye so e. on us? *Acts* 3:12*
Paul e. beholding council. 23:1*
but covet e. best gifts. *1 Cor* 12:31
in this we groan, e. *2 Cor* 5:2*
Elias prayed e. that. *Jas* 5:17*
that ye should e. contend. *Jude* 3

earneth

he that e. wages, e. to. *Hag* 1:6

earring

the man took a golden e. *Gen* 24:22*
when Laban saw e. and. 30
I put the e. upon her face. 47*
gave Job an e. of gold. *Job* 42:11*
as an e. of gold. *Pr* 25:12

earrings

gave to Jacob all their e. *Gen* 35:4*
break off the golden e. *Ex* 32:2*
brought e. for their offerings. 35:22
we have brought e. to. *Num* 31:50
give every man the e. *Judg* 8:24
Lord will take away e. *Isa* 3:20*
I put e. in thine ears. *Ezek* 16:12
decked herself with her e. *Hos* 2:13

ears

a word in my lord's e. *Gen* 44:18
in the e. of Pharaoh. 50:4
tell it in e. of thy son. *Ex* 10:2
rehearse it in e. of Joshua. 17:14
for ye have wept in e. *Num* 11:18
Moses spake in the e. *Deut* 31:30
declare cause in the e. of. *Josh* 20:4
in the e. of the men of. *Judg* 9:2, 3
the e. of every one that heareth shall. *1 Sam* 3:11; *2 Ki* 21:12; *Jer* 19:3
rehearseth them in e. of. *1 Sam* 8:21
according to all we have heard with our e. *2 Sam* 7:22; *1 Chr* 17:20
cry did enter into his e. *2 Sam* 22:7
sound is in his e. in. *Job* 15:21
the fame thereof with our e. 28:22
he openeth the e. of men. 33:16
cry came even into his e. *Ps* 18:6
and his e. are opened to. 34:15
we have heard with our e. 44:1
e. but hear not. 115:6; 135:17
whoso stoppeth his e. at. *Pr* 21:13
speak not in the e. of a fool. 23:9
that taketh a dog by e. 26:17
after the hearing of his e. *Isa* 11:3
the e. of them that hear. 32:3
that stoppeth his e. from. 33:15
e. of deaf shall be unstopped. 35:5
opening the e. but he heareth not. 42:20
blind and deaf that have e. 43:8
go, and cry in the e. of. *Jer* 2:2
people, which have e. and. 5:21
Zephaniah read in the e. of. 29:29
sit down and read it in our e. 36:15
Jehudi read it in the e. of. 21
come to governor's e. *Mat* 28:14
put his fingers into his e. *Mark* 7:33
straightway his e. were opened. 35
having e. hear ye not? 8:18
in heart and e. resist. *Acts* 7:51
tidings came to the e. of. 11:22
strange things to our e. 17:20
hath given e. that they. *Rom* 11:8
having itching e. *2 Tim* 4:3
are entered into e. of Lord. *Jas* 5:4
and his e. are open to. *1 Pet* 3:12

ears *to hear*

not given you e. *to hear.* *Deut* 29:4
they have e. *to hear.* *Ezek* 12:2
he that hath e. *to hear.* *Mat* 11:15
13:9, 43; *Mark* 4:9, 23; 7:16
Luke 8:8; 14:35

mine **ears**

spoken in *mine* e. I will. *Num* 14:28
thou spakest of in *mine* e. *Judg* 17:2
of sheep in mine e.? *1 Sam* 15:14
tumult come into *mine* e. *2 Ki* 19:28; *Isa* 37:29
and *mine* e. attent to. *2 Chr* 7:15
mine e. hast thou opened. *Ps* 40:6
mine e. hear my desire of. 92:11
in *mine* e. said the Lord. *Isa* 5:9
it was revealed in *mine* e. 22:14
cry in *mine* e. with loud. *Ezek* 8:18
cried also in *mine* e. with loud. 9:1
thy salutation sounded in *mine* e. *Luke* 1:44

ears *of the people*

speak now in e. *of the people.* *Ex* 11:2
spake in e. *of the people.* *Deut* 32:44
proclaim in the e. *of the people.* *Judg* 7:3
tidings in the e. *of the people.* *1 Sam* 11:4
talk not in the e. *of the people.* *2 Ki* 18:26; *Isa* 36:11
e. *of the people* were attentive. *Neh* 8:3
read in e. *of the people.* *Jer* 28:7
36:6, 10, 13, 14

their **ears**

these things in *their* e. *Gen* 20:8
earrings which were in *their* e. 35:4
brake off earrings in *their* e. *Ex* 32:3
these words in *their* e. *Deut* 31:28
read in *their* e. *2 Ki* 23:2
2 Chr 34:30; *Jer* 36:15
he openeth *their* e. in. *Job* 36:15
make heart fat, *their* e. heavy, lest they hear with *their* e. *Isa* 6:10
Mat 13:15; *Acts* 28:27
their e. shall be deaf. *Mi* 7:16
but they stopped *their* e. *Zech* 7:11
Acts 7:57
away *their* e. from truth. *2 Tim* 4:4

thine **ears**

let *thine* e. be attent. *2 Chr* 6:40
wilt cause *thine* e. to. *Ps* 10:17
let *thine* e. be attentive to. 130:2
apply *thine* e. to words. *Pr* 23:12
thine e. hear a word. *Isa* 30:21
children say again in *thine* e. 49:20
that I speak in *thine* e. *Jer* 28:7
and hear with *thine* e. *Ezek* 3:10
40:4; 44:5
earrings in *thine* e. and. 16:12
away thy nose and *thine* e. 23:25
thee to hear with *thine* e. 24:26

your **ears**

which I speak in *your* e. *Deut* 5:1
declaration with *your* e. *Job* 13:17
incline *your* e. to words. *Ps* 78:1
have heard with *your* e. *Jer* 26:11
sent me to speak in *your* e. 15
but blessed are *your* e. *Mat* 13:16
scripture is fulfilled in *your* e. *Luke* 4:21
sayings sink down in *your* e. 9:44

ears

e. of corn came up. *Gen* 41:5, 22
a meat offering green e. *Lev* 2:14
not eat green e. till ye bring. 23:14
mayest pluck the e. *Deut* 23:25
go and glean e. of corn. *Ruth* 2:2
man of God full e. of. *2 Ki* 4:42
wicked cut off as tops of e. *Job* 24:24
as when one reapeth e. *Isa* 17:5
an hungered, and began to pluck e. *Mat* 12:1; *Mark* 2:23; *Luke* 6:1
see **seven**

earth

[1] *The globe or planet which we inhabit*, Gen 1:10; Ps 24:1. [2] *The world in distinction from heaven or hell*, John 3:31; Col 3:1, 2. [3] *The people on the globe*, Gen 11:1, Ps 96:1. [4] *Certain parts of the earth—countries*, Ezra 1:2; Rom 9:28. [5] *The ground, in distinction from the water of the globe*, Gen 4:11; Num 6:30. *A man of the earth is taken as meaning a mortal, earthly-minded man*, Ps 10:18.

e. was without form. *Gen* 1:2
and God called the dry land e. 10
let e. bring forth grass. 11, 24
e. brought forth grass and herb. 12
be fruitful, replenish e. and. 28; 9:1
the e. also was corrupt before. 6:11
ark was lifted up above e. 7:17
in second month was the e. 8:14
while e. remaineth, seedtime. 22
covenant between me and e. 9:13
in his days was the e. divided. 10:25; *1 Chr* 1:19
nations of e. shall be blessed in. *Gen* 18:18; 22:18; 26:4; 28:14
give thee of fatness of the e. 27:28
in plenteous years e. brought. 41:47
the Lord in midst of the e. *Ex* 8:22
know that e. is the Lord's. 9:29
Deut 10:14; *Ps* 24:1; *1 Cor* 10:26
one cannot be able to see e. *Ex* 10:5
e. swallowed them. 15:12
an altar of e. thou shalt. 20:24
if e. open her mouth. *Num* 16:30*
the e. opened. 32; 26:10; *Ps* 106:17
lest the e. swallow us up. *Num* 16:34
above all nations of e. *Deut* 28:1
e. under thee shall be iron. 23
O e. the words of my mouth. 32:1
ride on high places of e. 13
a fire shall consume the e. 22
for the pillars of the e. *1 Sam* 2:8
so that the e. rang again. 4:5
trembled, and the e. quaked. 14:15
a man came out with e. upon his head. *2 Sam* 1:2; 15:32
then e. shook and. 22:8; *Ps* 18:7
so that the e. rent. *1 Ki* 1:40
two mules' burden of e. *2 Ki* 5:17
and let the e. rejoice. *1 Chr* 16:31
Ps 96:11
because God cometh to judge the e. *1 Chr* 16:33; *Ps* 96:13; 98:9
of God of heaven and e. *Ezra* 5:11
thou hast made the e. *Neh* 9:6
Isa 45:12
offspring as grass of e. *Job* 5:25
which shaketh the e. 9:6
the e. is given into the hand of. 24
thereof is longer than the e. 11:9
waters and they overturn e. 12:15
to whom alone the e. was. 15:19*
O e. cover not thou my. 16:18
shall the e. be forsaken? 18:4
and the e. shall rise up. 20:27
as for mighty man, he had e. 22:8
the poor of the e. hide. 24:4
he hangeth the e. upon nothing. 26:7
to dwell in caves of the e. 30:6
they were viler than the e. 8*
him a charge over the e.? 34:13
when he quieteth the e. by. 37:17
I laid the foundations of e. 38:4
perceived breadth of the e.? 18
uttermost parts of the e. *Ps* 2:8
be instructed, ye judges of e. 10
that the man of the e. may. 10:18
silver tried in a furnace of e. 12:6
his seed shall inherit the e. 25:13
e. is full of the goodness of. 33:5
looketh on all inhabitants of e. 14
those that wait upon the Lord shall inherit the e. 37:9*, 11*, 22*
not fear though e. be removed. 46:2
uttered his voice, e. melted. 6

for the shields of the e. Ps 47:9
the joy of the whole e. is. 48:2
hast made e. to tremble. 60:2*
into lower parts of the e. 63:9
in uttermost parts of the e. 65:8
thou visitest the e. and waterest. 9
then shall e. yield her increase. 67:6
Ezek 34:27
the e. shook, the heavens. Ps 68:8
sing unto God, ye kingdoms of e. 32
up from depths of the e. 71:20
as showers that water the e. 72:6
tongue walketh through e. 73:9
the e. and all the inhabitants are dissolved. 75:3; Isa 24:19
wicked of e. shall wring. Ps 75:8
the e. feared. 76:8
God arose to save meek of e. 9
the e. trembled. 77:18; 97:4
like e. which he hath. 78:69
O God, judge the e. thou. 82:8
ever thou hadst formed the e. 90:2
Lord reigneth, let e. rejoice. 97:1
Lord reigneth, let the e. be. 99:1
thou laid foundation of the e. 102:25
104:5; Pr 8:29; Isa 48:13
e. is satisfied with fruit. Ps 104:13
the e. is full of thy riches. 24
tremble, O e. at presence. 114:7
e. hath he given to the. 115:16
the e. O Lord, is full of. 119:64
thou hast established the e. 90
prepareth rain for the e. 147:8
his glory is above the e. 148:13
Lord hath founded the e. Pr 3:19
Isa 24:1
from everlasting, or ever e. Pr 8:23
had not made the e. nor fields. 26
e. for depth and heart of. 25:3
the e. that is not filled. 30:16
for three things the e. is. 21
the e. abideth for ever. Eccl 1:4
the profit of the e. is for all. 5:9
the fruit of the e. shall be. Isa 4:2*
that smiteth the e. with rod. 11:4
e. shall be full of the knowledge. 9
the e. shall remove out of. 13:13
man that made the e. to? 14:16
the e. mourneth and. 24:4; 33:9
the e. is defiled under the. 24:5
e. is utterly broken down, e. 19
e. shall reel. 20
e. shall cast out the dead. 26:19
the e. also shall disclose. 21
let the e. hear, and all. 34:1
sitteth on circle of the e. 40:22
the Creator of ends of the e. 28
that spread abroad the e. 44:24
let the e. open. 45:8
I have made the e. 12
be ye saved, all the ends of the e. 22
and be joyful, O e. 49:13
look on the e. the e. shall. 51:6
saith the Lord, the e. is my. 66:1
shall the e. be made to bring? 8*
I beheld the e. it was. Jer 4:23
for this shall the e. mourn. 28
hear, O e. I will bring evil. 6:19
at his wrath the e. shall. 10:10
O e. e. e. hear word of Lord, write. 22:29; Mi 1:2
go up and cover the e. Jer 46:8
the e. is moved at. 49:21; 50:46
made the e. by his power. 51:15
give it to wicked of the e. Ezek 7:21
the Lord hath forsaken the e. 9:9
and the e. shined with his. 43:2
the e. shall hear the corn. Hos 2:22
e. shall quake before. Joel 2:10
darken e. in clear day. Amos 8:9
the e. with her bars. Jonah 2:6
strong foundations of e. Mi 6:2
move out like worms of e. 7:17
the e. is burnt up at. Nah 1:5
e. filled with knowledge. Hab 2:14
the e. was full of his praise. 3:3
didst cleave the e. with rivers. 9
the e. is stayed from. Hag 1:10
sent to walk to and fro through the e. Zech 1:10; 6:7
eyes of Lord run through e. 4:10
smite the e. with a curse. Mal 4:6
for they shall inherit e. Mat 5:5
swear not by the e. it is God's. 35
had not much e. Mat 13:5
Mark 4:5
for the e. bringeth forth. Mark 4:28
he that is of the e. is earthly, and speaketh of the e. John 3:31
first man is of the e. 1 Cor 15:47
vessels of wood and of e. 2 Tim 2:20
the e. which drinketh in. Heb 6:7*
voice then shook the e. but. 12:26
for precious fruit of e. Jas 5:7
the e. brought forth her fruit. 18
the e. and works therein. 2 Pet 3:10
hurt not the e. nor sea. Rev 7:3
trees before the God of the e. 11:4
have power to smite the e. with. 6
the e. opened and swallowed. 12:16
causeth the e. to worship. 13:12
and the e. was lightened. 18:1
whore, which did corrupt e. 19:2
from whose face e. fled away. 20:11
see **beasts, dust, ends, face, heaven, kings, people, whole**

all the **earth**

dominion over all the e. Gen 1:26
seed alive on face of all the e. 7:3
confound language of all the e. 11:9
not Judge of all the e. do? 18:25
us after manner of all the e. 19:31
none like me in all the e. Ex 9:14
my name declared through all the e. 16; Rom 9:17
treasure; for all the e. is. Ex 19:5
not been done in all the e. 34:10
all the e. shall be filled. Num 14:21
the Lord of all the e. Josh 3:11
Zech 6:5
going way of all the e. Josh 23:14
1 Ki 2:2
be dry on all the e. Judg 6:37*
all the e. may know. 1 Sam 17:46
all the e. sought to. 1 Ki 10:24
no God in all the e. but. 2 Ki 5:15
judgements are in all the e.
1 Chr 16:14; Ps 105:7
sing to the Lord, all the e.
1 Chr 16:23; Ps 96:1
fear before him, all the e. 1 Chr 16:30
Ps 33:8; 96:9
thy name in all the e. Ps 8:1, 9
make princes in all the e. 45:16
great king over all the e. 47:2
Zech 14:9
let thy glory be above all the e.
Ps 57:5, 11; 108:5
all the e. shall worship thee. 66:4
most high over all the e. 83:18; 97:9
make a joyful noise, all the e. 98:4
I gathered all the e. Isa 10:14
excellent things, known in all e. 12:5
of his people, from all the e. 25:8
city a curse to all the e. Jer 26:6
an honour before all the e. 33:9
golden cup that made all the e. 51:7
O mountain, destroyest all the e. 25
shall fall the slain of all the e. 49*
bear rule over all the e. Dan 2:39
let all the e. keep silence. Hab 2:20
all the e. be devoured. Zeph 3:8
all the e. sitteth still. Zech 1:11
darkness over all the e. Luke 23:44*
sound went into all the e. Rom 10:18
of God sent into all the e. Rev 5:6

from the **earth**

up a mist from the e. Gen 2:6
cursed from the e. 4:11*
were destroyed from the e. 7:23
waters were abated from the e. 8:11
thou shalt be cut off from the e.
Ex 9:15; Josh 7:9; Ps 109:15
Pr 2:22; Nah 2:13
Saul arose from the e. 1 Sam 28:23
shall I not take you away from the e.? 2 Sam 4:11
to raise him from the e. 12:17
David arose from the e. 20
shall perish from the e. Job 18:17
their fruit from the e. Ps 21:10
remembrance of them from the e.
34:16
praise Lord from the e. 148:7
to devour poor from the e. Pr 30:14
shall perish from the e. Jer 10:11
were lifted up from e. Ezek 1:19, 21
it was lifted up from the e. Dan 7:4
up a snare from the e. Amos 3:5*
I be lifted up from the e. John 12:32
life is taken from the e. Acts 8:33
Saul arose from the e. 9:8
with such a fellow from the e. 22:22
to take peace from the e. Rev 6:4
were redeemed from the e. 14:3

in the **earth**

let fowl multiply in the e. Gen 1:22
a vagabond in the e. 4:12, 14
of man was great in the e. 6:5
Nimrod a mighty one in the e. 10:8
not a man in the e. to come. 19:31
you a posterity in the e. 45:7
that is in the e. beneath. Ex 20:4
they are hid in the e. Josh 7:21
any thing that is in the e. Judg 18:10
like to name of the great men in the e. 2 Sam 7:9; 1 Chr 17:8
what nation in e. like Israel?
2 Sam 7:23; 1 Chr 17:21
all things that are in the e.
2 Sam 14:20
all that is in the e. is. 1 Chr 29:11
no God like thee in the e. 2 Chr 6:14
to and fro in the e. Job 1:7; 2:2
none like him in the e. 1:8; 2:3
root thereof wax old in the e. 14:8
portion is cursed in the e. 24:18
leaveth her eggs in the e. 39:14
saints that are in the e. Ps 16:3
what desolations in the e. 46:8
I will be exalted in the e. 10
God that judgeth in the e. 58:11
handful of corn in the e. 72:16
I am a stranger in the e. 119:19
speaker be established in e. 140:11
be recompensed in the e. Pr 11:31
judgements are in the e. Isa 26:9
not wrought deliverance in the e. 18
not take root in the e. 40:24
have set judgement in the e. 42:4
Jerusalem a praise in the e. 62:7
who blesseth himself in the e. and he that sweareth in the e. 65:16
thee, be written in the e. Jer 17:13
created a new thing in the e. 31:22
sow her unto me in the e. Hos 2:23
shew wonders in the e. Joel 2:30
off righteousness in the e. Amos 5:7
digged in the e. and hid. Mat 25:18
and hid thy talent in the e. 25
when it is sown in the e. less than all seeds in the e. Mark 4:31
three that bear witness in the e.
1 John 5:8

on, or, upon the **earth**

had made man on the e. Gen 6:6
God looked upon the e. behold. 12
cause it to rain upon the e. 7:4
rain was upon the e. forty. 12, 17
and multiply upon the e. 8:17
sun was risen upon the e. 19:23
a ladder set upon the e. 28:12
day they were upon the e. Ex 10:6
things that creep upon the e.
Lev 11:29, 42, 44
live upon the e. Deut 4:10; 12:1, 19
upon the e. he shewed thee his. 4:36
shall pour it upon the e. 12:16, 24
David lay upon the e. 2 Sam 12:16
nor remainder upon the e. 14:7
but will God indeed dwell on the e.?
1 Ki 8:27; 2 Chr 6:18
sends rain upon the e. 1 Ki 17:14
our days on e. as a. 1 Chr 29:15
Job 8:9
time to man upon e.? Job 7:1
stand at latter day upon the e. 19:25
since man was placed on the e. 20:4
the snow, be thou on the e. 37:6
on e. there is not his like. 41:33
tread down my life on the e. Ps 7:5
he shall be blessed upon the e. 41:2
way may be known upon the e. 67:2
there is none upon e. I. 73:25
seed be mighty upon the e. 112:2
four things little upon the e. Pr 30:24
not a just man upon the e. Eccl 7:20
princes walking upon the e. 10:7
evil shall be done upon e. 11:2
empty themselves upon the e. 3
flowers appear on the e. S of S 2:12

determined *upon the e.* Isa 28:22
lift your eyes, look *upon the e.* 51:6
for truth *upon the e.* Jer 9:3*
liver is poured *upon the e.* Lam 2:11
not a man *on the e.* can. Dan 2:10
fall in snare *upon the e.* Amos 3:5
least grain fall *upon the e.* 9:9
not up treasures *upon e.* Mat 6:19
Son of man hath power *on e.* to. 9:6
Mark 2:10; *Luke* 5:24
come to send peace *on e.*
Mat. 10:34
thou shalt bind *on e.* 16:19; 18:18
two of you shall agree *on e.* 18:19
no man your father *upon the e.* 23:9
blood shed *upon the e.* 35
so as no fuller *on e.* can. *Mark* 9:3
glory to God, *on e.* *Luke* 2:14
that built a house *upon the e.* 6:49
come to send fire *on the e.* 12:49
come to give peace *on e.?* 51
shall he find faith *on e.?* 18:8
for things coming *on the e.* 21:26*
glorified thee *on the e.* *John* 17:4
short work will Lord make *on the e.*
Rom 9:28
not on things *on the e.* *Col* 3:2
mortify members *upon the e.* 5
if he were *on e.* he. *Heb* 8:4
they were strangers *on the e.* 11:13
refused him that spake *on e.* 12:25
lived in pleasure *on the e.* *Jas* 5:5
it rained not *on the e.* for. 17
that dwell *upon the e.* *Rev* 3:10
priests, we shall reign *on e.* 5:10
on them that dwell *on the e.* 6:10
wind should not blow *on the e.* 7:1
hail, and fire, cast *upon the e.* 8:7
which standeth *upon the e.* 10:8
dwell *on the e.* 11:10; 13:8, 14
14:6; 17:8
thrust in his sickle *on the e.* 14:16
first poured out vial *upon the e.* 16:2
blood of all slain *upon the e.* 18:24

out of the **earth**

ascending *out of the e.* *1 Sam* 28:13
springing *out of the e.* *2 Sam* 23:4
and *out of the e.* shall. *Job* 8:19
iron is taken *out of the e.* 28:2
as for the *e. out of* it cometh. 5
shall spring *out of the e.* *Ps* 85:11
bring food *out of the e.* 104:14
be consumed *out of the e.* 35
kings, arise *out of the e.* *Dan* 7:17
break battle *out of the e.* *Hos* 2:18
man perished *out of the e.* *Mi* 7:2
coming up *out of the e.* *Rev* 13:11

to, or, *unto the* **earth**

bowing himself *to the e.* *Gen* 24:52
bow down to thee, *to the e.* 37:10
bowed *to the e.* 42:6; 43:26
bowed with his face *to the e.* 48:12
Joshua fell on his face *to the e.*
Josh 5:14; 7:6
Dagon fallen on his face *to the e.*
1 Sam 5:3*
Goliath fell on face *to the e.* 17:49
David stooped face *to the e.* 24:8
she bowed herself *to the e.* 25:41
1 Ki 1:31
me smite him, *to the e.* *1 Sam* 26:8
not my blood fall *to the e.* 20
to David he fell *to the e.* *2 Sam* 1:2
not one hair shall fall *to the e.*
14:11; *1 Ki* 1:52
fall *to the e.* nothing. *2 Ki* 10:10
bodies fallen *to the e.* *2 Chr* 20:24
or speak *to the e.* *Job* 12:8
bowing down *to the e.* *Ps* 17:11
belly cleaveth *unto the e.* 44:25
he shall call *to the e.* that. 50:4
he returneth *to the e.* 146:4
beast that goeth *to the e.* *Eccl* 3:21
then shall dust return *to the e.* 12:7
they shall look *unto the e.* *Isa* 8:22
bring down strength *to the e.* 63:6
of contention *to the e.* *Jer* 15:10
and former rain *to the e.* *Hos* 6:3
their faces *to the e.* *Luke* 24:5
Saul fell *to the e.* and. *Acts* 9:4
great sheet, let down *to the e.* 10:11
we were all fallen *to the e.* 26:14
of heaven fell *to the e.* *Rev* 6:13

did not cast them *to the e.* *Rev* 12:4
saw he was cast *unto the e.* 13

earthen

the *e.* vessel wherein it. *Lev* 6:28
the *e.* vessel whereinto. 11:33
of birds killed in *e.* vessel. 14:5, 50
holy water in *e.* vessel. *Num* 5:17
brought beds, and *e.* *2 Sam* 17:28
and get a potter's *e.* bottle. *Jer* 19:1
put evidences in an *e.* vessel. 32:14
esteemed as *e.* pitchers. *Lam* 4:2
treasure in *e.* vessels. *2 Cor* 4:7

earthly

if I have told you *e.* *John* 3:12
he that is of the earth is *e.* 31
if our *e.* house of. *2 Cor* 5:1
walk, who mind *e.* things. *Phil* 3:19
this wisdom is *e.*, sensual. *Jas* 3:15

earthquake

The scripture speaks of several earthquakes. *One of the most remarkable occurred in the twenty-seventh year of Uzziah, king of Judah,* Zech 14:5.

Another very memorable earthquake, was that at the time of our Saviour's crucifixion, Mat 27:51.

Great alterations and changes are expressed in scripture by a shaking of the earth, Heb 12:26. *The delivering of the Israelites out of Egypt is called a moving, or shaking, of the earth,* Ps 68:8. *And an extraordinary and unexpected alteration in the state of affairs, civil or ecclesiastical, is represented by a great* earthquake, *Rev* 6:12 and 16:18.

an *e.* Lord was not in *e.* *1 Ki* 19:11
after the *e.* a fire, Lord was not. 12
visited of the Lord with *e.* *Isa* 29:6
saw two years before *e.* *Amos* 1:1
ye fled from before the *e.* *Zech* 14:5
when centurion saw the *e.* *Mat* 27:54
there was a great *e.*, the angel. 28:2
Acts 16:26; *Rev* 6:12; 11:13
thunderings and an *e.* *Rev* 8:5; 11:19
a great *e.* so mighty an *e.* 16:18

earthquakes

and *e.* in divers places. *Mat* 24:7
Mark 13:8; *Luke* 21:11

earthy

first man is of earth, *e.* *1 Cor* 15:47
e. such are they also that are *e.* 48
have borne the image of the *e.* 49

ease

nations shalt find no *e.* *Deut* 28:65
trod the Benjamites down with *e.*
Judg 20:43*
in thought of him at *e.* *Job* 12:5
I was at *e.* 16:12
dieth, being wholly at *e.* 21:23
his soul shall dwell at *e.* *Ps* 25:13
with scorning of those at *e.* 123:4
ye women that are at *e.* *Isa* 32:9
tremble, ye women that are at *e.* 11
Jacob shall return, be in rest, at *e.*
Jer 46:27
Moab hath been at *e.* from. 48:11
of a multitude being at *e.* *Ezek* 23:42
woe to them that are at *e.* *Amos* 6:1
with heathen at *e.* *Zech* 1:15
take thine *e.* eat, drink. *Luke* 12:19

ease, *verb*

when thou *e.* thyself. *Deut* 23:13*
e. thou somewhat the. *2 Chr* 10:4, 9
my couch *e.* my complaint. *Job* 7:13
ah, I will *e.* me of mine. *Isa* 1:24

eased

I forbear, what am I *e.?* *Job* 16:6
that other men be *e.* and. *2 Cor* 8:13

easier

so shall it be *e.* for. *Ex* 18:22
e. to say, thy sins be forgiven, or to.
Mat 9:5; *Mark* 2:9; *Luke* 5:23
e. for a camel to go. *Mat* 19:24
Mark 10:25; *Luke* 18:25
it is *e.* for heaven and. *Luke* 16:17

easily

charity is not *e.* provoked. *1 Cor* 13:5
sin which doth so *e.* beset. *Heb* 12:1

east

(*The Hebrews express the east, west, north, and south, by words which signify,* before, behind, left, and right, *according to the position of a man with his face turned towards the east. The term* Kedem (*before or east*), *as generally used, refers to the lands directly east of Palestine : Arabia, Mesopotamia, and Babylon. Another term,* Mizrach, *used of* far east, *has no definite signification*)

God placed at the *e.* of. *Gen* 3:24
removed to a mountain on *e.* 12:8
Lot chose plain, journeyed *e.* 13:11
abroad to the west and *e.* 28:14
into land of people of the *e.* 29:1
that encamp toward *e.* *Num* 3:38
Balak hath brought me out of *e.* 23:7
the children of the *e.* came. *Judg* 6:3
33; 7:12; 8:10; *1 Ki* 4:30
three looking toward *e.* *1 Ki* 7:25
2 Chr 4:4
porters towards the *e.* *1 Chr* 9:24
to flight them toward the *e.* 12:15
greatest of all men of *e.* *Job* 1:3
cometh not from *e.* nor. *Ps* 75:6
as far as *e.* is from west. 103:12
gathered them from the *e.* 107:3
be replenished from *e.* *Isa* 2:6
spoil them of *e.* 11:14; *Jer* 49:28
righteous man from the *e.* *Isa* 41:2
thy seed from the *e.* 43:5; *Zech* 8:7
ravenous bird from the *e.* *Isa* 46:11
their faces towards *e.* *Ezek* 8:16
deliver thee to men of *e.* 25:4, 10
to gate which looketh toward *e.*
40:6, 22; 43:1; 44:1; 46:1, 12
of God came from way of *e.* 43:2
waters issue out toward the *e.* 47:8
toward the *e.* ten thousand. 48:10
suburbs of city toward the *e.* 17
waxed great toward *e.* *Dan* 8:9
tidings out of the *e.* shall. 11:44
drive him toward *e.* sea. *Joel* 2:20
wander from north to *e.* *Amos* 8:12
mount cleave toward *e.* *Zech* 14:4
came wise men from *e.* *Mat* 2:1
we have seen star in the *e.* 2, 9
come from *e.* and. 8:11; *Luke* 13:29
lightning cometh out of *e.* *Mat* 24:27
angel ascending from *e.* *Rev* 7:2*
the way of kings of *e.* 16:12*
on the *e.* three gates, on the. 21:13

east border

point out *e. border.* *Num* 34:10
in *e. border* of Jericho. *Josh* 4:19
e. border was the salt sea. 15:5
west border to *e. border.* *Ezek* 45:7
oblation toward *e. border.* 48:21

Easter

(*The Passover. The name Easter was given later to the Christian celebration of this season*)

intending after *E.* to. *Acts* 12:4

east gate

the keeper of the *e. gate.* *Neh* 3:29
by entry of the *e. gate.* *Jer* 19:2*
stood at door of *e. gate.* *Ezek* 10:19
Spirit brought me unto *e. gate.* 11:1

east side

of court on the *e.-side.* *Ex* 27:13
and on the *e.-side* shall. *Num* 2:3
Ai, on *e.-side* of Beth-el. *Josh* 7:2
of inheritance on the *e.-side.* 16:5
came by *e.-side* of land. *Judg* 11:18
mountain on the *e.-side.* *Ezek* 11:23
he measured the *e.-side* with. 42:16
from the *e.-side* even unto the. 48:2
3, 4, 5, 6, 7, 8, 23, 24, 25, 26, 27
Jonah sat on the *e.-side.* *Jonah* 4:5

eastward

lift up thine eyes *e.* and. *Gen* 13:14
Deut 3:27
open the window *e.* and. *2 Ki* 13:17
e. were six Levites. *1 Chr* 26:17
with line went forth *e.* *Ezek* 47:3

east wind

blasted with the *e. wind.* *Gen* 41:6
23, 27

Lord brought an e.-wind. Ex 10:13 14:21
fill his belly with e.-wind. Job 15:2
e.-wind carrieth him away. 27:21
which scattereth e.-wind. 38:24
ships with an e.-wind. Ps 48:7
caused an e.-wind to blow. 78:26
wind in day of e.-wind. Isa 27:8
scatter them as with an e.-wind. Jer 18:17
wither when the e.-wind. Ezek 17:10
and the e.-wind drieth up. 19:12
the e.-wind hath broken. 27:26
followeth after e.-wind. Hos 12:1
he be fruitful, an e.-wind. 13:15
a vehement e.-wind. Jonah 4:8
faces sup up as the e.-wind. Hab 1:9

easy

knowledge is e. to him. Pr 14:6
my yoke is e. my burden. Mat 11:30
except ye utter words e. 1 Cor 14:9
wisdom from above is e. Jas 3:17

eat

The word is used in Scripture as we use it and its synonyms devour, consume, etc., both literally and figuratively. [1] *To chew and swallow food,* Gen 27:4. [2] *To waste, consume,* Eccl 5:11. [3] *To oppress and destroy,* Ps 14:4. [4] *To have close union with Christ, symbolized by eating his flesh,* John 6:56. [5] *To read closely and attentively, as we say devour a book,* Jer 15:16.

Eating with a person, in the East, is regarded almost as making a covenant of friendship which must not be broken; hence the scandal to the Jews of Jesus' eating with publicans and sinners, Mat 9:11; *and the special sin of the betrayal by Judas, who had so often eaten with his Master.*

of every tree freely e. Gen 2:16
in the day ye e. your eyes. 3:5
Eve took and did e. 6
and I did e. 12, 13
dust shalt thou e. all days. 14
in sorrow shalt thou e. of it all. 17
by angels, they did e. 18:8; 19:3
bring it to me, that I may e. 27:4
and they did e. there upon. 31:46
the birds did e. them out. 40:17
Egyptians did e. by themselves. 43:32
locusts shall e. every. Ex 10:5
the locusts may e. every herb. 12
with bitter herbs they shall e. it. 12:8
save that which every man e. 16
shall no stranger e. 43, 48; Lev 22:13
circumcised, then shall he e. Ex 12:44
e. that to-day, for to-day is. 16:25
children of Israel did e. manna forty. 35; John 6:31, 49, 58
poor of thy people may e. Ex 23:11
Aaron and sons shall e. 29:32
Lev 6:16; 8:31
thou e. of his sacrifice. Ex 34:15
males shall e. it. Lev 6:18, 29; 7:6
Num 18:10
priest that offereth it e. it. Lev 6:26
all that be clean e. 7:19; Num 18:11
shall in no wise e. of it. Lev 7:24
e. of it without leaven. 10:12
yet these ye may e. 11:21, 22
Deut 14:20
Aaron and his sons shall e. Lev 24:9
what shall we e. the seventh. 25:20
your enemies shall e. it. 26:16
remember fish we did e. Num 11:5
give us flesh, that we may e. 13
shall not lie down till he e. 23:24
the people did e. of their. 25:2
buy meat of them that ye may e. Deut 2:6
e. in gates. 12:15, 21; 15:22; 26:12
unclean and clean may e. 12:15, 22 15:22
e. before Lord. 12:18; 14:26; 15:20
I will e. flesh, thou mayest e. 12:20
give it to stranger that he e. 14:21
and another man e. of it. Deut 20:6*
then thou mayest e. grapes. 23:24
gather grapes, worms shall e. 28:39
e. fruit of own body. 53; Lam 2:20
which did e. the fat of. Deut 32:38
did e. of the old corn. Josh 5:11
vineyards ye planted not ye e. 24:13
they tarried, and did e. Judg 19:8
Hannah did e. and was. 1 Sam 1:18
and afterwards they e. 9:13
and e. and sin not against. 14:34
Jonathan did e. no meat. 20:34
and e. that thou mayest have. 28:22
he shall e. at my table. 2 Sam 9:11
1 Ki 2:7
of Jeroboam shall dogs e. 1 Ki 14:11
16:4; 21:23; 2 Ki 9:10, 36
that we may e. and die. 1 Ki 17:12
angel said, arise and e. 19:5
Acts 10:13; 11:7
they shall e. and leave. 2 Ki 4:43
they did e. and left thereof. 44
give thy son that we may e. him to-day, and we will e. my son. 6:28
we boiled my son, and did e. 29
ye e. every man of. 18:31; Isa 36:16
yet did they e. passover. 2 Chr 30:18
children of Israel did e. Ezra 6:21
take corn, that we may e. Neh 5:2
so they did e. and. 9:25; Ps 78:29
sighing cometh before I e. Job 3:24
let me sow, and let another e. 31:8
the meek shall e. and. Ps 22:26
they that be fat on earth shall e. 29
will I e. the flesh of bulls. 50:13
man did e. angels' food. 78:25
shalt e. the labour of thine. 128:2
e. the fruit of own way. Pr 1:31
Isa 3:10
soul of transgressors shall e. Pr 13:2
they that love it shall e. 18:21
my son, e. thou honey. 24:13
whoso keepeth fig-tree shall e. 27:18
and young eagles shall e. it. 30:17
for who can e. or hasten? Eccl 2:25
they are increased that e. 5:11
sleep is sweet, whether he e. 12
princes e. in the morning. 10:16
blessed, when thy princes e. in. 17
his garden and e. his. S of S 4:16
we will e. our own bread. Isa 4:1
butter and honey shall he e. 7:15
and honey shall every one e. 22
e. on the left hand. 9:20
lion shall e. straw. 11:7; 65:25
oxen and asses shall e. 30:24
plant vineyards, and e. fruit thereof. 37:30; 65:21; Jer 29:5, 28
the worm shall e. them. Isa 51:8
come ye, buy and e. yea. 55:1
hearken to me, and e. that which. 2
they that gathered it shall e. 62:9
a people which e. swine's. 65:4
my servants shall e. but ye shall. 13
shall not plant and another e. 22
words were found, and I did e. them. Jer 15:16
shall e. every one the flesh of. 19:9
open thy mouth and e. Ezek 2:8
e. that thou findest, e. this roll. 3:1
e. by weight. 4:10
fathers shall e. sons. 5:10
thou didst e. fine flour, and. 16:13
and in thee they e. upon the. 22:9
ye e. the fat, and clothe you. 34:3
Nebuchadnezzar did e. Dan 4:33
for they shall e. and not. Hos 4:10
Mi 6:14; Hag 1:6
shall e. unclean things. Hos 9:3
all that e. thereof shall be. 4
that e. the lambs out of. Amos 6:4
who also e. the flesh. Mi 3:3
let the rest e. every one. Zech 11:9
but he shall e. the flesh of the. 16
how David did e. the. Mat 12:4
did all e. and were filled. 14:20
15:37; Mark 6:42; 8:8; Luke 9:17
yet the dogs e. of the. Mat 15:27
Mark 7:28
that did e. were 4,000. Mat 15:38
as they did e. he said. 26:21
Mark 14:18, 22
brake it, and said, take e. Mat 26:26
Mark 14:22; 1 Cor 11:24
when they saw him e. Mark 2:16
they that did e. were above. 6:44
no man e. fruit of thee. 11:14
that thou mayest e. passover? 14:12
14; Luke 22:8, 11; John 18:28
and did e. rubbing them. Luke 6:1
him that he would e. with. 7:36
e. such things as are set. 10:8
let us e. and be merry. 15:23
took it, and did e. before. 24:43
prayed him, Master, e. John 4:31
because ye did e. of loaves. 6:26
that a man may e. thereof. 50
except ye e. the flesh of Son. 53
they did e. their meat. Acts 2:46
wentest in and didst e. with. 11:3
we will e. nothing till we. 23:14*
one believeth he may e. Rom 14:2
doubteth is damned if he e. 23
some e. it as a thing. 1 Cor 8:7
we e. are we better; if we e. not. 8
I will eat no flesh while the. 13
all e. the same spiritual meat. 10:3
who e. of the sacrifices. 18
whatsoever is sold, that e. 25
e. asking no question for. 27
if any man hunger, let him e. 11:34
not, neither should he e. 2 Thes 3:10
their word will e. as. 2 Tim 2:17
and shall e. your flesh. Jas 5:3
shall e. her flesh, and. Rev 17:16
that ye may e. flesh of kings. 19:18

see **blood, bread**

eat with *drink*

they did e. and drink. Gen 24:54
26:30; Ex 24:11; Judg 9:27; 19:4
sat down to e. and drink. Ex 32:6
1 Cor 10:7
nor e. bread, nor drink. Ex 34:28
Deut 9:9, 18
did e. bread and drink. 1 Sam 30:11
house to e. and drink? 2 Sam 11:11
did e. of his meat and drink. 12:3
taste what I e. or drink? 19:35
they e. and drink before. 1 Ki 1:25
neither will I e. bread nor drink water. 13:8, 9, 17, 22
will I e. bread nor drink. 16
get thee up, e. and drink. 18:41
they may e. and drink. 2 Ki 6:22
one tent did e. and drink. 7:8
e. own dung, drink. 18:27; Isa 36:12
and did e. and drink before Lord. 1 Chr 29:22
them to e. and drink. 2 Chr 28:15
e. no bread nor drink. Ezra 10:6
e. the fat and drink. Neh 8:10
nor e. nor drink three. Esth 4:16
sisters to e. and drink. Job 1:4
so is he, e. and drink. Pr 23:7
better than that he e. and drink. Eccl 2:24; 3:13; 5:18; 8:15
e., yea, drink abundantly. S of S 5:1
e. drink, ye princes. Isa 21:5
let us e. and drink, to-morrow we shall die. 22:13; 1 Cor 15:32
not father e. and drink? Jer 22:15
e. thy fruit and drink. Ezek 25:4
may e. flesh and drink blood. 39:17
pulse to e. and water to drink. Dan 1:12
e. and when ye did drink. Zech 7:6
what shall e. or drink. Mat 6:25, 31
Luke 12:29
to e. and drink with drunken. Mat 24:49; Luke 12:45
why do ye e. and d.? Luke 5:30
but thy disciples e. and d. 33
take thine ease, e. drink. 12:19
afterward thou shalt e. and drink. 17:8
they did e. they drank, they. 27, 28
e. and drink at my table. 22:30
Saul did neither e. nor drink. Acts 9:9
who did e. and drink with him. 10:41
e. nor drink till they. 23:12, 21
e. flesh nor drink wine. Rom 14:21
power to e. and to drink? 1 Cor 9:4
ye e. or drink, or whatever. 10:31
not houses to e. and drink in? 11:22
as ye e. this bread and drink. 26
shall e. and drink unworthily. 27
and so let him e. and drink. 28

he did eat
Eve gave, and *he did e.* *Gen* 3:6
loved Esau, because *he did e.* 25:28
near to Isaac, and *he did e.* 27:25
not aught, save bread *he did e.* 39:6
Egyptian bread, and *he did e.*
1 Sam 30:11
he did e. continually. *2 Sam* 9:13
bread before him, *he did e.* 12:20
John *did e.* locusts and. *Mark* 1:6
those days *he did e.* *Luke* 4:2
for before *he did e.* *Gal* 2:12

eat *not*
tree of knowledge of good and evil,
shalt *not e.* *Gen* 2:17; 3:1, 3
commanded thee *not* to *e.* 3:11, 17
blood thereof shall ye *not e.* 9:4
Lev 19:26; *Deut* 12:16, 23, 24, 25
15:23
I will *not e.* till I have. *Gen* 24:33
children of Israel *e. not.* 32:32
Egyptians might *not e.* with. 43:32
e. not of it raw, nor. *Ex* 12:9
a foreigner shall *not e.* 45; 29:33
these shall ye *not e.* *Lev* 11:4
Deut 14:3, 7
a leper *not e.* of. *Lev* 22:4, 6, 10, 12
that torn he shall *not e.* to. 8
ye shall *not e.* one day. *Num* 11:19
ye shall *not e.* of any thing that.
Deut 14:21; *Ezek* 44:31
ox slain, thou shalt *not e.* *Deut* 28:31
and *e. not* any unclean. *Judg* 13:4
7, 14
she wept and did *not e.* *1 Sam* 1:7
for the people will *not e.* till. 9:13
and said, I will *not e.* 28:23
and they could *not e.* *2 Ki* 4:40
with thy eyes, but *not e.* 7:2, 19
not e. of most holy things. *Ezra* 2:63
Neh 7:65
and let me *not e.* of. *Ps* 141:4
e not bread of him that. *Pr* 23:6
e. not bread of men. *Ezek* 24:17
except they wash, *e. not.* *Mark* 7:3, 4
I will not *e.* thereof. *Luke* 22:16
such an one *not* to *e.* *1 Cor* 5:11
neither if we *e. not* are we. 8:8
e. not, for his sake that. 10:28

shall ye **eat**
thus *shall ye e.* it. *Ex* 12:11
seven days *shall ye e.* 15, 20
nor *shall ye e.* flesh torn. 22:31
wave-breast *shall ye e.* *Lev* 10:14
cheweth the cud, that *shall ye e.*
11:3; *Deut* 14:4, 6
these *shall ye e.* of all that. *Lev* 11:9
in fifth year *shall ye e.* of. 19:25
flesh of daughters *shall ye e.* 26:29
fins and scales *shall ye e.* *Deut* 14:9

ye shall **eat**
and *ye shall e.* the fat. *Gen* 45:18
ye shall e. it in haste. *Ex* 12:11
first month at even *ye shall e.* 18
at even *ye shall e.* flesh. 16:12
ye shall e. no fat. *Lev* 7:23, 24
ye shall e. no blood. 26; 17:14
ye shall e. it in holy place. 10:13
ye shall e. neither bread nor. 23:14
ye shall e. the increase. 25:12
ye shall e. your fill. 19
ye shall e. of old store. 22; 26:10
ye shall e. and not be. 26:26
ye shall e. flesh of your sons. 29
Lord will give flesh, and *ye shall e.*
Num 11:18
and *ye shall e.* in every place. 18:31
ye shall e. before Lord. *Deut* 12:7
of all clean birds *ye shall e.* 14:11
go up, for *ye shall e.* *1 Sam* 9:19
a sign, *ye shall e.* this year such.
2 Ki 19:29; *Isa* 37:30
obedient *ye shall e.* good. *Isa* 1:19
ye shall e. the riches of the. 61:6
and *ye shall e.* fat till. *Ezek* 39:19
ye shall e. in plenty. *Joel* 2:26
thought what *ye shall e.* *Luke* 12:22

to **eat**
in evening flesh *to e.* *Ex* 16:8
who shall give us flesh *to e.*?
Num 11:4, 18
soul longeth *to e.* flesh. *Deut* 12:20
have like portions *to e.* 18:8
to the high place *to e.* *1 Sam* 9:13
king sat him down *to e.* meat. 20:24
to cause David *to e.* *2 Sam* 3:35
master's son have food *to e.* 9:10
but he refused *to e.* 13:9
fruit for the young men *to e.* 16:2
for people with him *to e.* 17:29
poured out for men *to e.* *2 Ki* 4:40
have had enough *to e.* *2 Chr* 31:10
land thou gavest, *to e.* the. *Neh* 9:36
manna on them *to e.* *Ps* 78:24
when thou sittest *to e.* *Pr* 23:1
not good *to e.* much honey. 25:27
given him power *to e.* *Eccl* 5:19
God giveth him not power *to e.* 6:2
shall be for them *to e.* *Isa* 23:18
cause them *to e.* flesh. *Jer* 19:9
he caused me *to e.* roll. *Ezek* 3:2
son of man, cause thy belly *to e.* 3
make thee *to e.* grass. *Dan* 4:25, 32
there is no cluster *to e.* *Mi* 7:1
as eagle that hasteth *to e.* *Hab* 1:8*
pluck ears of corn and *to e.* *Mat* 12:1
not lawful for him *to e.* 4
Mark 2:26; *Luke* 6:4
give ye them *to e.* *Mat* 14:16
Mark 6:37; *Luke* 9:13
to e. with unwashen. *Mat* 15:20
multitude have nothing *to e.* 32
Mark 8:1, 2
prepare *to e.* passover. *Mat* 26:17
should be given her *to e.* *Mark* 5:43
no leisure so much as *to e.* 6:31
to e. this passover. *Luke* 22:15
I have meat *to e.* that ye. *John* 4:32
any brought him aught *to e.*? 33
this man give us his flesh *to e.*? 6:52
broken it, he began *to e.* *Acts* 27:35
emboldened *to e.* things. *1 Cor* 8:10
ye come, this is not *to e.* 11:20
when ye come together *to e.* 33
have no right *to e.* *Heb* 13:10
will I give *to e.* of tree of. *Rev* 2:7
to e. things sacrificed unto. 14, 20
I will give *to e.* of hidden manna. 17

eat *up*
lean did *e. up* the. *Gen* 41:4, 20
land of enemies *e.* you *up.* *Lev* 26:38
he shall *e. up* nations. *Num* 24:8
nation thou knowest not shall *e. up.*
Deut 28:33
on me to *e. up* my flesh. *Ps* 27:2
did *e. up* all the herbs. 105:35
moth *e.* them *up.* *Isa* 50:9; 51:8
shall *e. up* thine harvest, *e. up* thy
flocks, *e. up* thy vines. *Jer* 5:17
wind shall *e. up* thy pastures. 22:22*
e. up the sin of my people. *Hos* 4:8*
and did *e. up* a part. *Amos* 7:4
it shall *e.* thee *up* like. *Nah* 3:15*
said, take it, and *e.* it *up.* *Rev* 10:9

eaten
hast thou *e.* of tree? *Gen* 3:11
that which young men have *e.* 14:24
rams of thy flock have I not *e.* 31:38
had *e.* them up, it could not be known
that they had *e.* them. 41:21
in one house shall it be *e.* *Ex* 12:46
no leavened bread be *e.* 13:3, 7
his flesh shall not be *e.* 21:28
a field or vineyard to be *e.* 22:5
it shall not be *e.* because. 29:34
be *e.* in the holy place. *Lev* 6:16
26; 7:6
burnt, it shall not be *e.* 6:23; 7:19
no sin-offering shall be *e.* 6:30
be *e.* the same day it. 7:15, 16
if sacrifice of peace-offering be *e.* 18
ye not *e.* the sin offering? 10:17
ye should indeed have *e.* it in. 18
if I had *e.* the sin-offering. 19
shall not be *e.* 11:13, 41; *Deut* 14:19
be *e.* the same day. *Lev* 19:6; 22:30
be *e.* at all on the third day. 19:7
unleavened bread be *e.* *Num* 28:17
Ezek 45:21
when thou shalt have *e.* and be full.
Deut 6:11; 8:10, 12
roe-buck and the hart is *e.* 12:22
vineyard, hath not *e.* of it. 20:6*
I have not *e.* thereof. 26:14
ye have not *e.* bread nor. 29:6
when they shall have *e.* and. 31:20
had *e.* of the old corn. *Josh* 5:12
when Boaz had *e.* and. *Ruth* 3:7
if people had *e.* freely. *1 Sam* 14:30
for he had *e.* no bread all. 28:20
had *e.* his spirit came again. 30:12
have we *e.* at all of? *2 Sam* 19:42
camest back, and hast *e.* *1 Ki* 13:22
the lion had not *e.* the carcase. 28
have not *e.* the bread. *Neh* 5:14
unsavoury be *e.* without salt. *Job* 6:6
have *e.* my morsel alone. 31:17
if I have *e.* the fruits thereof. 39
zeal of thine house hath *e.* me up.
Ps 69:9; *John* 2:17
I have *e.* ashes like bread. *Ps* 102:9
and bread *e.* in secret. *Pr* 9:17
morsel that thou hast *e.* shalt. 23:8
I have *e.* my honey-comb. *S of S* 5:1
have *e.* up the vineyard. *Isa* 3:14
they have *e.* up Jacob. *Jer* 10:25
figs could not be *e.* 24:2, 3, 8; 29:17
e. sour grapes. 31:29; *Ezek* 18:2
I have not *e.* that. *Ezek* 4:14
not *e.* upon mountains. 18:6, 15
even hath *e.* upon mountains. 11
ye have *e.* fruit of lies. *Hos* 10:13
locust hath left, canker-worm *e.*
Joel 1:4; 2:25
and they that had *e.* *Mat* 14:21
Mark 8:9
we have *e.* and drunk. *Luke* 13:26
e. afterward thou shalt *e.* 17:8
to them that had *e.* *John* 6:13
became hungry, and would have *e.*
Acts 10:10
Lord, I have never *e.* any. 14
he was *e.* of worms, and. 12:23
broken bread and *e.* departed. 20:11
when they had *e.* enough. 27:38
as soon as I had *e.* it. *Rev* 10:10

eater
out of the *e.* came meat. *Judg* 14:14
may give bread to the *e.* *Isa* 55:10
fall into mouth of the *e.* *Nah* 3:12

eaters
be not among riotious *e.* *Pr* 23:20

eatest
in the day thou *e.* thou. *Gen* 2:17
said Elkanah, why *e.*? *1 Sam* 1:8
spirit so sad that thou *e.*? *1 Ki* 21:5

eateth
e. leavened bread be. *Ex* 12:15, 19
the soul that *e.* *Lev* 7:18, 20, 25, 27
17:10, 15
every one that *e.* shall bear. 19:8
a land that *e.* up the. *Num* 13:32
cursed be the man that *e.*
1 Sam 14:24, 28
harvest the hungry *e.* up. *Job* 5:5
and another never *e.* with. 21:25*
behemoth which I made, he *e.* 40:15
similitude of ox that *e.* *Ps* 106:20
righteous *e.* to satisfying. *Pr* 13:25
she *e.* and wipeth her mouth. 30:20
and she *e.* not the bread. 31:27
fool foldeth hands and *e.* *Eccl* 4:5
all his days also he *e.* in. 5:17
but a stranger *e.* it, this is. 6:2
yet in his hand he *e.* it up. *Isa* 28:4
behold, he *e.* but awaketh. 29:8
with part thereof he *e.* flesh. 44:16
he that *e.* of their eggs dieth. 59:5
man that *e.* sour grape. *Jer* 31:30
why *e.* your master with publicans?
Mat 9:11; *Mark* 2:16; *Luke* 15:2
one of you who *e.* with me, shall betray me. *Mark* 14:18; *John* 13:18
whoso *e.* my flesh hath. *John* 6:54
he that *e.* my flesh dwelleth in. 56
so he that *e.* me, even he. 57
he that *e.* of this bread, shall. 58
another who is weak *e.* *Rom* 14:2
that *e.* despise him that *e.* not. 3
he that *e.*, *e.* to Lord; he that *e.* not,
to Lord he *e.* not. 6
evil for that man who *e.* with. 20
because he *e.* not of faith. 23
planteth vineyard, and *e.* not of fruit
thereof? and *e.* not of. *1 Cor* 9:7
e. unworthily, *e.* damnation. 11:29

eating
a lamb according to number of souls
to *e.* *Ex* 12:4; 16:16, 18, 21

Samson took thereof, and went on *e.* *Judg* 14:9
not against Lord in *e.* *1 Sam* 14:34
spread abroad on all earth *e.* 30:16
guests made an end of *e.* *1 Ki* 1:41
they were *e.* of pottage. *2 Ki* 4:40
upon him while he is *e.* *Job* 20:23
e. swine's flesh, and the. *Isa* 66:17
they made an end of *e.* *Amos* 7:2
were *e.* Jesus took bread. *Mat* 26:26
concerning *e.* of things. *1 Cor* 8:4
in *e.* every one taketh his. 11:21
see **drinking**

Ebal
put curse upon mount *E.* *Deut* 11:29
these stones in mount *E.* 27:4
stand upon mount *E.* to curse. 13
built an altar in mount *E.* *Josh* 8:30
half of them over-against *E.* 33

Ebed
words of Gaal son of *E.* *Judg* 9:30
E. the son of Jonathan. *Ezra* 8:6

Ebed-melech
E. spake to the king. *Jer* 38:8
speak to *E.* the Ethiopian. 39:16

Eben-ezer
Israel pitched beside *E.* *1 Sam* 4:1
Philistines brought ark from *E.* 5:1
Samuel called name of stone *E.* 7:12

Eber
Shem father of the children of *E.* *Gen* 10:21
unto *E.* were born two sons. 25
1 Chr 1:19
ships shall afflict *E.* *Num* 24:24

Ed
called the altar *E.* *Josh* 22:34

Eden
put man into garden of *E.* *Gen* 2:15
forth from the garden of *E.* 3:23
make her wilderness like *E.* *Isa* 51:3; *Ezek* 36:35
been in *E.* the garden. *Ezek* 28:13
so that all the trees of *E.* 31:9
the trees of *E.* be comforted. 16
brought down with trees of *E.* 18
land is as the garden of *E.* *Joel* 2:3
holds sceptre from *E.* *Amos* 1:5

edge
Etham in *e.* of wilderness. *Ex* 13:20
Num 33:6
make fifty loops in the *e.* *Ex* 26:10
and he do not whet the *e.* *Eccl* 10:10
see **teeth**

edge *of the sword*
slew Hamor with the *e. of sword.* *Gen* 34:26
Amalek with *e. of sword.* *Ex* 17:13
Sihon with *e. of sword.* *Num* 21:24
all with *e. of sword.* *Josh* 6:21
smote Ai with *e. of sword.* 8:24
Sisera with *e. of sword.* *Judg* 4:15
Jabesh-gilead with *e. of sword.* 21:10
servants slain with *e. of sword.* *Job* 1:15, 17
turned the *e. of the sword.* *Ps* 89:43
them with *e. of sword.* *Jer* 21:7
fall by the *e. of sword.* *Luke* 21:24
escaped the *e. of sword.* *Heb* 11:34

edged
and a two-*e.* sword in. *Ps* 149:6
sharp as a two-*e.* sword. *Pr* 5:4
sharper than two-*e.* *Heb* 4:12
out of mouth went two-*e.* *Rev* 1:16

edges
joined at the two *e.* *Ex* 28:7*; 39:4*
dagger had two *e.* *Judg* 3:16
sharp sword with two *e.* *Rev* 2:12

edification
(*Literally, a building up, constructing; hence edify meant to organize, establish; also to instruct and improve, especially morally*)
his neighbour to *e.* *Rom* 15:2
prohesieth speaketh to *e.* *1 Cor* 14:3
Lord hath given us for *e.* *2 Cor* 10:8*
which Lord hath given to *e.* 13:10*

edified
churches had rest, were *e.* *Acts* 9:31
but the other is not *e.* *1 Cor* 14:17

edifieth
but charity *e.* *1 Cor* 8:1
speaks in an unknown tongue *e.* himself; he that prophesieth *e.* 14:4

edify
wherewith one may *e.* *Rom* 14:19
things lawful, but *e.* not. *1 Cor* 10:23
e. one another, even. *1 Thes* 5:11*

edifying
that church may receive *e.* *1 Cor* 14:5
that ye may excel to the *e.* 12
let all things be done to *e.* 26
do all things for your *e.* *2 Cor* 12:19
for the *e.* of the body. *Eph* 4:12*
increase of the body to the *e.* 16*
which is good to use of *e.* 29
questions rather than *e.* *1 Tim* 1:4*

Edom
his name called *E.* *Gen* 25:30
Esau is *E.* 36:1
dukes of *E.* amazed. *Ex* 15:15
Moses sent messengers to the king of *E.* *Num* 20:14; *Judg* 11:17
E. refused to give Israel. *Num* 20:21
E. shall be a possession. 24:18
out of the field of *E.* *Judg* 5:4
against Moab and *E.* *1 Sam* 14:47
David put garrisons in *E.* *2 Sam* 8:14; *1 Chr* 18:13
Hadad of king's seed in *E.* *1 Ki* 11:14
he had cut off every male in *E.* 16
there was then no king in *E.* 22:47
water by the way of *E.* *2 Ki* 3:20
in his days *E.* revolted from. 8:20
thou hast indeed smitten *E.* 14:10
sought after gods of *E.* *2 Chr* 25:20
over *E.* will I cast out my shoe. *Ps* 60:8; 108:9
lead me into *E.*? 60:9; 108:10
the tabernacles of *E.* are. 83:6
remember the children of *E.* 137:7
shall lay their hand on *E.* *Isa* 11:14
who cometh from *E.*? 63:1
E. I will punish. *Jer* 9:26; 25:21
and yokes to king of *E.* 27:3
concerning *E.* saith Lord. 49:7; *Ob* 1
E. shall be a desolation. *Jer* 49:17
counsel he hath taken against *E.* 20
because *E.* hath dealt. *Ezek* 25:12
lay my vengeance upon *E.* 14
there is *E.* her kings and. 32:29
E. shall escape out of. *Dan* 11:41
E. shall be a wilderness. *Joel* 3:19
deliver them up to *E.* *Amos* 1:6, 9
burnt bones of the king of *E.* 2:1
possess the remnant of *E.* 9:12
destroy wise men out of *E.* *Ob* 8
whereas *E.* saith, we are. *Mal* 1:4
see **daughter**

Edomite, -s
Esau father of *E.* *Gen* 36:9, 43
shalt not abhor an *E.* *Deut* 23:7
stirred up Hadad the *E.* *1 Ki* 11:14
Joram smote the *E.* *2 Ki* 8:21
2 Chr 21:9
E. became David's. *1 Chr* 18:13
the *E.* revolted from. *2 Chr* 21:10
lo, thou hast smitten the *E.* 25:19
the *E.* had come and smitten. 28:17
see **Doeg**

effect
make her vow of no *e.* *Num* 30:8
spake to her to that *e.* *2 Chr* 34:22
of people of none *e.* *Ps* 33:10
the *e.* of righteousness. *Isa* 32:17
his lies shall not so *e.* it. *Jer* 48:30*
days are at hand, and *e.* *Ezek* 12:23
commandment of none *e.* *Mat* 15:6*
word of God of none *e.* *Mark* 7:13*
faith of God without *e.*? *Rom* 3:3
promise of none *e.* 4:14; *Gal* 3:17
word hath taken none *e.* *Rom* 9:6*
of Christ be of none *e.* *1 Cor* 1:17*
Christ become of no *e.* to. *Gal* 5:4*

effected
Solomon prosperously *e.* *2 Chr* 7:11

effectual
for a great door and *e.* *1 Cor* 16:9
e. in enduring the same. *2 Cor* 1:6*
e. working of his power. *Eph* 3:7
according to the *e.* working. 4:16*
thy faith may become *e.* *Philem* 6
the *e.* prayer of righteous. *Jas* 5:16*

effectually
that wrought *e.* in Peter. *Gal* 2:8
the word *e.* worketh in. *1 Thes* 2:13

effeminate
nor *e.* shall inherit the. *1 Cor* 6:9

egg
any taste in white of an *e.*? *Job* 6:6
if he ask an *e.* will offer. *Luke* 11:12

eggs
young ones or *e.* the dam sitting on the young or *e.* shall. *Deut* 22:6
ostrich leaveth her *e.* *Job* 39:14
one gathereth *e.* that are. *Isa* 10:14
cockatrice' *e.* he that eateth *e.* 59:5
as partridge sitteth on *e.* *Jer* 17:11

Eglah
Ithream, by *E.* David's wife. *2 Sam* 3:5

Eglaim
howling is gone unto *E.* *Isa* 15:8

Eglon
Israel served *E.* the king. *Judg* 3:14
brought presents to *E.* and *E.* 17

Egypt
from the river of *E.* to. *Gen* 15:18
God hath made me lord of all *E.* 45:9
I will smite *E.* *Ex* 3:20; *Jer* 9:26
46:25
I may lay my hand on *E.* *Ex* 7:4
stretched hand over waters of *E.* 8:6
between cattle of Israel and *E.* 9:4
knowest thou not that *E.* is? 10:7
thou camest out of *E.* 23:15; 34:18
thou hast forgiven this people from *E.* *Num* 14:19
is a people come out of *E.* 22:5
shewed great signs upon *E.* *Deut* 6:22
none of the diseases of *E.* on. 7:15
what he did unto army of *E.* 11:4
smite thee with botch of *E.* 28:27
on thee all diseases of *E.* 60
rolled away reproach of *E.* *Josh* 5:9
and I plagued *E.* 24:5
I am a young man of *E.* *1 Sam* 30:13
excelled wisdom of Egypt. *1 Ki* 4:30
thou trustest on *E.* *2 Ki* 18:21, 24
Isa 36:6, 9
E. was glad when. *Ps* 105:38
who smote firstborn of *E.* 135:8
wonders into midst of thee, O *E.* 9
to him that smote *E.* in. 136:10
bed with fine linen of *E.* *Pr* 7:16
after the manner of *E.* *Isa* 10:24
Amos 4:10
recover remnant from *E.* *Isa* 11:11
burden of *E.* the idols of *E.* 19:1
the spirit of *E.* shall fail in. 3
in that day shall *E.* be like. 16
shall Israel be third with *E.* 24
blessed be ye *E.* my people. 25
be ashamed of *E.* their glory. 20:5
as at report concerning *E.* so. 23:5
beat off from stream of *E.* 27:12
trust in the shadow of *E.* your. 30:3
I gave *E.* for thy ransom. 43:3
the labour of *E.* shall come. 45:14
what to do in way of *E.*? *Jer* 2:18
shalt be ashamed of *E.* as. 36
of Lord which came against *E.* 46:2
E. is like a fair heifer, but. 20
defile not yourselves with the idols of *E.* *Ezek* 20:7
nor left she her idols from *E.* 23:8
thou shalt not remember *E.* 27
with broidered work from *E.* 27:7
prophesy against him and all *E.* 29:2
bring again the captivity of *E.* 14
they also that uphold *E.* shall. 30:6
pain come as in day of *E.* 9
fury on Sin, strength of *E.* 15
shall spoil the pomp of *E.* 32:12
lament for ever, even for *E.* 16
wail for the multitude of *E.* 18
precious things of *E.* *Dan* 11:43
gone, *E.* shall gather them. *Hos* 9:6
E. shall be a desolation. *Joel* 3:19
as by the flood of *E.* *Amos* 8:8; 9:5
Ethiopia and *E.* were her. *Nah* 3:9
the sceptre of *E.* shall. *Zech* 10:11

if family of E. go not up. Zech 14:18
him governor over E. Acts 7:10
by faith he forsook E. Heb 11:27
is called Sodom and E. Rev 11:8
see **daughter**

in Egypt

tell of all my glory in E. Gen 45:13
me not, I pray thee in E. 47:29
affliction of my people in E. Ex 3:7
which is done to you in E. 16
hail, such as hath not been in E. 9:18
I wrought in E. 10:2; Josh 24:7
a great cry in E. Ex 12:30
no graves in E. 14:11
it was well with us in E. Num 11:18
and we have dwelt in E. a. 20:15
all that he did for you in E.
Deut 1:30; 4:34
all that he did in E. Josh 9:9
wrought his signs in E. Ps 78:43
smote all the firstborn in E. 51
not thy wonders in E. 106:7
had done great things in E. 21
famine shall follow after you in E.
Jer 42:16
declare ye in E. and publish. 46:14
whoredoms in E. Ezek 23:3
I have set a fire in E. 30:8, 16
will I execute judgements in E. 19
an angel appeared in E. Mat 2:19
dwellers in E. we do hear. Acts 2:10
than the treasures in E. Heb 11:26

into Egypt

countries came into E. Gen 41:57
I will go down with thee into E. 46:4
that came with Jacob into E. 26
better to return into E. Num 14:3, 4
Lord shall come into E. Isa 19:1
walk to go down into E. 30:2
fled and went into E. Jer 26:21
faces to go into E. 41:17; 42:15
go ye not into E. 42:19; 43:2
ambassadors into E. Ezek 17:15
carry captives into E. Dan 11:8
and oil is carried into E. Hos 12:1
flee into E. Mat 2:13
he departed into E. 14
sold Joseph into E. Acts 7:9
come, I will send thee into E. 34
hearts turned back again into E. 39
see **king**

land of Egypt

Sodom like land of E. Gen 13:10
Ishmael's wife out of land of E.
21:21
never saw in all the land of E. 41:19
plenty through land of E. 29, 30, 53
set over land of E. 41; 45:8, 26
in the land of E. was bread. 41:54
good of the land of E. 45:18, 20
the land of E. is before thee. 47:6
money failed in the land of E. 15
Joseph bought all the land of E. 20
made it a law over land of E. 26
all elders of the land of E. 50:7
blood in all land of E. Ex 7:19
frogs, lice, flies covered land of E.
8:6, 16, 24
blains, hail, locusts in land of E.
9:9, 22; 10:14
darkness over land of E. 10:21, 22
Moses was great in land of E. 11:3
Lord smote firstborn in land of E.
12:29; 13:15
would God we had died in land of E.
16:3; Num 14:2
you out of land of E. Ex 16:6
20:2; 29:46
strangers in land of E. 22:21; 23:9
Lev 19:34; Deut 10:19; Acts 13:17
gods which brought thee out of land
of E. Ex 32:4; 1 Ki 12:28; Neh 9:18
after doings of land of E. Lev 18:3
Lord thy God, who brought you out
of land of E. 19:36; 26:13
Num 15:41; Deut 5:6; 13:5, 10
20:1; Judg 2:12; 1 Sam 12:6
from day thou didst depart out of
land of E. Deut 9:7; Judg 19:30
Isa 11:16; Jer 7:22; 11:7; 34:13
Mi 7:15
goest is not land of E. Deut 11:10
camest out of the land of E. in. 16:3
things in the land of E. Ps 78:12
out through the land of E. 81:5
shall in land of E. speak. Isa 19:18
altar for witness in land of E. 19, 20
outcasts in the land of E. 27:13
will go into land of E. Jer 42:14
sword overtake you in land of E. 16
they came into the land of E. 43:7
array himself with land of E. 12
return out of the land of E. 44:28
to them in land of E. Ezek 20:5
the harlot in the land of E. 23:19
whoredom from the land of E. 27
the land of E. desolate. 29:9, 12
land of E. utterly waste. 10
given him the land of E. for. 20
no more prince of land of E. 30:13
land of E. not escape. Dan 11:42
derision in land of E. Hos 7:16
thy God from land of E. 12:9; 13:4
them out of land of E. Zech 10:10
lead them out of land of E. Heb 8:9
people out of land of E. Jude 5

out of Egypt

Abraham out of E. Gen 13:1
carry me out of E. 47:30
bring Israel out of E. Ex 3:11
they were thrust out of E. 12:39
with a strong hand hath the Lord
brought thee out of E. 13:9, 16
came we forth out of E.? Num 11:20
is a people come out of E. 22:11
of men that came out of E. 32:11
thou camest out of E. Deut 16:6
when ye came out of E. Josh 2:10
till all that came out of E. 5:6
I made you go out of E. Judg 2:1
1 Sam 10:18
Israel came out of E. 1 Sam 15:6
hast redeemed out of E. 1 Chr 17:21
came with him out of E. 2 Chr 12:3
princes come out of E. Ps 68:31
brought a vine out of E. 80:8
when Israel went out of E. 114:1
a highway out of E. Isa 19:23
set forth Urijah out of E. Jer 26:23
army was come out of E. 37:5
called my son out of E. Hos 11:1
Mat 2:15
tremble as a bird out of E. Hos 11:11
Lord brought Israel out of E. 12:13
when ye came out of E. Hag 2:5
not all that came out of E. Heb 3:16

to Egypt

the Edomites came to E. 1 Ki 11:18
Jehoahaz came to E. 2 Ki 23:34
2 Chr 36:4
Judah be a terror to E. Isa 19:17
Lord shall be known to E. 21
woe to them that go to E. for. 31:1
they call to E. they go. Hos 7:11
see **return**

Egyptian

handmaid an E. Gen 16:1, 3; 21:9
an E. bought Joseph of. 39:1
Lord blessed the E. house for. 5
Hebrews are not as E. Ex 1:19
Moses spied an E. smiting. 2:11
slew E. and hid him. 12; Acts 7:24
an E. delivered us out of the. Ex 2:19
whose father was an E. Lev 24:10
shalt not abhor an E. Deut 23:7
they found an E. in. 1 Sam 30:11
Benaiah slew an E., and the E. had a.
2 Sam 23:21; 1 Chr 11:23
had servant an E. Jarha. 1 Chr 2:34
Lord destroy tongue of E. Isa 11:15
and the E. shall come into. 19:23
art not thou that E. who? Acts 21:38

Egyptians

Pharaoh said to the E. Gen 41:55
abomination to E. 43:32; 46:34
the E. mourned for Jacob. 50:3
ye shall spoil the E. Ex 3:22; 12:36
sacrifice abomination of E.? 8:26
difference between E. and. 11:7
they borrowed of the E. 12:35
but the E. pursued them. 14:9, 10
E. whom ye have seen to-day. 13
E. said, let us flee from Israel...
fighteth for them against E. 25
the Lord overthrew E. in the. 27
seen what I did to the E. Ex 19:4
should the E. speak and say? 32:12
then the E. shall hear it. Num 14:13
E. vexed us and our fathers. 20:15
E. evil entreated and. Deut 26:6
darkness between you and the E.
Josh 24:7
deliver you from the E.? Judg 10:11
gods that smote the E. 1 Sam 4:8
why harden your hearts, as E.? 6:6
to abominations of E. Ezra 9:1
set the E. against the E. Isa 19:2
the E. will I give into hand of a. 4
the E. shall know the Lord in. 21
the E. shall serve with the. 23
king of Assyria lead away E. 20:4
the E. shall help in vain and. 30:7
now E. are men and not God. 31:3
houses of gods of the E. Jer 43:13
given the hand to the E. Lam 5:6
fornication with E. Ezek 16:26
in bruising thy teats by E. 23:21
and I will scatter the E. 29:12
30:23, 26
I will gather the E. from. 29:13
learned in wisdom of E. Acts 7:22
which E. assaying to do. Heb 11:29

Ehud

raised up E. the son of. Judg 3:15
E. made him a dagger. 16
E. went forth. 23
and E. escaped while they. 26
Israel again did evil, when E. 4:1
sons of Bilham, E. 1 Chr 7:10
the sons of E. 8:6

eight

is e. days old shall be circumcised.
Gen 17:12; 21:4; Luke 2:21
these e. Milcah did bear. Gen 22:23
they shall be e. boards. Ex 26:25
Moses gave e. oxen to. Num 7:8
on the sixth day e. bullocks. 29:29
Israel served Chushan-rishathaim
e. years. Judg 3:8
Abdon judged Israel e. years. 12:14
the Ephrathite had e. 1 Sam 17:12
was of stones of e. cubits. 1 Ki 7:10
Jehoram reigned e. 2 Ki 8:17
Josiah was e. years old when he.
22:1; 2 Chr 34:1
e. among sons of Ithamar.
1 Chr 24:4
sanctified house of Lord in e. days.
2 Chr 29:17
to seven, and also to e. Eccl 11:2
Ishmael escaped with e. Jer 41:15
going up had e. steps. Ezek 40:31
34, 37
e. tables, whereon slew sacrifices. 41
e. principal men. Mi 5:5
about an e. days after. Luke 9:28
after e. days disciples. John 20:26
had kept his bed e. years. Acts 9:33
wherein e. souls were. 1 Pet 3:20

eight hundred

begat Seth e. hun. years. Gen 5:4
he begat Enoch e. hun. years. 19
Adino slew e. hun. 2 Sam 23:8
array e. hun. thousand. 2 Chr 13:3

eighteen

served Eglon e. years. Judg 3:14
oppressed Israel e. years. 10:8
two pillars of brass e. 1 Ki 7:15
2 Ki 25:17; Jer 52:21
sons and brethren e. 1 Chr 26:9
Rehoboam took e. 2 Chr 11:21
those e. on whom tower. Luke 13:4
Satan hath bound these e. years. 16

eighteen thousand

of Israel e. thous. Judg 20:25
there fell of Benjamin e. thous. 44
of Manasseh, e. thous. 1 Chr 12:31
slew of Edomites e. thous. 18:12
princes gave of brass e. thous. 29:7
city round was e. thous. Ezek 48:35

eighteenth

in e. year of Jeroboam. 1 Ki 15:1
2 Chr 13:1
Jehoram reigned the e. 2 Ki 3:1
in the e. year of king Josiah. 22:3
23:23; 2 Chr 34:8; 35:19
the e. lot came forth. 1 Chr 24:15

the **e.** to Hanani, he. *1 Chr* 25:25
e. year of Nebuchadnezzar. *Jer* 32:1; 52:29

eighth

and ye shall sow the *e.* *Lev* 25:22
in Bul, which is *e.* *1 Ki* 6:38
ordained a feast in the *e.* 12:32
the *e.* lot came forth to. *1 Chr* 24:10
the *e.* to Jeshaiah. 25:15
Peulthaia the *e.* 26:5
the *e.* captain for the *e.* 27:11
in *e.* month word came. *Zech* 1:1
but saved Noah the *e.* *2 Pet* 2:5*
is not, even he is the *e.* *Rev* 17:11
the *e.* foundation was a beryl. 21:20
see **day, days**

either

Jacob *e.* good or bad. *Gen* 31:24, 29
Nadab and Abihu took *e.* his censer. *Lev* 10:1
other gods, *e.* sun or. *Deut* 17:3
nation shall not leave thee *e.* 28:51
e. he is talking, or. *1 Ki* 18:27
prosper, *e.* this or that. *Eccl* 11:6
ask a sign *e.* in depth or. *Isa* 7:11
for *e.* he will hate the one, and. *Mat* 6:24; *Luke* 16:13
e. make the tree good. *Mat* 12:33
e. how canst thou say to. *Luke* 6:42
e. what woman having ten. 15:8
crucified, on *e.* side one. *John* 19:18
except I speak to you *e.* *1 Cor* 14:6
e. can a vine bear figs? *Jas* 3:12
of *e.* side the river there. *Rev* 22:2

Ekron

as the ark came to *E.* *1 Sam* 5:10
restored to Israel from *E.* 7:14
Baal-zebub the god of *E.* *2 Ki* 1:2 3, 6, 16
mine hand against the *E.* *Amos* 1:8
E. shall be rooted up. *Zeph* 2:4
E. very sorrowful. *Zech* 9:5
E. a Jebusite. 7

Ekronites

the land of the *E.* not. *Josh* 13:3
ark came to Ekron, *E.* *1 Sam* 5:10

Elah

duke *E.* *Gen* 36:41
Shimei son of *E.* *1 Ki* 4:18
E. son of Baasha began. 16:8
Hoshea son of *E.* *2 Ki* 15:30; 17:1 18:1, 9
Caleb, *E.* the sons of *E.* *1 Chr* 4:15
E. the son of Uzzi, the son of. 9:8

Elah

pitched by valley of *E.* *1 Sam* 17:2
slew Goliath in valley of *E.* 21:9

Elam

of Shem, *E.* and Ashur. *Gen* 10:22
of Chedorlaomer king of *E.* 14:1
Hananiah and *E.* of. *1 Chr* 8:24
E. fifth son of Meshelemiah. 26:3
the children of *E.* *Ezra* 2:7, 31 8:7; *Neh* 7:12, 34
one of sons of *E.* answered. *Ezra* 10:2
chief of the people, *E.* *Neh* 10:14
Jehohanan and *E.* and Ezer. 12:42
recover people from *E.* *Isa* 11:11
go up, O *E.* 21:2
and *E.* bare the quiver. 22:6
made the kings of *E.* to. *Jer* 25:25
of Lord that came against *E.* 49:34
upon *E.* will I bring the four. 36
bring again the captivity of *E.* 39
there is *E.* and all her. *Ezek* 32:24
Shushan in province of *E.* *Dan* 8:2

Elamites

the *E.* wrote a letter to. *Ezra* 4:9
Parthians, *E.* we hear them. *Acts* 2:9

Elath

Azariah built *E.* *2 Ki* 14:22
that time Rezin recovered *E.* 16:6

El-bethel

altar, and called it *E.* *Gen* 35:7

Eldad

name of the one was *E.* *Num* 11:26
E. and Medad do prophesy. 27

elder

The original government of the Hebrews was patriarchal, where the head of the family exercised the supreme rule over all of his descendants; his married sons doing the same with their children and other descendants, but still remaining subordinate to the supreme head. At the father's death his firstborn succeeded him in supreme headship. Naturally only men of mature age came into these positions, hence the designation elder. In that way Jacob was the head of all who went to Egypt with him, although his sons had families of their own. From this came [1] *the great influence of the older people of the nation;* [2] *the division of the Israelites into tribes, with a head, chief, or prince over each as a whole;* [3] *the general use, in other nations as well as the Hebrews, of the term elder as an official title for those who as representatives of the people made all their decisions.*

The earliest mention of elders as a political body is at the time of the Exodus. The seventy elders mentioned in Exodus and Numbers were a sort of governing body, a parliament, and the origin of the tribunal of seventy elders called the Sanhedrin *or* Council. *There were also, after the founding of towns and cities, those who were put at the head of affairs who could not always derive their authority from their position in the tribe. These were also called elders, and they served as judges, to decide both civil and criminal causes.*

The Sanhedrin was a supreme council, serving as a court of appeal, and having a general oversight over the inferior courts, and the general affairs of the nation. In the New Testament Church the elders or presbyters were the same as the bishops. It was an office derived from the Jewish usage of elders or rulers of synagogues.

Shem the brother of Japhet the *e.* *Gen* 10:21*
e. serve younger. 25:23; *Rom* 9:12
my *e.* daughter Merab. *1 Sam* 18:17
kingdom, he is mine *e.* *1 Ki* 2:22
aged men, much *e.* than. *Job* 15:10
Elihu waited, they were *e.* 32:4
thy *e.* sister is Samaria. *Ezek* 16:46
names were Aholah the *e.* 23:4
his *e.* son was in field. *Luke* 15:25
intreat the *e.* women. *1 Tim* 5:2
younger, submit to the *e.* *1 Pet* 5:5

elder for *ruler*

rebuke not an *e.* but. *1 Tim* 5:1
against an *e.* receive not. 19
exhort, who am also an *e.* *1 Pet* 5:1
the *e.* to the elect lady. *2 John* 1
e. unto well-beloved. *3 John* 1

elders

e. of his house went. *Gen* 50:7
the *e.* of congregation. *Lev* 4:15
of Spirit to seventy *e.* *Num* 11:25
go to the gate to the *e.* *Deut* 25:7
stand before the Lord your *e.* 29:10
gather to me all *e.* of your. 31:28
ask thy father and *e.* and. 32:7
Israel served Lord all days of Joshua and *e.* *Josh* 24:31; *Judg* 2:7
described to him the *e.* *Judg* 8:14
e. of the town trembled. *1 Sam* 16:4
sent of the spoil to the *e.* of. 30:26
all the *e.* said to him. *1 Ki* 20:8
the *e.* did as Jezebel had. 21:11
Elisha sat in house, *e.* *2 Ki* 6:32
Jehu wrote letters and sent to *e.* 10:1
Hezekiah sent *e.* of priests to Isaiah the prophet. 19:2; *Isa* 37:2
eye of God upon the *e.* *Ezra* 5:5
the *e.* of the Jews builded. 6:14
counsel of the princes and *e.* 10:8
him in assembly of *e.* *Ps* 107:32
husband known among *e.* *Pr* 31:23
my priests and *e.* gave. *Lam* 1:19
e. of Zion sit upon the ground. 2:10
favoured not *e.* 4:16; 5:12
e. have ceased from gate. 5:14
and the *e.* of Judah. *Ezek* 8:1
sanctify a fast, gather *e.* *Joel* 1:14 2:16
the tradition of the *e.*? *Mat* 15:2
suffer many things of the *e.* 16:21 27:12
the *e.* sought false witness. 26:59
priests and *e.* persuaded the. 27:20
chief priests mocking with *e.* 41
they were assembled with *e.* 28:12
the tradition of the *e.* *Mark* 7:3
be rejected of *e.* 8:31; *Luke* 9:22
great multitude from *e.* *Mark* 14:43
priests held consultation with *e.* 15:1
unto the captains and *e.* *Luke* 22:52
their rulers and *e.* were. *Acts* 4:5
they reported all that *e.* had. 23
stirred up the people and *e.* 6:12
sent it to *e.* by Barnabas. 11:30
when they ordained *e.* in. 14:23
of the church and of the *e.* 15:4
apostles and *e.* came together. 6
the apostles, *e.* and brethren. 23
decrees ordained of the *e.* 16:4
he sent and called the *e.* of. 20:17
all the estate of the *e.* bear. 22:5
Ananias descended with *e.* 24:1
about whom the *e.* of Jews. 25:15
let *e.* that rule well be. *1 Tim* 5:17
thou shouldest ordain *e.* *Tit* 1:5
by faith the *e.* obtained. *Heb* 11:2
let him call for the *e.* *Jas* 5:14
e. which are among you. *1 Pet* 5:1
upon seats I saw 24 *e.* *Rev* 4:4
the 24 *e.* fall before him. 10 5:8, 14; 11:16; 19:4
one of *e.* saith unto me, weep. 5:5
in midst of the *e.* a Lamb. 6
voice of many angels about *e.* 11
all angels stood about *e.* 7:11
one of *e.* answered saying to me. 13
new song before throne and *e.* 14:3

elders with *city*

e. of his *city* shall fetch. *Deut* 19:12
e. of that *city* shall take and. 21:3
e. of that *city* wash their hands. 6
their son to *e.* of his *city.* 19
of virginity to *e.* of the *city.* 22:15
the *e.* of his *city* shall call. 25:8
declare his cause to *e.* *Josh* 20:4
took the *e.* of the *city.* *Judg* 8:16
ten men of *e.* of *city.* *Ruth* 4:2
them *e.* of every *city.* *Ezra* 10:14

elders *of Israel*

gather *e. of Israel* together. *Ex* 3:16
called for all the *e. of Israel.* 12:21
take with thee of *e. of Israel.* 17:5
e. of Israel came to eat with. 18:12
seventy of the *e. of Israel.* 24:1, 9 *Num* 11:16
e. of Israel commanded. *Deut* 27:1
this law to the *e. of Israel.* 31:9
e. of Israel put dust on. *Josh* 7:6
so all the *e. of Israel* came to king. *2 Sam* 5:3; *1 Ki* 8:3; *2 Chr* 5:4
pleased all *e. of Israel.* *2 Sam* 17:4
Ahithophel counsel *e. of Israel.* 15
e. of Israel came to king. *1 Chr* 11:3
David and *e. of Israel* fell. 21:16
came the *e. of Israel.* *Ezek* 14:1
e. of Israel came to inquire. 20:1
rulers of people, *e. of Israel.* *Acts* 4:8

elders with *people*

called for *e.* of the *people.* *Ex* 19:7
to be *e.* of the *people.* *Num* 11:16
70 men of the *e.* of the *people.* 24
buy it before *e.* of *people.* *Ruth* 4:4
before *e.* of my *people.* *1 Sam* 15:30
the *e.* of the *people* came. *Mat* 21:23; *Luke* 22:66
a multitude from *e.* of the *people.* *Mat* 26:47
e. of the *people* took counsel. 27:1
stirred up people and *e.* *Acts* 6:12

eldest

Abraham said to his *e.* *Gen* 24:2
Isaac called Esau his *e.* son. 27:1
searched, and began at the *e.* 44:12
Israel's *e.* son. *Num* 1:20; 26:5

three e. sons of Jesse followed.
1 Sam 17:13, 14
Eliab his e. brother heard. 28
he took his e. son and. 2 Ki 3:27
of men had slain the e. 2 Chr 22:1
drinking in their e. Job 1:13, 18
one by one, beginning at e. John 8:9

Elealeh

of Reuben built E. Num 32:37
Heshbon shall cry, and E. Isa 15:4
water thee with my tears, O E. 16:9
cry of Hesbon even to E. Jer 48:34

Eleazar

Aaron's son E. Ex 6:25; 28:1
Num 3:2; 26:60; 1 Chr 6:3; 24:1
Ezra 8:33
Moses was angry with E. Lev 10:16
E. ministered in priest's. Num 3:4
E. son of Aaron shall be chief. 32
to the office of E. pertaineth. 4:16
E. the priest took the. 16:39
put his garments upon E. 20:26
Moses and E. came down. 28
numbered by Moses and E. 26:63
he set Joshua before E. 27:22
brought spoil to Moses and E. 31:12
take sum of prey thou and E. 26
Moses gave tribute unto E. 41
E. and Joshua divide land. 34:17
came near before E. Josh 17:4
E. died. 24:33
sanctified E. to keep. 1 Sam 7:1
after him E. son of Dodo.
2 Sam 23:9; 1 Chr 11:12
son of E. was ruler. 1 Chr 9:20
sons of Mahli, E. 23:21; 24:28
E. died, and had no sons. 23:22
more chief men of sons of E. 24:4
governors were of sons of E. 5
Shemaiah and E. were. Neh 12:42
Eliud begat E. and E. Mat 1:15

elect

Or Chosen, is used, [1] *Of Christ,* Isa 42:1. [2] *Of good angels,* 1 Tim 5:21. [3] *Of the Israelites, who were God's chosen and peculiar people,* Isa 65:9, 22. [4] *Of those in whom Divine grace has achieved its supreme triumph, and who have passed from death unto life, and from the power of sin to the glad and eager service of God and our Lord Jesus Christ.*

behold mine e. in whom. Isa 42:1*
Israel mine e. I have called. 45:4*
mine elect shall inherit it. 65:9*
mine e. shall long enjoy work. 22*
but for the e.'s sake those days shall.
Mat 24:22; Mark 13:20
possible deceive very e. Mat 24:24
Mark 13:22
and they shall gather his e. from.
Mat 24:31; Mark 13:27
not God avenge his e.? Luke 18:7
any thing to charge of God's e.?
Rom 8:33
put on as the e. of God. Col 3:12
charge thee before the e. 1 Tim 5:21
endure all things for e.'s. 2 Tim 2:10
according to faith of God's e. Tit 1:1
e. according to foreknowledge.
1 Pet 1:2
Sion a chief corner-stone, e. 2:6
the elder to the e. lady. 2 John 1
the children of thy e. sister. 13

elected

church at Babylon e. 1 Pet 5:13

election

to e. might stand. Rom 9:11
a remnant according to e. of 11:5
the e. hath obtained it, the rest. 7
but as touching the e. they. 28
brethren, your e. of God. 1 Thes 1:4
your calling and e. sure. 2 Pet 1:10

El-elohe-Israel

called altar E.-Israel. Gen 33:20

elements

in bondage under e. of. Gal 4:3*
again to weak and beggarly e. 9*
the e. shall melt. 2 Pet 3:10, 12

elephant, *see* **ivory**

eleven

Jacob took his e. sons. Gen 32:22
sun, moon, and e. stars made. 37:9
curtains of goats' hair, e. Ex 26:7
the e. curtains shall be all of. 8
e. curtains he made. 36:14
e. of one size. 15
on third day e. bullocks. Num 29:20
are e. days' journey. Deut 1:2
e. cities with villages. Josh 15:51
give thee e. hundred pieces of silver.
Judg 16:5
I took the e. hundred shekels. 17:2
restored e. hundred shekels to. 3
Jehoiakim reigned e. years in.
2 Ki 23:36; 2 Chr 36:5
Zedekiah e. years. 2 Ki 24:18
2 Chr 36:11; Jer 52:1
then the e. disciples. Mat 28:16
he appeared to the e. Mark 16:14
all these things to the e. Luke 24:9
found the e. gathered together. 33
was numbered with the e. Acts 1:26
Peter standing up with e. 2:14

eleventh

in the e. year was house. 1 Ki 6:38
in e. year of Joram. 2 Ki 9:29
Jerusalem was besieged to the e.
2 Ki 25:2; Jer 52:5
the e. lot came forth. 1 Chr 24:12
the e. to Azareel, he, his. 25:18
e. captain for the e. month. 27:14
Jeremiah prophesied in e. Jer 1:3
in the e. year the city was. 39:2
word of the Lord came to Ezekiel in
e. year. Ezek 26:1; 30:20; 31:1
and about the e. hour. Mat 20:6
that were hired about the e. hour. 9
e. foundation of city was. Rev 21:20

Elhanan

E. slew brother of Goliath.
2 Sam 21:19; 1 Chr 20:5
E. the son of Dodo. 2 Sam 23:24
1 Chr 11:26

Eli

brought the child to E. 1 Sam 1:25
minister to Lord before E. 2:11; 3:1
now the sons of E. were sons. 2:12
came a man of God to E. and. 27
Samuel ran to E. and. 3:5; 6:8
in that day perform against E. 3:12
iniquity of E.'s house shall. 14
came in hastily and told E. 4:14
he spake concerning E. 1 Ki 2:27

Eli, Eli, *lama sabachthani*

E. E. lama sab. Mat 27:46
Eloi, Eloi, lama sab. Mark 15:34

Eliab

of tribe of Zebulon, E. Num 1:9
2:7; 7:24, 29; 10:16
Abiram sons of E. 16:1, 12; 26:9
sons of Pallu, E. 26:8
he did to sons of E. Deut 11:6
looked on E. 1 Sam 16:6
E. heard, and his anger. 17:28
begat his firstborn E. 1 Chr 2:13
E. the son of Nahath, the. 6:27
E. captain of the Gadites. 12:9
E. porter. 15:18, 20
E. with a psaltery. 16:5
took the daughter of E. 2 Chr 11:18

Eliada

E. a son of David. 2 Sam 5:16
1 Chr 3:8
of Benjamin, E. 2 Chr 17:17

Eliakim

came out E. the son of Hilkiah.
2 Ki 18:18; Isa 36:3
Hezekiah sent E. to Isaiah.
2 Ki 19:2; Isa 37:2
made E. son of Josiah king.
2 Ki 23:34; 2 Chr 36:4
E. and Maaseiah the. Neh 12:41
will call my servant E. Isa 22:20
Abiud begat E. and E. Mat 1:13
Jonan, the son of E. Luke 3:30

Eliam

the daughter of E. 2 Sam 11:3
E. the son of Ahithophel the. 23:34

Elias, *see* **Elijah**

Eliashib

E. and Pelaiah sons of. 1 Chr 3:24
eleventh lot came forth to E.
1 Chr 24:12
Johanan the son of E. Ezra 10:6
Neh 12:23
E. a singer. Ezra 10:24
E. the son of Zattu. 27
E. son of Bani. 36
E. the high priest. Neh 3:1
Joiakim begat E. and E. 12:10
E. was allied to Tobiah. 13:4
the evil E. did. 7
of sons of Joiada, son of E. 28

Eliezer

steward of my house is E. Gen 15:2
name of Moses' son was E.
Ex 18:4; 1 Chr 23:15
sons of Becher, E. and. 1 Chr 7:8
Benaiah and E. the priests. 15:24
son of E. was Rehabiah the. 23:17
ruler of Reubenites was E. 27:16
E. prophesied against. 2 Chr 20:37
then sent I for E. and. Ezra 8:16
E. had taken strange. 10:18, 23, 31
Jose, the son of E. Luke 3:29

Elihoreph

E. and Ahiah, sons of. 1 Ki 4:3

Elihu

of Jeroham, son of E. 1 Sam 1:1
E. fell to David out. 1 Chr 12:20
E. and Semachiah strong men. 26:7
of Judah, E. one of the. 27:18
wrath of E. the Buzite. Job 32:2
E. had waited. 4
E. answered. 6; 34:1; 35:1

Elijah, or Elias

E. the Tishbite said to. 1 Ki 17:1
did according to saying of E. 15
Lord heard the voice of E. 22
E. took the child, and brought. 23
E. went to shew himself. 18:2
art thou that my lord E.? 7
E. is here. 8
Ahab went to meet E. 16
E. mocked them. 27
E. slew all the prophets of Baal. 40
hand of the Lord was on E. 46
Ahab told Jezebel all that E. 19:1
what doest thou here, E.? 9, 13
and ran after E. 20, 21
Ahab said to E. hast thou? 21:20
it is E. the Tishbite. 2 Ki 1:8
third captain fell before E. 13
according to the word E. had. 17
when Lord would take up E. 2:1
E. took his mantle, and wrapt it. 8
E. went up by a whirlwind. 11
where is Lord God of E.? 14
spirit of E. doth rest on Elisha. 15
poured water on the hands of E. 3:11
which he spake by E. 9:36; 10:10, 17
a writing from E. 2 Chr 21:12
Maaseiah and E. sons of. Ezra 10:21
behold, I will send you E. Mal 4:5
this is Elias which was. Mat 11:14
some say, Elias. 16:14; Mark 6:15
Luke 9:8, 19
there appeared Elias. Mat 17:3
Mark 9:4; Luke 9:30
three tabernacles, one for Elias.
Mat 17:4; Mark 9:5; Luke 9:33
that Elias must first come.
Mat 17:10; Mark 9:11
Elias shall come and restore things.
Mat 17:11; Mark 9:12
Elias is come already. Mat 17:12
Mark 9:13
this man calleth for Elias.
Mat 27:47; Mark 15:35
let us see whether Elias will.
Mat 27:49; Mark 15:36
in the power of Elias. Luke 1:17
widows in the days of Elias. 4:25
fire to consume them as Elias. 9:54
art thou Elias? art thou? John 1:21
if thou be not Elias, why? 25
scripture saith of Elias. Rom 11:2
Elias was a man subject. Jas 5:17

Elim

came to E. Ex 15:27; Num 33:9
took their journey from E.
Ex 16:1; Num 33:10

Elimelech
name of man was *E.* *Ruth* 1:2
E. died. 3
Boaz a kinsman of family of *E.* 2:1
I have bought all that was *E.'s* 4:9

Eliphalet
Eliada and *E.* David's son. *2 Sam* 5:16; *1 Chr* 3:6, 8

Eliphaz
Adah bare to Esau, *E.* *Gen* 36:4, 10 *1 Chr* 1:35
the sons of *E.* *Gen* 36:11, 12, 15 *1 Chr* 1:36
E. came from his place. *Job* 2:11
E. the Temanite. 4:1; 15:1; 22:1
E. did as Lord commanded. 42:9

Elisabeth
Zacharias' wife *E.* *Luke* 1:5
E. was barren. 7
E. conceived. 24, 36
Mary saluted *E.* 40
E.'s full time came that she. 57

Elisha, Eliseus
thou shalt anoint *E.* *1 Ki* 19:16
escaped from Jehu, shall *E.* slay. 17
Elijah departed, and found *E.* 19
at Jericho came to *E.* *2 Ki* 2:5
E. saw it, and cried, my father. 12
spirit of Elijah doth rest on *E.* 15
is *E.* the son of Shaphat. 3:11
cried a certain woman unto *E.* 4:1
E. passed to Shunem, where was. 8
bare a son at that season that *E.* 17
when *E.* was come, behold. 32
came and stood at door of *E.* 5:9
E. telleth the words that. 6:12
E. prayed to the Lord . . . according to the word of *E.* 18
E. said, Lord, open eyes of. 20
if the head of *E.* stand on him. 31
the great things that *E.* hath. 8:4
the woman whose son *E.* restored. 5
what said *E.* to thee? 14
E. was fallen sick. 13:14
E. put his hands upon king's. 16
E. said, shoot. 17
cast man into sepulchre of *E.* 21
lepers in days of. *Luke* 4:27

Elishah
of Javan, *E.* *Gen* 10:4; 1 *Chr* 1:7
blue and purple from *E.* *Ezek* 27:7

Elishama
E. the son of Ammihud. *Num* 1:10 2:18; 7:48, 53; 10:22; *1 Chr* 7:26
E. David's son. *2 Sam* 5:16 *1 Chr* 3:6, 8; 14:7
and Jekamiah begat *E.* *1 Chr* 2:41
he sent with them *E.* *2 Chr* 17:8
E. scribe. *Jer* 36:12
E. of the seed royal. 41:1

Elisheba
Aaron took him *E.* *Ex.* 6:23

Elishua
E. David's. *2 Sam* 5:15; *1 Chr* 14:5

Eliud
Achim begat *E.* *Mat* 1:14
E. begat Eleazar. 15

Elkanah
sons of Korah; Assir, and *E.* *Ex* 6:24
his name was *E.* *1 Sam* 1:1
E. went up to offer sacrifice. 21
E. went to his house. 2:11
Eli blessed *E.* 20
the son of *E.* *1 Chr* 6:23, 27, 34 35; 9:16
the sons of *E.* 6:25, 26
E. the Korhite. 12:6
E. was doorkeeper for ark. 15:23
E. that was next to king. *2 Chr* 28:7

Elmodam
Cosam, the son of *E.* *Luke* 3:28

Elnathan
Nehushta daughter of *E.* *2 Ki* 24:8
I sent for *E.* and Jarib, *Ezra* 8:16
Jehoiakim sent *E.* into. *Jer* 26:22
E. the son of Achbor. 36:12
E. had made intercession to. 25

Elon
Bashemath daughter of *E.* *Gen* 26:34
Esau took Adah daughter of *E.* *Gen* 36:2
sons of Zebulun, Sered and *E.* 46:14
E. judged Israel. *Judg* 12:11
E. died. 12

eloquent
O my Lord, I am not *e.* *Ex* 4:10
doth take away *e.* orator. *Isa* 3:3*
named Apollos, an *e.* *Acts* 18:24*

else
give me children or *e.* I. *Gen* 30:1
doing any thing *e.* go. *Num* 20:19
the Lord he is God, there is none *e.* *Deut* 4:35, 39; *1 Ki* 8:60; *Isa* 45:5 6, 14, 18, 21, 22; 46:9; *Joel* 2:27
e. if ye in any wise go. *Josh* 23:12
nothing *e.* save sword. *Judg* 7:14
if I taste aught *e.* till. *2 Sam* 3:35
or *e.* three days sword. *1 Chr* 21:12
whoso *e.* cometh in. *2 Chr* 23:7
nothing *e.* but sorrow of. *Neh* 2:2
not sacrifice, *e.* would I. *Ps* 51:16
who *e.* can hasten here? *Eccl* 2:25
I am, none *e.* besides. *Isa* 47:8, 10
or *e.* believe me for. *John* 14:11
time in nothing *e.* but. *Acts* 17:21
accusing, or *e.* excusing. *Rom* 2:15
e. were your children. *1 Cor* 7:14
e. when thou shalt bless. 14:16
repent, or *e.* I will. *Rev* 2:5, 16

Elul
25th day of the month *E.* *Neh* 6:15

Elymas
but *E.* the sorcerer. *Acts* 13:8

embalm
physicians to *e.* his. *Gen* 50:2

embalmed
the physicians *e.* Israel. *Gen* 50:2
days of those that are *e.* 3
they *e.* Joseph, put him in a. 26

emboldened
conscience of weak be *e.* *1 Cor* 8:10

emboldeneth
what *e.* thee that thou? *Job* 16:3*

embrace
about this season thou shalt *e.* *2 Ki* 4:16
they *e.* the rock for want. *Job* 24:8
when thou dost *e.* her. *Pr* 4:8
why wilt thou *e.* bosom of? 5:20
a time to *e.* and refrain. *Eccl* 3:5
right hand doth *e.* *S of S* 2:6; 8:3
brought up in scarlet *e.* *Lam* 4:5

embraced
Laban *e.* Jacob. *Gen* 29:13
Esau ran and *e.* Jacob. 33:4
Jacob kissed and *e.* Joseph's. 48:10
Paul *e.* disciples and. *Acts* 20:1*
having seen and *e.* *Heb* 11:13*

embracing
and a time to refrain *e.* *Eccl* 3:5
Paul *e.* Eutychus said. *Acts* 20:10

embroider
thou shalt *e.* the coat. *Ex* 28:39*

embroiderer
manner of work of *e.* *Ex* 35:35
with him Aholiab, an *e.* in. 38:23

emerald, -s
second row an *e.* *Ex* 28:18; 39:11
in thy fairs with *e.* *Ezek* 27:16
precious stone thy covering, *e.* 28:13
in sight like unto *e.* *Rev* 4:3
fourth foundation was an *e.* 21:19

emerods
Lord will smite with *e.* *Deut* 28:27
smote Ashdod with *e.* *1 Sam* 5:6*
men of the city had *e.* 9*
that died not were smitten with *e.* 12*
five golden *e.* and five. 6:4*, 17*
make images of your *e.* 5*, 11*

Emims
came and smote the *E.* *Gen* 14:5
the *E.* dwelt therein in. *Deut* 2:10

eminent
built to thee an *e.* *Ezek* 16:24, 31
shall throw down thine *e.* place. 39
an high mountain and *e.* 17:22

Emmanuel
Or Immanuel, *is a* Hebrew *word, meaning* God with us. *A child whose birth is prophesied in* Isa 7:14 *as a sign from God. In its final fulfilment it has always been held to refer to the Messiah,* Mat 1:23, *and the name is applied to Christ by early Christian writers, and by modern writers down to our own day.*
shall call his name *Em.* *Isa* 7:14 *Mat* 1:23
fill breadth of thy land, O *Em.* *Isa* 8:8

Emmaus
that same day to *E.* *Luke* 24:13

Emmor
bought of sons of *E.* *Acts* 7:16

empire
published throughout all his *e.* *Esth* 1:20*

employ
tree is man's life, to *e.* *Deut* 20:19*

employed
these singers *e.* day and. *1 Chr* 9:33
and Jahaziah *e.* about. *Ezra* 10:15*

employment
out men of continual *e.* *Ezek* 39:14

emptied
hasted and *e.* her. *Gen* 24:20
came to pass as they *e.* sacks. 42:35
high priest's officer *e.* *2 Chr* 24:11
be he shaken out and *e.* *Neh* 5:13
brooks of defence shall be *e.* *Isa* 19:6*
land shall be utterly *e.* and. 24:3
Moab not been *e.* from. *Jer* 48:11
emptiers have *e.* them. *Nah* 2:2

emptiers
e. have emptied them out. *Nah* 2:2

emptiness
upon it the stones of *e.* *Isa* 34:11

empty
hadst sent me away *e.* *Gen* 31:42
the pit was *e.* there was no. 37:24
the seven *e.* ears blasted. 41:27
go, ye shall not go *e.* *Ex* 3:21
Egypt, none shall appear before me *e.* 23:15; 34:20; *Deut* 16:16
not let him go away *e.* *Deut* 15:13
in every man's hand *e.* *Judg* 7:16
brought me home *e.* *Ruth* 1:21
not *e.* to thy mother-in-law. 3:17
send not ark away *e.* *1 Sam* 6:3
thy seat will be *e.* 20:18, 25, 27
sword of Saul returned not *e.* *2 Sam* 1:22
borrow thee *e.* vessels. *2 Ki* 4:3
hast sent widows away *e.* *Job* 22:9
stretcheth north over *e.* place. 26:7
Lord maketh earth *e.* *Isa* 24:1
awaketh, and his soul is *e.* 29:8
make *e.* soul of the hungry. 32:6
returned with their vessels *e.* *Jer* 14:3
king of Babylon made me *e.* 51:34
then set it *e.* upon the. *Ezek* 24:11
Israel is an *e.* vine. *Hos* 10:1*
Nineveh is *e.* and void. *Nah* 2:10
is come, he findeth it *e.* *Mat* 12:44
and sent him away *e.* *Mark* 12:3 *Luke* 20:10, 11
rich he hath sent *e.* away. *Luke* 1:53

empty, *verb*
command that they *e.* *Lev* 14:36
clouds *e.* themselves. *Eccl* 11:3
wanderers shall *e.* his. *Jer* 48:12
fanners fan her and *e.* her. 51:2
they therefore *e.* their net. *Hab* 1:17
which *e.* the golden oil. *Zech* 4:12

emulation
if I may provoke to *e.* *Rom* 11:14*

emulations
works of the flesh are *e.* *Gal* 5:20*

enabled
Christ Jesus who hath *e.* *1 Tim* 1:12

encamp

e. before Pi-hahiroth. Ex 14:2
the Levites shall e. Num 1:50
as they e. so set forward. 2:17
but those that e. before the. 3:38
knowest how we are to e. 10:31
e. against Rabbah. 2 Sam 12:28
his troops come and e. Job 19:12
host should e. against me. Ps 27:3
I will e. about mine house. Zech 9:8

encamped

e. in Etham. Ex 13:20
e. by the waters. 15:27
where Moses e. at mount. 18:5
from Elim they e. by. Num 33:10
from Red Sea, and e. in the. 11
people came up and e. in Gilgal. Josh 4:19; 5:10
kings of the Amorites e. 10:5
Midianites e. against. Judg 6:4
Abimelech e. against Thebez. 9:50
children of Ammon e. in Gilead, Israel e. at Mizpeh. 10:17
Nahash e. against. 1 Sam 11:1
Philistines e. in Michmash. 13:16
the servants are e. in. 2 Sam 11:11
e. against Gibbethon. 1 Ki 16:15, 16
the Philistines e. in. 1 Chr 11:15
Sennacherib e. against. 2 Chr 32:1

encampeth

angel of the Lord e. Ps 34:7
scattered bones of him that e. 53:5

encamping

Egyptians overtook them e. Ex 14:9

enchanter

shall not be found an e. Deut 18:10

enchanters

not to dreamers nor e. Jer 27:9*

enchantments

magicians did so with e. Ex 7:11, 22; 8:7, 18
nor shall ye use e. nor. Lev 19:26
there is no e. against. Num 23:23
Balaam went not to seek for e. 24:1
used divination and e. 2 Ki 17:17
Manasseh used e. 21:6; 2 Chr 33:6
serpent will bite without e. Eccl 10:11*
for abundance of thine e. Isa 47:9
stand now with thine e. and. 12

encline, enclose, *see* **incline, inclose**

encountered

certain philosophers e. Acts 17:18

encourage

e. him, he shall cause to inherit it. Deut 1:38; 3:28
say to Joab, and e. 2 Sam 11:25
they e. themselves in an. Ps 64:5

encouraged

David e. himself in. 1 Sam 30:6*
priests and Levites be e. 2 Chr 31:4*
Josiah e. them to the service. 35:2
the carpenter e. goldsmith. Isa 41:7

end

[1] *A limit or boundary*, Job 37:3; 38:18. [2] *Termination, issue, or result*, 1 Sam 14:27. [3] *Death or destruction*, Gen 6:13; Amos 8:2; Mat 24:6. [4] *Purpose, aim*, Rom 10:4; 1 Tim 1:5.

the e. of all flesh is. Gen 6:13
e. of Egypt to the other e. 47:21
feast of in-gathering in the e. of year. Ex 23:16; 34:22
one cherub on the one e. the other cherub on other e. of. 25:19
scatter from one e. of. Deut 28:64
I will see what their e. shall. 32:20
angel put forth the e. Judg 6:21
the day groweth to an e. 19:9
Jonathan put forth e. of. 1 Sam 14:27
Baal was full from one e. 2 Ki 10:21
with blood from one e. 21:16
after the e. of two years. 2 Chr 21:19
uncleanness from one e. to. Ezra 9:11
what is my e. that I? Job 6:11
shall vain words have e.? 16:3
day and night come to an e. 26:10
he setteth an e. to darkness. 28:3
of wicked come to an e. Ps 7:9
destructions come to perpetual e. Ps 9:6
going forth is from the e. of. 19:6
for the e. of that man is. 37:37
the e. of the wicked shall be. 38†
make me to know mine e. 39:4
from the e. of the earth will. 61:2
I understood their e. 73:17*
and thy years have no e. 102:27
seen an e. of all perfection. 119:96
her e. is bitter. Pr 5:4*
but the e. thereof are. 14:12
there is an e. 23:18
not what to do in the e. 25:8
yet there is no e. of all. Eccl 4:8
there is no e. of all people. 16
the e. of all men. 7:2
better the e. of a thing. 8
e. of his talk is mischievous. 10:13
many books there is no e. 12:12
nor is there any e. of their treasures, nor any e. of their. Isa 2:7
his government shall be no e. 9:7
come from the e. of heaven. 13:5*
the extortioner is at an e. 16:4
after e. of 70 years Tyre. 23:15, 17
sing praise from e. of earth. 42:10
confounded world without e. 45:17
declaring the e. from the. 46:10
will you do in the e.? Jer 5:31
sword of Lord shall devour from one e. to the other e. 12:12; 25:33
at his e. he shall be a fool. 17:11
to give you an expected e. 29:11
there is hope in thine e. 31:17
till there be an e. of them. 44:27
his city is taken at one e. 51:31
our e. is near, our e. is. Lam 4:18
an e. the e. is come. Ezek 7:2, 3, 6
iniquity have an e. 21:25, 29; 35:5
hitherto is the e. of. Dan 7:28
time of e. shall be vision. 8:17
time appointed the e. 19*; 11:27
e. with a flood, and to e. 9:26
in the e. of years they shall. 11:6
purge them even to time of e. 35
at time of the e. king of south. 40
yet he shall come to his e. 45
seal book to time of the e. 12:4
shall be the e. of these things? 8*
words are closed, till time of the e. 9
go thou thy way till the e. be. 13
great houses have an e. Amos 3:15
to what e. is it for you? 5:18
the e. is come upon my people. 8:2
I will make the e. thereof. 10
for there is none e. of. Nah 2:9
there is none e. of their corpses. 3:3
the harvest is the e. of. Mat 13:39
shall be the sign of the e.? 24:3
gospel be preached, then shall e. 14
gather from one e. of heaven to. 31
went in and sat to see the e. 26:58
in the e. of the sabbath came. 28:1
cannot stand, hath an e. Mark 3:26
kingdom shall be no e. Luke 1:33
a parable to them, to this e. 18:1
things concerning me have e. 22:37
a king, to this e. was. John 18:37
for the e. of those. Rom 6:21
fruit to holiness, e. everlasting. 22
Christ is the e. of the law. 10:4
to this e. Christ both died. 14:9
for to this e. also. 2 Cor 2:9
e. shall be according to their. 11:15
glory world without e. Eph 3:21
many walk, whose e. is. Phil 3:19
e. of commandment is. 1 Tim 1:5
whose e. is to be burned. Heb 6:8
oath is to them an e. of all. 16
having neither beginning nor e. 7:3
but now once in the e. hath. 9:26
considering the e. of their. 13:7*
and ye have seen e. of. Jas 5:11
receiving e. of your faith. 1 Pet 1:9
what shall be the e. of them? 4:17
I am Alpha and Omega, the beginning and the e. Rev 21:6; 22:13

at the **end**

at the e. of forty days. Gen 8:6
at the e. of two years Pharaoh. 41:1
at the e. of 430 years. Ex 12:41
of consecration at an e. Lev 8:33
at the e. of 40 days. Deut 9:11
at the e. of three years. 14:28
at the e. of every seventh year a release. 15:1
at the e. of every seventh year read this law. 31:10
at the e. of three days. Josh 9:16
at the e. of two months. Judg 11:39
Boaz lay down at e. of. Ruth 3:7
at the e. of every year. 2 Sam 14:26
came to Jerusalem at the e. 24:8
at the e. of 3 years two. 1 Ki 2:39
at the e. of 7 years the. 2 Ki 8:3
at the e. of three years they. 18:10
find them at the e. of brook. 2 Chr 20:16
at the e. of year host of Syria. 24:23
stagger, and are at wits' e. Ps 107:27
go to meet Ahaz at the e. Isa 7:3
at the e. of seven years let go. Jer 34:14
at the e. of seven days. Ezek 3:16
at the e. they might stand. Dan 1:5
at the e. of 12 months he. 4:29
stand in the lot at the e. of. 12:13
at the e. it shall speak. Hab 2:3
in the e. of this world. Mat 13:40

but the **end**

seems right to a man, but the e. are ways of death. Pr 14:12; 16:25
but the e. thereof shall not. 20:21
but the e. is not yet. Mat 24:6
Mark 13:7; Luke 21:9
but the e. of all things. 1 Pet 4:7

last **end**

let my last e. be like. Num 23:10
shall not see our last e. Jer 12:4
remembereth not her last e. Lam 1:9
what shall be in last e. Dan 8:19

latter **end**

his latter e. shall be. Num 24:20
good at thy latter e. Deut 8:16
would consider their latter e. 32:29
kindness in the latter e. Ruth 3:10
bitterness in latter e. 2 Sam 2:26
yet thy latter e. should. Job 8:7
Lord blessed the latter e. of. 42:12
be wise in thy latter e. Pr 19:20
and know the latter e. Isa 41:22
remember the latter e. of it. 47:7
the latter e. is worse. 2 Pet 2:20

made an **end**

as Isaac had made an e. Gen 27:30
Jacob made an e. of. 49:33
made an e. of reconciling. Lev 16:20
made an e. of covering. Num 4:15
had made an e. of speaking. 16:31
Deut 20:9
made an e. of tithing. Deut 26:12
Moses had made an e. 31:24
made an e. of speaking. 32:45
Judg 15:17; 1 Sam 18:1; 24:16
2 Sam 13:36; 1 Ki 1:41; 3:1
Jer 26:8; 43:1; 51:63
made an e. of slaying. Josh 8:24
10:20
made an e. of dividing. 19:49, 51
had made an e. to offer. Judg 3:18
1 Sam 13:10
he had made an e. of. 1 Sam 10:13
made an e. of telling. 2 Sam 11:19
Hiram made an e. of. 1 Ki 7:40
Solomon made an e. of praying. 8:54; 2 Chr 7:1
made an e. of offering. 2 Ki 10:25
1 Chr 16:2; 2 Chr 29:29
made an e. of the. 2 Chr 20:23
till they had made an e. 24:10
made an e. with all that. Ezra 10:17
he had made an e. of measuring inner house. Ezek 42:15
thou hast made an e. of. 43:23
made an e. of eating. Amos 7:2
made an e. of commanding. Mat 11:1

make an **end**

I will also make an e. 1 Sam 3:12
will they make an e. in a? Neh 4:2
long ere you make an e.? Job 18:2
thou shalt make an e. to. Isa 33:1
thou make an e. of me. 38:12, 13
nor did I make an e. of. Ezek 20:17
to make an e. of sins. Dan 9:24
he will make an utter e. Nah 1:8, 9

make a full **end**
desolate, yet will I not *make a full e.*
Jer 4:27; 5:18; 30:11; 46:28
destroy, but *make* not *a full e.* 5:10
thou *make a full e.*? *Ezek* 11:13

to the **end**
to the e. thou mayest know that I.
Ex 8:22; *Ezek* 20:26
to the e. Israel may. *Lev* 17:5
to the e. that he should. *Deut* 17:16
to the e. that he may prolong. 20
their words *to the e.* of. *Ps* 19:4
to the e. my glory may sing. 30:12
thy statutes even *to the e.* 119:112
from beginning *to the e.* *Eccl* 3:11
to the e. man should find. 7:14
utter it even *to the e.* *Isa* 48:20
be my salvation *to the e.* 49:6
will he keep it *to the e.*? *Jer* 3:5
to the e. that none of. *Ezek* 31:14
sight thereof *to the e.* *Dan* 4:11
dominion reacheth *to the e.* of. 22
how long shall be *to the e.*? 12:6
to the e. that every one. *Ob* 9
endureth *to the e.* shall be saved.
Mat 10:22; 24:13; *Mark* 13:13
cast out, *to the e.* they. *Acts* 7:19
to the e. you may be. *Rom* 1:11
to the e. the promise might. 4:16
acknowledge *to the e.* *2 Cor* 1:13
look *to the e.* of that. 3:13
to the e. he may establish.
1 Thes 3:13
sober, and hope *to the e.* *1 Pet* 1:13

unto the **end**
beginning *unto the e.* *Deut* 11:12
the east border was *unto the e.*
Josh 15:5
to glean *unto the e.* of. *Ruth* 2:23
may be tried *unto the e.* *Job* 34:36
wars to cease *unto the e.* *Ps* 46:9
I shall keep it *unto the e.* 119:33
proclaimed *unto the e.* of. *Isa* 62:11
it came *unto the e.* of. *Jer* 1:3
dominion even *unto the e.* *Dan* 6:26
destroy his dominion *unto the e.* 7:26
and *unto the e.* of the war. 9:26
alway, even *unto the e.* *Mat* 28:20
loved them *unto the e.* *John* 13:1
confirm you *unto the e.* *1 Cor* 1:8
fast confidence *unto the e.* *Heb* 3:6
beginning stedfast *unto the e.* 14
assurance of hope *unto the e.* 6:11
my works *unto the e.* *Rev* 2:26

endamage
so thou shalt *e.* the. *Ezra* 4:13†

endanger
make me *e.* my head to. *Dan* 1:10

endangered
cleaveth wood shall be *e.* *Eccl* 10:9

endeavour
I will *e.* that you may. *2 Pet* 1:15*

endeavoured
we *e.* to go into Macedonia.
Acts 16:10*
we *e.* to see your face. *1 Thes* 2:17

endeavouring
e. to keep the unity of. *Eph* 4:3*

endeavours
to wickedness of their *e.* *Ps* 28:4*

ended
seventh day God *e.* work. *Gen* 2:2
years of plenteousness *e.* 41:53
words till they were *e.* *Deut* 31:30
mourning for Moses were *e.* 34:8
so they *e.* the matter. *2 Sam* 20:18
the words of Job are *e.* *Job* 31:40
prayers of David are *e.* *Ps* 72:20
days of thy mourning *e.* *Isa* 60:20
is past, summer is *e.* *Jer* 8:20
when Jesus had *e.* these. *Mat* 7:28
when forty days were *e.* *Luke* 4:2
when the devil had *e.* all. 13
supper being *e.* the devil. *John* 13:2

endeth
noise of them that rejoice *e.* *Isa* 24:8

ending
I am the beginning and *e.* *Rev* 1:8

endless
heed to *e.* genealogies. *1 Tim* 1:4
after power of an *e.* life. *Heb* 7:16

En-dor
Manasseh had *E.* *Josh* 17:11
a woman at *E.* hath a. *1 Sam* 28:7
Jabin, which perished at *E.* *Ps* 83:10

endow
he shall surely *e.* her. *Ex* 22:16*

ends
push the people to *e.* *Deut* 33:17
shall judge the *e.* of the. *1 Sam* 2:10
the *e.* of staves were seen. *1 Ki* 8:8
2 Chr 5:9
for he looketh to the *e.* *Job* 28:24
directeth his lightning to *e.* 37:3
it might take hold of the *e.* 38:13
and his circuit to the *e.* *Ps* 19:6
all the *e.* of the world shall. 22:27
thy praise to *e.* of the earth. 48:10
God ruleth in Jacob to the *e.* 59:13
confidence of all the *e.* of. 65:5
all the *e.* of the earth shall fear. 67:7
the *e.* of earth have seen the. 98:3
vapours to ascend from the *e.* of the
earth. 135:7; *Jer* 10:13; 51:16
eyes of a fool are in *e.* *Pr* 17:24
established all *e.* of the earth? 30:4
creator of the *e.* of earth. *Isa* 40:28
e. of the earth were afraid. 41:5
taken from *e.* of the earth. 9
daughters from *e.* of the earth. 43:6
to me and be saved, all the *e.* 45:22
all *e.* shall see the salvation. 52:10
Gentiles come from *e.* *Jer* 16:19
a noise shall come to the *e.* 25:31
fire devoureth both the *e.* *Ezek* 15:4
shall he be great to *e.* *Mi* 5:4
dominion to *e.* of earth. *Zech* 9:10
salvation to *e.* of earth. *Acts* 13:47*
words to *e.* of the world. *Rom* 10:18
on whom *e.* of the world. *1 Cor* 10:11

endued
God hath *e.* me with. *Gen* 30:20*
a wise son, *e.* with. *2 Chr* 2:12
have sent a cunning man, *e.* with. 13
till ye be *e.* with. *Luke* 24:49*
and *e.* with knowledge? *Jas* 3:13*

endure
[1] *To last,* Ps 72:12; 1 Pet 1:25.
[2] *To suffer patiently,* Mat 24:13.
[3] *To sustain or bear up under,*
Gen 33:14. [4] *To tolerate,* Esth
8:6.

as children be able to *e.* *Gen* 33:14*
thou shalt be able to *e.* *Ex* 18:23
for how can I *e.* to see evil. *Esth* 8:6
fast, but it shall not *e.* *Job* 8:15
I could not *e.* 31:23*
the Lord shall *e.* for ever. *Ps* 9:7*
102:12, 26; 104:31
weeping may *e.* for a night. 30:5
as long as sun and moon *e.* 72:5
his name shall *e.* for ever. 17
seed will I make to *e.* 89:29, 36
doth the crown *e.* to? *Pr* 27:24
can thy heart *e.* or? *Ezek* 22:14
that shall *e.* to the end. *Mat* 24:13
Mark 13:13
no root, and so *e.* but. *Mark* 4:17
tribulations that ye *e.* *2 Thes* 1:4
therefore *e.* hardness. *2 Tim* 2:3*
therefore I *e.* all things for. 10
will not *e.* sound doctrine. 4:3
watch in all things, *e.* afflictions. 5
if ye *e.* chastening. *Heb* 12:7
they could not *e.* what was. 20
count them happy who *e.* *Jas* 5:11
for conscience *e.* grief. *1 Pet* 2:19

endured
time should have *e.* for. *Ps* 81:15
if God *e.* with much. *Rom* 9:22
persecutions I *e.* *2 Tim* 3:11
after he had patiently *e.* *Heb* 6:15
ye *e.* a great fight of afflictions. 10:32
for Moses *e.* as seeing him. 11:27
he *e.* the cross. 12:2
he *e.* such contradiction. 3

endureth
for his anger *e.* but a. *Ps* 30:5
goodness of God *e.* continually. 52:1
peace so long as moon *e.* 72:7
truth *e.* to all generations. 100:5
dominion *e.* throughout all. 145:13
he that *e.* to the end. *Mat* 10:22
meat which *e.* unto life. *John* 6:27
hopeth all things, *e.* all. *1 Cor* 13:7
blessed is man that *e.* *Jas* 1:12

endureth *for ever*
his mercy *e. for ever.* *1 Chr* 16:34, 41
2 Chr 5:13; 7:3, 6; 20:21
Ezra 3:11; *Ps* 106:1; 107:1
118:1, 2, 3, 4; 136:1, 2, 3, etc.
138:8; *Jer* 33:11
his righteousness *e. for ever.*
Ps 111:3; 112:3, 9
his praise *e. for ever.* 111:10
his truth *e. for ever* 117:2
thy judgements *e. for ever.* 119:160
name, O Lord, *e. for ever.* 135:13
word of Lord *e. for ever.* *1 Pet* 1:25

enduring
fear of Lord is clean, *e.* *Ps* 19:9
is effectual in *e.* the. *2 Cor* 1:6
in heaven a better and *e.* *Heb* 10:34

Eneas, Aeneas
E. had kept his bed eight. *Acts* 9:33
E. Jesus maketh thee whole. 34

En-eglaim
from En-gedi to *E.* *Ezek* 47:10

enemies
(*The Revised Version frequently substitutes the words* adversaries, adversary, *which have slightly different meanings, but not so different as to make it worth while to star each reference so changed*)

avenged of the king's *e.* *1 Sam* 18:25
when Lord hath cut off *e.* 20:15
Lord require it of David's *e.* 16
so and more do God to *e.* 25:22
a present of the spoil of *e.* of. 30:26
to *e.* to blaspheme. *2 Sam* 12:14
the *e.* of my lord be as. 18:32
Lord fought against *e.* *2 Chr* 20:29
e. of the Jews hoped to. *Esth* 9:1
me from my deadly *e.* *Ps* 17:9
the *e.* of the Lord shall be. 37:20
sharp in heart of king's *e.* 45:5
speak with the *e.* in gate. 127:5
beloved into hands of *e.* *Jer* 12:7
the *e.* have heard a cry of. 48:5
her friends become her *e.* *Lam* 1:2
her *e.* prosper. 5
a man's *e.* are the men of. *Mi* 7:6
if when we were *e.* *Rom* 5:10
concerning gospel, they are *e.* 11:28
till he hath put all *e.* *1 Cor* 15:25
are the *e.* of the cross. *Phil* 3:18
were *e.* in your mind. *Col* 1:21

his **enemies**
possess the gate of *his e.* *Gen* 22:17
eat up nations *his e.* *Num* 24:8*
he hath driven out *his e.* 32:21
help to him from *his e.* *Deut* 33:7
him rest from *his e.* *2 Sam* 7:1
hath avenged him of *his e.* 18:19
him out of hand of *his e.* 22:1
him rest from all *his e.* *1 Chr* 22:9
counteth me as one of *his e.*
Job 19:11
as for all *his e.* he. *Ps* 10:5
not deliver him to will of *his e.* 41:2
let *his e.* be scattered. 68:1
God shall wound head of *his e.* 21
his e. shall lick the dust. 72:9
he smote *his e.* in the hinder. 78:66
made all *his e.* to rejoice. 89:42
a fire burneth up *his e.* 97:3
see his desire upon *his e.* 112:8
his e. will I clothe with. 132:18
he maketh *his e.* to be at. *Pr* 16:7
Lord shall join *his e.* *Isa* 9:11
shall prevail against *his e.* 42:13
repay, recompence to *his e.* 59:18
rendereth recompence to *his e.* 66:6
indignation known towards *his e.* 14
Pharaoh into hand of *his e.* *Jer* 44:30
reserveth wrath for *his e.* *Nah* 1:2
darkness shall pursue *his e.* 8
till *his e.* be made his footstool.
Heb 10:13

mine **enemies**
curse *mine e.* *Num* 23:11; 24:10
vengeance to *mine e.* *Deut* 32:41
enlarged over *mine e.* *1 Sam* 2:1

I be avenged on mine e. 1 Sam 14:24
Lord hath broken forth upon mine e. 2 Sam 5:20; 1 Chr 14:11
be saved from mine e. 2 Sam 22:4; Ps 18:3
have pursued mine e. 2 Sam 22:38; Ps 18:3
hast given me the necks of mine e. 2 Sam 22:41; Ps 18:40
me forth from mine e. 2 Sam 22:49
to betray to mine e. 1 Chr 12:17*
hast smitten all mine e. Ps 3:7
lead me, because of mine e. 5:8
eye waxeth old because of mine e. 6:7
let all mine e. be ashamed. 10
because of rage of mine e. 7:6
when mine e. are turned. 9:3
delivereth me from mine e. 18:48
table in presence of mine e. 23:5
let not mine e. triumph. 25:2; 35:19
consider mine e. for they. 25:19
mine e. came upon me. 27:2
head be lifted up above mine e. 6
plain path, because of mine e. 11
deliver me not to will of mine e. 12
a reproach among all mine e. 31:11
deliver me from mine e. 15
but mine e. are lively. 38:19
mine e. speak evil of me. 41:5
mine e. reproach. 42:10; 102:8
shall reward evil to mine e. 54:5
mine eye hath seen his desire upon mine e. 7; 59:10
mine e. would swallow me up. 56:2
then shall mine e. turn back. 9
deliver me from mine e. 59:1; 143:9
they being mine e. wrongfully. 69:4
deliver me because of mine e. 18
mine e. speak against me. 71:10
see my desire on mine e. 92:11
made me wiser than mine e. 119:98
because mine e. have forgotten. 139
many are mine e. yet do I not. 157
forth thy hand against mine e. 138:7
I count them mine e. 139:22
of thy mercy cut off mine e. 143:12
avenge me of mine e. Isa 1:24
all mine e. have heard. Lam 1:21
mine e. chased me sore like. 3:52
mine e. bring hither. Luke 19:27

our enemies

they join also to our e. Ex 1:10
our e. themselves being. Deut 32:31
out of hand of our e. 1 Sam 4:3
deliver us out of hand of our e. 12:10; 2 Sam 19:9; Ps 44:7
of the reproach of our e. Neh 5:9
when rest of our e. heard. 6:1, 16
will we push down our e. Ps 44:5
tread down our e. 60:12; 108:13
and our e. laugh among. 80:6
redeemed us from our e. 136:24
our e. have opened their. Lam 3:46
be saved from our e. Luke 1:71
delivered out of hands of our e. 74

their enemies

naked amongst their e. Ex 32:25
faintness in land of their e. Lev 26:36
when they be in land of their e. 44
backs before their e. Josh 7:8, 12
stood not a man of all their e; Lord delivered their e. into. 21:44
rest from their e. 23:1; Esth 9:16
sold into hand of their e. Judg 2:14
out of hand of their e. 18; 8:34
into the hand of their e. 2 Ki 21:14; 2 Chr 6:36; 25:20; Neh 9:27
sea overwhelmed their e. Ps 78:53
soon have subdued their e. 81:14
stronger than their e. 105:24
the waters covered their e. 106:11
their e. oppressed them. 42
to sword before their e. Jer 15:9
by sword before their e. 19:7; 20:4
their e. shall straiten them. 9
of Judah give into hands of their e. 20:5; 21:7; 34:20, 21; Ezek 39:23
out of their e. lands. Ezek 39:27
captivity before their e. Amos 9:4
which tread down their e. Zech 10:5
fire devoureth their e. Rev 11:5
ascended, and their e. beheld. 12

thine enemies

who delivered thine e. Gen 14:20
hand be in neck of thine e. 49:8
be an enemy to thine e. Ex 23:22
I will make thine e. to turn. 27
rise, Lord, let thine e. Num 10:35
cast out all thine e. Deut 6:19
goest against thine e. 20:1; 21:10
thine e. distress thee. 28:53, 55, 57
thine e. be found liars to. 33:29
not stand before thine e. Josh 7:13
so let all thine e. perish. Judg 5:31
vengeance for thee of thine e. 11:36
thine e. be as Nabal. 1 Sam 25:26
the souls of thine e. shall. 29
cut off all thine e. 2 Sam 7:9; 1 Chr 17:8
in that lovest thine e. 2 Sam 19:6
three months before thine e. 24:13
nor hast asked life of thine e. 1 Ki 3:11; 2 Chr 1:11
while sword of thine e. 1 Chr 21:12
strength because of thine e. Ps 8:2
hand find out all thine e. 21:8
power shall thine e. submit. 66:3
foot dipped in blood of thine e. 68:23
thine e. roar. 74:4
forget not the voice of thine e. 23
thine e. make a tumult. 83:2
thou hast scattered thine e. 89:10
wherewith thine e. have. 51
lo, thine e. O Lord, thine e. 92:9
make thine e. thy footstool. 110:1; Mat 22:44; Mark 12:36; Luke 20:43; Heb 1:13
rule in midst of thine e. Ps 110:2
thine e. take thy name in. 139:20
the fire of thine e. shall. Isa 26:11
corn to be meat for thine e. 62:8
thee pass with thine e. Jer 15:14
thine e. have opened. Lam 2:16
interpretation to thine e. Dan 4:19
redeem thee from thine e. Mi 4:10
all thine e. shall be cut off. 5:9
gate be set open to thine e. Nah 3:13
thine e. cast a trench. Luke 19:43

your enemies

ye shall chase your e. Lev 26:7
your e. shall fall before you. 8
sow in vain, for your e. shall. 16
ye shall be slain before your e. 17
no power to stand before your e. 37
be saved from your e. Num 10:9
be not smitten before your e. 14:42; Deut 1:42
rest from all your e. Deut 12:10
to battle against your e. 20:3
goeth to fight against your e. 4
ye shall be sold to your e. 28:68
Lord do to all your e. Josh 10:25
divide the spoil of your e. 22:8
delivered you out of hand of your e. 1 Sam 12:11; 2 Ki 17:39
but I say, love your e. Mat 5:44; Luke 6:27, 35

enemy

hand dashed in pieces e. Ex 15:6
the e. said, I will pursue. 9
then I will be an e. to. 23:22
go to war against the e. Num 10:9
and was not his e. nor. 35:23
I feared wrath of the e. Deut 32:27
the beginning of revenges upon e. 42
he shall thrust out the e. 33:27
hath delivered our e. Judg 16:23, 24
thou shalt see an e. 1 Sam 2:32*
Saul became David's e. 18:29
if a man find his e. will he? 24:19
thy people be smitten down before e. 1 Ki 8:33; 2 Chr 6:24
thou deliver them to e. 1 Ki 8:46
make thee fall before e. 2 Chr 25:8
e. could not countervail. Esth 7:4
the e. is this wicked Haman. 6
deliver me from e.'s hand? Job 6:23
he counteth me for his e. 33:10
let the e. persecute my. Ps 7:5
thou mightest still the e. 8:2
e. destructions are come to. 9:6
mourning because of e.? 42:9; 43:2
us turn back from the e. 44:10
because of voice of the e. 55:3
not an e. that reproached me. 12
a strong tower from the e. Ps 61:3
my life from fear of e. 64:1
even all that the e. hath. 74:3
shall e. blaspheme thy name? 10
e. hath reproached, O Lord. 18
when he delivered from e. 78:42
his glory into the e.'s hand. 61
e. shall not exact upon him. 89:22
for the e. hath persecuted. 143:3
kisses of an e. are. Pr 27:6
when the e. shall come in. Isa 59:19
he was turned to be their e. 63:10
the sword of the e. is. Jer 6:25
I will cause the e. to entreat. 15:11
them with east wind before e. 18:17
thee with wound of an e. 30:14
into captivity before e. Lam 1:5
for e. hath magnified himself. 9
children are desolate, because e. 16
drawn back his hand before e. 2:3
he hath bent his bow like an e. 4
the Lord was an e. he hath. 5
that e. should have entered. 4:12
because the e. had said. Ezek 36:2
the e. shall pursue him. Hos 8:3
people is risen up as an e. Mi 2:8
seek strength because of e. Nah 3:11
his e. came, sowed tares. Mat 13:25
said, an e. hath done this. 28
the e. that sowed them is. 39
tread over power of e. Luke 10:19
child of devil, thou e. of. Acts 13:10
last e. to be destroyed. 1 Cor 15:26
am I become your e.? Gal 4:16
count him not as an e. 2 Thes 3:15
a friend of world is the e. Jas 4:4

hand of the enemy

into the hand of the e. Lev 26:25; Neh 9:27
delivered us from the hand of the e. Ezra 8:31
not shut me up into hand of the e. Ps 31:8
his glory into the hand of e. 78:61
redeemed from the hand of the e. 106:10; 107:2
fell into hand of the e. Lam 1:7
given into the hand of the e. 2:7

mine enemy

sent away mine e.? 1 Sam 19:17
delivered me from my e. 2 Sam 22:18; Ps 18:17
found me, O mine e.? 1 Ki 21:20
mine e. sharpeneth his. Job 16:9
let mine e. be as wicked. 27:7
delivered him that is mine e. Ps 7:4
how long shall mine e. be? 13:2
lest mine e. say, I have prevailed. 4
because mine e. doth not. 41:11
I swaddled hath mine e. Lam 2:22
rejoice not, O mine e. Mi 7:8
then she that is mine e. shall. 10

thine enemy

if thou meet thine e. Ex 23:4
thine e. shall distress. Deut 28:57
deliver thine e. 1 Sam 24:4; 26:8
Lord is become thine e. 28:16
of Ish-bosheth thine e. 2 Sam 4:8
thou me for thine e.? Job 13:24
rejoice not when thine e. Pr 24:17
if thine e. hunger. 25:21; Rom 12:20
hath caused thine e. to. Lam 2:17
Lord hath cast out thine e. Zeph 3:15
thou shalt hate thine e. Mat 5:43

enflame, see inflame

engaged

who is this that e. his? Jer 30:21*

En-gedi

wilderness of Judah, E. Josh 15:62
David dwelt in the holds at E. 1 Sam 23:29; 24:1
Hazazon-tamar, is E. 2 Chr 20:2
in the vineyards of E. S of S 1:14
fishers stand from E. Ezek 47:10

engine, -s

Uzziah made e. 2 Chr 26:15
set e. of war against. Ezek 26:9

engrafted

with meekness e. word. Jas 1:21*

engrave

like a signet shalt e. Ex 28:11
I will e. the graving. Zech 3:9

engraven
ministration of death e. 2 Cor 3:7

engraver
with the work of an e. Ex 28:11
all manner of work of the e. 35:35
Aholiab, of tribe of Dan, an e. 38:23

engravings
like e. of a signet. Ex 28:11, 21, 36
39:14, 30

enjoin
to e. thee that which is. Philem 8

enjoined
Purim as Esther had e. Esth 9:31
who hath e. him his ways? Job 36:23
blood of testament God e. Heb 9:20*

enjoy
land e. her sabbaths. Lev 26:34, 43
that Israel may e. Num 36:8*
beget sons, not e. them. Deut 28:41
return to land and e. it. Josh 1:15*
e. pleasure, behold this. Eccl 2:1
make soul e. good. 24; 3:13; 5:18
elect shall long e. work. Isa 65:22
thee we e. great quietness. Acts 24:2
giveth us all things to e. 1 Tim 6:17
than e. the pleasures of. Heb 11:25

enjoyed
till the land e. her. 2 Chr 36:21

enlarge
God shall e. Japhet. Gen 9:27
cast out nations and e. Ex 34:24
when Lord shall e. thy. Deut 12:20
if the Lord e. thy coast as. 19:8
bless me, and e. coast. 1 Chr 4:10
thou shalt e. my heart. Ps 119:32
e. the place of thy tent. Isa 54:2
might e. their border. Amos 1:13
make bald, e. thy. Mi 1:16
and e. the borders of. Mat 23:5

enlarged
my mouth is e. over. 1 Sam 2:1
thou hast e. my steps. 2 Sam 22:37
Ps 18:36
thou hast e. me when I. Ps 4:1*
troubles of my heart are e. 25:17
hell hath e. herself. Isa 5:14
thou hast e. thy bed, and. 57:8
thine heart shall fear and be e. 60:5
our heart is e. 2 Cor 6:11
recompence in same, be ye also e. 13
we shall be e. by you. 10:15*

enlargement
then e. shall arise from. Esth 4:14*

enlargeth
blessed be he that e. Deut 33:20
he e. the nations, and. Job 12:23*
who e. his desire as hell. Hab 2:5

enlarging
and there was an e. Ezek 41:7*

enlighten
Lord will e. my darkness. Ps 18:28*

enlightened
Jonathan's eyes were e. 1 Sam 14:27
29
to be e. with the light of. Job 33:30
his lightnings e. the world. Ps 97:4*
understanding being e. Eph 1:18
for those who were e. Heb 6:4

enlightening
Lord is pure, e. the eyes. Ps 19:8

enmity
I will put e. between thee. Gen 3:15
or in e. smite him. Num 35:21
thrust him suddenly without e. 22
before they were at e. Luke 23:12
carnal mind is e. against. Rom 8:7
abolished in his flesh e. Eph 2:15
cross, having slain the e. 16
friendship of world is e. Jas 4:4

Enoch
Cain's wife bare E. Gen 4:17
Jared begat E. 5:18
E. walked with God. 22, 24
which was the son of E. Luke 3:37
by faith E. was translated. Heb 11:5
E. also prophesied of these. Jude 14

Enon
John was baptizing in E. John 3:23

Enos
Seth called son's name E. Gen 4:26
which was son of E. Luke 3:38

enough
straw and provender e. Gen 24:25
I have e. my brother. 33:9
my blessing, because I have e. 11
it is large e. for them. 34:21
it is e. Joseph is yet alive. 45:28
entreat Lord, for it is e. Ex 9:28
bring much more than e. for. 36:5
dwelt long e. in this mount. Deut 1:6
compassed this mountain long e. 2:3
the hill is not e. for us. Josh 17:16
it is e.: stay now thine hand.
2 Sam 24:16; 1 Ki 19:4; 1 Chr 21:15
Mark 14:41; Luke 22:38
we have had e. to eat. 2 Chr 31:10
have goats' milk e. for. Pr 27:27
he that followeth after vain persons
shall have poverty e. 28:19
four things say not, it is e. 30:15
the fire that saith not, it is e. 16
which can never have e. Isa 56:11
destroy till they have e. Jer 49:9
eat, and not have e. Hos 4:10
not have stolen till they had e. Ob 5
the lion did tear e. for. Nah 2:12
but ye have not e. ye. Hag 1:6
not be room e. to receive it. Mal 3:10
it is e. for the disciple. Mat 10:25
lest there be not e. for us. 25:9
servants have bread e. Luke 15:17
they had eaten e. Acts 27:38

enquire
call damsel, and e. at her. Gen 24:57
Rebekah went to e. of Lord. 25:22
the people come to e. of. Ex 18:15
and that thou e. not. Deut 12:30
then shalt thou e. and. 13:14
come unto the judge and e. 17:9
man doth come and e. of. Judg 4:20
when a man went to e of. 1 Sam 9:9
did I then begin to e. of God? 22:15
woman, that I may e. of her. 28:7
Jehoshaphat said, e. I pray thee, at.
1 Ki 22:5; 2 Chr 18:4
we may e. of. 1 Ki 22:7; 2 Chr 18:6
go, e. of Baal-zebub. 2 Ki 1:2
not here a prophet to e.? 3:11
meet the man, and e. of the. 8:8
altar shall be for me to e. 16:15
go ye, e. of Lord. 22:13; 2 Chr 34:21
which sent you to e. 2 Ki 22:18
2 Chr 34:26
a familiar spirit, to e. 1 Chr 10:13
Tou sent to David to e. of. 18:10*
David could not go to e. of. 21:30
to e. concerning Judah. Ezra 7:14
for e. I pray thee of the. Job 8:8
beauty of Lord and to e. in. Ps 27:4
thou dost not e. wisely. Eccl 7:10
if ye will e. e. ye. Isa 21:12
e. I pray thee, of Lord. Jer 21:2
of Judah that sent you to e. 37:7
cometh to prophet to e. Ezek 14:7
elders of Israel came to e. 20:1
saith Lord, are ye come to e.? 3
e. who in it is worthy. Mat 10:11*
to e. among themselves.
Luke 22:23*; John 16:19
e. for Saul. Acts 9:11
if ye e. concerning other. 19:39*
as though ye would e. 23:15*, 20
any do e. of Titus my. 2 Cor 8:23

enquired
heard of it, and e. Deut 17:4
children of Israel e. of. Judg 20:27
they e. of the Lord. 1 Sam 10:22
and he e. of the Lord. 22:10, 13
David e. of Lord. 23:2, 4; 30:8
2 Sam 2:1; 5:19, 23; 21:1*
1 Chr 14:10, 14
Saul e. Lord answered. 1 Sam 28:6
David sent and e. 2 Sam 11:3
as if a man had e. at the. 16:23
Saul e. not of the Lord. 1 Chr 10:14
for we e. not at the ark in. 13:3*
they returned and e. Ps 78:34*
should I be e. of at all? Ezek 14:3
saith the Lord, I will not be e. 20:3
shall I be e. of by you? as I live, saith
Lord God, I will not be e. of. 31
I will yet for this be e. of. Ezek 36:37
matters the king e. of. Dan 1:20
those that have not e. for. Zeph 1:6
Herod e. of wise men. Mat 2:7*, 16*
then e. he the hour he. John 4:52
or our brethren be e. of. 2 Cor 8:23
of salvation prophets e. 1 Pet 1:10*

enquirest
e. after mine iniquity and. Job 10:6

enquiry
after vows to make e. Pr 20:25
the men had made e. Acts 10:17

enrich
the king will e. him. 1 Sam 17:25
thou didst e. the kings. Ezek 27:33

enriched
in every thing ye are e. 1 Cor 1:5
being e. in every thing. 2 Cor 9:11

enrichest
thou greatly e. it with. Ps 65:9

En-rogel
Ahimaaz stayed by E. 2 Sam 17:17
slew sheep and oxen by E. 1 Ki 1:9

enrolled
This word is used in the Revisions in two places; in place of taxed *in* Luke 2:1; *and in place of* written *in* Heb 12:23. *The word was also put into the margin of the old version, previous to the revision.*
all the world should be e. Luke 2:1
church of firstborn e. in. Heb 12:23

ensample
as ye have us for an e. Phil 3:17
to make ourselves an e. 2 Thes 3:9
an e. to those that. 2 Pet 2:6*

ensamples
happened to them for e. 1 Cor 10:11*
so that ye were e. to all. 1 Thes 1:7
but being e. to the flock. 1 Pet 5:3

ensign
he will lift up an e. to. Isa 5:26
which shall stand for an e. 11:10
shall set up an e. for nations. 12
when he lifteth up an e. 18:3
left as an e. on an hill. 30:17
princes shall be afraid of e. 31:9
of a crown lifted as e. Zech 9:16

ensigns
they set up their e. for. Ps 74:4

ensnared
reign not, lest people be e. Job 34:30

ensue
seek peace, and e. it. 1 Pet 3:11*

entangle
(*Frequently used as meaning perplex, bewilder, or insnare*)
how they might e. him. Mat 22:15*

entangled
Pharaoh will say, they are e. Ex 14:3
be not e. again with yoke. Gal 5:1
are again e. therein and. 2 Pet 2:20

entangleth
e. himself with affairs of. 2 Tim 2:4

enter
not slothful to e. to. Judg 18:9
prince shall e. by the porch.
Ezek 44:3; 46:2, 8
also set his face to e. Dan 11:17
he shall e. peaceably on fattest. 24
some must e. therein. Heb 4:6

enter *in* or *into*
near to e. into Egypt. Gen 12:11
Moses not able to e. into. Ex 40:35
all that e. in to perform. Num 4:23
water that causeth curse shall e.
into the woman, and. 5:24, 27
children shall e. into. Deut 23:8
shouldest e. into covenant. 29:12
not to e. into their cities. Josh 10:19
cry did e. into his ears. 2 Sam 22:7
thy feet e. into city. 1 Ki 14:12
disguise myself and e into. 22:30
if we e. into the city. 2 Ki 7:4
third part of you that e. in. 11:5
will e. into lodgings of borders, and.
19:23; Isa 37:24
unclean should e. in. 2 Chr 23:19
e. into his sanctuary. 30:8

house that I shall *e. into*. *Neh* 2:8
none might *e. into* king's. *Esth* 4:2
will he *e.* with thee *into* ? *Job* 22:4
he should *e. into* judgement. 34:23
sword *e. into* their heart. *Ps* 37:15
e. into the king's palace. 45:15
e. into his gates with. 100:4
gate *into* which righteous shall *e.* 118:20
a fool's lips *e. into*. *Pr* 18:6
e. into the rock, and. *Isa* 2:10
Lord will *e. into* judgement. 3:14
righteous nation may *e. in*. 26:2
my people, *e.* thou *into* thy. 20
he shall *e. into* peace. 57:2
that *e. in* at these gates. *Jer* 7:2 17:20; 22:2
e. into defenced cities. 8:14
if I *e. into* the city, behold. 14:18
e. into gates kings. 17:25; 22:4
who shall *e. into* habitations ? 21:13
departed to go to *e. into*. 41:17
set your faces to *e. into*. 42:15
caused arrows to *e. into*. *Lam* 3:13
robbers shall *e. into* it. *Ezek* 7:22
nor shall they *e. into* land of. 13:9
shall *e. into* thy gates, as men *e. into* a city wherein is. 26:10
cause breath to *e. into* you. 37:5
the priests *e. therein*, then. 42:14
gate be shut, no man *e. in* by. 44:2
they shall *e. into* my sanctuary. 16
when they *e. in* at the gates of. 17
shall *e. into* the fortress. *Dan* 11:7
he shall *e. into* the countries. 40
shall *e.* also *into* glorious land. 41
like a thief they shall *e. in*. *Joel* 2:9
nor *e. into* Gilgal. *Amos* 5:5
Jonah began to *e. into*. *Jonah* 3:4
flying roll shall *e. into*. *Zech* 5:4
in no case *e. into* kingdom. *Mat* 5:20
prayest, *e. into* thy closet. 6:6
e. in at strait gate. 7:13; *Luke* 13:24
not every one shall *e. in*. *Mat* 7:21
into what city ye shall *e.* 10:11 *Luke* 10:8, 10
e. into a strong man's house. *Mat* 12:29; *Mark* 3:27
e. in and dwell there. *Mat* 12:45 *Luke* 11:26
better for thee to *e. into* life halt. *Mat* 18:8; *Mark* 9:43, 45, 47
wilt *e. into* life, keep. *Mat* 19:17
a rich man shall hardly *e. into*. 23
than for rich man to *e. into* kingdom. 24; *Mark* 10:25; *Luke* 18:25
e. into joy of thy Lord. *Mat* 25:21
no more openly *e. into*. *Mark* 1:45
may *e. into* the swine. 5:12 *Luke* 8:32
what house ye *e. into*. *Mark* 6:10 *Luke* 9:4; 10:5
and *e.* no more *into*. *Mark* 9:25
lest ye *e. into* temptation. 14:38 *Luke* 22:46
they which *e. in* may see. *Luke* 8:16
many will seek to *e. in* and. 13:24
and to *e. into* his glory ? 24:26
can he *e. into* his ? *John* 3:4
cannot *e. into* kingdom of God. 5
by me, if any man *e. in* he. 10:9
tribulation *e. into* the. *Acts* 14:22
grievous wolves shall *e. in*. 20:29
do *e. into* rest, if they *e. into* rest. *Heb* 4:3, 5
labour therefore to *e. into* rest. 11
boldness to *e. into* holiest by. 10:19
man was able to *e. into*. *Rev* 15:8
in no wise *e. into* it any. 21:27
may *e. in* through the gates. 22:14

enter *not*

e. not into judgement. *Ps* 143:2
e. not into the path. *Pr* 4:14
e. not into the fields of the. 23:10
e. not into house of. *Jer* 16:5
city of Samaritans *e. not*. *Mat* 10:5
that ye *e. not* into temptation. 26:41 *Luke* 22:40

not **enter**

Aaron shall *not e.* into. *Num* 20:24
not e. into congregation. *Deut* 23:1 2, 3
priests could *not e.* into. *2 Chr* 7:2
not e. into my rest. *Ps* 95:11
and equity *cannot e.* *Isa* 59:14
they should *not e.* into. *Lam* 1:10
shall *not e.* into the land. *Ezek* 20:38
nor uncircumcised *e.* into. 44:9
I will *not e.* into city. *Hos* 11:9
not e. into kingdom of. *Mat* 18:3
he shall *not e.* therein. *Mark* 10:15 *Luke* 18:17
shall *not e.* into rest. *Heb* 3:11, 18
we see they could *not e.* 19

see **kingdom of God**

entered

self-same day *e.* Noah. *Gen* 7:13
the angels turned in, and *e.* 19:3
sun was risen when Lot *e.* into. 23
Joseph *e.* into his chamber. 43:30
as Moses *e.* into the. *Ex* 33:9
bring men that are *e.* into. *Josh* 2:3
and they *e.* into the land. *Judg* 6:5
e. into an hold of god Berith. 9:46
e. into another tent. *2 Ki* 7:8
as Jehu *e.* in at the gate. 9:31
when king *e.* into the. *2 Chr* 12:11
e. into a covenant to seek. 15:12
Jotham *e.* not into the temple. 27:2
they *e.* into a curse. *Neh* 10:29
hast thou *e.* into springs ? *Job* 38:16
hast thou *e.* into treasures of ? 22
but when ye *e.* ye defiled. *Jer* 2:7
death is *e.* into our windows. 9:21
the people which had *e.* into. 34:10
when Jeremiah was *e.* into. 37:16
heathen *e.* her sanctuary. *Lam* 1:10
enemy should have *e.* gates. 4:12
spirit *e.* into me. *Ezek* 2:2; 3:24
I sware and *e.* into a covenant. 16:8
they *e.* unto the heathen. 36:20
the God of Israel hath *e.* 44:2
in day that foreigners *e.* *Ob* 11
shouldest not have *e.* into gate. 13
e. into my bones, I. *Hab* 3:16
when Jesus was *e.* into. *Mat* 8:5
he *e.* into a ship and passed. 9:1
how he *e.* into house of God. 12:4
day Noah *e.* into the ark. 24:38 *Luke* 17:27
the unclean spirits went out and *e.* *Mark* 5:13; *Luke* 8:33
whithersoever he *e.* *Mark* 6:56
Mary *e.* into house. *Luke* 1:40
I *e.* thine house, thou gavest. 7:44
feared as they *e.* into cloud. 9:34
woe to lawyers, ye *e.* not in. 11:52
then *e.* Satan into Judas. 22:3 *John* 13:27
when ye are *e.* the city. *Luke* 22:10
are *e.* into their labours. *John* 4:38
a garden, into the which he *e.* 18:1
Pilate *e.* into the judgement-hall. 33
Ananias *e.* and putting. *Acts* 9:17
nothing unclean hath *e.* into. 11:8
e. into castle and told Paul. 23:16
Agrippa was *e.* into place of. 25:23
to whom Paul *e.* in, and. 28:8
sin *e.* into the world. *Rom* 5:12
the law *e.* 20
neither have *e.* into heart. *1 Cor* 2:9
e. not in because of. *Heb* 4:6
for he that is *e.* into his rest. 10
forerunner is for us *e.* even. 6:20
e. in once into holy place. 9:12, 24
are *e.* into the ears of. *Jas* 5:4
many deceivers are *e.* *2 John* 7
Spirit of life from God *e.* *Rev* 11:11

entereth

number every one that *e.* into the. *Num* 4:30, 35, 39, 43
to every one that *e.* *2 Chr* 31:16
when wisdom *e.* into. *Pr* 2:10
reproof *e.* more into a wise. 17:10
sword *e.* into their. *Ezek* 21:14
he that *e.* in by the way of. 46:9
whatsoever *e.* in at the mouth. *Mat* 15:17*; *Mark* 7:18
and *e.* in where the. *Mark* 5:40
follow him where he *e.* *Luke* 22:10
e. not by the door into. *John* 10:1
he that *e.* in by the door. 2
which *e.* into that within. *Heb* 6:19
as the high priest *e.* every. 9:25

entering

cast it at the *e.* of gate. *Josh* 8:29
shall stand at the *e.* of gate. *Josh* 20:4
Gaal stood in the *e.* *Judg* 9:35
Abimelech stood in the *e.* 44
men of Dan stood by the *e.* 18:16
the priest stood in the *e.* of gate. 17
by *e.* into a town that. *1 Sam* 23:7
battle in array at *e.* in. *2 Sam* 10:8
for the *e.* of the oracle. *1 Ki* 6:31
Elijah stood in the *e.* in. 19:13
four leprous men at *e.* *2 Ki* 7:3
lay heads in two heaps at *e.* 10:8
that were in the *e.* of the gate. 23:8
kings sat at *e.* of gate. *2 Chr* 18:9*
there is no house, no *e.* *Isa* 23:1
thrones at the *e.* of. *Jer* 1:15; 17:27
mark well the *e.* in of. *Ezek* 44:5
nor suffer ye them that are *e.* to. *Mat* 23:13; *Luke* 11:52
lusts of other things *e.* *Mark* 4:19
nothing without *e.* into him. 7:15*
e. into the sepulchre they saw. 16:5
at your *e.* ye shall. *Luke* 19:30
Saul *e.* into every house. *Acts* 8:3
what manner of *e.* in. *1 Thes* 1:9
a promise left us of *e.* *Heb* 4:1

enterprise

hands cannot perform *e.* *Job* 5:12

entertain

be not forgetful to *e.* *Heb* 13:2*

entertained

some have *e.* angels. *Heb* 13:2

entice

To persuade, or allure, Judg 14:15; 16:5; 2 Chr 18:19. *In the Bible usually in the bad sense.*

if a man *e.* a maid not. *Ex* 22:16
if wife *e.* thee secretly. *Deut* 13:6
e. husband, that he may. *Judg* 14:15
lords said to Delilah, *e.* him. 16:5
who shall *e.* Ahab ? *2 Chr* 18:19
I will *e.* him. 20
thou shalt *e.* him and prevail. 21
if sinners *e.* thee. *Pr* 1:10

enticed

if heart been secretly *e.* *Job* 31:27
peradventure he will be *e.* *Jer* 20:10†
when drawn away and *e.* *Jas* 1:14

enticeth

a violent man *e.* his. *Pr* 16:29

enticing

was not with *e.* words. *1 Cor* 2:4*
man beguile you with *e.* *Col* 2:4*

entire

that ye be perfect and *e.* *Jas* 1:4

entrance

us the *e.* into the city. *Judg* 1:24
shewed them the *e.* they smote it. 25
ran before Ahab to *e.* of. *1 Ki* 18:46
the two kings sat in the *e.* 22:10
kept the *e.* of king's. *2 Chr* 12:10*
the *e.* of thy words. *Ps* 119:130*
yourselves know our *e.* *1 Thes* 2:1
so an *e.* shall be. *2 Pet* 1:11

entreat

In the Bible, frequently, to treat, deal with, use (obsolete elsewhere), Jer 15:11.

cause the enemy to *e.* *Jer* 15:11*
e. them evil 400 years. *Acts* 7:6

see **intreat**

entreated

he *e.* Abraham well for. *Gen* 12:16†
so evil *e.* this people ? *Ex* 5:22†
and Egyptians evil *e.* us. *Deut* 26:6†
and *e.* them spitefully. *Mat* 22:6 *Luke* 18:32
e. him shamefully. *Luke* 20:11*
same evil *e.* our fathers. *Acts* 7:19
Julius courteously *e.* Paul. 27:3*
we were shamefully *e.* *1 Thes* 2:2

entreateth

he evil *e.* the barren. *Job* 24:21*

entries

the chambers and *e.* *Ezek* 40:38*

entry

king's *e.* without turned. *2 Ki* 16:18
fathers were keepers of *e.* *1 Chr* 9:19

doors of *e.* of house. *2 Chr* 4:22
crieth at the gates, at *e.* *Pr* 8:3
Jeremiah into third *e.* *Jer* 38:14
hide the stones at the *e.* of. 43:9
image of jealousy in the *e.* *Ezek* 8:5

envied
the Philistines *e.* Isaac. *Gen* 26:14
Rachel *e.* her sister, and. 30:1
Joseph's brethren *e.* him. 37:11
they *e.* Moses also in. *Ps* 106:16
for this man is *e.* of. *Eccl* 4:4
trees in garden of God *e.* *Ezek* 31:9

envies
aside all malice, guile, *e.* *1 Pet* 2:1

enviest
Moses said, *e.* thou ? *Num* 11:29*

envieth
charity suffereth, and *e.* *1 Cor* 13:4

envious
nor be *e.* against workers. *Ps* 37:1
for I was *e.* at the foolish. 73:3
be not thou *e.* against. *Pr* 24:1
fret not, neither be thou *e.* 19

environ
Canaanites hear and *e.* *Josh* 7:9*

envy
(Discontent at the excellence or good fortune of another. Frequently in the Bible with the distinct idea of malice or spite. The Revisions often replace it by jealousy)
wrath killeth, and *e.* *Job* 5:2
e. is rottenness of bones. *Pr* 14:30
who is able to stand before *e.*? 27:4
love, hatred, and *e.* is. *Eccl* 9:6
the *e.* also of Ephraim. *Isa* 11:13
and be ashamed for their *e.* 26:11
do according to thine *e.* *Ezek* 35:11
for *e.* they delivered him. *Mat* 27:18
Mark 15:10
patriarchs moved with *e.* *Acts* 7:9
Jews filled with *e.* spake. 13:45
believed not, moved with *e.* 17:5
full of *e.* murder, debate. *Rom* 1:29
preach Christ, even of *e.* *Phil* 1:15
whereof cometh *e.* strife. *1 Tim* 6:4
living in malice and *e.* *Tit* 3:3
dwelleth in us lusteth to *e.* *Jas* 4:5

envy, *verb*
e. thou not oppressor. *Pr* 3:31
let not thine heart *e.* sinners. 23:17
Ephraim not *e.* Judah. *Isa* 11:13

envying
not in strife and *e.* *Rom* 13:13*
there is among you *e.* *1 Cor* 3:3*
provoking one another, *e.* *Gal* 5:26
but if ye have bitter *e.* *Jas* 3:14*
where *e.* is, there is confusion. 16*

envyings
there be debates, *e.* *2 Cor* 12:20*
works of the flesh are *e.* *Gal* 5:21

Epaphras
as ye learned of *E.* our. *Col* 1:7
E. saluteth you. 4:12; *Philem* 23

Epaphroditus
to send to you *E.* *Phil* 2:25
received of *E.* 4:18

Epenetus
salute my well-beloved *E.* *Rom* 16:5

ephah
(A Hebrew measure of the same capacity as the bath, *containing ten* homers. *About a bushel, dry measure, or nine gallons liquid measure)*
see **bath,** *and* **homer**
homer is tenth part of *e.* *Ex* 16:36
tenth part of an *e.* *Lev* 5:11; 6:20
have a just *e.* 19:36; *Ezek* 45:10
tenth part of an *e.* of. *Num* 5:15
unleavened cakes of an *e.* *Judg* 6:19
and it was about an *e.* *Ruth* 2:17
take now an *e.* of this. *1 Sam* 17:17
seed of an homer shall yield an *e.*
Isa 5:10
the *e.* and baths shall. *Ezek* 45:11
an hin of oil to an *e.* 46:5, 7, 11
making the *e.* small. *Amos* 8:5
he said, this is an *e.* *Zech* 5:6
cast it into midst of the *e.* 8

Ephah
E. the son of Midian. *Gen* 25:4
1 Chr 1:33
E. Caleb's concubine. *1 Chr* 2:46
sons of Jahdai, Pelet, *E.* 47
the dromedaries of *E.* *Isa* 60:6

Ephes-dammim
Philistines pitched in *E.* *1 Sam* 17:1

Ephesians
great is Diana of *E.* *Acts* 19:28, 34
the city of the *E.* is a worshipper. 35

Ephesus
Paul came to *E.* *Acts* 18:19
sailed from *E.* 21
Jew named Apollos came to *E.* 24
to Jews and Greeks at *E.* 19:17
not alone at *E.* but through Asia. 26
ye men of *E.* 35
Paul determined to sail by *E.* 20:16
fought with beasts at *E.* *1 Cor* 15:32
I will tarry at *E.* 16:8
thee to abide still at *E.* *1 Tim* 1:3
ministered to me at *E.* *2 Tim* 1:18
Tychicus have I sent to *E.* 4:12
send it to *E.* *Rev* 1:11
to the angel at *E.* 2:1

ephod
The upper garment worn by the Jewish priests. There were two sorts of ephods, one of plain linen for the priests, and another embroidered for the high priest. That for the high priest was of gold, blue, purple, crimson, and twisted linen. The shoulder pieces were held together by two onyx stones, each engraved with the names of six tribes of Israel, Ex 28:4, 5, 6, etc.
The Ephod worn by ordinary priests was of linen only, neither so rich, nor so much adorned.
to be set in. *e.* *Ex* 25:7; 35:9, 27
they shall make an *e.* and. 28:4, 6
curious girdle of *e.* 8*, 27, 28
39:5*, 20; *Lev* 8:7
on shoulders of *e.* *Ex* 28:12, 25
after the work of the *e.* 15; 39:8
robe of the *e.* of blue. 28:31; 39:22
he made the *e.* of gold, blue. 39:2
he put the *e.* upon him. *Lev* 8:7
and Gideon made an *e.* *Judg* 8:27
man Micah made an *e.* and. 17:5
there is in these houses an *e.* 18:14
girded with a linen *e.* *1 Sam* 2:18
choose him to wear an *e.* 28
the Lord's priest wearing an *e.* 14:3
sword is wrapt in cloth behind *e.* 21:9
85 persons that did wear *e.* 22:18
Abimelech fled with an *e.* in. 23:6
bring hither the *e.* 9; 30:7
danced before Lord, girded with linen *e.* *2 Sam* 6:14; *1 Chr* 15:27
shall abide without an *e.* *Hos* 3:4

Ephphatha
he saith to him, *E.* that. *Mark* 7:34

Ephraim, *a place*
had sheep-shearers beside *E.*
2 Sam 13:23
Abijah took *E.* and. *2 Chr* 13:19
into a city called *E.* *John* 11:54

mount **Ephraim**
if *mount E.* be too. *Josh* 17:15
Shechem in *mount E.* 20:7; 21:21
Joshua in *mount* of *E.* *Judg* 2:9
messengers through *mount E.* 7:24
Micah of *mount E.* 17:1
Levite came *to mount E.* 8
Danites passed unto *mount E.* 18:13
sojourning on side of *mount E.* 19:1
Elkanah of *mount E.* *1 Sam* 1:1
Saul passed through *mount E.* 9:4
Sheba of *mount E.* *2 Sam* 20:21
two men be come from *mount E.*
2 Ki 5:22
affliction from *mount E.* *Jer* 4:15
watchman upon *mount E.* 31:6
Israel be satisfied on *mount E.* 50:19

Ephraim, *a person,* or *people*
of Joseph's second son *E.* *Gen* 41:52
Israel laid right hand on *E.* *Gen* 48:14
saying, God make thee as *E,* and he set *E.* before Manasseh. 20
prince of *E.* was. *Num* 1:10; 7:48
on west side standard of *E.* 2:18
standard of the camp of *E.* 10:22
the sons of *E.* 26:35; *1 Chr* 7:20
the ten thousands of *E.* *Deut* 33:17
cities for the children of *E.*
Josh 16:9; 17:9
nor did *E.* drive out the. *Judg* 1:29
out of *E.* was there a root. 5:14
gleaning of the grapes of *E.* 8:2
fought with *E.* smote *E.* 12:4
Ish-bosheth king over *E.* *2 Sam* 2:9
E. their father mourned. *1 Chr* 7:22
dwelt of the children of *E.* 9:3
strangers out of *E.* fell. *2 Chr* 15:9
set garrisons in cities of *E.* 17:2
separated the army out of *E.* 25:10
Zichri a mighty man of *E.* 28:7
of *E.* had not cleansed. 30:18
all Israel brake images in *E.* 31:1
children of *E.* being armed. *Ps* 78:9
before *E.* stir up thy strength. 80:2
Syria is confederate with *E.* *Isa* 7:2
E. hath taken evil counsel. 5
sixty-five years shall *E.* 8
the head of *E.* is Samaria. 9
from the day that *E.* departed. 17
E. that say in the pride and. 9:9
Manasseh shall eat *E.* and *E.* 21
E. shall depart; *E.* not envy Judah, Judah not vex *E.* 11:13
fortress also shall cease from *E.* 17:3
woe to the drunkards of *E.* 28:1
drunkards of *E.* be trodden under. 3
cast out whole seed of *E.* *Jer* 7:15
I have heard *E.* bemoaning. 31:18
the stick of *E.* *Ezek* 37:16
stick of Joseph in hand of *E.* 19
a portion for *E.* 48:5
E. O *E.* thou committest. *Hos* 5:3
Israel and *E.* shall fall in iniquity. 5
E. shall be desolate. 9
I will be unto *E.* as a moth. 12
when *E.* saw his sickness, *E.* 13
E. as a lion. 14
O. *E.* what shall I do to thee ? 6:4
there is the whoredom of *E.* 10
the iniquity of *E.* 7:1
E. hath mixed himself among. 8
E. hired lovers. 8:9
E. made altars to sin. 11
E. shall eat unclean things. 9:3
watchmen of *E.* was with my God. 8
E. their glory shall fly away. 11
E. shall bring forth children to. 13
E. shall receive shame. 10:6
I will make *E.* to ride. 11
I taught *E.* to go. 11:3
how shall I give thee up, *E.*? 8
I will not return to destroy *E.* 9
E. compasseth me about with. 12
E. feedeth on wind. 12:1
E. said, I am rich. 8
E. provoked him to anger. 14
when *E.* spake trembling, he. 13:1
iniquity of *E.* is bound up. 12
E. say, what have I to do ? 14:8
shall possess the fields of *E.* *Ob* 19
cut off chariot from *E.* *Zech* 9:10
have filled the bow with *E.* 13
they of *E.* be like a mighty. 10:7
see **gate**

Ephraim *is*
E. *is* the strength. *Ps* 60:7; 108:8
E. *is* my firstborn. *Jer* 31:9
is *E.* my dear son ? 20
E. *is* joined to idols. *Hos* 4:17
E. *is* oppressed. 5:11
E. *is* a cake not turned. 7:8
E. *is* like a silly dove. 11
E. *is* smitten. 9:16
E. *is* as an heifer that is. 10:11

Ephraim with *tribe*
of the *tribe* of *E.* 40,500. *Num* 1:33
of the *tribe* of *E.* to spy. 13:8
of *tribe* of *E.* to divide. 34:24
inheritance of *tribe* of *E.* *Josh* 16:8
Kohathites had cities out of the *tribe* of *E.* 21:5, 20; *1 Chr* 6:66
chose not the *tribe* of *E.* *Ps* 78:67

Ephraimite, -s
art thou an E.? Judg 12:5
fell at that time of E. 42,000. 6

Ephratah
do thou worthily in E. Ruth 4:11
Hur, firstborn of E. 1 Chr 2:50; 4:4
lo, we heard of it at E. Ps 132:6
thou, Beth-lehem E. Mi 5:2

Ephrath
little way to come to E. Gen 35:16
Rachel buried in way to E. 19; 48:7
Caleb took to him E. 1 Chr 2:19

Ephrathite, -s
Mahlon, Chilion, E. of. Ruth 1:2
Elkanah was an E. 1 Sam 1:1
Jesse an E. 17:12
Jeroboam E. of Zereda. 1 Ki 11:26

Ephron
intreat for me to E. the. Gen 23:8
to E. weighed silver to E. 16
buried in the field of E. 25:9
bought with field of E. 49:30; 50:13

Epicureans
certain of E. encountered. Acts 17:18

epistle
(*A letter. In the New Testament, usually, a letter of an Apostle to a church or an individual*)
delivered the e. Acts 15:30; 23:33
Tertius who wrote this e. Rom 16:22
I wrote to you in an e. 1 Cor 5:9
e. written in our hearts. 2 Cor 3:2
declared to be the e. of Christ. 3
I perceive the same e. made. 7:8
when this e. is read, likewise read the e. from. Col 4:16
this e. be read to all. 1 Thes 5:27
by word or our e. 2 Thes 2:15
any obey not our word by this e. 3:14
which is the token in every e. 17
this second e. I now. 2 Pet 3:1

epistles
we e. of commendation. 2 Cor 3:1
as also in all his e. 2 Pet 3:16

equal
behold things that are e. Ps 17:2*
it was thou, a man, mine e. 55:13
legs of the lame are not e. Pr 26:7*
whom shall I be e.? Isa 40:25; 46:5
what shall I e. to thee. Lam 2:13
way of Lord not e. hear, is not my way e.? Ezek 18:25, 29; 33:17, 20
Israel, are not my ways e.? 18:29
for them, their way is not e. 33:17
hast made them e. to us. Mat 20:12
for they are e. to angels. Luke 20:36
himself e. with God. John 5:18
not robbery to be e. Phil 2:6*
your servants what is e. Col 4:1
and height of city are e. Rev 21:16

equal, *verb*
gold and crystal cannot e. Job 28:17
the topaz of Ethiopia not e. it. 19

equality
an e. that there be an e. 2 Cor 8:14

equally
two tenons e. distant. Ex 36:22

equals
above many my e. Gal 1:14*

equity
judge the people with e. Ps 98:9
thou dost establish e. 99:4
instruction of wisdom and e. Pr 1:3
understand judgement and e. 2:9
nor to strike princes for e. 17:26*
man whose labour is in e. Eccl 2:21*
with e. for meek of the. Isa 11:4
truth is fallen in street, and e. 59:14*
hear this, ye that pervert e. Mi 3:9
with me in peace and e. Mal 2:6*

Er
called his name E. Gen 38:3
took a wife for E. 6
E. was wicked. 7; 1 Chr 2:3
E. father of Lecah. 1 Chr 4:21
Elmodam, the son of E. Luke 3:28

Erastus
sent Timotheus and E. Acts 19:22
E. abode at Corinth. 2 Tim 4:20

ere
delivered e. midwives. Ex 1:19
long e. they believe me? Num 14:11
how long e. you make? Job 18:2
long e. thou be quiet? Jer 47:6
how long e. they attain? Hos 8:5
come down e. my child. John 4:49

erected
Jacob e. there an altar. Gen 33:20

err
(*To go astray; to fall into error*)
made Judah to e. 2 Chr 33:9
a people that do e. in. Ps 95:10
which do e. from thy. 119:21*
hast trodden them that e. 118
not e. that devise evil? Pr 14:22
instruction that causeth to e. 19:27
they which lead thee cause thee to e. Isa 3:12; 9:16
have caused Egypt to e. 19:14*
they e. in vision, they. 28:7
a bridle causing them to e. 30:28
the wayfaring men shall not e. 35:8
why hast thou made us to e.? 63:17
prophets in Baal, and caused people Israel to e. Jer 23:13; Mi 3:5
of whoredom caused them to e. Hos 4:12
lies caused them to e. Amos 2:4
ye do e. not knowing the scriptures. Mat 22:29; Mark 12:24, 27
always e. in their hearts. Heb 3:10
do not e. my brethren. Jas 1:16*
if any of you do e. from truth. 5:19

errand
eat till I have told e. Gen 24:33
I have a secret e. unto. Judg 3:19
I have an e. to thee, O. 2 Ki 9:5

erred
ignorance wherein he e. Lev 5:18
ye have e. and not. Num 15:22
I have e. exceedingly. 1 Sam 26:21
understand wherein I have e. Job 6:24
be it indeed that I have e. 19:4
yet I e. not from. Ps 119:110*
e. through wine and ... priest and the prophet have e. Isa 28:7*
they also that e. in spirit. 29:24
coveted they have e. 1 Tim 6:10*
some professing have e. 21
concerning truth have e. 2 Tim 2:18

erreth
he that refuseth reproof e. Pr 10:17
do for every one that e. Ezek 45:20

error
[1] *A mistake or oversight*, Eccl 5:6. [2] *False doctrine, which is not agreeable to the word of God*, 1 John 4:6. [3] *Sins of all sorts*, Ps 19:12; Heb 9:7.
smote Uzzah for his e. 2 Sam 6:7
if erred mine e. remaineth. Job 19:4
neither say that it was an e. Eccl 5:6
evil which I have seen as an e. 10:5
and to utter e. against. Isa 32:6
neither was there any e. found. Dan 6:4
last e. shall be worse. Mat 27:64
recompence of their e. Rom 1:27
converteth sinner from e. Jas 5:20
from them who live in e. 2 Pet 2:18
ye being led away with the e. 3:17
know we the spirit of e. 1 John 4:6
have ran greedily after e. Jude 11

errors
who can understand his e.? Ps 19:12
vanity, the work of e. Jer 10:15* 51:18*
he offered for e. of people. Heb 9:7

Esaias, *see* **Isaiah**

Esarhaddon
E. reigned in his stead. 2 Ki 19:37 Isa 37:38
since the days of E. king. Ezra 4:2

Esau
they called his name E. Gen 25:25
E. was a hunter. Gen 25:27
E. came from field. 29
thus E. dispised his birthright. 34
E. my brother is a hairy man. 27:11
whether thou be my son E. 21, 24
E. hated Jacob because of the. 41
these words of E. were told to. 42
then went E. to Ishmael. 28:9
Jacob sent messengers to E. 32:3
deliver me from hand of E. 11
a present sent unto my lord E. 18
E. ran to meet him. 33:4
E. said, I have enough, my. 9
thou fleddest from E. thy. 35:1
these are generations of E. 36:1
E. the father of the Edomites. 43
given mount Seir to E. Deut 2:5, 12 Josh 24:4
did to the children of E. Deut 2:22
unto Isaac, Jacob, and E. Josh 24:4 1 Chr 1:34
calamity of E. on him. Jer 49:8
I have made E. bare. 10
are things of E. searched out! Ob 6
house of E. shall be for stubble. 18
to judge the mount of E. 21
was not E. Jacob's? Mal 1:2
and I hated E. 3; Rom 9:13
blessed Jacob and E. Heb 11:20
be any profane person, as E. 12:16

escape
e. for thy life, e. to. Gen 19:17
O let me e. 20
haste thee, e. thither. 22
company which is left shall e. 32:8
none of them remain or e. Josh 8:22
e. into the land of the. 1 Sam 27:1
for we shall not else e. 2 Sam 15:14
get him fenced cities and e. 20:6
let none of them e. 1 Ki 18:40 2 Ki 9:15
if any I have brought e. 2 Ki 10:24
that e. out of Zion. 19:31; Isa 37:32
leave us a remnant to e. Ezra 9:8
think not thou shalt e. Esth 4:13
wicked shall not e. Job 11:20
shall they e. by iniquity? Ps 56:7
me, and cause me to e. 71:2*
wicked fall, whilst I e. 141:10
speaketh lies shall not e. Pr 19:5
pleaseth God shall e. Eccl 7:26
help, how shall we e.? Isa 20:6
I will send those that e. to. 66:19
shall not be able to e. Jer 11:11
nor principal of flock to e. 25:35
Zedekiah shall not e. 32:4; 34:3 38:18, 23
that go into Egypt e. 42:17; 44:14
return but such as shall e. 44:14
yet a small number that e. 28
swift flee, nor mighty man e. 46:6
spoiler shall come, no city e. 48:8
of them that flee and e. 50:28
let none thereof e. recompense. 29
some that shall e. the. Ezek 6:8
and they that e. of you shall. 9
they that e. shall e. and be. 7:16
e. that doth such things? 17:15
all these things, shall not e. 18
but these shall e. out. Dan 11:41*
land of Egypt shall not e. 42
and nothing shall e. them. Joel 2:3
off those of his that did e. Ob 14
can ye e. damnation of? Mat 23:33
accounted worthy to e. Luke 21:36
kill prisoners, lest any e. Acts 27:42
that thou shalt e. the? Rom 2:3
also make a way to e. 1 Cor 10:13
and they shall not e. 1 Thes 5:3
shall we e. if we neglect? Heb 2:3
much more shall not we e. 12:25

escape
I would hasten my e. Ps 55:8*

escaped
came one that had e. Gen 14:13
the locust eat what is e. Ex 10:5
given his sons that e. Num 21:29*
not deliver servant e. Deut 23:15
and Ehud e. while. Judg 3:26
there e. not a man. 29; 1 Sam 30:17
for them that be e. Judg 21:17
Jonathan taken, but people e. 1 Sam 14:41

David fled and e. 1 Sam 19:10, 12, 18
of camp of Israel I e. 2 Sam 1:3
and Baanah his brother e. 4:6
Ben-hadad the king e. 1 Ki 20:20
remnant that is e. of Judah take root. 2 Ki 19:30; Isa 37:31
smote rest that were e. 1 Chr 4:43
is the host of Syria e. 2 Chr 16:7
will return to you that are e. 30:6
for we remain yet e. Ezra 9:15
concerning Jews that had e. Neh 1:2
I only am e. Job 1:15, 16, 17, 19
am e. skin of my teeth. 19:20
is e. as a bird, the snare is broken and we are e. Ps 124:7
comely for them that are e. Isa 4:2
remnant and such as are e. 10:20
draw near, ye that are e. 45:20
son of Nethaniah e. Jer 41:15
ye that have e. remember. 51:50
that none in that day e. Lam 2:22
opened to him that is e. Ezek 24:27
one that had e. came. 33:21, 22
he e. out of their hands. John 10:39
to pass, they all e. safe. Acts 27:44
though he e. the sea, yet. 28:4
I was let down and e. 2 Cor 11:33
through faith e. edge of. Heb 11:34
if they e. not who refused. 12:25
e. the corruption that. 2 Pet 1:4
those that were clean e. 2:18*
after they have e. the pollutions. 20

escapeth

him that e. the sword of Hazael shall Jehu slay; him that e. 1 Ki 19:17
lions upon him that e. of. Isa 15:9
ask her that e. and ? Jer 48:19
he that e. in that day. Ezek 24:26
he that e. of them shall. Amos 9:1

escaping

be no remnant nor e. Ezra 9:14

eschew

e. evil and do good. 1 Pet 3:11*

eschewed

feared God and e. Job 1:1†, 8†; 2:3†

Esek

called name of well E. Gen 26:20

Eshcol

Amorite, brother of E. Gen 14:13
E. let them take their portion. 24
was called the brook E. Num 13:24
up unto the valley of E. 32:9

Esli

Naum, the son of E. Luke 3:25

especially *and* **specially**

s. the day thou stoodest. Deut 4:10
a reproach e. among. Ps 31:11*
and s. before thee. Acts 25:26
e. because I know thee expert. 26:3
e. to them of household. Gal 6:10
the Saviour, s. of those. 1 Tim 4:10
provide, s. for them of his. 5:8
e. they who labour in word. 17
the cloke bring, but e. 2 Tim 4:13
deceivers, s. they of the. Tit 1:10
brother beloved, s. to. Philem 16

espied

he e. his money in his. Gen 42:27
a land that I had e. for. Ezek 20:6
see **spy, spied**

espousals

him in day of his e. S of S 3:11
the love of thine e. Jer 2:2

espoused

Espousing, or betrothing, was done either by a formal contract in presence of witnesses; or without writing, by the man's giving a piece of silver to the bride before witnesses, and saying to her, Receive this piece of silver as a pledge that at such a time you shall become my spouse. *After the marriage was thus contracted, the young people had the liberty of seeing each other, which was not allowed them before. The union of believers with Christ is expressed under the figure of a marriage,* Isa 54:5; 2 Cor 11:2.

wife Michal whom I e. 2 Sam 3:14
his mother Mary was e. Mat 1:18
to a virgin e. to a man. Luke 1:27
to be taxed with Mary his e. 2:5
for I have e. you to one. 2 Cor 11:2

espy

Moses sent me to e. Josh 14:7*
stand by way, and e. Jer 48:19

Esrom

E. begat Aram. Mat 1:3; Luke 3:33

establish *and* **stablish**

Stablish is an obsolete form of establish, which word is most frequently substituted for it in the Revisions. Such passages are not here marked. [1] *To settle,* 1 Ki 9:5. [2] *To confirm,* Num 30:13. [3] *To perform, or make good,* Ps 119:38. [4] *To ordain, or appoint,* Hab 1:12.

thee will I e. my covenant. Gen 6:18
9:9; 17:7; Lev 26:9; Ezek 16:62
e. my covenant with. Gen 17:19, 21
her husband may e. it. Num 30:13
may e. his covenant he. Deut 8:18
the Lord shall e. thee an. 28:9
that he may e. thee to-day. 29:13
only Lord e. his word. 1 Sam 1:23
2 Sam 7:25*
I will e. his kingdom. 2 Sam 7:12
13; 1 Chr 17:11; 22:10; 28:7
I will e. throne of thy. 1 Ki 9:5
to set up his son, and to e. 15:4
and I will s. his throne. 1 Chr 17:12
as he went to s. his dominion. 18:3
then will I s. throne. 2 Chr 7:18
God loved Israel to e. them. 9:8
to s. among them days. Esth 9:21
yea he doth e. them for. Job 36:7*
but e. the just. Ps 7:9*
God will e. it. 48:8
the Highest himself shall e. 87:5
thy faithfulness shalt thou e. 89:2
thy seed will I e. for ever. 4
e. thou work of our hands, e. 90:17
thou dost e. equity, thou. 99:4
s. thy word to thy servant. 119:38
he will e. the border of. Pr 15:25
to e. it with judgement. Isa 9:7
give thee for a covenant to e. 49:8*
till he e. and make Jerusalem. 62:7
Lord that formed it, to e. it. Jer 33:2
I will e. an everlasting. Ezek 16:60
consulted to e. a royal. Dan 6:7
O king, e. the decree, and sign. 8
shall exalt themselves to e. 11:14
love the good, and e. Amos 5:15
yea, we e. the law. Rom 3:31
going about to e. their own. 10:3
to him that is of power to s. 16:25
Timothy our brother to e. 1 Thes 3:2
to the end he may s. your hearts. 13
s. you in every good. 2 Thes 2:17
the Lord shall s. you, and keep. 3:3
first, that he may e. Heb 10:9
also patient, s. your hearts. Jas 5:8
God of all grace s. 1 Pet 5:10

established, stablished

covenant which I have e. Gen 9:17
because the thing is e. by 41:32
have also e. my covenant. Ex 6:4
in sanctuary thy hands have e. 15:17
made thee, and e. thee ? Deut 32:6
Samuel was e. prophet. 1 Sam 3:20
now would Lord have e. thy. 13:13
not be e. nor thy kingdom. 20:31
perceived Lord had e. 2 Sam 5:12
let house of thy servant David be e. for ever. 7:26; 1 Chr 17:24
his kingdom was e. 1 Ki 2:12
Lord liveth, which hath e. me. 24
kingdom was e. in the hand. 46
let the thing be e. 1 Chr 17:23, 24
let thy promise be e. 2 Chr 1:9
when Rehoboam had e. the. 12:1
the Lord s. the kingdom in his. 17:5
when the kingdom was e. to. 25:3
so they e. a decree to keep. 30:5
their seed is e. in their. Job 21:8
he hath e. it upon floods. Ps 24:2
set my feet on a rock, and e. 40:2
he e. a testimony in Jacob. 78:5
earth he hath e. for, 69; 119:90
the world is e. 93:1
thy throne is e. of old. Ps 93:2
his heart is e. he shall not. 112:8
let not an evil speaker be e. 140:11
he hath s. the waters for. 148:6
by understanding, hath e. Pr 3:19
and let all thy ways be e. 4:26
when he e. the clouds above. 8:28*
man shall not be e. by. 12:3
of counsellors they are e. 15:22
for the throne is e. 16:12
purpose is e. by counsel. 20:18
by understanding is an house e. 24:3
e. all the ends of the earth. 30:4
believe, ye shall not be e. Isa 7:9
in mercy shall the throne be e. 16:5
God made earth, he hath e. it. 45:18
he e. the world. Jer 10:12; 51:15
I was e. in my kingdom. Dan 4:36
O mighty God, thou e. Hab 1:12
in the mouth of two witnesses every word be e. Mat 18:16
so were the churches e. Acts 16:5
to end you may be e. Rom 1:11
built up in him, and s. Col 2:7
which was e. upon better. Heb 8:6*
it is good that the heart be e. 13:9
though ye be e. in the. 2 Pet 1:12

shall be **established**

house *shall be e.* for. Lev 25:30*
2 Sam 7:16
of two or three witnesses *shall* matter *be e.* Deut 19:15; 2 Cor 13:1
kingdom *shall be e.* 1 Sam 24:20
thy kingdom, and thy throne, *shall be e.* for. 2 Sam 7:16*; 1 Ki 2:45
and his throne *shall be e.* for evermore. 1 Chr 17:14; Ps 89:37
believe in God, so *shall* ye *be e.* 2 Chr 20:20
decree, and it *shall be e.* Job 22:28
my hand *shall be e.* Ps 89:21
world *shall be e.* before thee. 96:10
and their seed *shall be e.* 102:28
of truth *shall be e.* for. Pr 12:19
thy thoughts *shall be e.* 16:3
his throne *shall be e.* 25:5; 29:14
of Lord's house *shall be e.* Isa 2:2
in mercy *shall* throne *be e.* 16:5
in righteousness *shalt be e.* 54:14
congregation *shall be e.* Jer 30:20
house of Lord *shall be e.* Mi 4:1
house, and it *shall be e.* Zech 5:11*

establisheth

he e. all her vows. Num 30:14
the king by judgement, e. Pr 29:4
no decree the king e. Dan 6:15
woe to him that e. city. Hab 2:12
he which e. us with you. 2 Cor 1:21

establishment

after e. Sennacherib. 2 Chr 32:1*

estate, state

[1] *Condition of life,* Gen 43:7. [2] *Social standing,* 1 Chr. 17:17. [3] *Pomp,* Esth 1:19.

man asked us of our s. Gen 43:7*
to the e. of a man of. 1 Chr 17:17*
set house of God in his s. 2 Chr 24:13
according to the s. of. Esth 1:7*
let the king give her royal e. to. 19
gifts according to the s. of. 2:18
every man at best s. Ps 39:5
remembered us in our low e. 136:23
diligent to know s. of thy. Pr 27:23
by a man of knowledge s. 28:2
lo, I am come to great e. Eccl 1:16
concerning the e. of sons of. 3:18*
from thy s. shall he pull. Isa 22:19
return to her former e. Ezek 16:55
stand up in his e. Dan 11:7*, 21*
then shall stand up in his e. 20*
but in his e. shall he honour. 38*
other spirits enter, the last s. of that man. Mat 12:45; Luke 11:26
hath regarded low e. of. Luke 1:48
all the e. of the elders. Acts 22:5
condescend to men of low e. Rom 12:16*
when I know your s. Phil 2:19
will naturally care for your s. 20
in whatsoever s. I am to be. 4:11
all my s. shall Tychicus. Col 4:7
sent, that he might know your e. 8
angels which kept not first e. Jude 6*

estates
you after your old *e*. *Ezek* 36:11
supper to his chief *e*. *Mark* 6:21*

esteem
will he *e*. thy riches ? *Job* 36:19*
I *e*. all thy precepts to. *Ps* 119:128
we did *e*. him smitten of. *Isa* 53:4
each *e*. other better than. *Phil* 2:3
to *e*. them highly for. *1 Thes* 5:13

esteemed
e. rock of his salvation. *Deut* 32:15
me shall be lightly *e*. *1 Sam* 2:30
a poor man and lightly *e*. 18:23
I have *e*. the words of. *Job* 23:12*
e. a man of understanding. *Pr* 17:28
turning shall be *e*. as the. *Isa* 29:16*
fruitful field shall be *e*. as a. 17*
despised, and we *e*. him not. 53:3
how are they *e*. as ! *Lam* 4:2
highly *e*. among men. *Luke* 16:15*
to judge who are least *e*. *1 Cor* 6:4*

esteemeth
he *e*. iron as straw. *Job* 41:27*
one *e*. one day above another; another *e*. every day. *Rom* 14:5
to him that *e*. any thing to. 14*

esteeming
e. reproach of Christ. *Heb* 11:26*

Esther
brought up Hadassah, *E*. *Esth* 2:7
the king loved *E*. 17
king made feast, even *E.'s* feast. 18
told it to *E*. 22
E.'s maids came, she sent. 4:4
told to Mordecai *E.'s* words. 12
Mordecai did all that E. had. 17
king held out to E. golden. 5:2; 8:4
what wilt thou, queen *E*.? 5:3
E. let no man come in with. 12
what is thy petition, queen *E*.? 7:2
to make request for life to *E*. 7
and *E*. spake yet again. 8:3
I have given *E*. the house. 7
E. the queen wrote with. 9:29
decree of *E*. confirmed these. 32

estimate
priest shall *e*. it good or bad, as the priest shall *e*. it. *Lev* 27:14

estimation
bring a ram with thy *e*. *Lev* 5:15
shall be for Lord, by thy *e*. 27:2
thy *e*. shall be of the male from. 3, 5
This word frequently occurs in this chapter
old, according to thy *e*. *Num* 18:16

estimations
all thy *e*. according to. *Lev* 27:25

estranged
mine acquaintance are *e*. *Job* 19:13
the wicked are *e*. from. *Ps* 58:3
were not *e*. from their lust. 78:30
because they have *e*. this. *Jer* 19:4
they are all *e*. from me. *Ezek* 14:5

Etam
Samson dwelt in top of *E*. *Judg* 15:8
men went to top of the rock *E*. 11

eternal
e. God is thy refuge. *Deut* 33:27
thee an *e*. excellency. *Isa* 60:15
is in danger of *e*. *Mark* 3:29
even his *e*. power and. *Rom* 1:20*
worketh an *e*. weight of. *2 Cor* 4:17
things which are not seen are *e*. 18
an house *e*. in the heavens. 5:1
according to *e*. purpose. *Eph* 3:11
unto the King *e*. be. *1 Tim* 1:17
salvation with *e*. glory. *2 Tim* 2:10
the author of *e*. salvation. *Heb* 5:9
doctrine of baptisms, and *e*. 6:2
having obtained *e*. redemption. 9:12
who through the *e*. Spirit offered. 14
the promise of *e*. inheritance. 15
us unto his *e*. glory. *1 Pet* 5:10
suffering the vengeance of *e*. *Jude* 7

eternal *life*
that I may have *e*. *life* ? *Mat* 19:16
righteous shall go into *life e*. 25:46
shall I do, that I may inherit *e*. *life* ? *Mark* 10:17; *Luke* 10:25; 18:18
in world to come *e*. *life*. *Mark* 10:30
in him should have *e*. *life*. *John* 3:15
gathereth fruit unto *life e*. 4:36
in them ye have *e*. *life*. 5:39
drinketh my blood hath *e*. *life*. 6:54
hast words of *e*. *life*. 68
I give unto them *e*. *life*. 10:28
his life, keep it to *e*. *life*. 12:25
he should give *e*. *life* to as. 17:2
this is *life e*. that they might. 3
were ordained to *e*. *life*. *Acts* 13:48
who seek glory, *e*. *life*. *Rom* 2:7
might grace reign to *e*. *life*. 5:21
but the gift of God is *e*. *life*. 6:23
lay hold on *e*. *life*. *1 Tim* 6:12, 19*
in hope of *e*. *life*. *Tit* 1:2
according to hope of *e*. *life*. 3:7
e. *life* which was with. *1 John* 1:2
promise he promised, *e*. *life*. 2:25
no murderer hath *e*. *life*. 3:15
God hath given to us *e*. *life*. 5:11
may know that ye have *e*. *life*. 13
is the true God, and *e*. *life*. 20
mercy of Lord unto *e*. *life*. *Jude* 21

eternity
One that inhabiteth *e*. *Isa* 57:15

Etham
encamped in *E*. *Ex* 13:20; *Num* 33:6
three days' journey in *E*. *Num* 33:8

Ethan
Solomon was wiser than *E*. *1 Ki* 4:31
Zerah, Zimri, and *E*. *1 Chr* 2:6

Ethanim
Israel assembled in the month *E*. *1 Ki* 8:2

Ethiopia
land of *E*. *Gen* 2:13; *Ezek* 29:10
heard say of Tirhakah king of *E*. *2 Ki* 19:9; *Isa* 37:9
Ahasuerus reigned from India to *E*. *Esth* 1:1; 8:9
the topaz of *E*. not equal. *Job* 28:19
E. stretch out hands to. *Ps* 68:31
Philistia and Tyre with *E*. 87:4
the rivers of *E*. *Isa* 18:1; *Zeph* 3:10
bare-foot for sign on *E*. *Isa* 20:3
they shall be ashamed of *E*. 5
gave Egypt for thy ransom, *E*. 43:3
the merchandise of *E*. shall. 45:14
great pain in *E*. *Ezek* 30:4
E. shall fall. 5; 38:5
E. and Egypt were the. *Nah* 3:9
a man of *E*. eunuch of. *Acts* 8:27

Ethiopian
because of *E*. woman. *Num* 12:1
Zerah the *E*. came out. *2 Chr* 14:9
can *E*. change his skin ? *Jer* 13:23
Ebed-melech the *E*. 38:7, 10, 12
39:16

Ethiopians
Lord smote *E*. the *E*. *2 Chr* 14:12
the *E*. and Lubims a huge ? 16:8
stirred Arabians near *E*. 21:16
shall lead the *E*. captives. *Isa* 20:4
E. that handle the shield. *Jer* 46:9
make careless *E*. afraid. *Ezek* 30:9
the Lybians and *E*. shall. *Dan* 11:43
ye not as children of *E*.? *Amos* 9:7
ye *E*. shall be slain. *Zeph* 2:12
under Candace of *E*. *Acts* 8:27

Eubulus
E. greeteth thee. *2 Tim* 4:21

Eunice
faith which dwelt in *E*. *2 Tim* 1:5

eunuch
Originally an impotent man. Since those put in charge of the harems of Eastern monarchs were as a general rule of this class, the name became practically synonymous with chamberlain, with no indication of his condition, although probably its use in scripture was strict. Eunuchs were not allowed by Jewish law to enter the house of God, Deut 23:1; *but they were present at the court,* 1 Chr 28:1, marg. *A eunuch was over the treasure of queen Candace of Ethiopia, and he was admitted to baptism,* Acts 8:27, 37.
neither let the *e*. say. *Isa* 56:3
an *e*. had come to. *Acts* 8:27
e. said, of whom speaks ? 34
e. said, what doth hinder me ? 36
Spirit caught Philip, *e*. saw. 39

eunuchs
looked out two or three *e*. *2 Ki* 9:32
and they shall be *e*. in palace. 20:18
Isa 39:7
Ahab called for one of *e*. *2 Chr* 18:8
saith the Lord to the *e*. *Isa* 56:4
after that the *e*. were. *Jer* 29:2
e. which passed between the. 34:19
when Ebed-melech one of *e*. 38:7
e. whom he had brought. 41:16
spake to master of his *e*. *Dan* 1:3
to whom the prince of the *e*. 7
Daniel requested of prince of *e*. 8
into favour with prince of *e*. 9
then prince of the *e*. brought. 18
e. who were so born, made *e*. of men. *Mat* 19:12

Euodias
I beseech *E*. and. *Phil* 4:2

Euphrates
the fourth river is *E*. *Gen* 2:14
unto great river, the river *E*. 15:18
go to great river *E*. *Deut* 1:7
Josh 1:4
yours from the river *E*. *Deut* 11:24
smote Hadadezer at the river *E*. *2 Sam* 8:3; *1 Chr* 18:3
Necho went up to *E*. *2 Ki* 23:29
2 Chr 35:20
took from Egypt to *E*. *2 Ki* 24:7
inhabited from river *E*. *1 Chr* 5:9
arise, go to *E*. *Jer* 13:4
so I hid it by *E*. 5
I went to *E*. 7
came against Pharaoh by *E*. 46:2
stumble and fall by river *E*. 6
hath a sacrifice by *E*. 10
cast it into midst of *E*. 51:63
bound in the river *E*. *Rev* 9:14
angel poured out vial on *E*. 16:12

euroclydon
(A tempestuous north-east wind of the Mediterranean, very dangerous to the sort of shipping used in the time of the Apostles. In the Revisions the name is given as Euraquilo)
arose tempestuous wind, called *e*. *Acts* 27:14

Eutychus
a young man named *E*. *Acts* 20:9

evangelist
house of Philip the *e*. *Acts* 21:8
do the work of an *e*. *2 Tim* 4:5

evangelists
some apostles, some *e*. *Eph* 4:11

Eve
called his wife's name *E*. *Gen* 3:20
Adam knew *E*. his wife. 4:1
as serpent beguiled *E*. *2 Cor* 11:3
first formed, then *E*. *1 Tim* 2:13

even
(The close of the day)
two angels to Sodom at *e*. *Gen* 19:1
fourteenth day of month at *e*. *Ex* 12:18
Moses said, at *e*. then shall. 16:6
at *e*. eat flesh. 12
at *e*. the quails came. 13
stand from morning to *e*. 18:14
Aaron lighteth lamps at *e*. 30:8
unclean until *e*. *Lev* 11:24, 25, 27, 28
31, 39, 40; 14:46; 15:5, 6, 7, etc.
17:15; 22:6; *Num* 19:7, 8, 10, 21
22
fourteenth day of first month, at *e*. *Lev* 23:5; *Num* 9:3; *Deut* 16:6
day of second month at *e*. *Num* 9:11
when cloud abode from *e*. to. 21
shall be clean at *e*. 19:19
would God it were *e*. *Deut* 28:67
wept before Lord till *e*. *Judg* 20:23
and fasted till *e*. 26; *2 Sam* 1:12
the people abode till *e*. 21:2
gleaned in field until *e*. *Ruth* 2:17
unto third day at *e*. *1 Sam* 20:5
Ahab died at *e*. *1 Ki* 22:35
2 Chr 18:34

praise Lord every morning and **e.** *1 Chr* 23:30
shalt go forth at *e.* in. *Ezek* 12:4
in the *e.* I digged through the wall. 7
and at *e.* my wife died. 24:18
when the *e.* was come. *Mat* 8:16
20:8; 26:20; 27:57; *Mark* 4:35
6:47; 11:19; 15:42
at *e.* they brought to. *Mark* 1:32
at *e.* at midnight, or cockcrow. 13:35
when **e.** was come. *John* 6:16

even

mine eyes *e.* seeing it. *1 Ki* 1:48
known to thee, *e.* to. *Pr* 22:19
flock of sheep that are **e.** *S of S* 4:2
e. saying to Jerusalem. *Isa* 44:28
e. to them will I give a name. 56:5
if a man do, he shall *e.* *Ezek* 20:11
if sword contemn *e.* the rod. 21:13
e. we ourselves groan. *Rom* 8:23
not *e.* nature itself ? *1 Cor* 11:14
kingdom to God, *e.* the. 15:24
e. the Father of our Lord. *2 Cor* 1:3
a measure to reach *e.* to you. 10:13
obedient to death, *e.* *Phil* 2:8

even, *adjective*

that net may be *e.* to. *Ex* 27:5
weighed in an *e.* balance. *Job* 31:6
my foot standeth in *e.* *Ps* 26:12
shall lay thee *e.* with. *Luke* 19:44

evening

came in to him in the **e.** *Gen* 8:11
came out of field in **e.** 30:16
of Israel kill it in *e.* *Ex* 12:6
but when *e.* cometh. *Deut* 23:11
hanging on trees until *e.* *Josh* 10:26
day draweth towards *e.* *Judg* 19:9
cursed that eateth till *e.* *1 Sam* 14:24
David smote them to the *e.* 30:17
in the *e.* she went. *Esth* 2:14
they return at **e.** they. *Ps* 59:6
at *e.* let them return and. 14
in the *e.* it is cut down. 90:6
forth to his labour until **e.** 104:23
went way to her house in **e.** *Pr* 7:9
in the *e.* withhold not. *Eccl* 11:6
the shadows of the *e.* *Jer* 6:4
of Lord was on me in *e.* *Ezek* 33:22
gate shall not be shut till *e.* 46:2
in Ashkelon lie down in *e.* *Zeph* 2:7
when **e.** was come. *Mat* 14:23
when it is *e.* ye say, **it.** 16:2
in the *e.* he cometh. *Mark* 14:17
abide with us, for it is **e.** *Luke* 24:29
same day at *e.* came. *John* 20:19

evening with *morning*

the *e.* and *morning* were first day.
Gen 1:5, 8, 13, 19, 23, 31
Moses from *morning* to *e.* *Ex* 18:13
shall order it from *e.* to *morning.*
27:21; *Lev* 24:3
Philistine drew near *morning* and *e.*
1 Sam 17:16
bread *morning* and *e.* *1 Ki* 17:6
offerings *morning* and *e.* *1 Chr* 16:40
2 Chr 2:4; 13:11; 31:3; *Ezra* 3:3
are destroyed from *morning* to *e.*
Job 4:20
e. and *morning*, and at. *Ps* 55:17
outgoings of *morning* and *e.* 65:8
vision of *e.* and *morning* is. *Dan* 8:26
persuading them from *morning* to *e.*
Acts 28:23

evening, *adjective*

prophesied till *e.* *1 Ki* 18:29
at time of offering of the *e.* 36
on great altar burn *e.* *2 Ki* 16:15
astonished until the *e.* *Ezra* 9:4
at *e.* sacrifice I arose from my. 5
let my prayer be as the *e.* *Ps* 141:2
the time of *e.* oblation. *Dan* 9:21
more fierce than the *e.* *Hab* 1:8
her judges are *e.* wolves. *Zeph* 3:3
at **e.** time shall be light. *Zech* 14:7

evenings

a wolf of the **e.** shall. *Jer* 5:6

event

one *e.* happeneth to. *Eccl* 2:14; 9:3
one *e.* to the righteous and. 9:2

eventide, *or* **eveningtide**

went out to meditate at *e.* *Gen* 24:63
Joshua fell on his face till *e.* *Josh* 7:6
of Ai he hanged on tree till *e.* 8:29
in an *e.* David walked. *2 Sam* 11:2
behold, at *e.* trouble. *Isa* 17:14
now the *e.* was come. *Mark* 11:11
him in hold, for it was **e.** *Acts* 4:3

ever

fire shall *e.* be burning. *Lev* 6:13
hast ridden on, *e.* since. *Num* 22:30
did *e.* people hear voice ? *Deut* 4:33
to love God, and to walk *e.* 19:9
e. fight against Israel ? *Judg* 11:25
Hiram was *e.* a lover. *1 Ki* 5:1
who *e.* perished, being ? *Job* 4:7
that trust, let them *e.* *Ps* 5:11
tender mercies have been **e.** 25:6
mine eyes are *e.* towards Lord. 25:15
he is *e.* merciful, and. 37:26*
and my sin is *e.* before me. 51:3
or *e.* thou hadst formed earth. 90:2
Pr 8:23
will *e.* be mindful of his. *Ps* 111:5
commandments are *e.* with. 119:98
or *e.* I was aware, my. *S of S* 6:12†
because he will not *e.* be. *Isa* 28:28
not one of the stakes shall *e.* 33:20
e. they came at bottom. *Dan* 6:24†
hath not been *e.* the like. *Joel* 2:2
was not, no, nor *e.* shall. *Mat* 24:21
him to do as he had *e.* *Mark* 15:8*
son, thou art *e.* with. *Luke* 15:31
told me all things *e.* I. *John* 4:29, 39
but the Son abideth *e.* 8:35
all that *e.* came before me. 10:8
I *e.* taught in the synagogue. 18:20
we, or *e.* he come, are. *Acts* 23:15
for no man *e.* yet hated. *Eph* 5:29
so shall we *e.* be with. *1 Thes* 4:17
but *e.* follow that which is. 5:15
e. learning, and never. *2 Tim* 3:7
because he continueth *e.* *Heb* 7:24
e. liveth to make intercession. 25
be glory, now and *e.* ***Jude*** **25**

***see* endureth**

for **ever**

(Many believe that the words **for** ever *or* everlasting *are not to be taken as synonymous with eternal, as being without end, but to be understood merely as meaning a very long time, to be left indeterminate. There seems to be a considerable amount of argument in favour of this in many cases, but it is not safe to conclude that it always should be so limited)*

give it and thy seed *for e.* *Gen* 13:15
me bear blame *for e.* 43:9; 44:32
this is my name *for e.* *Ex* 3:15
feast by an ordinance *for e.* 12:14, 17
to thee, and to thy sons *for e.* 24
see them again no more *for e.* 14:13
people may believe thee *for e.* 19:9
and he shall serve him *for e.* 21:6
between me and Israel *for e.* 31:17
and they shall inherit it *for e.* 32:13
land not be sold *for e.* *Lev* 25:23*
the house be established *for e.* 30*
shall be your bondmen *for e.* 46
for an ordinance *for e.* *Num* 10:8
15:15; 18:8
covenant of salt *for e.* 18:19
Amalek shall perish *for e.* 24:20
afflict Eber, he shall perish *for e.* 24
earth which God giveth thee *for e.*
Deut 4:40
be well with them *for e.* 5:29; 12:28
it shall be an heap *for e.* 13:16
shall be thy servant *for e.* 15:17
him and his sons *for e.* 18:5
not seek their peace *for e.* 23:6
upon thee for a sign *for e.* 28:46
revealed belong to us *for e.* 29:29
stones be a memorial *for e.* *Josh* 4:7
fear the Lord your God *for e.* 24
Ai, made it an heap *for e.* 8:28
land be thine inheritance *for e.* 14:9
before the Lord and abide *for e.*
1 Sam 1:22
house walk before me *for e.* 2:30
not be an old man in house *for e.* 32
walk before mine Anointed *for e.* 35
I will judge his house *for e.*
1 Sam 3:13
of Eli's house not purged *for e.* 14
not cut off thy kindness *for e.* 20:15
between thee and me *for e.* 23, 42
shall be my servant *for e.* 27:12
keeper of mine head *for e.* 28:2
sword devour *for e.?* *2 Sam* 2:26
and my kingdom guiltless *for e.* 3:28
confirmed Israel to thee *for e.* 7:24
let thy name be magnified *for e.* 26
his house may continue *for e.* 29
for thee to abide in *for e.* *1 Ki* 8:13
to put my name there *for e.* 9:3
the Lord loved Israel *for e.* 10:9
David's seed, but not *for e.* 11:39
will be thy servants *for e.* 12:7
2 Chr 10:7
leprosy cleave to thee *for e.*
2 Ki 5:27
make thine own *for e.* *1 Chr* 17:22
he and sons *for e.* to burn. 23:13
he will cast thee off *for e.* 28:9
God of Israel, keep this *for e.* 29:18
name may be there *for e.* *2 Chr* 7:16
to give a light to sons *for e.* 21:7
which he hath sanctified *for e.* 30:8
Jerusalem my name be *for e.* 33:4
congregation of God *for e.* *Neh* 13:1
they perish *for e.* without. *Job* 4:20
prevailest *for e.* against. 14:20
iron pen in the rock *for e.* 19:24
yet he shall perish *for e.* 20:7
should I be delivered *for e.* 23:7
he doth establish them *for e.* 36:7
Lord shall endure *for e.* *Ps* 9:7
of poor shall not perish *for e.* 18
thou shalt preserve them *for e.* 12:7
thou forget me, O Lord, *for e.?* 13:1
fear of Lord enduring *for e.* 19:9
made him most blessed *for e.* 21:6
in house of the Lord *for e.* 23:6
and lift them up *for e.* 28:9
the Lord sitteth king *for e.* 29:10
thanks to thee *for e.* 30:12; 79:13
counsel of Lord standeth *for e.* 33:11
their inheritance shall be *for e.* 37:18
his saints are preserved *for e.* 28
righteous shall dwell in land *for e.* 29
me before thy face *for e.* 41:12
and we praise thy name *for e.* 44:8
O Lord, cast us not off *for e.* 23
God hath blessed thee *for e.* 45:2
redemption of their soul ceaseth *for e.* 49:8
their houses continue *for e.* 11
God shall destroy thee *for e.* 52:5
I will praise thee *for e.* 9
abide in thy tabernacle *for e.* 61:4
he shall abide before God *for e.* 7
sing praise unto thy name *for e.* 8
he ruleth by his power *for e.* 66:7
Lord will dwell in it *for e.* 68:16
his name shall endure *for e.* 72:17
blessed be his glorious name *for e.* 19
my strength and portion *for e.* 73:26
hast thou cast us off *for e.?* 74:1
enemy blaspheme name *for e.?* 10
forget not thy poor *for e.* 19
I will declare *for e.* I will. 75:9
will Lord cast off *for e.?* 77:7
is mercy clean gone *for e.?* 8
wilt thou be angry *for e.?* 79:5
should have endured *for e.* 81:15
confounded and troubled *for e.* 83:17
thou be angry with us *for e.?* 85:5
sing of mercies of Lord *for e.* 89:1
mercy shall be built up *for e.* 2
his seed will I make to endure *for e.*
29, 36
wilt thou hide thyself *for e.?* 46
they should be destroyed *for e.* 92:7
holiness becometh house *for e.* 93:5
neither keep his anger *for e.* 103:9
remembered his covenant *for e.*
105:8
thou art a priest *for e.* after. 110:4
Heb 5:6; 6:20; 7:17, 21
commanded his covenant *for e.*
Ps 111:9
he shall not be moved *for e.* 112:6
for e. O Lord, thy word is. 119:89
from henceforth even *for e.* 125:2
131:3; *Isa* 9:7

this is my rest *for e.* *Ps* 132:14
Lord who keepeth truth *for e.* 146:6
the Lord shall reign *for e.* 10
for riches are not *for e.* *Pr* 27:24
wise more than fool *for e.* *Eccl* 2:16
God doth, it shall be *for e.* 3:14
have they more a portion *for e.* 9:6
trust ye in Lord *for e.* *Isa* 26:4
and assurance *for e.* 32:17
smoke shall go up *for e.* 34:10
shall possess it *for e.* from. 17
word of our God stand *for e.* 40:8
I shall be a lady *for e.* 47:7
my salvation shall be *for e.* 51:6
my righteousness shall be *for e.* 8
will not contend *for e.* nor. 57:16
words shall not depart *for e.* 59:21
people shall inherit land *for e.* 60:21
nor remember iniquity *for e.* 64:9
be glad and rejoice *for e.* 65:18
he reserve anger *for e.?* *Jer* 3:5
I will not keep anger *for e.* 12
a fire which shall burn *for e.* 17:4
and this city shall remain *for e.* 25
not be plucked up *for e.* 31:40
heart that they may fear *for e.* 32:39
ye shall drink no wine *for e.* 35:6
Jonadab shall not want a man to stand before me *for e.* 19
dragons and a desolation *for e.* 49:33
more inhabited *for e.* 50:39; 51:26 62
will not cast off *for e.* *Lam* 3:31
thou remainest *for e.* thy. 5:19
dost thou forget us *for e.?* 20
their children dwell *for e.* and David be their prince *for e.* *Ezek* 37:25
in midst of Israel *for e.* 43:7, 9
kingdom shall stand *for e.* *Dan* 2:44
honoured him that liveth *for e.* 4:34
living God and stedfast *for e.* 6:26
saints possess kingdom *for e.* 7:18
sware by him that liveth *for e.* 12:7
betroth thee unto me *for e.* *Hos* 2:19
Judah shall dwell *for e.* *Joel* 3:20
off pity kept wrath *for e.* *Amos* 1:11
Edom, shalt be cut off *for e.* *Ob* 10
with bars about me *for e.* *Jonah* 2:6
taken away my glory *for e.* *Mi* 2:9
Lord shall reign over them *for e.* 4:7
retaineth not anger *for e.* 7:18
Lord hath indignation *for e.* *Mal* 1:4
is power and glory *for e.* *Mat* 6:13
no fruit grow on thee *for e.* 21:19 *Mark* 11:14
reign over Jacob *for e.* *Luke* 1:33
to Abraham and seed *for e.* 55
abideth not in house *for e.* *John* 8:35
that Christ abideth *for e.* 12:34
may abide with you *for e.* 14:16
Creator, who is blessed *for e.* *Rom* 1:25
is over all, God blessed *for e.* 9:5
to whom be glory *for e.* 11:36; 16:27
righteousness remaineth *for e.* *2 Cor* 9:9
receive him *for e.* *Philem* 15
for *e.* sat down on the. *Heb* 10:12
perfected *for e.* them that are. 14
the same to-day and *for e.* 13:8
word of God, liveth *for e.* *1 Pet* 1:23
word of Lord endureth *for e.* 25
to whom mist of darkness is reserved *for e.* *2 Pet* 2:17; *Jude* 13
shall be with us *for e.* *2 John* 2
see **establish, established**

live for **ever**

tree of life, and *live for e.* *Gen* 3:22
hand and say, I *live for e.* *Deut* 32:40
king David *live for e.* *1 Ki* 1:31
let the king *live for e.* *Neh* 2:3
hearts shall *live for e.* *Ps* 22:26
that he should still *live for e.* 49:9
O king, *live for e.* *Dan* 2:4; 3:9 5:10; 6:6, 21
do they *live for e.?* *Zech* 1:5
if any man eat of this bread he shall *live for e.* *John* 6:51, 58

for **ever** *and* **ever**

Lord reign *for e. and e.* *Ex* 15:18
blessed be God *for e. and e.* people. *1 Chr* 16:36*; 29:10; *Dan* 2:20
bless your God *for e. and e.* *Neh* 9:5
out their name *for e and e.* *Ps* 9:5
Lord is King *for e. and e.* 10:16
him length of days *for e. and e.* 21:4
thy throne is *for e. and e.* 45:6
people praise thee *for e. and e.* 17
God is our God *for e. and e.* 48:14
in mercy of God *for e. and e.* 52:8
they stand fast *for e. and e.* 111:8
I keep thy law *for e. and e.* 119:44
bless thy name *for e. and e.* 145:1
praise thy name *for e. and e.* 2, 21
stablished them *for e. and e.* 148:6
time to come, *for e. and e.* *Isa* 30:8
pass through it *for e. and e.* 34:10
land I gave *for e. and e.* *Jer* 7:7*
you and fathers *for e. and e.* 25:5*
the kingdom *for e. and e.* *Dan* 7:18
shine as stars *for e. and e.* 12:3
walk in the name of God *for e and e.* *Mi* 4:5
whom be glory *for e. and e.* *Gal* 1:5 *Phil* 4:20; *1 Tim* 1:17 *2 Tim* 4:18; *Heb* 13:21
throne, O God, is *for e. and e.* *Heb* 1:8
to him who liveth *for e. and e.* *Rev* 4:9, 10; 5:14; 10:6; 15:7
be to the Lamb *for e. and e.* 5:13
power be unto God *for e. and e.* 7:12
Christ shall reign *for e. and e.* 11:15
ascendeth *for e. and e.* 14:11; 19:3
tormented day and night *for e. and e.* 20:10
shall reign *for e. and e.* 22:5

statute for **ever**

be a *statute for e.* *Ex* 27:21; 28:43 30:21; *Lev* 6:18; 10:9; 17:7 23:14, 21, 31, 41; 24:3 *Num* 18:23
a *statute for e.* *Ex* 29:28; *Lev* 7:34 36; 10:15; 16:31; *Num* 18:11, 19
a *statute for e.* unto Lord. *Lev* 6:22
stranger for *statute for e.* *Num* 19:10

everlasting

(See note on **for ever.** *The Revisions very frequently substitute the word* eternal *for everlasting)*

land of Canaan for an *e.* possession. *Gen* 17:8; 48:4
the *e.* God. 21:33; *Isa* 40:28 *Rom* 16:26
utmost bound of *e.* hills. *Gen* 49:26
an *e.* priesthood. *Ex* 40:15 *Num* 25:13
be an *e.* statute. *Lev* 16:34
e. arms. *Deut* 33:27
lift up, ye *e.* doors. *Ps* 24:7, 9
mercy *e.* 100:5
righteous in *e.* remembrance. 112:6
is an *e.* righteousness. 119:142, 144
and lead me in way *e.* 139:24
kingdom is an *e.* kingdom. 145:13 *Dan* 4:3; 7:27; *2 Pet* 1:11
righteous is an *e.* foundation. *Pr* 10:25
be called, the *e.* Father. *Isa* 9:6
Jehovah is *e.* strength. 26:4
dwell with *e.* burnings ? 33:14
they shall come with *e.* joy. 35:10 51:11; 61:7
with an *e.* salvation. 45:17
with *e.* kindness. 54:8
for an *e.* sign. 55:13
an *e.* name. 56:5; 63:12
unto thee an *e.* light. 60:19, 20
God is an *e.* King. *Jer* 10:10
e. confusion. 20:11
an *e.* reproach upon you. 23:40
I have loved thee with *e.* love. 31:3
dominion is an *e.* dominion. *Dan* 4:34 7:14
e. mountains were. *Hab* 3:6
cast into *e.* fire. *Mat* 18:8, 25, 41
go away into *e.* punishment. 25:46
you into *e.* habitations. *Luke* 16:9
with *e.* destruction. *2 Thes* 1:9
hath given us *e.* consolation. 2:16
be honour and power *e.* *1 Tim* 6:16
angels reserved in *e.* chains. *Jude* 6
having the *e.* gospel to. *Rev* 14:6
see **covenant**

from **everlasting**

blessed be God *from e.* *Ps* 41:13 106:48
even *from e.* to everlasting. 90:2
thou art *from e.* 93:2
mercy of Lord is *from e.* 103:17
I was set up *from e.* *Pr* 8:23
thy name is *from e.* *Isa* 63:16
forth have been *from e.* *Mi* 5:2
art thou not *from e.?* *Hab* 1:12

everlasting *life*

awake, some to *e. life.* *Dan* 12:2
shall inherit *e. life.* *Mat* 19:29
world to come *e. life.* *Luke* 18:30
believeth have *e. life.* *John* 3:16, 36
a well springing up to *e. life.* 4:14
heareth my words hath *e. life.* 5:24
meat which endureth to *e. life.* 6:27
who seeth Son may have *e. life.* 40
believeth on me hath *e. life.* 47
his commandment is *life e.* 12:50
unworthy of *e. life.* *Acts* 13:46
ye have the end *e. life.* *Rom* 6:22
of Spirit reap *life e.* *Gal* 6:8
believe on him to *life e.* *1 Tim* 1:16

evermore

oppressed and spoiled *e.* *Deut* 28:29
mercy unto David *e.* *2 Sam* 22:51
observe to do for *e.* *2 Ki* 17:37
throne shall be established for *e.* *1 Chr* 17:14
right hand pleasures for *e.* *Ps* 16:11
mercy to David and seed for *e.* 18:50
do good, and dwell for *e.* 37:27
doth his promise fail for *e.?* 77:8
and glorify thy name for *e.* 86:12
mercy I keep for him for *e.* 89:28
blessed be the Lord for *e.* 52
thou, Lord, most high for *e.* 92:8
seek his face *e.* 105:4
him for righteousness for *e.* 106:31
blessed be name of Lord for *e.* 113:2
we will bless the Lord for *e.* 115:18
going out and coming in *e.* 121:8
shall sit upon throne for *e.* 132:12
the blessing, life for *e.* 133:3
will set my sanctuary in the midst of them for *e.* *Ezek* 37:26, 28
e. give us this bread. *John* 6:34
of Lord blessed for *e.* *2 Cor* 11:31
rejoice *e.* pray. *1 Thes* 5:16
who is consecrated for *e.* *Heb* 7:28
was dead, I am alive for *e.* *Rev* 1:18

every

e. imagination of his heart. *Gen* 6:5
e. man-child be circumcised. 17:10
nor shalt gather *e.* *Lev* 19:10
put out of camp *e.* leper. *Num* 5:2
Samuel told him *e.* whit. *1 Sam* 3:18
refrained from *e.* evil. *Ps* 119:101
I hate *e.* false way. 104, 128
understand *e.* good path. *Pr* 2:9
she lieth in wait at *e.* corner. 7:12
the simple believeth *e.* word. 14:15
eyes of Lord in *e.* place. 15:3
but *e.* fool will be meddling. 20:3
e. word of God is pure. 30:5
e. knee shall bow, *e.* *Isa* 45:23 *Rom* 14:11
e. purpose of Lord shall. *Jer* 51:29
and effect of *e.* vision. *Ezek* 12:23
magnify himself above *e.* *Dan* 11:36
land mourn, *e.* family. *Zech* 12:12
e. place incense offered. *Mal* 1:11
by *e.* word that. *Mat* 4:4
put away his wife for *e.* 19:3
came to him from *e.* *Mark* 1:45
fame of him went into *e.* *Luke* 4:37
for *e.* tree is known by his. 6:44
and fear came upon *e.* *Acts* 2:43
Moses hath in *e.* city them. 15:21
teach *e.* where in *e.* *1 Cor* 4:17
bringing into captivity *e.* *2 Cor* 10:5
far above *e.* name named. *Eph* 1:21 *Phil* 2:9
e. joint supplieth, in measure of *e.* *Eph* 4:16
salute *e.* saint in Christ. *Phil* 4:21
e. creature of God is. *1 Tim* 4:4
prepared unto *e.* good. *2 Tim* 2:21
let us lay aside *e.* weight. *Heb* 12:1
e. good and perfect gift. *Jas* 1:17
submit to *e.* ordinance. *1 Pet* 2:13

believe not *e.* spirit, but. *1 John* 4:1
see **beast, city, day, man, morning, side, thing, way**

every *one*

that *e. one* that findeth. *Gen* 4:14
cursed be *e. one* that curseth. 27:29
are holy, *e. one* of them. *Num* 16:3
ye are alive *e. one* of you. *Deut* 4:4
hearken, *e. one* of you. *1 Ki* 22:28
eat ye *e. one* of his fig. *2 Ki* 18:31
Lord pardon *e. one.* *2 Chr* 30:18
of *e. one* that willingly. *Ezra* 3:5
were assembled to me *e. one.* 9:4
e. one that is proud. *Job* 40:11
look on *e. one* that is proud. 12
in temple *e. one* doth. *Ps* 29:9
for this shall *e. one* that is. 32:6
e. one that sweareth by him. 63:11
till *e. one* submit himself. 68:30
thy power to *e. one* that is. 71:18
is *e. one* that trusteth. 115:8; 135:18
e. one of thy judgements 119:160
blessed is *e. one* that feareth. 128:1
he saith to *e. one* that. *Eccl* 10:3
e. one beareth twins. *S of S* 4:2; 6:6
honey shall *e. one* eat. *Isa* 7:22
for *e. one* is an hypocrite. 9:17
vultures be gathered, *e. one.* 34:15
even *e. one* that is called by. 43:7
ho, *e. one* that thirsteth. 55:1
e. one that goeth out. *Jer* 5:6
e. one neighed after neighbour's. 8
e. one is given to covetousness. 6:13
derision daily, *e. one* mocketh. 20:7
turn ye now *e. one* from. 25:5
mourning, *e. one* for. *Ezek* 7:16
opened thy feet to *e. one.* 16:25
behold *e. one* were in thee to. 22:6
e. one that be found. *Dan* 12:1
they shall march *e. one.* *Joel* 2:7
e. one that stealeth shall. *Zech* 5:3
e. one that asketh. *Mat* 7:8
Luke 11:10
to me, *e. one* of you. *Mark* 7:14
to *e. one* which hath. *Luke* 19:26
so is *e. one* that is born of. *John* 3:8
e. one that is of truth. 18:37
and be baptized, *e. one* of. *Acts* 2:28
not far from *e. one* of us. 17:27
I ceased not to warn *e. one.* 20:31
e. one give account of. *Rom* 14:12
Lord hath called *e. one.* *1 Cor* 7:17
cursed is *e. one* that. *Gal* 3:10
e. one that nameth the. *2 Tim* 2:19
e. one that loveth is. *1 John* 4:7
white robes given to *e. one.* *Rev* 6:11

every *where*

to our brethren *e. where.* *1 Chr* 13:2
and preached *e. where.* *Mark* 16:20
preaching gospel *e. where.* *Luke* 9:6
Acts 8:4
all men *e. where* to. *Acts* 17:30
it is *e. where* spoken against. 28:22
as I teach *e. where* in. *1 Cor* 4:17
e. where, and in all. *Phil* 4:12
that men pray *e. where.* *1 Tim* 2:8

evidence

I subscribed the *e.* *Jer* 32:10*
so I took the *e.* 11*
I gave the *e.* to Baruch. 12*
e. both which is sealed, *e.* open. 14*
when I delivered the *e.* of the. 16*
faith is the *e.* of things. *Heb* 11:1*

evidences

take these *e.* *Jer* 32:14*
fields for money subscribe *e.* 44*

evident

it is *e.* to you if I lie. *Job* 6:28*
no man justified by law is *e.* *Gal* 3:11
an *e.* token of perdition. *Phil* 1:28
it is *e.* our Lord sprang. *Heb* 7:14
and it is yet far more *e.* for. 15

evidently

saw in a vision *e.* an. *Acts* 10:3*
Christ hath been *e.* set. *Gal* 3:1*

evil

[1] *Sin, moral evil,* 1 Ki 16:25; Eccl 9:3. [2] *Injurious or mischievous beasts or men,* Gen 37:20. [3] *Calamity,* Pr 22:3; Job 2:10.

The evil eye, according to ancient superstition, was one which could harm by merely looking at a person or his possessions. In the Bible, however, it more generally means the eye of envy, or of grudging benevolence, Pr 23:6; Mat 20:15.

lest some *e.* take me. *Gen* 19:19
ye have done *e.* in so doing. 44:5
lest I see the *e.* that shall come. 34
ye thought *e.* against me. 50:20
he hath done *e.* to people. *Ex* 5:23
look to it, for *e.* is before you. 10:10
the Lord repented of the *e.* 32:14
2 Sam 24:16; *1 Chr* 21:15
commit no more such *e.* *Deut* 19:20
shall separate him to *e.* out. 29:21
set before thee death and *e.* 30:15
and *e.* will befall you in. 31:29
if it seem *e.* to you to. *Josh* 24:15
hand of Lord against them for *e.*
Judg 2:15
e. of the men of Shechem. 9:57
but they knew not that *e.* was. 20:34
that *e.* is determined. *1 Sam* 20:7
if I knew certainly that *e.* were. 9
e. nor transgression in. 24:11
whereas I have rewarded thee *e.* 17
for *e.* is determined against. 25:17
they that seek *e.* to my lord. 26
e. hath not been found in thee. 28
what *e.* is in my hand ? 26:18
I have not found *e.* in thee. 29:6
shall reward doer of *e.* *2 Sam* 3:39
I will raise up *e.* against thee. 12:11
will be worse than all the *e.* 19:7
but hast done *e.* above. *1 Ki* 14:9
Omri wrought *e.* in eyes of. 16:25
and the Lord hath spoken *e.* concerning thee. 22:23; *2 Chr* 18:22
I am bringing such *e.* on. *2 Ki* 21:2
eyes shall not see all *e.* on. 22:20
have sinned and done *e.* *1 Chr* 21:17
if when *e.* cometh on us. *2 Chr* 20:9
there was *e.* determined. *Esth* 7:7
how can I endure to see *e.*? 8:6
feared God, eschewed *e.* *Job* 1:1, 8
2:3
in seven there shall no *e.* 5:19
lift up myself when *e.* found. 31:29
comforted him over all the *e.* 42:11
neither *e.* dwell with thee. *Ps* 5:4
if I have rewarded *e.* to him. 7:4
nor doth *e.* to his neighbour. 15:3
they intended *e.* against thee. 21:11
I will fear no *e.* thou art with. 23:4
e. shall slay wicked. 34:21
mischief, he abhorreth not *e.* 36:4
to shame that wish me *e.* 40:14
mine enemies speak *e.* of me. 41:5
should I fear in days of *e.*? 49:5
thou givest thy mouth to *e.* 50:19
reward *e.* unto mine enemies. 54:5
thoughts are against me for *e.* 56:5
years wherein we have seen *e.* 90:15
no *e.* befall thee. 91:10; *Jer* 23:17
that love the Lord, hate *e.* *Ps* 97:10
and of them that speak *e.* 109:20
e. shall hunt violent man to. 140:11
for their feet run to *e.* *Pr* 1:16
Isa 59:7
be quiet from fear of *e.* *Pr* 1:33
devise not *e.* against neighbour. 3:29
I was almost in all *e.* in midst. 5:14
he that pursueth *e.* pursueth. 11:19
heart of them that imagine *e.* 12:20
no *e.* happen to the just. 21
e. pursueth sinners. 13:21
the *e.* bow before the good. 14:19
that devise *e.* 22
even wicked for day of *e.* 16:4
ungodly man diggeth up *e.* fire. 27
moving his lips he bringeth *e.* 30
shall not be visited with *e.* 19:23
king scattereth away all *e.* 20:8
say not thou, I will recompense *e.* 22
soul of wicked desireth *e.* 21:10
prudent man foreseeth *e.* 22:3
27:12
if thou hast thought *e.* lay. 30:32
is vanity, and a great *e.* *Eccl* 2:21
there is a sore *e.* which I. 5:13, 16
an *e.* which I have seen. 6:1; 10:5
this is an *e.* among things. . .the heart of sons of men is full of *e.* 9:3
knowest not what *e.* shall be. 11:2
for they have rewarded *e.* *Isa* 3:9
punish world for their *e.* 13:11
shutteth eyes from seeing *e.* 33:15
I make peace and create *e.* 45:7
shall *e.* come upon thee. 47:11
keepeth his hand from any *e.* 56:2
is taken away from the *e.* 57:1
out of north *e.* break. *Jer* 1:14; 6:1
e. shall come upon them. 2:3
forth like fire, because of *e.* of.
4:4; 23:2; 26:3; 44:22
neither shall *e.* come upon us. 5:12
children of Judah have done *e.* 7:30
when thou dost *e.* then thou. 11:15
pronounced *e.* against thee for *e.* 17
thee well in time of *e.* 15:11
my hope in the day of *e.* 17:17
bring on them the day of *e.* 18
nation turn from *e.* I will repent of *e.*
18:8; 26:3, 13, 19; 42:10
I frame *e.* against you. 18:11
I will bring all *e.* that I. 19:15
my face against city for *e.* 21:10
e. shall go forth from. 25:32
prophesied of war and of *e.* 28:8
of peace and not of *e.* 29:11
children of Judah have done *e.* 32:20
because of all the *e.* of the. 32
on Judah and Jerusalem all the *e.*
I have. 35:17; 36:31
these men have done *e.* in. 38:9
against you for *e.* and cut off. 44:11
and were well, and saw no *e.* 17
I will watch over them for *e.* and. 27
words stand against you for *e.* 29
Heshbon they have devised *e.* 48:2
will render to Babylon all *e.* 51:24
wrote all *e.* that should come. 60
an *e.* an only *e.* behold. *Ezek* 7:5
comforted concerning the *e.* 14:22
hath watched upon *e.* *Dan* 9:14
repenteth him of the *e.* *Joel* 2:13
there be *e.* in a city ? *Amos* 3:6
who say, *e.* shall not overtake. 9:10
God repented of *e.* *Jonah* 3:10; 4:2
but *e.* came down from. *Mi* 1:12
woe to them that work *e.* 2:1
this family do I devise *e.* 3
no *e.* can come. 3:11
that imagineth *e.* against. *Nah* 1:11
purer eyes than to behold *e.* *Hab* 1:13
delivered from the power of *e.* 2:9
not see *e.* any more. *Zeph* 3:15
none imagine *e.* *Zech* 7:10; 8:17
and sick, is it not *e.*? *Mal* 1:8
every one that doeth *e.* is. 2:17
shall say all manner of *e.* *Mat* 5:11
more than these, cometh of *e.* 37*
that ye resist not *e.* 39*
sufficient for day is *e.* thereof. 6:34
wherefore think ye *e.* in your ? 9:4
what *e.* hath he done ? 27:23
Mark 15:14; *Luke* 23:22
lightly speak *e.* of me. *Mark* 9:39
evil man bringeth forth *e.* *Luke* 6:45
every one that doeth *e.* *John* 3:20
they that have done *e.* to. 5:29
e. bear witness of the *e.* 18:23
how much *e.* he hath. *Acts* 9:13
we find no *e.* in this man. 23:9
soul of man that doeth *e.* *Rom* 2:9
the *e.* which I would not. 7:19
abhor that which is *e.* 12:9
recompense to no man *e.* for *e.* 17
not overcome of *e.* overcome *e.* 21
wrath on him doeth *e.* 13:4
is *e.* for that man who eateth. 14:20
simple concerning *e.* 16:19
charity thinketh no *e.* *1 Cor* 13:5
none render *e.* for *e.* to. *1 Thes* 5:15
abstain from all appearance of *e.* 22
money is root of all *e.* *1 Tim* 6:10*
in mind to speak *e.* of no. *Tit* 3:2
tongue is an unruly *e.* *Jas* 3:8
not rendering *e.* for *e.* or. *1 Pet* 3:9
he that doeth *e.* hath not. *3 John* 11

evil, *adjective*

thoughts were only *e.* *Gen* 6:5; 8:21
e. beast devoured him. 37:20, 33
did see they were in *e.* case. *Ex* 5:19
people heard these *e.* tidings. 33:4
bear this *e.* congregation. *Num* 14:27
bring us in unto this *e.* place. 20:5

not one of *e.* generation. *Deut* 1:35
bring up an *e.* name. 22:14, 19
his eye shall be *e.* toward. 28:54
eye shall be *e.* toward her. 56
hear of your *e.* dealings. *1 Sam* 2:23
neither adversary nor *e.* *1 Ki* 5:4
that is come on us for *e.* *Ezra* 9:13
an *e.* disease cleaveth. *Ps* 41:8
encourage themselves in an *e.* 64:5
trouble by sending *e.* angels. 78:49
shall not be afraid of *e.* tidings. 112:7
let not an *e.* speaker be. 140:11
to keep thee from *e.* *Pr* 6:24
riches perish by *e.* travel. *Eccl* 5:14
vanity, and it is an *e.* disease. 6:2
as fishes taken in an *e.* net. 9:12
have taken *e.* counsel. *Isa* 7:5
instruments of churl are *e.* 32:7
remain of this *e.* family. *Jer* 8:3
against all mine *e.* neighbours. 12:14
this *e.* people refuse to hear. 13:10
their course is *e.* their force. 23:10
e. figs, very *e.* so *e.* 24:3, 8; 29:17
they have heard *e.* tidings. 49:23
send on them *e.* arrows. *Ezek* 5:16
send on you famine and *e.* beasts. 17
alas, for *e.* abominations of. 6:11
I will cause the *e.* beasts to. 34:25
shalt think an *e.* thought. 38:10
that coveteth an *e.* *Hab* 2:9
his sun to rise on *e.* *Mat* 5:45
if ye being *e.* 7:11; *Luke* 11:13
not bring forth *e.* fruit. *Mat* 7:18
how can ye being *e.* speak? 12:34
an *e.* generation seeketh a sign. 39
Luke 11:29
out of heart proceed *e.* thoughts, murders. *Mat* 15:19; *Mark* 7:21
if that *e.* servant shall say. *Mat* 24:48
cast out your name as *e.* *Luke* 6:22
kind to unthankful and to the *e.* 35
for their deeds were *e.* *John* 3:19
have found any *e.* doing. *Acts* 24:20
e. communications. *1 Cor* 15:33
might deliver us from *e.* *Gal* 1:4
let *e.* speaking be put. *Eph* 4:31
beware of *e.* workers. *Phil* 3:2
mortify *e.* concupiscence. *Col* 3:5
whereof cometh *e.* *1 Tim* 6:4
the Cretians are *e.* beasts. *Tit* 1:12
hearts sprinkled from *e.* *Heb* 10:22
become judges of *e.* *Jas* 2:4
all such rejoicing is *e.* 4:16
all malice and *e.* *1 Pet* 2:1
not bear them who are *e.* *Rev* 2:2

evil, *adverb*
why so *e.* entreated? *Ex* 5:22†
Egyptians *e.* entreated. *Deut* 26:6†
because it went *e.* *1 Chr* 7:23
he *e.* entreateth barren. *Job* 24:21*
if I have spoken *e.* *John* 18:23
entreat them *e.* 400 years. *Acts* 7:6
same *e.* entreated our fathers. 19
their minds *e.* affected. 14:2
but spake *e.* of that way. 19:9
shall not speak *e.* of ruler. 23:5
good be *e.* spoken of. *Rom* 14:16
why am I *e.* spoken of? *1 Cor* 10:30
e. one of another, he that speaks *e.* of brother, speaks *e.* of. *Jas* 4:11
whereas they speak *e.* *1 Pet* 3:16
for well-doing than for *e.* 17
think it strange, speaking *e.* 4:4
their part he is *e.* spoken of. 14
way of truth be *e.* *2 Pet* 2:2
are not afraid to speak *e.* 10; *Jude* 8
as natural brute beasts, speak *e.*
2 Pet 2:12; *Jude* 10

bring, brought **evil**
shall *bring* on you all *e.* *Josh* 23:15
overtake and *bring e.* *2 Sam* 15:14
that Lord might *bring e.* 17:14
I will *bring e.* on house. *1 Ki* 14:10
hast thou also *brought e.* on? 17:20
I will *bring e.* upon thee. 21:21
not *bring e.* in his days, but. 29
behold, I will *bring e.* upon this.
2 Ki 22:16; *2 Chr* 34:24
all the *e.* I will *bring.* *2 Chr* 34:28
I will *bring e.* and not. *Isa* 31:2
I will *bring e.* from north. *Jer* 4:6
will *bring e.* upon this people. 6:19
I will *bring e.* upon them. 11:11
I will *bring e.* upon men of. *Jer* 11:23
will *bring e.* on this place. 19:3, 15
I will *bring e.* even year of. 23:12
I begin to *bring e.* on city. 25:29
will *bring* on Judah *e.* 35:17; 36:31
bring my words on city for *e.* 39:16
will *bring e.* upon all flesh. 45:5
see **did, do**

evil joined with *good*
tree of knowledge of *good* and *e.*
Gen 2:9, 17
gods knowing *good* and *e.* 3:5, 22
ye rewarded *e.* for *good*? 44:4
no knowledge between *good* and *e.*
Deut 1:39
requited me *e.* for *good.* *1 Sam* 25:21
between *good* and *e.*? *2 Sam* 19:35
not prophesy *good* concerning me, but *e.* *1 Ki* 22:8, 18
never *good* to me, but *e.* *2 Chr* 18:7
not prophesy *good* to me, but *e.* 17
receive *good,* and not *e.*? *Job* 2:10
looked for *good,* then *e.* came. 30:26
rewarded me *e.* for *good.* *Ps* 35:12
109:5
that render *e.* for *good* are. 38:20
lovest *e.* more than *good.* 52:3
beholding *e.* and the *good.* *Pr* 15:3
whoso rewardeth *e.* for *good.* 17:13
will do him *good* and not *e.* 31:12
call *e. good,* and *good e.* *Isa* 5:20
to refuse *e.* choose *good.* 7:15, 16
e. be recompensed for *good*?
Jer 18:20
whether it be *good* or *e.* we. 42:6
proceedeth not *e.* and *good.*
Lam 3:38
seek *good* and not *e.* *Amos* 5:14
eyes on them for *e.* not for *good.* 9:4
who hate *good,* and love *e.* *Mi* 3:2
when I would do *good, e.* present.
Rom 7:21
neither having done *good* or *e.* 9:11
to discern *good* and *e.* *Heb* 5:14
is *e.* but what is *good.* *3 John* 11
see **great**

from **evil**
redeemed me *from* all *e.* *Gen* 48:16
kept his servant *from e.* *1 Sam* 25:39
wouldest keep me *from e.* *1 Chr* 4:10
and to depart *from e.* is. *Job* 28:28
keep thy tongue *from e.* *Ps* 34:13
depart *from e.* 14; 37:27; *Pr* 3:7
preserve thee *from* all *e.* 121:7
remove thy foot *from e.* *Pr* 4:27
to fools to depart *from e.* 13:19
and departeth *from e.* 14:16
of Lord men depart *from e.* 16:6
of upright is to depart *from e.* 17
that departeth *from e.* *Isa* 59:15
they proceed *from e.* to evil. *Jer* 9:3
have turned them *from* their *e.* way, and *from* the *e.* of. 23:22
Babylon not rise *from e.* 51:64
deliver us *from e.* *Mat* 6:13*
Luke 11:14
keep them *from e.* *John* 17:15*
stablish you, keep you *from e.*
2 Thes 3:3*
refrain his tongue *from e.* *1 Pet* 3:10

put away **evil**
put the *e. away* from. *Deut* 13:5
so thou shalt *put* the *e. away.* 17:7
19:19; 21:21; 22:21, 24; 24:7
put ye *away e.* from Israel. 17:12
22:21; *Judg* 20:13
put away e. from flesh. *Eccl* 11:10
put away e. of your doings. *Isa* 1:16

evil *in the sight of the Lord*
had done *e. in the sight of the Lord.*
Num 32:13; *Judg* 3:12
Israel did *e. in the sight of the Lord.*
Judg 2:11; 3:7, 12; 4:1; 6:1
10:6; 13:1; *1 Ki* 11:6; 14:22
15:26, 34; 16:7, 30; 22:52
2 Ki 8:18, 27; 13:2, 11; 14:24
15:9, 18, 24, 28; 17:2; 21:2, 20
2 Chr 22:4; 33:2, 22; 36:5, 9, 12
thou didst *e. in the sight of the Lord.*
1 Sam 15:19
in doing *e. in the sight of the Lord.*
1 Ki 16:19
sold to work *e. in the sight of the Lord.* *1 Ki* 21:20
he wrought *e. in the sight of the Lord.* *2 Ki* 3:2
sold themselves to do *e. in the sight of the Lord.* 17:17
to sin, doing *e. in the sight of the Lord.* 21:16; 23:32, 37; 24:9, 19
Er was *e. in the sight of the Lord.*
1 Chr 2:3
wrought much *e. in the sight of Lord.*
2 Chr 33:6

this **evil**
and repent of *this e.* *Ex* 32:12
done us *this* great *e.* *1 Sam* 6:9
we have added *this e.* to. 12:19
this e. in sending. *2 Sam* 13:16*
brought on them all *this e.* *1 Ki* 9:9
this e. is of the Lord. *2 Ki* 6:33
therefore he brought *this e.* on them.
2 Chr 7:22
God bring all *this e.* on? *Neh* 13:18
to you to do all *this* great *e.*? 27
friends heard of *this e.* *Job* 2:11
done *this e.* in thy sight. *Ps* 51:4
pronounced all *this e.* *Jer* 16:10
hast caused all *this e.* on. 32:23
like as I have brought all *this e.* 42
God hath pronounced *this e.* 40:2
why commit ye *this* great *e.*? 44:7
therefore *this e.* is happened. 23
it is written, all *this e.* is. *Dan* 9:13
for whose cause *this e.* *Jonah* 1:7, 8

evil *day* or *days*
few and *e.* have the *days.* *Gen* 47:9
days of the afflicted are *e.* *Pr* 15:15
while the *e. days* come not. *Eccl* 12:1
put far away the *e. day.* *Amos* 6:3
because *days* are *e.* *Eph* 5:16
be able to withstand in *e. day.* 6:13
day of **evil,** *see* **evil,** *substantive*

evil *doer,* or *doers*
neither help the *e. doers.* *Job* 8:20
hated the congregation of *e. doers.*
Ps 26:5
fret not because of *e. doers.* 37:1
e. doers shall be cut off. 9
up for me against *e. doers*? 94:16
depart from me, ye *e. doers.* 119:115
nation, a seed of *e. doers.* *Isa* 1:4
an hypocrite, an *e. doer.* 9:17
the seed of *e. doers* shall. 14:20
arise against house of *e. doers.* 31:2
soul of poor from *e. doers.* *Jer* 20:13
strengthen hands of *e. doers.* 23:14
trouble as an *e. doer.* *2 Tim* 2:9*
against you as *e. doers.* *1 Pet* 2:12
for the punishment of *e. doers.* 14
evil of you as of *e. doers.* 3:16
suffer as thief or an *e. doer.* 4:15
see **doings, eye**

evil *heart*
of man's *heart* is *e.* *Gen* 8:21
the imagination of *e. heart.* *Jer* 3:17
walked in imagination of *e. heart.*
7:24
every one in imagination of his *e. heart.* 11:8
every one after his *e. heart.* 16:12
do imagination of his *e. heart.* 18:12
be in any an *e. heart.* *Heb* 3:12

evil *man* or *men*
of pride of *e. men.* *Job* 35:12
arm of the *e. man.* *Ps* 10:15
deliver me from the *e. man.* 140:1
from way of the *e. man.* *Pr* 2:12
go not in the way of *e. men.* 4:14
wicked desireth net of *e. men.* 12:12
e. man seeketh only rebellion. 17:11
not envious against *e. men.* 24:1
fret not because of *e. men.* 19
be no reward to the *e. man.* 20
e. men understand not. 28:5
in transgression of an *e. man.* 29:6
e. man out of the evil treasure.
Mat 12:35; *Luke* 6:45
e. men shall wax worse. *2 Tim* 3:13
see **report**

evil *spirit* or *spirits*
e. sp. between Abimelech. *Judg* 9:23
an *e. sp.* from Lord. *1 Sam* 16:14, 15
when *e. sp.* from God is upon. 16

and the e. sp. departed from.
1 Sam 16:23
e. sp. from God came. 18:10; 19:9
cured many of e. sp. Luke 7:21
a woman healed of e. sp. 8:2
and the e. sp. went out. Acts 19:12
over them which had e. sp. 13
e. sp. said, Jesus I know. 15
man in whom the e. sp. was. 16

evil *thing*

what e. thing is this ? Neh 13:17
not heart to any e. thing. Ps 141:4
stand not in an e. thing. Eccl 8:3
shall feel no e. thing. 5
thing, whether good or e. 12:14
know that it is an e. thing. Jer 2:19
having no e. thing to say. Tit 2:8

evil *things*

bring on you e. things. Josh 23:15
poureth out e. things. Pr 15:28
hast done e. things. Jer 3:5
man bringeth e. things. Mat 12:35
all these e. things come. Mark 7:23
Lazarus e. things. Luke 16:25
inventors of e. things. Rom 1:30
not lust after e. things. 1 Cor 10:6

evil *time*

be ashamed in e. time. Ps 37:19
men snared in an e. time. Eccl 9:12
for it is an e. time. Amos 5:13
haughtily, for time is e. Mi 2:3

evil *way*

returned not from e. way. 1 Ki 13:33
feet from every e. way. Ps 119:101
fear of Lord to hate e. way. Pr 8:13
to go astray in e. way. 28:10
every one from his e. way. Jer 18:11
25:5; 26:3; 35:15; 36:3, 7
turned them from e. way. 23:22
every one from e. way. Jonah 3:8
they turned from e. way. 10

evil *ways*

turn from your e. ways. 2 Ki 17:13
Ezek 33:11
your own e. ways. Ezek 36:31
now from your e. ways. Zech 1:4

evil *work* or *works*

not seen e. work that is. Eccl 4:3
sentence against an e. work is. 8:11
the works thereof are e. John 7:7
terror to good works but e. Rom 13:3
me from every e. work. 2 Tim 4:18
and every e. work. Jas 3:16
his own works were e. 1 John 3:12

Evil-merodach

E. king of Babylon did lift up the.
2 Ki 25:27; Jer 52:31

evils

e. and troubles befall them, they say,
are not these e.? Deut 31:17
for all the e. which they have. 18
when many e. and troubles are. 21
innumerable e. compassed. Ps 40:12
people committed two e. Jer 2:13
lothe themselves for e. Ezek 6:9
lothe yourselves for all your e. 20:43
all the e. which Herod. Luke 3:19

ewe *or* ewes

Abraham set seven e. Gen 21:28
mean these seven e. lambs ? 29
e. and she goats have not. 31:38
two hundred e. and twenty. 32:14
take one e. lamb of. Lev 14:10
whether cow or e. ye. 22:28
save one e. lamb. 2 Sam 12:3
him from following the e. Ps 78:71

exact

not e. it of neighbour. Deut 15:2
of a foreigner thou mayest e. 3
you e. usury every one of. Neh 5:7
I likewise might e. of them. 10*
hundredth part of money ye e. 11
enemy shall not e. upon. Ps 89:22
in your fasts ye e. all. Isa 58:3
e. no more than what. Luke 3:13*

exacted

Menahem e. the money. 2 Ki 15:20
Jehoiakim e. the silver and. 23:35

exacteth

e. of thee less than. Job 11:6

exaction

we should leave the e. Neh 10:31

exactions

take away your e. Ezek 45:9

exactors

will also make thine e. Isa 60:17

exalt

my father's God, I will e. Ex 15:2
he shall e. the horn of. 1 Sam 2:10
shalt thou not e. them. Job 17:4
and let us e. his name. Ps 34:3
he shall e. thee to inherit. 37:34
let not rebellious e. themselves. 66:7
but my horn shalt thou e. 92:10
e. ye the Lord our God. 99:5, 9
let them e. him in the. 107:32
my God, I will e. thee. 118:28
lest wicked e. themselves. 140:8
e. her, and she shall. Pr 4:8
e. the voice unto them. Isa 13:2
I will e. my throne above. 14:13
thou art my God, I will e. 25:1
e. him that is low. Ezek 21:26
nor shall it e. itself any. 29:15
that none of the trees e. 31:14
robbers of people shall e. Dan 11:14
the king shall e. himself. 36
none at all would e. him. Hos 11:7
though thou e. thyself as. Ob 4*
whoso shall e. himself. Mat 23:12
if a man e. himself. 2 Cor 11:20
that he may e. in due. 1 Pet 5:6

exalted

his kingdom shall be e. Num 24:7
mine horn is e. in Lord. 1 Sam 2:1
Lord had e. his kingdom. 2 Sam 5:12
e. be the God of the rock of my.
22:47; Ps 18:46
then Adonijah e. himself. 1 Ki 1:5
I e. thee from people. 14:7; 16:2
against whom hast thou e. thy voice ?
2 Ki 19:22; Isa 37:23
and thou art e. as. 1 Chr 29:11
is e. above all blessings. Neh 9:5
who mourn may be e. Job 5:11
they are e. for a little while. 24:24
them for ever, they are e. 36:7
walk when vilest men are e. Ps 12:8
long shall my enemy be e.? 13:2
be thou e. Lord, in thine. 21:13
I will be e. among the heathen, I will
be e. in the earth. 46:10
he is greatly e. 47:9
be thou e. O God, above. 57:5, 11
horns of righteous shall be e. 75:10
righteousness shall they be e. 89:16
in thy favour our horn shall be e. 17
I have e. one chosen out. 19
in my name shall his horn be e. 24
thou, Lord, art e. far above. 97:9
be thou e. O God, above. 108:5
horn shall be e. with honour. 112:9
right hand of the Lord is e. 118:16
of the upright city is e. Pr 11:11
mountain of Lord's house shall be e.
Isa 2:2; Mi 4:1
be e. in that day. Isa 2:11, 17; 5:16
mention that his name is e. 12:4
will be e. that he may have. 30:18
the Lord is e. 33:5
now will I be e. 10
every valley shall be e. 40:4
my highways shall be e. 49:11
behold my servant shall be e. 52:13
Lord have e. the low. Ezek 17:24
and her stature was e. 19:11; 31:5
he e. himself in Israel. Hos 13:1
and their heart was e. 6
Capernaum e. to heaven. Mat 11:23
Luke 10:15
e. himself abased, humble himself e.
Mat 23:12; Luke 14:11; 18:14
e. them of low degree. Luke 1:52
right hand of God e. Acts 2:33
hath God e. with his right. 5:31
God of Israel e. people. 13:17
that you might be e. 2 Cor 11:7
lest I should be e. 12:7
God hath highly e. him. Phil 2:9
brother rejoice that he is e. Jas 1:9

exaltest

as yet e. thou thyself. Ex 9:17

exalteth

God e. by his power. Job 36:22*
he e. horn of his people. Ps 148:14
hasty of spirit e. folly. Pr 14:29
righteousness e. a nation. 34
he that e. his gate seeketh. 17:19
he that e. himself shall. Luke 14:11
18:14
every thing that e. itself. 2 Cor 10:5
who e. himself above all. 2 Thes 2:4

examination

that, after e. had, I. Acts 25:26

examine

sat down to e. matter. Ezra 10:16
e. me, O Lord, prove me. Ps 26:2
answer to them that e. 1 Cor 9:3
let a man e. himself. 11:28
e. yourselves, prove. 2 Cor 13:5

examined

I have e. him before you. Luke 23:14
if we this day be e. of. Acts 4:9
Herod e. keepers. 12:19
brought, that he should be e. 22:24
who should have e. him. 29
when they had e. me would. 28:18

examining

by e. of whom thou. Acts 24:8

example

not make her a publick e. Mat 1:19
have given you an e. John 13:15
but be thou an e. of. 1 Tim 4:12
man fall after same e. Heb 4:11
serve unto the e. of heavenly. 8:5
take prophets for an e. Jas 5:10
for us, leaving us an e. 1 Pet 2:21
set forth for an e., suffering. Jude 7

examples

these things were our e. 1 Cor 10:6
see **ensample, -s**

exceed

not e.: lest, if he should e., thy brother
seem vile to thee. Deut 25:3
except righteousness e. Mat 5:20
of righteousness doth e. 2 Cor 3:9

exceeded

wept, till David e. 1 Sam 20:41
Solomon e. all kings of. 1 Ki 10:23
transgressions that they e. Job 36:9*

exceedest

thou e. the fame that I. 2 Chr 9:6

exceedeth

thy wisdom e. the fame. 1 Ki 10:7

exceeding

and thy e. great reward. Gen 15:1
I will make thee e. fruitful. 17:6
Esau cried with an e. bitter. 27:34
Israel waxed e. mighty. Ex 1:7
voice of trumpet e. loud. 19:16
land we passed through e. Num 14:7
talk no more so e. 1 Sam 2:3
David took e. much brass.
2 Sam 8:8
rich man had e. many flocks. 12:2
gave Solomon wisdom e. 1 Ki 4:29
vessels unweighed, were e. 7:47
he brought e. much spoil. 1 Chr 20:2
house must be e. magnifical. 22:5
made cities e. strong. 2 Chr 11:12
there was e. much spoil. 14:14
until his disease waxed e. 16:12
Hezekiah had e. much riches. 32:27
thou hast made him e. Ps 21:6
I go unto God, my e. joy. 43:4
thy commandment is e. 119:96
four things which are e. Pr 30:24
that which is e. deep. Eccl 7:24
pride of Moab, he is e. Jer 48:29
iniquity of Israel e. great. Ezek 9:9
didst eat oil, and wast e. 16:13
e. in dyed attire upon heads. 23:15
upon feet an e. great army. 37:10
fish of the great sea, e. many. 47:10
the furnace was e. hot. Dan 3:22
then was the king e. glad. 6:23
fourth beast e. dreadful. 7:19
a little horn, which waxed e. 8:9
Nineveh was an e. great. Jonah 3:3
so Jonah was e. glad of 4:6
they rejoiced with e. great. Mat 2:10
Herod was e. wroth. 16
taketh him up into e. high. 4:8

rejoice and be e. glad. Mat 5:12
two possessed with devils, e. 8:28
kill him; they were e. sorry. 17:23
they were e. sorrowful. 26:22
soul e. sorrowful. 38; Mark 14:34
the king was e. sorry. Mark 6:26
raiment became e. white as. 9:3
Herod saw Jesus, was e. Luke 23:8
Moses born, and was e. Acts 7:20
that sin become e. sinful. Rom 7:13
worketh for us an e. 2 Cor 4:17
I am e. joyful in all our. 7:4
who long after you, for e. 9:14
what is the e. greatness. Eph 1:19
might shew the e. riches of. 2:7
able to do e. abundantly. 3:20
grace of our Lord e. 1 Tim 1:14
be glad also with e. joy. 1 Pet 4:13
given to us e. great and 2 Pet 1:4
faultless with e. joy. Jude 24
plague thereof was e. Rev 16:21

exceedingly

the waters prevailed e. Gen 7:19
men of Sodom were sinners e. 13:13
I will multiply thy seed e. 16:10
covenant and multiply thee e. 17:2
I will multiply Ishmael e. 20
Isaac trembled very e. and. 27:33
Jacob increased e. 30:43; 47:27
the fool and erred e. 1 Sam 26:21
Amnon hated her e. 2 Sam 13:15
the elders were e. afraid. 2 Ki 10:4
magnified Solomon e. 1 Chr 29:25
2 Chr 1:1
Jehoshaphat great e. 2 Chr 17:12
Uzziah strengthened himself e. 26:8
heard, it grieved them e. Neh 2:10
queen was e. grieved. Esth 4:4
rejoice e. when they can. Job 3:22
let the righteous e. rejoice. Ps 68:3
lusted e. in the wilderness. 106:14
testimonies, I love them e. 119:167
for we are e. filled with. 123:3, 4
earth is moved e. Isa 24:19
a fourth beast strong e. Dan 7:7
men were e. afraid. Jonah 1:10
then men feared the Lord e. 16
but it displeased Jonah e. 4:1
they were e. amazed. Mat 19:25
they feared e. and. Mark 4:41
cried out the more e. crucify. 15:14
these men do e. trouble. Acts 16:20
being e. mad against them. 26:11
and we being e. tossed. 27:18
and e. the more joyed. 2 Cor 7:13
being more e. zealous of. Gal 1:14
night and day praying e. 1 Thes 3:10
your faith groweth e. 2 Thes 1:3
I e. fear and quake. Heb 12:21

excel

thou shalt not e. Gen 49:4*
on the Sheminith to e. 1 Chr 15:21*
angels, that e. in. Ps 103:20*
graven images did e. Isa 10:10
seek that ye may e. 1 Cor 14:12*

excelled

Solomon's wisdom e. 1 Ki 4:30

excellency

the e. of dignity, and e. Gen 49:3†
in the greatness of thine e. Ex 15:7
who rideth in his e. Deut 33:26
who is the sword of thy e. 29
doth not their e. go? Job 4:21*
his e. make you afraid? 13:11
though his e. mount up. 20:6
thundereth with voice of his e. 37:4
thyself with majesty and e. 40:10
the e. of Jacob. Ps 47:4†
to cast him down from his e. 62:4†
his e. is over Israel. 68:34
the e. of knowledge is. Eccl 7:12
beauty of Chaldees' e. Isa 13:19*
e. of Carmel, Sharon; the e. 35:2
make thee an eternal e. 60:15
my sanctuary, the e. Ezek 24:21*
I abhor the e. of Jacob. Amos 6:8
Lord hath sworn by e. of Jacob. 8:7
Lord hath turned away e. of Jacob, as the e. of Israel. Nah 2:2
not with e. of speech. 1 Cor 2:1
e. of the power be of. 2 Cor 4:7*
all things loss for the e. Phil 3:8

excellent

Ahasuerus shewed e. Esth 1:4
Almighty is e. in power. Job 37:23
how e. is thy name in! Ps 8:1, 9
and to the e. in whom is all. 16:3
e. is thy lovingkindness! 36:7*
thou art more e. than the. 76:4
me, it shall be an e. oil. 141:5*
his name alone is e. 148:13*
according to e. greatness. 150:2
for I will speak of e. things. Pr 8:6
righteous is more e. than. 12:26*
e. speech becometh not a fool. 17:7
man of understanding is of an e. 27*
written to thee e. things? 22:20
his countenance e. as. S of S 5:15
fruit of earth shall be e. Isa 4:2
sing to Lord, he hath done e. 12:5
the Lord of hosts is e. in. 28:29
come to e. ornaments. Ezek 16:7
whose brightness was e. Dan 2:31
an e. majesty was added. 4:36
e. spirit found in Daniel. 5:12; 6:3
I heard that e. wisdom is. 5:14
to thee, e. Theophilus. Luke 1:3
to e. governor Felix. Acts 23:26
approvest things more e. Rom 2:18
Phil 1:10
shew you a more e. way. 1 Cor 12:31
obtained a more e. name. Heb 1:4
he obtained a more e. ministry. 8:6
Abel offered more e. sacrifice. 11:4
a voice from the e. 2 Pet 1:17†

excellest

virtuously, but thou e. all. Pr 31:29

excelleth

wisdom e. folly, as light e. Eccl 2:13
by reason of glory that e. 2 Cor 3:10

except

e. the God of my father. Gen 31:42
not let thee go, e. thou bless. 32:26
e. youngest brother. 42:15; 43:3, 5
e. we had lingered, we. 43:10
e. the land of the priests only. 47:26
e. thou make thyself a. Num 16:13
e. their Rock had. Deut 32:30
e. you destroy accursed. Josh 7:12
e. thou hadst hasted. 1 Sam 25:34
e. as the Lord hath. 2 Sam 3:9
e. thou first bring Michal. 13
e. thou take away the blind. 5:6
slack not thy riding, e. I. 2 Ki 4:24
e. the king delighted in. Esth 2:14
e. king hold out golden. 4:11
e. Lord build the house, e. Lord keep the city, the watchman. Ps 127:1
sleep not, e. they have. Pr 4:16
e. the Lord had left a. Isa 1:9
Rom 9:29
none other can shew it, e. Dan 2:11
nor worship any god, e. their. 3:28
e. we find it concerning the law. 6:5
two walk together, e.? Amos 3:3
e. your righteousness. Mat 5:20
e. he first bind the strong man. 12:29; Mark 3:27
e. ye be converted. Mat 18:3
put away his wife, e. for. 19:9
e. those days be shortened should no flesh be saved. 24:22; Mark 13:20
cup may not pass, e. I drink. Mat 26:42
Pharisees, e. they wash. Mark 7:3
e. we go and buy meat. Luke 9:13
e. ye repent, ye shall all. 13:3, 5
these miracles, e. God. John 3:2
e. a man be born again, he cannot. 3
e. a man be born of water and. 5
nothing, e. it be given from. 27
e. ye see signs and wonders. 4:48
e. the Father who hath sent. 6:44
e. ye eat the flesh of the Son. 53
e. it were given unto him of. 65
e. a corn of wheat fall. 12:24
cannot bear fruit, e. ye abide. 15:4
no power, e. it were given. 19:11
e. I shall see the prints of. 20:25
all scattered, e. apostles. Acts 8:1
how can I, e. some man? 31
e. ye be circumcised, ye. 15:1
e. it be for this one voice. 24:21
such as I am, e. these bonds. 26:29
e. these abide in ship, ye. 27:31
not known lust, e. the law. Rom 7:7
preach, e. they be sent? 10:15
not one another e. it. 1 Cor 7:5
speaketh with tongues, e. he. 14:5
e. I shall speak to you either. 6
e. they give a distinction in the. 7
e. ye utter words easy to be. 9
sowest is not quickened, e. 15:36
e. it be that I was not. 2 Cor 12:13
Christ is in you, e. ye be? 13:5
e. there come a falling. 2 Thes 2:3
he is not crowned, e. 2 Tim 2:5
remove thy candlestick, e. Rev 2:5
e. they repent their deeds. 22

excepted

he is e. who did put all. 1 Cor 15:27

excess

full of extortion and e. Mat 23:25
with wine, wherein is e. Eph 5:18*
walked in lusts, e. of. 1 Pet 4:3
run not with them to same e. 4

exchange

bread in e. for horses. Gen 47:17
then it and the e. thereof. Lev 27:10
and the e. of it shall not. Job 28:17
what shall a man give in e. for his soul? Mat 16:26; Mark 8:37

exchange

not sell of it, nor e. Ezek 48:14

exchangers

to put my money to e. Mat 25:27

exclude

they would e. you, that. Gal 4:17

excluded

is boasting? it is e. Rom 3:27

excommunicated

Excommunication is an ecclesiastical censure, whereby the person against whom it is pronounced is, for the time, cast out of the communion of the church.

The word is not used in the Bible, but the act is referred to in various ways, all easily recognizable. An example in the Jewish church is in John 9:34.

excuse

began to make e. Luke 14:18
that they are without e. Rom 1:20

excuse

that we e. ourselves? 2 Cor 12:19

excused

pray thee have me e. Luke 14:18, 19

excusing

thoughts accusing or else e. Rom 2:15

execration

and ye shall be an e. Jer 42:18
they shall be an e. and a. 44:12

execute

e. judgement on gods of. Ex 12:12
the priest shall e. upon. Num 5:30
that they may e. the service. 8:11
doth e. the judgement of. Deut 10:18
if thou e. my judgements. 1 Ki 6:12
when wilt thou e.? Ps 119:84
to e. vengeance upon. 149:7
to e. upon them the judgement. 9
take counsel, e. judgement. Isa 16:3
e. judgement between man. Jer 7:5
e. judgement in the morning. 21:12
e. judgement and. 22:3
branch e. judgement. 23:5; 33:15
I will e. judgements. Ezek 5:8, 10
when I shall e. judgements in. 15
will e. judgements among you. 11:9
they shall e. judgements. 16:41
and I will e. judgements. 25:11
and I will e. great vengeance. 17
fire in Zoan, e. judgements. 30:14
thus e. judgements in Egypt. 19
remove violence, e. judgement. 45:9
not e. fierceness of mine. Hos 11:9
and I will e. vengeance. Mi 5:15
plead my cause, e. judgement. 7:9
e. true judgement and. Zech 7:9
e. the judgement of truth and. 8:16
authority to e. judgement. John 5:27
minister of God to e. Rom 13:4
to e. judgement on all. Jude 15

executed
on their gods Lord *e.* *Num* 33:4
he *e.* justice of Lord. *Deut* 33:21
David *e.* judgement. *2 Sam* 8:15
1 Chr 18:14
that *e.* priest's office. *1 Chr* 6:10
Eleazar and Ithamar *e.* the. 24:2
they *e.* judgement. *2 Chr* 24:24
judgement be *e.* speedily. *Ezra* 7:26
Phinehas, *e.* judgement. *Ps* 106:30
sentence is not *e.* *Eccl* 8:11
not return till he have *e.* *Jer* 23:20
neither *e.* judgements. *Ezek* 11:12
20:24
hath *e.* true judgement. 18:8, 17
for they had *e.* judgement. 23:10
shall have *e.* judgements. 28:22, 26
heathen see judgement I have *e.*
39:21
Zacharias *e.* priest's office. *Luke* 1:8

executedst
nor *e.* his fierce wrath. *1 Sam* 28:18

executest
thou *e.* judgement and. *Ps* 99:4

executeth
known by judgement he *e.* *Ps* 9:16
the Lord *e.* righteousness. 103:6
the Lord *e.* judgement for. 146:7
man that *e.* my counsel. *Isa* 46:11
if any *e.* judgement. *Jer* 5:1
is strong that *e.* his word. *Joel* 2:11

executing
thou hast done well in *e.* *2 Ki* 10:30
cast them off from *e.* *2 Chr* 11:14
when Jehu was *e.* judgement. 22:8

execution
drew near to be put in *e.* *Esth* 9:1

executioner
king sent an *e.* and. *Mark* 6:27*

exempted
proclamation, none was *e.* *1 Ki* 15:22

exercise
bodily *e.* profiteth little. *1 Tim* 4:8

exercise
nor do I *e.* myself. *Ps* 131:1
Lord which *e.* loving. *Jer* 9:24
Gentiles *e.* dominion over them, and
they that are great *e.* *Mat* 20:25*
Mark 10:42*; *Luke* 22:25*
herein do I *e.* myself. *Acts* 24:16
and *e.* thyself rather. *1 Tim* 4:7

exercised
be *e.* therewith. *Eccl* 1:13; 3:10
of land have *e.* robbery. *Ezek* 22:29
senses *e.* to discern. *Heb* 5:14
to them which are *e.* thereby. 12:11
an heart *e.* with. *2 Pet* 2:14

exerciseth
he *e.* all the power of. *Rev* 13:12

exhort
did he testify and *e.* *Acts* 2:40
and now I *e.* you to be of. 27:22
it necessary to *e.* *2 Cor* 9:5*
beseech you and *e.* you. *1 Thes* 4:1
now we *e.* you, warn them. 5:14
we command and *e.* *2 Thes* 3:12
I *e.* that first of all. *1 Tim* 2:1
these things teach and *e.* 6:2
e. with all long suffering. *2 Tim* 4:2
may be able to *e.* and. *Tit* 1:9
young men likewise *e.* to be. 2:6
e. servants to be obedient to. 9
speak, *e.* rebuke with authority. 15
e. one another daily. *Heb* 3:13
elders among you, I *e.* *1 Pet* 5:1
for me to write and *e.* *Jude* 3

exhortation
other things in his *e.* *Luke* 3:18
have any word of *e.* say. *Acts* 13:15
when Paul had given them *e.* 20:2
let him wait on *e.* *Rom* 12:8
speaketh unto men to *e.* *1 Cor* 14:3*
he accepted the *e.* *2 Cor* 8:17
for our *e.* was not of. *1 Thes* 2:3
give attendance to *e.* *1 Tim* 4:13
ye have forgotten the *e.* *Heb* 12:5
suffer the word of *e.* 13:22

exhorted
Barnabas *e.* them to. *Acts* 11:23
they *e.* the brethren with. *Acts* 15:32
as you know how we *e.* *1 Thes* 2:11

exhorting
e. them to continue in. *Acts* 14:22
wrote, *e.* disciples to. 18:27*
but *e.* one another, and. *Heb* 10:25
I have written briefly, *e.* *1 Pet* 5:12

exile
stranger and also an *e.* *2 Sam* 15:19
the captive *e.* hasteneth. *Isa* 51:14

exorcists
(*This word comes from the Greek* exorkizein, *and means one who drives off an evil spirit by adjuration*)
of vagabond Jews, *e.* *Acts* 19:13

expectation
the *e.* of the poor shall. *Ps* 9:18
wait thou on God, for my *e.* 62:5
e. of wicked shall. *Pr* 10:28; 11:7
but the *e.* of the wicked is. 11:23
e. not be cut off. 23:18*; 24:14*
be ashamed of their *e.* *Isa* 20:5
behold, such is our *e.* 6
Ekron; for her *e.* shall. *Zech* 9:5
people were in *e.*, John. *Luke* 3:15
delivered me from *e.* of. *Acts* 12:11
for the *e.* of creature. *Rom* 8:19
to my earnest *e.* and. *Phil* 1:20

expected
to give you an *e.* end. *Jer* 29:11*

expecting
e. to receive something. *Acts* 3:5
e. till his enemies be. *Heb* 10:13

expedient
that it is *e.* for us. *John* 11:50
I tell you, it is *e.* for you that. 16:7
it was *e.* that one man die. 18:14
all things not *e.* *1 Cor* 6:12; 10:23
this is *e.* for you who. *2 Cor* 8:10
not *e.* for me doubtless to. 12:1

expel
God shall *e.* them. *Josh* 23:5*
did not ye hate me, *e.*? *Judg* 11:7*

expelled
Israel *e.* not Geshurites. *Josh* 13:13*
e. thence sons of Anak. *Judg* 1:20*
his banished be not *e.* *2 Sam* 14:14*
they *e.* them out of. *Acts* 13:50*

expences
e. be given out of king's. *Ezra* 6:4
decree that *e.* forthwith be given. 8

experience
by *e.* the Lord hath. *Gen* 30:27*
my heart had great *e.* *Eccl* 1:16
worketh *e.* and *e.* hope. *Rom* 5:4*

experiment
whiles by the *e.* of. *2 Cor* 9:13

expert
of Zebulun fifty thousand *e.* in war.
1 Chr 12:33*
of Danites 28,600. *e.* 35*
of Asher 40,000 *e.* 36*
swords, being *e.* in war. *S of S* 3:8
arrows as of an *e.* man. *Jer* 50:9
I know thee to be *e.* in. *Acts* 26:3

expired
the days were not *e.* *1 Sam* 18:26
after the year was *e.* *2 Sam* 11:1*
1 Chr 20:1*
come to pass days be *e.* *1 Chr* 17:11*
when year *e.* Nebuchadnezzar sent.
2 Chr 36:10*
when these days were *e.* *Esth* 1:5*
when these days are *e.* *Ezek* 43:27*
when forty years were *e.* *Acts* 7:30*
when 1000 years are *e.* *Rev* 20:7*

exploits
his land he shall do *e.* *Dan* 11:28*
people shall be strong and do *e.* 32

expound
not in three days *e.* *Judg* 14:14*

expounded
garments to them who *e.* the riddle.
Judg 14:19*
alone, he *e.* all things. *Mark* 4:34
he *e.* to them in all. *Luke* 24:27*
but Peter *e.* it by order. *Acts* 11:4
Aquila and Priscilla *e.* *Acts* 18:26
Paul *e.* and testified the. 28:23

express
being the *e.* image of. *Heb* 1:3*

expressed
men which are *e.* by. *Num* 1:17
of Manasseh 18,000, *e.* *1 Chr* 12:31
who were *e.* by name. 16:41
men *e.* took captives. *2 Chr* 28:15
men *e.* to give portions to. 31:19
Nethinims were *e.* by. *Ezra* 8:20

expressly
if I *e.* say to the lad. *1 Sam* 20:21
the word came *e.* to. *Ezek* 1:3
the Spirit speaketh *e.* *1 Tim* 4:1

extend
none to *e.* mercy to him. *Ps* 109:12
behold, I will *e.* peace. *Isa* 66:12

extended
e. mercy to me. *Ezra* 7:28
e. mercy to us. 9:9

extendeth
my goodness *e.* not to. *Ps* 16:2*

extinct
my days are *e.* the graves. *Job* 17:1
they are *e.* are quenched. *Isa* 43:17

extol
I will *e.* thee, O Lord. *Ps* 30:1
e. him that rideth upon. 68:4*
I will *e.* thee, my God. 145:1
Nebuchadnezzar *e.* King. *Dan* 4:37

extolled
and he was *e.* with. *Ps* 66:17
my servant shall be *e.* *Isa* 52:13*

extortion
greedily gained by *e.* *Ezek* 22:12*
they are full of *e.* *Mat* 23:25

extortioner
let the *e.* catch all. *Ps* 109:11
the *e.* is at an end. *Isa* 16:4
any man be drunkard, *e.* *1 Cor* 5:11

extortioners
not as other men are, *e.* *Luke* 18:11
not altogether with *e.* *1 Cor* 5:10
nor *e.* inherit kingdom of God. 6:10

extreme
shall smite thee with *e.* *Deut* 28:22*

extremity
knoweth it not in great *e.* *Job* 35:15*

eye
This is used [1] *literally, in many places.* [2] *Figuratively, for discernment, judgement, that by which the mind apprehends.*
e. for *e.* *Ex* 21:24; *Lev* 24:20
Deut 19:21; *Mat* 5:38
man smite *e.* of servant, or *e.*
Ex 21:26
hath a blemish in his *e.* *Lev* 21:20
his *e.* shall be evil. *Deut* 28:54
her *e.* shall be evil towards. 56
he kept him as apple of his *e.* 32:10
his *e.* was not dim, nor. 34:7
the *e.* of their God was. *Ezra* 5:5
e. that hath seen me. *Job* 7:8
given up ghost, and no *e.* had. 10:18
the *e.* which saw him, see. 20:9
e. of adulterer waiteth for twilight
saying, no *e.* shall see me. 24:15
a path which vulture's *e.* 28:7
and his *e.* seeth every precious. 10
when the *e.* saw me. 29:11
e. of the Lord is on them. *Ps* 33:18
neither wink with the *e.* 35:19
aha, aha, our *e.* hath seen it. 21
he that formed the *e.* shall? 94:9
that winketh with the *e.* *Pr* 10:10
the seeing *e.* hearing ear. 20:12
he that hath a bountiful *e.* shall. 22:9
the *e.* that mocketh at. 30:17
the *e.* is not satisfied. *Eccl* 1:8
neither is his *e.* satisfied. 4:8
their *e.* shall not spare. *Isa* 13:18
for they shall see *e.* to *e.* 52:8
neither hath the *e.* seen what he hath
prepared. 64:4; *1 Cor* 2:9
that were pleasant to the *e.* *Lam* 2:4
let not your *e.* spare. *Ezek* 9:5
none *e.* pitied, to do any of. 16:5

defiled, and let our e. Mi 4:11
light of the body is the e. Mat 6:22
Luke 11:34
mote in thy brother's e. and not beam
in own e. Mat 7:3; Luke 6:41, 42
e. offend thee, pluck it out. Mat 18:9
easier for camel to go through e. of.
19:24; Mark 10:25; Luke 18:25
because I am not the e. 1 Cor 12:16
if the whole body were an e. 17
e. cannot say. 21
in twinkling of an e. at last. 15:52
he cometh, and every e. Rev 1:7

evil eye

bread of him that hath an evil e.
Pr 23:6
to be rich hath an evil e. 28:22
but if thine e. be evil. Mat 6:23
Luke 11:34
is thine e. evil because? Mat 20:15
heart proceedeth evil e. Mark 7:22

mine eye

kill thee, but mine e. 1 Sam 24:10
mine e. no more see good. Job 7:7
mine e. hath seen all this. 13:1
mine e. poureth out tears. 16:20
doth mine e. continue in? 17:2
mine e. also is dim by. 7
but now mine e. seeth thee. 42:5
mine e. consumed. Ps 6:7; 31:9
I will guide thee with mine e. 32:8
mine e. hath seen his desire. 54:7
mine e. mourneth by reason. 88:9
mine e. shall see my desire. 92:11
mine e. mine e. runneth down.
Lam 1:16; 3:48
mine e. trickleth down and. 3:49
mine e. affecteth my heart. 51
shall mine e. spare. Ezek 5:11
7:4, 9; 8:18; 9:10
mine e. spared them. 20:17

right eye

sword shall be on arm, and his right
e.: his right e. utterly. Zech 11:17
if right e. offend thee. Mat 5:29

thine eye

thine e. shall not pity. Deut 7:16
13:8; 19:13, 21; 25:12
and thine e. be evil against. 15:9
apple of thine e. cease. Lam 2:18
if thine e. be single. Mat 6:22
Luke 11:34
beam in thine own e. Mat 7:3
Luke 6:41
if thine e. offend thee. Mat 18:9
Mark 9:47

see apple

eyebrows

shave all his hair off e. Lev 14:9

eyed

and Saul e. David. 1 Sam 18:9

tender eyed

Leah was tender e. Gen 29:17

eyelids

on mine e. is shadow of. Job 16:16
eyes are like e. of morning. 41:18
e. try the children of men. Ps 11:4
or slumber to mine e. 132:4
let thine e. look straight. Pr 4:25
to thine eyes, slumber to e. 6:4
let her take thee with her e. 25
their e. are lifted up. 30:13
that our e. may gush out. Jer 9:18

eyes

for food pleasant to e. Gen 3:6
e. of them both were opened. 7
mistress was despised in her e. 16:4
conceived, I was despised in her e. 5
is to thee a covering of e. 20:16
God opened Hagar's e. 21:19
Jacob laid rods before e. of. 30:41
master's wife cast her e. on. 39:7
good in the e. of Pharaoh. 41:37
the e. of Israel were dim. 48:10
to be abhorred in the e. of. Ex 5:21
glory of Lord like fire in e. 24:17
and the thing be hid from the e. of.
Lev 4:13
burning ague consume the e. 26:16
be hid from the e. of her. Num 5:13
thou mayest be to us e. 10:31
wilt thou put out the e. of? 16:14
sanctify me in e. of Israel. Num 20:12
Lord opened e. of Balaam. 22:31
man whose e. are open. 24:3, 15
a gift doth blind the e. Deut 16:19
Lord give thee failing of e. 28:65
Lord hath not given you e. to. 29:4
be avenged for my two e. Judg 16:28
uncovered himself in e. 2 Sam 6:20
that the e. of my lord the king. 24:3
e. of all Israel upon thee. 1 Ki 1:20
Lord opened the e. of the. 2 Ki 6:17
Lord, open the e. of these men. 20
put out e. of Zedekiah. 25:7
Jer 39:7; 52:11
was right in the e. of. 1 Chr 13:4
hast thou e. of flesh? Job 10:4
the e. of the wicked shall fail. 11:20
even the e. of his children. 17:5
seeing it is hid from the e. 28:21
I was e. to the blind. 29:15
caused e. of the widow to fail. 31:16
and her e. behold afar off. 39:29
in whose e. a vile person. Ps 15:4
pure, enlightening e. 19:8
e. have they, but. 115:5; 135:16
as the e. of servants, the. 123:2
the e. of all wait upon thee. 145:15
Lord openeth the e. of blind. 146:8
as smoke to the e. so is. Pr 10:26
light of the e. rejoiceth. 15:30
as a precious stone in e. of. 17:8
the e. of a fool are in ends. 24
who hath redness of e.? 23:29
e. of man are never satisfied. 27:20
the wise man's e. are. Eccl 2:14
better the sight of e. than. 6:9
pleasant for the e. to behold. 11:7
thou hast dove's e. S of S 1:15; 4:1
to provoke the e. of his. Isa 3:8
daughters walk with wanton e. 16
e. of the lofty be humbled. 5:15
the e. of the blind shall see. 29:18
the e. of them that see. 32:3
the e. of the blind shall be. 35:5
to open the blind e. to bring. 42:7
bring forth blind that have e. 43:8
Lord made bare his arm in e. 52:10
we grope as if we had no e. 59:10
which have e. and see not. Jer 5:21
Ezek 12:2
their rings were full of e. Ezek 1:18
the wheels were full of e. 10:12
as she saw them with her e. 23:16
known in e. of many nations. 38:23
in horn were e. like the e. Dan 7:8
even of that horn that had e. 20
of purer e. than to behold. Hab 1:13
upon one stone seven e. Zech 3:9
if it be marvellous in the e. 8:6
when the e. of man shall be. 9:1
rather than having two e. to be cast.
Mat 18:9; Mark 9:47
having e. see ye not? Mark 8:18
e. of all were fastened. Luke 4:20
blessed are the e. which see. 10:23
anointed the e. of blind. John 9:6
any opened e. of one born blind. 32
can a devil open e. of blind? 10:21
this man, which opened e.? 11:37
Dorcas opened her e. Acts 9:40
hath given them e. they. Rom 11:8
before whose e. Christ. Gal 3:1
e. of your understanding. Eph 1:18
things are open to e. of. Heb 4:13
having e. full of adultery. 2 Pet 2:14
the lust of the e. and. 1 John 2:16
of throne beasts full of e. Rev 4:6
each six wings, full of e. within. 8
a Lamb having seven e. 5:6

his eyes

old, and his e. were dim. Gen 27:1
his e. red with wine. 49:12
having his e. open. Num 24:4, 16
find no favour in his e. Deut 24:1
Philistines put out his e. Judg 16:21
Eli, his e. began to. 1 Sam 3:2; 4:15
he tasted, and his e. were. 14:27
Ahijah not see, his e. were. 1 Ki 14:4
put his e. on his e. 2 Ki 4:34
the child opened his e. 35
I pray thee, open his e. 6:17
slew sons of Zedekiah before his e.
25:7; Jer 39:6; 52:10
king do what is good in his e.
1 Chr 21:23
and I be pleasing in his e. Esth 8:5
enemy sharpeneth his e. Job 16:9
his e. shall see his destruction. 21:20
resteth, yet his e. are on. 24:23
the rich man openeth his e. 27:19
his e. are on the ways of. 34:21
he withdraweth not his e. 36:7
he taketh it with his e. 40:24*
his e. are like the eyelids. 41:18
his e. are privily set. Ps 10:8
his e. behold children of men. 11:4
no fear of God before his e. 36:1
ruleth by power, his e. behold. 66:7
he winketh with his e. Pr 6:13
he shutteth his e. to. 16:30
scattereth away evil with his e. 20:8
findeth no favour in his e. 21:10
he that hideth his e. shall. 28:27
sleepeth with his e. Eccl 8:16
his e. are as eyes of. S of S 5:12
in his e. as one that found. 8:10
after the sight of his e. Isa 11:3
his e. shall have respect to. 17:7
and shutteth his e. from. 33:15
his e. shall behold his e. Jer 32:4
see not the ground with his e.
Ezek 12:12
away abomination of his e. 20:7
horn between his e. Dan 8:5, 21
his e. were as lamps of fire. 10:6
he had spit on his e. Mark 8:23
he put his hands again on his e. 25
made clay, opened his e. John 9:14
or who hath opened his e. 21
Peter fastening his e. Acts 3:4
and when his e. were opened. 9:8
there fell from his e. as it had. 18
then Saul set his e. on him. 13:9
because darkness hath blinded his e.
1 John 2:11
his e. as a flame of fire. Rev 1:14
2:18; 19:12

lift or lifted up eyes

Lot lifted up his e. and. Gen 13:10
lift up now thine e. and. 14; 31:12
Deut 3:27; 2 Ki 19:22; Isa 49:18
60:4; Jer 3:2; Ezek 8:5; Zech 5:5
Abraham lift up his e.
Gen 18:2; 22:4, 13
Isaac lifted up his e. 24:63
Rebekah lifted up her e. 64
Jacob lifted up his e. 31:10; 33:1
Joseph lifted up his e. 43:29
lifted up their e. the Egyptians.
Ex 14:10
Balaam lifted up his e. Num 24:2
lest thou lift up thine e. Deut 4:19
Joshua lifted up his e. Josh 5:13
old man lifted up his e. Judg 19:17
lifted up their e. and. 1 Sam 6:13
young man that kept the watch lifted
up e. 2 Sam 13:34; 18:24
David lifted up his e. and. 1 Chr 21:16
they lifted up their e. and. Job 2:12
lift up mine e. to hills. Ps 121:1
unto thee lift I up mine e. 123:1
hast thou lifted up thy e.? Isa 37:23
lift up your e. 51:6; Ezek 33:25
John 4:35
lifted up e. to idols. Ezek 18:6, 15
hath lifted up his e. to idols. 12
thou shalt not lift up thine e. 23:27
Nebuchadnezzar lift. up e. Dan 4:34
then I lifted up mine e. 8:3; 10:5
Zech 1:18; 2:1; 5:1, 5, 9; 6:1
had lifted up their e. they. Mat 17:8
Jesus lifted up his e. Luke 6:20
John 6:5; 11:41; 17:1
in hell he lift up his e. Luke 16:23
not lift up so much as his e. 18:13

eyes of the Lord

grace in e. of the Lord. Gen 6:8
the e. of the Lord are. Deut 11:12
right in the e. of the Lord. 13:18
set by in e. of the Lord. 1 Sam 26:24
favour in e. of the Lord. 2 Sam 15:25
David did right in the e. of the Lord.
1 Ki 15:5, 11; 22:43; 2 Chr 14:2
e. of the Lord run to and fro through.
2 Chr 16:9; Zech 4:10

e. of the Lord are upon the righteous. Ps 34:15; 1 Pet 3:12
of man before e. of the Lord. Pr 5:21
the e. of the Lord are in. 15:3
e. of the Lord preserve. 22:12
glorious in e. of the Lord. Isa 49:5
the e. of the Lord are on the. Amos 9:8

mine eyes

departed from mine e. Gen 31:40
that I may set mine e. upon. 44:21
bribe to blind mine e. 1 Sam 12:3
see how mine e. have been. 14:29
life much set by in mine e. 26:24
one to sit, mine e. seeing. 1 Ki 1:48
hallowed house, mine e. and mine heart shall be. 9:3; 2 Chr 7:16
mine e. had seen it. 1 Ki 10:7
2 Chr 9:6
in my ways, to do right in mine e. 1 Ki 11:33; 14:8; 2 Ki 10:30
now mine e. be open. 2 Chr 7:15
hid not sorrow from mine e. Job 3:10
an image was before mine e. 4:16
mine e. shall behold. 19:27
made a covenant with mine e. 31:1
mine heart walked after mine e. 7
lighten mine e. lest I sleep. Ps 13:3
mine e. are toward the Lord. 25:15
lovingkindness before mine e. 26:3
as for the light of mine e. it. 38:10
mine e. fail, whilst I wait. 69:3
thou holdest mine e. waking. 77:4
no evil thing before mine e. 101:3
mine e. shall be on the faithful. 6
delivered mine e. from tears. 116:8
open mine e. 119:18
turn away mine e. 37
mine e. fail for thy word. 82
mine e. fail for thy salvation. 123
of waters run down mine e. 136
mine e. prevent night watches. 148
heart not haughty, nor mine e. 131:1
I will not give sleep to mine e. 132:4
but mine e. are unto thee. 141:8
mine e. desired, I kept not. Eccl 2:10
hide mine e. from you. Isa 1:15
away evil doings from mine e. 16
mine e. have seen the King. 6:5
mine e. fail with looking. 38:14
evil before mine e. 65:12; 66:4
they are hid from mine e. 65:16
O that mine e. were a. Jer 9:1
mine e. shall weep sore. 13:17
let mine e. run down with. 14:17
mine e. are on their ways, nor is their iniquity hid from mine e. 16:17
I will set mine e. upon them. 24:6
mine e. do fail with. Lam 2:11
be hid from mine e. Hos 13:14
I will set mine e. on. Amos 9:4
mine e. shall behold her. Mi 7:10
marvellous in mine e. Zech 8:6
now have I seen with mine e. 9:8
I will open mine e. on the. 12:4
mine e. seen salvation. Luke 2:30
anointed mine e. John 9:11, 15
yet he hath opened mine e. 30
I had fastened mine e. Acts 11:6

our eyes

manna before our e. Num 11:6
signs before our e. Deut 6:22
nor have our e. seen it. 21:7
O God, our e. are upon thee. 2 Chr 20:12
God may lighten our e. Ezra 9:8
it is marvellous in our e. Ps 118:23
Mat 21:42; Mark 12:11
so our e. wait upon the Lord. Ps 123:2
that our e. may run down. Jer 9:18
our e. as yet failed for. Lam 4:17
for these things our e. are. 5:17
meat cut off before our e. Joel 1:16
our e. may be opened. Mat 20:33
have seen with our e. 1 John 1:1

own eyes

not after you own e. Num 15:39
man whatsoever is right in own e. Deut 12:8; Judg 17:6; 21:25
cast down in their own e. Neh 6:16
righteous in his own e. Job 32:1
flattereth himself in his own e. Ps 36:2
not wise in thine own e. Pr 3:7
of a fool right in his own e. 12:15
of man are clean in his own e. 16:2
way of man right in his own e. 21:2
generation pure in their own e. 30:12
to them wise in own e. Isa 5:21
plucked out your own e. Gal 4:15

their eyes

Simeon before their e. Gen 42:24
Egyptians before their e. Ex 8:26
any ways hide their e. Lev 20:4
speak to rock before their e. Num 20:8
me at the water before their e. 27:14
the Lord opened their e. 2 Ki 6:20
was laid before their e. Ezra 3:12
their husbands in their e. Esth 1:17
offspring before their e. Job 21:8
have set their e. bowing. Ps 17:11
let their e. be darkened. 69:23
their e. stand out with fatness. 73:7
lighteneth both their e. Pr 29:13
O how lofty are their e. 30:13
beholding them with their e. Eccl 5:11
their e. lest they see with their e. Isa 6:10; Mat 13:15; Acts 28:27
to pieces before their e. Isa 13:16
for he hath shut their e. 44:18
their e. did fail, because. Jer 14:6
and with their e. Ezek 6:9
away abominations of their e. 20:8
their e. after father's idols. 24
bitterness sigh before their e. 21:6
and have hid their e. from. 22:26
from them desire of their e. 24:25
sanctified in you before their e. 36:23
in thy hand before their e. 37:20
sanctified in thee before their e. 38:16
their e. shall consume. Zech 14:12
then touched he their e. Mat 9:29
their e. were opened. 30
their e. they have closed. 13:15
Jesus touched their e., their e. 20:34
for their e. were heavy. 26:43
Mark 14:40
but their e. were holden. Luke 24:16
their e. were opened. 31
he hath blinded their e. John 12:40
to open their e. Acts 26:18
fear of God before their e. Rom 3:18
let their e. be darkened. 11:10
and God shall wipe away all tears from their e. Rev 7:17; 21:4

thine eyes

found favour in thine e. Gen 30:27
put his hand on thine e. 46:4
shall we die before thine e.? 47:19
memorial between thine e. Ex 13:9
frontlets between thine e. 16
Deut 6:8
thine e. have seen all. Deut 3:21
lift up thine e. behold with thine e. 27
forget things thine e. have. 4:9
temptations thine e. saw. 7:19; 29:3
terrible things thine e. seen. 10:21
ox be slain before thine e. 28:31
thine e. shall look, and. 32
mad for sight of thine e. 34, 67
thee to see it with thine e. 34:4
let thine e. be on field. Ruth 2:9
have I found grace in thine e.? 10
to consume thine e. 1 Sam 2:33
I have found grace in thine e. 20:3
I have found favour in thine e. 29
thine e. have seen how the. 24:10
men find favour in thine e. 25:8
soul was precious in thine e. 26:21
found grace in thine e. 27:5
take thy wives before thine e. 2 Sam 12:11
what is good in thine e. 19:27
thine e. are on the haughty. 22:28
that thine e. may be open toward. 1 Ki 8:29, 52; 2 Chr 6:20, 40
is pleasant in thine e. 1 Ki 20:6
shalt see it with thine e. 2 Ki 7:2
open, Lord, thine e. and see. 19:16; Isa 37:17
thine e. shall not see. 2 Ki 22:20
a small thing in thine e. 1 Chr 17:17
nor thine e. see all evil. 2 Chr 34:28
ear be attentive, thine e. Neh 1:6
thine e. are upon me. Job 7:8
I am clean in thine e. 11:4
dost thou open thine e. upon? 14:3
what do thine e. wink at? 15:12
cut off from before thine e. Ps 31:22
in order before thine e. 50:21
only with thine e. shalt thou. 91:8
thine e. did see my substance. 139:16
not depart from thine e. Pr 3:21, 4:21
let thine e. look right on. 4:25
give not sleep to thine e. nor. 6:4
open thine e. and thou. 20:13
wilt thou set thine e. on? 23:5
let thine e. observe my ways. 26
thine e. shall behold strange. 33
of prince thine e. have seen. 25:7
walk in sight of thine e. Eccl 11:9
my heart with thine e. S of S 4:9
turn away thine e. from me. 6:5
thine e. like the fishpools in. 7:4
thine e. shall see teachers. Isa 30:20
thine e. shall see the king in. 33:17
thine e. see Jerusalem a quiet. 20
not thine e upon truth? Jer 5:3
thine e. shall behold it. 20:4
thine e. are not but for thy. 22:17
and thine e. from tears. 31:16
thine e. are open on all. 32:19
thine e. shall behold king of. 34:3
we are but few, as thine e. do. 42:2
whom paintedst thine e. Ezek 23:40
from thee desire of thine e. 24:16
behold with thine e. 40:4; 44:5
open thine e. and behold. Dan 9:18
are hid from thine e. Luke 19:42
were thine e. opened? John 9:10, 26
he hath opened thine e.? 17
thine e. with eyesalve. Rev 3:18

your eyes

in day ye eat your e. Gen 3:5
to them as is good in your e. 19:8
let me find grace in your e. 34:11
your e. see and the eyes of my. 45:12
I have found grace in your e. 50:4
pricks in your e. thorns in sides. Num 33:55; Josh 23:13
he did before your e. Deut 1:30
4:34; 29:2
your e. have seen what the Lord. 4:3; 11:7; Josh 24:7
tables before your e. Deut 9:17
as frontlets between your e. 11:18
any baldness between your e. 14:1
Lord do before your e. 1 Sam 12:16
hissing, as ye see with your e. 2 Chr 29:8
Lord hath closed your e. Isa 29:10
lift up your e. 40:26; Jer 13:20
a den of robbers in your e. Jer 7:11
out of this place in your e. 16:9
slay them before your e. 29:21
the desire of your e. Ezek 24:21
captivity before your e. Zeph 3:20
in your e. in comparison. Hag 2:3
your e. shall see, Lord. Mal 1:5
but blessed are your e. Mat 13:16

right eyes

out all your right e. 1 Sam 11:2

eyesalve

anoint thine eyes with e. Rev 3:18

eyeservice

not with e. as menpleasers. Eph 6:6; Col 3:22

eyesight

according to my cleanness in his e. 2 Sam 22:25; Ps 18:24

eyewitnesses

from beginning were e. Luke 1:2
were e. of his majesty. 2 Pet 1:16

Ezekiel

E. is unto you a sign. Ezek 24:24

Ezel

remain by the stone E. 1 Sam 20:19

Ezra

sons of E. Jether and. 1 Chr 4:17

Artaxerxes king to E. Ezra 7:12
thou, E. after the wisdom of. 25
when E. had prayed and. 10:1
E. brought the law. Neh 8:2
and E. blessed the Lord. 6
priests, Seraiah, Jeremiah, E. 12:1
of E. Meshullam was priest. 13
were in days of E. the priest. 26
and E. the scribe before them. 36

F

fables

nor give heed to f. and. 1 Tim 1:4
refuse profane and old wives' f. 4:7
shall be turned unto f. 2 Tim 4:4
not giving heed to Jewish f. Tit 1:14
cunningly devised f. 2 Pet 1:16

face

[1] *The literal meaning, the face, the front part of the head,* Gen 3:19. [2] *Presence,* Lev 19:32. [3] Before the face of *means in the sight of,* Ps 41:12.

in sweat of thy f. shalt. Gen 3:19
I flee from the f. of mistress. 16:8
put the earring upon her f. 24:47*
fleddest from the f. of Esau. 35:1, 7
Esau went from f. of his. 36:6
sent to Joseph to direct his f. 46:28*
bowed with his f. to the earth. 48:12
Moses fled from the f. Ex 2:15
let us flee from the f. of. 14:25
the skin of f. shone. 34:29, 30, 35
he put a vail on his f. 33
hair fallen towards his f. Lev 13:41
honour the f. of old man. 19:32
father had spit in her f. Num 12:14
slay red heifer before his f. 19:3
shall not be afraid of f. Deut 1:17
them that hate him to f. 7:10
Lord destroyeth before your f. 8:20
wicked man be beaten before f. 25:2
and spit in his f. and say. 9
ass taken before thy f. 28:31
give them up before your f. 31:5
liest thou upon thy f.? Josh 7:10
Dagon was fallen on his f. 1 Sam 5:3, 4
David stooped with his f. to. 24:8
Abigail bowed on her f. and. 25:41
Saul stooped with his f. to. 28:14
should I hold up my f.? 2 Sam 2:22
Absalom bowed on his f. to. 14:33
bowed himself before the king on his f. 24:20; 1 Chr 21:21
Nathan bowed with his f. 1 Ki 1:23
Bath-sheba bowed with her f. 31
king turned f. about. 8:14; 2 Chr 6:3
put f. between knees. 1 Ki 18:42
wrapped his f. in his mantle. 19:13
himself with ashes on his f. 20:38*
Ahab turned away his f. and. 21:4
lay my staff upon f. of. 2 Ki 4:29
Gehazi laid staff on the f. of. 31
Hazael spread it on his f. so. 8:15
Jezebel painted her f. and. 9:30*
Jehu lifted his f. to the window. 32
Joash wept over his f. and. 13:14
wilt thou turn away f. of one. 18:24 Isa 36:9
Hezekiah turned f. to wall. 2 Ki 20:2 Isa 38:2
turn not away the f. of thine. 2 Chr 6:42; Ps 132:10
Lord will not turn away his f. from. 2 Chr 30:9
he returned with shame of f. 32:21
Josiah would not turn his f. 35:22
I blush to lift up my f. Ezra 9:6
to confusion of f. 7; Dan 9:8
will curse thee to thy f. Job 1:11; 2:5
a spirit passed before my f. 4:15
then shalt thou lift up thy f. 11:15
leanness beareth witness to f. 16:8
my f. is foul with weeping. 16
declare his way to his f.? 21:31
and thou shalt lift up thy f. 22:26
and disguiseth his f. 24:15
he holdeth back the f. of. 26:9
spare not to spit in my f. 30:10
who can discover the f. of? Job 41:13
who can open doors of his f.? 14
way straight before my f. Ps 5:8
behold thy f. in righteousness. 17:15
arrows against the f. of them. 21:12
thou settest me before thy f. 41:12
look upon the f. of thine. 84:9
and truth go before thy f. 89:14
beat down his foes before his f. 23
with an impudent f. said. Pr 7:13
wicked man hardeneth his f. 21:29
the boldness of his f. Eccl 8:1
covert from f. of the spoiler. Isa 16:4
destroy the f. of the covering. 25:7
he hath made plain the f. 28:25
neither his f. now wax pale. 29:22
bow down to thee with their f. 49:23
me continually to my f. 65:3
back, and not f. Jer 2:27; 32:33
though thou rentest thy f. 4:30*
I discover thy skirts upon thy f. that. 13:26; Nah 3:5
the back, and not the f. Jer 18:17
from hand of them whose f. 22:25
remove it from before my f. 32:31
the right of man before f. Lam 3:35
the f. of a man, the f. of a lion, f. of an ox, the f. of an eagle. Ezek 1:10
I made thy f. strong against. 3:8
my f. will I also turn from. 7:22
f. of a man, f. of a lion, f. of an eagle. 10:14; 41:19
stumblingblock before their f. 14:3
fury shall come up in my f. 38:18*
a deep sleep on f. Dan 8:18; 10:9
f. as appearance of lightning. 10:6
turn his f. unto the isles. 11:18
pride of Israel testifieth to his f. Hos 5:5; 7:10
they are before my f. 7:2
before their f. people be. Joel 2:6*
drive him with his f. toward. 20*
come before thy f. Nah 2:1
anoint head, wash thy f. Mat 6:17
I send my messenger before thy f. 11:10; Mark 1:2; Luke 7:27
angels behold f. of my. Mat 18:10
then did they spit in his f. 26:67
hast prepared before f. Luke 2:31
messengers before his f. 9:52; 10:1
his f. was as though he would. 9:53
they struck him on the f. 22:64
his f. was bound about. John 11:44
foresaw Lord always before my f. Acts 2:25
God drave out before the f. 7:45
so falling down on his f. 1 Cor 14:25
not stedfastly behold f. 2 Cor 3:7
as Moses, who put vail over f. 13
but we all with open f. beholding. 18
glory of God, in f. of Jesus. 4:6
if a man smite you on the f. 11:20
I was unknown by f. to. Gal 1:22
I withstood him to the f. 2:11
natural f. in a glass. Jas 1:23
third beast had a f. as a. Rev 4:7
his f. was as it were the sun. 10:1
were nourished from the f. 12:14
from whose f. the earth and. 20:11
see **seek, set, shine, sky, waters, wilderness, world**

face *with cover,* or *covered*

she *covered* her f. Gen 38:15
locusts *cover* f. of the earth. Ex 10:5, 15
they *cover* f. of the earth. Num 22:5
the king *covered* his f. 2 Sam 19:4
they *covered* Haman's f. Esth 7:8
covereth his f. with. Job 15:27
neither hath he *covered* darkness from my f. 23:17
shame of my f. hath *covered* me. Ps 44:15
sake shame hath *covered* my f. 69:7
nettles had *covered* f. Pr 24:31
with twain he *covered* his f. Isa 6:2
thou shalt *cover* thy f. Ezek 12:6
the prince shall *cover* his f. 12
spit on him, and *cover* his f. Mark 14:65

face *of the country*

scattered over f. *of the country.* 2 Sam 18:8

face *of the deep*

darkness upon f. *of the deep.* Gen 1:2
f. *of the deep* is frozen. Job 38:30
compass on f. *of the depth.* Pr 8:27

face *of the earth*

herb upon f. *of the earth.* Gen 1:29
driven me from f. *of the earth.* 4:14
to multiply on f. *of the earth.* 6:1
seed alive on f. *of* all *the earth.* 7:3
destroy from off f. *of the earth.* 4 Deut 6:15; 1 Ki 13:34; Amos 9:8
waters on f. *of the* whole *earth.* Gen 8:9
scattered on f. *of the earth.* 11:4
famine over f. *of the earth.* 41:56
consume them from f. *of the earth.* Ex 32:12
all people unto f. *of the earth.* 33:16
meek above all men on f. *of the earth.* Num 12:3
above all people on f. *of the earth.* Deut 7:6
cut off every one from f. *of the earth.* 1 Sam 20:15
renewest the f. *of the earth.* Ps 104:30
kingdoms on the f. *of the earth.* Isa 23:17
dung on the f. *of the earth.* Jer 8:2; 16:4
cast thee from f. *of the earth.* 28:16
men on the f. *of the earth* shake. Ezek 38:20
he goat came on the f. *of the earth.* Dan 8:5
poureth them on f. *of the earth.* Amos 5:8; 9:6
curse goeth over the f. *of the earth.* Zech 5:3
discern f. *of the earth.* Luke 12:56
dwell on f. *of the* whole *earth.* 21:35
dwell on f. *of the earth.* Acts 17:26

face *to* **face**

I have seen God f. *to* f. Gen 32:30
Lord spake to Moses f. *to* f. Ex 33:11
Lord, art seen f. *to* f. Num 14:14
talked with you f. *to* f. Deut 5:4
whom Lord knew f. *to* f. 34:10
seen an angel f. *to* f. Judg 6:22
in water f. answereth *to* f. Pr 27:19
plead with you f. *to* f. Ezek 20:35
have accusers f. *to* f. Acts 25:16
a glass, then f. *to* f. 1 Cor 13:12
to you, speak f. *to* f. 2 John 12
see thee and speak f. *to* f. 3 John 14

fell on **face** or **faces**

Joseph *fell on* father's f. Gen 50:1
brethren *fell down* before his f. 18
people saw, *fell on* their f. Lev 9:24
Moses and Aaron *fell on* f. Num 14:5 16:22, 45
Moses *fell on* f. 16:4
Balaam *fell* flat on his f. 22:31
Joshua *fell on* f. Josh 5:14; 7:6
and his wife *fell on* f. Judg 13:20
then she *fell on* her f. Ruth 2:10
Goliath *fell on* f. 1 Sam 17:49
David *fell on* his f. 20:41
Abigail *fell on* f. 25:23
Mephibosheth *fell on* f. 2 Sam 9:6
woman of Tekoah *fell on* f. 14:4
Joab *fell on* f. 22
Ahimaaz *fell on* his f. 18:28
Obadiah *fell on* f. 1 Ki 18:7
people *fell on* their f. 39
and elders *fell on* f. 1 Chr 21:16
I saw it I *fell upon* f. Ezek 1:28 3:23; 9:8; 11:13; 43:3; 44:4 Dan 8:17
Nebuchadnezzar *fell upon* his f. Dan 2:46
disciples *fell on* f. Mat 17:6
Jesus *fell on* his f. 26:39
leper *fell on* f. Luke 5:12
Samaritan *fell on* his f. 17:16
four and twenty elders *fell on* their f. Rev 11:16

face *of the field*

dung on f. *of the field.* 2 Ki 9:37

face *of the gate*
from *f. of the gate.* Ezek 40:15
face *of the ground*
mist watered the *f. of the ground.* Gen 2:6
was on the *f. of the ground.* 7:23
abated from *f. of the ground.* 8:8
the *f. of the ground* was dry. 13
hide, hideth, or *hid* **face**
from thy *f.* shall I *be hid.* Gen 4:14
and Moses *hid* his *f.* Ex 3:6
hide my *f.* from them. Deut 31:17
18; 32:20
wherefore *hidest* thou thy *f.* and? Job 13:24; Ps 44:24; 88:14
when he *hideth* his *f.* Job 34:29
he *hideth* his *f.* he will. Ps 10:11
how long wilt thou *hide* thy *f.*? 13:1
neither hath he *hid* his *f.* 22:24
hide not thy *f.* 27:9; 69:17; 102:2
143:7
thou didst *hide* thy *f.* 30:7; 104:29
hide thy *f.* from my sins. 51:9
hideth his *f.* from the. Isa 8:17
I *hid* not my *f.* from shame. 50:6
a little wrath I *hid* my *f.* 54:8
your sins have *hid* his *f.* 59:2
thou hast *hid* thy *f.* from us. 64:7
ways not *hid* from my *f.* Jer 16:17
hid my *f.* from this city. 33:5
therefore *hid* I my *f.* Ezek 39:23, 24
nor will I *hide* my *f.* any more. 29
will even *hide* his *f.* Mi 3:4
hide us from the *f.* of. Rev 6:16
face *of the house*
breadth of *f. of the house.* Ezek 41:14
face *of the Lord*
cry great before *f. of the Lord.* Gen 19:13
blood fall before *f. of Lord.* 1 Sam 26:20
entreat *f. of the* Lord. 1 Ki 13:6*
f. of the Lord is against them. Ps 34:16; 1 Pet 3:12
heart before *f. of the Lord.* Lam 2:19
go before *f. of the Lord.* Luke 1:76
face *of the porch*
f. of the porch were. Ezek 40:15*
thick planks on *f. of the p.* 41:25
face joined with *see, saw, seen*
afterward will *see* his *f.* Gen 32:20
therefore have I *seen* thy *f.* 33:10
not *see f.* except. 43:3, 5; 44:23
may not *see* man's *f.* 44:26
me die, I have *seen* thy *f.* 46:30
not thought to *see* thy *f.* 48:11
Pharaoh said, *see* my *f.* Ex 10:28
I will *see* thy *f.* again no more. 29
thou canst not *see* my *f.* 33:20
my *f.* shall not be *seen.* 23
children of Israel *saw f.* of. 34:35
not *see* my *f.* except. 2 Sam 3:13
let him not *see* my *f.* 14:24
dwelt and *saw* not king's *f.* 28
now let me *see* the king's *f.* 32
let us *look* one another in the *f.* 2 Ki 14:8; 2 Chr 25:17
looked one another in *f.* 2 Ki 14:11
princes who *saw* king's *f.* Esth 1:14
he shall *see* his *f.* with. Job 33:26
saw his *f.* as it had been *f.* Acts 6:15
shall *see* my *f.* no more. 20:25, 38
as have not *seen* my *f.* Col 2:1
endeavoured to *see* your *f.* 1 Thes 2:17
that we might *see* your *f.* 3:10
and they shall *see* his *f.* Rev 22:4
seek **face**
seek his *f.* continually. 1 Chr 16:11
Ps 105:4
people pray and *seek* my *f.* 2 Chr 7:14
generation that *seek* thy *f.* Ps 24:6
seek ye my *f.* my heart said, thy *f.* Lord will I *seek.* 27:8
diligently to *seek* thy *f.* Pr 7:15
return, till they *seek* my *f.* Hos 5:15
set **face**
Jacob *set* his *f.* toward. Gen 31:21
I will *set* my *f.* against that soul. Lev 17:10; 20:6
set my *f.* against that man. Lev 20:3, 5; Ezek 14:8
set my *f.* against you. Lev 26:17
Jer 44:11
Balaam *set* his *f.* toward. Num 24:1
Hazael *set* his *f.* to. 2 Ki 12:17
I have *set* my *f.* like a. Isa 50:7
set my *f.* against this city. Jer 21:10
set thy *f.* against it. Ezek 4:3
thou shalt set thy *f.* towards. 7
set thy *f.* towards mountains. 6:2
set thy *f.* against daughters. 13:17
I will *set* my *f.* against them. 15:7
set thy *f.* toward south. 20:46
set thy *f.* toward Jerusalem. 21:2
go whithersoever thy *f.* is *set.* 16
set thy *f.* against Ammonites. 25:2
set thy *f.* against Zidon. 28:21
set thy *f.* against Pharaoh. 29:2
set thy *f.* against mount Seir. 35:2
set thy *f.* against Gog. 38:2
I *set* my *f.* unto Lord. Dan 9:3
I *set* my *f.* toward ground and. 10:15
he shall *set* his *f.* to enter. 11:17
stedfastly *set* his *f.* to. Luke 9:51
face *shine*
his *f.* to *shine* upon thee. Num 6:25
make thy *f.* to *shine* on thy. Ps 31:16; 119:135
cause his *f.* to *shine* on us. 67:1
cause thy *f. shine.* 80:3, 7, 19
oil to make his *f.* to *shine.* 104:15
wisdom maketh *f.* to *shine.* Eccl 8:1
cause thy *f.* to *shine* on. Dan 9:17
his *f.* did *shine* as sun. Mat 17:2
face *of the sky*
ye can discern the *f. of the sky.* Mat 16:3; Luke 12:56
face *of the waters*
moved on *f. of the waters.* Gen 1:2
ark went upon *f. of the waters.* 7:18
face *of the wilderness*
on *f. of the wilderness.* Ex 16:14
face *of the world*
commandeth on *f. of world.* Job 37:12
nor fill *f. of the world.* Isa 14:21
Israel shall fill *f. of the world.* 27:6
faces
their *f.* were backward. Gen 9:23
set *f.* of the flocks toward. 30:40
bowed with *f.* to the earth. 42:6
Moses laid before their *f.* Ex 19:7
fear may be before your *f.* 20:20
and their *f.* shall look one. 25:20
mercy seatward were *f.* of. 37:9
turned their *f.* and said. Judg 18:23
thou hast shamed the *f.* 2 Sam 19:5
all Israel set their *f.* on. 1 Ki 2:15
whose *f.* were like the *f.* 1 Chr 12:8
their *f.* were inward. 2 Chr 3:13
fathers have turned away *f.* 29:6
worshipped with their *f.* Neh 8:6
covereth *f.* of the judges. Job 9:24
and bind their *f.* in secret. 40:13
and *f.* were not ashamed. Ps 34:5
fill their *f.* with shame. 83:16
ye grind the *f.* of the poor. Isa 3:15
amazed, their *f.* shall be as. 13:8
wipe away tears from off all *f.* 25:8
hid as it were our *f.* from him. 53:3
be not afraid of their *f.* Jer 1:8
be not dismayed at their *f.* 17
their *f.* harder than a rock. 5:3
to confusion of their own *f.* 7:19
all *f.* are turned into paleness. 30:6
set their *f.* to enter Egypt. 42:15
17; 44:12
with their *f.* thitherward. 50:5
shame hath covered our *f.* 51:51
the *f.* of elders were not. Lam 5:12
every one four *f.* Ezek 1:6, 10, 11, 15
face strong against their *f.* 3:8
shame shall be on their *f.* 7:18
men, with *f.* toward the east. 8:16
turn away your *f.* from. 14:6
all *f.* shall be burnt therein. 20:47
every cherub had two *f.* 41:18
he see your *f.* worse. Dan 1:10
but unto us confusion of *f.* as. 9:7
be much pained, all *f.* Joel 2:6
f. of them all gather. Nah 2:10
their *f.* shall sup up as. Hab 1:9
spread dung on your *f.* Mal 2:3
hypocrites disfigure their *f.* Mat 6:16
bowed down their *f.* to. Luke 24:5
before throne on their *f.* Rev 7:11
f. of the locusts were as *f.* 9:7
fade
strangers *f.* away. 2 Sam 22:46
Ps 18:45
we all *f.* as a leaf. Isa 64:6
them, and leaf shall *f.* Jer 8:13
whose leaf shall not *f.* Ezek 47:12
rich man shall *f.* away. Jas 1:11
fadeth
an oak, whose leaf *f.* Isa 1:30
mourneth and *f.*, the world *f.* 24:4
grass withereth, the flower *f.* 40:7, 8
inheritance that *f.* not. 1 Pet 1:4
a crown of glory that *f.* not. 5:4
fading
glorious beauty a *f.* flower. Isa 28:1
beauty shall be a *f.* flower. 4
fail
will without *f.* drive out. Josh 3:10
f. deliver Ammon. Judg 11:30*
shalt without *f.* recover. 1 Sam 30:8
day by day without *f.* Ezra 6:9
fail, *verb*
your cattle, if money *f.* Gen 47:16
eyes shall *f.* with longing. Deut 28:32
he will not *f.* thee nor forsake thee. 31:6, 8; Josh 1:5; 1 Chr 28:20
not *f.* to burn fat. 1 Sam 2:16*
let no man's heart *f.* him. 17:32
I should not *f.* to sit with. 20:5
not *f.* from house of. 2 Sam 3:29
not *f.* thee a man on. 1 Ki 2:4
8:25; 9:5; 2 Chr 6:16
neither cruse of oil *f.* 1 Ki 17:14, 16
take heed that ye *f.* not. Ezra 4:22*
let nothing *f.* of all. Esth 6:10
not *f.* to keep these days. 9:27, 28
eyes of the wicked *f.* Job 11:20
as waters *f.* from the sea. 14:11
even eyes of children shall *f.* 17:5
caused eyes of widow to *f.* 31:16
for the faithful *f.* from. Ps 12:1
mine eyes *f.* while I wait. 69:3
doth his promise *f.* for? 77:8
nor my faithfulness to *f.* 89:33
mine eyes *f.* for thy word. 119:82
mine eyes *f.* for thy salvation. 123
rod of his anger shall *f.* Pr 22:8
desire *f.* because man. Eccl 12:5
spirit of Egypt shall *f.* Isa 19:3*
waters shall *f.* 5
glory of Kedar *f.* 21:16
and they all shall *f.* together. 31:3
cause drink of the thirsty to *f.* 32:6
troubled, for vintage shall *f.* 10
no one of these shall *f.* nor. 34:16*
mine eyes *f.* with. 38:14
he shall not *f.* nor be. 42:4
that his bread should not *f.* 51:14
for the spirit should *f.* 57:16
spring whose waters *f.* not. 58:11
their eyes did *f.* because. Jer 14:6
unto me as waters that *f.*? 15:18
I caused wine to *f.* from. 48:33*
Hos 9:2
eyes do *f.* with tears. Lam 2:11
his compassions *f.* not. 3:22
poor of the land to *f.* Amos 8:4
labour of olive shall *f.* Hab 3:17
that when ye *f.* they. Luke 16:9
than one tittle of the law to *f.* 17*
prayed that thy faith *f.* not. 22:32
prophecies, they shall *f.* 1 Cor 13:8*
thy years shall not *f.* Heb 1:12
the time would *f.* me to tell. 11:32
looking lest any man *f.* of. 12:15*
failed
their heart *f.* them. Gen 42:28
and when money *f.* in the. 47:15*
waters *f.* were cut off. Josh 3:16*
f. not any good thing which Lord. 21:45; 23:14; 1 Ki 8:56
my kinsfolk have *f.* and. Job 19:14
refuge *f.* me, no man. Ps 142:4
my soul *f.* when he. S of S 5:6
their might *f.* they. Jer 51:30
our eyes as yet *f.* for. Lam 4:17

falleth
should we die ? money *f.* Gen 47:15
bull gendereth and *f.* not. Job 21:10
my strength *f.* me. Ps 31:10; 38:10
my heart *f.* me. 40:12; 73:26
forsake me not when strength *f.* 71:9
knees are weak, my flesh *f.* 109:24
O Lord, my spirit *f.* 143:7
his wisdom *f.* him. Eccl 10:3
the grass *f.* there is. Isa 15:6
strong in power, not one *f.* 40:26*
seek water, their tongue *f.* 41:17
hungry and his strength *f.* 44:12
truth *f.* and he that. 59:15*
and every vision *f.* Ezek 12:22
judgement to light, *f.* not. Zeph 3:5
treasure in the heavens that *f.* not. Luke 12:33
charity never *f.* but. 1 Cor 13:8

failing
Lord shall give thee *f.* Deut 28:65
men's hearts *f.* them. Luke 21:26

fain
he would *f.* flee. Job 27:22
f. have filled his belly. Luke 15:16

faint
field, and he was *f.* Gen 25:29, 30
smote thee when thou wast *f.* Deut 25:18
f. yet pursuing. Judg 8:4
bread to people, for they be *f.* 5
people were very *f.* 1 Sam 14:28, 31
so *f.* they could not go. 30:10, 21
wine, that such as be *f.* 2 Sam 16:2
David fought and waxed *f.* 21:15
the whole heart is *f.* Isa 1:5
therefore shall all hands be *f.* 13:7*
awaketh, and behold he is *f.* 29:8
he giveth power to the *f.* 40:29
he drinketh no water, and is *f.* 44:12
my heart is *f.* Jer 8:18
are many, my heart is *f.* Lam 1:22
for this our heart is *f.* our. 5:17

faint, *verb*
let not your hearts *f.* Deut 20:3
lest his brethren's heart *f.* 8*
inhabitants of land *f.* Josh 2:9*
all the inhabitants of country *f.* 24*
if thou *f.* in the day of. Pr 24:10
even the youths shall *f.* Isa 40:30
Amos 8:13
not be weary, walk, not *f.* Isa 40:31
lest your hearts *f.* Jer 51:46
he hath made me *f.* all. Lam 1:13
young children *f.* 2:19
every spirit shall *f.* Ezek 21:7
their heart may *f.* and. 15*
send fasting, lest they *f.* Mat 15:32
them fasting, they will *f.* Mark 8:3
ought to pray, not to *f.* Luke 18:1
received mercy we *f.* not. 2 Cor 4:1
for which cause we *f.* not. 16
shall reap, if we *f.* not. Gal 6:9
that ye *f.* not at my. Eph 3:13
lest ye be wearied and *f.* Heb 12:3
nor *f.* when thou art rebuked. 5

fainted
Jacob's heart *f.* for he. Gen 45:26
all the land of Canaan *f.* by. 47:13
I had *f.* unless I had. Ps 27:13
hungry and thirsty, soul *f.* 107:5
thy sons *f.* they lie at. Isa 51:20
I *f.* in my sighing. Jer 45:3*
trees of the field *f.* for. Ezek 31:15
I Daniel *f.* and was sick. Dan 8:27
soul *f.* I remembered. Jonah 2:7
that he *f.* and wished in. 4:8
compassion on them, because they *f.* Mat 9:36*
laboured and hast not *f.* Rev 2:3*

faintest
come upon thee, and thou *f.* Job 4:5

fainteth
my soul *f.* for courts. Ps 84:2
my soul *f.* for thy salvation. 119:81
a standardbearer *f.* Isa 10:18
Creator of ends of earth *f.* not. 40:28

fainthearted
who is fearful and *f.* let. Deut 20:8
fear not, nor be *f.* for. Isa 7:4
Hamath and Arpad *f.* Jer 49:23*

faintness
I will send a *f.* into. Lev 26:36

fair
daughters of men were *f.* Gen 6:2
Sarah was *f.* 12:11, 14
Rebekah was *f.* 24:16; 26:7
David was of *f.* countenance. 1 Sam 17:42
Tamar was *f.* 2 Sam 13:1; 14:27
Abishag a *f.* damsel. 1 Ki 1:4
Vashti the queen was *f.* Esth 1:11
let *f.* virgins be sought for. 2:2
gather the *f.* young virgins. 3
Esther was *f.* and beautiful. 7
f. weather cometh out. Job 37:22*
no women found so *f.* as. 42:15
with *f.* speech she. Pr 7:21
so is a *f.* woman without. 11:22
when he speaketh *f.* believe. 26:25
thou art *f.* S of S 1:15, 16; 4:1, 7
rise up, my love, my *f.* one. 2:10, 13
how *f.* is thy love, my sister! 4:10
f. as the moon. 6:10
how *f.* art thou, O love. 7:6
many houses great and *f.* Isa 5:9
thy stones with *f.* colours. 54:11
in vain make thyself *f.* Jer 4:30
and olive tree *f.* and of fruit. 11:16
though they speak *f.* words. 12:6
Egypt is like a very *f.* heifer. 46:20
also taken thy *f.* jewels. Ezek 16:17
shall take thy *f.* jewels. 39; 23:26
a cedar in Lebanon with *f.* 31:3
thus was he *f.* in his greatness. 7
I have made him *f.* by multitude. 9
leaves were *f.* fruit. Dan 4:12, 21
passed over her *f.* neck. Hos 10:11
f. virgins shall faint for. Amos 8:13
set a *f.* mitre upon his. Zech 3:5†
it will be *f.* weather, for. Mat 16:2
Moses was born, exceeding *f.* Acts 7:20
by *f.* speeches deceive. Rom 16:18
a desire to make a *f.* shew. Gal 6:12

fair *havens*
place called *f. havens.* Acts 27:8

fairer
is not younger sister *f.*? Judg 15:2
thou art *f.* than the. Ps 45:2
countenances appeared *f.* Dan 1:15

fairest
f. among women. S of S 1:8; 5:9
6:1

fairs
(*Revisions*, wares)
traded in *f.* Ezek 27:12, 14, 16, 19, 22
thy riches and thy *f.* shall. 27

faith
Faith is a dependence on the veracity of another; firm belief or trust in a person, thing, doctrine, or statement. And one is said to keep faith when he performs a promise made to another.

I. *Historical faith is a belief in the truthfulness and accuracy of the Scriptural narrative and teachings,* Jas 2:17, 24.

II. *Saving faith is the acceptance by the intellect, affection, and will of God's favour extended to man through Christ. This faith produces a sincere obedience in the life and conversation. The firm foundation of faith is the essential supreme perfection of God; his unerring knowledge, immutable truth, infinite goodness, and almighty power.*

By this faith, we are said to be justified, Rom 5:1. *Not formally, as if it were our righteousness before God. It is called the faith through which we are saved,* Eph 2:8. *Faith is, as it were, a condition on our part whereby we come to be partakers of the blessings of the new covenant. It is a faith which worketh by love,* Gal 5:6. *It is not an idle, inactive grace, but shews itself by producing in us love to God and our neighbour.*

Faith, in scripture, is also taken for the truth and faithfulness of God, Rom 3:3. *Faith is also used for the doctrine of the gospel, which is the object of faith,* Acts 24:24; Gal 1:23.

children in whom is no *f.* Deut 32:20
O ye of little *f.* Mat 6:30; 8:26
14:31; 16:8; Luke 12:28
so great *f.* no, not in Israel.
Mat 8:10; Luke 7:9
f. as a grain of mustard seed.
Mat 17:20
if ye have *f.* ye shall not. 21:21
judgement, mercy, and *f.* 23:23
how is it ye have no *f.*? Mark 4:40
have *f.* in God. 11:22
Lord, increase our *f.* Luke 17:5
if ye had *f.* ye might say to. 6
shall he find *f.*? 18:8
f. which is by him. Acts 3:16
Stephen, a man full of *f.* 6:5, 8
of priests obedient to the *f.* 7
Barnabas a good man, full of *f.* 11:24
to turn the deputy from the *f.* 13:8
perceiving that he had *f.* 14:9
them to continue in the *f.* 22
he had opened door of *f.* 27
churches established in the *f.* 16:5
f. toward our Lord Jesus. 20:21
Felix heard Paul concerning the *f.*
24:24
grace for obedience to *f.* Rom 1:5
revealed from *f.* to *f.* 17
unbelief make *f.* without effect. 3:3*
is excluded by law of *f.* 27
f. counted for righteousness. 4:5, 9
a seal of righteousness of *f.* 11
also walk in steps of that *f.* 12
through the righteousness of *f.* 13
if they of law be heirs, *f.* is. 14
it is of *f.* . . . which is of the *f.* of. 16
righteousness, which is of *f.* 9:30
10:6
that is the word of *f.* which. 10:8
f. cometh by hearing, hearing. 17*
God hath dealt measure of *f.* 12:3
according to proportion of *f.* 6
hast thou *f.*? have it to. 14:22
of *f.* what is not of *f.* is sin. 23
to nations for obedience of *f.* 16:26
to another *f.* by the. 1 Cor 12:9
though I have all *f.* and have. 13:2
now abideth *f.* hope, charity. 13
having same Spirit of *f.* 2 Cor 4:13
now preached *f.* which. Gal 1:23
or by the hearing of *f.* 3:2, 5
that they which are of *f.* 7, 9
law is not of *f.* but the man. 12
before *f.* came. 23
after that *f.* is come. 25
but *f.* which worketh by love. 5:6
fruit of Spirit is love, joy, *f.* 22*
who are of household of *f.* 6:10
one Lord, one *f.* one. Eph 4:5
all come in the unity of the *f.* 13
taking the shield of *f.* 6:16
peace to brethren, with *f.* from. 23
furtherance and joy of *f.* Phil 1:25
striving together for the *f.* of the. 27
remembering work of *f.* 1 Thes 1:3
putting on breastplate of *f.* 5:8
glory for patience and *f.* 2 Thes 1:4
would fulfil the work of *f.* 11
for all men have not *f.* 3:2
f. unfeigned. 1 Tim 1:5
grace of Lord abundant with *f.* 14
f. and a good conscience; some put away, concerning *f.* have. 19
holding the mystery of *f.* in a. 3:9
some shall depart from the *f.* 4:1
nourished up in words of *f.* 6
he hath denied the *f.* 5:8
they have cast off their first *f.* 12†
erred from the *f.* 6:10, 21
and follow after *f.* 11
fight the good fight of *f.* 12
the unfeigned *f.* that is. 2 Tim 1:5
overthrow the *f.* of some. 2:18
follow *f.* 22
reprobate concerning the *f.* 3:8
hast fully known my *f.*, charity. 3:10
finished my course, kept *f.* 4:7
according to the *f.* of. Tit 1:1
mine own son, after common *f.* 4

hearing of thy f. toward. Philem 5
not being mixed with f. Heb 4:2
not laying again foundation of f. 6:1
heart in full assurance of f. 10:22
hold fast profession of our f. 23*
f. is substance of things hoped. 11:1
without f. it is impossible to. 6
the author and finisher of our f. 12:2
whose f. follow, considering 13:7
have not f. with respect. Jas 2:1
a man say he hath f. can f. save ? 14
f. without works is dead. 17, 20, 26
a man say, thou hast f. and. 2:18
how f. wrought with his works, and
by works was f. made. 22
the prayer of f. shall save. 5:15
obtained like precious f. 2 Pet 1:1
the world, even our f. 1 John 5:4
earnestly contend for f. Jude 3
building up on your most holy f. 20
and hast not denied my f. Rev 2:13
I know thy works, and f. and. 19
the patience and the f. of. 13:10
they that keep f. of Jesus. 14:12

by faith

just shall live by his f. Hab 2:4
Rom 1:17; Gal 3:11; Heb 10:38
purifying hearts by f. Acts 15:9
who are sanctified by f. 26:18
comforted by mutual f. Rom 1:12
the righteousness of God by f. 3:22
justified by f. 28; 5:1; Gal 2:16
3:24
justify circumcision by f. Rom 3:30
by whom we have access by f. 5:2
they sought it not by f. 9:32
standest by f. 11:20; 2 Cor 1:24
for we walk by f. not. 2 Cor 5:7
I live by the f. of the Son. Gal 2:20
the promise by f. 3:22
ye are children of God by f. 26
for hope of righteousness by f. 5:5
whom have access by f. Eph 3:12
Christ dwell in your hearts by f. 17
righteousness of God by f. Phil 3:9
by f. Abel. Heb 11:4
by f. Enoch. 5
by f. Noah. 7
by f. Abraham. 8, 9, 17
by f. Isaac blessed Jacob. 20
by f. Jacob. 21
by f. Joseph made mention. 22
by f. Moses. 23, 24, 27
by f. passed through Red sea. 29
by f. walls of Jericho fell down. 30
by f. Rahab. 31
by works a man is justified, not by f.
only. Jas 2:24

in faith

being not weak in f. Rom 4:19
staggered not, was strong in f. 20
him that is weak in the f. 14:1
stand fast in the f. 1 Cor 16:13
as ye abound in f. 2 Cor 8:7
examine whether ye be in the f. 13:5
if ye continue in the f. Col 1:23
and stablished in the f. 2:7
Timothy my own son in f. 1 Tim 1:2
godly edifying which is in f. 4
a teacher of the Gentiles in f. 2:7
saved, if they continue in f. 15
purchase great boldness in f. 3:13
an example of believers in f. 4:12
hold fast form in f. 2 Tim 1:13
be found in the f. Tit 1:13; 2:2
greet them that love us in f. 3:15
these all died in f. Heb 11:13
but let him ask in f. Jas 1:6
poor of this world, rich in f. 2:5
resist, stedfast in the f. 1 Pet 5:9

their faith

Jesus seeing their f. Mat 9:2
Mark 2:5; Luke 5:20

through faith

through f. in his name. Acts 3:16
a propitiation through f. Rom 3:25
uncircumcision through f. 30
make void law through f.? 31
justify heathen through f. Gal 3:8
promise of Spirit through f. 14
grace saved through f. Eph 2:8
righteousness which is through f.
Phil 3:9
risen through the f. of. Col 2:12
to salvation through f. 2 Tim 3:15
who through f. inherit. Heb 6:12
through f. we understand. 11:3
through f. Sara received. 11
through f. he kept passover. 28
through f. subdued kingdoms. 33
a good report through f. 39
power of God through f. 1 Pet 1:5

thy faith

thy f. made thee whole. Mat 9:22
Mark 5:34; 10:52; Luke 8:48
17:19
O woman, great is thy f. Mat 15:28
thy f. hath saved. Luke 7:50; 18:42
prayed that thy f. fail not. 22:32
communication of thy f. Philem 6
shew me thy f. without. Jas 2:18

your faith

according to your f. be. Mat 9:29
where is your f.? Luke 8:25
your f. is spoken of. Rom 1:8
your f. should not stand. 1 Cor 2:5
your f. is also vain. 15:14, 17
dominion over your f. 2 Cor 1:24
having hope when your f. is. 10:15
after I heard of your f. Eph 1:15
on service of your f. Phil 2:17
since we heard of your f. Col 1:4
stedfastness of your f. in Christ. 2:5
your f. toward God. 1 Thes 1:8
comfort you concerning your f. 3:2
I sent to know your f. 5
Timothy brought tidings of your f. 6
comforted over you by your f. 7
perfect what is lacking in your f. 10
that your f. groweth. 2 Thes 1:3
trying of your f. worketh. Jas 1:3
the trial of your f. being. 1 Pet 1:7
end of your f. even salvation. 9
that your f. and hope might be. 21
add to your f. virtue, to. 2 Pet 1:5

faithful

Moses is f. in mine house.
Num 12:7; Heb 3:2, 5
the f. God who keepeth. Deut 7:9
raise me up a f. priest. 1 Sam 2:35
who is so f. as David ? 22:14
one of them f. in Israel. 2 Sam 20:19
Hananiah was a f. man. Neh 7:2
foundest his heart f. before. 9:8
for they were counted f. 13:13
for the f. fail from among. Ps 12:1
for Lord preserveth the f. 31:23
as a f. witness in heaven. 89:37
eyes shall be on the f. of. 101:6
all thy commandments are f. 119:86
testimonies righteous and very f. 138
a f. spirit concealeth. Pr 11:13
a f. ambassador is health. 13:17
a f. witness will not lie, but. 14:5
a f. man who can find ? 20:6
as snow in harvest, so is a f. 25:13
f. are the wounds of a friend. 27:6
a f. man shall abound with. 28:20
how is the f. city become ! Isa 1:21
afterwards be called f. city. 26
I took unto me f. witnesses. 8:2
because of the Lord that is f. 49:7
Lord be a f. witness. Jer 42:5
forasmuch as he was f. Dan 6:4
but Judah is f. with. Hos 11:12
who then is a f. and ? Mat 24:45
well done, thou good and f. 25:21
f. in a few things. 23; Luke 19:17
who then is that f. and ? Luke 12:42
is f. in the least is f. also. 16:10
not been f. in unrighteous. 11
have not been f. in what is. 12
judged me f. to Lord. Acts 16:15
God is f. by whom. 1 Cor 1:9; 10:13
in stewards, that a man be f. 4:2
sent you Timothy f. in Lord. 17
mercy of Lord to be f. 7:25†
blessed with f. Abraham. Gal 3:9
to the saints and f. in. Eph 1:1
Tychicus a f. minister. 6:21
saints and f. brethren. Col 1:2
Epaphras, for you f. minister. 7; 4:7
Onesimus, a f. brother. 4:9
f. is he that calleth you. 1 Thes 5:24
the Lord is f. who shall. 2 Thes 3:3
that he counted me f. 1 Tim 1:12
is a f. saying. 1 Tim 1:15; 4:9; Tit 3:8
must be sober, and f. 1 Tim 3:11
service because they are f. 6:2*
same commit to f. men. 2 Tim 2:2
it is a f. saying. 11
yet he abideth f. 13
blameless, having f. Tit 1:6*
holding fast the f. word. 9
might be a f. high priest. Heb 2:17
f. to him that appointed him. 3:2
is f. that promised. 10:23; 11:11
souls, as unto a f. 1 Pet 4:19
by Silvanus a f. brother. 5:12
he is f. to forgive us. 1 John 1:9
Christ the f. witness. Rev 1:5; 3:14
be f. unto death, I will give. 2:10
wherein Antipas was f. martyr. 13
with him, are called, and f. 17:14
that sat upon him was called F. 19:11
words are true and f. 21:5; 22:6

faithfully

for they dealt f. 2 Ki 12:15; 22:7
do in fear of Lord f. 2 Chr 19:9
they brought in offerings f. 31:12
the men did the work f. 34:12
the king that f. judgeth. Pr 29:14
him speak my word f. Jer 23:28
doest f. whatsoever thou. 3 John 5

faithfulness

render to every man f. 1 Sam 26:23
there is no f. in their mouth. Ps 5:9
thy f. reacheth unto clouds. 36:5
I have declared thy f. and. 40:10
or shall thy f. be declared ? 88:11
I will make known thy f. 89:1
thy f. shalt thou establish. 2
thy f. also in the congregation. 5
who is like to thee, or to thy f.? 8
but my f. and my mercy shall. 24
nor will I suffer my f. to fail. 33
good to shew forth thy f. 92:2
thou in f. hast afflicted me. 119:75
thy f. is unto all generations. 90
in thy f. answer me. 143:1
and f. the girdle of his. Isa 11:5
thy counsels of old are f. 25:1
great is thy f. Lam 3:23
betroth thee unto me in f. Hos 2:20

faithless

O f. generation. Mat 17:17
Mark 9:19; Luke 9:41
be not f. but believing. John 20:27

fall, *substantive*

haughty spirit before a f. Pr 16:18
righteous shall see their f. 29:16
moved at noise of their f. Jer 49:21
isles shake at sound of their f.
Ezek 26:15
isles tremble in day of thy f. 18
to shake at sound of his f. 31:16
for his life in day of thy f. 32:10
and great was the f. of it. Mat 7:27
child is set for the f. Luke 2:34
through their f. salvation. Rom 11:11
if the f. of them be riches of. 12

fall, *verb*

a deep sleep to f. upon. Gen 2:21
occasion against us, and f. 43:18
see that ye f. not out by way. 45:24
so that rider f. backward. 49:17
fear and dread shall f. Ex 15:16
dig a pit, ox or ass f. therein. 21:33
on whatsoever any f. Lev 11:32
if their carcase f. on any. 37, 38
lest land f. to whoredom. 19:29
they shall f. before you. 26:7, 8
shall f. when none pursueth. 36
shall f. one upon another. 37*
let them f. by the camp. Num 11:31
your carcases shall f. in. 14:29, 32
is the land that shall f. to. 34:2
if any man f. from. Deut 22:8
rise thou, and f. upon us. Judg 8:21
swear ye will not f. upon me. 15:12
and f. into the hand of the. 18
let f. some handfuls of. Ruth 2:16*
know how matter will f. 3:18
none of his words f. 1 Sam 3:19
not one hair of his head f. to. 14:45
2 Sam 14:11; 1 Ki 1:52; Acts 27:34
to make David f. 1 Sam 18:25
would not f. on the priests. 22:17

turn thou, and f. on priests. 1 Sam 22:18
therefore let not my blood f. 26:20
near and f. on him. 2 Sam 1:15
1 Ki 2:29, 31
let us f. into the hand of God, not f.
2 Sam 24:14; 1 Chr 21:13
shall persuade Ahab to go up and f.
1 Ki 22:20; 2 Chr 18:19
let us f. unto the host. 2 Ki 7:4
shall f. nothing of word of. 10:10
meddle, that thou shouldst f.? 14:10
f. to his master Saul. 1 Chr 12:19
till thy bowels f. out. 2 Chr 21:15
God shall make thee f. 25:8*
that thou shouldest f. and Judah. 19
thou hast begun to f. shall not prevail, but shalt surely f. Esth 6:13
not his dread f. upon you? Job 13:11
let thine arm f. from my. 31:22
let them f. by their own. Ps 5:10
mine enemies shall f. and. 9:3*
that the poor may f. by. 10:10
into that destruction let him f. 35:8
f. shall not be utterly cast. 37:24
arrows, whereby people f. 45:5
make their tongue to f. 64:8*
and he let it f. in midst of. 78:28
but ye shall f. like one of the. 82:7
a thousand shall f. at thy side. 91:7
thrust at me that I might f. 118:13
burning coals f. upon them. 140:10
let wicked f. into their own. 141:10
Lord upholdeth all that f. 145:14
unless they cause some to f. Pr 4:16
a prating fool shall f. 10:8, 10
the wicked shall f. by his. 11:5
where no counsel is people f. 14
trusteth in his riches shall f. 28
of the Lord shall f. therein. 22:14
wicked shall f. into mischief. 24:16*
whoso diggeth a pit shall f. therein.
26:27; Eccl 10:8
causeth to go astray shall f. Pr 28:10
that hardeneth his heart shall f. 14
he that is perverse shall f. at. 18
if they f. one will lift. Eccl 4:10
if the tree f. toward the south. 11:3
shall stumble and f. Isa 8:15
they shall f. under the slain. 10:4
and Lebanon shall f. by a. 34
nail fastened in sure place f. 22:25
fleeth from fear f. into pit. 24:18
the earth shall f. and not rise. 20
that they might go and f. 28:13
as a breach ready to f. 30:13
of slaughter, when towers f. 25
young men shall utterly f. 40:30
therefore mischiefs shall f. 47:11
whoso gather against shall f. 54:15
anger to f. on you. Jer 3:12*
f. amongst them that f. 6:15; 8:12
the fathers and sons shall f. 6:21*
shall they f. and not arise? 8:4
the carcases of men shall f. 9:22
I have caused him to f. 15:8
shall be driven out and f. 23:12
a whirlwind f. on head. 19*; 30:23*
be drunken, and spue, and f. 25:27
ye shall f. like a pleasant vessel. 34
it is false; I f. not away to. 37:14
shall all f. in the land of. 44:12*
they shall stumble and f. 46:6
made many to f. yea one. 16*
fleeth shall f. into the pit. 48:44
her young men f. in. 49:26; 50:30
most proud stumble and f. 50:32
the slain shall f. in land. 51:4, 47, 49
wall of Babylon shall f. 51:44
Babylon caused slain of Israel to f. 49
made my strength to f. Lam 1:14*
the slain shall f. in the. Ezek 6:7
that it shall f. and ye, O great hail-stones, shall f. and a. 13:11
foundation discovered, it shall f. 14
let no lot f. on it. 24:6
all thy company shall f. 27:27, 34
thou shalt f. upon. 29:5; 39:5
when slain shall f. in Egypt. 30:4
they that uphold Egypt shall f. 6
I will cause the sword to f. out. 22
I cause multitude to f. 32:12
not f. thereby in the day. 33:12
in all thy rivers shall they f. 35:8
steep places shall f., every wall shall f. Ezek 38:20
arrows to f. 39:3
shalt f. on the mountains. 4
they caused Israel to f. 44:12
this land shall f. to you for. 47:14
robbers of thy people shall f.
Dan 11:14
but he shall stumble and f. 19
when they shall f. 34
some f. to try them. 35
shalt thou f. in the day, the prophet also shall f. with thee. Hos 4:5*
that doth not understand shall f. 14*
and Ephraim f. Judah shall f. 5:5*
shall say to the hills, f. on us. 10:8
transgressors shall f. therein. 14:9
can a bird f. in a snare? Amos 3:5
the horns of the altar shall f. 14
even they shall f. and never. 8:14
shall not the least grain f. to. 9:9
rejoice not, when I f. Mi 7:8
they shall f. into mouth. Nah 3:12
not one sparrow f. to. Mat 10:29
if it f. into a pit on sabbath. 12:11
both shall f. into the ditch. 15:14
Luke 6:39
crumbs which f. from. Mat 15:27
whoso f. on this stone be broken, on whom it f. it. 21:44; Luke 20:18
and the stars shall f. from heaven.
Mat 24:29; Mark 13:25
Satan as lightning f. Luke 10:18
to say to mountains, f. on us. 23:30
except a corn f. into. John 12:24
fearing lest they should f. into.
Acts 27:17*
soldiers cut ropes and let her f. 32
shall not an hair f. from head. 34*
stumbled that they should f.
Rom 11:11
put an occasion to f. in his. 14:13
take heed lest he f. 1 Cor 10:12
he f. into condemnation. 1 Tim 3:6
a good report, lest he f. into. 7
they that be rich f. 6:9
lest any f. after the. Heb 4:11
fearful to f. into hands of. 10:31
when ye f. into temptation. Jas 1:2
lest ye f. into condemnation. 5:12
things ye shall never f. 2 Pet 1:10*
beware lest ye f. from your. 3:17
mountains and rocks, f. on. Rev 6:16
I saw a star f. from heaven. 9:1

fall *away*

of temptation f. away. Luke 8:13
if they f. away to renew. Heb 6:6

fall *down*

brother's ass f. down. Deut 22:4
of city shall f. down flat. Josh 6:5
David let his spittle f. down.
1 Sam 21:13
all kings shall f. down. Ps 72:11
that is holpen shall f. down. Isa 31:3
their host shall f. down as. 34:4
f. down to stock of a tree? 44:19
Sabeans shall f. down unto. 45:14
they f. down, they worship. 46:6
of Pharaoh f. down. Ezek 30:25
ye f. down and worship. Dan 3:5, 10
if ye f. down and worship image. 15
many shall f. down slain. 11:26
these things will I give thee, if thou wilt f. down. Mat 4:9; Luke 4:7
twenty-four elders f. down. Rev 4:10

fall, joined with *sword*

f. on us with pestilence or sword.
Ex 5:3
this land to f. by sword. Num 14:3
ye shall f. by the sword. 43
Sennacherib f. by sword. 2 Ki 19:7
they shall f. by the sword.
Ps 63:10*; Ezek 6:11
thy men shall f. by sword. Isa 3:25
every one shall f. by sword. 13:15
Assyrian f. with the sword. 31:8
I will cause him to f. by the sword in.
37:7; Jer 19:7
friends f. by sword. Jer 20:4
thou shalt not f. by the sword. 39:18
third part f. by sword. Ezek 5:12
that is near f. by the sword. 6:12
ye shall f. by the sword. 11:10
fugitives shall f. by sword.
Ezek 17:21
remnant shall f. by the sword. 23:25
and daughters f. by sword. 24:21
of Dedan shall f. by sword. 25:13
men in league f. by the sword. 30:5
tower of Syene, f. by the sword. 6
young men shall f. by the sword. 17
I will cause the sword to f. 22
in wastes shall f. by sword. 33:27
understand f. by sword. Dan 11:33
princes f. by the sword. Hos 7:16
Samaria shall f. by the sword. 13:16
when they f. on sword. Joel 2:8
sons and daughters f. by sword.
Amos 7:17
f. by edge of the sword. Luke 21:24

fallen

why is thy countenance f.? Gen 4:6
that hath his hair f. off. Lev 13:41
if thy brother be f. in decay. 25:35*
all Ai were f. on edge of. Josh 8:24
lord was f. down dead. Judg 3:25
inheritance had not f. unto. 18:1
the woman was f. at the. 19:27
Dagon was f. 1 Sam 5:3
a deep sleep f. 26:12
found Saul and his sons f. 31:8
1 Chr 10:8
not live after he was f. 2 Sam 1:10
mourned, because they were f. 12
there is a great man f. this. 3:38
now Elisha was f. sick. 2 Ki 13:14
dead bodies f. to earth. 2 Chr 20:24
our fathers have f. by sword. 29:9
Haman was f. on bed. Esth 7:4
brought down and f. Ps 20:8
there are workers of iniquity f. 36:12
how art thou f. from! Isa 14:12
nor inhabitants of world f. 26:18
f. by the sword. Ezek 32:22, 23, 24
hast f. by thine iniquity. Hos 14:1
of you have an ox f.? Luke 14:5
the Holy Ghost was f. Acts 8:16
Eutychus being f. into a. 20:9*
when we were all f. I heard. 26:14
lest they should have f. 27:29*
when Paul should have f. 28:6
f. out to the furtherance. Phil 1:12
from whence thou art f. Rev 2:5

are **fallen**

are f. and dead. 2 Sam 1:4
how are the mighty f.! 19, 25, 27
are f. under feet. 22:39; Ps 18:38
the lines are f. to me. Ps 16:6
terrors of death are f. upon. 55:4
midst whereof they are f. 57:6
reproaches of them are f. 69:9
the bricks are f. down. Isa 9:10
the Jews that are f. to. Jer 38:19
mighty men, they are f. 46:12
Babylon's foundations are f. 50:15
my virgins are f. by. Lam 2:21
his branches are f. his. Ezek 31:12
not lie with mighty that are f. 32:27
all their kings are f. Hos 7:7
some are f. asleep. 1 Cor 15:6, 18
ye are f. from grace. Gal 5:4
seven kings, five are f. Rev 17:10

is **fallen**

man whose hair is f. Lev 13:40
our lot is f. on this. Num 32:19
your terror is f. upon us. Josh 2:9
fire of God is f. from. Job 1:16
and is f. into the ditch. Ps 7:15
and Judah is f. Isa 3:8
for thy harvest is f. 16:9
Babylon is f. is f. 21:9
Rev 14:8; 18:2
truth is f. in the streets. Isa 59:14
the spoiler is f. on thy. Jer 48:32
Babylon is suddenly f. 51:8
crown is f. from our. Lam 5:16
lo, when the wall is f. Ezek 13:12
virgin of Israel is f. Amos 5:2
raise up tabernacle that is f. 9:11
for the cedar is f. Zech 11:2
tabernacle of David which is f.
Acts 15:16

fallest

f. away to Chaldeans. Jer 37:13

falleth

when there f. out any. Ex 1:10

vessel whereinto any f. Lev 11:33
whereupon their carcase f. 35
inheritance where lot f. Num 33:54
not fail one that f. on. 2 Sam 3:29
as a man f. before wicked men. 34
will light on him as dew f. 17:12
when deep sleep f. on men. Job 4:13
33:15
wicked messenger f. Pr 13:17
perverse tongue f. into. 17:20
a just man f. seven times. 24:16
rejoice not when thine enemy f. 17
to him alone when he f. Eccl 4:10
of men are snared when it f. 9:12
where tree f. there shall it be. 11:3
leaf f. off from vine. Isa 34:4*
and f. down thereto. 44:15, 17
he that f. to Chaldeans. Jer 21:9
whoso f. not down. Dan 3:6, 11
oft-times he f. into fire. Mat 17:15
a house divided f. Luke 11:17
give me the portion that f. 15:12
own master standeth or f. Rom 14:4
the flower thereof f. Jas 1:11
1 Pet 1:24

falling

f. into a trance. Num 24:4, 16
upholden him that was f. Job 4:4
the mountain f. cometh to. 14:18
deliver feet from f. Ps 56:13; 116:8
a righteous man f. Pr 25:26*
and as a f. fig from. Isa 34:4*
came trembling and f. Luke 8:47
great drops of blood f. down. 22:44
and Judas f. headlong. Acts 1:18
and f. into a place where. 27:41*
and so f. down, he. 1 Cor 14:25
except there come a f. 2 Thes 2:3
able to keep you from f. Jude 24*

fallow

break up your f. ground. Jer 4:3
Hos 10:12

see **deer**

false

shalt not raise a f. report. Ex 23:1
keep thee far from a f. matter. 7
it is f. tell us now. 2 Ki 9:12
my words shall not be f. Job 36:4
hate every f. way. Ps 119:104, 128
done to thee, thou f. tongue ? 120:3*
a f. balance is an. Pr 11:1
wicked doer giveth heed to f. 17:4*
and f. balance is not good. 20:23
whoso boasteth of a f. gift. 25:14
they prophesy a f. vision. Jer 14:14*
them that prophesy f. 23:32*
it is f. I fall not away. 37:14
have seen f. burdens. Lam 2:14*
them as a f. divination. Ezek 21:23*
love no f. oath. Zech 8:17
diviners have told f. dreams. 10:2
swift witness against f. Mal 3:5
there arise f. Christs and f. prophets.
Mat 24:24; Mark 13:22
taken by f. accusation. Luke 19:8*
for such are f. apostles. 2 Cor 11:13
in perils among f. brethren. 26
because of f. brethren. Gal 2:4
without affection, f. 2 Tim 3:3
they be not f. accusers. Tit 2:3*
f. teachers among you. 2 Pet 2:1

see **prophet**

false *prophets*

beware of f. prophets. Mat 7:15
many f. prophets rise. 24:11, 24
f. prophets shall rise. Mark 13:22
fathers to f. prophets. Luke 6:26
f. prophets among people. 2 Pet 2:1
f. prophets are gone out. 1 John 4:1

false *witness*

shalt not bear f. witness against thy.
Ex 20:16; Deut 5:20; Mat 19:18
if a f. witness rise up. Deut 19:16*
if witness be a f. witness. 18
a f. witness that speaketh. Pr 6:19
f. witness sheweth forth. 12:17; 14:5
f. witness not be unpunished. 19:5, 9
a f. witness shall perish. 21:28
man that beareth f. witness. 25:18
heart proceed f. witness. Mat 15:19
elders sought f. witness. 26:59
bare f. witness against him.
Mark 14:56, 57

false *witnesses*

f. witnesses are risen up. Ps 27:12
f. witnesses did rise. 35:11*
f. witnesses came, at last came two
f. witnesses. Mat 26:60
set up f. witnesses. Acts 6:13
f. witnesses of God. 1 Cor 15:15

falsehood

wrought f. against my. 2 Sam 18:13*
in answers remaineth f. Job 21:34
he hath brought forth f. Ps 7:14
them down, deceit is f. 119:118
is a right hand of f. 144:8, 11
under f. have we hid. Isa 28:15
are ye not a seed of f.? 57:4
words of f. 59:13
his molten image is f.
Jer 10:14; 51:17
forgotten me, and trusted in f. 13:25
they commit f. and thief. Hos 7:1
walking in spirit and f. Mi 2:11

falsely

thou wilt not deal f. Gen 21:23
was lost, sweareth f. Lev 6:3
which he hath sworn f. 5
neither deal f. nor lie. 19:11
shall not swear by my name f. 12
witness have testified f. Deut 19:18
nor have we dealt f. Ps 44:17
they swear f. Jer 5:2
prophets prophesy f. 31; 29:9
every one dealeth f. 6:13; 8:10
steal, murder, and swear f.? 7:9
thou speakest f. of Ishmael. 40:16
speakest f. the Lord hath. 43:2
swearing f. in making. Hos 10:4
house that sweareth f. Zech 5:4
say evil against you f. Mat 5:11
nor accuse any f. Luke 3:14*
oppositions of science, f. 1 Tim 6:20
f. accuse conversation. 1 Pet 3:16

falsifying

and f. the balances. Amos 8:5*

fame

f. heard in Pharaoh's. Gen 45:16
nations heard f. of thee. Num 14:15
Joshua's f. was noised. Josh 6:27
we heard the f. of God. 9:9
his f. was in all nations. 1 Ki 4:31
queen heard f. of. 10:1; 2 Chr 9:1
wisdom exceedeth f. 1 Ki 10:7
2 Chr 9:6
the f. of David went to. 1 Chr 14:17
house must be of f. and of. 22:5
Mordecai's f. went. Esth 9:4
heard f. with our ears. Job 28:22*
isles that have not heard my f.
Isa 66:19
have heard the f. our hands. Jer 6:24
and I will get them f. Zeph 3:19*
the f. of Jesus went. Mat 4:24*
Mark 1:28*; Luke 4:14, 37*; 5:15*
f. thereof went abroad. Mat 9:26
departed, spread abroad his f. 31
Herod heard of f. of Jesus. 14:1*

familiar

f. friends have forgotten. Job 19:14
my f. friend hath lifted up. Ps 41:9

familiar *spirit*

woman of a f. spirit. Lev 20:27
a f. spirit to enquire of her; a f. spirit
at Endor. 1 Sam 28:7
divine to me by the f. spirit. 8
of one that had f. spirit. 1 Chr 10:13
Manasseh dealt with a f. spirit.
2 Chr 33:6
of one that hath a f. spirit. Isa 29:4

familiar *spirits*

that have f. spirits. Lev 19:31
that turneth after f. spirits. 20:6
consulter with f. spirits. Deut 18:11
put away those that had f. spirits.
1 Sam 28:3
cut off those that have f. spirits. 9
Manasseh dealt with f. spirits.
2 Ki 21:6
workers with f. spirits Josiah. 23:24
say, seek f. spirits. Isa 8:19
to them that have f. spirits. 19:3

familiars

all my f. watched for. Jer 20:10*

families

isles of Gentiles divided after f.
Gen 10:5
were the f. of the Canaanites. 18
the sons of Ham after their f. 20
f. of Shem. 31
all f. of earth blessed. 12:3; 28:14
dukes of Esau according to f. 36:40
nourished brethren with f. 47:12
these be f. of Reuben. Ex 6:14
Num 26:7; Josh 13:15, 23
these are the f. of Simeon. Ex 6:15
Num 26:12, 14; Josh 19:1, 8
f. of Gershon. Ex 6:17; Num 3:18
21; 4:22, 24, 38, 40, 41; Josh 21:33
f. of Levi. Ex 6:19, 25; Num 4:46
26:57, 58; Josh 21:27; 1 Chr 6:19
lamb according to your f. Ex 12:21
of the f. of strangers. Lev 25:45
of Israel after their f. Num 1:2
sons of Kohath by their f. 3:19
27, 29, 30; 4:37; Josh 21:4, 10
sons of Merari, by f. Num 3:20, 33, 35
4:33, 42, 44, 45; Josh 21:34, 40
1 Chr 6:63
cut not off tribe of f. of. Num 4:18
heard them weep through f. 11:10
the f. of Gad. 26:15, 18
Josh 13:24, 28
the f. of Judah. Num 26:20, 22
Josh 15:1, 12, 20
sons of Issachar after f. Num 26:23
25; Josh 19:17, 23; 21:6
1 Chr 6:62; 7:5
f. of Zebulun. Num 26:26, 27
Josh 19:10, 16
Joseph after f. Num 26:28; 36:1
the f. of Manasseh. 26:34; 36:12
Josh 13:29; 17:2
Ephraim after f. Num 26:35, 37
Josh 16:5, 8; 21:5, 20; 1 Chr 6:66
of Benjamin after f. Num 26:38, 41
Josh 18:11, 20, 21; 1 Sam 10:21
sons of Dan after their f. Num 26:42
Josh 19.40, 48
sons of Asher after f. Num 26:44
Josh 19:24, 31
sons of Naphtali after f. Num 26:48
50; Josh 19:32
of Zelophehad of Manasseh's f.
Num 27:1
divide land by lot among f. 33:54
chief fathers of f. of Gilead. 36:1
come according to f. Josh 7:14
half children of Machir, by f. 13:31
tribe of Dan according to f. 19:40, 48
least of f. of Benjamin. 1 Sam 9:21
f. of Kirjath-jearim. 1 Chr 2:53
f. of scribes which dwelt at Jabez. 55
these are f. of Zorathites. 4:2
f. of them that wrought fine. 21
mentioned princes in their f. 38
according to divisions of the f.
2 Chr 35:5*, 12*
set people after their f. Neh 4:13
contempt of f. terrify me ? Job 31:34
God setteth solitary in f. Ps 68:6
maketh him f. like a flock. 107:41
I will call all the f. of. Jer 1:15
hear, all ye f. of the house. 2:4
fury on the f. that call not on. 10:25
I will take all f. of the north. 25:9
I will be God of all the f. of. 31:1
the two f. which Lord hath. 33:24
we will be as the f. of. Ezek 20:32
you have I known of all f. Amos 3:2
that selleth f. through. Nah 3:4
all the f. that remain. Zech 12:14
will not come up of the f. 14:17

family

my face against his f. Lev 20:5
return every man to his f. 25:10, 41
himself to stock of stranger's f. 47
his uncle or any of his f. may. 49
of Gershon was the f. Num 3:21
of Kohath was the f. of. 27
f. of Hanochites, f. of Palluites. 26:5
family *mentioned often to the*
59th verse
name done away from f.? 27:4
inheritance to next of his f. 11
marry to f. of father's. 36:6, 8, 12
lest a f. turn away. Deut 29:18

the *f*. which the Lord. Josh 7:14
took the *f*. of the Zarhites. 17
go man and all his *f*. Judg 1:25
my *f*. is poor in Manasseh. 6:15
communed with the *f*. of his. 9:1
Manoah a man of *f*. of the. 13:2
a Levite of the *f*. of Judah. 17:7
Danites sent of their *f*. five. 18:2
be a priest to a *f*. in Israel. 19
departed every man to his *f*. 21:24
a kinsman of the *f*. of. Ruth 2:1
f. least of Benjamin. 1 Sam 9:21
f. of Matri was taken. 10:21
my life, or my father's *f*. 18:18
yearly sacrifice for all *f*. 20:6, 29
whole *f*. is risen against. 2 Sam 14:7
a man of the *f*. of Saul. 16:5
neither did *f*. multiply. 1 Chr 4:27
to *f*. of Kohath cities. 6:61, 70
ark remained with *f*. of. 13:14
of Purim kept by every *f*. Esth 9:28
a city, and two of a *f*. Jer 3:14
chosen by residue of this evil *f*. 8:3
against *f*. I brought out. Amos 3:1
every *f*. mourn. Zech 12:12, 13, 14
if the *f*. of Egypt go not up. 14:18
whole *f*. in heaven and. Eph 3:15

famine

Famines of more or less intensity frequently occurred in Palestine because of its dependence upon the rain, and in Egypt because of its dependence on a proper overflow of the Nile. Not until modern times has it been possible to store rain, or to regulate the flow of rivers, to any appreciable extent. Famine also came naturally when locusts or other insects destroyed the crops. The worst famine named in the Bible is that in Egypt and the surrounding countries in the time of Joseph, Gen 41.

for the *f*. was grievous. Gen 12:10
a *f*. in land, besides first *f*. 26:1
empty ears seven years of *f*. 41:27
the *f*. shall consume the land. 30
not be known by reason of *f*. 31
to Joseph two sons before the *f*. 50
the *f*. was over all the face of. 56
land fainted by reason of *f*. 47:13
there was a *f*. Ruth 1:1
a *f*. in days of David. 2 Sam 21:1
shall seven years of *f*. come? 24:13
if there be in land *f*. 1 Ki 8:37
2 Chr 20:9
a sore *f*. in Samaria. 1 Ki 18:2
2 Ki 6:25
then *f*. is in the city. 2 Ki 7:4
the Lord hath called for a *f*. 8:1
the *f*. prevailed in Jerusalem. 25:3
you to die by *f*. 2 Chr 32:11
in *f*. he shall redeem thee. Job 5:20
at destruction and *f*. thou. 22
for want and *f*. were solitary. 30:3
keep them alive in *f*. Ps 33:19
in the days of *f*. they shall be. 37:19
he called for a *f*. on land. 105:16
I will kill thy root with *f*. Isa 14:30
destruction, *f*. and sword. 51:19
see sword, nor *f*. Jer 5:12; 14:13, 15
sword and *f*. shall prophets. 14:15
people cast out, because of *f*. 16
behold them that are sick with *f*. 18
as are for the *f*. to the *f*. 15:2
deliver up their children to *f*. 18:21
from *f*. to Nebuchadnezzar. 21:7
send the *f*. among. 24:10; 29:17
nation will I punish with the *f*. 27:8
persecute with sword and *f*. 29:18
to Chaldeans because of *f*. 32:24
a liberty for you to the *f*. 34:17
f. shall follow close after. 42:16
the *f*. was sore in the city. 52:6
was black, because of *f*. Lam 5:10
part consumed with *f*. Ezek 5:12
send on them evil arrows of *f*. 16
so will I send on you *f*. 17; 14:13
f. within, *f*. and pestilence. 7:15
leave a few men from *f*. 12:16
and I will lay no *f*. upon you. 36:29
receive no more reproach of *f*. 30
a *f*. not of bread, but of. Amos 8:11
great *f*. was through the. Luke 4:25
there arose a mighty *f*. 15:14
shall *f*. separate us from? Rom 8:35
in one day, death, *f*. Rev 18:8

by the **famine**

sons and daughters die *by the f*. Jer 11:22
consume them *by the f*. 14:12, 15
shall be consumed *by f*. 16:4
44:12, 18, 27
abideth in city die *by the f*. 21:9
why will ye die *by the f*.? 27:13
to king of Babylon *by the f*. 32:36
remaineth in city die *by f*. 38:2
Ezek 6:12
die *by f*. and pestilence. Jer 42:17
know that ye shall die *by the f*. 22
punished Jerusalem *by the f*. 44:13
they shall fall *by the f*. Ezek 6:11

famines

there shall be *f*. pestilences, and.
Mat. 24:7; Mark 13:8; Luke 21:11

famish *and* **famished**

all land of Egypt was *f*. Gen 41:55
suffer righteous to *f*. Pr 10:3
honourable men are *f*. Isa 5:13
he will *f*. all gods of the. Zeph 2:11

famous

princes *f*. in. Num 16:2*; 26:9*
thou *f*. in Beth-lehem. Ruth 4:11
his name may be *f*. in Israel. 14
were *f*. men. 1 Chr 5:24; 12:30
a man was *f*. as he had. Ps 74:5*
thanks to him who slew *f*. 136:18
and she became *f*. Ezek 23:10*
daughters of the *f*. nations. 32:18

fan, *substantive*

winnowed with the *f*. Isa 30:24
I will fan them with a *f*. Jer 15:7
whose *f*. is in his hand. Mat 3:12
Luke 3:17

fan, *verb*

shalt *f*. them, wind shall. Isa 41:16†
a dry wind not to *f*. nor. Jer 4:11†
I will *f*. them with a fan. 15:7
fanners that shall *f*. her. 51:2†

far

that be *f*. from thee to. Gen 18:25
you shall not go very *f*. Ex 8:28
keep thee *f*. from false matter. 23:7
if the place be too *f*. Deut 12:21
14:24
stranger come from a *f*. land. 29:22
waters stood very *f*. Josh 3:16
go not very *f*. from the city. 8:4
we are *f*. from you, when ye. 9:22
father adventured life *f*. Judg 9:17
f. from the Zidonians. 18:7, 28
by Jebus, day was *f*. spent. 19:11
f. be it from thee. 1 Sam 20:9
they carry them away *f*. 1 Ki 8:46
his name spread *f*. 2 Chr 26:15
now therefore be ye *f*. Ezra 6:6
separated one *f*. from. Neh 4:19
all Jews both nigh and *f*. Esth 9:20
children are *f*. from safety. Job 5:4
put iniquity *f*. away. 11:14; 22:23
f. be it from God to do. 34:10
judgements are *f*. out of. Ps 10:5
why art thou so *f*. from? 22:1
they that are *f*. from thee. 73:27
thou art exalted *f*. above all. 97:9
as *f*. as the east is from the west, so
f. hath he removed. 103:12
let blessing be *f*. from him. 109:17
that follow mischief are *f*. 119:150
salvation is *f*. from wicked. 155
perverse lips put *f*. from. Pr 4:24
remove thy way *f*. from her. 5:8
Lord is *f*. from wicked. 15:29
his friends go *f*. from him. 19:7
his soul shall be *f*. from them. 22:5
rod of correction shall drive it *f*. 15
price is *f*. above rubies. 31:10
as *f*. as light excelleth. Eccl 2:13
Lord have removed men *f*. Isa 6:12
shall turn the rivers *f*. away. 19:6
removed the nations *f*. 26:15
hear ye that are *f*. from. 46:12
swallowed thee be *f*. away. 49:19
shalt be *f*. from oppression. 54:14
therefore is judgement *f*. from. 59:9
thou art *f*. from their. Jer 12:2
all the kings of the north *f*. 25:26
to remove you *f*. from land. 27:10
upon all cities of Moab *f*. or. 48:24
thus *f*. is judgement of Moab. 47
thus *f*. are words of Jeremiah. 51:64
my soul *f*. from peace. Lam 3:17
have I set it *f*. from. Ezek 7:20
said, get ye *f*. from Lord. 11:15
the fourth king *f*. richer. Dan 11:2
ye might remove them *f*. Joel 3:6
that put *f*. away evil day. Amos 6:3
in that day decree be *f*. Mi 7:11
be it *f*. from thee, Lord. Mat 16:22
when day was now *f*. Mark 6:35
not *f*. from the kingdom of. 12:34
is as a man taking *f*. journey. 13:34
was not *f*. from house. Luke 7:6
Jesus said, suffer ye thus *f*. 22:51
abide with us, for day is *f*. 24:29
led them out as *f*. as to. 50
were not *f*. from land. John 21:8
travelled as *f*. as Phenice. Acts 11:19
Barnabas go as *f*. as Antioch. 22
he be not *f*. from every one. 17:27
I will send thee *f*. hence to. 22:21
came to meet us as *f*. as. 28:15
the night is *f*. spent, the. Rom 13:12
a *f*. more exceeding. 2 Cor 4:17
we are come as *f*. as to you. 10:14
f. above all principality. Eph 1:21
that ascended up *f*. above all. 4:10
Christ, which is *f*. better. Phil 1:23
it is yet *f*. more evident. Heb 7:15*
see **country, countries**

far *from me*

saith, be it *f. from me*. 1 Sam 2:30
22:15; 2 Sam 20:20; 23:17
withdraw hand *f. from me*. Job 13:21
my brethren *f. from me*. 19:13
of wicked *f. from me*. 21:16; 22:18
they flee *f. from me*. 30:10
not *f. from me*, for trouble. Ps 22:11
19; 35:22; 38:21; 71:12
hide not thy face *f. from me*. 27:9
mine acquaintance *f. from me*. 88:8
lover and friend *f. from me*. 18
remove *f. from me* vanity. Pr 30:8
but it was *f. from me*. Eccl 7:23
their heart *f. from me*. Isa 29:13
they are gone *f. from me*. Jer 2:5
comforter is *f. from me*. Lam 1:16
of kings *f. from me*. Ezek 43:9
Levites gone *f. from me*. 44:10
heart is *f. from me*. Mat 15:8
Mark 7:6

from **far**

against thee *from f*. Deut 28:49
Jer 5:15
fetch my knowledge *from f*. Job 36:3
up an ensign *from f*. Isa 5:26
which shall come *from f*. 10:3
bound which are fled *from f*. 22:3
name of Lord cometh *from f*. 30:27
bring my sons *from f*. 43:6; 60:9
hearken, ye people, *from f*. 49:1
these shall come *from f*. 12
thy sons shall come *from f*. 60:4
I will save thee *from f*. Jer 30:10
for men to come *from f*. Ezek 23:40
horsemen shall come *from f*.
Hab 1:8
divers of them came *from f*.
Mark 8:3

far *off*

gone, and not yet *f. off*. Gen 44:4
shall pitch *f. off* about. Num 2:2
gods of people *f. off*. Deut 13:7
do to all the cities *f. off*. 20:15
neither is commandment *f. off*. 30:11
king tarried in a place *f. off*.
2 Sam 15:17
captives to a land *f. off*. 2 Chr 6:36
lo, I would wander *f. off*. Ps 55:7
than a brother *f. off*. Pr 27:10
f. off who can find out? Eccl 7:24
they shall flee *f. off*. Isa 17:13
hear, ye that are *f. off*. 33:13
shall behold land that is *f. off* 17
righteousness not be *f. off*. 46:13
send thy messengers *f. off*. 57:9
peace to him that is *f. off*. 19
look for salvation, it is *f. off*. 59:11

he that is *f. off* shall die. *Ezek* 6:12
that I should go *f. off*. 8:6
although I cast them *f. off*. 11:16
prophesieth of times *f. off*. 12:27
those that be *f. off* from thee. 22:5
to Israel near and *f. off*. *Dan* 9:7
I will remove *f. off* the. *Joel* 2:20
sell them to Sabeans *f. off*. 3:8
her that was cast *f. off*. *Mi* 4:7
f. off shall come and. *Zech* 6:15
ye who were *f. off* made. *Eph* 2:13

fare

look how thy brethren *f.* *1 Sam* 17:18

fare

so he paid the *f.* thereof. *Jonah* 1:3

fared

the rich man *f.* *Luke* 16:19

farewell

first go bid them *f.* at. *Luke* 9:61
yourselves, ye do well, *f.* *Acts* 15:29
Paul bade them *f.* saying. 18:21
they had to say against him, *f.* 23:30
finally, brethren, *f.* be. *2 Cor* 13:11

farm

their ways, one to his *f.* *Mat* 22:5

farther

f. though a wise man. *Eccl* 8:17
f. and fell on his face. *Mat* 26:39
had gone a little *f.* thence. *Mark* 1:19
see **further**

farthing, -s

paid the uttermost *f.* *Mat* 5:26
two sparrows sold for a *f.*? 10:29†
in two mites, a *f.* *Mark* 12:42
sparrows sold for two *f.*? *Luke* 12:6†

fashion

this is the *f.* thou shalt. *Gen* 6:15*
f. of the tabernacle. *Ex* 26:30
bowls made he after the *f.* 37:19*
according to all the *f.* *1 Ki* 6:38
Ahaz sent the *f.* of. *2 Ki* 16:10
shew them form and *f.* *Ezek* 43:11
never saw it on this *f.* *Mark* 2:12
f. of his countenance. *Luke* 9:29
tabernacle according to *f.* *Acts* 7:44*
f. of this world passeth. *1 Cor* 7:31
found in *f.* as a man. *Phil* 2:8
grace of *f.* of it perisheth. *Jas* 1:11

fashion

one *f.* us in the womb? *Job* 31:15

fashioned

Aaron *f.* the calf. *Ex* 32:4
thine hands have *f.* me. *Job* 10:8
Ps 119:73
in continuance were *f.* *Ps* 139:16
respect to him that *f.* it. *Isa* 22:11
thy breasts are *f.*, thine. *Ezek* 16:7
that it may be *f.* like. *Phil* 3:21*

fashioneth

he *f.* their hearts alike. *Ps* 33:15
the smith *f.* it with the. *Isa* 44:12
clay say to him that *f.* it? 45:9

fashioning

not *f.* yourselves to. *1 Pet* 1:14

fashions

were according to *f.* *Ezek* 42:11

fast, *adverb*

the Lord had *f.* closed. *Gen* 20:18
Sisera was *f.* asleep and. *Judg* 4:21
but we will bind thee *f.* 15:13
if they bind me *f.* with. 16:11*
here *f.* by my maidens. *Ruth* 2:8
Boaz said to me, keep *f.* by. 21
this work goeth *f.* on. *Ezra* 5:8*
clods cleave *f.* together. *Job* 38:38
he commanded, it stood *f.* *Ps* 33:9
his strength setteth *f.* 65:6
f. hold of instruction. *Pr* 4:13
of Moab hasteth *f.* *Jer* 48:16
took captives held them *f.* 50:33
in ship, and was *f.* asleep. *Jonah* 1:5
who made their feet *f.* *Acts* 16:24
forepart stuck *f.* remained. 27:41*

fast

Fasting has, in all ages, and among all nations, been much in use in times of mourning, sorrow, and afflictions. It is in some sort inspired by nature, which, in these circumstances, denies itself nourishment, and takes off the edge of hunger. There is no example of fasting, properly so called, to be seen before Moses; yet it is presumable that the patriarchs fasted, since we see that there were very great mournings among them, such as that of Abraham for Sarah, Gen 23:2; *and that of Jacob for his son Joseph,* Gen 37:34.

Moses enjoins no particular fast, excepting that upon the day of atonement, which was generally and strictly observed, Lev 23:27, 29. *Since the time of Moses, examples of fasting have been very common among the Jews. Joshua and the elders of Israel remained prostrate before the ark from morning until evening, without eating, after the Israelites were defeated by the men of Ai,* Josh 7:6. *The eleven tribes which had taken arms against that of Benjamin, seeing they could not hold out against the inhabitants of Gibeah, fell down before the ark upon their faces, and so continued till the evening without eating,* Judg 20:26. *The Israelites perceiving themselves to be pressed by the Philistines, assembled before the Lord at Mizpeh, and fasted in his presence till the evening,* 1 Sam 7:6. *And David fasted while the first child he had by Bath-sheba, the wife of Uriah, was sick,* 2 Sam 12:16.

Moses fasted forty days on mount Horeb, Ex 34:28. *Elijah passed as many days without eating any thing,* 1 Ki 19:8. *And our Saviour fasted in the wilderness forty days and forty nights,* Mat 4:2. *These fasts were out of the common rules of nature.*

It does not appear by our Saviour's own practice, or any commands that he gave to his disciples, that he instituted any particular fasts, or enjoined any to be kept out of pure devotion. It is however inferred from such statements as those in Luke 5:33–35, *that he expected his followers would do so. The one condition he made was that it be sincere,* Mat. 6:16.

proclaim a *f.*, set Naboth. *1 Ki* 21:9
they proclaimed a *f.* and set. 12
Jehoshaphat proclaimed a *f.*
2 Chr 20:3
Ezra proclaimed a *f.* at. *Ezra* 8:21
in the day of your *f.* you. *Isa* 58:3
such *f.* I have chosen? call this *f.*? 5
is not this *f.* that I have chosen? 6
they proclaimed a *f.* *Jer* 36:9
sanctify a *f.* *Joel* 1:14; 2:15
Nineveh proclaimed a *f.* *Jonah* 3:5
f. of the fourth month, of. *Zech* 8:19
f. was now already past. *Acts* 27:9

fast, *verb*

thou didst *f.* and weep. *2 Sam* 12:21
is dead, wherefore should I *f.*? 23
I and my maidens *f.* *Esth* 4:16
ye *f.* for strife, not *f.* as. *Isa* 58:4
when they *f.* I will not. *Jer* 14:12
did ye at all *f.* unto me? *Zech* 7:5
f. be not as hypocrites of a sad . . .
appear to men to *f.* *Mat* 6:16
thou appear not to men to *f.* 18
why do we *f.* disciples *f.* not? 9:14
Mark 2:18
then shall they *f.* *Mat* 9:15
Mark 2:20; *Luke* 5:35
disciples of John used to *f.*
Mark 2:18
f. while bridegroom with them? they cannot *f.* 19; *Luke* 5:35
of John *f.* often? *Luke* 5:33
I *f.* twice in the week. 18:12

fasted

the people *f.* that day. *Judg* 20:26
drew water, and *f.* *1 Sam* 7:6
buried them, and *f.* seven days. 31:13
1 Chr 10:12
and *f.* for Saul. *2 Sam* 1:12
David *f.* 12:16
while the child was alive I *f.* 22
Ahab *f.* *1 Ki* 21:27
so we *f.* *Ezra* 8:23
Nehemiah *f.* and prayed. *Neh* 1:4
why have we *f.* say they? *Isa* 58:3
when ye *f.* in fifth and. *Zech* 7:5
Jesus *f.* forty days and. *Mat* 4:2
ministered to Lord and *f.* *Acts* 13:2
when they had *f.* they laid hands. 3

fasten

shalt *f.* the chains. *Ex* 28:14*, 25*
to *f.* the plate on high. 39:31
I will *f.* him as a nail. *Isa* 22:23
they *f.* it with nails. *Jer* 10:4

fastened

ends of chains they *f.* *Ex* 39:18*
Moses *f.* his sockets, set up. 40:18*
Jael *f.* the nail into. *Judg* 4:21*
Delilah *f.* it with a pin, and. 16:14
f. Saul's body to wall. *1 Sam* 31:10
with a sword *f.* upon. *2 Sam* 20:8
beams should not be *f.* *1 Ki* 6:6*
f. his head in temple. *1 Chr* 10:10
six steps were *f.* to. *2 Chr* 9:18
hangings *f.* with cords of. *Esth* 1:6
are the foundations *f.* *Job* 38:6
as nails *f.* by masters. *Eccl* 12:11
nail *f.* in the sure place. *Isa* 22:25
f. it with nails that it should. 41:7
within were hooks *f.* *Ezek* 40:43
the eyes of all were *f.* on. *Luke* 4:20
when I had *f.* mine eyes. *Acts* 11:6
a viper out of heat and *f.* on. 28:3

fastening

Peter *f.* his eyes upon him. *Acts* 3:4

fastest

thou *f.* anoint thy head. *Mat* 6:17

fasting

were assembled with *f.* *Neh* 9:1
decree came, was *f.* *Esth* 4:3
humbled my soul with *f.* *Ps* 35:13
and chastened soul with *f.* 69:10
knees are weak through *f.* 109:24
words of Lord on the *f.* *Jer* 36:6
king passed the night *f.* *Dan* 6:18
himself to seek by prayer and *f.* 9:3
turn ye with *f.* weeping. *Joel* 2:12
not send them away *f.* *Mat* 15:32
goeth not out but by *f.* 17:21
Mark 9:29
if I send them away *f.* *Mark* 8:3
four days ago I was *f.* *Acts* 10:30
ordained elders, and prayed *f.* 14:23
fourteenth day ye continued *f.* 27:33
may give yourselves to *f.* *1 Cor* 7:5

fastings

the matters of the *f.* *Esth* 9:31
Anna served God with *f.* *Luke* 2:37
approving ourselves in *f.* *2 Cor* 6:5
in *f.* often, in cold and. 11:27

fat

The Mosaic law declared that to the Lord belongs all the fat of sacrificial animals, Lev 3:16, 17. *Neither it nor the blood was eaten, but was burned as an offering to God,* Ex 29:13, 22; Lev 4:8, 9. *The ground of this law was that the fat was the richest part of the animal, and therefore belonged to God.*

The word is used figuratively to mean the best part of a thing, or the richest productions, Neh 9:25; Ps 63:5; Isa 25:6; Rom 11:17.

Abel also brought of *f.* *Gen* 4:4
the *f.* of sacrifice remain. *Ex* 23:18
take *f.* that covereth the inwards, and *f.* upon kidneys. 29:13, 22
Lev 3:3, 4, 9, 10, 14, 15; 4:8; 7:3, 4
head and *f.* in order. *Lev* 1:8, 12
sweet savour, the *f.* is Lord's. 3:16
he shall take off the *f.* of. 4:8, 31, 35
burn his *f.* 26; 6:12; 7:3, 31; 17:6
Num 18:17
f. of beast dieth of itself. *Lev* 7:24
the *f.* with breast, it shall he. 30

he that offereth f. shall have. Lev 7:33
Moses burnt head and f. of. 8:20
one wafer and put them on f. 26
but the f. he burnt. 9:10, 20
fire from Lord consumed f. 24
the f. of sin offering shall. 16:25
f. of lambs with f. of Deut 32:14
and the f. closed upon. Judg 3:22
before they burnt f. 1 Sam 2:15
let them not fail to burn the f. 16
to hearken is better than f. of. 15:22
from f. of mighty. 2 Sam 1:22
altar too little to receive f. 1 Ki 8:64
offered f. of. 2 Chr 7:7; 29:35
priests busied in offering f. 35:14
he maketh collops of f. Job 15:27
inclosed in their own f. Ps 17:10
enemies of Lord as the f. of. 37:20
full of f. of fed beasts. Isa 1:11
made f. with the f. of kidneys. 34:6
nor hast filled me with f. of. 43:24
when ye offer the f. and. Ezek 44:7
stand to offer to me the f. 15

fat, *adjective*

came seven kine f. Gen 41:2
did eat up seven f. kine. 4, 20
out of Asher bread shall be f. 49:20
land is, whether f. or. Num 13:20
waxen f. then they turn. Deut 31:20
f. and kicked, thou waxen f. 32:15
Eglon was a very f. man. Judg 3:17
to make yourselves f. 1 Sam 2:29
the woman had a f. calf. 28:24
Adonijah slew f. cattle. 1 Ki 1:9
19, 25
provision for one day ten f. 4:23
they found f. pasture. 1 Chr 4:40
a f. land became f. Neh 9:25
not served thee in large and f. 35
that be f. on earth shall. Ps 22:29
shall be f. and flourishing. 92:14*
their heart as f. as grease. 119:70
soul shall be made f. Pr 11:25
soul of diligent be made f. 13:4
a good report maketh bones f. 15:30
in Lord shall be made f. 28:25
waste places of f. ones. Isa 5:17
make heart of this people f. 6:10
Lord shall send among his f. 10:16
make a feast of f. things. 25:6
on the head of f. valleys. 28:1
on the head of the f. valley. 4
and bread shall be f. and. 30:23
sword of Lord is made f. 34:6
and their dust shall be made f. 7
Lord shall make f. thy. 58:11*
they are waxen f. they. Jer 5:28
grown f. as the heifer at. 50:11*
in a f. pasture shall feed. Ezek 34:14
but I will destroy the f. and. 16
I will judge between the f. 20
one lamb out of f. pastures. 45:15†
offering of f. beasts. Amos 5:22
by them their portion is f. Hab 1:16

eat **fat**

and ye shall eat the f. Gen 45:18
a statute that ye eat no f.
Lev 3:17; 7:23
whoso eateth f. of the beast. 7:25
which did eat the f. Deut 32:38
eat the f. and drink sweet. Neh 8:10
ye eat f. and clothe you. Ezek 34:3
eat f. till ye be full and. 39:19
eat the flesh of the f. Zech 11:16

father

In addition to its common use, this word is also used [1] *in the sense of seniors,* Acts 7:2; 22:1; *and of parents in general, or ancestors,* Dan 5:2; Jer 27:7; Mat 23:30, 32. [2] *The founder of a trade or profession, and the head of the inhabitants of a town,* Gen 4:20–22; 1 Chr 2:51; 4:14, 18. [3] *God, either as the Creator of the human race or as the loving guardian of his spiritual children, or in his relation to Jesus Christ,* Mal 2:10; Rom 8:15; Mark 14:36.

Jabal was f. of such as. Gen 4:20
Jubal was the f. of all such as. 21
and Ham is the f. of. 9:18
f. of nations. 17:4, 5; Rom 4:17, 18
have ye a f.? Gen 44:19
and we said, we have a f. 20
God made me f. to Pharaoh. 45:8
whose f. was an Egyptian. Lev 24:10
as a nursing f. beareth. Num 11:12
statutes between f. and. 30:16
f. shall bring forth. Deut 22:15
man give damsel's f. fifty. 29
of house of mother's f. Judg 9:1
with me, and be to me a f. 17:10
go with us, and be to us a f. 18:19
the f. of the damsel saw him. 19:3
damsel's f. retained him, he. 4
Kish was the f. of Saul. 1 Sam 9:3
14:51
Salem the f. of. 1 Chr 2:51
of Hemath the f. of house of. 55
Joab the f. of the valley of. 4:14
at Gibeon dwelt f. of. 8:29; 9:35
Esther had neither f. nor. Esth 2:7
I was a f. to the poor. Job 29:16
up with me, as with a f. 31:18
hath the rain a f.? 38:28
f. of fatherless, and judge. Ps 68:5
as a f. pitieth his children. 103:13
correcteth, even as a f. Pr 3:12
hear the instruction of a f. 4:1
son maketh a glad f. 10:1; 15:20
f. of a fool hath no joy. 17:21
f. of the righteous rejoice. 23:24
called, the everlasting F. Isa 9:6
Eliakim shall be a f. to. 22:21
the f. to child shall make. 38:19
for I am a f. to Israel. Jer 31:9
as the soul of the f. so. Ezek 18:4
son bear the iniquity of f.? 19
son shall not bear iniquity of f. 20
in thee they set light by f. 22:7
for f. or mother they may. 44:25
the son dishonoureth f. Mi 7:6
if I then be a f. where? Mal 1:6
have we not all one f.? 2:10
f. deliver up the child. Mat 10:21
Mark 13:12
he that loveth f. or. Mat 10:37
I thank thee, O F. Lord of. 11:25
so F. it seemed good. 26; Luke 10:21
John 11:41
knoweth Son, but the F. Mat 11:27
that curseth f. let him die. 15:4
Mark 7:10
leave f. and mother, and. Mat 19:5
that hath forsaken f. mother, or.
29; Mark 10:29
baptizing in name of F. Mat 28:19
taketh f. of damsel. Mark 5:40
Luke 8:51
the f. of the child cried. Mark 9:24
knoweth no man, but the F. 13:32
Abba, F., all things are. 14:36
Simon f. of Alexander. 15:21
no man knows who F. is. Luke 10:22
ask bread of any that is a f. 11:11
f. shall be divided against the son, the son against the f. 12:53
f. I have sinned against. 15:21
f. said, bring forth best robe. 22
I pray thee, f. send to my. 16:27
F. if thou be willing, remove. 22:42
F. forgive them, they know. 23:34
F. into thy hands I commend. 46
of the only begotten of F. John 1:14
Son which is in bosom of the F. 18
the F. loveth the Son. 3:35; 5:20
nor at Jerusalem worship F. 4:21
shall worship the F. in spirit. 23
the f. knew that it was at the. 53
but what he seeth F. do. 5:19
for as the F. raiseth up dead. 21
F. judgeth no man, but hath. 22
they honour the F.: he that honoureth not Son, honoureth not F. 23
for as the F. hath life in himself. 26
seek not mine own, but will of F. 30
works which F. hath given me bear witness that the F. hath sent. 36
F. which sent me, hath borne. 37
8:16; 12:49; 14:24; 1 John 4:14
think not that I accuse you to the F.
John 5:45
him hath God the F. sealed. 6:27
all that the F. giveth me shall. 37
and this is the F.'s will, that. 39
is not this Jesus, whose f. and? 42
no man can come, except F.
John 6:44
that hath learned of the F. 45
any hath seen F. he hath seen F. 46
F. hath sent me, and I live by F. 57
not alone, but I and the F. 8:16
the F. that sent me beareth. 18
understood not he spake of F. 27
F. hath not left me alone. 29
we have one F. even God. 41
devil is a liar, and the f. of it. 44
F. knoweth me, so know I F. 10:15
say ye of him whom the F. 36
believe that the F. is in me. 38
F. save me from this hour. 12:27
F. glorify thy name; then came. 28
even as the F. said unto me. 50
he should depart unto F. 13:1
knowing that the F. had given all. 3
I am the way, truth, and life, no man cometh to the F. but by me. 14:6
Lord, shew us the F. and. 8
hath seen me, hath seen the F. 9
I am in the F. and F. in. 11; 17:21
that the F. may be glorified. 14:13
I will pray the F. for you. 16; 16:26
Comforter whom the F. will. 14:26
I love the F.: as the F. gave me. 31
as the F. hath loved me, so. 15:9
whatsoever ye shall ask of the F. in my name, he may. 16; 16:23
from the F. the Spirit who proceedeth from the F. 15:26
they have not known the F. 16:3
all things that the F. hath are. 15
because I go the the F. 16, 17
shew you plainly of the F. 25
the F. loveth you, because ye. 27
forth from the F. and go to the F. 28
not alone, because the F. is. 32
F. the hour is come. 17:1
O F. glorify thou me with. 5
Holy F. keep those whom thou. 11
F. I will that they also, whom. 24
O righteous F. the world hath. 25
for promise of the F. Acts 1:4
the F. hath put in his own power. 7
received of the F. the promise. 2:33
he might be f. of all. Rom 4:11
and the f. of circumcision to them. 12
faith of Abraham, the f. of. 16
raised from the dead by the F. 6:4
whereby we cry, Abba, F. 8:15
are beloved for F.'s sake. 11:28
glorify God the F. of our. 15:6
2 Cor 1:3; 11:31; Eph 1:3
1 Pet 1:3
but one God, the F. 1 Cor 8:6
up kingdom to God the F. 15:24
F. of mercies, the God. 2 Cor 1:3
I will be a F. unto you. 6:18
Paul an apostle by Jesus Christ and God the F. Gal 1:1
peace from God the F. 3; 2 Tim 1:2
Tit 1:4
will of God and our F. Gal 1:4
until time appointed of the F. 4:2
Spirit into your hearts, crying, F. 6
our Lord Jesus, the F. Eph 1:17
access by one Spirit to the F. 2:18
for this cause I bow unto F. 3:14
one God and F. of all. 4:6
giving thanks to the F. 5:20
Col 1:3, 12; 3:17
faith from God the F. Eph 6:23
to the glory of the F. Phil 2:11
as a son with the f. he hath. 22
it pleased F. that in him. Col 1:19
of the mystery of the F. 2:2
church which is in God F. 1 Thes 1:1
we charged you, as a f. doth. 2:11
entreat him as a f. 1 Tim 5:1
will be to him a F. Heb 1:5
Melchisedec without f. 7:3
whom the F. chasteneth not? 12:7
be in subjection to F. of spirits. 9
good gift cometh from F. Jas 1:17
religion before God and F. 27
therewith bless God, even F. 3:9
foreknowledge of God F. 1 Pet 1:2
if ye call on the F. who. 17
received from God the F. 2 Pet 1:17
life, which was with F. 1 John 1:2
our fellowship is with the F. 3

father—the F. that dwelleth in me, He doeth the works. John 14:10

have an Advocate with the *F.*
1 John 2:1
because ye have known the *F.* 13
the love of *F.* is not in him. 15
pride of life is not of the *F.* 16
he is antichrist that denieth *F.* 22
denieth the Son, hath not *F.*: he that
acknowledgeth Son hath *F.* 23
continue in Son and in the *F.* 24
what manner of love *F.* hath. 3:1
three bear record, *F.* the Word. 5:7
the *F.* and from Lord Jesus Christ
the Son of the *F.* *2 John* 3
a commandment from the *F.* 4
he that abideth in Christ hath *F.* 9
sanctified by God the *F.* *Jude* 1
see **Abraham**

her **father**

in and lay with her *f.* *Gen* 19:33
Rachel came with *her f.'s.* 29:9
her f.'s brother, told *her f.* 12
images that were *her f.'s.* 31:19
Tamar dwelt in *her f.'s.* 38:11
if *her f.* utterly refuse. *Ex* 22:17
she profaneth *her f.* *Lev* 21:9
returned to *her f.'s* house as in youth,
shall eat of *her f.'s* meat. 22:13
her f. had but spit in. *Num* 12:14
woman vow a vow in *her f.'s.* 30:3
and *her f.* hear her, and shall hold. 4
if *her f.* disallow her in the day. 5
her youth, in *her f.'s* house. 16
wife to one of tribe of *her f.* 36:8
bewail *her f.* and mother a month.
Deut 21:13
to door of *her f.'s* house, to play
whore in *her f.'s* house. 22:21
brought Rahab and *her f.* *Josh.* 6:23
he saved *her f.'s* household. 25
to ask of *her f.* a field. 15:18
Judg 1:14
months returned to *her f.* *Judg* 11:39
but *her f.* would not suffer. 15:1
Philistines burnt her and *her f.* 6
brought him into *her f.'s.* 19:3
when *her f.* and *mother.* *Esth* 2:7

his **father**

shall a man leave *his f.* and mother.
Gen 2:24; *Mark* 10:7; *Eph* 5:31
saw nakedness of *his f.* *Gen* 9:22
Haran died before *his f.* 11:28
blessing wherewith *his f.* 27:41
Jacob obeyed *his f.* and. 28:7
Jacob sware by fear of *his f.* 31:53
in the land wherein *his f.* 37:1
Joseph brought to *his f.* their. 2
told the dream to *his f. his f.* 10
brethren envied, but *his f.* 11
rid him, to deliver him to *his f.* 22
the lad cannot leave *his f.* 44:22
sacrifices to the God of *his f.* 46:1
went up to meet Israel *his f.* 29
Joseph nourished *his f.* and. 47:12
made a mourning for *his f.* 50:10
Amram took *his f.'s* sister. *Ex* 6:20
he that smiteth *his f.* shall. 21:15
curseth *his f.* shall die. 17; *Lev* 20:9
fear every man his mother and *his f.*
Lev 19:3
man that lieth with *his f.'s.* 20:11
if a man take *his f.'s* daughter. 17
of Aaron be defiled for *his f.* 21:2
priest not defile himself for *his f.* 11
Nazarite not unclean for *his f.*
Num 6:7
inheritance to *his f.'s.* 27:10
if *his f.* have no brethren. 11
will not obey *his f.* *Deut* 21:18
his f. bring him to the elders. 19
man shall not take *his f.'s.* 22:30
he that setteth light by *his f.* 27:16
lieth with daughter of *his f.* 22
said to *his f.* I have not seen. 33:9
Gideon feared *his f.'s.* *Judg* 6:27
buried in sepulchre of *his f.* 8:32
wickedness he did to *his f.* 9:56
his f. knew not that it was of. 14:4
Jonathan told not *his f.* *1 Sam* 14:1
heard not when *his f.* charged. 27
spake good of David to *his f.* 19:4
it was determined of *his f.* 20:33
because *his f.* had done shame. 34
in sepulchre of *his f.* *2 Sam* 2:32

I will be *his f.* and he. *2 Sam* 7:14
as *his f.* shewed kindness. 10:2
1 Chr 19:2
Absalom went in unto *his f.'s.*
2 Sam 16:22
Ahithophel buried in sepulchre of *his
f.* 17:23
Saul buried in sepulchre of *his f.*
21:14
his f. was a man of Tyre. *1 Ki* 7:14
2 Chr 2:14
his f. had dedicated. *1 Ki* 7:51
15:15; *2 Chr* 15:18
as heart of David *his f.* *1 Ki* 11:4
Solomon went not fully after Lord,
as did David *his f.* 6; 15:11
2 Ki 18:3; *2 Chr* 28:1; 29:2
not as did David *his f.* *1 Ki* 11:33
2 Ki 14:3; 16:2
walked in all sins of *his f.* *1 Ki* 15:3
Nadab did evil and walked in way of
his f. 26; 22:43, 52; *2 Ki* 21:21
did evil, not like *his f.* *2 Ki* 3:2
together after Ahab *his f.* 9:25
cities taken out of hand of *his f.*
13:25
son of Joash, slew servants who had
slain *his f.* 14:5; *2 Chr* 25:3
king instead of *his f.* *2 Ki* 14:21
23:30, 34
Reuben defiled *his f.'s.* *1 Chr* 5:1
I will be *his f.* he shall. 17:13; 28:6
not firstborn, yet *his f.* 26:10
appeared to David *his f.* *2 Chr* 3:1
to order of David *his f.* 8:14
walked in first ways of *his f.* 17:3
Jehoshaphat sought God of *his f.* 4
walked in way of Asa *his f.* 20:32
counsellors after death of *his f.* 22:4
in ways of David *his f.* 34:2, 3
heareth instruction of *his f.* *Pr* 13:1
fool despiseth *his f.'s* instruction.
15:5
foolish son is a grief to *his f.* 17:25
foolish son calamity of *his f.* 19:13
he that wasteth *his f.*, is a son. 26
whoso curseth *his f.* his lamp. 20:20
of riotous men shameth *his f.* 28:7
whoso robbeth *his f.* or mother. 24
wisdom, rejoiceth *his f.* 29:3
ravens pick out eye that mocketh *his
f.* 30:17
to him that saith to *his f.* *Isa* 45:10
a son that seeth *his f.'s.* *Ezek* 18:14
not die for iniquity of *his f.* 17
as for *his f.* because he cruelly. 18
bring golden vessels *his f.* *Dan* 5:2
a man and *his f.* go in to. *Amos* 2:7
his f. and mother shall. *Zech* 13:3
a son honours *his f.* a. *Mal* 1:6
at variance against his *f.* *Mat* 10:35
whoso shall say to *his f.* it. 15:5
Mark 7:11
and honour not *his f.* or. *Mat* 15:6
of man come in glory of *his F.* 16:27
Mark 8:38; *Luke* 9:26
did the will of *his f.*? *Mat* 21:31
he asked *his f.* how? *Mark* 9:21
him the throne of *his f.* *Luke* 1:32
called him after name of *his f.* 59
they made signs unto *his f.* 62
his f. Zacharias was filled with. 67
Jesus delivered him to *his f.* 9:42
to me, and hate not *his f.* 14:26
younger of them said to *his f.* 15:12
arose and came to *his f. his f.* saw. 20
therefore came *his f.* and. 28
said, God was *his F.* *John* 5:18
but *his f.* was a Greek. *Acts* 16:1
have *his f.'s* wife. *1 Cor* 5:1
was yet in loins of *his f.* *Heb* 7:10
priests to God and his *F.* *Rev* 1:6
his F.'s name written in. 14:1
see **house**

my **father**

yesternight with my *f.* *Gen* 19:34
she is daughter of *my f.* not. 20:12
my f. peradventure will feel. 27:12
bless me, even me also, O *my f.* 34
the God of *my f.* 31:5, 42; 32:9
Ex 18:4
came to thy servant *my f.*
Gen 44:24, 27, 30

surety for the lad to *my f.* *Gen* 44:32
doth *my f.* yet live? 45:3
haste to go up to *my f.* 9
tell *my f.* 13
my f. and brethren are come. 47:1
not so, *my f.* for this is. 48:18
ready to perish *my f.* *Deut* 26:5
will save alive *my f.* *Josh* 2:13
my f. fought for you. *Judg* 9:17
my f. if thou hast opened. 11:36
not told it *my f.* nor my. 14:16
lest *my f.* leave caring. *1 Sam* 9:5
my f. troubled the land. 14:29
and what is *my f.'s* family? 18:18
Saul *my f.* seeketh to kill. 19:2
I will commune with *my f.* of thee. 3
my f. will do nothing, but he. 20:2
as he hath been with *my f.* 13
let my *f.* and my mother be. 22:3
hand of Saul *my f.* shall not. 28:17
the kingdom of *my f.* *2 Sam* 16:3
buried by grave of *my f.* 19:37
ark of Lord before David *my f.* in all
wherein *my f.* was. *1 Ki* 2:26
my f. David not knowing. 32
that thou didst to David *my f.* 44
thou hast shewed to David *my f.* 3:6
thy servant king instead of *my f.* 7
David *my f.* could not build. 5:3
Lord spake to David *my f.* saying. 5
in the heart of David *my f.* to. 8:17
kept with thy servant David *my f.* 24
let my word be verified to *my f.* 26
2 Chr 6:16
shall be thicker than my *f.'s.* loins.
1 Ki 12:10; *2 Chr* 10:10
my f. did lade you with. *1 Ki* 12:11
2 Chr 10:11
my f. chastised you. *1 Ki* 12:14
2 Chr 10:14
league between *my f.* *1 Ki* 15:19
2 Chr 16:3
kiss *my f.* and mother. *1 Ki* 19:20
cities *my f.* took I will. 20:34
saw it, cried, *my f. my f.* *2 Ki* 2:12
my f. shall I smite them? 6:21
my f. my f. the chariot of. 13:14
chose me before house of *my f.* and
among sons of *my f.* *1 Chr* 28:4
didst deal with *my f.* *2 Chr* 2:3
of *my f.'s* sepulchres. *Neh* 2:3
send me to city of *my f.s'.* 5
corruption, thou art *my f.* *Job* 17:14
my f. and my mother. *Ps* 27:10
cry unto me, thou art *my F.* 89:26
for I was *my f.'s* son. *Pr* 4:3
knowledge to cry, *my f.* *Isa* 8:4
stock, thou art *my f.* *Jer* 2:27
not cry unto me, *my f.*? 3:4, 19
who brought tidings to *my f.* 20:15
whom *my f.* brought out. *Dan* 5:13
doeth the will of *my F.* *Mat* 7:21
12:50
go and bury *my f.* 8:21; *Luke* 9:59
I confess before *my F.* *Mat* 10:32
him will I deny before *my F.* 33
are delivered to me of *my F.* 11:27
Luke 10:22
plant *my* heavenly *F.* *Mat* 15:13
my F. who is in heaven. 16:17
angels behold face of *my F.* 18:10
it shall be done of *my F.* 19
so shall *my* heavenly *F.* also. 35
whom prepared of *my F.* 20:23
no man but *my F.* only. 24:36
come ye blessed of *my F.* 25:34
new with you in *my F.'s.* 26:29
O *my F.* if it be possible, let. 39
my F. if this cup may not pass. 42
thinkest I cannot pray to *my F.*? 53
must be about *my F.'s.* *Luke* 2:49
many hired servants of *my f.* 15:17
arise, and go to *my f.* and say, *f.* 18
send him to *my f.'s* house. 16:27
as *my F.* hath appointed. 22:29
I send the promise of *my F.* 24:49
my F. worketh hitherto. *John* 5:17
but the will of *my F.* 30
I am come in *my F.'s* name. 43
my F. giveth you true bread. 6:32
except it be given of *my F.* 65
neither know me, nor *my F.* 8:19
my F. hath taught me, I speak. 28
which I have seen with *my F.* 38

but I honour *my F.* and ye. *John* 8:49
it is *my F.* that honoureth me. 54
therefore doth *my F.* love. 10:17
commandment received of *my F.* 18
works I do in *my F.'s* name bear. 25
my F. who gave them, none is able to pluck them out of *my F.'s.* 29
I and *my F.* are one. 30
works I shewed from *my F.* 32
if I do not works of *my F.* 37
me, him will *my F.* honour. 12:26
should have known *my F.* 14:7
because I go to *my F.* 12; 16:10
know that I am in *my F.* 14:20
loveth me, be loved of *my F.* 21, 23
my F. is greater than I. 28
I am the vine, *my F.* is the. 15:1
herein is *my F.* glorified. 8
kept *my F.'s* commandments. 10
all that I heard of *my F.* I have. 15
hateth me, hateth *my F.* 23, 24
the cup *my F.* hath given. 18:11
for I am not yet ascended to *my F.* I ascend to *my F.* and. 20:17
as *my F.* hath sent me. 21
as I received of *my F.* *Rev* 2:27
confess his name before *my F.* 3:5

***our* father**

our f. is old. *Gen* 19:31
make *our f.* drink wine. 32
away all that was *our f.'s.* 31:1, 16
youngest is this day with *our f.* 42:13, 32
thy servant *our f.* is in. 43:28
bring *our f.* with sorrow. 44:31
our f. died in wilderness. *Num* 27:3
why should the name of *our f.?* 4
God of Israel *our F.* *1 Chr* 29:10
thou art *our F.*, Abraham. *Isa* 63:16
O Lord, thou art *our F.* 64:8
our f. commanded us. *Jer* 35:6
obeyed the voice of *our f.* 8, 10
our F. which art in heaven. *Mat* 6:9; *Luke* 11:2
kingdom of *our f.* David. *Mark* 11:10
sware to *our f.* Abraham. *Luke* 1:73
we have Abraham to *our f.* 3:8
art thou greater than *our f.?* *John* 4:12; 8:53
of glory appeared to *our f.* *Acts* 7:2
and peace from God *our F.* *Rom* 1:7
1 Cor 1:3; *2 Cor* 1:2; *2 Thes* 1:2
1 Tim 1:2; *Philem* 3
even by *our f.* Isaac. *Rom* 9:10
will of God, and *our F.* *Gal* 1:4
peace from God *our F.* *Eph* 1:2
Phil 1:2; *Col* 1:2; *1 Thes* 1:1
unto God *our F.* be. *Phil* 4:20
sight of God and our *F.* *1 Thes* 1:3
now God *our F.* direct our. 3:11
you in holiness before *our F.* 13
Paul unto church in God *our F.* *2 Thes* 1:1
now God, even *our F.* comfort. 2:16

***their* father**

nakedness of *their f.* and saw not nakedness of *their f.* *Gen* 9:23
made *their f.* drink wine. 19:33
daughters with child by *their f.* 36
went to feed *their f.'s* flock. 37:12
to water *their f.'s* flock. *Ex* 2:16
anoint them as thou didst *their f.* 40:15
to the tribe of *their f.* *Num* 36:6
after Dan *their f.* *Josh* 19:47
Judg 18:29
to voice of *their f.* *1 Sam* 2:25
one said, who is *their f.?* 10:12
prophet's sons told *their f.* *1 Ki* 13:11
Ephraim *their f.* *1 Chr* 7:22
died before *their f.* 24:2
under hands of *their f.* 25:3, 6
their f. gave them gifts. *2 Chr* 21:3
their f. gave inheritance. *Job* 42:15
a generation that curseth *their f.* *Pr* 30:11
consolation for *their f.* *Jer* 16:7
Jonadab's sons obeyed *their f.'s.* 35:14, 16
their f.'s nakedness. *Ezek* 22:10
ship with Zebedee *their f.* *Mat* 4:21
they left ship and *their f.* and. 22
shine in kingdom of *their f.* *Mat* 13:43

***thy* father**

thee from *thy f.'s* house. *Gen* 12:1
I heard *thy f.* speak to Esau. 27:6
thou shalt bring it to *thy f.* 10
remain a widow at *thy f.'s.* 38:11
I am the God of *thy f.*, fear. 46:3
by the God of *thy f.* 49:25
the blessings of *thy f.* have. 26
thy f. commanded before he. 50:16
forgive servants of God of *thy f.* 17
honour *thy f.* and mother. *Ex* 20:12
Deut 5:16; *Mat* 15:4; 19:19
brethren of tribe of *thy f.* *Num* 18:2
God of *thy f.* promised. *Deut* 6:3
is not he *thy f.?* 32:6
ask *thy f.* and he will shew thee. 7
hast left *thy f.* and. *Ruth* 2:11
is my sin before *thy f.?* *1 Sam* 20:1
if *thy f.* miss me, then say. 6
chose me before *thy f.* *2 Sam* 6:21
David doth honour *thy f.* that he sent comforters to? 10:3; *1 Chr* 19:3
served in *thy f.'s* presence. *2 Sam* 16:19
do it for David *thy f.'s.* *1 Ki* 11:12
thy f. made yoke grievous. 12:4, 10
2 Chr 10:4
a league between my father and *thy f.* *1 Ki* 15:19
cities my father took from *thy f.* 20:34
thee to prophets of *thy f.* *2 Ki* 3:13
Lord, the God of David *thy f.* 20:5
2 Chr 21:12; *Isa* 38:5
know thou the God of *thy f.* *1 Chr* 28:9
walk before me as *thy f.* *2 Chr* 7:17
aged men elder than *thy f.* *Job* 15:10
instruction of *thy f.* *Pr* 1:8; 23:22
keep *thy f.'s* commandment. 6:20
thy f. and mother be glad. 23:25
thine own and *thy f.'s.* friend. 27:10
thy first *f.* hath sinned. *Isa* 43:27
thee with heritage of *thy f.* 58:14
house of *thy f.* dealt. *Jer* 12:6
did not *thy f.* eat, drink, and? 22:15
thy f. was an Amorite. *Ezek* 16:3
of *thy f.* the king, *thy f.* *Dan* 5:11
God gave *thy f.* a kingdom. 18
thy F. which seeth. *Mat* 6:4, 6, 18
shut thy door, pray to *thy F.* 6
honour *thy f.* and mother. *Mark* 7:10
10:19; *Luke* 18:20; *Eph* 6:2
thy f. and I sought. *Luke* 2:48
thy f. hath killed the fatted. 15:27
said they, where is *thy f.?* *John* 8:19

***your* father**

power I served *your f.* *Gen* 31:6
your f. hath deceived me. 7
is *your f.* alive? 43:7
you up in peace to *your f.* 44:17
you wagons, bring *your f.* 45:19
hearken unto Israel *your f.* 49:2
obeyed Jonadab *your f.* *Jer* 35:18
your f. an Amorite. *Ezek* 16:45
may glorify *your F.* who. *Mat* 5:16
may be children of *your F.* 45
be ye perfect, as *your F.* in. 48
have no reward of *your F.* 6:1
your F. knoweth what things ye. 8, 32; *Luke* 12:30
forgive, *your* heavenly *F.* *Mat* 6:14
if ye forgive not, neither will *your F.* 15; *Mark* 11:25, 26
sparrow fall without *your F.* *Mat* 10:29
it is not the will of *your F.* 18:14
call no man *your f.* upon earth, one is *your F.* which is in heaven. 23:9
your F. also is merciful. *Luke* 6:36
it is *your F.'s* pleasure to. 12:32
have seen with *your f.* *John* 8:38
ye do the deeds of *your f.* then. 41
if God were *your F.* ye would. 42
ye are of *your f.* the devil, the lusts of *your f.* ye will do. 44
I ascend to my Father and *your F.* 20:17

father-in-law

thy *f.-in-law* goeth to Timnath. *Gen* 38:13
she went to her *f.-in-law.* *Gen* 38:25
flock of Jethro his *f.-in-law.* *Ex* 3:1; 4:18
Moses' *f.-in-law.* 18:1, 8, 14, 17
Judg 1:16*; 4:11*
let his *f.-in-law* depart. *Ex* 18:27
Raguel, Moses' *f.-in-law.* *Num* 10:29
f.-in-law retained him. *Judg* 19:4
rose to depart, his *f.-in-law* urged. 7
f.-in-law was dead. *1 Sam* 4:19, 21
Annas was *f.-in-law* to. *John* 18:13

fatherless

not afflict any *f.* child. *Ex* 22:22
be widows, and children *f.* 24
execute the judgement of the *f.* and. *Deut* 10:18; *Ps* 82:3; *Isa* 1:17
ye overwhelm the *f.* and *Job* 6:27
the arms of the *f.* have been. 22:9
they drive away the ass of *f.* 24:3
pluck the *f.* from the breast. 9
delivered the poor and the *f.* 29:12
eaten alone, and *f.* have not. 31:17
lifted up my hand against the *f.* 21
art the helper of the *f.* *Ps* 10:14
to judge the *f.* and the oppressed. 18
a father of the *f.* a judge of. 68:5
let his children be *f.* 109:9
nor any favour his *f.* children. 12
not into fields of the *f.* *Pr* 23:10
judge not the *f.* *Isa* 1:23; *Jer* 5:28
not have mercy on their *f.* *Isa* 9:17
that they may rob the *f.* 10:2
leave thy *f.* children. *Jer* 49:11
we are orphans and *f.* *Lam* 5:3
have they vexed the *f.* *Ezek* 22:7
in thee *f.* findeth mercy. *Hos* 14:3
those that oppress the *f.* *Mal* 3:5
pure religion to visit *f.* and. *Jas* 1:27

fatherless with *stranger*

the *stranger*, the *f.*, the widow come. *Deut* 14:29; 24:19, 20, 21; 26:12, 13
stranger and *f.* rejoice. 16:11, 14
judgement of *stranger* nor *f.* 24:17
judgement of *stranger* and *f.* 27:19
they slay *stranger*, murder the *f.* *Ps* 94:6
preserveth *strangers* and *f.* 146:9
oppressed not *stranger*, *f.* and. *Jer* 7:6; 22:3; *Zech* 7:10

fathers

heads of their *f.'* houses. *Ex* 6:14, 25
Josh 14:1; 19:51; 21:1
1 Chr 8:10, 13, 28
thy father, nor thy *f.* *Ex* 10:6
iniquity of the *f.* upon the. 20:5
34:7; *Num* 14:18; *Deut* 5:9
f. shall not be put to death . . . for *f.* *Deut* 24:16; *2 Ki* 14:6
whose *f.* I would have. *Job* 30:1
and riches inheritance of *f.* *Pr* 19:14
kings be thy nursing *f.* *Isa* 49:23
f. and sons shall fall. *Jer* 6:21; 13:14
children gather wood, *f.* 7:18
f. eaten sour grapes. 31:29
Ezek 18:2
iniquity of the *f.* on. *Jer* 32:18
the *f.* shall not look back to. 47:3
f. shall eat the sons in. *Ezek* 5:10
the *f.* to children, and children to *f.* *Mal* 4:6; *Luke* 1:17
not of Moses, but of the *f.* *John* 7:22
and *f.* hearken. *Acts* 7:2; 22:1
promise made unto the *f.* 13:32
of the law of the *f.* 22:3
whose are the *f.* of whom. *Rom* 9:5
yet have not many *f.* *1 Cor* 4:15
f. provoke not children. *Eph* 6:4
Col 3:21
in times past to the *f.* *Heb* 1:1
we had *f.* of our flesh who. 12:9
since the *f.* fell asleep. *2 Pet* 3:4
I write unto you *f.* *1 John* 2:13, 14
see **buried, chief**

***his* fathers**

removed the idols *his f.* *1 Ki* 15:12
the things *his f.* had. *2 Ki* 12:18
did what was evil as *his f.* 15:9
forsook Lord God of *his f.* 21:22
2 Chr 21:10
according to all *his f.* had done. *2 Ki* 23:32, 37; 24:9

like burning of his f. 2 Chr 21:19
Ahaz provoked God of his f. 28:25
heart to seek God of his f. 30:19
himself before God of his f. 33:12
to generation of his f. Ps 49:19
let the iniquity of his f. be. 109:14
do what his f. have not. Dan 11:24
regard the God of his f. 37
and a god whom his f. knew not. 38
David was laid to his f. Acts 13:36

my fathers

to the years of my f. Gen 47:9
I will lie with my f. 30
the name of my f. be named. 48:16
bury me with my f. in the. 49:29
he is my f.' God, I will. Ex 15:2
no better than my f. 1 Ki 19:4
inheritance of my f. to thee. 21:3, 4
have gods delivered them my f.?
2 Ki 19:12; 2 Chr 32:14; Isa 37:12
not what I and my f. 2 Chr 32:13
sojourner as all my f. Ps 39:12
praise thee, O God of my f. Dan 2:23
worship I God of my f. Acts 24:14
of traditions of my f. Gal 1:14

our fathers

now both we and also our f.
Gen 46:34; 47:3
how our f. went down. Num 20:15
not covenant with our f. Deut 5:3
land which he sware to our f. 6:23
26:3, 15
cried to the God of our f. 26:7
pattern of altar our f. Josh 22:28
brought our f. out of Egypt. 24:17
miracles which our f. told of ?
Judg 6:13
with us, as with our f. 1 Ki 8:57
which he commanded our f. 58
because our f. have not. 2 Ki 22:13
the God of our f. look. 1 Chr 12:17
sojourners, as were all our f. 29:15
Lord God of our f. keep in thoughts
of thy people. 18; 2 Chr 20:6
thou gavest our f. 2 Chr 6:31
Neh 9:36
for our f. have trespassed. 2 Chr 29:6
our f. have fallen by the sword. 9
our f. have not kept word of. 34:21
our f. provoked God. Ezra 5:12
blessed be the God of our f. 7:27
since the days of our f. in a. 9:7
affliction of our f. in Egypt. Neh 9:9
our f. dealt proudly, and. 16
our f. trusted in thee. Ps 22:4
our f. have told us. 41:1; 78:3
we have sinned with our f. 106:6
our f. understood not thy wonders. 7
where our f. praised thee. Isa 64:11
devoured labour of our f. Jer 3:24
we and our f. have not obeyed. 25
our f. have inherited lies. 16:19
have done, we and our f. 44:17
our f. have sinned, and. Lam 5:7
confusion of face to our f. Dan 9:8
our sins and iniquities of our f. 16
sworn to our f. from. Mi 7:20
the covenant of our f. Mal 2:10
had been in days of our f. Mat 23:30
as he spake to our f. Luke 1:55
mercy promised to our f. 72
our f. worshipped in. John 4:20
our f. did eat manna in the. 6:31
God of our f. hath glorified his Son.
Acts 3:13
covenant God made with our f. 25
God of our f. raised up Jesus. 5:30
our f. found no sustenance. 7:11
Jacob died, and our f. 15
and evil entreated our f. and. 19
spake in Sinai and with our f. 38
to whom our f. would not obey. 39
our f. had the tabernacle of. 44
God of Israel chose our f. 13:17
a yoke which our f. nor we. 15:10
promise made to our f. 26:6
spake Holy Ghost to our f. 28:25
our f. were under cloud. 1 Cor 10:1

slept with fathers

David slept with his f. 1 Ki 2:10
11:21
Solomon slept with his f. 2:43
2 Chr 9:31
Jeroboam slept with f. 1 Ki 14:20
2 Ki 14:29
Rehoboam slept with f. 1 Ki 14:31
2 Chr 12:16
Abijam slept with his f. 1 Ki 15:8
2 Chr 14:1
Asa slept with his f. 1 Ki 15:24
2 Chr 16:13
so Baasha slept with f. 1 Ki 16:6
Omri slept with f. 28
Ahab slept with f. 22:40
Jehoshaphat slept with f. 50
2 Chr 21:1
Joram slept with his f. 2 Ki 8:24
Jehu slept with his f. 10:35
Jehoahaz slept with his f. 13:9
Joash slept with his f. 13; 14:16
that the king slept with his f. 14:22
2 Chr 26:2
Azariah slept with his f. 2 Ki 15:7
Menahem slept with his f. 22
Jotham slept with f. 38; 2 Chr 27:9
Ahaz slept with his f. 2 Ki 16:20
2 Chr 28:27
Hezekiah slept with f. 2 Ki 20:21
2 Chr 32:33
Manasseh slept with f. 2 Ki 21:18
2 Chr 33:20
Jehoiakim slept with f. 2 Ki 24:6
Uzziah slept with his f. 2 Chr 26:23

their fathers

God of their f. hath. Ex 4:5
heads of their f. 6:14, 25; Josh 14:1
19:51; 21:1; 1 Chr 5:24; 7:2, 7
8:6; 9:9, 13
in iniquity of their f. Lev 26:39
confess iniquity of their f. 40
land thou swarest to give to their f.
Num 11:12; 14:23; Deut 10:11
31:20; Josh 1:6; 5:6; 21:43, 44
Jer 32:22
the covenant of their f. Deut 29:25
children ask their f. Josh 4:6, 21
head of house of their f. 22:14
were gathered to their f. Judg 2:10
forsook the Lord God of their f. 12
turned out of way their f. walked. 17
corrupted more than their f. 19
covenant I commanded their f. 20
keep way of Lord, as their f. 22
which he commanded their f. 3:4
again to land thou gavest to their f.
1 Ki 8:34, 48; 2 Chr 6:25, 38
their f. out of Egypt. 1 Ki 9:9
of land he gave to their f. 14:15
2 Ki 21:8; Jer 16:15; 24:10
above all that their f. 1 Ki 14:22
since day their f. came. 2 Ki 21:15
house of their f. increased greatly.
1 Chr 4:38
against God of their f. 5:25
blessed the God of their f. 29:20
forsook God of their f. 2 Chr 7:22
24:24; 28:6
sacrifice to God of their f. 11:16
relied on Lord God of their f. 13:18
to seek God of their f. 14:4; 15:12
them to the God of their f. 19:4
hearts to God of their f. 20:33
trespassed against God of their f.
30:7
confession to God of their f. 22
covenant of God of their f. 34:32
following the God of their f. 33
God of their f. sent by his. 36:15
confessed sins of their f. Neh 9:2
into land promisedst to their f. 23
to the search of their f. Job 8:8
men have told from their f. 15:18
as their f. a stubborn. Ps 78:8
things did he in sight of their f. 12
dealt unfaithfully like their f. 57
of children are their f. Pr 17:6
for iniquity of their f. Isa 14:21
did worse than their f. Jer 7:26
after Baalim, which their f. 9:14
whom they nor their f. have. 16; 19:4
covenant I made with their f.
11:10; 31:32; Heb 8:9
as their f. have forgotten. 23:27
against Lord, hope of their f. Jer 50:7
they and their f. have. Ezek 2:3
eat sons, and sons eat their f. 5:10
know abominations of their f.
Ezek 20:4
eyes were after their f.' idols. 24
which their f. walked. Amos 2:4
heart of children to their f. Mal 4:6
like manner did their f. Luke 6:23
for so did their f. to the false. 26

thy fathers

go to thy f. in peace. Gen 15:15
thy f.' children shall bow. 49:8
land which he sware to thy f.
Ex 13:5, 11; Deut 6:10, 18; 7:12
13; 8:18; 9:5; 13:17; 19:8; 28:11
29:13; 30:20
it, as God of thy f. said. Deut 1:21
nor forget covenant of thy f. 4:31
because he loved thy f. 37; 10:15
with manna which thou knewest not,
neither did thy f. 8:3, 16
thy f. went into Egypt. 10:22
the God of thy f. giveth thee. 12:1
gods thou nor thy f. 13:6; 28:64
land he promised thy f. 19:8; 27:3
nation thou nor thy f. have. 28:36
multiply thee above thy f. 30:5
rejoice over thee, as over thy f. 9
sleep with thy f. 31:16; 2 Sam 7:12
to sepulchre of thy f. 1 Ki 13:22
what thy f. laid up. 2 Ki 20:17
I will gather thee to thy f. 22:20
2 Chr 34:28
go to be with thy f. 1 Chr 17:11
book of records of thy f. Ezra 4:15
instead of thy f. shall be. Ps 45:16
not land-mark thy f. set. Pr 22:28
with burnings of thy f. Jer 34:5
I am God of thy f. the. Acts 7:32

your fathers

you to land of your f. Gen 48:21
God of your f. sent me. Ex 3:13
Deut 1:11; 4:1; Josh 18:3
2 Chr 28:9; 29:5
did your f. Num 32:8; Neh 13:18
risen up in your f.' stead. Num 32:14
land Lord sware to your f. Deut 1:8
35; 7:8; 8:1; 11:9, 21; Judg 2:1
sacrificed to gods whom your f.
Deut 32:17
your f. dwelt on other. Josh 24:2
I brought your f. out of Egypt. 6
put away gods your f. served. 14
the gods which your f. served. 15
did to you and your f. 1 Sam 12:7
your f. cried, Lord brought your f. 8
Lord against you as against your f. 15
I commanded your f. 2 Ki 17:13
fight not against God of your f.
2 Chr 13:12
not like your f. and brethren. 30:7, 8
Zech 1:4
of land appointed for your f.
2 Chr 33:8
offering to God of your f. Ezra 8:28
confession to God of your f. 10:11
when your f. tempted me. Ps 95:9
Heb 3:9
and iniquities of your f. Isa 65:7
what iniquity have your f.? Jer 2:5
to land I have given to your f. 3:18
dwell in land I gave to your f. 7:7
14; 23:39; 25:5; 35:15
Ezek 20:42; 36:28; 47:14
I spake not to your f. in. Jer 7:22
since the day your f. came. 25
I commanded your f. 11:4; 17:22
earnestly protested unto your f. 11:7
your f. have forsaken me. 16:11
done worse than your f. 12
ye nor your f. 13
made covenant with your f. 34:13
but your f. hearkened not unto. 14
not, neither they nor your f. 44:3
forgotten wickedness of your f.? 9
I set before you and your f. 10
the incense ye, your f. and. 21
not in statutes of your f. Ezek 20:18
in this your f. have blasphemed. 27
polluted after manner of your f.? 30
like as I pleaded with your f. 36
in land wherein your f. dwelt. 37:25
I saw your f. as the first. Hos 9:10
been in days of your f.? Joel 1:2
displeased with your f. Zech 1:2

be not as your f. Zech 1:4
your f. where are they? 5
my words take hold of your f.? 6
when your f. provoked me to. 8:14
from days of your f. Mal 3:7
the measure of your f. Mat 23:32
prophets, and your f. Luke 11:47
ye allow the deeds of your f. 48
your f. did eat manna. John 6:49
not as your f. did eat manna. 58
ye resist Holy Ghost as your f. did. Acts 7:51
who of prophets have not your f.? 52
by tradition from your f. 1 Pet 1:18

fathoms
twenty f. again fifteen f. Acts 27:28

fatling
calf, young lion, and f. Isa 11:6

fatlings
Agag and best of the f. 1 Sam 15:9
sacrificed oxen and f. 2 Sam 6:13
offer burnt sacrifices of f. Ps 66:15
all of them f. of Bashan. Ezek 39:18
my oxen and my f. are. Mat 22:4

fatness
God give thee of f. of. Gen 27:28
thy dwelling shall be the f. of. 39
thick and covered with f. Deut 32:15
should I leave my f.? Judg 9:9
his face with his f. Job 15:27
thy table should be full of f. 36:16
be satisfied with the f. Ps 36:8
as with marrow and f. 63:5
all thy paths drop f. 65:11
eyes stand out with f. 73:7
my flesh faileth of f. 109:24
f. of his flesh wax lean. Isa 17:4
sword of Lord is made fat with f. 34:6
dust shall be made fat with f. 7
let your soul delight itself in f. 55:2
the soul of priests with f. Jer 31:14
with them partakest of f. Rom 11:17

fats
(*Revisions*, vats)
the f. shall overflow with. Joel 2:24
press is full, the f. overflow. 3:13

fatted
oxen, harts, f. fowl. 1 Ki 4:23
hired men are like f. Jer 46:21*

see **calf**

fatter, *see* **countenances**

fattest
wrath of God slew the f. Ps 78:31
shall enter on f. places. Dan 11:24

fault, -s
I remember my f. this. Gen 41:9
f. is in thine own people. Ex 5:16
be beaten according to f. Deut 25:2*
I have found no f. in. 1 Sam 29:3
me this day with f. 2 Sam 3:8
cleanse me from secret f. Ps 19:12
and prepare without my f. 59:4
find no occasion or f. Dan 6:4
if thy brother trespass, tell him his f. Mat 18:15
they found f. Mark 7:2
I find no f. in this man. Luke 23:4
14; John 18:38*; 19:4, 6*
why doth he yet find f.? Rom 9:19
now there is utterly a f. 1 Cor 6:7*
man be overtaken in a f. Gal 6:1*
finding f. with them, he. Heb 8:8
confess your f. one to. Jas 5:16*
be buffeted for your f. 1 Pet 2:20*
without f. before throne. Rev 14:5*

faultless
first covenant had been f. Heb 8:7
is able to present you f. Jude 24

faulty
doth speak as one which is f. 2 Sam 14:13*
shall they be found f. Hos 10:2*

favour
gave Joseph f. in sight of. Gen 39:21
f. in sight of the Egyptians, not go empty. Ex 3:21; 11:3; 12:36
which shall not shew f. Deut 28:50
O Naphtali, satisfied with f. 33:23
that they might have no f. Josh 11:20
Samuel was in f. with. 1 Sam 2:26
granted me life and f. Job 10:12†
with f. wilt compass him. Ps 5:12
his f. is life, weeping may. 30:5
thy f. thou hast made mountain to. 7
thou hadst a f. unto them. 44:3
even rich shall entreat thy f. 45:12
in thy f. horn shall be exalted. 89:17
remember me with the f. Ps 106:4
a good man sheweth f. and. 112:5*
I entreated thy f. with my. 119:58
seeketh good procureth f. Pr 11:27
good understanding giveth f. 13:15
among the righteous there is f. 14:9*
king's f. is toward a wise. 35
his f. is as a cloud of the. 16:15
many will entreat the f. of. 19:6
the king's f. is as dew upon. 12
his neighbour findeth no f. 21:10
loving f. rather to be chosen. 22:1
may seek the ruler's f. 29:26
f. is deceitful, beauty is vain. 31:30†
race not to swift, nor f. Eccl 9:11
f. be shewed to wicked. Isa 26:10
them will shew them no f. 27:11
but in my f. have I had. 60:10
I will not shew you f. Jer 16:13
had brought Daniel into f. Dan 1:9†
Jesus increased in f. Luke 2:52
having f. with all people. Acts 2:47
God gave Moses f. in sight of. 7:10
high priest desired f. against. 25:3

find, or *found* **favour**
have found f. in thy sight. Gen 18:3
30:27; Num 11:15; 1 Sam 20:29
Neh 2:5; Esth 5:8; 7:3; 8:5
have I not found f.? Num 11:11
to pass she find no f. Deut 24:1
let me find f. in thy sight. Ruth 2:13
David hath found f. in. 1 Sam 16:22
let the young men find f. in. 25:8
shall find f. in eyes of. 2 Sam 15:25
Hadad found f. in sight. 1 Ki 11:19
so shalt thou find f. in. Pr 3:4
shall find more f. than he. 28:23
as one that found f. S of S 8:10*
hast found f. with God. Luke 1:30
David found f. before. Acts 7:46

obtain, or *obtained* **favour**
Esther obtained f. Esth 2:15, 17† 5:2
findeth me, shall obtain f. Pr 8:35
a good man obtaineth f. of. 12:2
findeth a wife, obtaineth f. 18:22

favour, *verb*
the lords f. thee not. 1 Sam 29:6
glad, that f. my righteous. Ps 35:27
the set time to f. her is. 102:13*
thy servants f. dust thereof. 14*
let any to f. his fatherless. 109:12*

favourable
be f. unto them for our. Judg 21:22*
and God will be f. unto. Job 33:26
cast off, be f. no more? Ps 77:7
thou hast been f. to thy land. 85:1

favoured
beautiful and well f. Gen 29:17
Joseph was well f. 39:6
well f. kine. 41:2, 4, 18
of river ill f. kine. 3, 4, 19, 21, 27
they f. not the elders. Lam 4:16
children well f. and. Dan 1:4
whoredoms of well f. harlot. Nah 3:4
thou art highly f. Lord. Luke 1:28

evil **favouredness**
bullock wherein any evil f. Deut 17:1

favourest
I know that thou f. me. Ps 41:11*

favoureth
he that f. Joab, let him. 2 Sam 20:11

fear
(*The fear of God means that reverence for God which leads to obedience because of one's realization of his power, as well as of his love to man*)
the f. of you shall be. Gen 9:2
except the f. of Isaac had. 31:42
Jacob sware by the f. of his. 53
f. and dread fall upon. Ex 15:16*
I will send my f. before thee. 23:27*
I will put the f. of thee. Deut 2:25
Lord shall lay the f. of you. 11:25
Lord brought f. of him. 1 Chr 14:17
f. was on them because. Ezra 3:3
them that put me in f. Neh 6:14, 19
the f. of the Jews. Esth 8:17; 9:2
the f. of Mordecai fell on. 9:3
this thy f. thy confidence? Job 4:6
f. came upon me and trembling. 14
forsaketh f. of the Almighty. 6:14
let not his f. terrify me. 9:34*
yea, thou castest off f. and. 15:4
houses safe from f. nor. 21:9
snares round about, sudden f. 22:10
dominion and f. are with him. 25:2
he mocketh at f. and is not. 39:22
in thy f. will I worship. Ps 5:7
put them in f. O Lord. 9:20
there were they in great f. 14:5
a f. to mine acquaintance. 31:11
f. was on every side. 13*
f. took hold upon them. 48:6*
in f. where no f. was. 53:5
preserve my life from f. of. 64:1
to thy f. so is thy wrath. 90:11
f. of them fell upon them. 105:38
who is devoted to thy f. 119:38
mock when your f. cometh. Pr 1:26
your f. cometh as desolation. 27
shall be quiet from f. of evil. 33
be not afraid of sudden f. nor. 3:25
the f. of the wicked shall. 10:24
the f. of a king is as roaring. 20:2*
f. of man bringeth a snare. 29:25
his sword because of f. S of S 3:8
not come the f. of briers. Isa 7:25
neither f. ye their f. nor. 8:12
the Lord, let him be your f. and. 13
give thee rest from thy f. 14:3*
of pleasure turned unto f. 21:4*
f. and the pit, and the snare. 24:17
that fleeth from f. 18; Jer 48:44
f. toward me is taught. Isa 29:13
our heart from thy f. 63:17
evil thing, that my f. is not. Jer 2:19
sword and f. on every. 6:25*; 20:10
have heard a voice of f. not. 30:5
will put my f. in their hearts. 32:40
f. and the pit shall be upon. 48:43
I will bring a f. upon thee. 49:5
hath seized on Damascus. 24*
cry to them, f. is on every side. 29*
f. and a snare is come. Lam 3:47
a f. in land of Egypt. Ezek 30:13
if master, where is my f.? Mal 1:6
Zacharias saw him, f. Luke 1:12
f. came on all. 65; 7:16; Acts 2:43
5:5, 11; 19:17; Rev 11:11
f. to whom f. is due. Rom 13:7
in weakness and in f. 1 Cor 2:3
what f.! what desire! 2 Cor 7:11
not given us spirit of f. 2 Tim 1:7
them who through f. of. Heb 2:15
God with reverence, godly f. 12:28*
your sojourning here in f. 1 Pet 1:17
answer with meekness and f. 3:15
no f. in love, love casteth out f. 1 John 4:18

for **fear**
for the f. wherewith. Deut 28:67
not rather done it for f. Josh 22:24*
dwelt for f. of Abimelech. Judg 9:21
fled that day for f. of. 1 Sam 21:10
to get away for f. of Saul. 23:26
he reprove thee for f. of? Job 22:4
over to strong hold for f. Isa 31:9*
for f. of the army of. Jer 35:11
army broken up for f. 37:11
Asa had made for f. of Baasha. 41:9
for f. was round about. 46:5*
for f. of the oppressing. 50:16
for the f. wherewith he. Mal 2:5
disciples cried out for f. Mat 14:26
for f. of him keepers did shake. 28:4
hearts failing for f. Luke 21:26
no man spake openly for f. John 7:13
but secretly for f. of the Jews. 19:38
disciples assembled for f. of Jews. 20:19
off for f. of torment. Rev 18:10, 15

fear *of God*
surely f. of God is not. Gen 20:11
ruling in the f. of God. 2 Sam 23:3
the f. of God was on. 2 Chr 20:29

to walk in f. of God? Neh 5:9
because of the f. of God. 15
is no f. of God before his Ps 36:1
no f. of God before their. Rom 3:18
holiness in the f. of God. 2 Cor 7:1
to another in f. of God. Eph 5:21

fear of the Lord

f. of Lord fell on people.
1 Sam 11:7*; 2 Chr 17:10
f. of the Lord came. 2 Chr 14:14
let the f. of the Lord be upon. 19:7
thus do, in the f. of the Lord. 9
the f. of Lord is wisdom. Job 28:28
the f. of Lord is clean. Ps 19:9
will teach you f. of the Lord. 34:11
f. of the Lord is beginning of 111:10
f. of Lord beginning of knowledge.
Pr 1:7; 9:10
did not choose f. of the Lord. 1:29
understand the f. of the Lord. 2:5
f. of the Lord is to hate evil. 8:13
f. of the Lord prolongeth days. 10:27
in the f. of the Lord is strong. 14:26
the f. of the Lord is fountain of. 27
better little with f. of the Lord. 15:16
f. of the Lord is instruction of. 33
by f. of the Lord men depart. 16:6
the f. of the Lord tendeth. 19:23
by the f. of the Lord are riches. 22:4
f. of the Lord all day long. 23:17
in dust for f. of the Lord. Isa 2:10
into caves for f. of the Lord. 19
clefts of rocks for f. of the Lord. 21
knowledge, and of the f. of the Lord.
11:2
understanding in f. of the Lord 3
f. of the Lord is his treasure. 33:6
walking in f. of the Lord. Acts 9:31

with fear

serve Lord with f. Ps 2:11
they departed with f. Mat 28:8
were all filled with f. Luke 5:26
were taken with great f. 8:37
how with f. ye received. 2 Cor 7:15
to masters with f. and. Eph 6:5
work out salvation with f. Phil 2:12
Noah moved with f. Heb 11:7
subject to masters with f. 1 Pet 2:18
conversation coupled with f. 3:2
and others save with f. Jude 23

without fear

labour is in vain without f. Job 39:16
like, who is made without f. 41:33
serve him without f. Luke 1:74
be with you without f. 1 Cor 16:10
to speak word without f. Phil 1:14
feeding themselves without f.
Jude 12

fear, verb

shall f. every man his. Lev 19:3
neither f. ye the people. Num 14:9
they may learn to f. me. Deut 4:10
O that they would f. me. 5:29
f. this glorious name. 28:58
thou shalt f. day and night. 66
of heart wherewith thou shalt f. 67
if thou f. to go down. Judg 7:10
that they may f. thee. 1 Ki 8:40
2 Chr 6:31
may know thy name to f. 1 Ki 8:43
2 Chr 6:33
neither f. other gods. 2 Ki 17:38
but Lord your God ye shall f. 39
f. before him all earth. 1 Chr 16:30*
Ps 96:9
servants who desire to f. Neh 1:11
did I f. a great multitude? Job 31:34
I will f. no evil. Ps 23:4
whom shall I f.? 27:1
laid up for them that f. 31:19
and f. and shall trust in Lord. 40:3
wherefore should I f. in days? 49:5
righteous also shall see, and f. 52:6
given a banner to them that f. 60:4
heritage of those that f. 61:5
shall f. and declare the work. 64:9
shall f. thee as long as the sun. 72:5
unite my heart to f. thy name. 86:11
heathen shall f. thy name. 102:15
my reproach which I f. 119:39
a companion of them that f. 63
they that f. thee will be glad. 74
those that f. thee turn unto me. 79

men should f. before him. Eccl 3:14
neither f. ye their fear. Isa 8:12
like to women, afraid and f. 19:16
city of terrible nations shall f. 25:3
the workmen shall f. and be. 44:11
f. the name of the Lord. 59:19
thine heart shall f. and be. 60:5*
who would not f. thee? Jer 10:7
and they shall f. no more. 23:4
them one heart that may f. 32:39
they shall f. and tremble for. 33:9
your heart faint, and ye f. for. 51:46
I f. my lord the king. Dan 1:10
that men f. before God of. 6:26
inhabitants of Samaria f. Hos 10:5*
move as worms, and f. Mi 7:17
surely thou wilt f. me. Zeph 3:7
the people did f. before. Hag 1:12
Ashkelon shall see it and f. Zech 9:5
to you that f. my name. Mal 4:2
say, of men, we f. the. Mat 21:26
forewarn you whom ye shall f.
Luke 12:5
of bondage again to f. Rom 8:15
be not highminded, but f. 11:20
I f. lest as the serpent. 2 Cor 11:3
I f. lest I shall not find you. 12:20
rebuke that others may f. 1 Tim 5:20
let us f. lest promise. Heb 4:1
I exceedingly f. and quake. 12:21
f. none of those things. Rev 2:10
reward to them that f. thy. 11:18

fear God

and live, for I f. God. Gen 42:18
men, such as f. God. Ex 18:21
but thou shalt f. thy God. Lev 19:14
32; 25:17, 36, 43
Job f. God for nought? Job 1:9
hear, all ye that f. God. Ps 66:16
but f. thou God. Eccl 5:7
be well with them that f. God. 8:12
f. God and keep his. 12:13
shall f. God of Israel. Isa 29:23*
dost not f. God? Luke 23:40
f. God give audience. Acts 13:16
f. God, honour king. 1 Pet 2:17
f. God, and give glory to. Rev 14:7

hear and fear

Israel shall hear and f. Deut 13:11
21:21
the people shall hear and f. 17:13
those shall hear and f. 19:20

fear him

for I f. him. Gen 32:11
after God, and f. him. Deut 13:4
him shall ye f. him shall. 2 Ki 17:36
men therefore f. him. Job 37:24
and f. him, seed of. Ps 22:23*
vows before them that f. him. 25
Lord with them that f. him. 25:14
of Lord on them that f. him. 33:18
angel encampeth about them that f.
him. 34:7
no want to them that f. him. 9
ends of earth shall f. him. 67:7
is nigh them that f. him. 85:9
mercy to them that f. him. 103:11
Lord pitieth them that f. him. 13
mercy of the Lord is upon them that
f. him. 17; Luke 1:50
meat to them that f. him. Ps. 111:5
desire of them that f. him. 145:19
pleasure in them that f. him. 147:11
f. him who is able to. Mat 10:28
Luke 12:5
praise God, ye that f. him. Rev 19:5

fear the Lord

that thou mightest f. the Lord.
Deut 6:2
thou shalt f. Lord thy. 13; 10:20
2 Ki 17:39
to f. the Lord our God. Deut 6:24
f. the Lord, walk in his ways. 10:12
learn to f. the Lord. 14:23; 17:19
31:12, 13
that ye might f. the Lord. Josh 4:24
now therefore f. the Lord. 24:14
if ye will f. the Lord. 1 Sam 12:14
only f. the Lord and serve him. 24
I thy servant f. the Lord. 1 Ki 18:12
2 Ki 4:1
taught them f. Lord. 2 Ki 17:28
honoureth them that f. the Lord.
Ps 15:4
ye that f. the Lord, praise. 22:23
let all the earth f. the Lord. 33:8
O f. the Lord, ye his saints. 34:9
ye that f. the Lord trust. 115:11
will bless them that f. the Lord. 13
that f. the Lord, say, his. 118:4
that f. the Lord, bless the. 135:20
f. the Lord, depart from. Pr 3:7
my son, f. thou the Lord. 24:21
say, let us f. the Lord. Jer 5:24
did he not f. the Lord, and? 26:19
shall Israel f. the Lord. Hos 3:5
and I f. the Lord, the. Jonah 1:9

fear not

f. not, Abram, I am thy. Gen 15:1
f. not, God hath heard voice. 21:17
f. not, I am with thee. 26:24
midwife said to Rachel, f. not. 35:17
said, peace be to you, f. not. 43:23
f. not to go down into Egypt. 46:3
Joseph said, f. not, for am I? 50:19
f. not, I will nourish you and your. 21
f. not, stand and see. Ex 14:13
Moses said, f. not, God is. 20:20
Lord is with us, f. them not.
Num 14:9
Lord said to Moses, f. him not. 21:34
possess the land, f. not. Deut 1:21
f. not Og. 3:2, 22
f. not your enemies. 20:3
f. not the Canaanites. 31:6
Josh 10:8, 25
Lord will go before thee, f. not.
Deut 31:8; Josh 8:1; 1 Chr 28:20
turn in to me, f. not. Judg 4:18
f. not gods of the Amorites. 6:10
peace be to thee, f. not. 23
now, my daughter, f. not. Ruth 3:11
women that stood by said, f. not.
1 Sam 4:20
Samuel said to people, f. not. 12:20
abide thou with me, f. not. 22:23
said unto David, f. not. 23:17
to Mephibosheth, f. not. 2 Sam 9:7
servants, kill Amnon, f. not. 13:28
Elijah said to widow, f. not.
1 Ki 17:13
f. not: for they that be. 2 Ki 6:16
unto this day, they f. not. 17:34
f. not to serve. 25:24; Jer 40:9
will be with you, f. not. 2 Chr 20:17
therefore they f. not God. Ps 55:19
do they shoot, and f. not. 64:4
f. not the tails of firebrands. Isa 7:4
are of a fearful heart, f. not. 35:4
f. thou not, I am with. 41:10; 43:5
thy God will hold thy right hand, saying to thee, f. not. 41:13
f. not, thou worm Jacob. 14
f. not, I have redeemed thee. 43:1
f. not, O Jacob, and Jeshurun I have.
44:2; Jer 30:10; 46:27, 28
f. ye not, nor be afraid. Isa 44:8
f. not the reproach of men. 51:7
f. not, thou shalt not be. 54:4
f. ye not me? Jer 5:22
thou saidst, f. not. Lam 3:57
f. not, nor be dismayed. Ezek 3:9
f. not, Daniel. Dan 10:12, 19
f. not, O land, be glad. Joel 2:21
said to Jerusalem, f. not. Zeph 3:16
Spirit remaineth, f. not. Hag 2:5
shall be a blessing, f. not. Zech 8:13
do well to Judah, f. ye not. 15
against them that f. not me. Mal 3:5
f. not to take to thee Mary. Mat 1:20
f. them not, there is nothing. 10:26
f. not them which kill the body. 28
f. not, ye are of. 31; Luke 12:7
angel said to women, f. not. Mat 28:5
f. not, Zacharias. Luke 1:13
f. not, Mary. 30
to the shepherds f. not. 2:10
Simon, f. not. 5:10
Jairus, f. not. 8:50
f. not, little flock. 12:32
though I f. not God, nor. 18:4
f. not, daughter of Sion. John 12:15
f. not, Paul, thou must. Acts 27:24
f. not, I am the first and. Rev 1:17

not fear

I know ye will *not* yet *f.* *Ex* 9:30
not f. other gods. *2 Ki* 17:35, 37
I speak, and *not f.* him. *Job* 9:35
far away, thou shalt *not f.* 11:15
my heart shall *not f.* *Ps* 27:3
we will *not f.* though earth be. 46:2
I will *not f.* what. 56:4; 118:6
oppression, shalt *not f.* *Isa* 54:14
who would *not f.* thee? *Jer* 10:7
roared, who will *not f.*? *Amos* 3:8
dost *not* thou *f.* God? *Luke* 23:40
not f. what man shall do. *Heb* 13:6
who shall *not f.* thee? *Rev* 15:4

feared

Lot *f.* to dwell in Zoar. *Gen* 19:30
Isaac *f.* to say of Rebekah. 26:7
Moses *f.* and said, this. *Ex* 2:14
he that *f.* the word of Lord. 9:20
Amalek smote thee, *f.* *Deut* 25:18
gods whom your fathers *f.* 32:17*
were it not that I *f.* the wrath. 27
f. Joshua as they did. *Josh* 4:14
Gideon *f.* *Judg* 6:27
Jether *f.* to slay them. 8:20
Samuel *f.* to shew Eli. *1 Sam* 3:15
honey dropped, for people *f.* 14:26
because I *f.* the people. 15:24
answer, he *f.* Abner. *2 Sam* 3:11
the Syrians *f.* to help. 10:19
David's servants *f.* to tell. 12:18
Adonijah *f.* because of. *1 Ki* 1:50
Israel heard judgement, and *f.* 3:28
f. other gods. *2 Ki* 17:7
they *f.* not the Lord. 25
to be *f.* above all gods. *1 Chr* 16:25
Ps 96:4
Jehoshaphat *f.* and. *2 Chr* 20:3
even thou, art to be *f.* *Ps* 76:7
the earth *f.* 8
presents to him that ought to be *f.* 11
safely, so that they *f.* not. 78:53
that thou mayest be *f.* 130:4
the isles saw it and *f.* *Isa* 41:5
and hast *f.* continually. 51:13
whom hast thou *f.* that thou. 57:11
sister Judah *f.* not. *Jer* 3:8
the sword which ye *f.* shall. 42:16
humbled, nor have they *f.* 44:10
ye have *f.* the sword. *Ezek* 11:8
all people and nations *f.* *Dan* 5:19
fear wherewith he *f.* me. *Mal* 2:5
Herod *f.* the multitude. *Mat* 14:5
21:46
and they *f.* exceedingly. *Mark* 4:41
Herod *f.* John, knowing he. 6:20
and chief priests *f.* Jesus. 11:18
of men, they *f.* people. 32; 12:12
Luke 20:19; 22:2; *Acts* 5:26
and they *f.* as they. *Luke* 9:34
and they *f.* to ask him. 45
a city a judge which *f.* not. 18:2
I *f.* thee because thou art. 19:21
because they *f.* the Jews. *John* 9:22
the magistrates *f.* when. *Acts* 16:38
Christ was heard in that he *f.*
Heb 5:7

feared *God*

but the midwives *f. God.* *Ex* 1:17
because they *f. God,* he made. 21
was faithful, and *f. God.* *Neh* 7:2
Job was one that *f. God.* *Job* 1:1
Cornelius *f. God* with his. *Acts* 10:2

feared *greatly*

the Canaanites *f. greatly.* *Josh* 10:2
all people *greatly f.* the. *1 Sam* 12:18
Obadiah *f.* Lord *greatly.* *1 Ki* 18:3
the thing I *greatly f.* is. *Job* 3:25
God is *greatly* to be *f.* *Ps* 89:7
they with him *f. greatly.* *Mat* 27:54

feared *the Lord*

the people *f. the Lord.* *Ex* 14:31
so they *f. the Lord.* *2 Ki* 17:32, 33, 41
we *f.* not *the Lord.* *Hos* 10:3
the men *f. the Lord.* *Jonah* 1:16
that *f. Lord* spake one to another . . .
that *f. the Lord.* *Mal* 3:16

fearest

I know that thou *f.* God. *Gen* 22:12
have not I held my peace even of old,
and thou *f.* me not? *Isa* 57:11
hand of them thou *f.* *Jer* 22:25

feareth

behold, Adonijah *f.* king. *1 Ki* 1:51
Job, one that *f.* God. *Job* 1:8; 2:3
what man *f.* the Lord? *Ps* 25:12
blessed is man that *f.* Lord. 112:1
blessed is every one that *f.* 128:1
shall the man be blessed that *f.* 4
that *f.* commandment. *Pr* 13:13
walketh in his uprightness *f.* 14:2
a wise man *f.* and departeth. 16
happy is man that *f.* always. 28:14
woman that *f.* Lord shall be. 31:30
that *f.* God shall come. *Eccl* 7:18
because the wicked *f.* not. 8:13
as he that *f.* an oath. 9:2
among you *f.* the Lord? *Isa* 50:10
Cornelius, one that *f.* *Acts* 10:22
he that *f.* him, is accepted. 35
whosoever among you *f.* God. 13:26
he that *f.* is not perfect. *1 John* 4:18

fearful

who is like thee, *f.* in? *Ex* 15:11
what man is *f.* let him. *Deut* 20:8
Judg 7:3
mayest fear this *f.* name. *Deut* 28:58
say to them of a *f.* heart. *Isa* 35:4
why are ye *f.* O ye of? *Mat* 8:26
why are ye so *f.*? *Mark* 4:40
f. sights in divers. *Luke* 21:11*
a certain *f.* looking for. *Heb* 10:27
f. to fall into the hands of. 31
f. have their part in the. *Rev* 21:8

fearfully

f. and wonderfully made. *Ps* 139:14

fearfulness

f. and trembling are. *Ps* 55:5
heart panteth, *f.* affrighted. *Isa* 21:4*
f. hath surprised hypocrites. 33:14*

fearing

children cease from *f.* *Josh* 22:25
the woman *f.* and. *Mark* 5:33
the chief captain *f.* lest. *Acts* 23:10
f. lest they fall into the. 27:17, 29
f. them which were of. *Gal* 2:12
in singleness of heart *f.* *Col* 3:22
forsook Egypt, not *f.* *Heb* 11:27

fears

delivered me from all my *f.* *Ps* 34:4
and when *f.* shall be in. *Eccl* 12:5*
will bring their *f.* upon. *Isa* 66:4
were fightings, within *f.* *2 Cor* 7:5

feast

The Hebrews had a great number of feasts. The first, and most ancient of all, was the sabbath, or the seventh day of the week, instituted to preserve the memory of the world's creation, Gen 2:3.

The Passover celebration began on the evening of the fourteenth day of the first month in the ecclesiastical year, which was the seventh of the civil year. It lasted seven days, but the first and last days only were days of rest, Ex 12:14, etc.

The feast of Pentecost was celebrated on the fiftieth day after the Passover, or seven complete weeks after the consecration of the harvest season by the offering of the sheaf of the first ripe barley, Ex 23:16; Lev 23:15–22; Num 28.

The feast of Trumpets was celebrated on the first day of the civil year, in the month Tisri, *answering to our September. This day was kept solemn; all manual labour was forbidden to be done upon it; and particular sacrifices were offered,* Lev 23:24, 25.

The new moons, or first days of every month, were also celebrated as minor feasts.

The feast of Tabernacles, the feast of ingathering or real harvest festival, was kept for a week in the month Tisri, *beginning five days after the day of atonement.*

Besides these feasts mentioned by Moses, we find the feasts of lots, *or* Purim, *which celebrated the escape of the Jews from Haman; the feast of Dedication, or rather of the restoration of the temple after it had been profaned by Antiochus Epiphanes, which is thought to be the feast mentioned in the gospel,* John 10:22, *was celebrated in the winter. Josephus says it was called* the feast of lights.

The Day of Atonement, which was not a feast but a fast, was kept upon the tenth day of the month Tisri, *or September. The Hebrews call it* Kippur, *that is, pardon or expiation, because it was instituted for the expiation of all the sins, irreverences, and pollutions of all the Israelites, from the high priest to the lowest of the people, committed by them throughout the whole year.*

Lot made a *f.* *Gen* 19:3
Abraham made a *f.* 21:8
Isaac made a *f.* 26:30
Laban made a *f.* 29:22
Pharaoh made a *f.* to servants. 40:20
they may hold a *f.* *Ex* 5:1; 10:9
keep it a *f.* 12:14; *Lev* 23:39, 41
the seventh day shall be a *f.* *Ex* 13:6
three times thou shalt keep a *f.* 23:14
the *f.* of harvest, the firstfruits. 16
Aaron said, to-morrow is a *f.* 32:5
fifteenth day is the *f.* *Num* 28:17
ye shall keep a *f.* to the Lord. 29:12
shalt rejoice in thy *f.* *Deut* 16:14
Samson made there a *f.* *Judg* 14:10
within the seven days of the *f.* 12
wept before him while *f.* lasted. 17
Nabal held a *f.* in his. *1 Sam* 25:36
David made Abner a *f.* *2 Sam* 3:20
Solomon made a *f.* *1 Ki* 3:15; 8:65
all Israel assembled at the *f.* 8:2
a *f.* like to the *f.* in Judah. 12:32
he ordained a *f.* to the children. 33
f. in the seventh month. *2 Chr* 5:3
Neh 8:14
Solomon kept the *f.* seven. *2 Chr* 7:8
9; 30:22; *Neh* 8:18; *Ezek* 45:25
Ahasuerus made *f.* *Esth* 1:3, 5; 2:18
Vashti made a *f.* 1:9
the Jews had a *f.* 8:17
heart hath continual *f.* *Pr* 15:15
f. is made for laughter. *Eccl* 10:19
make to all people a *f.* *Isa* 25:6
seven days of the *f.* *Ezek* 45:23
Belshazzar made a great *f.* *Dan* 5:1
at that *f.* the governor was wont to
release. *Mat* 27:15; *Mark* 15:6
up after custom of the *f.* *Luke* 2:42
Levi made him a great *f.* 5:29
but when thou makest a *f.* call. 14:13
release one unto them at *f.* 23:17
bear to governor of the *f.* *John* 2:8
when the ruler of the *f.* tasted. 9
things he did at Jerusalem at the *f.*,
for they also went to the *f.* 4:45
after this a *f.* of the Jews. 5:1
the passover, a *f.* of the Jews. 6:4
to this *f.* I go not up yet to *f.* 7:8
then went he also up to the *f.* 10
the Jews sought him at the *f.* 11
about midst of the *f.* Jesus. 14
that great day of the *f.* 37
at Jerusalem the *f.* of. 10:22
that he will not come to *f.*? 11:56
much people were come to *f.* 12:12
Greeks among them that came *f.* 20
we have need of against the *f.* 13:29
I must keep this *f.* *Acts* 18:21
let us keep the *f.* not. *1 Cor* 5:8
believe not bid you to a *f.* 10:27
sporting while they *f.* *2 Pet* 2:13
spots, when they *f.* with you. *Jude* 12*

feasted

his sons went and *f.* *Job* 1:4

feast *of the passover*

nor sacrifice of *f. of passover* be left.
Ex 34:25
two days *f. of passover.* *Mat* 26:2
Mark 14:1
year at *f. of passover.* *Luke* 2:41
before the *f. of passover* when Jesus
knew his hour was come. *John* 13:1

solemn feast
days keep a solemn f. Deut 16:15
trumpet on solemn f. day. Ps 81:3
noise as in solemn f. day. Lam 2:7*

feast of tabernacles
fifteenth day f. of taber. Lev 23:34
shalt observe f. of taber. Deut 16:13
three times appear in f. of taber.
16; 31:10; 2 Chr 8:13
kept f. of taber. as it. Ezra 3:4
go up to keep f. of taber. Zech 14:16
not to keep f. of taber. 18, 19
Jews' f. of taber. was at. John 7:2

feast of unleavened bread
observe f. of unl. br. Ex 12:17
23:15; 34:18
fifteenth day is f. of unl. br.
Lev 23:6
appear in f. of unl. br. Deut 16:16
2 Chr 8:13
to keep f. of unl. br. 2 Chr 30:13
children of Israel kept f. of unl. br. 21
f. of unl. br. seven days. 35:17
Ezra 6:22; Ezek 45:21
first day of f. of unl. br. Mat 26:17
after two days was f. of unl. br.
Mark 14:1; Luke 22:1

feast of weeks
shalt observe f. of weeks. Ex 34:22
Deut 16:10
appear in f. of weeks. Deut 16:16
burnt offerings in f. of weeks.
2 Chr 8:13

feast day, -s
will also cause her f. days. Hos 2:11
will ye do in day of the f. of? 9:5
I despise your f. days. Amos 5:21
said, not on the f. day. Mat 26:5
Mark 14:2
in the f. day many. John 2:23

feasting
made it a day of f. Esth 9:17, 18
should make them days of f. 22
days of their f. were gone. Job 1:5
than to go to house of f. Eccl 7:2
not go into house of f. Jer 16:8

feasts
these are my f. Lev 23:2, 4, 37, 44
hypocritical mockers in f. Ps 35:16
pipe, and wine in their f. Isa 5:12
I will make their f. Jer 51:39
part to give offerings in f. Ezek 45:17
in f. the meat offering shall. 46:11
I will turn your f. into. Amos 8:10
joy, gladness, cheerful f. Zech 8:19
love uppermost rooms at f. Mat 23:6
Mark 12:39; Luke 20:46
spots in your f. of charity. Jude 12

appointed feasts
your appointed f. my soul. Isa 1:14

set feasts
things do in your set f. Num 29:39
to offer on the set f. 1 Chr 23:31
Ezra 3:5
king's portion for set f. 2 Chr 31:3
for offering in the set f. Neh 10:33

solemn feasts
offering in your solemn f. Num 15:3
house for offering on solemn f.
2 Chr 2:4
offering on solemn f. three. 8:13
none come to solemn f. Lam 1:4*
caused the solemn f. to be. 2:6*
Jerusalem in solemn f. Ezek 36:38
come before Lord in solemn f. 46:9
to cease her solemn f. Hos 2:11*
dwell as in days of solemn f. 12:9
Judah, keep thy solemn f. Nah 1:15
even dung of your solemn f. Mal 2:3

feathered, see fowl

feathers
away crop with his f. Lev 1:16*
goodly wings to peacock? or wings
and f. to the ostrich? Job 39:13
f. covered with yellow. Ps 68:13*
shall cover thee with his f. 91:4*
long-winged, full of f. Ezek 17:3, 7
were grown like eagle's f. Dan 4:33

fed
Jacob f. Laban's flock. Gen 30:36
he f. the asses of Zibeon. 36:24
the seven kine f. in a. Gen 41:2, 18
he f. them with bread for. 47:17
the God who f. me all my. 48:15
bread wherewith I have f. Ex 16:32
he f. thee with manna. Deut 8:3
who f. thee in the wilderness. 16
concubines in ward, f. 2 Sam 20:3*
f. them with bread. 1 Ki 18:4, 13
over the herds that f. 1 Chr 27:29
in Lord, thou shalt be f. Ps 37:3*
so he f. them, according to. 78:72
he should have f. them with. 81:16
full of fat of f. beasts. Isa 1:11
I had f. them to the full. Jer 5:7
were as f. horses in the morning. 8
honey wherewith I f. Ezek 16:19
and kill them that are f. 34:3
shepherds f. themselves, f. not. 8
all flesh was f. with it. Dan 4:12
they f. Nebuchadnezzar with. 5:21
two staves, and I f. flock. Zech 11:7
thee hungered, and f.? Mat 25:37
that f. the swine fled. Mark 5:14
Luke 8:34
desiring to be f. with. Luke 16:21
I have f. you with milk. 1 Cor 3:2

feeble
when cattle were f. he. Gen 30:42
Amalekites smote all f. Deut 25:18
many children, waxen f. 1 Sam 2:5
Ish-bosheth's hands were f.
2 Sam 4:1
carried all the f. of. 2 Chr 28:15
what do these f. Jews? Neh 4:2
hast strengthened the f. Job 4:4
I am f. and sore broken. Ps 38:8*
not one f. person amongst. 105:37
the conies are but a f. folk. Pr 30:26
remnant very small and f. Isa 16:14*
confirm f. knees. 35:3
fame, our hands wax f. Jer 6:24
Damascus is waxed f. and. 49:24
of Babylon's hands waxed f. 50:43
all hands shall be f. Ezek 7:17
21:7
he that is f. be as David. Zech 12:8
which seem to be f. 1 Cor 12:22
comfort the f.-minded. 1 Thes 5:14
hands and f. knees. Heb 12:12*

feebler
so the f. were Laban's. Gen 30:42

feebleness
not look back for f. Jer 47:3

feed
brethren went to f. Gen 37:12
where they f. their flocks. 16
trade hath been to f. cattle. 46:32*
shall f. in another man's. Ex 22:5
neither let flocks f. before. 34:3
thou shalt f. my people. 2 Sam 5:2†
I commanded to f. Israel. 7:7†
1 Chr 17:6†
commanded ravens to f. 1 Ki 17:4
take away flocks and f. Job 24:2
the worms shall f. sweetly on. 20
f. them, and lift them up. Ps 28:9†
in grave, death f. on them. 49:14*
he brought David to f. Jacob. 78:71
lips of the righteous f. Pr 10:21
like two roes which f. S of S 4:5
my beloved is gone to f. in. 6:2
f. after their manner. Isa 5:17
the cow and the bear shall f. 11:7
firstborn of poor shall f. 14:30
there shall the calf f. and. 27:10
cattle f. in large pastures. 30:23
f. his flock as a shepherd. 40:11
they shall f. in the ways. 49:9
strangers shall stand and f. 61:5
wolf and the lamb shall f. 65:25
pastors who shall f. you. Jer 3:15
f. every one in his place. 6:3
pastors that f. my people. 23:2
shepherds which shall f. them. 4
Israel shall f. on Carmel. 50:19
they that f. delicately. Lam 4:5
woe to shepherds that f. Ezek 34:2
eat the fat, but ye f. not flock. 3
neither shall shepherds f. 10
my servant David shall f. them. 23
that f. of his meat. Dan 11:26*
now the Lord will f. them. Hos 4:16
the flour and winepress not f. 9:2
let them not f. nor drink. Jonah 3:7
f. in strength of the Lord. Mi 5:4
they shall f. thereupon. Zeph 2:7
they shall f. none make afraid. 3:13
I will not f. you. Zech 11:9
the shepherd shall not f. that. 16
sent him to fields to f. Luke 15:15
take heed to f. church of. Acts 20:28
all my goods to f. poor. 1 Cor 13:3
for the Lamb shall f. Rev 7:17*
that they should f. her there. 12:6*

feed, imperatively
f. me with that red. Gen 25:30
water the sheep, go and f. 29:7
f. him with bread and water.
1 Ki 22:27; 2 Chr 18:26
f. me with food convenient. Pr 30:8
f. thy kids beside the. S of S 1:8
f. thy people with thy rod. Mi 7:14
saith Lord, f. the flock. Zech 11:4
f. my lambs. John 21:15
f. my sheep. 16*, 17
if enemy hunger, f. him. Rom 12:20
f. the flock of God. 1 Pet 5:2*

I will feed
I will again f. and keep. Gen 30:31
I will f. thee with me. 2 Sam 19:33
I will f. them that oppress. Isa 49:26
I will f. thee with heritage of. 58:14
I will f. them with wormwood.
Jer 9:15; 23:15
I will f. them upon the mountains.
Ezek 34:13
I will f. them in a good pasture. 14
I will f. my flock, and cause. 15
I will f. the fat and the strong. 16
I will f. the flock of. Zech 11:7

feedest
f. them with bread of tears. Ps 80:5
me where thou f. flock. S of S 1:7

feedeth
mouth of fools f. on. Pr 15:14
my beloved f. among lilies.
S of S 2:16; 6:3
he f. on ashes, a deceived. Isa 44:20
Ephraim f. on wind. Hos 12:1
your heavenly Father f. Mat 6:26
ravens sow not, yet God f. them.
Luke 12:24
who f. a flock, and. 1 Cor 9:7

feeding
Joseph was f. his flock. Gen 37:2
plowing, the asses f. by. Job 1:14
to cease from f. flock. Ezek 34:10
where is the f. place? Nah 2:11
an herd of swine f. Mat 8:30
Mark 5:11; Luke 8:32
a servant f. cattle. Luke 17:7*
f. themselves without fear. Jude 12*

feel
peradventure will f. me. Gen 27:12
come near, that I may f. thee. 21
suffer me that I may f. Judg 16:26
he shall not f. quietness. Job 20:20*
before pots can f. thorns. Ps 58:9
commandment f. no evil. Eccl 8:5*
if haply they might f. Acts 17:27

feeling
being past f. have given. Eph 4:19
touched with the f. of. Heb 4:15

feet
lawgiver from between his f.
Gen 49:10
Jacob gathered up f. in the bed. 33
thy shoes from off thy f. Ex 3:5
Acts 7:33
passover with shoes on f. Ex 12:11
have legs above their f. Lev 11:21
will pass through on f. Deut 2:28
cometh from between her f. 28:57
they sat down at thy f. every. 33:3
the f. of the priests were. Josh 3:15
old shoes, and clouted upon f. 9:5
put your f. on the necks of. 10:24
land whereon thy f. have. 14:9
he covereth his f. in. Judg 3:24
Sisera fled away on his f. 4:15, 17
at her f. bowed, at her f. fell. 5:27
go in, uncover his f. and. Ruth 3:4
behold a woman lay at his f. 8
he will keep the f. of 1 Sam 2:9

Jonathan climbed on hands and f. 1 Sam 14:13
Saul went in to cover his f. 24:3
rode with five damsels at f. 25:42
thy f. put into fetters. 2 Sam 3:34
Jonathan's son lame of f. 4:4; 9:3, 13
cut off their hands and their f. 4:12
Mephibosheth had neither dressed his f. 19:24
he maketh my f. like hinds' f. 22:34
Ps 18:33; Hab 3:19
my f. did not slip. 2 Sam 22:37
Ps 18:36
of war in shoes on his f. 1 Ki 2:5
Ahijah heard sound of her f. 14:6
when thy f. enter the city, the. 12
Asa was diseased in his f. 15:23
2 Chr 16:12
came, caught him by f. 2 Ki 4:27
not sound of his master's f.? 6:32
no more of her than the f. 9:35
man revived, stood upon his f. 13:21
nor make the f. of Israel. 21:8
David king stood on his f. 1 Chr 28:2
not old, their f. swelled. Neh 9:21
ready to slip with his f. Job 12:5
puttest my f. in stocks, thou settest a print upon heels of my f. 13:27
cast into a net by his own f. 18:8
and drive him to his f. 11
blind, f. was I to the lame. 29:15
youth rise, push away my f. 30:12
he putteth my f. in the stocks. 33:11
my hands and my f. Ps 22:16
for he shall pluck my f. out. 25:15
hast set my f. in large room. 31:8
he set my f. on rock, and. 40:2
deliver my f. from falling? 56:13
suffereth not our f. to be. 66:9
my f. were almost gone. 73:2
lift up thy f. unto perpetual. 74:3
f. they hurt with fetters. 105:18
f. have they, but they walk not. 115:7
hast delivered my f. from. 116:8
my f. unto thy testimonies. 119:59
I refrained my f. from every. 101
thy word is a lamp to my f. 105
f. shall stand within thy gates. 122:2
their f. run to evil. Pr 1:16; 6:18
Isa 59:7
ponder the path of thy f. Pr 4:26
her f. go down to death. 5:5
wicked man speaketh with his f. 6:13
on coals and his f. not be burnt? 28
her f. abide not in her house. 7:11
hasteth with his f. sinneth. 19:2
cutteth off the f. and drinketh. 26:6
spreadeth a net for his f. 29:5*
beautiful are thy f. with. S of S 7:1
a tinkling with their f. Isa 3:16
away ornaments about their f. 18
with twain covered his f., with. 6:2
Lord shall shave hair of the f. 7:20
own f. shall carry her afar. 23:7
f. of the poor shall tread. 26:6
send forth the f. of the ox. 32:20
he had not gone with his f. 41:3
shall lick up dust of thy f. 49:23
f. of him that bringeth tidings. 52:7
Nah 1:15
place of my f. glorious. Isa 60:13
before your f. stumble. Jer 13:16
not refrained their f. 14:10
and hid snares for my f. 18:22
thy f. are sunk in the mire. 38:22
spread a net for my f. Lam 1:13
their f. were straight f. Ezek 1:7
son of man, stand upon thy f. 2:1
Spirit set me upon my f. 2; 3:24
hast opened thy f. to. 16:25
put on thy shoes upon thy f. 24:17
your heads, shoes on your f. 23
thou hast stamped with f. 25:6
troubledst waters with thy f. 32:2
foul residue with your f. 34:18
trodden and fouled with f. 19
and stood upon their f. 37:10
f. part of iron. Dan 2:33, 42
stone smote image upon his f. 34
thou sawest the f. and toes. 41
stamped residue with f. of it. 7:7, 19
his f. like polished brass. 10:6
Rev 1:15; 2:18
clouds are dust of his f. Nah 1:3
his f. shall stand upon. Zech 14:4
depart, shake off the dust of your f. Mat 10:14; Mark 6:11; Luke 9:5
lame and blind at Jesus' f. Mat 15:30
rather than having two f. to. 18:8
they held him by the f. and. 28:9
to guide our f. into way. Luke 1:79
she kissed his f. and. 7:38
woman not ceased to kiss my f. 45
man sitting at the f. of Jesus. 8:35
Jairus fell down at Jesus' f. 41
Mary, who sat at Jesus' f. 10:39
ring on hand, shoes on his f. 15:22
behold my hands and my f. 24:39
shewed them his hands and f. 40
wiped his f. with. John 11:2; 12:3
Mary anointed the f. of Jesus. 12:3
angel at head, the other at f. 20:12
immediately his f. received strength. Acts 3:7
laid them down at apostles' f. 4:35
37; 5:2
f. of them who have buried. 5:9
their clothes at young man's f. 7:58
shoes of his f. I am not. 13:25
they shook off the dust of their f. 51
Lystra a man impotent in his f. 14:8
stand upright on thy f. he. 10
who made their f. fast in. 16:24
Agabus bound hands and f. 21:11
brought up at f. of Gamaliel. 22:3
rise, and stand upon thy f. 26:16
f. are swift to shed. Rom 3:15
the f. of them that preach. 10:15
nor head to the f. I. 1 Cor 12:21
your f. shod with the. Eph 6:15
straight paths for f. Heb 12:13
and worship before thy f. Rev 3:9
mighty angel, his f. as pillars. 10:1
witnesses stood upon their f. 11:11
his f. were as f. of a bear. 13:2
to worship before his f. 22:8

at his **feet**

cast foreskin at his f. Ex 4:25
ten thousand at his f. Judg 4:10
she lay at his f. until. Ruth 3:14
Abigail fell at his f. 1 Sam 25:24
of Shunem fell at his f. 2 Ki 4:37
Esther fell down at his f. Esth 8:3
coals went forth at his f. Hab 3:5
servant fell at his f. Mat 18:29
Jairus fell at his f. Mark 5:22
Syrophenician woman fell at his f. 7:25
stood at his f. behind. Luke 7:38
Mary fell down at his f. John 11:32
Sapphira fell at his f. Acts 5:10
Cornelius met him, fell at his f. 10:25
I fell at his f. as dead. Rev 1:17
fell at his f. to worship him. 19:10

feet joined with *sole* or *soles*

soles of your f. tread. Deut 11:24
as soles of priests' f. Josh 3:13; 4:18
them under soles of his f. 1 Ki 5:3
sole of my f. dried. 2 Ki 19:24
Isa 37:25
bow at the soles of thy f. Isa 60:14
the sole of their f. was. Ezek 1:7
the place of soles of my f. 43:7
be ashes under soles of f. Mal 4:3

under **feet**

under his f. as it were. Ex 24:10
darkness under his f. 2 Sam 22:10
Ps 18:9
fallen under my f. 2 Sam 22:39
put all things under his f. Ps 8:6
1 Cor 15:27; Eph 1:22
subdue nations under our f. Ps 47:3
dragon shalt trample under f. 91:13
carcase trodden under f. Isa 14:19
drunkards trodden under f. 28:3
to crush under his f. all. Lam 3:34
trample them under their f. Mat 7:6
bruise Satan under your f. Rom 16:20
all enemies under his f. 1 Cor 15:25
in subjection under his f. Heb 2:8
sun, moon under her f. Rev 12:1

feet with *wash*, or *washed*

fetched, wash your f. Gen 18:4
tarry all night, wash your f. 19:2
gave water to wash his f. 24:32
and they washed their f. Gen 43:24
Aaron and his sons shall wash hands and f. Ex 30:19, 21; 40:31
and concubine washed f. Judg 19:21
to wash the f. of. 1 Sam 25:41
thy house, wash thy f. 2 Sam 11:8
wash his f. in blood of. Ps 58:10
have washed my f. how. S of S 5:3
began to wash his f. Luke 7:38
hath washed my f. with tears. 44
to wash disciples' f. John 13:5
Lord dost thou wash my f.? 6
thou shalt never wash my f. 8
needeth not save to wash his f. 10
after he had washed their f. 12
if I have washed your f. 14
have washed saints' f. 1 Tim 5:10

feign

f. thyself to be a mourner. 2 Sam 14:2
f. herself to be another. 1 Ki 14:5
should f. themselves. Luke 20:20

feigned

David f. himself mad. 1 Sam 21:13
prayer that goeth not out of f. lips. Ps 17:1
with f. words make. 2 Pet 2:3

feignedly

turned to me but f. Jer 3:10

feignest

f. thou to be another? 1 Ki 14:6
but thou f. them out of. Neh 6:8

Felix

bring Paul safe to F. Acts 23:24
Lysias to excellent governor F. 26
accepted always, most noble F. 24:3
when F. came with his wife. 24
Paul reasoned of judgement, F. 25
certain man left in bonds by F. 25:14

fell

and his countenance f. Gen 4:5
of Sodom and Gomorrah f. 14:10
a deep sleep f. on Abram. 15:12
Esau ran, and f. on his. 33:4
Joseph's brethren f. before. 44:14
Joseph f. on Benjamin's neck. 45:14
Jacob f. on Joseph's neck. 46:29
f. of the people 3000. Ex 32:28
goat on which the Lord's lot f. Lev 16:9, 10
mixt multitude f. lusting. Num 11:4
dew f. on the camp, the manna f. 9
Moses and Aaron f. 14:5; 16:22, 45
20:6
that f. that day, 12,000. Josh 8:25
Joshua came and f. upon. 11:7
and wrath f. on all the. 22:20
Sisera's host f. on edge. Judg 4:16
Sisera f. 5:27
of bread smote tent that it f. 7:13
for there f. 120,000 men. 8:10
there f. of Ephraimites 42,000. 12:6
the house f. on the lords. 16:30
there f. of Benjamin 18,000. 20:44
f. of Israel 30,000. 1 Sam 4:10
Eli f. from his seat backward. 18
fear of the Lord f. on people. 11:7
Philistines f. before Jonathan. 14:13
Doeg turned, and f. upon. 22:18
Abigail f. at David's feet. 25:24
Saul f. straightway along on. 28:20
no fault in him since he f. 29:3
three days agone I f. sick. 30:13
Saul took a sword and f. 31:4
armourbearer f. 5; 1 Chr 10:4, 5
Mephibosheth f. and. 2 Sam 4:4
f. some of the people of. 11:17
Amnon f. sick for his sister. 13:2
Joab's sword f. out as he. 20:8
they f. all seven together. 21:9
f. by hand of David. 22; 1 Chr 20:8
Benaiah f. on Adonijah. 1 Ki 2:25
who f. upon two men better than. 32
Benaiah f. on Joab. 34
Benaiah f. on Shimei. 46
Abijah son of Jeroboam f. 14:1
the son of the woman f. sick. 17:17
fire of Lord f. and consumed. 18:38
a wall f. on 27,000 men. 20:30
third captain f. on knees. 2 Ki 1:13
mantle of Elijah that f. from. 2:13
it f. on a day Elisha passed. 4:8, 11

it *f.* on a day the child went. *2 Ki* 4:18
Shunammite *f.* at his feet. 37
the axe head *f.* into water. 6:5
man of God said, where *f.* it? 6
so it *f.* out to him, the. 7:20*
the fugitives that *f.* away. 25:11
f. some of Manasseh. *1 Chr* 12:19
there *f.* of Israel 70,000. 21:14
because there *f.* wrath for. 27:24*
for they *f.* to David. *2 Chr* 15:9
the fear of Lord *f.* on all. 17:10
inhabitants of Jerusalem *f.* 20:18
bowels *f.* out by reason of. 21:19
the soldiers of Israel *f.* on. 25:13
I *f.* on my knees and. *Ezra* 9:5
fear of Jews *f.* on. *Esth* 8:17; 9:2
the fear of Mordecai *f.* upon. 9:3
Sabeans *f.* on the asses. *Job* 1:15
Chaldeans *f.* on camels, and. 17
the house *f.* on young men, and. 19
to eat my flesh, they *f.* *Ps* 27:2
their priests *f.* by sword. 78:64
the fear of Israel *f.* on. 105:38
that *f.* away, *f.* to. *Jer* 39:9; 52:15
one *f.* upon another. 46:16
her people *f.* into hand. *Lam* 1:7
and children *f.* under wood. 5:13*
hand of the Lord *f.* *Ezek* 8:1; 11:5
so *f.* they all by the sword. 39:23
f. a voice from heaven. *Dan* 4:31
came up, before whom three *f.* 7:20
a great quaking *f.* upon them. 10:7
and the lot *f.* on Jonah. *Jonah* 1:7
the house *f.* not. *Mat* 7:25
house, and it *f.* 27; *Luke* 6:49
seed *f.* by way side. *Mat* 13:4
Mark 4:4; *Luke* 8:5
f. upon stony places. *Mat* 13:5
Mark 4:5; *Luke* 8:6
some *f.* among thorns. *Mat* 13:7
Mark 4:7; *Luke* 8:7
other *f.* into good. *Mat* 13:8
Mark 4:8; *Luke* 8:8
Jairus *f.* at his feet. *Mark* 5:22
Syrophenician woman came, *f.* 7:25
he *f.* on the ground and. 9:20
Jesus *f.* on the ground. 14:35
fear *f.* upon Zacharias. *Luke* 1:12
as they sailed, Jesus *f.* asleep. 8:23
a certain man *f.* among. 10:30, 36
upon whom tower in Siloam *f.* 13:4
his father *f.* on his neck. 15:20
crumbs which *f.* from rich. 16:21
went backward and *f.* to. *John* 18:6
Judas by trangression *f.* *Acts* 1:25
gave forth lots, and the lot *f.* 26
he had said this, he *f.* asleep. 7:60
Saul *f.* to the earth and. 9:4
there *f.* from his eyes as it had. 18
Peter became hungry, *f.* into. 10:10
Holy Ghost *f.* on them. 44; 11:15
chains *f.* from Peter's hands. 12:7
there *f.* on him a mist and. 13:11
David *f.* on sleep and saw. 36
and fear *f.* on all the Jews. 19:17
Paul went down, *f.* on. 20:10
they all *f.* on Paul's neck. 37
I *f.* unto the ground, and. 22:7
them which *f.* severity. *Rom* 11:22
reproaches of them *f.* on me. 15:3
and *f.* in one day. *1 Cor* 10:8
whose carcases *f.* in the. *Heb* 3:17
since fathers *f.* asleep. *2 Pet* 3:4
when I saw him I *f.* at. *Rev* 1:17
the stars of heaven *f.* unto. 6:13
there *f.* a great star from. 8:10
and great fear *f.* on them who. 11:11
the tenth part of the city *f.* by. 13
and there *f.* a noisome and. 16:2
and cities of nations *f.* 19
there *f.* upon men, great hail out. 21
I *f.* at his feet to worship him. 19:10

see **face, faces**

fell *down*

ass saw angel, she *f. down.*
Num 22:27*
and I *f. down* before. *Deut* 9:18, 25
shouted, wall *f. down.* *Josh* 6:20
there he *f. down* dead. *Judg* 5:27
concubine *f. down* at door. 19:26
Philistines *f.* down. *1 Sam* 17:52
Israel *f. down* in Gilboa. 31:1
1 Chr 10:1
so they *f. down* together. *2 Sam* 2:16
Asahel *f. down* there, and. 23
Ahimaaz *f. down.* 18:28*
Shimei *f. down.* 19:18
and Ahaziah *f. down.* *2 Ki* 1:2
f. down many slain. *1 Chr* 5:22
there *f. down* of Israel. *2 Chr* 13:17
Esther *f. down* at. *Esth* 8:3
Job *f. down* on ground. *Job* 1:20
f. down there was none. *Ps* 107:12
all nations *f. down* and. *Dan* 3:7
these three *f. down* bound in. 23
wise men *f. down* and. *Mat* 2:11
servant therefore *f. down,* saying.
18:26, 29
unclean spirits *f. down.* *Mark* 3:11
with issue of blood *f. down.* 5:33
Simon Peter *f. down* at. *Luke* 5:8
which had devils *f. down.* 8:28
Jairus *f. down.* 41
the Samaritan *f. down.* 17:16
Mary *f. down* at feet. *John* 11:32
Ananias *f. down.* *Acts* 5:5
Sapphira *f. down.* 10
Cornelius *f. down* at his feet. 10:25
keeper *f. down* before Paul. 16:29
image which *f. down* from. 19:35
Eutychus *f. down* from third. 20:9
walls of Jericho *f. down.* *Heb* 11:30
elders *f. down* before the Lamb.
Rev 5:8, 14; 19:4
John *f. down* to worship. 22:8

fell

shall *f.* every good tree. *2 Ki* 3:19

felled

and they *f.* all good trees. *2 Ki* 3:25

feller

no *f.* is come up against. *Isa* 14:8

fellest

before wicked men, so *f.* *2 Sam* 3:34

felling

as one was *f.* a beam. *2 Ki* 6:5

felloes

their *f.* and their spokes. *1 Ki* 7:33

fellow

this one *f.* came in to. *Gen* 19:9
smitest thou thy *f.*? *Ex* 2:13
told a dream to his *f.* *Judg* 7:13
Lord set every man's sword against
his *f.* through. 22; *1 Sam* 14:20
brought this *f.* to play the madman;
shall this *f.* come. *1 Sam* 21:15
in vain have I kept all this *f.* 25:21
make this *f.* return. 29:4
caught every one his *f.* *2 Sam* 2:16
put this *f.* in prison. *1 Ki* 22:27
2 Chr 18:26
wherefore came this mad *f.* to?
2 Ki 9:11
one will lift up his *f.* *Eccl* 4:10
the satyr shall cry to his *f.* *Isa* 34:14
said every one to his *f.* *Jonah* 1:7
awake, O sword, against the man
that is my *f.*, saith Lord. *Zech* 13:7
f. doth not cast out. *Mat* 12:24*
this *f.* said, I am able to. 26:61*
this *f.* was also with Jesus. 71*
Luke 22:59*
found this *f.* perverting. *Luke* 23:2*
as for this *f.* we know. *John* 9:29*
Didymus said to *f.* disciples. 11:16
this *f.* persuadeth men. *Acts* 18:13*
away with such a *f.* from. 22:22
this man a pestilent *f.* 24:5

fellow-citizens

but *f.-citizens* with saints. *Eph* 2:19

fellow-heirs

Gentiles be *f.-heirs.* *Eph* 3:6

fellow-helper

Titus my *f.-helper.* *2 Cor* 8:23

fellow-helpers

we might be *f.-helpers.* *3 John* 8

fellow-labourer

Timotheus our *f.-labourer.*
1 Thes 3:2
Philemon our *f.-labourer.* *Philem* 1

fellow-labourers

other my *f.-labourers.* *Phil* 4:3
Lucas, my *f.-labourers.* *Philem* 24

fellow-prisoner

Aristarchus my *f.-prisoner.* *Col* 4:10
Epaphras my *f.-prisoner.* *Philem* 23

fellow-prisoners

Andronicus and Junia *f.-prisoners.*
Rom 16:7

fellows

virginity, I and my *f.* *Judg* 11:37*
lest angry *f.* run on thee. 18:25
as one of the vain *f.* *2 Sam* 6:20
with oil of gladness above *f.*
Ps 45:7; *Heb* 1:9
his *f.* shall be ashamed. *Isa* 44:11
tribes of Israel his *f.* *Ezek* 37:19*
sought Daniel and his *f.* *Dan* 2:13*
that Daniel and his *f.* not. 18*
was more stout than his *f.* 7:20
thou and thy *f.* that set. *Zech* 3:8
children calling to their *f.* *Mat* 11:16
Jews took lewd *f.* of. *Acts* 17:5

fellow-servant, or *servants*

found one of his *f.-serv.* *Mat* 18:28
his *f.-serv.* fell at his feet. 29
so when his *f.-serv.* saw what. 31
have had compassion on *f.-serv.* 33
begin to smite his *f.-serv.* 24:49
of Epaphras our *f.-serv.* *Col* 1:7
Tychicus, who is a *f.-serv.* in. 4:7
till their *f.-serv.* should. *Rev* 6:11
it not, I am thy *f.-serv.* 19:10; 22:9

fellowship

him to keep, or in *f.* *Lev* 6:2
of iniquity have *f.* with? *Ps* 94:20
apostles' doctrine and *f.* *Acts* 2:42
called to the *f.* of his Son. *1 Cor* 1:9
not that ye should have *f.* 10:20*
what *f.* hath righteousness with?
2 Cor 6:14
take on us the *f.* of ministering. 8:4
gave to me right hand of *f.* *Gal* 2:9
make men see what is *f.* *Eph* 3:9*
have no *f.* with works of. 5:11
for your *f.* in the gospel. *Phil* 1:5
if there be any *f.* of the spirit. 2:1
that I may know the *f.* of. 3:10
also may have *f.* with us, and our *f.*
is with Father, and. *1 John* 1:3
if we say that we have *f.* with. 6
if we walk in light, we have *f.* 7

fellow-soldier

Epaphroditus my *f.-soldier.*
Phil 2:25
Paul to Archippus our *f.-soldier.*
Philem 2

fellow-workers

only are my *f.-workers.* *Col* 4:11

felt

and Isaac *f.* him. *Gen* 27:22
darkness that may be *f.* *Ex* 10:21
beaten me, and I *f.* it not. *Pr* 23:35
she *f.* she was healed. *Mark* 5:29
shook off the beast and *f.* *Acts* 28:5*

female

male and *f.* created. *Gen* 1:27; 5:2
they shall be male and *f.* 6:19
sevens, the male and his *f.* 7:2, 3
went in two and two, male and *f.* 9
went in, went in male and *f.* 16
whether it be male or *f.* *Lev* 3:1
offering be of flock, male or *f.* 6
a *f.* without blemish. 4:28, 32; 5:6
that hath born a male or *f.* 12:7
if it be a *f.* thy estimation shall. 27:4
thy estimation for the *f.* ten. 5, 7
for the *f.* from a month old. 6
both male and *f.* shall. *Num* 5:3
the likeness of male or *f.* *Deut* 4:16
not be a male or *f.* barren. 7:14
made them male and *f.* *Mat* 19:4
Mark 10:6
in Christ neither male nor *f.*
Gal 3:28

fence

wall and a tottering *f.* *Ps* 62:3

fenced, *verb*

f. me with bones and. *Job* 10:11
he hath *f.* up my way that. 19:8
hath a vineyard, *f.* it. *Isa* 5:2

fenced

till thy high and *f.* walls. *Deut* 28:52
must be *f.* with iron. *2 Sam* 23:7
ye shall smite every *f.* *2 Ki* 3:19

there are with you a *f.* city. *2 Ki* 10:2
tower to the *f.* city. 17:9; 18:8
day of Lord on every *f.* *Isa* 2:15
make thee a *f.* brasen. *Jer* 15:20
ruined cities become *f.* *Ezek* 36:35

fenced *cities*
(*American Revision uses here the word* fortified)

ones dwell in *f. cities.* *Num* 32:17
all these *cities* were *f.* *Deut* 3:5
to possess *cities* great and *f.* 9:1
rest entered into *f. cities. Josh* 10:20
the *cities* were great and *f.* 14:12
number of *f. cities.* *1 Sam* 6:18
lest he get *f. cities.* *2 Sam* 20:6
Sennacherib came against all the *f. cities* of. *2 Ki* 18:13; *2 Chr* 12:4
lay waste *f. cities.* *2 Ki* 19:25
Solomon built *f. cities.* *2 Chr* 8:5
Shishak took the *f. cities.* 12:4
Asa built *f. cities* in Judah. 14:6
placed forces in *f. cities.* 17:2, 19
judges throughout all *f. cities.* 19:5
gave them *f. cities* in Judah. 21:3
put captains in *f. cities.* 33:14
impoverish thy *f. cities.* *Jer* 5:17
of north take *f. cities.* *Dan* 11:15
Judah multiplied *f. cities. Hos* 8:14
alarm against *f. cities.* *Zeph* 1:16

fens

in covert of reed and *f.* *Job* 40:21

ferret

f. chameleon and lizard. *Lev* 11:30*

ferry boat

there went a *f. boat.* *2 Sam* 19:18

fervent

Apollos, being *f.* in spirit. *Acts* 18:25
f. in spirit, serving Lord. *Rom* 12:11
he told us your *f.* mind. *2 Cor* 7:7*
f. prayer of a righteous. *Jas* 5:16*
above all things *f.* charity. *1 Pet* 4:8
elements melt with *f.* heat. *2 Pet* 3:10, 12

fervently

Epaphras labouring *f.* *Col* 4:12
love one another with a pure heart *f.* *1 Pet* 1:22

Festus

Porcius *F.* come into. *Acts* 24:27
F. willing to do Jews a pleasure. 25:9
came to Caesarea to salute *F.* 13
F. declared Paul's cause unto. 14
at *F.*' commandment Paul was. 23
not mad, most noble *F.* 26:25

fetch

I will *f.* a morsel of bread. *Gen* 18:5
go, *f.* me two good kids. 27:9, 13
then I will send and *f.* thee. 45
ark, sent maid to *f.* it. *Ex* 2:5
must we *f.* water out ? *Num* 20:10*
elders shall send and *f.* *Deut* 19:12
shalt not go to *f.* pledge. 24:10, 19
from thence will Lord *f.* thee. 30:4
of Gilead went to *f.* *Judg* 11:5
take men to *f.* victuals. 20:10
let us *f.* the ark. *1 Sam* 4:3
come ye down, and *f.* it up. 6:21
Samuel said, Send and *f.* him. 16:11
20:31
let us come over and *f.* 26:22
f. a compass behind. *2 Sam* 5:23*
doth king not *f.* home his. 14:13
to *f.* about this form of speech. 20*
f. me, I pray thee, a. *1 Ki* 17:10
as she was going to *f.* it. 11
he is, that I may *f.* him. *2 Ki* 6:13
f. quickly Micaiah the. *2 Chr* 18:8
f. olive branches, pine. *Neh* 8:15
I will *f.* my knowledge. *Job* 36:3
say they, I will *f.* wine. *Isa* 56:12
king sent Jehudi to *f.* *Jer* 36:21
come and *f.* us out. *Acts* 16:37*

fetched

water, I pray you, be *f.* *Gen* 18:4
Abraham *f.* a calf tender and. 7
Jacob went and *f.* the kids. 27:14
they *f.* carved image. *Judg* 18:18
men came and *f.* up ark. *1 Sam* 7:1
they ran, and *f.* Saul thence. 10:23
they would have *f.* wheat. *2 Sam* 4:6
David sent and *f.* Mephibosheth. 9:5
David sent and *f.* Bath-sheba. 11:27*
Joab *f.* from Tekoah a. *2 Sam* 14:2
king Solomon *f.* Hiram. *1 Ki* 7:13
f. from Ophir gold, 420 talents. 9:28
f. a compass of seven. *2 Ki* 3:9
Jehoiada sent and *f.* rulers. 11:4
f. from Egypt a chariot. *2 Chr* 1:17
guard came and *f.* the. 12:11*
and they *f.* forth Urijah. *Jer* 26:23
and from thence *f.* a. *Acts* 28:13*

fetcheth

and his hand *f.* a stroke. *Deut* 19:5

fetters

bound Samson with *f.* *Judg* 16:21
hands were not bound, nor thy feet put into *f.* *2 Sam* 3:34
put out eyes of Zedekiah, and bound him with *f.* of brass. *2 Ki* 25:7
Manasseh was bound with *f.* *2 Chr* 33:11
Jehoiakim bound with *f.* to. 36:6
feet they hurt with *f.* *Ps* 105:18
their nobles with *f.* of iron. 149:8
being often bound with *f.* *Mark* 5:4
Luke 8:29

fever

shall smite thee with a *f. Deut* 28:22
Peter's wife's mother sick of a *f.* *Mat* 8:14; *Mark* 1:30; *Luke* 4:38
at 7th hour *f.* left him. *John* 4:52
of Publius sick of a *f.* *Acts* 28:8

few

damsel abide a *f.* days. *Gen* 24:55
tarry a *f.* days till thy. 27:44
I being *f.* in number, they. 34:30
f. and evil the days of my life. 47:9
I will make you *f.* *Lev* 26:22
Deut 4:27; 28:62
the cloud was a *f.* days. *Num* 9:20
see people whether they be *f.* 13:18
to *f.* shall give less. 26:54; 35:8
divided between many and *f.* 26:56
sojourned there with a *f. Deut* 26:5
live, let not his men be *f.* 33:6
to save by many or *f.* *1 Sam* 14:6
whom hast thou left *f.* sheep ? 17:28
but priests were too *f.* *2 Chr* 29:34
I and some *f.* men with. *Neh* 2:12
large, but the people were *f.* 7:4
are not my days *f.*? *Job* 10:20
man is of *f.* days and full. 14:1
when a *f.* years are come. 16:22
let his days be *f.* and let. *Ps* 109:8
therefore let words be *f.* *Eccl* 5:2
a little city, and *f.* men in it. 9:14
cease, because they are *f.* 12:3
trees of forest shall be *f.* *Isa* 10:19
inhabitants are burned, and *f.* 24:6
shalt also take a *f.* in. *Ezek* 5:3
I will leave a *f.* men from. 12:16
f. days be destroyed. *Dan* 11:20
strait is gate, and *f.* *Mat* 7:14
labourers are *f.* 9:37; *Luke* 10:2
seven, and a *f.* little fishes. *Mat* 15:34; *Mark* 8:7
f. are chosen. *Mat* 20:16; 22:14
faithful in a *f.* things. 25:21, 23
laid hands on a *f.* sick. *Mark* 6:5
be beaten with *f.* stripes. *Luke* 12:48
are there *f.* that be saved ? 13:23
hear us a *f.* words. *Acts* 24:4
as I wrote in *f.* words. *Eph* 3:3
for a *f.* days chastened. *Heb* 12:10
written unto you in *f.* words. 13:22
wherein *f.* that is, eight. *1 Pet* 3:20
a *f.* things against. *Rev* 2:14, 20
hast a *f.* names even in. 3:4

but a **few**

to him *but a few* days. *Gen* 29:20
but f. years to jubile. *Lev* 25:52
the men of Ai are *but f.* *Josh* 7:3
when ye were *but f.* *1 Chr* 16:19
Ps 105:12
we are left *but a f.* of. *Jer* 42:2

not a **few**

vessels, borrow *not a f.* *2 Ki* 4:3
cut off nations *not a f.* *Isa* 10:7
and they shall *not be f.* *Jer* 30:19
chief women *not a f.* *Acts* 17:4
of men *not a f.* 12

fewer

to *f.* ye shall give less. *Num* 33:54

fewest

ye were *f.* of all people. *Deut* 7:7

fewness

according to *f.* of years. *Lev* 25:16

fidelity

servants shewing good *f.* *Tit* 2:10

field

the *f.* give I thee. *Gen* 23:11
the *f.* and cave were made sure. 20
of my son is as smell of a *f.* 27:27
called Rachel and Leah to *f.* 31:4
in *f.* which Abraham. 49:30; 50:13
a man shall cause a *f.* to. *Ex* 22:5
that the corn or *f.* be consumed. 6
shalt not sow thy *f.* with. *Lev* 19:19
six years shalt sow thy *f.* 25:3
seventh year shalt not sow thy *f.* 4
if he sanctify his *f.* from. 27:17, 18
redeem the *f.* or if he sold the *f.* 20
covet thy neighbour's *f.* *Deut* 5:21
ask of her father a *f.* *Josh* 15:18
Judg 1:14
not to glean in another *f.* *Ruth* 2:8
what day thou buyest *f.* of. 4:5
Joab's *f.* is near mine. *2 Sam* 14:30
servants set my *f.* on fire ? 31
upper pool, in highway of fuller's *f.* *2 Ki* 18:17; *Isa* 7:3; 36:2
fled every one to his *f.* *Neh* 13:10
let the *f.* be joyful. *Ps* 96:12
I went by the *f.* of slothful. *Pr* 24:30
and goats the price of *f.* 27:26
considereth a *f.* and buyeth. 31:16
king himself is served by *f. Eccl* 5:9
woe to them that lay *f.* to *f. Isa* 5:8
joy is taken out of plentiful *f.* 16:10
herbs of every *f.* wither. *Jer* 12:4
Zion plowed like a *f.* 26:18; *Mi* 3:12
my *f.* in Anathoth. *Jer* 32:7, 8, 25
have we vineyard, nor *f.* 35:9
gladness is taken from plentiful *f.* 48:33
the *f.* is wasted, the. *Joel* 1:10
good seed in his *f.* *Mat* 13:24, 31
the *f.* is the world, good seed. 38
of heaven is like to treasure hid in a *f.*; he selleth all, buyeth that *f.* 44
with them the potter's *f.* 27:7, 10
f. was called *f.* of blood. 8; *Acts* 1:19
when come from the *f.* *Luke* 17:7
man purchased a *f.* with. *Acts* 1:18

fruitful **field**

glory of his *fruitful f.* *Isa* 10:18
Lebanon turned into *fruitful f.* 29:17
till wilderness be a *fruitful f.* and the *fruitful f.* be counted a. 32:15
righteousness in the *fruitful f.* 16
the seed in a *fruitful f.* *Ezek* 17:5

in the **field**

when they were *in the f.* *Gen* 4:8
out to meditate *in the f.* 24:63
and behold a well *in the f.* 29:2
Joseph was wandering *in the f.* 37:15
gather all thou hast *in the f. Ex* 9:19
hail smote all that was *in the f.* 25
ye shall not find it *in the f.* 16:25
found slain, lying *in the f. Deut* 21:1
find a betrothed damsel *in f.* 22:25
blessed in city and *in the f.* 28:3
cursed in city and *in the f.* 16
angel came to woman *in f. Judg* 13:9
stone remaineth *in f.* of. *1 Sam* 6:18
stand beside my father *in the f.* 19:3
found an Egyptian *in the f.* 30:11
they two strove *in the f. 2 Sam* 14:6
two were alone *in the f. 1 Ki* 11:29
dieth of Jeroboam *in the f.* 14:11
dieth of Ahab *in the f.* fowls. 21:24
kings by themselves *in f. 1 Chr* 19:9
over them that did work *in f.* 27:26
every one his corn *in f.* *Job* 24:6
marvellous things *in f.* of Zoan. *Ps* 78:12, 43
it fit for thyself *in the f.* *Pr* 24:27
the hind calved *in the f.* *Jer* 14:5
O my mountain *in the f.* 17:3
we have treasures *in the f.* 41:8
is *in the f.* shall die. *Ezek* 7:15
slay thy daughters *in the f.* 26:6, 8
shalt dwell *in the f.* and. *Mi* 4:10
every one grass *in the f.* *Zech* 10:1

nor vine cast her fruit in the f. Mal 3:11
let him who is in f. return to. Mat 24:18; Mark 13:16
Luke 17:31
shall two be in the f. Mat 24:40
Luke 17:36
shepherds abiding in f. Luke 2:8
grass which is to-day in the f. 12:28
his elder son was in the f. 15:25

into the **field**

and went into the f. Num 22:23
people went into the f. Judg 9:42
cart came into the f. 1 Sam 6:14
come let us go into the f. 20:11
men came out into f. 2 Sam 11:23
removed Amasa into the f. 20:12
one went into f. and. 2 Ki 4:39
let us go forth into f. S of S 7:11
go not forth into f. nor. Jer 6:25
if I go forth into the f. 14:18

of the **field**

plant and herb of the f. Gen 2:5
sons of Jacob came out of f. 34:7
four parts, for seed of the f. 47:24
trees of the f. yield fruit. Lev 26:4
no devoted thing of the f. 27:28
for the tree of the f. is. Deut 20:19
marchedst out of the f. Judg 5:4
old man from work out of f. 19:16
on a part of the f. Ruth 2:3
Saul came out of the f. 1 Sam 11:5
of the f. of Naboth. 2 Ki 9:25
as dung upon the face of the f. 37
league with stones of the f. Job 5:23
as a flower of the f. Ps 103:15
charge you by the roes of the f. S of S 2:7; 3:5
were as grass of the f. Isa 37:27
as the flower of the f. 40:6
beast of the f. honour me. 43:20
trees of the f. shall clap. 55:12
as keepers of the f. are. Jer 4:17
of Lebanon from rock of the f. 18:14
want of fruits of the f. Lam 4:9
multiply as bud of the f. Ezek 16:7
all trees of the f. shall know. 17:24
tree of the f. shall yield fruit. 34:27
multiply increase of the f. 36:30
take no wood out of the f. 39:10
in tender grass of the f. Dan 4:15
hemlock in furrows of f. Hos 10:4
altars as heaps in furrows of f. 12:11
harvest of the f. is. Joel 1:11
even all the trees of the f. are. 12
flame hath burnt all trees of f. 19
Samaria as an heap of f. Mi 1:6
consider lilies of the f. Mat 6:28
if God so clothe grass of the f. 30
parable of the tares of the f. 13:36

see **beast, beasts**

open **field**

bird loose into open f. Lev 14:7
sacrifices which they offer in open f. 17:5
carcases as dung upon the open f. Jer 9:22
cast out in the open f. Ezek 16:5
cast thee forth upon open f. 32:4
him that is in the open f. I. 33:27
thou shalt fall upon the open f. 39:5

fields

died out of houses and f. Ex 8:13
shall be counted as the f. Lev 25:31
which is not of the f. of. 27:22
us inheritance of f. Num 16:14
not pass through f. or. 20:17; 21:22
send grass into thy f. Deut 11:15
might eat increase of the f. 32:13
vine is as vine of the f. of. 32
f. and villages gave they. Josh 21:12
he will take your f. 1 Sam 8:14
of Jesse give each of you f.? 22:7
wall to us when we were in f. 25:15
Anathoth, to thine own f. 1 Ki 2:26
that dieth of Baasha in f. 16:4
let the f. rejoice, and. 1 Chr 16:32
over storehouses in the f. 27:25
sendeth waters upon f. Job 5:10
sow the f. and plant. Ps 107:37
we found it in the f. of wood. 132:6
yet he had not made the f. Pr 8:26
into f. of the fatherless. Pr. 23:10
for f. of Heshbon. Isa 16:8
lament for pleasant f. 32:12
their f. turned to. Jer 6:12; 8:10
seen abominations in the f. 13:27
f. shall be possessed again. 32:15
f. bought. 43
men shall buy f. for money. 44
Nebuzar-adan gave them f. 39:10
captains of forces in the f. 40:7, 13
shall possess f. of Ephraim. Ob 19
they covet f. and take. Mi 2:2
turning away, hath divided our f. 4
although f. yield no meat. Hab 3:17
went through the corn f. Mark 2:23
Luke 6:1
your eyes, look on the f. John 4:35
which reaped down your f. Jas 5:4

open **fields**

living bird into open f. Lev 14:53
with sword in open f. Num 19:16
encamped in the open f. 2 Sam 11:11
shalt fall upon open f. Ezek 29:5

fierce

be their anger, it was f. Gen 49:7
nation of f. countenance. Deut 28:50
the voice of f. lion and. Job 4:10
huntest me as a f. lion. 10:16
nor the f. lion passed by it. 28:8
none is so f. that dare stir. 41:10
a f. king shall rule over. Isa 19:4
shalt not see a f. people. 33:19
king of f. countenance. Dan 8:23
horses are more f. than. Hab 1:8
with devils, exceeding f. Mat 8:28
and they were more f. Luke 23:5
shall be incontinent, f. 2 Tim 3:3
ships which are driven of f. winds. Jas 3:4*

see **anger, wrath**

fierceness

swalloweth ground with f. and. Job 39:24
land desolate for the f. Jer 25:38

fiercer

words of Judah f. than. 2 Sam 19:43

fiery

the Lord sent f. serpents. Num 21:6
make thee a f. serpent, and set. 8
wherein were f. serpents. Deut 8:15
from his right hand a f. law. 33:2
make them as a f. oven. Ps 21:9
fruit a f. flying serpent. Isa 14:29
into midst of f. furnace. Dan 3:6, 11
15, 21
God is able to deliver us from f. 17
three men into midst of f. furnace. 23
came near to mouth of f. furnace. 26
his throne was like the f. flame. 7:9
a f. stream issued and came. 10
able to quench f. darts. Eph 6:16
of judgement, and f. Heb 10:27*
not strange concerning f. 1 Pet 4:12

fifteen

f. cubits upwards did. Gen 7:20
hangings to be f. cubits. Ex 27:14
15; 38:14
shall be f. shekels. Lev 27:7
now Ziba had f. sons. 2 Sam 9:10
Ziba and his f. sons went. 19:17
on forty-five pillars, f. 1 Ki 7:3
Amaziah lived after Jehoash f. years. 2 Ki 14:17
I will add to thy days f. years. 20:6
2 Chr 25:25; Isa 38:5
f. shekels shall be. Ezek 45:12
bought her to me for f. Hos 3:2
Bethany was f. furlongs. John 11:18
and found it f. fathoms. Acts 27:28
I abode with Peter f. days. Gal 1:18

fifteenth

in f. year of Amaziah. 2 Ki 14:23
f. to Bilgah. 1 Chr 24:14
f. to Jerimoth. 25:22
to Jerusalem in f. year. 2 Chr 15:10
in the f. year of reign. Luke 3:1

fifteenth *day*

came to Sin, on f. day. Ex 16:1
on f. day of the same month. Lev 23:6; Num 28:17; 33:3
f. day of this seventh month feast of. Lev 23:34, 39; Num 29:12
on f. day of the eighth month was Jeroboam's. 1 Ki 12:32, 33
on f. day they rested. Esth 9:18, 21
f. day of twelfth year. Ezek 32:17
in f. day do like in feast 45:25

fifth

Leah bare Jacob the f. Gen 30:17
f. lot came out for Asher. Josh 19:24
smote Asahel under f. 2 Sam 2:23*
Abner under the f. rib. 3:27*
Joab smote Amasa in the f. 20:10*
Sanballat sent f. time. Neh 6:5
when he had opened f. seal. Rev 6:9
the f. angel sounded, and I saw. 9:1
f. angel poured out his vial. 16:10
the f. a sardonyx. 21:20

see **day, part**

fifth *month*

Aaron died first day of f. month. Num 33:38
f. month came Nebuzar-adan. 2 Ki 25:8; Jer 52:12
fifth captain for f. month. 1 Chr 27:8
Ezra came in f. month. Ezra 7:8, 9
Jerusalem captive in the f. month. Jer 1:3
in f. month Hananiah spake. 28:1
in f. month the elders. Ezek 20:1
I weep in f. month? Zech 7:3
fasted and mourned in f. month. 5
fast of fourth and of f. month. 8:19

fifth *year*

in f. year ye shall eat. Lev 19:25
f. year of king Rehoboam Shishak came. 1 Ki 14:25; 2 Chr 12:2
in the f. year of Joram. 2 Ki 8:16
in f. year of Jehoiakim. Jer 36:9
f. year of Jehoiachin's. Ezek 1:2

fifties

place rulers of f. Ex 18:21, 25
Deut 1:15
appoint captains over f. 1 Sam 8:12
burnt two captains of f. 2 Ki 1:14

fiftieth

ye shall hallow f. year. Lev 25:10
a jubile shall that f. year be to. 11
in f. year of Azariah. 2 Ki 15:23

fifty

breadth of ark f. cubits. Gen 6:15
not spare the place for f.? 18:24, 26
f. loops shalt thou make. Ex 26:5
10; 36:12, 17
make f. taches of gold. 26:6, 11
36:13, 18
hangings of f. cubits. 27:12; 38:12
two hundred and f. shekels, of sweet calamus two hundred f. 30:23
7th sabbath, number f. Lev 23:16
males thy estimation f. shekels. 27:3
homer of barley seed valued at f. 16
from thirty years old even to f. years. Num 4:3, 23, 30, 35, 39
from age of f. shall serve no. 8:25
two hundred and f. princes of. 16:2
bring two hundred and f. censers. 17
fire devoured two hundred f. 26:10
one portion of f. for Levites. 31:30
Moses took one portion of f. of. 47
give damsel's father f. Deut 22:29
a wedge of gold of f. Josh 7:21
Absalom had f. men to. 2 Sam 15:1
Adonijah had f. men to. 1 Ki 1:5
breadth of house of forest f. 7:2
hid them by f. in a cave. 18:4, 13
captain of f. with his f. 2 Ki 1:9
11, 13
fire consume thee and thy f. 10, 12
f. men of sons of the prophets. 2:7
they sent therefore f. men to. 17
left to Jehoahaz but f. 13:7
Menahem exacted of each f. 15:20
but Pekah slew f. men of. 25
weight of nails was f. 2 Chr 3:9
Ebed went up with f. Ezra 8:6
Tirshatha gave f. basons. Neh 7:70
gallows f. cubits. Esth 5:14; 7:9
Lord will take captain of f. Isa 3:3
to face of porch f. Ezek 40:15
length f. cubits. 21, 25, 29, 33, 36
42:7

of north door f. cubits. Ezek 42:2
to draw out f. vessels. Hag 2:16
owed 500 pence, other f. Luke 7:41
sit down quickly, and write f. 16:6
art not yet f. years old. John 8:57

fifty-two

Azariah reigned f.-two. 2 Ki 15:2
children of Nebo f.-two. Ezra 2:29; Neh 7:33
wall finished in f.-two days. Neh 6:15

fifty-six

of Netophah, f. and six. Ezra 2:22

fifty thousand

of people f. thousand. 1 Sam 6:19
of camels f. thousand. 1 Chr 5:21
of Zebulun f. thousand. 12:33
price of books f. thousand pieces of silver. Acts 19:19

fifty-three thousand

of Naphtali numbered f.-three thousand. Num 1:43; 2:30; 26:47

fifty-four thousand

of Issachar f.-four thousand four hundred. Num 1:29; 2:6

fifty-seven thousand

Zebulun f.-seven thousand four. Num 1:31; 2:8

fifty-nine thousand

of Simeon numbered f.-nine thousand three hundred. Num 1:23

fig, -s

The fig tree and its fruit are well known; they were very common in Palestine, and there is mention often made of them in scripture. Our first parents clothed themselves with fig leaves, Gen 3:7. *The prophet Isaiah gave orders to apply a lump of figs to Hezekiah's boil; and immediately after he was cured,* 2 Ki 20:7.

The cursing of the fig tree, in Mat 21:19, *is explained by the fact that the fruit of this tree appears before the leaves, and a tree so full of leaves indicated that ripe figs should be there, even though it was not yet the regular season. The meaning is then, that when one has the outward show of a good character, without its fruits, he is but a hypocrite, and of no value to the kingdom of God.*

To dwell under one's own vine, or fig tree, *represents in scripture a time of happiness and prosperity, safety and security,* 1 Ki 4:25.

sewed f. leaves together. Gen 3:7
of pomegranates and f. Num 13:23
no place of seed, or of f. or. 20:5
Abigail took cakes of f. 1 Sam 25:18
gave Egyptian a cake of f. 30:12
said, take a lump of f. 2 Ki 20:7; Isa 38:21
that were nigh brought f. 1 Chr 12:40
sabbath some brought f. Neh 13:15
putteth forth green f. S of S 2:13
as a falling f. from. Isa 34:4*
there shall be no f. on. Jer 8:13
of f. one had very good f. 24:1, 2, 3
as the evil f. that cannot be eaten. 8
I will make them like vile f. 29:17
fig trees with first ripe f. Nah 3:12
men gather f. of thistles? Mat 7:16; Luke 6:44
bear berries, or a vine f.? Jas 3:12
casteth her untimely f. Rev 6:13

fig tree

trees said to the f. come, reign. Judg 9:10, 11
dwelt safely under his f. 1 Ki 4:25; Mi 4:4
eat every one of his f. 2 Ki 18:31; Isa 36:16
whoso keepeth f. shall eat. Pr 27:18
fathers as firstripe in the f. Hos 9:10
he hath barked my f. Joel 1:7
vine is dried, the f. languisheth. 12
the f. and vine do yield. 2:22
the f. shall not blossom. Hab 3:17
as yet the f. hath not. Hag 2:19
call every man under f. Zech 3:10
when he saw a f. in way. Mat 21:19; Mark 11:13
how soon is f. withered! Mat 21:20; Mark 11:20, 21
a parable of the f. Mat 24:32; Mark 13:28
a man had a f. planted. Luke 13:6
I come, seeking fruit on this f. 7
behold the f. and all trees. 21:29
under the f. I saw. John 1:48, 50

fig trees

of wheat, vines, and f. Deut 8:8
smote their vines also and f. Ps 105:33
eat up thy vines and f. Jer 5:17
destroy her vines and f. Hos 2:12
when your gardens and f. Amos 4:9
strong holds shall be like f. Nah 3:12

fight, *substantive*

as host was going forth to the f. 1 Sam 17:20
fight the good f. of faith. 1 Tim 6:12
I have fought a good f. 2 Tim 4:7
ye endured a great f. Heb 10:32*
strong, waxed valiant in f. 11:34*

fight, *verb*

we will go up and f. Deut 1:41
go not up, nor f., I am not among. 42
Sihon and his people came to f. 2:32*
art come against me to f. Judg 11:12
yourselves like men, f. 1 Sam 4:9
me a man that we may f. 17:10
nigh when ye did f.? 2 Sam 11:20
f. not small nor great. 1 Ki 22:31; 2 Chr 18:30
about Jehoshaphat to f. 2 Chr 18:31
ye shall not need to f. in. 20:17
teacheth my fingers to f. Ps 144:1
men have forborn to f. Jer 51:30
shall f. because Lord is. Zech 10:5
Judah also shall f. at. 14:14
would my servants f. John 18:36
so f. I, not as one that. 1 Cor 9:26
f. the good fight of faith. 1 Tim 6:12
ye kill, ye f. and war. Jas 4:2
see **battles**

fight *against*

join enemies, f. against us. Ex 1:10
to a city to f. against it. Deut 20:10
to enemies against whom ye f. Josh 10:25
pitched to f. against Israel. 11:5
Danites went up to f. against. 19:47
first to f. against them? Judg 1:1
that we may f. against Canaanites. 3
over Jordan to f. against Judah. 10:9
to f. against Ammon. 11:8, 9
against Israel, or f. against them? 25
come ye to f. against me? 12:3
set themselves to f. against. 20:20
f. against Amalekites. 1 Sam 15:18
Philistines f. against Keilah. 23:1
not f. against enemies of king. 29:8
Judah with Benjamin to f. against Israel. 1 Ki 12:21; 2 Chr 11:1
not f. against your brethren. 1 Ki 12:24; 2 Chr 11:4
let us f. against them in plain. 1 Ki 20:23, 25
to f. against Jehoshaphat. 22:32
kings were come to f. against them. 2 Ki 3:21
he is come out to f. against. 19:9
O Israel, f. not against. 2 Chr 13:12
Sennacherib to f. against. 32:2
Necho came to f. against. 35:20
and f. against Jerusalem. Neh 4:8
f. against them that f. against me. Ps 35:1
be many that f. against me. 56:2
f. every one against his brother. Isa 19:2
nations that f. against Ariel. 29:7
nations that f. against Zion. 8
f. against thee, not prevail. Jer 1:19; 15:20
wherewith ye f. against king. 21:4
I myself will f. against you. 5
city is given to the Chaldeans that f. against it. 32:24, 29; 34:22; 37:8
Chaldeans that f. against you. 37:10
Lord shall f. against. Zech 14:3
found to f. against God. Acts 5:39
let us not f. against God. 23:9
f. against them with sword. Rev 2:16*

fight *for*

f. for you. Ex 14:14; Deut 1:30; 3:22; 20:4
f. for your master's. 2 Ki 10:3
f. for your brethren, sons. Neh 4:14
our God shall f. for us. 20
Lord shall come to f. for. Isa 31:4

fight *with*

go out, f. with Amalek. Ex 17:9
gathered to f. with Joshua. Josh 9:2
to f. with the Midianites. Judg 8:1
go out and f. with Abimelech. 9:38
may f. with children of Ammon. 11:6
gathered to f. with Israel. 1 Sam 13:5; 28:1
if he be able to f. with me. 17:9
servant will f. with this Philistine. 32
disguised himself to f. with him. 2 Chr 35:22
of shaking f. with it. Isa 30:32
ye f. with Chaldeans. Jer 32:5
came to f. with Chaldeans. 33:5
went to f. with Ishmael. 41:12
return to f. with prince of. Dan 10:20
south come and f. with him. 11:11

fighteth

Lord f. for them against. Ex 14:25
the Lord God, that f. for. Josh 23:10
my lord f. the battles. 1 Sam 25:28

fighting

were f. Philistines. 1 Sam 17:19
Uzziah had host of f. 2 Chr 26:11
O God, he f. oppresseth. Ps 56:1

fightings

without were f. within. 2 Cor 7:5
whence come wars and f.? Jas 4:1

figure

similitude of any f. Deut 4:16
maketh it after the f. of. Isa 44:13
who is the f. of him. Rom 5:14
I have in a f. transferred. 1 Cor 4:6
which was a f. of the time. Heb 9:9
whence he received him in a f. 11:19
the like f. whereunto. 1 Pet 3:21*

figures

carved with carved f. 1 Ki 6:29
f. ye made to worship. Acts 7:43
holy places, f. of the true. Heb 9:24*

file

had a f. for mattocks. 1 Sam 13:21

fill, *substantive*

shall eat f. in safety. Lev 25:19
mayest eat grapes thy f. Deut 23:24
let us take our f. of love. Pr 7:18

fill, *verb*

multiply, and f. waters. Gen 1:22
Joseph commanded to f. 42:25; 44:1
locusts shall f. thy houses. Ex 10:6
Moses said, f. an homer. 16:32*
f. thine horn with oil. 1 Sam 16:1
f. four barrels with. 1 Ki 18:33
till he f. thy mouth with. Job 8:21
a wise man f. belly with east. 15:2
when he is about to f. his. 20:23
f. my mouth with arguments. 23:4
f. appetite of young lions. 38:39*
canst thou f. his skin with? 41:7
thy mouth and I will f. it. Ps 81:10
f. their faces with shame. 83:16
shall f. places with dead. 110:6
shall f. our houses with. Pr 1:13
I will f. their treasures. 8:21
wings shall f. breadth of. Isa 8:8
nor f. face of world with. 14:21
f. face of the world with fruit. 27:6
we will f. ourselves with. 56:12
I will f. inhabitants with. Jer 13:13
not I f. heaven and earth? 23:24
it is to f. them with the dead. 33:5
surely I will f. thee with. 51:14
f. thy bowels with this roll. Ezek 3:3
not satisfy their souls nor f. 7:19
f. the courts with the slain. 9:7
f. thine hand with coals of fire. 10:2
gather pieces, f. it with choice. 24:4
shall f. the land with slain. 30:11

f. beasts of whole earth. *Ezek* 32:4*
I will *f.* the valleys with thy. 5
f. his mountains with slain. 35:8
f. masters' house with. *Zeph* 1:9
I will *f.* this house with. *Hag* 2:7
which is put in to *f.* it up. *Mat* 9:16
have bread to *f.* such a ? 15:33
f. ye up then the measure of. 23:32
f. the water-pots with. *John* 2:7
God of hope *f.* you with. *Rom* 15:13
ascended, that he might *f.* all. *Eph* 4:10
f. up what is behind of. *Col* 1:24
Jews, to *f.* up their sins. *1 Thes* 2:16
cup she hath filled, *f.* *Rev* 18:6*

filled

earth is *f.* with violence. *Gen* 6:13
Hagar went and *f.* the bottle. 21:19
Rebekah *f.* her pitcher. 24:16
Philistines had *f.* the wells. 26:15
children of Israel *f.* land. *Ex* 1:7
f. the troughs to water flock. 2:16
I have *f.* with wisdom. 28:3; 35:35
I have *f.* him with Spirit. 31:3; 35:31
of Lord *f.* tabernacle. 40:34, 35
within thy gates and be *f.* *Deut* 26:12
have eaten and *f.* themselves. 31:20
these bottles we *f.* were. *Josh* 9:13
cloud *f.* house of Lord. *1 Ki* 8:10
glory of Lord *f.* house. 11
2 Chr 5:14; 7:1, 2
he *f.* the trench also with. 18:35
but Syrians *f.* the country. 20:27
man his stone and *f.* it. *2 Ki* 3:25
Manasseh *f.* Jerusalem. 21:16; 24:4
Josiah *f.* places with bones. 23:14
which have *f.* it from end. *Ezra* 9:11
with princes who *f.* their. *Job* 3:15
hast *f.* me with wrinkles. 16:8*
yet he *f.* their houses with. 22:18
are *f.* with loathsome. *Ps* 38:7
let my mouth be *f.* with thy. 71:8
let the whole earth be *f.* 72:19
to take deep root, it *f.* the. 80:9
openest thine hand, *f.* with. 104:28*
exceedingly *f.* with contempt. 123:3
our soul is *f.* with scorning. 4
lest strangers be *f.* with. *Pr* 5:10
lest thou be *f.* with honey. 25:16
earth that is not *f.* with. 30:16*
a fool when he is *f.* with meat. 22
nor the ear *f.* with hearing. *Eccl* 1:8
his soul be not *f.* with good. 6:3
and yet the appetite is not *f.* 7
my head is *f.* with dew. *S of S* 5:2
and his train *f.* temple. *Isa* 6:1
are my loins *f.* with pain. 21:3
Lord hath *f.* Zion with. 33:5
sword of Lord is *f.* with blood. 34:6
nor *f.* me with the fat of thy. 43:24
old man that hath not *f.* 65:20
thou hast *f.* me with. *Jer* 15:17
they *f.* mine inheritance. 16:18
f. this place with blood of. 19:4
Ishmael *f.* the pit with them. 41:9
and thy cry hath *f.* the land. 46:12
he hath *f.* his belly with. 51:34
hath *f.* me with bitterness. *Lam* 3:15
he is *f.* full with reproach. 30
have *f.* the land with. *Ezek* 8:17
and the cloud *f.* the inner. 10:3
have *f.* the streets with slain. 11:6
f. the midst of thee with. 28:16
waste cities be *f.* with. 36:38
glory of Lord *f.* the house. 43:5
44:4
the stone cut out *f.* the. *Dan* 2:35
lion *f.* his holes with. *Nah* 2:12
thou art *f.* with shame. *Hab* 2:16
but are not *f.* with drink. *Hag* 1:6
I have *f.* the bow with. *Zech* 9:13
and *f.* a spunge with. *Mat* 27:48
Mark 15:36; *John* 19:29
new piece that *f.* it up. *Mark* 2:21
let the children first be *f.* 7:27
he hath *f.* the hungry. *Luke* 1:53
strong in spirit, *f.* with wisdom. 2:40
they came and *f.* both ships. 5:7
come, that my house be *f.* 14:23
f. his belly with husks. 15:16
they *f.* them up to brim. *John* 2:7
they *f.* twelve baskets with. 6:13
sorrow hath *f.* your heart. 16:6
rushing mighty wind, *f.* *Acts* 2:2
Peter, *f.* with Holy Ghost. *Acts* 4:8
why hath Satan *f.* thine heart ? 5:3
f. Jerusalem with your doctrine. 28
mightest be *f.* with Holy Ghost. 9:17
Paul, *f.* with the Holy Ghost. 13:9
being *f.* with all unrighteousness. *Rom* 1:29
are *f.* with all knowledge. 15:14
if first I be somewhat *f.* with. 24*
I am *f.* with comfort. *2 Cor* 7:4
f. with the fulness of God. *Eph* 3:19
not drunk with wine, be *f.* with. 5:18
f. with the fruits of. *Phil* 1:11
might be *f.* with knowledge. *Col* 1:9
that I may be *f.* with joy. *2 Tim* 1:4
in peace, be warmed and *f.* *Jas* 2:16
angel *f.* the censer with. *Rev* 8:5
for in them is *f.* up the wrath. 15:1*
cup which she hath *f.* fill. 18:6*

shall be **filled**

morning ye *shall be f.* *Ex* 16:12
earth *shall be f.* with. *Num* 14:21
valley *shall be f.* with. *2 Ki* 3:17
shall be f. with own. *Pr* 1:31
shall thy barns *be f.* with plenty. 3:10
wicked *shall be f.* with. 12:21
the backslider *shall be f.* 14:14
increase of lips *shall* he *be f.* 18:20*
his mouth *shall be f.* with. 20:17
knowledge *shall* chambers *be f.* 24:4
every bottle *shall be f.* *Jer* 13:12
shalt be f. with drunkenness. *Ezek* 23:33
ye *shall be f.* at my table. 39:20
earth *shall be f.* with. *Hab* 2:14
shall be f. like bowls. *Zech* 9:15
blessed they that hunger, they *shall be f.* *Mat* 5:6
John *shall be f.* with. *Luke* 1:15
every valley *shall be f.* 3:5
ye that hunger, ye *shall be f.* 6:21

was **filled**

earth *was f.* with violence. *Gen* 6:11
Hiram *was f.* with. *1 Ki* 7:14
country *was f.* with water. *2 Ki* 3:20
house *was f.* with a. *2 Chr* 5:13
was f. with sweet odours. 16:14
our mouth *was f.* with. *Ps* 126:2
house *was f.* with smoke. *Isa* 6:4
land *was f.* with sin. *Jer* 51:5
house *was f.* with cloud. *Ezek* 10:4
Elisabeth *was f.* with Holy Ghost. *Luke* 1:41
Zacharias *was f.* with Holy Ghost. 67
house *was f.* with odour. *John* 12:3
city *was f.* with confusion. *Acts* 19:29
temple *was f.* with smoke. *Rev* 15:8

were **filled**

so were they *f.* they *were f.* *Hos* 13:6
they *were f.* with wrath. *Luke* 4:28
were f. with fear, saying. 5:26
they *were f.* with madness. 6:11
they *were f.* with water. 8:23
when they *were f.* he. *John* 6:12
did eat of loaves, and *were f.* 26
they *were* all *f.* with the Holy Ghost. *Acts* 2:4; 4:31
they *were f.* with wonder. 3:10
and *were f.* with indignation. 5:17
the Jews *were f.* with envy. 13:45
disciples *were f.* with joy and. 52
fowls *were f.* with their. *Rev* 19:21
see **eat**

filledst

houses, which thou *f.* not. *Deut* 6:11
thou *f.* many people. *Ezek* 27:33

fillest

belly thou *f.* with hid. *Ps* 17:14

fillet

a *f.* of twelve cubits. *Jer* 52:21*

filleth

he *f.* me with bitterness. *Job* 9:18
the rain also *f.* pools. *Ps* 84:6*
he *f.* hungry soul with. 107:9
the mower *f.* not his hand. 129:7
f. thee with finest of wheat. 147:14
fulness of him that *f.* all. *Eph* 1:23

fillets

hooks of the pillars, and their *f.* be. *Ex* 27:10, 11; 38:10, 11, 12, 17, 19
chapiters and *f.* with gold. 36:38

filletted

f. with silver. *Ex* 27:17; 38:17
overlaid chapiters and *f.* 38:28

filling

f. our hearts with food. *Acts* 14:17

filth

Lord washed away *f.* of. *Isa* 4:4
cast abominable *f.* upon. *Nah* 3:6
made as the *f.* of world. *1 Cor* 4:13
putting away *f.* of flesh. *1 Pet* 3:21

filthiness

f. out of the holy place. *2 Chr* 29:5
had separated from *f.* of. *Ezra* 6:21
an unclean land with the *f.* 9:11
is not washed from their *f.* *Pr* 30:12
are full of vomit and *f.* *Isa* 28:8
her *f.* is in her skirts. *Lam* 1:9
thy *f.* was poured out. *Ezek* 16:36
and I will consume thy *f.* 22:15
that the *f.* of it may be. 24:11
in thy *f.* is lewdness, shalt not be purged from thy *f.* 13
from all *f.* will I cleanse you. 36:25
cleanse ourselves from all *f.* of. *2 Cor* 7:1*
nor let *f.* be once named. *Eph* 5:4
wherefore lay apart all *f.* *Jas* 1:21
of abomination and *f.* of. *Rev* 17:4*

filthy

more abominable and *f.* *Job* 15:16*
altogether become *f.* *Ps* 14:3; 53:3
righteousness as *f.* rags. *Isa* 64:6*
woe to her that is *f.* *Zeph* 3:1*
Joshua clothed with *f.* *Zech* 3:3
take away *f.* garments from him. 4
you also put off *f.* communication. *Col* 3:8*
nor greedy of *f.* lucre. *1 Tim* 3:3*, 8
not given to *f.* lucre. *Tit* 1:7
teaching things for *f.* lucre's sake. 11
1 Pet 5:2
Lot vexed with *f.* *2 Pet* 2:7*
these *f.* dreamers defile. *Jude* 8
he that is *f.* let him be *f.* *Rev* 22:11

finally

f. my brethren, farewell. *2 Cor* 13:11
Eph 6:10; *Phil* 3:1; 4:8
2 Thes 3:1; *1 Pet* 3:8

find

wearied themselves to *f.* *Gen* 19:11
speak to Esau, when you *f.* 32:19
sin shall *f.* you out. *Num* 32:23
the revenger of blood *f.* him. 35:27
a man *f.* a damsel. *Deut* 22:25, 28
sojourn where he could *f.* a place. *Judg* 17:8, 9
Lord grant ye may *f.* rest. *Ruth* 1:9
go, *f.* out arrows. *1 Sam* 20:21, 36
if a man *f.* his enemy. 24:19
peradventure we may *f.* *1 Ki* 18:5
to *f.* out every device. *2 Chr* 2:14*
Assyria come and *f.* much. 32:4
I knew where I might *f.* *Job* 23:3
every man to *f.* according to. 34:11
seek out his wickedness till thou *f.* *Ps* 10:15
thou shalt *f.* knowledge. *Pr* 2:5
words are like to those that *f.* 4:22
right to them that *f.* knowledge. 8:9
I *f.* out knowledge of inventions. 12
a man should *f.* nothing. *Eccl* 7:14
counting one by one, to *f.* out the. 27
sought to *f.* acceptable. 12:10
if *f.* my beloved, tell him. *S of S* 5:8
screech owl shall *f.* a. *Isa* 34:14
in the day of fast you *f.* 58:3
that they may *f.* it so. *Jer* 10:18*
like harts that *f.* no. *Lam* 1:6
her prophets also *f.* no vision. 2:9
sought to *f.* occasion against Daniel, but could *f.* none. *Dan* 6:4
not *f.* except we *f.* it concerning. 5
and few there be that *f.* it. *Mat* 7:14
and if so be that he *f.* it. 18:13
if haply he might *f.* any. *Mark* 11:13
coming suddenly, *f.* you. 13:36
that they might *f.* an. *Luke* 6:7
and *f.* them so, blessed are. 12:38
I come seeking fruit and *f.* 13:7
that which is lost, till he *f.* it. 15:4
seek diligently till she *f.* it ? 8
go in and out and *f.* *John* 10:9

f. a tabernacle for God. Acts 7:46
might feel after him and f. 17:27
we f. no evil in this man. 23:9
why doth he yet f. fault ? Rom 9:19
and f. you unprepared. 2 Cor 9:4
he may f. mercy of Lord. 2 Tim 1:18
see **favour**

can or *canst* **find**

can we f. such a one as ? Gen 41:38
straw where you *can* f. it. Ex 5:11
and gold thou *canst* f. Ezra 7:16
when they *can* f. the grave. Job 3:22
canst thou by searching f. out God ?
canst thou f. out Almighty ? 11:7
faithful man who *can* f.? Pr 20:6
who *can* f. virtuous woman ? 31:10
no man *can* f. out work. Eccl 3:11
exceeding deep, who *can* f. it ? 7:24
can f. a man that seeketh. Jer 5:1

cannot **find**

said, I *cannot* f. her. Gen 38:22
if he *cannot* f. thee, will slay me. 1 Ki 18:12
I *cannot* f. one wise man. Job 17:10
Almighty, we *cannot* f. him. 37:23
a man cannot f. out work. Eccl 8:17

find *grace*

may f. *grace* in thy sight. Gen 32:5
Ex 33:13
are to f. *grace* in sight. Gen 33:8
let me f. *grace*. 15
let me f. *grace* in your eyes. 34:11
f. *grace* in sight of my lord. 47:25
in whose sight I f. *grace*. Ruth 2:2
thy handmaid f. *grace*. 1 Sam 1:18
f. *grace* in thy sight. 2 Sam 16:4
we may f. *grace* to help. Heb 4:16

I **find**

if *I* f. in Sodom fifty. Gen 18:26
if *I* f. there forty-five. 28
if I f. thirty there. 30
till *I* f. out a place for. Ps 132:5
and *I* f. more bitter than. Eccl 7:26
when *I* should f. thee. S of S 8:1
sighing, and *I* f. no. Jer 45:3
Pilate said, *I* f. no fault. Luke 23:4
John 18:38; 19:4, 6
to perform good, *I* f. not. Rom 7:18*
I f. then a law, that when I. 21

not **find**, or **find** *not*

to-day ye shall *not* f. it. Ex 16:25
Saul shall *not* f. thee. 1 Sam 23:17
sought, could *not* f. 2 Sam 17:20
but they shall *not* f. me. Pr 1:28
Hos 5:6; John 7:34, 36
soul seeketh, but I f. *not*. Eccl 7:28
him, could *not* f. him. S of S 5:6
seek, but shalt *not* f. them. Isa 41:12
Hos 2:7
not f. any occasion. Dan 6:5
shall *not* f. her paths. Hos 2:6
seek the word, *not* f. it. Amos 8:12
not f. what way they. Luke 5:19
could *not* f. what they might. 19:48
that we shall *not* f. him. John 7:35
that which is good, I f. *not*. Rom 7:18
I shall *not* f. you such. 2 Cor 12:20
death, and shall *not* f. it. Rev 9:6

shall, or *shalt* **find**

seek Lord thou *shalt* f. Deut 4:29
shalt f. no ease among these. 28:65
do as thou *shalt* f. Judg 9:33
ye *shall* f. him before. 1 Sam 9:13
there *shall* f. two men by. 10:2
ye *shall* f. them at end. 2 Chr 20:16
children *shall* f. compassion. 30:9
thou *shalt* f. in book of. Ezra 4:15
tried me, and *shalt* f. Ps 17:3
shall f. out thine enemies. 21:8
shall f. precious substance. Pr 1:13
that seek me early *shall* f. me. 8:17
Jer 29:13
matter wisely, *shall* f. good. Pr 16:20
understanding *shall* f. good. 19:8
for thou *shalt* f. it after. Eccl 11:1
in her month *shall* f. her. Jer 2:24
ye *shall* f. rest to your souls. 6:16
Mat 11:29
shall f. none iniquity in. Hos 12:8
seek and ye *shall* f. Mat 7:7
Luke 11:9

life for my sake *shall* f. it. Mat 10:39
thou *shalt* f. a piece of money. 17:27
ye *shall* f. an ass tied, and a colt.
21:2; Mark 11:2
as many as ye *shall* f. Mat 22:9
cometh, *shall* f. so doing. 24:46
Luke 12:37, 43
ye *shall* f. babe wrapt. Luke 2:12
shall he f. faith on earth ? 18:8
cast the net on the right side, ye *shall* f. John 21:6
shalt f. them no more. Rev 18:14

findest

with whomsover thou f. Gen 31:32
eat thou f. eat this roll. Ezek 3:1

findeth

every one that f. me. Gen 4:14
he f. occasions against. Job 33:10
as one that f. spoil. Ps 119:162
happy is man that f. Pr 3:13
whoso f. me, f. life. 8:35
scorner seeketh wisdom, f. it. 14:6
a froward heart, f. no good. 17:20
whoso f. a wife f. good. 18:22
his neighbour f. no favour. 21:10
that followeth after mercy f. life. 21
whatsoever thy hand f. Eccl 9:10
heathen, she f. no rest. Lam 1:3
in thee the fatherless f. Hos 14:3
and he that seeketh f. Mat 7:8
Luke 11:10
f. his life shall lose it. Mat 10:39
walketh, seeking rest, f. none. 12:43
f. it empty, swept. 44; Luke 11:25
he f. his disciples asleep. Mat 26:40
Mark 14:37
f. his own brother Simon. John 1:41
Jesus f. Philip. 43
Philip f. Nathanael. 45
afterward Jesus f. him in. 5:14

finding

any f. Cain kill him. Gen 4:15
who doeth things past f. Job 9:10
f. thine own pleasure. Isa 58:13
seeking rest, and f. Luke 11:24
f. nothing how they. Acts 4:21
Paul came f. certain. 19:1; 21:4
f. ship sailing over to. 21:2
his ways past f. out. Rom 11:33*
for f. fault with them. Heb 8:8

fine

for gold where they f. it. Job 28:1*

fine

and two vessels of f. Ezra 8:27
they that work in f. flax. Isa 19:9*
feet like unto brass. Rev 1:15; 2:18

fine *flour*

offering of f. *flour*. Lev 2:1; 24:5
cakes of f. f. mingled with oil. 2:4, 5, 7
7:12; 14:10, 21; 23:13; Num 6:15
7:13, 19, 25, 31, 37, 43, 49, 55, 61
8:8
tenth part of an ephah of f. *flour*.
Lev 5:11; 6:20
measures of f. *flour* in. 1 Ki 4:22
measure f. *flour* sold for shekel.
2 Ki 7:1, 16, 18
appointed to oversee f. *flour*.
1 Chr 9:29; 23:29
didst eat f. *flour*, honey. Ezek 16:13
I gave thee f. *flour*, and oil. 19
of oil to temper with f. *flour*. 46:14
merchandise of f. *flour*. Rev 18:13

fine *gold*

he overlaid with f. *gold*. 2 Chr 3:5
most holy he overlaid with f. *gold*. 8
be for jewels of f. *gold*. Job 28:17
or said to f. *gold*, thou. 31:24
desired than f. *gold*. Ps 19:10
thy commandments above f. *gold*.
119:127
of wisdom than f. *gold*. Pr 3:14
better than gold, than f. *gold*. 8:19
as an ornament of f. *gold*. 25:12
head is as most f. *gold*. S of S 5:11
pillars set on sockets of f. *gold*. 15
more precious than f. *gold*. Isa 13:12
most f. *gold* changed! Lam 4:1*
of Zion comparable to f. *gold*. 2
image's head f. *gold*. Dan 2:32
loins were girded with f. *gold*. 10:5*
Tyrus heaped f. *gold*. Zech 9:3

fine *linen*

in vestures of f. *linen*. Gen 41:42
offering ye shall take, f. *linen*.
Ex 25:4
ten curtains of f. twined *linen*. 26:1
the vail of f. *linen*. 31; 36:35
2 Chr 3:14
hanging of f. twined *linen*. Ex 26:36
27:9, 16, 18; 36:37; 38:9, 16, 18
take gold and f. *linen*. 28:5
the ephod of f. *linen*. 28:6; 39:2
girdle f. *linen*. 28:8; 39:5, 29
breastplate f. *linen*. 28:15; 39:8
the coat of f. *linen*, thou shalt make
mitre of f. *linen*. 28:39
bring an offering of f. *linen*. 35:6
with whom was found f. *linen*. 23
brought scarlet and f. *linen*. 25
with wisdom to work all manner of f. *linen*. 35; 38:23, 2 Chr 2:14
curtains of f. *linen* and. Ex 36:8
coats of f. *linen* for Aaron. 39:27
of f. *linen*, bonnets of f. *linen*. 28
that wrought f. *linen*. 1 Chr 4:21
clothed with robe of f. *linen*. 15:27
with cords of f. *linen*. Esth 1:6
Mordecai with garment of f. *linen*.
8:15
my bed with f. *linen*. Pr 7:16*
she maketh f. *linen*. 31:24*
take away f. *linen*. Isa 3:23
girded thee with f. *linen*. Ezek 16:10
thy raiment was of f. *linen*. 13
f. *linen* from Egypt was. 27:7
occupied in thy fairs with f. *linen*. 16
Joseph bought f. *linen*. Mark 15:46*
in purple and f. *linen*. Luke 16:19
merchandise of f. *linen*. Rev 18:12
that city clothed in f. *linen* is. 16
to be arrayed in f. *linen*. 19:8
in heaven clothed in f. *linen*. 14

fine *meal*

measures of f. *meal*. Gen 18:6

finer

forth a vessel for the f. Pr 25:4†

finest

fed thee with the f. of. Ps 81:16
filleth thee with f. of wheat. 147:14

finger

The finger of God is used to mean his power, his working. Pharaoh's magicians discovered the finger of God in the miracles which Moses wrought, Ex 8:19. *This legislator gave the law written with the finger of God to the Hebrews,* Ex 31:18.

magicians said, this is f. of. Ex 8:19
blood on altar with thy f. 29:12
written with the f. of God. 31:18
Deut 9:10
priest dip his f. in blood. Lev 4:6
17, 25, 30, 34; 8:15; 9:9; 16:14, 19
his right f. in the oil, and sprinkle of the oil with his f. 14:16, 27
take of blood with his f. Num 19:4
my little f. thicker. 1 Ki 12:10
2 Chr 10:10
the putting forth of the f. Isa 58:9
if I with the f. of God. Luke 11:20
he dip tip of his f. in water. 16:24
and with his f. wrote. John 8:6
put my f. into the print. 20:25
reach hither thy f. and behold. 27

fingers

on every hand six f. 2 Sam 21:20
1 Chr 20:6
heavens, work of thy f. Ps 8:3
who teacheth my f. to fight. 144:1
man teacheth with his f. Pr 6:13
bind them on thy f. write. 7:3
f. with sweetsmelling. S of S 5:5
which their own f. have made.
Isa 2:8; 17:8
hands defiled with blood, and f. 59:3
thickness of pillar four f. Jer 52:21
came forth f. of a man's. Dan 5:5
but will not move them with one of their f. Mat 23:4; Luke 11:46
and he put his f. into. Mark 7:33

fining

f. pot is for silver. Pr 17:3†; 27:21

finish

in a cubit shalt thou *f.* *Gen* 6:16
to *f.* transgression. *Dan* 9:24
Zerubbabel's hands shall *f.* *Zech* 4:9
have sufficient to *f.* *Luke* 14:28*
laid foundation, is not able to *f.* 29
to build, was not able to *f.* 30
his will, and *f.* his work. *John* 4:34
Father hath given me to *f.* 5:36*
I might *f.* my course. *Acts* 20:24*
for he will *f.* the work. *Rom* 9:28
f. in you the same grace. *2 Cor* 8:6*

finished

heavens and earth were *f.* *Gen* 2:1
thus was the work *f.* *Ex* 39:32; 40:33
till they were *f.* *Deut* 31:24
till every thing was *f.* *Josh* 4:10
till he have *f.* the thing. *Ruth* 3:18
Solomon built house and *f.* *1 Ki* 6:9
14, 22, 38; *2 Chr* 5:1; 7:11
Solomon *f.* all his house. *1 Ki* 7:1
9:1, 25; *2 Chr* 8:16
so was work of pillars *f.* *1 Ki* 7:22
to number, but *f.* not. *1 Chr* 27:24
not fail thee, till thou hast *f.* 28:20
they had *f.* repairing. *2 Chr* 24:14
sang, till burnt offering was *f.* 29:28
they *f.* the heaps in the. 31:7
and yet it is not *f.* *Ezra* 5:16*
elders of Jews built and *f.* 6:14, 15
so the wall was *f.* in. *Neh* 6:15
numbered thy kingdom and *f.* it. *Dan* 5:26
all these things shall be *f.* 12:7
when Jesus had *f.* these. *Mat* 13:53
Jesus *f.* these sayings. 19:1; 26:1
I have *f.* the work thou. *John* 17:4*
it is *f.* and he bowed his head. 19:30
we had *f.* our course. *Acts* 21:7
I have *f.* my course. *2 Tim* 4:7
were *f.* from foundation. *Heb* 4:3
sin, when it is *f.* bringeth. *Jas* 1:15*
mystery of God should be *f.* *Rev* 10:7
witnesses have *f.* their testimony. 11:7
till the thousand years were *f.* 20:5

finisher

Jesus, author and *f.* of. *Heb* 12:2*

fins

hath *f.* and scales eat. *Lev* 11:9 *Deut* 14:9
all that hath not *f.* shall be an abomination. *Lev* 11:10, 12

fir

concerning timber of *f.* *1 Ki* 5:8
covered floor with planks of *f.* 6:15
are cedar, rafters of *f.* *S of S* 1:17

fire

Fire is often used as a symbol of God, Deut 4:24; Ps 18:12, 13, 14; Ezek 1:4; Rev 1:14. *And it is said that Jesus will appear in the midst of fire at his second coming,* 2 Thes 1:8. *The wrath of God is compared to fire,* Ps 18:8.

Our Saviour is compared to fire, Mal 3:2. *The Holy Ghost is likewise compared to fire,* Mat 3:11. *The angels themselves, as the ministers of God, are compared to a burning fire, speedy and irresistible in the execution of his commands,* Ps. 104:4.

Fire from heaven fell frequently on the victims sacrificed to the Lord, as a mark of his presence and approbation. It is thought that God in this manner expressed his acceptance of Abel's sacrifices, Gen 4:4. *When the Lord made a covenant with Abraham, a fire, like that of a furnace, passed through the divided pieces of the sacrifices, and consumed them,* Gen 15:17. *Fire fell upon the sacrifices which Moses offered at the dedication of the tabernacle,* Lev 9:24; *and upon those of Manoah, Samson's father,* Judg 13:19, 20; *upon Solomon's, at the dedication of the temple,* 2 Chr 7:1; *and upon Elijah's, at mount Carmel,* 1 Ki 18:38.

The word of God is compared to fire, Jer 23:29.

Abraham took *f.* in his. *Gen* 22:6
behold the *f.* and the wood, but. 7
the bush burned with *f.* *Ex* 3:2
Lord sent hail and the *f.* along. 9:23
hail, and *f.* mingled with hail. 24
flesh in that night roast with *f.* 12:8, 9
upon mount Sinai in *f.* 19:18
if *f.* break out, and catch. 22:6
then I cast gold into *f.* and. 32:24
f. was on the tabernacle by night. 40:38; *Num* 9:16; *Deut* 1:33
the priest put *f.* on the altar, and lay wood in order upon *f.* *Lev* 1:7
upon the wood in *f.* 8, 12, 17; 3:5
green ears of corn dried by *f.* 2:14
f. of the altar be burning. 6:9, 10 12, 13
came a *f.* out from before. 9:24
the sons of Aaron put *f.* in. 10:1
there went out *f.* from Lord. 2
shall put incense upon *f.* 16:13
pass through *f.* to Molech. 18:21
Deut 18:10; *2 Ki* 17:17; 23:10
hair, and put it in the *f.* *Num* 6:18
Moses prayed, the *f.* was. 11:2
censers, and put *f.* therein. 16:7, 18
take the censers, and scatter *f.* 37
take a censer, and put *f.* therein. 46
holy things reserved from *f.* 18:9
for there is a *f.* gone out. 21:28
may abide *f.* go through *f.* 31:23
mountain burnt with *f.* *Deut* 4:11 9:15
earth he shewed his great *f.* 4:36
afraid by reason of the *f.* 5:5
nor let me see this great *f.* 18:16
burned Achan with *f.* *Josh* 7:25
there rose up *f.* out of. *Judg* 6:21
let *f.* come out of bramble. 9:15
tow when it toucheth the *f.* 16:9
lay it on wood, put no *f.* under. *1 Ki* 18:23, 25
the God that answereth by *f.* 24
then *f.* of Lord fell. 38; *2 Chr* 7:1, 3
after earthquake a *f.*, Lord was not in *f.*, after *f.* a still small. *1 Ki* 19:12
then let *f.* come down. *2 Ki* 1:10
and the *f.* of God came down. 12
a chariot and horses of *f.* 2:11
mountain, full of chariots of *f.* 6:17
Ahaz made son pass through *f.* 16:3
have cast their gods into *f.* 19:18
made son pass through *f.* 21:6 *2 Chr* 33:6
make son pass through *f.* *2 Ki* 23:10
answered him from heaven by *f.* *1 Chr* 21:26
roasted passover with *f.* *2 Chr* 35:13
the gates are consumed with *f.* *Neh* 2:3, 13
the *f.* of God is fallen. *Job* 1:16
the spark of his *f.* shall not. 18:5
is turned up as it were *f.* 28:5
and sparks of *f.* leap out. 41:19
while I was musing the *f.* *Ps* 39:3
he burneth chariot in the *f.* 46:9
we went through *f.* and. 66:12
as wax melteth before *f.* so. 68:2
cast *f.* into thy sanctuary. 74:7
with a light of *f.* 78:14; 105:39
as the *f.* burneth the wood. 83:14
a *f.* goeth before him and. 97:3
gave hail and flaming *f.* in. 105:32
they are quenched as *f.* 118:12
be cast into the *f.* into deep. 140:10
f. and hail, stormy wind. 148:8
can a man take *f.* in bosom. *Pr* 6:27
in his lips as a burning *f.* 16:27
where no wood is, the *f.* 26:20
as wood is to *f.* so is contentious. 21
the grave and the *f.* saith not. 30:16
burning and fuel of *f.* *Isa* 9:5
wickedness burneth as the *f.* 18
the people shall be as fuel of *f.* 19
a burning like burning of a *f.* 10:16
light of Israel shall be for a *f.* 17
not be found a sherd to take *f.* 30:14
the pile thereof is *f.* and wood. 33
whose *f.* is in Zion. 31:9
of Assyria cast gods into *f.* 37:19
walkest through *f.* not be. *Isa* 43:2
in the *f.* he warmeth himself, saith, I have seen the *f.* 44:16
as stubble, the *f.* shall burn. 47:14
walk in light of your *f.* and. 50:11
when the melting *f.* burneth, the *f.* causeth the waters to boil. 64:2
a *f.* that burneth all the day. 65:5
the Lord will come with *f.* 66:15
by *f.* will Lord plead with all. 16
worm not die, neither *f.* be. 24
fury come forth like *f.* *Jer* 4:4
my words in thy mouth *f.* 5:14
his word was as a *f.* shut up. 20:9
lest my fury go out like *f.* 21:12
cut down choice cedars, cast in *f.* 22:7
king of Babylon roasted in *f.* 29:22
sons to pass through *f.* to Molech. 32:35; *Ezek* 16:21; 20:26, 31
was a *f.* on the hearth. *Jer* 36:22
Jehudi cut roll, cast it into *f.* 23
but a *f.* shall come forth. 48:45
labour in vain and in the *f.* 51:58
against Jacob like flaming *f.* *Lam* 2:3
bent his bow, poured out fury like *f.* 4
I looked, behold, a *f.* *Ezek* 1:4
the *f.* was bright, out of the *f.* 13
take *f.* from between wheels. 10:6
cherub stretched forth hand to *f.* 7
blow against thee in *f.* 21:31; 22:21
thou shalt be for fuel to *f.* 21:32
to blow *f.* upon it. 22:20
I will even make pile for *f.* 24:9
her scum shall be in the *f.* 12
will I bring forth a *f.* from. 28:18
in *f.* of my jealousy have I spoken. 36:5; 38:19
bodies the *f.* had no power, nor the smell of *f.* passed on. *Dan* 3:27
wheels like burning *f.* 7:9
his eyes as lamps of *f.* 10:6
burneth as a flaming *f.* *Hos* 7:6
blood, *f.* and pillars of smoke. *Joel* 2:30; *Acts* 2:19
lest he break out like *f.* *Amos* 5:6
Lord God called to contend by *f.* 7:4
house of Jacob shall be a *f.* *Ob* 18
under him as wax before *f.* *Mi* 1:4
fury poured out like *f.* *Nah* 1:6
people shall labour in *f.* *Hab* 2:13
be unto her a wall of *f.* *Zech* 2:5
brand plucked out of *f.*? 3:2
hearth of *f.* and like torch of *f.* 12:6
the third part through the *f.* 13:9
he is like a refiner's *f.* *Mal* 3:2
bringeth not forth good fruit is cast into *f.* *Mat* 3:10; 7:19; *Luke* 3:9 *John* 15:6
baptize with Holy Ghost, and *f.* *Mat* 3:11; *Luke* 3:16
cast them into a furnace of *f.* *Mat* 13:42, 50
ofttimes falleth into *f.* *Mat* 17:15 *Mark* 9:22
or two feet, be cast into everlasting *f.* *Mat* 18:8; *Mark* 9:43, 46
me, into everlasting *f.* *Mat* 25:41
f. is not quenched. *Mark* 9:44, 45
Peter warmed himself at *f.* 14:54
command *f.* to come? *Luke* 9:54
the same day it rained *f.* 17:29
beheld him as he sat by *f.* 22:56
cloven tongues like as of *f.* *Acts* 2:3
when Paul laid sticks on the *f.* 28:3
he shook off the beast into *f.* 5
revealed by *f.* and the *f.* shall try every man's work. *1 Cor* 3:13
shall be saved, yet so as by *f.* 15
in flaming *f.* taking. *2 Thes* 1:8
his ministers a flame of *f.* *Heb* 1:7
faith quenched violence of *f.* 11:34
to mount that burned with *f.* 12:18
how great matter a little *f.* *Jas* 3:5
and the tongue is a *f.*, a world of. 6
eat your flesh as it were *f.* 5:3
gold, though it be tried with *f.* *1 Pet* 1:7
reserved unto *f.* against. *2 Pet* 3:7
heavens being on *f.* be dissolved. 12
vengeance of eternal *f.* *Jude* 7
others save, pulling out of the *f.* 23
of me gold tried in the *f.* *Rev* 3:18
seven lamps of *f.* burning. 4:5
angel filled the censer with *f.* 8:5

there followed hail and *f.* *Rev* 8:7
great mountain burning with *f.* 8
of their mouths issued *f.* 9:17; 11:5
part of men killed by the *f.* 9:18
he maketh *f.* come down. 13:13
angel which had power over *f.* 14:18
sea of glass mingled with *f.* 15:2
him to scorch men with *f.* 16:8
and *f.* came down from God. 20:9
the devil was cast into lake of *f.* 10
hell cast into the lake of *f.* 14
in book of life, cast into *f.* 15
lake which burneth with *f.* 21:8
see **brimstone, burn** *or* **burnt, coals, consume, consuming, devour, devoured, devouring, flame, hell, midst**

kindle, or *kindled* **fire**

he that *kindled* the *f.* *Ex* 22:6
kindle no *f.* on sabbath day. 35:3
a *f.* is *kindled* in my anger, and. *Deut* 32:22; *Jer* 15:14; 17:4
him coals of *f. kindled.* *2 Sam* 22:13
so a *f.* was *kindled* against Jacob. *Ps* 78:21
f. kindled in their company. 106:18
kindle a burning like a *f.* *Isa* 10:16
behold, all ye that *kindle* a *f.* 50:11
fathers *kindled f.* *Jer* 7:18
hath *kindled f.* on green. 11:16
then will I *kindle* a *f.* in gates. 17:27
I will *kindle* a *f.* in forest. 21:14
I will *kindle* a *f.* in houses of. 43:12
I will *kindle* a *f.* in the wall. 49:27
I will *kindle* a *f.* in his cities. 50:32
Lord hath *kindled* a *f.* in. *Lam* 4:11
kindle a *f.* in the forest. *Ezek* 20:47
heap on wood, *kindle f.* 24:10
I will *kindle* a *f.* in wall of Rabbah. *Amos* 1:14
neither do ye *kindle f.* on my altar. *Mal* 1:10
f. on the earth; and what if it be already *kindled*? *Luke* 12:49
when they had *kindled* a *f.* 22:55
barbarians *kindled* a *f.* *Acts* 28:2

made with **fire**

an offering *made* by *f.* unto Lord. *Ex* 29:18, 25, 41; *Lev* 1:9, 13, 17 2:2, 9, 16; 3:3, 5, 9, 11, 14, 16 7:5, 25, 8:21, 28; 21:6, 22:27 23:8, 13, 18, 25, 27, 36, 37; 24:7 *Num* 15:3, 10, 13, 14; 18:17; 28:3
the offerings of Lord *made* by *f.* *Lev* 2:3, 10; 4:35; 5:12; 6:17, 18 7:30, 35; 10:12, 15; 21:21; 24:9 *Deut* 18:1; *1 Sam* 2:28
sacrifices *made* by *f.* *Lev* 10:13 *Num* 28:2; *Josh* 13:14
bring sacrifice *made* by *f.* unto Lord. *Num* 15:25; 28:6, 8, 13, 19, 24 29:6, 13, 36

pillar of **fire**

Lord looked through *pillar of f.* *Ex* 14:24
his feet as *pillars of f.* *Rev* 10:1
see, by **night**

send, or *sent* **fire**

from above he *sent f.* *Lam* 1:13
and I will *send* a *f.* *Ezek* 39:6
send a *f.* upon his cities. *Hos* 8:14
send a *f.* into house of. *Amos* 1:4
I will *send* a *f.* on the wall. 7
I will *send* a *f.* on wall of Tyrus. 10
send f. on Teman. 12
I will *send* a *f.* on Moab. 2:2
send f. on Judah. 5
I am come to *send f.* on. *Luke* 12:49

set **fire**

set on *f.* foundations of. *Deut* 32:22
set city of Ai on *f.* *Josh* 8:8
hasted, and *set* the city on *f.* 19
had *set* Jerusalem on *f.* *Judg* 1:8
the people *set* the hold on *f.* 9:49
had *set* the brands on *f.* and. 15:5
set on *f.* all the cities of. 20:48
set Joab's field on *f.* *2 Sam* 14:30
have thy servants *set* field on *f.*? 31
set strong holds on *f.* *2 Ki* 8:12
them that are *set* on *f.* *Ps* 57:4
women *set* them on *f.* *Isa* 27:11
hath *set* him on *f.* round. 42:25
set up a sign of *f.* in. *Jer* 6:1
Chaldeans shall *set* on *f.* this. 32:29
when I have *set* a *f.* in. *Ezek* 30:8
I will *set f.* in Zoan. 14
set f. in Egypt. 16
set on *f.* and burn weapons. 39:9
tongue is a fire, *setteth* on *f.* . . . it is *set* on *f.* of hell. *Jas* 3:6

strange **fire**

Abihu offered *strange f.* *Lev* 10:1
died when they offered *strange f.* *Num* 3:4; 26:61

firebrand, -s

took *f.* and put a *f.* in. *Judg* 15:4
mad man who casteth *f.* *Pr* 26:18
tails of these smoking *f.* *Isa* 7:4
ye were as a *f.* plucked. *Amos* 4:11

firepans

make basons and *f.* *Ex* 27:3
f. and all vessels of brass. 38:3
f. carried he away. *2 Ki* 25:15 *Jer* 52:19

fires

glorify ye the Lord in *f.* *Isa* 24:15*

firkins

waterpots containing two or three *f.* *John* 2:6

firm

priests stood *f.* on dry. *Josh* 3:17
place where priests' feet stood *f.* 4:3
are *f.* in themselves. *Job* 41:23
his heart is as *f.* as a stone. 24
no bands in death, their strength is *f.* *Ps* 73:4
to make a *f.* decree. *Dan* 6:7*
rejoicing of the hope *f.* *Heb* 3:6

firmament

By the word firmament (Hebrew, rakiah), the Hebrews understood the heavens, which they thought to be like a solid arch between the upper and lower waters. They also believed that the stars are set in this arch, like so many precious stones in gold and silver, Gen 1:17.

let there be a *f.* in midst. *Gen* 1:6
f. waters under and above *f.* 7
God called the *f.* Heaven. 8
let there be lights in the *f.* 14, 15
God set them in *f.* of heaven. 17
fowl that fly above open *f.* 20
f. sheweth his handy work. *Ps* 19:1
praise him in *f.* of his power. 150:1
of *f.* was as crystal. *Ezek* 1:22
a voice from the *f.* over their. 25
above the *f.* was the likeness of. 26
in *f.* above the cherubims. 10:1
shine as brightness of *f.* *Dan* 12:3

fir tree

the two doors were of *f.* *1 Ki* 6:34
house he cieled with *f.* *2 Chr* 3:5
I will set in desert the *f.* *Isa* 41:19
instead of the thorn the *f.* 55:13
the *f.* the pine tree and box. 60:13
I am like a green *f.* *Hos* 14:8
howl, *f.* *Zech* 11:2

fir trees

so Hiram gave Solomon *f.* *1 Ki* 5:10; 9:11
I will cut down tall *f.* *2 Ki* 19:23 *Isa* 37:24
send me *f.* *2 Chr* 2:8
the *f.* rejoice. *Isa* 14:8
the stork the *f.* are her. *Ps* 104:17
ship boards of *f.* of Senir. *Ezek* 27:5
the *f.* were not like his boughs. 31:8
f. shall be terribly shaken. *Nah* 2:3

fir wood

on instruments of *f.* *2 Sam* 6:5

first

the *f.* came out red. *Gen* 25:25
a famine beside the *f.* famine. 26:1
midwife said, this came out *f.* 38:28
not hearken to *f.* sign. *Ex* 4:8
the *f.* of the firstfruits bring. 23:19
the *f.* row a sardius. 28:17; 39:10
two tables like to the *f.* 34:1, 4 *Deut* 10:1, 3
what is for sin offering *f.* *Lev* 5:8
Judah, these shall *f.* set. *Num* 2:9
and they *f.* took their journey. 10:13
time of the *f.* ripe grapes. *Num* 13:20
offer up a cake of the *f.* of your. 15:20, 21; *Ezek* 44:30
whatsoever is *f.* ripe. *Num* 18:13
Amalek was *f.* of nations. 24:20
according to the *f.* time. *Deut* 10:10
I will give thee *f.* rain. 11:14*
thine hand shall be *f.* upon. 13:9
hands of witnesses be *f.* upon. 17:7
f. of the fleece of thy sheep. 18:4
provided *f.* part for himself. 33:21
theirs was *f.* lot. *Josh* 21:10 *1 Chr* 24:7; 25:9
who shall go up *f.* *Judg* 1:1; 20:18
Israel are smitten as in *f.* 20:39
f. slaughter twenty. *1 Sam* 14:14
same was *f.* altar Saul built. 35
thou *f.* bring Michal. *2 Sam* 3:13
I am come the *f.* this day to. 19:20
that advice should not be *f.* 43
captain, howbeit he attained not unto *f.* 23:19, 23; *1 Chr* 11:21, 25
thereof a little cake *f.* *1 Ki* 17:13
and dress it *f.* for ye are. 18:25
men of princes went out *f.* 20:17
now *f.* inhabitants that. *1 Chr* 9:2
smiteth the Jebusites *f.* 11:6
day David delivered *f.* this. 16:7
length by cubits after *f.* *2 Chr* 3:3
had seen glory of the *f.* *Ezra* 3:12
sat *f.* in the kingdom. *Esth* 1:14
art thou *f.* man born? *Job* 15:7
that is *f.* in his own cause. *Ps* 18:17
the *f.* shall say to Zion. *Isa* 41:27
thy *f.* father hath sinned. 43:27
ships of Tarshish *f.* to bring. 60:9
bringeth forth her *f.* child. *Jer* 4:31
f. I will recompense iniquity. 16:18
like the figs that are *f.* ripe. 24:2
words that were in *f.* roll. 36:28
f. king of Assyria devoured. 50:17
Daniel was *f.* president. *Dan* 6:2*
the *f.* beast was like a lion. 7:4 *Rev* 4:7*
be diverse from the *f.* *Dan* 7:24*
horn between eyes is *f.* king. 8:21
return to my *f.* husband. *Hos* 2:7
f. ripe in fig tree at *f.* time. 9:10
go captive with the *f.* *Amos* 6:7
to thee shall come *f.* *Mi* 4:8*
like fig trees with *f.* ripe. *Nah* 3:12
that saw house in *f.* glory? *Hag* 2:3*
in the *f.* chariot red. *Zech* 6:2
shall save tents of Judah *f.* 12:7
f. be reconciled to thy. *Mat* 5:24
seek ye *f.* the kingdom of. 6:33
f. cast beam out of. 7:5; *Luke* 6:42
suffer me *f.* to go and bury. *Mat* 8:21 *Luke* 9:59
f. bind the strong man. *Mat* 12:29 *Mark* 3:27
state worse than the *f.* *Mat* 12:45 *Luke* 11:26
gather ye together *f.* tares. *Mat* 13:30
Elias *f.* come. 17:10, 11; *Mark* 9:12
take up fish that *f.* *Mat* 17:27
but when the *f.* came, they. 20:10
he came to the *f.* and said. 21:28
they say unto him, the *f.* 31
other servants more than *f.* 36
f. when married. 22:25 *Mark* 12:20; *Luke* 20:29
this is *f.* commandment. *Mat* 22:38 *Mark* 12:28, 29, 30
cleanse *f.* that which is. *Mat* 23:26
f. the blade, then ear. *Mark* 4:28
let the children *f.* be filled. 7:27
desire to be *f.* he shall be last. 9:35
and the gospel must *f.* be. 13:10
appeared *f.* to Mary. 16:9
perfect understanding from the *f.* *Luke* 1:3
was *f.* made when Cyrenius. 2:2
second sabbath after the *f.* he. 6:1
f. say, Peace be to this house. 10:5
that he had not *f.* washed. 11:38
sitteth not down *f.* and. 14:28
f. must he suffer many. 17:25
things must *f.* come to pass. 21:9
f. findeth his brother. *John* 1:41
whosoever *f.* stepped in, made. 5:4
without sin, let him *f.* cast. 8:7
where John at *f.* baptized. 10:40
led him away to Annas *f.* 18:13

brake the legs of the f. John 19:32
disciple came f. to the. 20:4, 8
to you f. God sent him. Acts 3:26
Jacob sent out our fathers f. 7:12*
called Christians f. at. 11:26
past the f. and second ward. 12:10
when John had f. preached. 13:24
it should f. have been spoken. 46
f. unto them of Damascus. 26:20
Christ f. that should rise from. 23
cast themselves f. into sea. 27:43
f. I thank my God. Rom 1:8
of the Jew f. and also of. 2:9, 10
who hath f. given to him ? 11:35
if f. I be somewhat filled. 15:24
f. apostles, secondarily. 1 Cor 12:28
let the f. hold his peace. 14:30
for I delivered f. of all that. 15:3
the f. man Adam a living soul. 45
howbeit that was not f. which. 46
the f. man is of the earth. 47
f. gave their own selves. 2 Cor 8:5
for if there be f. a willing mind. 12
who f. trusted in Christ. Eph 1:12
descended f. into lower parts. 4:9
which is the f. commandment. 6:2
in Christ shall rise f. 1 Thes 4:16
come a falling away f. 2 Thes 2:3
that in me f. Christ. 1 Tim 1:16*
for Adam was f. formed. 2:13
let these also f. be proved. 3:10
learn f. to shew piety at home. 5:4
have cast off their f. faith. 12
faith dwelt f. in thy grandmother. 2 Tim 1:5
husbandman be f. partaker of. 2:6
at my f. answer no man stood. 4:16
after f. and second. Tit 3:10
to whom it was f. preached. Heb 4:6*
teach you which be the f. 5:12
f. being by interpretation, king. 7:2
offer f. for his own sins. 27
the f. covenant. 8:7, 13; 9:1, 15, 18
f. tabernacle, wherein. 9:2, 6, 8
he taketh away the f. that. 10:9
wisdom from above, is f. Jas 3:17
if judgement f. begin at. 1 Pet 4:17
knowing this f. that no prophecy. 2 Pet 1:20; 3:3
because he f. loved us. 1 John 4:19
who kept not their f. estate. Jude 6*
thou hast left thy f. love. Rev 2:4
repent, and do the f. works. 5
the power of the f. beast. 13:12
this is the f. resurrection. 20:5
f. heaven and f. earth were. 21:1
the f. foundation was jasper. 19

see **day, last**

at the first

made the altar at the f. Gen 13:4
city was called Luz at the f. 28:19
of money returned at the f. 43:18
down at the f. to buy food. 20
down before Lord as at the f. Deut 9:18, 25
come against us at the f. Josh 8:5
they flee before us as at the f. 6
of city Laish at the f. Judg 18:29
smitten before us as at the f. 20:32
be overthrown at the f. 2 Sam 17:9
send for to thy servant at f. 1 Ki 20:9
ye did it not at the f. 1 Chr 15:13
which came up at the f. Neh 7:5
thy judges as at the f. Isa 1:26
when at the f. he lightly. 9:1*
I set my name at the f. Jer 7:12
I will build them as at the f. 33:7
return captivity of land, as at the f. 11
which appeared at the f. Dan 8:1
understood not at the f. John 12:16
which at the f. came by night. 19:39
God at the f. did visit. Acts 15:14
at the f. among mine own. 26:4
gospel unto you, at the f. Gal 4:13*
at the f. began to be spoken by. Heb 2:3

first *month*

f. month, the f. day of the month. Gen 8:13
the f. month of year to. Ex 12:2
f. month eat unleavened bread. 18
Lev 23:5
day of f. month set up. Ex 40:2, 17
f. month keep passover. Num 9:1
28:16; 2 Chr 35:1; Ezra 6:19
Ezek 45:21
desert of Zin in f. month. Num 20:1
from Rameses in f. month. 33:3
of Jordan in f. month. Josh 4:19
over Jordan in f. month. 1 Chr 12:15
captain that served f. month. 27:2, 3
f. month opened doors. 2 Chr 29:3
first day of f. month to sanctify and sixteenth day of f. month. 17
f. month began he to go. Ezra 7:9
the f. month we departed. 8:31
end with them by f. month. 10:17
in f. month cast Pur, on thirteenth day of the f. month. Esth 3:7, 12
f. month take a young. Ezek 45:18
and latter rain in f. month. Joel 2:23

first *year*

(In the giving of the age, as lamb of the first year, *the American Revision changes to* lamb a year old)

lambs male of the f. year. Ex 12:5
offer two lambs of f. year day by. 29:38; Lev 23:19; Num 28:3, 9
take a kid of the f. year. Lev 9:3
bring a lamb of the f. year. 12:6
Num 6:12; 7:15, 21, 27, 33, 39, 45
51, 57, 63, 69, 75, 81; Ezek 46:13
take an ewe lamb of the f. year. Lev 14:10; Num 6:14
an he lamb of f. year. Lev 23:12
Num 6:14
seven lambs of f. year. Lev 23:18
Num 28:11, 19, 27; 29:2, 8, 36
peace offering five lambs of f. year. Num 7:17, 23, 29, 35, 41, 47, 53, 59
lambs of the f. year twelve. 87
the lambs of the f. year sixty. 88
a she goat of the f. year. 15:27
a burnt offering, fourteen lambs of f. year. 29:13, 17, 20, 23, 26, 29, 32
Hezekiah in f. year of. 2 Chr 29:3
in f. year of Cyrus. 36:22
Ezra 1:1; 5:13; 6:3
f. year of Nebuchadnezzar. Jer 25:1
f. year of Evil-merodach. 52:31
to the f. year of Cyrus. Dan 1:21
in the f. year of Belshazzar. 7:1
in the f. year of Darius I. Daniel. 9:1, 2; 11:1

first begotten

when he bringeth in the f. b. Heb 1:6
Jesus, who is f. b. of dead. Rev 1:5

firstborn

The firstborn of both man and beast was considered as belonging to God. If of man, the child was redeemed, Ex 13:13, 15; 34:20. *If of a clean beast it was sacrificed, and if unclean either had the neck broken or was replaced by a lamb,* Ex 13:13, 15; 22:30; 34:20. *Later the Levites were substituted for the Israelites' firstborn,* Num 3:12, 41, 46; 8:13–19.

To the firstborn son belonged the birthright, which included the headship of the family or tribe, and a double portion of his father's property.

f. said to younger. Gen 19:31, 34
f. went in, lay with her father. 33
f. bare a son, called name Moab. 37
said, I am Esau, thy f. 27:19, 32
to give younger before f. 29:26
f. according to his birthright. 43:33
not so my father, this is f. 48:18
Israel is my son, even my f. Ex 4:22
I will slay thy son, even thy f. 23
all the f. in Egypt shall die. 11:5
and I will smite all the f. 12:12
Lord smote all the f. in. 29; 13:15
sanctify unto me all the f. 13:2
the f. of thy sons shalt thou. 22:29
f. of thy sons. 34:20; Num 18:15
instead of all the f. Num 3:12
41, 45; 8:17, 18
the f. of Israel are mine, I hallowed to me all the f. of. 3:13
number the f. of the males of. 40
Moses numbered f. of Israel. 42
of f. of Israel took he money. Num 3:50
the Egyptians buried all their f. 33:4
if f. son be her's that. Deut 21:15
for the right of f. is his. 17
f. which she beareth, succeed. 25:6
lay foundation in his f. Josh 6:26
foundation in Abiram f. 1 Ki 16:34
Reuben f. he was the f. 1 Chr 5:1
though he was not the f. yet. 26:10
Jehoram, the f. 2 Chr 21:3
the f. to the house of. Neh 10:36
the f. of death shall. Job 18:13
he smote all the f. in. Ps 78:51
105:36; 135:8; 136:10
my f. higher than kings. 89:27
f. of the poor shall feed. Isa 14:30
Israel, Ephraim is my f. Jer 31:9
my f. for my transgression ? Mi 6:7
in bitterness for his f. Zech 12:10
Mary brought forth her f. son. Mat 1:25; Luke 2:7
f. among many brethren. Rom 8:29
the f. of every creature. Col 1:15
the beginning, f. from the dead. 18
lest he that destroyed f. Heb 11:28
ye are come to the church of f. 12:23

firstfruits

The firstfruits were to be given as an offering to Jehovah, Lev 23:10, 17; Ex 23:19. *The term is used figuratively also,* Rom 8:23; Jas 1:18.

to offer f. ripe fruits. Ex 22:29
f. of thy labour thou hast. 23:16
first of f. 23:19; 34:26; Deut 26:2
of f. of wheat harvest. Ex 34:22
oblation of the f. offer. Lev 2:12
the meat offering of f. green. 14
a sheaf of the f. of harvest. 23:10
they are the f. unto the Lord. 17
wave them with bread of the f. 20
f. of oil, wine, wheat. Num 18:12
in the day of f. when ye. 28:26
the f. of thy corn, wine. Deut 18:4
brought the f. of the land. 26:10
brought man of God f. 2 Ki 4:42
brought in abundance f. 2 Chr 31:5
bring f. of our ground. Neh 10:35
should bring the f. of our dough. 37
over, chambers for f. 12:44; 13:31
honour Lord with the f. Pr 3:9
Israel was the f. of his. Jer 2:3
there will I require f. Ezek 20:40
the first of all the f. 44:30
nor exchange the f. of land. 48:14
have the f. of the Spirit. Rom 8:23
if the f. be holy. 11:16
who is the f. of Achaia. 16:5
1 Cor 16:15
Christ the f. of them that slept. 1 Cor 15:20, 23
f. of his creatures. Jas 1:18
being the f. unto God. Rev 14:4

firstling

(*The same as firstborn, but confined to the firstborn of beasts*)

shalt set apart every f. of beast, males shall be. Ex 13:12; 34:19
every f. of an ass. 13:13; 34:20
the Lord's f. no man. Lev 27:26
f. of unclean beasts. Num 18:15
the f. of a cow, sheep, or goat. 17
all the f. males sanctify. Deut 15:19
Joseph's glory is like f. of. 33:17

firstlings

Abel brought f. of his flock. Gen 4:4
instead of all the f. Num 3:41
ye shall bring f. of your. Deut 12:6
not eat within thy gates the f. 17
eat the f. in place Lord shall. 14:23
f. of our herds bring to. Neh 10:36

fish

dominion over f. Gen 1:26, 28
f. in river shall die. Ex 7:18, 21
f. we did eat in Egypt. Num 11:5
all the f. of the sea be gathered ? 22
nor likeness of any f. in. Deut 4:18
of Tyre, which brought f. Neh 13:16
his head with f. spears ? Job 41:7
thou hast put the f. under. Ps 8:8
waters into blood, slew f. 105:29

sluices and ponds for *f.* *Isa* 19:10*
their *f.* stinketh because there. 50:2
will cause the *f.* to stick. *Ezek* 29:4
and all the *f.* of thy rivers. 5
very great multitude of *f.* 47:9
their *f.* as the *f.* of the great sea. 10
a great *f.* to swallow Jonah, in belly
of *f.* three days. *Jonah* 1:17
to Lord out of the *f.'s* belly. 2:1
Lord spake to the *f.* and it. 10
if he ask a *f.* will he give? *Mat* 7:10
take up *f.* that first cometh. 17:27
a piece of a broiled *f.* *Luke* 24:42
they saw *f.* laid thereon. *John* 21:9
bring of *f.* ye have now caught. 10
Jesus taketh bread, and *f.* 13

fish, *verb*

fishers, they shall *f.* *Jer* 16:16

fishermen

but the *f.* were gone out. *Luke* 5:2

fisher, -s

the *f.* also shall mourn. *Isa* 19:8
I will send for many *f.* *Jer* 16:16
that the *f.* shall stand. *Ezek* 47:10
for they were *f.* *Mat* 4:18
Mark 1:16
make you *f.* of men. *Mat* 4:19
Mark 1:17
Peter girt *f.'s* coat to him. *John* 21:7

fishes

you shall be on all *f.* *Gen* 9:2
creeping things and *f.* *1 Ki* 4:33
f. of the sea shall. *Job* 12:8
the *f.* that are taken in. *Eccl* 9:12
the *f.* of the sea. *Ezek* 38:20
f. of the sea shall be taken. *Hos* 4:3
makest men as *f.* of sea. *Hab* 1:14
consume the *f.* of the sea. *Zeph* 1:3
five loaves and two *f.* *Mat* 14:17
Mark 6:38; *Luke* 9:13; *John* 6:9
seven loaves and a few *f.* *Mat* 15:34
Mark 8:7
a great multitude of *f.* *Luke* 5:6
astonished at the draught of *f.* 9
not able to draw it for *f.* *John* 21:6
drew net to land full of great *f.* 11
of beasts, another of *f.* *1 Cor* 15:39

fish gate

on entering of *f. gate.* *2 Chr* 33:14
f. gate did the sons of. *Neh* 3:3
after them from above *f. gate.* 12:39
noise of a cry from *f. gate.* *Zeph* 1:10

fishhooks

your posterity with *f.* *Amos* 4:2

fishing

Peter saith unto them, I go a *f.*
John 21:3

fishpools

thine eyes like the *f.* in. *S of S* 7:4

fist, -s

smite another with his *f.* *Ex* 21:18
gathered wind in his *f.*? *Pr* 30:4
with *f.* of wickedness. *Isa* 58:4

fit

him away by a *f.* man. *Lev* 16:21*
f. to go out to war and battle.
1 Chr 7:11*; 12:8*
is it *f.* to say to a king? *Job* 34:18
make it *f.* for thyself. *Pr* 24:27*
vine made *f.* for no. *Ezek* 15:5
f. for kingdom of God. *Luke* 9:62
it is not *f.* for the land nor. 14:35
not *f.* that he should live. *Acts* 22:22
submit as it is *f.* in Lord. *Col* 3:18

fitches

he not cast abroad the *f.*? *Isa* 28:25
f. are not threshed, *f.* are. 27
wheat, barley, millet, *f.* *Ezek* 4:9*

fitly

a word *f.* spoken is like. *Pr* 25:11
eyes washed with milk, *f.* *S of S* 5:12
in whom building *f.* *Eph* 2:21
from whom the whole body *f.* 4:16

fitted

with gold *f.* upon carved. *1 Ki* 6:35
they shall withal be *f.* *Pr* 22:18*
vessels of wrath *f.* to. *Rom* 9:22

fitteth

the carpenter *f.* it. *Isa* 44:13*

five

Siddim, four kings with *f.* *Gen* 14:9
destroy all for lack of *f.*? 18:28
Benjamin's mess was *f.* 43:34
f. years in which no earing. 45:6, 11
to Benjamin he gave *f.* changes. 22
presented *f.* of his brethren. 47:2
thief restore *f.* oxen for. *Ex* 22:1
other *f.* curtains coupled. 26:3, 9
36:10, 16
make *f.* bars for the boards. 26:26
27; 36:31, 32
f. pillars. 26:37; 36:38
an altar *f.* cubits long, *f.* 27:1
height of hangings *f.* 18; 38:18
f. sockets of brass. 36:38
f. cubits breadth, *f.* the length. 38:1
f. of you chase an hundred. *Lev* 26:8
estimation be from *f.* years. 27:5
from a month old to *f.* years. 6
take *f.* shekels apiece. *Num* 3:47
18:16
of peace offerings, *f.* rams, *f.* goats,
f. 7:17, 23, 29, 35, 41, 47, 53
slew *f.* kings of Midian. 31:8
f. kings of Amorites. *Josh* 10:5
these *f.* kings fled and hid. 16
f. kings hid. 17
bring out the *f.* kings. 22
brought out these *f.* kings unto. 23
hanged them on *f.* trees. 26
f. lords of the Philistines. 13:3
Judg 3:3
children of Dan sent *f.* *Judg* 18:2
f. golden emerods, *f.* *1 Sam* 6:4
when *f.* lords of Philistines had. 16
David chose *f.* smooth stones. 17:40
give me *f.* loaves of bread. 21:3
f. sheep, *f.* measures of corn. 25:18
Abigail rode on an ass with *f.* 42
Mephibosheth was *f.* *2 Sam* 4:4
David took the *f.* sons of. 21:8
f. bases on the right, *f.* *1 Ki* 7:39
f. on right side, *f.* on. 49; *2 Chr* 4:7
cab of dove's dung sold *f.* *2 Ki* 6:25
let some take *f.* of the horses. 7:13
have smitten *f.* or six times. 13:19
f. men in king's presence. 25:19
the sons of Zera, *f.* of. *1 Chr* 2:6
Benaiah slew an Egyptian *f.* 11:23
four or *f.* in fruitful. *Isa* 17:6
f. cities in Egypt speak. 19:18
at the rebuke of *f.* shall ye. 30:17
but *f.* loaves and two. *Mat* 14:17
Mark 6:38; *Luke* 9:13
f. loaves of the *f.* thousand.
Mat 16:9; *Mark* 8:19
f. were wise, *f.* foolish. *Mat* 25:2
unto one he gave *f.* talents. 15, 16
are not *f.* sparrows sold? *Luke* 12:6
f. in one house divided. 52
I have bought *f.* yoke of. 14:19
I have *f.* brethren 16:28
thy pound hath gained *f.* 19:18
be thou also over *f.* cities. 19
hast had *f.* husbands. *John* 4:18
pool Bethesda having *f.* porches 5:2
lad which had *f.* barley loaves. 6:9
fragments of *f.* barley loaves. 13
rather speak *f.* words. *1 Cor* 14:19
f. times received I forty stripes.
2 Cor 11:24
seven kings, *f.* are fallen. *Rev* 17:10

fixed

my heart is *f.* *Ps* 57:7; 108:1
his heart is *f.*, trusting. 112:7
there is a gulf *f.* *Luke* 16:26

flag, -s

she laid the ark in the *f.* *Ex* 2:3
when she saw the ark among *f.* 5
f. grow without water? *Job* 8:11
the reeds and *f.* shall. *Isa* 19:6

flagon

each a *f.* of wine. *2 Sam* 6:19*
1 Chr 16:3*

flagons

stay me with *f.* *S of S* 2:5*
to all the vessels of *f.* *Isa* 22:24
to other gods, love *f.* *Hos* 3:1*

flakes

the *f.* of his flesh joined. *Job* 41:23

flame

angel appeared in a *f.* *Ex* 3:2
Acts 7:30
a *f.* from the city of. *Num* 21:28
Jer 48:45
f. went up, angel went in the *f.*
Judg 13:20
make a great *f.* to rise. 20:38*
the *f.* of the city ascended up. 40*
the *f.* shall dry up his. *Job* 15:30
a *f.* goeth out of his mouth. 41:21
f. setteth mountains on. *Ps* 83:14
the *f.* burnt up the wicked. 106:18
which hath a vehement *f.* *S of S* 8:6
f. consumeth the chaff. *Isa* 5:24
Holy One shall be for a *f.* 10:17
with *f.* of devouring fire. 29:6
with *f.* of a devouring fire. 30:30
neither the *f.* kindle upon thee. 43:2
not deliver themselves from *f.* 47:14
flaming *f.* not quenched. *Ezek* 20:47
f. slew those men that. *Dan* 3:22
his throne was like fiery *f.* 7:9
body was given to burning *f.* 11*
shall fall by sword and by *f.* 11:33
the *f.* hath burnt all trees. *Joel* 1:19
and behind them a *f.* burneth. 2:3
like the noise of a *f.* of fire. 5
house of Joseph shall be a *f.* *Ob* 18
am tormented in this *f.* *Luke* 16:24
maketh his ministers a *f.* *Heb* 1:7
eyes as a *f.* *Rev* 1:14; 2:18; 19:12

flames

of Lord divideth the *f.* *Ps* 29:7
their faces shall be as *f.* *Isa* 13:8
to render rebuke with *f.* 66:15

flaming

at Eden a *f.* sword. *Gen* 3:24
the *f.* flame shall not be quenched.
Ezek 20:47
chariots with *f.* torches. *Nah* 2:3
see **fire**

flanks

(*Revised Version,* loins)
the fat which is by the *f.* shall he.
Lev 3:4, 10, 15; 4:9; 7:4
collops of fat on his *f.* *Job* 15:27

flash

as the appearance of a *f.* *Ezek* 1:14

flat

hath a *f.* nose shall not. *Lev* 21:18
Balaam bowed, fell *f.* *Num* 22:31
of city shall fall down *f.* *Josh* 6:5
people shouted, wall fell down *f.* 20

flatter

they *f.* with their tongue. *Ps* 5:9
they did *f.* him with their. 78:36

flattereth

f. himself in his own eyes. *Ps* 36:2
stranger who *f.* with. *Pr* 2:16; 7:5
meddle not with him that *f.* 20:19*
more favour than he that *f.* 28:23
a man that *f.* spreadeth a net. 29:5

flatteries

obtain the kingdom by *f.* *Dan* 11:21
do wickedly be corrupt by *f.* 32
shall cleave to them with *f.* 34

flattering

neither let me give *f.* titles to man.
Job 32:21
for I know not to give *f.* titles. 22
with *f.* lips and double. *Ps* 12:2
the Lord shall cut off all *f.* lips. 3
with the *f.* of her lips. *Pr* 7:21
a *f.* mouth worketh ruin. 26:28
no more *f.* divination. *Ezek* 12:24
neither used we *f.* *1 Thes* 2:5

flattery

speaketh *f.* to his friends. *Job* 17:5*
from *f.* of strange woman. *Pr* 6:24

flax

f. and barley smitten, *f.* *Ex* 9:31
hid them with stalks of *f.* *Josh* 2:6
cords became as *f.* that. *Judg* 15:14
she seeks wool and *f.* *Pr* 31:13
they that work in fine *f.* *Isa* 19:9
the smoking *f.* shall he not quench.
42:3; *Mat* 12:20
a man with a line of *f.* *Ezek* 40:3
lovers that give me *f.* *Hos* 2:5
I will recover my wool and my *f.* 9

flay
f. their skins from off them. *Mi* 3:3

flayed
the Levites *f.* them. *2 Chr* 35:11

flea
is king come after a *f.*? *1 Sam* 24:14
26:20

fled
kings of Sodom and Gomorrah *f.*
Gen 14:10
Hagar *f.* 16:6
Jacob *f.* 31:22; *Hos* 12:12
Moses *f.* from Pharaoh. *Ex* 2:15
4:3; *Acts* 7:29
king of Egypt that people *f.* *Ex* 14:5
Egyptians *f.* against the sea. 27
f. at the cry of them. *Num* 16:34
Israel *f.* by way of the. *Josh* 8:15
these five kings *f.* and hid. 10:16
Adoni-bezek *f.* *Judg* 1:6
Sisera *f.* away. 4:15
host ran and cried, and *f.* 7:21*, 22
Zalmunna *f.* 8:12
Jotham ran and *f.* 9:21
to the tower *f.* men and. 51
Jephthah *f.* 11:3
the Benjamites *f.* 20:45, 47
and I *f.* to-day out of. *1 Sam* 4:16
heard that Philistines *f.* 14:22
men of Israel *f.* from Goliath. 17:24
David *f.* and escaped. 19:10
12, 18; 20:1; 21:10
Abiathar escaped and *f.* 22:20; 23:6
four hundred which rode and *f.* 30:17
Israel *f.* from Philistines. 31:1, 7
2 Sam 19:8
Beerothites *f.* to Gittaim. *2 Sam* 4:3
and his nurse *f.* 4
the Syrians *f.* 10:14, 18
Absalom and king's sons *f.* 13:29
34:37, 38
all Israel *f.* every one to tent. 18:17
came to me when I *f.* *1 Ki* 2:7
Joab *f.* to the tabernacle. 28, 29
Hadad *f.* 11:17
Rezon *f.* from his lord. 23
Jeroboam *f.* 40
the Syrians *f.* 20:20; *1 Chr* 19:18
2 Ki 7:7
the people *f.* to their. *2 Ki* 8:21
prophet opened door and *f.* 9:10
Joram *f.* 23
all the men of war *f.* by night. 25:4
Jer 52:7
the men of Israel *f.* *1 Chr* 10:1
11:13; *2 Chr* 13:16
Ethiopians and they *f.* *2 Chr* 14:12
the Levites *f.* every one. *Neh* 13:10
they that did see me *f.* *Ps* 31:11
the sea saw it and *f.* 114:3
with bread him that *f.* *Isa* 21:14
all thy rulers are *f.* together. 22:3
noise of tumult the people *f.* 33:3
birds of the heavens were *f.* *Jer* 4:25
the fowl and beast are *f.* 9:10
Urijah heard and *f.* 26:21
Egyptians are *f.* 46:5
also her hired men are *f.* 21
I *f.* before to Tarshish. *Jonah* 4:2
flee as ye *f.* before the. *Zech* 14:5
they that kept them *f.* *Mat* 8:33
disciples forsook him and *f.* 26:56
Mark 14:50
they went out and *f.* *Mark* 16:8
the prisoners had been *f.* *Acts* 16:27*
f. for refuge to lay hold. *Heb* 6:18
the woman *f.* *Rev* 12:6
every island *f.* away. 16:20
earth and heaven *f.* away. 20:11

he **fled**
told him not that *he f.* *Gen* 31:20
so *he f.* 21
when *he f.* from his brother. 35:7
he left his garment and *f.* 39:12
13, 15, 18
to the city of his refuge, whither *he* was *f.* *Num* 35:25; *Josh* 20:6
Abimelech chased Gaal, and *he f.*
Judg 9:40
they knew when *he f.* *1 Sam* 22:17
Ahaziah fled, and *he f.* *2 Ki* 9:27
he f. to Lachish. 14:19; *2 Chr* 25:27
he f. from presence of. *Jonah* 1:10
he left linen cloth, and *f.* naked.
Mark 14:52

is **fled**
no satisfaction for him that *is f.*
Num 35:32
is f. before Philistines. *1 Sam* 4:17
David *is f.* out of the. *2 Sam* 19:9
Gibeah of Saul *is f.* *Isa* 10:29

they **fled**
they that remained *f.* *Gen* 14:10
they f. from before men of Ai.
Josh 7:4
as *they f.* Lord cast down. 10:11
Israel was smitten, *they f.* every man to. *1 Sam* 4:10; *2 Ki* 14:12
champion dead *they f.* *1 Sam* 17:51
slew Philistines, and *they f.* 19:8
Joab drew nigh, *they f.* *2 Sam* 10:13
1 Chr 19:14
Moabites, *they f.* before them.
2 Ki 3:24
Israel saw that *they f.* *1 Chr* 10:7
at thy rebuke *they f.* *Ps* 104:7
they f. from swords. *Isa* 21:15
they f. and went forth. *Jer* 39:4
when *they f.* away. *Lam* 4:15
they f. to save themselves. *Dan* 10:7
for *they* have *f.* from me. *Hos* 7:13*
what was done, *they f.* *Luke* 8:34
they f. out of that house. *Acts* 19:16

fleddest
thou *f.* from Esau. *Gen* 35:1
ailed thee, O sea, thou *f.*? *Ps* 114:5

flee
I *f.* from the face of. *Gen* 16:8
this city is near to *f.* unto. 19:20
arise, *f.* to Laban my. 27:43
us *f.* from face of Israel. *Ex* 14:25
a place whither he shall *f.* 21:13
f. when none pursueth. *Lev* 26:17, 36
hate thee *f.* before thee. *Num* 10:55
Ps 68:1
now *f.* thou to thy place. *Num* 24:11
that the manslayer may *f.* 35:6
11, 15; *Deut* 4:42; 19:3, 4, 5
Josh 20:3, 4, 9
and *f.* before thee. *Deut* 28:7, 25
first we *f.* before them. *Josh* 8:5, 6
had no power to *f.* this way or. 20
let us *f.* and draw them. *Judg* 20:32
but didst *f.* on spoil. *1 Sam* 15:19
nurse made haste to *f.* *2 Sam* 4:4
f. else we shall not escape. 15:14
men steal away when they *f.* 19:3
f. three months before? 24:13
made speed to get to chariot, and *f.*
1 Ki 12:18; *2 Chr* 10:18
then open door, and *f.* *2 Ki* 9:3
such a man as I *f.*? *Neh* 6:11
f. from the iron weapon. *Job* 20:24
would fain *f.* out of hand. 27:22
abhor me, they *f.* far from. 30:10*
arrow cannot make him *f.* 41:28
f. as bird to your? *Ps* 11:1
kings of armies *f.* apace. 68:12
I *f.* from thy presence? 139:7
O Lord, I *f.* to thee to hide. 143:9
wicked *f.* when no man. *Pr* 28:1
he shall *f.* to the pit. 17
whom will ye *f.* for help? *Isa* 10:3
f. every one into his own. 13:14
his fugitives shall *f.* unto Zoar. 15:5
they shall *f.* far off. 17:13
expectation whither we *f.* for. 20:6
no, for we will *f.* on horses. 30:16
at rebuke of five shall ye *f.* 17
f. ye from the Chaldeans. 48:20
the city shall *f.* for noise. *Jer* 4:29
to *f.* out of Jerusalem. 6:1
shepherds have no way to *f.* 25:35
f. save your lives, and be. 48:6
wings to Moab, that it may *f.* 9
Edom shall *f.* 49:8
Damascus turned to *f.* 24
f. dwell deep, inhabitants of. 30
f. every one to his own land. 50:16
voice of them that *f.* and escape. 28
f. out of midst of Babylon. 51:6
Zech 2:6
man did *f.* from a lion. *Amos* 5:19
Jonah rose up to *f.* to. *Jonah* 1:3
that look on, shall *f.* *Nah* 3:7
take young child and *f.* *Mat* 2:13
hath warned you *f.* from wrath? 3:7
Luke 3:7
persecute you in city *f.* *Mat* 10:23
be in Judea *f.* to the mountains.
24:16; *Mark* 13:14; *Luke* 21:21
stranger not follow, but *f.* *John* 10:5
shipmen were about to *f.* *Acts* 27:30
f. fornication. *1 Cor* 6:18
f. from idolatry. 10:14
O man of God, *f.* these. *1 Tim* 6:11
f. also youthful lusts. *2 Tim* 2:22
devil, he will *f.* from you. *Jas* 4:7
death shall *f.* from them. *Rev* 9:6
that the woman might *f.* into. 12:14

flee *away*
wherefore didst thou *f. away*?
Gen 31:27
if *f. away*, they will not. *2 Sam* 18:3
my days *f. away*. *Job* 9:25
f. away as a dream. 20:8
that see, shall *f. away*. *Ps* 64:8*
day break, and shadows *f. away*.
S of S 2:17; 4:6
sighing *f. away*. *Isa* 35:10; 51:11
let not swift *f. away*. *Jer* 46:6
courageous shall *f. away*. *Amos* 2:16
O thou seer, go, *f. away* into. 7:12
fleeth of them, shall not *f. away*. 9:1
Nineveh shall *f. away*. *Nah* 2:8
grasshoppers in hedges *f. away*. 3:17

fleece
first of *f.* of sheep give. *Deut* 18:4
a *f.* of wool in floor. *Judg* 6:37
Gideon wringed dew out of *f.* 38
let it be dry only upon the *f.* 39
not warmed with *f.* of. *Job* 31:20

fleeing
flee as *f.* from sword. *Lev* 26:36
that *f.* to one of these. *Deut* 4:42
for want and famine *f.* to. *Job* 30:3*

fleeth
smite him mortally, *f.* *Deut* 19:11
he *f.* as a shadow. *Job* 14:2
he who *f.* from noise of. *Isa* 24:18
ask him that *f.* and. *Jer* 48:19
he that *f.* from the fear, shall. 44
f. shall not flee away. *Amos* 9:1*
that is an hireling *f.* *John* 10:12, 13

flesh
[1] *The muscles and other soft parts of the animal body, whether of man, beast, bird, or fish,* Ex 12:8; Mat 26:41. [2] *All beings possessed of flesh, man and the inferior animals, especially man; often in contrast with God, who is spirit,* Gen 6:13. [3] *Human nature considered as unregenerate and unsanctified,* Rom 7:5. [4] *The word is also used for one of near kindred,* Gen 37:27; 2 Sam 19:12, 13.

To be one flesh, denotes an intimate communion, as if the two were but one person or one body, Gen 2:24. *This phrase is used by the Apostle to shew the union between Christ and believers,* Eph 5:30, 31. *Flesh also signifies the human nature of Christ,* Heb 10:20.

God closed up the *f.* *Gen* 2:21
to his wife, they shall be one *f.* 24
not strive with man, he is *f.* 6:3
ye shall circumcise the *f.* of. 17:11
whose *f.* is not circumcised. 14
Abraham circumcised *f.* of. 23
he is our brother and our *f.* 37:27
turned again as his other *f.* *Ex* 4:7
burn the *f.* 29:14; *Lev* 9:11; 16:27
Num 19:5
man's *f.* not be poured. *Ex* 30:32
what shall touch *f* thereof. *Lev* 6:27
as for *f.*, all that be clean shall. 7:19
boil the *f.* at the door of. 8:31
be quick raw *f.* 13:10, 14, 15, 16, 24
if skin of their *f.* have bright. 38, 39
that toucheth the *f.* of him. 15:7
if her issue in her *f.* be blood. 19
make any cuttings in their *f.* 21:5

while *f.* was between. *Num* 11:33
whom *f.* is half consumed. 12:12
the *f.* of them shall be thine. 18:18
my sword shall devour *f. Deut* 32:42
take *f.* and unleavened cakes. *Judg* 6:20
fire out of rock, and consumed *f.* 21
while *f.* was in seething. *1 Sam* 2:13
give *f.* to roast for the priest. 15
David dealt to each *f.* *2 Sam* 6:19
1 Chr 16:3
him bread and *f.* in morning, bread and *f.* in evening. *1 Ki* 17:6
boiled *f.* with instruments of. 19:21
f. of the child waxed. *2 Ki* 4:34
with him is an arm of *f.* *2 Chr* 32:8
yet our *f.* is as the *f.* of. *Neh* 5:5
hast thou eyes of *f.*? *Job* 10:4
clothed me with skin and *f.* 11
I will not fear what *f.* can. *Ps* 56:4
he provide *f.* for his people? 78:20
rained *f.* also upon them as dust. 27
remembered they were but *f.* 39
the *f.* of thy saints given to. 79:2
sayings are health to their *f. Pr* 4:22
not among riotous eaters of *f.* 23:20
and their horses are *f.* 31:3
I will feed them with own *f.* 49:26
and the holy *f.* is passed. *Jer* 11:15
spoilers come, no *f.* have. 12:12
cursed be man that maketh *f.* 17:5
nor came abominable *f.* *Ezek* 4:14
city is caldron, and we be *f.* 11:3
slain in midst of it, they are the *f.* 7
nor ye be the *f.* in the midst. 11
give them a heart of *f.* 19; 36:26
great of *f.* and hast increased. 16:26
whose *f.* is as *f.* of asses. 23:20
consume the *f.*, spice it well. 24:10
I will bring *f.* upon you. 37:6, 8
dwelling is not with *f.* *Dan* 2:11
arise, devour much *f.* 7:5
neither came *f.* nor wine. 10:3
sacrifice *f.* for sacrifices. *Hos* 8:13
f. from off their bones. *Mi* 3:2
their *f.* shall be poured. *Zeph* 1:17
if one bear holy *f.* in. *Hag* 2:12
f. shall consume away. *Zech* 14:12
f. and blood hath not. *Mat* 16:17
and they twain be one *f.* 19:5, 6
Mark 10:8; *1 Cor* 6:16; *Eph* 5:31
should no *f.* be saved. *Mat* 24:22
Mark 13:20
spirit willing, *f.* is weak. *Mat* 26:41
Mark 14:38
spirit hath not *f.* and. *Luke* 24:39
the Word was made *f.* *John* 1:14
the *f.* profiteth nothing. 6:63
of David according to *f.* *Acts* 2:30
Rom 1:3
shall no *f.* be justified. *Rom* 3:20
Abraham as pertaining to *f.* 4:1
with *f.* I serve the law of sin. 7:25
law was weak through *f.*, God sent own Son in likeness of sinful *f.* 8:3
and kinsmen according to *f.* 9:3
of whom as concerning the *f.* 5
make not provision for the *f.* 13:14
that no *f.* should glory. *1 Cor* 1:29
there is one *f.* of men, and. 15:39
f. and blood cannot inherit. 50
purpose according to *f.*? *2 Cor* 1:17
of Jesus manifest in our *f.* 4:11
our *f.* had no rest, but. 7:5
walked according to the *f.* 10:2
conferred not with *f.* and. *Gal* 1:16
by works of law no *f.* justified. 2:16
are ye made perfect by the *f.*? 3:3
not liberty for occasion to the *f.* 5:13
f. lusteth against the Spirit, Spirit against *f.* 17
Christ's have crucified the *f.* 24
in lusts of our *f.* *Eph* 2:3
masters according to the *f.* 6:5
Col 3:22
wrestle not against *f.* and. *Eph* 6:12
children partakers of *f.* *Heb* 2:14
we had fathers of our *f.* who. 12:9
going after strange *f.* are. *Jude* 7
these filthy dreamers defile the *f.* 8
hating even garment spotted by *f.* 23
eat *f.* of captains, *f.* of. *Rev* 19:18
all the fowls filled with their *f.* 21
see **eat, eateth**

after the **flesh**

ye judge *after the f.* *John* 8:15
who walk not *after the f. Rom* 8:1, 4
are *after the f.* mind things of *f.* 5
debtors to flesh to live *after the f.* 12
if ye live *after the f.* ye shall die. 13
many wise men *after f.* *1 Cor* 1:26
behold Israel *after the f.* 10:18
no man *after the f.*: though we have known Christ *after f.* *2 Cor* 5:16
we do not war *after the f.* 10:3
many glory *after the f.* I also. 11:18
Ishmael born *after the f. Gal* 4:23, 29
them that walk *after f.* *2 Pet* 2:10

all **flesh**

for *all f.* had corrupted. *Gen* 6:12
God said, the end of *all f.* is. 13
of *all f.* two of every sort bring into the ark to keep. 19; 7:15
all f. died that moved upon. 7:21
bring forth of *all f.* both of. 8:17
nor *all f.* cut off any more. 9:11, 15
covenant between me and *all f.* 16, 17
the life of *all f.* is blood. *Lev* 17:14
shave *all* their *f.* and. *Num* 8:7
God of spirits of *all f.* 16:22; 27:16
that openeth matrix of *all f.* 18:15
who of *all f.* heard word. *Deut* 5:26
all f. shall perish together. *Job* 34:15
to thee shall *all f.* come. *Ps* 65:2
who giveth food to *all f.* 136:25
let *all f.* bless his holy name. 145:21
all f. shall see it together. *Isa* 40:5
all f. is grass. 6; *1 Pet* 1:24
all f. shall know I am thy Saviour. *Isa* 49:26; *Ezek* 21:5
by fire will Lord plead with *all f.* *Isa* 66:16
all f. shall come to worship. 23
an abhorring to *all f.* 24
will plead with *all f.* *Jer* 25:31
I am Lord the God of *all f.* 32:27
I will bring evil on *all f.* 45:5
all f. shall see that I. *Ezek* 20:48
sword go forth against *all f.* 21:4
and *all f.* was fed of it. *Dan* 4:12
will pour out my Spirit on *all f.* *Joel* 2:28; *Acts* 2:17
be silent, O *all f.* *Zech* 2:13
all f. shall see salvation. *Luke* 3:6
given him power over *all f. John* 17:2
all f. is not same flesh. *1 Cor* 15:39

his **flesh**

his f. shall not be eaten. *Ex* 21:28
seethe *his f.* in holy place. 29:31
burn all *his f.* with. *Lev* 4:11; 8:17
linen breeches on *his f.* 6:10; 16:4
a rising in the skin of *his f.* 13:2
look on plague in skin of *his f.* 3
spot be white in skin of *his f.* 4
old leprosy in skin of *his f.* 11, 13
also wash *his f.* in water. 14:9
15:16; 16:24, 28; *Num* 19:7
running issue out of *his f.* *Lev* 15:2
whether *his f.* run with his issue. 3
wash them not, nor bathe *his f.* 17:16
unclean, unless he wash *his f.* 22:6
Ahab put sackcloth on *his f.* *1 Ki* 21:27
his f. came again, and. *2 Ki* 5:14
Joram had sackcloth on *his f.* 6:30
touch his bone and *his f.* *Job* 2:5
his f. upon him shall have. 14:22
O that we had of *his f.* 31:31
his f. is consumed away. 33:21
his f. be fresher than a child's. 25
flakes of *his f.* are joined. 41:23
cruel troubleth *his f.* *Pr* 11:17
foldeth hands, eateth *his f. Eccl* 4:5
fatness of *his f.* wax lean. *Isa* 17:4
man give us *his f.* to eat? *John* 6:52
his f. did see corruption. *Acts* 2:31
he that soweth to *his f.* *Gal* 6:8
abolished in *his f.* the. *Eph* 2:15
no man yet hated *his* own *f.* 5:29
members of his body, of *his f.* 30
reconciled in body of *his f. Col* 1:22
in days of *his f.* when. *Heb* 5:7
that is to say, *his f.* 10:20

in the **flesh**, or *in* **flesh**

Abraham was circumcised *in the f.* *Gen* 17:24
Ishmael circumcised *in the f.* 25
uncircumcised *in the f.* *Ezek* 44:7
uncircumcised *in the f.* not enter. 9
fairer and fatter *in f.* *Dan* 1:15
circumcision outward *in the f.* *Rom* 2:28
for when we were *in the f.* 7:5
for sin condemned sin *in the f.* 8:3
are *in the f.* cannot please God. 8
but ye are not *in the f.* but. 9
have trouble *in the f.* *1 Cor* 7:28
in the f. not war after f. *2 Cor* 10:3
given to me a thorn *in the f.* 12:7
which I now live *in the f.* *Gal* 2:20
to make a fair shew *in the f.* 6:12
Gentiles *in the f.* called the circumcision *in the f.* made. *Eph* 2:11
if I live *in the f.* this is. *Phil* 1:22
to abide *in the f.* more needful. 24
have no confidence *in the f.* 3:3
might have confidence *in the f.* 4
not seen my face *in the f.* *Col* 2:1
though I be absent *in the f.* 5
God manifest *in the f.* *1 Tim* 3:16
more to thee, both *in the f. Philem* 16
put to death *in the f.* *1 Pet* 3:18
Christ suffered for us *in the f.*: he that hath suffered *in the f.* 4:1
no longer live *in the f.* 2
judged according to men *in the f.* 6
denieth Christ *in the f. 1 John* 4:2, 3
not Christ is come *in the f. 2 John* 7

my **flesh**

my bread and *my f.*? *1 Sam* 25:11
the hair of *my f.* stood. *Job* 4:15
or is *my f.* brass? 6:12
my f. is clothed with worms. 7:5
I take *my f.* in my teeth? 13:14
cleaveth to skin, and *my f.* 19:20
and not satisfied with *my f.*? 22
yet in *my f.* shall I see God. 26
trembling taketh hold of *my f.* 21:6
my f. shall rest in hope. *Ps* 16:9
Acts 2:26
no soundness in *my f.* *Ps* 38:3, 7
my f. longeth for thee in a dry. 63:1
my f. faileth, but God is my. 73:26
my heart and *my f.* crieth out. 84:2
my knees are weak, *my f.* 109:24
my f. trembleth for fear. 119:120
done to me, and to *my f.* *Jer* 51:35
my f. and my skin hath. *Lam* 3:4
bread I will give is *my f.* *John* 6:51
eateth *my f.* hath eternal. 54, 56
my f. is meat indeed. 55
in *my f.* dwelleth no. *Rom* 7:18
provoke them which are *my f.* 11:14
temptation which was in *my f.* *Gal* 4:14
afflictions of Christ in *my f. Col* 1:24

see **bone**

of the **flesh**

carry forth aught *of the f.* *Ex* 12:46
if aught *of the f.* remain. 29:34
nor give *of the f.* *Deut* 28:55
sound heart is life *of the f. Pr* 14:30
study weariness *of the f. Eccl* 12:12
not of the will *of the f.* *John* 1:13
is born *of the f.* is flesh. 3:6
do mind the things *of the f. Rom* 8:5
which are children *of the f.* 9:8
for destruction *of the f.* *1 Cor* 5:5
cleanse from all filthiness *of the f.* *2 Cor* 7:1
through infirmity *of the f.* *Gal* 4:13
shall not fulfil the lust *of the f.* 5:16
now works *of the f.* are manifest. 19
soweth to flesh *of the f.* reap. 6:8
in lusts *of* our *f.* desires *of the f.* *Eph* 2:3
putting off sins *of the f.* *Col* 2:11
to the satisfying *of the f.* 23
to the purging *of the f.* *Heb* 9:13
away the filth *of the f.* *1 Pet* 3:21
through lusts *of the f.* *2 Pet* 2:18
the lust *of the f.* the. *1 John* 2:16

thy **flesh**

birds shall eat *thy f.* *Gen* 40:19
give *thy f.* unto fowls. *1 Sam* 17:44
are thy bone and *thy f.* *2 Sam* 5:1
1 Chr 11:1
wash, *thy f.* shall come. *2 Ki* 5:10
when *thy f.* is consumed. *Pr* 5:11

not mouth to cause *thy f.* Eccl 5:6
put away evil from *thy f.* 11:10
hide not thyself from *thine* own *f.* Isa 58:7
lay *thy f.* on mountains. Ezek 32:5

your flesh

make cuttings in *your f.* Lev 19:28
then I will tear *your f.* Judg 8:7
stony heart out of *your f.* Ezek 36:26
of the infirmity of *your f.* Rom 6:19
they may glory in *your f.* Gal 6:13
uncircumcision of *your f.* Col 2:13
rust shall eat *your f.* Jas 5:3

fleshhook

servant came with a *f.* 1 Sam 2:13
all that the *f.* brought up. 14

fleshhooks

shalt make his *f.* and. Ex 27:3
made vessels and the *f.* 38:3
upon purple cloth the *f.* Num 4:14
pure gold for the *f.* 1 Chr 28:17
also the pots and *f.* 2 Chr 4:16

fleshly, fleshy

simplicity, not *f.* wisdom. 2 Cor 1:12
but in *f.* tables of the heart. 3:3
puffed up by his *f.* mind. Col 2:18
abstain from *f.* lusts. 1 Pet 2:11

flesh pots

we sat by the *f. pots.* Ex 16:3

flew

people *f.* upon spoil. 1 Sam 14:32
f. one of the seraphims. Isa 6:6

flies

swarms of *f.* upon thee. Ex 8:21
he removed the swarms of *f.* 31
he sent divers sorts of *f.* Ps 78:45
there came divers sorts of *f.* 105:31
dead *f.* cause ointment. Eccl 10:1

flieth

any winged fowl that *f.* Deut 4:17
every creeping thing that *f.* 14:19*
a nation swift as the eagle *f.* 28:49
for arrow that *f.* by day. Ps 91:5
cankerworm spoileth and *f.* Nah 3:16

flight

go out with haste nor *f.* Isa 52:12
the *f.* shall perish from. Amos 2:14
pray *f.* be not in winter. Mat 24:20
Mark 13:18
to *f.* armies of aliens. Heb 11:34
see **put**

flint

water out of rock of *f.* Deut 8:15
turning *f.* into a fountain. Ps 114:8
horses be counted like *f.* Isa 5:28
have I set my face like a *f.* 50:7
harder than *f.* have I. Ezek 3:9

flinty

to suck oil out of the *f.* rock. Deut 32:13

floats

by sea in *f.* 1 Ki 5:9; 2 Chr 2:16

flock

Abel brought firstlings of his *f.* Gen 4:4
Abraham set ewe lambs of *f.* 21:28
go to *f.* and fetch two good. 27:9
Jacob watered the *f.* of Laban. 29:10
again feed and keep thy *f.* 30:31
I will pass through all thy *f.* 32
Jacob fed rest of Laban's *f.* 36
separate all the brown in the *f.* 40
Rachel and Leah to his *f.* 31:4
rams of thy *f.* have I not eaten. 38
overdrive them, the *f.* will die. 33:13
Joseph was feeding the *f.* with. 37:2
brethren went to feed their *f.* 12, 13
I will send a kid from the *f.* 38:17
water their father's *f.* Ex 2:16
Moses helped, watered *f.* 17, 19
Moses led the *f.* to the desert. 3:1
of your offering for the *f.* Lev 1:2
bring a female from the *f.* 5:6
ram without blemish out of *f.* 18
6:6; Ezra 10:19; Ezek 43:23, 25
concerning tithe of the *f.* Lev 27:32
savour of the herd or *f.* Num 15:3
kill of thy herd and *f.* Deut 12:21
him liberally out of thy *f.* 15:14
all the firstling males of thy *f.* 19
sacrifice to Lord of the *f.* Deut 16:2
lion took lamb out of *f.* 1 Sam 17:34
spared to take of own *f.* 2 Sam 12:4
gave to people of the *f.* 2 Chr 35:7
to set with dogs of my *f.* Job 30:1
makest thy *f.* to rest at. S of S 1:7
go by the footsteps of the *f.* 8
hair is as a *f.* of goats. 4:1; 6:5
teeth are like *f.* of sheep. 4:2; 6:6
feed his *f.* like a shepherd. Isa 40:11
them with shepherd of his *f.* 63:11
Lord's *f.* is carried. Jer 13:17
where is the *f.*, thy beautiful *f.*? 20
ye have scattered my *f.* and. 23:2
gather the remnant of my *f.* 3
ye principal of the *f.* 25:34
nor principal of the *f.* to escape. 35
an howling of principal of the *f.* 36
him as a shepherd doth his *f.* 31:10
shall sing for the young of the *f.* 12
least of *f.* draw them. 49:20; 50:45
in pieces shepherd and his *f.* 51:23
take the choice of the *f.* Ezek 24:5
eat the fat, ye feed not the *f.* 34:3*
my *f.* was scattered on the face. 6*
my *f.* became a prey, my *f.* meat. 8*
require my *f.* I will deliver my *f.* 10*
as a shepherd seeketh out his *f.* 12
I will feed my *f.* 15*
as for you, O my *f.* 17
therefore will I save my *f.* 22
ye my *f.* the *f.* of my pasture. 31*
the holy *f.* as *f.* of Jerusalem. 36:38
offer one lamb out of the *f.* 45:15
eat lambs out of the *f.* Amos 6:4
Lord took me as I followed *f.* 7:15
let not herd nor *f.* taste. Jonah 3:7
as the *f.* in the midst. Mi 2:12
O tower of the *f.* the strong. 4:8
thy people, *f.* of thine heritage. 7:14
the *f.* shall be cut off. Hab 3:17
save them as the *f.* of. Zech 9:16
they went their way as a *f.* 10:2*
Lord of hosts hath visited his *f.* 3
will feed *f.* of slaughter. 11:4, 7
poor of the *f.* that waited on. 7, 11
woe to shepherd, that leaveth *f.* 17
deceiver which hath in his *f.* a male. Mal 1:14
sheep of *f.* be scattered. Mat 26:31
keeping watch over their *f.* Luke 2:8
fear not little *f.* it is your. 12:32
take heed to all the *f.* Acts 20:28
wolves enter, not sparing *f.* 29
who feedeth a *f.* and. 1 Cor 9:7
feed the *f.* of God. 1 Pet 5:2
but being ensamples to the *f.* 3

***like a* flock**

their little ones *like a f.* Job 21:11
leddest thy people *like a f.* Ps 77:20
guided them in wilderness *like a f.* 78:52
that leadest Joseph *like a f.* 80:1
maketh him families *like a f.* 107:41
them with men *like a f.* Ezek 36:37

flocks

f. of sheep lying by well, out of that they watered the *f.* Gen 29:2
thither were all the *f.* gathered. 3
we cannot until the *f.* be gathered. 8
Jacob set rods before the *f.* 30:38
the *f.* conceived before the rods. 39
faces of the *f.* towards the ringstraked, he put his own *f.* by. 40*
I have oxen, asses, *f.* and. 32:5
he divided the *f.* and herds. 7
whether it be well with *f.* 37:14
tell me where they feed their *f.* 16
have no pasture for their *f.* 47:4
in exchange for horses and *f.* 17
if his offering be of the *f.* Lev 1:10
ram without blemish out of *f.* 5:15
took spoil of all their *f.* Num 31:9
take one portion of the *f.* 30
our wives, our *f.* and cattle. 32:26
also bless *f.* of thy sheep. Deut 7:13
blessed be the *f.* of thy sheep. 28:4
cursed be the *f.* of thy sheep. 18
not leave the *f.* of thy sheep. 51
hear bleatings of the *f.* Judg 5:16
like two little *f.* of kids. 1 Ki 20:27
seek pasture for their *f.* 1 Chr 4:39
there was pasture for their *f.* 41
and over the *f.* was Jaziz. 1 Chr 27:31
Arabians brought him *f.* 2 Chr 17:11
violently take away *f.* Job 24:2
pastures are clothed with *f.* Ps 65:13
their *f.* to hot thunderbolts. 78:48
turn aside by the *f.* of. S of S 1:7
cities of Aroer be for *f.* Isa 17:2
palaces be a pasture of *f.* 32:14
all the *f.* of Kedar shall be. 60:7
strangers shall feed your *f.* 61:5
Sharon shall be a fold for *f.* 65:10
the shepherds with their *f.* Jer 6:3
all *f.* shall be scattered. 10:21
Judah they that go forth with *f.* 31:24
shepherds causing *f.* to lie. 33:12
the *f.* shall pass again under rod. 13
tents and *f.* shall take away. 49:29
as the he goats before the *f.* 50:8
a couching place for *f.* Ezek 25:5
not the shepherds feed the *f.*? 34:2*
the waste cities filled with *f.* 36:38
f. of sheep are desolate. Joel 1:18
as a young lion among *f.* of. Mi 5:8
sea coast be folds for *f.* Zeph 2:6
f. lie down in midst of Nineveh. 14*

flocks with *herds*

Lot also had *f.* and *herds.* Gen 13:5
given Abraham *f.* and *herds.* 24:35
possession of *f.* and *herds.* 26:14
Jacob divided *f.* and *herds.* 32:7
the *f.* and *herds* with young. 33:13
me, thou, thy *f.* and *herds.* 45:10
brethren, their *f.* and *herds.* 47:1
their *f.* and *herds* left they. 50:8
will go with *f.* and *herds.* Ex 10:9
let your *f.* and your *herds* be. 24
take your *f.* and your *herds.* 12:32
neither let *f.* nor *herds* feed. 34:3
f. and *herds* be slain. Num 11:22
thy *herds* and *f.* multiply. Deut 8:13
firstling of *herds* and *f.* 12:6, 17
14:23; Neh 10:36
took all *f.* and *herds.* 1 Sam 30:20
had exceeding many *f.* and *herds.* 2 Sam 12:2
possessions of *f.* and *herds.* 2 Chr 32:29
thy *f.* look to thy *herds.* Pr 27:23
devoured *f.* and *herds.* Jer 3:24
nation eat thy *f.* and *herds.* 5:17
go with *f.* and *herds* to. Hos 5:6

flood

[1] *A great flow of water; inundation.* [2] *Figuratively, of dangers or sorrows or temptations which come like a flood of water.* [3] *Specifically, the great flood of Noah's time.*

I bring a *f.* of water on. Gen 6:17
when the *f.* of waters was. 7:6
because of the waters of the *f.* 7
after seven days *f.* was on earth. 10
f. was forty days on earth. 17
any more a *f.* to destroy. 9:11
lived after the *f.* 350 years. 28
to them were sons born after *f.* 10:1
nations divided in earth after *f.* 32
your fathers dwelt on other side of the *f.* Josh 24:2*, 3* 14*, 15*
as the *f.* decayeth and. Job 14:11*
foundation overthrown with *f.* 22:16*
f. breaketh out from the. 28:4*
Lord sitteth upon the *f.* Ps 29:10
went through the *f.* on foot. 66:6
let not the water-*f.* overflow. 69:15
cleave fountain and the *f.* 74:15
them away as with a *f.* 90:5
strong one, which as a *f.* Isa 28:2*
enemy come in like a *f.* 59:19*
who cometh up as a *f.*? Jer 46:7*
Egypt riseth up like a *f.* 8*
waters be an overflowing *f.* 47:2*
end shall be with a *f.* Dan 9:26
with arms of a *f.* shall be. 11:22
it shall rise up wholly as a *f.* Amos 8:8*; 9:5*
be drowned as by the *f.* of. 9:5*
with an overrunning *f.* Nah 1:8
in days before the *f.* Mat 24:38
and knew not till the *f.* came. 39
Luke 17:27
when the *f.* arose the. Luke 6:48
bringing in the *f.* on world. 2 Pet 2:5

dragon poured out water as a f. Rev 12:15*
earth helped, swallowed up the f. 16*

floods

the f. stood upright. Ex 15:8
f. of ungodly made me afraid. 2 Sam 22:5; Ps 18:4
not see rivers and f. Job 20:17*
bindeth f. from overflowing. 28:11*
established it upon the f. Ps 24:2
surely in f. of great waters. 32:6*
deep waters, where the f. 69:2
turned their f. into blood. 78:44*
f. have lifted up, O Lord, f. 93:3
let the f. clap their hands. 98:8
neither can f. drown love. S of S 8:7
f. upon the dry ground. Isa 44:3*
I restrained the f. Ezek 31:15*
f. compassed me about. Jonah 2:3
the f. came, winds. Mat 7:25, 27

floor, *substantive*

the threshing f. of Atad. Gen 50:10
inhabitants saw mourning in f. 11
priests take dust in f. Num 5:17
heave offering of threshing f. 15:20
as the corn of the threshing f. 18:27
as increase of threshing f. 30
furnish him out of thy f. Deut 15:14*
a fleece of wool in the f. Judg 6:37*
winnoweth in threshing f. Ruth 3:2
came to Nachon's threshing f. 2 Sam 6:6; 1 Chr 13:9
altar in threshing f. of. 2 Sam 24:18
David said, to buy threshing f. 21
he overlaid the f. of. 1 Ki 6:30
cedar from one side of the f. 7:7
out of the barn-f. or the. 2 Ki 6:27
answered in threshing f. 1 Chr 21:28
prepared in threshing f. of. 2 Chr 3:1
and the corn of my f. Isa 21:10
is like a threshing f. Jer 51:33
a reward on every corn f. Hos 9:1
the f. and winepress shall not. 2*
as chaff driven out of the f. 13:3*
them as sheaves into f. Mi 4:12*
he will throughly purge his f. Mat 3:12*; Luke 3:17*

floor, *verb*

timber to f. the houses. 2 Chr 34:11*

floors

rob the threshing f. 1 Sam 23:1
of summer threshing f. Dan 2:35
f. shall be full of wheat. Joel 2:24

flour

of wheaten f. make them. Ex 29:2
his handful of the f. Lev 2:2; 6:15
tenth part of ephah of f. for a meat-. Num 28:5, 20, 28; 29:3, 9, 14
cakes of an ephah of f. Judg 6:19
1 Sam 1:24
she took f. and kneaded it. 1 Sam 28:24; 2 Sam 13:8*
brought f. parched corn. 2 Sam 17:28
see **deal, fine**

flourish

in his days the righteous f. Ps 72:7
they of the city shall f. like. 16
the workers of iniquity f. 92:7
the righteous shall f. like the. 12
f. in the courts of our God. 13
himself shall his crown f. 132:18
the righteous shall f. Pr 11:28
tabernacle of upright shall f. 14:11
the almond tree shall f. Eccl 12:5*
let us see if vine f. S of S 7:12*
shalt make thy seed to f. Isa 17:11*
your bones shall f. like an. 66:14
made the dry tree to f. Ezek 17:24

flourished

to see whether vine f. S of S 6:11*
your care of me hath f. Phil 4:10*

flourisheth

in the morning it f. Ps 90:6
as a flower of field, so he f. 103:15

flourishing

in old age, fat and f. Ps 92:14*
I was at rest, and f. in. Dan 4:4

flow

his goods shall f. away. Job 20:28
wind blow, and waters f. Ps 147:18
spices thereof may f. out. S of S 4:16
all nations shall f. unto it. Isa 2:2
waters to f. out of the rock. 48:21
shalt see and f. together. 60:5*
mountains might f. down at. 64:1
f. to goodness of Lord. Jer 31:12
nations shall not f. together. 51:44
the hills shall f. with milk, the rivers of Judah f. with waters. Joel 3:18
people shall f. to mountain. Mi 4:1
out of his belly f. living. John 7:38

flowed

Jordan f. over all banks. Josh 4:18
the mountains f. down. Isa 64:3
the waters f. over mine. Lam 3:54

floweth

land that f. with milk and honey. Lev 20:24; Num 13:27; 14:8
16:13, 14; Deut 6:3; 11:9; 26:15
27:3; 31:20; Josh 5:6

flowing

to a land f. with milk and honey. Ex 3:8, 17; 13:5; 33:3; Jer 11:5
32:22; Ezek 20:6, 15
wellspring of wisdom as a f. Pr 18:4
glory of Gentiles like a f. Isa 66:12
or shall cold f. waters? Jer 18:14
gloriest thou in thy f. valley? 49:4

flower

increase shall die in f. 1 Sam 2:33
if she pass f. of her age. 1 Cor 7:36

flower

with knop and f. in one branch. Ex 25:33; 37:19
he cometh forth as a f. Job 14:2
he shall cast off his f. as. 15:33
as a f. of field, so he. Ps 103:15
sour grape is ripening in f. Isa 18:5
glorious beauty is a fading f. 28:1, 4
goodliness thereof is as f. of. 40:6
f. fadeth. 7, 8; Nah 1:4; Jas 1:10
11; 1 Pet 1:24

flowers

his f. shall be of same. Ex 25:31
37:17
his knops and his f. 37:20
if her f. be upon him, he. Lev 15:24*
of her that is sick of her f. of. 33*
to the f. thereof was. Num 8:4
of house within carved with open f. 1 Ki 6:18, 29, 32, 35; 7:26, 49
like brim of cup with f. 2 Chr 4:5
the f. lamps, and tongs made. 21
the f. appear on earth. S of S 2:12
cheeks as a bed of spices, sweet f. 5:13*

flute

ye hear the f. Dan 3:5, 7, 10, 15

fluttereth

eagle f. over her young. Deut 32:11

flux

of Publius sick of a f. Acts 28:8

fly

Lord shall hiss for the f. in. Isa 7:18

fly, *verb*

and fowl that may f. Gen 1:20
rode upon a cherub, and did f. 2 Sam 22:11; Ps 18:10
born to trouble as sparks f. Job 5:7
doth the hawk f. by thy? 39:26*
he did f. upon the wings. Ps 18:10
for then would I f. away. 55:6
is soon cut off, we f. away. 90:10
riches f. away as an eagle. Pr 23:5
with twain he did f. Isa 6:2
shall f. upon the shoulders of. 11:14
who are these that f. as a cloud. 60:8
he shall f. as an eagle. Jer 48:40
hunt the souls to make them f. Ezek 13:20
Gabriel being caused to f. Dan 9:21
their glory shall f. away. Hos 9:11
they shall f. as the eagle. Hab 1:8
I saw another angel f. Rev 14:6
to all the fowls that f. in. 19:17
see **flee, flieth**

flying

eat of every f. creeping. Lev 11:21*
but all other f. creeping things. 23*
all cattle and f. fowl. Ps 148:10
as the swallow by f. so. Pr 26:2
fruit shall be a fiery f. Isa 14:29
come viper and fiery f. serpent. 30:6
as birds f. so will the Lord. 31:5†
and behold, a f. roll. Zech 5:1, 2
fourth beast like a f. eagle. Rev 4:7
heard an angel f. through. 8:13

foal, -s

bulls, twenty asses, ten f. Gen 32:15
binding his f. to the vine. 49:11
f. of an ass. Zech 9:9; Mat 21:5

foam

of Samaria cut off as f. Hos 10:7

foameth

f. gnasheth with his teeth. Mark 9:18
Luke 9:39

foaming

on ground wallowed f. Mark 9:20
raging waves of sea, f. Jude 13

fodder

or loweth the ox over his f. Job 6:5

foes

destroyed before thy f. 1 Chr 21:12
the Jews slew of their f. Esth 9:16
mine enemies and f. Ps 27:2
thou hast not made my f. to. 30:1
I will beat down his f. 89:23
a man's f. shall be they. Mat 10:36
make thy f. thy footstool. Acts 2:35

fold

as vesture shalt thou f. Heb 1:12*

fold

shepherds make their f. Isa 13:20*
Sharon shall be f. for flocks. 65:10
on mountains their f. be. Ezek 34:14
as flock in midst of their f. Mi 2:12*
flock be cut off from the f. Hab 3:17
hundred, some sixty, some thirty f. Mat 13:8, 23; Mark 4:8, 20
shall receive 100 f. Mat 19:29
other sheep which are not of this f. there shall be one f. John 10:16*

folden

while they be f. together. Nah 1:10

foldeth

the fool f. his hands. Eccl 4:5

folding

leaves of one door were f. 1 Ki 6:34
a little f. of hands. Pr 6:10; 24:33

folds

build ye f. for. Num 32:24, 36
no he goats out of thy f. Ps 50:9
bring them again to their f. Jer 23:3
the sea coast shall be f. Zeph 2:6

folk

leave with thee some of f. Gen 33:15
conies are but a feeble f. Pr 30:26
the f. shall labour in fire. Jer 51:58*
hands upon few sick f. Mark 6:5
multitude of impotent f. John 5:3*
a multitude bringing sick f. Acts 5:16

follow

woman not willing to f. Gen 24:8
Joseph said, f. after the men. 44:4
out, and people that f. Ex 11:8
harden Pharaoh that he shall f. 14:4
the Egyptians shall f. them. 17*
a woman, and no mischief f. 21:22
and if any mischief f. then. 23
not f. a multitude to do evil. 23:2
what is altogether just f. Deut 16:20
if the thing f. not. 18:22
inclined to f. Abimelech. Judg 9:3
men, who f. my lord. 1 Sam 25:27
faint they could not f. David. 30:21
people that f. Absalom. 2 Sam 17:9
then I will f. thee. 1 Ki 19:20
I f. the thing that good is. Ps 38:20
virgins her companions that f. 45:14
upright in heart shall f. it. 94:15
they draw nigh that f. 119:150
that they f. strong drink. Isa 5:11
ye that f. after righteousness. 51:1
being a pastor to f. thee. Jer 17:16
the famine shall f. close. 42:16
prophets that f. own spirit. Ezek 13:3
shall f. after her lovers. Hos 2:7
if we f. on to know the Lord. 6:3
Master, I will f. thee. Mat 8:19
Luke 9:57, 61
these signs f. them. Mark 16:17

not after them, nor f. Luke 17:23
about him saw what would f. 22:49
a stranger will they not f. John 10:5
why cannot I f. thee now? 13:37
from Samuel, and that f. Acts 3:24
f. things that make for peace.
Rom 14:19
f. after charity. 1 Cor 14:1
but I f. after. Phil 3:12*
f. that which is good. 1 Thes 5:15
know how ye ought to f. 2 Thes 3:7*
ourselves an ensample to you to f. 9*
some men they f. after. 1 Tim 5:24
f. righteousness. 6:11; 2 Tim 2:22
f. peace with all men. Heb 12:14
whose faith f. considering end. 13:7*
the glory that should f. 1 Pet 1:11
that ye should f. his steps. 2:21
f. their pernicious ways. 2 Pet 2:2
f. not that which is evil. 3 John 11*
are they that f. Lamb. Rev 14:4
they may rest from their labours, and
their works do f. them. 13

follow him

if Lord be God, f. him. 1 Ki 18:21
suffered no man to f. him. Mark 5:37
out, and his disciples f. him. 6:1
f. him into the house. Luke 22:10
Mark 14:13
before, the sheep f. him. John 10:4

follow me

woman will not be willing to f. me.
Gen 24:5, 39
Ehud said, f. after me. Judg 3:24
bread, to the people that f. me. 8:5
handfuls for people that f. me.
1 Ki 20:10
f. me, I will bring you to. 2 Ki 6:19
and mercy shall f. me. Ps 23:6
Jesus saith, f. me, I. Mat 4:19*
8:22; 9:9; Mark 2:14; Luke 5:27
take up his cross, f. me. Mat 16:24
Mark 8:34; 10:21; Luke 9:23
sell that thou hast, f. me. Mat 19:21
Luke 18:22
he said, f. me. Luke 9:59
John 1:43; 21:22
sheep hear my voice and f. me.
John 10:27
if any serve me, let him f. me. 12:26
thou canst not f. me now. 13:36
garment about thee, f. me. Acts 12:8

followed

Rebekah and her damsels f. the.
Gen 24:61
so commanded he all that f. 32:19
they have wholly f. the Lord.
Num 32:12; Deut 1:36
the men that f. Baal-peor. Deut 4:3
ark of the covenant f. Josh 6:8
but I wholly f. Lord. 14:8, 9, 14
forsook the Lord, f. other. Judg 2:12
cut down bough, f. Abimelech 9:49
f. hard after Philistines. 1 Sam 14:22
Jesse's three sons f. Saul. 17:13, 14
Philistines f. Saul. 31:2; 2 Sam 1:6
1 Chr 10:2
house of Judah f. David. 2 Sam 2:10
king David himself f. the bier. 3:31
Ahithophel saw counsel was not f.
17:23
Israel f. Sheba the son of. 20:2
none f. house of David. 1 Ki 12:20
of people f. Tibni, half f. 16:21, 22
forsaken Lord, thou hast f. 18:18
and the army which f. them. 20:19
no water for cattle that f. 2 Ki 3:9
Elisha rose and f. her. 4:30
so Gehazi f. after Naaman. 5:21
Jehu f. after Ahaziah. 9:27
Jehoahaz f. sins of Jeroboam. 13:2
and they f. vanity. 17:15
players on instruments f. Ps 68:25
head looked, they f. it. Ezek 10:11
Lord took me as I f. Amos 7:15
women which f. Jesus. Mat 27:55
we left all and f. thee. Mark 10:28
Luke 18:28
they f. they were afraid. Mark 10:32
Peter f. afar off. Luke 22:54
religious proselytes f. Acts 13:43
the same f. Paul and us. 16:17

f. not after righteousness. Rom 9:30
who f. after law of righteousness. 31
drank that rock that f. 1 Cor 10:4
diligently f. every good. 1 Tim 5:10
not f. cunningly devised. 2 Pet 1:16
was Death, and hell f. Rev 6:8
there f. hail and fire mingled. 8:7
and there f. another angel. 14:8
and the third angel f. them. 9

followed him

elders of Israel f. him. Num 16:25
and light persons f. him. Judg 9:4
and all people f. him. 1 Sam 13:7
f. him a mess of meat. 2 Sam 11:8
they left their nets and f. him.
Mat 4:20; Mark 1:18
left the ship and f. him. Mat 4:22
f. him great multitudes. 25; 8:1
12:15; 19:2; 20:29; Mark 2:15
5:24; Luke 23:27; John 6:2
when entered, his disciples f. him.
Mat 8:23; Luke 22:39
two blind men f. him. Mat 9:27
but Peter f. him afar off. 26:58
Mark 14:54
f. him a young man. Mark 14:51
forsook all and f. him. Luke 5:11, 28
said unto the people that f. him. 7:9
Peter went out and f. him. Acts 12:9
armies f. him on white. Rev 19:14

followed me

Caleb hath f. me fully. Num 14:24
have not wholly f. me. 32:11
David who f. me with all. 1 Ki 14:8
of the guard which f. me. Neh 4:23
f. me, in the regeneration. Mat 19:28

followedst

thou f. not young men. Ruth 3:10

followers

I beseech you, be f. of me.
1 Cor 4:16*; 11:1*; Phil 3:17*
be ye f. of God as dear. Eph 5:1*
ye became f. of us and. 1 Thes 1:6*
became f. of the churches. 2:14*
f. of them who through. Heb 6:12*
f. of that which is good. 1 Pet 3:13*

followeth

that f. her be killed. 2 Ki 11:15
2 Chr 23:14
my soul f. hard after. Ps 63:8
but he that f. vain persons.
Pr 12:11; 28:19
that f. righteousness. 15:9; 21:21
one loveth gifts and f. Isa 1:23
none f. thee to commit. Ezek 16:34
Ephraim feeds on wind, f. Hos 12:1
not up his cross and f. Mat 10:38
because he f. not us. Mark 9:38
Luke 9:49
f. me shall not walk in. John 8:12

following

by reason of famine f. Gen 41:31
turn away thy son from f. Deut 7:4
thou be not snared by f. them. 12:30
from f. the Lord. Josh 22:16, 18, 23
29; 1 Sam 12:20; 2 Ki 17:21
2 Chr 25:27; 34:33
corrupted in f. other. Judg 2:19
to return from f. after. Ruth 1:16
if ye continue f. Lord. 1 Sam 12:14
went up from f. Philistines. 14:46
Saul is turned back from f. 15:11
Saul was returned from f. 24:1
Asahel turned not from f. Abner.
2 Sam 2:19, 30
bid people return from f. their. 26
I took thee from f. the sheep, to.
7:8; 1 Chr 17:7; Ps 78:71
and they f. Adonijah. 1 Ki 1:7
if you shall at all turn from f. 9:6
Ahab did abominably in f. 21:26
tell it to the generation f. Ps 48:13
in generation f. name be. 109:13
the word with signs f. Mark 16:20
to-morrow, and day f. Luke 13:33
Jesus turned, saw them f. John 1:38
the day f. 43
the day f. when the people. 6:22
seeth disciple Jesus loved f. 21:20
we came day f. unto. Acts 21:1, 18
night f. Lord stood by him. 23:11
gone astray, f. way of. 2 Pet 2:15

folly

Shechem had wrought f. Gen 34:7
f. by playing the whore. Deut 22:21
because Achan wrought f. Josh 7:15
I pray you, do not this f. Judg 19:23
committed lewdness and f. in. 20:6
according to f. that they wrought. 10
Nabal his name, and f. 1 Sam 25:25
do not thou this f. 2 Sam 13:12
angels he charged with f. Job 4:18
God layeth not f. to them. 24:12
lest I deal with you after f. 42:8
their way is their f. Ps 49:13
let them not turn again to f. 85:8
in the greatness of his f. Pr 5:23
but a fool layeth open his f. 13:16
but the f. of fools is deceitful. 14:8
the simple inherit f. 18
foolishness of fools is f. 24
hasty of spirit exalteth f. 29
f. is joy to him destitute of. 15:21
the instruction of fools is f. 16:22
rather than a fool in his f. 17:12
is f. and shame to him. 18:13
not a fool according to his f. 26:4
answer a fool according to his f. 5
so a fool returneth to his f. 11
my heart to know wisdom and f.
Eccl 1:17
in my heart to lay hold on f. 2:3
turned to behold f. 12
wisdom excelleth f. 13
to know wickedness of f. 7:25
so doth a little f. him that. 10:1
f. is set in great dignity. 6
every mouth speaketh f. Isa 9:17
seen f. in the prophets of. Jer 23:13
bear with me a little in my f.
2 Cor 11:1
their f. shall be made. 2 Tim 3:9

food

pleasant and that is good for f.
Gen 2:9
woman saw tree was good for f. 3:6
take thou to thee of all f. 6:21
gather all f. of those good. 41:35
came to buy f. 42:7, 10; 43:2, 4
20, 22; 44:25
take f. for the famine. 42:33*
commanded to fill sacks with f. 44:1
your f. and for f. for your. 47:24
her f. not be diminished. Ex 21:10
the f. of the offering. Lev 3:11, 16
all manner of trees for f. 19:23
eat holy things, it is his f. 22:7*
him f. and raiment. Deut 10:18
cursed that eateth f. 1 Sam 14:24, 28
that master's son have f. to eat.
2 Sam 9:10*
my desire, in giving f. for. 1 Ki 5:9
gave Hiram wheat for f. to his. 11
more than necessary f. Job 23:12
wilderness yieldeth f. for. 24:5†
provideth for raven f.? 38:41†
mountains bring him forth f. 40:20
man did eat angels' f. Ps 78:25*
he may bring forth f. out. 104:14
who giveth f. to all flesh. 136:25
Lord who giveth f. to the. 146:7
he giveth to the beast his f. 147:9
ant gathereth her f. in. Pr 6:8
much f. is in the tillage of. 13:23
goats' milk enough for thy f. 27:27
rain which leaveth no f. 28:3
feed me with f. convenient for. 30:8
she bringeth her f. from afar. 31:14†
I have diminished thine ordinary f.
Ezek 16:27
increase thereof shall be for f. 48:18
filling our hearts with f. Acts 14:17
minister bread for your f. 2 Cor 9:10
having f. and raiment. 1 Tim 6:8
and destitute of daily f. Jas 2:15

fool

I have played f. and. 1 Sam 26:21
f. hath said in heart. Ps 14:1; 53:1
likewise the f. and brutish. 49:10
neither doth a f. understand. 92:6
prating f. shall fall. Pr 10:8, 10
it is a sport to a f. to do mischief. 23
the f. shall be servant to. 11:29*
way of a f. right in own eyes. 12:15*
a f.'s wrath is presently known. 16

but f. layeth open his folly. Pr 13:16
the f. rageth and is confident. 14:16
f. despiseth father's instruction. 15:5
speech becometh not a f. 17:7
than a hundred stripes into a f. 10
a bear meet a man rather than f. 12
price in hand of a f. to get. 16
begetteth a f. doth it to sorrow. 21
f. when he holdeth his peace. 28
f. hath no delight in understanding. 18:2
a f.'s lips enter into contention. 6
but every f. will be meddling. 20:3
answer not a f. 26:4
answer a f. 5
so is he that giveth honour to a f. 8
the great God rewardeth the f. 10
as a dog so a f. returneth to his. 11
but a f.'s wrath is heavier. 27:3
though thou bray a f. in a mortar. 22
f. uttereth all his mind. 29:11
f. walketh in darkness. Eccl 2:14
as it happeneth to the f. so. 15
of wise man more than of f. 16
whether he be wise or a f.? 19
the f. foldeth his hands. 4:5
a f.'s voice is known by. 5:3
hath wise more than the f.? 6:8
but a f.'s heart is at his left. 10:2
f. is full of words. 14
at his end he shall be a f. Jer 17:11
whosoever shall say, Thou f. shall be in danger. Mat 5:22
f., this night thy soul. Luke 12:20*
let him become a f. 1 Cor 3:18
thou f., that thou sowest is. 15:36*
no man think me a f. 2 Cor 11:16*
to glory, I shall not be a f. 12:6*
I am become a f. in glorying. 11*

as a fool

died Abner as a f. dieth? 2 Sam 3:33
as a f. to correction of. Pr 7:22
how dieth wise? as the f. Eccl 2:16
yet as a f. receive me. 2 Cor 11:16
I speak as a f. I am more. 23

for a fool

delight not seemly for a f. Pr 19:10
wisdom is too high for a f. 24:7
honour is not seemly for a f. 26:1
and a rod for the f.'s back. 3
for a f. when filled with meat. 30:22

is a fool

uttereth slander is a f. Pr 10:18
perverse in lips, and is a f. 19:1
in his own heart is a f. 28:26
he that is a f. walketh, saith to every one that he is a f. Eccl 10:3
the prophet is a f., the. Hos 9:7

of a fool

way of a f. is right in. Pr 12:15
the father of a f. hath no joy. 17:21
eyes of a f. in ends of the earth. 24
speak not in the ears of a f. 23:9
a message by hand of a f. 26:6
more hope of a f. than. 12; 29:20
so laughter of the f. Eccl 7:6
lips of a f. will swallow. 10:12

foolish

thus requite Lord, O f.? Deut 32:6
provoke them with a f. nation. 21
Rom 10:19
speakest as one of f. Job 2:10
for wrath killeth the f. man. 5:2
I have seen the f. taking root. 3
the f. shall not stand. Ps 5:5*
make me not reproach of f. 39:8
for I was envious at the f. 73:3*
so f. was I and ignorant. 22*
f. people have blasphemed. 74:18
remember how the f. man. 22
forsake the f. and live. Pr 9:6*
a f. woman is clamorous. 13
f. son is heaviness of his. 10:1
mouth of f. is near destruction. 14
but the f. plucketh it down. 14:1
in the mouth of the f. is a rod. 3
go from presence of a f. man. 7
heart of the f. doeth not so. 15:7
f. man despiseth his mother. 20
a f. son is a grief to his father. 17:25
a f. son is the calamity of. 19:13
a f. man spendeth a treasure. 21:20
wise man contendeth with f. Pr 29:9
better is a wise child than a f. king. Eccl 4:13
neither be thou f. 7:17
labour of the f. wearieth. 10:15
maketh knowledge f. Isa 44:25
for my people are f. Jer 4:22
surely these are poor, they are f. 5:4
hear now this, O f. people. 21
are altogether brutish and f. 10:8
seen vain and f. things. Lam 2:14
woe unto f. prophets. Ezek 13:3
instruments of a f. shepherd. Zech 11:15
likened unto a f. man. Mat 7:26
five virgins were wise, five f. 25:2
f. heart was darkened. Rom 1:21*
an instructor of the f. 2:20
hath not God made f.? 1 Cor 1:20
O f. Galatians, who? Gal 3:1
are ye so f.? having begun. 3
filthiness, nor f. talking. Eph 5:4
be rich fall into f. lusts. 1 Tim 6:9
but f. questions avoid. 2 Tim 2:23
Tit 3:9
were sometimes f. deceived. Tit 3:3
put to silence ignorance of f. men. 1 Pet 2:15

foolishly

thou hast now done f. Gen 31:28
1 Sam 13:13; 2 Chr 16:9
wherein we have done f. Num 12:11
I have done very f. 2 Sam 24:10
1 Chr 21:8
not, nor charged God f. Job 1:22
said to fools, deal not f. Ps 75:4
soon angry dealeth f. Pr 14:17
if thou hast done f. in lifting. 30:32
I speak it as it were f. 2 Cor 11:17
I speak f. I am bold also. 21

foolishness

of Ahithophel into f. 2 Sam 15:31
stink because of my f. Ps 38:5
thou knowest my f. 69:5
of fools proclaimeth f. Pr 12:23
but the f. of fools is folly. 14:24
mouth of fools poureth out f. 15:2
mouth of fools feedeth on f. 14
the f. of man perverteth way. 19:3
f. is bound in heart of child. 22:15
the thought of f. is sin. 24:9
yet will not his f. depart. 27:22
know wickedness of f. Eccl 7:25
of the words of his mouth is f. 10:13
thefts, pride, f. come. Mark 7:22
preaching of cross to them that perish f. 1 Cor 1:18
pleased God by f. of preaching. 21
Christ crucified, to the Greeks f. 23
because the f. of God is wiser. 25
of Spirit of God are f. to him. 2:14
wisdom of world is f. with God. 3:19

fools

be as one of the f. in. 2 Sam 13:13
he maketh the judges f. Job 12:17
they were children of f. 30:8
I said to f. deal not. Ps 75:4*
ye f. when will ye be wise? 94:8
f. because of transgression. 107:17
but f. despise wisdom. Pr 1:7*
how long, f. hate knowledge? 22
prosperity of f. destroy them. 32
shame be the promotion of f. 3:35
ye f. be ye of an understanding. 8:5
f. die for want of wisdom. 10:21*
heart of f. proclaimeth. 12:23
abomination to f. to depart. 13:19
companion of f. be destroyed. 20
folly of f. is deceit. 14:8
f. make a mock at sin. 9*
foolishness of f. is folly. 24
what is in the midst of f. is. 33
mouth of f. poureth foolishness. 15:2
mouth of f. feedeth on foolishness. 14
instruction of f. is folly. 16:22
stripes are prepared for f. 19:29
a parable in mouth of f. 26:7, 9
than give sacrifice of f. Eccl 5:1
he hath no pleasure in f. 4
heart of f. is in house of. 7:4
than for man to hear the song of f. 5
anger resteth in the bosom of f. 9
of him that ruleth among f. 9:17
princes of Zoan are f. Isa 19:11*, 13
wayfaring men, though f. 35:8
ye f. and blind. Mat 23:17, 19
ye f. did not he that? Luke 11:40*
O f. and slow of heart to. 24:25*
wise, they became f. Rom 1:22
we are f. for Christ's. 1 Cor 4:10
for ye suffer f. gladly. 2 Cor 11:19*
that ye walk not as f. Eph 5:15*

foot

thee no man lift up his f. Gen 41:44
six hundred thousand on f. Ex 12:37
give f. for f. 21:24; Deut 19:21
shalt make a laver of brass and his f. 30:18, 28; 31:9*; 35:16*; 38:8*
39:39*; 40:11*; Lev 8:11*
leprosy cover from head to f. Lev 13:12
ass crushed Balaam's f. Num 22:25
nor did thy f. swell. Deut 8:4
and wateredst it with thy f. 11:10
loose his shoe from off his f. 25:9
shoe not waxen old upon thy f. 29:5
their f. shall slide in due. 32:35
let Asher dip his f. in oil. 33:24
every place your f. Josh 1:3
loose thy shoe from off thy f. 5:15
Barak was sent on f. to. Judg 5:15
Asahel was as light of f. as a roe. 2 Sam 2:18
every f. six toes. 21:20; 1 Chr 20:6
trod Jezebel under f. 2 Ki 9:33
any more remove the f. 2 Chr 33:8
my f. hath held his steps. Job 23:11
even waters forgotten of the f. 28:4
or if my f. hath hasted to. 31:5
forgetteth that f. may crush. 39:15
in net they hid is their f. Ps 9:15
my f. standeth in even place. 26:12
let not the f. of pride come. 36:11
when my f. slippeth. 38:16
went through the flood on f. 66:6
thy f. be dipped in blood. 68:23
lest thou dash thy f. against a stone. 91:12; Mat 4:6; Luke 4:11
I said my f. slippeth, thy. Ps 94:18
not suffer thy f. to be moved. 121:3
refrain thy f. from their. Pr 1:15
safely, thy f. shall not stumble. 3:23
the Lord shall keep thy f. from. 26
remove thy f. from. 4:27
withdraw thy f. from thy. 25:17
is like f. out of joint. 19
keep thy f. when goest. Eccl 5:1
mountains tread under f. Isa 14:25
meted out trodden under f. 18:7*
off thy shoe from off thy f. 20:2
the f. shall tread it down. 26:6
called righteous man to his f. 41:2
if thou turn away thy f. from. 58:13
withhold thy f. from. Jer 2:25
trodden my portion under f. 12:10
hath trodden under f. Lam 1:15*
stamp with thy f. and. Ezek 6:11
no f. of man, no f. of beast. 29:11
neither shall the f. of man. 32:13
give host to be trodden under f. Dan 8:13
that is swift of f. shall. Amos 2:15
salt trodden under f. of. Mat 5:13
the people followed him on f. 14:13
if thy f. offend thee. 18:8; Mark 9:45
bind him hand and f. Mat 22:13
many ran a f. thither. Mark 6:33
forth bound hand and f. John 11:44
so much as to set his f. on. Acts 7:5
minding himself to go a-f. 20:13
if the f. say, because I. 1 Cor 12:15
trodden under f. the Son. Heb 10:29
with a garment to the f. Rev 1:13
holy city shall tread under f. 11:2

sole of foot

no rest for sole of her f. Gen 8:9
a botch from sole of f. Deut 28:35
not set sole of her f. on ground. 56
nor the sole of thy f. have rest. 65
sole of your f. shall tread. Josh 1:3
Absalom, from sole of f. 2 Sam 14:25
with boils from sole of f. Job 2:7
from sole of f. to head. Isa 1:6
sole of f. like sole of a calf's f. Ezek 1:7

***left* foot**
he set his *left f.* upon. *Rev* 10:2
***right* foot**
he set his *right f.* on sea. *Rev* 10:2
foot breadth
not so much as *f. breadth. Deut* 2:5*
footed
whatsoever is cloven *f.* *Lev* 11:3
though he be cloven *f.* is unclean. 7
a man that is broken *f.* shall. 21:19
all manner of four *f.* beasts.
Acts 10:12; 11:6
birds and four *f.* beasts. *Rom* 1:23
footmen
six hundred thousand *f. Num* 11:21
Saul said to the *f.* *1 Sam* 22:17*
if thou hast run with *f.* and. *Jer* 12:5
footsteps
up my goings that my *f.* *Ps* 17:5*
thy way is in sea, thy *f.* are. 77:19
they reproached the *f.* of. 89:51
go thy way by the *f.* of. *S of S* 1:8
footstool
an house for *f.* of our. *1 Chr* 28:2
six steps to throne with *f.* of gold.
2 Chr 9:18
worship at his *f.* *Ps* 99:5; 132:7
hand till I make thine enemies thy *f.*
110:1; *Mat* 22:44; *Mark* 12:36
Luke 20:43; *Acts* 2:35; *Heb* 1:13
earth is my *f.* *Isa* 66:1; *Acts* 7:49
remembered not his *f.* *Lam* 2:1
swear not by earth, his *f.* *Mat* 5:35
enemies be made his *f.* *Heb* 10:13
poor, sit here under my *f.* *Jas* 2:3
for
all things we call on him *f. Deut* 4:7
all Joab had sent him *f. 2 Sam* 11:22
f. piece of bread that. *Pr* 28:21
f. he maketh his sun to. *Mat* 5:45
to be heard *f.* much speaking. 6:7
f. I was hungry, and ye. 25:35, 42
we received grace *f.* *John* 1:16
f. f. this cause ye pay. *Rom* 13:6
f. we know, if this house. *2 Cor* 5:1
f. we can do nothing against but *f.* the truth. 13:8
looking *f.* the coming of. *2 Pet* 3:12
forasmuch
f. as God hath shewed. *Gen* 41:39
f. as he hath no inheritance with.
Deut 12:12
f. as the Lord hath taken. *Judg* 11:36
f. as we have sworn. *1 Sam* 20:42
f. as my lord is come. *2 Sam* 19:30
f. as thou hast disobeyed. *1 Ki* 13:21
f. as Reuben defiled. *1 Chr* 5:1
f. as this people draw. *Isa* 29:13
f. as there is none like. *Jer* 10:6
f. among all wise men of nations. 7
f. as iron breaketh. *Dan* 2:40
f. as he also is son of. *Luke* 19:9
f. then as God gave them. *Acts* 11:17
f. then as we are offspring. 17:29
f. as I know that thou hast. 24:10
f. as he is the image. *1 Cor* 11:7
f. as ye are zealous of. 14:12*
f. as ye know your labour is. 15:58
f. as we know ye were. *1 Pet* 1:18
f. then as Christ suffered for us. 4:1
forbad
whatsoever Lord *f.* us. *Deut* 2:37
but John *f.* him, saying. *Mat* 3:14*
casting out devils in thy name, we *f.* him. *Mark* 9:38; *Luke* 9:49
the ass *f.* the madness. *2 Pet* 2:16*
forbare
escaped, and Saul *f.* *1 Sam* 23:13
then the prophet *f.* and. *2 Chr* 25:16
Ishmael *f.* and slew. *Jer* 41:8
forbear
if see his ass, and would *f. Ex* 23:5
if thou shalt *f.* to vow. *Deut* 23:22
shall I go, or *f.*? *1 Ki* 22:6
2 Chr 18:5, 14
f. why shouldest thou be smitten?
2 Chr 25:16
f. thee from meddling with 35:21
many years didst thou *f. Neh* 9:30*
and though I *f.* what? *Job* 16:6
thou *f.* to deliver them. *Pr* 24:11*
seem ill to thee to come, *f. Jer* 40:4
whether they will hear or *f.*
Ezek 2:5, 7; 3:11
he that forbeareth, let him *f.* 3:27
f. to cry, make no mourning. 24:17*
give me my price, if *f.* *Zech* 11:12
have not we power to *f.*? *1 Cor* 9:6
f. lest any should think. *2 Cor* 12:6
we could no longer *f.* *1 Thes* 3:1
forbearance
thou the riches of his *f.*? *Rom* 2:4
of sins, through the *f.* of God. 3:25
forbeareth
that *f.* keep passover. *Num* 9:13
he that *f.* let him forbear. *Ezek* 3:27
forbearing
by long *f.* is prince. *Pr* 25:15
I was weary with *f.* *Jer* 20:9
f. one another in love. *Eph* 4:2
Col 3:13
do the same things, *f.* *Eph* 6:9
forbid
my lord Moses, *f.* *Num* 11:28
Lord *f.* I should do. *1 Sam* 24:6
f. I should stretch forth hand. 26:11
Naboth said, the Lord *f.* *1 Ki* 21:3
my God *f.* it me. *1 Chr* 11:19
Jesus said, *f.* him not. *Mark* 9:39
Luke 9:50
suffer little children, and *f.* them not.
Mark 10:14; *Luke* 18:16
f. not to take coat also. *Luke* 6:29*
can any *f.* water? *Acts* 10:47
f. none acquaintance to come. 24:23
f. not to speak with. *1 Cor* 14:39
***God* forbid**
(*American Revision renders this* far be it from me)
God f. Gen 44:7, 17; *Josh* 22:29
24:16; *1 Sam* 12:23; 14:45; 20:2
Job 27:5; *Luke* 20:16; *Rom* 3:4, 6
31; 6:2, 15; 7:7, 13; 9:14; 11:1
11; *1 Cor* 6:15; *Gal* 2:17; 3:21
6:14
forbidden
commit any of things *f.* *Lev* 5:17*
of what Lord hath *f.* *Deut* 4:23
and were *f.* to preach the. *Acts* 16:6
forbiddeth
f. them that would. *3 John* 10
forbidding
f. to give tribute to. *Luke* 23:2
preaching kingdom of God, no man *f.*
Acts 28:31
f. us to speak to the. *1 Thes* 2:16
f. to marry. *1 Tim* 4:3
forborn
men of Babylon *f.* to. *Jer* 51:30
force
wouldest take by *f.* *Gen* 31:31
nor was his natural *f.* *Deut* 34:7
if not, I will take it by *f. 1 Sam* 2:16
made them to cease by *f. Ezra* 4:23
by great *f.* of my disease. *Job* 30:18
and his *f.* is in the navel. 40:16
out their blood by *f.* *Jer* 18:21*
and their *f.* is not right. 23:10
under shadow, because of *f.* 48:45*
with *f.* and cruelty have. *Ezek* 34:4
hast shed blood by *f.* of. 35:5*
shall not strengthen his *f. Amos* 2:14
violent take it by *f.* *Mat* 11:12
would take him by *f.* *John* 6:15
to take Paul by *f.* *Acts* 23:10
for a testament is of *f.* *Heb* 9:17
force, *verb*
if the man *f.* her and. *Deut* 22:25
brother, do not *f.* me. *2 Sam* 13:12
will he *f.* the queen? *Esth* 7:8
forced
Ammonites *f.* children. *Judg* 1:34
my concubine have they *f.* 20:5
I *f.* myself therefore. *1 Sam* 13:12
Amnon *f.* Tamar and. *2 Sam* 13:14
hated Amnon, because he *f.* his. 22
determined from day he *f.* his. 32
flattering of lips she *f.* *Pr* 7:21
forces
placed *f.* in fenced. *2 Chr* 17:2
will not esteem all the *f.* *Job* 36:19
the *f.* of the Gentiles. *Isa* 60:5*
men may bring to thee the *f.* 11*
the captains of the *f.* that. *Jer* 40:7
13; 41:11, 13, 16; 42:1, 8; 43:4, 5
a multitude of great *f.* *Dan* 11:10
in his estate honour God of *f.* 38*
carried away captive his *f.* *Ob* 11*
forcible
how *f.* right words. *Job* 6:25
forcing
not destroy trees by *f.* *Deut* 20:19*
so the *f.* of wrath. *Pr* 30:33
ford, -s
Jacob passed over the *f.* *Gen* 32:22
men pursued spies to *f.* *Josh* 2:7
Israel took the *f.* of. *Judg* 3:28
daughters of Moab at *f.* *Isa* 16:2
forecast
shall *f.* devices. *Dan* 11:24*, 25*
forefathers
the iniquities of their *f.* *Jer* 11:10
whom I serve from my *f. 2 Tim* 1:3
forefront
six curtains in the *f.* *Ex* 26:9
on the *f.* of the mitre it shall. 28:37
upon his *f.* did he put. *Lev* 8:9*
f. of one rock was. *1 Sam* 14:5*
set Uriah in the *f.* of. *2 Sam* 11:15
the brazen altar from *f.* *2 Ki* 16:14
Jehoshaphat in the *f.* *2 Chr* 20:27
f. of lower gate to *f.* of. *Ezek* 40:19
the *f.* of the house stood. 47:1
forehead
plate shall be on Aaron's *f. Ex* 28:38
he is *f.* bald: yet is he. *Lev* 13:41
a leprosy sprung up in bald *f.* 42
if rising be reddish in bald *f.* 43
smote the Philistine in *f.*, stone sunk in his *f.* *1 Sam* 17:49
leprosy rose up in Uzziah's *f.*
2 Chr 26:19
behold he was leprous in his *f.* 20
thou hadst a whore's *f.* *Jer* 3:3
have made thy *f.* strong. *Ezek* 3:8
harder than flint have made thy *f.* 9
put a jewel upon thy *f.* and. 16:12*
mark of beast in his *f.* *Rev* 14:9
and upon her *f.* was a name. 17:5
foreheads
forehead strong against their *f.*
Ezek 3:8
set a mark on the *f.* of them. 9:4
sealed servants of God in their *f.*
Rev 7:3
not seal of God in their *f.* 9:4
all to receive mark in their *f.* 13:16
Father's name written in their *f.* 14:1
received the mark upon their *f.* 20:4
his name shall be in their *f.* 22:4
foreigner
f. and hired servant not. *Ex* 12:45*
of a *f.* thou mayest. *Deut* 15:3
foreigners
in the day that *f.* entered. *Ob* 11
no more strangers and *f. Eph* 2:19*
foreknew
away people which he *f.* *Rom* 11:2
foreknow
whom he did *f.* he also. *Rom* 8:29
foreknowledge
being delivered by the *f.* *Acts* 2:23
elect according to *f.* of. *1 Pet* 1:2
foremost
Jacob commanded the *f. Gen* 32:17
put handmaids and children *f.* 33:2
the running of the *f.* is. *2 Sam* 18:27
foreordained
who verily was *f.* *1 Pet* 1:20*
forepart
two rings towards *f.* of. *Ex* 28:27
39:20
the oracle in the *f.* *1 Ki* 6:20*
wall on *f.* of chambers. *Ezek* 42:7
the *f.* of ship stuck. *Acts* 27:41*
forerunner
whither the *f.* is for us. *Heb* 6:20
foresaw
I *f.* the Lord always. *Acts* 2:25*

foreseeing
the scripture *f.* God. *Gal* 3:8
foreseeth
a prudent man *f.* the evil. *Pr* 22:3*
27:12*
foreship
cast anchors out of *f.* *Acts* 27:30
foreskin
circumcise flesh of your *f.* *Gen* 17:11
flesh of his *f.* is not circumcised. 14
circumcised flesh of their *f.* 23, 24, 25
Zipporah cut off the *f.* *Ex* 4:25
the flesh of his *f.* shall. *Lev* 12:3
circumcise therefore *f.* *Deut* 10:16
let thy *f.* be uncovered. *Hab* 2:16*
foreskins
circumcised Israel at hill of the *f.*
Josh 5:3
but an hundred *f.* of. *1 Sam* 18:25
David brought their *f.* 27
to me for an hundred *f.* *2 Sam* 3:14
take away *f.* of your heart. *Jer* 4:4
forest
David came into the *f.* *1 Sam* 22:5
Solomon built house of *f.* *1 Ki* 7:2
them in the house of the *f.* 10:17
2 Chr 9:16
into the *f.* of his Carmel. *2 Ki* 19:23
Isa 37:24
Asaph, keeper of king's *f.* *Neh* 2:8
every beast of the *f.* is. *Ps* 50:10
wherein all beasts of the *f.* 104:20
kindle in thickets of *f.* *Isa* 9:18
shall consume glory of his *f.* 10:18
the rest of the trees of his *f.* 19
in the *f.* of Arabia ye lodge. 21:13
didst look to armour of the *f.* 22:8
field be esteemed as a *f.* 29:17
32:15
hail, coming down on the *f.* 32:19
cypress from among trees of *f.* 44:14
break forth into singing, O *f.* 23
all ye beasts of the *f.* come. 56:9
a lion out of *f.* shall slay. *Jer* 5:6
one cutteth a tree out of *f.* 10:3
heritage is to me as a lion in *f.* 12:8
I will kindle a fire in the *f.* 21:14
become as high places of the *f.*
26:18; *Mi* 3:12
they shall cut down her *f.* *Jer* 46:23
vine tree among the trees of the *f.*
Ezek 15:6
prophesy against the *f.* of the. 20:46
say unto the *f.* of the south. 47
I will make them a *f.* *Hos* 2:12
will lion roar in the *f.*? *Amos* 3:4
as lion among beasts of the *f.* *Mi* 5:8
the *f.* of the vintage is. *Zech* 11:2
forests
Jotham built castles in *f.* *2 Chr* 27:4
voice of the Lord discovereth the *f.*
Ps 29:9
cut down thickets of the *f.* *Isa* 10:34
cut down any out of *f.* *Ezek* 39:10
foretell
I *f.* you as if I were. *2 Cor* 13:2*
foretold
I have *f.* you all things. *Mark* 13:23
prophets have likewise *f.* *Acts* 3:24*
forewarn
but I will *f.* you whom. *Luke* 12:5*
forewarned
as we also have *f.* you. *1 Thes* 4:6
forfeited
his substance should be *f.* *Ezra* 10:8
forgat
remember Joseph, but *f.* *Gen* 40:23
children of Israel *f.* Lord. *Judg* 3:7
and when they *f.* Lord. *1 Sam* 12:9
and they *f.* his works. *Ps* 78:11
soon *f.* his works. 106:13
f. God their Saviour. 21
far from peace, I *f.* *Lam* 3:17
after her lovers and *f.* me. *Hos* 2:13
forgave
he *f.* their iniquity. *Ps* 78:38
loosed him, and *f.* him. *Mat* 18:27
I *f.* thee all that debt. 32
he frankly *f.* them. *Luke* 7:42
he to whom he *f.* most. 43

if I *f.* any thing to whom I *f.* it for
your sakes *f.* I it in. *2 Cor* 2:10
even as Christ *f.* you. *Col* 3:13
forgavest
thou *f.* the iniquity of. *Ps* 32:5
thou wast a God that *f.* them. 99:8
forged
the proud have *f.* a lie. *Ps* 119:69
forgers
ye are *f.* of lies, are all. *Job* 13:4
forget
till he *f.* that which thou. *Gen* 27:45
for God hath made me *f.* 41:51
lest thou *f.* the things. *Deut* 4:9
lest ye *f.* covenant of the Lord. 23
the Lord will not *f.* the covenant. 31
lest thou *f.* Lord. 6:12; 8:11, 14, 19
f. not how thou provokedst. 9:7
out Amalek, thou shalt not *f.* 25:19
if thou wilt not *f.* thine. *1 Sam* 1:11
covenant I made ye shall not *f.*
2 Ki 17:38
paths of all that *f.* God. *Job* 8:13
if I say, I will *f.* my complaint. 9:27
thou shalt *f.* thy misery. 11:16
the womb shall *f.* him. 24:20
all the nations that *f.* God. *Ps* 9:17
O Lord, *f.* not the humble. 10:12
how long wilt thou *f.* me? 13:1
f. also thine own people. 45:10
consider this, ye that *f.* God. 50:22
lest my people *f.*: scatter. 59:11
f. not the congregation of thy. 74:19
f. not the voice of thine enemies. 23
might not *f.* the works of God. 78:7
so that I *f.* to eat my bread. 102:4
f. not all his benefits. 103:2
I will not *f.* thy word. 119:16
do I not *f.* thy statutes. 83, 109, 141
I will never *f.* thy precepts. 93
for I do not *f.* thy law. 153
I do not *f.* thy commandments. 176
if I *f.* thee let my hand *f.* 137:5
my son, *f.* not my law. *Pr* 3:1
wisdom, get understanding, *f.* 4:5
lest they drink and *f.* the law. 31:5
let him drink and *f.* poverty. 7
f. her sucking child? yea, they may *f.*
yet will I not *f.* thee. *Isa* 49:15
shalt *f.* the shame of thy youth. 54:4
they that *f.* my holy mountain. 65:11
can maid *f.* ornaments? *Jer* 2:32
think to cause my people to *f.* 23:27
I, even I, will utterly *f.* you. 39
thou *f.* us for ever? *Lam* 5:20
forgotten law, I will also *f.* *Hos* 4:6
never *f.* any of their works. *Amos* 8:7
is not unrighteous to *f.* *Heb* 6:10
good and communicate *f.* not. 13:16
forgetful
not *f.* to entertain. *Heb* 13:2
he be not a *f.* hearer. *Jas* 1:25
forgetfulness
righteousness in land of *f.* *Ps* 88:12
forgettest
f. thou our affliction? *Ps* 44:24
and *f.* the Lord thy maker. *Isa* 51:13
forgetteth
and *f.* that the foot. *Job* 39:15
he *f.* not the cry of. *Ps* 9:12
f. the covenant of her God. *Pr* 2:17
f. what manner of man. *Jas* 1:24
forgetting
f. those things behind. *Phil* 3:13
forgive
f. I pray, the trespass, *f.* the trespass
of servants of God. *Gen* 50:17
f. I pray thee, my sin. *Ex* 10:17
if thou wilt *f.* their sin. 32:32
Lord shall *f.* her. *Num* 30:5, 8, 12
he will not *f.* your sins. *Josh* 24:19
I pray, *f.* the trespass. *1 Sam* 25:28
when thou hearest, *f.* *1 Ki* 8:30, 39
2 Chr 6:21, 30
f. the sin of thy people. *1 Ki* 8:34
f. the sin of thy servants. 36
2 Chr 6:25, 27, 39
f. thy people have sinned. *1 Ki* 8:50
then will I hear and *f.* *2 Chr* 7:14
look on my pain, and *f.* *Ps* 25:18
Lord, art good and ready to *f.* 86:5

man boweth, therefore *f.* *Isa* 2:9
f. not their iniquity nor. *Jer* 18:23
for I will *f.* their iniquity. 31:34
that I may *f.* their iniquity. 36:3
O Lord *f.* Lord hearken. *Dan* 9:19
O Lord God, *f.* I beseech. *Amos* 7:2
f. us, as we *f.* our debtors.
Mat 6:12; *Luke* 11:4
f. men trespasses, Father will *f.*
Mat 6:14
if ye *f.* not, nor will your Father *f.* 15
hath power to *f.* sin. 9:6
Mark 2:10; *Luke* 5:24
how oft my brother sin, and I *f.* him?
Mat 18:21
if ye from your hearts *f.* not. 35
who can *f.* sins but God only?
Mark 2:7; *Luke* 5:21
f. that your Father may *f.* you.
Mark 11:25
not *f.* your Father will not *f.* 26
f. and ye shall be. *Luke* 6:37*
if thy brother repent, *f.* him. 17:3, 4
Father, *f.* them, they know. 23:34
ye ought rather to *f.* *2 Cor* 2:7
to whom ye *f.* any thing, I *f.* also. 10
not burdensome, *f.* me this. 12:13
faithful and just to *f.* *1 John* 1:9
forgiven
atonement, and it shall be *f.* them.
Lev 4:20, 26, 31, 35; 5:10, 13, 16
18; 6:7; 19:22; *Num* 15:25, 26
28; *Deut* 21:8
thou hast *f.* from Egypt. *Num* 14:19
blessed, whose transgression is *f.*
Ps 32:1; *Rom* 4:7
hast *f.* the iniquity of thy. *Ps* 85:2
the people shall be *f.* *Isa* 33:24
cheer, thy sins be *f.* *Mat* 9:2, 5
Mark 2:5, 9; *Luke* 5:20, 23; 7:48
blasphemy be *f.*; against Holy Ghost
not be *f.* *Mat* 12:31, 32
Mark 3:28; *Luke* 12:10
their sins be *f.* them. *Mark* 4:12
forgive, and ye shall be *f.* *Luke* 6:37
sins are *f.* but to whom little is *f.* 7:47
of heart may be *f.* thee. *Acts* 8:22
for Christ's sake hath *f.* *Eph* 4:32
he quickened, having *f.* *Col* 2:13
sins, they shall be *f.* him. *Jas* 5:15
because your sins are *f.* *1 John* 2:12
forgiveness
f. with thee that be. *Ps* 130:4
hath never *f.* but is in. *Mark* 3:29
God exalted to give *f.* *Acts* 5:31*
him is preached unto you *f.* 13:38*
to God, that they receive *f.* 26:18*
in whom we have *f.* of. *Eph* 1:7
Col 1:14
forgivenesses
God belong mercies and *f.* *Dan* 9:9
forgiveth
heals thy diseases, who *f.* *Ps* 103:3
say, who is this *f.* sins? *Luke* 7:49
forgiving
f. iniquity, transgression. *Ex* 34:7
Num 14:18
forbearing, *f.* one another.
Eph 4:32; *Col* 3:13
forgot
and hast *f.* a sheaf in. *Deut* 24:19
forgotten
all the plenty shall be *f.* *Gen* 41:30
nor have I *f.* them. *Deut* 26:13
not be *f.* out of mouths. 31:21
hast *f.* God that formed thee. 32:18
familiar friends have *f.* *Job* 19:14
flood breaks out, even waters *f.* 28:4
needy shall not alway be *f.* *Ps* 9:18
said in his heart, God hath *f.* 10:11
I am *f.* as a dead man. 31:12
rock, why hast thou *f.* me? 42:9
is come, yet have we not *f.* 44:17
if we have *f.* name of our God. 20
hath God *f.* to be gracious? 77:9
I have not *f.* thy law. 119:61
because mine enemies have *f.* 139
days to come all be *f.* *Eccl* 2:16
and the wicked were *f.* in the. 8:10
for the memory of them is *f.* 9:5
thou hast *f.* God of thy. *Isa* 17:10
Tyre shall be *f.* seventy years. 23:15

thou harlot that hast been *f.* *Isa* 23:16
thou shalt not be *f.* of me. 44:21
my Lord hath *f.* me. 49:14
the former troubles are *f.* 65:16
my people have *f.* me. *Jer* 2:32
13:25; 18:15
have *f.* the Lord their God. 3:21
confusion never be *f.* 20:11; 23:40
as their fathers have *f.* my. 23:27
all thy lovers have *f.* thee. 30:14
f. wickedness of your fathers. 44:9
covenant that shall not be *f.* 50:5
they turned away, have *f.* 6
caused Sabbath to be *f.* *Lam* 2:6
thou hast *f.* me. *Ezek* 22:12
because thou hast *f.* me. 23:35
seeing thou hast *f.* the law. *Hos* 4:6
for Israel hath *f.* Maker. 8:14
exalted, therefore have *f.* me. 13:6
they had *f.* to take bread. *Mat* 16:5
Mark 8:14
and not one of them is *f.* *Luke* 12:6
have *f.* the exhortation. *Heb* 12:5
f. that he was purged. *2 Pet* 1:9

forks

they had a file for *f.* *1 Sam* 13:21

form

the earth was without *f.* *Gen* 1:2*
what *f.* is he of ? *1 Sam* 28:14
about this *f.* of speech. *2 Sam* 14:20*
I could not discern *f.* *Job* 4:16*
I *f.* the light and create. *Isa* 45:7
his *f.* more than sons of. 52:14
he hath no *f.* nor comeliness. 53:2
and, lo, it was without *f.* *Jer* 4:23*
appeared the *f.* of man's. *Ezek* 10:8
shew them the *f.* of the house. 43:11
and the *f.* of his visage. *Dan* 3:19
the *f.* of the fourth is like the. 25*
appeared in another *f.* *Mark* 16:12
hast *f.* of knowledge. *Rom* 2:20
ye have obeyed that *f.* of. 6:17
who being in the *f.* of God. *Phil* 2:6
took upon him the *f.* of a servant. 7
hold fast *f.* of sound. *2 Tim* 1:13
having *f.* of godliness. 3:5

formed

the Lord God *f.* man of. *Gen* 2:7
out of the ground God *f.* every. 19
forgotten God that *f.* *Deut* 32:18*
I have *f.* it. *2 Ki* 19:25; *Isa* 37:26
dead things are *f.* from. *Job* 26:5*
hand hath *f.* crooked serpent. 13*
I also am *f.* out of the clay. 33:6
or ever thou hadst *f.* earth. *Ps* 90:2
he that *f.* the eye. 94:9
sea is his, his hands *f.* the. 95:5
the great God that *f.* all. *Pr* 26:10*
he that *f.* them will shew. *Isa* 27:11
thus saith he that *f.* thee. 43:1
I have *f.* him, yea, I have. 7
before me there was no god *f.* nor. 10
this people have I *f.* for myself. 21
that made thee, and *f.* thee 44:2
who hath *f.* a god ? 10*
art my servant, I have *f.* thee. 21
thus saith he that *f.* thee. 24
God that *f.* the earth, he *f.* it. 18
Lord that *f.* me from womb to. 49:5
no weapon *f.* against thee. 54:17
before I *f.* thee I knew. *Jer* 1:5
Lord that *f.* it to establish it. 33:2
behold, he *f.* grasshoppers. *Amos* 7:1
shall the thing *f.* say to him that *f.* it ?
Rom 9:20
in birth, till Christ be *f.* in. *Gal* 4:19
Adam was first *f.*, then. *1 Tim* 2:13

former

deliver cup after the *f.* *Gen* 40:13
fought against the *f.* king of Moab.
Num 21:26
her *f.* husband which. *Deut* 24:4
was the manner in *f.* time. *Ruth* 4:7
answered after the *f.* *1 Sam* 17:30
the two captains of *f.* *2 Ki* 1:14
do after the *f.* manner. 17:34, 40
the *f.* governors were. *Neh* 5:15
inquire, I pray, of *f.* age. *Job* 8:8
the wilderness in *f.* time. 30:3*
O remember not *f.* iniquities.
Ps 79:8
where are thy *f.* loving- ? 89:49
no remembrance of *f.* *Eccl* 1:11
f. days were better than these. 7:10
shew the *f.* things. *Isa* 41:22; 43:9
the *f.* things are come to pass. 42:9
remember ye not the *f.* 43:18
remember *f.* things of old. 46:9
I have declared *f.* things. 48:3
raise up the *f.* desolations. 61:4
I will measure their *f.* work. 65:7*
the *f.* troubles are forgotten. 16
f. shall not be remembered. 17
that giveth the *f.* and latter rain.
Jer 5:24; *Hos* 6:3; *Joel* 2:23
is *f.* of all things. *Jer* 10:16; 51:19
the *f.* kings before thee. 34:5
write in it all the *f.* words. 36:28
thy daughter return to *f.* *Ezek* 16:55
multitude greater than *f.* *Dan* 11:13
but it shall not be as the *f.* or. 29
glory greater than of the *f.* *Hag* 2:9
the *f.* prophets have cried. *Zech* 1:4
7:7, 12
not be to people as in *f.* days. 8:11
waters go half toward the *f.* 14:8*
pleasant to Lord as in *f.* *Mal* 3:4*
the *f.* treatise have I made. *Acts* 1:1
concerning *f.* conversation. *Eph* 4:22
not according to *f.* lusts. *1 Pet* 1:14
f. things are passed. *Rev* 21:4*

formeth

lo, he that *f.* mountains. *Amos* 4:13
and *f.* the spirit of man. *Zech* 12:1

fornication

This word is taken [1] *For the sin of impurity*, Mat 5:32; 1 Cor 7:2. [2] *For the sin of idolatry, which is infidelity to and forsaking of the true God for false gods*, 2 Chr 21:11.

caused Jerusalem to commit *f.*
2 Chr 21:11
Tyre shall commit *f.* with. *Isa* 23:17
hast multiplied thy *f.* *Ezek* 16:29
saving for cause of *f.* *Mat* 5:32; 19:9
we be not born of *f.* *John* 8:41
that they abstain from *f.* *Acts* 15:20
29; 21:25
being filled with all *f.* *Rom* 1:29
f. among you, and such *f.* *1 Cor* 5:1
the body is not for *f.* but for. 6:13
flee *f.* 18
nevertheless, to avoid *f.* 7:2
not repented of their *f.* *2 Cor* 12:21
works of the flesh, *f.* *Gal* 5:19
f. let it not be named. *Eph* 5:3
mortify therefore *f.* *Col* 3:5
will of God that ye abstain from *f.*
1 Thes 4:3
cities giving themselves over to *f.*
Jude 7
space to repent of her *f.* *Rev* 2:21
neither repented they of their *f.* 9:21
the wine of wrath of her *f.* 14:8
made drunk with wine of her *f.* 17:2
golden cup full of filthiness of *f.* 4
with wine of wrath of her *f.* 18:3
did corrupt earth with her *f.* 19:2

fornications

pouredst out thy *f.* on. *Ezek* 16:15
out of heart proceed *f.* thefts.
Mat 15:19; *Mark* 7:22
see **commit, committed**

fornicator

called a brother be a *f.* *1 Cor* 5:11
lest there be any *f.* or. *Heb* 12:16

fornicators

you not to company with *f.* *1 Cor* 5:9
yet not altogether with the *f.* of. 10
nor shall *f.* inherit the kingdom. 6:9

forsake

this people will *f.* me. *Deut* 31:16
in that day I will *f.* them. 17
God forbid we should *f.* *Josh* 24:16
if ye *f.* the Lord and serve. 20
should I *f.* my sweetness? *Judg* 9:11*
I will *f.* remnant of. *2 Ki* 21:14*
if thou *f.* him, cast thee. *1 Chr* 28:9
if ye turn away, and *f.* *2 Chr* 7:19
but if ye *f.* him, he will *f.* you. 15:2
wrath is against them that *f.* him.
Ezra 8:22
father and mother *f.* me. *Ps* 27:10
cease from anger and *f.* wrath. 37:8
if his children *f.* my law. *Ps* 89:30
will he *f.* his inheritance. 94:14
because wicked *f.* law. 119:53
let not mercy and truth *f.* *Pr* 3:3
f. the foolish, and live. 9:6*
they that *f.* the law. 28:4
they that *f.* the Lord. *Isa* 1:28
let wicked *f.* his way. 55:7
ye are they that *f.* Lord. 65:11
all that *f.* the Lord. *Jer* 17:13
I will even *f.* you. 23:33*, 39*
f. her, and let us go every one. 51:9
wherefore dost thou *f.*? *Lam* 5:20
that *f.* the holy covenant. *Dan* 11:30
f. their own mercy. *Jonah* 2:8
teachest the Jews to *f.* *Acts* 21:21

forsake *not*

thou *f.* *not* the Levite. *Deut* 12:19
wickedness and *f.* it *not.* *Job* 20:13*
f. me *not*, O. *Ps* 38:21; 71:9, 18
thy statutes, O *f.* me *not.* 119:8
f. *not* works of thine own. 138:8
f. *not* law of mother. *Pr* 1:8; 6:20
good doctrine, *f.* ye *not* my. 4:2
f. her *not*, she shall preserve thee. 6
and father's friend *f.* *not.* 27:10

not **forsake**

he will *not* *f.* thee. *Deut* 4:31*
31:6, 8; *1 Chr* 28:20
Levite, thou shalt *not* *f.* *Deut* 14:27
not fail nor *f.* thee. *Josh* 1:5
Heb 13:5
Lord will *not* *f.* his people.
1 Sam 12:22; *1 Ki* 6:13
not leave us, nor *f.* us. *1 Ki* 8:57
didst *not* consume, nor *f.* *Neh* 9:31
we will *not* *f.* the house of. 10:39
neither *f.* me, O God of. *Ps* 27:9
God of Israel, will *not* *f.* *Isa* 41:17
will I do, and *not* *f.* them. 42:16
nor did they *f.* the idols. *Ezek* 20:8

forsaken

because he had *f.* the Lord.
2 Chr 21:10; 24:24; 28:6
why is house of God *f.*? *Neh* 13:11
shall earth be *f.* for thee ? *Job* 18:4
not seen righteous *f.* *Ps* 37:25
the land shall be *f.* of. *Isa* 7:16
the cities of Aroer are *f.* 17:2
shall be as a *f.* bough, and an. 9
the habitation shall be *f.* 27:10
because palaces shall be *f.* 32:14
hath called thee as a woman *f.* 54:6
shalt no more be termed *f.* 62:4
every city shall be *f.* *Jer* 4:29
cold waters from another place be *f.*?
18:14*
saith Lord to cities *f.* *Ezek* 36:4
the virgin of Israel is *f.* *Amos* 5:2*
Gaza shall be *f.* and. *Zeph* 2:4

have, hast, hath **forsaken**

whereby thou *hast* *f.* *Deut* 28:20
have *f.* the Lord. 29:25; *Judg* 10:10
now the Lord *hath* *f.* us. *Judg* 6:13*
yet ye *have* *f.* me. 10:13
works wherewith they *have* *f.* me.
1 Sam 8:8
sinned, because we *have* *f.* 12:10
because they *have* *f.* me. *1 Ki* 11:33
ye *have* *f.* commandments of. 18:18
Israel *have* *f.* thy covenant. 19:10, 14
have *f.* me and burnt. *2 Ki* 22:17
2 Chr 34:25; *Jer* 16:11; 19:4
ye *have* *f.* me, I have. *2 Chr* 12:5
charge of Lord ye *have* *f.* 13:11
ye *have* *f.* the Lord, he *hath* *f.* 24:20
have done evil, *have* *f.* him. 29:6
for we *have* *f.* thy commandments.
Ezra 9:10
he *hath* oppressed and *f.* *Job* 20:19
my God, my God, why *hast* thou *f.*?
Ps 22:1; *Mat* 27:46; *Mark* 15:34
saying, God *hath* *f.* him. *Ps* 71:11
they *have* *f.* the Lord. *Isa* 1:4
the Lord *hath* *f.* me. 49:14
for a small moment *have* I *f.* 54:7
have *f.* me, burnt. *Jer* 1:16
they *have* *f.* me, the fountain. 2:13
in that thou *hast* *f.* the Lord. 17, 19
thy children *have* *f.* me. 5:7
answer, like as ye *have* *f.* me. 19
saith, because they *have* *f.* 9:13
confounded, because ye *have* *f.* 19

have f. my house. Jer 12:7
thou hast f. me, saith Lord. 15:6*
have f. fountain of living. 17:13
because they have f. covenant. 22:9
he hath f. his covert as lion. 25:38
Lord hath f. earth. Ezek 8:12; 9:9
we have f. all and. Mat 19:27*
every one that hath f. houses. 29*
Demas hath f. me. 2 Tim 4:10
which have f. right way. 2 Pet 2:15

not forsaken

the Lord is our God, we have not f. 2 Chr 13:10
yet God hath not f. us. Ezra 9:9
thou hast not f. them. Ps 9:10
sought out, a city not f. Isa 62:12
Israel hath not been f. Jer 51:5
persecuted, but not f. 2 Cor 4:9

forsaketh

f. the fear of the Almighty. Job 6:14
for the Lord f. not his. Ps 37:28
from her f. the guide of. Pr 2:17
grievous to him that f. way. 15:10
confesseth and f. have mercy. 28:13
whoso f. not all that. Luke 14:33*

forsaking

until there be a great f. Isa 6:12
not f. the assembling of. Heb 10:25

forsook

he f. God that made. Deut 32:15
they f. the Lord God. Judg 2:12, 13
10:6
f. their cities and fled. 1 Sam 31:7
1 Chr 10:7
because they f. the Lord. 1 Ki 9:9
Rehoboam f. the counsel of old men.
12:8, 13; 2 Chr 10:8, 13
Amon f. the God of his. 2 Ki 21:22
f. God of their fathers. 2 Chr 7:22
Rehoboam f. law of Lord. 12:1
he f. tabernacle of Shiloh. Ps 78:60
but I f. not thy precepts. 119:87
f. not ordinance of God. Isa 58:2
hind calved in field and f. Jer 14:5
disciples f. him and fled.
Mat 26:56*; Mark 14:50*
they f. their nets and. Mark 1:18*
they f. all and followed. Luke 5:11*
all men f. me. 2 Tim 4:16
by faith Moses f. Egypt. Heb 11:27

forsookest

God slow to anger, f. not. Neh 9:17
thou in thy mercies f. them not. 19

forswear

thou shalt not f. thyself. Mat 5:33

fort, -s

so David dwelt in the f. 2 Sam 5:9*
they built f. against Jerusalem.
2 Ki 25:1; Jer 52:4
high f. of walls bring. Isa 25:12
and I will raise f. against. 29:3*
the f. and towers shall be. 32:14*
and built a f. against it. Ezek 4:2
21:22; 26:8
building f. to cut off. 17:17
for Jerusalem to build a f. 21:22
he shall make a f. against. 26:8
they that be in the f. shall die. 33:27*
shall turn toward the f. Dan 11:19

forth

that time f. servants. Neh 4:16
from that time f. came they. 13:21
name of the Lord, from this time f.
Ps 113:2; 115:18; 121:8
out every man right f. Jer 49:5
from that time f. began. Mat 16:21
nor durst from that day f. 22:46
from that day f. took. John 11:53

forthwith

that f. expences be. Ezra 6:8*
f. sprung up, because. Mat 13:5*
he f. came to Jesus and. 26:49*
f. when they were. Mark 1:29*
charged him, and f. sent him. 43*
and f. Jesus gave unclean. 5:13*
and f. came thereout. John 19:34*
he received sight f. and. Acts 9:18*
and f. the angel departed. 12:10*
drew Paul out, and f. doors. 21:30*

fortieth

Aaron died there in f. Num 33:38
in f. year Moses spake. Deut 1:3
in f. year of reign of. 1 Chr 26:31
Asa died in one and f. 2 Chr 16:13

fortify

they f. the city against. Judg 9:31*
will these feeble Jews f.? Neh 4:2
houses broken down to f. Isa 22:10
she should f. height of. Jer 51:53
watch the way, f. thy. Nah 2:1
waters for siege, f. strong. 3:14*

fortified

Rehoboam f. the strong. 2 Chr 11:11
Uzziah built towers and f. 26:9
they f. Jerusalem to broad. Neh 3:8
shall come from f. cities. Mi 7:12*

fortress, -es

the Lord is my rock and my f.
2 Sam 22:2; Ps 18:2; 31:3; 71:3
91:2; 144:2
the f. also shall cease. Isa 17:3
the f. of the high fort shall. 25:12
brambles come up in the f. 34:13
I have set thee for a f. Jer 6:27
wares, O inhabitant of the f. 10:17*
O Lord, my f. in day of. 16:19*
enter into the f. of king. Dan 11:7
and be stirred up even to his f. 10
all thy f. be spoiled. Hos 10:14
spoiled come against f. Amos 5:9
day come to thee from f. Mi 7:12*

Fortunatus

glad of the coming of F. 1 Cor 16:17

forty

there shall be f. found; he said, I will
not do it for f.'s sake. Gen 18:29
shalt make f. sockets. Ex 26:19
f. sockets of silver. 21; 36:24, 26
Abdon had f. sons and. Judg 12:14
Hazael went and took f. 2 Ki 8:9
governors had taken f. Neh 5:15
more than f. made. Acts 23:13, 21
see **days**

forty *baths*

one contained f. baths. 1 Ki 7:38

forty *cubits*

house before it was f. cubits long.
1 Ki 6:17
the length f. cubits. Ezek 41:2
courts joined of f. cubits. 46:22

forty *kine*

f. kine, ten bulls. Gen 32:15

forty *stripes*

f. stripes he may give. Deut 25:3
f. stripes save one. 2 Cor 11:24

forty *years*

Isaac was f. years. Gen 25:20
Esau f. years when he took. 36:34
Israel did eat manna f. years.
Ex 16:35; Neh 9:21
wander in wilderness f. years.
Num 14:33; 32:13
your iniquities f. years. 34
thy walking these f. years. Deut 2:7
God led thee f. years. 8:2; 29:5
thy foot swell these f. years. 4
Israel walked f. years in. Josh 5:6
f. years old was I when. 14:7
the land had rest f. years.
Judg 3:11; 5:31; 8:28
hand of Philistines f. years. 13:1
Eli judged f. years. 1 Sam 4:18
Ish-bosheth f. years old. 2 Sam 2:10
David reigned f. years. 5:4
1 Ki 2:11
after f. years Absalom. 2 Sam 15:7
Solomon reigned f. years. 1 Ki 11:42
Jehoash reigned f. years. 2 Ki 12:1
Joash reigned f. years. 2 Chr 24:1
f. years was I grieved. Ps 95:10
it be inhabited f. years. Ezek 29:11
cities be desolate f. years. 12
at the end of f. years I will. 13
I led you f. years in the. Amos 2:10
ye offered sacrifices f. years. 5:25
Acts 7:42
healed was above f. years. Acts 4:22
Moses was f. years old, he. 7:23
when f. years expired, there. 30
wonders in wilderness f. years. 36
the time of f. years suffered. 13:18
them Saul by space of f. years. 21
saw my works f. years. Heb 3:9
with whom he grieved f. years ? 17

forty-one *years*

Rehoboam f.-one years old when he.
1 Ki 14:21; 2 Chr 12:13
Asa reigned f.-one years. 1 Ki 15:10
Jeroboam reigned f.-one years.
2 Ki 14:23

forty-two

cities add f.-two cities. Num 35:6
two bears tare f. and two. 2 Ki 2:24
them alive, f. and two men. 10:14
f.-two years old Ahaz. 2 Chr 22:2
of Azmaveth f. and two. Ezra 2:24
Beth-azmaveth f. and two. Neh 7:28
holy city tread f.-two. Rev 11:2
to continue f.-two months. 13:5

forty-five

if I find f.-five, I will. Gen 18:28
me alive f.-five years. Josh 14:10
that lay on f.-five pillars. 1 Ki 7:3

forty-six

f.-six years was temple. John 2:20

forty-eight

cities of Levites f.-eight. Num 35:7
Josh 21:41

forty-nine

space be to thee f.-nine years.
Lev 25:8

forty *thousand*

tribe of Ephraim were f. thousand.
Num 1:33; 2:19; 26:18
about f. thousand prepared for war.
Josh 4:13
shield or spear seen among f. thousand.
Judg 5:8
David slew f. thousand horsemen.
2 Sam 10:18; 1 Chr 19:18
Solomon had f. thousand. 1 Ki 4:26
of Asher expert in war f. thousand.
1 Chr 12:36

forty-one *thousand*

Asher were f. and one thousand.
Num 1:41; 2:28

forty-two *thousand*

fell of Ephraimites f.-two thousand.
Judg 12:6

forward

not inherit on yonder side or f.
Num 32:19
backward and not f. Jer 7:24
upon eighth day and so f. Ezek 43:27
helped f. the affliction. Zech 1:15
also to be f. year ago. 2 Cor 8:10*
but being more f. of own. 17*
same which I also was f. Gal 2:10*
whom if thou bring f. on. 3 John 6
see that **day, go, set, went**

forwardness

by occasion of the f. 2 Cor 8:8*
for I know f. of your mind. 9:2*

fought

then came Amalek and f. Ex 17:8
so Joshua f. with Amalek. 10
then king Arad f. against Israel.
Num 21:1
Sihon came and f. against Israel. 23
Judg 11:20
Sihon f. against former. Num 21:26
Lord f. for Israel. Josh 10:14, 42
23:3
all Israel f. against Libnah. 10:29
f. against Lachish. 31
Amorites on the other side f. 24:8
men of Jericho f. against you. 11
found Adoni-bezek and f. Judg 1:5
Judah had f. against Jerusalem. 8
kings came, then f. kings of. 5:19
f. from heaven, stars in courses f. 20
my father f. for you and. 9:17
Gaal went out and f. with. 39
the men of Gilead f. with. 12:4
Philistines f. 1 Sam 4:10; 1 Chr 10:1
Saul f. against all his. 1 Sam 14:47
David f. with Philistines. 19:8; 23:5
people stood still, nor f. 2 Sam 2:28
f. against Hadadezer. 8:10
1 Chr 18:10
the Syrians f. against David.
2 Sam 10:17; 1 Chr 19

David f. against Rabbah and took. 2 Sam 12:29
Joram f. Hazael. 2 Ki 8:29; 9:15
Hazael f. against Gath. 12:17
Joash f. against Amaziah. 13:12
14:15
Lord f. against enemies. 2 Chr 20:29
f. against me without a. Ps 109:3
Tartan f. against Ashdod. Isa 20:1
turned their enemy and f. 63:10
f. against Jerusalem. Jer 34:1, 7
when he f. in day of. Zech 14:3
smite them that f. against. 12*
I have f. with beasts at. 1 Cor 15:32
I have f. a good fight. 2 Tim 4:7
Michael and his angels f. Rev 12:7*

foul, adj.

my face is f. with. Job 16:16
it will be f. weather. Mat 16:3
he rebuked the f. spirit. Mark 9:25*
Babylon, the hold of every f. spirit. Rev 18:2*

foul, -ed

ye must f. the residue. Ezek 34:18
they drink that ye have f. with. 19

fouledst

troubledst waters and f. Ezek 32:2

found

for Adam not f. an help. Gen 2:20
dove f. no rest for sole of her. 8:9
Isaac's servants digged and f. 26:19
Isaac's servants said we have f. 32
is it that thou hast f. it so? 27:20
Reuben went and f. mandrakes in. 30:14
tents, but f. not images. 31:33
what hast thou f. of all thy stuff? 37
Anah that f. the mules in. 36:24
coat, said, this have we f. 37:32
kid, and thou hast not f. her. 38:23
money which we f. in our. 44:8
God hath f. out the iniquity of. 16
went three days and f. no. Ex 15:22
went to gather manna and f. 16:27
or if he have f. that. Lev 6:3
f. a man that gathered. Num 15:32
f. him brought him to Moses. 33
with what thou hast f. Deut 22:3
came to her I f. her not a maid. 14, 17
f. her in field, and the. 22:27
he hath f. some uncleanness. 24:1
he f. him in a desert land. 32:10
pursuers sought, but f. them not. Josh 2:22
five kings are f. hid in a cave. 10:17
they f. Adoni-bezek and. Judg 1:5
not plowed with heifer, not f. 14:18
he f. a new jawbone of ass. 15:15
f. four hundred young virgins. 21:12
but they f. not asses. 1 Sam 9:4
they f. young maidens going to. 11
asses, they are f. 9:20; 10:2, 16
Lord is witness ye have not f. 12:5
was no smith f. in Israel. 13:19
no sword nor spear f. in hand. 22
evil hath not been f. with. 25:28
I have f. no fault in him. 29:3
they f. an Egyptian in field. 30:11
f. Saul and his three sons. 31:8
thy servant f. in his heart to pray. 2 Sam 7:27; 1 Chr 17:25
nor was weight of brass f. 1 Ki 7:47
prophet Ahijah f. Jeroboam. 11:29
he went and f. his carcase. 13:28
an oath that they f. thee not. 18:10
Elijah departed and f. Elisha. 19:19
a lion f. him and slew him. 20:36
f. me, O mine enemy? have f. 21:20
sought Elijah, but f. not. 2 Ki 2:17
f. no more of her than skull. 9:35
I f. the book of the law in. 22:8
sixty men that were f. in city. 25:19
they f. fat pasture and. 1 Chr 4:40
whom precious stones were f. 29:8
there are good things f. 2 Chr 19:3
by genealogy, but they were not f. Ezra 2:62; Neh 7:64
f. there none of sons of. Ezra 8:15
f. nothing to answer. Neh 5:8
they f. written in the law of. 8:14
nor is wisdom f. in land. Job 28:13
up myself when evil f. mine. 31:29
because they had f. no answer. 32:3
lest ye say, we have f. wisdom. Job 32:13
I have f. a ransom. 33:24
no women f. so fair as the. 42:15
looked for comforters, f. Ps 69:20
none of men of might f. their. 76:5
yea sparrow hath f. an house. 84:3
I have f. David my servant. 89:20
wandered and f. no city. 107:4
we f. it in the fields of wood. 132:6
seek thy face, and I have f. Pr 7:15
wisdom be when thou hast f. 24:14
hast thou f. honey? 25:16
this have I f. saith the preacher. Eccl 7:27
man among a thousand have I f. but woman have I not f. 28
f. that God made man upright. 29
sought him, f. him not. S of S 3:1, 2
the watchmen f. me. 3; 5:7
f. him whom my soul loveth. 3:4
hand hath f. kingdoms. Isa 10:10
my hand hath f. the riches of. 14
all that are f. in thee are. 22:3
hast f. the life of thine hand. 57:10
f. of them that sought me not. 65:1
iniquity have your fathers f.? Jer 2:5
in thy skirts is f. the blood of. 34
among my people are f. 5:26
to the pits and f. no water. 14:3
words were f. and I did eat. 15:16
house I f. their wickedness. 23:11
ten men were f. that said. 41:8
all that f. them devoured. 50:7
this is the day we have f. Lam 2:16
for man, but I f. none. Ezek 22:30
excellent spirit was f. in Daniel. Dan 5:12
weighed, and art f. wanting. 27
nor any fault f. in Daniel. 6:4
these men f. Daniel praying. 11
I f. Israel like grapes. Hos 9:10
he f. him in Beth-el, and. 12:4
Ephraim said, I have f. me out. 8
from me is thy fruit f. 14:8
he f. a ship for Tarshish. Jonah 1:3
transgressions of Israel f. Mi 1:13
when ye have f. him. Mat 2:8
I have not f. so great faith. 8:10
Luke 7:9
when a man hath f. he. Mat 13:44
when he had f. one pearl of. 46
and f. one of his fellow. 18:28
went on and f. others standing. 20:6
f. nothing thereon. 21:19
Mark 11:13; Luke 13:6
gathered all as many as they f. Mat 22:10
he f. them asleep. 26:43
Mark 14:40; Luke 22:45
sought witnesses, yet f. they none. Mat 26:60; Mark 14:55
f. a man of Cyrene. Mat 27:32
when they had f. him. Mark 1:37
ate with defiled hands, f. fault. 7:2
when she was come, f. devil gone. 30
they f. the colt tied by door. 11:4
f. the babe in a manger. Luke 2:16
after three days they f. him. 46
f. the place where it was. 4:17
returning f. the servant whole. 7:10
they f. man clothed and in. 8:35
when he hath f. the sheep. 15:5
for I have f. my sheep. 6
when she hath f. the piece. 9
are not any f. that returned. 17:18
they f. even as he had. 19:32; 22:13
f. this fellow perverting nation. 23:2
I have f. no fault in this man. 14
f. the stone rolled away. 24:2
they f. not the body of Lord Jesus. 3
when they f. not his body. 23
and they f. the eleven gathered. 33
we have found Messias. John 1:41
45
Jesus f. in the temple those. 2:14
young men came in, f. her. Acts 5:10
when the officers f. them not. 22
our fathers f. no sustenance. 7:11
that if he f. any of this way. 9:2
Peter f. many come together. 10:27
Herod sought Peter, f. him. 12:19
they f. a certain sorcerer. 13:6
I have f. David, a man after. 22
I f. an altar with this. Acts 17:23
f. this man a pestilent fellow. 24:5
if they have f. any evil doing. 20
I f. he hath done nothing. 25:25
came to Puteoli, where we f. 28:14
Abraham our father hath f. Rom 4:1
ordained to life, I f. to be to. 7:10
yea, we are f. false. 1 Cor 15:15
because I f. not Titus. 2 Cor 2:13
ourselves are f. sinners. Gal 2:17
being f. in fashion as a man. Phil 2:8
the office, f. blameless. 1 Tim 3:10
Onesiphorus sought me, f. 2 Tim 1:17
f. no place of repentance. Heb 12:17
your faith might be f. 1 Pet 1:7
I f. of thy children. 2 John 4
tried them, and hast f. Rev 2:2
I have not f. thy works perfect. 3:2
nor was their place f. any. 12:8
and mountains were not f. 16:20

be found

there shall be forty f. Gen 18:29
with whomsoever it be f. 44:9
no leaven be f. in houses. Ex 12:19
stealeth a man, if he be f. in. 21:16
if a thief be f. breaking up. 22:2, 7
if theft be certainly f. in his hand. 4
lie with her, they be f. Deut 22:28
him, he could not be f. 1 Sam 10:21
on him where he be f. 2 Sam 17:12
if wickedness be f. in. 1 Ki 1:52
if thou seek him, he will be f. of thee. 1 Chr 28:9; 2 Chr 15:2
fly away and not be f. Job 20:8
but where shall wisdom be f.? 28:12
pray in time when thou mayest be f. Ps 32:6
till his iniquity be f. to be. 36:2
him, but he could not be f. 37:36
if he be f. he shall restore. Pr 6:31
be f. in way of righteousness. 16:31
reprove thee and thou be f. a. 30:6
curse thee, and thou be f. guilty. 10
not be f. a sherd to take. Isa 30:14
nor beast shall be f. there. 35:9
joy and gladness shall be f. 51:3
seek Lord while he may be f. 55:6
I will be f. of you. Jer 29:14
sins of Judah be sought for, not be f. 50:20
shalt thou never be f. Ezek 26:21
and fall, and not be f. Dan 11:19
every one shall be f. written in. 12:1
now shall they be f. faulty. Hos 10:2
deceitful tongue be f. in. Zeph 3:13
place shall not be f. for. Zech 10:10
be f. to fight against God. Acts 5:39
that a steward be f. 1 Cor 4:2
we shall not be f. naked. 2 Cor 5:3
they may be f. even as we. 11:12
that I shall be f. such as ye. 12:20
be f. in him, not having my. Phil 3:9
that ye may be f. of him. 2 Pet 3:14
city of Babylon be f. no. Rev 18:21
no craftsman shall be f. any. 22

see favour

found grace

Noah f. grace in eyes of. Gen 6:8
thy servant hath f. grace. 19:19
f. grace in thy sight. 33:10; 47:29
50:4
Joseph f. grace in his sight. 39:4
hast also f. grace in. Ex 33:12, 17
if I have f. grace in thy sight. 13
34:9; Judg 6:17; 1 Sam 27:5
thy people have f. grace? Ex 33:16
if we have f. grace in thy sight. Num 32:5
why have I f. grace in? Ruth 2:10
father knoweth I f. grace. 1 Sam 20:3
thy servant knoweth I have f. grace. 2 Sam 14:22
the people f. grace in. Jer 31:2

is found

with whom it is f. be my servant. Gen 44:10, 16
people that is f. shall. Deut 20:11
is f. some good thing. 1 Ki 14:13
this book that is f. 2 Ki 22:13
2 Chr 34:21
is f. city hath been. Ezra 4:19
seeing root of matter is f. Job 19:28
in lips of him wisdom is f. Pr 10:13

every one that *is f.* shall. *Isa* 13:15
as new wine *is f.* in cluster. 65:8
thief is ashamed when he *is f.* *Jer* 2:26
in thy skirts *is f.* the blood. 34
a conspiracy *is f.* among the. 11:9
excellent wisdom *is f.* *Dan* 5:12, 14
from me *is* thy fruit *f.* *Hos* 14:8
my son lost and *is f.* *Luke* 15:24, 32
our boasting which I made *is f.* a truth. *2 Cor* 7:14

was **found**

cup *was f.* in Benjamin's. *Gen* 44:12
gathered money that *was f.* 47:14
with whom *was f.* purple. *Ex* 35:23
with whom *was f.* shittim wood. 24
and Jonathan *was f.* *1 Sam* 13:22
told the money that *was f.* *2 Ki* 12:10
shewed all that *was f.* in treasury. 20:13; *Isa* 39:2
gathered the money that *was f.* *2 Ki* 22:9; *2 Chr* 34:17
read book which *was f.* *2 Ki* 23:2; *2 Chr* 34:30
sought him, he *was f.* *2 Chr* 15:4, 15
away substance that *was f.* 21:17
was f. at Achmetha a roll. *Ezra* 6:2
was f. in it a poor wise. *Eccl* 9:15
was he *f.* among thieves? *Jer* 48:27
perfect till iniquity *was f.* *Ezek* 28:15
none *was f.* like Daniel. *Dan* 1:19
clay broken, no place *was f.* 2:35
like wisdom of the gods *was f.* 5:11
before him innocency *was f.* 6:22
she *was f.* with child of. *Mat* 1:18
past, Jesus *was f.* alone. *Luke* 9:36
Philip *was f.* at Azotus. *Acts* 8:40
I *was f.* of them that. *Rom* 10:20
neither *was* guile *f.* in. *1 Pet* 2:22
no man *was f.* worthy. *Rev* 5:4
in their mouth *was f.* no guile. 14:5
in her *was f.* the blood of. 18:24
there *was f.* no place for them. 20:11

was not **found**

iniquity *was not f.* in his. *Mal* 2:6
Enoch *was not f.* because. *Heb* 11:5
was not f. written in. *Rev* 20:15

foundation

not been in Egypt since *f.* *Ex* 9:18
he shall lay the *f.* in his. *Josh* 6:26
hewn stones to lay the *f.* *1 Ki* 5:17
in fourth year was *f.* of house. 6:37
of costly stones even from *f.* 7:9, 10
he laid the *f.* of Jericho in. 16:34
work was prepared of *f.* *2 Chr* 8:16
they began to lay the *f.* of. 31:7
f. of temple not yet laid. *Ezra* 3:6
when the builders laid *f.* of. 10, 12
Sheshbazzar laid *f.* of house. 5:16
much less in them whose *f.* *Job* 4:19
whose *f.* was overflown. 22:16
his *f.* is in holy mountains. *Ps* 87:1
of old thou hast laid the *f.* 102:25
Rase it, even to the *f.* thereof. 137:7
righteous an everlasting *f.* *Pr* 10:25
I lay in Zion for a *f.* *Isa* 28:16
to temple, thy *f.* shall be. 44:28
my hand hath laid the *f.* of. 48:13
f. thereof be discovered. *Ezek* 13:14
discovering the *f.* to neck. *Hab* 3:13
from day the *f.* was laid. *Hag* 2:18
Zerubbabel hath laid *f.* *Zech* 4:9
prophets which were when *f.* 8:9
Lord, which layeth the *f.* of. 12:1
and laid the *f.* on a rock. *Luke* 6:48
like a man that without a *f.* built. 49
lest haply after he hath laid *f.* 14:29
build on another man's *f.* *Rom* 15:20
as a wise masterbuilder I laid the *f.* *1 Cor* 3:10
for other *f.* can no man lay than. 11
if any man build on this *f.* gold. 12
built on *f.* of prophets. *Eph* 2:20
up in store a good *f.* *1 Tim* 6:19
f. of God standeth sure. *2 Tim* 2:19
thou, Lord, hast laid the *f.* *Heb* 1:10
not laying the *f.* of repentance. 6:1
the first *f.* jasper. *Rev* 21:19

foundation *of the world*

kept secret from the *f. of the world.* *Mat* 13:35
prepared from *f. of the world.* 25:34
blood shed from the *f. of the world.* *Luke* 11:50
lovedst me before *f. of the world.* *John* 17:24
chosen us in him before the *f. of the world.* *Eph* 1:4
finished from *f. of world.* *Heb* 4:3
oft suffered since *f. of world.* 9:26
foreordained before *f. of the world.* *1 Pet* 1:20
slain from *f. of the world.* *Rev* 13:8
not written from *f. of the world.* 17:8

foundations

and set on fire the *f.* *Deut* 32:22
the *f.* of heaven moved. *2 Sam* 22:8
f. of the world were discovered. 16; *Ps* 18:7, 15
set up walls and joined *f.* *Ezra* 4:12
let the *f.* thereof be strongly. 6:3
wast thou when I laid *f.*? *Job* 38:4
whereupon are the *f.* fastened. 6
if *f.* be destroyed, what? *Ps* 11:3
all the *f.* of the earth are out. 82:5
laid the *f.* of earth not to be. 104:5
when he appointed the *f.* *Pr* 8:29
for *f.* of Kir-hareseth. *Isa* 16:7*
the *f.* of the earth do shake. 24:18
have ye not understood from *f.* of earth? 40:21
Lord that laid *f.* of earth. 51:13
that I may lay *f.* of the earth. 16
I will lay thy *f.* with sapphires. 54:11
thou shalt raise up the *f.* of. 58:12
f. of earth can be searched. *Jer* 31:37
her *f.* are fallen, her walls. 50:15*
not take of thee a stone for *f.* 51:26
and it hath devoured the *f.* *Lam* 4:11
Egypt's *f.* shall be broken. *Ezek* 30:4
the *f.* of the side chambers. 41:8
and I will discover the *f.* *Mi* 1:6
and ye strong *f.* of earth. 6:2
f. of prison were shaken. *Acts* 16:26
for a city that hath *f.* *Heb* 11:10
walls of city had twelve *f.* *Rev* 21:14
f. garnished with precious stones. 19

founded

for he hath *f.* it upon seas. *Ps* 24:2
fulness thereof, thou hast *f.* 89:11
to place which thou hast *f.* 104:8
testimonies thou hast *f.* 119:152
Lord by wisdom *f.* earth. *Pr* 3:19
that Lord hath *f.* Zion. *Isa* 14:32
people was not till Assyrian *f.* 23:13†
and he hath *f.* his troop. *Amos* 9:6
fell not, for it was *f.* on a rock. *Mat* 7:25
it was *f.* on a rock. *Luke* 6:48

founder

mother gave them to *f.* *Judg* 17:4
bellows are burnt, *f.* *Jer* 6:29
work of the hands of the *f.* 10:9*
every *f.* confounded by. 14*; 51:17*

foundest

and *f.* his heart faithful. *Neh* 9:8

fountain

Is properly the source or spring-head of waters. It is often used of a well. Metaphorically, God is called the fountain of living waters, Jer 2:13. *Springs or fountains are called living, when they never cease, but are always sending forth their waters. All spiritual graces and refreshments communicated by the Spirit, are also compared to a fountain,* Joel 3:18; Zech 13:1.

found Hagar by a *f.* *Gen* 16:7
a *f.* wherein is water. *Lev* 11:36
he discovered her *f.* the *f.* of. 20:18
f. of Jacob shall be on a. *Deut* 33:28
Israelites pitched by a *f.* *1 Sam* 29:1
for with thee is *f.* of life. *Ps* 36:9
bless the Lord from the *f.* 68:26
didst cleave the *f.* and the. 74:15
turned flint into a *f.* of water. 114:8
let thy *f.* be blessed. *Pr* 5:18
law of the wise is a *f.* of life. 13:14
the fear of Lord is a *f.* of life. 14:27
is a troubled *f.* and corrupt. 25:26
pitcher be broken at *f.* *Eccl* 12:6
a *f.* sealed. *S of S* 4:12
a *f.* of gardens. *S of S* 4:15
forsaken *f.* of living. *Jer* 2:13; 17:13
as a *f.* casteth out her waters. 6:7*
oh that mine eyes were a *f.* of. 9:1
a *f.* shall come forth of. *Joel* 3:18
in that day a *f.* shall be. *Zech* 13:1
the *f.* of her blood. *Mark* 5:29
doth a *f.* send forth sweet waters? *Jas* 3:11
no *f.* can yield salt water and. 12
I will give of the *f.* of life. *Rev* 21:6

fountains

f. of the great deep. *Gen* 7:11
the *f.* also of the deep were. 8:2
God bringeth thee into a land of *f.* *Deut* 8:7
go into land, to all *f.* *1 Ki* 18:5
took counsel to stop waters of *f.* *2 Chr* 32:3
much people, who stopped all the *f.* 4
let thy *f.* be dispersed. *Pr* 5:16*
there were no *f.* abounding. 8:24
when he strengthened the *f.* 28
I will open *f.* in midst. *Isa* 41:18
and his *f.* shall be dried. *Hos* 13:15
he shall lead them to living *f.* *Rev* 7:17
star fell upon *f.* of waters. 8:10
worship him that made the *f.* 14:7
third angel poured vial upon *f.* 16:4

four

river became *f.* heads. *Gen* 2:10
f. kings joined battle with five. 14:9
and *f.* parts shall be your. 47:24
he shall restore *f.* sheep. *Ex* 22:1
shalt make for it *f.* rings. 25:26
shall be *f.* bowls made like. 34
of one curtain *f.* cubits. 26:2, 8
their pillars *f.* their sockets *f.* 27:16; 38:19
in candlestick were *f.* bowls. 37:20
he cast *f.* rings for the *f.* ends. 38:5
f. rows of stones set in the. 39:10
fowls that creep going on all *f.* *Lev* 11:20
of beasts that go on all *f.* 27, 42
two wagons, *f.* oxen to. *Num* 7:7
f. wagons, eight oxen to sons of. 8
fringes on the *f.* quarters. *Deut* 22:12
a custom to lament *f.* *Judg* 11:40
these *f.* were born. *2 Sam* 21:22
fill *f.* barrels with water. *1 Ki* 18:33
there were *f.* leprous men. *2 Ki* 7:3
saw his son's sons, even *f.* *Job* 42:16
f. things say not, it is. *Pr* 30:15
be *f.* things which I know not. 18
f. things which it cannot bear. 21
there be *f.* things which are little. 24
f. things are comely in going. 30:29
f. or five in the utmost. *Isa* 17:6
appoint over them *f.* kinds. *Jer* 15:3
Jehudi read three or *f.* leaves. 36:23
likeness of *f.* living creatures. *Ezek* 1:5
every one had *f.* faces. 6, 15; 10:14, 21
they *f.* had one likeness. 1:16; 10:10
went upon their *f.* sides. 1:17; 10:11
every one had *f.* wings. 10:21
send my *f.* sore judgements. 14:21
and say, come from *f.* winds. 37:9
f. tables were on this side, *f.* 40:41
altar *f.* cubits; and *f.* horns. 43:15
these *f.* children, God. *Dan* 1:17
lo, I see *f.* men loose, walking. 3:25
the *f.* winds of heaven strove. 7:2
f. great beasts came from sea. 3
these *f.* beasts are *f.* kings. 17
f. notable horns towards *f.* 8:8
whereas *f.* stood up, *f.* kingdoms. 22
kingdom divided towards *f.* winds. 11:4
f. I will not turn away punishment. *Amos* 1:3, 6, 9, 11, 13; 2:1, 4, 6
I saw, and behold *f.* horns. *Zech* 1:18
the Lord shewed me *f.* carpenters. 20
there came *f.* chariots out. 6:1
and they shall gather elect from *f.* winds. *Mat* 24:31; *Mark* 13:27
sick of palsy borne of *f.* *Mark* 2:3
are yet *f.* months, then. *John* 4:35
Lazarus had lain in grave *f.* 11:17
the soldiers made *f.* parts. 19:23

f. days ago I was fasting. *Acts* 10:30
Philip had *f.* daughters. 21:9
have *f.* men which have a vow. 23
cast *f.* anchors out of stern. 27:29
about throne were *f.* beasts. *Rev* 4:6
the *f.* beasts had each of them. 8
the *f.* beasts said, amen. 5:14
a voice in the midst of *f.* beasts. 6:6
f. angels, on *f.* corners, holding *f.* 7:1
a voice from the *f.* horns of. 9:13
loose the *f.* angels bound in. 14
sung new song before *f.* beasts. 14:3
one of *f.* beasts gave seven. 15:7
elders and the *f.* beasts fell. 19:4
see **corners, days, footed, twenty, hundred, thousand**

four *times*
they sent to me *f. times.* *Neh* 6:4

fourfold
shall restore lamb *f.* *2 Sam* 12:6
taken any thing, I restore *f.* *Luke* 19:8

fourscore
Moses was *f.* years old, Aaron *f.* and three, when they spake. *Ex* 7:7
land had rest *f.* years. *Judg* 3:30
Barzillai was *f.* old. *2 Sam* 19:32, 35
ass's head was sold for *f.* *2 Ki* 6:25
Jehu appointed *f.* men. 10:24
Eliel chief, his brethren *f.* *1 Chr* 15:9
with him *f.* priests. *2 Chr* 26:17
Zebadiah, and with him *f.* *Ezra* 8:8
if by strength they be *f.* *Ps* 90:10
threescore queens, *f.* *S of S* 6:8
came from Samaria, *f.* *Jer* 41:5
widow about *f.* and four. *Luke* 2:37
take thy bill, and write *f.* 16:7

fourscore *and five*
I am this day *f. and five* years old. *Josh* 14:10
Doeg slew *f. and five.* *1 Sam* 22:18

fourscore *and six*
Abram was *f. and six.* *Gen* 16:16

one hundred and **fourscore**
days of Isaac were *one hundred and f.* *Gen* 35:28

four hundred and **fourscore**
in *four hundred f.* years after Israel were come out of Egypt. *1 Ki* 6:1

fourscore *thousand*
f. thousand hewers in mountains. *1 Ki* 5:15; *2 Chr* 2:18

fourscore *and seven thousand*
Issachar reckoned in all *f. and seven thousand.* *1 Chr* 7:5

one hundred **fourscore** *and five thousand*
angel smote in camp *one hundred f. and five thousand.* *2 Ki* 19:35

foursquare
altar shall be *f.* *Ex* 27:1
the breastplate *f.* 28:16
he measured court *f.* *Ezek* 40:47
ye shall offer holy oblation *f.* 48:20
and the city lieth *f.* *Rev* 21:16

fourteen
I served *f.* years for. *Gen* 31:41
born to Jacob, all souls were *f.* 46:22
offer for burnt offering *f.* lambs of. *Num* 29:13, 17, 20, 23, 26, 29, 32
tribe of Judah had in valley *f.* cities with their. *Josh* 15:36; 18:28
and Israel held a feast *f.* *1 Ki* 8:65
God gave to Heman *f.* *1 Chr* 25:5
waxed mighty, married *f.* wives. *2 Chr* 13:21
settle be *f.* cubits long. *Ezek* 43:17
to David *f.* from David to carrying to Babylon *f.* to Christ *f.* *Mat* 1:17
a man above *f.* years. *2 Cor* 12:2
then *f.* years after I went. *Gal* 2:1

fourteen *thousand*
Job had *f. thousand* sheep. *Job* 42:12

fourteen *thousand seven hundred*
died in plague were *f. thousand seven hundred.* *Num* 16:49

fourteenth
in the *f.* year came Chedorlaomer. *Gen* 14:5

in *f.* year of Hezekiah. *2 Ki* 18:13
Isa 36:1
the *f.* lot came forth to. *1 Chr* 24:13
f. lot came forth to Mattithiah. 25:21
in the *f.* year after city. *Ezek* 40:1
but when the *f.* night was come. *Acts* 27:27
see **day**

fourth
f. river is Euphrates. *Gen* 2:14
in *f.* generation they shall. 15:16
iniquity of fathers to the *f.* *Ex* 20:5
34:7; *Num* 14:18; *Deut* 5:9
and *f.* row a beryl. 28:20; 39:13
in *f.* year fruit shall be. *Lev* 19:24
f. lot came to Issachar. *Josh* 19:17
David's *f.* son, Adonijah. *2 Sam* 3:4
1 Chr 3:2
thy children of *f.* generation. *2 Ki* 10:30; 15:12
f. had the face of eagle. *Ezek* 10:14
f. kingdom strong as. *Dan* 2:40
form of *f.* is like Son of God. 3:25
a *f.* beast dreadful and strong. 7:7
then I would know truth of *f.* 19
the *f.* beast shall be the *f.* 23
the *f.* shall be far richer. 11:2
in the *f.* chariot were. *Zech* 6:3
Jesus came in *f.* watch. *Mat* 14:25
f. beast was like a flying eagle. *Rev* 4:7
when he had opened the *f.* seal. 6:7
the *f.* angel sounded, the sun. 8:12
the *f.* angel poured out his vial. 16:8
third, a chalcedony; *f.* an. 21:19
see **day, month, part**

fourth *year*
in the *f. year* of Solomon's reign he began. *1 Ki* 6:1, 37; *2 Chr* 3:2
Jehoshaphat began to reign in *f. year* of Ahab. *1 Ki* 22:41
in the *f. year* of Hezekiah Shalmaneser came up against. *2 Ki* 18:9
word came to Jeremiah in *f. year* of Jehoiakim. *Jer* 25:1
in the *f. year* of Zedekiah. 28:1
in the *f. year* of Jehoiakim this word came to. 36:1; 45:1; 46:2
commanded Seraiah in *f. year.* 51:59
in *f. year* of Darius. *Zech* 7:1

fowl
have dominion over *f.* *Gen* 1:26, 28
of ground God formed every *f.* 2:19
the *f.* of the heaven destroyed. 7:23
bring forth of all flesh, of *f.* 8:17
fear of you shall be on every *f.* 9:2
I establish my covenant with *f.* 10
no blood, whether of *f.* or. *Lev* 7:26
law of the beasts and *f.* 11:46
likeness of any winged *f.* *Deut* 4:17
there is a path which no *f.* *Job* 28:7*
dominion over *f.* of air. *Ps* 8:8
beasts and flying *f.* praise. 148:10
f. of heavens and beast. *Jer* 9:10
under it shall dwell all *f.* *Ezek* 17:23
speak to every feathered *f.* 39:17*
priest not eat any thing torn, *f.* 44:31
back of it four wings of a *f.* *Dan* 7:6

fowler
deliver thee from snare of *f.* *Ps* 91:3
a bird from hand of the *f.* *Pr* 6:5
prophet is a snare of a *f.* *Hos* 9:8

fowlers
escaped out of snare of *f.* *Ps* 124:7

fowls
take of *f.* also of air by. *Gen* 7:3
when the *f.* came down on. 15:11*
if the burnt sacrifice to Lord be of *f.* *Lev* 1:14
these *f.* ye shall have in. 11:13
of all clean *f.* ye may. *Deut* 14:20
carcase be meat to all *f.* of. 28:26
thy flesh to the *f.* *1 Sam* 17:44, 46
spake of beasts and of *f.* *1 Ki* 4:33
that dieth in fields, *f.* eat. 14:11
16:4; 21:24
f. were prepared for me. *Neh* 5:18
ask the *f.* they shall tell. *Job* 12:7
know all *f.* of mountains. *Ps* 50:11
he rained *f.* like as the sand. 78:27
left to the *f.* of the mountains, and the *f.* summer upon. *Isa* 18:6*

let *f.* get from branches. *Dan* 4:14
f. sow not, neither reap. *Mat* 6:26*
the *f.* devoured the seed. 13:4*
Mark 4:4*; *Luke* 8:5*
that *f.* may lodge under it. *Mark* 4:32*; *Luke* 13:19*
much better than *f.* *Luke* 12:24*
a sheet wherein were *f.* *Acts* 10:12
11:6
an angel cried to all the *f.* *Rev* 19:17*
and all the *f.* were filled with. 21*

fowls *of the heaven*
wiser than *f. of heaven.* *Job* 35:11
bodies of thy servants meat to *f. of the heaven.* *Ps* 79:2
by them the *f. of heaven.* 104:12
of people meat for *f. of the heaven.* *Jer* 7:33; 16:4; 19:7; 34:20
will appoint *f. of the heaven.* 15:3
given Pharaoh for meat to *f. of heaven.* *Ezek* 29:5
f. of heaven made their nests in Assyria. 31:6
ruin all *f. of heaven* remain. 13
will cause all *f. of heaven* to. 32:4
the *f. of heaven* shall shake. 38:20
f. of heaven given to Nebuchadnezzar. *Dan* 2:38
covenant for them with *f. of heaven.* *Hos* 2:18
languish with *f. of heaven.* 4:3
down as the *f. of heaven.* 7:12
consume *f. of the heaven.* *Zeph* 1:3
f. of heaven lodged in. *Luke* 13:19

fox
The Hebrew word Shual *is used generally of any sort of fox or of jackal, which really belongs to the dog family. Most probably jackals are intended in* Judg 15:4, *as they were much more numerous, and remained in packs, which made them easier to capture. Although several species of foxes are found in Palestine, it is impossible to decide with certainty in any particular case which species is intended, if it is not the jackal.*

a *f.* break down stone. *Neh* 4:3
go and tell that *f.* I cast. *Luke* 13:32

foxes
caught three hundred *f.* *Judg* 15:4
shall be a portion for *f.* *Ps* 63:10
take the *f.* the little *f.* *S of S* 2:15
Zion is desolate, *f.* walk. *Lam* 5:18
thy prophets are like *f.* *Ezek* 13:4
f. have holes. *Mat* 8:20; *Luke* 9:58

fragments
(*Revisions substitute for this* broken pieces)
up *f.* twelve baskets full. *Mat* 14:20
Mark 6:43; *Luke* 9:17; *John* 6:13
baskets full of *f.*? *Mark* 8:19, 20
gather up *f.* that remain. *John* 6:12

frail
I may know how *f.* I am. *Ps* 39:4

frame
he knoweth our *f.* *Ps* 103:14
which was as *f.* of a city. *Ezek* 40:2

frame, *verb*
could not *f.* to pronounce. *Judg* 12:6
behold, I *f.* evil against. *Jer* 18:11
will not *f.* their doings. *Hos* 5:4*

framed
thing *f.* say to him that *f.* it? *Isa* 29:16†
building fitly *f.* groweth. *Eph* 2:21
worlds *f.* by word of God. *Heb* 11:3

frameth
evil, thy tongue *f.* deceit. *Ps* 50:19
f. mischief by a law. 94:20

frankincense
spices with pure *f.* *Ex* 30:34
put *f.* thereon. *Lev* 2:1, 15; 5:11
24:7; *Num* 5:15
oil with all the *f.* thereof. *Lev* 2:2
priest shall burn the oil with all *f.* 16; 6:15
appointed to oversee *f.* *1 Chr* 9:29
where they laid the *f.* *Neh* 13:5
brought I the vessels and the *f.* 9

comes perfumed with *f.*? *S of S* 3:6
I will get me to the hill of *f.* 4:6
cinnamon, with all trees of *f.* 14
presented to him gold, *f.* *Mat* 2:11
no man buyeth *f.* wine. *Rev* 18:13

frankly

nothing to pay, he *f.* *Luke* 7:42*

fraud

his mouth is full of cursing and *f.*
Ps 10:7*
kept back by *f.* crieth. *Jas* 5:4

fray

(*American Revision substitutes for this* frighten)
no man shall *f.* them away.
Deut 28:26; *Jer* 7:33
these are come to *f.* them. *Zech* 1:21

freckled

a *f.* spot that groweth. *Lev* 13:39*

free

an Hebrew servant, in the seventh year shall go out *f.* *Ex* 21:2
Deut 15:12; *Jer* 34:9, 14
say, I will not go out *f.* *Ex* 21:5
then shall she go out *f.* 11*
he shall let him go *f.* for his. 26
he shall let him go *f.* for tooth's. 27
not be put to death because not *f.*
Lev 19:20
f. from this bitter water. *Num* 5:19
woman be not defiled, shall be *f.* 28
thou sendest him out *f.* *Deut* 15:13
hard when thou sendest him *f.* 18
but he shall be *f.* at home. 24:5
his father's house *f.* *1 Sam* 17:25
the singers, who remaining were *f.*
1 Chr 9:33
as many as were of *f.* *2 Chr* 29:31*
the servant is *f.* from. *Job* 3:19
who sent out the wild ass *f.*? 39:5
uphold me with thy *f.* *Ps* 51:12†
f. among the dead, like slain. 88:5*
king loosed him, let him go *f.* 105:20
to let the oppressed go *f.* *Isa* 58:6
man let his servant go *f.* *Jer* 34:9
caused them whom they let go *f.* 11
and honour not his father or his mother, he shall be *f.* *Mat* 15:6
saith, then are the children *f.* 17:26
it is Corban, he shall be *f.* *Mark* 7:11
truth shall make you *f.* *John* 8:32
sayest thou, ye shall be made *f.*? 33
make you *f.* ye shall be *f.* indeed. 36
but I was *f.* born. *Acts* 22:28*
offence, so is the *f.* gift. *Rom* 5:15
but *f.* gift is of many offences. 16
even so the *f.* gift came upon. 18
being made *f.* from sin. 6:18, 22
servants of sin ye were *f.* 20
her husband be dead, she is *f.* 7:3
Spirit of life made me *f.* 8:2
mayest be made *f.* use. *1 Cor* 7:21
not an apostle? am I not *f.*? 9:1
though I be *f.* from all men. 19
whether bond or *f.* 12:13
there is neither bond nor *f.* *Gal* 3:28
Col 3:11
Jerusalem above, is *f.* *Gal* 4:26
children of bondwoman, but of *f.* 31
wherewith Christ hath made us *f.* 5:1
receive of Lord, bond or *f.* *Eph* 6:8
that word may have *f.* *2 Thes* 3:1*
as *f.* and not using your liberty.
1 Pet 2:16
causeth all, *f.* and bond. *Rev* 13:16
eat flesh of both bond and *f.* 19:18

free *offerings*

brought *f. offerings.* *Ex* 36:3
and publish *f. offerings.* *Amos* 4:5

freed

shall none of you be *f.* *Josh* 9:23*
that is dead is *f.* from sin. *Rom* 6:7*

freedom

with a woman, not *f.* *Lev* 19:20
great sum obtained *f.* *Acts* 22:28*

freely

of every tree *f.* eat. *Gen* 2:16
the fish we did eat *f.* *Num* 11:5
of people had eaten *f.* *1 Sam* 14:30
of chief fathers offered *f.* *Ezra* 2:68
which king hath offered *f.* to. 7:15
I will *f.* sacrifice unto thee. *Ps* 54:6
I will love them *f.* *Hos* 14:4
f. ye have received *f.* give. *Mat* 10:8
let me *f.* speak. *Acts* 2:29
before whom I speak *f.* 26:26
justified *f.* by his grace. *Rom* 3:24
will with him also *f.* give us. 8:32
know things *f.* given us. *1 Cor* 2:12
preached the gospel of God *f.*
2 Cor 11:7
give of fountain of life *f.* *Rev* 21:6
whosoever will, let him take *f.* 22:17

freeman

called, is the Lord's *f.* *1 Cor* 7:22
every bondman and *f.* *Rev* 6:15

freewill

f. to go up to Jerusalem. *Ezra* 7:13

freewill *offering*

who offereth *f. off.* it. *Lev* 22:21
bullock thou mayest offer *f. off.* 23
make sacrifice in *f. off.* *Num* 15:3
with a tribute of *f. off.* *Deut* 16:10
a *f. off.* shalt thou keep. 23:23
beasts besides *f. off.* *Ezra* 1:4
that willingly offered a *f. off.* 3:5
silver thou canst find with *f. off.* 7:16
silver and gold are a *f. off.* 8:28

freewill *offerings*

offer oblation for *f. off.* *Lev* 22:18
beside all your *f. off.* 23:38
Num 29:39
thither bring your *f. off.* *Deut* 12:6
not eat within thy gates *f. off.* 17
Kore was over *f. off.* of. *2 Chr* 31:14
accept the *f. off.* of my. *Ps* 119:108

freewoman

two sons, by bondmaid, and by a *f.*
Gal 4:22
but he of the *f.* was by promise. 23
not be heir with son of the *f.* 30
children of bondwoman, but of *f.* 31

frequent

in prisons more *f.* *2 Cor* 11:23*

fresh

manna was as taste of *f.* *Num* 11:8
my glory was *f.* in me. *Job* 29:20
anointed with *f.* oil. *Ps* 92:10
yield salt water and *f.* *Jas* 3:12*

fresher

flesh shall be *f.* than a. *Job* 33:35

fret

burn it in the fire, it is *f.* *Lev* 13:55

fret, *verb*

provoked her to make her *f.*
1 Sam 1:6
f. not thyself. *Ps* 37:1, 7, 8
Pr 24:19
be hungry, they shall *f.* *Isa* 8:21

fretted

but thou hast *f.* me in. *Ezek* 16:43†

fretteth

and his heart *f.* against. *Pr* 19:3

fretting

the plague is a *f.* leprosy.
Lev 13:51, 52; 14:44

fried

cakes mingled with oil of flour *f.*
Lev 7:12*
Levites to wait about that which is *f.*
1 Chr 23:29*

friend

The friend of the king was a high court official, probably the king's confidential adviser, Gen 26:26; 1 Ki 4:5.

The friend of God is a title given to Abraham because of his close relations with God and his faithfulness, 2 Chr. 20:7; Jas 2:23.

The word friend was used as a general salutation, whether to friend or foe, Mat 22:12; 26:50.

sent kid by hand of his *f.* *Gen* 38:20
God spake to Moses as a man to *f.*
Ex 33:11
or if thy wife or *f.* entice. *Deut* 13:6
companion whom he used as his *f.*
Judg 14:20
Amnon had a *f.* his. *2 Sam* 13:3
Hushai David's *f.* came into city.
15:37; 16:16
this thy kindness to thy *f.*? why wentest thou not with thy *f.*? 16:17
Zabud was principal officer, the king's *f.* *1 Ki* 4:5
gavest to the seed of Abraham thy *f.*
2 Chr 20:7
pity be shewed from his *f.* *Job* 6:14
and ye dig a pit for your *f.* 27
as though he had been my *f.*
Ps 35:14
my familiar *f.* hath lifted up. 41:9
lover and *f.* hast thou put far. 88:18
be surety for thy *f.* *Pr* 6:1*
hand of thy *f.*; make sure thy *f.* 3*
f. loveth at all times. 17:17
surety in the presence of his *f.* 18
a *f.* that sticketh closer. 18:24
every man is a *f.* to him that. 19:6
the king shall be his *f.* 22:11
faithful are the wounds of a *f.* 27:6
so doth sweetness of man's *f.* 9
thine own *f.* and father's *f.* 10
blesseth his *f.* with a loud voice. 14
sharpeneth countenance of his *f.* 17
this is my *f.* O daughter. *S of S* 5:16
seed of Abraham my *f.* *Isa* 41:8
neighbour and his *f.* *Jer* 6:21
eat every one flesh of his *f.* 19:9
beloved of her *f.* yet an. *Hos* 3:1
trust ye not in a *f.* put. *Mi* 7:5
behold, a *f.* of publicans. *Mat* 11:19
Luke 7:34
f. I do thee no wrong. *Mat* 20:13
f. how camest thou hither? 22:12
f. wherefore art thou come? 26:50
which of you have a *f.* and go at midnight and say, *f.* lend. *Luke* 11:5
for a *f.* of mine in his journey. 6
not give him because he is his *f.* 8
bade thee say, *f.* go up higher. 14:10
the *f.* of the bridegroom. *John* 3:29
our *f.* Lazarus sleepeth. 11:11
this man go, art not Cesar's *f.* 19:12
made Blastus their *f.* *Acts* 12:20
Abraham called *f.* of God. *Jas* 2:23
will be a *f.* of the world. 4:4

friendly

Levite went to speak *f.* *Judg* 19:3*
thou hast spoken *f.* to. *Ruth* 2:13*
must shew himself *f.* *Pr* 18:24*

friends

David sent spoil to his *f.* *1 Sam* 30:26
shew kindness to Saul's *f.* *2 Sam* 3:8
thine enemies, hatest thy *f.* 19:6*
left him not one of his *f.* *1 Ki* 16:11
sent and called for his *f.* *Esth* 5:10
said his wife and all his *f.* 14
Haman told his wife and *f.* 6:13
when Job's three *f.* heard. *Job* 2:11
my *f.* scorn me, but mine eye. 16:20
speaketh flattery to his *f.* 17:5
familiar *f.* have forgotten me. 19:14
all my inward *f.* abhorred me. 19
have pity on me, O ye *f.* 21
Elihu's wrath kindled against *f.* 32:3
Lord's wrath kindled against *f.* 42:7
Lord turned when he prayed for *f.* 10
my *f.* stand aloof. *Ps* 38:11
is hated, rich hath *f.* *Pr* 14:20
whisperer separateth chief *f.* 16:28
a matter, separateth *f.* 17:9
hath *f.* shew himself friendly. 18:24
wealth maketh many *f.* but. 19:4
how much more do his *f.* go. 7
eat, O *f.*; drink, yea. *S of S* 5:1
thee a terror to thy *f.* *Jer* 20:4
shalt be buried there, thou and *f.* 6
thy *f.* have set thee on. 38:22*
f. have dealt treacherously. *Lam* 1:2
wounded in house of my *f.* *Zech* 13:6
when his *f.* heard of it. *Mark* 3:21
go home to thy *f.* 5:19
centurion sent *f.* to him. *Luke* 7:6
my *f.* be not afraid of them. 12:4
a dinner, call not thy *f.* 14:12
he calleth together his *f.* 15:6
she calleth her *f.* and neighbours. 9
make merry with my *f.* 29

yieldeth peaceable *f.* of *Heb* 12:11
the tree *yielded* her *f.* *Rev* 22:2

fruitful

saying, Be *f.* and multiply. *Gen* 1:22
28; 8:17; 9:7; 35:11
I will make thee exceeding *f.* 17:6
I will make Ishmael *f.* 20
room for us, we shall be *f.* 26:22
bless thee, and make thee *f.* 28:3
make Jacob *f.* 48:4
Joseph is a *f.* bough, a *f.* 49:22
children of Israel were *f.* *Ex* 1:7
I will make you *f.* and. *Lev* 26:9
he turneth a *f.* land into. *Ps* 107:34
thy wife shall be as a *f.* vine. 128:3
mountains and *f.* trees, praise. 148:9
beloved hath vineyard in a *f.* hill. *Isa* 5:1
four or five in the outmost *f.* 17:6
shall lament for the *f.* vine. 32:12
f. place was a wilderness. *Jer* 4:26
they shall be *f.* and increase. 23:3
was *f.* and full of. *Ezek* 19:10
though he be *f.* an east. *Hos* 13:15
gave us rain and *f.* *Acts* 14:17
being *f.* in every good. *Col* 1:10
see **field**

fruits

take of the best *f.* in land. *Gen* 43:11
to offer first of ripe *f.* *Ex* 22:29
six years gather in the *f.* 23:10
according to years of the *f.* *Lev* 25:15*, 16*
till her *f.* come in. 22
neither the trees yield their *f.* 26:20
precious *f.* brought forth. *Deut* 33:14
thy sons shall bring in *f.* *2 Sam* 9:10
restore to her all the *f.* of. *2 Ki* 8:6
and eat the *f.* thereof. 19:29
if I have eaten the *f.* *Job* 31:39
fields, which may yield *f.* *Ps* 107:37
I planted trees of all kind of *f.* *Eccl* 2:5
orchard with pleasant *f.* *S of S* 4:13
my beloved eat his pleasant *f.* 16
I went down to see the *f.* of. 6:11*
gates all manner of pleasant *f.* 7:13
and Carmel shake off *f.* *Isa* 33:9*
pine away for want of *f.* *Lam* 4:9
not destroy the *f.* of your. *Mal* 3:11
bring *f.* meet for repentance. *Mat* 3:8; *Luke* 3:8
know them by their *f.* *Mat* 7:16, 20
that they receive the *f.* of it. 21:34
who shall render him the *f.* in. 41
given to a nation bringing *f.* 43
I have no room where to bestow my *f.* *Luke* 12:17
there will I bestow all my *f.* 18*
increase the *f.* of your. *2 Cor* 9:10
filled with the *f.* of. *Phil* 1:11
husbandman first partaker of the *f.* *2 Tim* 2:6
wisdom from above full of good *f.* *Jas* 3:17
f. thy soul lusted after. *Rev* 18:14
of life bare twelve manner of *f.* 22:2
see **first**

summer **fruits**

hundred of *summer f.* *2 Sam* 16:1
summer f. and harvest. *Isa* 16:9
ye wine and *summer f.* *Jer* 40:10
wine and *summer f.* very much. 12
spoiler is fallen on *summer f.* 48:32
when they gathered the *summer f.* *Mi* 7:1

fruit trees

and possessed *f. trees.* *Neh* 9:25

frustrate

hired counsellors to *f.* *Ezra* 4:5
I do not *f.* grace of God. *Gal* 2:21*

frustrateth

that *f.* the tokens of liars. *Isa* 44:25

fryingpan

be a meat offering in the *f.* *Lev* 2:7
all that is dressed in the *f.* 7:9

fuel

be with burning and *f.* of. *Isa* 9:5
people shall be as *f.* of the fire. 19
vine tree is cast into the fire for *f.* *Ezek* 15:4, 6
thou shalt be for *f.* to the fire, 21:32

fugitive

a *f.* and a vagabond. *Gen* 4:12
I shall be a *f.* and a vagabond. 14

fugitives

Gileadites *f.* of Ephraim. *Judg* 12:4
and the *f.* that fell away. *2 Ki* 25:11
cry for Moab, his *f.* shall. *Isa* 15:5*
all his *f.* shall fall by. *Ezek* 17:21

fulfil

f. her week, and we will. *Gen* 29:27
f. your works. *Ex* 5:13
number of thy days I will *f.* 23:26
he might *f.* the word. *1 Ki* 2:27
if thou takest heed to *f.* *1 Chr* 22:13*
to *f.* threescore and. *2 Chr* 36:21
canst thou number months they *f.*? *Job* 39:2
Lord grant thee, and *f.* all. *Ps* 20:4
the Lord *f.* all thy petitions. 5
he will *f.* the desire of them. 145:19
becometh us to *f.* all. *Mat* 3:15
not come to destroy, but to *f.* 5:17
David, who shall *f.* my. *Acts* 13:22*
if it *f.* the law. *Rom* 2:27
for the flesh, to *f.* the lusts. 13:14
ye shall not *f.* the lust. *Gal* 5:16
and so *f.* the law of Christ. 6:2
f. ye my joy, that ye be. *Phil* 2:2
given to me, to *f.* word. *Col* 1:25
heed ministry, that thou *f.* 4:17
f. good pleasure of his. *2 Thes* 1:11
if ye *f.* the royal law. *Jas* 2:8
put in their hearts to *f.* *Rev* 17:17*

fulfilled

to be delivered were *f.* *Gen* 25:24
my wife, for my days are *f.* 29:21
forty days were *f.* for so are *f.* 50:3
have ye not *f.* your task? *Ex* 5:14
seven days *f.* after Lord hath. 7:25
till purification be *f.* *Lev* 12:4, 6
of his separation are *f.* *Num* 6:13
when days be *f.* and. *2 Sam* 7:12
in that the king *f.* request. 14:22
hath with his hand *f.* it. *1 Ki* 8:15
hast *f.* it with hand. 24; *2 Chr* 6:15
the Lord hath *f.* that. *2 Chr* 6:4
word of Lord might be *f.* *Ezra* 1:1
thou hast *f.* judgement. *Job* 36:17*
and your wives have *f.* *Jer* 44:25
he hath *f.* his word he. *Lam* 2:17
our days are *f.* our end is. 4:18
when days of siege are *f.* *Ezek* 5:2
the same hour was thing *f.* *Dan* 4:33
till three whole weeks were *f.* 10:3
that it might be *f.* *Mat* 1:22; 2:15
23; 8:17; 12:17; 13:35; 21:4
27:35; *John* 12:38; 15:25; 17:12
18:9, 32; 19:24, 28, 36
f. that which was spoken. *Mat* 2:17
27:9
pass from law till all be *f.* 5:18
in them is *f.* the prophecy. 13:14
not pass till these things be *f.* 24:34
the time is *f.* kingdom. *Mark* 1:15
sign when these things be *f.*? 13:4*
words which shall be *f.* *Luke* 1:20
when they had *f.* the days. 2:43
all things written may be *f.* 21:22
until times of Gentiles be *f.* 24
not eat till it be *f.* in kingdom. 22:16
all things must be *f.* 24:44
this my joy therefore is *f.* *John* 3:29†
they might have my joy *f.* in. 17:13†
God shewed, he hath *f.* *Acts* 3:18
after many days were *f.* Jews. 9:23
and Barnabas *f.* their ministry. 12:25
and as John *f.* his course. 13:25
have *f.* them in condemning. 27
had *f.* all that was written of. 29
God hath *f.* the same to us. 33
grace of God for work they *f.* 14:26
righteousness of law might be *f.* in. *Rom* 8:4
loveth another hath *f.* the law. 13:8
when obedience is *f.* *2 Cor* 10:6
law is *f.* in one word. *Gal* 5:14
killing of brethren be *f.* *Rev* 6:11
plagues of seven angels *f.* 15:8*
till words of God be *f.* 17:17*
no more, till 1000 years be *f.* 20:3*
see **scripture**

fulfilling

fire, hail, stormy wind *f.* *Ps* 148:8
love is the *f.* of the law. *Rom* 13:10
f. the desires of the flesh. *Eph* 2:3*

full

of Amorites not yet *f.* *Gen* 15:16
Abraham an old man, and *f.* 25:8
Isaac old and *f.* of days. 35:29
at the end of two *f.* years. 41:1
thin ears devoured seven *f.* 7, 22
money in his sack *f.* weight. 43:21
be *f.* of swarms of flies. *Ex* 8:21
an homer *f.* of manna therein. 16:33
he should make *f.* restitution. 22:3
corn beaten out of *f.* ears. *Lev* 2:14
censer *f.* of coals, hands *f.* of. 16:12
land became *f.* of wickedness. 19:29
within a *f.* year redeem it. 25:29
if not redeemed in a *f.* year. 30
both *f.* of fine flour. *Num* 7:13, 19
25, 31, 37, 43, 49, 55, 61, 67, 73, 79
spoon of ten shekels *f.* of. 14, 20, 26
32, 38, 44, 50, 56, 62, 68, 74, 80, 86
Balak give house *f.* of. 22:18; 24:13
houses *f.* of good things, have eaten and be *f.* *Deut* 6:11; 8:10, 12
will send grass, that thou mayest eat and be *f.* 11:15
bewail her father a *f.* month. 21:13
Naphtali *f.* of the blessing. 33:23
Joshua was *f.* of Spirit of. 34:9
dew, a bowl *f.* of water. *Judg* 6:38
house was *f.* of men and. 16:27
I went out *f.* and Lord. *Ruth* 1:21
and a *f.* reward be given thee. 2:12
they that were *f.* hired. *1 Sam* 2:5
they gave them in *f.* tale. 18:27
in country of Philistines a *f.* 27:7
and with one *f.* line to. *2 Sam* 8:2
make valley *f.* of ditches. *2 Ki* 3:16
when vessels were *f.* she said. 4:6
mountain was *f.* of horses. 6:17
all the way was *f.* of garments. 7:15
house of Baal was *f.* from one. 10:21
grant it me for *f.* price. *1 Chr* 21:22
I will verily buy it for a *f.* price. 24
David old and *f.* of. 23:1; 29:28
was Haman *f.* of wrath. *Esth* 3:5
f. of indignation against. 5:9
come to grave in a *f.* age. *Job* 5:26
I am *f.* of tossings to and fro. 7:4
I am *f.* of confusion. 10:15
a man *f.* of talk be justified? 11:2
man is of few days *f.* of trouble. 14:1
bones are *f.* of sins of youth. 20:11
one dieth in his *f.* strength. 21:23
his breasts are *f.* of milk, his. 24
I am *f.* of matter, the Spirit. 32:18
on thy table should be *f.* of. 36:16
Job died, old and *f.* of days. 42:17
they are *f.* of children. *Ps* 17:14*
broken my heart, I am *f.* of. 69:20
waters of a *f.* cup are wrung. 73:10
dark places *f.* of habitations of. 74:20
sent meat to the *f.* 78:25
trees of Lord are *f.* of sap. 104:16*
happy that hath quiver *f.* of. 127:5
that our garners may be *f.* 144:13
an house *f.* of sacrifices. *Pr* 17:1
the *f.* soul loatheth honeycomb. 27:7
hell and destruction are never *f.* 20
lest I be *f.* and deny thee. 30:9
yet the sea is not *f.* *Eccl* 1:7
all things are *f.* of labour. 8
than both hands *f.* with travel. 4:6*
if the clouds be *f.* of rain. 11:3
I am *f.* of burnt offerings. *Isa* 1:11
your hands are *f.* of blood. 15
faithful city *f.* of judgement. 21
earth shall be *f.* of knowledge. 11:9
houses shall be *f.* of doleful. 13:21
waters of Dimon *f.* of blood. 15:9
thou art *f.* of stirs 22:2
valleys shall be *f.* of chariots. 7
a feast *f.* of marrow. 25:6
tables are *f.* of vomit and. 28:8
his lips are *f.* of indignation. 30:27
they are *f.* of the fury of. 51:20
a *f.* wind from those. *Jer* 4:12
when I had fed them to the *f.* 5:7
I am *f.* of the fury of the Lord. 6:11
within two *f.* years will I. 28:3, 11
the Rechabites pots *f.* of wine. 35:5

city sit solitary that was f. Lam 1:1
he is filled f. with reproach. 3:30
their wings were f. of. Ezek 1:18
court was f. of the brightness. 10:4
the wheels were f. of eyes. 12
great eagle with wings f. of. 17:3
fruitful and f. of branches. 19:10
the sum, f. of wisdom and. 28:12
rivers shall be f. of thee. 32:6
in midst of valley which was f. 37:1
ye shall eat fat till ye be f. and. 39:19
then was Nebuchadnezzar f. of fury. Dan 3:19
transgressors are come to f. 8:23
Daniel mourned three f. weeks. 10:2
floors shall be f. of wheat. Joel 2:24
but truly I am f. of power. Mi 3:8
the rich men are f. of violence. 6:12
earth was f. of his praise. Hab 3:3
streets shall be f. of boys. Zech 8:5
thy body shall be f. of light. Mat 6:22; Luke 11:36
when it was f. they drew. Mat 13:48
twelve baskets f. 14:20; Mark 6:43
left seven baskets f. Mat 15:37
but within are f. of extortion. 23:25
within f. of dead men's bones. 27
within ye are f. of hypocrisy. 28
f. well ye reject commandment of. Mark 7:9
filled a spunge f. of vinegar. 15:36
now Elizabeth's f. time. Luke 1:57
Jesus being f. of the Holy Ghost. 4:1
behold a man f. of leprosy fell. 5:12
woe unto you that are f. 6:25
Lazarus laid at his gate f. of. 16:20
among us, f. of grace. John 1:14
for my time is not yet f. come. 7:8
that your joy be f. 15:11; 16:24
was set a vessel f. of vinegar. 19:29
men are f. of new wine. Acts 2:13
shalt make me f. of joy. 28
look out men f. of Holy Ghost. 6:3
Stephen f. of faith and. 5, 8; 7:55
Moses was f. forty years old. 7:23
Dorcas f. of good works. 9:36
Barnabas f. of the Holy Ghost. 11:24
O f. of all subtilty and. 13:10
they were f. of wrath and. 19:28
being f. of envy, murder. Rom 1:29
ye also are f. of goodness. 15:14
now ye are f. now ye are. 1 Cor 4:8
and was f. of heaviness. Phil 2:26*
I am instructed to be f. and. 4:12
I have all and abound, I am f. 18
f. proof of thy ministry. 2 Tim 4:5
meat to them of f. age. Heb 5:14*
tongue an unruly evil, f. Jas 3:8
wisdom from above is pure, f. 17
with joy unspeakable, f. of. 1 Pet 1:8
eyes f. of adultery. 2 Pet 2:14
that your joy may be f. 1 John 1:4
that we receive a f. reward. 2 John 8
to face, that our joy may be f. 12
four beasts f. of eyes. Rev 4:6, 8
every one golden vials f. of. 5:8
seven golden vials f. of wrath. 15:7
kingdom was f. of darkness. 16:10*
I saw a woman f. of names of. 17:3
a golden cup f. of abominations. 4
seven vials f. of seven last. 21:9
see **assurance, compassion**

is full

set aside that which is f. 2 Ki 4:4
his mouth is f. of cursing. Ps 10:7
Rom 3:14
right hand is f. of bribes. Ps 26:10
of the Lord is f. of majesty. 29:4
earth is f. of goodness of the. 33:5
hand is f. of righteousness. 48:10
river of God, which is f. of. 65:9
wine is red, it is f. of mixture. 75:8
my soul is f. of troubles. 88:3
the earth is f. of thy riches. 104:24
earth is f. of thy mercy. 119:64
heart of sons of men is f. of. Eccl 9:3
a fool is f. of words. 10:14*
land is f. of silver, is f. of. Isa 2:7
their land also is f. of idols. 8
the whole earth is f. of his. 6:3
as a cage is f. of birds. Jer 5:27
with him that is f. of days. 6:11
the land is f. of adulterers. 23:10
land is f. of crimes, city is f. of. Ezek 7:23
land is f. of blood, city is f. of. 9:9
for the press is f. the fats. Joel 3:13
cart is pressed, that is f. of sheaves. Amos 2:13
it is all f. of lies and. Nah 3:1
body is f. of light, is f. of. Luke 11:34
inward part is f. of ravening. 39

to the **full**

and did eat bread to the f. Ex 16:3
when Lord shall give bread in morning to the f. 8
eat your bread to the f. Lev 26:5

fuller, -s

and stood in the highway of the f.'s field. 2 Ki 18:17; Isa 7:3; 36:2
like a refiner's fire, and f.'s. Mal 3:2
so as no f. on earth can. Mark 9:3

fully

Caleb followed me f. Num 14:24
Boaz said, it hath f. been. Ruth 2:11
Solomon went not f. after. 1 Ki 11:6
heart of men is f. set to. Eccl 8:11
devoured as stubble f. Nah 1:10*
day of Pentecost f. come. Acts 2:1
being f. persuaded, that. Rom 4:21
let every man be f. persuaded. 14:5
I have f. preached the gospel. 15:19
thou hast f. known my. 2 Tim 3:10
by me preaching might be f. 4:17
thrust in sickle, grapes f. Rev 14:18

fulness

the f. of the winepress. Num 18:27
precious things of the earth, f. Deut 33:16
the sea roar and the f. thereof. 1 Chr 16:32; Ps 96:11; 98:7
in f. of sufficiency shall. Job 20:22
in thy presence is f. of joy. Ps 16:11
earth is the Lord's and the f. 24:1
1 Cor 10:26, 28
the world is mine, and f. thereof. Ps 50:12; 89:11
iniquity of Sodom, f. of. Ezek 16:49
of his f. have we received grace for. John 1:16
how much more their f.? Rom 11:12
till f. of Gentiles be come in. 25
come in the f. of the gospel. 15:29
when f. of time was come. Gal 4:4
that in the f. of times he. Eph 1:10
the f. of him that filleth all in all. 23
be filled with the f. of God. 3:19
come to stature of f. of Christ. 4:13
in him should all f. dwell. Col 1:19
in him dwelleth f. of Godhead. 2:9

furbish

f. the spears, put on the. Jer 46:4

furbished

a sword is sharpened and also f. Ezek 21:9, 10
given to be f. 11
sword f. to consume. 28

furious

(*Revisions substitute* wrathful)
with f. man thou shalt. Pr 22:24
a f. man aboundeth in. 29:22
execute judgement in f. rebukes. Ezek 5:15; 25:17
Nebuchadnezzar the king was very f. Dan 2:12
Lord revengeth, and is f. Nah 1:2

furiously

of Jehu, he driveth f. 2 Ki 9:20
they shall deal f. with. Ezek 23:25*

furlongs

(*A furlong was about an eighth of a mile*)
from Jerusalem sixty f. Luke 24:13
rowed about five and twenty f. John 6:19
nigh Jerusalem about fifteen f. 11:18
out by space of 1600 f. Rev 14:20
the city with reed, 12,000 f. 21:16

furnace

[1] *An oven for smelting iron from the ore,* Deut 4:20; 1 Ki 8:51. [2] *A crucible for refining gold and silver,* Pr 17:3; Ezek 22:20. [3] *A bake oven,* Neh 3:11; Isa 31:9.

a smoking f. and a. Gen 15:17
went up as the smoke of a f. 19:28
handfuls of ashes of the f. Ex 9:8
and they took ashes of the f. 10
ascended as the smoke of a f. 19:18
taken you out of the f. Deut 4:20
from the midst of the f. 1 Ki 8:51
Jer 11:4
pure words, as silver tried in a f. of earth. Ps 12:6
as the f. for gold. Pr 17:3; 27:21
his f. in Jerusalem. Isa 31:9
chosen thee in f. of affliction. 48:10
dross in midst of the f. Ezek 22:18
gather you as tin in midst of f. 20
silver melted in midst of the f. 22
be cast into midst of a burning fiery f. Dan 3:6, 11
cast them into a f. Mat 13:42, 50
brass, as if burned in a f. Rev 1:15
a smoke, as smoke of a great f. 9:2

furnaces

Hashub repaired tower of f. Neh 3:11
from the tower of the f. to. 12:38

furnish

shalt f. him liberally. Deut 15:14
can God f. a table in ? Ps 78:19*
that f. the drink offering. Isa 65:11*
f. thyself to go into. Jer 46:19

furnished

Hiram f. Solomon with. 1 Ki 9:11
she hath also f. her table. Pr 9:2
wedding f. with guests. Mat 22:10*
will shew you a room f. Mark 14:15
Luke 22:12
throughly f. unto all. 2 Tim 3:17

furniture

(*General meaning, fittings*)
put them in camels' f. Gen 31:34
tabernacle and his f. Ex 31:7; 39:33
table and his f. 8*
altar with all his f. 9*
the candlestick and his f. 35:14*
none end of all pleasant f. Nah 2:9

furrow

bind the unicorn in the f.? Job 39:10

furrows

or the f. thereof likewise. Job 31:38
thou settlest the f. Ps 65:10
plowed, made long their f. 129:3
might water it by f. of. Ezek 17:7*
it shall wither in the f. where. 10*
as hemlock in the f. of. Hos 10:4
bind themselves in their two f. 10*
their altars as heaps in the f. 12:11

further

angel went f. and stood. Num 22:26
officers shall speak f. to. Deut 20:8
inquired of the Lord f. 1 Sam 10:22
shalt thou come, but no f. Job 38:11
yea, twice, will proceed no f. 40:5
f. by these, my son, be admonished. Eccl 12:12
f. need have we of witnesses ? Mat 26:65; Mark 14:63; Luke 22:71
why troublest Master f.? Mark 5:35
as he would have gone f. Luke 24:28
that it spread no f. Acts 4:17
when they had f. threatened them. 21
Herod proceeded f. to take. 12:3
f. he brought Greeks also. 21:28
that I be not f. tedious. 24:4
they had gone a little f. 27:28*
they shall proceed no f. 2 Tim 3:9
f. need another priest. Heb 7:11

further, *verb*

f. not his wicked device. Ps 140:8

furtherance

things which happened have fallen out unto f. of gospel. Phil 1:12*
shall abide with you for your f. 25*

furthered

f. the people and house of. Ezra 8:36

furthermore

the Lord said f. to Moses. Ex 4:6
Lord said f. to Ezekiel. Ezek 8:6

fury
(*American Revision usually substitutes* wrath)
tarry, till brother's *f.* *Gen* 27:44
walk contrary to you in *f.* *Lev* 26:28
God shall cast the *f.* of. *Job* 20:23*
f. is not in me, who. *Isa* 27:4
his *f.* is upon all their armies. 34:2
feared because of *f.* of the oppressor; where is the *f.* of the ? 51:13
which hast drunk cup of his *f.* 17
they are full of the *f.* of the Lord. 20
even the dregs of cup of my *f.* 22
repay *f.* to his adversaries. 59:18
I will trample them in my *f.* 63:3
arm brought salvation, my *f.* it. 5
I will make them drunk in my *f.* 6
to render his anger with *f.* 66:15†
lest my *f.* come forth like. *Jer* 4:4
I am full of the *f.* of the Lord. 6:11
I will fight against you in *f.* 21:5
lest *f.* go out like fire and burn. 12
a whirlwind is gone forth in *f.* 23:19
30:23
take the wine cup of this *f.* 25:15
city hath been a provocation of my *f.* 32:31
slain in mine anger and *f.* 33:5
great is the *f.* the Lord hath. 36:7
hath accomplished his *f.* *Lam* 4:11
cause my *f.* to rest on them ... I have accomplished my *f.* *Ezek* 5:13
when I execute judgements in *f.* 15
thus will I accomplish my *f.* 6:12
therefore will I deal in *f.* 8:18
with a stormy wind in my *f.* 13:13
I will give thee blood in *f.* 16:38
make my *f.* towards thee to rest. 42
she was plucked up in my *f.* 19:12
with *f.* poured out will I rule. 20:33
I will cause my *f.* to rest. 21:17
gather you in mine anger and *f.* 22:20
that it might cause *f.* to come. 24:8
till I have caused my *f.* to rest. 13
do in Edom according to my *f.* 25:14
in my jealousy and in my *f.* 36:6
f. shall come up in my face. 38:18
Nebuchadnezzar in his *f.* *Dan* 3:13
was Nebuchadnezzar full of *f.* 19
ran unto him in the *f.* of his. 8:6
let thy *f.* be turned away from. 9:16
shall go forth with great *f.* to. 11:44
will execute *f.* on heathen. *Mi* 5:15
jealous for her with great *f.* *Zech* 8:2
see **pour, poured**

G

Gaal
Zebul thrust out *G.* *Judg* 9:41

Gabbatha
pavement, in Hebrew, *G.* *John* 19:13

Gabriel
G. make this man understand. *Dan* 8:16
while I was praying, the man *G.* 9:21
I am *G.* that stand in. *Luke* 1:19
the angel *G.* was sent from God. 26

Gad
she called his name *G.* *Gen* 30:11
sons of Zilpah, *G.* and Asher. 35:26
sons of *G.* 46:16; *Num* 1:24; 26:15
18; *1 Chr* 12:14
G. troop shall overcome. *Gen* 49:19
prince of *G.* *Num* 1:14; 2:14; 7:42
children of *G.* had a multitude. 32:1
children of *G.* came and spake. 2
children of *G.* will pass over. 29
Moses gave to *G.* the kingdom of. 33
tribe of the children of *G.* have.
34:14; *Josh* 13:28; 18:7
mount Ebal to curse *G.* *Deut* 27:13
and of *G.* he said, Blessed be he that enlargeth *G.* 33:20
the children of *G.* passed. *Josh* 4:12
the children of *G.* returned out. 22:9
went to land of *G.* *1 Sam* 13:7
the midst of river of *G.* *2 Sam* 24:5
to the prophet *G.* David's seer. 11
1 Chr 21:9, 18
David said unto *G.* I am in a. 14
according to the saying of *G.* 19
are in the book of *G.* *1 Chr* 29:29
to command of *G.* *2 Chr* 29:25
their king inherit *G.*? *Jer* 49:1
a portion for *G.* *Ezek* 48:27
one gate of *G.* 34

tribe of **Gad**
of *tribe of G.* 45,650. *Num* 1:25
then the *tribe of G.* shall set forward, captain of *G.* shall. 2:14; 10:20
of *tribe of G.* to spy the land. 13:15
tribe of the children of *G.* have.
34:14; *Josh* 13:24
assigned Ramoth in Gilead out of the *tribe of G.* *Josh* 20:8; 21:7
38; *1 Chr* 6:63, 80
tribe of G. were sealed 12,000.
Rev 7:5

Gadarenes
into country of the *G.* *Mark* 5:1
Luke 8:26
country of *G.* besought. *Luke* 8:37

gaddest
why *g.* thou about to ? *Jer* 2:36

Gadite, -s
gave I unto the *G.* *Deut* 3:12, 16
the Reubenites and *G.* *Josh* 22:1
Bani *G.* one of David's. *2 Sam* 23:36
Hazael smote the *G.* *2 Ki* 10:33
of the *G.* there separated. *1 Chr* 12:8
made rulers over the *G.* 26:32

gain
kings of Canaan took no *g.* *Judg* 5:19
is it *g.* to him to make ? *Job* 22:3
of every one greedy of *g.* *Pr* 1:19
the *g.* thereof is better than. 3:14
that is greedy of *g.* troubleth. 15:27
that by usury and unjust *g.* 28:8*
he that despiseth the *g.* of. *Isa* 33:15
every one for his *g.* from his. 56:11
hand at thy dishonest *g.* *Ezek* 22:13
like as wolves to get dishonest *g.* 27
divide the land for *g.* *Dan* 11:39
I will consecrate their *g.* *Mi* 4:13
her masters much *g.* *Acts* 16:16
brought no small *g.* to the. 19:24*
did I make a *g.* of you? *2 Cor* 12:17*
did Titus make a *g.* of you ? 18*
Christ, and to die is *g.* *Phil* 1:21
what things were *g.* to me. 3:7
supposing that *g.* is. *1 Tim* 6:5
with contentment is great *g.* 6
there buy, sell and get *g.* *Jas* 4:13

gain, *verb*
I know that ye would *g.* *Dan* 2:8
g. the whole world, and ? *Mat* 16:26
Mark 8:36; *Luke* 9:25
to all, that I might *g.* the. *1 Cor* 9:19
that I might *g.* the Jews. 20
that I might *g.* them that are. 21
g. the weak. 22

gained
what is the hope of the hypocrite, though he hath *g.*? *Job* 27:8
thou hast greedily *g.* by. *Ezek* 22:12
if he hear, thou hast *g.* *Mat* 18:15
received two had also *g.* 25:17, 22
have *g.* besides them five talents. 20
much every man had *g.* *Luke* 19:15
thy pound hath *g.* ten pounds. 16
thy pound hath *g.* five pounds. 18
and to have *g.* this harm. *Acts* 27:21*

gains
hope of their *g.* was. *Acts* 16:19

gainsay
shall not be able to *g.* *Luke* 21:15

gainsayers
be able to convince the *g.* *Tit* 1:9

gainsaying
came I to you without *g.* *Acts* 10:29
forth my hands to a *g.* *Rom* 10:21
they have perished in the *g.* *Jude* 11

Gaius
having caught *G.* a man. *Acts* 19:29
G. of Derbe accompanied Paul. 20:4
G. mine host saluteth. *Rom* 16:23
none but Crispus and *G.* *1 Cor* 1:14
unto the wellbeloved *G.* *3 John* 1

Galatia
had gone through the region of *G.*
Acts 16:6; 18:23
order to churches of *G.* *1 Cor* 16:1
is departed to *G.* *2 Tim* 4:10
through Pontus, *G.* *1 Pet* 1:1

Galatians
O foolish *G.* who hath ? *Gal* 3:1

galbanum
spices, onycha, and *g.* *Ex* 30:34

Galeed
Jacob called the heap *G.* *Gen* 31:47
was the name of it called *G.* 48

Galilean, -s
art a *G.* *Mark* 14:70; *Luke* 22:59
some told him of the *G.* *Luke* 13:1
these *G.* were sinners above all *G.*? 2
whether the man were a *G.*? 23:6
he was come, the *G.* *John* 4:45
all these that speak, *G.*? *Acts* 2:7

Galilee
Kedesh in *G.* for a city. *Josh* 20:7
Kedesh in *G.* to. 21:32; *1 Chr* 6:76
Hiram 20 cities in *G.* *1 Ki* 9:11
took Ijon and *G.* *2 Ki* 15:29
grievously afflict her in *G.* *Isa* 9:1
turned into parts of *G.* *Mat* 2:22
cometh Jesus from *G.* to John. 3:13
Mark 1:9
G. of the Gentiles. *Mat* 4:15
walking by sea of *G.* 18; *Mark* 1:16
there followed multitudes from *G.*
Mat 4:25; *Mark* 3:7
nigh unto the sea of *G.* *Mat* 15:29
Jesus of *G.* 21:11
I will go before you into *G.* 26:32
Mark 14:28
followed Jesus from *G.* *Mat* 27:55
Mark 15:41; *Luke* 23:49, 55
he goeth before you into *G.*
Mat 28:7; *Mark* 16:7
he preached throughout all *G.*
Mark 1:39
power of Spirit into *G.* *Luke* 4:14
he preached in synagogues of *G.* 44
beginning from *G.* to this place. 23:5
of *G.* he asked whether Galilean ? 6
to you when he was in *G.* 24:6
Jesus walked in *G.* *John* 7:1, 41
art thou of *G.*? out of *G.* ariseth. 52
who was of Bethsaida in *G.* 12:21
ye men of *G.* *Acts* 1:11
Judas of *G.* rose up. 5:37
churches rest through all *G.* 9:31
know which began from *G.* 10:37
them that came from *G.* 13:31
see **Cana**

gall
[1] *The bitter secretion from the liver, bile,* Job 16:13; 20:25. [2] *A poisonous, bitter herb, called in the Hebrew,* rosh, Deut 29:18. [3] *Used metaphorically for bitter affliction,* Jer 8:15.
be a root that beareth *g.* *Deut* 29:18
their grapes are grapes of *g.* 32:32
he poureth out my *g.* on. *Job* 16:13
his meat is the *g.* of asps. 20:14
sword cometh out of his *g.* 25
they gave me also *g.* for. *Ps* 69:21
hath given us water of *g.* *Jer* 8:14
give them water of *g.* 9:15; 23:15
hath compassed me with *g.* *Lam* 3:5
the wormwood and the *g.* 19
turned judgement into *g.* *Amos* 6:12
vinegar mingled with *g.* *Mat* 27:34
I perceive thou art in *g.* *Acts* 8:23

gallant
no galley, nor shall *g.* ship. *Isa* 33:21

galleries
king is held in the *g.* *S of S* 7:5*
measured the *g.* thereof. *Ezek* 41:15

gallery
the pavement was *g.* against *g.*
Ezek 42:3

galley
wherein shall go no *g.* *Isa* 33:21

Gallim
Michal to Phalti of *G.* *1 Sam* 25:44
O daughter of *G.* *Isa* 10:30

Gallio
when *G.* was the deputy. *Acts* 18:12
and *G.* cared for none of those. 17

gallows
to hang Mordecai on *g*. *Esth* 6:4
hanged Haman on the *g*. 7:10; 8:7
sons be hanged on the *g*. 9:13, 25

Gamaliel
of Manasseh, *G*. son of. *Num* 1:10
2:20; 7:54, 59; 10:23
a Pharisee named *G*. *Acts* 5:34
brought up at the feet of *G*. 22:3

Gammadims
and the *G*. were in thy. *Ezek* 27:11

gap
man that should stand in *g*. before. *Ezek* 22:30

gaped
have *g*. upon. *Job* 16:10; *Ps* 22:13

gaps
not gone up into the *g*. *Ezek* 13:5

garden
man and put him in *g*. *Gen* 2:15
sent him forth from the *g*. 3:23
plain of Jordan was as the *g*. 13:10
and wateredst it as a *g*. *Deut* 11:10
I may have it for a *g*. *1 Ki* 21:2
shooteth forth in his *g*. *Job* 8:16
g. inclosed is my sister. *S of S* 4:12
my beloved come into his *g*. 16
I am come into my *g*. my sister. 5:1
is gone down into his *g*. 6:2, 11
Zion is as a lodge in a *g*. *Isa* 1:8
ye shall be as a *g*. which hath. 30
desert like the *g*. of God. 51:3
shalt be like a watered *g*. 58:11
as the *g*. causeth things sown. 61:11
shall be as a watered *g*. *Jer* 31:12
away his tabernacle, as it were of a *g*. *Lam* 2:6
in Eden the *g*. of God. *Ezek* 28:13
cedars in *g*. of God could not. 31:8
all the trees in the *g*. of God. 9
land is become like the *g*. of. 36:35
land is as the *g*. of Eden. *Joel* 2:3
took and cast into his *g*. *Luke* 13:19
Cedron, where was a *g*. *John* 18:1
did not I see thee in the *g*.? 26
there was a *g*. and in the *g*. 19:41

gardener
he had been the *g*. *John* 20:15

gardens
thy tents as *g*. by the. *Num* 24:6
I made me *g*. and orchards. *Eccl* 2:5
a fountain of *g*. a well. *S of S* 4:15
to feed in the *g*. and to gather. 6:2
thou that dwellest in the *g*. 8:13
be confounded for the *g*. *Isa* 1:29
a people that sacrificeth in *g*. 65:3
purify themselves in the *g*. 66:17
g. and eat the fruit. *Jer* 29:5, 28
sent blasting, when your *g*. *Amos* 4:9
they shall also make *g*. and 9:14

garlands
brought oxen and *g*. *Acts* 14:13

garlick
we remember the *g*. we. *Num* 11:5

garment
and Japhet took a *g*. *Gen* 9:23
came out red, like a hairy *g*. 25:25
by his *g*. he left his *g*. 39:12
he left his *g*. with me. 15, 18
she laid up his *g*. till her lord. 39:16
blood thereof on any *g*. *Lev* 6:27
g. wherein is the plague. 13:47, 49
if plague be spread in the *g*. in. 51
plague of leprosy in a *g*. 59; 14:55
every *g*. whereon is the seed. 15:17
nor *g*. mingled. 19:9; *Deut* 22:11*
not put on a woman's *g*. *Deut* 22:5
goodly Babylonish *g*. *Josh* 7:21
Achan, the silver, and the *g*. 24
they spread a *g*. and. *Judg* 8:25
Tamar had a *g*. of. *2 Sam* 13:18
she rent her *g*. and went on. 19
clad himself with a new *g*. *1 Ki* 11:29
took every man his *g*. *2 Ki* 9:13
I heard this I rent my *g*. *Ezra* 9:3
having rent my *g*. and mantle I. 5
Mordecai went with a *g*. *Esth* 8:15
consumeth, as a *g*. that. *Job* 13:28
force of my disease is my *g*. 30:18
when I made the cloud the *g*. 38:9
clay to seal, they stand as a *g*. 14
discover the face of his *g*.? *Job* 41:13
sackcloth also my *g*. *Ps* 69:11
violence covereth them as *g*. 73:6
yea all of them shall wax old like a *g*.
102:26; *Isa* 50:9; 51:6, *Heb* 1:11
with light, as with a *g*. *Ps* 104:2
it with the deep as with a *g*. 6
himself with cursing as a *g*. 109:18
as the *g*. which covereth him. 19
g. that is surety. *Pr* 20:16; 27:13
as he that taketh away a *g*. in. 25:20
bound the waters in a *g*.? 30:4
eat them up like a *g*. *Isa* 51:8
to give *g*. of praise for spirit. 61:3
shepherd putteth on his *g*. *Jer* 43:12
the naked with a *g*. *Ezek* 18:7, 16
whose *g*. was white as. *Dan* 7:9
ye pull off robe with the *g*. *Mi* 2:8
holy flesh in skirt of his *g*. *Hag* 2:12
shall wear a rough *g*. *Zech* 13:4*
violence with his *g*. *Mal* 2:16
new cloth to old *g*. *Mat* 9:16
Mark 2:21; *Luke* 5:36
touched the hem of his *g*. *Mat* 9:20
21; 14:36; *Mark* 5:27; *Luke* 8:44
not on a wedding *g*. *Mat* 22:11, 12
back again to take up his *g*. *Mark* 13:16
clothed with a long white *g*. 16:5
sell his *g*. and buy one. *Luke* 22:36
cast thy *g*. about thee. *Acts* 12:8
hating even the *g*. spotted. *Jude* 23
of man clothed with a *g*. *Rev* 1:13

garments
and change your *g*. *Gen* 35:2
Tamar put her widow's *g*. 38:14
washed his *g*. in wine, his. 49:11
may make Aaron's *g*. to. *Ex* 28:3
sprinkled the blood on Aaron's *g*.
29:21; *Lev* 8:30
them wisdom to make *g*. *Ex* 31:10
put off his *g*. put on other *g*.
Lev 6:11; 16:23, 24
borders of their *g*. *Num* 15:38
strip Aaron of his *g*. put. 20:26
Moses stripped Aaron of *g*. put. 28
Gibeonites brought old *g*. *Josh* 9:5
you thirty changes of *g*. *Judg* 14:12
gave David his *g*. *1 Sam* 18:4
cut off their *g*. in the middle.
2 Sam 10:4; *1 Chr* 19:4
David tare his *g*. *2 Sam* 13:31
to receive money and *g*.? *2 Ki* 5:26
all the way was full of *g*. and. 7:15
Jehoiakim's *g*. 25:29; *Jer* 52:33
one hundred priests' *g*. *Ezra* 2:69
gave 530 priests' *g*. *Neh* 7:70
gave sixty-seven priests' *g*. 72
how thy *g*. are warm. *Job* 37:17
they part my *g*. among. *Ps* 22:18
all thy *g*. smell of myrrh. 45:8
went down to skirts of his *g*. 133:2
let thy *g*. be always white. *Eccl* 9:8
smell of thy *g*. is like. *S of S* 4:11
every battle is with *g*. *Isa* 9:5
put on thy beautiful *g*. 52:1
their webs shall not become *g*. 59:6
he put on the *g*. of vengeance. 17
he hath clothed me with *g*. 61:10
that cometh with dyed *g*. 63:1
shall be sprinkled upon my *g*. 3
not afraid, nor rent *g*. *Jer* 36:24
could not touch their *g*. *Lam* 4:14
tookest thy broidered *g*. *Ezek* 16:18
there shall lay their *g*. they. 42:14
sanctify people with their *g*. 44:19
in their coats and other *g*. *Dan* 3:21
heart, and not your *g*. *Joel* 2:13
clothed with filthy *g*. *Zech* 3:3
take the filthy *g*. from him. 4
spread their *g*. in the way. *Mat* 21:8
Mark 11:8
the borders of their *g*. *Mat* 23:5
they parted his *g*. casting lots.
27:35; *Mark* 15:24
casting away his *g*. *Mark* 10:50
g. on the colt. 11:7; *Luke* 19:35
by them in shining *g*. *Luke* 24:4*
he laid aside his *g*. *John* 13:4
shewing coats and *g*. *Acts* 9:39
and your *g*. are motheaten. *Jas* 5:2
have not defiled their *g*. *Rev* 3:4
watcheth and keepeth his *g*. 16:15

***holy* garments**
make *holy g*. for Aaron. *Ex* 28:2, 4
put wisdom to make *holy g*. 31:10
holy g. he shall wash. *Lev* 16:4, 32
lay their *holy g*. *Ezek* 42:14

garner
gather his wheat into the *g*.
Mat 3:12; *Luke* 3:17

garners
our *g*. may be full. *Ps* 144:13
the *g*. are laid desolate. *Joel* 1:17

garnish, -ed
he *g*. the house with. *2 Chr* 3:6
by his Spirit he hath *g*. *Job* 26:13
findeth it swept and *g*. *Mat* 12:44
Luke 11:25
you *g*. the sepulchres of. *Mat* 23:29
of the wall are *g*. *Rev* 21:19*

garrison, -s
to hill where is *g*. of. *1 Sam* 10:5
Jonathan smote the *g*. of the. 13:3
over to the Philistines' *g*. 14:1, 6
the *g*. and the spoilers, they also. 15
David put *g*. in Syria. *2 Sam* 8:6
1 Chr 18:6
David put *g*. in Edom. *2 Sam* 8:14
1 Chr 18:13
g. of Philistines in Beth-lehem.
2 Sam 23:14; *1 Chr* 11:16
Jehoshaphat set *g*. in Judah.
2 Chr 17:2
strong *g*. shall go down. *Ezek* 26:11
kept the city with a *g*. *2 Cor* 11:32

gat
Moses *g*. him up into. *Ex* 24:18
g. up from tabernacle. *Num* 16:27
and *g*. them up to the top. *Judg* 9:51
and David *g*. him a. *2 Sam* 8:13
covered him, but he *g*. *1 Ki* 1:1
the pains of hell *g*. hold. *Ps* 116:3
I *g*. men singers, and. *Eccl* 2:8
we *g*. our bread with the. *Lam* 5:9

gate
The gates were the important part of an ancient city. They gave the only means of passing through the wall and were usually closed at night and were strengthened by bars of brass or iron. The gate was the place of public concourse, partly because it was an open space, not usually found elsewhere in a city. Much of the legal business of the city was done there, Ruth 4:11.
The word gate is sometimes used to mean power or dominion. God promises Abraham, that his posterity should possess the gates of their enemies, their towns, their fortresses, Gen 22:17. *They should conquer them, they should have dominion over them.*
The gates of death are the brink, or mouth of the grave, Ps 9:13.

thy seed possess the *g*. of enemies.
Gen 22:17; 24:60
Jacob said, this is the *g*. of. 28:17
go in and out from *g*. to *g*. *Ex* 32:27
bring him to the *g*. *Deut* 21:19
bring them both out to the *g*. 22:24
brother's wife go up to *g*. 25:7
they shut the *g*. *Josh* 2:7
took the doors of the *g*. *Judg* 16:3
then went Boaz to the *g*. *Ruth* 4:1
dead be not cut off from the *g*. 10
by the side of the *g*. *1 Sam* 4:18
beside the way of the *g*. *2 Sam* 15:2
to the chamber over the *g*. 18:33
water by *g*. 23:15, 16; *1 Chr* 11:18
when Elijah came to *g*. *1 Ki* 17:10
have the charge of the *g*. *2 Ki* 7:17
cast lots for every *g*. *1 Chr* 26:13
porters at every *g*. *2 Chr* 8:14
the *g*. should be shut. *Neh* 13:19
before the king's *g*. *Esth* 4:2; 6:12
when I went out to the *g*. *Job* 29:7
this *g*. of the Lord, the. *Ps* 118:20
the fish pools by the *g*. *S of S* 7:4
howl, O *g*. cry, O city. *Isa* 14:31
the *g*. is smitten with. 24:12

to turn the battle to the *g.* *Isa* 28:6
at the entry of new *g.* *Jer* 36:10
have ceased from the *g.* *Lam* 5:14
to door of the inner *g.* *Ezek* 8:3
at the door of the *g.* twenty-. 11:1
Lord come by way of the *g.* 43:4
this *g.* shall be shut, none. 44:2
enter by way of *g.* 3; 46:2, 8
blood on the posts of the *g.* 45:19
the *g.* of the inner court shall. 46:1
but the *g.* shall not be shut till. 2
open the *g.* one shall shut the *g.* 12
g. of Reuben, one *g.* of Judah. 48:31
the *g.* of my people. *Ob* 13
he is come into the *g.* of. *Mi* 1:9
from Lord to the *g.* of Jerusalem. 12
have passed through the *g.* 2:13
strait *g.* wide is the *g.* and broad is. *Mat* 7:13, 14; *Luke* 13:24*
when he came nigh *g.* *Luke* 7:12
a beggar Lazarus laid at his *g.* 16:20
Cornelius stood before *g.* *Acts* 10:17
they came to the iron *g.* 12:10
Rhoda opened not the *g.* for. 14
suffered without the *g.* *Heb* 13:12
every several *g.* was of. *Rev* 21:21
see **entereth, entering**

gate
he that exalteth his *g.* *Pr* 17:19

at the **gate**
of all that went in *at the g.* of city. *Gen* 23:10, 18
Jehu entered in *at the g.* *2 Ki* 9:31
at the g. of Sur, and a third *at the g.* 11:6; *2 Chr* 23:5
man's left hand *at the g.* *2 Ki* 23:8
set a chest *at the g.* of. *2 Chr* 24:8
I see Mordecai sitting *at the* king's *g.* *Esth* 5:13
in array *at the g.* *Isa* 22:7
they laid daily *at the g.* *Acts* 3:2*
who sat for alms *at* beautiful *g.* 10
see **fish gate**

high **gate**
through the *high g.* *2 Chr* 23:20
Jotham built the *high g.* of. 27:3
in stocks in the *high g.* *Jer* 20:2
see **horse gate**

in the **gate**
and Lot sat *in the g.* *Gen* 19:1
Moses stood *in the g.* of. *Ex* 32:26
virginity to elders *in g.* *Deut* 22:15
wait for Samson *in the g.* *Judg* 16:2
people *in the g.* said, we. *Ruth* 4:11
near to Samuel *in the g.* *1 Sam* 9:18
Abner aside *in the g.* *2 Sam* 3:27
king sat *in the g.* they told all. 19:8
a shekel *in the g.* *2 Ki* 7:1, 18
the people trod on him *in the g.* 20
sat *in the* king's *g.* *Esth* 2:19, 21
saw him *in the* king's *g.* 5:9
his children are crushed *in the g.* *Job* 5:4
when I saw my help *in the g.* 31:21
that sit *in the g.* speak. *Ps* 69:12
speak with the enemies *in g.* 127:5
the afflicted *in the g.* *Pr* 22:22
openeth not his mouth *in the g.* 24:7
him that reproveth *in g.* *Isa* 29:21
stand *in the g.* of the Lord's. *Jer* 7:2
stand *in the g.* of children. 17:19
when he was *in the g.* of. 37:13
king then sitting *in the g.* of. 38:7
princes of Babylon sat *in the g.* 39:3
but Daniel sat *in the g.* *Dan* 2:49
that rebuketh *in the g.* *Amos* 5:10
turn aside the poor *in the g.* 12
establish judgement *in the g.* 15

old **gate**
old g. repaired Jehoiada. *Neh* 3:6
priests went above the *old g.* 12:39

prison **gate**
stood still in the *prison g.* *Neh* 12:39

sheep **gate**
went even unto *sheep g.* *Neh* 12:39

valley **gate**
towers at the *valley g.* *2 Chr* 26:9
out by *g.* of the *valley.* *Neh* 2:13
entered by the *g.* of the *valley.* 15
the *valley g.* repaired Hanun. 3:13

water **gate**
over against *water g.* *Neh* 3:26
the street before the *water g.* 8:1
in the law before the *water g.* 3
in the street of the *water g.* 16
even to the *water g.* eastward. 12:37

gates
Levite within your *g.* *Deut* 12:12
son set up *g.* *Josh* 6:26; *1 Ki* 16:34
gods, then was war in *g.* *Judg* 5:8
the Lord shall go to the *g.* 5:11
appointed to praise in *g.* *2 Chr* 31:2
g. are burnt. *Neh* 1:3; 2:3, 13, 17
let not the *g.* of Jerusalem be. 7:3
and Levites purified the *g.* 12:30
my servants set I at the *g.* 13:19*
the Levites to keep the *g.* 22
thy praise in the *g.* *Ps* 9:14
lift up your heads, O ye *g.* 24:7, 9
the Lord loveth the *g.* of Zion. 87:2
enter into his *g.* with. 100:4
for he hath broken the *g.* of. 107:16
open to me the *g.* of. 118:19
in openings of *g.* *Pr* 1:21; 8:3
watching daily at my *g.* 8:34
the wicked at the *g.* of the. 14:19
husband is known in the *g.* 31:23
works praise her in the *g.* 31
our *g.* are all manner. *S of S* 7:13*
and her *g.* shall lament. *Isa* 3:26
they may go into the *g.* of the. 13:2
open ye the *g.* that righteous. 26:2
I shall go to the *g.* of the. 38:10
before him the two leaved *g.* 45:1*
I will break in pieces the *g.* of. 2*
go through, go through the *g.* 62:10
hear the word, all ye that enter in at the *g.* *Jer* 7:2; 17:20; 22:2
Judah mourneth, and the *g.* 14:2
fan them with a fan in *g.* of. 15:7
go and stand in all the *g.* of. 17:19
on the sabbath by the *g.* 21, 24
there enter into the *g.* 25; 22:4
I will kindle a fire in the *g.* of. 27
and cast forth beyond the *g.* 22:19
Zion's *g.* are desolate. *Lam* 1:4
her *g.* are sunk into the ground. 2:9
should have entered the *g.* 4:12
of sword against their *g.* *Ezek* 21:15
battering rams against the *g.* 22
she is broken that was the *g.* of. 26:2
at the east side three *g.* one. 48:32
foreigners entered his *g.* *Ob* 11
the *g.* of the rivers shall. *Nah* 2:6
the *g.* of thy land shall be set. 3:13
truth and peace in your *g.* *Zech* 8:16
g. of hell shall not prevail. *Mat* 16:18
and they watched the *g.* *Acts* 9:24
priests brought oxen to the *g.* 14:13
the city had twelve *g.* at *g.* *Rev* 21:12
three *g.* on the north three *g.* 13
the twelve *g.* were twelve pearls. 21
the *g.* of it shall not be shut at. 25
see **bars, death**

thy **gates**
thy stranger within *thy g.* *Ex* 20:10
Deut 5:14
thou shalt write them on *thy g.*
Deut 6:9; 11:20
eat flesh in *thy g.* 12:15, 21
mayest not eat within *thy g.* the. 17
thou and Levite in *thy g.* 18
the stranger that is in *thy g.* 14:21
Levite within *thy g.* thou shalt. 27
up the tithe within *thy g.* 28
the widow within *thy g.* shall. 29
poor man within any of *thy g.* 15:7
eat the firstling within *thy g.* 22
the passover within *thy g.* 16:5
Levite in *thy g.* 11, 14; 26:12
shalt thou make in all *thy g.* 16:18
that man or woman to *thy g.* 17:5
Levite come from any of *thy g.* 18:6
escaped dwell in one of *thy g.* 23:16
not oppress within *thy g.* 24:14
besiege thee in all *thy g.* 28:52
distress thee in all *thy g.* 55
gather the people within *thy g.* 31:12
stand within *thy g.* O. *Ps* 122:2
I will make *thy g.* of. *Isa* 54:12
therefore *thy g.* shall be open. 60:11
thy walls salvation, and *thy g.* 18
enter *thy g.* as men. *Ezek* 26:10

Gath
ark be carried about to *G.* *1 Sam* 5:8
golden emerods, for *G.* one. 6:17
that David was fled to *G.* 27:4
tell it not in *G.* publish. *2 Sam* 1:20
giant in *G.* and fell by the hand of David and. 21:22; *1 Chr* 20:8
Shimei ran to *G.* *1 Ki* 2:39
Shimei went to *G.* to seek. 40
and fought against *G.* *2 Ki* 12:17
drove away inhabitants of *G.*
1 Chr 8:13
David took *G.* from the. 18:1
brake down wall of *G.* *2 Chr* 26:6
then go down to *G.* of. *Amos* 6:2
declare ye it not at *G.* *Mi* 1:10

gather
Jacob said, *g.* stones, and. *Gen* 31:46
let them *g.* all the food of. 41:35
let them go and *g.* straw. *Ex* 5:7
g. stubble. 12
g. thy cattle. 9:19*
shall *g.* a certain rate. 16:4
g. twice as much. 5
six days *g.* it. 26
sow thy land and *g.* 23:10; *Lev* 25:3
not *g.* the gleanings. *Lev* 19:9; 23:22
thou shalt not *g.* every grape of. 10
nor *g.* grapes of the vine. 25:5, 11
we shall not sow, nor *g.* in our. 20
trumpet, then princes *g.* *Num* 10:4
g. seventy men of the elders. 11:16
a man that is clean shall *g.* 19:9
rain that thou mayest *g.* *Deut* 11:14
thou shalt *g.* all the spoil of. 13:16
vineyard and not *g.* grapes. 28:30, 39
carry much seed out, and *g.* but. 38
g. thee from all nations. 30:3
Ezek 36:24
into the field to *g.* herbs. *2 Ki* 4:39
g. thee to thy 22:20; *2 Chr* 34:28
Levites to *g.* *1 Chr* 13:2
g. money to repair. *2 Chr* 24:5
yet will I *g.* them from. *Neh* 1:9
some appointed to *g.* for the. 12:44
they *g.* the vintage of the. *Job* 24:6*
if he *g.* to himself his spirit. 34:14
will he bring seed, and *g.* it? 39:12
g. not my soul with sinners. *Ps* 26:9
and knoweth not who shall *g.* 39:6
that thou givest them they *g.* 104:28
save us, and *g.* us from 106:47
shall *g.* for him that will. *Pr* 28:8
to sinner travail, to *g.* *Eccl* 2:26
gone down to *g.* lilies. *S of S* 6:2
there the owl *g.* under. *Isa* 34:15
he shall *g.* the lambs with. 40:11
fear not, I will *g.* thee from. 43:5
great mercies will I *g.* thee. 54:7
yet will I *g.* others to him. 56:8
cast up the highway, *g.* out. 62:10
I will *g.* all nations and. 66:18
g. to flee. *Jer* 6:1*
the children *g.* wood. 7:18
none shall *g.* them. 9:22
g. up thy wares. 10:17
I will *g.* the remnant of my. 23:3
I will *g.* you from all the. 29:14
I will *g.* them from coasts of. 31:8
32:37; *Ezek* 20:34, 41; 34:13
he that scattered Israel will *g.*
Jer 31:10
g. ye wine, and summer. 40:10
and none shall *g.* up him that. 49:5
I will even *g.* you from. *Ezek* 11:17
I will *g.* all thy lovers against. 16:37
I will *g.* you into the midst of. 22:19
as they *g.* silver, so will I *g.* 20, 21
g. the pieces. 24:4
I will *g.* the Egyptians. 29:13
I will *g.* them on every. 37:21; 39:17
among nations, I will *g.* *Hos* 8:10
Egypt shall *g.* them up. 9:6
g. the elders and the. *Joel* 1:14
much pained, all faces shall *g.* 2:6*
g. the people, *g.* the children. 16
I will *g.* all nations, and bring. 3:2
will surely *g.* remnant. *Mi* 2:12
g. her that was driven out. 4:6
Zeph 3:19
he shall *g.* them as sheaves into. 12
g. thyself in troops, O daughter. 5:1
the faces of them all *g.* *Nah* 2:10*

they shall *g.* captivity as. *Hab* 1:9
they catch them, and *g.* them in. 15
my determination is to *g.* *Zeph* 3:8
I will *g.* them that are sorrowful. 18
even in the time that I *g.* you. 20
I will hiss for them and *g.* *Zech* 10:8
I will *g.* them out of Assyria. 10
I will *g.* all nations against. 14:2
g. his wheat into his garner.
Mat 3:12; *Luke* 3:17
they sow not, nor do they *g.* *Mat* 6:26
do men *g.* grapes ? 7:16; *Luke* 6:44
wilt that we go and *g.*? *Mat* 13:28
he said, nay, lest while ye *g.* up. 29
burn tares, but *g.* the wheat into. 30
shall *g.* out of his kingdom all. 41
and that *g.* where I have not. 25:26
as a hen doth *g.* her. *Luke* 13:34
g. up the fragments that. *John* 6:12
men *g.* them and cast them. 15:6
g. the clusters of vine. *Rev* 14:18
g. them to the battle of that. 16:14

gather *together*

few they shall *g. tog.* *Gen* 34:30
g. yourselves *tog.* ye sons. 49:1, 2*
g. the elders of Israel *tog.* *Ex* 3:16
g. congregation of Israel *tog.*
Lev 8:3*; *Num* 8:9*
g. thou the assembly *tog.* *Num* 20:8*
g. the people *tog.* 24:16; *Deut* 4:10*
31:12*
g. the rest *tog.* and. *2 Sam* 12:28
O God, and *g.* us *tog.* *1 Chr* 16:35
David commanded to *g. tog.* 22:2
in my heart to *g. tog.* *Neh* 7:5
may *g. tog.* all the fair. *Esth* 2:3
g. tog. the Jews present in. 4:16
if he *g. tog.* who can ? *Job* 11:10*
g. my saints *tog.* unto me. *Ps* 50:5
they *g.* themselves *tog.* to. 56:6
they *g. together* against the. 94:21
they *g.* themselves *tog.* 104:22*
time to *g.* stones *tog.* *Eccl* 3:5
shall *g. tog.* the dispersed. *Isa* 11:12
these *g. tog.* and. 49:18; 60:4
they shall surely *g. tog.* but. 54:15
the trumpet, cry, *g. tog.* *Jer* 4:5*
g. ye *tog.* and come against. 49:14
king sent to *g. tog.* *Dan* 3:2
g. yourselves *tog.* round. *Joel* 3:11
g. tog. yea, *g. tog.* O. *Zeph* 2:1
g. tog. first the tares. *Mat* 13:30
they shall *g. tog.* his elect. 24:31
Mark 13:27
he should *g. tog.* in one. *John* 11:52
Eph 1:10*
g. tog. to the supper of. *Rev* 19:17
g. Gog and Magog *tog.* to. 20:8

gathered

Abraham died and was *g.* *Gen* 25:8
Ishmael was *g.* 17
Isaac was *g.* to people. 35:29
Jacob was *g.* to his people. 49:29, 33
and they *g.* some more. *Ex* 16:17
that *g.* much, he that *g.* little. 18
2 Cor 8:15
they *g.* it every morning. *Ex* 16:21
hast *g.* in thy labours. 23:16
ye have *g.* in the fruits. *Lev* 23:39
the people *g.* quails. *Num* 11:32
g. sticks. 15:32
g. congregation against. 16:19*, 42*
Aaron shall be *g.* to. 20:24, 26
Moses *g.* to his people. 27:13
31:2; *Deut* 32:50
kings *g.* their meat. *Judg* 1:7
that generation was *g.* to. 2:10
and Abiezer was *g.* after. 6:34
there were *g.* vain men to. 11:3
they *g.* all the lords of. *1 Sam* 5:8
every one that was in distress *g.* 22:2
which cannot be *g.* up. *2 Sam* 14:14
they *g.* all able to put. *2 Ki* 3:21
Josiah be *g.* to grave in peace. 22:20
2 Chr 34:28
all my servants were *g.* *Neh* 5:16
down, but shall not be *g.* *Job* 27:19
the mighty are *g.* against. *Ps* 59:3
and he *g.* them out of lands. 107:3
of the mountains are *g.* *Pr* 27:25
who hath *g.* the winds in his ? 30:4
I *g.* me also silver. *Eccl* 2:8
I have *g.* my myrrh with. *S of S* 5:1
he fenced it, and *g.* out. *Isa* 5:2
one gathereth eggs, have I *g.* 10:14
ye shall be *g.* one by one. 27:12
vultures be *g.* 34:15
his Spirit *g.* them. 16
though Israel be not *g.* yet. 49:5
besides those that are *g.* 56:8
but they that have *g.* it shall. 62:9*
and all nations shall be *g.* *Jer* 3:17
they shall not be *g.* 8:2; 25:33
all people *g.* against Jeremiah. 26:9
all the Jews *g.* to thee should. 40:15
I shall have *g.* house. *Ezek* 28:25
be brought together nor *g.* 29:5
hast thou *g.* thy company to ? 38:13*
have *g.* them out of their. 39:27
but I have *g.* them to their own. 28
the people shall be *g.* *Hos* 10:10
I am as when they *g.* *Mi* 7:1
tares are *g.* and burnt. *Mat* 13:40
a net cast into the sea, and *g.* of. 47
before him shall be *g.* all. 25:32
and *g.* to him the whole band. 27:27
g. chief priests a council. *John* 11:47
g. a company, set city. *Acts* 17:5
when Paul had *g.* a bundle of. 28:3
the angel *g.* the vine of. *Rev* 14:19

gathered *together*

they *g.* them *tog.* upon. *Ex* 8:14
congregation to be *g. tog.* *Num* 10:7
fish of the sea be *g. tog.*? 11:22
congregation was *g. tog.* *Judg* 20:1*
11; *Ezra* 3:1; *Neh* 8:1
Judah *g. tog.* to ask. *2 Chr* 20:4
they *g.* themselves *tog.* *Job* 16:10
under nettles were they *g. tog.* 30:7
abjects *g.* themselves *tog.* *Ps* 35:15
of the people are *g. tog.* 47:9
when people are *g. tog.* to. 102:22
are they *g. tog.* for war. 140:2
children of Judah be *g. tog.* *Hos* 1:11
nations are *g. tog.* against. *Mi* 4:11*
all people be *g. tog.* *Zech* 12:3
two or three are *g. tog.* *Mat* 18:20
I have *g.* thy children *tog.*, as a hen.
23:37; *Luke* 13:34
there will eagles be *g. tog.*
Mat 24:28; *Luke* 17:37
all the city was *g. tog.* *Mark* 1:33
younger son *g.* all *tog.* *Luke* 15:13
they found the eleven *g. tog.* 24:33
rulers were *g. tog.* *Acts* 4:26
where many were *g. tog.* 12:12
had *g.* the church *tog.* 14:27
when ye are *g. tog.* and. *1 Cor* 5:4
g. tog. into a place called. *Rev* 16:16
beast and his army *g. tog.* 19:19

gatherer, -s

thy hand as a grape *g.* *Jer* 6:9
grape *g.* come to thee. 49:9; *Ob* 5
I was a *g.* of sycamore. *Amos* 7:14*

gatherest

when thou *g.* the grapes. *Deut* 24:21

gathereth

that *g.* the ashes shall. *Num* 19:10
he *g.* the waters of sea. *Ps* 33:7
his heart *g.* iniquity to itself. 41:6
he *g.* the outcasts. 147:2; *Isa* 56:8
the ant *g.* her food in the. *Pr* 6:8
he that *g.* in summer is a wise. 10:5
but he that *g.* by labour shall. 13:11
one *g.* eggs that are left. *Isa* 10:14
as when the harvestman *g.* 17:5*
scattered, and no man *g.* *Nah* 3:18
but *g.* to him all nations. *Hab* 2:5
he that *g.* not scattereth. *Mat* 12:30
Luke 11:23
as a hen *g.* her chickens. *Mat* 23:37
he that reapeth *g.* fruit. *John* 4:36

gathering

to him shall the *g.* of. *Gen* 49:10*
they that found him *g.* *Num* 15:33
was there *g.* sticks. *1 Ki* 17:10
were three days in *g.* *2 Chr* 20:25*
vintage shall fail, the *g.* *Isa* 32:10*
your spoil like the *g.* of the. 33:4
g. where thou hast not. *Mat* 25:24
g. that the Lord had. *Acts* 16:10*
and by our *g.* together. *2 Thes* 2:1

gatherings

that there be no *g.* *1 Cor* 16:2*

gave

Adam *g.* names to all. *Gen* 2:20
the woman *g.* me of the tree. 3:12
he *g.* him tithes. 14:20; *Heb* 7:2, 4
Abraham *g.* all that he. *Gen* 25:5
land which God *g.* 28:4; 35:12
Lord *g.* the people favour. *Ex* 11:3
12:36
the cloud *g.* light by night to. 14:20
took of Spirit, and *g.* *Num* 11:25
I *g.* my daughter to. *Deut* 22:16
they *g.* him the city. *Josh* 19:50
the Lord *g.* to Israel all the. 21:43
the Lord *g.* them rest. 44
2 Chr 15:15; 20:30
I drave them out, and *g.* *Judg* 6:9
Lord *g.* her conception. *Ruth* 4:13
God *g.* to Saul another. *1 Sam* 10:9
I *g.* thee thy master's. *2 Sam* 12:8
Lord *g.* Solomon. *1 Ki* 4:29; 5:12
and the Lord *g.* Israel. *2 Ki* 13:5
God *g.* to Heman. *1 Chr* 25:5
and God *g.* Hezekiah. *2 Chr* 32:24
read book, *g.* the sense. *Neh* 8:8
Lord *g.* and the Lord. *Job* 1:21
God *g.* Job twice as much as. 42:10
and the Highest *g.* his. *Ps* 18:13
the Lord *g.* the word, great. 68:11
g. me also gall, they *g.* me. 69:21
for he *g.* them their. 78:29; 106:15
return to God that *g.* it. *Eccl* 12:7
who *g.* Jacob for a spoil ? *Isa* 42:24
I *g.* Egypt for thy ransom. 43:3
I *g.* my back to the smiters. 50:6
my meat also which I *g.* *Ezek* 16:19
I *g.* them my statutes. 20:11
moreover also, I *g.* them my. 12
I *g.* them also statutes that were. 25
God *g.* these four children. *Dan* 1:17
Daniel prayed and *g.* thanks. 6:10
she did not know that I *g.* *Hos* 2:8
g. thee a king in mine anger. 13:11
ye *g.* the Nazarites wine. *Amos* 2:12
I *g.* my covenant to Levi. *Mal* 2:5
Jesus *g.* them power against unclean.
Mat 10:1; *Mark* 6:7; *Luke* 9:1
he brake and *g.* loaves. *Mat* 14:19
15:36; 26:16; *Mark* 6:41; 8:6
14:22; *Luke* 9:16; 22:19
who *g.* thee authority ? *Mat* 21:23
Mark 11:28; *Luke* 20:2
ye *g.* me meat, ye *g.* me. *Mat* 25:35
ye *g.* me no meat, and ye *g.* me. 42
husks, and no man *g.* *Luke* 15:16
to them *g.* he power to. *John* 1:12
God so loved world that he *g.* 3:16
he *g.* them bread from heaven. 6:31
my Father who *g.* them me. 10:29
Father *g.* me commandment. 14:31
to speak as Spirit *g.* them. *Acts* 2:4
and he *g.* them no inheritance. 7:5
God *g.* Joseph favour and. 10
Cornelius *g.* much alms to the. 10:2
as God *g.* them the like gift. 11:17
smote him, because he *g.* not. 12:23
afterward God *g.* them Saul. 13:21
he did good, and *g.* us rain. 14:17
to whom we *g.* no such. 15:24
when put to death, I *g.* my. 26:10
God *g.* them over to a. *Rom* 2:28
even as the Lord *g.* to. *1 Cor* 3:5
Apollos watered, but God *g.* the. 6
but first *g.* their own. *2 Cor* 8:5
who *g.* himself. *Gal* 1:4; *Tit* 2:14
who loved me, and *g.* *Gal* 2:20
but God *g.* it to Abraham by. 3:18
and *g.* him to be head. *Eph* 1:22
he led captivity captive and *g.* 4:8
and he *g.* some apostles; some. 11
Christ loved the church, and *g.* 5:25
commandment we *g.* *1 Thes* 4:2
who *g.* himself a ransom. *1 Tim* 2:6
corrected us, we *g.* them. *Heb* 12:9
and the heavens *g.* rain. *Jas* 5:18
love one another, as he *g.* us.
1 John 3:23
believeth not the record God *g.* 5:10
Jesus Christ which God *g.* *Rev* 1:1
g. her space to repent of her. 2:21
the dragon *g.* him his power. 13:2, 4

gave *up*

Abraham *g. up* ghost. *Gen* 25:8
Isaac *g. up* the ghost. 35:29

Joab g. up the sum of. 2 Sam 24:9
g. them up to desolation. 2 Chr 30:7
he g. up their cattle. Ps 78:48
I g. them up to their own. 81:12*
my elders g. up ghost. Lam 1:19
a loud voice, and g. up. Mark 15:37
39; Luke 23:46; John 19:30
Ananias g. up the ghost. Acts 5:5
God g. them up to worship. 7:42
God also g. them up to. Rom 1:24
for this cause God g. them up to. 26
the sea g. up the dead. Rev 20:13

gavest

the woman whom thou g. Gen 3:12
land which thou g. 1 Ki 8:34, 40, 48
2 Chr 6:25, 31, 38; Neh 9:35
thou g. him the name of. Neh 9:7
thou g. them right judgements. 13
g. them bread from heaven. 15
g. also thy good Spirit, g. water. 20
g. them kingdoms and nations. 22
thou g. them saviours who saved. 27
g. the goodly wings to? Job 39:13*
life of thee; thou g. it him. Ps 21:4
thou g. him to be meat to. 74:14
thou g. me no water for. Luke 7:44
g. me no kiss, but this woman. 45
yet thou never g. me a kid, to. 15:29
finished work thou g. John 17:4
men whom thou g. me out of world,
thine they were, and thou g. 6
the words which thou g. me. 8
those that thou g. me I have kept. 12
the glory which thou g. me. 22
of them whom thou g. me. 18:9

gay

that weareth g. clothing. Jas 2:3*

Gaza

Samson went to G. and. Judg 16:1
brought Samson down to G. 21
Pharaoh smote G. Jer 47:1
baldness is come upon G. 5
three transgressions of G. Amos 1:6
will send a fire on the wall of G. 7
G. shall be forsaken. Zeph 2:4
G. shall see it, king shall perish from
G. Zech 9:5
from Jerusalem to G. Acts 8:26

gaze

through unto the Lord to g. Ex 19:21

gazing

I will set thee as a g.-stock. Nah 3:6
why stand ye g. up into? Acts 1:11
ye were made a g.-stock. Heb 10:33

Geba

G. with her suburbs. Josh 21:17
1 Chr 6:60
king Asa built G. 1 Ki 15:22
2 Chr 16:6
Josiah defiled the high places from
G. 2 Ki 23:8
taken up lodging at G. Isa 10:29
be as a plain from G. Zech 14:10

Gebal

G. and Ammon are. Ps 83:7
the ancients of G. were. Ezek 27:9

Gebim

inhabitants of G. gather. Isa 10:31

Gedaliah

and G. sware to them. 2 Ki 25:24
Jer 40:9
Jeduthun, G. and Zeri. 1 Chr 25:3
second lot came forth to G. 9
Jarib and G. had taken. Ezra 10:18
G. the son of Pashur. Jer 38:1
G. son of Ahikam believed not. 40:14
Ishmael smote G. with sword. 41:2
took all that were left with G. 43:6
son of Cushi, son of G. Zeph 1:1
see **Ahikam**

Gehazi

Elisha said to G. 2 Ki 4:12, 36
but G. came near to thrust. 27
G. followed after Naaman. 5:21
to him, Whence comest thou, G.? 25
the king talked with G. servant. 8:4

Gemariah

Jeremiah sent by G. Jer 29:3
G. made intercession not to. 36:25

gender

shalt not let cattle g. Lev 19:19
knowing that they do g. 2 Tim 2:23

gendereth

their bull g. and faileth not. Job 21:10
frost of heaven, who hath g.? 38:29
which g. to bondage. Gal 4:24

genealogies

Comes from the Greek word Genealogia, which signifies a history of the descent of an individual or family from an ancestor. The Jews were very exact in their genealogies, partly in order that family honours and family property should descend properly; partly to keep the line wherein the Messiah was to come.

Even the Babylonian Exile did not prevent the keeping of these, as a rule, for we find that some, who claimed Jewish descent but could not produce their genealogy, were not allowed part in the Return as were the others.

were reckoned by g. 1 Chr 9:1
Shemaiah concerning g. 2 Chr 12:15
to all reckoned by g. 31:9
fables and endless g. 1 Tim 1:4
avoid foolish questions, g. Tit 3:9

genealogy

and the g. is not to be. 1 Chr 5:1
these sought their g. Ezra 2:62
Neh 7:64
the g. of them that went. Ezra 8:1
I found a register of g. Neh 7:5

general

g. of the king's army. 1 Chr 27:34*
to g. assembly and. Heb 12:23

generally

I counsel that Israel be g. gathered.
2 Sam 17:11*
lamentation g. on house. Jer 48:38

generation

[1] *A begetting or producing, or the person or thing produced,* Gen 2:4; 5:1. [2] *Each succession of persons from a common ancestor,* Gen 50:23; Deut 23:2. [3] *An age or period, not meaning as now the average lifetime of man, but the average period of the activity of any body of contemporaries,* Ex 1:6; Num 32:13; Judg 2:10.

seen righteous in this g. Gen 7:1
Joseph died, and all that g. Ex 1:6
war with Amalek from g. to g. 17:16
till that g. was consumed.
Num 32:13; Deut 2:14
not one of this evil g. Deut 1:35
enter even to his tenth g. 23:2
an Ammonite to tenth g. shall not. 3
Edomite and Egyptian in third g. 8
so that the g. to come shall. 29:22
perverse and crooked g. 32:5, 20
g. were gathered to their fathers, and
there arose another g. Judg 2:10
remembered in every g. Esth 9:28
preserve them from this g. Ps 12:7
for God is in the g. of the. 14:5
to the Lord for a g. 22:30
this is the g. of them that. 24:6
that ye may tell it to the g. 48:13
he shall go to the g. of his. 49:19
shewed thy strength to this g. 71:18
I should offend against the g. 73:15
shewing to the g. to come the. 78:4
that the g. to come might know. 6
a stubborn and rebellious g. 8
forty years grieved with this g.
95:10; Heb 3:10
this shall be written for g. 102:18
in g. following let their. 109:13
the g. of the upright shall be. 112:2
one g. shall praise thy works. 145:4
crown endure to every g.? Pr 27:24
there is a g. that curseth. 30:11
there is a g. that are pure in. 12
a g. lofty. 13
a g. whose teeth are swords. 14
g. passeth away, another g. Eccl 1:4

not dwelt in from g. to g. Isa 13:20
Jer 50:39
from g. to g. it shall lie. Isa 34:10
from g. to g. they shall dwell. 17
salvation shall be from g. to g. 51:8
who declare his g.? 53:8; Acts 8:33
O g. see ye the word of. Jer 2:31
the Lord hath rejected g. 7:29
remains from g. to g. Lam 5:19
and his dominion is from g. to g.
Dan 4:3, 34
children tell another g. Joel 1:3
shall dwell from g. to g. 3:20
the g. of Jesus Christ. Mat 1:1
O g. of vipers. 3:7*; 12:34*; 23:33*
Luke 3:7*
whereto shall I liken this g.?
Mat 11:16; Luke 7:31
evil and adulterous g. Mat 12:39
16:4; Mark 8:12; Luke 11:29
shall rise in judgement with this g.
Mat 12:41; Luke 11:32
queen of the south rise up with g.
Mat 12:42; Luke 11:31
also to this wicked g. Mat 12:45
O perverse g. 17:17; Mark 9:19
Luke 9:41
shall come on this g. Mat 23:36
this g. shall not pass. 24:34
Mark 13:30; Luke 21:32
of me in this sinful g. Mark 8:38
on them from g. to g. Luke 1:50
Son of man be to this g. 11:30
prophets required of this g. 50, 51
children of this world in their g. 16:8
must be rejected of this g. 17:25
from this untoward g. Acts 2:40
he had served his own g. 13:36
ye are a chosen g. a. 1 Pet 2:9*
see **fourth**

generations

g. of the heavens and. Gen 2:4
the g. of Adam. 5:1
the g. of Noah. 6:9; 10:1
just man and perfect in his g. 6:9
I make for perpetual g. 9:12
these are the g. of Shem. 11:10
g. of Terah. 27
me and thy seed in their g. 17:7
thy seed after thee in their g. 9
every man child in your g. must. 12
g. of Ishmael. 25:12, 13; 1 Chr 1:29
these the g. of Isaac. Gen 25:19
the g. of Esau. 36:1
g. of Jacob, Joseph. 37:2
memorial unto all g. Ex 3:15
of Levi according to their g. 6:16
to Lord throughout your g. 12:14
observe this day in your g. 17
observed by Israel in their g. 42
to be kept for your g. 16:32, 33
statute for ever to their g. 27:21
30:21; Lev 3:17; 6:18; 7:36
10:9; 17:7; 23:14, 21, 31, 41
throughout your g. Ex 29:42
burn incense throughout your g. 30:8
oil throughout your g. 31
a sign throughout your g. 31:13, 16
priesthood through their g. 40:15
of thy seed in their g. Lev 21:17
your g. may know that I. 23:43
for ever in g. 24:3; Num 10:8
18:23
covenant to a thousand g. Deut 7:9
consider the years of many g. 32:7
between you and our g. Josh 22:27
when they should say to our g. 28
g. of Israel might teach. Judg 3:2
now these are the g. of. Ruth 4:18
word which he commanded to a
thousand g. 1 Chr 16:15; Ps 105:8
sons' sons, even four g. Job 42:16
his heart to all g. Ps 33:11
to be remembered in all g. 45:17
places continue to all g. 49:11
the king's years as many g. 61:6
fear thee throughout all g. 72:5
shew forth thy praise to all g. 79:13
out thine anger to all g.? 85:5
known thy faithfulness to all g. 89:1
build up thy throne to all g. 4
our dwelling place in all g. 90:1
his truth endureth to all g. 100:5

remembrance unto all *g.* *Ps* 102:12
thy years are throughout all *g.* 24
him for righteousness to all *g.* 106:31
thy faithfulness is unto all *g.* 119:90
memorial throughout all *g.* 135:13
dominion throughout all *g.* 145:13
O Zion, shall reign to all *g.* 146:10
calling the *g.* from the. *Isa* 41:4
O arm of the Lord as in the *g.* 51:9
up the foundations of many *g.* 58:12
make thee a joy of many *g.* 60:15
the desolations of many *g.* 61:4
to the years of many *g.* *Joel* 2:2
g. from Abraham to David are 14 *g.* *Mat* 1:17
behold, all *g.* shall call. *Luke* 1:48
been hid from ages and *g.* *Col* 1:26

Gennesaret

land of *G.* *Mat* 14:34; *Mark* 6:53
Jesus stood by lake of *G.* *Luke* 5:1

Gentile

The Hebrews call the Gentiles by the general name of Goiim, *which signifies the nations that have not received the faith, or law of God. All who are not Jews and circumcised, are comprised under the word* Goiim. *Those who were converted, and embraced Judaism, they called Proselytes.*

The apostle Paul *generally includes all Gentiles under the name of* Greeks, Rom 1:16.

The old prophets declared in a very particular manner the calling of the Gentiles. Jacob foretold, that when Shiloh, or the Messiah should come, to him should the gathering of the people be; that is, the Gentiles should yield obedience to Christ, and acknowledge him for their Lord and Saviour.

and also of the *g.* *Rom* 2:9*, 10*

Gentiles

(*The Revisions very often substitute for this the word* nations)

by these the isles of the *g.* *Gen* 10:5
dwelt in Harosheth of *g.* *Judg* 4:2
Jesse, to it shall the *g.* *Isa* 11:10
judgement to the *g.* 42:1; *Mat* 12:18
light to *g.* *Isa* 42:6; 49:6
Luke 2:32; *Acts* 13:47
will lift up mine hand to *g.* *Isa* 49:22
thy seed shall inherit the *g.* 54:3
and the *g.* shall come to thy. 60:3
the forces of the *g.* shall come. 5, 11
also suck the milk of the *g.* 16
ye shall eat the riches of the *g.* 61:6
seed shall be known among the *g.* 9
and the *g.* shall see thy. 62:2
the glory of the *g.* like a. 66:12
declare my glory among the *g.* 19
destroyer of the *g.* is on. *Jer* 4:7
any of the vanities of the *g.*? 14:22*
the *g.* shall come to thee from. 16:19
came to Jeremiah against *g.* 46:1
princes are among the *g.* *Lam* 2:9
defiled bread among *g.* *Ezek* 4:13
shall they be among the *g.* *Hos* 8:8
proclaim ye this among *g.* *Joel* 3:9
Jacob shall be among the *g.* *Mi* 5:8
cast out the horns of *g.* *Zech* 1:21
be great among the *g.* *Mal* 1:11
Jordan, Galilee of the *g.* *Mat* 4:15
these things do the *g.* seek. 6:32
go not into the way of the *g.* 10:5
testimony against them and the *g.* 18
his name shall the *g.* trust. 12:21
deliver him to the *g.* to mock. 20:19
Mark 10:33; *Luke* 18:32
of *g.* exercise dominion. *Mat* 20:25
Luke 22:25
g., until the times of *g.* *Luke* 21:24
among *g.* and teach *g.* *John* 7:35
Pilate with *g.* were. *Acts* 4:27
into the possession of the *g.* 7:45
to bear my name before the *g.* 9:15
on the *g.* also was poured out. 10:45
heard that the *g.* received. 11:1
God to *g.* granted repentance? 18
g. besought these words. 13:42
Barnabas said, lo, we turn to *g.* 46
when the *g.* heard this, they. 48
Jews stirred up the *g.* *Acts* 14:2*
assault made both of Jews and *g.* 5
opened the door of faith to the *g.* 27
conversion of the *g.* great joy. 15:3
the *g.* by my mouth should hear. 7
God had wrought among the *g.* 12
how God at first did visit *g.* 14
all the *g.* on whom my name. 17
them, which from among the *g.* 19
greeting to the brethren of the *g.* 23
henceforth I will go to the *g.* 18:6
Paul into the hands of the *g.* 21:11
God wrought among the *g.* by. 19
teachest the Jews among *g.* to. 21
as touching the *g.* which believe. 25
send thee far hence to the *g.* 22:21
thee from the people and *g.* 26:17
shewing to the *g.* that they. 20
Christ should shew light to the *g.* 23
salvation of God is sent to *g.* 28:28
fruit, as among other *g.* *Rom* 1:13
when the *g.* which have not. 2:14
God is blasphemed among the *g.* 24
have proved both Jews and *g.* 3:9
also of the *g.*? yes, of the *g.* 29
Jews only, but also of the *g.* 9:24
g. which followed not after. 30
salvation is come to the *g.* 11:11
of them the riches of the *g.* 12
you *g.* as the apostle of the *g.* 13
till the fulness of the *g.* be come. 25
g. might glorify God . . . I will confess to thee among the *g.* 15:9
he saith, rejoice, ye *g.* with his. 10
praise Lord, all ye *g.* and laud him. 11
reign over the *g.* in him shall *g.* 12
minister of Jesus Christ to the *g.* that the offering up of the *g.* 16
to make the *g.* obedient by word. 18
for if the *g.* have been made. 27
but all the churches of the *g.* 16:4
as named among the *g.* *1 Cor* 5:1
things which the *g.* sacrifice. 10:20
offence, neither to Jews nor *g.* 32
ye know ye were *g.* carried. 12:2
whether we be Jews or *g.* 13
I preach among the *g.* *Gal* 2:2
mighty in me towards the *g.* 8
he did eat with the *g.* 12
manner of *g.*, why compellest *g.*? 14
Jews, and not sinners of the *g.* 15
Abraham might come on the *g.* 3:14
ye being in time past *g.* in. *Eph* 2:11
of Jesus Christ for you *g.* 3:1
that *g.* should be fellowheirs of. 6
among the *g.* the unsearchable. 8
henceforth walk not as other *g.* 4:17
this mystery among the *g.* *Col* 1:27
to speak to the *g.* *1 Thes* 2:16
lust of concupiscence, as the *g.* 4:5
a teacher of the *g.* *1 Tim* 2:7
preached to the *g.* believed on. 3:16
apostle and teacher of *g.* *2 Tim* 1:11
and that all the *g.* might hear. 4:17
honest among the *g.* *1 Pet* 2:12
wrought the will of the *g.* 4:3
taking nothing of the *g.* *3 John* 7
court is given to the *g.* *Rev* 11:2

gentle

we were *g.* among you. *1 Thes* 2:7
of the Lord must be *g.* *2 Tim* 2:24
g. shewing all meekness. *Tit* 3:2
above is pure and *g.* *Jas* 3:17
only to the good and *g.* *1 Pet* 2:18

gentleness

g. hath made me. *2 Sam* 22:36
Ps 18:35
I beseech you by the *g.* *2 Cor* 10:1
the fruit of the Spirit is *g.* *Gal* 5:22*

gently

deal *g.* with the young. *2 Sam* 18:5
he will *g.* lead those with. *Isa* 40:11

Gera

Ehud the son of *G.* *Judg* 3:15
son of *G.* *2 Sam* 16:5; 19:16, 18
1 Ki 2:8

gerahs

a shekel is twenty *g.* *Ex* 30:13
Lev 27:25; *Num* 3:47; 18:16
Ezek 45:12

Gerar

Abraham sojourned in *G.* *Gen* 20:1
Abimelech king of *G.* 2
Isaac dwelt in *G.* *Gen* 26:6
the herdmen of *G.* 20

Gergesenes

into the country of the *G.* *Mat* 8:28

Gerizim

blessing on mount *G.* *Deut* 11:29
these shall stand on mount *G.* 27:12
over against mount *G.* *Josh* 8:33
stood on top of mount *G.* *Judg* 9:7

Gershom, Gershon

sons of Levi, *G.* Kohath. *Gen* 46:11
Ex 6:16; *Num* 3:17; *1 Chr* 6:1, 16
23:6
of Moses' son was *G.* *Ex* 2:22
of *G.* Libni, Shimei. 6:17; *Num* 3:18
of *G.* was the family of. *Num* 3:21
charge of the sons of *G.* 25
sum of the sons of *G.* 4:22, 38
service of the sons of *G.* 28
four oxen gave to sons of *G.* 7:7
the sons of *G.* bearing the. 10:17
children of *G.* had. *Josh* 21:6, 27
Jonathan the son of *G.* *Judg* 18:30
of the sons of Phinehas, *G.* *Ezra* 8:2

Geshur

fled and went to *G.* *2 Sam* 13:37, 38
Joab went to *G.* 14:23
why I come from *G.* 32
thy servant vowed a vow at *G.* 15:8
Jair took *G.* and Aram. *1 Chr* 2:23

Geshurites

the *G.* dwell among the. *Josh* 13:13
his men invaded the *G.* *1 Sam* 27:8

get

saying, *g.* me this damsel. *Gen* 34:4
and so *g.* them out of the. *Ex* 1:10
and I will *g.* me honour upon. 14:17
he be poor and cannot *g.* *Lev* 14:21
such as he is able to *g.* 22, 30, 31
whose hand is not able to *g.* 32
that his hand shall *g.* *Num* 6:21
now therefore I will *g.* me. 22:34
giveth thee power to *g.* *Deut* 8:18
strangers shall *g.* up above. 28:43
g. her for me to wife. *Judg* 14:2, 3
let me *g.* away and. *1 Sam* 20:29
David made haste to *g.* 23:26
lest Sheba *g.* fenced. *2 Sam* 20:6
lord the king may *g.* *1 Ki* 1:2
Rehoboam made speed to *g.* up to his chariot. 12:18; *2 Chr* 10:18
catch them alive, and *g.* *2 Ki* 7:12
through thy precepts I *g.* *Ps* 119:104
g. wisdom, *g.* *Pr* 4:5, 7
dishonour shall he *g.* 6:33
better it is to *g.* wisdom . . . to *g.* understanding rather to be. 16:16
price in the hand of a fool to *g.* 17:16
thou learn his ways and *g.* 22:25
there is a time to *g.* and. *Eccl* 3:6
I will *g.* me to the mountains.
S of S 4:6
let us *g.* up early to vineyards. 7:12
I will *g.* me to great men. *Jer* 5:5
g. a potter's earthen bottle. 19:1
harness the horses, and *g.* up. 46:4
wings to Moab, that it may *g.* 48:9
hedged me about, I cannot *g.* out.
Lam 3:7
to destroy souls, to *g.* *Ezek* 22:27
let the beasts *g.* away. *Dan* 4:14
I will *g.* them praise. *Zeph* 3:19
to *g.* into ship. *Mat* 14:22
Mark 6:45
they may lodge and *g.* *Luke* 9:12
into sea, and *g.* to land. *Acts* 27:43
lest Satan should *g.* *2 Cor* 2:11
buy, sell, and *g.* gain. *Jas* 4:13

get *thee*

g. thee out of. *Gen* 12:1; *Acts* 7:3
g. thee into the land. *Gen* 22:2
g. thee out from this land. 31:13
g. thee to Pharaoh in. *Ex* 7:15
g. thee from me, take heed. 10:28
g. thee out, and all people. 11:8
Moses, away, *g. thee* down and thou shalt. 19:24; 32:7; *Deut* 9:12
g. thee up to mount. *Num* 27:12
Deut 33:49
g. thee up to the top. *Deut* 3:27
g. thee up to the place the. 17:8
g. thee up, wherefore? *Josh* 7:10

g. thee up to the wood. *Josh* 17:15
arise, *g. thee* down unto. *Judg* 7:9
wash thyself, *g. thee.* *Ruth* 3:3
depart, *g. thee* into. *1 Sam* 22:5
g. thee in to king David. *1 Ki* 1:13
g. thee to Anathoth to thine. 2:26
g. thee to Shiloh, behold there. 14:2
arise therefore, *g. thee* to thine. 12
g. thee hence. 17:3
g. thee to Zarephath. 9
Elijah said, *g. thee* up, eat. 18:41
g. thee down, that the rain stop. 44
g. thee to the prophets of. *2 Ki* 3:13
so didst thou *g. thee* a. *Neh* 9:10
g. thee to this treasurer, *Isa* 22:15
thou shalt say unto it, *g. thee.* 30:22
O Zion, *g. thee* up into the. 40:9
sit thou silent, and *g. thee.* 47:5
g. thee a linen girdle, put. *Jer* 13:1
son of man, *g. thee* to the. *Ezek* 3:4
and go, *g. thee* to them of the. 11
Jesus saith to him, *g. thee. Mat* 4:10
Peter, *g. thee* behind me, Satan.
16:23; *Mark* 8:33; *Luke* 4:8
g. thee out, for Herod. *Luke* 13:31
arise, *g. thee* down, go. *Acts* 10:20
g. thee quickly out of. 22:18

get ye

Lot said, up, *g. ye* out. *Gen* 19:14
g. ye out of the way, turn. *Isa* 30:11
arise, *g. ye* up to the. *Jer* 49:31
said, *g. ye* far from. *Ezek* 11:15
come, *g. ye* down, for the. *Joel* 3:13
he said, *g. ye* hence, walk. *Zech* 6:7

get you

g. you possessions. *Gen* 34:10
g. you down thither and buy. 42:2
rise up, *g. you* up in peace. 44:17
the king said, *g. you* to. *Ex* 5:4
go you, *g. you* straw where you. 11
rise up, *g. you* forth from. 12:31
turn you, *g. you* into. *Num* 14:25
g. you up from tabernacle. 16:24
Balaam said, *g. you* into your. 22:13
g. you into your tents. *Deut* 5:30
Josh 22:4
g. you to the mountain. *Josh* 2:16
to-morrow *g. you* early. *Judg* 19:9
g. you up, for ye shall. *1 Sam* 9:13
g. you down from among the. 15:6
g. you up to Carmel, and go. 25:5
flee, *g. you* off, dwell. *Jer* 49:30

Gethsemane

to a place called *G.* *Mat* 26:36
Mark 14:32

getteth

whosoever *g.* up to the. *2 Sam* 5:8
happy is the man that *g.* *Pr* 3:13
reproveth a scorner *g.* shame, rebuketh a wicked man *g.* blot. 9:7
he that heareth reproof *g.* 15:32
the heart of the prudent *g.* 18:15
he that *g.* wisdom loveth his. 19:8
so he that *g.* riches. *Jer* 17:11
he that *g.* out of the pit shall. 48:44

getting

away the cattle of his *g.* *Gen* 31:18
with all thy *g.* get. *Pr* 4:7
g. of treasures by a lying. 21:6

ghost

(*American Revision renders this* spirit)

Jacob yielded up the *g.* *Gen* 49:33
I had given up the *g.* *Job* 10:18
shall be as the giving up of *g.* 11:20
yea, man giveth up the *g.* 14:10
she hath given up the *g.* *Jer* 15:9
cried, and yielded up *g.* *Mat* 27:50
down and yielded up *g.* *Acts* 5:10
see **gave, give, holy**

Giah

Ammah that lieth before *G.*
2 Sam 2:24

giant

The Hebrew Nephel *may signify a monster, or a terrible man, who beats and bears down other men. The Scripture speaks of Giants who lived before the flood; they are called* Nephilim, *mighty men which were of old, men of renown,* Gen 6:4. *The words* Emim *and* Rephaim *are also used to denote these unusual men.*

The Anakims, *or the sons of Anak, were the most famous giants of Palestine. They dwelt near Hebron. Their stature was so much above what was common, that the Israelites, who were sent to view the promised land, told the people at their return, that they had seen giants of the race of Anak in that country, who were of so monstrous a size, that the Israelites, in comparison, were* but *grasshoppers,* Num 13:33.

sons of the *g.* *2 Sam* 21:16, 18
1 Chr 20:4
the son of the *g.* *1 Chr.* 20:6
born to the *g.* 8
runneth upon me like a *g. Job* 16:14

giants

(*The Revisions replace this word in all passages by the Hebrew word, using it as a proper name*)

were *g.* in the earth. *Gen* 6:4
the *g.* the sons of Anak. *Num* 13:33
Emims were counted *g.* *Deut* 2:11
remained of the remnant of *g.* 3:11*
Josh 12:4; 13:12
was called the land of *g.* *Deut* 3:13
the end of the valley of *g. Josh* 15:8
up to the land of the *g.* 17:15
came to the valley of the *g.* 18:16

Gibeah

when they were by *G.* *Judg* 19:14
of mount Ephraim sojourned in *G.* 16
the thing we will do to *G.* 20:9
the children of Belial in *G.* 13
themselves in array against *G.* 30
went home to *G. 1 Sam* 10:26; 15:34
in the uttermost part of *G.* 14:2
up to the Lord in *G.* *2 Sam* 21:6
Ramah is afraid, *G.* of Saul.
Isa 10:29
blow ye the cornet in *G.* *Hos* 5:8
themselves as in the days of *G.* 9:9
days of *G.* the battle of *G.* 10:9

Gibeon

feared, because *G.* was. *Josh* 10:2
help me, that we may smite *G.* 4
sun, stand thou still upon *G.* 12
by the pool of *G.* *2 Sam* 2:13
he had slain Asahel at *G.* 3:30
at the great stone in *G.* 20:8
in *G.* Lord appeared. *1 Ki* 3:5; 9:2
at *G.* dwelt father of *G.* *1 Chr* 8:29
9:35
burnt offering was at *G.* 21:29
as in the valley of *G.* *Isa* 28:21
the son of Azur in *G.* *Jer* 28:1
Ishmael by the waters in *G.* 41:12

Gibeonites

because Saul slew *G. 2 Sam* 21:1, 2
See 2 Sam 21:3, 4, 9. *1 Chr* 12:4. *Neh* 3:7

Gideon

G. threshed wheat by. *Judg* 6:11
G. built an altar there unto the. 24
Spirit of the Lord came upon *G.* 34
Jerubbaal, who is *G.* rose up. 7:1
nothing else, save sword of *G.* 14
sword of the Lord and of *G.* 18, 20
G. slew Zeba. 8:21
G. made an ephod thereof. 27
G. had 70 sons. 30
G. died in a good old age. 32
nor kindness to the house of *G.* 35
fail me to tell of *G.* *Heb* 11:32

Gideoni

prince of Benjamin, Abidan the son of *G.* *Num* 1:11; 2:22; 7:60, 65

gier eagle

abomination, the *g. e.* *Lev* 11:18*
Deut 14:17*

gift

so much dowry and *g.* *Gen* 34:12
take no *g.* a *g.* blindeth. *Ex* 23:8
Deut 16:19
the Levites as a *g. Num* 8:19; 18:6
office as a service of *g.* 18:7
the heave offering of their *g.* 11
given us any *g.*? *2 Sam* 19:42
Tyre shall be there with *g. Ps* 45:12
a *g.* is as a precious stone. *Pr* 17:8
a wicked man taketh a *g.* out. 23
a man's *g.* maketh room for. 18:16
a *g.* in secret pacifieth anger. 21:14
boasteth himself of a false *g.* 25:14
enjoy good, it is *g.* *Eccl* 3:13; 5:19
and a *g.* destroyeth the heart. 7:7
if a prince give a *g.* to. *Ezek* 46:16
if he give a *g.* to one of his. 17
if thou bring thy *g.* to. *Mat* 5:23
leave there thy *g.* before the. 24
and offer the *g.* that Moses. 8:4
it is a *g.* by me. 15:5; *Mark* 7:11
sweareth by the *g.* is. *Mat* 23:18, 19
if thou knewest the *g.* *John* 4:10
ye shall receive the *g.* *Acts* 2:38
thought the *g.* of God may be. 8:20
also was poured out the *g.* 10:45
God gave them the like *g.* as. 11:17
to you some spiritual *g.* *Rom* 1:11
is free *g.* of God and the *g.* by grace abounded. 5:15
so is the *g.* the free *g.* is of. 16
receive the *g.* of righteousness. 17
the free *g.* came on all men. 18
the *g.* of God is eternal life. 6:23
ye come behind in no *g.* *1 Cor* 1:7
man hath his proper *g.* of God. 7:7
though I have the *g.* of. 13:2
that for the *g.* bestowed. *2 Cor* 1:11
that we would receive the *g.* 8:4*
God for his unspeakable *g.* 9:15
it is the *g.* of God. *Eph* 2:8
a minister, according to the *g.* 3:7
the measure of the *g.* of Christ. 4:7
not because I desire a *g.* *Phil* 4:17
neglect not the *g.* that. *1 Tim* 4:14
stir up the *g.* that is in. *2 Tim* 1:6
tasted of the heavenly *g.* *Heb* 6:4
good *g.* and perfect *g.* *Jas* 1:17
man hath received the *g. 1 Pet* 4:10

gifts

Abraham gave *g.* to sons. *Gen* 25:6
shall hallow in their *g.* *Ex* 28:38
feasts, besides your *g.* *Lev* 23:38
out of all your *g.* offer. *Num* 18:29
David's servants, and brought *g.*
2 Sam 8:2, 6; *1 Chr* 18:2
Lord is no taking of *g.* *2 Chr* 19:7
Jehoshaphat gave great *g.* of. 21:3
Ammonites gave *g.* to Uzziah. 26:8
and many brought *g.* unto. 32:23
a feast and gave *g.* *Esth* 2:18
make them days of sending *g.* 9:22
hast received *g.* for men. *Ps* 68:18
Sheba and Seba shall offer *g.* 72:10
though thou givest many *g.* *Pr* 6:35
he that hateth *g.* shall live. 15:27
is friend to him that giveth *g.* 19:6
that receiveth *g.* overthroweth. 29:4
every one loveth *g.* *Isa* 1:23
g. to whores, *g.* to lovers. *Ezek* 16:33
polluted them in their own *g.* 20:26
when ye offer your *g.* ye pollute. 31
holy name no more with your *g.* 39
in thee have they taken *g.* 22:12
dream, ye shall receive *g.* *Dan* 2:6
king gave Daniel many great *g.* 48
then Daniel said, let thy *g.* be. 5:17
they presented to him *g.* *Mat* 2:11
how to give good *g.* 7:11
Luke 11:13
rich casting their *g.* into. *Luke* 21:1
adorned with goodly stones and *g.* 5
g. of God are without. *Rom* 11:29
having *g.* differing according. 12:6
concerning spiritual *g.* *1 Cor* 12:1
there are diversities of *g.* but the. 4
to another the *g.* of healing. 9, 28, 30
but covet earnestly the best *g.* 12:31
charity, and desire spiritual *g.* 14:1
ye are zealous of spiritual *g.* 12
captive, gave *g.* to men. *Eph* 4:8
bearing witness with *g.* *Heb* 2:4
he may offer *g.* and sacrifices. 5:1
high priest ordained to offer *g.* 8:3
there are priests that offer *g.* 4
which were offered, both *g.* and. 9:9
God testifying of Abel's *g.* 11:4
dwell on earth shall send *g. Rev* 11:10

Gihon

the second river is *G.* *Gen* 2:13

Gibeon—*Josh* 9:3, 17; 10:1, 5, 6, 10, 41; 11:19; 18:25; 21:17; *2 Sam* 2:12, 16, 24; *1 Ki* 3:4; *1 Chr* 14:16; 16:39; *2 Chr* 1:3, 13; *Neh* 3:7; 7:25; *Jer* 41:16

Solomon down to G. 1 Ki 1:33, 38
anointed him king in G. 45

Gilboa

all Israel pitched in G. 1 Sam 28:4
Saul fell down slain in mount G. 31:1
8; 2 Sam 21:12; 1 Chr 10:1, 8
by chance on mount G. 2 Sam 1:6
ye mountains of G. let there be. 21

Gilead

saw the land of G. was. Num 32:1
G. to Machir. 40; Deut 3:15
shewed him land of G. Deut 34:1
a man of war, had G. Josh 17:1
Phinehas into the land of G. 22:13
the inhabitants of G. Judg 10:18
went with the elders of G. 11:11
Ish-bosheth king over G. 2 Sam 2:9
Absalom pitched in land of G. 17:26
Tishbite, who was of G. 1 Ki 17:1
G. is mine. Ps 60:7; 108:8
of goats from G. S of S 4:1; 6:5
is there no balm in G.? Jer 8:22
thou art G. to me. 22:6
go up into G. 46:11
shall be satisfied on mount G. 50:19
G. is the city of them. Hos 6:8
is there iniquity in G.? they 12:11
they have threshed G. Amos 1:3
up women with child of G. 13
Benjamin shall possess G. Ob 19
feed in Bashan and G. Mi 7:14
them into the land of G. Zech 10:10
see **Ramoth**

Gileadite, -s

G. judged Israel. Judg 10:3
Jephthah the G. 11:1
ye G. are fugitives of. 12:4
and the G. took the passages. 5
Barzillai the G. 2 Sam 17:27
see **Barzillai**

Gilgal

up and encamped in G. Josh 4:19
Joshua unto the camp at G. 9:6
of G. sent to the camp at. 10:6
an angel came up from G. Judg 2:1
went in circuit to G. 1 Sam 7:16
go down before me to G. 10:8
let us go to G. and renew. 11:14
Saul was in G. 13:7
Samuel came not to G. 8
hewed Agag in pieces in G. 15:33
come not ye to G. nor. Hos 4:15
their wickedness is in G. 9:15
they sacrifice bullocks in G. 12:11
G. multiply transgression. Amos 4:4
enter not into G. for G. shall. 5:5
him from Shittim to G. Mi 6:5

Gilonite

the G. 2 Sam 15:12; 23:34

gin

the g. shall take him by. Job 18:9
for a g. to the inhabitants. Isa 8:14
fall into a snare where no g is?
Amos 3:5

gins

they spread a net, they set g. for me.
Ps 140:5
keep me from the g. of the. 141:9

gird

g. him with the curious. Ex 29:5, 9
Ehud did g. his dagger. Judg 3:16
g. ye on every man his. 1 Sam 25:13
g. thy sword on thy thigh. Ps 45:3
g. yourselves, and ye shall. Isa 8:9
not g. with what. Ezek 44:18
g. yourselves, and lament. Joel 1:13
shall g. himself, and. Luke 12:37
g. thyself, and serve me, till. 17:8
another shall g. thee. John 21:18
g. thyself and bind on. Acts 12:8
see **loins, sackcloth**

girded

g. him with the girdle. Lev 8:7
when ye g. on every man. Deut 1:41
six hundred men g. Judg 18:11
Samuel g. with a linen. 1 Sam 2:18
David danced, was g. 2 Sam 6:14
Joab's garment was g. unto. 20:8
thou hast g. me with. 22:40; Ps 18:39
they g. sackcloth on. 1 Ki 20:32
thou hast g. me with. Ps 30:11
setteth fast mountains, being g. 65:6
strength wherewith he hath g. 93:1
girdle wherewith he is g. 109:19
I g. thee, though thou. Isa 45:5
elders of Zion g. with. Lam 2:10
I g. thee about with fine. Ezek 16:10
images of the Chaldeans g. 23:15
lament like a virgin g. with. Joel 1:8
he took a towel and g. John 13:4
the towel wherewith he was g. 5
seven angels, breasts g. Rev 15:6
see **loins, sword**

girdedst

young thou g. thyself. John 21:18

girdeth

let not him that g. on. 1 Ki 20:11
he g. their loins with. Job 12:18*
it is God that g. me. Ps 18:32
g. her loins with strength. Pr 31:17

girding

instead of a stomacher, a g. Isa 3:24
the Lord did call to g. with. 22:12

girdle

With the long loose robes which were commonly worn in the East a girdle was very necessary when a man wished to do any active work. When men were at ease the robes fell loosely around them, but the first thing in preparing for walking or for work was to tighten the girdle and tuck up the long skirts of the robe, 1 Ki 18:46.

The girdle was sometimes of leather, but more usually a long piece of soft cloth, or silk that could be easily wrapped around the body and tied tightly.

they shall make a g. Ex 28:4
g. of the ephod which is. 8*, 27*
28*; 29:5*; 39:5*, 20*; Lev 8:7*
make g. of needlework. Ex 28:39*
they made a g. of fine twined. 39:29
David his bow and g. 1 Sam 18:4
have given thee a g. 2 Sam 18:11
blood of war on his g. 1 Ki 2:5
Elijah was girt with a g. 2 Ki 1:8
loins of kings with a g. Job 12:18
for a g. wherewith he. Ps 109:19
instead of a g. there shall. Isa 3:24
nor shall the g. of their loins. 5:27
shall be the g. of his loins, and faithfulness the g. of his reins. 11:5
strengthen Eliakim with thy g. 22:21
get thee a linen g. put it. Jer 13:1
this people shall be as this g. 10
a leathern g. Mat 3:4; Mark 1:6
g. man that owneth this g. Acts 21:11
the paps with a golden g. Rev 1:13

girdles

make for Aaron's sons g. Ex 28:40
gird Aaron and sons with g. 29:9
gird Aaron's sons with g. Lev 8:13
she delivereth g. to the. Pr 31:24
of Chaldeans girded with g.
Ezek 23:15
girded with golden g. Rev 15:6

Girgashite, -s

begat the G. Gen 10:16; 1 Chr 1:14
land of the G. Gen 15:21; Neh 9:8
Lord hath cast out the G. Deut 7:1
without fail drive out G. Judg 3:10

girl, -s

have sold a g. for wine. Joel 3:3
city be full of boys and g. Zech 8:5

girt

they that stumbled are g. 1 Sam 2:4
he was g. with a girdle. 2 Ki 1:8
Peter g. his fisher's coat. John 21:7
stand, having your loins g. Eph 6:14
g. about the paps with a. Rev 1:13

Gittite

Obed-edom the G. 2 Sam 6:10, 11
Ittai the G. 15:19, 22; 18:2
Goliath the G. 21:19

Gittith

This is the title prefixed to Psalms 8, 81, *and* 84.

It probably means either a musical instrument in use in Gath, or a vintage song to the tune of which the psalm should be sung, or a march of the Gittite guard, 2 Sam 15:18.

give

g. me the persons, and. Gen 14:21
what wilt g. me, seeing? 15:2
the field I g. thee, and the. 23:11
therefore God g. thee of dew. 27:28
all thou shalt g. me I will g. 28:22
better I g. her thee, than g. 29:19
g. me my wife. 21
g. me children or else I die. 30:1
g. me my wives and my. 26
will we g. our daughters. 34:16
thou must g. us also. Ex 10:25
her father utterly refuse to g. 22:17
on the eighth day thou shalt g. 30
then they shall g. every man. 30:12
this they shall g. every one half. 13
thou shalt g. the Levites. Num 3:9
Lord g. thee peace. 6:26
said, who shall g. us flesh? 11:4, 18
if Balak would g. me. 22:18; 24:13
I g. to Phinehas my covenant. 25:12
g. thou the more inheritance, to few thou shalt g. 26:54; 33:54
ye shall g. to Levites suburbs. 35:2
thou shalt g. him. Deut. 15:10, 14
every man g. as he is able. 16:17
Ezek 46:5, 11
day thou shalt g. him. Deut 24:15
forty stripes he may g. him. 25:3
swear to me, and g. me. Josh 2:12
now therefore g. me this. 14:12
g. me a blessing, g. springs. 15:19
Judg 1:15
that fleeth, they shall g. Josh 20:4
to g. the Midianites into. Judg 7:2
answered, we will willingly g. 8:25
nay, but thou shalt g. 1 Sam 2:16
wealth which God shall g. Israel. 32
they said g. us a king. 8:6
g. me a man that we may. 17:10
king will g. him his daughter. 25
David said, g. it me. 21:9
will the son of Jesse g. every? 22:7
shall I then g. it to men whom. 25:11
would g. me drink of the water of the well. 2 Sam 23:15; 1 Chr 11:17
these did Araunah g. 2 Sam 24:23
1 Chr 21:23
g. thy servant an. 1 Ki 3:9
O my lord, g. her the living. 26, 27
g. every man according to. 8:39*
if thou wilt g. me half. 13:8
he said, G. me thy son, and. 17:19
I said, G. thy son, that. 2 Ki 6:29
if it be, g. me thine hand. 10:15
saying, G. thy daughter to my. 14:9
g. to Lord, ye kindreds of the people.
1 Chr 16:28, 29; Ps 29:1, 2; 96:7, 8
Lord g. thee wisdom. 1 Chr 22:12
g. me now wisdom. 2 Chr 1:10
hand of God was to g. them. 30:12
and to g. us a nail in his. Ezra 9:8
to g. us a reviving, to g. us a wall. 9
g. them for a prey in land. Neh 4:4
all that a man hath will he g. Job 2:4
g. flattering titles to man. 32:21
ask of me, and I shall g. Ps 2:8
g. them according to. 28:4
he shall g. thee the desires. 37:4
none can g. to God a ransom. 49:7
not sacrifice, else would I g. 51:16
g. us help from. 60:11; 108:12
can he g. bread also? can he? 78:20
O turn, g. thy strength to. 86:16
shall g. his angels. 91:11; Mat 4:6
but I g. myself unto. Ps 109:4
g. me. 119:34, 73, 125, 144, 169
g. instruction to a wise. Pr 9:9
my son, g. me thine heart. 23:26
if enemy hunger, g. him. 25:21
Rom 12:20
the rod and reproof g. Pr 29:15
shall g. thee rest, shall g. delight. 17
g. me neither poverty nor 30:8
two daughters, crying, g. 15
that he may g. to him. Eccl 2:26
g. a portion to seven. 11:2
man would g. substance. S of S 8:7
then he shall g. the rain. Isa 30:23
g. place to me, that I. 49:20

may g. seed to the sower. Isa 55:10
g. unto them beauty for ashes. 61:3
g. him no rest till he establish. 62:7
shall I g. thee a pleasant? Jer 3:19
to whom shall I speak and g.? 6:10*
to g. man according. 17:10; 32:19
g. heed to me, O Lord. 18:19
I think to g. you an expected. 29:11
bring them, and g. them wine. 35:2
tears run down, g. thyself. Lam 2:18
g. them sorrow of heart, thy. 3:65
mouth, eat that I g. thee. Ezek 2:8
with this roll that I g. thee. 3:3
and g. them warning. 17
thy children, which didst g. 16:36
to land, I lifted up mine hand to g. it to them. 20:28, 42; 47:14
if wicked g. again that he. 33:15
prince g. a gift to his sons. 46:16, 17
and g. thy rewards to. Dan 5:17
I am come forth to g. 9:22*
with shame do love, g. ye. Hos 4:18
g. O Lord, what wilt thou g.? 9:14
thou saidst, g. me a king and. 13:10
shall I g. my firstborn? Mi 6:7
g. her fruit, the ground shall g. increase, and heavens g. Zech 8:12
g. me my price, if not. 11:12
g. to him that asketh thee. Mat 5:42
g. us this day our. 6:11; Luke 11:3
if he ask bread, will he g.? Mat 7:9
will he g. a serpent? 10; Luke 11:11
g. gifts unto your children, your Father g. to them that ask him? Mat 7:11; Luke 11:13
g. place. Mat 9:24
freely ye received, freely g. 10:8
shall g. to drink a cup. 42
he promised to g. her what. 14:7
g. ye them to eat. 16; Mark 6:37
Luke 9:13
what g. in exchange for his soul? Mat 16:26; Mark 8:37
and g. to them for. Mat 17:27
command to g. a writing? 19:7
g. to the poor. 19:21; Mark 10:21
call the labourers, and g. Mat 20:8
is not mine to g. 20:23; Mark 10:40
g. us of your oil, for our. Mat 25:8
what will ye g. me? 26:15
I will that thou g. me. Mark 6:25
and he will g. the vineyard. 12:9
whomsoever I will, I g. it. Luke 4:6
g. and it shall be given . . . good measure shall men g. 6:38
he will g. him as many as he. 11:8
g. alms of such things. 41; 12:33
he that bade thee say, g. this. 14:9
younger said, g. me the. 15:12
who shall g. you that which? 16:12
Jesus saith, G. me. John 4:7, 10
drinketh water I shall g. 14
the Son of man shall g. you. 6:27
said, Lord, evermore g. us. 34
how can this man g. us his? 52
g. God the praise, this man. 9:24
I g. to them eternal life. 10:28
thou wilt ask, God will g. 11:22
that he should g. something. 13:29
g. you another Comforter. 14:16
my peace I g. unto you not as world giveth, g. I unto you. 27
shall ask, he may g. it. 15:16
whatsoever ye ask he will g. 16:23
that he should g. eternal life. 17:2
such as I have g. I thee. Acts 3:6
we will g. ourselves to prayer. 6:4*
he promised he would g. it for. 7:5
Simon said, G. me also. 8:19
it is more blessed to g. than. 20:35
with him also freely g. us. Rom 8:32
avenge not, but rather g. 12:19
ye may g. yourselves. 1 Cor 7:5
g. none offence, neither. 10:32
let him g. not grudgingly. 2 Cor 9:7
God may g. you the. Eph 1:17
that he may have to g. to him. 4:28
g. to your servants that. Col 4:1*
g. attendance to reading. 1 Tim 4:13
meditate, g. thyself wholly to. 15
righteous Judge shall g. 2 Tim 4:8
we ought to g. the more. Heb 2:1
g. life for them that sin. 1 John 5:16
g. me the little book. Rev. 10:9
he had power to g. life. Rev 13:15
to g. her the cup of the wine. 16:19
torment and sorrow g. her. 18:7
to g. every man according. 22:12*

see **account, charge, ear, glory, light, sware**

I will **give**

I will g. to thee and thy seed the land. Gen 17:8; 48:4; Deut 34:4
I will g. thee a son also. Gen 17:16
I will surely g. the tenth to. 28:22
shall say to me I will g. 34:11, 12
and I will g. this people. Ex 3:21
with thee, and I will g. 33:14
I will g. you rain in due season. Lev 26:4; Deut 11:14
I will g. peace in the land. Lev 26:6
I will g. him to the. 1 Sam 1:11
I will g. her, that she may be. 18:21
I will g. thy wives to. 2 Sam 12:11
not rend all, but I will g. 1 Ki 11:13
I will g. ten tribes to thee. 31
come home, and I will g. thee. 13:7
I will g. thee for it a better. 21:2
I will g. thee the vineyard of. 7
I will g. him rest, I will g. 1 Chr 22:9
I will g. thee riches. 2 Chr 1:12
O Lord, I will g. thanks. Ps 30:12
I will sing and g. 57:7*; 108:1*
to-morrow I will g. when. Pr 3:28
I will g. them children to. Isa 3:4
Zion, behold, and I will g. 41:27
I will g. thee for. 42:6; 49:8
I will g. thee the treasures. 45:3
I will g. thee for a light to the. 49:6
I will g. them an everlasting. 56:5
I will g. pastors according. Jer 3:15
I will g. them waters of gall. 9:15
I will g. you assured peace. 14:13
I will g. thy substance to the. 17:3
I will g. them an heart to. 24:7
I will g. them one heart. 32:39
Ezek 11:19
I will g. men that have. Jer 34:18
I will g. it into the hand. Ezek 7:21
and I will g. you the land of. 11:17
I will g. thee blood in fury. 16:38*
I will also g. thee into their. 39
I will g. them to thee for. 61
whose right it is, I will g. 21:27
I will g. them to be removed. 23:46
I will g. land of Egypt to. 29:19
I will g. thee the opening of the. 21
and I will g. you an heart. 36:26
I will g. her vineyards. Hos 2:15
unto me, and I will g. Mat 11:28
I will g. to thee the keys of. 16:19
is right, I will g. you. 20:4
I will g. to this last even as. 14
what thou wilt, I will g. Mark 6:22
for I will g. you a mouth. Luke 21:15
I will g. is my flesh, which I will g. for the life of the world. John 6:51
I will g. you the sure. Acts 13:34
be faithful, I will g. thee. Rev 2:10
I will g. him a white stone and. 17
I will g. to every one according. 23
I will g. him the morning star. 28
and I will g. power to my two. 11:3
I will g. to him that is athirst. 21:6

will I **give**

will I g. this land. Gen 12:7; 13:15
24:7; 28:13; 35:12; Ex 32:13
33:1
Caleb, to him will I g. Deut 1:36
go in thither, to them will I g. 39
to him will I g. Achsah. Josh 15:16
Judg 1:12
will I g. to the man of. 1 Sam 9:8
Merab, her will I g. thee. 18:17
to thee will I g. land. 1 Chr 16:18
Ps 105:11
therefore will I g. thanks. Ps 18:49
there will I g. thee my. S of S 7:12
therefore will I g. men for. Isa 43:4
them will I g. in mine house. 56:5
so will I g. Zedekiah. Jer 24:8
thy life will I g. to thee for a. 45:5
so will I g. inhabitants. Ezek 15:6
new heart also will I g. you. 36:26
and in this place will I g. Hag 2:9
all these things will I g. Mat 4:9
all this power will I g. Luke 4:6
overcometh will I g. Rev 2:7, 17, 26

Lord **give**

land which Lord will g. you. Ex 12:25
Lev 14:34; 23:10; 25:2; Num 15:2
the Lord shall g. you flesh. Ex 16:8
therefore the Lord will g. Num 11:18
Lord delight in us, he will g. 14:8
Lord refuseth to g. me leave. 22:13
Lord commanded to g. nine. 34:13
Lord commanded to g. the land. 36:2
land the Lord doth g. Deut 1:25
the Lord shall g. thee a. 28:65
Lord commanded Moses to g. Josh 9:24
Lord commanded to g. us. 17:4
the Lord commanded to g. us cities. 21:2
which the Lord shall g. Ruth 4:12
the Lord his God did g. 1 Ki 15:4
the Lord is able to g. 2 Chr 25:9
the Lord will g. strength. Ps 29:11
the Lord will g. grace and. 84:11
the Lord shall g. that which. 85:12
the Lord himself shall g. Isa 7:14
the Lord shall g. thee rest. 14:3
though the Lord g. you bread. 30:20
Lord shall g. them showers. Zech 10:1
Lord shall g. him the. Luke 1:32
Lord g. mercy to house. 2 Tim 1:16

not **give**, *or* **give** *not*

said, thou shalt not g. Gen 30:31
I will not g. you straw. Ex 5:10
shall not g. more, poor not g. 30:15
shalt not g. thy money. Lev 25:37
I will not g. you of. Deut 2:5; 9:19
thy daughter thou shalt not g. 7:3
he will not g. of the flesh of. 28:55
shall not any of us g. Judg 21:1
we have sworn we will not g. 7
we will not g. them. 1 Sam 30:22
I will not g. inheritance. 1 Ki 21:4
g. not your daughters. Ezra 9:12
Neh 10:30; 13:25
not g. sleep to mine. Ps 132:4
g. not sleep to thine eyes. Pr 6:4
g not thy strength unto. 31:3
constellations shall not g. Isa 13:10
my glory will I not g. 42:8; 48:11
I will no more g. thy corn. 62:8
let us not g. heed to any. Jer 18:18
not g. Jeremiah into the hand. 26:24
a cloud, the moon shall not g. her light. Ezek 32:7; Mat 24:29
Mark 13:24
to whom not g. honour. Dan 11:21
g. not thine heritage to. Joel 2:17
g. not that which is holy. Mat 7:6
g. or shall we not g.? Mark 12:15
neither g. place to the. Eph 4:27
g. not those things they. Jas 2:16

give *thanks*

I will g. thanks. 2 Sam 22:50
Ps 18:49
g. thanks to the Lord, call upon. 1 Chr 16:8; Ps 105:1; 106:1
107:1; 118:1, 29; 136:1, 3
God of our salvation, that we may g. thanks. 1 Chr 16:35; Ps 106:47
by name, to g. thanks. 1 Chr 16:41
with a harp to g. thanks. 25:3
appointed Levites to g. thanks. 2 Chr 31:2
who shall g. thee thanks? Ps 6:5
g. thanks at the remembrance of his holiness. 30:4; 97:12
Lord, I will g. thanks to thee. 30:12
I will g. thanks in the great. 35:18
do we g. thanks, do g. thanks. 75:1
people will g. thee thanks. 79:13
it is a good thing to g. thanks. 92:1
save us to g. thanks to thy. 106:47
I will rise to g. thanks. 119:62
the tribes go up to g. thanks. 122:4
g. thanks unto God of gods. 136:2
O g. thanks unto God of heaven. 26
righteous shall g. thanks to. 140:13
not only I g. thanks. Rom 16:4
for which I g. thanks. 1 Cor 10:30
I cease not to g. thanks. Eph 1:16
we g. thanks to God and. Col 1:3

g. thanks to God always. 1 Thes 1:2
in every thing g. thanks. 5:18
bound to g. thanks. 2 Thes 2:13
g. thee thanks, Lord God. Rev 11:17

give up

the Lord walketh, to g. up thine enemies. Deut 23:14; 31:5
he shall g. Israel up. 1 Ki 14:16
did not I g. up the ghost? Job 3:11
hold my tongue, I shall g. up. 13:19
I will say to north, g. up. Isa 43:6
how shall I g. thee up? Hos 11:8
therefore will he g. them up. Mi 5:3
thou deliverest will I g. up. 6:14

given

Sarah should have g. Gen 21:7
because he hath g. his. Lev 20:3
they are g. as a gift for. Num 18:6
to the blessing g. Deut 12:15; 16:17
a full reward be g. thee. Ruth 2:12
thought I would have g. 2 Sam 4:10
would have g. thee such and. 12:8*
I would have g. thee ten. 18:11
hath the king g. us any gift? 19:42
the man of God had g. 1 Ki 13:5
thine own have we g. 1 Chr 29:14
let it be g. them day by. Ezra 6:9
the silver is g. to thee. Esth 3:11
let my life be g. me at my. 7:3
why is light g. to him? Job 3:20
why is light g. to a man whose? 23
whom alone the earth was g. 15:19
bodies of thy servants g. Ps 79:2
he hath g. to the. 112:9; 2 Cor 9:9
the earth hath he g. to the. Ps 115:16
that which he hath g. will. Pr 19:17
deliver those that are g. Eccl 8:8
are g. from one shepherd. 12:11
Child is born, to us Son is g. Isa 9:6
therefore hear, thou that art g. 47:8
g. to covetousness. Jer 6:13; 8:10
he said to all who had g. him. 44:20
we have g. the hand to. Lam 5:6
is this land g. Ezek 11:15; 33:24
they are desolate, they are g. 35:12
beasts, fowls hath he g. Dan 2:38
lion, and a man's heart was g. 7:4
she shall be g. up, and they. 11:6
it is g. to you to know the mysteries. Mat 13:11; Mark 4:11; Luke 8:10
save they to whom it is g. Mat 19:11
be g. to a nation bringing. 21:43
are g. in marriage. 22:30
Mark 12:25; Luke 20:35
sold for much and g. Mat 26:9
Mark 14:5
all power is g. to me in. Mat 28:18
hear more shall be g. Mark 4:24
to whom much is g. of. Luke 12:48
nothing, except it be g. John 3:27
hath g. to the Son to have life. 5:26
of all he hath g. me, I should. 6:39
come to me, except it were g. 65
except it were g. thee from. 19:11
is none other name g. Acts 4:12
hoped that money should be g. 24:26
Holy Ghost which is g. Rom 5:5
who hath first g. to him. 11:35
because of the grace that is g. 15:15
freely g. us of God. 1 Cor 2:12
that thanks may be g. 2 Cor 1:11
law g. which could have g. Gal 3:21*
dispensation, which is g. Eph 3:2
unto me, the least, is this grace g. 8
who have g. themselves over. 4:19
Christ hath loved us, and g. 5:2
to you it is g. in behalf. Phil 1:29*
and hath g. him a name above. 2:9
if Jesus had g. them rest. Heb 4:8
Spirit which he hath g. 1 John 3:24
because he hath g. us of his. 4:13
white robes were g. to. Rev 6:11
power was g. to him to. 13:5
it was g. unto him to make war. 7

God or Lord hath, had given

the Lord hath g. Abraham flocks. Gen 24:35
and Rachel said, God hath g. 30:6
and Leah said, God hath g. me. 18
God hath g. me your father's. 31:9
G. hath graciously g. me. 33:5
God hath g. you treasure in. 43:23
the children God hath g. me. 48:9
the Lord hath g. you. Ex 16:15
for that the Lord hath g. you the. 29
land which the Lord hath g. them. Num 32:7, 9; Deut 3:18; 28:52
Josh 2:9, 14; 23:13, 15; Jer 25:5
shout, for Lord hath g. Josh 6:16
land which the Lord hath g. 18:3
Lord hath g. me my. 1 Sam 1:27
Lord hath g. it to a neighbour. 15:28; 28:17
with what the Lord hath g. 30:23
the kingdom hath God g. me. 2 Chr 36:23; Ezra 1:2
man to whom God hath g. Eccl 5:19
children Lord hath g. Isa 8:18
Heb 2:13
Lord hath g. a command. Isa 23:11
Lord hath g. me the tongue. 50:4
Lord hath g. knowledge. Jer 11:18
seeing the Lord hath g. it. 47:7
the Lord had g. thanks. John 6:23
whom God hath g. to. Acts 5:32
God hath g. thee all that. 27:24
God hath g. them spirit. Rom 11:8
the Lord hath g. us for edification. 2 Cor 10:8; 13:10
but God who hath g. us. 1 Thes 4:8
the record God hath g. 1 John 5:11
see **rest**

I have, or have I given

brethren have I g. him. Gen 27:37
I have g. thee that thou. 1 Ki 3:13
therefore I have g. Jacob. Isa 43:28*
I have g. him for a witness. 55:4
things I have g. shall pass. Jer 8:13
I have g. it to whom it seemed. 27:5
I have g. thee cow's dung. Ezek 4:15
I have g. him land of Egypt. 29:20
I have g. you cleanness. Amos 4:6
be pulled out of land I have g. 9:15
I have g. you example. John 13:15
I have g. them the words. 17:8, 14
gavest me, I have g. them. 22
I have g. order to the. 1 Cor 16:1

not given

and she was not g. unto. Gen 38:14
I have not g. ought. Deut 26:14
Lord hath not g. you an heart. 29:4
hath he not g. you rest? 1 Chr 22:18
Levites had not been g. Neh 13:10
thou hast not g. water to. Job 22:7
maidens were not g. Ps 78:63
but he hath not g. me over. 118:18
who hath not g. us as a prey. 124:6
Jerusalem not be g. into. Isa 37:10
thou shalt not be g. into. Jer 39:17
because thou hast not g. Ezek 3:20
he that hath not g. forth upon. 18:8
to them it is not g. Mat 13:11
Holy Ghost was not yet g. John 7:39
bishop not g. to wine. 1 Tim 3:3*
Tit 1:7*
not g. to much wine. 1 Tim 3:8
God hath not g. us the. 2 Tim 1:7
women likewise not g. to. Tit 2:3*

shall be given

shall inheritance be g. Num 26:54
thy sheep shall be g. to. Deut 28:31
thy sons shall be g. to another. 32
commandment shall be g. Ezra 4:21
it shall be g. to half of. Esth 5:3
to him shall be g. of gold. Ps 72:15
what shall be g. to thee? 120:3
reward shall be g. him. Isa 3:11
bread shall be g. him, waters. 33:16
glory of Lebanon shall be g. 35:2
this city shall be g. into the hand of king. Jer 21:10; 38:3, 18
marishes, they shall be g. Ezek 47:11
the saints shall be g. into. Dan 7:25
the kingdom shall be g. to the. 27
ask and it shall be g. you in that same hour. Mat 7:7; Luke 11:9
shall be g. you in same. Mat 10:19
Mark 13:11
no sign shall be g. Mat 12:39
Mark 8:12; Luke 11:29
hath, to him shall be g. and more abundance. Mat 13:12; 25:29
Mark 4:25; Luke 8:18
it shall be g. them for. Mat 20:23
kingdom of God shall be g. 21:43
give, and it shall be g. Luke 6:38
your prayers I shall be g. Philem 22
God, and it shall be g. him. Jas 1:5

thou hast, or hast thou given

thou hast g. no seed. Gen 15:3
which thou hast g. us. Deut 26:15
thou hast g. me south. Josh 15:19*
Judg 1:15*
why hast thou g. me? Josh 17:14
thou hast g. this great. Judg 15:18
thou hast g. him bread. 1 Sam 22:13
this deed thou hast g. 2 Sam 12:14
thou hast g. me the shield of thy salvation. 22:36; Ps 18:35
thou hast g. me the necks. 2 Sam 22:41; Ps 18:40
thou hast g. him a son to. 1 Ki 3:6
land thou hast g. 8:36; 2 Chr 6:27
are these thou hast g.? 1 Ki 9:13
possession thou hast g. 2 Chr 20:11
thou hast g. us such. Ezra 9:13
thou hast g. him his heart's. Ps 21:2
thou hast g. us like sheep. 44:11
thou hast g. a banner to them. 60:4
thou hast g. me the heritage. 61:5
thou hast g. commandment to. 71:3
thou hast g. him power. John 17:2
that all things thou hast g. me. 7
but for them which thou hast g. 9
thy name those thou hast g. me. 11
thou hast g. them blood. Rev 16:6

giver

taker of usury, so with g. Isa 24:2
God loveth a cheerful g. 2 Cor 9:7

givest

thou g. him nought, and. Deut 15:9
not be grieved when thou g. him. 10
if righteous, what g. thou? Job 35:7
thou g. thy mouth to evil. Ps 50:19
thou g. them tears to drink. 80:5
thou g. them, they gather. 104:28
thou g. them their meat in. 145:15
rest content, though thou g. Pr 6:35
thou g. not warning, to. Ezek 3:18
but thou g. thy gifts to all. 16:33
that thou g. a reward, and none. 34
thou verily g. thanks. 1 Cor 14:17

giveth

he g. you on sixth day. Ex 16:29
in land which Lord thy God g. thee. 20:12; Deut 4:40; 5:16; 25:15
every man that g. willingly. Ex 25:2*
all that any man g. Lev 27:9
the Lord our God g. thee. Deut 2:29
4:1, 21; 11:17, 31; 12:1, 10*
15:4, 7; 16:20; 17:14; 18:9; 19:1
2, 10, 14; 21:1, 23; 24:4; 26:1, 2
27:2, 3; 28:8; Josh 1:11, 15
he that g. thee power. Deut 8:18
God g. not this land for thy. 9:6
g. you rest from. 12:10; 25:19
if a prophet g. thee a sign or. 13:1
gates which Lord g. 16:5, 18; 17:2
who g. rain upon the earth. Job 5:10
he g. no account of any of his. 33:13
when he g. quietness. 34:29
who g. songs. 35:10
but g. right to the poor. 36:6
he g. meat. 31
great deliverance g. he. Ps 18:50
righteous sheweth mercy, g. 37:21
God of Israel is he that g. 68:35
of thy words g. light. 119:130
for so he g. his beloved. 127:2
who g. food to all flesh. 136:25
146:7; 147:9
g. salvation to kings. 144:10
he g. snow. 147:16
the Lord g. wisdom out. Pr 2:6
he g. grace to the lowly. 3:34
Jas 4:6; 1 Pet 5:5
good understanding g. Pr 13:15
g. and spareth not. 21:26; 22:9
he that g. to the poor shall. 28:27
g. to a man that is good, but to the sinner he g. travail. Eccl 2:26
yet God g. him not power to. 6:2
he g. power to the faint. Isa 40:29
g. breath. 42:5
g. rain. Jer 5:24
woe to him that g. him not. 22:13
g. the sun for a light. 31:35
he g. his cheek to him. Lam 3:30

he *g.* wisdom to the wise. *Dan* 2:21
and *g.* it to whomsover. 4:17, 25, 32
woe to him that *g.* his. *Hab* 2:15
it *g.* light to all that are. *Mat* 5:15
God *g.* not the Spirit. *John* 3:34
but my Father *g.* you the true. 6:32
who cometh down and *g.* life. 33
all that the Father *g.* me shall. 37
the good shepherd *g.* his. 10:11
not as the world *g.* give I. 14:27
he *g.* to all life, breath. *Acts* 17:25
he that *g.* let him do it. *Rom* 12:8
he eateth to the Lord, for he *g.* 14:6
but God that *g.* the. *1 Cor* 3:7
he that *g.* her in marriage. 7:38
God *g.* it a body as it hath. 15:38
but thanks be to God who *g.* us. 57
killeth, but the Spirit *g.* *2 Cor* 3:6
g. us richly all things. *1 Tim* 6:17
ask of God, that *g.* to. *Jas* 1:5
g. more grace, God *g.* grace to. 4:6
as of ability that God *g.* *1 Pet* 4:11*
for the Lord God *g.* *Rev* 22:5

giving
loveth the stranger in *g.* *Deut* 10:18
by *g.* him a double portion of. 21:17
visited his people in *g.* *Ruth* 1:6
my desire, in *g.* food. *1 Ki* 5:9
by *g.* him according to. *2 Chr* 6:23
their hope be as the *g.* *Job* 11:20
were marrying and *g.* *Mat* 24:38
g. out that himself was. *Acts* 8:9
g. them the Holy Ghost, as he. 15:8
was strong in faith, *g.* *Rom* 4:20
g. of the law, and the service. 9:4
things *g.* sound. *1 Cor* 14:7
at thy *g.* of thanks. 16
g. no offence in any thing. *2 Cor* 6:3
concerning *g.* and. *Phil* 4:15
g. heed to seducing. *1 Tim* 4:1
g. honour to the wife as. *1 Pet* 3:7
g. all diligence, add to. *2 Pet* 1:5
g. themselves over to. *Jude* 7
see **thanks**

glad
seeth thee, he will be *g.* *Ex* 4:14
the priest's heart was *g.* *Judg* 18:20
men of Jabesh were *g.* *1 Sam* 11:9
Israel went to tents *g.* *1 Ki* 8:66
2 Chr 7:10
Haman *g.* *Esth* 5:9
the city Shushan was *g.* 8:15
are *g.* when they can find. *Job* 3:22
see it and are *g.* 22:19; *Ps* 64:10
therefore my heart is *g.* *Ps* 16:9
thou hast made him *g.* with. 21:6
shall hear and be *g.* 34:2; 69:32
them be *g.* that favour my. 35:27
they have made thee *g.* 45:8
the streams shall make *g.* the. 46:4
let the nations be *g.* and sing. 67:4
make us *g.* 90:15
thou, Lord, hast made me *g.* 92:4
let the isles be *g.* 97:1
Zion heard, and was *g.* 8
wine that maketh *g.* the. 104:15
I will be *g.* in the Lord. 34*
Egypt was *g.* 105:38
then are they *g.* because. 107:30
they that fear thee will be *g.* 119:74
I was *g.* when they said unto. 122:1
whereof we are *g.* 126:3
a wise son maketh a *g.* father.
Pr 10:1; 15:20
but a good word maketh it *g.* 12:25
that is *g.* at calamities, not. 17:5
and thy mother shall be *g.* 23:25
let not thy heart be *g.* when. 24:17
wise, and make my heart *g.* 27:11
wilderness shall be *g.* *Isa* 35:1
Hezekiah was *g.* of them, and. 39:2
is born, making him very *g.* *Jer* 20:15
because ye were *g.* O ye. 50:11
they are *g.* that thou. *Lam* 1:21
was the king exceeding *g.* *Dan* 6:23
they make the king *g.* *Hos* 7:3
Jonah was *g.* because of. *Jonah* 4:6
shall see it and be *g.* *Zech* 10:7
were *g.* and promised money.
Mark 14:11; *Luke* 22:5
I am sent to shew thee these *g.* tidings. *Luke* 1:19*
shewing the *g.* tidings of the. 8:1*

make merry and be *g.* *Luke* 15:32
saw my day and was *g.* *John* 8:56
I am *g.* for your sakes that I. 11:15
seen grace of G. he was *g.* *Acts* 11:23
heard this, they were *g.* 13:48
I am *g.* therefore on. *Rom* 16:19*
I am *g.* of the coming. *1 Cor* 16:17*
then that maketh me *g.*? *2 Cor* 2:2
we are *g.* when we are weak. 13:9*
glory revealed, ye may be *g.* also.
1 Pet 4:13*

glad joined with *rejoice*
be *g.* and let the earth *rejoice.*
1 Chr 16:31; *Ps* 96:11
I will be *g.* and *rejoice.* *Ps* 9:2
rejoice, Israel shall be *g.* 14:7; 53:6
I will be *g.* and *rejoice* in thy. 31:7
be *g.* and *rejoice,* ye righteous.
32:11; 68:3
that seek thee, be *g.* and *rejoice.*
40:16; 70:4
rejoice, daughters of Judah be *g.*
48:11*
that we may be *g.* and *rejoice.* 90:14
we will *rejoice* and be *g.* in it. 118:24
we will be *g.* and *rejoice* in thee.
S of S 1:4
we will *rejoice* and be *g.* in his salvation. *Isa* 25:9
but be you *g.* and *rejoice* for. 65:18
rejoice ye with Jerusalem, and be *g.*
66:10
rejoice and be *g.* O Edom. *Lam* 4:21
O land, be *g.* and *rejoice.* *Joel* 2:21
g. ye children of Zion, and *rejoice.* 23
they *rejoice* and are *g.* *Hab* 1:15
be *g.* and *rejoice,* O. *Zeph* 3:14
rejoice and be *g.* great. *Mat* 5:12
rejoice, my tongue was *g.* *Acts* 2:26*
be *g.* and *rejoice,* the. *Rev* 19:7*

gladly
Herod heard John *g.* *Mark* 6:20
people heard Christ *g.* 12:37
that *g.* received the word. *Acts* 2:41
the brethren received us *g.* 21:17
ye suffer fools *g.* seeing. *2 Cor* 11:19
most *g.* therefore will I rather. 12:9
I will very *g.* spend and be. 15

gladness
in the day of your *g.* ye. *Num* 10:10
not the Lord with *g.* of. *Deut* 28:47
brought up ark with *g.* *2 Sam* 6:12*
strength and *g.* are in. *1 Chr* 16:27
drink that day with great *g.* 29:22
sang praises with *g.* *2 Chr* 29:30
of unleavened bread with *g.* 30:21
kept other seven days with *g.* 23
there was very great *g.* *Neh* 8:17
keep the dedication with *g.* 12:27
light, and *g.* and joy. *Esth* 8:16, 17
a day of feasting and *g.* 9:17, 18, 19
thou hast put *g.* in my heart. *Ps* 4:7
thou hast girded me with *g.* 30:11
thee with oil of *g.* 45:7; *Heb* 1:9
with *g.* and rejoicing shall. *Ps* 45:15
make me to hear joy and *g.* 51:8
and *g.* is sown for the upright. 97:11
serve the Lord with *g.*: come. 100:2
forth his chosen with *g.* 105:43*
that I may rejoice in the *g.* 106:5
the righteous shall be *g.* *Pr* 10:28
and in the day of the *g.* *S of S* 3:11
joy and *g.* is taken away. *Isa* 16:10
behold joy and *g.* 22:13
ye shall have a song and *g.* 30:29
obtain joy and *g.* 35:10; 51:11
joy and *g.* shall be found. 51:3
cease voice of mirth and *g.* *Jer* 7:34
16:9; 25:10
sing with *g.* for Jacob, shout. 31:7
heard a voice of joy and *g.* 33:11
joy and *g.* taken from the. 48:33
joy and *g.* from house. *Joel* 1:16
house of Judah joy and *g.* *Zech* 8:19
receive it with *g.* *Mark* 4:16*
shalt have joy and *g.* *Luke* 1:14
did eat their meat with *g.* *Acts* 2:46
opened not the gate for *g.* 12:14*
our hearts with food and *g.* 14:17
in the Lord with all *g.* *Phil* 2:29*

glass
see through a *g.* darkly. *1 Cor* 13:12*

beholding as in a *g.* *2 Cor* 3:18*
his natural face in a *g.* *Jas* 1:23*
there was a sea of *g.* like. *Rev* 4:6
I saw a sea of *g.* mingled. 15:2
pure gold, like clear *g.* 21:18, 21

glasses
Lord will take away *g.* *Isa* 3:23*
see **looking**

glean
thou shalt not *g.* vineyard.
Lev 19:10; *Deut* 24:21
go to field and *g.* ears. *Ruth* 2:2
they shall thoroughly *g.* *Jer* 6:9

gleaned
g. of them in highways. *Judg* 20:45
she came and *g.* after. *Ruth* 2:3

gleaning, -s
the *g.* of harvest. *Lev* 19:9; 23:22
is not the *g.* of grapes? *Judg* 8:2
yet *g.* grapes shall be left. *Isa* 17:6
the *g.* grapes when vintage is. 24:13
they not leave some *g.*? *Jer* 49:9
I am as the grape *g.* of the. *Mi* 7:1

glede
ye shall not eat the *g.* *Deut* 14:13

glistering
now I have prepared *g.* *1 Chr* 29:2*
the *g.* sword cometh out. *Job* 20:25
raiment was white and *g.* *Luke* 9:29*

glitter, -ing
if I whet my *g.* sword. *Deut* 32:41
g. spear rattleth against. *Job* 39:23*
furbished that it may *g.* *Ezek* 21:10*
to consume, because of the *g.* 28*
lifteth up the *g.* spear. *Nah* 3:3
shining of thy *g.* spear. *Hab* 3:11

gloominess
a day of darkness and *g.* *Joel* 2:2
Zeph 1:15

gloriest
wherefore *g.* thou in the? *Jer* 49:4

glorieth
let him that *g.* *Jer* 9:24
1 Cor 1:31; *2 Cor* 10:17

glorified
all the people I will be *g.* *Lev* 10:3
hast increased nation, thou art *g.*
Isa 26:15
for the Lord hath *g.* himself. 44:23
O Israel, in whom I will be *g.* 49:3
of Israel he hath *g.* thee. 55:5; 60:9
my hands, that I may be *g.* 60:21
of the Lord that he might be *g.* 61:3
said, let the Lord be *g.* 66:5
I will be *g.* in midst. *Ezek* 28:22
in the day I shall be *g.* 39:13
hast thou not *g.* *Dan* 5:23
pleasure in it, and be *g.* *Hag* 1:8
marvelled, and *g.* God. *Mat* 9:8
Mark 2:12; *Luke* 5:26
they *g.* the God of Israel. *Mat* 15:31
synagogues, being *g.* of. *Luke* 4:15
fear on all, and they *g.* God. 7:16
made straight, and *g.* God. 13:13
the leper *g.* God. 17:15
the centurion *g.* God. 23:47
Holy Ghost was not yet given, because Jesus not *g.* *John* 7:39
Son of God might be *g.* 11:4
but when Jesus was *g.* 12:16
the Son of man should be *g.* 23
I have both *g.* it, and will. 28
Son of man *g.* God is *g.* in. 13:31
if God be *g.* in him, God shall. 32
that the Father may be *g.* in. 14:13
herein is my Father *g.* that ye. 15:8
I have *g.* thee on earth. 17:4
and thine are mine, and I am *g.* 10
God of our fathers hath *g.* *Acts* 3:13
for all men *g.* God for what. 4:21
they held their peace, and *g.* 11:18
Gentiles heard this, they *g.* 13:48
they of Jerusalem *g.* the Lord. 21:20
they knew God, they *g.* *Rom* 1:21
with him, that we may be *g.* 8:17
whom he justified, them he also *g.* 30
and they *g.* God in me. *Gal* 1:24
come to be *g.* in saints. *2 Thes* 1:10
the name of Jesus may be *g.* 12
word of the Lord may be *g.* 3:1
so Christ *g.* not himself. *Heb* 5:5

that God in all things may be g. through Jesus Christ. 1 Pet 4:11
spoken of, but on your part he is g. 14
how much she hath g. Rev 18:7

glorifieth, -ing

whoso offereth praise g. Ps 50:23
shepherds returned, g. Luke 2:20
he departed to his own house, g. 5:25
the blind man followed him, g. 18:43

glorify

all ye seed of Jacob g. Ps 22:23
thee, and thou shalt g. me. 50:15
all nations shall come and g. 86:9
and I will g. thy name for ever. 12
wherefore g. ye the Lord. Isa 24:15
shall the strong people g. thee. 25:3
and I will g. the house of. 60:7
multiply, I will also g. Jer 30:19
g. your Father which is. Mat 5:16
g. thy name, I will g. it. John 12:28
God shall also g. him in. 13:32
he shall g. me; for he shall. 16:14
g. thy Son, that thy Son also may g. 17:1
now, O Father, g. me with thine. 5
what death he should g. God. 21:19
with one mind and mouth g. God. Rom 15:6
that the Gentiles might g. God. 9
g. God in body and. 1 Cor 6:20
g. God for your professed. 2 Cor 9:13
may g. God in the day. 1 Pet 2:12
let him g. God on this behalf. 4:16
fear thee, and g. thy name. Rev 15:4

glorious

hand, O Lord, is become g. Ex 15:6
who is like thee, O Lord, g. in. 11
mayest fear this g. Deut 28:58
g. was king of Israel! 2 Sam 6:20
thank and praise thy g. 1 Chr 29:13
blessed be thy g. name. Neh 9:5
the king's daughter is all g. Ps 45:13
his honour, make his praise g. 66:2
and blessed be his g. name. 72:19
more g. than the mountains. 76:4
g. things are spoken of thee. 87:3
his work is honourable and g. 111:3*
I will speak of the g. honour. 145:5
to make known the g. majesty of. 12*
of the Lord shall be g. Isa 4:2
Jesse, and his rest shall be g. 11:10
he shall be for a g. throne. 22:23
whose g. beauty is a fading. 28:1
the g. beauty which is on head of. 4
Lord shall cause his g. voice. 30:30
the g. Lord will be to us a. 33:21*
yet shall I be g. in the eyes. 49:5*
make the place of my feet g. 60:13
who is this that is g. in his? 63:1
led them by Moses with his g. 12
people to make thyself a g. name. 14
a g. high throne from. Jer 17:12
made very g. in midst. Ezek 27:25
he shall stand in the g. Dan 11:16
he shall enter also into the g. 41
between the seas in the g. holy. 45
people rejoiced for g. Luke 13:17
into the g. liberty of the. Rom 8:21
engraven in stones was g. 2 Cor 3:7
of the Spirit be rather g. 3:8
lest light of g. gospel should. 4:4
it to himself a g. church. Eph 5:27
like to his g. body. Phil 3:21
according to his g. power. Col 1:11
according to g. gospel. 1 Tim 1:11
looking for g. appearing. Tit 2:13

gloriously

he hath triumphed g. Ex 15:1
reign before his ancients g. Isa 24:23

glory

hath he gotten all this g. Gen 31:1
for Aaron for g. Ex 28:2, 40
inherit the throne of g. 1 Sam 2:8
g. is departed from Israel. 4:21, 22
for Lord must be of g. 1 Chr 22:5
thine is greatness, power, and g. 29:11; Mat 6:13
Haman told of the g. of. Esth 5:11
the g. of his nostrils is. Job 39:20
and array thyself with g. and. 40:10*
King of g. shall come in. Ps 24:7, 9
who is this King of g.? the Lord. 10
the God of g. thundereth. Ps 29:3
when the g. of his house. 49:16
afterward receive me to g. 73:24
help us, O God, for the g. of. 79:9
that g. may dwell in our land. 85:9
for thou art the g. of their. 89:17
they changed their g. into. 106:20
speak of the g. of thy. 145:11
let the saints be joyful in g. 149:5
the wise shall inherit g. Pr 3:35
the g. of children are their. 17:6
the g. of young men is their. 20:29
search their own g. is not g. 25:27
men rejoice there is g. 28:12
hide thee in the dust, for the g. of his majesty. Isa 2:10, 19, 21
for upon all the g. shall be a. 4:5
their g. and pomp shall descend. 5:14
where will ye leave your g.? 10:3
I will punish the g. of his high. 12
and shall consume the g. of his. 18
Babylon the g. of kingdom. 13:19
all of them lie in g. each in. 14:18
the g. of Moab shall be. 16:14
they shall be as the g. of the. 17:3
g. of Jacob shall be made thin. 4
be ashamed of Egypt their g. 20:5
and all the g. of Kedar shall. 21:16
g. of his Father's house. 22:24
to stain the pride of all g. 23:9
we heard songs, even g. to. 24:16
the g. of Lebanon shall be. 35:2
in their g. ye shall boast. 61:6
with the abundance of her g. 66:11
the g. of the Gentiles as a. 12
have changed their g. Jer 2:11
might be to me for a g. 13:11
even the crown of your g. 18
g. of all lands. Ezek 20:6, 15
take from them joy of their g. 24:25
I will open the g. of the. 25:9
I shall set g. in the land of. 26:20
whom art thou thus like in g.? 31:18
hath given thee power and g. Dan 2:37; 7:14
the g. of my kingdom returned. 4:36
and increase with g. 11:39
I will change their g. Hos 4:7
as for Ephraim, their g. shall. 9:11
priests that rejoiced for the g. 10:5
come to Adullam the g. Mi 1:15
end of the store and g. Nah 2:9
filled with shame for g. Hab 2:16
this house in her first g.? Hag 2:3
I will fill this house with g. saith. 7
g. of this latter house greater. 9
will be the g. in midst. Zech 2:5
after the g. hath he sent me to. 8
temple, he shall bear the g. 6:13
their g. is spoiled, a voice of. 11:3
g. of the house of David, g. of. 12:7
kingdoms of world, and g. Mat 4:8
trumpet, that they may have g. 6:2
shall come in the g. of his Father. Mat 16:27; Mark 8:38
Son of man coming with power and great g. Mat 24:30; Mark 13:26 Luke 21:27
saying, G. to God in the highest. Luke 2:14; 19:38
light to Gentiles, and the g. 2:32
will I give thee, and the g. 4:6
who appeared in g. and spake. 9:31
with the g. which I had. John 17:5
the g. thou gavest me, I have. 22
the God of g. appeared. Acts 7:2
he gave not God the g. 12:23
could not see for the g. of. 22:11
strong in faith, giving g. Rom 4:20
raised from the dead by the g. 6:4
to be compared with the g. 8:18
to whom pertaineth the g. and. 9:4
had afore prepared unto g. 23
of him are all things, to whom be g. 11:36; Gal 1:5; 2 Tim 4:18 Heb 13:21; 1 Pet 5:11
to God only wise be g. Rom 16:27 1 Tim 1:17
hath ordained to our g. 1 Cor 2:7
have crucified the Lord of g. 8
but the woman is the g. of the. 11:7
woman have long hair, it is a g. 15
g. of celestial is one, the g. of. 15:40
one g. of the sun, another g. of. 41
dishonour, it is raised in g. 1 Cor 15:43
for the g. of his countenance, which g. 2 Cor 3:7
be g. the ministration of righteousness doth exceed in g. 9
had no g. by reason of the g. 10
we are all changed from g. to g. 18
us an eternal weight of g. 4:17
administered to us to the g. of. 8:19
they are messengers, and the g. 23
to the praise of the g. of. Eph 1:6
the Father of g. may give you. 17
what is the riches of the g. 18
for you, which is your g. 3:13
to him be g. in the church by. 21
are by Christ to g. of. Phil 1:11
and whose g. is in their shame. 3:19
according to his riches in g. by. 4:19
now to God and our Father be g. 20
the g. of this mystery, which is Christ in you, the hope of g. Col 1:27
ye appear with him in g. 3:4
nor of men sought we g. 1 Thes 2:6
called you to his kingdom and g. 12
for ye are our g. and joy. 20
punished from the g. of. 2 Thes 1:9
to the obtaining of the g. of. 2:14
seen of angels, received up into g. 1 Tim 3:16
in Christ, with eternal g. 2 Tim 2:10
in bringing many sons to g. Heb 2:10
was counted worthy of more g. 3:3
over it the cherubims of g. 9:5
Lord Jesus, the Lord of g. Jas 2:1
joy unspeakable, full of g. 1 Pet 1:8
it testified the g. that should. 11
raised him up, and gave him g. 21
all the g. of man, as the flower. 24
for what g. is it, if when ye be? 2:20
the Spirit of g. and of God. 4:14
a partaker of the g. that shall. 5:1
hath called us to eternal g. by. 10
that hath called us to g. 2 Pet 1:3
voice to him from the excellent g. 17
g. both now and ever. 3:18; Rev 1:6
wise God our Saviour be g. Jude 25
worthy to receive g. Rev 4:11; 5:12
blessing and g. and wisdom. 7:12
affrighted, and gave g. to God. 11:13
see **crown, honour, vain**

***give* glory**

my son, *give* g. to God. Josh 7:19
ye shall *give* g. to God. 1 Sam 6:5
give to Lord g. 1 Chr 16:28, 29 Ps 29:1, 2; 96:7, 8; Jer 13:16
will *give* grace and g. Ps 84:11
but to thy name *give* the g. 115:1
let them *give* g. unto the. Isa 42:12
not lay it to heart to *give* g. Mal 2:2
that returned to *give* g. Luke 17:18
when those beasts *give* g. Rev 4:9
fear God, and *give* g. to him. 14:7
and repented not to *give* g. 16:9

glory *of God*

declare the g. *of God.* Ps 19:1
the g. *of God* to conceal. Pr 25:2
g. of the *God* of Israel. Ezek 8:4
the g. *of God* was gone up from. 9:3
the g. *of God* was over them. 10:19 11:22
the g. *of God* came from the. 43:2
is for the g. *of God.* John 11:4
thou shouldest see the g. *of God.* 40
up and saw the g. *of God.* Acts 7:55
come short of g. *of God.* Rom 3:23
in hope of the g. *of God.* 5:2
received us to the g. *of God.* 15:7
do all to the g. *of God.* 1 Cor 10:31
man is image and g. *of God.* 11:7
and amen, to g. *of God.* 2 Cor 1:20
the knowledge of the g. *of God.* 4:6
many redound to g. *of God.* 15
by Christ to the g. *of God.* Phil 1:11
Jesus is Lord to the g. *of God.* 2:11
smoke from g. *of God.* Rev 15:8
Jerusalem, having g. *of God.* 21:11
no need of the sun, g. *of God.* 23

***his* glory**

God hath shewed us *his* g. Deut 5:24
his g. like the firstling of. 33:17*
declare *his* g. among. 1 Chr 16:24 Ps 96:3

his *g.* is great in thy. *Ps* 21:5
doth every one speak of *his g.* 29:9
his g. shall not descend after. 49:17
earth be filled with *his g.* 72:19
delivered *his g.* into the. 78:61
thou hast made *his g.* to. 89:44*
and all the people see *his g.* 97:6
Zion, he shall appear in *his g.* 102:16
and *his g.* above the. 113:4; 148:13
it is *his g.* to pass over. *Pr* 19:11
provoke the eyes of *his g.* *Isa* 3:8
the whole earth is full of *his g.* 6:3
the king of Assyria and *his g.* 8:7
under *his g.* he shall kindle. 10:16
shall fear *his g.* from rising. 59:19
and *his g.* shall be seen upon. 60:2
Ah lord, or, Ah *his g.* *Jer* 22:18
earth shined with *his g.* *Ezek* 43:2
and they took *his g.* *Dan* 5:20
God came, *his g.* covered. *Hab* 3:3
Solomon in all *his g.* *Mat* 6:29
Luke 12:27
shall sit in *his g.* *Mat* 19:28
Luke 9:26
awake, they saw *his g.* *Luke* 9:32
and to enter into *his g.* 24:26
we beheld *his g.* glory as. *John* 1:14
and manifested forth *his g.* 2:11
but he that seeketh *his g.* that. 7:18
Esaias, when he saw *his g.* 12:41
through my lie unto *his g.* *Rom* 3:7
make known riches of *his g.* 9:23
to the praise of *his g.* *Eph* 1:12, 14
according to riches of *his g.* 3:16
being brightness of *his g.* *Heb* 1:3
that when *his g.* shall be. *1 Pet* 4:13
before the presence of *his g.* *Jude* 24
was lightened with *his g.* *Rev* 18:1

***my* glory**

tell my father of all *my g.* *Gen* 45:13
be sanctified by *my g.* *Ex* 29:43
while *my g.* passeth by. 33:22
which have seen *my g.* *Num* 14:22
he hath stript me of *my g.* *Job* 19:9
my g. was fresh in me, my. 29:20
thou art *my g.* and lifter. *Ps* 3:3
how long will ye turn *my g.*? 4:2
my g. rejoiceth. 16:9
my g. may sing. 30:12
awake up *my g.* 57:8
in God is *my g.* 62:7
sing and give praise with *my g.* 108:1
my g. will I not give to another.
Isa 42:8; 48:11
have created him for *my g.* 43:7
salvation for Israel, *my g.* 46:13
glorify the house of *my g.* 60:7
shall come and see *my g.* 66:18
my g. they shall declare *my g.* 19
I will set *my g.* among. *Ezek* 39:21
have ye taken away *my g.* *Mi* 2:9
I seek not *mine* own *g.* *John* 8:50
that they may behold *my g.* 17:24

glory *of the Lord*

ye shall see *g. of the Lord.* *Ex* 16:7
g. of Lord appeared. 10; *Lev* 9:23
Num 14:10; 16:19, 42; 20:6
the *g. of the Lord* abode. *Ex* 24:16
the *g. of Lord* was like. 17
the *g. of the Lord* filled. 40:34, 35
the *g. of the Lord* shall. *Lev* 9:6
filled with *g. of the Lord.* *Num* 14:21
the *g. of the Lord* filled. *1 Ki* 8:11
2 Chr 5:14; 7:1, 2, 3; *Ezek* 43:5
44:4
g. of Lord shall endure. *Ps* 104:31
great is the *g. of the Lord.* 138:5
shall see *g. of the Lord.* *Isa* 35:2
g. of the Lord be revealed. 40:5
g. of the Lord shall be thy. 58:8
and the *g. of the Lord* is risen. 60:1
the likeness of *g. of Lord.* *Ezek* 1:28
blessed be the *g. of the Lord.* 3:12
and behold, the *g. of the Lord.* 23
the *g. of the Lord* went up. 10:4
g. of the Lord departed from. 18
the *g. of the Lord* stood upon. 11:23
g. of the Lord came into. 43:4
knowledge of *g. of Lord.* *Hab* 2:14
g. of the Lord shone. *Luke* 2:9
as in a glass *g. of the Lord.*
2 Cor 3:18

***thy* glory**

I beseech thee shew me *thy g.*
Ex 33:18
who hast set *thy g.* above. *Ps* 8:1
sword on thy thigh with *thy g.* 45:3
let *thy g.* be above. 57:5, 11; 108:5
to see thy power and *thy g.* 63:2
let *thy g.* appear unto their. 90:16
kings of the earth *thy g.* 102:15
the chariots of *thy g.* *Isa* 22:18
thy God *thy g.* 60:19
kings shall see *thy g.* 62:2
from the habitation of *thy g.* 63:15
disgrace throne of *thy g.* *Jer* 14:21
come down from *thy g.* and. 48:18
shall be on *thy g.* *Hab* 2:16
thy left hand in *thy g.* *Mark* 10:37

glory, *verb*

g. over me, when shall I. *Ex* 8:9
g. of this, and tarry at. *2 Ki* 14:10
g. ye in his holy name. *1 Chr* 16:10
Ps 105:3
give thanks, and *g.* *1 Chr* 16:35
sweareth by him shall *g.* *Ps* 63:11
upright in heart shall *g.* 64:10
that I may *g.* with thine. 106:5
shalt *g.* in Holy One of. *Isa* 41:16
shall all the seed of Israel *g.* 45:25
and in him shall they *g.* *Jer* 4:2
let not the rich man *g.* 9:23
let him *g.* in this, that he. 24
he hath whereof to *g.* *Rom* 4:2
but we *g.* in tribulations also. 5:3*
whereof I may *g.* through. 15:17
that no flesh should *g.* *1 Cor* 1:29
he that glorieth, let him *g.* in the
Lord. 31; *2 Cor* 10:17
therefore, let no man *g.* *1 Cor* 3:21
why dost thou *g.* as if thou? 4:7
preach, I have nothing to *g.* of. 9:16
to *g.* on our behalf, to answer them
who *g.* *2 Cor* 5:12
wherein they *g.* they may be. 11:12
many *g.* after the flesh, I will *g.* 18
if I must needs *g.* I will *g.* of. 30
expedient for me doubtless to *g.* 12:1
will I *g.* of myself I will not *g.* 5
for though I would desire to *g.* I. 6
therefore I will rather *g.* in. 9
circumcised, that they may *g.* in.
Gal 6:13
should *g.* save in the cross of. 14
that we ourselves *g.* in. *2 Thes* 1:4
envying in hearts, *g.* not. *Jas* 3:14

glorying

your *g.* is not good. *1 Cor* 5:6
man should make my *g.* void. 9:15
great is my boldness, great my *g.*
of you. *2 Cor* 7:4
I am become a fool in *g.* 12:11

glutton, -s

this our son, is a *g.* *Deut* 21:20*
drunkard and *g.* shall. *Pr* 23:21

gluttonous

they said, behold a man *g.*
Mat 11:19; *Luke* 7:34

gnash

he shall *g.* with his teeth. *Ps* 112:10
thine enemies hiss and *g.* *Lam* 2:16

gnashed

they *g.* upon me with. *Ps* 35:16
and they *g.* on him with. *Acts* 7:54

gnasheth

he *g.* on me with his teeth.
Job 16:9; *Ps* 37:12
he foameth and *g.* *Mark* 9:18*

gnashing

weeping and *g.* of teeth. *Mat* 8:12
13:42, 50; 22:13; 24:51; 25:30
Luke 13:28

gnat

who strain at a *g.* and. *Mat* 23:24

gnaw

her judges *g.* not bones. *Zeph* 3:3*

gnawed

they *g.* their tongues. *Rev* 16:10

go

on thy belly shalt thou *go.* *Gen* 3:14
whither wilt thou *go*? 16:8
prosper my way which I *go.*
Gen 24:42
after that Rebekah shall *go.* 55
that I may *go* to my master. 56
go with this man? she said, I will *go.*
58
Abimelech said to Isaac, *go.* 26:16
keep me in this way that I *go.* 28:20
send me away that I may *go.* 30:25
me *go*, for the day breaketh... said,
I will not let thee *go.* 32:26
and I, whither shall I *go*? 37:30
and we will arise, and *go.* 43:8
will not let you *go.* *Ex* 3:19; 4:21
he will let you *go.* 3:20; 11:1
go, ye shall not *go* empty. 3:21
go; if thou refuse to let him *go*, I.
4:23; 8:2, 21; 9:2; 10:4
he let him *go*, then she said. 4:26*
let my people *go.* 5:1; 7:16; 8:1
20; 9:1, 13; 10:3
nor will I let Israel *go.* 5:2
he refuseth to let the people *go.*
7:14; 8:32; 9:35; 10:27
will let the people *go.* 8:8, 28; 9:28
let the men *go.* 10:7
who are they that shall *go*? 8
we will *go* with our young and. 9
light to *go* by day and night. 13:21
Neh 9:12, 19
we have let Israel *go* from. *Ex* 14:5
Lord said to Moses, *go* on. 17:5
shall *go* before thee. 23:23; 32:34
gods to *go* before us. 32:23
Acts 7:40
my presence shall *go.* *Ex* 33:14
have found grace in sight, *go.* 34:9
shall be, if thou *go* with. *Num* 10:32
go by the king's highway. 20:17, 19
to give me leave to *go.* 22:13
men call thee, rise up, and *go.* 20, 35
and now behold, I *go* unto. 24:14
shall make it *go* through fire. 31:23
shall your brethren *go* to war? 32:6
but we will *go* ready armed. 17
by what way ye should *go.* *Deut* 1:33
in land whither ye *go.* 4:5, 26
11:8, 11; 30:18
it may *go* well. 4:40; 5:16; 19:13
ye *go* after other gods. 11:28; 28:14
go and return to his house. 20:5, 6
7, 8
then thou shalt let her *go.* 21:14
in anywise let the dam *go.* 22:7
she may *go* and be another. 24:2
thy God, he it is that doth *go.* 31:6
for thou must *go* with this people. 7
the Lord, he it is that doth *go.* 8
the land whither they *go* to be. 16
know their imagination they *go.* 21*
sendest us we will *go.* *Josh* 1:16
the way by which ye must *go.* 3:4
but they let *go* the man. *Judg* 1:25
go with me, then I will *go.* 4:8
the Lord said to him, *go* in. 6:14
this shall *go*, the same shall *go.* 7:4
to thee, that thou mayest *go.* 11:8
then my strength will *go.* 16:17
whether our way we *go* shall? 18:5
is your way wherein ye *go.* 6
be not slothful to *go* to possess. 9
when ye *go.* 10
hold thy peace, *go* with us. 19
to spring, they let her *go.* 19:25
again, why will ye *go*? *Ruth* 1:11
she was stedfastly minded to *go.* 18
let me *go* to field and glean, *go.* 2:2
let it *go* again to its. *1 Sam* 5:11
did they not let people *go*? 6:6
ark, send it away that it may *go.* 8
let us *go* thither, he can shew. 9:6
if we *go* what shall we bring the? 7
go up before me, to-morrow I will let
thee *go.* 19
when he turned his back to *go.* 10:9
for then should ye *go.* 12:21
how can I *go*? if Saul hear it. 16:2
thou art not able to *go* against. 17:33
Saul would let him *go* no more. 18:2
he said, let me *go*, why? 19:17
but let me *go*, that I may hide. 20:5
David went whither could *go.* 23:13
driven me out, saying, *go.* 26:19
a woman, that I may *go* and. 28:7

shall go to him, he. 2 Sam 12:23
I cause my shame to go? 13:13
Absalom said, let me go and. 15:7
seeing I go whither I may. 20
that thou go to battle in thy. 17:11
thy servant will go a little. 19:36
that is for David, let him go. 20:11
go the way of all the. 1 Ki 2:2
let me depart, that I may go. 11:21
nothing, howbeit, let me go in. 22
shall kill me, and go to. 12:27*
nor turn to go by the way. 13:17
because thou hast let go a. 20:42
wilt thou go with me to battle? 22:4
2 Chr 18:3
wilt thou go with me? 2 Ki 3:7
wherefore wilt thou go to? 4:23
water, that they may go and. 6:22
he that letteth him go, his life. 10:24
it will go into hand. 18:21; Isa 36:6
in thy name we go. 2 Chr 14:11*
let not the army of Israel go. 25:7
if thou wilt go, do it, be strong. 8
go to nothing and perish. Job 6:18
before I go whence I shall not return.
10:21; 16:22
it shall go ill with him that. 20:26*
ye not asked them that go by? 21:29
righteousness I will not let go. 27:6
in the way thou shalt go. Ps 32:8
before I go hence, and be. 39:13
God, why go I mourning? 42:9; 43:2
he shall go to the generation. 49:19
they go from strength to. 84:7
righteousness shall go before. 85:13
mercy and truth shall go. 89:14
that they might go to a city. 107:7
we will go into his tabernacles. 132:7
whither shall I go from thy? 139:7
none that go unto her. Pr 2:19
go and come again, to-morrow. 3:28
can one go on hot coals? 6:28
to call passengers who go right. 9:15
go from the presence of a. 14:7
neither will the scorner go. 15:12
much more do his friends go. 19:7
child in the way he should go. 22:6
that go to seek mixed wine. 23:30
be three things which go well. 30:29
all go unto one place. Eccl 3:20
return to go as he came. 5:15, 16
hath seen no good, do not all go? 6:6
it is better to go to the house. 7:2
after that, they go to the dead. 9:3
not how to go to city. 10:15
and the mourners go about. 12:5
I would not let him go. S of S 3:4
mincing as they go. Isa 3:16
and who will go for us? 6:8
he said, go and tell. 9; Acts 28:26
I would go through them. Isa 27:4
that they might go and fall. 28:13
he shall let go my captives. 45:13
the way thou shouldest go. 48:17
thy righteousness shall go. 58:8
go through, go through the. 62:10
thou shalt go to all that. Jer 1:7
I might leave my people, and go. 9:2
ye shall go and pray to me. 29:12
how long wilt thou go about? 31:22
go to Babylon. 34:3; Mi 4:10
good to go, there go. Jer 40:4, 5
reward, and let him go. 5
saying, let me go, and I will. 15
place whither ye desire to go. 42:22
the voice thereof shall go like. 46:22
they shall go and seek Lord. 50:4
they refused to let them go. 33
the Spirit was to go. Ezek 1:12, 20
that I should go far from my. 8:6
go through the midst of. 9:4, 5
high place whereto ye go? 20:29
go thee one way or other. 21:16
they shall go with flocks. Hos 5:6
they call to Egypt, they go to. 7:11
when they shall go I will spread. 12
I taught Ephraim also to go. 11:3
who, if he go through. Mi 5:8
and sought to go. Zech 6:7
these that go toward the north. 8
inhabitants of one city shall go. 8:21
we will go with you, for we. 23
and shall g. with whirlwinds. 9:14
Joseph was afraid to go. Mat 2:22
compel thee to go a mile, go twain.
Mat 5:41; Luke 7:8
and I say to this man, go. Mat 8:9
he said to them, go, they went. 32
but go ye learn what that. 9:13
go rather to the lost sheep of. 10:6
he answered, I go sir, and. 21:30
but go rather to them that sell. 25:9
sit ye here, while I go and. 26:36
go, tell my brethren that they go to Galilee. 28:10
go ye therefore and teach all. 19
go and see. Mark 6:38
and they let them go. 11:6
shall go before him in. Luke 1:17
he stedfastly set his face to go. 9:51
but go thou and preach the. 60
then said Jesus, go and do. 10:37
ground and must needs go. 14:18
I am ready to go with thee. 22:33
not answer me, nor let me go. 68
chastise him, and let him go. 23:22
to whom shall we go? John 6:68
and then I go unto him that. 7:33
whence I came and whither I go. 8:14
I go my way, whither I go ye. 21
loose him, and let him go. 11:44
whither I go thou canst not. 13:36
I go to prepare a place for. 14:2
whither I go ye know, the way. 4
I go unto my Father. 12; 16:10
I go to the Father. 14:28; 16:17, 28
cried, if thou let this man go. 19:12
I go a fishing, they say, we also go.
21:3
that he might go to his. Acts 1:25
determined to let him go. 3:13
them, they let them go. 4:21
being let go they went to their. 23
not speak, and let them go. 5:40
should go as far as Antioch. 11:22
essayed to go into Bithynia. 16:7
saying, let those men go. 35
taken Jason, they let them go. 17:9
I go bound in the Spirit to. 20:22
Cesar, to Cesar shalt thou go. 25:12
would have let me go. 28:18
now I go to Jerusalem. Rom 15:25
dare you go to law? 1 Cor 6:1
bid, and ye be disposed to go. 10:27
that I go also, they shall go. 16:4
brethren that they go. 2 Cor 9:5
I shall see how it will go. Phil 2:23
will go into such a city. Jas 4:13
see **free**

go aside

if any man's wife go aside. Num 5:12
shalt not go aside from. Deut 28:14
who shall go aside to ask? Jer 15:5
commanded them to go aside.
Acts 4:15

go astray

brother's ox go astray. Deut 22:1
go astray as soon as they. Ps 58:3
folly he shall go astray. Pr 5:23
not to her ways, go not astray. 7:25
righteous to go astray. 28:10
caused them to go astray. Jer 50:6
may go no more astray. Ezek 14:11

go away

not go very far away. Ex 8:28
let him go away empty. Deut 15:13
if he say, I will not go away. 16
Samuel turned about to go away.
1 Sam 15:27
will he let him go away? 24:19
their excellency go away? Job 4:21*
his mouth shall he go away. 15:30
ye that escaped the sword, go away.
Jer 51:50
I will tear and go away. Hos 5:14
suffer us to go away. Mat 8:31
go away into everlasting. 25:46
will ye also go away? John 6:67
how I said, I go away. 14:28; 16:7

go back

caused the sea to go back. Ex 14:21
do in any wise go back. Josh 23:12
mouth, I cannot go back. Judg 11:35
go back again, what? 1 Ki 19:20
shall the shadow go back? 2 Ki 20:9
so will not we go back. Ps 80:18
go back to Gedaliah. Jer 40:5
I will not go back, nor. Ezek 24:14

go down

let us go down and confound their.
Gen 11:7
I will go down now, and see. 18:21
the Lord said, go not down. 26:2
send him, we will not go down. 43:5
we cannot go down, then will we go down. 44:26
fear not, Jacob, to go down. 46:3
Lord said, go down. Ex 19:21
and they go down quick. Num 16:30
nor shall sun go down. Deut 24:15
the sun hasted not to go down about a whole day. Josh 10:13
if thou fear to go down. Judg 7:10
thou shalt go down. 1 Sam 10:8
go down after Philistines by. 14:36
go down to Keilah, I will. 23:4
who will go down with me? 26:6
let him not go down with us. 29:4
David said, go down to. 2 Sam 11:8
why didst thou not go down? 10
make thee go up and down. 15:20
go down to meet Ahab. 1 Ki 21:18
go down with him, be. 2 Ki 1:15
for the shadow to go down. 20:10*
to-morrow go down. 2 Chr 20:16
in a moment go down to. Job 21:13
that go down to the dust. Ps 22:29
become like them that go down. 28:1
and let them go down quick. 55:15
they that go down to the sea. 107:23
neither any that go down. 115:17
I be like them that go down. 143:7
her feet go down to death. Pr 5:5
as those that go down. Isa 14:19
woe to them that walk to go down.
30:2; 31:1
they that go down into pit. 38:18
sun shall not go down, nor. 60:20
let them go down to. Jer 50:27
garrisons shall go down. Ezek 26:11
with them that go down to the pit.
20; 31:14; 32:18, 24, 25, 29, 30
these waters go down into. 47:8
then go down to Gath. Amos 6:2
I will cause the sun to go down. 8:9
the sun shall go down. Mi 3:6
is on housetop not go down.
Mark 13:15
which are able to go down. Acts 25:5
let not the sun go down on. Eph 4:26

go forth

go forth of the ark, thou. Gen 8:16
not go forth hence, except. 42:15
the priest shall go forth. Lev 14:3
all able to go forth to war.
Num 1:3; 2 Chr 25:5
have a place to go forth. Deut 23:12
forbare to go forth. 1 Sam 23:13
when kings go forth to. 2 Sam 11:1
I will surely go forth with you. 18:2
thou go not forth, there will. 19:7
and go not forth thence. 1 Ki 2:36
said, I will go forth; go forth. 22:22
minds, let none go forth. 2 Ki 9:15
Jerusalem shall go forth a remnant.
19:31; Isa 37:32
as wild asses go they forth. Job 24:5
own people to go forth. Ps 78:52
wilt not thou go forth with? 108:11
go not forth hastily to. Pr 25:8
no king, yet go they forth. 30:27
go forth, O ye daughters. S of S 3:11
come, let us go forth into the. 7:11
out of Zion shall go forth the law.
Isa 2:3; Mi 4:2
the Lord shall go forth. Isa 42:13
go forth of Babylon. 48:20; Jer 50:8
say to prisoners, go forth. Isa 49:9
made thee waste shall go forth. 17
righteousness thereof go forth. 62:1
go not forth into the field. Jer 6:25
if I go forth into the field. 14:18
let them go forth. 15:1
whither shall we go forth? 2
evil shall go forth from. 25:32
O Israel, thou shalt go forth. 31:4
measuring line shall yet go forth. 39
if thou wilt go forth to the king. 38:17
but if thou wilt not go forth to. 18, 21

he shall *go forth* from. *Jer* 43:12
go forth as they that *go forth*. *Ezek* 12:4
the prince shall *go forth*. 12
my sword shall *go forth*. 21:4
messengers shall *go forth*. 30:9
and he shall *go forth* by the. 46:8
shall *go forth* over against it. 9
shall *go forth* with great. *Dan* 11:44
let bridegroom *go forth*. *Joel* 2:16
judgement doth never *go forth*. *Hab* 1:4
four spirits which *go forth*. *Zech* 6:5
black horses *go forth* into the. 6
then shall the Lord *go forth*. 14:3
ye shall *go forth* and grow. *Mal* 4:2
behold, he is in the desert, *go* not *forth*. *Mat* 24:26
Paul have to *go forth*. *Acts* 16:3
let us *go forth* to him. *Heb* 13:13
devils which *go forth*. *Rev* 16:14

go *forward*

Israel that they *go forward*. *Ex* 14:15
they shall *go forward* in. *Num* 2:24
shall shadow *go forward*? *2 Ki* 20:9
behold, I *go forward*, but. *Job* 23:8

go *his way*

and went to *go his way*. *Judg* 19:27

go *their way*

let these *go their way*. *John* 18:8

go *thy way*

thy wife, take her, *go thy way*. *Gen* 12:19
go thy way, the Lord. *1 Sam* 20:22
my staff, and *go thy way*. *2 Ki* 4:29
go thy way, eat thy bread. *Eccl* 9:7
go thy way forth by. *S of S* 1:8
go thy way, for words. *Dan* 12:9
go thy way till the end be, for. 13
go thy way, be reconciled. *Mat* 5:24
go thy way, shew thyself to. 8:4
that thine is, and *go thy way*. 20:14
this saying, *go thy way*. *Mark* 7:29
go thy way, sell whatsoever. 10:21
go thy way; thy faith hath made thee whole. 52; *Luke* 17:19
Jesus saith, *go thy way*. *John* 4:50
go thy way, for he is a. *Acts* 9:15
Felix answered, *go thy way*. 24:25

go *your way, -s*

up and *go* on *your ways*. *Gen* 19:2
afterward *go your way*. *Josh* 2:16; *Judg* 19:5
daughters, *go your way*. *Ruth* 1:12
go your way, eat the fat. *Neh* 8:10
go your way, make it as. *Mat* 27:65
go your way into village. *Mark* 11:2
go your way, tell his disciples. 16:7
go your way, tell John. *Luke* 7:22
go your ways, I send you as. 10:3
receive you not, *go your ways*. 10
go your ways, pour out. *Rev* 16:1

go *in*, or *into*, or *not* **go** *in*

from Ur, to *go into* land of Canaan. *Gen* 11:31; 12:5
when *go into* tabernacle. *Ex* 30:20
go in and out from gate to. 32:27
wine, when ye *go into*. *Lev* 10:9
house, before the priest *go in*. 14:36
neither shall he *go in* to any. 21:11
only he shall not *go in* to the vail. 23
his sons shall *go in*. *Num* 4:19
but they shall not *go in* to see. 20
that shall the Levites *go in*. 8:15
which may go out, and *go in*. 27:17
that they should not *go into*. 32:9
thou also shalt not *go in* thither. *Deut* 1:37; 4:21
son of Nun he shall *go in*. 1:38
live, and *go in* and possess. 4:1; 8:1
go in and possess. 6:18; 10:11
strong, and *go in* and possess. 11:8
not *go into* his house to fetch. 24:10
turned aside to *go in*. *Judg* 19:15
shalt *go in*, and uncover. *Ruth* 3:4
shall I then *go into*? *2 Sam* 11:11
I will not *go in*, nor eat. *1 Ki* 13:8
I may not return, nor *go in* with. 16
may *go in*, and dress it for. 17:12
look out Jehu, and *go in*. *2 Ki* 9:2
go in and slay them, let none. 10:25
shalt *go into* an inner. *2 Chr* 18:24
of the Levites shall *go in*. 23:6*
would *go into* the temple to save his life? I will not *go in*. *Neh* 6:11
turn was come to *go in*. *Esth* 2:15
her that she should *go in*. 4:8
and so will I *go in* unto the king. 16
then *go* thou *in* merrily unto. 5:14
nor will I *go in* with. *Ps* 26:4
open the gates, I will *go in*. 118:19
make me *go in* path of thy. 119:35
we will *go into* his tabernacle. 132:7
nor *go into* thy brother's *Pr* 27:10
they shall *go into* holes. *Isa* 2:19
and let us *go into* the. *Jer* 4:5
I cannot *go into* the house of. 36:5
but we will *go into* the land. 42:14
go ye not *into* Egypt. 19
when they *go in* shall *go in*. *Ezek* 46:10
go into clay, and tread. *Nah* 3:14
go into house of Josiah. *Zech* 6:10
take the young child, and *go into* the land of Israel. *Mat* 2:20
and many there be that *go in*. 7:13
go into the vineyard, and. 20:4, 7
go into village. 21:2; *Luke* 19:30
harlots *go into* kingdom. *Mat* 21:31
go ye *into* the highways. 22:9
go in, nor suffer others to *go in*. 23:13
go into the city, to such a man. 26:18; *Mark* 14:13
that they may *go into*. *Mark* 6:36
nor *go into* the town, nor tell. 8:26
go into all the world, preach. 16:15
suffered no man to *go in*. *Luke* 8:51
angry, and would not *go in*. 15:28
he shall *go in* and out. *John* 10:9
see him *go into* heaven. *Acts* 1:11
shall *go into* perdition. *Rev* 17:8
see **captivity**

go *in*

Sarai said, I pray thee, *go in* unto. *Gen* 16:2
drink wine, and *go* thou *in*. 19:34
behold my maid Bilhah, *go in*. 30:3
go in unto thy brother's wife. 38:8
that thou shalt *go in*. *Deut* 21:13
if take a wife, and *go in* unto. 22:13
husband's brother shall *go in*. 25:5
marriages, and *go in*. *Josh* 23:12
I will *go in* to my wife. *Judg* 15:1
go in unto thy father's. *2 Sam* 16:21
shall not *go in* to them. *1 Ki* 11:2
went to her as they *go in*. *Ezek* 23:44
a man and his father *go in*. *Amos* 2:7

go *in peace*

go to thy fathers *in peace*. *Gen* 15:15
to Moses, *go in peace*. *Ex* 4:18
shall *go* to their place *in peace*. 18:23
to Danites, *go in peace*. *Judg* 18:6
to Hannah, *go in peace*. *1 Sam* 1:17
to David, *go in peace*. 20:42
to Abigail, *go* up *in peace*. 25:35
Achish said to David, *go in peace*. 29:7
to Absalom, *go in peace*. *2 Sam* 15:9
let not his hoary head *go* down *in peace*. *1 Ki* 2:6
to Naaman, *go in peace*. *2 Ki* 5:19
go in peace, and be whole of thy. *Mark* 5:34
faith hath saved thee, *go in peace*. *Luke* 7:50; 8:48
they were let *go in peace*. *Acts* 15:33

let us **go**

say, *let us go* to Dothan. *Gen* 37:17
let us go three days'. *Ex* 3:18; 5:3
say, *let us go* sacrifice. 5:8, 17
would hardly *let us go*. 13:15
let us go after. *Deut* 13:2, 6, 13
he spake, *let us go*. *1 Sam* 9:9, 10
let us go to Gilgal and renew. 11:14
let us go over to Philistines'. 14:1, 6
let us go to Jordan. *2 Ki* 6:2
let us go into the house. *Ps* 122:1
let us go up to mountain. *Isa* 2:3
let us go into defenced. *Jer* 4:5
let us go by night and destroy. 6:5
let us go to Jerusalem for. 35:11
let us go again to our own. 46:16
let us go, every one to his own. 51:9
let us go to pray before. *Zech* 8:21
let us go into next towns. *Mark* 1:38
let us go, he that betrayeth. 14:42
let us go to Bethlehem. *Luke* 2:15
then saith he, *let us go*. *John* 11:7
let us go to him. 15
let us go that we may die. 16
even so I do; arise, *let us go*. 14:31
let us go again and. *Acts* 15:36
let us go on to perfection. *Heb* 6:1

I will **go**

I will go to the right, *I will go* to the. *Gen* 13:9
with this man? *I will go*. 24:58
let us go, *I will go*. 33:12; *Isa* 45:2
son is alive, *I will go* see. *Gen* 45:28
I will only *go* through. *Num* 20:19
thy burnt offering, and *I will go*. 23:3
I will go along by the. *Deut* 2:27
I will go likewise with. *Judg* 1:3
go with me, then *will I go*. 4:8
and she said, *I will* surely *go* with. 9
I will go out as at other. 16:20
thou goest, *I will go*. *Ruth* 1:16
he answered, *I will go*. *2 Ki* 6:3
he said, *I will go*. *2 Chr* 18:29
then *will I go* to the altar. *Ps* 43:4
I will go into thy house with. 66:13*
I will go in the strength of. 71:16*
of righteousness, *I will go* in. 118:19*
after them *I will go*. *Jer* 2:25
I will go to them that. *Ezek* 38:11
for she said, *I will go* after. *Hos* 2:5
I will go and return to my first. 7
I will go to my place, till they. 5:15
I will wail, *I will go*. *Mi* 1:8
seek the Lord; *I will go*. *Zech* 8:21
I will go before you into Galilee. *Mat* 26:32; *Mark* 14:28
I will arise and *go* to. *Luke* 15:18
henceforth *I will go* to. *Acts* 18:6

go *near*

go near, and hear all. *Deut* 5:27
David said, *go near*. *2 Sam* 1:15
prince would I *go near*. *Job* 31:37
go near, join thyself to. *Acts* 8:29

go *not*, or *not* **go**

if thy presence *go not*. *Ex* 33:15
Hobab said, I will *not go*. *Num* 10:30
he said, thou shalt *not go*. 20:20
Balaam, shalt *not go*. 22:12
I *cannot go* beyond word. 18; 24:13
thou shalt *not go* over. *Deut* 3:27
ye shall *not go* after other gods. 6:14; *1 Ki* 11:10
if he say, I will *not go*. *Deut* 15:16
thou shalt *not go* again to. 24:19
but thou shalt *not go* thither to. 32:52
go not far from the city. *Josh* 8:4
if wilt *not go* with me, I will *not go*. *Judg* 4:8
not go, the same shall *not go*. 7:4
we will *not* any of us *go* to his. 20:8
go not empty to thy mother-in-law. *Ruth* 3:17
David said, I *cannot go* with these. *1 Sam* 17:39
I may *not go* fight against. 29:8
let *not* all *go*, howbeit he would *not go*. *2 Sam* 13:25
not say to you, *go not*? *2 Ki* 2:18
David could *not go*. *1 Chr* 21:30
should *not go* to battle. *2 Chr* 25:13
instruction, let her *not go*. *Pr* 4:13
and *go not* into the way of evil. 14
furious man thou shalt *not go*. 22:24
for ye shall *not go* out. *Isa* 52:12
because they *cannot go*. *Jer* 10:5
thou shalt *not go* into house. 16:8
go not after other gods. 25:6; 35:15
that the vessels left *go not*. 27:18
go not into Egypt. 42:19; 43:2
thou shalt *not go* unpunished. 49:12
steps, that we *cannot go*. *Lam* 4:18
priests shall *not go* out. *Ezek* 42:14
go not into the way of. *Mat* 10:5
go not from house to. *Luke* 10:7
see here or there: *go not*. 17:23; 21:8

go *over*

I pray thee let me *go over*. *Deut* 3:25
Joshua shall *go over* before. 28; 31:3
land whither ye *go over*. 4:14, 26; 31:13; 32:47
go over Jordan, ye shall *go over*. 4:22
thou shalt not *go over* the. 24:20

who shall go over sea for us? Deut 30:13
the Lord thy God will go over. 31:3
but thou shalt not go over. 34:4
therefore arise, go over. Josh 1:2
said, let me go over. Judg 12:5
come, let us go over. 1 Sam 14:1, 6
faint, they could not go over. 30:10
me go over and take. 2 Sam 16:9
Chimham, let him go over. 19:37
he shall come and go over. Isa 8:7
make men go over dryshod. 11:15
down, that we may go over. 51:23
Noah should no more go over. 54:9
Ishmael departed to go over to. Jer 41:10
let us go over to other. Luke 8:22

go *out*

from all that go out of. Gen 9:10
time that women go out to. 24:11
cause every man to go out. 45:1
children of Israel go out. Ex 6:11
behold, I go out from thee, I. 8:29
after that I will go out, and. 11:8
let the children of Israel go out. 10
none of you shall go out at the. 12:22
people shall go out and gather. 16:4
let no man go out of his place on. 29
seventh year he shall go out. 21:2
go out by himself; if married, his wife shall go out with him. 3
her master's, and he shall go out. 4
if the servant say, I will not go out. 5
a maidservant not go out as. 7
then shall she go out free. 11
fire on altar never go out. Lev 6:13
shall not go out of tabernacle in. 8:33
ye shall not go out at the door. 10:7
then the priest shall go out. 14:38
seed of copulation go out. 15:16
shall go out to the altar. 16:18
he go out of the sanctuary. 21:12
jubile it shall go out. 25:28, 31, 33
it shall not go out in jubile. 30
he shall go out. 54
he shall not go out to war. Deut 24:5
thou shalt go out one way. 28:25
who shall go out, his blood. Josh 2:19
go out, I pray now, and. Judg 9:38
he said, I will go out as at. 16:20
shall I yet again go out to. 20:28
it is good thou go out. Ruth 2:22
I will go out and stand. 1 Sam 19:3
come, let us go out into field. 20:11
Achish said, thou shalt go out. 28:1
then Lord shall go out. 2 Sam 5:24
thou shalt go no more out. 21:17
not suffer any to go out, or come in to Asa. 1 Ki 15:17; 2 Chr 16:1
put ropes on heads, and go out to. 1 Ki 20:31
at the time kings go out. 1 Chr 20:1
go out and be a lying spirit, go out. 2 Chr 18:21
fear not, to-morrow go out. 20:17
go out of sanctuary, for thou. 26:18
himself hasted also to go out. 20
lettest such words go out. Job 15:13
which didst not go out with. Ps 60:10
scorner, contention go out. Pr 22:10
be not hasty to go out of. Eccl 8:3
depart ye, go ye out. Isa 52:11
ye shall not go out with haste. 12
ye shall go out with joy, and. 55:12
lest my fury go out like. Jer 21:12
my people, go ye out of the. 51:45
they shall go out from. Ezek 15:7
prince shall go out the same. 44:3
entereth by north, shall go out. 46:9
and ye shall go out at. Amos 4:3
living waters go out from. Zech 14:8
bridegroom cometh, go ye out to. Mat 25:6
ye go out of city, shake off. Luke 9:5
go out quickly into the streets. 14:21
go out into the highways and. 23
must ye needs go out. 1 Cor 5:10
he was called to go out. Heb 11:8
shall go no more out. Rev 3:12
and shall go out to deceive. 20:8

go *to*

go to, let us make brick. Gen 11:3
go to, let us build. 4
go to, let us confound. Gen 11:7
go to now, I will prove. Eccl 2:1
go to, I will tell you what. Isa 5:5
go to now, ye that say. Jas 4:13
go to now, ye rich men, weep. 5:1

go *up*

arise, go up to Beth-el. Gen 35:1, 3
and let the lad go up with. 44:33
how shall I go up to? 34; 45:9
Pharaoh said, go up and. 50:6
frogs shall go up and. Ex 8:3
take heed ye go not up into. 19:12
nor shalt thou go up by steps. 20:26
neither shall people go up. 24:2
a great sin, I will go up. 32:30
depart and go up, thou and. 33:1
for I will not go up in the midst. 3
land, when thou shalt go up. 34:24
shalt not go up and down. Lev 19:16
let us go up at once and. Num 13:30
we be not able to go up against. 31
lo, we be here, and will go up. 14:40 Deut 1:41
go not up. Num 14:42
but they presumed to go up. 44
his brother's wife go up. Deut 25:7
shall go up for us to heaven. 30:12
go up, let 3000 men go up. Josh 7:3
did not intend to go up against. 22:33
who shall go up for us to? Judg 1:1
said, Judah shall go up. 2; 20:18
an angel said, I made you go up. 2:1
that I may go up and down on. 11:37
arise, that we may go up. 18:9
we will go up by lot against. 20:9
which of us shall go up first to? 18
shall I go up again? 23
go up against him. 28
not go up till the child. 1 Sam 1:22
if it go up by the way of his. 6:9
and to whom shall he go up? 20
shall find him before he go up. 9:13
Samuel came to go up to. 14, 19
say, Tarry; we will not go up. 14:9
come up unto us, we will go up. 10
shall I go up to any of cities of Judah? the Lord said, go up. 2 Sam 2:1
shall I go up against the? 5:19
should I make thee go up? 15:20
I to live, that I should go up. 19:34
go up, rear an altar in floor. 24:18 1 Chr 21:18
ye shall not go up. 1 Ki 12:24 2 Chr 11:4
if this people go up to. 1 Ki 12:27
it is too much for you to go up. 28
go up, look towards the sea. 18:43
go up, for the Lord shall deliver. 22:6 12; 2 Chr 18:11, 14
may go up and fall at Ramoth. 1 Ki 22:20; 2 Chr 18:19
go up, meet messengers. 2 Ki 1:3
go up thou bald head, go up. 2:23
wilt thou go up with me? 3:7
which way shall we go up? 8
Hazael set his face to go up to. 12:17
Lord said, go up against the land. 18:25; Isa 36:10
third day thou shalt go up. 2 Ki 20:5
sign that I shall go up? 8; Isa 38:22
go up to Hilkiah. 2 Ki 22:4
shall I go up? 1 Chr 14:10
go not up after them. 14
we go up to Ramoth? 2 Chr 18:5
let him go up. 36:23; Ezra 1:3
he began to go up from. Ezra 7:9
all which are minded to go up. 13
if a fox go up he shall. Neh 4:3
go up by the mountains. Ps 104:8
surely I will not go up into. 132:3
flock of sheep that go up. S of S 6:6
I will go up to the palm tree. 7:8
let us go up to mountain of Lord. Isa 2:3; Mi 4:2
let us go up against Judah. Isa 7:6
weeping shall they go it up. 15:5
go up, O Elam. 21:2
the smoke shall go up. 34:10
ravenous beast shall go up. 35:9
go up against this land, and. 36:10
go ye up upon her walls. Jer 5:10
arise, and let us go up at noon. 6:4
Nebuchadnezzar may go up. 21:2
go up to Lebanon, and cry. Jer 22:20
let us go up to Zion, to the. 31:6
he saith, I will go up and. 46:8
go up into Gilead, and take. 11
continual weeping shall go up. 48:5
go up to Kedar, and spoil men. 49:28
go up against the land of. 50:21
I will go up to land of Ezek 38:11
were seven steps to go up. 40:26
neither go up to Beth-aven. Hos 4:15
go up to the mountain. Hag 1:8
go up from year to year. Zech 14:16
we go up to Jerusalem. Mat 20:18 Mark 10:33; Luke 18:31
friend, go up higher. Luke 14:10
go ye up to this feast, I go not up. John 7:8
go up to Jerusalem. Acts 15:2
that Paul should not go up to. 21:4
we besought him not to go up to. 12
wilt thou go up to Jerusalem? 25:9

go *a whoring*

lest they go a whoring. Ex 34:15
and thy sons go a whoring after. 16
cut off all that go a whoring. Lev 20:5
I will cut off such as go a whoring. 6
ye use to go a whoring. Num 15:39
people will go a whoring. Deut 31:16
Judah go a whoring. 2 Chr 21:13
destroyed all that go a whoring. Ps 73:27
eyes which go a whoring. Ezek 6:9

goad, -s

slew 600 men with an ox g. Judg 3:31
a file to sharpen the g. 1 Sam 13:21
words of wise are as g. Eccl 12:11

goat

take a heifer, a she g. Gen 15:9
if his offering be a g. Lev 3:12
lay his hand on the head of g. 4:24
eat no fat of ox, sheep, or of g. 7:23
he took the g. which was the. 9:15
Moses sought the g. of the. 10:16
Aaron shall bring the g. on. 16:9
the g. in the wilderness. 22
whosoever killeth a g. in the. 17:3
when a g. is brought forth. 22:27
he shall bring a g. Num 15:27
the firstling of a g. thou shalt. 18:17
one g. for a sin offering, to. 28:22
29:22, 28, 31, 34, 38
eat the ox, sheep, and g. Deut 14:4
prepare every day a g. Ezek 43:25
g. had a notable horn. Dan 8:5
rough g. is the king of Grecia. 21

***he* goat**

comely in going, an he g. Pr 30:31
down like rams with he g. Jer 51:40
behold, an he g. came. Dan 8:5
therefore the he g. waxed very. 8

***live* goat**

bring live g. Lev 16:20
lay both hands on live g. 21

***scape*goat**

other lot for the scapegoat. Lev 16:8
to let him go for a scapegoat. 10
let go scapegoat shall wash. 26

***wild* goat**

ye shall eat the wild g. Deut 14:5

goats

from thence two kids of g. Gen 27:9
she put the skins of the g. on. 16
and speckled among the g. 30:32
is not speckled among g. 33
he removed g. 35
thy she g. have not cast. 31:38
she g. and twenty he g. 32:14
brethren killed a kid of the g. 37:31
take it from sheep or g. Ex 12:5
offering be of sheep or g. Lev 1:10
knowledge, he shall bring his offering, a kid of the g. 4:23, 28; 5:6
take a kid of g. for a sin offering. 9:3
two kids of the g. 16:5
two g. and present them. 7
offer a male of sheep or g. 22:19
sacrifice one kid of the g. for a sin offering. 23:19; Num 7:16; 15:24
five he g. five lambs. Num 7:17, 23 29, 35, 41, 47, 53, 59, 65, 71, 77, 83
kids of the g. for a sin offering. 7:87
he g. sixty, the lambs of first. 88

rams and he *g.* of breed. *Deut* 32:14
Nabal had a thousand *g.* *1 Sam* 25:2
brought 7,700 he *g.* *2 Chr* 17:11
they brought seven he *g.* for. 29:21
the dedication twelve he *g.* *Ezra* 6:17
of captivity offered 12 he *g.* 8:35
I will take no he *g.* out. *Ps* 50:9
or will I drink the blood of *g.*? 13
offer to thee bullocks with *g.* 66:15
the *g.* are the price of. *Pr* 27:26
thou shalt have *g.*' milk enough. 27
hair is as a flock of *g.* *S of S* 4:1; 6:5
not in the blood of he *g.* *Isa* 1:11
fat with the blood of *g.* 34:6
and be as the he *g.* before. *Jer* 50:8
occupied with thee in *g.* *Ezek* 27:21
between the rams and he *g.* 34:17
drink the blood of lambs and *g.* 39:18
second day offer a kid of the *g.* 43:22
a kid of the *g.* daily for a. 45:23
kindled, I punished the *g.* *Zech* 10:3
divideth sheep from *g.* *Mat* 25:32
shall set the *g.* on his left hand. 33
nor entered by blood of *g.* *Heb* 9:12
blood of bulls and *g.* sanctifieth. 13
blood of *g.* and sprinkled book. 19
not possible that the blood of *g.* **10**:4

wild **goats**

David on rocks of *wild g.* *1 Sam* 24:2
knowest thou when the *wild g.* bring. *Job* 39:1
are a refuge for *wild g.* *Ps* 104:18

goats' hair

offering ye shall take *gs.' hair.* *Ex* 25:4
shalt make curtains of *gs.' hair.* 26:7
willing, let him bring *gs.' hair.* 35:6
with whom was found *gs.' hair.* 23
and all the women spun *gs.' hair.* 26
made curtains of *gs.' hair* for. 36:14
purify all works of *gs.' hair* and wood. *Num* 31:20
gs.' hair for bolster. *1 Sam* 19:13, 16

goatskins

in sheepskins and *g.* *Heb* **11**:37

Gob

with Philistines at *G.* *2 Sam* **21**:18

goblet

thy navel is like a round *g.* *S of S* **7**:2

god referred to *man*

made thee a *g.* to Pharaoh. *Ex* **7**:1

god for *idol*

with that which is not *g.* *Deut* 32:21
if he be a *g.* let him plead. *Judg* 6:31
they made Baal-berith their *g.* 8:33
went into house of their *g.* 9:27
which Chemosh thy *g.* giveth. 11:24
Philistines' *g.* was Dagon. 16:23, 24
sore on us, and our *g.* *1 Sam* 5:7
Israel worshipped the *g.* *1 Ki* 11:33
he is a *g.* either talking, or. 18:27
Baal-zebub the *g.* of Ekron. *2 Ki* 1:2, 3, 6, 16
house of Nisroch his *g.*, his sons. 19:37; *2 Chr* 32:21; *Isa* 37:38
hasten after other *g.* *Ps* 16:4
formed a *g.* or molten? *Isa* 44:10
maketh a *g.* and worshippeth. 15, 17
and that pray to a *g.* that. 45:20
he maketh it a *g.*: they fall. 46:6
vessels into house of his *g.* *Dan* 1:2
according to the name of my *g.* 4:8
magnify self above every *g.* 11:36
the star of your *g.* ye made. *Amos* 5:26; *Acts* 7:43
swear, and say, thy *g.* O. *Amos* 8:14
cried, every man to his *g.* *Jonah* 1:5
will walk in name of his *g.* *Mi* 4:5
this his power to his *g.* *Hab* 1:11
it is the voice of a *g.* *Acts* 12:22
the *g.* of this world hath blinded. *2 Cor* **4**:4

any **god**

that sacrifice to *any g.* *Ex* 22:20
nor is there *any G.* beside. *2 Sam* 7:22; *1 Chr* 17:20
might not worship *any g.* *Dan* 3:28
ask a petition of *any g.* or. 6:7, 12
neither shall he regard *any g.* 11:37

other **god**

shalt worship no *other g.* *Ex* **34**:14
because there is no *other g.* can deliver. *Dan* 3:29
there is none *other g.* *1 Cor* 8:4

strange **god**

there was no *strange g.* *Deut* 32:12
our hands to a *strange g.* *Ps* 44:20
no *strange g.* be in thee, nor worship *strange g.* 81:9
there was no *strange g.* *Isa* 43:12
he do with a *strange g.* *Dan* 11:39

God

The Creator and Father of all things, supreme Ruler of the world. The usual name given to God by the Hebrews was that which is rendered into English by the word Jehovah. *Where the older version has the word* GOD *printed in capitals the American Revision has substituted the word* Jehovah.

This word Jehovah *was so reverenced by the ancient Hebrews that it was not generally pronounced, its place being taken, in speaking, by* Adonai, *Lord,* Elohim, *or* El-Shaddai, *all of which are really expressions for the attributes of God.*

Lord, thou *G.* seest me. *Gen* 16:13
to be a *G.* to thee and thy. 17:7
I am the *G.* of Beth-el, where. 31:13
what is this that *G.* hath? 42:28
you that sent me hither, but *G.* 45:8
behold, I die, but *G.* shall be. 48:21
be to Aaron instead of *G.* *Ex* 4:16
to me, and be to you a *G.* 6:7
and *G.* shall be with thee. 18:19
what hath *G.* wrought? *Num* 23:23
alas, who shall live when *G.*? 24:23
what nation which hath *G.*? *Deut* 4:7
that he may be to thee a *G.* 29:13
G. do so and more also. *1 Sam* 3:17
14:44; 25:22; *2 Sam* 3:9, 35
19:13; *1 Ki* 2:23; *2 Ki* 6:31
know that there is a *G.* *1 Sam* 17:46
till I know what *G.* will do for. 22:3
who is *G.* save the Lord? *2 Sam* 22:32; *Ps* 18:31
if the Lord be *G.* *1 Ki* 18:21
the *G.* the Lord, he is the *G.* 39
thou art the *G.* even. *2 Ki* 19:15
G., art not thou *G.* in? *2 Chr* 20:6
G. be with him, he is the *G.* *Ezra* 1:3
art a *G.* ready to pardon. *Neh* 9:17
sayest, how doth *G.* know? *Job* 22:13; *Ps* 73:11
art not a *G.* that hast. *Ps* 5:4
the man that made not *G.* his. 52:7
art great, thou art *G.* alone. 86:10 *Isa* 37:16
behold, *G.* is my salvation. *Isa* 12:2
a *G.* besides me? yea, there is no *G.* 44:8
look unto me, I am *G.* there is. 45:22
I am *G.* there is none else. 46:9
I will be their *G.* they my people. *Jer* 31:33; 32:38
a god, I sit in seat of *G.* *Ezek* 28:2
shalt be a man, and no *G.* 9
therefore it is not *G.* *Hos* 8:6
for I am *G.* and not man, the. 11:9
who is a *G.* like unto thee? *Mi* 7:18
Emmanuel, which is *G.* *Mat* 1:23
ye cannot serve *G.* and mammon. 6:24; *Luke* 16:13
good but one, that is *G.* *Mat* 19:17 *Mark* 10:18; *Luke* 18:19
there is one *G.* and. *Mark* 12:32
with *G.* and Word was *G.* *John* 1:1
can do miracles, except *G.* be. 3:2
we have one Father, even *G.* 8:41
forth, and came from *G.* 42
know thee, the only true *G.* 17:3
by wonders, which *G.* did. *Acts* 2:22
we ought to obey *G.* rather. 5:29
patriarchs sold Joseph, but *G.* 7:9
I perceive *G.* is no respecter. 10:34
let *G.* be true, and. *Rom* 3:4
if *G.* be for us, who can be? 8:31
now the *G.* of patience and. 15:5
to us there is but one *G.* *1 Cor* 8:6
that *G.* may be all in all. 15:28
hath anointed us, is *G.* *2 Cor* 1:21
G. of love and peace shall. 13:11
called *G.* so that he as *G.* *2 Thes* 2:4
G. was manifest in the. *1 Tim* 3:16
profess that they know *G.* *Tit* 1:16
that built all things is *G.* *Heb* 3:4
ceased from his works, as *G.* 4:10
I will be to them a *G.*, they to. 8:10
G. is light, in him is no. *1 John* 1:5
no man hath seen *G.* at any. 4:12
and *G.* himself shall be. *Rev* 21:3
G. shall wipe away all tears. 4
I will be his *G.* and he shall be. 7

against **God**

wickedness, and sin *against G.*? *Gen* 39:9
the people spake *against G.* *Num* 21:5; *Ps* 78:19
transgressed *against G.* *1 Chr* 5:25
spake *against* the *G.* of. *2 Chr* 32:19
thy spirit *against G.* *Job* 15:13
stretcheth out his hand *against G.* 25
multiplieth his words *against G.* 34:37
speak amiss *against G.* *Dan* 3:29
marvellous things *against G.* 11:36
rebelled *against* her *G.* *Hos* 13:16
found to fight *against G.* *Acts* 5:39
blasphemous words *against G.* 6:11
let us not fight *against G.* 23:9
mind is enmity *against G.* *Rom* 8:7
thou that repliest *against G.*? 9:20
in blasphemy *against G.* *Rev* 13:6

see **almighty**

before **God**

was corrupt *before G.* *Gen* 6:11
Moses' father *before G.* *Ex* 18:12
themselves *before G.* *Josh* 24:1
abode till even *before G.* *Judg* 21:2
Israel played *before G.* *1 Chr* 13:8
and there Uzza died *before G.* 10
burnt sacrifices *before G.* 16:1
Manasseh humbled himself *before G.* *2 Chr* 33:12
heart was humbled *before G.* 34:27
deliver *before* the *G.* of. *Ezra* 7:19
restrainest prayer *before G.* *Job* 15:4
shall I appear *before G.*? *Ps* 42:2
may walk *before G.* in light. 56:13
he shall abide *before G.* for. 61:7
let righteous rejoice *before G.* 68:3
in Zion appeareth *before G.* 84:7
him that is good *before G.* *Eccl* 2:26
to utter any thing *before G.* 5:2
he feareth not *before G.* 8:13
gave thanks *before his G.* *Dan* 6:10
making supplication *before G.* 11
that men tremble *before G.* 26
both righteous *before G.* *Luke* 1:6
of them is forgotten *before G.* 12:6
in deed and word *before G.* 24:19
found favour *before G.* *Acts* 7:46
come for a memorial *before G.* 10:4
we are all here present *before G.* 33*
all good conscience *before G.* 23:1
of law are just *before G.* *Rom* 2:13
may become guilty *before G.* 3:19
to glory, but not *before G.* 4:2
have it to thyself *before G.* 14:22
we speak *before G.* in. *2 Cor* 12:19
behold, *before G.* I lie not. *Gal* 1:20
your hearts *before G.* *1 Thes* 3:13
and acceptable *before G.* *1 Tim* 5:4
thee *before G.* 21:1; *2 Tim* 4:1
and undefiled *before G.* *Jas* 1:27
words perfect *before G.* *Rev* 3:2
the horns of the altar *before G.* 9:13
which accused them *before G.* 12:10
in remembrance *before G.* 16:19
and great, stand *before G.* 20:12*

see **called, chosen, commanded**

eternal **God**

eternal G. is thy refuge. *Deut* 33:27

everlasting **God**

called on name of *ever. G.* *Gen* 21:33
the *ever. G.* fainteth not. *Isa* 40:28
to commandment of *ever. G.* *Rom* 16:26

see **father, fear, forbid, gave, glorify**

high God
was priest of the most high G. Gen 14:18; Heb 7:1
Abraham of most high G. Gen 14:19
blessed be the most high G. 20
up my hand to the most high G. 22
cry unto G. most high. Ps 57:2
G. was their rock, the high G. 78:35
provoked the most high G. 56
servants of most high G. Dan 3:26
shew the wonders the high G. 4:2
high G. gave Nebuchadnezzar. 5:18
that the most high G. ruled. 21
before the most high G. Mi 6:6
thou Son of the most high G. Mark 5:7; Luke 8:28
servants of most high G. Acts 16:17

holy God
he is an holy G. he is. Josh 24:19
stand before this holy G.? 1 Sam 6:20
the Lord our G. is holy. Ps 99:9
G. that is holy shall be. Isa 5:16

God of heaven
all earth hath the Lord G. of heaven given. 2 Chr 36:23; Ezra 1:2
servants of G. of heaven. Ezra 5:11
provoked G. of heaven. 12
offerings of the G. of heaven. 6:9, 10
law of the G. of heaven. 7:12, 21
commanded by the G. of heaven. 23
prayed before G. of heaven. Neh 1:4
so I prayed to the G. of heaven. 2:4
to the G. of heaven. Ps 136:26
desire mercies of G. of heaven. Dan 2:18
Daniel blessed the G. of heaven. 19
the G. of heaven shall set up a. 44
Lord, the G. of heaven. Jonah 1:9
glory to G. of heaven. Rev 11:13
blasphemed the G. of heaven. 16:11

God of hosts
again, O G. of hosts. Ps 80:7, 19
we beseech thee, O G. of hosts. 14
name is the G. of hosts. Amos 5:27
see **Lord God**

God is
G. is with thee in all. Gen 21:22
see, G. is witness betwixt me. 31:50
fear not, for G. is come. Ex 20:20
G. is not a man, that. Num 23:19
G. is there in heaven? Deut 3:24
the eternal G. is thy refuge. 33:27
our holy G. is a jealous God. Josh 24:19; Nah 1:2
G. is come into the camp. 1 Sam 4:7
for G. is come. 10:7; 1 Chr 17:2
G. is departed from me. 1 Sam 28:15
G. is my strength and. 2 Sam 22:33
G. is gone forth before. 1 Chr 14:15
G. himself is with us. 2 Chr 13:12
I answer thee, G. is. Job 33:12
G. is mighty and despiseth. 36:5
behold, G. is great, and we know. 26
G. is angry with wicked. Ps 7:11
G. is not in all his thoughts. 10:4
for G. is in the generation of. 14:5
whose G. is Lord. 33:12; 144:15
G. is our refuge and. 46:1; 62:8
G. is in midst of her, she shall. 46:5
G. is gone up with a shout. 47:5
for G. is King. 7
G. is known in her palaces. 48:3
for G. is judge himself. 50:6; 75:7
behold, G. is my helper, Lord. 54:4
this I know, for G. is for me. 56:9
for G. is my defence. 59:9, 17
in G. is my salvation and glory. 62:7; Isa 12:2
of the fatherless is G. Ps 68:5
truly G. is good to Israel. 73:1
G. is strength of my heart, and. 26
G. is my King of old, working. 74:12
G. is greatly to be feared in. 89:7
gracious is the Lord, our G. is. 116:5
G. is the Lord that hath. 118:27
for G. is in heaven, and. Eccl 5:2
G. that is holy shall be. Isa 5:16
for G. is with us. 8:10
surely G. is in thee. 45:14
we have heard that G. is. Zech 8:23
G. is able of these stones to raise. Mat 3:9; Luke 3:8
G. is not God of dead. Mat 22:32
to his seal that G. is. John 3:33
G. is a Spirit. 4:24
G. is glorified in him. 13:31
G. is no respecter of. Acts 10:34
for G. is my witness. Rom 1:9
for G. is able to graff them. 11:23
for G. is able to make him. 14:4*
G. is faithful, by whom. 1 Cor 1:9
G. is faithful who will not. 10:13
and report that G. is in you. 14:25
G. is not author of confusion, but. 33
as G. is true, our word. 2 Cor 1:18
G. is able to make all grace. 9:8
but G. is one. Gal 3:20
G. is not mocked. 6:7
but G. who is rich in. Eph 2:4
G. is my record, how. Phil 1:8
whose g. is their belly. 3:19
G. is witness. 1 Thes 2:5
G. is not unrighteous to. Heb 6:10
G. is not ashamed to be. 11:16
for our G. is a consuming fire. 12:29
for with such sacrifices G. is. 13:16
G. is light. 1 John 1:5
for G. is love. 4:8, 16
G. is greater than our heart. 3:20

God of Israel
and saw the G. of Israel. Ex 24:10
the G. of Israel hath. Num 16:9
to give glory to the G. of Israel. Josh 7:19; 1 Sam 6:5
G. of Israel was their. Josh 13:33
ye committed against G. of Israel. 22:16
to do with the G. of Israel? 24
heart to the G. of Israel. 24:23
G. of Israel dispossessed the. Judg 11:23
given thee of G. of Israel. Ruth 2:12
the G. of Israel grant. 1 Sam 1:17
the ark of the G. of Israel. 5:11
Lord G. of Israel, no God like thee. 1 Ki 8:23; 2 Chr 6:14
thing toward G. of Israel. 1 Ki 14:13
called on G. of Israel. 1 Chr 4:10
of hosts is the G. of Israel. 17:24
not seek G. of Israel? 2 Chr 15:13
offered to G. of Israel. Ezra 7:15
words of the G. of Israel. 9:4
blessed be the Lord G. of Israel. Ps 41:13; 72:18; 106:48; Luke 1:68
I the G. of Israel will. Isa 41:17
call thee by name, G. of Israel. 45:3
themselves on the G. of Israel. 48:2
glory of the G. of Israel. Ezek 8:4
glorified the G. of Israel. Mat 15:31

living God
voice of the living G. Deut 5:26
hereby know living G. is. Josh 3:10
armies of living G. 1 Sam 17:26, 36
Assyria hath sent to reproach living G. 2 Ki 19:4, 16; Isa 37:4, 17
soul thirsteth for God, the living G. Ps 42:2
flesh crieth out for living G. 84:2
living G. an everlasting. Jer 10:10
the words of the living G. 23:36
living G. and stedfast. Dan 6:26
ye are sons of living G. Hos 1:10
art Christ, Son of living G. Mat 16:16; John 6:69
I adjure thee by the living G. 26:63
vanities to living G. Acts 14:15
children of living G. Rom 9:26
Spirit of the living G. 2 Cor 3:3
the temple of the living G. 6:16
serve living and true G. 1 Thes 1:9
church of the living G. 1 Tim 3:15
trust in the living G. 4:10; 6:17
in departing from living G. Heb 3:12
conscience to serve living G. 9:14
to fall into hands of living G. 10:31
Zion, the city of living G. 12:22
the seal of the living G. Rev 7:2
For combinations of **Lord** *with* **God**, *see in divisions under* **Lord**

merciful God
Lord, the Lord G. merciful. Ex 34:6
God is a merciful G. Deut 4:31
Lord your G. is merciful if ye turn. 2 Chr 30:9
gracious and merciful G. Neh 9:31
gracious is the Lord, our G. is merciful. Ps 116:5
thou art a G. merciful. Jonah 4:2

mighty God
by hands of mighty G. Gen 49:24
Lord is among you, a mighty G. Deut 7:21; 10:17
our God, the mighty G. Neh 9:32
G. is mighty, and. Job 36:5
the mighty G. the Lord. Ps 50:1
how he vowed to mighty G. 132:2
I find an habitation for mighty G. 5
be called the mighty G. Isa 9:6
shall return to the mighty G. 10:21
mighty G. Lord of hosts. Jer 32:18
O mighty G. thou hast. Hab 1:12

my God
then shall Lord be my G. Gen 28:21
he is my G. my father's G. Ex 15:2
my people, thy God my G. Ruth 1:16
I cried to my G. he heard. 2 Sam 22:7; Ps 18:6
and have not departed from my G. 2 Sam 22:22; Ps 18:21
by my G. I have leaped over a. 2 Sam 22:30; Ps 18:29
for God, even my G. 1 Chr 28:20
what my G. saith, that. 2 Chr 18:13
think upon me, my G. for good. Neh 5:19; 13:31
remember me, my G. 13:14, 22
my G. my G. why hast thou forsaken me? Ps 22:1; Mat 27:46
thou art my G. from my. Ps 22:10
I said, Thou art my G. 31:14
O my G. be not far. 38:21; 71:12
thou art my Father, my G. 89:26
sing praise to my G. 104:33; 146:2
thou art my G. and I will. 118:28
I will extol thee, my G. O. 145:1
and take name of my G. Pr 30:9
but will ye weary my G.? Isa 7:13
is passed over from my G. 40:27
deliver me, for thou art my G. 44:17
soul shall be joyful in my G. 61:10
my G. hath sent his angel. Dan 6:22
they shall say, Thou art my G. Hos 2:23; Zech 13:9
Israel shall cry to me, my G. Hos 8:2
my G. will cast them away. 9:17
I will wait, for my G. will. Mi 7:7
ascend to my G. and. John 20:17
and said, My Lord and my G. 28
I thank my G. Rom 1:8; 1 Cor 1:4; 14:18; Phil 1:3; Philem 4
lest when I come, my G. 2 Cor 12:21
my G. shall supply all. Phil 4:19
on him the name of my G. Rev 3:12

no God
I am he, there is no G. Deut 32:39
there is no G. like thee. 1 Ki 8:23; 2 Chr 6:14
there is no G. in Israel? 2 Ki 1:16
now I know there is no G. in. 5:15
no g. of any nation. 2 Chr 32:15
said, There is no G. Ps 14:1; 53:1
before me there was no G. Isa 43:10
beside me there is no G. 44:6, 8; 45:5, 14, 21
shalt be a man, and no G. Ezek 28:9
shalt know no G. but me. Hos 13:4

O God
heal her now, O G. Num 12:13
only this once, O G. Judg 16:28
hear me, O G. of my. Ps 4:1
redeem Israel, O G. out of. 25:22
from bloodguiltiness, O G. 51:14
thy vows are upon me, O G. 56:12
nor hath eye seen, O G. Isa 64:4
to do thy will, O G. Heb 10:7, 9

of God
for the cause was of G. 2 Chr 10:15
not hear, for it came of G. 25:20
my defence is of G. who. Ps 7:10
esteem him smitten of G. Isa 53:4
savourest not things of G. Mat 16:23; Mark 8:33
of will of man, but of G. John 1:13
he which is of G. hath seen. 6:46
of doctrine whether it be of G. 7:17
of G. heareth: ye are not of G. 8:47
this man is not of G. 9:16

if he were not *of G.* *John* 9:33
praise of men more than *of G.* 12:43
if it be *of G.* ye cannot. *Acts* 5:39
is not of men, but *of G.* *Rom* 2:29
but *of G.* that sheweth mercy. 9:16
of G. powers ordained *of G.* 13:1
of G. is made unto us. *1 Cor* 1:30
which ye have *of G.* ye are. 6:19
things are *of G.* 11:12; *2 Cor* 5:18
as *of G.* in the sight *of G.* *2 Cor* 2:17
our sufficiency is *of G.* 3:5
salvation, and that *of G.* *Phil* 1:28
righteousness which is *of G.* 3:9
he that was called *of G.* *Heb* 5:4
not righteousness, is not *of G.*
1 John 3:10
spirits whether they are *of G.* 4:1
not that Christ is come, is not *of G.* 3
we are *of G.* 6
we know that we are *of G.* 5:19
he that doeth good is *of G.* *3 John* 11
see **angel, ark, born, children, chosen, church, counsel, fear, glory, grace, hand, house, kingdom, knowledge, love, man, people, power, servant, sight, son, sons, spirit, will, words, work, works, world, wrath**

our **God**

go and sacrifice to *our G.* *Ex* 5:8
because *our G.* is not. *Deut* 31:17
ye greatness unto *our G.* 32:3
serve Lord, he is *our G.* *Josh* 24:18
have forsaken *our G.* *Judg* 10:10
any rock like *our G.* *1 Sam* 2:2
people, and for the cities of *our G.*
2 Sam 10:12; *1 Chr* 19:13
who is a rock, save *our G.*?
2 Sam 22:32; *Ps* 18:31
now therefore, *our G.* *1 Chr* 29:13
for great is *our G.* *2 Chr* 2:5
O Lord, thou art *our G.* 14:11
art not thou *our G.* who didst? 20:7
now, O *our G.* what? *Ezra* 9:10
hear, O *our G.* *Neh* 4:4
our G. shall fight for us. 20
work was wrought of *our G.* 6:16
our G. the great, mighty God. 9:32
our G. turned the curse into a. 13:2
song, even praise to *our G.* *Ps* 40:3
this God is *our G.* for ever. 48:14
our G. shall come and not. 50:3
and God, even *our* own *G.* 67:6
he that is *our G.* is the God. 68:20
so great a God as *our G.*? 77:13
he is *our G.* 95:7
our G. is in the heavens. 115:3
gracious is the Lord, *our G.* 116:5
lo, this is *our G.* we. *Isa* 25:9
to *our G.* for he will. 55:7
departing away from *our G.* 59:13
day of vengeance of *our G.* 61:2
our G. whom we serve. *Dan* 3:17
remaineth be for *our G.* *Zech* 9:7
by the Spirit of *our G.* *1 Cor* 6:11
our G. is a consuming. *Heb* 12:29
hast made us to *our G.* *Rev* 5:10
salvation to *our G.* who sitteth. 7:10
honour, and power be to *our G.* 12
see **peace, said, saith, serve, sent, speak, speed, spoken**

their **God**

I will be *their G.* *Gen* 17:8
Ex 29:45; *Jer* 24:7; 31:33; 32:38
Ezek 11:20; 34:24; 37:23, 27
Zech 8:8; *2 Cor* 6:16; *Rev* 21:3
to *their G.* for offerings of the Lord, and bread of *their G.* *Lev* 21:6
might be *their G.* 26:45; *Ezek* 14:11
thou art become *their G.*
2 Sam 7:24; *1 Chr* 17:22
the eye of *their G.* was. *Ezra* 5:5
where is *their G.*? *Ps* 79:10
115:2; *Joel* 2:17
people seek to *their G.*? *Isa* 8:19
and curse their king, and *their G.* 21
not the ordinance of *their G.* 58:2
judgement of *their G.* *Jer* 5:4, 5
people that know *their G.* *Dan* 11:32
gone a whoring from under *their G.*
Hos 4:12
their doings to turn to *their G.* 5:4
in Lord of hosts *their G.* *Zech* 12:5

not ashamed to be called *their G.*
Heb 11:16

thy **God**

fear *thy G.* *Lev* 19:14; 25:17, 36, 43
praise, and he is *thy G.* *Deut* 10:21
this day the Lord to be *thy G.* 26:17
my people, *thy G.* my. *Ruth* 1:16
let not *thy G.* deceive thee.
2 Ki 19:10; *Isa* 37:10
peace to thee, for *thy G.* *1 Chr* 12:18
because *thy G.* loved Israel made he thee king. *2 Chr* 9:8
to law of *thy G.* in thy. *Ezra* 7:14
wisdom of *thy G.* laws of *thy G.* 25
this is *thy G.* that brought. *Neh* 9:18
to me, Where is *thy G.*? *Ps* 42:3, 10
God, *thy G.* hath anointed thee.
45:7; *Heb* 1:9
I am God, even *thy G.* *Ps* 50:7
thy G. commanded strength. 68:28
praise the Lord, praise *thy G.* 147:12
dismayed, for I am *thy G.* *Isa* 41:10
full of the rebuke of *thy G.* 51:20
that saith to Zion, *Thy G.* 52:7
Lord be a light, and *thy G.* 60:19
shall *thy G.* rejoice over thee. 62:5
thy G. whom thou servest. *Dan* 6:16
is *thy G.* whom thou servest? 20
chasten thyself before *thy G.* 10:12
forgotten the law of *thy G.* *Hos* 4:6
gone a whoring from *thy G.* 9:1
to *thy G.* and wait on *thy G.* 12:6
prepare to meet *thy G.* *Amos* 4:12
arise, call upon *thy G.* *Jonah* 1:6
to walk humbly with *thy G.* *Mi* 6:8

to, or *unto* **God**

interpretations belong *to G.*?
Gen 40:8
their cry came up *unto G.* *Ex* 2:23
for he is holy *unto* his *G.* *Lev* 21:7
sacrifice to devils, not *to G.*
Deut 32:17; *1 Cor* 10:20
none like *unto* the *G.* of. *Deut* 33:26
shall be a Nazarite *unto G.*
Judg 13:5, 7; 16:17
three men going up *to G.* *1 Sam* 10:3
matter pertaining *to G.* *1 Chr* 26:32
man be profitable *unto G.*? *Job* 22:2
meet to be said *unto G.* I. 34:31
power belongeth *unto G.* *Ps* 62:11
to G. the Lord belong issues. 68:20
shall stretch her hands *to G.* 31
for me to draw near *to G.* 73:28
I cried *to G.* even *to G.* with. 77:1
spirit shall return *unto G.* *Eccl* 12:7
in approaching to *G.* *Isa* 58:2
our heart with hands *to G.* *Lam* 3:41
render *unto G.* the things. *Mat* 22:21
Mark 12:17; *Luke* 20:25
from God, went *to G.* *John* 13:3
you more than *unto G.* *Acts* 4:19
not lied unto men, but *unto G.* 5:4
from power of Satan *unto G.* 26:18
turn *to G.* and do works meet. 20
he liveth *unto G.* *Rom* 6:10
but alive *unto G.* 11
yield yourselves *unto G.* as alive. 13
should bring forth fruit *unto G.* 7:4
a living sacrifice *unto G.* 12:1
give account of himself *to G.* 14:12
not unto men but *unto G.* *1 Cor* 14:2
delivered up kingdom *to G.* 15:24
unto G. and our Father. *Phil* 4:20
them that come *unto G.* *Heb* 7:25
to G. must believe that he is. 11:6
ye are come *to G.* the Judge. 12:23
yourselves therefore *to G.* *Jas* 4:7
might bring us *to G.* *1 Pet* 3:18
but live according *to G.* in the. 4:6
hast redeemed us *to G.* *Rev* 5:9
child was caught up *unto G.* 12:5
being the firstfruits *unto G.* 14:4
see **true**

with **God**

Enoch walked *with G.* *Gen* 5:22, 24
Noah walked *with G.* 6:9
thou hast power *with G.* 32:28
people to meet *with G.* *Ex* 19:17
hath wrought *with G.* *1 Sam* 14:45
house be not so *with G.* *2 Sam* 23:5
from meddling *with G.* *2 Chr* 35:21
man be just *with G.*? *Job* 9:2
and I desire to reason *with G.* 13:3

might plead for a man *with G.*
Job 16:21
a man be justified *with G.*? 25:4
portion of a wicked man *with G.*
27:13
should delight himself *with G.* 34:9
enter into judgement *with G.* 23
with G. is terrible majesty. 37:22
is not stedfast *with G.* *Ps* 78:8
Judah yet ruleth *with G.* *Hos* 11:12
his strength had power *with G.* 12:3
but *with G.* all things are possible.
Mat 19:26; *Mark* 10:27
Luke 1:37; 18:27
found favour *with G.* *Luke* 1:30
increased in favour *with G.* 2:52
Word was *with G.* the. *John* 1:1
himself equal *with G.* 5:18; *Phil* 2:6
respect of persons *with G.* *Rom* 2:11
faith, we have peace *with G.* 5:1
there unrighteousness *with G.*? 9:14
labourers together *with G.* *1 Cor* 3:9
this world is foolishness *with G.* 19
man therein abide *with G.* 7:24
righteous thing *with G.* *2 Thes* 1:6
of world is enmity *with G.* *Jas* 4:4
this is acceptable *with G.* *1 Pet* 2:20
would **God**, *see* **would**

your **God**

your G. hath given you. *Gen* 43:23
go ye, sacrifice to *your G.* *Ex* 8:25
of Egypt to be *your G.* *Lev* 11:45
22:33; 25:38; *Num* 15:41
I will be *your G.* and ye. *Lev* 26:12
Jer 7:23; 11:4; 30:22; *Ezek* 36:28
memorial before *your G.* *Num* 10:10
be holy to *your G.* 15:40
lest ye deny *your G.* *Josh* 24:27
day rejected *your G.* *1 Sam* 10:19
your G. should deliver. *2 Chr* 32:14
how much less shall *your G.*? 15
we seek *your G.* as ye do. *Ezra* 4:2
your G. will come with. *Isa* 35:4
ye my people, saith *your G.* 40:1
cities of Judah, behold *your G.* 9
between you and *your G.* 59:2
your G. saith the Lord. *Ezek* 34:31
of a truth it is, *your G.* *Dan* 2:47
I will not be *your G.* *Hos* 1:9
say that he is *your G.* *John* 8:54
to my God and *your G.* 20:17

goddess

after *g.* of Zidonians. *1 Ki* 11:5
worshipped Ashtoreth, the *g.* 33
temple of great *g.* Diana. *Acts* 19:27
worshippers of the *g.* Diana. 35
nor yet blasphemers of your *g.* 37

godhead

think that *g.* is like to. *Acts* 17:29
eternal power and *g.* *Rom* 1:20*
dwelleth the fulness of *g.* *Col* 2:9

godliness

lead a quiet life in all *g.* *1 Tim* 2:2
becometh women professing *g.* 10
great is the mystery of *g.* 3:16
exercise thyself rather unto *g.* 4:7
g. is profitable unto all things. 8
doctrine which is according to *g.* 6:3
men, supposing that gain is *g.* 5
g. with contentment is great gain. 6
follow after righteousness, *g.* 11
having a form of *g.* but. *2 Tim* 3:5
the truth which is after *g.* *Tit* 1:1
that pertain to life and *g.* *2 Pet* 1:3
add to patience *g.* to *g.* brotherly. 6, 7
of persons ought to be in all *g.* 3:11

godly

set apart him that is *g.* *Ps* 4:3
help, Lord, for the *g.* man. 12:1
every one that is *g.* pray. 32:6
he might seek a *g.* seed. *Mal* 2:15
in *g.* sincerity had our. *2 Cor* 1:12
sorry after a *g.* manner. 7:9, 11
g. sorrow worketh repentance. 10
I am jealous over you with *g.* 11:2
will live *g.* in Christ. *2 Tim* 3:12
that ye should live *g.* in. *Tit* 2:12
God with reverence and *g.* fear.
Heb 12:28*
how to deliver the *g.* *2 Pet* 2:9
forward after a *g.* sort. *3 John* 6

gods
ye shall be as *g.* knowing. *Gen* 3:5
hast thou stolen my *g.*? 31:30
against all *g.* of Egypt. *Ex* 12:12
shalt not make with me *g.* of. 20:23
thou shalt not revile the *g.* 22:28
not bow down to their *g.* 23:24
covenant with them nor their *g.* 32
up, make us *g.* to go before us.
32:1, 23; *Acts* 7:40
these be thy *g.* O Israel. *Ex* 32:4, 8
they have made them *g.* of gold. 31
go a whoring after their *g.* 34:15
the sacrifices of their *g.* *Num* 25:2
upon the Egyptians' *g.* also. 33:4
Jer 43:12, 13; 46:25
images of their *g.* shall. *Deut* 7:25
Lord your God is God of *g.* 10:17
down the images of their *g.* 12:3
thou enquire not after their *g.* 30
their *g.* burnt their sons and daughters in the fire to their *g.* 31
entice thee to the *g.* of people. 13:7
they have done to their *g.* 20:18
say, where are their *g.*? 32:37
Lord God of *g.* knoweth. *Josh* 22:22
mention of the name of their *g.* 23:7
they chose new *g.* then. *Judg* 5:8
I said, fear not the *g.* of the. 6:10
go and cry to the *g.* which ye. 10:14
Micah had an house of *g.* 17:5
ye have taken away my *g.* 18:24
is gone back to her *g.* *Ruth* 1:15
are the *g.* that smote. *1 Sam* 4:8
hand from off you and your *g.* 6:5
cursed David by his *g.* 17:43
she said, I saw *g.* ascending. 28:13
from Egypt and their *g.* *2 Sam* 7:23
your heart after their *g.* *1 Ki* 11:2
incense and sacrificed to their *g.* 8
to go up, behold thy *g.* 12:28
the name of your *g.* 18:24, 25
let the *g.* do so to me. 19:2; 20:10
their *g.* are *g.* of the hills. 20:23
every nation made *g.* *2 Ki* 17:29
and served their own *g.* 33
g. delivered his land? 18:33; 19:12
2 Chr 32:13, 14; *Isa* 36:18; 37:12
where are the *g.* of Hamath?
2 Ki 18:34; *Isa* 36:19
g. into fire they were no *g.* *2 Ki* 19:18
went a whoring after *g.* *1 Chr* 5:25
armour in the house of their *g.* 10:10
their *g.* David burnt them. 14:12
Jeroboam made for *g.* *2 Chr* 13:8
be a priest to them that are no *g.* 9
g. of Seir to be his *g.* 25:14
Ahaz sacrificed to the *g.* of. 28:23
the *g.* of the nations have not. 32:17
vessels in house of his *g.* *Ezra* 1:7
he judgeth among the *g.* *Ps* 82:1
said, ye are *g.* 6; *John* 10:34
thanks unto the God of *g.* *Ps* 136:2
before *g.* will I sing praise. 138:1
fallen, and her *g.* broken. *Isa* 21:9
may know that ye are *g.* 41:23
molten images, ye are our *g.* 42:17
changed her *g.* are no *g.*? *Jer* 2:11
g. thou hast made? . . . number of thy cities are thy *g.* 28; 11:13
sworn by them that are no *g.* 5:7
the *g.* that have not made the. 10:11
cry to the *g.* to whom they. 11:12
make *g.* and they are no *g.*? 16:20
that burneth incense to his *g.* 48:35
can shew it, except the *g.* *Dan* 2:11
that your God is a God of *g.* 47
is the spirit of the holy *g.* 4:8
of holy *g.* is in thee. 9, 18; 5:14
the *g.* of gold and silver. 5:4, 23
like the wisdom of the *g.* 11
carry captives into Egypt *g.* 11:8
things against God of *g.* 36
say any more, ye are our *g.* *Hos* 14:3
out of the house of thy *g.* *Nah* 1:14
if he called them *g.* to. *John* 10:35
the *g.* are come down to. *Acts* 14:11
they be no *g.* which are made. 19:26
are called *g.* there be *g.* *1 Cor* 8:5
which by nature are no *g.* *Gal* 4:8
see **serve**

all **gods**
Lord is greater than *all g.* *Ex* 18:11
to be feared above *all g.*
1 Chr 16:25; *Ps* 96:4
all g. of the people are idols.
1 Chr 16:26; *Ps* 96:5
great is God above *all g.* *2 Chr* 2:5
Ps 135:5
a great King above *all g.* *Ps* 95:3
worship him, *all* ye *g* 97:7
exalted above *all g.* 9
he will famish *all* the *g.* *Zeph* 2:11

among the **gods**
among the g. who is like. *Ex* 15:11
who *among the g.* could deliver?
2 Ki 18:35; *2 Chr* 32:14; *Isa* 36:20
among the g. there is. *Ps* 86:8

molten **gods**
no *molten g.* *Ex* 34:17; *Lev* 19:4

other **gods**
shalt have no *other g.* before me.
Ex 20:3; *Deut* 5:7
of names of *other g.* *Ex* 23:13
ye shall not go after *other g.*
Deut 6:14; 11:28; 28:14
1 Ki 11:10; *Jer* 25:6; 35:15
thy son to serve *other g.* *Deut* 7:4
if thou walk after *other g.* 8:19
let us go after *other g.* 13:2, 6, 13
hath gone and served *other g.* 17:3
29:26; *Josh* 23:16; *Judg* 10:13
1 Sam 8:8; *Jer* 11:10
speak in name of *other g.* *Deut* 18:20
away, and worship *other g.* and serve them. *Deut* 30:17; *Jer* 22:9
they turned to *other g.* *Deut* 31:18
then will they turn to *other g.* 20
and followed *other g.* *Judg* 2:12
went a whoring after *other g.* 17
in following *other g.* to serve. 19
go serve *other g.* *1 Sam* 26:19
upon *other g.* *1 Ki* 9:9; *2 Chr* 7:22
his heart after *other g.* *1 Ki* 11:4
gone and made thee *other g.* 14:9
offer sacrifice to *other g.* *2 Ki* 5:17
sinned, and had feared *other g.* 17:7
ye shall not fear *other g.* 35, 37, 38
burnt incense to *other g.* 22:17
2 Chr 34:25; *Jer* 1:16; 19:4
incense to *other g.* *2 Chr* 28:25
nor walk after *other g.* *Jer* 7:6
walk after *other g.* whom. 9; 13:10
and walked after *other g.* 16:11
burn no incense to *other g.* 44:5
burning incense to *other g.* in. 8, 15
look to *other g.* and love. *Hos* 3:1
see **serve**

strange **gods**
the *strange g.* *Gen* 35:2; *1 Sam* 7:3
they gave Jacob the *strange g.*
Gen 35:4; *Josh* 24:23
jealousy with *strange g.* *Deut* 32:16
and serve *strange g.* *Josh* 24:20
away their *strange g.* *Judg* 10:16
away altar of *strange g.* *2 Chr* 14:3
away the *strange g.* and idol. 33:15
as ye served *strange g.* so. *Jer* 5:19
setter forth of *strange g.* *Acts* 17:18

God-ward
be thou for people to *G.* *Ex* 18:19
we through Christ to *G.* *2 Cor* 3:4
your faith to *G.* is. *1 Thes* 1:8

goest
in places whither thou *g.* *Gen* 28:15
whither *g.* thou? 32:17; *Judg* 19:17
Zech 2:2; *John* 13:36; 16:5
is it not in that thou *g.*? *Ex* 33:16
inhabitants whither thou *g.* 34:12
thou *g.* before them by. *Num* 14:14
God shall bring thee into the land whither thou *g.* *Deut* 7:1; 11:29
the land whither thou *g.* is. 11:10
cut off nations whither thou *g.* 12:29
when thou *g.* to battle. 20:1; 21:10
thou settest thine hand to, whither thou *g.* 23:20; *Josh* 1:7
shalt thou be when thou *g.* *Deut* 28:6
cursed shalt thou be when thou *g.* 19
cleave to thee whither thou *g.* 21
plucked off land whither thou *g.* 63
die in mount whither thou *g.* 32:50
with thee whither thou *g.* *Josh* 1:9
thou *g.* to take a wife of. *Judg* 14:3
whither thou *g.* I will go. *Ruth* 1:16
wherefore *g.* thou also? *2 Sam* 15:19
thou *g.* over brook. *1 Ki* 2:37, 42
but thou *g.* not forth with. *Ps* 44:9
when thou *g.* steps shall. *Pr* 4:12
when thou *g.* it shall lead thee. 6:22
keep thy foot when thou *g.* *Eccl* 5:1
in grave whither thou *g.* 9:10
a prey whither thou *g.* *Jer* 45:5
I will follow thee whither *g.*
Mat 8:19; *Luke* 9:57
when thou *g.* with thine. *Luke* 12:58
sought to stone thee, *g.* *John* 11:8
we know not whither thou *g.* 14:5

goeth
lo, he *g.* out unto the. *Ex* 7:15
deliver it by that the sun *g.* 22:26
shall bear them when he *g.* 28:29
on Aaron's heart when he *g.* 30
shall be heard when he *g.* in. 35
these ye may eat that *g.* *Lev* 11:21
he that *g.* into the house. 14:46
him whose seed *g.* from. 15:32; 22:4
the tabernacle when he *g.* in. 16:17
who *g.* to holy things having. 22:3
when it *g.* out in jubile. 27:21
when a wife *g.* aside. *Num* 5:29
the Lord which *g.* before. *Deut* 1:30
thy God is he that *g.* over. 9:3
as when a man *g.* into wood. 19:5
Lord your God is he that *g.* 20:4
when the host *g.* forth against. 23:9
pledge when the sun *g.* down. 24:13
as the sun when he *g.* *Judg* 5:31
as David, who *g.* at. *1 Sam* 22:14
as his part is that *g.* down to. 30:24
thy master *g.* to house of. *2 Ki* 5:18
be with the king as he *g.* out. 11:8
2 Chr 23:7
this work *g.* fast on. *Ezra* 5:8
that *g.* down to grave. *Job* 7:9
lo, he *g.* by me, and I see. 9:11
when *g.* in company with. 34:8
hear the sound that *g.* out of. 37:2
g. on to meet the armed men. 39:21
prayer that *g.* not out of. *Ps* 17:1
when he *g.* abroad, he telleth. 41:6
such a one as *g.* on in his. 68:21
thy fierce wrath *g.* over me. 88:16
a fire *g.* before him, and. 97:3
man *g.* forth to his work. 104:23
he that *g.* forth and weepeth. 126:6
his breath *g.* forth; he. 146:4
so he that *g.* in to his. *Pr* 6:29
g. after her, as an ox *g.* to the. 7:22
when it *g.* well with righteous. 11:10
pride *g.* before destruction. 16:18
g. about as a talebearer. 20:19
as a thorn *g.* up into hand of. 26:9
no wood is, there the fire *g.* out. 20
her candle *g.* not out by. 31:18
sun *g.* down, and hasteth. *Eccl* 1:5
man *g.* up, spirit of beast *g.* 3:21
because man *g.* to his long. 12:5
that *g.* down sweetly. *S of S* 7:9
from the time it *g.* forth. *Isa* 28:19
when one *g.* with a pipe to. 30:29
so shall my word be that *g.* 55:11
whoso *g.* therein shall not. 59:8
as a beast *g.* down into the. 63:14
every one that *g.* out. *Jer* 5:6
woe unto us, for the day *g.* 6:4
that *g.* out to Chaldeans. 21:9; 38:2
but weep sore for him that *g.* 22:10
whirlwind of the Lord *g.* 30:23
we will do what *g.* out of our. 44:17
every one that *g.* by it. 49:17; 50:13
have blown, but none *g.* *Ezek* 7:14
their heart *g.* after their. 33:31
in the day that he *g.* into the. 44:27
as the early dew, it *g.* *Hos* 6:4
thy judgements are as light that *g.* 5
this is the curse that *g.* *Zech* 5:3
he said, this is an ephah that *g.* 6
I say to this man go, and he *g.*
Mat 8:9; *Luke* 7:8
then *g.* he and taketh. *Mat* 12:45
Luke 11:26
for joy thereof *g.* and. *Mat* 13:44
not that which *g.* into mouth. 15:11
this kind *g.* not out but by. 17:21
Son of man *g.* as it is written. 26:24
Mark 14:21; *Luke* 22:22
he *g.* before you into Galilee.
Mat 28:7; *Mark* 16:7

not tell whither it g. John 3:8
thou hast a devil; who g.? 7:20
g. before them, the sheep. 10:4
she g. unto the grave to weep. 11:31
not whither he g. 12:35; 1 John 2:11
brother g. to law with. 1 Cor 6:6
who g. a warfare any time at. 9:7
beholdeth himself and g. Jas 1:24
Lamb whithersoever he g. Rev 14:4
and is of the seven, and g. 17:11
and out of his mouth g. a. 19:15

Gog

G. his son, Shimei his. 1 Chr 5:5
set thy face against G. Ezek 38:2
I am against thee, O G. 3; 39:1
be sanctified in thee, O G. 38:16
when G. shall come against. 18
give to G. a place of graves. 39:11
G. and Magog, to gather. Rev 20:8

Golan, *see* **Bashan**

going

sun g. down, a deep. Gen 15:12
his hands steady, to g. Ex 17:12
thou meet thine enemy's ox g. 23:4
g. forth of border from. Num 34:4
sacrifice the passover at g. Deut 16:6
rejoice, Zebulun, in thy g. 33:18
and smote them in the g. Josh 7:5
as they were in the g. down. 10:11
at the g. down of the sun carcases. 27
I am g. the way of all the. 23:14
I am now g. to house of. Judg 19:18
up, let us be g. but none. 28
meet thee three men g. 1 Sam 10:3
in g. turned not from. 2 Sam 2:19
heareth a sound of g. in trees. 5:24
1 Chr 14:15
as she was g. to fetch. 1 Ki 17:11
went a proclamation at g. 22:36
g. by the way, children. 2 Ki 2:23
they smote Ahaziah at the g. 9:27
time of sun g. down, he. 2 Chr 18:34
from g. to and fro in. Job 1:7; 2:2
deliver him from g. down to. 33:24
he will deliver his soul from g. 28
his g. forth is from end. Ps 19:6
calleth earth, from rising of sun to g.
down. 50:1; 113:3; Mal 1:11
sun knoweth his g. down. Ps 104:19
g. down to the chambers. Pr 7:27
man looketh well to his g. 14:15
yea, four are comely in g. 30:29
shall be darkened in his g. Isa 13:10
g. up to Luhith, continual weeping
shall g. up; in the g. Jer 48:5
g. and weeping they shall. 50:4
g. up had eight. Ezek 40:31, 34, 37
with every g. forth of the. 44:5
after his g. forth, one shut. 46:12
and laboured till g. down. Dan 6:14
g. forth of the commandment. 9:25
his g. forth is prepared. Hos 6:3
rise, let us be g. Mat 26:46
what king g. to war. Luke 14:31
g. through midst of. John 8:59
these g. before, tarried. Acts 20:5
g. about to establish. Rom 10:3
some men's sins g. 1 Tim 5:24
disannulling of command g. before.
Heb 7:18
g. after strange flesh are. Jude 7

see **coming**

goings

and Moses wrote their g. Num 33:2
the g. out of their borders. 34:5
8, 9, 12; Josh 15:4, 7, 11; 16:3, 8
18:12, 14
man, he seeth all his g. Job 34:21
hold up my g. in thy paths. Ps 17:5
on a rock, established my g. 40:2
seen thy g. even the g. of. 68:24
purposed to overthrow my g. 140:4
and he pondereth all his g. Pr 5:21
man's g. are of the Lord. 20:24
is no judgement in their g. Isa 59:8
there g. out were. Ezek 42:11
shew them the g. out thereof. 43:11
whose g. forth have been. Mi 5:2

gold

Havilah, where there is g. Gen 2:11
the g. of that land is good. 12
chain of g. on Joseph's neck. 41:42
make you gods of g. Ex 20:23
cast four rings of g. for. 25:12, 26
26:29; 28:23, 26, 27; 37:3, 13
overlay them with g. 25:13, 28
26:29, 37; 30:5; 37:4, 15, 28
two cherubims of g. 25:18; 37:7
make fifty taches of g. 26:6; 36:13
hooks shall be of g. 26:32, 37; 36:38
ephod of g. 28:6
girdle of g. 8
ouches of g. 11, 13; 39:6, 13, 16
breastplate of g. 15
chains of g. 28:24
thou shalt make bells of g. 33
who hath any g. let him. 32:24
have made them gods of g. 31
jewels of g. an offering of g. 35:22
the boards with g. bars with g. 36:34
their chapiters and fillets with g. 38
all the g. that was occupied. 38:24
they did beat the g. into thin. 39:3
thou shalt set the altar of g. 40:5
ten shekels of g. Num 7:14, 20
the altar twelve spoons of g. 84
all the g. of the spoons was 120. 86
captains' oblation, jewels of g. 31:50
a wedge of g. of 50. Josh 7:21
Achan and the wedge of g. 24
1700 shekels of g. Judg 8:26
and put the jewels of g. 1 Sam 6:8
laid coffer and the mice of g. 11
the coffer with the jewels of g. 15
David took shields of g. 2 Sam 8:7
1 Chr 18:7
altar, he overlaid with g. 1 Ki 6:22
cherubims with g. 28; 2 Chr 3:10
the altar and table of g. 1 Ki 7:48
lamps and tongs of g. 49
hinges of g. 50
Tyre furnished Solomon with g. and.
9:11; 10:11; 2 Chr 9:10
queen of Sheba came with g.
1 Ki 10:2; 2 Chr 9:1
the weight of g. came in one year.
1 Ki 10:14; 2 Chr 9:13
200 targets of beaten g. 1 Ki 10:16
made three hundred shields of g. 17
the throne with the best g. 18
made two calves of g. 12:28
made ships to go for g. 22:48
Hezekiah cut off g. 2 Ki 18:16
of g. by weight for g. 1 Chr 28:14
and the g. was g. of. 2 Chr 3:6
ten candlesticks of g. 4:7
basons of g. 8
censers, and spoons of pure g. 22
throne, with a footstool of g. 9:18
carried away the shields of g. 12:9
g. copper precious as g. Ezra 8:27
thousand drachms of g. Neh 7:70
chief of the fathers gave g. 71
people gave g. 72
lay up g. as dust, the g. Job 22:24*
I shall come forth like g. 23:10
earth, it hath the dust of g. 28:6
wisdom cannot be gotten for g. 15
it cannot be valued with the g. 16
the g. and the crystal cannot. 17
g. my hope, or said to fine g. 31:24
esteem thy riches? no, not g. 36:19*
gave Job an earring of g. 42:11
desired are they than g. Ps 19:10
stand the queen in g. of Ophir. 45:9
be given of the g. of Sheba. 72:15
as a jewel of g. in a. Pr 11:22
it is to get wisdom than g. 16:16
there is g. and a multitude of. 20:15
comely with chains of g. S of S 1:10*
his hands are as g. rings set. 5:14
of thy images of g. Isa 30:22
spreadeth it over with g. 40:19
for brass I will bring g. for. 60:17
thee with ornaments of g. Jer 4:30
g. become dim! fine g. Lam 4:1
Sheba occupied with g. Ezek 27:22
art head of g. Dan 2:38
Nebuchadnezzar made image of g.
3:1
hast praised the gods of g. 5:23
they put a chain of g. about. 29
a candlestick all of g. Zech 4:2
and I will try them as g. is. 13:9
they presented to him g. Mat 2:11
whoso shall swear by the g. of. 23:16
for whether is greater, the g. or the
temple? Mat 23:17
not adorned with g. or pearls.
1 Tim 2:9; 1 Pet 3:3
round about with g. Heb 9:4
come a man with a g. ring. Jas 2:2
faith more precious than g. 1 Pet 1:7
thee to buy of me g. tried. Rev 3:18
their heads crowns of g. 4:4; 9:7
woman was decked with g. 17:4
city that was decked with g. 18:16

see **beaten, crown, fine**

pure **gold**

overlay the ark with pure g. within.
Ex 25:11, 24; 30:3; 37:2, 11, 26
a mercy seat of pure g. 25:17; 37:6
dishes, spoons and covers of pure g.
25:29; 37:16, 23
make a candlestick of pure g. 25:31
37:17; 1 Ki 7:49
snuffdishes pure g. Ex 25:38
1 Ki 7:50; 2 Chr 4:22
two chains of pure g. at ends.
Ex 28:14, 22; 39:15
a plate of pure g. 28:36; 39:30
he overlaid with pure g. 1 Ki 6:20
vessels of Lebanon of pure g. 10:21
2 Chr 9:20
pure g. for fleshhooks. 1 Chr 28:17
porch within with pure g. 2 Chr 3:4
the throne with pure g. 9:17
to be valued with pure g. Job 28:19
settest a crown of pure g. Ps 21:3
city was pure g. Rev 21:18
street of pure g. 21

gold with *silver*

Abram was rich in silver and g.
Gen 13:2; 24:35
my lord's house silver or g. 44:8
jewels of silver and g. Ex 3:22
11:2; 12:35
offering, take silver and g. 25:3
to work in g. silver. 31:4; 35:32
his house full of silver and g.
Num 22:18; 24:13
only g. and silver that may. 31:22
not desire silver and g. Deut 7:25
when thy silver and g. is. 8:13
greatly multiply silver and g. 17:17
seen their idols, silver and g. 29:17
silver and g. are consecrated to.
Josh 6:19, 24
your tents with silver and g. 22:8
silver and g. David dedicated.
2 Sam 8:11; 1 Ki 7:51
will have no silver or g. 2 Sam 21:4
house of Lord silver and g. he had.
1 Ki 15:15; 2 Chr 15:18
Asa took all the silver and g.
1 Ki 15:18; 2 Chr 16:2
I have sent a present of silver and g.
1 Ki 15:19; 2 Chr 16:3
silver and g. is mine. 1 Ki 20:3
deliver silver and g. 5
thence silver and g. 2 Ki 7:8
Jehoash took the silver and g.
2 Ki 14:14; 2 Chr 25:24
Ahaz took silver and g. 2 Ki 16:8
Hezekiah shewed them silver and g.
20:13; Isa 39:2
Jehoiakim gave silver and g. exacted
silver and g. 2 Ki 23:35
things of g. in g. of silver in silver.
25:15; Jer 52:19
good, of g. and silver. 1 Chr 29:3
king made silver and g. 2 Chr 1:15
place help with silver and g. Ezra 1:4
gave silver and g. 2:69
to carry silver and g. 7:15
weighed them silver and g. 8:25, 33
beds were of g. and silver. Esth 1:6
for silver, a place for g. Job 28:1
silver her feathers with g. Ps 68:13
them out with silver and g. 105:37
are silver and g. 115:4; 135:15
is better than g. and silver. 119:72
silver receive knowledge rather than
g. Pr 8:10
silver, furnace for g. 17:3; 27:21
favour rather than silver or g. 22:1
of g. in pictures of silver. 25:11
me also silver and g. Eccl 2:8

ot g. with studs of silver. S of S 1:11
pillars of silver, bottom of g. 3:10
is full of silver and g. Isa 2:7
cast his idols of silver and g. 20; 31:7
shall not regard silver or g. 13:17
g. out of the bag, and weigh silver. 46:6
their silver and g. with them. 60:9
deck it with silver and g. Jer 10:4
away their silver and g. silver and g. not able. Ezek 7:19; Zeph 1:18
wast thou decked with g. and silver. Ezek 16:13
silver and g. broken. Dan 2:35, 45
the gods of silver and g. 5:4, 23
he honour with g. and silver. 11:38
over treasures of g. and silver. 43
I multiplied her silver and g. Hos 2:8
of their silver and g. have they. 8:4
taken my silver and g. Joel 3:5
of silver and spoil of g. Nah 2:9
laid over with silver and g. Hab 2:19
silver is mine, and the g. Hag 2:8
then take silver and g. Zech 6:11
purge them as g. and silver. Mal 3:3
provide neither g. nor silver. Mat 10:9
Peter said, silver and g. Acts 3:6
Godhead like to silver and g. 17:29
coveted no man's silver or g. 20:33
this foundation g. silver. 1 Cor 3:12
vessels of silver and g. 2 Tim 2:20
your g. and silver cankered. Jas 5:3
were not redeemed with silver and g. 1 Pet 1:18
of idols of silver and g. Rev 9:20

talent and talents of gold

of a talent of pure g. Ex 25:39
of a talent of pure g. made. 37:24
weight of crown a talent of g. 2 Sam 12:30; 1 Chr 20:2
Solomon 120 talents of g. 1 Ki 9:14
from Ophir 420 talents of g. 28
she gave Solomon 120 talents of g. 10:10; 2 Chr 9:9
came to Solomon 666 talents of g. 1 Ki 10:14
put the land to a talent of g. 2 Ki 23:33; 2 Chr 36:3
100,000 talents of g. 1 Chr 22:14
proper good 3000 talents of g. 29:4
fathers gave 5000 talents of g. 7
Ophir 450 talents of g. 2 Chr 8:18
of g. vessels 100 talents. Ezra 8:26

vessels of gold

Toi sent to David vessels of g. 2 Sam 8:10; 1 Chr 18:10
Solomon's drinking vessels were of g. 1 Ki 10:21; 2 Chr 9:20
every man brought present, vessels of g. 1 Ki 10:25; 2 Chr 9:24
for house of Lord vessels of g. 2 Ki 12:13
cut in pieces vessels of g. 24:13
of rest of money made they vessels of g. 2 Chr 24:14
the vessels of g. and silver 5400. Ezra 1:11
vessels of g. Cyrus deliverd. 5:14
I weighed of vessels of g. 100. 8:26
drink in vessels of g. Esth 1:7
into Egypt vessels of g. Dan 11:8
not only vessels of g. 2 Tim 2:20

golden

a g. crown to the border. Ex 25:25
a g. bell. 28:34
two g. rings, 30:4; 39:20
Aaron said, break off the g. 32:2
upon forefront he put g. Lev 8:9
one g. spoon of ten. Num 7:26
had g. earrings, because. Judg 8:24
the weight of g. earrings he. 26
g. emerods, five g. 1 Sam 6:4, 17, 18
departed not from the g. 2 Ki 10:29
for the g. basons he. 1 Chr 28:17
there are with you g. 2 Chr 13:8
and also let the g. vessels. Ezra 6:5
king shall hold out a g. sceptre. Esth 4:11; 5:2; 8:4
or the g. bowl be broken. Eccl 12:6
more precious than the g. Isa 13:12
how hath the g. city ceased ! 14:4
Babylon hath been g. Jer 51:7
and worship g. image. Dan 3:5, 12
commanded to bring the g. 5:2
they brought the g. vessels taken. 3
g. pipes, empty the g. oil. Zech 4:12
g. censer and ark where was g. pot. Heb 9:4
turned, I saw seven g. Rev 1:12
girt about the paps with a g. 13
the mystery of the seven g. 20
who walketh in midst of the g. 2:1
g. vials. 5:8; 15:7
having a g. censer. 8:3
on his head a g. crown. 14:14
a g. cup full. 17:4
had a g. reed to measure the. 21:15
see **altar**

goldsmith, -s

Uzziel of the g. repaired. Neh 3:8
the g.'s son. 31
and merchants repaired and g. 32
the g. spreadeth it over. Isa 40:19
carpenter encouraged the g. 41:7
they hire a g. and he maketh. 46:6

Golgotha

come to a place called G. Mat 27:33
Mark 15:22; John 19:17

Goliath

G. of Gath a. 1 Sam 17:4, 23
sword of G. the Philistine. 21:9
he gave him the sword of G. 22:10
slew the brother of G. 2 Sam 21:19
1 Chr 20:5

Gomer

sons of Japheth, G. Magog. Gen 10:2; 1 Chr 1:5
the sons of G. Ashkenaz, Riphath. Gen 10:3; 1 Chr 1:6
G. and all his bands. Ezek 38:6
he took G. the daughter. Hos 1:3

Gomorrah

destroyed Sodom and G. Gen 13:10
goods of Sodom and G. 14:11
cry of Sodom and G. is. 18:20
the Lord rained on G. fire. 19:24
looked towards Sodom and G. 28
like the overthrow of Sodom and G. Deut 29:23; Isa 1:9; 13:19
Jer 23:14; 49:18; 50:40
Amos 4:11; Rom 9:29
2 Pet 2:6; Jude 7
vine is of fields of G. Deut 32:32
the law, ye people of G. Isa 1:10
of Ammon shall be as G. Zeph 2:9
be more tolerable for G. Mat 10:15
Mark 6:11

gone

thou wouldest needs be g. Gen 31:30
daughter, and we will be g. 34:17
for your households, and be g. 42:33
flocks and herds, and be g. Ex 12:32
seeth their power is g. Deut 32:36
not Jonathan was g. 1 Sam 14:3
number now, and see who is g. 17
I have g. the way which the. 15:20
as soon as the lad was g. 20:41
g. in to my father's ? 2 Sam 3:7
he is quite g. 24
Amnon said, Arise, be g. 13:15
that Shimei had g. from. 1 Ki 2:41
when he was g. a lion met. 13:24
away dung till it be all g. 14:10
as soon as I am g. Spirit. 18:12
busy here and there, he was g. 20:40
messenger that was g. to call. 22:13
but have g. from tent to. 1 Chr 17:5
I rise, and the night be g.? Job 7:4
destroyed me, and I am g. 19:10
exalted for a while, but are g. 24:24
are dried up and g. away. 28:4*
of mine eyes, it also is g. Ps 38:10
I had g. with the multitude to. 42:4
me, my feet were almost g. 73:2
is his mercy clean g. for ever ? 77:8
passeth over it, and it is g. 103:16
I am g. like the shadow that. 109:23
good man is g. a long. Pr 7:19
when he is g. his way, then. 20:14
who had come and g. Eccl 8:10*
the rain is over and g. S of S 2:11
had withdrawn, and was g. 5:6
whither is thy beloved g. O ? 6:1
therefore my people are g. Isa 5:13
the mirth of the land g. Isa 24:11
the way he had not g. 41:3
in me, that they are g. Jer 2:5
I have not g. after Baalim ? 23
this people are revolted and g. 5:23
beasts are g. 9:10
thou art g. backward. 15:6
none that are g. into Egypt. 44:14
all remnant that are g. shall. 28
they have g. from mountain. 50:6
Judah is g. Lam 1:3
Zion's children are g. 5
g. without strength. 6
my virgins are g. 18
from heathen whither g. Ezek 37:21
the thing is g. from me. Dan 2:5, 8
lo, they are g. because of. Hos 9:6
will new moon be g. Amos 8:5
angels were g. from. Luke 2:15
as if he would have g. further. 24:28
for his disciples were g. John 4:8
behold, the world is g. after. 12:19
saw hope of gains was g. Acts 16:19
among whom I have g. 20:25
who is g. into heaven. 1 Pet 3:22
have g. in the way of Cain. Jude 11

gone about

Saul is g. about and. 1 Sam 15:12
feastings were g. about. Job 1:5
city is g. about the. Isa 15:8
hath g. about to profane. Acts 24:6*

gone aside

if thou hast not g. aside. Num 5:19
if hast g. aside to another. 20
they are all g. aside, they. Ps 14:3
they were g. aside, they. Acts 26:31

gone astray

I have g. astray like. Ps 119:176
like sheep have g. astray. Isa 53:6
one of them be g. astray, he seeketh that which is g. astray. Mat 18:12
way, and are g. astray. 2 Pet 2:15

gone away

Abner was g. away. 2 Sam 3:22, 23
men of Israel were g. away. 23:9
the waters were g. away. Job 28:4
they are g. away backward. Isa 1:4
Levites which are g. away from. Ezek 44:10
are g. away from mine. Mal 3:7*
disciples are g. away. John 6:22

gone back

sister-in-law is g. back. Ruth 1:15
nor have I g. back. Job 23:12
every one is g. back. Ps 53:3
he was not yet g. back, he. Jer 40:5

gone down

passed, and g. down. 1 Sam 15:12
Adonijah is g. down. 1 Ki 1:25
Ahab g. down to possess. 21:18
shadow had g. down in the dial of Ahaz. 2 Ki 20:11; Isa 38:8
my beloved is g. down. S of S 6:2
her sun is g. down while. Jer 15:9
his young men are g. down. 48:15
all people g. down. Ezek 31:12
the strong are g. down, slain. 32:21
Tubal g. down. 27
Zidonians g. down. 30
Jonah was g. down to. Jonah 1:5

gone forth

when Israel was g. forth. Ex 19:1
of Elisha was g. forth. 2 Ki 6:15
God is g. forth before. 1 Chr 14:15
my salvation is g. forth. Isa 51:5
g. forth to make thy land. Jer 4:7
my children are g. forth of me. 10:20
is profaneness g. forth into. 23:15
whirlwind of Lord is g. forth. 19
brethren that are not g. forth. 29:16
the morning is g. forth. Ezek 7:10
of the Lord and are g. forth. 36:20
g. forth to slay wise men. Dan 2:14
when I am g. forth, prince. 10:20
when he was g. forth. Mark 10:17

gone out

as soon as I am g. out I. Ex 9:29
there is wrath g. out. Num 16:46
certain men g. out. Deut 13:13
which is g. out of thy lips. 23:23
is not the Lord g. out ? Judg 4:14

hand of Lord is g. out. Ruth 1:13
when wine was g. out. 1 Sam 25:37
the Syrians had g. out. 2 Ki 5:2
therefore they are g. out. 7:12
afore Isaiah was g. out into. 20:4
their line is g. out. Ps 19:4
alter the thing that is g. out. 89:34
the word is g. out of my. Isa 45:23
scum is not g. out of it. Ezek 24:6
when unclean spirit is g. out.
Mat 12:43; Luke 11:24
our lamps are g. out. Mat 25:8
that virtue had g. out of him.
Mark 5:30; Luke 8:46
devil is g. out of daughter.
Mark 7:29, 30; Luke 11:14
he was g. out, Jesus. John 13:31
are all g. out of way. Rom 3:12*
false prophets are g. out. 1 John 4:1

gone *over*

be g. over the brook. 2 Sam 17:20
iniquities are g. over. Ps 38:4
and billows are g. over me. 42:7
then the stream had g. over. 124:4
the proud waters had g. over. 5
they are g. over passage. Isa 10:29
g. over the sea. 16:8; Jer 48:32
shall not have g. over. Mat 10:23

gone *up*

my son, thou art g. up. Gen 49:9
bed on which g. up. 2 Ki 1:4, 6, 16
God is g. up with a shout. Ps 47:5
he is g. up to Bajith. Isa 15:2
than me, and art g. up. 57:8
she is g. up on every. Jer 3:6
cry of Jerusalem is g. up. 14:2
army, which are g. up. 34:21
Moab is spoiled, and g. up. 48:15
God of Israel was g. up. Ezek 9:3
ye have not g. up into the gaps. 13:5
are g. up to Assyria. Hos 8:9
his brethren were g. up. John 7:10
had g. up and saluted. Acts 18:22

gone *a whoring*

they have g. a whoring. Lev 17:7
thou hast g. a whoring. Ezek 23:30
g. a whoring from under. Hos 4:12
for thou hast g. a whoring from. 9:1

good, *substantive*

done to thee nothing but g. Gen 26:29
I will surely do thee g. 32:12
I will give you the g. of the. 45:18
for the g. of the land of Egypt. 20
God meant it unto g. to bring. 50:20
Lord hath spoken g. Num 10:29
after he hath done you g. Josh 24:20
behold, if there be g. 1 Sam 20:12
for thou hast rewarded me g. 24:17
Lord rewarded thee g. 19
according to all the g. he. 25:30
it had been g. for me. 2 Sam 14:32
Lord will requite g. for his. 16:12
prophets declare g. to the king.
1 Ki 22:13; 2 Chr 18:12
of mine own proper g. 1 Chr 29:3*
because he had done g. 2 Chr 24:16
be strong, and eat the g. Ezra 9:12
who had spoken g. for. Esth 7:9
shall we receive g. at? Job 2:10
know thou it for thy g. 5:27
mine eye shall no more see g. 7:7
flee away, they see no g. 9:25
wherewith he can do no g. 15:3
lo, their g. is not in their. 21:16*
be at peace: thereby g. shall. 22:21
he doeth not g. to the widow. 24:21
who will shew us any g.? Ps 4:6
none doeth g., no, not one. 14:1, 3
53:1, 3; Rom 3:12
days, that he may see g. Ps 34:12
held my peace even from g. 39:2
hand, they are filled with g. 104:28
that I may see the g. of. 106:5*
of Lord I will seek thy g. 122:9
shall see the g. of Jerusalem. 128:5
withhold not g. from them. Pr 3:27
the merciful man doth g. to. 11:17
he that diligently seeketh g. 27
a man satisfied with g. by. 12:14
a man shall eat g. by fruit. 13:2
but to the righteous g. shall be. 21
truth be to them that devise g. 14:22
matter wisely, shall find g. 16:20
a froward heart findeth no g.
Pr 17:20
a merry heart doeth g. like a. 17:22
understanding shall find g. 19:8
soul enjoy g. Eccl 2:24; 3:13; 5:18
I know that there is no g. in. 3:12*
and bereave my soul of g.? 4:8
and what g. is there to the? 5:11*
his soul be not filled with g. 6:3
yet hath he seen no g. all go. 6
not a man just, that doeth g. 7:20
one sinner destroyeth much g. 9:18
ye shall eat the g. of. Isa 1:19
bringeth good tidings of g. 52:7
we looked for peace, no g. came.
Jer 8:15; 14:19
shall not see when g. cometh. 17:6
evil, I will repent of the g. 18:10
I stood before thee to speak g. 20
shall he behold the g. I will. 29:32
I will bring all the g. I have. 32:42
which shall hear all the g. that. 33:9
them away as I saw g. Ezek 16:50
I said, if ye think g. Zech 11:12
been g. for that man. Mat 26:24
that have done g. to the. John 5:29
who went about doing g. Acts 10:38
in that he did g. and gave us. 14:17
every man that worketh g. Rom 2:10
thought it g. to be left. 1 Thes 3:1
hath this world's g. and. 1 John 3:17

for **good**

fear the Lord for our g. Deut 6:24
thee this day for thy g. 10:13
again rejoice over thee for g. 30:9
God on all of them for g. Ezra 8:22
think upon me, O my God, for g.
Neh 5:19; 13:31
and know thou it for thy g. Job 5:27
shew me a token for g. Ps 86:17
surety for thy servant for g. 119:122
this people for their g. Jer 14:11
out of this place for their g. 24:5
set mine eyes on them for g. 6
me for ever, for the g. of. 32:39
waited carefully for g. Mi 1:12
things work together for g. Rom 8:28
minister of God to thee for g. 13:4
please his neighbour for g. 15:2
see **bad, evil**

good, *adjective*

Hagar sat her down a g. Gen 21:16
I pray thee, send me g. 24:12
Rebekah said, what g. shall? 27:46
g. ears. 41:5
g. kine. 26
g. years. 35
our father is in g. health. 43:28
on his father's neck a g. 46:29
for g.-will of him that. Deut 33:16
sons, it is no g. report. 1 Sam 2:24
I will teach you the g. and. 12:23
men were very g. to us, we. 25:15
I know that thou art g. in my. 29:9
see thy matters are g. 2 Sam 15:3
what the king thought g. 19:18
teach them the g. way. 1 Ki 8:36
not failed one word of all his g. 56
speak g. words. 12:7; 2 Chr 10:7
g. is the word of the Lord.
2 Ki 20:19*; Isa 39:8
Lord be with the g. 2 Chr 19:11
saying, the g. Lord pardon. 30:18
the g. hand of his God on him.
Ezra 7:9; Neh 2:8
the g. hand of our God. Ezra 8:18
them true laws, g. Neh 9:13
gavest thy g. Spirit to instruct. 20
is it g. that thou shouldest? Job 10:3
is it g. that he should search? 13:9
their young ones are in g. 39:4
g. and upright is the Lord. Ps 25:8
steps of a g. man are ordered. 37:23
heart is inditing a g. matter. 45:1
Lord, art g., ready. 86:5; 119:68
a g. man sheweth favour. 112:5*
thy judgements are g. 119:39
teach me g. judgement and. 66
understand every g. path. Pr 2:9
mayest walk in the way of g. men. 20
g. word maketh the heart. 12:25
evil bow before the g. and. 14:19
in due season, how g. is it! 15:23
g. report maketh bones fat. Pr 15:30
with g. advice make war. 20:18*
a g. name rather to be chosen. 22:1
they have a g. reward. Eccl 4:9
what g. is there to the owners? 5:11
there is one event to the g. and. 9:2
they both shall be alike g. 11:6
where is the g. way. Jer 6:16
g. figs. 24:2
the good figs, very g. 3
like g. figs, so will I. 5
I will perform my g. word. 29:10
planted in a g. soil. Ezek 17:8
gather every g. piece, thigh. 24:4
I thought it g. to shew. Dan 4:2
the angel with g. words. Zech 1:13
receiveth it with g.-will. Mal 2:13
know how to give g. gifts.
Mat 7:11; Luke 11:13
g. tree bringeth forth g. Mat 7:17, 18
daughter, be of g. 9:22; Luke 8:48
fell in g. ground. Mat 13:8, 23
Mark 4:8, 20; Luke 8:8, 15
g. seed. Mat 13:24
g. Master, what g. thing. 19:16
why callest thou me g.? none g. 17
eye evil because I am g.? 20:15
well done, thou g. and. 25:21
peace on earth, g.-will. Luke 2:14*
g. measure, pressed down. 6:38
Mary hath chosen that g. 10:42
it is your Father's g. pleasure. 12:32
hast kept the g. wine. John 2:10
I am the g. Shepherd, the g. 10:11
ye know how that a g. Acts 15:7
is holy, and just, and g. Rom 7:12
what is that g. and perfect. 12:2
corrupt g. manners. 1 Cor 15:33
g. remembrance of us. 1 Thes 3:6*
of those that are g. 2 Tim 3:3
must be a lover of g. men. Tit 1:8
that have tasted the g. Heb 6:5
every g. gift. Jas 1:17
sit in a g. place. 2:3
subject not only to g. 1 Pet 2:18
will love life, and see g. days. 3:10
see **bad, cheer, conscience, courage, day, do, old** age

as **good**

of one, and him as g. Heb 11:12

good *heed*

take ye g. heed. Deut 2:4; 4:15
Josh 23:11
preacher gave g. heed. Eccl 12:9

is **good**

gold of that land is g. Gen 2:12
thou hast spoken is g. Deut 1:14
do that which is g. in sight. 6:18
me in the host is g. 1 Sam 29:6
said, the saying is g. 1 Ki 2:38
word that I have heard is g. 42
and speak that which is g. 22:13
I have done that which is g.
2 Ki 20:3; Isa 38:3
Lord is g. 1 Chr 16:34; 2 Chr 5:13
7:3; Ezra 3:11; Ps 100:5; 106:1
107:1; 118:1, 29; 135:3; 136:1
145:9; Jer 33:11; Lam 3:25
Nah 1:7
which is g. in his sight. 1 Chr 19:13
ourselves what is g. Job 34:4
see that the Lord is g. Ps 34:8
thy lovingkindness is g. 69:16
truly God is g. to Israel, to. 73:1
Lord shall give that which is g. 85:12
because thy mercy is g. 109:21
thy Spirit is g.; lead me into. 143:10
the righteous is only g. Pr 11:23
so is g. news from a far. 25:25
her merchandise is g. 31:18*
man that is g. in his sight, may give
to him that is g. Eccl 2:26*
who knoweth what is g. for? 6:12
wisdom is g. with an. 7:11
as is the g. so is the sinner. 9:2
eat ye that which is g. Isa 55:2
this girdle which is g. Jer 13:10
shadow thereof is g. Hos 4:13
thee, O man, what is g. Mi 6:8
one that doeth evil is g. Mal 2:17
salt is g. but if the salt. Mark 9:50
Luke 14:34

forth that which is g. Luke 6:45
none is g. save one, that. 18:19
then that which is g. Rom 7:13
but how to perform that is g. I. 18
cleave to that which is g. 12:9
you wise to that which is g. 16:19
that this is g. for the. 1 Cor 7:26
but that is g. Eph 4:29
follow that which is g. 1 Thes 5:15
3 John 11
hold fast that which is g. 1 Thes 5:21
know that the law is g. 1 Tim 1:8
is g. and acceptable in sight. 2:3
for every creature of God is g. 4:4
for that is g. and acceptable. 5:4
be followers of that which is g.
1 Pet 3:13

it is good

wait on thy name, for it is g.
Ps 52:9; 54:6
it is g. for me to draw near. 73:28
it is a g. thing to give thanks. 92:1
it is g. for me that I have. 119:71
it is g. to sing praises unto. 147:1
thou honey, because it is g. Pr 24:13
it is g. and comely for. Eccl 5:18
it is g. that thou shouldest. 7:18
it is g. that a man should. Lam 3:26
it is g. that a man bear the yoke. 27
it is g. for nothing but. Mat 5:13
it is g. for us to be here. 17:4
Mark 9:5; Luke 9:33
unto the law that it is g. Rom 7:16
it is g. neither to eat. 14:21
it is g. for a man not to touch a.
1 Cor 7:1, 8
I say, it is g. for a man so to be. 26
it is g. to be zealously. Gal 4:18

good land

come to bring them to g. land.
Ex 3:8; Deut 8:7
we searched is a g. land. Num 14:7
is a g. land which Lord. Deut 1:25
generation see that g. land. 35
over, and see the g. land. 3:25
not go unto that g. land. 4:21
over and possess that g. land. 22
go in and possess the g. land. 6:18
God bringeth thee into a g. land. 8:7
Lord thy God for the g. land. 10
giveth not this g. land for thy. 9:6
lest ye perish from off g. land. 11:17
until ye perish from this g. land.
Josh 23:13, 15
perish from off the g. land. 16
land, and it is very g. Judg 18:9
Israel out of this g. land. 1 Ki 14:15
g. piece of land. 2 Ki 3:19, 25
possess this g. land. 1 Chr 28:8

good with make

the owner of pit shall make it g.
Ex 21:34; 22:14*
shall not make it g. 22:11*, 13, 15
shall make it g.; beast for. Lev 24:18
shall he not make it g.? Num 23:19
make your ways and your doings g.
Jer 18:11*

good man

Ahimaaz is a g. man. 2 Sam 18:27
steps of a g. man are. Ps 37:23
a g. man sheweth favour. 112:5
the g. man is not at home. Pr 7:19
g. man obtaineth favour of. 12:2
a g. man satisfied. 12:14; 14:14
a g. man leaveth an. 13:22
the g. man is perished. Mi 7:2*
g. man out of good treasure.
Mat 12:35; Luke 6:45
against the g. man. Mat 20:11*
if the g. man of the house had known.
24:43*; Luke 12:39*
Joseph was a g. man. Luke 23:50
some said, he is a g. man. John 7:12
Barnabas was a g. man. Acts 11:24
for a g. man some would. Rom 5:7

not good

it is not g. that man. Gen 2:18
the counsel is not g. 2 Sam 17:7
in a way that is not g. Ps 36:4
into way that is not g. Pr 16:29
punish the just is not g. 17:26
is not g. to accept the person. 18:5
without knowledge is not g. 19:2
and a false balance is not g. Pr 20:23
not g. to have respect. 24:23; 28:21
it is not g. to eat much honey. 25:27
in a way that is not g. Isa 65:2
did that which is not g. Ezek 18:18
statutes that were not g. 20:25
doings that were not g. 36:31
case be so, it is not g. Mat 19:10*
Paul thought not g. to. Acts 15:38
your glorying is not g. 1 Cor 5:6

seem, seemed, seemeth good

as it seemeth g. to thee. Josh 9:25
Judg 10:15; 1 Sam 14:36, 40
Ezra 7:18; Esth 3:11; Jer 26:14
40:4
do to them what seemeth g. unto.
Judg 19:24
do what seemeth g. 1 Sam 1:23
3:18; 11:10; 24:4
Abner spake all seemed g. to.
2 Sam 3:19
the Lord do that seemeth him g.
10:12; 15:26
Chimham what seem g. 19:37, 38
and offer up what seemeth g. 24:22
if it seem g. to thee. 1 Ki 31:2
Jer 40:4
if it seem g. to you, let. 1 Chr 13:2
if it seem g. to the king. Ezra 5:17
Esth 5:4
as seemed g. to potter. Jer 18:4
so it seemed g. in sight.
Mat 11:26*; Luke 10:21*
it seemed g. to me. Luke 1:3
it seemed g. unto us. Acts 15:25
it seemed g. to the Holy Ghost. 28

good with thing

the thing that thou doest is not g.
Ex 18:17
rejoice in every g. thing. Deut 26:11
aught of any g. thing. Josh 21:45
the thing is not g. 1 Sam 26:16
is found some g. thing. 1 Ki 14:13
Hazael took of every g. thing of.
2 Ki 8:9
Lord not want any g. thing. Ps 34:10
I follow the thing that g. is. 38:20
no g. thing will he withhold. 84:11
it is a g. thing to give thanks. 92:1
a wife, findeth a g. thing. Pr 18:22
I will perform g. thing. Jer 33:14
cast off the thing that is g. Hos 8:3
what g. thing shall I do? Mat 19:16
can any g. thing come? John 1:46
flesh, dwelleth no g. thing. Rom 7:18
affected in a g. thing. Gal 4:18
his hands thing which is g. Eph 4:28
knowing that what g. thing any. 6:8
that g. thing committed. 2 Tim 1:14
acknowledging every g. thing in you.
Philem 6
it is a g. thing the heart. Heb 13:9

good things

houses full of all g. things. Deut 6:11
failed of all the g. things. Josh 23:14
that as all g. things are come. 15
there were g. things. 2 Chr 12:12
there are g. things found. 19:3
houses with g. things. Job 22:18
thy mouth with g. things. Ps 103:5
the upright shall have g. things.
Pr 28:10
have withholden g. things. Jer 5:25
give g. things to them? Mat 7:11
ye being evil speak g. things? 12:34
good man bringeth forth g. things. 35
the hungry with g. things. Luke 1:53
time receivedst thy g. things. 16:25
glad tidings of g. things. Rom 10:15
unto him in all g. things. Gal 6:6
be teachers of g. things. Tit 2:3
these things are g. and. 3:8
high priest of g. things. Heb 9:11
a shadow of g. things to come. 10:1

good tidings

have brought g. tidings. 2 Sam 4:10
and cometh with g. tidings. 18:27
and bringest g. tidings. 1 Ki 1:42
is a day of g. tidings. 2 Ki 7:9
that bringest g. tidings. Isa 40:9
one that bringeth g. tidings. 41:27
him that bringeth g. tidings. 52:7
me to preach g. tidings. Isa 61:1
who bringeth g. tidings. Nah 1:15
I bring you g. tidings of. Luke 2:10
brought us g. tidings of. 1 Thes 3:6

was good

God saw that it was g. Gen 1:4, 10
12, 18, 21, 25
thing, behold it was very g. 31
woman saw that the tree was g. 3:6
saw the interpretation was g. 40:16
thing was g. in eyes of. 41:37
Issachar saw that rest was g. 49:15
spared all that was g. 1 Sam 15:9
did that which was g. 2 Chr 14:2
wrought that which was g. 31:20
hand of God which was g. Neh 2:18
see what was that g. for. Eccl 2:3

good understanding

woman of g. unders. 1 Sam 25:3
g. unders. have all that. Ps 111:10
find favour and g. unders. Pr 3:4
g. unders. giveth favour. 13:15

good work

hands for this g. work. Neh 2:18
she hath wrought a g. work.
Mat 26:10; Mark 14:6
for a g. work we stone. John 10:33
abound to every g. work. 2 Cor 9:8
hath begun a g. work. Phil 1:6
fruitful in every g. work. Col. 1:10
every g. word and work. 2 Thes 2:17
bishop, desireth a g. work. 1 Tim 3:1
followed every g. work. 5:10
unto every g. work. 2 Tim 2:21
every g. work reprobate. Tit 1:16
to be ready to every g. work. 3:1
perfect in every g. work. Heb 13:21

good works

his works to thee have been very g.
1 Sam 19:4
may see your g. works. Mat 5:16
many g. works have I. John 10:32
Dorcas full of g. works. Acts 9:36
not a terror to g. works. Rom 13:3
Christ Jesus unto g. works. Eph 2:10
adorned with g. works. 1 Tim 2:10
well reported of for g. works. 5:10
the g. works of some are. 25
that they be rich in g. works. 6:18
furnished to all g. works. 2 Tim 3:17
a pattern of g. works. Tit 2:7
people, zealous of g. works. 14
to maintain g. works. 3:8, 14
unto love and g. works. Heb 10:24
may by your g. works. 1 Pet 2:12

goodlier

not in Israel a g. person. 1 Sam 9:2

goodliest

he will take your g. 1 Sam 8:16
thy children, even the g. 1 Ki 20:3

goodliness

the g. thereof as flower of. Isa 40:6

goodly

Rebekah took g. raiment. Gen 27:15
Joseph was a g. person and. 39:6*
hind let loose, giveth g. words. 49:21
when she saw he was a g. Ex 2:2
they made g. bonnets of. 39:28
day of boughs, the g. Lev 23:40
how g. are thy tents. Num 24:5
they burnt all their g. castles. 31:10*
me see that g. mount. Deut 3:25
great and g. cities which thou. 6:10
lest when thou hast built g. 8:12
I saw a g. Babylonish. Josh 7:21
young man, and a g. 1 Sam 9:2
David was ruddy and g. to. 16:12
Egyptian, a g. man. 2 Sam 23:21
also was a very g. man. 1 Ki 1:6
Babylon the g. vessels. 2 Chr 36:10
and destroyed the g. vessels. 19
gavest thou g. wings? Job 39:13
yea, I have a g. heritage. Ps 16:6
boughs were like the g. 80:10*
how shall I give thee a g.? Jer 3:19
olive tree, fair, and of g. fruit. 11:16
that it might be a g. Ezek 17:8
shall bear fruit, and be a g. 23
have made g. images. Hos 10:1
temples my g. things. Joel 3:5
as his g. horse in battle. Zech 10:3
g. price that I was prized. 11:13

man seeking *g.* pearls. *Mat* 13:45
adorned with *g.* stones. *Luke* 21:5
if there come a man in *g.* *Jas* 2:2*
all things dainty and *g.* *Rev* 18:14*

goodness

Jethro rejoiced for all *g.* *Ex* 18:9
I will make all my *g.* pass. 33:19
the Lord God abundant in *g.* 34:6
what *g.* the Lord shall. *Num* 10:32
thou promisedst this *g.* *2 Sam* 7:28
1 Chr 17:26
joyful for all the *g.* that the Lord had done. *1 Ki* 8:66; *2 Chr* 7:10
thy saints rejoice in *g.* *2 Chr* 6:41
Hezekiah his *g.* 32:32
Josiah and his *g.* 35:26
themselves in thy *g.* *Neh* 9:25
not served thee in thy great *g.* 35
my *g.* extendeth not to. *Ps* 16:2
him with blessings of *g.* 21:3
g. and mercy shall follow me. 23:6
remember thou me, for thy *g.* 25:7
I had believed to see the *g.* 27:13
O how great is thy *g.* thou. 31:19
the earth is full of the *g.* of. 33:5
the *g.* of God endureth. 52:1
shall be satisfied with the *g.* of. 65:4
crownest the year with thy *g.* 11
thou hast prepared of thy *g.* 68:10
praise the Lord for his *g.* 107:8, 15, 21, 31
and filleth the hungry soul with *g.* 9
my *g.* and my fortress, my. 144:2
utter the memory of thy *g.* 145:7
proclaim every one his *g.* *Pr* 20:6
g. toward house of Israel. *Isa* 63:7
I brought you to eat the *g.* *Jer* 2:7
shall flow together to the *g.* 31:12
satisfied with my *g.* saith Lord. 14
and tremble for all the *g.* 33:9
fear the Lord and his *g.* *Hos* 3:5
your *g.* is as a morning cloud. 6:4
according to *g.* of his land. 10:1
for how great is his *g.* *Zech* 9:17
riches of his *g.* not knowing that the *g.* of God leadeth thee. *Rom* 2:4
g. and severity of God, toward thee *g.* if thou continue in his *g.* 11:22
that you are full of *g.* 15:14
the fruit of the Spirit is *g.* *Gal* 5:22
Eph 5:9
good pleasure of his *g.* *2 Thes* 1:11

goods

back all the *g.* and Lot. *Gen* 14:16
the persons, and take the *g.* 21
the *g.* of his master were in. 24:10
carried away all his *g.* 31:18*; 46:6
to his neighbour's *g.* *Ex* 22:8, 11
earth swallowed them and their *g* *Num* 16:32
spoil of Midian and their *g.* 31:9
be for Levites' cattle and *g.* 35:3*
thee plenteous in *g.* *Deut* 28:11
smite thy wives, thy *g.* *2 Chr* 21:14*
let men help him with *g.* *Ezra* 1:4
strengthened their hands with *g.* 6
that of king's *g.* expenses be. 6:8
or to confiscation of *g.* 7:26
houses full of all *g.* *Neh* 9:25*
shall restore their *g.* *Job* 20:10*
shall no man look for his *g.* 21*
his *g.* shall flow away in the day. 28
when *g.* increase, they. *Eccl* 5:11
gotten cattle and *g.* *Ezek* 38:12
to take away cattle and *g.*? 13
their *g.* shall become a. *Zeph* 1:13*
man's house, and spoil his *g.* *Mat* 12:29; *Mark* 3:27
ruler over all his *g.* *Mat* 24:47
delivered to them his *g.* 25:14
that taketh away thy *g.* *Luke* 6:30
keepeth his palace, his *g.* are. 11:21
all my fruits and my *g.* 12:18
thou hast much *g.* laid up for. 19
give me the portion of *g.* that. 15:12*
him that he had wasted his *g.* 16:1
the half of my *g.* I give to. 19:8
sold their *g.* and parted. *Acts* 2:45
though I bestow all my *g.* *1 Cor* 13:3
the spoiling of your *g.* *Heb* 10:34*
rich, and increased with *g.* *Rev* 3:17*

gopher *wood*

an ark of *g. wood.* *Gen* 6:14

gore, -d

an ox *g.* man or woman. *Ex* 21:28
whether he have *g.* a son or a. 31

gorgeous

arrayed Jesus in a *g.* *Luke* 23:11

gorgeously

clothed most *g.* *Ezek* 23:12
are *g.* apparelled in. *Luke* 7:25

Goshen

dwell in G. *Gen* 45:10; 46:34; 47:4, 6, 27
that day the land of G. *Ex* 8:22
only in the land of G. was. 9:26
smote the country of G. *Josh* 10:41
Joshua took all the land of G. 11:16
inheritance of Judah, G. 15:51

gospel

The English word gospel comes from the Anglo-Saxon gōdspel *which meant good tidings, through* gōdspel, *or god-story. The word in the original (Greek) in the New Testament is* euaggelion, *from which, through the Latin* evangelium, *comes our word* evangel, *with its derivatives. In the New Testament it is the Christ-message, not the books which were written to spread that message. Later it was applied to the four books which tell of the earthly life of Jesus—Matthew, Mark, Luke, and John.*

of the *g.* of Jesus Christ. *Mark* 1:1
came, saying, repent and believe *g.* 15
lose his life for my sake and *g.*'s. 8:35
his house for my sake and *g.*'s. 10:29
the *g.* must be published. 13:10
by my mouth hear *g.* *Acts* 15:7
testify the *g.* of grace of God. 20:24
apostle, separated to *g.* *Rom* 1:1
whom I serve with my spirit in *g.* 9
for I am not ashamed of *g.* of. 16
secrets of men according to my *g.* 2:16
have not all obeyed the *g.* 10:16
as concerning the *g.* they. 11:28
ministering the *g.* of God. 15:16
fulness of the blessing of the *g.* 29
stablish you according to *g.* 16:25
begotten you through *g.* *1 Cor* 4:15
lest we should hinder the *g.* 9:12
a dispensation of the *g.* 17*
g. I may make the *g.* of Christ without charge . . . my power in *g.* 18
this I do for the *g.*'s sake. 23
if our *g.* be hid, it is hid. *2 Cor* 4:3
lest light of glorious *g.* of Christ. 4
brother, whose praise is in *g.* 8:18
your professed subjection to *g.* 9:13
another Spirit or *g.* 11:4; *Gal* 1:6
and would pervert the *g.* *Gal* 1:7
I communicated to them the *g.* 2:2
that the truth of the *g.* might. 5
they saw the *g.* of uncircumcision. 7
according to the truth of the *g.* 14
of truth the *g.* of your. *Eph* 1:13
his promise in Christ by the *g.* 3:6
preparation of the *g.* of peace. 6:15
known the mystery of the *g.* 19
fellowship in the *g.* till now. *Phil* 1:5
and confirmation of the *g.* 7, 17
to the furtherance of the *g.* 12
becometh the *g.* striving together for the faith of the *g.* 27
served with me in the *g.* 2:22
laboured with me in the *g.* 4:3
that in the beginning of the *g.* 15
in word of truth of the *g.* *Col* 1:5
away from the hope of the *g.* 23
g. came not in word but. *1 Thes* 1:5
we were bold to speak the *g.* 2:2
allowed to be put in trust with *g.* 4
to have imparted not the *g.* only. 8
our fellow-labourer in the *g.* 3:2
on them that obey not the *g.* *2 Thes* 1:8; *1 Pet* 4:17
he called you by our *g.* *2 Thes* 2:14
g. of the blessed God. *1 Tim* 1:11
of the afflictions of the *g.* *2 Tim* 1:8
immortality to light through *g.* 10
raised according to my *g.* 2:8
to me in bonds of the *g.* *Philem* 13

gospel joined with *preach, preached, preaching*

Jesus went *preaching g.* *Mat* 4:23; 9:35; *Mark* 1:14
the poor have the *g. preached.* *Mat* 11:5*; *Luke* 7:22
this *g.* shall be *preached.* *Mat* 24:14; 26:13; *Mark* 14:9
go, *preach* the *g.* to. *Mark* 16:15
me to *preach* the *g.* *Luke* 4:18*
they departed, *preaching* the *g.* 9:6
taught, and *preached the g.* 20:1
and *preached* the *g.* to. *Acts* 8:25
and there they *preached* the *g.* 14:7
when they had *preached* the *g.* 21
called us to *preach* the *g.* 16:10
preach the *g.* at Rome. *Rom* 1:15
feet of them that *preach g.* 10:15
I have fully *preached* the *g.* 15:19
I strived to *preach* the *g.* not. 20
baptize, but to *preach g.* *1 Cor* 1:17
that *preach* the *g.* should live. 9:14
I *preach* the *g.* have nothing to glory, woe to me if I *preach* not *g.* 16
that when I *preach* the *g.* I may. 18
the *g.* which I *preached.* 15:1
Troas to *preach* the *g.* *2 Cor* 2:12
as to you in *preaching* the *g.* 10:14
preached to you freely the *g.* 11:7
angel *preach* any other *g.* *Gal* 1:8, 9
the *g. preached* of me is not. 11
preached before the *g.* to. 3:8
of flesh I *preached* the *g.* 4:13
preached to you the *g.* *1 Thes* 2:9
to us was the *g. preached.* *Heb* 4:2*
that *preached* the *g.* to. *1 Pet* 1:12
which by *g.* is *preached* to you. 25
this cause was the *g. preached.* 4:6
g. to *preach* to them. *Rev* 14:6†

got

her and *g.* him out. *Gen* 39:12, 15
they *g.* not the land by. *Ps* 44:3
I *g.* me servants and. *Eccl* 2:7
I *g.* a girdle according. *Jer* 13:2*
take the girdle that thou hast *g.* 4*

gotten

she said, I have *g.* a. *Gen* 4:1
was our father's hath he *g.* all. 31:1
when I have *g.* me honour. *Ex* 14:18
he hath deceitfully *g.* *Lev* 6:4
what every man hath *g.* *Num* 31:50
of my hand hath *g.* this. *Deut* 8:17
moreover if he be *g.* *2 Sam* 17:13
wisdom cannot be *g.* *Job* 28:15
because my hand had *g.* 31:25
his holy arm hath *g.* *Ps* 98:1
wealth *g.* by vanity shall. *Pr* 13:11
an inheritance may be *g.* 20:21
have *g.* more wisdom. *Eccl* 1:16
the abundance *g.* they. *Isa* 15:7
because riches he hath *g.* *Jer* 48:36
thou hast *g.* riches. *Ezek* 28:4
thou hast *g.* thee renown. *Dan* 9:15
I saw them that had *g.* *Rev* 15:2*

gourd

[1] *Hebrew* Kikayon, *used only in* Jonah 4:6. *It may mean the castor-oil plant, or a genuine gourd.* [2] *Wild gourd of* 2 Ki 4:39 *was a poisonous gourd, supposed to be the* colocynth, *which might be mistaken for the wholesome globe cucumber.*

a *g.* Jonah glad of the *g.* *Jonah* 4:6
a worm smote the *g.* that it. 7
thou hast had pity on the *g.* for. 10

wild **gourds**

one gathered *wild g.* his. *2 Ki* 4:39

govern

dost thou now *g.* the. *1 Ki* 21:7
he that hateth right *g.*? *Job* 34:17
for thou shalt *g.* the nations. *Ps* 67:4

government, -s

and the *g.* shall be upon. *Isa* 9:6
of the increase of his *g.* there. 7
I will commit thy *g.* into his. 22:21
helps, *g.* diversities of. *1 Cor* 12:28
them that despise *g.* *2 Pet* 2:10*

governor

Joseph was *g.* *Gen* 42:6; 45:26*
Obadiah was *g.* over. *1 Ki* 18:3*
Solomon to be chief *g.* *1 Chr* 29:22*

the vessels to the g. Ezra 5:14
not eaten bread of the g. Neh 5:14
I required not bread of the g. 18
he is the g. among the. Ps 22:28*
their g. shall proceed. Jer 30:21*
back also to Gedaliah the g. 40:5
smote Gedaliah the g. 41:2, 18
stirred up Zerubbabel g. Hag 1:14
the g. and to Joshua. 2:2, 21
and he shall be as a g. Zech 9:7*
offer it now to thy g. Mal 1:8
of thee shall come a g. Mat 2:6
him to Pontius Pilate the g. 27:2
if this come to the g.'s ears. 28:14
and bear to the g. of. John 2:8*
informed the g. against. Acts 24:1
g. under Aretas king. 2 Cor 11:32
ships turned whither g. Jas 3:4*

governors

heart is towards the g. Judg 5:9
out of Machir came down g. 14
king's commissions to g. Ezra 8:36
letters be given me to g. Neh 2:7
the former g. were chargeable. 5:15
Daniel chief of the g. Dan 2:48
the g. of Judah shall. Zech 12:5*
I will make the g. of Judah. 6*
shall be brought before g. Mat 10:18
heir is under tutors and g. Gal 4:2*
submit yourselves to g. 1 Pet 2:14

Gozan

placed Israel by the river of G.
2 Ki 17:6; 18:11; 1 Chr 5:26
my fathers have destroyed, as G.
2 Ki 19:12; Isa 37:12

grace

[1] *The free mercy of God, or the enjoyment of his favour,* Rom 11:6; 2 Tim 1:9. [2] *A Christian virtue,* 2 Cor 8:7.

for a little space g. hath. Ezra 9:8
Esther obtained g. in. Esth 2:17*
g. is poured into lips. Ps 45:2
Lord is a sun, he will give g. 84:11
shall be an ornament of g. Pr 1:9
so shall they be life and g. to. 3:22
but he giveth g. to. 34; Jas 4:6
head an ornament of g. Pr 4:9
for the g. of his lips the king. 22:11
shoutings, crying, g. g. Zech 4:7
I will pour the Spirit of g. 12:10
of Father, full of g. and. John 1:14
we have all received, g. for g. 16
but g. and truth came by Jesus. 17
and great g. was on. Acts 4:33
testimony to word of his g. 14:3
had believed through g. 18:27
you to the word of his g. 20:32
whom we received g. and. Rom 1:5
g. and peace to you from God. 7
1 Cor 1:3; 2 Cor 1:2; Gal 1:3
Eph 1:2; Phil 1:2; Col 1:2
1 Thes 1:1; 2 Thes 1:2; Philem 3
justified freely by his g. Rom 3:24
reward is not reckoned of g. but. 4:4
faith, that it might be by g. 16
have access into this g. wherein. 5:2
who receive abundance of g. 17
where sin abounded g. did much. 20
even so might g. reign through. 21
shall we continue in sin, that g.? 6:1
not under law, but under g. 14
shall we sin, because under g.? 15
according to the election of g. 11:5
and if by g. then it is no more. 6
for I say, through the g. given. 12:3
gifts differing according to the g. 6
because of the g. given to. 15:15
I by g. be a partaker. 1 Cor 10:30
his g. bestowed upon me was. 15:10
abundant g. might redound to.
2 Cor 4:15
finish in you the same g. also. 8:6
see that ye abound in this g. 7
to travel with us with this g. 19
God is able to make all g. 9:8
said my g. is sufficient for thee. 12:9
him who called you to g. Gal 1:6
God, who called me by his g. 15
when James perceived the g. 2:9
the law, ye are fallen from g. 5:4
praise of the glory of his g. Eph 1:6
according to the riches of his g. 7
by g. ye are saved. Eph 2:5, 8
the exceeding riches of his g. 7
least of all saints is this g. 3:8
every one of us is given g. 4:7
that it may minister g. to the. 29
g. be with all that love our. 6:24
ye are all partakers of my g. Phil 1:7
singing with g. in your. Col 3:16
let speech be alway with g. 4:6
g. be with you. 18; 2 Tim 4:22
Tit 3:15; Heb 13:25
us good hope through g. 2 Thes 2:16
g. mercy, and peace from. 1 Tim 1:2
2 Tim 1:2; Tit 1:4; 2 John 3
g. of our Lord was. 1 Tim 1:14
g. be with thee. Amen. 6:21
us according to his g. 2 Tim 1:9
be strong in the g. that is in. 2:1
being justified by his g. Tit 3:7
boldly to the throne of g. Heb 4:16
done despite to the Spirit of g. 10:29
let us have g. to serve God. 12:28
heart be established with g. 13:9
the g. of the fashion of. Jas 1:11
he giveth more g. giveth g. to. 4:6
g. and peace. 1 Pet 1:2; 2 Pet 1:2
who prophesied of the g. 1 Pet 1:10
hope to the end for the g. 13
as being heirs of g. 3:7
God resisteth proud, giveth g. 5:5
the God of g. who hath called. 10
grow in g. and. 2 Pet 3:18
turning the g. of God into. Jude 4
g. and peace from him. Rev 1:4
see **find, found**

grace *of God*

and the g. of God was. Luke 2:40
he had seen g. of God. Acts 11:23
to continue in the g. of G. 13:43
recommended to g. of G. 14:26
15:40
gospel of the g. of God. 20:24
much more g. of God. Rom 5:15
the g. of God given you. 1 Cor 1:4
according to g. of God which. 3:10
g. of God I am what I am, yet not I, but the g. of God which. 15:10
by the g. of God we had. 2 Cor 1:12
ye receive not the g. of God in. 6:1
of the g. of God bestowed on. 8:1
for the exceeding g. of God in. 9:14
frustrate the g. of God. Gal 2:21
dispensation of g. of God. Eph 3:2
to gift of the g. of God given me. 7
day ye knew g. of God. Col 1:6
according to g. of God. 2 Thes 1:12
g. of God that bringeth. Tit 2:11
that he by g. of God. Heb 2:9
any man fail of g. of God. 12:15
of the manifold g. of God. 1 Pet 4:10
this is true g. of God. 5:12

grace *of our Lord Jesus*

through g. of Lord Jesus we shall.
Acts 15:11
the g. of our Lord Jesus. Rom 16:20
24; 1 Cor 16:23; Phil 4:23
1 Thes 5:28; 2 Thes 3:18
know g. of our Lord Jesus. 2 Cor 8:9
the g. of our Lord Jesus Christ, love of God, and communion. 13:14
g. of our Lord Jesus Christ be with your spirit. Gal 6:18; Philem 25
g. of Lord Jesus Christ be with you.
Rev 22:21

gracious

he said, God be g. to. Gen 43:29
I will hear, for I am g. Ex 22:27
be g. to whom I will be g. 33:19
the Lord, the Lord God, g. 34:6
2 Chr 30:9; Ps 103:8; 116:5
145:8; Joel 2:13
his face shine, and be g. Num 6:25
whether God will be g.? 2 Sam 12:22
the Lord was g. unto them. 13:23
to pardon, g. merciful. Neh 9:17, 31
then he is g. to him. Job 33:24
hath God forgotten to be g.? Ps 77:9
thou, O Lord, art a God g. 86:15
111:4; 112:4
a g. woman retaineth. Pr 11:16
wise man's mouth are g. Eccl 10:12
wait that he may be g. Isa 30:18
he will be very g. to thee. 19
be g. to us. Isa 33:2
how g. when pangs. Jer 22:23*
may be the Lord will be g. Amos 5:15
that thou art a g. God. Jonah 4:2
God that he will be g. to. Mal 1:9
wondered at g. words. Luke 4:22
tasted that the Lord is g. 1 Pet 2:3

graciously

children which G. hath g. Gen 33:5
because God hath dealt g. with. 11
and grant me thy law g. Ps 119:29
iniquity, and receive us g. Hos 14:2*

graft, -ed

olive tree wert g. in. Rom 11:17
broken that I might be g. in. 19
g. in, for God is able to g. them. 23
and g. much more these be g. 24

grain

yet shall not least g. fall. Amos 9:9*
is like a g. of mustard. Mat 13:31
Mark 4:31; Luke 13:19
faith as a g. of mustard seed, ye shall say unto this mountain.
Mat 17:20; Luke 17:6
bare g. wheat, or some other g.
1 Cor 15:37*

grandmother

dwelt first in thy g. Lois. 2 Tim 1:5

grant

according to the g. they. Ezra 3:7

grant

ye shall g. a redemption. Lev 25:24
Lord g. you that you. Ruth 1:9
God of Israel g. thee. 1 Sam 1:17
g. me place of this threshingfloor; thou shalt g. it me. 1 Chr 21:22*
but I will g. them some. 2 Chr 12:7
and g. him mercy in. Neh 1:11
it please the king to g. Esth 5:8
that God would g. the. Job 6:8
g. thee according to thine. Ps 20:4
us thy mercy, O Lord, g. us. 85:7
and g. me thy law graciously. 119:29
g. not, O Lord, the desires. 140:8
g. my two sons may sit. Mat 20:21*
Mark 10:37
g. to us, that we being. Luke 1:74
g. that with boldness we. Acts 4:29
God g. you be likeminded.
Rom 15:5
g. you to be strengthened. Eph 3:16
the Lord g. that he may. 2 Tim 1:18
will I g. to sit with me. Rev 3:21*

granted

God g. him that which. 1 Chr 4:10
knowledge is g. thee. 2 Chr 1:12
and the king g. him all. Ezra 7:6
g. according to good hand. Neh 2:8
what is thy petition? and it shall be g.
Esth 5:6; 7:2; 9:12
let it be g. to the Jews in. 9:13
thou hast g. me life and. Job 10:12
of righteous shall be g. Pr 10:24
a murderer to be g. you. Acts 3:14
God also to the Gentiles g. 11:18
who g. signs to be done by. 14:3
to her was g. she should. Rev 19:8*

grape

There was an abundance of vineyards in Palestine from the earliest times. The vines were celebrated both for luxuriant growth and for the immense clusters of grapes which they produced which were sometimes carried on a staff between two men as in the case of the spies, Num 13:23, 24, *and as has been done in some instances in modern times.*

From the abundance and excellence of the vines, it may readily be understood how frequently this plant is the subject of metaphor in the Holy Scriptures.

nor gather every g. of. Lev 19:10*
drink the blood of the g. Deut 32:14
shake off his unripe g. Job 15:33
vines with tender g. S of S 2:13*
us see whether the tender g. 7:12*
the sour g. is ripening in. Isa 18:5
have eaten a sour g. Jer 31:29

that eateth the sour *g*. *Jer* 31:30
I am as the *g*.-gleanings. *Mi* 7:1

grapegatherer

turn back thy hand as a *g*. *Jer* 6:9
g. come, would they ? 49:9; *Ob* 5

grapes

brought forth ripe *g*. *Gen* 40:10
his clothes in blood of *g*. 49:11
nor gather the *g*. of thy. *Lev* 25:5
in jubile, nor gather *g*. of thy. 11
shall he eat moist *g*. or. *Num* 6:3
the time of the firstripe *g*. 13:20
a branch with one cluster of *g*. 23
then thou mayest eat *g*. *Deut* 23:24
when thou gatherest the *g*. of. 24:21
vineyard, not gather the *g*. 28:30*, 39
their *g*. are *g*. of gall, their. 32:32
is not gleaning of the *g*.? *Judg* 8:2
they trode the *g*. and cursed. 9:27
bringing in wine and *g*. *Neh* 13:15
our vines have tender *g*. *S of S* 2:15*
breasts are like to clusters of *g*. 7:7
it should bring forth *g*. *Isa* 5:2
forth *g*. brought it forth wild *g*.? 4
yet gleaning *g*. shall be left. 17:6
as gleaning *g*. when vintage. 24:13
there shall be no *g*. on. *Jer* 8:13
as they that tread the *g*. 25:30
leave some gleaning *g*. 49:9; *Ob* 5
fathers have eaten sour *g*. *Ezek* 18:2
I found Israel like *g*. in the. *Hos* 9:10
treader of *g*. shall overtake the. *Amos* 9:13
men gather *g*. of thorns ? *Mat* 7:16
bush gather they *g*. *Luke* 6:44
thrust in sickle, her *g*. *Rev* 14:18

grass

let earth bring forth *g*. *Gen* 1:11
and the earth brought forth *g*. 12
as the ox licketh up *g*. *Num* 22:4
I will send *g*. in thy. *Deut* 11:15
not sown, not any *g*. 29:23
distil as showers upon the *g*. 32:2
as the *g*. springeth out. *2 Sam* 23:4
peradventure find *g*. to. *1 Ki* 18:5
the *g*. of the field, as green herb, as *g*. on. *2 Ki* 19:26; *Isa* 37:27
thine offspring is the *g*. of. *Job* 5:25
wild ass bray when he hath *g*.? 6:5
behold, behemoth eateth *g*. 40:15
be cut down like the *g*. *Ps* 37:2
down like rain upon mown *g*. 72:6
they of city shall flourish like *g*. 16
in the morning they are like *g*. 90:5
when wicked spring as the *g*. 92:7
smitten, and withered like *g*. 102:4
a shadow; I am withered like *g*. 11
as for man, his days are as *g*. 103:15
he causeth *g*. to grow for. 104:14
of an ox that eateth *g*. 106:20
let them be as the *g*. upon. 129:6
who maketh *g*. to grow upon. 147:8
is as dew upon the *g*. *Pr* 19:12
hay appeareth, the tender *g*. 27:25
g. faileth, there is no. *Isa* 15:6
of dragons, shall be *g*. 35:7
cry, all flesh is *g*. 40:6; *1 Pet* 1:24
g. withereth, surely the people is *g*. *Isa* 40:7, 8
spring up as among the *g*. 44:4
man which shall be made as *g*. 51:12
because there was no *g*. *Jer* 14:5, 6
grown fat as the heifer at *g*. 50:11
stump in tender *g*. *Dan* 4:15, 23
make thee eat *g*. 25, 32, 33; 5:21
made an end of eating *g*. *Amos* 7:2
as showers upon the *g*. *Mi* 5:7
shall give every one *g*. *Zech* 10:1
if God so clothe the *g*. *Mat* 6:30
Luke 12:28
the multitude to sit down on *g*. *Mat* 14:19; *Mark* 6:39
now there was much *g*. *John* 6:10
as the flower of the *g*. he. *Jas* 1:10
sun risen, but it withereth the *g*. 11
and all green *g*. was. *Rev* 8:7
they should not hurt the *g*. of. 9:4

grasshopper, -s

(*Grasshoppers or locusts are frequently mentioned in the Bible as very destructive agents. They came over the land in huge numbers, eating every green leaf, and very often leaving famine in their path*)

these ye may eat, the *g*. *Lev* 11:22
in our own sight as *g*. *Num* 13:33
as *g*. for multitude. *Judg* 6:5*; 7:12*
make him afraid as a *g*.? *Job* 39:20*
and the *g*. shall be a. *Eccl* 12:5
thereof are as *g*. *Isa* 40:22
they are more than *g*. *Jer* 46:23*
behold, he formed *g*. in. *Amos* 7:1*
captains are as great *g*. *Nah* 3:17

grave, *substantive*

(*The Revisions very frequently substitute for* grave *the Hebrew word* Sheol, *which means the place of the dead*)

pillar upon her *g*. that is the pillar of Rachel's *g*. unto this. *Gen* 35:20
I will go down to *g*. to my. 37:35
hairs with sorrow to *g*. 42:38; 44:31
bury me in the *g*. which I. 50:5
whosoever toucheth a *g*. *Num* 19:16
that touched one dead, or a *g*. 18
bringeth down to the *g*. *1 Sam* 2:6
wept at Abner's *g*. *2 Sam* 3:32
and be buried by the *g*. of. 19:37
his head go to the *g*. in. *1 Ki* 2:6
his head bring down to the *g*. 9
laid his carcase in his own *g*. 13:30
Jeroboam shall come to *g*. 14:13
thou shalt be gathered into thy *g*. *2 Ki* 22:20; *2 Chr* 34:28
when they can find the *g*. *Job* 3:22
thou shalt come to thy *g*. in. 5:26
so he that goeth to *g*. shall. 7:9
been carried from womb to *g*. 10:19
wouldest hide me in the *g*. 14:13
if I wait, the *g*. is my house. 17:13
they go down to the *g*. 21:13
yet shall he be brought to the *g*. 32
so doth the *g*. those that have. 24:19
stretch out his hand to the *g*. 30:24
soul draweth near to the *g*. 33:22*
in the *g*. who shall give? *Ps* 6:5
brought up my soul from the *g*. 30:3
the wicked be silent in the *g*. 31:17
laid in the *g*.: consume in the *g*. 49:14
my soul from the power of *g*. 15
life draweth nigh to the *g*. 88:3
like slain that lie in the *g*. 5
be declared in the *g*. 11
his soul from hand of *g*.? 89:48
scattered at the *g*.'s mouth. 141:7
them alive as the *g*. *Pr* 1:12
g. and barren womb, say not. 30:16
no wisdom in *g*. whither. *Eccl* 9:10
jealousy is cruel as the *g*. *S of S* 8:6
pomp is brought down to *g*. *Isa* 14:11
thou art cast out of thy *g*. like. 19
go to the gates of the *g*. 38:10
the *g*. cannot praise thee, death. 18
he made his *g*. with wicked. 53:9
might have been my *g*. *Jer* 20:17
he went down to the *g*. *Ezek* 31:15
company is round about her *g*. 32:23
from the power of *g*.; I will redeem from death: O *g*. I will. *Hos* 13:14
I will make thy *g*. for. *Nah* 1:14
he had lain in the *g*. *John* 11:17*
saying, she goeth to the *g*. to. 31*
again groaning, cometh to the *g*. 38*
called Lazarus out of his *g*. 12:17*
g. where is thy victory? *1 Cor* 15:55*

grave, *adjective*

deacons must be *g*. *1 Tim* 3:8
wives must be *g*. 11
aged men be sober, *g*. *Tit* 2:2

grave, *verb*

g. on the onyx stones. *Ex* 28:9
a plate of pure gold, and *g*. on it. 36
a man that can skill to *g*. *2 Chr* 2:7
sent a cunning man to *g*. any. 14

graveclothes

came forth bound with *g*. *John* 11:44

graved

on the borders he *g*. *1 Ki* 7:36
and he *g*. cherubims on. *2 Chr* 3:7

gravel

mouth be filled with *g*. *Pr* 20:17
of thy bowels like *g*. *Isa* 48:19*
broken my teeth with *g*. *Lam* 3:16

graven

was writing of God *g*. *Ex* 32:16
g. as signets are *g*. with the. 39:6
g. with an iron pen. *Job* 19:24
I have *g*. thee on palms of. *Isa* 49:16
g. upon the table of their. *Jer* 17:1
maker thereof hath *g*. it. *Hab* 2:18
Godhead is like gold *g*. *Acts* 17:29

graven *image*

make unto thee any *g*. *image*. *Ex* 20:4; *Lev* 26:1; *Deut* 5:8
corrupt and make a *g*. *image*. *Deut* 4:16, 25
that maketh any *g*. *image*. 27:15
son to make a *g*. *image*. *Judg* 17:3
founder, who made a *g*. *image*. 4
in these houses a *g*. *image*. 18:14
the *g*. *image*. 17
Dan set up the *g*. *image*. 30, 31
Manasseh set up *g*. *image*. *2 Ki* 21:7
melteth a *g*. *image*. *Isa* 40:19
workman to prepare a *g*. *image*. 20
they that make a *g*. *image* are. 44:9
who hath molten a *g*. *image*? 10
thereof he maketh his *g*. *image*. 17
the wood of their *g*. *image*. 45:20
my *g*. *image* hath commanded. 48:5
founder confounded by *g*. *image*. *Jer* 10:14; 51:17
cut off the *g*. and molten *image*. *Nah* 1:14
profiteth the *g*. *image*? *Hab* 2:18

graven *images*

burn their *g*. *images* with fire. *Deut* 7:5, 25
hew down the *g*. *images* of. 12:3
nations feared the Lord, and served their *g*. *images*. *2 Ki* 17:41
set up *g*. *images* before. *2 Chr* 33:19
he had beaten the *g*. *images*. 34:7
to jealousy with *g*. *images*. *Ps* 78:58
they that serve *g*. *images*. 97:7
whose *g*. *images* did excel. *Isa* 10:10
fallen, and all the *g*. *images*. 21:9
covering of thy *g*. *images*. 30:22
I give my praise to *g*. *images*. 42:8
ashamed that trust in *g*. *images*. 17
anger with their *g*. *images*. *Jer* 8:19
it is the land of *g*. *images*. 50:38
judgement on *g*. *images*. 51:47, 52
incense to *g*. *images*. *Hos* 11:2
g. *images* shall be beaten. *Mi* 1:7
thy *g*. *images* also will I cut. 5:13

graves

were no *g*. *in* Egypt. *Ex* 14:11
cast powder on the *g*. *2 Ki* 23:6
strowed it upon the *g*. *2 Chr* 34:4
days extinct, the *g*. are. *Job* 17:1
remain among the *g*. *Isa* 65:4
priests' bones out of their *g*. *Jer* 8:1
and cast his dead body into *g*. 26:23
his *g*. are about him. *Ezek* 32:22
23, 25, 26
I will open your *g*. and cause you to come up out of your *g*. 37:12
opened your *g*. brought out of *g*. 13
give Gog a place of *g*. in. 39:11*
the *g*. were opened. *Mat* 27:52*
bodies of saints came out of *g*. 53*
for ye are as *g*. which. *Luke* 11:44
all that are in the *g*. *John* 5:28*
bodies to be put in *g*. *Rev* 11:9*

graveth

that *g*. an habitation in. *Isa* 22:16

graving

golden calf with a *g*. tool. *Ex* 32:4
grave any manner of *g*. *2 Chr* 2:14
I will engrave *g*. thereof. *Zech* 3:9

gravings

on mouth of laver were *g*. *1 Ki* 7:31

gravity

subjection with all *g*. *1 Tim* 3:4
in doctrine shewing *g*. *Tit* 2:7

gray, *see* **hairs** *and* **head**

grayheaded

I am old and *g*. my. *1 Sam* 12:2
with us are the *g*. *Job* 15:10
when I am old and *g*. *Ps* 71:18

grease

heart is as fat as *g*. *Ps* 119:70

great

[1] *Large in size,* 2 Chr 2:5. [2] *Considerable in degree of qualities or feelings,* Gen 39:9; Ps 14:5. [3] *Eminent or important,* Gen 24:35; 2 Chr 17:12.

and make thy name *g.* *Gen* 12:2
my master is become *g.* 24:35
with *g.* wrestlings have I. 30:8
can I do this *g.* wickedness? 39:9
to save your lives by a *g.* 45:7
my son, he also shall be *g.* 48:19
unwalled towns a *g.* many. *Deut* 3:5
God is a *g.* God. 10:17; *2 Chr* 2:5
eyes have seen *g.* acts. *Deut* 11:7
neither let me see this *g.* fire. 18:16
meaneth the heat of his *g.*? 29:24
wilt thou do unto thy *g.*? *Josh* 7:9
thou heardest cities were *g.* 14:12
there a *g.* altar by Jordan. 22:10
for he did those *g.* signs in. 24:17
divisions of Reuben *g.* *Judg* 5:15
your wickedness is *g.* *1 Sam* 12:17
David went on, and grew *g.* and the Lord was with him. *2 Sam* 5:10
I have made thee a *g.* name. 7:9
thou art *g.* O Lord God, none is. 22
given *g.* occasion to enemies. 12:14
gentleness hath made me *g.* 22:36
Ps 18:35
shall hear of thy *g.* name. *1 Ki* 8:42
2 Chr 6:32
the journey is too *g.* for. *1 Ki* 19:7
Shunem, where a *g.* woman. *2 Ki* 4:8
g. is the wrath of the Lord. 22:13
g. is the Lord, and. *1 Chr* 16:25
Ps 48:1; 96:4; 135:5; 145:3
Lord's hand, for very *g.* *1 Chr* 21:13
thine hand it is to make *g.* 29:12
house I build is *g.* for *g.* *2 Chr* 2:5
I am to build shall be wonderful *g.* 9
Jehoshaphat waxed *g.* 17:12
our trespass is *g.* 28:13
g. wrath poured. 34:21
Lord who is *g.* and terrible. *Neh* 4:14
now therefore our God, the *g.* 9:32
his empire, for it is *g.* *Esth* 1:20
that thy seed shall be *g.* *Job* 5:25
is not thy wickedness *g.*? 22:5
by *g.* force of my disease. 30:18
yet he knoweth it not in *g.* 35:15
a *g.* ransom. 36:18
God is *g.*, and we know him not. 26
the number of thy days is *g.* 38:21
in him, because strength is *g.*? 39:11
were they in *g.* fear. *Ps* 14:5; 53:5
keeping of them there is *g.* 19:11
his glory is *g.* in thy salvation. 21:5
mine iniquity, for it is *g.* 25:11
O how *g.* is thy goodness! 31:19
art *g.* and doest wondrous. 86:10
how *g.* are thy works! 92:5
O God, how *g.* is the sum! 139:17
this wisdom seemed *g.* *Eccl* 9:13
houses even *g.* and fair. *Isa* 5:9
people that walked in darkness have seen *g.* light. 9:2; *Mat* 4:16
g. is the Holy One of. *Isa* 12:6
send them a Saviour and a *g.* 19:20*
divide him a portion with *g.* 53:12
and *g.* shall be the peace of. 54:13
are become *g.* and rich. *Jer* 5:27
art *g.* and thy name is *g.* in. 10:6
her womb to be always *g.* 20:17
the *G.*, the mighty God is his. 32:18
g. in counsel, and mighty in. 19
I have sworn by my *g.* name. 44:26
they are new, *g.* is thy. *Lam* 3:23
increased and waxed *g.* *Ezek* 16:7
a *g.* eagle with *g.* wings. 17:3, 7
even make the pile for fire *g.* 24:9
to serve a *g.* service against. 29:18
the waters made him *g.* 31:4*
I will sanctify my *g.* name. 36:23
how *g.* his signs, how. *Dan* 4:3
ram pushing, and he became *g.* 8:4*
for their wickedness is *g.* *Joel* 3:13
go to Hamath the *g.* *Amos* 6:2
shall he be *g.* unto the ends. *Mi* 5:4
g. his goodness, how *g.* *Zech* 9:17
my name shall be *g.* *Mal* 1:11
exceeding glad, for *g.* is your reward. *Mat* 5:12; *Luke* 6:23, 35
shall be called *g.* in the. *Mat* 5:19
if light be darkness, how *g.* is! 6:23
one pearl of *g.* price. 13:46
g. is thy faith. 15:28
g. possessions. 19:22; *Mark* 10:42
they that are *g.* exercise. *Mat* 20:25
be *g.* among you. 26; *Mark* 10:43
Master, which is the *g.*? *Mat* 22:36
is the first and *g.* commandment. 38
g. in sight of Lord. *Luke* 1:15, 32
you, the same shall be *g.* 9:48
the harvest truly is *g.* but. 10:2*
us and you there is a *g.* gulf. 16:26
out that he was some *g.* *Acts* 8:9
g. is Diana of the. 19:28, 34
g. is my boldness, *g.* is. *2 Cor* 7:4
that he hath a *g.* zeal for. *Col* 4:13
g. is mystery of. *1 Tim* 3:16
in *g.* house not only. *2 Tim* 2:20
appearing of the *g.* God. *Tit* 2:13
now consider how *g.* this. *Heb* 7:4
how *g.* a matter a little. *Jas* 3:5*
another sign in heaven, *g.* *Rev* 15:1
g. Babylon came in. 16:19
Babylon the *g.* mother. 17:5; 18:2
unto supper of the *g.* God. 19:17
see **city, company, congregation, cry, day, destruction**

great *evil*

hath done us *g. evil.* *1 Sam* 6:9
to do all this *g. evil.* *Neh* 13:27
vanity, and a *g. evil.* *Eccl* 2:21
pronounced this *g. evil.* *Jer* 16:10
thus might we procure *g. evil.* 26:19
I have brought this *g. evil.* 32:42
why commit this *g. evil*? 44:7
bringing upon us a *g. evil.* *Dan* 9:12
see **exceeding, joy**

great *king* or *kings*

thus saith the *g. king.* *2 Ki* 18:19
28; *Isa* 36:4, 13
which a *g. king* of Israel. *Ezra* 5:11
the Lord is a *g. King.* *Ps* 47:2
Zion, the city of the *g. King.* 48:2
the Lord is a *g. King* above. 95:3
to him that smote *g. kings.* 136:17
there came a *g. king.* *Eccl* 9:14
g. kings shall serve. *Jer* 25:14; 27:7
for I am a *g. King,* saith. *Mal* 1:14
is city of the *g. King.* *Mat* 5:35

great *men*

like name of *g. men* in earth.
2 Sam 7:9; *1 Chr* 17:8
sons were with *g. men.* *2 Ki* 10:6
Jehu slew all Ahab's *g. men* and. 11
son of one of *g. men.* *Neh* 11:14*
g. men are not always wise. *Job* 32:9
him before *g. men.* *Pr* 18:16
stand not in place of *g. men.* 25:6
get me unto the *g. men.* *Jer* 5:5
all houses of the *g. men.* 52:13
is sword of the *g. men.* *Ezek* 21:14
all her *g. men* were bound. *Nah* 3:10
g. men hid themselves. *Rev* 6:15*
merchants were the *g. men.* 18:23*

great *multitude, multitudes*

Gad had a *g. multitude.* *Num* 32:1
hast thou seen all this *g. multitude*? *1 Ki* 20:13
I will deliver this *g. multitude.* 28
be ye a *g. multitude.* *2 Chr* 13:8
there cometh a *g. multitude.* 20:2
by reason of this *g. multitude.* 15
carried a *g. multitude* captives. 28:5
did I fear a *g. multitude*? *Job* 31:34
all that *g. multitude.* *Isa* 16:14
by, even a *g. multitude.* *Jer* 44:15
very *g. multitude* of fish. *Ezek* 47:9
set forth a *g. multitude.* *Dan* 11:11
g. multitudes followed him.
Mat 4:25; 8:1; 12:15*; 19:2
20:29; *Mark* 3:7; *John* 6:2
when Jesus saw *g. multitude.*
Mat 8:18; 14:14; *Mark* 9:14
g. multitudes came. *Mat* 15:30
bread as to fill so *g. multitude.* 33
a *g. multitude* spread their. 21:8
with Judas a *g. multitude* with.
26:47; *Mark* 14:43
inclosed a *g. multitude.* *Luke* 5:6
a *g. multitude* came together to. 15
in these lay a *g. multitude.* *John* 5:3
a *g. multitude* of Jews. *Acts* 14:1
Greeks a *g. multitude.* *Acts* 17:4
a *g. multitude* which no. *Rev* 7:9
the voice of a *g. multitude.* 19:6

great *nation* and *nations*

a *g. nation,* and will bless. *Gen* 12:2
18:18; 46:3; *Ex* 32:10
Ishmael a *g. nation.* 17:20; 21:18
surely this *g. nation* is. *Deut* 4:6
he became there a *nation g.* 26:5
before you *g. nations.* *Josh* 23:9
who smote *g. nations.* *Ps* 135:10*
a *g. nation* shall be raised. *Jer* 6:22
Babylon an assembly of *g. nations.*
50:9
from the north, a *g. nation.* 41
dwelt all *g. nations.* *Ezek* 31:6

great *people*

therein, a *people g.* *Deut* 2:10
Zamzummims, a *people g.* many. 21
a *people g.* and tall, children. 9:2
seeing I am a *g. people.* *Josh* 17:14
if thou be a *g. people.* 15
thou art a *g. people.* 17
g. people that cannot be. *1 Ki* 3:8
judge this *g. people*? 9; *2 Chr* 1:10
son over this *g. people.* *1 Ki* 5:7
mountains like as of *g. people.*
Isa 13:4
g. people hath not been. *Joel* 2:2

great *power*

out of Egypt with *g. power.* *Ex* 32:11
2 Ki 17:36; *Neh* 1:10
power of my lord be *g.* *Num* 14:17
people and hast *g. power.* *Josh* 17:17
against me with *g. power*? *Job* 23:6
Lord, and of *g. power.* *Ps* 147:5
man and beast upon the ground, by my *g. power.* *Jer* 27:5; 32:17
wither even without *g. power.*
Ezek 17:9*
slow to anger, *g.* in *power.* *Nah* 1:3
clouds with *g. power.* *Mark* 13:26
g. power gave the. *Acts* 4:33
saying, this man is the *g. power.* 8:10
to thee thy *g. power.* *Rev* 11:17
from heaven, having *g. power.* 18:1

great *sea*

shall have the *g. sea.* *Num* 34:6
wilderness unto *g. sea.* *Josh* 1:4
kings in the coasts of *g. sea.* 9:1
border was to the *g. sea.* 15:12
inheritance of Judah, to *g. sea.* 47
I have cut off to the *g. sea.* 23:4
as fish of the *g. sea.* *Ezek* 47:10
land toward north from *g. sea.* 15
winds strove upon *g. sea.* *Dan* 7:2
see **sin**

great *slaughter*

with a *g. s.* at Gibeon. *Josh* 10:10
end of slaying them with *g. s.* 20
Ammonites with *g. s.* *Judg* 11:33
smote Philistines with *g. s.* 15:8
Israel with *g. s.* *1 Sam* 4:10, 17
smitten people with a *g. s.* 6:19
David slew Philistines with a *g. s.*
19:8; 23:5
a *g. s.* that day. *1 Sam* 18:7
slew Assyrians with *g. s.* *1 Ki* 20:21
slew Israel with a *g. s.* *2 Chr* 13:17
smote Ahaz with a *g. s.* 28:5
in day of *g. s.* when. *Isa* 30:25
Lord hath a *g. s.* in the land. 34:6

so **great**

hast brought *so g.* a sin. *Ex* 32:21
what nation *so g.* hath? *Deut* 4:7, 8
who is able to judge *so g.* a people?
1 Ki 3:9; *2 Chr* 1:10
who is *so g.* a God as? *Ps* 77:13
so g. in his mercy to them. 103:11
I have not found *so g.* faith, no, not in Israel. *Mat* 8:10; *Luke* 7:9
bread as to fill *so g.* *Mat* 15:33
delivered us from *so g.* *2 Cor* 1:10
we neglect *so g.* salvation? *Heb* 2:3
are compassed with *so g.* a. 12:1
ships though *so g.* yet. *Jas* 3:4
earthquake and *so g.* *Rev* 16:18
in one hour *so g.* riches come. 18:17

small and **great**

blindness *small and g.* *Gen* 19:11
hear *small* as well as *g.* *Deut* 1:17
divers weights, a *g. and small.* 25:13

measures, a g. and small. Deut 25:14
smote men small and g. 1 Sam 5:9
do nothing g. or small. 20:2
not any either g. or small. 30:2
lacking neither small nor g. 19
fight not with small nor g.
1 Ki 22:31; 2 Chr 18:30
small and g. went to house.
2 Ki 23:2; 2 Chr 34:30
people small and g. 2 Ki 25:26
lots, as well small as g. 1 Chr 26:13
he put to death, whether small or g.
2 Chr 15:13
by courses, g. and small. 31:15
hand vessels, g. and small. 36:18
feast unto g. and small. Esth 1:5
husbands honour g. and small. 20
small and g. are there. Job 3:19
the small rain, and to g. rain. 37:6*
creeping, small and g. Ps 104:25
fear the Lord, small and g. 115:13
possessions of g. and small. Eccl 2:7
g. and small shall die. Jer 16:6
ephah small, shekel g. Amos 8:5
witnessing to small and g. Acts 26:22
fear him, small and g. Rev 11:18
he caused small and g. to. 13:16
ye that fear him, small and g. 19:5
flesh of all men, small and g. 18
I saw dead, small and g. 20:12

great *stone* and *stones*

a g. stone was upon the. Gen 29:2
that set up g. stones. Deut 27:2
cast down g. stones. Josh 10:11
roll g. stones upon the mouth of. 18
Joshua took a g. stone, and. 24:26
there was a g. stone. 1 Sam 6:14
Levites put them on the g. stone. 15
to the g. stone of Abel, whereon. 18
transgressed, roll a g. stone. 14:33
were at g. stone in. 2 Sam 20:8
they brought g. stones to. 1 Ki 5:17
was of g. stones. 7:10; Ezra 5:8
to shoot g. stones. 2 Chr 26:15
three rows of g. stones. Ezra 6:4
take g. stones and hide. Jer 43:9
he rolled a g. stone to. Mat 27:60

great *thing* and *things*

thing as this g. thing is. Deut 4:32
God that hath done g. things. 10:21
and see this g. thing. 1 Sam 12:16
consider how g. things he hath. 24
shalt both do g. things and. 26:25*
hast done g. things. 2 Sam 7:21*
and to do for you g. things and. 23
bid thee do some g. thing. 2 Ki 5:13
tell me all the g. things Elisha. 8:4
he should do this g. thing? 13
known these g. things. 1 Chr 17:19
to God who doeth g. things.
Job 5:9; 9:10, 37:5
hast done g. things, who. Ps 71:19
God who had done g. things. 106:21
done g. things for them. 126:2, 3
g. and mighty things. Jer 33:3
and seekest thou g. things? 45:5
a mouth speaking g. things.
Dan 7:8, 20; Rev 13:5
I have written g. things. Hos 8:12*
he hath done g. things. Joel 2:20
the Lord will do g. things. 21
heard what g. things he. Mark 3:8
tell them how g. things the Lord
hath done. 5:19; Luke 8:39
hath done g. things. Luke 1:49
he published how g. things. 8:39
will shew how g. things. Acts 9:16*
a g. thing if we reap? 1 Cor 9:11
no g. thing if his ministers be.
2 Cor 11:15
member boasteth g. things. Jas 3:5

very **great**

till he became very g. Gen 26:13
man Moses was very g. Ex 11:3
people with a very g. plague.
Num 11:33
cities are walled and very g. 12:28
promote thee unto very g. 22:17
of young men was very g. 1 Sam 2:17
there was a very g. slaughter. 4:10
very g. trembling. 14:15
very g. discomfiture. 20
Nabal was a very g. man, he. 25:2
laid a very g. heap. 2 Sam 18:17
for Barzillai was a very g. 19:32
came with a very g. train. 1 Ki 10:2
very g. are his mercies. 1 Chr 21:13
very g. burning for Asa. 2 Chr 16:14
very g. host into their hand. 24:24
a very g. congregation. 30:13
Ezra 10:1
up wall a very g. height. 2 Chr 33:14
and there was a very g. Neh 8:17
Job a very g. household. Job 1:3
that his grief was very g. 2:13
God, thou art very g. Ps 104:1
there shall be a very g. multitude
of fish. Ezek 47:9
he goat waxed very g. Dan 8:8
up with a very g. army. 11:25
for his camp is very g. Joel 2:11
shall be a very g. valley. Zech 14:4
very g. multitude spread. Mat 21:8
multitude very g. having. Mark 8:1
rolled away, for it was very g. 16:4

was **great**

wickedness of man was g. Gen 6:5
their substance was g. so that. 13:6
to Gibeon, that was g. 1 Ki 3:4
there was g. indignation. 2 Ki 3:27
where decree came was g. Esth 4:3
Mordecai was g. in the. 9:4; 10:3
because my wealth was g. Job 31:25
I was g. and increased. Eccl 2:9
she that was g. among. Lam 1:1
tree's height was g. Dan 4:10
it fell, and g. was the fall of it.
Mat 7:27; Luke 6:49

great *waters*

in floods of g. waters. Ps 32:6
sea, thy path in g. waters. 77:19
do business in g. waters. 107:23
deliver me out of g. waters. 144:7
and by g. waters the seed. Isa 23:3
Ishmael by g. waters. Jer 41:12
do roar like g. waters. 51:55*
their wings like g. waters. Ezek 1:24
of the seed by g. waters, set. 17:5*
in a good soil by g. waters. 8*
when g. waters shall cover. 26:19
brought thee into g. waters. 27:26
his root was by g. waters. 31:7*
floods, the g. waters were stayed. 15
all beasts beside g. waters. 32:13
through heap of g. waters. Hab 3:15

great *while*

of thy servant's house for a g. while.
2 Sam 7:19; 1 Chr 17:17
rising up a g. while. Mark 1:35
g. while ago repented. Luke 10:13
barbarians looked a g. while.
Acts 28:6

great *work* and *works*

Israel saw that g. work. Ex 14:31
had seen all g. works. Judg 2:7
young, and work is g. 1 Chr 29:1
the work is g. and we. Neh 4:19
I am doing a g. work, I cannot. 6:3
the works of the Lord are g.
Ps 111:2; Rev 15:3
I made g. works, I builded. Eccl 2:4

greater

God made the g. light to. Gen 1:16
my punishment is g. than I can. 4:13
there is none g. in this house. 39:9
only in throne will I be g. than. 41:40
younger brother shall be g. 48:19
know the Lord is g. than. Ex 18:11
make of thee g. nation. Num 14:12
Deut 9:14
people is g. and taller. Deut 1:28
drive nations g. than thou. 4:38
7:1; 9:1; 11:23
because Gibeon was g. Josh 10:2
there been a much g. 1 Sam 14:30
the hatred was g. than. 2 Sam 13:15
this evil is g. than the other. 16*
make his throne g. 1 Ki 1:37, 47
David waxed g. and g. 1 Chr 11:9
the g. house he cieled. 2 Chr 3:5
Mordecai waxed g. and g. Esth 9:4
answer, that God is g. Job 33:12
is g. than the punishment. Lam 4:6
g. abominations. Ezek 8:6, 13, 15
set forth a multitude g. Dan 11:13
or their border g. than. Amos 6:2
glory of latter house g. Hag 2:9
hath not risen a g. than John the
Baptist. Mat 11:11; Luke 7:28
in this place is one g. Mat 12:6
g. than Jonas is. 41; Luke 11:32
behold a g. than Solomon is here.
Mat 12:42; Luke 11:31
receiving g. damnation. Mat 23:14
Mark 12:40; Luke 20:47
whether is g. the gold or? Mat 23:17
for whether is g. the gift or the? 19
sown, it becometh g. Mark 4:32
is no other commandment g. 12:31
my barns, and build g. Luke 12:18
whether is g. he that sitteth? 22:27
thou shalt see g. things.
John 1:50; 5:20; 14:12
art thou g. than our father? 4:12
I have a g. witness than that. 5:36
art thou g. than our father? 8:53
Father is g. than all. 10:29; 14:28
the servant is not g. 13:16; 15:20
g. love hath no man than this. 15:13
delivered me to thee hath g. 19:11
to lay upon you no g. Acts 15:28
g. is he that prophesieth. 1 Cor 14:5
of whom the g. part remain. 15:6
he could swear by no g. Heb 6:13
men verily swear by the g. 16
by a g. and more perfect. 9:11
reproach of Christ g. riches. 11:26
we shall receive g. Jas 3:1*
angels which are g. in. 2 Pet 2:11
God is g. than our. 1 John 3:20
g. is he that is in you, than he. 4:4
witness of God is g. this is the. 5:9
I have no g. joy than to. 3 John 4

greatest

was over 100, g. over. 1 Chr 12:14
hitherto the g. part had kept the. 29
this man was the g. of. Job 1:3
from least to g. given. Jer 6:13; 8:10
from least to the g. 31:34; Heb 8:11
people from least to the g. Jer 42:1
called people from least to g. 8
die, from the least to the g. 44:12
sackcloth, from the g. Jonah 3:5
when grown, it is the g. Mat 13:32
who is the g. in the kingdom? 18:1
as this little child, same is g. 4
but he that is g. shall be. 23:11
disputed who should be g.
Mark 9:34; Luke 9:46
strife who should be g. Luke 22:24
but he that is g. let him be as. 26
heed from least to the g. Acts 8:10
but the g. of these is. 1 Cor 13:13

greatly

I will g. multiply thy. Gen 3:16
Lot pressed upon them g. and. 19:3
hath blessed my master g. 24:35
then Jacob was g. afraid and. 32:7
whole mount quaked g. Ex 19:18
of Lord was kindled g. Num 11:10
and the people mourned g. 14:39
Lord shall g. bless thee. Deut 15:4*
nor shall he g. multiply silver. 17:17
they were g. distressed. Judg 2:15*
Israel was g. impoverished. 6:6*
anger was kindled g. 1 Sam 11:6
all men of Israel rejoiced g. 15
the people g. feared the Lord. 12:18
he loved him g. became his. 16:21
Philistine, they were g. 17:11
Philistines his heart trembled g. 28:5
David was g. distressed, for. 30:6
the men were g. ashamed.
2 Sam 10:5; 1 Chr 19:5
David's anger was g. kindled.
2 Sam 12:5
David said, I have sinned g. 24:10
1 Chr 21:8
kingdom was established g. 1 Ki 2:12
Solomon's words, he rejoiced g. 5:7
now Obadiah feared the Lord g. 18:3
fathers increased g. 1 Chr 4:38
great is the Lord, g. to be. 16:25*
Ps 48:1; 96:4; 145:3
their anger was g. 2 Chr 25:10
Manasseh humbled himself g. 33:12
latter end should g. Job 8:7
in thy salvation how g. Ps 21:1

my heart g. rejoiceth, I will. Ps 28:7
bowed down g. go mourning. 38:6
so shall the king g. desire. 45:11
earth belong to God, he is g. 47:9
my defence, I shall not be g. 62:2
thou g. enrichest it with river. 65:9
my lips shall g. rejoice when. 71:23
wroth, and g. abhorred. 78:59
his people g. 105:24; 107:38
I will g. praise the Lord. 109:30
blessed that delighteth g. in. 112:1
I was g. afflicted, I said in. 116:10
proud have had me g. in. 119:51
of righteous shall g. Pr 23:24
be g. ashamed that. Isa 42:17†
I will g. rejoice in the Lord. 61:10
shall not that land be g.? Jer 3:1
surely thou hast g. deceived. 4:10
we are g. confounded, have. 9:19
persecutors shall be g. 20:11·†
my sabbaths they g. Ezek 20:13
because that Edom hath g. 25:12
was king Belshazzar g. Dan 5:9
thou art g. beloved. 9:23; 10:11, 19
made thee small, thou art g. Ob 2
day of Lord hasteth g. Zeph 1:14
g. O daughter of Zion. Zech 9:9
governor marvelled g. Mat 27:14
Jairus besought him g. Mark 5:23
them that wept and wailed g. 38
beheld, they were amazed g. 9:15
the living, ye therefore do g. 12:27
rejoiceth g. because of. John 3:29
people ran to porch, g. Acts 3:11
disciples multiplied in Jerusalem g. 6:7
I g. desired Apollos. 1 Cor 16:12
how g. I long after you all. Phil 1:8
I rejoiced in the Lord g. that. 4:10
desiring g. to see us, as. 1 Thes 3:6
g. desiring to see thee. 2 Tim 1:4
for he hath g. withstood our. 4:15
ye g. rejoice though now. 1 Pet 1:6
I rejoiced g. that I found. 2 John 4
I rejoiced g. when the. 3 John 3
see **feared**

greatness
in g. of thy excellency. Ex. 15:7
by g. of thine arm they shall be. 16
pardon according to g. Num 14:19
to shew thy servant thy g. Deut 3:24
shewed us his glory and g. 5:24
hast redeemed through thy g. 9:26
who have not seen his g. 11:2
ascribe ye g. unto our God. 32:3
hast done all this g. 1 Chr 17:19
to make thee a name of g. and. 21
O Lord is the g., the power. 29:11
half of g. of thy wisdom. 2 Chr 9:6
and the g. of the burdens. 24:27
spare me according to g. Neh 13:22
the declaration of the g. Esth 10:2
by g. of thy power. Ps 66:3
thou shalt increase my g. 71:21
according to the g. of thy. 79:11
his g. is unsearchable. 145:3
I declare thy g. 6
according to his excellent g. 150:2
in the g. of his folly he. Pr 5:23
calleth by name, by g. Isa 40:26
thou art wearied in the g. 57:10*
travelling in the g. of his. 63:1
for g. of iniquity thy. Jer 13:22
art thou like in thy g.? Ezek 31:2
thus was he fair in his g. 7
thy g. is grown and. Dan 4:22
the g. of the kingdom shall. 7:27
what is exceeding g. of. Eph 1:19

greaves
Goliath had g. of brass. 1 Sam 17:6

Grecia
rough goat is king of G. Dan 8:21
when I am gone, prince of G. 10:20
stir up all against realm of G. 11:2

Grecians
Judah sold to the G. Joel 3:6
a murmuring of the G. Acts 6:1
and disputed against the G. 9:29
spoke to the G. preaching. 11:20

Greece
against thy sons, O G. Zech 9:13
Paul came to G. and abode. Acts 20:2

greedily
he coveteth g. all day. Pr 21:26
hast g. gained of thy. Ezek 22:12
they ran g. after the error. Jude 11*

greediness
all uncleanness with g. Eph 4:19

greedy
as a lion that is g. of. Ps 17:12
every one that is g. of. Pr 1:19
he that is g. of gain troubleth. 15:27
they are g. dogs, can. Isa 56:11
not g. of filthy lucre. 1 Tim 3:3, 8

Greek
superscription written in G. Luke 23:38; John 19:20
canst thou speak G.? Acts 21:37
G. tongue hath his name. Rev 9:11

Greek
the woman was a G. Mark 7:26
Timotheus was a G. Acts 16:1, 3
Jew first, and also to G. Rom 1:16
no difference between Jew and G. 10:12; Gal 3:28; Col 3:11
was with me, being a G. Gal 2:3
see appellatives

Greeks
certain G. came to. John 12:20
a multitude of G. believed. Acts 14:1; 17:4, 12
persuaded the Jews and the G. 18:4
then the G. took Sosthenes. 17
Jews and G. heard the word. 19:10
this was known to all the G. 17
testifying to Jews and G. 20:21
he brought the G. also into. 21:28
both to G. and Barbarians. Rom 1:14
G. seek after wisdom. 1 Cor 1:22
preach Christ crucified, to the G. 23
unto called, Jews and G., Christ. 24

green
have given every g. herb. Gen 1:30
as the g. herb have I given you. 9:3
Jacob took rods of g. poplar. 30:37*
remained not any g. Ex 10:15
for thy firstfruits g. ears. Lev 2:14*
eat no g. ears, till ye have. 23:14*
bind me with seven g. Judg 16:7
brought to her seven g. withs. 8
inhabitants were as g. herbs. 2 Ki 19:26; Isa 37:27
where were white, g., blue. Esth 1:6
he is g. before the sun. Job 8:16
and his branch shall not be g. 15:32
searcheth after every g. thing. 39:8
maketh me lie down in g. Ps 23:2
they shall wither as the g. herb. 37:2
wicked spreading like a g. bay. 35
fair, also our bed is g. S of S 1:16
fig tree putteth forth her g. 2:13
grass faileth, there is no g. Isa 15:6
called thy name, a g. Jer 11:16
her roots, leaf shall be g. 17:8
I am like a g. fir tree. Hos 14:8
companies on g. grass. Mark 6:39
hail and fire, and all g. Rev 8:7
commanded not to hurt any g. 9:4

green tree
under every g. tree. Deut 12:2
images under every g. tree. 1 Ki 14:23; 2 Ki 17:10
Ahaz sacrificed under every g. tree. 2 Ki 16:4; 2 Chr 28:4
I am like a g. olive tree. Ps 52:8
under every g. tree. Isa 57:5
under every g. tree thou. Jer 2:20
under every g. tree, there played. 3:6
thy ways under every g. tree. 13
be under every g. tree. Ezek 6:13
I have dried up the g. tree. 17:24
it shall devour every g. tree. 20:47
things in a g. tree. Luke 23:31

green trees
groves by g. trees. Jer 17:2

greenish
if the plague be g. in. Lev 13:49
be with hollow strakes g. or. 14:37

greenness
it is yet in his g. and. Job 8:12

greet
(The Revisions change this word to salute when used in the New Testament)
go to Nabal and g. 1 Sam 25:5
g. Priscilla and Aquila. Rom 16:3
g. church. 5
g. Mary who bestowed labour. 6
g. Amplias. 8
g. the household of Narcissus. 11
all the brethren g. you. 1 Cor 16:20
Phil 4:21
g. ye one another. 1 Cor 16:20
2 Cor 13:12; 1 Pet 5:14
and Demas g. you. Col 4:14
g. the brethren with an. 1 Thes 5:26
g. them that love us in. Tit 3:15
of thy elect sister g. thee. 2 John 13
peace be to thee, g. the. 3 John 14

greeteth
Eubulus g. thee. 2 Tim 4:21*

greeting, -s
g. in markets. Mat 23:7*
Luke 11:43*; 20:46*
and brethren, send g. Acts 15:23
Lysias to Felix sendeth g. 23:26
tribes scattered abroad, g. Jas 1:1

grew
every herb before it g. Gen 2:5*
he overthrew that which g. 19:25
Isaac g. 21:8; 26:13
Ishmael g. and dwelt in. 21:20
the boys g. 25:27
Israel g. and multiplied. 47:27*
afflicted, more they g. Ex 1:12*
Moses g. 2:10
his wife's sons g. up. Judg 11:2
Samson g. and the Lord. 13:24
the child Samuel g. 1 Sam 2:21, 26
David went on and g. 2 Sam 5:10
lamb g. up together with him. 12:3
it g. and became a. Ezek 17:6
tree g. and was strong. Dan 4:11
and the thorns g. up. Mark 4:7
bettered, but rather g. worse. 5:26
child g. and waxed. Luke 1:80; 2:40
it g. and waxed a great tree. 13:19
people g. and multiplied. Acts 7:17
word of God g. and multiplied. 12:24
so mightily g. the word of. 19:20

greyhound
for comely in going, a g. Pr 30:31

grief, -s
a g. unto Isaac and. Gen 26:35
out of abundance of g. 1 Sam 1:16*
be no g. to thee, or offence. 25:31
shall know his own g. 2 Chr 6:29*
they saw that his g. was. Job 2:13
oh that my g. were throughly. 6:2*
lips should assuage your g. 16:5
speak, my g. is not assuaged. 6
my eye is consumed because of g. Ps 6:7; 31:9
my life is spent with g. my. 31:10ᵘ
they talk to g. of those thou. 69:26*
a foolish son is a g. to. Pr 17:25
much wisdom is much g. Eccl 1:18
are sorrows, and his travail g. 2:23
be a heap in day of g. Isa 17:11
and acquainted with g. 53:3
he hath borne our g. and carried. 4
bruise him, he put him to g. 10
before me continually is g. Jer 6:7*
truly this is a g. and I must. 10:19
for the Lord hath added g. 45:3*
though he cause g. he will. Lam 3:32
a gourd, a shadow to deliver him from g. Jonah 4:6*
if any caused g. he hath. 2 Cor 2:5*
with joy and not with g. Heb 13:17
toward God endure g. 1 Pet 2:19

grievance
cause me to behold g.? Hab 1:3*

grieve
man shall be to g. 1 Sam 2:33
that it may not g. me. 1 Chr 4:10*
how oft did they g.? Ps 78:40
doth not willingly g. Lam 3:33
g. not the Holy Spirit of. Eph 4:30

grieved

the earth, and it *g.* him. *Gen* 6:6
sons heard and were *g.* and. 34:7
now be not *g.* that ye sold me. 45:5
archers have sorely *g.* him. 49:23
and they were *g.* because. *Ex* 1:12
shall not be *g.* when. *Deut* 15:10
soul was *g.* for misery. *Judg* 10:16
why is thy heart *g.*? *1 Sam* 1:8
it *g.* Samuel, and he cried. 15:11*
Jonathan know this lest he be *g.* 20:3
arose, for he was *g.* for David. 34
soul of all the people was *g.* 30:6
heard how king was *g.* *2 Sam* 19:2
it *g.* them exceedingly. *Neh* 2:10
it *g.* me sore, and I cast forth. 13:8
was queen exceedingly *g.* *Esth* 4:4
commune, wilt thou be *g.*? *Job* 4:2
was not my soul *g.* for the? 30:25
thus my heart was *g.*, I. *Ps* 73:21
forty years was I *g.* with. 95:10
wicked shall see it, and be *g.* 112:10
transgressors and was *g.* 119:158
am not I *g.* with those that? 139:21
called thee as a woman *g.* *Isa* 54:6
therefore thou wast not *g.* 57:10*
them, they have not *g.* *Jer* 5:3
I Daniel was *g.* in spirit. *Dan* 7:15
therefore he shall be *g.* and. 11:30
not *g.* for the affliction. *Amos* 6:6
being *g.* for the hardness. *Mark* 3:5
he went away *g.* for he had. 10:22
Peter was *g.* because. *John* 21:17
being *g.* that they taught. *Acts* 4:2
Paul being *g.* said to spirit. 16:18*
if thy brother be *g.* *Rom* 14:15
that ye should be *g.* *2 Cor* 2:4*
caused grief, he hath not *g.* me. 5
wherefore I was *g.* with. *Heb* 3:10*
but with whom was he *g.* forty? 17*

grieveth

for it *g.* me much for. *Ruth* 1:13
it *g.* him to bring it. *Pr* 26:15

grieving

shall be no more a *g.* *Ezek* 28:24

grievous

for the famine was *g.* *Gen* 12:10*
because their sin is very *g.* 18:20
the thing was very *g.* in. 21:11
God said, let it not be *g.* in thy. 12
famine shall be very *g.* 41:31
this is a *g.* mourning to the. 50:11
came a *g.* swarm of flies. *Ex* 8:24
a *g.* murrain. 9:3
to rain a very *g.* hail. 18, 24
locusts were very *g.* before. 10:14
Shimei cursed me with a *g.* *1 Ki* 2:8
g. service lighter. 12:4; *2 Chr* 10:4
his ways always *g.* *Ps* 10:5*
speak *g.* things against. 31:18*
but *g.* words stir up anger. *Pr* 15:1
correction is *g.* unto him that. 10
wrought under sun is *g.* *Eccl* 2:17
his life shall be *g.* unto. *Isa* 15:4*
g. vision is declared unto me. 21:2
they are all *g.* revolters. *Jer* 6:28
my hurt, my wound is *g.* 10:19
people broken with a *g.* blow. 14:17
they shall die of *g.* deaths. 16:4
a *g.* whirlwind shall fall on. 23:19*
thy wound is *g.* 30:12; *Nah* 3:19
bind heavy burdens and *g.*
Mat 23:4; *Luke* 11:46
shall *g.* wolves enter in. *Acts* 20:29
Jews laid many *g.* complaints. 25:7
to me indeed is not *g.* but. *Phil* 3:1*
seemeth joyous, but *g.* *Heb* 12:11
commandments are not *g.* *1 John* 5:3
a *g.* sore on men that. *Rev* 16:2

grievously

afterward did more *g.* *Isa* 9:1*
it shall fall *g.* upon head. *Jer* 23:19*
Jerusalem hath *g.* sinned. *Lam* 1:8
turned, for I have *g.* rebelled. 20
land sinneth by trespassing *g.*
Ezek 14:13*
g. tormented. *Mat* 8:6
daughter *g.* vexed. 15:22

grievousness

that write *g.* which they. *Isa* 10:1*
they fled from the *g.* of war. 21:15

grind

Samson did *g.* in the. *Judg* 16:21
then let my wife *g.* unto. *Job* 31:10
what mean ye to *g.* the? *Isa* 3:15
take millstones and *g.* meal. 47:2
took the young men to *g.* *Lam* 5:13*
it will *g.* him to powder.
Mat 21:44*; *Luke* 20:18*

grinders

the *g.* cease, because. *Eccl* 12:3

grinding

when sound of the *g.* is. *Eccl* 12:4
two women *g.* at the mill.
Mat 24:41; *Luke* 17:35

grisled

were speckled and *g.* *Gen* 31:10, 12
in fourth chariot were *g.* *Zech* 6:3
the *g.* go forth toward the south. 6

groan

men *g.* from out of city. *Job* 24:12
her land wounded shall *g.* *Jer* 51:52
Pharaoh shall *g.* before. *Ezek* 30:24
how do the beasts *g.*! *Joel* 1:18
we ourselves *g.* within. *Rom* 8:23
in this we *g.* desiring to. *2 Cor* 5:2
we in this tabernacle do *g.* being. 4

groaned

he *g.* in the spirit. *John* 11:33

groaneth

the whole creation *g.* *Rom* 8:22

groaning, -s

God heard their *g.* and. *Ex* 2:24
the *g.* of Israel. 6:5; *Acts* 7:34
Lord because of their *g.* *Judg* 2:18
is heavier than my *g.* *Job* 23:2
I am weary with *g.* all. *Ps* 6:6
my *g.* is not hid from thee. 38:9
by reason of my *g.* my bones. 102:5
to hear the *g.* of the prisoner, to. 20
with the *g.* of a deadly. *Ezek* 30:24
Jesus *g.* in himself. *John* 11:38
for us with *g.* that. *Rom* 8:26

grope, -eth

shalt *g.* at noonday as the blind *g.*
Deut 28:29
they *g.* in noonday as. *Job* 5:14
they *g.* in the dark without. 12:25
g. for the wall like the blind, we *g.*
Isa 59:10

gross

g. darkness shall cover. *Isa* 60:2
for light, make it *g.* *Jer* 13:16
people's heart is waxed *g.*
Mat 13:15; *Acts* 28:27

ground

he *g.* the calf to powder. *Ex* 32:20
Deut 9:21
the people *g.* the manna. *Num* 11:8

ground *corn*

spread *g.* *corn* on the. *2 Sam* 17:19*

ground

not a man to till the *g.* *Gen* 2:5
formed man of the dust of the *g.* 7
out of the *g.* the Lord formed. 19
he said, cursed is the *g.* for. 3:17
but Cain a tiller of *g.* 4:2
blood crieth to me from the *g.* 10
because of the *g.* the Lord. 5:29
I will not again curse the *g.* 8:21
bowed himself toward the *g.* 18:2*
with his face toward *g.* 19:1*
where thou standest is holy *g.*
Ex 3:5; *Acts* 7:33
g. whereon they are shall. *Ex* 8:21
the *g.* clave asunder. *Num* 16:31
be the fruit of thy *g.* *Deut* 28:4, 11
fastened the nail into *g.* *Judg* 4:21
set them to ear his *g.* *1 Sam* 8:12
his spear stuck in the *g.* at. 26:7
was a piece of *g.* full. *2 Sam* 23:11
he stood in midst of the *g.* and. 12*
water is naught, and *g.* *2 Ki* 2:19*
cast him into the plat of *g.* 9:26
where was a parcel of *g.* *1 Chr* 11:13
did cast them in clay *g.* *2 Chr* 4:17
the firstfruits of our *g.* *Neh* 10:35
bring the tithes of our *g.* to. 37
trouble spring out of the *g.* *Job* 5:6
the stock thereof die in the *g.* 14:8
snare is laid for him in the *g.* 18:10
the desolate and waste *g.* 38:27
he swallows the *g.* with. *Job* 39:24
devoured fruit of their *g.* *Ps* 105:35
watersprings into dry *g.* 107:33
he turneth dry *g.* into water. 35*
break clods of his *g.*? *Isa* 28:24
shalt speak out of the *g.* 29:4
seed that thou shalt sow the *g.* 30:23
oxen and young asses that ear *g.* 24
and the parched *g.* shall. 35:7*
laid thy body as the *g.* 51:23
break up your fallow *g.* *Jer* 4:3
Hos 10:12
poured on fruit of the *g.* *Jer* 7:20
because the *g.* is chapt, there. 14:4
gates are sunk into the *g.* *Lam* 2:2
face, thou see not *g.* *Ezek* 12:6, 12
cieled from the *g.* up to the. 41:16
and touched not the *g.* *Dan* 8:5
face was towards *g.* 18; 10:9, 15
with them for things of *g.* *Hos* 2:18
and the *g.* shall give her. *Zech* 8:12
not destroy fruits of your *g.* *Mal* 3:11
but other fell into good *g.* *Mat* 13:8
Luke 8:8
he that received seed into good *g.*
Mat 13:23; *Luke* 8:15
cast seed into the *g.* *Mark* 4:26*
the *g.* of a certain rich. *Luke* 12:16
why cumbereth it the *g.*? 13:7
I have bought a piece of *g.* 14:18*
lay thee even with the *g.* 19:44
near the parcel of *g.* *John* 4:5
corn of wheat fall into *g.* 12:24*

see **dry, face**

on or upon the **ground**

he spilled it *on the g.* *Gen* 38:9
fell before him *on the g.* 44:14
cast the rod *on the g.* he cast it *on the g.* *Ex* 4:3
and fire ran along *upon the g.* 9:23*
on dry *g.* through the sea. 14:16, 22
as the hoar frost *on the g.* 16:14
pour blood *upon the g.* *Deut* 15:23
nest chance to be *on the g.* 22:6
would not set her foot *upon g.* 28:56
upon all *the g.* let there. *Judg* 6:39
there was dew *upon* all *the g.* 40
was honey *upon the g.* *1 Sam* 14:25
slew oxen and calves *on the g.* 32
son of Jesse liveth *on the g.* 20:31
water spilt *on the g.* *2 Sam* 14:14
him as dew falleth *on the g.* 17:12
said, Smite *upon the g.* *2 Ki* 13:18
Job fell *upon the g.* and. *Job* 1:20
down with him *upon the g.* 2:13
out my gall *upon the g.* 16:13
shall sit *on the g.* *Isa* 3:26
of Babylon, sit *on the g.* 47:1
be dung *upon the g.* *Jer* 25:33
man and beast *upon the g.* 27:5*
of Zion sit *on the g.* *Lam* 2:10
young and old lie *on the g.* in. 21
poured it not *upon the g.* *Ezek* 24:7
princes shall sit *upon the g.* 26:16
the multitude to sit *on the g.*
Mat 15:35; *Mark* 8:6
some fell *on* stony *g.* *Mark* 4:5, 16*
fell *on* good *g.* 8, 20; *Luke* 8:8, 15
and he fell *on* the *g.* *Mark* 9:20
forward, and fell *on g.* and. 14:35
he wrote *on the g.* *John* 8:6, 8
he spat *on the g.* 9:6

to or unto the **ground**

till thou return *unto the g.* *Gen* 3:19
Jacob bowed himself *to the g.* 33:3
his wife fell *to the g.* *Judg* 13:20
Benjamin destroyed *to the g.* 20:21
and destroyed *to the g.* of Israel. 25
bowed and fell *to the g.* *Ruth* 2:10
his words fall *to the g.* *1 Sam* 3:19
fallen on his face *to the g.* 5:4
not one hair fall *to the g.* 14:45
and fell on his face *to the g.* 20:41
Abigail bowed *to the g.* before. 25:23
with his face *to the g.* 28:14
I smite thee *to the g.*? *2 Sam* 2:22
casting him down *to the g.* 8:2
fell on her face *to the g.* 14:4
Joab fell *to the g.* 22
Absalom bowed *to the g.* 33
not thou smite him *to the g.*? 18:11
out Amasa's bowels *to the g.* 20:10
Nathan bowed *to the g.* *1 Ki* 1:23

prophets bowed to the g. 2 Ki 2:15
she bowed herself to the g. 4:37
Ornan bowed to the g. 1 Chr 21:21
Israel bowed with their faces to g. 2 Chr 7:3
bowed with his face to the g. 20:18
with their faces to the g. Neh 8:6
casting down the dwelling place of thy name to the g. Ps 74:7
crown, by casting it to the g. 89:39
cast his throne down to the g. 44
smitten my life down to the g. 143:3
the wicked down to the g. 147:6
thou cut down to the g.! Isa 14:12
images he hath broken to the g. 21:9
bring to the g. even to dust. 25:12
city he layeth even to the g. 26:5
languish, are black to the g. Jer 14:2
strong holds of Judah to g. Lam 2:2
hang their heads to the g. 10
down the wall to the g. Ezek 13:14
mother was cast down to the g. 19:12
garrison shall go down to g. 26:11
I will cast thee to the g. 28:17
cast the ram down to the g. Dan 8:7
some of hosts and stars to the g. 10
and cast down the truth to the g. 12
altar shall fall to the g. Amos 3:14
bring me down to the g.? Ob 3
shall not fall to the g. Mat 10:29
blood falling to the g. Luke 22:44
went backward, and fell to the g. John 18:6
I fell to the g. and heard. Acts 22:7

ground

is the pillar and g. of. 1 Tim 3:15

grounded

in every place where g. Isa 30:32*
ye being rooted and g. Eph 3:17
continue in the faith, g. Col 1:23

grove

[1] *A tamarisk tree*, Gen 21:33 (R.V.). [2] *The* Asherah (R.V.) *is in all other places, for singular,* Asherim, *for plural.*

Abraham planted a g. Gen 21:33
shalt not plant a g. Deut 16:21
and cut down the g. Judg 6:25
g. was cut down that was by. 28
she had made an idol in a g. 1 Ki 15:13; 2 Chr 15:16
Ahab made a g. and. 1 Ki 16:33
there remained the g. 2 Ki 13:6
Israel made a g. and served. 17:16
up altars, and made a g. 21:3
the vessels made for the g. 23:4
he brought out the g. from house. 6
burnt the high place and the g. 15

groves

ye shall cut down their g. Ex 34:13
Deut 7:5
ye shall burn their g. Deut 12:3
forgat Lord and served g. Judg 3:7; 2 Chr 24:18
out of this good land, because they have made their g. 1 Ki 14:15
built them g. on. 23; 2 Ki 17:10
the prophets of the g. 1 Ki 18:19
Hezekiah cut down g. 2 Ki 18:4
cut down the g. 23:14; 2 Chr 34:3, 4
and cut down the g. 2 Chr 14:3
Jehoshaphat took away the g. 17:6
thou hast taken away the g. 19:3
all Israel cut down the g. 31:1
Manasseh made g. 33:3
where he set up g. 19
to purge Judah from the g. 34:3
broken down the altars and g. 7
nor shall he respect the g. Isa 17:8
the g. and the images shall. 27:9
remember altars and g. Jer 17:2
I will pluck up thy g. Mi 5:14

grow

God made every tree to g. Gen 2:9
them g. into a multitude. 48:16
let locks of his hair g. Num 6:5
hair of head began to g. Judg 16:22
he make it not to g. 2 Sam 23:5
eat such things as g. 2 Ki 19:29
why should damage g.? Ezra 4:22
can the rush g. up? Job 8:11
out of the earth shall others g. 19*
washest away things that g. Job 14:19*
thistles g. instead of wheat. 31:40
they g. up with corn, they go. 39:4
he shall g. like a cedar. Ps 92:12
causeth grass to g. 104:14; 147:8
nor how the bones g. in. Eccl 11:5
and a branch shall g. Isa 11:1*
shalt thou make thy plant g. 17:11*
he shall g. up before him. 53:2
they g. yea, they bring. Jer 12:2
Branch to g. up unto David. 33:15
suffer their locks to g. Ezek 44:20
by the river shall g. all trees. 47:12
shall g. as the lily, cast. Hos 14:5*
shall revive as the corn, and g. as. 7*
nor madest it g. which. Jonah 4:10
the Branch, he shall g. up. Zech 6:12
ye shall g. up as calves. Mal 4:2*
consider the lilies how they g. Mat 6:28; Luke 12:27
let both g. together until. Mat 13:30
let no fruit g. on thee. 21:19
seed should g. up, he. Mark 4:27
whereunto this would g. Acts 5:24
may g. up into him in all. Eph 4:15
of word, that ye may g. 1 Pet 2:2
g. in grace and in. 2 Pet 3:18

groweth

shall eat every tree that g. Ex 10:5
freckled spot that g. in. Lev 13:39*
which g. of its own accord. 25:5, 11
nor any grass g. therein. Deut 29:23
behold, the day g. to. Judg 19:9
the dust g. into hardness. Job 38:38*
like grass which g. up. Ps 90:5, 6
which withereth afore it g. up. 129:6
eat this year such as g. Isa 37:30
when it is sown, it g. up. Mark 4:32
g. unto an holy temple. Eph 2:21
because your faith g. 2 Thes 1:3

grown

till Shelah be g. Gen 38:11
Shelah was g. 14
when Moses was g. he. Ex 2:11
for they were not g. up. 9:32
thou art g. thick. Deut 32:15
for them till they were g. Ruth 1:13
tarry until your beards be g. 2 Sam 10:5; 1 Chr 19:5
with young men g. 1 Ki 12:8, 10
when the child was g. up. 2 Ki 4:18
as corn blasted before it be g. 19:26
Isa 37:27
our trespass is g. up to. Ezra 9:6
sons may be as plants g. Ps 144:12
and lo, it was all g. over. Pr 24:31
because ye are g. fat as. Jer 50:11*
fashioned, thy hair is g. Ezek 16:7
art g. strong, thy greatness is g. Dan 4:22
his hairs were g. like eagles'. 33
when g. it is the greatest. Mat 13:32

growth

g. lo, it was latter g. Amos 7:1

grudge

nor bear any g. against. Lev 19:18
let them g. if they be. Ps 59:15*
g. not one against. Jas 5:9*

grudging

to another without g. 1 Pet 4:9*

grudgingly

let him give, not g. or. 2 Cor 9:7

guard

a captain of the g. Gen 37:36; 39:1
servant to a captain of the g. 41:12
David set him over his g. 2 Sam 23:23; 1 Chr 11:25
shields to captain of g. 1 Ki 14:27
2 Chr 12:10
g. bare them and brought them. 1 Ki 14:28; 2 Chr 12:11
part at gate behind g. 2 Ki 11:6
captain of g. came to Jerusalem. 25:8; Jer 52:12
captain of g. brake down walls. 2 Ki 25:10; Jer 52:14
rest of people captain of g. 2 Ki 25:11
the captain of the g. left of poor. 12
in night they may be a g. Neh 4:22
nor I nor men of the g. put off. 23
captain of g. concerning. Jer 39:11
when the captain of g. had. Jer 40:1
captain of the g. gave him. 5
the captain of the g. took. 52:30
and be a g. to them. Ezek 38:7
answered captain of g. Dan 2:14
prisoners to captain of g. Acts 28:16

guard chamber

guard bare them to g. chamber. 1 Ki 14:28; 2 Chr 12:11

guest

he was gone to be g. Luke 19:7*

guestchamber

where is the g.? Mark 14:14
Luke 22:11

guests

Adonijah and all the g. 1 Ki 1:41
all g. with Adonijah were afraid. 49
her g. are in the depths. Pr 9:18
hath prepared and bid g. Zeph 1:7
was furnished with g. Mat 22:10
the king came in to see the g. 11

guide, -s

he will be our g. even. Ps 48:14
it was thou, a man, my g. 55:13
who forsaketh the g. of. Pr 2:17
which having no g., overseer. 6:7
my father, thou art the g. Jer 3:4
put ye not confidence in g. Mi 7:5
to you, ye blind g. Mat 23:16, 24
who was g. to them. Acts 1:16
confident thou art a g. of. Rom 2:19

guide, *verb*

canst thou g. Arcturus? Job 38:32
the meek will he g. in. Ps 25:9
lead me and g. me. 31:3
I will teach and g. thee with. 32:8*
thou shalt g. me with thy. 73:24
he will g. his affairs with. 112:5*
of the upright shall g. Pr 11:3
be wise, and g. thine heart in. 23:19
of water shall he g. them. Isa 49:10
is none to g. her among. 51:18
the Lord shall g. thee. 58:11
to g. our feet into the way. Luke 1:79
he will g. you into all. John 16:13
except some man g. me? Acts 8:31
bear children, g. house. 1 Tim 5:14*

guided, -ing

Israel g. his hands. Gen 48:14
thou hast g. them in thy. Ex 15:13
the Lord g. them on. 2 Chr 32:22
I have g. her from my. Job 31:18
g. them in the wilderness. Ps 78:52
hast g. them by the skilfulness. 72

guile

if a man slay with g. Ex 21:14
in whose spirit there is no g. Ps 32:2
keep lips from speaking g. 34:13
1 Pet 3:10
deceit and g. depart not. Ps 55:11
indeed, in whom is no g. John 1:47
I caught you with g. 2 Cor 12:16
exhortation was not in g. 1 Thes 2:3
aside all malice and g. 1 Pet 2:1
who did no sin, neither was g. 22
mouth was found no g. Rev 14:5*

guilt

g. of innocent. Deut 19:13; 21:9

guiltiness

have brought g. on us. Gen 26:10
me from blood-g. O God. Ps 51:14

guiltless

Lord will not hold him g. Ex 20:7
Deut 5:11
then shall the man be g. Num 5:31
shall return and be g. 32:22
on him, and he will be g. Josh 2:19
anointed and be g. 1 Sam 26:9
my kingdom are g. 2 Sam 3:28
king and his throne be g. 14:9
hold him not g. for thou. 1 Ki 2:9
not have condemned the g. Mat 12:7

guilty

verily g. concerning. Gen 42:21
will by no means clear g. Ex 34:7
Num 14:18
not be done are g. Lev 4:13; 22:27
he shall be unclean and g. 5:2
knoweth of it, he shall be g. 3, 4
he shall be g., he shall confess. 5

he wist it not, yet is he g. Lev 5:17
because he sinned and is g. he. 6:4
the slayer shall not be g. Num 35:27
no satisfaction for a murderer g. 31
that you should be g. Judg 21:22
being g. offered a ram. Ezra 10:19
and thou be found g. Pr 30:10
become g. in blood. Ezek 22:4
hold themselves not g. Zech 11:5
by the gift on it, he is g. Mat 23:18*
they said, he is g. of death. 26:66*
Mark 14:64*
world may become g. Rom 3:19*
shall be g. of the body. 1 Cor 11:27
in one point, he is g. Jas 2:10

gulf
us and you is a great g. Luke 16:26

Gur
smote Ahaziah at the going up to G.
2 Ki 9:27

gush, -ed
till the blood g. out. 1 Ki 18:28
rock, the waters g. out. Ps 78:20
opened rock, waters g. out. 105:41
clave the rock, and the waters g. out.
Isa 48:21
and our eyelids g. out. Jer 9:18
and his bowels g. out. Acts 1:18

gutter, -s
Jacob set rods in the g. Gen 30:38
before the eyes of the cattle in g. 41
who getteth up to the g. 2 Sam 5:8*

H

ha
the trumpets, ha, ha. Job 39:25

habergeon
hole of an h. Ex 28:32*; 39:23*
spear, the dart, the h. Job 41:26*

habergeons
h. and bows (Uzziah). 2 Chr 26:14*
servants held bows and h. Neh 4:16*

habitable
rejoicing in the h. part. Pr 8:31

habitation
I will prepare him an h. Ex 15:2*
camp shall his h. be. Lev 13:46
even to his h. shall ye. Deut 12:5
why kick at offering, commanded in
my h.? 1 Sam 2:29
thou shalt see an enemy in my h. 32
me both it, and his h. 2 Sam 15:25
built an house of h. for. 2 Chr 6:2
and have turned from the h. 29:6
God of Israel whose h. is. Ezra 7:15
but suddenly I cursed h. Job 5:3
thou shalt visit thy h. and shalt. 24
make h. of thy righteousness. 8:6
be scattered upon his h. 18:15
I have loved the h. of thy. Ps 26:8
from the place of his h. he. 33:14
let their h. be desolate. 69:25
thou my strong h. whereunto. 71:3
and judgement the h. 89:14; 97:2
made the most High thy h. 91:9
fowls of heaven have their h. 104:12
might go to a city of h. 107:7, 36
find an h. for the mighty God. 132:5
for Lord hath desired it for his h. 13
but he blesseth the h. of. Pr 3:33
and that graveth an h. Isa 22:16
and the h. shall be forsaken. 27:10
shall dwell in a peaceable h. 32:18
see Jerusalem a quiet h. 33:20
it shall be an h. of dragons. 34:13
in the h. of dragons shall be. 35:7
and behold from the h. of. 63:15
thine h. is in midst of. Jer 9:6
have made his h. desolate. 10:25
mightily roar upon his h. 25:30
thee, O h. of justice. 31:23; 50:7
cities thereof be an h. of. 33:12
they dwelt in the h. of. 41:17
against h. of strong. 49:19; 50:44
Israel again to his h. 50:19
surely he shall make their h. 45
Egypt to return to their h. Ezek 29:14
whose h. is high, that saith. Ob 3
moon stood still in their h. Hab 3:11
it is written, let his h. be. Acts 1:20
the bounds of their h. 17:26
for an h. of God through. Eph 2:22
which left their own h. Jude 6
Babylon is become the h. Rev 18:2

holy **habitation**
guided them to thy holy h. Ex 15:13
down from thy holy h. Deut 26:15
is God in his holy h. Ps 68:5
his voice from holy h. Jer 25:30
up out of his holy h. Zech 2:13

habitations
cruelty are in their h. Gen 49:5*
in all your h. eat unleaven. Ex 12:20
kindle no fire through your h. 35:3
ye be come into the h. Num 15:2
places of earth full of h. Ps 74:20
fall round about their h. 78:28
forth curtains of thy h. Isa 54:2
for h. of the wilderness. Jer 9:10
who shall enter into our h.? 21:13
and the peaceable h. are cut. 25:37
surely he shall make their h. 49:20
swallowed up the h. of. Lam 2:2
in all their h. make land. Ezek 6:14
the h. of the shepherds. Amos 1:2
you into everlasting h. Luke 16:9*

Hachilah
hid in hill of H. 1 Sam 23:19; 26:1
Saul pitched in the hill of H. 26:3

had
ruled over all that he h. Gen 24:2
he knew not aught he h. save. 39:6
he that gathered much h. Ex 16:18
the Lord h. a delight in. Deut 10:15
Rahab and all that she h. Josh 6:25
Achan and all that he h. 7:24
of them shall I be h. in. 2 Sam 6:22
did this thing, and h. no pity. 12:6
mighty men whom David h. 23:8
she said, h. Zimri peace. 2 Ki 9:31
house and all he h. 1 Chr 13:14
as for me, I h. in my heart to. 28:2
and pattern of all that he h. by. 12
in safety, neither h. I rest. Job 3:26
if men said not, oh that we h. 31:31
him twice as much as he h. 42:10
I said, O that I h. wings. Ps 55:6
I h. rather be a doorkeeper. 84:10
to be h. in reverence of all. 89:7
proud have h. me greatly. 119:51
as were oppressed, they h. Eccl 4:1
behold, for peace I h. Isa 38:17
we grope as if we h. no eyes. 59:10
in my favour have I h. mercy. 60:10
and they h. no light. Jer 4:23
then h. we plenty of victuals. 44:17
pleasant things she h. in. Lam 1:7
she came down wonderfully: h. no. 9
yet h. he no wages for. Ezek 29:18
but I h. pity for mine holy. 36:21
by his strength Jacob h. Hos 12:3
yea he h. power over the angel. 4
against which thou hast h. Zech 1:12
yet h. he the residue of. Mal 2:15
he sold all that he h. Mat 13:46
seven, for they all h. her? 22:28
did cast in all she h. Mark 12:44
thou hast h. five husbands. John 4:18
of whatsoever disease he h. 5:4
Judas h. the bag, and bare. 12:6
if I h. not come, they h. not h. 15:22
the glory I h. with thee before. 17:5
all that believed h. all. Acts 2:44
shorn his head, for he h. 18:18
that after examination h., I. 25:26
faith he h. yet being. Rom 4:11, 12
what fruit h. ye in those things? 6:21
wives be as though they h. none.
1 Cor 7:29
but we h. the sentence of. 2 Cor 1:9
of entering in we h. 1 Thes 1:9
and blessed him that h. Heb 7:6
old commandment which ye h. from.
1 John 2:7
that which we h. from. 2 John 5

Hadadezer, Hadarezer
David smote H. 2 Sam 8:3; 9:10
1 Chr 18:3
came to succour H. 2 Sam 8:5
shields of gold on servants of H. 7
cities of H. 8
H. had wars with Toi. 2 Sam 8:10
the spoil of H. 12
H. sent and brought out the. 10:16
Rezon fled from H. 1 Ki 11:23

Hadadrimmon
the mourning of H. in. Zech 12:11

Hadassah
H. his uncle's daughter. Esth 2:7

Hadoram
begat H. Gen 10:27; 1 Chr 1:21
Tou sent H. his son. 1 Chr 18:10
Rehoboam sent H. 2 Chr 10:18

Hadrach
word of Lord in land of H. Zech 9:1

hadst
for it was little thou h. Gen 30:30
because thou h. a favour. Ps 44:3
thou h. a whore's forehead. Jer 3:3
neither h. pleasure therein. Heb 10:8

haft
and the h. also went in. Judg 3:22

Hagar
H. an Egyptian. Gen 16:1, 3, 8
H. bare Abram a son. 15, 16; 25:12
Sarah saw son of H. the. 21:9
Abraham gave H. bread. 14
called to H., What aileth thee, H.? 17
see **Agar**

Hagarenes
the H. are confederate. Ps 83:6

Hagarites
made war with H. 1 Chr 5:10, 19
H. were delivered into their. 20

Haggai
son of Gad, H. Shuni. Gen 46:16
H. prophesied to the Jews. Ezra 5:1
prophesying of H. the prophet. 6:14
word of the Lord by H. Hag 1:1, 3
2:1, 10, 20

Haggith
Adonijah the son of H. 2 Sam 3:4
1 Ki 1:5, 11; 2:13; 1 Chr 3:2

hail
rain a very grievous h. Ex 9:18
Lord sent thunder and h., fire. 23
of Israel were, was there no h. 26
nor shall there be any more h. 29
h. ceased. 33
remaineth from the h. 10:5, 12, 15
the treasures of the h.? Job 38:22
their vines with h. Ps 78:47
gave up their cattle also to the h. 48
he gave them h. for rain. 105:32
fire, h. snow and vapour. 148:8
which as a tempest of h. Isa 28:2
the h. shall sweep away the. 17
I smote you with h. in all. Hag 2:17
there followed h. and fire. Rev 8:7
and there was great h. 11:19
fell on men a great h. out of. 16:21

hail, *verb*
dwell when it shall h. Isa 32:19

hail
Judas said, H. master. Mat 26:49
H. King of the Jews. 27:29
Mark 15:18; John 19:3
to Mary, and said, H. Luke 1:28

hailstones
which died with h. Josh 10:11
clouds passed, h. and. Ps 18:12, 13
shew indignation with h. Isa 30:30
and ye, O great h. shall. Ezek 13:11
there shall be great h. in my. 13
I will rain great h. fire, and. 38:22

hair
when the h. in the plague. Lev 13:3
if in plague a yellow h. 30
no black h. in it. 31
there is black h. grown. 37
shave off h. 14:8, 9
the h. of his separation. Num 6:19*
sling stones h.'s breadth. Judg 20:16
not one h. of thy son. 2 Sam 14:11
because the h. was heavy on. 26
there shall not an h. of. 1 Ki 1:52
I plucked off their h. Neh 13:25
spirit passed, h. of my. Job 4:15
thy h. is as a flock. S of S 4:1; 6:5

and instead of well set *h.* *Isa* 3:24
shave the head and *h.* of feet. 7:20
to them that plucked off *h.* 50:6
cut off thy *h.* O. *Jer* 7:29
and divide the *h.* *Ezek* 5:1
thy *h.* is grown. 16:7
John had raiment of camel's *h.*
Mat 3:4; *Mark* 1:6
canst not make one *h.* *Mat* 5:36
his feet with her *h.* *John* 11:2; 12:3
if a man have long *h.* *1 Cor* 11:14
a woman have long *h.* it is a. 15
not with broidered *h.* or. *1 Tim* 2:9
not of plaiting the *h.* *1 Pet* 3:3
black as sackcloth of *h.* *Rev* 6:12
had *h.* as the *h.* of women. 9:8
see **goats, head**

hairs

ye shall bring down my *h.*
Gen 42:38; 44:29, 31
if there be no white *h.* *Lev* 13:21
also with man of gray *h.* *Deut* 32:25
are more than the *h.* of my head.
Ps 40:12; 69:4
and even to hoar *h.* will. *Isa* 46:4
h. were grown like eagles'. *Dan* 4:33
gray *h.* are here and there. *Hos* 7:9
the very *h.* of your head are all
numbered. *Mat* 10:30; *Luke* 12:7
did wipe them with *h.* *Luke* 7:38, 44
head and *h.* were white. *Rev* 1:14

hairy

red, all over like an *h.* *Gen* 25:25
Esau is an *h.* man. 27:11
his hands were *h.* 23
Elijah was an *h.* man. *2 Ki* 1:8
the *h.* scalp of such an one. *Ps* 68:21

hale

lest adversary *h.* thee. *Luke* 12:58†

half

Moses took *h.* the blood. *h.* *Ex* 24:6
of sweet cinnamon *h.* so much. 30:23
h. of it in morning, and *h.* *Lev* 6:20
of whom the flesh is *h.* *Num* 12:12
take it of their *h.* and give it. 31:29
h. of them over against. *Josh* 8:33
within as it were an *h.* *1 Sam* 14:14
Hanun shaved off one *h.* *2 Sam* 10:4
nor if *h.* of us die, will they. 18:3
h. the people of Israel. 19:40
h. of the child to one, *h.* *1 Ki* 3:25
h. was not told. 10:7; *2 Chr* 9:6
give me *h.* thine house. *1 Ki* 13:8
h. of people followed Tibni, *h.* 16:21
the ruler of the *h.* part. *Neh* 3:9, 12
h. part of Bethzur. 16
h. of Keilah. 17, 18
children spake *h.* in speech. 13:24
to the *h.* of the kingdom. *Esth* 5:3
7:2; *Mark* 6:23
bloody men shall not live *h.* *Ps* 55:23
Samaria committed *h.* *Ezek* 16:51
be for time, times, and an *h.*
Dan 12:7; *Rev* 12:14
I bought her for *h.* an. *Hos* 3:2
h. of the city shall go. *Zech* 14:2
h. of mount toward the south. 4
h. toward the sea. 8
leaving him *h.* dead. *Luke* 10:30
behold, the *h.* of my goods. 19:8
silence about space of *h.* *Rev* 8:1
bodies three days and an *h.* 11:9, 11
see **shekel, tribe**

haling

Saul *h.* men and women. *Acts* 8:3†

hall

Jesus into common *h.* *Mat* 27:27*
led him away to the *h.* *Mark* 15:16*
fire in midst of the *h.* *Luke* 22:55*
see **judgement**

hallow

children of Israel shall *h.* *Ex* 28:38
h. them to minister to me in. 29:1
things which they *h.* to. *Lev* 22:2, 3
hallowed, I am the Lord which *h.* 32
h. the fiftieth year, proclaim. 25:10
and he shall *h.* his head. *Num* 6:11
same day did king *h.* court.
1 Ki 8:64; *2 Chr* 7:7
h. ye sabbath. *Jer* 17:22, 24, 27
and *h.* my sabbaths. *Ezek* 20:20
keep laws and *h.* my sabbaths. 44:24

hallowed

the sabbath day and *h.* it. *Ex* 20:11
Aaron shall be *h.* and his. 29:21
she shall touch no *h.* *Lev* 12:4
he hath profaned the *h.* 19:8*
I will be *h.* among children. 22:32
h. me all the firstborn. *Num* 3:13
and every man's *h.* things. 5:10
censers, for they are *h.* 16:37*, 38*
of all the *h.* things I have. 18:8
the *h.* part thereof out of it. 29
have brought away *h.* *Deut* 26:13
common, but there is *h.* *1 Sam* 21:4*
the priest gave him *h.* bread. 6*
I have *h.* this house. *1 Ki* 9:3, 7
Jehoash took all the *h.* *2 Ki* 12:18
polluted the house of Lord which he
had *h.* *2 Chr* 36:14
h. be thy name. *Mat* 6:9; *Luke* 11:2

halt

(Lame, limping)
is better to enter into life *h.*
Mat 18:8*; *Mark* 9:45
bring in hither the *h.* *Luke* 14:21*
of *h.* waiting for moving. *John* 5:3

halt

how long *h.* ye between? *1 Ki* 18:21†
ready to *h.*, my sorrow is. *Ps* 38:17†

halted

Jacob passed, he *h.* *Gen* 32:31
I will make her that *h.* *Mi* 4:7

halteth

will assemble her that *h.* *Mi* 4:6†
I will save her that *h.* *Zeph* 3:19†

halting

familiars watched for my *h.*
Jer 20:10†

Ham

Noah begat Shem, *H.* *Gen* 5:32
6:10; 9:18; 10:1; *1 Chr* 1:4
selfsame day *H.* *Gen* 7:13
H. is the father of Canaan. 9:18
sons of *H.* 10:6, 20; *1 Chr* 1:8
smote the Zuzims in *H.* *Gen* 14:5
they of *H.* had dwelt. *1 Chr* 4:40
in the tabernacles of *H.* *Ps* 78:51
sojourned in the land of *H.* 105:23
wonders in land of *H.* 27; 106:22

Haman

king promoted *H.* *Esth* 3:1
king's servants reverenced *H.* 2
H. full of wrath. 5
wherefore *H.* sought to destroy. 6
cast the lot before *H.* 7
and the king and *H.* sat down. 15
H. promised to pay. 4:7
H. came to banquet. 5:4, 5, 8; 7:1
went *H.* forth that day joyful. 5:9
H. told them of the glory of his. 11
the thing pleased *H.* 14
H. standeth in the court. 6:5
H. thought in his heart. 6
then *H.* took the apparel. 11
H. hasted to his house mourning. 12
H. told Zeresh his wife. 13
this wicked *H.* 7:6
H. made request. 7
H. was fallen on the bed. 8
so they hanged *H.* 10
gave Esther the house of *H.* 8:1
slew the sons of *H.* 9:10
they hanged *H.*'s ten sons. 14

Hamath

as men come to *H.* *Num* 13:21
Hor to the entrance of *H.* 34:8
Josh 13:5; *Judg* 3:3; *1 Ki* 8:65
2 Ki 14:25; *2 Chr* 7:8
king of *H.* *2 Sam* 8:9; *1 Chr* 18:9
Jeroboam recovered *H.* *2 Ki* 14:28
Assyria brought men from *H.* 17:24
the men of *H.* made Ashima. 30
the gods of *H.*? 18:34; *Isa* 36:19
where is the king of *H.*? *2 Ki* 19:13
Isa 37:13
put in bands in the land of *H.*
2 Ki 23:33; 25:21
smote Hadarezer to *H.* *1 Chr* 18:3
built store cities in *H.* *2 Chr* 8:4
is not *H.* as Arpad? *Isa* 10:9
recover his people from *H.* 11:11
to *H.* where he gave. *Jer* 39:5; 52:9
Damascus, *H.* is confounded. 49:23

on the north, *H.* *Ezek* 47:16, 17
till a man come over against *H.* 20
H. also shall border. *Zech* 9:2

Hammedatha

the son of *H.* *Esth* 8:5; 9:10, 24

hammer

then Jael took an *h.* in. *Judg* 4:21
with *h.* she smote Sisera. 5:26
neither *h.* nor axe heard. *1 Ki* 6:7
smootheth with the *h.* *Isa* 41:7
like a *h.* that breaketh. *Jer* 23:29
how is the *h.* of whole earth. 50:23

hammers

the carved work with *h.* *Ps* 74:6
fashioneth it with *h.* *Isa* 44:12
fasten it with nails and *h.* *Jer* 10:4

Hamon-Gog

call it the valley of *H.* *Ezek* 39:11
have buried it in the valley of *H.* 15

Hamor

field of the children of *H.* Shechem's
father. *Gen* 33:19; *Josh* 24:32
H. went out to commune.
Gen 34:6, 8
to *H.* and Shechem hearkened all. 24
they slew *H.* and Shechem. 26
serve the men of *H.* *Judg* 9:28

Hanameel

H. thine uncle's son. *Jer* 32:7, 8
bought the field of *H.* my uncle's. 9
evidence to Baruch in sight of *H.* 12

Hananeel

tower of *H.* *Neh* 3:1; 12:39
Jer 31:38; *Zech* 14:10

Hanani

to Jehu son of *H.* the. *1 Ki* 16:1
H. son of Heman. *1 Chr* 25:4
18th lot to *H.* 25
at that time *H.* the seer. *2 Chr* 16:7
Jehu son of *H.* went to meet. 19:2
in book of Jehu son of *H.* 20:34
of the sons of Imman, *H.* *Ezra* 10:20
H. one of my brethren. *Neh* 1:2
I gave my brother *H.* charge. 7:2
H. with the musical. 12:36

Hananiah

Meshullam and *H.* and. *1 Chr* 3:19
the sons of *H.* 21
H. Benjamite. 8:24
H. son of Heman. 25:4
sixteenth lot to *H.* 23
Uzziah had an host under *H.*
2 Chr 26:11
sons of Bebai; *H.* Zabbai. *Ezra* 10:28
H. the son of an. *Neh* 3:8
I gave *H.* ruler of palace. 7:2
H. sealed. 10:23
chief fathers: *H.* 12:12, 41
H. son of Azur the prophet. *Jer* 28:1
H. spake in the presence of all. 11
after that *H.* had broken. 12
H. died that year in the seventh. 17
Zedekiah son of *H.* sat in. 36:12
Irijah the son of *H.* took. 37:13
of Judah, Daniel, *H.* *Dan* 1:6
he gave to *H.* the name of. 7
Melzar was set over Daniel, *H.* 11
was found none like Daniel, *H.* 19
made the thing known to *H.* 2:17

hand

The word hand is sometimes used for power, as in 1 Sam 5:6, 7. *This is especially the case where the expression right hand is used.*

To pour water on any one's hands, meant to serve him, 2 Ki 3:11.

To wash one's hands, denoted that the person was innocent of crime, Deut 21:6, 7; Mat 27:24.

To kiss one's hand, is an act of adoration, Job 31:27.

To lift up one's hand, is a way of taking an oath in use with all nations, Gen 14:22. *It was likewise a posture used in praying for a blessing,* Lev 9:22. *To lift up the hand against one, is to rebel against him,* 2 Sam 20:21.

To give one's hand, means to swear friendship, to promise security, to make alliance, 2 Ki 10:15.

The right hand *denotes power, strength. The scripture generally imputes to God's right hand all the effects of his omnipotence,* Ex 15:6; Ps 17:7; 20:6; 44:3.

Often, to be at one's right hand signifies to defend, to protect, to support, Ps 16:8; 109:31.

Laying on of hands is understood in different ways both in the Old and New Testaments. [1] *It is often taken for ordination and consecration of priests and ministers, as well among the Jews as the Christians,* Num 8:10; Acts 6:6; 13:3; 1 Tim 4:14. [2] *It is sometimes also made use of to signify the establishment of judges and magistrates,* Gen 48:14; Num 27:18.

into your *h.* are they. *Gen* 9:2
all that he had in Joseph's *h.* 39:6
man in whose *h.* the cup. 44:17
with a strong *h.* shall he. *Ex* 6:1
by strength of *h.* Lord brought. 13:3
Israel went out with an high *h.* 14:8 *Num* 33:3
stretch out thine *h.* over. *Ex* 14:16
there shall not a *h.* touch it. 19:13
h. for *h.*, foot for. 21:24; *Deut* 19:21
testimony in Moses' *h.* *Ex* 34:29
on this *h.* and that *h.* 38:15
remain in the *h.* of him. *Lev* 25:28
afterwards the *h.* of all. *Deut* 13:9
thou shalt cut off her *h.* 25:12
on our head if any *h.* *Josh* 2:19
h. of the house of Joseph. *Judg* 1:35
Lord shall sell Sisera into *h.* 4:9
now fall into the *h.* of the. 15:18
smote all that came to *h.* of. 20:48*
of whose *h.* have I? *1 Sam* 12:3
nor spear found in the *h.* of. 13:22
was no sword in the *h.* of. 17:50
when the business was in *h.* 20:19
their *h.* also is with David. 22:17
and eat it at her *h.* *2 Sam* 13:5, 6
is not the *h.* of Joab with? 14:19
h. six fingers. 21:20; *1 Chr* 20:6
let me not fall into *h.* of men. *2 Sam* 24:14; *1 Chr* 21:13
kingdom established in *h.* *1 Ki* 2:46
and the king's *h.* was restored. 13:6
a cloud like a man's *h.* 18:44
Lord shall deliver it into the king's *h.* 22:6, 12, 15; *2 Chr* 28:5
lord on whose *h.* the. *2 Ki* 7:2, 17
went out from under the *h.* 13:5
hath Lord left you in *h.* *2 Chr* 12:5
according to good *h.* of his. *Ezra* 7:9
the *h.* of princes hath been. 9:2
earth is given into *h.* of. *Job* 9:24
into whose *h.* God bringeth. 12:6
in whose *h.* is the soul of every. 10
every *h.* of the wicked shall. 20:22
their good is not in their *h.* 21:16
mighty taken away without *h.* 34:20
he sealeth up the *h.* of every. 37:7
hast not shut me into *h.* *Ps* 31:8
let not the *h.* of the wicked. 36:11
deliver me out of *h.* of wicked. 71:4; 82:4; 97:10
servants look to the *h.* 123:2
as arrows are in the *h.* of. 127:4
two-edged sword be in their *h.* 149:6
thou art come into *h.* *Pr* 6:3
with a slack *h.* but the *h.* of. *Pr* 10:4
though *h.* join in *h.*, the wicked shall not be unpunished. 11:21; 16:5
the *h.* of the diligent shall. 12:24
why a price in *h.* of a fool? 17:16
as a thorn goeth up into the *h.* 26:9
the staff in their *h.* is. *Isa* 10:5
shake the *h.* that they may go. 13:2
this is the *h.* that is stretched. 14:26
I will give over into the *h.* 19:4
down to the earth with the *h.* 28:2
dearly beloved into *h.* of. *Jer* 12:7
vessel was marred in the *h.* 18:4
as clay in the potter's *h.* so are. 6
with an outstretched *h.* I will. 21:5
h. of Ahikam was with Jeremiah, not to give him into *h.* of people. 26:24
she hath given her *h.* 50:15*
we have given the *h.* to. *Lam* 5:6
princes are hanged up by their *h.* 12
an *h.* was sent me, and lo. *Ezek* 2:9
forth the form of an *h.* 8:3; 10:8
nor did she strengthen *h.* of. 16:49
shall be taken with the *h.* 21:24
no god in the *h.* of him that. 28:9
require my flock at their *h.* 34:10
stick which is in the *h.* of. 37:19
in man's *h.* a measuring reed. 40:5
forth fingers of a man's *h.* *Dan* 5:5
God in whose *h.* thy breath is. 23
he shall be broken without *h.* 8:25
behold, an *h.* touched me. 10:10
and daughters into *h.* *Joel* 3:8
in the power of their *h.* *Mi* 2:1
shall see plummet in *h.* *Zech* 4:10
he touched her *h.* *Mat* 8:15
bind him *h.* and foot. 22:13
a man who had a withered *h.* *Mark* 3:1, 3; *Luke* 6:8
is betrayed into *h.* *Mark* 14:41
as many have taken in *h.* *Luke* 1:1
being delivered out of the *h.* 74
the *h.* of him that betrayeth. 22:21
escaped out of their *h.* *John* 10:39
dead came forth, bound *h.* 11:44
beckoning to them with *h.* *Acts* 12:17
because I am not the *h.* *1 Cor* 12:15
eye cannot say to the *h.* I have. 21
ordained by angels in the *h.* *Gal* 3:19
take little book open in *h.* *Rev* 10:8
having a golden cup in her *h.* 17:4
blood of his servants at her *h.* 19:2

at **hand**, *or at the* **hand**

at the h. of every beast, *at the h.* of man, *at the h.* of man's. *Gen* 9:5
days of mourning for my father are *at h.* 27:41
field Jacob bought *at h.* of. 33:19
year of release is *at h.* *Deut* 15:9
day of their calamity is *at h.* 32:35
I have here *at h.* fourth. *1 Sam* 9:8
Lord require it *at h.* of. 20:16
avenge blood *at the h.* of. *2 Ki* 9:7
was *at the* king's *h.* in. *Neh* 11:24
day of Lord is *at h.* *Isa* 13:6 *Joel* 1:15; *Zeph* 1:7
am I a God *at h.* and? *Jer* 23:23
the days are *at h.* and. *Ezek* 12:23
I require *at* watchman's *h.* 33:6
fruit, for they are *at h.* to. 36:8
cometh, it is nigh *at h.* *Joel* 2:1
kingdom of heaven is *at h.* *Mat* 3:2; 4:17; 10:7
my time is *at h.* 26:18
the hour is *at h.* 45
he is *at h.* that doth. 46; *Mark* 14:42
kingdom of God is *at h.* *Mark* 1:15 *Luke* 21:31
summer is now nigh *at h.* *Luke* 21:30
and the Jews' passover was *at h.* *John* 2:13; 11:55
feast of tabernacles was *at h.* 7:2
sepulchre was nigh *at h.* 19:42
spent, the day is *at h.* *Rom* 13:12
be known, Lord is *at h.* *Phil* 4:5
the day of Christ is *at h.* *2 Thes* 2:2*
my departure is *at h.* *2 Tim* 4:6*
end of all things is *at h.* *1 Pet* 4:7
for time is *at h.* *Rev* 1:3; 22:10

by the **hand**

send *by h.* of him whom. *Ex* 4:13
of tabernacle counted *by h.* 38:21
Lord commanded *by h.* *Lev* 8:36 10:11; 26:46; *Num* 4:37, 45, 49 9:23; 10:13; 15:23; 16:40; 27:23 36:13; *Josh* 14:2; 20:2; 21:2, 8 22:9; *Judg* 3:4; *1 Ki* 8:53, 56 *2 Chr* 33:8; 35:6; *Neh* 9:14 *Ps* 77:20
send him away *by the h.* *Lev* 16:21
by the h. of avenger of. *Josh* 20:9
lad that held *by the h.* *Judg* 16:26
David fall *by the h. of.* *1 Sam* 18:25
one day perish *by the h.* of. 27:1
by the h. of my servant. *2 Sam* 3:18
comfort him *by h.* of servants. 10:2
letter, sent it *by h.* of Uriah. 11:14
sent *by the h.* of Nathan the. 12:25
these fell *by the h.* of David. 21:22 *1 Chr* 20:8
Solomon sent *by the h.* *1 Ki* 2:25
by the h. of his servant. *1 Ki* 14:18
by the h. of Jehu came. 16:7
spake *by the h.* of Jonah. *2 Ki* 14:25
by the h. of Jeroboam. 27
spake *by h.* of Ahijah. *2 Chr* 10:15
not pour out wrath *by the h.* 12:7
out vessels *by the h.* of. *Ezra* 1:8
weighed *by the h.* of. 8:33
sendeth a message *by h.* *Pr* 26:6
taketh her *by the h.* *Isa* 51:18
send yokes *by the h.* of. *Jer* 27:3
in the day I took them *by the h.* 31:32 *Heb* 8:9
on Edom *by h.* of Israel. *Ezek* 25:14
lay the land waste *by h.* of. 30:12
took her *by the h.* *Mat* 9:25 *Mark* 1:31; 5:41; *Luke* 8:54
took the blind man *by h.* *Mark* 8:23
that was possessed *by the h.* 9:27
to be a deliverer *by h.* *Acts* 7:35
they led him *by the h.* 9:8
some to lead him *by the h.* 13:11
the salutation *by the h.* *Col* 4:18

see **Chaldeans, enemy**

hand joined with *enemies.*

may save us out of the *h.* of our *e.* *1 Sam* 4:3; 12:10; *2 Sam* 3:18
deliver you out of *h.* of *e.* *1 Sam* 12:11; *2 Ki* 17:39
saved us out of the *h.* of our *e.* *2 Sam* 19:9
into the *h.* of their *e.* *2 Ki* 21:14 *2 Chr* 25:20; *Neh* 9:27
them in *h.* of their *e.* *Neh* 9:28
me from *h.* of mine *e.* *Ps* 31:15
this city into *h.* of their *e.* *Jer* 20:5 21:7; 34:20, 21; *Ezek* 39:23
give Pharaoh into *h.* of his *e.* 44:30
thee from the *h.* of thy *e.* *Mi* 4:10
out of the *h.* of our *e.* *Luke* 1:74

from the **hand**

deliver me *from h.* of my. *Gen* 32:11
redeemed you *from the h.* *Deut* 7:8
delivered us *from h.* of. *Judg* 8:22
my reproach *from h.* of. *1 Sam* 25:39
saveth the poor *from the h.* *Job* 5:15
redeem me *from the h.* of the. 6:23
deliver his soul *from the h.* *Ps* 89:48
from the h. of him that hated, and redeemed them *from h.* 106:10
me *from h.* of strange. 144:7, 11
thyself as a roe *from h.* of. *Pr* 6:5
poor *from h.* of evil. *Jer* 20:13
from h. of him that was. 31:11
be saved *from the h.* *Luke* 1:71

hand *of God*

h. of God was heavy. *1 Sam* 5:11
h. of God was to give. *2 Chr* 30:12
according to the good *h. of God.* *Ezra* 7:9; *Neh* 2:8
by good *h. of God* upon us. 8:18
h. of God is upon all them for. 22
the *h. of God* is upon us. 31
told them of *h. of God.* *Neh* 2:18
good at the *h. of God?* *Job* 2:10
pity on me, *h. of God* hath. 19:21
teach you by the *h. of God.* 27:11
it was from the *h. of God.* *Eccl* 2:24
works are in the *h. of God.* 9:1
diadem in *h. of* thy *God.* *Isa* 62:3
heaven, and sat on right *h. of God.* *Mark* 16:19; *Rom* 8:34; *Col* 3:1 *Heb* 10:12; *1 Pet* 3:22
by the right *h. of God.* *Acts* 2:33
standing on right *h. of G.* 7:55, 56
under the *h. of God.* *1 Pet* 5:6

his **hand**

lest he put forth *his h.* *Gen* 3:22
his h. will be against every. 16:12
men laid hold on *his h.* 19:16
of his master were in *his h.* 24:10
that which came to *his h.* 32:13*
that he did prosper in *his h.* 39:3
Pharaoh took ring off *his h.* 41:42
his h., and caught it and it became a rod in *his h.* *Ex* 4:4
when he took it out, *his h.* was. 6
took the rod of God in *his h.* 20
out *his h.* over the waters. 8:6, 17
Moses stretched forth *his h.* 10:22
held up *his h.* let down *his h.* 17:11
God delivered him into *his h.* 21:13

if found in *his h.* *Ex* 21:16
he die under *his h.* 20
theft be certainly found in *his h.* 22:4
he hath put *his h.* to goods. 8, 11
on the nobles he laid not *his h.* 24:11
testimony were in *his h.* 32:15; 34:4
shall put *his h.* on head. *Lev* 1:4
priest shall have in *his h.* *Num* 5:18
beside that that *his h.* shall. 6:21*
all his land out of *his h.* 21:26
his sword drawn in *his h.* 22:23, 31
1 Chr 21:16
took a javelin in *his h.* *Num* 25:7
his h. fetcheth a stroke. *Deut* 19:5
man with his sword drawn in *his h.*
Josh 5:13
Joshua drew not *his h.* back. 8:26
deliver the slayer up into *his h.* 20:5
end of the staff in *his h.* *Judg* 6:21
into *his h.* hath God delivered. 7:14
his h. is not removed. *1 Sam* 6:3
it is not *his h.* that smote us. 9
no man put *his h.* to his. 14:26
Jonathan put *his h.* to his. 27
he shall play with *his h.* 16:16
harp and played with *his h.* 23; 18:10
staff and his sling in *his h.* 17:40
head of the Philistine in *his h.* 57
he put his life in *his h.* and. 19:5
strengthened *his h.* in God. 23:16
Uzzah put *his h.* to ark. *2 Sam* 6:6
1 Chr 13:10
and hath with *his h.* *1 Ki* 8:15
whole kingdom out of *his h.* 11:34
his h. which he put forth. 13:4
strike *his h.* over place. *2 Ki* 5:11
he gave *his h.* took him up. 10:15
every man with his weapons in *his h.*
11:8, 11; *2 Chr* 23:7
was confirmed in *his h.* *2 Ki* 14:5
his h. might be with him to. 15:19
man lean, it will go into *his h.* 18:21
save us out of *his h.* 19:19
understand by *his h.* *1 Chr* 28:19
had a censer in *his h.* *2 Chr* 26:19
he gave them all into *his h.* 36:17
with open letter in *his h.* *Neh* 6:5
he would let loose *his h.* *Job* 6:9
darkness is ready at *his h.* 15:23
he stretcheth out *his h.* against. 25
his h. hath formed the. 26:13
would fain flee out of *his h.* 27:22
he putteth forth *his h.* upon. 28:9
upholdeth him with *his h.* *Ps* 37:24
will not leave him in *his h.* 33
they remembered not *his h.* 78:42
I will set *his h.* also in sea. 89:25
in *his h.* are the deep places. 95:4
sheep of *his h.* To-day, if ye will. 7
therefore he lifted up *his h.* 106:26
the mower filleth not *his h.* 129:7
a slothful man hideth *his h.* *Pr* 19:24
26:15
and nothing is in his *h.* *Eccl* 5:14
he may carry away in *his h.* 15
beloved put in *his h.* *S of S* 5:4
his h. is stretched out still. *Isa* 5:25
9:12, 17, 21; 10:4; 14:27
shall shake *his h.* against. *Isa* 10:32
Lord shall set *his h.* again. 11:11
shake *his h.* over the river. 15
thy government into *his h.* 22:21
while it is yet in *his h.* he. 28:4
Lord shall stretch out *his h.* 31:3
Lord, save us from *his h.* 37:20
waters in hollow of *his h.* 40:12
shall subscribe with *his h.* to. 44:5
in the shadow of *his h.* hath. 49:2
of Lord shall prosper in *his h.* 53:10
keepeth *his h.* from doing. 56:2
consumed them by *his h.* *Jer* 27:8
my transgression bound by *his h.*
Lam 1:14
he hath not withdrawn *his h.* 2:8
he turneth *his h.* against me. 3:3
with his censer in *his h.* *Ezek* 8:11
his destroying weapon in *his h.* 9:1
lo, he had given *his h.* 17:18
the sword to fall out of *his h.* 30:22
I will put my sword in *his h.* 24
according as *his h.* shall. 46:7*
none can stay *his h.* or. *Dan* 4:35
could deliver out of *his h.* 8:4, 7
cause craft to prosper in *his h.* 25
multitude be given into *his h.*
Dan 11:11
but these shall escape out of *his h.* 41
he stretched out *his h.* *Hos* 7:5
balances of deceit are in *his h.* 12:7
horns coming out of *his h.* *Hab* 3:4
hiss, and wag *his h.* *Zeph* 2:15
man with staff in *his h.* *Zech* 8:4
his h. rise up against hand. 14:13
whose fan is in *his h.* *Mat* 3:12
Luke 3:17
he that dippeth *his h.* *Mat* 26:23
and *his h.* was restored whole.
Mark 3:5; *Luke* 6:10
beseech him to put *his h.* *Mark* 7:32
man having put *his h.* to. *Luke* 9:62
a ring on *his h.*, and shoes. 15:22
all things into *his h.* *John* 3:35
him with the palm of *his h.* 18:22
how God by *his h.* *Acts* 7:25
a viper fastened on *his h.* 28:3
hang on *his h.* 4
pair of balances in *his h.* *Rev* 6:5
and he had in *his h.* a little. 10:2
in his forehead, or in *his h.* 14:9
crown, and in *his h.* sharp sickle. 14
with a great chain in *his h.* 20:1

hand *of the Lord*, or *Lord's* **hand**

the *h. of the Lord* is upon. *Ex* 9:3
had died by *h. of the Lord.* 16:3
is *Lord's h.* waxed? *Num* 11:23
h. of the Lord was against them to destroy. *Deut* 2:15
know that *h. of Lord* is. *Josh* 4:24
Israel out of *h. of the Lord.* 22:31
the *h. of the Lord* was against them for evil. *Judg* 2:15
h. of the Lord is gone. *Ruth* 1:13
h. of Lord was heavy. *1 Sam* 5:6
h. of Lord was against the city. 9
the *h. of the Lord* was against the Philistines. 7:13
then shall *h. of the Lord* be. 12:15
let us now fall into *h. of the Lord.*
2 Sam 24:14; *1 Chr* 21:13
h. of the Lord was on. *1 Ki* 18:46
h. of the Lord came upon. *2 Ki* 3:15
according to *h. of Lord.* *Ezra* 7:6
h. of Lord hath wrought this.
Job 12:9; *Isa* 40:20
in *h. of the Lord* there. *Ps* 75:8
heart is in *h. of the Lord.* *Pr* 21:1
shaking of the *h. of Lord.* *Isa* 19:16
mountain shall *h. of the Lord.* 25:10
received *of the Lord's h.* 40:2
hast drunk at *h. of Lord* cup. 51:17
Lord's h. is not shortened. 59:1
a crown of glory in *h. of Lord.* 62:3
h. of Lord shall be known. 66:14
the cup at the *Lord's h.* *Jer* 25:17
been a golden cup in *Lord's h.* 51:7
h. of the Lord was there. *Ezek* 1:3
the *h. of the L.* was upon me. 3:14
22; 8:1; 37:1
h. of the Lord was on me. 33:22
selfsame day the *h. of Lord.* 40:1
and the *h. of the Lord* was with him.
Luke 1:66; *Acts* 11:21
behold, the *h. of the Lord* is.
Acts 13:11

see lay, *or* **laid**

left **hand**

if thou wilt take *left h.* I. *Gen* 13:9
Hobah which is on *left h.* of. 14:15
to the right *h.* or to the *left.* 24:49
his right hand toward Israel's *left h.* and Manasseh in his *left h.* 48:13
Israel laid his *left h.* upon. 14
wall on right *h.* and *left.* *Ex* 14:22
oil into his own *left h.* *Lev* 14:15, 27
we will not turn to the right *h.* nor to the *left.* *Num* 20:17; *Deut* 2:27
5:32; 17:11, 20; 28:14
either to right *h.* or *left.* *Num* 22:26
from it to right *h.* or to *left.* *Josh* 1:7
23:6; *1 Sam* 6:12; *Pr* 4:27
Ehud put forth *left h.* *Judg* 3:21
held lamps in their *left h.* 7:20
hold of other pillar with *left h.* 16:29
he turned not to *left h.* *2 Sam* 2:19
none can turn to right *h.* or to *left.*
14:19
were on right *h.* and *left.* 16:6
host of heaven on his *left h.*
1 Ki 22:19; *2 Chr* 18:18
Josiah turned not to the right *h.* or *left.* *2 Ki* 22:2
which were on a man's *left h.* 23:8
Merari stood on *left h.* *1 Chr* 6:44
use both right *h.* and *left* in. 12:2
name of that on *left h.* *2 Chr* 3:17
and he put five on the *left h.* 4:6
on the right, five on the *left h.* 7
on pulpit, on his *left h.* *Neh* 8:4
on *left h.* he doth work. *Job* 23:9
and in her *left h.* riches. *Pr* 3:16
fool's heart is at his *left h.* *Eccl* 10:2
his *left h.* is under my head.
S of S 2:6; 8:3
he shall eat on *left h.* and. *Isa* 9:20
when ye turn to the *left h.* 30:21
forth on the right *h.* and *left.* 54:3
dwell at thy *left h.* *Ezek* 16:46
on the right *h.* or on the *left.* 21:16
smite thy bow out of thy *left h.* 39:3
he held up his *left h.* to. *Dan* 12:7
between right *h.* and *left.* *Jonah* 4:11
all people on right *h.* and *left.*
Zech 12:6
let not *left h.* know what. *Mat* 6:3
one on right *h.* other on *left.* 20:21
Mark 10:37
to sit on right *h.* and *left* not mine.
Mat 20:23; *Mark* 10:40
right *h.*, goats on *left.* *Mat* 25:33
shall say to them on *left h.* 41
crucified on right *h.* other on *left.*
27:38; *Mark* 15:27; *Luke* 23:33
Cyprus on the *left h.* *Acts* 21:3
righteousness on right *h.* and *left.*
2 Cor 6:7

see lift *hand* or *hands*

mighty **hand**

go, no not with *mighty h.* *Ex* 3:19
forth with *mighty h.* 32:11
servant thy *mighty h.* *Deut* 3:24
him a nation by a *mighty h.* 4:34
God brought thee out of Egypt through a *mighty h.* 5:15; 6:21
7:8, 19; 9:26; 11:2
26:8; 34:12
come for thy *mighty h.* *2 Chr* 6:32
a *mighty h.* will I rule. *Ezek* 20:33
bring you out with a *mighty h.* 34
you out of Egypt with *mighty h.*
Dan 9:15
under *mighty h.* of God. *1 Pet* 5:6

mine and *my* **hand**

I have lifted up *mine h.* *Gen* 14:22
lambs shalt thou take of *my h.* 21:30
it is in power of *my h.* to do. 31:29
I bear loss, of *my h.* didst thou. 39
receive my present at *my h.* 33:10
deliver him into *my h.* I will. 42:37
I will be surety, of *my h.* shalt. 43:9
with rod that is in *mine h.* *Ex* 7:17
my h. shall destroy them. 15:9
rod in *mine h.* 17:9
will cover thee with *mine h.* 33:22
I will take away *mine h.* and thou. 23
this people into *my h.* *Num* 21:2
there were a sword in *mine h.* 22:29
might of *my h.* hath. *Deut* 8:17
the two tables in *mine h.* 10:3
neither any that can deliver out of *my h.* 32:39; *Isa* 43:13
I lift up *my h.* to heaven. *Deut* 32:40
and if *mine h.* take hold on. 41
save Israel by *my h.* *Judg* 6:36, 37
lest vaunt, saying, *mine* own *h.* 7:2
delivered Zeba into *mine h.* 8:7
this people were under *my h.* 9:29
Lord delivered them into *my h.* 12:3
silver unto Lord from *my h.* 17:3
not found aught in *my h.* *1 Sam* 12:5
this day into *mine h.* 17:46
let not *mine h.* be upon him. 18:17
common bread under *mine h.* 21:4
delivered him into *mine h.* 23:7
stretch *mine h.* against Lord's. 24:6
see the skirt in *my h.*, no transgression in *mine h.* 11
mine h. shall not be upon. 12, 13
into *mine h.* to day. 24:10; 26:23
what evil is in *mine h.*? 26:18
I have put my life in *my h.* 28:21

my h. shall be with. 2 Sam 3:12
deliver Philistines into mine h.? 5:19; 1 Chr 14:10
forth mine h. against Absalom. 2 Sam 18:12
that my h. may be. 1 Ki 13:6
leaneth on my h. in. 2 Ki 5:18
Samaria out of my h.? 18:34
out of mine h., that Lord should deliver Jerusalem out of mine h.? 35
of land into my h. 1 Chr 22:18
you out of my h.? 2 Chr 32:15, 17
put my life into mine h.? Job 13:14
bow was renewed in my h. 29:20
rejoiced because mine h. had. 31:25
or my mouth hath kissed my h. 27
neither shall my h. be heavy. 33:7*
turned my h. against. Ps 81:14
with whom my h. shall be. 89:21
soul is continually in my h. 119:109
stretched out my h. Pr 1:24
I will turn my h. upon. Isa 1:25
as my h. hath found the. 10:10
by the strength of my h. I have. 13
my h. hath found as a nest the. 14
Samaria out of my h.? 36:19
deliver Jerusalem out of my h. 20
mine h. also hath laid. 48:13
is my h. shortened at all? 50:2
this ye have of my h. 11
in the shadow of mine h. 51:16
mine h. made. 66:2; Acts 7:50
I will stretch out my h. Jer 6:12
15:6; 51:25
cause them to know mine h. 16:21
so are ye in mine h. O house. 18:6
wine cup of this fury at my h. 25:15
will I stretch out my h. Ezek 6:14
digged through wall with my h. 12:7
mine h. shall be upon prophets. 13:9
mine h., saying I am the Lord. 20:5, 6
23, 28, 42; 36:7; 44:12; 47:14
withdrew my h. and wrought. 20:22
I have smitten mine h. at thy. 22:13
they shall be one in mine h. 37:19
deliver her out of mine h. Hos 2:10
I will turn mine h. Amos 1:8
into hell, thence shall mine h. 9:2
I will shake mine h. Zech 2:9
I will turn mine h. upon the. 13:7
pluck them out of my h. John 10:28
pluck them out of my Father's h. 29
except I shall thrust my h. 20:25
salutation of me Paul with mine own h. 1 Cor 16:21; 2 Thes 3:17
I have written with my h. Gal 6:11
Philem 19

our hand

let not our h. be on him. Gen 37:27
have brought it again in our h. 43:21
say, Our h. is high. Deut 32:27
Samson into our h. Judg 16:23
Lord hath delivered them into our h. 1 Sam 14:10; 30:23
thou die not by our h. Jer 11:21
made ready to our h. 2 Cor 10:16

out of hand, or out of the hand

I took out of the h. of. Gen 48:22
Egyptian delivered us out of h. of. Ex 2:19
out of h. of Egyptians. 3:8; 14:30
offering out of woman's h. Num 5:25
kill me, I pray thee, out of h. 11:15
deliver him out of h. of the. 35:25
out of the h. of Israel. Josh 9:26
judges which delivered them out of the h. Judg 2:16
delivered you out of the h. 6:9
out of the h. of the Philistines. 13:5
out of h. of these gods? 1 Sam 4:8
me out of h. of this Philistine. 17:37
I delivered thee out of h. of Saul. 2 Sam 12:7; 22:1
spear out of the Egyptian's h. 23:21
kingdom out of h. of. 1 Ki 11:12, 31
we take it not out of h. of. 22:3
took again out of h. of. 2 Ki 13:25
out of h. of the king of Assyria. 20:6
Isa 38:6
deliver me out of h. of. Ps 71:4
rid them out of the h. of. 82:4
he delivereth them out of h. 97:10
out of h. of the wicked. Jer 15:21
spoiled out of h. of. Jer 21:12; 22:3
not escape out of h. 32:4; 38:18, 23
deliver us out of their h. Lam 5:8
out of their h. I will not. Zech 11:6
escaped out of their h. John 10:39
out of the h. of Herod. Acts 12:11
ascended before God out of angel's h. Rev 8:4; 10:10

right hand

right h. on Ephraim's. Gen 48:14, 18
thy right h. O Lord, is. Ex 15:6
the thumb of their right h. 29:20
Lev 8:23, 24; 14:14, 17, 25, 28
from his right h. went. Deut 33:2
right h. to workman's. Judg 5:26
Amasa with right h. 2 Sam 20:9
on Solomon's right h. 1 Ki 2:19
on right h. of mount. 2 Ki 23:13
himself on the right h. Job 23:9
upon my right h. rise the. 30:12
that thine own right h. can. 40:14
he is at my right h. I. Ps 16:8
at thy right h. are pleasures for. 11
savest by thy right h. them. 17:7
thy right h. hath holden me. 18:35
saving strength of his right h. 20:6
thy right h. shall find out. 21:8
their right h. is full of bribes. 26:10
but thy right h. and thy arm. 44:3
thy right h. shall teach thee. 45:4
on thy right h. did stand queen. 9
thy right h. is full of. 48:10
save with thy right h. and. 60:5
my soul followeth, thy right h. 63:8
holden me by my right h. 73:23
withdrawest thou thy right h.? 74:11
remember years of the right h. 77:10
mountain which his right h. 78:54
the vineyard which thy right h. 80:15
upon the man of thy right h. 17
thy hand, high is thy right h. 89:13
I will also set his right h. in the. 25
thou hast set up the right h. of his. 42
shall fall at thy right h. 91:7
his right h. hath gotten him. 98:1
save with thy right h. and. 108:6
let Satan stand at his right h. 109:6
he shall stand at the right h. of. 31
sit thou at my right h. until I. 110:1
Luke 20:42; Acts 2:34; Heb 1:13
the Lord at thy right h. Ps 110:5
the right h. of the Lord. 118:15
right h. of the Lord is exalted. 16
thy shade upon thy right h. 121:5
I forget, let my right h. forget. 137:5
and thy right h. shall save. 138:7
even there thy right h. shall. 139:10
looked on my right h., no man. 142:4
right h. is a right h. of falsehood. 144:8, 11
of days is in her right h. Pr 3:16
the ointment of his right h. 27:16
heart is at his right h. Eccl 10:2
and his right h. doth. S of S 2:6
his right h. should embrace me. 8:3
thee with right h. of. Isa 41:10
Lord thy God will hold thy right h. 13
is there not a lie in my right h.? 44:20
to Cyrus whose right h. I have. 45:1
my right h. hath spanned the. 48:13
hath sworn by his right h. 62:8
that led them by the right h. 63:12
the signet on my right h. Jer 22:24
drawn back his right h. Lam 2:3
he stood with his right h. as an. 4
at right h. divination. Ezek 21:22
cup of Lord's right h. Hab 2:16
standing at his right h. Zech 3:1
if thy right h. offend thee. Mat 5:30
not left know what thy right h. 6:3
Son of man sitting on the right h. of power. Mark 14:62; Luke 22:69
to heaven, sat on right h. of God. Mark 16:19; Heb 1:3; 8:1
10:12; 12:2; 1 Pet 3:22
man whose right h. was. Luke 6:6
he is on my right h. I. Acts 2:25
the right h. of God exalted. 33; 5:31
he took him by the right h. and. 3:7
standing on right h. of God. 7:55, 56
is even at the right h. Rom 8:34
right h. in heavenly. Eph 1:20
sitteth on the right h. of. Col 3:1
in his right h. seven stars. Rev 1:16
20; 2:1
laid right h. upon me, saying. 1:17
I saw in his right h. a book. 5:1, 7
receive mark in their right h. 13:16
see left hand

to stretch forth or out hand

Abraham stretched forth his h. to slay. Gen 22:10
I will stretch out my h. on Egypt. Ex 3:20; 7:5; 9:15
stretch out thy h. over the sea. 14:16; 26:7, 19
Moses stretched out his h. 14:21, 27
who can stretch forth hand against the Lord's anointed? 1 Sam 26:9
not afraid to stretch forth thy h. 2 Sam 1:14
stretch forth thy hand. Ps 138:7
she stretcheth out her h. Pr 31:20
I will stretch out my h. Ezek 14:9
will I stretch out mine h. upon. 13
I will stretch out mine h. upon. 25:7
I will also stretch out mine h. 13
I will stretch out mine h. on the. 16
I will stretch out mine h. against. 35:3
shall stretch forth his h. Dan 11:42
stretch out mine h. upon Judah. Zeph 1:4
stretch out his h. against Assyria. 2:13
see strong

thine or thy hand

blood from thy h. Gen 4:11
thy maid is in thy h., do to. 16:6
he said, lay not thine h. upon. 22:12
thy h. under my thigh. 24:2; 47:29
thy h. shall be in the neck. 49:8
what is that in thine h.? Ex 4:2
this rod in thine h. 17; 7:15; 17:5
stretch forth thine h. over. 8:5; 9:22
10:12, 21; Mat 12:13; Mark 3:5
it shall be for a sign on thine h. Ex 13:9, 16; Deut 6:8
put not thine h. with. Ex 23:1
delivered Og into thy h. Num 21:34
in works of thy h. Deut 2:7; 14:29
15:10; 23:20; 28:8, 12, 20
I have given into thy h. 2:24
Og and his people into thy h. 3:2
thy h. shall be first on him. 13:9
nought of cursed thing to thine h. 17
bind up money in thine h. 14:25
nor shut thine h. from thy. 15:7
thou shalt open thine h. wide to. 8
pluck the ears with thine h. 23:25
be no might in thine h. 28:32
in every work of thine h. 30:9
all the saints are in thy h. 33:3
I have given into thine h. Josh 6:2
for I will give Ai into thine h. 8:18
behold, we are in thine h. to. 9:25
slack not thy h. from thy. 10:6
kings of Canaan into thy h. 8
Sisera into thine h. Judg 4:7
the Midianites into thine h. 7:7
and Zalmunna in thine h.? 8:15
hold thy peace, lay thine h. 18:19
Benjamin into thine h. 20:28
priest, withdraw thy h. 1 Sam 14:19
what is under thine h.? give. 21:3
deliver Philistines into thine h. 23:4; 2 Sam 5:19
I may eat of thine h. 2 Sam 13:10
stay thine h. 24:16; 1 Chr 21:15
let thine h., I pray thee, be against me. 2 Sam 24:17; 1 Chr 21:17
hast fulfilled it with thine h. 1 Ki 8:24; 2 Chr 6:15
of bread in thine h. 2 Ki 17:11
Syrians into thine h. 20:13, 28
hast let go out of thy h. a man. 42
take my staff in thine h. 2 Ki 4:29
take a present in thine h. 8:8
take this box of oil in thine h. 9:1
give me thine h. and he gave. 10:15
he said, put thine h. upon. 13:16
and that thine h. might. 1 Chr 4:10
in thine h. is power and might. 29:12
for house cometh of thine h. 16
in thine h. is there not? 2 Chr 20:6
law which is in thine h. Ezra 7:14

wisdom that is in *thine h. Ezra* 7:25
but put forth *thine h.* and touch.
Job 1:11; 2:5
himself put not forth *thine h.* 1:12
behold, he is in *thine h.* but. 2:6
can deliver out of *thine h.* 10:7
if iniquity be in *thine h.* put. 11:14
withdraw *thine h.* far from. 13:21
what receiveth he of *thine h.*? 35:7
O God, lift up *thine h.* *Ps* 10:12
spite, to requite it with *thy h.* 14
from men which are *thy h.* 17:14
thine h. shall find out all. 21:8
into *thine h.* I commit my. 31:5
my times are in *thy h.*: deliver. 15
for day and night *thy h.* was. 32:4
thy h. presseth me. 38:2
by blow of *thine h.* 39:10
why withdrawest thou *thy h.*? 74:11
thy h. be upon the man of *thy* right *h.* 80:17
they are cut off from *thy h.* 88:5
thou openest *thy h.* 104:28; 145:16
know that this is *thy h.* 109:27
let *thine h.* help me. 119:173
laid *thine h.* on me. 139:5
even there shall *thy h.* lead. 10
send *thine h.* from above. 144:7
is in power of *thine h.* *Pr* 3:27
if thou hast stricken *thy h.* 6:1
if thought evil, lay *thy h.* upon. 30:32
withdraw not *thine h.* *Eccl* 7:18
whatsoever *thy h.* findeth to do. 9:10
evening withhold not *thine h.* 11:6
ruin be under *thy h.* *Isa* 3:6
when *thy h.* is lifted up, they. 26:11
I the Lord will hold *thine h.* 42:6
my inheritance into *thine h.* 47:6
I have taken out of *thy h.* cup. 51:22
found the life of *thine h.* 57:10
we are the work of *thy h.* 64:8
thine h. as a grape. *Jer* 6:9
I sat alone because of *thy h.* 15:17
to take the cup at *thine h.* 25:28
take in *thy h.* the roll. 36:14
chains which were upon *thine h.* 40:4
his blood will I require at *thine h.*
Ezek 3:18, 20; 33:8
smite with *thine h.* and. 6:11
and fill *thine h.* with coals. 10:2
I will give her cup into *thine h.* 23:31
took hold of thee by *thy h.* 29:7
shall become one in *thine h.* 37:17
to turn *thine h.* upon the. 38:12
he given into *thine h.* *Dan* 2:38
deliver us out of *thine h.* 3:17
thine h. shall he lift up on. *Mi* 5:9
cut off witchcrafts out of *thine h.* 12
if *thy h.* or foot offend thee.
Mat 18:8; *Mark* 9:43
reach *thy h.* and thrust. *John* 20:27
thine h. and counsel. *Acts* 4:28
stretching forth *thine h.* to heal. 30

your hand

your h. are they delivered. *Gen* 9:2
take double money in *your h.* 43:12
your feet, staff in *your h.* *Ex* 12:11
of the land into *your h.* 23:31
rejoice in all ye put *your h.* to.
Deut 12:7
deliver it into *your h.* *Josh* 8:7, 20
delivered them into *your h.* 10:19
Amorites into *your h.* 24:8, 11
Moabites into *your h.* *Judg* 3:28
Midianites into *your h.* 7:15
his blood of *your h.*? *2 Sam* 4:11
be delivered into *your h. 2 Chr* 18:14
hath delivered them into *your h.* 28:9
required this at *your h.*? *Isa* 1:12
I am in *your h.*: do with. *Jer* 26:14
said, behold, he is in *your h.* 38:5
and fulfilled with *your h.* 44:25
be no more in *your h.* *Ezek* 13:21
deliver my people out of *your h.* 23
an offering at *your h.* *Mal* 1:10
should I accept this of *your h.*? 13
it with good will at *your h.* 2:13

handbreadth

a border of an *h.* round about.
Ex 25:25; 37:12
a molten sea *h.* thick. *1 Ki* 7:26
2 Chr 4:5
made my days as an *h.* *Ps* 39:5

six cubits long, and an *h. Ezek* 40:5
the cubit is a cubit and an *h.* 43:13

hand broad

hooks an *h. broad.* *Ezek* 40:43

handful

take thereout an *h.* of flour. *Lev* 2:2
5:12; 6:15; 9:17*; *Num* 5:26
an *h.* of meal in a barrel. *1 Ki* 17:12
there shall be an *h.* of. *Ps* 72:16*
better is *h.* with quietness. *Eccl* 4:6
and as the *h.* after the. *Jer* 9:22

handfuls

earth brought forth by *h. Gen* 41:47
take to you *h.* of ashes of. *Ex* 9:8
fall also some *h.* of. *Ruth* 2:16*
if dust of Samaria shall suffice for *h.*
1 Ki 20:10
ye pollute me for *h.* of? *Ezek* 13:19

handkerchiefs

were brought unto sick *h. Acts* 19:12

handle

father of such as *h.* the. *Gen* 4:21
they that *h.* the pen of. *Judg* 5:14
men that could *h.* shield. *1 Chr* 12:8
2 Chr 25:5
hands, but they *h.* not. *Ps* 115:7
they that *h.* the law knew. *Jer* 2:8
Lybians that *h.* the shield. 46:9
all that *h.* the oar, and. *Ezek* 27:29
h. me and see. *Luke* 24:39
taste not, *h.* not. *Col* 2:21

handled

that it may be *h.* *Ezek* 21:11
him away shamefully *h.* *Mark* 12:4
our hands have *h.* of the. *1 John* 1:1

handleth

he that *h.* matter wisely. *Pr* 16:20
cut off him that *h.* sickle. *Jer* 50:16
shall he stand that *h.* *Amos* 2:15

handling

all of them *h.* swords. *Ezek* 38:4
not *h.* the word of God. *2 Cor* 4:2

handmaid

Sarai had an *h.* whose. *Gen* 16:1
Zilpah to be Leah's *h.* 29:24; 35:26
to be Rachel's *h.* 29:29; 30:4; 35:25
that son of thy *h.* may. *Ex* 23:12
wine for me and thy *h.* *Judg* 19:19
spoken friendly to thy *h.* *Ruth* 2:13
answered, I am Ruth thine *h.* 3:9
on affliction of thine *h.* *1 Sam* 1:11
count not thine *h.* for a daughter. 16
Hannah said, let thy *h.* find. 18*
let thy *h.* speak. 25:24
remember thy *h.* 31
let thy *h.* be a servant to wash. 41
thy *h.* had two sons. *2 Sam* 14:6
hear the words of thy *h.* 20:17
didst swear to thy *h.*? *1 Ki* 1:13
the Lord thy God to thy *h.* 17
she took my son while thine *h.* 3:20
thy *h.* hath not any thing. *2 Ki* 4:2
man of God, do not lie to thine *h.* 16
save the son of thy *h.* *Ps* 86:16
and the son of thy *h.* 116:16
and an *h.* that is heir to. *Pr* 30:23
caused every man his *h.* *Jer* 34:16
behold the *h.* of the. *Luke* 1:38

handmaiden

the low estate of his *h.* *Luke* 1:48

handmaids

children to the two *h.* *Gen* 33:1
he put the *h.* and their children. 2
not like to one of thy *h.* *Ruth* 2:13
himself in eyes of *h.* *2 Sam* 6:20
the *h.* to return for *h.* *Jer* 34:11
on the *h.* will I pour my spirit.
Joel 2:29; *Acts* 2:18

hands

thyself under her *h.* *Gen* 16:9
the *h.* are the *h.* of Esau. 27:22
h. were made strong by *h.* of. 49:24
but Moses' *h.* were. *Ex* 17:12
thou shalt put all in the *h.* of. 29:24
h. and on his son's *h.* *Lev* 8:27
of memorial in her *h.* *Num* 5:18
and shall put them on the *h.* 6:19
the work of men's *h.* *Deut* 4:28
27:15; *2 Ki* 19:18; *2 Chr* 32:19

of the covenant were in my two *h.*
Deut 9:15
I cast them out of my two *h.* 17
the *h.* of the witnesses shall. 17:7
through the work of your *h.* 31:29
delivered them into *h.* of. *Judg* 2:14
into *h.* of Midianites. 6:13
are *h.* of Zeba and Zalmunna? 8:6, 15
delivered them out of *h.* of enemies.
34; *1 Sam* 14:48
into *h.* of Philistines. *Judg* 10:7
given Laish into your *h.* 18:10
and her *h.* were upon the. 19:27
nor deliver me into *h.* *1 Sam* 30:15
let your *h.* be strong. *2 Sam* 2:7
Zech 8:9, 13
then the *h.* of all with. *2 Sam* 16:21
delivered them into the *h.* of. 21:9
they cannot be taken with *h.* 23:6
into the *h.* of the guard. *1 Ki* 14:27
2 Chr 12:10
poured water on the *h.* *2 Ki* 3:11
skull and the palms of her *h.* 9:35
whom I brought into your *h.* 10:24
Asaph under the *h.* of. *1 Chr* 25:2
under the *h.* of Jeduthun. 3
h. of their father. 6
let not your *h.* be weak. *2 Chr* 15:7
weakened the *h.* of people. *Ezra* 4:4
strengthened the weak *h.* *Job* 4:3
God hath turned me into the *h.* 16:11
who is he that will strike *h.*? 17:3
that hath clean *h.* shall be. 9
he that hath clean *h.* *Ps* 24:4
in whose *h.* is mischief. 26:10
clap your *h.* 47:1
ye weigh the violence of your *h.* 58:2
shall stretch out her *h.* unto. 68:31
idols, the work of men's *h.* 115:4
135:15; *Isa* 37:19
h. but handle not, feet. *Ps* 115:7
lift up your *h.* in sanctuary. 134:2
me, O Lord, from the *h.* of. 140:4
folding of the *h.* to sleep. *Pr* 6:10
24:33
h. that shed innocent blood. 6:17
the recompence of man's *h.* 12:14
plucketh it down with her *h.* 14:1
a man striketh *h.* and. 17:18
one of them that strike *h.* 22:26
spider taketh hold with her *h.* 30:28
worketh willingly with her *h.* 31:13
h. to the spindle, her *h.* hold. 19
yea, she reacheth forth her *h.* to. 20
give her the fruit of her *h.* and. 31
then both *h.* full with. *Eccl* 4:6*
her *h.* are as bands. 7:26
the idleness of *h.* 10:18
the work of the *h.* of a. *S of S* 7:1
forth your *h.* I will hide my eyes from
you; your *h.* are full. *Isa* 1:15
worship work of their own *h.* 2:8
therefore shall all *h.* be faint. 13:7
idols which your own *h.* have. 31:7
strengthen ye the weak *h.* 35:3
thy work say, he hath no *h.* 45:9
h. are defiled with blood. 59:3
that spreadeth her *h.* *Jer* 4:31
a tree, the work of the *h.* of. 10:3
and of the *h.* of the founder, blue. 9
cause them to fall by *h.* that. 19:7
weapons that are in your *h.* 21:4
the *h.* of evildoers, that none return.
23:14; *Ezek* 13:22
not with works of your *h. Jer* 25:6, 7
shall pass under *h.* of him. 33:13
weakeneth *h.* of men of war, *h.* 38:4
upon all the *h.* shall be. 48:37
Zion spreadeth her *h.* *Lam* 1:17
how esteemed as work of *h.* 4:2
that was overthrown, and no *h.* 6
h. of pitiful women have sodden. 10
h. shall be feeble. *Ezek* 7:17; 21:7
was cut out without *h. Dan* 2:34, 45
may do evil with both *h.* *Mi* 7:3
all shall clap the *h.* over. *Nah* 3:19
in all labour of your *h.* *Hag* 2:17
the *h.* of Zerubbabel laid. *Zech* 4:9
to eat with unwashen *h.* *Mat* 15:20
Mark 7:2, 5
betrayed into *h.* of men. *Mat* 17:22
26:45; *Mark* 9:31; *Luke* 9:44
having two *h.* to be cast into fire.
Mat 18:8; *Mark* 9:43

h., another without h. Mark 14:58
ye stretched forth no h. Luke 22:53
must be delivered into the h. 24:7
wicked h. have crucified. Acts 2:23
by h. of the apostles were. 5:12
in temples made with h. 48; 17:24
laying on of the apostles' h. 8:18
elders by the h. of Barnabas. 11:30
is worshipped with men's h. 17:25
gods which are made with h. 19:26
these h. have ministered to. 20:34
shall deliver him into the h. 21:11
house not made with h. 2 Cor 5:1
in flesh made by h. Eph 2:11
circumcision made without h. Col 2:11
work with your own h. 1 Thes 4:11
pray, lifting up holy h. 1 Tim 2:8
of h. of presbytery. 4:14; Heb 6:2
tabernacle not with h. Heb 9:11
into holy place made with h. 24
fearful to fall into the h. of. 10:31
wherefore lift up the h. 12:12
cleanse your h. ye sinners. Jas 4:8

see clap

his hands

his h. were hairy. Gen 27:23
guiding his h. 48:14
Hur stayed up his h. Ex 17:12
cast the tables out of his h. 32:19
his own h. shall bring. Lev 7:30
and hath not rinsed his h. in. 15:11
his h. full of sweet incense. 16:12
Aaron shall lay both his h. on. 21
Balak smote his h. Num 24:10
let his h. be sufficient. Deut 33:7
and accept the work of his h. 11
for Moses had laid his h. 34:9
the deserving of his h. Judg 9:16
both the palms of his h. 1 Sam 5:4
climbed up on his h. and his. 14:13
went and strengthened his h. 23:16
heard, his h. were feeble. 2 Sam 4:1
spread his h. toward heaven. 1 Ki 8:22; 38:54; 2 Chr 6:12, 13, 29
with the work of his h. 1 Ki 16:7
put his h. upon his h. 2 Ki 4:34
in not receiving at his h. 5:20
Elisha put his h. upon the. 13:16
who hath with his h. 2 Chr 6:4
with one of his h. Neh 4:17
blessed the work of his h. Job 1:10
he woundeth, and his h. make. 5:18
and his h. shall restore their. 20:10
all are the works of his h. 34:19
for he clappeth his h. amongst. 37
snared in work of his h. Ps 9:16
not the operation of his h. 28:5
by the skilfulness of his h. 78:72
his h. were delivered from. 81:6
the sea is his, and his h. 95:5
the works of his h. are verity. 111:7
his h. refuse to labour. Pr 21:25
foldeth his h. together. Eccl 4:5
his h. are as gold rings. S of S 5:14
the reward of his h. shall. Isa 3:11
consider the operation of his h. 5:12
to altars, the work of his h. 17:8
his h. in midst of them, as he that swimmeth spreadeth his h. 25:11
that shaketh his h. from. 33:15
every man with his h. on? Jer 30:6
king heard the report, his h. 50:43
the deep lifted up his h. Hab 3:10
his h. shall also finish. Zech 4:9
he should put his h. on them. Mat 19:13; Mark 10:16
washed his h. before the. Mat 27:24
are wrought by his h. Mark 6:2
put his h. on his eyes. 8:23, 25
shewed them his h. and feet. Luke 24:40; John 20:20
and he lifted up his h. Luke 24:50
given all things into his h. John 13:3
except I see in his h. the. 20:25
putting his h. on him. Acts 9:17
Herod stretched forth his h. 12:1
and his chains fell off from his h. 7
wall, and escaped his h. 2 Cor 11:33
working with his h. Eph 4:28

see lay, laid

mine hands, my hands

in innocency of my h. Gen 20:5
seen the labour of my h. Gen 31:42
I will spread abroad my h. Ex 9:29; Ezra 9:5
I put my life in my h. Judg 12:3
according to cleanness of my h. 2 Sam 22:21; Ps 18:20, 24
he teacheth my h. to war. 2 Sam 22:35; Ps 18:34; 144:1
is no wrong in mine h. 1 Chr 12:17
O God, strengthen my h. Neh 6:9
and if I make my h. Job 9:30
any injustice in mine h. 16:17
blot hath cleaved to mine h. 31:7
there be iniquity in my h. Ps 7:3
they pierced my h. and my. 22:16
I will wash mine h. in. 26:6
when I lift up my h. toward. 28:2
I will lift up my h. in thy name. 63:4
in vain, I have washed my h. 73:13
I have stretched out my h. 88:9
my h. will I lift to thy. 119:48
lifting up of my h. as the. 141:2
I stretch forth my h. to thee. 143:6
the works that my h. Eccl 2:11
I rose, and my h. S of S 5:5
Assyria the work of my h. Isa 19:25
he seeth the work of mine h. 29:23
concerning the work of my h. 45:11
even my h. have stretched out. 12
graven thee on palms of my h. 49:16
people also the work of my h. 60:21
I have spread out my h. all. 65:2
I will also smite mine h. Ezek 21:17
you out of my h.? Dan 3:15
set me on the palms of my h. 10:10
behold my h. and my feet. Luke 24:39; John 20:27
but also my h. and head. John 13:9
stretched forth my h. Rom 10:21
by putting on of my h. 2 Tim 1:6

our hands

concerning toil of our h. Gen 5:29
have we brought in our h. 43:22
into our h. Og king of. Deut 3:3
shall say, our h. have not shed. 21:7
delivered into our h. all. Josh 2:24
meat offering at our h. Judg 13:23
into our h. our enemy. 16:24
will give you into our h. 1 Sam 17:47
stretched out our h. to a. Ps 44:20
thou the work of our h. upon. 90:17
fame, our h. wax feeble. Jer 6:24
heart with our h. to God. Lam 3:41
say to work of our h. Hos 14:3
him away out of our h. Acts 24:7
working with our own h. 1 Cor 4:12
our h. have handled. 1 John 1:1

right hands

they gave to me and Barnabas the right h. of fellowship. Gal 2:9

their hands

him out of their h. Gen 37:21, 22
shall put their h. on head. Ex 29:10
shall put their h. on the. 15, 19
shalt receive them of their h. 25 Lev 8:28
Israel shall put their h. Num 8:10
the Levites shall lay their h. 12
fruit of land in their h. Deut 1:25
the elders shall wash their h. 21:6
Midianites into their h. Judg 7:2
me not out of their h. 12:2
they cut off their h. 2 Sam 4:12
they clapped their h. 2 Ki 11:12
me to anger with all the works of their h. 22:17; 2 Chr 34:25
their h. with vessels of. Ezra 1:6
on and prospereth in their h. 5:8
their h. in the work of the. 6:22
they gave their h. that they. 10:19
strengthened their h. for. Neh 2:18
their h. shall be weakened. 6:9
gavest them into their h. 9:24
their h. cannot perform. Job 5:12
strength of their h. profit me. 30:2
after work of their h. Ps 28:4
have not found their h. 76:5
bear thee up in their h. 91:12
forth their h. to iniquity. 125:3
the spoils of their h. Isa 25:11
act of violence is in their h. 59:6
shall enjoy work of their h. 65:22
works of their own h. Jer 1:16
the works of their h. Jer 25:14 Lam 3:64
with works of their h. Jer 32:30
delivered me into their h. Lam 1:14
their h. and wings. Ezek 10:12
blood is in their h. 23:37, 45
violence that is in their h. Jonah 3:8
every work of their h. Hag 2:14
with their h. they should bear thee. Mat 4:6; Luke 4:11
they wash not their h. Mat 15:2
palms of their h. 26:67; Mark 14:65
except they wash their h. Mark 7:3
rubbing them in their h. Luke 6:1
smote him with their h. John 19:3
in the works of their h. Acts 7:41
wonders to be done by their h. 14:3
and palms in their h. Rev 7:9
not of the works of their h. 9:20
received his mark in their h. 20:4

thine or thy hands

sanctuary which thy h. Ex 15:17
bless thee in all works of thine h. Deut 16:15; 24:19
afterward shall thine h. Judg 7:11
thy h. were not bound. 2 Sam 3:34
despise work of thine h.? Job 10:3
thine h. have made and fashioned. 8
desire to work of thine h. 14:15
by pureness of thine h. 22:30
over the works of thy h. Ps 8:6
triumph in the works of thy h. 92:4
heavens are work of thy h. 102:25
thy h. have made me and. 119:73
shalt eat labour of thine h. 128:2
the works of thine own h. 138:8
I muse on the work of thy h. 143:5
destroy work of thine h. Eccl 5:6
and thine h. on thy head. Jer 2:37
lift up thy h. for the life. Lam 2:19
smite thine h. together. Ezek 21:14
can thine h. be strong in the? 22:14
worship work of thine h. Mi 5:13
let not thine h. be slack. Zeph 3:16
these wounds in thine h.? Zech 13:6*
Father, into thy h. I. Luke 23:46
stretch forth thy h. John 21:18
are the works of thine h. Heb 1:10
him over the works of thy h. 2:7

handstaves

and shall burn the h. Ezek 39:9

hand weapon

him with a h. weapon. Num 35:18

handwriting

blotting out the h. Col 2:14*

handywork

firmament showeth his h. Ps 19:1

hang

Pharaoh shall h. thee. Gen 40:19
h. them before the Lord. Num 25:4
if thou h. him on a tree. Deut 21:22
thy life shall h. in doubt. 28:66
we will h. them up. 2 Sam 21:6
to speak to the king to h. Esth 6:4
then the king said, H. him. 7:9
there h. a thousand. S of S 4:4
they shall h. upon him all. Isa 22:24
virgins of Jerusalem h. Lam 2:10
take pin of it to h. any? Ezek 15:3
on these two h. all law. Mat 22:40
saw venomous beast h. Acts 28:4
lift up hands h. down. Heb 12:12

hanged

h. the chief baker. Gen 40:22; 41:13
for he that is h. is. Deut 21:23
and the king of Ai he h. Josh 8:29
the five kings h. he on. 10:26
Rechab and Baanah h. 2 Sam 4:12
Ahithophel h. himself. 17:23
Absalom h. 18:10
seven sons of Saul h. they. 21:9
set up, let him be h. Ezra 6:11
chamberlains were h. Esth 2:23
they h. Haman. 7:10
they h. his ten sons. 9:14
we h. our harps on the. Ps 137:2
princes are h. up by their. Lam 5:12
they h. the shield and. Ezek 27:10
h. their shields upon thy walls. 11
millstone were h. about. Mat 18:6 Mark 9:42; Luke 17:2
Judas went and h. Mat 27:5

thieves who were *h*. *Luke* 23:39
and *h*. on a tree. *Acts* 5:30; 10:39

hangeth

and he *h*. the earth upon. *Job* 26:7
is every one that *h*. on. *Gal* 3:13

hanging

they were *h*. on trees. *Josh* 10:26

hanging

(*Revised Versions substitute for this the word* screen)
thou shalt make an *h*. *Ex* 26:36
thou shalt make for the *h*. five. 37
h. for court gate. 27:16; 38:18
39:40; 40:8, 33
the *h*. for the door at the. 35:15
36:37; 39:38; 40:5, 28

hangings

h. of an hundred cubits. *Ex* 27:9; 11
38:9, 11
shall be *h*. of fifty. 27:12; 38:12
the *h*. on either side of gate. 27:14
15; 38:14, 15
the *h*. of court. 35:17; 38:9
16, 18; 39:40; *Num* 3:26; 4:26
women wove *h*. for the. *2 Ki* 23:7
blue *h*. fastened with. *Esth* 1:6

Hannah

Elkanah's wife *H*. had. *1 Sam* 1:2
H. why weepest thou? 8
so *H*. rose up. 9
H. spake in her heart, only her. 13
Elkanah knew *H*. 19
after *H*. conceived. 20
but *H*. went not up. 22
H. prayed, and said. 2:1
the Lord visited *H*. so that. 21

Hanoch

sons of Midian, Ephah, *H*.
Gen 25:4; *1 Chr* 1:33
H. son of Reuben. *Gen* 46:9
Ex. 6:14; *Num* 26:5; *1 Chr* 5:3

Hanun

H. his son reigned in. *2 Sam* 10:1
kindness unto *H*. 2; *1 Chr* 19:2
H. took David's servants, and.
2 Sam 10:4; *1 Chr* 19:4
the valley gate repaired *H*. *Neh* 3:13
H. sixth son of Zalaph repaired. 30

hap

and her *h*. was to light. *Ruth* 2:3

haply

if *h*. the people had. *1 Sam* 14:30
if *h*. he might find any. *Mark* 11:13
lest *h*. after he hath laid. *Luke* 14:29
lest *h*. ye be found to. *Acts* 5:39
if *h*. they might feel after. 17:27
h. if they of Macedonia. *2 Cor* 9:4*

happen

no punishment *h*. to. *1 Sam* 28:10
there shall no evil *h*. to. *Pr* 12:21
shew us what shall *h*. *Isa* 41:22
what things should *h*. *Mark* 10:32

happened

it was a chance that *h*. *1 Sam* 6:9
as I *h*. by chance upon. *2 Sam* 1:6
there *h*. to be there a man. 20:1
him of all that had *h*. *Esth* 4:7
therefore this evil is *h*. to. *Jer* 44:23
of all things that had *h*. *Luke* 24:14
wonder at that which *h*. *Acts* 3:10
blindness in part is *h*. *Rom* 11:25*
now all things *h*. to. *1 Cor* 10:11
the things which *h*. to me. *Phil* 1:12
some strange thing *h*. *1 Pet* 4:12
is *h*. to them according. *2 Pet* 2:22

happeneth

that one event *h*. to. *Eccl* 2:14
as it *h*. to the fool, so it *h*. 15
wicked men to whom it *h*. 8:14
but time and chance *h*. to. 9:11

happier

but she is *h*. if she so. *1 Cor* 7:40

happy

h. am I, for daughters. *Gen* 30:13
h. art thou, O Israel. *Deut* 33:29
h. thy men, *h*. thy servants.
1 Ki 10:8; *2 Chr* 9:7
h. is the man whom God. *Job* 5:17
h. is man who hath quiver. *Ps* 127:5
h. shalt thou be, it shall be. 128:2
h. he be that rewardeth. *Ps* 137:8, 9
h. is that people that is in such a case, yea *h*. is that. 144:15
h. is he that hath God of. 146:5
h. is man that findeth. *Pr* 3:13
h. is every one that retaineth. 18
h. is he that hath mercy on. 14:21
trusteth in the Lord, *h*. is he. 16:20
h. is the man that feareth. 28:14
he that keepeth the law, *h*. is. 29:18
are they *h*. that deal? *Jer* 12:1
now we call the proud *h*. *Mal* 3:15
know these things, *h*. *John* 13:17
I think myself *h*. king. *Acts* 26:2
h. is he that condemneth. *Rom* 14:22
behold, we count them *h*. *Jas* 5:11
righteousness' sake, *h*. *1 Pet* 3:14
for name of Christ *h*. are ye. 4:14

Haran, *a man*

Terah begat *H*. *Gen* 11:26, 27
H. died before Terah. 28
Milcah, the daughter of *H*. 29
Terah took Lot the son of *H*. his. 31
Caleb's concubine, bare *H*. and Moza, and *H*. begat. *1 Chr* 2:46
Shimei, *H*. Shelomith. 23:9

Haran, *a place*

Terah came to *H*. *Gen* 11:31
Terah died in *H*. 32
at 75 years departed out of *H*. 12:4
souls that they had gotten in *H*. 5
flee to *H*. 27:43
from Beer-sheba toward *H*. 28:10
they said, of *H*. are we. 29:4
my fathers destroyed *H*. *2 Ki* 19:12
Isa 37:12

Harbonah

H. was one of the. *Esth* 1:10; 7:9

hard

is any thing too *h*. for? *Gen* 18:14
travailed, and had *h*. 35:16, 17
their lives bitter with *h*. *Ex* 1:14
h. causes they brought unto. 18:26
cause that is too *h*. *Deut* 1:17
it shall not seem *h*. to thee. 15:18
if there arise matter too *h*. for. 17:8
laid upon us *h*. bondage. 26:6
of Zeruiah be too *h*. *2 Sam* 3:39
Amnon thought it *h*. to do. 13:2
to prove him with *h*. questions.
1 Ki 10:1; *2 Chr* 9:1
thou hast asked a *h*. *2 Ki* 2:10
as *h*. as a piece of the. *Job* 41:24*
hast shewed thy people *h*. *Ps* 60:3
thy wrath lieth *h*. on me. 88:7
long shall wicked speak *h*.? 94:4*
way of transgressors is *h*. *Pr* 13:15*
give thee rest from *h*. *Isa* 14:3
there is nothing too *h*. *Jer* 32:17
Lord: is there any thing too *h*.? 27
art not sent to a people of *h*.
Ezek 3:5, 6
shewing *h*. sentences. *Dan* 5:12*
that thou art an *h*. man. *Mat* 25:24
h. for them that trust. *Mark* 10:24
this is an *h*. saying. *John* 6:60
h. for thee to kick. *Acts* 9:5; 26:14
things to say, and *h*. *Heb* 5:11
which are things *h*. to. *2 Pet* 3:16
all ungodly of their *h*. *Jude* 15

hard, *adverb*

rump, shall he take off *h*. by. *Lev* 3:9
Abimelech went *h*. to. *Judg* 9:52*
Israel pursued *h*. after. 20:45
h. after Philistines in. *1 Sam* 14:22
followed *h*. upon Saul, and upon.
31:2; *2 Sam* 1:6; *1 Chr* 10:2
Naboth had a vineyard *h*. *1 Ki* 21:1
cut off garments *h*. by. *1 Chr* 19:4*
my soul followeth *h*. after. *Ps* 63:8
the men rowed *h*. to. *Jonah* 1:13
whose house joined *h*. *Acts* 18:7

harden

I will *h*. Pharaoh's heart. *Ex* 4:21
7:3; 14:4
I will *h*. the hearts of the. 14:17
shalt not *h*. thy heart. *Deut* 15:7
it was of Lord to *h*. *Josh* 11:20
wherefore then do ye *h*.? *1 Sam* 6:6
yea, I would *h*. myself. *Job* 6:10*
h. not your hearts. *Ps* 95:8
Heb 3:8, 15; 4:7

hardened

Lord *h*. Pharaoh's heart. *Ex* 7:13
9:12; 10:1, 20, 27; 11:10; 14:8
Pharaoh's heart is *h*. 7:14*
was *h*. 22; 8:19; 9:7*, 35
he *h*. his heart. 8:15, 32; 9:34
Lord thy God *h*. his. *Deut* 2:30
as Egyptians and Pharaoh *h*. their.
1 Sam 6:6
they *h*. their necks. *2 Ki* 17:14
Zedekiah *h*. heart from. *2 Chr* 36:13
they and our fathers *h*. their necks.
Neh 9:16; 17:29
who hath *h*. himself. *Job* 9:4
she is *h*. against her young. 39:16†
hast thou *h*. our heart? *Isa* 63:17
hearkened not, but *h*. *Jer* 7:26*
have *h*. their necks not to. 19:15*
when his mind was *h*. *Dan* 5:20
for their heart was *h*. *Mark* 6:52
have ye your heart yet *h*.? 8:17
blinded their eyes, *h*. *John* 12:40
but when divers were *h*. *Acts* 19:9
lest any of you be *h*. *Heb* 3:13

hardeneth

a wicked man *h*. his. *Pr* 21:29
he that *h*. his heart shall fall. 28:14
that being often reproved *h*. 29:1
whom he will he *h*. *Rom* 9:18

harder

brother offended *h*. to. *Pr* 18:19
have made their faces *h*. *Jer* 5:3
h. than flint have I made. *Ezek* 3:9

hardhearted

house of Israel are *h*. *Ezek* 3:7*

hardly

when Sarai dealt *h*. *Gen* 16:6
when Pharaoh would *h*. *Ex* 13:15
h. bestead and hungry. *Isa* 8:21†
rich man shall *h*. enter. *Mat* 19:23*
Mark 10:23; *Luke* 18:24
bruising him, *h*. departeth. *Luke* 9:39
h. passing it, we came. *Acts* 27:8*

hardness

dust groweth into *h*. *Job* 38:38*
because of *h*. of your hearts.
Mat 19:8; *Mark* 10:5
grieved for the *h*. of. *Mark* 3:5
upbraided them with their *h*. 16:14
but after thy *h*. and. *Rom* 2:5
endure *h*. as a good. *2 Tim* 2:3*

hare

the *h*. is unclean to you. *Lev* 11:6
Deut 14:7

harlot

our sister as with *h*.? *Gen* 34:31
her, he took her to be an *h*. 38:15
daughter in law hath played *h*. 24
priest shall not take an *h*. *Lev* 21:14
spies came into an *h*.'s. *Josh* 2:1
only Rahab the *h*. shall live. 6:17
Jephthah was son of an *h*. *Judg* 11:1
Samson saw there an *h*. and. 16:1
him with attire of an *h*. *Pr* 7:10
faithful city become an *h*.? *Isa* 1:21
years shall Tyre sing as an *h*. 23:15
take an harp, thou *h*. that hast. 16
wanderest, playing the *h*. *Jer* 2:20
thou hast played the *h*. with. 3:1
tree, and there hath played *h*. 6
feared not, but went and played *h*. 8
playedst the *h*. because. *Ezek* 16:15
playedst *h*. thereon. 16
playedst not *h*. with them. 28
hast not been as an *h*. 31
O *h*. hear the word. 35
thee to cease from playing the *h*. 41
Aholah played the *h*. when. 23:5
wherein she had played the *h*. 19
a woman that playeth the *h*. 44
mother hath played the *h*. *Hos* 2:5
thou shalt not play the *h*. 3:3
tho' Israel play the *h*., let not. 4:15
have given a boy for an *h*. *Joel* 3:3
thy wife shall be an *h*. *Amos* 7:17
return to hire of an *h*. *Mi* 1:7
of the well favoured *h*. *Nah* 3:4
the members of an *h*.? *1 Cor* 6:15
that he who is joined to an *h*. is. 16
by faith the *h*. Rahab. *Heb* 11:31
not Rahab the *h*. justified? *Jas* 2:25

harlots
came two women h. 1 Ki 3:16
keepeth company with h. Pr 29:3
assemble in h.' houses. Jer 5:7
whores, sacrifice with h. Hos 4:14
publicans and h. go. Mat 21:31
but the publicans and the h. 32
thy living with h. Luke 15:30
Babylon, mother of h. Rev 17:5

harm
this pillar unto me, for h. Gen 31:52
shall make amends for h. Lev 5:16
enemy, nor sought his h. Num 35:23
will no more do thee h. 1 Sam 26:21
shall Sheba do more h. 2 Sam 20:6
and there was no h. in. 2 Ki 4:41
do my prophets no h. 1 Chr 16:22
Ps 105:15
if he have done thee no h. Pr 3:30
him, and do him no h. Jer 39:12
do thyself no h. Acts 16:28
gained this h. 27:21
he felt no h. 28:5
saw no h. come to him. 6
spake any h. of thee. 21

harm
will h. you, if followers? 1 Pet 3:13

harmless
wise as serpents and h. Mat 10:16
ye may be h., the sons. Phil 2:15
is holy, h., undefiled. Heb 7:26*

harness, *substantive*
(*Revised Versions substitute for this the word* armour)
him that girdeth on h. 1 Ki 20:11
joints of his h. 22:34; 2 Chr 18:33
brought every man h. 2 Chr 9:24

harness, *verb*
h. the horses, and get. Jer 46:4

harnessed
Israel went up h. out of. Ex 13:18*

Harod
pitched beside well of H. Judg 7:1

Harosheth, *see* **gentiles**

harp
of them that handle h. Gen 4:21
thee away with tabret and h. 31:27
of prophets with a h. 1 Sam 10:5
is a cunning player on an h. 16:16
David took an h. and played. 23
prophesied with a h. to. 1 Chr 25:3
take the timbrel and h. Job 21:12
h. also is turned to mourning. 30:31
praise Lord with the h. Ps 33:2; 150:3
yea, on the h. will I praise thee. 43:4
my dark sayings upon the h. 49:4
awake psaltery and h. 57:8; 108:2
sing with h. 71:22; 92:3; 98:5
147:7; 149:3
bring hither the pleasant h. 81:2
the h. and the viol are in. Isa 5:12
sound like an h. for Moab. 16:11
take an h. 23:16
the joy of the h. ceaseth. 24:8
at sound of h. Dan 3:5, 7, 10, 15
whether pipe or h. 1 Cor 14:7

harped
known what is piped or h.? 1 Cor 14:7

harpers
the voice of h. harping. Rev 14:2
the voice of h. shall be heard. 18:22

harps
all Israel played on h. 2 Sam 6:5
made of almug trees h. 1 Ki 10:12
we hanged our h. upon. Ps 137:2
be with tabrets and h. Isa 30:32
the sound of thy h. Ezek 26:13
every one of them h. Rev 5:8
harping with their h. 14:2
the h. of God. 15:2
see **cymbal**

harrow
or will he h. the valleys? Job 39:10

harrows
under saws and h. of. 2 Sam 12:31
with saws and h. of iron. 1 Chr 20:3

hart
may eat flesh as of the h. Deut 12:15
14:5; 15:22
as the h. panteth after. Ps 42:1
lame man leap as an h. Isa 35:6

harts
ten fat oxen, besides h. 1 Ki 4:23
princes become like h. Lam 1:6

harvest
(*This, the time for reaping, or the ingathering of the crops, is used both literally and figuratively in Scripture. The day of judgement is called the harvest time for the world*)
while earth remaineth, h. Gen 8:22
went in days of wheat h. 30:14
neither be earing nor h. 45:6
keep the feast of h. Ex 23:16; 34:22
in earing time and in h. 34:21
when ye reap h. Lev 19:9; 23:10
22; Deut 24:19
own accord of h. not reap. Lev 25:5
in beginning of barley h. Ruth 1:22
my maidens till end of h. 2:21, 23
of Beth-shemesh reaping their h.
1 Sam 6:13
will set them to reap his h. 8:12
is it not wheat h. to-day? 12:17
death in h. in barley h. 2 Sam 21:9
her from beginning of barley h. 10
whose h. the hungry eateth. Job 5:5
gathereth her food in the h. Pr 6:8
he that sleepeth in h. causeth. 10:5
as rain in h. so honour is not. 26:1
according to joy in h. Isa 9:3
for the shouting for thy h. is. 16:9
but the h. shall be a heap in. 17:11
cloud of dew in the heat of h. 18:4
for afore the h. when the bud. 5
the h. of the river is her. 23:3
they shall eat up thy h. Jer 5:17
to us the appointed weeks of h. 24
the h. is past, summer is. 8:20
O Judah, he hath set an h. Hos 6:11
because h. of the field. Joel 1:11
put in the sickle, for the h. 3:13
yet three months to h. Amos 4:7
h. is plenteous, the. Mat 9:37
pray ye Lord of h. 38; Luke 10:2
grow together until h.: in time of h.
Mat 13:30
h. is end of the world, reapers. 39
in the sickle because h. Mark 4:29
said unto them, the h. Luke 10:2
cometh h.? the fields are white to h.
John 4:35
time is come, for the h. Rev 14:15

harvestman
it shall be as when the h. Isa 17:5
fall as handful after h. Jer 9:22

harvest time
overfloweth all *time* of h. Josh 3:15
in *time* of wheat h. Judg 15:1
to David in h. *time*. 2 Sam 23:13
of snow in the *time* of h. Pr 25:13
handleth sickle in h. *time*. Jer 50:16
a little while *time* of her h. 51:33
in the *time* of h. I will. Mat 13:30

hast
Lot, h. thou here any besides? whatsoever thou h. in. Gen 19:12
Esau said, H. thou but one? 27:38
as a prince h. thou power. 32:28
Esau said, keep that thou h. 33:9
thy flock, and all that thou h. 45:10
and gather all that thou h. Ex 9:19
every firstling thou h. shall. 13:12
gold, and all thou h. is. Deut 8:13
makest thou? what h.? Judg 18:3
and all that thou h. 1 Sam 25:6
h. thou not here with? 2 Sam 15:35
tell me, what h. in house. 2 Ki 4:2
h. thou eyes of flesh, or? Job 10:4
h. thou an arm like God? 40:9
say not, Go, when thou h. Pr 3:28
what h. thou here? whom h. thou?
Isa 22:16
go and sell that thou h. Mat 19:21
Mark 10:21; Luke 18:22
thou h. that is thine. Mat 25:25
from whence then h.? John 4:11
to whom thou now h. is not. 18
thou h. words of eternal life. 6:68
said, thou h. a devil. 7:20; 8:48, 52
if I wash thee not, thou h. John 13:8
thou h. neither part nor. Acts 8:21
thou who h. the form of. Rom 2:20
h. thou faith? have it to. 14:22
what h. thou that thou? 1 Cor 4:7
may say, thou h. faith. Jas 2:18
thou h. patience, and for. Rev 2:3
but this thou h. 6
thou h. a name to live. 3:1, 4
thou h. a little strength. 8
hold that fast which thou h. 11

haste, *substantive*
for Moses and Aaron in h. Ex 10:16
ye shall eat in h. with your. 12:11
out of land in h. 33; Deut 16:3
business required h. 1 Sam 21:8
cast away in their h. 2 Ki 7:15
they went up in h. to. Ezra 4:23
I said in my h., I am cut. Ps 31:22
I said in my h., All men. 116:11
shall not go out with h. Isa 52:12
Daniel before king in h. Dan 2:25
king rose up in h. and spake. 3:24
the king went in h. unto the. 6:19
in straightway with h. Mark 6:25
the hill country with h. Luke 1:39
the shepherds came with h. 2:16

haste
h. thee, escape thither. Gen 19:22
h. ye and go up to my. 45:9, 13
speed, h., stay not. 1 Sam 20:38
h. thee, for Philistines have. 23:27
O my Strength, h. thee. Ps 22:19
see **make** *haste*

hasted
young man, and he h. Gen 18:7
drink, my lord, and she h. 24:18, 20
and taskmasters h. them. Ex 5:13
people h. and passed. Josh 4:10
the king of Ai saw it, they h. 8:14
the ambush h. and set the city. 19
the sun h. not to go down. 10:13
liers in wait h. and. Judg 20:37
David h. 1 Sam 17:48
Abigail h. 25:23, 42
except thou hadst h. and. 34
the witch at En-dor h. and. 28:24
who was of Bahurim, h. 2 Sam 19:16
the prophet h. and took. 1 Ki 20:41
they h. and put garments. 2 Ki 9:13
yea, himself h. also. 2 Chr 26:20
Haman h. to his house. Esth 6:12
they h. to bring Haman unto. 14
or if my foot hath h. to. Job 31:5
were troubled and h. away.
Ps 48:5; 104:7
Paul h. to be at. Acts 20:16

hasten
h. hither Micaiah the. 1 Ki 22:9*
and see that ye h. the. 2 Chr 24:5
sorrows multiplied that h. Ps 16:4*
I would h. my escape from. 55:8
or who else can h.? Eccl 2:25*
let him h. his work that. Isa 5:19
I the Lord will h. it in his. 60:22
I will h. my word to. Jer 1:12*

hastened, -eth
Abraham h. into the tent. Gen 18:6
angels h. Lot, saying, arise. 19:15
howbeit the Levites h. 2 Chr 24:5
posts went out, being h. by king.
Esth 3:15; 8:14
captive exile h. to. Isa 51:14
I have not h. from. Jer 17:16

hasteth
as the eagle that h. Job 9:26*
drinketh up a river, and h. 40:23*
as a bird h. to snare. Pr 7:23
and he that h. with his feet. 19:2
he that h. to be rich, hath an. 28:22
the sun h. to the place. Eccl 1:5
the affliction of Moab h. Jer 48:16
fly as eagle that h. to eat. Hab 1:8
great day of the Lord h. Zeph 1:14

hastily
brought Joseph h. out. Gen 41:14
driving them out h. Judg 2:23
Abimelech called h. unto his. 9:54
and the man came in h. 1 Sam 4:14
the men did h. catch it. 1 Ki 20:33*
may be gotten h. Pr 20:21

go not forth *h.* to strive, lest. *Pr* 25:8
Mary that she rose *h.* *John* 11:31*

hasting

judgement, and *h.* righteousness. *Isa* 16:5*
and *h.* unto the coming. *2 Pet* 3:12*

hasty

he that is *h.* of spirit. *Pr* 14:29
every one that is *h.* only. 21:5
seest thou a man that is *h.* 29:20
let not thy heart be *h.* *Eccl* 5:2
be not *h.* in thy spirit to be. 7:9
be not too *h.* to go out of his. 8:3
as the *h.* fruit before. *Isa* 28:4*
why is decree so *h.*? *Dan* 2:15*
that bitter and *h.* nation. *Hab* 1:6

hatch

owl shall *h.* and gather. *Isa* 34:15
they *h.* cockatrice' eggs, weave. 59:5

hatcheth

sitteth on eggs and *h.* not. *Jer* 17:11*

hate

This word is used in the Bible frequently, as it is now, not for literal hatred, but a dislike, or even a lesser degree of love for one than for another, Deut 21:15; Pr 13:24; Luke 14:26.

gate of those that *h.* *Gen* 24:60
Joseph will peradventure *h.* 50:15
shalt not *h.* thy brother. *Lev* 19:17
they that *h.* you shall reign. 26:17
them that *h.* thee flee. *Num* 10:35
repayeth them that *h.* *Deut* 7:10
lay them upon them that *h.* 15; 30:7
if any man *h.* his neighbour. 19:11
and go in unto her and *h.* her. 22:13
if the latter husband *h.* her. 24:3
the loins of them that *h.* him. 33:11
and love them that *h.*? *2 Chr* 19:2
that *h.* thee shall be. *Job* 8:22
shall find those that *h.* thee. *Ps* 21:8
they that *h.* the righteous. 34:21
they which *h.* us spoil for. 44:10
let them also that *h.* him flee. 68:1
they that *h.* thee have lifted. 83:2
and I will plague them that *h.* 89:23
ye that love the Lord *h.* evil. 97:10
he turned their heart to *h.* 105:25
them be turned back that *h.* 129:5
how long, fools, will ye *h.*? *Pr* 1:22
six things doth the Lord *h.* 6:16
Lord is to *h.* evil; pride do I *h.* 8:13
reprove not a scorner, lest he *h.* 9:8
brethren of the poor do *h.* 19:7
weary of thee, and so *h.* thee. 25:17
bloodthirsty *h.* the upright. 29:10
love and a time to *h.* *Eccl* 3:8
unto will of them that *h.* *Ezek* 16:27
to them that *h.* thee. *Dan* 4:19
h. him that rebuketh. *Amos* 5:10
h. the evil, and love the good. 15
who *h.* the good, and love. *Mi* 3:2
love thy neighbour, *h.* *Mat* 5:43
do good to them that *h.* you. 44
Luke 6:27
either he will *h.* the one. *Mat* 6:24
Luke 16:13
shall betray and shall *h.* *Mat* 24:10
hand of all that *h.* us. *Luke* 1:71
are ye when men shall *h.* you. 6:22
h. not his father, and mother. 14:26
world cannot *h.* you, but. *John* 7:7
if the world *h.* you, ye know that it hated me. 15:18; *1 John* 3:13
ten horns, these shall *h.* *Rev* 17:16

***I* hate**

there is one man, but *I h.* him. *1 Ki* 22:8; *2 Chr* 18:7
I h. the work of them. *Ps* 101:3
I h. every false way. 119:104, 128
I h. vain thoughts. 113
I h. and abhor lying. 163
do not *I h.* them, O Lord? 139:21
I h. them with perfect hatred. 22
froward mouth do *I h.* *Pr* 8:13
I h. robbery for burnt. *Isa* 61:8
abominable thing that *I h.* *Jer* 44:4
I h. I despise your feast. *Amos* 5:21
I h. his palaces, therefore. 6:8
these are things that *I h.* *Zech* 8:17

what I *h.* that do I. *Rom* 7:15
the Nicolaitans *I h.* *Rev* 2:6, 15*

hate *me*

me, seeing ye *h. me*? *Gen* 26:27
and fourth generation of them that *h. me.* *Ex* 20:5; *Deut* 5:9
reward them that *h. me.* *Deut* 32:41
do not ye *h. me*? *Judg* 11:7
thou dost *h. me.* 14:16
destroy them that *h. me.* *2 Sam* 22:41; *Ps* 18:40
I suffer of them that *h. me.* *Ps* 9:13
they *h. me* with cruel hatred. 25:19
let them wink that *h. me.* 35:19
that *h. me* wrongfully. 38:19; 69:4
all that *h. me* whisper. 41:7
upon me, in wrath *h. me.* 55:3*
from them that *h. me.* 69:14
they which *h. me* may see. 86:17
desire upon them that *h. me.* 118:7
all they that *h. me* love. *Pr* 8:36

hated

Esau *h.* Jacob, because. *Gen* 27:41
the Lord saw Leah was *h.* 29:31
that I was *h.* 33
h. Joseph yet the more. 37:4, 5, 8
shot at him and *h.* him. 49:23*
and said, because the Lord *h.* us. *Deut* 1:27; 9:28
h. him not in times past. 4:42
19:4, 6; *Josh* 20:5
one loved and another *h.* *Deut* 21:15
before the son of the *h.* 16
shall acknowledge the son of *h.* 17
thou hadst utterly *h.* her. *Judg* 15:2
and blind that are *h.* *2 Sam* 5:8
Amnon *h.* Tamar. 13:15
Absalom *h.* Amnon. 22
from my strong enemy, and from them that *h.* me. 22:18; *Ps* 18:17
rule over them that *h.* *Esth* 9:1
would unto those that *h.* them. 5
destruction of him that *h.* *Job* 31:29
I have *h.* congregation of. *Ps* 26:5
I have *h.* them that regard. 31:6
put them to shame that *h.* us. 44:7
neither was it he that *h.* me. 55:12
saved them from him that *h.* 106:10
and they that *h.* them ruled. 41
they *h.* knowledge, and. *Pr* 1:29
and say, how have I *h.* 5:12
man of wicked devices is *h.* 14:17
the poor is *h.* even of his own. 20
therefore I *h.* life. *Eccl* 2:17
I *h.* labour. 18
been forsaken and *h.* *Isa* 60:15
brethren that *h.* you said. 66:5
therefore have I *h.* mine. *Jer* 12:8
them that thou hast *h.* *Ezek* 16:37
sith thou hast not *h.* blood. 35:6
I *h.* them for wickedness. *Hos* 9:15
I loved Jacob, and *h.* Esau. *Mal* 1:3; *Rom* 9:13
ye shall be *h.* *Mat* 10:22
Mark 13:13; *Luke* 21:17
shall be *h.* of all nations. *Mat* 24:9
his citizens *h.* him, and. *Luke* 19:14
it *h.* me before it *h.* you. *John* 15:18
have both seen and *h.* both me. 24
written in their law, They *h.* me. 25
world hath *h.* them, because. 17:14
no man ever yet *h.* his. *Eph* 5:29
righteousness and *h.* *Heb* 1:9

hateful

iniquity be found to be *h.* *Ps* 36:2
we were *h.* and hating. *Tit* 3:3
every unclean and *h.* bird. *Rev* 18:2

hatefully

shall deal with thee *h.* *Ezek* 23:29

haters

the *h.* of Lord should. *Ps* 81:15
backbiters, *h.* of God. *Rom* 1:30

hatest

thine enemies, and *h.* *2 Sam* 19:6
thou *h.* all workers of. *Ps* 5:5
lovest righteousness, and *h.* 45:7
thou *h.* instruction, and. 50:17
into hand whom thou *h.* *Ezek* 23:28
thou *h.* the deeds of the. *Rev* 2:6

hateth

if thou see ass of him that *h.* *Ex* 23:5

be slack to him that *h.* *Deut* 7:10
every abomination he *h.* 12:31
any image which the Lord *h.* 16:22
daughter unto this man, he *h.* 22:16
me in his wrath, who *h.* *Job* 16:9
shall even he that *h.* right? 34:17
loveth violence, his soul *h.* *Ps* 11:5
dwelt with him that *h.* peace. 120:6
and he that *h.* suretyship. *Pr* 11:15
but he that *h.* reproof is. 12:1
a righteous man *h.* lying, but. 13:5
he that spareth his rod *h.* his. 24
he that *h.* reproof shall die. 15:10
but he that *h.* gifts shall live. 27
he that *h.* dissembleth with. 26:24
a lying tongue *h.* those that. 28
he that *h.* covetousness. 28:16
is partner with a thief *h.* his. 29:24
feasts my soul *h.* *Isa* 1:14
Lord saith, that he *h.* *Mal* 2:16
one that doeth evil *h.* *John* 3:20
but me the world *h.* because. 7:7
that *h.* his life in this world. 12:25
world, therefore world *h.* you. 15:19
he that *h.* me *h.* my Father also. 23
he that *h.* his brother. *1 John* 2:9, 11
whosoever *h.* his brother is. 3:15
I love God, and *h.* his brother. 4:20

hath

h. he given all that he *h.* *Gen* 24:36
uncleanness he *h.* *Lev* 22:5
no devoted thing of all he *h.* 27:28
h. the strength of. *Num* 23:22; 24:8
done away because he *h.* no. 27:4
inherit that which he *h.* *Deut* 21:16
a double portion of all he *h.* 17
woman and all she *h.* *Josh* 6:22
burnt with fire, and all he *h.* 7:15
h. the Lord as great? *1 Sam* 15:22
thine handmaid *h.* not. *2 Ki* 4:2
she *h.* no child, her husband is. 14
hedge about all he *h.* *Job* 1:10
touch all he *h.* 11
behold, all that he *h.* is in thy. 12
all that a man *h.* will he give. 2:4
so the poor *h.* hope. 5:16
h. the rain a father? 38:28
righteous man *h.* is better. *Ps* 37:16
catch all that he *h.* 109:11
happy is the man *h.* his quiver. 127:5
happy he that *h.* God of. 146:5
despised and *h.* a servant. *Pr* 12:9
the sluggard desireth, and *h.* 13:4
maketh himself rich, yet *h.* 7
is life unto him who *h.* it. 16:22
stone in eyes of him that *h.* it. 17:8
he that *h.* it, shall abide. 19:23
who *h.* woe? who *h.* sorrow? who *h.* wounds? 23:29
yea, he *h.* neither child. *Eccl* 4:8
for he *h.* not another to help. 10
for what *h.* the wise more? 6:8
neither *h.* he the power in the. 8:8
and she *h.* no breasts. *S of S* 8:8
and his soul *h.* appetite. *Isa* 29:8
he *h.* no hands. 45:9
and *h.* no light. 50:10
he *h.* no form nor comeliness. 53:2
he that *h.* no money, come. 55:1
prophet that *h.* a dream, let him tell, and he that *h.* my word. *Jer* 23:28
h. Israel no sons? *h.* he no? 49:1
deceiver which *h.* in flock. *Mal* 1:14
h. not where to lay head. *Mat* 8:20
Luke 9:58
he that *h.* ears to hear, let him hear. *Mat* 11:15; 13:9, 43; *Mark* 4:9
Luke 8:8; 14:35; *Rev* 2:7
they say he *h.* a devil. *Mat* 11:18
h. to him shall be given, who *h.* not, from him shall be taken that he *h.* 13:12; 25:29; *Mark* 4:25
Luke 8:18; 19:26
selleth all that he *h.* and. *Mat* 13:44
whence *h.* this man? 56; *Mark* 6:2
h. Beelzebub, and. *Mark* 3:22
because they said, he *h.* an. 30
and ye say, he *h.* a devil. *Luke* 7:33
John 10:20
ruler over all that he *h.* *Luke* 12:44
forsaketh not all that he *h.* 14:33
whose superscription *h.* it? 20:24
h. a purse, he that *h.* no. 22:36

spirit *h.* not flesh and bones. *Luke* 24:39
he that *h.* the bride, is. *John* 3:29
he that believeth on the Son *h.* everlasting life. 36; 5:24; 6:47, 54
Father *h.* life in himself, so *h.* 5:26
h. one that judgeth him. 12:48
he that *h.* my commandments. 14:21
prince of this world *h.* nothing. 30
greater love *h.* no man than. 15:13
all things that the Father *h.* 16:15
delivered thee unto me, *h.* 19:11
what advantage then *h.*? *Rom* 3:1
by works, he *h.* whereof to. 4:2
h. not the potter power over? 9:21
the wife *h.* not power of. *1 Cor* 7:4
but every man *h.* his proper gift. 7
h. a psalm, *h.* a doctrine, *h.* a. 14:26
h. righteousness with unrighteousness? what communion *h.* *2 Cor* 6:14
what concord *h.* Christ? 15
what agreement *h.* temple of God? 16
according to that a man *h.* 8:12
desolate *h.* more children. *Gal* 4:27
nor idolater *h.* any. *Eph* 5:5
if any thinketh he *h.* *Phil* 3:4
builder *h.* more honour. *Heb* 3:3
man *h.* an unchangeable. 7:24
your confidence, which *h.* great. 10:35
a man say he *h.* faith, and? *Jas* 2:14
denieth Son, same *h.* *1 John* 2:23
every man that *h.* this hope. 3:3
ye know that no murderer *h.* 15
whoso *h.* this world's good, and. 17
believed the love that God *h.* 4:16
no fear in love, because fear *h.* 18
believeth on Son of God *h.* 5:10
h. the Son *h.* life, *h.* not Son *h.* 12
not in the doctrine of Christ, *h.* not God. He that abideth *h.* *2 John* 9
that *h.* key of David. *Rev* 3:7
where she *h.* a place prepared. 12:6
because he knoweth that he *h.* 12
beast which *h.* the seven heads. 17:7
and there is the mind which *h.* 9
on such the second death *h.* 20:6

hating

provide men of truth, *h.* *Ex* 18:21
times past hateful, and *h.* *Tit* 3:3
h. even garment spotted by. *Jude* 23

hatred

if he thrust him off *h.* *Num* 35:20
h. wherewith he hated. *2 Sam* 13:15
hate me with cruel *h.* *Ps* 25:19
compassed me about with *h.* 109:3
they have rewarded me *h.* 5
I hate them with perfect *h.* I. 139:22
h. stirs up strifes, love. *Pr* 10:12
he that hideth *h.* with lying lips. 18
than a stalled ox, and *h.* 15:17
whose *h.* is covered by deceit. 26:26
knoweth either love or *h.* *Eccl* 9:1
their love, their *h.* and envy is. 6
destroy it for the old *h.* *Ezek* 25:15
thou hast had a perpetual *h.* 35:5
to envy thou hast used out of *h.* 11
iniquity, and for great *h.* *Hos* 9:7
but the prophet is *h.* in the house. 8
works of flesh; witchcraft, *h.* *Gal* 5:20

hats

in their hosen and *h.* *Dan* 3:21*

haughtily

neither shall ye go *h.* *Mi* 2:3

haughtiness

h. of men shall be bowed. *Isa* 2:11
and the *h.* of men shall be. 17
I will lay low the *h.* of the. 13:11
of the *h.* of Moab. 16:6; *Jer* 48:29

haughty

thine eyes are upon *h.* *2 Sam* 22:28
Lord, my heart is not *h.* *Ps* 131:1
an *h.* spirit before a fall. *Pr* 16:18
before destruction heart is *h.* 18:12
proud and *h.* scorner is his. 21:24
daughters of Zion are *h.* *Isa* 3:16
high hewn down, and *h.* 10:33*
the *h.* people of the earth. 24:4*
were *h.* before me, I. *Ezek* 16:50
no more be *h.* because. *Zeph* 3:11

haunt

his place where his *h.* *1 Sam* 23:22
men were wont to *h.* *1 Sam* 30:31
to be on all that *h.* it. *Ezek* 26:17

have

they *h.* all one language. *Gen* 11:6
h. ye another brother? 43:7
h. ye a father? 44:19
have brought all that they *h.* 46:32
thou shalt *h.* no other gods. *Ex* 20:3 *Deut* 5:7
the priest shall *h.* it. *Lev* 7:7, 8
the sons of Aaron shall *h.* 10
and a just hin, shall ye *h.* 19:36
priest's daughter *h.* no child. 22:13 *Num* 27:8, 9
whence should I *h.* flesh? *Num* 11:13
h. I now any power at all to? 22:38
peace he and his seed shall *h.* 25:13
that *h.* many, them that *h.* few. 35:8
voice of God, as we *h.*? *Deut* 5:26
father and all they *h.* *Josh* 2:13
though they *h.* iron chariots. 17:18
what *h.* you to do with Lord? 22:24
h. ye called us to take that we *h.*? *Judg* 14:15
h. taken my gods, and what *h.*? 18:24
I am too old to *h.* an husband, if I should *h.* an husband. *Ruth* 1:12
but we will *h.* a king. *1 Sam* 8:19
present to bring; what *h.* we? 9:7
utterly destroy all that they *h.* 15:3
what can he *h.* more but the? 18:8
h. I need of mad men, that ye *h.*? 21:15
Amnon said, *h.* out all. *2 Sam* 13:9
they *h.* there with them their. 15:36
what *h.* I to do with you, ye? 16:10
I *h.* no son to keep my name. 18:18
what right *h.* I yet to cry? 19:28
said unto king, how long *h.* I to? 34
Israel said, we *h.* ten parts in. 43
h. thou respect unto. *1 Ki* 8:28
saying, What portion *h.* we? 12:16
I *h.* not a cake, but an handful. 17:12
king, I am thine, and all I *h.* 20:4
that I may *h.* it for a garden. 21:2
scattered as sheep that *h.* no. 22:17
h. her forth without. *2 Ki* 11:15 *2 Chr* 23:14
this sign shalt thou *h.* *2 Ki* 20:9
shall any after thee *h.* *2 Chr* 1:12
from henceforth thou shalt *h.* 16:9
what *h.* I to do with thee? 35:21
he said, *H.* me away, for I am. 23
other men *h.* our lands. *Neh* 5:5
let it look for light but *h.* *Job* 3:9
O that I might *h.* my request. 6:8
then should I yet *h.* comfort. 10
what profit should we *h.* if? 21:15
they mar my path, they *h.* no. 30:13
profit shall I *h.* if be cleansed? 35:3
the Lord shall *h.* them. *Ps* 2:4
h. workers of iniquity? 14:4; 53:4
in pleasant places, I *h.* a. 16:6
say, Ah! so would we *h.* it. 35:25
whom *h.* I in heaven but? 73:25
sing to my God while I *h.* 104:33
a good understanding *h.* all. 111:10
they *h.* mouths; eyes *h.* they. 115:5
they *h.* ears; noses *h.* they. 6, 7 135:16, 17
so shall I *h.* wherewith to. 119:42
great peace *h.* they which love. 165
praises unto my God while I *h.* 146:2
this honour *h.* all his saints. 149:9
lot, let us all *h.* one purse. *Pr* 1:14
shall beg in harvest and *h.* 20:4
shall *h.* him become his son. 29:21
and I *h.* not the understanding. 30:2
nor *h.* the knowledge of the holy. 3
they *h.* all one breath. *Eccl* 3:19
giveth life to them that *h.* it. 7:12
h. they any more a reward. 9:5
neither *h.* they any more portion. 6
we *h.* a little sister and. *S of S* 8:8
thou, O Solomon, must *h.* a. 12
gone, because they *h.* no. *Isa* 5:13
also shalt thou *h.* no rest. 23:12
h. a strong city, salvation will. 26:1
ye shall *h.* a song as in night. 30:29
blind that *h.* eyes, deaf that *h.* 43:8
h. not I the Lord? there is no. 45:21
in the Lord *h.* I righteousness. 24
children which thou shalt *h.* 49:20
hand shortened? *h.* I no? *Isa* 50:2
h. of my hand, ye shall lie down. 11
now therefore what *h.* I here? 52:5
dogs, which can never *h.* 56:11
for your shame you shall *h.* 61:7
h. eyes and see not; which *h.* ears, and hear not. *Jer* 5:21
people love to *h.* it so, what. 31
no flesh shall *h.* peace. 12:12
h. sons nor daughters in. 16:2
said, ye shall *h.* peace. 23:17; 29:7
plant vineyard, nor *h.* any. 35:7
he shall *h.* none to sit upon. 36:30
he shall *h.* his life for a prey. 38:2
to the which they *h.* a desire. 44:14
they will destroy till they *h.* 49:9
the nation which *h.* neither gates. 31
mind, therefore *h.* I hope. *Lam* 3:21
neither will I *h.* any pity. *Ezek* 5:11 7:4; 8:18; 9:10
eye spare, neither *h.* ye pity. 9:5
h. I any pleasure that the? 18:23
I *h.* no pleasure in death. 32; 33:11
when iniquity shall *h.* 21:25, 29
any wisdom that I *h.* *Dan* 2:30
loose, and they *h.* no hurt. 3:25
shall *h.* a chain of gold. 5:7, 16
the king should *h.* no damage. 6:2
now they shall say, We *h.* *Hos* 10:3
unto you, ye shall not *h.* *Mi* 3:6
this shall they *h.* for. *Zeph* 2:10
but ye *h.* not enough. *Hag* 1:6
h. we not all one father? *Mal* 2:10
we *h.* Abraham to our father. *Mat* 3:9; *Luke* 3:8
thy coat, let him *h.* thy. *Mat* 5:40
love you, what reward *h.* ye? 46
they *h.* their reward. 6:2; 5:16
the foxes *h.* holes, birds *h.* nests. 8:20; *Luke* 9:58
what *h.* we to do with thee, Jesus? *Mat* 8:29; *Mark* 1:24; *Luke* 4:34
and he shall have more abundance. *Mat* 13:12; 25:29
it is not lawful for thee to *h.* her. 14:4; *Mark* 6:18
we *h.* so much bread? *Mat* 15:33
how many loaves *h.* ye? 34 *Mark* 6:38; 8:5
h. faith as a grain. *Mat* 17:20; 21:21
what shall I do, that I may *h.*? 19:16
followed thee what shall we *h.*? 27
h. poor always with you, but me ye *h.* 26:11; *Mark* 14:7; *John* 12:8
need *h.* we of witnesses? *Mat* 26:65
h. nothing to do with that. 27:19
deliver him now, if he will *h.* him. 43
the whole *h.* no need of. *Mark* 2:17
long as they *h.* the bridegroom. 19
if any man *h.* ears to hear. 4:23 7:16; *Rev* 13:9
so fearful, how is it ye *h.*? *Mark* 4:40
saying, It is because we *h.* 8:16
h. salt in yourselves, *h.* peace. 9:50
thou shalt *h.* treasure in heaven. 10:21; *Luke* 18:22
shall *h.* whatsoever he. *Mark* 11:23
receive them, and ye shall *h.* 24
what thank *h.* ye? *Luke* 6:32, 33, 34
taken what he seemeth to *h.* 8:18
which of you shall *h.* a friend? 11:5
alms of such things as ye *h.* 41
and after that *h.* no more. 12:4
which neither *h.* storehouse nor. 24
sell that ye *h.* and give alms. 33
I pray thee *h.* me excused. 14:18, 19
ever with me, all that I *h.* 15:31
we will not *h.* this man to. 19:14
Satan hath desired to *h.* you. 22:31
what communications ye *h.*? 24:17
flesh and bones, as ye see me *h.* 39
h. ye here any meat? 41; *John* 21:5
said, They *h.* no wine. *John* 2:3
woman, what *h.* I to do with thee? 4
but *h.* everlasting life. 3:15, 16
answered and said, I *h.* no. 4:17
hath given the Son to *h.* life. 5:26
and ye *h.* not his word abiding. 38
I know that ye *h.* not the love. 42
believeth on him, may *h.* 6:40
except ye eat his flesh, ye *h.* no. 53
tempting, that they might *h.* to. 8:6
he that followeth me, shall *h.* 12
h. one father even God. 41

I *h.* not a devil. *John* 8:49
ye were blind, ye should *h.* no. 9:41
I am come that they might *h.* 10:10
other sheep I *h.* which are not. 16
walk while ye *h.* light. 12:35, 36
might *h.* peace. In the world ye shall
h. tribulation: I *h.* overcome. 16:33
but ye *h.* a custom that I. 18:39
we *h.* a law. 19:7
we *h.* no king but Cesar. 15
that believing ye might *h.* life. 20:31
silver and gold *h.* I none, but such as
I *h.* *Acts* 3:6
said, Lord, what wilt thou *h.*? 9:6
in him we live, move, and *h.* 17:28
know that by this craft we *h.* 19:25
h. four men which *h.* a vow. 21:23
when Gentiles, which *h.* *Rom* 2:14
ye *h.* your fruit unto holiness. 6:22
if any man *h.* not the Spirit. 8:9
I will come, and Sara shall *h.* 9:9
and all members *h.* not the. 12:4
hast thou faith ? *h.* to thyself. 14:22
I *h.* whereof I may glory. 15:17
but we *h.* the mind of. *1 Cor* 2:16
are naked, and *h.* no certain. 4:11
instructors, yet *h.* ye not many. 15
that one should *h.* his father's. 5:1
is in you, which ye *h.* of God. 6:19
let every man *h.* his own wife, let
every woman *h.* her own. 7:2
yet such shall *h.* trouble in the. 28
they that *h.* wives be as though. 29
h. you without carefulness. 32
I think also that I *h.* the Spirit. 40
that we all *h.* knowledge. 8:1
h. we not power to eat ? 9:4, 5, 6
if a man *h.* long hair, it is. 11:14
if a woman *h.* long hair, it is a. 15
we *h.* no such custom, nor the. 16
what, *h.* ye not houses to eat in? 22
eye not say to hand, I *h.* no. 12:21
h. all the gifts of healing ? 30
h. not charity, I am become. 13:1
I *h.* all faith and *h.* not charity. 2, 3
your rejoicing which I *h.* 15:31
for some *h.* not the knowledge. 34
such trust *h.* we through. *2 Cor* 3:4
seeing we *h.* this ministry, we. 4:1
out of that which ye *h.* 8:11
he may *h.* to give to him. *Eph* 4:28
h. no fellowship with the. 5:11
I *h.* you in my heart. *Phil* 1:7
but I *h.* all. 4:18
love which ye *h.* to all. *Col* 1:4
what great conflict I *h.* for you. 2:1
if any man *h.* a quarrel. 3:13
ye also *h.* a Master in. 4:1
ye suffered, as they *h.* *1 Thes* 2:14
for all men *h.* not faith. *2 Thes* 3:2
not because we *h.* not power. 9
who will *h.* all men to. *1 Tim* 2:4
him with whom we *h.* to. *Heb* 4:13
seeing then that we *h.* a great. 14
by reason of use *h.* their senses. 5:14
which hope we *h.* as an. 6:19
we *h.* such a High Priest, set. 8:1
that this man *h.* somewhat also. 3
that ye *h.* in heaven a better. 10:34
with such things as ye *h.* 13:5
we *h.* an altar whereof they *h.* no. 10
here *h.* we no continuing city. 14
but let patience *h.* her. *Jas* 1:4
h. not faith of Christ with. 2:1
and *h.* not works, can faith ? 14
even so faith, if it *h.* not works. 17
thou hast faith, and I *h.* works. 18
if ye *h.* bitter envy, and strife. 3:14
ye lust and *h.* not, ye desire to *h.* ye
fight and war, yet ye *h.* not. 4:2
above all things *h.* *1 Pet* 4:8
we *h.* a more sure word. *2 Pet* 1:19
a heart they *h.* exercised. 2:14
if we say, we *h.* no sin. *1 John* 1:8
h. an Advocate with the Father. 2:1
but we *h.* an unction from the. 20
and this commandment *h.* we. 4:21
that ye may know that ye *h.* 5:13
this is the confidence that we *h.* 14
we *h.* the petitions we desired. 15
I *h.* no greater joy than. *3 John* 4
Diotrephes, who loveth to *h.* the. 9
I *h.* the keys of hell. *Rev* 1:18
I *h.* somewhat against. 2:4; 14:20
and ye shall *h.* tribulation. *Rev* 2:10
to you, and to as many as *h.* not. 24
but what ye *h.* already, hold. 25
which *h.* not the seal of God. 9:4
h. the testimony of Jesus. 12:17
they *h.* no rest day nor night. 14:11
these *h.* one mind, and give. 17:13
brethren that *h.* the testimony. 19:10
liars shall *h.* their part in lake. 21:8
that they may *h.* right to tree. 22:14
see **compassion, dominion**

haven

dwell at the *h.* an *h.* *Gen* 49:13
them to their desired *h.* *Ps* 107:30
h. not commodious, an *h.* *Acts* 27:12

fair **havens**

place which is called *fair h.* *Acts* 27:8

having

h. his uncleanness. *Lev* 7:20; 22:3
h. her sickness. 20:18
h. a wen or scurvy. 22:22
into a trance, but *h.* *Num* 24:4, 16
stay for them from *h.* *Ruth* 1:13
h. a drawn sword in. *1 Chr* 21:16
h. Judah and Benjamin. *2 Chr* 11:12
mourning, and *h.* his. *Esth* 6:12
h. no guide, overseer. *Pr* 6:7
and *h.* neither bars nor. *Ezek* 38:11
pass ye away, *h.* thy. *Mi* 1:11
king cometh to thee, *h.* *Zech* 9:9
he taught as one *h.* *Mat* 7:29
h. soldiers under me. 8:9; *Luke* 7:8
were as sheep *h.* no shepherd.
Mat 9:36; *Mark* 6:34
rather than *h.* two hands or. *Mat* 18:8
rather than *h.* two eyes to be cast.
9; *Mark* 9:43
not *h.* wedding garment ? *Mat* 22:12
if a man die, *h.* no children. 24
Luke 20:28
and *h.* no issue, left. *Mat* 22:25
woman *h.* an alabaster box. 26:7
Mark 14:3
h. nothing to eat, Jesus. *Mark* 8:1
h. eyes, see ye not ? *h.* ears ? 18
a fig tree *h.* leaves. 11:13
h. one son. 12:6
woman *h.* an issue of. *Luke* 8:43
man of you *h.* an hundred ? 15:4
either what woman *h.* ten pieces ? 8
but which of you, *h.* a servant ? 17:7
how knows he letters, *h.*? *John* 7:15
Simon Peter *h.* a sword. 18:10
h. land, sold it, and. *Acts* 4:37
h. a good report of the Jews. 22:12
h. more perfect knowledge of. 24:22
h. not the law, are a law. *Rom* 2:14
h. then gifts differing according. 12:6
h. a matter against. *1 Cor* 6:1
he that standeth stedfast, *h.* 7:37
h. the same spirit of. *2 Cor* 4:13
h. nothing, and yet possessing. 6:10
h. therefore these promises. 7:1
ye always *h.* all sufficiency in. 9:8
h. in a readiness to revenge. 10:6
but *h.* hope, when your faith is. 15
h. no hope. *Eph* 2:12
not *h.* spot or wrinkle. 5:27
h. your loins girt about. 6:14
h. a desire to depart. *Phil* 1:23
h. this confidence. 25
h. the same conflict. 30
h. the same love. 2:2
not *h.* my own righteousness. 3:9
h. made peace through. *Col* 1:20
h. nourishment ministered. 2:19
h. his children in. *1 Tim* 3:4
h. the promise of the life that. 4:8
h. damnation, because they. 5:12
and *h.* food and raiment, let. 6:8
h. this seal, the Lord. *2 Tim* 2:19
h. a form of godliness, but. 3:5
they shall heap teachers, *h.* 4:3
h. faithful children, not. *Tit* 1:6
h. conversation honest. *1 Pet* 2:12
h. a good conscience, they. 3:16
h. eyes full of adultery. *2 Pet* 2:14
these be sensual, *h.* not. *Jude* 19
h. seven horns. *Rev* 5:6
h. every one harps. 8
I saw an angel, *h.* the seal of. 7:2
h. a golden censer. 8:3
h. breastplates. 9:17
h. seven heads. *Rev* 12:3
h. great wrath. 12
h. the everlasting gospel 14:6
h. the harps of God. 15:2
h. a golden cup. 17:4
h. great power. 18:1
h. the key of the pit. 20:1
holy Jerusalem, *h.* the glory. 21:11

havock

as for Saul. he made *h.* of. *Acts* 8:3*

hawk

h. had in. *Lev* 11:16; *Deut* 14:15
doth the *h.* fly by thy ? *Job* 39:26

hay

h. appeareth, and tender. *Pr* 27:25
the *h.* is withered away. *Isa* 15:6*
on this foundation, *h.* *1 Cor* 3:12

Hazael

H. to be king. *1 Ki* 19:15, 17
H. went to meet Elisha. *2 Ki* 8:8, 9
Ben-hadad died, and *H.* reigned. 15
went with Joram against *H.* 28, 29
kept Ramoth because of *H.* 9:14
H. smote them in all coasts. 10:32
H. set his face to Jerusalem. 12:17
sent the hallowed things to *H.* 18
Israel into the hand of *H.* 13:3, 22
so *H.* died. 24
Ben-hadad son of *H.* took cities. 25
fire into the house of *H.* *Amos* 1:4

hazarded

men that have *h.* lives. *Acts* 15:26

hazel

took him rods of *h.* and. *Gen* 30:37*

Hazelelponi

of their sister was *H.* *1 Chr* 4:3

Hazeroth

abode at *H.* *Num* 11:35; 33:17
removed from *H.* 12:16; 33:18

Hazor

Joshua took *H.* head of. *Josh* 11:10
and he burnt *H.* with fire. 11, 13
Kedesh and *H.* cities of. 15:23, 25
Ramah and *H.* cities of. 19:36
Jabin who reigned in *H.* *Judg* 4:2
raised a levy to build *H.* *1 Ki* 9:15
king of Syria took *H.* *2 Ki* 15:29
the kingdoms of *H.* *Jer* 49:28
O ye inhabitants of *H.* 30
and *H.* shall be a dwelling for. 33

he

he shall rule over thee. *Gen* 3:16
strive with man, for *he* is flesh. 6:3
he with whom it is found. 44:10
brother be greater than *he.* 48:19
art *he* whom thy brethren. 49:8
he shall be thy spokesman to the
people, and *he* shall be. *Ex* 4:16
and hardened his heart, *he.* 9:34
he hath put in his heart that *he* may
teach both *he* and. 35:34
he among the sons of. *Lev* 7:33
shall go out in jubile, *he* and. 25:54
cursed is *he* that. *Num* 24:9
came, *he* and all his. *Deut* 3:1
it is *he* that giveth power to. 8:18
cursed be *he.* 27:16
So to the end of the chapter
he that doth go with thee, *he* will.
31:6, 8
is not *he* thy Father that ? 32:6
I, even I am *he,* and there is. 39
Isa 41:4; 43:10, 13; 46:4; 48:12
Lord your God is *he.* *Josh* 23:3, 10
what man is *he* will ? *Judg* 10:18
I am *he* that came. *1 Sam* 4:16
not a goodlier person than *he.* 9:2
this is *he.* 16:12
as his name is so is *he.* 25:25
two men better than *he.* *1 Ki* 2:32
she and *he* and her house. 17:15
thou *he* that troubleth Israel ? 18:17
is not that *he* whose places.
2 Ki 18:22; *Isa* 36:7
he in first year of reign. *2 Chr* 29:3
where, and who is *he* ? *Job* 9:24
who is *he* that will plead ? 13:19
man dieth, and where is *he* ? 14:10
20:7; *Isa* 63:11
thou art *he* that took me. *Ps* 22:9

he it is shall tread. Ps 60:12; 108:13
he that is our God is the God. 68:20
he is God, it is he that. 100:3
is he that giveth salvation. 144:10
Lord, happy is he. Pr 16:20; 29:18
he that is higher than. Eccl 5:8
untimely birth is better than he. 6:3
he sitteth on the circle. Isa 40:22
he that comforteth. 51:12; 52:6
John 18:5, 6, 8; Rev 1:18; 2:23
and said, it is not he. Jer 5:12
art not thou he, O Lord our? 14:22
the king is not he that can do. 38:5
he also shall be in derision. 48:26
art thou he of whom? Ezek 38:17
is more righteous than he. Hab 1:13
where is he that is born? Mat 2:2
this is he that was spoken of. 3:3
art thou he that should come? 11:3
Luke 7:19, 20
he that is not with me is against me,
and he that. Mat 12:30; Luke 11:23
Christ? whose son is he? Mat 22:42
he is in the desert, he is in. 24:26
the same is he. 26:48; Mark 14:44
is none other but he. Mark 12:32
he to whom the Son. Luke 10:22
and he from within shall. 11:7
who is he that gave thee this? 20:2
he that sitteth at meat, or he? 22:27
they said, he is not here, but. 24:6
we trusted he should have. 21
this was he of whom. John 1:15, 30
I that speak to thee, am he. 4:26
where is he? 7:11
is not this he they seek to kill? 25
believe not that I am he, ye. 8:24
then shall ye know that I am he. 28
they said, is not this he that? 9:8
this is he, but he said, I am he. 9
who is he, Lord? 36
he that talketh with thee. 37
ye may believe that I am he. 13:19
they knew it was he who. Acts 3:10
this is he that was in church. 7:38
is not this he that destroyed? 9:21
Peter said, I am he whom. 10:21
he that was ordained of God. 42
ye that I am? I am not he. 13:25
he is not a Jew that is. Rom 2:28
he is a Jew that is one inwardly. 29
he that in these things. 14:18
are we stronger than he? 1 Cor 10:22
that as he is Christ's. 2 Cor 10:7
faithful is he that. 1 Thes 5:24
he who now letteth will let, until he
be taken. 2 Thes 2:7
son is he whom the father? Heb 12:7
he for our profit, that we might. 10
as he which hath called. 1 Pet 1:15
we walk in light, as he is. 1 John 1:7
when he shall appear, we may. 2:28
is righteous, even as he is. 3:7
dwelleth in him, and he. 24; 4:15
he that is in you, than he in. 4:4
because as he is, so are we in. 17
he that hath the Son, hath life; and
he that hath not the Son. 5:12
follow not evil, he that doeth good is
of God; he that doeth. 3 John 11
holy is he that hath part. Rev 20:6
he that is unjust, he that is. 22:11

head

it shall bruise thy h. Gen 3:15
shall lift up thy h. 40:13, 19
on the h. of Joseph, and on the top of
the h. of him. 49:26; Deut 33:16
Aaron and his sons put their hands
upon h. Ex 29:10; Lev 4:4; 8:14
put hands upon the h. of the ram.
Ex 29:15, 19; Lev 8:18, 22
shall put hand on the h. Lev 1:4
shall lay his hand on the h. of. 3:2
hand on h. of sin offering. 4:29, 33
leprous, his plague is in his h. 13:44
shall be rent, and his h. bare. 45
not make baldness on their h. 21:5
shall not uncover his h. nor rend. 10
uncover the woman's h. Num 5:18
shall no razor come upon his h. 6:5
of his God is on his h. 7
shall shave his h. 9, 18; Deut 21:12
and he shall hallow his h. Num 6:11
on his h., blood on our h. Josh 2:19
she smote off Sisera's h. Judg 5:26
no razor shall come on his h. 13:5
Goliath's h. 1 Sam 17:57
of Nabal on his own h. 25:39
thee keeper of my h. for ever. 28:2
cut off Saul's h. 31:9
earth upon his h. 2 Sam 1:2; 15:32
blood be upon thy h. 1:16; 1 Ki 2:37
and said, Am I a dog's h.? 2 Sam 3:8
let it rest on the h. of Joab, and. 29
go over, and take off his h. 16:9
take thy master from thy h. to-day.
2 Ki 2:3, 5
unto his father, My h. my h. 4:19
if the h. of Elisha shall. 6:31
murderer sent to take away my h. 32
daughter of Jerusalem hath shaken
her h. 19:21; Isa 37:22
did lift up the h. of Jehoiachin.
2 Ki 25:27; Jer 52:31
his way on his h. 2 Chr 6:23
are increased over our h. Ezra 9:6
reproach on their own h. Neh 4:4
return on his own h. Esth 9:25
Job arose, shaved his h. Job 1:20
yet will not I lift up my h. 10:15
I could shake my h. at you. 16:4
the lifter up of mine h. Ps 3:3
shall return on his own h. 7:16
out the lip, they shake the h. 22:7
thou anointest my h. with oil. 23:5
now shall my h. be lifted up. 27:6
iniquities are gone over mine h. 38:4
a shaking of the h. among. 44:14
is strength of mine h. 60:7; 108:8
God shall wound the h. of. 68:21
hate thee, have lift up the h. 83:2
therefore shall he lift up the h. 110:7
as for the h. of those that. 140:9
which shall not break my h. 141:5
blessings are on the h. of. Pr 10:6
blessing on the h. of him. 11:26
heap coals of fire on his h. 25:22
Rom 12:20
man's eyes are in his h. Eccl 2:14
hand is under my h. S of S 2:6; 8:3
my h. is filled with dew, my. 5:2
his h. as most fine gold. 11
thy h. as Carmel. 7:5
whole h. is sick and heart. Isa 1:5
joy shall be on their h. 51:11
is it to bow down his h. as a? 58:5
helmet of salvation on his h. 59:17
and thine hands on thy h. Jer 2:37
O that my h. were waters. 9:1
fall grievously on the h. 23:19; 30:23
their way on their h. Ezek 9:10
h. was made bald, shoulder. 29:18
O king, thou art this h. Dan 2:38
recompense on your h. Joel 3:4, 7
pant after dust on the h. Amos 2:7
will bring baldness on every h. 8:10
cut them in the h. all of them. 9:1
no man did lift up his h. Zech 1:21
then set the crowns on the h. 6:11
thou swear by thy h. Mat 5:36
smote him on h. 27:30; Mark 15:19
she said, The h. of John. Mark 6:24
my h. with oil thou didst. Luke 7:46
but also my hands and h. John 13:9
his h. covered, dishonoureth his h.
1 Cor 11:4
ought to have power on her h. 10
the h. to the feet, I have no. 12:21
and gave him as h. to the church.
Eph 1:22; 4:15; Col 1:18
not holding the h. from. Col 2:19
eyes flame of fire, and h. Rev 19:12
see **bald, beard, bow, bowed, cover, covered, crown**

head *of the corner*

the h. of the corner. Mat 21:42
Mark 12:10; Luke 20:17
Acts 4:11; 1 Pet 2:7

head, for *ruler, governor*

one rod shall be for the h. Num 17:3
he was h. over a people of a. 25:15
Lord will make thee h. Deut 28:13
he shall be the h. and thou shalt. 44
each one an h. of house. Josh 22:14
he shall be h. over all Gilead.
Judg 10:18; 11:8
shall I be your h.? Judg 11:9
the people made him h. 11
thou not made the h.? 1 Sam 15:17
thou hast kept me to be h. of the
heathen. 2 Sam 22:44; Ps 18:43
thou art exalted as h. 1 Chr 29:11
h. of Damascus is Rezin, h. of.
Isa 7:8, 9
will cut off from Israel h. 9:14
and honourable, he is the h. 15
nor work which h. or tail, or. 19:15
art Gilead to me, h. of. Jer 22:6
themselves one h. Hos 1:11
woundedst the h. out of. Hab 3:13
thou didst strike through the h. 14
h. of every man is Christ; the h. of
the woman is the man; and the
h. of Christ is God. 1 Cor 11:3
is the h. of the wife, even as Christ is
h. of the church, and. Eph 5:23
h. of all principality. Col 2:10

head, for *top, chief*

the h. of fat valleys. Isa 28:1, 4
they lie at the h. of all the. 51:20*
built high places at h. Ezek 16:25
choose it at the h. of the. 21:19
king of Babylon stood at the h. of. 21

head with *hair* or *hairs*

hair is fallen off his h. Lev 13:40, 41
shave all his hair off his h. 14:9
locks of hair of his h. Num 6:5
and shalt take the hair of h. of. 18
the hair of his h. began. Judg 16:22
not an hair of his h. 1 Sam 14:45
weighed hair of his h. 2 Sam 14:26
plucked off hair of my h. Ezra 9:3
they are more than hairs of my h.
Ps 40:12; 69:4
the hair of thine h. S of S 7:5
nor was an hair of their h. Dan 3:27
hair of his h. like the pure. 7:9
hairs of your h. are numbered.
Mat 10:30; Luke 12:7
with hairs of her h. Luke 7:38, 44
not an hair of your h. perish. 21:18
not an hair fall from h. Acts 27:34
his h. and his hairs were. Rev 1:14

axe **head**

the axe h. slippeth. Deut 19:5
axe h. fell into water. 2 Ki 6:5

bed's **head**

himself on the bed's h. Gen 47:31

hoary **head**

rise before the hoary h. Lev 19:32

spear's **head**

spear's h. weighed 600 shekels.
1 Sam 17:7; 2 Sam 21:16

headbands

Lord will take away h. Isa 3:20*

headlong

of froward is carried h. Job 5:13
might cast him down h. Luke 4:29
falling h. he burst. Acts 1:18

heads

they bowed down their h. Gen 43:28
Ex 4:31
uncover not your h. lest. Lev 10:6
and put dust upon their h. Josh 7:6
Job 2:12
they lifted up their h. no. Judg 8:28
did God render upon their h. 9:57
it not be with the h. 1 Sam 29:4
put ropes on our h. 1 Ki 20:31
put ropes on their h. and came. 32
take ye the h. of your. 2 Ki 10:6
they have brought the h. of the. 8
lift up your h. O ye gates. Ps 24:7, 9
caused men to ride over our h. 66:12
brakest the h. of the dragons. 74:13
thou brakest the h. of leviathan. 14
on me, they shaked their h. 109:25
their h. shall be baldness. Isa 15:2
everlasting joy on their h. 35:10
and covered their h. Jer 14:3
ashamed, they covered their h. 4
shall be on all their h. Ezek 7:18
their way on their h. 11:21; 22:31
their swords under their h. 32:27
have linen bonnets on their h. 44:18
they shall poll their h. 20

reviled, wagging their *h.* *Mat* 27:39
Mark 15:29
up, and lift up your *h.* *Luke* 21:28
blood be upon your own *h.* *Acts* 18:6
on their *h.* were as it were. *Rev* 9:7
were like to serpents, and had *h.* 19
having seven *h.* and on his *h.* 13:1
his *h.* as it were wounded to. 3
seven *h.* are seven mountains. 17:9
they cast dust on their *h.* 18:19

heads for *governors*

and made them *h.* over. *Ex* 18:25
were *h.* of thousands. *Num* 1:16
take all the *h.* of the people. 25:4*
and Gad answered the *h.* *Josh* 22:21
Joshua called for their *h.* and. 23:2
the *h.* of Israel were. *1 Chr* 12:32
assembled all the *h.* to. *2 Chr* 5:2
certain of the *h.* of Ephraim. 28:12
shall wound the *h.* over. *Ps* 110:6
O *h.* of Jacob, and. *Mi* 3:1, 9
h. thereof judge for reward. 11
see **fathers**

headstone

is become the *h.* of the. *Ps* 118:22
bring forth the *h.* with. *Zech* 4:7†

heady

for men shall be *h.* *2 Tim* 3:4*

heal

h. her now, O God. *Num* 12:13
alive, I wound, I *h.* *Deut* 32:39
I will *h.* thee, and add. *2 Ki* 20:5
sign that the Lord will *h.* me ? 8
their sin, and will *h.* *2 Chr* 7:14
O Lord, *h.* me, for my. *Ps* 6:2
h. my soul, for I have sinned. 41:4
h. the breaches thereof, for. 60:2
to kill, and a time to *h.* *Eccl* 3:3
smite and *h.* it, and he shall *h.* them.
Isa 19:22
his ways, and will *h.* him. 57:18, 19
return, and I will *h.* your. *Jer* 3:22
h. me, O Lord, and I shall be. 17:14
I will *h.* thee of thy wounds. 30:17
breach is great, who can *h.* thee ?
Lam 2:13
yet could he not *h.* you. *Hos* 5:13
he hath torn, and will *h.* us. 6:1
I will *h.* their backsliding, I. 14:4
he shall not *h.* that that. *Zech* 11:16
I will come and *h.* him. *Mat* 8:7
to *h.* all manner of sickness. 10:1
Mark 3:15
h. the sick, cleanse the lepers.
Mat 10:8; *Luke* 9:2; 10:9
is it lawful to *h.* on the sabbath days ?
Mat 12:10; *Luke* 14:3
I should *h.* them. *Mat* 13:15
John 12:40; *Acts* 28:27
whether he would *h.* on sabbath.
Mark 3:2; *Luke* 6:7
he hath sent me to *h.* the. *Luke* 4:18
ye will surely say, Physician, *h.* 23
the Lord was present to *h.* 5:17
that he would come and *h.* his. 7:3*
would come down and *h.* *John* 4:47
forth thine hand to *h.* *Acts* 4:30

healed

God *h.* Abimelech and. *Gen* 20:17
him to be thoroughly *h.* *Ex* 21:19
was a boil and is *h.* *Lev* 13:18
the scall is *h.* 37
the plague of leprosy be *h.* 14:3, 48
thou canst not be *h.* *Deut* 28:27
then he shall be *h.* *1 Sam* 6:3
have *h.* the waters. *2 Ki* 2:21
waters were *h.* 22
king Joram went to be *h.* in. 8:29
Joram was returned to be *h.* 9:15
2 Chr 22:6
Lord hearkened and *h.* *2 Chr* 30:20
thee, and thou hast *h.* me. *Ps* 30:2
sent his word, and *h.* them. 107:20
and convert, and be *h.* *Isa* 6:10
and with his stripes we are *h.* 53:5
have *h.* the hurt. *Jer* 6:14; 8:11
which refuseth to be *h.* 15:18
O Lord, and I shall be *h.* 17:14
balm, if so be she may be *h.* 51:8
h. Babylon, but she is not *h.* 9
not be bound up to be *h.* *Ezek* 30:21
neither have ye *h.* that which. 34:4
the waters shall be *h.* *Ezek* 47:8, 9
marishes thereof shall not be *h.* 11
I would have *h.* Israel. *Hos* 7:1
but they knew not that I *h.* 11:3
the palsy, and he *h.* *Mat* 4:24
speak, and my servant shall be *h.*
Mat 8:8; *Luke* 7:7
multitudes followed him, he *h.*
Mat 12:15; 14:14
that she may be *h.* and. *Mark* 5:23*
all, nor could be *h.* of. *Luke* 8:43
therefore come and be *h.* and. 13:14
when he saw that he was *h.* 17:15
touched his ear, and *h.* him. 22:51
he that was *h.* wist not. *John* 5:13
the man who was *h.* *Acts* 4:14
and they were *h.* every one. 5:16
that he had faith to be *h.* 14:9*
Paul prayed, and *h.* father of. 28:8
but let it rather be *h.* *Heb* 12:13
another, that ye may be *h.* *Jas* 5:16
whose stripes ye were *h.* *1 Pet* 2:24
deadly wound was *h.* *Rev* 13:3, 12

healer

I will not be an *h.* *Isa* 3:7

healeth

the Lord that *h.* thee. *Ex* 15:26
who *h.* all thy diseases. *Ps* 103:3
he *h.* the broken in heart. 147:3
and he *h.* the stroke. *Isa* 30:26

healing, *substantive*

no *h.* for us, the time of *h.* *Jer* 14:19
is no *h.* of thy bruise. *Nah* 3:19*
Sun of righteousness arise with *h.*
Mal 4:2
that had need of *h.* *Luke* 9:11
on whom this miracle of *h.* *Acts* 4:22
another the gift of *h.* *1 Cor* 12:9, 28
have all the gifts of *h.*? 30
leaves of tree were for *h.* *Rev* 22:2

healing

thou hast no *h.* medicine. *Jer* 30:13
went about *h.* all manner. *Mat* 4:23
preaching gospel, and *h.* *Luke* 9:6
h. all that were oppressed of the.
Acts 10:38

health

our father is in good *h.* *Gen* 43:28
Joab said, Art thou in *h.*? *2 Sam* 20:9
who is the *h.* of my countenance.
Ps 42:11†; 43:5†
thy saving *h.* may be known. 67:2
it shall be *h.* to thy navel. *Pr* 3:8
they are *h.* to all their flesh. 4:22
the tongue of the wise is *h.* 12:18
but a faithful ambassador is *h.* 13:17
sweet to the soul, and *h.* to. 16:24
thy *h.* shall spring forth. *Isa* 58:8
looked for a time of *h.* *Jer* 8:15
why is not the *h.* of my people ? 22
I will restore *h.* unto thee. 30:17
I will bring it *h.* and cure. 33:6
for this is for your *h.* *Acts* 27:34*
mayest be in *h.* as thy soul. *3 John* 2

heap, *substantive*

h. and did eat on the *h.* *Gen* 31:46
this *h.* be witness, and this pillar. 52
floods stood upright as an *h.* *Ex* 15:8
Josh 3:13, 16; *Ps* 33:7; 78:13
shall be an *h.* for ever. *Deut* 13:16
over him a great *h.* of. *Josh* 7:26
burnt Ai, and made it an *h.* 8:28
raise on the king of Ai a great *h.* 29
down at the end of the *h.* *Ruth* 3:7
they laid very great *h.* *2 Sam* 18:17
thy belly is like an *h.* of. *S of S* 7:2
shall be a ruinous *h.* *Isa* 17:1
harvest shall be an *h.* in the. 11*
thou hast made of a city an *h.* 25:2
builded on her own *h.* *Jer* 30:18
Rabbah shall be a desolate *h.* 49:2
make Samaria as an *h.* *Mi* 1:6
didst walk through the *h.* *Hab* 3:15
one came to an *h.* of. *Hag* 2:16

heap

I will *h.* mischiefs upon. *Deut* 32:23
I could *h.* up words. *Job* 16:4*
though he *h.* up silver as. 27:16
the hypocrites in heart, *h.* 36:13*
thou shalt *h.* coals of fire. *Pr* 25:22
Rom 12:20
to gather and to *h.* up. *Eccl* 2:26
h. on wood, kindle fire. *Ezek* 24:10
for they shall *h.* dust. *Hab* 1:10
h. to themselves teachers. *2 Tim* 4:3

heaped

Tyrus *h.* up silver as. *Zech* 9:3
ye have *h.* treasure. *Jas* 5:3*

heapeth

he *h.* up riches, and. *Ps* 39:6
he *h.* unto him all people. *Hab* 2:5

heaps

them together on *h.* *Ex* 8:14
bone of an ass, *h.* on *h.* *Judg* 15:16
lay ye them in two *h.* *2 Ki* 10:8
fenced cities into ruinous *h.* 19:25
and laid them by *h.* *2 Chr* 31:6
month they began to lay the *h.* 7
princes came and saw the *h.* 8
revive stones out of the *h.*? *Neh* 4:2
are ready to become *h.* *Job* 15:28
have laid Jerusalem on *h.* *Ps* 79:1
make Jerusalem *h.* *Jer* 9:11; 26:18
way marks, make thee high *h.* 31:21
cast Babylon up as *h.* and. 50:26
and Babylon shall become *h.* 51:37
their altars are as *h.* in. *Hos* 12:11
Jerusalem shall become *h.* *Mi* 3:12

hear

(*This word is often used for listening to the word of God with a firm purpose to obey his commands. It is also used of God hearing prayer, in the sense of answering, or granting it*)

that all that *h.* will laugh. *Gen* 21:6
h. us, my lord, thou art a. 23:6
that the people may *h.* *Ex* 19:9
noise of them that sing do I *h.* 32:18
h. I pray you, ye sons. *Num* 16:8
rise up, Balak, and *h.* 23:18
and her father *h.* her vow. 30:4
h. the cause between. *Deut* 1:16
and I will make them *h.* my. 4:10
h. Israel the statutes. 5:1; 6:3; 9:1
20:3; *Isa* 48:1; *Mark* 12:29
and *h.* all that the Lord. *Deut* 5:27
h. all these words which I. 12:28
if thou shalt *h.* say in one. 13:12
bring it, that we may *h.* 30:12, 13
that they may *h.* and fear Lord.
31:12, 13; *Jer* 6:10
h. the words of the Lord. *Josh* 3:9
when ye hear the sound of trumpet.
6:5; *Neh* 4:20; *Dan* 3:5, 15
h. O ye kings, give ear. *Judg* 5:3
why abodest, to *h.* bleatings of ? 16
riddle, that we may *h.* it. 14:13
for I *h.* of your evil. *1 Sam* 2:23
it is no good report that I *h.* 24
lowing of the oxen which I *h.* 15:14
how can I go ? if Saul *h.* it. 16:2
h. the words of thy handmaid. 25:24
2 Sam 20:17
let my lord the king *h.* *1 Sam* 26:19
no man deputed of the king to *h.*
2 Sam 15:3
as soon as ye *h.* the sound of. 10
what thing soever thou shalt *h.* 35
send to me every thing that ye *h.* 36
h. likewise what Hushai saith. 17:5
woman cried out of city, *h. h.* 20:16
as soon as they *h.*, they shall be obedient. 22:45; *Ps* 18:44
to *h.* the wisdom of Solomon.
1 Ki 4:34; 10:8, 24; *2 Chr* 9:7, 23
Mat 12:42; *Luke* 11:31
and *h.* thou in heaven. *1 Ki* 8:30
32, 34, 36, 39, 43, 45, 49; *2 Chr* 6:21
saying, O Baal, *h.* us. *1 Ki* 18:26
made the host to *h.* a. *2 Ki* 7:6
h. the word of the great king. 18:28
Isa 36:13
h. the words of Sennacherib.
2 Ki 19:16; *Isa* 37:17
when thou shalt *h.* a. *1 Chr* 14:15
thou mayest *h.* prayer. *Neh* 1:6*
h. O our God, for we are. 4:4
and all that could *h.* with. 8:2
h. it, and know thou it. *Job* 5:27
h. diligently my speech. 13:17; 21:2
will God *h.* his cry ? 27:9
h. my words. 34:2
h. I beseech thee, and I will. 42:4

have mercy upon me, *h.* *Ps* 4:1
39:12; 54:2; 84:8; 102:1; 143:1
the Lord *h.* thee in the day. 20:1*
save, Lord, let the king *h.* us. 9*
h. O Lord, when I cry with. 27:7
h. O Lord, and have mercy. 30:10
h. this, all ye people, give ear. 49:1
h. O my people, and. 50:7; 81:8
make me to *h.* joy and. 51:8
for who, say they, doth *h.*? 59:7
h. my cry, O God, attend to. 61:1
come, and *h.*, all ye that fear. 66:16
h. groaning of the prisoner. 102:20
when they *h.* the words of. 138:4
me to *h.* thy lovingkindness. 143:8
my son, *h.* the instruction. *Pr* 1:8
h. ye children, the instruction. 4:1
h. O my son, and receive. 10; 19:20
h. for I will speak of excellent. 8:6
h. instruction, and be wise. 33
cease to *h.* instruction. 19:27
bow thine ear, *h.* the words. 22:17
h. thou, my son, be wise. 23:19
and be more ready to *h.* *Eccl* 5:1
it is better to *h.* the rebuke. 7:5
let us *h.* the conclusion of. 12:13
voice, cause me to *h.* it. *S of S* 8:13
h. O heavens, and give ear. *Isa* 1:2
h. ye indeed, but. 6:9; *Mark* 4:12
when he bloweth, *h.* ye. *Isa* 18:3
h. ye that are afar off what. 33:13
let the earth *h.* and all that. 34:1
h. ye deaf. 42:18
who will *h.* for time to come? 23
or let them *h.* and say, It is. 43:9
assemble yourselves and *h.* 48:14
h. ye this, I have not spoken. 16
h. and your soul shall live. 55:3
John 5:25
shall I *h.* the sound of? *Jer* 4:21
therefore *h.* ye nations. 6:18
h. O earth. 19
h. ye the words of this. 11:2, 6
who refused to *h.* 10; 13:10
h. ye, give ear, for the Lord. 13:15
then I will cause thee to *h.* 18:2
caused my people to *h.* my. 23:22
if the princes *h.* that I have. 38:25
therefore *h.* counsel of. 49:20; 50:45
h. I pray you, all. *Lam* 1:18
h. what I say. *Ezek* 2:8
h. at my mouth. 3:17; 33:7
he that heareth, let him *h.* 3:27
lying to my people, that *h.* 13:19
h. what is the word that. 33:30
they *h.* thy words, but will not. 31, 32
O God, *h.* the prayer of. *Dan* 9:17*
O Lord, *h.* O Lord, forgive. 19
h. ye this, O priests. *Hos* 5:1
h. this, ye old men. *Joel* 1:2
h. this word that the Lord hath
spoken. *Amos* 3:1; 4:1; 5:1; 8:4
h. all ye people, hearken. *Mi* 1:2
I said, *h.* I pray you, O. 3:1, 9
h. ye, O mountains. 6:2
h. ye the rod and him. 9
all that *h.* the bruit of. *Nah* 3:19
lest they should *h.* law. *Zech* 7:12
the things which ye *h.* *Mat* 11:4
lame walk, and deaf *h.* 5
Mark 7:37; *Luke* 7:22
to *h.* those things that ye *h.*
Mat 13:17; *Luke* 10:24
he said to multitude *h.* *Mat* 15:10
beloved Son, *h.* him. 17:5; *Mark* 9:7
neglect to *h.* them, to *h.* *Mat* 18:17
are such as *h.* the word. *Mark* 4:18
20; *Luke* 8:12, 13
heed what ye *h.* you that *h.* more.
Mark 4:24
pressed on him to *h.* *Luke* 5:1
multitudes came together to *h.* 15
which came to *h.* him, and to. 6:17
I say to you which *h.* love your. 27
heed therefore how ye *h.* 8:18
which *h.* the word and. 21; 11:28
but who is this of whom I *h.*? 9:9
publicans and sinners to *h.* him. 15:1
said, How is it that I *h.* this? 16:2
and prophets let them *h.* them. 29
Lord said, *H.* what the unjust. 18:6
were very attentive to *h.* him. 19:48*
to him in temple, for to *h.* him. 21:38
as I *h.* I judge. *John* 5:30
who can *h.* it? *John* 6:60
law judge a man before it *h.*? 7:51
wherefore would ye *h.* it again? 9:27
sheep *h.* his voice, and he. 10:3
if any man *h.* my words. 12:47
and the word which ye *h.* is. 14:24
how *h.* we every man? *Acts* 2:8
this, which ye now see and *h.* 33
send for thee, and to *h.* 10:22
to *h.* all things that are. 33
desired to *h.* the word of God. 13:7
whole city came together to *h.* 44
by my mouth should *h.* the. 15:7
either to tell or to *h.* some. 17:21
ye *h.* Paul hath turned. 19:26
h. ye my defence which I make. 22:1
that thou wouldest *h.* us of. 24:4
Agrippa said, I would *h.* 25:22
but we desire to *h.* what. 28:22
I *h.* there be divisions. *1 Cor* 11:18
or else be absent, I may *h.* *Phil* 1:27
we *h.* that some walk. *2 Thes* 3:11
thyself and them that *h.* *1 Tim* 4:16
all the Gentiles might *h.* *2 Tim* 4:17
let every one be swift to *h.* *Jas* 1:19
we know that he *h.* us. *1 John* 5:15
than to *h.* my children. *3 John* 4
blessed that *h.* words of. *Rev* 1:3
which neither can see, nor *h.* 9:20
see **ear, ears, voice**

hear *me*

shall Pharaoh *h. me*? *Ex* 6:12
h. me, O Lord, *h. me*. *1 Ki* 18:37
h. me, my brethren. *1 Chr* 28:2
h. me, thou Jeroboam. *2 Chr* 13:4
h. me, Asa. 15:2
and he said, *h. me*, O Judah. 20:20
h. me, ye Levites, sanctify. 29:5
I will shew thee, *h. me*, I. *Job* 15:17
O that one would *h. me*, my. 31:35
h. me when I call, O God. *Ps* 4:1*
consider, and *h. me*, O Lord. 13:3*
upon thee, for thou wilt *h. me*. 17:6*
h. me, lest they should rejoice. 38:16
attend unto me, and *h. me*. 55:2*
thy right hand, and *h. me*. 60:5*
multitude of thy mercy *h. me*. 69:13*
trouble, *h. me* speedily. 17*; 143:7
God, my God will *h. me*. *Mi* 7:7
I beseech thee to *h. me*. *Acts* 26:3
also all that *h. me*, were such. 29
that will they not *h. me*. *1 Cor* 14:21

hear *not*, or *not* **hear**

wilt *not h.* but worship. *Deut* 30:17
the Lord will *not h.* *1 Sam* 8:18*
and thou dost *not h.* me. *Job* 30:20*
surely God will *not h.* vanity. 35:13
Lord will *not h.* me. *Ps* 66:18
the ear, shall he *not h.*? 94:9
many prayers, I will *not h.* *Isa* 1:15
Jer 7:16; 11:14; 14:12
Ezek 8:18; *Amos* 5:23
children that will *not h.* law. *Isa* 30:9
ear heavy that it *cannot h.* 59:1
he will *not h.* 2
when I spake ye did *not h.* 65:12
when I spake, they did *not h.* 66:4
Zech 1:4
have ears and *h. not*. *Jer* 5:21
Ezek 12:2; *Mark* 8:18
but if ye will *not h.* *Jer* 13:17
22:5; *Mal* 2:2
that they might *not h.* *Jer* 17:23
19:15; *Zech* 7:11
thou saidst, I will *not h.* *Jer* 22:21
praised the gods of silver, which see
not, nor *h.* *Dan* 5:23; *Rev* 9:20
Lord, but he will *not h.* *Mi* 3:4
I cry, and thou wilt *not h.* *Hab* 1:2
not receive you, *nor h.* *Mat* 10:14
if he will *not h.* thee, then. 18:16
if they *h. not* Moses. *Luke* 16:31
even because ye *cannot h.* *John* 8:43
therefore *h.* them *not*, because. 47
I told you, and ye did *not h.* 9:27
but the sheep did *not h.* them. 10:8
soul which will *not h.* *Acts* 3:23
will they *not h.* me. *1 Cor* 14:21
do ye *not h.* the law? *Gal* 4:21

would not **hear**

besought us, we *would not h.*
Gen 42:21
against the child, ye *would not h.* 22
thou *wouldest not h.* *Ex* 7:16
Israel *would not h.* *Deut* 1:43; 3:26
2 Ki 17:14; 18:12; *Neh* 9:29
Zech 7:13
Amaziah *would not h.* *2 Ki* 14:11
2 Chr 25:20
this is the refreshing: yet they *would
not h.* *Isa* 28:12
might be for praise, they *would not h.*
Jer 13:11; 29:19
he *would not h.* 36:25
I *would not h.* *Zech* 7:13

hear *now*, or *now* **hear**

and he said, *h. now* my words.
Num 12:6; 20:10
Saul said, *h. now*, ye. *1 Sam* 22:7
h. now, thou son of Ahitub. 12
h. now my reasoning. *Job* 13:6
h. me *now*, therefore, O. *Pr* 5:7
and he said, *h.* ye *now*. *Isa* 7:13
now h. O Jacob my servant. 44:1
h. now, thou that art given to. 47:8
therefore, *h. now* this, thou. 51:21
h. now this, O foolish. *Jer* 5:21
h. now, Hananiah. 28:15
h. now, O Joshua. *Zech* 3:8
h. now, I pray thee, O my. 37:20
h. ye *now* what the Lord. *Mi* 6:1
which ye *now* see and *h.* *Acts* 2:33
in me, and *now h.* to be in. *Phil* 1:30

shall **hear**

the people *shall h.* and. *Ex* 15:14
Deut 13:11; 17:13; 19:20; 21:21
the Egyptians *shall h.* it. *Num* 14:13
ye *shall h.* small as well. *Deut* 1:17
who *shall h.* report of thee. 2:25
which *shall h.* all these statutes. 4:6
of the land *shall h.* of it. *Josh* 7:9
and thou *shalt h.* what. *Judg* 7:11
Israel *shall h.* that. *2 Sam* 16:21
shall h. of thy great. *1 Ki* 8:42
and he *shall h.* a rumour. *2 Ki* 19:7
Isa 37:7
prayer to him, he *shall h.* *Job* 22:27
humble *shall h.* thereof. *Ps* 34:2
cry, and he *shall h.* my voice. 55:17
God *shall h.* and afflict them. 19
mine ears *shall h.* desire of. 92:11
they *shall h.* my words. 141:6
day *shall* the deaf *h.* *Isa* 29:18
when he *shall h.* it he will. 30:19
thine ears *shall h.* a word. 21
shall h. all the good. *Jer* 33:9
and the heaven *shall h.* *Hos* 2:21
the earth *shall h.* the corn and. 22
by hearing, ye *shall h.* *Mat* 13:14
Acts 28:26
if he *shall h.* thee thou. *Mat* 18:15
ye *shall h.* of wars. 24:6
Mark 13:7; *Luke* 21:9
dead *shall h.* voice of. *John* 5:25
whatsoever he *shall h.* that. 16:13
him *shall* ye *h.* in all things.
Acts 3:22; 7:37
said he, thou *shalt h.* him. 25:22
shall they *h.* without a. *Rom* 10:14

will **hear**

speak unto us, we *will h.* *Ex* 20:19
Deut 5:27
cry, I *will* surely *h.* *Ex* 22:23, 27
I *will h.* what the Lord. *Num* 9:8
king *will h.* to deliver. *2 Sam* 14:16
be thy God *will h.* the. *2 Ki* 19:4
then *will* I *h.* from heaven.
2 Chr 7:14; *Ps* 20:6
wilt h. and help. *2 Chr* 20:9; *Ps* 38:15
the Lord *will h.* *Ps* 4:3
thou *wilt h.* me. 17:6
I *will h.* what God the Lord. 85:8
he also *will h.* their cry, and. 145:19
man *will h.* and increase. *Pr* 1:5
the Lord *will h.* them. *Isa* 41:17*
are yet speaking, I *will h.* 65:24
house of Judah *will h.* *Jer* 36:3
whether they *will h.* or forbear.
Ezek 2:5, 7; 3:11
I *will h.* the heavens. *Hos* 2:21
God, my God *will h.* me. *Mi* 7:7
I am their God and *will h.* them.
Zech 10:6; 13:9
we *will h.* thee again of. *Acts* 17:32
for they *will h.* that thou. 21:22

I will h. thee, when thy. Acts 23:35
to the Gentiles, they will h. 28:28

hear the word of the Lord
h. therefore the word of the Lord.
1 Ki 22:19; 2 Chr 18:18
Jer 29:20; 42:15; Amos 7:16
Elisha said h. ye word of the Lord.
2 Ki 7:1; Jer 17:20; 21:11
Hezekiah, H. the word of Lord.
2 Ki 20:16; Isa 39:5
h. word of the Lord, ye rulers of Sodom. Isa 1:10
h. the word of the Lord, ye scornful men. 28:14
h. word of Lord, ye that tremble. 66:5
h. word of Lord, O house of Jacob.
Jer 2:4; 10:1
h. the word of the Lord, all ye of. 7:2
yet h. word of the Lord, O ye. 9:20
h. word of Lord, O kings of Judah.
19:3; 22:2
earth, h. the word of the Lord. 22:29
h. the word of Lord, O ye nations.
31:10
h. word of Lord, O Zedekiah. 34:4
h. the word of the Lord, all Judah.
44:24, 26
of Israel, h. the word of the Lord, I will bring a. Ezek 6:3; 36:1, 4
prophets h. ye the word of the Lord.
13:2
O harlot, h. the word of the Lord.
16:35
forest of the south, H. the word of the Lord. 20:47
Ammonites, h. the word of the Lord.
25:3
shepherds, h. the word of the Lord.
34:7, 9
dry bones, h. the word of the Lord.
37:4
h. word of the Lord, ye children.
Hos 4:1
Amaziah, h. thou the word of the Lord. Amos 7:16

heard
because Lord hath h. Gen 16:11
neither yet h. I of it, but. 21:26
because the Lord hath h. that. 29:33
aloud, and the Egyptians h. 45:2
God h. their groaning. Ex 2:24
he hath h. your murmurings. 16:9
neither let it be h. out of thy. 23:13
sound shall be h. when he. 28:35
people h. these evil tidings. 33:4
let all that h. him lay. Lev 24:14
complained, the Lord h. Num 11:1
against Moses, the Lord h. it. 12:2
they have h. thou art among. 14:14
nations which have h. the fame. 15
in the day that he h. it. 30:7, 14
they h. that they were. Josh 9:16
Samuel cried, and the Lord h. him.
1 Sam 7:9*
come, as thy servant hath h.? 23:11
hast not h. that Adonijah? 1 Ki 1:11
nor was any tool of iron h. in. 6:7
and prosperity exceedeth fame which I h. 10:7; 2 Chr 9:6
hast thou not h. long ago?
2 Ki 19:25; Isa 37:26
make one sound to be h. 2 Chr 5:13
he was entreated and h. his. 33:13
the noise was h. afar. Ezra 3:13
the joy of Jerusalem h. Neh 12:43
h. the secret of God? Job 15:8
of wrong, but I am not h. 19:7
but how little a portion is h. 26:14
when the ear h. me, then it. 29:11
the Lord hath h. my. Ps 6:9
thou hast h. the desire of. 10:17
save me, for thou hast h. 22:21*
but when he cried he h. 24; 34:6
40:1; 120:1
I sought the Lord, and he h. 34:4*
but I as a deaf man h. not. 38:13
thou, O God, hast h. my vows. 61:5
verily God hath h. me, he. 66:19
cause judgement to be h. 76:8
therefore the Lord h. this and. 78:21
when God h. this, was wroth. 59
where I h. a language that I. 81:5
Zion h. and was glad, and. 97:8
their affliction, when he h. Ps 106:44
for thou hast h. me, and. 118:21*
lo, we h. of it at Ephratah. 132:6
cry himself, but not be h. Pr 21:13
to be h. unto Laish. Isa 10:30
have ye not h.? hath it not? 40:21
hast thou not h. everlasting God? 28
thou hast h. see all this, will? 48:6
which they had not h. shall. 52:15
violence shall no more be h. in. 60:18
men have not h. what he hath. 64:4
weeping shall be no more h. 65:19
who hath h. such a thing? 66:8
isles afar off, that have not h. 19
thou hast h. the sound. Jer 4:19
wickedness, spoil is h. in her. 6:7
rising early, but ye h. not. 7:13
hearkened and h. but they. 8:6
ask the heathen, who hath h. 18:13
let cry be h. from houses when. 22
howling of the flock shall be h. 25:36
prophesied as ye have h. 26:11
h. every one should let his. 34:10
spoken, but they have not h. 35:17
the nations have h. of thy. 46:12
and the cry is h. among. 50:46
a rumour that shall be h. in. 51:46
they have h. that I sigh. Lam 1:21
thou hast h. their reproach. 3:61
the nations h. of him. Ezek 19:4
thy harps shall be no more h. 26:13
h. the sound of the trumpet. 33:5
and I h. but I understood. Dan 12:8
their congregation hath h. Hos 7:12
unto Lord, and he h. me. Jonah 2:2*
such as they have not h. Mi 5:15
I h., my belly trembled. Hab 3:16
Lord hearkened and h. it. Mal 3:16
ye have h. it was said. Mat 5:21
27, 33, 38, 43
they shall be h. for their much. 6:7
ye hear, and have not h. them.
13:17; Luke 10:24
offended after they h. Mat 15:12
when the king h. thereof. 22:7
ye have h. his blasphemy. 26:65
Mark 14:64
but when they have h. Mark 4:15
and when they h. it they. 14:11
fear not, thy prayer is h. Luke 1:13
Acts 10:31
have spoken, shall be h. Luke 12:3
when they h. it, they said. 20:16
what he hath h. that. John 3:32
every man that hath h. of the. 6:45
on ground, as though he h. not. 8:6
since world began was it not h. 9:32
I thank thee that thou hast h. 11:41
ask them which h. me, what. 18:21
when Simon Peter h. that it. 21:7
for the promise ye have h. Acts 1:4
h. this, they were pricked. 2:37
many of them which h. the. 4:4
fear came on all them that h. 5:5
when the Gentiles h. this. 13:48
the same h. Paul speak, who. 14:9
which worshipped God, h. us. 16:14
and the prisoners h. them. 25*
h. this, they were baptized. 19:5
of what thou hast seen and h. 22:15
h. him concerning the faith. 24:24
of whom they have not h. Rom 10:14
but I say, have they not h.? 18
they that have not h. shall. 15:21
not seen, nor ear h. 1 Cor 2:9
h. of my conversation. Gal 1:13
after that ye h. the word. Eph 1:13
h. of your faith in the Lord. 15
if so be ye have h. him and. 4:21
that ye had h. that he. Phil 2:26
things ye have h. and seen. 4:9
since we h. of your faith. Col 1:4
since day ye h. of it, and knew. 6
since day we h. it, do not cease. 9
things thou hast h. of me. 2 Tim 2:2
to us by them that h. him. Heb 2:3
for some when they had h. 3:16
with faith in them that h. 4:2
offered up prayers, and was h. 5:7
h. of the patience of Job. Jas 5:11
ye h. that antichrist shall come.
1 John 2:18; 4:3
have h. from the beginning. 2:24
3:11; 2 John 6
therefore how thou hast h. Rev 3:3
and all that are in them h. 5:13
I h. the number of them which. 7:4
and I h. the number of the. 9:16
I h. the angel of the waters. 16:5
of trumpeters shall be h. no. 18:22
the voice of bride shall be h. no. 23
things, and h. them, when I h. 22:8

I have **heard**
Ishmael I have h. thee. Gen 17:20
dreamed a dream: I have h. say that thou canst. 41:15; Dan 5:14, 16
I have h. there is corn. Gen 42:2
I have h. their cry. Ex 3:7
I have h. the groaning. 6:5
I have h. the murmuring. 16:12
Num 14:27
I have h.' the voice of. Deut 5:28
now I have h. that thou. 1 Sam 25:7
word that I have h. is. 1 Ki 2:42
I have h. thy prayer thou hast. 9:3
2 Ki 20:5; 2 Chr 7:12; Isa 38:5
which thou hast prayed I have h.
2 Ki 19:20
I also have h. thee, saith Lord.
22:19; 2 Chr 34:27
I have h. many such things. Job 16:2
I have h. the check of my. 20:3
I have h. of thee by the hearing. 42:5
for I have h. slander. Ps 31:13
twice I have h. this, power. 62:11
that which I have h. of. Isa 21:10
I have h. from the Lord a. 28:22
in an acceptable time have I h. 49:8*
2 Cor 6:2
I have h. what prophets. Jer 23:25
I have h. Ephraim bemoaning. 31:18
I have h. you, behold, I will. 42:4
I have h. a rumour from. 49:14
know I have h. all. Ezek 35:12
I have h. him and. Hos 14:8*
Lord, I have h. thy speech. Hab 3:2
I have h. the reproach. Zeph 2:8
those things I have h. John 8:26
truth, which I have h. of God. 40
all things that I have h. of. 15:15
I have h. their groaning. Acts 7:34
Lord, I have h. by many of this. 9:13

heard joined with voice
h. voice of the Lord walking. Gen 3:8
I h. thy voice, and was afraid. 10
God h. the voice of the lad. 21:17
God hath h. my voice, and. 30:6
h. that I lifted up my voice. 39:15
then he h. the voice of. Num 7:89
we cried, he h. our voice. 20:16
the Lord h. the voice of. Deut 1:34
similitude, only he h. a voice. 4:12
v. of God as thou hast h. 33; 5:26
ye h. the voice out of the. 5:23
have h. his voice out of the. 24
and the Lord h. the voice of your. 28
we cried, the Lord h. our voice. 26:7
let not thy voice be h. Judg 18:25
her voice was not h. 1 Sam 1:13
the Lord h. the voice. 1 Ki 17:22
voice was h. prayer. 2 Chr 30:27
was silence, I h. a voice. Job 4:16
I have h. the voice of thy. 33:8
stay them when his voice is h. 37:4
Lord with my voice, he h. Ps 3:4
the Lord hath h. the voice of. 6:8
I called, he h. my voice out of. 18:6
no speech where their voice is not h.
19:3
because he hath h. the voice of. 28:6
the voice of his praise to be h. 66:8
love the Lord, because he hath h. my voice. 116:1
voice of the turtle is h. S of S 2:12
h. the voice of the Lord. Isa 6:8
their voice shall be h. even. 15:4
his glorious voice to be h. 30:30
nor cause his voice to be h. 42:2
to make your voice be h. on. 58:4
voice of weeping shall no more be h.
65:19
a voice was h. upon the. Jer 3:21
h. a voice of a woman in. 4:31
voice of wailing is h. out of. 9:19
h. a voice of trembling. 30:5
a voice was h. in Ramah. 31:15
Mat 2:18

hast *h.* my *voice,* hide. Lam 3:56
and I *h.* a *voice* of one. Ezek 1:28
I *h.* behind me a *voice* of. 3:12
voice should no more be *h.* 19:9
cause their *voice* to be *h.* 27:30
I *h.* a man's *voice* between. Dan 8:16
yet *h.* I the *voice* of his words, when I *h.* 10:9
voice of thy messengers no more be *h.* Nah 2:13
neither *h.* his *voice.* John 5:37
h. a *voice,* saying, Saul, Saul. Acts 9:4; 22:7; 26:14
h. a *voice* saying to me, arise. 11:7
they *h.* not the *voice* of him. 22:9
which *voice* they that *h.* Heb 12:19
voice which came from heaven we *h.* 2 Pet 1:18
I *h.* a great *voice.* Rev 1:10; 16:1; 19:1; 21:3
the first *voice* I *h.* was as it. 4:1
I beheld, and *h.* the *voice* of. 5:11
I *h.* a *voice* in the midst of the. 6:6
I *h.* the *voice* of the fourth beast. 7
I *h.* a *voice* from the four. 9:13
I *h.* a *voice* from heaven. 10:4, 8; 14:2, 13; 18:4
and I *h.* a loud *voice,* saying. 12:10
I *h.* the *voice* of harpers. 14:2
I *h.* as it were the *voice* of a. 19:6

we have **heard**

we have h. how the Lord. Josh 2:10
as soon as *we had h.* these. 11
we have h. the fame of him. 9:9
thee according to all *we have h.* 2 Sam 7:22; 1 Chr 17:20
we have h. kings of Israel are. 1 Ki 20:31
we have h. the fame thereof. Job 28:22; Jer 6:24
we have h. with our ears. Ps 44:1
as *we have h.* so have we. 48:8
dark sayings which *we have h.* 78:3
we have h. of pride of Moab. Isa 16:6; Jer 48:29
we have h. songs, glory. Isa 24:16
we have h. a voice. Jer 30:5
because *we have h.* reproach. 51:51
we have h. a rumour from. Ob 1
for *we have h.* that God. Zech 8:23
we have h. him say, I. Mark 14:58
whatsoever *we have h.* done in Capernaum. Luke 4:23
we ourselves *have h.* of his. 22:71
we believe, *we have h.* John 4:42
we have h. out of the law. 12:34
speak things *we have h.* Acts 4:20
we have h. him speak. 6:11
we have h. him say, this Jesus. 14
we have h. that certain. 15:24
we have not *h.* whether there. 19:2
to things which *we have h.* Heb 2:1
that which *we have h.* 1 John 1:1, 3
message which *we have h.* of him. 5

heard joined with *word* or *words*

when he *h.* the *words* of. Gen 24:30
Abraham's servant *h.* their *words.* 52
and when Esau *h.* the *words.* 27:34
Jacob *h.* the *words* of Laban's. 31:1
when his master *h.* the *words.* 39:19
h. words of God. Num 24:4, 16
heads of Israel *h. words.* Josh 22:30
for it hath *h.* all the *words* of. 24:27
when Zebul *h.* the *words.* Judg 9:30
Samuel *h.* all the *words.* 1 Sam 8:21
Israel *h.* Goliath's *words.* 17:11
the same *words,* and David *h.* 23
words were *h.* which David. 31
the *word* that I have *h.* is good. 1 Ki 2:42
Hiram *h.* Solomon's *words.* 5:7
when Ahab *h.* those *words.* 21:27
when the king *h. words.* 2 Ki 6:30
be not afraid of *words* thou hast *h.* 19:6; Isa 37:6
h. the *words* of book of law, he rent. 2 Ki 22:11, 18; 2 Chr 34:19
Asa *h.* these *words.* 2 Chr 15:8
I *h.* these *words,* I sat. Neh 1:4
angry when I *h.* these *words.* 5:6
wept, when they *h. words.* 8:9
h. the voice of thy *words,* saying. Job 33:8
man's *words* are not *h.* Eccl 9:16
the *words* of wise men are *h.* in. 17
words which God hath *h.* Isa 37:4
marked, and *h.* his *word.* Jer 23:18
ye have not *h.* my *words.* 25:8
city all the *words* ye have *h.* 26:12
all the princes *h.* his *words.* 21
them all the *words* he had *h.* 36:13
not afraid that *h.* these *words.* 24
Pashur *h.* the *words* Jeremiah. 38:1
Darius *h.* these *words.* Dan 6:14
thy *words* were *h.,* and I am. 10:12
they *h.* these *words.* Mat 22:22
as soon as Jesus *h.* the *word.* Mark 5:36
Jesus' feet, and *h.* his *words.* Luke 10:39
fell on them who *h. word.* Acts 10:44
h. unspeakable *words.* 2 Cor 12:4
ye *h.* the *word* of truth. Eph 1:13
ye *h.* in the *word* of the. Col 1:5
word which ye *h.* of us. 1 Thes 2:13
sound *words* thou hast *h.* of me. 2 Tim 1:13
h. intreated that *word.* Heb 12:19
the *word* ye have *h.* from the. 1 John 2:7

heardest

and thou *h.* his words. Deut 4:36
for thou *h.* in that day. Josh 14:12
h. what I spake against this place. 2 Ki 22:19; 2 Chr 34:27
and thou *h.* their cry by. Neh 9:9
thou *h.* them from heaven. 27, 28
thou *h.* the voice of my. Ps 31:22
my ways, and thou *h.* me. 119:26*
the day when thou *h.* Isa 48:7
yea, thou *h.* not, yea, thou. 8
of hell I cried, thou *h.* Jonah 2:2

hearer

if any be a *h.* of the word. Jas 1:23
he being not a forgetful *h.* but. 25

hearers

the *h.* of the law are. Rom 2:13
minister grace unto *h.* Eph 4:29
the subverting of the *h.* 2 Tim 2:14
doers of word, and not *h.* Jas 1:22

hearest

Boaz to Ruth, *h.* thou? Ruth 2:8
h. thou men's words? 1 Sam 24:9
when *h.* sound in the. 2 Sam 5:4
when thou *h.* forgive. 1 Ki 8:30; 2 Chr 6:21
daytime, but thou *h.* not. Ps 22:2*
thou that *h.* prayer, unto thee. 65:2
said unto him, *h.* thou? Mat 21:16
h. thou not how many things? 27:13
wind bloweth, and thou *h.* John 3:8
and I knew that thou *h.* me. 11:42

heareth

for that he *h.* your murmurings. Ex 16:7, 8
disallow her in day that he *h.* Num 30:5
when he *h.* the words of. Deut 29:19
for thy servant *h.* 1 Sam 3:9, 10
at which ears of every one that *h.* 11; 2 Ki 21:12; Jer 19:3
whosoever *h.* it will say. 2 Sam 17:9
and he *h.* the cry of the. Job 34:28
cry, and the Lord *h.* Ps 34:17
thus I was as a man that *h.* not. 38:14
Lord *h.* poor, and despiseth. 69:33
blessed is the man that *h.* Pr 8:34
a wise son *h.* his father's. 13:1
ransom his riches, but the poor *h.* 8
but he *h.* the prayer of. 15:29
that *h.* the reproof of life. 31, 32
a matter before he *h.* it. 18:13
the man that *h.* speaketh. 21:28
lest he that *h.* it put thee. 25:10
h. cursing, and bewrayeth it. 29:24
there is none that *h.* Isa 41:26
opening the ears, but he *h.* not. 42:20
shalt say, he that *h.* Ezek 3:27
whosoever *h.* the sound of the. 33:4
whoso *h.* these sayings. Mat 7:24, 26; Luke 6:47, 49
when any one *h.* word. Mat 13:19
is he that *h.* the word. 20, 22, 23
he that *h.* you *h.* me. Luke 10:16
and *h.* him rejoiceth. John 3:29
h. my word, and believeth. 5:24
that is of God *h.* God's words. 8:47
h. not sinners, but if any man be a worshipper of God, him he *h.* 9:31
one that is of the truth, *h.* 18:37
me above that he *h.* of. 2 Cor 12:6
and the world *h.* them. 1 John 4:5
he that knoweth God *h.* us. 6
according to his will, he *h.* us. 5:14
let him that *h.* say, Come. Rev 22:17
I testify to every man that *h.* 18

hearing

law to Israel in their *h.* Deut 31:11
for in our *h.* the king. 2 Sam 18:12
was neither voice nor *h.* 2 Ki 4:31
hast spoken in my *h.* Job 33:8
I have heard of thee by the *h.* 42:5
nor reprove after the *h.* of. Isa 11:3
I was bowed down at the *h.* 21:3
that stoppeth his ears from *h.* 33:15
to others he said in my *h.* Ezek 9:5
cried unto them in my *h.* O. 10:13
a famine of *h.* the word. Amos 8:11
to be reserved to the *h.* Acts 25:21*
entered into the place of *h.* 23
faith cometh by *h.* and *h.* Rom 10:17
the *h.*? if whole were *h.* 1 Cor 12:17
or by the *h.* of faith. Gal 3:2, 5
seeing ye are dull of *h.* Heb 5:11

hearing, *verb*

the *h.* ear, the Lord. Pr 20:12
turneth away the ear from *h.* 28:9
nor is the ear filled with *h.* Eccl 1:8
and *h.* they hear not. Mat 13:13
by *h.* ye shall hear, and shall. 14
their ears dull of *h.* 15; Acts 28:27; Heb 5:11
h. him were astonished. Mark 6:2
h. them and asking. Luke 2:46
Ananias *h.* these words. Acts 5:5
h. and seeing the miracles which. 8:6
men stood, *h.* a voice, but. 9:7
many of the Corinthians *h.* 18:8
h. of thy love and faith. Philem 5
Lot in seeing and *h.* 2 Pet 2:8

hearken

how shall Pharaoh *h.*? Ex 6:30
if ye *h.* to these judgements. Deut 7:12
if ye will *h.* diligently to my. 11:13
if thou carefully *h.* to voice of. 15:5; Jer 17:24
to him ye shall *h.* Deut 18:15
if thou *h.* to commandments. 28:13; 1 Ki 11:38
as to Moses, so will we *h.* Josh 1:17
to *h.* than the fat of. 1 Sam 15:22
for who will *h.* to you in? 30:24
have thou respect to *h.* to cry. 1 Ki 8:28
mayest *h.* to the prayer. 29, 52; 2 Chr 6:19, 20
shall we *h.* then to you? Neh 13:27
Israel, if thou wilt *h.* Ps 81:8
if ruler *h.* to lies, servants. Pr 29:12
them that hear shall *h.* Isa 32:3
h. and hear for the time. 42:23
if so be they will *h.* and. Jer 26:3
to *h.* to the prophets whom I. 5
pray to me, and I will *h.* unto. 29:12
not receive instruction to *h.* 35:13
refused to *h.,* stopped. Zech 7:11
to *h.* unto you more than. Acts 4:19
knocked, a damsel came to *h.* 12:13*

hearken, *imperatively*

wives of Lamech, *h.* to. Gen 4:23
my lord, *h.* to me. 23:15
h. to Israel your father. 49:2
rise up, *h.* unto me, thou son of. Num 23:18
h. O Israel, to statutes. Deut 4:1
take heed, and *h.* O Israel. 27:9
he cried, *h.* to me, ye. Judg 9:7
h. to the supplication. 1 Ki 8:30; 2 Chr 6:21
he said, *h.* O people. 1 Ki 22:28
and he said, *h.* all ye. 2 Chr 18:27
h. ye, all Judah, and ye. 20:15
and *h.* to the pleadings of. Job 13:6

Job, h. unto me. Job 32:10; 33:31
h. to all my words. 33:1
h. unto me, ye men of, 34:10
let a wise man h. 34
h. to this, O Job. 37:14
h. I will teach you. Ps 34:11
h. O daughter. 45:10
h. to me, therefore, O children.
Pr 7:24; 8:32
hear my voice, h. and. Isa 28:23
come near, ye nations, h. 34:1; 49:1
h. to me, O house of Jacob. 46:3
48:12; Hos 5:1
h. to me, stouthearted. Isa 46:12
h. to me, ye that follow after. 51:1
h. unto me, my people, give ear. 4
h. to me, ye that know. 7
h. diligently unto me, eat. 55:2
saying, h. to the sound. Jer 6:17
O Lord, h. and do; defer. Dan 9:19
h. O earth, and all that. Mi 1:2
he said, h. to me, every. Mark 7:14
ye men of Judah, h. to. Acts 2:14
men, brethren, and fathers, h. 7:2
saying, men and brethren, h. 15:13
h. my beloved brethren. Jas 2:5
see **voice**

hearken *not*, or *not* **hearken**

if ye will *not h.*, to be. Gen 34:17
Pharaoh shall *not h.* to you. Ex 7:4
22; 11:9
but if ye will *not h.* to me. Lev 26:14
18, 21, 27
thou shalt *not h.* to that. Deut 13:3
not h. unto him, nor shall thine. 8
the man that will *not h.* to. 17:12
that whosoever will *not h.* 18:19
chastened, he will *not h.* to. 21:18
not h. to Balaam. 23:5; Josh 24:10
will *not h.* to thy words. Josh 1:18
yet they would *not h.* to. Judg 2:17
king of Edom would *not h.* 11:17
men of Gibeah would *not h.* 19:25
of Benjamin would *not h.* 20:13
elders said, *h. not* to him. 1 Ki 20:8
did *not h.* but did after. 2 Ki 17:40
h. not to Hezekiah. 18:31; Isa 36:16
Rehoboam would *not h.* 2 Chr 10:16
spake, but they would *not h.* 33:10
if *not h.* hold thy peace, I. Job 33:33
not h. to the voice of. Ps 58:5
but my people would *not h.* 81:11
ear is uncircumcised, they *cannot h.*
Jer 6:10
said, we will *not h.* 17; 44:16
shalt speak, they will *not h.* 7:27
they cry to me, I will *not h.* 11:11
that they may *not h.* to me. 16:12
if ye will *not h.* to me. 17:27
26:4; Ezek 20:39
h. not to words of the prophets.
Jer. 23:16; 27:9, 14, 16, 17; 29:8
counsel, wilt thou *not h.*? 38:15
not h. to thee, for they will *not h.*
Ezek 3:7
rebelled, and would *not h.* 20:8
because they did *not h.* to him.
Hos 9:17; Zech 1:4

hearkened

Abraham h. to Ephron. Gen 23:16
God h. to Leah. 30:17
God h. to Rachel. 22
to Hamor h. all that went out. 34:24
that Joseph h. not to her. 39:10
h. not to Moses. Ex 6:9; 16:20
Israel have not h. to me. 6:12
Pharaoh h. not to them. 7:13
8:15, 19; 9:12
Lord h. to me. Deut 9:19; 10:10
these nations h. to observers. 18:14
h. to Joshua as to Moses. 34:9
Josh 1:17
king of Ammonites h. Judg 11:28
the woman of Endor h. 1 Sam 28:21
king h. not to people. 1 Ki 12:15
16; 2 Chr 10:15
h. therefore to the word. 1 Ki 12:24
Ben-hahad h. to king Asa. 15:20
2 Chr 16:4
and the Lord h. to. 2 Ki 13:4
king of Assyria h. to Asa. 16:9
Hezekiah h. to messengers. 20:13
Judah h. not to the law. 21:9
fathers h. not to words. 2 Ki 22:13
Joash h. to princes. 2 Chr 24:17
Amaziah h. not to the. 25:16
Lord h. to Hezekiah, and. 30:20
Josiah h. not to Pharaoh-necho. 35:22
and h. not to thy commandments.
Neh 9:16, 29, 34; Jer 34:14
now when Mordecai h. Esth 3:4
that my people had h. Ps 81:13
and he h. diligently with. Isa 21:7
O that thou hadst h. to my. 48:18
they have not h. to my word.
Jer 6:19; 7:24, 26; 25:3, 4, 7
26:5; 29:19; 32:33; 34:17; 35:14
15, 16; 36:31; 44:5
Irijah h. not to Jeremiah. 37:14
they would have h. to thee. Ezek 3:6
neither have we h. to thy. Dan 9:6
the Lord h. and heard it. Mal 3:16
Jer 8:6
sirs, ye should have h. Acts 27:21
see **voice**

hearkenedst

h. not to voice of Lord. Deut 28:45

hearkeneth

but whoso h. to me. Pr 1:33
he that h. to counsel is wise. 12:15

hearkening

angels h. to the voice of. Ps 103:20

heart

(*The word heart is used in Scripture as the seat of life or strength; hence it means mind, soul, spirit, or one's entire emotional nature and understanding. It is also used as the centre or inner part of a thing*)

Jacob's h. fainted, for. Gen 45:26
for ye know the h. of a. Ex 23:9
they shall be on Aaron's h. 28:30
whoso is of a willing h. let. 35:5
he filled with wisdom of h. 35
eyes, cause sorrow of h. Lev 26:16*
discourage ye the h.? Num 32:7
they discouraged the h. of the. 9
there were such an h. Deut 5:29
smite with astonishment of h. 28:28
the Lord with gladness of h. 47
give thee there a trembling h. 65
Lord hath not given you an h. to. 29:4
h. of the people melt. Josh 14:8
great thoughts of h. Judg 5:15
there were great searchings of h. 16
the priest's h. was glad, he. 18:20
now Hannah, she spake in her h.
1 Sam 1:13
that God gave him another h. 10:9
but the Lord looketh on the h. 16:7
let no man's h. fail because. 17:32
David's h. smote him, because. 24:5
no grief, nor offence of h. 25:31
and Nabal's h. was merry within. 36
she despised him in her h. 2 Sam 6:16
1 Chr 15:29
Amnon's h. is merry. 2 Sam 13:28
that the king's h. was toward. 14:1
thrust darts through the h. 18:14
he bowed the h. of all men. 19:14
an understanding h. 1 Ki 3:9
given thee an understanding h. 12
Solomon wisdom and largeness of h.
4:29
the h. of David. 8:17; 2 Chr 6:7
people went to tents glad of h.
1 Ki 8:66; 2 Chr 7:10
communed with him of all that was
in her h. 1 Ki 10:2; 2 Chr 9:1
perfect, as was the h. of. 1 Ki 11:4
shall the h. of this people. 12:27
h. of king of Assyria. 2 Ki 6:11
into any man's h. 12:4; 2 Chr 29:31
were not of double h. 1 Chr 12:33
let the h. of them rejoice. 16:10
Ps 105:3
I know thou triest the h. 1 Chr 29:17
18; Jer 11:20
came into Solomon's h. 2 Chr 7:11
turned the h. of king of. Ezra 6:22
a thing as this in the king's h. 7:27
else but sorrow of h. Neh 2:2
when the h. of the king. Esth 1:10
forth that day with a glad h. 5:9
he is wise in h. and. Job 9:4
he taketh away the h. of. Job 12:24†
I caused the widow's h. to. 29:13
but the hypocrites in h. heap. 36:13
not any that are wise of h. 37:24
given understanding to h. 38:36*
and with double h. do. Ps 12:2
are right, rejoicing the h. 19:8
them that are of a broken h. 34:18
knoweth the secrets of the h. 44:21
arrows are sharp in the h. 45:5
in h. ye work wickedness. 58:2
the h. is deep. 64:6
have more than h. could wish. 73:7
a froward h. shall depart. 101:4
an high look, and a proud h. will. 5
glad the h. of man, bread, which
strengtheneth man's h. 104:15
a h. that deviseth wicked. Pr 6:18
met him a woman subtle of h. 7:10
ye of an understanding h. 8:5
the wise in h. will receive. 10:8
h. of the wicked is little worth. 20
froward h. are abomination. 11:20
be servant to the wise of h. 29
but he that is of perverse h. 12:8
deceit is in the h. of them who. 20
heaviness in the h. of man. 25
hope deferred maketh the h. 13:12
the h. knoweth his own. 14:10
in laughter the h. is sorrowful. 13
backslider in h. be filled with. 14
a sound h. is the life of the flesh. 30
wisdom resteth in h. of him. 33
but the h. of the foolish doeth. 15:7
a merry h. maketh a cheerful countenance; but by sorrow of the h. 13
h. of him that hath understanding. 14
a merry h. hath a continual feast. 15
the h. of the righteous studieth. 28
of the eyes rejoiceth the h. 30
the preparation of h. in man. 16:1
proud in h. is an abomination. 5
a man's h. deviseth his way. 9
h. of wise teacheth his mouth. 23
seeing he hath no h. to it. 17:16
hath a froward h. findeth no. 20
a merry h. doeth good like a. 22
before destruction the h. of. 18:12
the h. of the prudent getteth. 15
many devices in a man's h. 19:21
counsel in h. of man is like. 20:5
the king's h. is in the hand of. 21:1
high look, and a proud h. is sin. 4
he that loveth pureness of h. 22:11
foolishness is bound in the h. 15
doth not he that pondereth h.? 24:12
and the h. of kings is. 25:3
singeth songs to an heavy h. 20
a wicked h. is like a potsherd. 26:23
perfume rejoice the h. 27:9
h. of man answereth to man. 19
that is of a proud h. stirreth. 28:25*
the h. of her husband doth. 31:11
sadness of countenance h. Eccl 7:3
the h. of the wise is in the house of
mourning, but the h. of fools. 4
and a gift destroyeth the h. 7*
wise man's h. discerneth both. 8:5
the h. of men is fully set in. 11
the h. of the sons of men is. 9:3
drink thy wine with merry h. 7
wise man's h. is at right hand, fool's
h. at left. 10:2
make their h. fat. Isa 6:10
Mat 13:15; Acts 28:27
pride and stoutness of h. Isa 9:9
punish fruit of the stout h. 10:12
all hands faint, every man's h. 13:7
ye shall have gladness of h. 30:29
h. of rash shall understand. 32:4
to them that are of fearful h. 35:4
yet he laid it not to h. 42:25
a deceived h. hath turned. 44:20
and no man layeth it to h. 57:1
Jer 12:11
and to revive the h. of the. Isa 57:15
uttering from the h. words of. 59:13
servants shall sing for joy of h., but
ye shall cry for sorrow of h. 65:14
the h. of the king and princes. Jer 4:9
people hath a rebellious h. 5:23
Israel are uncircumcised in h. 9:26
triest the reins and the h. 11:20
the h. is deceitful above all. 17:9

I the Lord search the *h.* *Jer* 17:10
that seest the reins and *h.* 20:12
long shall this be in the *h.*? 23:26
and I will give them an *h.* to. 24:7
be as the *h.* of a woman in her. 48:41; 49:22
give them sorrow of *h.* *Lam* 3:65
with their whorish *h.* *Ezek* 6:9
I will take the stony *h.* out. 11:19
with lies ye made *h.* of the. 13:22
and make you a new *h.* and. 18:31
every *h.* shall melt, all hands. 21:7
rejoiced in *h.* with all thy. 25:6
vengeance with a despiteful *h.* 15*
for thee with bitterness of *h.* 27:31*
and I will give you an *h.* of. 36:26
strangers uncircumcised in *h.* 44:7
9; *Acts* 7:51
let a beast's *h.* be given. *Dan* 4:16
a man's *h.* was given to it. 7:4
wine take away the *h.* *Hos* 4:11*
like a silly dove without *h.* 7:11*
h. melteth, and the knees. *Nah* 2:10
city that said in her *h.* *Zeph* 2:15
not lay it to *h.* to give glory, because ye do not lay it to *h.* *Mal* 2:2
turn the *h.* of fathers, and *h.* 4:6
meek and lowly in *h.* *Mat* 11:29
out of the abundance of the *h.* 12:34
Luke 6:45
out of the treasure of the *h.*
Mat 12:35; *Luke* 6:45
come forth from the *h.* *Mat* 15:18
out of *h.* proceed evil thoughts. 19
Mark 7:21
with hardness of *h.* *Mark* 16:14
pondered them in her *h.* *Luke* 2:19
kept these sayings in her *h.* 51
which in a good *h.* having. 8:15
O fools, slow of *h.* to believe. 24:25
devil having put into the *h.* *John* 13:2
eat with singleness of *h.* *Acts* 2:46
were cut to the *h.* 5:33; 7:54
purpose of *h.* they would. 11:23
impenitent *h.* treasurest. *Rom* 2:5
circumcision is that of the *h.* 29
ye have obeyed from the *h.* 6:17
with the *h.* man believeth unto. 10:10
entered into *h.* of man. *1 Cor* 2:9
so decreed in his *h.* that he. 7:37
of much anguish of *h.* I. *2 Cor* 2:4
written in fleshly tables of *h.* 3:3
appearance, and not in *h.* 5:12
earnest care in the *h.* of Titus. 8:16
will of God from the *h.* *Eph* 6:6
but in singleness of *h.* *Col* 3:22
in presence, not in *h.* *1 Thes* 2:17
of the intents of the *h.* *Heb* 4:12
us draw near with a true *h.* 10:22
h. be established with grace. 13:9
the hidden man of the *h.* *1 Pet* 3:4
an *h.* exercised with. *2 Pet* 2:14
she saith in her *h.* I sit. *Rev* 18:7

heart

depths were congealed in *h.* *Ex* 15:8
h. of Egypt shall melt in. *Isa* 19:1
so shall the Son of man be . . . in the *h.* of the earth. *Mat* 12:40

heart with *all*

serve him with *all* your *h.* and with.
Deut 11:13; *Josh* 22:5
1 Sam 12:20, 24
love the Lord with *all* your *h.* and.
Deut 13:3; 30:6; *Mat* 22:37
Mark 12:30, 33; *Luke* 10:27
do them with *all* thy *h.* *Deut* 26:16
return to the Lord with *all* thine *h.*
30:2; *Joel* 2:12
told her *all* his *h.* *Judg* 16:17, 18
walk before me with *all* their *h.*
1 Ki 2:4; 8:23
return unto thee with *all* their *h.* and all. 8:48; *2 Ki* 23:25; *2 Chr* 6:38
followed me with *all* his *h.* *1 Ki* 14:8
heed to walk with *all h.* *2 Ki* 10:31
walk before the Lord with *all* their *h.*
23:3; *2 Chr* 34:31
seek God of fathers with *all* their *h.*
2 Chr 15:12
they had sworn with *all* their *h.* 15
sought the Lord with *all* his *h.* 22:9
he did it with *all* his *h.* and. 31:21
O Lord, with *all* my *h.* *Ps* 86:12
Lord with *all* thy *h.*, lean not. *Pr* 3:5
search for me with *all* your *h.*
Jer 29:13
with the joy of *all* their *h.* *Ezek* 36:5
be glad with *all* the *h.* *Zeph* 3:14
believest with *all* thy *h.* *Acts* 8:37

see **apply, broken, clean, evil, harden, hardened**

his **heart**

imagination of *his h.* *Gen* 6:5
Lord and grieved him at *his h.* 6
Lord said in *his h.* 8:21
Abraham in *his h.* 17:17
Esau said in *his h.*, The days. 27:41
he will be glad in *his h.* *Ex* 4:14
neither did he set *his h.* to. 7:23
that giveth willingly with *his h.* 25:2
of judgement upon *his h.* 28:29
he hath put in *his h.* that he. 35:34
made *his h.* obstinate. *Deut* 2:30
multiply wives, that *his h.* 17:17
his h. be not lifted up above his. 20
avenger pursue, while *his h.* 19:6
heart faint as well as *his h.* 20:8
he is poor, and setteth *his h.* 24:15
that he bless himself in *his h.* 29:19
his h. was merry, he went. *Ruth* 3:7
his h. trembled for the. *1 Sam* 4:13
laid up these words in *his h.* 21:12
it came to pass that *his h.* 25:37
David said in *his h.* 27:1
his h. trembled. 28:5
found in *his h.* to pray this prayer.
2 Sam 7:27; *1 Chr* 17:25
take the thing to *his h.* *2 Sam* 13:33
which God had put in *his h.*
1 Ki 10:24; *2 Chr* 9:23
wives turned away *his h.*
1 Ki 11:3, 4, 9
Jeroboam said in *his h.* 12:26
arrow went out at *his h.* *2 Ki* 9:24
prepared not *his h.* to. *2 Chr* 12:14
his h. was lifted up in ways. 17:6
his h. was lifted up to his. 26:16
that prepareth *his h.* to seek. 30:19
for *his h.* was lifted up. 32:25
himself for the pride of *his h.* 26
know all that was in *his h.* 31
Ezra prepared *his h.* to. *Ezra* 7:10
foundest *his h.* faithful. *Neh* 9:8
Haman thought in *his h.* *Esth* 6:6
that durst presume in *his h.* 7:5
if he set *his h.* upon man. *Job* 34:14
his h. is as firm as a stone. 41:24
wicked boasteth of *his h.'s.* *Ps* 10:3
he hath said in *his h.* 6; 11:13
14:1; 53:1
that speaketh truth in *his h.* 15:2
hast given him *his h.'s* desire. 21:2
the thoughts of *his h.* to all. 33:11
law of his God is in *his h.* 37:31
his h. gathereth iniquity to. 41:6
smooth, but war was in *his h.* 55:21
according to integrity of *his h.* 78:72
his h. is fixed, trusting in. 112:7
his h. is established, he shall not. 8
frowardness is in *his h.* *Pr* 6:14
but that *his h.* may discover. 18:2
and *his h.* fretteth against. 19:3
thinketh in *his h.* so is he; eat and drink, saith he, but *his h.* 23:7
but he that hardeneth *his h.* 28:14
yea *his h.* taketh not rest. *Eccl* 2:23
him in the joy of *his h.* 5:20
day of gladness of *his h.* *S of S* 3:11
his h. was moved, and the h. *Isa* 7:2
neither doth *his h.* think so, but it is in *his h.* to destroy and. 10:7
his h. will work iniquity, to. 32:6
none considereth in *his h.* 44:19*
frowardly in the way of *his h.* 57:17
but in *h.* he layeth *his.* *Jer* 9:8
performed thoughts of *his h.* 23:20
engaged *his h.* to approach. 30:21*
performed the intents of *his h.* 24
heard the haughtiness of *his h.* 48:29
up his idols in *his h.* *Ezek* 14:4, 7
his h. lifted up in his height. 31:10
Dan 5:20
Daniel purposed in *his h.* *Dan* 1:8
let *his h.* be changed. 4:16; 5:21
the king set *his h.* on Daniel. 6:14
shall magnify himself in *his h.* 8:25
his h. shall be lifted up. *Dan* 11:12
his h. shall be against the holy. 28
that saith in *his h.*, Who shall? *Ob* 3
adultery with her in *his h.* *Mat* 5:28
away that was sown in *his h.* 13:19
if evil servant shall say in *his h.*
24:48; *Luke* 12:45
entereth not into *his h.* *Mark* 7:19
shall not doubt in *his h.* but. 11:23
of *his h.*; an evil man out of the evil treasure of *his h.* *Luke* 6:45
it came into *his h.* to. *Acts* 7:23
standeth stedfast in *his h.* *1 Cor* 7:37
thus are the secrets of *his h.* 14:25
as he purposeth in *his h.* *2 Cor* 9:7

mine or *my* **heart**

the integrity of *my h.* *Gen* 20:5
speaking in *mine h.* Rebekah. 24:45
imagination of *mine h.* *Deut* 29:19
word as it was in *mine h.* *Josh* 14:7
my h. is toward the. *Judg* 5:9
said, *My h.* rejoiceth. *1 Sam* 2:1
to that which is in *mine h.* 35
my eyes and *mine h.* shall be there.
1 Ki 9:3; *2 Chr* 7:16
went not *mine h.* with? *2 Ki* 5:26
h. right as *my h.* is with thy h.? 10:15
to all that was in *mine h.* 30
if to help, *mine h.* shall. *1 Chr* 12:17
mine h. to build an house of. 28:2
it is in *mine h.* to make. *2 Chr* 29:10
what God had put in *my h.* to do.
Neh 2:12; 7:5
thoughts of *my h.* are. *Job* 17:11
God maketh *my h.* soft, and. 23:16
my h. shall not reproach me. 27:6
and *mine h.* walked after mine. 31:7
mine h. have been deceived by. 9
and *my h.* hath been secretly. 27
of the uprightness of *my h.* 33:3
at this also *my h.* trembleth. 37:1
hast put gladness in *my h.* *Ps* 4:7
take counsel, sorrow in *my h.* 13:2
but I trusted, *my h.* shall rejoice. 5
my h. is glad. 16:9
thou hast proved *mine h.* 17:3
let the meditation of *my h.* 19:14
my h. is like wax. 22:14
try my reins and *my h.* 26:2
troubles of *my h.* are enlarged. 25:17
my h. shall not fear though. 27:3
my h. said to thee, Thy face, Lord. 8
my h. trusted in him, *my h.* 28:7
of the wicked saith in *my h.* 36:1
of the disquietness of *my h.* 38:8
my h. panteth, my strength faileth.
10; *Isa* 21:4
my h. was hot within me. 39:3
yea, thy law is within *my h.* 40:8
hid thy righteousness within *my h.* 10
able to look up, therefore *my h.* 12
my h. is inditing a good matter. 45:1
the meditation of *my h.* be of. 49:3
my h. is sore pained within me. 55:4
my h. is fixed, O God, *my h.* is.
57:7; 108:1
I will cry, when *my h.* is. 61:2
if I regard iniquity in *my h.* 66:18
reproach hath broken *my h.* 69:20
verily I have cleansed *my h.* 73:13
my h. was grieved, I was pricked. 21
my h. faileth, but God is the strength of *my h.* 26
my h. and flesh crieth out for. 84:2
unite *my h.* to fear thy name. 86:11
my h. is smitten and withered. 102:4
my h. is wounded within me. 109:22
word have I hid in *mine h.* 119:11
when thou shalt enlarge *my h.* 32
incline *my h.* to thy testimonies. 36
my h. be sound in thy statutes. 80
are the rejoicing of *my h.* 111
inclined *mine h.* to perform. 112
Lord, *my h.* is not haughty. 131:1
search me, and know *my h.* 139:23
incline not *my h.* to any evil. 141:4
my h. within me is desolate. 143:4
how hath *my h.* despised? *Pr* 5:12
can say, I have made *my h.*? 20:9
if thine heart be wise, *my h.* 23:15
I gave *my h.* to seek. *Eccl* 1:13
my h. had great experience of. 16
I gave *my h.* to know wisdom. 17

I said in *mine h.* I will prove thee. *Eccl* 2:1, 15; 3:17, 18
mine h. to give myself to wine, yet acquainting *mine h.* with. 2:3
I withheld not *my h.* from any. 10
to cause *my h.* to despair of all. 20
mine h. to know and search. 7:25
8:9, 16
this I considered in *my h.* 9:1
hast ravished *my h.* *S of S* 4:9
I sleep, but *my h.* waketh. 5:2
my h. shall cry out for. *Isa* 15:5
day of vengeance is in *mine h.* 63:4
according to *mine h.* *Jer* 3:15
pained at *my h.* *my h.* maketh. 4:19
neither came it into *my h.* 7:31*
when I comfort myself, *my h.* 8:18
hast seen me and tried *mine h.* 12:3
joy and rejoicing of *mine h.* 15:16
his word was in *mine h.* as a. 20:9
mine h. is broken. 23:9
mine h. shall mourn. 48:31
therefore *mine h.* shall sound. 36
behold, *mine h.* is turned. *Lam* 1:20
my sighs are many, and *my h.* 22
mine eye affecteth *mine h.* 3:51
kept the matter in *my h.* *Dan* 7:28
mine h. is turned within. *Hos* 11:8
did *my h.* rejoice. *Acts* 2:26
to weep, and break *mine h.*? 21:13
continual sorrow in *my h.* *Rom* 9:2
my h.'s desire to God for Israel. 10:1
because I have you in *my h.* *Phil* 1:7

see **applied**

one **heart**

was to give them *one h.* *2 Chr* 30:12
I will give them *one h.* *Jer* 32:39
Ezek 11:19
believed were of *one h.* *Acts* 4:32

own **heart**

not after your *own h.* *Num* 15:39
sought man after his *own h.* *1 Sam* 13:14; *Acts* 13:22
according to thine *own h.* hast thou. *2 Sam* 7:21; *1 Chr* 17:19
man plague of his *own h.* *1 Ki* 8:38
had devised of his *own h.* 12:33
them out of thine *own h.* *Neh* 6:8
your *own h.* on your bed. *Ps* 4:4
according to thine *own h.* 20:4
shall enter into their *own h.* 37:15
I commune with my *own h.* and. 77:6
trusteth in his *own h.* *Pr* 28:26
communed with mine *own h.* *Eccl* 1:16
thy *own h.* knoweth thou hast. 7:22
after imagination of their *own h.* *Jer* 9:14; 23:17
a vision of their *own h.* 23:16
prophesy the deceit of their *own h.* 26; *Ezek* 13:17
of Israel in their *own h.* *Ezek* 14:5
but deceiveth his *own h.* *Jas* 1:26

our **heart**

have discouraged *our h.* *Deut* 1:28
for *our h.* shall rejoice. *Ps* 33:21
our h. is not turned back. 44:18
let us lift up *our h.* with. *Lam* 3:41
the joy of *our h.* is ceased. 5:15
our h. is faint. 17
did not *our h.* burn? *Luke* 24:32
our mouth is open, *our h.* *2 Cor* 6:11
if *our h.* condemn us. *1 John* 3:20
if *our h.* condemn us not, we. 21

perfect **heart**

let your *h.* be *perfect.* *1 Ki* 8:61
his *h.* was not *perfect.* 11:4; 15:3
Asa's *h.* was *perfect* with the Lord. 15:14; *2 Chr* 15:17
have walked before thee with a *perfect h.* *2 Ki* 20:3; *Isa* 38:3
came with *perfect h.* to. *1 Chr* 12:38
serve God with a *perfect h.* 28:9
with *perfect h.* they offered. 29:9
give Solomon my son a *perfect h.* 19
them whose *h.* is *perfect.* *2 Chr* 16:9
in fear of Lord with *perfect h.* 19:9
right, but not with a *perfect h.* 25:2
my house with *perfect h.* *Ps* 101:2

pure **heart**

ascend? that hath a *pure h.* *Ps* 24:4
blessed are the *pure* in *h.* *Mat* 5:8
is charity out of *pure h.* *1 Tim* 1:5
the Lord out of a *pure h.* *2 Tim* 2:22
another with a *pure h.* *1 Pet* 1:22

their **heart**

their h. failed them. *Gen* 42:28
their h. melted, neither was there spirit in them. *Josh* 5:1
thou hast turned *their h.* *1 Ki* 18:37
and prepare *their h.* *1 Chr* 29:18
utter words out of *their h.*? *Job* 8:10
thou hast hid *their h.* from. 17:4
wilt prepare *their h.* *Ps* 10:17
generation that set not *their h.* 78:8
they tempted God in *their h.* 18
their h. was not right with him. 37
people that do err in *their h.* 95:10
he turned *their h.* to hate. 105:25
he brought down *their h.* 107:12
their h. is as fat as grease. 119:70
imagine mischief in *their h.* 140:2
for *their h.* studieth. *Pr* 24:2
set the world in *their h.* *Eccl* 3:11
madness is in *their h.* while. 9:3
ears and understand with *their h.* *Isa* 6:10; *Mat* 13:15; *Acts* 28:27
their h. is far from me. *Isa* 29:13
Mat 15:8; *Mark* 7:6
neither say they in *their h.* *Jer* 5:24
in the imagination of *their h.* 13:10
prophesy the deceit of *their h.* 14:14
is graven on table of *their h.* 17:1
their h. cried to Lord. *Lam* 2:18
up their idols in *their h.* *Ezek* 14:3
for *their h.* went after their. 20:16
that *their h.* may faint, ruins. 21:15
but *their h.* goeth after. 33:31
they set *their h.* on their. *Hos* 4:8
they have made ready *their h.* 7:6
not cried unto me with *their h.* 14
their h. is divided. 10:2
their h. was exalted. 13:6
I will rend the caul of *their h.* 8
men that say in *their h.* *Zeph* 1:12
their h. shall rejoice. *Zech* 10:7
Judah shall say in *their h.* 12:5
their h. was hardened. *Mark* 6:52
Rom 1:21
the thought of *their h.* *Luke* 9:47
their h.; they should not see, nor understand with *their h.* *John* 12:40
were pricked in *their h.* *Acts* 2:37
the vail is upon *their h.* *2 Cor* 3:15
the blindness of *their h.* *Eph* 4:18

thine, thy **heart**

in the integrity of *thy h.* *Gen* 20:6
my plagues upon *thine h.* *Ex* 9:14
not hate thy brother in *thine h.* *Lev* 19:17
they depart from *thy h.* *Deut* 4:9
if thou seek him with all *thy h.* 29
consider it in *thine h.* 4:39; 8:5
love Lord with all *thine h.* 6:5
in *thine h.* these nations are more. 7:17; 8:17; 18:21; *Jer* 13:22
know what was in *thine h.* *Deut* 8:2
then *thine h.* be lifted up, and. 14
speak not thou in *thine h.* after. 9:4
not for uprightness of *thine h.* 5
serve thy God with all *thy h.* 10:12
a thought in *thy* wicked *h.* 15:9
thine h. shall not be grieved. 10
fear of *thine h.* wherewith. 28:67
circumcise *thine h.* and the *h.* 30:6
is very nigh unto thee, in *thy h.* 14
if *thine h.* turn, so that thou. 17
when *thine h.* is not. *Judg* 16:15
and let *thine h.* be merry. 19:6, 9
1 Ki 21:7
father said, Comfort *thine h.* *Judg* 19:8
why is *thy h.* grieved? *1 Sam* 1:8
thine shall be to grieve *thine h.* 2:33
tell thee all that is in *thine h.* 9:19
do all that is in *thine h.* *1 Sam* 14:7
2 Sam 7:3; *1 Chr* 17:2
thee, according to *thy h.* *1 Sam* 14:7
pride and naughtiness of *thy h.* 17:28
reign over all that *thine h.* *2 Sam* 3:21
wickedness *thine h.* is *1 Ki* 2:44
in *thine h.* to build. 8:18
2 Chr 1:11; 6:8
Jehu said, Is *thine h.* right, as my *h.* is with *thy h.*? *2 Ki* 10:15
thine h. hath lifted thee up. 14:10
2 Chr 25:19
because *thine h.* was tender. *2 Ki* 22:19; *2 Chr* 34:27
hast prepared *thine h.* *2 Chr* 19:3
thou shouldest set *thine h.* *Job* 7:17
things hast thou hid in *thine h.* 10:13
if thou prepare *thine h.* and. 11:13
why doth *thine h.* carry thee? 15:12
lay up his words in *thine h.* 22:22
shall strengthen *thine h.* *Ps* 27:14
give thee the desires of *thine h.* 37:4
thine h. to understanding. *Pr* 2:2
wisdom entereth into *thine h.* 10
my son, let *thine h.* keep my. 3:1
upon the table of *thine h.* 3; 7:3
he said, let *thine h.* retain. 4:4, 21
keep *thy h.* with all diligence. 23
them continually upon *thine h.* 6:21
after her beauty in *thine h.* 25
let not *thine h.* incline to her. 7:25
if *thine h.* be wise, my *h.* 23:15
let not *thine h.* envy sinners. 17
hear, my son, and guide *thine h.* 19
my son, give me *thine h.* 26
thine h. shall utter perverse. 33
let not *thine h.* be glad when. 24:17
let not *thine h.* be hasty to. *Eccl* 5:2
thy h. cheer thee; walk in ways of *thy h.* 11:9
remove sorrow from *thy h.* 10
thou hast said in *thine h.* *Isa* 14:13
thine h. shall meditate terror. 33:18
these things to *thy h.* 47:7; 57:11
that sayest in *thine h.* I am. 47:8, 10
shalt thou say in *thine h.* 49:21
O Jerusalem, wash *thine h.* *Jer* 4:14
because it reacheth unto *thine h.* 18
thine h. are not but for thy. 22:17
set *thine h.* toward the. 31:21
thine h. deceived thee. 49:16; *Ob* 2
pour out *thine h.* like. *Lam* 2:19
receive in *thine h.* hear. *Ezek* 3:10
how weak is *thine h.* saith. 16:30
can *thine h.* endure in days. 22:14
because *thine h.* is lifted up. 28:2, 5
hast set *thine h.* as the heart. 6
thine h. was lifted up because. 17
set *thine h.* upon all that I. 40:4
know the thoughts of *thy h.* *Dan* 2:30
hast not humbled *thine h.* 5:22
thou didst set *thine h.* to. 10:12
filled *thine h.* to lie. *Acts* 5:3
thou conceived this in *thine h.*? 4
for *thy h.* is not right in the. 8:21
thought of *thine h.* may. 22
say not in *thine h.*, Who? *Rom* 10:6
and shalt believe in *thine h.* that. 9

upright in **heart**

were more *upright in h.* *2 Chr* 29:34
saveth the *upright in h.* *Ps* 7:10
may shoot at the *upright in h.* 11:2
joy, ye that are *upright in h.* 32:11
righteousness to *upright in h.* 36:10
the *upright in h.* shall glory. 64:10
the *upright in h.* shall follow. 94:15
sown for the *upright in h.* 97:11

uprightness of **heart**

he walketh in *uprightness of h.* *1 Ki* 3:6; 9:4
I will praise thee with *uprightness of h.* *Ps* 119:7

whole **heart**

I will praise thee, O Lord, with my *whole h.* *Ps* 9:1; 111:1; 138:1
seek him with the *whole h.* 119:2
with my *whole h.* have I. 10
observe it with my *whole h.* 34
thy favour with my *whole h.* 58
thy precepts with my *whole h.* 69
I cried with my *whole h.* hear. 145
head is sick, the *whole h.* *Isa* 1:5
not turned with *whole h.* *Jer* 3:10
unto me with their *whole h.* 24:7
them in land with my *whole h.* 32:41

whose **heart**

whose h. stirred him up. *Ex* 35:21
29; 36:2
all the women, *whose h.* 35:26
whose h. turneth away. *Deut* 29:18
whose h. is as the heart. *2 Sam* 17:10

whose h. thou knowest. *1 Ki* 8:39 *2 Chr* 6:30
behalf of them *whose h. 2 Chr* 16:9
in *whose h.* are the ways. *Ps* 84:5
woman *whose h.* is snares and nets. *Eccl* 7:26
in *whose h.* is my law. *Isa.* 51:7
whose h. departeth from. *Jer* 17:5
whose h. walketh after. *Ezek* 11:21
whose h. the Lord. *Acts* 16:14

your **heart**

circumcise foreskin of *your h.* *Deut* 10:16; *Jer* 4:4
your h. be not deceived. *Deut* 11:16
lay up these my words in *your h.* 18
will turn away *your h.* *1 Ki* 11:2
set *your h.* and soul. *1 Chr* 22:19
your h. shall live. *Ps* 22:26
he shall strengthen *your h.* 31:24
ye people, pour out *your h.* 62:8
if riches increase, set not *your h.* 10
your h. shall live that seek. 69:32
ye see this, *your h.* shall. *Isa* 66:14
and lest *your h.* faint. *Jer* 51:46
and rend *your h.* and not. *Joel* 2:13
you imagine evil in *your h. Zech* 7:10
there will *your h.* be also. *Mat* 6:21 *Luke* 12:34
have ye *your h.* yet? *Mark* 8:17
for the hardness of *your h.* 10:5
not *your h.* be troubled. *John* 14:1, 27
sorrow hath filled *your h.* 16:6
I will see you, and *your h.* shall. 22
in singleness of *your h.* *Eph* 6:5

hearted

many as were willing *h.* *Ex* 35:22
the stout *h.* are spoiled. *Ps* 76:5
all the merry *h.* do sigh. *Isa* 24:7
me to bind up the broken *h.* 61:1
of Israel are hard *h.* *Ezek* 3:7

faint **hearted**

is there that is *faint h.*? *Deut* 20:8

tender **hearted**

Rehoboam was young and *tender h.* *2 Chr* 13:7
and be kind one to another, *tender h.* *Eph* 4:32

wise **hearted**

unto all that are *wise h.* *Ex* 28:3
hearts of all that are *wise h.* 31:6
and every *wise h.* among you. 35:10
all the women that were *wise h.* 25
then wrought every *wise h.* man. 36:1, 2, 8

hearth

make cakes upon the *h.* *Gen* 18:6
bones are burnt as an *h.* *Ps* 102:3*
to take fire from the *h.* *Isa* 30:14
a fire on the *h.* burning. *Jer* 36:22*
roll into fire that was on the *h.* 23*
of Judah like *h.* of fire. *Zech* 12:6*

heartily

what ye do, do it *h.* as to. *Col* 3:23

hearts

they discouraged the *h.* *Num* 32:9
wherefore the *h.* of the. *Josh* 7:5
of men, whose *h.* God. *1 Sam* 10:26
so Absalom stole the *h.* *2 Sam* 15:6
the *h.* of the men of Israel. 13
thou only knowest the *h.* *1 Ki* 8:39 *2 Chr* 6:30
the Lord searcheth all *h. 1 Chr* 28:9
the righteous God trieth the *h.* *Ps* 7:9; *Pr* 17:3
more then the *h.* of men? *Pr* 15:11
but the Lord pondereth the *h.* 21:2
wine to those that be of heavy *h.* 31:6*
mighty men's *h.* of Moab. *Jer* 48:41
I will also vex the *h.* *Ezek* 32:9
both these kings' *h.* shall. *Dan* 11:27
turn the *h.* of the fathers. *Luke* 1:17
that the thoughts of *h.* may be. 2:35
signs in the sun, men's *h.* 21:26
which knowest the *h.* of all men. *Acts* 1:24; 15:8
he that searcheth the *h.* *Rom* 8:27
by fair speeches deceive the *h.* 16:18
the counsels of the *h.* *1 Cor* 4:5
searcheth the reins and *h.* *Rev* 2:23

our **hearts**

soon as we heard, *our h.* *Josh* 2:11
incline *our h.* to him. *1 Ki* 8:58
filling *our h.* with food. *Acts* 14:17
love of God is shed abroad in *our h.* *Rom* 5:5
of the Spirit in *our h.* *2 Cor* 1:22
our epistle written in *our h.* 3:2
God hath shined in *our h.* 4:6
that you are in *our h.* to die. 7:3
God, who trieth *our h.* *1 Thes* 2:4
our h. sprinkled from. *Heb* 10:22
and shall assure *our h.* *1 John* 3:19

their **hearts**

a faintness into *their h.* *Lev* 26:36
if then *their* uncircumcised *h.* 41
their h. inclined to follow. *Judg* 9:3
when *their h.* were merry. 16:25
they were making *their h.* 19:22
thee with all *their h.* *2 Chr* 6:14
such as set *their h.* to seek. 11:16
people had not prepared *their h.* to. 20:33
my sons have cursed God in *their h.* *Job* 1:5
but mischief is in *their h.* *Ps* 28:3
he fashioneth *their h.* alike. 33:15
let them not say in *their h.*, Ah. 35:25
said in *their h.*, Let us destroy. 74:8
gave them up to *their* own *h.* 81:12
that are upright in *their h.* 125:4
hath shut *their h.* they. *Isa* 44:18
and write my law in *their h.* *Jer* 31:33; *Heb* 8:10
put my fear in *their h.* *Jer* 32:40
out of *their* own *h.* *Ezek* 13:2
consider not in *their h.* *Hos* 7:2
yea, they made *their h.* *Zech* 7:12
and reasoning in *their h.* *Mark* 2:6
for the hardness of *their h.* 3:5
taketh away word sown in *their h.* 4:15; *Luke* 8:12
in imagination of *their h.* *Luke* 1:51
heard laid them up in *their h.* 66
all men mused in *their h.* of. 3:15
in *their h.* turned back. *Acts* 7:39
through lust of *their h.* *Rom* 1:24
work of law written in *their h.* 2:15
their h. might be comforted. *Col* 2:2
always err in *their h.* *Heb* 3:10
God hath put in *their h.* *Rev* 17:17

your **hearts**

comfort ye *your h.* after. *Gen* 18:5
O Israel, let not *your h.* *Deut* 20:3
set *your h.* to all the words. 32:46
ye know in all *your h.* *Josh* 23:14
incline *your h.* to the Lord. 24:23
do ye harden *your h.*? *1 Sam* 6:6
the Lord with all *your h.* and prepare *your h.* to the Lord to serve. 7:3
ye dissembled in *your h.* *Jer* 42:20*
imagine evil in *your h.* *Zech* 8:17
think ye evil in *your h.*? *Mat* 9:4
if ye from *your h.* forgive not. 18:35
of the hardness of *your h.* 19:8
these things in *your h.*? *Mark* 2:8
what reason ye in *your h.*? *Luke* 5:22
God knoweth *your h.* 16:15
settle it in *your h.* not to. 21:14
lest at any time *your h.* be. 34
thoughts arise in *your h.*? 24:38
of his Son into *your h.* *Gal* 4:6
Christ may dwell in *your h.* *Eph* 3:17
melody in *your h.* to. 5:19; *Col* 3:16
that he might comfort *your h.* 6:22
keep *your h.* and minds. *Phil* 4:7
peace of God rule in *your h.* *Col* 3:15
your estate and comfort *your h.* 4:8
may establish *your h.* *1 Thes* 3:13
comfort *your h.* and. *2 Thes* 2:17
Lord direct *your h.* into love. 3:5
if ye have strife in *your h.* *Jas* 3:14
your h. ye double minded. 4:8
ye have nourished *your h.* 5:5
be ye also patient, stablish *your h.* 8
the Lord God in *your h.* *1 Pet* 3:15
day star arise in *your h.* *2 Pet* 1:19

hearty

sweetness of a friend by *h.* *Pr* 27:9

heat

h., summer and winter. *Gen* 8:22
sat in the tent door in the *h.* of. 18:1
what meaneth the *h.* of? *Deut* 29:24
be devoured with burning *h.* 32:24
slew Ammonites till *h.* *1 Sam* 11:11
they came about the *h.* *2 Sam* 4:5
but he gat no *h.* *1 Ki* 1:1
my lord may get *h.* 2
drought and *h.* consume. *Job* 24:19
my bones are burnt with *h.* 30:30
hid from the *h.* thereof. *Ps* 19:6
together, then they have *h.* *Eccl* 4:11
a shadow in the daytime from the *h.* *Isa* 4:6; 25:4
like a clear *h.* on herbs, and like a cloud of dew in the *h.* 18:4
h. in a dry place, even the *h.* 25:5
neither shall the *h.* nor sun. 49:10
shall not see when *h.* *Jer* 17:8
dead body shall be cast in the day to *h.* 36:30
in their *h.* I will make their. 51:39
and I went in the *h.* of. *Ezek* 3:14
borne the burden and *h.* *Mat* 20:12
blow, there will be *h.* *Luke* 12:55
came a viper out of the *h.* *Acts* 28:3
no sooner risen with a burning *h.* *Jas* 1:11
shall melt with fervent *h.* *2 Pet* 3:10

heat

h. the furnace more. *Dan* 3:19

heated

more than wont to be *h.* *Dan* 3:19
adulterers, as an oven *h.* *Hos* 7:4

heath

he shall be like the *h.* in. *Jer* 17:6
flee, and be like the *h.* in the. 48:6

heathen

(*Most frequently this word merely means the other nations as distinguished from the Hebrews, without intending any reference to religion. But it generally means idolaters. The Revisions very frequently substitute the word* nations *for heathen*)

bondmen shall be of the *h.* round. *Lev* 25:44
forth in sight of the *h.* 26:45
be head of *h.* *2 Sam* 22:44; *Ps* 18:43
to abominations of the *h.* *2 Ki* 16:3 17:15; 21:2; *2 Chr* 28:3; 36:14
walked in statutes of *h.* *2 Ki* 17:8
as did the *h.* whom the Lord. 11
deliver us from the *h.* *1 Chr* 16:35
over all kingdoms of *h.* *2 Chr* 20:6
the abominations of the *h.* 33:2
made Judah to do worse than *h.* 9
from filthiness of the *h.* *Ezra* 6:21
Jews who were sold to *h.* *Neh* 5:8
because of the reproach of the *h.* 9
all the *h.* that were about us. 6:16
why do the *h.* rage? *Ps* 2:1 *Acts* 4:25
shall give thee the *h.* for thy. *Ps* 2:8
thou hast rebuked the *h.* thou. 9:5
the *h.* are sunk in the pit that. 15
arise, let the *h.* be judged in. 9:19
the *h.* are perished out of his. 10:16
Lord bringeth the counsel of *h.* 33:10
how thou didst drive out the *h.* 44:2
the *h.* raged, the kingdoms. 46:6
God reigneth over the *h.* 47:8
awake to visit all the *h.* 59:5
shalt have all the *h.* in derision. 8
he cast out the *h.* also. 78:55; 80:8
the *h.* are come into thine. 79:1
thy wrath upon the *h.* 6; *Jer* 10:25
the *h.* say, where is their God? let him be known among *h.* *Ps* 79:10 115:2
he that chastiseth the *h.* 94:10
openly shewed in the sight of *h.* 98:2
h. shall fear the name of the. 102:15
gave them the lands of the *h.* 105:44
gave them into hand of the *h.* 106:41
gave them heritage of the *h.* 111:6
the idols of the *h.* are silver. 135:15
execute vengeance upon the *h.* 149:7
the lords of the *h.* have. *Isa* 16:8
of the *h.* be not dismayed at signs of heaven, for the *h.* *Jer* 10:2
ambassador is sent to the *h.* 49:14
seen that the *h.* entered. *Lam* 1:10
bring the worst of the *h.* *Ezek* 7:24

after the manners of *h.* *Ezek* 11:12
polluted before the *h.* 20:9, 14, 22
ye say, we will be as the *h.* 32
be sanctified before the *h.* 41; 28:25
thee a reproach to the *h.* 22:4
inheritance in sight of the *h.* 16
gone a whoring after the *h.* 23:30
deliver thee for a spoil to *h.* 25:7
house of Judah is like to all the *h.* 8
it shall be the time of the *h.* 30:3
hand of the mighty one of *h.* 31:11
his shadow in midst of the *h.* 17
no more be a prey to the *h.* 34:28
neither bear the shame of the *h.* 29
possession to the residue of *h.* 36:3
a derision to the residue of the *h.* 4
ye have borne the shame of the *h.* 6
when they entered unto the *h.* 20
h. know I am Lord. 23, 36; 37:28
38:16; 39:7
and all the *h.* shall see my. 39:21
that the *h.* should rule. *Joel* 2:17
and come, all ye *h.* and gather. 3:11
h. be wakened, and come up to valley
of Jehoshaphat... to judge all *h.* 12
possess remnant of all *h.* *Amos* 9:12
the Lord is near on all the *h.* *Ob* 15
all the *h.* drink continually. 16
execute fury upon the *h.* *Mi* 5:15
thou didst thresh the *h.* *Hab* 3:12
all the isles of the *h.* *Zeph* 2:11
destroy the strength of *h.* *Hag* 2:22
sore displeased with *h.* *Zech* 1:15
shall speak peace to the *h.* 9:10
the wealth of all the *h.* shall. 14:14
wherewith Lord will smite the *h.* 18
repetitions as the *h.* do. *Mat* 6:7
let him be to thee as an *h.* 18:17*
in perils by the *h.* *2 Cor* 11:26
we should go unto the *h.* *Gal* 2:9
that God would justify the *h.* 3:8

among the **heathen**

among the h. and land. *Lev* 26:33
Jer 9:16; *Ezek* 20:23; 22:15
perish *among the h.* and. *Lev* 26:38
few in number *among h.* *Deut* 4:27
thee, O Lord, *among h.* and sing
praises. *2 Sam* 22:50; *Ps* 18:49
declare his glory *among h.*
1 Chr 16:24; *Ps* 96:3
to us from *among the h.* *Neh* 5:17
it is reported *among the h.* 6:6
scattered us *among the h.* *Ps* 44:11
us a byword *among the h.* 14
I will be exalted *among the h.* 46:10
known *among the h.* in sight. 79:10
say *among the h.* that Lord. 96:10
were mingled *among the h.* 106:35
and gather us from *among h.* 47
judge *among the h.* he shall. 110:6
said *among the h.* Lord hath. 126:2
ask *among the h.*, who. *Jer* 18:13
make thee small *among the h.* 49:15
she dwelleth *among the h.* *Lam* 1:3
said *among the h.* they shall. 4:15
shadow we shall live *among the h.* 20
have cast them far off *among the h.*
Ezek 11:16
abominations *among the h.* 12:16
went forth *among the h.* 16:14
scatter them *among the h.* 36:19
profaned *among the h.* 21, 22, 23
you from *among the h.* 24, 37:21
reproach of famine *among the h.* 30
set my glory *among the h.* 39:21
be led into captivity *among h.* 28
a reproach *among the h.* *Joel* 2:19
ambassador sent *among the h.* *Ob* 1
made thee small *among the h.* 2
behold ye *among the h.* *Hab* 1:5
a curse *among the h.* *Zech* 8:13
be great *among the h.* *Mal* 1:11
name is dreadful *among the h.* 14
preach him *among the h.* *Gal* 1:16

heave

as ye do the *h.* offering, so shall ye *h.*
it. *Num* 15:20

heaved

is *h.* of the ram of. *Ex* 29:27
ye have *h.* the best. *Num* 18:30, 32
see **offering, shoulder**

heaven

This word is used of the abode of the redeemed after death and the second resurrection. It is also used for God, without whom there would be no heaven.
It is sometimes used of the air, as in the phrase birds *or* fowls of heaven. *And for the sky, wherein the sun, moon, and stars are placed.*

the beginning God created *h.* *Gen* 1:1
and God called the firmament *h.* 8
lights in the firmament of *h.* 14, 15
fly in the open firmament of *h.* 20
and the windows of *h.* were. 7:11
windows of *h.* were stopped. 8:2
possessor of *h.* and earth. 14:19, 22
fire from the Lord out of *h.* 19:24
God called to Hagar out of *h.* 21:17
called to Abraham out of *h.* 22:11, 15
give thee of the dew of *h.* 27:28, 39
said, this is the gate of *h.* 28:17
blessings of *h.* above. 49:25
six days Lord made *h.* and earth.
Ex 20:11; 31:17
as it were the body of *h.* in. 24:10
I will make your *h.* as. *Lev* 26:19
burned to the midst of *h.* *Deut* 4:11
I call *h.* and earth. 26; 30:19; 31:28
ask from the one side of *h.* to. 4:32
out of *h.* he made thee hear his. 36
behold, the *h.* and *h.* of heavens.
10:14; *Ps* 115:16
water of the rain of *h.* *Deut* 11:11
he shut up *h.* 17; *1 Ki* 8:35
2 Chr 6:26; 7:13
multiplied as days of *h.* *Deut* 11:21
open the *h.* to give the rain. 28:12
h. that is over thy head shall. 23
scatter thee to the utmost part of *h.*
30:4; *Neh* 1:9
precious things of *h.* *Deut* 33:13
of Jeshurun rideth upon the *h.* 26
of *h.* shall he thunder. *1 Sam* 2:10
taken up between *h.* *2 Sam* 18:9
dropped on them out of *h.* 21:10
the foundations of *h.* moved. 22:8
h. and the *h.* of heavens cannot.
1 Ki 8:27; *2 Chr* 2:6; 6:18
when *h.* is shut up, and. *1 Ki* 8:35
mean while the *h.* was black. 18:45
of all kingdoms, thou hast made *h.*
2 Ki 19:15; *2 Chr* 2:12; *Neh* 9:6
angel stood between *h.* *1 Chr* 21:16
it is as high as *h.* *Job* 11:8
h. shall reveal his iniquity. 20:27
is not God in height of *h.*? 22:12
walketh in the circuit of *h.* 14
the pillars of *h.* tremble at. 26:11
the hoary frost of *h.* who? 38:29
thou the ordinances of *h.*? 33
who can stay the bottles of *h.*? 37
forth is from the end of *h.* *Ps* 19:6
hear him from his holy *h.* 20:6
let *h.* and earth praise him. 69:34
he opened the doors of *h.* 78:23
given them of the corn of *h.* 24
to endure as the days of *h.* 89:29
h. is high above the earth. 103:11
them with the bread of *h.* 105:40
the Lord who made *h.* and earth.
115:15; 121:2; 124:8; 134:3
146:6; *Isa* 37:16; *Jer* 32:17
Acts 4:24; 14:15; *Rev* 14:7
covereth *h.* with clouds. *Ps* 147:8
glory is above earth and *h.* 148:13
the *h.* for height, the earth. *Pr* 25:3
far, from the end of *h.* *Isa* 13:5
who hath meted out *h.* with. 40:12
sing, O *h.* and be. 49:13; *Rev* 18:20
h. my throne, earth my footstool.
Isa 66:1; *Acts* 7:49
cakes to the queen of *h.* *Jer* 7:18
not dismayed at the signs of *h.* 10:2
do not I fill *h.* and earth? 23:24
if *h.* above can be measured. 31:37
appointed ordinances of *h.* 33:25
to burn incense to queen of *h.* 44:17
18, 19, 25
from the four quarters of *h.* 49:36
hath stretched out the *h.* by. 51:15
the *h.* and earth shall sing for. 48
swifter than eagles of *h.* *Lam* 4:19
me between earth and *h.* *Ezek* 8:3
I will cover the *h.* and make. 32:7
the lights of *h.* will I make dark. 8
be wet with dew of *h.* *Dan* 4:15
23, 25, 33; 5:21
his will in the army of *h.* 4:35
extol and honour the King of *h.* 37
thyself against the Lord of *h.* 5:23
the four winds of *h.* strove. 7:2
of man, came with clouds of *h.* 13
towards the four winds of *h.* 8:8
divided toward four winds of *h.* 11:4
buildeth his stories in *h.* *Amos* 9:6
the *h.* over you is stayed. *Hag* 1:10
as the four winds of *h.* *Zech* 2:6
ephah between earth and *h.* 5:9
not open windows of *h.* *Mal* 3:10
till *h.* and earth pass. *Mat* 5:18
neither swear by *h.*; for it is God's
throne. 34; *Jas* 5:12
I thank thee, Father, Lord of *h.*
Mat 11:25; *Luke* 10:21
swear by *h.* sweareth by. *Mat* 23:22
coming in the clouds of *h.* 24:30
26:64; *Mark* 14:62
elect from one end of *h.* *Mat* 24:31
h. and earth shall pass away. 35
Mark 13:31; *Luke* 21:33
the angels of *h.* but my. *Mat* 24:36
from utmost part of *h.* *Mark* 13:27
Jesus praying, the *h.* *Luke* 3:21
when the *h.* was shut up. 4:25
I have sinned against *h.* 15:18, 21
it is easier for *h.* and earth. 16:17
for the powers of *h.* shall be. 21:26
hereafter ye shall see *h.* *John* 1:51
the *h.* must receive. *Acts* 3:21
I saw *h.* opened, and a vessel.
10:11; *Rev* 19:11
seeing he is Lord of *h.* *Acts* 17:24
prayed again, and the *h.* *Jas* 5:18
cometh down out of *h.* *Rev* 3:12
h. departed as a scroll when. 6:14
an angel flying through the midst of *h.*
8:13; 14:6
who created *h.* and the things. 10:6
have power to shut *h.* that. 11:6
voice out of the temple of *h.* 16:17
fell on men a great hail out of *h.* 21
rejoice over her, thou *h.* 18:20
fowls that fly in midst of *h.* 19:17
came down from God out of *h.* 20:9
earth and *h.* fled away, and. 11
a new *h.* and earth, the first *h.* 21:1
Jerusalem descending out of *h.* 10
see **fowl, fowls**

from **heaven**

and the rain *from h.* was. *Gen* 8:2
rain bread *from h.* for you. *Ex* 16:4
I have talked with you *from h.*
20:22; *Neh* 9:13
look down *from h.* *Deut* 26:15
Isa 63:15; *Lam* 3:50
as dust *from h.* shall it. *Deut* 28:24
cast great stones *from h.* *Josh* 10:11
they fought *from h.* *Judg* 5:20
Lord thundered *from h.* *2 Sam* 22:14
down *from h.* and there came down
fire *from h.* *2 Ki* 1:10, 12, 14
answered him *from h.* *1 Chr* 21:26
hear thou *from h.* *2 Chr* 6:21, 23
27, 30
the fire came down *from h.* 7:1
then will I hear *from h.* and. 14
bread *from h.* for hunger. *Neh* 9:15
heardest them *from h.* 27, 28
of God is fallen *from h.* *Job* 1:16
the Lord looked down *from h.*
Ps 14:2; 53:2
the Lord looketh *from h.* *Ps* 33:13
shall send *from h.* and save. 57:3
judgement to be heard *from h.* 76:8
O God, look down *from h.* 80:14
shall look down *from h.* 85:11
from h. did the Lord behold. 102:19
from h. O Lucifer! *Isa* 14:12
as snow falleth *from h.* and. 55:10
Lord cast down *from h.* *Lam* 2:1
came down *from h.* *Dan* 4:13
an holy one coming down *from h.* 23
fell a voice *from h.* saying. 31
Mat 3:17; *Luke* 3:22; *John* 12:28
shew them a sign *from h.* *Mat* 16:1
John, whence was it? *from h.* or of?
21:25, *Mark* 11:30; *Luke* 20:4
for the angel descended *from h.*
Mat 28:2; *Rev* 10:1; 18:1; 20:1

seeking of him a sign from h.
Mark 8:11; Luke 11:16
fire to come down from h. Luke 9:54
as lightning fall from h. 10:18
fire and brimstone from h. 17:29
signs shall there be from h. 21:11
appeared an angel from h. 22:43
Spirit descending from h. John 1:32
came down from h. 3:13; 6:33
except it be given him from h. 3:27
he that cometh from h. is above. 31
he gave them bread from h. to. 6:31
gave you not that bread from h. 32
I came from h. not to do. 38, 42
came down from h. 41, 50, 51, 58
came a sound from h. Acts 2:2
a light from h. shined about him.
9:3; 22:6; 26:13
sheet let down from h. 11:5
voice answered me again from h. 9
good, and gave us rain from h. 14:17
God is revealed from h. Rom 1:18
man is the Lord from h. 1 Cor 15:47
our house that is from h. 2 Cor 5:2
an angel from h. preach. Gal 1:8
wait for his Son from h. 1 Thes 1:10
himself shall descend from h. 4:16
Lord Jesus shall be revealed from
h. 2 Thes 1:7
him that speaketh from h. Heb 12:25
gospel to you with the Holy Ghost
sent down from h. 1 Pet 1:12
fell a great star from h. Rev 8:10
and I saw a star fall from h. 9:1
voice from h., Seal up those things.
10:4, 8; 11:12; 14:2, 13; 18:4
fire come down from h. 13:13

see God of heaven

host, or, *hosts of* heaven

seest the host of h. Deut 4:19
and worshipped the host of h. 17:3
Lord sitting on the throne and the
host of h. 1 Ki 22:19; 2 Chr 18:18
Israel worshipped the host of h.
2 Ki 17:16
Manasseh worshipped host of h.
21:3; 2 Chr 33:3
built altars for the host of h.
2 Ki 21:5; 2 Chr 33:5
vessels made for host of h. 2 Ki 23:4
that burnt incense to host of h. 5
made the h. of heavens with their
host, and the host of h. Neh 9:6
all the host of h. shall be. Isa 34:4
them before the host of h. Jer 8:2
incense to all the host of h. 19:13
as the host of h. cannot be. 33:22
even to the host of h. Dan 8:10
them that worship host of h. Zeph 1:5
up to worship the host of h. Acts 7:42

in heaven

nor likeness of any thing in h.
Ex 20:4; Deut 5:8
what God in h. can do? Deut 3:24
that the Lord he is God in h. 4:39
in h. that thou shouldest say. 30:12
God he is God in h. Josh 2:11
is no God like thee in h. 1 Ki 8:23
2 Chr 6:14
hear thou in h. 1 Ki 8:30, 32, 34
36, 39, 43, 45, 49
make windows in h. 2 Ki 7:2, 19
all that is in h. and. 1 Chr 29:11
art not thou God in h.? 2 Chr 20:6
my witness is in h. Job 16:19
the Lord's throne is in h. Ps 11:4
whom have I in h. but thee? 73:25
thy thunder was in the h. 77:18*
an east wind to blow in the h. 78:26
who in h. can be compared to? 89:6*
as a faithful witness in h. 37*
himself to behold things in h. 113:6
thy word is settled in h. 119:89
that did he in h. and earth. 135:6
for God is in h. and thou. Eccl 5:2
sword shall be bathed in h. Isa 34:5
the stork in h. knoweth her. Jer 8:7
there is a God in h. that. Dan 2:28
signs and wonders in h. and. 6:27
buildeth his stories in h. Amos 9:6
great is your reward in h. Mat 5:12
your Father who is in h. 16
of your Father who is in h. Mat 5:45
be perfect as your Father in h. 48
which art in h. 6:9; Luke 11:2
will be done on earth, as it is in h.
Mat 6:10; Luke 11:2
yourselves treasures in h. Mat 6:20
shall your Father in h. give. 7:11
will of my Father in h. 21; 12:50
before my Father in h. 10:32
I deny before my Father in h. 33
but my Father which is in h. 16:17
shall be bound in h.: shall be loosed
in h. 19; 18:18
in h. their angels do always behold
the face of my Father in h. 18:10
for them of my Father in h. 19
thou shalt have treasure in h. 19:21
Luke 18:22
are as the angels of God in h.
Mat 22:30; Mark 12:25
your Father who is in h. Mat 23:9
sign of the Son of man in h. 24:30
all power is given to me in h. 28:18
will your Father in h. Mark 11:26
the powers that are in h. 13:25
no, not the angels which are in h. 32
reward is great in h. Luke 6:23
your names are written in h. 10:20
joy shall be in h. over one. 15:7
peace in h. and glory in. 19:38
Son of man who is in h. John 3:13
wonders in h. above and. Acts 2:19
whether in h. or in earth. 1 Cor 8:5
gather in one, things in h. Eph 1:10
of whom the whole family in h. 3:15
your master is in h. 6:9; Col 4:1
should bow, of things in h. Phil 2:10
is in h. from whence we look. 3:20
is laid up for you in h. Col 1:5
all things created that are in h. 16
him to reconcile all things in h. 20
ye have in h. a better. Heb 10:34
born which are written in h. 12:23
inheritance reserved in h. 1 Pet 1:4
there are three that bear record in h.
1 John 5:7
door was opened in h. Rev 4:1
a throne was set in h. and one. 2
no man in h. or earth was. 5:3
creature in h. saying, Blessing. 13
was silence in h. 8:1
great voices in h. 11:15
temple of God was opened in h. 19
a great wonder in h. 12:1, 3
there was war in h.: Michael. 7
place found any more in h. 8
loud voice saying in h. 10; 19:1
them that dwell in h. 13:6
of the temple which is in h. 14:17
I saw another sign in h. great. 15:1
the tabernacle of testimony in h. 5
the armies that were in h. 19:14

into heaven

take up Elijah into h. 2 Ki 2:1
up by a whirlwind into h. 11
if I ascend into h. thou. Ps 139:8
who hath ascended into h.? Pr 30:4
Rom 10:6
said, I will ascend into h. Isa 14:13
was received up into h. Mark 16:19
angels were gone away into h.
Luke 2:15
from them, carried up into h. 24:51
into h. taken from you into h. Jesus
shall come . . . go into h. Acts 1:11
looked up stedfastly into h. 7:55
was received up into h. 10:16; 11:10
into h. itself, to appear. Heb 9:24
who is gone into h. on. 1 Pet 3:22

see kingdom

heaven *joined with stars*

stars in the firmament of h. Gen 1:17
thy seed as stars of h. 22:17; 26:4
Ex 32:13; 1 Chr 27:23; Neh 9:23
you are this day as stars of h.
Deut 1:10; 10:22
whereas ye were as stars of h. 28:62
the stars of h. shall not. Isa 13:10
cover h. and make stars. Ezek 32:7
merchants as stars of h. Nah 3:16
the stars shall fall from h.
Mat 24:29; Mark 13:25
and the stars of h. fell. Rev 6:13
the third part of stars of h. 12:4

to heaven, or *unto* heaven

top may reach unto h. Gen 11:4
and the top of it reached to h. 28:12
the cities great and walled up to h.
Deut 1:28; 9:1
thou lift up thine eyes unto h. 4:19
who shall go up for us to h.? 30:12
I lift up my hand to h. and. 32:40
smoke of the city ascended up to h.
Josh 8:20
flame of the city ascended up to h.
Judg 20:40
cry of city went up to h. 1 Sam 5:12
hands spread up to h. 1 Ki 8:54
that reacheth up unto h. 2 Chr 28:9
prayer came up even unto h. 30:27
Isaiah prayed and cried to h. 32:20
they mount up to h. Ps 107:26
her judgement reacheth unto h.
Jer 51:9
height reached to h. Dan 4:11, 20
held up his left hand unto h. 12:7
they climb up to h. Amos 9:2
which art exalted to h. Mat 11:23
and looking up to h. 14:19
Mark 6:41; Luke 9:16
looking up to h. he. Mark 7:34
much as his eyes unto h. Luke 18:13
and no man hath ascended up to h.
John 3:13
Jesus lifted up his eyes to h. 17:1
caught up to the third h. 2 Cor 12:2
lifted up his hand to h. Rev 10:5
and they ascended up to h. 11:12
sins have reached unto h. 18:5

toward heaven

look now toward h. Gen 15:5
sprinkle it toward the h. Ex 9:8
Moses sprinkled it up toward h. 10
thine hand toward h. 22; 10:21
forth his rod toward h. 9:23
forth his hand toward h. 10:22
flame went up toward h. Judg 13:20
Solomon spread forth his hands toward h. 1 Ki 8:22; 2 Chr 6:13
dust on their heads toward h.
Job 2:12
as an eagle toward h. Pr 23:5
stedfastly toward h. Acts 1:10

under heaven

let the waters under h. Gen 1:9
destroy all flesh from under h. 6:17
high hills under the whole h. 7:19
remembrance of Amalek from under
h. Ex 17:14; Deut 25:19
thee on nations under h. Deut 2:25
divided to all nations under h. 4:19
their name from under h. 7:24; 9:14
out his name from under h. 29:20
of Israel from under h. 2 Ki 14:27
seeth under the whole h. Job 28:24
directeth it under the whole h. 37:3
is under the whole h. is mine. 41:11
all things done under h. Eccl 1:13
good they should do under h. 2:3
every purpose under the h. 3:1
out of one part under h. Luke 17:24
of every nation under h. Acts 2:5
none other name under h. 4:12
every creature under h. Col 1:23

heavenly

h. Father will forgive you. Mat 6:14
yet your h. Father feedeth them. 26
your h. Father knoweth that ye. 32
every plant my h. Father. 15:13
so shall my h. Father do also. 18:35
a multitude of the h. host. Luke 2:13
your h. Father shall give the. 11:13
believe, if I tell you of h. John 3:12
not disobedient to the h. Acts 26:19
the h. such are they that are h.
1 Cor 15:48
also bear the image of the h. 49
spiritual blessings in h. Eph 1:3
right hand in h. places. 1:20; 2:6
unto the powers in h. places. 3:10
preserve me to his h. 2 Tim 4:18
partakers of the h. Heb 3:1
and have tasted of the h. gift. 6:4
example and shadow of h. 8:5

h. things with better sacrifices. *Heb* 9:23
an *h.* country. 11:16
the *h.* Jerusalem. 12:22

heavens

thus the *h.* and the earth. *Gen* 2:1
generations of the *h.* and the earth in the day that the Lord made the *h.* 4
give ear, O *h.* I will speak. *Deut* 32:1; *Isa* 1:2
also his *h.* shall drop. *Deut* 33:28
earth trembled, the *h.* *Judg* 5:4
he bowed the *h.* and came. *2 Sam* 22:10; *Ps* 18:9
the heaven of *h.* cannot. *1 Ki* 8:27
the Lord made the *h.* *1 Chr* 16:26
Neh 9:6; *Ps* 96:5; 102:25; 136:5
let the *h.* be glad, let. *1 Chr* 16:31
then hear from the *h.* *2 Chr* 6:25
33, 35, 39
is grown up to the *h.* *Ezra* 9:6
spreadeth out the *h.* *Job* 9:8
man riseth not till the *h.* be. 14:12
yea, the *h.* are not clean in. 15:15
excellency mount up to the *h.* 20:6
Spirit he hath garnished the *h.* 26:13
look to the *h.* and see, and. 35:5
thou hast set thy glory above the *h.* *Ps* 8:1; 113:4
I consider thy *h.* the work. *Ps* 8:3
the *h.* declare the glory of God. 19:1
the Lord were the *h.* made. 33:6
shall call to the *h.* from above. 50:4
h. shall declare his righteousness. 6
exalted, O God, above *h.* 57:5, 11
108:5
mercy is great unto the *h.* 57:10
108:4
him that rideth upon the *h.* 68:4, 33
h. also dropped at the presence. 8
their mouth against the *h.* 73:9
thy *h.* shall praise thy wonders. 89:5
the *h.* are thine, the earth also. 11
let the *h.* rejoice, earth be glad. 96:11; *Rev* 12:12
h. declare his righteousness. *Ps* 97:6
who stretchest out the *h.* 104:2
Isa 40:22
mercy is great above the *h.* *Ps* 108:4
the heaven, even the *h.* are. 115:16
bow thy *h.* O Lord, and come. 144:5
praise ye the Lord from the *h.* 148:1
ye *h.* of *h.* and waters above the *h.* 4
he established the *h.* *Pr* 3:19
when he prepared the *h.* I was. 8:27
will shake the *h.* and earth. *Isa* 13:13
Hag 2:6, 21
the *h.* shall be rolled. *Isa* 34:4
he that created the *h.* 42:5; 45:18
sing, O ye *h.* for the Lord. 44:23
Lord, that stretcheth forth the *h.* 24
45:12; 51:13; *Jer* 10:12; *Zech* 12:1
drop down ye *h.* from above. *Isa* 45:8
hand hath spanned the *h.* 48:13
sing, O *h.* and be joyful, O. 49:13
clothe *h.* with blackness, I. 50:3
eyes to the *h.* and look, the *h.* 51:6
that I may plant the *h.* and lay. 16
for as the *h.* are higher than. 55:9
thou wouldest rend the *h.* and. 64:1
behold, I create new *h.* and. 65:17
for as the new *h.* which I. 66:22
astonished, O ye *h.* and. *Jer* 2:12
I beheld the *h.* and they had. 4:23
birds of the *h.* were fled. 25; 9:10
shall the earth mourn, *h.* 4:28
the *h.* and the earth shall perish, and from under these *h.* 10:11
or can the *h.* give showers? 14:22
from under *h.* of the Lord. *Lam* 3:66
that the *h.* were opened. *Ezek* 1:1
Mat 3:16
known that the *h.* do. *Dan* 4:26
I will hear the *h.*, they. *Hos* 2:21
the *h.* shall tremble, sun. *Joel* 2:10
and the *h.* and the earth. 3:16
his glory covered the *h.* *Hab* 3:3
four spirits of the *h.* *Zech* 6:5
and the *h.* shall give their dew. 8:12
powers of the *h.* shall be. *Mat* 24:29
coming up, he saw the *h.* *Mark* 1:10
not ascended into the *h.* *Acts* 2:34
whom the *h.* must receive until. 3:21
behold, I see the *h.* opened *Acts* 7:56
h. are the work of thine. *Heb* 1:10
Priest that is passed into *h.* 4:14
Priest made higher than the *h.* 7:26
by word of God the *h.* *2 Pet* 3:5
but the *h.* which are now, are. 7
h. shall pass away with a great. 10
wherein the *h.* being on fire. 12

in the **heavens**

that sitteth *in the h.* *Ps* 2:4
Lord also thundered *in the h.* 18:13
mercy, O Lord, is *in the h.* 36:5
shalt thou establish *in the h.* 89:2
prepared his throne *in the h.* 103:19
God is *in the h.* he hath done. 115:3
O thou that dwellest *in the h.* 123:1
light is darkened *in the h.* *Isa* 5:30*
a multitude of waters *in the h.* *Jer* 10:13; 51:16
hearts to God *in the h.* *Lam* 3:41
shew wonders *in the h.* *Joel* 2:30
a treasure *in the h.* *Luke* 12:33
hands, eternal *in the h.* *2 Cor* 5:1
of the Majesty *in the h.* *Heb* 8:1
patterns of things *in the h.* 9:23

heavier

be *h.* than the sand of. *Job* 6:3
my stroke is *h.* than my. 23:2
a fool's wrath is *h.* than. *Pr* 27:3

heavily

so that drave them *h.* *Ex* 14:25
I bowed down *h.* as one. *Ps* 35:14*
on ancient hast thou *h.* laid. *Isa* 47:6

heaviness

sacrifice I rose from my *h.* *Ezra* 9:5*
I will leave off my *h.* *Job* 9:27*
heart, and I am full of *h.* *Ps* 69:20
soul melteth for *h.* 119:28
a foolish son is the *h.* of. *Pr* 10:1
h. in the heart of man. 12:25
the end of that mirth is *h.* 14:13
there shall be *h.* and. *Isa* 29:2*
of praise for spirit of *h.* 61:3
that I have great *h.* and. *Rom* 9:2*
come again to you in *h.* *2 Cor* 2:1*
my brother was full of *h.* *Phil* 2:26*
your joy be turned into *h.* *Jas* 4:9
if need be, ye are in *h.* *1 Pet* 1:6*

heavy

Moses' hands were *h.* *Ex* 17:12
for this thing is too *h.* for. 18:18
because it is too *h.* for. *Num* 11:14
was an old man and *h.* *1 Sam* 4:18
was *h.* on them of Ashdod. 5:6, 11
the hair was *h.* on. *2 Sam* 14:26
father's *h.* yoke lighter. *1 Ki* 12:4
10, 11, 14; *2 Chr* 10:4, 10, 11, 14
sent to thee with *h.* *1 Ki* 14:6
went to his house *h.* 20:43; 21:4
the bondage was *h.* *Neh* 5:18
shall my hand be *h.* *Job* 33:7
and night thy hand was *h.* *Ps* 32:4
h. burden they are too *h.* 38:4
singeth songs to an *h.* *Pr* 25:20
stone is *h.* and sand weighty. 27:3
wine to those that be of *h.* 31:6*
make their ears *h.*, shut. *Isa* 6:10
transgression thereof shall be *h.* 24:20
and the burden thereof is *h.* 30:27*
carriages were *h.* loaden. 46:1*
this the fast, to undo the *h.*? 58:6*
neither his ear *h.* that it. 59:1
hath made my chain *h.* *Lam* 3:7
all ye that are *h.* laden. *Mat* 11:28
for they bind *h.* burdens. 23:4
sorrowful, and very *h.* 26:37*
for their eyes were very *h.* 43
Mark 14:33*, 40*
were with him, were *h.* *Luke* 9:32

Heber

the sons of Beriah, *H.* *Gen* 46:17
1 Chr 7:31
H. the Kenite. *Judg* 4:11, 17; 5:24
which was the son of *H.* *Luke* 3:35

Hebrew, *language*

written over him in *H.* *Luke* 23:38
John 19:20
a pool called in the *H.* *John* 5:2
called in *H.* Gabbatha. 19:13
called in *H.* Golgotha. 17
Paul spake to them in *H.* *Acts* 21:40; 22:2
a voice saying in the *H.* *Acts* 26:14
in *H.* Abaddon. *Rev* 9:11
in the *H.* Armageddon. 16:16

Hebrew *man*

an *H. man,* be sold. *Deut* 15:12

Hebrew, *servant*

the *H. servant* came in. *Gen* 39:17
if thou buy an *H. servant.* *Ex* 21:2

Hebrew *woman, women*

a midwife to *H. women.* *Ex* 1:16
H. women are not as the. 19
thee a nurse of the *H. women*? 2:7
if any *H. woman* be. *Deut* 15:12

Hebrewess

man should let an *H.* *Jer* 34:9

Hebrew

told Abraham the *H.* *Gen* 14:13
see he hath brought in an *H.* 39:14
with us a young man, an *H.* 41:12
Egyptian smiting an *H.* *Ex* 2:11
H. or Hebrewess go free. *Jer* 34:9
I am an *H.* *Jonah* 1:9

Hebrews

out of the land of the *H.* *Gen* 40:15
might not eat with the *H.* 43:32
this is one of the *H.* *Ex* 2:6
two men of the *H.* strove. 13
God of the *H.* 3:18; 5:3; 7:16
9:1, 13; 10:3
shout in camp of the *H.* *1 Sam* 4:6
ye be not servants to the *H.* 9
let the *H.* hear. 13:3
lest the *H.* make swords. 19
behold the *H.* come forth. 14:11
the *H.* that were with the. 21
princes said, What do these *H.*? 29:3
Grecians against the *H.* *Acts* 6:1
they *H.* or Israelites? *2 Cor* 11:22
an Hebrew of the *H.* *Phil* 3:5

Hebron, *place*

Sarah died in Kirjath-arba, the same is *H.* *Gen* 23:2; 35:27; *Josh* 14:15
20:7; *Judg* 1:10
out of the vale of *H.* *Gen* 37:14
H. was built seven. *Num* 13:22
as he did to *H.* so he. *Josh* 10:39
Joshua gave to Caleb *H.* 14:13, 14
Judg 1:20
them which were in *H.* *1 Sam* 30:31
Go up? he said, Unto *H.* *2 Sam* 2:1
David was king in *H.* 11; 5:5
1 Ki 2:11; *1 Chr* 29:27
Joab and his men came to *H.* *2 Sam* 2:32
to David were sons born in *H.* 3:2, 5
1 Chr 3:1, 4
they buried Abner in *H.* *2 Sam* 3:32
head of Ish-bosheth in *H.* 4:12
to *H.* and David made a league with them in *H.* 5:3; *1 Chr* 11:3
wives after he was come from *H.* *2 Sam* 5:13
vowed to the Lord in *H.* 15:7
Absalom reigneth in *H.* 10
cities of Judah *H.* a. *1 Chr* 6:57
with a perfect heart to *H.* 12:38
built Zorah, *H.* in. *2 Chr* 11:10

Hebron, *person*

Amram, *H.* and Uzziel. *Ex* 6:18
Num 3:19; *1 Chr* 6:2, 18; 23:12
Mareshah father of *H.* *1 Chr* 2:42
the sons of *H.* 43; 15:9; 23:19; 24:23

hedge

hast thou not made an *h.* *Job* 1:10
of slothful is an *h.* *Pr* 15:19
breaketh a *h.*, a serpent. *Eccl* 10:8*
I will take away the *h.* *Isa* 5:5
nor made up the *h.* for. *Ezek* 13:5*
man that should make up *h.* 22:30*
sharper than a thorn *h.* *Mi* 7:4
h. about it, digged for. *Mark* 12:1

hedge

behold, I will *h.* up thy. *Hos* 2:6

hedged

whom God hath *h.* in. *Job* 3:23
hath *h.* me about, I. *Lam* 3:7*
a vineyard, and *h.* it. *Mat* 21:33

hedges

amongst plants and *h.* *1 Chr* 4:23

hast thou broken down her h.?
Ps 80:12; 89:40
run to and fro by the h. Jer 49:3*
which camp in the h. Nah 3:17
the highways and h. Luke 14:23

heed

Amasa took no h. to. 2 Sam 20:10
Jehu took no h. to. 2 Ki 10:31
by taking h. according. Ps 119:9
wicked doer giveth h. Pr 17:4
preacher gave good h. Eccl 12:9*
diligently with much h. Isa 21:7
let us not give h. to any. Jer 18:18
h. to me, O Lord, and hearken. 19
he gave h. unto them. Acts 3:5
the people of Samaria gave h. 8:6
they gave h. to Simon from least. 10
neither give h. to fables. 1 Tim 1:4
Tit 1:14
h. to seducing spirits. 1 Tim 4:1
give the more earnest h. Heb 2:1
see take

heel, -s

thou shalt bruise his h. Gen 3:15
hold on Esau's h. 25:26; Hos 12:3
that biteth the horses' h. Gen 49:17
settest a print on the h. Job 13:27*
gin shall take him by the h. 18:9
friend, hath lifted up his h. against
me. Ps 41:9; John 13:18
when iniquity of my h. Ps 49:5
iniquity are thy h. made. Jer 13:22

Hege

unto the custody of H. Esth 2:3

heifer

take me an h. of three. Gen 15:9
bring me a red h. Num 19:2
burn the h. in his sight. 5
gather up the ashes of the h. 9
that city shall take an h. Deut 21:3
shall strike off h.'s neck. 4
wash hands over the h. 6
not plowed with my h. Judg 14:18
Lord said, Take an h. 1 Sam 16:2
out for Moab as an h. of. Isa 15:5*
Egypt is like a fair h. Jer 46:20
uttered their voice as an h. 48:34
ye are grown fat as an h. 50:11
back, as a backsliding h. Hos 4:16
Ephraim is as an h. that is. 10:11
the ashes of an h. Heb 9:13

height

the h. of the ark shall. Gen 6:15
ark of shittim wood, a cubit and a
half be h. Ex 25:10, 23; 37:1, 10
h. of the altar shall. Ex 27:1; 38:1
h. of court shall be. 27:18; 38:18
h. of altar of incense. 30:2; 37:25
look not on the h. of. 1 Sam 16:7
Goliath's h. was six cubits. 17:4
the h. of house of God. 1 Ki 6:2
oracle twenty cubits in the h. 20
the h. of the one cherub was. 26
the h. of the house of Lebanon. 7:2
h. of the one chapiter was five. 16
the h. of the molten sea was. 23
h. of one base was three cubits. 27
with chariots I am come up to the h.
of. 2 Ki 19:23; Isa 37:24
the h. of one pillar was. 2 Ki 25:17
it up a very great h. 2 Chr 33:14
the h. of God's house. Ezra 6:3
is not God in the h. of heaven? and
behold the h. of the. Job 22:12
Lord looked from h. of. Ps 102:19
the heaven for h., and earth. Pr 25:3
in the depth, or in the h. Isa 7:11
come and sing in the h. Jer 31:12
O thou that holdest the h. 49:16
though she should fortify h. 51:53
in mountain of the h. of Israel.
Ezek 17:23; 20:40
she appeared in her h. with. 19:11
therefore his h. was exalted. 31:5*
thou hast lifted up thyself in h. 10*
trees exalt themselves for h. 14*
fill the valleys with thy h. 32:5
image of gold whose h. Dan 3:1
saw and beheld a tree whose h. 4:10
and the h. thereof reached. 11, 20
whose h. was like the h. Amos 2:9
nor h. nor depth shall be. Rom 8:39
what is the h. of the love? Eph 3:18
breadth and h. of the city. Rev 21:16

heights

Lord, praise him in the h. Ps 148:1
I will ascend above the h. Isa 14:14

heinous

for this is an h. crime. Job 31:11

heir, -s

in my house is mine h. Gen 15:3
saying, This shall not be thine h. 4
Ishmael shall not be h. with. 21:10
we will destroy the h. 2 Sam 14:7
an handmaid that is h. Pr 30:23
no sons? hath he no h.? Jer 49:1
be h. unto them that were his h. 2*
yet will I bring an h. Mi 1:15*
this is the h. Mat 21:38
Mark 12:7; Luke 20:14
that he should be h. of. Rom 4:13
which are of the law be h. 14
children, then h.; h. of God, and
joint-h. with Christ; if we. 8:17
ye are h. according to the. Gal 3:29
I say, that the h. as long as. 4:1
if a son, then an h. of God. 7
bondwoman shall not be h. 30
Gentiles should be fellow-h. Eph 3:6
h. according to the hope. Tit 3:7
whom he appointed h. of Heb 1:2
for them who shall be h. of. 14
God willing to shew unto the h. 6:17
h. of the righteousness by. 11:7
and Jacob, h. with him of the. 9
h. of the kingdom he hath. Jas 2:5
as h. together of grace. 1 Pet 3:7

Helam

the river came to H. 2 Sam 10:16

Helbon

merchant in wine of H. Ezek 27:18

held

Joseph h. up his father's. Gen 48:17
when Moses h. up hand. Ex 17:11
the loops h. one curtain to. 36:12*
and h. the lamps in. Judg 7:20
Samson said unto lad that h. 16:26
she h. it, he measured. Ruth 3:15
Nabal h. a feast in his. 1 Sam 25:36
for Joab h. back the. 2 Sam 18:16
time Solomon h. a feast. 1 Ki 8:65
sea h. three thousand. 2 Chr 4:5
them h. both spears. Neh 4:16, 21
and with the other hand he h. 17
the king h. out the golden. Esth 5:2
if we have been sold, I had h. 7:4
my foot h. his steps, his. Job 23:11
mouth must be h. in. Ps 32:9
thy mercy, O Lord, h. me up. 94:18
I h. him, and would not. S of S 3:4
the king is h. in the galleries. 7:5
took them captives, h. Jer 50:33
he h. up his right hand. Dan 12:7
h. a council against him. Mat 12:14
Mark 15:1
the men that h. Jesus. Luke 22:63
same man that was healed, h. Peter.
Acts 3:11
part h. with Jews, part with. 14:4
dead wherein we were h. Rom 7:6
testimony which they h. Rev 6:9

held peace

at her, h. his peace. Gen 24:21
Jacob h. his peace until they. 34:5
and Aaron h. his peace. Lev 10:3
her husband h. his peace at her.
Num 30:7; 11:14
Saul, he h. his peace. 1 Sam 10:27
people h. their peace. 2 Ki 18:36
they h. their peace, and found.
Neh 5:8
nobles h. their peace. Job 29:10
I was dumb, I h. my peace. Ps 39:2
h. their peace. Isa 36:21; Mark 3:4
9:34; Luke 14:4; 20:26
Acts 11:18; 15:13
have not I h. my peace? Isa 57:11
but Jesus h. his peace. Mat 26:63

Heldai

captivity even of H. Zech 6:10

Heli

which was the son of H. Luke 3:23

Helkath-hazzurim

place was called H. 2 Sam 2:16

hell

This word is generally used in the Old Testament to translate the Hebrew word Sheol, *which really means simply the place of the dead, without reference to happiness or the reverse, see* Gen 37:35; 42:38; 1 Sam 2:6; Job 14:13.

In other passages there is an idea of punishment. The American Revision retains the Hebrew word in all places.

In the New Testament the word hell is used to translate two words, [1] *Hades, generally meaning the same as Sheol, the place of the dead,* **Acts 2:27; 1 Cor 15:55; Rev 20:13.** [2] **Gehenna,** *the place of retribution for evil deeds.*

Note.—*Where this last is the meaning of a verse it is here starred.*

burn unto the lowest h. Deut 32:22
sorrows of h. compassed me.
2 Sam 22:6; Ps 18:5
deeper than h. what canst? Job 11:8
h. is naked before him. 26:6
shall be turned into h. Ps 9:17
thou wilt not leave my soul in h.
16:10; Acts 2:27
go down quick into h. Ps 55:15
my soul from the lowest h. 86:13
and the pains of h. gat hold. 116:3
if I make my bed in h. thou. 139:8
her steps take hold on h. Pr 5:5
her house is the way to h. 7:27
guests are in the depths of h. 9:18
h. and destruction are before. 15:11
depart from h. beneath. 24
shalt deliver his soul from h. 23:14
h. and destruction are never. 27:20
therefore h. hath enlarged. Isa 5:14
h. from beneath is moved. 14:9
shalt be brought down to h. 15
and with h. are we at. 28:15
debase thyself even unto h. 57:9
I cast him down to h. Ezek 31:16
they also went down unto h. 17
him out of the midst of h. 32:21
which are going down to h. with. 27
though they dig into h. Amos 9:2
out of the belly of h. Jonah 2:2
enlargeth his desire as h. Hab 2:5
shall be in danger of h. Mat 5:22*
body should be cast into h. 29*, 30*
to destroy soul and body in h.
10:28*; Luke 12:5*
Capernaum brought down to h.
Mat 11:23; Luke 10:15
gates of h. shall not. Mat 16:18
having two eyes, to be cast into h.
18:9*; Mark 9:47*
twofold more child of h. Mat 23:15*
escape the damnation of h.? 33*
h. he lifted up his eyes. Luke 16:23
soul was not left in h. Acts 2:31
tongue is set on fire of h. Jas 3:6*
cast angels down to h. 2 Pet 2:4*
and I have the keys of h. Rev 1:18
was Death, and h. followed. 6:8
death and h. delivered up the. 20:13
death and h. were cast into the. 14

helm

about with a small h. Jas 3:4*

helmet

he had a h. of brass. 1 Sam 17:5, 38
and an h. of salvation. Isa 59:17
against shield and h. Ezek 23:24
they hanged the shield and h. 27:10
all of them with shield and h. 38:5
take h. of salvation, and. Eph 6:17
and for an h. the hope of. 1 Thes 5:8

helmets

prepared spears and h. 2 Chr 26:14
forth with your h. Jer 46:4

help, *substantive*

I will make him an h. Gen 2:18
there was not found an h. meet. 20
father, said he, was my h. Ex 18:4
be thou an h. to him. Deut 33:7

upon the heavens in thy *h.* *Deut* 33:26
saved by Lord the shield of thy *h.* 29
they came not to the *h.* *Judg* 5:23
hot, ye shall have *h.* *1 Sam* 11:9
gathered to ask *h.* of. *2 Chr* 20:4
is not my *h.* in me ? *Job* 6:13
my hand, when I saw my *h.* 31:21
soul, there is no *h.* for him. *Ps* 3:2
the Lord send thee *h.* from. 20:2
thou hast been my *h.* leave. 27:9
waits for Lord, he is our *h.* 33:20
stand up for mine *h.* 35:2; 44:26
thou art my *h.* and my. 40:17; 70:5
praise him for the *h.* of his. 42:5
God is a very present *h.* in. 46:1
h. for vain is the *h.* 60:11; 108:12
because thou hast been my *h.* 63:7
my God, make haste for my *h.* 71:12
I have laid *h.* upon one that. 89:19
Lord had been my *h.* 94:17
he is their *h.* and their. 115:9, 10, 11
from whence cometh my *h.* 121:1
my *h.* cometh from Lord which. 2
our *h.* is in name of Lord. 124:8
man, in whom there is no *h.* 146:3
hath the God of Jacob for his *h.* 5
to whom will ye flee for *h.*? *Isa* 10:3
we flee for *h.* to be delivered. 20:6
nor be an *h.* nor profit, but. 30:5
that go down to Egypt for *h.* 31:1
against the *h.* of them that work. 2
failed for our vain *h.* *Lam* 4:17
holpen with a little *h.* *Dan* 11:34
but in me is thine *h.* *Hos* 13:9
having obtained *h.* of. *Acts* 26:22

help, *verb*
father, who shall *h.* thee. *Gen* 49:25
forbear to *h.* him, thou shalt surely *h.* him. *Ex* 23:5*; *Deut* 22:4
let them rise and *h.* *Deut* 32:38
your brethren, and *h.* *Josh* 1:14
come unto me, and *h.* me. 10:4
us quickly, and save us, and *h.* us. 6
king of Gezer came up to *h.* 33
then *h.* me: then I will *h.* thee. *2 Sam* 10:11; *1 Chr* 19:12
Syrians feared to *h.* Ammon. *2 Sam* 10:19; *1 Chr* 19:19
woman said, *H.*, O king. *2 Sam* 14:4; *2 Ki* 6:26
come unto me to *h.* me. *1 Chr* 12:17
day there came to David to *h.* 22
of Damascus came to *h.* 18:5
David commanded to *h.* 22:17
it is nothing with thee to *h.*, *h.* us, O Lord our God, we rest. *2 Chr* 14:11
shouldest thou *h.* the ungodly. 19:2
then thou wilt hear and *h.* 20:9
for God hath power to *h.* and. 25:8
war with mighty power to *h.* 26:13
kings of Assyria to *h.* him. 28:16
Syria *h.* them, that they may *h.* 23
the Levites did *h.* them. 29:34
and his mighty men did *h.* him. 32:3
is the Lord our God, to *h.* us. 8
the men of his place *h.* *Ezra* 1:4
to require horsemen to *h.* 8:22
will he *h.* the evil doers. *Job* 8:20*
him that had none to *h.* him. 29:12
h. Lord. *Ps* 12:1
for there is none to *h.* 22:11
haste thee to *h.* me. 22:19; 38:22; 40:13; 70:1
Lord shall *h.* them. 37:40
God shall *h.* her. 46:5
awake to *h.* me. 59:4
h. us, O God of salvation. 79:9
was none to *h.* 107:12; *Isa* 63:5
h. me, O Lord my God. *Ps* 109:26
my part with them that *h.* 118:7
h. thou me. 119:86
let thine hand *h.* me. 173
and let thy judgements *h.* me. 175
hath not another to *h.* *Eccl* 4:10
the Egyptians shall *h.* *Isa* 30:7
fear not, I will *h.* 41:10, 13, 14; 44:2
Lord God will *h.* me. 50:7, 9
army, which is come to *h.* *Jer* 37:7
people fell, and none did *h.* *Lam* 1:7
scatter all about to *h.* *Ezek* 12:14
out of hell with them that *h.* 32:21
princes came to *h.* me. *Dan* 10:13
his end, and none shall *h.* 11:45
him, saying, Lord *h.* me. *Mat* 15:25
on us and *h.* us. *Mark* 9:22
Lord, I believe, *h.* thou mine. 24
they should come and *h.* *Luke* 5:7
bid her therefore that she *h.* 10:40
into Macedonia, and *h.* us. *Acts* 16:9
crying out, men of Israel, *h.* 21:28
h. those women which. *Phil* 4:3
we may find grace to *h.* *Heb* 4:16

helped
Moses stood up and *h.* *Ex* 2:17
hath the Lord *h.* us. *1 Sam* 7:12
following Adonijah, *h.* *1 Ki* 1:7
and two kings that *h.* him. 20:16
and they were *h.* *1 Chr* 5:20
but they *h.* them not, for the. 12:19
they *h.* David against the band. 21
when God *h.* the Levites that. 15:26
the Lord *h.* Jehoshaphat. *2 Chr* 18:31
every one *h.* to destroy. 20:23
God *h.* him against the. 26:7
for he was marvellously *h.* till. 15
king of Assyria *h.* him not. 28:21
Shabbethai the Levite *h.* *Ezra* 10:15
officers of the king *h.* *Esth* 9:3
how hast thou *h.* him that ? *Job* 26:2
and I am *h.* *Ps* 28:7
brought low, and he *h.* me. 116:6
but the Lord *h.* me. 118:13
they *h.* every one his. *Isa* 41:6
day of salvation have I *h.* thee. 49:8
and they *h.* forward the. *Zech* 1:15
when he was come, *h.* *Acts* 18:27
the earth *h.* the woman. *Rev* 12:16

helper
nor was there any *h.* *2 Ki* 14:26
my path, they have no *h.* *Job* 30:13
thou art the *h.* of the. *Ps* 10:14
Lord, be thou my *h.* 30:10
God is my *h.* 54:4
deliver him that hath no *h.* 72:12
and Zidon every *h.* *Jer* 47:4
salute Urbane, our *h.* *Rom* 16:9*
the Lord is my *h.* I will. *Heb* 13:6

helpers
among the mighty men, *h.* *1 Chr* 12:1
and peace be to thine *h.* 18
the proud *h.* do stoop. *Job* 9:13
when all her *h.* shall be. *Ezek* 30:8
and Lubim were thy *h.* *Nah* 3:9
and Aquila my *h.* in. *Rom* 16:3*
but are *h.* of your joy. *2 Cor* 1:24
we might be fellow-*h.* *3 John* 8

helpeth
for thy God *h.* thee. *1 Chr* 12:18
both he that *h.* shall fall. *Isa* 31:3
the Spirit also *h.* our. *Rom* 8:26
submit to every one that *h.* with us. *1 Cor* 16:16

helping
the prophets of God *h.* *Ezra* 5:2
thou so far from *h.* me ? *Ps* 22:1
ye also *h.* together by. *2 Cor* 1:11

helps
used *h.* undergirding. *Acts* 27:17
gifts of healings, *h.* *1 Cor* 12:28

helve
head slippeth from the *h.* *Deut* 19:5

hem, -s
upon the *h.* of it thou shalt make. *Ex* 28:33*, 34*; 39:24*, 25*, 26*
woman touched *h.* of his garment. *Mat* 9:20*; 14:36*

Heman
wiser than Ethan, *H.* *1 Ki* 4:31
Zerah, *H.* and Calcol. *1 Chr* 2:6
H. a singer, son of Joel. 6:33; 15:17, 19; 16:42
the sons of Asaph and of *H.* 25:1; 4, 6; *2 Chr* 5:12; 29:14; 35:15
H. God gave *H.* 14 sons. *1 Chr* 25:6

hemlock
springeth up as *h.* in. *Hos* 10:4
of righteousness into *h.* *Amos* 6:12

hen
as a *h.* gathereth chickens. *Mat* 23:37; *Luke* 13:34

Hen
crown shall be for *H.* *Zech* 6:14

hence
said, they are departed *h.* *Gen* 37:17
ye shall not go forth *h.* 42:15
carry up my bones from *h.* 50:25; *Ex* 13:19
go *h.* thrust you out *h.* *Ex* 11:1
depart and go *h.* thou and. 33:1
not with me, carry us not up *h.* 15
thee down quickly from *h.* *Deut* 9:12
h. out of Jordan twelve. *Josh* 4:3
depart not *h.* I pray thee. *Judg* 6:18
nor go *h.* but abide fast by. *Ruth* 2:8
get thee *h.* *1 Ki* 17:3; *Isa* 30:22; *Mat* 4:10
O spare me, before I go *h.* *Ps* 39:13
take from *h.* thirty. *Jer* 38:10
he said, Get you *h.*, walk. *Zech* 6:7
shall say, Remove *h.* to. *Mat* 17:20
cast thyself down from *h.* *Luke* 4:9
out, and depart *h.* 13:31; *John* 7:3
pass from *h.* to you. *Luke* 16:26
take things *h.*; make not. *John* 2:16
arise, let us go *h.* 14:31
my kingdom not *h.* 18:36
sir, if thou have borne him *h.* 20:15
the H. G. not many days *h.* *Acts* 1:5
I will send thee far *h.* unto. 22:21
come they not *h.* even ? *Jas* 4:1

henceforth
the ground not *h.* yield. *Gen* 4:12
neither must Israel *h.* *Num* 18:22
ye shall *h.* return no. *Deut* 17:16
shall *h.* commit no more. 19:20
I will not *h.* drive out. *Judg* 2:21
thy servant will *h.* not. *2 Ki* 5:17
from *h.* thou shalt have. *2 Chr* 16:9
about his people from *h.* *Ps* 125:2*
hope in the Lord from *h.* 131:3*
it with justice from *h.* *Isa* 9:7
h. there shall no more come. 52:1
mouth of thy seed's seed *h.* 59:21
thou shalt no more *h.* *Ezek* 36:12
in mount Zion from *h.* *Mi* 4:7
ye shall not see me *h.* *Mat* 23:39
I will not drink *h.* of this. 26:29
h. all generations shall. *Luke* 1:48
fear not, from *h.* thou shalt. 5:10
h. there shall be five in one. 12:52
h. ye know him, and. *John* 14:7
h. I call you not servants. 15:15
they speak *h.* to no man. *Acts* 4:17
I am clean, *h.* I will go unto. 18:6
that *h.* we should not. *Rom* 6:6*
should not *h.* live unto. *2 Cor* 5:15*
h. know we no man, *h.* know. 16*
from *h.* let no man. *Gal* 6:17
h. be no more children. *Eph* 4:14*
that ye *h.* walk not as other 17
h. there is laid up for. *2 Tim* 4:8
h. expecting till enemies. *Heb* 10:13
who die in Lord, from *h.* *Rev* 14:13

henceforward
and *h.* among your. *Num* 15:23*
no fruit grow on thee *h.* *Mat* 21:19

Hephzi-bah
mother's name was *H.* *2 Ki* 21:1
thou shalt be called *H.* *Isa* 62:4

herald
then an *h.* cried aloud. *Dan* 3:4

herb
the *h.* yielding seed. *Gen* 1:11, 12
I have given you every *h.* 29
made every *h.* 2:5
thou shalt eat the *h.* 3:18
even as the *h.* I have given. 9:3
hail smote every *h.* of. *Ex* 9:22, 25
the locusts eat every *h.* 10:12, 15
rain upon the tender *h.* *Deut* 32:2
were as the green *h.* *2 Ki* 19:26; *Isa* 37:27
before any other *h.* *Job* 8:12
the bud of the tender *h.* 38:27*
wither as the green *h.* *Ps* 37:2
he causeth *h.* to grow for. 104:14
shall flourish like an *h.* *Isa* 66:14*

herbs
and with bitter *h.* eat it. *Ex* 12:8; *Num* 9:11
it as a garden of *h.* *Deut* 11:10
have it for garden of *h.* *1 Ki* 21:2
into field to gather *h.* *2 Ki* 4:39
and did eat up all the *h.* *Ps* 105:35

better is a dinner of *h*. *Pr* 15:17
and *h*. of the mountains are. 27:25
a clear heat upon *h*. *Isa* 18:4*
thy dew is as the dew of *h*. 26:19
I will dry up all their *h*. 42:15
how long the *h*. of every. *Jer* 12:4
is greatest among all *h*. *Mat* 13:32
Mark 4:32
tithe all manner of *h*. *Luke* 11:42
who is weak eateth *h*. *Rom* 14:2
and bringeth forth *h*. *Heb* 6:7

herd, -s

Abraham ran to the *h*. *Gen* 18:7
Jacob divided his *h*. into two. 32:7
my lord also hath our *h*. 47:18
our flocks and *h*. will. *Ex* 10:9
your offering of the *h*. *Lev* 1:2
h. male or female. 3:1; *Num* 15:3
the tithe of the *h*. or. *Lev* 27:32
shalt kill of thy *h*. *Deut* 12:21
males that come of thy *h*. 15:19
Saul came after the *h*. *1 Sam* 11:5*
spared to take of his *h*. *2 Sam* 12:4
the *h*. in Sharon, *h*. in. *1 Chr* 27:29
Achor a place for the *h*. *Isa* 65:10
for young of the *h*. *Jer* 31:12
h. of cattle are perplexed. *Joel* 1:18
let not the *h*. nor flock. *Jonah* 3:7
there shall be no *h*. in. *Hab* 3:17
h. of swine feeding. *Mat* 8:30
Mark 5:11; *Luke* 8:32
whole *h*. ran violently. *Mat* 8:32
Mark 5:13; *Luke* 8:33
see **flocks**

herdman

prophet, but I was an *h*. *Amos* 7:14

herdmen

the *h*. of Abram and Lot. *Gen* 13:7
no strife between my *h*. and thy *h*. 8
h. of Gerar did strive with Isaac's *h*. 26:20
chiefest of *h*. belonged. *1 Sam* 21:7
who was among the *h*. *Amos* 1:1

here

men said, hast thou *h*.? *Gen* 19:12
thy two daughters which are *h*. 15
therefore swear unto me *h*. by. 21:23
h. I am. 22:1, 7, 11; 27:1, 18; 31:11
37:13; 46:2; *Ex* 3:4; 1 *Sam* 3:4, 5
6, 8, 16; *2 Sam* 1:7; 15:26; *Isa* 6:8
abide ye *h*. with the ass. *Gen* 22:5
I stand *h*. by the well. 24:13
set it *h*. before my brethren. 31:37
and *h*. also have I done. 40:15
one of your brethren *h*. with. 42:33
lo, *h*. is seed for you, ye shall. 47:23
Tarry ye *h*. for us, until. *Ex* 24:14
saying, Lo, we be *h*. *Num* 14:40
lodge *h*. this night, I will. 22:8, 19
h. seven altars, prepare *h*. 23:1, 29
go to war, and you sit *h*.? 32:6
we will build sheepfolds *h*. for. 16
who are all of us *h*. alive. *Deut* 5:3
after all the things we do *h*. 12:8
h. and with him that is not *h*. 29:15
cast lots for you *h*. *Josh* 18:6, 8
is there any man *h*.? *Judg* 4:20
and what hast thou *h*.? 18:3
lodge *h*. 19:9
behold, *h*. is my daughter. 24
give *h*. your advice and. 20:7
but abide *h*. fast by. *Ruth* 2:8
turn aside, sit down *h*. 4:1, 2
I am the woman that stood by thee *h*. *1 Sam* 1:26
hill and said, Is the seer *h*.? 9:11
behold, *h*. I am. 12:3; 22:12
Isa 58:9
slay them *h*. and eat. *1 Sam* 14:34
Samuel said to Jesse, Are *h*.? 16:11
is there not *h*. under thine? 21:8
h. wrapped in a cloth, none save *h*. 9
behold, we be afraid *h*. in. 23:3
what do these Hebrews *h*.? 29:3
tarry *h*. to-day. *2 Sam* 11:12
turn aside *h*. 18:30
be thou *h*. present. 20:4
h. be oxen. 24:22
nay, but I will die *h*. *1 Ki* 2:30
behold, Elijah is *h*. 18:8; 11:14
what doest thou *h*. Elijah? 19:9, 13
as thy servant was busy *h*. 20:40
not *h*. a prophet? 22:7; *2 Ki* 3:11
Elijah said, Tarry *h*. *2 Ki* 2:2, 6
h. is Elisha. 3:11
why sit we *h*. until we die? 7:3
lepers said, If we sit still *h*. 4
look there be *h*. none of the. 10:23
joy thy people present *h*. *1 Chr* 29:17
h. shall thy proud. *Job* 38:11
may say unto thee, *H*. we are. 35
this is my rest, *h*. will. *Ps* 132:14
behold, *h*. cometh a. *Isa* 21:9
thou *h*.? whom hast thou *h*.? 22:16
h. a little, and there. 28:10, 13
therefore, what have I *h*.? 52:5
Israel committeth *h*. *Ezek* 8:6, 17
gray hairs are *h*. and. *Hos* 7:9
a greater than Jonas is *h*. *Mat* 12:41
Luke 11:32
a greater than Solomon is *h*.
Mat 12:42; *Luke* 11:31
give me *h*. John Baptist's. *Mat* 14:8
we have *h*. but five loaves. 17
there be some standing *h*. 16:28
Luke 9:27
to be *h*. let us make *h*. *Mat* 17:4
shall not be left *h*. one stone. 24:2
you, Lo, *h*. is Christ. 23; *Mark* 13:21
sit ye *h*. while I go and pray.
Mat 26:36 *Mark* 14:32
tarry ye *h*. and watch. *Mat* 26:38
he is not *h*., he is risen. 28:6
Mark 16:6; *Luke* 24:6
are not his sisters *h*.? *Mark* 6:3
stones and buildings are *h*. 13:1
heard done, do *h*. in thy. *Luke* 4:23
for we are *h*. in a desert place. 9:12
neither shall they say, Lo *h*.! 17:21
say to you, See *h*.; or, see there. 23
behold, *h*. is thy pound. 19:20
h. are two swords, he said. 22:38
unto them, Have ye *h*. any? 24:41
there is a lad *h*. which. *John* 6:9
Lord, if thou hadst been *h*. 11:21, 32
h. is water. *Acts* 8:36
behold, I am *h*. Lord. 9:10
and *h*. he hath authority from. 14
are we all *h*. present before. 10:33
no harm: for we are all *h*. 16:28
who ought to have been *h*. 24:19
and all men which are *h*. 25:24
unto you all things done *h*. *Col* 4:9
h. men that die receive. *Heb* 7:8
for *h*. have we no continuing. 13:14
sit *h*. in a good place, or sit *h*. under.
Jas 2:3
of your sojourning *h*. *1 Pet* 1:17
h. is the patience of the saints.
Rev 13:10; 14:12
h. is wisdom; let him that. 13:18
h. are they that kept the. 14:12
and *h*. is the mind which hath. 17:9
see **stand**

hereafter

things that are to come *h*. *Isa* 41:23
h. also, if ye will not. *Ezek* 20:39
should come to pass *h*. *Dan* 2:29, 45
h. shall ye see the Son. *Mat* 26:64
man eat fruit of thee *h*. *Mark* 11:14
h. shall Son of man sit. *Luke* 22:69
I say, *H*. ye shall see. *John* 1:51
not now, thou shalt know *h*. 13:7
h. I will not talk much with. 14:30
pattern to them which *h*. *1 Tim* 1:16
things which shall be *h*. *Rev* 1:19
thee things which must be *h*. 4:1
there come two woes more *h*. 9:12

hereby

h. ye shall be proved, by. *Gen* 42:15
h. shall I know that ye are. 33
h. know that the Lord. *Num* 16:28
h. know that the living. *Josh* 3:10
nothing, yet am I not *h*. *1 Cor* 4:4
h. we do know that we. *1 John* 2:3
keepeth word, *h*. know we that. 5
h. perceive we the love of God. 3:16
and *h*. we know that we are of. 19
and *h*. we know that he abideth. 24
h. know ye the Spirit of God. 4:2
h. know we the Spirit of truth. 6
h. know we that we dwell in him. 13

herein

only *h*. will the men. *Gen* 34:22*
h. thou hast done foolishly.
2 Chr 16:9
h. is that saying true. *John* 4:37
h. is a marvellous thing, that. 9:30
h. is my Father glorified. 15:8
h. do I exercise myself. *Acts* 24:16
h. I give my advice, for. *2 Cor* 8:10
h. is love. *1 John* 4:10
h. is love made perfect. 17

heresies

(This word never appears in the New Testament in its strict modern meaning, but means sects, factions)

also *h*. among you. *1 Cor* 11:19†
the flesh, wrath, strife, *h*. *Gal* 5:20
bring in damnable *h*. *2 Pet* 2:1

heresy

way which they call *h*. *Acts* 24:14*

heretick

an *h*. after the second. *Tit* 3:10*

heretofore

am not eloquent, neither *h*. *Ex* 4:10
straw to make brick as *h*. 5:7
not passed this way *h*. *Josh* 3:4
thou knewest not *h*. *Ruth* 2:11
not been such a thing *h*. *1 Sam* 4:7
which *h*. have sinned. *2 Cor* 13:2

hereunto

or who else can hasten *h*.? *Eccl* 2:25*
for even *h*. were ye. *1 Pet* 2:21

herewith

wast not satisfied *h*. *Ezek* 16:29
be meat in mine house, and prove me now *h*. saith the. *Mal* 3:10

heritage

I will give it you for an *h*. *Ex* 6:8
and the *h*. appointed by. *Job* 20:29
the *h*. of oppressors which. 27:13
yea, I have a goodly *h*. *Ps* 16:6
give me the *h*. of those that. 61:5
people, they afflict thy *h*. 94:5
he may give them the *h*. of. 111:6
have I taken as an *h*. 119:111
lo, children are an *h*. of the. 127:3
and gave their land for an *h*.
135:12; 136:21, 22
is the *h*. of the servants. *Isa* 54:17
I will feed thee with the *h*. 58:14
and ye made mine *h*. *Jer* 2:7
I give thee a goodly *h*.? 3:19
I have left mine *h*. 12:7
mine *h*. is as a lion. 8
mine *h*. is unto me as a speckled. 9
them again every man to his *h*. 15
discontinue from thine *h*. 17:4
O destroyers of mine *h*. 50:11
and give not thine *h*. to. *Joel* 2:17
plead with them for my *h*. 3:2
oppress a man and his *h*. *Mi* 2:2
feed the flock of thine *h*. 7:14
by the transgression of his *h*. 18
Esau's mountains and *h*. *Mal* 1:3
being lords over God's *h*. *1 Pet* 5:3*

heritages

to inherit the desolate *h*. *Isa* 49:8

Hermas, Hermes

salute *Hermas*, Patrobas, *Hermes*.
Rom 16:14

Hermogenes

are Phygellus and *H*. *2 Tim* 1:15

Hermon

mount Sion, which is *H*. *Deut* 4:48
all mount *H*. Reuben. *Josh* 13:11
Tabor and *H*. shall. *Ps* 89:12
the dew of *H*. that descended. 133:3
top of Shenir and *H*. *S of S* 4:8

Hermonites

from the land of *H*. *Ps* 42:6

Herod

should not return to *H*. *Mat* 2:12
was there till the death of *H*. 15
H. slew all the children in. 16
for *H*. had laid hold on John. 14:3
Mark 6:17
but when *H*.'s birthday was kept.
Mat 14:6; *Mark* 6:21
H. feared John. *Mark* 6:20
beware of the leaven of *H*. 8:15
and *H*. being tetrarch. *Luke* 3:1
all the evils which *H*. had done. 19
H. heard of all that was done. 9:7

depart thence, for *H*. *Luke* 13:31
Pilate sent Jesus to *H*. 23:7
H. was glad. 8
H. with his men of war set. 11
Pilate and *H*. were made. 12
no fault in this man, nor yet *H*. 15
both *H*. and Pilate. *Acts* 4:27
H. vexed the church. 12:1
when *H*. would have brought. 6
out of the hand of *H*. 11
day *H*. made an oration to them. 21
had been brought up with *H*. 13:1
him to be kept in *H*.'*s*. 23:35

Herodians
see **sect**
their disciples, with *H*. saying, we.
Mat 22:16; *Mark* 12:13
took counsel with the *H*. *Mark* 3:6

Herodias
John in prison for *H*.'*s* sake.
Mat 14:3; *Mark* 6:17
the daughter of *H*. danced.
Mat 14:6; *Mark* 6:22
H. had a quarrel. *Mark* 6:19
reproved by John for *H*. *Luke* 3:19

Herodion
salute *H*. my kinsman. *Rom* 16:11

heron
the stork, the *h*. unclean. *Lev* 11:19
Deut 14:18

herself
number to *h*. seven days. *Lev* 15:28
if she profane *h*. by playing. 21:9
if a woman bind *h*. by a. *Num* 30:3
she returned answer to *h*. *Judg* 5:29
bowed *h*. and travailed. *1 Sam* 4:19
Abigail bowed *h*. to the earth. 25:41
a woman washing *h*. *2 Sam* 11:2
she shall feign *h*. another. *1 Ki* 14:5
she lifteth up *h*. on high. *Job* 39:18
swallow found a nest for *h*. *Ps* 84:3
h. coverings of tapestry. *Pr* 31:22
hell hath enlarged *h*. *Isa* 5:14
screech owl find for *h*. a place. 34:14
as a bride adorneth *h*. with. 61:10
Israel hath justified *h*. *Jer* 3:11
of Zion that bewaileth *h*. 4:31
is feeble and turneth *h*. to. 49:24
maketh idols against *h*. *Ezek* 22:3
their idols she defiled *h*. 23:7
she hath wearied *h*. with lies. 24:12
she decked *h*. with her. *Hos* 2:13
Tyrus did build *h*. a. *Zech* 9:3
she said within *h*. If I. *Mat* 9:21
earth bringeth forth fruit of *h*.
Mark 4:28
Elisabeth hid *h*. five. *Luke* 1:24
woman could in no wise lift up *h*.
13:11
through faith Sarah *h*. *Heb* 11:11
Jezebel who calleth *h*. a. *Rev* 2:20
she hath glorified *h*. and lived. 18:7
and his wife hath made *h*. 19:7
see **himself**

Heshbon
Israel dwelt in *H*. *Num* 21:25
H. was the city of Sihon. 26
come into *H*. 27
a fire gone out of *H*. 28
H. is perished. 30
children of Reuben built *H*. 32:37
given Sihon king of *H*. *Deut* 2:24
while Israel dwelt in *H*. *Judg* 11:26
land of the king of *H*. *Neh* 9:22
like the fish pools of *H*. *S of S* 7:4
H. shall cry. *Isa* 15:4
for field of *H*. languish. 16:8
water thee with my tears, O *H*. 9
in *H*. they have devised. *Jer* 48:2
from cry of *H*. even to Elealeh. 34
stood under the shadow of *H*., but a fire shall come out of *H*. 45
howl, O *H*. 49:3
see **Sihon**

Heth
Canaan begat Sidon and *H*.
Gen 10:15; *1 Chr* 1:13
before the children of *H*. *Gen* 23:7
Abraham purchased of the sons of *H*.
25:10; 49:32
because of the daughters of *H*.
Gen 27:46

hew
h. thee two tables of stone. *Ex* 34:1
Deut 10:1
shall *h*. down the graven. *Deut* 12:3
man goeth with neighbour to *h*. 19:5
they *h*. me cedar trees. *1 Ki* 5:6
and Hiram's builders did *h*. 18*
David set masons to *h*. *1 Chr* 22:2
Solomon told 80,000 to *h*. *2 Chr* 2:2
h. ye down trees and. *Jer* 6:6
cried aloud, *H*. down. *Dan* 4:14, 23

hewed
he *h*. two tables like the first.
Ex 34:4; *Deut* 10:3
Saul *h*. oxen in pieces. *1 Sam* 11:7
and Samuel *h*. Agag in pieces. 15:33
h. stones to lay. *1 Ki* 5:17*
three rows of *h*. stone. 6:36; 7:12
measures of *h*. stones. 7:9, 11
buy *h*. stone to repair. *2 Ki* 12:12
thou hast *h*. thee out. *Isa* 22:16
my people have *h*. them. *Jer* 2:13
therefore have I *h*. them. *Hos* 6:5

hewer
h. of wood, unto drawer. *Deut* 29:11

hewers
be *h*. of wood and. *Josh* 9:21, 23
made them that day *h*. of wood. 27
80,000 *h*. in mountains. *1 Ki* 5:15
2 Chr 2:18
money to masons and *h*. *2 Ki* 12:12
are *h*. with thee in. *1 Chr* 22:15
to thy servants the *h*. *2 Chr* 2:10
come against Egypt as *h*. *Jer* 46:22

heweth
boast against him that *h*.? *Isa* 10:5
that *h*. him out a sepulchre. 22:16
he *h*. him down cedars, and. 44:14

hewn
she hath *h*. out her seven. *Pr* 9:1
of stature shall be *h*. down. *Isa* 10:33
Lebanon is ashamed, and *h*. 33:9*
the rock whence ye are *h*. 51:1
h. down and cast into fire. *Mat* 3:10
7:19; *Luke* 3:9
he had *h*. out in the rock. *Mat* 27:60
Mark 15:46; *Luke* 23:53
see **stone**

Hezekiah, *called* **Ezekias**
H. Ahaz's son reigned. *2 Ki* 16:20
H. sent to the king of Assyria. 18:14
H. gave him all the silver in. 15
H. hath taken away. 22; *Isa* 36:7
let not *H*. deceive you. *2 Ki* 18:29
2 Chr 32:15; *Isa* 36:14
hearken not to *H*. *2 Ki* 18:31, 32
Isa 36:16
king *H*. heard it, he rent his.
2 Ki 19:1; *Isa* 37:1
H. prayed. *2 Ki* 19:15; *2 Chr* 30:18
Isa 37:15
H. was sick to death. *2 Ki* 20:1
2 Chr 32:24; *Isa* 38:1
H. wept sore. *2 Ki* 20:3; *Isa* 38:3
turn again, tell *H*. *2 Ki* 20:5
Berodach sent a present to *H*. 12
Isa 39:1
nothing, that *H*. shewed them not.
2 Ki 20:13; *Isa* 39:2
H. said, Good is the word of the.
2 Ki 20:19; *Isa* 39:8
H. slept with his fathers. *2 Ki* 20:21
2 Chr 32:3
built what *H*. had destroyed.
2 Ki 21:3; *2 Chr* 33:3
Neariah, *H*. and. *1 Chr* 3:23
came in days of *H*. and smote. 4:41
H. commanded to offer. *2 Chr* 29:27
H. rejoiced, and all the people. 36
the Lord hearkened to *H*. 30:20
H. spake comfortably to all. 22
H. gave the congregation 1000. 24
H. appointed the courses of. 31:2
then *H*. commanded to prepare. 11
rested on the words of *H*. 32:8
so shall not the God of *H*. deliver. 17
saved *H*. from Sennacherib. 22
H. rendered not again according. 25
not on them in the days of *H*. 26
H. prospered in all his. *2 Chr* 32:30
the children of Ater of *H*. *Ezra* 2:16
Neh 7:21
which the men of *H*. copied. *Pr* 25:1
Manasseh the son of *H*. *Jer* 15:4
in days of *H*. 26:18; *Mi* 1:1
H. and all Judah put. *Jer* 26:19
to Hosea in days of *H*. *Hos* 1:1
Achaz begat *H*. *Mat* 1:9
H. begat Manasses. 10

Hezron
sons of Reuben, *H*. Carmi.
Gen 46:9; *Ex* 6:14
son of Pharez, *H*. *Gen* 46:12
Ruth 4:18; *1 Chr* 2:5; 4:1
H. begat Ram, Ram. *Ruth* 4:19
the sons of *H*. *1 Chr* 2:9
Caleb the son of *H*. 18
H. begat Segub. 21
after that *H*. was dead. 24
Jerahmeel the firstborn of *H*. 25

hid, *verb*
and Adam and his wife *h*. *Gen* 3:8
because I was naked, and I *h*. 10
Jacob *h*. them under the oak. 35:4
goodly child, she *h*. Moses. *Ex* 2:2
Moses slew the Egyptian, and *h*. 12
Moses *h*. his face, for he was. 3:6
Rahab *h*. the spies with. *Josh* 2:4, 6
because she *h*. messengers. 6:17, 25
and behold they are *h*. in the. 7:21
the five kings *h*. themselves. 10:16
Jotham was left, for he *h*. *Judg* 9:5
Samuel told Eli and *h*. *1 Sam* 3:18
Saul *h*. himself. 10:22
David *h*. himself. 20:24
Obadiah *h*. the. *1 Ki* 18:4, 13
and the Lord hath *h*. *2 Ki* 4:27
give thy son, she hath *h*. 6:29
and *h*. it, carried thence, and *h*. 7:8
h. him and his. 11:2; *2 Chr* 22:11
Ornan and four sons *h*. *1 Chr* 21:20
h. sorrow from mine eyes. *Job* 3:10
these things hast thou *h*. 10:13
thou hast *h*. their heart from. 17:4
young men saw me and *h*. 29:8
in net which they *h*. is their. *Ps* 9:15
neither hath he *h*. his face. 22:24
without cause they *h*. for me. 35:7
net that he hath *h*. catch himself. 8
I would have *h*. myself. 55:12
thy word have I *h*. in. 119:11*
the proud have *h*. a snare. 140:5
falsehood have we *h*. *Isa* 28:15
his hand, in quiver he *h*. me. 49:2
I *h*. not my face from shame. 50:6
and we *h*. as it were our. 53:3
in a little wrath I *h*. my face. 54:8
I *h*. me and was wroth, and. 57:17
your sins have *h*. his face. 59:2
for thou hast *h*. thy face from. 64:7
because they are *h*. from. 65:16
so I went and *h*. it by. *Jer* 13:5
from the place where I had *h*. it. 7
for they have *h*. snares for. 18:22
I have *h*. my face from this. 33:5
to take them, but the Lord *h*. 36:26
on these stones I have *h*. 43:10
have *h*. their eyes from. *Ezek* 22:26
h. I my face from them. 39:23, 24
thou hast *h*. from the wise.
Mat 11:25; *Luke* 10:21
h. in three measures of meal.
Mat 13:33; *Luke* 13:21
went and *h*. his lord's. *Mat* 25:18
I went and *h*. thy talent in the. 25
Elisabeth *h*. herself five. *Luke* 1:24
but Jesus *h*. himself. *John* 8:59
free man *h*. themselves. *Rev* 6:15

hid
suck of treasures *h*. in. *Deut* 33:19
and behold, it was *h*. in. *Josh* 7:22
the five kings are found *h*. 10:17
behold, he is *h*. now in. *2 Sam* 17:9
no matter *h*. from king. 18:13
1 Ki 10:3; *2 Chr* 9:2
he was *h*. in house of God.
2 Ki 11:3; *2 Chr* 22:12
Ahaziah was *h*. in. *2 Chr* 22:9
dig for it more than for *h*. *Job* 3:21
given to a man whose way is *h*.? 23
brooks, wherein the snow is *h*. 6:16
the thing that is *h* bringeth. 28:11

seeing it is *h.* from eyes. *Job* 28:21
the waters are *h.* as with a. 38:30
belly thou fillest with *h.* *Ps* 17:14
nothing is *h.* from the heat. 19:6
searchest for her as for *h.* *Pr* 2:4
why sayest, My way is *h.* *Isa* 40:27
they are *h.* in prison houses. 42:22
nor their iniquity *h.* from. *Jer* 16:17
bound up, his sin is *h.* *Hos* 13:12*
h. that shall not be known. *Mat* 10:26
Mark 4:22; *Luke* 8:17; 12:2
this saying was *h.* *Luke* 9:45; 18:34
but now they are *h.* from. 19:42
beginning hath been *h.* in. *Eph* 3:9
mystery which hath been *h.* *Col* 1:26
in whom are *h.* all treasures. 2:3
and your life is *h.* with Christ. 3:3
by faith Moses was *h.* *Heb* 11:23

be hid

thy face shall I *be h.* *Gen* 4:14
thing *be h.* from. *Lev* 4:13; 5:3, 4
't *be h.* from the eyes. *Num* 5:13
shalt *be h.* from scourge. *Job* 5:21
darkness shall *be h.* in his. 20:26
of prudent men *be h.* *Isa* 29:14
repentance shall *be h.* *Hos* 13:14
though they *be h.* *Amos* 9:3
drunken, thou shalt *be h.* *Nah* 3:11
shall *be h.* in the day. *Zeph* 2:3
if our gospel *be h.* it is. *2 Cor* 4:3*

not be hid

on an hill *cannot be h.* *Mat* 5:14
he entered into an house, but he could
not be h. *Mark* 7:24
otherwise *cannot be h.* *1 Tim* 5:25

not hid

fathers, and *not h.* it. *Job* 15:18
iniquity have I *not h.* *Ps* 32:5
and my groaning is *not h.* 38:9
not h. thy righteousness. 40:10
and my sins are *not h.* from. 69:5
substance was *not h.* when. 139:15
they are *not h.* from my face, neither
is iniquity hid from. *Jer* 16:17
Israel is *not h.* from me. *Hos* 5:3
saw that she was *not h.* *Luke* 8:47

Hiddekel

the third river is *H.* *Gen* 2:14
the side of the river *H.* *Dan* 10:4

hidden

if it be *h.* from him, he. *Lev* 5:2
it is not *h.* from thee. *Deut* 30:11
as an *h.* untimely birth. *Job* 3:16
number of years is *h.* to the. 15:20*
seeing times are not *h.* from. 24:1
in *h.* part shalt make me. *Ps* 51:6
wicked rise, a man is *h.* *Pr* 28:12
I will give thee *h.* riches. *Isa* 45:3
shewed thee new things, *h.* 48:6
how are his *h.* things sought! *Ob* 6
of these things are *h.* *Acts* 26:26
h. wisdom which God. *1 Cor* 2:7
will bring to light the *h.* things. 4:5
have renounced *h.* things. *2 Cor* 4:2
but let it be the *h.* man. *1 Pet* 3:4
I give to eat of the *h.* *Rev* 2:17

hidden *ones*

against thy *h. ones.* *Ps* 83:3

hide, *substantive*

his *h.* and flesh he. *Lev* 8:17*; 9:11*

hide

shall I *h.* from Abraham? *Gen* 18:17
we will not *h.* it from my. 47:18
she could not longer *h.* him. *Ex* 2:3
any ways *h.* their eyes. *Lev* 20:4
go astray, *h.* thyself. *Deut* 22:1, 4
lost things, thou mayest not *h.* 3
and *h.* yourselves there. *Josh* 2:16
tell what thou hast done, *h.* it. 7:19
to *h.* the wheat from. *Judg* 6:11
h. it not from me, if thou *h.*
1 Sam 3:17; *2 Sam* 14:18
secret place, and *h.* *1 Sam* 19:2
why should my father *h.*? 20:2
let me go, that I may *h.* myself. 5
the place where thou didst *h.* 19
h. thyself by the brook. *1 Ki* 17:3
chamber to *h.* 22:25; *2 Chr* 18:24
then will I not *h.* myself. *Job* 13:20
O that thou wouldest *h.* me. 14:13
he *h.* it under his tongue. 20:12
from his purpose, and *h.* *Job* 33:17
h. them in the dust together. 40:13
h. me under the shadow. *Ps* 17:8
h. me in his pavilion, in secret of his
tabernacle shall he *h.* me. 27:5*
thou didst *h.* thy face and I. 30:7
thou shalt *h.* them in secret. 31:20
and *h.* not thyself from my. 55:1
h. me from the secret counsel. 64:2
we will not *h.* them from their. 78:4
O Lord, wilt thou *h.* thyself? 89:46
h. not thy commandments. 119:19
I flee to thee to *h.* me. 143:9
h. my commandments. *Pr* 2:1*
I will *h.* my eyes from you. *Isa* 1:15
and *h.* thee in the dust, for. 2:10
they *h.* not their sin. 3:9
h. the outcasts. 16:3
h. thyself as it were for a. 26:20
to them that seek deep to *h.* 29:15
that thou *h.* not thyself from. 58:7
and *h.* it there in a hole. *Jer* 13:4
I commanded thee to *h.* there. 6
h. thee, thou, and Jeremiah. 36:19
ask thee a thing, *h.* nothing. 38:14
h. it not from us. 25
h. them in the clay. 43:9
h. not thine ear at my. *Lam* 3:56
no secret they can *h.* *Ezek* 28:3
garden of God could not *h.* 31:8
neither will I *h.* my face. 39:29
and shall *h.* a multitude. *Jas* 5:20
h. us from the face of him. *Rev* 6:16
see **face**

hide *himself*

doth not David *h. himself*?
1 Sam 23:19; 26:1
can any *h. himself* in? *Jer* 23:24
not be able to *h. himself.* 49:10
Jesus did *h. himself.* *John* 12:36

hide *themselves*

they that *h. themselves.* *Deut* 7:20
people did *h. themselves* in caves.
1 Sam 13:6
to *h. themselves* in field. *2 Ki* 7:12
the earth *h. themselves.* *Job* 24:4
iniquity may *h. themselves.* 34:22
they *h. themselves,* they. *Ps* 56:6
rise, men *h. themselves.* *Pr* 28:28
fled to *h. themselves.* *Dan* 10:7
h. themselves in top of. *Amos* 9:3

hidest

wherefore *h.* thou thy face?
Job 13:24; *Ps* 44:24; 88:14
why *h.* thyself in times? *Ps* 10:1
thou *h.* thy face, they are. 104:29
art a God that *h.* thyself. *Isa* 45:15

hideth

places where he *h.* *1 Sam* 23:23
he *h.* himself on the right. *Job* 23:9
when he *h.* his face, who? 34:29
who is he that *h.* counsel? 42:3
he *h.* his face, he will. *Ps* 10:11
yea, the darkness *h.* not. 139:12
he that *h.* hatred with. *Pr* 10:18
slothful *h.* his hand. 19:24*; 26:15*
man foreseeth and *h.* 22:3; 27:12
whosoever *h.* her, *h.* the. 27:16*
he that *h.* his eyes shall. 28:27
that *h.* his face from the. *Isa* 8:17
a man hath found, he *h.* *Mat* 13:44

hiding

by *h.* mine iniquity in. *Job* 31:33
my *h.* place. *Ps* 32:7; 119:114
shall overflow the *h.* *Isa* 28:17
man shall be as an *h.* place. 32:2
and there was the *h.* of. *Hab* 3:4

Hiel

H. the Beth-elite built. *1 Ki* 16:34

Higgaion

snared in his work *H.* *Ps* 9:16

high

[1] *Lofty, tall, elevated,* Deut 3:5; Esth 5:14. [2] *Advanced,* Gen 29:7. [3] *Exalted in rank or dignity,* Deut 26:19; Ps 62:9. [4] *Arrogant, boastful,* Ps 18:27; Isa 10:12. [5] *High places were the altars built, according to custom, on conspicuous places. They are usually thought of as places of idolatry, and certainly were such in later times.*

lo, it is yet *h.* day. *Gen* 29:7
Israel went out with *h.* hand.
Ex 14:8; *Num* 33:3
quails as it were two cubits *h.*
Num 11:31*
were fenced with *h.* walls. *Deut* 3:5
gods on the *h.* mountains. 12:2
and to make thee *h.* above. 26:19
get up above thee very *h.* 28:43*
till thy *h.* and fenced walls. 52
should say, our hand is *h.* 32:27*
at this house which is *h.* *1 Ki* 9:8
estate of a man of *h.* *1 Chr* 17:17
this house is *h.* shall be. *2 Chr* 7:21
a gallows be made of fifty cubits *h.*
Esth 5:14; 7:9
it is as *h.* as heaven. *Job* 11:8
he judgeth those that are *h.* 21:22
behold the stars, how *h.* 22:12
and the *h.* arm shall be. 38:15
he beholdeth all *h.* things. 41:34
wilt bring down *h.* looks. *Ps* 18:27*
give ear, both low and *h.* 49:2
men of *h.* degree are a lie. 62:9
also, O God, is very *h.* 71:19
built his sanctuary like *h.* 78:69*
strong is thy hand, *h.* is thy. 89:13
thou, Lord, art *h.* above earth. 97:9
99:2; 113:4
him that hath an *h.* look and. 101:5
for as the heaven is *h.* 103:11
I exercise in things too *h.* 131:1*
though the Lord be *h.* yet. 138:6
such knowledge, it is *h.* 139:6
let the *h.* praises of God be in. 149:6
praise him on *h.* sounding. 150:5
and as an *h.* wall in his. *Pr* 18:11
an *h.* look, and a proud heart. 21:4
wisdom is too *h.* for a fool. 24:7
afraid of that which is *h.* *Eccl* 12:5
on all cedars that are *h.* *Isa* 2:13
and upon all the *h.* mountains. 14
Lord sitting on a throne *h.* 6:1
the glory of his *h.* looks. 10:12
the *h.* ones of stature shall be. 33
of the *h.* ones that are on *h.* 24:21
the fortress of *h.* fort shall. 25:12
breach swelling out in an *h.* 30:13
my servant shall be very *h.* 52:13
for thus saith the *h.* and. 57:15
a glorious *h.* throne. *Jer* 17:12
waymarks, make thee *h.* 31:21*
thou makest thy nest *h.* 49:16
h. gates shall be burnt with. 51:58
their rings they were so *h.* *Ezek* 1:18
brought down the *h.* tree. 17:24
low, and abase him that is *h.* 21:26
behold the Assyrian was of *h.* 31:3
I will feed them on the *h.* 34:14
the two horns were *h.* *Dan* 8:3
whose habitation is *h.* that. *Ob* 3
against the *h.* towers. *Zeph* 1:16
sabbath day was an *h.* *John* 19:31
with an *h.* arm brought. *Acts* 13:17
mind not *h.* things. *Rom* 12:16
it is *h.* time. 13:11
casting down every *h.* *2 Cor* 10:5
for the prize of the *h.* *Phil* 3:14
had a wall great and *h.* *Rev* 21:12
see **gate, God, hill, hills**

most High

knowledge of *most H.* *Num* 24:16
when the *most H.* divided to the.
Deut 32:8
the *most H.* uttered. *2 Sam* 22:14
sing praise to the name of the Lord
most H. *Ps* 7:17; 9:2; 92:1
through mercy of the *most H.* 21:7
the tabernacle of the *most H.* 46:4
the Lord *most H.* is terrible. 47:2
pay thy vows to the *most H.* 50:14
against me, O thou *most H.* 56:2*
I will cry unto God *most H.* 57:2
knowledge in the *most H.*? 73:11
the right hand of the *most H.* 77:10
by provoking the *most H.* 78:17, 56
the children of the *most H.* 82:6
that thou art *most H.* over. 83:18
secret place of the *most H.* 91:1
thou hast made the *most H.* thy. 9
but thou, Lord, art *most H.* 92:8

the counsel of the *most H.* *Ps* 107:11
I will be like the *most H.* *Isa* 14:14
the face of the *most H.* *Lam* 3:35
of mouth of *most H.* proceedeth. 38
that the *most H.* ruleth. *Dan* 4:17
this is the decree of the *most H.* 24
most H. ruleth in kingdom. 25, 32
and I blessed the *most H.* and. 34
the saints of *most H.* shall. 7:18
was given to the saints of *most H.* 22
great words against the *most H.* 25
of the saints of the *most H.* 27
but not to the *most H.* *Hos* 7:16
called them to the *most H.* 11:7
the *most H.* dwelleth not. *Acts* 7:48
***see* mountain**

***on* high**
stretch wings *on h.* *Ex* 25:20; 37:9
of blue, to fasten it *on h.* 39:31*
God will set thee *on h.* *Deut* 28:1
hast lifted me up *on h.* *2 Sam* 22:49
man who was raised up *on h.* 23:1
set Naboth *on h.* *1 Ki* 21:9, 12
hast thou lifted up thine eyes *on h.*? *2 Ki* 19:22; *Isa* 37:23
kingdom was lifted up *on h.* *1 Chr* 14:2
praise God of Israel *on h.* *2 Chr* 20:19*
to set up *on h.* those. *Job* 5:11
and my record is *on h.* 16:19
of the Almighty from *on h.*? 31:2
she lifteth up herself *on h.* 39:18
up and make her nest *on h.*? 27
sakes therefore return *on h.* *Ps* 7:7
thou hast ascended *on h.* 68:18
O God, set me up *on h.* 69:29
lift not up your horn *on h.* 75:5
I will set him *on h.* because. 91:14
the Lord *on h.* is mightier. 93:4
setteth he the poor *on h.* 107:41
our God, who dwelleth *on h.*? 113:5
out a sepulchre *on h.* *Isa* 22:16
for the windows from *on h.* 24:18
host of high ones that are *on h.* 21
down them that dwell *on h.* 26:5
be poured on us from *on h.* 32:15
he dwelleth *on h.* 33:5
he shall dwell *on h.* 16
lift up your eyes *on h.* and. 40:26
voice to be heard *on h.* 58:4
shall roar from *on h.* *Jer* 25:30
deep set him up *on h.* *Ezek* 31:4*
may set his nest *on h.* *Hab* 2:9
lifted up his hands *on h.* 3:10
dayspring from *on h.* *Luke* 1:78
endued with power from *on h.* 24:49
he ascended up *on h.* *Eph* 4:8
of the Majesty *on h.* *Heb* 1:3
***see* place, places, priest, tower**

higher
his king shall be *h.* *Num* 24:7
Saul was *h.* than any of. *1 Sam* 9:2
Jotham built *h.* gate of. *2 Ki* 15:35*
on the *h.* places, I even. *Neh* 4:13*
clouds, which are *h.* *Job* 35:5
to the rock that is *h.* than I. *Ps* 61:2
make him *h.* than kings. 89:27*
regardeth, and there be *h.* *Eccl* 5:8
are *h.* than earth, so my ways *h.* than your ways, thoughts. *Isa* 55:9
read Baruch in the *h.* *Jer* 36:10*
from the way of the *h.* *Ezek* 9:2*
for the galleries were *h.* than. 42:5
and this shall be the *h.* place. 43:13*
one horn *h.* than other, *h.* *Dan* 8:3
to thee, Friend, go up *h.* *Luke* 14:10
soul be subject to the *h.* *Rom* 13:1
an High Priest made *h.* *Heb* 7:26

highest
Lord thundered, the *H.* *Ps* 18:13
H. himself shall establish her. 87:5
nor the *h.* part of the dust. *Pr* 8:26*
she crieth upon the *h.* places. 9:3
is higher than the *h.* *Eccl* 5:8
and took the *h.* branch. *Ezek* 17:3
I will take of the *h.* branch. 22
from lowest chamber to the *h.* 41:7
saying, Hosanna in the *h.* *Mat* 21:9
Mark 11:10
called the Son of the *H.* *Luke* 1:32
the power of the *H.* shall. 35
called the prophet of the *H.* 76

glory to God in the *h.* *Luke* 2:14
19:38
shall be the children of the *H.* 6:35
sit not down in the *h.* room. 14:8
and love the *h.* seats in. 20:46*

highly
angel said, thou art *h.* *Luke* 1:28
that which is *h.* esteemed. 16:15*
Herod was *h.* displeased. *Acts* 12:20
think of himself more *h.* *Rom* 12:3
wherefore God also hath *h.* *Phil* 2:9
to esteem them very *h.* *1 Thes* 5:13

highminded
be not *h.* but fear. *Rom* 11:20
1 Tim 6:17
traitors, heady, *h.* *2 Tim* 3:4*

highness
by reason of his *h.* I. *Job* 31:23*
that rejoice in my *h.* *Isa* 13:3*

highway, -s
and your *h.* shall be. *Lev* 26:22
by king's *h.* *Num* 20:17, 19; 21:22
Deut 2:27
in days of Jael *h.* were. *Judg* 5:6
to kill the people in the *h.* 20:31
and draw them unto the *h.* 32
gleaned of them in the *h.* 45
kine went along the *h.* *1 Sam* 6:12
wallowed in blood in *h.* *2 Sam* 20:12
h. of fuller's field. *2 Ki* 18:17
Isa 7:3; 36:2
h. of upright to depart. *Pr* 16:17
an *h.* for the remnant. *Isa* 11:16
shall be *h.* out of Egypt to. 19:23
h. lie waste, wayfaring man. 33:8
and an *h.* shall be there. 35:8
make in the desert a *h.* for. 40:3
and my *h.* shall be exalted. 49:11
cast up, cast up the *h.* 62:10
heart toward the *h.* *Jer* 31:21
shall say in all the *h.* *Amos* 5:16*
go therefore into the *h.* *Mat* 22:9
Luke 14:23
Bartimaeus sat by *h.* *Mark* 10:46

Hilkiah
Eliakim son of *H.* *2 Ki* 18:18
Eliakim son of *H.* to Hezekiah. 37
Isa 36:22
saying, Go up to *H.* *2 Ki* 22:4
H. gave book to. 8, 10; *2 Chr* 34:15
H. to enquire of the Lord for him. *2 Ki* 22:12; *2 Chr* 34:20
so *H.* went to Huldah. *2 Ki* 22:14
2 Chr 34:22
commanded *H.* to bring *2 Ki* 23:4
Shallum begat *H.* and *H.* *1 Chr* 6:13
H. son of Amaziah. 45
H. son of Meshullam. 9:11
H. the second son of Hosah. 26:11
H. the son of Shallum. *Ezra* 7:1
H. stood on Ezra's right. *Neh* 8:4
Seraiah the son of *H.* dwelt. 11:11
H. the priest went up with. 12:7
of *H.*, Hashabiah were priests. 21
servant Eliakim son of *H.* *Isa* 22:20
Jeremiah the son of *H.* *Jer* 1:1
son of *H.* was sent to Babylon. 29:3

hill
built an altar under the *h.* *Ex* 24:4*
which dwelt in that *h.* *Num* 14:45*
were ready to go up into the *h.* *Deut* 1:41*, 43*
circumcised Israel at *h.* *Josh* 5:3
they said, The *h.* is not. 17:16*
Joshua buried on the *h.* Gaash. 24:30*; *Judg* 2:9
Eleazar was buried in *h.* *Josh* 24:33
Midianites were by *h.* *Judg* 7:1
house of Abinadab in *h.* *1 Sam* 7:1
his servants went up the *h.* 9:11*
shalt come to *h.* of God. 10:5, 10
hid in *h.* of Hachilah. 23:19; 26:1
came down by covert of *h.* 25:20*
they were come to *h.* *2 Sam* 2:24
much people came by the *h.* 13:34
Shimei went along on the *h.* 16:13
they hanged them in the *h.* 21:9*
Solomon built in the *h.* *1 Ki* 11:7*
the *h.* Samaria, built on *h.* 16:24
to man of God to the *h.* *2 Ki* 4:27
who shall ascend into the *h.*? *Ps* 24:3
remember thee from the *h.* 42:6

h. of God is as the *h.* of. *Ps* 68:15*
this is the *h.* which God. 16*
I will get me to the *h.* *S of S* 4:6
vineyard in a very fruitful *h.* *Isa* 5:1
shake his head against *h.* 10:32
be left an ensign on an *h.* 30:17
hosts shall fight for the *h.* 31:4
every mountain and *h.* shall. 40:4
hunt them from every *h.* *Jer* 16:16
measuring line upon the *h.* 31:39
holdest the height of the *h.* 49:16
gone from mountain to *h.* 50:6
make places about my *h.* *Ezek* 34:26
city that is set on an *h.* *Mat* 5:14
and every *h.* shall be. *Luke* 3:5
led him unto the brow of the *h.* 4:29
were come down from the *h.* 9:37*
the midst of Mars' *h.* *Acts* 17:22*

***high* hill, -s**
all *high h.* under heaven. *Gen* 7:19
groves on every *high h.* *1 Ki* 14:23
2 Ki 17:10
is a *high h.* as the hill. *Ps* 68:15
why leap ye, ye *high h.*? this is. 16
high h. are a refuge for the. 104:18
every *high h.*, rivers. *Isa* 30:25
when on every *high h.* *Jer* 2:20, 23
remember groves on *high h.* 17:2
idols on every *high h.* *Ezek* 6:13
then they saw every *high h.* 20:28
wandered on every *high h.* 34:6

***holy* hill**
on my *holy h.* of Zion. *Ps* 2:6
he heard me out of his *holy h.* 3:4
shall dwell in thy *holy h.*? 15:1
me, bring me to thy *holy h.* 43:3
worship at his *holy h.* the. 99:9

hill, with *top*
stand on *top* of the *h.* *Ex* 17:9
Hur, went to *top* of the *h.* 10
to go up to the *h. top.* *Num* 14:44
them to the *top* of an *h.* *Judg* 16:3*
David stood on the *top* of an *h.* *1 Sam* 26:13*
Abner stood on the *top* of an *h.* *2 Sam* 2:25
little past the *top* of the *h.* 16:1*
sat on the *top* of an *h.* *2 Ki* 1:9

hill country
inhabitants of *h. country.* *Josh* 13:6
of Aaron, Arba in *h. country.* 21:11
down into *h. country.* *Luke* 1:39
noised through all the *h. country.* 65

hills
of the everlasting *h.* *Gen* 49:26
and from the *h.* I behold. *Num* 23:9
out of the valleys and *h.* *Deut* 8:7
out of whose *h.* thou mayest. 9
it is a land of *h.* and valleys. 11:11
precious things of lasting *h.* 33:15
smote all country of *h.* *Josh* 10:40*
took all that land, the *h.* 11:16*
the gods of the *h.* *1 Ki* 20:23, 28
all Israel scattered on the *h.* 22:17*
burnt incense on the *h.* *2 Ki* 16:4
2 Chr 28:4
thou made before the *h.*? *Job* 15:7
foundations also of the *h.* *Ps* 18:7*
cattle on a thousand *h.* are. 50:10
the little *h.* rejoice on every. 65:12
the little *h.* by righteousness. 72:3
h. were covered with shadow. 80:10*
strength of the *h.* is his also. 95:4
the *h.* melted like wax at. 97:5†
let the *h.* be joyful together. 98:8
springs, which run among *h.* 104:10*
he watereth the *h.* from his. 13*
he toucheth the *h.* and they. 32*
and the little *h.* skipped. 114:4, 6
I will lift up mine eyes to *h.* 121:1
mountains and all *h.* praise. 148:9
before the *h.* was I brought. *Pr* 8:25
skipping upon the *h.* *S of S* 2:8
be exalted above the *h.* *Isa* 2:2
day of the Lord shall be on all *h.* 14
h. did tremble, their carcases. 5:25
on all *h.* shall not come the. 7:25
who hath weighed the *h.* in? 40:12
and thou shalt make the *h.* 41:15
make waste mountains and *h.* 42:15
mountains shall depart, *h.* 54:10
the *h.* shall break forth. 55:12

blasphemed me upon the h. Isa 65:7
salvation hoped for from h. Jer 3:23
I beheld, and lo, the h. moved. 4:24
thy abominations on the h. 13:27
saith Lord to the h. Ezek 6:3; 36:4
in thy h. shall slain fall. 35:8
and say to the h. to the rivers. 36:6
burn incense on the h. Hos 4:13
and they shall say to the h. 10:8
and the h. shall flow with. Joel 3:18
wine, and all the h. Amos 9:13
be exalted above the h. Mi 4:1
arise, and let the h. hear thy. 6:1
the h. melt, and earth. Nah 1:5
perpetual h. did bow. Hab 3:6
great crashing from the h. Zeph 1:10
begin to say to the h. Luke 23:30

him

me he restored, and h. Gen 41:13
whosoever hath sinned, h. Ex 32:33
Caleb, h. will I bring. Num 14:24
to come near, even h. whom. 16:5
h. shalt thou serve, and to h.
Deut 10:20
the Lord hath chosen h. and. 18:5
see ye h. whom Lord. 1 Sam 10:24
h. that dieth in city. 1 Ki 14:11
16:4; 21:24
h. that pisseth against the wall.
21:21; 2 Ki 9:8
they hid h. even h. and. 2 Ki 11:2
and h. that followed her, kill. 15
h. shall ye fear, h. shall ye. 17:36
h. did outlandish women. Neh 13:26
h. they have hanged on. Esth 8:7
not h. that is deceived. Job 15:31
h. that had none to help h. 29:12
behold, who teacheth like h.? 36:22
thunder with a voice like h.? 40:9
Job shall pray for you, for h. 42:8
Lord hath set apart h. Ps 4:3
h. shall he teach in the way. 25:12
worship h. 45:11
h. that hath no helper. 72:12
h. will I cut off, h. that hath. 101:5
h. that soweth discord. Pr 6:19
h. shall the people curse. 24:24
a little folly h. that is in. Eccl 10:1
h. that offereth in the. Jer 48:35
and cut off from it h. Ezek 35:7
and h. that holdeth the. Amos 1:5
cut off h. that offereth. Mal 2:12
h. only shalt thou serve. Mat 4:10
Luke 4:8
confess me before men, h. will I confess also. Mat 10:32; Luke 12:8
h. will I deny before my. Mat 10:33
h. that sent me. 40; Mark 9:37
this is my Son, hear ye h.
Mat 17:5; Acts 3:22; 7:37
go tell h. between h. and. Mat 18:15
nor let h. in the field return.
24:18; Mark 13:6
h. they compelled to. Mat 27:32
let h. that readeth. Mark 13:14
let h. that is on the housetop. 15
h. that for sedition and. Luke 23:25
but h. they saw not. 24:24
whom he hath sent, h. John 5:38
come in his own name, h. ye. 43
h. hath God the Father sealed. 6:27
h that cometh unto me, I will. 37
h. he heareth. 9:31
h. will my Father honour. 12:26
God shall also glorify h. in. 13:32
h. being delivered. Acts 2:23
h. God exalted. 5:31
h. God raised up the third. 10:40
h. would Paul have to go forth with h. 16:3
whom ye worship h. declare. 17:23
h. that is weak in faith. Rom 14:1
let not h. that eateth, despise h. 3
defile temple, h. shall. 1 Cor 3:17
h. that thinketh he standeth. 10:12
for he hath made h. to. 2 Cor 5:21
let h. that is taught in the. Gal 6:6
let h. that stole steal no. Eph 4:28
h. therefore I hope to. Phil 2:23
receive h. therefore in the Lord. 29
h. whose coming is. 2 Thes 2:9
might destroy h. that. Heb 2:14
sprang there of one, and h. 11:12

about him

his servants were standing about h.
1 Sam 22:6, 7
the footmen that stood about h. 17
wars which were about h. 1 Ki 5:3
compassed about h. to. 2 Chr 18:31
made an hedge about h.? Job 1:10
let all round about h. Ps 76:11
in reverence of all about h. 89:7
all ye that are about h. Jer 48:17
be a dismaying to all about h. 39
devour all round about h. 50:32
shall be round about h. Lam 1:17
scatter all that are about h. to help him. Ezek 12:14
his graves are round about h.
32:22, 25, 26
great multitudes about h. Mat 8:18
multitude sat about h. Mark 3:32
the Jews round about h. John 10:24
each six wings about h. Rev 4:8

above him

shall be strong above h. Dan 11:5

after him

with his seed after h. Gen 17:19
his household after h. 18:19
be a statute for his seed after h.
Ex 28:43
shall be his son's after h. 29:29
that go a whoring after h. Lev 20:5
turn away from after h. Num 32:15
of blood pursue after h. Josh 20:5
fled, they pursued after h. Judg 1:6
they went after h. and took. 3:28
was gathered after h. 6:34, 35
armourbearer after h. 1 Sam 14:13
I went out after h. and. 17:35
saw that Saul came after h. 26:3
followed hard after h. 2 Sam 1:6
and all the people after h. 15:17
the people returned after h. 23:10
on the throne of my lord after h.
1 Ki 1:20, 27
to set up his son after h. 15:4
I will run after h. and. 2 Ki 5:20
Jehu followed after h. and. 9:27
sent after h. to. 14:19; 2 Chr 25:27
so that after h. was none like him.
2 Ki 18:5; 23:25
Zebadiah his son after h. 1 Chr 27:7
priest went in after h. 2 Chr 26:17
after h. repaired. Neh 3:16
So to the 31st verse
they that come after h. Job 18:20
he in his house after h. 21:21
every man shall draw after h. 33
a path to shine after h. 41:32
not descend after h. Ps 49:17
children are blessed after h. Pr 20:7
bring to see what shall be after h.
Eccl 3:22; 6:12
should find nothing after h. 7:14
what shall be after h. who? 10:14
after h. through the city. Ezek 9:5
sent a message after h. Luke 19:14
world is gone after h. John 12:19
much people after h. Acts 5:37
to him, and to his seed after h. 7:5
if haply they might feel after h. 17:27
which should come after h. 19:4

against him

man's hand against h. Gen 16:12
he prevailed not against h. 32:25
they conspired against h. 37:18
1 Ki 15:27; 16:9; 2 Ki 14:19
15:10, 25; 21:23
which ye murmur against h.
Ex 16:8; Num 14:36; 16:11
an adversary against h. Num 22:22
man rise up against h. Deut 19:11
witness rise to testify against h. 16
loins that rise against h. 33:11
a man over against h. Josh 5:13
lion roared against h. Judg 14:5
Philistines shouted against h. 15:14
Lord said, Go up against h. 20:23
battle was against h. 2 Sam 10:9
put forth against h. dried. 1 Ki 13:4
to bear witness against h. 21:10
went up against h. 2 Ki 23:29
Lord sent against h. bands of. 24:2
to speak against h. 2 Chr 32:17
not prevail against h. Esth 6:13
movedst me against h. Job 2:3
have sinned against h. 8:4
hardened himself against h. 9:4
prevailest for ever against h. 14:20
thou strive against h.? 33:13
what doest thou against h.? 35:6
sinned yet more against h. Ps 78:17
messenger shall be sent against h.
Pr 17:11
if one prevail against h. Eccl 4:12
axe boast against h., or saw magnify itself against h.? Isa 10:15
are called forth against h. 31:4
that are incensed against h. 45:24
lift up a standard against h. 59:19
we shall prevail against h. Jer 20:10
for since I spake against h. I. 31:20
against h. that bendeth, let. 51:3
prophesy against h. and Egypt.
Ezek 29:2; 38:2
call for a sword against h. 38:21
I will plead against h. with. 22
have sinned against h. Dan 9:11
but he that cometh against h. 11:16
prepare war against h. Mi 3:5
I have sinned against h. 7:9
up a parable against h.? Hab 2:6
and held a counsel against h.
Mat 12:14; Mark 3:6
that cometh against h. Luke 14:31
they cried so against h. Acts 22:24
what they had against h. 23:30
priest desired favour against h. 25:3
to have judgement against h. 15
not bring against h. a. Jude 9
sinners have spoken against h. 15
make war against h. Rev 19:19

at him

the archers shot at h. Gen 49:23
Saul cast a javelin at h. 1 Sam 20:33
threw stones at h. and. 2 Sam 16:13
shall clap their hands at h. Job 27:23
him that puffeth at h. Ps 12:5
the Lord shall laugh at h. 37:13
shall see and laugh at h. 52:6
do they shoot at h. and. 64:4
shut their mouths at h. Isa 52:15
south shall push at h. Dan 11:40
the mountains quake at h. Nah 1:5
they were offended at h. Mark 6:3
at h. they cast stones, and. 12:4
and they marvelled at h. 17
he marvelled at h. and. Luke 7:9
they could not come at h. for. 8:19
Jews then murmured at h. John 6:41
took up stones to cast at h. 8:59

before him

meat before h. to eat. Gen 24:33
messengers before h. to. 32:3
so went the present over before h. 21
and they cried before h. 41:43
they sat before h. 43:33
fell before h. 44:14
Lord passed by before h. Ex 34:6
have wept before h. Num 11:20
man straight before h. Josh 6:5
service of the Lord before h. 22:27
chased, he fled before h. Judg 9:40
wife wept before h. and. 14:16, 17
anointed is before h. 1 Sam 16:6
came to Saul and stood before h. 21
a shield went before h. 17:7
they fled before h. 2 Sam 10:13
1 Chr 19:14
eat and drink before h. 2 Sam 11:13
they set bread before h. 12:20
and fifty men to run before h.
15:1; 1 Ki 1:5
I was also upright before h.
2 Sam 22:24; Ps 18:23
harlots, stood before h. 1 Ki 3:16
Omri worse than all before h. 16:25
Ahab evil above all before h. 30, 33
men, sons of Belial, before h. 21:10
to the ground before h. 2 Ki 2:15
when called, stood before h. 4:12
prophets were sitting before h. 38
king sent a man from before h. 6:32
kings stood not before h. how? 10:4
kings that were before h. 17:2
nor any that were before h. 18:5
did, which were before h. 21:11
there was no king before h. 23:25

did eat bread continually *before h.* *2 Ki* 25:29; *Jer* 52:33
and come *before h.* *1 Chr* 16:29
fear *before h.* 30; *Ps* 96:9
Eccl 3:14; 8:12
before h. like Solomon. *1 Chr* 29:5
to burn *before h.* sweet. *2 Chr* 2:4, 6
kingdom was quiet *before h.* 14:5
chosen you to stand *before h.* 29:11
that wine was *before h.* *Neh* 2:1
make a request *before h.* *Esth* 4:8
proclaim *before h.* 6:9, 11
fall *before h.* 13
I will maintain my ways *before h.* *Job* 13:15
shall not come *before h.* 16
are innumerable *before h.* 21:33
order my cause *before h.* 23:4
hell is naked *before h.* and. 26:6
judgement is *before h.* 35:14
is turned into joy *before h.* 41:22
cry came *before h.* *Ps* 18:6
brightness that was *before h.* 12
shall bow *before h.* 22:29
a fire shall devour *before h.* 50:3
pour out your heart *before h.* 62:8
that hate him flee *before h.* 68:1
God, sing and rejoice *before h.* 4
wilderness shall bow *before h.* 72:9
kings shall fall *before h.*, nations shall serve *h.* 11
righteousness shall go *before h.* 85:13
and majesty are *before h.* 96:6
worship the Lord, fear *before h.* 9
goeth *before h.* and burneth. 97:3
his chosen stood *before h.* 106:23
showed *before h.* my trouble. 142:2
rejoicing always *before h.* *Pr* 8:30
wisdom is *before h.* that hath. 17:24
reward with him, work *before h.* *Isa* 40:10; 62:11
nations *before h.* are as. 40:17
gave nations *before h.* and. 41:2
to subdue nations *before h.* 45:1
supplications *before h.* *Jer* 42:9
wilt thou say *before h.* *Ezek* 28:9
shall groan *before h.* with. 30:24
10,000 stood *before h.* *Dan* 7:10
no beasts might stand *before h.* 8:4
no power in ram to stand *before h.* 7
none shall stand *before h.* 11:16
be overflown from *before h.* 22
shall I come *before h.*? *Mi* 6:6
keep silence *before h.* *Hab* 2:20
before h. went the pestilence. 3:5
a book of remembrance written *before h.* *Mal* 3:16
before h. be gathered. *Mat* 25:32
bowed the knee *before h.* 27:29
fell down *before h.* *Mark* 3:11; 5:33
before h. in the spirit. *Luke* 1:17
and righteousness *before h.* 75
means to lay him *before h.* 5:18
I have nothing to set *before h.* 11:6
that I am sent *before h.* *John* 3:28
Paul also *before h.* *Acts* 23:33
before h. whom he believed, even. *Rom* 4:17
without blame *before h.* *Eph* 1:4
joy that was set *before h.* *Heb* 12:2
not ashamed *before h.* *1 John* 2:28
assure our hearts *before h.* 3:19
first beast *before h.* *Rev* 13:12
wrought miracles *before h.* 19:20

behind **him**

in the tent door *behind h.* *Gen* 18:10
spear came out *behind h.* *2 Sam* 2:23
his master's feet *behind h.*? *2 Ki* 6:32
leave a blessing *behind h.* *Joel* 2:14
behind h. were red horses. *Zech* 1:8
diseased with an issue of blood came *behind h.* *Mat* 9:20; *Luke* 8:44
leave his wife *behind h.* *Mark* 12:19
at his feet *behind h.* *Luke* 7:38

beside **him**

there is none *beside h.* *Deut* 4:35
his servants passed on *beside h.* *2 Sam* 15:18
beside h. stood Mattithiah. *Neh* 8:4

between **him**

Lord made *between h.* *Lev* 26:46
shall discern *between h.* *Mal* 3:18

beyond **him**

an arrow *beyond h.* *1 Sam* 20:36

by **him**

not let us pass *by h.* *Deut* 2:30
shall dwell in safety *by h.* 33:12
by h. children of Israel. *Judg* 3:15
all that stood *by h.* went out. 19
and *by h.* actions are. *1 Sam* 2:3
that evil is determined *by h.* 20:7
of heaven standing *by h.* *1 Ki* 22:19
we may enquire of the Lord *by h.* *2 Ki* 3:11; 8:8
by h. the Lord had given. 5:1
hundred slain *by h.* *1 Chr* 11:11
queen also sitting *by h.* *Neh* 2:6
the Ammonite was *by h.* 4:3
sweareth *by h.* shall glory. *Ps* 63:11
that are slain *by h.* *Isa* 27:7
by h. daily sacrifice was. *Dan* 8:11
sware *by h.* that liveth for ever. 12:7; *Rev* 10:6
rocks are thrown down *by h.* *Nah* 1:6
sweareth *by h.* who. *Mat* 23:21
sweareth *by h.* that sitteth. 22
Herod being reproved *by h.* shut up John. *Luke* 3:19
heard all that was done *by h.* 9:7
things that were done *by h.* 13:17
all things were made *by h.* *John* 1:3
the world was made *by h.* and. 10
wonders God did *by him.* *Acts* 2:22
the faith which is *by h.* 3:16; 4:10
by h. all that believe. 13:39
following the Lord stood *by h.* 23:11
ye are enriched *by h.* *1 Cor* 1:5
are all things, and we *by h.* 8:6
have been taught *by h.* *Eph* 4:21
for *by h.* were all things. *Col* 1:16
he is before all things, *by h.* all. 17
by h. to reconcile all things to himself *by h.* 20
to God the Father *by h.* 3:17
are taken captive *by h.* *2 Tim* 2:26
that come to God *by h.* *Heb* 7:25
by h. let us offer the sacrifice. 13:15
who *by h.* do believe in. *1 Pet* 1:21
are sent *by h.* for punishment. 2:14

concerning **him**

made an oath *con. h.* *Judg* 21:5
word Lord hath spoken *con. h.* *2 Ki* 19:21; *Isa* 37:22
so commanded *con. h.* *Esth* 3:2
a proclamation *con. h.* *Dan* 5:29
among people *con h.* *John* 7:12, 32
Jews did not believe *con. h.* 9:18
David speaketh *con. h.* *Acts* 2:25
enquire something *con. h.* 23:15
con. h. that hath so done. *1 Cor* 5:3

see **fear**

for **him**

an help meet *for h.* *Gen* 2:18, 20
Joseph's father wept *for h.* 37:35
I will be surety *for h.* of. 43:9
no blood shed *for h.* *Ex* 22:2
blood shed *for h.* 3
accepted *for h.* to make atonement *for h.* *Lev* 1:4; 4:26, 31; 5:13
14:18, 19, 20, 31; 15:15; 19:22
Num 5:8; 6:11; 15:28
shall ask counsel *for h.* *Num* 27:21
take no satisfaction *for h.* 35:32
lie in wait *for h.* and. *Deut* 19:11
his hands be sufficient *for h.* 33:7
he that will plead *for h.* *Judg* 6:31
shall entreat *for h.*? *1 Sam* 2:25
how he laid wait *for h.* in. 15:2
them, and Saul sent *for h.* 17:31
enquired of Lord *for h.* 22:10, 15
sought no more again *for h.* 27:4
till the land *for h.* *2 Sam* 9:10
for h. the kingdom, even *for h.* *1 Ki* 2:22
saddled *for h.* the ass, to wit. 13:23
all Israel shall mourn *for h.* 14:13
very great burning *for h.* *2 Chr* 16:14
people made no burning *for h.* 21:19
I have prepared *for h.* *Esth* 5:4
saw that he moved not *for h.* 9
there is nothing done *for h.* 6:3
gallows he had prepared *for h.* 4
talk deceitfully *for h.*? *Job* 13:7
did not I weep *for h.* that ? 30:25
there is no help *for h.* *Ps* 3:2
Lord, and wait patiently *for h.* 37:7
give to God a ransom *for h.* 49:7
prayer also be made *for h.* 72:15
as *for h.* that wanteth. *Pr* 9:4, 16
he shall gather it *for h.* that. 28:8
bowels were moved *for h.* *S of S* 5:4
the Lord and look *for h.* *Isa* 8:17
for h. he will save us. 25:9
a snare *for h.* that reproveth. 29:21
are all they that wait *for h.* 30:18
his arm shall rule *for h.* 40:10
what he hath prepared *for h.* that waiteth *for h.* 64:4
shall not lament *for h.* *Jer* 22:18
my bowels are troubled *for h.* 31:20
to them that wait *for h.* *Lam* 3:25
Pharaoh make *for h.* in. *Ezek* 17:17
for h. I caused Lebanon to mourn *for h.*, and all the trees of the field fainted *for h.* 31:15
so shalt thou do *for h.* that. 45:20
nor shall she be *for h.* *Dan* 11:17
where no gin is *for h.* *Amos* 3:5
Lord nor enquired *for h.* *Zeph* 1:6
shall mourn *for h.* be in bitterness *for h.* *Zech* 12:10
not lawful *for h.* to eat. *Mat* 12:4
better *for h.* that a millstone. 18:6
Mark 9:42; *Luke* 17:2
when he looketh not *for h.* *Mat* 24:50; *Luke* 12:46
Jesus had done *for h.* *Mark* 5:20
child Jesus, to do *for h.* *Luke* 2:27
they were all waiting *for h.* 8:40
went to make ready *for h.* 9:52
made unto God *for h.* *Acts* 12:5
for I look *for h.* with. *1 Cor* 16:11
created by him and *for h.* *Col* 1:16
them that look *for h.* *Heb* 9:28

from **him**

and God went up *from h.* *Gen* 35:13
it be hid *from h.* when. *Lev* 5:3
by him, went out *from h.* *Judg* 3:19
locks, his strength went *from h.* 16:19
hid nothing *from h.* *1 Sam* 3:18
retire *from h.* *2 Sam* 11:15
went out *from h.* 13:9
thing would come *from h.* *1 Ki* 20:33
were scattered *from h.* *2 Ki* 25:5
the Lord turned *from h.* *2 Chr* 12:12
turn *from h.* that he may. *Job* 14:6
he hid his face *from h.* *Ps* 22:24
the poor *from h.* that spoileth. 35:10
have hid myself *from h.* 55:12
waiteth on God: *from h.* 62:1
of the righteous *from h.* *Isa* 5:23
hid as it were our faces *from h.* 53:3
she go *from h.* and become. *Jer* 3:1
part of hand sent *from h.* *Dan* 5:24
ye take *from h.* burdens. *Amos* 5:11
and laid his robe *from h.* *Jonah* 3:6
from h. that would borrow of thee. *Mat* 5:42
from h. shall be taken. 13:12
Mark 4:25; *Luke* 8:18
from h. that hath not shall be taken. *Mat* 25:29; *Luke* 19:26
hour might pass *from h.* *Mark* 14:35
he taketh *from h.* all. *Luke* 11:22
I am *from h.* *John* 7:29
but will flee *from h.* 10:5
soon removed *from h.* *Gal* 1:6
if we turn away *from h.* *Heb* 12:25
of compassion *from h.* *1 John* 3:17
commandment have we *from h.* 4:21
peace *from h.* which is. *Rev* 1:4

see **depart, departed**

in **him**

nations of earth shall be blessed *in h.* *Gen* 18:18
for my name is *in h.* *Ex* 23:21
Shechem put confidence *in h.* *Judg* 9:26
was no strength *in h.* *1 Sam* 28:20
no fault *in h.* 29:3; *John* 19:4, 6
in h. will I trust. *2 Sam* 22:3
Ps 91:2
he is a buckler to all that trust *in h.* *2 Sam* 22:31; *Isa* 36:6

if wickedness be in h. 1 Ki 1:52
the wisdom of God was in h. 3:28
because in h. there is found. 14:13
there was no breath left in h. 17:17
put their trust in h. 1 Chr 5:20
me, yet will I trust in h. Job 13:15
before him, trust thou in h. 35:14
that put their trust in h. Ps 2:12
all those that trust in h. 18:30
my heart trusted in h. and I. 28:7
our heart shall rejoice in h. 33:21
66:6; 149:2
man that trusteth in h. 34:8
none of them that trust in h. 22
trust also in h.; and he shall. 37:5
because they trust in h. 40
trust in h. at all times, ye. 62:8
shall be glad and trust in h. 64:10
men shall be blessed in h. 72:17
is no unrighteousness in h. 92:15
John 7:18
perceivest not in h. lips. Pr 14:7
them that put their trust in h. 30:5
shall not rejoice in h. Eccl 4:16
bless themselves in h. Jer 4:2
all them that trust in h. 46:25
his taste remained in h. 48:11
therefore will I hope in h. Lam 3:24
servants who trusted in h. Dan 3:28
nor any error or fault found in h. 6:4
none understanding in h. Ob 7
them that trust in h. Nah 1:7
soul is not upright in h. Hab 2:4
they were offended in h. Mat 13:57
do shew themselves in h. 14:2
no cause of death in h. Luke 23:22
in h. was life; and the life. John 1:4
whosoever believeth in h. 3:15, 16
Acts 10:43
shall be in h. a well of. John 4:14
dwelleth in me, and I in h. 6:56
10:38; 15:5
his brethren believe in h. 7:5
there is no truth in h. 8:44
made manifest in h. 9:3
no light in h. 11:10
God is glorified in h. 13:31
if God be glorified in h. 32
in h. we live, move. Acts 17:28
they believe in h. of. Rom 10:14
in h. shall the Gentiles trust. 15:12
of man which is in h. 1 Cor 2:11
all things, we in h. 8:6; 1 John 5:20
nay, but in h. was yea. 2 Cor 1:19, 20
righteousness of God in h. 5:21
for we are weak in h. but. 13:4
chosen us in h. Eph 1:4
gather together; even in h. 10
Christ, and be found in h. Phil 3:9
that in h. should all. Col 1:19; 2:9
so walk ye in h. 2:6
rooted and built up in h. 7
in h. dwelleth the fulness of the. 9
ye are complete in h. who is the. 10
I will put my trust in h. Heb 2:13
shall have no pleasure in h. 10:38
the truth is not in h. 1 John 2:4
in h. verily is love of God perfected,
hereby know we that we are in h. 5
he that saith he abideth in h. 6
thing is true in h. and in you. 8
none occasion of stumbling in h. 10
the Father is not in h. 15; 3:17
you, ye shall abide in h. 27, 28
man that hath this hope in h. 3:3
in h. is no sin. 5
who abideth in h. sinneth not. 6
for his seed remaineth in h. he. 9
hath eternal life abiding in h. 15
dwelleth in h. and he in h. 24; 4:13
15, 16
confidence that we have in h. 5:14

into **him**

child's soul come into h. 1 Ki 17:21
soul of the child came into h. 22
many devils were entered into h.
Luke 8:30
Satan entered into h. John 13:27
may grow up into h. in. Eph 4:15

of **him**

Lord was entreated of h. Gen 25:21
beware of h. and obey. Ex 23:21
not what is become of h. 32:1, 23
flesh of h. hath issue. Lev 15:7, 33
take thou no usury of h. 25:36
but by the blood of h. Num 35:33
I will require it of h. Deut 18:19
not be afraid of h. 22; 2 Ki 1:15
heart fail because of h. 1 Sam 17:32
and take somewhat of h. 2 Ki 5:20
shall be for the life of h. 10:24
of h. came the chief. 1 Chr 5:2
they were the ruin of h. 2 Chr 28:23
he was entreated of h. 33:13, 19
to seek of h. a right way. Ezra 8:21
eye of h. hath seen me. Job 7:8
despised in the thought of h. 12:5
is the place of h. that knoweth. 18:21
consider, I am afraid of h. 23:15
not thyself because of h. Ps 37:7
mouth craveth it of h. Pr 16:26
wise child, shall have joy of h. 23:24
of a fool than of h. 26:12; 29:20
take a pledge of h. for a. 27:13
shall the work say of h. Isa 29:16
feet of h. bringeth good tidings.
52:7; Nah 1:15
will not make mention of h. Jer 20:9
be not afraid of h. saith the. 42:11
as the punishment of h. Ezek 14:10
Babylon hath taken oath of h. 17:13
no pleasure in the death of h. 18:32
nations also heard of h. he. 19:4
in the hand of h. that slayeth. 28:9
take hold of skirt of h. Zech 8:23
I will encamp because of h. 9:8
as it is written of h. Mat 26:24
Mark 9:13; 14:21
in a dream because of h. Mat 27:19
should tell no man of h. Mark 8:30
of h. shall Son of man be ashamed.
38; Luke 9:26
of h. that taketh thy. Luke 6:30
much given, of h. shall much. 12:48
ye of h. whom Father. John 10:36
the justifier of h. that. Rom 3:26
not of works but of h. that. 9:11
it is not of h. that willeth, but. 16
for of h. and through him. 11:36
of h. are ye in Christ. 1 Cor 1:30
shew forth praises of h. 1 Pet 2:9
ye may be found of h. 2 Pet 3:14
we have heard of h. 1 John 1:5
which we have received of h. 2:27
doeth righteousness is born of h. 29
all kindreds of the earth shall wail
because of h. Rev 1:7

on, or upon **him**

whatsoever is laid upon h. Ex 21:30
his uncleanness upon h. Lev 7:20
if her flowers be upon h. he. 15:24
and not suffer sin upon h. 19:17
his blood shall be upon h. 20:9
oil of his God is upon h. 21:12
spirit that was upon h. Num 11:25
his iniquity shall be upon h. 15:31
seeing him not, cast it upon h. 35:23
shall be first upon h. Deut 13:9
witnesses shall be first upon h. 17:7
written in this book upon h. 29:20
if any hand be upon h. Josh 2:19
the Spirit of the Lord came upon h.
Judg 3:10; 14:6, 19; 15:14
Num 24:2; 1 Sam 10:10, 19:23
Philistines be upon h. 1 Sam 18:17
I will come upon h. 2 Sam 17:2
an oath be laid upon h. 1 Ki 8:31
2 Chr 6:22
saying, Lay hold on h. 1 Ki 13:4
shut the door upon h. 2 Ki 4:21
head of Elisha stand on h. 6:31
the people trode upon h. in. 7:17, 20
there was wrath upon h. 2 Chr 32:25
Lord his God upon h. Ezra 7:6, 9
set thy heart upon h. Job 7:17
destroyer shall come upon h. 15:21
wicked shall come upon h. 20:22
and shall rain it upon h. while. 23
cometh, terrors are upon h. 25
when trouble cometh upon h.? 27:9
I will call upon h. as. Ps 116:2
nigh to all that call upon h. 145:18
I will pour water upon h. Isa 44:3
of our peace was upon h. 53:5
seek the Lord, call ye upon h. 55:6
and he will have mercy upon h. 7
have mercy upon h. Jer 31:20
will I spread upon h. Ezek 12:13
be upon h., wickedness of the wicked
shall be upon h. 18:20
gray hairs are here and there upon h.
Hos 7:9
shall leave his blood upon h. 12:14
put my Spirit upon h. Mat 12:18
and they spit upon h. and. 27:30
and on h. they laid the. Luke 23:26
it abode upon h. John 1:32
remaining on h. 33
on h. is not condemned. 3:18; 5:24
6:40; Rom 9:33; 1 Pet 2:6
look on h. whom they. John 19:37
Saul set his eyes on h. Acts 13:9
not only to believe on h. Phil 1:29
had mercy on h. and not on h. 2:27
took not on h. the nature. Heb 2:16
that sat on h. Rev 6:2, 5, 8; 19:11
and he set a seal upon h. 20:3

over **him**

thou shalt rule over h. Gen 4:7
and confess over h. all. Lev 16:21
thou shalt not rule over h. 25:43, 53
people wept again over h. 2 Sam 3:34
they mourned over h. 1 Ki 13:30
burnt the king's house over h. 16:18
a wicked man over h. Ps 109:6
spread their net over h. Ezek 19:8
times pass over h. Dan 4:16, 23
made lamentation over h. Acts 8:2
no more dominion over h. Rom 6:9
let them pray over h. Jas 5:14

through **him**

that all men through h. John 1:7
that the world through h. 3:17
be saved from wrath, through h.
Rom 5:9
than conquerors through h. 8:37
of him, through h. and to him. 11:36
through h. we have access. Eph 2:18
sent his Son, that we might live
through h. 1 John 4:9

to, or unto **him**

to Seth, to h. also there. Gen 4:26
Lord, who appeared unto h. 12:7
shall a child be born unto h.? 17:17
of which God had spoken to h. 21:2
unto h. hath he given all that. 24:36
unto h. shall the gathering. 49:10
thou shalt be to h. Ex 4:16
not be to h. as an usurer. 22:25
it shall be a statute for ever unto h.
28:43; 30:21
and to h. will I give the. Deut 1:36
raise up a Prophet, unto h. 18:15
to do to h. as he hath. Judg 15:10
Lord hath done to h. 1 Sam 28:17
David, even so I do to h. 2 Sam 3:9
wilt thou go to h. to-day? 2 Ki 4:23
so it fell out unto h. for the. 7:20
even to h. and his sons. 2 Chr 13:5
king, so shall ye say unto h. 34:26
to h. that is afflicted. Job 6:14
what doest thou unto h.? 35:6
to h. that rideth on. Ps 68:33
to h. shall be given of gold. 72:15
to h. that made great lights. 136:7
to h. that smote great kings, for. 17
one event to h. that sacrificeth, and to
h. that sacrificeth not. Eccl 9:2
people turneth not to h. Isa 9:13
turn to h. from whom Israel. 31:6
they are counted to h. less. 40:17
will ye compare unto h.? 18
even to h. shall men come. 45:24
thus saith the Lord to h. whom. 49:7
to h. that is far off, and to h. 57:19
look, even to h. that is poor. 66:2
to h. that knocketh, it. Mat 7:8
to h. that smiteth thee. Luke 6:29
whosoever hath, to h. shall be. 8:18
to h. that blasphemeth against. 12:10
living, for all live unto h. 20:38
then I go unto h. John 7:33; 16:5
to h. the porter openeth, the. 10:3
to h. they agreed, and. Acts 5:40
to h. they had regard, because. 8:11
to h. give all the prophets. 10:43
now to h. that worketh. Rom 4:4
to h. that worketh not, but. 5
even to h. who is raised. 7:4
and to h. are all things, to. 11:36

to h. that esteemeth, *to h. Rom* 14:14
now *to h.* that is of power to. 16:25
be *to h.* who speaketh a. *1 Cor* 14:11
it was accounted *to h.* for. *Gal* 3:6
unto h. be glory in the. *Eph* 3:21
I will be *to h.* a Father. *Heb* 1:5
to h. that was able to save him. 5:7
it was imputed *unto h.* *Jas* 2:23
to h. that knoweth to do good, *to h.* 4:17
unto h. that loved us. *Rev* 1:5
to h. that overcometh. 2:7, 17; 3:21
to h. will I give power over. 2:26
will give *unto h.* that is athirst. 21:6

toward **him**

it was not *toward h.* *Gen* 31:2
anger was abated *toward h. Judg* 8:3
heart is perfect *toward h. 2 Chr* 16:9
stretch out thine hands *toward h.* *Job* 11:13
lift up thy hands *toward h. Lam* 2:19
branches turned *toward h. Ezek* 17:6
your love *toward h.* *2 Cor* 2:8

under **him**

stone and put it *under h. Ex* 17:12
mule that was *under h. 2 Sam* 18:9
helpers do stoop *under h. Job* 9:13
spread sackcloth and ashes *under h.* *Isa* 58:5
the roots thereof were *under h.* *Ezek* 17:6
all things put *under h.* *1 Cor* 15:27
28; *Heb* 2:8

with **him**

saw that Lord was *with h. Gen* 39:3
I have given *with h.* Aholiab. *Ex* 31:6; 38:23
with h. will I speak mouth to mouth. *Num* 12:8; *Jer* 32:4
his God is *with h.* and. *Num* 23:21
with h. that standeth here with us, also *with h.* that is. *Deut* 29:15
was no strange god *with h.* 32:12
and the Lord was *with h.* *1 Sam* 3:19; 18:12, 14
the Lord is *with h.* 16:18
folly is *with h.* 25:25
Lord of hosts was *with h.* *2 Sam* 5:10; *1 Chr* 11:9
will I be, and *with h.* *2 Sam* 16:18
Solomon held a feast, and all Israel *with h.* *1 Ki* 8:65; *2 Chr* 7:8
word of Lord is *with h.* *2 Ki* 3:12
his hand might be *with h.* 15:19
the Lord was *with h.* and he. 18:7
1 Chr 9:20; *2 Chr* 1:1; 15:9
while ye be *with h.* *2 Chr* 15:2
with h. fourscore priests of. 26:17
be more with us than *with h.* 32:7
with h. is an arm of flesh, with. 8
the Lord his God be *with h.* 36:23
Ezra 1:3
with h. 150 males. *Ezra* 8:3
with h. 200 males. 4
with h. 50 males. 6
with h. is wisdom. *Job* 12:13, 16
candle shall be put out *with h.* 18:6
acquaint thyself *with h.* and. 22:21
mercy shall be *with h.* *Ps* 89:24
I will be *with h.* in trouble. 91:15
and *with h.* is plenteous. 130:7
one brought up *with h.* *Pr* 8:30
that shall abide *with h.* *Eccl* 8:15
righteous, it shall be well *with h.* *Isa* 3:10
wicked, it shall be ill *with h.* 11
his reward is *with h.* 40:10; 62:11
with h. also that is of a. 57:15
it was well *with h.* *Jer* 22:15, 16
he shall deal *with h.* *Ezek* 31:11
covenant was *with h.* of. *Mal* 2:5
art in the way *with h.* *Mat* 5:25
they should be *with h.* *Mark* 3:14
he might be *with h.* 5:18; *Luke* 8:38
hand of Lord was *with h. Luke* 1:66
this man was also *with h.* 22:56
except God be *with h.* *John* 3:2
and make our abode *with h.* 14:23
but God was *with h.* *Acts* 7:9; 10:38
him is accepted *with h.* 10:35
did eat and drink *with h.* 10:41
crying, Away *with h.* 21:36

we are buried *with h.* by baptism. *Rom* 6:4; *Col* 2:12
live *with h.* *Rom* 6:8; *2 Cor* 13:4
1 Thes 5:10; *2 Tim* 2:11
shall he not *with h.* give? *Rom* 8:32
will God bring *with h.* *1 Thes* 4:14
we also shall reign *with h.* *2 Tim* 2:12; *Rev* 20:6
the heirs *with h.* of the. *Heb* 11:9
when we were *with h.* *2 Pet* 1:18
and I will sup *with h.* *Rev* 3:20
with h. 144,000 having his. 14:1
they that are *with h.* are. 17:14

within **him**

his soul *within h.* mourn. *Job* 14:22
the gall of asps *within h.* 20:14
layeth up deceit *within h.* *Pr* 26:24
his Holy Spirit *within h.* *Isa* 63:11
spirit of man *within h.* *Zech* 12:1

without **him**

and *without h.* was not. *John* 1:3

himself

set on for him by *h.* *Gen* 43:32
if he came in by *h.* he shall go out by *h.* *Ex* 21:3
sin offering which was for *h.* *Lev* 9:8; 16:6, 11
shall make an atonement for *h.* 16:11, 17, 24
to bring you near to *h.* *Num* 16:9
taken spoil, every man for *h.* 31:53
Lord hath chosen thee to *h. Deut* 7:6
14:2; 28:9; 29:13; *2 Sam* 7:23
provided the first part for *h.* *Deut* 33:21
let the Lord *h.* require. *Josh* 22:23
he *h.* turned again. *Judg* 3:19
David encouraged *h.* *1 Sam* 30:6
Elijah *h.* went a day's journey, and he requested *for h.* *1 Ki* 19:4
God *h.* is with us for. *2 Chr* 13:12
thrust him out, yea, *h.* hasted. 26:20
h. separated from the. *Ezra* 10:8
only on *h.* put not forth. *Job* 1:12
wise may be profitable to *h.* 22:2
will he delight *h.* in the? 27:10
because he justified *h.* rather. 32:2
that he should delight *h.* with. 34:9
when he raiseth *h.* the. 41:25
him that is godly for *h.* *Ps* 4:3
the poor committeth *h.* unto. 10:14
net that he hath hid catch *h.* 35:8
he setteth *h.* in a way that is. 36:4
for God is judge *h.* 50:6
and the Highest *h.* shall. 87:5
but on *h.* shall his crown. 132:18
Lord hath chosen Jacob to *h.* 135:4
shall take wicked *h.* *Pr* 5:22
shall be watered also *h.* 11:25
h. rich, that maketh *h.* poor. 13:7
man shall be satisfied from *h.* 14:14
hath made all things for *h.* 16:4
that laboureth, laboureth for *h.* 26
he also shall cry *h.* but shall. 21:13
the evil, and hideth *h.* 22:3; 27:12
child left to *h.* bringeth. 29:15
beloved hath withdrawn *h. S of S* 5:6
the Lord *h.* shall give you. *Isa* 7:14
he hath spoken, and *h.* hath. 38:15
another shall call *h.* by the. 44:5
departeth from evil, maketh *h.* 59:15
make *h.* an everlasting name? 63:12
way of man is not in *h.* *Jer* 10:23
that is mad, and maketh *h.* 29:26
hath sworn by *h.* 51:14; *Amos* 6:8
prince prepare for *h.* *Ezek* 45:22
be cut off, but not for *h.* *Dan* 9:26
he hath withdrawn *h.* *Hos* 5:6
vine, bringeth forth fruit to *h.* 10:1
the mighty deliver *h.* *Amos* 2:14
swift of foot shall not deliver *h.* 15
h. shall reward thee. *Mat* 6:4
h. took our infirmities, bare. 8:17
he not root in *h.* but dureth. 13:21
he saved others; *h.* he cannot save. 27:42; *Mark* 15:31
said, He is beside *h.* *Mark* 3:21
let him deny *h.*, and take up his cross. 8:34; *Luke* 9:23
love his neighbour as *h. Mark* 12:33
sent them, whither he *h.* *Luke* 10:1
spirits more wicked than *h.* 11:26
lord's will, and prepared not *h.* 12:47

he came to *h.* he said. *Luke* 15:17
nobleman went to receive for *h.* 19:12
saying, that he *h.* is Christ. 23:2
also *h.* waited for the kingdom. 51
the things concerning *h.* 24:27
Jesus *h.* stood in the midst of. 36
Jesus *h.* baptized not. *John* 4:2
God was his Father, making *h.* 5:18
I say, the Son can do nothing of *h.* 19
for as the Father hath life in *h.* 26
for he *h.* knew what he would. 6:6
when Jesus knew in *h.* that his. 61
and he *h.* seeketh to be known. 7:4
he that speaketh of *h.* seeketh. 18
him, he shall speak for *h.* 9:21
this spake he not of *h.* but. 11:51
God shall glorify him in *h.* 13:32
he shall not speak of *h.* but. 16:13
Father *h.* loveth you, because. 27
maketh *h.* a king, speaketh. 19:12
Jesus shewed *h.* again. 21:1, 14
durst no man join *h.* to. *Acts* 5:13
rose up Theudas, boasting *h.* 36
giving out that *h.* was some. 8:9
speaketh the prophet this? of *h.*? 34
while Peter doubted in *h.* 10:17
when Peter was come to *h.* 12:11
he left not *h.* without witness. 14:17
while he answered for *h.* 25:8; 26:1
as he spake for *h.* Festus said. 26:24
was suffered to dwell by *h.* 28:16
think of *h.* more highly. *Rom* 12:3
to *h.*, no man dieth to *h.* 14:7
for even Christ pleased not *h.* 15:3
yet he *h.* is judged of. *1 Cor* 2:15
but he *h.* shall be saved, yet. 3:15
let a man examine *h.*, and so. 11:28
then shall the Son *h.* be. 15:28
reconciled us to *h.* by Jesus. *2 Cor* 5:18, 19
man trust to *h.* let him of *h.* 10:7
for ye suffer if a man exalt *h.* 11:20
who gave *h.* for our sins. *Gal* 1:4
gave *h.* for me. 2:20
think *h.* to be something. 6:3
he have rejoicing in *h.* 4
to make in *h.* of twain. *Eph* 2:15
Jesus *h.* being the chief corner-. 20
hath given *h.* for us. 5:2
gave *h.* for it. 25
present it to *h.* a glorious church. 27
loveth *h.* 28
so love his wife, even as *h.* 33
reconcile all things to *h.* *Col* 1:20
sitteth, shewing *h.* that. *2 Thes* 2:4
who gave *h.* a ransom. *1 Tim* 2:6
h. for us, to purify to *h.* *Tit* 2:14
being condemned of *h.* 3:11
when he had by *h.* purged. *Heb* 1:3
he also *h.* likewise took part. 2:14
in that he *h.* hath suffered. 18
for that he *h.* also is compassed. 5:2
as for the people, so also for *h.* 3
no man taketh this honour to *h.* 4
Christ glorified not *h.* to be made. 5
he sware by *h.* 6:13
when he offered up *h.* 7:27
away sin by the sacrifice of *h.* 9:26
but committed *h.* to. *1 Pet* 2:23
ought to walk, even as. *1 John* 2:6
hath this hope, purifieth *h.* even. 3:3
believeth hath the witness in *h.* 5:10
nor doth he *h.* receive. *3 John* 10
that no man knew but *h.* *Rev* 19:12
God *h.* shall be with them. 21:3
see **bowed, hide**

hin

(*A liquid measure of the Hebrews. It was the sixth part of a* Bath *or* Ephah, *and held about one gallon and three pints*)

fourth part of an *h.* of oil. *Ex* 29:40
unto thee of oil olive an *h.* 30:24
a just ephah and an *h.* shall. *Lev* 19:36
shall be of wine, fourth part of an *h.* 23:13; *Num* 15:4; 28:14
part of an *h.* of wine. *Num* 15:5
the third part of an *h.* of oil. 6
half an *h.* 9
drink sixth part of an *h.* *Ezek* 4:11
an *h.* of oil for an ephah. 45:24
46:5, 7, 11
third part of an *h.* of oil to. 46:14

hind, -s
Naphtali is a *h.* let loose. *Gen* 49:21
my feet like *hs.*' feet, and setteth me.
2 Sam 22:34; *Ps* 18:33; *Hab* 3:19
thou mark when the *h.*? *Job* 39:1
of Lord maketh the *h.* *Ps* 29:9
her be as the loving *h.* *Pr* 5:19
I charge you by the *h.* of the field.
S of S 2:7; 3:5
the *h.* calved in the field. *Jer* 14:5

hinder
h. me not, seeing the. *Gen* 24:56
let nothing *h.* thee from. *Num* 22:16
come and fight, and *h.* the. *Neh* 4:8*
away, who can *h.* him? *Job* 9:12
and shut up, who can *h.* him? 11:10
what doth *h.* me to be? *Acts* 8:36
should *h.* the gospel of. *1 Cor* 9:12
who did *h.* you, that? *Gal* 5:7

hinder *end*
Abner smote him with *h. end* of.
2 Sam 2:23

hinder *part*
and his *h. part* toward. *Joel* 2:20
Jesus was in the *h. part.* *Mark* 4:38
the *h. part* was broken. *Acts* 27:41*

hinder *parts*
their *h. parts* were inward.
1 Ki 7:25; *2 Chr* 4:4
enemies in the *h. parts.* *Ps* 78:66*

hinder *sea*
them toward the *h. sea.* *Zech* 14:8*

hindered
given, that they be not *h.* *Ezra* 6:8
were entering in, ye *h.* *Luke* 11:52
have been much *h.* *Rom* 15:22
have come, but Satan *h.* *1 Thes* 2:18
that your prayers be not *h.* *1 Pet* 3:7

hindereth
is persecuted, and none *h.* *Isa* 14:6*

hindermost, or hindmost
put Rachel and Joseph *h.* *Gen* 33:2
shall go *h.* with their. *Num* 2:31
and smote the *h.* of thee. *Deut* 25:18
pursue, and smite the *h.* *Josh* 10:19
the *h.* of the nations. *Jer* 50:12

hinges
and the *h.* of gold for. *1 Ki* 7:50
door turneth upon his *h.* *Pr* 26:14

Hinnom
went up by valley of *H.* *Josh* 15:8
is in the valley of *H.* *2 Ki* 23:10
incense in the valley of *H.* *2 Chr* 28:3
to pass through fire in *H.* 33:6
the valley of the son of *H.* *Jer* 19:2
places in the valley of *H.* 32:35

hip
he smote them *h.* and. *Judg* 15:8

Hiram
H. king of Tyre sent messengers to.
2 Sam 5:11; *1 Chr* 14:1
H. king of Tyre sent servants to Solomon, for *H.* was ever. *1 Ki* 5:1, 8
H. gave Solomon cedar trees. 10
Solomon gave *H.* 20,000. 11
peace between *H.* and Solomon. 12
Solomon sent and fetched *H.* 7:13
H. made the lavers, *H.* made. 40
H. came to see the cities. 9:12
H. sent in the navy his. 27
the navy of *H.* brought in. 10:11
at sea a navy, with the navy of *H.* 22

hire, *substantive*
God hath given me my *h.* *Gen* 30:18
and of such shall be my *h.* 32
when it shall come for thy *h.* 33
ringstraked shall be thy *h.* 31:8*
thing, it came for his *h.* *Ex* 22:15
shalt not bring the *h.* *Deut* 23:18
thou shalt give him his *h.* 24:15
to thee will I give *h.* *1 Ki* 5:6
she shall turn to her *h.* *Isa* 23:17
and her *h.* shall be holiness to. 18
in that thou scornest *h.* *Ezek* 16:31
and thou also shalt give no *h.* 41
it of the *h.* of an harlot, return to the *h.* of an harlot. *Mi* 1:7
priests thereof teach for *h.* 3:11
no *h.* for man, nor any *h.* *Zech* 8:10
give them their *h.* *Mat* 20:8
labourer is worthy of his *h.*
Luke 10:7
the *h.* of the labourers is. *Jas* 5:4

hire
h. a goldsmith, and he. *Isa* 46:6
went out to *h.* labourers. *Mat* 20:1

hired
h. thee with my son's. *Gen* 30:16
if it be an *h.* thing it. *Ex* 22:15
wages of him that is *h.* *Lev* 19:13
they *h.* against thee Balaam.
Deut 23:4; *Neh* 13:2
Abimelech *h.* vain persons. *Judg* 9:4
Micah hath *h.* me, and I am. 18:4
that were full, have *h.* *1 Sam* 2:5
Ammon *h.* the Syrians. *2 Sam* 10:6
1 Chr 19:7
king of Israel hath *h.* *2 Ki* 7:6
h. masons and. *2 Chr* 24:12
Amaziah *h.* 100,000 mighty. 25:6
h. counsellors against. *Ezra* 4:5
Sanballat had *h.* him. *Neh* 6:12, 13
with a razor that is *h.* *Isa* 7:20
h. men are like fatted. *Jer* 46:21
up, Ephraim hath *h.* *Hos* 8:9
yea, though they have *h.* among. 10
no man hath *h.* us. *Mat* 20:7
when they came that were *h.* 9
Paul dwelt two years in his own *h.* house. *Acts* 28:30

hired *servant*
an *h. servant* not eat thereof.
Ex 12:45; *Lev* 22:10
be meat for thy *h. servant.* *Lev* 25:6
but as an *h. servant* he shall be. 40
the time of an *h. servant* shall. 50
as a yearly *h. servant* shall he. 53
a double *h. servant.* *Deut* 15:18*
not oppress an *h. servant.* 24:14

hired *servants*
the ship with *h. servants.* *Mark* 1:20
many *h. servants* have. *Luke* 15:17
as one of thy *h. servants.* 19

hireling
days like the days of an *h.*? *Job* 7:1
as an *h.* looketh for the reward. 2
he shall accomplish as an *h.* 14:6
in three years as the years of an *h.*
Isa 16:14; 21:16
those that oppress the *h.* *Mat* 3:5
he that is an *h.* and not. *John* 10:12
the *h.* fleeth, because he is an *h.* 13

hires
all the *h.* thereof shall. *Mi* 1:7

hirest
thou *h.* them, that they. *Ezek* 16:33

his
(*As the neuter possessive pronoun* its *was hardly come into use in* 1611 *when the Authorised Version* ("*King James's Version*") *was translated, the possessive* his *was often used where modern usage would require* its. *In these places the Revisions change the pronoun to the modern form*)
the seed should not be *h.* *Gen* 38:9
dead beast shall be *h.* *Ex* 21:34
another challengeth to be *h.* 22:9
part, and it shall be *h.* *Lev* 27:15
hallowed thing shall be *h.* *Num* 5:10
the Lord will shew who are *h.* 16:5
and let my last end be like *h.* 23:10
of the firstborn is *h.* *Deut* 21:17
h. will I be, with him. *2 Sam* 16:18
for it was *h.* from the. *1 Ki* 2:15
a captain of *h.* conspired. *2 Ki* 15:25
is one law of *h.* to put. *Esth* 4:11
and the deceiver are *h.* *Job* 12:16
because it is none of *h.* 18:15
Lord, all ye saints of *h.* *Ps* 30:4
strength of the hills is *h.* also. 95:4
ye ministers of *h.* that do. 103:21
is mine, and I am *h.* *S of S* 2:16
passed by; *h.* it was. *Ezek* 16:15
then it shall be *h.* to the year. 46:17
wisdom and might are *h.* *Dan* 2:20
h. that did escape, nor have delivered up those of *h.* *Ob* 14
him increaseth that which is not *h.*
Hab 2:6
is not mine, but *h.* that. *John* 7:16
baptized, he and all *h.* *Acts* 16:33
Spirit, he is none of *h.* *Rom* 8:9
knoweth them that are *h.* *2 Tim* 2:19
works, as God did from *h.* *Heb* 4:10

hiss
(*Hiss, or hissing is generally used in the Bible with the idea of contempt or scorn. Occasionally the the word has the idea of anger*)
house every one shall *h.* *1 Ki* 9:8
men shall *h.* him out of. *Job* 27:23
he will *h.* to them from. *Isa* 5:26
the Lord shall *h.* for the fly. 7:18
passeth thereby shall *h.* *Jer* 19:8
49:17; 50:13
they *h.* at the daughter. *Lam* 2:15
thy enemies *h.* and gnash the. 16
the merchants shall *h.* *Ezek* 27:36
passeth by her shall *h.* *Zeph* 2:15
I will *h.* for them and. *Zech* 10:8

hissing
delivered them to *h.* *2 Chr* 29:8
their land a perpetual *h.* *Jer* 18:16
make this city an *h.* 19:8
make them an *h.* 25:9, 18; 29:18
Babylon shall be an *h.* 51:37
inhabitants thereof an *h.* *Mi* 6:16

hit
and the archers *h.* him. *1 Sam* 31:3*
1 Chr 10:3*

hither
angry that ye sold me *h.* *Gen* 45:5
it was not you that sent me *h.* 8
bring down my father *h.* 13
draw not nigh *h.*: put off. *Ex* 3:5
there came men in *h.* *Josh* 2:2
bring the description *h.* to me. 18:6
him, who brought thee *h.*? *Judg* 18:3
we will not turn aside *h.* 19:12
bring *h.* a burnt offering *1 Sam* 13:9
Saul said, bring *h.* the ark. 14:18
bring me *h.* every man his ox. 34
let us draw near *h.* unto God. 36
bring *h.* Agag. 15:32
why camest thou *h.*? 17:28
Abiathar, bring *h.* the. 23:9; 30:7
I have brought them *h.* *2 Sam* 1:10
hasten *h.* Micaiah *1 Ki* 22:9*
Jordan divided *h.* and. *2 Ki* 2:8, 14
not bring in captives *h.* *2 Chr* 28:13
which brought us up *h.* *Ezra* 4:2
his people return *h.* *Ps* 73:10
take a psalm, and bring *h.* 81:2
let him turn in *h.* *Pr* 9:4, 16
draw near *h.* ye sons of. *Isa* 57:3
he said, bring them *h.* *Mat* 14:18
Jesus said, bring him *h.* to me.
17:17; *Luke* 9:41
how camest thou in *h.*? *Mat* 22:12
bring in *h.* the poor. *Luke* 14:21
bring *h.* the fatted calf and. 15:23
bring *h.* and slay them. 19:27
colt tied, loose him, bring him *h.* 30
Rabbi, when camest thou *h.*?
John 6:25
reach *h.* thy finger, reach *h.* 20:27
that came *h.* for that. *Acts* 9:21
call *h.* Simon, whose surname. 10:32
have brought *h.* these men. 19:37
see **come**

hitherto
behold, *h.* thou wouldest. *Ex* 7:16
Lord hath blessed me *h.* *Josh* 17:14
h. thou hast mocked. *Judg* 16:13
grief have I spoken *h.* *1 Sam* 1:16
and saying, *H.* hath the Lord. 7:12
thou hast brought me *h.* *2 Sam* 7:18
1 Chr 17:16
thy father's servant *h.* *2 Sam* 15:34
who *h.* waited in the. *1 Chr* 9:18
h. the greatest part kept. 12:29
h. shalt thou come, but. *Job* 38:11
h. have I declared thy. *Ps* 71:17
terrible from their beginning *h.*
Isa 18:2, 7
my Father worketh *h.* *John* 5:17
h. have ye asked nothing. 16:24
to come, but was let *h.* *Rom* 1:13
for *h.* ye were not able. *1 Cor* 3:2

Hittite
the field of Ephron the *H.* *Gen* 25:9

daughter of Beeri the *H.* *Gen* 26:34
Elon the *H.* 36:2
Abraham bought of Ephron the *H.* 49:30; 50:13
I will drive out the *H.* *Ex* 23:28 33:2; 34:11
the *H.* and Amorite. *Josh* 9:1; 11:3
to Abimelech the *H.* *1 Sam* 26:6
send me Uriah the *H.* *2 Sam* 11:6
thy servant Uriah the *H.* 21, 24
hast killed Uriah the *H.* 12:9
taken the wife of Uriah the *H.* 10
Uriah the *H.* thirty-seven. 23:39
matter of Uriah the *H.* *1 Ki* 15:5
thy mother an *H.* *Ezek* 16:3, 45

Hittites

unto thy seed have I given land of *H.* *Gen* 15:20; *Josh* 1:4
Canaanites, *H.* Amorites. *Ex* 3:8, 17 13:5; 23:23; *Deut* 7:1; 20:17 *Josh* 3:10; 12:8; 24:11; *Judg* 3:5 *1 Ki* 9:20; *Neh* 9:8
into the land of the *H.* *Judg* 1:26
Israel dwelt among the *H.* 3:5
loved women of the *H.* *1 Ki* 11:1
hired the kings of the *H.* *2 Ki* 7:6
left of *H.*, Solomon made. *2 Chr* 8:7
abominations of the *H.* *Ezra* 9:1

Hivite, much in **Hittite**

ho

to whom he said, *Ho.* *Ruth* 4:1
ho every one that thirsteth. *Isa* 55:1
ho, ho, come forth. *Zech* 2:6

hoar, *see* **frost, hairs, head**

hoary

think the deep to be *h.* *Job* 41:32

Hobab

Moses said to *H.* come. *Num* 10:29
of the children of *H.* *Judg* 4:11

hoised

they *h.* up the mainsail. *Acts* 27:40*

hold, *substantive*

(*In the Old Testament the American Revision renders this* stronghold)

they entered into a *h.* *Judg* 9:46
put them to the *h.* and set the *h.* 49
David in *h.* *1 Sam* 22:4; 24:22 *2 Sam* 5:17; 23:14
abide not in the *h.* *1 Sam* 22:5
came of Judah to *h.* *1 Chr* 12:16
and put them in *h.* unto. *Acts* 4:3*
is become the *h.* of every. *Rev* 18:2
see **strong**

hold

lift up the lad, *h.* him. *Gen* 21:18
that they may *h.* a feast. *Ex* 5:1
to let them go, and wilt *h.* 9:2
for we must *h.* a feast unto. 10:9
Lord will not *h.* 20:7; *Deut* 5:11
bring the vail, and *h.* it. *Ruth* 3:15
how should I *h.* up my? *2 Sam* 2:22
his hand to ark of God, and took *h.* of it, oxen shook it. 6:6; *1 Chr* 13:9
now therefore *h.* him. *1 Ki* 2:9
the king shall *h.* out. *Esth* 4:11
teach me, and I will *h.* *Job* 6:24
I know that thou wilt not *h.* 9:28
if I *h.* my tongue, I shall. 13:19
the righteous also shall *h.* on. 17:9
dart, the habergeon cannot *h.* 41:26
h. up my goings in thy. *Ps* 17:5
horror hath taken *h.* upon. 119:53
h. thou me up, and I shall. 117
and thy right hand shall *h.* 139:10
and her hands *h.* the. *Pr* 31:19
they all *h.* swords, being. *S of S* 3:8
I the Lord will *h.* thy. *Isa* 41:13
and I will *h.* thine hand. 42:6
broken cisterns, can *h.* *Jer* 2:13
astonishment hath taken *h.* 8:21
they shall *h.* the bow. 50:42
anguish took *h.* of him, and. 43
to make it strong to *h.* *Ezek* 30:21
might have *h.*, they had not *h.* 41:6
then shall he say, *H.* *Amos* 6:10
them, and *h.* themselves. *Zech* 11:5
else he will *h.* to the one. *Mat* 6:24 *Luke* 16:13
all *h.* John as a prophet. *Mat* 21:26
they have received to *h.* *Mark* 7:4
ye *h.* the tradition of men. *Mark* 7:8
who *h.* the truth in. *Rom* 1:18*
receive him, and *h.* such. *Phil* 2:29
h. the traditions ye. *2 Thes* 2:15
if we *h.* the beginning. *Heb* 3:14
them that *h.* the doctrine. *Rev* 2:14
that *h.* doctrine of Nicolaitanes. 15
see **caught, take**

hold *fast*

he shall *h.* it *fast*, but. *Job* 8:15
my righteousness I *h. fast*, I. 27:6
they *h. fast* deceit, they. *Jer* 8:5
prove all things, *h. fast*. *1 Thes* 5:21
h. fast the form of sound. *2 Tim* 1:13
if we *h. fast* the confidence. *Heb* 3:6
h. fast our profession. 4:14; 10:23
ye have already *h. fast*. *Rev* 2:25
h. fast and repent. 3:3
h. fast which thou hast. 11

hold *peace*

ye shall *h.* your *peace*. *Ex* 14:14
her father *h.* his *peace*. *Num* 30:4
husband altogether *h.* his *peace*. 14
h. thy *peace*, lay hand. *Judg* 18:19
h. thy *peace*, my sister. *2 Sam* 13:20
I know it, *h.* ye your *peace*. *2 Ki* 2:3, 5
tidings, and we *h.* our *peace*. 7:9
saying, *H.* your *peace*. *Neh* 8:11
lies make men *h.* their *peace*? *Job* 11:3
altogether *h.* your *peace*. 13:5
h. your *peace*, let me alone. 13
mark well, *h.* thy *peace* and. 33:31
h. thy *peace*, and I will teach. 33
O God, *h.* not thy *peace*, be not still. *Ps* 83:1; 109:1
will I not *h.* my *peace*. *Isa* 62:1
which shall never *h.* their *peace*. 6
wilt thou *h.* thy *peace* and? 64:12
I cannot *h.* my *peace*. *Jer* 4:19
h. thy *p.* at the presence. *Zeph* 1:7
because they should *h.* their *peace*. *Mat* 20:31; *Mark* 10:48; *Luke* 18:39
h. thy *peace* come out of him. *Mark* 1:25; *Luke* 4:35
should *h.* their *peace*. *Luke* 19:40
to them to *h.* their *peace*. *Acts* 12:17
but speak, and *h.* not thy *peace*. 18:9
let the first *h.* his *peace*. *1 Cor* 14:30

holden

there was not *h.* such a passover. *2 Ki* 23:22*, 23*
if they be *h.* in cords. *Job* 36:8*
thy right hand hath *h.* *Ps* 18:35
by thee have I been *h.* up. 71:6
thou hast *h.* me up by my. 73:23
shall be *h.* with the cords. *Pr* 5:22
I have long *h.* my peace. *Isa* 42:14
whose right hand I have *h.* to. 45:1
eyes were *h.* they. *Luke* 24:16
possible he should be *h.* *Acts* 2:24
yea, he shall be *h.* up. *Rom* 14:4*

holdest

if thou altogether *h.* thy. *Esth* 4:14
wherefore *h.* thou me? *Job* 13:24
h. my eyes waking, I. *Ps* 77:4
O thou that *h.* the height. *Jer* 49:16
h. thy tongue when the. *Hab* 1:13
thou *h.* fast my name. *Rev* 2:13

holdeth

and still he *h.* fast his. *Job* 2:3
h. back the face of his throne. 26:9
bless God who *h.* our. *Ps* 66:9
a man of understanding *h.* *Pr* 11:12
a fool when he *h.* his peace. 17:28
and none *h.* with me. *Dan* 10:21
I will cut off him that *h.* *Amos* 1:5, 8
that *h.* the seven stars. *Rev* 2:1

holding

shaketh his hands from *h.* *Isa* 33:15
I am weary with *h.* in, I. *Jer* 6:11
eat not, *h.* the tradition. *Mark* 7:3
h. forth the word of life. *Phil* 2:16
not *h.* the head, from. *Col* 2:19
h. faith and a good. *1 Tim* 1:19
h. the mystery of faith in a pure. 3:9
h. fast faithful word, as he. *Tit* 1:9
I saw four angels *h.* the. *Rev* 7:1

holds

have remained in their *h.* *Jer* 51:30*
brought him into *h.* *Ezek* 19:9*
see **strong**

hole

there shall be an *h.* in the. *Ex* 28:32
Jehoiada bored an *h.* in. *2 Ki* 12:9
put in his hand by the *h.* *S of S* 5:4
child shall play on the *h.* *Isa* 11:8
look to *h.* of the pit whence. 51:1
and hide it there in a *h.* of. *Jer* 13:4
I looked, behold a *h.* *Ezek* 8:7

holes

come forth out of the *h.* *1 Sam* 14:11
h. of the rocks. *Isa* 2:19; 7:19
all of them snared in *h.* 42:22
hunt them out of the *h.* *Jer* 16:16
her nest in sides of the *h.* 48:28
not move out of their *h.* *Mi* 7:17*
lion filled his *h.* with prey. *Nah* 2:12*
to put it in a bag with *h.* *Hag* 1:6
shall consume in their *h.* *Zech* 14:12*
Jesus saith, The foxes have *h.* *Mat* 8:20; *Luke* 9:58

holier

come not near, for I am *h.* *Isa* 65:5

holiest

which is called the *h.* *Heb* 9:3
the way into the *h.* was not yet. 8
enter into the *h.* by blood of. 10:19*

holily

are witnesses how *h.* *1 Thes* 2:10

holiness

like thee, glorious in *h.*? *Ex* 15:11
h. to the Lord. 28:36*; 39:30* *Zech* 14:20*, 21*
worship the Lord in the beauty of *h.* *1 Chr* 16:29; *Ps* 29:2; 96:9
praise the beauty of *h.* *2 Chr* 20:21
sanctified themselves in *h.* 31:18
at the remembrance of his *h.* *Ps* 30:4*; 97:12
sitteth upon throne of his *h.* 47:8*
praised in mountain of his *h.* 48:1
hath spoken in his *h.* 60:6; 108:7
once I have sworn by my *h.* 89:35
h. becometh thine house, O. 93:5
be willing, in beauties of *h.* 110:3
and her hire shall be *h.* *Isa* 23:18
shall be called the way of *h.* 35:8
drink it in the courts of my *h.* 62:9*
from habitation of thy *h.* 63:15
the people of thy *h.* have. 18*
Israel was *h.* to the Lord. *Jer* 2:3
of the words of his *h.* 23:9
bless thee, O mountain of *h.* 31:23
God hath sworn by his *h.* *Amos* 4:2
mount Zion there shall be *h.* *Ob* 17*
Judah hath profaned the *h.* *Mal* 2:11
might serve him in *h.* *Luke* 1:75
as though by our *h.* made. *Acts* 3:12*
according to Spirit of *h.* *Rom* 1:4
servants to righteousness unto *h.* 6:19
ye have your fruit unto *h.* 22
perfecting *h.* in the fear. *2 Cor* 7:1
created in righteousness and *h.* *Eph* 4:24
your hearts unblameable, in *h.* *1 Thes* 3:13
us unto uncleanness, but to *h.* 4:7*
continue in faith and *h.* *1 Tim* 2:15
in behaviour as becometh *h.* *Tit* 2:3
be partakers of his *h.* *Heb* 12:10
follow peace with men, and *h.* 14*

hollow

the *h.* of his thigh. *Gen* 32:25, 32
shalt make the altar *h.* with boards. *Ex* 27:8; 38:7
plague be in walls with *h.* *Lev* 14:37
God clave an *h.* place. *Judg* 15:19
measured waters in *h.* *Isa* 40:12
the pillar, it was *h.* *Jer* 52:21

holpen

(*American Revision,* helped)

have *h.* the children. *Ps* 83:8
thou, Lord, hast *h.* me. 86:17
and he that is *h.* shall. *Isa* 31:3
they shall be *h.* with a. *Dan* 11:34
hath *h.* his servant Israel. *Luke* 1:54

holy
[1] *Godly,* Deut 33:8; Ps 86:2.
[2] *Dedicated,* 2 Chr 31:6, *or sacred* 1 Cor 9:13. [3] *The holy place, the inner room of the tabernacle or temple where none but priests could enter.* [4] *The Holy of Holies, the innermost part of the house of God, where only the High Priest entered, and he but once a year, on the Day of Atonement.*
thou standest is *h.* ground. *Ex* 3:5
the rest of the *h.* sabbath. 16:23
to me a *h.* nation. 19:6; *1 Pet* 2:9
sabbath day to keep it *h.* *Ex* 20:8
hallow in all their *h.* gifts. 28:38
and put the *h.* crown upon the. 29:6
because they are *h.* 33
because it is *h.* 34
make it an oil of *h.* ointment. 30:25
it is *h.* and it shall be *h.* unto. 32
tempered together, pure and *h.* 35
for it is *h.* unto you. 31:14, 15
upon Aaron the *h.* crown. *Lev* 8:9
may put difference between *h.* 10:10
he shall put on the *h.* linen. 16:4
make atonement for the *h.* 33
Lord your God am *h.* 19:2; 21:8
be ye *h.* 20:7
for he is *h.* unto his God. 21:7
man sanctify his house to be *h.* 27:14
the tithe of the land is *h.* unto. 30
the priest shall take *h.* *Num* 5:17
ye may remember, and be *h.* 15:40
all the congregation are *h.* 16:3
shew who are his, and who is *h.* 5
not redeem them, they are *h.* 18:17
sent Phinehas with the *h.* 31:6*
for there is none *h.* as. *1 Sam* 2:2
vessels of the young men are *h.* 21:5
ark and the tabernacle, and all the *h.* *1 Ki* 8:4; *2 Chr* 5:5
I perceive this is an *h.* *2 Ki* 4:9
bring the *h.* vessels into. *1 Chr* 22:19
I have prepared for the *h.* 29:3
go in, for they are *h.* *2 Chr* 23:6
Levites which were *h.* to the Lord, put the *h.* ark into the. 35:3
the other *h.* offerings sod they in. 13
h. to the Lord, vessels are *h.* also. *Ezra* 8:28
the *h.* seed mingled themselves. 9:2
known unto them thy *h.* *Neh* 9:14
hear him from his *h.* heaven. *Ps* 20:6
art *h.* O thou that inhabitest. 22:3
lift my hands towards thy *h.* 28:2
preserve my soul, for I am *h.* 86:2*
his *h.* arm hath gotten him. 98:1
his footstool, for he is *h.* 99:5
and worship at his *h.* hill. 9
remembered his *h.* promise. 105:42
the Lord is *h.* in all his. 145:17*
the knowledge of the *h.* is. *Pr* 9:10
devoureth that which is *h.* 20:25
I the knowledge of the *h.* 30:3*
Jerusalem shall be called *h.* *Isa* 4:3
one cried, *H. h. h.* is the Lord. 6:3
h. seed shall be the substance. 13
worship in the *h.* mountain. 27:13
as when a *h.* solemnity is. 30:29
Lord hath made bare his *h.* 52:10
sabbath, the *h.* of the Lord. 58:13
thy *h.* cities are a wilderness. 64:10
our *h.* and beautiful house is. 11
the *h.* flesh is passed. *Jer* 11:15
no difference between *h.* *Ezek* 22:26
increase them as the *h.* flock. 36:38*
they be *h.* chambers, where. 42:13
their garments, for they are *h.* 14
and lay them in the *h.* 44:19
shall teach difference between *h.* 23
an *h.* portion of the land. 45:1, 4
oblation of *h.* portion. 6, 7; 48:18
into the *h.* chambers of the. 46:19
for the priests shall be this *h.* 48:10
not sell firstfruits, for it is *h.* 14
shall offer the *h.* oblation. 20, 21
came in before me, in whom is the spirit of the *h.* *Dan* 4:8, 9, 18; 5:11
heart shall be against the *h.* 11:28
the *h.* covenant, intelligence with them that forsake the *h.* 30
h. flesh, and with his skirt touch bread or oil, shall it be *h.*? *Hag* 2:12
inherit Judah in the *h.* *Zech* 2:12
Lord is raised up out of his *h.* 13
give not that which is *h.* *Mat* 7:6
and all the *h.* angels with. 25:31
he was a just man and *h.* *Mark* 6:20
he shall come in his own glory, and of *h.* angels. 8:38; *Luke* 9:26
by the mouth of *h.* prophets. *Luke* 1:70; *Acts* 3:21
and to remember his *h.* *Luke* 1:72
male shall be called *h.* to. 2:23
h. Father, keep those. *John* 17:11
against thy *h.* child. *Acts* 4:27
done by name of thy *h.* child. 30
thou standest is *h.* ground. 7:33
warned from God by an *h.* 10:22
had promised in the *h.* *Rom* 1:2
the commandment is *h.*, just. 7:12
fruit be *h.* if the root be *h.* 11:16
ye present your bodies a *h.* 12:1
salute one another with an *h.* kiss. 16:16; *1 Cor* 16:20; *2 Cor* 13:12 *1 Thes* 5:26; *1 Pet* 5:14
temple of God is *h.* *1 Cor* 3:17
but now are they *h.* 7:14
that she may be *h.* 34
h. and without blame. *Eph* 1:4; 5:27
to present you *h.* and. *Col* 1:22
put on, as the elect of God, *h.* 3:12
epistle be read to all *h.* *1 Thes* 5:27
lifting up *h.* hands. *1 Tim* 2:8
hath called us with an *h.* *2 Tim* 1:9
hast known *h.* scriptures. 3:15*
bishop must be sober, *h.* *Tit* 1:8
h. brethren, partakers of. *Heb* 3:1
priest became us, who is *h.* 7:26
h. in all conversation. *1 Pet* 1:15, 16
a *h.* priesthood, to offer up. 2:5
the *h.* women also who trusted. 3:5
we were with him in *h.* *2 Pet* 1:18
but *h.* men spake as moved by. 21
than to turn from the *h.* 2:21
words spoken before by the *h.* 3:2
what persons to be in all *h.* 11
things, saith he that is *h.* *Rev* 3:7
H. h. h. Lord God Almighty. 4:8
How long, O Lord, *h.* and? 6:10
tormented in presence of *h.* 14:10
not fear thee? for thou art *h.* 15:4
rejoice over her, ye *h.* 18:20*
h. is he that hath part in first. 20:6
and he shewed me the *h.* 21:10
Lord God of the *h.* prophets. 22:6*
he that is *h.* let him be *h.* still. 11
see **convocation, habitation, hill**

holy *day*
day shall be an *h. day.* *Ex* 35:2
this *day* is *h.* unto. *Neh* 8:9, 10, 11
them on sabbath or *h. day.* 10:31
multitude that kept *h. day.* *Ps* 42:4
thy pleasure on my *h. day.* *Isa* 58:13
in respect of an *h. day.* *Col* 2:16*
see **garments**

Holy *Ghost*
(*American Revision substitutes for this the words* Holy Spirit. *The starred references here refer to other changes*)
with child of the *H. Ghost.* *Mat* 1:18
conceived in her is of *H. Ghost.* 20
baptize you with *H. Ghost.* 3:11 *Mark* 1:8; *Luke* 3:16 *John* 1:33; *Acts* 1:5
blasphemy against the *H. Ghost.* *Mat* 12:31*; *Mark* 3:29 *Luke* 12:10
speaketh against the *H. Ghost.* *Mat* 12:32
baptize in name of Father, Son, and *H. Ghost.* 28:19
David said by the *H. Ghost.* *Mark* 12:36; *Acts* 1:16
speak, but the *H. Ghost.* *Mark* 13:11
filled with *H. Ghost.* *Luke* 1:15
the *H. Ghost* shall come upon. 35
and Elisabeth was filled with the *H. Ghost.* 41
Zacharias was filled with the *H. Ghost.* 67
Simeon; *H. Ghost* was upon. 2:25
revealed unto him by *H. Ghost.* 26
the *H. Ghost* descended in a. 3:22
being full of the *H. Ghost.* 4:1
H. Ghost shall teach you. *Luke* 12:12
for the *H. Ghost* was. *John* 7:39*
who is the *H. Ghost.* 14:26
he saith, receive ye the *H. Ghost.* 20:22; *Acts* 2:38
he through the *H. Ghost.* *Acts* 1:2
after that the *H. Ghost* is come. 8
filled with the *H. Ghost.* 2:4; 4:31
the promise of the *H. Ghost.* 2:33
Peter, filled with the *H. Ghost.* 4:8
heart to lie to the *H. Ghost.* 5:3
witnesses, so is also *H. Ghost.* 32
look out men full of *H. Ghost.* 6:3*
Stephen, a man full of *H. Ghost.* 5
ye always resist the *H. Ghost.* 7:51
he being full of *H. Ghost* looked. 55
might receive the *H. Ghost.* 8:15
and they received the *H. Ghost.* 17
when Simon saw that *H. Ghost.* 18
hands, he may receive *H. Ghost.* 19
be filled with the *H. Ghost.* 9:17
the comfort of the *H. Ghost.* 31
anointed Jesus with *H. Ghost.* 10:38
H. Ghost fell on all which. 44
poured the gift of the *H. Ghost.* 45
have received the *H. Ghost.* 47
H. Ghost fell on them as on. 11:15
shall be baptized with *H. Ghost.* 16
Barnabas, full of the *H. Ghost.* 24
the *H. Ghost* said, separate. 13:2
being sent forth by *H. Ghost.* 4
Paul, filled with the *H. Ghost.* 9
were filled with the *H. Ghost.* 52
giving them the *H. Ghost* as. 15:8
it seemed good to the *H. Ghost.* 28
were forbidden of *H. Ghost.* 16:6
the *H. Ghost*? ... not heard whether there be any *H. Ghost.* 19:2
laid hands on them, the *H. Ghost.* 6
save that the *H. Ghost.* 20:23
over which *H. Ghost* hath made. 28
thus saith the *H. Ghost,* so. 21:11
well spake the *H. Ghost* by. 28:25
love of God is shed abroad in hearts by *H. Ghost.* *Rom* 5:5
me witness in the *H. Ghost.* 9:1
God is joy in the *H. Ghost.* 14:17
through power of *H. Ghost.* 15:13
being sanctified by *H. Ghost.* 16
words which *H. Ghost.* *1 Cor* 2:13*
the temple of the *H. Ghost.* 6:19
Lord, but by the *H. Ghost.* 12:3
kindness, by *H. Ghost.* *2 Cor* 6:6
communion of the *H. Ghost.* 13:14
gospel came in *H. Ghost.* *1 Thes* 1:5
word with joy of the *H. Ghost.* 6
thing keep by *H. Ghost.* *2 Tim* 1:14
renewing of the *H. Ghost.* *Tit* 3:5
with gifts of the *H. Ghost.* *Heb* 2:4
as the *H. Ghost* saith, To-day. 3:7
made partakers of the *H. Ghost.* 6:4
the *H. Ghost* this signifying. 9:8
whereof the *H. Ghost* is a. 10:15
the *H. Ghost* sent down. *1 Pet* 1:12
moved by the *H. Ghost.* *2 Pet* 1:21
Word, and the *H. Ghost.* *1 John* 5:7
praying in the *H. Ghost.* *Jude* 20
see **God**

most **holy**
place and the *most h.* *Ex* 26:33
of the testimony in the *most h.* 34
be an altar *most h.* 29:37; 40:10
it is *most h.* 30:10
that they may be *most h.* 29
perfume shall be to you *most h.* 36
offering shall be Aaron's, it is *most h.* *Lev* 2:3, 10; 6:17; 10:12
the sin offering is *most h.* 6:25, 29 10:17
trespass offering is *most h.* 7:1, 6 14:13
bread of God, both of *most h.* 21:22
cakes of fine flour are *most h.* 24:9
devoted thing is *most h.* to. 27:28
be service about *most h.* *Num* 4:4
they approach the *most h.* things. 19
render to me shall be *most h.* 18:9
in the *most h.* place shalt thou. 10
them for the *most h.* place. *1 Ki* 6:16
made vessels for the *most h.* 7:50
brought the ark unto *most h.* place. 8:6; *2 Chr* 5:7
sons for work of *most h.* *1 Chr* 6:49

to sanctify most h. 1 Chr 23:13
made the most h. house. 2 Chr 3:8
in the most h. house he made. 10
doors thereof for the most h. 4:22
Kore to distribute the most h. 31:14
not eat of the most h. things.
Ezra 2:63; Neh 7:65
limit shall be most h. Ezek 43:12
near in the most h. place. 44:13
be the sanctuary and most h. 45:3
oblation be a thing most h. 48:12
weeks to anoint the most h. Dan 9:24
yourselves on your most h. Jude 20

holy mountain, -s

foundation is in the h. mountains.
Ps 87:1
nor destroy in my h. mountain.
Isa 11:9; 65:25
will I bring to my h. mountain. 56:7
shall inherit my h. mountain. 57:13
that forget my h. mountain. 65:11
beasts to my h. mountain. 66:20
in my h. mountain they. Ezek 20:40
wast upon the h. mountain. 28:14
turned from thy h. mountain.
Dan 9:16
supplication for the h. mountain. 20
in glorious h. mountain. 11:45
alarm in my h. mountain. Joel 2:1
in Zion, my h. mountain. 3:17
drunk on my h. mountain. Ob 16
because of h. mountain. Zeph 3:11
Lord called h. mountain. Zech 8:3

holy name

to profane my h. name. Lev 20:3
profane not my h. name. 22:2
ye profane my h. name. 32
glory ye in his h. name. 1 Chr 16:10
Ps 105:3
we give thanks to thy h. name.
1 Chr 16:35; Ps 106:47
house for thy h. name. 1 Chr 29:16
trusted in his h. name. Ps 33:21
terrible name, for it is h. 99:3
bless the Lord, bless his h. name.
103:1; 145:21
h. and reverend is his name. 111:9
Luke 1:49
One, whose name is h. Isa 57:15
my h. name no more. Ezek 20:39
they profaned my h. name. 36:20
but I had pity for mine h. name. 21
sakes, but for my h. name's sake. 22
h. name known in . . . not let them pollute my h. name any more. 39:7
will be jealous for my h. name. 25
my h. name shall Israel no. 43:7
they have defiled my h. name by. 8
to profane my h. name. Amos 2:7

holy oil

an h. anointing oil. Ex 30:25, 31
made the h. anointing oil. 37:29
was anointed with h. oil. Num 35:25
with my h. oil have I. Ps 89:20

holy One

Urim be with thy h. one. Deut 33:8*
words of the H. One. Job 6:10
in hell, nor suffer thine H. One to.
Ps 16:10; Acts 2:27; 13:35
in vision to thy h. one. Ps 89:19*
and his H. One shall be. Isa 10:17
shall sanctify the H. One of. 29:23
I be equal ? saith the H. One. 40:25
I am the Lord your H. One. 43:15
Redeemer of Israel his H. One. 49:7
an h. one came down. Dan 4:13, 23
for I am the H. One in. Hos 11:9
from everlasting, O Lord my H. One.
Hab 1:12
the H. One came from mount. 3:3
I know thee who thou art, the H. One.
Mark 1:24; Luke 4:34
ye denied the H. One. Acts 3:14
unction from the H. One. 1 John 2:20

holy One of Israel

lifted thy eyes against the H. One of Isr. 2 Ki 19:22; Isa 37:23
sing, O thou H. One of Isr. Ps 71:22
limited the H. One of Isr. 78:41
the H. One of Isr. is our king. 89:18
provoked the H. One of Isr. Isa 1:4
counsel of the H. One of Isr. 5:19
the word of the H. One of Isr. 24
the Lord, the H. One of Isr. Isa 10:20
43:3; 45:11
great is the H. One of Isr. in. 12:6
have respect to H. One of Isr. 17:7
rejoice in the H. One of Isr. 29:19
cause the H. One of Isr. to. 30:11
saith the H. One of Isr. 12, 15
not unto the H. One of Isr. 31:1
Redeemer, the H. One of Isr. 41:14
glory in the H. One of Isr. 16
and the H. One of Isr. hath. 20
your Redeemer, the H. One of Isr.
43:14
is his name, the H. One of Isr. 47:4
saith thy Redeemer, the H. One of Isr. 48:17; 54:5
of Isr. and his H. One. 49:7
unto thee, for the H. One of Isr. 55:5
gold to the H. One of Isr. 60:9
the Zion of the H. One of Isr. 14
Babylon proud against the H. One of Isr. Jer 50:29
sin against the H. One of Isr. 51:5
Lord, the H. One in Isr. Ezek 39:7

holy ones

the word of the h. ones. Dan 4:17

holy people

thou art an h. people to the Lord.
Deut 7:6; 14:2, 21
thou mayest be an h. people. 26:19
establish thee an h. people. 28:9
call them, the h. people. Isa 62:12
and destroy the h. people. Dan 8:24
the power of the h. people. 12:7

holy place

in unto the h. place. Ex 28:29, 35
minister in the h. place. 43; 29:30
seeth his flesh in the h. place. 29:31
sweet incense for the h. place. 31:11
service in h. place. 35:19; 39:1, 41
all the work of the h. place. 38:24*
with unleavened bread . . . in h. place.
Lev 6:16, 26; 7:6; 10:13; 24:9
wash that in the h. place. 6:27
reconcile withal in the h. place. 30
eaten sin offering in h. place? 10:17*
not brought in within h. place. 18*
slay burnt offering in h. place. 14:13*
not at all times into the h. place. 16:2
Aaron come into the h. place. 3
atonement for the h. place. 16
atonement in the h. place. 17, 27
end of reconciling the h. place. 20
when he went into the h. place. 23
flesh with water in the h. place. 24
place whereon thou standest is h.
Josh 5:15
seen out in the h. place. 1 Ki 8:8
priests come out of the h. place. 10
2 Chr 5:11
charge of the h. place. 1 Chr 23:32
carry filthiness out of the h. place.
2 Chr 29:5
burnt offerings in the h. place. 7
up to his h. dwelling-place. 30:27
stand in the h. place according. 35:5
us a nail in his h. place. Ezra 9:8
stand in his h. place ? Ps 24:3
make glad the h. place. 46:4
as in Sinai, in the h. place. 68:17
from the place of the h. Eccl 8:10
in the high and h. place. Isa 57:15
this is the most h. place. Ezek 41:4
place is h. 42:13
not go out of the h. place. 14
it shall be an h. place for the. 45:4
the abomination stand in h. place.
Mat 24:15
blasphemous words against this h. place. Acts 6:13
hath polluted this h. place. 21:28
once into the h. place. Heb 9:12
entered every year into h. place. 25

holy places

because places are h. 2 Chr 8:11
out of thy h. places. Ps 68:35
h. places shall be defiled. Ezek 7:24
thy word toward the h. places. 21:2*
not entered into h. places. Heb 9:24

shall be **holy**

ye shall be h. men unto. Ex 22:31
toucheth altar shall be h. 29:37
toucheth them shall be h. Ex 30:29
Lev 6:18
holy, and it shall be h. Ex 30:32, 37
tabernacle, and it shall be h. 40:9
flesh thereof shall be h. Lev 6:27
ye shall be h. for I am holy. 11:44
45; 19:2; 20:26
fruit thereof shall be h. to. 19:24
the priests shall be h. unto. 21:6
they shall be h. to the Lord. 23:20
it is the jubile: it shall be h. 25:12
man giveth to Lord shall be h. 27:9
exchange thereof shall be h. 10, 33
field in the jubile shall be h. 21
the tenth shall be h. unto the. 32
Nazarite shall be h. unto. Num 6:5
doth choose he shall be h. 16:7
male shall eat it, it shall be h. 18:10
shall thy camp be h. Deut 23:14
towards east shall be h. Jer 31:40
holy portion shall be h. Ezek 45:1
then shall Jerusalem be h. Joel 3:17

holy Spirit

take not thy h. Spirit. Ps 51:11
and vexed his h. Spirit. Isa 63:10
is he that put his h. Spirit ? 11
Father give h. Spirit. Luke 11:13
h. Spirit of promise. Eph 1:13
grieve not h. Spirit of God. 4:30
given us his h. Spirit. 1 Thes 4:8

holy temple

toward thy h. temple. Ps 5:7; 138:2
the Lord is in his h. temple. 11:4
the goodness of thy h. temple. 65:4
h. temple have they defiled. 79:1
toward thy h. temple. Jonah 2:4
in unto thee, to thy h. temple. 7
Lord from his h. temple. Mi 1:2
Lord is in his h. temple. Hab 2:20
groweth to an h. temple in. Eph 2:21

holy thing

eat of the h. thing. Lev 22:10
if a man eat of the h. thing. 14
thy estimation as an h. thing. 27:23
not touch any h. thing. Num 4:15*
to them a thing most h. Ezek 48:12
therefore that h. thing. Luke 1:35

holy things

bear iniquity of h. things. Ex 28:38
ignorance in the h. things. Lev 5:15
from the h. things of Israel. 22:2
that goeth unto the h. things. 3
h. things till he be clean. 4, 6, 12
shall afterward eat of the h. things. 7
shall not profane the h. things. 15
when they eat h. things. 16
not go in to see, when h. things are.
Num 4:20
of h. things shall be his. 5:9; 18:19
shall ye pollute the h. things. 18:32
thy h. things take and. Deut 12:26
in purifying h. things. 1 Chr 23:28
the tithe of h. things. 2 Chr 31:6*
ordinances for h. things. Neh 10:33
the h. things to the Levites. 12:47
I require your h. things. Ezek 20:40
despised mine h. things. 22:8
have profaned my h. things. 26
not kept charge of my h. things. 44:8
near to any of my h. things. 13
minister about h. things. 1 Cor 9:13*

home

until her lord came h. Gen 39:16
bring these men h. slay and. 43:16*
beast not brought h. Ex 9:19
thou shalt bring her h. Deut 21:12
but he shall be free at h. one. 24:5
father's household h. to thee.
Josh 2:18*
if ye bring me h. again. Judg 11:9
way, that thou mayest go h. 19:9
Lord hath brought me h. Ruth 1:21
went unto their own h. 1 Sam 2:20
and bring their calves h. from. 6:7
men shut up their calves at h. 10
went h. to Gibeah. 10:26; 24:22
no more h. to his father's. 18:2
David sent h. to Tamar. 2 Sam 13:7
the king doth not fetch h. 14:13
Ahithophel gat him h. to. 17:23
Lebanon, two months at h. 1 Ki 5:14
h. with me and refresh. 13:7, 15

and tarry at *h.* *2 Ki* 14:10
2 Chr 25:19
bring the ark of God *h.* *1 Chr* 13:12
so David brought not ark *h.* to. 13
the army of Ephraim to go *h.*: they returned *h.* in great. *2 Chr* 25:10
Haman came *h.*, called. *Esth* 5:10
believe he will bring *h.* *Job* 39:12
she that tarried at *h.* *Ps* 68:12
good man is not at *h.* *Pr* 7:19
come *h.* at the day appointed. 20
man goeth to his long *h.* *Eccl* 12:5
that Gedaliah should carry him *h.* *Jer* 39:14
abroad the sword, *h.* there. *Lam* 1:20
neither keepeth at *h.* *Hab* 2:5
when ye brought it *h.* I. *Hag* 1:9
servant lieth at *h.* sick. *Mat* 8:6
go *h.* to thy friends. *Mark* 5:19
farewell which are at *h.* *Luke* 9:61
he cometh *h.* he calleth his. 15:6
took her to his own *h.* *John* 19:27
went away to their own *h.* 20:10
and they returned *h.* *Acts* 21:6
hunger let him eat at *h.* *1 Cor* 11:34
ask their husbands at *h.* 14:35
at *h.* in the body. *2 Cor* 5:6
learn to show piety at *h.* *1 Tim* 5:4*
chaste, keepers at *h.* *Tit* 2:5

homeborn

be to him that is *h.* *Ex* 12:49
sister whether *born* at *h.* *Lev* 18:9
Israel a servant ? is he a *h.*? *Jer* 2:14

homer

(A measure of capacity used in both liquid and dry measure. It was equal to ten ephahs or baths, or approximately 90 *gallons or* 11 *bushels. This word is frequently confused with omer, which was one-tenth of an ephah or about* 7 *pints)* [*Numb* 11:32]
h. of barley seed at fifty. *Lev* 27:16
seed of an *h.* shall yield. *Isa* 5:10
shall be after the *h.* *Ezek* 45:11
the sixth part of an ephah of an *h.* 13
of a bath, for ten baths are an *h.* 14
for an *h.* and half an *h.* *Hos* 3:2

honest

in an *h.* and good heart. *Luke* 8:15
you seven men of *h.* *Acts* 6:3*
provide things *h.* in the. *Rom* 12:17*
providing *h.* things in. *2 Cor* 8:21*
should do that which is *h.* 13:7*
whatsoever things are *h.* *Phil* 4:8*
our conversation *h.* *1 Pet* 2:12*

honestly

let us walk *h.* as in day. *Rom* 13:13
may walk *h.* toward. *1 Thes* 4:12†
things willing to live *h.* *Heb* 13:18†

honesty

life in godliness and *h.* *1 Tim* 2:2*

honey

Palestine is often referred to in the Bible as a land flowing with milk and honey, Ex 3:8. *Bees are still abundant even in the remote parts of the wilderness, where they deposit their honey in the crevices of rocks or in hollow trees. In some places the word which is translated honey may mean a decoction of the juice of the grape,* Gen 43:11; Ezek 27:17. *Honey was not to be used in sacrifices,* Lev 2:11; *but the firstfruits of honey as of other things were to be presented to the Lord, for the use of his priests.*
carry a little *h.*, spices. *Gen* 43:11
like wafers made with *h.* *Ex* 16:31
no leaven, nor any *h.* *Lev* 2:11
a land of oil olive and *h.* *Deut* 8:8
2 Ki 18:32
he made him to suck *h.* *Deut* 32:13
there was *h.* in carcase. *Judg* 14:8, 9
what sweeter than *h.*? what? 18
and there was *h.* upon. *1 Sam* 14:25
h. dropped. 26
I tasted a little *h.* 29, 43
brought *h.* and butter. *2 Sam* 17:29
take a cruse of *h.* and. *1 Ki* 14:3
brought firstfruits of *h.* *2 Chr* 31:5
see the brooks of *h.* and. *Job* 20:17
sweeter than *h.* *Ps* 19:10; 119:103
with *h.* out of the rock. 81:16
my son, eat *h.* *Pr* 24:13; 25:16
it is not good to eat much *h.* 25:27
h. and milk are under. *S of S* 4:11
my honeycomb with my *h.* 5:1
butter and *h.* shall he eat. *Isa* 7:15
for butter and *h.* shall everyone. 22
we have treasures of *h.* *Jer* 41:8
was in my mouth as *h.* for. *Ezek* 3:3
eat fine flour, *h.* and oil. 16:13 19
Judah traded in *h.* and balm. 27:17
and his meat was locusts and wild *h.*
Mat 3:4; *Mark* 1:6
in thy mouth sweet as *h.* *Rev* 10:9
see **floweth, flowing**

honeycomb

rod, and dipped it in a *h.* *1 Sam* 14:27
also than honey and *h.* *Ps* 19:10
strange woman drop as *h.* *Pr* 5:3
words are as an *h.* sweet. 16:24
eat the *h.* which is sweet. 24:13
full soul loatheth an *h.* 27:7
Thy lips drop as the *h.* *S of S* 4:11
I have eaten my *h.* with. 5:1
him a piece of an *h.* *Luke* 24:42

honour

to their assembly, my *h.* *Gen* 49:6*
will get me *h.* upon Pharaoh. *Ex* 14:17
when I have gotten me *h.* upon. 18
I will promote thee unto great *h.*
Num 22:17, 37
hath kept thee back from *h.* 24:11
shalt put some of thine *h.* 27:20
above all nations in *h.* *Deut* 26:19
shall not be for thine *h.* *Judg* 4:9
to pass, we may do thee *h.* 13:17
shall I be had in *h.* *2 Sam* 6:22
given thee riches and *h.* *1 Ki* 3:13
glory and *h.* are in his. *1 Chr* 16:27
can David say more for *h.* 17:18
both riches and *h.* come of. 29:12
in old age, full of riches and *h.* 28
not asked riches or *h.* *2 Chr* 1:11
thee riches, and wealth, and *h.* 12
had *h.* in abundance. 17:5; 18:1
nor shall it be for thy *h.* 26:18
had much riches and *h.* 32:27
of Jerusalem did him *h.* 33
the *h.* of his excellent. *Esth* 1:4
shall give to their husbands *h.* 20
h. hath been done Mordecai ? 6:3
light and gladness, joy and *h.* 8:16
sons come to *h.* he. *Job* 14:21
the enemy lay mine *h.* in. *Ps* 7:5*
crowned him with *h.* 8:5; *Heb* 2:7, 9
h. and majesty. *Ps* 21:5
loved the place where thine *h.* 26:8*
nevertheless man being in *h.* 49:12
in *h.* and understandeth not. 20
sing forth the *h.* of his name. 66:2*
thy mouth be filled with thy *h.* 71:8
h. and majesty are before him. 96:6
thou art clothed with *h.* 104:1
horn shall be exalted with *h.* 112:9
I will speak of the *h.* of thy. 145:5
h. have all his saints, praise. 149:9
left hand are riches and *h.* *Pr* 3:16
and she shall bring thee to *h.* 4:8
lest thou give thine *h.* to others. 5:9
riches and *h.* are with me. 8:18
a gracious woman retaineth *h.* 11:16
of the people is the king's *h.* 14:28*
before *h.* is humility. 15:33; 18:12
it is an *h.* for a man to cease. 20:3
followeth mercy, findeth *h.* 21:21
of the Lord are riches and *h.* 22:4
the *h.* of kings is to search. 25:2*
so *h.* is not seemly for a fool. 26:1
so is he that giveth *h.* to a fool. 8
h. shall uphold the humble. 29:23
and *h.* are her clothing. 31:25*
whom God hath given *h.* *Eccl* 6:2
that is in reputation for *h.* 10:1
h. before all nations of. *Jer* 33:9*
rewards and great *h.* *Dan* 2:6
I have built for the *h.* of my. 4:30*
mine *h.* and brightness returned. 36*
gave thy father glory and *h.* 5:18*
they shall not give the *h.* of. 11:21
father, where is mine *h.*? *Mal* 1:6
prophet is not without *h.* save in his.
Mat 13:57; *Mark* 6:4; *John* 4:44
receive not *h.* from men. *John* 5:41*
h. one of another, and seek not *h.* 44*
if I honour myself, my *h.* is. 8:54*
seek for glory and *h.* *Rom* 2:7
but *h.* to every man that. 10
lump to make one vessel to *h.* 9:21
kindly affectioned, in *h.* 12:10
render therefore *h.* to whom *h.* 13:7
we bestow more *h.* *1 Cor* 12:23, 24
by *h.* and dishonour, by. *2 Cor* 6:8*
not in any *h.* to satisfying. *Col* 2:23*
possess his vessel in *h.* *1 Thes* 4:4
the only wise God be *h.* *1 Tim* 1:17
counted worthy of double *h.* 5:17
own masters worthy of all *h.* 6:1
to whom be *h.* and power. 16
vessels, some to *h.* *2 Tim* 2:20, 21
builded, hath more *h.* *Heb* 3:3
no man taketh this *h.* to. 5:4
be found to praise, *h.* *1 Pet* 1:7
giving *h.* to the wife as to the. 3:7
from God the Father *h.* *2 Pet* 1:17
beasts give glory and *h.* *Rev* 4:9
to receive glory and *h.* 11; 5:12
h. power and might be to him. 5:13
7:12; 19:1
be glad, rejoice, and give *h.* 19:7*
bring their glory and *h.* 21:24, 26

honour, *verb*

h. thy father and thy mother.
Ex 20:12; *Deut* 5:16; *Mat* 15:4
19:19; *Mark* 7:10; 10:19
Luke 18:20; *Eph* 6:2
shalt not *h.* the person. *Lev* 19:15
thou shalt *h.* the face of the old. 32
they *h.* God and man. *Judg* 9:9
that *h.* me I will *h.* *1 Sam* 2:30
yet *h.* me now, I pray thee. 15:30
David doth *h.* thy father, that he.
2 Sam 10:3; *1 Chr* 19:3
whom the king delighteth to *h.*
Esth 6:6, 7, 9, 11
I will deliver him and *h.* *Ps* 91:15
h. Lord with thy substance. *Pr* 3:9
with their lips do *h.* me. *Isa* 29:13
the beast of the field shall *h.* 43:20
and shalt *h.* him, not doing. 58:13
I extol and *h.* the King. *Dan* 4:37
he *h.* the God . . . a god whom his fathers knew not, shall he *h.* 11:38
and *h.* not his father or. *Mat* 15:6
should *h.* Son as they *h.* *John* 5:23
but I *h.* my Father, and ye. 8:49
if I *h.* myself, my *h.* is nothing. 54
him will my Father *h.* 12:26
h. widows that are. *1 Tim* 5:3
h. all men, fear God, *h.* *1 Pet* 2:17

honourable

Shechem was more *h.* *Gen* 34:19
sent princes more *h.* *Num* 22:15
the city a man of God, and he is an *h.* man, all he saith. *1 Sam* 9:6
faithful as David, who is *h.* in. 22:14
was he not most *h.* of three ?
2 Sam 23:19; *1 Chr* 11:21
was more *h.* than the thirty, but. 23
now Naaman was *h.* with. *2 Ki* 5:1
Jabez was more *h.* than. *1 Chr* 4:9
behold, was *h.* among thirty. 11:25
had the earth, and the *h.* *Job* 22:8
king's daughters among thy *h.*
Ps 45:9
his work is *h.* and glorious. 111:3
doth take away the *h.* man. *Isa* 3:3
behave proudly against the *h.* 5
and their *h.* men are famished. 5:13
ancient and *h.* he is the head. 9:15
whose traffickers are the *h.* of. 23:8
bring into contempt all the *h.* of. 9
magnify the law and make it *h.* 42:21
thou hast been *h.* 43:4
the holy of the Lord *h.* 58:13
cast lots for her *h.* men. *Nah* 3:10
of Arimathaea an *h.* *Mark* 15:43*
lest a more *h.* man be. *Luke* 14:8
Jews stirred up the *h.* *Acts* 13:50*
also of *h.* women not a few. 17:12
ye are strong, ye are *h.* *1 Cor* 4:10
members we think less *h.* 12:23
marriage is *h.* in all. *Heb* 13:4

honoured
I will be *h.* upon Pharaoh. *Ex* 14:4
reproof shall be *h.* *Pr* 13:18
on his master shall be *h.* 27:18
nor hast thou *h.* me with. *Isa* 43:23
all that *h.* her, despise. *Lam* 1:8
of the elders were not *h.* 5:12
I praised and *h.* him that. *Dan* 4:34
who also *h.* us with. *Acts* 28:10
or one member be *h.* *1 Cor* 12:26

honourest
and *h.* thy sons above. *1 Sam* 2:29

honoureth
but he *h.* them that fear. *Ps* 15:4
is better than he that *h.* *Pr* 12:9
he that *h.* him hath mercy. 14:31
a son *h.* his father, where? *Mal* 1:6
and *h.* me with their lips. *Mat* 15:8
Mark 7:6
he that *h.* not the Son, *h.* not the. *John* 5:23
it is my Father that *h.* me, of. 8:54*

honours
honoured us with many *h.* *Acts* 28:10

hoods
I will take away the *h.* *Isa* 3:23*

hoof
there shall not an *h.* be. *Ex* 10:26
whatever parteth *h.* and. *Lev* 11:3
divide the *h.* but divideth not *h.* 4
divideth not the *h.* 5, 6; *Deut* 14:7
the swine, though he divide the *h.*
Lev 11:7, 26; *Deut* 14:6, 8

hoofs
were the horse *h.* broken. *Judg* 5:22
than an ox with *h.* *Ps* 69:31
horses' *h.* shall be counted. *Isa* 5:28
of the stamping of the *h.* *Jer* 47:3
with *h.* of horses shall. *Ezek* 26:11
nor shall the *h.* of beasts. 32:13
I will make thy *h.* brass. *Mi* 4:13

hook
I will put my *h.* in thy nose.
2 Ki 19:28; *Isa* 37:29
thou draw leviathan with an *h.*?
Job 41:1, 2*
go, and cast an *h.* and. *Mat* 17:27

hooks
their *h.* shall be of gold. *Ex* 26:32
37; 36:36
the *h.* of the pillars shall be. 27:10
11, 17; 38:10, 11, 12, 17, 19
their spears into pruning *h.* *Isa* 2:4
Mi 4:3
off the sprigs with pruning *h.* 18:5
but I will put *h.* *Ezek* 29:4; 38:4
and within were *h.*, an hand. 40:43
beat your pruning *h.* into. *Joel* 3:10
take you away with *h.* *Amos* 4:2

hope
should say, I have *h.*, if. *Ruth* 1:12
there is *h.* in Israel. *Ezra* 10:2
fear, confidence, thy *h.*? *Job* 4:6
poor hath *h.*, and iniquity. 5:16
my days are spent without *h.* 7:6
hypocrite's *h.* shall perish. 8:13, 14*
be secure, because there is *h.* 11:18
their *h.* shall be as the giving up. 20
for there is *h.* of a tree if it. 14:7
thou destroyest the *h.* of man. 19
what is *h.* of hypocrite though? 27:8
the *h.* of him is in vain. 41:9
might set their *h.* in. *Ps* 78:7
happy is he whose *h.* is in. 146:5
the *h.* of the righteous. *Pr* 10:28
h. of unjust men perisheth. 11:7
h. deferred maketh the. 13:12
but the righteous hath *h.* 14:32
thy son while there is *h.* 19:18
more *h.* of a fool than. 26:12; 29:20
to living, there is *h.* *Eccl* 9:4
is no *h.* *Isa* 57:10; *Jer* 2:25; 18:12
O the *h.* of Israel. *Jer* 14:8; 17:13
blessed is the man whose *h.* 17:7*
there is *h.* in the end, saith. 31:17
even the Lord, the *h.* of their. 50:7
therefore have I *h.* *Lam* 3:21
the dust, if so be there may be *h.* 29
she saw that her *h.* was. *Ezek* 19:5
our bones dried, our *h.* lost. 37:11
Achor for a door of *h.* *Hos* 2:15
the Lord will be the *h.* *Joel* 3:16*
hold ye prisoners of *h.* *Zech* 9:12
the *h.* of their gains. *Acts* 16:19
of the *h.* and resurrection of. 23:6
I have *h.* toward God which. 24:15
now I am judged for the *h.* 26:6
for which *h.'s* sake, I am accused. 7
h. that we should be saved. 27:20
for *h.* of Israel I am bound. 28:20
experience; experience, *h.* *Rom* 5:4
h. maketh not ashamed, because. 5
saved by *h.*: but *h.* seen is not *h.* 8:24
through patience might have *h.* 15:4
that ye may abound in *h.* through. 13
be partaker of his *h.* *1 Cor* 9:10
now abideth faith, *h.*, charity. 13:13
this life only we have *h.* in. 15:19
h. of you is stedfast. *2 Cor* 1:7
seeing that we have such *h.* 3:12
having *h.* when your faith is. 10:15
we thro' the Spirit wait for *h.* *Gal* 5:5
may know what is the *h.* *Eph* 1:18
having no *h.* and without God. 2:12
even as ye are called in one *h.* 4:4
for the *h.* laid up for you. *Col* 1:5
be not moved away from the *h.* 23
which is Christ in you, the *h.* of. 27
your patience of *h.* in. *1 Thes* 1:3
for what is our *h.* and joy? 2:19
even as others who have no *h.* 4:13
and for an helmet the *h.* of. 5:8
hath given us good *h.* *2 Thes* 2:16
Jesus, who is our *h.* *1 Tim* 1:1
looking for that blessed *h.* *Tit* 2:13
made heirs according to the *h.* 3:7
rejoicing of the *h.* firm to. *Heb* 3:6
to the full assurance of *h.* 6:11
who have fled to lay hold on *h.* 18
which *h.* we have as an anchor of. 19
bringing in of a better *h.* did. 7:19
us again to a lively *h.* *1 Pet* 1:3
that your faith and *h.* might be. 21
asketh a reason of the *h.* that. 3:15
man that hath this *h.* *1 John* 3:3

hope, *verb*
strength, that I should *h.*? *Job* 6:11*
didst make me *h.* when. *Ps* 22:9*
of courage, all ye that *h.* in. 31:24
h. in his mercy. 33:18; 147:11
on us, according as we *h.* in. 33:22
in thee, O Lord, do I *h.* 38:15
h. thou in God. 42:5, 11; 43:5
but I will *h.* continually. 71:14
thou hast caused me to *h.* 119:49
I *h.* in thy word. 81, 114; 130:5
let Israel *h.* in Lord. 130:7; 131:3
in the pit cannot *h.* for. *Isa* 38:18
therefore will I *h.* in him. *Lam* 3:24
good that a man should both *h.* 26
have made others to *h.* *Ezek* 13:6
if ye lend to them of whom ye *h.*
Luke 6:34
promise our tribes *h.* to. *Acts* 26:7
why doth he *h.* for? *Rom* 8:24
if we *h.* for that we see not. 25
him I *h.* to send presently. *Phil* 2:23
be sober, and *h.* to the. *1 Pet* 1:13

in **hope**
my flesh shall rest in *h.* *Ps* 16:9*
Acts 2:26
against hope believed *in h.* *Rom* 4:18
and rejoice *in h.* of the glory. 5:2
hath subjected the same *in h.* 8:20
rejoicing *in h.* patient in. 12:12
may abound *in h.* through. 15:13
ploweth *in h.*; that thresheth *in h.*
1 Cor 9:10
in h. of eternal life which. *Tit* 1:2

my **hope**
is now *my h.*? as for *my h.* *Job* 17:15
and *my h.* hath he removed. 19:10
if I have made gold *my h.* or. 31:24
what wait I for? *my h.* is. *Ps* 39:7
for thou art *my h.* O Lord God. 71:5
Jer 17:17
not be ashamed of *my h.* *Ps* 119:116
and *my h.* is perished. *Lam* 3:18*
according to *my h.* that in. *Phil* 1:20

hoped
enemies of the Jews *h.* *Esth* 9:1
confounded because they had *h.*
Job 6:20
have *h.* in thy judgements. *Ps* 119:43
I have *h.* in thy word. 74, 147
I have *h.* for thy salvation. 166
in vain is salvation *h.* for. *Jer* 3:23
he *h.* to have seen some. *Luke* 23:8
h. money should have. *Acts* 24:26
they did, not as we *h.* *2 Cor* 8:5
substance of things *h.* for. *Heb* 11:1

hopeth
charity *h.* all things. *1 Cor* 13:7

Hophni
two sons of Eli, *H.* *1 Sam* 1:3; 4:4
H. and Phinehas shall both. 2:34
H. and Phinehas were slain. 4:11, 17

hoping
do good, and lend, *h.* *Luke* 6:35*
I write, *h.* to come. *1 Tim* 3:14

Hor, *see* **mount**

Horeb
came to the mountain of God, even to *H.* *Ex* 3:1; *1 Ki* 19:8
before thee on the rock in *H.* *Ex* 17:6
of ornaments by mount *H.* 33:6
spake to us in *H.* *Deut* 1:6; 4:15
stoodest before the Lord in *H.* 4:10
a covenant with us in *H.* 5:2; 29:1
also in *H.* ye provoked the. 9:8
desiredst of the Lord in *H.* 18:16
two tables which Moses put in ark at *H.* *1 Ki* 8:9; *2 Chr* 5:10
they made a calf in *H.* *Ps* 106:19
commanded unto him in *H.* *Mal* 4:4

Hor-hagidgad
encamped at *H.* *Num* 33:32
went from *H.* 33

Hormah
discomfited them to *H.* *Num* 14:45
called the name of place *H.* 21:3
you in Seir, even unto *H.* *Deut* 1:44
of Judah, Eltolad, *H.* *Josh* 15:30
out of Judah, Bethul, *H.* 19:4
the city was called *H.* *Judg* 1:17
them that were in *H.* *1 Sam* 30:30
Shimei's sons dwelt at *H.* *1 Chr* 4:30

horn
This word is often used metaphorically to signify strength and honour, because horns are the chief weapons and ornaments of the animals which possess them; hence they are also used as a type of victory. In the sense of honour, the word stands both for the abstract, Lam 2:3; *and so for supreme authority, or for the concrete,* Dan 7:8, *whence it comes to mean king or kingdom.*

wont to push with his *h.* *Ex* 21:29
Hannah said, mine *h.* is. *1 Sam* 2:1
and he shall exalt the *h.* of. 10
fill thine *h.* with oil, go, I will. 16:1
Samuel took the *h.* of oil. 13
the *h.* of my salvation. *2 Sam* 22:3
Ps 18:2
priest took an *h.* of oil. *1 Ki* 1:39
God, to lift up the *h.* *1 Chr* 25:5
I have defiled my *h.* in. *Job* 16:15
lift not up the *h.* *Ps* 75:4, 5
and in thy favour our *h.* 89:17
and in my name shall his *h.* 24
h. shalt thou exalt like *h.* 92:10
his *h.* shall be exalted with. 112:9
make the *h.* of David to. 132:17
he also exalteth the *h.* of. 148:14
h. of Moab is cut off. *Jer* 48:25
cut off all the *h.* of Israel. *Lam* 2:3
he hath set up the *h.* of thine. 17
I will cause the *h.* of. *Ezek* 29:21
little *h.*; in this *h.* *Dan* 7:8, 20
the great words which the *h.* 11
the same *h.* made war with the. 21
goat had a notable *h.* between. 8:5
he was strong, the great *h.* 8
of them came forth a little *h.* 9
the great *h.* that is between his. 21
lift up their *h.* over the. *Zech* 1:21
hath raised up an *h.* of. *Luke* 1:69

hornet
(*The large species of wasp, whose sting is very severe*)

Lord will send the *h*. *Deut* 7:20
I sent the *h*. before you. *Josh* 24:12

hornets

I will send *h*. before thee. *Ex* 23:28

horns

in a thicket by his *h*. *Gen* 22:13
h. of it on the four corners, his *h*.
Ex 27:2; 30:2; 37:25; 38:2
put of the blood on the *h*. 29:12
Lev 4:7, 18, 25, 30, 34; 8:15; 9:9
16:18
shalt overlay the *h*. *Ex* 30:3; 37:26
make an atonement on *h*. of. 30:10
his *h*. are like the *h*. *Deut* 33:17
Joab caught hold on *h*. of. *1 Ki* 2:28
Zedekiah made *h*. of iron. 22:11
2 Chr 18:10
heard me from the *h*. of. *Ps* 22:21
than a bullock that hath *h*. 69:31
h. of the wicked will I cut off, but the
h. of the righteous shall. 75:10
bind the sacrifice to the *h*. 118:27
brought for a present *h*. *Ezek* 27:15
all the diseased with your *h*. 34:21
the altar and upward shall be four *h*.
43:15
fourth beast had ten *h*. *Dan* 7:7, 20
I considered the *h*., three *h*. were. 8
the ten *h*. are ten kings that shall. 24
ram had two *h*.: the two *h*. were. 8:3
came to the ram which had two *h*. 6
the ram, and brake his two *h*. 7
two *h*. are the kings of Media. 20
have we not taken *h*. by. *Amos* 6:13
for I will make thy *h*. iron. *Mi* 4:13
he had *h*. coming out of. *Hab* 3:4
I saw, and behold, four *h*. *Zech* 1:18
the *h*. which have scattered. 19, 21
are come to cast out the *h*. 21
a Lamb having seven *h*. *Rev* 5:6
having seven heads and ten *h*. 12:3
beast having ten *h*. and on his *h*. 13:1
another beast had two *h*. like a. 11
coloured beast, having ten *h*. 17:3
hath the seven heads and ten *h*. 7
the ten *h*. thou sawest are. 12, 16
see **rams**

Horonaim

in the way of *H*. they shall. *Isa* 15:5
crying shall be from *H*. *Jer* 48:3
in going down of *H*. the enemies. 5
from Zoar to *H*. they uttered. 34

Horonite, *see* Sanballat

horrible

wicked he shall rain a *h*. *Ps* 11:6*
me up also out of a *h*. pit. 40:2
a *h*. thing is committed. *Jer* 5:30
virgin of Israel hath done a *h*. 18:13
seen in the prophets a *h*. 23:14
I have seen a *h*. thing in. *Hos* 6:10

horribly

be *h*. afraid, O ye heavens. *Jer* 2:12
their kings shall be *h*. *Ezek* 32:10

horror

a *h*. of great darkness. *Gen* 15:12
h. hath overwhelmed me. *Ps* 55:5
h. hath taken hold on me. 119:53*
h. shall cover them, and. *Ezek* 7:18

horse

The most striking feature of the notices of this animal in the Bible is that it invariably means a war-horse. The principal use of the horse in war was in the chariot, and because of the hilly nature of Palestine only certain localities allowed the use of chariots. The possession of a large number of horses, or their breeding, was forbidden in early times, Deut 17:16, *and was held to apply to later periods as well. David first gathered a force of cavalry or chariots,* 2 Sam 8:4, *but Solomon was the first to have them in great numbers,* 1 Ki 4:26. *They were not shod, and those with naturally hard hoofs were greatly desired,* Isa 5:28. *Horses and chariots were used in idolatrous processions,* 2 Ki 23:11.

adder that biteth the *h*. heels.
Gen 49:17
the *h*. and rider hath he. *Ex* 15:21
were *h*. hoofs broken. *Judg* 5:22
a *h*. for 150 shekels. *1 Ki* 10:29
2 Chr 1:17
Ben-hadad king escaped on *h*. with.
1 Ki 20:20
like the army lost, *h*. for *h*. 25
let *h*. the king rideth upon. *Esth* 6:8
let this *h*. be delivered to one. 9
take the apparel and *h*. as thou. 10
Haman the apparel and the *h*. 11
she scorneth the *h*. *Job* 39:18
hast thou given *h*. strength? 19
be ye not as the *h*. or as. *Ps* 32:9
h. is a vain thing for safety. 33:17
the chariot and *h*. are cast. 76:6
not in the strength of the *h*. 147:10
the *h*. is prepared against. *Pr* 21:31
a whip for the *h*. a rod for the. 26:3
forth the chariot and *h*. *Isa* 43:17
through the deep, as a *h*. 63:13
as the *h*. rusheth into. *Jer* 8:6
will I break in pieces the *h*. 51:21
nor shall he that rideth *h*. *Amos* 2:15
a man riding upon a red *h*. *Zech* 1:8
and I will cut off the *h*. from. 9:10
made them as his goodly *h*. 10:3
I will smite every *h*. with. 12:4
shall be the plague of the *h*. 14:15
behold, a white *h*. *Rev* 6:2; 19:11
h. that was red. 6:4
a black *h*. 5
behold, a pale *h*. 8
blood came even to the *h*. 14:20
against him that sat on the *h*. 19:19
sword of him that sat on the *h*. 21

horseback

there went one on *h*. to. *2 Ki* 9:18
then he sent out a second on *h*. 19
and bring him on *h*. *Esth* 6:9
Haman brought him on *h*. 11
sent letters by posts on *h* 8:10

horse gate

to entering of *h*. *gate*. *2 Chr* 23:15
above *h*. *gate* repaired. *Neh* 3:28
corner of the *h*. *gate*. *Jer* 31:40

horseleech

the *h*. hath two daughters. *Pr* 30:15

horseman

Joram said, take an *h*. *2 Ki* 9:17
h. lifteth up the bright. *Nah* 3:3

horsemen

Joseph chariots and *h*. *Gen* 50:9
the *h*. of Pharaoh pursued. *Ex* 14:9
me honour on Pharaoh and his *h*. 17
Pharaoh and *h*. went into sea. 15:19
Josh 24:6
your sons to be his *h*. *1 Sam* 8:11
Philistines gathered 6000 *h*. 13:5
lo, the *h*. followed hard. *2 Sam* 1:6
and David took 700 *h*. 8:4
David slew 40,000 *h*., smote. 10:18
prepared chariots and *h*. *1 Ki* 1:5
Solomon had 12,000 *h*. 4:26; 10:26
store for his chariots, and cities for
his *h*. 9:19, 22; *2 Chr* 8:6, 9
escaped on an horse with his *h*. 20:20
chariots of Israel and *h*. *2 Ki* 2:12
leave to Jehoahaz but fifty *h*. 13:7
Joash said, O my father, the *h*. 14
in Egypt for chariots and *h*. 18:24
came up with 60,000 *h*. *2 Chr* 12:3
a huge host with many *h*. 16:8
ashamed to require *h*. *Ezra* 8:22
sent captains and *h*. with. *Neh* 2:9
chariot with a couple of *h*. *Isa* 21:7, 9
h. shall set themselves in array. 22:7
not bruise them with his *h*. 28:28*
and trust in *h*. because they. 31:1
put thy trust on Egypt for *h*. 36:9
flee for the noise of the *h*. *Jer* 4:29
get up, ye *h*. and stand with. 46:4
all of them *h*. riding. *Ezek* 23:6, 12
against Tyrus with *h*. 26:7
shake at the noise of the *h*. 10
Togarmah traded in fairs with *h*.
27:14*
thee forth, horses and *h*. 38:4
north shall come with *h*. *Dan* 11:40

I will not save them by horses, nor by
h. *Hos* 1:7
as *h*. so shall they run. *Joel* 2:4
h. shall spread themselves, and their
h. shall come from far. *Hab* 1:8
make ready *h*. threescore. *Acts* 23:23
morrow they left the *h*. to go. 32
number of the army of *h*. *Rev* 9:16

horses

bread in exchange for *h*. *Gen* 47:17
hand of Lord is upon the *h*. *Ex* 9:3
h. to himself, to the end that he
should multiply *h*. *Deut* 17:16
also and straw for the *h*. *1 Ki* 4:28
they brought *h*. and mules. 10:25
2 Chr 9:24
Solomon had *h*. out of Egypt.
1 Ki 10:28; *2 Chr* 1:16, 17; 9:28
find grass to save the *h*. *1 Ki* 18:5
and my *h*. are as thy *h*. 22:4
2 Ki 3:7
there appeared *h*. of fire. *2 Ki* 2:11
Naaman came with his *h*. and. 5:9
they left their *h*. and fled for. 7:7
but *h*. tied. 10
some take five of the *h*. 13
blood was sprinkled on the *h*. 9:33
brought Amaziah on *h*. 14:20
2 Chr 25:28
I will deliver thee 2000 *h*.
2 Ki 18:23; *Isa* 36:8
Josiah took away the *h*. *2 Ki* 23:11
h. were 736. *Ezra* 2:66; *Neh* 7:68
I have seen servants on *h*. *Eccl* 10:7
land is also full of *h*. *Isa* 2:7
their *h*.' hoofs shall be counted. 5:28
no, for we will flee upon *h*. 30:16
and stay on *h*. and trust in. 31:1
and their *h*. are flesh, and not. 3
his *h*. are swifter than. *Jer* 4:13
as fed *h*. in the morning. 5:8
they ride on *h*. set in array. 6:23
snorting of his *h*. was heard. 8:16
canst thou contend with *h*.? 12:5
harness the *h*. and get up, ye. 46:4
stamping of the hoofs of his *h*. 47:3
and they shall ride upon *h*. 50:42
cause the *h*. to come up as. 51:27
they might give him *h*. *Ezek* 17:15
horsemen riding on *h*. 23:6, 12
issue is like the issue of *h*. 20
all of them riding on *h*. 23; 38:15
the abundance of his *h*. 26:10
traded in thy fairs with *h*. 27:14
forth, and all thy army, *h*. 38:4
nor by battle, by *h*. *Hos* 1:7
not save, we will not ride on *h*. 14:3
as the appearance of *h*. *Joel* 2:4
have taken away your *h*. *Amos* 4:10
shall *h*. run upon the rock? 6:12
that I will cut off thy *h*. *Mi* 5:10
their *h*. also are swifter. *Hab* 1:8
that thou didst ride on thy *h*. 3:8
walk through the sea with thy *h*. 15
I will overthrow the *h*. *Hag* 2:22
him there were red *h*. *Zech* 1:8
chariot red *h*., in the second black *h*.
6:2
white *h*., in fourth chariot bay *h*. 3
h. go forth into the north country. 6
the riders on *h*. shall be. 10:5
on bells of *h*. HOLINESS UNTO
THE LORD. 14:20
we put bits in the *h*.' mouths. *Jas* 3:3
locusts were like *h*. *Rev* 9:7
h., the heads of *h*. as heads of. 17
buyeth the merchandise of *h*. 18:13
followed him upon white *h*. 19:14
may eat flesh of kings and *h*. 18
see **chariots**

hosanna

An Hebrew *word, meaning*, Save, we pray. *It is taken from the* 118*th Psalm, and was the cry of the multitudes as they thronged in our Lord's triumphal procession into Jerusalem*, Mat 21:9, 15; Mark 11:9, 10; John 12:13.

Hosea

(*One of the Minor Prophets. The same name as* **Hoshea**)

hosen

men were bound in their *h*. *Dan* 3:21

Hoshea

H. son of Nun. Deut 32:44
H. made a conspiracy. 2 Ki 15:30
H. son of Elah began to reign. 17:1
H. became Assyria's servant. 3
ninth year of H. Samaria. 6; 18:10
ruler of Ephraim was H. 1 Chr 27:20
H. sealed the covenant. Neh 10:23

hospitality

This virtue has always been very much esteemed by civilized peoples. The Jewish laws with regard to strangers are framed in accordance with the spirit of hospitality, Lev 19:33, 34, etc.; *and before the giving of the law there were many instances of the entertaining of strangers,* Gen 18:2, 3; Heb 13:2. *It was more necessary in those times of difficult travel and few inns, but the spirit of modern hospitality is the same.*

In Apostolic times the virtue was strongly enjoined on the followers of Christ, although the higher civilization and larger population made it less of a necessity than in patriarchal times.

distributing, given to h. Rom 12:13
1 Tim 3:2
but a lover of h. a lover. Tit 1:8
use h. one to another. 1 Pet 4:9

host

two pence, gave them to h. Luke 10:35
Gaius mine h. and of. Rom 16:23

host

[1] *The word very frequently means camp or army. In these passages, easily discovered by the context, the Revisions use these other words.* [2] *It means in some cases merely a vast number.*

earth was finished, and all h. Gen 2:1
chief captain of his h. 21:22, 32
he said, This is God's h. 32:2
honoured on all his h. Ex 14:4, 17
h. of Egyptians through pillar of fire and of cloud, and troubled h. 24
the waters covered all the h. 28
dew lay round about the h. 16:13
h. and those that were numbered. Num 2:4, 6, 8, 11, 13, 15, 19, 21, 23
all that entered into h. Num 4:3*
over the h. of Judah. 10:14
the h. of Issachar. 15
over h. of Zebulun. 16
over h. of Reuben. 18
over h. of Simeon. 19
wroth with the officers of h. 31:14
the officers of the h. came near. 48
war were wasted from h. Deut 2:14
to destroy them from among h. 15
when the h. goeth forth against. 23:9
pass through the h. and. Josh 1:11
the officers went through the h. 3:2
as captain of the h. of the Lord. 5:14
came again to Joshua to the h. 18:9
the captain of whose h. Judg 4:2
and all the h. of Sisera fell on. 16
the h. of Midian was beneath. 7:8
arise, get thee down unto the h. 9, 10
cake of bread tumbled into the h. 13
and all the h. ran, and cried 21
up and smote the h., the h. 8:11
pursued and discomfited all the h. 12
Saul came into the h. 1 Sam 11:11
there was trembling in the h. 14:15
the noise of the h. went on and. 19
the captain of Saul's h. was Abner. 50
David came as the h. was. 17:20
when Saul saw the h. of the. 28:5
deliver the h. of Israel to. 19
coming in with me in the h. is. 29:6
Lord shall smite the h. 2 Sam 5:24
David had smitten all the h. of Hadadezer. 8:9; 1 Chr 18:9
David smote Shobach captain of their h. 2 Sam 10:18; 1 Chr 19:18
Amasa captain of h. 2 Sam 17:25
if thou be not captain of h. 19:13
Joab was over all the h. 20:23
1 Chr 18:15
these three brake through the h. 2 Sam 23:16; 1 Chr 11:18
son of Ner captain of h. of Israel and Amasa captain of h. 1 Ki 2:32
Benaiah over the h. 35, 4:4
Omri captain of the h., king. 16:16
gathered all his h. together. 20:1
hand and carry me out of h. 22:34
was no water for the h. 2 Ki 3:9
spoken for to captain of the h.? 4:13
sent he horses and great h. 6:14
Ben-hadad gathered his h. and. 24
come and let us fall unto the h. 7:4
h. to hear the noise of a great h. 6
behold the captains of the h. 9:5
Sennacherib sent a great h. 18:17
Nebuchadnezzar came and his h. 25:1
scribe of the h. 19; Jer 52:25
their fathers over the h. 1 Chr 9:19
was a great h. like the h. 12:22
of all the captains of the h. 27:3
Zerah came with an h. 2 Chr 14:9
not relied, therefore is the h. 16:7
Ethiopians and Lubims a huge h.? 8
and carry me out of the h. 18:33
delivered a great h. into. 24:24
Uzziah had an h. of fighting. 26:11
Oded went out before the h. 28:9
though an h. should encamp. Ps 27:3
all h. of them made by breath. 33:6
by the multitude of an h. 16
Pharaoh and h. in Red sea. 136:15
hosts mustereth the h. of. Isa 13:4
Lord shall punish the h. of. 24:21
that bringeth out their h. 40:26
and all their h. have I. 45:12
destroy ye utterly all her h. Jer 51:3
speech, as noise of an h. Ezek 1:24
cast down some of the h. Dan 8:10
himself to the prince of the h. 11
an h. was given him against the. 12
to give the h. to be trodden. 13
the captivity of this h. shall. Ob 20
multitude of heavenly h. Luke 2:13
see **heaven**

hostages

all the gold and silver and h. and. 2 Ki 14:14; 2 Chr 25:24

hosts

the h. of Lord went out. Ex 12:41
of Canaan and all their h. Josh 10:5
11:4
Zalmunna with their h. Judg 8:10
sent the captains of the h. 1 Ki 15:20
the Lord, all ye his h. Ps 103:21
O God, go forth with h.? 108:11
all his angels, all his h. 148:2
a goodly heritage of the h. Jer 3:19
see **God, Lord**

hot

when the sun waxed h. Ex 16:21
there is a h. burning. Lev 13:24
afraid of anger and h. Deut 9:19
pursue, while his heart is h. 19:6
this our bread we took h. Josh 9:12
Lord was h. against Israel, and he. Judg 2:14*, 20*; 3:8*; 10:7*
not thine anger be h. against. 6:39*
time sun be h., ye. 1 Sam 11:9
put h. bread in day when it. 21:6
be opened till the sun be h. Neh 7:3
when it is h. they are. Job 6:17
neither chasten in thy h. Ps 6:1; 38:1
my heart was h. within me. 39:3
he gave their flocks to h. 78:48
can one go upon h. coals ? Pr 6:28
brass of it may be h. Ezek 24:11
furnace was exceeding h. Dan 3:22
they are all h. as an oven. Hos 7:7
seared with a h. iron. 1 Tim 4:2
thou art neither cold nor h.: I would thou wert cold or h. Rev 3:15, 16
see **wax, verb**

hotly

thou hast so h. pursued. Gen 31:36

hottest

Uriah in forefront of h. 2 Sam 11:15

hough

Lord said, thou shalt h. Josh 11:6

houghed

h. their horses, burnt. Josh 11:9
and David h. all the. 2 Sam 8:4

hour

(The day was not divided into hours by the ancient Hebrews. Only the natural divisions of morning, noon, and evening were noted. After the Exile there was a somewhat clearer division which, it is supposed, was learned from the Babylonians. The length of the hour was dependent usually upon the season, as people commonly reckoned it as the twelfth part of the natural day, from sunrise to sunset, and this would differ according to season)

was astonied for one h. Dan 4:19*
made whole from that h. Mat 9:22
made whole from that very h. 15:28
was cured from that very h. 17:18
about the third h. and saw. 20:3
about the sixth and ninth h. 5
the eleventh h. 6
have wrought but one h. 12
that h. knoweth no man. 24:36, 42
Mark 13:32
such an h. as ye think not. Mat 24:44, 50; Luke 12:40, 46
neither the day nor the h. Mat 25:13
could ye not watch one h.? 26:40
Mark 14:37
the h. is at hand, the. Mat 26:45
h. was darkness over land to ninth h. 27:45; Mark 15:33; Luke 23:44
about the ninth h. Jesus cried. Mat 27:46; Mark 15:34
be given you in that h. Mark 13:11
that if possible the h. might. 14:35
it was the third h. and they. 15:25
in that h. Jesus rejoiced. Luke 10:21
had known what h. the thief. 12:39
and when the h. was come. 22:14
but this is your h. and the power. 53
space of one h. after another. 59
for it was about tenth h. John 1:39
Jesus saith, Woman, mine h. is. 2:4
it was about the sixth h. 4:6; 19:14
believe me, the h. cometh. 4:21, 23
he the h. when he began to amend, yesterday at seventh h. 52
h. is coming, and. 5:25, 28; 16:32
his h. was not yet come. 7:30; 8:20
the h. is come, Son. 12:23; 17:1
Father, save me from this h.: but for this cause came I to this h. 12:27
when Jesus knew that his h. 13:1
hath sorrow, because her h. 16:21
from that h. that disciple. 19:27
seeing it is third h. of. Acts 2:15
h. of prayer being the ninth h. 3:1
about the ninth h. an angel. 10:3
up to pray about the sixth h. 9
ago I was fasting until this h. 30
make ready at the third h. of. 23:23
to this present h. both. 1 Cor 4:11
conscience of idol unto this h. 8:7
stand we in jeopardy every h.? 15:30
gave place, no not for an h. Gal 2:5
not know what h. I will. Rev 3:3
I will keep thee from the h. of. 10
silence about space of half an h. 8:1
which were prepared for an h. 9:15
the h. of his judgement is come. 14:7
receive power as kings one h. 17:12
for in one h. is thy judgement. 18:10
in one h. so great riches come. 17
that great city in one h. she is. 19

same **hour**

the same h. be cast. Dan 3:6, 15
the same h. was the thing. 4:33
the same h. came forth fingers. 5:5
was healed the same h. Mat 8:13
it shall be given you the same h. 10:19; Luke 12:12
the same h. said Jesus. Mat 26:55
that same h. cured many. Luke 7:21
scribes same h. sought to lay. 20:19
they rose up the same h. 24:33
that it was at the same h. John 4:53
he came out the same h. Acts 16:18
he took them same h. of night. 33

the same h. I looked up. Acts 22:13
the same h. was there a. Rev 11:13

hours

are there not twelve h.? John 11:9
about space of three h. Acts 5:7
about two h., Great is Diana. 19:34

house

[1] *A place to dwell in,* Gen 19:3; *hence used also of the body as the dwelling place of the soul of man.* 2 Cor 5:1. [2] *The household, or persons dwelling in the house,* Acts 10:2; Heb 11:7. [3] *Kindred or lineage,* 2 Sam 7:18; Luke 1:27. [4] *Wealth, riches, or estates,* Mat 23:14. [5] *The grave,* Job 30:23; Isa 14:18. [6] *The house of God, the building erected for the worship of God, in which his spirit is most frequently considered as dwelling,* Judg 18:31; 2 Chr 5:14; 1 Tim 3:15.

Sodom compassed the h. Gen 19:4
to the h. of my master's. 24:27
I have prepared the h. 31
go to the h. of Bethuel, thy. 28:2
Lord blessed the Egyptian's h. 39:5
the Egyptians and the h. of. 45:2
frogs shall come into h. of. Ex 8:3
a lamb according to the h. of. 12:3*
not an h. where there was not. 30
carry of the flesh out of the h. 46
came out from Egypt, out of h. of bondage. 13:3, 14; Deut 5:6; 6:12
shalt not covet neighbour's h.
Ex 20:17; Deut 5:21
command they empty h. Lev 14:36
priest shall go out of the h. 38
break down h. and mortar of h. 45
he that goeth into the h. shall. 46
he shall take to cleanse the h. 49
h. sold in walled city, not go. 25:30
if she vowed in her husband's h.
Num 30:10
redeemed you out of h. Deut 7:8
of the land of Egypt, from the h. of.
8:14; 13:5, 10; Josh 24:17
Judg 6:8; Jer 34:13; Mi 6:4
h. of him that hath his shoe loosed.
Deut 25:10
for her h. was upon the. Josh 2:15
neither shewed kindness to h. of.
Judg 8:35
h. of Millo made Abimelech. 9:6
let fire come from h. of Millo. 20
Ammon fought against the h. 10:9
may feel pillars whereon h. 16:26
the h. was full of men. 27
h. fell on the lords. 30
Micah had an h. of gods. 17:5
and they came unto the h. 18:13
no man receiveth me to h. 19:18
Belial beset the h. round. 22; 20:5
sworn unto h. of Eli. 1 Sam 3:14
brought the ark into the h. 5:2
and brought the ark into the h. 7:1
thee, where the seer's h. is. 9:18
Nabal was churlish, and of h. 25:3
certainly make my lord a sure h. 28
war between h. of Saul and h. of David. 2 Sam 3:1
shew kindness to the h. of Saul. 8
let there not fail from the h. of. 29
came to h. of Ish-bosheth, who. 4:5
lame shall not come into the h. 5:8
h. of Obed-edom, David brought ark from his h. 6:11,12; 1 Chr 13:14
I have not dwelt in any h.
2 Sam 7:6; 1 Chr 17:5
he will make thee an h. 2 Sam 7:11
to bless the h. of thy servant. 29
1 Chr 17:27
is left of the h. of Saul? 2 Sam 9:1
I gave thee thy master's h. 12:8
now to thy brother Amnon's h. 13:7
a man of the family of the h. 16:5
who made me an h. as. 1 Ki 2:24
which he spake concerning the h. 27
and the whole h. he overlaid. 6:22
so Solomon finished the h. 9:25
Pharaoh, who gave him an h. 11:18
made an h. of his high places. 12:31
bring an evil on the h. of. 14:10, 14
Baasha smote all the h. of. 15:29
Zimri slew all the h. of. 1 Ki 16:11
and he, and her h. did eat. 17:15
I will make thy h. like the h. 21:22
cry to king for her h. and. 2 Ki 8:3
as did the h. of Ahab. 18, 27
2 Chr 21:6; 22:4
for the whole h. of Ahab. 2 Ki 9:8
best, fight for your master's h. 10:3
h. of Baal was full from one end. 21
made the h. of Baal a draught h. 27
for all that was laid out for h. 12:12
h. of his precious things, all the h. of his armour. 20:13; Isa 39:2
h. of which I said, My. 2 Ki 23:27
every great man's h. he burnt. 25:9
of Salma; Ataroth the h. 1 Chr 2:54*
sons, the h. of Asuppim. 26:15*
glory of Lord filled the h. 2 Chr 7:1
Ezek 43:4, 5
chosen this place to myself for h. of.
2 Chr 7:12
so the h. of Ahaziah had no. 22:9
but against the h. wherewith. 35:21
that we went to the h. of. Ezra 5:8
let the h. be builded, the place. 6:3
and for the h. which I. Neh 2:8
gather all virgins to the h. Esth 2:3
king did give h. of Haman. 8:1, 7
drinking wine in eldest brother's h.
Job 1:13, 18
and smote the corners of the h. 19
hath taken away a h. which. 20:19
for ye say, Where is the h. of? 21:28
and to the h. appointed for. 30:23
shouldest know paths to the h. 38:20
whose h. I have made the. 39:6
my rock be for a h. of. Ps 31:2
the sparrow hath found an h. 84:3
stork, fir trees are her h. 104:17
her h. inclineth to death. Pr 2:18
young man went way to her h. 7:8
her feet abide not in her h. 11
her h. is the way to hell. 27
wisdom hath builded her h. 9:1
but the h. of the righteous shall. 12:7
the h. of the wicked shall be. 14:11
the Lord will destroy the h. of. 15:25
than an h. full of sacrifices. 17:1
h. and riches are inheritance. 19:14
dwell in corner of h. top. 21:9; 25:24
wisely considereth the h. 21:12
through wisdom is an h. built. 24:3
foot from thy neighbour's h. 25:17
nor go into brother's h. in day. 27:10
to go to h. of mourning, than h. of feasting. Eccl 7:2
through idleness of hands h. 10:18
when the keepers of the h. 12:3
the beams of our h. are. S of S 1:17
me to the banqueting h. his. 2:4
brought him into my mother's h. 3:4
bring thee into my mother's h. 8:2
woe to them that join h. to h., field.
Isa 5:8
the h. was filled with smoke. 6:4
that opened not the h. of. 14:17*
so that there is no h. 23:1
every h. shut. 24:10
he will arise against the h. of. 31:2
and I will glorify the h. of. 60:7
our holy and beautiful h. is. 64:11
enter not into the h. of. Jer 16:5
thou shalt not go into h. of. 8
h. of the king of Judah. 21:11; 22:1
go to the h. of the Rechabites. 35:2
to h. of Jonathan. 37:20; 38:26
rebellious h. yet shall know a.
Ezek 2:5; 3:9, 26, 27; 12:3
rebellious like that rebellious h. 2:8
he said to them, Defile the h. go. 9:7
the midst of a rebellious h. 12:2
in your days, O rebellious h. 25
say now to the rebellious h. 17:12
a parable to the rebellious h. 24:3
shew them the form of the h. 43:11
this is the law of h.; Upon the top. 12
so shall ye reconcile the h. 45:20
which he carried to the h. Dan 1:2
blood of Jezreel on the h. Hos 1:4
a fire into the h. of Hazael. Amos 1:4
that holdeth the sceptre from the h. 5
the winter h. with summer h. 3:15
or went into h. and leaned his. 5:19
the great h. and the little h. 6:11
I will rise against h. of. Amos 7:9
drop not thy word against the h. 16
the h. of Esau shall be for. Ob 18
heaps, and the mountain of the h. shall be as high places. Mi 3:12
let us go up to the h. of the. 4:2
works of the h. of Ahab. 6:16
out of the h. of thy gods. Nah 1:14
enter into the h. of the thief, into h. of him that sweareth. Zech 5:4
family of the h. of Nathan. 12:12
and beat upon that h. Mat 7:25, 27
Luke 6:48
when ye come into a h. Mat 10:12
if h. be worthy, let. 13; Luke 10:5
every h. divided against itself.
Mat 12:25; Mark 3:25
how can one enter into a strong man's h.? Mat 12:29; Mark 3:27
against good man of h. Mat 20:11*
your h. is left to you desolate.
Mat 23:38; Luke 13:25
man of the h. had known in what watch. Mat 24:43; Luke 12:39
h. divided against itself, that h.
Mark 3:25
that hath left h. or brethren. 10:29
is the guestchamber? say ye to the good man of h. 14:14; Luke 22:11
that h. remain, go not from h. to h.
Luke 10:7
Martha, received him into her h. 38
not light candle and sweep h.? 15:8
h. was filled with odour. John 12:3
from heaven filled all h. Acts 2:2
breaking bread from h. to h. 46*
every h. ceased not to teach. 5:42*
Simon a tanner, whose h. is. 10:6
entered into the man's h. 11:12
he came to the h. of Mary. 12:12
but the Jews assaulted the h. 17:5
whose h. joined hard to the. 18:7
they fled out of that h. naked. 19:16
publicly, and from h. to h. 20:20
entered into the h. of Philip. 21:8
greet the church in their h. Rom 16:5
1 Cor 16:19
which are of the h. of. 1 Cor 1:11*
ye know the h. of Stephanas. 16:15
earthly h. be dissolved, we have an h.
2 Cor 5:1
desiring to be clothed upon with h. 2*
wandering about from h. to h. and.
1 Tim 5:13
younger women guide the h. 14*
Lord give mercy to h. of. 2 Tim 1:16
in a great h. there are vessels. 2:20
he who built the h. more honour than h. Heb 3:3
h. is built by some man, he. 4
whose h. are we, if we hold fast. 6
receive him not into your h. nor.
2 John 10
see **Aaron, born, build, built, chief, David, door, dwell**

house joined with *father*

get thee from thy father's h.
Gen 12:1
to wander from father's h. 20:13
took me from my father's h. 24:7
thou shalt go to my father's h. 38
wife for my son of my father's h. 40
portion for us in our father's h.?
31:14
at thy father's h. till Shelah be grown ... dwell in her father's h. 38:11
made me forget my father's h. 41:51
my brethren and father's h. 46:31
in Egypt, he and his father's h. 50:22
a lamb, according to h. of their fathers. Ex 12:3
returned to her father's h. Lev 22:13
Israel by h. of their fathers, with.
Num 1:2, 18, 20, 22, 24
tribe, every one head of the h. of his fathers. 1:4, 44; Josh 22:14
numbered by the h. of their fathers.
Num 1:45
pitch with ensign of their father's h.
2:2
children of Levi after the h. of their fathers, by. 3:15, 20; 4:46
Gershon by h. of their fathers. 4:38

Merari after h. of their fathers.
Num 4:42
according to h. of their fathers
twelve rods. 17:2, 3
and father's h. bear iniquity of. 18:1
vow a vow, being in her father's h.
30:3, 16
Reuben, Gad, according to the h. of
their fathers. 34:14
whore in her father's h. Deut 22:21
kindness to my father's h. Josh 2:12
the least in my father's h. Judg 6:15
risen up against my father's h. 9:18
not inherit in our father's h. 11:2
burn thee and thy father's h. 14:15
all the h. of his father came. 16:31
went to his father's h. 19:2
brought him into her father's h. 3
plainly appear to h. of thy father.
1 Sam 2:27
said the h. of thy f. should walk. 30
thee, and on all thy father's h.? 9:20
king will make his father's h. 17:25
no more home to his father's h. 18:2
king sent to call all his father's h.
22:11
thou and all thy father's h. shall. 16
destroy my name out of father's h.
24:21
rest on Joab and all his father's h.
2 Sam 3:29
iniquity be on me, and on my father's
h. 14:9
my father's h. were but dead. 19:28
pray thee, be against me and against
my father's h. 24:17; 1 Chr 21:17
innocent blood from me and father's
h. 1 Ki 2:31
father's h. have troubled Israel.
18:18
Hemath father of the h. of Rechab.
1 Chr 2:55
h. of their fathers increased. 4:38
son of Guni, chief of h. of their
fathers. 5:15, 24; 7:2, 7, 9, 40
with them after the h. of fathers. 7:4
chief in the h. of their fathers. 9:9
13; 12:30
of Zadok, his father's h. 12:28
me before the h. of my father. 28:4
slain thy brethren of thy father's h.
2 Chr 21:13
could not shew their father's h.
Ezra 2:59; Neh 1:6
chief of h. of their father. Ezra 10:16
both I and my father's h. Neh 1:6
thou and thy father's h. shall be destroyed. Esth 4:14
forget thy people and thy father's h.
Ps 45:10
take hold of his brother of the h. of
his father. Isa 3:6
bring on thy father's h. days. 7:17
throne to his father's h. 22:23
all the glory of his father's h. 24
the h. of thy fathers dealt treacherously. Jer 12:6
send him to my father's h.
Luke 16:27
not my Father's h. a house of merchandise. John 2:16
Father's h. are many mansions. 14:2
nourished in his father's h. Acts 7:20

house of God

other but the h. of God. Gen 28:17
stone which I set shall be God's h. 22
drawers of water for h. of God.
Josh 9:23
all the time h. of God. Judg 18:31
and went up to the h. of God. 20:18*
people came unto the h. of God. 26*
21:2*
which one goeth up to h. of God. 31*
Azariah ruler of h. of God.
1 Chr 9:11; Neh 11:11
governors of h. of God. 1 Chr 24:5
glory filled the h. of God. 2 Chr 5:14
with them hid in h. of God. 22:12
they set the h. of God in. 24:13
a carved image in the h. of God. 33:7
they burnt the h. of God. 36:19
to the h. of the great God. Ezra 5:8
let the h. of God be builded. 15; 6:7
needed for the h. of God? Ezra 7:20
it be done for the h. of the God. 23
let us meet in h. of God. Neh 6:10
I said, Why is the h. of God? 13:11
I went with them to the h. of God.
Ps 42:4; 55:14
olive tree in the h. of God. 52:8
be doorkeeper in h. of God. 84:10
thou goest to h. of God. Eccl 5:1
let us go up to the h. of God.
Isa 2:3; Mi 4:2
is hated in the h. of God. Hos 9:8
withholden from h. of God. Joel 1:13
cut off from the h. of God. 16
to h. of God men to pray. Zech 7:2*
into the h. of God, and did eat the.
Mat 12:4; Mark 2:26; Luke 6:4
to behave thyself in the h. of God.
1 Tim 3:15
high priest over the h. of God.
Heb 10:21
begin at the h. of God. 1 Pet 4:17

his house

Lord plagued Pharaoh and his h.
Gen 12:17
of his h. were circumcised. 17:27
him overseer over his h. 39:4, 5
made me lord of all his h. 45:8
Acts 7:10
atonement for his h. Lev 16:6, 11
a man shall sanctify his h. 27:14
sanctified it will redeem his h. 15
would give me his h. full of silver.
Num 22:18; 24:13
let him go and return to his h.
Deut 20:5, 6, 7, 8
him send her out of his h. 24:1
go into his h. to fetch his pledge. 10
became a snare to his h. Judg 8:27
with Jerubbaal and his h. 9:16, 19
spoken concerning his h. 1 Sam 3:12
I will judge his h. for ever. 13
Ramah, for there was his h. 7:17
Israel buried Samuel in his h. 25:1
departed every one to his h.
2 Sam 6:19
before thy father and his h. 21
pass, when the king sat in his h. 7:1
concerning his h. 25; 1 Chr 17:23
went not down to his h. 11:9, 10, 13
fetched her to his h. became. 27
bring the king back to his h.? 19:11
it is for Saul and his bloody h. 21:1
silver nor gold of Saul, nor of his h. 4
his h. there shall be peace. 1 Ki 2:33
building, and finished all his h. 7:1
man to his h. for thing. 12:24; 22:17
1 Chr 16:43; 2 Chr 11:4; 18:16
did eat bread in his h. 1 Ki 13:19
sword against Baasha and his h. 16:7
of Israel went to his h. 20:43; 21:4
Elisha sat in his h. and. 2 Ki 6:32
nothing in his h. Hezekiah. 20:13
it went evil with his h. 1 Chr 7:23
Saul, his sons, and all his h. 10:6
the ark remained in his h. 13:14
toward God and his h. 2 Chr 24:16
his h. be made a dunghill. Ezra 6:11
one repaired over against his h.
Neh 3:28
out every man from his h. 5:13
to be over against his h. 7:3
an hedge about his h.? Job 1:10
shall return no more to his h. 7:10
he shall lean on his h. it shall. 8:15
the increase of his h. shall. 20:28
pleasure hath he in his h.? 21:21
he buildeth his h. as a moth. 27:18
when the glory of his h. Ps 49:16
made him Lord of his h. 105:21
and riches shall be in his h. 112:3
give the substance of his h. Pr 6:31
S of S 8:7
not depart from his h. Pr 17:13
even punish that man and his h.
Jer 23:34
oppress a man and his h. Mi 2:2
evil covetousness to his h. Hab 2:9
in the midst of his h. Zech 5:4
then he shall spoil his h. Mat 12:29
Mark 3:27
to take any thing out of his h.
Mat 24:17; Mark 13:15
not have suffered his h. Mat 24:43
he would come into his h. Luke 8:41
went down to his h. justified. 18:14
believed and his whole h. John 4:53
feared God with all his h. Acts 10:2
to send for thee into his h. 22
he had seen an angel in his h. 11:13
to him and to all in his h. 16:32
into his h. he rejoiced, believing in
God with all his h. 34; 18:8
church which is in his h. Col 4:15
faithful in all his h. Heb 3:2, 5
an ark for the saving of his h. 11:7
also Mark 2:15

house of Israel

let h. of Israel bewail. Lev 10:6
be of h. of Israel that killeth an ox or
lamb. 17:3, 8, 10; 22:18
all h. of Israel mourned. Num 20:29
h. of Israel lamented. 1 Sam 7:2
they mourned for the h. of Israel.
2 Sam 1:12
all the h. of Israel played. 6:5
David and the h. of Israel. 15
the h. of Israel and Judah. 12:8
shall h. of Israel restore the. 16:3
kings of h. of Israel are. 1 Ki 20:31
truth toward h. of Israel. Ps 98:3
us, he will bless h. of Israel. 115:12
bless ye Lord, O h. of Israel. 135:19
vineyard of Lord is the h. of Israel.
Isa 5:7
the h. of Israel shall possess. 14:2
remnant of the h. of Israel. 46:3
goodness toward h. of Israel. 63:7
families of h. of Israel. Jer 2:4
as a thief, so is the h. of Israel. 26
Judah shall walk with h. of Israel.
3:18
treacherously, h. of Israel. 20; 5:11
h. of Israel are uncircumcised. 9:26
the h. of Israel have broken. 11:10
evil for evil, of the h. of Israel. 17
cleave to me the whole h. of Israel.
13:11
liveth, who led the h. of Israel. 23:8
I will sow the h. of Israel. 31:27
covenant with h. of Israel. 31, 33
I promised to the h. of Israel. 33:14
the h. of Israel was ashamed. 48:13
speak to h. of Israel. Ezek 3:1; 17:2
20:27, 30; 24:21; 33:10; 36:22
get thee unto the h. of Israel. 3:4
thou art sent to the h. of Israel. 5
h. of Israel will not hearken to me,
for all the h. of Israel are. 7
watchman to h. of Israel. 17; 33:7
be a sign to the h. of Israel. 4:3
iniquity of the h. of Israel upon. 4
bear iniquity of the h. of Israel. 5
a fire shall come forth into the h. of
Israel. 5:4
abominations of the h. of Israel. 6:11
all the idols of the h. of Israel. 8:10
the ancients of h. of Israel. 11, 12
the iniquity of the h. of Israel. 9:9
ye said, O h. of Israel, for. 11:5
the h. of Israel wholly are they. 15
the h. of Israel said. 12:9, 27; 18:29
divination within h. of Israel. 12:24
hedge for the h. of Israel. 13:5
the writing of the h. of Israel. 9
h. of Israel that setteth up idols.
14:4, 7
h. of Israel may go no more. 11
eyes to idols of h. of Israel. 18:6, 15
O h. of Israel, is not my way? 25
will I judge you, O h. of Israel. 30
ye die, O h. of Israel? 31; 33:11
but the h. of Israel rebelled. 20:13
O h. of Israel, go ye, serve ye every
one his idols, if ye will not. 39
all the h. of Israel serve me. 40
corrupt doings, O h. of Israel. 44
h. of Israel is to me become. 22:18
briar to the h. of Israel. 28:24
have gathered the h. of Israel. 25
staff of a reed to h. of Israel. 29:6
the confidence of h. of Israel. 16
the horn of the h. of Israel to. 21
that they, even the h. of Israel. 34:30
multiply all the h. of Israel. 36:10
when the h. of Israel dwelt in. 17
which the h. of Israel profaned. 21

your sakes, O h. of Israel. Ezek 36:22
for your ways, O h. of Israel. 32
be enquired of by the h. of Israel. 37
bones are whole h. of Israel. 37:11
write on it, for the h. of Israel. 16
months shall h. of Israel be. 39:12
the h. of Israel shall know I. 22
h. of Israel went into captivity. 23
mercy on whole h. of Israel. 25
poured my Spirit on h. of Israel. 29
thou seest to the h. of Israel. 40:4
shew house to h. of Israel. 43:10
rebellious, even to h. of Israel. 44:6
caused the h. of Israel to fall. 12
of the seed of the h. of Israel. 22
for the whole h. of Israel. 45:6
land shall they give to h. of Israel. 8
reconciliation for the h. of Israel. 17
kingdom of h. of Israel. Hos 1:4
have mercy on the h. of Israel. 6
and hearken, ye h. of Israel. 5:1
horrible thing in h. of Israel. 6:10
h. of Israel compasseth me. 11:12
leave ten to h. of Israel. Amos 5:3
saith the Lord to the h. of Israel. 4
sacrifices 40 years, O h. of Israel? 25
nations, to whom h. of Israel. 6:1
you a nation, O h. of Israel. 14
against thee in the h. of Israel. 7:10
I will sift the h. of Israel. 9:9
sins of the h. of Israel. Mi 1:5
princes of the h. of Israel. 3:1, 9
a curse, O h. of Israel. Zech 8:13
go to lost sheep of the h. of Israel. Mat 10:6; 15:24
all the h. of Israel know. Acts 2:36
O h. of Israel, have ye offered? 7:42
a new covenant with h. of Israel. Heb 8:8, 10

house of Jacob

souls of h. of Jacob. Gen 46:27
say to the h. of Jacob. Ex 19:3
h. of Jacob from people. Ps 114:1
O h. of Jacob, let us walk. Isa 2:5
forsaken thy people, h. of Jacob. 6
his face from h. of Jacob. 8:17
escaped of the h. of Jacob. 10:20
cleave to the h. of Jacob. 14:1
Lord concerning h. of Jacob. 29:22
O h. of Jacob and Israel. 46:3
hear ye this, O h. of Jacob. 48:1
shew the h. of Jacob their sins. 58:1
word of Lord, O h. of Jacob. Jer 2:4
declare this in the h. of Jacob. 5:20
my hand to h. of Jacob. Ezek 20:5
testify in h. of Jacob. Amos 3:13
utterly destroy the h. of Jacob. 9:8
the h. of Jacob shall possess. Ob 17
h. of Jacob shall be a fire. 18
named the h. of Jacob. Mi 2:7
pray, ye heads of the h. of Jacob. 3:9
reign over h. of Jacob. Luke 1:33

house of Joseph

men into Joseph's h. Gen 43:17
h. of Joseph shall abide. Josh 18:5
the h. of Joseph went up. Judg 1:22
the h. of Joseph sent to descry. 23
hand of the h. of Joseph. 35
I am come the first this day of all the h. of Joseph. 2 Sam 19:20
charge of h. of Joseph. 1 Ki 11:28
break out like fire in h. of Joseph. Amos 5:6
h. of Joseph shall be a flame. Ob 18
will save the h. of Joseph. Zech 10:6

house of Judah

David king over h. of Judah. 2 Sam 2:4, 7, 11; 1 Chr 2:84
I gave thee h. of Judah. 2 Sam 12:8
he assembled all the h. of Judah. 1 Ki 12:21
speak to all the h. of Judah. 23
escaped of the h. of Judah shall take. 2 Ki 19:30; Isa 37:31
ruler of h. of Judah. 2 Chr 19:11
behind the h. of Judah. Neh 4:16
a father to h. of Judah. Isa 22:21
h. of Judah shall walk. Jer 3:18
the h. of Judah hath dealt. 5:11
the h. of Judah hath broken. 11:10
for evil of the h. of Judah that. 17
I will pluck h. of Judah. 12:14
cleave to me the h of Judah. 13:11
I will sow the h. of Judah. Jer 31:27
a new covenant with h. of Judah. 31
I promised to h. of Judah. 33:14
may be h. of Judah will hear. 36:3
bear the iniquity of h. of Judah forty days. Ezek 4:6
light thing to h. of Judah? 8:17
iniquity of h. of Judah is great. 9:9
Aha, against the h. of Judah. 25:3
the h. of Judah is like to all the. 8
dealt against the h. of Judah. 12
mercy upon h. of Judah. Hos 1:7
I will be to the h. of Judah. 5:12
young lion to the h. of Judah. 14
for remnant of h. of Judah. Zeph 2:7
a curse, O h. of Judah. Zech 8:13
to do well to the h. of Judah. 15
the fast shall be to h. of Judah. 19
Lord hath visited h. of Judah. 10:3
strengthen the h. of Judah. 6
eyes unto the h. of Judah. 12:4
covenant with h. of Judah. Heb 8:8

king's **house**

on roof of the king's h. 2 Sam 11:2
departed out of the king's h. 8
hear out of the king's h. 15:35
finished the king's h. 1 Ki 9:1
treasure of king's h. 14:26; 15:18
2 Ki 16:8; 2 Chr 12:9; 25:24
Zimri burnt the king's h. 1 Ki 16:18
told it to the king's h. 2 Ki 7:11*
he burnt the king's h. 25:9
Jer 39:8; 52:13
shall be at the king's h. 2 Chr 23:5
son was over the king's h. 26:21
portion out of h. of the king. 28:21
given out of the king's h. Ezra 6:4
maidens out of king's h. Esth 2:9
shalt escape in the king's h. 4:13
was great in the king's h. 9:4
give ear, O h. of the king. Hos 5:1

house of Levi

a man of the h. of Levi. Ex 2:1
rod of Aaron for h. of Levi was. Num 17:8
the Lord, O h. of Levi. Ps 135:20
family of the h. of Levi. Zech 12:13

in the **house**

of Esau that were in h. Gen 27:15
even all that was in the h. 34:29
blessing was on all in the h. 39:5
not what is with me in the h. 8
was heard in Pharaoh's h. 45:16
in one h. shall passover. Ex 12:46
of leprosy in a h. Lev 14:34, 35
again and break out in the h. 43
the plague be spread in the h. 44
he that lieth, that eateth in the h. 47
plague hath not spread in the h. 48
whoso with thee in the h. Josh 2:19
all that are with her in the h. 6:17
in the h. of Micah. Judg 17:4, 12
find rest, each in h. of. Ruth 1:9
she tarried a little in the h. 2:7
had a fat calf in the h. 1 Sam 28:24
sent to publish it in the h. of. 31:9
they put his armour in the h. of. 10
dwell in one h.... of a child with her in the h. 1 Ki 3:17
any tool of iron heard in the h. 6:7
is found some good in the h. 14:13
drinking himself drunk in the h. 16:9
in the h.? thine handmaid hath not any thing in the h. 2 Ki 4:2
he returned, and walked in the h. 35
leaneth on my hand, bow in h. 5:18
and bestowed them in the h. 24
in h. of Nisroch. 19:37; Isa 37:38
a graven image in the h. 2 Ki 21:7
slew young men in the h. 2 Chr 36:17
had put them in the h. of. Ezra 1:7
search was made in the h. of. 6:1
the queen also in the h.? Esth 7:8
the gallows standeth in the h. of. 9
my songs in the h. of my. Ps 119:54
curse of Lord is in the h. Pr 3:33
thy labours be in the h. of a. 5:10
her feet abide not in her h. 7:11
in the h. of the righteous is. 15:6
wise is in h. of mourning ... fools is in the h. of mirth. Eccl 7:4
it may remain in the h. Isa 44:13
set their abominations in the h. Jer 7:30; 32:34
covenant before me in the h. 34:15
put him in the h. of Jonathan. 37:15
remain ten men in one h. Amos 6:9
in the h. of Aphrah roll. Mi 1:10*
of wickedness in the h. of. 6:10
I was wounded in the h. Zech 13:6
unto all that are in the h. Mat 5:15
that he was in the h. Mark 2:1
being in the h. he asked them. 9:33
in the h. his disciples asked. 10:10
in Bethany, in the h. of Simon. 14:3
nor abode in any h. but. Luke 8:27
abideth not in the h. John 8:35
Mary sat still in the h. 11:20
enquire in the h. of Judas. Acts 9:11
Peter is lodged in the h. of. 10:32

house joined with Lord

shalt bring into the h. of the Lord. Ex 23:19; 34:26; Neh 10:35
of a dog into h. of Lord. Deut 23:18
treasury of h. of the Lord. Josh 6:24
going to h. of the Lord. Judg 19:18
up to the h. of the Lord. 1 Sam 1:7
unto h. of the Lord. 24; 2 Ki 12:4
9, 13; 22:4; 2 Chr 34:14
came into h. of Lord. 2 Sam 12:20
of building h. of Lord. 1 Ki 3:1
foundation of h. of Lord laid. 6:37
2 Chr 8:16; Ezra 3:11; Zech 8:9
made for h. of the Lord. 1 Ki 7:40
45:51; 2 Chr 4:16; 5:1; 24:14
cloud filled h. of Lord. 1 Ki 8:10, 11
2 Chr 5:13; 7:2; Ezek 44:4
dedicated h. of the Lord. 1 Ki 8:63
he went up unto the h. of Lord. 10:5; 2 Chr 9:4
hid in the h. of Lord six. 2 Ki 11:3
oath of them in h. of the Lord. 4
let her not be slain in h. of Lord. 15
2 Chr 23:14
appointed officers over h. of Lord. 2 Ki 11:18; 2 Chr 23:18
brought from the h. of the Lord. 2 Ki 11:19; 23:6
found in h. of the Lord. 12:10
14:14; 16:8; 18:15
oversight of the h. of the Lord. 12:11
was not brought into h. of Lord. 16
turned he from h. of Lord. 16:18
shalt go up unto h. of Lord. 20:5
will heal me, and that I shall go up to the h. of the Lord. 8; Isa 38:22
covenant which were found in h. of Lord. 2 Ki 23:2, 24; 2 Chr 34:17, 30
Sodomites that were by h. of Lord. 2 Ki 23:7
entering in of h. of the Lord. 11
burnt the h. of the Lord. 25:9
Jer 52:13
song in the h. of the Lord. 1 Chr 6:31
said, This is the h. of the Lord. 22:1
build the h. of the Lord thy God. 11
prepared for the h. of the Lord. 14
the work of the h. of the Lord. 23:4
minister in the h. of the Lord. 26:12
so the h. of the Lord. 2 Chr 8:16
he was cut off from h. of Lord. 26:21; Joel 1:9
sanctify h. of the Lord. 2 Chr 29:5
cleanse the h. of the Lord. 15
the idol out of h. of Lord. 33:15
book of the law in h. of Lord. 34:15
polluted the h. of the Lord. 36:14
beautify h. of the Lord. Ezra 7:27
will dwell in the h. of Lord. Ps 23:6
I may dwell in the h. of Lord. 27:4
planted in the h. of the Lord. 92:13
vows in courts of Lord's h. 116:19
you out of the h. of Lord. 118:26
let us go into h. of the Lord. 122:1
because of the h. of Lord I will. 9
stand in the h. of the Lord. 134:1
135:2
mountain of the Lord's h. Isa 2:2
Mi 4:1
up into h. of the Lord. Isa 37:14
praise to h. of the Lord. Jer 17:26
governor in the h. of the Lord. 20:1
which was by h. of the Lord. 2
to worship in the Lord's h. 26:2
words in the h. of the Lord. 7

spake to me in *h.* of *Lord. Jer* 28:1
that stood in the *h.* of the *Lord.* 5
officers in the *h.* of the *Lord.* 29:26
Rechabites into *h.* of the *Lord.* 35:2
I cannot go into *h.* of *Lord.* 36:5
read in the *Lord's h.* upon the. 6
entry that is in *h.* of the *Lord.* 38:14
them to the *h.* of the *Lord.* 41:5
the sanctuaries of *Lord's h.* 51:51
a noise in the *h.* of the *Lord. Lam* 2:7
the time that the *Lord's h. Hag* 1:2
see **court, door, gate, treasures, vessels**

mine, or *my* **house**
the steward of *my h.* is. *Gen* 15:2
one born in *my h.* is mine heir. 3
be destroyed, I and *my h.* 34:30
thou shalt be over *my h.* 41:40
faithful in all *mine h.* *Num* 12:7
things out of *mine h.* *Deut* 26:13
my h. we will serve Lord. *Josh* 24:15
forth of doors of *my h.* *Judg* 11:31
this man come into *mine h.* 19:23
kindness from *my h.* *1 Sam* 20:15
fellow come into *my h.*? 21:15
what is my *h.* that thou hast ?
2 Sam 7:18; *1 Chr* 17:16
go into *mine h.* to eat ? *2 Sam* 11:11
my h. be not so with God. 23:5
it is near to my *h.* *1 Ki* 21:2
all in *mine h.* have they seen.
2 Ki 20:15; *Isa* 39:4
settle him in *mine h.* *1 Chr* 17:14
the grave is *mine h.* *Job* 17:13
I will walk in *my h.* with. *Ps* 101:2
into the tabernacle of *my h.* 132:3
at the window of *my h.* *Pr* 7:6
in *my h.* is neither bread. *Isa* 3:7
them will I give in *mine h.* 56:5
in *my h.* of prayer, *mine h.* shall be called an *h.* of. 7; *Mat* 21:13
Mark 11:17; *Luke* 19:46
beloved to do in *mine h.*? *Jer* 11:15
forsaken *mine h.* I left mine. 12:7
in *my h.* have I found their. 23:11
I sat in *mine h.* and. *Ezek* 8:1
done in midst of *mine h.* 23:39
to pollute it, even *my h.* 44:7
was at rest in *mine h.* *Dan* 4:4
drive them out of *mine h.* *Hos* 9:15
why ? because of *mine h.* *Hag* 1:9
shalt also judge *my h.* *Zech* 3:7
I will encamp about *mine h.* 9:8
may be meat in *mine h.* *Mal* 3:10
I will return into *my h.* *Mat* 12:44
Luke 11:24
them farewell at *my h.* *Luke* 9:61
compel them, that *my h.* 14:23
hour I prayed in *my h.* *Acts* 10:30
saying, Come into *my h.* and. 16:15

own **house**
servants born in *own h.* *Gen* 14:14
I provide for mine *own h.* 30:30
bring it unto thine *own h.* *Deut* 22:2
and come unto his *own h.* *Josh* 20:6
and dwelt in his *own h.* *Judg* 8:29
person in his *own h.* *2 Sam* 4:11
against thee out of thy *own h.* 12:11
own h. and not see my face, so Absalom returned to *own h.* 14:24
again in peace to his *own h.* 19:30
Joab buried in his *own h.* *1 Ki* 2:34
an end of building his *own h.* 3:1
building his *own h.* 13 years. 7:1
a levy to build his *own h.* 9:15
own h. David. 12:16; *2 Chr* 10:16
thee into thine *own h.* *1 Ki* 14:12
was buried in the garden of his *own h.* *2 Ki* 21:18; *2 Chr* 33:20
slew the king in his *own h.*
2 Ki 21:23; *2 Chr* 33:24
came in his heart to make in his *own h.* *2 Chr* 7:11
wherein Solomon had built the house of the Lord and his *own h.* 8:1
bear rule in his *own h.* *Esth* 1:22
troubleth his *own h.* shall. *Pr* 11:29
of gain troubleth his *own h.* 15:27
every one in his *own h.* *Isa* 14:18
are the men of his *own h.* *Mi* 7:6
run every man to his *own h.* *Hag* 1:9
a prophet is not without honour, save in his *own h.* *Mat* 13:57; *Mark* 6:4
to his *own h.* *Luke* 1:23; 5:25
Mary returned to her *own h.* 1:56
a great feast in his *own h.* 5:29
return to thy *own h.* and shew. 8:39
man went unto his *own h.* *John* 7:53
two years in his *own h.* *Acts* 28:30*
that ruleth well his *own h.* *1 Tim* 3:4
know not how to rule his *own h.* 5
for those of his *own h.* 5:8
as a Son over his *own h.* *Heb* 3:6

this **house**
greater in *this h.* than I. *Gen* 39:9
and bring me out of *this h.* 40:14
this h. thou art building. *1 Ki* 6:12
how much less *this h.* that I. 8:27
opened toward *this h.* 29; *2 Chr* 6:20
before thine altar in *this h.*
1 Ki 8:31; *2 Chr* 6:22
make supplication to thee in *this h.*
1 Ki 8:33, 42; *2 Chr* 6:24, 32
his hands towards *this h.* *1 Ki* 8:38
hallowed *this h.* 9:3; *2 Chr* 7:16, 20
at *this h.* every one shall hiss.
1 Ki 9:8; *2 Chr* 7:21
this h. which I have chosen.
2 Ki 21:7; *2 Chr* 33:7
upon us we stand before *this h.* for thy name is in this *h.* *2 Chr* 20:9
foundation of *this h.* was. *Ezra* 3:12
who destroyed *this h.* 5:12
this h. was finished on third. 6:15
stand before me in *this h.* *Jer* 7:10
is *this h.* become a den of ? 11
therefore will I do to *this h.* 14
enter in by the gates of *this h.* 22:4
this h. shall become a desolation. 5
will I make *this h.* like Shiloh. 26:6
this h. shall be like Shiloh. 9
me to prophesy against *this h.* 12
and *this h.* lie waste. *Hag* 1:4
who is left that saw *this h.* in ? 2:3
I will fill *this h.* with glory, saith. 7
the glory of *this* latter *h.* greater. 9
laid foundation of *this h.* *Zech* 4:9
say, Peace be to *this h.* *Luke* 10:5
is salvation come to *this h.* 19:9

thine or *thy* **house**
all *thy h.* into the ark. *Gen* 7:1
been twenty years in *thy h.* 31:41
up and come into *thine h.* *Ex* 8:3
that is clean in *thy h.* *Num* 18:11, 13
when thou sittest in *thine h.*
Deut 6:7; 11:19
on the posts of *thy h.* 6:9; 11:20
an abomination into *thine h.* 7:26
he loveth thee and *thine h.* 15:16
bring her home to *thine h.* 21:12
remain in *thine h.* and bewail. 13
bring not blood upon *thine h.* 22:8
not have in *thine h.* divers. 25:14
given to thee and *thine h.* 26:11
are entered into *thine h.* *Josh* 2:3
shall go out of doors of *thy h.* 19
we will burn *thine h.* on. *Judg* 12:1
man that came into *thine h.* 19:22
woman that is come into *thine h.*
Ruth 4:11
let *thy h.* be like the house. 12
that *thy h.* should walk. *1 Sam* 2:30
not be an old man in *thine h.* 31
the increase of *thine h.* shall die. 33
one in *thine h.* shall crouch to. 36
is honourable in *thine h.* 22:14
peace be to *thine h.* and to. 25:6
her, Go up in peace to *thine h.* 35
thine h. shall be established for.
2 Sam 7:16
go down to *thy h.* and wash. 11:8
didst not thou go down to *thine h.*? 10
never depart from *thine h.* 12:10
go to *thine h.* 14:8; *1 Ki* 1:53
give me half *thine h.* *1 Ki* 13:8
back with thee into *thine h.* 18
make *thy h.* like the *h.* of Jeroboam.
16:3; 21:22
they shall search *thine h.* 20:6
set *thine h.* in order. *2 Ki* 20:1
Isa 38:1
what have they seen in *thine h.*?
2 Ki 20:15; *Isa* 39:4
all in *thine h.* shall be carried.
2 Ki 20:17; *Isa* 39:6
come to *thy h.* in multitude. *Ps* 5:7
loved the habitation of *thy h.* *Ps* 26:8
satisfied with fatness of *thy h.* 36:8
no bullock out of *thy h.* 50:9
satisfied with goodness of *thy h.* 65:4
will go into *thy h.* with burnt. 66:13
zeal of *thine h.* hath eaten me up.
69:9; *John* 2:17
holiness becometh *thine h.* *Ps* 93:5
fruitful vine by sides of *thine h.* 128:3
that are cast out to *thy h.* *Isa* 58:7
thou shalt live and *thine h.* *Jer* 38:17
shut thyself within *thine h.*
Ezek 3:24
blessing to rest in *thine h.* 44:30
consulted shame to *thy h.* *Hab* 2:10
arise, go unto *thine h.* *Mat* 9:6
Mark 2:11; *Luke* 5:24
the passover at *thy h.* *Mat* 26:18
I entered *thine h.* thou. *Luke* 7:44
to-day I must abide at *thy h.* 19:5
thou and all *thy h.* shall be saved.
Acts 11:14; 16:31
to the church in *thy h.* *Philem* 2
see **tops**

household, *or* **households**
he will command his *h.* *Gen* 18:19
Jacob said to his *h.* Put away. 35:2
famine of your *h.* be gone. 42:33*
lest thou and thy *h.* come to. 45:11
take your father and your *h.* and. 18
nourished his father's *h.* 47:12
shall be food for your *h.* 24
man and his *h.* came. *Ex* 1:1
if the *h.* be too little for the. 12:4
made an atonement for his *h.*
Lev 16:17
every place, and your *h.* *Num* 18:31
wonders upon all his *h.* *Deut* 6:22*
swallowed them and their *h.* 11:6
rejoice, thou and thy *h.* 14:26
eat it before the Lord, thou and thy *h.*
15:20
bring all thy father's *h.* *Josh* 2:18
Rahab, her father's *h.* and all. 6:25
and the family shall come by *h.* 7:14
brought his *h.* man by man. 18
he feared his father's *h.* *Judg* 6:27
life, with the lives of thy *h.* 18:25
evil is determined against his *h.*
1 Sam 25:17*
man with his *h.* 27:3; *2 Sam* 2:3
Lord blessed him and all his *h.*
2 Sam 6:11*
David returned to bless his *h.* 20
king went forth and all his *h.* 15:16
asses be for the king's *h.* to. 16:2
put his *h.* in order, and. 17:23*
to carry over the king's *h.* 19:18
Judah brought the king and his *h.* 41
Abishai was over the *h.* *1 Ki* 4:6
victuals for the king and his *h.* 7
in giving food for my *h.* 5:9
Hiram wheat for food to his *h.* 11
Genubath was in Pharaoh's *h.* 11:20*
go and tell the king's *h.* *2 Ki* 7:9
go and thine *h.* to sojourn. 8:1
Eliakim son of Hilkiah who was over *h.* 18:18; 19:2; *Isa* 36:22; 37:2
principal *h.* being taken. *1 Chr* 24:6*
camels and a great *h.* *Job* 1:3
milk for food of thy *h.* *Pr* 27:27
and giveth meat to her *h.* 31:15
not afraid of the snow for her *h.*: for all her *h.* are clothed with scarlet. 21
well to the ways of her *h.* 27
they call them of his *h.*? *Mat* 10:25
foes shall be they of his own *h.* 36
ruler over his *h.* 24:45; *Luke* 12:42
was baptized and her *h.* *Acts* 16:15
are of Aristobulus' *h.* *Rom* 16:10
that be of the *h.* of Narcissus. 11
I baptized also the *h.* of. *1 Cor* 1:16
to them who are of the *h.* *Gal* 6:10
no more strangers, but of the *h.* of God. *Eph* 2:19
that are of Cesar's *h.* *Phil* 4:22
salute the *h.* of. *2 Tim* 4:19*

householder
so the servants of the *h.* *Mat* 13:27
unto a man that is an *h.* 52; 20:1
was a certain *h.* planted. 21:33

household servants
two of his *h. servants.* *Acts* 10:7

household stuff

found of all thy *h. stuff*? *Gen* 31:37
I cast out all the *h. stuff*. *Neh* 13:8

houses

carry corn for the famine of your *h.* *Gen* 42:19
God, he made them *h.* *Ex* 1:21†
heads of their fathers' *h.* 6:14
frogs from thee and thy *h.* 8:9, 11
and the frogs died out of the *h.* 13
swarms of flies into thy *h.* 21, 24
and cattle flee into the *h.* 9:20
fill thy *h.* and the *h.* of all thy servants, and the *h.* of all. 10:6
on the upper door post of the *h.* 12:7
blood be for a token upon the *h.* 13
away leaven out of your *h.* 15
no leaven found in your *h.* 19
destroyer to come in unto your *h.* 23
passed over and delivered our *h.* 27
h. of villages be counted. *Lev* 25:31
the *h.* of the cities of their. 32, 33
sum of the sons of Gershon throughout their *h.* *Num* 4:22
swallowed them up and their *h.* 16:32*
according to their father's *h.* 17:6
we will not return unto our *h.* 32:18
to give thee *h.* full of all. *Deut* 6:11
when hast built goodly *h.* and. 8:12
dwellest in their cities and *h.* 19:1
Neh 9:25
hot provision out of our *h.* *Josh* 9:12
that there is in these *h.* *Judg* 18:14
men that were in the *h.* near. 22
he cried against the *h.* *1 Ki* 13:32
they shall search the *h.* of thy. 20:6
put them in the *h.* of. *2 Ki* 17:29
which sacrificed in the *h.* of the. 32
he brake down the *h.* of the. 23:7
the *h.* of the high places, Josiah. 19
he burnt all the *h.* of Jerusalem. 25:9; *Jer* 52:13
David made *h.* in city. *1 Chr* 15:1
Solomon pattern of the *h.* 28:11
to overlay the walls of the *h.* 29:4
timber to floor the *h.* *2 Chr* 34:11
and prepare yourselves by *h.* 35:4
your wives and your *h.* *Neh* 4:14
mortgaged our lands and *h.* 5:3
them their vineyards and *h.* 11
the people were few, and *h.* not. 7:4
we cast lots after the *h.* of our. 10:34
and feasted in their *h.* *Job* 1:4
princes, who filled their *h.* 3:15
them that dwell in *h.* of clay. 4:19
he dwelleth in *h.* which no. 15:28
their *h.* are safe from fear, nor. 21:9
yet he filled their *h.* with. 22:18
the dark they dig through *h.* 24:16
that their *h.* shall continue. *Ps* 49:11
let us take the *h.* of God. 83:12*
fill our *h.* with spoil. *Pr* 1:13
make they their *h.* in rocks. 30:26
I builded me *h.* I planted. *Eccl* 2:4
the poor is in your *h.* *Isa* 3:14
of a truth, many *h.* shall. 5:9; 6:11
rock of offence to both *h.* of. 8:14
h. be spoiled, their wives. 13:16
their *h.* shall be full of doleful. 21
shall cry in their desolate *h.* 22
on the tops of their *h.* every. 15:3
the *h.* of Jerusalem, and the *h.* 22:10
yea, upon all the *h.* of joy in. 32:13
shall build *h.* and inhabit. 65:21
troops in the harlots' *h.* *Jer* 5:7
as cage is full of birds, are their *h.* 27
and their *h.* shall be turned. 6:12
cry be heard from their *h.* 18:22
the *h.* of Jerusalem and the *h.* of. 19:13
build ye *h.* and dwell in. 29:5, 28
h. and fields shall be possessed. 32:15
h. on whose roofs they offered. 29
concerning *h.* of this city, and *h.* 33:4
they burnt the *h.* of the people. 39:8
I will kindle a fire in *h.* of. 43:12, 13
h. are turned to aliens. *Lam* 5:2
shall possess their *h.* *Ezek* 7:24
it is not near, let us build *h.* 11:3
burn thine *h.* with fire. 16:41; 23:47
destroy thy pleasant *h.* 26:12
shall build *h.* and plant. *Ezek* 28:26
thee in the doors of the *h.* 33:30
shall be a place for their *h.* 45:4
your *h.* shall be made a dunghill. *Dan* 2:5
their *h.* shall be made a dunghill. 3:29
I will place them in their *h.* saith. *Hos* 11:11
climb up upon the *h.* *Joel* 2:9
and summer house, *h.* of ivory shall perish, great *h.* shall. *Amos* 3:15
the *h.* of Achzib shall be. *Mi* 1:14
and they covet *h.* and take. 2:2
cast out from their pleasant *h.* 9
which fill their masters' *h.* *Zeph* 1:9
h. shall become a desolation, they shall build *h.* but not inhabit. 13
in the *h.* of Ashkelon shall. 2:7
to dwell in your cieled *h.*? *Hag* 1:4
h. shall be rifled, and the. *Zech* 14:2
wear soft clothing are in kings' *h.* *Mat* 11:8
one that hath forsaken *h.* or. 19:29
devour widows' *h.* 23:14*
Mark 12:40; *Luke* 20:47
fasting to their own *h.* *Mark* 8:3*
receive me into their *h.* *Luke* 16:4
were possessors of *h.* sold. *Acts* 4:34
have ye not *h.* to eat in? *1 Cor* 11:22
ruling their own *h.* well. *1 Tim* 3:12
they which creep into *h.* *2 Tim* 3:6
who subvert whole *h.* *Tit* 1:11

how

and *h.* saidst thou, she? *Gen* 26:29
h. is it thou hast found it? 27:20
Jacob said, *h.* dreadful is. 28:17
h. then can I do this great? 39:9
h. then should we steal out? 44:8
what shall we speak? *h.* shall? 16
h. shall I go to my father, lad? 34
h. is that ye are come so? *Ex* 2:18
h. then shall Pharaoh hear? 6:12
and *h.* shall Pharaoh hearken? 30
Moses told *h.* the Lord. 18:8
seen *h.* I bare you. 19:4; *Deut* 1:31
h. we are to encamp in. *Num* 10:31
h. shall I curse, whom God hath not cursed? *h.* 23:8
h. goodly are thy tents, O! 24:5
h. can I myself bear? *Deut* 1:12
if thou shalt say, *H.* can I? 7:17
h. the earth opened her mouth. 11:6
h. did these nations serve? 12:30
h. he met thee by the way. 25:18
h. we have dwelt in Egypt, and *h.* we came through nations. 29:16
h. should one chase a. 32:30
h. shall we make a league with? *Josh* 9:7
h. shall we order the child, *h.* do to him? *Judg* 13:12
she said, *H.* canst thou say? 16:15
they said, Tell us, *h.* was this? 20:3
h. do for wives for them? 21:7, 16
know *h.* the matter will. *Ruth* 3:18
said, *H.* shall this man? *1 Sam* 10:27
see *h.* mine eyes have been. 14:29
h. can I go? if Saul hear he. 16:2
h. went the matter, I. *2 Sam* 1:4
h. knowest thou that Saul and? 5
h. are the mighty fallen! 19, 25, 27
h. Joab did, *h.* the people did, and *h.* 11:7
h. then will he vex himself? 12:18
I know not *h.* to go out. *1 Ki* 3:7
h. do you advise, that I may? 12:6
h. Jeroboam warred, and *h.* 14:19
h. I hid an hundred men of. 18:13
and see *h.* the man seeketh. 20:7
h. he seeketh a quarrel. *2 Ki* 5:7
two kings stood not, *h.* then? 10:4
taught them *h.* they should. 17:28
h. then wilt thou turn away? 18:24
Isa 36:9
heard long ago, *h.* I have done it. *2 Ki* 19:25; *Isa* 37:26
h. I have walked before thee. *2 Ki* 20:3; *Isa* 38:3
behold, I say, *H.* they. *2 Chr* 20:11
his prayer, and *h.* God was. 33:19
to know *h.* Esther did. *Esth* 2:11
h. can I endure to see evil that? 8:6
h. should a man be just? *Job* 9
and thou sayest, *H.* doth? 22:1
h. hast thou helped him that is without power? *h.* savest thou? 26:2
h. little a portion is heard of! 14
h. say ye to my soul, Flee. *Ps* 11:1
h. thou didst drive out heathen, *h.* 44:2
say to God, *H.* terrible art thou. 66:3
h. doth God know? 73:11
h. amiable are thy tabernacles. 84:1
h. short my time is. 89:47
O Lord, *h.* manifold are! 104:24
O *h.* love I thy law, it is. 119:97
h. sweet are thy words unto. 103
consider *h.* I love thy precepts. 159
h. he sware unto the Lord. 132:2
h. precious are thy thoughts. 139:17
a word in due season, *h.* good! *Pr* 15:23
there is a generation, O *h.* 30:13
he knoweth not *h.* to go. *Eccl* 10:15
knowest not *h.* the bones. 11:5
h. fair is thy love, my sister, my spouse! *S of S* 4:10; 7:6
I have put off my coat, *h.* shall? 5:3
h. beautiful are thy feet with. 7:1
h. art thou fallen from! *Isa* 14:12
shall say in that day, and *h.*? 20:6
for *h.* should my name be? 48:11
h. to speak a word in season. 50:4
h. beautiful are the feet of him. 52:7; *Rom* 10:15
h. canst thou say, I am? *Jer* 2:23
I said, *h.* shall I put thee? 3:19
h. shall I pardon thee for this? 5:7
h. do ye say? 8:8; 48:14
h. are we spoiled? 9:19
to ask *h.* thou doest? 15:5
h. can it be quiet, seeing the? 47:7
h. is the hammer of the whole? 50:23
h. doth city sit solitary. *Lam* 1:1
h. weak is thy heart. *Ezek* 16:30
if we pine away in sins, *h.*? 33:10
h. shall I give thee up, Ephraim? *h.* deliver thee? *h.* make? *Hos* 11:8
h. do the beasts groan? *Joel* 1:18
if thieves came to thee, *h.* art. *Ob* 5
h. is she become a desolation. *Zeph* 2:15
h. do you see it now? *Hag* 2:3
h. great is his goodness! *Zech* 9:17
if light be darkness *h.* *Mat* 6:23
h. wilt thou say to thy brother? 7:4
if ye know *h.* to give good gifts. 11
Luke 11:13
take no thought *h.* or. *Mat* 10:19
h. they might destroy him. 12:14
Mark 3:6; 11:18
h. shall his kingdom stand? *Mat* 12:26; *Luke* 11:18
h. can ye, being evil, speak? *Mat* 12:34
h. is it that ye do not understand that I spake it not? 16:11
h. think ye? if a man have. 18:12
h. soon is the fig tree. 21:20
h. camest thou in hither not? 22:12
if call him Lord, *h.* is he his son? 45
Luke 20:44
h. can ye escape the? *Mat* 23:33
h. then shall the scriptures? 26:54
h. is it that he eateth? *Mark* 2:16
h. he went into house. 26; *Luke* 6:4
grow up, he knoweth not *h.* *Mark* 4:27
he said, *H.* is it that ye have? 40
h. hardly shall they that. 10:23
sought *h.* they might take him. 14:1
sought *h.* he might betray him. 11
Luke 22:4
h. shall this be, seeing I? *Luke* 1:34
h. is it that ye sought me? 2:49
take heed *h.* ye hear. 8:18
h. readest thou? 10:26
and *h.* am I straitened till it. 12:50
h. is it that ye do not discern? 56
he said, *h.* is it that I hear? 16:2
remember *h.* he spake unto? 24:6
h. he was known of them in. 35
h. can a man be born? *John* 3:4
h. can these things be? 9
h. can ye believe? 5:44
if not his writing, *h.* believe? 47
h. can this man give us his? 6:52

h. knoweth this man? John 7:15
h. were thy eyes opened? 9:10
h. opened eyes? 26
h. loved him. 11:36
h. can we know the way? 14:5
h. is it thou wilt manifest? 22
finding nothing h. they. Acts 4:21
h. is it that ye have agreed? 5:9
h. God by his hand would. 7:25
h. can I, except some man? 8:31
told, h. he had seen the Lord. 9:27
h. God anointed Jesus of. 10:38
h. he had seen an angel. 11:13
h. he had opened the door. 14:27
let us go again, and see h. 15:36
h. I kept back nothing that. 20:20
h. so labouring, ye ought to. 35
h. shall God judge the? Rom 3:6
h. we that are dead to sin? 6:2
h. to perform what is good. 7:18
h. shall he not with him freely? 8:32
h. shall they call? h. shall they believe? h. shall they hear? 10:14
h. he maketh intercession to. 11:2
h. unsearchable his judgements. 33
take heed h. he buildeth. 1 Cor 3:10
unmarried careth h. he may. 7:32
that is married careth h. he. 33
she careth h. she may please. 34
h. shall it be known what is piped? 14:7
h. shall be known what is spoken? 9
h. say some that there is no? 15:12
man will say, h. are the dead? 35
h. with fear and. 2 Cor 7:15
h. that in a great trial of. 8:2
know ye not h. that Jesus? 13:5
h. turn ye again to weak? Gal 4:9
ye see h. large a letter I have. 6:11
also may know h. I do. Eph 6:21
see h. it will go with me. Phil 2:23
h. to be abased, and know h. to. 4:12
h. ye ought to answer. Col 4:6
and h. ye turned to God. 1 Thes 1:9
h. holily we behaved ourselves. 2:10
h. we exhorted you. 11
h. ye ought to walk. 4:1
should know h. to possess his. 4:4
h. ye ought to follow us. 2 Thes 3:7
not h. to rule his own house, h. shall he take care of the? 1 Tim 3:5
know h. thou oughtest to behave. 15
h. shall we escape if we? Heb 2:3
now consider h. great this man. 7:4
ye see h. that by works. Jas 2:24
h. great a matter a little fire. 3:5
Lord knoweth h. to. 2 Pet 2:9
h. dwelleth the love of? 1 John 3:17
h. can he love God whom he? 4:20
h. that the Lord having. Jude 5
h. thou canst not bear them. Rev 2:2
h. thou hast received. 3:3
see **do**

how *long*

h. long wilt refuse to? Ex 10:3
h. long shall this man be a snare? 7
h. long refuse to keep my? 16:28
h. long will this people provoke me? h. long will it be ere? Num 14:11
h. long shall I bear with this? 27
h. long are ye slack to? Josh 18:3
Eli said, H. long wilt? 1 Sam 1:14
h. long wilt thou mourn for? 16:1
Barzillai said, H. long? 2 Sam 19:34
h. long halt ye between? 1 Ki 18:21
for h. long shall thy journey be? Neh 2:6
h. long wilt thou not depart from? Job 7:19
h. long wilt thou speak? h. long shall words of thy mouth be like? 8:2
h. long will it be ere you? 18:2
h. long will ye vex my soul? 19:2
h. long will ye turn my glory into shame? h. long will ye? Ps 4:2
vexed; but thou, O Lord, h. long? 6:3
h. long wilt thou forget me? 13:1
h. long shall I take counsel in my soul? h. long shall my enemy? 2
Lord, h. long wilt thou look? 35:17
h. long will ye imagine? 62:3
among us that knoweth h. long. 74:9
h. long shall adversary? Ps 74:10
h. long wilt thou be angry for? 79:5; 80:4
h. long will ye judge unjustly? 82:2
h. long, Lord, wilt thou hide? 89:46
return, O Lord, h. long? let. 90:13
the proud, Lord, h. long shall the wicked, h. long shall? 94:3
h. long shall they utter and? 4
h. long, simple ones, will? Pr 1:22
h. long wilt thou sleep, O? 6:9
then said I, Lord, h. long? Isa 6:11
h. long shall vain? Jer 4:14
h. long shall I see standard? 21
h. long shall land mourn? 12:4
h. long shall this be in heart? 23:26
baldness on Gaza, h. long wilt? 47:5
O sword of the Lord, h. long ere? 6
h. long shall be vision? Dan 8:13
h. long shall it be to end of? 12:6
h. long will it be ere they? Hos 8:5
h. long shall I cry, and? Hab 1:2
increaseth what not his, h. long? 2:6
h. long wilt thou not have mercy on Jerusalem? Zech 1:12
h. long shall I be with you, h. long? Mat 17:17; Mark 9:19; Luke 9:41
h. long is it ago since? Mark 9:21
h. long dost thou make? John 10:24
h. long, O Lord, holy and? Rev 6:10

how *many*

h. many are mine iniquities and? Job 13:23
h. many are the days? Ps 119:84
h. many loaves have ye? Mat 15:34 Mark 6:38; 8:5
h. many baskets ye took up? Mat 16:9; Mark 8:19, 20
h. many things they. Mark 15:4
h. many hired servants. Luke 15:17
in h. many things he. 2 Tim 1:18

how *many times*

h. many times shall I adjure thee? 1 Ki 22:16; 2 Chr 18:15

how *much*

h. much rather when. 2 Ki 5:13
without prescribing h. much. Ezra 7:22
h. much better is it to get. Pr 16:16
h. much better is thy love. S of S 4:10
h. much is a man better? Mat 12:12
h. much owest thou to? Luke 16:5, 7
h. much every man hath. 19:15
h. much evil he hath. Acts 9:13
h. much he is the Mediator. Heb 8:6
of h. much sorer punishment. 10:29
h. much she hath glorified. Rev 18:7

how *much less*

contain thee, h. much less this house? 1 Ki 8:27; 2 Chr 6:18
h. much less shall your God? 2 Chr 32:15
h. much less in them that dwell in houses of clay? Job 4:19
h. much less shall I answer? 9:14
h. much less is man that is? 25:6
h. much less to him that accepteth? 34:19
h. much less shall it be meet for? Ezek 15:5

how *much more*

and h. much more after my death? Deut 31:27
h. much more if people? 1 Sam 14:30
h. much more then if we? 23:3
h. much more when wicked men? 2 Sam 4:11
h. much more now may this? 16:11
h. much more abominable and? Job 15:16
h. much more then the hearts of? Pr 15:11
h. much more do his friends? 19:7
h. much more when with a? 21:27
h. much more when I send my four sore judgements? Ezek 14:21
h. much more shall your heavenly Father? Mat 7:11; Luke 11:13
h. much more shall call? Mat 10:25
h. much more are ye better than? Luke 12:24
h. much more will he clothe you? Luke 12:28
h. much more their fulness? Rom 11:12
h. much more these which be? 24
h. much more things that pertain to? 1 Cor 6:3
brother to me, h. much more to? Philem 16

how *oft, often*

h. oft is the candle of the wicked put out? h. oft cometh? Job 21:17
h. oft did they provoke? Ps 78:40
h. oft shall my brother? Mat 18:21
h. often would I have gathered thy children as a. 23:37; Luke 13:34

howbeit

h. Sisera fled on his feet. Judg 4:17
h. the king of Ammonites. 11:28
h. the hair of his head began. 16:22
h. the name of the city was. 18:29
h. we may not give them wives of. 21:18
h. there is a kinsman. Ruth 3:12
h. yet protest solemnly. 1 Sam 8:9
h. Asahel refused to. 2 Sam 2:23
h. because by this deed hast. 12:14
h. he would not hearken. 13:14
h. he would not go, but blessed. 25
h. he attained not unto the first three. 23:19; 1 Chr 11:21
h. the kingdom is turned. 1 Ki 2:15
h. I believed not the words. 10:7 2 Chr 9:6
h. I will not rend all the kingdom. 1 Ki 11:13, 34
I have lacked nothing, h. let. 11:22
h. slingers went about it. 2 Ki 3:25
h. Lord shewed me, that he. 8:10
h. from sins of Jeroboam, Jehu. 10:29
h. there were not made for. 12:13
h. high places were not taken away. 14:4; 15:35; 2 Chr 20:33
h. every nation made. 2 Ki 17:29
h. they did not hearken, but. 40
h. there was no reckoning. 22:7
h. the Lord God of Israel. 1 Chr 28:4
h. the king of Israel stayed himself. 2 Chr 18:34
h. the Levites hastened it not. 24:5
h. he entered not into temple. 27:2
h. in business of ambassadors. 32:31
h. thou art just in all. Neh 9:33
h. our God turned the curse. 13:2
h. he will not stretch out. Job 30:24
h. he meaneth not so. Isa 10:7
h. I sent to you all my. Jer 44:4
h. this kind goeth not. Mat 17:21
h. Jesus suffered him. Mark 5:19
h. in vain do they worship me. 7:7
h. there came boats from. John 6:23
h. no man spake openly of. 7:13
h. we know this man whence he. 27
h. Jesus spake of his death. 11:13
h. when he the Spirit of truth. 16:13
h. many who heard the. Acts 4:4
h. the Most High dwelleth not. 7:48
h. he rose up and came into. 14:20
h. certain men clave to him. 17:34
h. we must be cast upon a. 27:26
h. they looked when he should have swollen. 28:6
h. we speak wisdom. 1 Cor 2:6
h. there is not in every man. 8:7
h. in the Spirit he speaketh. 14:2
h. in malice be children, in. 20
h. that was not first which. 15:46
h. wherein soever any is. 2 Cor 11:21
h. when ye knew not God. Gal 4:8
h. for this cause I obtained mercy. 1 Tim 1:16
h. not all that came out of. Heb 3:16

howl

(*American Revision usually substitutes the word* wail)

h. ye, for the day of the. Isa 13:6
h. O gate. 14:31
Moab shall h. 15:2, 3; 16:7
h. ye ships of Tarshish, for it. 23:1
pass over to Tarshish, h. ye. 6
make them to h. 52:5
h. for vexation. 65:14
lament and h. Jer 4:8; 48:20

h. ye shepherds. *Jer* 25:34
inhabitants of the land shall *h.* 47:2
I will *h.* for Moab. 48:31
they shall *h.* 39
h. O Heshbon. 49:3
h. for Babylon. 51:8
cry and *h.* son of man. *Ezek* 21:12
prophesy and say, *H.* ye, woe. 30:2
h. ye drinkers. *Joel* 1:5
h. ye vinedressers. 11
lament and *h.* ye ministers of. 13
I will wail and *h.*, will go. *Mi* 1:8
h. ye inhabitants of. *Zeph* 1:11
h. fir tree, *h.* O ye oaks. *Zech* 11:2
ye rich men, weep and *h.* *Jas* 5:1

howled

not cried to me, when they *h.* on. *Hos* 7:14

howling

in waste *h.* wilderness. *Deut* 32:10
h. thereof is gone to Eglaim and. *Isa* 15:8
an *h.* of principal of the. *Jer* 25:36
h. from the second gate. *Zeph* 1:10
there is a voice of the *h.* *Zech* 11:3

howlings

songs of the temple shall be *h.* *Amos* 8:3

huge

and Lubims a *h.* host. *2 Chr* 16:8

humble

[1] *Not proud or assertive. The word does not have its modern sense of undue self-depreciation.* [2] *To humble is to humiliate.*

and he shall save the *h.* *Job* 22:29
not the cry of the *h.* *Ps* 9:12*
O God, forget not the *h.* 10:12*
hast heard the desire of the *h.* 17*
the *h.* shall hear thereof and. 34:2
h. shall see this and be glad. 69:32
better be of a *h.* spirit. *Pr* 16:19*
honour shall uphold the *h.* 29:23*
of a contrite and *h.* spirit, to revive the spirit of the *h.* *Isa* 57:15
but giveth grace to the *h.* *Jas* 4:6
1 Pet 5:5

humble

refuse to *h.* thyself? *Ex* 10:3
to *h.* thee and to prove. *Deut* 8:2, 16
h. ye them, and do. *Judg* 19:24
my people shall *h.* *2 Chr* 7:14
because thou didst *h.* thyself. 34:27
go, *h.* thyself, and make. *Pr* 6:3
h. yourselves, sit down. *Jer* 13:18
shall *h.* himself. *Mat* 18:4; 23:12
my God will *h.* me. *2 Cor* 12:21
h. yourselves in the sight. *Jas* 4:10
h. yourselves under. *1 Pet* 5:6

humbled

if their uncircumcised hearts be *h.* *Lev* 26:41
h. thee and suffered thee. *Deut* 8:3
because thou hast *h.* her. 21:14
22:29
hath *h.* his neighbour's wife. 22:24
because hast *h.* thyself. *2 Ki* 22:19
princes and the king *h.* *2 Chr* 12:6
when the Lord saw that they *h.* 7
he *h.* himself, wrath turned. 12
divers of Asher and Zebulun *h.* 30:11
Hezekiah *h.* himself for pride. 32:26
Manasseh *h.* himself greatly. 33:12
graven images before he was *h.* 19
Amon *h.* not himself before the Lord, as Manasseh his father *h.* 23
Zedekiah *h.* not himself. 36:12
as for me, I *h.* my soul. *Ps* 35:13*
looks of man shall be *h.* *Isa* 2:11*
h., eyes of the lofty shall be *h.* 5:15
and the haughty shall be *h.* 10:33*
they are not *h.* even to. *Jer* 44:10
remembrance and is *h.* *Lam* 3:20*
in thee have they *h.* *Ezek* 22:10
and another in thee hath *h.* 11
thou his son hast not *h.* *Dan* 5:22
he *h.* himself and became. *Phil* 2:8

humbledst

because thou *h.* thyself. *2 Chr* 34:27

humbleness

put on kindness, *h.* of. *Col* 3:12

humbleth

seest thou how Ahab *h.*? because he *h.* himself. *1 Ki* 21:29
he croucheth and *h.* *Ps* 10:10*
who *h.* himself to behold. 113:6
man boweth, great man *h.* *Isa* 2:9*
he that *h.* himself shall be exalted. *Luke* 14:11; 18:14

humbly

I *h.* beseech thee that. *2 Sam* 16:4
love mercy, and to walk *h.* *Mi* 6:8

humiliation

in his *h.* his judgement. *Acts* 8:33

humility

before honour is *h.* *Pr* 15:33; 18:12
by *h.* are riches, and honour. 22:4
Lord with all *h.* of mind. *Acts* 20:19*
beguile you in a voluntary *h.* *Col* 2:18
wisdom in will worship and *h.* 23
another, clothed with *h.* *1 Pet* 5:5

hundred

Shem was an *h.* years. *Gen* 11:10
child be born to him that is an *h.*? 17:17; 21:5; *Rom* 4:19
Jacob bought for an *h.* pieces. *Gen* 33:19; *Josh* 24:32
hangings *h.* cubits long. *Ex* 27:9, 11
38:9, 11
the court shall be an *h.* cubits. 18
h. sockets were cast of the *h.* 38:27
five shall chase an *h.* and an *h.* put to. *Lev* 26:8
shall amerce him in an *h.* *Deut* 22:19
so Gideon and the *h.* men. *Judg* 7:19
ten of an *h.* an *h.* of a 1000. 20:10
of Benjamin 25,000 and an *h.* 35
but an *h.* foreskins. *1 Sam* 18:25
2 Sam 3:14
an *h.* clusters of raisins. *1 Sam* 25:18
2 Sam 16:1
reserved for an *h.* chariots. *2 Sam* 8:4; *1 Chr* 18:4
provision for one day *h.* *1 Ki* 4:23
house of the forest an *h.* cubits. 7:2
Obadiah took *h.* prophets. 18:4, 13
this before an *h.* men? *2 Ki* 4:43
Jehoahaz in bands, and put land to a tribute of an *h.* 23:33; *2 Chr* 36:3
least was over an *h.* *1 Chr* 12:14
Simeon seven thousand and one *h.* 25
Lord make his people an *h.* 21:3
Solomon made an *h.* *2 Chr* 3:16
made an *h.* basons of gold. 4:8
men for an *h.* talents of silver. 25:6
what shall we do for the *h.* talents? 9
Jotham an *h.* talents of silver. 27:5
brought an *h.* rams. 29:32
they gave one *h.* priests'. *Ezra* 2:69
offered at the dedication an *h.* 6:17
an *h.* talents of silver, *h.* measures of wheat and wine, and an *h.* 7:22
h. talents of gold, an *h.* 8:26
restore to them the *h.* *Neh* 5:11
more than an *h.* stripes. *Pr* 17:10
man beget an *h.* children. *Eccl* 6:3
though sinner do evil *h.* times. 8:12
h. years old, but the sinner being an *h.* years old shall. *Isa* 65:20
measured an *h.* cubits. *Ezek* 40:19
gate to gate an *h.* cubits. 23, 27
h. cubits long, an *h.* cubits broad. 47
house an *h.* cubits long. 41:13
place toward east, an *h.* cubits. 14
one side and other, an *h.* cubits. 15
the temple were an *h.* cubits. 42:8
shall leave an *h.*, that which went forth by an *h.* shall. *Amos* 5:3
if a man have an *h.* sheep. *Mat* 18:12; *Luke* 15:4
owed him an *h.* pence. *Mat* 18:28
an *h.* measures of oil. *Luke* 16:6
thou? an *h.* measures of wheat. 7
myrrh and aloes, an *h.* *John* 19:39

hundredfold, *see* **fold**

one **hundred** *and five*

Seth lived *one h. and five* years. *Gen* 5:6

one **hundred** *and ten*

Joseph lived *one h. and ten* years. *Gen* 50:22, 26
Joshua died, being an *h. and ten* years old. *Josh* 24:29; *Judg* 2:8
Johanan an *h. and ten.* *Ezra* 8:12

one **hundred** *and twelve*

Uzziel an *h. and twelve.* *1 Chr* 15:10
Jorah, an *h. and twelve.* *Ezra* 2:18
Hariph, an *h. and twelve.* *Neh* 7:24

one **hundred** *and nineteen*

Terah *h. and nineteen.* *Gen* 11:25

one **hundred** *and twenty*

his days shall be *h. and twenty* years. *Gen* 6:3
the gold of the spoons was an *h. and twenty* shekels. *Num* 7:86
an *h. and twenty* years. *Deut* 31:2
Moses an *h. and twenty* years. 34:7
an *h. and twenty* talents of gold. *1 Ki* 10:10; *2 Chr* 9:9
and brethren an *h. and twenty.* *1 Chr* 15:5
porch an *h. and twenty.* *2 Chr* 3:4
an *h. and twenty* priests. 5:12
kingdom an *h. and twenty.* *Dan* 6:1
names were about an *h. and twenty.* *Acts* 1:15

one **hundred** *twenty two*

men of Michmash, *h. twenty two.* *Ezra* 2:27; *Neh* 7:31

one **hundred** *twenty three*

Aaron *h. twenty three.* *Num* 33:39
of captivity an *h. twenty and three.* *Ezra* 2:21; *Neh* 7:32

one **hundred** *and twenty seven*

Sarah was an *h. twenty seven.* *Gen* 23:1
reigned over an *h.* and *twenty seven.* *Esth* 1:1; 8:9; 9:30

one **hundred** *and twenty eight*

men of Anathoth *h. twenty eight.* *Ezra* 2:23; *Neh* 7:27
Asaph an *h. twenty eight.* *Ezra* 2:41
brethren an *h.* and *twenty eight.* *Neh* 11:14

one **hundred** *and thirty*

Adam lived *h. thirty* years. *Gen* 5:3
pilgrimage are an *h. and thirty.* 47:9
weight thereof was an *h. and thirty.* *Num* 7:13, 19, 25
charger weighing an *h. and thirty.* 85
brethren an *h. and thirty.* *1 Chr* 15:7
Jehoiada was an *h. and thirty* years. *2 Chr* 24:15

one **hundred** *thirty three*

Kohath an *h. thirty three.* *Ex* 6:18

one **hundred** *thirty seven*

Ishmael an *h.* and *thirty seven.* *Gen* 25:17
of Levi were *h.* and *thirty seven.* *Ex* 6:16
Amram were an *h. thirty seven.* 20

one **hundred** *thirty eight*

children of Shobai of Ater, *h. thirty eight.* *Neh* 7:45

one **hundred** *thirty nine*

of Shobai in all an *h. thirty nine.* *Ezra* 2:42

one **hundred** *forty*

Job an *h. forty* years. *Job* 42:16

one **hundred** *forty four*

the wall an *h. forty four* cubits. *Rev* 21:17

one **hundred** *forty seven*

Jacob an *h. forty seven.* *Gen* 47:28

one **hundred** *forty eight*

the children of Asaph *h. forty eight.* *Neh* 7:44

one **hundred** *and fifty*

waters prevailed an *h. and fifty* days. *Gen* 7:24; 8:3
and an horse for an *h. and fifty.* *1 Ki* 10:29; *2 Chr* 1:17
sons' sons an *h. and fifty.* *1 Chr* 8:40
reckoned of males, an *h. and fifty.* *Ezra* 8:3
table an *h. and fifty* Jews. *Neh* 5:17

one **hundred** *fifty three*

net full of fishes an *h. and fifty and three.* *John* 21:11

one **hundred** *fifty six*
Magbish, and *h. fifty six.* Ezra 2:30
one **hundred** *sixty*
with him *h. sixty* males. *Ezra* 8:10
one **hundred** *sixty two*
Jared lived *h. sixty two* years. *Gen* 5:18
one **hundred** *seventy two*
brethren *h. seventy two. Neh* 11:19
one **hundred** *seventy five*
life was an *h. seventy five. Gen* 25:7
one **hundred** *eighty*
of Isaac an *h.* and *eighty* years. *Gen* 35:28
feast for an *h.* and *eighty* days. *Esth* 1:4
one **hundred** *eighty two*
Lamech lived *h. eighty two* and. *Gen* 5:28
one **hundred** *eighty seven*
Methuselah lived *h. eighty seven. Gen* 5:25
one **hundred** *eighty eight*
of Beth-lehem an *h. eighty eight. Neh* 7:26
hundred *thousand*
Judah were an *h. thous. Num* 2:9
the camp of Reuben an *h. thous.* 16
slew of Syrians *h. thous. 1 Ki* 20:29
to king of Israel an *h. thous.* lambs, an *h. thous.* rams. *2 Ki* 3:4
from Hagarites an *h. thous.* men. *1 Chr* 5:21
thousand and *h. thous.* 21:5
for house of Lord *h. thous.* 22:14
an *h. thous.* talents of iron. 29:7
he hired an *h. thous. 2 Chr* 25:6
one **hundred** *and eight thousand and an* **hundred**
of camp of Ephraim, 108,100. *Num* 2:24
an **hundred** *twenty thousand*
the Midianites 120,000. *Judg* 8:10
a sacrifice of an 120,000 sheep. *1 Ki* 8:63; *2 Chr* 7:5
Gad, and Manasseh, 120,000. *1 Chr* 12:37
slew in Judah in one day 120,000. *2 Chr* 28:6
Nineveh were about 120,000 persons. *Jonah* 4:11
an **hundred** *forty four thousand*
were sealed 144,000 of all. *Rev* 7:4
with him 144,000, having his. 14:1
learn that song but the 144,000. 3
an **hundred** *fifty thousand*
strangers in the land of Israel were found 150,000. *2 Chr* 2:17
an **hundred** *eighty thousand*
with Benjamin 180,000. *1 Ki* 12:21 *2 Chr* 11:1
with Jehozabad were 180,000, for. *2 Chr* 17:18
an **hundred** *eighty five thousand*
of the Lord smote of the Assyrians, 185,000. *2 Ki* 19:35; *Isa* 37:36
two **hundred**
begat Nahor *two h.* years. *Gen* 11:23
two h. she goats, and *two h.* 32:14
Achan saw *two h.* shekels. *Josh* 7:21
his mother took *two h. Judg* 17:4
slew of Philistines *two h.* men. *1 Sam* 18:27
two h. abode by. 25:13; 30:10, 21
two h. loaves, *two h.* cakes. 25:18
weighed hair *two h. 2 Sam* 14:26
with Absalom went *two h.* 15:11
Ziba brought David *two h.* 16:1
pomegranates were *two h. 1 Ki* 7:20
Solomon made *two h.* targets. 10:16 *2 Chr* 9:15
burnt offerings *two h. 2 Chr* 29:32
were among them *two h. Ezra* 2:65
offered at dedication *two h.* 6:17
the fruit thereof *two h. S of S* 8:12
one lamb out of *two h. Ezek* 45:15
two h. pennyworth is not. *John* 6:7
make ready *two h.* soldiers, and spearmen *two h. Acts* 23:23

two **hundred** *five*
the days of Terah were *two h. five* years. *Gen* 11:32
two **hundred** *seven*
Reu lived *two h. seven. Gen* 11:21
two **hundred** *nine*
Peleg lived *two h. nine. Gen* 11:19
two **hundred** *twelve*
gates were *two h. twelve. 1 Chr* 9:22
two **hundred** *eighteen*
Obadiah *two h. eighteen. Ezra* 8:9
two **hundred** *twenty*
service of Levites *two h. twenty. Ezra* 8:20
two **hundred** *twenty three*
Beth-el and Ai *two h. twenty three. Ezra* 2:28
two **hundred** *thirty two*
of provinces *two h. thirty two. 1 Ki* 20:15
two **hundred** *forty two*
fathers *two h. forty two. Neh* 11:13
two **hundred** *forty five*
their mules *two h.* and *forty five. Ezra* 2:66; *Neh* 7:68
and *two h. forty five* singing men. *Neh* 7:67
two **hundred** *fifty*
cinnamon *two h.* and *fifty,* of calamus *two h.* and *fifty. Ex* 30:23
two h. and *fifty* princes. *Num* 16:2
two h. and *fifty* censers. 17
consumed the *two h.* and *fifty.* 35
two h. and *fifty* that bare. *2 Chr* 8:10
north *two h. fifty. Ezek* 48:17
two **hundred** *seventy six*
ship *two h. seventy six* souls. *Acts* 27:37
two **hundred** *eighty four*
in the holy city *two h. eighty four. Neh* 11:18
two **hundred** *eighty eight*
songs *two h. eighty eight. 1 Chr* 25:7
two **hundred** *fifty thousand*
sheep *two h. fifty thous. 1 Chr* 5:21
three **hundred**
Enoch walked with God *three h. Gen* 5:22
the ark shall be *three h.* 6:15
Benjamin *three h.* pieces of. 45:22
lapped were *three h.* men. *Judg* 7:6
and he retained those *three h.* 8
the *three h.* men that were. 8:4
coast of Arnon *three h.* years. 11:26
and caught *three h.* foxes. 15:4
spear weighed *three h.* shekels. *2 Sam* 21:16
Abishai lifted up his spear against *three h.* 23:18; *1 Chr* 11:11, 20
made *three h.* shields. *1 Ki* 10:17
Solomon had *three h.* 11:3
Hezekiah *three h.* talents. *2 Ki* 18:14
three h. shekels of gold. *2 Chr* 9:16
against Asa with *three h.* 14:19
passover offerings *three h.* 35:8
with Shechaniah *three h. Ezra* 8:5
the Jews slew *three h. Esth* 9:15
sold for *three h.* pence. *John* 12:5
three **hundred** *eighteen*
with *three h. eighteen* servants. *Gen* 14:14
three **hundred** *twenty*
Harim *three h.* and *twenty. Ezra* 2:32; *Neh* 7:35
three **hundred** *twenty three*
the children of Bezai 323. *Ezra* 2:17 *Neh* 7:23
three **hundred** *twenty eight*
of Hashum *three h. twenty eight. Neh* 7:22
three **hundred** *forty five*
children of Jericho 345. *Ezra* 2:34 *Neh* 7:36
three **hundred** *fifty*
flood *three h. fifty* years. *Gen* 9:28

three **hundred** *sixty*
of Israel *three h. sixty* men died. *2 Sam* 2:31
three **hundred** *sixty five*
Enoch's days were *three h. sixty five* years. *Gen* 5:23
three **hundred** *seventy two*
the children of Shephatiah 372. *Ezra* 2:4; *Neh* 7:9
three **hundred** *ninety*
to number of days 390. *Ezek* 4:5, 9
three **hundred** *thousand*
went out to war 300,000. *Num* 31:36
Israel were 300,000. *1 Sam* 11:8 *2 Chr* 14:8
with Adnah mighty men 300,000. *2 Chr* 17:14
and Benjamin to be 300,000. 25:5
three **hundred** *and seven thousand five* **hundred**
an army of 307,500. *2 Chr* 26:13
three **hundred** *and thirty seven thousand five* **hundred**
pertained unto the congregation was 337,500 sheep. *Num* 31:43
four **hundred**
afflict them *four h.* years. *Gen* 15:13; *Acts* 7:6
four h. shekels of silver. 23:15, 16
Esau cometh to thee with *four h.* 32:6; 33:1
found *four h.* virgins of. *Judg* 21:12
there were with David about *four h.* men. *1 Sam* 22:2; 25:13; 30:10
save *four h.* young men on. 30:17
four h. pomegranates. *1 Ki* 7:42
prophets of the groves *four h.* 18:19
gathered of the prophets about *four h.* and said. 22:6; *2 Chr* 18:5
brake down wall of Jerusalem *four h.* cubits. *2 Ki* 14:13; *2 Chr* 25:23
of house *four h.* lambs. *Ezra* 6:17
to whom about *four h. Acts* 5:36
four **hundred** *and three*
Arphaxad lived 403. *Gen* 11:13
lived after he begat Eber 403. 15
four **hundred** *and ten*
second sort *four h. ten. Ezra* 1:10
four **hundred** *and twenty*
from thence gold, 420. *1 Ki* 9:28
four **hundred** *and thirty*
Eber lived 430 years. *Gen* 11:17
in Egypt 430 years. *Ex* 12:40, 41
law which was 430 years. *Gal* 3:17
four **hundred** *thirty five*
their camels were 435. *Ezra* 2:67 *Neh* 7:69
four **hundred** *and fifty*
prophets of Baal 450. *1 Ki* 18:19, 22
gave judges about *four h. fifty* years. *Acts* 13:20
four **hundred** *fifty four*
Adin *four h. fifty four. Ezra* 2:15
four **hundred** *sixty eight*
of Perez were 468 men. *Neh* 11:6
four **hundred** *eighty*
in 480 years Solomon. *1 Ki* 6:1
four **hundred** *thousand*
Benjamin 400,000. *Judg* 20:2, 17
array with 400,000 men. *2 Chr* 13:3
four **hundred** *seventy thousand*
Judah was 470,000 that. *1 Chr* 21:5
five **hundred**
Noah was *five h.* years. *Gen* 5:32
Shem lived after *five h.* years. 11:11
of pure myrrh *five h. Ex* 30:23
of cassia *five h.* shekels after. 24
levy one soul of *five h. Num* 31:28
offerings *five h.* oxen. *2 Chr* 35:9
Shushan *five h.* men. *Esth* 9:6, 12
five h. yoke of oxen, *five h.* she asses. *Job* 1:3
he measured *five h.* reeds. *Ezek* 42:16, 17, 18, 19, 20
be for the sanctuary *five h.* in length, with *five h.* in breadth. 45:2
one owed *five h.* pence. *Luke* 7:41
above *five h.* brethren at. *1 Cor* 15:6

five **hundred** *and thirty*
gave *five h. and thirty* priests'. *Neh* 7:70
five **hundred** *and fifty*
five hundred fifty bare rule over. *1 Ki* 9:23
five **hundred** *thousand*
men of Judah were 500,000 men. *2 Sam* 24:9
slain of Israel 500,000 men. *2 Chr* 13:17
six **hundred**
Noah *six h.* years old when flood. *Gen* 7:6, 11
Pharaoh took *six h.* *Ex* 14:7
slew with an ox goad *six h.* *Judg* 3:31
out of Eshtaol *six h.* 18:11, 16, 17
six h. Benjamites fled to. 20:47
Saul numbered the people *six h.* *1 Sam* 13:15; 14:2
spear head weighed *six h.* 17:7
David and his men about *six h.* 23:13; 27:2; 30:9
all the Gittites were *six h.* men. *2 Sam* 15:18
six h. shekels of gold went to one target. *1 Ki* 10:16; *2 Chr* 9:15
a chariot went for *six h.* shekels. *1 Ki* 10:29; *2 Chr* 1:17
Ornan *six h.* shekels. *1 Chr* 21:25
house with gold to *six h.* talents. *2 Chr* 3:8
consecrated things were *six h.* oxen. 29:33
six **hundred** *twenty one*
children of Ramah *six h. twenty one.* *Ezra* 2:26; *Neh* 7:30
six **hundred** *twenty three*
Bebai *six h. twenty three.* *Ezra* 2:11
six **hundred** *twenty eight*
Bebai, *six h. twenty eight.* *Neh* 7:16
six **hundred** *forty two*
of Bani, *six h. forty two.* *Ezra* 2:10
Nekoda, *six h. forty two.* *Neh* 7:62
six **hundred** *forty eight*
Binnui, *six h. forty eight.* *Neh* 7:15
six **hundred** *and fifty*
weighed unto their hand *six h. fifty* talents. *Ezra* 8:26
six **hundred** *fifty two*
Nekoda, *six h. fifty two.* *Ezra* 2:60
Arah, *six h.* and *fifty two.* *Neh* 7:10
six **hundred** *sixty six*
gold to Solomon in year 666 talents. *1 Ki* 10:14
of Adonikam, 666. *Ezra* 2:13
and his number is 666. *Rev* 13:18
six **hundred** *sixty seven*
of Adonikam, 667. *Neh* 7:18
six **hundred** *seventy five*
tribute of sheep was 675. *Num* 31:37
six **hundred** *ninety*
Jeuel and brethren 690. *1 Chr* 9:6
six **hundred** *thousand*
journeyed about 600,000. *Ex* 12:37
for every man for 600,000. 38:26
numbered were 600,000. *Num* 1:46
people are 600,000 footmen. 11:21
six **hundred** *seventy five thousand*
prey was 675,000 sheep. *Num* 31:32
seven **hundred**
of Gibeah were *seven h.* chosen. *Judg* 20:15, 16
David took from him *seven h.* *2 Sam* 8:4
David slew men of *seven h.* 10:18
had *seven h.* wives. *1 Ki* 11:3
Moab took *seven h.* *2 Ki* 3:26
the Lord *seven h.* oxen. *2 Chr* 15:11
seven **hundred** *twenty one*
Lod, Hadid, Ono, 721. *Neh* 7:37
seven **hundred** *twenty five*
Lod, Hadid, Ono, 725. *Ezra* 2:33
seven **hundred** *thirty six*
their horses were 736. *Ezra* 2:66 *Neh* 7:68
seven **hundred** *forty three*
of Kirjath-arim, 743. *Ezra* 2:25
seven **hundred** *forty five*
captive of the Jews 745. *Jer* 52:30
seven **hundred** *sixty*
of Zaccai 760. *Ezra* 2:9; *Neh* 7:14
seven **hundred** *seventy five*
children of Arah, 775. *Ezra* 2:5
seven **hundred** *seventy seven*
of Lamech were 777. *Gen* 5:31
seven **hundred** *eighty two*
Methuselah lived 782. *Gen* 5:26
eight **hundred**
he begat Seth lived 800. *Gen* 5:4
after he begat Enoch lived 800. 19
his spear against 800. *2 Sam* 23:8
with 800,000 chosen men. *2 Chr* 13:3
eight **hundred** *seven*
after he begat Enos 807. *Gen* 5:7
eight **hundred** *fifteen*
after he begat Cainan 815. *Gen* 5:10
eight **hundred** *twenty two*
that did work were 822. *Neh* 11:12
eight **hundred** *thirty*
he begat Jared 830 years. *Gen* 5:16
eight **hundred** *thirty two*
carried captive 832. *Jer* 52:29
eight **hundred** *forty*
he begat Mahalaleel 840. *Gen* 5:13
eight **hundred** *forty five*
children of Zattu were 845. *Neh* 7:13
eight **hundred** *ninety five*
Mahalaleel were 895. *Gen* 5:17
nine **hundred**
Jabin had *nine h.* *Judg* 4:3, 13
nine **hundred** *five*
days of Enos were 905. *Gen* 5:11
nine **hundred** *ten*
days of Cainan 910 years. *Gen* 5:14
nine **hundred** *twelve*
days of Seth were 912. *Gen* 5:8
nine **hundred** *twenty eight*
him Gabbai, Sallai, 928. *Neh* 11:8
nine **hundred** *thirty*
that Adam lived were 930. *Gen* 5:5
nine **hundred** *forty five*
children of Zattu 945. *Ezra* 2:8
nine **hundred** *fifty*
of Noah were 950 years. *Gen* 9:29
nine **hundred** *fifty six*
brethren according to generations 956. *1 Chr* 9:9
nine **hundred** *sixty two*
Jared were 962 years. *Gen* 5:20
nine **hundred** *sixty nine*
days of Methuselah were 969 years. *Gen* 5:27
nine **hundred** *seventy three*
the children of Jedaiah 973. *Ezra* 2:36; *Neh* 7:39

hundreds

be rulers of *h.* and tens. *Ex* 18:21 25; *Deut* 1:15
was wroth with captains over *h.* *Num* 31:14
took gold of the captains of *h.* 54
will son of Jesse make you captains of *h.*? *1 Sam* 22:7
the Philistines passed on by *h.* 29:2
set captains of *h.* over. *2 Sam* 18:1
all the people came out by *h.* 4
and set the rulers over *h.* *2 Ki* 11:4
captains over *h.* did the priest give spears and. 10; *2 Chr* 23:9
with the captains of *h.* *1 Chr* 13:1
which the captains over *h.* 26:26
the captains over the *h.* 28:1
then the captains of *h.* offered. 29:6
Jehoiada took captains of *h.* into. *2 Chr* 23:1
made them captains over *h.* 25:5
sat down in ranks by *h.* *Mark* 6:40

hunger, *substantive*

whole assembly with *h.* *Ex* 16:3
serve thine enemies in *h.* *Deut* 28:48
they shall be burnt with *h.* 32:24
bread from heaven for their *h.* *Neh* 9:15
young lions do lack and suffer *h.* *Ps* 34:10
an idle soul shall suffer *h.* *Pr* 19:15
he is like to die for *h.* *Jer* 38:9*
see no war, nor have *h.* of. 42:14
that faint for *h.* in top of. *Lam* 2:19
than they that be slain with *h.* 4:9
be no more consumed with *h.* *Ezek* 34:29
and I perish with *h.* *Luke* 15:17
been in *h.* and thirst. *2 Cor* 11:27
given them to kill with *h.* *Rev* 6:8

hunger, *verb*

he suffered thee to *h.* *Deut* 8:3
shall not *h.* nor thirst. *Isa* 49:10
blessed are they that *h.* *Mat* 5:6 *Luke* 6:21
are full, for ye shall *h.* *Luke* 6:25
he that cometh to me shall never *h.* *John* 6:35
if thine enemy *h.* feed. *Rom* 12:20
we both *h.* and thirst. *1 Cor* 4:11
and if any man *h.* let him eat. 11:34
they shall *h.* no more. *Rev* 7:16

hungerbitten

his strength shall be *h.* *Job* 18:12

hungred, hungered

he was afterwards an *h.* *Mat* 4:2 *Luke* 4:2
his disciples were an *h.* *Mat* 12:1
did when he was an *h.* 3; *Mark* 2:25
returned into city, he *h.* *Mat* 21:18
for I was an *h.* and ye gave. 25:35
Lord, when saw we thee an *h.*? 37, 44
for I was an *h.* and ye gave. 42
did when himself was an *h.* *Luke* 6:3

hungry

they that were *h.* ceased. *1 Sam* 2:5
the people is *h.*, weary. *2 Sam* 17:29
they know that we be *h.* *2 Ki* 7:12
h. eateth up and taketh it. *Job* 5:5
withholden bread from the *h.* 22:7
away the sheaf from the *h.* 24:10
if I were *h.* I would not. *Ps* 50:12
h. and thirsty, their soul. 107:5
filleth the *h.* soul with goodness. 9
and there he maketh the *h.* to. 36
who giveth food to the *h.* 146:7
satisfy his soul when he is *h.* *Pr* 6:30
if thine enemy be *h.* give. 25:21
to the *h.* soul every bitter. 27:7
bestead and *h.*: when they shall be *h.*, they shall fret. *Isa* 8:21
snatch on right hand, and be *h.* 9:20
it shall even be as when a *h.* 29:8
empty the soul of the *h.* 32:6
yea, he is *h.* and his strength. 44:12
to deal thy bread to the *h.*? 58:7
draw out thy soul to the *h.* 10
shall eat, but ye shall be *h.* 65:13
his bread to the *h.* *Ezek* 18:7, 16
from Bethany he was *h.* *Mark* 11:12
he hath filled the *h.* with. *Luke* 1:53
Peter became very *h.* *Acts* 10:10
one is *h.* and another is. *1 Cor* 11:21
to be full and to be *h.* *Phil* 4:12

hunt

(Hunting as a matter of necessity, whether for the extermination of dangerous beasts or for procuring food, betokens a rude and semi-civilized state; as an amusement, it indicates an advanced state. As a pastoral people the Hebrews did little hunting as a sport; and their rules of eating prevented their doing so for food, after the Law was given)

Esau went to field to *h.* *Gen* 27:5
as when one doth *h.* *1 Sam* 26:20
wilt thou *h.* the prey? *Job* 38:39
evil shall *h.* violent man. *Ps* 140:11
the adulteress will *h.* *Pr* 6:26
shall *h.* them from every. *Jer* 16:16
they *h.* our steps that we. *Lam* 4:18
will ye *h.* the souls? *Ezek* 13:18
pillows wherewith ye there *h.* 20
h. every man his brother. *Mi* 7:2

hunted

in your hand to be *h.* *Ezek* 13:21

hunter, -s
mighty *h.* before the Lord: even as Nimrod the mighty *h.* *Gen* 10:9
Esau was a cunning *h.* 25:27
a roe from hand of the *h.* *Pr* 6:5
will I send for many *h.* *Jer* 16:16

huntest
yet thou *h.* my soul. *1 Sam* 24:11
h. me as a fierce lion. *Job* 10:16

hunteth
which *h.* and catcheth. *Lev* 17:13

hunting
brother came in from *h.* *Gen* 27:30
roasteth not that which he took in *h.* *Pr* 12:27

Hur
Moses, Aaron, *H.* went up. *Ex* 17:10
Aaron and *H.* stayed up his. 12
Aaron and *H.* are with you. 24:14
Bezaleel, the son of Uri, son of *H.* 31:2; 35:30; 38:22
they slew Evi, Rekem, Zur, *H.* and. *Num* 31:8; *Josh* 13:21
of *H.* in mount Ephraim. *1 Ki* 4:8
Ephratah, which bare *H.* *1 Chr* 2:19
H. begat Uri. 20
sons of Caleb the son of *H.* 50
sons of Judah, *H.* Shobal. 4:1
sons of *H.* Ephratah, Ashur. 4
Rephaiah son of *H.* *Neh* 3:9

hurl
if *h.* at him by lying in. *Num* 35:20

hurleth
and as a storm *h.* him. *Job* 27:21*

hurling
right hand and left in *h.* *1 Chr* 12:2*

hurt, *substantive*
a young man to my *h.* *Gen* 4:23
that thou wilt do us no *h.* 26:29
power of my hand to do you *h.* 31:29
he turn and do you *h.* *Josh* 24:20*
peace to thee, and no *h.* *1 Sam* 20:21
behold, David seeketh thy *h.* 24:9
that rise to do *h.* be. *2 Sam* 18:32
why meddle to thy *h.* that thou? *2 Ki* 14:10; *2 Chr* 25:19
why damage grow to *h.*? *Ezra* 4:22
such as sought their *h.* *Esth* 9:2
that sweareth to his *h.* *Ps* 15:4
that devise my *h.* 35:4; 70:2
ashamed that rejoice at my *h.* 26
my *h.* speak mischievous. 38:12
do they devise my *h.* 41:7
with reproach that seek my *h.* 71:13
brought to shame that seek my *h.* 24
for the owners to their *h.* *Eccl* 5:13
ruleth over another to his own *h.* 8:9
have healed *h.* of my people. *Jer* 6:14; 8:11
walk after other gods to your *h.* 7:6
for *h.* of my people am I *h.* 8:21
woe is me for my *h.*! 10:19
to be removed for their *h.* 24:9*
and I will do you no *h.* 25:6
provoke me to your own *h.* 7
welfare of this people, but the *h.* 38:4
they have no *h.* *Dan* 3:25
I have done no *h.* 6:22
and no manner of *h.* was. 23
voyage will be with *h.* *Acts* 27:10

hurt, *participle*
if a beast be *h.* no man. *Ex* 22:10
if it be *h.* or die, the owner. 14
were good and we were not *h.* *1 Sam* 25:15
whoso removeth stones shall be *h.* *Eccl* 10:9
for the *h.* of my people am I *h.* *Jer* 8:21
not be *h.* of second death. *Rev* 2:11

hurt, *verb*
suffered him not to *h.* me. *Gen* 31:7
men strive and *h.* woman. *Ex* 21:22
if one man's ox *h.* another's that. 35
neither have I *h.* one. *Num* 16:15
shepherds with us, we *h.* *1 Sam* 25:7
thy wickedness may *h.* a. *Job* 35:8
whose feet *h.* with fetters. *Ps* 105:18
not *h.* nor destroy in all my holy. *Isa* 11:9; 65:25
lest any *h.* it, I will keep it. 27:3
lions have not *h.* me. *Dan* 6:22
it shall not *h.* them. *Mark* 16:18
came out of him, and *h.* *Luke* 4:35
shall by any means *h.* you. 10:19
set on thee to *h.* thee. *Acts* 18:10
see thou *h.* not the oil. *Rev* 6:6
given to *h.* earth and sea. 7:2
saying, *H.* not the earth, neither. 3
they should not *h.* the grass. 9:4
and their power was to *h.* men. 10
heads, and with them they do *h.* 19
if any *h.* them, fire proceedeth. 11:5

hurtful
this city is *h.* to kings. *Ezra* 4:15
David from the *h.* sword. *Ps* 144:10
be rich fall into *h.* lusts. *1 Tim* 6:9

hurting
kept me from *h.* thee. *1 Sam* 25:34

husband
a bloody *h.* art thou to. *Ex* 4:25, 26
as the woman's *h.* will lay. 21:22
that is betrothed to a *h.* *Lev* 19:20 *Deut* 22:23
his sister which hath had no *h.* *Lev* 21:3; *Ezek* 44:25
if she had at all an *h.* *Num* 30:6
woman married to a *h.* *Deut* 22:22
and if the latter *h.* hate her or. 24:3
her former *h.* may not take her. 4
perform the duty of a *h.* 25:5
eye shall be evil toward *h.* 28:56
the *h.* of the woman slain. *Judg* 20:4
Naomi's *h.* died, she. *Ruth* 1:3
to have an *h.* if I should have an *h.* 12
the *h.* with the wife shall. *Jer* 6:11
although I was an *h.* to them. 31:32
with sackcloth for *h.* of. *Joel* 1:8
begat Joseph the *h.* of. *Mat* 1:16
she had lived with an *h.* *Luke* 2:36
I have no *h.* Thou hast well said, I have no *h.* *John* 4:17
if *h.* be dead, she is loosed from her *h.* *Rom* 7:2, 3
h. render to wife due benevolence, also wife to the *h.* *1 Cor* 7:3
also the *h.* hath not power of his. 4
let not the *h.* put away his wife. 11
woman who hath an *h.* that. 13
h. is sanctified by wife, and unbelieving wife is sanctified by *h.* 14
espoused you to one *h.* *2 Cor* 11:2
than she which hath an *h.* *Gal* 4:27
the *h.* is head of wife as. *Eph* 5:23
bishop be blameless, *h.* of one wife. *1 Tim* 3:2; *Tit* 1:6

***her* husband**
fruit, and gave to *her h.* *Gen* 3:6
wife gave Hagar to *her h.* 16:3
not take a woman put away from *her h.* *Lev* 21:7
hid from eyes of *her h.* *Num* 5:13
done trespass against *her h.* 27
aside to another instead of *her h.* 29
and *her h.* heard it, and. 30:7, 11, 14
if *her h.* disallow her on the day. 8
and if she vowed in *her h.'s* house. 10
if *her h.* hath utterly made. 12
her h. may establish it or make. 13
unto her, and be *her h.* *Deut* 21:13
her h.'s brother shall go in. 25:5
draweth near to deliver *her h.* 11
woman came and told *her h.* *Judg* 13:6
Manoah *her h.* was not with her. 9
made haste, and shewed *her h.* 10
her h. arose and went after. 19:3
her two sons and *her h.* *Ruth* 1:5
each of you in the house of *her h.* 9
Naomi had kinsman of *her h.* 2:1
Elkanah *her h.* to her. *1 Sam* 1:8, 23
she said unto *her h.* I will not go. 22
when she came up with *her h.* 2:19
father and *her h.* were dead. 4:19
because of *her h.* 21
she told not *her h.* 25:19
took her from *her h.* *2 Sam* 3:15
her h. went with her along. 16
wife of Uriah heard that *her h.* was dead, mourned for *her h.* 11:26
said to *her h.*, Behold now. *2 Ki* 4:9
hath no child, and *her h.* is old. 14
she called unto *her h.* and said. 22
wife is a crown to *her h.* *Pr* 12:4
heart of *her h.* doth safely. 31:11
her h. is known in the gates. 23
her h. also riseth up, and he. 28
wife departeth from *her h.* *Jer* 3:20
taketh strangers instead of *her h.* *Ezek* 16:32
that loatheth *her h.* and her. 45
wife, neither am I *her h.* *Hos* 2:2
now Joseph *her h.* being. *Mat* 1:19
shall put away *her h.* *Mark* 10:12
marrieth her put away from *her h.* *Luke* 16:18
buried her by *her h.* *Acts* 5:10
by law to *her h.* so long. *Rom* 7:2
if *her h.* be dead, she is free from. 3
woman have *her* own *h.* *1 Cor* 7:2
and likewise the wife to *her h.* 3
let not wife depart from *her h.* 10
or be reconciled to *her h.* 11
how she may please *her h.* 34
the law as long as *her h.* liveth. 39
that she reverence *her h.* *Eph* 5:33
a bride adorned for *her h.* *Rev* 21:2

***my* husband**
now therefore *my h.* *Gen* 29:32
this time will *my h.* be joined. 34
that thou hast taken *my h.*? 30:15
given my maiden to *my h.* 18
Leah said, Now will *my h.* dwell. 20
my h.'s brother refuseth. *Deut* 25:7
am a widow, *my h.* is dead. *2 Sam* 14:5; *2 Ki* 4:1
not leave to *my h.* a. *2 Sam* 14:7
go and return to *my* first *h.* *Hos* 2:7

***thy* husband**
desire shall be to *thy h.* *Gen* 3:16
instead of *thy h.* *Num* 5:19, 20
said to Samson's wife, entice *thy h.* *Judg* 14:15
since death of *thy h.* *Ruth* 2:11
is it well with *thy h.*? *2 Ki* 4:26
thy Maker is *thine h.* *Isa* 54:5
go, call *thy h.* *John* 4:16
he is not *thy h.* 18
that have buried *thy h.* *Acts* 5:9
thou shalt save *thy h.* *1 Cor* 7:16

husbandman
Noah began to be an *h.* *Gen* 9:20
I break in pieces the *h.* *Jer* 51:23
alas! they shall call the *h.* *Amos* 5:16
no prophet, I am a *h.* *Zech* 13:5*
vine, my Father is the *h.* *John* 15:1
h. that laboureth must. *2 Tim* 2:6
h. waiteth for precious. *Jas* 5:7

husbandmen
captain left of the poor to be *h.* *2 Ki* 25:12; *Jer* 52:16
Uzziah had *h.* also in. *2 Chr* 26:10
dwell in Judah itself *h.* *Jer* 31:24
ashamed, O ye *h.* howl. *Joel* 1:11
let it out to *h.* and went into a far. *Mat* 21:33; *Luke* 20:9
sent his servants to *h.* *Mat* 21:34 *Mark* 12:2; *Luke* 20:10
when *h.* saw the son. *Mat* 21:38 *Mark* 12:7; *Luke* 20:14
what will he do to those *h.*? *Mat* 21:40
his vineyard to other *h.* 41
might receive from *h.* *Mark* 12:2
he will come and destroy the *h.* 9

husbandry
Uzziah had husbandmen also: for he loved *h.* *2 Chr* 26:10
ye are God's *h.* ye are. *1 Cor* 3:9

husbands
they may be your *h.*? *Ruth* 1:11
stay for them from having *h.*? 13
shall despise their *h.* in. *Esth* 1:17
wives shall give to their *h.* honour. 20
give your daughters to *h.* *Jer* 29:6
which loathed their *h.* *Ezek* 16:45
thou hast had five *h.* *John* 4:18
let them ask their *h.* *1 Cor* 14:35
yourselves to your *h.* *Eph* 5:22, 24
h. love your wives, even as Christ. 25; *Col* 3:19
yourselves to your own *h.* *Col* 3:18
let deacons be the *h.* *1 Tim* 3:12
women to love their *h.* *Tit* 2:4
chaste, obedient to their own *h.* 5

subjection to your own h. 1 Pet 3:1
ye h. dwell with them according. 7

Hushai

H. the Archite came. 2 Sam 15:32
so H. David's friend came into. 37
H. came to Absalom and. 16:16
said to H., Is this thy kindness ? 17
call H. 17:5
for, said H. thou knowest thy. 8
the counsel of H. is better than. 14
then said H. to Zadok and to. 15
Baanah the son of H. 1 Ki 4:16
and H. was the king's. 1 Chr 27:33

husk, -s

kernels even to the h. Num 6:4
full ears of corn in h. 2 Ki 4:42
filled his belly with h. Luke 15:16

Huzzab

H. be led away captive. Nah 2:7

Hymenaeus

of whom is H. and. 1 Tim 1:20
is H. and Philetus. 2 Tim 2:17

hymn, -s

when they had sung an h. Mat 26:30
Mark 14:26
to yourselves in psalms and h.
Eph 5:19
one another in psalms and h. Col 3:16

hypocrisies

aside all malice and h. 1 Pet 2:1

hypocrisy

(*A false assumption of virtue; canting pretence of goodness or religion. The word is frequently used in the Bible with the meaning of godlessness*)
iniquity, to practise h. Isa 32:6
within ye are full of h. Mat 23:28
knowing their h. said. Mark 12:15
of Pharisees, which is h. Luke 12:1
speaking lies in h. their. 1 Tim 4:2
is pure and without h. Jas 3:17

hypocrite

the h.'s hope shall perish. Job 8:13*
for an h. shall not come. 13:16*
shall stir up himself against h. 17:8*
and the joy of the h. is but. 20:5*
what is the hope of the h.? 27:8*
h. reign not, lest the people. 34:30*
an h. with his mouth destroyeth.
Pr 11:9*
for every one is an h. Isa 9:17*
thou h., first cast out beam. Mat 7:5
thou h., cast beam out. Luke 6:42
thou h., doth not each one ? 13:15

hypocrites

congregation of h. shall. Job 15:34*
the h. in heart heap up. 36:13*
fearfulness hath surprised the h.
Isa 33:14*
not sound a trumpet, as h. Mat 6:2
prayest, thou shalt not be as h. 5
when ye fast, be not as the h. 16
ye h. well did Esaias prophesy. 15:7
Mark 7:6
O ye h. ye can discern the face of.
Mat 16:3; Luke 12:56
why tempt ye me, ye h.? Mat 22:18
scribes and Pharisees, h. ye shut up.
23:13, 14, 15, 23, 25, 27, 29
him his portion with the h. 24:51
scribes and Pharisees, h. Luke 11:44

hypocritical

with h. mockers in feasts. Ps 35:16*
him against an h. nation. Isa 10:6*

hyssop

(*A bushy herb in common use among the Hebrews. It is not known whether it was or was not the shrub now known by the name*)
shall take a bunch of h. Ex 12:22
take cedar wood, scarlet, and h.
Lev 14:4, 6, 49, 51
cleanse the house with the h. 52
shall cast h. into midst. Num 19:6
a clean person shall take h. 18
cedar tree even unto the h. 1 Ki 4:33
purge me with h. and I. Ps 51:7
spunge, and put it on h. John 19:29
he took blood with h. Heb 9:19

I

I

behold I, even I, do bring a flood.
Gen 6:17
I, behold I, establish my. 9:9
I shall be destroyed, I and. 34:30
shall I, thy mother and ? 37:10
and I, whither shall I go ? 30
in this house greater than I. 39:9
who am I, that I should go to ?
Ex 3:11
Lord is righteous, I and my. 9:27
and I, behold I will harden. 14:17
I thy father in law Jethro am. 18:6
I, behold I, have given with. 31:6
I, even I, will chastise. Lev 26:28
I, behold I, have taken the Levites.
Num 3:12; 18:6
nations more than I, how can I.?
Deut 7:17
I, even I, am he, there is no. 32:39
forty years old was I. Josh 14:7
I, even I, will sing to the. Judg 5:3
till I Deborah arose, that I arose. 7
when I blow, I and all that. 7:18
may bewail my virginity, I. 11:37
I and my people were at strife. 12:2
I came to Gibeah, I and my. 20:4
more righteous than I. 1 Sam 24:17
I and my kingdom are. 2 Sam 3:28
I, whither shall I cause my ? 13:13
I and my son Solomon be. 1 Ki 1:21
I, even I, only remain a prophet.
18:22; 19:10, 14
who am I, and what my people that
we should ? 1 Chr 29:14; 2 Chr 2:6
what I and fathers have. 2 Chr 32:13
I, even I Artaxerxes. Ezra 7:21
but so did not I, because. Neh 5:15
I also and my maidens. Esth 4:16
I only am escaped to tell thee.
Job 1:15, 16, 17, 19
condemneth thee, and not I. 15:6
refuse or choose, and not I. 34:33
rock that is higher than I. Ps 61:2
they are stronger than I. 142:6
hereunto more than I? Eccl 2:25
I am the rose of Sharon. S of S 2:1
I am my beloved's. 6:3; 7:10
I am a wall. 8:10
I and children Lord hath given me.
Isa 8:18; Heb 2:13
I the Lord, the first; I am he.
Isa 41:4; 43:11, 25
I am with thee, for I. 41:10; 43:5
I am the first, I am the last. 44:6
48:12; Rev 1:17
who as I shall call, and ? Isa 44:7
I, even my hands have. 45:12
even to your old age I am he, I. 46:4
I am God, and there is none else, I. 9
I, even I have spoken, I have. 48:15
it was, there am I. 16; Mat 18:20
yet shall I be glorious in. Isa 49:5
I, even I am he. 51:12; 52:6
behold, it is I. 52:6
stand by thyself, for I am. 65:5
thou art stronger than I. Jer 20:7
behold I, even I, will utterly. 23:39
behold I, even I, am against thee.
Ezek 5:8
behold I, even I, will bring a. 6:3
behold I, even I, will search. 34:11
I, even I, will judge between fat. 20
I am their inheritance, I am. 44:28
when I, even I Daniel. Dan 8:15
I, even I, will tear, I will. Hos 5:14
Haggai spoke, I am with. Hag 1:13
I was but little displeased. Zech 1:15
I accept of your hands ? Mal 1:13
after me is mightier than I.
Mat 3:11; Mark 1:7
it is I, be not afraid. Mat 14:27
Mark 6:50; John 6:20
men say that I the Son ? Mat 16:13
two or three, there am I in. 18:20
in name, saying, I am Christ. 24:5
began to say, Lord, is it I ? 26:22
offended, yet will not I. Mark 14:29
father and I sought thee. Luke 2:48
if I by Beelzebub cast out. 11:19
if I with the finger of God cast. 20
name saying, I am Christ. Luke 21:8
but I am among you as he. 22:27
that it is I myself, handle me. 24:39
he confessed, I am not the Christ.
John 1:20; 3:28
I knew him not. 33
I that speak am he. 4:26
I am not alone, but I and. 8:16
I am from above, I am not of. 23
I am he, I do nothing of myself. 28
verily, before Abraham was, I. 58
I and my Father are one. 10:30
the Father in me, and I in him. 38
17:21
and I, if I be lifted up, will. 12:32
if I then your Lord and. 13:14
I in my Father. 14:20
I go unto Father: for my Father is
greater than I. 28
abide in me, and I in you. 15:4
I in them. 17:23, 26
but I have known thee. 25
Pilate answered, am I a Jew ? 18:35
what was I, that I could ? Acts 11:17
I obtained this freedom; I was. 22:28
no more I, that do it. Rom 7:17, 20
I am of Paul, I of Apollos, I of.
1 Cor 1:12; 3:4
and I, brethren, when I came to. 2:1
and I, brethren, could not speak. 3:1
I would that all men even as I. 7:7
if they abide even as I. 8
yet not I, but Lord. 10
or I only and Barnabas, have. 9:6
I therefore so run, so fight I, not. 26
of me, even as I am of Christ. 11:1
I am what I am, yet not I. 15:10
whether it were I or they, so. 11
work of Christ, even as I. 16:10
Hebrews ? so am I. 2 Cor 11:22
I am more. 23
I burn not ? 29
dead to the law, that I. Gal 2:19
I live, yet not I, but Christ liveth. 20
brethren, be as I am, for I am. 4:12
I, brethren, if I yet preach. 5:11
I should glory in cross, and I to. 6:14
I also, after I heard of. Eph 1:15
I therefore, prisoner of the Lord. 4:1
be ye holy, for I am. 1 Pet 1:16
I love in the truth, and not I only.
2 John 1
I am Alpha and Omega. Rev 1:8
as many as I love, I rebuke. 3:19
as I also overcame. 21
I John saw. 21:2; 22:8
see thou do it not, I am thy. 22:9
I Jesus have sent my angel to testify
these things, I am the root and. 16

Ibhar

David's son I. 2 Sam 5:15
1 Chr 3:6; 14:5

ice

blackish by reason of ice. Job 6:16
womb came the ice and frost. 38:29
forth his ice like morsels. Ps 147:17

Ichabod

child I. glory departed. 1 Sam 4:21
Ahiah, the son of Ahitub, I. 14:3

Iconium

Barnabas came unto I. Acts 13:51
in I. they went both into the. 14:1
thither certain Jews from I. 19
of by the brethren at I. 16:2
which came to me at I. 2 Tim 3:11

Iddo

Abinadab son of I. had. 1 Ki 4:14
Joash his son, I. his. 1 Chr 6:21
half tribe of Manasseh I. 27:21
acts of Solomon written in visions of
I. the. 2 Chr 9:29; 12:15; 13:22
Zechariah son of I. prophesied.
Ezra 5:1; Zech 1:1, 7
prophesying of Zechariah son of I.
Ezra 6:14
I. the chief, and told them what they
should say to I. and his. 8:17
I. with priests went up. Neh 12:4

idle

[1] *One who is slothful or lazy,* Ex 5:8, 17. [2] *One that would*

work, but is not hired, Mat 20:3, 6.
[3] *Unprofitable,* Mat 12:36.
they be *i.*; therefore they cry. *Ex* 5:8
are *i.* ye are *i.*: ye say, Let us go. 17
and *i.* soul shall suffer. *Pr* 19:15
every *i.* word that men. *Mat* 12:36
standing *i.* in marketplace. 20:3, 6
words seemed *i.* tales. *Luke* 24:11
they learn to be *i.* and not only *i.*
1 Tim 5:13

idleness
eateth not the bread of *i.* *Pr* 31:27
i. the house droppeth. *Eccl* 10:18
and abundance of *i.* *Ezek* 16:49*

idol
woe to the *i.* shepherd. *Zech* 11:17

idol
she made an *i.* in grove. *1 Ki* 15:13
2 Chr 15:16
he set the *i.* in house of. *2 Chr* 33:7
he took the *i.* out of the house. 15
say my *i.* hath done them. *Isa* 48:5
incense as if he blessed an *i.* 66:3
a despised broken *i.* *Jer* 22:28*
offered sacrifice to the *i.* *Acts* 7:41
we know an *i.* is nothing in world.
1 Cor 8:4; 10:19
some with conscience of the *i.* 8:7

idolater
a brother be an *i.* not to. *1 Cor* 5:11
an *i.* hath any inheritance. *Eph* 5:5

idolaters
with the covetous or *i.* *1 Cor* 5:10
i. shall not inherit the kingdom. 6:9
neither be ye *i.* as were some. 10:7
but *i.* shall have their part. *Rev* 21:8
without are murderers and *i.* 22:15

idolatries
walked in abominable *i.* *1 Pet* 4:3

idolatrous
Josiah put down the *i.* *2 Ki* 23:5

idolatry
is as iniquity and *i.* *1 Sam* 15:23*
city wholly given to *i.* *Acts* 17:16*
beloved, flee from *i.* *1 Cor* 10:14
works of the flesh are *i.* *Gal* 5:20
covetousness, which is *i.* *Col* 3:5

idols
turn ye not unto *i.* *Lev* 19:4
shall make no *i.* 26:1
carcases upon carcases of your *i.* 30
their *i.* wood and stone. *Deut* 29:17
in the house of their *i.* *1 Sam* 31:9
Asa removed the *i.* his. *1 Ki* 15:12
abominable in following *i.* 21:26
for they served *i.* *2 Ki* 17:12
2 Chr 24:18
Judah to sin with his *i.* *2 Ki* 21:11
Amon served the *i.* that his. 21
the *i.* that were spied in the. 23:24
carry tidings to their *i.* *1 Chr* 10:9
gods of the people are *i.* 16:26
Asa put away abominable *i.* out.
2 Chr 15:8
Josiah cut down all the *i.* in. 34:7*
gods of the nations are *i.* *Ps* 96:5
that boast themselves of *i.* 97:7
they served their *i.* that. 106:36
whom they sacrificed to the *i.* of. 38
their *i.* are silver. 115:4; 135:15
their land is full of *i.* *Isa* 2:8
the *i.* he shall utterly abolish. 18
cast away his *i.* of silver. 20; 31:7
hath found kingdoms of *i.* 10:10
i., so do to Jerusalem and her *i.*? 11
i. of Egypt shall be moved at. 19:1
they shall seek to the *i.* and to. 3
the makers of *i.* shall go to. 45:16
their *i.* were on the beasts. 46:1
inflaming yourselves with *i.* 57:5
her *i.* are confounded. *Jer* 50:2*
and they are mad upon their *i.* 38
I will cast down your slain men
before your *i.* *Ezek* 6:4, 5, 13
laid waste, your *i.* may be broken. 6
go a whoring after their *i.* 9
offer sweet savour to all their *i.* 13
the *i.* of Israel pourtrayed. 8:10
up their *i.* in their heart. 14:3, 4, 7
estranged from me through their *i.* 5
repent, and turn from your *i.* 6
i. of thy abominations. *Ezek* 16:36
eyes to the *i.* of Israel. 18:6, 15
hath lifted up his eyes to the *i.* 12
yourselves with *i.* of Egypt. 20:7, 18
nor did they forsake the *i.* of. 8
for their heart went after *i.* 16
their eyes went after father's *i.* 24
pollute yourselves with all your *i.*
20:31; 22:4; 23:7, 30, 37
my holy name no more with *i.* 20:39
city maketh *i.* against herself. 22:3
slain their children to their *i.* 23:39
ye shall bear the sins of your *i.* 49
I will destroy *i.* and will. 30:13
up your eyes towards your *i.* 33:25
i. wherewith they polluted it. 36:18
from *i.* will I cleanse you. 25; 37:23
astray from me after their *i.* 44:10
ministered to them before their *i.* 12
Ephraim is joined to *i.* *Hos* 4:17
gold have they made them *i.* 8:4
have made *i.* according to. 13:2
I to do any more with *i.* 14:8
i. thereof will I lay. *Mi* 1:7
therein to make dumb *i.* *Hab* 2:18
i. have spoken vanity. *Zech* 10:2*
I will cut off names of the *i.* 13:2
from pollutions of *i.* *Acts* 15:20
from meats offered to *i.* 29; 21:25
thou that abhorrest *i.* *Rom* 2:22
things offered to *i.* *1 Cor* 8:1, 4, 10
10:19, 28; *Rev* 2:14, 20
carried away to dumb *i.* *1 Cor* 12:2
temple of God with *i.*? *2 Cor* 6:16
ye turned to God from *i.* *1 Thes* 1:9
keep yourselves from *i.* *1 John* 5:21
not worship devils and *i.* *Rev* 9:20

Idumea
shall come down on *I.* *Isa* 34:5, 6
I. shall be desolate. *Ezek* 35:15
have I spoken against all *I.* 36:5
followed him from *I.* *Mark* 3:8

if
she said, *if* it be so ? *Gen* 25:22
if he said thus. 31:8
if ye will be as we be. 34:15
if it must be so now, take of. 43:11
if so be the Lord will. *Josh* 14:12
if they say to us, Tarry. *1 Sam* 14:9
if we say thus, it is well. 20:7
2 Sam 15:26
if we say, *if* we sit still here; *if* they
save us, *if* they kill us. *2 Ki* 7:4
if ye be mine, *if* ye will. 10:6
if I be wicked. *Job* 9:29; 10:15
if it be not so. 24:25
if I have done this, *if* there. *Ps* 7:3
if they be prophets, *if*. *Jer* 27:18
take balm for her pain, *if* so. 51:8
if it be so, our God is. *Dan* 3:17
if it may be a lengthening. 4:27
if so be it yield, strangers. *Hos* 8:7
if thou be the Son of God. *Mat* 4:3
27:40; *Luke* 4:3
if it be thou, bid me come. *Mat* 14:28
let him deliver him, *if* he. 27:43
if thou wilt, thou canst. *Mark* 1:40
if we shall say, Of men. 11:32
if he be Christ. *Luke* 23:35, 39
John 10:24
if thou be not Elias. *John* 1:25
if the world hate you. 15:18
1 John 3:13
if thou let this man go. *John* 19:12
if it be of God ye cannot. *Acts* 5:39
if in this life only we. *1 Cor* 15:19
if a son, then an heir of. *Gal* 4:7
if any consolation, *if* any. *Phil* 2:1
if they shall enter. *Heb* 4:3, 5
if they had been of us. *1 John* 2:19

if *not*
if not I will know. *Gen* 18:21
if not tell me. 24:49
if not, blot me, I pray. *Ex* 32:32
if not, let fire come out. *Judg* 9:15, 20
and *if not*, I will take. *1 Sam* 2:16
if not, then we shall know it is. 6:9
if not, I pray thee. *2 Sam* 13:26
after his saying? *if not* speak. 17:6
but *if not*, it shall not. *2 Ki* 2:10
if not, where, and who? *Job* 9:24
if not, hearken unto me, hold. 33:33
if not, be it known to. *Dan* 3:18
give me my price; *if not*. *Zech* 11:12
but *if not*, it shall turn. *Luke* 10:6
if not, after that thou shalt. 13:9

if *now*
if now I have found favour. *Gen* 18:3
O God, *if now* thou do. 24:42
if now ye will deal kindly with. 49
if now I have found grace in thy.
33:10; 47:29; *Ex* 34:9; *Judg* 6:17
if now thou didst receive it.
1 Cor 4:7

ignominy
and with *i.* reproach. *Pr* 18:3

ignorance
if a soul shall sin through *i.* *Lev* 4:2*
5:15; *Num* 15:24*, 27*, 28*, 29*
of Israel sin through *i.* *Lev* 4:13*
hath done somewhat through *i.* 22*
common people sin through *i.* 27*
forgiven them, for it is *i.* *Num* 15:25*
I wot that through *i.* ye. *Acts* 3:17
and the times of this *i.* God. 17:30
alienated through the *i.* *Eph* 4:18
to former lusts in your *i.* *1 Pet* 1:14
ye may put to silence *i.* of. 2:15

ignorant
foolish was I, and *i.*; I was. *Ps* 73:22
they are all *i.* they are. *Isa* 56:10*
though Abraham be *i.* of us. 63:16
that they were *i.* men. *Acts* 4:13
I would not have you *i.* brethren.
Rom 1:13; *1 Cor* 10:1; 12:1
2 Cor 1:8; *1 Thes* 4:13
i. of God's righteousness. *Rom* 10:3
should be *i.* of this mystery. 11:25
man be *i.* let him be *i.* *1 Cor* 14:38
not *i.* of Satan's devices. *2 Cor* 2:11
have compassion on the *i.* *Heb* 5:2
they are willingly *i.* of. *2 Pet* 3:5*
but, beloved, be not *i.* of this one. 8

ignorantly
soul that sinneth *i.* *Num* 15:28*
killeth his neighbour *i.* *Deut* 19:4*
ye *i.* worship, declare I. *Acts* 17:23
because I did it *i.* in. *1 Tim* 1:13

ill
kine came up *i.* favoured. *Gen* 41:3
4, 19, 20, 21
why dealt ye so *i.* with me? 43:6
hath any *i.* blemish. *Deut* 15:21
it shall go *i.* with him. *Job* 20:26*
it went *i.* with Moses. *Ps* 106:32
the wicked, it shall be *i.* *Isa* 3:11
if it seem *i.* to thee to. *Jer* 40:4
his stink and his *i.* *Joel* 2:20
behaved themselves *i.* *Mi* 3:4*
love worketh no *i.* to. *Rom* 13:10

illuminated
ye were *i.* ye endured. *Heb* 10:32*

Illyricum
round about unto *I.* *Rom* 15:19

image
make man in our *i.* *Gen* 1:26, 27
9:6
a son in his own *i.* after his *i.* 5:3
nor rear up a standing *i.* *Lev* 26:1*
Deut 16:22*
Michal took an *i.* and. *1 Sam* 19:13*
behold there was an *i.* in bed. 16*
put away the *i.* of Baal. *2 Ki* 3:2*
they brake down the *i.* and. 10:27*
Manasseh set carved *i.* *2 Chr* 33:7
an *i.* was before mine. *Job* 4:16*
shalt despise their *i.* *Ps* 73:20
seat of the *i.* of jealousy. *Ezek* 8:3, 5
behold, a great *i.* stood. *Dan* 2:31
stone that smote *i.* became a. 35
the king made an *i.* of gold. 3:1
worship the golden *i.* 5, 10, 15
many days without an *i.* *Hos* 3:4*
whose is this *i.*? *Mat* 22:20
Mark 12:16; *Luke* 20:24
of the *i.* which fell down. *Acts* 19:35
glory of God into an *i.* *Rom* 1:23
to be conformed to the *i.* of. 8:29
bowed the knee to *i.* of Baal. 11:4
is the *i.* and glory of God. *1 Cor* 11:7
as we have borne the *i.* of. 15:49
changed into same *i.* *2 Cor* 3:18

the i. of God. 2 Cor 4:4; Col 1:15
after the i. of him that. Col 3:10
by his Son, the express i. Heb 1:3
a shadow, not the very i. of. 10:1
they should make an i. Rev 13:14
had power to give life unto the i. 15
man worship beast and his i. 14:9
rest, who worship beast and his i. 11
victory over beast and his i. 15:2
fell on them that worshipped i. 16:2
them that worshipped his i. 19:20
not worshipped beast nor his i. 20:4
see **graven**

molten **image**
made them a *molten i.* Deut 9:12
son to make a *molten i.* Judg 17:3
and worshipped *molten i.* Ps 106:19
for his *molten i.* is falsehood.
Jer 10:14; 51:17
graven and *molten i.* Hab 2:18

imagery
in the chambers of his i. Ezek 8:12

images
Rachel had stolen her father's i.
Gen 31:19*, 34*
searched but found not the i. 35*
quite break down their i. Ex 23:24*
34:13*; Deut 7:5*; Num 33:52
I will cut down your i. Lev 26:30
make i. of your emerods. 1 Sam 6:5
they laid the i. of their emerods. 11
they left their i., David. 2 Sam 5:21
hast made molten i. to. 1 Ki 14:9
built them high places, i. and. 23*
i. out of house of Baal. 2 Ki 10:26
his i. brake they in pieces. 11:18
18:4*; 23:14*
set up i. 17:10*
they made molten i. 16
Josiah put away i. that were. 23:24*
broke down the i. 2 Chr 14:3, 5
Jehoiada brake i. 23:17
Hezekiah brake i. 31:1*
Ahaz made also molten i. 28:2
sacrificed to all the carved i. 33:22
down carved and molten i. 34:3, 4
not look to groves or i. Isa 17:8
the groves and i. shall not. 27:9
the ornament of molten i. 30:22
their molten i. are wind and. 41:29
he shall break the i. Jer 43:13*
idols confounded, her i. are. 50:2
altars desolate, and your i. Ezek 6:4
idols broken, and that your i. may. 6
but they made the i. of their. 7:20
madest to thyself i. of men. 16:17
of Babylon consulted with i. 21:21
the i. of the Chaldeans. 23:14
cause their i. to cease out of. 30:13
they have made goodly i. Hos 10:1*
their altars, spoil their i. 2*
have made their molten i. of. 13:2
the tabernacle of your i. Amos 5:26
graven and standing i. Mi 5:13*

image work
he made two cherubims of *i. work.*
2 Chr 3:10

imagination
(An old meaning of the word is a plotting or a devising of evil. Another, which is much used in the Bible, is stubbornness)
every i. of his heart was. Gen 6:5
the i. of man's heart is evil. 8:21
though I walk in the i. Deut 29:19*
for I know their i. 31:21
1 Chr 28:9
this for ever in the i. 1 Chr 29:18
the i. of his own heart. Jer 23:17*
scattered the proud in i. Luke 1:51

imaginations
Lord understandeth all i. 1 Chr 28:9
heart that deviseth wicked i. Pr 6:18
hast seen all their i. Lam 3:60*
thou hast heard all their i. 61*
became vain in their i. Rom 1:21*
casting down i. that. 2 Cor 10:5
see **heart**

imagine
do ye i. to reprove words? Job 6:26
the devices ye wrongfully i. 21:27
why do the people i. a? Ps 2:1
they seek my hurt and i. 38:12
how long will ye i. mischief? 62:3*
i. mischief in their heart. 140:2†
heart of them that i. evil. Pr 12:20*
yet do they i. mischief. Hos 7:15†
what do ye i. against? Nah 1:9†
let none i. evil against neighbour.
Zech 7:10†; 8:17†
why do the people i.? Acts 4:25

imagined
which they have i. Gen 11:6*
in devices they have i. Ps 10:2†
they i. mischievous device. 21:11†

imagineth
there is one that i. evil. Nah 1:11†

Imlah, *see* **Micaiah; Immanuel,** *see* **Emmanuel**

immediately
they i. left the ship and. Mat 4:22
i. his leprosy was cleansed. 8:3
Mark 1:42; Luke 5:13
i. received sight. Mat 20:34
Mark 10:52; Luke 18:43
i. the cock crew. Mat 26:74
Luke 22:60; John 18:27
i. the Spirit driveth him. Mark 1:12
he lifted her up, and i. the. 31
Satan cometh i. and taketh. 4:15
when affliction ariseth, i. they. 17
mouth was opened i. Luke 1:64
i. it fell. 6:49
i. her issue of blood staunched. 8:44
i. she was made straight. 13:13
kingdom of God should i. 19:11
and i. the man was made. John 5:9
Aeneas arose i. Acts 9:34
I sent i. to thee. 10:33
i. the angel of the Lord smote. 12:23
and i. all the doors were. 16:26
i. I conferred not with. Gal 1:16
and i. I was in the Spirit. Rev 4:2

immortal
King eternal, i., invisible. 1 Tim 1:17*

immortality
to them who seek for i. Rom 2:7*
mortal must put on i. 1 Cor 15:53
this mortal shall have put on i. 54
only hath i. dwelling. 1 Tim 6:16
who brought i. to light. 2 Tim 1:10*

immutability
the i. of his counsel. Heb 6:17

immutable
that by two i. things, in. Heb 6:18

impart
two coats, let him i. to. Luke 3:11
that I may i. to you some. Rom 1:11

imparted
nor hath he i. to her. Job 39:17
were willing to have i. 1 Thes 2:8

impediment
bring one that had i. in. Mark 7:32

impenitent
thou, after thy i. heart. Rom 2:5

imperious
work of an i. whorish. Ezek 16:30

implacable
without natural affection, i. Rom 1:31

implead
law is open, let them i. Acts 19:38*

importunity
of his i. he will rise and. Luke 11:8

impose
it shall not be lawful to i. Ezra 7:24

imposed
in carnal ordinances i. on. Heb 9:10

impossible
and nothing shall be i. Mat 17:20
with men this is i.; but. 19:26
Mark 10:27; Luke 18:27
for with God nothing shall be i.
Luke 1:37*; 18:27
it is i. but that offences will. 17:1
it is i. for those who were. Heb 6:4*
it was i. for God to lie. 18
without faith it is i. to please. 11:6

impotent
a great multitude of i. John 5:3*
deed done to the i. man. Acts 4:9
there sat a man at Lystra i. in. 14:8

impoverish
shall i. thy fenced cities. Jer 5:17*

impoverished
Israel was greatly i. Judg 6:6*
he that is so i. chooseth. Isa 40:20
Edom saith, We are i. but. Mal 1:4*

imprisoned
they know that I i. Acts 22:19

imprisonment
death, banishment, or i. Ezra 7:26
of mockings, bonds, i. Heb 11:36

imprisonments
in stripes, in i., in tumults. 2 Cor 6:5

impudent
and with an i. face she. Pr 7:13
for they are i. children Ezek 2:4
the house of Israel are i. 3:7*

impute
[1] *To charge or credit another with,* 2 Sam 19:19. [2] *To ascribe vicariously,* Rom 4:11. *The Revisions frequently substitute* reckon.
let not the king i. any. 1 Sam 22:15
let not my lord i. 2 Sam 19:19
the Lord will not i. sin. Rom 4:8

imputed
nor shall it be i. to him. Lev 7:18
blood shall be i. to that man. 17:4
righteousness might be i. Rom 4:11
i. to him for righteousness. 22, 23
Jas 2:23
shall be i. if we believe. Rom 4:24
but sin is not i. when there. 5:13

imputeth
blessed, to whom Lord i. not. Ps 32:2
God i. righteousness. Rom 4:6

imputing
pass over, i. his power. Hab 1:11*
Christ, not i. their trespasses unto.
2 Cor 5:19

in
and the Lord shut him *in.* Gen 7:16
I am *in* Father. John 14:10, 11, 20

inasmuch
i. as he hated him not. Deut 19:6
i. as thou followedst not. Ruth 3:10
i. as have done it to one. Mat 25:40
i. as ye did it not to one of the. 45
i. as both in bonds. Phil 1:7
i. as he who builded. Heb 3:3
i. as ye are partakers of. 1 Pet 4:13

incense
A rich perfume used in sacrifices, Ex 37:29.
shall burn a perpetual i. Ex 30:8
ye shall offer no strange i. thereon. 9
he made the pure i. of sweet. 37:29
set the altar of gold for i. 40:5
his censer, and put i. Lev 10:1
he shall put i. on the fire. 16:13
ten shekels full of i. Num 7:14, 86
put i. in them before Lord. 16:7, 17
the 250 men that offered i. 35
Moses said to Aaron, put on i. 46
on i. and made an atonement. 47
shall put i. before thee. Deut 33:10
the altars of i. took. 2 Chr 30:14
forsaken me, and burned i. 34:25
I will offer to thee the i. Ps 66:15
be set forth before thee as i. 141:2
i. is an abomination to me. Isa 1:13
not wearied thee with i. 43:23*
bring gold and i. and shew. 60:6*
sacrificeth and burneth i. on. 65:3
burneth i. as if he blessed. 66:3*
cometh there to me i.? Jer 6:20*
the gods to whom they offer i. 11:12
provoke me to anger, in offering i. 17
offerings and i. in their. 41:5*
and him that burneth i. to. 48:35
and a thick cloud of i. Ezek 8:11
thou hast set mine oil and i. 16:18
thou hast set mine i. and oil. 23:41
i. shall be offered to my. Mal 1:11
praying at time of i. Luke 1:10

given to him much *i.* to. *Rev* 8:3
the smoke of thy *i.* ascended up. 4
see **altar, burn, burnt**

sweet incense
spices for *sweet i.* *Ex* 25:6
35:8, 28; *Num* 4:16
to make oil and *sweet i.* *Ex* 31:11
brought the oil and *sweet i.* 39:38
a censer, hands full of *sweet i.* *Lev* 16:12

incensed
are *i.* against thee be ashamed. *Isa* 41:11
all that are *i.* against him. 45:24

incline
i. your heart to Lord. *Josh* 24:23
he may *i.* our hearts. *1 Ki* 8:58
i. your ears to the words. *Ps* 78:1
i. my heart unto thy testimonies. 119:36
i. not my heart to any thing. 141:4
see **ear**

inclined
i. to follow Abimelech. *Judg* 9:3
Lord *i.* unto me, and heard my cry. *Ps* 40:1; 116:2
I have *i.* mine heart to. 119:112
nor *i.* mine ear to them. *Pr* 5:13
nor *i.* ear. *Jer* 7:24, 26; 11:8; 17:23
34:14
but ye have not *i.* your ear. 25:4
35:15; 44:5

inclineth
her house *i.* to death. *Pr* 2:18

inclose
we will *i.* her with cedar. *S of S* 8:9

inclosed
onyx stones *i.* in ouches. *Ex* 39:6, 13
Israel *i.* the Benjamites. *Judg* 20:43
they are *i.* in their own fat. *Ps* 17:10
of the wicked have *i.* me. 22:16
a garden *i.* is my sister. *S of S* 4:12*
he hath *i.* my ways with. *Lam* 3:9*
i. great multitude of fishes. *Luke* 5:6

inclosings
stones shall be set in gold in *i.* *Ex* 28:20*; 39:13*

incontinency
tempt you not for your *i.* *1 Cor* 7:5

incontinent
natural affection, *i.* *2 Tim* 3:3*

incorruptible
the glory of the *i.* God. *Rom* 1:23
to obtain an *i.* crown. *1 Cor* 9:25
the dead shall be raised *i.* 15:52
us to an inheritance, *i.* *1 Pet* 1:4
being born of *i.* seed, by the. 23

incorruption
it is raised in *i.* *1 Cor* 15:42
neither doth corruption inherit *i.* 50
this corruptible must put on *i.* 53
corruptible shall have put on *i.* 54

increase, *substantive*
yield you the *i.* thereof. *Lev* 19:25
for thy cattle shall all the *i.* 25:7
take thou no usury of him or *i.* 36
usury, lend him victuals for *i.* 37
the land shall yield her *i.* 26:4
land shall not yield her *i.* or. 20
i. of the threshingfloor. *Num* 18:30
risen up in father's stead an *i.* 32:14
I will also bless the *i.* of thy kine. *Deut* 7:13; 28:4
shalt truly tithe all the *i.* 14:22
shall bring forth all tithe of the *i.* 28
shall bless thee in all thy *i.* 16:15
be the *i.* of thy kine. 28:18, 51
i. of thy house shall die. *1 Sam* 2:33
it yieldeth much *i.* to. *Neh* 9:37
i. of his house shall. *Job* 20:28
would root out all mine *i.* 31:12
earth shall yield her *i.* *Ps* 67:6
he gave also their *i.* to the. 78:46
and our land shall yield her *i.* 85:12
much *i.* is by the strength. *Pr* 14:4
and with the *i.* of his lips he. 18:20
not be satisfied with *i.* *Eccl* 5:10
of the *i.* of his government. *Isa* 9:7
firstfruits of his *i.* was. *Jer* 2:3
nor hath taken any *i.* *Ezek* 18:8, 17
upon usury, and taken *i.* 18:13; 22:12
earth shall yield her *i.* *Ezek* 34:27
ground shall give her *i.* *Zech* 8:12
but God gave the *i.* *1 Cor* 3:6, 7
maketh *i.* of the body to. *Eph.* 4:16
increaseth with *i.* of God. *Col* 2:19

increase, *verb*
by years thou shalt *i.* *Lev* 25:16
O Israel, that ye may *i.* *Deut* 6:3
lest beasts of the field *i.* on. 7:22
i. thy army, and come. *Judg* 9:29
he would *i.* Israel like. *1 Chr* 27:23
strange wives to *i.* *Ezra* 10:10
latter end should greatly *i.* *Job* 8:7
dost not *i.* thy wealth by. *Ps* 44:12
if riches *i.* set not your heart. 62:10
thou shalt *i.* my greatness. 71:21
in the world, they *i.* in riches. 73:12
the Lord shall *i.* you more. 115:14
a wise man will *i.* *Pr* 1:5; 9:9
that oppresseth poor to *i.* 22:16
they perish, the righteous *i.* 28:28
goods *i.* they are increased that. *Eccl* 5:11
there be many things that *i.* 6:11
meek shall *i.* their joy. *Isa* 29:19
and didst *i.* thy perfumes. 57:9
I will *i.* the famine on. *Ezek* 5:16
will *i.* it, and lay no famine. 36:29
I will *i.* them with men like a. 37
he shall *i.* with glory. *Dan* 11:39
commit whoredom, and shall not *i.* *Hos* 4:10
they shall *i.* as they have. *Zech* 10:8
unto Lord, *I.* our faith. *Luke* 17:5
he must *i.*, but I must. *John* 3:30
and *i.* the fruits of your. *2 Cor* 9:10
make you to *i.* in love. *1 Thes* 3:12
we beseech you, that ye *i.* 4:10*
they will *i.* to more. *2 Tim* 2:16*

increased
the waters *i.* and bare. *Gen* 7:17, 18
thou hadst, and it is now *i.* 30:30
Jacob *i.* 43
Israel *i.* abundantly. *Ex* 1:7
till thou be *i.* and inherit. 23:30
the host went on and *i.* *1 Sam* 14:19
people *i.* with Absalom. *2 Sam* 15:12
the battle *i.* that day. *1 Ki* 22:35
2 Chr 18:34
house of their fathers *i.* *1 Chr* 4:38
for our iniquities are *i.* *Ezra* 9:6
are they *i.* that trouble me. *Ps* 3:1
that their corn and wine *i.* 4:7
glory of his house is *i.* 49:16
and he *i.* his people greatly. 105:24
years of thy life shall be *i.* *Pr* 9:11
I *i.* more than all before. *Eccl* 2:9
goods increase, they are *i.* that. 5:11
nation, and not *i.* the joy. *Isa* 9:3
thou hast *i.* the nation. 26:15
their backslidings are *i.* *Jer* 5:6
widows are *i.* above the sand. 15:8
take wives, that ye may be *i.* 29:6
because thy sins were *i.* 30:14, 15
i. in daughter of Judah. *Lam* 2:5*
and hast *i.* thy whoredoms. *Ezek* 16:26*; 23:14
wisdom hast thou *i.* thy riches. 28:5
and knowledge shall be *i.* *Dan* 12:4
were *i.* so they sinned. *Hos* 4:7*
according to fruit, he hath *i.* 10:1*
increase, as they have *i.* *Zech* 10:8
fruit, that sprang up and *i.* *Mark* 4:8
Jesus *i.* in wisdom and. *Luke* 2:52*
and the word of God *i.* *Acts* 6:7
Saul *i.* the more in strength. 9:22
churches *i.* in number daily. 16:5
when your faith is *i.* *2 Cor* 10:15*
rich, and *i.* with goods. *Rev* 3:17*

increasest
i. thine indignation upon. *Job* 10:17

increaseth
my affliction *i.* *Job* 10:16*
he *i.* the nations. 12:23
the tumult of those *i.* *Ps* 74:23*
scattereth, and yet *i.* *Pr* 11:24
she *i.* the transgressors. 23:28
man of knowledge *i.* strength. 24:5
he that by unjust gain *i.* his. 28:8*
multiplied, transgression *i.* 29:16
i. knowledge, *i.* sorrow. *Eccl* 1:18
no might, he *i.* strength. *Isa* 40:29
he daily *i.* lies and. *Hos* 12:1*
woe to him that *i.* that. *Hab* 2:6
body *i.* with the increase. *Col* 2:19

increasing
i. in the knowledge of God. *Col* 1:10

incredible
thought *i.* God should ? *Acts* 26:8

incurable
him with an *i.* disease. *2 Chr* 21:18
my wound is *i.* without. *Job* 34:6
why is my wound *i.*? *Jer* 15:18
thy bruise is *i.* 30:12
thy sorrow is *i.* 15
for her wound is *i.*; for it is. *Mi* 1:9

indebted
every one that is *i.* to us. *Luke* 11:4

indeed
wife shall bear a son *i.* *Gen* 17:19
yet *i.* she is my sister. 20:12
i. reign over us, shalt thou *i.*? 37:8
mother and brethren *i.* come. 10
for *i.* I was stolen away out. 40:15
if you will obey my voice *i.* *Ex* 19:5; 23:22
ye should *i.* have eaten it. *Lev* 10:18
hath the Lord *i.* spoken ? *Num* 12:2
if thou wilt *i.* deliver this. 21:2
am I not able *i.* to promote ? 22:37
i. the hand of the Lord. *Deut* 2:15
son of the hated, which is *i.* 21:16
i. I have sinned against. *Josh* 7:20
if thou wilt *i.* look on. *1 Sam* 1:11
but will God *i.* dwell on the earth ? *1 Ki* 8:27, *2 Chr* 6:18
thou hast *i.* smitten. *2 Ki* 14:10
wouldest bless me *i.* *1 Chr* 4:10
have sinned and done evil *i.* 21:17
i. that I have erred. *Job* 19:4
i. speak righteousness. *Ps* 58:1
hear ye *i.*, see ye *i.* but. *Isa* 6:9
for if ye do this thing *i.* *Jer* 22:4
I *i.* baptize. *Mat* 3:11; *Mark* 1:8
Luke 3:16
that he was a prophet *i.* *Mark* 11:32
we *i.* justly. *Luke* 23:41
the Lord is risen *i.* 24:34
behold an Israelite *i.* *John* 1:47
that this is *i.* the Christ. 4:42
meat *i.*, my blood is drink *i.* 6:55
the rulers know *i.* that this is ? 7:26
then are ye my disciples *i.* 8:31
make you free, ye shall be free *i.* 36
that *i.* a notable miracle. *Acts* 4:16
law, neither *i.* can be. *Rom* 8:7
all things *i.* are pure, but it. 14:20
and *i.* bear with me. *2 Cor* 11:1
some *i.* preach Christ. *Phil* 1:15
you to me *i.* is not grievous. 3:1
i. have a shew of wisdom. *Col* 2:23
i. ye do it towards all. *1 Thes* 4:10
honour widows that are widows *i.* *1 Tim* 5:3
she that is a widow *i.* 5, 16
disallowed *i.* of men. *1 Pet* 2:4

indignation
great *i.* against Israel. *2 Ki* 3:27
Sanballat took great *i.* *Neh* 4:1
Haman was full of *i.* *Esth* 5:9
there increasest thine *i.* *Job* 10:17
pour out thy *i.* on them. *Ps* 69:24
he cast upon them wrath, *i.* 78:49
thine *i.* and thy wrath. 102:10
in their hand is mine *i.* *Isa* 10:5
for yet a little while, and the *i.* 25
even the Lord, and the weapons of his *i.* 13:5, *Jer* 50:25
hide thyself till the *i.* be. *Isa* 26:20
full of *i.* his tongue as fire. 30:27
with the *i.* of his anger. 30
for the *i.* of the Lord is on. 34:2
i. shall be known towards. 66:14
not be able to abide his *i.* *Jer* 10:10
for thou hast filled me with *i.* 15:17
despised in *i.* of his anger. *Lam* 2:6
I will pour out mine *i.* *Ezek* 21:31
not rained on in day of his *i.* 22:24
therefore I poured out mine *i.* 31
i. against holy covenant. *Dan* 11:30
will bear the *i.* of the Lord. *Mi* 7:9
who can stand before his *i.*? *Nah* 1:6
march through land in *i.* *Hab* 3:12
i. these seventy years. *Zech* 1:12

whom the Lord hath *i.* *Mal* 1:4
they were moved with *i.* *Mat* 20:24
they had *i.* saying, To what? 26:8
ruler of synagogue answered with *i.* *Luke* 13:14
they were filled with *i.* *Acts* 5:17*
obey unrighteousness, *i.* *Rom* 2:8
what *i.*, yea, what fear! *2 Cor* 7:11
looking for of fiery *i.* *Heb* 10:27
into the cup of his *i.* *Rev* 14:10

inditing

my heart is *i.* a good. *Ps* 45:1*

industrious

man that he was *i.* *1 Ki* 11:28

inexcusable

therefore thou art *i.* O. *Rom* 2:1*

infallible

himself by many *i.* proofs. *Acts* 1:3

infamous

mock thee which art *i.* *Ezek* 22:5

infamy

thine *i.* turn not away. *Pr* 25:10
an *i.* of the people. *Ezek* 36:3*

infant

slay man, woman, *i.* *1 Sam* 15:3
no more thence an *i.* of. *Isa* 65:20

infants

as *i.* which never saw light. *Job* 3:16
i. shall be dashed in. *Hos* 13:16
brought also *i.* to him. *Luke* 18:15

inferior

I am not *i.* to you. *Job* 12:3; 13:2
another kingdom *i.* to thee. *Dan* 2:39
ye *i.* to other churches? *2 Cor* 12:13

infidel

believeth with an *i.*? *2 Cor* 6:15*
and is worse than an *i.* *1 Tim* 5:8*

infinite

not thine iniquities *i.*? *Job* 22:5*
his understanding is *i.* *Ps* 147:5
her strength, and it was *i.* *Nah* 3:9

infirmities

himself took our *i.* and. *Mat* 8:17
healed by him of their *i.* *Luke* 5:15
cured many of their *i.* 7:21; 8:2
Spirit also helpeth our *i.* *Rom* 8:26
strong ought to bear the *i.* of. 15:1
which concern mine *i.* *2 Cor* 11:30
I glory not, but in mine *i.* 12:5*, 9
I take pleasure in mine *i.* 10
wine for thine often *i.* *1 Tim* 5:23
with the feeling of our *i.* *Heb* 4:15

infirmity

(Disease or disability, ordinarily applied to the body, but in the Bible used frequently for mental or moral weakness)

separation for her *i.* *Lev* 12:2
this is mine *i.* but I will. *Ps* 77:10
a man will sustain his *i.* *Pr* 18:14
which had a spirit of *i.* *Luke* 13:11
thou art loosed from thine *i.* 12
an *i.* thirty-eight years. *John* 5:5
of the *i.* of your flesh. *Rom* 6:19
ye know how through *i.* I. *Gal* 4:13
also is compassed with *i.* *Heb* 5:2
high priests which have *i.* 7:28

inflame

continue till wine *i.* them. *Isa* 5:11

inflaming

i. yourselves with idols. *Isa* 57:5

inflammation

an *i.* of the burning. *Lev* 13:28*
smite thee with an *i.* *Deut* 28:22

inflicted

punishment which was *i.* *2 Cor* 2:6

influences

canst thou bind the *i.*? *Job* 38:31*

infolding

a fire *i.* itself, and a. *Ezek* 1:4

inform

to all that they *i.* thee. *Deut* 17:10*

informed

i. me, and talked with. *Deut* 9:22*
are *i.* of thee that thou teachest. *Acts* 21:21, 24
i. the governor. 24:1; 25:2, 15

ingathering

feast of the *i.* in the end. *Ex* 23:16

ingrafted

with meekness the *i.* word. *Jas* 1:21

inhabit

land which ye shall *i.* *Num* 35:34
the wicked shall not *i.* *Pr* 10:30
villages that Kedar doth *i.* *Isa* 42:11
shall build houses and *i.* 65:21
shall not build, and another *i.* 22
shall *i.* the parched. *Jer* 17:6
thou daughter, that dost *i.* 48:18
i. those wastes of Israel. *Ezek* 33:24
waste cities and *i.* them. *Amos* 9:14
houses, but not *i.* them. *Zeph* 1:13

inhabitant

great and fair without *i.* *Isa* 5:9
cities be wasted without *i.* 6:11
Ephraim and the *i.* of Samaria. 9:9
cry out and shout, thou *i.* of. 12:6
the *i.* of this isle shall say in. 20:6
snare, are upon thee, O *i.* of. 24:17
i. shall not say, I am sick. 33:24
cities are burned without *i.* *Jer* 2:15
cities shall be laid waste without an *i.* 4:7; 9:11; 26:9; 33:10; 34:22
gather thy wares, O *i.* of the. 10:17*
i. of the valley. 21:13
i. of Lebanon. 22:23
is a curse, without an *i.* 44:22
desolate, without *i.* 46:19; 51:29, 37
O *i.* of Aroer. 48:19
O *i.* of Moab. 43
be upon Babylon, shall the *i.* 51:35
I will cut off the *i.* from plain of Aven. *Amos* 1:5
I will cut off the *i.* from Ashdod. 8
i. of Saphir, *i.* of Zaanan. *Mi* 1:11
the *i.* of Maroth waited carefully. 12
O thou *i.* of Lachish, bind the. 13
will bring an heir to thee, O *i.* 15
destroy, that there shall be no *i.* *Zeph* 2:5
destroyed, so that there is none *i.* 3:6

inhabitants

he overthrew all the *i.* *Gen* 19:25
take hold of the *i.* of. *Ex* 15:14
all the *i.* of Canaan shall melt. 15
itself vomiteth out her *i.* *Lev* 18:25
proclaim liberty to all the *i.* 25:10
land that eateth up the *i.* *Num* 13:32
have withdrawn the *i.* *Deut* 13:13
thou shalt surely smite the *i.* of. 15
even the *i.* of the country. *Josh* 2:24
peace, save the *i.* of Gibeon. 11:19
drive out the *i.* 17:12; *Judg* 1:19, 27
no league with the *i.* of. *Judg* 2:2
the *i.* of the villages ceased. 5:7*
curse ye bitterly the *i.* thereof. 23
be head over all the *i.* of Gilead. 10:18; 11:8
the *i.* of Jabesh-gilead there. 21:9
smite the *i.* of Jabesh-gilead. 10
buy it before the *i.* and. *Ruth* 4:4*
Elijah who was of the *i.* *1 Ki* 17:1*
i. were of small power. *2 Ki* 19:26
first *i.* that dwelt in. *1 Chr* 9:2
the *i.* of mount Seir. *2 Chr* 20:23
from under the *i.* thereof. *Job* 26:5
all the *i.* of world stand. *Ps* 33:8
looketh on all the *i.* of the earth. 14
give ear, all ye *i.* of the world. 49:1
all the *i.* thereof are dissolved. 75:3
put down the *i.* like a. *Isa* 10:13*
all ye *i.* of the world, see ye. 18:3
be still, ye *i.* of the isle. 23:2, 6
and scattereth abroad the *i.* 24:1
the earth is defiled under the *i.* 5
therefore the *i.* of the earth are. 6
the *i.* of the world will learn. 26:9
have the *i.* of the world fallen. 18
behold man no more with the *i.* 38:11
i. thereof are as grasshoppers. 40:22
isles and *i.* sing to the Lord. 42:10
let the *i.* of the rock sing, let. 11
too narrow by reason of the *i.* 49:19
fill the *i.* with drunkenness. *Jer* 13:13
will I do to the *i.* thereof. 19:12
I will smite the *i.* of this city. 21:6
as Sodom, and the *i.* thereof. 23:14
for a sword upon the *i.* thereof. 25:29
50:35
innocent blood on the *i.* *Jer* 26:15
dwell deep, O *i.* of Dedan. 49:8, 30
the Lord will disquiet the *i.* 50:34
and my blood upon the *i.* of. 51:35
i. of the world would not. *Lam* 4:12
i. of Egypt shall know. *Ezek* 29:6
i. of earth are reputed as. *Dan* 4:35
i. thereof have spoken lies. *Mi* 6:12
I should make the *i.* thereof an. 16
come *i.* of many cities. *Zech* 8:20
the *i.* of one city shall go to. 21
the *i.* of the earth have. *Rev* 17:2
see **Jerusalem**

inhabitants *of the land*

stink among the *i. of land.* *Gen* 34:30
I will deliver *i. of land.* *Ex* 23:31
a covenant with *i. of land.* 34:12, 15
because of the *i. of land.* *Num* 32:17
shall drive out the *i. of land.* 33:52
55; *2 Chr* 20:7
all the *i. of the land* faint. *Josh* 2:9
all the *i. of land* shall hear of. 7:9
to destroy all the *i. of the land.* 9:24
of old the *i. of land.* *1 Sam* 27:8
he hath given *i. of land.* *1 Chr* 22:18
forth on all *i. of land.* *Jer* 1:14
will fling out the *i. of land.* 10:18
and the *i. of land* shall howl. 47:2
controversy with *i. of land.* *Hos* 4:1
the *i. of the land* tremble. *Joel* 2:1
no more pity *i. of the l.* *Zech* 11:6

inhabited

till they came to a land *i.* *Ex* 16:35
iniquities to a land not *i.* *Lev* 16:22
it shall never be *i.* nor. *Isa* 13:20
thou shalt be *i.* 44:26
formed it to be *i.* 45:18
the desolate cities to be *i.* 54:3
make thee a land not *i.* *Jer* 6:8
in a salt land and not *i.* 17:6
thee cities which are not *i.* 22:6
afterward it shall be *i.* as in. 46:26
it shall not be *i.* 50:13
no more *i.* for ever. 39
the cities that are *i.* *Ezek* 12:20
set thee, that thou be not *i.* 26:20
nor shall it be *i.* forty years. 29:11
the cities shall be *i.* and the. 36:10
desolate places that are now *i.* 38:12
Jerusalem be *i.* as towns. *Zech* 2:4
and Askelon shall not be *i.* 9:5
Jerusalem shall be *i.* again. 12:6
it shall be lifted up, and *i.* in. 14:10
but Jerusalem shall be safely *i.* 11

inhabiters

woe, woe, woe, to *i.* of. *Rev* 8:13
woe to the *i.* of the earth. 12:12

inhabitest

thou that *i.* the praises. *Ps* 22:3

inhabiteth

houses which no man *i.* *Job* 15:28
lofty One that *i.* eternity. *Isa* 57:15

inhabiting

be meat to the people *i.* *Ps* 74:14

inherit

know that I shall *i.* it? *Gen* 15:8
and they shall *i.* it for ever. *Ex* 32:13
it to the Levites to *i.* *Num* 18:24
names of tribes they shall *i.* 26:55
we will not *i.* on yonder side. 32:19
cause Israel to *i.* it. *Deut* 1:38
Lord God giveth you to *i.* 12:10
he maketh his sons to *i.* 21:16
not *i.* in our father's. *Judg* 11:2
them *i.* the throne of. *1 Sam* 2:8
seed shall *i.* the earth. *Ps* 25:13
that wait on the Lord shall *i.* 37:9
but the meek shall *i.* the earth. 11
Mat 5:5
be blessed of him shall *i.* *Ps* 37:22
also of his servants shall *i.* it. 69:36
O God, for thou shalt *i.* all. 82:8
the wise shall *i.* glory. *Pr* 3:35
cause those who love me to *i.* 8:21
own house, shall *i.* the wind. 11:29
the simple *i.* folly, but the. 14:18
to cause to *i.* the desolate. *Isa* 49:8
thy seed shall *i.* the Gentiles. 54:3*
and mine elect shall *i.* it, and. 65:9
my people Israel to *i.* *Jer* 12:14
doth their king *i.* Gad? 49:1*
ye shall *i.* it, one as well. *Ezek* 47:14

the Lord shall *i.* Judah. *Zech* 2:12
shall *i.* everlasting life. *Mat* 19:29
i. the kingdom prepared for. 25:34
i. eternal life. *Mark* 10:17
Luke 10:25; 18:18
unrighteous not *i.* the. *1 Cor* 6:9
neither shall extortioners *i.* 10
Gal 5:21
cannot *i.* the kingdom of God, nor
doth corruption *i.* *1 Cor* 15:50
who through faith *i.* the. *Heb* 6:12
called, that ye should *i.* *1 Pet* 3:9
he that overcometh shall *i.* *Rev* 21:7

inherit *land*

give thee this *land* to *i.* it. *Gen* 15:7
that thou mayest *i.* land. 28:4
ye shall *i.* their *land.* *Lev* 20:24
land ye shall *i.* by lot. *Num* 34:13
thou mayest *i.* his *land.* *Deut* 2:31
i. land Lord giveth thee. 16:20; 19:3
righteous shall *i.* the *land.* *Ps* 37:29
shall exalt thee to *i.* the *land.* 34
they *i.* the *land* for ever. *Isa* 60:21
border, whereby ye shall *i.* the *land.*
Ezek 47:13

inheritance

any portion or *i.* for us? *Gen* 31:14
of their brethren in their *i.* 48:6
in mountain of thine *i.* *Ex* 15:17
take them as an *i.* for. *Lev* 25:46
or given us *i.* of fields. *Num* 16:14
i. for I am thy part and thine *i.* 18:20
shall cause his *i.* to pass to. 27:8
i. to brethren. 9
i. to father's brethren. 10
our *i.* is fallen. 32:19, 32; 34:15
prince, to divide the land by *i.* 34:18
put to the *i.* of the tribe. 36:3, 4
Israel may enjoy the *i.* 8
nor *i.* remove from one tribe to. 9
a people of *i.* as ye are. *Deut* 4:20
destroy not thine *i.* 9:26
they are thine *i.* 29
Jacob is the lot of his *i.* 32:9
sacrifices of Lord their *i.* *Josh* 13:14
18:7
God of Israel was their 13:33
by lot was their *i.* 14:2; *Ps* 78:55
Hebron therefore became the *i.* of.
Josh 14:14
daughters of Manasseh had *i.* 17:6
every man to his *i.* 24:28; *Judg* 2:6
21:24
i. for them that escaped. *Judg* 21:27
lest I mar mine own *i.* *Ruth* 4:6
thee captain over his *i.* *1 Sam* 10:1
from abiding in the *i.* of. 26:19
neither *i.* in son of Jesse. *2 Sam* 20:1
1 Ki 12:16
that ye may bless the *i.* *2 Sam* 21:3
thy people and thy *i.* *1 Ki* 8:51, 53
give the *i.* of my fathers. 21:3, 4
the remnant of mine *i.* *2 Ki* 21:14
Canaan, the lot of your *i.* *1 Chr* 16:18
every one in his *i.* *Neh* 11:20
what *i.* of the Almighty? *Job* 31:2
is the portion of mine *i.* *Ps* 16:5
bless thine *i.* 28:9
chosen for his *i.* 33:12
their *i.* shall be for ever. 37:18
he shall choose our *i.* for us. 47:4
thou didst confirm thine *i.* 68:9
the rod of thine *i.*, thou hast. 74:2
and was wroth with his *i.* 78:62
him to feed Israel his *i.* 71
heathen are come into thine *i.* 79:1
neither will he forsake his *i.* 94:14
Canaan, the lot of your *i.* 105:11
that I may glory with thine *i.* 106:5
he abhorred his own *i.* 40
good man leaveth an *i.* *Pr* 13:22
have part of the *i.* among. 17:2
house and riches are the *i.* of. 19:14
an *i.* may be gotten hastily. 20:21
wisdom is good with an *i.* *Eccl* 7:11
blessed be Israel mine *i.* *Isa* 19:25
I have polluted mine *i.* and. 47:6
sake, the tribes of thine *i.* 63:17
Israel is the rod of his *i.* *Jer* 10:16
51:19
right of *i.* is thine, redemption. 32:8
i. is turned to strangers. *Lam* 5:2
thou shalt be their *i.* *Ezek* 36:12
for an *i.*: I am their *i.* *Ezek* 44:28
i. thereof shall be his son's.
46:16, 17
shall not take of the people's *i.* 18
i. among you with tribes. 47:22, 23
let us seize on his *i.* *Mat* 21:38
and the *i.* shall be ours. *Mark* 12:7
Luke 20:14
that he divide the *i.* *Luke* 12:13
to give you an *i.* among. *Acts* 20:32
and *i.* among them sanctified. 26:18
if the *i.* be of the law, it. *Gal* 3:18
we have obtained an *i.* *Eph* 1:11
which is the earnest of our *i.* 14
the riches of the glory of his *i.* in. 18
i. in the kingdom of Christ. 5:5
to be partakers of the *i.* of. *Col* 1:12
shall receive the reward of *i.* 3:24
as he hath by *i.* obtained. *Heb* 1:4
the promise of eternal *i.* 9:15
begotten us to an *i.* *1 Pet* 1:4

for **inheritance**

and take us *for* thine *i.* *Ex* 34:9
all the tenth in Israel *for* an *i.*
Num 18:21, 26
shall be divided *for* an *i.* 26:53
33:54; 34:2; 36:2; *Deut* 4:21, 38
15:4; 19:10; *Josh* 13:6, 7, 32
14:1; 19:49, 51; *Ezek* 45:1
47:22; 48:29
the Lord doth give thee *for* an *i.*
Deut 20:16; 21:23; 24:4; 25:19
26:1; *Josh* 11:23; 13:6; 14:13
1 Ki 8:36; *2 Chr* 6:27; *Jer* 3:18
leave it *for* an *i.* for children.
1 Chr 28:8; *Ezra* 9:12
give thee heathen *for* thine *i.* *Ps* 2:8
is given us *for* an *i.* *Ezek* 33:24
it shall be to them *for* an *i.* I. 44:28
shall fall unto you *for* an *i.* 47:14
after receive *for* an *i.* *Heb* 11:8

no or *none* **inheritance**

thou shalt have *no i.* *Num* 18:20
23:24; 26:62; *Deut* 10:9; 14:27
29; 18:1, 2; *Josh* 13:14, 33; 14:3
no i. in the son of Jesse. *2 Chr* 10:16
he gave him *none i.* in it. *Acts* 7:5

inheritances

these are the *i.* Joshua. *Josh* 19:51

inherited

return till Israel have *i.* *Num* 32:18
children of Israel *i.* in. *Josh* 14:1
they *i.* the labour of. *Ps* 105:44
our fathers have *i.* lies. *Jer* 16:19
one, and he *i.* the land. *Ezek* 33:24
have *i.* the blessing. *Heb* 12:17

inheriteth

inheriting which he *i.* *Num* 35:8

inheritor

out of Judah an *i.* of my. *Isa* 65:9

iniquities

over the goat all the *i.* *Lev* 16:21
in the *i.* of their fathers shall. 26:39
our *i.* are increased over. *Ezra* 9:6
for our *i.* have we, our kings. 7
punished us less than our *i.* 13
Israel confessed the *i.* *Neh* 9:2
how many are mine *i.*? *Job* 13:23
thou makest me to possess the *i.* 26
great, and thine *i.* infinite. 22:5
and mine *i.* are gone over. *Ps* 38:4
i. have taken hold on me. 40:12
my sins, and blot out all *i.* 51:9
they search out *i.* 64:6
i. prevail against. 65:3
not against us former *i.* 79:8
hast set our *i.* before thee. 90:8
Lord, who forgiveth all thine *i.* 103:3
rewarded us according to our *i.* 10
if thou, Lord shouldest mark *i.* 130:3
redeem Israel from all his *i.* 8
his own *i.* shall take the. *Pr* 5:22
wearied me with thine *i.* *Isa* 43:24
but he was bruised for our *i.* 53:5
as for our *i.* we know them. 59:12
our *i.* like the wind have taken. 64:6
consumed us because of our *i.* 7
turned back to *i.* of their. *Jer* 11:10
O Lord, though our *i.* testify. 14:7
for *i.* of her priests that. *Lam* 4:13
multitude of thine *i.* *Ezek* 28:18
break off thine *i.* by. *Dan* 4:27
from our *i.* and understand. 9:13
for our sins, and for the *i.* of. 16
turn, he will subdue our *i.* *Mi* 7:19
bless in turning every one from his *i.*
Acts 3:26
blessed are they whose *i.* *Rom* 4:7
hath remembered her *i.* *Rev* 18:5

their **iniquities**

bear on him all *their i.* *Lev* 16:22
fools because of *their i.* *Ps* 107:17
he shall bear *their i.* *Isa* 53:11
will pardon all *their i.* *Jer* 33:8
sinned, we have borne *their i.*
Lam 5:7
their i. shall be on their. *Ezek* 32:27
may be ashamed of *their i.* 43:10
their i. will I remember no more.
Heb 8:12; 10:17

your **iniquities**

shall ye bear *your i.* *Num* 14:34
for *your i.* have you sold. *Isa* 50:1
your i. separated between you. 59:2
your i. I will recompense. 65:7
your i. have turned away. *Jer* 5:25
pine away for *your i.* *Ezek* 24:23
loathe youselves for *your i.* 36:31
cleansed you from all *your i.* 33
punish you for all *your i.* *Amos* 3:2

iniquity

i. of the Amorites is not. *Gen* 15:16
thou be consumed in the *i.* of. 19:15
God hath found out the *i.* of. 44:16
visiting the *i.* of fathers. *Ex* 20:5
34:7; *Num* 14:18; *Deut* 5:9
forgiving *i.* and transgression.
Ex 34:7; *Num* 14:18
and pardon our *i.* and. *Ex* 34:9
therefore I do visit the *i.* *Lev* 18:25
an offering bringing *i.* to. *Num* 5:15
shall the man be guiltless from *i.* 31
pray thee, the *i.* of this people. 14:19
he hath not beheld *i.* in Jacob. 23:21
against a man for any *i.* *Deut* 19:15
God of truth and without *i.* 32:4
i. of Peor too little for? *Josh* 22:17
judge for the *i.* which. *1 Sam* 3:13
the *i.* of Eli's house shall not. 14
and stubbornness is as *i.* 15:23*
if there be in me *i.* slay me. 20:8
upon me let this *i.* be. 25:24
2 Sam 14:9
if there be *i.* in me, let. *2 Sam* 14:32
let not my lord impute *i.* to. 19:19
to take away *i.* of thy servant.
24:10; *1 Chr* 21:8
for there is no *i.* with. *2 Chr* 19:7
they that plow *i.* reap. *Job* 4:8
poor hath hope, and *i.* stoppeth. 5:16
I pray you, let it not be *i.* 6:29*
is there *i.* in my tongue? 30*
God exacteth less than thine *i.* 11:6
if *i.* be in thy hand, put it far. 14
for thy mouth uttereth thine *i.* 15:5
filthy is man which drinketh *i.* 16
thou shalt put away *i.* far. 22:23
it is an *i.* to be punished. 31:11, 28
innocent, nor is there *i.* in me. 33:9
if I have done *i.* I will do. 34:32
that they return from *i.* 36:10
take heed, regard not *i.* for this. 21
can say, Thou hast wrought *i.*? 23
O Lord, if there be *i.* in. *Ps* 7:3
behold, he travaileth with *i.* 14
whom the Lord imputeth not *i.* 32:2
thou forgavest the *i.* of my sin. 5
the words of his mouth are *i.* 36:3
thou dost correct man for *i.* 39:11
heart gathereth *i.* to itself. 41:6
when the *i.* of my heels shall. 49:5
behold I was shapen in *i.* and. 51:5
and have done abominable *i.* 53:1
they cast *i.* upon me, and in. 55:3
shall they escape by *i.*? 56:7
if I regard *i.* in my heart. 66:18
thou hast forgiven the *i.* of thy. 85:2
throne of *i.* have fellowship. 94:20
all *i.* shall stop her mouth. 107:42
let the *i.* of his fathers be. 109:14
they also do no *i.*: they walk. 119:3
let not any *i.* have dominion. 133
put forth their hands to *i.* 125:3
by mercy and truth *i.* *Pr* 16:6

of the wicked devoureth i. Pr 19:28
he that soweth i. shall reap. 22:8
of righteousness that i. Eccl 3:16
a people laden with i. a. Isa 1:4
it is i. even the solemn meeting. 13
woe to them that draw i. 5:18
i. is taken away, and thy sin. 6:7
prepare for the i. of their. 14:21
this i. shall not be purged. 22:14
by this shall the i. of Jacob. 27:9
all that watch for i. are cut off. 29:20
this i. shall be to you as a. 30:13
cry unto her, her i. is pardoned. 40:2
Lord hath laid on him the i. 53:6
for the i. of his covetousness. 57:17
fingers are defiled with i. 59:3
they bring forth i. 4
their works are works of i. 6
their thoughts are thoughts of i. 7
not wroth, nor remember i. 64:9
what i. have your fathers ? Jer 2:5
thine i. is marked before me. 22
only acknowledge thine i. 3:13
the greatness of thine i. are. 13:22
we acknowledge the i. of our. 14:20
what is our i.? 16:10
i. hid from mine eyes. 17
for multitude of thine i. 30:14, 15
Hos 9:7
recompensest i. of fathers. Jer 32:18
the i. of Israel be sought for. 50:20
Babylon, be not cut off in her i. 51:6
not discovered thine i. Lam 2:14
for the punishment of the i. of. 4:6
thine i. is accomplished, he will visit thine i. O daughter of Edom. 22
lay i. of the house of. Ezek 4:4
nor strengthen himself in i. 7:13
the i. of the house of Israel. 9:9
this was the i. of thy sister. 16:49
withdrawn his hand from i. 18:8
he shall not die for the i. of his. 17
repent, so i. shall not be your. 30
to remembrance your i. 21:23, 24
i. shall have an end. 25, 29; 35:5
wast perfect, till i. was found. 28:15
defiled thy sanctuaries by i. of. 18
house of Israel to fall into i. 44:12
make reconciliation for i. Dan 9:24
the i. of Ephraim was. Hos 7:1
against children of i. 10:9
ye reaped i. 13
find no i. in me. 12:8
is there i. in Gilead ? 11
the i. of Ephraim is bound up. 13:12
for thou hast fallen by thine i. 14:1
take away all i. and receive us. 2
woe to them that devise i. Mi 2:1
they build up Jerusalem with i. 3:10
who is a God like to thee, that pardoneth i.? 7:18
why dost thou shew me i.? Hab 1:3
and thou canst not look on i. 13*
that establisheth a city by i. 2:12
Lord, he will not do i. Zeph 3:5
of Israel shall not do i. 13
I have caused thine i. to. Zech 3:4
I will remove the i. of that land. 9
i. was not found in his lips, did turn many away from i. Mal 2:6
gather them which do i. Mat 13:41
ye are full of hypocrisy and i. 23:28
because i. shall abound, love. 24:12
field with the reward of i. Acts 1:18
thou art in the bond of i. 8:23
servants to i. unto i. Rom 6:19
rejoiceth not in i. but in. 1 Cor 13:6
the mystery of i. doth. 2 Thes 2:7*
Christ, depart from i. 2 Tim 2:19
redeem us from all i. Tit 2:14
hast hated i. therefore God. Heb 1:9
tongue is a fire, a world of i.
Jas 3:6
see **bear, commit, committed**

his **iniquity**
his i. shall be upon him. Num 15:31
that man perished not alone in his i.
Josh 22:20
heavens shall reveal his i. Job 20:27
God layeth up his i. for his. 21:19
until his i. be found to be. Ps 36:2
die for his i. Jer 31:30; Ezek 3:18
19; 7:16; 18:26
the stumblingblock of his i.
Ezek 14:7, 14
shall die in his i. 18:18; 33:8, 9
he is taken away in his i. but. 33:6
was rebuked for his i. 2 Pet 2:16*

mine **iniquity**
what is mine i. and ? 1 Sam 20:1
I kept myself from mine i.
2 Sam 22:24; Ps 18:23
thou not take away mine i.? Job 7:21
thou enquirest after mine i. 10:6
not acquit me from mine i. 14
bag, thou sewest up mine i. 14:17
if I covered, by hiding mine i. 31:33
pardon mine i. for it is. Ps 25:11
faileth because of mine i. 31:10
and mine i. have I not hid. 32:5
for I will declare mine i. I. 38:18
me throughly from mine i. 51:2

their **iniquity**
pine away in their i. Lev 26:39
confess their i. and iniquity of. 40
the punishment of their i. 41, 43
cover not their i. let not. Neh 4:5
add iniquity unto their i. Ps 69:27
he forgave their i. 78:38
I will visit their i. 89:32
bring upon them their i. 94:23
brought low for their i. 106:43
punish wicked for their i. Isa 13:11
inhabitants of earth for their i. 26:21
people shall be forgiven their i. 33:24
now remember their i. Jer 14:10
I will recompense their i. 16:18
forgive not their i. nor blot. 18:23
punish that nation for their i. 25:12
for I will forgive their i. 31:34
cleanse them from all their i. 33:8
I may forgive their i. and sin. 36:3
punish his servants for their i. 31
thee the years of their i. Ezek 4:5
may consume away for their i. 17
the stumblingblock of their i. 7:19
14:3
bear the punishment of their i. 14:10
which bringeth their i. to. 29:16
went into captivity for their i. 39:23
set their heart on their i. Hos 4:8
Israel fall in their i. 5:5
he will remember their i. he. 9:9

work **iniquity**
with men that work i. Ps 141:4
help of them that work i. Isa 31:2
heart will work i. to practise. 32:6
a city of them that work i. Hos 6:8
from me, ye that work i. Mat 7:23

workers of **iniquity**
punishment to the w. of i. Job 31:3
company with the w. of i. 34:8
where the w. of i. may hide. 22
stand, thou hatest all w. of i. Ps 5:5
depart from me all ye w. of i. 6:8
Luke 13:27
have all w. of i. no ? Ps 14:4; 53:4
not away with the w. of i. 28:3
there are the w. of i. fallen. 36:12
envious against the w. of i. 37:1
deliver me from the w. of i. 59:2
insurrection of the w. of i. 64:2
all the w. of i. do flourish. 92:7
the w. of i. shall be scattered. 9
the w. of i. boast themselves. 94:4
stand up for me against the w. of i. 16
them forth with the w. of i. 125:5
from the gins of the w. of i. 141:9
destruction shall be to w. of i.
Pr 10:29; 21:15

injured
ye have not i. me at all. Gal 4:12

injurious
a persecutor and i. 1 Tim 1:13

injustice
not for i. in my hands. Job 16:17

ink
I wrote them with i. Jer 36:18
written not with i. but. 2 Cor 3:3
I would not write with i. 2 John 12
3 John 13

inkhorn
with a writer's i. Ezek 9:2, 3, 11

inn
ass provender in the i. Gen 42:27*
we came to the i. we opened. 43:21*
by the way in the i., the. Ex 4:24*
no room for them in the i. Luke 2:7
brought him to an i. and took. 10:34

inner
cherubims in i. house. 1 Ki 6:27
gave patterns of the i. 1 Chr 28:11
to the king into the i. court. Esth 4:11
Esther stood in the i. court. 5:1
and the cloud filled the i. Ezek 10:3
end of measuring the i. house. 42:15
the gate of the i. court shall be. 46:1
thrust them into the i. Acts 16:24
with might in the i. man. Eph 3:16
see **chamber**

innermost
into the i. parts of the belly.
Pr 18:8; 26:22

innocency
in the i. of my hands. Gen 20:5
wash my hands in i. so. Ps 26:6
have washed my hands in i. 73:13
before him i. was found. Dan 6:22
be ere they attain to i.? Hos 8:5

innocent
the i. and the righteous. Ex 23:7
reward to slay the i. Deut 27:25
whoever perished being i.? Job 4:7
laugh at the trial of the i. 9:23
that thou wilt not hold me i. 28
i. shall stir up the hypocrite. 17:8
i. laugh them to scorn. 22:19
deliver the island of the i. 30
i. shall divide the silver. 27:17
I am i. nor is iniquity in me. 33:9
doth he murder the i. Ps 10:8
taketh reward against the i. 15:5
I shall be i. from the great. 19:13*
let us lurk privily for the i. Pr 1:11
toucheth her shall not be i. 6:29*
haste to be rich shall not be i. 28:20*
sayest, Because I am i. Jer 2:35
I am i. of the blood of. Mat 27:24
see **blood**

innocents
the blood of the poor i. Jer 2:34
place with the blood of i. 19:4

innumerable
after him, as there are i. Job 21:23
i. evils have compassed. Ps 40:12
are things creeping i. 104:25
grasshoppers, and are i. Jer 46:23
i. multitude gathered. Luke 12:1
is by the sea shore i. Heb 11:12
an i. company of angels. 12:22

inordinate
corrupt in her i. love. Ezek 23:11*
fornication, i. affection. Col 3:5*

inquisition
shall make diligent i. Deut 19:18
when i. was made of the. Esth 2:23
he maketh i. for blood. Ps 9:12

inscription
found an altar with this i. Acts 17:23

inside
covered the walls on i. 1 Ki 6:15

inspiration
i. of Almighty giveth. Job 32:8*
all scripture is given by i. 2 Tim 3:16

instant
[1] *A short moment of time*, Isa 29:5. [2] *Very eager, or pressing*, Luke 23:23.
yea, it shall be at an i. Isa 29:5
cometh suddenly at an i. 30:13
at what i. I speak. Jer 18:7, 9
she coming in that i. Luke 2:38*
and they were i. with loud. 23:23*
patient, continuing i. Rom 12:12*
preach the word, be i. 2 Tim 4:2

instantly
instantly Luke 7:4*; Acts 26:7*

instead see **stead**

instruct
that he might i. thee. Deut 4:36
thy good Spirit to i. Neh 9:20
that contendeth i. him ? Job 40:2*

my reins also *i.* me in. *Ps* 16:7
I will *i.* thee and teach thee. 32:8
mother's house, who will *i. S of S* 8:2
his God doth *i.* him to. *Isa* 28:26
understand shall *i.* many. *Dan* 11:33
Lord, that he may *i.* *1 Cor* 2:16

instructed

led him about, he *i.* *Deut* 32:10*
Jehoiada the priest *i.* him. *2 Ki* 12:2
Chenaniah *i.* about the. *1 Chr* 15:22
that were *i.* in the songs of. 25:7
Solomon was *i.* for the. *2 Chr* 3:3*
behold thou hast *i.* many. *Job* 4:3
be *i.* ye judges of the. *Ps* 2:10
mine ear to them that *i.* *Pr* 5:13
the wise is *i.* he receiveth. 21:11
spake thus to me and *i.* *Isa* 8:11
who *i.* him, and taught him? 40:14
be *i.* O Jerusalem, lest my. *Jer* 6:8
after that I was *i.* I smote. 31:19
every scribe who is *i.* to. *Mat* 13:52
and she, being before *i.* of. 14:8*
wherein thou hast been *i.* *Luke* 1:4
man was *i.* in the way. *Acts* 18:25
his will, being *i.* out of. *Rom* 2:18
and in all things, I am *i.* *Phil* 4:12*

instructing

i. those that oppose. *2 Tim* 2:25

instruction

the ears, and sealeth *i.* *Job* 33:16
seeing thou hatest *i.* and. *Ps* 50:17
to know wisdom and *i.* *Pr* 1:2
to receive the *i.* of wisdom. 3
despise wisdom and *i.* 7; 15:5
hear the *i.* of thy father. 1:8; 4:1
take fast hold of *i.*, let her. 4:13
how have I hated *i.* and my. 5:12
he shall die without *i.* and. 23
and reproofs of *i.* are the. 6:23
receive my *i.* 8:10
hear *i.* and be wise. 33
give *i.* to a wise man and he. 9:9
way of life that keepeth *i.* 10:17*
loveth *i.* loveth knowledge. 12:1*
son heareth his father's *i.* 13:1
shall be to him that refuseth *i.* 18*
he that refuseth *i.* hateth his. 15:32*
the fear of the Lord is the *i.* of. 33
but the *i.* of fools is folly. 16:22*
hear counsel, and receive *i.* 19:20
cease to hear the *i.* that causeth. 27
apply thy heart to *i.* and. 23:12
buy the truth, also *i.* and. 23
upon it and received *i.* 24:32
not hear, nor receive *i.* *Jer* 17:23
not hearkened to receive *i.* 32:33
receive *i.* to hearken to my. 35:13
a reproach, a taunt, an *i.* *Ezek* 5:15
surely thou wilt receive *i.* *Zeph* 3:7*
all scripture is profitable for *i.* *2 Tim* 3:16

instructor

Tubal-Cain, an *i.* of. *Gen* 4:22*
i. of foolish, a teacher. *Rom* 2:20*

instructors

ye have 10,000 *i.* in. *1 Cor* 4:15

instrument

smite him with an *i.* of. *Num* 35:16
sing to him with an *i.* of ten strings. *Ps* 33:2; 92:3
new song, O God, on an *i.* 144:9
threshed with a threshing *i.* *Isa* 28:27
thee a sharp threshing *i.* 41:15
that bringeth forth an *i.* for. 54:16*
one that can play on an *i.* *Ezek* 33:32

instruments

i. of cruelty are in their. *Gen* 49:5*
pattern of all the *i.* *Ex* 25:9*
shall keep all the *i.* of. *Num* 3:8
they shall take all the *i.* of. 4:12*
sanctified all the *i.* 7:1*
with the holy *i.* 31:6*
make *i.* of war, and *i.* *1 Sam* 8:12
king Saul with *i.* of music. 18:6
their flesh with *i.* of oxen. *1 Ki* 19:21
to oversee all the *i.* of. *1 Chr* 9:29*
make a sound with musical *i.* 16:42
singing with loud *i.* to. *2 Chr* 30:21
Hanani with musical *i.* *Neh* 12:36
prepared for him the *i.* *Ps* 7:13
players on *i.* followed after. 68:25*
as the players on *i.* shall be. 87:7*
praise him with stringed *i.* *Ps* 150:4
as musical *i.* and that of. *Eccl* 2:8†
i. also of the churl are evil. *Isa* 32:7
my songs to the stringed *i.* 38:20
nor *i.* of music brought. *Dan* 6:18
Gilead with threshing *i.* *Amos* 1:3
and invent to themselves *i.* of. 6:5
singer on my stringed *i.* *Hab* 3:19
take thee *i.* of a foolish. *Zech* 11:15
yield members *i.* of unrighteousness, members as *i.* of. *Rom* 6:13

insurrection

this city hath made *i.* *Ezra* 4:19
from the *i.* of the workers. *Ps* 64:2*
that had made *i.* who had committed murder in the *i.* *Mark* 15:7
Jews made *i.* with one. *Acts* 18:12*

integrity

in *i.* of my heart I have. *Gen* 20:5
I know that thou didst this in the *i.* 6
thy father walked in *i.* *1 Ki* 9:4
he holdeth fast his *i.* *Job* 2:3
dost thou still retain thine *i.* 9
I will not remove my *i.* from. 27:5
that God may know my *i.* 31:6
according to my *i.* that. *Ps* 7:8
i. and uprightness preserve. 25:21
I walked in my *i.* 26:1
I will walk in *i.* 11
thou upholdest me in my *i.* 41:12
he fed them according to *i.* 78:72
the *i.* of the upright shall. *Pr* 11:3
poor that walketh in his *i.* 19:1
just man walketh in his *i.* 20:7

intelligence

i. with them that forsake covenant. *Dan* 11:30*

intend

did not *i.* to go up. *Josh* 22:23*
ye *i.* to add more to. *2 Chr* 28:13
ye *i.* to bring this man's. *Acts* 5:28
what ye *i.* to do as touching. 35

intended

for they *i.* evil against. *Ps* 21:11

intendest

i. thou to kill me, as the? *Ex* 2:14

intending

which of you *i.* to build? *Luke* 14:28
i. after Easter to bring. *Acts* 12:4
sailed to Assos, there *i.* to. 20:13

intent

to the *i.* the Lord might. *2 Sam* 17:14
to *i.* he might destroy. *2 Ki* 10:19
to the *i.* he might let. *2 Chr* 16:1
to the *i.* that I might. *Ezek* 40:4
to the *i.* that the living. *Dan* 4:17
not there to the *i.* ye. *John* 11:15
for what *i.* he spake this to. 13:28
and came hither for that *i.* *Acts* 9:21
I ask for what *i.* ye have? 10:29
to the *i.* we should not. *1 Cor* 10:6
to the *i.* that now to the. *Eph* 3:10

intents

till he have performed *i.* *Jer* 30:24
is a discerner of the *i.* *Heb* 4:12

intercession

and made *i.* for the. *Isa* 53:12
cry, nor make *i.* to me. *Jer* 7:16
let them now make *i.* to the. 27:18
Gemariah had made *i.* 36:25
but the Spirit maketh *i.* for us. *Rom* 8:26, 27, 34
how he maketh *i.* to God. 11:2*
he ever liveth to make *i.* *Heb* 7:25

intercessions

that prayers and *i.* be. *1 Tim* 2:1

intercessor

he wondered that there was no *i.* *Isa* 59:16

intermeddle

a stranger doth not *i.* *Pr* 14:10

intermeddleth

seeketh and *i.* with all. *Pr* 18:1*

intermission

ceaseth not without any *i.* *Lam* 3:49

interpret

none that could *i.* them. *Gen* 41:8
according to his dream he did *i.* 12
do all *i.*? *1 Cor* 12:30
except [illegible] *i.* 14:5
pray that he may *i.* *1 Cor* 14:13
let one *i.* 27

interpretation

[1] *A translation, or turning from one language into another,* 1 Cor 12:10. [2] *The gift of explaining visions and dreams, etc.,* Gen 40:8; 2 Pet 1:20.

each man according to the *i.* of his dream. *Gen* 40:5; 41:11
the *i.* of it. 40:12, 18; *Dan* 4:24; 5:26
baker saw that the *i.* *Gen* 40:16
when Gideon heard the *i.* *Judg* 7:15
a proverb and the *i.* *Pr* 1:6*
we shall shew the *i.* *Dan* 2:4, 7, 36
the dream is certain, and the *i.* 45
and the *i.* thereof be to thy. 4:19
he will shew the *i.* 5:12
not shew the *i.* 15
and he made me to know the *i.* 7:16
Cephas, which is by *i.* a. *John* 1:42
of Siloam, which is by *i.* Sent. 9:7
by *i.* is called Dorcas. *Acts* 9:36
sorcerer, so is his name by *i.* 13:8
to another the *i.* of. *1 Cor* 12:10
every one of you hath an *i.* 14:26
being by *i.* king of. *Heb* 7:2
is of any private *i.* *2 Pet* 1:20

interpretations

Joseph said, do not *i.*? *Gen* 40:8
that thou canst make *i.* *Dan* 5:16

interpreted

as Joseph had *i.* *Gen* 40:22; 41:13
written and *i.* in the. *Ezra* 4:7*
being *i.* is, God with us. *Mat* 1:23
being *i.*, Damsel, arise. *Mark* 5:41
which is, being *i.* the place of. 15:22
i. My God, my God, why hast? 34
being *i.* Master. *John* 1:38
which is, being *i.*, the Christ. 41
is, being *i.* the son of. *Acts* 4:36

interpreter

and there is no *i.* of it. *Gen* 40:8
spake to them by an *i.* 42:23
i., one among a thousand. *Job* 33:23
but if there be no *i.* let. *1 Cor* 14:28

interpreting

i. of dreams was found. *Dan* 5:12

intreat

[1] *To supplicate or pray to,* Ex 8:8; Judg 13:8. [2] *To intercede, or speak in one's behalf,* Gen 23:8; 1 Sam 2:25. [3] *To seek,* Pr 19:6.

i. for me to Ephron the. *Gen* 23:8
called for Moses, and said, *i.* the. *Ex* 8:8, 28; 9:28; 10:17
when shall I *i.* for thee? 8:9
I will *i.* the Lord that the flies. 29
i. me not to leave thee. *Ruth* 1:16
who shall *i.* for him? *1 Sam* 2:25
i. the face of the Lord. *1 Ki* 13:6
among the people, shall *i.* *Ps* 45:12
many will *i.* the favour of. *Pr* 19:6
being defamed, we *i.* *1 Cor* 4:13
I *i.* thee also, true yoke-. *Phil* 4:3*
rebuke not, but *i.* him. *1 Tim* 5:1*

intreated

i. for his wife, Lord was *i.* *Gen* 25:21
out and *i.* the Lord. *Ex* 8:30; 10:18
then Manoah *i.* the Lord. *Judg* 13:8
after that God was *i.* *2 Sam* 21:14
Lord was *i.* for the land. 24:25
cried and he was *i.* of. *1 Chr* 5:20
prayed, and God was *i.* *2 Chr* 33:13
God, and he was *i.* of us. *Ezra* 8:23
I called, I *i.* him with. *Job* 19:16
though I *i.* for the children's. 17*
I *i.* thy favour with my. *Ps* 119:58
he shall be *i.* of them. *Isa* 19:22
his father out, and *i.* *Luke* 15:28
i. the word should not. *Heb* 12:19
from above is easy to be *i.* *Jas* 3:17
see also **entreat, etc.**

intreaties

the poor useth *i.* but the. *Pr* 18:23
praying us with much *i.* *2 Cor* 8:4

intruding

i. into things he hath not. *Col* 2:18*

invade

wouldest not let Israel *i.* *2 Chr* 20:10
will *i.* them with troops. *Hab* 3:16

invaded
the Philistines have *i.* *1 Sam* 23:27
David and his men *i.* the. 27:8
the Amalekites *i.* the south. 30:1
bands of Moabites *i.* *2 Ki* 13:20
Philistines had *i.* the. *2 Chr* 28:18

invasion
we made an *i.* on. *1 Sam* 30:14

invent
i. instruments of music. *Amos* 6:5*

invented
Uzziah made engines, *i.* by cunning men, to shoot arrows. *2 Chr* 26:15

inventions
vengeance of their *i.* *Ps* 99:8*
him to anger with their *i.* 106:29*
whoring with their own *i.* 39*
out knowledge of witty *i.* *Pr* 8:12*
have sought out many *i.* *Eccl* 7:29

inventors
i. of evil things. *Rom* 1:30

invisible
the *i.* things of him are. *Rom* 1:20
the image of the *i.* God. *Col* 1:15
heaven and earth, visible and *i.* 16
the King immortal, *i.* *1 Tim* 1:17
as seeing him who is *i.* *Heb* 11:27

invited
since I said, I have *i.* *1 Sam* 9:24
Absalom *i.* all king's. *2 Sam* 13:23
to-morrow am I *i.* to her. *Esth* 5:12

inward
it in the fire; it is fret *i.* *Lev* 13:55
their hinder parts were *i.* *1 Ki* 7:25
and their faces were *i.* *2 Chr* 3:13
my *i.* friends abhorred. *Job* 19:19
who hath put wisdom in the *i.*? 38:36
i. part is very wickedness. *Ps* 5:9
i. thought is, that their houses. 49:11
desirest truth in the *i.* parts. 51:6
i. thought of every one of. 64:6
searching all the *i.* parts. *Pr* 20:27
so do stripes the *i.* parts of the. 30
my *i.* parts sound for Kir-. *Isa* 16:11
my law in their *i.* parts. *Jer* 31:33
your *i.* part is full of. *Luke* 11:39
the law of God after *i.* *Rom* 7:22
the *i.* man is renewed. *2 Cor* 4:16
i. affection is more abundant. 7:15

inwardly
their mouth, but curse *i.* *Ps* 62:4
but *i.* they are ravening. *Mat* 7:15
is a Jew who is one *i.* *Rom* 2:29

inwards
fat that covereth the *i.* *Ex* 29:13, 22
Lev 3:3, 9, 14; 4:8; 7:3; 9:19
thou shalt wash the *i.* *Ex* 29:17
Lev 1:9, 13; 9:14
his *i.* and dung burn in. *Lev* 4:11
the fat on the *i.* Moses burnt. 8:16
washed the *i.* and the legs with. 21

iron
(*The word is used*: [1] *Literally, of the metal so named.* [2] *As a symbol of hardness and strength*)
with an instrument of *i.* *Num* 35:16
was a bedstead of *i.* *Deut* 3:11
out of the *i.* furnace, out of Egypt. 4:20; *1 Ki* 8:51; *Jer* 11:4
a land whose stones are *i.* *Deut* 8:9
not lift up any *i.* tool on. 27:5
is under thee shall be *i.* 28:23
put a yoke of *i.* on. 48; *Jer* 28:14
over which no man lift *i.* *Josh* 8:31
have chariots of *i.* 17:16; *Judg* 1:19
though they have *i.* chariots, and. *Josh* 17:18
hundred chariots of *i.* *Judg* 4:3, 13
weighed 600 shekels of *i.* *1 Sam* 17:7
under harrows of *i.* *2 Sam* 12:31
1 Chr 20:3
must be fenced with *i.* *2 Sam* 23:7
nor any tool of *i.* heard. *1 Ki* 6:7
Zedekiah made him horns of *i.* 22:11; *2 Chr* 18:10
and the *i.* did swim. *2 Ki* 6:6
David prepared *i.* in. *1 Chr* 22:3
i. for the things of *i.* 29:2, 7
graven with an *i.* pen. *Job* 19:24
shall flee from the *i.* weapon. 20:24
i. is taken out of the earth. *Job* 28:2
bones are like bars of *i.* 40:18
he esteemeth *i.* as straw. 41:27
break them with a rod of *i.* *Ps* 2:9
they hurt, he was laid in *i.* 105:18*
being bound in *i.* 107:10
cut bars of *i.* 16
their nobles with fetters of *i.* 149:8
i. sharpeneth *i.* so a. *Pr* 27:17
if the *i.* be blunt, and he. *Eccl* 10:10
thickets of forest with *i.* *Isa* 10:34
I will cut asunder the bars of *i.* 45:2
thy neck is an *i.* sinew, thy. 48:4
for *i.* I will bring silver, for stones *i.* 60:17
thee this day an *i.* pillar. *Jer* 1:18
shall *i.* break northern *i.*? 15:12
Judah is written with a pen of *i.* 17:1
make for them yokes of *i.* 28:13
i. pan, and set it for a wall of *i.* *Ezek* 4:3
was thy merchant with *i.* 27:12
Javan occupied with bright *i.* 19
his legs of *i.*, feet part *i.* *Dan* 2:33
34, 41, 42
then was the *i.* and clay broken. 35
kingdom shall be strong as *i.* 40
it had great *i.* teeth, it. 7:7
beast, whose teeth were of *i.* 19
with instruments of *i.* *Amos* 1:3
for I will make thy horn *i.* *Mi* 4:13
they came to the *i.* gate. *Acts* 12:10
seared with a hot *i.* *1 Tim* 4:2
rule them with a rod of *i.* *Rev* 2:27
12:5; 19:15
were breastplates of *i.* *Rev* 9:9
see **brass**

irons
fill his skin with barbed *i.*? *Job* 41:7

is *there*
is there yet any portion? *Gen* 31:14
God *is there* in heaven? *Deut* 3:24
what nation *is there* so great? 4:7, 8
who *is there* of all flesh that? 5:26
man *is there* that hath? 20:5; 7:8
is there any understanding. 32:28
is there any man? *Judg* 4:20
is there never a? 14:3
who *is there* among all the? 21:5, 8
neither *is there* any rock. *1 Sam* 2:2
and David said, *is there* not? 17:29
nor *is there* any God beside thee. *2 Sam* 7:22; *Isa* 44:8
is there any that is left of Saul's? *2 Sam* 9:1, 3
is there not here a prophet? *1 Ki* 22:7
2 Ki 3:11; *2 Chr* 18:6
in thy hand *is there* not? *2 Chr* 20:6
who *is there* among you of all his people? 36:23; *Ezra* 1:3
who *is there* being as I? *Neh* 6:11
is there iniquity in? *Job* 6:30; 33:9
is there any secret thing? 15:11*
what profit *is there* in my blood? *Ps* 30:9
is there a price in the? *Pr* 17:16
is there any thing whereof it may be? *Eccl* 1:10
what good *is there* to? 5:11
nor *is there* any end of their treasures, nor *is there* any. *Isa* 2:7
nor *is there* knowledge to. 44:19
nor say, *Is there* not a lie in? 20
is there no balm in Gilead, *is there*? *Jer* 8:22
I am Lord, *is there* any thing? 32:27
asked him, *Is there* any word? 37:17
is there iniquity in Gilead? surely they are vanity. *Hos* 12:11
is there yet any with thee? *Amos* 6:10
what man *is there* of you? *Mat* 7:9
nor *is there* salvation in. *Acts* 4:12
what profit *is there* of? *Rom* 3:1
is there unrighteousness with? 9:14

there **is**
there is as it were a plague in. *Lev* 14:35
there is nothing at all. *Num* 11:6
and *there is* no god. *Deut* 32:39
yet *there is* both straw. *Judg* 19:19
there is a feast of the Lord. 21:19
for *there is* no restraint. *1 Sam* 14:6
that *there is* a God in. *1 Sam* 17:46
there is but a step between. 20:3
then come thou, for *there is*. 21
there is neither adversary. *1 Ki* 5:4
there is no God like thee in heaven. 8:23; *2 Chr* 6:14
there is no man that sinneth not. *1 Ki* 8:46; *2 Chr* 6:36
behold, *there is* Ahijah. *1 Ki* 14:2
there is yet one man. 22:8
there is a prophet in. *2 Ki* 5:8
yet *there is* hope in Israel. *Ezra* 10:2; *Job* 11:18
there is a certain people. *Esth* 3:8
ye may know *there is* a. *Job* 19:29
shalt say, *There is* lifting up. 22:29
but *there is* a spirit in man. 32:8
fool hath said, *There is* no God. *Ps* 14:1; 53:1
in keeping them *there is* great. 19:11
there is no want to them that. 34:9
there is a river whose streams. 46:4
verily *there is* a reward for. 58:11
there is little Benjamin. 68:27
man, in whom *there is* no help. 146:3
there is that scattereth. *Pr* 11:24
there is that maketh himself. 13:7
the righteous *there is* favour. 14:9
there is a way that seemeth right. 12; 16:25
in all labour *there is* profit. 23
there is an end. 23:18
there is a generation that curseth. 30:11, 12, 13, 14
to every thing *there is* a. *Eccl* 3:1
there is a just man, *there is* a. 7:15
word of a king is, *there is*. 8:4
there is that neither day nor. 16
there is one event. 9:2
for to him *there is* hope. 4
me *there is* no Saviour. *Isa* 43:11
me *there is* no God. 44:6, 8; 45:5
there is no throne, O daughter. 47:1
there is no peace to wicked. 48:22
57:21; *Jer* 6:14
because *there is* no water. *Isa* 50:2
there is no beauty. 53:2
but thou saidst, *There is* no hope. 57:10; *Jer* 2:25; 18:12
there is hope in thy end. *Jer* 31:17
Jeremiah said, *There is*. 37:17
there is a conspiracy of. *Ezek* 22:25
there is Elam. 32:24
there is Edom, her kings. 29
because *there is* no shepherd. 34:5
there is a God that revealeth. *Dan* 2:28
there is a man in thy kingdom. 5:11
because *there is* no truth. *Hos* 4:1
there is no healing of. *Nah* 3:19
there is no resurrection. *Mat* 22:23
Mark 12:18; *1 Cor* 15:12
there is none good but. *Mark* 10:18
and yet *there is* room. *Luke* 14:22
there is joy in presence of. 15:10
because *there is* no truth. *John* 8:44
stumbleth, because *there is*. 11:10
there is among you envying and. *1 Cor* 3:3
reported *there is* fornication. 5:1
to us *there is* but one God. 8:6
there is a natural body, *there is* a. 15:44
against such *there is* no law. *Gal* 5:23
there is no respect of. *Col* 3:25
there is no fear in love. *1 John* 4:18
there is a sin unto death. 5:16
there is a sin not unto death. 17
see **none, one**

there **is** *not*
there is not aught left in. *Gen* 47:18
king's sons *there is not*. *2 Sam* 13:30
there is not among us. *1 Ki* 5:6
there is not a God in. *2 Ki* 1:3, 6
to birth, and *there is not*. 19:3
upon earth *there is not*. *Job* 41:33
and *there is not* a second. *Eccl* 4:8
there is not one barren. *S of S* 6:6
there is not a greater. *Luke* 7:28
that *there is not* a wise. *1 Cor* 6:5
there is not in every man that. 8:7

Isaac
call his name *I.* *Gen* 17:19; 21:3

will I establish with *I.* *Gen* 17:21
heir with my son, even *I.* 21:10
for in *I.* shall thy seed be called.
12; *Rom* 9:7; *Heb* 11:18
take thine only son *I.* *Gen* 22:2
Abraham bound *I.* 9
take a wife for *I.* 24:4
appointed for *I.* 14
I. went out to meditate in the. 63
I. was comforted after his. 67
all that he had unto *I.* 25:5
his sons *I.* and Ishmael buried. 9
God blessed *I.* 11
I. forty years old when he took. 20
I. intreated the Lord for his wife. 21
I. was sixty years old when. 26
I. loved Esau. 28
I. went to Abimelech king of. 26:1
I. was sporting with Rebekah his. 8
I. sowed and received an. 12
I.'s servants digged in valley and. 19
grief of mind to *I.* and Rebekah. 35
as *I.* had made an end of. 27:30
I. called Jacob, blessed him. 28:1
I. sent Jacob away, he went to. 5
except the fear of *I.* had. 31:42
the God of *I.* 32:9; *Ex* 3:6, 15, 16
4:5; *1 Ki* 18:36; *1 Chr* 29:18
2 Chr 30:6; *Mat* 22:32
Mark 12:26; *Luke* 20:37
Acts 3:13; 7:32
Jacob came to *I.* *Gen* 35:27
I. gave up the ghost. 29
to the God of his father *I.* 46:1
God, before whom my father *I.* 48:15
let the name of my father *I* 16
there they buried *I.* 49:31
he sware to *I.* 50:24
remembered his covenant with Abraham, with *I.* *Ex* 2:24; *Lev* 26:42
his seed and gave him *I.* *Josh* 24:3
I gave unto *I.* Jacob and Esau. 4
his oath unto *I.* *1 Chr* 16:16; *Ps* 105:9
rulers over the seed of *I.* *Jer* 33:26
high places of *I.* shall be desolate.
Amos 7:9
word against the house of *I.* 16
I., and *I.* begat Jacob. *Mat* 1:2
Luke 3:34; *Acts* 7:8
shall sit down with *I.* in. *Mat* 8:11
when ye shall see *I.* in. *Luke* 13:28
conceived by our father *I.* *Rom* 9:10
we, brethren, as *I.* was. *Gal* 4:28
in tabernacles with *I.* and. *Heb* 11:9
Abraham offered up *I.* 17; *Jas* 2:21
by faith *I.* blessed Jacob. *Heb* 11:20

Isaiah *or* **Esaias**
Hezekiah sent Eliakim to *I.*
2 Ki 19:2; *Isa* 37:2
Hezekiah was sick, *I.* came to him.
2 Ki 20:1; *Isa* 38:1
and *I.* cried unto the Lord.
2 Ki 20:11; *2 Chr* 32:20
acts did *I.* write. *2 Chr* 26:22; 32:32
I. hath walked naked. *Isa* 20:3
spoken by the prophet *E.* *Mat* 3:3
4:14; 8:17; 12:17; 13:14
Luke 3:4; *John* 1:23; 12:38
well did *E.* prophesy of you.
Mat 15:7; *Mark* 7:6
him book of prophet *E.* *Luke* 4:17
because that *E.* said. *John* 12:39
these things said *E.* when he. 41
the eunuch read *E.* *Acts* 8:28, 30
spake the Holy Ghost by *E.* 28:25
E. also crieth concerning. *Rom* 9:27
E. said before, Except the Lord. 29
E. saith, Lord, who hath ? 10:16
E. is very bold, and saith, I. 20
again *E.* saith, There shall be. 15:12

Iscariot, *see* **Judas**

Ish-bosheth
Abner took *I.* and set. *2 Sam* 2:8
wroth for the words of *I.* 3:8
David sent messengers to *I.* 14
they brought the head of *I.* 4:8
but they took the head of *I.* 12

Ishmael
call his name *I.* *Gen* 16:11, 15
old when Hagar bare *I.* 16
said to God, O that *I.* might. 17:18
as for *I.* I have heard thee, I. 20
I. was 13 years old when. 25
his sons Isaac and *I.* buried. *Gen* 25:9
the generations of *I.* 12, 13, 16
1 Chr 1:29, 31
years of the life of *I.* 137. *Gen* 25:17
went Esau unto *I.* and took. 28:9
I. came to Gedaliah. *2 Ki* 25:23
Jer 40:8
I. came and ten men with him.
2 Ki 25:25; *Jer* 41:1
Abraham, Isaac and *I.* *1 Chr* 1:28
and *I.* were sons of Azel. 8:38; 9:44
Zebadiah son of *I.* the. *2 Chr* 19:11
Jehoiada took *I.* into covenant. 23:1
I. Elasah, had taken. *Ezra* 10:22
Ammonites hath sent *I.* *Jer* 40:14
I will slay *I.* 15
for thou speakest falsely of *I.* 16
I. smote Gedaliah. 41:2
I. went forth to meet them. 6
then *I.* carried away captive. 10
then Johanan went to fight with *I.* 12
but *I.* escaped from Johanan. 15

Ishmaelites
let us sell him to the *I.* *Gen* 37:27
bought him of the hand of *I.* 39:1
because they were *I.* *Judg* 8:24
Edomites and *I.* confederate against.
Ps 83:6

Island
he shall deliver the *i.* of. *Job* 22:30
the wild beasts of the *i.* *Isa* 34:14
under a certain *i.* Clauda. *Acts* 27:16
must be cast on a certain *i.* 26
the *i.* was called Melita. 28:1
of the chief man of the *i.* 7
others who had diseases in the *i.* 9
every *i.* was moved out. *Rev* 6:14
every *i.* fled away, mountains. 16:20

Islands
his people from the *i.* of. *Isa* 11:11
wild beasts of the *i.* shall. 13:22
keep silence before me, O *i.* 41:1
his praise in the *i.* 42:12
I will make the rivers *i.* and. 15
i. he will repay recompence. 59:18
wild beasts of the *i.* shall. *Jer* 50:39

Isle
inhabitants of the *i.* say. *Isa* 20:6
be still, ye inhabitants of the *i.* 23:2
Tarshish, howl, inhabitants of the *i.* 6
through the *i.* to Paphos. *Acts* 13:6
which had wintered in the *i.* 28:11
I John was in the *i.* that is. *Rev* 1:9

Isles
the *i.* of the Gentiles. *Gen* 10:5
laid a tribute on the *i.* *Esth* 10:1
the kings of the *i.* shall. *Ps* 72:10
let the multitude of the *i.* be. 97:1
ye the Lord in the *i.* of. *Isa* 24:15
he taketh up the *i.* as a very. 40:15
the *i.* saw it and feared, the. 41:5
the *i.* shall wait for his law. 42:4
the *i.* and the inhabitants thereof. 10
listen, O *i.* unto me, and. 49:1
the *i.* shall wait upon me. 51:5; 60:9
the *i.* afar off that have not. 66:19
over the *i.* of Chittim. *Jer* 2:10
the kings of the *i.* shall drink. 25:22
hear and declare it in the *i.* 31:10
shall not *i.* shake at ? *Ezek* 26:15
the *i.* tremble, the *i.* shall. 18
of the people for many *i.* 27:3
benches of ivory, brought out of *i.* 6
blue and purple from the *i.* of. 7
many *i.* were the merchandise. 15
inhabitants of the *i.* shall be. 35
dwell carelessly in the *i.* 39:6
turn his face to the *i.* *Dan* 11:18
all the *i.* of the heathen. *Zeph* 2:11

Israel
be no more Jacob but *I.* *Gen* 32:28
but *I.* shall be thy name. 35:10
1 Ki 18:31
I. dwelt in land of Egypt. *Gen* 47:27
and *I.* bowed himself upon the. 31
in thee shall *I.* bless, saying. 48:20
the shepherd, the stone of *I.* 49:24
I. is my son. *Ex* 4:22
obey his voice to let *I.* go ? 5:2
that we have let *I.* go from. 14:5
from *I.*, for Lord fighteth. 25
Lord saved *I.* that day from. 30
I. prevailed. *Ex* 17:11
Isaac, and *I.* thy servant. 32:13
her son and a man of *I.* *Lev* 24:10
good concerning *I.* *Num* 10:29
to the many thousands of *I.* 36
thus saith thy brother *I.*, Let. 20:14
I. vowed a vow unto the Lord. 21:2
then *I.* sang this song, Spring up. 17
defy *I.* 23:7
shall be said of *I.* What hath! 23
a Sceptre rise out of *I.* 24:17
Edom a possession, and *I.* 18
Phinehas went after man of *I.* 25:8
name be not put out of *I.* *Deut* 25:6
shall teach *I.* thy law, Jacob. 33:10
I. then shall dwell in safety. 28
when *I.* turned their backs. *Josh* 7:8
I. hath sinned. 11
took the mountain of *I.* 11:16
and *I.* he shall know. 22:22
I. served the Lord all days. 24:31
it came to pass when *I.* *Judg* 1:28
them I may prove *I.* 2:22; 3:1, 4
toward the governors of *I.* 5:9
I. was greatly impoverished by. 6:1
save *I.* 14, 15, 36, 37
lest *I.* vaunt themselves. 7:2
so that *I.* was sore distressed. 10:9
grieved for the misery of *I.* 16
because *I.* took away my land. 11:13
smote Benjamin before *I.* 20:35
I. was smitten. *1 Sam* 4:2, 10
I. is fled. 17
on whom is the desire of *I.*? 9:20
heard that *I.* also was had. 13:4
also the strength of *I.* will. 15:29
of the God of the armies of *I.* 17:45
the beauty of *I.* is slain. *2 Sam* 1:19
broughtest in *I.* 5:2; *1 Chr* 11:2
nation is like thy people *I.*? *2 Sam* 7:23
the ark, and *I.* and Judah. 11:11
for *I.* had fled every man to. 19:8
Judah and *I.* were many. *1 Ki* 4:20
I. dwelt safely. 25; *Jer* 23:6
I. shall be a proverb among. *1 Ki* 9:7
he abhorred *I.* 11:25
so *I.* rebelled. 12:19
Lord shall smite *I.* as a reed. 14:15
art thou he that troubleth *I.*? 18:17
began to cut *I.* short. *2 Ki* 10:32
was put to the worse before *I.* 14:12
would blot out the name of *I.* 27
carried *I.* away into Assyria. 17:6
23, 27
of Jacob, whom he named *I.* 34
the Lord concerning *I.* *1 Chr* 11:10
they of *I.* were a thousand. 21:5
the God of *I.* 29:18; *1 Ki* 18:36
2 Chr 6:16; 30:6; *Jer* 31:1
because thy God loved *I.* *2 Chr* 9:8
whether they were of *I.* *Ezra* 2:59
Neh 7:61
for ever towards *I.* *Ezra* 3:11
to increase the trespass of *I.* 10:10
Jacob shall rejoice, *I.* shall be glad.
Ps 14:7; 53:6
fear him, all ye seed of *I.* 22:23
redeem *I.* O God, out of all. 25:22
Lord, from the fountain of *I.* 68:26
heard this, he abhorred *I.* 78:59
would not hearken, *I.* would. 81:11
O that my people *I.* had walked. 13
that name of *I.* may be no more. 83:4
Judah was his sanctuary, *I.* 114:2
he that keepeth *I.* shall. 121:4
peace shall be upon *I.* 125:5; 128:6
I. hope in the Lord. 130:7; 131:3
Lord hath chosen *I.* for his. 135:4
together the outcasts of *I.* 147:2
let *I.* rejoice in him that made. 149:2
but *I.* doth not know nor. *Isa* 1:3
blessed be *I.* mine inheritance. 19:25
I. shall blossom and bud. 27:6
but thou *I.* art my servant. 41:8
who gave *I.* to robbers ? 42:24
have given *I.* to reproaches. 43:28
himself by the name of *I.* 44:5
for *I.* mine elect's sake, I. 45:4
I. shall be saved in Lord with. 17
in the Lord shall the seed of *I.* 25
called by the name of *I.* 48:1
though *I.* be not gathered, *I.* 49:5
to restore the preserved of *I.* 6
gathereth the outcasts of *I.* 56:8

I. acknowledge us not. *Isa* 63:16
I. was holiness to the Lord. *Jer* 2:3
is *I.* a servant ? 14
the salvation of *I.* 3:23
I. is the rod of his. 10:16; 51:19
of *I.*, saviour in trouble. 14:8; 17:13
for was not *I.* a derision ? 48:27
hath *I.* no sons ? hath he no ? 49:1
I. shall be heir to them that were. 2
I. is a scattered sheep, lions. 50:17
I will bring *I.* again to his. 19
iniquity of *I.* be sought for and. 20
I. hath not been forsaken of. 51:5
Lord hath swallowed up *I.* *Lam* 2:5
you in the border of *I.* *Ezek* 11:10
wilt thou make a full end of *I.*? 13
I the Lord do sanctify *I.* 37:28
are gone from me, when *I.* 44:10
though thou *I.* play harlot. *Hos* 4:15
I. slideth back as a backsliding. 16
I. is not hid from me, *I.* 5:3; 6:10
I. shall fall. 5:5
I. shall cry to me, My God. 8:2
I. hath cast off the thing that. 3
I. is swallowed up. 8
I. shall know it. 9:7
I. hath forgotten his Maker. 14
I found *I.* like grapes in the. 9:10
I. is an empty vine. 10:1
I. shall be ashamed of his own. 6
the sin of *I.* be destroyed. 8
when *I.* was a child, then I. 11:1
how shall I deliver thee, *I.*? 8
I. served and kept sheep. 12:12
with them for my heritage *I.* *Joel* 3:2
I. shall surely be led. *Amos* 7:11, 17
Adullam the glory of *I.* *Mi* 1:15
they shall smite the judge of *I.* 5:1
holpen his servant *I.* *Luke* 1:54
art thou a master of *I.*? *John* 3:10
that for the hope of *I.* *Acts* 28:20
not all *I.* which are of *I.* *Rom* 9:6
concerning *I.* though number of *I.* 27
I. which followed the law of. 31
but I say, did not *I.* know ? 10:19
I. hath not obtained what he. 11:7
behold *I.* after the flesh. *1 Cor* 10:18
on them and on *I.* of God. *Gal* 6:16
of the stock of *I.* of the. *Phil* 3:5
see **children, congregation, elders, God, Holy** *One of Israel,* **house**

against **Israel**

Arad fought *ag. I.* *Num* 21:1
Sihon fought *ag. I.* 23
is there any divination *ag. I.*? 23:23
anger of Lord was kindled *ag. I.* 25:3
32:13; *Judg* 2:14, 20; 3:8; 10:7
2 Sam 24:1; *2 Ki* 13:3; *1 Chr* 27:24
2 Chr 28:13; *Ps* 78:21
of Canaan *ag. I.* *Josh* 8:14; 11:5
Balak of Moab warred *ag. I.* 24:9
Eglon *ag. I.* *Judg* 3:12
Midian *ag. I.* 6:2
Ammon made war *ag. I.* 11:4, 5, 20
Balak, did he ever strive *ag. I.*? 25
Philistines put themselves in array *against I.* *1 Sam* 4:2; 7:7, 10
31:1; *1 Chr* 10:1
Ben-hadad *ag. I.* *1 Ki* 20:26
2 Ki 6:8
Moab rebelled *ag. I.* *2 Ki* 1:1
was great indignation *ag. I.* 3:27
yet the Lord testified *ag. I.* 17:13
stood up *against I.* *1 Chr* 21:1
Rehoboam went out *ag. I.* *2 Chr* 11:1
words I have spoken *ag. I.* *Jer* 36:2
prophesy not *ag. I.* *Amos* 7:16
maketh intercession *ag. I.* *Rom* 11:2

all **Israel**

able men out of *all I.* *Ex* 18:25
all I. round about fled. *Num* 16:34
all I. shall hear. *Deut* 13:11; 21:21
all I. stoned Achan with. *Josh* 7:25
all I. went a whoring. *Judg* 8:27
that his sons did to *all I.* *1 Sam* 2:22
all I. knew that Samuel was. 3:20
word of Samuel came to *all I.* 4:1
lay it for a reproach on *all I.* 11:2
but *all I.* and Judah loved. 18:16
all I. had lamented Samuel. 28:3
to bring about *all I.* *2 Sam* 3:12
all I. understood that it was not. 37
will do this thing before *all I.*
2 Sam 12:12
in *all I.* none so much praised. 14:25
all I. shall hear that thou art. 16:21
all I. know thy father. 17:10
and *all I.* fled every one to. 18:17
speech of *all I.* is come to me. 19:11
the eyes of *all I.* are. *1 Ki* 1:20
thou knowest that *all I.* set. 2:15
all I. heard of the judgement. 3:28
king and *all I.* offered sacrifice. 8:62
all I. stoned Adoram with. 12:18
all I. shall mourn for him. 14:13
gather to me *all I.* unto. 18:19
I saw *all I.* scattered. 22:17
2 Chr 18:16
David and *all I.* went to. *1 Chr* 11:4
David and *all I.* played. 13:8
all I. brought up the ark of. 15:28
I have walked with *all I.* 17:6
all I. and the princes obeyed. 29:23
all I. forsook the law. *2 Chr* 12:1
hear me, Jeroboam, and *all I.* 13:4
God smote Jeroboam and *all I.* 15
ruin of him and of *all I.* 28:23
to make an atonement for *all I.*
29:24; *Ezra* 6:17
all I. went out and brake. *2 Chr* 31:1
all I. dwelt in their cities. *Ezra* 2:70
Neh 7:73
made *all I.* swear to do. *Ezra* 10:5
all I. gave the portions. *Neh* 12:47
belongeth to us, to *all I.* *Dan* 9:7
yea, *all I.* have transgressed. 11
the law of Moses for *all I.* *Mal* 4:4
not *all I.* which are of *I.* *Rom* 9:6
so *all I.* shall be saved, as it. 11:26

camp of **Israel**

went before the *camp of I.* *Ex* 24:19
Egyptians and the *camp of I.* 20
the *camp of I.* a curse. *Josh* 6:18
them without the *camp of I.* 23
out of the *camp of I.* am I escaped.
2 Sam 1:3
came to the *camp of I.* *2 Ki* 3:24

for **Israel**

God had done *for I.* *Ex* 18:1, 8
Josh 24:31; *Judg* 2:7, 10; *1 Ki* 8:66
Lord fought *for I.* *Josh* 10:14, 42
left no sustenance *for I.* *Judg* 6:4
cried unto Lord *for I.* *1 Sam* 7:9
made it an ordinance *for I.* 30:25
not any helper *for I.* *2 Ki* 14:26
atonement *for I.* as Moses had.
1 Chr 6:49; 22:1; *Neh* 10:33
statute *for I.*, a law of God. *Ps* 81:4
salvation in Zion *for I.* *Isa* 46:13
word of the Lord *for I.* *Zech* 12:1
my prayer to God *for I.* *Rom* 10:1

from **Israel**

shalt be cut off *from I.* *Ex* 12:15
Num 19:13
be turned away *from I.* *Num* 25:4
put evil *from I.* *Deut* 17:12; 22:22
Judg 20:13
one tribe cut off *from I.* *Judg* 21:6
the glory is departed *from I.*
1 Sam 4:21, 22
the cities taken *from I.* were. 7:14
away the reproach *from I.* 17:26
the plague was stayed *from I.*
2 Sam 24:25
they separated *from I.* all the mixed multitude. *Neh* 13:3
cut off *from I.* head and. *Isa* 9:14
for *from I.* was it also, the. *Hos* 8:6

in **Israel**

he had wrought folly *in I.* *Gen* 34:7
Deut 22:21; *Josh* 7:15
Judg 20:6, 10
Jacob, scatter them *in I.* *Gen* 49:7
strangers sojourn *in I.* *Lev* 20:2
22:18; *Ezek* 14:7
able to go forth to war *in I.*
Num 1:3, 45; 26:2
heads of thousands *in I.* 1:16; 10:4
to me all the firstborn *in I.* 3:13
every thing devoted *in I.* 18:14
given all the tenth *in I.* for an. 21
nor seen perverseness *in I.* 23:21
abomination is wrought *in I.*
Deut 17:4; 22:21
up his brother a name *in I.* 25:7
his name be called *in I.* *Deut* 25:10
arose not a prophet since *in I.* 34:10
Rahab dwelleth *in I.* *Josh* 6:25
in I. till that I Deborah arose, that I arose a mother *in I.* *Judg* 5:7
spear seen among 40,000 *in I.*? 8
in I. to lament Jephthah. 11:39
was no king *in I.* 17:6, 18:1
19:1; 21:25
be priest to a family *in I.* 18:19
in I., one tribe lacking *in I.*? 21:3
times *in I.* concerning redeeming, this was a testimony *in I.* *Ruth* 4:7
his name may be famous *in I.* 14
I will do a thing *in I.* *1 Sam* 3:11
beforetime *in I.* when a man. 9:9
wrought salvation *in I.* 11:13; 14:45
father's house free *in I.* 17:25
know that there is a God *in I.* 46
is my father's family *in I.* 18:18
who is like to thee *in I.*? 26:15
great man fallen *in I.* *2 Sam* 3:38
ought to be done *in I.* 13:12
be as one of the fools *in I.* 13
put to death this day *in I.*? 19:22
and peaceable *in I.*, thou seekest to destroy a mother *in I.* 20:19
shalt thou kill any man *in I.* 21:4
cut off him that is shut up and left *in I.* *1 Ki* 14:10; 21:21; *2 Ki* 9:8
that thou art God *in I.* *1 Ki* 18:36
left me seven thousand *in I.* 19:18
because there is not a God *in I.*
2 Ki 1:3, 6, 16
that there is a prophet *in I.* 5:8
no God in all the earth but *in I.* 15
the prophet *in I.* telleth the. 6:12
for there was joy *in I.* *1 Chr* 12:40
a man to be ruler *in I.* *2 Chr* 7:18
because he had done good *in I.* 24:16
for them that are left *in I.* 34:21
Josiah made all present *in I.* to. 33
passover like to that kept *in I.* 35:18
made them an ordinance *in I.* 25
yet there is hope *in I.* *Ezra* 10:2
Judah, his name is great *in I.* *Ps* 76:1
and he appointed law *in I.* 78:5
signs and for wonders *in I.* *Isa* 8:18
hath glorified himself *in I.* 44:23
committed villany *in I.* *Jer* 29:23
set signs and wonders *in I.* 32:20
it as a proverb *in I.* *Ezek* 12:23
18:3
I am the holy One *in I.* 39:7
Gog a place of graves *in I.* 11
give them no possession *in I.* 44:28
every dedicated thing *in I.* 29
shall be his possession *in I.* 45:8
oblation for the prince *in I.* 16
he exalted himself *in I.* *Hos* 13:1
that is to be ruler *in I.* *Mi* 5:2
is committed *in I.* *Mal* 2:11
so great faith, no not *in I.* *Mat* 8:10
Luke 7:9
it was never so seen *in I.* *Mat* 9:33
and rising of many *in I.* *Luke* 2:34
many widows were *in I.* 4:25
lepers *in I.* 27
see **king, kings**

land of **Israel**

no smith found in all the *land of I.*
1 Sam 13:19
little maid out of *land of I.* *1 Ki* 5:2
came no more into *land of I.* 6:23
brethren left in *land of I.* *1 Chr* 13:2
strangers that were in *land of I.*
22:2; *2 Chr* 2:17; 30:25
idols through *land of I.* *2 Chr* 34:7
the Lord to the *land of I.* *Ezek* 7:2
I will give you the *land of I.* 11:17
the Lord of the *land of I.* 12:19
enter into *land of I.* 13:9; 20:38
bring you into the *land of I.* 20:42
37:12
prophesy against the *land of I.* 21:2
Aha, against the *land of I.* 25:3
with despite against *land of I.* 6
Judah and *land of I.* were. 27:17
shall come against *land of I.* 38:18
great shaking in the *land of I.* 19
brought me into *land of I.* 40:2
go into the *land of I.* for. *Mat* 2:20
and came into the *land of I.* 21

made **Israel** *sin*
Jeroboam *made I.* to *sin. 1 Ki* 14:16
15:26, 30, 34; 16:19, 26; 22:52
Baasha *made* my people *I.* to *sin.*
16:2, 13
Ahab *made I.* to *sin.* 21:22
son of Nebat who *made I.* to *sin.*
2 Ki 3:3; 10:29, 31; 13:2, 6, 11
14:24; 15:9, 18, 24, 28; 23:15

men of **Israel**
called for all *men of I.* *Josh* 10:24
men of I. gathered. *Judg* 20:11
men of I. went out. 20
men of I. encouraged themselves. 22
the *men of I.* gave place to the. 36
men of I. were distressed that day.
1 Sam 14:24
the *men of I.* fled from the. 31:1
beaten and the *men of I.* *2 Sam* 2:17
hearts of the *men of I.* are. 15:13
whom the *men of I.* choose. 16:18
words of men of Judah fiercer than
of the *men of I.* 19:43
men of I. were gone away. 23:9
down the chosen *men of I.* *Ps* 78:31
fear not, ye *men of I.* I. *Isa* 41:14
ye *men of I.* hear these. *Acts* 2:22
ye *men of I.* why marvel? 3:12
ye *men of I.* take heed to. 5:35
Paul said, *Men of I.* give. 13:16
crying out, *Men of I.* help. 21:28

O **Israel**
these be thy gods, *O I.* *Ex* 32:4
are thy tabernacles, *O I.* *Num* 24:5
hearken, *O I.* *Deut* 4:1; 27:9
Isa 48:12
hear, *O I.*, the statutes. *Deut* 5:1
6:3, 4; 9:1; 20:3; *Ps* 50:7
81:8; *Isa* 44:1; *Mark* 12:29
happy art thou, *O I.* *Deut* 33:29
in the midst of thee, *O I.* *Josh* 7:13
every man to his tents, *O I.*
2 Sam 20:1; *1 Ki* 12:16
2 Chr 10:16
behold thy gods, *O I.* *1 Ki* 12:28
O I. trust thou in Lord. *Ps* 115:9
why speakest thou, *O I.*? *Isa* 40:27
O I. fear not. 43:1; *Jer* 30:10
46:27
been weary of me, *O I.* *Isa* 43:22
O I. for thou art my servant, *O I.*
thou shalt not be. 44:21; 49:3
if thou wilt return, *O I.* *Jer* 4:1
Hos 14:1
O I. thy prophets are. *Ezek* 13:4
rejoice not, *O I.* for joy. *Hos* 9:1
O I. thou hast sinned from. 10:9
O I. thou hast destroyed. 13:9
to meet thy God, *O I.* *Amos* 4:12
shout, *O I.* be glad and. *Zeph* 3:14

over **Israel**
Abimelech reigned three years *over*
I. *Judg* 9:22
had dominion *over I.* 14:4
his sons judges *over I.* *1 Sam* 8:1
reigned two years *over I.* 13:1
thee from being king *over I.* 13:26
Ish-bosheth Saul's son reigned *over*
I. *2 Sam* 2:10
throne of David *over I.* 3:10
5:2, 3, 17; 6:21; *1 Chr* 11:3
hosts is the God *over I.* *2 Sam* 7:26
Solomon king *over I.* *1 Ki* 1:34
Jeroboam king *over I.* 11:37
shall raise up a king *over I.* 14:14
Nadab reigned *over I.* 15:25
Elah reigned *over I.* 16:8
Omri king *over I.* 16
Ahab reigned *over I.* 29
Ahaziah reigned *over I.* 22:51
Jehoram reigned *over I.* *2 Ki* 3:1
Jehu king *over I.* 9:3, 6, 12; 10:36
Jehoahaz reigned *over I.* 13:1
Jehoash reigned *over I.* 10
Zechariah reigned *over I.* 15:8
Menahem reigned *over I.* 15:17
Pekahiah reigned *over I.* 23
Hoshea reigned *over I.* 17:1
Chenaniah for outward business *over*
I. *1 Chr* 26:29
times that went *over I.* are. 29:30
his excellency is *over I.* *Ps* 68:34
preacher was king *over I.* *Eccl* 1:12

Israel joined with *people*
much *people* of *I.* died. *Num* 21:6
O Lord, to thy *people I.* *Deut* 21:8
and bless thy *people I.* 26:15
should bless *people* of *I.* *Josh* 8:33
before his *people I.* *Judg* 11:23
offerings of *I.* my *people.* *1 Sam* 2:29
Saul captain over my *people I.* 9:16
made his *people I.* utterly. 27:12
I will save my *people I.* *2 Sam* 3:18
to feed my *people I.* 5:2; 7:7
1 Chr 11:2
for his *people I.'s* sake. *2 Sam* 5:12
for my *people I.* that they may dwell
and move no. 7:10; *1 Chr* 17:9
to thyself thy *people I.* *2 Sam* 7:24
not forsake my *people I.* *1 Ki* 6:13
when thy *people I.* be smitten. 8:33
2 Chr 6:24
what prayer soever be made by all
thy *people I.* *1 Ki* 8:38
fear thee, as do thy *people I.* 43
given rest to his *people I.* 56
because of his *people I.* *1 Chr* 14:2
be ruler over my *people I.* 17:7
2 Chr 6:5
earth is like thy *people I.* *1 Chr* 17:21
people I. didst thou make. 22
shewed *I.* his *people.* *2 Chr* 7:10
blessed Lord and his *people I.* 31:8
serve now the Lord your God and his
people I. 35:3
all they of the *people* of *I.* *Ezra* 7:13
people of *I.* have not separated. 9:1
heritage to *I.* his *people.* *Ps* 135:12
people I. be as the sand. *Isa* 10:22
wickedness of my *people I.* *Jer* 7:12
which I caused my *people I.* 12:14
caused my *people I.* to err. 23:13
again the captivity of my *people I.*
and Judah. 30:3; *Amos* 9:14
Edom by my *people I.* *Ezek* 25:14
your fruit to my *people I.* 36:8
will cause my *people I.* to walk. 12
when my *people I.* dwelleth. 38:14
come up against my *people I.* 16
the sin of my *people I.* *Dan* 9:20
go, prophesy unto my *people I.*
Amos 7:15
is come upon my *people I.* 8:2
shall rule my *people I.* *Mat* 2:6
glory of thy *people I.* *Luke* 2:32
people of *I.* were gathered against.
Acts 4:27
God of this *people I.* chose. 13:17
repentance to all *people* of *I.* 24

princes of **Israel**
the *princes of I.* being. *Num* 1:44
the *princes of I.* heads and princes of
the tribes offered at the. 7:2, 84
princes of I. to help. *1 Chr* 22:17
David assembled the *princes of I.*
23:2; 28:1
princes of I. humbled. *2 Chr* 12:6
slew divers of *princes of I.* 21:4
lamentation for the *princes of I.*
Ezek 19:1
be upon all the *princes of I.* 21:12
the *princes of I.* were on thee. 22:6
it suffice you, O *princes of I.* 45:9

to or *unto* **Israel**
God spake *unto I.* in. *Gen* 46:2
hear and hearken *unto I.* 49:2
the Lord hath done *to I.* *Ex* 18:9
Joshua gave it for inheritance *to I.*
Josh 11:23; 21:43
Lord hath given rest *unto I.* 23:1
he hath shewed *unto I.* *Judg* 8:35
what Amalek did *to I.* *1 Sam* 15:2
that seemed good *to I.* *2 Sam* 3:19
an adversary *to I.* *1 Ki* 11:25
for a law, and *to I.* for an everlasting
covenant. *1 Chr* 16:17; *Ps* 105:10
a cause of trespass *to I.*? *1 Chr* 21:3
I will give quietness *to I.* in. 22:9
ordinance for ever *to I.* *2 Chr* 2:4
scribe of his statutes *to I.* *Ezra* 7:11
Lord had commanded *to I.* *Neh* 8:1
truly God is good *to I.* *Ps* 73:1
heritage *unto I.* 135:12; 136:22
sheweth his judgements *to I.* 147:19
as it was *to I.* in the day. *Isa* 11:16
a wilderness *unto I.*? *Jer* 2:31
a father *to I.* Ephraim is. *Jer* 31:9
I will be as the dew *to I.* *Hos* 14:5
to declare *to I.* his sin. *Mi* 3:8
the word of the Lord *to I.* *Mal* 1:1
day of his shewing *unto I.* *Luke* 1:80
be made manifest *to I.* *John* 1:31
restore the kingdom *to I.*? *Acts* 1:6
to give repentance *to I.* 5:31
God hath raised *unto I.* 13:23
to I. he saith, All day. *Rom* 10:21
in part is happened *to I.* 11:25

tribes of **Israel**
Dan shall judge as one of *tribes of I.*
Gen 49:16
are the twelve *tribes of I.* 28
according to 12 *tribes of I.* *Ex* 24:4
through all *tribes of I.* to war.
Num 31:4
to any of the other *tribes of I.* 36:3
every one of *tribes of I.* shall keep. 9
evil out of *tribes of I.* *Deut* 29:21
when the *tribes of I.* were. 33:5
men out of *tribes of I.* *Josh* 3:12
to number of *tribes of I.* 4:5, 8
brought *I.* by their *tribes.* 7:16
Joshua gave to the *tribes of I.* 12:7
fathers of *tribes of I.* divided. 19:51
princes through *tribes of I.* 22:14
Joshua gathered all *tribes of I.* 24:1
Dan not among *tribes of I.* *Judg* 18:1
chief of *tribes of I.* presented. 20:2
of an 100 out of all *tribes of I.* 10
tribes of I. came not up. 21:5, 8
a breach in the *tribes of I.* 15
him out of all *tribes of I.* *1 Sam* 2:28
the smallest of the *tribes of I.* 9:21
Samuel caused all *tribes of I.* 10:20
made head of the *tribes of I.*? 15:17
came all the *tribes of I.* to David.
2 Sam 5:1
word with any of *tribes of I.* 7:7
servant is of one of *tribes of I.* 15:2
spies through all the *tribes of I.* 10
strife through the *tribes of I.* 19:9
all the *tribes of I.* and number. 24:2
no city out of all the *tribes of I.* to
build. *1 Ki* 8:16; *2 Chr* 6:5
Jerusalem out of all the *tribes of I.*
1 Ki 11:32; 14:21; *2 Ki* 21:7
2 Chr 12:13; 33:7
out of all the *tribes of I.* *2 Chr* 11:16
goats according to *tribes of I.*
Ezra 6:17
made *tribes of I.* to dwell. *Ps* 78:55
I will take *tribes of I.* *Ezek* 37:19
the twelve *tribes of I.* 47:13, 21, 22
city out of all the *tribes of I.* 48:19
after the names of the *tribes of I.* 31
among *tribes of I.* have I. *Hos* 5:9
the eyes of all *tribes of I.* *Zech* 9:1
judging the twelve *tribes of I.*
Mat 19:28; *Luke* 22:30
with names of twelve *tribes of I.*
Rev 21:12

with **Israel**
Amalek fought *with I.* *Ex* 17:8
a covenant *with* thee and *I.* 34:27
have no inheritance *with I.* *Deut* 18:1
his judgements *with I.* 33:21
of Canaan fought *with I.* *Josh* 9:2
Gibeon made peace *with I.* 10:1
themselves together to fight *with I.*
1 Sam 13:5; 28:1; *2 Sam* 21:15
Syrians made peace *with I.*
2 Sam 10:19
was very angry *with I.* *2 Ki* 17:18
for Lord is not *with I.* *2 Chr* 25:7
Lord will plead *with I.* *Mi* 6:2

Israelite
the *I.* was slain, Zimri. *Num* 25:14
the son of Ithra an *I.* *2 Sam* 17:25
behold an *I.* indeed, in. *John* 1:47
I also am an *I.* of seed. *Rom* 11:1

Israelites
the cattle of the *I.* dead. *Ex* 9:7
I. born shall dwell in. *Lev* 23:42
all the *I.* passed over on. *Josh* 3:17
only divide it by lot to the *I.* 13:6
destroyed of the *I.* *Judg* 20:21
servants did to all *I.* *1 Sam* 2:14
I. went to the Philistines to. 13:20
turned to be with the *I.* 14:21
all the *I.* lamented Samuel. 25:1

the *I.* pitched by a. *1 Sam* 29:1
the *I.* were troubled at. *2 Sam* 4:1
the *I.* rose and smote. *2 Ki* 3:24
as all the multitude of the *I.* 7:13
inhabitants were the *I.* *1 Chr* 9:2
who are *I.*; to whom. *Rom* 9:4
are they *I.*? so am I. *2 Cor* 11:22

Israelitish

the son of an *I.* woman. *Lev* 24:10
I. woman's son blasphemed the. 11

Issachar

Leah called his name *I.* *Gen* 30:18
Leah's son, *I.* 35:23
sons of *I.* 46:13; *1 Chr* 7:1
I. is a strong ass. *Gen* 49:14
Israel's sons, *I.*, Zebulun. *Ex* 1:3
1 Chr 2:1
the princes of *I.*, Nethaneel.
Num 1:8; 2:5; 7:18
I. and Joseph shall stand to bless.
Deut 27:12
rejoice, Zebulun and *I.* in. 33:18
they met together in *I.* *Josh* 17:10
Manasseh had in *I.* and Asher. 11
the princes of *I.* were with Deborah,
even *I.* and also. *Judg* 5:15
Tola a man of *I.* arose to. 10:1
was an officer in *I.* *1 Ki* 4:17
Ahijah of the house of *I.* 15:27
they that were nigh to *I.* *1 Chr* 12:40
I. the seventh son of. 26:5
captain of *I.* Omri the son of. 27:18
of *I.* had not cleansed. *2 Chr* 30:18
of Simeon, *I.* a portion. *Ezek* 48:25
by the border of *I.*, Zebulun a. 26
south side, one gate of *I.*, one. 33

tribe of **Issachar**

were numbered of the *tribe of I.*
Num 1:29
Judah shall be the *tribe of I.* 2:5
over the *tribe of I.* was. 10:15
of the *tribe of I.* to spy the. 13:7
prince of the *tribe of I.* 34:26
inheritance of the *tribe of I.*
Josh 19:23
lot out of the families of the *tribe of I.*
21:6, 28; *1 Chr* 6:62, 72
of *tribe of I.* were sealed. *Rev* 7:7

issue

[1] *A passage, way, or outlet*, Ps 68:20. [2] *Children or posterity*, Gen 48:6. [3] *A flux or running*, Lev 12:7. [4] *To flow*, Ezek 47:8. [5] *To come forth hastily and violently*, Josh 8:22.

issue, *substantive*

i. which thou begettest. *Gen* 48:6
the *i.* of her blood. *Lev* 12:7; 15:25
Mat 9:20; *Mark* 5:25
Luke 8:43, 44
running *i.* *Lev* 15:2, 3; 22:4
hath the *i.* 15:8, 28
of Joab, one hath an *i.* *2 Sam* 3:29
on him the offspring and *i.* *Isa* 22:24
whose *i.* is like the *i.* *Ezek* 23:20
having no *i.* left his wife. *Mat* 22:25

issue

thy sons that *i.* from thee. *2 Ki* 20:18
Isa 39:7
these waters *i.* toward. *Ezek* 47:8*

issued

other *i.* out of the city. *Josh* 8:22
break forth as if it *i.* *Job* 38:8
waters *i.* from under. *Ezek* 47:1
because their waters *i.* out of. 12
a fiery stream *i.* and. *Dan* 7:10
of their mouths *i.* fire. *Rev* 9:17, 18

issues

to God belong the *i.* *Ps* 68:20
out of it are the *i.* of life. *Pr* 4:23

Italian

a centurion of the *I.* band. *Acts* 10:1

Italy

Jew lately come from *I.* *Acts* 18:2
that we should sail into *I.* 27:1
they of *I.* salute you. *Heb* 13:24

itch

will smite thee with *i.* *Deut* 28:27

itching

teachers having *i.* ears. *2 Tim* 4:3

Ithamar

Aaron's sons, Abihu, and *I.*
Ex 6:23; *1 Chr* 6:3
counted by the hand of *I.* 38:21
charge under hand of *I.* *Num* 4:28
Ahimelech of sons of *I.* *1 Chr* 24:3
chief men among the sons of *I.* 4
of the sons of *I.* Daniel. *Ezra* 8:2
see **Eleazar**

Ithiel

I. son of Jesaiah dwelt. *Neh* 11:7
man spake to *I.* even to *I.* *Pr* 30:1

itself

the fruit tree, whose seed is in *i.*
Gen 1:11
the beast that dieth of *i.* *Lev* 7:24
17:15; 22:8; *Deut* 14:21
land *i.* vomiteth out. *Lev* 18:25
nor reap what groweth of *i.* 25:11
Isa 37:30
undersetters were of the base *i.*
1 Ki 7:34
darkness, as darkness *i.* *Job* 10:22
gathereth iniquity to *i.* *Ps* 41:6
even Sinai *i.* was moved at. 68:8
his heart may discover *i.* *Pr* 18:2
wine when it moveth *i.* aright. 23:31
ointment which bewrayeth *i.* 27:16
the tender grass sheweth *i.* 25
shall axe boast *i.* against him that
heweth, saw magnify *i.*, rod shake
i., staff lift up *i.* *Isa* 10:15
your soul delight *i.* in fatness. 55:2
shall thy moon withdraw *i.* 60:20
shall dwell in Judah *i.* *Jer* 31:24
a fire unfolding *i.* and. *Ezek* 1:4
not eaten what dieth of *i.* 4:14; 44:31
be base, that it might not lift *i.* 17:14
nor exalt *i.* any more above. 29:15
it raised up *i.* on the one. *Dan* 7:5
thought for the things of *i.* *Mat* 6:34
every kingdom divided against *i.*
12:25; *Mark* 3:24, 25; *Luke* 11:17
branch cannot bear fruit of *i.*
John 15:4
together in a place by *i.* 20:7
i. could not contain the books. 21:25
Spirit *i.* beareth witness. *Rom* 8:16
creature *i.* also shall be delivered. 21
Spirit *i.* maketh intercession for. 26
there is nothing unclean of *i.* 14:14
not even nature *i.* teach? *1 Cor* 11:14
charity vaunteth not *i.*, is not. 13:4
charity doth not behave *i.* 5
every thing that exalts *i.* *2 Cor* 10:5
edifying of *i.* in love. *Eph* 4:16
into heaven *i.* to appear. *Heb* 9:24
good report of truth *i.* *3 John* 12

Iturea

brother Philip tetrarch of *I.* *Luke* 3:1

Ivah

the gods of Hena and *I.*? *2 Ki* 18:34
is the king of *I.*? 19:13; *Isa* 37:13

ivory

king made a throne of *i.* *1 Ki* 10:18
2 Chr 9:17
bringing gold, silver, and *i.*
1 Ki 10:22; *2 Chr* 9:21
the *i.* house which Ahab. *1 Ki* 22:39
out of the *i.* palaces. *Ps* 45:8
his belly is as bright *i.* *S of S* 5:14
thy neck is as a tower of *i.* 7:4
made thy benches of *i.* *Ezek* 27:6
thee for a present horns of *i.* 15
houses of *i.* shall perish. *Amos* 3:15
lie upon beds of *i.* and stretch. 6:4
man buyeth vessels of *i.* *Rev* 18:12

J

Jaazaniah

J. came to Gedaliah. *2 Ki* 25:23
J. of the house of the. *Jer* 35:3
J. stood with his censer. *Ezek* 8:11
J. and Pelatiah princes of. 11:1

Jabal

J. was the father of such. *Gen* 4:20

Jabbok

passed over the ford *J.* *Gen* 32:22
not to any place of river *J.* *Deut* 2:37
Reuben and Gad border to *J.* 3:16
Gilead to the river *J.* *Josh* 12:2

Jabesh

told Saul the tidings of men of *J.*
1 Sam 11:5
shewed to the men of *J.* and. 9
came to *J.* and burned the. 31:12
their bones at *J.* 13; *1 Chr* 10:12
Shallum the son of *J.* conspired.
2 Ki 15:10
Shallum the son of *J.* began to. 13
smote Shallum the son of *J.* 14

Jabesh-gilead

none to the camp from *J.* *Judg* 21:8
smite the inhabitants of *J.* 10
found 400 young virgins of *J.* 12
Benjamites wives of women of *J.* 14
Nahash came and encamped against
J. *1 Sam* 11:1
the inhabitants of *J.* heard what.
31:11; *1 Chr* 10:12
men of *J.* were they that buried Saul.
2 Sam 2:4
bones of Saul from men of *J.* 21:12

Jabez

scribes who dwelt at *J.* *1 Chr* 2:55

Jabez

honourable than his brethren, mother
called his name *J.* *1 Chr* 4:9
J. called on God of Israel, saying. 10

Jabin

when *J.* king of Hazor. *Josh* 11:1
sold them into hand of *J.* *Judg* 4:2
peace between *J.* and the house. 17
God subdued that day, *J.* king. 23
of Israel prevailed against *J.* 24
do to them as unto *J.* *Ps* 83:9

Jachin

he called the pillar on the right hand
J. *1 Ki* 7:21; *2 Chr* 3:17

jacinth

breastplates of fire, *j.* *Rev* 9:17*
foundation of city was a *j.* 21:20

Jacob

he was called *J.* *Gen* 25:26
J. was a plain man. 27
J. sod pottage. 29
J. gave Esau pottage. 34
the voice is *J.'s*. 27:22
J. was scarce gone out. 30
is not he rightly named *J.*? 36
Esau hated *J.* 41
if *J.* take a wife of Heth. 46
Isaac sent away *J.* 28:5
J. obeyed his father. 7
J. awaked out of sleep. 16
J. vowed a vow. 20
J. saw Rachel the daughter. 29:10
J. served seven years for Rachel. 20
and *J.* did so, and fulfilled her. 28
J. came out of the field in. 30:16
and J. took him rods of green. 37
were Laban's, the stronger *J.'s*. 42
J. hath taken all that was. 31:1
J. stole away unawares to Laban. 20
J. sware by the fear of his father. 53
J. sent messengers before. 32:3
J. saith, Thus have I sojourned. 4
then *J.* was greatly afraid. 7
say, They be thy servant *J.'s*. 18
J. was left alone, and there. 24
be no more *J.* but Israel. 28; 35:10
J. called the name of place. 32:30
J. looked, and behold, Esau. 33:1
J. journeyed to Succoth. 17
J. came to Shalem. 18
J. held his peace until they. 34:5
sons of *J.* 7, 13, 25; 35:26; 49:1, 2
1 Ki 18:31
J. came to Luz. *Gen* 35:6
J. called the place Beth-el. 15
these are the generations of *J.* 37:2
J. rent his clothes, put sackcloth. 34
J.'s heart fainted, for he. 45:26
J. and all his seed came into. 46:6
that came with *J.* were sixty-six. 26
J. blessed Pharaoh. 47:10
the whole age of *J.* 28
the mighty God of *J.* 49:24; *Ex* 3:6
15, 16; 4:5; *2 Sam* 23:1; *Ps* 20:1

remembered his covenant with *J.*
Ex 2:24; *Lev* 26:42
come, curse me *J.* and. *Num* 23:7
can count dust of *J.* and number? 10
enchantment against *J.* it shall be
said of *J.* and Israel, what? 23
shall come a star out of *J.* 24:17
out of *J.* come he that shall have. 19
J. is the lot of his. *Deut* 32:9
they shall teach *J.* thy. 33:10
fountain of *J.* shall be on land. 28
Israel his servant, ye children of *J.*
1 Chr 16:13; *Ps* 105:6
J. shall rejoice. *Ps* 14:7; 53:6
the name of the God of *J.* 20:1
all ye seed of *J.* glorify him. 22:23
command deliverances for *J.* 44:4
the god of *J.* 46:7, 11; 75:9; 76:6
81:1, 4; 84:8; 94:7; 114:7; 132:2
5; 146:5
the excellency of *J.* whom he loved.
47:4; *Nah* 2:2
fire was kindled against *J.* *Ps* 78:21
he brought him to feed *J.* his. 71
for they have devoured *J.* and. 79:7
brought back the captivity of *J.* 85:1
gates of Zion more than all the dwellings of *J.* 87:2
J. sojourned in the land of. 105:23
the Lord hath chosen *J.* 135:4
the God of *J.* *Isa* 2:3; 41:21
Mi 4:2; *Mat* 22:32; *Mark* 12:26
Luke 20:37; *Acts* 3:13; 7:32, 46
remnant of *J.* shall return. *Isa* 10:21
Lord will have mercy on *J.* 14:1
in that day the glory of *J.* shall. 17:4
shall cause them that come of *J.* 27:6
by this shall the iniquity of *J.* be. 9
sanctify the Holy One of *J.* 29:23
J. whom I have chosen, the. 41:8
fear not, thou worm *J.* and ye. 14
who gave *J.* for a spoil? 42:24
therefore I have given *J.* to. 43:28
call himself by the name of *J.* 44:5
Lord hath redeemed *J.* 23; *Jer* 31:11
for *J.* my servant's sake. *Isa* 45:4
hath redeemed his servant *J.* 48:20
that formed me to bring *J.* 49:5
servant to raise up the tribes of *J.* 6
the mighty One of *J.* 26; 60:16
feed thee with heritage of *J.* 58:14
bring forth a seed out of *J.* 65:9
the portion of *J.* not like them.
Jer 10:16; 51:19
they have eaten up *J.* and. 10:25
even the time of *J.'s* trouble. 30:7
fear thou not, O my servant *J.* 10
bring again the captivity of *J.* 18
sing with the gladness for *J.* 31:7
will I cast away the seed of *J.* 33:26
J. shall return to be in rest. 46:27
commanded concerning *J.* *Lam* 1:17
he burned against *J.* like a. 2:3
Judah shall plow, *J.* shall. *Hos* 10:11
I will punish *J.* 12:2
J. fled into Syria. 12
abhor the excellency of *J.* *Amos* 6:8
shall *J.* arise, for he is small? 7:2, 5
sworn by the excellency of *J.* 8:7
for the transgression of *J.* *Mi* 1:5
hear, I pray you, O heads of *J.* 3:1
remnant of *J.* shall be among. 5:8
Esau *J.'s* brother? yet I loved *J.*
Mal 1:2
therefore, ye sons of *J.* are not. 3:6
Isaac begat *J.* *Mat* 1:2
Matthan begat *J.* 15
sit down with Abraham, Isaac, and *J.*
8:11
J. in kingdom of God. *Luke* 13:28
now *J.'s* well was there. *John* 4:6
Joseph called his father *J.* *Acts* 7:14
J. have I loved, but. *Rom* 9:13
turn away ungodliness from *J.* 11:26
in tabernacles with *J.* *Heb* 11:9
by faith Isaac blessed *J.* 20
J. blessed the sons of Joseph. 21

see **house**

in **Jacob**

I will divide them *in J.* *Gen* 49:7
not beheld iniquity *in J.* *Num* 23:21
know that God ruleth *in J.* *Ps* 59:13
established a testimony *in J.* 78:5
and righteousness *in J.* *Ps* 99:4
from transgression *in J.* *Isa* 59:20

O **Jacob**

how goodly are thy tents, *O J.!*
Num 24:5
that seek thy face, *O J.* *Ps* 24:6
why sayest thou, *O J.?* *Isa* 40:27
Lord that created thee, *O J.* 43:1
hast not called upon me, *O J.* 22
yet hear, *O J.* 44:1
fear not, *O J.* my servant. 2
Jer 46:27, 28
remember these, *O J.* for. *Isa* 44:21
hearken unto me, *O J.* 48:12
I will surely assemble, *O J.* *Mi* 2:12

to or *unto* **Jacob**

speak not *to J.* *Gen* 31:24, 29
God appeared *unto J.* and. 35:9
land which he sware to give *to J.*
50:24; *Ex* 6:8; 33:1; *Num* 32:11
Deut 6:10; 29:13; 30:20; 34:4
Ezek 37:25
confirmed the same *to J.* for a law.
1 Chr 16:17; *Ps* 105:10
shewed his word *unto J.* *Ps* 147:19
Lord sent a word *unto J.* *Isa* 9:8
declare *unto J.* his transgression.
Mi 3:8
wilt perform truth *to J.* and. 7:20

Jael

fled away to tent of *J.* *Judg* 4:17
J. took a nail of the tent and. 21
J. came out to meet Barak. 22
in days of *J.* the highways. 5:6
blessed above women shall *J.* 24

Jah

extol him by his name *J.* *Ps* 68:4

Jahaz

his people and came and fought at *J.*
Num 21:23; *Deut* 2:32
Judg 11:20
shall be heard even to *J.* *Isa* 15:4
to *J.* have they uttered. *Jer* 48:34

Jahazah

out of Reuben *J.* given. *Josh* 21:36
judgement is come upon Holon and
J. *Jer* 48:21

jailer

charging the *j.* to keep. *Acts* 16:23

Jair

J. took the small towns. *Num* 32:41
Deut 3:14
J. the Gileadite judged. *Judg* 10:3
J. died. 5
Segub begat *J.* *1 Chr* 2:22
Elhanan the son of *J.* slew. 20:5
Mordecai the son of *J.* *Esth* 2:5

Jairus

J. a ruler of the synagogue.
Mark 5:22; *Luke* 8:41

Jakeh, *see* **Agur**

Jambres

as Jannes and *J.* withstood Moses.
2 Tim 3:8

James

saw two brethren *J.* and John.
Mat 4:21; *Mark* 1:19
J. the son of Zebedee. *Mat* 10:2
Mark 3:17
J. the son of Alpheus. *Mat* 10:3
Mark 3:18; *Acts* 1:13
and his brethren *J.* and Joses.
Mat 13:55; *Mark* 6:3
after six days Jesus taketh Peter, *J.*
and John. *Mat* 17:1; *Mark* 5:37
9:2; 14:33; *Luke* 8:51
Mary mother of *J.* *Mat* 27:56
Mark 15:40; 16:1; *Luke* 24:10
much displeased with *J.* *Mark* 10:41
Peter, *J.* and John asked him. 13:3
J. was astonished at. *Luke* 5:10
abode both Peter, *J.* and. *Acts* 1:13
Herod killed *J.* brother of. 12:2
Peter said, shew these things to *J.* 17
J. answered, saying, Hearken. 15:13
Paul went in with us unto *J.* 21:18
after that was seen of *J.* *1 Cor* 15:7
save *J.* the Lord's brother. *Gal* 1:19
J. perceived the grace given. 2:9
before certain came from *J.* did. 12

jangling

turned aside to vain *j.* *1 Tim* 1:6

Janna

Melchi the son of *J.* *Luke* 3:24

Jannes, *see* **Jambres**

Japheth

J. the sons of Noah. *Gen* 5:32
6:10; 7:13; 9:18; *1 Chr* 1:4
Shem and *J.* took a garment and.
Gen 9:23
God shall enlarge *J.* he shall. 27
unto *J.* were sons born. 10:1
1 Chr 1:4, 5
Eber, brother of *J.* *Gen* 10:21

Jareb

saw, and sent to king *J.* *Hos* 5:13
for a present to king *J.* 10:6

Jared

begat *J.* *Gen* 5:15; *Luke* 3:37

Jasher

written in the book of *J.* *Josh* 10:13
2 Sam 1:18

Jashubites

the family of the *J.* *Num* 26:24

Jason

assaulted the house of *J.* *Acts* 17:5
they drew *J.* 6
whom *J.* hath received. 7
had taken security of *J.* 9
Lucius, *J.* and Sosipater. *Rom* 16:21

jasper

fourth row an onyx and a *j.*
Ex 28:20; 39:13
topaz, the diamond and *j.* *Ezek* 28:13
was to look upon like a *j.* *Rev* 4:3
light was like to a *j.* stone. 21:11
of the wall of city was of *j.* 18
stones, the first foundation was *j.* 19

Javan

sons of Japheth, *J.*, Tubal. *Gen* 10:2
1 Chr 1:5
those that escape to *J.* *Isa* 66:19
J. and Tubal were. *Ezek* 27:13, 19

javelin

(*A variety of spear. Revisions use the general word* spear)
and Phinehas took a *j.* *Num* 25:7
there was a *j.* in Saul's hand.
1 Sam 18:10; 19:9
Saul cast the *j.* for he said. 18:11
he smote the *j.* into the wall. 19:10

jaw

an hollow place in the *j.* *Judg* 15:19*
canst thou bore his *j.*? *Job* 41:2

jawbone

Samson found a new *j.* *Judg* 15:15
with the *j.* of an ass have. 16
he cast away the *j.* out of his. 17

jaws

and I brake the *j.* of. *Job* 29:17
tongue cleaveth to my *j.* *Ps* 22:15
shall be a bridle in *j.* *Isa* 30:28
off the yoke on their *j.* *Hos* 11:4

jaw teeth

their *j. teeth* as knives. *Pr* 30:14

Jazer

saw the land of *J.* *Num* 32:1, 3
are come even unto *J.* *Isa* 16:8
I will bewail with weeping of *J.* 9

jealous

Lord thy God am a *j.* God. *Ex* 20:5
34:14; *Deut* 4:24; 5:9; 6:15
Josh 24:19
j. of his wife. *Num* 5:14, 30
j. for Lord of hosts. *1 Ki* 19:10, 14
and will be *j.* for my. *Ezek* 39:25
will the Lord be *j.* for. *Joel* 2:18
God is *j.* and the Lord. *Nah* 1:2
I am *j.* for Jerusalem. *Zech* 1:14
was *j.* for Zion. 8:2
for I am *j.* over you. *2 Cor* 11:2

jealousies

is law of *j.* when a wife. *Num* 5:29

jealousy

(*In addition to its modern meaning, this word also used to mean zeal, solicitude*)
the spirit of *j.* come. *Num* 5:14, 30
for it is an offering of *j.* and. 15, 18

then priest shall take *j.* offering.
Num 5:25
consumed not Israel in my *j.* 25:11
j. shall smoke against. *Deut* 29:20
they provoked him to *j.* 32:16
1 Ki 14:22
moved me to *j.*: I will move them
to *j.* *Deut* 32:21
they moved him to *j.* *Ps* 78:58
how long, Lord, shall thy *j.*? 79:5
for *j.* is the rage of man. *Pr* 6:34
j. is cruel as the grave. *S of S* 8:6
he shall stir up *j.* like. *Isa* 42:13
seat of the image of *j.*? *Ezek* 8:3
gate of altar this image of *j.* in. 5
give thee blood in fury and *j.* 16:38
my *j.* shall depart from thee. 42
I will set my *j.* against thee. 23:25
in the fire of *j.* have I spoken. 36:5
6; 38:19
whose land devoured by fire of his *j.*
Zeph 1:18; 3:8
for Zion with great *j.* *Zech* 1:14; 8:2
provoke you to *j.* by them. *Rom* 10:19
Gentiles, to provoke them to *j.* 11:11
provoke the Lord to *j.*? *1 Cor* 10:22
over you with godly *j.* *2 Cor* 11:2

Jebusite
Canaan begat the *J.* *Gen* 10:16
1 Chr 1:14
drive out the *J.* *Ex* 33:2; 34:11
the threshingplace of Araunah the *J.*
2 Sam 24:16; *1 Chr* 21:15
Judah, and Ekron as a *J.* *Zech* 9:7

Jebusites
the *J.* dwell in the. *Num* 13:29
J. dwell with the children of Judah.
Josh 15:63
drive *J.* that inhabited. *Judg* 1:21
turn into this city of the *J.* 19:11
up and smiteth the *J.* *2 Sam* 5:8
see **Hittites**

Jeconiah
sons of Jehoiakim, *J.* *1 Chr* 3:16
the sons of *J.* Assir and. 17
away captive *J.* *Jer* 24:1; 27:20
will bring again to this place *J.* 28:4

Jedidiah
called Solomon *J.* *2 Sam* 12:24, 25

Jeduthun
Heman and *J.* to give. *1 Chr* 16:41
the sons of *J.* 42; 25:3; *2 Chr* 29:14
the king's order to *J.* *1 Chr* 25:6

Jegar-sahadutha
Laban called the heap *J.* *Gen* 31:47

Jehoahaz, *called* **Ahaziah**
J. son of Jehu reigned. *2 Ki* 10:35
J. son of Jehu began to reign. 13:1
people of the land took *J.* the son of
Josiah. 23:30; *2 Chr* 36:1
Pharaoh-necho took *J.* away.
2 Ki 23:34; *2 Chr* 36:4
never a son save *J.* *2 Chr* 21:17

Jehoash, *or* **Joash**
J. seven years old when. *2 Ki* 11:21
J. did what was right in sight. 12:2
J. sent all the hallowed things. 18
his servant slew *J.* in the house. 20
J. the son of Jehoahaz. 13:10
sent messengers to *J.* 14:8
J. slept with his fathers and. 16

Jehoiachin
J. was 18 years old. *2 Ki* 24:8
J. king of Judah went to. 12
up the head of *J.* 25:27; *Jer* 52:31
J. was eight years old. *2 Chr* 36:9

Jehoiada
Benaiah the son of *J.* *2 Sam* 8:18
20:23; 23:20, 22; *1 Chr* 11:22, 24
18:17
king sent Benaiah son of *J.* *1 Ki* 1:44
Benaiah the son of *J.* was over. 4:4
J. made a covenant. *2 Ki* 11:17
2 Chr 23:16
J. the priest instructed. *2 Ki* 12:2
J. was leader of the. *1 Chr* 12:27
after Ahithophel was *J.* a. 27:34
right all the days of *J.* *2 Chr* 24:2
after the death of *J.* came the. 17
remembered not the kindness *J.* 22
for the blood of the sons of *J.* 25

old gate repaired *J.* son. *Neh* 3:6
thee priest instead of *J.* *Jer* 29:26

Jehoiakim
turned his name to *J.* *2 Ki* 23:34
2 Chr 36:4
J. gave silver and gold. *2 Ki* 23:35
J. became his servant three. 24:1
the Lord concerning *J.* *Jer* 22:18
J. sent men after Urijah into. 26:22
the roll which *J.* the king. 36:28
thus saith the Lord of *J.* king of. 30
Zedekiah did what was evil as *J.*
52:2
and the Lord gave *J.* *Dan* 1:2

Jehonadab
lighted on *J.* the son. *2 Ki* 10:15
Jehu and *J.* went into the house. 23

Jehoram
J. son of Jehoshaphat. *1 Ki* 22:50
2 Ki 8:16
J. the son of Ahab. *2 Ki* 1:17
Elishama and *J.* priests. *2 Chr* 17:8
J. went forth and smote the. 21:9
the Lord stirred up against *J.* 16
went with *J.* to war against. 22:5
Ahaziah went out with *J.* against. 7

Jehoshaphat
J. the son of Ahilud. *2 Sam* 8:16, 20
24; *1 Ki* 4:3; *1 Chr* 18:15
J. son of Paruah was. *1 Ki* 4:17
J. the son of Asa. 15:24; *2 Chr* 17:1
J. came down to Ahab. *1 Ki* 22:2
Ahab and *J.* sat each on his throne.
10; *2 Chr* 18:9
J. went up to Ramoth-gilead.
1 Ki 22:29; *2 Chr* 18:28
J. cried out. *1 Ki* 22:32
J. slept with his fathers. 50
let my servants go, but *J.* would. 49
I regard presence of *J.* *2 Ki* 3:14
look out there Jehu the son of *J.* 9:2
J. blew with trumpet. *1 Chr* 15:24
Lord was with *J.* because. *2 Chr* 17:3
they made no war against *J.* 10
J. waxed great exceedingly. 12
J. had riches and honour in. 18:1
J. feared and set himself to. 20:3
returned, and *J.* in the forefront. 27
after this did *J.* join with Ahaziah. 35
Eliezer prophesied against *J.* 37
walked in the ways of *J.* 21:12
said they, He is the son of *J.* 22:9
down to the valley of *J.* *Joel* 3:2
come up to the valley of *J.* 12

Jehoshua
Oshea, son of Nun, *J.* *Num* 13:16
Non his son, *J.* his son. *1 Chr* 7:27

Jehovah
by my name *J.* was I not. *Ex* 6:3
whose name alone is *J.* *Ps* 83:18
Lord *J.* is my strength. *Isa* 12:2
Lord *J.* is everlasting strength. 26:4

Jehovah-jireh
called the name of the place *J.*
Gen 22:14

Jehovah-nissi
name of the altar *J.* *Ex* 17:15

Jehovah-shalom
and called the altar *J.* *Judg* 6:24

Jehu
J. son of Hanani. *1 Ki* 16:1, 7, 12
J. son of Nimshi shalt thou. 19:16
J. slay; that escapeth sword of *J.* 17
look out there *J.* *2 Ki* 9:2
J. is king. 13
J. son of Nimshi conspired. 14
a watchman spied company of *J.* 17
driving is like the driving of *J.* 20
J. drew a bow with his full. 24
J. slew all that remained of. 10:11
Ahab served Baal, *J.* shall serve. 18
J. departed not from the sins. 29
J. took no heed to walk in the. 31
word which he spake to *J.* 15:12
Obed begat *J.* and *J.* *1 Chr* 2:38
J. son of Josibiah. 4:35
J. son of Azmaveth. 12:3
J. went out to meet. *2 Chr* 19:2
written in the book of *J.* son. 20:34
J. was executing judgement. 22:8
the blood of Jezreel on *J.* *Hos* 1:4

jeoparded
were people that *j.* their. *Judg* 5:18

jeopardy
went in *j.* of their lives. *2 Sam* 23:17
1 Chr 11:19
will fall to Saul, to *j.* *1 Chr* 12:19
with water, and were in *j.* *Luke* 8:23
and why stand we in *j.*? *1 Cor* 15:30

Jephthah
J. the Gileadite was a mighty . . . and
Gilead begat *J.* *Judg* 11:1
J. fled from his brethren, and. 3
J. uttered all his words before. 11
hearkened not to words of *J.* 28
the Spirit came on *J.* 29
J. vowed a vow. 30
to lament the daughter of *J.* 40
J. judged Israel six years, then died
J. 12:7
the Lord sent *J.* and. *1 Sam* 12:11
would fail me to tell of *J.* *Heb* 11:32

Jephunneh
Caleb the son of *J.* *Num* 13:6
the sons of Jether, *J.* *1 Chr* 7:38
see **Caleb**

Jerahmeel
Hezron, *J.* and Ram. *1 Chr* 2:9
the sons of *J.* 33
J. the son of Kish. 24:29
king commanded *J.* to. *Jer* 36:26

Jeremiah
Hamutal, the daughter of *J.* of.
2 Ki 23:31; 24:18; *Jer* 52:1
J. a mighty. *1 Chr* 5:24; 12:4, 10, 13
and *J.* lamented for. *2 Chr* 35:25
humbled not himself before *J.* 36:12
of Lord by the mouth of *J.* till land
enjoyed her. 21, 22; *Ezra* 1:1
Azariah, *J.* sealed the. *Neh* 10:2
Seraiah, *J.* went up with. 12:1
days of Joiakim, of *J.*, Hananiah. 12
J. and Shemaiah went after. 34
the words of *J.* the son. *Jer* 1:1
the word that came to *J.* 7:1; 11:1
14:1; 18:1
devise devices against *J.* 18:18
Pashur smote *J.* and put him. 20:2
the Lord, What seest thou, *J.*? 24:3
people were gathered against *J.* 26:9
the hand of Ahikam was with *J.* 24
yoke from the prophet *J.* 28:10
why hast thou not reproved *J.*? 29:27
J. was shut up in court of. 32:2
J. spake all these words to. 34:6
Jaazaniah the son of *J.* 35:3
said, Go hide thee, thou and *J.* 36:19
Lord hid Baruch the scribe and *J.* 26
J. came in and went out. 37:4
so Irijah took *J.* and brought. 14
princes were wroth with *J.* 15
when *J.* was entered into the. 16
to commit *J.* into the court of. 21
they cast *J.* into the dungeon. 38:6
drew up *J.* with cords out of the. 13
the king sware secretly to *J.* 16
gave charge concerning *J.* 39:11
then went *J.* to Gedaliah son of. 40:6
J. wrote in a book all the evil. 51:60
thus far are the words of *J.* 64
was spoken by *J.* *Mat* 2:17; 27:9
others say Thou art *J.* or one. 16:14

Jericho
go view *J.* *Josh* 2:1
passed over right against *J.* 3:16
J. was straitly shut up. 6:1
I have given into thine hand *J.* 2
the man that buildeth the city *J.* 26
Joshua sent men from *J.* to. 7:2
to *J.* and the men of *J.* fought. 24:11
tarry at *J.* till your beard be grown.
2 Sam 10:5; *1 Chr* 19:5
days did Hiel build *J.* *1 Ki* 16:34
Lord hath sent me to *J.* *2 Ki* 2:4
Chaldees overtook him in the plains
of *J.* 25:5; *Jer* 39:5; 52:8
the captives to *J.* *2 Chr* 28:15
man went down to *J.* *Luke* 10:30
by faith the walls of *J.* *Heb* 11:30

Jeroboam
J. was a mighty man of. *1 Ki* 11:28
Solomon sought to kill *J.* and *J.* 40
J. dwelt in Egypt. 12:2

J. was come again. 1 Ki 12:20
J. built Shechem and dwelt. 25
J. ordained a feast in the eighth. 32
J. stood by the altar to burn. 13:1
after this J. returned not from. 33
became sin to the house of J. 34
at that time Abijah the son of J. 14:1
come in, thou wife of J. 6
bring evil upon the house of J. 10
him that dieth of J. shall the. 11
for he only of J. shall come to. 13
of the sins of J. 16; 15:30
between Rehoboam and J. 14:30
Baasha left not to J. any. 15:29
evil and walked in the way of J. 34
2 Ki 10:31; 13:6; 14:24; 17:22
J. son of Joash sat on. 2 Ki 13:13
saved Israel by the hand of J. 14:27
J. drave Israel from following. 17:21
genealogies in days of J. 1 Chr 5:17
J. had cast off Levites. 2 Chr 11:14
golden calf which J. made for. 13:8
God smote J. and all Israel. 15
neither did J. recover strength. 20
prophesied in the days of J. Hos 1:1
Amos 1:1
rise against house of J. Amos 7:9
thus Amos saith, J. shall die. 11

Jeroboam joined with *Nebat*
J. son of Nebat lifted. 1 Ki 11:26
spake by Ahijah the Shilonite to J. son of Nebat. 12:15; 2 Chr 10:15
like house of J. the son of Nebat.
1 Ki 16:3; 21:22; 2 Ki 9:9
in all the way of J. the son of Nebat.
1 Ki 16:26, 31; 22:52; 2 Ki 3:3
Jehu departed not from the sins of J. son of Nebat. 2 Ki 10:29; 13:2
11; 14:24; 15:9, 18, 24, 28

Jerubbaal
he called him J. saying. Judg 6:32
then J. (who is Gideon) rose up. 7:1
and J. went and dwelt in his. 8:29
they kindness to the house of J. 35
either that all sons of J. reign. 9:2
slew his brethren the sons of J. 5
if ye dealt well with J. 16
if sincerely with J. 19
is not he the son of J.? 28
the Lord sent J. and. 1 Sam 12:11

Jerubbesheth
Abimelech son of J. 2 Sam 11:21

Jerusalem, *or* Hierusalem
Jebusi, which is J. Josh 18:28
Judg 19:10
Goliath's head to J. 1 Sam 17:54
and his men went to J. 2 Sam 5:6
the shields of gold to J. 8:7
all the people returned to J. 12:31
shall bring me again to J. 15:8
carried the ark of God again to J. 29
my lord went out of J. 19:19
they came to J. at the end of. 24:8
stretched out his hand on J. to. 16
1 Chr 21:15
of building the wall of J. 1 Ki 3:1
she came to J. with a very. 10:2
for J.'s sake which I have chosen.
11:13; 2 Chr 6:6
him and to establish J. 1 Ki 15:4
country, that Lord should deliver J.
2 Ki 18:35; Isa 36:20
out of J. shall go forth a remnant.
2 Ki 19:31; Isa 37:32
bring such evil upon J. 2 Ki 21:12
I will wipe J. as a man wipeth a. 13
blood till he had filled J. 16; 24:4
I will cast off J. when. 2 Ki 23:27
he carried away all J. and. 24:14
burnt all the houses of J. 25:9
not be poured on J. 2 Chr 12:7
came to J. with psalteries. 20:28
wrath was upon J. 24:18; 29:8
32:25
altars in every corner of J. 28:24
spake against the God of J. 32:19
Josiah began to purge J. from. 34:3
to inquire concerning J. Ezra 7:14
thou before the God of J. 19
so I came to J. Neh 2:11; 7:6; 13:7
merchants lodged without J. 13:20
Zion, build thou walls of J. Ps 51:18
the heathen have laid J. on. Ps 79:1
have they shed round about J. 3
J. is builded as a city. 122:3
pray for the peace of J. they. 6
mountains are round about J. 125:2
thou shalt see the good of J. 128:5
if I prefer not J. above my. 137:6
children of Edom in the day of J. 7
the Lord doth build up J. he. 147:2
comely, O my love, as J. S of S 6:4
he saw concerning J. Isa 1:1; 2:1
for J. is ruined. 3:8
have purged the blood of J. 4:4
so will I do to J. 10:11
performed whole work on J. 12
numbered the houses of J. 22:10
Lord of hosts defend J. 31:5
thine eyes see J. a quiet. 33:20
speak ye comfortably to J. 40:2
give to J. one that bringeth. 41:27
that saith to J. Thou shalt. 44:26
of J. for Lord hath comforted his people, he hath redeemed J. 52:9
for J.'s sake I will not rest till. 62:1
give him no rest till he make J. 7
Zion is a wilderness, J. a. 64:10
for behold, I create J. a. 65:18
rejoice ye with J. and be glad. 66:10
and cry in the ears of J. Jer 2:2
they shall call J. the throne of. 3:17
fro through the streets of J. 5:1
to flee out of the midst of J. 6:1
why then is this people of J.? 8:5
I will make J. heaps, and a. 9:11
words in the streets of J. 11:6
great pride of Judah and J. 13:9
Judah mourneth, the cry of J. 14:2
come from the places about J. 17:26
make void the counsel of J. 19:7
the houses of J. shall be defiled. 13
have seen in prophets of J. an. 23:14
J. shall become heaps. 26:18
Mi 3:12
about J. shall flocks pass. Jer 33:13
in those days J. shall dwell. 16
let us go to J. for fear of. 35:11
till day that J. was taken. 38:28
brake down the walls of J. 39:8
the evil I have brought on J. 44:2
was kindled in the streets of J. 6
let J. come into your mind. 51:50
J. hath grievously sinned. Lam 1:8
J. is as a menstruous woman. 17
this is J. Ezek 5:5
go through the midst of J. 9:4
son of man cause J. to know. 16:2
of Babylon is come to J. 17:12
sword may come to Judah in J. 21:20
right hand the divination for J. 22
gather you into the midst of J. 22:19
one that had escaped out of J. 33:21
flock of J. in her solemn. 36:38
being open toward J. Dan 6:10
as hath been done upon J. 9:12
of the commandment to build J. 25
again the captivity of J. Joel 3:1
then shall J. be holy. 17
J. shall dwell. 20
entered and cast lots upon J. Ob 11
are they not J.? Mi 1:5
build up Zion with blood, J. 3:10
search J. with candles. Zeph 1:12
not have mercy on J.? Zech 1:12
I am jealous for J. and Zion. 14
comfort Zion, and choose J. 17; 2:12
horns which have scattered J. 1:19
goest thou? I go to measure J. 2:2
J. shall be inhabited as towns. 4
I will dwell in the midst of J. 8:3
have I thought to do well to J. 15
behold, I will make J. a cup. 12:2
make J. a burdensome stone. 3
J. shall be safely inhabited. 14:11
the offering of J. shall be. Mal 3:4
then went out to him J. Mat 3:5
Mark 1:5
neither swear by J. Mat 5:35
to shew how he must go to J. 16:21
when he was come into J. 21:10
parents brought him to J. Luke 2:22
they turned back again to J. 45
a great multitude out of J. 6:17
as though he would go to J. 9:53
that a prophet perish out of J. 13:33
because he was nigh to J. Luke 19:11
ye shall see J. compassed. 21:20
J. shall be trodden down of the. 24
tarry ye in J. till ye be. 24:49
and they returned to J. with. 52
Jesus was coming to J. John 12:12
ye have filled J. with. Acts 5:28
might bring them bound unto J. 9:2
bound in the Spirit to J. 20:22
tidings came that all J. was. 21:31
get thee quickly out of J. 22:18
him whether he would go to J.? 25:20
that my service for J. Rom 15:31
your liberality unto J. 1 Cor 16:3
Agar answereth to J. Gal 4:25
J. which is above is free. 26
the new J. Rev 3:12; 21:2
the holy J. 21:10
see **dwell**

against **Jerusalem**
Judah had fought ag. J. Judg 1:8
Shishak came ag. J. 1 Ki 14:25
2 Chr 12:9
Sennacherib ag. J. 2 Ki 18:17
2 Chr 32:2
the king of Babylon came ag. J.
2 Ki 24:10; 25:1; Jer 34:1, 7
39:1; 52:4; Ezek 24:2
Shimshai, wrote ag. J. Ezra 4:8
to come and fight ag. J. Neh 4:8
publish ag. J. Jer 4:16
cast a mount ag. J. 6:6
that Tyrus hath said ag. J. Ezek 26:2
destroy nations that come ag. J.
Zech 12:9; 14:12

at **Jerusalem**
dwelt with Judah at J. Josh 15:63
came to his house at J. 2 Sam 20:3
sacrifice in house of the Lord at J.
1 Ki 12:27; 2 Chr 9:25; Isa 27:13
fathers dwelt at J. 1 Chr 9:34, 38
to build the house of the Lord at J.
2 Chr 3:1; Ezra 1:2; 5:2
offered themselves to dwell at J.
Neh 11:2
this time was not I at J. 13:6
because of thy temple at J. Ps 68:29
the Lord who dwelleth at J. 135:21
shall dwell in Zion at J. Isa 30:19
into J., so we dwell at J. Jer 35:11
also shall fight at J. Zech 14:14
should accomplish at J. Luke 9:31
Herod himself was also at J. 23:7
all nations, beginning at J. 24:47
nor yet at J. shall ye worship.
John 4:21
all things that he did at J. 45
to all the dwellers at J. Acts 1:19
against the church at J. 8:1
hath done to thy saints at J. 9:13
they that dwell at J. have. 13:27
be at J. the day of Pentecost. 20:16
so shall the Jews at J. bind. 21:11
but also to die at J. for the name. 13
to them of Damascus at J. 26:20
for the saints at J. Rom 15:26
see **daughters**

from **Jerusalem**
Shimei had gone from J. 1 Ki 2:41
Hazael went away from J. 2 Ki 12:18
carried into captivity from J. to.
24:15; Esth 2:6; Jer 24:1; 27:20
29:1; 52:29
the word of the Lord from J.
Isa 2:3; Mi 4:2
take away from J. the stay. Isa 3:1
the Lord utter his voice from J.
Joel 3:16; Amos 1:2
cut off the horse from J. Zech 9:10
waters shall go out from J. 14:8
followed him from J. Mat 4:25
man went down from J. Luke 10:30
which was from J. about sixty. 24:13
should not depart from J. Acts 1:4
way that goeth down from J. 8:26
there came prophets from J. 11:27
from J. to Illyricum I. Rom 15:19

in **Jerusalem**
dwell with Benjamin in J. Judg 1:21
feed thee with me in J. 2 Sam 19:33
thee an house in J. 1 Ki 2:36
a light alway before me in J. 11:36
15:4

worship before this altar *in J.* *2 Ki* 18:22
Lord said, *In J.* will I put. 21:4
now Huldah dwelt *in J.* in. 22:14
these dwelt *in J.* *1 Chr* 8:28, 32; 9:3
that they may dwell *in J.* 23:25
king made silver *in J.* *2 Chr* 9:27
away the altars that were *in J.* 30:14
great joy *in J.* not the like *in J.* 26
house of the Lord which is *in J.* *Ezra* 1:3
Israel, whose habitation is *in J.* 7:15
us a wall in Judah and *in J.* 9:9
no right nor memorial *in J.* *Neh* 2:20
let every one lodge *in J.* 4:22
bring one of ten to dwell *in J.* 11:1
Zion and his praises *in J.* *Ps* 102:21
that have been before me *in J.* *Eccl* 1:16; 2:7, 9
that remaineth *in J.* be. *Isa* 4:3
Lord of hosts shall reign *in J.* 24:23
scornful men that rule *in J.* 28:14
is in Zion, his furnace *in J.* 31:9
I will rejoice *in J.* and joy. 65:19
shall be comforted *in J.* 66:13
publish *in J.* and say. *Jer* 4:5
which Manasseh did *in J.* 15:4
the staff of bread *in J.* *Ezek* 4:16
in mount Zion and *in J.* *Joel* 2:32
J. be inhabited in her place, even *in J.* *Zech* 12:6
every pot *in J.* shall be. 14:21
is committed *in J.* *Mal* 2:11
a man *in J.* whose name. *Luke* 2:25
that looked for redemption *in J.* 38
Jesus tarried behind *in J.* 43
sinners above all that dwell *in J.* 13:4
art thou only a stranger *in J.*? 24:18
in J. is the place where. *John* 4:20
shall be witnesses to me *in J.* *Acts* 1:8; 10:39
the disciples multiplied *in J.* 6:7
hast testified of me *in J.* 23:11
which thing I also did *in J.* 26:10

inhabitants of **Jerusalem**

ye *inhabitants of J.* be not afraid. *2 Chr* 20:15
Lord saved *inhabitants of J.* 32:22
inhabitants of J. did him honour. 33
inhabitants of J. did according to. 34:32
O *inhabitants of J.* judge. *Isa* 5:3
snare to *inhabitants of J.* 8:14
father to the *inhabitants of J.* 22:21
inhabitants of J. shall remain for. *Jer* 17:25
and tell Judah and *inhabitants of J.* 35:13
to whom *inhabitants of J.* have said. *Ezek* 11:15
I give the *inhabitants of J.* for. 15:6
the *inhabitants of J.* shall be my strength. *Zech* 12:5
the glory of the *inhabitants of J.* 7
shall defend the *inhabitants of J.* 8
pour upon *inhabitants of J.* the. 10
opened to the *inhabitants of J.* 13:1

O **Jerusalem**

vows in midst of thee, *O J.* *Ps* 116:19
stand within thy gates, *O J.* 122:2
if I forget thee, *O J.* 137:5
praise the Lord, *O J.* 147:12
O J. that bringest good. *Isa* 40:9
stand up, *O J.* 51:17
beautiful garments, *O J.* 52:1
arise, and sit down, *O J.* 2
O J. wash thy heart from. *Jer* 4:14
be thou instructed, *O J.* lest. 6:8
cut off thine hair, *O J.* and. 7:29
woe to thee, *O J.* Wilt thou not? 13:27
who have pity upon thee, *O J.*? 15:5
O J. J. thou that killest the prophets. *Mat* 23:37; *Luke* 13:34

up to **Jerusalem**

up with the king *to J.* *2 Sam* 19:34
for you to go *up to J.* *1 Ki* 12:28
his face to go *up to J.* *2 Ki* 12:17
Pekah came *up to J.* to war. 16:5
let him go *up to J.* *Ezra* 1:3; 7:13
we go *up to J.*; Son of man. *Mat* 20:18; *Mark* 10:33 *Luke* 18:31
the way going *up to J.* *Mark* 10:32
ascending *up to J.* *Luke* 19:28
Peter was come *up to J.* *Acts* 11:2
go *up to J.* to the apostles. 15:2
he should not go *up to J.* 21:4, 12
wilt thou go *up to J.* and ? 25:9
neither went I *up to J.* to. *Gal* 1:17
I went *up to J.* to see Peter and. 18
I went *up to J.* with Barnabas. 2:1

Jeshua

came with Zerubbabel, *J.* *Ezra* 2:2
stood up *J.* son of Jozadak. 3:2

Jeshurun

but *J.* waxed fat and. *Deut* 32:15
he was king in *J.* when Israel. 33:5
none like to the God of *J.* 26
fear not, thou *J.* whom. *Isa* 44:2

Jesse

Obed, he is the father of *J.* *Ruth* 4:17; *Mat* 1:5
Obed begat *J.* and *J.* begat David. *Ruth* 4:22; *Mat* 1:6
I will send thee to *J.* *1 Sam* 16:1
he sanctified *J.* and his sons and. 9
I have seen a son of *J.* that is. 18
Saul sent messengers unto *J.* 19
I am the son of thy servant *J.* 17:58
hast chosen the son of *J.* 20:30
as long as the son of *J.* liveth. 31
will the son of *J.* give every.? 22:7
made a league with the son of *J.* 8
Doeg said, I saw the son of *J.* 9
and who is the son of *J.*? 25:10
inheritance in son of *J.* *2 Sam* 20:1 *1 Ki* 12:16; *2 Chr* 10:16
to David the son of *J.* *1 Chr* 10:14
thine are we, thou son of *J.* 12:18
rod out of the stem of *J.* *Isa* 11:1
shall be a root of *J.* 10; *Rom* 15:12
found David the son of *J.* *Acts* 13:22

jesting

nor filthiness, nor *j.* not. *Eph* 5:4

Jesus

J. for he shall save his people from. *Mat* 1:21, 25; *Luke* 1:31; 2:21
J. was led up of the Spirit. *Mat* 4:1
from that time *J.* began to. 17
J. put forth his hand and. 8:3
when *J.* heard it, he marvelled. 10
do with thee, *J.* thou Son of God ? 29; *Mark* 1:24; 5:7; *Luke* 8:28
city came out to meet *J.* *Mat* 8:34
J. seeing their faith. 9:2
as *J.* sat at meat. 10
J. turned him about. 22
J. departed thence. 27
J. knew their thoughts. 12:25
these things spake *J.* to the. 13:24
Herod heard of the fame of *J.* 14:1
walked on the water, to go to *J.* 29
they saw no man save *J.* only. 17:8 *Mark* 9:8
J. rebuked the devil and. *Mat* 17:18
when come into the house, *J.* 25
J. called a little child to him. 18:2
two blind men heard that *J.* 20:30
J. had compassion on them. 34
is *J.* the prophet of Nazareth. 21:11
J. perceived their wickedness. 22:18
they might take *J.* by subtilty. 26:4
the disciples did as *J.* had. 19
J. took bread and. 26; *Mark* 14:22
thou also wast with *J.* *Mat* 26:69 71; *Mark* 14:67
remembered words of *J.* *Mat* 26:75
written, This is *J.* the king. 27:37
J. cried with a loud voice. 46 *Mark* 15:37
Joseph, who also himself was *J.*' disciple. *Mat* 27:57
fear not ye, I know ye seek *J.* *Mat* 28:5; *Mark* 16:6
J. met them. *Mat* 28:9
J. came and spake to them. 18
J. could no more enter. *Mark* 1:45
J. withdrew himself with his. 3:7
J. gave them leave. 5:13
J. suffered him not. 19
J. knowing that virtue had gone. 30
Elias and Moses talking with *J.* 9:4
then *J.* beholding him. 10:21
J. saw that he answered. *Mark* 12:34
bound *J.* and carried him. 15:1
in the midst before *J.* *Luke* 5:19
what they might do to *J.* 6:11
who sat at *J.*' feet and heard. 10:39
Zacchaeus sought to see *J.* who. 19:3
bear the cross after *J.* 23:26
J. himself drew near and. 24:15
they said, Is not this *J.*? *John* 6:42
that is called *J.* made clay. 9:11
J. spake of his death. 11:13
J. wept. 35
sir, we would see *J.* 12:21
when *J.* knew that his hour. 13:1
leaning on *J.*' bosom. 23
whom seek ye ? they said, *J.* 18:7
officers that stood by struck *J.* 22
came *J.* forth, wearing crown. 19:5
there stood by the cross of *J.* 25
J. knowing that all things were. 28
took the body of *J.* 40
there laid they *J.* 42
knew not that it was *J.* 20:14; 21:4
of all that *J.* began to. *Acts* 1:1
this same *J.* which is taken up. 11
was guide to them who took *J.* 16
this *J.* hath God raised up. 2:32 3:26; 5:30
hath glorified his Son *J.* 3:13
through *J.* resurrection from. 4:2
that they had been with *J.* 13
not to teach in the name of *J.* 18
against thy holy child *J.* 27
the name of thy holy child *J.* 30
not speak in the name of *J.* 5:40
this *J.* shall destroy this place. 6:14
he saw *J.* standing on the right. 7:55
Philip preached unto him *J.* 8:35
I am *J.* whom thou persecutest. 9:5 22:8; 26:15
even *J.*, that appeared to thee. 9:17
at Damascus in the name of *J.* 27
how God anointed *J.* with. 10:38
raised to Israel a Saviour *J.* 13:23
there is another king, one *J.* 17:7
because he preached *J.* and the. 18
adjure you by *J.* whom Paul. 19:13
J. I know, and Paul I know, but. 15
had questions of one *J.* who. 25:19
persuading them concerning *J.* 28:23
of him that believeth in *J.* *Rom* 3:26
Spirit of him that raised up *J.* 8:11
by Spirit calleth *J.* *1 Cor* 12:3
your servants for *J.*' sake. *2 Cor* 4:5
the life of *J.* might be made. 10
we are delivered to death for *J.* 11
J. shall raise up us also by *J.* 14
that cometh, preach another *J.* 11:4
him as the truth is in *J.* *Eph* 4:21
at name of *J.* every knee. *Phil* 2:10
J. who delivered us. *1 Thes* 1:10
them that sleep in *J.* will God. 4:14
we see *J.* who was made. *Heb* 2:9
great high priest, *J.* son. 4:14; 6:20
was *J.* made surety of better. 7:22
the holiest by the blood of *J.* 10:19
looking unto *J.* the author of. 12:2
to *J.* the Mediator of the new. 24
wherefore *J.* suffered without. 13:12
confess *J.* is Son of God. *1 John* 4:15
that *J.* is the Son of God. 5:5
that keep the faith of *J.* *Rev* 14:12
with blood of martyrs of *J.* 17:6
beheaded for the witness of *J.* 20:4
I *J.* have sent mine angel to. 22:16

see **Christ**

Jesus joined with *Lord*

all the time the *Lord J.* *Acts* 1:21
same *J.* both *Lord* and Christ. 2:36
Stephen saying, *Lord J.* 7:59
in the name of the *Lord J.* 8:16
boldly in the name of *Lord J.* 9:29
Grecians, preaching *Lord J.* 11:20
believe on the *Lord J.* Christ. 16:31
heard the word of the *Lord J.* 19:10
and the name of the *Lord J.* was. 17
the words of the *Lord J.* 20:35
Lord J. same night he. *1 Cor* 11:23
no man can say that *J.* is *Lord.* 12:3
are ours in the day of the *Lord J.* *2 Cor* 1:14
about the dying of *Lord J.* 4:10
the marks of *Lord J.* *Gal* 6:17

who both killed *Lord J. 1 Thes* 2:15
exhort you by the *Lord J.* 4:1
we gave you by *Lord J.* 2
Lord J. shall be revealed. *2 Thes* 1:7
from dead our *Lord J.* *Heb* 13:20
knowledge of *J.* our *Lord. 2 Pet* 1:2
even so, come *Lord J.* *Rev* 22:20
see **grace, name**

Jesus *said*
mind the word *J. said.* *Mark* 14:72
believed the word *J. said. John* 2:22
the same hour in which *J. said.* 4:53
when *J.* had thus *said*, he was. 13:21
yet *J. said* not unto him. 21:23

Jesus, for *Joshua*
with *J.* into possession. *Acts* 7:45
if *J.* had given them rest. *Heb* 4:8

Jesus
J. who is called Justus. *Col* 4:11

Jethro, called *Reuel*
Moses kept the flock of *J.* *Ex* 3:1
Moses returned to *J.* his. 4:18
when *J.* heard of all that God. 18:1
J. came with his sons and his wife. 5
I thy father in law *J.* am come. 6
J. rejoiced for the goodness. 9, 10
J. took a burnt offering and. 12

Jew
a certain *J.* whose name. *Esth* 2:5
told them that he was a *J.* 3:4
do even so to Mordecai the *J.* 6:10
of them, to wit, of a *J.* *Jer* 34:9
take hold of skirt of a *J. Zech* 8:23
is it that thou, being a *J.*? *John* 4:9
Pilate answered am I a *J.*? 18:35
for a man that is a *J.* *Acts* 10:28
sorcerer, a *J.* named Bar-jesus. 13:6
certain *J.* named Aquila. 18:2
a *J.* named Apollos. 24
sons of Sceva a *J.* 19:14
Alexander a *J.* 33, 34
Paul a *J.* 21:39; 22:3
to the *J.* first. *Rom* 1:16; 2:9, 10
behold, thou art called a *J.*, and. 2:17
he is not a *J.* 28
he is a *J.* who is one inwardly. 29
what advantage then hath the *J.*? 3:1
no difference between the *J.* and.
10:12; *Gal* 3:28; *Col* 3:11
to the *J.* I became as a *J. 1 Cor* 9:20
if thou being a *J.* livest as. *Gal* 2:14

jewel
as a *j.* of gold in a. *Pr* 11:22
of knowledge are a precious *j.* 20:15
put a *j.* on thy forehead. *Ezek* 16:12*

jewels
servant brought forth *j.* *Gen* 24:53
shall borrow *j.* of gold. *Ex* 3:22
11:2; 12:35
they brought all *j.* of gold. 35:22
Num 31:50
gold, even all wrought *j. Num* 31:51
put the *j.* of gold in. *1 Sam* 6:8, 15
riches and precious *j.* *2 Chr* 20:25
for all manner of pleasant *j.* 32:27*
of it shall not be for *j.* *Job* 28:17
comely with rows of *j.* *S of S* 1:10*
joints of thy thighs are like *j.* 7:1
bride adorneth herself with her *j.*
Isa 61:10
taken thy *j.* of my gold. *Ezek* 16:17
shall take thy fair *j.* 39; 23:26
with earrings and *j.* *Hos* 2:13
when I make up my *j.* *Mal* 3:17*

Jewess
Timotheus was son of a *J. Acts* 16:1
Felix' wife Drusilla was a *J.* 24:24

Jewish
not giving heed to *J.* *Tit* 1:14

Jewry
my father brought out of *J. Dan* 5:13

Jews
king Rezin drave the *J.* *2 Ki* 16:6
the *J.* are come up to. *Ezra* 4:12
I asked concerning the *J.* *Neh* 1:2
what do these feeble *J.*? 4:2
table one hundred and fifty *J.* 5:17
thou and the *J.* think to rebel. 6:6
I saw *J.* that married wives. 13:23
mourning among the *J.* *Esth* 4:3
deliverance arise unto *J.* *Esth* 4:14
Mordecai be of seed of the *J.* 6:13
laid his hand upon the *J.* 8:7
write ye for the *J.*, in king's name. 8
J. had light, and gladness. 16, 17
for the fear of the *J.* fell upon. 17
officers of the king helped the *J.* 9:3
should not fail from among *J.* 28
was great among the *J.* 10:3
said, I am afraid of the *J. Jer* 38:19
captive 3023 of the *J.* 52:28, 30
near and accused the *J.* *Dan* 3:8
is reported among the *J. Mat* 28:15
John's disciples and *J.* *John* 3:25
the *J.* have no dealings with. 4:9
salvation is of the *J.* 22
feast of the *J.* 5:1
did the *J.* persecute Jesus. 16
J. sought the more to kill him. 18
the *J.* therefore strove among. 6:52
openly of him, for fear of *J.* 7:13
the *J.* did not believe that. 9:18
the *J.* took up stones again. 10:31
master, the *J.* of late sought. 11:8
when Jesus saw her and the *J.* 33
J. went away and believed. 12:11
I taught in temple, whither *J.* 18:20
not be delivered to the *J.* 36
of Jesus as the manner of *J.* 19:40
to none, but the *J.* only. *Acts* 11:19
Herod saw it pleased the *J.* 12:3
because of the *J.* that were. 16:3
these men being *J.* do trouble. 20
J. and Greeks heard the word. 19:10
certain of the vagabond *J.* 13
the *J.* laid wait for him. 20:3, 19
so shall the *J.* at Jerusalem. 21:11
certain of the *J.* banded. 23:12
this man was taken of the *J.* 27
certain *J.* from Asia found. 24:18
to the *J.* have done no wrong. 25:10
is he God of *J.* only ? *Rom* 3:29
Christ, to the *J.* a. *1 Cor* 1:23
to *J.* I became as a Jew, that. 9:20
of *J.* five times received. *2 Cor* 11:24
and not as do the *J.* *Gal* 2:14
we who are *J.* by nature, and. 15
have suffered of the *J. 1 Thes* 2:14
which say they are *J.* and are not.
Rev 2:9; 3:9
see **Gentiles**

all the **Jews**
Haman sought to destroy *all the J.*
Esth 3:6, 13
more than *all the J.* 4:13
go, gather *all the J.* 16
when *all the J.* in Moab. *Jer* 40:11
even *all the J.* returned out of. 12
Ishmael slew *all the J.* that. 41:3
the word concerning *all the J.* 44:1
all the J. except they wash, they.
Mark 7:3
all the Jews to depart. *Acts* 18:2
this was known to *all the J.* 19:17
thou teachest *all the J.* to. 21:21
a good report of *all the J.* 22:12
of sedition among *all the J.* 24:5
manner of life at Jerusalem know *all the J.* 26:4

King of the **Jews**
that is born *King of the J.? Mat* 2:2
Jesus, Art thou *King of the J.*?
27:11; *Mark* 15:2; *Luke* 23:3
John 18:33
Hail, *King of the J.* *Mat* 27:29
Mark 15:18; *John* 19:3
accusation, This is the *King of the Jews.* *Mat* 27:37; *Mark* 15:26
Luke 23:38; *John* 19:19
will ye that I release to you *King of the J.*? *Mark* 15:9; *John* 18:39
call the *King of the J.*? *Mark* 15:12
if thou be the *King of the J.* save thyself. *Luke* 23:37
the *King of the J.* but that he said, I am *King of the J.* *John* 19:21

Jezebel
Ahab took to wife *J.* *1 Ki* 16:31
when *J.* cut off the prophets. 18:4
when *J.* slew the prophets of. 13
of Baal which eat at *J.*'s table. 19
Ahab told *J.* all that Elijah. 19:1
the elders did as *J.* had sent. 21:11
when *J.* heard Naboth. *1 Ki* 21:15
dogs shall eat *J.* 23; *2 Ki* 9:10, 36
none like Ahab, whom *J. 1 Ki* 21:25
avenge at the hand of *J.* *2 Ki* 9:7
whoredoms of thy mother *J.* 22
J. shall be as dung upon face of field, so they shall not say, this is *J.* 37
sufferest that woman *J.* *Rev* 2:20

Jezreel, name of place and person
pitched in the valley of *J. Judg* 6:33
also took Ahinoam of *J. 1 Sam* 25:43
by a fountain which is in *J.* 29:1
Ish-bosheth king over *J. 2 Sam* 2:9
rode and went to *J.* *1 Ki* 18:45
before Ahab to entrance of *J.* 46
a vineyard which was in *J.* 21:1
dogs shall eat Jezebel by the wall of *J.* 23; *2 Ki* 9:10, 36
Joram went back to *J.* *2 Ki* 8:29
2 Chr 22:6
in a chariot and went to *J. 2 Ki* 9:16
come to me to *J.* by to-morrow. 10:6
heads of the king's sons to *J.* 7
of the father of Etam, *J.* *1 Chr* 4:3
call his name *J.* for I will avenge the blood of *J.* on house. *Hos* 1:4
break bow of Israel in valley of *J.* 5
for great shall be the day of *J.* 11
wine and oil shall hear *J.* 2:22

Jezreelite, *see* **Naboth**

Joab
three sons of Zeruiah, *J. 2 Sam* 2:18
should I hold up my face to *J.*? 22
J. also and Abishai pursued. 24
of Abner rest on the head of *J.* 3:29
so *J.* and Abishai his brother. 30
J. son of Zeruiah was. 8:16; 20:23
1 Chr 11:6; 18:15; 27:34
demanded of Uriah how *J.* did.
2 Sam 11:7
abide in tents, and my lord *J.* 11
David wrote a letter to *J.* 14
J. fought against Rabbah of. 12:26
J. put the words in widow's. 14:3
is not the hand of *J.* with thee ? 19
Absalom sent for *J.* 29
J.'s field is near. 30
J. killed Amasa. 20:9
woman said, Art thou *J.*? 17
the king's word prevailed against *J.*
24:4; *1 Chr* 21:4
Adonijah conferred with *J. 1 Ki* 1:7
moreover thou knowest what *J.* 2:5
J. fled to tabernacle of Lord. 28
six months *J.* remain, every. 11:16
Seraiah begat *J.* *1 Chr* 4:14
J. led the army. 20:1
word was abominable to *J.* 21:6
all that Abner and *J.* had. 26:28
of children of Jeshua and *J.*
Ezra 2:6; *Neh* 7:11
of the sons of *J.* Obadiah. *Ezra* 8:9

Joah
J. son of Asaph the recorder.
2 Ki 18:18; *Isa* 36:3
J. son of Zimmah. *1 Chr* 6:21
J. son of Obed-edom. 26:4

Joanna
which was the son of *J.* *Luke* 3:27
J. the wife of Chuza. 8:3; 24:10

Joash
that pertaineth to *J.* the. *Judg* 6:11
sword of Gideon the son of *J.* 7:14
carry him back to Amon and *J.* the.
1 Ki 22:26; *2 Chr* 18:25
Jehosheba stole *J.* *2 Ki* 11:2
2 Chr 22:11
J. the son of Jehoahaz. *2 Ki* 13:9
J. the king of Israel wept over. 14
J. beat Ben-hadad three times. 25
of Jeroboam the son of *J.* 14:27
Becher, Zemira, and *J.* *1 Chr* 7:8
J. the son of Shemaiah the. 12:3
over the cellars of oil was *J.* 27:28
J. remembered not the. *2 Chr* 24:22
executed judgement against *J.* 24

Job
the sons of Issachar, *J.* *Gen* 46:13
in the land of Uz whose name was *J.*
Job 1:1
considered my servant *J.*? 8; 2:3
Satan said, Doth *J.* fear God ? 1:9

J. sinned not with his lips. Job 1:22; 2:10
Satan went and smote J. with. 2:7
three men ceased to answer J. 32:1
against J. was Elihu's wrath. 2
no answer and condemned J. 3
none of you that convinced J. 12
mark well, O J. hearken. 33:31
man is like J. who drinketh? 34:7
J. hath spoken without. 35
my desire is that J. may be tried. 36
doth J. open his mouth in vain? 35:16
spoken as my servant J. hath. 42:7, 8
bullocks and go to my servant J. 8
the Lord also accepted J. 9
the Lord gave J. twice as much. 10
Lord blessed the latter end of J. 12
so fair as the daughters of J. 15
after this lived J. 140 years. 16
so J. died, being old and full. 17
Noah, Daniel and J. Ezek 14:14, 20
heard of the patience of J. Jas 5:11

Joel

Samuel's firstborn was J. 1 Sam 8:2
Simeon, J. and Jehu. 1 Chr 4:35
Reubenites, the sons of J. 5:4, 8
of the Gadites, J. the chief, and. 12
Heman, a singer, son of J. 6:33
Elkanah the son of J. a. 36
Michael, Obadiah and J. 7:3
J. and Mibhar were valiant. 11:38
of the sons of Gershom, J. 15:7
David called for Isaiah and J. 11
Laadan, the chief was J. 23:8
Jehuli, Zetham and J. 26:22
half tribe of Manasseh, J. 27:20
J. and Benaiah had. Ezra 10:43
J. son of Zichri was. Neh 11:9
word came to J. the son. Joel 1:1
spoken by the prophet J. Acts 2:16

Johanan

J. came to Gedaliah. 2 Ki 25:23
Jer 40:8, 13
Josiah, the firstborn J. 1 Chr 3:15
into the chamber of J. Ezra 10:6
but when J. heard of all. Jer 41:11
so J. obeyed not the voice of. 43:4

John son of *Zacharias*

J. had raiment of camel's hair. Mat 3:4; Mark 1:6
came to be baptized, but J. Mat 3:14
when J. was cast into prison. 4:12
Mark 1:14
then came to him the disciples of J. Mat 9:14; Mark 2:18; Luke 5:33
7:18; 11:1; John 3:25
J. had heard the works of Christ. Mat 11:2; Luke 7:19
go and shew J. these things. Mat 11:4; Luke 7:22
Jesus began to say concerning J. Mat 11:7; Luke 7:24
the law prophesied till J. Mat 11:13
Luke 16:16
Herod beheaded J. Mat 14:10
Mark 6:16; Luke 9:9
all hold J. as a prophet. Mat 21:26
Mark 11:32; Luke 20:6
J. came in way of righteousness. Mat 21:32
Herod feared J. knowing. Mark 6:20
thou shalt call his name J. Luke 1:13, 60
mused in their hearts of J. 3:15
it was said, that J. was risen. 9:7
a man, whose name was J. John 1:6
and this is the record of J. 19, 32
next day J. seeth Jesus coming. 29
J. also was baptizing in Enon. 3:23
for J was not yet cast into. 24
made more disciples than J. 4:1
sent to J. and he bare witness. 5:33
greater witness than that of J. 36
J. did no miracle; but all that J. spake. 10:41
for J. truly baptized with water. Acts 1:5; 11:16
J. had first preached before. 13:24
and as J. fulfilled his course, he. 25
see **baptism, baptist**

John *the apostle*

James and J. the sons of. Mat 4:21
10:2; Mark 1:19; 3:17
Jesus sent Peter and J. Luke 22:8
Peter and J. went up. Acts 3:1
lame man held Peter and J. 11
the boldness of Peter and J. 4:13
sent to Samaria Peter and J. 8:14
James the brother of J. 12:2
his angel to his servant J. Rev 1:1
J. to the seven churches which. 4
J. who also am your brother. 9:1
I J. saw the holy city. 21:2
see **James**

John

J. and Alexander. Acts 4:6

John, surnamed *Mark*

Peter came to house of J. Acts 12:12
with them J. whose surname. 25
and they had also J. to their. 13:5
J. departing from them, returned. 13
to take with them J. 15:37

join

they j. to our enemies. Ex 1:10
did Jehoshaphat j. 2 Chr 20:35
and j. in affinity with. Ezra 9:14
hand j. in hand. Pr 11:21; 16:5
woe to them that j. house. Isa 5:8
the Lord shall j. his enemies. 9:11*
sons of stranger that j. 56:6
come, let us j. ourselves. Jer 50:5
j. them one to another. Ezek 37:17
they shall j. in the end. Dan 11:6
the rest durst no man j. Acts 5:13
go near and j. thyself to this. 8:29
Saul assayed to j. himself. 9:26

joined

kings were j. together in. Gen 14:3
they j. battle with them in the. 8*
will my husband be j. to me. 29:34
of Levi be j. to thee. Num 18:2, 4
they j. battle, Israel. 1 Sam 4:2
day the battle was j. 1 Ki 20:29
Jehoshaphat j. affinity. 2 Chr 18:1
he j. with Ahaziah to. 20:36, 37
set up walls, and j. the. Ezra 4:12*
all the wall was j. Neh 4:6
j. should keep these days. Esth 9:27
let it not be j. to the days. Job 3:6*
Leviathan's scales are j. one. 41:17
the flakes of his flesh are j. 23
Assur also is j. with them. Ps 83:8
to him that is j. to all. Eccl 9:4
every one j. to them. Isa 13:15*
and the strangers shall be j. 14:1
thou shalt not be j. with them. 20
nor him that hath j. to the. 56:3
their wings were j. one. Ezek 1:9
were courts j. of forty. 46:22*
Ephraim is j. to idols. Hos 4:17
many nations shall be j. Zech 2:11
what God hath j. together. Mat 19:6; Mark 10:9
he went and j. himself. Luke 15:15
about four hundred j. Acts 5:36
whose house j. hard to the. 18:7
ye be perfectly j. in. 1 Cor 1:10
he which is j. to an harlot. 6:16
he that is j. to the Lord is one. 17
the whole body fitly j. Eph 4:16*
and shall be j. to his wife. 5:31*
see **Baal-peor**

joining, -s

prepared iron for the j. 1 Chr 22:3*
j. to the wing of the. 2 Chr 3:12

joint

thigh was out of j. Gen 32:25*
all my bones are out of j. Ps 22:14
is like a foot out of j. Pr 25:19
by that which every j. Eph 4:16

joint-heirs

heirs of God, and j.-heirs. Rom 8:17

joints

king of Israel between the j. of the. 1 Ki 22:34; 2 Chr 18:33
the j. of thy thighs are. S of S 7:1†
that the j. of his loins. Dan 5:6
all the body by j. knit. Col 2:19
to dividing asunder of j. Heb 4:12

Jonadab, *called* **Jehonadab**

J. was Amnon's friend. 2 Sam 13:3
J. son of Rechab came. 2 Ki 10:15
J. our father commanded. Jer 35:6
obeyed the voice of J. Jer 35:8, 18
J. shall not want a man to stand. 19

Jonah, *or* **Jonas**

spake by his servant J. 2 Ki 14:25
J. rose to flee to Tarshish. Jonah 1:3
lots, and the lot fell upon J. 7
they cast J. into the sea, the. 15
J. was in the belly of the fish. 17
J. prayed. 2:1
the fish vomited out J. 10
J. went to Nineveh. 3:3
it displeased J. 4:1
the gourd to come up over J. 4:6
to it, but the sign of the prophet J. Mat 12:39; 16:4; Luke 11:29, 30
as J. was three days in. Mat 12:40
repented at the preaching of J. 41
Simon son of J. lovest thou me? John 21:15, 16, 17

Jonathan

J. and his sons were. Judg 18:30
men were with J. in. 1 Sam 13:2
with Saul and J. were swords. 22
knew not that J. was gone. 14:3
J. climbed up upon his hands. 13
J. heard not when his father. 27
though it be in J. my son, he. 39
I and J. my son will be on the. 40
J. was taken. 42
thou shalt surely die, J. 44
so the people rescued J. that he. 45
the soul of J. was knit with. 18:1
but J. Saul's son delighted. 19:2
J. spake good of David to Saul. 4
let not J. know this lest he. 20:3
do so and much more to J. 13
J. made a covenant with the. 16
anger was kindled against J. 30
J. knew it was determined to. 33
J. cried after the lad. 37
J. and David knew. 39
J. arose and went to David. 23:16
the Philistines slew J. 31:2
1 Chr 10:2
Saul and J. his son. 2 Sam 1:4
the bow of J. turned not back. 22
Saul and J. were lovely in. 23
distressed for thee, my brother J. 26
J. had a son that was lame. 4:4; 9:3
shew thee kindness for J.'s sake. 9:7
J. the son of Abiathar. 15:27, 36
1 Ki 1:42, 43
now J. and Ahimaaz. 2 Sam 17:17
Mephibosheth the son of J. 21:7
took the bones of Saul and J. 12
J. the son of Shimea slew him. 21
1 Chr 20:7
of sons of Jashen, J. 2 Sam 23:32
Jada, Jether and J. 1 Chr 2:32
sons of Hashem, J. Ahiam. 11:34
also J. David's uncle was a. 27:32
Ebed the son of J. went. Ezra 8:6
only J. and Jehaziah were. 10:15
Joiada begat J. Neh 12:11
of Melicu, J. 14
Zechariah the son of J. with a. 35
in prison in the house of J. Jer 37:15
return to the house of J. 20; 38:26
Johanan and J. came to. 40:8
see **David, Saul**

Joppa

bring it by sea in floats to J. 2 Chr 2:16; Ezra 3:7
Jonah went down to J. Jonah 1:3
at J. a disciple named. Acts 9:36
it was known throughout all J. 42
Peter tarried many days in J. 43
send men to J. and call. 10:5, 32
certain brethren from J. 23
I was in the city of J. praying. 11:5

Joram, *called* **Jehoram**

Toi sent J. his son to. 2 Sam 8:10
J. of Ahab; J. son of. 2 Ki 8:16
Syrians wounded J. 28
J. went to Jezreel. 29
Jehoshaphat conspired against J. 9:14
a bow and smote J. between. 24
Jehosheba the daughter of J. 11:2
of the Levites, J. over. 1 Chr 26:25
destruction of Ahaziah was of God by coming to J. 2 Chr 22:7
Josaphat begat J. and J. Mat 1:8

Jordan
him all the plain of *J.* *Gen* 13:11
go down to *J.* and goings out at the.
Num 34:12; *Josh* 13:27; 18:12
come to *J.* stand still in *J. Josh* 3:8
passeth over before you into *J.* 11
J. overfloweth all his banks in. 15
stones out of the midst of *J.* 4:3
priests, come ye up out of *J.* 17
God dried the waters of *J.* 23
Lord hath made *J.* a border. 22:25
they took the fords of *J.* *Judg* 3:28
7:24; 12:5
slew him at the passages of *J.* 12:6
king returned and came to *J.*
2 Sam 19:15
down to meet me at *J.* *1 Ki* 2:8
in plain of *J.* did the king cast them
in clay ground. 7:46; *2 Chr* 4:17
brook Cherith before *J. 1 Ki* 17:3, 5
Lord hath sent me to *J.* *2 Ki* 2:6
they two stood by *J.* 7
Elisha stood by *J.* 13
go and wash in *J.* seven times. 5:10
dipped himself seven times in *J.* 14
let us go, we pray thee, to *J.* 6:2
went after the Syrians to *J.* 7:15
that he can draw up *J.* *Job* 40:23
thee from the land of *J.* *Ps* 42:6
sea fled, *J.* was driven. 114:3, 5
do in the swelling of *J.*? *Jer* 12:5
from the swelling of *J.* 49:19; 50:44
pride of *J.* is spoiled. *Zech* 11:3
were baptized of him in *J.* *Mat* 3:6
Mark 1:5, 9
cometh Jesus from Galilee to *J.*
Mat 3:13

beyond **Jordan**
Atad which is *beyond J.* *Gen* 50:10
Abel-mizraim, which is *beyond J.* 11
land that is *beyond J.* *Deut* 3:25
kings of Amorites *beyond J.*
Josh 9:10
gave them *beyond J.* 13:8; 18:7
Gilead abode *beyond J.* *Judg* 5:17
Zebulun and land of Naphtali *beyond*
J. in. *Isa* 9:1; *Mat* 4:15
in Bethabara *beyond J.* *John* 1:28
he that was with thee *beyond J.* 3:26

on the other side **Jordan**
Ebal, are they not *on other side J.*?
Deut 11:30
content and dwelt *on the other side*
J. *Josh* 7:7
and half the tribe *on the other side J.*
12:1; 13:27, 32; 14:3; 17:5; 22:4
on other side J. Bezer. 20:8
who dwelt *on the other side J.* 24:8
of Oreb, Zeeb *on other side J.*
Judg 7:25
Israel *on other side J.* oppressed.
10:8
on other side J. forsook. *1 Sam* 31:7
of Merari cities *on other side J.*
1 Chr 6:78
on the other side J. 120,000. 12:37

on this side **Jordan**
is fallen *on this side J.* *Num* 32:19
32; 34:15; *Josh* 1:14, 15; 22:7
give three cities *on this side J.*
Num 35:14; *Deut* 4:41
on this side J. Moses. *Deut* 1:5
we took the land *on this side J.* 3:8
kings *on this side J.* *Josh* 9:1
1700 officers *this side J. 1 Chr* 26:30

over **Jordan**
I passed *over* this *J.* *Gen* 32:10
land, bring us not *over J. Num* 32:5
go all of you armed *over J.* 21
we will pass *over J.* armed. 32
passed *over J.* into the land. 33:51
35:10; *Deut* 12:10; 27:4, 12
thou shalt not go *over J.* *Deut* 3:27
4:21; 31:2
this land, I must not go *over J.* 4:22
pass *over J.* this day. 9:1; 11:31
go *over J.* thou and all. *Josh* 1:2
three days ye shall pass *over J.* 11
were passed clean *over J.* 3:17; 4:1
Israel came *over* this *J.* on. 4:22
brought this people *over J.* to. 7:7
ye went *over J.* and came. 24:11
Ammon passed *over J.* *Judg* 10:9
Hebrews went *over J.* *1 Sam* 13:7
his men passed *over J.* *2 Sam* 2:29
the people passed *over J.* 17:22
and all Israel passed *over J.* 24
conduct the king *over J.* 19:15, 31
they that passed *over J. 1 Chr* 12:15
David passed *over J.* against. 19:17

Jorim, Jose
Jose the son of Eliezer, the son of
Jorim. *Luke* 3:29

Josedech, *see* **Joshua**

Joseph
she called his name *J.* *Gen* 30:24
Jacob put Rachel and *J.* 33:2
the sons of Rachel, *J.* and Benjamin.
35:24; 46:19; *1 Chr* 2:2
J. brought to his father. *Gen* 37:2
Israel loved *J.* 3
J. dreamed a dream. 5
his brethren sold *J.* 28
J. is rent in pieces. 33
but the Lord was with *J.* 39:2, 21
Egyptian's house for *J.'s* sake. 5
wife cast her eyes upon *J.* 7
J.'s master took him and put him. 20
butler told his dream to *J.* 40:9
not the chief butler remember *J.* 23
they brought *J.* out of the. 41:14
Pharaoh put his ring on *J.'s* hand. 42
J. 30 years old when he stood. 46
J. gathered corn as the sand of. 49
go to *J.* 41:55
J. knew his brethren. 42:8
J. is not. 36
the man did as *J.* bade. 43:17
J. made haste, for his bowels. 30
I am J. 45:3, 4
say, Thus saith thy son *J.* 9
they told him, saying, *J.* is. 26, 28
J. shall put his hand upon thine. 46:4
J. went up to meet Israel his. 29
J. nourished his father and. 47:12
all the Egyptians came to *J.* 15
die, and he called his son *J.* 29
one told Jacob, thy son *J.* 48:2
J. brought them from between. 12
Jacob blessed *J.* and said, God. 15
J. is a fruitful bough, even a. 49:22
blessings shall be on head of *J.* 26
J. went up to bury his father. 50:7
J. will peradventure hate us. 15
and they sent a messenger to *J.* 16
J. wept when they spake unto. 17
J. took an oath of the children. 25
new king which knew not *J.*
Ex 1:8; *Acts* 7:18
Moses took the bones of *J. Ex* 13:19
sons of *J.* Manasseh. *Num* 26:28, 37
these on Gerizim to bless, Judah, *J.*
Deut 27:12
of *J.* he said, Blessed of the. 33:13
blessing come upon head of *J.* 16
but the birthright was *J.'s. 1 Chr* 5:2
sons of Jacob and *J.* *Ps* 77:15
refused the tabernacle of *J.* 78:67
give ear, thou that leadest *J.* 80:1
this he ordained in *J.* for a. 81:5
even *J.* who was sold for a. 105:17
write for *J.* the stick. *Ezek* 37:16, 19
tribes of Israel, *J.* shall have. 47:13
one gate of *J.* one gate of. 48:32
be gracious to the remnant of *J.*
Amos 5:15
not grieved for the affliction of *J.* 6:6
near the ground that Jacob gave to *J.*
John 4:5
the patriarchs sold *J.* into. *Acts* 7:9
at the second time *J.* was made. 13
then *J.* called his father Jacob. 14
Jacob blessed sons of *J.* *Heb* 11:21
J. made mention of Israel's. 22
see **house**

Joseph with *tribe* and *children*
of the *children* of *J.* of Ephraim.
Num 1:10, 32
of the *tribe* of *J.* namely of. 13:11
princes of the *children* of *J.* 34:23
the *tribe* of the sons of *J.* hath. 36:5
the *children* of *J.* two tribes.
Josh 14:4; 16:4
the lot of *children* of *J.* fell. 16:1
the *children* of *J.* spake. 17:14, 16
dwelt the *children* of *J.* *1 Chr* 7:29
of the *tribe* of *J.* were sealed 12,000.
Rev 7:8

Joseph, husband of *Mary*
Jacob begat *J.* the. *Mat* 1:16
mother Mary was espoused to *J.* 18
J. her husband being a just man. 19
J. did as angel of the Lord hath. 24
the Lord appeared to *J.* 2:13, 19
name was *J.* of house. *Luke* 1:27
J. also went up from Galilee. 2:4
the shepherds found Mary, *J.* 16
and *J.* and his mother knew. 43
as we supposed, the son of *J.* 3:23
this *J.'s* son? 4:22; *John* 1:45; 6:42

Joseph, the name of divers men
Issachar, Igal son of *J.* *Num* 13:7
of Asaph, Zaccur, *J.* *1 Chr* 25:2, 9
Shallum, *J.* had taken. *Ezra* 10:42
of Shebaniah, *J.* was a. *Neh* 12:14
J. of Arimathaea, Jesus' disciple.
Mat 27:57, 59; *Mark* 15:43, 45
Luke 23:50; *John* 19:38
Janna, son of *J.* *Luke* 3:24, 26, 30
two, *J.* called Barsabas. *Acts* 1:23

Joses
James and *J. Mat* 13:55; *Mark* 6:3
Mary the mother of *J.* *Mat* 27:56
Mark 15:40, 47
J. by apostles was surnamed.
Acts 4:36

Joshua, called **Jehoshua,** and **Oshea**
J. discomfited Amalek. *Ex* 17:13
rehearse it in the ears of *J.* 14
rose up and his minister *J.* 24:13
when *J.* heard the noise of. 32:17
J. departed not out of the. 33:11
of the tribe of Ephraim, *Oshea* son
of Nun. *Num* 13:8
Oshea the son of Nun, Jehoshua. 16
save Caleb and *J.* 14:30, 38; 26:65
32:12
take thee *J.* 27:18
he set *J.* before Eleazar. 22
Eleazar and *J.* shall divide. 34:17
but *J.* shall go in. *Deut* 1:38; 31:3
charge *J.* and encourage him. 3:28
31:23
J. was full of the spirit of. 34:9
J. commanded officers. *Josh* 1:10
J. sent two men to spy secretly. 2:1
Lord said to *J.* 3:7; 5:9; 6:2
7:10; 8:18; 10:8
children of Israel did so as *J.* 4:8
day the Lord magnified *J.* in. 14
children, them *J.* circumcised. 5:7
J. fell on his face to the earth. 14
and *J.* did so. 15
so the Lord was with *J.* 6:27
J. rent his clothes. 7:6
pursued after *J.* 8:16
then *J.* built an altar to the. 30
which *J.* read not before all the. 35
then spake *J.* Sun, stand still. 10:12
their land did *J.* take at one. 42
J. did unto them as the Lord. 11:9
now *J.* was old and. 13:1; 23:1
so *J.* blessed Caleb and gave. 14:13
J. cast lots for them before. 18:10
gave an inheritance to *J* 19:49
J. blessed the Reubenites. 22:6
J. gathered the tribes of. 24:1
so *J.* made a covenant with. 25
J. the servant of the Lord died. 29
Judg 2:8
days of *J.* and of elders that overlived *J.* *Josh* 24:31; *Judg* 2:7
into the field of *J.* *1 Sam* 6:14, 18
which he spake by *J.* *1 Ki* 16:34
in of the gate of *J.* *2 Ki* 23:8
J. son of Josedech. *Hag* 1:1, 12, 14
2:2, 4
and he shewed me *J.* the. *Zech* 3:1
now *J.* was clothed with filthy. 3
stone that I have laid before *J.* 9
set them upon the head of *J.* 6:11

Josiah
a child shall be born, *J.* *1 Ki* 13:2
the people made *J.* king. *2 Ki* 21:24
2 Chr 33:25
J. was eight years old. *2 Ki* 22:1

did *J.* take away. *2 Ki* 23:19, 24
2 Chr 34:33
J. went. *2 Ki* 23:29; *2 Chr* 35:22
sons of *J.* were Johanan. *1 Chr* 3:15
J. kept a passover. *2 Chr* 35:1
keep such a passover as *J.* 18
in the 18th year of *J.* was this. 19
archers shot at king *J.* and. 23
and Jerusalem mourned for *J.* 24
lamented for *J.*.. men spake of *J.* 25
came in days of *J.* *Jer* 1:2; 3:6
Zephaniah in days of *J.* *Zeph* 1:1
go into the house of *J.* *Zech* 6:10
Amon begat *J.* *Mat* 1:10
J. begat Jechonias. 11

jot

one *j.* or tittle shall in. *Mat* 5:18

Jotham

J. youngest son of. *Judg* 9:5, 21
on them came the curse of *J.* 57
J. judged the people. *2 Ki* 15:5
2 Chr 26:21
of Jahdai, Regem and *J.* *1 Chr* 2:47
Azariah his son, *J.* his son. 3:12
genealogies in the days of *J.* 5:17
J. became mighty. *2 Chr* 27:6
in the days of *J.* *Isa* 1:1; *Hos* 1:1
Mi 1:1
Ozias begat *J.* and *J.* *Mat* 1:9

journey

Lord hath made his *j.* *Gen* 24:21
Jacob went on his *j.* and. 29:1
after him seven days' *j.* 31:23
let us take our *j.* 33:12
Israel took his *j.* 46:1
they took their *j.* from. *Ex* 13:20
Israelites took their *j.* from. 16:1
a *j.* yet shall keep the. *Num* 9:10
is not in a *j.* and forbeareth to. 13
they first took their *j.* 10:13
there are eleven days' *j.* *Deut* 1:2
arise, take thy *j.* before the. 10:11
take victuals with you for your *j.*
Josh 9:11
by reason of the very long *j.* 13
the *j.* thou takest is not. *Judg* 4:9
Lord sent thee on a *j.* *1 Sam* 15:18
thou not from thy *j.*? *2 Sam* 11:10
or he is in a *j.* *1 Ki* 18:27
the *j.* is great. 19:7
compass of seven days' *j.* *2 Ki* 3:9
for how long shall thy *j.* be? *Neh* 2:6
man is gone a long *j.* *Pr* 7:19
nor scrip for your *j.* nor. *Mat* 10:10
take nothing for their *j.* *Mark* 6:8
Luke 9:3
a friend of mine in his *j.* *Luke* 11:6
the younger took his *j.* into a. 15:13
Jesus wearied with his *j.* *John* 4:6
might have a prosperous *j.* *Rom* 1:10
I trust to see you in my *j.* 15:24*
may bring me on my *j.* *1 Cor* 16:6
and Apollos on their *j.* *Tit* 3:13
bring forward on their *j.* *3 John* 6

day's **journey**

the quails fall a *day's j.* *Num* 11:31
himself went a *day's j.* *1 Ki* 19:4
to enter city a *day's j.* *Jonah* 3:4
went a *day's j.* among. *Luke* 2:44
from Jerusalem a sabbath *day's j.*
Acts 1:12

see three **days**

journeyed

that as they *j.* they. *Gen* 11:2
Abram *j.* going on toward. 12:9, 20:1
Lot *j.* east. 13:11
Jacob *j.* to Succoth. 33:17
Israel *j.* toward Beth-el. 35:5
j. from Beth-el. 16
j. to the tower of Edar. 21
cloud not taken up, then they *j.* not.
Ex 40:37; *Num* 9:21
after that the children of Israel *j.*
Num 9:17, 18
charge of the Lord, and *j.* not. 19
commandment of Lord they *j.* 20, 23
j. not till Miriam was brought. 12:15
house of Micah as he *j.* *Judg* 17:8
as Saul *j.* he came near. *Acts* 9:3
which *j.* with him stood. 7; 26:13

journeying

make trumpets for *j.* of. *Num* 10:2
we are *j.* to the place. *Num* 10:29
as he was *j.* towards. *Luke* 13:22
in *j.* often, in perils. *2 Cor* 11:26

journeyings

were the *j.* of Israel's. *Num* 10:28

journeys

Abram went on his *j.* *Gen* 13:3
j. according to the. *Ex* 17:1
cloud was taken up, they went on in
their *j.* 40:36; *Num* 10:12
for the cloud was upon the tabernacle through all their *j.* *Ex* 40:38
blow an alarm for their *j.* *Num* 10:6
these are the *j.* of Israel. 33:1, 2

joy, *substantive*

to meet Saul with *j.* *1 Sam* 18:6
for there was *j.* in. *1 Chr* 12:40
by lifting up the voice with *j.* 15:16
bring ark of the covenant with *j.* 25
now have I seen with *j.* the. 29:17
to Jerusalem with *j.* *2 Chr* 20:27
noise of the shout of *j.* *Ezra* 3:43
of the house of God with *j.* 6:16
the feast seven days with *j.* 22
the *j.* of the Lord is. *Neh* 8:10
j. of Jerusalem was heard. 12:43
the Jews had light, *j.* *Esth* 8:16
sorrow to *j.* they should make them
days of feasting and *j.* 9:22*
this is the *j.* of his way. *Job* 8:19
the *j.* of the hypocrite is but. 20:5
widow's heart to sing for *j.* 29:13
he will see his face with *j.* 33:26
and sorrow is turned into *j.* 41:22*
presence is fulness of *j.* *Ps* 16:11
his tabernacles sacrifices of *j.* 27:6
but *j.* cometh in the morning. 30:5
I went with the voice of *j.* and. 42:4
unto God my exceeding *j.* 43:4
the *j.* of the whole earth is. 48:2
restore to me the *j.* of thy. 51:12
nations be glad and sing for *j.* 67:4
forth his people with *j.* 105:43
sow in tears shall reap in *j.* 126:5
Jerusalem above my chief *j.* 137:6
counsellors of peace is *j.* *Pr* 12:20
not intermeddle with his *j.* 14:10
folly is *j.* to him destitute. 15:21
a man hath *j.* by the answer of. 23
father of a fool hath no *j.* 17:21
it is *j.* to the just to do. 21:15
a wise child shall have *j.* 23:24
not my heart from *j.* *Eccl* 2:10
him wisdom, knowledge, and *j.* 26
God answereth him in the *j.* 5:20
way, eat thy bread with *j.* 9:7
the *j.* according to the *j.* *Isa* 9:3
Lord shall have no *j.* in their. 17*
with *j.* shall ye draw water. 12:3
j. is taken out of the plentiful. 16:10
j. of the harp ceaseth. 24:8
j. is darkened. 11
meek shall increase their *j.* 29:19
on all houses of *j.* 32:13
a *j.* of wild asses. 14
and rejoice even with *j.* and. 35:2
j. on their heads. 10; 51:11
break forth into *j.* 52:9
go out with *j.* 55:12
I will make thee a *j.* of many. 60:15
to give them the oil of *j.* for. 61:3
everlasting *j.* shall be unto them. 7
my servants shall sing for *j.* 65:14
I create her people a *j.* 18
but he shall appear to your *j.* 66:5
rejoice for *j.* with her, all ye. 10
the word was to me the *j.* *Jer* 15:16
turn their mourning into *j.* 31:13
to me a name of *j.*, a praise. 33:9
shall be heard the voice of *j.* 11
spakest, thou skippedst for *j.* 48:27*
j. is taken from the plentiful. 33
praise, the city of my *j.* 49:25
city, the *j.* of the whole. *Lam* 2:15
the *j.* of our heart is ceased. 5:15
take from them the *j.* *Ezek* 24:25
appointed, with the *j.* of all. 36:5
rejoice not, O Israel, for *j.* *Hos* 9:1
because *j.* is withered. *Joel* 1:12
rejoice over thee with *j.* *Zeph* 3:17
anon with *j.* receiveth it. *Mat* 13:20
Luke 8:13
for *j.* thereof goeth and. *Mat* 13:44
enter thou into the *j.* *Mat* 25:21, 23
leaped in my womb for *j.* *Luke* 1:44
in that day, and leap for *j.* 6:23
seventy returned again with *j.* 10:17
j. shall be in heaven over one. 15:7
there is *j.* in the presence of. 10
they yet believed not for *j.* 24:41
this my *j.* therefore is. *John* 3:29
to you, that my *j.* might remain in
you, and that your *j.* might. 15:11
sorrow shall be turned into *j.* 16:20
for *j.* that a man is born into. 21
and your *j.* no man taketh from. 22
ye shall receive, that your *j.* 24
might have my *j.* fulfilled. 17:13
make me full of *j.* with. *Acts* 2:28*
disciples filled with *j.* in the. 13:52
might finish my course with *j.* 20:24
kingdom of God is *j.* in. *Rom* 14:17
God fill you with all *j.* in. 15:13
may come to you with *j.* by the. 32
are helpers of your *j.* *2 Cor* 1:24
that my *j.* is the *j.* of you all. 2:3
joyed we for the *j.* of Titus. 7:13
the abundance of their *j.* 8:2
Spirit is love, *j.* peace. *Gal* 5:22
making request with *j.* *Phil* 1:4
furtherance and *j.* of faith. 25
fulfil ye my *j.* 2:2
my *j.* and crown. 4:1
received the word with *j.* *1 Thes* 1:6
what is our hope or *j.*? 2:19
ye are our *j.* 20
for the *j.* wherewith we joy. 3:9
I may be filled with *j.* *2 Tim* 1:4
let me have *j.* of thee. *Philem* 20
who for the *j.* that was. *Heb* 12:2
they may do it with *j.* and. 13:17
count it *j.* when ye fall into. *Jas* 1:2
and your *j.* be turned into. 4:9
ye rejoice with *j.* *1 Pet* 1:8
be glad also with exceeding *j.* 4:13
that your *j.* may be full. *1 John* 1:4
2 John 12
I have no greater *j.* than. *3 John* 4
you faultless with exceeding *j.*
Jude 24

see gladness

joy, *verb*

the king shall *j.* in thy. *Ps* 21:1
j. before thee according. *Isa* 9:3
I will rejoice and *j.* in my. 65:19
I will *j.* in the God of my. *Hab* 3:18
he will *j.* over thee with. *Zeph* 3:17
we also *j.* in God through. *Rom* 5:11*
I *j.* and rejoice with you. *Phil* 2:17
for the same cause also do ye *j.* 18
wherewith we *j.* for you. *1 Thes* 3:9

great **joy**

the people rejoiced with *great j.*
1 Ki 1:40
David the king rejoiced with *great j.*
1 Chr 29:9
so there was *great j.* *2 Chr* 30:26
them rejoice with *great j.* *Neh* 12:43
they rejoiced with *great j.* *Mat* 2:10
sepulchre with fear and *great j.* 28:8
good tidings of *great j.* *Luke* 2:10
to Jerusalem with *great j.* 24:52
and there was *great j.* in. *Acts* 8:8
they caused *great j.* to all. 15:3
for we have *great j.* in thy. *Philem* 7

shout, or *shouted for* **joy**

many *shouted* aloud *for j.* *Ezra* 3:12
sons of God *shouted for j.* *Job* 38:7
trust in thee rejoice: let them ever
shout for j. *Ps* 5:11; 35:27
shout for j. all ye that are. 32:11
the valleys *shout for j.* they. 65:13
thy saints *shout for j.* 132:9, 16

joyed

more *j.* we for the joy. *2 Cor* 7:13

joyful

went to their tents *j.* *1 Ki* 8:66
Lord hath made them *j.* *Ezra* 6:22
went forth that day *j.* *Esth* 5:9
let no *j.* voice come therein. *Job* 3:7
love thy name be *j.* in. *Ps* 5:11
soul shall be *j.* in the Lord. 35:9
shall praise thee with *j.* lips. 63:5
make a *j.* noise to God, all. 66:1
make a *j.* noise to the God of. 81:1

that know the j. sound. Ps 89:15
make a j. noise to the rock of. 95:1
a j. noise to him. 2; 98:4; 100:1
make a j. noise before the. 98:6
let the hills be j. together before. 8*
the barren to be a j. mother. 113:9
let the children of Zion be j. 149:2
let the saints be j. in glory; let. 5*
of prosperity be j. but in. Eccl 7:14
heavens, and be j. earth. Isa 49:13
make them j. in my house of. 56:7
soul shall be j. in my God. 61:10
I am exceeding j. in all. 2 Cor 7:4*

joyfully

live j. with the wife. Eccl 9:9
down and received him j. Luke 19:6
ye took j. the spoiling of. Heb 10:34

joyfulness

not the Lord with j. Deut 28:47
to longsuffering with j. Col 1:11

joying

with you in the spirit, j. Col 2:5

joyous

art full of stirs, a j. city. Isa 22:2
is this your j. city, whose. 23:7
houses of joy in the j. city. 32:13
no chastening seemeth to be j.
Heb 12:11

jubile

cause trumpet of the j. to. Lev 25:9
j. it shall be holy to you. 10, 12
a j. shall that fiftieth year be. 11
in the year of j. ye shall return. 13
a field shall go out in the year of j.
25:28; 27:21, 24
house shall not go out in the j. 25:30
they shall go out in the year of j.
31, 33, 54
his field from year of j. 27:17, 18
j. then their inheritance. Num 36:4

Judah

called his name J. Gen 29:35
sons of Leah, J. Issachar. 35:23
J. thought Tamar to be an. 38:15
J. acknowledged the signet and. 26
sons of J. 46:12; Num 26:19
1 Chr 2:3; 4:1
Jacob sent J. before him. Gen 46:28
J. thou art he whom thy. 49:8
J. is a lion's whelp, he couched. 9
sceptre shall not depart J. until. 10
the sons of Israel, Levi, J. Ex 1:2
1 Chr 2:1
J. Nashan son of. Num 1:7
the camp of J. shall pitch on. 2:3
numbered in the camp of J. 9
Simeon, Levi, J. shall. Deut 27:12
blessing of J. the voice of J. 33:7
brought the family of J. Josh 7:17
J. shall abide in their coast. 18:5
the Lord said, J. shall go. Judg 1:2
the Lord was with J. 19
fight against J. 10:9
whom Tamar bare to J. Ruth 4:12
search him out throughout all the
thousands of J. 1 Sam 23:23
J. do shew kindness. 2 Sam 3:8
David reigned over J. seven. 5:5
the ark, Israel, and J. abide. 11:11
J. came to Gilgal to meet. 19:15
go number Israel and J. 24:1
captain of host of J. 1 Ki 2:32
J. and Israel were many, as. 4:20
J. and Israel dwelt safely. 25
of God out of J. by the word of the
Lord to Beth-el. 13:1; 2 Ki 23:17
J. did evil in the sight of. 1 Ki 14:22
Abijam reigned over J. 15:1
reigned Asa over J. 9
went up against J. 17; 2 Chr 16:1
Jehoshaphat began to reign over J.
1 Ki 22:41
Lord would not destroy J. 2 Ki 8:19
Edom revolted from J. 20, 22
2 Chr 21:8, 10
Ahaziah began to reign over J.
2 Ki 9:29
to fall, thou and J. with thee. 14:10
2 Chr 25:19
J. was put to the worse.
2 Ki 14:12; 2 Chr 25:22
Azariah restored Elath to J.
2 Ki 14:22; 2 Chr 26:2
to send against J. Rezin. 2 Ki 15:37
testified against Israel and J. 17:13
J. kept not the commandments. 19
Manasseh made J. to sin. 21:11, 16
2 Chr 33:9
bringing such evil upon J. 2 Ki 21:12
his anger kindled against J. 23:26
2 Chr 25:10
I will remove J. also. 2 Ki 23:27
bands of Chaldees against J. 24:2
of the Lord came this on J. 3
so J. was carried away. 25:21
1 Chr 6:15
J. prevailed above his. 1 Chr 5:2
of J., Elihu, one of David's. 27:18
for he hath chosen J. to be. 28:4
so they were before J. 2 Chr 13:13
children of Israel fled before J. 16
Asa commanded J. to seek. 14:4
took the groves out of J. 17:6
Jehoram compelled J. to. 21:11
hast made J. and Jerusalem. 13
wrath came upon J. 24:18; 28:9
29:8; 32:25
Lord brought J. low, made J. 28:19
lambs for a sin offering for J. 29:21
all the congregation of J. 30:25
Manasseh commanded J. to. 33:16
Josiah began to purge J. 34:3, 5
sons of J. to set forward. Ezra 3:9
sent to enquire concerning J. 7:14
J. and Eliezer had taken. 10:23
wouldst send me to J. Neh 2:5
convey me till I come into J. 7
the nobles of J. sent letters. 6:17
J. son of Senuah was second. 11:9
for J. rejoiced for the priests. 12:44
Gilead is mine, J. Ps 60:7; 108:8
J. was his sanctuary, Israel. 114:2
he saw concerning J. Isa 1:1; 2:1
Lord doth take from J. the stay. 3:1
J. is fallen. 8
let us go up against J. 7:6
that Ephraim departed from J. 17
pass through J. shall overflow. 8:8
together shall be against J. 9:21
together the dispersed of J. 11:12
J. shall be cut off; Ephraim shall not
envy J. and J. not vex. 13
discovered the covering of J. 22:8
forth out of the waters of J. 48:1
and out of J. an inheritor of. 65:9
cities are thy gods, O J. Jer 2:28
treacherous sister J. saw it. 3:7, 8
Egypt, and J. and Edom. 9:26
will I mar the pride of J. 13:9
J. shall be carried away captive. 19
J. mourneth. 14:2
hast thou utterly rejected J. 19
the sin of J. is written with. 17:1
I will void the counsel of J. 19:7
J. shall be saved. 23:6
do this to cause J. to sin. 32:35
I will cause the captivity of J. 33:7
I have spoken against J. 36:2
the Lord, ye remnant of J. 42:15
in mouth of any man of J. 44:26
sins of J. shall not be found. 50:20
J. hath not been forsaken of. 51:5
J. was carried away captive. 52:27
Lam 1:3
sword may come to J. Ezek 21:20
J. and Israel were thy. 27:17
write upon it for J. and for. 37:16
of Reuben, a portion for J. 48:7
gate of Reuben, one gate of J. 31
harlot, yet let not J. Hos 4:15
J. shall fall. 5:5
when J. saw his wound. 13
O J. what shall I do unto thee? 6:4
J. shall plow, Jacob shall. 10:11
but J. ruleth yet with God. 11:12
also a controversy with J. 12:2
but J. shall dwell for ever. Joel 3:20
three transgressions of J. Amos 2:4
I will send a fire on J., it shall. 5
incurable, it is come to J. Mi 1:9
little among the thousands of J. 5:2
out mine hand upon J. Zeph 1:4
have scattered J. Zech 1:19, 21
Lord shall inherit J. his. 2:12
when I have bent J. for me. 9:13
save the tents of J. first. Zech 12:7
J. also shall fight at. 14:14
J. hath dealt treacherously; J. hath
profaned the holiness. Mal 2:11
then shall the offering of J. 3:4
Jacob begat J. Mat 1:2
J. begat Phares. 3
which was the son of J. Luke 3:33
our Lord sprang of J. Heb 7:14

all **Judah**

but all Israel and *all* J. 1 Sam 18:16
33 years over *all* J. 2 Sam 5:5
all J. rejoiced at the. 2 Chr 15:15
all J. stood before the Lord. 20:13
all J. did honour Hezekiah. 32:33
all J. and Jerusalem mourned. 35:24
all J. brought the tithe. Neh 13:12
give *all* J. to the king of. Jer 20:4
set my face to cut off *all* J. 44:11
see **Benjamin, Beth-lehem, children, cities, daughter, daughters, house**

in **Judah**

be afraid here *in* J. 1 Sam 23:3
the feast that is *in* J. 1 Ki 12:32
it came to pass *in* Jerusalem and J.
2 Ki 24:20; Jer 52:3
cunning men that are with me *in* J.
2 Chr 2:7
in J. things went well. 12:12
they taught *in* J. and had book. 17:9
Pekah slew *in* J. 120,000 in. 28:6
in J. hand of God was to give. 30:12
for them that are left *in* J. 34:21
the Jews that were *in* J. Ezra 5:1
mercy to give us a wall *in* J. 9:9
saying, There is a king *in* J. Neh 6:7
I saw *in* J. some treading. 13:15
in J. is God known. Ps 76:1
declare ye *in* J. publish in Jerusalem.
Jer 4:5; 5:20
prosper, ruling any more *in* J. 22:30
shall be as a governor *in* J. Zech 9:7
every pot *in* J. be holiness. 14:21
see **king, kings**

land of **Judah**

Lord shewed him all the *land of* J.
Deut 34:2
went to return unto the *land of* J.
Ruth 1:7
thee into the *land of* J. 1 Sam 22:5
remained in *land of* J. 2 Ki 25:22
garrisons in *land of* J. 2 Chr 17:2
the *land of* J. shall be a. Isa 19:17
shall be sung in the *land of* J. 26:1
speech in the *land of* J. Jer 31:23
had nothing in the *land of* J. 39:10
committed in the *land of* J. 44:9
should return into the *land of* J. 14
seer, into the *land of* J. Amos 7:12
horn over the *land of* J. Zech 1:21
Bethlehem, in the *land of* J. Mat 2:6

men of **Judah**

men of J. said, Why are? Judg 15:10
the *men of* J. anointed. 2 Sam 2:4
the heart of all the *men of* J. 19:14
the words of the *men of* J. 43
men of J. clave to their king. 20:2
assemble the *men of* J. within. 4
men of J. were five hundred. 24:9
men of J. gave a shout. 2 Chr 13:15
men of J. gathered. Ezra 10:9
men of J. are his pleasant. Isa 5:7
your hearts, ye *men of* J. Jer 4:4
is found among the *men of* J. 11:9
bring upon the *men of* J. all. 36:31
the sight of the *men of* J. 43:9
men of J. shall be consumed. 44:27
belongeth to the *men of* J. Dan 9:7
see **princes**

tribe of **Judah**

Bezaleel of the *tribe of* J. Ex 31:2
35:30; 38:22
numbered of *tribe of* J. Num 1:27
the prince of the *tribe of* J. 7:12
of the *tribe of* J. Caleb. 13:6; 34:19
Achan of *tribe of* J. took. Josh 7:1
and the *tribe of* J. was taken. 16, 18
lot of the *tribe of* J. 15:1, 20
Levites out of the *tribe of* J. 21:4, 9
1 Chr 6:65
the *tribe of* J. only. 1 Ki 12:20

left but tribe of J. only. 2 Ki 17:18
but he chose the tribe of J. Ps 78:68
Lion of the tribe of J. hath. Rev 5:5
of the tribe of J. were sealed. 7:5

Judas

Joses, Simon, and J. Mat 13:55
J. one of the twelve came, and a. 26:47; Mark 14:43
Luke 22:47; John 18:3, 5
then J. repented himself. Mat 27:3
some thought because J. John 13:29
J. said unto him, not Iscariot. 14:22
spake before concerning J. Acts 1:16
J. by transgression, fell. 25
after this man rose up J. of. 5:37
enquire in the house of J. for. 9:11
J. surnamed Barsabas. 15:22, 27
J. and Silas exhorted the. 32

Judas *Iscariot*

J. Iscariot, who betrayed him. Mat 10:4; Mark 3:19
Luke 6:16; John 6:71; 12:4; 13:2
J. Iscariot went to chief priests. Mat 26:14; Mark 14:10
Satan into J. Iscariot. Luke 22:3
the sop to J. Iscariot. John 13:26

Judaea

into the province of J. Ezra 5:8
in J. flee into mountains. Mat 24:16
Mark 13:14; Luke 21:21
he left J. and departed. John 4:3
depart hence and go into J. again. 7:3; 11:7
in J. ye shall be witnesses. Acts 1:8
ye men of J. be this known. 2:14
had rest throughout J. 9:31
was published through J. 10:37
went down from J. to Cesarea. 12:19
received letters out of J. 28:21
that do not believe in J. Rom 15:31
on my way toward J. 2 Cor 1:16
churches which are in J. are in Christ. 1 Thes 2:14

judge, *substantive*

shall not the J. of all? Gen 18:25
came, and will needs be a j. 19:9
who made thee a j. over us? Ex 2:14
Acts 7:27, 35
come to the j. that shall. Deut 17:9
will not hearken to the j. 12
that the j. shall cause him to. 25:2
the Lord was with the j. Judg 2:18
the j. was dead, they corrupted. 19
the Lord the J. be j. this. 11:27
if a man sin, the j. 1 Sam 2:25*
O that I were made j. 2 Sam 15:4
supplication to my j. Job 9:15*
delivered for ever from my j. 23:7
to be punished by the j. 31:28
declare, for God is j. Ps 50:6
a j. of the widows. 68:5
God is the j. 75:7
lift up thyself, thou J. of. 94:2
away from Jerusalem the j. Isa 3:2
I will cut off the j. from. Amos 2:3
shall smite the J. of Israel. Mi 5:1
prince asketh, and the j. asketh. 7:3
deliver thee to the j., the j. deliver. Mat 5:25; Luke 12:58
man, who made me a j.? Luke 12:14
saying, There was in a city a j. 18:2
hear what the unjust j. saith. 6
be the j. of quick and. Acts 10:42
for I will be no j. of such. 18:15
hast been of many years a j. 24:10
the Lord, the righteous j. 2 Tim 4:8
come to God the J. of. Heb 12:23
a doer of the law, but a j. Jas 4:11
behold, the J. standeth before. 5:9

judge, *verb, applied to* **God** *and* **Christ**

j. between me and thee. Gen 16:5
1 Sam 24:12, 15
God of their father j. Gen 31:53
Lord look on you, and j. Ex 5:21
Lord shall j. his people. Deut 32:36
Ps 50:4; 135:14; Heb 10:30
Lord shall j. the ends. 1 Sam 2:10
hear and j. thy servants. 1 Ki 8:32
2 Chr 6:23
cometh to j. the earth. 1 Chr 16:33
Ps 96:13; 98:9
wilt thou not j. them? 2 Chr 20:12
sayest, Can he j. through? Job 22:13
Lord shall j. the people righteously. Ps 7:8; 9:8; 50:4; 96:10
j. the fatherless and poor. 10:18
Isa 11:4
j. me, O Lord. Ps 7:8; 26:1; 35:24
43:1; 54:1; Lam 3:59
arise, O God, j. the earth. Ps 82:8
shall j. the world with righteousness. 96:13; 98:9; Acts 17:31
shall j. among the heathen. Ps 110:6
God shall j. the righteous. Eccl 3:17
and he shall j. among the. Isa 2:4
the Lord standeth to j. the. 3:13
he shall not j. after the sight. 11:3
mine arm shall j. the people. 51:5
and will j. thee according. Ezek 7:3
I j. between cattle and cattle. 34:17
there will I sit to j. the. Joel 3:12
j. among many people. Mi 4:3
I hear, I j.: my judgement. John 5:30
I j. no man. 8:15
and yet if I j. 16
things to say and to j. of you. 26
I j. him not, I came not to j. 12:47
when God shall j. the. Rom 2:16
how shall God j. the world? 3:6
who shall j. quick and dead. 2 Tim 4:1; 1 Pet 4:5
and adulterers God will j. Heb 13:4
dost thou not j. and? Rev 6:10
in righteousness he doth j. 19:11

see further, I *will* **judge**

judge, *applied to* **man,** *or other things*

that they may j. betwixt. Gen 31:37
Dan shall j. his people as. 49:16
that Moses sat to j. the. Ex 18:13
I j. between one and another. 16
small matter they shall j. 22
in righteousness shalt thou j. thy. Lev 19:15; Deut 1:16; 16:18
the congregation j. Num 35:24
the judges may j. them. Deut 25:1
sin, the judge shall j. 1 Sam 2:25
make us a king to j. us. 8:5, 6, 20
heart to j. thy people: for who is able to j. this? 1 Ki 3:9; 2 Chr 1:10
throne where he might j. 1 Ki 7:7
mayest j. my people. 2 Chr 1:11
for ye j. not for man, but for. 19:6
set judges which may j. Ezra 7:25
do ye j. uprightly, O ye? Ps 58:1
he shall j. thy people with. 72:2
he shall j. the poor of. 4; Pr 3:9
how long will ye j. unjustly? Ps 82:2
j. the fatherless, plead. Isa 1:17
j. not the fatherless. 23; Jer 5:28
j. I pray you betwixt me. Isa 5:3
wilt thou j. them? Ezek 20:4; 22:2
they shall j. thee. 23:24, 45; 24:14
Son of man, wilt j. Aholah? 23:36
they shall j. it according to. 44:24
saviours come to j. the. Ob 21
the heads thereof j. for. Mi 3:11
then thou shalt also j. Zech 3:7
j. not that ye be not. Mat 7:1
what judgement ye j. 2; Luke 6:37
yea, and why j. ye not? Luke 12:57
j. not according to the appearance, but j. righteous. John 7:24
doth our law j. any man before? 51
ye j. after flesh. 8:15
same shall j. him. 12:48
take and j. him according to. 18:31
j. ye. Acts 4:19
j. yourselves unworthy. 13:46
for sittest thou to j. me after? 23:3
if it fulfil the law, j. thee. Rom 2:27
j. him that eateth. 14:3
why dost thou j. thy brother? 10
let us not j. one another, but j. 13
I j. not mine own self. 1 Cor 4:3
j. nothing before the time. 5
I to do to j. them that are without? do not ye j. them that are within? 5:12
not know that saints shall j.? 6:2
know ye not that we shall j.? 3
to j. who are least esteemed. 4
shall be able to j. between. 5*
j. ye what I say. 10:15
j. in yourselves. 11:13
we would j. ourselves. 1 Cor 11:31*
speak, and the other j. 14:29*
because we thus j. that. 2 Cor 5:14
let no man therefore j. Col 2:16
but if thou j. the law. Jas 4:11

I will **judge**

I told him that I will j. 1 Sam 3:13
receive, I will j. uprightly. Ps 75:2
I will j. thee according to thy ways. Ezek 7:3, 8, 27; 33:20
I will j. you in the border. 11:10, 11
I will j. thee as women that. 16:38
therefore I will j. you, O. 18:30
I will j. thee in the place. 21:30
I, even I, will j. between. 34:20, 22

will I **judge**

the nation they shall serve will I j. Gen 15:14; Acts 7:7
own mouth will I j. thee. Luke 19:22

judged

God hath j. me and. Gen 30:6
j. the people, small matter they j. Ex 18:26
Othniel j. Israel. Judg 3:10
Deborah j. Israel. 4:4
Tola j. Israel. 10:2
Jair j. Israel. 3
Jephthah j. Israel. 12:7
Ibzan j. Israel. 8
Elon j. Israel. 11
Abdon j. Israel. 14
Samson j. Israel. 15:20; 16:31
Eli j. Israel. 1 Sam 4:18
Samuel j. Israel. 7:6, 15, 16, 17
judgement the king had j. 1 Ki 3:28
of the judges that j. 2 Ki 23:22
let the heathen be j. in. Ps 9:19
condemn him when he is j. 37:33
when he shall be j. let him. 109:7
j. the cause of the poor. Jer 22:16
that shed blood are j. Ezek 16:38
thou also who hast j. thy sisters. 52
and the wounded shall be j. 28:23
known, when I have j. thee. 35:11
to their doings I j. them. 36:19
our judges that j. us. Dan 9:12
that ye be not j. Mat 7:1
shall be j. 2; Luke 6:37
him, thou hast rightly j. Luke 7:43
prince of this world is j. John 16:11
if ye have j. me to be. Acts 16:15
we would have j. according. 24:6
and there be j. of these. 25:9, 20
stand, where I ought to be j. 25:10
and am j. for the hope of the. 26:6
shall be j. by the law. Rom 2:12
Jas 2:12
overcome when thou art j. Rom 3:4
why yet am I also j. as a sinner? 7
yet he himself is j. of. 1 Cor 2:15
a small thing that I should be j. 4:3
I have j. already, as though I. 5:3
and if the world shall be j. by. 6:2
for why is my liberty j. of? 10:29
judge we should not be j. 11:31
when we are j. we are chastened. 32
convinced of all, he is j. of. 14:24
she j. him faithful. Heb 11:11*
be j. according to men. 1 Pet 4:6
time of the dead, that they should be j. Rev 11:18
because thou hast j. thus. 16:5
righteous, for he hath j. the. 19:2
the dead were j. out of those. 20:12
were j. every man according to. 13

judgement

[1] *The sentence, or decision of a judge,* 1 Ki 3:28. [2] *The spirit of wisdom and prudence, enabling to know and discern right from wrong, and good from evil,* Ps 72:1. [3] *The righteous statutes and commandments of God,* Ps 119:7, 20. [4] *Justice and equity,* Isa 1:17; Luke 11:42. [5] *God's decrees and purposes concerning nations, or persons,* Rom 11:33. [6] *Courts of judgement,* Mat 5:21. [7] *The last judgement,* Mat. 25:31-46.

gods I will execute j. Ex 12:12
according to this j. be it done. 21:31
after many, to wrest j. 23:2, 6

make the breastplate of j. Ex 28:15
names in breastplate of j. 29, 30
a statute of j. Num 27:11; 35:29
after the j. of Urim before the. 27:21
afraid of man, for the j. Deut 1:17
he doth execute the j. of the. 10:18
judge the people with just j. 16:18
not wrest j. 19
shew thee sentence of j. 17:9
according to the j. 11
thou shalt not pervert the j. 24:17
and they come unto j. 25:1
cursed be he that perverteth j. 27:19
for all his ways are j.; a God. 32:4†
if my hand take hold on j. I. 41
the congregation for j. Josh 20:6
up to Deborah for j. Judg 4:5
bribes and perverted j. 1 Sam 8:3
David executed j. 2 Sam 8:15
1 Chr 18:14
came to king for j. 2 Sam 15:2, 6
understanding to discern j. 1 Ki 3:11
all Israel heard of the j. the. 28
the porch of j. 7:7
so shall thy j. be. 20:40
took king and gave j. 2 Ki 25:6
chief of fathers for j. 2 Chr 19:8
cometh on us as the sword, j. 20:9
when Jehu was executing j. 22:8
executed j. against Joash. 24:24
let j. be executed. Ezra 7:26
all that knew law and j. Esth 1:13
doth God pervert j.? Job 8:3
if I speak of j. 9:19
but there is no j. 19:7
that ye may know there is a j. 29
do the aged understand j. 32:9
let us choose to us j. 34:4
will the Almighty pervert j. 12
yet j. is before him, trust. 35:14*
fulfilled the j. of the wicked, j. and justice take hold on thee. 36:17
awake for me to the j. thou. Ps 7:6
hath prepared his throne for j. 9:7
shall minister j. to the people. 8
the Lord is known by the j. he. 16
he loveth righteousness and j. 33:5†
37:28
he shall bring forth thy j. as. 37:6
and his tongue talketh of j. 30
shall judge thy poor with j. 72:2
thou didst cause j. to be heard. 76:8*
when God arose to j. to save the. 9
justice and j. are the. 89:14†; 97:2†
but j. shall return to. 94:15
also loveth j.; thou executest j. and. 99:4†
I will sing of mercy and j. to. 101:1
Lord executeth j. for. 103:6; 146:7
blessed are they that keep j. 106:3
Phinehas stood up and executed j. 30
the works are verity and j. 111:7
teach me good j. and. 119:66
I have done j. and justice. 121†
quicken me according to thy j. 149
for there are set thrones of j. 122:5
to execute upon them the j. 149:9
instruction of wisdom and j. Pr 1:3†
he keepeth the paths of j. and. 2:8†
then shalt thou understand j. and. 9†
the midst of the paths of j. 8:20
that is destroyed for want of j. 13:23
gift to pervert the ways of j. 17:23
an ungodly witness scorneth j. 19:28
that sitteth in the throne of j. 20:8
evil men understand not j. but. 28:5
the king by j. establisheth the. 29:4
every man's j. cometh from. 26
nor pervert the j. of any of. 31:5
the sun the place of j. Eccl 3:16
violent perverting of j. and. 5:8
man discerneth both time and j. 8:5
every purpose there is time and j. 6
seek j. Isa 1:17
it was full of j. 21
Zion shall be redeemed with j. 27†
purged Jerusalem by spirit of j. 4:4
and looked for j. 5:7†
and to establish it with j. 9:7
to turn aside the needy from j. 10:2†
execute j. 16:3; Jer 21:12; 22:3
Ezek 18:8; 45:9; Zech 7:9; 8:12
seeking j. Isa 16:5
for a spirit of j. 28:6
I will lay j. to the line. Isa 28:17†
for the Lord is a God of j. 30:18
then j. shall dwell in the. 32:16†
Lord hath filled Zion with j. 33:5†
the people of my curse to j. 34:5
taught him in the path of j.? 40:14
let us come near together to j. 41:1
he shall bring forth j. to the. 42:1
he shall bring forth j. unto truth. 3
he shall not fail, till he have set j. 4
from prison and from j. 53:8
keep ye j. and do justice. 56:1
Hos 12:6†
is no j. in their goings. Isa 59:8†
therefore is j. far from us. 9†
we look for j. but there is none. 11†
j. is turned away backward. 14†
him that there was no j. 15†
I the Lord love j. I hate. 61:8†
be any that executeth j. Jer 5:1
not the j. of their God. 4; 8:7*
they have known the j. of their. 5:5
if ye throughly execute j. 7:5
exercise j. and righteousness. 9:24†
correct me, but with j. not in. 10:24
execute j. in the morning. 21:12
branch shall execute j. 23:5; 33:15
to Riblah, where he gave j. upon Zedekiah. 39:5; 52:9
and j. is come upon the. 48:21
thus far is the j. of Moab. 47
whose j. was not to drink. 49:12*
forsake her, for her j. reacheth. 51:9
for they had executed j. Ezek 23:10
I will set j. before them, they. 24
all whose ways are j. Dan 4:37
j. was set. 7:10
but the j. shall sit. 26
j. was given to the saints of the. 22
give ye ear, for j. is. Hos 5:1
thus j. springeth up as hemlock. 10:4
turn j. into wormwood. Amos 5:7
love the good, and establish j. in. 15
but let j. run down as waters and. 24
for ye have turned j. into gall. 6:12
is it not to know j.? Mi 3:1
I am full of j. 8
that abhor j. 9
and execute j. for me. 7:9
law is slacked, j. doth. Hab 1:4
j. shall proceed of themselves. 7
thou hast ordained them for j. 12
have wrought his j. Zeph 2:3
every morning doth he bring j. 3:5
where is the God of j.? Mal 2:17
in danger of the j. Mat 5:21, 22
with what j. ye judge, ye shall. 7:2
shew j. to the Gentiles. 12:18
till he send forth j. unto victory. 20
and have omitted j., mercy. 23:23†
pass over j. and love of. Luke 11:42†
but hath committed all j. John 5:22
him authority to execute j. also. 27
but judge righteous j. 7:24
j. I am come into this world. 9:39
now is the j. of this world. 12:31
reprove the world of j. 16:8, 11
in his humiliation his j. Acts 8:33
as he reasoned of j., Felix. 24:25
the Jews desiring to have j. 25:15
knowing the j. of God. Rom 1:32*
sure that the j. of God is. 2:2
that thou shalt escape the j. of ? 3
and revelation of the righteous j. 5
for the j. was by one to. 5:16
j. came on all men to. 18
be joined together in j. 1 Cor 1:10
should be judged of man's j. 4:3
token of the righteous j. 2 Thes 1:5
open, going before to j. 1 Tim 5:24
and of eternal j. Heb 6:2
after this the j. 9:27
certain fearful looking for of j. 10:27
j. without mercy, shewed no mercy, mercy rejoiceth against j. Jas 2:13
we shall receive greater j. 3:1
that j. must begin at the. 1 Pet 4:17
whose j. lingereth not. 2 Pet 2:3*
angels reserved unto j. 4
to j. of the great day. Jude 6
to execute j. 15
fear God, for the hour of his j. is come. Rev 14:7
will shew thee j. of the great. 17:1
for in one hour is thy j. come. Rev 18:10
and j. was given to them. 20:4
see **bear, day**

do judgement

to do justice and j. Gen 18:19†
1 Ki 10:9; Pr 21:3†; Jer 22:15
God was in him to do j. 1 Ki 3:28
them to do justice and j. 2 Chr 9:8
they refuse to do j. Pr 21:7†
it is joy to the just to do j. but. 15†
I will do j. on the graven images. Jer 51:47
I will do j. on her graven images. 52

in judgement

unrighteousness in j. Lev 19:15, 35
the congregation in j. Num 35:12
not respect persons in j. Deut 1:17
matter too hard for thee in j. 17:8
ye that sit in j. and. Judg 5:10*
who is with you in j. 2 Chr 19:6
come together in j. Job 9:32
excellent in power and in j. 37:23
shall not stand in j. Ps 1:5
the meek will he guide in j. 25:9
trangresseth not in j. Pr 16:10
overthrow the righteous in j. 18:5
have respect of persons in j. 24:23
hosts shall be exalted in j. Isa 5:16
him that sitteth in j. 28:6
they stumble in j. 7
behold princes shall rule in j. 32:1
that shall rise against thee in j. 54:17
Lord liveth in righteousness and in j. Jer 4:2†
they stand in j. Ezek 44:24
betroth thee to me in j. Hos 2:19
oppressed and broken in j. 5:11
come near to you in j. Mal 3:5
Nineveh shall rise in j. Mat 12:41
queen of south shall rise in j. 42
Luke 11:31, 32
your love may abound in j. Phil 1:9*

into judgement

bringest me into j. with. Job 14:3
will he enter with thee into j.? 22:4
that he should enter into j. 34:23
enter not into j. with. Ps 143:2
God will bring thee into j. Eccl 11:9
bring every work into j. 12:14
Lord will enter into j. Isa 3:14

my judgement

taken away my j. Job 27:2*; 34:5*
my j. was as a robe. 29:14*
wilt thou also disannul my j.? 40:8
up thyself, awake to my j. Ps 35:23
my j. is passed over from. Isa 40:27
yet surely my j. is with Lord. 49:4
I will make my j. to rest for a. 51:4
heathen shall see my j. Ezek 39:21
and my j. is just. John 5:30
my j. is true. 8:16
yet I give my j. 1 Cor 7:25
happier in my j. 40

judgement hall

Jesus to the hall of j. . . . went not into the j. hall. John 18:28*
Pilate entered into the j. hall. 33*
into the j. hall, and saith. 19:9*
kept in Herod's j. hall. Acts 23:35*

judgements

I will redeem you with great j. Ex 6:6; 7:4
these are the j. thou shalt set. 21:1
told the people all the j. 24:3
gods the Lord executed j. Num 33:4
judge according to these j. 35:24
are the j. which the Lord. 36:13
if ye hearken to these j. Deut 7:12
they shall teach Jacob thy j. 33:10
he executed the j. of the Lord. 21
his j. were before me. 2 Sam 22:23
Ps 18:22
remember j. of his mouth. 1 Chr 16:12; Ps 105:5
his j. are in all the earth. 1 Chr 16:14; Ps 105:7
but sinned against thy j. Neh 9:29
thy j. are far above out. Ps 10:5
the j. of the Lord are true. 19:9
thy j. are a great deep. 36:6
be glad because of thy j. 48:11

give the king thy *j.* O God. *Ps* 72:1
Judah rejoiced, because of thy *j.* 97:8
learned thy righteous *j.* 119:7
with my lips I declared all *j.* of. 13
longing that it hath unto thy *j.* 20
thy *j.* have I laid before me. 30
away my reproach, for thy *j.* are. 39
I hoped in thy *j.* 43
I remembered thy *j.* 52
because of thy righteous *j.* 62, 164
I know, O Lord, that thy *j.* are. 75
I have not departed from thy *j.* 102
I will keep thy righteous *j.* 106
teach me thy *j.* 108
I am afraid of thy *j.* 120
art thou, and upright are thy *j.* 137
quicken me according to thy *j.* 156
every one of thy righteous *j.* 160
let my soul live, and let thy *j.* 175
his *j.* they have not known. 147:20
j. are prepared for. *Pr* 19:29
way of thy *j.* we waited. *Isa* 26:8
for when thy *j.* are in the earth. 9
me talk with thee of thy *j.* *Jer* 12:1*
nor done according to *j.* *Ezek* 5:7*
j. in midst of thee. 8; 10:15; 11:9
execute *j.* on thee in sight. 16:41
shall judge thee according to their *j.* 23:24
I will execute *j.* on Moab. 25:11
executed *j.* on all those that. 28:26
I will execute *j.* in No. 30:14
thus will I execute *j.* in Egypt. 19
I will feed them with *j.* 34:16
by departing from thy *j.* *Dan* 9:5
thy *j.* are as the light that. *Hos* 6:5
hath taken away thy *j.* *Zeph* 3:15
unsearchable are his *j.* *Rom* 11:33
if ye have *j.* of things. *1 Cor* 6:4
j. are made manifest. *Rev* 15:4*
righteous are thy *j.* 16:7; 19:2

my judgements

ye shall do *my j.* I am. *Lev* 18:4
therefore keep *my j.* 5; 25:18
if your soul abhor *my j.* so. 26:15
because they despised *my j.* 43
constant to do *my j.* *1 Chr* 28:7
children walk not in *my j.* *Ps* 89:30
I will utter *my j.* against. *Jer* 1:16
she changed *my j.* into wickedness. *Ezek* 5:6
neither have kept *my j.* nor. 5:7
when I send *my* four sore *j.* 14:21
and ye shall keep *my j.* 36:27
judge it according to *my j.* 44:24

statutes and judgements

keep my *st. and* my *j.* *Lev* 18:5, 26
20:22; *Deut* 7:11; 11:1; 26:16, 17
30:16; *1 Ki* 2:3; 8:58; 9:4; 11:33
observe all my *st. and j.* *Lev* 19:37
Deut 11:32; 12:1; *2 Chr* 7:17
these are the *st. and j.* Lord made. *Lev* 26:46; *Deut* 4:45
hearken to *st. and j.* *Deut* 4:1; 5:1
I have taught you *st. and j.* 4:5
hath *st. and j.* so righteous as all ? 8
commanded to teach *st. and j.* 14
6:1; *Ezra* 7:10
I will speak the *st. and j.* *Deut* 5:31
thee, What mean the *st. and j.*? 6:20
forget Lord in not keeping his *st. and j.* 8:11; *Neh* 1:7
my *st. and* execute my *j.* *1 Ki* 6:12
heed to fulfil *st. and j.* *1 Chr* 22:13
come between *st. and j.* *2 Chr* 19:10
thou gavest them right *st. and j.* *Neh* 9:13
a curse, to do all his *st. and j.* 10:29
sheweth his *st. and j.* to. *Ps* 147:19
refused my *j. and* my *st.* *Ezek* 5:6
not walked in my *st.* nor executed my *j.* 11:12; 20:13, 16, 21
walked in my *st. and j.* 18:9, 17
20:19; 37:24
my *st. and* shewed my *j.* 20:11
st. of fathers, nor observe their *j.* 18
them *st.* not good, *and j.* 25
of Moses with *st. and j.* *Mal* 4:4

judgement seat

he was set down on *j. seat.* *Mat* 27:19; *John* 19:13
brought him to the *j. seat.* *Acts* 18:12
drave them from the *j. seat.* 16
beat Sosthenes before the *j. seat.* 17
I stand at Cesar's *j. seat.* 25:10
I sat on *j. seat.* 17
we shall all stand before the *j. seat* of Christ. *Rom* 14:10; *2 Cor* 5:10
draw you before *j. seats.* *Jas* 2:6

judges

shall bring him to the *j.* *Ex* 21:6*
and he shall pay as the *j.* 22
shall be brought to the *j.* 22:8*
both shall come before the *j.* 9*
Moses said to the *j.* Slay. *Num* 25:5
I charged your *j.* at that. *Deut* 1:16
j. shalt thou make in all. 16:18
stand before priests and *j.* 19:17
the *j.* shall make diligent. 18
thy elders and thy *j.* shall. 21:2
they come, that the *j.* may. 25:1
enemies themselves being *j.* 32:31
their *j.* stood on this side. *Josh* 8:33
Joshua called for their heads and *j.* 23:2; 24:1
Lord raised up *j.* *Judg* 2:16, 18
would not hearken to their *j.* 17
when the *j.* ruled a famine. *Ruth* 1:1
he made his sons *j.* *1 Sam* 8:1, 2
I commanded *j.* to be. *2 Sam* 7:11
from the days of the *j.* *2 Ki* 23:22
word to any of the *j.* *1 Chr* 17:6, 10
thousand were officers and *j.* 23:4
and his sons were for *j.* 26:29
Solomon spake to the *j.* *2 Chr* 1:2
he set *j.* in the land. 19:5
said to the *j.* 6
set *j.* which may judge. *Ezra* 7:25
and with them the *j.* of every. 10:14
covereth the face of the *j.* *Job* 9:24
and he maketh the *j.* fools. 12:17
iniquity to be punished by *j.* 31:11
be instructed, ye *j.* of the. *Ps* 2:10
when *j.* are overthrown in. 141:6
princes, and all *j.* of the earth. 148:11
princes rule, and all *j.* of. *Pr* 8:16
I will restore thy *j.* as at. *Isa* 1:26
he maketh the *j.* of the earth. 40:23
sent to gather the *j.* *Dan* 3:2, 3
his words against our *j.* that. 9:12
they have devoured their *j.* *Hos* 7:7
where are thy *j.* of whom ? 13:10
her *j.* are evening wolves. *Zeph* 3:3
they shall be your *j.* *Mat* 12:27
Luke 11:19
that he gave to them *j.* *Acts* 13:20
and are become *j.* of evil. *Jas* 2:4

judgest

be clear when thou *j.* *Ps* 51:4
Lord of hosts, that *j.* *Jer* 11:20
whosoever thou art that *j.* *Rom* 2:1
O man, that *j.* them which do. 3
that *j.* another man's servant ? 14:4
who art thou that *j.*? *Jas* 4:12

judgeth

seeing he *j.* those that. *Job* 21:22
for by them *j.* he the people. 36:31
God *j.* the righteous, is. *Ps* 7:11
verily he is a God that *j.* in. 58:11
in congregation of mighty, he *j.* 82:1
king that faithfully *j.* *Pr* 29:14
for the Father *j.* no man. *John* 5:22
there is one that *j.* 8:50
one that *j.* him. 12:48
he that is spiritual *j.* all. *1 Cor* 2:15
but he that *j.* me is the Lord. 4:4
that are without, God *j.* 5:13
he that *j.* his brother, *j.* *Jas* 4:11
respect of persons *j.* *1 Pet* 1:17
committed himself to him that *j.* 2:23
strong is the Lord that *j.* *Rev* 18:8

judging

j. the people of the land. *2 Ki* 15:5
2 Chr 26:21
satest in the throne *j.* right. *Ps* 9:4
he shall sit *j.* and seeking. *Isa* 16:5
j. the twelve tribes. *Mat* 19:28
Luke 22:30

juice

to drink wine of the *j.* *S of S* 8:2

jumping

noise of horses and the *j.* *Nah* 3:2†

juniper

and sat under a *j.* tree. *1 Ki* 19:4, 5
who cut up *j.* roots. *Job* 30:4*
the mighty with coals of *j.* *Ps* 120:4

Jupiter

called Barnabas, *J.* *Acts* 14:12
then the priests of *J.* brought. 13
image which fell down from *J.* 19:35

jurisdiction

he belonged to Herod's *j.* *Luke* 23:7

just

[1] *One who is righteous before God,* Gen 6:9. [2] *Exact, accurate,* Lev 19:36. [3] *Honest, upright,* Luke 23:50. *The word is in most places replaced in the Revisions by the word* righteous.

Noah was a *j.* man. *Gen* 6:9
j. balances, *j.* weights, a *j.* ephah, and a *j.* hin shall ye have. *Lev* 19:36; *Deut* 25:15; *Ezek* 45:10
judge people with *j.* *Deut* 16:18
that is altogether *j.* shalt thou. 20
a God without iniquity, *j.* and. 32:4
over men must be *j.* *2 Sam* 23:3
thou art *j.* in all that is. *Neh* 9:33
mortal man be more *j.*? *Job* 4:17
but how should man be *j.* with ? 9:2
j. upright man is laughed to. 12:4
he may prepare it, but the *j.* 27:17
in this thou art not *j.* 33:12
end, but establish the *j.* *Ps* 7:9
wicked plotteth against the *j.* 37:12
the habitation of the *j.* *Pr* 3:33
the path of the *j.* is as the. 4:18
a *j.* man, and he will increase. 9:9
are upon the head of the *j.* 10:6
the memory of the *j.* is blessed. 7
tongue of the *j.* is as choice. 20
the mouth of the *j.* bringeth forth. 31
but *j.* weight is his delight. 11:1
but through knowledge shall the *j.* 9
but the *j.* shall come out of. 12:13
shall no evil happen to the *j.* 21
the sinner is laid up for the *j.* 13:22
a *j.* weight and balance are. 16:11
he that condemneth the *j.* is. 17:15
also to punish the *j.* is not good. 26
in his own cause seemeth *j.* 18:17
j. man walketh in his integrity. 20:7
joy to the *j.* to do judgement. 21:15
a *j.* man falleth seven times. 24:16
hate the upright, but the *j.* 29:10
man is an abomination to the *j.* 27
j. man that perisheth in. *Eccl* 7:15
not a *j.* man upon earth that. 20
there be *j.* men to whom it. 8:14
j. is uprightness, thou most upright dost weigh path of *j.* *Isa* 26:7
turn aside the *j.* for a thing. 29:21
I the Lord, a *j.* God, and a. 45:21
shed the blood of the *j.* *Lam* 4:13
but if a man be *j.* and. *Ezek* 18:5
he is *j.* he shall surely live. 9
ways of Lord right, *j.* *Hos* 14:9
they afflict the *j.* they. *Amos* 5:12
the *j.* shall live by faith. *Hab* 2:4
Rom 1:17; *Gal* 3:11; *Heb* 10:38
j. Lord is in the midst. *Zeph* 3:5
j. and having salvation. *Zech* 9:9
husband, being a *j.* man. *Mat* 1:19
sendeth rain on the *j.* and on. 5:45
the wicked from among the *j.* 13:49
to do with that *j.* man. 27:19
innocent of the blood of this *j.* 24
knowing that he was a *j.* *Mark* 6:20
the wisdom of the *j.* *Luke* 1:17
Simeon was *j.* and devout. 2:25
the resurrection of the *j.* 14:14
over ninety and nine *j.* persons. 15:7
should feign themselves *j.* 20:20
Joseph was a good man and *j.* 23:50
and my judgement is *j.* *John* 5:30
the centurion a *j.* man. *Acts* 10:22
shall be resurrection both of *j.* 24:15
hearers of the law are *j.* *Rom* 2:13
whose damnation is *j.* 3:8
he might be *j.* 26
the commandment holy, *j.* 7:12
whatsoever things are *j.* *Phil* 4:8
give servants that which is *j.* *Col* 4:1

a bishop must be *j.*, holy. *Tit* 1:8
received a *j.* recompence. *Heb* 2:2
spirits of *j.* men made perfect. 12:23
condemned and killed the *j. Jas* 5:6
Christ suffered, the *j.* *1 Pet* 3:18
delivered *j.* Lot, vexed. *2 Pet* 2:7
if we confess, he is *j.* to. *1 John* 1:9
j. and true are thy ways. *Rev* 15:3

most **just**

condemn him that is *most j.*?
Job 34:17

Just *One*

Holy One and the *J.* *Acts* 3:14
of the coming of the *J. One.* 7:52
his will, and see that *J. One.* 22:14

justice

(*Uprightness, just treatment. The Revisions often change this word to* righteousness)
keep way of Lord to do *j. Gen* 18:19
he executeth *j.* of Lord. *Deut* 33:21
David executed *j.* *2 Sam* 8:15
1 Chr 18:14
judge, I would do *j.* *2 Sam* 15:4
Almighty pervert *j.*? *Job* 8:3
judgement and *j.* take hold. 36:17
is excellent in plenty of *j.* 37:23
do *j.* to the afflicted and. *Ps* 82:3
j. and judgement are habitation.
89:14
have done judgement and *j.* 119:121
receive the instruction of *j.* *Pr* 1:3
reign, and princes decree *j.* 8:15
seest the perverting of *j.* *Eccl* 5:8
establish his throne with *j.* *Isa* 9:7
keep ye judgement, and do *j.* 56:1
ask of me the ordinances of *j.* 58:2
none calleth for *j.* 59:4
neither doth *j.* overtake us. 9
j. standeth afar off, truth is. 14
execute judgement and *j.* in earth.
Jer 23:5
bless thee, O habitation of *j.* 31:23
the Lord, the habitation of *j.* 50:7
princes, execute judgement and *j.*
Ezek 45:9

see do **judgement,** before

justification

raised again for our *j.* *Rom* 4:25
gift is of many offences to *j.* 5:16
free gift came upon all men to *j.* 18

see **sanctify**

justified

a man full of talk be *j.*? *Job* 11:2
I know that I shall be *j.* 13:18
then can man be *j.* with God? 25:4
because he *j.* himself rather. 32:2
thou mightest be *j.* when. *Ps* 51:4
sight shall no man living be *j.* 143:2
they may be *j.* *Isa* 43:9
thou mayest be *j.* 26
all the seed of Israel be *j.* 45:25
backsliding Israel hath *j.* *Jer* 3:11
j. thy sisters in all. *Ezek* 16:51, 52
wisdom is *j.* of her children.
Mat 11:19; *Luke* 7:35
thy words thou shalt be *j. Mat* 12:37
and publicans *j.* God. *Luke* 7:29
this man went down *j.* rather. 18:14
are *j.* from all things from which ye could not be *j.* by. *Acts* 13:39
doers of the law shall be *j. Rom* 2:13
mightest be *j.* in thy sayings. 3:4
shall no flesh be *j.* in his sight. 20
j. freely by his grace. 24; *Tit* 3:7
a man is *j.* by faith. *Rom* 3:28; 5:1
Gal 2:16; 3:24
if Abraham were *j.* by. *Rom* 4:2
being *j.* by faith we have peace. 5:1
being now *j.* by his blood, we. 9
he *j.* them he also glorified. 8:30
yet am I not hereby *j.* *1 Cor* 4:4
ye are *j.* in the name of Lord. 6:11
a man is not *j.* by the works of the law. *Gal* 2:16; 3:11
whosoever of you is *j.* by law. 5:4
God manifest in the flesh, *j.* in the spirit. *1 Tim* 3:16
our father *j.* by works? *Jas* 2:21
that by works a man is *j.* 24
was not Rahab the harlot *j.* by? 25

justifier

j. of him who believeth. *Rom* 3:26

justifieth

he that *j.* the wicked is. *Pr* 17:15
he is near that *j.* me. *Isa* 50:8
believeth on him that *j.* *Rom* 4:5
of God's elect? it is God that *j.* 8:33

justify

(*To show to be just or righteous; to vindicate*)
I will not *j.* the wicked. *Ex* 23:7
then they shall *j.* the. *Deut* 25:1
if I *j.* myself, my own. *Job* 9:20
God forbid that I should *j.* 27:5
speak, for I desire to *j.* thee. 33:32
which *j.* the wicked for. *Isa* 5:23
my righteous servant *j.* many. 53:11
he willing to *j.* himself. *Luke* 10:29
are they which *j.* yourselves. 16:15
God shall *j.* circumcision. *Rom* 3:30
foreseeing that God would *j. Gal* 3:8

justifying

and *j.* the righteous. *1 Ki* 8:32
2 Chr 6:23

justle

the chariots shall *j.* one. *Nah* 2:4†

justly

Lord require but to do *j.*? *Mi* 6:8
indeed *j.* for we receive. *Luke* 23:41
how holily and *j.* we. *1 Thes* 2:10

Justus

Joseph, who was surnamed *J.* and.
Acts 1:23
certain man's house, named *J.* 18:7
Jesus, who is called *J.* *Col* 4:11

K

Kadesh

Enmishpat, which is *K.* *Gen* 14:7
to wilderness of Paran to *K.*
Num 13:26
behold, we are in *K.* a city. 20:16
me at water of Meribah in *K.* 27:14
Deut 32:51; *Ezek* 47:19; 48:28
of Zin, which is *K.* *Num* 33:36
abode in *K.* many days. *Deut* 1:46
shaketh the wilderness of *K. Ps* 29:8

Kadesh-barnea

I sent them from *K.* to see the land.
Num 32:8; *Deut* 9:23; *Josh* 14:7
them from *K.* to Gaza. *Josh* 10:41
concerning me and thee in *K.* 14:6

Kareah, *see* **Johanan**

Kedar

the son of Ishmael, *K.* *Gen* 25:13
1 Chr 1:29
I dwell in the tents of *K.* *Ps* 120:5
comely as the tents of *K. S of S* 1:5
glory of *K.* shall fail. *Isa* 21:16, 17
the villages that *K.* doth. 42:11
the flocks of *K.* shall be. 60:7
send to *K.* and consider. *Jer* 2:10
K., thus saith the Lord; Arise ye, go up to *K.* 49:28
princes of *K.* occupied. *Ezek* 27:21

keep

[1] *To retain or hold fast,* 2 Tim 1:14. [2] *To defend and protect,* Ps 127:1. [3] *To observe and practise,* Ps 119:4; Acts 16:4. [4] *To celebrate,* Mat 26:18. [5] *To perform as a duty; observe,* Mat 19:17.
the garden of Eden to *k.* *Gen* 2:15
and they shall *k.* the way of. 18:19
I am with thee, to *k.* thee. 28:15, 20
I will again feed and *k.* thy. 30:31
my brother, *k.* that thou hast. 33:9
and let them *k.* food in the. 41:35
whom the Egyptians *k.* *Ex* 6:5
shall *k.* it till the fourteenth. 12:6
k. it a feast to the Lord through.
14; 23:15; 34:18; *Lev* 23:41
that ye shall *k.* this service.
Ex 12:25; 13:5
of Israel shall *k.* it. 12:47
thou shalt *k.* this ordinance in. 13:10
sabbath day to *k.* it holy. 20:8
31:13, 14, 16; *Deut* 5:12, 15
money or stuff to *k.* *Ex* 22:7, 10
k. thee far from a false matter. 23:7
three times shalt thou *k.* a feast. 14
I send an Angel to *k.* thee in. 20
that delivered him to *k.* *Lev* 6:2, 4
ye shall *k.* my ordinances, I am the Lord. 18:4, 30; 22:9; *Ezek* 11:20
shall *k.* my sabbaths. *Lev* 19:3, 30
26:2; *Isa* 56:4
shall *k.* a feast seven days.
Lev 23:39; *2 Chr* 30:13
ye shall *k.* my judgements and do.
Lev 25:18
Lord bless thee and *k.* *Num* 6:24
14th day at even ye shall *k.* it. 9:3
month at even they shall *k.* it. 11
thy sons shall *k.* your priests'. 18:7
ye shall *k.* a feast to the. 29:12
k. himself to inheritance. 36:7*, 9*
k. therefore and do them. *Deut* 4:6
5:1*
loved you, would *k.* the oath. 7:8
if ye *k.* them, the Lord shall *k.* 12
k. the feast of weeks to the. 16:10
shalt *k.* a solemn feast to Lord. 15
may learn to *k.* all the words. 17:19
k. thee from every wicked. 23:9
gone out of thy lips thou shalt *k.* 23*
k. therefore the words of this. 29:9
k. yourselves from the. *Josh* 6:18
set men by the cave, for to *k.* 10:18
to *k.* all that is written in the. 23:6
whether they will *k.* the. *Judg* 2:22
thou shalt *k.* fast by my. *Ruth* 2:21
he will *k.* the feet of his. *1 Sam* 2:9
Eleazar his son, to *k.* the ark. 7:1
women which were concubines to *k.*
2 Sam 15:16; 16:21; 20:3
no son to *k.* my name. 18:18
k. with thy servant David.
1 Ki 8:25; *2 Chr* 6:16
man to me and said, *K.* *1 Ki* 20:39
that thou wouldest *k.* me. *1 Chr* 4:10
which could *k.* rank. 12:33*, 38*
that thou mayest *k.* the law. 22:12
k. this for ever in imagination. 29:18
had no power to *k.* still the kingdom.
2 Chr 22:9*
ye purpose to *k.* under the. 28:10
for they could not *k.* it at. 30:3
assembly took counsel to *k.* other. 23
watch and *k.* them till. *Ezra* 8:29
to *k.* the dedication with. *Neh* 12:27
that the Levites should *k.* 13:22
nor *k.* they the king's. *Esth* 3:8
that they would *k.* those two. 9:27
that thou wouldest *k.* me. *Job* 14:13
though he *k.* it still within. 20:13
k. them, O Lord. *Ps* 12:7; 31:20
k. me as the apple of the eye. 17:8
k. back thy servant also from presumptuous sins. 19:13
O *k.* my soul, and deliver me. 25:20
k. thy tongue from evil, and. 34:13
and *k.* his way. 37:34
I will *k.* my mouth. 39:1
my mercy will I *k.* for him. 89:28
his angels charge, to *k.* thee. 91:11
nor chide, nor will he *k.* his. 103:9
observe and *k.* his laws. 105:45
blessed are they that *k.* judgement.
106:3
barren woman to *k.* house. 113:9
blessed are they that *k.* his. 119:2
thou hast commanded us to *k.* 4
may live and *k.* thy word. 17, 101
teach me, and I shall *k.* it to. 33
I shall *k.* thy law. 34, 44
I have said, that I would *k.* 57
I am a companion of them that *k.* 63
I will *k.* thy precepts with. 69, 134
so shall I *k.* the testimony of thy. 88
I understand, because I *k.* thy. 100
k. thy righteous judgements. 106
therefore doth my soul *k.* them. 129
down my eyes, because they *k.* 136
save me, and I shall *k.* thy. 146
except the Lord *k.* the city. 127:1
k. me from the hands of the. 140:4
k. the door of my lips. 141:3
k. me from the snares they have. 9
understanding shall *k.* thee. *Pr* 2:11
thou mayest *k.* the paths of the. 20
my son, *k.* sound wisdom and. 3:21

Lord shall k. thy foot from. Pr 3:26
love wisdom, and she shall k. 4:6
k. instruction, let her not go, for. 13
k. my sayings in the midst of. 21
k. thy heart with all diligence. 23
and that thy lips may k. 5:2
when thou sleepest it shall k. 6:22
to k. thee from the evil woman. 24
my son, k. my words, and lay. 7:1
may k. thee from the strange. 5
for blessed are they that k. 8:32
he that doth k. his soul shall. 22:5
it is pleasant if thou k. them. 18
such as k. the law contend. 28:4
there is a time to k. and. Eccl 3:6
k. thy foot when thou goest to. 5:1
k. the fruit thereof, two. S of S 8:12
wilt k. him in perfect. Isa 26:3
I the Lord do k. it, I will k. it. 27:3
have called thee, I will k. thee. 42:6
k. not back. 43:6
k. ye judgement. 56:1
k. his anger to the end? Jer 3:5
and I will not k. anger for ever. 12
k. him as a shepherd doth. 31:10
I will k. nothing back from. 42:4
k. my judgements and do them.
Ezek 20:19; 36:27
that they may k. the whole. 43:11
k. mercy and judgement. Hos 12:6
k. the doors of thy mouth. Mi 7:5
k. thy feasts. Nah 1:15
k. the munition. 2:1
shalt also k. my courts. Zech 3:7
man taught me to k. cattle. 13:5*
k. the feast of tabernacles. 14:16
18, 19
the priests' lips should k. Mal 2:7
k. your own tradition. Mark 7:9
his angels charge to k. Luke 4:10
having heard the word k. it. 8:15
that hear the word and k. it. 11:28
thy enemies shall k. thee in. 19:43
if k. my saying shall. John 8:51, 52
but I know him, and k. his. 55
his life in this world shall k. 12:25
if a man love me he will k. 14:23
my saying, they will k. yours. 15:20
k. through thy name. 17:11
k. from the evil. 15
and to k. back part of the. Acts 5:3
for a man that is a Jew to k. 10:28
him to soldiers to k. him. 12:4
command them to k. the law. 15:5
ye must be circumcised, and k. 24
from which, if ye k. yourselves. 29
them the decrees for to k. 16:4
charging the jailer to k. them. 23
I must by all means k. this. 18:21
k. themselves from things. 21:25
a centurion to k. Paul. 24:23*
if thou k. the law. Rom 2:25
k. the righteousness of law. 26
let us k. the feast. 1 Cor 5:8
not k. company. 11
decreed that he will k. his. 7:37
I k. under my body and bring. 9:27*
that ye k. the ordinances, as. 11:2
if ye k. in memory what I. 15:2*
and so will I k. myself. 2 Cor 11:9
neither do circumcised k. Gal 6:13
endeavouring to k. unity. Eph 4:3
peace of God shall k. Phil 4:7
who shall stablish and k. 2 Thes 3:3
nor partaker of sins, k. 1 Tim 5:22
k. that which is committed to. 6:20
able to k. that which I have committed unto him. 2 Tim 1:12
good thing committed to thee k. 14
and to k. himself unspotted. Jas 1:27
whosoever shall k. whole law. 2:10
k. yourselves from idols. 1 John 5:21
k. yourselves in the love. Jude 21
to him that is able to k. you. 24
blessed are they that hear and k.
Rev 1:3
I will k. thee from the hour of. 3:10
of them who k. the sayings of. 22:9

keep *alive*

ark to k. them alive. Gen 6:19, 20
to k. seed alive on the face of. 7:3
women, children k. alive. Num 31:18
full line to k. alive. 2 Sam 8:2
none can k. alive his own soul.
Ps 22:29
deliver and k. them alive in. 33:19
preserve him and k. him alive. 41:2

keep *charge*

and k. the charge of the Lord.
Lev 8:35; 1 Ki 2:3
k. charge of tabernacle. Num 1:53
18:4; 31:30; 1 Chr 23:32
they shall k. his charge. Num 3:7
8:26; 18:3; Deut 11:1
k. the charge of children of Israel.
Num 3:8
k. charge of the sanctuary. 32
18:5; 1 Chr 23:32
to me, and k. my charge. Ezek 44:16
if thou wilt k. my charge. Zech 3:7

keep *commandments*

refuse ye to k. my com.? Ex 16:28
to them that k. my com. 20:6
Deut 5:10; 7:9; Dan 9:4
ye k. my com. and do them.
Lev 22:31; Deut 4:40; 6:17; 7:11
if ye k. my com. Lev 26:3
Deut 11:22; 19:9; 28:9; 30:10
1 Ki 3:14
may k. the com. of Lord. Deut 4:2
would fear me and k. my com. 5:29
thou wouldest k. his com. 8:2
thou shalt k. the com. 6; 11:1, 8
13:4, 18
to k. the com. of the Lord. 10:13
27:1; 30:16
avouched Lord to k. his com. 26:17
thee, that thou shouldest k. com. 18
hearkenedst not to k. his com. 28:45
to k. his com. to cleave. Josh 22:5
charge of Lord to k. his com. 1 Ki 2:3
k. my com. 6:12; 2 Ki 17:13
Pr 4:4; 7:2
incline our hearts to k. his com.
1 Ki 8:58
be perfect to k. his com. 61
if ye will not k. my com. I will. 9:6
if thou wilt k. my com. 11:38
Neh 1:9; John 15:10
made a covenant to k. com.
2 Ki 23:3; 2 Chr 34:31
k. and seek for all the com. of the.
1 Chr 28:8
a perfect heart to k. thy com. 29:19
of God, but k. his com. Ps 78:7
delayed not to k. thy com. 119:60
for I will k. com. of my God. 115
let thy heart k. my com. Pr 3:1
my son, k. thy father's com. 6:20
to k. the king's com. Eccl 8:2
fear God and k. his com. this. 12:13
enter into life, k. the com. Mat 19:17
love me, k. my com. John 14:15
k. this com. without spot. 1 Tim 6:14
we do know that we know him if we k. his com. 1 John 2:3
receive, because we k. his com. 3:22
love God and k. his com. 5:2
love of God, that we k. his com. 3
her seed which k. com. Rev 12:17
are they which k. the com. 14:12
see **covenant**

keep *passover*

k. pass. to Lord . . . be circumcised, then let him k. pass. Ex 12:48
of Israel k. pass. in its season.
Num 9:2, 4; Deut 16:1
2 Ki 23:21
could not k. the pass. Num 9:6
yet he shall k. pass. 10
ordinances of pass. they shall k. 12
and forbeareth to k. the pass. 13
if a stranger will k. the pass. to. 14
come to k. the pass. to. 2 Chr 30:1
taken counsel, to k. pass. in the. 2
was prepared to k. pass. 35:16
kings of Israel k. such a pass. 18
say to him, I will k. pass. Mat 26:18

keep *silence*

who said, K. silence, and. Judg 3:19
k. not silence. Ps 35:22; 83:1
come and not k. silence. 50:3
a time to k. silence and. Eccl 3:7
k. silence before me, O. Isa 41:1
k. not silence. 62:6
behold, I will not k. silence. Isa 65:6
elders of daughter of Zion k. silence.
Lam 2:10
prudent shall k. silence. Amos 5:13
let the earth k. silence. Hab 2:20
let him k. silence in the. 1 Cor 14:28
let your women k. silence in the. 34

keep *statutes*

if thou wilt k. all his stat. Ex 15:26
Deut 30:10; 1 Ki 9:4; 11:38
k. my stat. and judgements.
Lev 18:5, 26; 19:19; 20:8, 22
Ezek 44:24
thou shalt k. therefore his stat.
Deut 4:10; 26:16
fear Lord to k. his stat. 6:2
avouched Lord to k. his stat. 26:17
hearkenedst not to k. his stat. 28:45
in my ways to k. my stat. 1 Ki 11:33
were directed to k. thy stat. Ps 119:5
I will k. thy stat., forsake. 8, 145
will turn and k. my stat. Ezek 18:21

keeper

Abel was a k. of sheep. Gen 4:2
am I my brother's k.? 9
Joseph favour in sight of k. 39:21
the k. of the prison committed. 22
the k. of the prison looked not to. 23
left sheep with a k. 1 Sam 17:20
carriage in the hand of the k. 22
I will make thee k. of mine. 28:2
k. of the wardrobe. 2 Ki 22:14
2 Chr 34:22
Asaph the k. of the king's. Neh 2:8
after him Shemaiah k. of the. 3:29
Hege k. of women. Esth 2:3, 8, 15
and as a booth that the k. Job 27:18
Lord is thy k., the Lord. Ps 121:5
they made me the k. of. S of S 1:6
the son of Shallum k. of Jer 35:4
k. of prison awaking. Acts 16:27*
the k. of the prison told this. 36*

keepers

a third part shall be k. 2 Ki 11:5
k. of the gates of the. 1 Chr 9:19
when the k. of the house. Eccl 12:3
k. took away my vail. S of S 5:7
let out the vineyard to k. 8:11
as k. of the field are. Jer 4:17
k. of charge of house. Ezek 40:45
46; 44:8, 14
for fear of him the k. Mat 28:4
k. standing before doors. Acts 5:23
k. kept the prison. 12:6*
Herod examined the k. 19*
discreet, chaste, k. at home. Tit 2:5*
see **door**

keepest

who k. covenant and. 1 Ki 8:23
2 Chr 6:14; Neh 9:32
orderly and k. the law. Acts 21:24

keepeth

and he die not, but k. Ex 21:18
faithful God which k. covenant.
Deut 7:9; Neh 1:5
behold he k. the sheep. 1 Sam 16:11
he k. back his soul from. Job 33:18
he k. all his bones, none. Ps 34:20
he that k. thee will not. 121:3, 4
Lord God, which k. truth. 146:6
he k. the paths of. Pr 2:8
is in the way of life that k. 10:17*
he that k. his mouth k. 13:3; 21:23
righteousness k. him upright in. 13:6
k. his way preserveth. 16:17; 19:16
he that k. understanding. 19:8
that k. thy soul, doth not he. 24:12
whoso k. the fig tree shall. 27:18
whoso k. the law is a wise. 28:7
that k. company with harlots. 29:3
but a wise man k. it in till. 11
but he that k. the law, happy. 18
k. the commandments. Eccl 8:5
nation which k. truth. Isa 26:2
k. the sabbath from polluting it, and k. his hand from doing. 56:2, 6
that k. back his sword. Jer 48:10
he sitteth alone and k. Lam 3:28
man, neither k. at home. Hab 2:5
a strong man armed k. Luke 11:21
yet none of you k. the. John 7:19
is not of God, because he k. 9:16

that hath my commandments and *k.* them. *John* 14:21
he that loveth me not, *k.* not. 24
I know him, and *k.* not. *1 John* 2:4
whoso *k.* his word, in him. 5; 3:24
he that is begotten of God *k.* 5:18
that overcometh and *k.* *Rev* 2:26
blessed is he that *k.* his. 16:15
blessed is he that *k.* sayings. 22:7

keeping

Lord God *k.* mercy for. *Ex* 34:7
k. the charge of the. *Num* 3:28, 38
forget not God, in not *k.* *Deut* 8:11
with them *k.* sheep. *1 Sam* 25:16
were porters *k.* the ward. *Neh* 12:25
and in *k.* of them is great. *Ps* 19:11
by *k.* of his covenant. *Ezek* 17:14
O Lord the great God, *k.* *Dan* 9:4
there were shepherds *k.* *Luke* 2:8
k. the commandments. *1 Cor* 7:19
commit the *k.* of their. *1 Pet* 4:19

Keilah

K. and Achzib, cities. *Josh* 15:44
Philistines fight against *K.* *1 Sam* 23:1
arise, go down to *K.* 4
David saved *K.* 5
son of Ahimelech fled to *K.* 6
K. deliver me to Saul ? 11, 12
part of *K.* repaired. *Neh* 3:17, 18

Kenaz, *see* **Othniel** (*Gen* 36:11. 15, 42; *1 Chr* 1:36, 53; 4:15)

Kenites

seed have I given the *K.* *Gen* 15:19
Balaam looked on the *K.* *Num* 24:21
Saul said to the *K.* *1 Sam* 15:6
road against south of the *K.* 27:10

kept

Abraham *k.* my charge. *Gen* 26:5
with sheep, for she *k.* them. 29:9
nor hath he *k.* back any thing. 39:9
send one, and ye shall be *k.* 42:16
now Moses *k.* the flock. *Ex* 3:1
lay up for you to be *k.* until. 16:23
pot of manna *k.* for. 32, 33, 34
the owner hath not *k.* 21:29, 36
and it be *k.* close, and. *Num* 5:13
they *k.* the passover. 9:5
why are we *k.* back ? 7
then Israel *k.* the charge. 19, 23
bring Aaron's rod to be *k.* 17:10
k. for a water of separation. 19:9
Lord hath *k.* thee back. 24:11
which *k.* the charge of the. 31:47
k. them as the apple. *Deut* 32:10
they observed thy word, and *k.* 33:9
Israel *k.* the passover. *Josh* 5:10
k. me alive these 45 years. 14:10
ye have *k.* all that Moses. 22:2
ye have *k.* the charge of. 3
k. fast by the maidens. *Ruth* 2:23
time it hath been *k.* *1 Sam* 9:24
not *k.* the commandment. 13:13, 14
David said, Thy servant *k.* his. 17:34
k. themselves from women. 21:4
surely in vain have I *k.* all. 25:21
blessed be thou who hast *k.* me. 33
the Lord God hath *k.* me. 34, 39
why hast thou not *k.* thy ? 26:15
because ye have not *k.* your. 16
the young man that *k.* *2 Sam* 13:34
I have *k.* the ways of the Lord. 22:22
Ps 18:21
I have *k.* myself from iniquity. *2 Sam* 22:24; *Ps* 18:23
hast *k.* me to be head of the heathen. *2 Sam* 22:44
not *k.* the oath of Lord ? *1 Ki* 2:43
thou hast *k.* for him this great. 3:6
k. with thy servant David my father. 8:24; *2 Chr* 6:15
Solomon *k.* not that the Lord. *1 Ki* 11:10
thou hast not *k.* my covenant and. 11
because David *k.* my commandments. 34; 14:8
man of God from Judah not *k.* 13:21
Judah *k.* not the. *2 Ki* 17:19
Hezekiah *k.* commandments. 18:6
the word of the Lord Saul *k.* not. *1 Chr* 10:13
while David *k.* himself close. 12:1
Solomon *k.* the feast. *2 Chr* 7:8
k. the dedication of altar. 9
k. feast of unleavened bread. 30:21; *Ezra* 6:22
and they *k.* other seven days. *2 Chr* 30:23
our fathers have not *k.* the. 34:21
Josiah and Israel *k.* the passover. 35:1, 17, 19
was no passover like to that *k.* 18
they *k.* also the feast of. *Ezra* 3:4
k. the dedication of this house. 6:16
children of the captivity *k.* the. 19
we have not *k.* the commandments. *Neh* 1:7
they *k.* the feast seven days. 8:18
nor our fathers *k.* thy law. 9:34
days of Purim be *k.* *Esth* 9:28
ways have I *k.* and not. *Job* 23:11
k. close from the fowls of air. 28:21
I have *k.* me from paths. *Ps* 17:4
hast *k.* me alive. 30:3
a multitude that *k.* holy day. 42:4
they *k.* not the covenant of. 78:10
they tempted God, and *k.* not. 56
they *k.* his testimonies and. 99:7
have *k.* thy testimonies. 119:22, 167
I have *k.* thy law. 55
because I *k.* thy precepts. 56, 168
now have I *k.* thy word. 67
they *k.* not thy word. 158
eyes desired, I *k.* not. *Eccl* 2:10
riches *k.* for owners thereof. 5:13
vineyard have I not *k.* *S of S* 1:6
a holy solemnity is *k.* *Isa* 30:29
not *k.* my laws. *Jer* 16:11
and *k.* his precepts. 35:18
neither have *k.* my judgements. *Ezek* 5:7; 20:21
hath *k.* my judgements. 18:9
hath *k.* my statutes. 19
ye have not *k.* the charge of. 44:8
that *k.* the charge of my. 15; 48:11
would, he *k.* alive, he set. *Dan* 5:19
I *k.* the matter in my heart. 7:28
for a wife, and *k.* sheep. *Hos* 12:12
and Edom *k.* his wrath. *Amos* 1:11
Judah hath not *k.* his. 2:4
statutes of Omri are *k.* *Mi* 6:16
as ye have not *k.* my ways. *Mal* 2:9; 3:7
what profit is it that we have *k.*? 3:14
they that *k.* the swine. *Mat* 8:33
which have been *k.* secret. 13:35
Herod's birthday was *k.* 14:6
these have I *k.* from my youth. 19:20; *Luke* 18:21
nor was any thing *k.* secret, but. *Mark* 4:22
and they *k.* that saying. 9:10
Luke 9:36
Mary *k.* these things. *Luke* 2:19, 51
he was *k.* bound with chains. 8:29
thy pound, which I have *k.* 19:20
but thou hast *k.* good. *John* 2:10
of my burying hath she *k.* this. 12:7
as I have *k.* my father's. 15:10
if they have *k.* my saying. 20
thine they were, and have *k.* 17:6
k. in thy name, those thou gavest me I have *k.* 12
and spake to her that *k.* the. 18:16
saith the damsel that *k.* the door. 17
sold, and *k.* back part of. *Acts* 5:2
law, and have not *k.* it. 7:53
Eneas had *k.* his bed eight. 9:33
Peter was *k.* in prison. 12:5
keepers *k.* the prison. 6
I *k.* back nothing profitable. 20:20
and *k.* the raiment of them. 22:20
and he commanded him to be *k.* 23:35; 25:21
that Paul should be *k.* 25:4
the centurion *k.* them from. 27:43
with a soldier that *k.* him. 28:16
mystery *k.* secret since. *Rom* 16:25
I *k.* myself from being. *2 Cor* 11:9
the governor *k.* the city with. 32
we were *k.* under law. *Gal* 3:23
my course, I *k.* the faith. *2 Tim* 4:7
through faith Moses *k.* *Heb* 11:28
the hire that is *k.* back. *Jas* 5:4
who are *k.* by the power. *1 Pet* 1:5
by the same word are *k.* *2 Pet* 3:7
angels which *k.* not their. *Jude* 6
hast *k.* my word, and not. *Rev* 3:8
because thou hast *k.* the word. 10

kept *silence*

men gave ear, and *k. sil.* *Job* 29:21
great multitude, that I *k. sil.* 31:34
when I *k. sil.* my bones. *Ps* 32:3
hast thou done, and I *k. sil.* 50:21
the multitude *k. sil.* *Acts* 15:12
Hebrew, they *k.* the more *sil.* 22:2

kerchiefs

k. on head of every. *Ezek* 13:18
your *k.* will I tear, and deliver. 21

Kerioth

judgement is come on *K.* *Jer* 48:24
K. is taken. 41
devour the palaces of *K.* *Amos* 2:2

kernels

eat nothing from the *k.* *Num* 6:4

kettle

servant struck into the *k.* *1 Sam* 2:14

Keturah

wife, her name was *K.* *Gen* 25:1
children of *K.* 4; *1 Chr* 1:32, 33

key

therefore they took a *k.* *Judg* 3:25
k. of house of David lay. *Isa* 22:22
have taken away the *k.* *Luke* 11:52
saith he that hath the *k.* *Rev* 3:7
given *k.* of bottomless pit. 9:1; 20:1

keys

give the *k.* of kingdom. *Mat* 16:19
k. of hell and of death. *Rev* 1:18

kick

wherefore *k.* ye at my ? *1 Sam* 2:29
it is hard to *k.* against the pricks. *Acts* 9:5; 26:14

kicked

but Jeshurun waxed fat and *k.* *Deut* 32:15

kid

(*Kid of the goats is frequently changed in Revisions to* he goat)

brethren killed a *k.* of. *Gen* 37:31
I will send thee a *k.* from. 38:17
not seethe the *k.* in his mother's milk. *Ex* 23:19; 34:26; *Deut* 14:21
bring his offering, a *k.* of the goats. *Lev* 4:23, 28; 9:3; *Ezek* 43:22
45:23
or a *k.* for a sin offering. *Lev* 5:6
then ye shall sacrifice one *k.* 23:19
Num 7:16, 22, 28; 15:24; 28:15
30; 29:5, 11, 16, 19, 25
done for a lamb or a *k.* *Num* 15:11
and made ready a *k.* *Judg* 6:19
so Manoah took a *k.* with a. 13:19
Samson rent lion as a *k.* 14:6
visited his wife with a *k.* 15:1
an ass laden, and a *k.* *1 Sam* 16:20
lie down with the *k.* *Isa* 11:6
never gavest me a *k.* *Luke* 15:29

kidneys

thou shalt take the two *k.* and burn. *Ex* 29:13, 22; *Lev* 3:4, 10, 15; 4:9
7:4; 8:16, 25
but fat and *k.* burnt on. *Lev* 9:10, 19
rams, with the fat of *k.* *Deut* 32:14
the sword of Lord, with fat of *k.* of rams. *Isa* 34:6

Kidron, *see* **brook**

kids

fetch me from thence two *k.* *Gen* 27:9
she put the skins of the *k.* on. 16
take two *k.* of the goats. *Lev* 16:5
the *k.* of the goats for. *Num* 7:87
one carrying three *k.* *1 Sam* 10:3
two little flocks of *k.* *1 Ki* 20:27
Josiah gave lambs and *k.* *2 Chr* 35:7
feed thy *k.* beside the. *S of S* 1:8

kill

Cain, should *k.* him. *Gen* 4:15
they will *k.* me, but will save. 12:12
men of the place should *k.* me. 26:7
himself, purposing to *k.* thee. 27:42
and said, Let us not *k.* him. 37:21
a son, then ye shall *k.* him. *Ex* 1:16
thou to *k.* me ? 2:14; *Acts* 7:28
him, and sought to *k.* him. *Ex* 4:24

of Israel shall *k.* it. *Ex* 12:6, 21
to *k.* this whole assembly. 16:3
to *k.* us and our children. 17:3
thou shalt not *k.* 20:13*; *Deut* 5:17*
Mat 5:21; *Rom* 13:9
steal an ox or sheep, and *k.* *Ex* 22:1
I will *k.* you with the sword. 24
k. bullock before the Lord. 29:11
Lev 1:5; 4:4
then thou shalt *k.* the ram. *Ex* 29:20
shall *k.* it on the side of the altar.
Lev 1:11; 16:15
and *k.* it at the door of the. 3:2
shall *k.* it before the tabernacle. 8, 13
k. it in the place where they *k.* 4:24
k. the burnt offering. 33; 7:2
k. the sin offering. 14:13; 16:11
he shall *k.* the lamb of the. 14:25
shall *k.* the one of the birds. 50
seed to Molech, and *k.* him not. 20:4
thou shalt *k.* the woman and the. 16
cow or ewe, ye shall not *k.* it. 22:28
thus with me, *k.* me. *Num* 11:15
if thou *k.* all this people as. 14:15
hast brought us to *k.* us in. 16:13
for now would I *k.* thee. 22:29
k. every male among the little ones,
k. every woman that hath. 31:17
revenger of blood *k.* slayer. 35:27
should *k.* his neighbour unawares.
Deut 4:42
thou mayest *k.* and eat flesh. 12:15
then thou shalt *k.* of thy herd. 21
but thou shalt surely *k.* him. 13:9
I *k.* and I make alive, I. 32:39
if Lord were pleased to *k.* *Judg* 13:23
saying, Surely we will not *k.* 15:13
it is day, we shall *k.* him. 16:2
they began to *k.* as at other times.
20:31, 39
hear it, he will *k.* me. *1 Sam* 16:2
if he be able to *k.* me, then. 17:9
that they should *k.* David. 19:1
Saul my father seeketh to *k.* thee. 2
why should I *k.* thee? 17
bade me *k.* thee. 24:10
swear thou wilt neither *k.* me. 30:15
smite Amnon, then *k.* *2 Sam* 13:28
that we may *k.* him, for the life. 14:7
iniquity be in me, let him *k.* me. 32
nor for us shalt thou *k.* any. 21:4
Solomon sought to *k.* *1 Ki* 11:40
and they shall *k.* me, and go. 12:27
am I God, to *k.* and? *2 Ki* 5:7
and if they *k.* us, we shall. 7:4
him that followeth her *k.* 11:15
k. the passover, sanctify. *2 Chr* 35:6
by posts to *k.* all Jews. *Esth* 3:13
a time to *k.* and a time. *Eccl* 3:3
and I will *k.* thy root. *Isa* 14:30
year to year, let them *k.* 29:1*
ye *k.* them that are fed. *Ezek* 34:3
shall *k.* shall be in danger. *Mat* 5:21
fear not them which *k.* the body.
10:28; *Luke* 12:4
and they shall *k.* him. *Mat* 17:23
Mark 9:31; 10:34
come let us *k.* him. *Mat* 21:38
Mark 12:7; *Luke* 20:14
ye shall *k.* and crucify. *Mat* 23:34
deliver you up, and shall *k.* you. 24:9
take Jesus by subtilty and *k.* 26:4
to save life, or to *k.*? *Mark* 3:4
do not *k.* 10:19; *Luke* 18:20
Jas 2:11
for Herod will *k.* thee. *Luke* 13:31
hither the fatted calf and *k.* it. 15:23
and scribes sought how to *k.* 22:2
Jews sought the more to *k.* him.
John 5:18; 7:1
why go ye about to *k.* me? 7:19
who goeth about to *k.* thee? 20
he whom they seek to *k.*? 25
will he *k.* himself? 8:22
ye seek to *k.* me. 37, 40
not but to steal and *k.* 10:10
Jews took counsel to *k.* Paul.
Acts 9:23; 26:21
day and night to *k.* him. 9:24
to him, Rise, Peter, *k.* and eat. 10:13
they went about to *k.* him. 21:31
near, are ready to *k.* him. 23:15
laying wait in the way to *k.* 25:3
soldiers' counsel was to *k.* 27:42
no adultery, yet if thou *k.* *Jas* 2:11
ye *k.* and desire to have, and. 4:2
I will *k.* her children. *Rev* 2:23
that they should *k.* one another. 6:4
power was given them to *k.* with. 8
that they should not *k.* them. 9:5
overcome them and *k.* them. 11:7

killed

Joseph's coat, and *k.* a kid.
Gen 37:31
the beast hath *k.* a man. *Ex* 21:29
bullock shall be *k.* before. *Lev* 4:15
where the burnt offering is *k.* shall
the sin offering be *k.* before. 6:25
the ram he *k.* 8:19
one of the birds be *k.* 14:5
in the blood of the bird *k.* 6
ye have *k.* the people. *Num* 16:41
whosoever hath *k.* any person. 31:19
skirt of thy robe, and *k.* *1 Sam* 24:11
take my flesh I have *k.* for. 25:11
woman hasted and *k.* the calf. 28:24
thou hast *k.* Uriah with. *2 Sam* 12:9
smote the Philistine and *k.* 21:17
and because he *k.* him. *1 Ki* 16:7
and smote Ela, and *k.* him. 10
hast thou *k.* and also taken? 21:19
Pekah *k.* Pekahiah. *2 Ki* 15:25
David *k.* Shophach. *1 Chr* 19:18
Ahab *k.* sheep and. *2 Chr* 18:2
he slew those that had *k.* the. 25:3
so they *k.* the bullocks, rams. 29:22
the priests *k.* them and made. 24
k. the passover. 30:15; 35:1, 11
Ezra 6:20
for thy sake are we *k.* *Ps* 44:22
k. her beasts, mingled. *Pr* 9:2
hast *k.* and not pitied. *Lam* 2:21
and be *k.* and be raised again.
Mat 16:21; *Mark* 8:31; 9:31
beat one, and *k.* another. *Mat* 21:35
Mark 12:5
oxen and my fatlings are *k.* *Mat* 22:4
are children of them that *k.* 23:31
Herodias would have *k.* *Mark* 6:19
k. him and cast him out of the. 12:8
the first day, when they *k.* 14:12
fathers *k.* them. *Luke* 11:47, 48
after he hath *k.* hath power. 12:5
hath *k.* the fatted calf. 15:27, 30
when the passover must be *k.* 22:7
k. the Prince of life. *Acts* 3:15
he *k.* James. 12:2
and would have *k.* himself. 16:27
drink till they had *k.* Paul. 23:12
Jews, and should have been *k.* 27
for thy sake we are *k.* all. *Rom* 8:36
Lord, they have *k.* thy prophets. 11:3
as chastened and not *k.* *2 Cor* 6:9
who *k.* the Lord Jesus. *1 Thes* 2:15
ye have condemned and *k.* *Jas* 5:6
brethren who should be *k.* *Rev* 6:11
was the third part of men *k.* 9:18
the rest which were not *k.* by. 20
he must in this manner be *k.* 11:5
killeth with sword, must be *k.* 13:10
image of the beast, should be *k.* 15

killedst

to kill me, as thou *k.* the. *Ex* 2:14
forasmuch as thou *k.* *1 Sam* 24:18

killest

Jerusalem, which *k.* the prophets.
Mat 23:37; *Luke* 13:34

killeth

k. an ox, or lamb, or goat, in the
camp, or *k.* it out. *Lev* 17:3
k. any man shall surely be put to
death. 24:17, 21; *Num* 35:30
he that *k.* a beast. *Lev* 24:18, 21
k. any person unawares. *Num* 35:11
15; *Deut* 19:4; *Josh* 20:3, 9
the Lord *k.* and maketh. *1 Sam* 2:6
man who *k.* him, king. 17:25; 26:27
wrath *k.* the foolish man. *Job* 5:2
the murderer *k.* the poor and. 24:14
of the slothful *k.* him. *Pr* 21:25
he that *k.* an ox, as if he. *Isa* 66:3
who *k.* you will think. *John* 16:2
letter *k.*, but the Spirit. *2 Cor* 3:6
he that *k.* with sword. *Rev* 13:10

killing

which aided him in *k.* *Judg* 9:24
charge of *k.* passover. *2 Chr* 30:17
oxen, and *k.* sheep. *Isa* 22:13
by swearing, lying, *k.* and. *Hos* 4:2
beating some, and *k.* *Mark* 12:5

kin

approach to any near of *k.* *Lev* 18:6
uncovereth his near *k.* 20:19
for his *k.* that is near, he. 21:2
if any of his *k.* come to. 25:25*, 49
the man is near of *k.* to. *Ruth* 2:20
the king is near of *k.* *2 Sam* 19:42
not, but among his own *k.* *Mark* 6:4

kind, *substantive*

herb yielding seed, and the fruit tree
yielding fruit after his *k.*
Gen 1:11, 12
forth abundantly after their *k.* and
every winged fowl after his *k.* 21
beast of earth after their *k.* 24
beast of the earth after his *k.* 25
k. and of cattle after their *k.*, every
creeping thing after his *k.* 6:20
cattle and fowl, after their *k.* 7:14
raven, hawk after his *k.* *Lev* 11:14
15, 16, 19; *Deut* 14:14
and tortoise after his *k.* *Lev* 11:29
cattle gender with a diverse *k.* 19:19
instruments of every *k.* *1 Chr* 28:14
sellers of all *k.* of ware. *Neh* 13:20
I planted trees of all *k.* *Eccl* 2:5
the multitude of all *k.* of. *Ezek* 27:12
and gathered of every *k.* *Mat* 13:47
this *k.* goeth not out but by prayer.
17:21; *Mark* 9:29
there is one *k.* of flesh. *1 Cor* 15:39
that we should be a *k.* *Jas* 1:18
for every *k.* of beasts and birds. 3:7

kind

saying, If thou be *k.* to. *2 Chr* 10:7
God is *k.* to unthankful. *Luke* 6:35
suffereth long and is *k.* *1 Cor* 13:4
be *k.* one to another. *Eph* 4:32

kindle

a contentious man to *k.* *Pr* 26:21*
k. in the thickets of the. *Isa* 9:18
k. a burning like the burning. 10:16
breath of the Lord doth *k.* it. 30:33
nor shall the flame *k.* upon. 43:2
never want a man to *k.* *Jer* 33:18*
fire and flame shall *k.* in. *Ob* 18

kindled

Potiphar's wrath was *k.* *Gen* 39:19
burning the Lord hath *k.* *Lev* 10:6
wrath of the Lord was *k.* *Num* 11:33
Deut 11:17; *2 Ki* 22:13, 17
Ps 106:40
coals were *k.* by it. *2 Sam* 22:9
Ps 18:8
also *k.* his wrath against. *Job* 19:11
k. the wrath of Elihu, against Job
was his wrath *k.* because. 32:2
three friends was his wrath *k.* 3, 5
my wrath is *k.* against thee. 42:7
when his wrath is *k.* but. *Ps* 2:12
when their wrath is *k.* 124:3
the sparks that ye have *k.* *Isa* 50:11
wrath was *k.* in the cities. *Jer* 44:6
I the Lord have *k.* it. *Ezek* 20:48
my repentings are *k.* *Hos* 11:8
if it be already *k.* *Luke* 12:49
see **anger, fire**

kindleth

his breath *k.* coals. *Job* 41:21
yea, he *k.* it, and baketh. *Isa* 44:15
a matter a little fire *k.*! *Jas* 3:5*

kindly

if you will deal *k.* with me.
Gen 24:49; 47:29
Shechem spake *k.* to the. 34:3
Joseph spake *k.* to his. 50:21
deal *k.* and truly with. *Josh* 2:14
the Lord deal *k.* with you. *Ruth* 1:8
thou shalt deal *k.* with. *1 Sam* 20:8
spake *k.* to Jehoiachin. *2 Ki* 25:28
Jer 52:32
be *k.* affectioned one. *Rom* 12:10*

kindness

this is thy *k.* thou shalt. *Gen* 20:13
according to the *k.* I have. 21:23
O Lord, shew *k.* to my master. 24:12
know that thou hast shewed *k.* 14
think on me, and shew *k.* 40:14

I have shewed you *k.* that ye will also
shew *k.* to my father's. *Josh* 2:12
nor shewed *k.* to house. *Judg* 8:35
not left off his *k.* to living. *Ruth* 2:20
thou hast shewed more *k.* 3:10
ye shewed *k.* to Israel. *1 Sam* 15:6
thou shalt shew me the *k.* of. 20:14
thou shalt not cut off thy *k.* 15
this *k.* unto your lord. *2 Sam* 2:5
k. to you, I also will requite you this
k. because ye have done this. 6
against Judah shew *k.* to house. 3:8
that I may shew him *k.* for. 9:1
any, that I may shew the *k.* of. 3
shew thee *k.* for Jonathan's sake. 7
k. to Hanun son of Nahash, as his
father shewed *k.* 10:2; *1 Chr* 19:2
Absalom said, Is this thy *k.* to thy?
2 Sam 16:17
shew *k.* to the sons of. *1 Ki* 2:7
kept for David this great *k.* 3:6
Joash remembered not *k.* of.
2 Chr 24:22
God gracious, of great *k.* *Neh* 9:17*
the maiden obtained *k.* of. *Esth* 2:9
me his marvellous *k.* *Ps* 31:21
for his merciful *k.* is great. 117:2
let thy merciful *k.* be for. 119:76
smite me, it shall be a *k.* 141:5
desire of a man is his *k.* *Pr* 19:22
in her tongue is the law of *k.* 31:26
with everlasting *k.* will I. *Isa* 54:8
but my *k.* shall not depart. 10
I remember thee, the *k.* of. *Jer* 2:2
for he is gracious, of great *k.*
Joel 2:13* *Jonah* 4:2*
people shewed us no little *k.*
Acts 28:2
by longsuffering, by *k.* *2 Cor* 6:6
in his *k.* toward us. *Eph* 2:7
put on *k.* humbleness of. *Col* 3:12
k. of God our Saviour. *Tit* 3:4
godliness brotherly *k.*; to *k.* charity.
2 Pet 1:7

see **lovingkindness**

kindred

God said, Get thee from thy *k.*
Gen 12:1; *Acts* 7:3
go to *k.* and take a wife.
Gen 24:4; 38:40
Lord who took me from my *k.* 7*
when thou comest to my *k.* if they. 41
the Lord said, Return to thy *k.* 31:3
13*; 32:9
asked us straitly of our *k.* 43:7
to my own land and *k.* *Num* 10:30
brought out all her *k.* *Josh* 6:23
of the *k.* of Elimelech. *Ruth* 2:3; 3:2
the *k.* of Saul 3000. *1 Chr* 12:29
Esther shewed not her people or *k.*
Esth 2:10, 20
to see the destruction of my *k.* 8:6
Elihu, of the *k.* of Ram. *Job* 32:2
men of thy *k.* said, Get. *Ezek* 11:15
none of thy *k.* called by. *Luke* 1:61
the *k.* of the high priest. *Acts* 4:6
Joseph's *k.* was made known. 7:13
Jacob to him and all his *k.* 14
dealt subtilly with our *k.* 19
redeemed us out of every *k.* and.
Rev 5:9
gospel to preach to every *k.* 14:6

kindreds

give to the Lord, ye *k.* *1 Chr* 16:28
Ps 96:7
all *k.* of nations shall. *Ps* 22:27
k. of the earth be blessed. *Acts* 3:25
k. of the earth shall wail. *Rev* 1:7
a great multitude of all *k.* 7:9
of *k.* shall see their dead. 11:9
was given him over all *k.* 13:7

kinds

creepeth after their *k.* *Gen* 8:19*
divers *k.* of spices. *2 Chr* 16:14
appoint over them four *k.* *Jer* 15:3
be according to their *k.* *Ezek* 47:10
dulcimer, and all *k.* of music.
Dan 3:5, 7, 10, 15
to another divers *k.* of. *1 Cor* 12:10
are, it may be, so many *k.* of. 14:10

kine

Is taken, [1] *Literally, for cows.*
Deut 7:13. [2] *Figuratively, for*
the proud and wealthy rulers of
Israel, Amos 4:4.

forty *k.* ten bulls, a. *Gen* 32:15
up seven well favoured *k.* 41:2, 18
seven other *k.* came out. 3, 4, 19, 20
seven good *k.* are seven years. 26
the seven thin ill favoured *k.* are. 27
bless the increase of thy *k.* *Deut* 7:13
blessed shall be the increase of thy
k. 28:4
cursed shall be the increase of thy *k.*
18
not leave the increase of thy *k.* 51
butter of *k.*, milk of sheep. 32:14
milch *k.* and tie the *k.* *1 Sam* 6:7
took two *k.* 10
the *k.* took the straight way. 12
wood of cart, and offered the *k.* 14
butter, and cheese of *k.* *2 Sam* 17:29
hear ye this word, ye *k.* *Amos* 4:1

king

Melchizedek *k.* of Salem.
Gen 14:18; *Heb* 7:1
in Edom, before there reigned any *k.*
Gen 36:31; *1 Chr* 1:43
arose up a new *k.* over. *Ex* 1:8
the shout of a *k.* is. *Num* 23:21
and his *k.* shall be higher. 24:7
I will set a *k.* over me. *Deut* 17:14
shalt in any wise set him *k.* over. 15
bring thee, and thy *k.* which. 28:36
and he was *k.* in Jeshurun. 33:5
the children of a *k.* *Judg* 8:18
the trees went to anoint a *k.* 9:8
no *k.* in Israel, but every man did.
17:6; 18:1; 19:1; 21:25
give strength to his *k.* *1 Sam* 2:10
go make us a *k.* to judge us. 8:5
give us a *k.* 6
shew the manner of the *k.* 8:9, 11
cry in that day because of your *k.* 18
we will have a *k.* 19
that our *k.* may judge us, and. 20
and make them a *k.* 22
nay, but set a *k.* over us. 10:19
God save the *k.* 24; *2 Sam* 16:16
2 Ki 11:12; *2 Chr* 23:11
I have made a *k.* over. *1 Sam* 12:1
the *k.* walketh before you. 2
nay; but a *k.* shall reign over us: when
Lord your God was your *k.* 12
behold the *k.* whom ye have. 13
wickedness is great in asking a *k.* 17
our sins this evil, to ask us a *k.* 19
consumed, both you and your *k.* 25
sent me to anoint thee to be *k.* 15:1
rejected thee from being *k.* 23, 26
I have provided me a *k.* 16:1
let not the *k.* sin against his. 19:4
I should not fail to sit with *k.* 20:5
let not the *k.* impute any. 22:15
that thou shalt surely be *k.* 24:20
a feast like the feast of a *k.* 25:36
enemies of my lord the *k.* 29:8
he made Ish-bosheth *k.* *2 Sam* 2:9
what the *k.* did, pleased all. 3:36
not of the *k.* to slay Abner. 37
Lord had established him *k.* over.
5:12
him a mess of meat from *k.* 11:8
I anointed thee *k.* over. 12:7
I pray thee, speak to the *k.* 13:13
and the *k.* and his throne be. 14:9
of God so is my Lord the *k.* 17; 19:27
controversy, came to the *k.* 15:2
there is none deputed of the *k.* 3
abide with the *k.* for thou art. 19
in what place my lord the *k.* 21
this dead dog curse the *k.*? 16:9
flee, I will smite the *k.* only. 17:2
is no matter hid from the *k.* 18:13
k. saved us out of the hand of. 19:9
of all Israel is come to the *k.* 11
the *k.* should take it to his heart. 19
I know that I am this day *k.* 22
I yet to cry any more to the *k.*? 28
because the *k.* is near of kin. 42
we have ten parts in the *k.* 43
tower of salvation for his *k.* 22:51
Araunah as a *k.* give to *k.* 24:23
Adonijah said, I will be *k.* *1 Ki* 1:5
for Solomon shall be *k.* in my. 35
I will speak for thee to the *k.* 2:18
as *k.* hath said, so will thy. *1 Ki* 2:38
made thy servant *k.* instead of. 3:7
women spake before the *k.* 22
Israel heard the judgement the *k.* 28
k. and all Israel offered. 8:62
not any thing hid from the *k.* 10:3
lifted up his hand against *k.* 11:26
thou shalt reign and shalt be *k.* 37
who told me I should be *k.* 14:2
the Lord shall raise up a *k.* over. 14
conspired and hath slain the *k.* 16:16
blaspheme God and the *k.* 21:10
prophets declare good to the *k.* 22:13
2 Chr 18:12
there was then no *k.* in Edom: a
deputy was *k.* *1 Ki* 22:47
O man of God, *k.* said. *2 Ki* 1:9, 11
be spoken for to the *k.*? 4:13
lord on whose hand the *k.* 7:2
she went to cry to the *k.* for. 8:3
shewed that thou shalt be *k.* 13
Edom revolted, made a *k.* over. 20
we will not make any *k.* 10:5
with the *k.* as he goeth out and. 11:8
a covenant between the Lord and *k.*,
between the *k.* also and the. 17
had slain the *k.* his father. 14:5
2 Chr 25:3
brought the *k.* word. *2 Ki* 22:9
20; *2 Chr* 34:16, 28
Shaphan read it before the *k.*
2 Ki 22:10; *2 Chr* 34:18
they took the *k.* and brought him.
2 Ki 25:6; *Jer* 52:9
they dwelt with the *k.* *1 Chr* 4:23
Shemaiah wrote them before *k.* 24:6
worshipped the Lord and *k.* 29:20
hath made thee *k.* *2 Chr* 2:11; 9:8
so the *k.* hearkened not to. 10:15
for he thought to make him *k.* 11:22
him at the command of the *k.* 24:21
thou made of the *k.'s* counsel? 25:16
be it known to the *k.* *Ezra* 4:12
13; 5:8
and pray for the life of *k.* and. 6:10
who will not do the law of the *k.* 7:26
who hath put in the *k.'s* heart to. 27
to require of the *k.* a band of. 8:22
was the *k.'s* cupbearer. *Neh* 1:11
will ye rebel against the *k.*? 2:19
mayest be their *k.* according to. 6:6
to preach, saying, There is a *k.* 7
nations was there no *k.* like him, God
made him *k.* over all Israel. 13:26
so I will go in unto the *k.* *Esth* 4:16
whom the *k.* delighteth to. 6:6, 7
as the word went out of the *k.* 7:8
who had spoken good for the *k.* 9
prevail, as a *k.* ready to. *Job* 15:24
bring him to the *k.* of terrors. 18:14
I sat chief, and dwelt as a *k.* in. 29:25
is it fit to say to the *k.*, Thou? 34:18
he is a *k.* over all children. 41:34
I set my *k.* upon my holy. *Ps* 2:6
hearken to my cry, my *K.* 5:2; 84:3
the Lord is *K.* for ever. 10:16; 29:10
deliverance giveth he to his *k.* 18:50
let the *k.* hear us when we call. 20:9
k. shall joy in thy strength. 21:1
for the *k.* trusteth in the Lord. 7
and the *K.* of glory shall come. 24:7, 9
K. of glory? the Lord strong. 8
the Lord of hosts, he is the *K.* 10
no *k.* saved by the multitude. 33:16
art my *K.* O God, command. 44:4
I have made touching the *k.* 45:1
so shall the *k.* greatly desire. 11
she shall be brought to the *k.* 14
sing praises to our *K.* 47:6
God is the *K.* 7
thou wilt prolong the *k.'s* life. 61:6
the *k.* shall rejoice in God. 63:11
the goings of my God, my *K.* 68:24
give the *k.* thy judgements. 72:1
God is my *K.* of old, working. 74:12
Holy One of Israel is our *k.* 89:18
noise before the Lord, the *K.* 98:6
the *k.'s* strength also loveth. 99:4
the *k.* sent and loosed him. 105:20
of Zion be joyful in their *K.* 149:2
of people is the *k.'s* honour. *Pr* 14:28
the *k.'s* favour is toward a wise. 35
and truth preserve the *k.* 20:28
for grace of his lips, the *k.* 22:11

fear thou the Lord, and k. Pr 24:21
the wicked from before the k. 25:5
the locusts have no k. yet go. 30:27
and a k. against whom there is. 31
what can the man do that cometh after the k.? Eccl 2:12
the k. himself is served by the. 5:9
where the word of a k. is, there. 8:4
O land, when thy k. is a child. 10:16
blessed when thy k. is the son. 17
curse not the k. no, not in thy. 20
the k. brought me into. S of S 1:4
while the k. sitteth at his table. 12
k. Solomon with the crown. 3:11
the k. is held in the galleries. 7:5
mine eyes have seen the K. Isa 6:5
let us set a k. in the midst of it. 7:6
curse their k. and their God. 8:21
and a fierce k. shall rule over. 19:4
according to days of one k. 23:15
for Tophet; yea, for the k. it. 30:33
behold, a k. shall reign in. 32:1
thine eyes shall see the k. 33:17
Lord is our k., he will save us. 22
your reasons, saith the k. of. 41:21
Creator of Israel, your K. 43:15
and thou wentest to the k. 57:9
the heart of k. shall perish. Jer 4:9
Lord in Zion ? is not her k. in ? 8:19
the true God, an everlasting k. 10:10
to the k. and queen, Humble. 13:18
a K. shall reign and prosper. 23:5
thus saith the Lord, of the k. 29:16
for the k. is not he that can do. 38:5
hast said to the k. the k. . . to thee. 25
saith the K. whose name is the Lord. 46:18; 48:15; 51:57
why doth their k. inherit Gad ? 49:1*
I will destroy from thence the k. 38
Lord hath despised the k. Lam 2:6
the k. shall mourn and. Ezek 7:27
taken the k. and the princes. 17:12
hath taken of the k.'s seed and. 13
k. dwelleth that made him k. 16
I will bring a k. of kings from. 26:7
k. shall be k. to them all. 37:22, 24
there is no k. asked such. Dan 2:10
none that can shew it before k. 11
before the k. and I will shew the k. 24
these men before the k. 3:13
is come upon my lord the k. 4:24
while the word was in the k.'s. 31
and honour the K. of heaven. 37
the k. saw the part of the hand. 5:5
assembled together to the k. 6:6
k. of fierce countenance shall. 8:23
and a mighty k. shall stand. 11:3
the k. shall do according to his. 36
many days without a k. Hos 3:4
seek the Lord, and David their k. 5
sent to k. Jareb. 5:13; 10:6
they made the k. glad with. 7:3
in the day of our k. princes made. 5
no k.; what then should a k. do ? 10:3
her k. is cut off, as the foam. 7
the Assyrian shall be his k. 11:5
I will be thy k.; give me a k. 13:10
I gave thee a k. in mine anger. 11
k. shall go into captivity. Amos 1:15
for it is the k.'s chapel, the k.'s. 7:13
and their k. shall pass. Mi 2:13
cry ? is there no k. in thee ? 4:9
k. shall perish from Gaza. Zech 9:5
thy K. cometh to thee. 9; Mat 21:5
into the hand of his k. Zech 11:6
shall be k. over all the earth. 14:9
even go up to worship the K. 16, 17
kingdom likened to a certain k. Mat 18:23; 22:2
k. came in to see the guests. 22:11
with haste to the k. Mark 6:25
what k. going to war against another k.? Luke 14:31
K. that cometh in name of. 19:38
he himself is Christ, a K. 23:2
to make him a k. John 6:15
thy K. cometh. 12:15
to him, Art thou a k. then ? 18:37
maketh himself a k. speaketh. 19:12
saith to the Jews, Behold your K. 14
crucify your K.? have no k. but. 15
till another k. arose, who. Acts 7:18
afterward they desired a k. 13:21
that there is another k. one. 17:7
the k. knoweth of these. Acts 26:26
now to the K., eternal. 1 Tim 1:17
who is the K. of kings, and. 6:15
and not afraid of the k.'s. Heb 11:23
not fearing the wrath of the k. 27
to the k. as supreme. 1 Pet 2:13
fear God, honour the k. 17
they had a k. over them. Rev 9:11
just are thy ways, thou K. 15:3
of lords, K. of kings. 17:14; 19:16
see **David, great, house, Jews**

king of the Amorites, see **Sihon**

king of Assyria
Pul the k. of A. came. 2 Ki 15:19
exacted money to give k. of A. 20
from house of Lord to k. of A. 16:18
Hoshea k. of A. took Samaria. 17:6
k. of A. did carry away Israel. 18:11
thus saith great king the k. of A. 19
land out of hand of k. of A. 33
saith Lord concerning k. of A. 19:32 Isa 37:33
turned heart of k. of A. to. Ezra 6:22
bring upon thee the k. of A. Isa 7:17
shave by k. of A. the head and. 20
k. of A. hath devoured. Jer 50:17
will punish Babylon as I punished k. of A. 18
shepherds slumber, O k. of A. Nah 3:18
see **Bashan, Babylon**

king of Egypt
midwives did not as k. of E. Ex 1:17
sure the k. of E. will not let. 3:19
them a charge to the k. of E. 6:13
k. of E. came not again any more . . . pertained to k. of E. 2 Ki 24:7
k. of E. came up. 2 Chr 12:2
the k. of E. put him down. 36:3
k. of E. made Eliakim his brother. 4
so is the k. of E. to all that. Isa 36:6
see **Pharaoh**

king of Israel
after whom is the k. of Isr. come ? 1 Sam 24:14
k. of Isr. is come out to. 26:20
glorious was the k. of Isr. to day! 2 Sam 6:20
thee, go out to k. of Isr. 1 Ki 20:31
not, save only with k. of Isr. 22:31 2 Chr 18:30
they said, Surely it is k. of Isr. 1 Ki 22:32; 2 Chr 18:31
shew me which of us is for k. of Isr.? 2 Ki 6:11
out of the hand of k. of Isr. 16:7
that it was not k. of Isr. 2 Chr 18:32
son of David k. of Isr. did build. 35:3 Ezra 5:11
not Solomon k. of Isr. sin? Neh 13:26
saith the Lord, the k. of Isr. Isa 44:6
the k. of Isr. be cut off. Hos 10:15
k. of Isr. is in the midst. Zeph 3:15
if he be k. of Isr. let him descend. Mat 27:42; Mark 15:32
thou art the k. of Isr. John 1:49
blessed is the k. of Isr. 12:13

king of Judah
being then k. of J. 2 Ki 8:16
to k. of J. which sent you to. 22:18
as for k. of J. who sent. 2 Chr 34:26
to do with thee, thou k. of J.? 35:21
hear the word of the Lord O k. of J. Jer 34:4
thus shall ye say to k. of J. 37:7

king of Moab
Balak k. of M. brought. Num 23:7
the k. of M. warred. Josh 24:9
Israel served the k. of M. Judg 3:14
like manner sent to k. of M. 11:17
better than Balak k. of M.? 25
into hand of k. of M. 1 Sam 12:9
father and mother to k. of M. 22:4
and Mesha k. of M. 2 Ki 3:4
k. of M. rebelled against Israel. 5, 7
when the k. of M. saw battle. 26
and yokes to the k. of M. Jer 27:3

O **king**
Abner said, O k. I. 1 Sam 17:55
therefore, O k. come down. 23:20
lord, O k. 1 Sam 26:17; 2 Sam 14:9 22; 16:4; 19:26; 1 Ki 1:13, 20, 24 20:4; 2 Ki 6:12, 26; 8:5
Tekoah said, Help, O k. 2 Sam 14:4
I will be thy servant, O k. 15:34
O k. let not the army. 2 Chr 25:7
extol thee, my God, O k. Ps 145:1
would not fear thee, O k.? Jer 10:7
O k. live for ever. Dan 2:4; 3:9 5:10; 6:21
as for thee, O k. 2:29
thou O k. sawest an image. 31
thou O k. art a king of kings, for. 37
O k. hast made a decree. 3:10
deliver us out of thy hand, O k. 17
be it known to thee, O k. 18
true, O k. 24
it is thou, O k. 4:22
O k. let my counsel be. 27
O k. Nebuchadnezzar, to thee it. 31
O thou k., the most high God. 5:18
a petition save of thee, O k. 6:7
now, O k. establish the decree. 8
regardeth not thee, O k. 13
know, O k. 15
also before thee, O k. have I. 22
at midday, O k. I saw. Acts 26:13
O k. I was not disobedient. 19

king of Persia
as Cyrus, k. of P. hath. Ezra 4:3
till the reign of Darius k. of P. 5
Bishlam wrote unto Artaxerxes k. of P. 7; 6:14
mercy in sight of the k. of P. 9:9
see **Cyrus**

king of Syria
Ben-hadad k. of S. 1 Ki 20:20
k. of S. will come up against. 22
captain of host of k. of S. 2 Ki 5:1
k. of S. was sick. 8:7
k. of S. hath sent me to thee. 9
the k. of S. oppressed them. 13:4
k. of S. had destroyed them. 7
out of the hand of the k. of S. 16:7
hast relied on k. of S. the host of the k. of S. is escaped. 2 Chr 16:7
see **Ben-hadad, Hazael, Rezin**

king of Tyre
Hiram k. of T. sent messengers to. 2 Sam 5:11; 1 Chr 14:1
the k. of T. sent servants. 1 Ki 5:1
Hiram the k. of T. had. 9:11
sent to Huram the k. of T. 2 Chr 2:3
Huram the k. of T. answered. 11

kingdom
ye shall be to me a k. Ex 19:6
Gad, Reuben, and Manasseh the k. of Sihon and the k. of. Num 32:33 Deut 3:13; Josh 13:12, 21, 27, 30
took the k. of Og in. Deut 3:4
matter of k. he told. 1 Sam 10:16
Samuel told the manner of the k. 25
renew the k. there. 11:14
Saul took k. 14:47
rent the k. of Israel. 15:28; 28:17
can he have more but the k.? 18:8
to translate the k. 2 Sam 3:10
Israel shall restore me the k. 16:3
hath delivered the k. into hand. 8
thou knowest that the k. 1 Ki 2:15
ask for him the k. for he is my. 22
not like made in any k. 10:20 2 Chr 9:19
I will surely rend the k. from thee. 1 Ki 11:11; 31:35
not rend away all k. 11:13, 34
to bring k. again to Rehoboam. 12:21; 2 Chr 11:1
k. return again to house. 1 Ki 12:26
I rent the k. away from the. 14:8
no k. where my lord hath not. 18:10
dost thou now govern the k.? 21:7
as the k. was confirmed. 2 Ki 14:5
with him, to confirm the k. 15:19
and turned the k. to David. 1 Chr 10:14; 12:23
from one k. to another people. 16:20; Ps 105:13
earth is thine, thine is the k. O Lord. 1 Chr 29:11; Ps 22:28; Mat 6:13
think to withstand the k. 2 Chr 13:8
and the k. was quiet before. 14:5

k. gave he to Jehoram. 2 Chr 21:3
Jehoram was risen up to the k. 4
no power to keep still the k. 22:9
for a sin offering for the k. 29:21
no god of any nation or k. 32:15
not served thee in their k. Neh 9:35
which sat first in the k. Esth 1:14
thou art come to the k. for. 4:14
given to the half of the k. 5:3, 6; 7:2
shall fight, k. against k. Isa 19:2
Mat 24:7; Mark 13:8; Luke 21:10
call nobles thereof to k. Isa 34:12
the k. that will not serve thee. 60:12
Jer 27:8
I speak concerning a k. Jer 18:7
concerning a k., to build and to. 9
he hath polluted the k. and. Lam 2:2
didst prosper into a k. Ezek 16:13
that the k. might be base. 17:14
shall be there a base k. 29:14
heaven hath given thee a k. Dan 2:37
shall God of heaven set up a k. 44
Most High ruleth in k. 4:17, 25, 32
O king, the k. is departed. 31
Daniel concerning the k. 6:4
take the k. and possess the k. 7:18
the saints possessed the k. 22
whose k. is an everlasting k. 27
give the honour of the k. 11:21
cause to cease the k. of. Hos 1:4
Lord are upon sinful k. Amos 9:8
the k. shall be the Lord's. Ob 21
k. shall come to daughter. Mi 4:8
the gospel of the k. Mat 4:23
9:35; 24:14
the children of the k. shall. 8:12
k. divided against itself is brought.
12:25; Mark 3:24; Luke 11:17
seed are children of k. Mat 13:38
shall shine as the sun in the k. 43
inherit the k. prepared for. 25:34
drink it new in my Father's k. 26:29
blessed be k. of our. Mark 11:10
pleasure to give you k. Luke 12:32
to receive for himself a k. 19:12
having received the k. 15
I appoint unto you a k. as. 22:29
thou restore again the k.? Acts 1:6
have delivered up the k. 1 Cor 15:24
translated us into the k. Col 1:13
we receiving a k. that. Heb 12:28
heirs of the k. which he. Jas 2:5
an entrance ministered into everlasting k. 2 Pet 1:11
k. and patience of Jesus. Rev 1:9
have received no k. as yet. 17:12
to agree, and give their k. to. 17
see **establish, established, throne**

kingdom *of God*

but seek ye first the k. of God.
Mat 6:33; Luke 12:31
k. of God is come unto. Mat 12:28
Luke 10:9, 11; 11:20
eye of a needle, than for a rich man to enter into k. of God. Mat 19:24
Mark 10:23; Luke 18:24
harlots go into k. of God. Mat 21:31
k. of God shall be taken from. 43
preaching k. of God. Mark 1:14
Acts 8:12; 20:25; 28:31
k. of God is at hand. Mark 1:15
to know the mystery of k. of God.
4:11; Luke 8:10
so is the k. of God as if. Mark 4:26
whereunto shall liken k. of God?
30; Luke 13:18, 20
have seen k. of God. Mark 9:1
better to enter into the k. of God. 47
children, for of such is k. of God.
Mat 19:14; Luke 18:16
whoso shall not receive k. of God.
Mark 10:15; Luke 18:17
trust in riches to enter into k. of God.
Mark 10:24, 25; Luke 18:25
far from the k. of God. Mark 12:34
I drink it new in the k. of God. 14:25
which waited for the k. of God.
15:43; Luke 23:51
I must preach k. of God. Luke 4:43
poor, for yours is the k. of God. 6:20
that is least in the k. of God. 7:28
glad tidings of k. of God. 8:1
them to preach k. of God. 9:2, 60
and spake to them of k. of God.
Luke 9:11
of death, till they see k. of God. 27
back, is fit for the k. of God. 62
the prophets in the k. of God. 13:28
sit down in the k. of God. 29
shall eat bread in k. of God. 14:15
since that time the k. of God. 16:16
demanded when k. of God. 17:20
the k. of God cometh not with. 20
behold the k. of God is within. 21
children for k. of God's sake. 18:29
that k. of God should appear. 19:11
the k. of God is nigh at hand. 21:31
it be fulfilled in the k. of God. 22:16
I will not drink until k. of God. 18
cannot see the k. of God. John 3:3
cannot enter into the k. of God. 5
things pertaining to k. of God.
Acts 1:3; 8:12; 19:8
much tribulation enter into k. of God.
14:22
and testified k. of God. 28:23
k. of God is not meat. Rom 14:17
k. of God is not in word. 1 Cor 4:20
shall not inherit the k. of God. 6:9
nor extortioners inherit k. of God.
10; Gal 5:21; Eph 5:5
cannot inherit k. of God. 1 Cor 15:50
workers unto the k. of God. Col 4:11
worthy of the k. of God. 2 Thes 1:5
come the k. of our God. Rev 12:10

kingdom *of heaven*

repent, for k. of h. is at hand.
Mat 3:2; 4:17; 10:7
in spirit, their's is k. of h. 5:3, 10
least in k. of h. great in k. of h. 19
no case enter into k. of h. 20; 18:3
Lord, shall enter into k. of h. 7:21
with Abraham in k. of h. 8:11
in k. of h. is greater than. 11:11
k. of h. suffereth violence, violent. 12
know mysteries of the k. of h. 13:11
the k. of h. is like. 24, 31, 33, 44, 45
47, 52; 18:23; 20:1; 22:2; 25:1, 14
to thee the keys of k. of h. 16:19
is the greatest in k. of h.? 18:1, 4
for ye shut up the k. of h. 23:13

his **kingdom**

the beginning of his k. Gen 10:10
his k. shall be exalted. Num 24:7
on the throne of his k. Deut 17:18
may prolong his days in his k. 20
he had exalted his k. 2 Sam 5:12
with him in his k. 1 Chr 11:10
for his k. was lifted up on high. 14:2
strengthened in his k. 2 Chr 1:1
to build a house for his k. 2:1, 12
again to Jerusalem into his k. 33:13
his k. ruleth over all. Ps 103:19
glorious majesty of his k. 145:12
that is born in his k. Eccl 4:14
upon his k. to order and. Isa 9:7
his k. is an everlasting k. Dan 4:3
his k. from generation to generation.
34; 6:26; 7:14
his k. shall be broken and. 11:4
south shall come into his k. 9
how shall his k. stand? Mat 12:26
Luke 11:18
gather out of his k. all. Mat 13:41
Son of man coming in his k. 16:28
of his k. there shall be. Luke 1:33
hath called you to his k. 1 Thes 2:12
at his appearing and his k. 2 Tim 4:1
and his k. was full of. Rev 16:10

my **kingdom**

brought on me and my k. Gen 20:9
I and my k. are guiltless. 2 Sam 3:28
settle him in my k. for. 1 Chr 17:14
glory of my k. in my k. Dan 4:36
in every dominion of my k. 6:26
it to the half of my k. Mark 6:23
eat and drink at my table in my k.
Luke 22:30
my k. is not of this world, if my k. were, but now my k. John 18:36

thy **kingdom**

but now thy k. shall. 1 Sam 13:14
sceptre of thy k. a right sceptre.
Ps 45:6; Heb 1:8
speak of glory of thy k. Ps 145:11
thy k. is an everlasting kingdom. 13
thy k. shall be sure to. Dan 4:26
there is a man in thy k. 5:11
God numbered thy k. 26
thy k. is divided. 28
thy k. come, thy will be done.
Mat 6:10; Luke 11:2
on the left in thy k. Mat 20:21
thou comest to thy k. Luke 23:42

kingdoms

Lord do to all the k. Deut 3:21
be removed into all the k. of. 28:25
the head of all those k. Josh 11:10
you out of hand of all k. 1 Sam 10:18
reigned over all k. from. 1 Ki 4:21
the God of all the k. of. 2 Ki 19:15
all the k. may know. 19; Isa 37:20
went over all the k. 1 Chr 29:30
know the service of the k. 2 Chr 12:8
fear fell upon all the k. 17:10; 20:29
thou rulest over all the k. of. 20:6
all k. hath the Lord. 36:23; Ezra 1:2
thou gavest them k. and. Neh 9:22
the heathen raged, the k. Ps 46:6
sing unto God, ye k. of the. 68:32
thy wrath on the k. that have. 79:6
k. are gathered to serve. 102:22
smote all the k. of Canaan. 135:11
my hand hath found the k. Isa 10:10
the noise of the k. of nations. 13:4
Babylon the glory of k. 19; 47:5
man that did shake k.? 14:16
he shook the k. 23:11
God of all k. 37:16
and over the k. I have. Jer 1:10
and in all their k. none like. 10:7*
to be removed into all k. 15:4; 24:9
34:17
all the k. of the world shall. 25:26
prophesied against great k. 28:8
them a terror to all k. 29:18
all the k. fought against. 34:1
concerning Kedar and the k. 49:28
with thee will I destroy k. 51:20
call together against her the k. 27
be the basest of the k. Ezek 29:15
neither be divided into two k. 37:22
consume all these k. Dan 2:44
shall be diverse from all k. 7:23
four k. shall stand up out of. 8:22
better than these k.? Amos 6:2
and I will shew the k. thy. Nah 3:5
I may assemble the k. to. Zeph 3:8
throne of k. and I will destroy the strength of the k. of. Hag 2:22
shewed him all the k. of world.
Mat 4:8; Luke 4:5
through faith subdued k. Heb 11:33
k. of this world become k. Rev 11:15

kingly

he was deposed from his k. throne.
Dan 5:20

kings

k. shall come out of thee. Gen 17:6
16; 35:11
these are the k. that reigned. 36:31
slew the k. of Midian. Num 31:8
hath done to these two k. Deut 3:21
he shall deliver their k. into. 7:24
five k. of Amorites. Josh 10:5
these five k. fled. 16
bring out those five k. 22
put your feet on necks of these k. 24
Joshua smote all their k. 40; 11:17
all these k. thirty and one. 12:24
seventy k. having their thumbs cut off. Judg 1:7
hear, O ye k. 5:3
the k. came and fought. 19
time when k. go forth to. 2 Sam 11:1
not be any among the k. 1 Ki 3:13
10:23; 2 Chr 1:12; 9:22
Solomon over all the k. on. 1 Ki 4:24
Ben-hadad and thirty-two k. 20:1
these three k. together. 2 Ki 3:10
this is blood, the k. are surely. 23
hired against us the k. of the. 7:6
behold, two k. stood not before. 10:4
he reproved k. for them. 1 Chr 16:21
Ps 105:14
k. sought the presence of. 2 Chr 9:23
but not in the sepulchres of the k.
21:20; 24:25
burial which belonged to k. 26:23

the revenue of the *k.* *Ezra* 4:13
this city hath been hurtful to *k.* 15
made insurrection against *k.* 19
there have been mighty *k.* over. 20
God destroy *k.* that shall. 6:12
Artaxerxes, king of *k.* to Ezra. 7:12
k. and priests have been delivered. 9:7; *Neh* 9:24
little to us and our *k.* *Neh* 9:32
nor have our *k.* or princes. 34
had I been at rest with *k.* *Job* 3:14
he looseth the bond of *k.* 12:18
with *k.* are they on the throne. 36:7
k. of the earth set themselves. *Ps* 2:2; *Acts* 4:26
be wise, therefore, O ye *k.* *Ps* 2:10
k.' daughters among thy. 45:9
lo, the *k.* were assembled. 48:4
k. of armies did flee apace. 68:12
when the Almighty scattered *k.* 14
shall *k.* bring presents to thee. 29
yea, all *k.* shall fall down. 72:11
he is terrible to the *k.* of. 76:12
make him higher than the *k.* 89:27
the *k.* of the earth shall fear. 102:15
he shall strike through *k.* in. 110:5
of thy testimonies before *k.* 119:46
nations, and slew mighty *k.* 135:10
which smote great *k.* 136:17, 18
all *k.* of the earth. 138:4; 148:11
that giveth salvation to *k.* 144:10
to bind their *k.* with chains. 149:8
by me *k.* reign, and princes. *Pr* 8:15
abomination for *k.* to commit. 16:12
righteous lips are the delight of *k.* 13
the diligent in business shall stand before *k.* 22:29
honour of *k.* to search a. 25:2
heart of *k.* is unsearchable. 3
the spider is in *k.*' palaces. 30:28
to that which destroyeth *k.* 31:3
it is not for *k.* O Lemuel, to drink. 4
the peculiar treasure of *k.* *Eccl* 2:8
be forsaken of both her *k.* *Isa* 7:16
my princes altogether *k.*? 10:8
raised all the *k.* of the nations. 14:9
all the *k.* of the nations lie in. 18
I am the son of ancient *k.* 19:11
Lord shall punish the *k.* of. 24:21
and made him ruler over *k.* 41:2
I will loose the loins of *k.* to. 45:1
k. shall see and arise, princes. 49:7
k. shall be thy nursing fathers. 23
the *k.* shall shut their mouths. 52:15
and *k.* to the brightness of. 60:3
their *k.* shall minister to thee. 10
thy gates open, that their *k.* 11
also suck the breast of *k.* 16
and all *k.* shall see thy glory. 62:2
they, their *k.* and princes. *Jer* 2:26
even *k.* that sit upon David's. 13:13
into the gates of this city, *k.* 17:25
k. sitting upon the throne of. 22:4
I made Judah and *k.* drink. 25:18
k. of Tyrus. 22
all the *k.* of Arabia. 24
the *k.* of Zimri. 25
all the *k.* of the north. 26
me to anger, they, their *k.* 32:32
burnings of former *k.* before. 34:5
as we, our *k.* and princes to. 44:17
your *k.* and princes burnt. 21
I will punish their *k.* and. 46:25
k. shall go into captivity. 49:3
many *k.* shall be raised up. 50:41
the spirit of *k.* of the Medes. 51:11
k. of the earth would not. *Lam* 4:12
their *k.* shall be sore afraid. *Ezek* 27:35; 32:10
I will lay thee before *k.* to. 28:17
there is Edom, her *k.* and. 32:29
their *k.* shall no more defile. 43:7
k. and setteth up *k.* *Dan* 2:21
these *k.* shall God set up a. 44
that your God is a Lord of *k.* 47
the four beasts are four *k.* 7:17
ten *k.*; he shall subdue three *k.* 24
spake in thy name to our *k.* 9:6
to our *k.* and princes belongs. 8
I remained there with the *k.* 10:13
stand up three *k.* 11:2
both these *k.*' hearts. 27
hot as an oven, all their *k.* *Hos* 7:7
they have set up *k.* but not. 8:4
they shall scoff at *k.* *Hab* 1:10
brought before governors and *k.* for my sake. *Mat* 10:18; *Mark* 13:9; *Luke* 21:12
clothing are in *k.*' houses. *Mat* 11:8
of whom do *k.* of the earth? 17:25
prophets and *k.* have. *Luke* 10:24
k. of Gentiles exercise. 22:25
a chosen vessel to bear my name before *k.* *Acts* 9:15
ye have reigned as *k.* *1 Cor* 4:8
prayers be made for *k.* *1 Tim* 2:2
King of *k.*, Lord of lords. 6:15; *Rev* 17:14; 19:16
from slaughter of the *k.* *Heb* 7:1
Christ the prince of the *k.* *Rev* 1:5
hath made us *k.* and priests. 6*; 5:10*
k. of the earth hid themselves. 6:15
prophesy again before *k.* 10:11
way of the *k.* of east might. 16:12
spirits which go forth to the *k.* 14
whom *k.* of earth committed. 17:2
there are seven *k.*, five are fallen. 10
ten *k.* which receive power as *k.* 12
city which reigneth over *k.* of. 18
k. of earth have committed. 18:3
k. of earth who shall bewail her. 9
ye may eat the flesh of *k.* 19:18
k. of the earth gathered to make. 19
the *k.* of the earth do bring. 21:24

kings *of the Amorites*
two *k.* of *Am.* *Deut* 4:47; 31:4; *Josh* 2:10; 9:10; 24:12
when all *k. of Am.* heard. *Josh* 5:1
five *k. of Am.* gathered. 10:5, 6
see **book, great**

kings *of Israel*
book of the Chronicles of the *k. of Isr.* *1 Ki* 14:19; 15:31; 16:5, 14, 20, 27; 22:39; *2 Ki* 1:18; 10:34; 13:8, 12; 14:15, 28; 15:11, 15, 21, 26, 31
more than all *k. of Isr.* *1 Ki* 16:33
we heard that *k. of Isr.* are. 20:31
Jehoram walked in way of *k. of Isr.* *2 Ki* 8:18
Joash was buried with the *k. of Isr.* 13:13; 14:16
Jeroboam slept with his fathers *k. of Isr.* 14:29
Ahaz walked in the way of the *k. of Isr.* 16:3
Hoshea did evil, but not as the *k. of Isr.* 17:2
Israel walked in the statutes of the *k. of Isr.* 8
away houses the *k. of Isr.* 23:19
passover in days of the *k. of Isr.* 22
written in book of *k. of Isr.* *1 Chr* 9:1; *2 Chr* 16:11; 25:26; 27:7; 28:26; 32:32; 33:18
is mentioned in the book of the *k. of Isr.* *2 Chr* 20:34; 35:27; 36:8
Ahaz was not brought into sepulchres of *k. of Isr.* 28:27
houses of Achzib shall be a lie to *k. of Isr.* *Mi* 1:14

kings *of Judah*
Ziklag pertained to the *k. of J.* *1 Sam* 27:6
acts of Rehoboam in the Chronicles of the *k. of J.* *1 Ki* 14:29; 15:7, 23; 22:45; *2 Ki* 8:23; 15:6, 36; 16:19; 20:20; 21:17, 25; 23:28; 24:5
hallowed things the *k. of J.* had dedicated. *2 Ki* 12:18, 19
written in the Chronicles of the *k. of J.* 14:18; *2 Chr* 25:26; 28:26; 32:32; 35:27; 36:8
like him of all the *k. of J.* *2 Ki* 18:5
priests *k. of J.* ordained. 23:5
took horses *k. of J.* had given. 11
beat down altars which *k. of J.* 12
passover in all days of *k. of J.* 22
floor houses *k. of J.* *2 Chr* 34:11
Isaiah in days of the *k. of J.* *Isa* 1:1
iron pillar against *k. of J.* *Jer* 1:18
bring out bones of the *k. of J.* 8:1
in gate, whereby *k. of J.* 17:19
word of Lord ye *k. of J.* 20; 19:3
burnt incense to gods *k. of J.* 19:4
houses of the *k. of J.* shall. 13
treasures of *k. of J.* will. 20:5
concerning houses of *k. of J.* *Jer* 33:4
wickedness of *k. of J.*? 44:9
word of Lord that came to Hosea in days of *k. of J.* *Hos* 1:1; *Mi* 1:1
see **kings** *of Israel*

kinsfolk
my *k.* have failed and. *Job* 19:14
Jesus among their *k.* *Luke* 2:44

kinsfolks
left none of Baasha's *k.* *1 Ki* 16:11
Jehu slew Ahab's *k.* *2 Ki* 10:11*
shall be betrayed by *k.* *Luke* 21:16

kinsman
if the man have no *k.* to. *Num* 5:8
give his inheritance to his *k.* 27:11
Naomi had a *k.* his name. *Ruth* 2:1
thou art a near *k.* 3:9
near *k.*: a *k.* nearer than I. 12
to thee the part of a *k.* well; if not, I will do the part of a *k.* to thee 13
behold the *k.* of whom Boaz. 4:1
the *k.* said, I cannot redeem it. 6
the *k.* said unto Boaz, Buy it. 8
not left thee this day without a *k.* 14
being his *k.* whose ear. *John* 18:26
salute Herodion my *k.* *Rom* 16:11

kinsmen
of kin one of our next *k.* *Ruth* 2:20
my lovers and *k.* stood. *Ps* 38:11
friends, brethren, nor *k.* *Luke* 14:12
called together his *k.* *Acts* 10:24
accursed, for my *k.* according to the. *Rom* 9:3
salute my *k.* 16:7
my *k.* salute you. 21

kinswoman
is my father's near *k.* *Lev* 18:12
she is thy mother's near *k.* 13
call understanding thy *k.* *Pr* 7:4

kinswomen
they are her near *k.* *Lev* 18:17

Kir
the people captive to *K.* *2 Ki* 16:9
in the night *K.* of Moab. *Isa* 15:1
Elam bare the quiver, *K.* 22:6
go into captivity to *K.* *Amos* 1:5
brought the Assyrians from *K.*? 9:7

Kir-haraseth
only in *K.* left they. *2 Ki* 3:25
for the foundations of *K.* *Isa* 16:7
inward parts shall sound for *K.* 11

Kiriathaim
smote Emims in Shavah *K.* *Gen* 14:5
saith Lord, *K.* is confounded and. *Jer* 48:1
judgement is come upon *K.* and. 23

Kirjath-arba
Sarah died in *K.* the. *Gen* 23:2; *Josh* 14:15; 20:7; *Judg* 1:10

Kirjath-jearim
K. a city of the Hivites. *Josh* 9:17
was to Baalah, which is *K.* 15:9, 60
K. a city of Judah. 18:14; *1 Chr* 13:6
the men of *K.* came. *1 Sam* 7:1
ark of God from *K.* *1 Chr* 13:5
brought the ark from *K.* *2 Chr* 1:4

Kish
a man of Benjamin whose name was *K.* *1 Sam* 9:1
asses of *K.* Saul's father. 3; 14:51
that is come to the son of *K.*? 10:11
and Saul the son of *K.* was. 21
Saul in sepulchre of *K.* *2 Sam* 21:14
K. the son of Gibeon. *1 Chr* 8:30
Ner begat *K.* 33
K. son of Mahli. 23:21
K. son of Abdi. *2 Chr* 29:12
of Shimei, son of *K.* *Esth* 2:5
them Saul the son of *K.* *Acts* 13:21

kiss, -es
In the Bible times and countries the kiss was given as a sign. [1] *Of reverence and subjection to a superior,* 1 Sam 10:1. [2] *Of love and affection,* Gen 27:26, 27; 1 Sam 20:41. [3] *Of idolatrous reverence and adoration,* Hos 13:2.
the *k.* of an enemy are. *Pr* 27:6
k. me with the *k.* of. *S of S* 1:2
thou gavest me no *k.* *Luke* 7:45

Son of man with a *k.*? *Luke* 22:48
another with an holy *k.* *Rom* 16:16
greet with an holy *k.* *1 Cor* 16:20
2 Cor 13:12
brethren with an holy *k.* *1 Thes* 5:26
one another with a *k.* *1 Pet* 5:14

kiss, *verb*

come near now and *k.* *Gen* 27:26
not suffered me to *k.* my sons. 31:28
Amasa by beard to *k.* *2 Sam* 20:9
let me *k.* my father. *1 Ki* 19:20
k. the Son, lest he be angry. *Ps* 2:12
every man shall *k.* his. *Pr* 24:26
him *k.* me with kisses. *S of S* 1:2
I would *k.* thee, yea I should. 8:1
let men that sacrifice *k.* *Hos* 13:2
saying, Whomsoever I *k.* the same.
Mat 26:48; *Mark* 14:44
not ceased to *k.* my feet. *Luke* 7:45
drew near to Jesus to *k.* him. 22:47

kissed

Jacob came near and *k.* *Gen* 27:27
Jacob *k.* Rachel and wept. 29:11
Laban *k.* Jacob. 13
Laban *k.* his sons and his. 31:55
Esau *k.* Jacob. 33:4
Joseph *k.* all his brethren. 45:15
Jacob *k.* and embraced. 48:10
on his father's face and *k.* him. 50:1
Moses in the mount and *k.* *Ex* 4:27
his father in law and *k.* him. 18:7
k. her daughters in law. *Ruth* 1:9
Orpah *k.* her mother in law. 14
poured oil and *k.* Saul. *1 Sam* 10:1
Jonathan and David *k.* one. 20:41
the king *k.* Absalom. *2 Sam* 14:33
Absalom *k.* any man that. 15:5
the king *k.* Barzillai, and. 19:39
which hath not *k.* him. *1 Ki* 19:18
mouth hath *k.* my hand. *Job* 31:27
righteousness and peace *k.* *Ps* 85:10
she caught him and *k.* him. *Pr* 7:13
hail, Master, and *k.* him. *Mat* 26:49
Mark 14:45
Mary *k.* his feet and. *Luke* 7:38
fell on his neck and *k.* him. 15:20
Paul's neck and *k.* him. *Acts* 20:37

kite

the *k.* after his kind unclean.
Lev 11:14*; *Deut* 14:13*

Kittim

sons of Javan, Tarshish, *K.*
Gen 10:4; *1 Chr* 1:7
see **Chittim**

knead

k. it, and make cakes. *Gen* 18:6
women *k.* their dough. *Jer* 7:18

kneaded

Endor took flour and *k.* *1 Sam* 28:24
Tamar took flour and *k.* *2 Sam* 13:8
the baker *k.* the dough. *Hos* 7:4

kneadingtroughs

frogs shall come into thy *k.* *Ex* 8:3
their *k.* being bound up in. 12:34

knee

before him, bow the *k.* *Gen* 41:43
every *k.* shall bow, every tongue.
Isa 45:23; *Rom* 14:11; *Phil* 2:10
they bowed the *k.* before him.
Mat 27:29*; *Mark* 15:19
who have not bowed the *k.* *Rom* 11:4

kneel

he made his camels *k.* *Gen* 24:11
let us *k.* before the Lord. *Ps* 95:6

kneeled

Solomon *k.* down on. *2 Chr* 6:13
Daniel *k.* three times. *Dan* 6:10
and Jesus *k.* down and. *Luke* 22:41
Stephen *k.* and cried with. *Acts* 7:60
Peter *k.* and prayed. 9:40
Paul *k.* and prayed. 20:36
and we *k.* down on the shore. 21:5

kneeling

Solomon rose up from *k.* *1 Ki* 8:54
a man *k.* to him saying. *Mat* 17:14
Mark 10:17
there came a leper *k.* *Mark* 1:40

knees

Bilhah shall bear on my *k.* *Gen* 30:3
out from between his *k.* 48:12
brought up on Joseph's *k.* *Gen* 50:23
shall smite thee in the *k.* *Deut* 28:35
on his *k.* to drink. *Judg* 7:5, 6
made Samson sleep on her *k.* 16:19
from kneeling on his *k.* *1 Ki* 8:54
put his face between his *k.* 18:42
k. which have not bowed. 19:18
third captain fell on his *k.* *2 Ki* 1:13
sat on his mother's *k.* till noon. 4:20
kneeled down on his *k.* *2 Chr* 6:13
I fell on my *k.* and spread. *Ezra* 9:5
why did the *k.* prevent? *Job* 3:12
strengthened the feeble *k.* 4:4
my *k.* are weak through. *Ps* 109:24
confirm the feeble *k.* *Isa* 35:3
and be dandled upon her *k.* 66:12
all *k.* shall be weak as water.
Ezek 7:17; 21:7
the waters were to the *k.* 47:4
his *k.* smote one against. *Dan* 5:6
kneeled on his *k.* three times. 6:10
an hand set me upon my *k.* 10:10
she is empty, and the *k.* *Nah* 2:10
bowing their *k.* worshipped him.
Mark 15:19
Simon Peter fell down at Jesus' *k.*
Luke 5:8
for this cause I bow my *k.* *Eph* 3:14
hang down and feeble *k.* *Heb* 12:12

knew

Adam *k.* Eve his wife. *Gen* 4:1, 25
Cain *k.* his wife. 17
Judah *k.* her no more. 38:26
Jephthah's daughter *k.* no man.
Judg 11:39
they *k.* her and abused her. 19:25
Elkanah *k.* Hannah his. *1 Sam* 1:19
but the king *k.* her not. *1 Ki* 1:4
Joseph *k.* her not, till. *Mat* 1:25

knew

Adam and Eve *k.* that. *Gen* 3:7
Noah *k.* what his younger. 9:24
Jacob *k.* it, and said, It is. 37:33
Onan *k.* the seed should not. 38:9
Joseph saw and *k.* his. 42:7, 8
and *k.* the knowledge. *Num* 24:16
from the day I *k.* you. *Deut* 9:24
a prophet whom the Lord *k.* 34:10
such as before *k.* nothing. *Judg* 3:2
Manoah *k.* that he was an. 13:21
they *k.* the voice of the. 18:3
all Israel *k.* Samuel. *1 Sam* 3:20
Saul *k.* that the Lord was. 18:28
for if I *k.* then would I not. 20:9
Jonathan *k.* that it was. 33
only David and Jonathan *k.* 39
for the servant *k.* nothing of. 22:15
slay the priests, because they *k.* 17
David said to Abiathar, I *k.* it. 22
David *k.* that Saul secretly. 23:9
Saul *k.* David's voice, and. 26:17
he *k.* that valiant men. *2 Sam* 11:16
Obadiah *k.* Elijah, and. *1 Ki* 18:7
then Manasseh *k.* the. *2 Chr* 33:13
manner to all that *k.* law. *Esth* 1:13
O that I *k.* where I might! *Job* 23:3
because I *k.* that thou. *Isa* 48:4
shouldest say, Behold, I *k.* them. 7
I *k.* that thou wouldest deal very. 8
I formed thee, I *k.* thee. *Jer* 1:5
then I *k.* this was the word of. 32:8
Gedaliah, and no man *k.* it. 41:4
men which *k.* their wives. 44:15
I *k.* that they were the cherubims.
Ezek 10:20
he *k.* their desolate palaces. 19:7
he *k.* that the most high. *Dan* 5:21
when Daniel *k.* the writing was. 6:10
I *k.* thou art a gracious. *Jonah* 4:2
k. that it was the word of. *Zech* 11:11
profess I never *k.* you. *Mat* 7:23
when Jesus *k.* he withdrew. 12:15
Jesus *k.* their thoughts. 25; *Luke* 6:8
I *k.* thee that thou art an. *Mat* 25:24
he *k.* that for envy they. 27:18
speak because they *k.* *Mark* 1:34
ship, straightway they *k.* him. 6:54
k. he had spoken the parable. 12:12
the devils, for they *k.* *Luke* 4:41
servant which *k.* his lord's. 12:47
nor *k.* they the things that. 18:34
were opened, and they *k.* 24:31
but the servants *k.* *John* 2:9
not commit himself unto them, be cause he *k.* *John* 2:24
and testify, for he *k.* what was. 25
the father *k.* it was at the. 4:53
Jesus *k.* he had been long in. 5:6
for he himself *k.* what he. 6:6
Jesus *k.* that his disciples. 61
Jesus *k.* from the beginning who. 64
I *k.* that thou hearest me. 11:42
that if any man *k.* where he. 57
when Jesus *k.* that his hour. 13:1
for he *k.* who should betray him. 11
no man at the table *k.* for what. 28
Jesus *k.* that they were. 16:19
Judas which betrayed him *k.* 18:2
k. that it was he that sat. *Acts* 3:10
which when the brethren *k.* 9:30
when Rhoda *k.* Peter's voice. 12:14
they *k.* all that his father was. 16:3
they *k.* that he was a Jew. 19:34
k. that he was a Roman. 22:29
which *k.* me from the beginning. 26:5
k. the island was called Melita. 28:1
that when they *k.* God. *Rom* 1:21
the princes of this world *k.* *1 Cor* 2:8
to be sin, who *k.* no sin. *2 Cor* 5:21
I *k.* a man in Christ. 12:2, 3
in you since ye *k.* grace of. *Col* 1:6
you *k.* what great conflict I. 2:1
though ye once *k.* this. *Jude* 5
written that no man *k.* *Rev* 19:12

knew *not*

place, and I *k.* it *not.* *Gen* 28:16
Jacob *k. not* that Rachel had. 31:32
Judah *k. not* she was his. 38:16
he *k. not* aught he had. 39:6
but they *k. not* him. 42:8
king which *k. not* Joseph. *Ex* 1:8
I *k. not* that thou stoodest.
Num 22:34
which thy fathers *k. not.* *Deut* 8:16
thy fathers *k. not.* 29:26; 32:17
a generation which *k. not* the Lord.
Judg 2:10
Manoah *k. not* that he was. 13:16
his father *k. not* that it was. 14:4
Benjamin *k. not* that evil. 20:34
of Eli *k. not* the Lord. *1 Sam* 2:12
people *k. not* that Jonathan. 14:3
the lad *k. not* any thing. 20:39
sent messengers after Abner, but David *k.* it *not.* *2 Sam* 3:26
k. ye *not* they would shoot? 11:20
simplicity, and *k. not* any. 15:11
I saw a tumult, but I *k. not.* 18:29
a people which I *k. not* shall. 22:44
gathered gourds for they *k.* them *not.* *2 Ki* 4:39
the rulers *k. not* whither. *Neh* 2:16
Job's friends *k.* him *not.* *Job* 2:12
the cause which I *k. not* I. 29:16
things which I *k. not.* 42:3
my charge things I *k. not.* *Ps* 35:11
against me, and I *k.* it *not.* 15
behold, we *k.* it *not.* *Pr* 24:12
blind by a way they *k. not.* *Isa* 42:16
set him on fire, yet he *k. not.* 25
and nations that *k. not* thee. 55:5
handle the law *k.* me *not.* *Jer* 2:8
k. not that they had devised. 11:19
other gods whom they *k. not.* 44:3
honour a god whom his fathers *k. not.* *Dan* 11:38
made princes and I *k.* it *not.* *Hos* 8:4
but they *k. not* that I healed. 11:3
nations whom they *k. not.* *Zech* 7:14
and they *k.* him *not.* *Mat* 17:12
k. not till flood came. 24:39
his mother *k. not* of it. *Luke* 2:43
that *k. not* and did commit. 12:48
the world *k.* him *not.* *John* 1:10
I *k.* him *not.* 31, 33
governor *k. not* whence it was. 2:9
yet they *k. not* the scriptures. 20:9
k. not that it was Jesus. 14; 21:4
because they *k.* him *not.* *Acts* 13:27
more part *k. not* wherefore. 19:32
when it was day, they *k. not.* 27:39
world by wisdom *k. not.* *1 Cor* 1:21
howbeit then, when ye *k. not* God.
Gal 4:8
world knoweth us not, because it *k.* him *not.* *1 John* 3:1

knewest
manna, which thou *k.* not. *Deut* 8:3
people which thou *k. not. Ruth* 2:11
thou *k.* that they dealt. *Neh* 9:10
then thou *k.* my path in. *Ps* 142:3
heardest not, yea, thou *k. Isa* 48:8
thy heart, thou *k.* all this. *Dan* 5:22
thou *k.* I reaped where. *Mat* 25:26
Luke 19:22
thou *k.* not the time of. *Luke* 19:44
if thou *k.* the gift of God. *John* 4:10

knife
Abraham took the *k. Gen* 22:6, 10
took a *k.* and laid hold. *Judg* 19:29
put a *k.* to thy throat. *Pr* 23:2
take thee a sharp *k. Ezek* 5:1
and smite about it with a *k.* 2

knit
Israel were *k.* together. *Judg* 20:11
soul of Jonathan was *k. 1 Sam* 18:1
my heart shall be *k. 1 Chr* 12:17
I saw a sheet *k.* at the. *Acts* 10:11
hearts being *k.* together. *Col* 2:2
body *k.* together increaseth with. 19

knives
make thee sharp *k.* and. *Josh* 5:2
Joshua made him sharp *k.* and. 3
cut themselves with *k. 1 Ki* 18:28
nine and twenty *k.* Cyrus. *Ezra* 1:9
jaw teeth as *k.* to devour. *Pr* 30:14

knock
k. and it shall be opened. *Mat* 7:7
Luke 11:9
ye begin to *k.* at door. *Luke* 13:25
stand at the door and *k. Rev* 3:20

knocked
and as Peter *k.* at door. *Acts* 12:13

knocketh
of my beloved that *k. S of S* 5:2
to him that *k.* shall be opened.
Mat 7:8; *Luke* 11:10
when he cometh and *k. Luke* 12:36

knocking
Peter continued *k.* and. *Acts* 12:16

knop, -s
his *k.* and his flowers. *Ex* 25:31, 34
36; 37:17
with a *k.* and flower in. 25:33; 37:19
and *k.* branches of the same. 25:36
37:17, 20, 22
cedar carved with *k. 1 Ki* 6:18
were *k.* compassing it, *k.* cast. 7:24

know
God doth *k.* that your eyes. *Gen* 3:5
man is become as one of us, to *k.* 22
said to Abram, *K.* thy seed. 15:13
and see, and if not, I will *k.* 18:21
if thou restore her not, *k.* 20:7
make them *k.* the statutes. *Ex* 18:16
hast not let me *k.* whom thou. 33:12
they shall *k.* the land. *Num* 14:31
k. this day and. *Deut* 4:39; 11:2
to prove thee and *k.* what was. 8:2
fathers *k.* he might make thee *k.* 3
proveth you, to *k.* whether ye. 13:3
shall let your children *k. Josh* 4:22
and Israel he shall *k.* 22:22
k. whether they would. *Judg* 3:4
city of my people doth *k. Ruth* 3:11
she rose up before one could *k.* 14*
sit still, my daughter, till thou *k.* 18
this assembly shall *k. 1 Sam* 17:47
he saith, Let not Jonathan *k.* 20:3
let no man *k.* any thing of. 21:2
k. and see that there is no. 24:11
therefore *k.* and consider. 25:17
Achish said to David, *k.* 28:1
surely thou shalt *k.* what thy. 2
to *k.* thy going out, to *k. 2 Sam* 3:25
things to make thy servant *k.* 7:21
to *k.* all things that are in. 14:20
thy servant doth *k.* that I. 19:20
k. every man the plague. *1 Ki* 8:38
2 Chr 6:29
he shall *k.* that there is. *2 Ki* 5:8
they *k.* that we be hungry. 7:12
k. now that there shall fall. 10:10
Issachar, to *k.* what Israel ought.
1 Chr 12:32
my son, *k.* thou the God of. 28:9
ought ye not to *k.* that. *2 Chr* 13:5
k. that this city is a. *Ezra* 4:15
all such as *k.* the laws of thy. 7:25
Mordecai walked to *k. Esth* 2:11
to *k.* what it was, and why it. 4:5
people *k.* whosoever shall come. 11
shalt *k.* thy tabernacle. *Job* 5:24
shalt *k.* that thy seed shall. 25
hear it, and *k.* thou it for thy. 27
nor shall his place *k.* him. 7:10
but of yesterday, and *k.* 8:9
k. therefore that God exacteth. 11:6
than hell, what canst thou *k.*? 8
to *k.* my transgression. 13:23
k. that God hath overthrown. 19:6
him, and he shall *k.* it. 21:19
sayest, How doth God *k.*? 22:13
do they that *k.* him not see? 24:1
one *k.* them, they are in terrors. 17
let us *k.* among ourselves. 34:4
dost thou *k.* when God? 37:15
dost thou *k.* the balancings of? 16
caused the dayspring to *k.* 38:12
that thou shouldest *k.* the paths. 20*
k. the Lord hath set apart. *Ps* 4:3
that *k.* thy name put their. 9:10
lovingkindness to them *k.* 36:10
Lord, make me to *k.* mine end. 39:4
be still, and *k.* that I am God. 46:10
part thou shalt make me to *k.* 51:6
k. that God ruleth in Jacob. 59:13
How doth God *k.*? 73:11
I thought to *k.* this. 16
Babylon to them that *k.* me. 87:4
blessed are they that *k.* the. 89:15
the place thereof shall *k.* it. 103:16
k. my heart, try me, and *k.* 139:23
no man that would *k.* me. 142:4
cause me to *k.* the way wherein. 143:8
k. wisdom and instruction. *Pr* 1:2
attend to *k.* understanding. 4:1
the lips of righteous *k.* what. 10:32
be thou diligent to *k.* the. 27:23
I gave my heart to *k. Eccl* 1:17
I applied my heart to *k.* 7:25
when I applied my heart to *k.* 8:16
though a wise man think to *k.* 17
the living *k.* they shall die, but. 9:5
but *k.* that God will bring thee. 11:9
before the child shall *k. Isa* 7:16
and all the people shall *k.* even. 9:9
Egyptians shall *k.* the Lord. 19:21
that they may see and *k.* 41:20
that we may *k.* the latter end. 22
all flesh shall *k.* that I am. 49:26
k. how to speak in season. 50:4
therefore my people shall *k.* 52:6
seek me, and delight to *k.* my. 58:2
thou shalt *k.* that I the Lord. 60:16
k. and see that it is an evil. *Jer* 2:19
see thy way in valley, *k.* what. 23
and *k.* O congregation, what is. 6:18
through deceit they refuse to *k.* 9:6
k. that for thy sake I have. 15:15
to *k.* my hand and my might, and
they shall *k.* that my name. 16:21
deceitful, who can *k.* it? 17:9
was not this to *k.* me? saith. 22:16
give them an heart to *k.* me. 24:7
they shall all *k.* me. 31:34; *Heb* 8:11
go, hide thee, let no man *k. Jer* 36:19
he said, Let no man *k.* of. 38:24
and no man shall *k.* it. 40:15
Judah shall *k.* whose words. 44:28
k. that there hath been a prophet.
Ezek 2:5; 33:33
k. that I the Lord hath spoken. 5:13
k. her abomination. 16:2; 20:4
they shall *k.* my vengeance. 25:14
all that *k.* thee shall be. 28:19
thus shall they *k.* that I am. 34:30
heathen shall *k.* 37:28; 39:23
givest knowledge to them who *k.*
Dan 2:21
k. that the Most High. 4:25, 32
made me *k.* the interpretation. 7:16
k. the truth of the fourth beast. 19
make thee *k.* what shall be. 8:19
k. therefore and understand. 9:25
people that *k.* their God. 11:32
thou shalt *k.* the Lord. *Hos* 2:20
Israel shall *k.* it. 9:7
and thou shalt *k.* no god. 13:4
prudent, and he shall *k.* them. 14:9
is it not for you to *k.*? *Mi* 3:1
thou shalt *k.* that the Lord sent me.
Zech 2:11; 4:9
shall *k.* that I have sent. *Mal* 2:4
let not thy left hand *k. Mat* 6:3
if ye *k.* how to give good gifts. 7:11
Luke 11:13
see no man *k.* it. *Mat* 9:30
Mark 5:43; 7:24; 9:30
it is given unto you to *k. Mat* 13:11
Mark 4:11; *Luke* 8:10
k. that it [desolation] is near.
Mat 24:33; *Mark* 13:29; *Luke* 21:20
k. this, if the goodman. *Mat* 24:43
Luke 12:39
k. that this is indeed. *John* 4:42
if any do his will, he shall *k.* 7:17
do the rulers *k.* indeed. 26
and *k.* what he doeth? 51
sheep follow him, for they *k.* 10:4
I *k.* my sheep. 14
thou shalt *k.* hereafter. 13:7
by this shall all men *k.* ye are. 35
behold, they *k.* what I said. 18:21
not for you to *k.* times. *Acts* 1:7
let all the house of Israel *k.* 2:36
shouldest *k.* his will and see. 22:14
they *k.* I imprisoned them that. 19
life from my youth *k.* all Jews. 26:4
I speak to them that *k. Rom* 7:1
but I say, Did not Israel *k.*? 10:19
neither can he *k.* them. *1 Cor* 2:14
nothing as he ought to *k.* 8:2
but I would have you *k.* that. 11:3
to *k.* the love of Christ. *Eph* 3:19
for this cause I sent to *k. 1 Thes* 3:5
one should *k.* how to possess. 4:4
to *k.* them who labour among. 5:12
them which believe and *k. 1 Tim* 4:3
this *k.* also that in last. *2 Tim* 3:1
they profess that they *k. Tit* 1:16
but wilt thou *k.* O vain? *Jas* 2:20
let him *k.* he which converteth. 5:20
but what they *k.* naturally. *Jude* 10
all churches shall *k.* that. *Rev* 2:23
I will make them to *k.* that I. 3:9
see **certain, certainly, certainty**

***I* know**
now *I k.* that thou art a. *Gen* 12:11
whereby shall *I k.* that I shall? 15:8
I k. that he will command. 18:19
I k. thou didst this in integrity. 20:6
now *I k.* that thou fearest. 22:12
thereby shall *I k.* that thou 24:14
I k. it, my son, *I k.* it. 48:19
Lord said, *I k.* their sorrows. *Ex* 3:7
Aaron thy brother *I k.* he can. 4:14
I k. that ye will not yet fear. 9:30
I k. that the Lord is greater. 18:11
thou hast said, *I k.* thee. 33:12, 17
I k. their imagination. *Deut* 31:21
for *I k.* thy rebellion and thy. 27
I k. that after my death ye will. 29
I k. the Lord hath given. *Josh* 2:9
I k. that thou wilt save. *Judg* 6:37
now *k. I* that the Lord will. 17:13
I k. thy pride and. *1 Sam* 17:28
do not *I k.* thou hast chosen? 20:30
till *I k.* what God will do for. 22:3
I k. well that thou shalt. 24:20
I k. that thou art good in my. 29:9
yea *I k.* it, hold you. *2 Ki* 2:3, 5
I k. that there is no God. 5:15
I k. the evil that thou wilt do. 8:12
I k. thy abode and. 19:27; *Isa* 37:28
I k. that thou triest. *1 Chr* 29:17
I k. that God hath. *2 Chr* 25:16
I k. it is so of a truth, but. *Job* 9:2
I k. thou wilt not hold me. 28
things hast hid, *I k.* that this. 10:13
what ye know, the same do *I k.* 13:2
behold, *I k.* that I shall be. 18
I k. that my Redeemer liveth. 19:25
I k. your thoughts and devices. 21:27
for *I k.* that thou wilt bring. 30:23
I k. that thou canst do every. 42:2
I k. that the Lord saveth. *Ps* 20:6
this *I k.* that thou favourest. 41:11
I k. all the fowls of the. 50:11
this *I k.* for God is for me. 56:9
I k. O Lord, that thy. 119:75
for *I k.* the Lord is great and. 135:5
I k. the Lord will maintain. 140:12
I k. that there is no good. *Eccl* 3:12

I k. that whatsoever God. *Eccl* 3:14
I k. it shall be well with. 8:12
nor shall *I k.* the loss of. *Isa* 47:8
and *I k.* that I shall not. 50:7
I k. their works and their. 66:18
I k. the way of man is. *Jer* 10:23
given me knowledge, and *I k.* 11:18
for *I k.* the thoughts that I. 29:11
I k. and am a witness, saith. 23
I k. his wrath, saith the. 48:30
I k. things that come. *Ezek* 11:5
the dream, and *I* shall *k.* *Dan* 2:9
I k. Ephraim, and Israel. *Hos* 5:3
I did *k.* thee in the wilderness. 13:5
I k. your manifold. *Amos* 5:12
I k. that for my sake. *Jonah* 1:12
fear not ye, *I k.* that ye. *Mat* 28:5
I k. thee who thou art. *Mark* 1:24
Luke 4:34
whereby shall *I k.* this. *Luke* 1:18
I k. that Messias cometh. *John* 4:25
but *I k.* you. 5:42
I k. whence I came. 8:14
I k. that ye are Abraham's. 37
but *I k.* him. 55
one thing *I k.* 9:25
Father knoweth me, so *I k.* 10:15
I k. my sheep, and they follow. 27
I k. that what thou wilt ask. 11:22
Martha said, *I k.* that he shall. 24
I k. his commandment is. 12:50
I speak not of all, *I k.* whom. 13:18
now *I k.* of a surety. *Acts* 12:11
Jesus *I k.* and Paul *I k.* 19:15
I k. that ye shall see my face. 20:25
I k. this, that after my departing. 29
I will *k.* the uttermost of. 24:22
because *I k.* thee to be expert. 26:3
king Agrippa, *I k.* that thou. 27
I k. that in me dwelleth. *Rom* 7:18
I k. nothing by myself. *1 Cor* 4:4
I k. in part, then shall *I k.* as. 13:12
I k. the forwardness of. *2 Cor* 9:2
I k. this shall turn to. *Phil* 1:19
I k. that I shall abide with you. 25
be of good comfort, when *I k.* 2:19
I k. how to be abased, *I k.* 4:12
for *I k.* whom I have believed. *2 Tim* 1:12
I k. him, and keepeth. *1 John* 2:4
I k. thy works. *Rev* 2:2, 9, 13, 19
3:1, 8, 15
I k. the blasphemy of them. 2:9

know *not*, or *not* **know**

is Abel? he said, I *k. not.* *Gen* 4:9
I am old, I *k. not* the day. 27:2
I *k. not* the Lord, nor will. *Ex* 5:2
we *k. not* with what we must. 10:26
or if thou *k.* him *not.* *Deut* 22:2
Samuel did *not* yet *k.* *1 Sam* 3:7
give to men whom I *k. not*? 25:11
I *k. not* how to go out. *1 Ki* 3:7
carry thee whither I *k. not.* 18:12
they *k. not* the manner. *2 Ki* 17:26
them that *k.* them *not.* *Ezra* 7:25
they shall *not k.* nor see. *Neh* 4:11
would I *not k.* my soul. *Job* 9:21*
knowest thou that we *k. not*? 15:9
do ye *not k.* their tokens? 21:29
they *k. not* the ways thereof. 24:13
the dark, they *k. not* the light. 16
for I *k. not* to give flattering. 32:22
great, and we *k.* him *not.* 36:26
for I *k. not* the numbers. *Ps* 71:15
they *k. not*, neither will they. 82:5
teacheth man, shall he *not k.*? 94:10
I will *not k.* a wicked person. 101:4
k. not at what they stumble. *Pr* 4:19
that thou canst *not k.* them. 5:6
doth *not* he *k.* it, and shall? 24:12
k. not what to do in the end. 25:8
wicked regardeth *not* to *k.* it. 29:7
four things which I *k. not.* 30:18
dead *k. not* any thing. *Eccl* 9:5
if thou *k. not*, O fairest. *S of S* 1:8
Israel doth *not k.* nor. *Isa* 1:3
shall ye *not k.* it? 43:19
there is no God; I *k. not* any. 44:8
thou shalt *not k.* from whence. 47:11
and thou didst *not k.* them. 48:6
they *k. not*, shall *not k.* peace. 59:8
for they *k. not* the way. *Jer* 5:4
other gods, whom ye *k. not*? 7:9
k. not the judgements of. *Jer* 8:7
k. not me, saith the Lord. 9:3
the heathen that *k.* thee *not.* 10:25
into a land that they *k. not.* 14:18
22:28
dwelleth safely shalt thou *not k.* it? *Ezek* 38:14
she did *not k.* that I gave. *Hos* 2:8
they *k. not* to do right. *Amos* 3:10
k. not the thoughts of. *Mi* 4:12
unto you, I *k.* you *not.* *Mat* 25:12
Peter said, I *k. not* what thou sayest. 26:70; *Luke* 22:60
curse and swear, saying, I *k. not.* *Mat* 26:72, 74; *Mark* 14:68, 71
Jesus said, Ye *k. not.* *Mark* 10:38
ye err, because ye *k. not* the. 12:24
seeing I *k. not* a man. *Luke* 1:34
I *k. not* whence you are. 13:25, 27
woman, I *k.* him *not.* 22:57
forgive them; for they *k. not.* 23:34
that they should *not k.* him. 24:16
standeth one among you whom ye *k. not.* *John* 1:26
if I should say, I *k.* him *not.* 8:55
blind man said, I *k. not.* 9:12, 25
opened his eyes, we *k. not.* 21
for this fellow, we *k. not* from. 29
for they *k. not* the voice of. 10:5
Lord, we *k. not* whither thou. 14:5
because they *k. not* him that. 15:21
we *k. not* where they have laid. 20:2
I *k. not* where they have laid. 13
could *not k.* the certainty. *Acts* 21:34
for we *k. not* what we should pray for. *Rom* 8:26
I *k. not* whether I baptized any other. *1 Cor* 1:16
I determined *not* to *k.* any. 2:2
if I *k. not* the meaning of. 14:11
which *k. not* God. *1 Thes* 4:5
vengeance on them that *k. not* God. *2 Thes* 1:8
k. not how to rule his. *1 Tim* 3:5
evil of things they *k. not.* *Jude* 10
shalt *not k.* what hour I. *Rev* 3:3
see, ye **know**

know *that I am the Lord*

ye shall *k. that I am the Lord.* *Ex* 6:7
16:12; *1 Ki* 20:28; *Ezek* 6:7, 13
7:4, 9; 11:10, 12; 12:20; 13:9, 14
21, 23; 14:8; 15:7; 20:38, 42, 44
23:49; 24:24; 25:5; 35:9; 36:11
37:6, 13; *Joel* 3:17
Egyptians shall *k. that I am Lord.* *Ex* 7:5; 14:4, 18
thou shalt *k. I am Lord.* *Ex* 7:17
1 Ki 20:13; *Isa* 49:23; *Ezek* 16:62
22:16; 25:7; 35:4, 12
to the end that thou mayest *k. that I am the Lord.* *Ex* 8:22
that ye may *k. that I am Lord.* 10:2; 31:13; *Ezek* 20:20
they shall *k. that I am the Lord.*
Ex 29:46; *Ezek* 6:10, 14; 7:27
12:15, 16; 24:27; 25:11, 17; 26:6
28:22, 23, 24, 26; 29:9, 16, 21
30:8, 19, 25, 26; 32:15; 33:29
34:27; 35:15; 36:38; 38:23
39:6, 28
that ye might *k. that I am the Lord.* *Deut* 29:6
I will give them an heart to *k.* me *that I am the Lord.* *Jer* 24:7
my sabbaths that they might *k. that I am the Lord.* *Ezek* 20:12, 26
and the heathen shall *k. that I am the Lord.* 36:23; 39:7
the house of Israel shall *k. that I am the Lord.* 39:22

may, mayest, or *might* **know**

mayest k. there is none like God. *Ex* 8:10; 9:14
mayest k. that the earth. 9:29
ye *may k.* the Lord doth put. 11:7
that I *may k.* what to do to. 33:5
thy way, that I *may k.* thee. 13
generations *may k.* that. *Lev* 23:43
may k. what the Lord. *Num* 22:19
that thou *mightest k.* that the Lord he is God. *Deut* 4:35
ye *may k.* the way by. *Josh* 3:4
may k. that as I was with Moses. 7
people *might k.* the hand. *Josh* 4:24
Israel *might k.* to teach. *Judg* 3:2
we *may k.* whether our way. 18:5
tell me, that I *may k.* *Ruth* 4:4
that all the earth *may k.* there is a God in Israel. *1 Sam* 17:46
1 Ki 8:43, 60; *2 Ki* 19:19
I *may k.* the number. *2 Sam* 24:2
this people *may k.* that. *1 Ki* 18:37
may k. thy name, and *may k.* that this house is. *2 Chr* 6:33
his servants, that they *may k.* 12:8
that ye *may k.* there is. *Job* 19:29
be weighed, that God *may k.* 31:6
that all men *may k.* his work. 37:7
nations *may k.* themselves. *Ps* 9:20
measure of days, that *may k.* 39:4
generation to come *might k.* 78:6
that men *may k.* that thou. 83:18
may k. that this is thy hand. 109:27
I *may k.* thy testimonies. 119:125
draw nigh that we *may k.* *Isa* 5:19
may k. to refuse the evil. 7:15
that all *may k.* that thou art. 37:20
that we *may k.* ye are gods. 41:23
declared, that we *may k.* and. 26
ye *may k.* and believe me. 43:10
that thou *mayest k.* that I am. 45:3
that they *may k.* from the rising. 6
thou *mayest k.* and try. *Jer* 6:27
that ye *may k.* that my words. 44:29
flesh *may k.* that I have. *Ezek* 21:5
that heathen *may k.* me. 38:16
mightest k. the thoughts. *Dan* 2:30
intent that the living *may k.* 4:17
cast lots, that we *may k.* *Jonah* 1:7
ye *may k.* the righteousness. *Mi* 6:5
that ye *may k.* that the Son of man. *Mat* 9:6; *Mark* 2:10; *Luke* 5:24
ye *may k.* and believe. *John* 10:38
the world *may k.* 14:31; 17:23
might k. thee the only true God. 17:3
ye *may k.* that I find no fault. 19:4
may we *k.* what this new? *Acts* 17:19
all *may k.* that those things. 21:24
we *might k.* the things. *1 Cor* 2:12
that ye *might k.* the love. *2 Cor* 2:4
that I *might k.* the proof of you. 9
that ye *may k.* the hope. *Eph* 1:18
whom I sent, that ye *might k.* 6:22
may k. him and the power. *Phil* 3:10
may k. how to answer. *Col* 4:6
whom I sent, that he *might k.* 8
thou *mayest k.* how thou oughtest to behave. *1 Tim* 3:15
may k. ye have eternal. *1 John* 5:13
that we *may k.* him that is true. 20

we **know**, or **know** *we*

Laban? they said, *We k.* *Gen* 29:5
shall *we k.* the word? *Deut* 18:21
we k. it is not his hand. *1 Sam* 6:9
nor *k. we* what to do. *2 Chr* 20:12
God is great, and *we k.* him not. *Job* 36:26
our iniquities, *we k.* them. *Isa* 59:12
we k. if we follow on to. *Hos* 6:3
cry to me, My God, *we k.* thee. 8:2
we k. thou art true, and. *Mat* 22:16
Mark 12:14; *Luke* 20:21
we k. thou art a teacher. *John* 3:2
to thee, we speak that *we* do *k.* 11
we k. what we worship. 4:22
father and mother *we k.*? 6:42
howbeit, *we k.* whence this. 7:27
we k. that thou hast a devil. 8:52
we k. that this is our son and. 9:20
said to him, *we k.* that this man. 24
we k. that God spake to Moses. 29
now *we k.* that God heareth. 31
Lord *we k.* not whither thou goest, and how can *we k.* the way? 14:5
and *we k.* that his testimony. 21:24
we would *k.* what these. *Acts* 17:20
we k. it is every where. 28:22
we k. that what things. *Rom* 3:19
we k. that the law is spiritual. 7:14
we k. that the whole creation. 8:22
we k. that all things work. 28
we k. that we all have. *1 Cor* 8:1
we k. that an idol is nothing in. 4
we k. in part, and prophesy. 13:9
we k. that if our earthly. *2 Cor* 5:1
k. we no man after flesh, *k. we.* 16

we k. that the law is. 1 Tim 1:8
for we k. him that hath. Heb 10:30
hereby we k. that we k. 1 John 2:3
hereby k. we that we are in him. 5
we k. that it is the last time. 18
but we k. that when he shall. 3:2
we k. that we have passed from. 14
hereby we k. that we are of the. 19
hereby we k. that he abideth. 24
hereby k. we the spirit of. 4:6
hereby k. we that we dwell in. 13
by this we k. that we love the. 5:2
we k. that he heareth us, we k. that we have petitions that we. 15
we k. whosoever is born of God. 18
we k. that we are of God, and. 19
we k. that the Son of God is come, that we may k. him that. 5:20

ye know, or know ye

he said, K. ye Laban the? Gen 29:5
ye k. that with all my power. 31:6
ye k. that my wife bare me. 44:27
at even ye shall k. the. Ex 16:6
ye k. the heart of a stranger. 23:9
ye shall k. my breach. Num 14:34
ye shall k. that the Lord. 16:28
ye shall k. the living God is among. Josh 3:10
and ye k. in all your hearts. 23:14
ye k. there is in these houses an ephod. Judg 18:14
k. ye that Ramoth is? 1 Ki 22:3
ye k. the man and his. 2 Ki 9:11
what ye k. the same do. Job 13:2
k. ye that the Lord he is God. Ps 100:3
hearken, ye that k. Isa 51:7
k. ye for certain, if ye. Jer 26:15
all ye that k. his name, say. 48:17
ye shall k. that I have not done. Ezek 14:23
ye shall k. I the Lord have spoken. 17:21; 37:14
ye shall k. that I am in. Joel 2:27
ye shall k. the Lord hath sent me. Zech 2:9; 6:15
ye shall k. them by their fruits. Mat 7:16, 20
ye k. that the princes of the Gentiles. 20:25; Mark 10:42
ye k. that summer is nigh. Mat 24:32
Mark 13:28; Luke 21:30
watch, for ye k. neither. Mat 25:13
k. ye not this parable? Mark 4:13
k. ye that the kingdom of God. Luke 21:31
ye both k. me, and know. John 7:28
ye shall k. that I am he. 8:28
ye shall k. the truth. 32
k. ye nothing. 11:49
k. ye what I have done. 13:12
if ye k. these things, happy. 13:17
I go ye k. and the way ye k. 14:4
from henceforth ye k. him. 7, 17
ye shall k. I am in my Father. 20
ye k. that it hated me before. 15:18
as ye yourselves also k. Acts 2:22
ye k. how that it is unlawful. 10:28
brethren, ye k. how that a good. 15:7
ye k. that by this craft we. 19:25
ye k. from the first day that. 20:18
ye k. that ye were Gentiles, carried. 1 Cor 12:2
ye k. your labour is not in. 15:58
brethren, ye k. the house of. 16:15
ye k. the grace of our Lord. 2 Cor 8:9
I trust ye shall k. we are not. 13:6
k. ye that they which are of faith. Gal 3:7
ye k. how through infirmities. 4:13
ye k. that no whoremonger. Eph 5:5
ye k. the proof of him. Phil 2:22
as ye k. what manner. 1 Thes 1:5
shamefully entreated, as ye k. 2:2
neither flattering words, as ye k. 5
ye k. how we exhorted and. 11
it came to pass, and ye k. 3:4
ye k. what commandments we. 4:2
and now ye k. what withholdeth. 2 Thes 2:6
ye k. how when he would have inherited the blessing. Heb 12:17
k. ye that our brother. 13:23
ye k. that ye were not redeemed. 1 Pet 1:18
put you in remembrance, though ye k. them. 2 Pet 1:12
seeing ye k. these things. 3:17
ye k. all things. 1 John 2:20
because ye k. it. 21
if ye k. he is righteous, ye k. 29
ye k. he was manifested to. 3:5
ye k. no murderer hath eternal. 15
hereby k. ye the Spirit of God. 4:2
and ye k. that our record. 3 John 12

ye know not, or know ye not

k. ye not that there is a prince fallen? 2 Sam 3:38
k. ye not what I and my fathers? 2 Chr 32:13
do ye not k. their tokens. Job 21:29
k. ye not what these things mean? Ezek 17:12
Jesus said, Ye k. not what ye ask. Mat 20:22
ye k. not what hour your Lord. 24:42
K. ye not this parable? Mark 4:13
ye err, because ye k. not. 12:24
watch, for ye k. not when. 13:33, 35
ye k. not what manner. Luke 9:55
standeth one among you, whom ye k. not. John 1:26
ye worship ye k. not what. 4:22
meat ye k. not of. 32
is true, whom ye k. not. 7:28
ye neither k. me nor my. 8:19
that ye k. not from whence. 9:30
k. ye not that so many? Rom 6:3*
k. ye not that to whom ye yield? 16
k. ye not, brethren, for I speak. 7:1*
k. ye not that ye are the temple of God? 1 Cor 3:16; 6:15, 19
k. ye not that a little leaven? 5:6
do ye not k. the saints shall? 6:2
k. ye not that we shall judge? 3
k. ye not, the unrighteous shall? 9
k. ye not that he which is? 16
do ye not k. that they which? 9:13
k. ye not that they which run? 24
k. ye not yourselves? 2 Cor 13:5
k. ye not that the friendship of? Jas 4:4
ye k. not what shall be on the. 14
not written, because ye k. not the truth. 1 John 2:21

knowest

thou k. my service that. Gen 30:26
thou k. how I have served thee. 29
thou k. any man of activity. 47:6
k. thou not yet that Egypt? Ex 10:7
thou k. the people are set on. 32:22
for thou k. how we are. Num 10:31
thou k. the travel that hath. 20:14
Egypt, which thou k. Deut 7:15
the Anakims, whom thou k. 9:2
nation thou k. not, shall eat. 28:33
thou k. the thing that the. Josh 14:6
k. thou not Philistines? Judg 15:11
woman said, Thou k. what Saul hath done. 1 Sam 28:9
how k. thou that Saul? 2 Sam 1:5
k. thou not that it will be? 2:26
thou k. Abner the son of Ner. 3:25
thou, Lord, k. thy servant. 7:20
1 Chr 17:18
For, said Hushai, thou k. 2 Sam 17:8
the king, thou k. it not. 1 Ki 1:18
thou k. also what Joab did to. 2:5
thou k. what thou oughtest to do. 9
thou k. that the kingdom was. 15
thou k. all the wickedness. 44
whose heart thou k. thou only k. 8:39
2 Chr 6:30
k. thou the Lord will? 2 Ki 2:3, 5
thou k. that thy servant did. 4:1
k. that I am not wicked. Job 10:7
k. thou that we know not? 15:9
k. thou not this of old, since? 20:4
therefore speak what thou k. 34:33
measures thereof, if thou k.? 38:5
earth, declare, if thou k. it all. 18
k. thou it, because thou wast? 21
k. thou the ordinances of heaven? 33
k. thou when the wild goats. 39:1, 2
not refrained, O Lord thou k. Ps 40:9; Jer 15:15
thou k. my foolishness. Ps 69:5
thou k. my downsitting and. 139:2
O Lord, thou k. it altogether. 4
k. not what a day may. Pr 27:1
k. not what evil shall. Eccl 11:2
k. not what is the way of the Spirit, even so thou k. not the works. 5
k. not whether shall prosper. 6
a nation that thou k. not. Isa 55:5
whose language thou k. not. Jer 5:15
but thou, O Lord, k. me. 12:3
land which thou k. not. 15:14; 17:4
desired woeful day, thou k. 17:16
thou k. all their counsel to. 18:23
thee things which thou k. not. 33:3
O Lord God, thou k. Ezek 37:3
k. thou wherefore I? Dan 10:20
angel said, K. thou not? Zech 4:5, 13
k. thou that Pharisees? Mat 15:12
thou k. commandments. Mark 10:19
Luke 18:20
deny that thou k. me. Luke 22:34
Nathanael said, Whence k. thou me? John 1:48
art thou a master, and k. not? 3:10*
Jesus said, What I do, thou k. 13:7
we are sure thou k. 16:30; 21:17
k. thou not I have power? 19:10
thou k. that I love thee. 21:15, 16
which k. the hearts of. Acts 1:24
no wrong, as thou very well k. 25:10
k. his will, and approvest. Rom 2:18
what k. thou, O wife, k.? 1 Cor 7:16
k. that all they in Asia. 2 Tim 1:15
how he ministered to me, thou k. 18
and k. not that thou art. Rev 3:17
I said unto him, Sir, thou k. 7:14

knoweth

my lord k. the children. Gen 33:13
when he k. of it, he shall. Lev 5:3, 4
he k. thy walking through. Deut 2:7
no man k. of Moses' sepulchre. 34:6
Lord God of gods, he k. Josh 22:22
the iniquity which he k. 1 Sam 3:13
thy father certainly k. that. 20:3
that also Saul my father k. 23:17
thy servant k. that I. 2 Sam 14:22
all Israel k. thy father is a. 17:10
he k. vain men, he seeth. Job 11:11
he k. the day of darkness is. 15:23
he k. the way that I take. 23:10
there is a path which no fowl k. 28:7
God understandeth and k. the. 23
therefore he k. their works. 34:25
Lord k. way of righteous. Ps 1:6
the Lord k. the days of the. 37:18
for he k. the secrets of the. 44:21
is there any among us that k. 74:9
Lord k. the thoughts of man. 94:11
k. our frame, remembereth. 103:14
moon for seasons, the sun k. 104:19
but the proud he k. afar off. 138:6
that my soul k. right well. 139:14
woman is simple and k. Pr 9:13
heart k. his own bitterness. 14:10
poor, that k. to walk. Eccl 6:8
thine own heart k. thou hast. 7:22
no man k. either love or hatred. 9:1
the ox k. his owner, the ass. Isa 1:3
the stork k. her appointed. Jer 8:7
he understandeth and k. me. 9:24
k. what is in the darkness. Dan 2:22
Lord is good, he k. them. Nah 1:7
the unjust k. no shame. Zeph 3:5
your Father k. what. Mat 6:8
k. ye have need of. 32; Luke 12:30
no man k. the Son but the Father, nor any k. Mat 11:27; Luke 10:22
of that day k. no man. Mat 24:36
Mark 13:32
ye justify, but God k. Luke 16:15
how k. this man letters? John 7:15
when Christ cometh, no man k. 27
as the Father k. me. 10:15
nor k. him. 14:17
he saw it, and he k. that he. 19:35
God which k. the hearts. Acts 15:8
for the king k. of these things. 26:26
he k. what is the mind. Rom 8:27
k. the things of a man, even so the things of God k. no. 1 Cor 2:11
he k. any thing, he k. nothing. 8:2
I love you not? God k. 2 Cor 11:11

God *k.* I lie not. *2 Cor* 11:31
I cannot tell, God *k.* 12:2, 3
the Lord *k.* them that. *2 Tim* 2:19
him that *k.* to do good. *Jas* 4:17
Lord *k.* how to deliver. *2 Pet* 2:9
and *k.* all things. *1 John* 3:20
he that *k.* God. 4:6
loveth is born of God, and *k.* 7
written, which no man *k.* *Rev* 2:17
because he *k.* that he hath. 12:12

who **knoweth,** or **knoweth** *not*

David our lord *k.* it *not.* *1 Ki* 1:11
who k. whether thou art? *Esth* 4:14
who k. not such things? *Job* 12:3
who k. not in all these, that the? 9
come to honour, he *k.* it *not.* 14:21
place of him that *k. not* God. 18:21
man *k. not* the price thereof. 28:13
in anger, yet he *k.* it *not.* 35:15*
riches, and *k. not* who. *Ps* 39:6
who k. the power of thine? 90:11
a brutish man *k. not,* nor a fool. 92:6
k. not that it is for his life. *Pr* 7:23
but he *k. not* that the dead. 9:18
and *who k.* the ruin of them? 24:22
*who k.*whether he be wise? *Eccl* 2:19
who k. the spirit of man that? 3:21
for *who k.* what is good for? 6:12
who k. the interpretation of? 8:1
for he *k. not* that which shall be. 7
for man also *k. not* his time. 9:12
because he *k. not* how to go. 10:15
who seeth us? *who k.* us? *Isa* 29:15
and there, yet he *k. not.* *Hos* 7:9
who k. if he will return? *Joel* 2:14
grow up, he *k. not* how. *Mark* 4:27
this people, who *k. not.* *John* 7:49
walketh in darkness, *k. not.* 12:35
servant *k. not* what his lord. 15:15
k. not that Ephesians. *Acts* 19:35
walketh in darkness, *k. not.* whither. *1 John* 2:11
therefore the world *k.* us *not.* 3:1
he that loveth not, *k. not* God. 4:8

knowing

ye shall be as gods, *k.* *Gen* 3:5
my father David not *k.* *1 Ki* 2:32
Jesus *k.* their thoughts. *Mat* 9:4
Luke 11:17
ye err, not *k.* scriptures. *Mat* 22:29
Jesus immediately *k.* in. *Mark* 5:30*
the woman *k.* what was done. 33
feared John, *k.* that he was. 6:20
but he *k.* their hypocrisy. 12:15
they laughed, *k.* that she. *Luke* 8:53
and one for Elias, not *k.* what. 9:33
Jesus *k.* the Father had. *John* 13:3
Jesus *k.* all things that should. 18:4
Jesus *k.* that all things were. 19:28
none durst ask him, *k.* that it. 21:12
k. that God had sworn. *Acts* 2:30
his wife not *k.* what was done. 5:7
he taught, *k.* only the baptism. 18:25
not *k.* the things that shall. 20:22
who *k.* the judgement of. *Rom* 1:32
not *k.* that the goodness of God. 2:4
k. that tribulation worketh. 5:3
k. this, that our old man is. 6:6
k. Christ being raised from dead. 9
k. the time, now it is high. 13:11
k. that as ye are partakers. *2 Cor* 1:7
k. that he which raised Lord. 4:14
k. that whilst we are at home. 5:6
k. the terror of the Lord, we. 11
k. that a man is not. *Gal* 2:16
k. that whatsoever good. *Eph* 6:8
k. that your master is. 9; *Col* 4:1
k. that I am set for. *Phil* 1:17
k. that of the Lord ye. *Col* 3:24
k. beloved, your election. *1 Thes* 1:4
k. this, that the law is. *1 Tim* 1:9
is proud, *k.* nothing, but doting. 6:4
k. that they do gender. *2 Tim* 2:23
k. of whom thou hast learned. 3:14
k. that he that is such. *Tit* 3:11
k. that thou wilt do more. *Philem* 21
k. ye have in heaven a. *Heb* 10:34
he went out, not *k.* whither. 11:8
k. this, that the trying of. *Jas* 1:3
k. we shall receive greater. 3:1
blessing, *k.* that ye are. *1 Pet* 3:9*
k. that the same afflictions are. 5:9
k. that shortly I must put. *2 Pet* 1:14
k. this, that no prophecy. *2 Pet* 1:20
k. there shall come scoffers in. 3:3

knowledge

tree of *k.* of good and. *Gen* 2:9, 17
filled Bezaleel in *k.* *Ex* 31:3; 35:31
sin come to his *k.* *Lev* 4:23, 28
and knew the *k.* of the. *Num* 24:16
thou shouldest take *k.* *Ruth* 2:10
blessed be he that did take *k.* 19
the Lord is a God of *k.* *1 Sam* 2:3
take *k.* of all the lurking. 23:23
shipmen that had *k.* of sea. *1 Ki* 9:27; *2 Chr* 8:18
give me *k.* that I may. *2 Chr* 1:10
but hast asked *k.* 11
k. is granted thee. 12
every one having *k.* *Neh* 10:28
wise man utter vain *k.*? *Job* 15:2
for we desire not the *k.* of. 21:14
shall any teach God *k.* seeing? 22
and my lips shall utter *k.* 33:3*
ear unto me, ye that have *k.* 34:2
I will fetch my *k.* from afar. 36:3
he that is perfect in *k.* is. 4; 37:16
night unto night sheweth *k.* *Ps* 19:2
is there *k.* in the most High? 73:11
he that teacheth man *k.* shall. 94:10
me good judgement and *k.* 119:66
such *k.* is too wonderful for. 139:6
that thou takest *k.* of him? 144:3
to give the young man *k.* *Pr* 1:4
fear of Lord is the beginning of *k.* 7
fools hate *k.* 22
if thou criest after *k.* 2:3*
for that they hated *k.* and did. 29
out of his mouth cometh *k.* and. 2:6
and when *k.* is pleasant to thy. 10
his *k.* the depths are broken. 3:20
and that thy lips may keep *k.* 5:2
right to them that find *k.* 8:9
k. rather than gold. 10
and find out *k.* 12
k. of the holy is understanding. 9:10
wise men lay up *k.*: but the. 10:14
but through *k.* shall the just. 11:9
loveth instruction loveth *k.* 12:1
a prudent man concealeth *k.* 23
prudent man dealeth with *k.* 13:16
k. is easy to him that. 14:6
not in him the lips of *k.* 7
prudent are crowned with *k.* 18
the tongue of the wise useth *k.* 15:2
the lips of the wise disperse *k.* 7
hath understanding seeketh *k.* 14
he that hath *k.* spareth his. 17:27
the prudent getteth *k.* and the ear of the wise seeketh *k.* 18:15
and he will understand *k.* 19:25
to err from the words of *k.* 27
lips of *k.* are a precious jewel. 20:15
when the wise is instructed, he receiveth *k.* 21:11
eyes of the Lord preserve *k.* 22:12
and apply thine heart unto my *k.* 17
excellent things in counsels and *k.* 20
thine ears to the words of *k.* 23:12
by *k.* shall the chambers be. 24:4
man of *k.* increaseth strength. 5
so shall the *k.* of wisdom be to. 14
by a man of *k.* the state. 28:2
wisdom, nor have *k.* of holy. 30:3
heart had experience of *k.* *Eccl* 1:16
he that increaseth *k.* increaseth. 18
is a man whose labour is in *k.* 2:21
God giveth to a man wisdom, *k.* 26
but the excellency of *k.* is. 7:12
nor *k.* in the grave, whither. 9:10
still taught the people *k.* 12:9
before the child shall have *k.* *Isa* 8:4
spirit of *k.* and of the fear. 11:2
whom shall he teach *k.*? them. 28:9
the rash shall understand *k.* 32:4
wisdom and *k.* shall be stability. 33:6
who taught him *k.* 40:14
nor is there *k.* 44:19
and maketh their *k.* foolish. 25
thy wisdom and thy *k.* hath. 47:10
by his *k.* my righteous. 53:11
which shall feed you with *k.* *Jer* 3:15
every man is brutish in his *k.* 10:14
51:17
Lord hath given me *k.* of it. 11:18
favoured and cunning in *k.* *Dan* 1:4
God gave them *k.* *Dan* 1:17
he giveth *k.* to them. 2:21
excellent spirit and *k.* were. 5:12
many run to and fro, and *k.* 12:4
destroyed for lack of *k.*: because thou hast rejected *k.*, I will. *Hos* 4:6
the earth filled with the *k.* *Hab* 2:14
priest's lips should keep *k.* *Mal* 2:7
that place had *k.* of him. *Mat* 14:35
k. of salvation by remission of sins. *Luke* 1:77
taken away the key of *k.* 11:52
marvelled and took *k.* *Acts* 4:13
having more perfect *k.* of. 24:22
to retain God in their *k.* *Rom* 1:28
which hast the form of *k.* 2:20
justified, for by law is the *k.* 3:20
zeal, but not according to *k.* 10:2
ye also are filled with all *k.* 15:14
in all utterance and all *k.* *1 Cor* 1:5
we know that we all have *k.* *K.* 8:1
there is not in every man that *k.* 7
if any man see thee which hast *k.* 10
through thy *k.* shall thy weak. 11
to another the word of *k.* by the. 12:8
understand all mysteries and all *k.* 13:2
whether there be *k.* it shall vanish. 8
speak to you by revelation or *k.* 14:6
the savour of his *k.* *2 Cor* 2:14
to give the light of the *k.* of the. 4:6
by *k.*, by longsuffering, by. 6:6
abound in faith, utterance, and *k.* 8:7
I be rude in speech, yet not in *k.* 11:6
give you wisdom in the *k.* *Eph* 1:17
ye may understand my *k.* 3:4*
love of Christ which passeth *k.* 19
we come in the unity of the *k.* 4:13
love may abound more in *k.* *Phil* 1:9
things but loss for *k.* of Christ. 3:8
ye might be filled with *k.* *Col* 1:9
hid treasures of wisdom and *k.* 2:3
new man which is renewed in *k.* 3:10
all men to come to the *k.* *1 Tim* 2:4
never able to come to *k.* *2 Tim* 3:7
after we have received *k.* *Heb* 10:26
man, and endued with *k.*? *Jas* 3:13*
husbands dwell with them according to *k.* *1 Pet* 3:7
through the *k.* of him. *2 Pet* 1:3
add to virtue *k.* and to *k.* 5
nor unfruitful in the *k.* of our. 8
grow in grace and in the *k.* of. 3:18

knowledge *of God*

shalt thou find the *k. of God.* *Pr* 2:5
is no truth, nor *k. of God.* *Hos* 4:1
desired the *k. of God* more. 6:6
the riches both of the wisdom and *k. of God.* *Rom* 11:33
have not the *k. of God.* *1 Cor* 15:34
exalteth itself against *k. of God.* *2 Cor* 10:5
increasing in the *k. of God.* *Col* 1:10
through the *k. of God.* *2 Pet* 1:2

knowledge *of the Lord*

the good *k. of the Lord.* *2 Chr* 30:22*
full of the *k. of the Lord.* *Isa* 11:9
escaped pollution through the *k. of the Lord.* *2 Pet* 2:20

no **knowledge**

your children which in that day had *no k.* *Deut* 1:39
have all the workers of iniquity *no k.*? *Ps* 14:4; 53:4
captivity because they have *no k.* *Isa* 5:13
have *no k.* that set up their images. 45:20
our soul, and thou takest *no k.* 58:3
do good, they have *no k.* *Jer* 4:22

without **knowledge**

committed *without k.* of. *Num* 15:24
Job hath spoken *without k.* and. *Job* 34:35
multiplieth words *without k.* 35:16
perish by sword, and die *without k.* 36:12
by words *without k.* 38:2; 42:3
the soul be *without k.* *Pr* 19:2

known

nor had any man *k.* her. *Gen* 24:16
surely this thing is *k.* *Ex* 2:14

if it be *k.* that the ox hath. *Ex* 21:36
for wherein shall it be *k.* 33:16
sin they have sinned is *k.* *Lev* 4:14
whether he hath seen or *k.* of it. 5:1
woman that hath *k.* man. *Num* 31:17
take wise men, and *k.* *Deut* 1:13, 15
be not *k.* who hath slain him. 21:1
which had *k.* the works. *Josh* 24:31
k. to you why his hand. *1 Sam* 6:3
let it be *k.* that thou art God in. *1 Ki* 18:36
it *k.* to the king. *Ezra* 4:12, 13; 5:8
enemies heard it was *k.* to. *Neh* 4:15
thing was *k.* to Mordecai. *Esth* 2:22
Lord is *k.* by the judgement. *Ps* 9:16
hast *k.* my soul in adversities. 31:7
God is *k.* in her palaces for. 48:3
thy way may be *k.* on earth. 67:2
thou hast *k.* my reproach. 69:19
in Judah is God *k.*: his name. 76:1
sea, thy footsteps are not *k.* 77:19
which we have heard and *k.* 78:3
be *k.* among the heathen in. 79:10
shall thy wonders be *k.* in? 88:12
because he hath *k.* my name. 91:14
that have *k.* thy testimonies. 119:79
I have *k.* of old thou hast. 152
hast searched me, and *k.* me. 139:1
that perverteth his ways shall be *k.* *Pr* 10:9
a fool's wrath is presently *k.* 12:16
a child is *k.* by his doings. 20:11
her husband is *k.* in the gates. 31:23
a fool's voice is *k.* by. *Eccl* 5:3
and it is *k.* that it is man, nor. 6:10
excellent things, this is *k.* *Isa* 12:5
and the Lord shall be *k.* to. 19:21
their seed shall be *k.* among. 61:9
hand of the Lord shall be *k.* to. 66:14
they have *k.* the way of. *Jer* 5:5
then shall prophet be *k.* the. 28:9
saith Lord God, be it *k.* *Ezek* 36:32
Acts 4:10; 13:38; 28:28
I will be *k.* in the eyes. *Ezek* 38:23
but if not, be it *k.* to thee. *Dan* 3:18
after thou shalt have *k.* the. 4:26
have I *k.* of all families. *Amos* 3:2
a day which shall be *k.* *Zech* 14:7
ye had *k.* what this meant. *Mat* 12:7
tree is *k.* by his fruit. 33; *Luke* 6:44
goodman of house had *k.* *Mat* 24:43
Luke 12:39
prophet, he would have *k.* *Luke* 7:39
saying, If thou hadst *k.* in. 19:42
how he was *k.* of them in. 24:35
himself seeketh to be *k.* *John* 7:4
nor my Father: if ye had *k.* me, ye should have *k.* my. 8:19; 14:7
I know my sheep, and am *k.* 10:14
now they have *k.* 17:7
and have *k.* surely. 8
I have *k.* thee, these have *k.* 25
that disciple which was *k.* 18:15, 16
was *k.* to all dwellers. *Acts* 1:19
this *k.* unto you, and hearken. 2:14
but their laying await was *k.* of. 9:24
it was *k.* throughout all Joppa. 42
k. unto God are all his works. 15:18
this was *k.* to all the Jews and. 19:17
have *k.* the certainty. 22:30; 23:28
which may be *k.* of God. *Rom* 1:19
for who hath *k.* the mind of the Lord? 11:34; *1 Cor* 2:16
for had they *k.* it. *1 Cor* 2:8
same is *k.* of him. 8:3
know, even as I also am *k.* 13:12
how shall it be *k.* what is piped? 14:7
how shall it be *k.* what is spoken? 9
Ye are our epistle, *k.* and. *2 Cor* 3:2
though we have *k.* Christ. 5:16
as unknown, and yet well *k.*; as. 6:9
have *k.* God or are *k.* of. *Gal* 4:9
might be *k.* by church the. *Eph* 3:10
let your moderation be *k.* *Phil* 4:5
thou hast fully *k.* my. *2 Tim* 3:10
from a child thou hast *k.* the. 15
preaching might be fully *k.* 4:17
because ye have *k.* him. *1 John* 2:13
we have *k.* and believed the. 4:16
that have *k.* the truth. *2 John* 1:1

made or *madest* known

Joseph *made* himself *k.* *Gen* 45:1
and *madest* *k.* to them. *Neh* 9:14
the Lord hath *made* *k.* his. *Ps* 98:2
make *k.* his ways to Moses. 103:7
that which is in the midst of fools is *made* *k.* *Pr* 14:33
have *made* *k.* to thee this day. 22:19
made myself *k.* to. *Ezek* 20:5, 9
Arioch *made* the thing *k.* *Dan* 2:15
Daniel *made* the thing *k.* to. 17
hast *made* *k.* to me, *made* *k.* to. 23
God hath *made* *k.* to the king. 45
made *k.* that which shall surely be. *Hos* 5:9
Lord hath *made* *k.* to us. *Luke* 2:15
seen it, they *made* *k.* abroad. 17
I have *made* *k.* to you. *John* 15:15
made *k.* to me the ways. *Acts* 2:28
Joseph was *made* *k.* to his brethren; and Joseph's kindred *made* *k.* 7:13
made *k.* to all nations. *Rom* 16:26
made *k.* to us the mystery. *Eph* 1:9
how by revelation he *made* *k.* 3:3
requests be *made* *k.* to. *Phil* 4:6
we *make* *k.* the coming. *2 Pet* 1:16

make known

I will *make* myself *k.* *Num* 12:6
thou mayest *make* *k.* to me what I. *1 Sam* 28:15
make *k.* his deeds among people. *1 Chr* 16:8; *Ps* 105:1
in *making* *k.* all these great. 17:19
they should *make* them *k.* *Ps* 78:5
with my mouth will I *make* *k.* 89:1
that he might *make* *k.* his. 106:8
to *make* *k.* to sons of men. 145:12
I will *make* *k.* my words. *Pr* 1:23
the father to children shall *make* *k.* thy truth. *Isa* 38:19
to *make* thy name *k.* to thy. 64:2
I will *make* myself *k.* *Ezek* 35:11
I *make* my holy name *k.* in. 39:7
a man that will *make* *k.* *Dan* 2:25
art thou able to *make* *k.* to me? 26
Lord *maketh* *k.* to the king. 28, 29
shall *make* *k.* the interpretation. 30
5:15, 16, 17
midst of the years *make* *k.* *Hab* 3:2
God willing to *make* his power *k.* *Rom* 9:22
that he might *make* *k.* riches of. 23
to *make* *k.* the mystery of. *Eph* 6:19
Tychicus shall *make* *k.* to you. 21
whom God will *make* *k.* *Col* 1:27
shall *make* *k.* to you all things. 4:9

not known

I have two daughters which have not *k.* man. *Gen* 19:8; *Num* 31:18
35; *Judg* 21:12
not be *k.* they had. *Gen* 41:21
and the plenty shall *not* be *k.* in. 31
Jehovah was I *not* *k.* *Ex* 6:3
with children which have *not* *k.* *Deut* 11:2; 31:13
to go after gods which ye have *not* *k.* 11:28; 13:6, 13
nor thy fathers have *k.* 28:36, 64
as had *not* *k.* the wars. *Judg* 3:1
withs, so his strength was *not* *k.* 16:9
but make *not* thyself *k.* *Ruth* 3:3
let it *not* be *k.* that a woman. 14
and the thing was *not* *k.* *2 Sam* 17:19
be *not* *k.* to be the wife. *1 Ki* 14:2
people whom I have *not* *k.* *Ps* 18:43
and thy footsteps are *not* *k.* 77:19
heathen that have *not* *k.* thee. 79:6
not *k.* my ways. 95:10; *Heb* 3:10
they have *not* *k.* them. *Ps* 147:20
he hath not seen the sun, *nor* *k.* any thing. *Eccl* 6:5
have ye *not* *k.*? *Isa* 40:21
hast thou *not* *k.*? 28
paths that they have *not* *k.* 42:16
have *not* *k.* nor understood. 44:18
though thou hast *not* *k.* me. 45:4, 5
foolish, they have *not* *k.* me. *Jer* 4:22
countries thou hast *not* *k.* *Ezek* 32:9
not make *k.* the dream. *Dan* 2:5, 9
they did *not* make *k.* to. 4:7; 5:8
they have *not* *k.* the Lord. *Hos* 5:4
their place is *not* *k.* *Nah* 3:17
for there is nothing hid that shall *not* be *k.* *Mat* 10:26; *Luke* 8:17; 12:2
they should *not* make him *k.* *Mat* 12:16; *Mark* 3:12
a stranger, and hast *not* *k.* the things which? *Luke* 24:18
yet ye have *not* *k.* him. *John* 8:55
and yet hast thou *not* *k.* me. 14:9
because they have *not* *k.* the. 16:3
the world hath *not* *k.* thee. 17:25
of peace have they *not* *k.* *Rom* 3:17
I had *not* *k.* sin but by the law: for I had *not* *k.* 7:7
other ages was *not* made *k.* *Eph* 3:5
been better *not* to have *k.* *2 Pet* 2:21
hath not seen *nor* *k.* him. *1 John* 3:6
which have *not* *k.* depths. *Rev* 2:24

Kohath

the sons of Levi, Gershon, *K.* and. *Gen* 46:11; *Ex* 6:16; *Num* 3:17
the sons of *K.* *Ex* 6:18; *Num* 3:19
27, 29, 30; 16:1; *1 Chr* 6:2, 22, 61
life of *K.* were 133 years. *Ex* 6:18
sum of the sons of *K.* of. *Num* 4:2
service of the sons of *K.* 4, 15; 7:9
the sons of *K.* Uriel. *1 Chr* 15:5

Kohathites

off the family of the *K.* *Num* 4:18
Aaron numbered sons of *K.* 34, 37
the *K.* set forward bearing. 10:21
the lot came out for *K.* *Josh* 21:4
1 Chr 6:54
sons of *K.* sanctified. *2 Chr* 29:12
the sons of the *K.* to set the. 34:12

Korah

Aholibamah bare *K.* *Gen* 36:5
duke *K.* 16, 18
sons of Izhar, *K.* Nepheg. *Ex* 6:21
Num 16:1
take censers, *K.* and all. *Num* 16:6
K. gathered all the congregation. 19
from about the tabernacle of *K.* 24
that he be not as *K.* and as. 40
strove in the company of *K.* 26:9
the children of *K.* died not. 11
not in the company of *K.* 27:3
Esau, Joalam and *K.* *1 Chr* 1:35
sons of Hebron, *K.* 2:43
Amminadab his son, *K.* his. 6:22
son of *K.* and his brethren. 9:19
in the gainsaying of *K.* *Jude* 11

L

Laban

a brother, his name was *L.* *Gen* 24:29
flee thou to *L.* my brother. 27:43
a wife of the daughters of *L.* 28:2
know ye *L.*? 29:5
L. gave Rachel, Bilhah. 29
Jacob fed the rest of *L.*'s flocks. 30:36
so the feebler were *L.*'s, the. 42
beheld the countenance of *L.* 31:2
seen all that *L.* doth to thee. 12
Jacob stole away unawares to *L.* 20
God came to *L.* in a dream by. 24
L. searched all the tent, but. 34
Jacob chode with *L.* 36
L. kissed his sons. 55
I have sojourned with *L.* and. 32:4

Laban

between Paran and *L.* *Deut* 1:1

labour, *substantive*

God hath seen the *l.* *Gen* 31:42
travailed and had hard *l.* 35:16, 17
and looked on our *l.* *Deut* 26:7
out every man from his *l.* *Neh* 5:13
or wilt thou leave thy *l.*? *Job* 39:11
her *l.* is in vain without fear. 16
he gave their *l.* to locust. *Ps* 78:46
yet is their strength *l.* and. 90:10
man goeth to his *l.* until. 104:23
they inherited the *l.* of the people. 105:44
down their heart with *l.* 107:12
let the stranger spoil his *l.* 109:11
thou shalt eat the *l.* of thy. 128:2
the *l.* of the righteous. *Pr* 10:16
he that gathereth by *l.* shall. 13:11
in all *l.* there is profit, but. 14:23
what profit hath a man of all his *l.*? *Eccl* 1:3
all things are full of *l.*; man. 8*
all my *l.* my portion of all my *l.* 2:10

I hated all my *l.* which I. *Eccl* 2:18
he have rule over all my *l.* 19
my heart to despair of the *l.* I. 20
a man whose *l.* is in wisdom. 21
what hath man of all his *l.* under? 22
soul enjoy good in *l.* 24; 3:13; 5:18
yet there is no end of all his *l.* 4:8
have a good reward for their *l.* 9
nothing of his *l.* which he may. 5:15
to rejoice in his *l.*; this is the gift. 19
all the *l.* of man is for his mouth. 6:7
shall abide with him of his *l.* 8:15
thy portion in thy *l.* under. 9:9
the *l.* of the foolish wearieth. 10:15
l. of Egypt shall come. *Isa* 45:14
spend your *l.* for that which? 55:2
shame devoured the *l.* of. *Jer* 3:24
came I forth to see *l.* and? 20:18
take away all thy *l.* *Ezek* 23:29
the land of Egypt for his *l.* 29:20*
though the *l.* of the olive. *Hab* 3:17
a drought on all the *l.* *Hag* 1:11
whereon ye bestowed no *l.* *John* 4:38
who bestowed much *l.* on. *Rom* 16:6
every man shall receive according to his *l.* *1 Cor* 3:8
that your *l.* is not in vain. 15:58
lest I bestowed *l.* in vain. *Gal* 4:11
flesh, this is fruit of my *l.* *Phil* 1:22
my brother and companion in *l.* 2:25
remembering your *l.* of. *1 Thes* 1:3
for ye remember, brethren, our *l.* 2:9
you, and our *l.* be in vain. 3:5
but wrought with *l.* and. *2 Thes* 3:8
to forget your *l.* of love. *Heb* 6:10
I know thy works, and *l.* *Rev* 2:2

labour, *verb*

work, that they may *l.* *Ex* 5:9
days shalt thou *l.* 20:9; *Deut* 5:13
not all the people to *l.* *Josh* 7:3
a land, for which he did not *l.* 24:13
be a guard to us, and *l.* *Neh* 4:22
I be wicked, why then *l.*? *Job* 9:29
Lord build, they *l.* in vain. *Ps* 127:1
oxen may be strong to *l.* 144:14*
his hands refuse to *l.* *Pr* 21:25
L. not to be rich, cease from. 23:4*
he, For whom do I *l.*? *Eccl* 4:8
though a man *l.* to seek it out. 8:17
I will weep bitterly, *l.* not. *Isa* 22:4
they shall not *l.* in vain, nor. 65:23
the people shall *l.* in vain. *Jer* 51:58
under persecution we *l.* *Lam* 5:5*
be in pain, and *l.* to bring. *Mi* 4:10
that the people should *l.* *Hab* 2:13
come unto me all ye that *l.* *Mat* 11:28
l. not for the meat that. *John* 6:27
and Tryphosa who *l.* *Rom* 16:12
and *l.* working with our. *1 Cor* 4:12
we *l.* to be accepted of. *2 Cor* 5:9*
but rather *l.* working. *Eph* 4:28
whereunto I also *l.* striving. *Col* 1:29
to know them which *l.* *1 Thes* 5:12
therefore we both *l.* and. *1 Tim* 4:10
especially they that *l.* in word. 5:17
let us *l.* therefore to. *Heb* 4:11*

laboured

so we *l.* in the work. *Neh* 4:21
that which he *l.* for. *Job* 20:18
on the labour I had *l.* to. *Eccl* 2:11
all my labour wherein I have *l.* 19
yet to a man that hath not *l.* 21
of his heart wherein he hath *l.* 22
what profit hath he that hath *l.*? 5:16
thy sorceries wherein thou hast *l.* *Isa* 47:12
to thee with whom thou hast *l.* 15
I said, I have *l.* in vain. 49:4
drink, for which thou hast *l.* 62:8
king *l.* to deliver Daniel. *Dan* 6:14
for which thou hast not *l.* *Jonah* 4:10
other men *l.* and ye are. *John* 4:38
salute Persis, who *l.* *Rom* 16:12
but I *l.* more abundantly. *1 Cor* 15:10
I have not run nor *l.* in. *Phil* 2:16
help those that *l.* with me in. 4:3
and for my name's sake *l.* *Rev* 2:3

labourer

the *l.* is worthy of his hire. *Luke* 10:7
l. is worthy of his reward. *1 Tim* 5:18

labourers

harvest plenteous, but *l.* few. *Mat* 9:37; *Luke* 10:2
pray the Lord that he will send *l.* *Mat* 9:38; *Luke* 10:2
went out early to hire *l.* *Mat* 20:1
when he had agreed with the *l.* 2
call the *l.* 8
for we are *l.* together. *1 Cor* 3:9*
behold the hire of the *l.* *Jas* 5:4

laboureth

he that *l.* *l.* for himself. *Pr* 16:26*
in that wherein he *l.*? *Eccl* 3:9
one that helpeth and *l.* *1 Cor* 16:16
the husbandman that *l.* *2 Tim* 2:6

labouring

the sleep of a *l.* man. *Eccl* 5:12
l. ye ought to support. *Acts* 20:35
l. for you in prayer. *Col* 4:12*
l. night and day we. *1 Thes* 2:9

labours

of thy *l.* when thou hast gathered in thy *l.* out of the field. *Ex* 23:16
all thy *l.* shall a nation. *Deut* 28:33
and thy *l.* be in the house. *Pr* 5:10
fast, ye exact all your *l.* *Isa* 58:3
I will deliver all their *l.* *Jer* 20:5*
in my *l.* shall they find no. *Hos* 12:8
I smote you in all the *l.* *Hag* 2:17
entered into their *l.* *John* 4:38
in tumults, in *l.* in. *2 Cor* 6:5
not boasting of other men's *l.* 10:15
in *l.* more abundant, in. 11:23
may rest from their *l.* *Rev* 14:13

lace

breastplate with *l.* of blue. *Ex* 28:28
thou shalt put it on a blue *l.* 37
tied it to a *l.* of blue to fasten. 39:31

Lachish

the Lord delivered *L.* *Josh* 10:32
the king of *L.* one. 12:11
Judah had *L.* 15:39
Amaziah fled to *L.* *2 Ki* 14:19
2 Chr 25:27
king of Assyria to *L.* *2 Ki* 18:14
Assyria sent Rab-shakeh from *L.* with a great host. 17; *Isa* 36:2
Rehoboam built *L.* and. *2 Chr* 11:9
Babylon fought against *L.* *Jer* 34:7
O inhabitant of *L.* bind. *Mi* 1:13

lack, *substantive*

destroy all for *l.* of five? *Gen* 18:28
that gathered little had no *l.* *Ex* 16:18; *2 Cor* 8:15
old lion perisheth for *l.* *Job* 4:11
ones wander for *l.* of meat. 38:41
my people are destroyed for *l.* of. *Hos* 4:6
his life to supply your *l.* *Phil* 2:30
that ye may have *l.* of. *1 Thes* 4:12

lack, *verb*

there shall *l.* five of? *Gen* 18:28
not *l.* any thing in it. *Deut* 8:9
the young lions do *l.* *Ps* 34:10
to the poor shall not *l.* *Pr* 28:27
thy head *l.* no ointment. *Eccl* 9:8
have I kept, what *l.* I yet? *Mat* 19:20
if any of you *l.* wisdom. *Jas* 1:5

lacked

thou hast *l.* nothing. *Deut* 2:7
l. of David's servants. *2 Sam* 2:30
provided victual, they *l.* *1 Ki* 4:27
but what hast thou *l.* with me? 11:22
sustain them, they *l.* *Neh* 9:21
because it *l.* moisture. *Luke* 8:6
without purse, *l.* ye any? 22:35
any among them that *l.* *Acts* 4:34
more honour to that part which *l.* *1 Cor* 12:24
ye were careful, but *l.* *Phil* 4:10

lackest

but one thing thou *l.* *Mark* 10:21
Luke 18:22

lacketh

there *l.* not one man of. *Num* 31:49
not fail one that *l.* bread. *2 Sam* 3:29
committeth adultery, *l.* *Pr* 6:32*
honoureth himself, and *l.* bread. 12:9
he that *l.* these things. *2 Pet* 1:9

lacking

thou suffer salt to be *l.* *Lev* 2:13
a lamb that hath any thing *l.* 22:23
should be one tribe *l.* in. *Judg* 21:3
there was nothing *l* to. *1 Sam* 30:19
they shall fear no more, nor shall be *l.* *Jer* 23:4
for that which was *l.* *1 Cor* 16:17
was *l.* to me the brethren. *2 Cor* 11:9
might perfect what is *l.* *1 Thes* 3:10

lad, -s

This word is used [1] *Of a boy of about thirteen,* Gen 21:12, 17. [2] *Of a boy of about seventeen,* Gen 37:2. [3] *Of a married man,* Gen 43:8 *compared with* 46:21. [4] *Of a servant,* 1 Sam 20:36.

grievous because of the *l.* *Gen* 21:12
God heard the voice of the *l.* 17
arise, lift up the *l.* 18
she gave the *l.* drink. 19
God was with the *l.* and he. 20
I and the *l.* will go yonder. 22:5
lay not thine hand upon the *l.* 12
l. was with the sons of Bilhah. 37:2
send the *l.* with me, and we. 43:8
we said, The *l.* cannot leave. 44:22
the *l.* be not with us, his life is bound up in the *l.*'s life. 30, 31, 34
became surety for the *l.* 32
abide instead of the *l.*; let the *l.* 33
who redeemed me, bless the *l.* 48:16
Samson said to the *l.* *Judg* 16:26
behold I will send a *l.* *1 Sam* 20:21
unto the *l.* Run, and as the *l.* ran. 36
Jonathan cried after the *l.* 37, 38
l. knew not any thing, only. 39
gave his artillery to his *l.* 40
a *l.* saw them and told. *2 Sam* 17:18
a *l.* here hath five barley. *John* 6:9

ladder

dreamed, and behold a *l.* *Gen* 28:12

lade

l. your beasts and go to. *Gen* 45:17
my father did *l.* you. *1 Ki* 12:11
ye *l.* men with grievous. *Luke* 11:46

laded

they *l.* their asses with the corn. *Gen* 42:26; 44:13
those that *l.* wrought. *Neh* 4:17
l. us with such things. *Acts* 28:10*

laden

sent ten asses *l.* with. *Gen* 45:23
Jesse took an ass *l.* with bread. *1 Sam* 16:20
a people *l.* with iniquity. *Isa* 1:4
labour and are heavy *l.* *Mat* 11:28
silly women, *l.* with sins. *2 Tim* 3:6

ladeth

woe to him that *l.* himself. *Hab* 2:6

lading

on the sabbath *l.* asses. *Neh* 13:15
damage not only of *l.* *Acts* 27:10

ladies

wise *l.* answered her, yea. *Judg* 5:29
shall *l.* of Persia and. *Esth* 1:18*

lady

no more be called a *l.* *Isa* 47:5†
and thou saidst, I shall be a *l.* 7†
the elder to the elect *l.* *2 John* 1
now I beseech thee, *l.*, that we. 5

laid

and *l.* it on both their. *Gen* 9:23
Abraham took wood and *l.* it. 22:6
Jacob *l.* the rods before. 30:41
she went away, and *l.* by her. 38:19
right hand, and *l.* it on. 48:14
she *l.* it in the flags by. *Ex* 2:3
let more work be *l.* on the men. 5:9
he shall give whatsoever is *l.* 21:30
Egyptians *l.* on us hard. *Deut* 26:6
stalks of flax she had *l.* *Josh* 2:6
they took and *l.* them out. 7:23
blood be *l.* on Abimelech. *Judg* 9:24
took the child and *l.* it in. *Ruth* 4:16
l. a great heap of stones on Absalom. *2 Sam* 18:17*
my son and *l.* it in her bosom, and *l.* her dead child in my. *1 Ki* 3:20
an oath be *l.* on him. 8:31; *2 Chr* 6:22
the prophet *l.* the carcase. *1 Ki* 13:29
l. his carcase in his own grave. 30
he carried him up, and *l.* him. 17:19
she went and *l.* him on. *2 Ki* 4:21
Lord *l.* this burden on him. 9:25
took and *l.* it on the boil. 20:7

l. upon Israel in the. 2 Chr 24:9
where they l. the meat. Neh 13:5
and my calamity l. in. Job 6:2
the snare is l. for him in. 18:10*
or who l. the corner-stone. 38:6
and majesty hast l. on. Ps 21:5
out of the net they have l. for. 31:4
like sheep they are l. in the. 49:14
to be l. in the balance, they. 62:9
they have l. Jerusalem on. 79:1
l. me in the lowest pit. 88:6
I have l. help upon one that. 89:19
hurt with fetters, he was l. 105:18
thy judgements have I l. 119:30
wicked have l. a snare. 110; 141:19
thou hast l. thine hand upon. 139:5
they have privily l. a snare. 142:3
he l. it upon my mouth. Isa 6:7*
burned him, yet l. it. 42:25; 57:11
thou hast very heavily l. 47:6
Lord l. on him the iniquity of. 53:6
I have l. a snare for thee. Jer 50:24
be thou l. with the uncircumcised.
Ezek 32:19
when I have l. the land. 33:29
spoken, saying, They are l. 35:12
I drew them, and I l. Hos 11:4
garners are l. desolate. Joel 1:17
on clothes l. to pledge. Amos 2:8
they have l. a wound. Ob 7
he arose and l. his robe. Jonah 3:6
now gather, he hath l. siege. Mi 5:1
it is l. over with gold. Hab 2:19
from before a stone was l. Hag 2:15
the stone that I have l. Zech 3:9
for they l. the pleasant land. 7:14
now the axe is l. to the root.
Mat 3:10; Luke 3:9
l. it in his own new tomb. Mat 27:60
and her daughter l. on. Mark 7:30
Mary beheld where he was l. 15:47
behold the place where they l. 16:6
her firstborn, and l. Luke 2:7
Lazarus was l. at his gate. 16:20
wherein never man before was l.
23:53; John 19:41
said, Where have ye l.? John 11:34
l. aside his garments, and. 13:4
there l. they Jesus therefore. 19:42
not where they have l. him. 20:2, 13
whom they l. at the gate. Acts 3:2
and l. the money at the. 4:37; 5:2
l. them on beds and couches. 5:15
when washed, they l. her in. 9:37
David was l. to his fathers. 13:36
nothing l. to his charge. 23:29
l. many complaints they could. 25:7
concerning the crime l. against. 16
necessity is l. upon me. 1 Cor 9:16
I pray it be not l. to. 2 Tim 4:16
see **foundation**

laid *down*
before they were l. down. Josh 2:8
carried them, and l. them down. 4:8
his feet and l. her down. Ruth 3:7
Eli was l. down. 1 Sam 3:2
Samuel l. down to sleep. 3
Amnon was l. down. 2 Sam 13:8
did eat, and l. him down. 1 Ki 19:6
Ahab came and l. him down. 21:4
I l. me down and slept. Ps 3:5
since thou art l. down no feller is.
Isa 14:8
up that I l. not down. Luke 19:22
l. them down at the. Acts 4:35
witnesses l. down their clothes. 7:58
for my life l. down their. Rom 16:4
he l. down his life for. 1 John 3:16

laid *hand*
nobles he l. not his hand. Ex 24:11
Tamar l. her hand on. 2 Sam 13:19
because he l. his hand on. Esth 8:7
l. not their hand on spoil. 9:10, 15, 16
princes l. their hand on. Job 29:9
thou hast l. thine hand. Ps 139:5
my hand that I have l. Ezek 39:21
he l. his right hand upon. Rev 1:17

laid *hands*
his sons l. their h. Lev 8:14, 18, 22
Moses l. his hands on Joshua.
Num 27:23; Deut 34:9
and they l. hands on her.
2 Ki 11:16; 2 Chr 23:15*
l. their hands on the he goats.
2 Chr 29:23
nor have l. hands on their. Ob 13
l. hands, and took him. Mat 18:28
and he l. his hands on them. 19:15
they came and l. hands on Jesus.
26:50; Mark 14:46
save that he l. hands on. Mark 6:5
he l. his hands on every. Luke 4:40
he l. his hands on her, she. 13:13
but no man l. hands on him.
John 7:30, 44; 8:20
and they l. hands on the apostles.
Acts 4:3; 5:18
and prayed, they l. hands on. 6:6
then l. they their hands on. 8:17
they l. their hands on Paul. 13:3
when Paul had l. his hands. 19:6
up the people, and l. hands. 21:27
Paul l. hands on Publius'. 28:8

laid *hold*
men l. hold on Lot's. Gen 19:16
took a knife, and l. hold. Judg 19:29
Saul l. hold on Samuel's skirt, and.
1 Sam 15:27
l. hold on other gods. 2 Chr 7:22
Herod had l. hold on John.
Mat 14:3; Mark 6:17
l. no hold on me. Mat 26:55
l. hold on Jesus. 57; Mark 14:51
l. hold on one Simon. Luke 23:26
he l. hold on the dragon. Rev 20:2

laid *up*
she l. up his garments. Gen 39:16
Joseph l. up food in the. 41:48
l. it up till the morning. Ex 16:24
Aaron l. up the pot of manna. 34
Moses l. up the rods. Num 17:7
not this l. up in store? Deut 32:34
Samuel l. it up before. 1 Sam 10:25
David l. up these words. 21:12
which thy fathers l. up. 2 Ki 20:17
treasures were l. up. Ezra 6:1
thou hast l. up for them. Ps 31:19
wealth of sinners is l. up. Pr 13:22
fruits which I have l. up. S of S 7:13
at Michmash he l. up. Isa 10:28
that l. up shall they carry. 15:7
shall not be treasured or l. up. 23:18
which fathers l. up be carried. 39:6
they l. up the roll in the. Jer 36:20
l. them up in their hearts. Luke 1:66
hast much goods l. up for. 12:19
thy pound I have kept l. up in. 19:20
for the hope which is l. up. Col 1:5
is l. up for me a crown. 2 Tim 4:8

laid *wait*
l. wait against Shechem. Judg 9:34
l. wait all night for Samson. 16:2
Amalek l. wait for him. 1 Sam 15:2
Saul came and l. wait in the valley. 5
l. wait at my neighbour's. Job 31:9
they l. wait for us in the wilderness.
Lam 4:19
when the Jews l. wait for him.
Acts 20:3; 23:30

laid *waste*
l. waste his dwelling place. Ps 79:7
Ar and Kir l. waste. Isa 15:1
Tyre, it is l. waste. 23:1
your strength is l. waste. 23:14
kings of Assyria l. waste all. 37:18
pleasant things are l. waste. 64:11
thy cities shall be l. waste. Jer 4:7
Ezek 6:6; 12:20; 19:7; 29:12
should this city be l. waste?
Jer 27:17
now she is l. waste. Ezek 26:2
l. my vine waste, and. Joel 1:7
Israel shall be l. waste. Amos 7:9
say, Nineveh is l. waste. Nah 3:7
I l. his heritage waste. Mal 1:3

laidest
l. affliction on our loins. Ps 66:11
takest up that thou l. Luke 19:21

lain
he had l. in the grave. John 11:17
the body of Jesus had l. 20:12
see **lien**

Laish
to spy the country of L. Judg 18:14
the name of the city was L. 29
cause thy voice to be heard unto L.
Isa 10:30

Laish, *person*
given to Phalti son of L. 1 Sam 25:44
Ish-bosheth took her from the son of
L. 2 Sam 3:15

lake
Jesus stood by the l. Luke 5:1
two ships standing by the l. 2
over to the other side of the l. 8:22
down a storm of wind on the l. 23
violently down a steep place into l. 33
were cast into a l. of fire. Rev 19:20
devil was cast into l. of fire. 20:10
hell were cast into the l. of. 14
not in the book of life, cast into l. 15
their part in the l. burneth. 21:8

lamb
(The word is used most often literally, of a young sheep. Jesus is called the Lamb of God because he was sacrificed for us, as was the lamb in the Jewish ritual)
where is the l. for a? Gen 22:7
God will provide himself a l. 8
to them every man a l. Ex 12:3, 21
your l. shall be without blemish. 5
thou redeem with a l. 13:13; 34:20
l. thou shalt offer in morning, and the
other l. 29:39, 41; Num 28:4
with a l. a tenth deal of. Ex 29:40
Num 28:21, 29; 29:4, 10, 15
if he offer a l. Lev 3:7; 4:32; 5:6
22:23; 23:12
as the fat of a l. is taken away. 4:35
if not able to bring a l. 5:7; 12:8
take a l. of the first year. 9:3
14:10; Num 6:12; 7:15, 21
the priest shall take the l. Lev 14:12
slay the l. 13, 25
l. of trespass offering. 24
that killeth an ox, or a l. or. 17:3
offer a l. without blemish. 23:12
one he l. of first year for a burnt
offering, ewe l. of. Num 6:14
prepare with sacrifice for one l. 15:5
thus done for one l. 11; 28:7, 13
14; Ezek 46:15
offered a sucking l. to. 1 Sam 7:9
lion and bear and took a l. 17:34
took the poor man's l. 2 Sam 12:4
he shall restore the l. fourfold. 6
shall dwell with the l. Isa 11:6
send ye the l. to the ruler of. 16:1
l. to the slaughter. 53:7; Jer 11:19
wolf and the l. shall feed. 65:25
that sacrificeth a l. as if he. 66:3
one l. out of flock for. Ezek 45:15
a l. of the first year thou. 46:13
Lord will feed them as l. Hos 4:16
behold l. of God that. John 1:29, 36
l. dumb before the shearer. Acts 8:32
as of a l. without blemish 1 Pet 1:19
the elders stood a l. slain. Rev 5:6
beasts fell down before the l. 8
saying, Worthy is the l. that was. 12
glory, and power, be to the l. for. 13
I saw when the l. opened one. 6:1
hide us from the wrath of the l. 16
multitude stood before the l. 7:9
salvation to our God and to the l. 10
white in the blood of the l. 14
for the l. shall feed and lead. 17
by the blood of the l. 12:11
l. slain from the foundation. 13:8
he had two horns like a l. and. 11
I looked, and lo, a l. stood on. 14:1
these are they that follow the l. 4
presence of angels and the l. 10
of Moses and song of the l. 15:3
war with the l. and the l. shall. 17:14
for the marriage of the l. is. 19:7
the marriage supper of the l. 9
I will shew thee the bride, the l.'s
wife. 21:9
the twelve apostles of the l. 14
God Almighty and the l. are the. 22
God did lighten it, and the l. is. 23
but they are written in the l.'s book. 27
of throne of God and of l. 22:1, 3

lambs

did separate the l. Gen 30:40
rams twelve, l. of the. Num 7:87
sixty l. 88
fourteen l. 29:13, 17, 20, 23
for the bullocks, l. and rams. 29:18
with fat of l. and rams. Deut 32:14
spared the best of the l. 1 Sam 15:9
to Israel 100,000 l. 2 Ki 3:4
to the Lord a thousand l. 1 Chr 29:21
priests killed l. and. 2 Chr 29:22
burnt offerings two hundred l. 32
Josiah gave to the people l. 35:7
mayest buy speedily l. Ezra 7:17
shall be as the fat of l. Ps 37:20
little hills skipped like l. 114:4
ye little hills that skipped like l. 6
l. are for thy clothing. Pr 27:26
delight not in blood of l. Isa 1:11
then shall the l. feed after. 5:17
sword filled with blood of l. 34:6
he shall gather the l. with. 40:11
I will bring them like l. Jer 51:40
occupied with thee in l. Ezek 27:21
ye shall drink the blood of l. 39:18
in the sabbath six l. 46:4
in new moons six l. 6
and meat offering for the l. 5, 7
eat the l. out of the flock. Amos 6:4
I send you forth as l. Luke 10:3
to Peter, Feed my l. John 21:15

five **lambs**

five l. of the first year. Num 7:17
23, 29, 35, 41, 47

seven **lambs**

Abraham set seven ewe l. Gen 21:28
what mean these seven ewe l. set? 29
these seven ewe l. thou shalt. 30
offer with bread seven l. Lev 23:18
seven l. of the first year without.
Num 28:11, 19, 27; 29:2, 8, 36
a tenth deal throughout seven l.
28:21, 29; 29:4, 10
they brought seven l. 2 Chr 29:21

two **lambs**

two l. of the first year offer.
Ex 29:38; Num 28:3
day he shall take two l. Lev 14:10
then ye shall sacrifice two l. of. 23:19
and on the sabbath two l. Num 28:9

lame

a blind or l. man shall. Lev 21:18
if it be l. thou shalt. Deut 15:21
Jonathan had a son that was l. of his
feet. 2 Sam 4:4; 9:3, 13
away the blind and the l. 5:6
whosoever smiteth the l. 8
because thy servant is l. 19:26
to the blind, feet to the l. Job 29:15
legs of the l. are not equal. Pr 26:7
then is prey divided, the l. Isa 33:23
then shall the l. man leap as. 35:6
them the blind and the l. Jer 31:8
offer the l. for sacrifice. Mal 1:8
that which was torn and l. 13
the l. walk. Mat 11:5; 15:31
21:14; Luke 7:22
call the poor, the l. and. Luke 14:13
certain man, l. from womb. Acts 3:2
l. man held Peter and John. 11
with palsies and that were l. 8:7
lest the l. be turned out. Heb 12:13

Lamech

Methusael begat L. Gen 4:18
L. took two wives. 19
Methuselah begat L. 5:25
1 Chr 1:3
Noe, which was son of L. Luke 3:36

lament

Israel went yearly to l. Judg 11:40*
and her gates shall l. Isa 3:26
fishers also shall mourn and l. 19:8
l. for the teats and pleasant. 32:12*
for this l. and howl, for. Jer 4:8
to l. nor bemoan them. 16:5, 6
they shall not l. for him. 22:18
l. thee saying, Ah Lord. 34:5
ye daughters of Rabbah, l. and. 49:3
rampart and the wall to l. Lam 2:8
they shall l. over Tyrus. Ezek 27:32
of the nations shall l. her. 32:16
l. like a virgin girded. Joel 1:8
gird yourselves, and l. ye priests. 13
l. with a doleful lamentation, and.
Mi 2:4
say, ye shall weep and l. John 16:20
kings of the earth shall l. Rev 18:9*

lamentable

king cried with a l. voice. Dan 6:20

lamentation

mourned with a sore l. Gen 50:10
lamented with this l. 2 Sam 1:17
their widows made no l. Ps 78:64
in ashes, make bitter l. Jer 6:26
and take up a l. on the high. 7:29
habitations of wilderness a l. 9:10
every one her neighbour l. 20
in Ramah l. and weeping. 31:15
Mat 2:18
shall be l. generally on. Jer 48:38
increased mourning and l. Lam 2:5
take thou up a l. for. Ezek 19:1
this is a l. and shall be for a l. 14
they shall take up a l. for Tyrus.
26:17; 27:2, 32
a l. upon the king of Tyrus. 28:12
take up a l. for Pharaoh. 32:2, 16
l. against you, O house. Amos 5:1
shall call such as are skilful of l. 16
turn all your songs into l. 8:10
lament with a doleful l. Mi 2:4
great l. over Stephen. Acts 8:2

lamentations

Josiah in their l. and, behold, they are
written in the l. 2 Chr 35:25
was written therein l. Ezek 2:10

lamented

people l. because the. 1 Sam 6:19
all the house of Israel l. after. 7:2
Israelites l. Samuel. 25:1; 28:3
David l. over Saul. 2 Sam 1:17
king l. over Abner and said. 3:33
and Jeremiah l. for. 2 Chr 35:25
die and not be l. Jer 16:4; 25:33
to you, but ye have not l. Mat 11:17
company of people l. Luke 23:27

lamp

In Bible times [1] *a small cup-like vessel, usually of earthenware, containing oil in which a cotton wick floated. It gave a very faint light.* [2] *A torch,* Judg 7:16, 20. *The word is frequently used symbolically, the special meaning being easily gained from the context.*

a burning l. that passed. Gen 15:17
to cause the l. to burn. Ex 27:20
ere l. went out, Samuel. 1 Sam 3:3
thou art my l. O Lord. 2 Sam 22:29
God gave him a l. in. 1 Ki 15:4
a l. despised in thought. Job 12:5*
thy word is a l. to my. Ps 119:105
I have ordained a l. for. 132:17
commandment is a l. the. Pr 6:23
l. of the wicked shall be put. 13:9
curseth his father, his l. shall. 20:20
salvation thereof as a l. Isa 62:1
star burning as it were a l. Rev 8:10

lamps

light the l. thereof. Ex 25:37; 40:4
dresseth the l. burn incense on. 30:7
when Aaron lighteth the l. at even. 8
and his l. with the oil for. 35:14
and they brought l. to Moses. 39:37
he lighted the l. before the Lord.
40:25; Num 8:2, 3
l. to burn continually. Lev 24:2
2 Chr 13:11
order the l. Lev 24:4
and cover his l. Num 4:9
l. within the pitchers. Judg 7:16
and held the l. in their left hand. 20
he made l. of gold. 1 Ki 7:49
2 Chr 4:20, 21
of his mouth go burning l. Job 41:19
like the appearance of l. Ezek 1:13
and his eyes as l. of fire. Dan 10:6
which took their l. Mat 25:1; 3:4
arose and trimmed their l. 7
give us of your oil; for our l. 8

seven **lamps**

make the seven l. thereof. Ex 25:37
his seven l. of pure gold. 37:23
seven l. shall give light. Num 8:2
a candlestick and seven l. Zech 4:2
seven l. of fire burning. Rev 4:5

lance

they that hold the l. are. Jer 50:42

lancets

cut themselves with l. 1 Ki 18:28

land

[1] *The earth, as distinguished from sea,* Mat 23:15. [2] *One particular country,* Mat 9:26. [3] *Arable ground,* Gen 26:12. [4] *The inhabitants of a country,* Isa 37:11. [5] *A certain possession,* 2 Sam 19:29; Acts 4:37.

gold of that l. is good. Gen 2:12
out of that l. went forth Ashur. 10:11
get thee into a l. I will shew. 12:1
Acts 7:3
and the l. was not able to. Gen 13:6
is not the whole l. before thee? 9
I will give thee and seed the l. 17:8
28:13; 35:12
behold, my l. is before thee. 20:15
of the Canaanite, in whose l. 24:37
Isaac sowed in that l. and. 26:12
bought the l. so the l. became. 47:20
only the l. of the priests bought. 22
the l. was corrupted by. Ex 8:24
so that l. was darkened. 10:15
days may be long upon the l. 20:12
goat bear iniquities into a l. not.
Lev 16:22
and the l. is defiled. 18:25, 27
that the l. spue not you. 28; 20:22
then shall the l. keep. 25:2; 26:34
l. shall yield her fruit. 25:19; 26:4
l. shall not be sold, for the l. 25:23
l. of your enemies shall eat. 26:38
and I will remember the l. 42
the l. also shall be left of them. 43
see the l. what it is, and. Num 13:18
the l. is a l. that eateth up the. 32
surely they shall not see the l. 14:23
Caleb will I bring to the l. 24
when ye be come into the l. 15:2, 18
Deut 17:14; 18:9; 26:1
delivered into thy hand his l.
Num 21:34; Deut 3:2
country Lord smote is a l. for cattle.
Num 32:4
blood defileth the l. and the l. 35:33
to him will I give the l. Deut 1:36
accounted a l. of giants. 2:20; 3:13
a l. of wheat, and barley, and. 8:8
l. wherein eat bread, l. whose. 9
not able to bring them into the l. 9:28
to Jotbath, a l. of rivers. 10:7
a l. which the Lord thy God. 11:12
whole l. thereof is brimstone. 29:23
cast them into another l. as at. 28
he found him in a desert l. 32:10
he will be merciful to his l. 43
blessed of the Lord be his l. 33:13
Lord shewed him all the l. 34:1
saying, Go view the l. Josh 2:1
Lord hath given you the l. 9; 21:43
Joshua took all that l. 11:16, 23
and the l. had rest from war. 14:15
given you a l. for which ye did. 24:13
l. had rest forty. Judg 3:11; 5:31
l. had rest fourscore years. 30
to fight against me in my l. 11:12
ye shall come to a large l. 18:10
day of the captivity of the l. 30
hath troubled the l. 1 Sam 14:29
David the king of the l.? 21:11
saying, Whose is the l.? 2 Sam 3:12
restore thee all the l. of Saul. 9:7
entreated for the l. 21:14; 24:25
them the l. of Cabul. 1 Ki 9:13
victuals, and gave him l. 11:18
cry to the king for her l. 2 Ki 8:3
since the day that she left the l. 6
manner of the God of l. 17:26, 27
take you to a l. of corn and wine.
18:32; Isa 36:17
hath any of the gods delivered at all
his l. 2 Ki 18:33; Isa 36:18

neither move any more out of the *l.* *2 Ki* 21:8; *2 Chr* 33:8
the king of Egypt came no more out of his *l.* *2 Ki* 24:7
left of the poor of the *l.* 25:12 *Jer* 52:16
and the *l.* was wide. *1 Chr* 4:40
Gath, who were born in that *l.* 7:21
pluck them out of my *l.* *2 Chr* 7:20
make walls, while the *l.* is. 14:7
when he had purged the *l.* 34:8
that ye may eat the good of *l.* *Ezra* 9:12; *Isa* 1:19
nor brought we any *l.* *Neh* 5:16
l. behold, we are servants in. 9:36
if my *l.* cry against me. *Job* 31:38
for correction, or his *l.*, or for. 37:13
barren *l.* his dwellings. 39:6
are perished out of his *l.* *Ps* 10:16
remember thee from the *l.* of. 42:6
got not the *l.* in possession. 44:3
root thee out of the *l.* of the. 52:5
deep root, and it filled the *l.* 80:9
be on the faithful of the *l.* 101:6
destroy all the wicked of the *l.* 8
called for a famine on the *l.* 105:16
the *l.* brought forth frogs in. 30
despised the pleasant *l.* 106:24
l. was polluted with blood. 38
he turneth the fruitful *l.* into. 107:34
thirsts after thee as a thirsty *l.* 143:6
into the *l.* of uprightness. 10
that tilleth his *l.* shall be. *Pr* 12:11 28:19
for the trangression of a *l.* 28:2
woe to thee, O *l.* when. *Eccl* 10:16
blessed art thou, O *l.* when thy. 17
if one look unto the *l.* *Isa* 5:30
l. that thou abhorrest shall be. 7:16
all *l.* shall become briers. 24
l. of Zebulun, *l.* of Naphtali. 9:1 *Mat* 4:15
thro' wrath of the Lord is *l.* *Isa* 9:19
come to destroy the whole *l.* 13:5
break the Assyrian in my *l.* 14:25
woe to the *l.* shadowing with. 18:1
whose *l.* the rivers have spoiled. 2, 7
blessing in the midst of the *l.* 19:24
the desert, from a terrible *l.* 21:1
l. of Chittim it is revealed. 23:1
the *l.* shall be utterly emptied. 24:3
darkened, the mirth of the *l.* 11
l. of trouble and anguish. 30:6
of a great rock in a weary *l.* 32:2
the *l.* of my people shall come. 13
behold the *l.* that is very. 33:17
the *l.* thereof shall become. 34:9
thirsty *l.* springs of water. 35:7
these from the *l.* of Sinim. 49:12
the *l.* of thy destruction be too. 19
he was cut off out of the *l.* of. 53:8
pillar against the whole *l.* *Jer* 1:18
wentest after me, in a *l.* that. 2:2
led us through a *l.* of deserts, a *l.* 6
ye entered, ye defiled my *l.* 7; 3:9
young lions made his *l.* waste. 2:15
I give thee a pleasant *l.*? 3:19
for the whole *l.* is spoiled. 4:20
serve strangers in a *l.* that is. 5:19
make thee a *l.* not inhabited. 6:8
l. trembled at the sound. 8:16
l. perisheth and is burnt. 9:12
we have forsaken the *l.* 19
let us cut him off from *l.* 11:19
the *l.* mourn, herbs wither? 12:4
from the one end of the *l.* even to. 12
bring again every man to his *l.* 15
brought Israel from *l.* of the north. 16:15; 31:16
because they defiled my *l.* 16:18
inhabit wilderness into a salt *l.* 17:6
the *l.* whereunto they desire. 22:27
is profaneness gone forth into the *l.* 23:15
I will bring on that *l.* all my. 25:13
very time of his *l.* come. 27:7
all the *l.* is before thee. 40:4
and thy cry hath filled the *l.* 46:12
the king of Babylon and his *l.* 50:18
for it is the *l.* of graven images. 38
a dry *l.*, a *l.* wherein no man. 51:43
her whole *l.* shall be confounded. 47
l. is full of bloody. *Ezek* 7:23
filled the *l.* with violence. 8:17
l. is full of blood, and city. *Ezek* 9:9
the *l.* sinneth against me 14:13
bring a sword on *l.* 17
a pestilence into *l.* 19
took also of the seed of the *l.* 17:5
hath taken the mighty of the *l.* 13
shall come forth out of one *l.* 21:19
thou art the *l.* is not cleansed. 22:24
in the gap before me for the *l.* 30
will I leave thee upon the *l.* 32:4
I bring the sword upon a *l.* 33:2
seeth the sword come upon the *l.* 3
l. is given us for inheritance. 24
have appointed my *l.* into their. 36:5
thou *l.* devourest up men, and. 13
like a cloud to cover the *l.* 38:9, 16
I will go up to the *l.* of unwalled. 11
I will bring thee against my *l.* 16
they may cleanse the *l.* 39:12
thus shall they cleanse the *l.* 16
shall be the border of the *l.* 47:15
he shall stand in the glorious *l.* *Dan* 11:16, 41
shall the *l.* mourn and. *Hos* 4:3
for a nation is come up upon my *l.* *Joel* 1:6
the *l.* is as the garden of Eden. 2:3
the Lord be jealous for his *l.* 18
fear not, O *l.* be glad. 21
and parted my *l.* 3:2
she is forsaken upon her *l.* *Amos* 5:2
the *l.* is not able to bear all. 7:10
make the poor of the *l.* to fail 8:4
shall not the *l.* tremble for this? 8
hosts is he that toucheth the *l.* 9:5
all things from off the *l.* *Zeph* 1:2*
whole *l.* shall be devoured by fire. 18
praise and fame in every *l.* 3:19*
Ho, ho, flee from the *l.* of. *Zech* 2:6
remove the iniquity of that *l.* in. 3:9
up, as an ensign upon his *l.* 9:16
l. shall mourn, every family. 12:12
unclean spirit to pass out of *l.* 13:2
in all the *l.* two parts therein. 8
all the *l.* shall be turned as a. 14:10
shall be a delightsome *l.* *Mal* 3:12
went abroad into all that *l.* *Mat* 9:26
for the *l.* of Sodom. 10:15; 11:24
ye compass sea and *l.* to. 23:15
was darkness over all the *l.* 27:45 *Mark* 15:33
sea, and he alone on the *l.* *Mark* 6:47
neither fit for the *l.* nor. *Luke* 14:35
a great famine in that *l.* 15:14
the ship was at the *l.* *John* 6:21
Peter drew the net to *l.* full. 21:11
having *l.* sold it, and. *Acts* 4:37
tell me whether ye sold the *l.* for? 5:8
day, they knew not the *l.* 27:39
into the sea, and get to *l.* 43
that they escaped all safe to *l.* 44
see **Benjamin, Canaan, Chaldeans, darkness, desolate, divide, divided, inhabitants, inherit, Israel, Judah, strange**

***dry* land**

let *dry l.* appear. *Gen* 1:9
called *dry l.* earth. 10
that was in the *dry l.* died. 7:22
water on *dry l.* and the waters shall become blood on *dry l.* *Ex* 4:9
Lord made the sea *dry l.* 14:21
Israel walked on *dry l.* 29; 15:19 *Neh* 9:11
the priests' feet were lifted up on *dry l.* *Josh* 4:18
came over this Jordan on *dry l.* 22
longeth for thee in a *dry l.* *Ps* 63:1
he turned the sea into *dry l.* 66:6
rebellious dwell in a *dry l.* 68:6
and his hands formed the *dry l.* 95:5
I will make *dry l.* springs. *Isa* 41:18
of nations shall be a *dry l.* *Jer* 50:12
her cities are a *dry l.* and. 51:43
lest I set her as a *dry l.* *Hos* 2:3
who made sea and *dry l.* *Jonah* 1:9
vomited out Jonah on the *dry l.* 2:10
shake the sea and *dry l.* *Hag* 2:6
the Red sea as by *dry l.* *Heb* 11:29
see **dwelt, Egypt, good**

***in the* land**

Canaanite dwelt then *in the l.* *Gen* 13:7
shall be fruitful *in the l.* *Gen* 26:22
plenty not be known *in the l.* 41:31
and ye shall traffick *in the l.* 42:34
for to sojourn *in the l.* are. 47:4
go ye, sacrifice to your God *in the l.* *Ex* 8:25
Lord shall do this thing *in the l.* 9:5
they are entangled *in the l.* 14:3
give peace *in the l.* and. *Lev* 26:6
ye may do them *in the l.* *Deut* 4:14
go well with thee *in the l.* 5:16
that ye may prolong days *in the l.* 11:9, 21; 25:15
hath given thee rest *in the l.* 25:19
bless thee *in the l.* 28:8, 11; 30:16
as long as ye live *in the l.* 31:13
no magistrate *in the l.* *Judg* 18:7
and if he be *in the l.* I. *1 Sam* 23:23
made judge *in the l.* *2 Sam* 15:4
if there be famine *in the l.* *1 Ki* 8:37 *2 Chr* 6:28
long as they live *in the l.* *2 Chr* 6:31
set judges *in the l.* 19:5
wonder that was done *in the l.* 32:31
nor is it found *in the l.* of. *Job* 28:13
goodness of the Lord *in the l.* of the. *Ps* 27:13
devise deceitful matter *in the l.* 35:20
the synagogues of God *in the l.* 74:8
walk before the Lord *in the l.* 116:9
thou art my portion *in the l.* 142:5
shall every one eat *in the l.* *Isa* 7:22
in the l. of uprightness he. 26:10
not see the Lord *in the l.* of. 38:11
them *in the l.* serve me. *Ezek* 20:40
I shall set glory *in the l.* of. 26:20
caused terror *in the l.* of the living. 32:23; 24:32
make them one nation *in the l.* 37:22
in the l. shall be his possession. 45:8
there is no truth *in the l.* *Hos* 4:1
up a Shepherd *in the l.* *Zech* 11:16
great distress *in the l.* *Luke* 21:23
by faith he sojourned *in the l.* of. *Heb* 11:9

***our* land**

buy us and *our l.* for bread, and we and *our l.* *Gen* 47:19
and *our l.* shall yield her. *Ps* 85:12
turtle is heard in *our l.* *S of S* 2:12
the Assyrian shall come into *our l.* *Mi* 5:5
us when he cometh into *our l.* 6

***own* land**

Jethro went into his *own l.* *Ex* 18:27 *Num* 10:30
a true report I heard in mine *own l.* *1 Ki* 10:6; *2 Chr* 9:5
carried out of their *own l.* *2 Ki* 17:23
take you to a land like your *own l.* 18:32; *Isa* 36:17
shall return to his *own l.* *2 Ki* 19:7
with shame to his *own l.* *2 Chr* 32:21
every one to his *own l.* *Isa* 13:14
and set them in their *own l.* 14:1
fall by the sword in his *own l.* 37:7
they that dwell in their *own l.* *Jer* 25:8; 27:11
Egypt, into their *own l.* 37:7; 42:12
flee every one to his *own l.* 50:16
them into their *own l.* *Ezek* 34:13 36:24; 37:14, 21; 39:28
Israel dwelt in their *own l.* 36:17
captive out of their *own l.* *Amos* 7:11
see **people, possess, possession**

***their* land**

people sold not *their l.* *Gen* 47:22
ye shall inherit *their l.* *Lev* 20:24
no inheritance in *their l.* *Num* 18:20
not give you of *their l.* *Deut* 2:5, 9
bring thee, and give thee *their l.* 4:38 *Judg* 6:9
we took *their l.* and gave it. *Deut* 29:8; *Josh* 10:42
Lord rooted them out of *their l.* *Deut* 29:28
and pray unto thee toward *their l.* *1 Ki* 8:48
sin and heal *their l.* *2 Chr* 7:14
flaming fire in *their l.* *Ps* 105:32

and gave their l. for an heritage.
Ps 135:12; 136:21
their l. is full of silver. Isa 2:7
their l. also is full of idols. 8
their l. shall be soaked with. 34:7
I will pluck them out of their l.
Jer 12:14
bring them again into their l. 16:15
forsaken, though their l. was. 51:5
shall be safe in their l. Ezek 34:27
they dwelt safely in their l. 39:26
will plant them on their l. Amos 9:15

this land

the Lord said, Unto thy seed I will give this l. Gen 12:7; 15:18; 24:7
48:4; Ex 32:13
thee again into this l. Gen 28:15
get thee out from this l. and. 31:13
will bring you out of this l. 50:24
brought us unto this l. Num 14:3
then he will bring us into this l. 8
this l. be given to thy servants. 32:5
this l. shall be your possession. 22
this l. shall fall to you. 34:2, 13
Josh 13:2
but I must die in this l. Deut 4:22
and he hath given us this l. 26:9
Josh 1:13
Lord done thus to this l.? Deut 29:24
27; 1 Ki 9:8; 2 Chr 7:21
the inhabitants of this l. Judg 2:2
Lord said, Go up against this l.
2 Ki 18:25; Isa 36:10
come again into this l. 2 Chr 30:9
sword shall not be in this l. Jer 14:15
that begat them in this l. 16:3
and small shall die in this l. 6
I will cast you out of this l. 13
he shall see this l. no more. 22:12
will bring them again to this l. 24:6
bring them against this l. 25:9
and this whole l. shall be a. 11
prophesied against this l. 26:20
be possessed again in this l. 32:15
and I will plant them in this l. 41
Babylon shall destroy this l. 36:29
come against you, nor this l. 37:19
if ye will abide in this l. I. 42:10
we will not dwell in this l. 13
pluck up even this whole l. 45:4
to us is this l. given in. Ezek 11:15
this l. shall fall unto you for. 47:14
this is the l. which ye shall. 48:29
removed him into this l. Acts 7:4

thy land

years thou shalt sow thy l. Ex 23:10
cast their young in thy l. 26
they shall not dwell in thy l. 33
nor shall any man desire thy l. 34:24
let me pass through thy l. Num 21:22
Deut 2:27; Judg 11:17, 19
bless the fruit of thy l. Deut 7:13
bury him; that thy l. be not. 21:23
give the rain to thy l. in. 28:12
shall be the fruit of thy l. 18, 42
do great things for thy l. 2 Sam 7:23
famine come to thee in thy l.? 24:13
been favourable to thy l. Ps 85:1
fill the breadth of thy l. Isa 8:8
thou hast destroyed thy l. 14:20
through thy l. as a river, O. 23:10
no more be heard in thy l. 60:18
thy l. be termed desolate; the Lord delighteth in thee, and thy l. 62:4
set darkness upon thy l. Ezek 32:8
thy l. shall be divided. Amos 7:17
cut off the cities of thy l. Mi 5:11
the gates of thy l. shall. Nah 3:13

your land

bought you and your l. Gen 47:23
when ye reap the harvest of your l.
Lev 19:9; 23:22
which they begat in your l. 25:45
and dwell in your l. safely. 26:5
nor the sword go through your l. 6
for your l. shall not yield her. 20
you go to war in your l. Num 10:9
get into your l. 22:13
this shall be your l. 34:12
give you rain of your l. Deut 11:14
his hand from off your l. 1 Sam 6:5
strange gods in your l. Jer 5:19
remove you far from your l. Jer 27:10
is your l. a desolation and. 44:22

landed

we had l. at Caesarea. Acts 18:22
into Syria, and l. at Tyre. 21:3

landing

l. at Syracuse we. Acts 28:12*

landmark, -s

not remove thy neighbour's l.
Deut 19:14; Pr 22:28; 23:10
removeth neighbour's l. Deut 27:17
some remove the l. and. Job 24:2

lands

dearth was in all l. Gen 41:45
left but our bodies and l. 47:18
wherefore they sold not their l. 22
restore those l. again. Judg 11:13
the kings of Assyria have done to all l. 2 Ki 19:11; Isa 37:11
David went into all l. 1 Chr 14:17
the manner of other l. 2 Chr 13:9
fear fell on all l. round about. 17:10
as the gods of other l. have. 32:17
separated from people of l. Ezra 9:1
with the people of those l. 2, 11
have mortgaged our l. Neh 5:3, 4
men have our l. and vineyards. 5
I pray you, this day their l. 11
separated from people of the l. 10:28
they call their l. after their. Ps 49:11
a joyful noise, all ye l. 66:1; 100:1
and gave them the l. of. 105:44
hand, to scatter them in the l. 106:27
gathered them out of the l. 107:3
brought up Israel from l. Jer 16:15
all these l. to Nebuchadnezzar. 27:6
into a land which is the glory of all l.
Ezek 20:6, 15
them out of their enemies' l. 39:27
hath forsaken houses, l. Mat 19:29
Mark 10:29
an hundredfold, l. Mark 10:30
were possessors of l. sold. Acts 4:34

lanes

go out quickly into the l. Luke 14:21

language

whole earth was of one l. Gen 11:1
one, and they have all one l. 6
and there confound their l. 7, 9
speak in the Syrian l. 2 Ki 18:26
Isa 36:11
Rab-shakeh cried in the Jews' l.
2 Ki 18:28; Isa 36:13
could not speak in the Jews' l. but according to the l. of. Neh 13:24
to every people after their l.
Esth 1:22; 3:12; 8:9
no l. where their voice is. Ps 19:3
where I heard a l. that I. 81:5
from a people of strange l. 114:1
five cities speak the l. of. Isa 19:18
a nation, whose l. thou. Jer 5:15
not sent to a people of hard l.
Ezek 3:5, 6
I decree, every l. that. Dan 3:29
turn to the people a pure l. Zeph 3:9
them speak in his own l. Acts 2:6

languages

O people, nations, and l. Dan 3:4
all l. fell down and worshipped. 7
Nebuchadnezzar to all l. 4:1
all l. trembled and feared. 5:19
Darius to all l. 6:25
all people, nations, and l. 7:14
ten men out of all l. Zech 8:23

languish

for the fields of Hebron l. Isa 16:8
spread nets on waters shall l. 19:8
haughty people of the earth do l. 24:4
gates of Judah l. and. Jer 14:2
that dwelleth therein shall l. Hos 4:3

languished

and wall to lament, l. Lam 2:8

languisheth

the world l. and fadeth. Isa 24:4
the vine l. 7
the earth mourneth and l. 33:9
she that hath borne seven l. Jer 15:9
the oil l. Joel 1:10
the fig tree l. 12
l. and Carmel, the flower l. Nah 1:4

languishing

Lord will strengthen him on the bed of l. Ps 41:3

lanterns

Judas cometh with l. John 18:3

Laodicea

conflict I have for them at L. Col 2:1
zeal for them that are in L. 4:13
salute brethren which are in L. 15
likewise read the epistle from L. 16

Laodiceans

read in the church of the L. Col 4:16
angel of church of the L. Rev 3:14

lap

wild gourds, his l. full. 2 Ki 4:39
I shook my l. and said. Neh 5:13
the lot is cast into the l. Pr 16:33

lapped

the number that l. were. Judg 7:6
the Lord said, By them that l. I. 7

lappeth

that l. of the water as. Judg 7:5

large

the land, behold it is l. Gen 34:21
them into a good and l. land. Ex 3:8
shall come into a l. land. Judg 18:10
he brought me forth also into a l. place. 2 Sam 22:20; Ps 18:19
the work is great and l. Neh 4:19
the city was l. and great. 7:4*
have not served thee in the l. 9:35
set my feet in a l. room. Ps 31:8
and set me in a l. place. 118:5
he will toss thee into a l. Isa 22:18
shall thy cattle feed in l. 30:23
ordained, he made it deep and l. 33
I will build l. chambers. Jer 22:14*
sister's cup deep and l. Ezek 23:32
as a lamb in a l. place. Hos 4:16
they gave l. money to. Mat 28:12
will shew you a l. upper room.
Mark 14:15; Luke 22:12
ye see how l. a letter I. Gal 6:11
the length is as l. as. Rev 21:16*

largeness

God gave Solomon l. 1 Ki 4:29

lasciviousness

heart of men proceed l. Mark 7:22
not repented of the l. 2 Cor 12:21
of the flesh are manifest, l. Gal 5:19
given themselves over to l. Eph 4:19
walked in l., lusts, excess. 1 Pet 4:3
grace of our God into l. Jude 4

last

(Frequently used where modern writers would use latter)

shall overcome at the l. Gen 49:19*
my l. end be like his. Num 23:10
why are ye the l. to bring the king back? 2 Sam 19:11, 12
now these be the l. words of. 23:1
for by the l. words of. 1 Chr 23:27
David the king, first and l. 29:29
of Solomon, first and l. 2 Chr 9:29
of Rehoboam, first and l. 12:15
the acts of Asa, first and l. 16:11
acts of Jehoshaphat, first and l. 20:34
acts of Amaziah, first and l. 25:26
the acts of Uzziah, first and l. 26:22
the acts of Ahaz, first and l. 28:26
Josiah's deeds, first and l. 35:27
the l. sons of Adonikam. Ezra 8:13
from the first day to the l. Neh 8:18
and thou mourn at the l. Pr 5:11*
the l. it biteth like a serpent. 23:32
the Lord, the first, and with the l.
Isa 41:4; 44:6; 48:12; Rev 1:11
17; 2:8; 22:13
he shall not see our l. end. Jer 12:4
at l. Nebuchadnezzar hath. 50:17
remembered not her l. Lam 1:9
at the l. Daniel came in. Dan 4:8
and the higher came up l. 8:3
what shall be in the l. end. 19
I will slay the l. of them. Amos 9:1
l. state of that man is worse.
Mat 12:45; Luke 11:26
many that are first shall be l. and the l. first. Mat 19:30; 20:16
Mark 10:31; Luke 13:30
beginning from the l. to. Mat 20:8

l. have wrought one hour. *Mat* 20:12
I will give to this *l.* even as unto. 14
l. of all he sent his son, saying.
21:37*; *Mark* 12:6
l. of all the woman died. *Mat* 22:27
Mark 12:22; *Luke* 20:32*
at the *l.* came two false. *Mat* 26:60*
the *l.* error shall be worse. 27:64
desire to be first, the same shall be *l.*
Mark 9:35
hast paid the *l.* mite. *Luke* 12:59
the eldest even to the *l.* *John* 8:9
set forth us the apostles *l.* *1 Cor* 4:9
and *l.* of all he was seen of. 15:8
the *l.* enemy is death. 26
the *l.* Adam. 45
changed in a moment, at the *l.* 52
at *l.* your care of me. *Phil* 4:10*
the *l.* works to be more. *Rev* 2:19
having the seven *l.* plagues. 15:1
seven vials full of the seven *l.* 21:9

last *day, days*

befall you in the *l. days.* *Gen* 49:1
come to pass in *l. days.* *Isa* 2:2
Mi 4:1; *Acts* 2:17
should raise it up at the *l. day.*
John 6:39, 40, 44, 54
in the *l. day,* the great day. 7:37
he shall rise again at the *l. day.* 11:24
judge him in the *l. day.* 12:48
in *l. days* perilous times. *2 Tim* 3:1
hath spoken in these *l. days* by his Son. *Heb* 1:2
treasure for the *l. days.* *Jas* 5:3
come in *l. days* scoffers. *2 Pet* 3:3

last *time, times*

revealed in the *l. time.* *1 Pet* 1:5
manifest in these *l. times* for. 20
is the *l. time*: are there many antichrists . . . it is the *l. time.*
1 John 2:18
be mockers in the *l. time.* *Jude* 18

lasted

wept while the feast *l.* *Judg* 14:17

lasting

things of the *l.* hills. *Deut* 33:15

latchet

nor the *l.* of their shoes. *Isa* 5:27
the *l.* of whose shoes. *Mark* 1:7
Luke 3:16

late

is vain for you to sit up *l.* *Ps* 127:2
of *l.* my people is risen up. *Mi* 2:8
the Jews of *l.* sought to. *John* 11:8

lately

Aquila a Jew *l.* come. *Acts* 18:2

Latin

written in Hebrew, and Greek, and *L.*
Luke 23:38*; *John* 19:20

latter

the voice of the *l.* sign. *Ex* 4:8
give thee the first rain, and *l.* rain.
Deut 11:14
if her *l.* husband hate her or. 24:3
stand at the *l.* day. *Job* 19:25
their mouth as for the *l.* rain. 29:23
as a cloud of the *l.* rain. *Pr* 16:15
mayest be wise in the *l.* end. 19:20
and there hath been no *l.* *Jer* 3:3
both the former and *l.* rain in. 5:24
in the *l.* years thou shalt. *Ezek* 38:8
in the *l.* time of their. *Dan* 8:23
not be as the former or the *l.* 11:29
as the *l.* and former rain. *Hos* 6:3
l. rain in the first month. *Joel* 2:23
beginning of the *l.* growth. *Amos* 7:1
the glory of the *l.* house. *Hag* 2:9
the time of the *l.* rain. *Zech* 10:1
that in the *l.* times. *1 Tim* 4:1
see **days, end**

lattice

cried through the *l.* *Judg* 5:28
fell down through the *l.* *2 Ki* 1:2
shewing himself through the *l.*
S of S 2:9

laud

praise the Lord, and *l.* *Rom* 15:11

laugh

(Used both for the laugh of joy and the laugh of derision)

wherefore did Sarah *l.*? *Gen* 18:13
said, Nay, but thou didst *l.* *Gen* 18:15
hath made me to *l.*, all will *l.* 21:6
and famine thou shalt *l.* *Job* 5:22
he will *l.* at the trial of the. 9:23*
and the innocent *l.* them to. 22:19
in the heavens shall *l.* *Ps* 2:4
all they that see me *l.* me to. 22:7
the Lord shall *l.* at him, for. 37:13
righteous also shall *l.* at him. 52:6
but thou, O Lord, shalt *l.* at. 59:8
and our enemies *l.* among. 80:6
will *l.* at your calamity. *Pr* 1:26
whether he rage or *l.* there is. 29:9
weep, and a time to *l.* *Eccl* 3:4
ye that weep, ye shall *l.* *Luke* 6:21
woe unto you that *l.* now! for ye. 25

laughed

Abraham *l.* *Gen* 17:17
Sarah *l.* in herself. 18:12
Sarah denied, saying, I *l.* not. 15
daughter of Zion hath *l.* *2 Ki* 19:21
Isa 37:22
they *l.* them to scorn. *2 Chr* 30:10
they *l.* us to scorn, and. *Neh* 2:19
just and upright man is *l.* *Job* 12:4
if I *l.* on them, they. 29:24
thou shalt be *l.* to scorn. *Ezek* 23:32
they *l.* him to scorn. *Mat* 9:24
Mark 5:40; *Luke* 8:53

laugheth

he *l.* at the shaking of. *Job* 41:29

laughing

till he fill thy mouth with *l.* *Job* 8:21

laughter

our mouth filled with *l.* *Ps* 126:2
even in *l.* the heart is. *Pr* 14:13
I said of *l.* It is mad. *Eccl* 2:2
sorrow is better than *l.* 7:3
so is *l.* of the fool. 6
let your *l.* be turned to. *Jas* 4:9

launch

he said to Simon, *L.* out. *Luke* 5:4*

launched

go over, and they *l.* forth. *Luke* 8:22
after we had *l.* *Acts* 21:1*; 27:2*, 4*

laver

make a *l.* of brass. *Ex* 30:18
the *l.* and his foot. 28; 31:9
35:16; 39:39
he made the *l.* of brass and. 38:8
thou shalt set the *l.* 40:7
and he set the *l.* 30
anoint the *l.* and his foot. 11
he anointed both the *l.* and. *Lev* 8:11
under the *l.* were undersetters.
1 Ki 7:30
l. was forty baths, and every *l.* 38
Ahaz removed the *l.* *2 Ki* 16:17

lavers

then made he ten *l.* of. *1 Ki* 7:38
Hiram make the *l.* and shovels. 40
l. on the bases. 43; *2 Chr* 4:6, 14

lavish

l. gold out of the bag. *Isa* 46:6

law

(When used alone it most frequently refers to the Mosaic Law, and, in the New Testament, the additions to that Law made by the Jewish teachers)

Joseph made it a *l.* over. *Gen* 47:26
l. to him that is homeborn. *Ex* 12:49
Lev 24:22; *Num* 15:16, 29
I will give thee a *l.* and. *Ex* 24:12
to the sentence of the *l.* *Deut* 17:11
hand went a fiery *l.* for them. 33:2
Moses commanded us a *l.* even. 4
according to all the *l.* *Josh* 1:7
stones a copy of the *l.* of Moses. 8:32
he read the words of the *l.* 34
take heed to the *l.* 22:5
2 Ki 17:13, 37; 21:8
nor do after the *l.* and. *2 Ki* 17:34
perform the words of the *l.* 23:24
according to all the *l.* of Moses. 25
to Jacob for a *l.* *1 Chr* 16:17
that thou mayest keep the *l.* 22:12
Judah to do the *l.* *2 Chr* 14:4
l. and commandment. 19:10
in their place according to *l.* 30:16
in every work, and in the *l.* 31:21
do according to the whole *l.* 33:8
heard the words of the *l.* 34:19
ready scribe in the *l.* *Ezra* 7:6, 12, 21
according to the *l.* of thy God. 14
will not do the *l.* of God and *l.* of. 26
be done according to the *l.* 10:3
the priest brought the *l.* *Neh* 8:2
the people to understand the *l.* 7
when they heard the words of *l.* 9
together to understand the *l.* 13
themselves to *l.* of God. 10:28
an oath to walk in God's *l.* 29
into them the portions of the *l.* 12:44
when they had heard the *l.* 13:3
was according to the *l.* *Esth* 1:8
queen Vashti according to *l.*? 15
one *l.* of his to put him to death. 4:11
which is not according to the *l.* 16
receive the *l.* from his. *Job* 22:22
in his *l.* he meditates day. *Ps* 1:2
l. of his God is in his heart. 37:31
he appointed a *l.* in Israel. 78:5
and they refused to walk in his *l.* 10
was a *l.* of the God of Jacob. 81:4
frameth mischief by a *l.* 94:20
the same to Jacob for a *l.* 105:10
the *l.* of thy mouth is better. 119:72
forsake not the *l.* of thy mother.
Pr 1:8; 6:20
is a lamp, and the *l.* is light. 6:23
l. of the wise is a fountain. 13:14
the *l.* praise the wicked, but such as keep the *l.* contend with. 28:4
keepeth the *l.* is a wise son. 7
away his ear from hearing the *l.* 9
but he that keepeth the *l.* 29:18
they drink and forget the *l.* 31:5
her tongue is the *l.* of kindness. 26
and give ear to the *l.* of. *Isa* 1:10
out of Zion shall go forth the *l.* 2:3
Mi 4:2
seal the *l.* *Isa* 8:16
to the *l.* and the testimony. 20
the isles shall wait for his *l.* 42:4
the Lord will magnify the *l.* 21
were they obedient to his *l.* 24
for a *l.* shall proceed from me. 51:4
they that handle the *l.* *Jer* 2:8
the *l.* shall not perish from. 18:18
was sealed according to *l.* 32:11
obeyed, nor walked in his *l.* 44:23
the *l.* is no more, prophets. *Lam* 2:9
the *l.* shall perish from. *Ezek* 7:26
concerning the *l.* of his God. *Dan* 6:5
according to *l.* of the Medes. 12, 15
thou hast forgotten the *l.* *Hos* 4:6
therefore the *l.* is slacked. *Hab* 1:4
done violence to the *l.* *Zeph* 3:4
priests concerning the *l.* *Hag* 2:11
they should hear the *l.* *Zech* 7:12
the *l.* of truth was in his. *Mal* 2:6
and they should seek the *l.* at. 7
caused many to stumble at the *l.* 8
ways, but have been partial in *l.* 9
remember the *l.* of Moses my. 4:4
am come to destroy the *l.* *Mat* 5:17
shall in no wise pass from the *l.* 18
any man will sue thee at the *l.* 40
the *l.* prophesied until John. 11:13
Luke 16:16
have ye not read in the *l.*? *Mat* 12:5
the great commandment in *l.* 22:36
commandments hang all the *l.* 40
the weightier matters of the *l.* 23:23
after the custom of the *l.* *Luke* 2:27
there were doctors of the *l.* 5:17
than for one tittle of the *l.* to. 16:17
l. was given by Moses. *John* 1:17
of whom Moses in the *l.* did. 45
give you the *l.* and yet none of you keepeth the *l.*? Why go ye? 7:19
l. of Moses should not be broken. 23
people who knoweth not the *l.* 49
doth our *l.* judge any man before? 51
Moses in the *l.* commanded. 8:5
is it not written in your *l.*? 10:34
we have heard out of the *l.* 12:34
what is written in their *l.* 15:25
judge him according to your *l.* 18:31
we have a *l.* and by our *l.* he. 19:7

Gamaliel, a doctor of the *l.* *Acts* 5:34
blasphemous words against *l.* 6:13
received the *l.* by angels. 7:53
reading of the *l.* and prophets. 13:15
could not be justified by the *l.* 39
to command them to keep the *l.* 15:5
circumcised and keep the *l.* 24
God contrary to the *l.* 18:13
but if it be a question of your *l.* 15
the *l.* is open. 19:38
zealous of the *l.* 21:20
thou thyself keepest the *l.* 24
man that teacheth against the *l.* 28
to the manner of the *l.* 22:3
devout man according to the *l.* 12
me after the *l.* and commandest me to be smitten contrary to *l.*? 23:3
have judged according to our *l.* 24:6
nor against the *l.* of the Jews. 25:8
persuading them out of the *l.* 28:23
without *l.*: ... have sinned in the *l.* shall be judged by the *l.* *Rom* 2:12
not the hearers of the *l.* are just. 13
Gentiles, which have not *l.*, do by nature things contained in *l.*, these, having not *l.*, are a *l.* unto. 14
shew the work of the *l.* written. 15
called a Jew, and restest in the *l.* 17
being instructed out of the *l.* 18
the form of the truth in *l.* 20
makest thy boast of the *l.* through breaking the *l.* dishonourest? 23
profiteth if thou keep the *l.* but if thou be a breaker of the *l.* 25
keep the righteousness of the *l* 26
it fulfil the *l.* judge thee who by circumcision dost trangress the *l.* 27
what things soever the *l.* saith. 3:19
l. no flesh be justified, for by the *l.* is the knowledge. 20, 28; *Gal* 2:16
righteousness of God is witnessed by the *l.* *Rom* 3:21
by what *l.* excluded? by the *l.* 27
void the *l.*? we establish the *l.* 31
promise was not through the *l.* 4:13
for if they which are of the *l.* 14
l. worketh wrath, for where no *l.* 15
not to that only which is of the *l.* 16
l. sin was in the world, but sin is not imputed when there is no *l.* 5:13
the *l.* entered, that the offence. 20
speak to them which know the *l.*, the *l.* hath dominion over a man. 7:1
the *l.* to her husband; if he be dead, she is loosed from the *l.* 2, 3
ye also are become dead to the *l.* 4
of sins which were by the *l.* 5
now we are delivered from the *l.* 6
is the *l.* sin? I had not known sin, but by *l.* nor lust, except *l.* had said. 7
for without the *l.* sin was dead. 8
the *l.* is holy, and commandment. 12
the *l.* is spiritual. 14
the *l.* is good. 16; *1 Tim* 1:8
I find then a *l.* *Rom* 7:21
I delight in the *l.* of God. 22
l. warring against the *l.* of my mind, bringing me into captivity to *l.* 23
I serve *l.* of God: flesh *l.* of sin. 25
l. of life made me free from the *l.* 8:2
for what the *l.* could not do, in. 3
righteousness of the *l.* might be. 4
carnal mind is not subject to the *l.* 7
pertaineth the giving of the *l.* 9:4
Israel followed after the *l.* of. 31
sought it by the works of the *l.* 32
Christ is the end of the *l.* for. 10:4
righteousness which is of the *l.* 5
loveth another, hath fulfilled *l.* 13:8
love is the fulfilling of the *l.* 10
dare any of you go to *l.*? *1 Cor* 6:1
brother goeth to *l.* with brother. 6
because ye go to *l.* one with. 7
wife is bound by the *l.* as long. 7:39
saith not the *l.* the same also? 9:8
obedience, as also saith the *l.* 14:34
sin, and strength of sin is the *l.* 15:56
not justified by the works of the *l.* *Gal* 2:16
I through the *l.* am dead to the *l.* 19
righteousness come by the *l.* then. 21
Spirit by the works of the *l.*? 3:2
doeth he it by the works of the *l.*? 5
as are of the works of the *l.* 10
no man is justified by the *l.* *Gal* 3:11
l. is not of faith, but the man. 12
redeemed us from the curse of *l.* 13
covenant in Christ, the *l.* cannot. 17
if the inheritance be of the *l.* not. 18
wherefore then serveth the *l.*? 19
l. ... promises? if a *l.* had been given, righteousness had been by the *l.* 21
the *l.* was our schoolmaster to. 24
tell me, do ye not hear the *l.*? 4:21
he is a debtor to do the whole *l.* 5:3
of you are justified by the *l.* 4
all the *l.* is fulfilled in one word. 14
against such there is no *l.* 23
bear ye, and so fulfil the *l.* of. 6:2
nor themselves keep the *l.* but. 13
abolished in his flesh the *l.* *Eph* 2:15
as touching the *l.* a. *Phil* 3:5
touching the righteousness in the *l.* 6
mine own righteousness, of the *l.* 9
to be teachers of the *l.* *1 Tim* 1:7
the *l.* is not made for a righteous. 9
contentions about the *l.* *Tit* 3:9
people according to the *l.* *Heb* 7:5
it the people received the *l.* 11
of necessity a change of the *l.* 12
not after the *l.* of a carnal. 16
for the *l.* made nothing perfect. 19
l. maketh men high priests, but word of the oath which was since *l.* 28
priests offer gifts according to *l.* 8:4
had spoken according to the *l.* 9:19
are by the *l.* purged with blood. 22
the *l.* having a shadow of good. 10:1
he that despised Moses' *l.* died. 28
into perfect *l.* of liberty. *Jas* 1:25
if ye fulfil the royal *l.* 2:8
and are convinced of the *l.* as. 9
shall keep the whole *l.* 10
thou art a transgressor of the *l.* 11
they that shall be judged by the *l.* 12
evil of the *l.* and judgeth the *l.* 4:11
sin transgresseth also the *l.* for sin is the transgression of *l.* *1 John* 3:4

see **book**

law *of the Lord*

that *the Lord's* *l.* may be. *Ex* 13:9
Jehu took no heed to walk in *l.* *of Lord.* *2 Ki* 10:31
Rehoboam forsook *l.* *of Lord* and. *2 Chr* 12:1
be encouraged in the *l.* *of Lord.* 31:4
Josiah's goodness according to the *l.* *of Lord.* 35:26
prepared his heart to seek the *l.* *of Lord.* *Ezra* 7:10
his delight is in the *l.* *of L.* *Ps* 1:2
the *l.* *of the Lord* is perfect. 19:7
who walk in the *l.* *of the Lord.* 119:1
cast away the *l.* *of Lord.* *Isa* 5:24
will not hear the *l.* *of the Lord.* 30:9
l. *of the Lord* is with us. *Jer* 8:8
despised the *l.* *of the Lord.* *Amos* 2:4
according to the *l.* *of Lord.* *Luke* 2:39

my **law**

will walk in *my l.* or no. *Ex* 16:4
children walk in *my l.* *2 Chr* 6:16
O my people, to *my l.* *Ps* 78:1
if his children forsake *my l.* 89:30
forget not *my l.* but keep. *Pr* 3:1
forsake not *my l.* 4:2
keep *my l.* as the apple. 7:2
in whose heart is *my l.* *Isa* 51:7
not hearkened unto *my l.* *Jer* 6:19
they have forsaken *my l.* 9:13
and have not kept *my l.* 16:11
not hearken to walk in *my l.* 26:4
put *my l.* in their inward parts. 31:33
feared nor walked in *my l.* 44:10
her priests have violated *my l.* *Ezek* 22:26
trespassed against *my l.* *Hos* 8:1
to him the great things of *my l.* 12

this **law**

this shall be the *l.* of leper. *Lev* 14:2
execute on her *this l.* *Num* 5:30
this is the ordinance of the *l.* 19:2; 31:21
Moses to declare *this l.* *Deut* 1:5
all *this l.* which I set before you. 4:8
shall write him a copy of *this l.* 17:18
to keep all the words of *this l.* 19
them the words of *this l.* 27:3, 8
confirmeth not the words of *this l.* *Deut* 27:26
not observe words of *this l.* 28:58
all the words of *this l.* 29:29; 31:12
Moses wrote *this l.* 31:9
thou shalt read *this l.* 11
of writing the words of *this l.* in. 24
children to do the words of *this l.* 32:46
read the words of *this l.* *Josh* 8:34

this is the **law**

this is the l. of the burnt offering. *Lev* 6:9; 7:37
this is the l. of meat offering. 6:14
this is the l. of sin offering. 25
this is the l. of the trespass. 7:1
this is the l. of the beasts. 11:46
this is the l. of her that hath. 12:7
this is the l. of the plague of leprosy. 13:59; 14:32, 57
this is the l. for all manner. 14:54
this is the l. of him that hath an issue. 15:32
this is the l. of jealousies. *Num* 5:29
this is the l. of the Nazarite. 6:13
this is the l. when a man dieth. 19:14
this is the l. which Moses. *Deut* 4:44
this is the l. of the house. *Ezek* 43:12
this is the l. and prophets. *Mat* 7:12

thy **law**

shall teach Israel *thy l.* *Deut* 33:10
they cast *thy l.* behind. *Neh* 9:26
bring them again to *thy l.* 29
kings, nor our princes kept *thy l.* 34
yea, *thy l.* is within my. *Ps* 40:8
teachest him out of *thy l.* 94:12
things out of *thy l.* 119:18
way of lying, and grant me *thy l.* 29
give me understanding, and I shall keep *thy l.* 34
I keep *thy l.* continually for ever. 44
have I not declined from *thy l.* 51
the wicked that forsake *thy l.* 53
thy name, and kept *thy l.* 55
but I have not forgotten *thy l.* 61
is fat, but I delight in *thy l.* 70
I may live, for *thy l.* is my delight. 77, 92, 174
pits, which are not after *thy l.* 85
O how I love *thy l.* 97
yet do I not forget *thy l.* 109
but *thy l.* do I love. 113, 163
made void *thy l.* 126
down, because they keep not *thy l.* 136
and *thy l.* is the truth. 142
are far from *thy l.* 150
peace have they who love *thy l.* 165
not, nor walked in *thy l.* *Jer* 32:23
have transgressed *thy l.* *Dan* 9:11

under the **law**

them that are *under the l.* *Rom* 3:19
for ye are not *under the l.* 6:14
because we are not *under l.* 15
under the l. as *under the l.* that I ... that are *under the l.* *1 Cor* 9:20
without law to God, but *under l.* 21
we were kept *under the l.* *Gal* 3:23
made *under the l.* 4:4
redeem them that were *under l.* 5
ye that desire to be *under the l.* 21
if ye be led of the Spirit, ye are not *under the l.* 5:18

without **law**

a long season, Israel hath been *without l.* *2 Chr* 15:3
as many as sinned *without l.* perish *without l.* *Rom* 2:12
righteousness of God *without l.* 3:21
for *without l.* sin was dead. 7:8
I was alive *without* the *l.* once. 9
that are *without l.*, as *without l.*, not *without l.* to God. *1 Cor* 9:21

written in the **law**

as it is *w. in the l.* of Moses. *1 Ki* 2:3; *2 Chr* 23:18; 25:4; 31:3; *Ezra* 3:2; *Neh* 10:34, 36; *Dan* 9:13; *Luke* 2:23
do according to all *w. in the l.* *1 Chr* 16:40; *2 Chr* 35:26
found *w. in the l.* that. *Neh* 8:14
oath that is *w. in l.* of. *Dan* 9:11

what is *w. in the l.*? *Luke* 10:26
fulfilled, which were *w. in l.* 24:44
things that are *w. in l.* *Acts* 24:14
it is *w. in the l.* *1 Cor* 9:9
in the l. it is *w.* 14:21

lawful

shall not be *l.* to impose. *Ezra* 7:24
shall the *l.* captive be? *Isa* 49:24
do that which is *l.* *Ezek* 18:5
21:27; 33:14, 19
the son hath done that which is *l.*
18:19; 33:16
do what is not *l.* *Mat* 12:2
Mark 2:24; *Luke* 6:2
was not *l.* for him to eat. *Mat* 12:4
Mark 2:26; *Luke* 6:4
l. to heal on the sabbath? *Mat* 12:10
12; *Mark* 3:4; *Luke* 6:9; 14:3
it is not *l.* for thee to have her.
Mat 14:4; *Mark* 6:18
is it *l.* for man to put away wife?
Mat 19:3; *Mark* 10:2
l. to give tribute to? *Mat* 22:17
Mark 12:14; *Luke* 20:22
it is not *l.* to put them in the treasury.
Mat 27:6
not *l.* for thee to carry. *John* 5:10
not *l.* for us to put any man. 18:31
which are not *l.* to receive. *Acts* 16:21
shall be determined in a *l.* 19:39
is it *l.* for you to scourge? 22:25
all things are *l.* unto me: all things *l.*
for me. *1 Cor* 6:12; 10:23
is not *l.* for a man to. *2 Cor* 12:4

lawfully

good, if a man use it *l.* *1 Tim* 1:8
yet is not crowned, except he strive *l.*
2 Tim 2:5

lawgiver

l. from between his feet. *Gen* 49:10*
digged the well by direction of the *l.*
Num 21:18*
in a portion of the *l.* *Deut* 33:21
Judah is my *l.* *Ps* 60:7*; 108:8*
the Lord is our *l.* and. *Isa* 33:22
there is one *l.* who is able. *Jas* 4:12

lawless

the law is for the *l.* and. *1 Tim* 1:9

laws

my statutes and my *l.* *Gen* 26:5
refuse ye to keep my *l.*? *Ex* 16:28
I do make them know the *l.* 18:16
teach them ordinances and *l.* 20
l. which the Lord made. *Lev* 26:46
know the *l.* of thy God. *Ezra* 7:25
thou gavest them true *l.* *Neh* 9:13
commandedst them statutes and *l.* 14
written among the *l.* of. *Esth* 1:19
their *l.* are diverse from all people,
neither keep they the king's *l.* 3:8
they might keep his *l.* *Ps* 105:45
have transgressed the *l.* *Isa* 24:5
shew them all the *l.* *Ezek* 43:11
hear all the *l.* 44:5
they shall keep my *l.* 24
to change times and *l.* *Dan* 7:25
we obeyed to walk in his *l.* 9:10
I will put my *l.* into their. *Heb* 8:10
put my *l.* into their hearts. 10:16

lawyer

(*One skilled in the interpretation of the Mosaic Law*)
one that was a *l.* asked him.
Mat 22:35; *Luke* 10:25
bring Zenas the *l.* and. *Tit* 3:13

lawyers

l. rejected the counsel. *Luke* 7:30
then answered one of the *l.* 11:45
woe unto you, *l.* 46, 52
Jesus spake to *l.*. 14:3

lay, *as with a woman*

the firstborn *l.* with her father.
Gen 19:33, 34, 35
and Jacob *l.* with Leah. 30:16
Shechem *l.* with Dinah. 34:2
Reuben went and *l.* with. 35:22
man that *l.* with woman. *Deut* 22:22
the man only that *l.* with her. 25
man that *l.* with her give fifty. 29
Eli heard they *l.* with. *1 Sam* 2:22
she came, and he *l.* with her.
2 Sam 11:4; 12:24
Amnon forced Tamar and *l.*
2 Sam 13:14
for in her youth they *l.* *Ezek* 23:8

lay

tale of bricks ye shall *l.* *Ex* 5:8
as woman's husband will *l.* 21:22
neither shalt thou *l.* upon. 22:25
and *l.* the wood in order. *Lev* 1:7
the priests shall *l.* the parts. 8, 12
thou shalt *l.* the frankincense. 2:15
and *l.* the burnt offering in. 6:12
Lord, *l.* not the sin upon. *Num* 12:11
l. them on them that hate. *Deut* 7:15
shall *l.* the fear of you upon. 11:25
l. not innocent blood to thy. 21:8*
l. thee an ambush for the city.
Josh 8:2
Samson *l.* till midnight. *Judg* 16:3
behold, a woman *l.* at his. *Ruth* 3:8
and Samuel *l.* till the. *1 Sam* 3:15
and *l.* it for a reproach on. 11:2
Saul *l.* in the trench, people. 26:5, 7
Ish-bosheth, who *l.* on a. *2 Sam* 4:5*
lamb eat of his meat, and *l.* 12:3
David *l.* all night on the. 16; 13:31
l. my bones beside his. *1 Ki* 13:31
l. it on wood and put no fire. 18:23
and as he *l.* and slept under. 19:5
Ahab fasted and *l.* in. 21:27
he went up and *l.* upon. *2 Ki* 4:34
l. ye them in two heaps at. 10:8
long as she *l.* desolate. *2 Chr* 36:21
many *l.* in sackcloth and. *Esth* 4:3
the dew *l.* all night. *Job* 29:19
he will not *l.* on man more. 34:23*
let him *l.* mine honour in. *Ps* 7:5
they that seek my life, *l.* 38:12
found a nest, where she may *l.* 84:3
and the living will *l.* it to. *Eccl* 7:2
woe to them that *l.* field. *Isa* 5:8
to *l.* the land desolate. 13:9
Ezek 33:28
I will *l.* low haughtiness. *Isa* 13:11
key of house of David *l.* on. 22:22
fortress shall he *l.* low. 25:12
behold, I will *l.* in Zion a. 28:16
judgement will I *l.* to the line. 17*
that *l.* a snare for him that. 29:21
staff which the Lord shall *l.* 30:32
there shall the great owl *l.* 34:15
a lump of figs, and *l.* it for. 38:21
thou didst not *l.* these things. 47:7
I will *l.* thy stones with fair. 54:11
I will *l.* stumblingblocks. *Jer* 6:21
Ezek 3:20
take thee a tile, and *l.* it. *Ezek* 4:1
l. siege against it. 2, 3
l. the iniquity of the house of. 4
I will *l.* bands upon thee. 8
I will *l.* my vengeance on. 25:14, 17
I will *l.* thee before kings. 28:17
l. thy flesh on the mountains. 32:5
and I will *l.* no famine upon. 35:29
be tilled, whereas it *l.* desolate. 34
I will *l.* sinews upon you. 37:6
there *l.* the most holy things. 42:13
14; 44:19
O Lord, *l.* not on us. *Jonah* 1:14
idols thereof will I *l.* *Mi* 1:7
l. it to heart, I will send a curse upon
you; because ye do not *l.* *Mal* 2:2
hath not where to *l.* his head.
Mat 8:20; *Luke* 9:58
and lay them on men's. *Mat* 23:4
see the place where the Lord *l.* 28:6
the sick of the palsy *l.* *Mark* 2:4
shall *l.* thee even with. *Luke* 19:44*
l. impotent folk, blind. *John* 5:3
it was a cave, and a stone *l.* 11:38
Lord, *l.* not this sin to. *Acts* 7:60
l. on you no greater burden. 15:28
and no small tempest *l.* on. 27:20
l. any thing to the charge. *Rom* 8:33
I *l.* in Sion a stumblingstone. 9:33
let every one *l.* by him. *1 Cor* 16:2
l. aside every weight. *Heb* 12:1
wherefore *l.* apart all. *Jas* 1:21
I *l.* in Sion a chief. *1 Pet* 2:6
see **foundation**

lay *down*

before they *l. down* men. *Gen* 19:4
and Lot perceived not when she *l.*
down. 33, 35
Jacob *l. down* in that place. *Gen* 28:11
he *l. down* as a lion. *Num* 24:9
he *l. down* at her feet. *Judg* 5:27
his feet, and *l.* thee *down.* *Ruth* 3:4
lie down, and Samuel went and *l.*
down. *1 Sam* 3:5, 9
Saul *l. down* naked all that. 19:24
Jonadab said, *L.* thee *down* on thy.
2 Sam 13:5
so Amnon *l. down* and made. 6
l. down now, put me in surety with.
Job 17:3*
l. me *down* in peace. *Ps* 4:8
young lions *l.* them *down.* 104:22
thy mother *l. down.* *Ezek* 19:2*
l. themselves *down* on clothes.
Amos 2:8
and I *l. down* my life for my sheep.
John 10:15, 17
l. it *down* of myself, have power to *l.*
it *down.* 18
I will *l. down* my life for. 13:37, 38
that a man *l. down* his life. 15:13
to *l. down* our lives. *1 John* 3:16

lay *hand*

l. not thy *hand* on the lad. *Gen* 22:12
shed no blood, *l.* no *hand.* 37:22
l. my *hand* upon Egypt. *Ex* 7:4
l. his *hand* on the head of his offering. *Lev* 3:2, 8
l. his *hand* on the head of the goat.
13; 4:24
he shall *l.* his *hand* on the bullock's
head. 4:4, 15
he shall *l.* his *hand* on the sin offering. 29, 33
l. thy *hand* on Joshua. *Num* 27:18
l. thy *hand* upon thy mouth, and go.
Judg 18:19
to *l. hand* on the king. *Esth* 2:21
to *l. hand* on such as sought. 9:2
daysman might *l.* his *hand.* *Job* 9:33
mark me, and *l.* your *hand.* 21:5
I will *l.* my *hand* on my mouth. 40:4
l. thy *hand* upon him. 41:8
thought evil, *l. hand* upon. *Pr* 30:32
l. their *hand* on Edom. *Isa* 11:14
shall *l.* their *hand* on their mouth.
Mi 7:16
and *l.* thy *hand* on her. *Mat* 9:18

lay *hands*

Aaron shall *l.* both his *hands* on.
Lev 16:21
him *l.* their *hands* on head. 24:14
the Levites *l.* their *h.* *Num* 8:12
I will *l. hands* on you. *Neh* 13:21
scorn to *l. hands* on. *Esth* 3:6
they sought to *l. hands* on him.
Mat 21:46; *Luke* 20:19
come and *l.* thy *hands.* *Mark* 5:23
l. hands on the sick, and they. 16:18
shall *l. hands* on you. *Luke* 21:12
on whomsoever I *l. hands.* *Acts* 8:19
l. hands suddenly on. *1 Tim* 5:22

lay *hold*

shall his father *l. hold.* *Deut* 21:19
and *l. hold* on her, and lie. 22:28
l. thee *hold* on one of. *2 Sam* 2:21
hand, saying, *L. hold* on. *1 Ki* 13:4
life to them that *l. hold.* *Pr* 3:18
I sought to *l. hold* on folly. *Eccl* 2:3
shall roar, and *l. hold* on. *Isa* 5:29
they shall *l. hold* on bow. *Jer* 6:23
l. hold on his neighbour. *Zech* 14:13
will he not *l. hold* on it? *Mat* 12:11
out to *l. hold* on him. *Mark* 3:21
they sought to *l. hold* on him. 12:12
l. hold on eternal life. *1 Tim* 6:12, 19
to *l. hold* on the hope. *Heb* 6:18

lay *up*

l. up corn under the hand. *Gen* 41:35
l. up manna for you till. *Ex* 16:23
l. up a pot of manna to be kept. 33
l. them *up* in tabernacle. *Num* 17:4
l. them *up* without the camp. 19:9
l. up these my words. *Deut* 11:18
shall *l.* it *up* within thy gates. 14:28
l. up his words in thy. *Job* 22:22
then shalt *l. up* gold as dust and. 24
l. up my commandments. *Pr* 7:1
wise men *l. up* knowledge. 10:14
l. not *up* for yourselves treasures
upon earth. *Mat* 6:19

l. up for yourselves treasures in heaven. *Mat* 6:20
children not to *l. up* for. *2 Cor* 12:14

lay *wait*

from such as *l.* in *wait.* *Ezra* 8:31
that *l. wait* for my soul. *Ps* 71:10
let us *l. wait* for blood. *Pr* 1:11
l. wait for their own blood. 18
l. not *wait* against the. 24:15
they *l. wait* as he that. *Jer* 5:26

lay *waste*

that shouldest be to *l. waste.* *2 Ki* 19:25; *Isa* 37:26
I will *l.* it *waste,* it shall. *Isa* 5:6
I will *l.* thy cities *waste.* *Ezek* 35:4

layest

thou *l.* the burden of. *Num* 11:11
l. thou a snare for my ? *1 Sam* 28:9

layeth

God *l.* up his iniquity. *Job* 21:19
soul crieth out, yet God *l.* 24:12*
the sword of him that *l.* at. 41:26
he *l.* up the depth in. *Ps* 33:7
l. the beams of his chambers. 104:3
he *l.* up wisdom for the. *Pr* 2:7
with knowledge, but a fool *l.* 13:16*
dissembleth, and *l.* up deceit. 26:24
l. her hands to the spindle. 31:19
the lofty city he *l.* low to. *Isa* 26:5
blessed is the man that *l.* 56:2*
perisheth, and no man *l.* it to. 57:1
but in heart he *l.* his wait. *Jer* 9:8
l. it to heart. 12:11
Lord *l.* the foundation. *Zech* 12:1
he that *l.* up treasure. *Luke* 12:21
he *l.* it on his shoulders. 15:5

laying

hurl at him by *l.* wait. *Num* 35:20
him any thing without *l.* wait. 22
commune of *l.* snares. *Ps* 64:5
l. aside the commandment of God. *Mark* 7:8
l. wait for him, and. *Luke* 11:54
l. on of the apostles'. *Acts* 8:18
but their *l.* wait was known. 9:24*
kinsmen heard of their *l.* in. 23:16
l. wait in the way to kill him. 25:3
with *l.* on of the hands. *1 Tim* 4:14
l. up in store a good foundation. 6:19
not *l.* again the foundation. *Heb* 6:1
doctrine of baptisms, and of *l.* on. 2
l. aside all malice, guile. *1 Pet* 2:1

Lazarus

certain beggar named *L.* *Luke* 16:20
seeth *L.* in Abraham's bosom. 23
send *L.* that he may dip the tip. 24
likewise *L.* received evil things. 25
Mary whose brother *L.* *John* 11:2
Jesus loved *L.* 5
our friend *L.* sleepeth. 11
L. is dead. 14
he cried, *L.* come forth. 43
L. was one of them that sat. 12:2
came that they might see *L.* 9
when he called *L.* out of grave. 17

lead, *substantive*

sank as *l.* in the mighty. *Ex* 15:10
l. that may abide fire. *Num* 31:22
graven with iron and *l.* *Job* 19:24
l. is consumed of the fire. *Jer* 6:29
they are *l.* in the midst. *Ezek* 22:18
as they gather *l.* so will I gather. 20
with iron, tin, and *l.* Tarshish. 27:12
lifted up a talent of *l.* *Zech* 5:7
he cast the weight of *l.* on the. 8

lead

I will *l.* on softly as the. *Gen* 33:14
a pillar of cloud to *l.* *Ex* 13:21
go, *l.* the people to the place. 32:34
l. them out and bring. *Num* 27:17
whither the Lord shall *l.* you. *Deut* 4:27; 28:37
shall make captains to *l.* the. 20:9
so the Lord alone did *l.* him. 32:12
Barak, *l.* thy captivity. *Judg* 5:12
they may *l.* them away. *1 Sam* 30:22
find compassion before them that *l.* *2 Chr* 30:9
pillar of cloud to *l.* *Neh* 9:19
l. me, O Lord, in thy. *Ps* 5:8
l. me in thy truth. 25:5
l. me in a plain path. 27:11
for thy name's sake *l.* me. *Ps* 31:3
light and truth, let them *l.* me. 43:3
l. me into Edom ? 60:9*; 108:10
l. me to the rock that is. 61:2
l. them forth with workers of. 125:5
there shall thine hand *l.* me. 139:10
l. me in the way everlasting. 24
l. me into the land of. 143:10
goest, it shall *l.* thee. *Pr* 6:22
l. in way of righteousness. 8:20*
l. thee to my mother's. *S of S* 8:2
l. thee cause thee to err. *Isa* 3:12
a little child shall *l.* them. 11:6
the king of Assyria *l.* 20:4
gently *l.* those that are with. 40:11
I will *l.* them in paths not. 42:16
hath mercy on them, shall *l.* 49:10
I will *l.* him, and restore. 57:18
so didst thou *l.* thy people. 63:14
with supplications will I *l.* *Jer* 31:9
shall *l.* Zedekiah to Babylon. 32:5
maids *l.* her, as with voice. *Nah* 2:7*
l. us not into temptation. *Mat* 6:13*; *Luke* 11:4*
if the blind *l.* the blind. *Mat* 15:14 *Luke* 6:39
when they shall *l.* you. *Mark* 13:11
take him and *l.* him away. 14:44
loose his ox and *l.* him. *Luke* 13:15
seeking some to *l.* him. *Acts* 13:11
have we not power to *l.*? *1 Cor* 9:5
we may *l.* a quiet life. *1 Tim* 2:2
l. captive silly women. *2 Tim* 3:6*
to *l.* them out of the land. *Heb* 8:9
shall feed and *l.* them. *Rev* 7:17

leader

Jehoiada was *l.* of the. *1 Chr* 12:27
David consulted with captains and every *l.* 13:1
I have given him a *l.* *Isa* 55:4

leaders

angel which cut off *l.* *2 Chr* 32:21
the *l.* of this people. *Isa* 9:16
they be blind *l.* of the. *Mat* 15:14*

leadest

that *l.* Joseph like a flock. *Ps* 80:1

leadeth

turned to the way that *l.* *1 Sam* 13:17
he *l.* counsellors away. *Job* 12:17
he *l.* princes away spoiled, and. 19
he *l.* me beside the still. *Ps* 23:2
he *l.* me in the paths of. 3
l. him into the way that. *Pr* 16:29
Lord thy God which *l.* *Isa* 48:17
wide is the way that *l.* to. *Mat* 7:13
narrow is the way that *l.* to life. 14
Jesus *l.* them into a high. *Mark* 9:2*
he calleth his sheep and *l.* *John* 10:3
the iron gate that *l.* *Acts* 12:10
the goodness of God *l.* to. *Rom* 2:4
he that *l.* shall go into. *Rev* 13:10

leaf

her mouth was an olive *l.* *Gen* 8:11
sound of a shaken *l.* *Lev* 26:36
wilt thou break a *l.* driven to and fro ? *Job* 13:25
his *l.* also shall not wither. *Ps* 1:3
be as an oak, whose *l.* *Isa* 1:30
their host fall as a *l.* 34:4
we all do fade as a *l.* 64:6
no grapes, the *l.* shall. *Jer* 8:13
but her *l.* shall be green, and. 17:8
l. shall not fade, the *l.* *Ezek* 47:12

league

(*The Revisions frequently change this word to* covenant)

make therefore a *l.* *Josh* 9:6, 11
Joshua made a *l.* with the. 15, 16
no *l.* with the inhabitants. *Judg* 2:2
my son hath made a *l.* *1 Sam* 22:8
king David made a *l.* *2 Sam* 5:3
Solomon made a *l.* *1 Ki* 5:12
is a *l.* between me and thee. 15:19
go break thy *l.* with. *2 Chr* 16:3
be in *l.* with the stones. *Job* 5:23
men of the land that is in *l.* shall. *Ezek* 30:5
after the *l.* he shall work. *Dan* 11:23

Leah

elder daughter was *L.* *Gen* 29:16
L. was tender eyed, but Rachel. 17
in the morning, behold it was *L.* 25
the Lord saw that *L.* *Gen* 29:31
L. conceived and bare. 32; 30:19
out of the field, *L.* met him. 30:16
Jacob called Rachel and *L.* 31:4
Jacob put *L.* and her children. 33:2
Dinah the daughter of *L.* went. 34:1
L.; Reuben, Simeon. 35:23; 46:15
Abraham, there I buried *L.* 49:31
make this woman like *L.* *Ruth* 4:11

lean

kine came out of the river *l.*fleshed. *Gen* 41:3, 19
the *l.*fleshed eat up the. 4, 20
land is, whether fat or *l.* *Num* 13:20
being the king's son *l.* *2 Sam* 13:4
of his flesh shall wax *l.* *Isa* 17:4
between fat cattle and *l.* *Ezek* 34:20

lean, *verb*

I may *l.* on the pillars. *Judg* 16:26
on which if a man *l.* *2 Ki* 18:21 *Isa* 36:6
shall *l.* on his house. *Job* 8:15
l. not to thine own. *Pr* 3:5
yet will they *l.* on the Lord. *Mi* 3:11

leaned

behold, Saul *l.* upon. *2 Sam* 1:6
on whose hand the king *l.* *2 Ki* 7:2
when they *l.* on thee. *Ezek* 29:7
l. his hand on the wall. *Amos* 5:19
who also *l.* on his breast. *John* 21:20

leaneth

not fail one that *l.* on. *2 Sam* 3:29
l. on my hand in the. *2 Ki* 5:18

leaning

that cometh up *l.* on. *S of S* 8:5
there was *l.* on Jesus'. *John* 13:23
Jacob worshipped, *l.* on. *Heb* 11:21

leanness

my *l.* rising up in me. *Job* 16:8
gave request, but sent *l.* *Ps* 106:15
among his fat ones *l.* *Isa* 10:16
but I said, My *l.*, my *l.*, woe. 24:16*

leap

all the rams which *l.* on. *Gen* 31:12
have legs to *l.* withal. *Lev* 11:21
and of Dan, he shall *l.* *Deut* 33:22
and sparks of fire *l.* out. *Job* 41:19
why *l.* ye, ye high hills ? *Ps* 68:16*
then shall the lame man *l.* *Isa* 35:6
of chariots shall they *l.* *Joel* 2:5
shall punish those that *l.* *Zeph* 1:9
in that day, and *l.* for joy. *Luke* 6:23

leaped

the rams which *l.* upon. *Gen* 31:10
by my God, I *l.* over a wall. *2 Sam* 22:30; *Ps* 18:29
they *l.* upon the altar. *1 Ki* 18:26
babe *l.* in her womb. *Luke* 1:41, 44
stand upright, and he *l.* *Acts* 14:10
he in whom evil spirit was, *l.* 19:16

leaping

Michal saw David *l.* *2 Sam* 6:16
behold he cometh *l.* on. *S of S* 2:8
l. up, stood and walked. *Acts* 3:8

learn

that they may *l.* to fear me. *Deut* 4:10; 14:23
that ye may *l.* them, and keep. 5:1
therein, that he may *l.* to fear. 17:19
shalt not *l.* to do after the. 18:9
they may hear, and *l.* and. 31:12
that their children may *l.* to. 13
I might *l.* thy statutes. *Ps* 119:71, 73
lest thou *l.* his ways. *Pr* 22:25
l. to do well, seek. *Isa* 1:17
neither shall they *l.* war. 2:4; *Mi* 4:3
the inhabitants of world shall *l.* righteousness. *Isa* 26:9
not the wicked *l.* righteousness. 10
murmured shall *l.* doctrine. 29:24†
l. not the way of heathen. *Jer* 10:2
if they will diligently *l.* ways. 12:16
but go and *l.* what that. *Mat* 9:13
l. of me, for I am meek and. 11:29
l. a parable of the fig tree. 24:32 *Mark* 13:28
l. in us not to think. *1 Cor* 4:6
one by one, that all may *l.* 14:31
if they will *l.* any thing, let them. 35
would *l.* of you, received ye ? *Gal* 3:2

l. not to blaspheme. 1 Tim 1:20*
let the woman l. in silence. 2:11
let them l. first to shew piety. 5:4
and withal they l. to be idle. 13
let ours l. to maintain. Tit 3:14
no man could l. that song. Rev 14:3

learned

tarry, for I have l. by. Gen 30:27*
among the heathen, and l. Ps 106:35
l. thy righteous judgements. 119:7
I neither l. wisdom, nor. Pr 30:3
deliver to one that is l. Isa 29:11
is not l. he saith, I am not l. 12
given me tongue of the l. he wakeneth mine ear to hear as l. 50:4*
it l. to catch the prey. Ezek 19:3, 6
every man that hath l. John 6:45
man letters, having never l. 7:15
Moses was l. in all. Acts 7:22*
the doctrine ye have l. Rom 16:17
have not so l. Christ. Eph 4:20
those things ye have l. and. Phil 4:9
l., therewith to be content. 11
as ye l. of Epaphras our. Col 1:7
in the things thou hast l. knowing of whom thou hast l. 2 Tim 3:14
though he were a son, yet l. Heb 5:8

learning

will hear and increase l. Pr 1:5
man, and he will increase in l. 9:9
of the lips increaseth l. 16:21
the heart of the wise addeth l. 23
whom they might teach l. Dan 1:4
God gave them skill in all l. 17
Festus said, Much l. Acts 26:24
were written for our l. Rom 15:4
ever l. and never able. 2 Tim 3:7

leasing

long will ye seek after l.? Ps 4:2*
destroy them that speak l. 5:6*

least

[1] *The smallest quantity,* Num 11:32. [2] *Most humble and lowly,* Luke 9:48. [3] *The meanest person, or one of the least judgement, skill, and experience,* Judg 6:15.

not worthy of the l. of. Gen 32:10
gathered l. gathered. Num 11:32
l. in my father's house. Judg 6:15
my family, the l. of. 1 Sam 9:21
one captain of l. of. 2 Ki 18:24
l. of flock shall draw them. Jer 49:20*; 50:45*
not the l. grain fall upon. Amos 9:9
art not the l. among the princes of Judah. Mat 2:6
of these l. commandments, shall be called the l. in the kingdom. 5:19
that is l. in the kingdom of heaven, is greater. 11:11*; Luke 7:28*
is the l. of all seeds. Mat 13:32*
have done it to the l. 25:40, 45
he that is l. among you. Luke 9:48
not able to do that which is l. 12:26
faithful in the l.: unjust in l. 16:10*
them to judge who are l. 1 Cor 6:4*
for I am the l. of the apostles. 15:9
who am less than the l. Eph 3:8

see **greatest**

at the **least**

damsel abide with us, at the l. Gen 24:55
at the l. such as before. Judg 3:2
if kept themselves at l. 1 Sam 21:4*
hadst known at l. in. Luke 19:42
that at the l. the shadow of Peter. Acts 5:15

leather

man, girt with a girdle of l. 2 Ki 1:8

leathern

John had a l. girdle. Mat 3:4

leave

[1] *Permission,* Num 22:13; Mark 5:13. [2] *To depart from,* John 16:28. [3] *Farewell,* Acts 18:18. [4] *To lay down,* Mat 5:24.

leave, *substantive*

refuseth to give me l. Num 22:13
asked l. of me. 1 Sam 20:6, 28
certain days obtained I l. Neh 13:6
Jesus gave them l. Mark 5:13
Pilate gave him l. to. John 19:38
Paul took his l. of the. Acts 18:18
when we had taken our l. one. 21:6
l. I went to Macedonia. 2 Cor 2:13

leave

l. father and mother and. Gen 2:24
Mat 19:5; Mark 10:7; Eph 5:31
let me l. with thee some of the folk. Gen 33:15
l. one of your brethren here. 42:33
cannot l. his father, if he l. 44:22
let no man l. manna till. Ex 16:19
what they l. the beasts of. 23:11
not l. any of the peace offering. Lev 7:15; 22:30
shall put off garments and l. 16:23
thou shalt l. them for the poor. 19:10; 23:22
l. none of the passover. Num 9:12
he said, L. us not, I pray. 10:31
will yet again l. them in the. 32:15
not l. thee either corn. Deut 28:51
of children which he shall l. 54
and l. them in the lodging. Josh 4:3*
olive said, Should I l. my? Judg 9:9
vine said, Should I l. my vine? 13
Entreat me not to l. Ruth 1:16
lest my father l. caring. 1 Sam 9:5
Saul said, Let us not l. a. 14:36
if I l. of all that pertain to. 25:22
shall not l. to my husband neither name nor. 2 Sam 14:7
let him not l. us nor. 1 Ki 8:57
shall eat and shall l. 2 Ki 4:43
did he l. of the people but fifty. 13:7
this good land, and l. it. 1 Chr 28:8
to l. us a remnant to. Ezra 9:8
l. it for an inheritance to your. 12
I pray you let us l. off this. Neh 5:10
the work cease whilst I l. it? 6:3
would l. the seventh year. 10:31*
wilt thou l. thy labour? Job 39:11
thou wilt not l. my soul in hell. Ps 16:10; Acts 2:27
they l. their substance to. Ps 17:14
thou hast been my help, l. me not. 27:9; 119:121
they die and l. their wealth. 49:10
O God, my trust, l. not my. 141:8
l. the paths of uprightness. Pr 2:13
l. off contention, before it be. 17:14
I should l. it to the man. Eccl 2:18
yet shall he l. it for his portion. 21
if ruler rise up against thee, l. 10:4
will ye l. your glory? Isa 10:3
shall l. your name for a curse. 65:15
I might l. my people, and. Jer 9:2
called by thy name, l. us not. 14:9
riches, he shall l. them in. 17:11
will a man l. the snow of? 18:14
child and suckling, to l. you. 44:7
l. the cities, and dwell in. 48:28
not l. some gleaning grapes? 49:9
l. thy fatherless children, I will. 11
and l. thee naked and bare. Ezek 16:39; 23:29
will turn thee, and l. but a. 39:2*
l. the stump of his. Dan 4:15, 23, 26
he l. his blood upon him. Hos 12:14
return, and l. a blessing. Joel 2:14
l. an hundred, shall l. Amos 5:3
who l. off righteousness in the. 7*
would they not l. grapes? Ob 5
it shall l. them neither. Mal 4:1
l. there thy gift before. Mat 5:24
doth he not l. the ninety and nine? 18:12; Luke 15:4
to have done, and not l. Mat 23:23
and l. his wife, and l. Mark 12:19
they shall not l. in thee. Luke 19:44
my peace I l. with you. John 14:27
I l. the world and go to the. 16:28
ye shall l. me alone, yet I am not. 32
not reason we should l. Acts 6:2
her, let her not l. him. 1 Cor 7:13
I will never l. thee, nor. Heb 13:5*
the court l. out, and. Rev 11:2

I will, or will I **leave**

if I say, I will l. off my. Job 9:27
I will l. my complaint upon. 10:1*
yet will I l. a remnant. Ezek 6:8
but I will l. a few. 12:16
I will l. you there, and melt. 22:20*
I will l. thee thrown into. Ezek 29:5†
I will l. thee upon the land. 32:4
I will l. in midst of thee. Zeph 3:12

I will not **leave**

I will not l. thee until I. Gen 28:15
as the Lord liveth, I will not l. thee. 2 Ki 2:2; 4:30
As thy soul liveth, I will not l. 2:4, 6
Lord I will not l. him in. Ps 37:33
I will not l. thee together. Jer 30:11
46:28
I will not l. you comfortless. John 14:18

leaved

before him the two-l. gates. Isa 45:1

leaven

A piece of dough salted and soured, to ferment and relish a mass of dough for bread, Hos 7:4; 1 Cor 5:6. *The word is also used figuratively in the New Testament for* teachings.

ye shall put away l. Ex 12:15, 19
neither shall be l. seen in all. 13:7
blood of my sacrifice with l. 34:25
shall be made with l. Lev 2:11
it shall not be baken with l. 6:17
eat meat offering without l. 10:12
they shall be baken with l. 23:17
of thanksgiving with l. Amos 4:5
kingdom of heaven is like l. Mat 13:33; Luke 13:21
the l. of the Pharisees. Mat 16:6
11; Mark 8:15; Luke 12:1
not beware of the l. Mat 16:12
little l. leaveneth the whole lump. 1 Cor 5:6; Gal 5:9
purge out therefore the old l. that. 1 Cor 5:7
let us keep the feast, not with old l. 8

leavened

for whosoever eateth l. Ex 12:15, 19
shall eat nothing l. in all your. 20
their dough before it was l. 34, 39
there shall no l. be eaten. 13:3, 7
after he hath kneaded the dough till it be l. Hos 7:4
till the whole was l. Mat 13:33
Luke 13:21

see **bread**

leaveneth

little leaven l. the whole lump. 1 Cor 5:6; Gal 5:9

leaves

sewed fig l. and made. Gen 3:7
when they cast their l. Isa 6:13*
read three or four l. Jer 36:23
it shall wither in all the l. Ezek 17:9
l. thereof fair. Dan 4:12, 21
shake off his l. 14
nothing thereon but l. Mat 21:19
Mark 11:13
his branch putteth forth l. Mat 24:32; Mark 13:28
l. were for the healing of. Rev 22:2

leaves *for doors*

the two l. of the one door. 1 Ki 6:34
two l. apiece, two l. for. Ezek 41:24

leaveth

the ostrich l. her eggs. Job 39:14
a good man l. an. Pr 13:22
like a sweeping rain which l. 28:3
idol shepherd, that l. Zech 11:17
then the devil l. him. Mat 4:11
the hireling l. the sheep. John 10:12

leaving

Jesus l. Nazareth, dwelt. Mat 4:13
thieves departed, l. Luke 10:30
men l. the natural use. Rom 1:27
l. the principles of the. Heb 6:1*
Christ suffered for us, l. 1 Pet 2:21

Lebanon

goodly mountain and L. Deut 3:25
that dwelt in mount L. Judg 3:3
ten thousand a month to L. 1 Ki 5:14
the forest of L. 7:2; 10:17, 21
was in L. sent to cedar in L. give thy. 2 Ki 14:9; 2 Chr 25:18
I am come up to the sides of L. 2 Ki 19:23; Isa 37:24
skill to cut timber in L. 2 Chr 2:8
L. and Sirion like a. Ps 29:6

Baasha *l. off* building. *1 Ki* 15:21
2 Chr 16:5
they *l. off* speaking. *Job* 32:15*
he hath *l. off* to be wise. *Ps* 36:3
so they *l. off* speaking. *Jer* 38:27
since we *l. off* to burn incense. 44:18
have *l off* to take heed. *Hos* 4:10

left *corner*
guard stood to the *l. corner* about.
2 Ki 11:11

lefthanded
raised Ehud, a man *l.* *Judg* 3:15
seven hundred chosen men *l.* 20:16

left *pillar*
he set up the *l. pillar.* *1 Ki* 7:21

left *side*
five bases on the *l. side.* *1 Ki* 7:39
five candlesticks on the *l. side.* 49
with his weapon from right to *l. side.*
2 Chr 23:10
had the face of an ox on the *l. side.*
Ezek 1:10
lie also on thy *l. side*, and lay. 4:4
olive tree upon *l. side. Zech* 4:3, 11

leg, -s
with fire his head and *l.* *Ex* 12:9
wash the inwards and his *l.* 29:17
Lev 9:14
his head, and his *l.* burn. *Lev* 4:11
he washed the inwards and *l.* 8:21
which have *l.* above their feet. 11:21
shall smite thee in the knees and *l.*
Deut 28:35
of brass upon his *l.* *1 Sam* 17:6
pleasure in the *l.* of a man. *Ps* 147:10
the *l.* of the lame are not. *Pr* 26:7
his *l.* are as pillars of. *S of S* 5:15
take away ornaments of *l. Isa* 3:20*
make bare the *l.* uncover the. 47:2*
his *l.* of iron, his feet. *Dan* 2:33
two *l.*, or piece of an ear. *Amos* 3:12
their *l.* might be broken. *John* 19:31
and brake the *l.* of the first. 32
he was dead, brake not his *l.* 33

Legion
my name is *L.* for we are many.
Mark 5:9; *Luke* 8:30

legions
me more than twelve *l.* *Mat* 26:53

leisure
had no *l.* so much as to. *Mark* 6:31

Lemuel
the words of king *L.* *Pr* 31:1
not for kings, O *L.* to drink. 4

lend
if thou *l.* money to any. *Ex* 22:25
not *l.* him thy victuals. *Lev* 25:37*
shalt *l.* to many nations. *Deut* 15:6
thou shalt surely *l.* him sufficient. 8
thou shalt not *l.* upon usury. 23:19
to a stranger thou mayest *l.* 20
thou dost *l.* thy brother any. 24:10
the man to whom thou dost *l.* 11
thou shalt *l.* to many nations. 28:12
l. to thee, thou shalt not *l.* him. 44
if ye *l.* to them of whom ye . . . for sinners also *l.* to sinners.
Luke 6:34
your enemies, do good and *l.* 35
and say to him, Friend, *l.* me. 11:5

lender
is servant to the *l.* *Pr* 22:7
as with the *l.* so with. *Isa* 24:2

lendeth
every creditor that *l.* *Deut* 15:2
merciful, and *l.*; his seed. *Ps* 37:26
man sheweth favour and *l.* 112:5
pity on the poor *l.* to Lord. *Pr* 19:17

length
through the land in the *l. Gen* 13:17
he is thy life, and the *l. Deut* 30:20
l. of days, understanding. *Job* 12:12
even *l.* of days for ever. *Ps* 21:4
for *l.* of days shall they. *Pr* 3:2
l. of days is in her right hand. 16
and to see what is the *l.* *Zech* 2:2
l. of the roll is twenty cubits. 5:2
be able to comprehend *l. Eph* 3:18
l. as large as the breadth. *Rev* 21:16

at **length**
him become his son *at l.* *Pr* 29:21
if now at *l.* I may have a journey.
Rom 1:10

lengthen
then will I *l.* thy days. *1 Ki* 3:14
l. thy cords and strengthen. *Isa* 54:2

lengthened
that thy days may be *l. Deut* 25:15*

lengthening
a *l.* of thy tranquillity. *Dan* 4:27

lent
they *l.* to them such as. *Ex* 12:36*
thing that is *l.* on usury. *Deut* 23:19
I *l.* him to the Lord, he shall be *l.*
1 Sam 1:28*
for the loan which is *l.* to. 2:20†
I have not *l.* on usury nor have men *l.* me. *Jer* 15:10

lentiles
gave Esau pottage of *l.* *Gen* 25:34
piece of ground full of *l. 2 Sam* 23:11
see **beans**

leopard
(*A large and ferocious spotted animal*)
the *l.* shall lie down with. *Isa* 11:6
a *l.* watch over their cities. *Jer* 5:6
can the *l.* change his spots ? 13:23
and lo, another like a *l.* *Dan* 7:6
I will be to them as a *l.* *Hos* 13:7
the beast was like to a *l.* *Rev* 13:2

leopards
the mountains of the *l.* *S of S* 4:8
horses are swifter than *l.* *Hab* 1:8

leper
l. in whom the plague is. *Lev* 13:45
shall be the law of the *l.* in. 14:2
the leprosy be healed in the *l.* 3
man of the seed of Aaron is a *l.* 22:4
out of the camp every *l.* *Num* 5:2
from the house of Joab, one that is a *l.* *2 Sam* 3:29
Naaman was a *l.* *2 Ki* 5:1
recover the *l.* 11
went from his presence a *l.* as. 27
Azariah was a *l.* to the day. 15:5
the king was a *l.* *2 Chr* 26:21
him, for they said, He is a *l.* 23
and behold, there came a *l.*
Mat 8:2; *Mark* 1:40
in the house of Simon the *l.*
Mat 26:6; *Mark* 14:3

lepers
when the *l.* came to the. *2 Ki* 7:8
heal the sick, cleanse *l.* *Mat* 10:8
the lame walk, the *l.* are cleansed.
11:5; *Luke* 7:22
many *l.* were in Israel. *Luke* 4:27
met him ten men that were *l.* 17:12

leprosy
skin like the plague of *l.* *Lev* 13:2
it is a plague of *l.* 3, 8, 11, 15, 25
27, 30, 42, 49
when the plague of *l.* is in a man. 9
if a *l.* break out. 12
if the *l.* covered his flesh. 13
as the *l.* appeareth in the skin. 43
that the plague of *l.* is in. 47
this is the law of the plague of *l.*
59; 14:54, 55, 57
if the plague of *l.* be healed. 14:3
him that is to be cleansed from *l.* 7
him in whom is the plague of *l.* 32
heed in the plague of *l.* *Deut* 24:8
recover him of his *l.* *2 Ki* 5:3, 7
mayest recover him of his *l.* 6
the *l.* of Naaman shall cleave. 27
the *l.* rose up in his. *2 Chr* 26:19
his *l.* was cleansed. *Mat* 8:3
Mark 1:42; *Luke* 5:13
behold, a man full of *l.* *Luke* 5:12
see **fretting**

leprous
behold, his hand was *l.* *Ex* 4:6
l. man he is unclean. *Lev* 13:44
Miriam became *l.* behold she was *l.*
Num 12:10
there were four *l.* men. *2 Ki* 7:3
and Uzziah was *l.* in. *2 Chr* 26:20

less
some more, some *l.* *Ex* 16:17
the poor shall not give *l.* than. 30:15
word of the Lord to do *l. Num* 22:18
to few thou shalt give *l.* inheritance.
26:54; 33:54
thy servant knew nothing *l.* or more.
1 Sam 22:15
Abigail told him nothing *l.* 25:36
punished us *l.* than our. *Ezra* 9:13
exacteth *l.* than iniquity. *Job* 11:6
much *l.* do lying lips a. *Pr* 17:7
much *l.* for a servant to rule. 19:10
all nations are counted *l.* *Isa* 40:17
when it is sown is *l.* *Mark* 4:31
mother of James the *l.* 15:40
members we think *l.* *1 Cor* 12:23
the more I love, the *l.* *2 Cor* 12:15
l. than the least of all. *Eph* 3:8
and that I may be the *l.* *Phil* 2:28
the *l.* is blessed of better. *Heb* 7:7

lesser
made the *l.* light to rule. *Gen* 1:16
for the treading of *l.* *Isa* 7:25*
l. settle to the greater. *Ezek* 43:14

lest
ye touch it, *l.* ye die. *Gen* 3:3
Lev 10:6, 7, 9; *Num* 18:32
l. we be scattered abroad. *Gen* 11:4
l. thou say, I have made. 14:23
l. thou be consumed in the. 19:15
l. I die. 19; 26:9
l. he come and smite me. 32:11
l. he die, as his brethren did. 38:11
Deut 20:5, 6, 7
let her take it to her, *l.* *Gen* 38:23
l. thou and thy household. 45:11
go, *l.* he fall on us with. *Ex* 5:3
l. peradventure the people. 13:17
l. they break through to the. 19:21
sanctify, *l.* the Lord break forth. 22
let not God speak with us, *l.* 20:19
I will not go, *l.* I consume thee. 33:3
shall not go in to see, *l.* they die.
Num 4:20; 18:22
l. ye perish quickly. *Deut* 11:17
l. he cry against thee to. 24:15
l. if he should exceed and. 25:3
let them live, *l.* wrath. *Josh* 9:20
shall be a witness, *l.* ye deny. 24:27
l. Israel vaunt themselves. *Judg* 7:2
let him not know, *l.* he. *1 Sam* 20:3
l. I take the city, and. *2 Sam* 12:28
l. he take thee away. *Job* 36:18
l. I deal with you after your. 42:8
kiss the Son *l.* he be angry. *Ps* 2:12
lighten mine eyes, *l.* I sleep. 13:3
consider this, *l.* I tear you. 50:22
l. thou dash thy foot. 91:12
Mat 4:6; *Luke* 4:11
Moses stood, *l.* he should. *Ps* 106:23
grant not, *l.* they exalt. 140:8
l. I be like them that go down. 143:7
reprove not a scorner, *l.* he. *Pr* 9:8
love not sleep, *l.* thou come. 20:13
l. thou learn his ways, and. 22:25
l. the Lord see it, and it. 24:18
l. thou know not what to do. 25:8
l. he that heareth it, put thee to. 10
l. he be weary of thee, and so. 17
answer not a fool, *l.* thou also. 26:4
add not to his words, *l.* he. 30:6
l. I be full and deny thee, or *l.* 9
l. they see with their eyes. *Isa* 6:10
Acts 28:27
l. any hurt it, I will keep it. *Isa* 27:3
not mockers, *l.* your bands. 28:22
l. thou shouldest say, My idol hath.
48:5, 7
be not dismayed, *l.* I. *Jer* 1:17
l. my fury come forth. 4:4; 21:12
instructed, *l.* my soul depart. 6:8
cause me not to return, *l.* I. 37:20
l. I strip her naked, and. *Hos* 2:3
seek the Lord, *l.* he break. *Amos* 5:6
as an adamant, *l.* they. *Zech* 7:12
l. I come and smite the. *Mal* 4:6
l. we should offend, go. *Mat* 17:27
l. there be not enough for us. 25:9
take heed, *l.* any man. *Mark* 13:5
l. coming suddenly, he find you. 36
watch and pray, *l.* ye enter. 14:38
l. they should believe. *Luke* 8:12

l. your hearts be overcharged.
Luke 21:34
sin no more, l. a worse. John 5:14
they went out l. they should. 18:28
l. ye be found to fight. Acts 5:39
beware therefore, l. that. 13:40
take heed, l. he spare not thee.
Rom 11:21, 25
l. we hinder the gospel. 1 Cor 9:12
standeth take heed l. he fall. 10:12
l. Satan should get. 2 Cor 2:11
l. I should be exalted above. 12:7
l. by any means I should. Gal 2:2
considering thyself, l. thou. 6:1
not of works, l. any man. Eph 2:9
l. any man beguile you. Col 2:4
provoke not children, l. they. 3:21
l. being lifted up with. 1 Tim 3:6
l. at any time we should let them slip.
Heb 2:1
l. there be in any an evil heart. 3:12
l. any of you be hardened. 13
l. any man fall after the same. 4:11
l. ye be weary and faint in. 12:3
l. what is lame be turned out. 13
l. any man fail of the grace. 15
grudge not, l. ye be. Jas 5:9
swear not, l. ye fall into. 12
beware, l. ye also being. 2 Pet 3:17
keepeth his garments, l. Rev 16:15

let

(*Used occasionally in the now obsolete sense of* hinder)
Naphtali is a hind l. Gen 49:21
king of Egypt will not l. you go.
Ex 3:19; 4:21; 7:14; 8:32; 9:7
17, 35; 10:20, 27; 11:10
after that he will l. you go. 3:20
l. my people go. 5:1; 7:16; 8:1, 20
9:1, 13; 10:3
why do ye l. the people from? 5:4*
I will l. you go. 8:28; 9:28; 13:17
why have we l. Israel go? 14:5
and Moses l. his father in law. 18:27
shall he l. her be redeemed. 21:8
l. him go free for his eye. 26, 27
seventh year thou shalt l. it. 23:11
hast not l. me know whom. 33:12
and shall l. the living bird. Lev 14:7
not l. seed pass through. 18:21*
not l. cattle gender with a. 19:19
thou shalt l. him go. Deut 15:12
thou shalt not l. him go away. 13
and all therein, he l. none remain.
Josh 10:28*, 30*
so Joshua l. the people. 24:28*
they l. the man go and. Judg 1:25
Saul would l. him go no. 1 Sam 18:2
to-morrow I will l. 2 Sam 11:12
I pray thee, l. Tamar my. 13:6
Elijah said, L. none of. 1 Ki 18:40
thou wouldest not l. 2 Chr 20:10
queen did l. no man. Esth 5:12
even that he would l. loose. Job 6:9
my righteousness I will not l. 27:6
l. not those that wait on thee be
ashamed, l. not those. Ps 69:6
and l. Satan stand at his right. 109:6
l. me not wander from thy. 119:10
and would not l. him go. S of S 3:4
l. out the vineyard to keepers. 8:11
work, and who shall l. it? Isa 43:13
those will I l. remain. Jer 27:11
I will not l. them pollute. Ezek 39:7
planted a vineyard and l. Mat 21:33
Mark 12:1; Luke 20:9
answer me nor l. me. Luke 22:68*
the Jews cried, If thou l. John 19:12
ship could not bear up, we l. her.
Acts 27:15*
you, but was l. hitherto. Rom 1:13*
who now letteth, will l. 2 Thes 2:7*
lest at any time we should l. Heb 2:1
see **alone**

let *down*

l. *down* thy pitcher, I pray thee.
Gen 24:14; 18:46
when he l. *down* his hands, Amalek.
Ex 17:11
Rahab l. them *down*. Josh 2:15, 18
Michal l. David *down*. 1 Sam 19:12
the man was l. *down*. 2 Ki 13:21
they l. *down* Jeremiah. Jer 38:6
they stood they l. *down* their wings.
Ezek 1:24, 25
they l. *down* the bed wherein.
Mark 2:4; Luke 5:19
and l. *down* your nets. Luke 5:4
at thy word I will l. *down* the net. 5
and l. him *down* in a basket.
Acts 9:25; 2 Cor 11:33
l. *down* to the earth. Acts 10:11
had l. *down* the boat. 27:30

letter

David wrote a l. to. 2 Sam 11:14
I will send a l. to the. 2 Ki 5:5
now when this l. is come to thee. 6
as soon as this l. cometh to. 10:2
Hezekiah received the l. 19:14
Isa 37:14
the l. was written in. Ezra 4:7
Rehum wrote a l. against. 8
now this is the copy of the l. 7:11
5:6, 7
a l. to Asaph the keeper. Neh 2:8
sent to me with an open l. in. 6:5
wrote to confirm this l. of. Esth 9:29
the words of the l. that. Jer 29:1
Zephaniah priest read this l. in. 29
Claudius wrote a l. to. Acts 23:25
the governor had read the l. he. 34
l. dost transgress the law. Rom 2:27
circumcision of heart, not in the l. 29
serve, not in the oldness of the l. 7:6
ministers not of the l. 2 Cor 3:6
you sorry with l. I do not repent. 7:8
ye see how large a l. I. Gal 6:11*
shaken by word or by l. 2 Thes 2:2
I have written a l. to. Heb 13:22

letters

l. in Ahab's name. 1 Ki 21:8, 9
Jehu wrote l. and sent. 2 Ki 10:1
Babylon sent l. to Hezekiah. 20:12
Hezekiah wrote l. also. 2 Chr 30:1
so the posts went with the l. 6
Sennacherib wrote l. to rail on. 32:17
let l. be given me to the. Neh 2:7
sent l. to Tobiah, and l. came. 6:17
and Tobiah sent l. to put me. 19
Ahasuerus sent l. to the. Esth 1:22
the l. were sent by posts. 3:13; 8:10
to reverse l. devised by Haman. 8:5
Mordecai sent l. to all. 9:20, 30
because thou hast sent l. Jer 29:25
was written in l. of. Luke 23:38
how knoweth this man l.? John 7:15
of him l. to Damascus. Acts 9:2
the apostles wrote l. after. 15:23*
I received l. to the brethren. 22:5
we neither received l. out of. 28:21
shall approve by your l. 1 Cor 16:3
we l. of commendation. 2 Cor 3:1
as if I would terrify you by l. 10:9
for his l. are weighty and. 10
such as we are in word, by l. 11

lettest

l. such words go out of. Job 15:13
with a cord thou l. down? 41:1*
now l. thou thy servant. Luke 2:29

letteth

he that l. him go, his life. 2 Ki 10:24
strife is as when one l. out. Pr 17:14
only he that now l. will. 2 Thes 2:7*

letting

deal deceitfully in not l. the people.
Ex 8:29

Levi

was his name called L. Gen 29:34
the sons of L. 46:11; Ex 6:16
Num 3:17
Simeon, L. are brethren. Gen 49:5
years of the life of L. Ex 6:16
upon you, ye sons of L. Num 16:7
Jochebed, daughter of L. 26:59
L. hath no part with his. Deut 10:9
priests the sons of L. shall. 21:5
L. he said, Let thy Thummim. 33:8
made priests which were not of L.
1 Ki 12:31
but L. and Benjamin. 1 Chr 21:6
none of the sons of L. Ezra 8:15
bless Lord, O house of L. Ps 135:20
the sons of Zadok among the sons of
L. Ezek 40:46
of Judah, one gate of L. Ezek 48:31
family of the house of L. Zech 12:13
covenant might be with L. Mal 2:4
corrupted the covenant of L. 8
purify the sons of L. 3:3
L. the son of Alpheus. Mark 2:14
Matthat, which was the son of L.
Luke 3:24, 29
he saw a publican named L. 5:27
L. made him a great feast in his. 29
L. who received tithes. Heb 7:9

***tribe of* Levi**

not number *tribe of* L. Num 1:49
bring the *tribe of* L. near and. 3:6
tribe of L. bring, that they. 18:2
separated the *tribe of* L. Deut 10:8
tribe of L. shall have no part nor.
18:1; Josh 13:14, 33
Moses' sons were named of the *tribe of* L. 1 Chr 23:14
of *tribe of* L. were sealed. Rev 7:7

leviathan

thou draw out l. with? Job 41:1
heads of l. in pieces. Ps 74:14
l. thou hast made to play. 104:26
punish l. even l. that crooked serpent. Isa 27:1

Levite

is not Aaron the l. thy? Ex 4:14
rejoice before the Lord your God,
ye and the l. Deut 12:12, 18
16:11, 14; 26:11, 13
l. shall come and eat. 14:29; 26:12
if a l. come from any of thy. 18:6
a young man a l. Judg 17:7, 9
so the l. went in. 10
the l. was content to dwell. 11
Micah consecrated the l. 12
a l. to my priest. 13
voice of the young man the l. 18:3
certain l. sojourning on mount. 19:1
the l. said, I came into Gibeah. 20:4
on Jahaziel a l. came. 2 Chr 20:14
Cononiah the l. was ruler. 31:12
Kore the l. over the freewill. 14
Shabbethai the l. helped. Ezra 10:15
likewise a l. came and. Luke 10:32
Barnabas a l. having. Acts 4:36

Levites

of the fathers of the l. Ex 6:25
for the service of the l. 38:21
cities of l. may redeem. Lev 25:32
the cities of the l. are their. 33
l. not numbered. Num 1:47; 2:33
shalt appoint the l. over the. 1:50
the l. shall take it down. 51
the l. shall pitch. 53
and thou shalt give the l. 3:9
I have taken the l.: the l. shall. 12
chief over chief of the l. 32
were numbered of the l. 39; 4:46
and thou shall take the l. for me.
3:41, 45; 8:14
shalt give wagons unto the l. 7:5
take the l. from Israel and. 8:6
bring the l. before tabernacle. 9, 10
Aaron shall offer the l. before the. 11
after that shall the l. go in. 15, 22
this is it that belongeth unto the l. 24
thou do to the l. touching their. 26
the l. to do service. 18:6, 23
tithes I have given to the l. 24
give to the l. cities round. 35:2, 8
minister, as his brethren the l. do.
Deut 18:7
to the l. he gave none. Josh 14:3
gave these cities to the l. 21:3, 8
all the cities of the l. were. 41
l. took down the ark. 1 Sam 6:15
Zadok and the l. were. 2 Sam 15:24
the children of the l. 1 Chr 15:15
when God helped the l. that. 26
l. wrote them before the king. 24:6
the l. which were singers stood.
2 Chr 5:12; 7:6
the l. left their suburbs and. 11:14
cast out the sons of Aaron and l. 13:9
also the l. shall be officers. 19:11
the l. shall compass the king. 23:6, 7
the l. hastened it not. 24:5
hear me, ye l. sanctify now. 29:5
spake comfortably to the l. 30:22
of the l. there were scribes. 34:13

Josiah said to *l.* which. 2 Chr 35:3
of the *l.* gave to the *l.* 500 oxen. 9
l. prepared for themselves. 14, 15
set the *l.* in their courses. Ezra 6:18
after him repaired the *l.* Neh 3:17
l. caused people to understand. 8:7
the *l.* stilled the people, saying. 11
the overseer of the *l.* was. 11:22
dedication they sought the *l.* 12:27
portions of *l.* had not been given them, for the *l.* were fled. 13:10
defiled the priesthood of the *l.* 29
I will multiply the *l.* Jer 33:22
l. that are gone shall bear iniquity. Ezek 44:10
went not astray when the *l.* 48:11

priests and Levites

shalt come to *p.* the *l.* Deut 17:9
to do all that *p.* and *l.* shall. 24:8
p. and l. bearing the ark. Josh 3:3
p. and l. brought up ark. 1 Ki 8:4
p. and l. shall be porters. 2 Chr 23:4
p. and l. were more upright. 29:34
p. and l. were ashamed, and. 30:15
l. and the *p.* praised the Lord. 21
then the *p. and l.* blessed the. 27
questioned with the *p. and l.* 31:9
gave willingly to the *p. and l.* 35:8
so *p. and l.* dwelt in. Ezra 2:70
for the *p. and l.* were purified. 6:20
went up of the *p. and* the *l.* 7:7
p. and l. have not separated. 9:1
made the *p. and l.* to swear. 10:5
our princes, *l. and p.* Neh 9:38
we cast lots among *p. and l.* 10:34
p. and l. purified themselves. 12:30
Judah rejoiced for the *p. and l.* 44
take of them for *p. and l.* Isa 66:21
p. and l. not want a man. Jer 33:18
with *l.* the *p.* my ministers. 21
the *p. and l.* that kept. Ezek 44:15
the Jews sent *p. and l.* John 1:19

Levitical

if perfection were by the *L.* Heb 7:11

levy, *substantive*

Solomon raised a *l.* of. 1 Ki 5:13
and Adoniram was over the *l.* 14
reason of the *l.* Solomon raised. 9:15

levy, *verb*

l. a tribute to the Lord. Num 31:28
did Solomon *l.* a tribute. 1 Ki 9:21*

lewd

ashamed of thy *l.* way. Ezek 16:27
unto Aholibah, the *l.* women. 23:44
l. fellows of baser sort. Acts 17:5*

lewdly

l. defiled his daughter. Ezek 22:11

lewdness

they have committed *l.* Judg 20:6
she hath wrought *l.* Jer 11:15
I have seen the *l.* of thy. 13:27
shalt not commit this *l.* Ezek 16:43
thou hast borne thy *l.* and. 58
in midst of thee they commit *l.* 22:9
calledst to remembrance *l.* 23:21
I make thy *l.* to cease. 27, 48
shall be discovered, both thy *l.* 29
therefore bear thou also thy *l.* and. 35
shall recompense your *l.* on you. 49
in thy filthiness is *l.* 24:13
now will I discover her *l.* Hos 2:10
murder in way, they commit *l.* 6:9
a matter of wicked *l.* Acts 18:14*

liar

who will make me a *l.*? Job 24:25
l. giveth ear to a naughty. Pr 17:4
poor man is better than a *l.* 19:22
and thou be found a *l.* 30:6
altogether to me as a *l.*? Jer 15:18*
he is a *l.* and the father. John 8:44
I shall be a *l.* like to. 55
and every man a *l.* Rom 3:4
sinned, we make him a *l.* 1 John 1:10
l. and truth is not in him. 2:4; 4:20
who is a *l.* but he that denieth? 22
not God, hath made him a *l.* 5:10

liars

shall be found *l.* to thee. Deut 33:29
in haste, all men are *l.* Ps 116:11
the tokens of the *l.* Isa 44:25

a sword is upon the *l.* Jer 50:36*
law is made for *l.* for. 1 Tim 1:10
the Cretians are alway *l.* Tit 1:12
and hast found them *l.* Rev 2:2
all *l.* shall have their part in. 21:8

liberal

l. soul shall be made fat. Pr 11:25
vile person shall not be called *l.* Isa 32:5†
the *l.* deviseth *l.* things, and by *l.* 8
for your *l.* distribution. 2 Cor 9:13*

liberality

your *l.* to Jerusalem. 1 Cor 16:3*
to the riches of their *l.* 2 Cor 8:2

liberally

furnish him *l.* out of. Deut 15:14
who giveth to all men *l.* Jas 1:5

Libertines

called synagogue of the *L.* Acts 6:9

liberty

ye shall proclaim *l.* Lev 25:10
and I will walk at *l.* Ps 119:45
he sent me to proclaim *l.* Isa 61:1
a covenant to proclaim *l.* Jer 34:8
in my sight, in proclaiming *l.* 15
his servant whom he had set at *l.* 16*
not hearkened to me in proclaiming *l.*: I proclaim a *l.* for you. 17
be his to the year of *l.* Ezek 46:17
l. them that are bruised. Luke 4:18
Paul, and let him have *l.* Acts 24:23*
man might have been set at *l.* 26:32
gave him *l.* to go to his friends. 27:3*
glorious *l.* of children of. Rom 8:21
she is at *l.* to marry. 1 Cor 7:39*
take heed lest this *l.* of yours. 8:9
for why is my *l.* judged of? 10:29
where the Spirit of the Lord is, there is *l.* 2 Cor 3:17
privily, to spy out our *l.* Gal 2:4
stand fast in the *l.* wherewith. 5:1*
called unto *l.*; only use not *l.* 13*
Timothy is set at *l.* Heb 13:23
looketh into the law of *l.* Jas 1:25
shall be judged by the law of *l.* 2:12
as free, and not using *l.* 1 Pet 2:16*
they promise them *l.* 2 Pet 2:19

Libnah

pitched in *L.* Num 33:20
removed from *L.* 21
passed to *L.* Josh 10:29
gave *L.* to Levites. 21:13
then *L.* revolted. 2 Ki 8:22
2 Chr 21:10
found the king of Assyria warring against *L.* 2 Ki 19:8; Isa 37:8
Hammutal, daughter of Jeremiah of *L.* 2 Ki 23:31; 24:18; Jer 52:1

Libya

L. shall fall with them. Ezek 30:5
parts of *L.* about Cyrene. Acts 2:10

Libyans

L. that handled the shield. Jer 46:9
L. and Ethiopians shall. Dan 11:43

lice

that dust may become *l.* Ex 8:16
smote dust, it became *l.* in man. 17
so with their enchantments to bring forth *l.*: so there were *l.* upon. 18
l. in all their coasts. Ps 105:31

licence

given him *l.* Paul stood. Acts 21:40*
accused have *l.* to answer. 25:16*

lick

now shall this company *l.* Num 22:4
dogs *l.* thy blood, even. 1 Ki 21:19
his enemies shall *l.* dust Ps 72:9
l. up the dust of thy feet. Isa 49:23
l. up the dust like a serpent. Mi 7:17

licked

fire *l.* up the water in. 1 Ki 18:38
dogs *l.* the blood of Naboth. 21:19
and the dogs *l.* up his blood. 22:38
the dogs came and *l.* his sores. Luke 16:21

licketh

lick up all, as the ox *l.* Num 22:4

lid

bored a hole in the *l.* 2 Ki 12:9

lie

drink wine, we will *l.* Gen 19:32
go thou in, and *l.* with him. 34
he shall *l.* with thee to-night. 30:15
she said, Come *l.* with me. 39:7, 12
2 Sam 13:11
he came in unto me to *l.* Gen 39:14
if a man *l.* with a maid. Ex 22:16
man shall *l.* with seed. Lev 15:18
if a man *l.* with her at all. 24
not *l.* carnally with thy. 18:20
shalt not *l.* with mankind. 22
nor *l.* with beasts. 23
l. with his daughter in law. 20:12
if *l.* with mankind. 13
if *l.* with a beast. 15
if a man *l.* with a woman having. 18
man *l.* with his uncle's wife. 20
if a man *l.* with her. Num 5:13
man find her, and *l.* Deut 22:23
if the man force her, and *l.* with. 25
damsel not betrothed, and *l.* with. 28
betroth a wife, and another *l.* 28:30
go to *l.* with my wife? 2 Sam 11:11
shall *l.* all night betwixt. S of S 1:13

lie

I will *l.* with my fathers. Gen 47:30*
let the ground *l.* still. Ex 23:11
curses in this book shall *l.* on him. Deut 29:20
went to *l.* in ambush. Josh 8:9*, 12
all thy wants *l.* on me. Judg 19:20
mark the place where he shall *l.* Ruth 3:4
let her *l.* in thy bosom. 1 Ki 1:2
I *l.* among them that are. Ps 57:4
like slain that *l.* in the grave. 88:5
if two *l.* together they have heat. Eccl 4:11
beasts of the desert shall *l.* there. Isa 13:21
kings of the nations *l.* in. 14:18*
thy sons *l.* at the head of all. 51:20
the young and old *l.* on. Lam 2:21
l. thou also upon thy left. Ezek 4:4
l. again on thy right side. 6
shalt *l.* 390 days. 9
shalt *l.* in the midst of the. 31:18
they *l.* uncircumcised. 32:21, 30
shall not *l.* with the mighty. 27
l. with the slain. 28
l. with uncircumcised. 29
shall they *l.* in a good fold. 34:14
come, *l.* all night in. Joel 1:13
that *l.* on beds of ivory. Amos 6:4
when Jesus saw him *l.* he. John 5:6
Peter seeth the linen clothes *l.* 20:6

lie *down*

before a beast, to *l. down* thereto. Lev 18:23; 20:16
ye shall *l. down* and none. 26:6
Israel shall not *l. down.* Num 23:24
cause him to *l. down.* Deut 25:2
Boaz went to *l. down* at. Ruth 3:7
tarry this night, *l. down* until. 13
Eli said, I called not, *l. down* again. 1 Sam 3:5, 6, 9
even he went to *l. down.* 2 Sam 11:13
when I *l. down* I say, When? Job 7:4
thou shalt *l. down* and none. 11:19
which shall *l. down* with him. 20:11
they shall *l. down* alike in. 21:26
the rich man shall *l. down.* 27:19
he maketh me *l. down* in. Ps 23:2
l. down and thy sleep be. Pr 3:24
leopard shall *l. down.* Isa 11:6
their young ones shall *l. down.* 7
and the needy shall *l. down.* 14:30
for flocks which shall *l. down.* 17:2
the calf feed and *l. down.* 27:10
power shall *l. down* together. 43:17
ye shall *l. down* in sorrow. 50:11
place for herds to *l. down* in. 65:10
we *l. down* in our shame. Jer 3:25
shepherds causing their flocks to *l. down.* 33:12
cause them to *l. down.* Ezek 34:15
them to *l. down* safely. Hos 2:18
l. down in the evening. Zeph 2:7
flocks shall *l. down.* 14
for beasts to *l. down* in. 15
Israel shall feed and *l. down.* 3:13

lie *in wait*
if a man l. not in wait. Ex 21:13
neighbour and l. in wait. Deut 19:11
l. in wait against the city . Josh 8:4
l. in wait in the field. Judg 9:32
saying, Go and l. in wait in. 21:20
hast stirred up my servant to l. in wait. 1 Sam 22:8, 13
in the covert to l. in wait. Job 38:40
for lo, they l. in wait. Ps 59:3
the wicked are to l. in wait. Pr 12:6
oven, whiles they l. in wait. Hos 7:6
all l. in wait for blood. Mi 7:2
l. in wait for him more. Acts 23:21
whereby they l. in wait to. Eph 4:14

lie *waste*
the highways l. waste. Isa 33:8
it shall l. waste. 34:10
and this house l. waste. Hag 1:4

lie, *verb*
soul l. to his neighbour. Lev 6:2*
ye shall not steal, nor l. 19:11
a man, that he should l. Num 23:19
Strength of Israel will not l. nor. 1 Sam 15:29
my lord, do not l. to thy. 2 Ki 4:16
is evident to you if I l. Job 6:28
should I l. against my right. 34:6
sworn that I will not l. Ps 89:35
faithful witness will not l. Pr 14:5
children that will not l. Isa 63:8*
walking in falsehood do l. Mi 2:11
shall speak and not l. Hab 2:3
filled thy heart to l.? Acts 5:3
I say the truth in Christ, I l. not. Rom 9:1; 1 Tim 2:7
Lord knoweth I l. not. 2 Cor 11:31
to you, behold I l. not. Gal 1:20
l. not one to another. Col 3:9
God, that cannot l., promised. Tit 1:2
impossible for God to l. Heb 6:18
glory not, l. not against. Jas 3:14
have fellowship with him and walk in darkness, we l. and. 1 John 1:6
say they are Jews, but do l. Rev 3:9

lie, *substantive*
men of high degree are a l. Ps 62:9
the proud have forged a l. 119:69
a l. in my right hand ? Isa 44:20
they prophesy a l. to you to remove. Jer 27:10, 14, 15*, 16; 29:21
this people to trust in a l. 28:15
caused you to trust in a l. 29:31
whilst they divine a l. Ezek 21:29
houses of Achzib shall be a l. to. Mi 1:14
for the diviners have seen a l. and. Zech 10:2
when he speaketh a l. he. John 8:44
truth of God into a l. Rom 1:25
more abounded through my l. 3:7
they should believe a l. 2 Thes 2:11
ye know that no l. is. 1 John 2:21
you of all things, and is no l. 27
whatsoever maketh a l. Rev 21:27
whosoever loveth and maketh a l. 22:15

lied
prophet, but he l. unto. 1 Ki 13:18
they l. unto him with. Ps 78:36
afraid, that thou hast l. Isa 57:11
thou hast not l. unto men. Acts 5:4

lien, *or* **lain**
one might have l. with. Gen 26:10
if no man have l. with. Num 5:19
if some man have l. with thee. 20
woman that hath l. Judg 21:11
for now should I have l. Job 3:13
though ye have l. among. Ps 68:13
thou hast not been l. with. Jer 3:2

liers *in wait*
there were l. in ambush. Josh 8:14
Shechem set l. in wait. Judg 9:25
there were l. in wait abiding. 16:12
Israel set l. in wait round. 20:29
the l. in wait came forth. 33
l. in wait hasted and rushed. 37
they trusted in the l. in wait. 36

lies
thou hast told me l. Judg 16:10, 13
should thy l. make men? Job 11:3*
ye are forgers of l. 13:4
such as turn aside to l. Ps 40:4
and go astray, speaking l. 58:3
they delight in l., they curse. 62:4
the mouth that speaketh l. 63:11
that telleth l. shall not tarry. 101:7
hates a false witness that speaketh l. Pr 6:19
but a false witness will utter l. 14:5
deceitful witness speaketh l. 25
and he that speaketh l. shall. 19:5
speaketh l. shall perish. 9
if a ruler hearken to l. his. 29:12
far from me vanity and l. 30:8
prophet that teacheth l. Isa 9:15
pride of Moab, but his l. 16:6*
we have made l. our refuge. 28:15
sweep away the refuge of l. 17
your lips have spoken l., your. 59:3
they trust in vanity, and speak l. 4
bend their tongues like their bow for l. Jer 9:3
taught their tongue to speak l. 5
prophesy l. 14:14; 23:25, 26
fathers have inherited l. 16:19
thou hast prophesied l. 20:6
adultery, and walk in l. 23:14
to err by their l. and lightness. 32
his l. shall not so affect it. 48:30*
spoken vanity and seen l. Ezek 13:8
upon the prophets that divine l. 9
my people that hear your l. 19
with l. ye have made the. 22
divining l. unto them, saying. 22:28
hath wearied herself with l. 24:12*
speak l. at one table. Dan 11:27
princes glad with their l. Hos 7:3
yet they have spoken l. against. 13
eaten the fruit of l. because. 10:13
compasseth me about with l. 11:12
increaseth l. and desolation. 12:1
and their l. caused them. Amos 2:4
thereof have spoken l. Mi 6:12
bloody city, it is full of l. Nah 3:1
image, and a teacher of l. Hab 2:18
Israel shall not speak l. Zeph 3:13
speakest l. in the name. Zech 13:3
speak l. in hypocrisy. 1 Tim 4:2

liest
the land whereon thou l. Gen 28:13
when thou l. down. Deut 6:7; 11:19
Get thee up; wherefore l. thou thus upon thy face ? Josh 7:10*
l. down, shalt not be afraid. Pr 3:24

lieth
doest not well, sin l. Gen 4:7*
of the deep that l. under. 49:25*
found that which was lost, and l. concerning it. Lev 6:3
he that l. in the house. 14:47
every bed whereon he l. is. 15:4
every thing that she l. upon shall be unclean. 20, 26
all the bed whereon he l. 24, 33
sabbaths, as long as it l. 26:34, 35
sabbaths, while she l. desolate. 43
his great strength l. Judg 16:5
wherein thy great strength l. 6, 15
l. under the shady trees. Job 40:21
he l. he shall rise no more. Ps 41:8
thy wrath l. hard on me, thou. 88:7
my servant l. at home sick. Mat 8:6
my daughter l. at point. Mark 5:23
as much as l. in you, live. Rom 12:18
the whole world l. in. 1 John 5:19

lieth *down*
it shall be when he l. down. Ruth 3:4
so man l. down and riseth. Job 14:12
that l. down in the midst. Pr 23:34

lieth *in wait*
l. in wait secretly as a lion: l. in wait to catch the poor. Ps 10:9*
and she l. in wait at every. Pr 7:12
she also l. in wait as for a. 23:28

lieth *waste*
the place of my fathers' sepulchres l. waste. Neh 2:3
you see how Jerusalem l. waste. 17

lieth, as with a woman
whoso l. with a beast. Ex 22:19
whoso l. carnally with a. Lev 19:20
man that l. with his father's. 20:11
lie with mankind as he l. with. 13
cursed be he that l. with. Deut 27:20
l. with beast. 21
l. with his sister. 22
l. with his mother in law 23
her that l. in thy bosom. Mi 7:5

lieutenants
(*Revised Versions*, satraps)
king's commissions to l. Ezra 8:36
commanded the king's l. Esth 3:12
had commanded to the l. 8:9
all the rulers and l. helped. 9:3

life
[1] *Literally, animate existence, as distinguished from dead matter,* Gen 1:20. [2] *Conscious existence with the powers derived from it,* Job 3:20. [3] *The existence of the soul after the death of the body,* John 5:29. *Other passages correspond with modern uses of the word, or are derived from these heads.*

creature that hath l. Gen 1:20
every thing wherein there is l. 30
into his nostrils the breath of l. 2:7
the tree of l. in the midst. 9; 3:22
keep the way of the tree of l. 3:24
wherein is the breath of l. 6:17; 7:22
flesh with the l. shall ye not eat. 9:4; Lev 17:14
man will I require l. of man. Gen 9:5
according to time of l. 18:10*, 14*
these were the years of the l. 23:1
the years of Abraham's l. 25:7
by the l. of Pharaoh. 42:15, 16
send me before to preserve l. 45:5
not attained to the years of l. 47:9
of the l. of Levi were 137. Ex 6:16
years of the l. of Kohath. 18
l. of Amram. 20
shall give l. for l. 21:23; Deut 19:21
for the l. of the flesh is. Lev 17:11
the other in her l. time. 18:18
blood is the l.; and thou mayest not eat the l. with flesh. Deut 12:23
tree of the field is man's l. 20:19
taketh a man's l. to pledge. 24:6
I have set before thee l. 30:15, 19
Jer 21:8
it is not a vain thing, because it is your l. Deut 32:47
the men answered, Our l. Josh 2:14
up in the bundle of l. 1 Sam 25:29
for the l. of his brother. 2 Sam 14:7
whether in death or l. there. 15:21
for thyself long l. nor asked the l. of. 1 Ki 3:11; 2 Chr 1:11
time of l. thou shalt. 2 Ki 4:16*, 17*
left camp, and fled for their l. 7:7
they may pray for the l. Ezra 6:10
Jews to stand for their l. Esth 8:11
why is l. given to the bitter in soul ? Job 3:20
thou hast granted me l. and. 10:12
and no man is sure of l. 24:22
owners thereof to lose their l. 31:39
the Almighty hath given me l. 33:4
he preserveth not the l. of the. 36:6
their l. is among the unclean. 14
shew me the path of l. Ps 16:11
he asked l. of thee, thou. 21:4
in his favour is l.: weeping. 30:5†
man is he that desireth l.? 34:12
with thee is the fountain of l. 36:9
thou wilt prolong the king's l. 61:6
kindness is better than l. 63:3
who holdeth our soul in l. 66:9
but gave their l. over to the. 78:50
with long l. will I satisfy him. 91:16
the blessing, even l. for. 133:3
which taketh away the l. Pr 1:19
nor take hold of the paths of l. 2:19
long l. and peace shall they. 3:2
she is a tree of l. to them that. 18
so shall they be l. to thy soul. 22
they are l. to those that find. 4:22
for out of it are the issues of l. 23
shouldest ponder the path of l. 5:6
of instruction are the way of l. 6:23
will hunt for the precious l. 26
whoso findeth me findeth l. and. 8:35
the righteous is a well of l. 10:11
is in the way of l. that keepeth. 17

the righteous is a tree of l. *Pr* 11:30
righteous regardeth the l. of. 12:10
in the way of righteousness is l. 28
the ransom of a man's l. are. 13:8
desire cometh, it is a tree of l. 12
law of the wise is a fountain of l. 14
of the Lord is a fountain of l. 14:27
a sound heart is the l. of the flesh. 30
wholesome tongue is a tree of l. 15:4
way of l. is above to the wise. 24
reproof of l. abideth among. 31
of the king's countenance is l. 16:15
understanding is wellspring of l. 22
death and l. are in the power. 18:21
followeth mercy, findeth l. 21:21
are riches, honour, and l. 22:4
good all the days of her l. 31:12
good they should do all the days of their l. *Eccl* 2:3
therefore I hated l. 17
wisdom giveth l. 7:12
in all these things is the l. *Isa* 38:16
sing songs all the days of our l. 20
found the l. of thy hand. 57:10*
and death shall be chosen rather than l. *Jer* 8:3
into the hand of those that seek their l. 21:7; 34:20, 21
I set before you the way of l. 21:8
dismayed before their enemies, before them that seek their l. 49:37
lift up thy hands for the l. *Lam* 2:19
strengthened the hands of wicked, by promising him l. *Ezek* 13:22*
walk in the statutes of l. 33:15
perish for this man's l. *Jonah* 1:14
my covenant was with him of l. and peace. *Mal* 2:5
which sought the child's l. *Mat* 2:20
take no thought for your l. 6:25
Luke 12:22
to enter into l. halt or maimed.
Mat 18:8; *Mark* 9:43, 45
enter into l. with one eye. *Mat* 18:9
if wilt enter into l. keep. *Mat* 19:17
is it lawful to save l. or to kill?
Mark 3:4; *Luke* 6:9
all the days of our l. *Luke* 1:75
for a man's l. consisteth not. 12:15
the l. is more than meat. 23
in him was l. and the l. *John* 1:4
believeth not, shall not see l. 3:36
Father hath l. in himself, so hath he given to the Son to have l. 5:26
good, to the resurrection of l. 29
to me that ye might have l. 40; 10:10
giveth l. unto the world. 6:33
I am the bread of l. 35, 48
which I will give for the l. of the. 51
and drink his blood, ye have no l. 53
words I speak to you, they are l. 63
but shall have the light of l. 8:12
resurrection and the l. 11:25; 14:6
believing ye might have l. 20:31
known to me the ways of l. *Acts* 2:28
killed the Prince of l. whom. 3:15
seeing he giveth to all l. 17:25
the manner of l. from my youth. 26:4
be no loss of any man's l. 27:22
in l. by one, Jesus Christ. *Rom* 5:17
all men to justification of l. 18
should walk in newness of l. 6:4
the Spirit of l. in Christ Jesus. 8:2
to be spiritually minded is l. 6
the Spirit is l. because of. 10
that neither death nor l. 38
the receiving them be but l.? 11:15
the world, or l., or death. *1 Cor* 3:22
things without l. giving sound. 14:7
we despaired even of l. *2 Cor* 1:8
the savour of l. unto l. 2:16
killeth, but the Spirit giveth l. 3:6
that the l. of Jesus might be. 4:10
death worketh in us, but l. in you. 12
might be swallowed up of l. 5:4
the l. which I now live. *Gal* 2:20
which could have given l. 3:21*
alienated from the l. *Eph* 4:18
whether it be by l. or by. *Phil* 1:20
holding forth the word of l. 2:16
l. is hid with Christ in God. *Col* 3:3
when Christ who is our l. shall. 4
may lead a peaceable l. *1 Tim* 2:2
having the promise of l. 4:8
the promise of l. in Christ. *2 Tim* 1:1
and he hath brought l. to light. 10
fully known my manner of l. 3:10
beginnning of days, nor end of l.
Heb 7:3
after the power of an endless l. 16
receive the crown of l. *Jas* 1:12
for what is your l.? it is even. 4:14
as being heirs together of the grace of l. *1 Pet* 3:7
for he that will love l. and see. 10
for the time past of our l. may. 4:3
all things pertaining to l. *2 Pet* 1:3
handled the word of l. *1 John* 1:1
for the l. was manifested, and we. 2
pride of l. is not of the Father. 2:16
hath Son hath l.; and he that hath not the Son of God hath not l. 5:12
he shall give him l. for them. 16
I give to eat of the tree of l. *Rev* 2:7
I will give thee a crown of l. 10
of the creatures that had l. died. 8:9
Spirit of l. from God entered. 11:11
he had power to give l. to. 13:15*
to thirsty of the water of l. 21:6
me a pure river of water of l. 22:1
tree of l. bare twelve manner of. 2
have right to the tree of l. 14
let him take the water of l. 17

see **book, eternal, everlasting**

his life

seeing *his* l. is bound. *Gen* 44:30
for the ransom of *his* l. *Ex* 21:30
read therein all the days of *his* l.
Deut 17:19
feared him all the days of *his* l.
Josh 4:14
father adventured *his* l. *Judg* 9:17
they which he slew in *his* l. 16:30
put *his* l. in his hand. *1 Sam* 19:5
was come out to seek *his* l. 23:15
this word against *his* l. *1 Ki* 2:23
he arose and went for *his* l. 19:3
thy life be for *his* l. 20:39, 42
his l. shall be for the life. *2 Ki* 10:24
the temple to save *his* l. *Neh* 6:11
to make request for *his* l. *Esth* 7:7
all that a man hath will he give for *his* l. *Job* 2:4
he is in thy hand, but save *his* l. 6
and *his* l. from perishing by. 33:18
his l. abhorreth bread. 20
his l. to destroyers. 22
he will deliver, and *his* l. shall. 28
not that it is for *his* l. *Pr* 7:23
his mouth, keepeth *his* l. 13:3
man to rejoice and do good in *his* l.
Eccl 3:12
man that prolongeth *his* l. 7:15
labours all the days of *his* l. 8:15
Moab, *his* l. shall be. *Isa* 15:4
his l. shall be to him for a prey.
Jer 21:9; 38:2
hand of them that seek *his* l. 44:30
to warn, to save *his* l. *Ezek* 3:18
himself in iniquity of *his* l. 7:13
tremble, every man for *his* l. 32:10
findeth *his* l. shall lose it; he that loseth *his* l. shall find it. *Mat* 10:39
16:25; *Mark* 8:35; *Luke* 9:24
17:33; *John* 12:25
to give *his* l. a ransom for many.
Mat 20:28; *Mark* 10:45
hate not *his* own l. also. *Luke* 14:26
good Shepherd giveth *his* l. for.
John 10:11
that a man lay down *his* l. for. 15:13
for *his* l. is taken from. *Acts* 8:33
trouble not yourselves, *his* l. 20:10
shall be saved by *his* l. *Rom* 5:10
regarding *his* l. to supply. *Phil* 2:30
he laid down *his* l. *1 John* 3:16

see **days**

my life

shewed in saving *my* l. *Gen* 19:19
of *my* l.: what good shall *my* l.? 27:46
my l. is preserved. 32:30
fed me all *my* l. 48:15
I put *my* l. in my hands. *Judg* 12:3
what is *my* l. or my father's family?
1 Sam 18:18
that he seeketh *my* l.? 20:1
he that seeketh *my* l. seeketh. 22:23
my l. be much set by. *1 Sam* 26:24
layest thou a snare for *my* l.? 28:9
I put *my* l. in my hand, and. 21
because *my* l. is yet whole in me.
2 Sam 1:9
my son of my bowels seeketh *my* l.
16:11
falsehood against *my* l. 18:13
now, take away *my* l. *1 Ki* 19:4
they seek *my* l. to take it away.
10, 14; *Rom* 11:3
let *my* l. be precious. *2 Ki* 1:13, 14
let *my* l. be given me at my petition.
Esth 7:3
I should prolong *my* l. *Job* 6:11
O remember that *my* l. is but. 7:7
chooseth death rather than *my* l. 15
yet I would despise *my* l. 9:21
my soul is weary of *my* l. 10:1
wherefore do I put *my* l. in? 13:14
let him tread down *my* l. *Ps* 7:5
follow me all the days of *my* l. 23:6
gather not *my* l. with bloody. 26:9
Lord is the strength of *my* l. 27:1
house of the Lord all days of *my* l. 4
my l. is spent with grief. 31:10
they devised to take away *my* l. 13
seek after *my* l. lay snares. 38:12
my prayer to the God of *my* l. 42:8
preserve *my* l. from fear of the. 64:1
and *my* l. draweth nigh to. 88:3
he hath smitten *my* l. to the. 143:3
cut off like a weaver *my* l. *Isa* 38:12
cut off *my* l. in dungeon. *Lam* 3:53
Lord, thou hast redeemed *my* l. 58
hast brought up *my* l. *Jonah* 2:6
take, I beseech thee, *my* l. 4:3
and I lay down *my* l. for the sheep.
John 10:15
me, because I lay down *my* l. 17
Lord, I will lay down *my* l. 13:37
nor count I *my* l. dear. *Acts* 20:24

this life

have their portion in *this* l. *Ps* 17:14
good for a man in *this* l. *Eccl* 6:12
this is thy portion in *this* l. and. 9:9
are choked with the cares of *this* l.
Luke 8:14
hearts overcharged with the cares of *this* l. 21:34
speak all words of *this* l. *Acts* 5:20
that pertain to *this* l. *1 Cor* 6:3
of things pertaining to *this* l. 4
if in *this* l. only we have hope. 15:19
entangleth himself with affairs of *this* l. *2 Tim* 2:4
eternal life, and *this* l. *1 John* 5:11

thy life

Escape for *thy* l.; look. *Gen* 19:17
dead which sought *thy* l. *Ex* 4:19
thy l. shall hang in doubt before thee, no assurance of *thy* l. *Deut* 28:66
thee, and thou lose *thy* l. *Judg* 18:25
thee a restorer of *thy* l. *Ruth* 4:15
if thou save not *thy* l. *1 Sam* 19:11
seeketh my life seeketh *thy* l. 22:23
thy l. was much set by this. 26:24
enemy that sought *thy* l. *2 Sam* 4:8
which this day saved *thy* l. 19:5
thou mayest save *thy* l. *1 Ki* 1:12
if I make not *thy* l. as the life. 19:2
peradventure he will save *thy* l. 20:31
if he be missing *thy* l. be. 39, 42
who redeemeth *thy* l. *Ps* 103:4
and the years of *thy* l. shall be.
Pr 4:10; 9:11
keep her, for she is *thy* l. 4:13
and the years of *thy* l. shall. 9:11
will I give people for *thy* l. 43:4
they will seek *thy* l. *Jer* 4:30
of the men that seek *thy* l. 11:21
22:25; 38:16
thy l. shall be for a prey to thee.
39:18; 45:5
wilt thou lay down *thy* l.? *John* 13:38

to or *unto* **life**

he had restored *to* l. *2 Ki* 8:1, 5
the righteous tendeth *to* l. *Pr* 10:16
as righteousness tendeth *to* l. 11:19
fear of the Lord tendeth *to* l. 19:23
the way that leadeth *unto* l. *Mat* 7:14
but is passed from death *unto* l.
John 5:24; *1 John* 3:14

granted repentance unto l. Acts 11:18
ordained to l. Rom 7:10
their dead raised to l. Heb 11:35

lift

To lift up the eyes, frequently means to direct and make known our desires to God by prayer, Ps 121; 123:1. *To lift up the head, is* [1] *To restore a person to his former dignity,* Gen 40:13. [2] *To recover former strength and courage, so as to oppress others,* Judg 8:28. [3] *To rejoice and be glad,* Luke 21:28. [4] *To be advanced above others, and obtain a complete victory over them,* Ps 27:6. *To lift up the hand, is* [1] *To swear, or by oath to confirm a thing,* Gen 14:22. [2] *To bless,* Lev 9:22. [3] *To pray,* Ps 28:2. [4] *To rise in rebellion,* 2 Sam 18:28; 20:21. [5] *To oppress, threaten, injure, or wrong in any way,* Job 31:21.

Hath lift up his heel against me, Ps 41:9. *Hath behaved himself insolently, contemptuously and injuriously towards me. It is a phrase taken from an unruly horse, who kicks at one who owns and feeds him.*

Lift not up the horn, Ps 75:4. *Carry not yourselves arrogantly, scornfully, or maliciously towards me or any of God's people.*

Lift up thy feet, Ps 74:3. *Come speedily to our help, and for our deliverance.*

To lift up one's self in height, that is to grow proud, insolent, and oppressive, Ezek 31:10.

the ark was l. up above. Gen 7:17
l. up the lad, and hold him in. 21:18
shall l. up thine head. 40:13, 19
if thou l. up a tool on it. Ex 20:25
Lord l. up his countenance upon thee. Num 6:26
wherefore then l. ye up? 16:3
l. up himself as a young lion. 23:24
shalt help him to l. Deut 22:4
not l. up an iron tool. 27:5; Josh 8:31
he l. up his spear against 800. 2 Sam 23:8
l. up thy prayer for the remnant. 2 Ki 19:4; Isa 37:4
l. up head of Jehoiachin. 2 Ki 25:27
were to l. up the horn. 1 Chr 25:5
I blush to l. up my face. Ezra 9:6
if righteous, yet will I not l. up. Job 10:15
then shalt thou l. up thy face. 11:15; 22:26
l. up the light of thy. Ps 4:6
arise, O Lord, in thine anger, l. 7:6
l. up your heads, O ye gates, be l. 24:7, 9
unto thee, O Lord, do I l. up my soul. 25:1; 86:4; 143:8
hear, when I l. up my hands. 28:2
feed them also, and l. them up. 9*
l. up thy feet to perpetual. 74:3
and to the wicked, l. not up. 75:4, 5
the floods l. up their waves. 93:3
l. up thyself, thou judge of. 94:2
shall he l. up the head. 110:7
I will l. up mine. 121:1; 123:1
if they fall, the one will l. Eccl 4:10
not l. up sword. Isa 2:4; Mi 4:3
he will l. up an ensign. Isa 5:26
as if staff should l. up itself. 10:15
smite, and shall l. up his staff. 24
so shall l. it up after the manner. 26
l. ye up a banner upon the. 13:2*
now will I rise, now will I l. 33:10
Lord shall l. up a standard. 59:19*
l. up a standard for the. 62:10
nor l. up cry nor prayer for them. Jer 7:16; 11:14
they shall l. up a shout. 51:14
let us l. up our heart. Lam 3:41
it might not l. itself up. Ezek 17:14
and shall l. up the buckler. 26:8
so that no man did l. up his head. Zech 1:21
will he not l. it out on the sabbath? Mat 12:11
in no wise l. up herself. Luke 13:11
l. up your heads; for your. 21:28
and he shall l. you up. Jas 4:10*
see **eyes**

lift *hand* or *hands*

I have l. up mine hand. Gen 14:22
shall no man l. up his hand. 41:44
I l. up my h., and say. Deut 32:40
l. up thine hand, forget. Ps 10:12
when I l. up my hands toward. 28:2
I will l. up my hands in thy. 63:4
my h. will I l. up to thy. 119:48
l. up your hands in sanctuary. 134:2
I will l. up mine hand to the Gentiles. Isa 49:22
l. up thy hands toward. Lam 2:19
wherefore l. up the h. Heb 12:12

lift *voice*

Hagar l. up her voice. Gen 21:16
canst thou l. up thy voice? Job 38:34
l. up thy voice, O daughter. Isa 10:30*
they shall l. up their voice. 24:14
l. up thy voice with strength. 40:9
not cry, nor l. up his voice. 42:2
and cities l. up their voice. 11
shall l. up the voice. 52:8
cry, spare not, l. up thy voice 58:1
cry, and l. up thy voice. Jer 22:20
to l. up the voice with. Ezek 21:22

lifted

Lot l. up his eyes and. Gen 13:10
Abraham l. up his eyes. 18:2; 22:13
Esau l. up voice. 27:38
and Jacob l. up his voice. 29:11
I l. up mine eyes, saw. 31:10; 33:1
l. up Joseph out of the pit. 37:28
as I l. up my voice. 39:18
Pharaoh l. up the head of. 40:20
l. up the rod and smote waters. Ex 7:20; 14:16
Aaron l. up his hand. Lev 9:22
the congregation l. up. Num 14:1
Moses l. up his hand and. 20:11
then thy heart be l. up. Deut 8:14
that his heart be not l. above. 17:20
of the priests' feet were l. Josh 4:18
the people l. up their voice and wept. Judg 2:4; 21:2; 1 Sam 11:4
so they l. up their heads. Judg 8:28
Jotham l. up his voice and. 9:7
Orpah and Ruth l. up their voice and wept. Ruth 1:9, 14
Saul l. up his voice and wept. 1 Sam 24:16
David and people l. up voice. 30:4
2 Sam 3:32
king's sons came and l. 2 Sam 13:36
Sheba hath l. up his hand. 20:21
also hast l. me up on high. 22:49
he l. up his spear against 300. 23:18
1 Chr 11:11
Jeroboam l. up hand against king. 1 Ki 11:26, 27
he l. up his face to the. 2 Ki 9:32
thine heart hath l. thee. 14:10
his kingdom was l. up. 1 Chr 14:2*
and singers l. up voice. 2 Chr 5:13
his heart was l. up in the ways. 17:6
heart was l. up to destruction. 26:16; 32:25
l. up their voice and wept. Job 2:12
if I have l. up my hand against. 31:21
or l. up myself when evil found. 29
who hath not l. up his soul. Ps 24:4
shall my head be l. up above. 27:6
for thou hast l. me up. 30:1
102:10
hath l. up his heel against me. 41:9
John 13:18
as he l. up axes upon the. Ps. 74:5
they that hate thee have l. up. 83:2
floods have l. up their voice. 93:3
therefore he l. up his hand. 106:26
and their eyelids are l. up. Pr 30:13
day of the Lord of hosts shall be on every one that is l. up. Isa 2:12
on cedars that are high and l. up. 13
mountains l. up. 14
sitting on a throne high and l. up. 6:1
when thy hand is l. up they. 26:11
against whom hast thou l. up thine eyes on high? Isa 37:23
her judgement is l. up to. Jer 51:9
creatures were l. up. Ezek 1:19
wheels were l. up. 20, 21; 10:17*
so the Spirit l. me up and. 3:14
Spirit l. me up between the earth. 8:3; 11:1
l. up their wings. 10:16, 19; 11:22
and l. up my hand to the. 20:5, 6
yet l. up mine hand in the. 15, 23
into the land for the which I l. up mine hand. 28, 42; 47:14
because thine heart is l. up. 28:2
5, 17; 31:10*
thus saith the Lord, I have l. 36:7
have I l. up my hand against. 44:12
when his heart was l. up. Dan 5:20
but hast l. up thyself against. 23
the first beast was l. up from. 7:4
then I l. up mine eyes. 8:3; 10:5
thine hand shall be l. up. Mi 5:9
his soul which is l. up is. Hab 2:4*
deep l. up his hands on high. 3:10
which l. up their horn. Zech 1:21
behold, there was l. up a. 5:7
they l. up the ephah between. 5:9
the stones of a crown, l. up. 9:16
the land shall be l. up. 14:10
by the hand, and l. her up. Mark 1:31
but Jesus l. him up, and. 9:27
he l. up his eyes on his. Luke 6:20
a certain woman l. up her. 11:27
ten lepers l. up their voices. 17:13
and he l. up his hands and. 24:50
l. up the serpent in the wilderness, ... the Son of man be l. John 3:14
when ye have l. up the Son. 8:28
I, if I be l. up, will draw all. 12:32
Son of man must be l. up. 34
Peter l. up his voice. Acts 2:14
l. up their voice to God with. 4:24
they l. up their voices saying. 14:11
and then l. up their voices. 22:22
being l. up with pride. 1 Tim 3:6*
the angel l. up his hand. Rev 10:5

lifter

my glory, and the l. up. Ps 3:3

liftest

thou l. me up to the wind. Job 30:22
l. me up from the gates. Ps 9:13
l. above those that rise up. 18:48
and l. up thy voice for. Pr 2:3

lifteth

bringeth low, and l. up. 1 Sam 2:7, 8
thine heart l. thee up. 2 Chr 25:19
what time the ostrich l. Job 39:18
wind which l. up the. Ps 107:25
he l. the needy out of the. 113:7
the Lord l. up the meek. 147:6*
when he l. up an ensign. Isa 18:3
that l. himself up in his. Jer 51:3
horseman l. up his bright. Nah 3:3*

lifetime

Absalom in his l. had. 2 Sam 18:18
thou in thy l. receivedst. Luke 16:25
were all their l. subject. Heb 2:15

lifting

Abishai chief, for l. up. 1 Chr 11:20
sounding, by l. up the voice. 15:16
answered, Amen, with l. Neh 8:6
shalt say, There is l. up. Job 22:29
l. up of my hands as. Ps 141:2
hast done foolishly in l. Pr 30:32
shall mount up like the l. Isa 9:18
at l. up of thyself nations were. 33:3
men pray every where, l. 1 Tim 2:8

light

morning was l., the men. Gen 44:3
of the house, till it was l. Judg 19:26
them till the morning l. 1 Sam 14:36
night shall be l. about. Ps 139:11
when morning is l. they. Mi 2:1
evening time it shall be l. Zech 14:7

light

our soul loatheth this l. Num 21:5
and my burden is l. Mat 11:30
our l. affliction worketh. 2 Cor 4:17

light

hired vain and l. persons. Judg 9:4
her prophets are l. and. Zeph 3:4

light, *adj.*
Asahel was *l.* of foot. *2 Sam* 2:18
light, *adv.*
cursed that setteth *l.* *Deut* 27:16
they set *l.* by father. *Ezek* 22:7
but made *l.* of it, and. *Mat* 22:5
light *thing*
seemeth it a *l. thing*? *1 Sam* 18:23
it had been a *l. thing*. *1 Ki* 16:31
a *l. thing* in sight of Lord. *2 Ki* 3:18
it is a *l. thing* for the shadow. 20:10
l. thing that thou shouldest. *Isa* 49:6
a *l. thing* they commit? *Ezek* 8:17
light
there be *l.* and there was *l.* *Gen* 1:3
God saw the *l.* 4
God called the *l.* day. 5
the greater *l.* to rule . . . lesser *l.* 16
Israel had *l.* in their. *Ex* 10:23
pillar gave *l.* by night to these. 14:20
offering, oil for the *l.* 25:6; 27:20
35:8, 14, 28; 39:37; *Lev* 24:2
pertaineth oil for the *l.* *Num* 4:16
as ye have *l.* depart. *1 Sam* 29:10
thou quench not the *l.* *2 Sam* 21:17*
he shall be as the *l.* of the. 23:4
l. was against *l.* in. *1 Ki* 7:4, 5
my servant may have a *l.* 11:36*
nor pillar of fire by night to shew them *l.* *Neh* 9:19
the Jews had *l.*, joy. *Esth* 8:16
neither let the *l.* shine. *Job* 3:4
let it look for *l.* but have none. 9
as infants which never saw *l.* 16
l. given to him in misery. 20, 23
without order, where the *l.* 10:22
bringeth out to *l.* the shadow. 12:22
they grope in the dark without *l.* 25
the *l.* of the wicked shall be. 18:5
the *l.* shall be dark in his. 6
l. shall shine on thy ways. 22:28
those that rebel against the *l.* 24:13
the murderer rising with the *l.* 14
daytime, they know not the *l.* 16
upon whom doth not his *l.*? 25:3
that is hid bringeth he to *l.* 28:11
and his life shall see the *l.* 33:28
to be enlightened with the *l.* of. 30
behold he spreadeth his *l.* 36:30
with clouds he covereth *l.* and. 32*
the *l.* of his cloud to shine? 37:15*
men see not the bright *l.* in. 21
wicked their *l.* is withholden. 38:15
where is way where *l.* dwelleth? 19
by what way is the *l.* parted? 24
his neesings a *l.* doth shine. 41:18
lift up the *l.* of thy. *Ps* 4:6
Lord is my *l.* and my salvation. 27:1
forth thy righteousness as *l.* 37:6
l. of mine eyes, it also is gone. 38:10
they shall never see *l.* 49:19
thou hast prepared the *l.* 74:16
all the night with a *l.* of fire. 78:14
l. is sown for the righteous. 97:11
who coverest thyself with *l.* 104:2
Lord, who hath shewed us *l.* 118:27
thy word is a lamp, and a *l.* 119:105
entrance of thy words giveth *l.* 130
darkness and *l.* are both. 139:12
sun, and all ye stars of *l.* 148:3
just is as the shining *l.* *Pr* 4:18
is a lamp, the law is *l.* 6:23
l. of righteous rejoiceth, but. 13:9
the *l.* of the eyes rejoiceth. 15:30
truly the *l.* is sweet. *Eccl* 11:7
while the sun or the *l.* be not. 12:2
put darkness for *l.* and *l.* *Isa* 5:20
the *l.* is darkened in the heavens. 30
it is because there is no *l.* 8:20*
a great *l.*; on them hath *l.* shined. 9:2
l. of Israel shall be for fire. 10:17
moon shall not cause her *l.* to shine. 13:10; *Mat* 24:29; *Mark* 13:24
l. of moon be as *l.* of sun, *l.* of sun as the *l.* of seven days. *Isa* 30:26
my judgement to rest for a *l.* 51:4
we wait for *l.* but behold. 59:9
be to thee an everlasting *l.* 60:19
heavens, and they had no *l.* *Jer* 4:23
I will take from them the *l.* 25:10
sun for a *l.* by day, and ordinances of the moon and stars for *l.* 31:35
and the *l.* dwelleth with. *Dan* 2:22
l. and understanding. *Dan* 5:11, 14
thy judgements as *l.* that. *Hos* 6:5
bring me forth to the *l.* *Mi* 7:9
brightness was as the *l.* *Hab* 3:4
at the *l.* of thine arrows they. 11
bring judgement to *l.* *Zeph* 3:5
in that day the *l.* shall. *Zech* 14:6
in darkness saw great *l.* *Mat* 4:16
ye are the *l.* of the world. 5:14
it giveth *l.* unto all that are in. 15*
let your *l.* so shine before men. 16
l. of body is the eye, if eye . . . full of *l.* 6:22*; *Luke* 11:34*, 36
raiment was white as the *l.* *Mat* 17:2
a *l.* to lighten Gentiles. *Luke* 2:32
enter in may see the *l.* 8:16; 11:33
wiser than the children of *l.* 16:8
and life was the *l.* of men. *John* 1:4
to bear witness of that *l.* 7, 8
that was the true *l.* which. 9
condemnation, that *l.* is come. 3:19
that doeth evil hateth the *l.* 20
doeth truth cometh to the *l.* 21
a shining *l.*: and ye were willing for a season to rejoice in his *l.* 5:35*
I am the *l.* of the world, he that followeth me shall have *l.* 8:12; 9:5
because he seeth the *l.* 11:9
stumbleth, because there is no *l.* 10
yet a little while is the *l.* 12:35
ye have *l.*, believe in the *l.* that. 36
I am come a *l.* into the world. 46
shined about him a *l.* *Acts* 9:3
a *l.* shined in the prison, and. 12:7
I have set thee to be a *l.* to. 13:47
he called for a *l.* and sprang. 16:29
there shone a great *l.* round. 22:6
were with me saw indeed the *l.* 9
not see for the glory of that *l.* 11
O king, I saw in the way a *l.* 26:13
should shew *l.* to the people and. 23
a *l.* of them which are in. *Rom* 2:19
put on the armour of *l.* 13:12
who will bring to *l.* hidden. *1 Cor* 4:5
lest the *l.* of the gospel. *2 Cor* 4:4
who commanded *l.* to shine out. 6
transformed into an angel of *l.* 11:14
now are ye *l.* in the Lord: walk as children of *l.* *Eph* 5:8
made manifest by the *l.*: for whatsoever doth make manifest is *l.* 13
inheritance of saints in *l.* *Col* 1:12
ye are all children of the *l.* and day. *1 Thes* 5:5
dwelling in *l.* no man. *1 Tim* 6:16
and immortality to *l.* *2 Tim* 1:10
into his marvellous *l.* *1 Pet* 2:9
take heed, as unto a *l.* that shineth in a dark place. *2 Pet* 1:19*
God is *l.* and in him. *1 John* 1:5
the *l.* of a candle shall. *Rev* 18:23
her *l.* was like a stone most. 21:11
lighten it, and the Lamb is the *l.* 23*
l. of the sun, the Lord giveth *l.* 22:5
see **countenance, darkness**

give **light**
and let them be to *give l.* *Gen* 1:15
and God set the stars to *give l.* 17
of fire to *give* them *l.* *Ex* 13:21
the lamps may *give l.* over against. 25:37; *Num* 8:2
he promised to *give* him alway a *l.* *2 Ki* 8:19*; *2 Chr* 21:7*
to *give* them *l.* in the way. *Neh* 9:12
and fire to *give l.* in the. *Ps* 105:39
stars of heaven shall not *give* their *l.* *Isa* 13:10
I will *give* thee for a *l.* to. 42:6; 49:6
nor shall the moon *give l.* to thee. 60:19; *Ezek* 32:7
it *giveth l.* unto all in the house. *Mat* 5:15; *Luke* 11:36
to *give* the *l.* of the knowledge of. *2 Cor* 4:6
Christ shall *give* thee *l.* *Eph* 5:14*
in the **light**
that I may walk *in the l.* *Ps* 56:13
come, let us walk *in the l.* *Isa* 2:5
walk *in the l.* of your fire. 50:11*
the light, believe *in the l.* *John* 12:36
we walk *in the l.* as he is *in the l.* *1 John* 1:7
he that saith he is *in the l.*, and. 2:9
brother, abideth *in the l.* *1 John* 2:10
saved shall walk *in l.* *Rev* 21:24
thy **light**
in *thy l.* shall we see light. *Ps* 36:9
O send out *thy l.* and thy truth. 43:3
then shall *thy l.* break forth. *Isa* 58:8
then shall *thy l.* rise in obscurity. 10
arise, shine, for *thy l.* is come. 60:1
the Gentiles shall come to *thy l.* 3
the sun shall be no more *thy l.* 19
Lord shall be *thy* everlasting *l.* 20
light, -ed
shall *l.* the lamps. *Ex* 25:37; 40:4
he *l.* the lamps before the Lord. 40:25; *Num* 8:3
for thou wilt *l.* my candle. *Ps* 18:28
nor do men *l.* a candle. *Mat* 5:15
no man when he hath *l.* a candle. *Luke* 8:16; 11:33
doth not *l.* a candle, and? 15:8
nor shall the sun *l.* on. *Rev* 7:16*
light (*to come upon*)
her hap was to *l.* on a. *Ruth* 2:3
and we will *l.* on him. *2 Sam* 17:12
lighted (*came down*)
she saw Isaac, she *l.* off. *Gen* 24:64
and she *l.* off her ass. *Josh* 15:18
Judg 1:14
Sisera *l.* off his chariot. *Judg* 4:15
Abigail hasted and *l.* off the ass. *1 Sam* 25:23
Naaman *l.* down from. *2 Ki* 5:21
lighted (*came upon*)
Jacob *l.* on a certain. *Gen* 28:11
Jehu *l.* on Jehonadab. *2 Ki* 10:15
word to Jacob and it *l.* on. *Isa* 9:8
lighten
the Lord will *l.* my. *2 Sam* 22:29
that our God may *l.* our. *Ezra* 9:8
l. mine eyes, lest I sleep. *Ps* 13:3
a light to *l.* the Gentiles. *Luke* 2:32
glory of God did *l.* it. *Rev* 21:23
lighten
peradventure he will *l.* *1 Sam* 6:5
cast wares into the sea, to *l.* it of. *Jonah* 1:5
lightened
looked unto him and were *l.* *Ps* 34:5
the lightnings *l.* the world. 77:18
earth was *l.* with his glory. *Rev* 18:1
see **enlightened**
lightened
being tossed, next day they *l.* ship. *Acts* 27:18*, 38
lighteneth
Lord *l.* both their eyes. *Pr* 29:13
for as lightning that *l.* *Luke* 17:24
lighter
make heavy yoke which he put upon us, *l.* *1 Ki* 12:4, 9, 10; *2 Chr* 10:10
altogether *l.* than vanity. *Ps* 62:9
lightest
say to him, When thou *l.* *Num* 8:2
lighteth
when Aaron *l.* the lamps. *Ex* 30:8
the true light which *l.* *John* 1:9
lighteth
axe head slippeth and *l.* *Deut* 19:5
lighting
Lord shall shew the *l.* down of his arm. *Isa* 30:30
like a dove, and *l.* on him. *Mat* 3:16
lightly
one might *l.* have lien. *Gen* 26:10
when at first he *l.* afflicted. *Isa* 9:1*
and all the hills moved *l.* *Jer* 4:24*
can *l.* speak evil of me. *Mark* 9:39*
see **esteemed**
lightness
l. of her whoredoms she. *Jer* 3:9
my people to err by their *l.* 23:32*
minded, did I use *l.*? *2 Cor* 1:17*
lightning
he sent *l.* and discomfited them. *2 Sam* 22:15
he made a way for the *l.* *Job* 28:26
he directeth his *l.* to the ends. 37:3
who divided a way for the *l.* 38:25
cast forth *l.* and scatter. *Ps* 114:6

out of fire went forth l. Ezek 1:13
ran as the appearance of l. 14
face as the appearance of l. Dan 10:6
his arrow shall go forth as the l.
Zech 9:14
as l. cometh out of the east.
Mat 24:27; Luke 17:24
his countenance was as l. Mat 28:3
I beheld Satan as l. fall. Luke 10:18

lightnings

thunders, l. and thick. Ex 19:16
all the people saw the l. and. 20:18
canst thou send l. that ? Job 38:35
he shot out l. and. Ps 18:14
l. lighted the world. 77:18; 97:4
he maketh l. for the rain. 135:7
he maketh l. with rain. Jer 10:13
51:16
chariots shall run like the l. Nah 2:4
out of throne proceeded l. Rev 4:5
were voices, thunderings, and l. 8:5
11:19
l. and a great earthquake. 16:18

lights

be l. in the firmament. Gen 1:14
let them be for l. in firmament. 15
God made two great l. greater. 16
windows of narrow l. 1 Ki 6:4*
that made great l. for. Ps 136:7
all the bright l. will I make dark.
Ezek 32:8
girded, your l. burning. Luke 12:35*
l. in the upper chamber. Acts 20:8
whom ye shine as l. in. Phil 2:15
from the Father of l. Jas 1:17

lign aloes

as the trees of l. a. which. Num 24:6

ligure

(Revised Versions, jacinth)
the third row a l., an agate and an amethyst. Ex 28:19; 39:12*

like

Sodom was l. the land. Gen 13:10
who is l. unto thee ? Ex 15:11
Deut 33:29; 1 Ki 8:23; 2 Chr 6:14
Ps 35:10; 71:19
manna was l. coriander. Ex 16:31
the glory of the Lord was l. 24:17
make any ointment l. it. 30:32
compoundeth any thing l. it. 33
of each shall there be a l. weight. 34
hew two tables l. unto the first. 34:1
Deut 10:1, 3
my last end be l. his. Num 23:10
hath been heard l. it. Deut 4:32
lest thou be a cursed thing l. it. 7:26
set king over me l. all nations.
17:14; 1 Sam 8:5, 20
they shall have l. portions to eat.
Deut 18:8
prophet of thy brethren l. me. 15
Acts 3:22; 7:37
raise a prophet from brethren l. to thee. Deut 18:18
l. the overthrow of Sodom. 29:23
not a prophet l. unto Moses. 34:10
no day l. that before. Josh 10:14
countenance l. an angel. Judg 13:6
brake them from his arms l. 16:12
I shall become weak and l. any. 17
though I be not l. to one of thy.
Ruth 2:13
woman l. Rachel and l. Leah. 4:11
let thy house be l. the house. 12
nor is there any rock l. 1 Sam 2:2
be strong, quit yourselves l. men. 4:9
1 Cor 16:13
staff of his spear was l. a. 17:7
Nabal held a feast l. the feast. 25:36
a valiant man, and who is l. 26:15
l. to name of great men. 2 Sam 7:9
what one nation in earth is l.? 23
he maketh my feet l. hinds'. 22:34
none l. thee before thee, nor after thee arise l. thee. 1 Ki 3:12, 13
there was not the l. made in. 10:20
Jeroboam ordained a feast l. 12:32
l. the house of Jeroboam. 16:3, 7
21:22; 2 Ki 9:9
ariseth a little cloud l. 1 Ki 18:44*
number thee an army l. the. 20:25
pitched before them l. two little. 27
word l. word of one of those.
1 Ki 22:13; 2 Chr 18:12
but not l. his father and l. 2 Ki 3:2
his flesh came again l. flesh of a. 5:14
l. the house of Baasha son of. 9:9
made them l. dust by threshing. 13:7
yet not l. David his father. 14:3
16:2; 2 Chr 28:1
the Lord charged they should not do l. them. 2 Ki 17:15
take you to a land l. your own.
18:32; Isa 36:17
l. to him was there no king.
2 Ki 23:25; Neh 13:26
host l. the host of God. 1 Chr 12:22
would increase Israel l. stars. 27:23
over a people l. the dust. 2 Chr 1:9
no burning for him l. burning. 21:19
be not ye l. your fathers and. 30:7
l. to the abominations of the. 33:2
there was no passover l. to. 35:18
to grave l. as a shock of. Job 5:26
hast thou not curdled me l.? 10:10
though man be born l. a wild. 11:12
he maketh them to stagger l. 12:25
your remembrances are l. 13:12*
he cometh forth l. a flower. 14:2
who drinketh iniquity l. water. 15:16
he runneth upon me l. a giant. 16:14
he shall perish for ever l. his. 20:7
they send their little ones l. 21:11
what man is l. Job, who ? 34:7
power: who teacheth l. him ? 36:22
gird up now thy loins l. a man. 38:3
40:7
hast thou an arm l. God ? or. 40:9
on earth there is not his l. 41:33
ye have not spoken right l. my. 42:8
he shall be l. a tree planted. Ps 1:3
ungodly are not so, but are l. 4
lest he tear my soul l. a lion. 7:2
l. a lion that is greedy of his. 17:12
out l. water, my heart l. wax. 22:14
I become l. them that go down. 28:1
I am forgotten, I am l. a. 31:12
thy righteousness is l. the. 36:6
shall be soon cut down l. grass. 37:2
spreading himself l. a green bay. 35
beauty to consume l. a moth. 39:11
thou hast given us l. sheep. 44:11
man is l. the beasts that. 49:12, 20
tongue is l. a sharp razor. 52:2
but I am l. a green olive tree. 8
O that I had wings l. a dove ! 55:6
l. the poison of a serpent, l. 58:4
make a noise l. a dog. 59:6, 14
whet their tongue l. a sword. 64:3
he shall come down l. rain. 72:6
neither plagued l. other men. 73:5
leddest thy people l. a flock. 77:20
78:52
unfaithfully l. their fathers. 78:57
their blood have shed l. water. 79:3
thereof l. the goodly cedars. 80:10
shall die l. men, and fall l. one. 82:7
make them l. a wheel. 83:13
who is a strong Lord l. unto thee ?
89:8; 113:5; Mi 7:18
flourish l. the palm tree, he shall grow l. a cedar in. Ps 92:12
heart withered l. grass. 102:4, 11
I am l. a pelican, l. an owl of the. 6
shall wax old l. a garment. 26
l. as a father pitieth his. 103:13
out the heavens l. a curtain. 104:2
the dry places l. a river. 105:41
stagger l. a drunken man. 107:27
l. water, and l. oil into. 109:18
they that make them are l. to them.
115:8; 135:18
we were l. them that dream. 126:1
lest I be l. them that go down. 143:7
man is l. to vanity, his days. 144:4
l. wool, hoar frost l. ashes. 147:16
l. the bars of a castle. Pr 18:19
counsel in the heart of man is l. 20:5
biteth l. a serpent, stingeth l. 23:32
unfaithful man is l. a broken tooth.
25:19
l. a city broken down, and. 28
fool, lest thou be l. to him. 26:4
my beloved is l. a roe. S of S 2:9
turn, my beloved, and be thou l. a roe.
17; 8:14
cometh l. pillars of smoke ? S of S 3:6
thy teeth are l. a flock of sheep. 4:2
thy lips l. scarlet, temples l. a. 3
thy neck is l. the tower of David. 4
breasts are l. two young. 5; 7:3
his lips l. lilies dropping sweet. 5:13
my soul made me l. chariots. 6:12
joints of thy thighs are l. jewels. 7:1
l. a goblet, thy belly is l. wheat. 2
stature l. a palm tree. 7
smell of thy nose l. apples. 8
would have been l. unto Gomorrah.
Isa 1:9; Rom 9:29
red l. crimson, shall be. Isa 1:18
inhabitants l. a valiant man. 10:13
lion shall eat straw l. the ox. 11:7
and shall be an highway, l. as it. 16
art thou become l. to us ? 14:10
I will be l. the most High. 14
out l. an abominable branch. 19
sound l. an harp for Moab. 16:11
in that day shall Egypt be l. 19:16
l. as my servant Isaiah hath. 20:3
will toss thee l. a ball into a. 22:18
l. a woman with child that. 26:17
breath of the Lord l. a stream. 30:33
Sharon is l. a wilderness. 33:9
I have cut off l. a weaver my. 38:12
l. a crane or swallow so did I. 14
will I cry l. a travailing. 42:14
to whom will ye compare me that we may be l.? 46:5
wicked are l. the troubled sea. 57:20
lift up thy voice l. a trumpet. 58:1
be l. a watered garden, and l. 11
for the wall l. the blind. 59:10
all l. bears, and mourn sore l. 11
enemy shall come in l. a flood. 19
l. him that treadeth in the. 63:2
our iniquities l. wind have. 64:6
peace to her l. a river. 66:12
lest my fury come forth l. fire.
Jer 4:4; 21:12
l. as ye have forsaken me. 5:19
portion of Jacob is not l. them. 10:16
I was l. a lamb brought to. 11:19
for he shall be l. the heath in. 17:6
word l. fire and l. a hammer? 23:29
make this house l. Shiloh. 26:6, 9
Zion shall be plowed l. a field. 18
l. Zedekiah and l. Ahab. 29:22
were added besides to them many l. words. 36:32
he is l. to die with hunger. 38:9
Egypt is l. a very fair heifer. 46:20
flee, be l. the heath in the. 48:6
be l. the dove that maketh nest. 28
shall come l. a lion. 49:19; 50:44
is l. me, who will appoint ? 49:19
of Jacob is not l. them. 51:19
not do any more the l. Ezek 5:9
l. as I have done, so shall. 12:11
and doeth the l. to any of. 18:10
the house of Judah is l. to all. 25:8
thou l. in thy greatness ? 31:2, 18
nor any tree was l. unto him in his. 8
month shall he do the l. 45:25
form of the fourth is l. the Son of God. Dan 3:25
made l. the beasts, l. oxen. 5:21
one l. the Son of man came. 7:13
shall be l. people, l. priest. Hos 4:9
princes l. them that remove. 5:10
they l. men have transgressed. 6:7
I am l. a green fir tree, from. 14:8
hath not been ever the l. Joel 2:2
lest he break out l. fire. Amos 5:6
instruments of music l. David. 6:5
l. as the Lord of hosts. Zech 1:6
the governors of Judah l. a. 12:6
l. a dove, and lighting. Mat 3:16
Mark 1:10; Luke 3:22; John 1:32
be not ye therefore l. unto. Mat 6:8
was not arrayed l. one of these.
29; Luke 12:27
l. children sitting in the market.
Mat 11:16; Luke 7:32
it was restored whole l. Mat 12:13
kingdom is l. to a grain of mustard.
13:31; Mark 4:31; Luke 13:19
kingdom of heaven is l. leaven.
Mat 13:33; Luke 13:21
is l. unto treasure. Mat 13:44
is l. unto a merchant. 45

is *l.* unto a net. *Mat* 13:47
is *l.* an householder. 52; 20:1
of heaven is *l.* unto a certain. 22:2
second is *l.* unto it. 39; *Mark* 12:31
l. to whited sepulchres. *Mat* 23:27
countenance was *l.* lightning. 28:3
shew you to whom he is *l. Luke* 6:47
and to what are they *l.*? 7:31
are *l.* unto children. 32
what is the kingdom of God *l.*? 13:18
never man spake *l.* this. *John* 7:46
I shall be a liar *l.* unto you. 8:55
others said, He is *l.* him. 9:9
l. a lamb dumb before. *Acts* 8:32
God gave them the *l.* gift. 11:17
we also are men of *l.* passions. 14:15
Godhead is *l.* gold or silver. 17:29
workmen of *l.* occupation. 19:25
l. to corruptible man. *Rom* 1:23
l. as Christ was raised up from. 6:4
fashioned *l.* unto his body. *Phil* 3:21
suffered *l.* things of. *1 Thes* 2:14
it behoved him to be made *l.* unto his brethren. *Heb* 2:17
all points tempted *l.* as we are. 4:15
but made *l.* unto the Son of God. 7:3
that wavereth is *l.* a wave *Jas* 1:6
he is *l.* a man beholding his. 23
Elias was a man subject to *l.* 5:17
l. figure whereunto even baptism doth now save us. *1 Pet* 3:21*
obtained *l.* precious faith. *2 Pet* 1:1
we shall be *l.* him. *1 John* 3:2
one *l.* the Son of man, clothed. *Rev* 1:13; 14:14
saying, Who is *l.* to the beast? 13:4
he had two horns *l.* a lamb, and. 11
three unclean spirits *l.* frogs. 16:13
city is *l.* to this great city? 18:18

like, *verb*

if the man *l.* not to. *Deut* 25:7, 8
did not *l.* to retain God. *Rom* 1:28

like *manner*

did in *l. man.* with their. *Ex* 7:11
in *l. man.* thou shalt deal. 23:11
in *l. man.* shalt thou do with his ass. *Deut* 22:3
in *l. man.* they sent to king of Moab. *Judg* 11:17
Samuel in *l. man.* *1 Sam* 19:24
Sanballat sent in *l. man.* *Neh* 6:5
shall die in *l. man.* *Isa* 51:6
ye in *l. man.* when ye. *Mark* 13:29
in *l. man.* did their fathers unto the prophets. *Luke* 6:23
third took her, in *l. man.* 20:31
shall so come in *l. man.* *Acts* 1:11
in *l. man.* that women adorn. *1 Tim* 2:9
in *l. man.* giving themselves to fornication. *Jude* 7

none **like**

there is *none l.* the Lord our God. *Ex* 8:10; 9:14; *Deut* 33:26 *2 Sam* 7:22; *1 Chr* 17:20
none l. the hail. *Ex* 9:24
none l. cry of Egypt. 11:6
none l. Saul among all. *1 Sam* 10:24
David said, There is *none l.* 21:9
was *none l.* Solomon. *1 Ki* 3:12
none l. Ahab. 21:25
after there was *none l.* Hezekiah. *2 Ki* 18:5
there is *none l.* him in. *Job* 1:8; 2:3
among the gods *none l.* unto thee. *Ps* 86:8; *Jer* 10:6, 7
I am God, and there is *none l.* me. *Isa* 46:9
is great, so that *none* is *l.* it. *Jer* 30:7
was found *none l.* Daniel. *Dan* 1:19

such **like**

and doeth not *such l.* *Ezek* 18:14
many other *such l.* things ye do. *Mark* 7:8, 13
drunkenness and such *l.* *Gal.* 5:21

like *wise*

I in *l. wise* will tell you. *Mat* 21:24

liked

of my father he *l.* me. *1 Chr* 28:4*

liken

to whom then will ye *l.* God? *Isa* 40:18, 25; 46:5
thing shall I *l.* to thee? *Lam* 2:13
doeth them, I will *l.* him. *Mat* 7:24
whereunto shall I *l.* this generation? 11:16; *Luke* 7:31
whereunto shall we *l.* the kingdom? *Mark* 4:30; *Luke* 13:20

likened

who can be *l.* unto the Lord? *Ps* 89:6
l. the daughter of Zion. *Jer* 6:2*
l. to a foolish man who. *Mat* 7:26
kingdom of heaven is *l.* 13:24 18:23; 25:1

likeness

let us make man after our *l.* *Gen* 1:26; 5:1
Adam begat a son in his own *l.* 5:3
not make the *l.* of any. *Ex* 20:4
a graven image, the *l.* of male or. *Deut* 4:16, 17, 18, 23*, 25*; 5:8
when I awake with thy *l.* *Ps* 17:15
l. will ye compare to him? *Isa* 40:18
l. of four living creatures. *Ezek* 1:5
as for the *l.* of their faces. 10; 10:22
l. of lamps. 1:13
the four had one *l.* 16; 10:10
the *l.* of the firmament was. 1:22
l. of a throne. 26; 10:1
the *l.* of the glory of the Lord. 1:28
lo, a *l.* as of fire. 8:2
l. of the hands of a man. 10:21
gods are come down in the *l.* of men. *Acts* 14:11
in the *l.* of his death, we shall be also in the *l.* of his. *Rom* 6:5
God sending his Son in the *l.* 8:3
made in the *l.* of men. *Phil* 2:7

likeminded

God of patience grant you to be *l.* *Rom* 15:5*
that ye be *l.* *Phil* 2:2*
I have no man *l.* who will care. 20

liketh

(*American Version*, pleaseth)
shall dwell where it *l.* *Deut* 23:16
also for the Jews as it *l.* *Esth* 8:8
for this *l.* you, O children. *Amos* 4:5

likewise

l. shalt thou do with thine oxen. *Ex* 22:30
gods, even so will I do *l.* *Deut* 12:30
maidservant thou shalt do *l.* 15:17
lost goods shalt thou do *l.* 22:3
look on me, and do *l.* *Judg* 7:17
and they prophesied *l.* *1 Sam* 19:21
fell *l.* on his sword, and died. 31:5
let us hear *l.* what he. *2 Sam* 17:5
l. did he for all his strange wives. *1 Ki* 11:8
l. fled before Abishai. *1 Chr* 19:15
praise every morning and *l.* 23:30
I *l.* might exact of them. *Neh* 5:10
my maidens will fast *l.* *Esth* 4:16
l. the fool and brutish. *Ps* 49:10
God shall *l.* destroy thee for. 52:5
l. hast cursed others. *Eccl* 7:22
they be quiet, and *l.* many. *Nah* 1:12
l. shall also Son of man. *Mat* 17:12
so *l.* shall my heavenly Father. 18:35
the sixth hour, and did *l.* 20:5
l. received every man a penny. 10
to the second and said *l.* 21:30
and they did unto them *l.* 36
l. the second and third died. 22:26 *Mark* 12:21
so *l.* when ye see these things. *Mat* 24:33; *Luke* 21:31
l. he that had received two talents. *Mat* 25:17
l. also said all his disciples. 26:35 *Mark* 14:31
l. the chief priests mocked. *Mat* 27:41; *Mark* 15:31
gave thanks *l.* to the Lord. *Luke* 2:38
let him do *l.* 3:11
do ye also to them *l.* 6:31
go and do thou *l.* 10:37
ye shall all *l.* perish. 13:3, 5
l., whoever forsaketh not all. 14:33
l. joy shall be in heaven. 15:7, 10
l. Lazarus received evil. 16:25
so *l.* when ye shall have done. 17:10
l. also the cup after supper. 22:20
also doeth the Son *l.* *John* 5:19
prophets have *l.* foretold. *Acts* 3:24
l. the men leaving the. *Rom* 1:27
l. reckon yourselves to be. 6:11
l. the Spirit helpeth our. 8:26
and *l.* also the wife to. *1 Cor* 7:3
other Jews dissembled *l.* *Gal* 2:13
l. the good works of. *1 Tim* 5:25
young men *l.* exhort to. *Tit* 2:6
he also himself *l.* took. *Heb* 2:14
arm yourselves *l.* with. *1 Pet* 4:1
l. these filthy dreamers. *Jude* 8
shone not, and the night *l.* *Rev* 8:12

liking

their young are in good *l.* *Job* 39:4
he see your faces worse *l.* *Dan* 1:10

lilies

wrought with flowers of *l.* *1 Ki* 7:26; *2 Chr* 4:5
feedeth among the *l.* *S of S* 2:16; 6:3
roes which feed among the *l.* 4:5
his lips like *l.* dropping sweet. 5:13
like wheat set about with *l.* 7:2
consider the *l.* how they grow. *Mat* 6:28; *Luke* 12:27

lily

Sharon, and *l.* of valleys. *S of S* 2:1
as the *l.* among thorns, so is my. 2
Israel shall grow as the *l.* *Hos* 14:5

lily *work*

chapiters were of *l. work.* *1 Ki* 7:19
top of the pillars was *l. work.* 22

lime

be as the burnings of *l.* *Isa* 33:12
of king of Edom to *l.* *Amos* 2:1

limit

l. thereof shall be most. *Ezek* 43:12

limited

they *l.* the Holy One. *Ps* 78:41*

limiteth

l. a certain day, saying. *Heb* 4:7*

line

bind this *l.* of scarlet. *Josh* 2:18
she bound the scarlet *l.* in the. 21
measured Moab with a *l.*; with one full *l.* to keep alive. *2 Sam* 8:2
a *l.* of twelve cubits. *1 Ki* 7:15
a *l.* of thirty cubits. 23; *2 Chr* 4:2
stretch over Jerusalem *l.* *2 Ki* 21:13
who hath stretched the *l.*? *Job* 38:5
their *l.* is gone out through. *Ps* 19:4
them an inheritance by *l.* 78:55
precept must be upon precept; *l.* upon *l.*, *l.* upon *l.* *Isa* 28:10, 13
judgement will I lay to the *l.* 17
shall stretch out on it the *l.* 34:11
hath divided it to them by *l.* 17
he marketh it out with a *l.* 44:13*
the measuring *l.* shall. *Jer* 31:39
hath stretched out a *l.* *Lam* 2:8
a man that had the *l.* of flax. *Ezek* 40:3
the man that had the *l.* went. 47:3
land shall be divided by *l.* *Amos* 7:17
a *l.* shall be stretched. *Zech* 1:16
a man with a measuring *l.* in. 2:1
not to boast in another man's *l.* *2 Cor* 10:16*

lineage

because he was of the *l.* of David. *Luke* 2:4*

linen

garment mingled of *l.* and woollen. *Lev* 19:19*; *Deut* 22:11
on him an ephod of *l.* *1 Chr* 15:27
wrapped him in the *l.* *Mark* 15:46 *Luke* 23:53
angels clothed in pure and white *l.* *Rev* 15:6*

linen, *adj.*

make them *l.* breeches. *Ex* 28:42
put on *l.* garment and *l.* breeches. *Lev* 6:10; 16:4
whether woollen or *l.* garment. 13:47, 48, 52, 59
Aaron shall put off the *l.* 16:23
l. clothes and *l.* garments. 32 *Ezek* 44:17, 18
Samuel ministered with a *l.* ephod. *1 Sam* 2:18

that did wear a l. ephod. 1 Sam 22:18
David was girded with a l. ephod. 2 Sam 6:14
l. yarn ... merchants received the l. 1 Ki 10:28*; 2 Chr 1:16*
get thee a l. girdle, put. Jer 13:1
wrapped it in a l. cloth. Mat 27:59
John 19:40
a l. cloth cast about his. Mark 14:51
left the l. cloth and fled naked. 52
Peter beheld the l. clothes. Luke 24:12; John 20:6
John saw the l. clothes. John 20:5
see **fine**

lines

with two l. measured. 2 Sam 8:2
l. are fallen in pleasant. Ps 16:6

lingered

while Lot l. the men. Gen 19:16
except we had l. surely we. 43:10

lingereth

whose judgement l. not. 2 Pet 2:3

lintel

and strike the l. and two. Ex 12:22
when he seeth blood on the l. he. 23
l. and side posts were. 1 Ki 6:31
smite l. that the posts. Amos 9:1*

lintels

lodge in the upper l. of it. Zeph 2:14

lion

(*This word is often used as a synonym of strength and power*)

Judah couched as a l. Gen 49:9
Israel lay down as a l., as a great l. Num 24:9
Gad dwelleth as a l. Deut 33:20
of l. there was a swarm of bees and honey in carcase of l. Judg 14:8
what is stronger than a l.? 18
a l. and took a lamb. 1 Sam 17:34
is as the heart of a l. 2 Sam 17:10
slew a l. in the midst of a pit. 23:20
1 Chr 11:22
a l. met him by the way and slew him, the l. also stood by. 1 Ki 13:24
l. standing by the carcase. 25, 28
hath delivered him to the l. 26
art departed from me, a l. shall slay thee; a l. found him and. 20:36
roaring of the l., and the voice of the fierce l. Job 4:10
huntest me as a fierce l. 10:16
nor the fierce l. passed by it. 28:8
hunt the prey for the l.? 38:39
lest he tear my soul like a l. Ps 7:2
he lieth in wait secretly as a l. 10:9
like a l. that is greedy of his. 17:12
gaped on me as a roaring l. 22:13
save me from the l.'s mouth. 21
thou shalt tread on the l. 91:13
king's wrath is as the roaring of a l. Pr 19:12
king is as the roaring of a l. 20:2
the slothful saith, There is a l. 22:13
there is a l. in the way, a l. 26:13
the righteous are bold as a l. 28:1
l. which is strongest among. 30:30
dog is better than a dead l. Eccl 9:4
their roaring shall be like a l. Isa 5:29
l. shall eat straw like the ox. 11:7
65:25
he cried, A l.: My lord, I stand. 21:8
no l. shall be there, nor. 35:9
as a l. so will be break all 38:13
your prophets like a l. Jer 2:30
l. is come up from his thicket. 4:7
a l. out of the forest shall slay. 5:6
my heritage is to me as a l. in. 12:8
forsaken his covert as the l. 25:38
shall come up like a l. 49:19; 50:44
as a l. in secret places. Lam 3:10
and the face of a l. on. Ezek 1:10
third was the face of a l. 10:14
prophets like a roaring l. 22:25
the first was like a l. and. Dan 7:4
will be to Ephraim as a l. Hos 5:14
he shall roar like a l. when. 11:10
I will be to them as l. 13:7
I will devour as a l. 8
cheek teeth of a great l. Joel 1:6
will a l. roar when he? Amos 3:4
l. hath roared, who will not? Amos 3:8
taketh out of mouth of l. 12
of Jacob shall be as a l. Mi 5:8
l. did tear in pieces enough for his. Nah 2:12
out of the mouth of the l. 2 Tim 4:17
the devil as a roaring l. 1 Pet 5:8
first beast was like a l. Rev 4:7
the l. of the tribe of Judah. 5:5
loud voice, as when a l. roareth. 10:3
mouth as the mouth of a l. 13:2
see **bear**

***old* lion**

as an *old* l. who shall rouse him? Gen 49:9
the *old* l. perisheth for. Job 4:11
come the young and *old* l.? Isa 30:6
lion, even *old* l. walked. Nah 2:11

***young* lion**

up himself as a *young* l. Num 23:24
behold, a *young* l. roared. Judg 14:5
young l. lurking in secret. Ps 17:12
young l. shalt thou trample. 91:13
calf and *young* l. lie down. Isa 11:6
like the *young* l. roaring on. 31:4
became a *young* l. and learned to catch the prey. Ezek 19:3, 6
another, and made him a *young* l. 5
thou art like a *young* l. of the. 32:2
face of a *young* l. was towards. 41:19
as a *young* l. to the house of Judah. Hos 5:14
will a *young* l. cry out of his den, if he has taken nothing? Amos 3:4
Jacob as a *young* l. among the flocks. Mi 5:8

lioness

what is thy mother? A l. Ezek 19:2

lionesses

lion strangled for his l. Nah 2:12

lionlike

slew two l. men of Moab. 2 Sam 23:20*; 1 Chr 11:22*

lions

Saul and Jonathan stronger than l. 2 Sam 1:23
on the borders were l., oxen: beneath the l. were. 1 Ki 7:29
cherubims, l. and palm trees. 36
two l. stood beside the stays. 10:19
2 Chr 9:18
twelve l. stood on the one side. 1 Ki 10:20; 2 Chr 9:19
the Lord sent l. among. 2 Ki 17:25
therefore he hath sent l. among. 26
were like faces of l. 1 Chr 12:8
rescue my darling from l. Ps. 35:17
my soul is among l.: I lie even. 57:4
look from top of Amana, from the l.' dens. S of S 4:8
l. upon him that escapeth. Isa 15:9
the l. have driven Israel. Jer 50:17
roar together like l. 51:38
she lay down among l. Ezek 19:2
went up and down among the l. 6
the l. had the mastery. Dan 6:24
Daniel from the power of the l. 27
the dwelling of the l.? Nah 2:11
her princes within are roaring l. Zeph 3:3
faith stopped the mouths of l. Heb 11:33
were as the teeth of l. Rev 9:8
the horses were as the heads of l. 17
see **den**

lion's *whelp, whelps*

Judah is a l. *whelp*. Gen 49:9
Dan is a l. *whelp*. Deut 33:22
the stout l. *whelps* are. Job 4:11
l. *whelps* have not trodden it. 28:8
they shall yell as l. *whelps*. Jer 51:38

***young* lions**

teeth of the *young* l. are. Job 4:10
the appetite of the *young* l.? 38:39
the *young* l. do lack and. Ps 34:10
great teeth of the *young* l. 58:6
young l. roar after their prey. 104:21
shall roar like *young* l. Isa 5:29
young l. roared upon him. Jer 2:15
whelps among *young* l. Ezek 19:2
with all the *young* l. shall. 38:13
the feedingplace of the *young* l.? Nah 2:11
sword shall devour thy *young* l. 13
voice of the roaring of *young* l. Zech 11:3

lip

put a covering on his l. Lev 13:45
they shoot out the l. Ps 22:7
the l. of truth shall be. Pr 12:19

lips

of uncircumcised l. Ex 6:12, 30
aught out of her l. Num 30:6; 8:12
heart, only her l. moved. 1 Sam 1:13
with flattering l. do they. Ps 12:2
shall cut off all flattering l. 3
our l. are our own, who is lord? 4
goeth not out of feigned l. 17:1
let lying l. be put to silence. 31:18
behold, swords are in their l. 59:7
for the words of their l. let. 12
praise thee with joyful l. 63:5
soul, O Lord, from lying l. 120:2
adders' poison is under their l. 140:3
mischief of their own l. cover. 9
and perverse l. put far. Pr 4:24
l. of a strange woman drop as. 5:3
with flattering of her l. she. 7:21
in the l. of him that hath. 10:13
hideth hatred with lying l. is a. 18
the l. of the righteous feed many. 21
the l. of righteous know what is. 32
lying l. are an abomination. 12:22
but the l. of the wise shall. 14:3
when perceivest not in him the l. 7
the talk of the l. tendeth only to. 23
the l. of the wise disperse. 15:7
a divine sentence is in the l. 16:10
righteous l. are the delight of. 13
sweetness of the l. increaseth. 21
doer giveth heed to false l. 17:4
less do lying l. become a prince. 7
a fool's l. enter into contention. 18:6
the l. of knowledge are a. 20:15
and their l. talk of mischief. 24:2
burning l. are like a potsherd. 26:23
l. of a fool will swallow himself. Eccl 10:12
causing the l. of those asleep to. S of S 7:9
undone, a man of unclean l. ... of a people of unclean l. Isa 6:5
for with stammering l. will. 28:11
this people with their l. do. 29:13
I create the fruit of the l. 57:19
your l. have spoken lies. 59:3
l. of those that rose. Lam 3:62
cover your l. nor eat. Ezek 24:22
taken up in the l. of talkers. 36:3
render the calves of our l. Hos 14:2
seers shall cover their l. Mi 3:7
priest's l. should keep. Mal 2:7
honoureth me with their l. Mat 15:8; Mark 7:6
of asps is under their l. Rom 3:13
other l. will I speak to. 1 Cor 14:21
fruit of our l. giving. Heb 13:15

***his* lips**

pronouncing with *his* l. Lev 5:4
did not Job sin with *his* l. Job 2:10
O that God would open *his* l. 11:5
from commandment of *his* l. 23:12
the request of *his* l. Ps 21:2
spake unadvisedly with *his* l. 106:33
he that refraineth *his* l. Pr 10:19
by transgression of *his* l. 12:13
openeth wide *his* l. shall have. 13:3
wise addeth learning to *his* l. 16:23
in *his* l. there is as a burning fire. 27
moving *his* l. he bringeth evil. 30
shutteth *his* l. is a man of. 17:28
his l. are the snare of his soul. 18:7
with the increase of *his* l. shall. 20
he that is perverse in *his* l. 19:1
that flattereth with *his* l. 20:19
for grace of *his* l. the king. 22:11
shall kiss *his* l. that giveth. 24:26
hateth dissembleth with *his* l. 26:24
his l. like lilies dropping. S of S 5:13
with breath of *his* l. shall. Isa 11:4
his l. are full of indignation. 30:27
was not found in *his* l. Mal 2:6
his l. that they speak. 1 Pet 3:10

my lips
to the pleading of *my l.* Job 13:6
moving of *my l.* should assuage. 16:5
my l. shall not speak wickedness. 27:4
I will speak, I will open *my l.* 32:20
my l. shall utter knowledge. 33:3
up their names into *my l.* Ps 16:4
lo, I have not refrained *my l.* 40:9
open thou *my l.* 51:15
my l. shall praise thee. 63:3
I will pay vows, which *my l.* 66:14
my l. shall greatly rejoice. 71:23
thing that is gone out of *my l.* 89:34
with *my l.* have I declared. 119:13
my l. shall utter thy praise. 171
Lord, keep the door of *my l.* 141:3
the opening of *my l.* Pr 8:6
is an abomination to *my l.* 7
which came out of *my l.* Jer 17:16
the sons of men touched *my l.* Dan 10:16
I heard, *my l.* quivered. Hab 3:16

thy lips
which is gone out of *thy l.* perform. Deut 23:23
I will put my bridle in *thy l.* 2 Ki 19:28; Isa 37:29
fill *thy l.* with rejoicing. Job 8:21
thy own *l.* testify against thee. 15:6
the word of *thy l.* I have. Ps 17:4
keep *thy l.* from speaking. 34:13
grace is poured into *thy l.* 45:2
thy l. may keep knowledge. Pr 5:2
withal be fitted in *thy l.* 22:18
rejoice when *thy l.* speak. 23:16
deceive not with *thy l.* 24:28
praise thee, and not *thine* own *l.* 27:2
thy l. are like a thread. S of S 4:3
thy l. O my spouse, drop as the. 11
this hath touched *thy l.* Isa 6:7
cover not *thy l.* and eat. Ezek 24:17

liquor
nor shall he drink any *l.* Num 6:3
a round goblet, which wanteth not *l.* S of S 7:2*

liquors
offer the first of thy *l.* Ex 22:29

listed
done unto him whatsoever they *l.* Mat 17:12; Mark 9:13

listen
l. O isles, unto me, and. Isa 49:1

listeth
wind bloweth where it *l.* John 3:8
whithersoever the governor *l.* Jas 3:4*

litters
bring your brethren in chariots and *l.* Isa 66:20

little
l. water, I pray you. Gen 18:4
let me drink a *l.* water of. 24:17
it was but *l.* thou hadst. 30:30
a *l.* way to Ephrath. 35:16; 48:7
buy us a *l.* food. 43:2; 44:25
a *l.* balm, a *l.* honey. 43:11
if the household be too *l.* Ex 12:4
he that gathered *l.* had no lack. 16:18 2 Cor 8:15
by *l.* and *l.* I will drive them out. Ex 23:30; Deut 7:22
and gather but *l.* in. Deut 28:38
Dan went out too *l.* for. Josh 19:47
is the iniquity of Peor too *l.*? 22:17
give me *l.* water to drink. Judg 4:19 1 Ki 17:10
that she tarried a *l.* in. Ruth 2:7
mother made him a *l.* 1 Sam 2:19
because I tasted a *l.* of this honey. 14:29, 43
when thou wast *l.* in thine. 15:17
save one *l.* ewe lamb. 2 Sam 12:3
if that had been too *l.* I would. 8
thy servant will go a *l.* way. 19:36*
brasen altar was too *l.* 1 Ki 8:64
my *l.* finger thicker than. 12:10 2 Chr 10:10
and a *l.* oil in a cruse. 1 Ki 17:12
make a *l.* cake. 13
there ariseth a *l.* cloud like. 18:44
like two *l.* flocks of kids. 20:27
l. children out of the city mocked. 2 Ki 2:23†
away captive a *l.* maid. 5:2
Ahab served Baal a *l.* but. 10:18
a *l.* space, give us a *l.* Ezra 9:8
all the trouble seem *l.* Neh 9:32
and my ear received a *l.* Job 4:12*
that I may take comfort a *l.* 10:20
but how *l.* a portion is heard? 26:14
suffer me a *l.* and I will shew. 36:2
wrath is kindled but a *l.* Ps 2:12*
made him a *l.* lower than the angels. 8:5; Heb 2:7
l. that righteous man hath. Ps 37:16
l. hills rejoice on every side. 65:12*
there is *l.* Benjamin, with. 68:27
l. hills by righteousness. 72:3*
l. hills skipped like lambs. 114:4, 6
a *l.* sleep, a *l.* slumber, a *l.* folding. Pr 6:10; 24:33
heart of the wicked is *l.* 10:20
better is a *l.* with the fear of. 15:16
better is a *l.* with righteousness. 16:8
four things that are *l.* on the. 30:24
sweet, whether he eat *l.* Eccl 5:12
there was a *l.* city, and few. 9:14
so doth a *l.* folly him that is in. 10:1
take us the foxes, the *l.* S of S 2:15
was but a *l.* that I passed. 3:4
we have a *l.* sister, and she. 8:8
hide thyself for a *l.* moment till. Isa 26:20
here a *l.* and there a *l.* 28:10, 13
the isles as a very *l.* thing. 40:15
in a *l.* wrath I hid my face. 54:8*
I will be to them a *l.* Ezek 11:16
but as if that were a very *l.* 16:47
and sent out her *l.* rivers. 31:4*
up another *l.* horn. Dan 7:8; 8:9
shall be holpen with a *l.* help. 11:34
they shall sorrow a *l.* Hos 8:10*
the *l.* house with clefts. Amos 6:11
l. among the thousands. Mi 5:2
sown much, and bring in *l.* Hag 1:6
for much, and lo, it came to *l.* 9
was but a *l.* displeased. Zech 1:15
clothe you, O ye of *l.* faith? Mat 6:30 8:26; 16:8; Luke 12:28
O thou of *l.* faith. Mat 14:31
seven, and a few *l.* fishes. 15:34
he went a *l.* further. 26:39 Mark 1:19; 14:35
my *l.* daughter lieth at. Mark 5:23
to whom *l.* is forgiven, the same loveth *l.* Luke 7:47
fear not, *l.* flock. 12:32
he was *l.* of stature. 19:3
been faithful in a very *l.* 19:17
of them may take a *l.* John 6:7
put the apostles forth a *l.* Acts 5:34
man alive, and were not a *l.* 20:12
barbarians shewed us no *l.* 28:2*
a *l.* leaven leaveneth the whole lump. 1 Cor 5:6; Gal 5:9
could bear with me a *l.* 2 Cor 11:1
that I may boast myself a *l.* 16
bodily exercise profiteth *l.* 1 Tim 4:8
use a *l.* wine for thy. 5:23
who was made a *l.* lower. Heb 2:9
tongue is a *l.* member . . . a *l.* Jas 3:5
vapour that appeareth for a *l.* 4:14
thou hast a *l.* strength. Rev 3:8
rest a *l.* season. 6:11
be loosed a *l.* season. 20:3
see **book, chambers, child, children**

little *one*, or *ones*
a *l. one*, is it not a *l. one*? Gen 19:20
l. ones took they captive. 34:29
we, and thou, and our *l. ones.* 43:8
l. one, and his brother is dead. 44:20
out of Egypt for your *l. ones.* 45:19
carried their *l. ones.* 46:5
food for your *l. ones.* 47:24
l. ones left they in Goshen. 50:8
will nourish you and your *l. ones.* 21
go, and your *l. ones.* Ex 10:10, 24
l. ones, them will I bring. Num 14:31
Midian captives and *l. ones.* 31:9
every male among the *l. ones.* 17
build cities for our *l. ones.* 32:16
our *l. ones* shall dwell in. 17, 26
we destroyed men, women, and *l. ones.* Deut 2:34
the women and *l. ones.* Deut 20:14
Joshua read before the women and *l. ones.* Josh 8:35
put the *l. ones* before. Judg 18:21
over and all the *l. ones.* 2 Sam 15:22
Judah stood before Lord and *l. ones.* 2 Chr 20:13
genealogy of all their *l. ones.* 31:18
right way for our *l. ones.* Ezra 8:21
cause to perish *l. ones.* Esth 8:11
their *l. ones* like a flock. Job 21:11
that dasheth thy *l. ones.* Ps 137:9
a *l. one* shall become a. Isa 60:22
nobles sent their *l. ones.* Jer 14:3
her *l. ones* have caused a cry. 48:4
my hand on the *l. ones.* Zech 13:7
give to drink to one of these *l. ones.* Mat 10:42
whoso shall offend one of these *l. ones.* 18:6; Mark 9:42
despise not one of these *l. ones.* Mat 18:10
of these *l. ones* should perish. 14
that he should offend one of these *l. ones.* Luke 17:2

little *while*
exalted for a *l. while.* Job 24:24
yet a *l. while* and wicked. Pr 37:10
l. while and indignation. Isa 10:25
a very *l. while*, and Lebanon. 29:17
possessed it but a *l. while.* 63:18
l. while and her harvest. Jer 51:33
yet a *l. while* and I will avenge the blood. Hos 1:4
a *l. while* and I will shake. Hag 2:6
and after a *l. while* another saw him. Luke 22:58
yet a *l. while* and I am with you. John 7:33; 13:33
yet a *l. while* is the light. 12:35
a *l. while*, and the world. 14:19
a *l. while*, and ye shall not see me, and again a *l. while.* 16:16, 17, 19
a *l. while*? we cannot tell. 18
for yet a *l. while* and he. Heb 10:37

live
they shall sell the *l.* ox. Ex 21:35
a seraphim, having a *l.* coal. Isa 6:6
see **goat**

live
tree of life, and *l.* for. Gen 3:22
and my soul shall *l.* because. 12:13
O that Ishmael might *l.*! 17:18
escape, and my soul shall *l.* 19:20
for thee, and thou shall *l.* 20:7
by sword shalt thou *l.* and. 27:40
thy goods, let him not *l.* 31:32
Joseph said, This do, and *l.* 42:18
Joseph, doth my father yet *l.*? 45:3
daughter, then she shall *l.* Ex 1:16
no man see me and *l.* 33:20
he shall *l.* in them, I am. Lev 18:5 Neh 9:29; Ezek 20:11, 13, 21
upon serpent, shall *l.* Num 21:8
alas, who shall *l.* when God? 24:23
all the days they shall *l.* Deut 4:10
people hear, as thou hast, and *l.*? 33
word of the Lord doth man *l.* 8:3
days that ye *l.* on the earth. 12:1
to one of these cities and *l.* 19:5
learn to fear Lord as long as ye *l.* 31:13; 1 Ki 8:40
let Reuben *l.* and not die. Deut 33:6
only Rahab harlot shall *l.* Josh 6:17
league with them to let them *l.* 9:15
we will let them *l.* lest wrath. 20, 21
not only while I *l.* shew. 1 Sam 20:14
l. thou and thy children. 2 Ki 4:7
they save us alive, we shall *l.* 7:4
ways so long as they *l.* 2 Chr 6:31
if a man die, shall he *l.*? Job 14:14
wherefore do the wicked *l.*? 21:7
your heart shall *l.* for ever. Ps 22:26
still *l.* and not see corruption. 49:9
will I bless thee while I *l.* 63:4
hearts shall *l.* that seek God. 69:32
he shall *l.* 72:15
I shall not die but *l.* 118:17
understanding and I shall *l.* 119:144
let my soul *l.* and it shall. 175
I *l.* will I praise the Lord. 146:2
commandments and *l.* Pr 4:4; 7:2

forsake the foolish and l. Pr 9:6
he that hateth gifts shall l. 15:27
if a man l. many years. Eccl 6:3, 6
11:8
madness is in their heart while they l.
9:3
l. joyfully with the wife whom. 9
thy dead men shall l. Isa 26:19
by these things men l.: make me
to l. 38:16
hear, and your soul shall l. 55:3
he that falleth to Chaldeans, shall l.
Jer 21:9; 27:12, 17; 38:2, 17
obey . . . and thy soul shall l. 38:20
his shadow we shall l. Lam 4:20
he shall surely l. Ezek 3:21; 18:9
17; 33:13, 15, 16
when thou wast in thy blood, L. 16:6
kept all my statutes, shall surely l.
18:19, 21, 22; 20:11, 25
shall he l. 18:24
turn yourselves and l. 32; 33:11
on us, how should we then l.? 33:10
is lawful and right, he shall l. 19
Son of man, can these bones l.? 37:3
enter you, and ye shall l. 5, 6, 14
which liveth and moveth shall l.;
every thing shall l. whither. 47:9
revive us, we shall l. in. Hos 6:2
seek me, and ye shall l. Amos 5:4, 6
me to die than to l. Jonah 4:3, 8
the just shall l. by his faith.
Hab 2:4; Rom 1:17
l. with their children. Zech 10:9
man shall not l. by bread alone.
Mat 4:4; Luke 4:4
lay thy hand upon her, and she shall l.
Mat 9:18; Mark 5:23
they which l. delicately. Luke 7:25
this do, and thou shalt l. 10:28
of dead, for all l. unto him. 20:38
dead shall hear voice of the Son of
God, and l. John 5:25
sent me, and I l. by Father: so he
that eateth me, even shall l. 6:57
he were dead, yet he shall l. 11:25
because I l. ye shall l. also. 14:19
in him we l. and move. Acts 17:28
not fit that he should l. 22:22
that are dead to sin, l. Rom 6:2
we believe that we shall also l. 8
we are debtors, not to l. after. 8:12
ye l. after flesh ye shall die . . . mortify deeds of body, ye shall l. 13
doeth these things shall l. by them.
10:5; Gal 3:12
if possible, l. peaceably. Rom 12:18*
l. we l. to the Lord; whether we l.
therefore or die, we are. 14:8
they l. of the things of. 1 Cor 9:13*
preach gospel, should l. of gospel. 14
l. are delivered to death. 2 Cor 4:11
as dying, and behold we l. 6:9
in our hearts to die and l. with. 7:3
we shall l. with him by the. 13:4
brethren, be of one mind, l. in. 11
Gentiles to l. as Jews. Gal 2:14
dead to the law, that I might l. 19
I l., yet not I, but Christ liveth in me,
the life I now l. in flesh, I l. by. 20
the just shall l. by faith. 3:11
Heb 10:38
if we l. in the Spirit, let. Gal 5:25
for me to l. is Christ. Phil 1:21
if I l. in the flesh, this is fruit. 22
now we l. if ye stand. 1 Thes 3:8
died, that we should l. 5:10
if dead, we shall also l. 2 Tim 2:11
all that will l. godly shall suffer. 3:12
that we should l. soberly. Tit 2:12
to Father of spirits and l.? Heb 12:9
things willing to l. honestly. 13:18
if the Lord will we shall l. Jas 4:15
should l. to righteousness. 1 Pet 2:24
no longer should l. in the flesh. 4:2
but l. according to God in spirit. 6
ensample to those that l. 2 Pet 2:6
escaped from them that l. in. 18
his Son, that we might l. 1 John 4:9
had the wound and did l. Rev 13:14
see for **ever**

as I **live**

as truly as I l., earth. Num 14:21, 28
so long as I l. Job 27:6; Ps 104:33
116:2
As I l. saith the Lord. Isa 49:18
Jer 22:24; Ezek 5:11; 14:16, 18
20; 16:48; 17:16, 19; 18:3; 20:3
33; 33:11, 27; 34:8; 35:6, 11
Zeph 2:9; Rom 14:11
As I l. saith the king. Jer 46:18

may, might, or mayest **live**

that we may l. and not die.
Gen 42:2; 43:8; 47:19
that he may l. with thee. Lev 25:35
no usury, that thy brother may l. 36
to them that they may l. Num 4:19
for to do to them, that ye may l.
Deut 4:1; 5:33; 8:1; 30:6, 16
one of these cities he might l. 4:42
follow, that thou mayest l. 16:20
that thou and thy seed may l. 30:19
that the child may l. 2 Sam 12:22
bread, that you may l. 2 Ki 18:32
sceptre, that he may l. Esth 4:11
bountifully, that I may l. Ps 119:17
mercies come to me, that I may l. 77
to thy word, that I may l. 116
dwell in tents, that ye may l. many.
Jer 35:7
slain, that they may l. Ezek 37:9
not evil, that ye may l. Amos 5:14
and thou mayest l. long. Eph 6:3

not **live**

the mountain shall not l. Ex 19:13
not suffer a witch to l. 22:18
not l. by bread only, but by the word.
Deut 8:3; Mat 4:4; Luke 4:4
sure that he could not l. 2 Sam 1:10
is wanting he shall not l. 2 Ki 10:19
set house in order, thou shalt not l.
20:1; Isa 38:1
I loath it, I would not l. Job 7:16
wicked shall not l. half. Ps 55:23
dead, they shall not l. Isa 26:14
souls that should not l. Ezek 13:19
then live ? he shall not l. 18:13
whereby they should not l. 20:25
to him, thou shalt not l. Zech 13:3
cast out children, that they might not
l. Acts 7:19
crying, that he ought not to l. 25:24
vengeance suffereth not to l. 28:4
not l. to themselves. 2 Cor 5:15

lived

his son, while he yet l. Gen 25:6
Jacob l. in the land of Egypt. 47:28
and Caleb l. still. Num 14:38
beheld the serpent of brass he l. 21:9
the voice of God and l. Deut 5:26
if Absalom had l. and. 2 Sam 19:6
before Solomon his father while he
yet l. 1 Ki 12:6; 2 Chr 10:6
Amaziah l. after death of Jehoash.
2 Ki 14:17; 2 Chr 25:25
while he l. he blessed. Ps 49:18
breath came into them, and they l.
Ezek 37:10
had l. with a husband. Luke 2:36
l. in all good conscience. Acts 23:1
sect of our religion I l. a. 26:5
ye also walked sometime, when ye
l. in them. Col 3:7
ye have l. in pleasure. Jas 5:5
how much she hath l. Rev 18:7, 9
they l. with Christ. 20:4
the rest l. not again. 5

lively

Hebrew women are l. Ex 1:19
but my enemies are l. Ps 38:19
received the l. oracles. Acts 7:38*
us again to a l. hope. 1 Pet 1:3*
ye, as l. stones, are built up a. 2:5*

liver

the caul above the l. Ex 29:13, 22
Lev 3:4, 10, 15; 4:9; 7:4; 8:16
25; 9:10, 19
strike through his l. Pr 7:23
my l. is poured upon. Lam 2:11
he looked in the l. Ezek 21:21
see **caul**

lives

your blood of your l. Gen 9:5
to save your l. by a great. 45:7
thou hast saved our l.: let us. 47:25
they made their l. bitter. Ex 1:14
deliver our l. from death. Josh 2:13
were sore afraid of our l. 9:24
that jeoparded their l. Judg 5:18
thou lose thy life with l. of. 18:25
Saul and Jonathan lovely in their l.
2 Sam 1:23
saved l. of thy sons, wives. 19:5
that went in jeopardy of their l.
23:17; 1 Chr 11:19
and stood for their l. Esth 9:16
they lurk privily for their l. Pr 1:18
fall by them which seek their l.
Jer 19:7; 46:26
seek their l. shall straiten them. 19:9
flee, save your l., be like the. 48:6
with the peril of our l. Lam 5:9
their l. were prolonged. Dan 7:12
Son of man is not come to destroy
men's l. Luke 9:56
hazarded their l. for our. Acts 15:26
will be with damage of our l. 27:10
to lay down our l. for. 1 John 3:16
they loved not their l. to. Rev 12:11

livest

Levite as long as thou l. Deut 12:19
if thou being a Jew l. after. Gal 2:14
a name that thou l. and. Rev 3:1

liveth

that l. shall be meat for. Gen 9:3
talk with man, and he l. Deut 5:24
have lent him to the Lord as long as
he l. 1 Sam 1:28
for as long as son of Jesse l. 20:31
thus shall say to him that l. 25:6
as God l. unless thou. 2 Sam 2:27
as my lord the king l. surely. 15:21
Lord l. blessed be my rock. 22:47
Ps 18:46
this is my son that l. 1 Ki 3:23
Elijah said, See thy son l. 17:23
that my Redeemer l. Job 19:25
as God l. who hath taken. 27:2
what man that l. and shall? Ps 89:48
shalt swear, the Lord l. Jer 4:2
though they say, The Lord l. they. 5:2
swear by my name, the Lord l. 12:16
no more be said, The Lord l. 16:14
15; 23:7, 8
Egypt, saying, The Lord l. 44:26
every thing that l. and. Ezek 47:9
nor swear, the Lord l. Hos 4:15
Thy God, O Dan, l.; and, The manner
of Beer-sheba l. Amos 8:14
Jesus said, Go thy way, thy son l.
John 4:50, 51, 53
whosoever l. and believeth in. 11:26
that he l. he l. to God. Rom 6:10
over man as long as he l. 7:1, 2
so if while her husband l. she be. 3
for none of us l. or dieth to. 14:7
wife is bound as long as her husband
l. 1 Cor 7:39
l. by the power of God. 2 Cor 13:4
yet not I, but Christ l. Gal 2:20
she that l. in pleasure is dead while
she l. 1 Tim 5:6*
it is witnessed that he l. Heb 7:8
he ever l. to make intercession. 25
no strength while testator l. 9:17
I am he that l. and was. Rev 1:18
see for **ever**

as the Lord **liveth**

as the Lord l. if ye have saved.
Judg 8:19
part of kinsman, as the Lord l.
Ruth 3:13
for, as the Lord l., . . . though it be in
Jonathan. 1 Sam 14:39
as the Lord l. 45; 19:6; 20:21
25:26; 26:10, 16; 28:10; 29:6
2 Sam 4:9; 12:5; 14:11; 1 Ki 1:29
2:24; 2 Ki 5:20; 2 Chr 18:13
Jer 38:16
as the Lord l. there is but a step.
1 Sam 20:3
as the Lord God of Israel l. 25:34
1 Ki 17:1; 18:15
as the Lord l. and as my lord the
king l. 2 Sam 15:21
as the Lord thy God l. 1 Ki 17:12
18:10

as the Lord l. and thy soul liveth. 2 Ki 2:2, 4, 6; 4:30
as the Lord of hosts l. before whom I stand. 3:14; 5:16

as thy soul liveth

as thy soul l. I am the woman who stood praying. 1 Sam 1:26
Abner said, As thy soul l. O. 17:55
as soul l. there is but one step. 20:3
as thy soul l. seeing Lord. 25:26
as thy soul l. I will not do this thing. 2 Sam 11:11
as thy soul l. none can turn to the right hand or left. 14:19
as thy soul l., I will not leave thee. So they went. 2 Ki 2:2

living

[1] *One who is alive, or enjoys life,* 1 Ki 3:22. [2] *Of a well, or water always running,* John 4:10; 7:38. [3] *Spiritual,* Rom 12:1. [4] *A person's wealth, goods, or estate,* Luke 15:12.

having dominion over every l. thing. Gen 1:28
man became a l. soul. 2:7
Eve, mother of all l. 3:20
every l. thing of all flesh, two. 6:19
and every l. substance I have. 7:4
and every l. substance was. 23
Noah and every l. thing. 8:1
any more every thing l. 21
of any l. thing which is in the water. Lev 11:10
as for the l. bird, he shall take it. 14:6, 7, 53
not made abominable by any l. 20:25
he stood between the dead and the l. Num 16:48
off his kindness to the l. Ruth 2:20
shut up l. in widowhood. 2 Sam 20:3
the l. is my son, the dead thy son. 1 Ki 3:22, 23
divide the l. child in two, and. 25
l. child was, give her the l. 26
king said, Give her the l. child. 27
in whose hand is soul of every l. thing. Job 12:10
found in the land of the l. 28:13
is hid from the eyes of all l. 21
house appointed for all l. 30:23
enlightened with light of l. 33:30
of the Lord in land of l. Ps 27:13
thee out of the land of the l. 52:5
walk in the light of the l. 56:13
away both l., and in his wrath. 58:9*
blotted out of the book of the l. 69:28
I will walk before the Lord in the land of the l. 116:9
thou art my portion in the land of the l. 142:5
in thy sight shall no man l. be justified. 143:2
the desire of every l. thing. 145:16
dead, more than the l. Eccl 4:2
I considered all the l. under the. 15
knoweth to walk before the l. 6:8
end of all men, and the l. will lay. 7:2
joined to all the l., for a l. dog is. 9:4
for the l. know that they shall die. 5
a well of l. water. S of S 4:15
is written among the l. in. Isa 4:3
seek to their God for the l. to. 8:19
Lord in the land of the l. 38:11
the l. the l. he shall praise thee. 19
out of the land of the l. 53:8
forsaken fountain of l. waters. Jer 2:13; 17:13
off from the land of the l. 11:19
wherefore doth a l. man? Lam 3:39
glory in the land of the l. 26:20
caused terror in the land of the l. Ezek 32:23, 24, 25, 26, 27, 32
I have more than any l. Dan 2:30
to the intent that the l. may. 4:17
l. waters shall go out. Zech 14:8
not the God of the dead, but of the l. Mat 22:32; Mark 12:27; Luke 20:38
she had, even all her l. Mark 12:44
woman had spent all her l. Luke 8:43
he divided unto them his l. 15:12
substance with riotous l. Luke 15:13, 30
why seek ye the l. among? 24:5
given thee l. water. John 4:10
whence hast thou that l. water? 11
I am the l. bread which came. 6:51
as the l. Father hath sent me. 57
shall flow rivers of l. water. 7:38
your bodies a l. sacrifice. Rom 12:1
be Lord both of dead and l. 14:9
first man Adam was made a l. soul. 1 Cor 15:45
l. in the world, are ye? Col 2:20
l. in malice, envy, and. Tit 3:3
enter by a new and l. Heb 10:20
coming as to a l. stone. 1 Pet 2:4
Lamb shall lead them to l. Rev 7:17*
every l. soul died in the sea. 16:3
see **bird, creature, God**

lizard

the l., snail, and mole. Lev 11:30

lo

l. Sarah thy wife shall. Gen 18:10
l. it is yet high day, water ye. 29:7
l. I die. 50:5
l. I come in a cloud. Ex 19:9
l. we be here, and will. Num 14:40
l. the Lord hath kept thee. 24:11
I did but taste honey, and l. I must die. 1 Sam 14:43
l. I have sinned and. 2 Sam 24:17
strength, l. he is strong. Job 9:19
away, and l. he was not. Ps 37:36
l. I come. 40:7
l. we heard it at Ephratah. 132:6
l. the man that made not God. 52:7
l. they that are far from. 73:27
l. thine enemies, for l. thine. 92:9
l. this only have I found. Eccl 7:29
l. the winter is past. S of S 2:11
l. this is our God, we. Isa 25:9
the earth, and l. it was. Jer 4:23
I beheld, and l. there was no. 25
l. certainly in vain made he it. 8:8
for l. I begin to bring evil. 25:29
when l. he had given. Ezek 17:18
for l. it cometh. 30:9
l. it will come. 33:33
for l. they are gone. Hos 9:6
l. the days shall come. Amos 4:2
ye looked for much, and l. Hag 1:9
and l. the heavens were. Mat 3:16
l., here is Christ, or there. 24:23
l. I have told you. 28:7
l. I am with you. 20
Satan bound, l. these. Luke 13:16
l. nothing worthy of death. 23:15
unworthy, l. we turn to. Acts 13:46
l. I come to do thy will. Heb 10:7, 9

loaden

carriages were heavy l. Isa 46:1*

loadeth

Lord, who daily l. us. Ps 68:19*

loaf

(A loaf in Palestine in Bible times was a round, flat, crisp cake of dough baked on the hearth)

one l. of bread, one cake. Ex 29:23
every one a l. of bread. 1 Chr 16:3
they more than one l. Mark 8:14

Lo-ammi

call his name L. for ye. Hos 1:9

loan

for the l. which is lent. 1 Sam 2:20†

loath, see **lothe**

loaves

take ten l. and run. 1 Sam 17:17
made haste and took 200 l. 25:18
take with thee ten l. 1 Ki 14:3
the man of God 20 l. 2 Ki 4:42
have here but five l. Mat 14:17
and he took the five l. 19; Mark 6:38; Luke 9:13
said, How many l. have ye? Mat 15:34; Mark 6:38; 8:5
he took the seven l. and the fishes. Mat 15:36; Mark 8:6
the five l. of the 5000. Mat 16:9
nor the seven l. of the 4000. 10
eat of the l. were 5000. Mark 6:44
not the miracle of the l. 52
Friend, lend me three l. Luke 11:5
who hath five barley l. John 6:9
Jesus took the l. and distributed. 11
fragments of the barley l. 13
because ye did eat of the l. 26
see **bread**

wave **loaves**

shall bring two wave l. Lev 23:17

lock

myrrh on the handles of the l. S of S 5:5*

locked

the doors and l. them. Judg 3:23
doors of the parlour were l. 24

locks

let the l. of the hair of his. Num 6:5
seven l. of my head. Judg 16:13
to shave off the seven l. 19
set up doors, and l. thereof. Neh 3:3*, 6*, 13*, 14*, 15*
doves' eyes within thy l. S of S 4:1*
pomegranate within thy l. 3*
my l. are filled with the drops. 5:2
his l. are bushy, and black as. 11
thy temples within thy l. 6:7*
uncover thy l., make bare. Isa 47:2
nor suffer their l. to. Ezek 44:20
see **bars**

locust

(An insect of the grasshopper family, which travels in swarms, and commits great ravages on vegetation. It has been used as food from the earliest times, and resembles the shrimp in taste. At the present time it is eaten by only the poorest people)

remained not one l. in. Ex 10:19
l. after his kind, and bald l. ye. Lev 11:22
all thy trees shall the l. Deut 28:42
if there be in the land l. 1 Ki 8:37; 2 Chr 6:28
also their labour to the l. Ps 78:46
tossed up and down as the l. 109:23
l. eaten, and that which l. Joel 1:4
restore the years that the l. 2:25

locusts

to-morrow I will bring l. Ex 10:4
hand over Egypt for the l. 12
the east wind brought the l. 13
no such l. 14
the west wind took away the l. 19
l. shall consume it. Deut 28:38
if I command the l. to. 2 Chr 7:13
he spake, and l. came. Ps 105:34
the l. have no king, yet. Pr 30:27
running to and fro of l. Isa 33:4
thyself many as the l. Nah 3:15
thy crowned are as the l. and. 17
his meat was l. and wild honey. Mat 3:4; Mark 1:6
came out of the smoke l. Rev 9:3
shapes of l. were like to horses. 7

lodge

daughter of Zion is left as a l. in garden. Isa 1:8

lodge

the house for us to l. in. Gen 24:23
enough, and room to l. 25
them, l. here this night. Num 22:8
place where ye shall l. Josh 4:3
l. here, that thy heart. Judg 19:9
to l. in Gibeah or in Ramah. 13, 15; 20:4
the old man said, Only l. not. 19:20
thou lodgest I will l. Ruth 1:16
thy father will not l. 2 Sam 17:8
l. not this night in the plains. 16
let every one l. within. Neh 4:22
why l. ye about the wall? 13:21
they cause the naked to l. Job 24:7*
stranger did not l. in street. 31:32
my beloved, let us l. S of S 7:11
of Arabia shall ye l. Isa 21:13
and l. in monuments, and eat. 65:4
shall thy vain thoughts l.? Jer 4:14
beasts shall l. in upper. Zeph 2:14
birds of the air come and l. in the. Mat 13:32; Mark 4:32
with whom we should l. Acts 21:16

lodged
Jacob l. there that same. Gen 32:13
and himself l. that night in the. 21
into harlot's house, and l. Josh 2:1*
he and all Israel, and l. there. 3:1
over to the place where they l. 4:8
came to the camp, and l. in. 6:11
but Joshua l. that night among. 8:9
of Micah, they l. there. Judg 18:2
eat and drink, and l. there. 19:4
urged him, therefore he l. 7
into a cave, and l. there. 1 Ki 19:9
they l. round about the. 1 Chr 9:27
merchants l. without. Neh 13:20
righteousness l. in it, but. Isa 1:21
to Bethany and l. there. Mat 21:17
Simon were l. there. Acts 10:18
called he them in, and l. them. 23
Publius l. us three days. 28:7*
if she have l. strangers. 1 Tim 5:10*

lodgest
Ruth said, Where thou l. Ruth 1:16

lodgeth
l. with one Simon a. Acts 10:6

lodging
leave them in the l. Josh 4:3
them to his house to l. Judg 19:15
have taken up their l. at. Isa 10:29
the wilderness a l. place. Jer 9:2
many to him into his l. Acts 28:23
prepare me also a l. Philem 22

lodgings
I will enter into the l. 2 Ki 19:23

loft
and carried him into a l. 1 Ki 17:19*
Eutychus fell down from the third l. Acts 20:9*

loftily
corrupt, they speak l. Ps 73:8

loftiness
l. of man shall be bowed. Isa 2:17
the pride of Moab, his l. Jer 48:29

lofty
haughty, nor mine eyes l. Ps 131:1
a generation, O how l. are I Pr 30:13
the l. looks of man shall. Isa 2:11
5:15
Lord be on every one that is l. 12*
the l. city he layeth low to. 26:5
on a l. mountain hast thou. 57:7
thus saith high and l. One. 15

log
(*A measure; two-thirds of a pint*)
the priest shall take a l. of oil. Lev 14:10, 12, 24
shall take some of the l. of oil. 15
then he shall take a l. of oil. 21

loins
(*The word is used often in the phrase to gird up the loins, which means to prepare for active work, since the eastern peoples commonly wore flowing garments and when they wished to be active tucked them up out of the way*)
shall come out of thy l. Gen 35:11
put sackcloth upon his l. 37:34
the souls which came out of his l. 46:26; Ex 1:5
eat it, with your l. girded. Ex 12:11
breeches reach from the l. 28:42
smite through the l. of. Deut 33:11
sword fastened on his l. 2 Sam 20:8
the girdle about his l. 1 Ki 2:5
son shall come forth of thy l. 8:19
2 Chr 6:9
thicker than my father's l. 1 Ki 12:10
2 Chr 10:10
Elijah girded up his l. 1 Ki 18:46
put sackcloth on our l. 20:31
girded sackcloth on their l. 32
girt with girdle of leather about his l. 2 Ki 1:8; Mat 3:4; Mark 1:6
gird up thy l. 2 Ki 4:29; 9:1
Job 38:3; 40:7; Jer 1:17
he girdeth the l. of kings. Job 12:18
if his l. have not blessed me. 31:20
his strength is in his l. 40:16
my l. are filled with a. Ps 38:7
affliction upon our l. 66:11
and make their l. continually. 69:23
girdeth her l. with strength. Pr 31:17
girdle of their l. be loosed. Isa 5:27
shall be the girdle of his l. 11:5
sackcloth from off thy l., put. 20:2
are my l. filled with pain. 21:3
gird sackcloth upon your l. 32:11
I will loose the l. of kings to. 45:1
girdle and put it upon thy l. Jer 13:1
as the girdle cleaveth to the l. 11
man with his hands on his l. 30:6
and upon the l. shall be. 48:37
appearance of his l. upward. Ezek 1:27
l. downward, fire; from his l. 8:2
sigh with the breaking of thy l. 21:6
with girdles upon their l. 23:15
thou madest all their l. to be. 29:7
have linen breeches on their l. 44:18
the waters were to the l. 47:4
so the joints of his l. were. Dan 5:6
l. were girded with fine gold. 10:5
bring sackcloth on your l. Amos 8:10
make thy l. strong. Nah 2:1
pain is in all l. 10
let your l. be girded. Luke 12:35
of his l. he would raise. Acts 2:30
having your l. girt about. Eph 6:14
they came out of the l. of. Heb 7:5
for he was yet in the l. of his. 10
wherefore gird up the l. 1 Pet 1:13

Lois
in thy grandmother L. 2 Tim 1:5

long
fed me all my life l. Gen 48:15
trumpet soundeth l. Ex 19:13, 19
that thy days may be l. on. 20:12
when the cloud tarried l. Num 9:19
ye dwelt l. enough. Deut 1:6; 2:3
and shalt have remained l. 4:25
if the way be too l. for thee. 14:24
overtake him, because way is l. 19:6
make great plagues and of l. 28:59
when they make a l. blast. Josh 6:5
old, by reason of the very l. 9:13
ye dwelt in the wilderness a l. 24:7*
there was l. war between. 2 Sam 3:1
and hast not asked l. life. 1 Ki 3:11
2 Chr 1:11
for a l. season Israel. 2 Chr 15:3
l. life will I satisfy him. Ps 91:16
forty years l. was I grieved. 95:10
my soul l. dwelt with him. 120:6
plowers made l. their furrows. 129:3
those that have been l. dead. 143:3
and l. life shall they. Pr 3:2*
the goodman is gone a l. 7:19
that tarry l. at the wine. 23:30
by l. forbearing is a prince. 25:15
man goeth to his l. home. Eccl 12:5
my elect shall l. enjoy. Isa 65:22
this captivity is l.: build. Jer 29:28
shall the women eat their children of a span l.? Lam 2:20*
a great eagle l.-winged. Ezek 17:3
his branches became l. because. 31:5
suffer their locks to grow l. 44:20
time appointed was l. Dan 10:1*
not stay l. in the place of. Hos 13:13
repented l. ago in sackcloth and. Mat 11:21
and for pretence make l. prayers. 23:14; Mark 12:40; Luke 20:47
who go in l. clothing. Mark 12:38
Luke 20:46
sitting clothed in a l. Mark 16:5
avenge, though he bear l. Luke 18:7*
to see him of a l. season. 23:8
as Paul was l. preaching. Acts 20:9*
l. after there arose a tempest. 27:14
but after l. abstinence Paul. 21
if a man have l. hair. 1 Cor 11:14
if a woman have l. hair it is a. 15
that thou mayest live l. Eph 6:3
if I tarry l. that thou. 1 Tim 3:15
the husbandman hath l. Jas 5:7*
***see* ago, cubits, day**

long, *verb*
which l. for death, but. Job 3:21
grant me thing that I l. for! 6:8
for I l. to see you, that. Rom 1:11
by their prayer which l. 2 Cor 9:14
how greatly I l. after you. Phil 1:8

as* long *as
as l. as she is put apart. Lev 18:19
enjoy sabbaths, as l. as it. 26:34, 35
as l. as the cloud abode. Num 9:18
forsake not the Levite as l. as thou. Deut 12:19
fear the Lord as l. as you live. 31:13
lent to the Lord, as l. as. 1 Sam 1:28
as l. as son of Jesse liveth. 20:31
any thing as l. as we were. 25:15
as l. as he sought the Lord he prospered. 2 Chr 26:5
as l. as she lay desolate she. 36:21
fear thee as l. as sun and. Ps 72:5
be continued as l. as the sun. 17
to the Lord as l. as I live. 104:33
call upon him as l. as I live. 116:2
as l. as they, and as broad as they. Ezek 42:11*
as l. as bridegroom is with them. Mat 9:15; Mark 2:19
as l. as I am in the world. I am the. John 9:5*
dominion over a man as l. as he. Rom 7:1
wife is bound as l. as her. 1 Cor 7:39
heir as l. as he is a child. Gal 4:1
daughters ye are as l. as. 1 Pet 3:6*
as l. as I am in this tabernacle. 2 Pet 1:13

***so* long**
is his chariot so l. in? Judg 5:28
found in thy servant, so l. 1 Sam 29:8
so l. as the whoredoms. 2 Ki 9:22
they may fear thee so l. 2 Chr 6:31
so l. as I see Mordecai. Esth 5:13
shall not reproach me so l. Job 27:6
peace so l. as the moon. Ps 72:7
that he tarried so l. Luke 1:21
bound to her husband so l. Rom 7:2
to-day, after so l. a time. Heb 4:7

long *time*
been there a l. time. Gen 26:8
dwelt in Egypt a l. time. Num 20:15
besiege a city a l. time. Deut 20:19
war a l. time with kings. Josh 11:18
a l. time after that Joshua. 23:1*
ark abode the time was l. 1 Sam 7:2
woman that had l. time. 2 Sam 14:2
not done it of a l. time. 2 Chr 30:5*
l. time holden my peace. Isa 42:14
and forsake us so l. time. Lam 5:20
after a l. time the lord of those servants. Mat 25:19; Luke 20:9
which had devils l. time. Luke 8:27
into a far country for a l. time. 20:9
that he had been a l. time. John 5:6
have I been so l. time with? 14:9
because of l. time he had. Acts 8:11
l. time abode they with. 14:3, 28
judgement of l. time. 2 Pet 2:3*

long *while*
he talked a l. while till. Acts 20:11

longed
David l. to go forth. 2 Sam 13:39
David l. and said, O that one. 23:15
1 Chr 11:17
behold, I have l. after. Ps 119:40
l. for thy commandments. 131
I have l. for thy salvation. 174
for he l. after you all. Phil 2:26
brethren dearly beloved and l. 4:1

longedst
thou sore l. after thy. Gen 21:30

longer
she could no l. hide him. Ex 2:3
you go, and ye shall stay no l. 9:28
could not any l. stand. Judg 2:14
he tarried l. than the. 2 Sam 20:5
wait for the Lord any l.? 2 Ki 6:33
the measure thereof is l. Job 11:9
Lord could no l. bear. Jer 44:22
for thou mayest be no l. Luke 16:2
desired him to tarry l. Acts 18:20
he ought not to live any l. 25:24
dead to sin, live any l. Rom 6:2
no l. under a schoolmaster. Gal 3:25
when we could no l. forbear. 1 Thes 3:1, 5
drink no l. water, but. 1 Tim 5:23
that he no l. live the rest. 1 Pet 4:2
should be time no l. Rev 10:6

longeth
my son Shechem *l.* for. *Gen* 34:8
because thy soul *l.* to. *Deut* 12:20
my flesh *l.* for thee in. *Ps* 63:1
my soul *l.* for the courts of. 84:2

longing
fail with *l.* for them. *Deut* 28:32
satisfieth the *l.* soul. *Ps* 107:9
my soul breaketh for the *l.* 119:20

longsuffering
Lord God merciful and gracious, *l.*
Ex 34:6*; *Num* 14:18*
Ps 86:15*; *2 Pet* 3:9
O Lord, take me not away in thy *l.*
Jer 15:15
thou the riches of his *l.* *Rom* 2:4
endured with much *l.* vessels. 9:22
by knowledge, by *l.* *2 Cor* 6:6
of the Spirit is love, *l.* *Gal* 5:22
l., forbearing one another. *Eph* 4:2
strengthened to all *l.* with. *Col* 1:11
as elect of God, meekness, *l.* 3:12
Christ might shew all *l.* *1 Tim* 1:16
fully known my faith, *l.* *2 Tim* 3:10
rebuke, exhort with all *l.* and. 4:2
when *l.* of God waited. *1 Pet* 3:20
l. of our Lord is salvation. *2 Pet* 3:15

look, -s
bring down high *l.* *Ps* 18:27
that hath a high *l.* I will not. 101:5
a proud *l.*, a lying tongue. *Pr* 6:17*
high *l.* and proud heart is sin. 21:4
the lofty *l.* of man shall be. *Isa* 2:11
punish the glory of his high *l.* 10:12
dismayed at their *l.* *Ezek* 2:6; 3:9
whose *l.* was more stout. *Dan* 7:20

look, *verb*
l. from the place where. *Gen* 13:14
l. towards heaven, and tell. 15:5
thy life, *l.* not behind thee. 19:17
l. ye so sadly to-day? 40:7
now let Pharaoh *l.* out a man. 41:33
Jacob said, Why *l.* ye one? 42:1
l. to it; for evil is. *Ex* 10:10
and their faces shall *l.* 25:20
l. that thou make them after. 40
then the priest shall *l.* *Lev* 13:39
priest shall *l.* and behold. 53, 56
shall *l.* if the plague. 14:3, 39, 44
l. not to the stubbornness. *Deut* 9:27
thine eyes shall *l.* and fail. 28:32
ruddy, and goodly to *l.* *1 Sam* 16:12
l. how thy brethren fare. 17:18
go up now, *l.* toward. *1 Ki* 18:43
I would not *l.* toward. *2 Ki* 3:14
l. when messenger cometh. 6:32
l. out there Jehu, and go in. 9:2
l. even out best and meetest. 10:3
l. there be none of the servants. 23
come, let us *l.* one another. 14:8
God of our fathers *l.* *1 Chr* 12:17
let it *l.* for light, but. *Job* 3:9
therefore shall no man *l.* 20:21*
l. to heavens and see, and. 35:5
my prayer to thee, and *l.* *Ps* 5:3*
that I am not able to *l.* up. 40:12
as the eyes of servants *l.* to. 123:2
let thine eyes *l.* right on. *Pr* 4:25
to know thy flocks, and *l.* well. 27:23
l. out at the windows. *Eccl* 12:3
l. from top of Amana. *S of S* 4:8
if one *l.* unto the land. *Isa* 5:30
on the Lord, I will *l.* for him. 8:17
curse their king and God, and *l.* 21
they shall *l.* unto earth, and. 22
in that day shall a man *l.* 17:7
he shall not *l.* to the altars. 8
l. away from me; I will weep. 22:4
l. in that day to the armour. 8
l. not to the Holy One of Israel. 31:1
hear ye deaf, *l.* ye blind, that. 42:18
l. unto me, and be saved, all. 45:22
l. to the rock whence ye are. 51:1
l. to Abraham your father and to. 2
they all *l.* to their own way. 56:11*
we *l.* for judgement, but. 59:11
but to this man will I *l.* that. 66:2
and while ye *l.* for light. *Jer* 13:16
take and *l.* well to him, do. 39:12
come with me and I will *l.* well. 40:4
mighty ones are fled, and *l.* 46:5
the fathers shall not *l.* back. 47:3
all of them princes to *l.* *Ezek* 23:15
remembrance when they *l.* 29:16
who *l.* to other gods, and. *Hos* 3:1
I will *l.* again towards. *Jonah* 2:4
I will *l.* unto the Lord. *Mi* 7:7
but none shall *l.* back. *Nah* 2:8
or do we *l.* for another? *Mat* 11:3
Luke 7:19, 20
hands on eyes, and made him *l.* up.
Mark 8:25
things begin, then *l.* up. *Luke* 21:28
search and *l.*: for out of. *John* 7:52
l. ye out seven men of. *Acts* 6:3
be a question of words, *l.* ye. 18:15
I *l.* for him with the brethren.
1 Cor 16:11
Israel could not stedfastly *l.* to the
end. *2 Cor* 3:13
while we *l.* not at things which. 4:18
from whence we *l.* for. *Phil* 3:20
to them that *l.* for him. *Heb* 9:28
angels desire to *l.* into. *1 Pet* 1:12
we *l.* for new heavens. *2 Pet* 3:13
seeing ye *l.* for such things, be. 14
l. to yourselves, that we. *2 John* 8
and no man was able to *l.* *Rev* 5:3
worthy to read the book nor *l.* 4

look *down*
l. down from thy holy. *Deut* 26:15
l. down, behold, and visit. *Ps* 80:14
righteousness shall *l. down*. 85:11
l. down from heaven, and. *Isa* 63:15
till Lord *l. down* and behold from
heaven. *Lam* 3:50

look *on*, or *upon*
be in cloud, and I will *l. upon* it.
Gen 9:16
art a fair woman to *l. upon*. 12:11
Rebekah was very fair to *l. upon*.
24:16; 26:7
afraid to *l. upon* God. *Ex* 3:6
Lord *l. upon* you and judge. 5:21
and Moses did *l. upon* all. 39:43
l. on the plague in the skin of the
flesh. *Lev* 13:3, 21, 25, 26, 31
32, 34, 43, 50
the priest shall *l. on* him. 3, 5, 6
27, 36
the priest shall *l. upon* it. 14:48
for a fringe, that ye may *l. upon* it.
Num 15:39
Gideon said, *L. on* me. *Judg* 7:17
if thou wilt indeed *l. on*. *1 Sam* 1:11
l. not *on* his countenance or. 16:7
l. upon such a dead dog. *2 Sam* 9:8
very beautiful to *l upon*. 11:2
Lord will *l. on* my affliction. 16:12
Lord *l. upon* it and require it.
2 Chr 24:22
queen was fair to *l. on*. *Esth* 1:11
be content, *l. upon* me. *Job* 6:28
l. on every one that is proud. 40:12
stare and *l. upon* me. *Ps* 22:17
l. upon mine affliction and. 25:18*
how long wilt thou *l. on*? 35:17
and *l. upon* the face of thine. 84:9
l. thou *upon* me, and be. 119:132*
let thine eyes *l.* right *on*. *Pr* 4:25
l. not thou *upon* the wine. 23:31
l. not *upon* me, because I am black.
S of S 1:6
return, that we may *l. upon*. 6:13
narrowly *l. upon* thee. *Isa* 14:16
l. upon Zion. 33:20
l. upon the earth beneath. 51:6
forth and *l. upon* the carcases. 66:24
let our eye *l. upon* Zion. *Mi* 4:11
l. upon thee, shall flee. *Nah* 3:7
purer eyes than to *l. upon* iniquity.
Hab 1:13
mayest *l. upon* their nakedness. 2:15
l. upon me whom they pierced.
Zech 12:10
I beseech thee, *l. upon*. *Luke* 9:38
your eyes, and *l. upon*. *John* 4:35
l. upon him whom they pierced.
19:37
Peter and John said, *L. on* us.
Acts 3:4, 12*
l. upon things after outward appearance. *2 Cor* 10:7
l. not every man *on* his. *Phil* 2:4
he that sat was to *l. upon*. *Rev* 4:3

looked
God *l.* on the earth and it. *Gen* 6:12
the men rose up, and *l.* 18:16
his wife *l.* back. 19:26
l. out at a window. 26:8
the Lord hath *l.* upon my. 29:32
the keeper of the prison *l.* not. 39:23
Joseph *l.* on them, behold they. 40:6
Moses went and *l.* on. *Ex* 2:11
he *l.* this way and that way. 12
and God *l.* upon the children. 25
Lord had *l.* on their affliction. 4:31
Deut 26:7
the Lord *l.* on the host of. *Ex* 14:24
l. toward the wilderness. 16:10
the people *l.* after Moses till. 33:8
Aaron *l.* on Miriam. *Num* 12:10
l. towards the tabernacle. 16:42
he *l.* on Amalek, he took up. 24:20
l. on the Kenites, and took up. 21
when the men of Ai *l.* *Josh* 8:20
mother of Sisera *l.* out. *Judg* 5:28
the Lord *l.* upon him, and said. 6:14
Manoah and his wife *l.* on. 13:19, 30
Benjamites *l.* behind them. 20:40
they had *l.* into the ark. *1 Sam* 6:19
I have *l.* on my people. 9:16
the watchmen of Saul *l.* and. 14:16
when they were come, he *l.* 16:6
the Philistines *l.* about, and. 17:42
Saul *l.* behind him, David stood.
24:8; *2 Sam* 1:7
Abner *l.* behind him. *2 Sam* 2:20
Michal *l.* through a window. 6:16
they *l.* but there was none. 22:42
servant went up and *l.* *1 Ki* 18:43
turned back and *l.* on. *2 Ki* 2:24
the people *l.* and behold he. 6:30
Jezebel painted, and *l.* out at. 9:30
l. one another in the face at. 14:11
when Judah *l.* back. *2 Chr* 13:14
l. on him, and behold he was. 26:20
sight of all who *l.* on her. *Esth* 2:15
troops of Tema *l.*, Sheba. *Job* 6:19
the Lord *l.* to see if any. *Ps* 14:2
l. to him, and were lightened. 34:5
God *l.* down on the children of. 53:2
l. down from his sanctuary. 102:19
l. they shaked their heads. 109:25
because the sun hath *l.* *S of S* 1:6*
he *l.* that it should bring. *Isa* 5:2
he *l.* for judgement, but behold. 7
ye have not *l.* to the maker. 22:11
terrible things which we *l.* not. 64:3
we *l.* for peace, no good came.
Jer 8:15; 14:19
certainly this is the day that we *l.* for.
Lam 2:16
whither the head *l.* they. *Ezek* 10:11
consulted with images, he *l.* 21:21
let our countenance be *l.* *Dan* 1:13
not have *l.* on the day. *Ob* 12
thou shouldest not have *l.* on. 13
ye *l.* for much, and lo it. *Hag* 1:9
when he *l.* round about. *Mark* 3:5
5:32; 10:23
he *l.* up to heaven, and blessed. 6:41
he *l.* and said, I see men as. 8:24
they *l.* they saw the stone. 16:4
l. on me to take away. *Luke* 1:25
to all that *l.* for redemption. 2:38
likewise a Levite came and *l.* 10:32
the Lord turned, and *l.* 22:61
then the disciples *l.* one. *John* 13:22
while they *l.* stedfastly. *Acts* 1:10
after they had *l.* a great while. 28:6*
for he *l.* for a city which. *Heb* 11:10
which we have *l.* upon. *1 John* 1:1

looked with *eyes*
Jacob lifted up his *eyes* and *l.*
Gen 33:1
lifted up their *eyes* and *l.* 37:25
I lifted up mine *eyes* and *l.* *Dan* 10:5
Zechariah lifted his *eyes* and *l.*
Zech 2:1; 5:9; 6:1

***I* looked**
have *I* also here *l.* after. *Gen* 16:13
I l. and behold ye had sinned.
Deut 9:16
when *I l.* for good, then. *Job* 30:26
I l. for some to take pity. *Ps* 69:20
I l. on my right hand, and. 142:4
at the window, *I l.* through. *Pr* 7:6

I l. upon it, and received. Pr 24:32
I l. on all the works that. Eccl 2:11
I l. that it should bring forth grapes. Isa 5:4
and I l. and there was none to. 63:5
I l. and behold. Ezek 1:4; 2:9; 8:7; 10:1, 9; 44:4
I Daniel l. and behold. Dan 12:5
I have l. and behold a candlestick. Zech 4:2
and the same hour I l. up. Acts 22:13
I l. and behold. Rev 4:1; 6:8; 14:1; 14; 15:5

lookest

thou l. narrowly to all. Job 13:27*
why l. on them that deal? Hab 1:13

looketh

if leprosy cover wheresoever priest l. Lev 13:12*
when he l. on the serpent. Num 21:8
Pisgah, which l. toward. 20; 23:28
man l. on the outward. 1 Sam 16:7
as an hireling l. for the. Job 7:2
l. to the ends of the earth. 28:24
he l. on men, and if any say. 33:27*
the Lord l. from heaven. Ps 33:13
he l. on all the inhabitants of. 14
he l. on the earth, and it. 104:32
the prudent l. well to. Pr 14:15
she l. well to the ways of. 31:27
he l. forth at the window. S of S 2:9
that l. forth as the morning? 6:10
as the tower which l. toward. 7:4
when he that l. upon it. Isa 28:4
the door that l. toward. Ezek 8:3
gate which l. eastward. 11:1; 40:6; 22*; 43:1; 44:1; 46:1, 12; 47:2
gate of the court that l. 40:20
l. on a woman to lust. Mat 5:28
lord come when that servant l. not for him. 24:50; Luke 12:46
l. into the perfect law of. Jas 1:25

looking

three oxen l. toward the north. 1 Ki 7:25
Michal l. out at a window, saw David. 1 Chr 15:29
three oxen l. toward the south. 2 Chr 4:4
mine eyes fail with l. upward. Isa 38:14
l. up to heaven, he blessed. Mat 14:19; Luke 9:16
and l. up to heaven, he. Mark 7:34
there were also women l. on. 15:40
l. round about them all. Luke 6:10
and l. back, is fit for the. 9:62
hearts failing them for l. 21:26*
John l. on Jesus saith. John 1:36
l. in, saw linen clothes lying. 20:5
l. stedfastly on him, saw. Acts 6:15
they ready, l. for a promise. 23:21
l. for that blessed hope. Tit 2:13
but a certain fearful l. for. Heb 10:27
l. unto Jesus the author and. 12:2
l. diligently, lest any fail of the. 15
l. for the coming of the. 2 Pet 3:12
l. for the mercy of our Lord. Jude 21

lookingglass, -es

(*Properly, as in Revisions,* mirror, mirrors, *as they were made of polished metal, not of glass*)
laver and foot of l.-glasses. Ex 38:8
sky as a molten l.-glass. Job 37:18

loops

make l. of blue. Ex 26:4, 5
l. shalt thou make. 5, 10
put taches in the l. 11
made l. of blue. 36:11
fifty l. made he. 12, 17

loose

Naphtali is a hind let l. Gen 49:21
let the living bird l. into. Lev 14:7
he would let l. his hand and cut me. Job 6:9
they have let l. the bridle. 30:11
lo I see four men l. Dan 3:25

loose, verb

and l. his shoe from. Deut 25:9
l. thy shoe from off thy. Josh 5:15
canst thou l. the bands of? Job 38:31
l. those that are appointed to death. Ps 102:20
go and l. the sackcloth. Isa 20:2
I will l. the loins of kings. 45:1
O Jerusalem, l. thyself from. 52:2
to l. the bands of wickedness. 58:6
and now behold I l. thee. Jer 40:4
whatsoever ye l. on earth. Mat 16:19; 18:18
an ass tied and colt, l. and bring. 21:2; Mark 11:2, 4; Luke 19:30
why do ye l. him? Luke 19:31, 33
Jesus said, L. him. John 11:44
shoes of his feet I am not worthy to l. Acts 13:25
been given, that he might l. 24:26
who is worthy to l. the seals? Rev 5:2
hath prevailed to l. the seven. 5
l. the four angels bound in. 9:14

loosed

that the breastplate be not l. Ex 28:28; 39:21
him that hath his shoe l. Deut 25:10
his bands l. from off. Judg 15:14
because he l. my cord. Job 30:11
l. the bands of the wild ass? 39:5
the king sent and l. him. Ps 105:20
thy servant, thou hast l. 116:16
silver cord be l., or bowl. Eccl 12:6
girdle of their loins be l. Isa 5:27
tacklings are l. they could. 33:23
hasteneth that he may be l. 51:14
joints of his loins were l. Dan 5:6
thou shalt loose on earth, shall be l. in heaven. Mat 16:19; 18:18
with compassion, and l. him. 18:27*
the string of his tongue was l. Mark 7:35; Luke 1:64
woman, thou art l. from. Luke 13:12
ought not this woman to be l.? 16
raised up, having l. the. Acts 2:24
when Paul and his company l. 13:13
every one's bands were l. 16:26
on the morrow he l. him from. 22:30
hearkened, and not have l. 27:21
l. the rudder bands, and hoised. 40
be dead, she is l. from. Rom 7:2*
art thou l. from wife? 1 Cor 7:27
the four angels were l. Rev 9:15
after that he must be l. a. 20:3, 7

looseth

he l. the bond of kings. Job 12:18
food to hungry, the Lord l. Ps 149:7

loosing

what do ye, l. the colt? Mark 11:5
as they were l. the colt. Luke 19:33
l. from Troas, we came. Acts 16:11*
l. thence, they sailed close. 27:13

lop

behold the Lord shall l. Isa 10:33

Lord

(*This word means, in general, one with power and authority, a master or ruler. The Hebrew word transliterated* Jehovah *is usually rendered in the Old Testament by* LORD *written in small capitals. This the American Revision changes to* Jehovah. *Otherwise the word is used for Jesus Christ, for the Holy Spirit, for a husband, and for any one whom it was desired to address deferentially*)
too hard for the L.? Gen 18:14
the L. before whom I walk. 24:40
we saw certainly the L. 26:28
again, then shall the L. be. 28:21
L. was with Joseph. 39:2, 21, 23
who is the L. that I should obey? Ex 5:2
and the L. did so, and there. 8:24
the earth is the L.'s. 9:29; Ps 24:1; 1 Cor 10:26
the L. be so with you, as I. Ex 10:10
because of that which the L. 13:8
beast the male shall be the L.'s. 12
be unto thee holy for the L. 30:37
on the L.'s side? let him come. 32:26
for L. whose name is jealous. 34:14
all the fat is the L.'s. Lev 3:16
Aaron shall cast one lot for the L. 16:8; 25:4; 27:2
thou L. art among this people, that thou L. art seen face. Num 14:14
therefore the L. will not be. 43
are given as a gift for the L. 18:6
that I may know what the L. 22:19
all that the L. speaketh that. 23:26
the L. hath kept thee back. 24:11
brought oblation for the L. 31:50
for they have wholly followed the L. 32:12; Deut 1:36
so shall the L. do to all kingdoms. Deut 3:21
know that the L. he is God. 4:35; 39; 1 Ki 18:39
I stood between the L. and you. Deut 5:5
heaven of heavens is the L.'s. 10:14
L. of lords, a great God, a. 17
ye have seen all that the L. 29:2
L. hath not given you an heart to. 4
hath the L. done thus to this land? 24; 1 Ki 9:8; 2 Chr 7:21
L. shall do to them as he did to Sihon. Deut 31:4
do ye thus requite the L.? 32:6
to flight, except the L. had. 30
O people, saved by the L. 33:29
swear unto me by the L. Josh 2:12; 1 Sam 24:21
even the L. of all the. Josh 3:11, 13
the L. do to all your enemies. 10:25
if so be the L. will be with me. 14:12
the L. was with Judah. Judg 1:19
and the L. was with the house. 22
which knew not the L. 2:10
is not the L. gone out before? 4:14
if the L. be with us, why is? 6:13
meet me shall surely be the L. 11:31
now know I that the L. will. 17:13
L. do so to me and more. Ruth 1:17; 1 Sam 20:13
the L. be with you. Ruth 2:4; 2 Chr 20:17; 2 Thes 3:16
none holy as the L. 1 Sam 2:2
pillars of the earth are the L.'s. 8
it is the L. let him do what seemeth. 3:18; John 21:7
Samuel grew, and the L. 1 Sam 3:19; 18:12, 14; 2 Ki 18:7; 1 Chr 9:20
this great thing which the L. will do. 1 Sam 12:16
the L. be with thee. 17:37; 20:13; 1 Chr 22:11, 16
the L. be between thee and me. 1 Sam 20:23, 42
L. art become their God. 2 Sam 7:24; 1 Chr 17:22
L. do what seemeth him good. 2 Sam 10:12; 1 Chr 19:13
if the L. be God, follow. 1 Ki 18:21
if the L. do not help. 2 Ki 6:27
what should I wait for the L.? 33
and see my zeal for the L. 10:16
am I now come up without the L.? 18:25; Isa 36:10
for great is the L. 1 Chr 16:25; Ps 48:1; 145:3
now L. thou art God. 1 Chr 17:26
that which is thine for the L. 21:24
for man, but for the L. 2 Chr 19:6
and the L. shall be with the good. 11
Manasseh knew that the L. 33:13
even that thou art L. alone. Neh 9:6; Isa 37:20
L. hath set apart the godly. Ps 4:3
nation, whose God is the L. 33:12
my bones say, L. who is? 35:10
for he is thy L.; worship. 45:11
if I regard iniquity, the L. will. 66:18
for thou L. art good, ready. 86:5
thou L. art most high for ever. 92:8; 97:9
know ye that the L. he is God. 100:3
do thou for me, O God the L. 109:21; 140:7
they may know that thou L. 109:27
gracious is the L. and. 116:5
this is the L.'s doing; it is. 118:23
God is the L. 27
if it had not been the L. 124:1, 2
L. shouldest mark iniquity. 130:3
find out a place for the L. 132:5
lest the L. see it, and it. Pr 24:18

thee, and say, Who is the L.? Pr 30:9
but shall stay upon the L. Isa 10:20
L. shall be known to Egypt. 19:21
the L. will be to us a place. 33:21
did not the L., he against whom we
 sinned? 42:24
sing, O heavens, for the L. 44:23
the L. will go before you. 52:12
where is the L. that brought us up
 out of Egypt? Jer 2:6, 8
for they are not the L.'s. 5:10
is not the L. in Zion? is not? 8:19
know that my name is the L. 16:21*
if so be that the L. will deal. 21:2
called, The L. our Righteousness.
 23:6; 33:16
saying, Know the L. 31:34
 Heb 8:11
the L. the hope of their. Jer 50:7
remember the L. afar off. 51:50
for the L. will not cast. Lam 3:31
till the L. look down, and. 50
possess it, whereas the L. was there.
 Ezek 35:10
your God is a L. of kings. Dan 2:47
face to shine, for the L.'s sake. 9:17
thou shalt know the L. Hos 2:20
have not known the L. 5:4
they shall walk after the L. 11:10
his reproach shall his L. 12:14
fear not, for the L. will. Joel 2:21
be evil in the city, and L. Amos 3:6
so the L. shall be with you. 5:14
kingdom shall be the L.'s. Ob 21
L. on the head of them. Mi 2:13
the L. and say, Is not the L.? 3:11
the L. shall reign over them in. 4:7
and what doth the L. require? 6:8
that swear by the L. and. Zeph 1:5
when eyes of man shall be toward
 the L. Zech 9:1
the L. shall be seen over them. 14
then shall the L. go forth. 14:3
in that day shall there be one L. 9
that saith, L. L. shall enter into the
 kingdom. Mat 7:21, 22
L. if thou wilt, thou canst make.
 8:2; Luke 5:12
L. save us. Mat 8:25
they said, Yea, L. 9:28; 13:51*
L. save me. 14:30
saying, L. help me. 15:25
she said, Truth, L.: yet the dogs. 27
L. that our eyes may. 20:33
L. hath need of. 21:3; Mark 11:3
 Luke 19:31, 34
doth David call him L.? Mat 22:43
 45; Mark 12:37; Luke 20:44
not what hour your L. Mat 24:42
whom his L. shall find so doing.
 46; Luke 12:43
the L. of that servant shall come.
 Mat 24:50; Luke 12:46
L. L. open to us. Mat 25:11
enter into the joy of thy L. 21
L. when saw thee an hungered?
 37, 44
L. is it I? 26:22
the place where the L. lay. 28:6
Son of man is L. of sabbath.
 Mark 2:28; Luke 6:5
how great things the L. Mark 5:19
L. I believe, help thou. 9:24*
 John 9:38; 11:27
L. that I might receive my sight.
 Mark 10:51*
L. working with them. Mark 16:20
ready a people for the L. Luke 1:17
thus L. dealt with me, to take. 25
Saviour, which is Christ the L. 2:11
why call ye me L. L. and do? 6:46
a man said to him, L. I. 9:57, 61
L. teach us to pray, as John. 11:1
L. let it alone this year, till. 13:8
apostles said unto the L. 17:5
where, L.? 37
L. remember me when thou. 23:42*
saying, The L. is risen indeed. 24:34
L., to whom shall we go? John 6:68
she said, No man, L. 8:11
who is he, L., that I might? 9:36
they said to him, L. come. 11:34
ye call me Master and L. 13:13
L. who is it? 25
they have taken the L. out. John 20:2
we have seen the L. 25
ask him, knowing it was the L. 21:12
Peter saith, L. what shall this? 21
whom ye crucified, both L. Acts 2:36
L. thou art God. 4:24
now L. behold threatenings. 29
who art thou, L.? 9:5; 26:15
and said, What is it, L.? 10:4
Not so L., for I have never. 14; 11:8
Jesus Christ, he is L. of all. 10:36
I said, What shall I do, L.? 22:10
short work will the L. Rom 9:28
same L. over all is rich unto. 10:12
he might be L. of the dead. 14:9
not have crucified the L. 1 Cor 2:8
the L. gave to every man. 3:5
he that judgeth me is the L. 4:4
to you, if the L. will. 19; Jas 4:15
body is for the L. 1 Cor 6:13
yet not I, but the L. 7:10
of administrations, but the same L.
 12:5
second man is the L. 15:47*
be present with the L. 2 Cor 5:8
I speak it not after the L. 11:17
one L., one faith, one. Eph 4:5
even as the L. the church. 5:29*
that Jesus Christ is L. Phil 2:11
the L. is at hand. 4:5
we ever be with the L. 1 Thes 4:17
the King of kings, and L. 1 Tim 6:15
that call on the L. 2 Tim 2:22
out of them all the L. delivered. 3:11
which the L. shall give me. 4:8
notwithstanding the L. stood. 17
began to be spoken by the L. Heb 2:3
saying, Know the L.: for all. 8:11
and the L. shall raise. Jas 5:15
one day is with the L. 2 Pet 3:8
Michael said, The L. rebuke. Jude 9
our L. was crucified. Rev 11:8
become the kingdoms of our L. 15
for he is L. of lords. 17:14; 19:16
see **anointed, appeared, bless, blessed, called, cast** *out,* **chosen, choose, commanded, fear, feared, give, given, liveth, made, rejoice, shewed, smite**

against the **Lord**

sinned ag. the L. your. Ex 10:16
 Josh 7:20; 2 Sam 12:13
murmurings ag. the L. Ex 16:7, 8
have trespassed ag. the L. Lev 5:19
 Num 5:6; 31:16
commit trespass ag. the L. Lev 6:2
only rebel not ag. the L. Num 14:9
 Josh 22:19
together ag. the L. Num 16:11
 27:3; Ps 2:2; Acts 4:26
we have spoken ag. the L. Num 21:7
when they strove ag. the L. 26:9
ye have sinned ag. the L. 32:23
 Jer 40:3; 44:23
have sinned ag. the L. Deut 1:41
 1 Sam 7:6; Jer 8:14
ye have been rebellious ag. the L.
 9:7, 24; 31:27
might rebel this day ag. the L.
 Josh 22:16
ye rebel this day ag. the L. 18
if in transgression ag. the L. 22
we should rebel ag. the L. 29
committed this trespass ag. the L. 31
if a man sin ag. the L. 1 Sam 2:25
sin ag. the L. in ceasing to. 12:23
the people sin ag. the L. in. 14:33
and eat, and sin not ag. the L. 34
Israel had sinned ag. the L. their
 God. 2 Ki 17:7
things not right ag. the L. God. 9
transgression he committed ag. the
 L. 1 Chr 10:13
because they had transgressed ag.
 the L. 2 Chr 12:2
warn them that they trespass not ag.
 the L. 19:10
offended already ag. the L. 28:13
transgressed sore ag. the L. 19
he trespass yet more ag. the L. 22
rulers take counsel ag. the L. Ps 2:2
heart fretteth ag. the L. Pr 19:3
wisdom nor counsel ag. the L. 21:30
doings are ag. the L. Isa 3:8
iniquity to utter error ag. the L. 32:6
and lying ag. the L. 59:13
taught rebellion ag. the L. Jer 28:16
 29:32
he magnified himself ag. the L 48:26
 42
because they have sinned ag. the L
 50:7
shoot at Babylon: for she hath sinned
 ag. the L. 14, 29
hast striven ag. the L. 24; Zeph 1:17
up thyself ag. the L. Dan 5:23
treacherously ag. the L. Hos 5:7
do ye imagine ag. the L.? Nah 1:9
that imagineth evil ag. the L. 11

before the **Lord**

mighty hunter bef. the L. Gen 10:9
well watered, bef. the L. 13:10
of Sodom were sinners bef. the L. 13
Abraham stood yet bef. the L. 18:22
eat and bless thee bef. the L. 27:7
come near bef. the L. Ex 16:9
lay it up bef. the L. to be kept. 33
 1 Sam 10:25
males appear bef. the L. Ex 23:17
 34:24; Deut 16:16; 1 Sam 1:22
order the lamps bef. the L.
 Ex 27:21; 40:25
bear their names bef. the L. 28:12
for a memorial bef. the L. 29
 30:16; Num 31:54
sprinkle seven times bef. the L.
 Lev 4:6, 17; 14:16, 27
a fire out from bef. the L. 9:24
they died bef. the L. 10:2; Num 3:4
bring her near, set her bef. the L.
 Num 5:16, 18, 30
remembered bef. the L. your. 10:9
of salt for ever bef. the L. 18:19
and hang them up bef. the L. 25:4
their cause bef. the L. 27:5
I fell down bef. the L. Deut 9:18
must eat them bef. the L. 12:18
which stand there bef. the L. 18:7
both shall stand bef. the L. 19:17
cursed be the man bef. the L. that
 buildeth. Josh 6:26
words bef. L. in Mizpeh. Judg 11:11
bef. the L. is your way. 18:6
all the people sat there bef. the L.
 20:26; 2 Sam 7:18
sin of men was very great bef. the
 L. 1 Sam 2:17
witness against me bef. the L. 12:3
reason with you bef. the L. 7
that day detained bef. the L. 21:7
men, cursed be they bef. L. 26:19
bef. the L. which chose. 2 Sam 6:21
them in the hill bef. the L. 21:9
Hezekiah spread it bef. the L.
 2 Ki 19:14; Isa 37:14
is subdued before the L. 1 Chr 22:18
did eat and drink bef. the L. 29:22
bef. the L. for he cometh to judge.
 Ps 96:13; 98:9
let them be bef. the L. 109:15
I will walk bef. the L. in. 116:9
destruction are bef. the L. Pr 15:11
that dwell bef. the L. Isa 23:18
supplications bef. the L. Jer 36:7
to eat bread bef. the L. Ezek 44:3
not our prayer bef. the L. Dan 9:13
shall I come bef. the L. Mi 6:6
O all flesh, bef. the L. Zech 2:13
to pray bef. the L. 7:2; 8:21, 22
mournfully bef. the L. Mal 3:14
charging them bef. the L. 2 Tim 2:14
accusation bef. the Lord. 2 Pet 2:11

from the **Lord**

gotten a man from the L. Gen 4:1
fire from the L. 19:24
proceedeth from the L. 24:50
forth a wind from the L. Num 11:31
came out a fire from the L. 16:35
wrath gone out from the L. 46
evil spirit from the L. troubled him.
 1 Sam 16:14; 19:9
a deep sleep from the L. 26:12
it was his from the L. 1 Ki 2:15
peace for ever from the L. 33
the blessing from the L. Ps 24:5
adversaries from the L. 109:20

my help cometh *from the L.* *Ps* 121:2
of the tongue is *from the L.* *Pr* 16:1
prudent wife is *from the L.* 19:14
but every man's judgement cometh *from the L.* 29:26
their counsel *from the L.* *Isa* 29:15
my way is hid *from the L.* 40:27
word came to Jeremiah *from the L.* *Jer* 7:1; 11:1; 18:1; 21:1; 26:1 27:1; 30:1; 32:1; 34:1, 8, 12 35:1; 36:1; 40:1
heart departeth *from the L.* 17:5
is there any word *from the L.*? 37:17
heard a rumour *from the L.* 49:14
no vision *from the L.* *Lam* 2:9
hope is perished *from the L.* 3:18
get ye far *from the L.* *Ezek* 11:15
word that cometh *from the L.* 33:30
whoredom, departing *from the L.* *Hos* 1:2
a rumour *from the L.* arise. *Ob* 1
evil came down *from the L.* *Mi* 1:12
Jacob shall be as dew *from the L.* 5:7
turned back *from the L.* *Zeph* 1:6
tumult *from the L.* shall. *Zech* 14:13
told her *from the L.* *Luke* 1:45
we are absent *from the L.* *2 Cor* 5:6

Lord *God*

blessed be the *L. God.* *Gen* 9:26
Abram said, *L. God,* what wilt? 15:2
L. God, whereby shall I know? 8
the *L. God* of my master. 24:27
I am the *L. God* of Abraham. 28:13
the *L. God* of Israel. *Ex* 32:27 *Josh* 9:18, 19; 10:40, 42; 13:14 33; 14:14
the *L. God* merciful and. 34:6
Joshua said, Alas, O *L. God.* *Josh* 7:7
L. God of gods, the *L. God* of. 22:22
ye to do with the *L. God* of? 24
the *L. God* of Israel. 24:2; *Judg* 4:6 5:3, 5; 11:21, 23; 21:3; *Ruth* 2:12 *1 Sam* 2:30; 14:41; 20:12; 23:10 25:32, 34; *1 Ki* 1:30; *1 Chr* 23:25 24:19
alas, O *L. God,* because. *Judg* 6:22
O *L. God,* remember me only. 16:28
who is able to stand before this holy *L. God*? *1 Sam* 6:20
L. God of hosts was with him. *2 Sam* 5:10
who am I, O *L. God,* and? 7:18
manner of man, O *L. God*? 19
for thou, *L. God,* knowest thy. 20
thou art great, O *L. God.* 22
the *L. God* of my lord the king. *1 Ki* 1:36
king said, Blessed be the *L. God.* 48; 8:15; *1 Chr* 16:36; 29:10
good thing toward the *L. God.* *1 Ki* 14:13
As the *L. God* of Israel liveth. 17:1
may know thou art *L. God.* 18:37 *2 Ki* 19:19
where is *L. God* of Elijah? *2 Ki* 2:14
state of a man of high degree, O *L. God.* *1 Chr* 17:17
fight ye not against *L. God* of fathers. *2 Chr* 13:12
house of the *L. God* of fathers. 24:18
for thy honour from *L. God.* 26:18
spake more against *L. God.* 32:16
thou art the *L. God,* who didst choose Abram. *Neh* 9:7
redeemed me, O *L. God* of. *Ps* 31:5
L. God of Israel from everlasting to. 41:13; 72:18; 106:48; *Luke* 1:68
L. God might dwell. *Ps* 68:18
thou art my hope, O *L. God.* 71:5
for *L. God* is a sun and. 84:11
I will hear what the *L. God.* 85:8
heard from the *L. God.* *Isa* 28:22
for the *L. God* will help me. 50:7, 9
for *L. God* shall slay thee. 65:15
saying, The *L. God* liveth. *Jer* 44:26
As I live, saith the *L. God.* *Ezek* 5:11, 14, 16
I am the *L. God.* 13:9; 23:49; 24:24
thus it was, saith the *L. God.* 16:19
Woe unto thee, saith the *L. God.* 23
to his ways, saith the *L. God.* 18:30
to pass, saith the *L. God.* *Ezek* 21:7
no more, saith the *L. God.* 13
forgotten me, saith the *L. God.* 22:12
wrought for me, saith *L. God.* 29:20
your God, saith the *L. God.* 34:31
am the Lord, saith the *L. God.* 36:23
sakes do I this, saith the *L. God.* 32
and I answered, O *L. God.* 37:3
spoken it, saith the *L. God.* 39:5 23:34; 26:14; 28:10
it is done, saith the *L. God.* 8
accept you, saith the *L. God.* 43:27
face unto the *L. God* to. *Dan* 9:3
even *L. God* of hosts is. *Hos* 12:5
Philistines shall perish, saith *L. God.* *Amos* 1:8
L. God will do nothing, but. 3:7
the *L. God* hath spoken, who? 8
liketh you, saith the *L. God.* 4:5
L. God of hosts is he that. 9:5
let the *L. God* be witness. *Mi* 1:2
L. God is my strength. *Hab* 3:19
sanctify the *L. God* in. *1 Pet* 3:15
holy, holy, *L. God* Almighty. *Rev* 4:8 11:17; 16:7
thy works, *L. God* Almighty. 15:3
for strong is the *L. God* who. 18:8
for the *L. God* omnipotent. 19:6
the *L. God* and the Lamb. 21:22
the *L. God* giveth them light. 22:5
see **fathers**

Lord *his God*

besought the *L. his God.* *Ex* 32:11
against the commandments of the *L. his God.* *Lev* 4:22
L. his God is with him. *Num* 23:21
learn to fear the *L. his G.* *Deut* 17:19
in name of the *L. his God.* 18:7
encouraged himself in *L. his G.* *1 Sam* 30:6
an house unto the name of *L. his G.* *1 Ki* 5:3
heart was not perfect with *L. his G.* 11:4; 15:3
L. his God give a lamp in. 15:4
the sight of *L. his God.* *2 Ki* 16:2
L. his God was with him. *2 Chr* 1:1
right in eyes of the *L. his God.* 14:2
Asa cried unto the *L. his God.* 11
when they saw that *L. his G.* 15:9
Uzziah transgressed against the *L. his G.* 26:16
his ways before *L. his God.* 27:6
L. his G. delivered Ahaz. 28:5
Hezekiah wrought right before *L. his God.* 31:20
Manasseh in affliction besought *L. his God.* 33:12
repair house of the *L. his God.* 34:8
evil in sight of *L. his God.* 36:5, 12
the *L. his G.* be with him, and. 23
to hand of *L. his G.* *Ezra* 7:6
happy he whose hope is in the *L. his God.* *Ps* 146:5
prayed to the *L. his God.* *Jonah* 2:1
of the name of *L. his God.* *Mi* 5:4

Lord *my God*

the word of *L. my God.* *Num* 22:18
L. my God commanded. *Deut* 4:5
again voice of *L. my God.* 18:16
hearkened to voice of *L. my God.* 26:14
followed the *L. my God.* *Josh* 14:8
offerings to *L. my God.* *2 Sam* 24:24
O *L. my G.* *1 Ki* 3:7; 8:28; 17:20, 21 *1 Chr* 21:17; *2 Chr* 6:19; *Ps* 7:1, 3 13:3; 30:2, 12; 35:24; 38:15 40:5; 86:12; 109:26; *Jonah* 2:6 *Hab* 1:12
the *L. my God* hath given. *1 Ki* 5:4
house unto the name of the *L. my God.* 5; *1 Chr* 22:7; *2 Chr* 2:4
hand of the *L. my God.* *Ezra* 7:28
out my hands to the *L. my God.* 9:5
the *L. my God* will. *Ps* 18:28
for thou art *L. my God.* *Jer* 31:18
I prayed unto the *L. my God.* *Dan* 9:4
supplication before *L. my God.* 20
L. my God, Feed the flock. *Zech* 11:4
and the *L. my God* shall come. 14:5

Lord *our God*

sacrifice to *L. our God.* *Ex* 3:18; 5:3 8:27; 10:25
there is none like to *L. our God.* *Ex* 8:10; *Ps* 113:5
to serve the *L. our God.* *Ex* 10:26
L. our God spake unto. *Deut* 1:6
all that wilderness, as the *L. our God* commanded us. 19, 41; 6:20
which *L. our God* doth give unto us. 1:20, 25; 2:29
L. our God delivered him. 2:33
unto whatsoever *L. our God.* 37
so nigh to them, as *L. our God.* 4:7
L. our God made a covenant. 5:2
the *L. our God* hath shewed. 24
hear the voice of *L. our God.* 25
hear all that the *L. our God.* 27
O Israel, *L. our God* is one Lord. 6:4; *Mark* 12:29
to fear *L. our God.* *Deut* 6:24
to do before *L. our God.* 25
day before the *L. our God.* 29:15
things belong to the *L. our God.* 29
you before the *L. our God.* *Josh* 18:6
the altar of *L. our God.* 22:19, 29
L. our God, he it is that brought us up. 24:17
the people said, The *L. our God.* 24
whomsoever *L. our God.* *Judg* 11:24
cry to the *L. our God* for. *1 Sam* 7:8
L. our God be with us. *1 Ki* 8:57
words be nigh unto *L. our God.* 59
we trust *Lord our God.* *2 Ki* 18:22
O *L. our God,* save thou us. 19:19
that it be of *L. our God.* *1 Chr* 13:2
the *L. our God* made a breach. 15:13
he is the *L. our God*; his judgements. 16:14; *Ps* 105:7
O *L. our God.* *1 Chr* 29:16 *2 Chr* 14:11; *Ps* 99:8; 106:47 *Isa* 26:13; 37:20; *Jer* 14:22 *Dan* 9:15
keep the charge of the *L. our God.* *2 Chr* 13:11
have sought the *L. our God.* 14:7
iniquity with the *L. our God.* 19:7
but with us is the *L. our God.* 32:8
L. our God shall deliver us. 11
been shewed from the *L. our God.* *Ezra* 9:8
name of the *L. our God.* *Ps* 20:7
beauty of the *L. our God.* 90:17
yea, the *L. our God* shall cut. 94:23
exalt ye the *L. our God.* 99:5, 9
for the *L. our God* is holy. 9
for he is the *Lord our God.* 105:7
house of the *L. our God.* 122:9
wait on the *L. our God.* 123:2
come to thee, for thou art the *L. our God.* *Jer* 3:22
L. our God is the salvation. 23
sinned against the *L. our God*... not obeyed voice of *L. our God.* 25
doeth *L. our God* these things? 5:19
let us now fear the *L. our God.* 24
for the *L. our God* hath put. 8:14
committed against the *L. our God.* 16:10
us in the name of *L. our God.* 26:16
up to Zion, to the *L. our God.* 31:6
pray now to *L. our God* for us. 37:3; 42:20
the voice of the *L. our God.* 42:6
the *L. our God* hath not sent. 43:2
vengeance of *L. our God.* 50:28
Zion the work of *L. our God.* 51:10
to the *L. our God* belong. *Dan* 9:9
obeyed voice of the *L. our God.* 10
for the *L. our God* is righteous in. 14
in the name of the *L. our G.* *Mi* 4:5
afraid of the *L. our God.* 7:17
as *L. our God* shall call. *Acts* 2:39
power to the *L. our God.* *Rev* 19:1

Lord *their God*

may serve *L. their God.* *Ex* 10:7 *2 Chr* 34:33; *Jer* 30:9
know that I am the *L. their God.* *Ex* 29:46; *Ezek* 28:26; 34:30 39:22, 28
break covenant, I am *L. their God* *Lev* 26:44; *Zech* 10:6
forgat *L. their God.* *Judg* 3:7 8:34; *1 Sam* 12:9; *Jer* 3:21
because they forsook *L. their God.* *1 Ki* 9:9; *Jer* 22:9

the *L. is* my strength.
Ps 28:7; 118:14
the *L. is* their strength, and he. 28:8
O taste and see that the *L. is.* 34:8
for the *L.* most high *is* terrible. 47:2
L. is our defence and Holy. 89:18
to shew that *L. is* upright. 92:15
the *L. is* clothed with strength. 93:1
the *L. is* my defence and. 94:22
the *L. is* a great God. 95:3; 96:4
99:2; 135:5
the *L. is* good. 100:5; 34:8; 135:3
145:9; *Jer* 33:11; *Lam* 3:25
Nah 1:7
L. is merciful and gracious.
Ps 103:8; 111:4; 145:8
the *L. is* high. 113:4
the *L. is* on my side. 118:6
the *L. is* thy keeper, the *L. is.* 121:5
so the *L. is* round about his. 125:2
L. is righteous. 129:4; 145:17
Lam 1:18; *Dan* 9:14
the *L. is* nigh to all them. *Ps* 145:18
L. is far from the wicked. *Pr* 15:29
the *L. is* the maker of them. 22:2
L. is a God of judgement. *Isa* 30:18
the *L. is* exalted. 33:5
L. is our judge, our. 22
L. is well pleased for his. 42:21
the *L. is* the true God. *Jer* 10:10
whose hope the *L. is.* 17:7
the *L. is* with me. 20:11
the *L. is* my portion. *Lam* 3:24
the city, the *L. is* there. *Ezek* 48:35
maketh the stars, the *L. is* his name.
Amos 5:8; 9:6
L. is in his holy temple. *Hab* 2:20
the just *L. is* in the midst thereof.
Zeph 3:5, 15
fight, because *L. is* with. *Zech* 10:5
shall say, The *L. is* my God. 13:9
the *L. is* risen indeed. *Luke* 24:34
the *L. is* that Spirit. *2 Cor* 3:17
known, the *L. is* at hand. *Phil* 4:5
the *L. is* the avenger of. *1 Thes* 4:6
but the *L. is* faithful. *2 Thes* 3:3
the *L. is* my helper, I. *Heb* 13:6
L. is very pitiful, and. *Jas* 5:11
tasted that *L. is* gracious. *1 Pet* 2:3
L. is not slack concerning. *2 Pet* 3:9

my **Lord**

said, Oh, not so, *my L.* *Gen* 19:18
Moses said, *O my L.* I. *Ex* 4:10
O *my L.* send by hand of whom. 13
let the power of *my L.* *Num* 14:17
saith *my L.* to his servant? *Josh* 5:14
O *my L.* if the *L.* be with us.
Judg 6:13
O *my L.* wherewith shall I? 15
O *my L.* let the man of God. 13:8
to the *L.* thou art *my L.* *Ps* 16:2
stir up thyself, my God, *my L.* 35:23
John 20:28
the *L.* said to *my L.* *Ps* 110:1
Mat 22:44; *Mark* 12:36
Luke 20:42; *Acts* 2:34
a lion: *My L.* I stand. *Isa* 21:8
but Zion said, *My L.* hath. 49:14
O *my L.* by the vision. *Dan* 10:16
of *my L.* talk with this *my L.*? 17
and I said, Let *my L.* speak. 19
O *my L.* what shall be end of? 12:8
said I, O *my L.* what are these?
Zech 1:9; 4:4; 6:4
knowest thou? No, *my L.* 4:5, 13
the mother of *my L.* *Luke* 1:43
have taken away *my L.* *John* 20:13
of Christ Jesus *my L.* *Phil* 3:8

O **Lord**

for thy salvation, *O L.* *Gen* 49:18
who is like to thee, *O L.*? *Ex* 15:11
return, *O L.* unto Israel. *Num* 10:36
Ps 6:4
O L. hast given me. *Deut* 26:10
O L. what shall I say? *Josh* 7:8
thine enemies perish, *O L.* *Judg* 5:31
O L. turn counsel of. *2 Sam* 15:31
thou art my lamp, *O L.* and. 22:29
be it far from me, *O L.* that. 23:17
O L. there is none like. *1 Chr* 17:20
O L. is greatness, thine, *O L.* 29:11
help us, *O L.* our God; *O L.* thou
art our God. *2 Chr* 14:11
arise, *O L.*; save me. *Ps* 3:7
lead me, *O L.* 5:8
O L. heal me. 6:2
but thou, *O L.* how long? 3
arise, *O L.* 7:6; 9:19; 10:12; 17:13
judge me, *O L.* according. 7:8; 26:1
O L. our *L.* 8:1, 9
I will praise thee, O *L.* 9:1
O L.: consider my trouble. 13
31:9; 86:3; 123:3
O L. my strength. 18:1; 19:14
be not thou far from me, *O L.* 22:19
35:22
hear, *O L.* 27:7; 30:10; 39:12
69:16; 86:6; 102:1; 119:145
140:6
I trusted in thee, *O L.* I said. 31:14
gods none like to thee, *O L.* 86:8
teach me thy way, *O L.* I walk. 11
25:4; 27:11
not unto us, *O L.* not unto. 115:1
O L. thy commandments. 119:151
hear my prayer, *O L.* 143:1, 7
Isa 37:17; *Dan* 9:19
O L. thou art my God. *Isa* 25:1
O L. art our Father. 63:16; 64:8
O L. thou art great. *Jer* 10:6
so be it, *O L.* 11:5
but thou, *O L.* knowest me. 12:3
O L. art in the midst of us. 14:9
O L. the hope of Israel. 17:13
heal me, *O L.* and I shall be. 14
see, *O L.*, and consider; for I am
become vile. *Lam* 1:11; 2:20
thou, *O L.* remainest for ever. 5:19
turn us unto thee, *O L.* we. 21
we beseech thee, *O L.* *Jonah* 1:14
O L. thou hast ordained. *Hab* 1:12
O L. revive thy work in. 3:2
O L. thou Son of David. *Mat* 15:22
20:30, 31
I am a sinful man, *O L.* *Luke* 5:8
thou art worthy, *O L.* to. *Rev* 4:11
saying, How long, *O L.*? 6:10
who shall not fear thee, *O L.*? 15:4
O L. which art, and wast. 16:5

see **Lord** *God*

anger of the **Lord**

anger of the L. was kindled against
Moses. *Ex* 4:14
anger of the L. was kindled against
Israel. *Num* 11:10; 25:3
Josh 7:1; *Judg* 2:14, 20; 3:8
10:7; *2 Sam* 24:1; *2 Ki* 13:3
Isa 5:25
anger of the L. kindled against
Aaron. *Num* 12:9
that the fierce *anger of L.* may. 25:4
augment yet the *anger of L.* 32:14
lest the *anger of L.* be. *Deut* 6:15
so will *anger of the L.* be. 7:4
anger of Lord shall smoke. 29:20
anger of the L. was kindled. 27
anger of L. be kindled against you.
Josh 23:16
anger of L. kindled against Uzzah.
2 Sam 6:7; *1 Chr* 13:10
through *anger of the L.* it came to.
2 Ki 24:20; *Jer* 52:3
anger of the L. kindled against
Amaziah. *2 Chr* 25:15
fierce *anger of the L.* is not turned
back from us. *Jer* 4:8
of the fierce *anger of the L.* 12:13
anger of the L. shall not return till.
23:20; 30:24
his soul from *anger of the L.* 51:45
in day of *L.'s anger* none. *Lam* 2:22
anger of L. hath divided them. 4:16
before the fierce *anger of L.* *Zeph* 2:2
hid in day of the *anger of the L.* 3
see **commandment, congregation, counsel, day, eyes, face, fear, feast, glory, hand, house, knowledge, law**

mouth of the **Lord**

word that proceedeth out of *mouth of L.* *Deut* 8:3
counsel at *mouth of L.* *Josh* 9:14
disobeyed *mouth of L.* *1 Ki* 13:21
for the *mouth of L.* hath spoken it.
Isa 1:20; 40:5; 58:14; *Jer* 9:12
Mi 4:4
by a new name, which the *mouth of the L.* shall name. *Isa* 62:2
speak not out of *mouth of the L.*
Jer 23:16

name of the **Lord**

Abram called on the *name of the L.*
Gen 12:8
she called the *name of L.* 16:13
Isaac called on *name of L.* 26:25
shall not take *name of L.* in vain.
Ex 20:7; *Deut* 5:11
proclaim *name of the L.* *Ex* 33:19
proclaimed the *name of the L.* 34:5
woman's son blasphemed the *name of the L.* *Lev* 24:11, 16
minister in *name of L.* *Deut* 18:5, 7
speaketh in the *name of the L.* 22
chosen to bless in *name of L.* 21:5
art called by the *name of L.* 28:10
publish *name of L.*: ascribe. 32:3
thy servants are come because of
name of the L. *Josh* 9:9
in *name of L.* of hosts. *1 Sam* 17:45
both of us in *name of L.* 20:42
called by *name of the L.* *2 Sam* 6:2
blessed the people in the *name of L.*
18; *1 Chr* 16:2
no house built to the *name of the L.*
1 Ki 3:2; 5:3, 5; 8:17, 20
1 Chr 22:7, 19; *2 Chr* 2:1, 4; 6:10
Sheba heard concerning *name of L.*
1 Ki 10:1
altar in the *name of the L.* 18:32
that which is true in *name of L.* 22:16
2 Chr 18:15
cursed them in *name of the L.*
2 Ki 2:24
which he spake in *name of L.*
1 Chr 21:19; *2 Chr* 33:18
blessed be the *name of the L.*
Job 1:21; *Ps* 113:2
sing praises to *name of L.* *Ps* 7:17
remember *name of the L.* our. 20:7
shall fear the *name of the L.* 102:15
to declare *name of the L.* in. 21
praise the *name of L.* 113:1; 135:1
148:5, 13; *Joel* 2:26
rising of sun *L.'s name* is. *Ps* 113:3
called I upon *name of L.* 116:4
in the *name of L.* will I destroy.
118:10, 11, 12
cometh in the *name of the L.* 26
thanks unto *name of the L.* 122:4
our help is in *name of L.* 124:8
we bless you in *name of L.* 129:8
name of L. is a strong. *Pr* 18:10
place of the *name of the L.* *Isa* 18:7
glorify the *name of the L.* in. 24:15
name of L. cometh from far. 30:27
which swear by *name of L.* 48:1
let him trust in *name of the L.* 50:10
and to love the *name of L.* to. 56:6
they fear the *name of L.* 59:19
and gold to *name of the L.* 60:9
all nations gathered to *name of the L.* *Jer* 3:17
prophesy not in the *name of L.* 11:21
prophesied in the *name of L.* 26:9
he hath spoken to us in the *name of L.* 16; 44:16
Urijah that prophesied in the *name of the L.* 26:20
mention of *name of L.* *Amos* 6:10
will walk in *name of Lord.* *Mi* 4:5
majesty of the *name of the L.* 5:4
trust in *name of the L.* *Zeph* 3:12
lies in *name of the L.* *Zech* 13:3
that cometh in the *name of L.*
Mat 21:9; 23:39; *Mark* 11:9, 10
Luke 13:35; 19:38; *John* 12:13
spake boldly in *name of the L.* Jesus.
Acts 9:29
to be baptized in *name of L.* 10:48
to call over them the *name of the L.*
19:13
and the *name of the L.* Jesus. 17
to die for the *name of L.* 21:13
sins, calling on the *name of L.* 22:16
that the *name of L.* Jesus may be
glorified. *2 Thes* 1:12
command you in the *name of L.* 3:6
have spoken in *name of L.* *Jas* 5:10
with oil in the *name of the L.* 14

of the **Lord**

of the L. to harden. Josh 11:20
asked him of the L. 1 Sam 1:20
them in the ears of the L. 8:21
Saul said, Blessed be ye of L. 23:21
2 Sam 2:5
his name Jedidiah because of the L. 2 Sam 12:25
the saying of the L. 1 Ki 15:29
this evil is of the L. 2 Ki 6:33
man of God and enquire of L. 8:8
saying of the L. to Elijah. 10:17
we may enquire of L. 2 Chr 18:7
go, enquire of the L. for me. 34:21
I will say of the L. He. Ps 91:2
disposing thereof is of the L. Pr 16:33
man's goings are of the L. 20:24
safety is of L. 21:31
worship, because of the L. Isa 49:7
O arm of the L. awake as. 51:9
pray thee, of the L. for us. Jer 21:2
it is of the L.'s mercies. Lam 3:22
salvation is of the L. Jonah 2:9
the will of L. be done. Acts 21:14
I have received of the L. 1 Cor 11:23
opened to me of the L. 2 Cor 2:12
shall he receive of the L. Eph 6:8
knowing that of the L. Col 3:24
may find mercy of the L. 2 Tim 1:18
receive any thing of the L. Jas 1:7
seen the end of the L. 5:11
longsuffering of the L. 2 Pet 3:15
see **angel**

prophet and *prophets of the* **Lord**

Samuel established to be a p. of the L. 1 Sam 3:20
Jezebel cut off p. of the L. 1 Ki 18:4
Jezebel slew the p. of the L. 13
I only remain a p. of the L. 22
is there not here a p. of the L. to? 22:7; 2 Ki 3:11; 2 Chr 18:6
a p. of the L. was there. 2 Chr 28:9
see **sabaoth, sabbath**

servant, servants of the **Lord**

Moses the s. of the L. died there. Deut 34:5
death of Moses s. of the L. Josh 1:1
which Moses the s. of the L. commanded. 1:13; 8:31, 33; 11:12
22:2, 5; 2 Ki 18:12
which Moses the s. of the L. gave. Josh 1:15; 12:6; 13:8; 18:7; 22:4
Moses the s. of the L. smite. 12:6
s. of L. sent me from Kadesh. 14:7
Joshua son of Nun the s. of the L. died. 24:29; Judg 2:8
blood of all the s. of the L. 2 Ki 9:7
here none of the s. of the L. 10:23
Moses s. of the L. made. 2 Chr 1:3
to commandment of Moses the s. of the L. 24:6
praise the Lord, praise, O ye s. of the L. Ps 113:1; 135:1
bless Lord, O all ye s. of L. 134:1
blind or deaf as the L.'s s. Isa 42:19
heritage of the s. of the L. 54:17
and the s. of the L. must not strive. 2 Tim 2:24

sight of the **Lord**

Er was wicked in s. of L. and he slew him. Gen 38:7
been accepted in s. of L. Lev 10:19
do that which is good in s. of L. Deut 6:18; 12:28
do what is right in s. of the L. 12:25
21:9; 2 Ki 12:2; 14:3; 15:3, 24
18:3; 22:2; 2 Chr 20:32; 24:2
25:2; 26:4; 27:2; 29:2; 34:2
wickedness is great ye have done in the s. of L. 1 Sam 12:17
1 Ki 21:25; 2 Ki 21:6
a light thing in s. of L. 2 Ki 3:18
did not what was right in s. of L. 16:2
2 Chr 28:1
precious in s. of L. is death of his saints. Ps 116:15
that doeth evil, is good in s. of L. Mal 2:17
great in the s. of the L. Luke 1:15
not only in s. of the L. 2 Cor 8:21
humble yourselves in the s. of the L. Jas 4:10
see **evil**

Spirit of the **Lord**

S. of L. came on Othniel. Judg 3:10
S. of L. came on Gideon. 6:34
S of L. came on Jephtha. 11:29
S. of L. began to move Samson. 13:25; 14:6, 19; 15:14
S. of L. will come on Saul. 1 Sam 10:6
S. of L. came upon David. 16:13
S. of L. departed from. 14
S. of L. spake by me. 2 Sam 23:2
S. of L. shall carry thee. 1 Ki 18:12
went S. of the L. from me to speak unto? 22:24; 2 Chr 18:23
S. of the L. hath taken. 2 Ki 2:16
Jahaziel came S. of L. 2 Chr 20:14
S. of L. shall rest upon. Isa 11:2
S. of L. bloweth upon it. 40:7
who hath directed S. of L.? 13
the S. of L. shall lift. 59:19
S. of L. is upon me, because the. 61:1; Luke 4:18
S. of L. caused him to rest. Isa 63:14
S. of L. fell upon me. Ezek 11:5
carried in S. of L. 37:1
house of Jacob, is the S. of L.? Mi 2:7
full of power by the S. of L. 3:8
agreed to tempt S. of L. Acts 5:9
the S. of L. caught away Philip. 8:39
where the S. of L. is, there is liberty. 2 Cor 3:17
glory, even as by the S. of L. 18

temple of the **Lord**

by a post of the t. of L. 1 Sam 1:9
lamp of God went out in the t. of the L. 3:3
people into t. of L. 2 Ki 11:13
gold off from doors of t. of L. 18:16
bring out of the t. of L. vessels. 23:4
Solomon had made in t. of L. 24:13
Uzziah went into t. of L. 2 Chr 26:16
not into the t. of the L. 27:2
uncleanness found in t. of L. 29:16
foundation of the t. of L. Ezra 3:6
laid foundation of t. of the L. 10
The t. of L., The t. of L. Jer 7:4
were set before the t. of the L. 24:1
t. of L. were 25 men, with their backs toward t. of L. and. Ezek 8:16
stone was laid in t. of L. Hag 2:15
and he shall build the t. of the L. Zech 6:12; 13:15
for a memorial in t. of L. 6:14
Zacharias went into t. of L. Luke 1:9

voice of the **Lord**

and obey v. of L. Deut 30:8
Jer 26:13; 38:20
obeyed not the v. of L. Josh 5:6
1 Sam 28:18; 1 Ki 20:36; Jer 3:25
7:28; 42:13, 21; 43:4, 7; 44:23
Dan 9:10
thou not obey v. of L.? 1 Sam 15:19
yea, I have obeyed the v. of the L. 20
in obeying the v. of the L. 22
the v. of the L. is upon. Ps 29:3
the v. of the L. is powerful. 4
the v. of the L. divideth the. 7
v. of L. shaketh the wilderness. 8
v. of the L. maketh the hinds. 9
not to the v. of the L. 106:25
I heard the v. of the L. Isa 6:8
v. of the L. shall Assyrians. 30:31
a v. of the L. that rendereth 66:6
v. of the L. our God that it may be well . . . obey the v. of L. Jer 42:6
the L.'s v. crieth unto the. Mi 6:9
people obeyed v. of the L. Hag 1:12
diligently obey the v. of L. Zech 6:15
v. of L. came to Moses. Acts 7:31

way of the **Lord**

command his household to keep w. of L. Gen 18:19
will keep the w. of the L. Judg 2:22
Amon walked not in the w. of the L. 2 Ki 21:22
who walk in w. of the L. Ps 119:1
w. of the L. is strength. Pr 10:29
prepare ye w. of the L. Isa 40:3
Mat 3:3; Mark 1:3; Luke 3:4
know not way of the L. Jer 5:4
they have known way of the L. 5
the w. of the L. is not equal. Ezek 18:25, 29; 33:17, 20
make straight way of L. John 1:23
instructed in w. of L. Acts 18:25

ways of the **Lord**

for I have kept the w. of L. 2 Sam 22:22; Ps 18:21
lifted up in w. of L. 2 Chr 17:6
sing in the w. of the L. Ps 138:5
the w. of the L. are right. Hos 14:9
cease to pervert the right w. of the L. Acts 13:10

word of the **Lord**

feared the w. of the L. Ex 9:20
regarded not the w. of the L. left. 21
according to w. of the L. Num 3:16
51; 4:45; 36:5; Deut 34:5
Josh 8:27; 19:50; 22:9; 1 Ki 12:24
13:26; 14:18; 16:12, 34; 17:5, 16
22:38; 2 Ki 1:17; 4:44; 7:16
9:26; 14:25
he hath despised the w. of the L. Num 15:31
beyond the w. of L. my God. 22:18
to shew you the w. of L. Deut 5:5
w. of L. was precious. 1 Sam 3:1
w. of the L. yet revealed to. 7
hast rejected the w. of L. 15:23, 26
the w. of L. is tried. 2 Sam 22:31
Ps 18:30
might fulfil w. of the L. 1 Ki 2:27
2 Chr 36:21
to the w. of the L. and returned. 1 Ki 12:24; 2 Chr 11:4; Jer 37:2
a man of God by w. of L. 1 Ki 13:1
the altar in the w. of the L. 2
man of God had given by w. of L. 5
charged me by w. of L. saying. 9
angel spake by w. of L. saying. 18
disobedient unto the w. of L. 26
he cried by the w. of the L. 32
according to the w. of L. 14:18
w. of the L. in my mouth. 17:24
prophet said, in w. of L., Smite. 20:35
enquire, I pray thee, at w. of L. 22:5; 2 Chr 18:4
Jehoshaphat said, W. of L. 2 Ki 3:12
this is w. of L. 9:36
nothing of the w. of the L. fall. 10:10
this was the w. of L. 15:12
good is the w. of L. 20:19; Isa 39:8
according to w. of L. 2 Ki 23:16
24:2; 1 Chr 11:3, 10; 12:23
15:15; Jer 13:2; 32:8; Jonah 3:3
against w. of the L. 1 Chr 10:13
of king by w. of L. 2 Chr 30:12
not kept the w. of the L. 34:21
that w. of L. might be accomplished. 36:22; Ezra 1:1
for the w. of L. is right. Ps 33:4
by w. of L. were heavens made. 6
word came, the w. of L. 105:19
and the w. of L. from Jerusalem. Isa 2:3; Mi 4:2
the w. of L. was to them. 28:13
see ye the word of the L. Jer 2:31
w. of the L. is to them a reproach. 6:10; 20:8
have rejected the w. of L. 8:9
to me, Where is the w. of L.? 17:15
to this day the w. of L. hath. 25:3
if the w. of L. be with them. 27:18
that this was the word of the L. 32:8
the w. of L. that came to Hosea. Hos 1:2
wander to seek w. of L. Amos 8:12
w. of L. is against you. Zeph 2:5
this is w. of the L. to Zerubbabel. Zech 4:6
w. of the L. in the land of Hadrach. 9:1; 12:1; Mal 1:1
poor of the flock knew that it was w. of L. Zech 11:11
Peter remembered w. of L. Luke 22:61; Acts 11:16
preached the w. of the L. Acts 8:25
13:49; 15:35, 36; 16:32
glorified the w. of the L. 13:48
heard the w. of the L. Jesus. 19:10

sounded out the w. of L. 1 Thes 1:8
say to you by the w. of the L. 4:15
pray that the w. of the L. may have free course. 2 Thes 3:1
w. of L. endureth for. 1 Pet 1:25

words of the **Lord**

Moses told people all w. of L. Ex 24:3; Num 11:24
Moses wrote all the w. of L. and. Ex 24:4
heard all the w. of the L. Josh 24:27
told people w. of the L. 1 Sam 8:10
the voice of the w. of the L. 15:1
came by w. of L. to cleanse the. 2 Chr 29:15
w. of the L. are pure. Ps 12:6
Baruch wrote all w. of L. Jer 36:4
roll thou hast written w. of L. 6, 8
of the book all the w. of the L. 11
hearing the w. of the L. Amos 8:11

see **came, hear**

work of the **Lord**

see the w. of the L. Ex 34:10
regard not the w. of L. Isa 5:12
cursed that doeth the w. of L. Jer 48:10
this is the w. of L. 50:25
declare the w. of L. 51:10
abounding in the w. of the L. 1 Cor 15:58
he worketh the w. of the L. 16:10

works of the **Lord**

known all the w. of the L. Josh 24:31
seen all the great w. of the L. Judg 2:7
regard not the w. of L. Ps 28:5
come, behold the w. of the L. 46:8
I will remember the w. of L. 77:11
these see the w. of the L. 107:24
the w. of L. are great. 111:2
declare w. of L. 118:17

wrath of the **Lord**

w. of L. was kindled. Num 11:33
the L.'s w. be kindled. Deut 11:17
for great is the w. of L. 2 Ki 22:13
2 Chr 34:21
the w. of L. turned. 2 Chr 12:12
the w. of L. was upon Judah. 29:8
so that the w. of the L. 32:26
until w. of the L. arose. 36:16
was w. of the L. kindled. Ps 106:40
through the w. of the L. Isa 9:19
remove in the w. of the L. 13:13
because of w. of the L. Jer 50:13
gold shall not be able to . . . day of w. of the L. Ezek 7:19; Zeph 1:18

see **praise**

Lord said

L. said in his heart. Gen 8:21
he hearkened not as the L. said. Ex 7:13; 22; 8:15, 19; Deut 9:3
Judg 2:15; 6:27
is that which the L. said. Ex 16:23
all the words the L. said. 24:3
all L. said we will do. 7; Num 32:31
place of which L. said. Num 10:29
as the L. said to him by the. 16:40
for the L. had said, They shall. 26:65
as the L. hath said. Deut 31:3
Josh 14:12; Joel 2:32
all the L. said to Moses. Josh 11:23
thing that the L. said. 14:6
what is the thing that L. said to thee? 1 Sam 3:17
tell thee what the L. said. 15:16
day of which the L. said to thee. 24:4
because the L. said to him, Curse David. 2 Sam 16:10
L. said he would dwell. 1 Ki 8:12
2 Chr 6:1
nations, concerning which L. said to Israel. 1 Ki 11:2
L. said not that he would blot out. 2 Ki 14:27
whereof the L. had said, Ye. 17:12
which L. said in Jerusalem. 21:4, 7
2 Chr 33:4
Solomon had made in temple as the L. said. 2 Ki 24:13
the L. hath said unto me. Ps 2:7
the L. said unto my Lord. 110:1
Mat 22:44; Mark 12:36
Luke 20:42; Acts 2:34
then said the L. Isa 7:3; 8:3
Ezek 44:2; Hos 3:1; Jonah 4:10
Luke 20:13
for so L. said unto me, I. Isa 18:4
thus hath L. said unto me. 21:16
Jer 4:27; 6:6
L. said, Forasmuch. Isa 29:13
rest, I the L. have said. Ezek 21:17
said the L. in a vision. Acts 9:10
the word of L. how he said. 11:16

saith the **Lord**

thus saith the L. Ex 4:22; 5:1
7:17; 1 Sam 2:27; 2 Sam 12:11
24:12
what the L. saith, that will I speak. Num 24:13
thus saith the L. God of. Josh 7:13
24:2; Judg 6:8; 2 Sam 12:7
but now the L. saith, Be it far from me. 1 Sam 2:30
saith L. of hosts. 15:2; 2 Sam 7:8
1 Chr 17:7; Jer 6:9; 7:3, 21
L. saith, that will I speak. 1 Ki 22:14
not be purged, saith the L. Isa 22:14
Jer 5:14; 35:17; 49:5; 50:31
now will I rise, saith the L.; now will I be exalted. Isa 33:10
Ps 12:5
now saith the L. that formed me. Isa 49:5
saith the L. that hath mercy. 54:10
for I am with thee, saith the L. Jer 1:8, 19; 30:11
fear is not in thee, saith the L. 2:19
yet return unto me, saith the L. 3:1
if thou wilt return, saith the L. 4:1
fear ye not me, saith L. 5:22
I have seen it, saith L. 7:11
evil, they know not me, saith the L. 9:3
to know me? saith the L. 22:16
I a God at hand, saith the L.? 23:23
I shall not see him, saith the L. 24
even forsake you, saith the L. 33
not sent him, saith the L. 27:15
not sent them, saith the L. 29:9
L. saith and the Lord hath not sent them. Ezek 13:6, 7
I am against you, saith L. 8
thus it was, saith L. 16:19
be no more, saith the L. God. 21:13
and I am your God saith L. 34:31
it is done, saith the L. God. 39:8
accept you, saith the L. God. 43:27
is it not even thus, O Israel? saith the L. Amos 2:11
this liketh you, saith the L. 4:5
shall not be, saith L. 7:3
called by my name, saith L. 9:12
the L. saith, Arise thou. Mi 6:1
behold, I am against thee, saith the L. Nah 2:13; 3:5
wait ye upon me, saith L. Zeph 3:8
why? saith L. of hosts. Hag 1:9
I am with you, saith L. 13
for I, saith the L. will be. Zech 2:5
but by my Spirit, saith the L. 4:6
loved you, saith the L. Mal 1:2
this of your hand, saith the L. 13
great King, saith the L. of hosts. 14
fear not me, saith the L. of. 3:5
now herewith, saith the L. of. 10
shall be mine, saith the L. of. 17
shall do this, saith the L. of. 4:3
saith the L. who doeth. Acts 15:17
I will repay, saith the L. Rom 12:19
hear me for all this, saith the L. 1 Cor 14:21
ye separate, saith the L. 2 Cor 6:17
regarded them not, saith the L. Heb 8:9
I will recompense, saith the L. 10:30
and the ending, saith the L. Rev 1:8

see **live, saved**

Lord joined with seek

thence thou shalt seek L. Deut 4:29
heart rejoice, that seek L. 1 Chr 16:10; Ps 105:3
seek the L. and his strength. 1 Chr 16:11; Ps 105:4
set your heart to seek the L. 1 Chr 22:19; 2 Chr 11:16
his heart to seek the L. 2 Chr 12:14
Judah to seek the L. God. 14:4
a covenant to seek the L. 15:12
would not seek the L. God. 13
set himself to seek the L. 20:3
Judah they came to seek L. 4
were come to seek the L. Ezra 6:21
praise the L. that seek. Ps 22:26
they that seek the L. shall not want any good. 34:10
that seek L. understand. Pr 28:5
neither do they seek L. Isa 9:13
31:1; Hos 7:10
ye that seek the L. look to. Isa 51:1
seek ye L. while he may be. 55:6
shall go and seek the L. Jer 50:4
return and seek the L. Hos 3:5
with their herds to seek the L. 5:6
to seek the L. till he come. 10:12
seek the L. and ye shall live, lest. Amos 5:6
seek ye the L. all ye meek. Zeph 2:3
go to seek the L. of hosts. Zech 8:21
people shall come to seek the L. 22
the L. whom ye seek shall suddenly come. Mal 3:1
of men might seek the L. Acts 15:17
seek the L. if haply they might. 17:27

Lord joined with sent

the L. sent him forth from the garden. Gen 3:23
the L. sent us to destroy it. 19:13
words of L. who had sent. Ex 4:28
L. God of the Hebrews sent. 7:16
and L. sent thunder and hail. 9:23
that the L. hath sent me. Num 16:28
death, then L. hath not sent. 29
cried, the L. sent an angel. 20:16
the L. sent fiery serpents. 21:6
L. sent you from Kadesh-barnea. Deut 9:23
wonders which the L. sent. 34:11
the L. sent a prophet. Judg 6:8
then the L. sent Moses. 1 Sam 12:8
and the L. sent Jerubbaal. 11
the L. sent thunder. 18
L. sent me to anoint thee. 15:1
the L. sent thee on a journey. 18
way which the L. sent me. 20
the L. hath sent thee away. 20:22
L. sent Nathan to David. 2 Sam 12:1
L. sent pestilence on Israel. 24:15
1 Chr 21:14
tarry, for the L. hath sent me to Beth-el. 2 Ki 2:2
L. hath sent me to Jericho. 4
L. sent me to Jordan. 6
therefore the L. sent lions. 17:25
the L. sent against him bands. 24:2
the L. sent an angel. 2 Chr 32:21
L. sent a word into Jacob. Isa 9:8
L. sent him to prophesy. Jer 19:14
L. hath sent to you all his servants. 25:4
drink to whom the L. had sent me. 17
L. sent me to prophesy. 26:12, 15
L. hath truly sent him. 28:9
the L. hath not sent thee. 15
L. hath not sent them. Ezek 13:6
the L. sent out a great wind into. Jonah 1:4
L. their God had sent him. Hag 1:12
L. hath sent to walk to. Zech 1:10
know L. of hosts hath sent me. 2:9
11; 4:9; 6:15
words which L. hath sent. 7:12
Saul, the L. Jesus hath sent me. Acts 9:17
the L. hath sent his angel. 12:11

serve the **Lord**

let the men go, that they may serve the L. their God. Ex 10:7
Pharaoh said, Go serve the L. your God. 8; 11:24; 12:31
take to serve the L. our God . . . with what we must serve the L. 10:26
ye shall serve the L. your. 23:25
to serve the L. thy God. Deut 10:12
fear and serve the L. Josh 24:14
seem evil unto you to serve the L. 15
will we serve the L.; he is our God. 18, 21, 24
Joshua said, Ye cannot serve L. 19

ye have chosen you the L. to serve
him. Josh 24:22
serve the L. with all your heart.
1 Sam 12:20
if the Lord shall bring me again, then
will I serve the L. 2 Sam 15:8
but yield, and serve the L. your God.
2 Chr 30:8; 35:3
Judah to serve the L. 33:16; 34:33
serve the L. with fear. Ps 2:11
serve the L. with gladness. 100:2
gathered to serve the L. 102:22
for ye serve the L. Christ. Col 3:24

Lord *spake*

name of L. that spake to. Gen 16:13
L. spake, saying, I will. Lev 10:3
in the day the L. spake with Moses.
Num 3:1; 9:1
as the L. spake unto Moses. 5:4
whereof L. spake to Moses. 21:16
L. spake to you out of the midst of
fire. Deut 4:12
similitude in the day the L. spake. 15
these words the L. spake to. 5:22
the words which the L. spake. 9:10
commandments which L. spake. 10:4
the L. spake this word to. Josh 14:10
this mountain whereof L. spake. 12
Samuel did that which the L. spake.
1 Sam 16:4
L. may continue his word which he
spake. 1 Ki 2:4
word of the L. which he spake. 27
as the L. spake to David my. 5:5
L. hath performed word he spake.
8:20; 2 Ki 10:10
perform his saying, which the L.
spake. 1 Ki 12:15; 2 Chr 10:15
to the word of the L. which he spake.
1 Ki 13:26; 14:18; 16:12, 34
17:16; 22:38; 2 Ki 10:10; 24:2
the L. which he spake by his servant
Ahijah. 1 Ki 15:29; 2 Ki 10:17
spake the L. saying, The dogs shall
eat Jezebel. 1 Ki 21:23
word of L. which he spake.
2 Ki 9:36
L. which he spake to Jehu. 15:12
L. spake by his servants. 21:10
L. spake unto Gad. 1 Chr 21:9
L. spake to Manasseh. 2 Chr 33:10
moreover, the L. spake. Isa 7:10
L. spake also unto me again. 8:5
for the L. spake thus to me with. 11
time spake the L. by Isaiah. 20:2
words that the L. spake. Jer 30:4
the word that the L. spake. 50:1
L. hath done that which he spake.
51:12
L. spake unto the fish. Jonah 2:10
then spake the L. to Paul. Acts 18:9

Lord joined with *spoken*

Abram departed as L. had spoken.
Gen 12:4; 21:1; 24:51; Ex 9:12
35; Deut 6:19
words the L. had spoken. Ex 4:30
all that the L. hath spoken. 19:8
gave in commandment all that the L.
had spoken. 34:32
statutes L. hath spoken. Lev 10:11
for L. had spoken to Moses, saying.
Num 1:48; 15:22
the L. hath spoken good. 10:29
hath the L. indeed spoken only by
Moses ? 12:2
what hath the L. spoken ? 23:17
L. hath not spoken. Deut 18:21, 22
failed not aught which L. had spoken.
Josh 21:45
L. have done the good he hath
spoken. 1 Sam 25:30
now then do it, for the L. hath
spoken. 2 Sam 3:18
for thou, O L. hath spoken it. 7:29
sign which L. hath spoken. 1 Ki 13:3
for the L. hath spoken it. 14:11
Isa 21:17; 22:25; 24:3; 25:8
Joel 3:8; Ob 18
after the L. had spoken these words
to Job. Job 42:7
the L. hath spoken, and called the
earth. Ps 50:1

for thus hath the L. spoken to me.
Isa 31:4
L. will do this thing that he hath
spoken. 38:7
mouth of L. hath spoken. Jer 9:12
proud, for the L. hath spoken. 13:15
say, What hath L. spoken ? 23:35, 37
L. hath spoken against nation. 27:13
destroyed, as L. hath spoken. 48:8
I the L. have spoken it. Ezek 5:13
15, 17; 17:21, 24; 21:32; 22:14
24:14; 26:14; 30:12; 34:24
36:36; 37:14
when the L. hath not spoken. 22:28
for I have spoken it, saith L.
26:5; 28:10; 39:5
hear this word that the L. hath
spoken. Amos 3:1
the L. God hath spoken, who ? 8
L. of hosts hath spoken it. Mi 4:4
fulfilled which was spoken of the L.
Mat 1:22; 2:15
so then after the L. had spoken to
them. Mark 16:19
had seen the L. and that he had
spoken. Acts 9:27
at the first began to be spoken by the
L. Heb 2:3

to or *unto the* **Lord**

I have lift up my hands to L. most
high. Gen 14:22
I have taken on me to speak to the L.
18:27, 31
let us go, and do sacrifice to L.
Ex 5:17; 8:8, 29
we must hold a feast to L. 10:9
12:14; Num 29:12
sing to the L. Ex 15:1, 21; Judg 5:3
1 Chr 16:23; Ps 13:6; 30:4; 68:32
95:1; 96:1, 2; 98:1, 5; 104:33
147:7; 149:1; Isa 12:5; 42:10
Jer 20:13
for to-day is a sabbath to the L.
Ex 16:25; 35:2; Lev 25:2
sacrificeth save unto the L. Ex 22:20
holy unto the L. 30:10; 31:15
Lev 23:20; 27:21, 30, 32
Num 6:8; Ezra 8:28
We have sinned ; pray unto L.
Num 21:7; Jer 29:7; Acts 8:24
do to the L. in feasts. Num 29:39
not do so to the L. thy. Deut 12:31
I have opened my mouth to the L.
Judg 11:35, 36
dedicated the silver to the L. 17:3
not up to the L. to Mizpeh. 21:8
Hannah prayed to the L. 1 Sam 1:10
and he prayed to the L. 8:6
is no restraint to the L. to. 14:6
hang them up to the L. 2 Sam 21:6
being priest to the L. 1 Ki 2:27
Elisha shut door, prayed to the L.
2 Ki 4:33; 6:18
Hezekiah clave to the L. 18:6
unto the wall, and prayed to L. 20:2
2 Chr 32:24; Isa 37:15; 38:2
passover holden to the L. 2 Ki 23:23
but poured it out to L. 1 Chr 11:18
give thanks to L., call upon his name.
16:8, 41; Ps 92:1
burn to L. morning and. 2 Chr 13:11
bring to the L. the collection. 24:9
but yield yourselves to the L. 30:8
salvation belongeth to the L. Ps 3:8
they cried unto the L. 18:41
and to the L. I made. 30:8; 142:1
compared to L. be likened to L.?
89:6
shall I render to the L. for ? 116:12
I said to the L. Thou art my. 140:6
abomination to the L. Pr 3:32
11:1, 20; 12:22; 15:8, 9, 26; 16:5
17:15; 20:10, 23
commit thy works to L. 16:3
giveth to poor lendeth to L. 19:17
vow a vow to the L. Isa 19:21
even to the L. and he shall heal. 22
shall be holiness to L. 23:18
Jer 2:3; Zech 14:20
to the L. for a name. Isa 55:13
joined himself to the L. 56:3, 6
acceptable day to the L. 58:5
Jeremiah prayed to the L. Jer 32:16

to take heed to the L. Hos 4:10
Jonah prayed to the L. Jonah 4:2
their gain unto the L. and their substance unto the L. of. Mi 4:13
therefore I will look to the L. I. 7:7
shall be known to the L. Zech 14:7
but shalt perform to the L. Mat 5:33
to present him to the L. Luke 2:22
shall be called holy to the L. 23
the more added to the L. Acts 5:14
they would cleave to the L. 11:23
they ministered unto the L. 13:2
commended them to the L. 14:23
judged me faithful to the L. 16:15
eateth, eateth to the L. Rom 14:6
live to the L.; we die to the L. 8
their own selves to the L. 2 Cor 8:5
is acceptable to the L. Eph 5:10
submit yourselves, as to the L. 22
6:7; Col 3:23

***see* cry, cried, give, turn**

lord, as applied to *man*

after I am old, my l. Gen 18:12
nay, my l. hear me. 23:11
my l. hearken to me. 15
Drink, my l.; and she hasted. 24:18
be l. over thy brethren, let. 27:29
I have made him thy l. 37
let it not displease my l. 31:35
shall ye speak to my l. Esau. 32:4
I have sent to tell my l. that I. 5
it is a present sent to my l. Esau. 18
his garment, until his l. 39:16*
had offended their l. the king. 40:1
nay, my l. but to buy food. 42:10
who is the l. of the land. 30, 33
is not this it, in which my l.? 44:5
should we steal out of thy l.'s house.8
will be my l.'s bondmen. 9
we told him the words of my l. 24
and he hath made me l. of all. 45:8
God hath made me l. of all. 9
my l. how that there is nothing left
in sight of my l. but our. 47:18
anger of my l. wax hot. Ex 32:22
and said, My l. Moses. Num 11:28
my l. I beseech thee, lay not. 12:11
as my l. commandeth. 32:25, 27
the Lord commanded my l. 36:2
their l. was fallen down. Judg 3:25
Turn in, my l., turn in to me. 4:18
fell down where her l. was. 19:26
and her l. rose up in morning. 27
favour in thy sight, my l. Ruth 2:13
l. I am of a sorrowful. 1 Sam 1:15
O my l. as thy soul liveth, my l. 26
here I am, my l. 22:12
Saul, saying, My l. the king. 24:8
on me, my l. on me let this. 25:24
let not my l. regard this man. 25
seek evil to my l. be as Nabal. 26
young men that follow my l. 27
shall have dealt with my l. 31
not kept thy l. the king ? 26:15
David said, It is my voice, my l. 17
why doth my l. thus pursue after? 18
fight against enemies of my l. 29:8
them hither to my l. 2 Sam 1:10
I will gather all Israel to my l. 3:21
according to all that my l. hath. 9:11
Uriah slept with all the servants of
his l. 11:9, 13
let not my l. suppose they. 13:32
handmaid speak to my l. 14:12
angel of God, so is my l. 17
none can turn from aught my l. 19
l. is wise according to wisdom. 20
dead dog curse my l. the king. 16:9
Cushi said, Tidings, my l. 18:31
let not my l. impute iniquity to me,
the day my l. the king. 19:19
first to go down to meet my l. 20
my l. is come again in peace. 30
be a burden to my l. 35
go over with my l. 37
take thou thy l.'s servants, and. 20:6
my l. the king may see it, but why
doth my l. delight in ? 24:3
let my l. take and offer what. 22
that my l. the king may. 1 Ki 1:2
thing done by my l. the king ? 27
the Lord God of my l. the king. 36
the Lord hath been with my l. 37

as my *l.* the king hath said. *1 Ki* 2:38
O my *l.* I and this woman. 3:17
O my *l.* give her the living child. 26
fled from his *l.* Hadadezer. 11:23
art thou that my *l.* Elijah? 18:7
was it not told my *l.* what I did? 13
Go tell thy *l.* Behold Elijah is. 14
my *l.* I am thine, and all. 20:4
tell my *l.* all thou didst send for. 9
pleasant as my *l.* seeth. *2 Ki* 2:19
nay, my *l.* do not lie to thine. 4:16
did I desire a son of my *l.*? 28
would God my *l.* were with the. 5:3
went in and told his *l.* saying. 4
servants said, None, my *l.* 6:12
saying, Help, my *l.* O king. 26
then a *l.* on whose hand. 7:2*, 17*
my *l.* O king, this is the woman. 8:5
said, Why weepeth my *l.*? 12
forth to the servants of his *l.* 9:11
thee, give pledges to my *l.* 18:23*
cunning men of my *l.* *2 Chr* 2:14
the counsel of my *l.* *Ezra* 10:3
our own, who is *l.* over us? *Ps* 12:4
Ah *l.*, or Ah his glory. *Jer* 22:18; 34:5
now, I pray thee, my *l.* 37:20
my *l.* the king, these men. 38:9
I fear my *l.* the king. *Dan* 1:10
is no king nor *l.* that asked. 2:10
my *l.* the dream be to them. 4:19
decree which is come upon my *l.* 24
servant above his *l.* *Mat* 10:24
that the servant be as his *l.* 25
L., have patience with me. 18:26
they came and told their *l.* all. 31
my *l.* delayeth his coming. 24:48
Luke 12:45
his *l.* *said* unto him, Well done.
Mat 25:21, 23
men that wait for their *l.* *Luke* 12:36
that servant shewed his *l.* 14:21
my *l.* taketh away from me. 16:3
and he said to the first, How much owest thou unto my *l.*? 5
not what his *l.* doeth. *John* 15:15
servant is not greater than his *l.* 20
thing to write to my *l.* *Acts* 25:26
a servant, though *l.* of all. *Gal* 4:1
Abraham, calling him *l.* *1 Pet* 3:6

lords

Behold now, my *l.*, turn in. *Gen* 19:2
consumed *l.* of high places of Arnon.
Num 21:28
is Lord of *l.* *Deut* 10:17
1 Tim 6:15; *Rev* 17:14
five *l.* of the Philistines. *Josh* 13:3
Judg 3:3
l. of the Philistines. *Judg* 16:5
and the house fell upon the *l.* 30
they gathered *l.* of the Philistines.
1 Sam 5:8, 11
plague on you all, and on your *l.* 6:4
l. of the Philistines went after 12
l. of the Philistines went up. 7:7
the *l.* passed on by hundreds. 29:2
nevertheless, the *l.* favour thee not. 6
that thou displease not the *l.* 7
offerings which *l.* offered. *Ezra* 8:25*
the *l.* of the heathen. *Isa* 16:8
other *l.* have had dominion. 26:13
say my people, We are *l.*? *Jer* 2:31*
great *l.* renowned, all. *Ezek* 23:23*
my counsellors and *l.* *Dan* 4:36
feast to a thousand of his *l.* 5:1
thy *l.* have drunk wine in them. 23
with his own signet and of his *l.* 6:17
made a supper to his *l.* *Mark* 6:21
gods many, and *l.* many. *1 Cor* 8:5
nor as being *l.* over God's. *1 Pet* 5:3

lordship

kings of Gentiles exercise *l.*
Mark 10:42; *Luke* 22:25

Lo-ruhamah

God said, Call her name *L.* *Hos* 1:6
weaned *L.* she conceived and. 8

lose

run on thee, and thou *l.* *Judg* 18:25
mules alive, that we *l.* *1 Ki* 18:5
caused owners to *l.* life. *Job* 31:39
shalt vomit up, and *l.* *Pr* 23:8
to get, and a time to *l.* *Eccl* 3:6
findeth his life shall *l.* it. *Mat* 10:39
16:25; *Mark* 8:35; *Luke* 9:24
he shall in no wise *l.* his reward.
Mat 10:42; *Mark* 9:41
and *l.* his own soul. *Mat* 16:26*
Mark 8:36*; *Luke* 9:25
if he *l.* one sheep. *Luke* 15:4
if she *l.* one piece. 8
whosoever shall *l.* his life. 17:33
Father's will I should *l.* *John* 6:39
loveth his life shall *l.* it. 12:25
look to yourselves, we *l.* *2 John* 8

loseth

and he that *l.* his life. *Mat* 10:39

loss

torn, I bare the *l.* of. *Gen* 31:39
pay for the *l.* of time. *Ex* 21:19
nor shall I know the *l.* *Isa* 47:8
come in one day *l.* of children. 9
gained this harm and *l.* *Acts* 27:21
there shall be no *l.* of any man's. 22
burned, he shall suffer *l.* *1 Cor* 3:15
I counted *l.* for Christ. *Phil* 3:7
and I count all things but *l.* for Christ, for whom I suffered the *l.* of. 8

lost

for any manner of *l.* thing. *Ex* 22:9
Deut 22:3
found that which was *l.* *Lev* 6:3
restore the *l.* thing he found. 4
the days that were before shall be *l.*
Num 6:12*
with all *l.* thing of thy brother's.
Deut 22:3
asses of Kish, Saul's father, were *l.*
1 Sam 9:3
as for thine asses that were *l.* 20
army like that thou hast *l.* *1 Ki* 20:25
astray like a *l.* sheep. *Ps* 119:176
thou hast *l.* the other. *Isa* 49:20*
seeing I have *l.* my children. 21*
people hath been *l.* sheep. *Jer* 50:6
saw that her hope was *l.* *Ezek* 19:5
sought that which was *l.* 34:4
I will seek that which was *l.* 16
they say, Our hope is *l.*, we. 37:11
if the salt have *l.* his savour. *Mat* 5:13
Mark 9:50; *Luke* 14:34
rather to the *l.* sheep. *Mat* 10:6
not sent but to the *l.* sheep. 15:24
Son of man is come to save that which was *l.* 18:11; *Luke* 19:10
go after that which is *l.* *Luke* 15:4
found my sheep which was *l.* 6
found the piece which I had *l.* 9
this my son was *l.* 24
thy brother was *l.* 32
Gather up fragments that nothing be *l.* *John* 6:12
none of them is *l.* but the. 17:12
them thou gavest me, I have *l.* 18:9
our gospel is hid, to them that are *l.*
2 Cor 4:3*

lot

Many things were decided in olden times by casting lots, and the term was used in rather a figurative sense in connection with other things. As examples, lots were cast, [1] *To find out a person,* 1 Sam 14:41; Jonah 1:7. [2] *To divide lands,* Num 26:55, 56. [3] *To choose a church officer,* Acts 1:26. [4] *To order and regulate the courses of men in office,* 1 Chr 24:5; 25:8. [5] *To decide a controversy,* Ps 22:18.

one *l.* for Lord, other for scapegoat.
Lev 16:8, 9, 10
land shall be divided by *l.*
Num 26:55; *Ezek* 48:29
divide the land by *l.* *Num* 33:54
36:2; *Josh* 13:6; *Ezek* 47:22
land ye shall inherit by *l.* *Num* 34:13
Jacob is the *l.* of his. *Deut* 32:9
was the *l.* of the tribe. *Josh* 15:1
the *l.* of Joseph. 16:1
was a *l.* for Manasseh. 17:1
thou given me but one *l.*? 14
thou shalt not have one *l.* only. 17
l. of the tribe of Benjamin. 18:11
and the second *l.* came forth. 19:1
the third *l.* came for the children. 10
fourth *l.* came out to Issachar. 17
fifth *l.* to Asher. *Josh* 19:24
sixth *l.* to Naphtali. 32
seventh *l.* came for tribe of Dan. 40
l. for families of Kohathites. 21:4
1 Chr 6:54
Gershon had by *l.* *Josh* 21:6
gave by *l.* to the Levites. 8
my *l.* to fight against Canaanites, likewise go . . . into thy *l.* *Judg* 1:3
we will go up by *l.* against it. 20:9
God, give a perfect *l.* *1 Sam* 14:41
Merari were given by *l.* *1 Chr* 6:63
I give the land of Canaan, the *l.* of.
16:18; *Ps* 105:11
they were divided by *l.* *1 Chr* 24:5
first *l.* came forth to Jehoiarib. 7
first *l.* came forth for Asaph. 25:9
Pur, that is *l.* before. *Esth* 3:7
cup, thou maintainest my *l.* *Ps* 16:5
shall not rest on the *l.* of the. 125:3
cast in thy *l.* among us. *Pr* 1:14
l. is cast into lap, but disposing. 16:33
l. causeth contentions to cease. 18:18
l. of them that rob us. *Isa* 17:14
and he hath cast the *l.* for. 34:17
stones of the stream are thy *l.* 57:6
this is thy *l.* from me. *Jer* 13:25
bring it out, let no *l.* fall. *Ezek* 24:6
stand in thy *l.* at end. *Dan* 12:13
none that shall cast a cord by *l.*
Mi 2:5
his *l.* was to burn incense. *Luke* 1:9
the *l.* fell on Matthias. *Acts* 1:26
no *l.* or part in this matter. 8:21
their land to them by *l.* 13:19*

Lot

Haran begat *L.* *Gen* 11:27
Terah took *L.* 31
L. went with him. 12:4; 13:1
L. had flocks. 13:5
strife between herdmen of Abram and *L.* 7
L. chose him all the plain of. 11
they took *L.* prisoner. 14:12
L. sat in the gate of Sodom; *L.* 19:1
pulled *L.* into house. 10
the angels hastened *L.* 15
God sent *L.* out of the midst of. 29
both the daughters of *L.* were. 36
I have given Ar to the children of *L.*
Deut 2:9, 19
holpen the children of *L.* *Ps* 83:8
was in the days of *L.* *Luke* 17:28
remember *L.*'s wife. 32
delivered just *L.* vexed. *2 Pet* 2:7

lothe (loathe)

Egyptians shall *l.* to drink. *Ex* 7:18
I *l.* it, I would not live. *Job* 7:16
l. themselves for evils. *Ezek* 6:9
ye shall *l.* yourselves in your. 20:43
l. yourselves for your iniquities.
36:31

lothed (loathed)

hath thy soul *l.* Zion? *Jer* 14:19
soul *l.* them, their soul. *Zech* 11:8*

lotheth (loatheth)

soul *l.* this light bread. *Num* 21:5
full soul *l.* an honeycomb. *Pr* 27:7
l. her husband and her. *Ezek* 16:45

lothing (loathing)

wast cast out to the *l.* *Ezek* 16:5*

lothsome (loathsome)

month, till it be *l.* to you. *Num* 11:20
skin is broken and become *l.* *Job* 7:5
are filled with a *l.* disease. *Ps* 38:7
a wicked man is *l.* and. *Pr* 13:5

lots

cast *l.* between me and Jonathan.
1 Sam 14:42
cast *l.* over against. *1 Chr* 24:31
parted garments, casting *l.*
Mat 27:35; *Mark* 15:24
they gave forth their *l.* *Acts* 1:26
see **cast**

loud

l. instruments to Lord. *2 Chr* 30:21
people shouted with a *l.* *Ezra* 3:13
the singers sang *l.* with. *Neh* 12:12
cried with a *l.* cry. *Esth* 4:1
play skilfully with a *l.* *Ps* 33:3
make a *l.* noise and rejoice. 98:4*
praise him on *l.* cymbals. 150:5

she is *l.* and stubborn. *Pr* 7:11*
angel cried with a *l.* cry. *Rev* 14:18

loud joined with *voice*

I cried with a *l. voice.* *Gen* 39:14
voice of the trumpet exceeding *l.* *Ex* 19:16
speak with a *l. voice.* *Deut* 27:14
wept with a *l. voice.* *2 Sam* 15:23
blessed congregation with a *l. voice.* *1 Ki* 8:55
sware to the Lord with a *l. voice.* *2 Chr* 15:14
to praise Lord with a *l. voice.* 20:19
Luke 19:37
many wept with a *l. voice.* *Ezra* 3:12
answered with a *l. voice.* 10:12
his friend with a *l. voice.* *Pr* 27:14
they cry with a *l. voice.* *Ezek* 8:18
he cried with a *l. voice*, saying. 9:1
spake out with a *l. voice.* *Luke* 1:42
unclean spirit cried with a *l. voice.* 8:28; *Acts* 8:7
back and with a *l. voice.* *Luke* 17:15
said with a *l. voice*, Stand. *Acts* 14:10
Festus said with a *l. voice.* 26:24
proclaiming with a *l. voice.* *Rev* 5:2*
with a *l. voice*, Worthy is. 12*
angel saying with a *l. voice*, Woe, woe. 8:13*; 14:7*, 9*, 15*
a *l. voice* saying in heaven. 12:10*

loud *voices*

instant with *l. voices.* *Luke* 23:23

louder

trumpet waxed *l.* and *l.* *Ex* 19:19

love

In a number of verses in the Authorized Version of the New Testament the word charity *is used where the true meaning is* love. *In the 17th century when the Bible was translated the word charity had this meaning, which the French* cher, chère, *from the same root* (*Latin,* carus, dear) *still retains. As charity now often means something quite different, both the Revisions substitute for it the word which expresses the true idea*—love. *These references are :* 1 Cor 8:1; 13:1, 2, 3, 4, 8, 13; 14:1; 16:14; Col. 3:14; 1 Thes 3:6; 2 Thes 1:3; 1 Tim 1:5; 2:15; 4:12; 2 Tim 2:22; 3:10; 1 Pet 4:8; 5:14; 2 Pet 1:7; 3 John 6; Jude 12; Rev 2:19. *See also* Rom 14:15.

a few days for the *l.* *Gen* 29:20
passing the *l.* of women. *2 Sam* 1:26
greater than the *l.* he had. 13:15
be thou ravished always with her *l.* *Pr* 5:19
let us take our fill of *l.* till. 7:18
hatred stirreth up strifes, but *l.* 10:12
dinner of herbs where *l.* is. 15:17
a transgression seeketh *l.* 17:9
rebuke is better than secret *l.* 27:5
no man knoweth either *l.* *Eccl* 9:1
also their *l.* and hatred is now. 6
banner over me was *l.* *S of S* 2:4
apples, for I am sick of *l.* 5; 5:8
thereof being paved with *l.* 3:10
how pleasant art thou, O *l.*! 7:6
l. is strong as death, jealousy. 8:6
many waters cannot quench *l.*: if a man would give all . . . for *l.* 7
I remember thee, the *l.* *Jer* 2:2
trimmest thy way to seek *l.*? 33
loved thee with everlasting *l.* 31:3
time was the time of *l.* *Ezek* 16:8
corrupt in her inordinate *l.* 23:11*
came to her into bed of *l.* 17
mouth they shew much *l.* 33:31
Daniel into tender *l.* *Dan* 1:9*
l. of Lord toward Israel. *Hos* 3:1
I drew them with bands of *l.* 11:4
l. of many shall wax cold. *Mat* 24:12
if ye have *l.* one to. *John* 13:35
greater *l.* hath no man than. 15:13
l. wherewith thou hast loved. 17:26
who shall separate us from the *l.* of Christ ? *Rom* 8:35
let *l.* be without dissimulation. 12:9
affectioned with brotherly *l.* 10
l. worketh no ill, therefore *l.* *Rom* 13:10
I beseech you for the *l.* of the. 15:30
you may know the *l.* *2 Cor* 2:4
that ye would confirm your *l.* 8
l. of Christ constraineth us. 5:14
Holy Ghost, by *l.* unfeigned. 6:6
prove the sincerity of your *l.* 8:8
churches the proof of your *l.* 24
and the God of *l.* shall be. 13:11
faith which worketh by *l.* *Gal* 5:6
but brethren, by *l.* serve one. 13
fruit of the Spirit is *l.*, joy. 22
after I heard of your *l.* *Eph* 1:15
l. of Christ, passeth knowledge. 3:19
and *l.* with faith, from God. 6:23
that your *l.* may abound. *Phil* 1:9
other of *l.* doth preach Christ. 17
therefore any comfort of *l.* 2:1
likeminded, having the same *l.* 2
l. which ye have to all the saints. *Col* 1:4
who declared to us your *l.* in. 1:8
your labour of *l.* *1 Thes* 1:3
touching brotherly *l.*, ye need. 4:9
breastplate of faith and *l.* 5:8
they received not the *l.* *2 Thes* 2:10
abundant with faith and *l.* *1 Tim* 1:14
the *l.* of money is the root. 6:10
righteousness, *l.*, patience. 11
not given the spirit of fear, but of *l.* *2 Tim* 1:7
yet for *l.*'s sake I rather beseech thee. *Philem* 9
work and labour of *l.* *Heb* 6:10
to provoke unto *l.* and to. 10:24
let brotherly *l.* continue. 13:1
to unfeigned *l.* of the. *1 Pet* 1:22
the *l.* of the Father is. *1 John* 2:15
behold what manner of *l.* the. 3:1
let us love one another, for *l.* 4:7
God is *l.* 8
herein is *l.* not that we loved God. 10
l. that God hath to us; God is *l.* 16
herein is our *l.* made perfect. 17
there is no fear in *l.*; perfect *l.* 18
this is *l.*, that we walk after. *2 John* 6
mercy to you, peace and *l.* *Jude* 2
hast left thy first *l.* *Rev* 2:4

love, *verb*

l. thy neighbour as. *Lev* 19:18, 34
Mat 19:19; 22:39; *Mark* 12:31
l. the Lord thy God with. *Deut* 6:5
10:12; 11:1, 13, 22; 19:9; 30:6
God, which keepeth covenant with them that *l.* him. 7:9; *Dan* 9:4
he will *l.* thee, bless thee. *Deut* 7:13
delight in thy fathers to *l.* 10:15
l. therefore the stranger, for ye. 19
know whether ye *l.* the Lord. 13:3
command thee to *l.* Lord thy. 30:16
that thou mayest *l.* the Lord. 20
take heed to *l.* the Lord your God. *Josh* 22:5; 23:11
l. him be as the sun. *Judg* 5:31
king's servants *l.* thee. *1 Sam* 18:22
shouldest thou *l.* them ? *2 Chr* 19:2
mercy for them that *l.* him. *Neh* 1:5
how long will ye *l.* vanity ? *Ps* 4:2
let them that *l.* thy name be. 5:11
I will *l.* thee, O Lord my. 18:1
O *l.* the Lord, all ye saints. 31:23
l. thy salvation say. 40:16; 70:4
they that *l.* his name shall. 69:36
ye that *l.* the Lord, hate evil. 97:10
usest to do to those that *l.* 119:132
great peace have they who *l.* 165
shall prosper that *l.* thee. 122:6
preserveth them that *l.* him. 145:20
long, ye simple, will ye *l.*? *Pr* 1:22
l. wisdom, and she shall keep. 4:6
all they that hate me, *l.* death. 8:36
a wise man and he will *l.* thee. 9:8
kings *l.* him that speaketh. 16:13
that *l.* it shall eat the fruit. 18:21
a time to *l.* and a time. *Eccl* 3:8
therefore do the virgins *l.* *S of S* 1:3
than wine, the upright *l.* thee. 4
to serve and *l.* the name. *Isa* 56:6
I the Lord *l.* judgement, I. 61:8
Jerusalem all ye that *l.* her. 66:10
and my people *l.* to have. *Jer* 5:31
l. a woman beloved, *l.* *Hos* 3:1
her rulers with shame, do *l.* *Hos* 4:18
drive them out, I will *l.* them. 9:15
I will *l.* them freely, for mine. 14:4
hate evil and *l.* the good. *Amos* 5:15
hate the good and *l.* the. *Mi* 3:2
to *l.* mercy and to walk. 6:8
l. no false oath. *Zech* 8:17
l. the truth. 19
it hath been said, *L.* thy. *Mat* 5:43
but I say, *L.* your enemies. 44
Luke 6:27, 35
if ye *l.* them which *l.* you. *Mat* 5:46; *Luke* 6:32
they *l.* to pray standing. *Mat* 6:5
hate the one and *l.* the other. 24
Luke 16:13
l. the Lord thy God with all thy heart. *Mat* 22:37; *Mark* 12:30, 33
Luke 10:27
l. the uppermost rooms. *Mat* 23:6
scribes, who *l.* to go. *Mark* 12:38
which of them will *l.*? *Luke* 7:42
ye *l.* greetings in the markets. *Luke* 11:43; 20:46
will *l.* him and manifest. *John* 14:21
l. me, my Father will *l.* him. 23
my commandment, That ye *l.* one another. 15:12, 17
the world would *l.* his own. 19
for good, to them *l.* God. *Rom* 8:28
owe nothing to any, but to *l.* 13:8
shalt *l.* thy neighbour as thyself. *Rom* 13:9; *Gal* 5:14; *Jas* 2:8
prepared for them that *l.* *1 Cor* 2:9
if any man *l.* God the same is. 8:3
husbands, *l.* your wives, as Christ also. *Eph* 5:25, 28, 33; *Col* 3:19
grace be with all them that *l.* our Lord Jesus. *Eph* 6:24
are taught of God to *l.* *1 Thes* 4:9
but to all them that *l.* *2 Tim* 4:8
teach young women to *l.* *Tit* 2:4
greet them that *l.* us in the. 3:15
Lord promised to them that *l.* him. *Jas* 1:12; 2:5
whom having not seen ye *l.* *1 Pet* 1:8
see ye *l.* one another with a. 22
l. the brotherhood. 2:17
l. as brethren. 3:8
he that will *l.* life. 10
l. not the world, if any man *l.* the. *1 John* 2:15
from the beginning that we should *l.* 3:11; 4:7, 11; *2 John* 5
to life, because we *l.* *1 John* 3:14
l. one another, as he gave us. 23
if we *l.* one another, God. 4:12
l. him, because he first loved us. 19
can he *l.* God whom he hath not ? 20
loveth God, *l.* his brother also. 21
l. the children of God, when we *l.* 5:2

love *of God*

ye pass over judgement and *l. of God.* *Luke* 11:42
not *l. of God* in you. *John* 5:42
l. of God is shed abroad. *Rom* 5:5
separate us from the *l. of God.* 8:39
l. of God be with you. *2 Cor* 13:14
hearts into the *l. of God.* *2 Thes* 3:5
kindness and *l. of God.* *Tit* 3:4
the *l. of God* perfected. *1 John* 2:5
hereby perceive we *l. of God.* 3:16
dwelleth the *l. of God* in him ? 17
was manifested the *l. of God.* 4:9
this is *l. of God* that we keep. 5:3
keep yourselves in the *l. of God.* *Jude* 21

his **love**

Lord did not set *his l.* *Deut* 7:7
because he hath set *his l.* *Ps* 91:14
in *his l.* and in his pity he. *Isa* 63:9
will rest in *his l.* he will. *Zeph* 3:17
and abide in *his l.* *John* 15:10
but God commendeth *his l.* *Rom* 5:8
if love one another *his l.* *1 John* 4:12

in **love**

clave unto these *in l.* *1 Ki* 11:2
in l. to my soul delivered. *Isa* 38:17
to you with a rod, or *in l.* *1 Cor* 4:21
as ye abound *in* your *l.* to. *2 Cor* 8:7
be without blame before him *in l.* *Eph* 1:4
rooted and grounded *in l.* 3:17

forbearing one another in l. Eph 4:2
the truth in l. may grow up to. 15
to edifying of itself in l. 16
walk in l. as Christ hath loved. 5:2
being knit together in l. Col 2:2
you to increase in l. 1 Thes 3:12
esteem them highly in l. 5:13
in faith and l. which is. 2 Tim 1:13
he that dwelleth in l. 1 John 4:16
no fear in l.: he that feareth is not made perfect in l. 18
Father in truth and l. 2 John 3

my love

for my l. they are mine. Ps 109:4
rewarded me hatred for my l. 5
compared thee, O my l. S of S 1:9
behold, thou art fair, my l. 15; 4:1
as lily, so is my l. among. 2:2
my l. till he please. 7; 3:5; 8:4
rise up, my l. 2:10, 13
all fair, my l.; there is no spot. 4:7
open to me, my l. my dove. 5:2
beautiful, O my l. as Tirzah. 6:4
continue ye in my l. John 15:9
abide in my l. 10
my l. be with you all in Christ Jesus. 1 Cor 16:24

thy love

thy l. was wonderful. 2 Sam 1:26
for thy l. is better. S of S 1:2; 4:10
we will remember thy l. more. 1:4
how fair is thy l. my sister! 4:10
hearing of thy l. and faith. Philem 5
joy and consolation in thy l. 7
hast left thy first l. Rev 2:4

I love

savoury meat, such as I l. Gen 27:4
if servant shall say, I l. Ex 21:5
canst thou say, I l. thee? Judg 16:15
I l. Tamar my brother. 2 Sam 13:4
I l. the Lord, because. Ps 116:1
O how l. I thy law. 119:97
thy law do I l. 113, 163
therefore I l. thy testimonies. 119
I l. thy commands above gold. 127
consider how I l. thy precepts. 159
thy testimonies I l. exceedingly. 167
I l. them that l. me. Pr 8:17
world may know that I l. John 14:31
knowest that I l. thee. 21:15, 16, 17
the more I l. you, the. 2 Cor 12:15
if a man say, I l. God. 1 John 4:20
I l. in the truth. 2 John 1; 3 John 1
as I l. I rebuke and. Rev 3:19

love me

my husband will l. me. Gen 29:32
showing mercy to thousands of them that l. me. Ex 20:6; Deut 5:10
I love them that l. me. Pr 8:17
cause those that l. me to inherit. 21
Father, ye would l. me. John 8:42
doth my Father l. me. 10:17
if ye l. me, keep my. 14:15
if a man l. me, he will keep. 23

love not

l. not sleep, lest thou. Pr 20:13
if any man l. not the. 1 Cor 16:22
because I l. you not? 2 Cor 11:11
l. not the world. 1 John 2:15
let us not l. in word. 3:18

loved

Rebekah to wife, and l. Gen 24:67
Isaac l. Esau, but Rebekah l. 25:28
meat such as his father l. 27:14
Jacob l. Rachel more. 29:18, 30
Shechem l. Dinah, and spake. 34:3
Israel l. Joseph more than. 37:3, 4
because he l. thy fathers. Deut 4:37
but because the Lord l. you. 7:8
23:5; 33:3
Samson l. a woman in. Judg 16:4
Elkanah l. Hannah. 1 Sam 1:5
Saul l. David. 16:21
Jonathan l. David as his own soul. 18:1, 3; 20:17
Israel and Judah l. David. 18:16
Saul's daughter, l. David. 20
Lord l. Solomon, and. 2 Sam 12:24
son of David, l. Tamar. 13:1
than love wherewith he l. her. 15
Solomon l. the Lord. 1 Ki 3:3
because the Lord l. Israel. 10:9
2 Chr 9:8
Solomon l. many strange. 1 Ki 11:1
the Lord l. his people. 2 Chr 2:11
Isa 48:14
Rehoboam l. Maacah. 2 Chr 11:21
Uzziah had husbandmen, he l. 26:10
the king l. Esther above. Esth 2:17
they whom I l. are turned against. Job 19:19
excellency of Jacob whom he l. Ps 47:4
the mount Zion which he l. 78:68
as he l. cursing, so let it. 109:17
heaven whom they have l. Jer 8:2
thus have they l. to wander. 14:10
them that thou hast l. Ezek 16:37
thou hast l. a reward on. Hos 9:1
their abominations were according as they l. 10
was a child, then I l. him. 11:1
wherein hast thou l. us.? Mal 1:2
holiness of Lord which he l. 2:11
beholding him, l. him. Mark 10:21
forgiven, for she l. much. Luke 7:47
God so l. the world. John 3:16
Jesus l. Martha, and her sister. 11:5
Jews, behold how he l. him. 36
for they l. praise of men more. 12:43
having l. his own, he l. them to. 13:1
disciple whom Jesus l. 23; 19:26
20:2; 21:7, 20
he that loveth me shall be l. 14:21
if ye l. me, ye would rejoice. 28
Father l. me, so have I l. you. 15:9
loveth you, because ye l. 16:27
l. them, as thou hast l. me. 17:23
love wherewith thou hast l. me. 26
more than conquerors through him that l. us. Rom 8:37
love you, the less I be l. 2 Cor 12:15
l. me, and gave himself. Gal 2:20
great love wherewith he l. Eph 2:4
as Christ also l. us. 5:2
Christ l. the church. 25
Father, which hath l. us. 2 Thes 2:16
Demas having l. this. 2 Tim 4:10
hast l. righteousness. Heb 1:9
Balaam l. the wages of. 2 Pet 2:15
l. God, but that he l. us. 1 John 4:10
if God so l. us. 11
because he first l. us. 19
to him that l. us and. Rev 1:5
l. not their lives to the death. 12:11

I have loved

I have l. the habitation. Ps 26:8
commandments I have l. 119:47, 48
I have l. thee, therefore. Isa 43:4
I have l. strangers, and. Jer 2:25
I have l. thee with an everlasting love. 31:3
I have l. you, yet ye say. Mal 1:2
as I have l. you, that ye also love. John 13:34; 15:12
Father loved me, so have I l. 15:9
written, Jacob I have l. Rom 9:13
make them know that I have l. Rev 3:9

lovedst

thou l. their bed where. Isa 57:8
l. me before foundation. John 17:24

lovely

and Jonathan were l. 2 Sam 1:23
he is altogether l. O. S of S 5:16
them as a very l. song. Ezek 33:32
whatsoever things are l. Phil 4:8

lover

for Hiram was ever a l. 1 Ki 5:1
l. and friend hast thou. Ps 88:18
a l. of hospitality, a l. of good men. Tit 1:8*

lovers

my l. and friends stand. Ps 38:11
the harlot with many l. Jer 3:1
thy l. will despise thee, they. 4:30
go up and cry, for all thy l. 22:20
thy l. shall go into captivity. 22
all thy l. have forgotten thee. 30:14
l. hath none to comfort. Lam 1:2
called for my l. but they deceived. 19
thy gifts to all thy l. Ezek 16:33
discovered with thy l. and idols. 36
I will gather thy l. 37
doted on her l. 23:5
her into the hand of her l. Ezek 23:9
behold, I will raise up thy l. 22
I will go after my l. Hos 2:5
shall follow her l. 7
her lewdness in the sight of l. 10
these rewards that my l. have. 12
and she went after her l. and. 13
Ephraim hath hired l. 8:9
be l. of their own selves. 2 Tim 3:2
l. of pleasures more than l. of. 4

loves

us solace ourselves with l. Pr 7:18
will I give thee my l. S of S 7:12

lovest

son Isaac whom thou l. Gen 22:2
thou dost but hate me, and l. me not. Judg 14:16
thou l. thine enemies. 2 Sam 19:6
thou l. righteousness. Ps 45:7
thou l. evil more than good. 52:3
thou l. all devouring words. 4
with wife whom thou l. Eccl 9:9
he whom thou l. is sick. John 11:3
Simon, son of Jonas, l. thou me? 21:15, 16, 17

loveth

for thy father, such as he l. Gen 27:9
little one, and his father l. him. 44:20
Lord l. the stranger in. Deut 10:18
go away because he l. thee. 15:16
daughter in law who l. Ruth 4:15
and him that l. violence. Ps 11:5
Lord l. righteousness. 7; 33:5
what man is he that l. many days? 34:12
Lord l. judgement. 37:28; 99:4
the Lord l. gates of Zion. 87:2
word is very pure, therefore thy servant l. 119:140
The Lord l. the righteous. 146:8
the Lord l. he correcteth. Pr 3:12
l. instruction, l. knowledge. 12:1
but he that l. him, chasteneth. 13:24
he l. him that followeth after. 15:9
a scorner l. not one that. 12
a friend l. at all times. 17:17
l. transgression that l. strife. 19
he that getteth wisdom l. his. 19:8
l. pleasure, he that l. wine. 21:17
he that l. pureness of heart. 22:11
whoso l. wisdom rejoiceth his. 29:3
that l. silver, he that l. Eccl 5:10
O thou whom my soul l. S of S 1:7
bed I sought him whom soul l. 3:1
seek him whom my soul l. 2
saw ye him whom my soul l.? 3
I found him whom my soul l. 4
every one l. gifts and. Isa 1:23
Ephraim as heifer l. to. Hos 10:11
he is a merchant, he l. to. 12:7
l. father or mother, he that l. son or daughter more than me. Mat 10:37
he l. our nation. Luke 7:5
the same l. little. 47
the Father l. the Son, and hath given all things. John 3:35; 5:20
l. his life shall lose it. 12:25
commandments, he it is that l. me, and he that l. me shall be. 14:21
he that l. me not, keepeth not. 24
Father himself l. you, because. 16:27
he that l. another hath. Rom 13:8
for God l. a cheerful giver. 2 Cor 9:7
that l. his wife, l. himself. Eph 5:28
for whom the Lord l. he. Heb 12:6
he that l. his brother. 1 John 2:10
he that l. not his brother, is not of God. 3:10
l. not his brother, abideth in death. 14; 4:8, 20
every one that l. is born of God. 4:7
that he who l. God, love his. 21
that l. him that begat, l. him. 5:1
Diotrephes l. to have. 3 John 9
l. and maketh a lie. Rev 22:15

loving

let her be as the l. hind. Pr 5:19
l. favour rather than silver. 22:1
lying down, l. to slumber. Isa 56:10

lovingkindness

thy marvellous l. Ps 17:7; 92:2
thy l. is before mine eyes. 26:3
how excellent is thy l. O God! 36:7

O continue thy *l.* to them. *Ps* 36:10
I have not concealed thy *l.* 40:10
let thy *l.* continually preserve. 11
the Lord will command his *l.* 42:8
we have thought of thy *l.* O. 48:9
mercy on me according to thy *l.* 51:1
because thy *l.* is better than. 63:3
O Lord, for thy *l.* is good. 69:16
l. be declared in the grave? 88:11
l. will I not utterly take. 89:33
to shew forth thy *l.* in the. 92:2
who crowneth thee with *l.* and. 103:4
shall understand *l.* of Lord. 107:43
quicken me after thy *l.* 119:88, 159
hear my voice according to thy *l.* 149
praise thy name for thy *l.* 138:2
cause me to hear thy *l.* in. 143:8
the Lord which exercise *l.* *Jer* 9:24
taken away my peace, even *l.* 16:5
with *l.* have I drawn thee. 31:3
shewest *l.* unto thousands. 32:18
betroth thee to me in *l.* *Hos* 2:19

lovingkindnesses
Lord thy mercies and *l.* *Ps* 25:6
where are thy former *l.*? 89:49
mention the *l.* of the Lord according to the multitude of his *l.* *Isa* 63:7

low
shalt come down very *l.* *Deut* 28:43
the Lord bringeth *l.* *1 Sam* 2:7
sycamore trees in the *l.* *2 Chr* 9:27
Uzziah had much cattle in *l.* 26:10
Philistines invaded cities of *l.* 28:18
on high those that be *l.* *Job* 5:11
look on proud, and bring him *l.* 40:12
high and *l.* rich and poor. *Ps* 49:2
surely men of *l.* degree. 62:9
remembered us in our *l.* 136:23
pride shall bring him *l.* *Pr* 29:23
rich sit in *l.* place. *Eccl* 10:6
sound of the grinding is *l.* 12:4
will lay *l.* the haughtiness. *Isa* 13:11
fort of thy walls shall he lay *l.* 25:12
the lofty city he layeth it *l.* to. 26:5
thy speech shall be *l.* out of. 29:4
city shall be *l.* in a *l.* place. 32:19
I called on thy name out of *l.* dungeon. *Lam* 3:55
spreading vine of *l.* *Ezek* 17:6
that I have exalted the *l.* tree. 24
exalt him that is *l.*, abase. 21:26
shall set thee in the *l.* parts. 26:20*
regarded *l.* estate of his. *Luke* 1:48
hath exalted them of *l.* degree. 52
condescend to men of *l.* *Rom* 12:16
let the brother of *l.* degree. *Jas* 1:9
but the rich in that he is made *l.* 10
***see* brought**

lower
l. second and third stories. *Gen* 6:16
if rising be in sight *l.* *Lev* 13:20
it be no *l.* than the skin. 21, 26
set in the *l.* places the. *Neh* 4:13
made him a little *l.* than the angels. *Ps* 8:5; *Heb* 2:7, 9
shall go into the *l.* parts of the. 63:9
put *l.* in presence of prince. *Pr* 25:7
waters of the *l.* pool. *Isa* 22:9
Shout, ye *l.* parts. 44:23
bottom even to the *l.* *Ezek* 43:14
descended first into the *l.* *Eph* 4:9

lower *parts of the earth*
[1] *The valley*, Isa 44:23. [2] *The state of the dead*, Ps 63:9. [3] *The mother's womb*, Ps 139:15. [4] *The earth, as the lowest part of the visible world, or the grave and state of the dead*, Eph 4:9.

lowest
shall burn to the *l* hell. *Deut* 32:22†
made priests *l.* *1 Ki* 12:31; 13:33 *2 Ki* 17:32
my soul from the *l.* hell. *Ps* 86:13†
thou hast laid me in the *l.* pit. 88:6
curiously wrought in the *l.* 139:15
increased from the *l.* *Ezek* 41:7
straitened more than the *l.* 42:6
shame to take *l.* room. *Luke* 14:9
sit down in the *l.* room. 10

loweth
wild ass bray, or *l.* the ox? *Job* 6:5

lowing
along the highway *l.* *1 Sam* 6:12
then the *l.* of the oxen? 15:14

lowliness
that ye walk with all *l.* *Eph* 4:2
but in *l.* of mind, let each. *Phil* 2:3

lowly
yet hath he respect to *l.* *Ps* 138:6
but he giveth grace to *l.* *Pr* 3:34
then cometh shame, but with *l.* 11:2
humble spirit with the *l.* 16:19*
he is just, *l.* and riding. *Zech* 9:9
for I am meek and *l.* *Mat* 11:29

lowring
for the sky is red and *l.* *Mat* 16:3

Lucas
Marcus, Demas, *L.* my. *Philem* 24

Lucifer
fallen from heaven, O *L.* *Isa* 14:12

Lucius
L. of Cyrene was a. *Acts* 13:1
L. Jason and Sosipater. *Rom* 16:21

lucre
Samuel's sons turned after *l.*, took. *1 Sam* 8:3
greedy of filthy *l.* *1 Tim* 3:3, 8
not be given to filthy *l.* *Tit* 1:7
they ought not for filthy *l.* 11
feed flock not for filthy *l.* *1 Pet* 5:2

Luke
L. the beloved physician. *Col* 4:14
only *L.* is with me. *2 Tim* 4:11

lukewarm
because thou art *l.* *Rev* 3:16

lump
take a *l.* of figs and lay. *2 Ki* 20:7* *Isa* 38:21*
of the same *l.* one vessel. *Rom* 9:21
firstfruit be holy the *l.* is. 11:16
a little leaven leaveneth the whole *l.* *1 Cor* 5:6; *Gal* 5:9
that ye may be a new *l.* *1 Cor* 5:7

lunatick
and those which were *l.* *Mat* 4:24*
mercy on my son, for he is *l.* 17:15*

lurk
come, let us *l.* privily. *Pr* 1:11
l. privily for their own lives. 18

lurking
knowledge of all the *l.* *1 Sam* 23:23
he sitteth in the *l.* places. *Ps* 10:8
as it were a young lion *l.* in. 17:12

lust
(Formerly often used with a general meaning of pleasure, desire, with no idea of evil)
my *l.* shall be satisfied. *Ex* 15:9
asking meat for their *l.* *Ps* 78:18
not estranged from their *l.* 30
to their own hearts' *l.* 81:12*
burned in their *l.* one. *Rom* 1:27
not known *l.* except the law. 7:7*
ye shall not fulfil *l.* of flesh. *Gal* 5:16
not in *l.* of concupiscence. *1 Thes* 4:5
he is drawn of his own *l.* *Jas* 1:14
l. hath conceived, it bringeth. 15
that is in world through *l.* *2 Pet* 1:4
that walk after flesh in the *l.* of. 2:10
l. of the flesh, the *l.* of. *1 John* 2:16
world passeth away, and the *l.* 17

lust, *verb*
l. not after her beauty. *Pr* 6:25
on a woman to *l.* after her. *Mat* 5:28
not *l.* after evil things. *1 Cor* 10:6
ye *l.* and have not, ye kill. *Jas* 4:2

lusted
buried the people that *l.* *Num* 11:34
but they *l.* exceedingly. *Ps* 106:14
not lust as they also *l.* *1 Cor* 10:6
fruits thy soul *l.* after. *Rev* 18:14

lusteth
what thy soul *l.* after. *Deut* 12:15 20, 21; 14:26
flesh *l.* against the Spirit. *Gal* 5:17
dwelleth in us *l.* to envy. *Jas* 4:5

lusting
mixed multitude fell a *l.* *Num* 11:4

lusts
the *l.* of other things. *Mark* 4:19
and the *l.* of your father. *John* 8:44
gave them up to uncleanness through *l.* *Rom* 1:24
obey it in the *l.* thereof. 6:12
provision for flesh, to fulfil *l.* 13:14
have crucified flesh with *l.* *Gal* 5:24
our conversation in the *l.* of. *Eph* 2:3
according to the deceitful *l.* 4:22
into foolish and hurtful *l.* *1 Tim* 6:9
flee youthful *l.* but. *2 Tim* 2:22
silly women led away with *l.* 3:6
own *l.* shall they heap teachers. 4:3
that denying worldly *l.* *Tit* 2:12
disobedient, serving divers *l.* 3:3
not hence, even of your *l.*? *Jas* 4:1
ye may consume it on your *l.* 3
according to former *l.* *1 Pet* 1:14
abstain from fleshly *l.* that. 2:11
no longer should live to the *l.* 4:2
in lasciviousness, *l.* excess of. 3
they allure through the *l.* *2 Pet* 2:18
walking after their own *l.* 3:3
complainers, walking after *l.* *Jude* 16
walk after their own ungodly *l.* 18

lusty
Moab 10,000 men, all *l.* *Judg* 3:29

Luz
the city was called *L.* at the first. *Gen* 28:19; *Judg* 1:23
Jacob came to *L.* in the. *Gen* 35:6
Almighty appeared to me at *L.* 48:3

Lycaonia
and Derbe, cities of *L.* *Acts* 14:6
voices, saying in the speech of *L.* 11

Lydda
down to the saints at *L.* *Acts* 9:32
dwelt at *L.* turned to the Lord. 35
forasmuch as *L.* was nigh. 38

Lydia
L. shall fall with them. *Ezek* 30:5

Lydia
L. whose heart the Lord. *Acts* 16:14
entered into the house of *L.* 40

lying
hated them that regard *l.* vanities, but I trust in the Lord. *Ps* 31:6
let the *l.* lips be put to silence. 18
thou lovest *l.* rather than. 52:3
and for cursing and *l.* which. 59:12
spoken against me with *l.* 109:2
remove from me the way of *l.* 119:29
I hate and abhor *l.* but thy law. 163
soul, O Lord, from *l.* lips. 120:2
hateth a proud look, a *l.* *Pr* 6:17
that hideth hatred with *l.* lips. 10:18
but a *l.* tongue is but for a. 12:19
l. lips are abomination to the. 22
a righteous man hateth *l.* but a wicked man is loathsome. 13:5
much less do *l.* lips become a. 17:7
getting of treasures by a *l.* 21:6
a *l.* tongue hateth those. 26:28
rebellious people, *l.* *Isa* 30:9
wicked devices with *l.* words. 32:7
in transgressing and *l.* against. 59:13
trust ye not in *l.* words. *Jer* 7:4
behold, ye trust in *l.* words that. 8
because have spoken *l.* words. 29:23
vanity and *l.* divination. *Ezek* 13:6
spoken a *l.* divination? 7
by your *l.* to my people that. 19
ye have prepared *l.* words. *Dan* 2:9
by swearing, *l.* and killing. *Hos* 4:2*
that observe *l.* vanities forsake. *Jonah* 2:8
away *l.* speak truth. *Eph* 4:25
whose coming is with *l.* *2 Thes* 2:9

lying *spirit*
l. spirit in the mouth of all his. *1 Ki* 22:22; *2 Chr* 18:21
Lord hath put a *l. spirit* in prophets. *1 Ki* 22:23; *2 Chr* 18:22

lying, *verb*
three flocks of sheep *l.* *Gen* 29:2
him that hateth thee, *l.* *Ex* 23:5
if one be found slain, *l.* *Deut* 21:1
my path and *l.* down. *Ps* 139:3
sleeping, *l.* down, loving. *Isa* 56:10

man sick of the palsy, *l.* *Mat* 9:2
where the damsel was *l.* *Mark* 5:40
babe *l.* in a manger. *Luke* 2:12, 16
then *l.* on Jesus' breast. *John* 13:25*
he saw the linen clothes *l.* yet. 20:5
napkin not *l.* with the linen. 7

lying *in wait*
rose up from *l. in wait.* *Judg* 9:35
now there were men *l. in wait.* 16:9
as a bear *l. in wait,* as. *Lam* 3:10
me by the *l. in wait* of Jews. *Acts* 20:19
when Paul's kinsmen heard of their *l. in wait.* 23:16

lying *with*
l. with Jacob's daughter. *Gen* 34:7
kill woman that hath known man by *l. with* him. *Num* 31:17
not known man by *l. with* him, keep alive. 18; *Judg* 21:12
women had not known man by *l. with* him. *Num* 31:35
if a man be found *l. with.* *Deut* 22:22

Lysanias
reign of Tiberius, *L.* *Luke* 3:1

Lysias
L. unto the most excellent Felix. *Acts* 23:26

Lystra
were ware of it, and fled unto *L.* *Acts* 14:6
a certain man at *L.* impotent. 8
Paul came to *L.* 16:1
by the brethren at *L.* 2
afflictions which came unto me at *L.* *2 Tim* 3:11

M

Maachah
Reumah Nahor's concubine bare *M.* *Gen* 22:24
M. mother of Absalom. *2 Sam* 3:3 *1 Chr* 3:2
M. the mother of Abijam, the daughter of. *1 Ki* 15:2, 10; *2 Chr* 11:22
M. Caleb's concubine. *1 Chr* 2:48
M. the wife of Machir bare. 7:16
Hanan the son of *M.* 11:43

Maaseiah
Zichri slew *M.* *2 Chr* 28:7
Rehum and *M.* sealed. *Neh* 10:25
Zephaniah the son of *M.* *Jer* 21:1 29:25; 37:3
Lord of Zedekiah son of *M.* 29:21
Neriah son of *M.* 32:12; 51:59
above the chamber of *M.* son. 35:4

Maath
which was the son of *M.* *Luke* 3:26

Macedonia
come over into *M.* and. *Acts* 16:9
Timotheus were come from *M.* 18:5
when he had passed through *M.* 19:21
hath pleased them of *M.* *Rom* 15:26
were come into *M.* *2 Cor* 7:5
bestowed on the churches of *M.* 8:1
boast of you to them of *M.* 9:2
lest if they of *M.* find you. 4
brethren which came from *M.* 11:9
to all that believe in *M.* *1 Thes* 1:7
sounded the word, not only in *M.* 8
the brethren that are in *M.* 4:10

Machir
M. the son of Manasseh. *Gen* 50:23; *Num* 32:39
M. begat Gilead. *Num* 26:29; 27:1 36:1; *Josh* 17:1
Moses gave Gilead unto *M.* *Num* 32:40; *Deut* 3:15
out of *M.* came down. *Judg* 5:14
M. the son of Ammiel. *2 Sam* 9:4 5; 17:27

Machpelah
give me cave of *M.* *Gen* 23:9, 17
buried Sarah in the cave of *M.* 19
buried Abraham in *M.* 25:9
buried Jacob in *M.* 49:30; 50:13

mad
be *m.* for the sight of. *Deut* 28:34
feigned himself *m.* *1 Sam* 21:13
servants, Ye see the man is *m.* 14
this *m.* fellow to thee? *2 Ki* 9:11
m. against me are sworn. *Ps* 102:8
I said of laughter, It is *m.* *Eccl* 2:2
maketh a wise man *m.* 7:7*
that maketh diviners *m.* *Isa* 44:25
be moved, and be *m.* *Jer* 25:16
for every man that is *m.* put. 29:26
they are *m.* upon their idols. 50:38
therefore the nations are *m.* 51:7
fool, the spiritual man is *m.* *Hos* 9:7
he hath a devil and is *m.* *John* 10:20
to Rhoda, Thou art *m.* *Acts* 12:15
being exceedingly *m.* against them. 26:11
learning doth make thee *m.* 24
I am not *m.* most noble Festus. 25
not say that ye are *m.*? *1 Cor* 14:23

made
who *m.* thee prince over us? *Ex* 2:14; *Acts* 7:27
hath *m.* man's mouth? *Ex* 4:11
m. his servants and cattle flee. 9:20
after he had *m.* it a molten. 32:4
Aaron had *m.* them naked. 25
m. them gods of gold. 31; *Hos* 8:4
of Israel *m.* all the work. *Ex* 39:42
why have ye *m.* us to come from Egypt? *Num* 20:5
and calf which he had *m.* *Deut* 9:21
Joshua and Israel *m.* as if. *Josh* 8:15
went and *m.* as if they had been. 9:4
m. the heart of the people. 14:8
altar which our fathers *m.* 22:28
m. Samson sleep upon. *Judg* 16:19
Samson *m.* the Philistines. 25, 27
away the gods which I *m.* 18:24
his sons *m.* themselves vile. *1 Sam* 3:13*
that Samuel *m.* his sons judges. 8:1
have *m.* a king over you. 12:1
wast thou not *m.* the head? 15:17
sword hath *m.* women childless. 33
Whither have ye *m.* road? 27:10
m. himself sick. *2 Sam* 13:6*
calves that he had *m.* *1 Ki* 12:32
idols which his fathers *m.* 15:12
she had *m.* an idol in a grove. 13 *2 Chr* 15:16
streets as my fathers *m.* in. 20:34
they *m.* him king and. *2 Ki* 11:12
so Urijah the priest *m.* it. 16:11
yet his father *m.* him. *1 Chr* 26:10
art thou *m.* of the king's counsel? *2 Chr* 25:16
for Ahab *m.* Judah naked. 28:19
set the idol he had *m.* in the. 33:7
Josiah *m.* all present to serve. 34:33
whom he *m.* governor. *Ezra* 5:14
we *m.* our prayer unto. *Neh* 4:9
Ahasuerus *m.* her queen. *Esth* 2:17
they *m.* it a day of feasting. 9:17, 18
wast thou *m.* before the? *Job* 15:7
m. a pit, and is fallen into pit he *m.* *Ps* 7:15
are sunk into the pit they *m.* 9:15
is the man that *m.* not God. 52:7
I *m.* me great works. *Eccl* 2:4
I *m.* me gardens. 5
I *m.* me pools of water. 6
they *m.* me the keeper. *S of S* 1:6
he *m.* the pillars of silver. 3:10
my soul *m.* me like chariots. 6:12
their own fingers have *m.* *Isa* 2:8
is this the man that *m.* earth? 14:16
for we have *m.* lies our refuge. 28:15
of him that *m.* it, he *m.* me not. 29:16
which your hands have *m.* unto. 31:7
they have *m.* them crooked. 59:8
gods that have not *m.* *Jer* 10:11
have *m.* my pleasant portion a wilderness. 12:10
vessel that *m.* was marred in hand of potter, so he *m.* it again. 18:4
had *m.* that the prison. 37:15
which Asa the king had *m.* 41:9
Nebuchadnezzar *m.* me an. 51:34
ye *m.* the heart of the. *Ezek* 13:22*
the king dwelleth that *m.* 17:16
m. their sweet savour. 20:28
ye have *m.* your iniquity to be. 21:24
waters *m.* him great, deep set. 31:4
thy father *m.* master of. *Dan* 5:11
yet *m.* we not prayer before. 9:13
princes have *m.* him sick. *Hos* 7:5
the workman *m.* it, therefore. 8:6
the god which ye *m.* *Amos* 5:26
they *m.* their hearts as. *Zech* 7:12
thy faith hath *m.* thee whole. *Mat* 9:22; *Mark* 5:34; 10:52 *Luke* 8:48; 17:19
have *m.* commandment of God of none effect. *Mat* 15:6
prayer, but ye have *m.* it a den of. 21:13; *Mark* 11:17; *Luke* 19:46
m. them other five talents. *Mat* 25:16
who *m.* me a judge? *Luke* 12:14
and his name hath *m.* *Acts* 3:16
as for Saul, he *m.* havock of. 8:3*
who had *m.* this conspiracy. 23:13
they hoised up sail, and *m.* 27:40
m. free from law of sin. *Rom* 8:2
concerning faith have *m.* *1 Tim* 1:19
law *m.* nothing perfect. *Heb* 7:19
believeth not, hath *m.* God a liar. *1 John* 5:10
m. them white in blood. *Rev* 7:14
m. all nations drink of wine. 14:8

***see* covenant, end, fire**

made, referring to *God, Lord, Christ*
God *m.* the firmament. *Gen* 1:7
m. two great lights, he *m.* stars. 16; *Ps* 136:7, 9
m. the beast of the earth. *Gen* 1:25
every thing that he had *m.* 31
from all his work he had *m.* 2:2
God *m.* the earth and heavens. 4 *Ex* 20:11; 31:17; *Ps* 146:6 *Isa* 45:18; *Jer* 10:12
m. to grow every tree. *Gen* 2:9
m. he a woman. 22
in the likeness of God *m.* 5:1; 9:6
Lord he had *m.* man. 6:6, 7
God *m.* a wind to pass over. 8:1
Sarah said, God hath *m.* me. 21:6
m. his journey prosperous. 24:21
Lord hath *m.* room for us. 26:22
the Lord *m.* all Joseph did. 39:3, 23
God hath *m.* me to forget. 41:51
God hath *m.* me a father. 45:8
God hath *m.* me lord of all. 9
feared God, he *m.* houses. *Ex* 1:21
Lord *m.* the sea dry land. 14:21
I *m.* Israel to dwell in. *Lev* 23:43
Lord your God and I have *m.* 26:13
he *m.* them wander in. *Num* 32:13
for the Lord *m.* his heart. *Deut* 2:30
out of heaven he *m.* thee to. 4:36
the Lord hath *m.* thee as. 10:22
m. the water of the Red sea. 11:4
nations which he hath *m.* 26:19
m. thee, and established thee. 32:6
he *m.* him ride, *m.* him suck. 13
then he forsook God which *m.* 15
Lord *m.* Jordan border. *Josh* 22:25
m. him have dominion. *Judg* 5:13*
the Lord had *m.* a breach in. 21:15
and *m.* them dwell in. *1 Sam* 12:8
Lord repented that he had *m.* 15:35
Lord had *m.* a breach. *2 Sam* 6:8*
he *m.* darkness pavilions. 22:12
thy gentleness hath *m.* me great. 36 *Ps* 18:35
who hath *m.* me a house. *1 Ki* 2:24
Lord loved Israel, therefore he *m.* 10:9; 14:7; 16:2; *2 Chr* 1:11
but the Lord *m.* the heavens. *1 Chr* 16:26; *Neh* 9:6; *Ps* 33:6 96:5; 121:2, 124:8; 134:3
Lord had *m.* them to rejoice. *2 Chr* 20:27
he sought the Lord, God *m.* 26:5
Lord had *m.* them joyful. *Ezra* 6:22; *Neh* 12:43
thy hands have *m.* me. *Job* 10:8
m. me weary, thou hast *m.* 16:7
he hath *m.* me a byword of. 17:6
he *m.* a decree for the rain. 28:26
that *m.* me in the womb make. 31:15
the Spirit of God *m.* me, and. 33:4
m. him can make his sword. 40:19
hast not *m.* my foes to. *Ps* 30:1
what desolations he hath *m.* in. 46:8
the sea is his and he *m.* it. 95:5
he *m.* us. 100:3
darkness, and *m.* it dark. 105:28

the day the Lord hath m. Ps 118:24
thy hands have m. me and. 119:73
that by wisdom m. the heavens. 136:5; Acts 14:15
m. Israel pass through. Ps 136:14
he hath m. a decree which. 148:6
rejoice in him that m. him. 149:2
the Lord m. all things. Pr 16:4
the Lord hath m. even both. 20:12
he hath m. every thing. Eccl 3:11
I found that God hath m. man. 7:29
he that m. them will not. Isa 27:11
he hath m. Tophet deep and. 30:33
thus saith the Lord that m. 44:2
he m. intercession for the. 53:12
things hath mine hand m. 66:2
lo, certainly in vain m. he it. Jer 8:8
Lord m. thee priest instead. 29:26
and hast m. thee a name as. 32:20
as the Lord liveth, that m. 38:16
he hath m. me desolate and faint. Lam 1:13; 3:11
the Lord hath m. my strength. 1:14
my skin hath he m. old. 3:4
hath m. my chain heavy. 7
m. my paths crooked. 9
he hath m. me drunken with. 15
I m. nations to shake at. Ezek 31:16
fear God who hath m. sea. Jonah 1:9
I m. their streets waste. Zeph 3:6
he m. them male and female. Mat 19:4; Mark 10:6
did not he that m. that? Luke 11:40
was not any thing m. John 1:3
Jesus m. more disciples. 4:1
he m. water wine. 46
he that m. me whole said. 5:11
m. clay of the spittle. 9:6; 11:14
m. himself the Son of God. 19:7
know that God hath m. Acts 2:36
know that God m. choice. 15:7
God that m. the world and. 17:24
hath m. of one blood all nations. 26
the Holy Ghost hath m. you. 20:28
m. foolish the wisdom. 1 Cor 1:20
m. us able ministers of. 2 Cor 3:6
hath m. him to be sin for us. 5:21
Christ hath m. us free. Gal 5:1
he hath m. us accepted. Eph 1:6
God hath m. us sit together. 2:6
he is our peace who hath m. 14
but m. himself of no. Philem 2:7
who hath m. us meet to. Col 1:12
he m. a shew of them openly. 2:15
by whom also he m. Heb 1:2
for when God m. promise to. 6:13
and hath m. us kings and. Rev 1:6
and worship him that m. 14:7

I have, or *have I* **made**

living substance I have m. Gen 7:4
lest thou say, I have m. 14:23
a father of nations have I m. thee. 17:5; Rom 4:17
Isaac said, Behold, I have m. him thy lord. Gen 27:37
see I have m. thee a god. Ex 7:1
I have m. thee a great name. 2 Sam 7:9; 1 Chr 17:8
I have m. supplication. 1 Ki 8:59
I have m. provision. 1 Chr 29:19
I Darius have made a decree. Ezra 6:11, 12
I have m. my bed in. Job 17:13
if I have m. gold my hope. 31:24
I have m. the wilderness. 39:6
things which I have m. Ps 45:1
who can say, I have m. my? Pr 20:9
I have m. their shouting. Isa 16:10
the sighing thereof have I m. 21:2
yea, I have m. him. 43:7; 46:4
I have m. the earth, and created. 45:12; Jer 27:5
the souls which I have m. Isa 57:16
behold I have m. thee a. Jer 1:18
but I have m. Esau bare. 49:10
behold, I have m. thy face strong. Ezek 3:8, 9
I have m. thee a watchman to. 17
whom I have not m. sad. 13:22
and I have m. the dry tree. 17:24
have I m. thee a reproach. 22:4
I have m. it for myself. 29:3, 9
I have m. him fair by multitude. 31:9
image which I have m. Dan 3:15
I have m. the stink of camps to. Amos 4:10
I have m. thee small among the. Obad 2
have I m. you contemptible. Mal 2:9
because I have m. a man every whit whole. John 7:23
yet have I m. myself. 1 Cor 9:19

thou hast **made**

plant them in the place which thou hast m. Ex 15:17
thou hast m. an atonement for. 29:36
this oath which thou hast m. us swear. Josh 2:17, 20
thou hast m. thy servant king instead of David. 1 Ki 3:7
supplication that thou hast m. 9:3
thou hast m. heaven and earth. 2 Ki 19:15; Isa 37:16; Jer 32:17
word came, saying, Thou hast m. great wars. 1 Chr 22:8
thou hast m. an hedge. Job 1:10
remember that thou hast m. 10:9
thou hast m. desolate all my. 16:7
thou hast m. him little lower than angels. Ps 8:5
thou hast m. me the head of. 18:43
thou hast m. him most blessed. 21:6
thou hast m. my mountain. 30:7
behold, thou hast m. my days. 39:5
thou hast m. the earth to tremble. 60:2
thou hast m. us drink the wine. 3
thou hast m. summer and. 74:17
all nations whom thou hast m. 86:9
thou hast m. me an abomination to them. 88:8
thou hast m. all his enemies. 89:42
thou hast m. his glory to cease. 44
hast thou m. all men in vain? 47
thou hast m. the Lord thy habitation. 91:9
thou, Lord, hast m. me glad. 92:4
wisdom hast thou m. them. 104:24
Leviathan, whom thou hast m. 26
thou hast m. me wiser than. 119:98
for thou hast m. of a city. Isa 25:2
but thou hast m. me to serve. 43:24
O Lord, why hast thou m. us to err from thy ways? 63:17
where are thy gods that thou hast m. thee? Jer 2:28
wait on thee, for thou hast m. 14:22
thou hast m. us as the offscouring and refuse. Lam 3:45
nor hast thou m. up the hedge in the house. Ezek 13:5
thou hast m. thee an high place in every street. 16:24
thou hast m. thy beauty to be. 25
thy idols which thou hast m. 22:4
at thy dishonest gain which thou hast m. 13
but one hour, and thou hast m. them equal to us. Mat 20:12
why hast thou m. me thus. Rom 9:20
thou hast m. us to our God kings and priests. Rev 5:10

made *haste*

Rebekah m. haste and. Gen 24:46
Joseph m. haste. 43:30
Moses m. haste. Ex 34:8
Manoah's wife m. haste. Judg 13:10
David made h. 1 Sam 23:26
Abigail m. haste. 25:18
nurse m. haste to flee. 2 Sam 4:4
I m. haste, and delayed. Ps 119:60
Zacchaeus m. haste. Luke 19:6
see **Israel, sin, known**

made *manifest*

secret that shall not be m. manifest. Luke 8:17
he should be m. manifest. John 1:31
his deeds may be m. manifest. 3:21
God should be m. manifest in. 9:3
I was m. manifest to them that asked not. Rom 10:20
m. manifest to all nations for the obedience of faith. 16:26
every man's work shall be m. manifest. 1 Cor 3:13
are approved may be m. manifest. 1 Cor 11:19
secrets of his heart m. manifest. 14:25
life of Jesus should be m. manifest. 2 Cor 4:10, 11
been throughly m. manifest. 11:6
m. manifest by the light. Eph 5:13
but now is m. manifest to. Col 1:26
now m. manifest by the appearing of Christ. 2 Tim 1:10
way into the holiest was not yet m. manifest. Heb 9:8
went out, that they they might be m. manifest. 1 John 2:19
judgements are m. manifest. Rev 15:4

made *peace*

and Joshua m. peace with them. Josh 9:15; 10:1, 4
was not a city that m. peace with Israel. 11:19
of Hadarezer were smitten, they m. peace. 2 Sam 10:19; 1 Chr 19:19
Jehoshaphat m. peace. 1 Ki 22:44

made *ready*

m. ready the present. Gen 43:25
Joseph m. ready his chariot. 46:29
m. ready his chariot, and. Ex 14:6
in and m. ready a kid. Judg 6:19
till we have m. ready a kid. 13:15
m. ready before it was. 1 Ki 6:7
chariot was m. ready. 2 Ki 9:21
m. ready for the building. 1 Chr 28:2
afterward they m. ready for themselves. 2 Chr. 35:14
his bow and m. it ready. Ps 7:12
have m. ready their heart. Hos 7:6
the disciples m. ready. Mat 26:19
Mark 14:16; Luke 22:13
they m. ready Peter fell. Acts 10:10
boast of things m. ready. 2 Cor 10:16
wife hath m. herself ready. Rev 19:7

made *speed*

Rehoboam m. speed to get. 1 Ki 12:18; 2 Chr 10:18

made *void*

hath utterly m. void. Num 30:12
thou hast m. void covenant. Ps 89:39
they have m. void thy law. 119:126
be heirs, faith is m. void. Rom 4:14

made, *passively*

hands were m. strong. Gen 49:24
may be m. unclean. Lev 22:5
shall bear all that is m. for them. Num 4:26
that is m. of the vine tree. 6:4
what supplication be m. 1 Ki 8:38
2 Chr 6:29
ears attend to prayer m. 2 Chr 6:40
let there be search m. in. Ezra 5:17
and search was m. in the house. 6:1
let his house be m. a dunghill. 11
gallows be m. of fifty. Esth 5:14
I am m. to possess months. Job 7:3
his like on earth, who is m. 41:33
when one is m. rich. Ps 49:16
fearfully and wonderfully m. 139:14
the righteous is m. plain. Pr 15:19
the simple is m. wise. 21:11
trust in Lord shall be m. fat. 28:25
cannot be m. straight. Eccl 1:15
countenance the heart is m. 7:3
a feast is m. for laughter. 10:19
which shall be m. as grass. Isa 51:12
shall earth be m. to bring forth. 66:8
a vessel that cannot be m. Jer 19:11
the word of the Lord was m. 20:8
his heart was m. like. Dan 5:21
these stones be m. bread. Mat 4:3
and the rent is m. worse. 9:16
Mark 2:21
and payment to be m. Mat 18:25
is m. ye make him twofold. 23:15
there was a cry m. behold. 25:6
rather a tumult was m. 27:24
the sepulchre be m. sure. 64
sabbath was m. for man. Mark 2:27
a recompence be m. thee. Luke 14:12
Pilate and Herod were m. 23:12
m. by him, and without him was not any thing m. that was m. John 1:3
the world was m. by him. 10

Word was *m.* flesh, and. *John* 1:14
the water that was *m.* wine. 2:9
wilt thou be *m.* whole? 5:6
Behold, thou art *m.* whole. 14
ye shall be *m.* free. 8:33
might be *m.* blind. 9:39
that they may be *m.* perfect. 17:23
distribution was *m.* to. *Acts* 4:35
prayer *m.* without ceasing. 12:5
promise which was *m.* 13:32; 26:6
prayer was wont to be *m.* 16:13
they be no gods which are *m.* 19:26
Jesus who was *m.* of the. *Rom* 1:3
by the things that are *m.* 20
thy circumcision is *m.* 2:25
were *m.* sinners, many *m.* 5:19
being *m.* free from sin. 6:18, 22
that which is good, *m.* death. 7:13
we had been *m.* like to Sodom. 9:29
the mouth confession is *m.* 10:10
let their table be *m.* a snare. 11:9
thy brother is *m.* weak. 14:21
cross of Christ be *m.* *1 Cor* 1:17
are in Christ, who of God is *m.* 30
m. a spectacle to the world. 4:9
we are *m.* as filth of world. 13
I am *m.* all things to all men. 9:22
have been all *m.* to drink. 12:13
in Christ shall all be *m.* alive. 15:22
first man Adam was *m.* a living soul,
last Adam was *m.* a. 45
which was *m.* glorious. *2 Cor* 3:10
an house not *m.* with hands. 5:1
might be *m.* the righteousness. 21
my strength is *m.* perfect in. 12:9
are ye now *m.* perfect by? *Gal* 3:3
Christ redeemed us, being *m.* 13
his seed were the promises *m.* 16
to whom the promise was *m.* 19
sent his Son, *m.* of a woman, *m.* 4:4
circumcision in flesh *m.* *Eph* 2:11
were far off, are *m.* nigh by the. 13
whereof I was *m.* a minister. 3:7
Col 1:23, 25
and was *m.* in the likeness. *Phil* 2:7
m. conformable to his death. 3:10
m. peace through blood. *Col* 1:20
with the circumcision *m.* 2:11
the law is not *m.* for a. *1 Tim* 1:9
and giving of thanks be *m.* for. 2:1
grace, we should be *m.* heirs. *Tit* 3:7
being *m.* so much better. *Heb* 1:4
it behoved him to be *m.* like. 2:17
for we are *m.* partakers of. 3:14
himself to be *m.* an high priest. 5:5
being *m.* perfect, he became the. 9
m. like to the Son of God. 7:3
m. of necessity a change. 12
m. not after law of a carnal. 16
an oath he was *m.* priest. 20
those priests were *m.* without. 21
Jesus was *m.* a surety of a better. 22
there was a tabernacle *m.* 9:2
a perfect tabernacle not *m.* 11
not entered into holy places *m.* 24
is a remembrance *m.* of sins. 10:3
expecting till his enemies be *m.* 13
ye were *m.* a gazingstock. 33
were not *m.* of things which. 11:3
weakness were *m.* strong. 34
us should not be *m.* perfect. 40
the spirits of just men *m* 12:23
rich, in that he is *m.* low. *Jas* 1:10
by works was faith *m.* perfect. 2:22
m. after similitude of God. 3:9
m. head of the corner. *1 Pet* 2:7
but these *m.* to be taken. *2 Pet* 2:12
they were *m.* bitter. *Rev* 8:11
been *m.* drunk with wine of. 17:2

madest

thou *m.* him to have dominion over.
Ps 8:6
visit the branch that thou *m.* 80:15
son of man, whom thou *m.* 17
m. to thyself images of. *Ezek* 16:17
thou *m.* all their loins to be. 29:7
neither *m.* it grow. *Jonah* 4:10
art not thou that Egyptian which *m.*
an uproar? *Acts* 21:38
thou *m.* him a little lower. *Heb* 2:7

madman

fellow to play the *m.* *1 Sam* 21:15
as a *m.* who casteth. *Pr* 26:18

madmen

have I need of *m.*? *1 Sam* 21:15
O *m.* the sword shall. *Jer* 48:2

madness

shall smite thee with *m.* *Deut* 28:28
heart to know wisdom and *m.*
Eccl 1:17
to behold wisdom and *m.* 2:12
wickedness of folly, and *m.* 7:25
m. is in their heart, while. 9:3
his talk is mischievous *m.* 10:13
horse and rider with *m.* *Zech* 12:4
were filled with *m.* *Luke* 6:11
dumb ass forbade the *m.* *2 Pet* 2:16

Magdala

into the coasts of *M.* *Mat* 15:39

magician

such things at any *m.* *Dan* 2:10

magicians

and called for the *m.* *Gen* 41:8
I told this to the *m.* but none. 24
m. of Egypt did so in like manner.
Ex 7:11, 22; 8:7, 18
the *m.* said to Pharaoh, This. 8:19
m. could not stand before. 9:11
ten times better than all *m.* *Dan* 1:20
king commanded to call the *m.* 2:2
the secret cannot the *m.* shew. 27
then came in the *m.* but did not. 4:7
master of the *m.* tell me. 9
father made master of the *m.* 5:11

magistrate

was no *m.* in the land. *Judg* 18:7
goest to the *m.* give. *Luke* 12:58

magistrates

set *m.* and judges, who. *Ezra* 7:25
bring you to the *m.* *Luke* 12:11*
Paul and Silas to the *m.* *Acts* 16:20
m. commanded to beat them. 22
the *m.* sent the serjeants. 35, 36
told these words to the *m.* 38
in mind to obey *m.* and. *Tit* 3:1*

magnifical

the house must be exceeding *m.*
1 Chr 22:5

magnificence

m. should be destroyed. *Acts* 19:27

magnified

thou hast *m.* thy mercy. *Gen* 19:19
Lord *m.* Joshua in sight. *Josh* 4:14
let thy name be *m.* *2 Sam* 7:26
1 Chr 17:24
and the Lord *m.* Solomon.
1 Chr 29:25; *2 Chr* 1:1
Hezekiah was *m.* in sight of all.
2 Chr 32:23*
say, Let the Lord be *m.* *Ps* 35:27
say continually, The Lord be *m.*
40:16; 70:4
thou hast *m.* thy word above. 138:2
for he *m.* himself against the Lord.
Jer 48:26, 42; *Dan* 8:11
the enemy hath *m.* himself. *Lam* 1:9
and *m.* themselves against their border.
Zeph 2:8
m. themselves against people. 10
Lord will be *m.* from the. *Mal* 1:5
but the people *m.* them. *Acts* 5:13
name of Lord Jesus was *m.* 19:17
Christ be *m.* in my body. *Phil* 1:20

magnify

[1] *To declare and shew forth one's greatness and glory,* Luke 1:46. [2] *To increase one's esteem, reputation, and authority,* Josh 3:7; 4:14; 1 Chr 29:25.

day will I begin to *m.* thee. *Josh* 3:7
thou shouldest *m.* him? *Job* 7:17
if indeed ye will *m.* yourselves. 19:5
remember that thou *m.* his. 36:24
O *m.* the Lord with me. *Ps* 34:3
clothed with shame that *m.* 35:26
my foot slippeth, they *m.* 38:16
did *m.* himself against me. 55:12
m. him with thanksgiving. 69:30
Shall the saw *m.* itself? *Isa* 10:15
he will *m.* the law and make. 42:21
thus will I *m.* myself. *Ezek* 38:23
and he shall *m.* himself. *Dan* 8:25
the king shall *m.* himself. 11:36
shall *m.* himself above all. 37

they *m.* not themselves. *Zech* 12:7
soul doth *m.* the Lord. *Luke* 1:46
tongues, and *m.* God. *Acts* 10:46
I am an apostle, I *m.* *Rom* 11:13*

Magog

the son of Japheth, *M.* *Gen* 10:2
1 Chr 1:5
against the land of *M.* *Ezek* 38:2
I will send a fire on *M.* and. 39:6
to gather Gog and *M.* *Rev* 20:8

Mahanaim

called name of place *M.* *Gen* 32:2
out of Gad to Levites, *M.*
Josh 21:38; *1 Chr* 6:80
Ish-bosheth to *M.* *2 Sam* 2:8
then David came to *M.* 17:24, 27
provided sustenance at *M.* 19:32
Shimei cursed me when I went to *M.*
1 Ki 2:8
the son of Iddo had *M.* 4:14

Maher-shalal-hash-baz

in the roll concerning *M.* *Isa* 8:1
then said Lord, Call his name *M.* 3

Mahlon

Elimelech's sons, *M.* *Ruth* 1:2
M. and Chilion died also both. 5
have bought all that was *M.* 4:9
wife of *M.* have I purchased. 10

maid

(*The Revisions frequently substitute for this word the word* handmaid. *The handmaids or maidservants of those days were usually slaves*)

go in unto my *m.* Hagar. *Gen* 16:2
behold, thy *m.* is in thy hand. 6
Hagar, Sarai's *m.* whence? 8
Laban gave Zilpah his *m.* 29:24
Bilhah, to be Rachel's *m.* 29
m. Bilhah, go in unto her. 30:3
Rachel's *m.* conceived. 7
gave Zilpah her *m.* 9
Zilpah, Leah's *m.* bare Jacob. 10, 12
she sent her *m.* to fetch. *Ex* 2:5
the *m.* went and called the. 8
smite his *m.* with a rod. 21:20
or the eye of his *m.* that it. 26
if a man entice a *m.* not. 22:16*
shall be meat for thy *m.* *Lev* 25:6
I came to her, I found her not a *m.*
Deut 22:14*, 17*
away captive a little *m.* *2 Ki* 5:2
thus said the *m.* that is of Israel. 4
m. was fair and beautiful. *Esth* 2:7
should I think upon a *m.*? *Job* 31:1
way of a man with a *m.* *Pr* 30:19
with *m.* so with mistress. *Isa* 24:2
m. forget her ornaments? *Jer* 2:32
the young man and the *m.* 51:22
father go in to the same *m.* *Amos* 2:7
for the *m.* is not dead. *Mat* 9:24
by the hand, and the *m.* arose. 25
another *m.* saw him. 26:71
Mark 14:69; *Luke* 22:56
called, saying, *M.*, arise. *Luke* 8:54

maid child

if she bear a *m. child.* *Lev* 12:5

maiden

I have given my *m.* to. *Gen* 30:18
is my daughter a *m.* *Judg* 19:24
on young man or *m.* *2 Chr* 36:17
every *m.* to the king. *Esth* 2:13
as the eyes of a *m.* to her mistress.
Ps 123:2
and mother of the *m.* *Luke* 8:51

maidens

her *m.* walked along by. *Ex* 2:5
abide here fast by my *m.* *Ruth* 2:8
that thou go out with his *m.* 22
kept fast by the *m.* of Boaz. 23
they found *m.* going to. *1 Sam* 9:11
I and my *m.* will fast. *Esth* 4:16
thou bind him for thy *m.*? *Job* 41:5
their *m.* were not given. *Ps* 78:63
young men and *m.* praise. 148:12
hath sent forth her *m.* *Pr* 9:3
maintenance for thy *m.* 27:27
giveth a portion to her *m.* 31:15
I got me servants and *m.* *Eccl* 2:7
m. of seed of Israel. *Ezek* 44:22*
begin to beat menservants and *m.*
Luke 12:45

maids

preferred her and her *m.* *Esth* 2:9
my *m.* count me for a. *Job* 19:15
ravished the *m.* in cities. *Lam* 5:11
slay utterly both *m.* and. *Ezek* 9:6
her *m.* shall lead her with. *Nah* 2:7
young men cheerful, and new wine the *m.* *Zech* 9:17

maidservant

the firstborn of the *m.* *Ex* 11:5
thy *m.* shall do no work. 20:10
Deut 5:14
not covet thy neighbour's wife, nor *m.* *Ex* 20:17
sell his daughter to be a *m.* 21:7
if he smite out his *m.'s* tooth. 27
if an ox push a *m.* he shall give. 32
that thy *m.* may rest as. *Deut* 5:14
desire thy neighbour's *m.* 21
eat them, thou and thy *m.* 12:18
16:11, 14
to thy *m.* thou shalt do. 15:17
son of his *m.* king. *Judg* 9:18
despise cause of my *m.* *Job* 31:13
his *m.* go free. *Jer* 34:9, 10

maidservants

Abram had *m.* and she asses.
Gen 12:16; 24:35
Abimelech's wife and *m.* 20:17
had much cattle and *m.* 30:43
entered into the two *m.'* tents. 31:33
rejoice, ye and your *m.* *Deut* 12:12
he shall take your *m.* *1 Sam* 8:16
of the *m.* shall I be had. *2 Sam* 6:22
time to receive *m.*? *2 Ki* 5:26

mail

he was armed with a coat of *m.*
1 Sam 17:5, 38

maimed

blind or *m.* ye shall not. *Lev* 22:22
them those that were *m.* *Mat* 15:30
wondered when they saw the *m.* 31
better to enter into life *m.* 18:8*
Mark 9:43
makest a feast, call *m.* *Luke* 14:13
bring in hither the poor and *m.* 21

main

hoised up the *m.*-sail. *Acts* 27:40*

maintain

[1] *To support and preserve*, 1 Chr 26:27; Ps 16:5. [2] *To defend by argument*, Job 13:15. [3] *To persevere in*, Tit 3:8, 14.

m. their cause. *1 Ki* 8:45, 49, 59
2 Chr 6:35, 39
they dedicate to *m.* the house of the Lord. *1 Chr* 26:27*
I will *m.* mine own ways. *Job* 13:15
Lord will *m.* the cause of. *Ps* 140:12
careful to *m.* good works. *Tit* 3:8
learn to *m.* good works for uses. 14

maintained

for thou hast *m.* my right. *Ps* 9:4

maintainest

portion, and thou *m.* my lot. *Ps* 16:5

maintenance

have *m.* from the king. *Ezra* 4:14*
the *m.* for thy maidens. *Pr* 27:27

majesty

is the power and *m.* *1 Chr* 29:11
upon him such royal *m.* 25
shewed the honour of his *m.* *Esth* 1:4
with God is terrible *m.* *Job* 37:22
deck thyself now with *m.* 40:10
honour and *m.* hast thou. *Ps* 21:5
voice of the Lord is full of *m.* 29:4
with thy glory and *m.* 45:3
in thy *m.* ride. 4
reigneth, he is clothed with *m.* 93:1
honour and *m.* are before him. 96:6
clothed with honour and *m.* 104:1
speak of the honour of thy *m.* 145:5
to make known the glorious *m.* 12
hide thee for the glory of his *m.*
Isa 2:10; 19:21
they shall sing for the *m.* of. 24:14
behold the *m.* of the Lord. 26:10
ornament he set it in *m.* *Ezek* 7:20
for the honour of my *m.* *Dan* 4:30
excellent *m.* was added unto me. 36
Nebuchadnezzar thy father *m.* 5:18
the *m.* he gave him, all people. 19
feed in *m.* of the name. *Mi* 5:4
on the right hand of *m.* *Heb* 1:3; 8:1
eyewitnesses of his *m.* *2 Pet* 1:16
wise God be glory and *m.* *Jude* 25

make

let us *m.* man. *Gen* 1:26
I will *m.* him an help. 2:18
and a tree to be desired to *m.* 3:6
m. coats of skins. 21
m. thee an ark. 6:14
let us *m.* brick. 11:3
let us *m.* us a name. 4
I will *m.* of thee a great nation.
12:2; 21:18; 46:3; *Ex* 32:10
let us *m.* a name, lest. *Gen* 12:4
I will *m.* thy seed as the dust. 13:16
I will *m.* thee exceeding fruitful.
17:6; 48:4
m. Ishmael fruitful, I will *m.* 17:20
let us *m.* our father drink wine.
19:32, 34
I will *m.* thy seed as the stars. 26:4
Isaac said, *M.* me savoury. 27:4
bless thee, and *m.* thee fruitful. 28:3
I will *m.* thy seed as the sand. 32:12
m. ye marriages with us and. 34:9
ye *m.* me to stink among the. 30
go to Beth-el, and *m.* there an. 35:1
m. there an altar unto God. 3
m. mention of me to Pharaoh. 40:14
land *m.* thy father to dwell. 47:6
God *m.* thee as Ephraim and. 48:20
they say to us, *M.* brick. *Ex* 5:16
m. your count for the lamb. 12:4
m. them know the statutes. 18:16
not *m.* unto thee any graven image.
20:4; *Lev* 26:1; *Deut* 5:8
not *m.* with me gods of. *Ex* 20:23
an altar of earth shalt thou *m.* 24
if thou wilt *m.* me an altar. 25
m. full restitution. 22:3, 5, 6, 12
m. no mention of other gods. 23:13
Josh 23:7
I will *m.* enemies turn. *Ex* 23:27
shall not dwell, lest they *m.* thee. 33
m. me a sanctuary. 25:8
so shall ye *m.* it. 9
shalt *m.* holy garments. 28:2, 4
garments which they shall *m.* 4
for Aaron's sons thou shalt *m.* 40
m. them linen breeches. 42
m. him an altar of shittim. 30:1
m. it an oil of holy ointment. 25
perfume, you shall not *m.* like. 37
that they *m.* all that. 31:6; 35:10
up, *m.* us gods which shall go before us. 32:1, 23; *Acts* 7:40
I will *m.* of thee a great. *Ex* 32:10
I will *m.* my goodness pass. 33:19
and *m.* thy sons go a whoring. 34:16
m. no molten gods. 17; *Lev* 19:4
neither man nor woman *m.* *Ex* 36:6
he shall *m.* amends for. *Lev* 5:16
not *m.* yourselves abominable.
11:43; 20:25
not *m.* any cuttings in your. 19:28
not *m.* baldness. 21:5; *Deut* 14:1
I will *m.* you fruitful. *Lev* 26:9
I will *m.* your heaven as iron. 19
beasts, which shall *m.* you few. 22
man shall *m.* a singular vow. 27:2
the Lord *m.* thee a curse, *m.* thy.
Num 5:21
he shall not *m.* himself unclean. 6:7
the Lord *m.* his face to shine. 25
so *m.* themselves clean. 8:7
let us *m.* a captain, and return. 14:4
will *m.* of thee a greater nation. 12
thou *m.* thyself a prince. 16:13
if the Lord *m.* a new thing. 30
let them *m.* them broad plates. 38
I will *m.* to cease from me. 17:5
m. thee a fiery serpent, and. 21:8
he shall *m.* her vow of none. 30:8
ye shall *m.* it go through fire. 31:23
Lord *m.* you a thousand. *Deut* 1:11
I will *m.* them rulers over you. 13
I will *m.* them hear my words. 4:10
ye *m.* you a graven image. 16, 23
nor shalt thou *m.* marriages.
Deut 7:3
m. thee know that man liveth. 8:3
if it *m.* thee answer of peace. 20:11
if it will *m.* no peace with thee. 12
m. thee high above all nations. 26:19
shall *m.* thee plenteous. 28:11; 30:9
Lord shall *m.* thee the head. 13
m. the remembrance of. 32:26
I kill, and I *m.* alive, I wound. 39
thou shalt *m.* thy way. *Josh* 1:8
m. yourselves accursed, and *m.* the camp of Israel a curse. 6:18
m. confession. 7:19; *Ezra* 10:11
so shall your children *m.* *Josh* 22:25
m. marriages with them. 23:12
Samson, that he may *m.* *Judg* 16:25
m. the woman like Rachel and Leah.
Ruth 4:11
provoked her sore, to *m.* *1 Sam* 1:6
m. them inherit the throne. 2:8
ye *m.* the Lord's people to. 2:24
to *m.* yourselves fat with. 29
ye shall *m.* images of your. 6:5
m. a new cart. 7
m. us a king to judge us. 8:5
hearken to them, and *m.* 22
because it hath pleased the Lord to *m.* you his. 12:22; *1 Chr* 17:22
Lord will *m.* my lord. *1 Sam* 25:28
I will *m.* thee keeper of mine. 28:2
m. this fellow return that he. 29:4
will *m.* thee an house. *2 Sam* 7:11
things, to *m.* thy servant know. 21
to *m.* him a name. 23
and *m.* thyself sick. 13:5
should I *m.* thee go up and? 15:20
all my desire, though he *m.* it. 23:5
m. his throne greater. *1 Ki* 1:37
God *m.* the name of Solomon. 47
did I not *m.* thee to swear? 2:42
prayer which thy servant shall *m.*
8:29; *2 Chr* 6:21
pray, and *m.* supplication to thee in.
1 Ki 8:33, 47; *2 Chr* 6:24
I will *m.* him prince all. *1 Ki* 11:34
m. the yoke lighter. 12:9, 10
2 Chr 10:10
m. thy house like the house of.
1 Ki 16:3; 21:22; *2 Ki* 9:9
and after *m.* for thee. *1 Ki* 17:13
if I *m.* not thy life as the life. 19:2
us *m.* a little chamber. *2 Ki* 4:10
am I God to kill and to *m.* alive? 5:7
let us *m.* a place, where we. 6:2
if Lord would *m.* windows. 7:2, 19
m. him arise up, and anoint. 9:2
we will not *m.* any king, do. 10:5
m. an agreement with me. 18:31
Isa 36:16
nor will I *m.* feet of Israel move.
2 Ki 21:8
m. his son or daughter to pass.
23:10; *Ezek* 20:31
all Israel to *m.* him king.
1 Chr 11:10; 12:31, 38
m. thee a name of greatness. 17:21
Lord *m.* his people 100 times. 21:3
he liked me to *m.* me king. 28:4
thine hand it is to *m.* great. 29:12
m. it a proverb among. *2 Chr* 7:20
thought to *m.* him king. 11:22
God shall *m.* thee fall before. 25:8
I *m.* a decree what ye shall do.
Ezra 6:8; 7:13, 21
branches of thick trees to *m.* booths.
Neh 8:15
the king to *m.* supplication. *Esth* 4:8
Haman stood up to *m.* request. 7:7
m. them days of feasting and. 9:22
and his hands *m.* whole. *Job* 5:18
m. thy supplication to. 8:5; 22:27
and if I *m.* my hands never. 9:30
should thy lies *m.* men hold? 11:3
m. me to know my transgression.
13:23
that ye *m.* yourselves strange. 19:3
now, who will *m.* me a liar? 24:25
made me in womb *m.* him? 31:15
quietness, who then can *m.*? 34:29
they *m.* the oppressed to cry. 35:9
can *m.* his sword to approach. 40:19
will he *m.* many supplications? 41:3
m. thy way straight before. *Ps* 5:8

night *m.* I my bed to swim. *Ps* 6:6
m. them as a fiery oven in. 21:9
shalt *m.* them turn their back. 12
m. me hope when on breasts. 22:9
m. thy face shine on thy servant.
31:16; 119:135
my soul shall *m.* her boast in. 34:2
m. me to know mine end. 39:4
m. me not the reproach of the. 8
m. no tarrying. 40:17; 70:5
will *m.* all his bed. 41:3
I will *m.* thy name to be. 45:17
the streams shall *m.* glad the. 46:4
in hidden part shalt *m.* me. 51:6
m. me to hear joy and gladness. 8
wings will I *m.* my refuge. 57:1
sing forth his name, *m.* his. 66:2
ye people, *m.* the voice of his. 8
thine enemies *m.* a tumult. 83:2
m. their nobles like Oreb. 11
O my God, *m.* them like a wheel. 13
valley of Baca, *m.* it a well. 84:6
will *m.* him my firstborn. 89:27
his seed also will I *m.* to endure. 29
m. us glad, according to the. 90:15
until I *m.* thine enemies thy. 110:1
Mat 22:44; *Mark* 12:36
Luke 20:43; *Acts* 2:35; *Heb* 1:13
they that *m.* them are like unto.
Ps 115:8; 135:18
m. me to understand the. 119:27
m. me go in the path of thy. 35
there will I *m.* the horn of. 132:17
if I *m.* my bed in hell, thou. 139:8
to the Lord did I *m.* my. 142:1
go humble thyself, and *m.* *Pr* 6:3
fools *m.* a mock at sin, but. 14:9
and with good advice *m.* war. 20:18
after vows to *m.* enquiry. 25
m. thee know the certainty. 22:21
m. no friendship with an angry. 24
riches certainly *m.* themselves. 23:5
be wise, and *m.* my heart glad. 27:11
yet *m.* they their houses. 30:26
who can *m.* that straight? *Eccl* 7:13
nor *m.* thyself over wise. 16
when ye *m.* many prayers. *Isa* 1:15
wash you, *m.* you clean. 16
m. me not a ruler. 3:7
m. the heart of this people fat. 6:10
let us *m.* a breach therein. 7:6
the Lord of hosts shall *m.* 10:23
and shall *m.* him of quick. 11:3
m. men go over dry shod. 15
m. mention that his name is. 12:4
will *m.* a man more precious. 13:12
m. thy shadow as the night. 16:3
Lord *m.* to all people a feast. 25:6
that he may *m.* peace with me. 27:5
m. to understand doctrine? 28:9
that *m.* a man an offender. 29:21
to *m.* empty the soul of the. 32:6
wilt thou recover me and *m.* 38:16
m. straight in the desert a. 40:3
Mat 3:3; *Mark* 1:3; *Luke* 3:4
I will *m.* the wilderness. *Isa* 41:18
I will *m.* the rivers islands. 42:15
I will *m.* darkness light before. 16
he will magnify and *m.* the law. 21
m. a way in the wilderness. 43:19
they that *m.* a graven image. 44:9
m. the crooked places straight. 45:2
m. peace and create evil, I the. 7
they shall *m.* supplication. 14
to whom will ye *m.* me equal? 46:5
m. bare the leg, uncover the. 47:2
m. his way prosperous. 48:15
m. all my mountains a way. 49:11
m. the rivers a wilderness. 50:2
I will *m.* my judgements to rest. 51:4
they that rule over them, *m.* 52:5
when thou shalt *m.* his soul. 53:10
m. thy windows of agates. 54:12
I will *m.* them joyful in my. 56:7
m. ye a wide mouth? 57:4
to *m.* your voice to be heard. 58:4
Lord shall *m.* fat thy bones. 11
I will *m.* the place of my feet. 60:13
m. thee an eternal excellency. 15
I will also *m.* thy officers peace. 17
till he *m.* Jerusalem a praise. 62:7
m. them drunk in my fury. 63:6
m. himself an everlasting name. 12
people to *m.* thyself a glorious. 14

to *m.* thy name known to thy. *Isa* 64:2
as new earth which I will *m.* 66:22
shalt thou *m.* thyself fair. *Jer* 4:30
m. my words in thy mouth. 5:14
m. thee mourning, as for an. 6:26
nor *m.* intercession to me. 7:16
m. Jerusalem heaps and den. 9:11
he turn it, and *m.* it gross. 13:16
m. thee a fenced brasen wall. 15:20
a man *m.* gods to himself. 16:20
good to the potter to *m.* it. 18:4
m. void counsel of Judah. 19:7
even *m.* this city as Tophet. 12
m. thee a terror to thyself. 20:4
I will *m.* thee a wilderness. 22:6
prophets, they *m.* you vain. 23:16
m. this house like Shiloh. 26:6
m. thee bonds and yokes, put. 27:2
now *m.* intercession to the Lord. 18
I will *m.* them like vile figs. 29:17
Lord *m.* thee like Zedekiah. 22
I will *m.* you be removed. 34:17
m. her cakes to worship her? 44:19
m. ye him drunken: for he. 48:26
I will *m.* thee small among. 49:15
m. thee a burnt mountain. 51:25
and *m.* her springs dry. 36
m. them drunken. 39
I will *m.* drunk her princes. 57
m. bread thereof. *Ezek* 4:9
m. a chain. 7:23
m. him a sign and a proverb. 14:8
I will *m.* my fury toward. 16:42
and *m.* you a new heart. 18:31
should we then *m.* mirth? 21:10
that should *m.* up the hedge. 22:30
m. no mourning for the dead. 24:17
m. her like the top of a. 26:4, 14
I will *m.* thee a terror, thou. 21
m. the stars thereof dark. 32:7, 8
I will *m.* them and places. 34:26
m. them one stick, shall be. 37:19
m. them one nation in the land. 22
m. them keepers of charge. 44:14
shall *m.* thee to eat grass as oxen.
Dan 4:25, 32
m. this man to understand the vision.
8:16; 10:14
weeks to *m.* reconciliation for. 9:24
fall to *m.* them white. 11:35
shall go utterly to purge and *m.* 44
I *m.* her as a wilderness. *Hos* 2:3
m. a wall, that she shall not find. 6
m. them to lie down safely. 18
m. the king glad with their. 7:3
m. Ephraim ride, Judah. 10:11
how shall I *m.* thee as Admah? 11:8
m. thee dwell in tabernacles. 12:9
nor will I *m.* you a reproach.
Joel 2:19
m. the poor of the land to. *Amos* 8:4
m. gardens, and eat fruit. 9:14
that *m.* my people err. *Mi* 3:5
her that halted a remnant. 4:7
I will *m.* thee sick in smiting. 6:13
I will *m.* thy grave, for. *Nah* 1:14
filth on thee, and *m.* thee vile. 3:6
m. thyself many, as the canker-. 15
write the vision, and *m.* *Hab* 2:2
m. my feet like hinds' feet. 3:19
shall *m.* even a speedy riddance.
Zeph 1:18
for I will *m.* you a name. 3:20
I will *m.* thee as a signet. *Hag* 2:33
m. bright clouds. *Zech* 10:1
I will *m.* Jerusalem a cup of. 12:2
I *m.* Jerusalem a burdensome. 3
did not he *m.* one? yet. *Mal* 2:15
when I *m.* up my jewels. 3:17
m. her a publick example. *Mat* 1:19
I will *m.* you fishers of men. 4:19
Mark 1:17
m. one hair white or black. *Mat* 5:36
Lord, if thou wilt, thou canst *m.* me.
8:2; *Mark* 1:40; *Luke* 5:12
m. the tree good, *m.* the. *Mat* 12:33
let us *m.* here three tabernacles.
17:4; *Mark* 9:5; *Luke* 9:33
for pretence *m.* long prayers.
Mat 23:14; *Mark* 12:40
to *m.* one proselyte, and. *Mat* 23:15
ye *m.* clean the outside of the cup.
25; *Luke* 11:39
I will *m.* thee ruler. *Mat* 25:21

your way, *m.* it as sure. *Mat* 27:65
why *m.* ye this ado? *Mark* 5:39
can ye *m.* children of? *Luke* 5:34
did he not *m.* that which is? 11:40
consent began to *m.* excuse. 14:18
m. me as one of thy hired. 15:19
m. friends of the mammon of. 16:9
m. straight the way of. *John* 1:23
m. not my Father's house. 2:16
by force to *m.* him a king. 6:15
the truth shall *m.* you free. 8:32
if the Son *m.* you free, ye shall. 36
dost thou *m.* us to doubt? 10:24
will come and *m.* our abode. 14:23
m. me full of joy with. *Acts* 2:28
him, arise and *m.* thy bed. 9:34
to *m.* thee a minister and a. 26:16
much learning doth *m.* thee mad. 24
m. the faith of God without effect.
Rom 3:3
do we then *m.* void the law? 31
power to *m.* one vessel unto. 9:21
short work will the Lord *m.* 28
m. not provision for the flesh. 13:14
God is able to *m.* him stand. 14:4
things which *m.* for peace. 19
to *m.* a certain contribution. 15:26
and *m.* them the members. *1 Cor* 6:15
meat *m.* my brother to offend. 8:13
temptation also *m.* a way to. 10:13
if I *m.* you sorry, who? *2 Cor* 2:2
m. up beforehand your bounty. 9:5
able to *m.* all grace abound. 8
did I *m.* gain of you by any? 12:17
m. myself a transgressor. *Gal* 2:18
m. the promise of none effect. 3:17
desire to *m.* a fair show in. 6:12
to *m.* in himself of twain. *Eph* 2:15
the Lord *m.* you to increase in love.
1 Thes 3:12
m. ourselves an ensample to you.
2 Thes 3:9
scriptures which are able to *m.* thee
wise unto salvation. *2 Tim* 3:15
m. full proof of thy ministry. 4:5
to *m.* the Captain of their. *Heb* 2:10
to *m.* reconciliation for the sins. 17
liveth to *m.* intercession. 7:25
m. all things according to. 8:5
could not *m.* him that did. 9:9
m. comers thereunto perfect. 10:1
m. straight paths for your. 12:13
m. you perfect in every good. 13:21
of them that *m.* peace. *Jas* 3:18
the God of all grace *m.* *1 Pet* 5:10
m. your calling and. *2 Pet* 1:10
we *m.* him a liar, his. *1 John* 1:10
I will *m.* them worship. *Rev* 3:9
m. a pillar in the temple of my. 12
eat it, and it shall *m.* thy belly. 10:9
shall *m.* war against them. 11:7
went to *m.* war with the. 12:17
saying, Who is able to *m.* war? 13:4
that they should *m.* an image. 14
he doth judge and *m.* war. 19:11
behold, I *m.* all things new. 21:5
see **afraid, atonement, covenant, desolate, desolation, end, fire, good, known, mention, noise**

make *haste*

come on them, *m. haste.* *Deut* 32:35
and said, *M. haste* and do as I have.
Judg 9:48
is before you, *m. haste.* *1 Sam* 9:12
me to *m. haste.* *2 Chr* 35:21
cause Haman to *m. haste.*
Esth 5:5; 6:10
for this I *m. haste.* *Job* 20:2
m. haste to help me, O Lord, my.
Ps 38:22; 40:13; 70:1; 71:12
I am poor and needy, *m. haste* unto
me. 70:5; 141:1
they *m. haste* to shed blood.
Pr 1:16; *Isa* 59:7
m. haste, my beloved. *S of S* 8:14
he that believeth shall not *m. haste.*
Isa 28:16
thy children shall *m. haste.* 49:17
let them *m. haste,* and. *Jer* 9:18
m. haste to the wall. *Nah* 2:5
said, Zacchaeus, *m. haste* *Luke* 19:5
m. haste and get quickly out.
Acts 22:18

make *manifest*
m. manifest the counsels. *1 Cor* 4:5
doth *m. manifest* is light. *Eph* 5:13
that I may *m.* it *manifest.* *Col* 4:4

make *ready*
m. ready three measures. *Gen* 18:6
m. ready, for these men. 43:16
and Joram said, *M. ready. 2 Ki* 9:21
m. ready their arrow on. *Ps* 11:2
m. ready thine arrows. 21:12
the trumpet to *m. ready. Ezek* 7:14
there *m. ready* for us. *Mark* 14:15
Luke 22:12
to *m. ready* a people. *Luke* 1:17
m. ready, wherewith I may sup. 17:8
m. ready 200 soldiers to. *Acts* 23:23

make *speed*
m. speed, haste. *1 Sam* 20:38
m. speed to depart. *2 Sam* 15:14
let him *m. speed* and. *Isa* 5:19

make *waste*
m. your cities *waste.* *Lev* 26:31
will *m. waste* mountains. *Isa* 42:15
will *m.* Jerusalem *waste. Ezek* 5:14
m. land of Egypt utterly *waste.*
29:10; 30:12

maker, or makers
more pure than his *M.*? *Job* 4:17
in so doing my *M.* will soon. 32:22
where is God my *M.*? 35:10
righteousness to my *M.* 36:3
before the Lord our *M.* *Ps* 95:6
oppresseth the poor, reproacheth his *M.* *Pr* 14:31
mocketh the poor reproacheth his *M.* 17:5
rich and poor, Lord is the *M.* 22:2
the *m.* of it as a spark. *Isa* 1:31*
shall a man look to his *M.* 17:7
ye have not looked to the *m.* 22:11*
that striveth with his *M.* 45:9
Holy One of Israel and his *M.* 11
confusion that are *m.* of idols. 16
forgettest the Lord thy *M.* 51:13
thy *m.* is thy husband, and. 54:5
saith the Lord the *M.* *Jer* 33:2
hath forgotten his *M.* *Hos* 8:14
graven image that *m.* hath graven, *m.* of his work? *Hab* 2:18
builder and *M.* is God. *Heb* 11:10

makest
and what *m.* thou in? *Judg* 18:3
m. me possess the iniquities of my youth. *Job* 13:26
is it gain to him that thou *m.*? 22:3
thou only *m.* me to dwell. *Ps* 4:8
m. his beauty to consume. 39:11
thou *m.* us to turn back. 44:10
thou *m.* us a reproach to our. 13
thou *m.* us a byword among. 14
m. the outgoings of morning. 65:8
m. the earth soft with showers. 10
thou *m.* us a strife to our. 80:6
thou *m.* darkness, and it. 104:20
that thou *m.* account of him? 144:3
m. thy flock to rest at. *S of S* 1:7
fashioneth it, what *m.* thou? *Isa* 45:9
that *m.* thy nest in cedars. *Jer* 22:23
thou *m.* this people to trust. 28:15
thou *m.* thy high place. *Ezek* 16:31
and *m.* men as the fishes. *Hab* 1:14
bottle to him, and *m.* him. 2:15
when thou *m.* a dinner. *Luke* 14:12
but when thou *m.* a feast, call. 13
prophets are dead, whom *m.* thou thyself? *John* 8:53
because thou being a man *m.* 10:33
and *m.* thy boast of God. *Rom* 2:17
m. thy boast of the law. 23

maketh
who *m.* the dumb, or deaf? *Ex* 4:11
priest that *m.* atonement clean.
Lev 7:7; 14:11
blood that *m.* an atonement. 17:11
that *m.* his son to pass. *Deut* 18:10
against the city that *m.* war. 20:20
he *m.* his sons to inherit. 21:16
m. merchandise of him. 24:7
cursed be the man that *m.* 27:15
cursed be he that *m.* the blind. 18
oath which the Lord *m.* with. 29:12
Lord killeth and *m.* *1 Sam* 2:6
the Lord *m.* poor, and *m.* rich.
1 Sam 2:7
God *m.* my way perfect.
2 Sam 22:33; *Ps* 18:32
he *m.* my feet like hinds' feet.
2 Sam 22:34; *Ps* 18:33
m. sore, and bindeth up. *Job* 5:18
Lord *m.* Arcturus, Orion. 9:9
he *m.* the judges fools. 12:17
he *m.* to stagger. 25
he *m.* collops of fat on his. 15:27
God *m.* my heart soft, and. 23:16
he *m.* peace in his high places. 25:2
booth that the keeper *m.* 27:18
m. us wiser than the fowls. 35:11
m. small the drops of water. 36:27
m. the deep to boil like a pot. 41:31
he *m.* a path to shine after him. 32
when he *m.* inquisition. *Ps* 9:12
he *m.* me to lie down in green. 23:2
Lord *m.* the hinds to calve. 29:9
he *m.* the devices of people of. 33:10
blessed is the man that *m.* the. 40:4
he *m.* wars to cease to the end. 46:9
who *m.* the clouds his chariot. 104:3
m. his angels spirits. 4; *Heb* 1:7
wine that *m.* glad heart. *Ps* 104:15
m. the storm a calm, the. 107:29
he *m.* the hungry to dwell. 36
m. him families like a flock. 41
he *m.* the barren woman to. 113:9
m. lightnings for rain, bringeth. 135:7
who *m.* grass to grow on the. 147:8
he *m.* peace in thy borders. 14
a wise son *m.* a glad father. *Pr* 10:1
15:20
but the hand of the diligent *m.* 10:4
blessing of the Lord, it *m.* rich. 22
m. ashamed is as rottenness. 12:4
heart of a man *m.* it to stoop, but a good word *m.* it glad. 25
m. himself rich, yet hath nothing, there is that *m.* himself. 13:7
hope deferred *m.* the heart sick. 12
a merry heart *m.* a cheerful. 15:13
good report *m.* the bones fat. 30
he *m.* even his enemies to be. 16:7
a man's gift *m.* room for. 18:16
wealth *m.* many friends, but. 19:4
she *m.* herself coverings. 31:22
she *m.* fine linen and selleth it. 24
the work that God *m.* *Eccl* 3:11
oppression *m.* a wise man mad. 7:7
wisdom *m.* his face to shine. 8:1
not works of God, who *m.* all. 11:5
Lord *m.* the earth empty. *Isa* 24:1
he *m.* the judges of the earth. 40:23
which *m.* a way in the sea. 43:16
he *m.* a god, and worshippeth it.
44:15, 17; 46:6
I am the Lord that *m.* all. 44:24
he *m.* diviners mad. 25
watereth earth, and *m.* it. 55:10
m. himself a prey. 59:15
he *m.* lightnings. *Jer* 10:13; 51:16
cursed be the man that *m.* 17:5
m. himself a prophet. 29:26, 27
m. idols against herself. *Ezek* 22:3
but *m.* his petition three. *Dan* 6:13
that *m.* desolate. 11:31; 12:11
that *m.* the morning. *Amos* 4:13
seek him that *m.* the seven stars. 5:8
sea, and *m.* it dry. *Nah* 1:4
he *m.* his sun to rise on. *Mat* 5:45
he *m.* both deaf to hear. *Mark* 7:37
m. himself a king. *John* 19:12
Aeneas, Jesus Christ *m.* *Acts* 9:34
hope *m.* not ashamed. *Rom* 5:5
Spirit *m.* intercession. 8:26, 27, 34
m. intercession to God. 11:2
who *m.* thee to differ? *1 Cor* 4:7
he that *m.* me glad, but? *2 Cor* 2:2
m. manifest the savour of his. 14
it *m.* no matter to me. *Gal* 2:6
m. increase of the body. *Eph* 4:16
m. men high priests, but the word of ... the law *m.* the Son. *Heb* 7:28
he *m.* fire come down. *Rev* 13:13
whatsoever *m.* a lie. 21:27; 22:15

maketh *haste*
m. haste to be rich. *Pr* 28:20

making
m. confession to the. *2 Chr* 30:22
testimony of Lord is sure, *m.* wise.
Ps 19:7
of *m.* many books there. *Eccl* 12:12
walking and *m.* a tinkling. *Isa* 3:16
that brought tidings, *m.* *Jer* 20:15
m. ephah small, and the. *Amos* 8:5
m. the word of God of. *Mark* 7:13
m. himself equal with. *John* 5:18
as poor, yet *m.* many. *2 Cor* 6:10
give thanks for you, *m.* mention of.
Eph 1:16; *1 Thes* 1:2; *Philem* 4
new man, so *m.* peace. *Eph* 2:15
m. melody in your heart. 5:19
you *m.* request with joy. *Phil* 1:4
m. them an ensample. *2 Pet* 2:6
compassion, *m.* a difference. *Jude* 22

making
wares of thy *m.* *Ezek* 27:16, 18

Malcham
by the Lord and by *M.* *Zeph* 1:5

Malchus
servant's name was *M.* *John* 18:10

male
every *m.* circumcised. *Gen* 17:23
34; 15:22, 24
for the passover a *m.* of. *Ex* 12:5
the *m.* shall be the Lord's. 13:12
34:19; *Luke* 2:23
a *m.* without blemish. *Lev* 1:3, 10
4:23; 22:19
every *m.* among the priests. 7:6
thy estimation shall be of the *m.* 27:3
5, 6, 7
every *m.* by their polls. *Num* 1:2
every *m.* from 20 years old. 20
every *m.* from a month old. 3:15
now kill every *m.* among. 31:17
smite every *m.* thereof. *Deut* 20:13
destroy every *m.* *Judg* 21:11
he had smitten every *m.* in Edom.
1 Ki 11:15, 16
hath in his flock a *m.* *Mal* 1:14
see **female**

male children
were the *m. children* of. *Josh* 17:2

malefactor
if he were not a *m.* *John* 18:30*

malefactors
there were two *m.* *Luke* 23:32
they crucified him, and the *m.* 33
one of the *m.* railed on him. 39

males
Levi slew all the *m.* *Gen* 34:25
m. be circumcised. *Ex* 12:48
to the Lord all being *m.* 13:15
three times a year all thy *m.* shall appear before. 23:17; *Deut* 16:16
all the *m.* of Aaron. *Lev* 6:18, 29
number of all *m.* from a month old.
Num 3:22; 28:34; 26:62
the firstborn of the *m.* 3:40, 43
Midianites, and slew the *m.* 31:7
all firstling *m.* sanctify. *Deut* 15:19
m. that came out of Egypt died.
Josh 5:4
their genealogy of *m.* *2 Chr* 31:16
to all the *m.* among priests. 19
by genealogy of the *m.* *Ezra* 8:3

malice
not with leaven of *m.* *1 Cor* 5:8
howbeit in *m.* be ye children. 14:20
from you with all *m.* *Eph* 4:31
also put off all these; *m.* *Col* 3:8
living in *m.* and envy. *Tit* 3:3
laying aside all *m.* *1 Pet* 2:1*

malicious
prating against us with *m.* *3 John* 10*

maliciousness
all unrighteousness, *m.* *Rom* 1:29
liberty for a cloke of *m.* *1 Pet* 2:16*

malignity
murder, debate, *m.* *Rom* 1:29

mallows
cut up *m.* by the bushes. *Job* 30:4

mammon
ye cannot serve God and *m.*
Mat 6:24; *Luke* 16:13
make friends of *m.* of. *Luke* 16:9
if not faithful in unrighteous *m.* 11

Mamre

Abram dwelt in the plain of *M*. *Gen* 13:18; 14:13
Eshcol, *M*. let them take. 14:24
appeared to Abraham in *M*. 18:1
Machpelah before *M*. 23:17, 19
49:30; 50:13
Jacob came to Isaac to *M*. 35:27

man

[1] *A human being*, 1 Cor 10:13. [2] *The human race; mankind*, Job 5:7. [3] *The adult male, as distinguished from a woman or a child*, Acts 4:22.

God said, Let us make *m*. in our image. *Gen* 1:26, 27; 9:6
God formed *m*. of the dust. 2:7
it is not good that *m*. should. 18
they were both naked, the *m*. 25
the *m*. is become as one of us. 3:22
not always strive with *m*. 6:3
I will destroy *m*. whom I have. 7
curse the ground for *m*.'s sake. 8:21
m.'s blood, by *m*. shall his. 9:6
which have not known *m*. 19:8
Num 31:35
restore the *m*. his wife. *Gen* 20:7
the *m*. wondering at her held. 24:21
Laban ran out to the *m*. to. 29
what *m*. is this that walketh? 65
give her to another *m*. 29:19
by the *m*. whose these are. 38:25
arise, go again to the *m*. 43:13
the *m*. in whose hand cup. 44:17
that ye have left the *m*.? *Ex* 2:20
content to dwell with the *m*. 21
who hath made *m*.'s mouth? 4:11
upon *m*., flesh shall it not be. 30:32
m. that brought us out of. 32:1, 23
be imputed to that *m*. and that *m*. shall be cut off from. *Lev* 17:4
m. bring his wife to. *Num* 5:15
but the *m*. that is clean, and. 9:13
the *m*. Moses was very meek. 12:3
the *m*. shall be put to death. 15:35
Deut 22:25
m. whom the Lord doth. *Num* 16:7
but *m*. that shall be unclean. 19:20
day that God created *m*. *Deut* 4:32
God doth talk with *m*. and he. 5:24
m. doth not live by bread only, but.
8:3; *Mat* 4:4; *Luke* 4:4
tree of the field is *m*.'s. *Deut* 20:19
and they shall come *m*. by *m*.
Josh 7:14, 17, 18
but they let go the *m*. *Judg* 1:25
I will shew thee the *m*. whom. 4:22
for as the *m*. is, so is his. 8:21
me they honour God and *m*. 9:9
cheereth God and *m*. 13
what *m*. will fight against? 10:18
m. hath appeared that came. 13:10
the *m*. spakest to the woman? 11
and as another *m*. 16:7, 11, 17
bring forth the *m*. that came. 19:22
the *m*. took her on an ass and. 28
m. was Elimelech. *Ruth* 1:2; 2:19
for the *m*. will not be in rest. 3:18
m. of thine whom I. *1 Sam* 2:33
m. came in hastily, and told. 4:14
a *m*. of God, and he is an honourable *m*. 9:6
behold the *m*. whom I spake. 17
if the *m*. should yet come. 10:22
Lord seeth not as *m*. seeth. 16:7
what be done to the *m*.? 17:26
lo, ye see the *m*. is mad. 21:14
anger kindled against the *m*. said to Nathan, the *m*. that. *2 Sam* 12:5
David, Thou art the *m*. 7
come out, thou bloody *m*. 16:7*, 8
the *m*. thou seekest is as if. 17:3
m. that consumed us, and. 21:5
the *m*. who was raised up on. 23:1
slew every one his *m*. *1 Ki* 20:20
when *m*. turned again. *2 Ki* 5:26
I will bring you to the *m*. 6:19
you know the *m*. and his. 9:11
tell the *m*. that sent you. 22:15
2 Chr 34:23
Levites *m*. by *m*. 38,000. *1 Chr* 23:3
the palace is not for *m*. but. 29:1
let not *m*. prevail. *2 Chr* 14:11
for ye judge not for *m*. but.
2 Chr 19:6
what shall be done unto the *m*.?
Esth 6:6, 7, 9
m. be more just than? *Job* 4:17
yet *m*. is born to trouble, as. 5:7
happy is the *m*. whom God. 17
appointed time for *m*. on earth? 7:1
what is *m*. that thou shouldest? 17
15:14; *Ps* 8:4; 144:3; *Heb* 2:6
but how should *m*. be just? *Job* 9:2
or seest thou as *m*. seeth? 10:4
days of *m*.? years as *m*.'s days? 5
vain *m*. would be wise, though *m*.
11:12
m. that is born of a woman. 14:1
m. dieth and wasteth away, *m*. 10
so *m*. lieth down, and riseth not. 12
first *m*. that was born? 15:7
what is *m*. that he should be? 14
abominable and filthy is *m*. 16
m. was first placed on the. 20:4
me is my complaint to *m*.? 21:4
can *m*. be justified with God? 25:4
m. that is a worm, and son of *m*. 6
but there is a spirit in *m*. 32:8
God thrusteth him down, not *m*. 13
that God is greater than *m*. 33:12
God speaketh, yet *m*. perceiveth it not. 14
that he may withdraw *m*. from purpose, and hide pride from *m*. 17
if a messenger, to shew to *m*. 23
worketh God often with *m*. 29
m. is like Job, who drinketh? 34:7
his heart upon *m*. if he gather. 14
for he will not lay on *m*. more. 23
arise, O Lord, let not *m*. *Ps* 9:19
that the *m*. of earth may no. 10:18
what *m*. is he that feareth? 25:12
what *m*. is he that desireth? 34:12
when thou dost correct *m*. 39:11
m. being in honour. 49:12, 20
I will not be afraid what *m*. 56:11
m. did eat angels' food, he. 78:25
thy hand be on the *m*. of. 80:17
what *m*. is he that liveth? 89:48
thou turnest *m*. to destruction. 90:3
that teacheth *m*. knowledge? 94:10
for *m*. his days are as grass. 103:15
m. goeth forth to his work. 104:23
I will not fear what *m*. can. 118:6
than put confidence in *m*. 8
m. is like to vanity, his days. 144:4
from *m*. that speaketh. *Pr* 2:12
come as an armed *m*. 6:11; 24:34
preparations of the heart in *m*. 16:1
m.'s goings are of the Lord, how can a *m*.? 20:24
so is the *m*. that deceiveth. 26:19
things full of labour, *m*. *Eccl* 1:8
can the *m*. do that cometh? 2:12
hath *m*. of all his labour? 22
it is known that it is *m*. 6:10
what is *m*. better? 11
what is good for *m*.? 12
because *m*. goeth to his long. 12:5
from *m*. whose breath is. *Isa* 2:22
I said, I shall behold *m*. no. 38:11
the *m*. that executeth my. 46:11
it is not in *m*. to direct. *Jer* 10:23
I am the *m*. that hath. *Lam* 3:1
cows' dung for *m*.'s dung.
Ezek 4:15
judgement between *m*. and *m*. 18:8
be changed from *m*.'s. *Dan* 4:16
O *m*. greatly beloved. 10:19
for I am God, and not *m*. *Hos* 11:9
declareth to *m*. what is. *Amos* 4:13
that tarrieth not for *m*. *Mi* 5:7
he hath shewed thee, O *m*. 6:8
the *m*. of wisdom shall see. 9
the wicked devoureth *m*. *Hab* 1:13
I will cut off the *m*. *Zeph* 1:3
the *m*. whose name is. *Zech* 6:12
m. taught me to keep cattle. 13:5*
awake, O sword, against *m*. that. 7
Lord will cut off the *m*. *Mal* 2:12
what *m*. is there of you, if his son?
Mat 7:9; 12:11; *Luke* 15:4
and they defile the *m*. *Mat* 15:18
let not *m*. put asunder. 19:6
Mark 10:9
I do not know the *m*. *Mat* 26:72, 74
sabbath was made for *m*. not *m*.
Mark 2:27
colt tied, whereon never *m*. sat. 11:2
he said, *M*. thy sins are. *Luke* 5:20
m. who made me a judge? 12:14
fear not God, nor regard *m*. 18:4
Peter said, *M*., I am not. 22:58
Peter said, *M*., I know not. 60
he asked, whether the *m*. was. 23:6
never *m*. was laid. 53; *John* 19:41
knew what was in *m*. *John* 2:25
what *m*. is that which said? 5:12
not testimony from *m*. 34
which none other *m*. did. 15:24
unto them, Behold the *m*. 19:5
for the *m*. was above. *Acts* 4:22
how can I, except some *m*.? 8:31
himself, or of some other *m*.? 34
the *m*. in whom the evil. 19:16
what *m*. is there that knoweth? 35
m. that owneth this girdle. 21:11
Jews laid wait for the *m*. 23:30
I would also hear the *m*. 25:22
inexcusable, O *m*. *Rom* 2:1
thinkest thou, O *m*. 3
of God after the inward *m*. 7:22
O wretched *m*. that I am, who? 24
but O *m*. who art thou that? 9:20
the *m*. who doeth. 10:5; *Gal* 3:12
with heart *m*. believeth. *Rom* 10:10
what *m*. knoweth the things of a *m*.?
1 Cor 2:11
how knowest thou, O *m*.? 7:16*
such as is common to *m*. 10:13
head of the woman is the *m*. 11:3
m. is not of the woman. 8
but woman for the *m*. 9
m. without the woman, nor the woman without the *m*. 11
the *m*. also by the woman. 12
by *m*. came death, by *m*. 15:21
the first *m*. Adam was made. 45
the first *m*. is of the earth, earthy; the second *m*. is the Lord. 47
outward *m*. perish, yet the inward *m*. is renewed day by. *2 Cor* 4:16
not of men, neither by *m*. *Gal* 1:1
I preached is not after *m*. 11
of twain one new *m*. *Eph* 2:15
his Spirit in the inner *m*. 3:16
that ye put on new *m*. created. 4:24
new *m*. which is renewed. *Col* 3:10
despiseth not *m*. but God. *1 Thes* 4:8
men, the *m*. Christ Jesus. *1 Tim* 2:5
usurp authority over the *m*. 12
Saviour toward *m*. appeared. *Tit* 3:4
house is built by some *m*. *Heb* 3:4
Lord pitched, and not *m*. 8:2
I will not fear what *m*. shall. 13:6
a double minded *m*. is unstable in all his ways. *Jas* 1:8
wilt thou know, O vain *m*.? 2:20
let it be the hidden *m*. *1 Pet* 3:4
see **beast, blessed, cursed, each, evil, foolish, good, old, poor, rich, understanding**

***a* man**

not *a m*. to till the ground. *Gen* 2:5
shall *a m*. leave his father. 24
Mat 19:5; *Mark* 10:7, *Eph* 5:31
I have gotten *a m*. from the Lord.
Gen 4:1
slain *a m*. to my wounding. 23
if *a m*. can number the dust. 13:16
there is not *a m*. to come in. 19:31
dead man; she is *a m*.'s wife. 20:3
Esau a cunning hunter, *a m*. 25:27
there wrestled *a m*. with him. 32:24
let Pharaoh look out *a m*. discreet and wise. 41:33
a m. in whom the Spirit of God. 38
wot ye not such *a m*. as I can? 44:15
in their anger they slew *a m*. 49:6
face, as *a m*. speaketh. *Ex* 33:11
plague of leprosy is in *a m*. *Lev* 13:9
if *a m*. do he shall live. 18:5
Neh 9:29; *Ezek* 20:11, 13, 21
and *a m*. of Israel strove. *Lev* 24:10
caused a blemish in *a m*. 20
no devoted thing *a m*. shall. 27:28
be *a m*. of every tribe. *Num* 1:4
tribe shall ye send *a m*. 13:2
a m. that gathered sticks. 15:32

is law when a m. dieth. Num 19:14
God is not a m. that he should lie.
23:19; 1 Sam 15:29
among these there was not a m. of.
Num 26:64
was not left a m. save Caleb. 65
a m. over the congregation. 27:16
take thee Joshua, a m. in whom. 18
Lord bare thee, as a m. Deut 1:31
after the cubit of a m. 3:11
that as a m. chasteneth his son. 8:5
shall not rise against a m. 19:15
take ye out of every tribe a m.
Josh 3:12; 4:2, 4
a m. over against him with. 5:13
shall not a m. of them stand. 10:8
hearkened to the voice of a m. 14
Arba was a great m. among. 14:15
not a m. of all their enemies. 21:44
the spies saw a m. Judg 1:24
escaped not a m. 3:29
was not a m. left. 4:16
was a m. that told a dream. 7:13
save the sword of Gideon a m. 14
Tola a m. of Issachar. 10:1
she called a m. 16:19
a m. plucked off his shoe. Ruth 4:7
I will send thee a m. 1 Sam 9:16
there shall not a m. be put. 11:13
the Lord hath sought him a m. 13:14
not leave a m. of them. 14:36
a m. who is a cunning player. 16:16
provide me a m. that can play. 17
choose you a m. for you, let. 17:8
give me a m. that we may fight. 10
such that a m. cannot speak. 25:17
and there escaped not a m. 30:17
as a m. falleth before. 2 Sam 3:34
prince and a great m. is fallen. 38
a m. enquired at the oracle. 16:23
happened to be there a m. 20:1*
and shew thyself a m. 1 Ki 2:2
not fail thee a m. on throne. 4; 8:25
a m. turned aside, and brought a m.
20:39
a m. whom I appointed to. 42
came a m. to meet us. 2 Ki 1:6
a m. from Baal-shalisha. 4:42
not a m. left that came not. 10:21
as they were burying a m.. 13:21
shall be a m. of rest. 1 Chr 22:9
there shall not fail thee a m.
2 Chr 6:16; 7:18
a m. to seek the welfare. Neh 2:10
should such a m. as I flee? 6:11
all that a m. hath will he. Job 2:4
why is light given to a m.? 3:23
shall a m. be more pure than? 4:17
he is not a m. as I am, that. 9:32
and should a m. full of talk? 11:2
he shutteth up a m. 12:14
if a m. die. 14:14
one might plead for a m. with God,
as a m. pleadeth for. 16:21
can a m. be profitable to God? 22:2
done against a nation or a m. 34:29
thy wickedness may hurt a m. 35:8
if a m. speak he shall be swallowed.
37:20
gird up now thy loins like a m. 38:3
40:7
I was as a m. that. Ps 38:14
but it was thou, a m. mine. 55:13
imagine mischief against a m.? 62:3
a m. was famous according. 74:5
a m. that hath no strength. 88:4
he sent a m. before them. 105:17
pleasure in the legs of a m. 147:10
strive not with a m. Pr 3:30
for jealousy is the rage of a m. 6:34
there is a way that seemeth right
unto a m. 14:12; 16:25
all ways of a m. are clean. 16:2
a m.'s ways please the Lord. 7
how can a m. understand? 20:24
a m. given to appetite. 23:2
so a contentious m. to kindle. 26:21
so is a m. that wandereth. 27:8
as the furnace, so is a m. to. 21
when the wicked rise a m. 28:12
he that rebuketh a m. shall find. 23
seest thou a m. that is hasty? 29:20
a m. whose labour is in wisdom and
knowledge, yet to a m. Eccl 2:21

God giveth to a m. that is good.
Eccl 2:26
for this a m. is envied of his. 4:4
a m. to whom God hath given. 6:2
who can tell a m. what shall? 12
a m. cannot tell what shall. 10:14
if a m. live many years. 11:8
if a m. would give all. S of S 8:7
I am a m. of unclean lips. Isa 6:5
a m. more precious than. 13:12
at that day shall a m. look. 17:7
than that a m. can stretch. 28:20
that make a m. an offender. 29:21
a m. shall be an hiding place. 32:2
not meet thee as a m. 47:3
he is a m. of sorrows and. 53:3
for a m. to afflict his soul? 58:5
an ox, is as if he slew a m. 66:3
forsaken, and not a m. Jer 4:29
places, if ye can find a m. 5:1
why shouldest thou be as a m.? 14:9
that thou hast borne me a m. 15:10
a m. made gods to himself? 16:20
a m. that shall not prosper. 22:30
I am like a m. whom wine. 23:9
see whether a m. doth travail? 30:6
a woman shall compass a m. 31:22
David shall never want a m. 33:17
shall the priests want a m. 18
Jonadab shall not want a m. 35:19
man put in array like a m. to. 50:42
good for a m. to hope. Lam 3:26
it is good for a m. that he bear. 27
complain, a m. for punishment. 39
sought for a m. among. Ezek 22:30
art a m. and not God. 28:2, 9
people of the land take a m. 33:2
not a m. on earth that. Dan 2:10
found a m. of the captives. 25
there is a m. in thy kingdom. 5:11
stand as a m. and a m.'s heart. 7:4
O Daniel, a m. greatly. 10:11
robbers wait for a m. Hos 6:9
there shall not be a m. left. 9:12
drew them with cords of a m. 11:4
a m. and his father go. Amos 2:7
as if a m. did flee from a lion. 5:19
a m. and his house, even a m. Mi 2:2
if a m. walking in spirit and. 11
a m.'s enemies are the men of his
own house. 7:6; Mat 10:36
as a m. spareth his own. Mal 3:17
I am a m. under authority. Mat 8:9
Luke 7:8
to set a m. at variance. Mat 10:35
how much is a m. better? 12:12
spirit is gone out of a m. 43
the mouth defileth a m. 15:11
unwashen hands defileth not a m. 20
is it lawful for a m. to put away?
19:3; Mark 10:2
if a m. die having no. Mat 22:24
the city, to such a m. and say to him.
26:18; Mark 14:13; Luke 22:10
seeing I know not a m.? Luke 1:34
depart, for I am a sinful m. 5:8
which a m. took and cast. 13:19
to be guest with a m. that is. 19:7
there was a m. sent from. John 1:6
after me cometh a m. who is. 30
except a m. be born again. 3:3, 5
how can a m. be born when? 4
a m. can receive nothing, except. 27
come, see a m. which told me. 4:29
I have made a m. whole. 7:23
a m. that hath told you the. 8:40
a m. that is called Jesus. 9:11
how can a m. a sinner, do such? 16
a m. makest thyself God. 10:33
if a m. love me, he will keep. 14:23
for joy that a m. is born into. 16:21
Jesus a m. approved of. Acts 2:22
I myself also am a m. 10:26
I found David, a m. after. 13:22
not believe, though a m. declare. 41
there stood a m. of Macedonia. 16:9
I am a m. who am a Jew. 21:39
preachest a m. should. Rom 2:21
sayest, a m. should not commit. 22
I speak as a m. 3:5
dominion over a m. 7:1
let a m. so account of us. 1 Cor 4:1
it is required, that a m. be found. 2
every sin that a m. doeth is. 6:18

it is good for a m. not to touch.
1 Cor 7:1
I say that it is good for a m. so. 26
say I these things as a m.? or. 9:8
a m. indeed ought not to. 11:7
if a m. have long hair, it is a. 14
but let a m. examine himself. 28
when I became a m., I put. 13:11
sufficient to such a m. is. 2 Cor 2:6
according to that a m. hath. 8:12
if a m. bring you into bondage, if a m.
smite. 11:20
I knew a m. in Christ caught. 12:2, 3
which it is not lawful for a m. 4
a m. is not justified by. Gal 2:16
brethren, if a m. be overtaken. 6:1
if a m. think himself to be. 3
found in fashion as a m. Phil 2:8
the law is good, if a m. 1 Tim 1:8
if a m. desire the office of a. 3:1
if a m. know not how to rule his. 5
if a m. also strive for. 2 Tim 2:5
if a m. therefore purge himself. 21
a m. that is a heretic. Tit 3:10
he is like a m. beholding. Jas 1:23
if there come a m. with a gold. 2:2
what profit, though a m. say. 14
a m. may say, Thou hast faith. 18
ye see how that by works a m. 24
Elias was a m. subject to like. 5:17
if a m. for conscience. 1 Pet 2:19
for of whom a m. is. 2 Pet 2:19
if a m. say, I love God. 1 John 4:20
beast had a face as a m. Rev 4:7
scorpion, when he striketh a m. 9:5

a certain man

a cer. m. found him. Gen 37:15
a cer. m. saw it, and. 2 Sam 18:10
a cer. m. drew a bow at a venture.
1 Ki 22:34; 2 Chr 18:33
a cer. m. had two sons. Mat 21:28
Luke 15:11
a cer. m. went down. Luke 10:30
the ground of a cer. rich m. 12:16
a cer. m. had a fig tree planted. 13:6
a cer. m. made a great supper.
14:16
there was a cer. m. which had. 16:1
a cer. blind m. sat by the way. 18:35
a cer. noble-m. went into a. 19:12
a cer. m. planted a vineyard. 20:9
a cer. noble-m. whose son was sick.
John 4:46
a cer. m. was sick, named. 11:1
a cer. m. lame from his. Acts 3:2
a cer. m. named Ananias, sold. 5:1
a cer. m. called Simeon, who. 8:9
there he found a cer. m. 9:33
there was a cer. m. in Caesarea. 10:1
there sat a cer. m. at Lystra. 14:8
entered into a cer. m.'s house. 18:7
a cer. m. named Demetrius. 19:24
a cer. m. left in bonds. 25:14

any man

a virgin, nor had any m. known her.
Gen 24:16
if thou knowest any m. of activity.
47:6
if any m. have any. Ex 24:14
nor let any m. be seen through. 34:3
nor shall any m. desire thy land. 24
any m. hath a running. Lev 15:2
if any m.'s seed of copulation go. 16
if any m. lie with her at all, he. 24
killeth any m. shall surely. 24:17
any m. giveth the priest. Num 5:10
if any m.'s wife go aside, and. 12
if any m. die very suddenly. 6:9
the dead body of any m. 19:11, 13
if a serpent had bitten any m. 21:9
if any m. hate his neighbour and.
Deut 19:11
witness rise up against any m. 16
blood on thy house, if any m. 22:8
be any m. among you that is not
clean. 23:10
not any m. be able to stand before.
Josh 1:5
remain courage in any m. 2:11
when any m. doth enquire, Is there
any m. here? Judg 4:20
weak and be like any other m. 16:17
no business with any m. 18:7, 28

that when *any m.* offered sacrifice. *1 Sam* 2:13
if *any m.* said, Fail not to burn. 16
taken aught at *any m.'s* hand. 12:4
when *any m.* that had a controversy. *2 Sam* 15:2
it was so, that when *any m.* came. 5
shall *any m.* be put to death. 19:22
for us shalt thou kill *any m.* 21:4
if *any m.* trespass. *1 Ki* 8:31
what supplication soever be made by *any m.* 38; *2 Chr* 6:29
if thou meet *any m.* *2 Ki* 4:29
chose I *any m.* to be ruler. *2 Chr* 6:5
nor told I *any m.* what God put in my heart. *Neh* 2:12
let me not accept *any m.* *Job* 32:21
more brutish than *any m.* *Pr* 30:2
marred more than *any m.* *Isa* 52:14
in mouth of *any m.* *Jer* 44:26
come not near *any m.* on. *Ezek* 9:6
ask a petition of *any* god or *m.* *Dan* 6:7, 12
if *any m.* sue thee at law. *Mat* 5:40
knoweth *any m.* the Father. 11:27
nor shall *any m.* hear his voice. 12:19
if *any m.* will come after me. 16:24 *Luke* 9:23
if *any m.* say aught to you, say. *Mat* 21:3; *Mark* 11:3; *Luke* 19:31
carest thou for *any m.* *Mat* 22:16
nor durst *any m.* from that day. 46
if *any m.* say, Lo, here is Christ. 24:23; *Mark* 13:21
nothing to *any m.* but go. *Mark* 1:44
if *any m.* hath ears to hear. 4:23 7:16; *Rev* 13:9
neither could *any m.* tame. *Mark* 5:4
not that *any m.* should know it. 9:30
if *any m.* desire to be first, the. 35
take heed, lest *any m.* deceive. 13:5
nor said any thing to *any m.* 16:8
art bidden of *any m.* to. *Luke* 14:8
if *any m.* come to me, and hate. 26
taken any thing from *any m.* 19:8
if *any m.'s* brother die, having. 20:28
hath *any m.* brought him aught to eat? *John* 4:33
not that *any m.* hath seen. 6:46
if *any m.* eat of this bread he. 51
if *any m.* do his will he shall. 7:17
if *any m.* thirst, let him come. 37
doth our law judge *any m.?* 51
never in bondage to *any m.* 8:33
if *any m.* did confess that he. 9:22
if *any m.* be a worshipper of. 31
that *any m.* opened the eyes of. 32
by me, if *any m.* enter in, he. 10:9
nor shall *any m.* pluck them out. 28
if *any m.* walk in the day. 11:9
if *any m.* knew where he were. 57
if *any m.* serve me, let him. 12:26
if *any m.* hear my words. 47
that *any m.* should ask thee. 16:30
for us to put *any m.* to death. 18:31
not call *any m.* common. *Acts* 10:28
can *any m.* forbid water, these? 47
matter against *any m.* law. 19:38
me disputing with *any m.* 24:12
Romans to deliver *any m.* 25:16
shall be no loss of *any m.'s* life. 27:22
if *any m.* have not the Spirit of. *Rom* 8:9
if *any m.* build on this. *1 Cor* 3:12
if *any m.'s* work abide. 14
if *any m.'s* work be burnt. 15
if *any m.* defile the temple of. 17
if *any m.* among you seemeth. 18
any m. that is called a brother. 5:11
is *any m.* called, being circumcised? 7:18
if *any m.* think that he knoweth. 8:2
if *any m.* love God. 3
if *any m.* see thee which hast. 10
that *any m.* should make my. 9:15
if *any m.* say that this is offered. 10:28
any m. seem to be contentious. 11:16
if *any m.* hunger let him. 34
any m. speak in an unknown. 14:27
if *any m.* think himself to be a. 37
if *any m.* be ignorant, let him. 38
if *any m.* love not the Lord. 16:22
if *any m.* be in Christ. *2 Cor* 5:17
if *any m.* trust to himself that. *2 Cor* 10:7
lest *any m.* should think of. 12:6
if *any m.* preach any other. *Gal* 1:9
not of works, lest *any m.* *Eph* 2:9
whatsoever good thing *any m.* 6:8
lest *any m.* should beguile. *Col* 2:4
beware lest *any m.* spoil you. 8
if *any m.* hath a quarrel. 3:13
none render evil for evil to *any m.* *1 Thes* 5:15
did eat *any m.'s* bread. *2 Thes* 3:8
if *any m.* obey not our word. 14
any m. teach otherwise. *1 Tim* 6:3
lest *any m.* fall after. *Heb* 4:11
but if *any m.* draw back, my. 10:38
lest *any m.* fail of the grace. 12:15
nor tempteth *any m.* *Jas* 1:13
if *any m.* among you seem. 26
if *any m.* offend not in word. 3:2
if *any m.* speak, let him. *1 Pet* 4:11
yet if *any m.* suffer as christian. 16
if *any m.* sin, we have. *1 John* 2:1
if *any m.* love the world, the. 15
and ye need not that *any m.* 27
if *any m.* see his brother sin. 5:16
if *any m.* hear my voice. *Rev* 3:20
if *any m.* will hurt them, fire. 11:5
if *any m.* worship the beast. 14:9
if *any m.* shall add to these. 22:18
if *any m.* shall take away from. 19

man child

every *m. child* shall be circumcised. *Gen* 17:10, 12
the uncircumcised *m. child* shall. 14
born a *m. child,* then. *Lev* 12:2
handmaid a *m. child.* *1 Sam* 1:11
said, There is a *m. child* conceived. *Job* 3:3; *Jer* 20:15
she was delivered of a *m. child.* *Isa* 66:7; *Rev* 12:5
brought forth a *m. child.* *Rev* 12:13

every man

on earth, and *every m.* *Gen* 7:21
at hand of *every m.'s* brother. 9:5
hand be against *every m.* and *every m.'s* hand. 16:12
to restore *every m.'s* money. 42:25
every m.'s money was in his sack. 35; 43:21
took down *every m.* his sack. 44:11
and laded *every m.* his ass, and. 13
Joseph cried, Cause *every m.* 45:1
the Egyptians sold *every m.* 47:20
every m. and his household. *Ex* 1:1
for they cast down *every m.* 7:12
let *every m.* borrow of his. 11:2
take to them *every m.* a lamb. 12:3
every m. according to his eating. 4 16:16; 18:21
that which *every m.* must eat. 12:16
abide ye *every m.* in his place. 16:29
every m. that giveth it. 25:2
give *every m.* a ransom for. 30:12
every m. a sword by his side, slay *every m.* his brother, *every m.* his. 32:27
stood *every m.* at his tent door. 33:8
they worshipped *every m.* in his. 10
came *every m.* from his work. 36:4
a bekah for *every m.* that is. 38:26
fear *every m.* his mother. *Lev* 19:3
ye shall return *every m.* 25:10, 13
pitch *every m.* by his standard. *Num* 1:52; 2:2, 17
every m.'s hallowed things. 5:10
give to *every m.* according to. 7:5
take *every m.* his censer. 16:17
they took *every m.* his censer. 18
write thou *every m.'s* name. 17:2
took *every m.* his rod. 9
men of war had taken spoil, *every m.* 31:53
Israel inherited *every m.* his. 32:18
pass over *every m.* armed. 27, 29
judge righteously between *every m.* *Deut* 1:16
shall ye return *every m.* to his. 3:20
not do *every m.* what is right. 12:8
every m. shall give as he. 16:17
every m. shall die for his own sin. *Deut* 24:16; *2 Ki* 14:6; *2 Chr* 25:4
every m. of you a stone. *Josh* 4:5
ascend *every m.* straight. 6:5, 20
every m. to his inheritance. 24:28 *Judg* 2:6
to *every m.* a damsel or. *Judg* 5:30
go *every m.* unto his place. 7:7, 8
and he put a trumpet in *every m.'s.* 16
set *every m.'s* sword against his fellow. 22; *1 Sam* 14:20
give me *every m.* his earrings. *Judg* 8:24, 25
the people cut down *every m.* 9:49
every m. did what was right in. 17:6; 21:25
catch you *every m.* his wife. 21:21
every m. to his tribe, *every m.* to. 24
every m. into his tent. *1 Sam* 4:10
Samuel said, Go ye *every m.* 8:22
every m. his ox, *every m.* his. 14:34
that break away *every m.* 25:10
David said, Gird you on *every m.* 13
the Lord render to *every m.* his righteousness. 26:23; *2 Chr* 6:30
grieved *every m.* for his sons. *1 Sam* 30:6
save to *every m.* his wife and. 22
they went out *every m.* *2 Sam* 13:9
every m. gat him upon his mule. 29
that *every m.* which hath any. 15:4
covered *every m.* his head, and. 30
for Israel hath fled *every m.* 19:8
Sheba said, *Every m.* to his. 20:1
dwelt safely *every m.* *1 Ki* 4:25
every m. the plague of heart. 8:38
give to *every m.* according to his. 39; *Job* 34:11; *Jer* 17:10
brought *every m.* his present. *1 Ki* 10:25; *2 Chr* 9:24
not go up, return *every m.* to his. *1 Ki* 12:24; 22:17, 36; *2 Chr* 11:4
take the kings, *every m.* *1 Ki* 20:24
thence *every m.* a beam. *2 Ki* 6:2
every m. with his weapons. 11:8
Judah fled *every m.* to their. 14:12
and then eat ye *every m.* of. 18:31
God shake out *every m.* *Neh* 5:13
do according to *every m.'s.* *Esth* 1:8
every m. should bear rule in his. 22
and *every m.* shall draw. *Job* 21:23
the hand of *every m.* that. 37:7
every m. at his best state is vanity. *Ps* 39:5, 11
every m. walketh in a vain shew. 6
renderest to *every m.* according to his work. 62:12; *Pr* 24:12
every m. is a friend to. *Pr* 19:6
every m. shall kiss his lips. 24:26
every m.'s judgement cometh. 29:26
eat *every m.* the flesh. *Isa* 9:20
therefore *every m.'s* heart shall. 13:7
in that day *every m.* shall cast. 31:7
every m. is brutish in knowledge. *Jer* 10:14; 51:17
turn *every m.* from his evil way. 26:3; 35:15; 36:3
for *every m.* that is mad, and. 29:26
teach no more *every m.* his neighbour. 31:34; *Heb* 8:11
in proclaiming liberty *every m.* to his neighbour. *Jer* 34:15, 17
rise up *every m.* in his tent. 37:10
deliver ye *every m.* his soul. 51:45
with *every m.* his censer. *Ezek* 8:11
every m. in the chambers. 12
every m. with his destroying. 9:1, 2
away *every m.* abominations. 20:7
they did not *every m.* cast away. 8
every m. shall tremble for. 32:10
not scattered *every m.* from. 46:18
every m. that shall hear. *Dan* 3:10
that *every m.* that shall ask. 6:12
mariners cried *every m.* *Jonah* 1:5
shall sit *every m.* under. *Mi* 4:4
hunt *every m.* his brother. 7:2
and ye run *every m.* to his own house. *Hag* 1:9
every m. his neighbour. *Zech* 3:10
every m. with his staff in his. 8:4
speak *every m.* truth to his neighbour. 16; *Eph* 4:25
why do we deal treacherously *every m.?* *Mal* 2:10

shall reward *every m.* according to.
Mat 16:27; *Rom* 2:6; *Rev* 22:12
received *every m.* a penny.
Mat 20:9, 10
he gave to *every m.* according. 25:15
saw *every m.* clearly. *Mark* 8:25
and gave to *every m.* his work. 13:34
casting lots, what *every m.* 15:24
give to *every m.* that. *Luke* 6:30
every m. presseth into it. 16:16
much *every m.* had gained. 19:15
which lighteth *every m.* *John* 1:9
every m. at beginning doth set. 2:10
every m. that hath heard and. 6:45
ye shall be scattered *every m.* 16:32
how hear we *every m.* in ? *Acts* 2:8
parted to all men, as *every m.* had need. 45; 4:35
every m. determined to send. 11:29
peace to *every m.* that. *Rom* 2:10
be true, but *every m.* a liar. 3:4
as God dealt to *every m.* the. 12:3
every m. be fully persuaded. 14:5
Lord gave to *every m.1 Cor* 3:5; 7:17
every m.'s work shall be made. 3:13
then shall *every m.* have praise. 4:5
nevertheless, let *every m.* have. 7:2
but *every m.* hath his proper gift. 7
let *every m.* abide in the. 20, 24
there is not in *every m.* that. 8:7
let *every m.* seek another's. 10:24*
know that the head of *every m.* 11:3
Spirit is given to *every m.* to. 12:7
every m. in his order, Christ. 15:23
commending ourselves to *every m.*
2 Cor 4:2
I testify again to *every m.* *Gal* 5:3
let *every m.* prove his own work. 6:4
for *every m.* shall bear his own. 5
look not *every m.* on his. *Phil* 2:4
teaching *every m.* in all wisdom; to present *every m.* *Col* 1:28
ye ought to answer *every m.* 4:6
taste death for *every m.* *Heb* 2:9
but *every m.* is tempted. *Jas* 1:14
let *every m.* be swift to hear. 19
who judgeth according to *every m.'s* work. *1 Pet* 1:17
to give reason to *every m.* that. 3:15
every m. hath received the gift. 4:10
every m. that hath this hope in him.
1 John 3:3
judged *every m.* according to their works. *Rev* 20:13
I testify to *every m.* that heareth.
22:18

man *of God*

Moses the *m. of God.* *Deut* 33:1
Josh 14:6
woman told, saying, A *m. of God* came to me. *Judg* 13:6
let the *m. of God* come again to. 8
a *m. of God* to Eli. *1 Sam* 2:27
is in this city a *m. of God.* 9:6
present to bring the *m. of God.* 7
give to the *m. of God* to tell us. 8
Shemaiah the *m. of God.* *1 Ki* 12:22
a *m. of God* out of Judah. 13:1
m. of God who was disobedient. 26
do with thee, O *m. of God* ? 17:18
I know that thou art a *m. of God.* 24
m. of God and spake to Ahab. 20:28
thou *m. of God,* king said, Come down. *2 Ki* 1:9, 11
O *m. of God,* I pray thee, let my life be precious. 13
she came and told *m. of God.* 4:7
this is *m. of God.* 9
thou *m. of God,* do not lie to. 16
that I may run to *m. of God.* 22
she came unto the *m. of God.* 25, 27
O thou *m. of God,* there is death. 40
brought the *m. of God* bread. 42
to the saying of *m. of God.* 5:14
of Elisha, the *m. of God.* 20; 8:4
to place which *m. of God.* 6:10
when the servant of the *m. of God.*
15
lord answered the *m. of God.* 7:2, 19
trode on him as the *m. of God* said.
17, 18
after the saying of *m. of God.* 8:2
m. of God is come hither. 7
the *m. of God* wept. *2 Ki* 8:11
and go, meet the *m. of God.* 8
and the *m. of God* was wroth. 13:19
word which the *m. of God.* 23:16
it is the sepulchre of *m. of God.* 17
Moses *m. of God.* *1 Chr* 23:14
2 Chr 30:16; *Ezra* 3:2
David the *m. of God.* *2 Chr* 8:14
Neh 12:24, 36
came a *m. of God* to Amaziah.
2 Chr 25:7
m. of God answered, The Lord is. 9
of Igdaliah a *m. of God.* *Jer* 35:4
thou, O *m. of God,* flee. *1 Tim* 6:11
that the *m. of God* may be perfect.
2 Tim 3:17

mighty **man**

Lord is with thee, thou *mighty m.*
Judg 6:12
now Jephthah was a *mighty m.* 11:1
a kinsman a *mighty m.* of. *Ruth* 2:1
Benjamite, a *mighty m.* of power
1 Sam 9:1
David a *mighty m.* and a man of war. 16:18; *2 Sam* 17:10
Jeroboam was a *mighty m.*
1 Ki 11:28
Naaman was also a *mighty m.*
2 Ki 5:1
Ismaiah a *mighty m.* among.
1 Chr 12:4
Eliada a *mighty m.* of valour.
2 Chr 17:17
Zichri, a *mighty m.* of. 28:7
as for the *mighty m.* he. *Job* 22:8
a *mighty m.* is not delivered by.
Ps 33:16
thou in mischief, O *mighty m.* 52:1
Lord awaked like a *mighty m.* 78:65
in the hand of a *mighty m.* 127:4
take away the *mighty m.* *Isa* 3:2
mighty m. shall be humbled. 5:15
the sword, not of a *mighty m.* 31:8
go forth as a *mighty m.* 42:13
nor let the *mighty m.* glory. *Jer* 9:23
shouldest be as a *mighty m.* 14:9
nor *mighty m.* escape. 46:6
mighty m. stumbled. 12
the *mighty m.* shall cry. *Zeph* 1:14
as sword of a *mighty m.* *Zech* 9:13
Ephraim shall be like a *mighty m.*
10:7

no **man**

no m. is with us, see. *Gen* 31:50
without thee shall *no m.* lift. 41:44
stood *no m.* while Joseph made. 45:1
saw that there was *no m.* *Ex* 2:12
let *no m.* leave of it till the. 16:19
let *no m.* go out of his place on. 29
hurt or driven away, *no m.* 22:10
no m. did put on him his. 33:4
shall *no m.* see me and live. 20
no m. shall come up with thee. 34:3
there shall be *no m.* in. *Lev* 16:17
no m. that hath a blemish. 21:21
no m. shall sanctify it, it is. 27:26
if *no m.* hath lain with. *Num* 5:19
no m. able to stand before thee.
Deut 7:24; 11:25
oppressed, and *no m.* shall save.
28:29, 68
no m. knoweth of his sepulchre. 34:6
no m. hath been able to stand before.
Josh 23:9
daughter knew *no m.* *Judg* 11:39
no m. that took them to his house.
19:15, 18
virgins that had known *no m.* 21:12
for by strength shall *no m.* *1 Sam* 2:9
and then if there be *no m.* 11:3
let *no m.'s* heart fail because. 17:32
let *no m.* know any thing of. 21:2
and *no m.* saw nor knew it. 26:12
no m. deputed of king. *2 Sam* 15:3
for there is *no m.* that sinneth not.
1 Ki 8:46; *2 Chr* 6:36
behold, there was *no m.* in camp.
2 Ki 7:5, 10
let him alone, let *no m.* move. 23:18
no m. do them wrong, he reproved.
1 Chr 16:21; *Ps* 105:14
queen did let *no m.* come. *Esth* 5:12
may *no m.* reverse. 8:8
no m. could withstand. *Esth* 9:2
shall *no m.* make thee ashamed ?
Job 11:3
in houses which *no m.* 15:28
therefore shall *no m.* look. 20:21
he riseth, and *no m.* is sure. 24:22
where *no m.* is, wherein there is *no m.* 38:26
I am a worm, and *no m.* *Ps* 22:6
there was *no m.* 142:4; *Isa* 41:28
59:16; *Jer* 4:25
in thy sight shall *no m.* be justified.
Ps 143:2
and *no m.* regarded. *Pr* 1:24
flee when *no m.* pursueth. 28:1
the pit, let *no m.* stay him. 17
no m. hath power over. *Eccl* 8:8
no m. knoweth either love. 9:1
no m. remembered that same. 15
no m. shall spare his. *Isa* 9:19
no m. may come in. 24:10
he regardeth *no m.* 33:8
when I came, was there *no m.* 50:2
and *no m.* layeth it to heart. 57:1
Jer 12:11
so that *no m.* went. *Isa* 60:15
and where *no m.* dwelt. *Jer* 2:6
no m. repented. 8:6
for *no m.* of his seed shall. 22:30
this is Zion, whom *no m.* 30:17
go hide, and let *no m.* know. 36:19
Zedekiah said, Let *no m.* 38:24
and *no m.* shall know it. 40:15
no m. knew it. 41:4
and *no m.* dwelleth. 44:2; 51:43
no m. shall abide there. 49:18, 33
50:40
ask bread, and *no m.* *Lam* 4:4
no m. may pass through. *Ezek* 14:15
no m. shall enter in by this. 44:2
yet let *no m.* strive or. *Hos* 4:4
is scattered, and *no m.* *Nah* 3:18
so that there is *no m.* *Zeph* 3:6
so that *no m.* did lift up. *Zech* 1:21
that *no m.* passed through nor. 7:14
no m. can serve two masters.
Mat 6:24; *Luke* 16:13
tell *no m.* *Mat* 8:4; 16:20
Mark 7:36; *Luke* 5:14; 9:21
see that *no m.* know it. *Mat* 9:30
Mark 5:43; 7:24; 8:30; 9:9
no m. knoweth the Son, but the Father. *Mat* 11:27; *Luke* 10:22
saw *no m.* save Jesus. *Mat* 17:8
tell the vision to *no m.* till the. 9
no m. was able to answer. 22:46
call *no m.* father on the earth. 23:9
that day and hour knoweth *no m.*
24:36; *Mark* 13:32
no m. that hath left house.
Mark 10:29; *Luke* 18:29
no m. eat fruit of thee. *Mark* 11:14
that thou carest for *no m.* 12:14
do violence to *no m.* *Luke* 3:14
salute *no m.* 10:4
with the husks, and *no m.* 15:16
no m. hath seen God. *John* 1:18
1 John 4:12
no m. can do these miracles. *John* 3:2
no m. hath ascended up to. 13
for the Father judgeth *no m.* 5:22
no m. can come to me. 6:44, 65
but *no m.* laid hands. 7:30, 44; 8:20
she said, *No m.* Lord. 8:11
I judge *no m.* 15
the night cometh when *no m.* 9:4
no m. taketh it from me. 10:18
no m. is able to pluck them out. 29
no m. at the table knew. 13:28
no m. cometh to the Father. 14:6
greater love hath *no m.* 15:13
and your joy *no m.* taketh. 16:22
let *no m.* dwell therein. *Acts* 1:20
that they speak to *no m.* 4:17
of the rest durst *no m.* join. 5:13
we had opened, we found *no m.* 23
voice, but seeing *no m.* 9:7, 8
no m. shall set on thee to. 18:10
preaching kingdom of God, *no m.*
28:31
recompense to *no m.* *Rom* 12:17
owe *no m.* any thing, but. 13:8
and *no m.* dieth to himself. 14:7
that *no m.* put a stumblingblock. 13

of God knoweth no m. 1 Cor 2:11
himself is judged of no m. 15
other foundation can no m. lay. 3:11
let no m. deceive himself. 18, 21
let no m. seek his own, but. 10:24
henceforth know we no m. after the flesh. 2 Cor 5:16
no m., we have corrupted no m. 7:2
God accepteth no m. Gal 2:6
but that no m. is justified by. 3:11
let no m. deceive you. Eph 5:6
2 Thes 2:3
for no m. ever yet hated. Eph 5:29
no m. likeminded, who. Phil 2:20
let no m. beguile you of. Col 2:18
that no m. go beyond. 1 Thes 4:6
suddenly on no m. 1 Tim 5:22
at my first answer no m. 2 Tim 4:16
to speak evil of no m. Tit 3:2
no m. taketh this honour. Heb 5:4
no m. gave attendance at. 7:13
without which no m. shall see. 12:14
let no m. say when he is. Jas 1:13
the tongue can no m. tame, it. 3:8
little children, let no m. 1 John 3:7
a new name, which no m. Rev 2:17
he that shutteth, and no m. 3:7
and no m. can shut it. 8
that no m. take thy crown. 11
and no m. was able to open. 5:3, 4
multitude which no m. could. 7:9
that no m. might buy or sell. 13:17
no m. could learn that song. 14:3
no m. was able to enter into. 15:8
no m. buyeth their merchandise. 18:11
a name written, that no m. 19:12

of man

of m. will I require life of m. Gen 9:5
all the firstborn of m. Ex 13:13
Num 18:15
afraid of the face of m. Deut 1:17
is this the manner of m.? 2 Sam 7:19
not fall into the hands of m. 24:14
1 Chr 21:13
what manner of m. was he ? 2 Ki 1:7
no man there, nor voice of m. 7:10
days as the days of m.? Job 10:5
destroyest the hope of m. 14:19
for vain is the help of m. Ps 60:11
108:12
wrath of m. shall praise thee. 76:10
the ways of m. are before. Pr 5:21
the spirit of m. will sustain. 18:14
the discretion of m. deferreth. 19:11
the desire of m. is his kindness. 22
so the heart of m. answereth. 27:19
fear of m. bringeth a snare. 29:25
not the understanding of m. 30:2
way of a m. with a maid. 19
all the labour of m. is. Eccl 6:7
misery of m. is great upon. 8:6
this is the whole duty of m. 12:13
after the figure of a m., according to the beauty of a m. Isa 44:13
shouldest be afraid of a m. 51:12
I know the way of m. is. Jer 10:23
aside the right of a m. Lam 3:35
they four had the face of a m.
Ezek 1:10; 10:14
no foot of m. shall pass. 29:11
neither shall the foot of m. 32:13
appearance of a m. Dan 8:15; 10:18
when the eyes of m. shall. Zech 9:1
who formeth the spirit of m. 12:1
of m. is this that the winds. Mat 8:27
Mark 4:41; Luke 8:25
of m. be so with his wife. Mat 19:10
he said, Come out of the m.
Mark 5:8; Luke 8:29
nor of the will of m. but. John 1:13
any should testify of m. 2:25
voice of a god, not of m. Acts 12:22
upon every soul of m. Rom 2:9
the blessedness of the m. 4:6
entered into heart of m. 1 Cor 2:9
knoweth the things of a m. save the spirit of m. which is in him, so. 11
judged of you, or of m. 4:3
woman is the glory of the m. 11:7
but the woman is of the m. 8, 12
neither received it of m. Gal 1:12
wrath of m. worketh not. Jas 1:20
forgetteth what manner of m. Jas 1:24
all the glory of m. as. 1 Pet 1:24
old time by the will of m. 2 Pet 1:21
is the number of a m. Rev 13:18
to the measure of a m. 21:17

one man

we all one m.'s sons. Gen 42:11, 13
two homers for one m. Ex 16:22
if one m.'s ox hurt another's. 21:35
this people as one m. Num 14:15
shall one m. sin, and wilt ? 16:22
lacketh not one m. of us. 31:49
one m. shall chase a. Josh 23:10
Midianites as one m. Judg 6:16
priest to the house of one m. 18:19
was gathered as one m. 20:1
all the people arose as one m. 8
if one m. sin against. 1 Sam 2:25
as the heart of one m. 2 Sam 19:14
there is yet one m. Micaiah.
1 Ki 22:8; 2 Chr 18:7
gathered together as one m.
Ezra 3:1; Neh 8:1
as one m. mocketh. Job 13:9
one m. among a thousand have.
Eccl 7:28
one m. ruleth over another. 8:9
shall take hold of one m. Isa 4:1
one m. was clothed with. Ezek 9:2
one m. should die for the people.
John 11:50; 18:14
by one m. sin entered into. Rom 5:12
grace, which is by one m. Jesus. 15
if by one m.'s offence death. 17
as by one m.'s disobedience many. 19
one m. esteemeth one day. 14:5
been the wife of one m. 1 Tim 5:9

son of man

nor son of m. that he Num 23:19
and the son of m. which. Job 25:6
may profit the son of m. 35:8
and son of m. that thou visitest.
Ps 8:4; Heb 2:6
on son of m. whom thou. Ps 80:17
son of m. that thou makest. 144:3
trust in the son of m. 146:3
not afraid of the son of m. Isa 51:12
blessed is the son of m. that. 56:2
nor shall son of m. dwell in it.
Jer 49:18, 33; 50:40
any son of m. pass thereby. 51:43
hast thou seen this, O son of m.?
Ezek 8:15, 17
sigh therefore, thou son of m. 21:6
one like the Son of m. Dan 7:13
Rev 1:13; 14:14
Son of m. hath not where to lay.
Mat 8:20; Luke 9:58
Son of m. hath power on earth to.
Mat 9:6; Mark 2:10; Luke 5:24
not gone over, till the Son of m. be.
Mat 10:23
the Son of m. came eating. 11:19
Luke 7:34
Son of m. is Lord even of sabbath.
Mat 12:8; Mark 2:28; Luke 5:5
whosoever speaketh against Son of m. Mat 12:32; Luke 12:10
shall Son of m. be three. Mat 12:40
good seed is the Son of m. 13:37
the Son of m. shall send forth. 41
say, that I, the Son of m. am ? 16:13
until the Son of m. be risen again.
17:9; Mark 9:9
the Son of m. shall be betrayed.
Mat 17:22; 20:18; 26:2, 45
Mark 14:41; Luke 9:44
also the coming of the Son of m.
Mat 24:27, 37, 39; Luke 17:26
see Son of m. coming. Mat 24:30
Mark 13:26; Luke 21:27
hour ye think not Son of m. cometh.
Mat 24:44; Luke 12:40
when the Son of m. shall. Mat 25:31
the Son of m. goeth. 26:24
Mark 14:21; Luke 22:22
Son of m. be ashamed. Mark 8:38
written of the Son of m. 9:12
the Son of m. is delivered. 31
10:33; Luke 24:7
Son of m. is as a man. Mark 13:34*
for the Son of m.'s sake. Luke 6:22
the Son of m. must suffer.
Luke 9:22, 26
S. of man is not come to destroy. 56
so shall Son of m. be to this generation. 11:30; 17:24
him shall the Son of m. confess. 12:8
of the days of the Son of m. 17:22
when the Son of m. cometh. 18:8
the Son of m. is come to seek. 19:10
stand before the Son of m. 21:36
betrayest thou the Son of m.? 22:48
descending on Son of m. John 1:51
even the Son of m. which is. 3:13
even so must the Son of m. be. 14
because he is the Son of m. 5:27
which the Son of m. shall give. 6:27
eat the flesh of the Son of m. 53
ye shall see the Son of m. ascend. 62
when ye have lifted up the Son of m. then shall. 8:28
Son of m. should be glorified. 12:23
Son of m. must be lifted up, who is this Son of m.? 34
now is the Son of m. glorified. 13:31
see the Son of m. standing. Acts 7:56
see son

that man

even that m. shall be cut off from.
Lev 17:9
I will set my face against that m.
20:3, 5; Ezek 14:8
brought not offering that m. shall.
Num 9:13
stone that m. or. Deut 17:5, 12
elders shall take that m. and. 22:18
so shall it be done to that m. 25:9
shall smoke against that m. 29:20
that m. perisheth not. Josh 22:20
and that m. was perfect. Job 1:1
for the end of that m. is. Ps 37:37
blessed is that m. who maketh. 40:4
this and that m. was born in. 87:5
for bread that m. will. Pr 28:21
that m. be as cities Lord. Jer 20:16
I will even punish that m. 23:34
last state of that m. is worse.
Mat 12:45; Luke 11:26
woe to that m. by whom. Mat 18:7
that m. by whom the Son of man is ... good were it for that m. 26:24
Mark 14:21; Luke 22:22
to do with that just m. Mat 27:19
by that m. whom he hath ordained.
Acts 17:31
evil for that m. who. Rom 14:20
that m. of sin be revealed, the son of perdition. 2 Thes 2:3
note that m. and have no. 3:14
let not that m. think he. Jas 1:7

this man

wilt thou go with this m.? Gen 24:38
he that toucheth this m. or. 26:11
how long shall this m. be ? Ex 10:7
gave my daughter to this m. to wife.
Deut 22:16
seeing this m. is come. Judg 19:23
to this m. do not so vile a thing. 24
this m. went up early. 1 Sam 1:3
said, How shall this m. save ? 10:27
seen this m. that is come ? 17:25
not my lord regard this m. 25:25
how this m. seeketh. 1 Ki 20:7
to me, and said, Keep this m. 39
this m. sends to me to. 2 Ki 5:7
mercy in sight of this m. Neh 1:11
this m. Mordecai waxed. Esth 9:4
this m. was the greatest. Job 1:3
this m. made not God. Ps 52:7
this m. was born there. 87:4, 5, 6
is this the m. that made ? Isa 14:16
this m. will I look, even to. 66:2
is this m. Coniah a despised broken idol ? Jer 22:28
Lord, Write ye this m. childless. 30
saying, This m. is worthy. 26:11, 16
let this m. be put to death, this m. seeketh not the welfare of. 38:4
make this m. understand. Dan 8:16
not perish for this m.'s life. Jonah 1:14
this m. shall be the peace. Mi 5:5
I say to this m. Go, and he. Mat 8:9
scribes said, This m. blasphemeth.
9:3; Mark 2:7

whence hath *this m.* this wisdom ? *Mat* 13:54; *Mark* 6:2
some said, *This m.* calleth. *Mat* 27:47
I know not *this m.* of. *Mark* 14:71
this m. was the Son of God. 15:39
this m. if he were a prophet. *Luke* 7:39
say to thee, Give *this m.* place. 14:9
saying, *This m.* began to build. 30
this m. receiveth sinners, and. 15:2
I tell you, *this m.* went down. 18:14
will not have *this m.* to reign. 19:14
said, *This m.* was also with. 22:56
I find no fault in *this m.* 23:4, 14
away with *this m.* 18
but *this m.* hath done nothing. 41
this m. went to Pilate and. 52
this m. give us his flesh ? *John* 6:52
how knoweth *this m.* letters ? 7:15
howbeit, we know *this m.* whence. 27
never man spake like *this m.* 46
Master, who did sin, *this m.*? 9:2
neither hath *this m.* sinned, nor. 3
this m. is not of God, he keepeth. 16
praise God, we know that *this m.* 24
if *this m.* were not of God he. 33
all that John spake of *this m.* 10:41
this m. which opened the eyes of blind, caused that *this m.*? 11:37
what do we ? for *this m.* doeth. 47
art not thou one of *this m.'s* ? 18:17
bring ye against *this m.*? 29
not *this m.* but Barabbas, now. 40
if let *this m.* go, thou art not. 19:12
and what shall *this m.* do ? 21:21
this m. purchased a field. *Acts* 1:18
had made *this m.* to walk. 3:12, 16
even by him doth *this m.* stand. 4:10
intend to bring *this m.'s* blood. 5:28
after *this m.* rose up Judas of. 37
this m. ceaseth not to speak. 6:13
saying, *This m.* is the great. 8:10
I heard of *this m.* how much. 9:13
of *this m.'s* seed hath God. 13:23
through *this m.* is preached to. 38
this m. was instructed in way. 18:25
this is the *m.* that teacheth all. 21:28
this m. is a Roman. 22:26
find no evil in *this m.* 23:9
this m. was taken of the Jews. 23:27
this m. a pestilent fellow. 24:5
accuse *this m.* if there be any. 25:5
ye see *this m.* about whom. 24
this m. doeth nothing worthy. 26:31
this m. might have been set at. 32
this m. is a murderer. 28:4
this m. was counted worthy. *Heb* 3:3
now consider how great *this m.* 7:4
this m. because he continueth. 24
that *this m.* have somewhat. 8:3*
this m. after he had offered. 10:12
this m. shall be blessed. *Jas* 1:25
but deceiveth, *this m.'s* religion. 26

man *of war*

the Lord is a *m. of war.* *Ex* 15:3
son of Manasseh, was a *m. of war.* *Josh* 17:1
David a *m. of war.* *1 Sam* 16:18
2 Sam 17:8; *1 Chr* 28:3
Goliath was a *m. of war* from his. *1 Sam* 17:33
take away the *m. of war.* *Isa* 3:2
jealousy like a *m. of war.* 42:13

wicked **man**

if the *wicked m.* be worthy to be. *Deut* 25:2
wicked m. travaileth. *Job* 15:20
the portion of a *wicked m.* from. 20:29; 27:13
set thou a *wicked m.* over. *Ps* 109:6
a *wicked m.* walketh with. *Pr* 6:12
he that rebuketh a *wicked m.* 9:7
when a *wicked m.* dieth, his. 11:7
a *wicked m.* is loathsome, and. 13:5
a *wicked m.* taketh a gift out. 17:23
wicked m. hardeneth his face. 21:29
lay not wait, O *wicked m.* 24:15
a *wicked m.* that prolongeth his. *Eccl* 7:15
wicked m. shall die in iniquity. *Ezek* 3:18
which *wicked m.* doeth. *Ezek* 18:24
when a *wicked m.* turneth from. 27
O *wicked m.* thou shalt surely die, that *wicked m.* shall die in. 33:8

wise **man**

m. discreet and *wise.* *Gen* 41:33
for thou art a *wise m.* *1 Ki* 2:9
David's uncle, was a *wise m.* *1 Chr* 27:32
a *wise m.* utter vain ? *Job* 15:2
I cannot find one *wise m.* 17:10
let a *wise m.* hearken to me. 34:34
a *wise m.* will hear and. *Pr* 1:5
rebuke a *wise m.* and he will. 9:8
give instruction to a *wise m.* he. 9
a *wise m.* feareth, and. 14:16
a *wise m.* will pacify wrath. 16:14
entereth more into a *wise m.* 17:10
a *wise m.* scaleth the city of. 21:22
seest thou a *m. wise* in his ? 26:12
if a *wise m.* contendeth with. 29:9
but a *wise m.* keepeth it in. 11
the *wise m.'s* eyes are in. *Eccl* 2:14
and how dieth the *wise m.*? 16
whether he shall be *wise m.* or. 19
maketh a *wise m.* mad. 7:7
who is as the *wise m.*? 8:1
a *wise m.'s* heart discerneth time. 5
though a *wise m.* think to know. 17
found in it a poor *wise m.* 9:15
a *wise m.'s* heart is at his right. 10:2
the words of a *wise m.'s* mouth. 12
who is the *wise m.* that ? *Jer* 9:12
let not the *wise m.* glory in. 23
liken him to a *wise m.* *Mat* 7:24
not a *wise m.* amongst. *1 Cor* 6:5
who is a *wise m.* endued ? *Jas* 3:13

man joined with *woman*

the *m.* said, the *woman* whom thou. *Gen* 3:12
dead *m.*, for the *woman* thou. 20:3
every *m.* and *woman.* *Ex* 35:29
let no *m.* nor *woman* make. 36:6
if a *m.* or *woman* have. *Lev* 13:29
if *m.* or *woman* have in the skin. 38
woman also with whom the *m.* 15:18
issue of the *m.* and *woman.* 33
if *m.* lie with a *woman.* 20:18
a *m.* or *woman* that hath a familiar spirit. 27
when *m.* or *woman* shall commit any sin. *Num* 5:6
when either *m.* or *woman* shall. 6:2
kill *woman* that hath known *m.* 31:17; *Judg* 21:11
m. or *woman* that hath. *Deut* 17:2
bring forth that *m.* or *woman.* 5
woman . . . that pertaineth to a *m.* nor shall *m.* put on a *woman's.* 22:5
if a *m.* . . . . with a *woman,* both *m.* that lay with *woman,* and *woman.* 22
be among you *m.* or *woman.* 29:18
utterly destroyed both *m.* and *woman.* *Josh* 6:21
but slay both *m., woman.* *1 Sam* 15:3
David left neither *m.* nor *woman* alive. 27:9, 11
m. and *woman* a loaf. *1 Chr* 16:3
m. or *woman* shall die. *2 Chr* 15:13
whether *m.* or *woman* come to the king. *Esth* 4:11
from you, *m.* and *woman.* *Jer* 44:7
in pieces *m.* and *woman.* 51:22
of the *woman* is the *m.* *1 Cor* 11:3
woman is the glory of the *m.* 7
the *m.* is not of the *woman,* but *woman* of the *m.* 8
nor is the *m.* without the *woman.* 11
as *woman* is of the *m.* so is the *m.* by the *woman.* 12
if any *m.* or *woman.* *1 Tim* 5:16

young **man**

I have slain a *young m.* *Gen* 4:23
Abraham gave it to a *young m.* 18:7*
the *young m.* deferred not to. 34:19
was with us a *young m.* an. 41:12
Joshua a *young m.* *Ex* 33:11
there ran a *young m.* *Num* 11:27
destroy both the *young m.* and. *Deut* 32:25
caught a *young m.* of the men of Succoth. *Judg* 8:14
hastily to the *young m.* and his *young m.* thrust him through. *Judg* 9:54
young m. of Beth-lehem-judah. 17:7
the *young m.* became his priest. 12
knew the voice of the *young m.* 18:3
Saul was a choice *young m.* and. *1 Sam* 9:2
Jonathan said to the *young m.* 14:1
whose son art thou, *young m.*? 17:58
I say thus to the *young m.* 20:22*
David, I am *young m.* of. 30:13
David said to the *young m.* that told. *2 Sam* 1:5, 13
bring the *young m.* Absalom. 14:21
for my sake with the *young m.* 18:5
young m. Absalom safe ? 29, 32
enemies be as that *young m.* is. 32
Solomon seeing *young m.* industrious. *1 Ki* 11:28
the eyes of the *young m.* *2 Ki* 6:17
so the *young m.* even *young m.* went to Ramoth. 9:4
and Zadok, a *young m.* *1 Chr* 12:28
compassion on *young m.* *2 Chr* 36:17
wherewith shall *young m.*? *Ps* 119:9
to *young m.* knowledge. *Pr* 1:4
discerned a *young m.* void of. 7:7
rejoice, O *young m.* in. *Eccl* 11:9
as *young m.* marrieth a. *Isa* 62:5
break in pieces the *young m.* and maid. *Jer* 51:22
speak to this *young m.* *Zech* 2:4
young m. said, All these. *Mat* 19:20
followed him a certain *young m.* *Mark* 14:51
saw a *young m.* sitting on the. 16:5
Young m. I say unto thee, arise. *Luke* 7:14
clothes at *young m.'s* feet. *Acts* 7:58
young m. named Eutychus. 20:9
brought the *young m.* alive. 12*
bring this *young m.* to the. 23:17, 18
captain then let the *young m.* 22

Manaen

M. who had been brought. *Acts* 13:1

Manasseh

called the firstborn *M.* *Gen* 41:51
thy two sons *M.* and Ephraim. 48:5
God make thee as Ephraim and *M.* and he set Ephraim before *M.* 20
of *M.* Gamaliel was. *Num* 1:10
Gamaliel prince of *M.* offered. 7:54
these are the families of *M.* 26:34
27:1
married into the family of *M.* 36:12
the thousands of *M.* *Deut* 33:17
two tribes, *M.* Ephraim. *Josh* 14:4
the male children of *M.* 17:2
Zelophehad son of *M.* had no. 3
there fell ten portions to *M.* 5
the daughters of *M.* had an. 6
M. had in Issachar, Beth-shean. 11
children of *M.* could not drive out. 12
my family is poor in *M.* *Judg* 6:15
Jonathan son of Gershom, son of *M.* 18:30
M. his son reigned. *2 Ki* 20:21
2 Chr 32:33
and *M.* seduced them to do more evil. *2 Ki* 21:9
M. shed innocent blood, till he. 16
the altars *M.* made did Josiah. 23:12
M. had provoked him withal. 26
for the sins of *M.* this came. 24:3
dwelt of the children of *M.* *1 Chr* 9:3
fell some of *M.* to David. 12:19
strangers out of *M.* fell. *2 Chr* 15:9
letters to Ephraim and *M.* 30:1
yet divers of *M.* humbled. 11
cut down the groves in *M.* 31:1
M. made Judah and Jerusalem. 33:9
Lord spake to *M.* he would not. 10
the captains took *M.* among. 11
then *M.* knew that the Lord he. 13
humbled not himself, as *M.* 23
so did Josiah in the cities of *M.* 34:6
M. had taken strange wives. *Ezra* 10:30, 33
Gilead is mine, *M.* *Ps* 60:7; 108:8
before *M.* stir up thy strength. 80:2
M. shall eat Ephraim. *Isa* 9:21
removed, because of *M.* *Jer* 15:4

side a portion for *M*. *Ezek* 48:4
Ezekias begat *M*. and *M*. *Mat* 1:10

tribe of **Manasseh**

numbered of the *tribe of M*. 32,200. *Num* 1:35
tribe of M. and the captain of the children of *M*. 2:20; 10:23
of the *tribe of M*., Gaddi. 13:11
to half *tribe of M*. the kingdom of Og. 32:33
half *tribe of M*. have received. 34:14
for the *tribe of M*., Hanniel. 23
half *tribe of M*. passed. *Josh* 4:12
nine tribes and half *tribe of M*. 13:7
tribe of M. this was possession of half *tribe of M*. 29; 12:6; 18:7
also a lot for the *tribe of M*. 17:1
gave Golan out of the *tribe of M*. 20:8; 21:27
the half *tribe of M*. built. 22:10
Gad, and half *tribe of M*. *1 Chr* 5:18
tribe of M. to the Levites. 6:70, 71
half *tribe of M*. 18,000 to. 12:31
rulers over Gad half *tribe of M*. 26:32; 27:20, 21
tribe of M. were sealed. *Rev* 7:6

mandrakes

(*The Hebrew word for mandrake means* love-plant, *and it is supposed to have power to excite vuluptuousness. Its roots are forked and sometimes bear a resemblance to a human being. It is a powerful narcotic*)
Reuben found *m*. Rachel said, Give me of thy *m*. *Gen* 30:14
son's *m*. also? Therefore he shall lie with thee for thy son's *m*. 15
hired thee with my son's *m*. 16
m. give a smell, and at. *S of S* 7:13

Maneh

shekels shall be your *M*. *Ezek* 45:12

manger

laid him in a *m*. *Luke* 2:7
shall find him in a *m*. 12
found the babe lying in a *m*. 16

manifest

that God might *m*. *Eccl* 3:18*
love him, and *m*. myself. *John* 14:21
m. thyself to us, and not unto? 22
the miracle is *m*. to all. *Acts* 4:16
known of God is *m*. in. *Rom* 1:19
m. counsels of hearts. *1 Cor* 4:5
it is *m*. that he is excepted. 15:27
makes *m*. the savour of. *2 Cor* 2:14
works of the flesh are *m*. *Gal* 5:19
my bonds in Christ are *m*. *Phil* 1:13
that I may make it *m*. *Col* 4:4
a *m*. token of righteous. *2 Thes* 1:5
God was *m*. in the flesh. *1 Tim* 3:16
good works of some are *m*. 5:25*
their folly shall be *m*. *2 Tim* 3:9
creature that is not *m*. *Heb* 4:13
but was *m*. in these last. *1 Pet* 1:20
children of God are *m*. *1 John* 3:10

see **made**

manifestation

waiteth for the *m*. of the. *Rom* 8:19
the *m*. of the Spirit is. *1 Cor* 12:7
but by *m*. of the truth. *2 Cor* 4:2

manifested

hid which shall not be *m*. *Mark* 4:22
miracles did Jesus, and *m*. forth his glory. *John* 2:11
I have *m*. thy name unto the. 17:6
the righteousness of God is *m*. *Rom* 3:21
but hath in due time *m*. *Tit* 1:3
the life was *m*. and we. *1 John* 1:2
that he was *m*. to take away. 3:5
purpose was the Son of God *m*. 8
in this was *m*. the love of God. 4:9

manifestly

are *m*. declared to be. *2 Cor* 3:3

manifold

in thy *m*. mercies forsookest them not. *Neh* 9:19
according to *m*. mercies gavest. 27
O Lord, how *m*. are thy! *Ps* 104:24
I know your *m*. transgressions and sins. *Amos* 5:12
shall not receive *m*. *Luke* 18:30
might be known the *m*. *Eph* 3:10
ye are in heaviness through *m*. temptations. *1 Pet* 1:6
good stewards of the *m*. grace. 4:10

mankind

shall not lie with *m*. as. *Lev* 18:22
if a man lie with *m*. as. 20:13
is the breath of all *m*. *Job* 12:10
them that defile with *m*. *1 Tim* 1:10
hath been tamed of *m*. *Jas* 3:7

manna

(*The word means* "what is this?" *It was the food by which Israel was sustained during the* 40 *years in the wilderness. There is a modern substance now called* manna, *but it does not answer all the conditions*)
to another, it is *m*. *Ex* 16:15
put a homer full of *m*. therein. 33
Israel did eat *m*. forty years. 35
nothing besides this *m*. *Num* 11:6
the *m*. was as coriander seed. 7
fell upon camp the *m*. fell on it. 9
and fed thee with *m*. *Deut* 8:3, 16 *Neh* 9:20; *Ps* 78:24
m. ceased, they had *m*. *Josh* 5:12
our fathers did eat *m*. *John* 6:31, 49
not as your fathers did eat *m*. 58*
golden pot that had *m*. *Heb* 9:4
give to eat of the hidden *m*. *Rev* 2:17

manner

two *m*. of people shall. *Gen* 25:23
was of all *m*. of bake-meats. 40:17
their lives bitter in all *m*. *Ex* 1:14
no *m*. of work shall be done. 12:16
all *m*. of trespass, any *m*. 22:9*
in wisdom, and in all *m*. of. 31:3, 5 35:31, 33, 35; 36:1; *1 Chr* 28:21
burnt offering according to *m*. *Lev* 5:10*; *Num* 9:14*
no *m*. of fat of ox or sheep. *Lev* 7:23
no *m*. of blood. 26, 27; 17:10, 14
law for all *m*. of plague. 14:54
ye shall do no *m*. of work. 23:31
ye shall have one *m*. of law. 24:22 *Num* 15:16*
she be taken with the *m*. *Num* 5:13
offering according to the *m*. 15:24*
do no *m*. of servile work. 28:18
saw no *m*. of similitude. *Deut* 4:15
this is the *m*. of the release. 15:2
that lieth with any *m*. of beast. 27:21
what *m*. of men were they? *Judg* 8:18
now this was the *m*. in. *Ruth* 4:7*
and shew them the *m*. of the king. *1 Sam* 8:9, 11
Samuel told the people the *m*. 10:25
bread is in a *m*. common. 21:5*
so will be his *m*. all the while. 27:11
is this the *m*. of man? *2 Sam* 7:19
what *m*. of man was he? *2 Ki* 1:7
by a pillar, as the *m*. was. 11:14
know not the *m*. of the God. 17:26
let him teach them the *m*. of God. 27
all *m*. of measure. *1 Chr* 23:29
for so was the king's *m*. *Esth* 1:13
abhorreth all *m*. of meat. *Ps* 107:18
full, affording all *m*. of store. 144:13
at our gates are all *m*. *S of S* 7:13
shall feed after their *m*. *Isa* 5:17*
this hath been thy *m*. *Jer* 22:21
and no *m*. of hurt was. *Dan* 6:23
the *m*. of Beer-sheba. *Amos* 8:14
and healing all *m*. of sickness. *Mat* 4:23; 10:1
shall say all *m*. of evil against. 5:11
What *m*. of man is this, that even wind? 8:27; *Mark* 4:41; *Luke* 8:25
all *m*. of sin shall be forgiven to. *Mat* 12:31
what *m* of stones are! *Mark* 13:1
what *m*. of salutation. *Luke* 1:29
saying, What *m*. of child shall? 66
have known what *m*. of woman. 7:39
ye know not what *m*. of spirit. 9:55
ye tithe mint, rue, and all *m*. 11:42
what *m*. of communications? 24:17
what *m*. of saying is this? *John* 7:36
m. of the Jews is to bury. 19:40*
Paul, as his *m*. was, went. *Acts* 17:2*
ye know after what *m*. I have. 20:18
to the perfect *m*. of the law. 22:3
it is not *m*. of Romans. *Acts* 25:16*
my *m*. of life from my youth. 26:4
wrought in me all *m*. of. *Rom* 7:8
sorry after a godly *m*. *2 Cor* 7:9*
m. of men we were. *1 Thes* 1:5
what *m*. of entering in we had. 9
known my *m*. of life. *2 Tim* 3:10*
assembling, as the *m*. *Heb* 10:25*
forgetteth what *m*. of man. *Jas* 1:24
m. of time the Spirit. *1 Pet* 1:11
holy in all *m*. of conversation. 15
what *m*. of persons. *2 Pet* 3:11
behold what *m*. of love. *1 John* 3:1
in this *m*. be killed. *Rev* 11:5
which bare twelve *m*. of fruits. 22:2

see **like**

after the **manner**

Sarah *after the m*. of women. *Gen* 18:11
to come in to us *after the m*. 19:31
after the former *m*. when. 40:13
deal with her *after the m*. *Ex* 21:9
number, *after the m*. *Num* 29:18
city *after the* same *m*. *Josh* 6:15
careless, *after the m*. of. *Judg* 18:17
turned and spake *after the* same *m*. *1 Sam* 17:30
after the m. of the nations. *2 Ki* 17:33; *2 Chr* 13:9
and I answered them *after the* same *m*. *Neh* 6:4
after the m. of Egypt. *Isa* 10:24 *Amos* 4:10
polluted *after the m*. *Ezek* 20:30
after the m. of Babylonians. 23:15
after the m. of adulteresses, and *after the m*. of women. 45*
after the m. of the purifying of the. *John* 2:6
circumcised *after the m*. *Acts* 15:1*
I speak *after the m*. of men. *Rom* 6:19; *1 Cor* 15:32; *Gal* 3:15
after the same *m*. also he took the cup. *1 Cor* 11:25
being a Jew, livest *after the m*. of. *Gal* 2:14*

after this **manner**

far from thee to do *after this m*. *Gen* 18:25
saying, *After this m*. did thy. 39:19
he sent *after this m*. ten asses. 45:23
after this m. ye shall offer daily. *Num* 28:24
spoken *after this m*. *2 Sam* 17:6
after this m. will I mar. *Jer* 13:9
after this m. therefore pray ye. *Mat* 6:9
one *after this m*. and. *1 Cor* 7:7
after this m. in old time. *1 Pet* 3:5

on this **manner**

saying, *On this m*. shall ye speak to. *Gen* 32:19
told Saul, saying, *On this m*. spake David. *1 Sam* 18:24
on this m. did Absalom. *2 Sam* 15:6
one said *on this m*., another on that *m*. *1 Ki* 22:20; *2 Chr* 18 19
persuade you *on this m*. *2 Chr* 32:15

manners

shall not walk in the *m*. *Lev* 20:23*
do after the former *m*. *2 Ki* 17:34†
have done after the *m*. *Ezek* 11:12*
suffered he their *m*. *Acts* 13:18†
corrupt good *m*. *1 Cor* 15:33†
God in divers *m*. spake. *Heb* 1:1

Manoah

M. intreated the Lord. *Judg* 13:8
God hearkened to the voice of *M*. 9
M. arose and went after his wife. 11
M. knew not that he was an angel. 16
M. took a kid, and offered it. 19
M. and his wife looked on it. 20
M. knew that he was an angel. 21
in the buryingplace of *M*. 16:31

manservant

not do any work, thou nor thy *m*. *Ex* 20:10; *Deut* 5:14
not covet thy neighbour's *m*. *Ex* 20:17; *Deut* 5:21
smite out his *m*.'s tooth. *Ex* 21:27
if the ox shall push a *m*. he shall. 32

must eat them, thou and thy *m.* *Deut* 12:18
rejoice, thou and *m.* 16:11, 14
despise cause of my *m.* *Job* 31:13
let his *m.* go free. *Jer* 34:9, 10

mansions

house are many *m.* *John* 14:2

manslayer

ye shall appoint for *m.* *Num* 35:6
the *m.* die not, until he stand. 12

manslayers

law was made for *m.* *1 Tim* 1:9

mantle

Sisera with a *m.* *Judg* 4:18*
and covered with a *m.* *1 Sam* 28:14
wrapped his face in his *m.* *1 Ki* 19:13
Elijah cast his *m.* upon Elisha. 19
Elijah took his *m.* and. *2 Ki* 2:8
Elisha took Elijah's *m.* that. 13, 14
heard this, I rent my *m.* *Ezra* 9:3, 5
arose and rent his *m.* *Job* 1:20
rent every one his *m.* 2:12
confusion, as with a *m.* *Ps* 109:29

mantles

I will take away the *m.* *Isa* 3:22

many

thou shalt be a father of *m.* nations. *Gen* 17:4, 5; *Rom* 4:17, 18
he made him a coat of *m.* colours. *Gen* 37:3; 23:32
to gaze, and *m.* perish. *Ex* 19:21
Moses said, Return, O Lord, to the *m.* thousands of. *Num* 10:36
whether they be few or *m.* 13:18
to *m.* thou shalt give more. 26:54
divided between *m.* and few. 56
have *m.* cities, shall give *m.* 35:8
hath cast out *m.* nations. *Deut* 7:1
lend to *m.* nations. 15:6; 28:12
and *m.* evils shall befall. 31:17, 21
and chariots very *m.* *Josh* 11:4
m. were overthrown. *Judg* 9:40
the destroyer which slew *m.* 16:24
she that hath *m.* children. *1 Sam* 2:5
the Lord to save by *m.* or few. 14:6
Judah and Israel were *m.* *1 Ki* 4:20
they were exceeding *m.* 7:47
dress it first, for ye are *m.* 18:25
witchcrafts are so *m.* *2 Ki* 9:22
Rehabiah were very *m.* *1 Chr* 23:17
hath given me *m.* sons. 28:5
Rehoboam desired *m.* *2 Chr* 11:23
to help whether with *m.* 14:11
there were *m.* in congregation. 30:17
m. of Ephraim and Manasseh. 18
we are *m.* that have. *Ezra* 10:13
and our daughters are *m.* *Neh* 5:2
there were *m.* in Judah sworn. 6:18
and feared God above *m.* 7:2
among *m.* nations was no king. 13:26
and *m.* lay in sackcloth. *Esth* 4:3
thou hast instructed *m.* *Job* 4:3
yea, *m.* shall make suit unto. 11:19
m. are they that rise up. *Ps* 3:1
there be *m.* that say of my. 2; 4:6
consider mine enemies, they are *m.* 25:19; 56:2
heard the slander of *m.* 31:13
m. sorrows shall be to the. 32:10
m. are the afflictions of the. 34:19
better than the riches of *m.* 37:16
m. shall see it and fear, and. 40:3
delivered, for there were *m.* 55:18
I am a wonder to *m.*; but thou. 71:7
m. are my persecutors. 119:157
years of thy life shall be *m.* *Pr* 4:10
for she hath cast down *m.* 7:26
the righteous feed *m.* 10:21
the rich hath *m.* friends. 14:20
wealth maketh *m.* friends. 19:4
for transgression of land *m.* are. 28:2
his eyes, shall have *m.* a curse. 27
darkness shall be *m.* *Eccl* 11:8
trust in chariots because they are *m.* *Isa* 31:1
knowledge shall he justify *m.* 53:11
he bare the sin of *m.* and made. 12
slain of the Lord shall be *m.* 66:16
their transgressions are *m.* *Jer* 5:6
for our backslidings are *m.* 14:7
for we are left but few of *m.* 42:2
he made *m.* to fall. 46:16
for my sighs are *m.* my. *Lam* 1:22
but we are *m.*; the land. *Ezek* 33:24
by peace shall destroy *m.* *Dan* 8:25
m. stand up against the king. 11:14
understand shall instruct *m.* 33
utterly to make away *m.* 44
m. that sleep in the dust shall. 12:2
m. shall run to and fro, and. 4
Ephraim hath made *m.* *Hos* 8:11
be quiet, and likewise *m.* *Nah* 1:12
inhabitants of *m.* cities. *Zech* 8:20
but did turn *m.* away. *Mal* 2:6
and *m.* there be that go. *Mat* 7:13
m. will say to me in that day. 22
m. shall come from the east. 8:11
he did not *m.* mighty works. 13:58
m. that are first shall be last. 19:30; *Mark* 10:31
for *m.* be called, but few chosen. *Mat* 20:16; 22:14
for *m.* shall come in my name, and shall deceive *m.* 24:5; *Mark* 13:6 *Luke* 21:8
love of *m.* shall wax. *Mat* 24:12
this is my blood, shed for *m.* 26:28
they appear to *m.* 27:53
name is Legion, for we are *m.* *Mark* 5:9; *Luke* 8:30
m. shall he turn to Lord. *Luke* 1:16
fall and rising of *m.* in Israel. 2:34
m. widows were in Israel. 4:25
m. lepers were in Israel. 27
and devils also came out of *m.* 41
her sins which are *m.* 7:47
great supper, and bade *m.* 14:16
are they among so *m.*? *John* 6:9
m. therefore of his disciples. 60, 66
and *m.* resorted to him, and. 10:41
for all so *m.*, the net was not. 21:11
I have heard by *m.* of this. *Acts* 9:13
where *m.* were gathered. 12:12
m. brought their books. 19:19
m. of the saints did I shut up. 26:10
m. be dead . . . the grace of God hath abounded unto *m.* *Rom* 5:15
m. were made sinners, *m.* be. 19
so we, being *m.* are one body. 12:5
she hath been a succourer of *m.* 16:2
not *m.* wise, not *m.* mighty are. *1 Cor* 1:26
yet have ye not *m.* fathers. 4:15
there be gods *m.* and lords *m.* 8:5
but with *m.* God was not. 10:5
we being *m.* are one bread. 17
seeking the profit of *m.* 33
m. are weak and *m.* sleep. 11:30
not one member, but *m.* 12:14
great door, and there are *m.* 16:9
may be given by *m.* *2 Cor* 1:11
punishment was inflicted of *m.* 2:6
m. which corrupt the word. 17
m. redound to glory. 4:15
as poor, yet making *m.* rich. 6:10
zeal hath provoked very *m.* 9:2
and profited above *m.* *Gal* 1:14
and to seeds, as of *m.* 3:16
m. brethren waxing confident by. *Phil* 1:14
m. walk, of whom I have told. 3:18
bringing *m.* sons to glory. *Heb* 2:10
they truly were *m.* priests. 7:23
offered to bear the sins of *m.* 9:28
sprang of one, so *m.* as stars. 11:12
my brethren be not *m.* *Jas* 3:1
m. shall follow pernicious. *2 Pet* 2:2
are there *m.* antichrists. *1 John* 2:18
because *m.* false prophets are. 4:1
see **believed, days, how, waters**

after **many**

cause to decline *after m.* *Ex* 23:2

as **many** *as*

and *as m. as* were willing. *Ex* 35:22
as m. as had not known. *Judg* 3:1
as m. as came to the place stood. *2 Sam* 2:23
as m. as were of free. *2 Chr* 29:31
as m. as ye find bid to. *Mat* 22:9
and gathered together *as m. as.* 10
as m. as touched him. *Mark* 6:56
rise and give *as m. as* he needeth. *Luke* 11:8
but *as m. as* received him. *John* 1:12
give eternal life to *as m. as.* 17:2
even to *as m. as* the Lord. *Acts* 2:39
as m. as have spoken have. 3:24
fear came upon *as m. as* heard. 5:11
and *as m. as* obeyed him. 36, 37
were astonished, *as m. as.* 10:45
as m. as were ordained to. 13:48
as m. as have sinned without law, and *as m. as* have. *Rom* 2:12
for *as m. as* are led by the Spirit. 8:14
as m. as are of the works. *Gal* 3:10
as m. as desire to make a fair shew in the flesh. 6:12
and *as m. as* walk according. 16
as m. as be perfect be. *Phil* 3:15
and for *as m. as* have not. *Col* 2:1
as m. servants *as* are. *1 Tim* 6:1
but to *as m. as* have not. *Rev* 2:24
as m. as I love I rebuke. 3:19
cause that *as m. as* would not. 13:15

many *people*

people of the land now are *m.* *Ex* 5:5
a *people* great and *m.* *Deut* 2:21
the *people* are too *m.* . . . yet too *m.* for me. *Judg* 7:2, 4
Lord had smitten *m.* of the *people.* *1 Sam* 6:19
m. of the *people* are fallen and dead. *2 Sam* 1:4
but the *people* are *m.* *Ezra* 10:13
m. people of land became. *Esth* 8:17
m. people shall go and say. *Isa* 2:3
judge and rebuke *m. people.* 4
multitude of *m. people.* 17:12
m. people of a strange. *Ezek* 3:6
without *m. people* to pluck it. 17:9
vex the hearts of *m. people.* 32:9
I will make *m. people* amazed. 10
and *m. people* with thee. 38:9, 15
judge among *m. people.* *Mi* 4:3
beat in pieces *m. people.* 13
shall be in midst of *m. people.* 5:7
m. people shall come. *Zech* 8:22
thou must prophesy before *m. peoples,* nations and tongues. *Rev* 10:11

many *things*

I have heard *m.* such *things.* *Job* 16:2
and *m.* such *things* are with. 23:14
there be *m. things* that. *Eccl* 6:11
seeing *m. things,* but. *Isa* 42:20
spake *m. things* to them. *Mat* 13:3
suffer *m. things* of the elders and chief priests. 16:21; *Mark* 8:31 9:12; *Luke* 9:22; 17:25
make thee ruler over *m. things.* *Mat* 25:21, 23
hearest thou not how *m. things* they witness? 27:13; *Mark* 15:4
have suffered *m. things* this day in a dream. *Mat* 27:19
suffered *m. things* of many physicians. *Mark* 5:26
he did *m. things,* and heard. 6:20
m. things there be, as washing of cups. 7:4, 8, 13
accused him of *m. things.* 15:3
thou art troubled about *m. things.* *Luke* 10:41
to speak of *m. things.* 11:53
I have *m. things* to say. *John* 8:26 16:12
there are *m.* other *things.* 21:25
that I ought to do *m. things* contrary. *Acts* 26:9
diligent in *m. things.* *2 Cor* 8:22
suffered so *m. things.* *Gal* 3:4
in how *m. things* he. *2 Tim* 1:18
have *m. things* to say. *Heb* 5:11
in *m. things* we offend. *Jas* 3:2
having *m. things* to write to you. *2 John* 12; *3 John* 13

many *a time*

m. a time turned he his. *Ps* 78:38
m. a time have they afflicted me. 129:1, 2

many *times*

how *m. times* shall I adjure thee? *1 Ki* 22:16
m. times didst deliver them. *Neh* 9:28; *Ps* 106:43

many years
if there be yet *m. years.* *Lev* 25:51
that was builded *m. years* ago.
Ezra 5:11
yet *m. years* didst thou. *Neh* 9:30
children, and live *m. years.* *Eccl* 6:3
man live *m. years,* and rejoice. 11:8
m. days and *years* shall. *Isa* 32:10
prophesied *m. years.* *Ezek* 38:17
done these so *m. years.* *Zech* 7:3
hast goods laid up for *m. years.*
Luke 12:19
he said, Lo, these *m. years.* 15:29
of *m. years* a judge. *Acts* 24:10
now after *m. years* I came to. 17
a great desire *m. years.* *Rom* 15:23

mar
nor *m.* the corners of. *Lev* 19:27
lest I *m.* mine own. *Ruth* 4:6
images of your mice that *m.* the land. *1 Sam* 6:5
and *m.* every good. *2 Ki* 3:19
they *m.* my path, they. *Job* 30:13
I *m.* the pride of Judah. *Jer* 13:9

Mara
not Naomi, call me *M.* *Ruth* 1:20

Marah
not drink of waters of *M.* *Ex* 15:23
days, and pitched in *M.* *Num* 33:8
removed from *M.* and came. 9

Maran-atha
(*An Aramaic or Syriac expression used by St. Paul at the conclusion of his First Epistle to the Corinthians,* 1 Cor 16:22, *meaning* our Lord cometh)

marble
I have prepared *m.* in. *1 Chr* 29:2
pillars of *m.*: pavement of red, blue, white, and black *m.* *Esth* 1:6
his legs are as pillars of *m.* set.
S of S 5:15
the vessels of *m.* no man. *Rev* 18:12

march
thou didst *m.* through. *Ps* 68:7
shall *m.* with an army. *Jer* 46:22
m. every one on his ways. *Joel* 2:7
which shall *m.* through. *Hab* 1:6
didst *m.* through the land. 3:12

marched
behold, the Egyptians *m.* *Ex* 14:10

marchedst
when thou *m.*, the earth. *Judg* 5:4

Marcus
M. sister's son to Barnabas. *Col* 4:10
M. saluteth. *Philem* 24; *1 Pet* 5:13

mariners
of Zidon were thy *m.* *Ezek* 27:8*
ships of the sea with their *m.* were. 9
thy *m.* shall fall into the midst of. 27
the *m.* shall come down from. 29
then the *m.* were afraid. *Jonah* 1:5

marishes
miry places and *m.* shall. *Ezek* 47:11

Mark
John, surnamed *M.* *Acts* 12:12
whose surname was *M.* 25; 15:37
Barnabas took *M.* and. 15:39
take *M.* and bring. *2 Tim* 4:11

mark, *substantive*
the Lord set a *m.* upon. *Gen* 4:15*
though I shot at a *m.* *1 Sam* 20:20
hast thou set me as a *m.* against thee? *Job* 7:20; 16:12; *Lam* 3:12
set a *m.* on the men. *Ezek* 9:4
any man on whom is the *m.* 6
I press toward the *m.* *Phil* 3:14*
all to receive a *m.* *Rev* 13:16
save he that had the *m.* 17
if any man receive his *m.* 14:9
whosoever receiveth his *m.* 11
his image, and over his *m.* 15:2
sore on them that had the *m.* 16:2
that received *m.* of beast. 19:20
nor received his *m.* upon their. 20:4

mark, *verb*
thou shalt *m.* the place. *Ruth* 3:4
m. when Amnon's heart is merry.
2 Sam 13:28
m. how this man. *1 Ki* 20:7
the prophet said, *M.* and see. 22
m. and afterwards we will. *Job* 18:2
m. me and be astonished, and. 21:5
m. well, O Job, hearken to me. 33:31
canst thou *m.* when the hinds? 39:1
m. the perfect man. *Ps* 37:37
m. well her bulwarks. 48:13
they *m.* my steps, when they. 56:6
if thou, Lord, shouldest *m.* 130:3
m. well, *m.* the entering. *Ezek* 44:5
m. them who cause. *Rom* 16:17
m. them who walk so. *Phil* 3:17

marked
as she prayed, Eli *m.* *1 Sam* 1:12
hast thou *m.* the old way? *Job* 22:15
which they had *m.* in the day. 24:16
yet thine iniquity is *m.* *Jer* 2:22
who hath *m.* his word and? 23:18
m. how they chose rooms. *Luke* 14:7

markest
if I sin, then thou *m.* *Job* 10:14

market
they traded in thy *m.* *Ezek* 27:13*
17*, 19*, 25*
standing idle in the *m.* *Mat* 20:3
they come from the *m.* *Mark* 7:4*
salutations in the *m.* places. 12:38
sitting in the *m.* place. *Luke* 7:32
is a pool at Jerusalem by the sheep *m.* *John* 5:2*
them into the *m.* place. *Acts* 16:19
he disputed in the *m.* daily. 17:17*

marketh
my feet in stocks, he *m.* *Job* 33:11
the carpenter *m.* it out. *Isa* 44:13

markets
(*Revisions,* marketplaces)
children sitting in the *m.* *Mat* 11:16
love greetings in the *m.* 23:7
Luke 11:43; 20:46

marks
ye shall not print any *m.* *Lev* 19:28
I bear in my body the *m.* *Gal* 6:17

marred
his visage was so *m.* *Isa* 52:14
girdle was *m.* *Jer* 13:7
the vessel was *m.* 18:4
m. their vine branches. *Nah* 2:2
the bottles will be *m.* *Mark* 2:22

marriage
(*The word marriage is used* [1] *literally; and* [2] *figuratively to represent the union of God with his people or of Christ with his church*)
her duty of *m.* shall he. *Ex* 21:10
were not given to *m.* *Ps* 78:63*
a king who made a *m.* *Mat* 22:2
come to the *m.* 4
all ye find, bid to the *m.* 9
not given in *m.* but as the angels.
22:30; *Mark* 12:25; *Luke* 20:35
given in *m.* until day. *Mat* 24:38
went in with him to the *m.* 25:10
they did eat, they were given in *m.*
Luke 17:27; 20:34
there was a *m.* in Cana. *John* 2:1
Jesus and his disciples to the *m.* 2
her in *m.* doeth well, but he that giveth her not in *m.* *1 Cor* 7:38
m. is honourable in all. *Heb* 13:4
m. of the Lamb is come. *Rev* 19:7
called to the *m.* supper of Lamb. 9

marriages
and make ye *m.* with us. *Gen* 34:9
neither shalt thou make *m.* *Deut* 7:3
else if he shall make *m.* *Josh* 23:12

married
Lot spake to them that *m.* *Gen* 19:14
if *m.* his wife shall go out. *Ex* 21:3
if *m.* to a stranger, she. *Lev* 22:12
woman whom he had *m.* *Num* 12:1
if they be *m.* to the sons of. 36:3
m. to their father's brothers'. 11
lying with a woman *m.* *Deut* 22:22
m. when sixty years old. *1 Chr* 2:21
Abijah *m.* fourteen. *2 Chr* 13:21
Jews that had *m.* wives. *Neh* 13:23
woman when she is *m.* *Pr* 30:23
of desolate than of *m.* *Isa* 54:1
in thee, thy land shall be *m.* 62:4
children, for I am *m.* to. *Jer* 3:14
hath *m.* the daughter of. *Mal* 2:11
the first when he had *m.* *Mat* 22:25
for he had *m.* her. *Mark* 6:17
be *m.* to another, committeth. 10:12
I have *m.* a wife, and. *Luke* 14:20
they drank, they *m.* wives. 17:27
husband liveth, she be *m.* *Rom* 7:3
dead, that ye should be *m.* 4
to the *m.* I command. *1 Cor* 7:10
he that is *m.* 33
she that is *m.* careth for. 34
to be *m.* to whom she will, only. 39

marrieth
young man *m.* a virgin. *Isa* 62:5
m. her who is put away, doth.
Mat 19:9; *Luke* 16:18

marrow
(*A soft tissue which fills the cavities of most bones; hence, the choicest of food*)
are moistened with *m.* *Job* 21:24
be satisfied as with *m.* *Ps* 63:5
it shall be health and *m.* *Pr* 3:8
feast of fat things full of *m.* *Isa* 25:6
asunder of joints and *m.* *Heb* 4:12

marry
brother's wife, and *m.* *Gen* 38:8*
m. to whom they think best...father's tribe shall they *m.* *Num* 36:6
wife of dead shall not *m.* *Deut* 25:5
so shall thy sons *m.* thee. *Isa* 62:5
m. her that is divorced committeth.
Mat 5:32; 19:9; *Mark* 10:11
so, it is not good to *m.* *Mat* 19:10
his brother shall *m.* his wife. 22:24
they neither *m.* nor are given. 30
Mark 12:25; *Luke* 20:35
let them *m.*, for it is better to *m.*
1 Cor 7:9
if thou *m.* if a virgin *m.*: she hath. 28
he sinneth not, let them *m.* 36
forbidding to *m.* and. *1 Tim* 4:3
to wax wanton, they will *m.* 5:11
the younger women *m.*, bear. 14

marrying
do this great evil in *m.* *Neh* 13:27
they were *m.* and giving. *Mat* 24:38

Mars' hill
in the midst of *M. hill.* *Acts* 17:22

mart
Tyre, and she is a *m.* of. *Isa* 23:3

Martha
a woman named *M.* *Luke* 10:38
M. was cumbered about. 40
M. M. thou art careful. 41
Mary and her sister *M.* *John* 11:1
now Jesus loved *M.* Mary, and. 5
Jesus was in that place where *M.* 30
made him a supper, and *M.* 12:2

martyr
blood of thy *m.* Stephen. *Acts* 22:20*
wherein Antipas was my faithful *m.*
Rev 2:13*

martyrs
drunken with blood of *m.* *Rev* 17:6

marvel
no *m.*; for Satan himself. *2 Cor* 11:14

marvel
if thou seest, *m.* not at. *Eccl* 5:8
and all men did *m.* *Mark* 5:20
m. not that I said, Ye must be born.
John 3:7
greater works, that ye may *m.* 5:20
m. not at this. 28
done one work, and ye *m.* 7:21
men of Israel, why *m.*? *Acts* 3:12
I *m.* that ye are so soon. *Gal* 1:6
m. not if the world. *1 John* 3:13
wherefore didst thou *m.*? *Rev* 17:7*

marvelled
and the men *m.* one. *Gen* 43:33
they saw it, and so they *m.* *Ps* 48:5
when Jesus heard it, he *m.* *Mat* 8:10
the men *m.* 27
m. and glorified God. 9:8*, 33
disciples saw it, they *m.* 21:20

they m., and left him. Mat 22:22
Mark 12:17; Luke 20:26
that the governor m. Mat 27:14
Mark 15:5, 44
m. because of their unbelief.
Mark 6:6
people m. that he tarried. Luke 1:21
his name is John, and they m. 63
Joseph and his mother m. at. 2:33
Jesus heard these things he m. 7:9
Pharisee saw it, he m. 11:38
disciples m. he talked. John 4:27
Jews m., How knoweth this ? 7:15
m. saying, Are not these ? Acts 2:7
they m. and took knowledge. 4:13

marvellous

who doeth m. things. Job 5:9
thou shewest thyself m. upon. 10:16
thy m. lovingkindness. Ps 17:7
he hath shewed me his m. 31:21
m. things did he in the sight. 78:12
for he hath done m. things. 98:1
Lord's doing; it is m. in our eyes.
118:23; Mat 21:42; Mark 12:11
shall speak m. things. Dan 11:36
will I shew unto him m. Mi 7:15
if it be m. should it be m.? Zech 8:6
herein is a m. thing. John 9:30
darkness into his m. light. 1 Pet 2:9
heaven, great and m. Rev 15:1

marvellous work

proceed to do a m. work. Isa 29:14

marvellous works

remember his m. works.
1 Chr 16:12; Ps 105:5
declare his m. works. 1 Chr 16:24
forth all thy m. works. Ps 9:1
great and m. are thy works. 139:14
Rev 15:3

marvellously

he was m. helped till. 2 Chr 26:15
God thundereth m. with. Job 37:5
regard, and wonder m. Hab 1:5

marvels

I will do m. such as have. Ex 34:10

Mary

Joseph the husband of M. Mat 1:16
his mother M. was espoused. 18
take unto thee M. thy wife. 20
saw the young child with M. 2:11
mother called M.? 13:55; Mark 6:3
M. the mother of James. Mat 27:56
Mark 15:40, 47; 16:1
virgin's name was M. Luke 1:27
fear not, M. 30
heard the salutation of M. 41
M. abode three months. 56
went to be taxed with M. his. 2:5
shepherds found M. and the. 16
but M. kept all these things in. 19
had a sister called M. 10:39
M. hath chosen that good part. 42
the town of M. John 11:1
M. that anointed the Lord. 2
but M. sat still. 20
she called M. her sister secretly. 28
M. took a pound of ointment. 12:3
M. the wife of Cleophas. 19:25
M. stood without at the. 20:11
Jesus saith to her, M. She turned. 16
in prayer with M. Acts 1:14
Peter came to house of M. 12:12
greet M. who bestowed. Rom 16:6

Mary Magdalene

women were there, among whom
was M. Magdalene. Mat 27:56
Mark 15:40; John 19:25
M. Magdalene sitting. Mat 27:61
came M. Magdalene to see the
sepulchre. 28:1; John 20:1
M. Magdalene and Mary the.
Mark 16:1; Luke 24:10
he appeared first to M. Magdalene.
Mark 16:9
M. Magdalene told the. John 20:18

masons

Hiram sent to David m. 2 Sam 5:11
1 Chr 14:1
gave money to m. and hewers of.
2 Ki 12:12; 22:6; Ezra 3:7
he set m. to hew. 1 Chr 22:2
they hired m. to repair. 2 Chr 24:12

Massah

name of the place M. Ex 17:7
shall not tempt the Lord, as ye tempted him in M. Deut 6:16; 9:22
whom thou didst prove at M. 33:8

mast, -s

lieth on the top of a m. Pr 23:34
not strengthen their m. Isa 33:23
Lebanon to make m. Ezek 27:5

master

Joseph's m. put him in. Gen 39:20
if she please not her m. Ex 21:8
give to their m. thirty shekels. 32
m. of the house shall be. 22:8
and spake to the m. of. Judg 19:22
the m. of the house went out. 23
David sent messengers to salute our
m. 1 Sam 25:14
determined against our m. 17
have not kept your m. 26:16*
m. Saul is dead. 2 Sam 2:7*
these have no m. 1 Ki 22:17
2 Chr 18:16
he cried, Alas, m. for it 2 Ki 6:5
drink, and go to their m. 22
and they went to their m. 23
seeing your m.'s sons are with. 10:2
look out the best of your m.'s sons. 3
take the heads of your m.'s sons. 6
ye say to your m. 19:6; Isa 37:6
and Chenaniah, m. of. 1 Chr 15:27
servant, so with his m. Isa 24:2
king spake to the m. Dan 1:3
m. of the magicians. 4:9; 5:11
and if I be a m. where is ? Mal 1:6
the Lord will cut off the m. 2:12*
m. I will follow thee. Mat 8:19
eateth your m. with publicans ? 9:11
they have called the m. 10:25
m. we would see a sign from. 12:38
fall from their m.'s table. 15:27
they said, Doth not your m.? 17:24
m. we know that thou art true.
22:16; Mark 12:14
one is your m. even. Mat 23:8*, 10
the m. saith, My time is at. 26:18
M. is it I? 25*
Hail, m. and kissed him. 49*
Mark 14:45*
why troublest thou the m. any more ?
Mark 5:35
m. it is good for us to be here. 9:5*
Luke 9:33
m. what shall I do ? Mark 10:17
Luke 10:25
for ye know not when the m.
Mark 13:35
the publicans said, M.? Luke 3:12
m. say on. 7:40
saying, M. we perish. 8:24
is dead; trouble not the m. 49
when once m. of the house. 13:25
thou a m. in Israel ? John 3:10*
the m. is come and calleth. 11:28
ye call me M. and ye say. 13:13
if I then your m. have washed. 14
believed the m. of ship. Acts 27:11
knowing your m. is in heaven.
Eph 6:9; Col 4:1
meet for the m.'s use. 2 Tim 2:21

his master

under the thigh of his m. Gen 24:9
of his m., for goods of his m. 10
Joseph was in house of his m. 39:2
when his m. heard the words. 19
if his m. have given him. Ex 21:4
his m. shall bore his ear through. 6
to his m. the servant which is escaped from his m. Deut 23:15
servant said to his m. Judg 19:11
the arrows and came to his m.
1 Sam 20:38
servants break away every one from
his m. 25:10
reconcile himself to his m. 29:4*
a great man with his m. 2 Ki 5:1
went in, and stood before his m. 25
not the sound of his m.'s feet ? 6:32
departed and came to his m. 8:14
Zimri peace, who slew his m.? 9:31
his m. hath sent to reproach God.
19:4; Isa 37:4
will fall to his m. Saul. 1 Chr 12:19
servant is free from his m. Job 3:19
that waiteth on his m. Pr 27:18
accuse not a servant to his m. 30:10
ass knoweth his m.'s crib. Isa 1:3
servant honoureth his m. Mal 1:6
the disciple is not above his m.
Mat 10:24; Luke 6:40
disciple be as his m. Mat 10:25
perfect shall be as his m. Luke 6:40
his own m. he standeth. Rom 14:4*

my master

my m. Abraham shew kindness to
my m. Gen 24:12, 27, 42, 48
shewed kindness to my m. 24:14
the Lord hath blessed my m. 35
Lord hath appointed for my m. 44
deal truly and kindly with my m. 49
send me away to my m. 54, 56
servant had said, It is my m. 65
my m. wotteth not what. 39:8
shall say, I love my m. Ex 21:5
should do this to my m. 1 Sam 24:6*
my m. left me because I fell. 30:13
me into the hands of my m. 15
my m. goeth into house of. 2 Ki 5:18
my m. hath spared Naaman. 20
my m. hath sent me, saying. 22
and he said, Alas, my m., how ? 6:15
I conspired against my m. 10:9
turn away one captain of the least of
my m.'s servants. 18:24; Isa 36:9
hath my m. sent me to thy master ?
2 Ki 18:27; Isa 36:12
I pray thee, to my m. Isa 36:8

thy master

be thy m.'s son's wife. Gen 24:51
rise up early with thy m.'s servants.
1 Sam 29:10
I give thy m.'s son all. 2 Sam 9:9
thy m.'s house, thy m.'s wives. 12:8
where is thy m.'s son ? 16:3
away thy m. to-day. 2 Ki 2:3, 5
we pray thee, and seek thy m. 16
the house of Ahab thy m. 9:7
master sent me to thy m. and. 18:27

masterbuilder

as wise m. I have laid. 1 Cor 3:10

masteries

if a man also strive for m., yet is he
not crowned. 2 Tim 2:5

masters

children shall be her m. Ex 21:4
eyes of servants look to their m.
Ps 123:2
refresheth soul of his m. Pr 25:13
as nails fastened by m. of. Eccl 12:11
them to say to their m. Jer 27:4
their m., Let us drink. Amos 4:1*
who fill their m.'s houses. Zeph 1:9
no man can serve two m. Mat 6:24
Luke 16:13
neither be ye called m. Mat 23:10
her m. much gain. Acts 16:16
her m. saw the hope of their gains. 19
to them that are your m. Eph 6:5
Col 3:22; Tit 2:9; 1 Pet 2:18
ye m. do the same things to them.
Eph 6:9; Col 4:1
count their m. worthy. 1 Tim 6:1
believing m., let them not despise. 2
be not many m. knowing. Jas 3:1*

mastery

them that shout for m. Ex 32:18
the lions had the m. of. Dan 6:24
that striveth for the m. 1 Cor 9:25*

mate

every one with her m. Isa 34:15
fail, none shall want her m. 16

matrix

set apart unto the Lord all that
openeth the m. Ex 13:12, 15
all that openeth the m. is. 34:19
firstborn that open the m. Num 3:12
every thing that openeth m. 18:15

Mattan

slew M. priest of Baal. 2 Ki 11:18
2 Chr 23:17

Mattathias

which was the son of M. Luke 3:25

matter
him concerning that m. Gen 24:9
small m. that thou hast taken. 30:15
when they have a m. they. Ex 18:16
every great m. they shall bring to thee, but every small m. they. 22
but every small m. they judged. 26
keep thee far from a false m. 23:7
that died about the m. of Korah. Num 16:49
you in m. of Peor, in m. 25:18
trespass in the m. of Peor. 31:16
arise a m. too hard. Deut 17:8
mouth of three witnesses m. 19:15
how the m. will fall out. Ruth 3:18
m. of the kingdom he. 1 Sam 10:16
touching the m. thou and I. 20:23
and David knew the m. 39
how went the m.? I pray. 2 Sam 1:4
no m. hid from the king. 18:13
they ended the m. 20:18
the m. is not so. 21
at all times as the m. 1 Ki 8:59*
save in the m. of Uriah the. 15:5
for every m. pertaining. 1 Chr 26:32
served the king in any m. 27:1
from command in any m. 2 Chr 8:15
see ye hasten the m. 24:5
to cease, till the m. Ezra 5:5
sat down to examine the m. 10:16
have m. for evil report. Neh 6:13
inquisition was made of the m. Esth 2:23
seeing the root of the m. Job 19:28
answer, for I am full of m. 32:18*
heart is inditing a good m. Ps 45:1
themselves in an evil m. 64:5*
spirit concealeth the m. Pr 11:13
that handleth a m. wisely. 16:20*
that repeateth a m. separateth. 17:9
that answereth a m. before. 18:13*
kings is to search out a m. 25:2
marvel not at the m. Eccl 5:8
wings shall tell the m. 10:20
the conclusion of the m. 12:13
the m. was not perceived. Jer 38:27
inkhorn, reported the m. Ezek 9:11
whoredoms a small m.? 16:20
can shew the king's m. Dan 2:10
known to us the king's m. 23
end of the m.: I kept the m. 7:28
understand the m. and. 9:23
to blaze abroad the m. Mark 1:45
him again of the same m. 10:10
Peter rehearsed the m. Acts 11:4
came to consider of this m. 15:6
Gallio said, If it were a m. of. 18:14
if Demetrius have a m. 19:38
the uttermost of your m. 24:22
any of you having a m.? 1 Cor 6:1
might be ready as a m. 2 Cor 9:5
it were, it maketh no m. Gal 2:6
defraud brother in any m. 1 Thes 4:6
great a m. a little fire! Jas 3:5*

this matter
speak no more to me of this m. Deut 3:26
his neighbour, so is this m. 22:26
who will hearken to you in this m.? 1 Sam 30:24
ye angry for this m.? 2 Sam 19:42
answer concerning this m. Ezra 5:5
pleasure to us concerning this m. 17
arise, for this m. belongeth. 10:4
sat trembling because of this m. 9
were employed about this m. 15
seen concerning this m. Esth 9:26
Melzar consented to them in this m. Dan 1:14
to answer thee in this m. 3:16
this m. is by the decree of. 4:17*
part nor lot in this m. Acts 8:21
hear thee again of this m. 17:32
approved yourselves clear in this m. 2 Cor 7:11

matters
if any have m. let him. Ex 24:14*
if arise m. of controversy. Deut 17:8
son of Jesse that is prudent in m. 1 Sam 16:18*
end of telling the m. 2 Sam 11:19
Absalom said, See thy m. are. 15:3
thou any more of thy m.? 19:29
you in m. of the Lord, and Zebadiah for all the king's m. 2 Chr 19:11
Pethahiah in all m. concerning. Neh 11:24
whether Mordecai's m. Esth 3:4
the m. of the fastings. 9:31, 32
not account of his m. Job 33:13
thus devise deceitful m. Ps 35:20*
exercise myself in great m. 131:1
in m. of wisdom he found. Dan 1:20
and told the sum of the m. 7:1
omitted the weightier m. Mat 23:23
be no judge of such m. Acts 18:15
any thing concerning other m. 19:39
there be judged of these m. 25:20
judge the smallest m.? 1 Cor 6:2
a busybody in other men's m. 1 Pet 4:15

Matthew
a man named M. and saith. Mat 9:9
Philip, Thomas, and M. the. 10:3
Mark 3:18; Luke 6:15; Acts 1:13

Matthias
called Barsabas, and M. Acts 1:23
the lot fell on M. and he was. 26

mattock
sharpen every man his axe and m. 1 Sam 13:20
be digged with the m. Isa 7:25

mattocks
had a file for the m. 1 Sam 13:21
Josiah with their m. 2 Chr 34:6*

maul
false witness, is a m. Pr 25:18

maw
two cheeks and the m. Deut 18:3

may
seeing I go whither I m. return thou. 2 Sam 15:20
she said, If I m. but touch. Mat 9:21
if this cup m. not pass away. 26:42
as I m. so say, Levi also. Heb 7:9

may *be*
that it m. be well with. Gen 12:13
it m. be that I may obtain. 16:2
that the Lord's law m. be. Ex 13:9
that his fear m. be before. 20:20
of all meat which m. be. Lev 11:34
for his sister a virgin he m. be. 21:3
that it m. be an holy. 23:21
m. be for a memorial. Num 10:10
the possession m. be ours. 32:32
m. be well with you. Deut 5:33; 6:3
18; 22:7; Ruth 3:1; Jer 7:23
m. be to thee a God. Deut 29:13
m. be there for a witness. 31:26
it m. be a witness between us. Josh 22:27
it m. be the Lord will. 1 Sam 14:6
m. be a snare, Philistines m. be. 18:21
it m. be that the king. 2 Sam 14:15
it m. be Lord will look on. 16:12
m. be Lord thy God will hear. 2 Ki 19:4; Isa 37:4
m. be before thee for. 1 Chr 17:27
that ye m. be strong. Ezra 9:12
it m. be that my sons have sinned. Job 1:5
consume them, that they m. not be. Ps 59:13
that Israel m. be no more. 83:4
our sons m. be as plants. 144:12
that our garners m. be full. 13
that our oxen m. be strong. 14
that thy trust m. be in. Pr 22:19
whereof it m. be said, See this is new. Eccl 1:10
that it m. be for the time. Isa 30:8
the Lord waiteth that he m. be. 18
that we m. be like. 46:5
I m. be glorified. 60:21
name m. be no more. Jer 11:19
it m. be the house of Judah. 36:3
it m. be they will present their. 7
that it m. be well with us. 42:6
take balm, if so be she m. 51:8
put his mouth in the dust; if so be there m. be hope. Lam 3:29
it m. be they will consider. Ezek 12:3
that they m. be my people. 14:11
it m. be a lengthening. Dan 4:27
that they m. be cut off. Hos 8:4
it m. be the Lord will. Amos 5:15
it m. be ye shall be hid. Zeph 2:3
that ye m. be children of. Mat 5:45
that thine alms m. be in secret. 6:4
it m. be they will reverence him. Luke 20:13
the inheritance m. be ours. 14
ye m. be the children. John 12:36
there ye m. be also. 14:3
that they m. be one. 17:11, 21, 22
that the love m. be in them. 26
that he m. be wise. 1 Cor 3:18
that ye m. be a new lump. 5:7
that she m. be holy in body. 7:34
are, it m. be, so many kinds. 14:10
be subject, that God m. be. 15:28
m. be that I will winter. 16:6
see that he m. be with you. 10
power m. be of God. 2 Cor 4:7
so there m. be a performance. 8:11
your abundance m. be a supply. 14
as I said, ye m. be ready. 9:3
that it m. be well with thee. Eph 6:3
that ye m. be blameless. Phil 2:15
that I m. be of good comfort. 19
I m. be the less sorrowful. 28
charge that they m. be. 1 Tim 5:7
man of God m. be. 2 Tim 3:17
that they m. be found in. Tit 1:13
that ye m. be perfect. Jas 1:4

mayest
with all thy heart thou m. Acts 8:37

mayest *be*
thou m. be a multitude. Gen 28:3
m. be to us instead of. Num 10:31
m. be an holy people. Deut 26:19
thou m. be their king. Neh 6:6
that thou m. be justified. Job 40:8
that thou m. be feared. Ps 130:4
sing songs, that thou m. be. Isa 23:16
that thou m. be my salvation. 49:6
that thou m. be saved. Jer 4:14
that thou m. be bound up. 30:13
for thou m. be no longer. Luke 16:2

Mazzaroth
canst thou bring forth M.? Job 38:32

me
serpent beguiled me. Gen 3:13
put in ward both me and. 41:10
me restored, and him he hanged. 13
me have ye bereaved of. 42:36
there is none like me in. Ex 9:14
they have rejected me. 1 Sam 8:7
when Joab sent me thy. 2 Sam 18:29
me, even me thy servant. 1 Ki 1:26
thyself to another than me. Isa 57:8
let not me be dismayed. Jer 17:18
me, and who will appoint me? 50:44
know no God but me. Hos 13:4
mother more than me. Mat 10:37
receiveth me, and he that receiveth me. 40; Mark 9:37; John 13:20
why callest thou me good? Mat 19:17; Luke 18:19
me ye have not always. Mat 26:11
Mark 14:7; John 12:8
he that despiseth me, despiseth him that sent me. Luke 10:16
would have believed me. John 5:46
world cannot hate you, but me. 7:7
ye neither know me, nor my. 8:19
though ye believe not me. 10:38
yet hast thou not known me? 14:9
hateth me hateth my Father. 15:23
hated both me and my Father. 24
known the Father nor me. 16:3
O Father, glorify thou me. 17:5
me? ask them who heard me. 18:21
if well, why smitest thou me? 23
he that delivered me to thee. 19:11
Simon, son of Jonas, lovest thou me? 21:15, 16, 17
Saul, why persecutest thou me? Acts 9:4; 22:7
what advantageth it me? 1 Cor 15:32

***about* me**
like the nations that are about me. Deut 17:14
children were about me. Job 29:5
came round about me daily. Ps 88:17
night shall be light about me. 139:11

the earth was *about me.* *Jonah* 2:6
shone a great light *about me.*
Acts 22:6; 26:13
above **me**
thy sons *above me.* *1 Sam* 2:29
after **me**
hotly pursued *after me.* *Gen* 31:36
them, Follow *after me.* *Judg* 3:28
to armourbearer, Come *after me.*
1 Sam 14:12
not cut off my seed *after me.* 24:21
Solomon shall reign *after me.*
1 Ki 1:13, 17, 30
Adonijah shall reign *after me.* 24
man that shall be *after me.* *Eccl* 2:18
shall there be *after me.* *Isa* 43:10
when thou wentest *after me.* *Jer* 2:2
after me is mightier. *Mat* 3:11
Mark 1:7; *John* 1:15, 27, 30
he that followeth not *after me.*
Mat 10:38; *Luke* 14:27
that will come *after me.* *Mat* 16:24
Mark 8:34; *Luke* 9:23
cometh one *after me.* *Acts* 13:25
that asked not *after me.* *Rom* 10:20
against **me**
from sinning *ag. me.* *Gen* 20:6
all these things are *ag. me.* 42:36
ye thought evil *ag. me.* 50:20
make thee sin *ag. me.* *Ex* 23:33
sinned *ag. me,* him will I blot. 32:33
they trespassed *ag. me.* *Lev* 26:40
murmur *ag. me.* *Num* 14:27, 29
gathered together *ag. me.* 35
abide over *ag. me.* 22:5
thou stoodest *ag. me.* 34
ye trespassed *ag. me.* *Deut* 32:51
Ezek 17:20; 20:27, 38; 39:23, 26
anger be hot *ag. me.* *Judg* 6:39
vaunt themselves *ag. me.* 7:2
doest me wrong to war *ag. me.* 11:27
Lord is gone out *ag. me.* *Ruth* 1:13
witness *ag. me* before. *1 Sam* 12:3
he arose *ag. me* I caught. 17:35
you have conspired *ag. me.* 22:8, 13
stirred thee up *ag. me.* 26:19
I pray thee, be *ag. me.* *2 Sam* 24:17
seeketh a quarrel *ag. me.* *2 Ki* 5:7
thy witnesses *ag. me.* *Job* 10:17
writest bitter things *ag. me.* 13:26
which is a witness *ag. me.* 16:8
I loved are turned *ag. me.* 19:19
will he plead *ag. me* with. 23:6
opposest thyself *ag. me.* 30:21
if my land cry *ag. me,* or. 31:38
findeth occasions *ag. me.* 33:10
many that rise up *ag. me.* *Ps* 3:1
18:39, 48
are risen up *ag. me.* 27:12; 54:3
their mouth wide *ag. me.* 35:21
ag. me do they devise my hurt,
whisper *ag. me.* 41:7
they are mad *ag. me,* they are sworn
ag. me. 102:8
did sit and speak *ag. me.* 119:23
he that sinneth *ag. me.* *Pr* 8:36
have rebelled *ag. me.* *Isa* 1:2
Ezek 2:3; 20:8, 13, 21
it crieth out *ag. me.* *Jer* 12:8
ag. me he is turned. *Lam* 3:3
their imaginations *ag. me.* 60
so they sinned *ag. me.* *Hos* 4:7
ag. me, spoken lies *ag. me.* 7:13
assemble and rebel *ag. me.* 14
imagine mischief *ag. me.* 15
O my people, testify *ag. me.* *Mi* 6:3
rejoice not *ag. me,* O mine. 7:8
have been stout *ag. me.* *Mal* 3:13
he that is not with me is *ag. me.*
Mat 12:30; *Luke* 11:23
my brother sin *ag. me?* 18:21
up his heel *ag. me.* *John* 13:18
have no power at all *ag. me.* 19:11
if they had aught *ag. me.* *Acts* 24:19
at **me**
thrust sore *at me* to fall. *Ps* 118:13
are ye angry *at me?* *John* 7:23
before **me**
all flesh is come *bef. me.* *Gen* 6:13
thee . . . righteous *bef. me.* 7:1
walk *bef. me,* and be thou perfect.
17:1; *1 Sam* 2:30; *1 Ki* 2:4
8:25; 9:4; *2 Chr* 7:17
a vine was *bef. me.* *Gen* 40:9
shalt have no other gods *bef. me.*
Ex 20:3; *Deut* 5:7
none shall appear *bef. me* empty.
Ex 23:15; 34:20
way is perverse *bef. me.* *Num* 22:32
go up *bef. me* to the high. *1 Sam* 9:19
go down *bef. me* to Gilgal. 10:8
I pray thee, stand *bef. me.* 16:22
go on *bef. me,* behold I come. 25:19
all his judgements were *bef. me.*
2 Sam 22:23; *Ps* 18:22; 119:30
as thou hast walked *bef. me.*
1 Ki 8:25; *2 Chr* 6:16
may have a light *bef. me.* *1 Ki* 11:36
humbleth himself *bef. me.* 21:29
because thou hast wept *bef. me.*
2 Ki 22:19; *2 Chr* 34:27
plainly read *bef. me.* *Ezra* 4:18
former governors that were *bef. me.*
Neh 5:15
the queen also *bef. me?* *Esth* 7:8
able to stand *bef. me?* *Job* 41:10
the Lord always *bef. me.* *Ps* 16:8
thou preparest a table *bef. me.* 23:5
is continually *bef. me.* 38:17
while the wicked is *bef. me.* 39:1
been continually *bef. me.* 50:8
my sin is ever *bef. me.* 51:3
endure as the sun *bef. me.* 89:36
all that have been *bef. me.*
Eccl 1:16; 2:7, 9
which is mine, is *bef. me.* *S of S* 8:12
come to appear *bef. me.* *Isa* 1:12
silence *bef. me,* O islands. 41:1
bef. me there was no god. 43:10
walls are continually *bef. me.* 49:16
spirit should fail *bef. me.* 57:16
behold, it is written *bef. me.* 65:6
shall remain *bef. me.* saith. 66:22
thine iniquity is marked *bef. me.*
Jer 2:22
bef. me continually is grief. 6:7
and come and stand *bef. me.* 7:10
Samuel stood *bef. me,* yet. 15:1
thou shalt stand *bef. me.* 19
prophets that have been *bef. me.*
28:8
have only done evil *bef. me.* 32:30
priests shall not want a man *bef. me.*
33:18; 35:19
had made a covenant *bef. me.* 34:15
will stand *bef. me?* 49:19; 50:44
elders of Judah sat *bef. me.*
Ezek 8:1
the elders of Israel sat *bef. me.*
14:1; 20:1
their way was *bef. me* as. 36:17
shall stand *bef. me* to offer. 44:15
Daniel came in *bef. me.* *Dan* 4:8
is come up *bef. me.* *Jonah* 1:2
violence are *bef. me.* *Hab* 1:3
and nation *bef. me.* *Hag* 2:14
shall prepare the way *bef. me.*
Mal 3:1; *Mat* 11:10
and slay them *bef. me.* *Luke* 19:27
preferred *bef. me,* for he was *bef. me.* *John* 1:15; 27:30
another steppeth down *bef. me.* 5:7
all that ever came *bef. me.* 10:8
of these things *bef. me.* *Acts* 25:9
were in Christ *bef. me.* *Rom* 16:7
were apostles *bef. me.* *Gal* 1:17
behind **me**
turn thee *behind me.* *2 Ki* 9:18, 19
heard *behind me* a voice. *Ezek* 3:12
get thee *behind me,* Satan, thou.
Mat 16:23; *Mark* 8:33; *Luke* 4:8
beside **me**
arose and took my son from *beside me.* *1 Ki* 3:20
beside me there is no Saviour.
Isa 43:11; *Hos* 13:4
and *beside me* there is no God.
Isa 44:6; 45:5, 6, 21
and none else *beside me.* 47:8, 10
between **me**
make *betw. me* and. *Gen* 9:12, 13
that is *betw. me* and every. 15, 17
no strife *betw. me* and thee. 13:8
Lord judge *betw. me* and thee.
16:5; *1 Sam* 24:12, 15
I will make my covenant *betw. me* and thee. *Gen* 17:2, 7, 10, 11
is that *betw. me* and thee? 23:15
witness *betw.* me and. 31:41, 48
Lord watch *betw. me* and thee. 49
God is witness *betw. me* and. 50
keep, for it is a sign *betw. me* and.
Ex 31:13, 17; *Ezek* 20:12, 20
cast lots *betw. me.* *1 Sam* 14:42
there is but a step *betw. me.* 20:3
saying, Lord be *betw. me* and. 42
there is a league *betw. me* and thee.
1 Ki 15:19; *2 Chr* 16:3
judge, I pray you, *betw. me.* *Isa* 5:3
and the wall *betw. me.* *Ezek* 43:8
by **me**
Rachel died *by me* in. *Gen* 48:7
there is a place *by me.* *Ex* 33:21
shalt not pass *by me.* *Num* 20:18
stand thou here *by me.* *Deut* 5:31
by me they honour God. *Judg* 9:9
as he spake *by me.* *1 Sam* 28:17
the Lord spake *by me.* *2 Sam* 23:2
Lord not spoken *by me.* *1 Ki* 22:28
2 Chr 18:27
the trumpet was *by me.* *Neh* 4:18
he goeth *by me,* and I. *Job* 9:11
by me kings reign. *Pr* 8:15
by me princes rule. 16
by me thy days shall be. 9:11
which are borne *by me.* *Isa* 46:3
but not *by me.* 54:15
up kings, but not *by me.* *Hos* 8:4
thou mightest be profited *by me.*
Mat 15:5; *Mark* 7:11
even he shall live *by me.* *John* 6:57
I am the door: *by me* if any. 10:9
to the Father but *by me.* 14:6
an angel stood *by me.* *Acts* 27:23
hath wrought *by me.* *Rom* 15:18
of God preached *by me.* *2 Cor* 1:19
which is made sorry *by me.* 2:2
that *by me* preaching. *2 Tim* 4:17
concerneth, concerning **me**
to Moses *conc. me.* *Josh* 14:6
word he spake *conc. me.* *1 Ki* 2:4
doth not prophesy good *conc. me.*
22:8, 18
will perfect that which *conc. me.*
Ps 138:8
a prophet to enquire *conc. me.*
Ezek 14:7
for the things *conc. me.* *Luke* 22:37
written in Psalms *conc. me.* 24:44
thy testimony *conc. me.* *Acts* 22:18
for **me**
entreat *for me* to Ephron. *Gen* 23:8
Ex 8:28
reserved a blessing *for me?*
Gen 27:36
wilt do this thing *for me.* 30:31
my righteousness answer *for me.* 33
which I have digged *for me.* 50:5
and nurse it *for me.* *Ex* 2:9
take the Levites *for me.* *Num* 3:41
it is too heavy *for me.* 11:14
for they are too mighty *for me.* 22:6
song may be a witness *for me.*
Deut 31:19
as *for me* and my house. *Josh* 24:15
too many *for me* to give. *Judg* 7:2
this thing be done *for me.* 11:37
get her *for me* to wife. 14:2, 3
and wine also *for me.* 19:19
as *for me.* *1 Sam* 12:23; *1 Chr* 22:7
28:2; 29:17; *Job* 21:4; *Ps* 5:7
17:15; 35:13
thou valiant *for me.* *1 Sam* 18:17
what God will do *for me.* 22:3
none of you that is sorry *for me.* 8
better *for me* than to escape. 27:1
the sons of Zeruiah be too hard *for me.* *2 Sam* 3:39
shalt thou build an house *for me.* 7:5
if Syrians be too strong *for me.*
10:11; *1 Chr* 19:12
good *for me* to have. *2 Sam* 14:32
mayest thou *for me* defeat. 15:34
they were too strong *for me.* 22:18
Ps 18:17
pray *for me,* that my hand be.
1 Ki 13:6
in and dress it *for me.* 17:12

not thy riding *for me.* *2 Ki* 4:24
the brasen altar be *for me* to. 16:15
enquire of the Lord *for me.* 22:13
2 Chr 34:21
was prepared *for me* daily. *Neh* 5:18
graves are ready *for me.* *Job* 17:1
thing appointed *for me.* 23:14
waited *for me* as for the rain. 29:23
things too wonderful *for me.* 42:3
art a shield *for me.* *Ps* 3:3
awake *for me.* 7:6
net they have laid privily *for me.*
31:4; 35:7; 119:110; 140:5
141:9; 142:3
as *for me.* 41:12; 55:16; 69:13
Isa 59:21; *Jer* 17:16; 26:14
40:10; *Ezek* 9:10; *Dan* 2:30
7:28; 10:17
this I know, God is *for me.* *Ps* 56:9
performeth all things *for me.* 57:2
hast been a shelter *for me.* 61:3
it was too painful *for me.* 73:16
rise up *for me,* who will stand up for *me?* 94:16
but do thou *for me,* O God. 109:21
it is good *for me.* 119:71
the proud digged pits *for me.* 85
wicked have waited *for me* to. 95
things too high *for me.* 131:1
is too wonderful *for me.* 139:6
food convenient *for me.* *Pr* 30:8
things too wonderful *for me.* 18
undertake *for me.* *Isa* 38:14
set it in order *for me?* 44:7
the place is too strait *for me.* 49:20
not be ashamed that wait *for me.* 23
the isles shall wait *for me.* 60:9
of them that asked not *for me.* 65:1
search *for me* with all. *Jer* 29:13
any thing too hard *for me?* 32:27
they wrought *for me.* *Ezek* 29:20
thou shalt abide *for me.* *Hos* 3:3
better *for me* to die. *Jonah* 4:3, 8
execute judgement *for me.* *Mi* 7:9
bent Judah *for me.* *Zech* 9:13
and give *for me* and. *Mat* 17:27
weep not *for me,* but. *Luke* 23:28
pray ye to the Lord *for me.* *Acts* 8:24
intent ye have sent *for me.* 10:29
prayers to God *for me.* *Rom* 15:30
are lawful *for me.* *1 Cor* 6:12; 10:23
it were better *for me* to die. 9:15
and gave himself *for me.* *Gal* 2:20
for me, that utterance. *Eph* 6:19
laid up *for me* a crown. *2 Tim* 4:8

from me

I pray thee, *from me.* *Gen* 13:9
thine only son *from me.* 22:12
steal away *from me?* 31:27
take thy daughters *from me.* 31
kept back any thing *from me.* 39:9
the one went out *from me.* 44:28
if ye take this also *from me.* 29
every man to go out *from me.* 45:1
get thee *from me,* see. *Ex* 10:28
tell me, hide it not *from me.*
Josh 7:19; *1 Sam* 3:17
strength will go *from me.* *Judg* 16:17
why should my father hide this thing *from me?* *1 Sam* 20:2
said, Have out all men *from me.*
2 Sam 13:9
put this woman out *from me.* 17
far be it *from me.* 20:20
this thing is *from me.* *1 Ki* 12:24
went Spirit of Lord *from me.* 22:24
2 Chr 18:23
Lord hath hid it *from me.* *2 Ki* 4:27
offended, return *from me.* 18:14
I chased him *from me.* *Neh* 13:28
driven quite *from me?* *Job* 6:13
his rod away *from me.* 9:34
thine hand far *from me.* 13:21
put my brethren far *from me.* 19:13
of the wicked is far *from me.* 21:16
mine integrity *from me.* 27:5
hide thy face *from me?* *Ps* 13:1
away his statutes *from me.* 18:22
O Lord, be not far *from me.* 35:22
light of eyes, gone *from me.* 38:10
thy stroke away *from me.* 39:10
tender mercies *from me.* 40:11
take not Holy Spirit *from me.* 51:11
turned his mercy *from me.* *Ps* 66:20
hidest thou thy face *from me?* 88:14
hide not thy face *from me* in trouble.
102:2; 143:7
commandments *from me.* 119:19
away my vail *from me.* *S of S* 5:7
turn away thine eyes *from me.* 6:5
look away *from me,* I will. *Isa* 22:4
age is removed *from me.* 38:12
a law shall proceed *from me.* 51:4
anger shall turn *from me.* *Jer* 2:35
shalt not turn away *from me.* 3:19
of thy measures *from me.* 13:25
hide nothing *from me.* 38:14
from me shall spoilers come. 51:53
warning *from me.* *Ezek* 3:17; 33:7
are all estranged *from me.* 14:5
separateth himself *from me.* 7
go no more astray *from me.* 11
went astray *from me* after. 44:10
Israel went astray *from me.* 15
thing is gone *from me.* *Dan* 2:5, 8
Israel is not hid *from me.* *Hos* 5:3
for they have fled *from me.* 7:13
bent to backsliding *from me.* 11:7
like a fir tree, *from me* is thy. 14:8
take away *from me* the noise of.
Amos 5:23
let this cup pass *from me.* *Mat* 26:39
Mark 14:36; *Luke* 22:22
not pass away *from me.* *Mat* 26:42
my lord taketh *from me.* *Luke* 16:3
man taketh it *from me.* *John* 10:18
all in Asia be turned away *from me.*
2 Tim 1:15
see **depart, departed**

in me

it is not *in me.* *Gen* 41:16
if there be iniquity *in me.*
1 Sam 20:8; *2 Sam* 14:32
life is yet whole *in me.* *2 Sam* 1:9
because he delighted *in me.* 22:20
Ps 18:19
is not my help *in me?* *Job* 6:13
the matter is found *in me.* 19:28
would put strength *in me.* 23:6
my breath is *in me.* 27:3
saith, It is not *in me.* 28:14
nor is there iniquity *in me.* 33:9
to mine integrity *in me.* *Ps* 7:8
arrows stick fast *in me.* 38:2
I pour out my soul *in me.* 42:4
why art thou disquieted *in me?* 5
be any wicked way *in me.* 139:24
fury is not *in me,* who. *Isa* 27:4
trust *in me* shall possess. 57:13
have fathers found *in me?* *Jer* 2:5
hast put thy trust *in me.* 39:18
thy widows trust *in me.* 49:11
soul is humbled *in me.* *Lam* 3:20
innocency found *in me.* *Dan* 6:22
no strength *in me.* 10:8, 17
find none iniquity *in me.* *Hos* 12:8
thyself, but *in me* is thy help. 13:17
shall not be offended *in me.*
Mat 11:6; *Luke* 7:23
little ones which believe *in me.*
Mat 18:6; *Mark* 9:42
be accomplished *in me.* *Luke* 22:37
he dwelleth *in me,* and I. *John* 6:56
he that believeth *in me.* 11:25, 26
believe also *in me.* 14:1
Father that dwelleth *in me.* 10
ye *in me,* and I in you. 20
prince hath nothing *in me.* 30
every branch *in me.* 15:2
abide *in me.* 4
he that abideth *in me.* 5
if a man abide not *in me* he is. 6
if ye abide *in me.* 7
in me ye might have peace. 16:33
as thou, Father, art *in me.* 17:21
I in them, and thou *in me,* that. 23
any evil doing *in me.* *Acts* 24:20
by faith that is *in me.* 26:18
no cause of death *in me.* 28:18
as *in me* is, I am ready. *Rom* 1:15
wrought *in me* all manner of. 7:8
sin working death *in me* by. 13
but sin that dwelleth *in me.* 17, 20
that *in me* dwelleth no good thing. 18
truth of Christ is *in me.* *2 Cor* 11:10
proof of Christ speaking *in me.* 13:3
to reveal his Son *in me.* *Gal* 1:16
and they glorified God *in me.* 24
was mighty *in me* towards. 2:8
but Christ liveth *in me.* 20
conflict which ye saw *in me,* and now hear to be *in me.* *Phil* 1:30
heard and seen *in me,* do. 4:9
which worketh *in me.* *Col* 1:29
that *in me* Christ Jesus. *1 Tim* 1:16

of me

of me, He is my brother. *Gen* 20:13
he will accept *of me.* 32:20
men say not *of me,* A woman slew.
Judg 9:54
take knowledge *of me.* *Ruth* 2:10
Saul shall despair *of me.* *1 Sam* 27:1
then dost thou ask *of me?* 28:16
this thing is done *of me.* *2 Chr* 11:4
not spoken *of me* the thing. *Job* 42:7
ask *of me,* and I shall give. *Ps* 2:8
in thy book it is written *of me.* 40:7
Heb 10:7
enemies speak evil *of me.* *Ps* 41:5
triumph thou because *of me.* 60:8
and Israel would none *of me.* 81:11
not take counsel *of me.* *Isa* 30:1
thou make an end *of me.* 38:12, 13
weary *of me,* O Israel. 43:22
not be forgotten *of me.* 44:21
and their righteousness *of me.* 54:17
they ask *of me* the ordinances. 58:2
are gone forth *of me.* *Jer* 10:20
sent you to enquire *of me.* 37:7
come to enquire *of me?* *Ezek* 20:3
say *of me,* Doth he not speak? 49
more than me, is not worthy *of me.*
Mat 10:37, 38
and learn *of me,* for I am. 11:29
ye shall be offended because *of me* this night. 26:31; *Mark* 14:27
whoso shall be ashamed *of me.*
Mark 8:38; *Luke* 9:26
lightly speak evil *of me.* *Mark* 9:39
virtue is gone out *of me.* *Luke* 8:46
do in remembrance *of me.* 22:19
Jew, askest drink *of me?* *John* 4:9
beareth witness *of me.* 5:32, 37
they which testify *of me.* 39
for Moses wrote *of me.* 46
this voice came not because *of me.*
12:30
he shall testify *of me.* 15:26
did others tell it thee *of me?* 18:34
promise ye have heard *of me.*
Acts 1:4
as thou hast testified *of me.* 23:11
be ye followers *of me.* *1 Cor* 4:16
11:1; *Phil* 3:17
this do in remembrance *of me.*
1 Cor 11:24, 25
he was seen *of me* also. 15:8
the salutation *of me* Paul. 16:21
Col 4:18
think *of me* above that which he . . . or heareth *of me.* *2 Cor* 12:6
which is preached *of me.* *Gal* 1:11
care *of me* hath flourished. *Phil* 4:10
the testimony *of me* his. *2 Tim* 1:8
which thou hast heard *of me.* 13
thou hast heard *of me,* commit. 2:2
had compassion *of me.* *Heb* 10:34

on me, or *upon* me

I have taken *upon me.* *Gen* 18:27, 31
thou hast brought *on me.* 20:9
I shall bring a curse *upon me.* 27:12
upon me be thy curse, my son. 13
custom of women is *upon me.* 31:35
think *on me* when it shall be. 40:14
ye will not fall *upon me.* *Judg* 15:12
all thy wants lie *upon me.* 19:20
come down *upon me.* *1 Sam* 13:12
upon me, my lord, *upon me.* 25:24
the iniquity be *on me.* *2 Sam* 14:9
set their faces *on me.* *1 Ki* 2:15
I pray thee, be *on me.* *1 Chr* 21:17
writing by his hand *upon me.* 28:19
hand of the Lord *upon me.*
Ezra 7:28; *Neh* 2:8, 18
think *upon me,* my God. *Neh* 5:19
feared is come *upon me.* *Job* 3:25
fear came *upon me.* 4:14
be content, look *upon me.* 6:28

thine eyes are upon me. Job 7:8
thyself marvellous upon me. 10:16
runneth upon me like a giant. 16:14
have pity upon me, O ye. 19:21
have mercy upon me. Ps 4:1; 6:2
9:13; 25:16; 27:7; 30:10; 31:9
51:1; 86:16
look and stare upon me. 22:17
thy hand was heavy upon me. 32:4
the Lord thinketh upon me. 40:17
they cast iniquity upon me. 55:3
thy vows are upon me. 56:12
hath set his love upon me. 91:14
he shall call upon me. 15
look thou upon me. 119:132
laid thine hand upon me. 139:5
look not upon me, sun hath looked
upon me. S of S 1:6
hast not called upon me. Isa 43:22
the isles shall wait upon me. 51:5
Spirit of the Lord God is upon me.
61:1; Luke 4:18
these things upon me? Jer 13:22
cast a stone upon me. Lam 3:53
Lord was strong upon me. Ezek 3:14
the hand of the Lord was there upon
me. 22; 33:22; 37:1; 40:1
hand fell there upon me. 8:1
Spirit of the Lord fell upon me. 11:5
therefore wait ye upon me. Zeph 3:8
then cried he upon me. Zech 6:8
flock that waited upon me. 11:11
they shall look upon me whom they
pierced. 12:10
have mercy upon me. Mat 15:22
Mark 10:47, 48; Luke 18:38, 39
wrought a good work upon me.
Mat 26:10; Mark 14:6
days wherein he looked on me.
Luke 1:25
that believeth on me. John 6:35
47; 7:38; 12:44, 46; 14:12
they believe not on me. 16:9
who shall believe on me. 17:20
things come upon me. Acts 8:24
reproaches of them that reproached
thee fell on me. Rom 15:3
necessity is laid upon me. 1 Cor 9:16
cometh upon me daily. 2 Cor 11:28
of Christ may rest upon me. 12:9
God had mercy on me. Phil 2:27
right hand upon me. Rev 1:17
see call

over me

to Pharaoh, Glory over me. Ex 8:9
will set a king over me. Deut 17:14
settest a watch over me. Job 7:12
enemy be exalted over me. Ps 13:2
let them not have dominion over me.
19:13; 119:133
enemies triumph over me. 25:2
doth not triumph over me. 41:11
billows are gone over me. 42:7
banner over me was love. S of S 2:4
waves passed over me. Jonah 2:3

to or unto me

blood crieth unto me. Gen 4:10
to me thou hast given no seed. 15:3
said he not unto me? 20:5
swear unto me by God. 21:23
spake the man unto me. 24:30
wherefore come ye to me? 26:27
Lord hath brought it to me. 27:20
thou hast done unto me? 29:25
hath given them to me. 31:9
unto me, Return to thy country. 32:9
what ye shall say unto me. 34:11, 12
shew kindness unto me. 40:14
brethren are come unto me. 46:31
the cry of the children of Israel is
come unto me. Ex 3:9
bloody husband art thou to me. 4:25
feast unto me in the wilderness. 5:1
take you to me for a people. 6:7
have not hearkened unto me. 12
sanctify unto me all firstborn. 13:2
criest thou unto me? 14:15
matter, they come unto me. 18:16
peculiar treasure unto me. 19:5
ye shall be unto me a kingdom. 6
they cry at all unto me. 22:23, 27
sons shalt thou give unto me. 29
shall be holy men unto me. Ex 22:31
that he may minister unto me. 28:1
3; 29:1; 30:30; 40:13; Jer 33:22
Ezek 43:19
let him come unto me. Ex 32:26
thou sayest unto me. 33:12
present thyself there to me. 34:2
for unto me Israel are. Lev 25:55
raise up a prophet like unto me
Deut 18:15; Acts 3:22; 7:37
to me belongeth vengeance and
recompence. Deut 32:35
are ye come unto me? Judg 11:7
as they did unto me, so have. 15:11
and be unto me a father. 17:10
Lord do so to me, and. Ruth 1:17
2 Sam 3:35; 19:13; 1 Ki 2:23
cry is come unto me. 1 Sam 9:16
anoint unto me him whom. 16:3
and to me they ascribed but. 18:8
very pleasant hast thou been unto
me. 2 Sam 1:26
he shall not return to me. 12:23
man might come unto me. 15:4
what Joab did to me. 1 Ki 2:5
so let the gods do to me and more.
19:2; 20:10
Lord saith unto me that will. 22:14
send unto me to recover a man of his
leprosy. 2 Ki 5:7
let him come now to me. 8
God do so to me. 6:31
thus and thus spake he to me. 9:12
and come to me to Jezreel. 10:6
tell the man that sent you to me.
22:15; 2 Chr 34:23
ark of God home to me? 1 Chr 13:12
prophesy good unto me. 2 Chr 18:17
extended mercy unto me. Ezra 7:28
then were assembled unto me. 9:4
but if ye turn unto me. Neh 1:9
afraid of is come unto me. Job 3:25
nights are appointed to me. 7:3
do not two things unto me. 13:20
unto me men gave ear. 29:21
declare unto me. 40:7; 42:4
lines are fallen unto me. Ps 16:6
incline thine ear unto me.
17:6; 31:2; 102:2
turn thee unto me. 25:16
merciful unto me. 26:11; 41:4, 10
56:1; 57:1; 86:3; 119:58, 132
be not silent to me. 28:1
he inclined unto me. 40:1; 77:1
what flesh can do unto me. 56:4
what man can do unto me. 11; 118:6
wilt hearken unto me. 81:8
he shall cry unto me, Thou. 89:26
wilt thou come unto me? 101:2
when they said unto me, Let. 122:1
are thy thoughts unto me! 139:17
thee, make haste unto me. 141:1
whoso hearkeneth unto me shall
dwell safely. Pr 1:33
will do so to him as he hath done to
me. 24:29
as to the fool, so it happeneth even to
me. Eccl 2:15
bundle of myrrh is my beloved unto
me. S of S 1:13, 14
abomination unto me. Isa 1:13
they are a trouble unto me. 14
he calleth to me out of Seir. 21:11
shall be unto me as Ariel. 29:2
unto me, for I have redeemed. 44:22
look unto me, and be saved. 45:22
unto me every knee shall bow. 23
let him come near to me. 50:8
as the waters of Noah unto me. 54:9
come not near to me, I am. 65:5
return, O Israel, unto me. Jer 4:1
though they shall cry unto me. 11:11
mine heritage is unto me. 12:8, 9
that they might be unto me. 13:11
thy word was unto me the joy. 15:16
be altogether unto me as a liar? 18
them unto me as Sodom. 23:14
this city hath been to me a. 32:31
shall be to me a name of joy. 33:9
who shall come unto me? 49:4
the violence done to me be. 51:35
shall be like unto me. Lam 1:21
as thou hast done unto me. 22
thou hast borne unto me. Ezek 16:20
house of Israel is to me. Ezek 22:18
they have done unto me. 23:38
she is turned unto me. 26:2
office of a priest unto me. 44:13
to me to minister unto me. 15
is not revealed to me. Dan 2:30
my reason returned unto me; lords
sought unto me. 4:36
betroth thee unto me. Hos 2:19, 20
and I will sow her unto me in. 23
I bought her to me for fifteen. 3:2
thou shalt be no priest to me. 4:6
them that calleth unto me. 7:7
they have not cried unto me with. 14
Israel shall cry unto me. 8:2
as Ethiopians unto me? Amos 9:7
shall come forth unto me. Mi 5:2
shall be a light unto me. 7:8
see what he will say unto me.
Hab 2:1
yet ye turned not to me. Hag 2:17
turn ye unto me, saith. Zech 1:3
at all fast unto me, even to me? 7:5
and comest thou to me? Mat 3:14
to me in that day, Lord. 7:22
come unto me all ye that. 11:28
bring them to me. 14:18; 17:17
21:2; Mark 9:19
forbid them not to come unto me.
Mat 19:14; Mark 10:14
and ye came unto me. Mat 25:36
ye have done it unto me. 40
not to these, ye did it not to me. 45
all power is given unto me. 28:18
it be unto me according. Luke 1:38
for that is delivered unto me. 4:6
whoso cometh to me. 6:47; 14:26
all things are delivered to me. 10:22
God be merciful to me a. 18:13
come to me to have life. John 5:40
he that cometh to me. 6:35, 37
no man can come to me. 44, 65
of the Father cometh unto me. 45
let him come unto me and. 7:37
I will draw all men unto me. 12:32
the Father said unto me. 50
speakest thou not unto me? 19:10
be witnesses unto me. Acts 1:8
known unto me the ways of life. 2:28
he is a chosen vessel unto me. 9:15
vessel descend, and it came even to
me. 11:5
a voice speaking unto me. 26:14
made death unto me? Rom 7:13
the grace given unto me. 12:3
1 Cor 3:10
things are lawful unto me. 1 Cor 6:12
should be so done unto me. 9:15
woe is unto me if I preach not. 16
gospel is committed unto me. 17
be a barbarian unto me. 14:11
a great door and effectual is open
unto me. 16:9; 2 Cor 2:12
was lacking to me. 2 Cor 11:9
maketh no matter to me. Gal 2:6
and have given them to me. 4:15
unto me who am less. Eph 3:8
for to me to live is Christ. Phil 1:21
to me indeed is not grievous. 3:1
but what things were gain to me. 7
been a comfort unto me. Col 4:11
not to me only. 2 Tim 4:8
is profitable to me. 11
now profitable to thee and to me.
Philem 11
especially to me. 16
thou owest to me thyself. 19
belongeth unto me, saith. Heb 10:30
what man shall do unto me. 13:6

toward me

countenance is not toward me as.
Gen 31:5
thy mercy toward me. Ps 86:13
all his benefits toward me. 116:12
I am my Beloved's, his desire is
toward me. S of S 7:10
fear toward me is taught. Isa 29:13
bowels and mercies toward me.
63:15
high God hath wrought toward me.
Dan 4:2
fervent mind toward me. 2 Cor 7:7
of service toward me. Phil 2:30

I will *m.* their former. *Isa* 65:7
them *m.* the pattern. *Ezek* 43:10
a measuring line to *m.* *Zech* 2:2
m. the temple of God. *Rev* 11:1
court leave out and *m.* not. 2
golden reed to *m.* the city. 21:15

measured

m. six measures of barley. *Ruth* 3:15
m. with a line, with two lines *m.* he. *2 Sam* 8:2
m. waters in hollow ? *Isa* 40:12
heaven above can be *m.* *Jer* 31:37
sand of the sea cannot be *m.* 33:22
he *m.* the breadth of. *Ezek* 40:5
m. the threshold. 6
he *m.* also the porch. 8, 9
he *m.* the entry. 11
m. the gate. 13, 24
m. the wall. 41:5
he *m.* the house. 13
he *m.* the length of the building. 15
he *m.* the east side with. 42:16
he *m.* north side. 17, 18, 19
he *m.* a thousand cubits. 47:3, 4
be as sand of sea which cannot be *m.* *Hos* 1:10
he stood and *m.* the earth. *Hab* 3:6
measure ye mete, it shall be *m.* to. *Mat* 7:2; *Mark* 4:24; *Luke* 6:38
he *m.* the city. *Rev* 21:16
he *m.* the wall. 17

measures

three *m.* of fine meal. *Gen* 18:6
not have divers *m.* *Deut* 25:14
Abigail took five *m.* of. *1 Sam* 25:18
provision for one day was thirty *m.* of flour, and sixty *m.* of. *1 Ki* 4:22
20 thousand *m.* of wheat, and twenty *m.* of pure oil. 5:11; *2 Chr* 2:10
m. of hewed stones. *1 Ki* 7:9, 11*
contain two *m.* of seed. 18:32
for all manner of *m.* *1 Chr* 23:29
done to an hundred *m.* *Ezra* 7:22
who hath laid the *m.*? *Job* 38:5
divers *m.* are like. *Pr* 20:10
is the portion of thy *m.* *Jer* 13:25
the arches according to these *m.* *Ezek* 40:24, 29
gate according to these *m.* 28, 32
are the *m.* of the altar. 43:13
the *m.* of the profane place. 48:16
to an heap of twenty *m.* *Hag* 2:16
leaven, which a woman hid in three *m.* of meal. *Mat* 13:33; *Luke* 13:21
an hundred *m.* of oil. *Luke* 16:6
he said, An hundred *m.* of wheat. 7
see **barley**

measuring

the *m.* line shall yet go. *Jer* 31:39
man with a *m.* reed. *Ezek* 40:3, 5
he had made an end of *m.* 42:15
he measured with *m.* reed. 16, 17 18, 19
a man with a *m.* line in. *Zech* 2:1
they *m.* themselves. *2 Cor* 10:12

meat

[1] *Food of any sort, especially any solid food. The Revisions generally change the word to food.* [2] *Flesh, as distinct from fish, fowl, or vegetables and grains.*

to you it shall be for *m.* *Gen* 1:29
I have given every herb for *m.* 30
every moving thing shall be *m.* 9:3
savoury *m.* such as I love. 27:4, 7
Esau also made savoury *m.* 31
bread and *m.* for his father. 45:23
of all *m.* which may be. *Lev* 11:34
his house, shall eat of his *m.* 22:11*
she shall eat of her father's *m.* 13*
sabbath of land shall be *m.* 25:6, 7
buy *m.* of them for money. *Deut* 2:6
thou shalt sell me *m.* for money. 28
destroy trees not for *m.* 20:20
kings gathered their *m.* *Judg* 1:7
out of the eater came forth *m.* 14:14
sit with the king at *m.* *1 Sam* 20:5
Jonathan did eat no *m.* the. 34
cause David to eat *m.* *2 Sam* 3:35
there followed him a mess of *m.* 11:8
eat of his own *m.* and drank. 12:3*
let Tamar dress the *m.* in. 13:5*
she saw the *m.* of his table. *1 Ki* 10:5; *2 Chr* 9:4
strength of that *m.* forty. *1 Ki* 19:8
were nigh brought *m.* *1 Chr* 12:40
they gave *m.* and drink. *Ezra* 3:7
are as my sorrowful *m.* *Job* 6:7
the mouth taste his *m.*? 12:11
m. in his bowels is turned. 20:14
shall none of his *m.* be left. 21*
juniper roots for their *m.* 30:4
soul abhorreth dainty *m.* 33:20
words, as the mouth tasteth *m.* 34:3
he giveth *m.* in abundance. 36:31
they wander for lack of *m.* 38:41
my tears have been my *m.* *Ps* 42:3
given us like sheep for *m.* 44:11
wander up and down for *m.* 59:15
gave me also gall for my *m.* 69:21
thou gavest him to be *m.* 74:14
tempted God by asking *m.* 78:18
he sent them *m.* to the full. 25
but while their *m.* was yet in. 30
the young lions seek their *m.* 104:21
thou mayest give them their *m.* 27
abhorreth all manner of *m.* 107:18
he hath given *m.* to them. 111:5
them *m.* in due season. 145:15
ant provideth her *m.* in. *Pr* 6:8
for they are deceitful *m.* 23:3
when he is filled with *m.* 30:22
yet they prepare their *m.* in the. 25
giveth *m.* to her household. 31:15
no more give thy corn to be *m.* for thine enemies. *Isa* 62:8
dust shall be the serpent's *m.* 65:25
pleasant things for *m.* *Lam* 1:11
while they sought their *m.* 19
children, they were their *m.* 4:10
m. shall be by weight. *Ezek* 4:10
my *m.* which I gave thee. 16:19
I have given thee for *m.* to beasts. 29:5; 34:5, 8
that they may not be *m.* 34:10
grow trees for *m.*, fruit for *m.* 47:12
would not defile himself with the king's *m.* *Dan* 1:8†
king who hath appointed your *m.* 10
and in it was *m.* for all. 4:12, 21
feed of his *m.*, shall destroy. 11:26†
and I laid *m.* unto them. *Hos* 11:4
not *m.* cut off before ? *Joel* 1:16
portion fat, *m.* plenteous. *Hab* 1:16
fields shall yield no *m.* 3:17
if one do touch any *m.*? *Hag* 2:12
in that ye say, His *m.* *Mal* 1:12
tithes, that there may be *m.* 3:10
and his *m.* was locusts. *Mat* 3:4
life more than *m.*? 6:25; *Luke* 12:23
as Jesus sat at *m.* in. *Mat* 9:10; 26:7 *Mark* 2:15; 14:3; 16:14 *Luke* 24:30
workman is worthy of his *m.* *Mat* 10:10
which sat with him at *m.* 14:9
took up of the broken *m.* 15:37* *Mark* 8:8*
to give them *m.* in due season. *Mat* 24:45; *Luke* 12:42
I was an hungered, and ye gave me *m.* *Mat* 25:35
hungered, and ye gave me no *m.* 42
that hath *m.*, let him do. *Luke* 3:11
commanded to give her *m.* 8:55
except we should go and buy *m.* 9:13
presence of them that sit at *m.* 14:10
servant, Go and sit down to *m.* 17:7
greater, he that sitteth at *m.*? 22:27
he said, Have ye here any *m.*? 24:41; *John* 21:5
were gone to buy *m.* *John* 4:8
m. to eat that ye know not of. 32
my *m.* is to do the will of him. 34
labour not for the *m.* which perisheth, but for that *m.* which. 6:27
my flesh is *m.* indeed, my. 55
they did eat their *m.* with. *Acts* 2:46
when he had received *m.* he. 9:19
jailor set *m.* before them. 16:34
them all to take *m.* 27:33, 34
and they also took some *m.* 36
be grieved with thy *m.*, destroy not him with thy *m.* for. *Rom* 14:15
for the kingdom of God is not *m.* 17*
for *m.* destroy not the work of. 20
milk, and not with *m.* *1 Cor* 3:2
m. commendeth us not to God. 8:8
if any man see thee sit at *m.* in. 10
if *m.* make my brother to offend. 13
did eat the same spiritual *m.* 10:3
let no man judge you in *m.* *Col* 2:16
of milk, not of strong *m.* *Heb* 5:12*
but strong *m.* belongeth to them. 14*
who for one morsel of *m.* sold. 12:16
see **fowls**

meat offering

(This offering did not contain flesh, but was usually a preparation of flour with spices and other ingredients. The Revisions usually change the word to meal offering)

according to *m. off.* of. *Ex* 29:41
offer no *m. off.* thereon. 30:9
Moses offered the *m. off.* 40:29
offer a *m. off.* *Lev* 2:1, 4, 5, 7, 14
remnant of *m. off.* 3, 10; 5:13
law of the *m. off.* 6:14; 7:37
deals of flour for a *m. off.* 14:10
pertaineth daily *m. off.* *Num* 4:16
fine flour mingled with oil for *m. off.* 7:13, 19; 28:12, 13
m. off. two tenths. 15:6; 28:9, 12
the *m. off.* of the morning. 28:8
when ye bring a new *m. off.* 26
besides his *m. off.* and burnt offering. 29:6, 22, 25, 34
to offer thereon *m. off.* *Josh* 22:23
took a kid with a *m. off.* *Judg* 13:19
not have received a *m. off.* 23
m. off. was offered. *2 Ki* 3:20*
wheat for the *m. off.* *1 Chr* 21:23
for continual *m. off.* *Neh* 10:33
thou offered a *m. off.* *Isa* 57:6
they lay the *m. off.* *Ezek* 42:13
they shall eat the *m. off.* 44:29
prepare the *m. off.* 45:17, 24
do like according to the *m. off.* 25
m. off. shall be an ephah for a ram. 46:5
a *m. off.* and an ephah for a bullock. 7, 11
they prepare the *m. off.* and. 15
m. off. and the drink offering is cut off. *Joel* 1:9
the *m. off.* and drink offering is withholden. 13
leave a blessing, even a *m. off.* 2:14

meat offerings

do for your *m. off.* *Num* 29:39
build an altar for *m. off.* *Josh* 22:29
because altar was too little to receive *m. off.* *1 Ki* 8:64; *2 Chr* 7:7
lambs with their *m. off.* *Ezra* 7:17
they laid their *m. off.* *Neh* 13:5
Judah to bring *m. off.* *Jer* 17:26
want a man to kindle *m. off.* 33:18
princes to give *m. off.* *Ezek* 45:17
though ye offer *m. off.* *Amos* 5:22

meats

desire thou his dainty *m.* *Pr* 23:6*
draught, purging all *m.* *Mark* 7:19
m. offered to idols. *Acts* 15:29*
m. for the belly, and the belly for *m.* *1 Cor* 6:13
to abstain from *m.*, which. *1 Tim* 4:3
which stood only in *m.* *Heb* 9:10
established with grace, not *m.* 13:9

Medad

told Moses, Eldad and *M.* prophesy in camp. *Num* 11:26, 27

meddle

m. not with them of mount Seir. *Deut* 2:5*
m. not with the children of. 19*
why *m.* to thy hurt ? *2 Ki* 14:10 *2 Chr* 25:19
m. not with him that. *Pr* 20:19
m. not with them that are. 24:21

meddled

contention before it be *m.* *Pr* 17:14*

meddleth

that *m.* with strife not. *Pr* 26:17*

meddling

forbear thee from *m.* *2 Chr* 35:21
but every fool will be *m.* *Pr* 20:3*

Mede, -s
cities of the M. 2 Ki 17:6; 18:11
the province of the M. Ezra 6:2
among the laws of the M. Esth 1:19
I will stir up M. against them.
Isa 13:17; Jer 51:11
all the kings of the M. Jer 25:25
kingdom is given to the M. Dan 5:28
the law of the M. 6:8, 12, 15
Ahasuerus of the seed of the M. 9:1
year of Darius the M. 11:1

Media
power of Persia and M. Esth 1:3
seven princes of Persia and M. 14
the ladies of M. shall say this. 18
book of the kings of M. 10:2
O M. all the sighing. Isa 21:2
two horns are kings of M. Dan 8:20

mediator
(This word, when applied to Moses, has the meaning of intermediary. When applied to Christ it has somewhat of that meaning, with probably a little of the meaning of intercessor)
angels in the hand of a m. Gal 3:19
a m. is not a m. of one, but. 20
one m. between God. 1 Tim 2:5
he is the m. of a better. Heb 8:6
for this cause he is m. of. 9:15
and to Jesus the m. of the. 12:24

medicine
heart doeth good like a m. Pr 17:22
thereof shall be for m. Ezek 47:12*

medicines
thou hast no healing m. Jer 30:13
in vain shalt thou use many m. 46:11

meditate
Isaac went out to m. Gen 24:63
shalt m. therein day. Josh 1:8
in his law doth he m. day. Ps 1:2
and m. on thee in the night. 63:6
I will m. also of all thy work. 77:12
will m. in thy precepts. 119:15, 78
did m. in thy statutes. 23
I will m. in thy statutes. 48
night watches, that I might m. 148
I m. on all thy works, I muse. 143:5
heart shall m. terror. Isa 33:18*
not to m. before what ye shall answer. Luke 21:14
m. upon these things. 1 Tim 4:15

meditation
my words, consider my m. Ps 5:1
let the m. of my heart be. 19:14
the m. of my heart shall be. 49:3
my m. of him shall be sweet. 104:34
I love thy law, it is my m. 119:97
for thy testimonies are my m. 99

meek
(Gentle, kind, not easily provoked, ready to yield rather than cause trouble; but not used in the Bible in the bad sense of tamely submissive and servile)
man Moses was very m. Num 12:3
the m. shall eat and. Ps 22:26
m. will he guide in judgement. 25:9
m. shall inherit the earth. 37:11
God arose to save all the m. 76:9
the Lord lifteth up the m. 147:6
he will beautify the m. with. 149:4
equity, for the m. of. Isa 11:4
the m. shall increase their. 29:19
preach good tidings to the m. 61:1
aside the way of the m. Amos 2:7
seek ye the Lord, all ye m. Zeph 2:3
blessed are the m. Mat 5:5
for I am m. and lowly. 11:29
thy king cometh to thee, m. 21:5
the ornament of a m. 1 Pet 3:4

meekness
because of truth and m. Ps 45:4
seek m. shall be hid. Zeph 2:3
come in the spirit of m.? 1 Cor 4:21†
by the m. of Christ. 2 Cor 10:1
fruit of the Spirit is m. Gal 5:23
restore in the spirit of m. 6:1
with all lowliness and m. Eph 4:2
put on therefore m., longsuffering. Col 3:12
faith, love, patience, m. 1 Tim 6:11
in m. instructing those. 2 Tim 2:25
gentle, shewing all m. Tit 3:2
receive with m. the ingrafted word. Jas 1:21
him shew his works with m. 3:13
of your hope with m. 1 Pet 3:15

meet
(As an adjective, fit, suitable)
I will make an help m. Gen 2:18
found an help m. for Adam. 20
Moses said, It is not m. Ex 8:26
pass over, all that are m. for war. Deut 3:18*
m. for the necks of them. Judg 5:30
it was not m. to see the king's dishonour. Ezra 4:14
surely it is m. to be said. Job 34:31*
more than is m. Pr 11:24
do with me as seemeth m. to you. Jer 26:14*
to whom it seemed m. to me. 27:5*
is it m. for any work? Ezek 15:4*
it was m. for no work. 5
fruits m. for repentance. Mat 3:8*
it is not m. to take the children's bread. 15:26; Mark 7:27
it was m. we should make merry. Luke 15:32
do works m. for repentance. Acts 26:20*
receiving that recompence which was m. Rom 1:27*
am not m. to be called an. 1 Cor 15:9
if it be m. that I go also. 16:4
is m. for me to think this. Phil 1:7*
made us m. to be partakers. Col 1:12
bound to thank God for you, as it is m. 2 Thes 1:3
he shall be vessel m. 2 Tim 2:21
herbs m. for them by. Heb 6:7
m. to stir you up. 2 Pet 1:13*

meet
Sodom went out to m. Gen 14:17
them, and ran to m. them. 18:2
Lot seeing them, rose up to m. 19:1
servant ran to m. Rebekah. 24:17
what man walketh to m. us? 65
Laban ran to m. Jacob. 29:13
Leah went out to m. Jacob. 30:16
Esau cometh to m. thee. 32:6; 33:4
Joseph went up to m. Israel. 46:29
Aaron cometh forth to m. Ex 4:14
go into wilderness to m. Moses. 27
Moses went out to m. his. 18:7
brought forth the people to m. 19:17
if thou m. thine enemy's ox. 23:4
there I will m. with thee. 25:22
29:42, 43; 30:6, 36; Num 17:4
Balak went out to m. Num 22:36
Lord will come to m. me. 23:3
stand here, while I m. the Lord. 15
went forth to m. them without. 31:13
lest the pursuers m. you. Josh 2:16*
with you, and go to m. them. 9:11
Jael went out to m. Sisera. Judg 4:18, 22
they came up to m. Gideon. 6:35
out of the doors to m. me. 11:31
his daughter came to m. him. 34
father of damsel rejoiced to m. 19:3
that they m. thee not in any other field. Ruth 2:22
shall m. thee three men. 1 Sam 10:3
m. a company of prophets. 5
Saul went to m. Samuel. 13:10
Samuel rose up early to m. 15:12
Philistine drew nigh to m. 17:48
the women came to m. Saul. 18:6
sent thee this day to m. me. 25:32
to m. David and to m. people. 30:21
Michal came out to m. 2 Sam 6:20
David sent to m. the men. 10:5
1 Chr 19:5
Archite came to m. him. 2 Sam 15:32
Mephibosheth came to m. 19:24
Shimei came down to m. 1 Ki 2:8
Solomon rose up to m. 19
went to m. Ahab, to m. Elijah. 18:16
arise, go down to m. Ahab. 21:18
go up to m. messengers. 2 Ki 1:3
there came a man to m. us. 6
what man came up to m. you? 7
prophets came to m. Elisha. 2 Ki 2:15
run now, I pray thee, to m. her. 4:26
if thou m. any man, salute. 29
the chariot to m. him. 5:21, 26
go m. the man of God. 8:8
Hazael went to m. him. 9
horseman, and send to m. 9:17
one on horseback to m. him. 18
Jonadab coming to m. him. 10:15
Ahaz went to m. the king. 16:10
let us m. together. Neh 6:2, 10
they m. with darkness. Job 5:14
the horse goeth on to m. 39:21
came I forth to m. thee. Pr 7:15
bear robbed of her whelps m. 17:12
rich and poor m. together. 22:2
poor and deceitful m. together. 29:13
go forth to m. Ahaz. Isa 7:3
hell is moved for thee to m. 14:9
beasts of desert shall also m. 34:14
vengeance, and I will not m. 47:3*
went forth to m. them. Jer 41:6
messenger run to m. another. 51:31
I will m. them as a bear bereaved. Hos 13:8
prepare to m. thy God. Amos 4:12
angel went out to m. Zech 2:3
city came out to m. Jesus. Mat 8:34
to m. the bridegroom. 25:1
cometh, go ye out to m. him. 6
there shall m. you a man.
Mark 14:13; Luke 22:10
with ten thousand to m. Luke 14:31
people went forth to m. John 12:13
to m. us as far as Appii-forum. Acts 28:15
clouds to m. the Lord. 1 Thes 4:17

meetest
look out the m. of your. 2 Ki 10:3
m. him that rejoiceth. Isa 64:5

meeteth
Esau my brother m. Gen 32:17
slay murderer when he m. him. Num 35:19, 21

meeting
afraid at m. of David. 1 Sam 21:1
even the solemn m. Isa 1:13

Megiddo
would dwell in M. Judg 1:27
Canaan fought by waters of M. 5:19
pertained Taanach and M. 1 Ki 4:12
raised a levy to build M. 9:15
Ahaziah fled to M. and. 2 Ki 9:27
Josiah was slain at M. 23:29, 30
2 Chr 35:22

Megiddon
in the valley of M. Zech 12:11

Melchi
which was the son of M. Luke 3:24

Melchizedek
king M. brought forth. Gen 14:18
priest for ever after the order of M.
Ps 110:4; Heb 5:6, 10; 6:20
7:17, 21
this M. king of Salem. Heb 7:1
loins of his father, when M. 10
should rise after the order of M. 11
after the similitude of M. ariseth. 15

melody
make sweet m. sing. Isa 23:16
found therein, the voice of m. 51:3
I will not hear the m. Amos 5:23
making m. in your heart. Eph 5:19

melons
we remember the m. Num 11:5

melt
(Frequently used in the old sense of to be prostrate because of fear)
of Canaan shall m. Ex 15:15
things, our hearts did m. Josh 2:11
made the heart of the people m. 14:8
lion, shall utterly m. 2 Sam 17:10
let them m. away as waters. Ps 58:7
with his teeth, and m. away. 112:10
every man's heart shall m. Isa 13:7
Ezek 21:7
the heart of Egypt shall m. Isa 19:1
behold, I will m. them. Jer 9:7
m. it; so will I m. you. Ezek 22:20
the land, and it shall m. Amos 9:5

all hills shall m. Amos 9:13; Nah 1:5
and the elements shall m. with heat. 2 Pet 3:10*, 12

melted

when sun waxed hot, it m. Ex 16:21
their heart m. Josh 5:1
hearts of Israel m. 7:5
the mountains m. before. Judg 5:5*
multitude m. away. 1 Sam 14:16
my heart is m. in midst. Ps 22:14
his voice, and the earth m. 46:6
the hills m. like wax. 97:5
their soul m. 107:26
mountains shall be m. Isa 34:3
ye shall be m. in the. Ezek 22:21
as silver is m. in the midst. 22

melteth

as a snail which m., let. Ps 58:8
as wax m. so let wicked perish. 68:2
my soul m. for heaviness. 119:28
out his word and m. them. 147:18
workman m. a graven. Isa 40:19†
burnt, the founder m. Jer 6:29
the heart of Nineveh m. Nah 2:10

melting

as when the m. fire. Isa 64:2

member

(*Generally used in the archaic sense of limb, or other part of the body. In this sense it is often also used figuratively*)
that hath his privy m. Deut 23:1
body is not one m. but. 1 Cor 12:14
if they were all one m., where? 19
whether one m. suffer, one m. 26
the tongue is a little m. Jas 3:5

members

my m. are as a shadow. Job 17:7
in thy book all my m. Ps 139:16
thy m. should perish. Mat 5:29, 30
nor your m. as instruments. Rom 6:13
as ye yielded your m. servants. 19
sins did work in our m. 7:5
another law in my m. . . . law of sin which is in my m. 23
many m. in one body, and all m. have not the same office. 12:4
every one m. one of another. 5
bodies are the m. of Christ? shall I then take the m. of? 1 Cor 6:15
body hath many m. and all m. 12:12
now hath God set the m. in. 18
are they many m., yet one body. 20
m. which seem more feeble. 22
but that the m. should have. 25
one member suffer, all the m. 26
ye are the body of Christ, and m. 27
for we are m. one of. Eph 4:25
m. of his body, of his flesh. 5:30
mortify your m. which are. Col 3:5
so is tongue among our m. Jas 3:6
lusts that war in your m. 4:1

memorial

this is my m. unto all. Ex 3:15
shall be to you for a m. 12:14
it shall be for a m. between. 13:9
write this for a m. in a book. 17:14
stones of m. to the children. 28:12
for a m. before the Lord. 29; 39:7
money may be for a m. 30:16
burn the m. of it on altar. Lev 2:2
9:16; 5:12; 6:15; Num 5:26
a m. of blowing trumpets. Lev 23:24; Num 10:10
on the bread for a m. Lev 24:7
for it is an offering of m. Num 5:15
priest put the offering of m. 18
took brasen censers to be a m. 16:40
gold of the captains for m. 31:54
stones shall be for a m. Josh 4:7
ye have no portion nor m. Neh 2:20
nor the m. of them perish. Esth 9:28
their m. is perished. Ps 9:6
and thy m. throughout all. 135:13
the Lord is his m. Hos 12:5
crowns be for a m. in. Zech 6:14
this be told for a m. of her. Mat 26:13; Mark 14:9
alms are come up for a m. Acts 10:4

memory

he may cut off the m. Ps 109:15
utter the m. of thy great. 145:7
m. of the just is blessed. Pr 10:7
m. of them is forgotten. Eccl 9:5
and made all their m. to. Isa 26:14
if ye keep in m. what. 1 Cor 15:2

Memphis

M. shall bury them. Hos 9:6

men

then began m. to call on. Gen 4:26
when m. began to multiply on. 6:1
looked, and lo, three m. stood. 18:2
the m. of the city, m. of Sodom. 19:4
where are m. which came into? 5
only to these m. do nothing. 8
smote the m. 11
power with God and m. 32:28
m. are peaceable with us. 34:21
only herein will the m. consent. 22
we are true m. 42:11, 31
bring these m. home. 43:16
said, Up, follow after the m. 44:4
m. are shepherds, for their. 46:32
saved the m.-children. Ex 1:17, 18
go now ye that are m. and. 10:11
thrice in the year shall m. 34:23
Aaron took these m. Num 1:17
all the people are m. of great. 13:32
m. that did bring evil report. 14:37
put out the eyes of these m.? 16:14
if these m. die the common death. 29
God said, What m. are these? 22:9
said to Balaam, Go with the m. 35
slay ye every one his m. that. 25:5
not one of these m. shall. Deut 1:35
to cease from among m. 32:26
Reuben live, let not his m. 33:6
there came m. in hither. Josh 2:2
bring forth the m. 3; 1 Sam 11:12
because he feared the m. Judg 6:27
Penuel answered as the m. 8:8
should give bread to thy m. 15
m. say not of me, A woman. 9:54
there were m. lying in wait. 16:9
therefore deliver us the m. 20:13
with the Lord and m. 1 Sam 2:26
he smote the m. of the city. 5:9
m. that died not were smitten. 12
hearest thou m.'s words? 24:9
but the m. were very good. 25:15
m. the sons of Zeruiah. 2 Sam 3:39
and let us play the m. for. 10:12
but dead men before my. 19:28
he that ruleth over m. must. 23:3
two lionlike m. of. 20; 1 Chr 11:22
happy thy m. that hear. 1 Ki 10:8
m. come out of Samaria. 20:17
now the m. did diligently. 33
open the eyes of these m. 2 Ki 6:20
they reckoned not with m. 12:15
the m. of Babylon . . . m. of Cuth, Nergal, m. of Hamath. 17:30
hath he not sent me to the m.? 18:27; Isa 36:12
what said these m.? 2 Ki 20:14
Isa 39:3
drink blood of these m.? 1 Chr 11:19
let m. say among the nations. 16:31
m. were greatly ashamed. 19:5
will God dwell with m.? 2 Chr 6:18
the m. expressed by name. 28:15
and the m. did the work. 34:12
let m. of his place help. Ezra 1:4
to cause these m. to cease. 4:21
expenses be given to these m. 6:8
nor m. of the guard. Neh 4:23
other m. have our lands and. 5:5
sleep falleth on m. Job 4:13; 33:15
they are gone away from m. 28:4
if the m. of my tabernacle. 31:31
m. do therefore fear him. 37:24
themselves to be but m. Ps 9:20
m. which are thy hand, from m. 17:14
m. will praise thee when. 49:18
m. of low degree are vanity, m. 62:9
hast received gifts for m. 68:18
and m. shall be blessed in. 72:17
as other m., neither are they plagued like other m. 73:5
but ye shall die like m. 82:7
that m. may know that thou. 83:18
O that m. would praise the Lord. 107:8, 15, 21, 31
on our side, when m. rose. 124:2
m. shall speak of the might. 145:6
m. do not despise a thief. Pr 6:30
to you, O m. I call. 8:4
m. depart from evil. 16:6
most m. proclaim each his own. 20:6
which the m. of Hezekiah. 25:1
m. to search their own glory. 27
when the wicked rise, m. hide. 28:28
God doeth it that m. may. Eccl 3:14
m. shall fall by the sword. Isa 3:25
the Lord have removed m. 6:12
thing for you to weary m.? 7:13
now the Egyptians are m. 31:3
by these things m. live. 38:16
wherefore I will give m. for. 43:4
even to him shall m. come. 45:24
and shew yourselves m. 46:8
that m. may bring to thee. 60:11
m. shall call you the ministers. 61:6
m. have not heard, nor. 64:4
set a trap, they catch m. Jer 5:26
horses set in array, as m. for. 6:23
neither can m. hear the voice. 9:10
let their m. be put to death. 18:21
I will give the m. that transgressed my covenant. 34:18
m. have done evil to prophet. 38:9
to Gedaliah, they and their m. 40:8
then the m. shall cry and. 47:2
arise ye, and spoil the m. of. 49:28
surely I will fill thee with m. 51:14
m. call the perfection. Lam 2:15
m. that devise mischief. Ezek 11:2
these m. set up their idols. 14:3
though these three m., Noah, Daniel, Job. 14, 16, 18
sent for m. to come from. 23:40
I will deliver thee to the m. 25:4, 10
ye are m., and I am God. 34:31
mountains with his slain m. 35:8
multiply m. upon you. 36:10, 37
m. have not regarded. Dan 3:12
fire slew those m. that took. 22
these m., upon whose bodies fire. 27
drive thee from m. 4:25, 32
m. we shall not find occasion. 6:5
that m. fear before the God. 26
but they like m. trangressed the covenant. Hos 6:7
m. that were at peace. Ob 7
pass securely, as m. averse. Mi 2:8
man's enemies are the m. of. 7:6
makest m. as the fishes. Hab 1:14
they are m. wondered at. Zech 3:8
had sent their m. to pray. 7:2
but lo, I will deliver the m. 11:6
light so shine before m. Mat 5:16
shall teach m. so, shall be called. 19
do not your alms before m. 6:1
they may appear to m. to fast. 16
thou appear not unto m. to fast. 18
that m. should do to you, do ye even so to them. 7:12; Luke 6:31
given such power to m. Mat 9:8
whoso shall confess me before m. 10:32; Luke 12:8
whoso shall deny me before m. Mat 10:33; Luke 12:9
but while m. slept, his enemy. Mat 13:25
whom do m. say that I am? 16:13
Mark 8:27
ye appear righteous to m. Mat 23:28
and said, I see m. as. Mark 8:24
with m. it is impossible. 10:27
Luke 18:27
good will toward m. Luke 2:14
thou shalt catch m. 5:10
shall rise up with the m. of. 11:31
to whom m. have committed. 12:48
I am not as other m. are. 18:11
not honour from m. John 5:41
manifested thy name to the m. 17:6
of these m. which have companied. Acts 1:21
others said, These m. are full. 2:13
what shall we do to these m.? 4:16
thou hast not lied unto m. 5:4
the m. ye put in prison are in. 25
obey God rather than m. 29
to do, as touching these m. 35
refrain from these m. 38
Spirit said, Behold three m. 10:19
also are m. of like passions. 14:15
m. that hazarded their lives. 15:26

these *m.* are servants of. *Acts* 16:17
serjeants, saying, Let those *m.* go. 35
brought hither these *m.* 19:37
also of yourselves shall *m.* 20:30
of offence toward God and *m.* 24:16
m. with *m.* working. *Rom* 1:27
condescend to *m.* of low. 12:16
we are made a spectacle unto world and to angels and *m.* *1 Cor* 4:9
for he speaketh not to *m.* 14:2
but in understanding be *m.* 20
with *m.* of other tongues and lips. 21
we persuade *m.* *2 Cor* 5:11
for I mean not that other *m.* 8:13
persuade *m.*? or seek to please *m.*? *Gal* 1:10
he gave gifts unto *m.* *Eph* 4:8
so ought *m.* to love their wives. 5:28
to Lord and not to *m.* 6:7; *Col* 3:23
not as pleasing *m.* but. *1 Thes* 2:4
I will that *m.* pray every. *1 Tim* 2:8
m. shall be lovers of. *2 Tim* 3:2
priest taken from among *m.* *Heb* 5:1
for *m.* verily swear by the. 6:16
here *m.* that die receive tithes. 7:8
as it is appointed unto *m.* 9:27
to the spirits of just *m.* 12:23
therewith curse we *m.* *Jas* 3:9
judged according to *m.* *1 Pet* 4:6
but holy *m.* of God. *2 Pet* 1:21
for there are certain *m.* crept. *Jude* 4
only those *m.* which have. *Rev* 9:4
their power was to hurt *m.* 10
redeemed from among *m.* 14:4
not since *m.* were on the earth. 16:18
tabernacle of God is with *m.* 21:3
see **brethren, chief, chosen, evil, great, Israel, Judah, old, rich, righteous, singing**

all **men**

all the *m.* of his house. *Gen* 17:27
all the *m.* are dead. *Ex* 4:19
die the common death of *all m.* *Num* 16:29
all the *m.* that followed. *Deut* 4:3
said, Have out *all m.* *2 Sam* 13:9
was wiser than *all m.* *1 Ki* 4:31
all m. may know his work. *Job* 37:7
all m. shall fear, and. *Ps* 64:9
thou made *all m.* in vain? 89:47
I said in my haste, *All m.* 116:11
that is the end of *all m.* *Eccl* 7:2
so with *all* the *m.* that set. *Jer* 42:17
I set *all m.* every one against his neighbour. *Zech* 8:10
ye shall be hated of *all m.* *Mat* 10:22
Mark 13:13; *Luke* 21:17
all m. cannot receive. *Mat* 19:11
tho' *all m.* shall be offended. 26:33
all m. seek thee. *Mark* 1:37
all m. did marvel. 5:20
all m. counted John a. 11:32
all m. speak well of you. *Luke* 6:26
sinners above *all m.* that dwelt. 13:4
that *all m.* through him. *John* 1:7
himself, because he knew *all m.* 2:24
the same baptizeth, and *all m.* 3:26
all m. should honour the Son. 5:23
if we let alone, *all m.* will. 11:48
I will draw *all m.* unto me. 12:32
by this shall *all m.* know that. 13:35
Lord, who knowest the hearts of *all m.* *Acts* 1:24
all m. glorified God for what. 4:21
but now commandeth *all m.* 17:30
hath given assurance to *all m.* 31
all the *m.* were about twelve. 19:7
burned their books before *all m.* 19
pure from the blood of *all m.* 20:26
be his witness to *all m.* 22:15
death passed upon *all m.* *Rom* 5:12
on *all m.* to condemnation, the free gift came on *all m.* to. 18
honest in the sight of *all m.* 12:17
live peaceably with *all m.* 18
is come abroad to *all m.* 16:19
I would that *all m.* were. *1 Cor* 7:7
for though I be free from *all m.* 9:19
I am made all things to *all m.* 22
even as I please *all m.* in. 10:33
of *all m.* most miserable. 15:19
known and read of *all m.* *2 Cor* 3:2
let us do good to *all m.* *Gal* 6:10
to make *all m.* see what is. *Eph* 3:9
let your moderation be known to *all m.* *Phil* 4:5
and contrary to *all m.* *1 Thes* 2:15
abound in love toward *all m.* 3:12
be patient toward *all m.* 5:14
follow that which is good to *all m.* 15
all m. have not faith. *2 Thes* 3:2
thanks be made for *all m.* *1 Tim* 2:1
who will have *all m.* to be saved. 4
who is the Saviour of *all m.* 4:10
but be gentle to *all m.* *2 Tim* 2:24
shall be made manifest to *all m.* 3:9
man stood with me, but *all m.* 4:16
God hath appeared to *all m.* *Tit* 2:11
shewing all meekness to *all m.* 3:2
follow peace with *all m.* *Heb* 12:14
God, that giveth to *all m.* *Jas* 1:5
Honour *all m.*, Love the. *1 Pet* 2:17
hath good report of *all m.* *3 John* 12

in **men**

let no man glory *in m.* *1 Cor* 3:21

like **men**

quit yourselves *like m.* *1 Sam* 4:9
1 Cor 16:13
but ye shall die *like m.* *Ps* 82:7
like m. have transgressed. *Hos* 6:7
yourselves *like* unto *m.* that wait for their lord. *Luke* 12:36

mighty **men**

mighty m. which were of old. *Gen* 6:4
mighty m. of Moab. *Ex* 15:15
the *mighty m.* of valour. *Josh* 1:14
Jericho and the *mighty m.* 6:2
thirty thousand *mighty m.* 8:3
m. of Gibeon were *mighty.* 10:2
ascended from Gilgal with *mighty m.* of valour. 7
bows of the *mighty m.* *1 Sam* 2:4
Joab and all the host of the *mighty m.* *2 Sam* 10:7; 20:7; *1 Chr* 19:8
mighty m. were on his right hand. *2 Sam* 16:6
his *m.*, that they be *mighty m.* 17:8
be names of the *mighty m.* 23:8
Eleazar one of the three *mighty m.* 9
the three *mighty m.* brake. 16, 17
name among three *mighty m.* 22
the *mighty m.* were not with Adonijah. *1 Ki* 1:8
the *mighty m.* and Solomon. 10
exacted of all *mighty m.* *2 Ki* 15:20
carried away all the *mighty m.* 24:14
these were *mighty m.* of valour. *1 Chr* 5:24; 7:7, 9, 11, 40
sons of Ulam were *mighty m.* 8:40
the chief of the *mighty m.* 11:10, 11
were among the *mighty m.* 12:1
were all *mighty m.* of valour. 21, 25
30; 26:6, 31
mighty m. submitted themselves to Solomon. 29:24
battle against Abijah, being *mighty m.* *2 Chr* 13:3; 14:8; 17:13, 14, 16
an hundred thousand *mighty m.* 25:6
counsel with his *mighty m.* 32:3
angel cut off all the *mighty m.* 21
their brethren *mighty m.* *Neh* 11:14
break in pieces *mighty m.* *Job* 34:24
more than ten *mighty m.* *Eccl* 7:19
all shields of *mighty m.* *S of S* 4:4
mighty m. of Kedar shall. *Isa* 21:17
quiver is an open sepulchre, they are all *mighty m.* *Jer* 5:16
king, with all his *mighty m.* 26:21
recovered *mighty m.* of war. 41:16
let *mighty m.* come forth. 46:9
we are *mighty m.* 48:14
hearts of *mighty m.* of Moab. 41
heart of *mighty m.* of Edom. 49:22
sword is upon her *mighty m.* 50:36
mighty m. of Babylon have. 51:30
mighty m. are taken, their bows. 56
I will make drunk her *mighty m.* 57
under foot my *mighty m.* *Lam* 1:15
table with *mighty m.* *Ezek* 39:20
mighty m. to bind. *Dan* 3:20
trust in the multitude of thy *mighty m.* *Hos* 10:13
shall run like *mighty m.* *Joel* 2:7
wake up the *mighty m.* 3:9
thy *mighty m.* O Teman. *Ob* 9
the shield of his *mighty m.* *Nah* 2:3
as *mighty m.* that tread. *Zech* 10:5
mighty m. hid themselves in the dens. *Rev* 6:15
eat the flesh of *mighty m.* 19:18

of **men**

saw the daughters *of m.* *Gen* 6:2
came in to the daughters *of m.* 4
none devoted *of m.* *Lev* 27:29
whether it be *of m.* *Num* 18:15
prey both *of m.* and beasts. 31:11
what manner *of m.* were. *Judg* 8:18
went with a band *of m.* *1 Sam* 10:26
him with the rod *of m.* *2 Sam* 7:14
spied a band *of m.* *2 Ki* 13:21
places with the bones *of m.* 23:14
they took away *of m.* *1 Chr* 5:21
the band *of m.* had slain. *2 Chr* 22:1
O thou Preserver *of m.*? *Job* 7:20
then he openeth the ears *of m.* 33:16
concerning the works *of m.* *Ps* 17:4
but I am a reproach *of m.* 22:6
haughtiness *of m.* shall be bowed down. *Isa* 2:11
the haughtiness *of m.* shall be made low. 17
taught by the precept *of m.* 29:13
workmen, they are *of m.* 44:11
fear ye not the reproach *of m.* 51:7
is despised and rejected *of m.* 53:3
carcases *of m.* shall fall. *Jer* 9:22
with the dead bodies *of m.* 33:5
to thyself images *of m.* *Ezek* 16:17
eat not the bread *of m.* 24:17, 22
traded the persons *of m.* in. 27:13
no more bereave them *of m.* 36:12
cities be filled with flocks *of m.* 38
mingle with the seed *of m.* *Dan* 2:43
Most High . . . *of m.* and setteth up . . . basest *of m.* 4:17, 25, 32; 5:21
by reason of multitude *of m.* *Mi* 2:12; *Zech* 2:4
make you fishers *of m.* *Mat* 4:19
trodden under foot *of m.* 5:13
they may have glory *of m.* 6:2
seen *of m.* 5; 23:5
beware *of m.* 10:17
for doctrines, commandments *of m.* 15:9; *Mark* 7:7
but the things that be *of m.* *Mat* 16:23; *Mark* 8:33
betrayed into hands *of m.* *Mat* 17:22
Mark 9:31; *Luke* 9:44; 24:7
made eunuchs *of m.* *Mat* 19:12
baptism of heaven or *of m.*? 21:25
if we say *of m.* 26; *Mark* 11:30
32; *Luke* 20:4, 6
regardest not person *of m.* *Mat* 22:16; *Mark* 12:14
be called *of m.* Rabbi. *Mat* 23:7
out of the heart *of m.* *Mark* 7:21
life was the light *of m.* *John* 1:4
they loved the praise *of m.* 12:43
Judas received a band *of m.* 18:3
to whom a number *of m.* *Acts* 5:36
if this work be *of m.* it will. 38
come down in likeness *of m.* 14:11
the residue *of m.* might seek. 15:17
honourable women, and *of m.* 17:12
unrighteousness *of m.* *Rom* 1:18
judge the secrets *of m.* 2:16
whose praise is not *of m.* 29
brethren, I speak after the manner *of m.* 6:19; *Gal* 3:15
Christ is approved *of m.* *Rom* 14:18
stand in the wisdom *of m.* *1 Cor* 2:5
learn in us not to think *of m.* 4:6
be not the servants *of m.* 7:23
speak with tongues *of m.* and. 13:1
if, after the manner *of m.*, I. 15:32
things in the sight *of m.* *2 Cor* 8:21
Paul an apostle, not *of m.* *Gal* 1:1
doctrine, by sleight *of m.* *Eph* 4:14
made in the likeness *of m.* *Phil* 2:7
after the tradition *of m.* *Col* 2:8
and doctrines *of m.* 22
manner *of m.* we were. *1 Thes* 1:5
nor *of m.* sought we glory. 2:6
it not as the word *of m.* 13
disputings *of m.* of. *1 Tim* 6:5
commandments *of m.* *Tit* 1:14
disallowed indeed *of m.* *1 Pet* 2:4
to silence ignorance *of* foolish *m.* 15
no longer live to the lusts *of m.* 4:2

receive the witness of m. 1 John 5:9
were as the faces of m. Rev 9:7
slay the third part of m. 15, 18
were slain of m. 7000. 11:13
fire come down in sight of m. 13:13
of slaves and souls of m. 18:13
see **children**

sons of **men**

ye sons of m. how long will ye turn my glory into? Ps 4:2; 58:1
thee, before the sons of m. 31:19
beholdeth all the sons of m. 33:13
I lie among the sons of m. 57:4
to make known to sons of m. 145:12
and my delights were with the sons of m. Pr 8:31
travail hath God given to the sons of m. Eccl 1:13; 3:10
good for sons of m. 2:3
delights of the sons of m. 8
the estate of the sons of m. 18
which befalleth the sons of m. 19
heart of sons of m. is set in. 8:11
the heart of the sons of m. 9:3
so are the sons of m. snared. 12
more than the sons of m. Isa 52:14
ways of the sons of m. Jer 32:19
driven from the sons of m. Dan 5:21
similitude of the sons of m. 10:16
joy is withered away from the sons of m. Joel 1:12
nor waiteth for the sons of m. Mi 5:7
be forgiven to sons of m. Mark 3:28
not known to sons of m. Eph 3:5

men of war

taken sum of m. of w. Num 31:49
till m. of w. came out of Egypt were. Deut 2:14, 16; Josh 5:6
the city, ye m. of w. Josh 6:3
drew sword, all these were m. of w. Judg 20:17
set over the m. of w. 1 Sam 18:5
they were m. of w. and chief captains. 1 Ki 9:22; 2 Chr 8:9
and all the m. of w. fled. 2 Ki 25:4; Jer 52:7
took an officer set over m. of w. 2 Ki 25:19; Jer 52:25
Gadites m. of w. came to. 1 Chr 12:8
these m. of w. came to Hebron. 38
set battle in array with m. of w. 2 Chr 13:3
and the m. of w. were in. 17:13
the hands of m. of w. Jer 38:4
Ishmael slew m. of w. 41:3
Johanan took the m. of w. 16
all the m. of w. shall be cut off. 49:26; 50:30
m. of w. are affrighted. 51:32
Phut were thy m. of w. Ezek 27:10
all thy m. of w. that are in thee. 27
at my table with m. of w. 39:20
climb wall like m. of w. Joel 2:7
all the m. of w. draw near. 3:9
Herod with his m. of w. Luke 23:11

wicked **men**

but the m. of Sodom were wicked. Gen 13:13
tents of these wicked m. Num 16:26
then answered all the wicked m. 1 Sam 30:22
as a man falleth before wicked m. 2 Sam 3:34*
when wicked m. have slain. 4:11
marked old way that wicked m. have trodden. Job 22:15
walketh with wicked m. 34:8
he striketh them as wicked m. 26
of his answers for wicked m. 36
there be wicked m. to whom it happeneth. Eccl 8:14
people are found wicked m. Jer 5:26
destroy those wicked m. Mat 24:41
be delivered from wicked m. 2 Thes 3:2

wise **men**

Pharaoh called for all wise m. Gen 41:8; Ex 7:11
wise m. that wrought. Ex 36:4
take ye wise m. and. Deut 1:13
chief of your tribes, wise m. 15
king said to wise m. Esth 1:13
then said Haman's wise m. 6:13
which wise m. have told. Job 15:18
hear my words, O ye wise m. 34:2
he seeth that wise m. die. Ps 49:10
wise m. lay up knowledge. Pr 10:14
he that walketh with wise m. 13:20
but wise m. turn away wrath. 29:8
the words of wise m. are. Eccl 9:17
where are thy wise m.? Isa 19:12
the wisdom of their wise m. 29:14
turneth wise m. backward. 44:25
the wise m. are ashamed. Jer 8:9
as among all the wise m. of. 10:7
Babylon, and on her wise m. 50:35
make drunken her wise m. 51:57
thy wise m. O Tyrus. Ezek 27:8
wise m. thereof were thy calkers. 9
destroy all the wise m. of. Dan 2:12
cannot the wise m. shew unto. 27
decree to bring in all the wise m. 4:6
king spake to the wise m. 5:7
even destroy the wise m. out. Ob 8
came wise m. from east. Mat 2:1
he had privily called the wise m. 7
was mocked of wise m. 16
I send wise m. 23:34
not many wise m. called. 1 Cor 1:26
speak as to wise m.; judge ye. 10:15

men joined with women

both m. and women brought bracelets. Ex 35:22
destroyed the m. and women and. Deut 2:34; Josh 8:25
thousand m. and women. Judg 9:49
fled all the m. and women. 51
m. and women, upon the roof about 3000 m and women. 16:27
well to the women as m. 2 Sam 6:19
brought the law before m. and women. Neh 8:2, 3
Jeremiah said to the m. and women. Jer 44:20
added to Lord both m. and women. Acts 5:14
Saul haling m. and women. 8:3
baptized, both m. and women. 12
whether m. or women he might bring them bound. 9:2
prison both m. and women. 22:24
men, women and children, see **children**

ye **men**

hearken unto me, ye m. Judg 9:7
ye m. of understanding. Job 34:10
ye m. of Galilee. Acts 1:11
ye m. of Judea. 2:14
ye m. of Israel. 5:35
ye m. and brethren, if ye. 13:15
ye m. of Athens. 17:22
ye m. of Ephesus, what man? 19:35

young **men**

that which the young m. Gen 14:24
Moses sent young m. Ex 24:5
Joshua one of the young m. Num 11:28
young m. that were spies. Josh 6:23
so used the young m. Judg 14:10
charged the young m. Ruth 2:9
followedst not young m. 3:10
the sin of the young m. 1 Sam 2:17
your goodliest young m. 8:16
the young m. kept themselves. 21:4
and the vessels of the young m. 5
ask thy young m. and they. 25:8
handmaid saw not the young m. 25
let one of the young m. come. 26:22
save 400 young m. which rode. 30:17
David called one of the young m. 2 Sam 1:15
let the young m. arise and. 2:14
hold on one of the young m. 21
have slain all the young m. 13:32
and ten young m. that bare. 18:15
consulted with young m. 1 Ki 12:8
spake after counsel of young m. 14
2 Chr 10:8, 14
by young m. of princes. 1 Ki 20:14
send, I pray thee, one of the young m. 2 Ki 4:22*
there be come two young m. 5:22
their young m. wilt thou slay. 8:12
slew their young m with. 2 Chr 36:17
it fell upon the young m. Job 1:19
the young m. saw me, and hid. 29:8
consumed their young m. Ps 78:63
praise the Lord, young m. 148:12
the glory of young m. is. Pr 20:29
no joy in their young m. Isa 9:17
bows also shall dash young m. 13:18
do I nourish up young m. 23:4
young m. shall be discomfited. 31:8
young m. shall utterly fall. 40:30
pour fury on assembly of young m. Jer 6:11
to cut off the young m. from. 9:21
the young m. shall die by. 11:22
against the mother of the young m. 15:8
let their young m. be slain. 18:21
young m. and old rejoice. 31:13
his chosen young m. are gone. 48:15
her young m. shall fall in the streets. 49:26; 50:30
spare ye not her young m. 51:3
assembly to crush my young m. Lam 1:15
my virgins and young m. are. 18
the young m. and old lie on. 2:21
took the young m. to grind. 5:13
the young m. have ceased from. 14
all of them desirable young m. Ezek 23:6, 12, 23
young m. of Aven shall fall. 30:17
your young m. shall see visions. Joel 2:28; Acts 2:17
and of your young m. Amos 2:11
your young m. have I slain. 4:10
your young m. shall faint. 8:13
the young m. cheerful. Zech 9:17
and the young m. laid. Mark 14:51
and the young m. arose. Acts 5:6
the young m. came in and found. 10
young m. likewise exhort. Tit 2:6
I write to you, young m. because. 1 John 2:13, 14

Menahem

M. smote Shallum in. 2 Ki 15:14
M. smote Tiphsah. 16
M. exacted money. 20

mend

brass to m. the house. 2 Chr 24:12
gave it the workmen to m. 34:10

mending

James and John, with Zebedee, m. their nets. Mat 4:21; Mark 1:19

Mene

M. M. God hath numbered thy. Dan 5:25, 26

menpleasers

not with eye service, as m. Eph 6:6
Col 3:22

menservants

Abram had m. and. Gen 12:16
Abimelech gave m. to. 20:14
God hath given my master m. 24:35
Jacob had m. and camels. 30:43
32:5
shall not go out as m. do. Ex 21:7
rejoice before Lord, ye and your m. Deut 12:12
king will take you m. 1 Sam 8:16
is it a time to receive m.? 2 Ki 5:26
shall begin to beat the m. Luke 12:45
see **two**

mensteales

law is made for m. 1 Tim 1:10

menstruous

cast them away as a m. Isa 30:22*
Jerusalem is as a m. Lam 1:17*
near to a m. woman. Ezek 18:6

mention

m. of me unto Pharaoh. Gen 40:14
make no m. of other gods. Ex 23:13
Josh 23:7
he made m. of the ark. 1 Sam 4:18
no m. shall be made of coral or of pearls. Job 28:18
m. of thy righteousness. Ps 71:16
m. of Rahab and Babylon. 87:4
make m. that his name. Isa 12:4
that maketh m. thereof shall. 19:17
by thee only we will make m 26:13

make m. of God of Israel. Isa 48:1
from bowels hath he made m. 49:1
ye that make m. of the Lord. 62:6
make ye m. to nations. Jer 4:16
I will not make m. of him. 20:9
we may not make m. of. Amos 6:10
I make m. of you always. Rom 1:9
Eph 1:16; 1 Thes 1:2
making m. of thee always. Philem 4
Joseph made m. of the. Heb 11:22

mention

I will m. the lovingkindnesses of. Isa 63:7
burden of the Lord shall ye m. no more. Jer 23:36

mentioned

these cities, which are m. Josh 21:9
these m. by name. 1 Chr 4:38
Jehu is m. in the book. 2 Chr 20:34*
sister Sodom was not m. Ezek 16:56
his transgressions shall not be m. 18:22*
his righteousness shall not be m. 24*
none of his sins shall be m. 33:16*

Mephibosheth

son, his name was M. 2 Sam 4:4
but M. shall eat bread at. 9:10, 11
M. had a young son Micha . . . of Ziba were servants to M. 12
are all that pertained unto M. 16:4
wentest thou not with me, M.? 19:25
but the king spared M. the. 21:7
sons of Rizpah, Armoni and M. 8

Merab

Saul's eldest daughter M. 1 Sam 14:49; 18:17
M. should have been given. 18:19

Merari

Gershon, Kohath, M. Gen 46:11
Ex 6:16; Num 3:17; 1 Chr 6:1, 16
23:6
sons of M. Ex 6:19; Num 3:20
1 Chr 6:19, 29; 23:21; 24:26
charge of the sons of M. Num 3:36
were numbered of M. 4:42
M. set forward. 10:17
oxen given to the sons of M. 7:8
cities given to M. Josh 21:7, 40
1 Chr 6:63, 77

merchandise

thou shalt not make m. Deut 21:14
and maketh m. of him. 24:7
m. of it is better than the m. Pr 3:14
perceiveth that her m. is good. 31:18
her m. shall be holiness. Isa 23:18
the m. of Ethiopia shall come. 45:14
make a prey of thy m. Ezek 26:12
were in thee to occupy thy m. 27:9
isles were the m. of thy hands. 15*
by the multitude of thy m. 28:16*
farm, another to his m. Mat 22:5
make not my Father's house an house of m. John 2:16
feigned words make m. 2 Pet 2:3
no man buyeth their m. Rev 18:11
the m. of gold, and silver. 12

merchant

current money with m. Gen 23:16
she is like the m. ships. Pr 31:14
delivereth girdles to the m. 24
all powders of the m. S of S 3:6
against the m. city. Isa 23:11*
art a m. of the people. Ezek 27:3
Tarshish was thy m. by reason. 12
Syria was thy m. 16, 18, 20*
he is a m., the balances. Hos 12:7*
for all the m. people. Zeph 1:11*

merchantman, men

passed by Midianites m. Gen 37:28
he had of the m. 1 Ki 10:15
like a m. seeking. Mat 13:45

merchants

traffic of spice m. 1 Ki 10:15
the king's m. received linen yarn. 28; 2 Chr 1:16
besides that which m. 2 Chr 9:14
the goldsmiths and the m. Neh 3:32
so the m. lodged without. 13:20
part him among the m.? Job 41:6
m. of Zidon replenished. Isa 23:2
city, whose m. are princes. 8
thy m. they shall wander. 47:15*
cropt the twigs, he set it in a city of m. Ezek 17:4
Meshech, were thy m. 27:13
Judah and Israel thy m. 17
in these were thy m. 21
m. of Sheba. 22, 23
there were thy m. in all sorts. 24
m. shall hiss at thee. 36
m. of Tarshish. 38:13
hast multiplied thy m. Nah 3:16
for the m. of the earth. Rev 18:3
the m. of the earth shall weep. 11
for thy m. were the great men. 23

Mercurius

called Paul, M., because. Acts 14:12

mercies

of the least of thy m. Gen 32:10
for his m. are great. 2 Sam 24:14
1 Chr 21:13
remember the m. of David thy servant. 2 Chr 6:42
in thy manifold m. Neh 9:19
according to thy m. thou gavest. 27
deliver according to thy m. 28
m. thou didst not consume. 31
according to thy m. blot out. Ps 51:1
in the multitude of thy m. 69:13
according to thy tender m. 16
I will sing of the m. of Lord. 89:1
not multitude of thy m. 106:7
according to multitude of his m. 45
let thy m. come also to me. 119:41
with great m. will I gather. Isa 54:7
sure m. of David. 55:3; Acts 13:34
on them according to his m. Isa 63:7
where is thy zeal and thy m.? 15*
I have taken away my m. Jer 16:5
shew m. to you, that he may. 42:12
it is of the Lord's m. we. Lam 3:22
according to multitude of his m. 32
desire m. concerning. Dan 2:18
to the Lord our God belong m. 9:9
righteousness, but thy great m. 18
betroth thee unto me in m. Hos 2:19
to Jerusalem with m. Zech 1:16
I beseech you by the m. Rom 12:1
the Father of m. and. 2 Cor 1:3
if any fellowship of the Spirit, if any bowels and m. Phil 2:1*
put on therefore, holy and beloved, bowels of m. Col 3:12*

***tender* mercies**

remember, O Lord, thy tender m. Ps 25:6; 51:1
withhold not thy tender m. 40:11
in anger shut up his tender m. 77:9
let thy tender m. speedily. 79:8
crowneth thee with tender m. 103:4
let thy tender m. come unto. 119:77
great are thy tender m. O Lord. 156
tender m. are over all his. 145:9
tender m. of the wicked. Pr 12:10

merciful

Lord being m. unto Lot. Gen 19:16
Lord God, m. and gracious. Ex 34:6*
be m. O Lord, to thy. Deut 21:8*
and will be m. to his land. 32:43*
with the m. thou wilt shew thyself m. 2 Sam 22:26; Ps 18:25
of Israel are m. kings. 1 Ki 20:31†
God is gracious and m. 2 Chr 30:9
pardon, gracious and m. Neh 9:17*
and be m. to me. Ps 26:11; 41:4
10; 56:1; 57:1; 86:3; 119:58, 132
the righteous is ever m. 37:26*
be not m. to any wicked. 59:5
God be m. to us, and bless us. 67:1
Lord is m. and gracious. 103:8*
for his m. kindness is great. 117:2
let thy m. kindness be for. 119:76
the m. man doeth good. Pr 11:17†
m. men are taken away. Isa 57:1†
Return, for I am m. saith. Jer 3:12
he is gracious and m. Joel 2:13*
that thou art a m. God. Jonah 4:2*
blessed are the m.: for they. Mat 5:7
be ye m. as your Father also is m. Luke 6:36
publican saying, God be m. 18:13
be a m. High Priest. Heb 2:17
m. to their unrighteousness. 8:12

see God

mercy

(Compassion; pity for the undeserving and the guilty. Used of both God and man. The word is frequently changed in the Revisions to lovingkindness)

not destitute of his m. Gen 24:27
and God give you m. before. 43:14
keeping m. for thousands. Ex 34:7
Dan 9:4
Lord is longsuffering and of great m. Num 14:18; Ps 103:11; 145:8
covenant and m. Deut 7:9, 12
my m. shall not depart. 2 Sam 7:15
1 Chr 17:13; Ps 89:24
m. and truth be with. 2 Sam 15:20
keepest covenant and m. 1 Ki 8:23
Neh 1:5; 9:32
m. endureth for ever. 1 Chr 16:34
41; 2 Chr 5:13; 7:3, 6; 20:21
Ezra 3:11; Ps 106:1; 107:1
118:1; 136:1, to the end
Jer 33:11
extended m. to me. Ezra 7:28
extended m. to us in sight of. 9:9
grant him m. in the sight. Neh 1:11
correction or for m. Job 37:13
and through the m. of. Ps 21:7
goodness and m. shall follow. 23:6
the paths of the Lord are m. 25:10
that trusteth in Lord, m. shall. 32:10
them that hope in his m. 33:18
I trust in the m. of God for. 52:8
God shall send forth his m. 57:3
the God of my m. shall prevent me. 59:10, 17
O prepare m. and truth. 61:7
O Lord, belongeth m. 62:12
which hath not turned his m. 66:20
is his m. clean gone for ever? doth m. fail? 77:8
m. and truth are met together. 85:10
art plenteous in m. 86:5, 15; 103:8
I said, m. shall be built up. 89:2
m. and truth shall go before. 14
my m. will I keep for him for. 28
he hath remembered his m. 98:3
the Lord is good, his m. is. 100:5
sing of m. and judgement. 101:1
the m. of the Lord is from. 103:17
there be none to extend m. 109:12
with the Lord there is m. and. 130:7
in those that hope in his m. 147:11
let not m. and truth forsake. Pr 3:3
he that hath m. on the poor. 14:21*
m. and truth shall be to them. 22
he that honoureth God hath m. 31
by m. and truth iniquity is. 16:6
m. and truth preserve the king . . . is upholden by m. 20:28; Isa 16:5
he that followeth after m. Pr 21:21
he that hath m. on them. Isa 49:10
saith the Lord that hath m. 54:10
in my favour have I had m. on. 60:10
are cruel, and have no m. Jer 6:23
there is no truth, nor m. Hos 4:1†
for I desired m. and not sacrifice. 6:6†
reap in m. 10:12†
keep m. and wait on God. 12:6†
the fatherless findeth m. 14:3
they forsake their own m. Jonah 2:8†
do justly, and to love m. Mi 6:8†
because he delighteth in m. 7:18
perform the m. to Abraham. 20
in wrath remember m. Hab 3:2
merciful, shall obtain m. Mat 5:7
omitted judgement and m. 23:23
m. is on them that fear. Luke 1:50
in remembrance of his m. 54
to perform the m. promised to. 72
remission through the tender m. 78
his glory on vessels of m. Rom 9:23
have now obtained m. 11:30
your m. they also may obtain m. 31
might glorify God for his m. 15:9
that hath obtained m. 1 Cor 7:25
as we have received m. 2 Cor 4:1
peace be on them, and m. Gal 6:16
God who is rich in m. Eph 2:4
death, but God had m. on. Phil 2:27
m. and peace from God. 1 Tim 1:2
2 Tim 1:2; Tit 1:4; 2 John 3
I obtained m. because I. 1 Tim 1:13
for this cause I obtained m. 16

Lord give *m.* to house. *2 Tim* 1:16
that he may find *m.* of the Lord. 18
but according to his *m.* *Tit* 3:5
that we may obtain *m.* *Heb* 4:16
Moses' law died without *m.* 10:28*
judgement without *m.* that shewed
no *m.* and *m.* rejoiceth. *Jas* 2:13
wisdom from above, full of *m.* 3:17
Lord is pitiful, and of tender *m.* 5:11
to his abundant *m.* hath. *1 Pet* 1:3
m. but now have obtained *m.* 2:10
m. to you, peace and love. *Jude* 2
looking for the *m.* of Lord Jesus. 21

have mercy

have m. upon me. *Ps* 4:1; 6:2
9:13; 25:16; 27:7; 30:10; 31:9
51:1; 86:16
shalt *have m.* on Zion. 102:13
have m. on us. 123:2, 3
his sins shall *have m.* *Pr* 28:13
neither *have m.* on their fatherless.
Isa 9:17*
Lord will *have m.* on Jacob. 14:1*
will not *have m.* on them. 27:11*
he may *have m.* on you. 30:18
for God will *have m.* upon. 49:13*
with kindness will I *have m.* 54:8
and he will *have m.* on him. 55:7
nor *have m.* but destroy them.
Jer 13:14*; 21:7
have m. on his dwelling-. 30:18*
I will surely *have m.* on. 31:20
33:26; *Ezek* 39:25; *Hos* 1:7; 2:23
he may *have m.* on you. *Jer* 42:12
no more *have m.* on the house of
Israel. *Hos* 1:6; 2:4
wilt thou not *have m.*? *Zech* 1:12
bring them again, for I *have m.* 10:6
I will *have m.* and not sacrifice.
Mat 9:13; 12:7
Son of David, *have m.* on me. 9:27
15:22; 20:30, 31; *Mark* 10:47, 48
Luke 18:38, 39
Lord, *have m.* on my son. *Mat* 17:15
Abraham, *have m.* on. *Luke* 16:24
Jesus, Master, *have m.* on. 17:13
I will *have m.* on whom I will *have
m.* *Rom* 9:15, 18
that he might *have m.* on all. 11:32

mercy joined with *shew, shewed sheweth, shewing*

Lord was with Joseph, and *shewed*
him *m.* *Gen* 39:21*
shewing m. to thousands. *Ex* 20:6
Deut 5:10
I will *shew m.* on whom I will *shew
m.* *Ex* 33:19
no covenant, nor *shew* them *m.*
Deut 7:2
may turn and *shew* thee *m.* 13:17
shew us city, and we will *shew* thee
m. *Judg* 1:24
sheweth m. to his anointed.
2 Sam 22:51; *Ps* 18:50
shewed to thy servant David . . .
great *m.* *1 Ki* 3:6; *2 Chr* 1:8
shewest m. to thy servants.
2 Chr 6:14
righteous *sheweth m.* *Ps* 37:21*
shew us thy *m.* O Lord, and. 85:7
remembered not to *shew m.* 109:16
didst *shew* them no *m.* *Isa* 47:6
cruel, and will not *shew m.* *Jer* 50:42
thy sins by *shewing m.* *Dan* 4:27
judgement, and *shew m.* *Zech* 7:9
Lord *shewed* great *m.* *Luke* 1:58
he that *shewed m.* on him. 10:37
God that *sheweth m.* *Rom* 9:16
sheweth m. with cheerfulness. 12:8
judgement without *m.* that hath
shewed no *m.* *Jas* 2:13

thy mercy

magnified *thy m.* to me. *Gen* 19:19
in *thy m.* hast led forth. *Ex* 15:13
the greatness of *thy m.* *Num* 14:19
according to *thy m.* *Neh* 13:22
in multitude of *thy m.* *Ps* 5:7
save me for *thy m.'s* sake. 6:4; 31:16
trusted in *thy m.* my heart. 13:5
according to *thy m.* remember. 25:7
rejoice in *thy m.* for thou. 31:7
let *thy m.* O Lord, be upon. 33:22
thy m. O Lord, is in the. 36:5
redeem us, for *thy m.'s* sake. *Ps* 44:26
for *thy m.* is great unto the. 57:10
I will sing aloud of *thy m.* 59:16
in the multitude of *thy m.* 69:13
shew us *thy m.* O Lord. 85:7
great is *thy m.* 86:13
O satisfy us early with *thy m.* 90:14
thy m. O Lord, held me up. 94:18
thy m. is great above heavens. 108:4
because *thy m.* is good. 109:21
save me according to *thy m.* 26
for *thy m.* and for thy truth's. 115:1
earth is full of *thy m.* 119:64
servant according to *thy m.* 124
thy m. endureth for ever. 138:8
and of *thy m.* cut off mine. 143:12

mercy seat

(*The golden covering of the ark of the covenant, in which the tables of the law were deposited*)
make a *m. seat* of gold. *Ex* 25:17
the cherubims covering the *m. seat*
with their wings. 20; *Heb* 9:5
m. seat between the cherubims.
Ex 25:22; *Lev* 16:2; *Num* 7:89
shalt put the *m. seat* upon the ark.
Ex 26:34; 40:20
made the *m. seat* of pure gold. 37:6
incense may cover *m. seat*. *Lev* 16:13
David gave Solomon the pattern of
the *m. seat*. *1 Chr* 28:11

Meribah

name of the place *M.* *Ex* 17:7
water of *M.* *Num* 20:13; 27:14
rebelled at water of *M.* 20:24
Deut 32:51; 33:8
thee at the waters of *M.* *Ps* 81:7

Merodach

Babylon taken, *M.* is. *Jer* 50:2

Merodach-baladan

M. sent letters and a. *Isa* 39:1

Merom

at the waters of *M.* *Josh* 11:5, 7

Meroz

Curse ye *M.* said angel. *Judg* 5:23

merrily

go in *m.* with the king. *Esth* 5:14

merry

they drank and were *m.* *Gen* 43:34
grapes, and made *m.* *Judg* 9:27*
when their hearts were *m.* 16:25
and let thine heart be *m.* 19:6
that thine heart may be *m.* 9
were making their hearts *m.* 22
Boaz, his heart was *m.* *Ruth* 3:7
Nabal's heart was *m.* *1 Sam* 25:36
Amnon's heart is *m.* *2 Sam* 13:28
Israel were making *m.* *1 Ki* 4:20
and let thine heart be *m.* 21:7
people away *m.* in heart. *2 Chr* 7:10*
heart of the king was *m.* *Esth* 1:10
m. heart maketh cheerful. *Pr* 15:13
he that is of a *m.* heart hath. 15*
a *m.* heart doeth good like a. 17:22
than to eat and be *m.* *Eccl* 8:15
drink thy wine with a *m.* heart. 9:7
laughter, wine maketh *m.* 10:19*
all the *m.*-hearted do sigh. *Isa* 24:7
them that make *m.* *Jer* 30:19
dances of them that make *m.* 31:4
eat, drink, and be *m.* *Luke* 12:19
let us eat and be *m.* 15:23, 24
I might make *m.* with my friends. 29
it was meet we should make *m.* 32
is any *m.*? let him sing. *Jas* 5:13*
over them and make *m.* *Rev* 11:10

Meshach, *see* **Abed-nego**

Meshech

M. the son of Japheth. *Gen* 10:2
1 Chr 1:5
Shem, Gether, and *M.* *1 Chr* 1:17
that I sojourn in *M.* *Ps* 120:5
Tubal and *M.* were thy. *Ezek* 27:13
there is *M.* 32:26
chief prince of *M.* 38:2, 3
the chief prince of *M.* and. 39:1

Mesopotamia

Eliezer went to *M.* to. *Gen* 24:10
they hired Balaam of *M.* *Deut* 23:4
Chushan-rishathaim king of *M.*
Judg 3:8
Lord delivered the king of *M.* 10
sent to hire chariots out of *M.*
1 Chr 19:6
the dwellers in *M.* we hear. *Acts* 2:9
God appeared to Abraham in *M.* 7:2

message

Ehud said, I have a *m.* from God.
Judg 3:20
had heard this *m.* *1 Ki* 20:12
that sendeth a *m.* by a fool. *Pr* 26:6
Haggai in the Lord's *m.* *Hag* 1:13
his citizens sent a *m.* *Luke* 19:14*
this is the *m.* which we have heard.
1 John 1:5; 3:11

messenger

sent a *m.* to Joseph. *Gen* 50:16*
the *m.* said, Israel. *1 Sam* 4:17
m. to David, saying. *2 Sam* 15:13
then Jezebel sent a *m.* *1 Ki* 19:2
the *m.* went to call Micaiah. 22:13
2 Chr 18:12
ere *m.* came to him, Elisha said,
When the *m.* cometh. *2 Ki* 6:32
the *m.* came to them, but. 9:18
there came a *m.* to Job. *Job* 1:14
a *m.* an interpreter of a. 33:23*
a wicked *m.* falleth into. *Pr* 13:17
a cruel *m.* shall be sent. 17:11
so is a faithful *m.* to them. 25:13
deaf, as my *m.* that I sent? *Isa* 42:19
one *m.* shall run to meet. *Jer* 51:31
unto whom a *m.* was sent. *Ezek* 23:40
Haggai, the Lord's *m.* *Hag* 1:13
for he is the *m.* of the Lord. *Mal* 2:7
will send my *m.* even the *m.* of. 3:1
Mat 11:10; *Mark* 1:2; *Luke* 7:27
the *m.* of Satan, to. *2 Cor* 12:7
in labour, but your *m.* *Phil* 2:25

messengers

Jacob sent *m.* before him. *Gen* 32:3
Moses sent *m.* from Kadesh.
Num 20:14; *Deut* 2:26
Israel sent *m.* unto Sihon, saying.
Num 21:21
Balak sent *m.* to Balaam. 22:5
spake I not also to thy *m.*? 24:12
Rahab hid the *m.* *Josh* 6:17, 25
Joshua sent *m.* to Achan's. 7:22
Gideon sent *m.* through. *Judg* 6:35
Jephthah sent *m.* to king. 11:12, 14
came the *m.* to Gibeah. *1 Sam* 11:4
Saul sent *m.* to Jesse, and. 16:19
Saul sent *m.* to David. 19:11, 14
15, 20, 21
David sent *m.* to salute our. 25:14
Abigail went after the *m.* 42
m. to Jabesh-gilead. *2 Sam* 2:5
Abner sent *m.* to David on. 3:12
David sent *m.* to Ish-bosheth. 14
Joab sent *m.* after Abner. 26
Hiram sent *m.* to David. 5:11
1 Chr 14:1
David sent *m.* to Bath-sheba, and.
2 Sam 11:4
Joab sent *m.* to David. 12:27
Ben-hadad sent *m.* to. *1 Ki* 20:2
go up to meet the *m.* *2 Ki* 1:3
sent *m.* to enquire of Baal-zebub. 16
Amaziah sent *m.* to Jehoash. 14:8
Ahaz sent *m.* to Tiglath-pileser. 16:7
Hoshea had sent *m.* to So. 17:4
Sennacherib sent *m.* to Hezekiah.
19:9; *Isa* 37:9
by thy *m.* hast thou reproached.
2 Ki 19:23
David sent *m.* to comfort Hanun.
1 Chr 19:2
sent to them by his *m.* *2 Chr* 36:15
but they mocked the *m.* of God. 16
wrath of a king is as *m.* *Pr* 16:14
what shall one answer *m.*? *Isa* 14:32
swift *m.* to nation scattered. 18:2
Hezekiah received letter from *m.*
37:14
the counsel of his *m.* 44:26
and thou didst send thy *m.* 57:9*
send by the hand of the *m.* *Jer* 27:3
sent *m.* unto them into. *Ezek* 23:16
in that day shall *m.* go forth. 30:9
the voice of thy *m.* be no. *Nah* 2:13
and when the *m.* of John. *Luke* 7:24
and sent *m.* before his face. 9:52
they are the *m.* of the. *2 Cor* 8:23
Rahab had received *m.* *Jas* 2:25

mess, or messes
sent *m.* to them, but Benjamin's *m.* five times so much. *Gen* 43:34
a *m.* of meat. *2 Sam* 11:8

Messiah
(*Literally, the Anointed One. It means the expected king and deliverer of the Hebrews, who should free them from the yoke of aliens, and make them a great nation ruling over the whole world.* Christ *is the same word in the Greek. Jesus of Nazareth, believed by his followers to be this long-promised Messiah of the Jews, is for that reason called Christ. The first promise of the Messiah, although not using that name, is that to Eve in* Gen 3:15. *The same promise was, in varying phraseology, repeated to many individuals through the ages, notably to Abraham and David*)
to build Jerusalem unto the *M.* the Prince. *Dan* 9:25*
and after 62 weeks shall *M.* be. 26*
found *M.* which is Christ. *John* 1:41
woman saith, I know that *M.* 4:25

met
and the angels of God *m.* *Gen* 32:1
thou by this drove I *m.*? 33:8
God of the Hebrews hath *m.* with us. *Ex* 3:18; 5:3
the Lord *m.* him, and sought. 4:24
Aaron went and *m.* Moses in. 27
they *m.* Moses and Aaron who. 5:20
God *m.* Balaam. *Num* 23:4, 16
because they *m.* you not. *Deut* 23:4 *Neh* 13:2
Amalek *m.* thee by way. *Deut* 25:18
all these kings were *m.* *Josh* 11:5
of prophets *m.* Saul. *1 Sam* 10:10
behold, Abigail *m.* David. 25:20
Ziba *m.* David with. *2 Sam* 16:1
Absalom *m.* the servants of. 18:9
a lion *m.* him. *1 Ki* 13:24
Elijah *m.* Obadiah, and he. 18:7
Ahaziah *m.* Jehu. *2 Ki* 9:21*
Jehu *m.* with the brethren. 10:13
mercy and truth are *m.* *Ps* 85:10
there *m.* him a woman. *Pr* 7:10
a lion, and bear *m.* him. *Amos* 5:19
m. him two possessed. *Mat* 8:28
behold, Jesus *m.* them, saying. 28:9
where two ways *m.* *Mark* 11:4*
much people *m.* him. *Luke* 9:37 *John* 12:18
there *m.* him ten men. *Luke* 17:12
then Martha went and *m.* him. *John* 11:20, 30
Cornelius *m.* him, and. *Acts* 10:25
damsel possessed *m.* us. 16:16
he disputed with them that *m.* 17:17
place where two seas *m.* 27:41
who *m.* Abraham. *Heb* 7:1
when Melchizedek *m.* him. 10

mete
when they did *m.* it with. *Ex* 16:18
I will *m.* out valley. *Ps* 60:6; 108:7
with what measure ye *m.* it shall be. *Mat* 7:2; *Mark* 4:24; *Luke* 6:38

meted
go to a nation *m.* out. *Isa* 18:2, 7
m. out heaven with a span. 40:12

meteyard
no unrighteousness in *m.* *Lev* 19:35

Metheg-ammah
David took *M.* from. *2 Sam* 8:1

Methuselah
Enoch begat *M.* *Gen* 5:21
M. begat Lamech. 25
days of *M.* were 969 years. 27
Henoch, *M.* Lamech. *1 Chr* 1:3
which was the son of *M.* *Luke* 3:37

Micah
mount Ephraim called *M.* *Judg* 17:1
man *M.* had an house of gods. 5
M. consecrated the Levite for. 12
thus dealeth *M.* 18:4
they set up *M.'s* graven image. 31
M. his son, Reaia his. *1 Chr* 5:5
Merib-baal begat *M.* 8:34; 9:40
sons of *M.* were Pithon, and Melech. *1 Chr* 8:35; 9:41
Mattaniah the son of *M.* 9:15
Abdon the son of *M.* *2 Chr* 34:20
M., Rehob, sealed the. *Neh* 10:11
M. the Morasthite prophesied in. *Jer* 26:18; *Mi* 1:1

Micaiah
M. the son of Imlah. *1 Ki* 22:8, 9 *2 Chr* 18:8
Zedekiah smote *M.* on. *1 Ki* 22:24
Take *M.*, and carry him back to Amon. 26; *2 Chr* 18:23, 25

mice
five golden *m.* *1 Sam* 6:4, 18
images of your emerods and *m.* 5

Michael
M. one of the chief. *Dan* 10:13
none holdeth with me but *M.* 21
at that time shall *M.* stand. 12:1
yet *M.* the archangel. *Jude* 9
M. and angels fought. *Rev* 12:7

Michaiah
mother was *M.* of Uriel. *2 Chr* 13:2
Jehoshaphat sent *M.* to teach. 17:7
son of *M.* to give. *Neh* 12:35, 41
M. heard what Baruch. *Jer* 36:11, 13

Michal
younger daughter *M.* *1 Sam* 14:49
M. Saul's daughter. 18:20, 28
so *M.* let David down. 19:12
M. took an image and laid. 13
Saul had given *M.* David's. 25:44
thou first bring *M.* *2 Sam* 3:13
deliver me my wife *M.* whom. 14
M. Saul's daughter looked . . . and despised. 6:16; *1 Chr* 15:29
M. had no child to. *2 Sam* 6:23
king took five sons of *M.* 21:8

midday
when *m.* was past. *1 Ki* 18:29
from morning to *m.* *Neh* 8:3
at *m.* O king, I saw in. *Acts* 26:13

middle
beginning of *m.* watch. *Judg* 7:19
there come people by the *m.* 9:37
hold of the two *m.* pillars. 16:29
of the *m.* of a sling. *1 Sam* 25:29
their garments in the *m.* *2 Sam* 10:4
the king did hallow the *m.* of the court. *1 Ki* 8:64; *2 Chr* 7:7
gone into the *m.* court. *2 Ki* 20:4
princes sat in the *m.* gate. *Jer* 39:3
were a wheel in the *m.* *Ezek* 1:16
broken down the *m.* wall. *Eph* 2:14

middlemost
higher than the *m.* *Ezek* 42:5, 6

Midian
dwelt in the land of *M.* *Ex* 2:15
Jethro priest of *M.* heard all. 18:1
said to the elders of *M.* *Num* 22:4
Zur of a chief house in *M.* 25:15
go and avenge the Lord of *M.* 31:3
they slew the kings of *M.* beside. 8
Israel took all the women of *M.* 9
delivered them to *M.* *Judg* 6:1, 2
hand hath God delivered *M.* 7:14
delivered us from *M.* 8:22; 9:17
M. subdued before Israel. 28
Edomites arose out of *M.* *1 Ki* 11:18
the yoke, as in day of *M.* *Isa* 9:4
the slaughter of *M.* at Oreb. 10:26
the dromedaries of *M.* shall. 60:6
curtains of the land of *M.* *Hab* 3:7

Midianites
by *M.* merchantmen. *Gen* 37:28
the *M.* sold him into Egypt to. 36
vex *M.* and smite them. *Num* 25:17
avenge Israel of the *M.* 31:2
to the Lord because of *M.* *Judg* 6:7
and thou shalt smite the *M.* 16
Israel pursued after the *M.* 7:23
princes of the *M.* Oreb, Zeeb. 25
wentest to fight with the *M.* 8:1
do to them as to the *M.* *Ps* 83:9

Midianitish
brought a *M.* woman. *Num* 25:6
of the *M.* woman was Cozbi. 15

midnight
at *m.* will I go into the. *Ex* 11:4
at *m.* the Lord smote the. 12:29
till *m.* and rose at *m.* *Judg* 16:3
at *m.* the man was afraid. *Ruth* 3:8
she arose at *m.* and. *1 Ki* 3:20
shall be troubled at *m.* *Job* 34:20
at *m.* I will rise to. *Ps* 119:62
at *m.* there was a cry. *Mat* 25:6
come at even, or *m.* *Mark* 13:35
at *m.* and say, Lend me. *Luke* 11:5
and at *m.* Paul and. *Acts* 16:25
continued his speech till *m.* 20:7

midst
dry through *m.* of sea. *Ex* 14:16 *Num* 33:8; *Neh* 9:11; *Ps* 136:14
take sickness from *m.* *Ex* 23:25
mountain burnt to the *m.* *Deut* 4:11
evil away from the *m.* of thee. 13:5
raise up a Prophet from *m.* 18:15
from the *m.* of the furnace of iron. *1 Ki* 8:51
brook that ran through the *m.* of. *2 Chr* 32:4
m. thereof being paved. *S of S* 3:10
purged blood from the *m.* *Isa* 4:4
breath shall reach to the *m.* 30:28
take away from the *m.* of thee. 58:9
proceed from the *m.* of. *Jer* 30:21
come from the *m.* of Sihon. 48:45
through the *m.* of the city. *Ezek* 9:4
glory went up from *m.* of city. 11:23
I will cut him off from *m.* 14:8, 9
m. of it is burnt, is it meet? 15:4
have filled the *m.* of thee. 28:16
I will bring forth a fire from *m.* of. 18
of the *m.* of the fire. *Dan* 3:26
judge from *m.* thereof. *Amos* 2:3
passing through the *m.* *Luke* 4:30
about the *m.* of the feast. *John* 7:14
going through the *m.* of them. 8:59
angel flying through the *m.* *Rev* 8:13

in the midst
be a firmament *in the m.* *Gen* 1:6
the tree of life *in the m.* 2:9; 3:3
Abram divided them *in the m.* 15:10
wonders I will do *in the m.* *Ex* 3:20
I am the Lord *in the m.* of. 8:22
overthrew Egyptians *in the m.* 14:27
walked on dry land *in the m.* of sea. 29; 15:19
for I will not go up *in the m.* 33:3
in the m. of their uncleanness. *Lev* 16:16
set forward *in the m.* of camp. *Num* 2:17
defile not the camp *in the m.* 5:3
and the city shall be *in the m.* 35:5 *Ezek* 48:15
acts which he did *in the m.* of. *Deut* 11:3
swallowed them up *in the m.* 6
separate three cities *in the m.* 19:2
God walketh *in the m.* of. 23:14
priests stood firm *in the m.* of Jordan. *Josh* 3:17; 4:10
set up twelve stones *in the m.* 4:9
accursed thing *in the m.* of. 7:13
are hid in the earth *in the m.* 21
anointed him *in the m.* *1 Sam* 16:13
was yet alive *in the m.* *2 Sam* 18:14
stood *in the m.* of the ground. 23:12
a lion *in the m.* of a pit in time. 20
they were *in the m.* of Samaria. *2 Ki* 6:20
their garments *in the m.* *1 Chr* 19:4
till we come *in the m.* *Neh* 4:11
it is melted *in the m.* of. *Ps* 22:14
will declare thy name: *in the m.* of the congregation. 22; *Heb* 2:12
God is *in the m.* of her, she. *Ps* 46:5
mischief *in the m.* 55:10
wickedness *in the m.* 11
enemies roar *in the m.* of. 74:4
working salvation *in the m.* 12
and he let it fall *in the m.* 78:28
take me not away *in the m.* 102:24
rule thou *in the m.* of thine. 110:2
pay vows *in the m.* of thee. 116:19
I walk *in the m.* of trouble. 138:7
keep them *in the m.* of. *Pr* 4:21
I was in all evil *in the m.* 5:14
I lead *in the m.* of the paths. 8:20
which is *in the m.* of fools. 14:33
he that lieth down *in the m.* 23:34
the way of a ship *in the m.* 30:19

a tower *in the m.* of it. *Isa* 5:2
I dwell *in the m.* of a people. 6:5
forsaking *in the m.* of the land. 12
set a king *in the m.* of it, the. 7:6
Holy One *in the m.* 12:6; *Hos* 11:9
in the m. of the noon day. *Isa* 16:3
blessing *in the m.* of the land. 19:24
fountains *in the m.* of thee. 41:18
oppression *in the m.* of her. *Jer* 6:6
is *in the m.* of deceit. 9:6
O Lord, art *in the m.* of us. 14:9
in the m. of his days. 17:11
in the m. of the people. 37:12
the just *in the m.* of her. *Lam* 4:13
in the m. of the nations. *Ezek* 5:5
will execute judgement *in the m.* 8
fall *in the m.* of you. 6:7; 11:7
in the m. of Babylon he. 17:16
sheddeth blood *in the m.* 22:3
ye shall be melted *in the m.* 21
as silver is melted *in the m.* of. 22
many widows *in the m.* thereof. 25
her princes *in the m.* thereof. 27
thus have they done *in the m.* 23:39
for spreading of nets *in the m.* 26:5
be glorified *in the m.* of thee. 28:22
profaned *in the m.* of them. 36:23
sanctuary *in the m.* of them. 37:26
my sanctuary shall be *in the m.* 28
dwell *in the m.* of Israel. 43:7, 9
and the prince *in the m.* 46:10
men walking *in the m.* *Dan* 3:25
in the m. of the week. 9:27
whoredoms is *in the m.* *Hos* 5:4
I am *in the m.* of Israel. *Joel* 2:27
conspired *in the m.* of. *Amos* 7:10
remnant be *in the m.* of. *Mi* 5:7, 8
thy casting down shall be *in the m.* of thee. 6:14
people *in the m.* of thee. *Nah* 3:13
in the m. of the years. *Hab* 3:2
lie down *in the m.* of her. *Zeph* 2:14
just Lord is *in the m.* thereof. 3:5
I will leave *in the m.* of thee a. 12
king of Israel, even the Lord, is *in the m.* of thee. 15, 17
glory *in the m.* of her. *Zech* 2:5
will dwell *in the m.* of thee. 10, 11
remain *in the m.* of his house. 5:4
sitteth *in the m.* of the ephah. 7
in the m. of Jerusalem. 8:3, 8
mount of Olives shall cleave *in the m.* thereof. 14:4
sheep *in the m.* of wolves. *Mat* 10:16
ship was *in the m.* of the sea. 14:24
Mark 6:47
set a little child *in the m.* of them.
Mat 18:2; *Mark* 9:36
am I *in the m.* of them. *Mat* 18:20
in the m. of the doctors. *Luke* 2:46
rise, and stand forth *in the m.* 6:8
let them which are *in the m.* 21:21
the vail was rent *in the m.* 23:45
Jesus himself stood *in the m.*
24:36; *John* 20:19, 26
had set her *in the m.* *John* 8:3, 9
one, and Jesus *in the m.* 19:18
Peter stood up *in the m.* *Acts* 1:15
falling, he burst asunder *in the m.* 18
then Paul stood up *in the m.* 17:22
blameless *in the m.* of a. *Phil* 2:15
in the m. of the seven candlesticks.
Rev 1:13; 2:1
in the m. of the Paradise of. 2:7
in the m. of the throne were. 4:6
in the m. of the throne stood. 5:6
7:17

***into the* midst**

Israel went *into the m.* *Ex* 14:22
and Moses went *into the m.* 24:18
I will come *into the m.* of thee. 33:5
Aaron ran *into the m.* *Num* 16:47
blood ran *into the m.* *1 Ki* 22:35
Mordecai went *into the m.* of the city. *Esth* 4:1
carried *into the m.* of sea. *Ps* 46:2
into the m. whereof they are. 57:6
I will assemble them *into the m.*
Jer 21:4
cast it *into the m.* of river. 51:63
into the m. of the fire. *Ezek* 5:4
I will gather you *into the m.* 22:19
into the m. of a fiery. *Dan* 3:6
and he cast it *into the m.* *Zech* 5:8

***out of the* midst**

sent Lot *out of the m.* *Gen* 19:29
angel appeared *out of the m.* of a bush. *Ex* 3:2
God called to him *out of the m.* of bush. 4; 24:16
spake unto you *out of the m.* of fire.
Deut 4:12; 15, 33, 36; 5:4, 22, 24
take him a nation *out of the m.* 4:34
take *out of the m.* of Jordan twelve stones. *Josh* 4:3, 8
they took them *out of the m.* 7:23
cometh *out of the m.* of pit. *Isa* 24:18
depart, go *out of the m.* of her. 52:11
Jer 50:8; 51:6, 45
forth *out of the m.* of it. *Ezek* 11:7
I will bring thee *out of the m.* 29:4
to him *out of the m.* of hell. 32:21
eat calves *out of the m.* *Amos* 6:4
cut off horses *out of the m.* *Mi* 5:10
pluck up groves *out of the m.* 14
take away *out of the m.* *Zeph* 3:11

midwive

the *m.* said unto Rachel. *Gen* 35:17
the *m.* bound on his hand a. 38:28
ye do the office of a *m.* *Ex* 1:16

midwives

but the *m.* feared God. *Ex* 1:17, 21
are delivered ere the *m.* come. 19
God dealt well with the *m.* 20

might, ***substantive***

art my firstborn, my *m.* *Gen* 49:3
this people in thy *m.* *Num* 14:13
according to thy *m.* *Deut* 3:24
love thy God with all thy *m.* 6:5
the *m.* of mine hand hath. 8:17
be no *m.* in thine hand. 28:32
goeth forth in his *m.* *Judg* 5:31
go in this thy *m.* 6:14
bowed with his *m.* 16:30
danced with all *his m.* *2 Sam* 6:14
Asa, and all his *m.* *1 Ki* 15:23
Baasha, and his *m.* 16:5
Omri and his *m.* 27
Jehoshaphat and his *m.* that. 22:45
Jehu and all his *m.* *2 Ki* 10:34
Jehoahaz and his *m.* 13:8
acts of Jehoash and his *m.* 14:15
Hezekiah and his *m.* 20:20
to the Lord with all his *m.* 23:25
captive all the men of *m.* 24:16
men of *m.* came to David. *1 Chr* 12:8
for the house with all my *m.* 29:2
in thine hand is power and *m.* 12
2 Chr 20:6
acts of David . . . with all his reign and his *m.* *1 Chr* 29:30
we have no *m.* against. *2 Chr* 20:12
his power and *m.* *Esth* 10:2
none of the men of *m.* *Ps* 76:5
men shall speak of the *m.* 145:6
to do, do it with thy *m.* *Eccl* 9:10
the spirit of counsel and *m.* *Isa* 11:2
near, acknowledge my *m.* 33:13
by the greatness of his *m.* 40:26
no *m.* he increaseth strength. 29
mighty man glory in his *m.* *Jer* 9:23
and thy name is great in *m.* 10:6
cause them to know my *m.* 16:21
break the chief of their *m.* 49:35
m. hath failed, they became. 51:30
ashamed of their *m.* *Ezek* 32:30
for wisdom and *m.* are. *Dan* 2:20
O God, who hast given me *m.* 23
that I have built by the *m.* 4:30
full of judgement and of *m.* *Mi* 3:8
be confounded at all their *m.* 7:16
not by *m.* nor by power, but. *Zech* 4:6
far above all *m.*, power. *Eph* 1:21
strengthened with *m.* 3:16; *Col* 1:11
and in power of his *m.* *Eph* 6:10
whereas angels, which are greater in *m.* *2 Pet* 2:11
m. be unto our God. *Rev* 7:12

might ***be***

I would it *m. be* according to.
Gen 30:34
tent, that it *m. be* one. *Ex* 36:18
it *m. be* above the curious. 39:21
that I *m. be* their God. *Lev* 26:45
fear me, that it *m. be*. *Deut* 5:29
that he *m. be* the king's. *1 Sam* 18:27
that my name *m. be*. *1 Ki* 8:16
windows, *m.* this thing *be*. *2 Ki* 7:2
silver, that his hand *m. be*. 15:19
my name *m. be* there. *2 Chr* 6:5, 6
m. not *be* as their fathers. *Ps* 78:8
that they *m. be* unto me. *Jer* 13:11
in good soil, that it *m. be*. *Ezek* 17:8
that ye *m. be* a possession to. 36:3
that my covenant *m. be*. *Mal* 2:4
prayed that he *m. be* with him.
Mark 5:18; *Luke* 8:38
what *m.* this parable *be*? *Luke* 8:9
that your joy *m. be* full. *John* 15:11
m. be the father of them. *Rom* 4:11
that it *m. be* of grace. 16
m. be Lord both of dead and. 14:9
m. not *be* chargeable. *2 Thes* 3:8
though I *m. be* much bold. *Philem* 8
m. be a merciful Priest. *Heb* 2:17
we *m. be* partakers of his. 12:10
and hope *m. be* in God. *1 Pet* 1:21
see **fulfilled**

mightier

for thou art much *m.* *Gen* 26:16
children of Israel are *m.* *Ex* 1:9
nation and *m.* than they. *Num* 14:12
Deut 4:38; 7:1; 9:1, 14; 11:23
the Lord on high is *m.* *Ps* 93:4
contend with him that is *m.* *Eccl* 6:10
he that cometh after me is *m.* than I.
Mat 3:11; *Mark* 1:7; *Luke* 3:16

mighties

one of the three *m.* *1 Chr* 11:12
these things did these three *m.* 19
had a name among the three *m.* 24

mightily

that ye may increase *m.* *Deut* 6:3
Jabin *m.* oppressed Israel. *Judg* 4:3
came *m.* on Samson. 14:6; 15:14
the Lord shall *m.* roar. *Jer* 25:30
let man and beast cry *m.* *Jonah* 3:8
fortify thy power *m.* *Nah* 2:1
m. convinced the Jews. *Acts* 18:28
so *m.* grew the word of God. 19:20
which worketh in me *m.* *Col* 1:29
cried *m.* saying, Babylon. *Rev* 18:2

mighty

he was a *m.* hunter. *Gen* 10:9
become a great and *m.* nation. 18:18
hear us: thou art a *m.* prince. 23:6
of Israel waxed *m.* *Ex* 1:7, 20
be no more *m.* thunderings. 9:28
the Lord turned a *m.* strong. 10:19
as lead in the *m.* waters. 15:10
nor shall honour the person of the *m.*
Lev 19:15
people, for they are too *m.* *Num* 22:6
he brought thee out with *m.* power.
Deut 4:37; 9:29
shall destroy them with a *m.* 7:23
great nation, *m.* and populous. 26:5
have dominion over the *m.* *Judg* 5:13
help of the Lord against the *m.* 23
hand of these *m.* gods. *1 Sam* 4:8
how are *m.* fallen! *2 Sam* 1:19, 25
the shield of the *m.* is vilely. 21
the slain, from fat of the *m.* 22
m. of the land carried. *2 Ki* 24:15
Nimrod was *m.* *1 Chr* 1:10
Zadok was *m.* 12:28
Benaiah was *m.* 27:6
Abijah was *m.* *2 Chr* 13:21
made war with *m.* power. 26:13
so Jotham became *m.* 27:6
there have been *m.* kings. *Ezra* 4:20
mercy to me before *m.* princes. 7:28
repaired to house of the *m.* *Neh* 3:16
a stone in the *m.* waters. 9:11
the poor from the *m.* *Job* 5:15
from the hand of the *m.*? 6:23
he is wise in heart, and *m.* 9:4
and he overthroweth the *m.* 12:19
the strength of the *m.* 21
the wicked *m.* in power? 21:7
draweth also the *m.* with. 24:22
the *m.* shall be taken away. 34:20
by reason of the arm of the *m.* 35:9
he raiseth himself, the *m.* 41:25
and *m.*, Lord *m.* in battle. *Ps* 24:8
give to the Lord, O ye *m.* 29:1
sword on thy thigh, O most *m.* 45:3
for lo, the *m.* are gathered. 59:3
his voice, and that a *m.* voice. 68:33

enemies wrongfully are *m.* *Ps* 69:4
thou driest up *m.* rivers. 74:15
in the congregation of the *m.* 82:1
among sons *m.* can be likened ? 89:6
thou hast a *m.* arm. 13
laid help upon one that is *m.* 19
bosom the reproach of the *m.* 50
mightier than the *m.* waves. 93:4
make his *m.* power known. 106:8
his seed shall be *m.* upon. 112:2
sharp arrows of the *m.* with. 120:4
nations, and slew *m.* kings. 135:10
he that is slow to anger is better than the *m.* *Pr* 16:32
the lot parteth between the *m.* 18:18
scaleth the city of the *m.* 21:22
for their Redeemer is *m.* 23:11*
m. shall fall in the war. *Isa* 3:25
that are *m.* to drink wine. 5:22
his *m.* wind shall he shake. 11:15
like the rushing of *m.* waters. 17:12
away with a *m.* captivity. 22:17
prey be taken from the *m.*? 49:24
in righteousness, *m.* to save. 63:1
a *m.* and an ancient nation. *Jer* 5:15
great in counsel and *m.* 32:19
shew thee great and *m.* things. 33:3
hath also taken the *m.* *Ezek* 17:13
by the swords of the *m.* will. 32:12
the strong among the *m.* shall. 21
shall not lie with the *m.* that. 27
with a great and *m.* army. 38:15
eat the flesh of the *m.* and. 39:18
how great and *m.* are his. *Dan* 4:3
his power shall be *m.* but not. 8:24
a *m.* king shall stand up that. 11:3
a very great and *m.* army. 25
the *m.* deliver himself. *Amos* 2:14
courageous among the *m.* 2:16
I know your *m.* sins. 5:12
righteousness as a *m.* stream. 24
a *m.* tempest in the sea. *Jonah* 1:4
howl, because the *m.* *Zech* 11:2
most of his *m.* works. *Mat* 11:20
if the *m.* works which were. 21, 23
this man these *m.* works ? 13:54
he did not many *m.* works there. 58 *Mark* 6:5
Baptist risen; therefore *m.* works do shew forth. *Mat* 14:2; *Mark* 6:14
m. works are wrought by. *Mark* 6:2
he that is *m.* hath done. *Luke* 1:49
he hath put down the *m.* from. 52
amazed at *m.* power of God. 9:43
there arose a *m.* famine in. 15:14
praised God for the *m.* works. 19:37
who was a prophet *m.* in deed. 24:19
as of a rushing *m.* wind. *Acts* 2:2
Moses was *m.* in words and. 7:22
Apollos, *m.* in the scriptures. 18:24
Gentiles obedient through *m.* signs. *Rom* 15:19
not many *m.* not many. *1 Cor* 1:26
weak, to confound things *m.* 27
weapons of our warfare are *m.* through God. *2 Cor* 10:4
is not weak, but *m.* in you. 13:3
same was *m.* in me toward. *Gal* 2:8
working of his *m.* power. *Eph* 1:19
Jesus shall be revealed with his *m.* angels. *2 Thes* 1:7
shaken of a *m.* wind. *Rev* 6:13
I saw another *m.* angel. 10:1; 18:21
so *m.* an earthquake and. 16:18
Alas, Babylon, that *m.* city ! 18:10
voice of *m.* thunderings. 19:6
see **acts, God, hand, man, men**

mighty *one*

Nimrod began to be a *m. one.* *Gen* 10:8
the *m. one* of Israel. *Isa* 1:24
30:29; 49:26; 60:16
Lebanon shall fall by *m. one.* 10:34
Lord hath a *m.* and strong *one.* 28:2
me as a *m.* terrible *one.* *Jer* 20:11
him into hand of *m. one.* *Ezek* 31:11

mighty *ones*

prancing of their *m. ones.* *Judg* 5:22
I have called my *m. ones.* *Isa* 13:3
their *m. ones* are beaten. *Jer* 46:5
thither cause thy *m. ones.* *Joel* 3:11

Milcah

M. daughter of Haran. *Gen* 11:29
M. also bare children. *Gen* 22:20, 23
Bethuel son of *M.* the wife. 24:15
daughter's name was *M.* *Num* 26:33

milch

thirty *m.* camels with. *Gen* 32:15
make a new cart, take two *m.* kine. *2 Sam* 6:7, 10

Milcom

Solomon went after *M.* *1 Ki* 11:5
they have worshipped *M.* god. 33
had builded for *M.* *2 Ki* 23:13

mildew, *see* **blasting**

mile

compel thee to go a *m.* *Mat* 5:41

Miletum

have I left at *M.* sick. *2 Tim* 4:20

Miletus

next day we came to *M.* *Acts* 20:15
from *M.* he sent to Ephesus to. 17

milk

An important article of food in the East. Not only the milk of cows, but also that of sheep, Deut 32:14, *of camels,* Gen 32:15, *and of goats,* Pr 27:27, *was used. The latter was most highly esteemed.*

took butter and *m.* *Gen* 18:8
teeth shall be white with *m.* 49:12
butter of kine and *m.* *Deut* 32:14
Jael opened a bottle of *m.* *Judg* 4:19
water, and she gave him *m.* 5:25
poured me out as *m.*? *Job* 10:10
his breasts are full of *m.* 21:24
thou shalt have goats' *m.* *Pr* 27:27
the churning of *m.* bringeth. 30:33
honey and *m.* are under. *S of S* 4:11
drunk my wine with my *m.* 5:1
his eyes washed with *m.* and. 12
for abundance of *m.* that. *Isa* 7:22
are weaned from the *m.* 28:9
come, buy wine and *m.* without. 55:1
thou shalt suck the *m.* of. 60:16
were whiter than *m.* *Lam* 4:7
fruit, and drink thy *m.* *Ezek* 25:4
hills shall flow with *m.* *Joel* 3:18
I have fed you with *m.* *1 Cor* 3:2
flock, and eateth not of the *m.*? 9:7
such as have need of *m.* *Heb* 5:12
that useth *m.* is a babe. 13
desire sincere *m.* of word. *1 Pet* 2:2
also Deut 14:21

milk

that ye may *m.* out and. *Isa* 66:11

mill, -s

that is behind the *m.* *Ex* 11:5
ground the manna in *m.* *Num* 11:8
shall be grinding at the *m.* *Mat* 24:41

millet

take lentiles, *m.* and. *Ezek* 4:9

millions

be thou mother of thousands of *m.* *Gen* 24:60

Millo

all the house of *M.* *Judg* 9:6
let fire devour the house of *M.* 20
built round about from *M.* *2 Sam* 5:9
of the levy to build *M.* *1 Ki* 9:15
did Solomon build *M.* 24; 11:27
Joash in the house of *M.* *2 Ki* 12:20

millstone

no man shall take the *m.* *Deut* 24:6
woman cast a piece of *m.* *Judg* 9:53 *2 Sam* 11:21
a piece of the nether *m.* *Job* 41:24
a *m.* were hanged about his neck. *Mat* 18:6; *Mark* 9:42; *Luke* 17:2
a stone like a great *m.* *Rev* 18:21
sound of a *m.* shall be heard. 22

millstones

the *m.* and grind meal. *Isa* 47:2
away the sound of the *m.* *Jer* 25:10

mincing

wanton eyes, walking and *m.* *Isa* 3:16

mind, *substantive*

a grief of *m.* to Isaac. *Gen* 26:35
m. of the Lord might. *Lev* 24:12*
all the desire of his *m.* *Deut* 18:6*
give thee sorrow of *m.* 28:65*
shalt call them to *m.* among. 30:1
him with a willing *m.* *1 Chr* 28:9
people had a *m.* to work. *Neh* 4:6
but he is in one *m.* who ? *Job* 23:13
dead man out of *m.* *Ps* 31:12
with a wicked *m.* *Pr* 21:27
all his *m.* but a wise man. 29:11*
perfect peace, whose *m.* *Isa* 26:3
bring it again to *m.* O ye. 46:8
shall not come into *m.* 65:17
covenant shall not come to *m.* *Jer* 3:16
and came it not into his *m.*? 44:21
his *m.* was hardened. *Dan* 5:20*
then shall his *m.* change. *Hab* 1:11
clothed, and in his right *m.* *Mark* 5:15; *Luke* 8:35
called to *m.* the words. *Mark* 14:72
Mary cast in her *m.* *Luke* 1:29
neither be ye of doubtful *m.* 12:29
received word with all readiness of *m.* *Acts* 17:11
serve with humility of *m.* 20:19
given up to a reprobate *m.* *Rom* 1:28
with the *m.* I serve the law. 7:25
carnal *m.* is enmity against. 8:7
he knoweth what is the *m.* of. 27
who hath known the *m.* of ? 11:34
be of the same *m.* one toward. 12:16
fully persuaded in his own *m.* 14:5
with one *m.* glorify God. 15:6
together in the same *m.* *1 Cor* 1:10
known the *m.* of the Lord ? . . . but we have the *m.* of Christ. 2:16
your fervent *m.* toward me. *2 Cor* 7:7
there be first a willing *m.* 8:12*
brethren, be of one *m.* 13:11 *Phil* 1:27*; 2:2
desires of the flesh and *m.* *Eph* 2:3
walk in vanity of their *m.* 4:17
in lowliness of *m.* let each. *Phil* 2:3
let this *m.* be in you which. 5
that they be of the same *m.* 4:2
puffed up by his fleshly *m.* *Col* 2:18
humbleness of *m.*, meekness. 3:12*
not soon shaken in *m.* *2 Thes* 2:2
God hath given us the spirit of a sound *m.* *2 Tim* 1:7*
their *m.* and conscience. *Tit* 1:15
put them in *m.* to be subject. 3:1
put my laws into their *m.* *Heb* 8:10
be ye all of one *m.* *1 Pet* 3:8
likewise with the same *m.* 4:1
not for lucre, but of a ready *m.* 5:2
here is the *m.* which hath. *Rev* 17:9
these have one *m.* and shall give. 13
see **alienated**

mine or *my* **mind**

not done them of *mine* own *m.* *Num* 16:28
good or bad of *mine* own *m.* 24:13
that which is in *my m.* *1 Sam* 2:35
was in *my m.* to build. *1 Chr* 22:7*
my m. could not be toward. *Jer* 15:1
nor came it into *my m.* 19:5; 32:35
this I recall to *my m.* *Lam* 3:21
another law warring against the law of *my m.* *Rom* 7:23

thy **mind**

not *thy m.* on the asses. *1 Sam* 9:20
be according to *thy m.*? *Job* 34:33
things come into *thy m.* *Ezek* 38:10
thoughts came into *thy m.* *Dan* 2:29
love the Lord thy God with all *thy m.* *Mat* 22:37; *Mark* 12:30 *Luke* 10:27
without *thy m.* would. *Philem* 14

your **mind**

if it be *your m.* I should. *Gen* 23:8
let Jerusalem come into *your m.* *Jer* 51:50
that come into *your m.* *Ezek* 11:5
which cometh into *your m.* 20:32
by renewing of *your m.* *Rom* 12:2
of *your* ready *m.* *2 Cor* 8:19
forwardness of *your m.* 9:2
in the spirit of *your m.* *Eph* 4:23
sometime alienated and enemies in *your m.* *Col* 1:21
up the loins of *your m.* *1 Pet* 1:13

mind, *verb*

are after flesh, *m.* things. *Rom* 8:5
m. not high things, but. 12:16
nevertheless let us *m.* *Phil* 3:16
for many walk, who *m.* earthly. 19

minded

stedfastly m. to go with. Ruth 1:18
Joash was m. to repair. 2 Chr 24:4
which are m. of their own free will. Ezra 7:13
Joseph was m. to put. Mat 1:19
for to be carnally m. is death, but to be spiritually m. is. Rom 8:6*
be not high-m. but fear. 11:20
grant you to be like m. one. 15:5
this confidence I was m. 2 Cor 1:15
when I was thus m. did I use. 17
will be no otherwise m. Gal 5:10
that ye be like m. having. Phil 2:2
no man like m. who will care. 20
be thus m. if in any thing ye be otherwise m. God will reveal. 3:15
comfort the feeble-m. 1 Thes 5:14
the rich be not high-m. 1 Tim 6:17
shall be heady, high-m. 2 Tim 3:4
exhort to be sober m. Tit 2:6
a double m. man is unstable. Jas 1:8
your hearts, ye double m. 4:8

mindful

be ye m. always of his. 1 Chr 16:15*
our fathers were not m. of. Neh 9:17
what is man, that thou art m. of him, and son of man? Ps 8:4; Heb 2:6
be m. of his covenant. Ps 111:5
Lord hath been m. of us, he. 115:12
not been m. of the rock. Isa 17:10
being m. of thy tears. 2 Tim 1:4*
if they had been m. of that country. Heb 11:15
m. of the words spoken. 2 Pet 3:2

minding

Paul m. himself to go afoot. Acts 20:13

minds

and speak your m. Judg 19:30
be chafed in their m. 2 Sam 17:8
if it be your m. let none go forth. 2 Ki 9:15
they set their m. Ezek 24:25*
with despiteful m. to cast it. 36:5*
and made their m. evil. Acts 14:2
they changed their m., and said. 28:6
but their m. were blinded. 2 Cor 3:14
world hath blinded the m. 4:4
your m. should be corrupted. 11:3
God shall keep your m. Phil 4:7
men of corrupt m. 1 Tim 6:5
2 Tim 3:8
in their m. will I write. Heb 10:16
wearied and faint in your m. 12:3*
I stir up your pure m. by. 2 Pet 3:1

mine

that thou seest is m. Gen 31:43
m. as Reuben and Simeon shall be m. 48:5
firstborn, both of man and beast, it is m. Ex 13:2; 34:19; Num 3:13
for all the earth is m. Ex 19:5
Ps 50:12
that ye should be m. Lev 20:26
Isa 43:1
the land is m. for ye are. Lev 25:23
the Levites shall be m. Num 3:12
45; 8:14
of children of Israel are m. 8:17
Joab's field is near m. 2 Sam 14:30
the kingdom was m. 1 Ki 2:15
let it be neither m. nor thine. 3:26
gold, and wives, are m. 20:3
if ye will be m. and if. 2 Ki 10:6
is under heaven is m. Job 41:11
myself from m. iniquity. Ps 18:23
beast of the forest is m. 50:10
wild beasts of field are m. 11
Gilead is m. and Manasseh is m. 60:7; 108:8
counsel is m. and sound. Pr 8:14
my beloved is m. and I am his. S. of S. 2:16; 6:3
my vineyard, which is m. 8:12
word shall stand, m. or. Jer 44:28
thee, thou becamest m. Ezek 16:8
souls are m.; soul of son is m. 18:4
and they were m. 23:4
when she was m. 5
the river is m. 29:9
these countries be m. 35:10
is m. and the gold is m. Hag 2:8
they shall be m. saith. Mal 3:17
heareth sayings of m. Mat 7:24
heareth these sayings of m. and. 26
my right hand and on my left, is not m. to give. 20:23; Mark 10:40
for a friend of m. in his journey is come to me. Luke 11:6
Jesus saith, M. hour. John 2:4
my doctrine is not m. 7:16
am known of m. 10:14
word which ye hear is not m. 14:24
he shall receive of m. 16:14
that the Father hath are m. 15
m. are thine, and thine are m. 17:10
vengeance is m., I will repay. Rom 12:19
in every prayer of m. Phil 1:4

mingle

men of strength to m. Isa 5:22
m. with the seed of. Dan 2:43

mingled

there was fire m. with. Ex 9:24
sow thy field with m. Lev 19:19
holy seed have m. Ezra 9:2
and m. my drink with. Ps 102:9
m. among the heathen. 106:35
she hath m. her wine. Pr 9:2
the wine which I have m. 5
Lord hath m. a perverse. Isa 19:14
cup to all m. people. Jer 25:20, 24
a sword on all the m. people. 50:37
Ezek 30:5
gave him vinegar m. Mat 27:34
gave him wine m. with. Mark 15:23
blood Pilate had m. Luke 13:1
followed hail and fire m. Rev 8:7
as it were a sea of glass m. 15:2

minish, -ed

(*American Revision*, diminish)
ye shall not m. aught of. Ex 5:19
are m. and brought low. Ps 107:39

minister

Used in the Bible mainly in the archaic sense of one who serves, waits on, or attends another, Ex 24:13; 1 Ki 10:5. *It is applied,* [1] *To Christ, when comparing him with the Hebrew high priest,* Heb 8:2. [2] *To those who were to care for the work of the gospel,* 1 Cor 4:1. [3] *To magistrates,* Rom 13:6. [4] *To the angels,* Ps 104:4.

rose, and his m. Joshua. Ex 24:13
spake to Joshua, Moses' m. Josh 1:1
let him be your m. Mat 20:26
Mark 10:43
book again to the m. Luke 4:20*
also John to their m. Acts 13:5*
to make thee a m. and a. 26:16
the m. of God to thee. Rom 13:4, 6
Christ was a m. of the. 15:8
I should be the m. of Jesus to. 16
is Christ the m. of sin? Gal 2:17
whereof I was made a m. Eph 3:7
Col 1:23, 25
Tychicus, a faithful m. of the Lord. Eph 6:21; Col 4:7
who is for you a faithful m. Col 1:7
brother and m. of God. 1 Thes 3:2
a good m. of Christ. 1 Tim 4:6
a m. of the sanctuary. Heb 8:2

minister, *verb*

m. to me in the priest's. Ex 28:1
3, 4, 41; 29:1, 44; 30:30; 31:10
35:19; 39:41; 40:13, 15
shall be upon Aaron to m. 28:35
when they come to altar to m. 43
29:30; 30:20
I will sanctify Aaron to m. 29:44
he presented them to m. Lev 7:35
whom he shall consecrate to m. 16:32; Num 3:3
m. with their brethren. Num 8:26
tribe of Levi to m. to. Deut 10:8
to stand to m. in the name. 18:5, 7
God hath chosen them to m. 21:5
child did m. to the. 1 Sam 2:11
could not stand to m. because of the. 1 Ki 8:11; 2 Chr 5:14
chosen to m. before him. 1 Chr 15:2
to m. and to give thanks. 1 Chr 23:13
2 Chr 31:2
priests which m. are. 2 Chr 13:10
he shall m. judgement to. Ps 9:8
rams of Nebaioth shall m. Isa 60:7
their kings shall m. to thee. 10
multiply Levites that m. Jer 33:22
which come near to m. Ezek 40:46
41:15, 16
stand before them to m. 44:11
not to be ministered unto, but to m. Mat 20:28; Mark 10:45
sick, and did not m.? Mat 25:44
his acquaintance to m. to him. Acts 24:23
I go to m. to the saints. Rom 15:25
duty is to m. to them in carnal. 27
they which m. about holy. 1 Cor 9:13
both m. bread for your. 2 Cor 9:10*
that it may m. grace. Eph 4:29*
which m. questions. 1 Tim 1:4
angels sent to m. to. Heb 1:14*
to the saints, and do m. 6:10
but to us they did m. the. 1 Pet 1:12
even so m. the same one to. 4:10
if any man m. let him do it as. 11

ministered

Eleazar and Ithamar m. Num 3:4
Deut 10:6
Samuel m. before. 1 Sam 2:18; 3:1
his servant that m. 2 Sam 13:17
Abishag m. to David. 1 Ki 1:4, 15
after Elijah, and m. to him. 19:21
snuffers, and all vessels wherewith they m. 2 Ki 25:14; Jer 52:18
m. to them before their. Ezek 44:12
thousand thousands m. Dan 7:10
angels came and m. to him. Mat 4:11; Mark 1:13
she arose and m. unto them. Mat 8:15; Mark 1:31
which m. to him of their substance. Luke 8:3
as they m. and fasted. Acts 13:2
these hands have m. to my. 20:34
epistle of Christ m. by us. 2 Cor 3:3
he that m. to my wants. Phil 2:25
having nourishment m. Col 2:19*
how many things he m. 2 Tim 1:18
stead he might have m. Philem 13
m. to the saints, and. Heb 6:10
an entrance shall be m. 2 Pet 1:11*

ministereth

now he that m. seed. 2 Cor 9:10
he that m. to you the Spirit. Gal 3:5*

ministering

charge of m. vessels. 1 Chr 9:28*
gates of house, m. to. Ezek 44:11
women followed Jesus m. to him. Mat 27:55
let us wait on our m. Rom 12:7
m. the gospel. 15:16
on us the m. to the saints. 2 Cor 8:4
for as touching m. to the saints. 9:1
are they not all m. spirits? Heb 1:14
priest standeth daily m. 10:11

ministers

the attendance of his m. 1 Ki 10:5
2 Chr 9:4
to impose toll on m. Ezra 7:24*
bring unto us m. for house. 8:17
ye m. of his that do. Ps 103:21
who maketh his m. a flaming fire. 104:4; Heb 1:7
men shall call you the m. Isa 61:6
covenant be broken with David my servant, and with my m. Jer 33:21
be m. in my sanctuary. Ezek 44:11
holy portion for the m. of. 45:4
the Lord's m. mourn. Joel 1:9
howl, ye m. 13
m. weep between the porch. 2:17
beginning were m. of word. Luke 1:2
God's m. attending. Rom 13:6
m. by whom ye believed. 1 Cor 3:5
us as of the m. of Christ. 4:1
who made us able m. 2 Cor 3:6
approving ourselves as the m. 6:4
no great thing, if his m. also be transformed as the m. of. 11:15
are they m. of Christ? I am more. 23

ministration
as the days of his *m.* *Luke* 1:23
neglected in the daily *m.* *Acts* 6:1
but if the *m.* of death. *2 Cor* 3:7
m. of the Spirit be rather? 8, 9
by the experiment of this *m.* 9:13

ministry
instruments of the *m.* *Num* 4:12
came to do the service of the *m.* 47
praised by their *m.* *2 Chr* 7:6
similitudes, by the *m.* of the prophets. *Hos* 12:10
obtained part of this *m.* *Acts* 1:17
that may take part of this *m.* 25
we will give ourselves to *m.* 6:4
they had fulfilled their *m.* 12:25
might finish my course, and *m.* 20:24
God had wrought by his *m.* 21:19
or *m.*, let us wait on our. *Rom* 12:7
to the *m.* of saints. *1 Cor* 16:15
seeing we have this *m.* *2 Cor* 4:1
hath given to us the *m.* of. 5:18
giving no offence, that the *m.* 6:3
for work of the *m.* for. *Eph* 4:12
take heed to the *m.* thou. *Col* 4:17
putting me into the *m.* *1 Tim* 1:12*
make full proof of thy *m.* *2 Tim* 4:5
profitable to me for the *m.* 11
he obtained a more excellent *m.* *Heb* 8:6
with blood the vessels of the *m.* 9:21

minstrel, -s
me a *m.* when *m.* played. *2 Ki* 3:15
when Jesus saw the *m.* *Mat* 9:23*

mint
pay tithe of *m.* anise. *Mat* 23:23
ye tithe *m.* and all. *Luke* 11:42

miracle
(*An event beyond the power of any known physical laws to produce; a supernatural occurrence produced by the power of God; a marvel, wonder. In the Revisions the word is generally rendered in the Old Testament* wonder, *or* mighty work; *and in the New Testament* sign)
speak, saying, Shew a *m.* *Ex* 7:9
considered not the *m.* *Mark* 6:52
no man which shall do a *m.* 9:39
hoped to have seen some *m.* done. *Luke* 23:8
this is the second *m.* *John* 4:54
and said, John did no *m.* 10:41
a notable *m.* hath been. *Acts* 4:16
forty years on whom this *m.* 22

miracles
which have seen *m.* *Num* 14:22
that have not seen his *m.* *Deut* 11:3
seen those signs and great *m.* 29:3
where be all his *m.* our. *Judg* 6:13
beginning of *m.* did. *John* 2:11
when they saw the *m.* he did. 23
no man can do these *m.* except. 3:2
because they saw his *m.* 6:2
not because ye saw the *m.* 26
will he do more *m.* than? 7:31
that is a sinner do such *m.*? 9:16
for this man doeth many *m.* 11:47
he had done so many *m.* 12:37
approved of God by *m.* *Acts* 2:22
Stephen did great *m.* among. 6:8
hearing and seeing the *m.* 8:6
wondered, beholding the *m.* 13
declaring what *m.* God had. 15:12
God wrought special *m.* by. 19:11
another the working *m.* *1 Cor* 12:10
after that *m.* 28
are all workers of *m.*? 29
he that worketh *m.* among. *Gal* 3:5
them witness with *m.* *Heb* 2:4
by the means of those *m.* *Rev* 13:14
spirits of devils working *m.* 16:14
false prophet that wrought *m.* 19:20

mire
I did stamp them as *m.* of the. *2 Sam* 22:43; *Isa* 10:6; *Mi* 7:10
rush grow up without *m.*? *Job* 8:11
he hath cast me into the *m.* 30:19
pointed things on the *m.* 41:30
I sink in deep *m.* where. *Ps* 69:2
deliver me out of the *m.*: let me. 14
whose waters cast up *m.* *Isa* 57:20
was no water, but *m.* *Jer* 38:6
thy feet are sunk in the *m.* 22
and fine gold as the *m.* *Zech* 9:3
tread their enemies in *m.* of. 10:5
her wallowing in the *m.* *2 Pet* 2:22

Miriam
M. took a timbrel. *Ex* 15:20
M. and Aaron spake. *Num* 12:1
M. became leprous white. 10
M. was shut up seven days. 15
M. died there. 20:1
were born Aaron, Moses, *M.* 26:59
remember what God did to *M.* by the way *Deut* 24:9
thee Moses, Aaron, and *M.* *Mi* 6:4

mirth
sent thee away with *m.* *Gen* 31:27
away to make great *m.* *Neh* 8:12
us desired of us *m.* *Ps* 137:3
and the end of that *m.* *Pr* 14:13
I will prove thee with *m.* *Eccl* 2:1
I said of *m.* What doeth it? 2
of fools is in the house of *m.* 7:4
then I commended *m.* because. 8:15
m. of tabrets, the joy of. *Isa* 24:8
joy is darkened, the *m.* of the. 11
the voice of *m.* from. *Jer* 7:34
16:9; 25:10; *Hos* 2:11
we then make *m.*? *Ezek* 21:10

miry
me out of the *m.* clay. *Ps* 40:2
the *m.* places shall not. *Ezek* 47:11
iron mixed with *m.* *Dan* 2:41, 43

miscarrying
give them a *m.* womb. *Hos* 9:14

mischief
(*Very frequently used to mean wickedness, iniquity*)
for he said, Lest some *m.* *Gen* 42:4
if *m.* befall him by the way in which ye go. 38; 44:29
depart, and yet no *m.* *Ex* 21:22
for *m.* did he bring them out. 32:12*
people that are set on *m.* 22*
that Saul practised *m.* *1 Sam* 23:9
art taken in thy *m.* *2 Sam* 16:8
the *m.* that Hadad did. *1 Ki* 11:25
see how this man seeketh *m.* 20:7
some *m.* will come upon us. *2 Ki* 7:9*
they thought to do me *m.* *Neh* 6:2
Esther besought to put away *m.* of. *Esth* 8:3
conceive *m.* and bring. *Job* 15:35
he conceived *m.* brought. *Ps* 7:14
his *m.* shall return upon his. 16
under his tongue is *m.* and. 10:7
thou beholdest *m.* and spite, to. 14
hands is *m.*, their hand is. 26:10
which speak peace, but *m.* 28:3
the wicked deviseth *m.* 36:4*
why boastest thyself in *m.*? 52:1
m. and sorrow are in the. 55:10
imagine *m.* against a man? 62:3
the throne, which frameth *m.*? 94:20
nigh that follow after *m.* 119:150*
let the *m.* of their own lips. 140:9
except they have done *m.* *Pr* 4:16
he deviseth *m.* continually. 6:14*
be swift in running to *m.* 18
sport to a fool to do *m.* 10:23*
he that seeketh *m.* it shall. 11:27
wicked shall be filled with *m.* 12:21
messenger falleth into *m.* 13:17*
perverse tongue falleth into *m.* 17:20
and their lips talk of *m.* 24:2
wicked shall fall into *m.* 16*; 28:14
therefore *m.* shall fall. *Isa* 47:11
in vanity, they conceive *m.* 59:4
m. shall come upon *m.* *Ezek* 7:26
are the men that devise *m.* 11:2*
kings' hearts shall be to do *m.* *Dan* 11:27
yet do they imagine *m.* *Hos* 7:15
full of all *m.* thou child. *Acts* 13:10*

mischiefs
I will heap *m.* on them. *Deut* 32:23
thy tongue deviseth *m.* *Ps* 52:2*
imagine *m.* in their heart. 140:2

mischievous
imagined a *m.* device. *Ps* 21:11
that seek my hurt, speak *m.* 38:12
he shall be called a *m.* *Pr* 24:8
the end of his talk is *m.* *Eccl* 10:13
man uttereth his *m.* desire. *Mi* 7:3

miserable
Job said, *m.* comforters. *Job* 16:2
of all men most *m.* *1 Cor* 15:19*
knowest not that thou art *m.* *Rev* 3:17

miserably
he will *m.* destroy those. *Mat* 21:41

miseries
Jerusalem remembered in days of her *m.* *Lam* 1:7
howl for your *m.* that shall. *Jas* 5:1

misery
was grieved for the *m.* *Judg* 10:16
given to him that is in *m.*? *Job* 3:20
thou shalt forget thy *m.* 11:16
remember his *m.* no more. *Pr* 31:7
the *m.* of a man is great. *Eccl* 8:6
mine affliction and *m.* *Lam* 3:19
destruction and *m.* are. *Rom* 3:16

Mishael
of Uzziel, *M.* Elzaphan and Zithri. *Ex* 6:22; *Lev* 10:4
Ezra's left hand stood *M.* *Neh* 8:4
children of Judah, *M.* *Dan* 1:6

miss
hair breadth and not *m.* *Judg* 20:16
if thy father at all *m.* *1 Sam* 20:6

missed
thou shalt be *m.* *1 Sam* 20:18
neither *m.* any thing as long. 25:15
nothing was *m.* of all that. 21

missing
neither was there aught *m.* unto them. *1 Sam* 25:7
any means he be *m.* *1 Ki* 20:39

mist
up a *m.* from the earth. *Gen* 2:6
there fell on him a *m.* *Acts* 13:11
to whom the *m.* of darkness is. *2 Pet* 2:17*

mistress
her *m.* was despised in. *Gen* 16:4
I flee from my *m.* Sarai. 8
return to thy *m.* 9
son of the *m.* of house. *1 Ki* 17:17
her *m.* Would God my lord. *2 Ki* 5:3
maiden to hand of her *m.* *Ps* 123:2
that is heir to her *m.* *Pr* 30:23
the maid so with her *m.* *Isa* 24:2
m. of witchcrafts, that. *Nah* 3:4

misused
they despised and *m.* *2 Chr* 36:16*

mite, -s
a widow threw in two *m.* *Mark* 12:42; *Luke* 21:2
paid the very last *m.* *Luke* 12:59

mitre
they shall make a *m.* *Ex* 28:4, 39
39:28
a blue lace upon the *m.* 28:37; 39:31
shalt put the *m.* upon his head. 29:6
the holy crown on the *m.* *Lev* 8:9
linen *m.* shall he be attired. 16:4
a fair *m.* on his head, so they set a fair *m.* *Zech* 3:5

mixed
a *m.* multitude went up. *Ex* 12:38
the *m.* multitude fell a. *Num* 11:4
they separated from Israel all *m.* *Neh* 13:3
that go to seek *m.* wine. *Pr* 23:30
thy wine *m.* with water. *Isa* 1:22
the iron *m.* with miry. *Dan* 2:41
Ephraim *m.* himself among. *Hos* 7:8
not being *m.* with faith. *Heb* 4:2*

mixture
wine red, it is full of *m.* *Ps* 75:8
Nicodemus, and brought a *m.* of myrrh and aloes. *John* 19:39
is poured out without *m.* *Rev* 14:10

Mizar
thee from the hill of *M.* *Ps* 42:6

Mizpah
the heap was called *M.* *Gen* 31:49

those stones Geba of Benjamin, and
M. *1 Ki* 15:22; *2 Chr* 16:6
son of Nethaniah came to Gedaliah
to *M.* *2 Ki* 25:23; *Jer* 41:1
men of Gibeon and *M.* *Neh* 3:7
Shallum ruler of *M.* 15
Ezer ruler of *M.* 19
went to Gedaliah to *M.* *Jer* 40:6
behold, I will dwell at *M.* 10
the Jews that were at *M.* 41:3
carried away captive from *M.* 14
been a snare on *M.* *Hos* 5:1

Mizpeh

Dilean and *M.* cities. *Josh* 15:38
M. Chephirah, cities of. 18:26
and encamped in *M.* *Judg* 10:17
uttered all his words in *M.* 11:11
gathered to the Lord in *M.* 20:1
up to the Lord to *M.* shall die. 21:5
gather all Israel to *M.* *1 Sam* 7:5
judged Israel in *M.* 6, 16
the people to the Lord to *M.* 10:17
David went thence to *M.* 22:3

Mnason

M. an old disciple. *Acts* 21:16

Moab

daughter's son was *M.* *Gen* 19:37
smote Midian in field of *M.* 36:35
1 Chr 1:46
take hold on men of *M.* *Ex* 15:15
woe to thee, *M.* *Num* 21:29
Jer 48:46
M. was sore afraid, and *M.* was
distressed. *Num* 22:3
smite the corners of *M.* 24:17
whoredom with daughters of *M.* 25:1
through the coast of *M.* *Deut* 2:18
Moses died in the land of *M.* 34:5
slew of *M.* about 10,000. *Judg* 3:29
so *M.* was subdued under the. 30
served gods of Syria and *M.* 10:6
took not away the land of *M.* 11:15
into the country of *M.* *Ruth* 1:2
took wives of the women of *M.* 4
Saul fought against *M.* and Ammon.
1 Sam 14:47
David smote *M.* and. *2 Sam* 8:2
slew two lionlike men of *M.* 23:20
the abomination of *M.* *1 Ki* 11:7
M. rebelled against. *2 Ki* 1:1
wilt thou go with me against *M.*? 3:7
kings are slain, therefore *M.* 23
had the dominion in *M.* *1 Chr* 4:22
gold he brought from *M.* 18:11
M. came against Jehoshaphat.
2 Chr 20:1
behold, how the children of *M.* 10
had married wives of *M.* *Neh* 13:23
M. is my washpot. *Ps* 60:8; 108:9
M. is confederate against thee. 83:6
lay their hand upon *M.* *Isa* 11:14
the burden of *M.* Ar of *M.* laid waste.
15:1; 16:13; *Jer* 48:1; *Ezek* 25:8
Amos 2:2
heart shall cry out for *M.* *Isa* 15:5
we have heard the pride of *M.* 16:6
Jer 48:29
like an harp for *M.* *Isa* 16:11
and the glory of *M.* shall be. 14
M. shall be trodden down. 25:10
I will punish Egypt, Judah, and *M.*
Jer 9:26
I made Edom and *M.* to. 25:21
Jews returned from *M.* 40:11
shall be no more praise of *M.* 48:2
give wings to *M.* that it may flee. 9
M. hath been at ease from his. 11
tell ye it in Arnon, that *M.* is. 20
M. shall wallow in his vomit. 26
gladness is taken from land of *M.* 33
how hath *M.* turned the back! 39
bring again the captivity of *M.* 47
send a fire upon *M.* *Amos* 2:2
M. shall be as Sodom. *Zeph* 2:9
see **king**

Moabite

a *M.* shall not enter into the congregation. *Deut* 23:3; *Neh* 13:1
Ithmah the *M.* a valiant. *1 Chr* 11:46

Moabites

is the father of the *M.* *Gen* 19:37
said, Distress not the *M.* *Deut* 2:9
delivered the *M.* to you. *Judg* 3:28
M. became David's servants and.
2 Sam 8:2; *1 Chr* 18:2
loved women of the *M.* *1 Ki* 11:1
Chemosh god of the *M.* 33
he will deliver the *M.* *2 Ki* 3:18
rose up and smote the *M.* 24
the bands of the *M.* invaded. 13:20
sent against him bands of *M.* 24:2
abominations of the *M.* *Ezra* 9:1

Moabitess, *see* **Ruth**

mock

[1] *To deride or laugh at*, 2 Chr 30:10. [2] *To speak in jest*, Gen 19:14. [3] *To disappoint, deceive*, Num 22:29.

Hebrew to *m.* us. *Gen* 39:14, 17
mocketh, do ye so *m.* him. *Job* 13:9
after I have spoken, *m.* on. 21:3
I will *m.* when your fear. *Pr* 1:26
fools make a *m.* at sin. 14:9
deliver me, and they *m.* *Jer* 38:19
adversary did *m.* at her. *Lam* 1:7
m. thee who art infamous. *Ezek* 22:5
deliver him to Gentiles to *m.* him.
Mat 20:19
they shall *m.* him and. *Mark* 10:34
behold, begin to *m.* him. *Luke* 14:29

mocked

seemed as one that *m.* to. *Gen* 19:14
thou hast *m.* me. *Num* 22:29
hast *m.* me, and told me lies.
Judg 16:10, 13, 15.
at noon, Elijah *m.* *1 Ki* 18:27
out of the city *m.* Elisha. *2 Ki* 2:23
them to scorn and *m.* *2 Chr* 30:10
but they *m.* the messengers. 36:16
wroth, and *m.* the Jews. *Neh* 4:1
I am as one *m.* of his. *Job* 12:4*
saw that he was *m.* he. *Mat* 2:16
they bowed the knee and *m.* 27:29
31; *Mark* 15:20
be *m.* and spitefully. *Luke* 18:32
men that held Jesus *m.* him. 22:63
Herod *m.* him. 23:11
the soldiers also *m.* him. 36
the resurrection, some *m.* *Acts* 17:32
deceived, God is not *m.* *Gal* 6:7

mocker

wine is a *m.*, strong drink. *Pr* 20:1

mockers

are there not *m.* with me? *Job* 17:2
with hypocritical *m.* *Ps* 35:16
be not *m.* lest bands be. *Isa* 28:22*
not in the assembly of *m.* *Jer* 15:17*
be *m.* in the latter times. *Jude* 18

mockest

when thou *m.* shall no man. *Job* 11:3

mocketh

as one *m.* another, do. *Job* 13:9*
he *m.* at fear, and is not. 39:22
m. poor reproacheth his. *Pr* 17:5
eye that *m.* at his father. 30:17
a derision, every one *m.* me. *Jer* 20:7

mocking, -s

saw the son of Hagar *m.* *Gen* 21:9
I made thee a *m.* to all. *Ezek* 22:4
the chief priests *m.* *Mat* 27:41
Mark 15:31
m. said, These men are. *Acts* 2:13
had trial of cruel *m.* *Heb* 11:36

moderately

you the former rain *m.* *Joel* 2:23*

moderation

m. be known to all men. *Phil* 4:5*

modest

themselves in *m.* apparel. *1 Tim* 2:9

moist

shall he eat *m.* grapes. *Num* 6:3*

moistened

and his bones are *m.* *Job* 21:24*

moisture

my *m.* is turned into. *Ps* 32:4
because it lacked *m.* *Luke* 8:6

mole

lizard, snail, and *m.* are. *Lev* 11:30*

Molech

pass through fire to *M.* *Lev* 18:21
that giveth of his seed to *M.* shall
surely be. 20:2; 3, 4; *Jer* 32:35
built an high place for *M.* *1 Ki* 11:7
son pass through to *M.* *2 Ki* 23:10

moles, *see* **bats**

mollified

neither bound up, nor *m.* *Isa* 1:6

Moloch

have borne the tabernacle of *M.*
Amos 5:26; *Acts* 7:43

molten

after he had made *m.* calf. *Ex* 32:4
8; *Deut* 9:12, 16; *Neh* 9:18
shalt make thee no *m.* gods.
Ex 34:17; *Lev* 19:4
chapiters of *m.* brass. *1 Ki* 7:16
he made a *m.* sea. 23
undersetters *m.* 30
their spokes were all *m.* 33
and brass is *m.* out of. *Job* 28:2
sky is strong, and as a *m.* 37:18
filthiness of it may be *m.* *Ezek* 24:11
the mountains shall be *m.* *Mi* 1:4

moment

midst of thee in a *m.* *Ex* 33:5
that I may consume them in a *m.*
Num 16:21, 45
try him every *m.* *Job* 7:18
hypocrite is but for a *m.* 20:5
and in a *m.* they go down to. 21:13
in a *m.* shall they die, people. 34:20
anger endureth but a *m.* *Ps* 30:5
into desolation as in a *m.* 73:19
tongue is but for a *m.* *Pr* 12:19
as it were for a *m.* *Isa* 26:20
I will water it every *m.* 27:3
two things shall come in a *m.* 47:9
small *m.* have I forsaken. 54:7
I hid my face from thee for a *m.* 8
my curtains in a *m.* *Jer* 4:20
was overthrown in a *m.* *Lam* 4:6
and shall tremble at every *m.*
Ezek 26:16; 32:10
kingdoms of world in a *m.* *Luke* 4:5
all be changed in a *m.* *1 Cor* 15:52
which is but for a *m.* *2 Cor* 4:17

money

(*Coined money was unknown until late in Bible times. Gold and silver in the form of rings or ingots were weighed in payment where we would count coins*)

give it for as much *m.* *Gen* 23:9*
I will give thee *m.* for the field. 13*
quite devoured also our *m.* 31:15
to restore every man's *m.* 42:25
he espied his *m.* 27
my *m.* is restored. 28
double *m.* in your hand. 43:12, 15
fear not, I had your *m.* 23
and put every man's *m.* in his. 44:1
Joseph gathered all the *m.* 47:14
for *m.* faileth. 15
how that our *m.* is spent. 18
go out free without *m.* *Ex* 21:11
for he is his *m.* 21
be laid on him a sum of *m.* 30*
and divide the *m.* 35*
deliver to his neighbour *m.* 22:7
if thou lend *m.* to any of my. 25
shalt take the atonement *m.* 30:16
not give him *m.* on usury.
Lev 25:37; *Deut* 23:19
took the redemption *m.* *Num* 3:49
meat and water for *m.* *Deut* 2:6, 28
turn it into *m.* 14:25
shalt bestow that *m.* 26
not sell her at all for *m.* 21:14
they took no gain of *m.* *Judg* 5:19
lords of Philistines brought *m.* 16:18
yet he restored the *m.* to his. 17:4
the worth of it in *m.* *1 Ki* 21:2
is it a time to receive *m.*? *2 Ki* 5:26
m. of the dedicated things. 12:4
therefore receive no more *m.* 7
m. in the chest, and told the *m.* that
was found 10; *2 Chr* 24:11
trespass *m.* and sin *m.* *2 Ki* 12:16
Menahem exacted the *m.* of. 15:20
Jehoiakim gave *m.* to. 23:35

gave m. also to masons. Ezra 3:7
buy speedily with this m. 7:17
we have borrowed m. Neh 5:4
servants might exact of them m. 10
of the sum of m. Haman. Esth 4:7
the fruits without m. Job 31:39
also gave him a piece of m. 42:11
put not out his m. to usury. Ps 15:5
he hath taken a bag of m. Pr 7:20
for wisdom and m. is a. Eccl 7:12
wine maketh merry, but m. 10:19
redeemed without m. Isa 52:3
no m., come, buy without m. 55:1
wherefore spend ye m. for that? 2
I weighed him the m. Jer 32:9, 10
men shall buy fields for m. and. 44
drunken our water for m. Lam 5:4
thereof divine for m. Mi 3:11
received the tribute m. Mat 17:24*
thou shalt find a piece of m. 27*
shew me the tribute m. 22:19
earth, and hid his lord's m. 25:18
to have put my m. to the exchangers, and at my. 27; Luke 19:23
large m. to the soldiers. Mat 28:12
so they took m. and did as they. 15
they took no m. in their purse. Mark 6:8; Luke 9:3
the people cast m. into. Mark 12:41
and promised to give him m. 14:11 Luke 22:5
changers of m. sitting. John 2:14
he poured out changers' m. 15
brought the m. and laid. Acts 4:37
sorcerer offered them m. 8:18
but Peter said, Thy m. perish. 20*
he hoped that m. should have. 24:26
the love of m. is the root. 1 Tim 6:10
see **brought**

moneychangers

overthrew tables of m. and seats of them. Mat 21:12; Mark 11:15

monsters

even the sea m. draw out. Lam 4:3*

month

(The Jews reckoned by the year of 360 days, and in all probability made an adjustment by adding a thirteenth month occasionally. They had two New Years, the Civil, in Tisri (October), and the Sacred, in Abib or Nisan, the month in which they left Egypt under Moses. The following table gives the months in order, beginning with the Sacred New Year. The numbers in parentheses are those of the civil reckoning; and the modern names given are approximately the corresponding months according to our calendar. The exact period in modern terms differs each year)

		Answering to our
(7)	1. Nisan, Abib,	April.
(8)	2. Iar, Zif,	May.
(9)	3. Sivan,	June.
(10)	4. Tammuz,	July.
(11)	5. Ab,	Aug.
(12)	6. Elul,	Sept.
(1)	7. Tisri, Ethanim,	Oct.
(2)	8. Marchesvan,	Nov.
(3)	9. Chisleu (Kislev),	Dec.
(4)	10. Tebeth,	Jan.
(5)	11. Sebat,	Feb.
(6)	12. Adar,	Mar.

Laban space of a m. Gen 29:14
ye out in the m. Abib. Ex 13:4
keep the feast in the m. Abib. 23:15
m. Abib thou camest out. 34:18 Deut 16:1; Josh 5:10
if it be from a m. old to. Lev 27:6
every male from m. old. Num 3:15 22, 28, 34, 39, 40, 43; 26:62
a m. or year that the cloud. 9:22
flesh, even a whole m. 11:20, 21
from a m. old shalt thou. 18:16
the burnt offering of every m. 28:14 29:6*
thine house a full m. Deut 21:13
each man his m. made provision. 1 Ki 4:7, 27
a m. they were in Lebanon. 5:14
in the m. Zif. 1 Ki 6:37
in the m. Bul. 38
feast in m. Ethanim. 8:2
in m. Chisleu. Neh 1:1
in m. Nisan. 2:1; Esth 3:7
m. Elul. Neh 6:15
Jews gathered in m. Adar. Esth 9:15, 17, 19, 21
m. which was turned from. 22
in her m. they shall find. Jer 2:24
now shall a m. devour. Hos 5:7*
I cut off in one m. Zech 11:8
prepared for a day and m. Rev 9:15
yielded her fruit every m. 22:2
see **first**

second **month**

in second m. the fountains were. Gen 7:11
second m. was the earth dried. 8:14
wilderness of Sin in second m. Ex 16:1
in second m. take sum. Num 1:1
in second m. shall keep passover. 9:11; 2 Chr 30:2
of second m. cloud was taken up. Num 10:11
second m. Solomon began to build. 1 Ki 6:1; 2 Chr 3:2
the course of second m. 1 Chr 27:4
second m. began Zerubbabel to. Ezra 3:8

third **month**

in third m. came into wilderness of. Ex 19:1
captain for third m. 1 Chr 27:5
gathered at Jerusalem in the third m. 2 Chr 15:10
in third m. they began to lay. 31:7
king's scribes were called in third m. Esth 8:9
in third m. word of Lord. Ezek 31:1

fourth **month**

fourth m. the famine. 2 Ki 25:3
fourth captain for fourth m. was. 1 Chr 27:5
fourth m. the city was. Jer 39:2
in fourth m. the famine was. 52:6
in fourth m. Ezekiel saw. Ezek 1:1
fast of the fourth m. Zech 8:19
see **fifth**

sixth **month**

captain for sixth m. 1 Chr 27:9
in sixth m. the elders of. Ezek 8:1
in sixth m. word of Lord. Hag 1:1
in sixth m. they did work in. 15
in sixth m. the angel. Luke 1:26
this is the sixth m. with her, who. 36
see **seventh**

eighth **month**

in eighth m. came word. Zech 1:1

ninth **month**

the ninth m. the people. Ezra 10:9
in the ninth m. they. Jer 36:9
winter house in the ninth m. 22
in ninth m. came word. Hag 2:10
from the ninth m. consider it. 18
to Zechariah in ninth m. Zech 7:1

tenth **month**

waters decreased until the tenth m. Gen 8:5
sat down in tenth m. Ezra 10:16
to the king in tenth m. Esth 2:16
tenth m. came Nebuchadrezzar. Jer 39:1; 52:4
in tenth m. came word. Ezek 24:1 29:1
in the tenth m. one that had escaped. 33:21

eleventh **month**

in the eleventh m. Moses. Deut 1:3
in eleventh m. came word. Zech 1:7

twelfth **month**

Haman to the twelfth m. Esth 3:7
thirteenth day of the twelfth m. 13 8:12; 9:1
twelfth m. Evil-merodach. Jer 52:31
in twelfth m. the word of. Ezek 32:1

this **month**

this m. shall be beginning. Ex 12:2
this m. shall take every man a. 3
keep this service in this m. Ex 13:5 Num 9:3; 28:17
tenth day of this m. an. Num 29:7
this m. Israel assembled. Neh 9:1

monthly

the m. prognosticators. Isa 47:13

months

in beginnings of your m. Num 10:10
in beginnings of m. offer a. 28:11
burnt offering through the m. 14
let me alone two m. Judg 11:37
at the end of two m. she returned. 39
was with her father four m. 19:2
in the rock Rimmon four m. 20:47
ark was in country of Philistines seven m. 1 Sam 6:1
Philistines a year and four m. 27:7
over Judah seven years and six m. 2 Sam 2:11; 5:5; 1 Chr 3:4
ark was with Obed-edom three m. 2 Sam 6:11
Jerusalem at end of nine m. 24:8
and two m. they were. 1 Ki 5:14
for six m. did Joab remain. 11:16
reigned over Israel six m. 2 Ki 15:8
by month through the m. 1 Chr 27:1
twelve m. purified, six m. with oil of myrrh, six m. with. Esth 2:12
into the number of the m. Job 3:6
so am I made to possess m. of. 7:3
number of his m. are with. 14:5
when the number of his m. 21:21
O that I were as in m. past, as. 29:2
canst thou number the m. that? 39:2
seven m. Israel shall be. Ezek 39:12
after the end of seven m. shall. 14
new fruit according to his m. 47:12
at the end of twelve m. Dan 4:29
and hid herself five m. Luke 1:24
heaven was shut up three years and six m. 4:25; Jas 5:17
are yet four m. then. John 4:35
there a year and six m. Acts 18:11
observe days, and m. Gal 4:10
tormented five m. Rev 9:5, 10
under foot forty-two m. 11:2
him to continue forty-two m. 13:5
see **three**

monuments

people which lodge in the m. Isa 65:4*

moon

the sun and the m. Deut 4:19; 33:14
m. in valley of Ajalon. Josh 10:12
m. and it shineth not. Job 25:5
when I consider the m. Ps 8:3
and peace so long as the m. 72:7
established for ever as the m. 89:37
he appointeth the m. for. 104:19
while the sun, m. or stars. Eccl 12:2
fair as m., clear as the. S of S 6:10
round tires like the m. Isa 3:18
see **sun**

new **moon**

is the new m. 1 Sam 20:5, 18
it is neither new m. 2 Ki 4:23
trumpet in the new m. Ps 81:3
that from one new m. to. Isa 66:23
in the day of new m. it. Ezek 46:1
in the day of new m. offer a. 6
will the new m. be gone? Amos 8:5
in respect of the new m. Col 2:16

new **moons**

sacrifices in the new m. 1 Chr 23:31 2 Chr 2:4; 31:3; Ezra 3:5 Neh 10:33; Ezek 46:3
new m. and sabbaths I. Isa 1:13
your new m. and feasts my soul. 14
offerings in the new m. Ezek 45:17
to cease her new m. Hos 2:11

Mordecai

M. came up with Zerubbabel. Ezra 2:2; Neh 7:7
Jew, whose name was M. Esth 2:5
M. sat in the king's gate. 19, 21
the thing was known to M. 22
Haman saw that M. bowed not. 3:5
shewed him the people of M. 6
M. rent his clothes, and put. 4:1
told Esther the words of M. 9
Esther bade them return M. 15
so long as I see M. the Jew. 5:13

gallows made, that M. Esth 5:14
honour hath been done to M.? 6:3
make haste, and do even so to M. 10
Haman had made for M. 7:9
his ring and gave it to M. Esther set
M. over the house of Haman. 8:2
M. went out from the king in. 15
because the fear of M. fell. 9:3
M. the Jew was next to king. 10:3

more

Jacob loved Rachel m. Gen 29:30
riches m. than that they might. 36:7
Israel loved Joseph m. than all. 37:3
brethren hated him yet the m. 5, 8
Israel are m. than we. Ex 1:9
the m. they afflicted them, the m. 12
let there m. work be laid upon. 5:9
Pharaoh sinned yet m. and. 9:34
yet will I bring one plague m. 11:1
they gathered some m. some. 16:17
rich shall not give m. nor. 30:15
add the fifth part m. thereto. Lev 6:5
shut him up seven days m. 13:5
33, 54
you seven times m. 26:18, 21
firstborn which are m. Num 3:46
princes m. honourable than. 22:15
word of Lord, to do less or m. 18
what the Lord will say to me m. 19
thou shalt give the m. 26:54; 33:54
a thousand times m. Deut 1:11
on you, not because ye were m. 7:7
nations are m. than I. 17; 20:1
add three cities m. for thee. 19:9
were m. which died. Josh 10:11
corrupted themselves m. Judg 2:19
m. than they which he slew. 16:30
and what have I m.? 18:24
Lord do so to me and m. Ruth 1:17
1 Sam 14:44; 2 Sam 3:35; 19:13
shewed m. kindness in. Ruth 3:10
God do so to thee and m. 1 Sam 3:17
what can ye have m. but the? 18:8
and much m. to Jonathan. 20:13
knew nothing less or m. 22:15
said, Thou art m. righteous. 24:17
m. do God to the enemies. 25:22
she told him nothing less or m. 36
to Abner, and m. also. 2 Sam 3:9
David took him m. concubines. 5:13
I will yet be m. vile than. 6:22
what can David say m. unto? 7:20
we have also m. right in. 19:43
God do so to me, and m. also.
1 Ki 2:23; 20:10; 2 Ki 6:31
Ahab did m. to provoke. 1 Ki 16:33
gods do to me, and m. also. 19:2
there is not a vessel m. 2 Ki 4:6
m. than they that be with them.
6:16; 2 Chr 32:7
seduced them to do m. evil. 2 Ki 21:9
his people so many m. 1 Chr 21:3
there were m. chief men found. 24:4
put m. to your yoke. 2 Chr 10:11
m. spoil than they could. 20:25
Lord is able to give thee m. 25:9
intend to add m. to our sins. 28:13
Ahaz did trespass yet m. against. 22
the Levites were m. upright. 29:34
his servants spake m. against. 32:16
Amon trespassed m. and m. 33:23
whatsoever m. shall be. Ezra 7:20
yet ye bring m. wrath. Neh 13:18
Esther obtained favour m. than all.
Esth 2:17
delight to do honour m. than? 6:6
dig for it m. than for hid. Job 3:21
m. than my necessary food. 23:12
nor regardeth the rich m. 34:19
for he will not lay on man m. 23
saidst, My righteousness is m. 35:2
teacheth us m. than the beasts. 11
latter end of Job m. than. 42:12
m. than when their corn. Ps 4:7
m. to be desired are they. 19:10
thy thoughts are m. than can. 40:5
iniquities are m. than the hairs. 12
lovest evil m. than good. 52:3
that hate me are m. than hairs. 69:4
yet praise thee m. and m. 71:14
they have m. than heart could. 73:7
they sinned yet m. against. 78:17
gates of Zion m. than all. 87:2
increase you m. and m. Ps 115:14
I have m. understanding. 119:99
understand m. than the ancients. 100
m. than they that watch for. 130:6
wisdom is m. precious. Pr 3:15
shineth m. and m. unto the. 4:18
there is that withholdeth m. 11:24
a reproof entereth m. into a. 17:10
there is m. hope of a fool than of him.
26:12; 29:20
I increased m. than all. Eccl 2:9
remembrance of wise m. than. 16
or who can hasten hereunto m.? 25
the dead m. than the living. 4:2
and be m. ready to hear than. 5:1
remember thy love m. S of S 1:4
what is thy beloved m.? 5:9
what could be done m. to? Isa 5:4
afterward did m. grievously. 9:1
I will bring m. upon Dimon. 15:9
his visage so marred m. than. 52:14
for m. are the children of the. 54:1
Israel justified herself m. Jer 3:11
because they are m. than the. 46:23
changed judgements into wickedness
m. than nations. Ezek 5:6
because he multiplied m. than the. 7
thou wast corrupted m. than they in
all thy ways. 16:47, 51, 52; 23:11
not for any wisdom that I have m.
than any living. Dan 2:30
the furnace seven times m. 3:19
continue m. years than the king. 11:8
knowledge of God m. Hos 6:6
now they sin m. and m. and. 13:2
wicked devoureth man m. Hab 1:13
what is m. than these. Mat 5:37
brethren only, what do you m.? 47
is not the life m. than meat? 6:25
Luke 12:23
of m. value than many sparrows.
Mat 10:31; Luke 12:7
loveth father or mother m. Mat 10:37
and m. than a prophet. 11:9
seven spirits m. wicked than. 12:45
he shall have m. abundance. 13:12
he rejoiceth m. of that sheep. 18:13
take with thee one or two m. 16
they should have received m. 20:10
cried the m. Have mercy. 31; 27:23
Mark 10:48; 15:14; Luke 18:39
give me m. than twelve. Mat 26:53
to you that hear shall m. Mark 4:24
m. he charged them, so much the m.
7:36
poor widow cast in m. than all.
12:43; Luke 21:3
have been sold for m. Mark 14:5
what thou spendest m. Luke 10:35
of him they will ask m. 12:48
not receive manifold m. in. 18:30
many m. believed. John 4:41
Jews sought the m. to kill. 5:18
will he do m. miracles than? 7:31
praise of men m. than. 12:43
that it may bring forth m. fruit. 15:2
Simon, lovest thou me m.? 21:15
to hearken to you m. Acts 4:19
believers were the m. added. 5:14
but Saul increased the m. in. 9:22
the m. part knew not why. 19:32
it is m. blessed to give. 20:35
there were m. than forty. 23:13, 21
believed the master m. than. 27:11
served the creature m. Rom 1:25
if the truth of God hath m. 3:7
we are m. than conquerors. 8:37
that I might gain the m. 1 Cor 9:19
I speak with tongues m. than. 14:18
so I rejoiced the m. 2 Cor 7:7
I boast the m. 10:8
am m.; in prisons m. frequent. 11:23
the desolate hath many m. Gal 4:27
love may abound m. and m.
Phil 1:9; 1 Thes 4:10
trust in the flesh, I m. Phil 3:4
God, abound m. and m. 1 Thes 4:1
lovers of pleasure m. 2 Tim 3:4
also do m. than I say. Philem 21
I m. say? time would fail. Heb 11:32
much m. shall not we escape. 12:25
yet once m. I shake not the. 26, 27
he giveth m. grace. Jas 4:6
m. sure word of prophecy. 2 Pet 1:19
and the last to be m. Rev 2:19
there come two woes m. 9:12
see **abundantly**

***any* more**

returned not again any m. Gen 8:12
curse the ground any m. 21; 9:11
nor shall thy name any m. 17:5
not any m. be called Jacob. 35:10
deal deceitfully any m. Ex 8:29
neither shall there be any m. 9:29
a cry, none like it any m. 11:6
man nor woman make any m. 36:6
not be redeemed any m. Lev 27:20
be no wrath any m. Num 18:5
voice of the Lord any m. Deut 5:25
see this great fire any m. 18:16
had Israel manna any m. Josh 5:12
nor will I be with you any m. 7:12
any m. sons in my womb? Ruth 1:11
Saul shall despair to seek me any m.
1 Sam 27:1
children of wickedness afflict any m.
2 Sam 7:10
feared to help Ammon any m.
10:19; 1 Chr 19:19
speakest thou any m.? 2 Sam 19:29
make the feet of Israel move any m.
2 Ki 21:8; 2 Chr 33:8
nor shall his place know him any m
Job 7:10; 20:9
I will not offend any m. 34:31
neither have they any m. Eccl 9:5
be stricken any m.? Isa 1:5
nor shall they learn war any m. 2:4
Mi 4:3
teachers be removed any m.
Isa 30:20
be termed desolate any m. 62:4
that be done any m. Jer 3:16
nor walk any m. after imagination. 17
stretch forth my tent any m. 10:20
I will not speak any m. in. 20:9
not return thither any m. 22:11
ruling any m. in Judah. 30
shall not sorrow any m. at. 31:12
thrown down any m. for ever. 40
themselves of them any m. 34:10
not do any m. the like. Ezek 5:9
words be prolonged any m. 12:28
shalt give no hire any m. 16:41
never open thy mouth any m. 63
shall not return any m. 21:5
not remember Egypt any m. 23:27
from thy filthiness any m. 24:13
thou shall be a terror, and never shalt
be any m. 27:36; 28:19
nor shall exalt itself any m. 29:15
nor foot of man trouble them any m.
32:13; 37:23
none of them any m. there. 39:28
hide my face any m. from them. 29
nor say any m. to the work. Hos 14:3
what I to do any m. with idols? 8
pass through her any m. Joel 3:17
not again pass by them any m.
Amos 7:8; 8:2
prophesy not again any m. at. 7:13
not see evil any m. Zeph 3:15
durst any ask him any m. Mat 22:46
not any m. than one loaf. Mark 8:14
they saw no man any m. save. 9:8
nor can they die any m. Luke 20:36
I will not eat any m. thereof. 22:16
let us not judge one another any m.
Rom 14:13
be spoken to them any m. Heb 12:19
shall they thirst any m. Rev 7:16
place in heaven found any m. 12:8
buyeth her merchandise any m. 18:11
nor shall there be any m. pain. 21:4

***much* more**

people being much m. Ex 36:5
much m. the wicked and. Pr 11:31
as this day, and much m. Isa 56:12
not much m. clothe you? Mat 6:30
so much m. went a fame. Luke 5:15
I say unto you, and much m. 7:26
much m. being now justified by his.
Rom 5:9
much m. being reconciled, we. 10
much m. they that receive. 17
grace did much m. abound. 20
much m. doth ministration. 2 Cor 3:9

much m. that which remaineth. 2 Cor 3:11
proved much m. diligent. 8:22
are much m. bold to. Phil 1:14
have obeyed, now much m. 2:12
so much m. as you see day. Heb 10:25
much m. shall not we escape. 12:25
being much m. precious. 1 Pet 1:7

no more

waters shall no m. Gen 9:15
be called no m. Jacob. 32:28
Judah knew her again no m. 38:26
ye shall see my face no m. 44:23
Ex 10:28
no m. give the people. Ex 5:7
see thy face again no m. 10:29
ye shall see them again no m. 14:13
shall no m. offer their. Lev 17:7
fifty they shall serve no m. Num 8:25
speak no m. to me of this. Deut 3:26
Lord spake, and added no m. 5:22
circumcise, and be no m. stiff-. 10:16
do no m. such wickedness. 13:11
17:13
henceforth return no m. 17:16
thou shalt see it no m. again. 28:68
I am 120 years, I can no m. go. 31:2
God will no m. drive out. Josh 23:13
up their heads no m. Judg 8:28
I will deliver you no m. 10:13
was no m. sad. 1 Sam 1:18
talk no m. so exceeding proudly. 2:3
came no m. into the coast of. 7:13
and Samuel came no m. to. 15:35
let him go no m. home to his. 18:2
return, for I will no m. do. 26:21
and he sought no m. again. 27:4
and answereth me no m. 28:15
after Israel no m. 2 Sam 2:28
dwell in a place of their own, and move no m. 7:10; 1 Chr 17:9
shalt go no m. out with us to battle. 2 Sam 21:17
there was no m. spirit in her. 1 Ki 10:5; 2 Chr 9:4
Elisha saw Elijah no m. 2 Ki 2:12
bands of Syria came no m. 6:23
no m. of her than the skull. 9:35
shall no m. carry the tabernacle. 1 Chr 23:26
us build, that we be no m. Neh 2:17
no m. on the sabbath. 13:21
Vashti came no m. Esth 1:19
she came no m. in to the king. 2:14
eyes shall no m. see good. Job 7:7
shall see me no m. 8
shall come up no m. 9
return no m. to his house. 10
till the heavens be no m. 14:12
saw him shall see him no m. 20:9
shall be no m. remembered. 24:20
they answered no m. 32:15, 16
iniquity, I will do no m. 34:32
the battle, do no m. 41:8
earth may no m. oppress. Ps 10:18
I go hence, and be no m. 39:13
he shall rise up no m. 41:8
see not signs, there is no m. 74:9
and be favourable no m. 77:7
name of Israel be no m. in. 83:4
thou rememberest no m. 88:5
thereof shall know it no m. 103:16
let the wicked be no m. 104:35
so is the wicked no m. Pr 10:25
remember his misery no m. 31:7
king, who will no m. be. Eccl 4:13
bring no m. vain oblations. Isa 1:13
shall no m. stay on him that. 10:20
driven away, and be no m. 19:7
there is no m. strength. 23:10
no m. rejoice. 12
the earth shall no m. cover. 26:21
shall weep no m. 30:19
vile person shall be no m. 32:5
I shall behold man no m. 38:11
shalt no m. be called tender. 47:1
shalt no m. be called the lady. 5
shalt no m. drink it again. 51:22
no m. come into thee the uncircumcised. 52:1
violence shall no m. be heard. 60:18
the sun shall be no m. thy light. 19
sun shall no m. go down. Isa 60:20
thou shalt no m. be termed. 62:4
I will no m. give thy corn to. 8
weeping shall be no m. heard. 65:19
there shall be no m. thence an. 20
will come no m. unto thee. Jer 2:31
they shall say no m. The ark. 3:16
no m. be called Tophet. 7:32; 19:6
his name may be no m. 11:19
shall no m. be said, The Lord liveth. 16:14; 23:7
shall return no m. 22:10
see this land no m. 12
fear no m. nor be dismayed. 23:4
of Lord shall ye mention no m. 36
fall and rise no m. because of. 25:27
teach no m. every man his neighbour, and I . . . their sin no m. 31:34
should be no m. a nation. 33:24
shall see this place no m. 42:18
name shall be no m. named. 44:26
saith Lord, Is wisdom no m.? 49:7
it shall no m. be inhabited. 50:39
law is no m. her prophets. Lam 2:9
he will no m. carry thee away. 4:22
no m. any vain vision. Ezek 12:24
and my word shall be no m. 25
the wall is no m. 13:15
and they shall be no m. in. 21
ye shall see no m. vanity. 23
go no m. astray. 14:11
and will be no m. angry. 16:42
that his voice should be no m. 19:9
ye my holy name no m. 20:39
it shall be no m. saith. 21:13, 27
shalt be no m. remembered. 32
speak, and be no m. dumb. 24:27
thou shalt be no m. built. 26:14
shalt be no m. 21
be no m. a pricking brier. 28:24
they shall no m. rule over. 29:15
shall be no m. the confidence of. 16
there shall be no m. a prince. 30:13
shall be no m. a prey. 34:22, 28, 29
shalt devour men no m. 36:14
shall be no m. two nations. 37:22
house of Israel no m. defile. 43:7
my princes shall no m. oppress. 45:8
I will no m. have mercy. Hos 1:6
shalt call me no m. Baali. 2:16
they shall no m. be remembered. 17
out, I will love them no m. 9:15
I will no m. make you a. Joel 2:19
fallen, she shall no m. rise. Amos 5:2
they shall no m. be pulled out. 9:15
have no m. soothsayers. Mi 5:12
thou shalt no m. worship work. 13
I will afflict thee no m. Nah 1:12
a command that no m. of thy. 14
the wicked shall no m. pass. 15
thy messengers shall no m. 2:13
shalt no m. be haughty. Zeph 3:11
I will no m. pity the. Zech 11:6
shall no m. be remembered. 13:2
be no m. utter destruction. 14:11
be no m. the Canaanite in the. 21
they are no m. twain, but one. Mat 19:6; Mark 10:8
and ye suffer him no m. Mark 7:12
and enter no m. into him. 9:25
I will drink no m. of the fruit. 14:25
exact no m. than what. Luke 3:13
we have no m. but five loaves. 9:13
after that have no m. that. 12:4
thou art made whole, sin no m. John 5:14; 8:11
back, and walked no m. with. 6:66
the world seeth me no m. 14:19
no m. can ye, except ye abide. 15:4
Father, and ye see me no m. 16:10
no m. the anguish, for joy. 21
when I shall no m. speak in. 25
now I am no m. in the world. 17:11
eunuch saw him no m. Acts 8:39
now no m. to return to corruption. 13:34
shall see my face no m. 20:25, 38
dieth no m.; death hath no m. Rom 6:9
now then it is no m. I that. 7:17, 20
no m. of works: otherwise grace is no m. grace. 11:6
know we him no m. 2 Cor 5:16
it is no m. of promise. Gal 3:18
thou art no m. a servant. Gal 4:7
ye are no m. strangers. Eph 2:19
we be no m. children tossed. 4:14
let him that stole steal no m. 28
iniquities I will remember no m. Heb 8:12; 10:17
had no m. conscience of sins. 10:2
no m. offering for sin. 18, 26
overcometh shall go no m. Rev 3:12
no m., neither thirst any more. 7:16
find them no m. at all. 18:14
be heard no m. in thee. 22, 23
deceive the nations no m. 20:3
no m. sea. 21:1
no m. death. 4
no m. curse. 22:3

moreover

m. by them is thy servant. Ps 19:11
he said, M. there shall be. Isa 39:8
thou hast m. multiplied. Ezek 16:29
m. this is their resemblance. Zech 5:6
mockings, m. of bonds. Heb 11:36

Moriah

into the land of M. Gen 22:2
the house of Lord in M. 2 Chr 3:1

morning

m. arose, the angels. Gen 19:15
servants rose up in the m. 24:54
they rose betimes in the m. 26:31
the m. behold it was Leah. 29:25
came in unto them in the m. 40:6
in the m. he shall devour. 49:27
thee to Pharaoh in the m. Ex 7:15
in the m. the east wind. 10:13
to his strength in the m. 14:27
in the m. ye shall see the glory. 16:7
shall give you in the m. bread. 8, 12
in the m. the dew lay round. 13
one lamb thou shalt offer in the m. 29:39; Num 28:4
meat offering of the m. Ex 29:41
m. and come up in the m. 34:2
nor sacrifice be left to the m. 25
altar all night to the m. Lev 6:9
taken up in the m. Num 9:21
Balaam rose in the m. and. 22:21, 22
in m., would God it were. Deut 28:67
death whilst it is yet m. Judg 6:31
in the m. when it is day, we. 16:2
her lord rose in the m. and. 19:27
Israel rose up in the m. 20:19
as the light of the m. when the sun riseth, even a m. 2 Sam 23:4
was up in the m. word came. 24:11
considered it in the m. 1 Ki 3:21
name of Baal from m. to noon. 18:26
some laboured from m. Neh 4:21
he read therein from m. to. 8:3
seek me in the m. but. Job 7:21
shine forth, and be as the m. 11:17
m. is to them as the shadow. 24:17
hast thou commanded the m.? 38:12
like eyelids of the m. 41:18
thou hear in the m., O Lord; in the m. will I direct my prayer. Ps 5:3
but joy cometh in the m. 30:5
dominion over them in the m. 49:14
sing of thy mercy in the m. 59:16
in the m. shall my prayer. 88:13
in the m. they are like grass. 90:5
in the m. it flourisheth and. 6
the dawning of the m. 119:147
they that watch for the m. 130:6
if I take the wings of the m. 139:9
thy lovingkindness in the m. 143:8
and princes eat in the m. Eccl 10:16
in m. sow thy seed, and in the. 11:6
looketh forth as the m.? S of S 6:10
O Lucifer, son of the m. Isa 14:12
before the m. he is not. 17:14
the watchman said, The m. 21:12
for m. by m. shall it pass. 28:19
he wakeneth m. by m. he. 50:4
thy light break forth as the m. 58:8
were as fed horses in the m. Jer 5:8
hear the cry in the m. 20:16
execute judgement in the m. 21:12
the m. is come on thee. Ezek 7:7*
the m. is gone forth, the rod. 10*
in the m. came the word of. 12:8
I spake to the people in the m.: . . . I did in the m. as I was. 24:18

came to me in the m. Ezek 33:22
is prepared as the m. Hos 6:3
for your goodness is as a m. 4
m. it burneth as a flaming fire. 7:6
a m. shall the king of Israel. 10:15*
as the m. spread upon the. Joel 2:2*
maketh the m. darkness. Amos 4:13
the shadow of death into the m. 5:8
a worm when the m. rose. Jonah 4:7
when the m. is light. Mi 2:1
in the m. it will be foul. Mat 16:3
when m. was come, the elders. 27:1
the m. as they passed. Mark 11:20
the cockcrowing, or in m. 13:35
see **cloud, evening**

early in the **morning**
Abraham gat up early in m.
Gen 19:27; 21:14; 22:3
Abimelech rose early in the m. 28:8
Jacob rose up early in m. 28:18
Laban rose early in m., kissed. 31:55
rise up early in m., stand. Ex 8:20
9:13
Moses rose early in m. 24:4; 34:4
Joshua rose early in m. Josh 3:1
6:12; 7:16; 8:10
city rose early in the m. Judg 6:28
Gideon rose early in m. 38
Levite rose early in m. 19:5, 8
they rose up early in the m.
1 Sam 1:19; 29:11; 2 Ki 3:22
19:35; 2 Chr 20:20; Isa 37:36
Samuel rose early in m. 1 Sam 15:12
David rose early in m. 17:20
wherefore rise up early in m. 29:10
Job rose up early in the m. Job 1:5
friend, rising early in m. Pr 27:14
rise early in m. to follow. Isa 5:11
arose early in m. they were. 37:36
king Darius rose very early in m.
Dan 6:19
went early in m. to hire. Mat 20:1
early in m. came to sepulchre.
Mark 16:2; Luke 24:1*
the people came early in m.
Luke 21:38; John 8:2
entered into the temple early in m.
Acts 5:21*

every **morning**
gathered manna every m. Ex 16:21
thereon sweet incense every m. 30:7
free offerings every m. 36:3
burn wood on it every m. Lev 6:12
opening every m. pertaineth to.
1 Chr 9:27
to stand every m. to thank. 23:30
they burn to the Lord every m.
2 Chr 13:11
visit him every m. Job 7:18
been chastened every m. Ps 73:14
be thou our arm every m. Isa 33:2
mercies are new every m. Lam 3:23
prepare a lamb every m. Ezek 46:13
meat offering every m. 14
every m. a burnt offering. 15
your sacrifices every m. Amos 4:4
every m. doth he bring judgement to
light. Zeph 3:5

morning *light*
let us spoil them until m. light.
1 Sam 14:36
pertain to him by m. light. 25:22
told him nothing until m. light. 36
over Jordan by m. light. 2 Sam 17:22
if we tarry until m. light. 2 Ki 7:9

morning *star* and *stars*
when m. stars sang together.
Job 38:7
give him the m. star. Rev 2:28
I am the bright and m. star. 22:16

until the **morning**
let nothing of it remain until the m.
Ex 12:10; 16:19; 23:18; 29:34
Lev 7:15; Num 9:12
at the door until the m. Ex 12:22
left of it until the m. 16:20
to be kept until the m. 23
not abide until the m. Lev 19:13
flesh remain until the m. Deut 16:4
her all night until the m. Judg 19:25
lie down until the m. Ruth 3:13
she lay until the m. 14
Samuel lay until the m. 1 Sam 3:15
heed to thyself until m. 1 Sam 19:2
kings in two heaps until m. 2 Ki 10:8
fill of love until the m. Pr 7:18
I reckoned until the m. Isa 38:13

morning *watch*
in m. watch the Lord. Ex 14:24
of host in m. watch. 1 Sam 11:11

morrow
Lord did that thing on the m. Ex 9:6
on m. the remainder. Lev 7:16; 19:6
none of it until the m. 22:30*
on m. after sabbath the priest. 23:11
ye shall count from the m. after. 15
on m. the congregation. Num 16:41
manna ceased on m. after. Josh 5:12
on the m. he took a thick. 2 Ki 8:15
not the bones till the m. Zeph 3:3
no thought for the m., for the m.
shall take thought for. Mat 6:34
to depart on the m. Acts 20:7
know not what shall be on the m.
Jas 4:14

*to-***morrow**
to-m shall this sign be. Ex 8:23
to-m. the Lord shall do this. 9:5
to-m. is the rest of the holy. 16:23
sanctify them to-day and to-m. 19:10
Aaron said, To-m. is a feast. 32:5
sanctify yourselves against to-m. ye.
Num 11:18; Josh 7:13
to-m. the Lord will shew. Num 16:5*
be thou, they and Aaron to-m. 16
to-m. Lord will do wonders. Josh 3:5
to-m. he will be wroth with. 22:18
to-m. get you early on. Judg 19:9
go up, for to-m. I will. 20:28
to-m. by that time sun. 1 Sam 11:9
to-m. is the new moon. 20:5, 18
to-m. shalt thou and thy. 28:19
my servants to thee to-m. 1 Ki 20:6
we will eat my son to-m. 2 Ki 6:28
to-m. a measure of fine flour be. 7:1
to Jezreel by to-m. this time. 10:6
to-m. go ye down against them.
2 Chr 20:16, 17
I will do to-m. as the king. Esth 5:8
to-m. am I invited to her with. 12
to-m. I will give, when. Pr 3:28
boast not thyself to-m. thou. 27:1
let us eat, for to-m. we die.
Isa 22:13; 1 Cor 15:32
to-m. shall be as this day. Isa 56:12
to-m. is cast into the oven. Mat 6:30
Luke 12:28
cures to-day and to-m. Luke 13:32
I must walk to-day and to-m. 33
to-m. said he, thou shalt. Acts 25:22
to-day or to-m. we will go. Jas 4:13

morsel
I will fetch a m. of bread. Gen 18:5
heart with a m. of bread. Judg 19:5
eat bread, and dip thy m. Ruth 2:14
or have eaten my m. Job 31:17
better is a dry m. and. Pr 17:1
the m. thou hast eaten shalt. 23:8
who for one m. sold his. Heb 12:16*
see **bread**

morsels
forth his ice like m. Ps 147:17

mortal
m. man be more just? Job 4:17
reign in your m. body. Rom 6:12
shall also quicken your m. 8:11
this m. must put on. 1 Cor 15:53, 54
manifest in our m. flesh. 2 Cor 4:11

mortality
m. might be swallowed. 2 Cor 5:4

mortally
smite his neighbour m. Deut 19:11

mortar
mills, or beat it in a m. Num 11:8
bray a fool in a m. Pr 27:22

morter (*mortar*)
slime had they for m. Gen 11:3
made them serve in m. Ex 1:14
take other m. and plaster. Lev 14:42
and shall break down the m. of. 45
upon princes as upon m. Isa 41:25
lo, others daubed it with untempered
m. Ezek 13:10, 11, 14, 15; 22:28
clay, and tread the m. Nah 3:14

mortgaged
also said, We have m. Neh 5:3

mortify
if ye m. deeds of body. Rom 8:13†
m. your members which. Col 3:5†

Moses
called his name M. Ex 2:10
M. feared, and said, This thing. 14
sought to slay M. but M. fled. 15
called to him and said, M. M. 3:4
M. hid his face, he was afraid. 6
anger was kindled against M. 4:14
go to meet M. 27
M. returned unto the Lord. 5:22
according to the word of M. 8:13, 31
9:12, 35; 12:35
M. stretched forth his hand. 10:22
M. was very great. 11:3
the Lord and his servant M. 14:31
the people murmured against M.
15:24; 17:3
they hearkened not to M. 16:20
M. cried to the Lord. 17:4
M. did so. 6; Num 17:11
M.' hands were heavy. Ex 17:12
M. built an altar. 15
M. sat to judge. 18:13
M. went up unto God. 19:3
M. returned the words of the. 8
called M. up to mount Sinai. 20
M. drew near unto the thick. 20:21
M. alone shall come near. 24:2
M. wrote all the words of the. 4
and M. went into the midst of. 18
as for M. we wot not what. 32:1, 23
M. besought the Lord. 11
M.' anger waxed hot. 19
the Lord talked with M. 33:9
M. went up. 34:4
M. put the vail upon his face. 34:35
M. did look on all work; M. 39:43
M. was not able to enter. 40:35
M. sought the goat of. Lev 10:16
the blasphemer to M. 24:11
as the Lord spake to M. Num 5:4
the people cried to M., and M. 11:2
M. heard people weep through. 10
indeed spoken only by M.? 12:2
M. was very meek above all. 3
M. is not so, who is faithful in. 7
ark and M. departed not out. 14:44
when M. heard it, he fell upon. 16:4
M. laid up the rods before the. 17:7
the people chode with M. 20:3
against God and against M. 21:5
M. made a serpent of brass and. 9
Midianitish woman in sight of M.
25:6
M. sent them to war, them. 31:6
M. was wroth with the officers. 14
M. wrote their goings out by. 33:2
M. charged the people. Deut 27:11
M. wrote this law and. 31:9
M. wrote this song, and taught. 22
wherewith M. the man of God. 33:1
M. the servant of the Lord. 34:5
since in Israel like to M. 10
as I was with M. so I. Josh 1:5; 3:7
as we hearkened to M. so. 1:17
Joshua, as they feared M. 4:14
Lord spake this word to M. 14:10
as I was in the day M. sent me. 11
as it is written in the law of M.
1 Ki 2:3; 2 Ki 23:25; 2 Chr 23:18
Ezra 3:2; Dan 9:11, 13
Luke 24:44; 1 Cor 9:9
the two tables which M. 1 Ki 8:9
M. the man of God. 1 Chr 23:14
the son of M. was ruler. 26:24
known his ways unto M. Ps 103:7
he sent M. his servant. 105:26
they envied M. also in the. 106:16
had not M. stood before him. 23
so that it went ill with M. for. 32
the right hand of M. Isa 63:12
though M. and Samuel. Jer 15:1
remember the law of M. Mal 4:4
appeared M. and Elias talking with.
Mat 17:3; Mark 9:4; Luke 9:30
let us make one tabernacle for M.
Mat 17:4; Mark 9:5
did M. then command? Mat 19:7
M. suffered you to put away. 8

Pharisees sit in M.' seat. Mat 23:2
did M. command you? Mark 10:3
M. wrote, If a man's brother die.
12:19; Luke 20:28
M. and the prophets. Luke 16:29
if they hear not M. and the. 31
dead are raised, M. shewed. 20:37
beginning at M. and all the prophets, he expounded. 24:27
law was given by M. John 1:17
have found him of whom M. 45
as M. lifted up the serpent. 3:14
one accuseth you, even M. 5:45
had ye believed M. ye had. 46
M. gave you not that bread. 6:32
did not M. give you the law? 7:19
not because it is of M. but of. 22
that the law of M. should not. 23
disciple, we are M.' disciples. 9:28
we know that God spake unto M. 29
for M. truly said unto. Acts 3:22
blasphemous words against M. 6:11
change the customs which M. 14
in which time M. was born. 7:20
then M. trembled and durst not. 32
this M. whom they refused, did. 35
M. that said unto Israel. 37
be justified by the law of M. 13:39
circumcised after manner of M. 15:1
them to keep the law of M. 5
M. hath in every city them that. 21
the Jews to forsake M. 21:21
things which M. did say. 26:22
out of the law of M. and. 28:23
from Adam to M. Rom 5:14
M. describeth righteousness of. 10:5
all baptized to M. in. 1 Cor 10:2
not behold the face of M. 2 Cor 3:7
not as M. who put a vail over. 13
when M. is read, the vail is. 15
and Jambres withstood M. 2 Tim 3:8
M. was faithful in all. Heb 3:2, 5
worthy of more glory than M. 3
that came out of Egypt by M. 16
which tribe M. spake nothing. 7:14
for when M. had spoken. 9:19
that despised M.' law. 10:28
by faith M. was hid three. 11:23
M. refused to be called son of. 24
M. said, I exceedingly fear. 12:21
about the body of M. Jude 9
song of M. and the Lamb. Rev 15:3
see **Aaron, book, commanded, law**

most

m. men proclaim every. Pr 20:6
m. of mighty works. Mat 11:20
them will love him m.? Luke 7:42
that he to whom he forgave m. 43
sorrowing m. of all for. Acts 20:38
it be by two, or at m. 1 Cor 14:27

mote

m. that is in thy brother's eye, but not beam? Mat 7:3; Luke 6:41
let me pull out the m. Mat 7:4
to cast out the m. out of thy brother's eye. 5; Luke 6:42

moth

are crushed before the m. Job 4:19
buildeth his house as a m. 27:18
beauty to consume like a m. Ps 39:11
the m. shall eat them up. Isa 50:9
51:8
I be to Ephraim as a m. Hos 5:12
treasures, where m. and rust doth corrupt. Mat 6:19
neither m. nor rust corrupt. 20
Luke 12:33

motheaten

garment that is m. Job 13:28
your garments m. Jas 5:2

mother

was the m. of all living. Gen 3:20
shall be a m. of nations. 17:16
told them of her m.'s house. 24:28
brother and m. precious things. 53
thou the m. of thousands of. 60
lest he smite the m. with. 32:11
called the child's m. Ex 2:8
to take a wife and her m. Lev 20:14
Deborah arose a m. Judg 5:7
m. of Sisera looked out. 28
go, return each to her m.'s. Ruth 1:8
to Zeruiah, Joab's m. 2 Sam 17:25
seekest to destroy a m. in. 20:19
be set for the king's m. 1 Ki 2:19
child, she is the m. thereof. 3:27
away the king's m. 2 Ki 24:15
and to be a joyful m. Ps 113:9
doth not bless their m. Pr 30:11
the only one of her m. S of S 6:9
of your m.'s divorcement? Isa 50:1
your m. shall be sore. Jer 50:12
as is the m. so is the. Ezek 16:44
your m. was an Hittite, father. 45
women the daughters of one m. 23:2
plead with your m. for she. Hos 2:2
their m. hath played the harlot. 5
m. was dashed in pieces upon. 10:14
up against her m. a man's enemies.
Mi 7:6; Mat 10:35; Luke 12:53
saw Peter's wife's m. sick.
Mat 8:14; Luke 4:38
instructed of her m. Mat 14:8
brought it to her m. 11; Mark 6:28
born from their m.'s womb.
Mat 19:12
m. of Zebedee's children. 20:20
the m. of my Lord should? Luke 1:43
the m. of Jesus was there. John 2:1
Acts 1:14
house of Mary m. of. Acts 12:12
Jerusalem which is the m. Gal 4:26
the m. of harlots. Rev 17:5
see **father**

***his* mother**

his m. took him a wife. Gen 21:21
into his m. Sarah's tent, and . . . after the death of his m. 24:67
brought them to his m. 27:14
brought mandrakes to his m. 30:14
brother Benjamin, his m.'s son. 43:29
he alone is left of his m. 44:20
seethe a kid in his m.'s milk.
Ex 23:19; 34:26; Deut 14:21
take his m.'s daughter. Lev 20:17
his m.'s name was Shelomith. 24:11
out of his m.'s womb. Num 12:12
the daughter of his m. Deut 27:22
Abimelech went to his m.'s. Judg 9:1
he said to his m. 17:2
he restored it to his m 3
his m. made him a little. 1 Sam 2:19
and his m. bare him. 1 Ki 1:6
his m. he removed from. 15:13
Elijah delivered him to his m. 17:23
walked in the way of his m. 22:52
lad, Carry him to his m. 2 Ki 4:19
his m. called his name. 1 Chr 4:9
his m. was his counsellor. 2 Chr 22:3
mourneth for his m. Ps 35:14
sin of his m. be blotted out. 109:14
is weaned of his m. 131:2
is the heaviness of his m. Pr 10:1
foolish man despiseth his m. 15:20
a child left bringeth his m. 29:15
prophecy that his m. taught. 31:1
forth of his m.'s womb. Eccl 5:15
crown wherewith his m. S of S 3:11
whom his m. comforteth. Isa 66:13
his m. was espoused. Mat 1:18
young child and his m. 2:13, 20
his m. stood without. 12:46
Mark 3:31; Luke 8:19
is not this the carpenter's son? is not his m. called Mary? Mat 13:55
with Holy Ghost from his m.'s womb.
Luke 1:15
his m. said, He shall be called. 60
Joseph and his m. knew not. 2:43*
but his m. kept these sayings. 51
the only son of his m. and. 7:12
he delivered him to his m. 15
second time into his m.'s womb?
John 3:4
his m. stood by the cross of. 19:25
saw his m. he saith to his m. 26
man lame from his m.'s womb.
Acts 3:2; 14:8
salute Rufus and his m. Rom 16:13

mother in law

lieth with his m. in law. Deut 27:23
kissed her m. in law. Ruth 1:14
hast done to thy m. in law. 2:11
Ruth dwelt with her m. in law. 23
all that her m. in law bade. 3:6
go not empty to thy m. in law.
Ruth 3:17
riseth up against the m. in law.
Mi 7:6; Mat 10:35; Luke 12:53

***my* mother**

the daughter of my m. Gen 20:12
even the sons of my m. Judg 8:19
Nazarite from my m.'s womb. 16:17
to her, Ask on, my m. 1 Ki 2:20
naked came I out of my m.'s. Job 1:21
up the doors of my m.'s womb. 3:10
the worm, Thou art my m. 17:14
guided her from my m.'s womb. 31:18
when on my m.'s breasts. Ps 22:9
thou art my God from my m.'s. 10
and in sin did my m. conceive. 51:5
become an alien to my m.'s. 69:8
he that took me out of my m.'s. 71:6
hast covered me in my m.'s. 139:13
beloved in sight of my m. Pr 4:3
my m.'s children were angry with me.
S of S 1:6
brought him to my m.'s house. 3:4
sucked the breasts of my m. 8:1
bring thee into my m.'s house. 2
the bowels of my m. he. Isa 49:1
woe is me, my m. that. Jer 15:10
not the day wherein my m. 20:14
or that my m. might have been. 17
Jesus said, Who is my m.?
Mat 12:48; Mark 3:33
behold my m. and my brethren.
Mat 12:49; Mark 3:34
my m. and my brethren are these.
Luke 8:21
separated me from my m.'s.
Gal 1:15

***thy* mother**

thy m.'s sons bow down. Gen 27:29
shall I and thy m. come to? 37:10
nakedness of thy m. Lev 18:7
nakedness of daughter of thy m. 9
not uncover nakedness of sister of thy m. 13; 20:19
the son of thy m. entice. Deut 13:6
so shall thy m. be childless among.
1 Sam 15:33
to the confusion of thy m.'s. 20:30
whoredoms of thy m. 2 Ki 9:22
thou slanderest thine own m.'s son.
Ps 50:20
forsake not the law of thy m.
Pr 1:8; 6:20
and despise not thy m. 23:22
thy m. brought thee forth. S of S 8:5
cast thee out, and thy m. Jer 22:26
father an Amorite, thy m. Ezek 16:3
thy m.'s daughter that loatheth. 45
and say, What is thy m.? 19:2
thy m. is like a vine in thy. 10
and I will destroy thy m. Hos 4:5
behold thy m. and thy brethren.
Mat 12:47; Mark 3:32
Luke 8:20; John 19:27
dwelt in thy m. Eunice. 2 Tim 1:5

mothers

shall be thy nursing m. Isa 49:23
Lord, concerning their m. Jer 16:3
m. where is corn and wine? soul was poured out into their m.' Lam 2:12
we are fatherless, our m. are. 5:3
hundredfold, sisters, m. Mark 10:30
for murderers of m. 1 Tim 1:9
elder women as m.; younger. 5:2

motions

the m. of sins did work. Rom 7:5*

mouldy

bread of provision was dry and m.
Josh 9:5, 12

mount, -ing

though his excellency m. Job 20:6
doth the eagle m. up at thy? 39:27
they m. up to heaven. Ps 107:26
shall m. up as the lifting. Isa 9:18*
by the m. of Luhith shall. 15:5
they shall m. up with wings. 40:31
though Babylon should m. up to.
Jer 51:53
when the cherubims lifted up wings to m. up. Ezek 10:16, 19

mount

(*This word very frequently means* hill country, *and is so rendered by the Revisions*)

sacrifice on the *m*. *Gen* 31:54
encamped at the *m*. of. *Ex* 18:5
whoso toucheth the *m*. shall. 19:12
Moses went down from the *m*. 14
32:15; 34:29
thick cloud upon the *m*. 16; 24:15
m. Sinai on a smoke. 18
bounds about the *m*. 23
Lord abode upon *m*. Sinai. 24:16
devouring fire on the top of *m*. 17
Lord gave Moses on *m*. Sinai. 31:18
brake them beneath the *m*. 32:19
in the morning to *m*. Sinai. 34:2
man be seen through all the *m*. 3
departed from the *m*. *Num* 10:33
and came unto *m*. Hor. 20:22
bring up to *m*. Hor. 25
Aaron died in *m*. Hor. 28
point out for you *m*. Hor. 34:7
long enough in this *m*. *Deut* 1:6
go to the *m*. of the Amorites. 7
the *m*. burned with fire. 9:15
shall stand upon *m*. Ebal. 27:13
get thee to *m*. Nebo, which. 32:49
shined forth from *m*. Paran. 33:2
draw towards *m*. Tabor. *Judg* 4:6
depart early from *m*. Gilead. 7:3
gat him up to *m*. Zalmon. 9:48
up by the ascent of *m*. *2 Sam* 15:30
the top of the *m*. where he. 32*
to Horeb, the *m*. of God. *1 Ki* 19:8
go and stand on the *m*. before. 11
on right hand the *m*. *2 Ki* 23:13
go to the *m*. and fetch. *Neh* 8:15
down also on *m*. Sinai. 9:13
of goats from *m*. Gilead. *S of S* 4:1
the *m*. of the daughter of Zion.
Isa 10:32; 16:1
I will sit on the *m*. of the. 14:13
shall worship in the holy *m*. 27:13
siege against thee with a *m*. 29:3
hew ye trees, and cast a *m*. against.
Jer 6:6; *Ezek* 4:2; 21:22; 26:8
north shall cast up a *m*. *Dan* 11:15
understanding out of *m*. Esau. *Ob* 8
come to judge the *m*. of Esau. 21
Holy One from *m*. Paran. *Hab* 3:3
in wilderness of *m*. Sinai. *Acts* 7:30
the one from the *m*. Sinai. *Gal* 4:24
Agar is *m*. Sinai in Arabia. 25
not come to the *m*. *Heb* 12:18
see **Carmel, Ephraim, Gerizim Gilboa, Seir, Zion**

before the **mount**

Israel camped *before the m*. *Ex* 19:2
the flocks feed *before the m*. 34:3

in, or *into the* **mount**

in the m. of the Lord. *Gen* 24:14
overtook Jacob *in the m*. Gilead.
31:23
and tarried all night *in the m*. 54
met him *in the m*. of God. *Ex* 4:27
go not up *into the m*. 19:12
Lord said to Moses, Come up to me
into the m. 24:12; *Deut* 10:1
Moses went up *into the m*. of God.
Ex 24:13, 15, 18
Moses was *in the m*. forty days.
24:18; *Deut* 9:9; 10:10
their pattern shewed thee *in the m*.
Ex 25:40; 26:30; 27:8; *Heb* 8:5
get thee up *into m*. *Num* 27:12
die *in the m*. as Aaron died *in m*.
Hor. *Deut* 32:50
altar to Lord *in m*. Ebal. *Josh* 8:30
the sepulchres *in the m*. *2 Ki* 23:16
to build house of Lord *in m*. Moriah.
2 Chr 3:1
rise up as *in m*. Perazim. *Isa* 28:21
spake to him *in m*. Sinai. *Acts* 7:38
with him *in the* holy *m*. *2 Pet* 1:18

mount *of Olives*

stand on the *m*. *of Olives*, and the *m*.
of Olives shall cleave. *Zech* 14:4
they were come to *m*. *of Olives*.
Mat 21:1; *Luke* 19:29
and as he sat upon *m*. *of Olives*.
Mat 24:3; *Mark* 13:3
sung an hymn, they went out into *m*.
of Olives. *Mat* 26:30
Mark 14:26; *Luke* 22:39
descent of *m*. *of Olives*. *Luke* 19:37
and abode in *m*. *of Olives*. 21:37
went unto *m*. *of Olives*. *John* 8:1
returned from the *m*. *of Olives*.
Acts 1:12

mountain

(*Used as now both literally and figuratively for a great mass, or a vast quantity. The Revisions frequently change it to* hill, *or* hill country)

A Catalogue of the most famous mountains mentioned in Scripture

Abarim, *on the East of Jordan, in Moab. Nebo and Pisgah were parts of this,* Num 27:12; Deut 34:1.

Ararat, *on which Noah's ark rested,* Gen 8:4.

Bashan, *probably a whole district of hill country.*

Carmel, *on the Mediterranean Sea on the border of Phoenicia,* 1 Ki 18:20–42.

Ebal, *in Samaria near Shechem,* Deut 11:26–29.

Gerizim, *separated by a valley from Ebal,* Deut 11:26–29.

Gilboa, *on which King Saul met his death,* 1 Sam 31:1.

Gilead, *a mountainous region east of Jordan.*

Hermon, *probably the scene of the Transfiguration,* Mat 17:1.

Hor, *on which Aaron died,* Num 20:25, 27.

Hor (*another*), Num 34:7, 8. *Probably Lebanon.*

Horeb *or* Sinai, *the Mount of God, or of the Law.*

Lebanon, *the most important range in Syria, to the north,* Josh 1:4; 1 Ki 5:2–7.

Moab, Mts. of, *a general term for the hill country east of Jordan.*

Moriah, *the site of the temple in Jerusalem.*

Nebo (Pisgah), *the place of Moses' death,* Deut. 34:1.

Olivet *or* Mt. of Olives, *near Jerusalem, associated much with our Saviour.*

Seir, *the mountainous district east of the Dead Sea,* Gen 14:6.

Sinai. *See* Horeb.

Tabor, *on the Plain of Esdraelon,* Judg 4:6–15; 19:22.

Zion *or* Sion, *one the mountains on which Jerusalem was built, the south-east corner.*

remained fled to the *m*. *Gen* 14:10
escape to the *m*. 19:17
I cannot escape to the *m*. 19
came to the *m*. of God. *Ex* 3:1
Egypt, shall serve God on this *m*. 12
to him out of the *m*. saying. 19:3
people saw the *m*. smoking. 20:18
up into top of the *m*. *Num* 14:40
ye are come to the *m*. *Deut* 1:20
ye have compassed this *m*. 2:3
goodly *m*. and Lebanon. 3:25
the *m*. burnt with fire. 4:11; 5:23
call the people to the *m*. 33:19
get ye to the *m*. and hide. *Josh* 2:16
plain and the *m*. of Israel. 11:16
give me this *m*. 14:12
the *m*. shall be thine. 17:18
drave out the inhabitants of the *m*.
Judg 1:19
forced children of Dan into *m*. 34
on a *m*. on the one side, and Israel
stood on a *m*. on. *1 Sam* 17:3
this side of the *m*. and David and his
men on that side of the *m*. 23:26
cast him on some *m*. *2 Ki* 2:16
the *m*. was full of horses. 6:17
surely the *m*. falling. *Job* 14:18
flee as a bird to your *m*.? *Ps* 11:1
thou hast made my *m*. to. 30:7
brought to this *m*. his right. 78:54
the *m*. of the Lord's house established. *Isa* 2:2; *Mi* 4:1
let us go up to the *m*. of the Lord.
Isa 2:3; *Mi* 4:2
a beacon on top of a *m*. *Isa* 30:17
goeth with a pipe to *m*. of Lord. 29
every *m*. shall be made low. 40:4
Luke 3:5
hunt them from every *m*. *Jer* 16:16
O my *m*. in the field, I will give. 17:3
the *m*. of the house as high places of.
26:18; *Mi* 3:12
people have gone from *m*. *Jer* 50:6
O *m*. saith the Lord . . . and I will
make thee a burnt *m*. 51:25
eyes are dim, because of *m*. of Zion.
Lam 5:18
Lord stood on the *m*. *Ezek* 11:23
as profane out of *m*. of God. 28:16
the house on top of the *m*. 43:12
stone became a great *m*. *Dan* 2:35
the stone was cut out of the *m*. 45
to thee from *m*. to *m*. *Mi* 7:12
go up to *m*., bring wood. *Hag* 1:8
who art thou, O great *m*.? *Zech* 4:7
m. of the Lord, the holy *m*. 8:3
half of *m*. shall remove. 14:4
he went up into a *m*. *Mat* 5:1
14:23; 15:29; *Mark* 3:13; 6:46
Luke 6:12; 9:28; *John* 6:3, 15
come down from the *m*. *Mat* 8:1
them into an high *m*. apart. 17:1
down from the *m*. 9; *Mark* 9:9
a grain of mustard, shall say to this
m. *Mat* 17:20; 21:21; *Mark* 11:23
into a *m*. where Jesus. *Mat* 28:16
swine feeding on *m*. *Luke* 8:32
as a beast touch the *m*. *Heb* 12:20
every *m*. and island were. *Rev* 6:14
as it were a great *m*. burning. 8:8
see **holy**

high **mountain**

banner upon the *high m*. *Isa* 13:2
upon every *high m*. rivers. 30:25
get thee up into the *high m*. 40:9
on a lofty and *high m*. hast. 57:7
gone up upon every *high m*. *Jer* 3:6
plant it on a *high m*. *Ezek* 17:22
set me on a very *high m*. 40:2
taketh him up into an exceeding *high*
m. and. *Mat* 4:8; *Luke* 4:5
Peter, James, and John, and bringeth
into *high m*. *Mat* 17:1; *Mark* 9:2
in the Spirit to *high m*. *Rev* 21:10

in the, or *in this* **mountain**

Zoar, and dwelt *in the m*. *Gen* 19:30
plant them *in the m*. *Ex* 15:17
go up *into the m*. *Num* 13:17
up *in this m*. Abarim. *Deut* 32:49
he blew a trumpet *in the m*. of.
Judg 3:27
David remained *in a m*. *1 Sam* 23:14
80,000 to hew *in the m*. *2 Chr* 2:2
God is to be praised *in the m*. of.
Ps 48:1
in this m. shall the Lord. *Isa* 25:6
he will destroy *in this m*. the face. 7
in this m. shall the hand of. 10
in the m. of Israel I. *Ezek* 17:23
ye kine, that are *in the m*. *Amos* 4:1
woe to them that trust *in the m*. 6:1
worshipped *in this m*. *John* 4:20
neither *in this m*. nor Jerusalem. 21

mountains

m. were covered. *Gen* 7:20
ark rested on the *m*. 8:4
in tenth month tops of the *m*. 5
departed from the *m*. *Num* 33:48
destroy places on the high *m*.
Deut 12:2
the Anakims from the *m*. *Josh* 11:21
the *m*. melted from. *Judg* 5:5
go up and down on the *m*. 11:37
her virginity upon the *m*. 38
ye *m*. of Gilboa, let. *2 Sam* 1:21
strong wind rent the *m*. *1 Ki* 19:11
as the roes on the *m*. *1 Chr* 12:8
all Israel scattered on the *m*.
2 Chr 18:16
which removeth the *m*. *Job* 9:5
he overturneth the *m*. by the. 28:9
m. bring forth food. 40:20
is like the great *m*. *Ps* 36:6

though the m. be carried into. Ps 46:2
though the m. shake with the. 3
strength setteth fast the m. 65:6
the m. shall bring peace. 72:3
glorious than m. of prey. 76:4
flames setteth the m. on fire. 83:14
before the m. were brought. 90:2
waters stood above the m. 104:6
they go up by the m.; go down by. 8
m. skipped like rams. 114:4, 6
as the m. are round about. 125:2
that descended on the m. 133:3
touch the m. and they shall. 144:5
grass to grow on the m. 147:8
m. and all hills praise the. 148:9
before the m. were settled. Pr 8:25
leaping on the m. S of S 2:8
be like a roe on the m. 17; 8:14
look from Amana and the m. 4:8
the day of the Lord shall be upon all the high m. Isa 2:14
and on my m. tread him. 14:25
up an ensign on the m. 18:3
the m. shall be melted with. 34:3
who hath weighed the m.? 40:12
thou shalt thresh the m. and. 41:15
and I will make waste m. 42:15
into singing, ye m. 44:23; 49:13
make all my m. a way. 49:11
how beautiful upon the m. are the feet of him that. 52:7; Nah 1:15
for the m. shall depart. Isa 54:10
m. shall break forth before. 55:12
the m. might flow down at. 64:1, 3
burnt incense on the m. 65:7
out of Judah an inheritor of my m. 9
I beheld the m. and. Jer 4:24
for the m. will I take up a. 9:10
stumble on the dark m. 13:16
from the m. bringing offerings. 17:26
vines on the m. of Samaria. 31:5
as Tabor among the m. so. 46:18
turned them away on the m. 50:6
pursued us on the m. Lam 4:19
set thy face toward the m. Ezek 6:2
and say, Ye m. of Israel, hear the. 3
shall be on the m. like doves. 7:16
not eaten upon the m. 18:6, 15
but hath eaten upon the m. 11
no more be heard on the m. 19:9
in thee they eat upon the m. 22:9
upon the m. his branches. 31:12
I will lay thy flesh on the m. 32:5
the m. of Israel shall be. 33:28
wandered through all the m. 34:6
feed them on the m. of Israel. 13, 14
I will fill his m. with his slain. 35:8
spoken against the m. of Israel. 12
m. of Israel, and say, Ye m. of Israel, hear the word of the. 36:1, 4
but ye, O m. of Israel, shall shoot. 8
one nation on the m. of Israel. 37:22
out against the m. of Israel. 38:8
m. shall be thrown down. 20
I will call for a sword against him throughout all my m. 21
and will bring thee on the m. 39:2
thou shalt fall on the m. of Israel. 4
even a great sacrifice on the m. 17
morning spread upon the m. Joel 2:2
m. shall drop down new wine. 3:18
assemble yourselves on the m. of. Amos 3:9
he that formeth the m. the. 4:13
the m. shall drop sweet wine. 9:13
the m. shall be molten. Mi 1:4
arise, contend thou before the m. 6:1
hear ye, O ye m. the Lord's. 2
the m. quake at him. Nah 1:5
people scattered on the m. 3:18
m. were scattered, the hills. Hab 3:6
m. saw thee, and they trembled. 10
a drought on the m. Hag 1:11
between the m. of brass. Zech 6:1
and laid his m. waste. Mal 1:3
goeth into the m. and. Mat 18:12
be in Judaea flee into the m. 24:16
that I could remove m. 1 Cor 13:2
the m. were not found. Rev 16:20
heads are seven m. on which. 17:9

in the **mountains**

to slay them in the m. Ex 32:12
pitched in m. of Abarim. Num 33:47
not to the cities in the m. Deut 2:37
kings that dwell in the m. Josh 10:6
made them dens in the m. Judg 6:2
as doth hunt a partridge in the m. 1 Sam 26:20
hewers in the m. 1 Ki 5:15
made high places in m. 2 Chr 21:11
had vine dressers in the m. 26:10
multitude in the m. like. Isa 13:4
day he was in the m. Mark 5:5
in deserts and in the m. Heb 11:38

of the **mountains**

tops of the m. were seen. Gen 8:5
offer him on one of m. I will. 22:2
Balak brought me out of the m. Num 23:7
foundations of the m. Deut 32:22
things of the ancient m. 33:15
liers in wait for him in top of the m. Judg 9:25
down from the top of the m. thou seest the shadow of the m. as. 36
I am come up to height of m. 2 Ki 19:23; Isa 37:24
with the showers of the m. Job 24:8
range of the m. is his pasture. 39:8
I know all the fowls of the m. Ps 50:11
of corn on top of the m. 72:16
and herbs of the m. Pr 27:25
shall be established in top of the m. Isa 2:2; Mi 4:1
as the chaff of the m. Isa 17:13
left to the fowls of the m. 18:6
shout from the top of the m. 42:11
the multitude of the m. Jer 3:23
cities of the m. shall flocks. 33:13
be in the tops of the m. Ezek 6:13
sounding again of the m. 7:7
on the tops of the m. Hos 4:13
chariots on tops of the m. Joel 2:5
to the bottom of the m. Jonah 2:6
flee to the valley of the m. Zech 14:5
in the rocks of the m. Rev 6:15

to the **mountains**

I will get me to the m. S of S 4:6
and crying to the m. Isa 22:5
thus saith the Lord to the m. Ezek 6:3; 36:4
thy blood even to the m. 32:6
man, prophesy to the m. 36:1, 6
they shall say to the m. Hos 10:8
nigh to the m. a herd. Mark 5:11
let them that be in Judaea flee to the m. 13:14; Luke 21:21
begin to say to m. Fall on us. Luke 23:30; Rev 6:16

mounts

(*American Revision*, mounds)
m. are come to the city. Jer 32:24
houses thrown down by the m. 33:4
him, by casting up m. Ezek 17:17

mourn

Abraham came to m. Gen 23:2
how long wilt thou m.? 1 Sam 16:1
rend clothes, and m. 2 Sam 3:31
came into the city to m. 1 Ki 13:29
all Israel shall m. for him. 14:13
holy to the Lord, m. not. Neh 8:9
an appointment to m. Job 2:11
that those which m. may be. 5:11
soul within him shall m. 14:22
I m. in my complaint. Ps 55:2*
and thou m. at the last. Pr 5:11
bear rule, the people m. 29:2*
a time to m. and a time. Eccl 3:4
gates shall lament and m. Isa 3:26
of Kir-hareseth shall ye m. 16:7
the fishers also shall m. 19:8
I did m. as a dove. 38:14
we roar like bears, we m. 59:11
sent me to comfort all that m. 61:2
m. in Zion, give beauty for ashes. 3
all ye that m. for her. 66:10
for this shall earth m. Jer 4:28
how long shall the land m.? 12:4
my heart shall m. for men. 48:31
ways of Zion do m. Lam 1:4
let not the seller m. Ezek 7:12
the king shall m. and the prince. 27
yet neither shalt thou m. nor. 24:16
ye shall pine away and m. one. 23
I caused Lebanon to m. Ezek 31:15
therefore shall the land m. Hos 4:3
for the people shall m. over. 10:5
the Lord's ministers m. Joel 1:9
of the shepherds shall m. Amos 1:2
every one m. that dwelleth. 8:8; 9:5
shall m. for him as one mourneth. Zech 12:10
and the land shall m. every. 12
blessed are they that m. Mat 5:4
children of bridechamber m.? 9:15
all the tribes of the earth m. 24:30
that laugh, for ye shall m. Luke 6:25
afflicted, and m. and weep. Jas 4:9
the merchants shall weep and m. Rev 18:11

mourned

Jacob m. for his son. Gen 37:34
Egyptians m. for Jacob. 50:3, 10
people heard these evil tidings, they m. Ex 33:4; Num 14:39
the congregation m. Num 20:29
nevertheless, Samuel m. for Saul. 1 Sam 15:35
and they m. for Saul. 2 Sam 1:12
Bath-sheba m. for Uriah. 11:26
David m. for his son. 13:37
as one that had long time m. 14:2
m. over the man of God. 1 Ki 13:30
all Israel m. for Jeroboam's. 14:18
Ephraim their father m. 1 Chr 7:22
and all Judah m. for. 2 Chr 35:24
m. for the transgression. Ezra 10:6
I sat down and m. Neh 1:4
when ye fasted and m. Zech 7:5
we have m. unto you, and ye have. Mat 11:17; Luke 7:32
told them as they m. Mark 16:10
and have not rather m. 1 Cor 5:2

mourner

feign thyself to be a m. 2 Sam 14:2

mourners

that comforteth the m. Job 29:25
m. go about the streets. Eccl 12:5
restore comforts to him and his m. Isa 57:18
be to them as bread of m. Hos 9:4

mourneth

behold, the king m. 2 Sam 19:1
I bowed as one that m. Ps 35:14
mine eye m. by reason of. 88:9*
the earth m. Isa 24:4; 33:9
the new wine m. 24:7
being desolate m. to me. Jer 12:11
Judah m. and the gates. 14:2
of swearing the land m. 23:10
the land m. for the corn. Joel 1:10
m. for his firstborn. Zech 12:10

mournfully

that we have walked m. Mal 3:14

mourning, *substantive*

days of m. for my father. Gen 27:41
and when the days of his m. 50:4
made a m. for his father Jacob. 10
m., this is a grievous m. 11
eaten thereof in my m. Deut 26:14
so the days of m. for Moses. 34:8
when the m. was past. 2 Sam 11:27
that day was turned into m. 19:2
there was great m. among. Esth 4:3
was turned to them from m. 9:22
to raise up their m. Job 3:8
my harp also is turned to m. 30:31
thou hast turned my m. Ps 30:11
to go to the house of m. Eccl 7:2
wise is in the house of m. 4
the Lord did call to m. Isa 22:12
and sorrow and m. shall flee. 51:11
and the days of thy m. shall. 60:20
them the oil of joy for m. 61:3
make thee m. as for. Jer 6:26
enter not into the house of m. 16:5
turn their m. into joy. 31:13
daughter of Judah m. Lam 2:5
our dance is turned into m. 5:15
written lamentations, m. and woe. Ezek 2:10
make no m. for the dead. 24:17
I caused a m. 31:15
with weeping and m. Joel 2:12
the husbandmen to m. Amos 5:16

turn your feasts into m. and I will
make it as the m. of an. Amos 8:10
came not forth in the m. Mi 1:11
m. in Jerusalem, as m. Zech 12:11
great m., Rachel weeping. Mat 2:18
us your desire, your m. 2 Cor 7:7
laughter be turned into m. Jas 4:9
in one day death and m. Rev 18:8

mourning, *verb*

to the grave to my son m. Gen 37:35
I pray thee, put on m. 2 Sam 14:2
hasted to his house m. Esth 6:12
went m. without the sun. Job 30:28
I am troubled, I go m. Ps 38:6
why go I m. because of oppression?
42:9; 43:2
call for the m. women. Jer 9:17
in m. to comfort them for. 16:7
all of them m. for their iniquities.
Ezek 7:16
I Daniel was m. 3 weeks. Dan 10:2
will make a m. as the owls. Mi 1:8

mouse

weasel and m. shall be. Lev 11:29
abomination, and the m. Isa 66:17

mouth

and lo, in her m. was. Gen 8:11
and enquire at her m. 24:57
stone was upon the well's m. 29:2
stone from the well's m. 3, 10
his money was in his sack's m.
42:27; 43:12, 21
who hath made man's m.? Ex 4:11
be to thee instead of a m. 16
will I speak m. to m. Num 12:8
the earth open her m. and. 16:30
put a word in Balaam's m. 23:5
put to death by the m. of witnesses.
35:30; Deut 17:6; 19:15
roll great stones on the m.
Josh 10:18, 27
open m. of cave, and bring out. 22
Eli marked her m. 1 Sam 1:12
the words in her m. 2 Sam 14:3, 19
a covering over the well's m. 17:19
every m. that hath not. 1 Ki 19:18
prophets declare good to the king
with one m. 22:13
a lying spirit in m. of his prophets.
22, 23; 2 Chr 18:21, 22
Necho from m. of God. 2 Chr 35:22
word of the Lord by the m. of Jeremiah. 36:21, 22; Ezra 1:1
went out of the king's m. Esth 7:8
iniquity stoppeth her m. Job 5:16
doth not the m. taste? 12:11*; 34:3*
there was no answer in the m. 32:5
out of the m. of babes hast. Ps 8:2
Mat 21:16
save me from the lion's m. Ps 22:21
whose m. must be held in. 32:9*
the m. of the righteous. 37:30
in whose m. are no reproofs. 38:14
but m. that speaketh lies. 63:11
let not the pit shut her m. 69:15
iniquity shall stop her m. 107:42
m. of wicked, m. of deceitful. 109:2
then was our m. filled with. 126:2
scattered at the grave's m. 141:7
whose m. speaketh vanity. 144:8, 11
from thee a froward m. Pr 4:24
and her m. is smoother than oil. 5:3
walketh with froward m. 6:12; 10:32
the froward m. do I hate. 8:13
violence covereth the m. of. 10:6, 11
the m. of the foolish is near. 14
the m. of the just bringeth. 31
the city is overthrown by m. 11:11
the m. of the upright shall. 12:6
in the m. of the foolish is a. 14:3
the m. of fools poureth out. 15:2
the m. of fools feedeth on. 14
the m. of the wicked poureth out. 28
the words of a man's m. are. 18:4
a fool's m. is his destruction. 7
m. of the wicked devoureth. 19:28
the m of a strange woman. 22:14
so is a parable in the m. 26:7, 9
and a flattering m. worketh ruin. 28
eateth, and wipeth her m. 30:20
words of a wise man's m. Eccl 10:12
Israel with open m. Isa 9:12
an evil doer, and every m. 17
make ye a wide m.? Isa 57:4
Spirit not depart out of m. 59:21
shall speak with him m. to m.
Jer 32:4; 34:3
Baruch wrote from m. of Jeremiah.
36:4, 27, 32; 45:1
goeth forth out of our m. 44:17
no more named in m. of any. 26
out of the m. of Most. Lam 3:38
to open the m. in the slaughter.
Ezek 21:22
thee the opening of the m. 29:21
came near to the m. of. Dan 3:26
word was in the king's m. 4:31
brought, and laid on the m. of. 6:17
it had three ribs in m. of it. 7:5
there was a m. speaking. 8, 20
of Baalim out of her m. Hos 2:17
taketh out of the m. Amos 3:12
shall even fall into the m. Nah 3:12
of lead on the m. of it. Zech 5:8
out of the m. of God. Mat 4:4
abundance of the heart the m. 12:34
goeth into the m. defileth not. 15:11
in the m. of two or three witnesses
every word. 18:16; 2 Cor 13:1
as he spake by m. of his. Luke 1:70
for I will give you a m. and. 21:15
Holy Ghost spake by m. of David.
Acts 1:16; 4:25
by m. of all his prophets. 3:18, 21
you the same things by m. 15:27
them to smite him on the m. 23:2
m. is full of cursing. Rom 3:14
that every m. may be stopped. 19
with the m. confession is. 10:10
that ye may with one m. 15:6
muzzle the m. of the ox. 1 Cor 9:9*
I was delivered out of m. 2 Tim 4:17
out of the same m. Jas 3:10
given to him a m. Rev 13:5
the spirits came out of m. of. 16:13
see **Lord**

his mouth

his m.: I will be with his m. Ex 4:15
put a word in his m. Num 23:16
proceedeth out of his m. 30:2
put my words in his m. Deut 18:18
no man put his hand to his m.
1 Sam 14:26, 27
delivered it out of his m. 17:35
there is tidings in his m. 2 Sam 18:25
and fire out of his m. devoured.
22:9; Ps 18:8
spake with his m. to David.
1 Ki 8:15; 2 Chr 6:4
he put his m. on his m. 2 Ki 4:34
judgements of his m. 1 Chr 16:12
by the breath of his m. Job 15:30
be sweet in his m. 20:12
keep it still within his m. 13
pray thee, the law from his m. 22:22
esteemed the words of his m. 23:12
sound that goeth out of his m. 37:2
draw up Jordan into his m. 40:23
out of his m. go burning. 41:19
and a flame goeth out of his m. 21
his m. is full of cursing. Ps 10:7
made by breath of his m. 33:6
words of his m. are iniquity. 36:3
man that openeth not his m. 38:13
words of his m. are smoother. 55:21
remember the judgements of his m.
105:5
his m. cometh knowledge. Pr 2:6
hypocrite with his m. 11:9
good by the fruit of his m. 12:14
eat good by the fruit of his m. 13:2
he that keepeth his m. keepeth. 3
joy by the answer of his m. 15:23
his m. transgresseth not. 16:10
of the wise teacheth his m. 23
for himself, for his m. craveth. 26
and his m. calleth for strokes. 18:6
satisfied with the fruit of his m. 20
not so much as bring it to his m.
19:24; 26:15
but his m. shall be filled. 20:17
whoso keepeth his m. 21:23
labour of a man is for his m. Eccl 6:7
beginning of words of his m. 10:13
with the kisses of his m. S of S 1:2
his m. is most sweet, this is. 5:16
earth with the rod of his m. Isa 11:4
was any deceit in his m. 53:9
peaceably with his m. Jer 9:8
ear receive the word of his m. 20
write all these words at his m. 36:17
bring out of his m. that. 51:44
putteth his m. in the dust. Lam 3:29
cleaveth to the roof of his m. 4:4
his blood out of his m. Zech 9:7
law of truth was in his m. Mal 2:6
should seek the law at his m. 7
and his m. was opened. Luke 1:64
words proceeded out of his m. 4:22
abundance of heart his m. 6:45
catch somewhat out of his m. 11:54
have heard of his own m. 22:71
filled a spunge and put it to his m.
John 19:29
hear the voice of his m. Acts 22:14
with the spirit of his m. 2 Thes 2:8
guile found in his m. 1 Pet 2:22
out of his m. went a sharp sword.
Rev 1:16; 19:15, 21
cast out of his m. water. 12:15
the dragon cast out of his m. 16
and his m. was as the mouth. 13:2

***my* mouth**

my m. that speaketh. Gen 45:12
the word God putteth in my m.
Num 22:38; 23:12
the words of my m. Deut 32:1
my m. is enlarged over. 1 Sam 2:1
I will not refrain my m. Job 7:11
mine own m. shall condemn. 9:20
strengthen you with my m. 16:5
my servant with my m. 19:16
fill my m. with arguments. 23:4
my m. hath kissed my hand. 31:27
neither have I suffered my m. 30
tongue hath spoken in my m. 33:2
will lay my hand upon my m. 40:4
purposed that my m. Ps 17:3
words of my m. be acceptable. 19:14
shall continually be in my m. 34:1
I said, I will keep my m. 39:1
he hath put a new song in my m. 40:3
hear this, my m. shall speak. 49:3
and my m. shall shew forth. 51:15
give ear to the words of my m. 54:2
my m. shall praise thee with. 63:5
my m. hath spoken, when I. 66:14
I cried to him with my m., he. 17
let my m. be filled with thy. 71:8
my m. shall shew forth thy. 15
ears to the words of my m. 78:1
I will open my m. in a parable. 2
with my m. will I make known. 89:1
praise the Lord with my m. 109:30
word of truth out of my m. 119:43
sweeter than honey to my m. 103
freewill offerings of my m. 108
cleave to the roof of my m. 137:6
O Lord, before my m. 141:3
my m. shall speak praise. 145:21
nor decline from the words of my m.
Pr 4:5; 5:7
attend to the words of my m. 7:24
for my m. shall speak truth. 8:7
the words of my m. are in. 8
he laid the coal on my m. Isa 6:7
and have not asked at my m. 30:2
my m. it hath commanded. 34:16
word is gone out of my m. 45:23
things went forth out of my m. 48:3
my m. like a sharp sword. 49:2
word that goeth out of my m. 55:11
hand and touched my m. Jer 1:9
shalt be as my m. 15:19
written from my m. 36:6
in my m. like honey for. Ezek 3:3
hear the word at my m. 17; 33:7
abominable flesh into my m. 4:14
flesh nor wine in my m. Dan 10:3
by the words of my m. Hos 6:5
open my m. in parables. Mat 13:35
time entered into my m. Acts 11:8
the Gentiles by my m. should. 15:7
I may open my m. boldly. Eph 6:19
with the sword of my m. Rev 2:16
I will spue thee out of my m. 3:16
the book was in my m. sweet. 10:10

mouth with *opened*

earth opened her m. to. Gen 4.11

earth *opened* her *m.* and swallowed.
Num 16:32; 26:10; *Deut* 11:6
opened the *m.* of ass. *Num* 22:28
I have *opened* my *m. Judg* 11:35, 36
opened Job his *m.* and. *Job* 3:1
and they *opened* their *m.* wide.
29:23; *Ps* 35:21
now I have *opened* my *m. Job* 33:2
I *opened* not my *m.* *Ps* 39:9
m. of the deceitful are *opened.* 109:2
I *opened* my *m.* and panted. 119:131
hell hath *opened* her *m.* *Isa* 5:14
there was none that *opened m.* 10:14
yet he *opened* not his *m.* 53:7
I *opened* my *m.* and he caused me.
Ezek 3:2
thy *m.* be *opened* to him which is.
24:27; 33:22
opened my *m.* and spake. *Dan* 10:16
opened his *m.* and taught. *Mat* 5:2
when thou hast *opened* his *m.* 17:27
his *m.* was *opened* immediately.
Luke 1:64
like a lamb dumb, so *opened* he not his *m.* *Acts* 8:32
Philip *opened* his *m.* 35
Peter *opened* his *m.* 10:34
our *m.* is *opened* to you. *2 Cor* 6:11
earth *opened* her *m.* and helped.
Rev 12:16
he *opened* his *m.* in blasphemy. 13:6

mouth with *openeth*

dumb man that *openeth* not his *m.*
Ps 38:13
a fool *openeth* not his *m.* *Pr* 24:7
openeth her *m.* with wisdom. 31:26

their **mouth**

their hand to *their m.* *Judg* 7:6
thy manna from *their m.* *Neh* 9:20
the poor from *their m.* *Job* 5:15
gaped upon me with *their m.* 16:10
laid their hand on *their m.* 29:9
cleaved to the roof of *their m.* 10
no faithfulness in *their m.* *Ps* 5:9
with *their m.* they speak. 17:10
O God, in *their m.*: break out. 58:6
they belch out with *their m.* 59:7
for the sin of *their m.* and words. 12
they bless with *their m.* but. 62:4
their m. against the heavens. 73:9
flatter him with *their m.* 78:36
praises of God be in *their m.* 149:6
draw near me with *their m. Isa* 29:13
cut off from *their m.* *Jer* 7:28
thou art near in *their m.* far. 12:2
enemies have opened *their m.*
Lam 2:16
with *their m.* they shew much love.
Ezek 33:31
my flock from *their m.* 34:10
is deceitful in *their m.* *Mi* 6:12
lay their hand on *their m.* 7:16
tongue found in *their m.* *Zeph* 3:13
shall consume away in *their m.*
Zech 14:12
nigh to me with *their m.* *Mat* 15:8
their m. speaketh great. *Jude* 16
power is in *their m.* and. *Rev* 9:19
fire proceedeth out of *their m.* 11:5
and in *their m.* was found. 14:5

thy **mouth**

I will be with *thy m.* *Ex* 4:12, 15
Lord's law may be in *thy m.* 13:9
of other gods out of *thy m.* 23:13
promised with *thy m.* *Deut* 23:23
word is nigh to thee, in *thy m.* 30:14
Rom 10:8
not depart out of *thy m.* *Josh* 1:8
where is now *thy m.*? *Judg* 9:38
if thou hast opened *thy m.* 11:36
lay thine hand upon *thy m.* 18:19
Pr 30:32
thy m. hath testified. *2 Sam* 1:16
thou spakest with *thy m.* *1 Ki* 8:24
2 Chr 6:15
word in *thy m.* is truth. *1 Ki* 17:24
words of *thy m.* be like a *Job* 8:2
till he fill *thy m.* with laughing. 21
thy m. uttereth thine iniquity. 15:5
thine own *m.* condemneth thee. 6
such words go out of *thy m.* 13
my covenant in *thy m.* *Ps* 50:16
thou givest *thy m.* to evil. 19
open *thy m.* *Ps* 81:10
who satisfieth *thy m.* with. 103:5†
all the judgements of *thy m.* 119:13
the law of *thy m.* is better. 72
the testimony of *thy m.* 88
hear the words of *thy m.* 138:4
snared with the words of *thy m.*
Pr 6:2
praise thee, and not *thine* own *m.*
27:2
open *thy m.* for the dumb, in. 31:8
open *thy m.*, judge righteously. 9
be not rash with *thy m.* *Eccl* 5:2
suffer not *thy m.* to cause thy. 6
roof of *thy m.* like the. *S of S* 7:9
I have put my words in *thy m.*
Isa 51:16; *Jer* 1:9
my words which I put in *thy m.* shall not depart out of *thy m.* *Isa* 59:21
my words in *thy m.* fire. *Jer* 5:14
open *thy m.* and eat. *Ezek* 2:8
tongue cleave to roof of *thy m.* 3:26
I will open *thy m.* and thou shalt. 27
was not mentioned by *thy m.* 16:56
never open *thy m.* any more. 63
set the trumpet to *thy m.* *Hos* 8:1
keep doors of *thy m.* *Mi* 7:5
out of *thine* own *m.* will I judge.
Luke 19:22
if thou confess with *thy m. Rom* 10:9
it shall be in *thy m.* sweet. *Rev* 10:9

your **mouth**

proceeded out of *your m. Num* 32:24
not arrogancy come out of *your m.*
1 Sam 2:3
lay your hand on *your m.* *Job* 21:5
thus with *your m.* ye have boasted.
Ezek 35:13
is cut off from *your m.* *Joel* 1:5
no corrupt communication proceed out of *your m. Eph* 4:29; *Col* 3:8

mouths

song, put it in their *m.* *Deut* 31:19
not be forgotten out of *m.* of. 21
they gaped upon me with their *m.*
Ps 22:13
meat was yet in their *m.* 78:30
they have *m.* but they speak not.
115:5; 135:16
there any breath in their *m.* 135:17
kings shall shut their *m.* at. *Isa* 52:15
ye and wives have spoken with your *m.* *Jer* 44:25
enemies opened their *m.* *Lam* 3:46
hath shut the lions' *m.* *Dan* 6:22
putteth not into their *m.* *Mi* 3:5
deceivers, whose *m.* must. *Tit* 1:11
stopped the *m.* of lions. *Heb* 11:33
put bits in the horses' *m.* *Jas* 3:3
their *m.* issued fire. *Rev* 9:17, 18

move

[1] *To change position,* 2 Ki 21:8. [2] *To rouse, or influence,* Deut 32:21; Judg 13:25. [3] *To affect, as by pity or other feeling,* Ruth 1:19.

not a dog *m.* his tongue. *Ex* 11:7
that *m.* in the waters. *Lev* 11:10
not *m.* a sickle into. *Deut* 23:25
I will *m.* them to jealousy. 32:21
Spirit of the Lord began to *m.*
Judg 13:25
may dwell and *m.* no more.
2 Sam 7:10; *2 Ki* 21:8*
let no man *m.* his bones. *2 Ki* 23:18
with nails that it *m.* not. *Jer* 10:4
m. out of their holes. *Mi* 7:17*
will not *m.* them. *Mat* 23:4
for in him we live, *m.* *Acts* 17:28
none of these things *m.* me. 20:24

moveable

her ways are *m.*, canst not. *Pr* 5:6*

moved

the Spirit of God *m.* on. *Gen* 1:2
all flesh died that *m.* on the. 7:21
have *m.* me to jealousy. *Deut* 32:21
none *m.* his tongue. *Josh* 10:21
she *m.* him to ask of her father a field. 15:18; *Judg* 1:14
that all the city was *m.* *Ruth* 1:19
heart, only her lips *m.* *1 Sam* 1:13
the king was much *m.* *2 Sam* 18:33
foundations of heaven *m.* *2 Sam* 22:8
m. David against them. 24:1
world shall be stable, that it be not *m.*
1 Chr 16:30; *Ps* 93:1; 96:10
dwell, and shall be *m.* no. *1 Chr* 17:9
God *m.* them to depart. *2 Chr* 18:31
they have *m.* sedition. *Ezra* 4:15
saw that Mordecai *m.* not. *Esth* 5:9
at this my heart is *m.* *Job* 37:1
flesh, they cannot be *m.* 41:23
I shall not be *m.* *Ps* 10:6; 16:8
30:6; 62:2, 6
those rejoice when I am *m.* 13:4
these things shall never be *m.* 15:5
foundations of the hills *m.* 18:7†
in Lord, and shall not be *m.* 21:7
she shall not be *m.* God shall. 46:5
the kingdoms were *m.* 6
suffer the righteous to be *m.* 55:22
suffereth not our feet to be *m.* 66:9
m. at the presence of God. 68:8*
they *m.* him to jealousy. 78:58
reigneth, let the earth be *m.* 99:1
surely he shall not be *m.* 112:6
not suffer thy foot to be *m.* 121:3
righteous shall not be *m.* *Pr* 12:3
and my bowels were *m.* *S of S* 5:4
the posts of the door *m.* *Isa* 6:4
heart was *m.* as trees are *m.* 7:2
and there was none that *m.* 10:14
hell from beneath is *m.* for. 14:9
the idols of Egypt shall be *m.* 19:1
earth is broken down, and *m.* 24:19
image that shall not be *m.* 40:20
it should not be *m.* 41:7
all the hills *m.* lightly. *Jer* 4:24
they shall drink, and be *m.* 25:16*
whose waters are *m.* as. 46:7*, 8*
earth is *m.* at the noise of. 49:21*
Babylon the earth is *m.* 50:46*
he was *m.* with choler. *Dan* 8:7
king of the south shall be *m.* 11:11
was *m.* with compassion. *Mat* 9:36
14:14; 18:27; *Mark* 1:41; 6:34
m. with indignation. *Mat* 20:24
all the city was *m.* saying. 21:10*
but the chief priests *m. Mark* 15:11*
that I should not be *m.* *Acts* 2:25
patriarchs, *m.* with envy. 7:9
but the Jews *m.* with envy. 17:5
the city was *m.* and people. 21:30
be not *m.* from the hope. *Col* 1:23
that no man be *m.* by. *1 Thes* 3:3
Noah *m.* with fear. *Heb* 11:7
kingdom which cannot be *m.* 12:28*
they spake as *m.* by. *2 Pet* 1:21
mountain and island *m.* *Rev* 6:14

movedst

though thou *m.* me against him.
Job 2:3

mover

found this fellow a *m.* of sedition.
Acts 24:5

moveth

living creature that *m.* *Gen* 1:21
every thing that *m.* on earth. 28
be on all that *m.* on earth. 9:2*
of every creature that *m. Lev* 11:46
Behemoth *m.* his tail. *Job* 40:17
thing that *m.* praise him. *Ps* 69:34
when it *m.* itself aright. *Pr* 23:31*
m. whithersoever the rivers come.
Ezek 47:9*

moving, *substantive*

the *m.* of my lips should. *Job* 16:5*
blind, waiting for the *m.* *John* 5:3

moving

the waters bring forth *m.* *Gen* 1:20
every *m.* thing shall be meat. 9:3
m. his lips, he bringeth. *Pr* 16:30*

mower

wherewith the *m.* filleth. *Ps* 129:7

mowings

growth after the king's *m.* *Amos* 7:1

mown

rain upon the *m.* grass. *Ps* 72:6

much

for thou art *m.* mightier. *Gen* 26:16
it is a night to be *m.* *Ex* 12:42
he that gathered *m.* 16:18; *2 Cor* 8:15
if the scab spread *m.* abroad.
Lev 13:7, 22, 27, 35

soul of people was m. Num 21:4
shall carry m. seed out. Deut 28:38
return with m. riches. Josh 22:8
it grieveth me m. for. Ruth 1:13
a m. greater slaughter. 1 Sam 14:30
his name was m. set by. 18:30
but Jonathan delighted m. in. 19:2
as thy life was m. set by this day, so let my life be m. set by. 26:24
had understanding exceeding m. 1 Ki 4:29
Jehu shall serve him m. 2 Ki 10:18
m. wickedness in sight of Lord. 21:6
of Ophel he built m. 2 Chr 27:3
Manasseh wrought m. evil in. 33:6
it is a time of m. rain. Ezra 10:13
it yieldeth m. increase. Neh 9:37
mine hand had gotten m. 31:25
m. less do lying lips. Pr 17:7
m. less for a servant to have. 19:10
whether he eat little or m. Eccl 5:12
he hath m. sorrow and wrath. 17
sinner destroyeth m. good. 9:18
thou take thee m. sope [soap]. Jer 2:22
it containeth m. Ezek 23:32
shew m. love. 33:31
fruit thereof was m. Dan 4:12, 21
ye have sown m. Hag 1:6
ye looked for m. 9
not m. better than they? Mat 6:26
where they had not m. earth. 13:5 Mark 4:5
might have been sold for m. Mat 26:9
sins are forgiven, for she loved m. Luke 7:47
m. is given, of him shall m. be required . . . committed m. 12:48
is faithful also in m.: unjust in least is unjust in m. 16:10
forth m. fruit. John 12:24; 15:5
I will not talk m. with you. 14:30
her masters m. gain. Acts 16:16
them m. which had believed. 18:27
Festus said, M. learning doth. 26:24
m. every way. Rom 3:2
laboured m. in the Lord. 16:12
out of m. affliction I. 2 Cor 2:4
m. rather be in subjection. Heb 12:9
m. more shall not we escape. 25
the righteous availeth m. Jas 5:16
I wept m. because no man. Rev 5:4
see **how** *much*, **how** *much less*, **how** *much more*, *much* **more**, **people**

as much

as m. money as it is worth. Gen 23:9
mess was five times as m. 43:34
fill sacks with food as m. 44:1
twice as m. as they gather daily. Ex 16:5, 22
sons have, one as m. as. Lev 7:10
for as m. as the Lord. Josh 17:14
take as m. as thy soul. 1 Sam 2:16
cut wood as m. as. 2 Chr 2:16
gave Job twice as m. as. Job 42:10
joy in testimonies, as m. Ps 119:14
to receive as m. again. Luke 6:34
likewise of fishes as m. John 6:11
as m. as in me is, I am. Rom 1:15
in as m. as I am the apostle. 11:13
as m. as lieth in you, live. 12:18
in as m. as not without an oath. Heb 7:20

so much

remained not so m. Ex 14:28
sweet cinnamon half so m. 30:23
poor and cannot get so m. Lev 14:21
not give you so m. as a. Deut 2:5
none to be so m. praised as Absalom. 2 Sam 14:25
there shall not be left so m. 17:12
the spoil, it was so m. 2 Chr 20:25
will not so m. as bring it. Pr 19:24
eat so m. as is sufficient for. 25:16
why gaddest thou so m.? Jer 2:36
have we spoken so m.? Mal 3:13
we have so m. bread? Mat 15:33
was no room, no, not so m. as about. Mark 2:2
not so m. as eat. 3:20; 6:31
so m. more a great deal they. 7:36
so m. the more went there a fame. Luke 5:15
have ye not read so m. as this? 6:3
would not lift up so m. as his. 18:13
he cried so m. the more, Have. 39
sold it for so m. she said, Yea, for so m. Acts 5:8
no inheritance, not so m. as to. 7:5
not so m. as heard whether. 19:2
not so m. as named. 1 Cor 5:1
being made so m. better. Heb 1:4
by so m. Jesus made surety. 7:22
so m. more as ye see day. 10:25
if so m. as a beast touch. 12:20
so m. torment and sorrow. Rev 18:7

too much

sufficient, and too m. Ex 36:7
them, ye take too m. Num 16:3, 7
the part of children of Judah was too m. for them. Josh 19:9
too m. for you to go up to. 1 Ki 12:28
arise too m. contempt. Esth 1:18

very much

corn as sand, very m. Gen 41:49
very m. cattle went up. Ex 12:38
remaineth very m. land. Josh 13:1
with very m. cattle, very m. 22:8
Sheba came with very m. 1 Ki 10:2
innocent blood very m. 2 Ki 21:16
David very m. brass. 1 Chr 18:8
away very m. spoil. 2 Chr 14:13
given him substance very m. 32:29
people transgressed very m. 36:14
I am afflicted very m. Ps 119:107
summer fruits very m. Jer 40:12

mufflers

away the chains, the m. Isa 3:19

mulberry trees

upon them over against the m. trees. 2 Sam 5:23; 1 Chr 14:14
the sound in tops of the m. trees. 2 Sam 5:24; 1 Chr 14:15

mule

gat him upon his m. 2 Sam 13:29
Absalom rode on a m., the m. 18:9
to ride on my m. 1 Ki 1:33; 38:44
not as the horse or m. Ps 32:9
plague of the horse, of the m. Zech 14:15

mules

Anah that found m. in. Gen 36:24*
brought horses and m., a rate year by year. 1 Ki 10:25; 2 Chr 9:24
grass to save the m. 1 Ki 18:5
to thy servant two m. 2 Ki 5:17
brought bread on camels and on m. 1 Chr 12:40
their m. were 245. Ezra 2:66 Neh 7:68
sent letters by riders on m. Esth 8:10*, 14*
your brethren on m. Isa 66:20
traded in thy fairs with m. Ezek 27:14

multiplied

Israel grew and m. Gen 47:27 Ex 1:7, 20
more afflicted, they m. Ex 1:12
my wonders may be m. in. 11:9
your God hath m. you. Deut 1:10
m. and all that thou hast is m. 8:13
that your days may be m. 11:21
I m. his seed, and gave. Josh 24:3
their cattle were m. 1 Chr 5:9
if his children be m. it is. Job 27:14
if thy transgressions be m. 35:6
their sorrows shall be m. Ps 16:4
hate me wrongfully are m. 38:19
them, so that they are m. 107:38
thy days shall be m. Pr 9:11
wicked are m. transgression. 29:16
thou hast m. the nation. Isa 9:3
for our transgressions are m. 59:12
when ye be m. they shall. Jer 3:16
m. more than the nations. Ezek 5:7*
ye have m. your slain in. 11:6
thou hast m. thy whoredoms. 16:25 23:19
m. thy fornication. 16:29
m. thine abominations. 51
faint, and ruins be m. Ezek 21:15
his boughs were m. 31:5
m. your words. 35:13
peace be m. to you. Dan 4:1; 6:25 1 Pet 1:2; 2 Pet 1:2; Jude 2
I m. her silver and gold. Hos 2:8
Judah hath m. fenced cities. 8:14
I have m. visions, and used. 12:10
hast m. thy merchants. Nah 3:16
when the number of the disciples was m. Acts 6:1, 7
people grew and m. in Egypt. 7:17
the fear of the Lord were m. 9:31
word of God grew and m. 12:24

multipliedst

children also m. thou as. Neh 9:23

multiplieth

he m. my wounds without. Job 9:17
he m. words against God. 34:37
m. words without knowledge. 35:16

multiply

be fruitful and m. Gen 1:22, 28 8:17; 9:7; 35:11
I will m. thy sorrow. 3:16
when men began to m. on. 6:1
I will m. Hagar's seed. 16:10; 17:20
and I will m. thee. 17:2; 48:4
I will m. thy seed. 22:17; 26:4, 24 Heb 6:14
bless thee, and m. thee. Gen 28:3
deal wisely with them; lest they m. Ex 1:10
I will m. my signs and. 7:3
lest the beast of the field m. 23:29
whom thou saidst, I will m. 32:13 Lev 26:9; Deut 7:13; 13:17 28:63; 30:5
that ye may live and m. and go in and possess. Deut 8:1; 30:16
the king shall not m. horses. 17:16
neither shall he m. wives, nor. 17
did all their family m. 1 Chr 4:27
I shall m. my days as. Job 29:18
I will m. them, they shall. Jer 30:19
so will I m. the seed of David. 33:22
I have caused thee to m. Ezek 16:7
I will m. men. 36:10
m. man and beast. 11
I will m. the fruit of the tree. 30
I will place them and m. 37:26
Gilgal m. transgression. Amos 4:4
and m. your seed sown. 2 Cor 9:10

multiplying

in m. I will multiply. Gen 22:17 Heb 6:14

multitude

[1] *A great company or number of persons or things*, Gen 30:30; 48:4. [2] *The common people*, Mat 9:33. [3] *The whole assembly, both common people and senators*, Acts 23:7. [4] *The church, or a company of the faithful*, Acts 15:12, 22; 21:22. [5] *Great store, or plenty*, Ps 5:7; Hos 9:7. [6] *Much variety*, Eccl 5:3, 7.

not numbered for m. Gen 16:10 32:12; 1 Ki 3:8
God Almighty make thee a m. Gen 28:3*
now increased unto a m. 30:30
I will make of thee a m. of people. 48:4*; 16:19
a mixed m. went up also. Ex 12:38
thou shalt not follow a m. 23:2
according to the m. of. Lev 25:16
mixed m. fell a lusting. Num 11:4
ye are as the stars for m. Deut 1:10 10:22; 28:62; Heb 11:12
as sand on sea shore for m. Josh 11:4; Judg 7:12; 1 Sam 13:5 2 Sam 17:11; 1 Ki 4:20
grasshoppers for m. Judg 6:5; 7:12
m. melted away. 1 Sam 14:16
he dealt among the whole m. of Israel. 2 Sam 6:19
could not be told for m. 1 Ki 8:5
they are as all the m. 2 Ki 7:13
hast said, With the m. of my chariots. 19:23; Isa 37:24
people like dust for m. 2 Chr 1:9
we go against this m. 14:11

the *m.* were dead bodies. *2 Chr* 20:24
for a *m.* had not cleansed. 30:18
be not afraid of all the *m.* 32:7
from Israel the mixed *m.* *Neh* 13:3
Haman told of the *m.* *Esth* 5:11
Mordecai accepted of the *m.* 10:3
should not the *m.* of words? *Job* 11:2
and *m.* of years should teach. 32:7
by reason of *m.* of oppressions. 35:9
he scorneth the *m.* of the city. 39:7*
I will come in the *m.* of. *Ps* 5:7
cast them out in *m.* of their. 10
no king saved by the *m.* of. 33:16
I had gone with the *m.* to the. 42:4
that boast themselves in *m.* 49:6
according to the *m.* of thy. 51:1
rebuke the *m.* of bulls, with. 68:30
O God, in the *m.* of thy. 69:13
turn to me, according to *m.* of. 16
deliver me not to the *m.* of. 74:19
in the *m.* of my thoughts. 94:19
they remembered not *m.* of. 106:7
and repented, according to *m.* 45
praise him among the *m.* 109:30
in the *m.* of words. *Pr* 10:19
in the *m.* of counsellors. 11:14; 24:6
in *m.* of people is the king's. 14:28
in *m.* of counsellors they are. 15:22
gold, and a *m.* of rubies. 20:15
the *m.* of business, a fool's voice is known by the *m.* of. *Eccl* 5:3
in the *m.* of dreams there are. 7
to what purpose is the *m.*? *Isa* 1:11
m. dried up with thirst. 5:13
m. and pomp shall descend. 14
woe to *m.* of many people. 17:12
so *m.* of nations be that fight. 29:8
when *m.* of shepherds is called. 31:4
shall come on thee for *m.* of. 47:9
stand now with the *m.* of thy. 12
thou art wearied in the *m.* of thy. 13
m. of camels shall cover thee. 60:6
according to *m.* of his loving. 63:7
is a *m.* of waters. *Jer* 10:13*; 51:16*
yea, they have called a *m.* 12:6*
I have wounded thee for *m.* 30:14
I will punish the *m.* of No. 46:25*
afflicted her, for *m.* of. *Lam* 1:5
compassion according to *m.* of. 3:32
wrath is on all the *m.* *Ezek* 7:12, 14
touching the whole *m.* thereof. 13
answer him according to the *m.* 14:4
by reason of the *m.* 27:12, 18, 33
the *m.* of the wares. 16, 18
Pharaoh and all his *m.* 31:18; 32:32
Elam and her *m.* 32:24
Tubal and all her *m.* 26
bury Gog, and all his *m.* 39:11
words like voice of a *m.* *Dan* 10:6
north shall set forth a *m.* 11:13
for *m.* of thine iniquity. *Hos* 9:7
thou didst trust in the *m.* 10:13
there is a *m.* of slain. *Nah* 3:3
the *m.* of the whoredoms of. 4
he feared the *m.* *Mat* 14:5; 21:46
I have compassion on the *m.* 15:32 *Mark* 8:2
thou seest the *m.* thronging thee. *Mark* 5:31; *Luke* 8:45
was with the angel a *m.* *Luke* 2:13
together an innumerable *m.* 12:1
him in the absence of the *m.* 22:6
yet spake, behold, a *m.* 47
whole *m.* of them arose. 23:1
a *m.* being present in. *John* 5:13
not able to draw it for the *m.* 21:6
m. that believed were of. *Acts* 4:32
saying pleased the whole *m.* 6:5
the *m.* rose up together. 16:22
m. must needs come together. 21:22
and shall hide a *m.* of sins. *Jas* 5:20
shall cover the *m.* of sins. *1 Pet* 4:8
see **great**

multitudes

draw her and all her *m.* *Ezek* 32:20
m. in the valley of decision. *Joel* 3:14
dumb spake; and the *m.* *Mat* 9:33
when he saw the *m.* he was. 36
m. cried, saying, Hosanna to. 21:9
m. were added both of. *Acts* 5:14
Jews saw *m.* they were. 13:45
the waters are *m.* *Rev* 17:15
see **great**

munition

against her and her *m.* *Isa* 29:7*
keep the *m.*, watch the. *Nah* 2:1†

munitions

his defence shall be *m.* *Isa* 33:16

murder

[1] *The taking away of a man's life unlawfully,* Mark 15:7. [2] *All cruelty in thought, word, or deed,* Mat 19:18; 1 John 3:15.
(*Intentional* murder *was always punished with death, but accidental* murder, *among the Hebrews, was only punished by banishment. Cities of refuge were appointed for manslaughter, whither a man might retire, and continue in safety, till the death of the high priest; then the offender was at liberty to return to his own city, and his own house, if he pleased. But as for the murderer, he was put to death without any remission, and the kinsmen of the murdered person might kill him with impunity*)

in secret doth he *m.* the. *Ps* 10:8
they slay the widow, and *m.* 94:6
ye steal, *m.* and commit? *Jer* 7:9
so priests *m.* in the way. *Hos* 6:9

murder

thou shalt do no *m.* *Mat* 19:18
who had committed *m.* *Mark* 15:7
and for *m.* was cast. *Luke* 23:19, 25
full of envy, *m.* debate. *Rom* 1:29

murderer

he is a *m.*: the *m.* shall surely be put to death. *Num* 35:16, 17, 18, 21
of blood shall slay the *m.* 19, 21
m. shall be put to death by. 30
no satisfaction for the life of a *m.* 31
see how this son of a *m.* *2 Ki* 6:32
m. rising with the light. *Job* 24:14
his children to the *m.* *Hos* 9:13
he was a *m.* from the. *John* 8:44
ye desired a *m.* to be. *Acts* 3:14
no doubt this man is a *m.* 28:4
of you suffer as a *m.* *1 Pet* 4:15
his brother is a *m.*; ye know that no *m.* hath eternal life. *1 John* 3:15

murderers

the children of the *m.* *2 Ki* 14:6
lodged in it, but now *m.* *Isa* 1:21
wearied, because of *m.* *Jer* 4:31
and destroyed those *m.* *Mat* 22:7
have been now the *m.* *Acts* 7:52
led 4000 men that were *m.* 21:38
law made for *m.* of fathers and. *1 Tim* 1:9
m. shall have their part. *Rev* 21:8
are whoremongers and *m.* 22:15

murders

out of the heart proceed *m.* *Mat* 15:19; *Mark* 7:21
the flesh are envyings, *m.* *Gal* 5:21
repented they of their *m.* *Rev* 9:21

murmur

that ye *m.* against us? *Ex* 16:7
murmurings ye *m.* 8; *Num* 14:27
the congregation to *m.* *Num* 14:36
what is Aaron, that ye *m.*? 16:11
of Israel, whereby they *m.* 17:5
Jesus said, *M.* not among. *John* 6:43
neither *m.* as some of. *1 Cor* 10:10

murmured

the people *m.* *Ex* 15:24; 17:3
congregation of Israel *m.* against. 16:2; *Num* 14:2; 16:41
years old, which have *m.* *Num* 14:29
ye *m.* in your tents. *Deut* 1:27
all the congregation *m.* *Josh* 9:18
believed not, but *m.* in. *Ps* 106:25
they that *m.* shall learn. *Isa* 29:24
received a penny, they *m.* *Mat* 20:11
and they *m.* against her. *Mark* 14:5
and Pharisees *m.* *Luke* 5:30
m. saying, This man receiveth. 15:2
m. that he was gone to be. 19:7
Jews *m.* at him, because. *John* 6:41
he knew that his disciples *m.* 61
heard that the people *m.* 7:32
as some of them *m.* *1 Cor* 10:10

murmurers

m. complainers, walking. *Jude* 16

murmuring

m. among the people. *John* 7:12
a *m.* of Grecians against. *Acts* 6:1

murmurings

he heareth your *m.* *Ex* 16:7, 8, 9 12; *Num* 14:27
your *m.* are not against us. *Ex* 16:8
cease the *m.* of Israel. *Num* 17:5
shalt quite take away their *m.* 10
do all things without *m.* *Phil* 2:14

murrain

be a very grievous *m.* *Ex* 9:3

muse

I *m.* on the work of thy. *Ps* 143:5

mused

men *m.* in their hearts. *Luke* 3:15*

music

to meet king Saul with *m.* *1 Sam* 18:6
with instruments of *m.* *1 Chr* 15:16 *2 Chr* 5:13; 23:13; 34:12
Levites with instruments of *m.* *2 Chr* 7:6
daughters of *m.* shall be. *Eccl* 12:4
rising, I am their *m.* *Lam* 3:63*
have ceased from their *m.* 5:14
ye hear the sound of cornet, and all kinds of *m.* *Dan* 3:5, 7, 10, 15
neither were instruments of *m.* 6:18
invent instruments of *m.* *Amos* 6:5
elder son heard *m.* and. *Luke* 15:25

musical

with *m.* instruments. *1 Chr* 16:42
with the *m.* instruments. *Neh* 12:36
as *m.* instruments, and. *Eccl* 2:8†

musicians

voice of *m.* shall be. *Rev* 18:22

musing

while I was *m.* the fire. *Ps* 39:3

must

m. I needs bring thy son? *Gen* 24:5
it *m.* not be so done in our. 29:26
thou *m.* come in to me. 30:16
if it *m.* be so. 43:11
it *m.* be put in water. *Lev* 11:32
seven days ye *m.* eat. 23:6
he *m.* do after the law. *Num* 6:21
m. we fetch you water out of? 20:10
m. I not take heed to speak? 23:12
Lord speaketh that I *m.* do. 26
by what way we *m.* go. *Deut* 1:22
I *m.* die in this land, I *m.* 4:22
thou *m.* eat them before. 12:18
approach that thou *m.* die. 31:14
way by which ye *m.* go. *Josh* 3:4
thou *m.* offer it to the. *Judg* 13:16
there *m.* be an inheritance. 21:17
a little, and lo I *m.* die. *1 Sam* 14:43
ruleth over men *m.* *2 Sam* 23:3
shall touch them *m.* be fenced. 7
he sleepeth, and *m.* be. *1 Ki* 18:27
hast said, so *m.* we do. *Ezra* 10:12
they *m.* needs be borne. *Jer* 10:5
fulfilled, that thus it *m.*? *Mat* 26:54
new wine *m.* be put into new bottles. *Mark* 2:22; *Luke* 5:38
Son of man *m.* suffer many things. *Mark* 8:31; 9:12
say the scribes that Elias *m.*? 9:11
of wars, be ye not troubled, for such things *m.* be. 13:7; *Luke* 21:9
gospel *m.* first be published. *Mark* 13:10
m. be about my Father's. *Luke* 2:49
I *m.* preach kingdom of God. 4:43
I bought ground, and *m.* go. 14:18
Zacchaeus, to-day I *m.* abide. 19:5
day when the passover *m.* 22:7
the things written *m.* be. 37; 24:44
he *m.* release one to them. 23:17
Son of man *m.* be delivered. 24:7
ye *m.* be born again. *John* 3:7
the serpent, so *m.* the Son of. 14
m. increase, but I *m.* decrease. 30
and he *m.* needs go through. 4:4
God is a spirit, *m.* worship him. 24
I *m.* work the works of him. 9:4
sheep I have, them also I *m.* 10:16
knew not that he *m.* rise again. 20:9

m. have been fulfilled. *Acts* 1:16
m. one be ordained to be a. 22
other name whereby we m. 4:12
told thee what thou m. do. 9:6
m. through much tribulation. 14:22
ye m. be circumcised and. 15:24
said, Sirs, what m. I do to? 16:30
I m. by all means keep this. 18:21
the multitude m. needs come. 21:22
so m. thou bear witness also. 23:11
fear not, thou m. be brought. 27:24
we m. be cast on a certain island. 26
wherefore ye m. needs. *Rom* 13:5
m. ye needs go out of. *1 Cor* 5:10
there m. also be heresies. 11:19
for he m. reign till he hath. 15:25
for we m. all appear. *2 Cor* 5:10
I m. needs glory, I will glory. 11:30
a bishop then m. be blameless.
1 Tim 3:2; *Tit* 1:7
he m. have a good report. *1 Tim* 3:7
likewise m. deacons be grave. 8
husbandman m. be first. *2 Tim* 2:6
the servant of the Lord m. not. 24
it remaineth that some m. *Heb* 4:6
there m. be the death of the. 9:16
cometh to God, m. believe that. 11:6
as they that m. give account. 13:17
shew thee things which m. *Rev* 4:1
if any will hurt, he m. in this. 11:5
that he m. be loosed a little. 20:3
to shew things which m. shortly. 22:6

mustard seed, *see* **grain**

mustered

he took the scribe which m. the people. *2 Ki* 25:19; *Jer* 52:25

mustereth

the Lord m. the host of. *Isa* 13:4

mutter, -ed

that peep, and that m. *Isa* 8:19
tongue hath m. perverseness. 59:3

mutual

comforted by the m. faith. *Rom* 1:12

muzzle

thou shalt not m. the ox. *Deut* 25:4
1 Cor 9:9; *1 Tim* 5:18

Myra

M. a city of Lycia. *Acts* 27:5

myrrh

bearing balm and m. *Gen* 37:25
the man a present, m., nuts. 43:11
pure m. five hundred. *Ex* 30:23
six months with oil of m. *Esth* 2:12
thy garments smell of m. *Ps* 45:8
perfumed my bed with m. *Pr* 7:17
a bundle of m. is my. *S of S* 1:13
perfumed with m. and. 3:6
get me to the mountain of m. 4:6
m. and aloes with all the chief. 14
I have gathered my m. with. 5:1
with m., my fingers with sweet m. 5
lilies, dropping sweet smelling m. 13
to him gifts, gold and m. *Mat* 2:11
wine mingled with m. *Mark* 15:23
brought a mixture of m. *John* 19:39

myrtle

fetch m. olive branches. *Neh* 8:15
in the wilderness the m. *Isa* 41:19
brier shall come up the m. 55:13

myrtle trees

and he stood among the *m. trees.*
Zech 1:8, 10, 11

myself

because naked, and hid m. *Gen* 3:10
by m. have I sworn, in blessing.
22:16; *Isa* 45:23; *Jer* 22:5; 49:13
brought you unto m. *Ex* 19:4
I sanctified them for m. *Num* 8:17
I the Lord will make m. known. 12:6
not able to bear you m. *Deut* 1:9, 12
go out and shake m. *Judg* 16:20
I cannot redeem it for m. *Ruth* 4:6
I forced m. therefore. *1 Sam* 13:12
that I may hide m. in the field. 20:5
kept me from avenging m. 25:33
go forth with you m. *2 Sam* 18:2
kept m. from mine iniquity. 22:24
shew m. unto him. *1 Ki* 18:15
I will disguise m. 22:30
2 Chr 18:29
I bow m. in the house of. *2 Ki* 5:18
chosen this place to m. *2 Chr* 7:12
I consulted with m. and. *Neh* 5:7
come with the king but m. *Esth* 5:12
do honour more than to m. 6:6
harden m. in sorrow. *Job* 6:10
so that I am a burden to m. 7:20
if I justify m. 9:20
I will comfort m. 27
if I wash m. with snow water. 30
leave my complaint upon m. 10:1
will I not hide m. from thee. 13:20
mine error remained with m. 19:4
whom I shall see for m. and eyes. 27
or have eaten my morsel m. 31:17
or if I lift up m. when evil found. 29
wherefore I abhor m. and. 42:6
I behaved m. as though he had been.
Ps 35:14
glory, I m. awake early. 57:8; 108:2
I will behave m. wisely in. 101:2
but I give m. to prayer. 109:4
I will delight m. in thy. 119:16
delight m. in thy commandments. 47
thy judgement and comforted m. 52
nor do I exercise m. in. 131:1
behaved and quieted m. as child. 2
heart to give m. to wine. *Eccl* 2:3
labour wherein I have shewed m. 19
now will I lift up m. *Isa* 33:10
people have I formed for m. 43:21
abroad the earth by m. 44:24
comfort m. against sorrow. *Jer* 8:18
I m. will fight against you. 21:5
will answer him by m. *Ezek* 14:7
in the day I made m. known. 20:5, 9
river is mine, I have made it for m.
29:3
will make m. known amongst. 35:11
I magnify m. and sanctify m. 38:23
nor did I anoint m. at all. *Dan* 10:3
bow m. before the high God. *Mi* 6:6
heard, I trembled in m. *Hab* 3:16
separated m. as I have. *Zech* 7:3
I m. worthy to come. *Luke* 7:7
I m.; handle me and see. 24:39
if I bear witness of m. *John* 5:31
know whether I speak of m. 7:17
I am not come of m. but he that. 28
though I bear record of m. 8:14
I am one that bear witness of m. 18
know that I do nothing of m. 28
nor came I of m. but he sent me. 42
if I honour m. my honour is. 54
I lay it down of m. 10:18
spoken of m.; Father sent me. 12:49
again, and receive you unto m. 14:3
that I speak, I speak not of m. 10
love him, and manifest m. to him. 21
for their sakes I sanctify m. 17:19
stand up, I m. also am. *Acts* 10:26
count I my life dear unto m. 20:24
more cheerfully answer for m. 24:10
herein do I exercise m. to have. 16
I would hear the man m. 25:22
I verily thought with m. I. 26:9
I could wish that m. were. *Rom* 9:3
I have reserved to m. 7000. 11:4
and I m. also am persuaded. 15:14
succourer of many, and of m. 16:2
for I know nothing by m. *1 Cor* 4:4
I have in a figure transferred to m. 6
that all men were even as I m. 7:7
yet have I made m. servant. 9:19
lest that I m. should be cast. 27
now I Paul m. beseech. *2 Cor* 10:1
an offence in abasing m.? 11:7
kept m. from being burdensome. 9
receive me, that I may boast m. a. 16
of m. I will not glory but. 12:5
m. was not burdensome to you. 13
I make m. a transgressor. *Gal* 2:18
I also m. shall come. *Phil* 2:24
not m. to have apprehended. 3:13
receive Onesimus as m. *Philem* 17

Mysia

come to *M.* *Acts* 16:7
they passing by *M.* came to Troas. 8

mysteries

(*Something secret, hidden, not known to all*)

you to know the m. of the kingdom.
Mat 13:11; *Luke* 8:10
as stewards of the m. *1 Cor* 4:1
though I understand all m. *1 Cor* 13:2
the Spirit he speaketh m. 14:2

mystery

know the m. of kingdom. *Mark* 4:11
be ignorant of this m. *Rom* 11:25
the revelation of the m. 16:25
wisdom of God in a m. *1 Cor* 2:7
I shew you a m.; We shall. 15:51
made known to us the m. *Eph* 1:9
made known to me the m. 3:3
knowledge in the m. of Christ. 4
what is the fellowship of the m. 9
this is a great m. but I speak. 5:32
boldly, to make known the m. of.
6:19; *Col* 1:26, 27; 4:3
acknowledgement of the m. *Col* 2:2
the m. of iniquity doth. *2 Thes* 2:7
holding m. of faith in. *1 Tim* 3:9
great is the m. of godliness. 16
the m. of the seven stars. *Rev* 1:20
m. of God should be finished. 10:7
m., Babylon the great. 17:5
m. of the woman. 7

N

Naaman

Benjamin, *N.* and. *Gen* 46:21
the son of Bela, *N.* *Num* 26:40
1 Chr 8:4
N. captain of Syria. *2 Ki* 5:1
N. was wroth and went away. 11
my master hath spared *N.* the. 20
the leprosy of *N.* shall cleave. 27
was cleansed, saving *N.* *Luke* 4:27

Naamathite, *see* **Zophar**

Naashon, or **Nahshon**

Elisheba the sister of *N.* *Ex* 6:23
N. son of Amminadab. *Num* 1:7
2:3; 10:14
offered the first day was *N.* 7:12
this was the offering of *N.* son. 17
Amminadab begat *N.* and *N.* begat.
Ruth 4:20; *1 Chr* 2:10, 11
Mat 1:4
which was the son of *N.* *Luke* 3:32

Nabal

name of the man was *N.* *1 Sam* 25:3
N. did shear his sheep. 4
go to *N.* and greet him. 5
N. is his name, and folly is. 25
Lord smote *N.* that he died. 38
returned the wickedness of *N.* 39
Abigail *N.*'s wife. 27:3; 30:5
2 Sam 2:2; 3:3

Naboth

N. the Jezreelite had. *1 Ki* 21:1
give thee vineyard of *N.* the. 7
set *N.* on high. 9, 12
heard *N.* was stoned. 14
Ahab heard that *N.* was dead. 16
Ahab is in the vineyard of *N.* 18
dogs licked the blood of *N.* 19
him in the portion of *N.* *2 Ki* 9:21, 25
seen yesterday the blood of *N.* 26

Nadab

the sons of Aaron, *N.* Abihu.
Ex 6:23; *Lev* 10:1
N. and Abihu, seventy. *Ex* 24:1, 9
N. and Abihu died. *Num* 3:4; 26:61
N. son of Jeroboam reigned.
1 Ki 14:20; 15:25
N. son of Shammai. *1 Chr* 2:28
the sons of *N.* 30
Baal and *N.* the sons. 8:30; 9:36

Nagge

was the son of *N.* *Luke* 3:25

Nahash

N. came up against Jabesh.
1 Sam 11:1; 12:12
shew kindness to Hanun the son of *N.* *2 Sam* 10:2; *1 Chr* 19:2
the daughter of *N.* *2 Sam* 17:25
Shobi son of *N.* brought beds. 27

Nahor

Serug begat *N.* *Gen* 11:22
N. lived 29 years. 24; *1 Chr* 1:26
Terah begat Abraham, *N.* and Haran.
Gen 11:26, 27

N.'s wife Milcah. *Gen* 11:29
hath born children to thy brother *N.* 22:20, 23; 24:15, 24
went to the city of *N.* 24:10
God of Abraham and *N.* 31:53

nail

(A finger-nail; a tent-peg, usually of wood; a metal pin, perhaps of gold)

n. of tent, and smote *n.* *Judg* 4:21
Sisera lay dead, the *n.* was. 22
she put her hand to the *n.* 5:26
give us a *n.* in his holy. *Ezra* 9:8
I will fasten him as a *n.* *Isa* 22:23
shall the *n.* that is fastened be. 25
out of him came the *n.* *Zech* 10:4

nailing

took it out of the way, *n.* *Col* 2:14

nails

her head, and pare her *n.* *Deut* 21:12
iron in abundance for *n.* *1 Chr* 22:3
the weight of the *n.* *2 Chr* 3:9
n. fastened by the. *Eccl* 12:11
he fastened his idol with *n.* *Isa* 41:7; *Jer* 10:4
his *n.* were grown like. *Dan* 4:33
fourth beast, whose *n.* were. 7:19
into the print of the *n.* *John* 20:25

Nain

into a city called *N.* *Luke* 7:11

Naioth

Samuel and David dwelt at *N.* *1 Sam* 19:18, 19, 22
Saul went to *N.* 23
David fled from *N.* 20:1

naked

[1] *Altogether unclothed or uncovered,* Gen 2:25; 3:7. [2] *With few clothes on, having put off the greatest part of them,* 1 Sam 19:24; John 21:7. [3] *Not clothed with the righteousness of Christ,* Rev 3:17. [4] *Destitute of all worldly goods,* Job 1:21. [5] *Discovered, known, and manifest,* Job 26:6; Heb 4:13.

they were *n.* and were. *Gen* 2:25
knew that they were *n.* 3:7, 10, 11
people were *n.* for Aaron had made them *n.* to their. *Ex* 32:25*
Saul lay down *n.* all. *1 Sam* 19:24
spoil clothed all the *n.* *2 Chr* 28:15
Ahaz made Judah *n.* and. 19*
n. came I out of my mother's womb, and *n.* shall I return. *Job* 1:21
thou hast stripped the *n.* of. 22:6
they cause the *n.* to lodge. 24:7, 10
hell is *n.* before him and. 26:6
n. shall he return, to go. *Eccl* 5:15
when thou seest the *n.* *Isa* 58:7
shalt make thyself *n.* *Lam* 4:21
hath covered the *n.* *Ezek* 18:7, 16
lest I strip her *n.* and set *Hos* 2:3
shall flee away *n.* in. *Amos* 2:16
I will go stripped and *n.* *Mi* 1:8
having thy shame *n.* 11*
bow was made quite *n.* *Hab* 3:9
I was *n.* and ye clothed. *Mat* 25:36 43
when saw we thee *n.* and? 38, 44
linen cloth about his *n.* *Mark* 14:51
linen cloth, fled from them *n.* 52
Peter was *n.* and cast. *John* 21:7
fled out of that house *n.* *Acts* 19:16
present hour we are *n.* *1 Cor* 4:11
we shall not be found *n.* *2 Cor* 5:3
but all things are *n.* to. *Heb* 4:13
if a brother or sister be *n.* *Jas* 2:15
poor, and blind, and *n.* *Rev* 3:17
garments, lest he walk *n.* 16:15
make her desolate and *n.* 17:16

see **bare**

nakedness

and Ham saw the *n.* of. *Gen* 9:22
n., they saw not their father's *n.* 23
to see the *n.* of the land. 42:9, 12
thy *n.* be not discovered. *Ex* 20:26
breeches to cover their *n.* 28:42
none shall uncover their *n.* *Lev* 18:6
the *n.* of father or mother. 7, 8, 11 15; 20:11
the *n.* of thy sister. *Lev* 18:9
n. of thy son's daughter. 10
n. of father's wife's daughter. 11
n. of father's sister. 12
n. of mother's sister. 13; 20:19
n. of father's brother. 18:14
n. of daughter in law. 15
n. of thy brother's wife, it is thy brother's *n.* 16
n. of a woman and her daughter. 17
n. of a woman as long as. 19; 20:18
sister's *n.* and she see his *n.* 20:17
uncovered his uncle's *n.* 20
uncovered his brother's *n.* 21
serve thine enemies in *n.* *Deut* 28:48
of thy mother's *n.* *1 Sam* 20:30
thy *n.* shall be uncovered. *Isa* 47:3
they have seen her *n.* *Lam* 1:8
I covered thy *n.*, yea. *Ezek* 16:8
thy *n.* discovered through. 36 23:18
and will discover thy *n.* 16:37
discovered their father's *n.* 22:10
these discovered her *n.* and. 23:10
the *n.* of thy whoredom shall. 29
flax given to cover her *n.* *Hos* 2:9
shew the nations thy *n.* *Nah* 3:5
mayest look on their *n.* *Hab* 2:15
who shall separate us from the love of Christ? shall *n.* *Rom* 8:35
often, in cold and *n.* *2 Cor* 11:27
that the shame of thy *n.* *Rev* 3:18

name

Name *is frequently used to designate the entire person, his individuality and his power. This is usually the case when the reference is to God.*

The word is also used to mean a race, as descended from some one man.

that was the *n.* thereof. *Gen* 2:19
call the *n.* of the city after *n.* 4:17
and called their *n.* Adam. 5:2
let us make us a *n.* lest we. 11:4
therefore the *n.* of the city. 19:22
the *n.* of the city was Luz. 28:19
shall be called after the *n.* of. 48:6
whose *n.* is Jealous. *Ex* 34:14
neither profane the *n.* of thy God. *Lev* 18:21; 19:12; 21:6; 22:2, 32
n. of one Eldad, of the. *Num* 11:26
write thou every man's *n.* 17:2
the *n.* of the Israelite that. 25:14
n. of Midianitish woman slain. 15
why should *n.* of our father? 27:4
Nobah, after his own *n.* 32:42
shalt destroy their *n.* *Deut* 7:24
and blot out their *n.* from. 9:14
bring up an evil *n.* on her. 22:14
he hath brought up an evil *n.* 19
firstborn shall succeed in *n.* 25:6
to raise up to his brother a *n.* 7
to make thee high in *n.* and in. 26:19
this glorious and fearful *n.* 28:58
nor make mention of *n.* *Josh* 23:7
man's *n.* with whom I. *Ruth* 2:19
raise up the *n.* of the dead. 4:5, 10
neighbours gave it a *n.* 17
n. of the man was Nabal. *1 Sam* 25:3
they spake to Nabal in the *n.* of. 9
whose *n.* is called by the *n.* of the Lord. *2 Sam* 6:2
a great *n.* like the *n.* of the great men in the earth. 7:9; *1 Chr* 17:8
God redeemed to make him a *n.* *2 Sam* 7:23; *1 Chr* 17:21
David gat him a *n.* when. *2 Sam* 8:13
to my husband neither *n.* nor. 14:7
Abishai had the *n.* among. 23:18
Benaiah, and had the *n.* among three mighty men. 22; *1 Chr* 11:20, 24
n. of Solomon better than thy *n.* and his throne greater. *1 Ki* 1:47
chose to put his *n.* there. 14:21 *2 Chr* 12:13
call ye on the *n.* of your gods. *1 Ki* 18:24, 25
wrote letters in Ahab's *n.* 21:8
not blot out the *n.* of. *2 Ki* 14:27
and was called after their *n.* *Ezra* 2:61; *Neh* 7:63
prophesied in the *n.* of. *Ezra* 5:1
and gavest him the *n.* of. *Neh* 9:7
so didst thou get thee a *n.* as. 10
the king in Mordecai's *n.* *Esth* 2:22
for the Jews in the king's *n.* 8:8
he shall have no *n.* in the. *Job* 18:17
thou hast put out their *n.* *Ps* 9:5
the *n.* of the God of Jacob. 20:1
in the *n.* of God we will set up. 5
if we have forgotten the *n.* 44:20
I will praise the *n.* of God. 69:30
the *n.* of Israel be no more. 83:4
whose *n.* alone is Jehovah 18
let them praise thy great *n.* 99:3
n. be blotted out. 109:13
Lord's *n.* is to be praised. 113:3
the *n.* of the wicked. *Pr* 10:7
n. of the Lord is a strong. 18:10
good *n.* is rather to be chosen. 22:1
lest I take the *n.* of my God. 30:9
a good *n.* is better than. *Eccl* 7:1
off from Babylon the *n.* *Isa* 14:22
it shall be to the Lord for a *n.* 55:13
them a *n.*, an everlasting *n.* 56:5
whose *n.* is holy. 57:15
called by a new *n.* 62:2
himself an everlasting *n.* 63:12
to make thyself a glorious *n.* 14
n. for a curse to my chosen, and call his servants by another *n.* 65:15
seed and your *n.* remain. 66:22
that they might be to me for a *n.* *Jer* 13:11; 33:9
which hast made thee a *n.* 32:20
this is the *n.* wherewith she. 33:16
saith the King, whose *n.* is the Lord. 46:18; 48:15; 51:57
n. thereof is called Bamah. *Ezek* 20:29
son of man, write thee the *n.* 24:2
the *n.* of the city shall be. 48:35
blessed be the *n.* of God. *Dan* 2:20
Daniel came, according to the *n.* 4:8
call her *n.* Lo-ruhamah. *Hos* 1:6
be remembered by their *n.* 2:17
saith Lord, whose *n.* is. *Amos* 5:27
every one in the *n.* of his god, we will walk in the *n.* of our. *Mi* 4:5
I will cut off the *n.* of the. *Zeph* 1:4
make you a *n.* and a praise. 3:20
whose *n.* is the Branch. *Zech* 6:12
prophet in the *n.* of a prophet, a righteous man in *n.* of. *Mat* 10:41
give a cup of water only in *n.* 42
baptizing them in the *n.* of. 28:19
kindred is called by this *n.* *Luke* 1:61
saying, His *n.* is John. 63
shall cast out your *n.* as evil. 6:22
from God, whose *n.* was. *John* 1:6
not believed in the *n.* of the. 3:18
I am come in my Father's *n.* 5:43
I do in my Father's *n.* 10:25
be baptized in the *n.* of. *Acts* 2:38
in the *n.* of Jesus Christ, rise up. 3:6
by what power or *n.* have ye? 4:7
there is none other *n.* under. 12
henceforth to no man in this *n.* 17, 18
may be done by the *n.* of Jesus. 30
should not teach in this *n.* 5:28, 40
preaching, concerning the *n.* 8:12
them that called on this *n.* 9:21
boldly in the *n.* of Jesus. 27
their lives for the *n.* of Jesus. 15:26
said, In the *n.* of Jesus. 16:18
they were baptized in the *n.* 19:5
contrary to the *n.* of Jesus of. 26:9
for the *n.* of God is. *Rom* 2:24
ye baptized in the *n.*? *1 Cor* 1:13
in the *n.* of our Lord Jesus. 5:4 *Eph* 5:20
are justified in the *n.* of. *1 Cor* 6:11
far above every *n.* that. *Eph* 1:21
him a *n.* above every *n.* *Phil* 2:9
at the *n.* of Jesus every knee. 10
do all in the *n.* of Lord. *Col* 3:17
that the *n.* of God be not. *1 Tim* 6:1
the *n.* of Christ, depart. *2 Tim* 2:19
obtained a more excellent *n.* *Heb* 1:4
blaspheme that worthy *n.*? *Jas* 2:7
if reproached for the *n.* *1 Pet* 4:14
should believe on *n.* of his Son. *1 John* 3:23; 5:13
a *n.* written, which no. *Rev* 2:17
thou hast a *n.* that thou livest. 3:1
I will write on him the *n.* of. 12

the *n.* of the star is called. *Rev* 8:11
n. in the Hebrew tongue is. 9:11
and on his heads the *n.* of. 13:1
his Father's *n.* written in. 14:1
blasphemed the *n.* of God. 16:9
was a *n.* written, Mystery. 17:5
a *n.* written no man knew but. 19:12
on his thigh a *n.* written, King of. 16
see **called**

name, *verb*

shalt anoint to me him whom I *n.*
1 Sam 16:3
bring him up whom I shall *n.* 28:8
mouth of the Lord shall *n.* *Isa* 62:2

by **name,** or *by the* **name**

I appeared *by the n.* of God. *Ex* 6:3
called *by n.* Bezaleel. 31:2; 35:30
I know thee *by n.* 33:12, 17
by n. ye shall reckon. *Num* 4:32
cities mentioned *by n.* *Josh* 21:9
of Gath, Goliath *by n.* *1 Sam* 17:23
Sheba, son of Bichri *by n.* hath lifted up his hand. *2 Sam* 20:21
be born, Josiah *by n.* *1 Ki* 13:2
these written *by n.* *1 Chr* 4:41
which were expressed *by n.* 12:31
16:41; *2 Chr* 28:15; 31:19
she were called *by n.* *Esth* 2:14
by the n. of Jacob, and surname himself *by the n.* *Isa* 44:5; 48:1
which call thee *by* thy *n.* 45:3
calleth his own sheep *by n.* *John* 10:3
by the n. of Jesus this. *Acts* 4:10
I beseech you *by the n.* *1 Cor* 1:10
our friends salute thee. Greet the friends *by n.* *3 John* 14
see **expressed**

his **name**

shall say, What is *his n.?* *Ex* 3:13
Pr 30:4
the Lord is *his n.* *Ex* 15:3
Jer 33:2; *Amos* 5:8; 9:6
not hold him guiltless that taketh *his n.* in vain. *Ex* 20:7; *Deut* 5:11
every stone with *his n.* shall they be.
Ex 28:21; 39:14
Jair called them after *his* own *n.*
Deut 3:14
and shalt swear by *his n.* 6:13
to bless in *his n.* to this day. 10:8
1 Chr 23:13
shall choose to put *his n.* *Deut* 12:5
21; *1 Ki* 14:21; *2 Chr* 12:13
choose to cause *his n.* *Deut* 12:11
choose to place *his n.* there. 14:23
16:6, 11; 26:2
shall choose to set *his n.* 14:24
that *his n.* be not put out. 25:6
his n. shall be called in Israel. 10
Lord shall blot out *his n.* 29:20
neither told he me *his n.* *Judg* 13:6
his n. may be famous. *Ruth* 4:14
for *his* great *n.'s* sake. *1 Sam* 12:22
Ps 23:3; 106:8; *1 John* 2:12
3 John 7
so that *his n.* was much. *1 Sam* 18:30
as *his n.* is, so is he, Nabal is *his n.*
25:25
give thanks to Lord, call upon *his n.*
1 Chr 16:8; *Ps* 105:1; *Isa* 12:4
give the glory due to *his n.*
1 Chr 16:29; *Ps* 29:2; 96:8
God that caused *his n.* *Ezra* 6:12
let us exalt *his n.* *Ps* 34:3; 66:2
when shall he die and *his n.?* 41:5
the heavens by *his n.* Jah. 68:4
they that love *his n.* shall. 69:36
his n. shall endure for ever. 72:17
and blessed be *his* glorious *n.* 19
his n. is great in Israel. 76:1
bless *his n.* 96:2; 100:4
among them that call on *his n.* 99:6
holy and reverend is *his n.* 111:9
sing praises to *his n.* for it. 135:3
praise *his n.*, for *his n.* alone. 148:13
praise *his n.* in the dance. 149:3
haughty scorner is *his n.* *Pr* 21:24
his n. shall be covered. *Eccl* 6:4
shall call *his n.* Immanuel. *Isa* 7:14
Mat 1:23
and *his n.* shall be called. *Isa* 9:6
make mention that ***his n.* is.** 12:4

the Lord of hosts is *his n.* *Isa* 47:4
48:2; 51:15; 54:5; *Jer* 10:16
31:35; 32:18; 50:34; 51:19
his n. should not have been cut off.
Isa 48:19
his n. may be no more. *Jer* 11:19
speak any more in *his n.* 20:9
this is *his n.* whereby he. 23:6
all ye that know *his n.* say. 48:17
God of hosts is *his n.* *Amos* 4:13
shall walk up and down in *his n.*
Zech 10:12
shall be one Lord, and *his n.* 14:9
thought on *his n.* a book. *Mal* 3:16
shalt call *his n.* Jesus. *Mat* 1:23
Luke 1:31; 2:21
his n. shall the Gentiles. *Mat* 12:21
for *his n.* was spread. *Mark* 6:14
thou shalt call *his n.* *Luke* 1:13
remission of sins should be preached in *his n.* 24:47
that believe on *his n.* *John* 1:12
many believed in *his n.* when. 2:23
shall come in *his* own *n.* 5:43
might have life through *his n.* 20:31
his n. through faith in *his n.* hath.
Acts 3:16
worthy to suffer for *his n.* 5:41
through *his n.* shall receive. 10:43
sorcerer, for so is *his n.* 13:8
them a people for *his n.* 15:14
all nations for *his n.* *Rom* 1:5
ye shewed towards *his n.* *Heb* 6:10
giving thanks to *his n.* 13:15
not blot out *his n.* but will confess *his n.* *Rev* 3:5
and *his n.* that sat on him. 6:8
hath *his n.* Apollyon. 9:11
to blaspheme *his n.* 13:6
number of *his n.* 17; 15:2
receiveth the mark of *his n.* 14:11
and *his n.* shall be in their. 22:4
see **holy, Lord**

my **name**

dost ask after *my n.?* *Gen* 32:29
let *my n.* be named on them. 48:16
this is *my n.* for ever. *Ex* 3:15
raised thee up, that *my n.* 9:16
where I record *my n.* I will. 20:24
provoke him not, for *my n.* 23:21
swear by *my n.* falsely. *Lev* 19:12
Molech, to profane *my* holy *n.* 20:3
my n. on the children. *Num* 6:27
shall speak in *my n.* *Deut* 18:19, 20
thou thus after *my n.?* *Judg* 13:18
wilt not destroy *my n.* *1 Sam* 24:21
Nabal, and greet him in *my n.* 25:5
an house for *my n.* *2 Sam* 7:13
1 Ki 5:5; 8:18, 19; *1 Chr* 22:10
lest I take the city, and it be called after *my n.* *2 Sam* 12:28
I have no son to keep *my n.* 18:18
my n. might be therein. *1 Ki* 8:16
29; 11:36; *2 Ki* 21:4, 7; *2 Chr* 6:5
6; 7:16; 33:4, 7
have hallowed for *my n.* *1 Ki* 9:7
not build an house to *my n.*
1 Chr 22:8; 28:3
it was in thine heart to build an house for *my n.* *2 Chr* 6:8
build the house for *my n.* 9
I have sanctified for *my n.* 7:20
I have chosen to set *my n.* there.
Neh 1:9; *Jer* 7:12
in *my n.* shall his horn. *Ps* 89:24
he hath known *my n.* 91:14
they shall sanctify *my n.* *Isa* 29:23
sun shall he call on *my n.* 41:25
I am the Lord, that is *my n.* 42:8
for *my n.'s* sake will I defer. 48:9
should *my n.* be polluted ? 11
made mention of *my n.* 49:1
my n. continually every day. 52:5
my people shall know *my n.* 6
cast you out for *my n.'s* sake. 66:5
they prophesy lies in *my n.*
Jer 14:14, 15; 23:25
know that *my n.* is the Lord. 16:21
to forget *my n.* as their fathers have forgotten *my n.* for Baal. 23:27
a lie in *my n.* 27:15; 29:9, 21, 23
turned and polluted *my n.* 34:16
sworn by ***my* great *n.*, *my n.* no.** 44:26

but I wrought for *my n.'s* sake.
Ezek 20:9, 14, 22, 44
sanctify *my* great *n.* 36:23
shall call on *my n.* I. *Zech* 13:9
priests, that despise *my n.* *Mal* 1:6
my n. shall be great among Gentiles, and ... shall be offered to *my n.* 11
my n. is dreadful among. 14
heart, to give glory unto *my n.* 2:2
and was afraid before *my n.* 5
to you that fear *my n.* shall. 4:2
hated of all men for *my n.'s* sake.
Mat 10:22; 24:9; *Mark* 13:13
Luke 21:17
receive a child in *my n.* *Mat* 18:5
Mark 9:37; *Luke* 9:48
gathered together in *my n.* *Mat* 18:20
forsaken houses for *my n.'s.* 19:29
many shall come in *my n.* 24:5
Mark 13:6; *Luke* 21:8
saying, *My n.* is Legion. *Mark* 5:9
do a miracle in *my n.* 9:39
cup of water to drink in *my n.* 41
in *my n.* shall they cast out. 16:17
rulers for *my n.'s* sake. *Luke* 21:12
ye shall ask in *my n.* *John* 14:13
14; 15:16; 16:23, 24, 26
whom he will send in *my n.* 14:26
will they do for *my n.'s* sake. 15:21
vessel to bear *my n.* *Acts* 9:15
he must suffer for *my n.'s* sake. 16
Gentiles upon whom *my n.* is. 15:17
my n. might be declared. *Rom* 9:17
I baptized in *mine* own *n.* *1 Cor* 1:15
and for *my n.'s* sake hast. *Rev* 2:3
thou holdest fast *my n.* and. 13
and hast not denied *my n.* 3:8
see **called**

thy **name**

and make *thy n.* great. *Gen* 12:2
thy n. Abram, but *thy n.* shall. 17:5
what is *thy n.?* 32:27, 29; *Judg* 13:17
thy n. shall be no more called Jacob.
Gen 32:28; 35:10; *1 Ki* 18:31
Pharaoh to speak in *thy n.* *Ex* 5:23
thou do to *thy* great *n.?* *Josh* 7:9
thy n. be magnified. *2 Sam* 7:26
will sing praise to *thy n.* 22:50
Ps 9:2; 18:49; 61:8; 66:4; 92:1
Solomon better than *thy n.* *1 Ki* 1:47
turn and confess *thy n.* 8:33
2 Chr 6:24, 26
but cometh for *thy n.'s* sake.
1 Ki 8:41; *2 Chr* 6:32
shall hear of *thy* great *n.* *1 Ki* 8:42
earth may know *thy n.*; this house is called by *thy n.* 43; *2 Chr* 6:33
house I built for *thy n.* *1 Ki* 8:44
48; *2 Chr* 6:34, 38
thy n. may be magnified. *1 Chr* 17:24
praise *thy n.* 29:13; *Ps* 44:8
wouldest put *thy n.* there. *2 Chr* 6:20
in *thy n.* we go against this. 14:11
a sanctuary for *thy n.* 20:8
before this house, for *thy n.* is. 9
who desire to fear *thy n.* *Neh* 1:11
blessed be *thy* glorious *n.* 9:5
let them that love *thy n.* *Ps* 5:11
how excellent is *thy n.* in. 8:1, 9
they that know *thy n.* will. 9:10
I will declare *thy n.* to my brethren.
22:22; *Heb* 2:12
for *thy n.'s* sake pardon. *Ps* 25:11
for *thy n.'s* sake lead me and. 31:3
through *thy n.* will we tread. 44:5
I will make *thy n.* to be. 45:17
according to *thy n.* so is. 48:10
I will wait on *thy n.* 52:9
save me by *thy n.* 54:1
heritage of those that fear *thy n.* 61:5
will lift up my hands in *thy n.* 63:4
defiled dwelling place of *thy n.* 74:7
enemy blaspheme *thy n.?* 10
people have blasphemed *thy n.* 18
needy praise *thy n.* 21
thy n. is near, thy works. 75:1
that have not called on *thy n.* 79:6
Jer 10:25
for the glory of *thy n.* and purge away our sins for *thy n.'s* sake. *Ps* 79:9
we will call upon *thy n.* 80:18
may seek *thy n.* O Lord. 83:16
come and glorify *thy n.* 86:9, 12

unite my heart to fear *thy n.* Ps 86:11
shall rejoice in *thy n.* 89:12, 16
O Lord, for *thy n.'s* sake. 109:21
but unto *thy n.* give glory. 115:1
I have remembered *thy n.* 119:55
do to those that love *thy n.* 132
thy n. O Lord, endureth. 135:13
n. for thy lovingkindness: for thou hast . . . word above all *thy n.* 138:2
take *thy n.* in vain. 139:20
shall give thanks to *thy n.* 140:13
that I may praise *thy n.* 142:7
O Lord, for *thy n.'s* sake. 143:11
I will bless *thy n.* for ever. 145:1, 2
praise *thy n.* for ever. 2; *Isa* 25:1
thy n. is as ointment. *S of S* 1:3
our soul is to *thy n.* *Isa* 26:8
will make mention of *thy n.* 13
thy n. is from everlasting. 63:16
make *thy n.* known to thine. 64:2
none that calleth on *thy n.* 7
art great and *thy n.* is. *Jer* 10:6
Lord calleth *thy n.* a green. 11:16
do thou it for *thy n.'s* sake. 14:7
do not abhor us for *thy n.'s* sake. 21
sent letters in *thy n.* to all. 29:25
I called upon *thy n.* *Lam* 3:55
prophets spake in *thy n.* *Dan* 9:6
wisdom shall see *thy n.* *Mi* 6:9
that no more of *thy n.* be. *Nah* 1:14
have we despised *thy n.*? *Mal* 1:6
hallowed be *thy n.* *Mat* 6:9
Luke 11:2
in *thy n.* have we cast out. *Mat* 7:22
he asked him, What is *thy n.*? *Mark* 5:9; *Luke* 8:30
casting out devils in *thy n.* *Mk.* 9:38
Luke 9:49
subject through *thy n.* *Luke* 10:17
Father, glorify *thy n.* *John* 12:28
I have manifested *thy n.* 17:6, 26
keep through *thine* own *n.* 11, 12
bind all that call on *thy n.* *Acts* 9:14
and sing unto *thy n.* *Rom* 15:9
to them that fear *thy n.* *Rev* 11:18
not fear and glorify *thy n.*? 15:4
see **called**

named, -eth

silver which he had *n.* *Gen* 23:16
Is not he rightly *n.* Jacob ? 27:36
my name be *n.* on them. 48:16
n. the child Ichabod. *1 Sam* 4:21
Jacob whom he *n.* Israel. *2 Ki* 17:34
Moses' sons *n.* of the. *1 Chr* 23:14
what hath been, is *n.* *Eccl* 6:10
ye shall be *n.* the priests. *Isa* 61:6
name shall no more be *n.* *Jer* 44:26
which are *n.* chief of. *Amos* 6:1
that art *n.* of the house. *Mi* 2:7
Jesus was so *n.* of the. *Luke* 2:21
twelve, whom he *n.* apostles. 6:13
not where Christ was *n.* *Rom* 15:20
such fornication not *n.* *1 Cor* 5:1
every name that is *n.* *Eph* 1:21
family in heaven and earth is *n.* 3:15
covetousness, let it not be once *n.* 5:3
let every one that *n.* *2 Tim* 2:19

namely

sore evil, *n.* riches kept. *Eccl* 5:13
razor that is hired, *n.* *Isa* 7:20
the second is like, *n.* *Mark* 12:31

names

Adam gave *n.* to all cattle. *Gen* 2:20
called their *n.* after the *n.* 26:18
make no mention of the *n.* of other. *Ex* 23:13; *Deut* 12:3
grave on them the *n.* of children of. *Ex* 28:9, 21
bear their *n.* before the. 12, 29
the number of their *n.* *Num* 1:2
n. of the men that shall stand. 5
number of *n.* of the Levites. 3:43
n. of the men which Moses. 13:16
n. of men which shall divide. 34:17
the *n.* of mighty men. *2 Sam* 23:8
what are the *n.* of the man ? *Ezra* 5:4
nor take up their *n.* into. *Ps* 16:4
lands after their own *n.* 49:11
the stars; he calleth them all by their *n.* 147:4; *Isa* 40:26
n. of them were Aholah. *Ezek* 23:4
I will take away the *n.* of. *Hos* 2:17
cut off the *n.* of the idols. *Zech* 13:2
your *n.* are written in. *Luke* 10:20
the number of the *n.* of 120. *Acts* 1:15
question of words and *n.* 18:15
whose *n.* are in the book. *Phil* 4:3
thou hast a few *n.* in Sardis. *Rev* 3:4
whose *n.* are not written. 13:8; 17:8
I saw a woman full of *n.* 17:3
n. written thereon, *n.* of the. 21:12
in them the *n.* of twelve apostles. 14

Naomi

Elimelech's wife was *N.* *Ruth* 1:2
is this *N.*? 19
call me not *N.*, call me Mara. 20
N. had a kinsman of her. 2:1
buyest the field of hand of *N.* 4:5
bought all at the hand of *N.* 9
there is a son born to *N.* 17

Naphtali

called his name *N.* *Gen* 30:8
Rachel's handmaid, Dan, *N.* 35:25
sons of *N.* 46:24; *Num* 1:42
26:48; *1 Chr* 7:13
N. is a hind let loose. *Gen* 49:21
Israel, *N.* Gad, and Asher. *Ex* 1:4
of *N.* Ahira was prince. *Num* 1:15
2:29; 7:78
Ebal to curse; Dan, *N.* *Deut* 27:13
of *N.* he said, O *N.* satisfied. 33:23
sixth lot came out to *N.* *Josh* 19:32
in Galilee, in mount *N.* 20:7
nor did *N.* drive out the. *Judg* 1:33
called Zebulun and *N.* to. 4:10
Zebulun and *N.* jeoparded. 5:18
Gideon sent messengers to *N.* 6:35
themselves together out of *N.* 7:23
was officer in *N.* *1 Ki* 4:15
Ben-hadad smote *N.* 15:20
2 Chr 16:4
carried *N.* captive to. *2 Ki* 15:29
N. brought bread on. *1 Chr* 12:40
captain of *N.* was Jerimoth. 27:19
Josiah in *N.* brake. *2 Chr* 34:6
princes of Zebulun and *N.* *Ps* 68:27
afflicted the land of *N.* *Isa* 9:1
a portion for *N.* *Ezek* 48:3
one gate of *N.* 34
dwelt in the borders of *N.* *Mat* 4:13
the land of *N.* by the way of. 15

***tribe of* Naphtali**

the *tribe of N.* 53,400 *Num* 1:43
host of the *tribe of N.* Ahira. 10:27
of the *tribe of N.* Nahbi. 13:14
of the *tribe of N.* Pedaheel. 34:28
inheritance of *tribe of N.* *Josh* 19:39
cities out of *tribe of N.* 21:32
1 Chr 6:62, 76
widow's son of *tribe of N.* *1 Ki* 7:14
tribe of N. were sealed. *Rev* 7:6

napkin

I have kept in a *n.* *Luke* 19:20
bound about with a *n.* *John* 11:44
n. that was about his head. 20:7

narrow

Lord stood in a *n.* way. *Num* 22:26
mount Ephraim be too *n.* *Josh* 17:15
made windows of *n.* *1 Ki* 6:4*
strange woman is a *n.* pit. *Pr* 23:27
destruction shall be too *n.* *Isa* 49:19*
n. is the way which. *Mat* 7:14*

narrowed

in wall he made *n.* rests. *1 Ki* 6:6*

narrower

covering *n.* than he can. *Isa* 28:20

narrowly

thou lookest *n.* to all. *Job* 13:27*
shall *n.* look upon thee. *Isa* 14:16

Nathan

son of David, *N.* *2 Sam* 5:14
N. the prophet. 7:2
so did *N.* speak. 17
the Lord sent *N.* 12:1, 25
Igal son of *N.* one of David's. 23:36
but *N.* the prophet he. *1 Ki* 1:10
talked with David, *N.* came in. 22
let Zadok and *N.* anoint him king. 34
Azariah son of *N.* was over. 4:5
Attai begat *N.* and *N.* *1 Chr* 2:36
Joel the brother of *N.* a. 11:38
written in the book of *N.* 29:29
Solomon in book of *N.* *2 Chr* 9:29
Ahava for *N.* and Ariel. *Ezra* 8:16
Shelemiah, *N.* had taken. 10:39
of the house of *N.* *Zech* 12:12
which was the son of *N.* *Luke* 3:31

Nathanael

Philip findeth *N.* *John* 1:45
N. of Cana. 21:2

nation

[1] *All the inhabitants of a particular country*, Deut 4:34. [2] *A country or kingdom*, Ex 34:10; Rev 7:9. [3] *Countrymen, natives of the same stock*, Acts 26:4. [4] *The heathen or Gentiles*, Isa 55:5.

also that *n.* they serve. *Gen* 15:14
wilt thou slay a righteous *n.*? 20:4
bondwoman I will make a *n.* 21:13
a *n.* and kings shall come. 35:11
Egypt, since it became a *n.* *Ex* 9:24
ye shall be unto me an holy *n.* 19:6
1 Pet 2:9
to sell her to a strange *n.* *Ex* 21:8*
that this *n.* is thy people. 33:13
have not been done in any *n.* 34:10
nor any of your *n.* commit abominations. *Lev* 18:26*
walk in the manners of the *n.* 20:23
I will make of thee a great *n.* *Num* 14:12; *Deut* 9:14
assayed to take him a *n.* from the midst of another *n.*? *Deut* 4:34
thy land shall a *n.* eat up. 28:33
bring thee and thy king to a *n.* 36
bring a *n.* against thee. 49
a *n.* of fierce countenance shall. 50
are a *n.* void of counsel. 32:28
what *n.* like thy people ? *2 Sam* 7:23
1 Chr 17:21
n. whither my lord hath not sent . . . took an oath of the *n.* *1 Ki* 18:10
every *n.* made gods. *2 Ki* 17:29
they went from *n.* to *n.* *1 Chr* 16:20
n. was destroyed of *n.* *2 Chr* 15:6
no god of any *n.* or kingdom. 32:15
it be done against a *n.* *Job* 34:29
blessed is *n.* whose God. *Ps* 33:12
my cause against an ungodly *n.* 43:1
cut them off from being a *n.* 83:4
they went from one *n.* to. 105:13
rejoice in gladness of thy *n.* 106:5
dealt so with any *n.* 147:20
righteousness exalteth a *n.* *Pr* 14:34
ah sinful *n.*, a people laden. *Isa* 1:4
n. shall not lift up sword against *n.* 2:4; *Mi* 4:3
thou hast multiplied the *n.* *Isa* 9:3
against an hypocritical *n.* 10:6
messengers of the *n.*? 14:32
swift messengers, to a *n.* scattered and peeled, a *n.* meted. 18:2, 7
open that the righteous *n.* may. 26:2
increased the *n.* O Lord, the *n.* 15
to him whom the *n.* abhorreth. 49:7
give ear to me, O my *n.* 51:4
thou shalt call a *n.* thou. 55:5
seek me, as a *n.* that did. 58:2
the *n.* that will not serve thee. 60:12
small one become a strong *n.* 22
a *n.* that was not called by. 65:1
or shall a *n.* be born at once ? 66:8
n. changed their gods ? *Jer* 2:11
avenged on such a *n.* 5:9, 29; 9:9
n. on you from far . . . it is a mighty *n.*, it is an ancient *n.* 5:15
a *n.* that obeyeth not the. 7:28
pluck up and destroy that *n.* 12:17
speak concerning a *n.* to. 18:7, 9
if that *n.* against whom I have. 8
punish that *n.* for their. 25:12, 27:8
shall go forth from *n.* to *n.* 25:32
n. which will not serve. 27:8, 13
cease from being a *n.* 31:36; 33:24
cut off Moab from being a *n.* 48:2
get you up to the wealthy *n.* 49:31
no *n.* whither Elam shall. 36
out of the north cometh a *n.* 50:3
have watched for a *n.* *Lam* 4:17
Israel, a rebellious *n.* *Ezek* 2:3
I will make them one *n.* in. 37:22
four kingdoms shall stand up out of the *n.* *Dan* 8:22
never was since there was a *n.* 12:1
for a *n.* is come up upon. *Joel* 1:6

raise up against you a *n.* *Amos* 6:14
was cast off a strong *n.* *Mi* 4:7
that bitter and hasty *n.* *Hab* 1:6
gather together, O *n.* *Zeph* 2:1
woe to the *n.* of the Cherethites. 5
so is this people and *n.* *Hag* 2:14
even this whole *n.* have. *Mal* 3:9
given to a *n.* bringing *Mat* 21:43
n. shall rise against *n.* 24:7
Mark 13:8; *Luke* 21:10
for he loveth our *n.* *Luke* 7:5
this fellow perverting the *n.* 23:2
come and take our *n.* *John* 11:48
one man die, that the whole *n.* 50
Jesus should die for that *n.* 51
and not for that *n.* only, but. 52
thine own *n.* hath delivered. 18:35
devout men out of every *n.* *Acts* 2:5
the *n.* to whom they shall be. 7:7
good report among all the *n.* 10:22
to come to one of another *n.* 28
but in every *n.* he that feareth. 35
deeds are done to this *n.* 24:2
thou hast been a judge to this *n.* 10
I came to bring alms to my *n.* 17
at first among mine own *n.* 26:4
aught to accuse my *n.* of. 28:19
my equals in my own *n.* *Gal* 1:14*
crooked and perverse *n.* *Phil* 2:15*
redeemed us out of every *n.* *Rev* 5:9
gospel to preach to every *n.* 14:6

see **foolish**

nations
(*Revisions, frequently* peoples)

were the *n.* divided. *Gen* 10:32
Tidal king of *n.* made war. 14:1*, 9*
shalt be a father of many *n.* 17:4
5; *Rom* 4:17, 18
and I will make *n.* of thee.
Gen 17:6; 35:11; 48:19
she shall be a mother of *n.* 17:16
two *n.* are in thy womb. 25:23
and let *n.* bow down to thee. 27:29
cast out the *n.* before thee. *Ex* 34:24
Deut 4:38; 7:22; 8:20
the *n.* are defiled. *Lev* 18:24
as it spued out the *n.* 28
reckoned among the *n.* *Num* 23:9
Israel shall eat up the *n.* 24:8
Amalek was the first of the *n.* 20
fear of thee on the *n.* *Deut* 2:25
wisdom in sight of the *n.* 4:6
scatter you among *n.* 27; *Neh* 1:8
hath cast out many *n.* *Deut* 7:1
to possess *n.* greater. 9:1; 11:23
God shall cut off *n.* 12:29; 19:1
lend to many *n.* 15:6; 28:12
set thee on high above all *n.* 28:1
Most High divided to the *n.* 32:8
rejoice, O ye *n.* with his people. 43
the Lord left those *n.* *Judg* 2:23
redeemest from the *n.* *2 Sam* 7:23
of the *n.* concerning. *1 Ki* 11:2
after the manner of *n.* *2 Ki* 17:33
hath any of the gods of the *n.*? 18:33
19:12; *2 Chr* 32:13, 14; *Isa* 36:18
say among the *n.*, The. *1 Chr* 16:31
driving out *n.* from before. 17:21
after the manner of *n.* *2 Chr* 13:9
among many *n.* was no. *Neh* 13:26
the *n.*: he enlargeth the *n.* *Job* 12:23
n. may know themselves. *Ps* 9:20
kindreds of *n.* shall worship. 22:27
Lord is governor among the *n.* 28
subdue the *n.* under our feet. 47:3
sing to thee among the *n.* 57:9; 108:3
his eyes behold the *n.* 66:7
let the *n.* be glad. 67:4
gods of the *n.* are idols. 96:5
their seed among the *n.* 106:27
they did not destroy the *n.* 34
the people curse, *n.* shall. *Pr* 24:24
shall judge among the *n.* *Isa* 2:4
an ensign to the *n.* from far. 5:26
in his heart to cut off *n.* 10:7
set up an ensign for the *n.* 11:12
he that ruled the *n.* in anger. 14:6
which didst weaken the *n.* 12
kings of the *n.* lie in glory. 18
Sihor, she is a mart of *n.* 23:3
the *n.* were scattered. 33:3
ye *n.* to hear. 34:1; *Jer* 31:10
n. are as a drop of a. *Isa* 40:15
shall he sprinkle many *n.* *Isa* 52:15
n. that knew not thee, shall. 55:5
yea, those *n.* shall be utterly. 60:12
that the *n.* may tremble at. 64:2
those that escape to the *n.* 66:19
thee a prophet to the *n.* *Jer* 1:5
this day set thee over the *n.* 10
n. shall bless themselves in. 4:2
make ye mention to *n.*, publish. 16
therefore hear ye *n.* 6:18; 31:10
fear thee, O King of *n.*? 10:7
the *n.* shall not be able to abide. 10
many *n.* shall pass by this city. 22:8
n. shall serve themselves of them.
25:14; 27:7
a controversy with the *n.* 25:31
n. have heard of thy shame. 46:12
ye among the *n.* Babylon is. 50:2
hindermost of the *n.* shall be a. 12
cry is heard among the *n.* 46
n. have drunken of her wine, *n.* 51:7
I break in pieces the *n.* 20
prepare the *n.* against her, call. 27
astonishment among the *n.* 41
the *n.* shall not flow together. 44
city that was great among *n.* *Lam* 1:1
my judgements into wickedness, more than the *n.* *Ezek* 5:6, 7
thee a reproach among the *n.* 14
remnant escape among the *n.* 6:8
remember me among the *n.* 9
scatter them among the *n.* 12:15
the *n.* also heard of him. 19:4
n. set against him on every side. 8
I will cause many *n.* to come. 26:3
shall become a spoil to the *n.* 5
strangers upon thee, the terrible of the *n.* 28:7; 30:11; 31:12
I will scatter Egyptians among *n.*
29:12; 30:23
no more rule over the *n.* 29:15
I made *n.* shake at the sound. 31:16
thou art like a lion of the *n.* 32:2
the daughters of the *n.* shall. 16, 18
thou hast said, These two *n.* 35:10
land hast bereaved thy *n.* 36:13
shall be no more two *n.* 37:22
forth out of the *n.* 38:8, 12
known in the eyes of many *n.* 23
sanctified in sight of many *n.* 39:27
have hired among the *n.* *Hos* 8:10
wanderers among the *n.* 9:17
scattered among the *n.* *Joel* 3:2
are named chief of *n.* *Amos* 6:1
many *n.* shall come and say. *Mi* 4:2
he shall rebuke strong *n.* afar off. 3
also many *n.* are gathered. 11
the *n.* shall see, be confounded. 7:16
that selleth *n.* through. *Nah* 3:4
I will shew the *n.* thy nakedness. 5
not spare continually to slay *n.*
Hab 1:17
hast spoiled many *n.* 2:8
and drove asunder the *n.* 3:6
I have cut off the *n.* *Zeph* 3:6
is to gather the *n.* 8
many *n.* shall be joined. *Zech* 2:11
and strong *n.* shall come to. 8:22
of all the languages of the *n.* 23
things do the *n.* seek. *Luke* 12:30
earth shall be distress of *n.* 21:25
destroyed seven *n.* in. *Acts* 13:19
I give power over the *n.* *Rev* 2:26
prophesy before many *n.* 10:11
n. shall see their dead bodies. 11:9
and the *n.* were angry, thy. 18
was given him over all *n.* 13:7
cities of the *n.* fell. 16:19
waters thou sawest are *n.* 17:15
that he should deceive the *n.* 20:3
n. of them which are saved. 21:24
the honour of the *n.* into it. 26
for the healing of the *n.* 22:2

see **great**

all **nations**

hath divided to *all n.* *Deut* 4:19
thee high above *all n.* 26:19; 28:1
a byword among *all n.* 28:37
his fame was in *all n.* *1 Ki* 4:31
fear of David on *all n.* *1 Chr* 14:17
marvellous works among *all n.* 16:24
Hezekiah magnified in sight of *all n.*
2 Chr 32:23
saving health among *all n.* *Ps* 67:2
kings fall down, *all n.* shall. 72:11
men blessed in him, *all n.* shall. 17
for thou shalt inherit *all n.* 82:8
all n. shall come and worship. 86:9
Lord is high above *all n.* 113:4
praise the Lord, *all* ye *n.* 117:1
all n. compassed me about. 118:10
all n. shall flow unto it. *Isa* 2:2
vail that is over *all n.* 25:7
indignation of Lord is on *all n.* 34:2
all n. before him are as nothing.
40:17
I will gather *all n.* and languages.
66:18; *Joel* 3:2
your brethren out of *all n.* *Isa* 66:20
and *all n.* shall serve him.
Jer 27:7; *Dan* 7:14
sift the house of Israel among *all n.*
Amos 9:9
but gathereth to him *all n.* *Hab* 2:5
all n. and the desire of *all n.* *Hag* 2:7
I will gather *all n.* *Zech* 14:2
punishment of *all n.* that come. 19
all n. shall call you blessed. *Mal* 3:12
ye shall be hated of *all n.* *Mat* 24:9
kingdom shall be preached to *all n.*
24:14; *Mark* 13:10; *Luke* 24:47
Rom 16:26
shall be gathered *all n.* *Mat* 25:32
go ye, and teach *all n.* 28:19
be called of *all n.* the. *Mark* 11:17
away captive into *all n.* *Luke* 21:24
suffered *all n.* to walk. *Acts* 14:16
one blood *all n.* of men. 17:26
the faith among *all n.* *Rom* 1:5
all n. for obedience of faith. 16:26
shall *all n.* be blessed. *Gal* 3:8
a multitude of *all n.* stood. *Rev* 7:9
was to rule *all n.* with a rod. 12:5
she made *all n.* drink of the wine.
14:8; 18:3
all n. shall come and worship. 15:4
sorceries were *all n.* deceived. 18:23

all the **nations**

all the n. of earth be blessed.
Gen 18:18; 22:18; 26:4
above *all the n.* on earth. *Deut* 14:2
set a king over me, as *all the n.*
17:14; *1 Sam* 8:5, 20
to mind among *all the n.* *Deut* 30:1
will gather thee from *all the n.* 3
into hell, and *all the n.* *Ps* 9:17
stretched out on *all the n.* *Isa* 14:26
the multitude of *all the n.* 29:7, 8
laid waste *all the n.* and. 37:18
let *all the n.* be gathered. 43:9
bare his holy arm in eyes of *all the n.*
52:10
spring forth before *all the n.* 61:11
and *all the n.* shall be gathered.
Jer 3:17
prophesied against *all the n.* 25:13
cause *all the n.* to drink it. 15
made *all the n.* drink. 17
this city a curse to *all the n.* 26:6
will gather you from *all the n.* 29:14
reproach among *all the n.* 18; 44:8
and honour before *all the n.* 33:9
make a full end of *all the n.* 46:28
them among *all the n.* *Zech* 7:14
destroy *all the n.* that come. 12:9
left of *all the n.* that came. 14:16

these **nations**

if thou say, *These n.* are more than I.
Deut 7:17
for wickedness of *these n.* 9:4, 5
Lord drive out all *these n.* 11:23
How did *these n.* serve? 12:30
these n. hearkened to. 18:14
cities which are not of *these n.* 20:15
among *these n.* shalt thou. 28:65
you serve the gods of *these n.* 29:18
Lord will destroy *these n.* 31:3
Lord hath done to *these n.* *Josh* 23:3
divided to you by lot *these n.* 4
that ye come not among *these n.* 7
to the remnant of *these n.* 12
no more drive out any of *these n.* 13
these n. the Lord left. *Judg* 3:1
so *these n.* feared Lord. *2 Ki* 17:41
these n. are uncircumcised. *Jer* 9:26
bring them against *these n.* 25:9

these n. shall serve king. Jer 25:11
of iron on neck of these n. 28:14

native

·:re see his n. country. Jer 22:10

nativity

died in the land of his n. Gen 11:28
left the land of thy n. Ruth 2:11
go to the land of our n. Jer 46:16
thy n. is of the land of. Ezek 16:3
as for thy n. in the day thou. 4
judge thee in land of thy n. 21:30*
Chaldea, the land of their n. 23:15

natural

not dim, nor his n. force. Deut 34:7
without n. affection. Rom 1:31
2 Tim 3:3
if God spared not the n. branches.
Rom 11:21, 24
n. man receiveth not. 1 Cor 2:14
sown a n. body. There is a n. 15:44
first that which is n. 46
his n. face in a glass. Jas 1:23
these as n. brute beasts. 2 Pet 2:12*

naturally

who will n. care for your state.
Phil 2:20*
know n. as brute beasts. Jude 10

nature

[1] *Natural endowment or instinct,* Rom 2:14. [2] *Birth, or natural descent,* Gal 2:15. [3] *The existing system of things in the world,* 1 Cor 11:14. [4] *The physical constitution or existence; the vital powers,* Heb 2:16. [5] *The state of the unregenerate soul,* Eph. 2:3

change to that against n. Rom 1:26
do by n. the things contained. 2:14
shall not uncircumcision by n.? 27
olive tree, which is wild by n. and wert graffed contrary to n. 11:24
not even n. itself teach ? 1 Cor 11:14
who are Jews by n. and. Gal 2:15
service unto them, which by n. 4:8
by n. children of wrath. Eph 2:3
took not on him the n. Heb 2:16*
on fire the course of n. Jas 3:6
partakers of the divine n. 2 Pet 1:4

naught, or **nought**

serve me for n.? Gen 29:15
n. of the cursed thing. Deut 13:17
and thou givest him n. 15:9
rejoice to bring you to n. 28:63*
pleasant, but the water n. 2 Ki 2:19
their counsel to n. Neh 4:15
doth Job fear God for n.? Job 1:9
wicked shall come to n. 8:22
mountain falling cometh to n. 14:18
pledge from thy brother for n. 22:6
counsel of heathen to n. Ps 33:10
sellest thy people for n. 44:12
set at n. all my counsel. Pr 1:25
n., it is n. saith the buyer. 20:14
counsel, it shall come to n. Isa 8:10
terrible one is brought to n. 29:20
aside the just for a thing of n. 21
as nothing, as a thing of n. 41:12
nothing, and your work of n. 24
have spent my strength for n. 49:4
ye have sold yourselves for n. 52:3
people is taken away for n. 5
vision, and a thing of n. Jer 14:14
Beth-el shall come to n. Amos 5:5
rejoice in a thing of n. 6:13
would shut the doors for n.? . . fire on mine altar for n. Mal 1:10
he must suffer many things, and be set at n. Mark 9:12; Luke 23:11
this is the stone set at n. Acts 4:11
scattered and brought to n. 5:36
of men, it will come to n. 38
in danger to be set at n. 19:27
set at n. thy brother ? Rom 14:10
to bring to n. things. 1 Cor 1:28
wisdom of this world that cometh to n. 1 Cor 2:6
any man's bread for n. 2 Thes 3:8
so great riches come to n. Rev 18:17

naughtiness

I know thy pride, and the n. of thy.
1 Sam 17:28
be taken in their own n. Pr 11:6*
and superfluity of n. Jas 1:21

naughty

a n. person walketh. Pr 6:12*
and a liar giveth ear to a n. 17:4*
other basket had very n. figs.
Jer 24:2*

Naum

which was the son of N. Luke 3:25

navel

his force is in the n. Job 40:16*
it shall be health to thy n. Pr 3:8
thy n. is like a round. S of S 7:2†
wast born, thy n. was. Ezek 16:4

naves

their n. and spokes. 1 Ki 7:33*

navy

Solomon made a n. of. 1 Ki 9:26
Hiram sent in the n. his. 27
the n. of Hiram brought gold. 10:11
king Solomon had at sea a n. of. 22

nay

for he will not say thee n. 1 Ki 2:17
not n. for I will not say thee n. 20*
communication be yea, yea, n. n.
Mat 5:37; Jas 5:12
I tell you N.; but rather. Luke 12:51
I tell you N., but except ye. 13:3, 5
he said, N. father Abraham. 16:30
n. verily, but let them. Acts 16:37
by law of works ? n. but. Rom 3:27
n. but O man, who art thou ? 9:20
should be yea, yea, n. n. 2 Cor 1:17
toward you was not yea and n. 18
Jesus Christ . . . was not yea, n. 19

Nazarene

he shall be called a N. Mat 2:23

Nazarenes

of the sect of the N. Acts 24:5

Nazareth

dwelt in a city called N. Mat 2:23
this is Jesus of N. 21:11; Mark 1:24
10:47; Luke 4:34; 18:37; 24:19
also with Jesus of N. Mark 14:67
ye seek Jesus of N. 16:6
Gabriel was sent to N. Luke 1:26
Jesus came to N. and. 2:51; 4:16
Jesus of N. John 1:45; 18:5, 7
19:19; Acts 2:22; 4:10; 6:14
22:8
good thing come out of N.? John 1:46
of Jesus of N. rise up. Acts 3:6
God anointed Jesus of N. 10:38
to the name of Jesus of N. 26:9

Nazarite

(Among the ancient Hebrews, a person who was consecrated to God, and pledged never to cut the hair, drink wine, or touch a corpse during the period of the vow. This could be taken for a limited period, or for life. The Revisions change the spelling to Nazirites)

a vow of a N. to separate. Num 6:2
the law of the N. when. 13, 21
the N. shall shave the head of. 18
put them on the hands of the N. 19
after that the N. may drink. 20
the child shall be a N. to God.
Judg 13:5, 7; 16:17

Nazarites

her N. purer than snow. Lam 4:7*
of your young men for N. Amos 2:11
ye gave the N. wine to drink. 12

Neapolis

ext day we came to N. Acts 16:11

near

this city is n. to flee to. Gen 19:20
Jacob went n. to Isaac. 27:22
bring it n., he brought it n. 25
Jacob went n. and rolled. 29:10
thou shalt be n. to me, thou. 45:10
he brought them n. and. 48:10
land of Philistines, although that was n. Ex 13:17
any that is n. of kin. Lev 18:6
thy father's n. kinswoman. 12
thy mother's n. kinswomen. 13, 17
for he uncovereth his n. kin. 20:19
his kin n. to him he may be defiled.
Lev 21:2
bring the tribe of Levi n. Num 3:6
bring her n. and set her. 5:16
to bring you n. to himself. 16:9, 10
cometh n. the tabernacle. 17:13
in plains of Moab, n. Jericho. 26:3
go thou n. and hear all. Deut 5:27
not plant a grove of trees n. 16:21
men n. Micah's house. Judg 18:22
not that evil was n. them. 20:34
the man is n. of kin to. Ruth 2:20
spread skirt, for thou art a n. 3:9, 12
Joab's field is n. mine. 2 Sam 14:30
because the king is n. of kin. 19:42
land of enemy far or n. 1 Ki 8:46
2 Chr 6:36
thy vineyard, because it is n. to.
1 Ki 21:2
one is so n. another, no. Job 41:16
for trouble is n. Ps 22:11
thy name is n. 75:1
thou art n. O Lord, thy. 119:151
horn of Israel, a people n. 148:14
through the street, n. her. Pr 7:8
the mouth of the foolish is n. 10:14
is a neighbour that is n. 27:10
that are n. acknowledge. Isa 33:13
tell ye, and bring them n. 45:21
bring n. my righteousness. 46:13
he is n. that justifieth me. 50:8
my righteousness is n. my. 51:5
upon the Lord while he is n. 55:6
my salvation is n. to come. 56:1
peace be to him that is n. 57:19
thou art n. in their mouth. Jer 12:2
kings of the north far and n. 25:26
our end is n., our days. Lam 4:18
he that is n. shall fall. Ezek 6:12
day of trouble is n. 7:7; 30:3
who say, It is not n., let us. 11:3
be n. and far shall mock thee. 22:5
to Israel that are n. Dan 9:7
the day of the Lord is n. Ob 15
Zech 1:14
know that it is n. even. Mat 24:33
that summer is n. Mark 13:28
together his n. friends. Acts 10:24

see **came, come, draw, drew**

nearer

there is a kinsman n. Ruth 3:12
our salvation n. than. Rom 13:11

Nebaioth

the son of Ishmael, N. Gen 25:13
1 Chr 1:29
rams of N. shall minister. Isa 60:7

Nebat, *see* **Jeroboam**

Nebo

Elealeh and N. is a land. Num 32:3
the children of Reuben built N. 38
get thee up unto mount N.
Deut 32:49; 34:1
in Aroer, even unto N. 1 Chr 5:8
the children of N. Ezra 2:29; 10:43
the men of the other N. Neh 7:33
Moab shall howl over N Isa 15:2
N. stoopeth. 46:1
woe unto N. Jer 48:1
is come upon Dibon and N. 22

Nebuchadnezzar, Nebuchadrezzar

in his days N. came up. 2 Ki 24:1
25:1; 2 Chr 36:6; Jer 39:1; 52:4
for the people whom N. 2 Ki 25:22
carried away Judah by N. 1 Chr 6:15
Jer 24:1; 29:1; 52:28
Cyrus brought forth the vessels N.
Ezra 1:7; 5:14; 6:5
which will not serve N. Jer 27:8
I break the yoke of N. 28:11
that they may serve N. king. 14
deliver them into hand of N. 29:21
this city into the hand of N. 32:28
N. gave charge concerning. 39:11
I will take N. my servant. 43:10
N. king of Babylon shall. 49:28
last this N. hath broken. 50:17
N. hath devoured me, he. 51:34
I will bring on Tyrus N. Ezek 26:7
I will give the land of Egypt to N.
29:19; 30:10
N. dreamed. Dan 2:1

N. the king made an image. *Dan* 3:1
N. was full of fury. 19
N. was astonished. 24
ame upon the king *N.* **4:28,** 33
t end of days I *N.* lifted up mine. 34
I *N.* praise and extol. 37
most high God gave *N.* a. **5:18**

Nebuzar-adan

N. captain of guard. *2 Ki* 25:8
N. left of the poor of. *Jer* 39:10

necessary

his words more than *n.* *Job* 23:12
was *n.* that the word first. *Acts* 13:46
greater burden than these *n.* 15:28
with such things as were *n.* 28:10*
which seem feeble are *n.* *1 Cor* 12:22
I thought it *n.* to exhort. *2 Cor* 9:5
I supposed it *n.* to send. *Phil* 2:25
good works for *n.* uses. *Tit* 3:14
n. patterns should be. *Heb* 9:23

necessities

have ministered to my *n.* *Acts* 20:34
ministers of God in *n.* *2 Cor* 6:4
I take pleasure in *n.*, in. 12:10

necessity

[1] *Something that must needs be, when it is contrary to its very nature and principles to be otherwise,* Heb 9:16. [2] *Poverty, or want of temporal good things,* Rom 12:13. [3] *Force or constraint,* 2 Cor 9:7.

of *n.* he must release. *Luke* 23:17
distributing to the *n.* *Rom* 12:13
having no *n.* and hath. *1 Cor* 7:37
for *n.* is laid upon me, yea. 9:16
not grudgingly, or of *n.* *2 Cor* 9:7
once and again to my *n.* *Phil* 4:16
not be as it were of *n.* *Philem* 14
made of *n.* a change of. *Heb* 7:12
n. this man have somewhat. 8:3
there must of *n.* be the death. **9:16**

neck

skins on smooth of his *n.* *Gen* **27:16**
break the yoke from off thy *n.* 40
Esau fell on his *n.* and. 33:4
gold chain about Joseph's *n.* 41:42
Ezek 16:11; *Dan* 5:7, 16, 29
fell on Benjamin's *n.* and. *Gen* 45:14
Jacob's *n.*; he wept on his *n.* 46:29
thy hand shall be on the *n.* 49:8
break his *n.* *Ex* 13:13; 34:20
off his head from his *n.* *Lev* 5:8
strike off the heifer's *n.* *Deut* 21:4
a yoke of iron upon thy *n.* 28:48
and his *n.* brake, and. *1 Sam* 4:18
Zedekiah stiffened his *n.* *2 Chr* 36:13
hardened their *n.* and. *Neh* 9:29
on him, even on his *n.* *Job* 15:26
he hath taken me by the *n.* 16:12
hast thou clothed his *n.* with? 39:19
in his *n.* remaineth strength. 41:22
speak not with a stiff *n.* *Ps* 75:5
be chains about thy *n.* *Pr* 1:9
bind them about thy *n.* 3:3; 6:21
life and grace to thy *n.* 3:22
thy *n.* is comely with. *S of S* **1:10**
thy *n.* is like the tower of. 4:4
my heart with one chain of thy *n.* 9
thy *n.* is a tower of ivory. 7:4
reach even to the *n.* *Isa* 8:8
be taken from off thy *n.* 10:27
to the midst of the *n.* 30:28
thy *n.* is an iron sinew. 48:4
from the bands of thy *n.* 52:2
as if he cut off a dog's *n.* 66:3
not, made their *n.* stiff. *Jer* 17:23
and put them on thy *n.* 27:2
will not put *n.* under yoke of. 8, 11
the yoke from off Jeremiah's *n.* 28:10, 12
I have put a yoke on the *n.* 14
break his yoke from off thy *n.* 30:8
are come upon my *n.* *Lam* 1:14
over on her fair *n.* *Hos* 10:11
the foundation unto the *n.* *Hab* 3:13
a millstone were hanged about his *n.*
Mat 18:6; *Mark* 9:42; *Luke* 17:2
his father fell on his *n.* *Luke* 15:20
put a yoke on the *n.* *Acts* 15:10
they fell on Paul's *n.* and. 20:37
see **harden**

necks

put your feet on the *n.* *Josh* 10:24
for the *n.* of them that. *Judg* 5:30
were on their camel's *n.* 8:21, 26
given me *n.* of enemies.
2 Sam 22:41*; *Ps* 18:40*
the nobles put not their *n.* *Neh* 3:5
walk with stretched forth *n.* *Isa* 3:16
bring your *n.* under yoke. *Jer* 27:12
n. are under persecution. *Lam* 5:5
to bring thee on the *n.* *Ezek* 21:29
shall not remove your *n.* *Mi* 2:3
life laid down their own *n.* *Rom* 16:4

necromancer

found among you a *n.* *Deut* **18:11**

need

him sufficient for his *n.* *Deut* 15:8
have I *n.* of madmen? *1 Sam* 21:15
much as thou shalt *n.* *2 Chr* 2:16
ye shall not *n.* to fight in. 20:17
and let what they have *n.* *Ezra* 6:9
so he shall have no *n.* *Pr* 31:11
I have *n.* to be baptized. *Mat* 3:14
Father knoweth what things ye have
n. of. 6:8, 32; *Luke* 12:30
that be whole *n.* not a physician.
Mat 9:12; *Mark* 2:17; *Luke* 5:31
they *n.* not depart, give. *Mat* 14:16
the Lord hath *n.* of them. 21:3
Mark 11:3; *Luke* 19:31, 34
n. have we of witnesses? *Mat* 26:65
Mark 14:63; *Luke* 22:71
David did when he had *n.* *Mark* 2:25
healed them that had *n.* *Luke* 9:11
over just persons which *n.* 15:7
things we have *n.* of. *John* 13:29
as every man had *n.* *Acts* 2:45; 4:35
her in what she hath *n.* *Rom* 16:2
if *n.* so require, let him. *1 Cor* 7:36
to the hand, I have no *n.* **12:21**
our comely parts have no *n.* 24
or *n.* we epistles of? *2 Cor* **3:1**
to abound and to suffer *n.* *Phil* **4:12**
God shall supply all your *n.* 19
so that we *n.* not speak. *1 Thes* 1:8
of brotherly love ye *n.* not that. 4:9
of the times ye have no *n.* that. 5:1
grace to help in time of *n.* *Heb* 4:16
have *n.* that one teach you again;
such as have *n.* of milk. 5:12
what *n.* that another priest? 7:11
for ye have *n.* of patience. 10:36
though now, if *n.* be. *1 Pet* 1:6
ye *n.* not that any man. *1 John* 2:27
and see his brother have *n.* 3:17
I am rich, and have *n.* *Rev* 3:17
the city had no *n.* of sun. 21:23
and they *n.* no candle, nor. 22:25

needed

he *n.* not that any should. *John* 2:25
as though he *n.* any thing. *Acts* 17:25

needest, -eth

Jacob said, What *n.* it. *Gen* 33:15
give him as many as he *n.* *Luke* 11:8
is washed, *n.* not save. *John* 13:10
and *n.* not that any man. 16:30
to give to him that *n.* *Eph* 4:28
a workman that *n.* not. *2 Tim* 2:15
who *n.* not daily to offer. *Heb* 7:27

needful

shall be *n.* for the house. *Ezra* 7:20
one thing is *n.* and Mary. *Luke* 10:42
n. to circumcise them. *Acts* 15:5
the flesh is more *n.* for you. *Phil* 1:24
these things which are *n.* *Jas* 2:16
it was *n.* for me to write. *Jude* 3

needle

for a camel to go through the eye of
a *n.* *Mat* 19:24; *Mark* 10:25
Luke 18:25

needlework

an hanging wrought with *n.*
Ex 26:36; 27:16; 36:37; 38:18
make the girdle of *n.* 28:39; 39:29
divers colours of *n.* *Judg* 5:30
brought in raiment of *n.* *Ps* 45:14

needs

must *n.* be circumcised. *Gen* 17:13
said, This one fellow will *n.* 19:9
must I *n.* bring thy son again? 24:5
thou wouldest *n.* be gone. 31:30
we must *n.* die, and. *2 Sam* 14:14
must *n.* be borne, because. *Jer* 10:5
it must *n.* be that offences. *Mat* 18:7
for such things must *n.* *Mark* 13:7
ground, and I must *n.* *Luke* 14:18
n. go through Samaria. *John* 4:4
this scripture must *n.* *Acts* 1:16
must *n.* have suffered. 17:3
the multitude must *n.* come. 21:22
ye must *n.* be subject. *Rom* 13:5
must *n.* go out of world. *1 Cor* 5:10
if I must *n.* glory. *2 Cor* 11:30

needy

open thy hand to the *n.* *Deut* 15:11
servant that is poor and *n.* 24:14
they turn the *n.* out of. *Job* 24:4
killeth the poor and *n.* 14
the *n.* shall not alway. *Ps* 9:18
for the sighing of the *n.* now. 12:5
the poor and *n.* 35:10; 72:4, 13
bow, to cast down the *n.* 37:14
I am poor and *n.*, make. 40:17; 70:5
he shall deliver the *n.* 72:12; 82:4
the poor and *n.*, save the *n.* 72:13
let the poor and *n.* praise. 74:21
justice to the afflicted and *n.* **82:3**
deliver the poor and *n.* rid from. 4
for I am poor and *n.* 86:1; 109:22
the poor and *n.* man. 109:16
he lifteth the *n.* out of the. 113:7
devour the *n.* from. *Pr* 30:14
cause of the poor and *n.* 31:9
forth her hands to the *n.* 20
to turn aside the *n.* *Isa* 10:2
n. shall lie down in safety. 14:30
been a strength to the *n.* in. 25:4
steps of the *n.* shall tread. 26:6
when the *n.* speaketh right. 32:7
when the poor and *n.* seek. 41:17
and the right of *n.* do. *Jer* 5:28
cause of the poor and *n.* 22:16
the hands of the *n.* *Ezek* 16:49
oppressed the poor and *n.* 18:12
vexed the poor and *n.* 22:29
Bashan, which crush the *n.* *Amos* **4:1**
O ye that swallow up the *n.* **8:4**
buy the *n.* for a pair of shoes. **6**

neesings

by his *n.* a light doth. *Job* **41:18†**

neglect

n. to hear them, tell it to the church,
but if he *n.* to hear. *Mat* 18:17*
n. not the gift that. *1 Tim* **4:14**
how shall we escape, if *n.*? *Heb* 2:3

neglected

their widows were *n.* *Acts* **6:1**

neglecting

n. the body, not in any. *Col* **2:23***

negligent

my sons, be not now *n.* *2 Chr* **29:11**
not be *n.* to put you in. *2 Pet* **1:12***

Nehelamite, *see* **Shemaiah**

Nehemiah

N. came with Zerubbabel. *Ezra* 2:2
Neh 7:7
the words of *N.* the son. *Neh* 1:1
N. son of Azbuk repaired. 3:16
N. which is the. 8:9; 10:1
Israel in the days of *N.* 12:47

Nehushtan

the brasen serpent *N.* *2 Ki* **18:4**

neighbour

[1] *One who dwells or is placed near to another,* 2 Ki 4:3. [2] *Every man, to whom we have an opportunity of doing good,* Mat 22:39. [3] *A fellow-labourer, of one and the same people,* Acts 7:27. [4] *One who does us good, and who pities and relieves us in distress,* Luke 10:36.

every woman borrow of her *n.*
Ex 3:22; 11:2
hath given it to a *n.* *1 Sam* 15:28
better is a *n.* that is near. *Pr* 27:10
the *n.* and his friends. *Jer* 6:21
and teach every one her *n.* 9:20
was *n.* to him that fell. *Luke* 10:36

neighbour, *adjective*

overthrow of Sodom and Gomorrah
and the *n.* *Jer* 49:18; 50:40

his neighbour
and his n. take a lamb. Ex 12:4
come on his n. to slay him. 21:14
if a man deliver to his n. 22:7
hand to his n.'s goods. 8, 11
deliver to his n. an ass or ox. 10
if borrow aught of his n. and it. 14
camp, slay every man his n. 32:27
or hath deceived his n. Lev 6:2
adultery with his n.'s wife, shall. 20:10; Deut 22:24
cause a blemish in his n. Lev 24:19
should kill his n. Deut 4:42; 19:4
lendeth aught to his n. he shall not exact of his n. or his. 15:2
if any hate his n. and lie. 19:11
a man riseth against his n. 22:26
removeth his n.'s landmark. 27:17
cursed be he that smiteth his n. 24
shoe, and gave to his n. Ruth 4:7
trespass against his n. 1 Ki 8:31
man sin against his n. 2 Chr 6:22
one mocked of his n. Job 12:4
as a man pleadeth for his n. 16:21
speak vanity with his n. Ps 12:2
nor doeth evil to his n. 15:3*
privily slandereth his n. 101:5
goeth in to his n.'s wife. Pr 6:29
his mouth destroyeth his n. 11:9
despiseth his n. 12; 14:21
is more excellent than his n. 12:26
poor is hated even of his n. 14:20
a violent man enticeth his n. 16:29
but his n. cometh and. 18:17
separated from his n. 19:4*
his n. findeth no favour. 21:10
false witness against his n. 25:18
man that deceiveth his n. 26:19
that flattereth his n. spreadeth. 29:5
a man is envied of his n. Eccl 4:4
oppressed every one by his n. Isa 3:5
fight every one against his n. 19:2
they helped every one his n. 41:6
neighed after his n.'s wife. Jer 5:8
between a man and his n. 7:5
every one of his n., trust not. 9:4
deceive every one his n. 5
speak peaceably to his n. 8
every man to his n. 22:8; 23:35
useth his n.'s service without. 22:13
tell every one to his n. 23:27
words every one from his n. 30
teach no more every man his n. 31:34; Heb 8:11*
liberty to his n. Jer 34:15, 17
defiled his n.'s wife. Ezek 18:6, 15
hath defiled his n.'s wife. 11; 22:11 33:26
that giveth his n. drink. Hab 2:15
call every man his n. Zech 3:10
every one against his n. 8:10
every man the truth to his n. 16
imagine evil against his n. 17
love his n. as himself. Mark 12:33
he that did his n. wrong. Acts 7:27
worketh no evil to his n. Rom 13:10
let every one please his n. 15:2
speak every man truth with his n. Eph 4:25

my neighbour
wait at my n.'s door. Job 31:9
to Jesus, Who is my n.? Luke 10:29

thy neighbour
not bear false witness against thy n. Ex 20:16; Deut 5:20
take thy n.'s raiment to. Ex 22:26
carnally with thy n.'s wife. Lev 18:20
thou shalt not defraud thy n. 19:13
shalt thou judge thy n. 15
stand against the blood of thy n. 16
in any wise rebuke thy n. 17
love thy n. as thyself. 18
buyest aught of thy n. 25:14, 15
or covet thy n.'s wife. Deut 5:21
thou shalt not remove thy n.'s. 19:14
comest into thy n.'s vineyard. 23:24
and given it to thy n. 1 Sam 28:17
give them to thy n. 2 Sam 12:11
say not to thy n. Go. Pr 3:28
devise not evil against thy n. 29
be not witness against thy n. 24:28
when thy n. hath put thee to. 25:8
debate thy cause with thy n. 9
withdraw thy foot from thy n.'s. Pr 25:17
shalt love thy n. Mat 5:43; 19:19 22:39; Mark 12:31; Luke 10:27 Rom 13:9; Gal 5:14; Jas 2:8

neighbours
that they were their n. Josh 9:16
her n. gave it a name. Ruth 4:17
borrow vessels abroad of all thy n. 2 Ki 4:3
speak peace to their n. Ps 28:3
reproach among all my n. 31:11
us a reproach to our n. 44:13
become a reproach to our n. 79:4
render unto our n. sevenfold. 12
makest us a strife to our n. 80:6
he is a reproach to his n. 89:41
against all my evil n. Jer 12:14
adultery with their n.' wives. 29:23
his seed is spoiled and his n. 49:10
fornication with Egypt, thy n. Ezek 16:26
gained of thy n. by extortion. 22:12
the Assyrians her n. 23:5, 12
n. and her cousins heard. Luke 1:58
a supper, call not thy rich n. 14:12
together his friends and n. 15:6, 9
n. and they who before had seen him blind. John 9:8

neighed
n. after his neighbour's wife. Jer 5:8

neighing, -s
land trembled at the n. Jer 8:16
seen thine adulteries and n. 13:27

neither
the tree, n. shall ye touch. Gen 3:3
fight n. with small nor. 1 Ki 22:31
n. tell I you by what. Mat 21:27

nephew
(*Most frequently this means son's son, grandchild, and is so rendered in Revisions*)
neither have son nor n. Job 18:19*
from Babylon son and n. Isa 14:22*

nephews
forty sons and thirty n. Judg 12:14*
have children or n. 1 Tim 5:4*

Ner
N. begat Kish. 1 Chr 8:33; 9:36, 39
see **Abner**

Nereus
salute Julia, N. and. Rom 16:15

Nergal
Cuth made N. their god. 2 Ki 17:30

Neriah, *see* **Baruch**

nest
thou puttest thy n. in a. Num 24:21
if a bird's n. chance to. Deut 22:6
as an eagle stirreth up her n. 32:11
I shall die in my n. Job 29:18
command, make n. on high? 39:27
swallow hath found a n. Ps 84:3
wandereth from her n. Pr 27:8
hath found as n. riches. Isa 10:14
bird cast out of the n. 16:2
the great owl made her n. 34:15
thy n. in the cedars. Jer 22:23
the dove makes her n. in the. 48:28
thy n. as high as the eagle. 49:16
set thy n. among the stars. Ob 4
he may set his n. on high. Hab 2:9

nests
the birds make their n. Ps 104:17
fowls of heaven made their n. Ezek 31:6
and the birds of the air have n. Mat 8:20; Luke 9:58

net
(*A woven fabric for catching fish or birds; hence a snare, trap. It is also used figuratively, as for difficulties in which one is caught; or the traps set by one's enemies*)
he is cast into a n. by. Job 18:8
compassed me with his n. 19:6
in the n. they hid, is. Ps 9:15
draweth him into his n. 10:9
pluck my feet out of n. 25:15; 31:4
they have hid for me their n. 35:7
let his n. that he hath hid catch. 8
they have prepared a n. for. Ps 57:6
thou broughtest us into the n. 66:11
they have spread a n. by. 140:5
surely in vain the n. Pr 1:17
the wicked desireth the n. of. 12:12
that flattereth spreadeth a n. 29:5
fishes are taken in an evil n. Eccl 9:12
as a wild bull in a n. Isa 51:20
he hath spread a n. Lam 1:13
my n. will I spread on him. Ezek 12:13; 17:20
nations shall spread their n. 19:8
I will spread out my n. over. 32:3
ye have been a n. spread. Hos 5:1
I will spread my n. upon them. 7:12
hunt his brother with a n. Mi 7:2
catch them in their n. Hab 1:15
therefore they sacrifice to their n. 16
therefore empty their n.? 17
casting n. into the sea. Mat 4:18 Mark 1:16
of heaven is like a n. cast. Mat 13:47
I will let down the n. Luke 5:5
multitude of fishes, and their n. 6
the n. on the right side. John 21:6
came in a ship, dragging the n. with. 8
n. to land, yet was not the n. 11

Nethaneel
N. the son of Zuar was prince. Num 1:8; 2:5; 7:18, 23; 10:15
N. the fourth son of. 1 Chr 2:14
N. and Amasai blew with. 15:24
the son of N. the scribe, one. 24:6
Obed-edom, Joah and N. 26:4
Jehoshaphat sent N. to. 2 Chr 17:7
N. gave to the Levites for. 35:9
Ishmael, N. had taken. Ezra 10:22
in days of Joiakim N. Neh 12:21
N. with musical instruments. 36

Nethaniah
Ishmael son of N. 2 Ki 25:23, 25 Jer 40:8; 41:1
Asaph, Joseph and N. 1 Chr 25:2
fifth lot came forth to N. he. 12
Levites to teach, even N. 2 Chr 17:8
princes sent the son of N. Jer 36:14
Ishmael the son of N. slew. 41:2
but Ishmael son of N. escaped. 15

nether
they stood at the n. part. Ex 19:17
no man shall take n. millstone to. Deut 24:6*
gave her the upper springs and the n. Josh 15:19; Judg 1:15
built Gezer and Beth-horon the n. 1 Ki 9:17; 1 Chr 7:24
as a piece of n. millstone. Job 41:24
delivered to death to n. parts. Ezek 31:14
be comforted in the n. parts. 16
shalt be brought down to n. parts. 18
them down to the n. parts. 32:18
Elam gone down to the n. parts. 24

nethermost
the n. chamber was. 1 Ki 6:6

Nethinims
inhabitants were the N. 1 Chr 9:2
the N. went up with. Ezra 2:43
N. and the children of Solomon's servant were 392. 58; Neh 7:60
the N. went to Jerusalem. Ezra 7:7
not lawful to impose toll on N. 24
to Iddo and brethren the N. 8:17
the N. whom David appointed. 20
N. dwelt in Ophel. Neh 3:26; 11:21
the N. had separated from. 10:28
and Gispa were over the N. 11:21

nets
n. of checker work. 1 Ki 7:17
wicked fall into their own n. Ps 141:10
heart is snares and n. Eccl 7:26
they that spread n. shall. Isa 19:8
spreading of n. in the. Ezek 26:5
place to spread n. on. 14; 47:10
James and John mending their n. Mat 4:21; Mark 1:19; Luke 5:2
they forsook their n. Mark 1:18
your n. for a draught. Luke 5:4

nettles
under the n. they were. Job 30:7

and n. had covered the. Pr 24:31
n. and brambles in the. Isa 34:13
n. shall possess the. Hos 9:6
shall be the breeding of n. Zeph 2:9

network

grate of n. of brass. Ex 27:4; 38:4
round about on n. 1 Ki 7:18, 42
n. on the chapiters. Jer 52:22
all the pomegranates on n. were. 23

networks

the two n. upon the. 1 Ki 7:41
pomegranates for the two n. 42
they that weave n. shall. Isa 19:9*

never

kine, such as I n. saw. Gen 41:19
the fire shall n. go out. Lev 6:13
upon which n. came yoke. Num 19:2
the poor shall n. cease. Deut 15:11
n. break my covenant. Judg 2:1
is there n. a woman among? 14:3
green withs that were n. dried. 16:7
if bind with new ropes that n. 11
sword shall n. depart. 2 Sam 12:10
he n. prophesieth good. 2 Chr 18:7
was n. a son left him, save. 21:17
infants which n. saw light. Job 3:16
make my hands n. so clean. 9:30
n. eateth with pleasure. 21:25
I shall n. be in adversity. Ps 10:6
his face, he will n. see it. 11
these things shall n. be moved. 15:5
in prosperity I said, I shall n. 30:6
in thee do I trust, let me n. 31:1
they shall n. see light. 49:19
Lord will n. suffer righteous. 55:22
O Lord, let me n. be put to. 71:1
I will n. forget thy precepts. 119:93
the righteous shall n. be. Pr 10:30
destruction are n. full, so the eyes of a man are n. satisfied. 27:20
three things that are n. 30:15
Babylon n. be inhabited. Isa 13:20
the seed of evil doers shall n. 14:20
no city, it shall n. be built. 25:2
are greedy dogs which can n. 56:11
watchmen that shall n. hold. 62:6
we are thine: Thou n. barest. 63:19
their confusion shall n. Jer 20:11
David shall n. want a man. 33:17
n. open thy mouth. Ezek 16:63
Tyrus shall n. be found. 26:21
terror and n. shall be. 27:36; 28:19
a kingdom that shall n. Dan 2:44
trouble, such as n. was. 12:1
my people shall n. be ashamed. Joel 2:26, 27
I will n. forget any of. Amos 8:7
they shall fall and n. rise. 14
judgement doth n. go. Hab 1:4
profess unto them, I n. Mat 7:23
it was n. so seen in Israel. 9:33
have ye n. read, Out of the mouth of babes? 21:16, 42; Mark 2:25
Peter said, Yet will I n. Mat 26:33
he answered him to n. a word. 27:14
we n. saw it on this. Mark 2:12
Holy Ghost, hath n. forgiveness. 3:29
into fire that n. shall be. 9:43, 45
colt tied, whereon n. man sat. 11:2; Luke 19:30
good for that man if he had n. been born. Mark 14:21
n. gavest me a kid to. Luke 15:29
the wombs that n. bare. 23:29
wherein n. man before was laid. 53
John 19:41
I give, shall n. thirst. John 4:14
shall n. hunger, and he that believeth on me shall n. thirst. 6:35
man, having n. learned? 7:15
n. man spake like this man. 46
and we were n. in bondage. 8:33
he shall n. see death. 51, 52; 10:28
11:26
thou shalt n. wash my feet. 13:8
I have n. eaten any. Acts 10:14
being a cripple, who n. had. 14:8
charity n. faileth, but. 1 Cor 13:8
n. able to come to. 2 Tim 3:7
n. with those sacrifices. Heb 10:1
the same sacrifices which can n. 11
I will n. leave thee, nor forsake. 13:5
things ye shall n. fall. 2 Pet 1:10

never *so*

charming n. so wisely. Ps 58:5

never *so much*

ask me n. so m. dowry. Gen 34:12

nevertheless

n. in the day when I. Ex 32:34
n. these ye shall not eat. Lev 11:4
Deut 14:7
n. a fountain or pit shall. Lev 11:36
n. the people be strong. Num 13:28
n. the ark of the covenant. 14:44
n. the firstborn of man shalt. 18:15
n. the Kenite shall be wasted. 24:22
n. it shall be purified with. 31:23
n. the Lord thy God. Deut 23:5
n. children of Israel expelled not. Josh 13:13
n. my brethren that went up. 14:8
n. the inhabitants of. Judg 1:33
n. the Lord raised up judges. 2:16
n. the people refused. 1 Sam 8:19
n. Samuel mourned for Saul. 15:35
n. Saul spake not any thing. 20:26
n. the lords favour thee not. 29:6
n. David took the strong. 2 Sam 5:7
n. a lad saw them and told. 17:18
n. he would not drink thereof. 23:16
n. thou shalt not build. 1 Ki 8:19
n. for David's sake did the. 15:4
n. Asa his heart was perfect. 14
n. in his old age he was. 23
n. the high places were not. 22:43
n. if thou see me when. 2 Ki 2:10
n. he cleaved to the sins of. 3:3
n. they departed not from sins. 13:6
n. the priests of the high. 23:9
n. David took the castle. 1 Chr 11:5
n. the king's word prevailed. 21:4
n. they shall be his. 2 Chr 12:8
n. the heart of Asa was. 15:17
n. there are good things found. 19:3
n. divers of Asher humbled. 30:11
n. the people did sacrifice in. 33:17
n. Josiah would not turn. 35:22
n. we made our prayer. Neh 4:9
n. they were disobedient. 9:26
n. for thy mercies' sake thou. 31
n. him did outlandish women. 13:26
n. Haman refrained. Esth 5:10
n. thou heardest my. Ps 31:22
n. man being in honour. 49:12
n. I am continually with thee. 73:23
n. they did flatter him with. 78:36
n. my lovingkindness will I not. 89:33
n. he saved them for his. 106:8
n. he regarded their affliction. 44
n. the counsel of the Lord. Pr 19:21
n. the poor man's wisdom. Eccl 9:16
n. the dimness shall not be. Isa 9:1
n. in those days I will not. Jer 5:18
n. the hand of Ahikam was. 26:24
n. hear thou this word that. 28:7
n. Elnathan and Delaiah. 36:25
n. if thou warn the. Ezek 3:21
n. I will remember my. 16:60
n. mine eye spared them. 20:17
n. I withdrew my hand, and. 22
n. if thou warn the wicked. 33:9
n. leave the stump of. Dan 4:15
n. the men rowed hard. Jonah 1:13
n. for the oath's sake. Mat 14:9
from me, n. not as I will, but. 26:39
n. hereafter ye shall see the. 64
n. not what I will. Mark 14:36
Luke 22:42
n. at thy word I will. Luke 5:5
n. I must walk to-day. 13:33
n. when Son of man cometh. 18:8
Lazarus is dead, n. let. John 11:15
n. among the chief rulers. 12:42
n. I tell you the truth; it is. 16:7
n. he left not himself. Acts 14:17
n. the centurion believed. 27:11
n. death reigned from. Rom 5:14
n. I have written more boldly. 15:15
n. to avoid fornication. 1 Cor 7:2
n. such shall have trouble in. 28
n. he that standeth stedfast. 37
n. we have not used this. 9:12
n. neither is the man. 11:11
n. when it shall turn. 2 Cor 3:16
n. God comforteth those that. 7:6
n. being crafty, I caught. 12:16
n. I live, yet not I, but. Gal 2:20
n. what saith scripture, cast. 4:30
n. let every one so love his wife. Eph 5:33
n. to abide in the flesh. Phil 1:24
n. whereto we have already. 3:16
n. I am not ashamed. 2 Tim 1:12
n. the foundation of God. 2:19
n. it yieldeth peaceable. Heb 12:11
n. we look for new. 2 Pet 3:13
n. I have somewhat. Rev 2:4

new

[1] *Fresh, newly made,* Judg 15:13; Mat 9:17. [2] *Sweet, as new wine, not yet fermented,* Joel 1:5. [3] *Undressed, as cloth,* Mat 9:16.

there arose up a n. king. Ex 1:8
offer a n. meat offering. Lev 23:16
Num 28:26
old, because of the n. Lev 26:10
Lord make a n. thing. Num 16:30
what man is there that hath built a n. house? Deut 20:5; 22:8
when taken a n. wife, he shall. 24:5
sacrificed to devils, to n. 32:17
bottles of wine were n. Josh 9:13
they chose n. gods, then. Judg 5:8
they bound him with n. cords. 15:13
16:11, 12
make a n. cart, and. 1 Sam 6:7
set the ark on a n. cart. 2 Sam 6:3
1 Chr 13:7
being girded with a n. 2 Sam 21:16
clad with a n. garment. 1 Ki 11:29
Ahijah caught the n. garment. 30
bring a n. cruse, and. 2 Ki 2:20
stood in the n. court. 2 Chr 20:5
it is ready to burst like n. Job 32:19
a n. song. Ps 33:3; 96:1; 98:1
144:9; 149:1; Isa 42:10
put a n. song in my mouth. Ps 40:3
is no n. thing under the. Eccl 1:9
whereof may be said, This is n.? 10
all pleasant fruits, n. S of S 7:13
behold n. things do. Isa 42:9; 48:6
behold, I will do a n. thing. 43:19
be called by a n. name. 62:2
n. heavens and a n. 65:17; 66:22
the n. gate of the Lord's house. Jer 26:10; 36:10
the Lord hath created a n. 31:22
mercies are n. every. Lam 3:23
I will put a n. spirit within you. Ezek 11:19; 36:26
a n. heart and n. spirit. 18:31
shall bring forth n. fruit. 47:12
a piece of n. cloth to an. Mat 9:16*
Mark 2:21*; Luke 5:36
but they put n. wine into n. bottles. Mat 9:17; Mark 2:22; Luke 5:38
of his treasure things n. Mat 13:52
for this is my blood of the n. 26:28
Mark 14:24; Luke 22:20
1 Cor 11:25
until I drink it n. with you. Mat 26:29; Mark 14:25
body in his own n. tomb. Mat 27:60
saying, What n. doctrine? Mark 1:27
speak with n. tongues. 16:17
a n. commandment give. John 13:34
a n. sepulchre, wherein. 19:41
what this n. doctrine is? Acts 17:19
to tell or to hear some n. thing. 21
ye may be a n. lump. 1 Cor 5:7
able ministers of the n. 2 Cor 3:6
in Christ, he is a n. creature; behold, all things are become n. 5:17
but a n. creature. Gal 6:15
of twain, one n. man. Eph 2:15
put on the n. man. 4:24; Col 3:10
the Mediator of the n. Heb 9:15
by a n. and living way hath. 10:20
as n. born babes desire. 1 Pet 2:2
n. heavens and a n. 2 Pet 3:13
I write no n. commandment unto. 1 John 2:7
a n. commandment I write. 8
I wrote a n. commandment. 2 John 5
n. name written, which. Rev 2:17
n. Jerusalem. 3:12; 21:2
I will write my n. name. 3:12
and they sung a n. song. 5:9; 14:3

n. heaven and a *n.* earth. *Rev* 21:1
I make all things *n.* 5
see **covenant, moon**

new *wine*
offering of the *n. wine.* *Neh* 10:39
chamber where the *n. wine.* 13:5
brought tithe of *n. wine* unto the. 12
burst out with *n. wine.* *Pr* 3:10
the *n. wine* mourneth, the. *Isa* 24:7
as the *n. wine* is found in. 65:8
wine and *n. wine* take. *Hos* 4:11
n. wine shall fail in her. 9:2
the *n. wine* is cut off. *Joel* 1:5
n. wine is dried up. 10
mountains shall drop *n. wine.* 3:18
drought on the *n. wine.* *Hag* 1:11
n. wine shall make the maids cheerful. *Zech* 9:17
n. wine into old bottles, but *n. wine.* *Mat* 9:17; *Mark* 2:22; *Luke* 5:37
men are full of *n. wine.* *Acts* 2:13

newly
gods that came *n.* up. *Deut* 32:17*
but *n.* set the watch. *Judg* 7:19

newness
should walk in *n.* of life. *Rom* 6:4
we should serve in *n.* of spirit. 7:6

news
so is good *n.* from afar. *Pr* 25:25

next
bear at this set time *n.* *Gen* 17:21
neighbour *n.* take a lamb. *Ex* 12:4
stood up all the *n.* day. *Num* 11:32
inheritance to his kinsman *n.* 27:11
the city which is *n.* to. *Deut* 21:3
the elders of the city *n.* to the. 6
is one of our *n.* kinsmen. *Ruth* 2:20
and I shall be *n.* to thee. *1 Sam* 23:17
them to the evening of *n.* day. 30:17
Elkanah that was *n.* *2 Chr* 28:7
Mordecai was *n.* to king. *Esth* 10:3
worm the *n.* day smote. *Jonah* 4:7
the *n.* day that followed. *Mat* 27:62
us go into the *n.* towns. *Mark* 1:38
the *n.* day John seeth. *John* 1:29
in hold unto the *n.* day. *Acts* 4:3
the *n.* day Moses shewed. 7:26
be preached *n.* sabbath. 13:42, 44

Nicanor
Stephen, Philip and *N.* *Acts* 6:5

Nicodemus
N. a ruler of the Jews. *John* 3:1
N. came to Jesus by. 7:50; 19:39

Nicolaitanes
hatest the deeds of the *N.* *Rev* 2:6
hold the doctrine of the *N.* 15

Nicopolis
to come unto me to *N.* *Tit* 3:12

Niger
Simeon who was called *N.* *Acts* 13:1

nigh
virgin that is *n.* to him. *Lev* 21:3
any that is *n.* of kin may. 25:49
him, but not *n.*, a star. *Num* 24:17
hath God so *n.* to them. *Deut* 4:7
gods of the people *n.* to the. 13:7
if thy brother be not *n.* 22:2
the word is *n.* unto thee. 30:14 *Rom* 10:8
wherefore approached ye so *n.*? *2 Sam* 11:20, 21
my words be *n.* to the. *1 Ki* 8:59
Lord is *n.* unto them that. *Ps* 34:18
his salvation is *n.* them that. 85:9
the Lord is *n.* unto all that. 145:18
day of the Lord is *n.* *Joel* 2:1
ye know that summer is *n.* *Mat* 24:32; *Luke* 21:30
that it is *n.* even at the. *Mark* 13:29
desolation thereof is *n.* *Luke* 21:20
your redemption draweth *n.* 28
kingdom of God is *n.* at hand. 31
a feast of Jews was *n.* *John* 6:4
passover was *n.* at hand. 11:55
sepulchre was *n.* at hand. 19:42
n. by the blood of Christ. *Eph* 2:13
peace to them that were *n.* 17
sick, *n.* unto death. *Phil* 2:27
is rejected, is *n.* unto. *Heb* 6:8
see **came, draw**

night
[1] *The time while the sun is below our horizon,* Ex 12:30, 31; Mat 27:64. [2] *A time of ignorance and unbelief,* Rom 13:12. [3] *Adversity and affliction,* Isa 21:12. [4] *Death,* John 9:4.

darkness he called *n.* *Gen* 1:5
lights, to divide the day from *n.* 14
lesser light to rule the *n.* 16
tarry all *n.* 19:2; *Num* 22:19 *Judg* 19:6, 9
men which came in to thee this *n.*? *Gen* 19:5
drink wine that *n.* 33, 34, 35
tarried all *n.* 24:54; 28:11; 31:54 32:13, 21
appeared to Isaac the same *n.* 26:24
shall lie with thee to-*n.* 30:15, 16
each man his dream in one *n.* 40:5 41:11
Israel in visions of the *n.* 46:2
and at *n.* he shall divide. 49:27*
eat the flesh that *n.* roast. *Ex* 12:8
the land of Egypt this *n.* 12
n. to be much observed to the Lord, this is that *n.* of the Lord to be. 42
not near the other all *n.* 14:20
the burning on the altar all *n.* *Lev* 6:9
not abide with thee all *n.* 19:13
the people stood up all that *n.* *Num* 11:32
and the people wept that *n.* 14:1
to them, Lodge here this *n.* 22:8, 19
God came to Balaam at *n.* 20
shall no leavened bread remain all *n.* *Deut* 16:4
body shall not remain all *n.* 21:23
came men in hither to-*n.* *Josh* 2:2
that *n.* for it was dry on. *Judg* 6:40
all *n.* and were quiet all *n.* 16:2
man would not tarry that *n.* 19:10
and abused her all the *n.* until. 25
an husband also to-*n.* *Ruth* 1:12
Boaz winnoweth barley to-*n.* 3:2
cried to the Lord all *n.* *1 Sam* 15:11
Lord hath said to me this *n.* 16
fled and escaped that *n.* 19:10
if thou save not thy life to-*n.* 11
rose up and went away that *n.* 28:25
men of Jabesh went all *n.* 31:12
men walked all *n.* *2 Sam* 2:29
Joab and his men went all *n.* 32
away through the plain all *n.* 4:7
David went and lay all *n.* 12:16
pursue after David this *n.* 17:1
lodge not this *n.* in the plain. 16
tarry one with thee this *n.* 19:7
that *n.* the angel of the. *2 Ki* 19:35
that *n.* did God appear. *2 Chr* 1:7
n. could not the king sleep. *Esth* 6:1
let the *n.* perish in which it. *Job* 3:3
let that *n.* be solitary. 7
the visions of the *n.* 4:13
arise, and the *n.* be gone? 7:4
and the dew lay all *n.* on my. 29:19
desire not the *n.* when people. 36:20
all the *n.* make I my bed. *Ps* 6:6
n. unto *n.* sheweth knowledge. 19:2
may endure for a *n.*, but joy. 30:5
he led them all *n.* with a. 78:14
forth thy faithfulness every *n.* 92:2
darkness, and it is *n.* 104:20
even the *n.* shall be light. 139:11
the black and dark *n.* *Pr* 7:9
ariseth also while it is yet *n.* 31:15
shall lie all *n.* between my breasts. *S of S* 1:13
with the drops of the *n.* 5:2
continue until *n.* till wine. *Isa* 5:11
make thy shadow as the *n.* 16:3
the *n.* of my pleasure he. 21:4*
what of the *n.*? what of the *n.*? 11
morning cometh, and also the *n.* 12
shall be a dream of a *n.* 29:7
aside to tarry for a *n.* *Jer* 14:8
secret revealed in a *n.* *Dan* 2:19
in that *n.* was Belshazzar. 5:30
king passed the *n.* fasting. 6:18
baker sleepeth all the *n.* *Hos* 7:6
howl, come, lie all *n.* in. *Joel* 1:13
the day dark with *n.* *Amos* 5:8
up in a *n.* perished in a *n.* *Jonah* 4:10
therefore *n.* shall be to you. *Mi* 3:6
fourth watch of *n.* Jesus went to. *Mat* 14:25; *Mark* 6:48
be offended because of me this *n.* *Mat* 26:31; *Mark* 14:27
this *n.* before cockcrow. *Mat* 26:34
we have toiled all *n.* *Luke* 5:5
continued all *n.* in prayer to. 6:12
this *n.* thy soul shall be. 12:20
in that *n.* two shall be in. 17:34
at *n.* he went out and abode. 21:37
the *n.* cometh when no. *John* 9:4
went out, and it was *n.* 13:30
that *n.* they caught nothing. 21:3
the same *n.* Peter was. *Acts* 12:6
the same hour of the *n.* 16:33
n. following the Lord stood. 23:11
soldiers at third hour of the *n.* 23
stood by me this *n.* the angel. 27:23
the *n.* is far spent, the. *Rom* 13:12
the same *n.* in which. *1 Cor* 11:23
we are not of the *n.* nor. *1 Thes* 5:5
there shall be no *n.* there. *Rev* 21:25; 22:5

by **night**
to Abimelech in a dream *by n.* *Gen* 20:3
to Laban in a dream *by n.* 31:24
stolen by day, or stolen *by n.* 39
consumed me, and the frost *by n.* 40
Moses and Aaron *by n.* *Ex* 12:31
before them *by n.* in a. 13:21, 22 14:20; 40:38; *Neh* 9:12
appearance of fire *by n.* *Num* 9:16
cloud taken up by day or *by n.* 21
in fire *by n.* to shew. *Deut* 1:33
forth out of Egypt *by n.* 16:1
that chanceth him *by n.* 23:10
Joshua sent them away *by n.* *Josh* 8:3
that he did it *by n.* *Judg* 6:27
up *by n.* thou and thy people. 9:32
house round about *by n.* 20:5
after Philistines *by n.* *1 Sam* 14:36
Abishai came to people *by n.* 26:7
Saul came to the woman *by n.* 28:8
beasts of the field *by n.* *2 Sam* 21:10
Lord appeared to Solomon *by n.* *1 Ki* 3:5; *2 Chr* 7:12
by n. and compassed. *2 Ki* 6:14
rose *by n.* and smote Edomites. 8:21; *2 Chr* 21:9
all the men of war fled *by n.* *2 Ki* 25:4; *Jer* 52:7
not be afraid of terror *by n.* *Ps* 91:5
nor the moon smite thee *by n.* 121:6
that *by n.* stand in the house. 134:1
moon and stars to rule *by n.* 136:9 *Jer* 31:35
candle goeth not out *by n.* *Pr* 31:18
by n. on my bed I. *S of S* 3:1
of a flaming fire *by n.* *Isa* 4:5
let us go *by n.* and destroy. *Jer* 6:5
forth out of the city *by n.* 39:4
if thieves *by n.* they will. 49:9
I saw in my vision *by n.* *Dan* 7:2
if robbers *by n.* came to thee. *Ob* 5
and his mother *by n.* *Mat* 2:14
lest his disciples come *by n.* 27:64 28:13
watch over their flock *by n.* *Luke* 2:8
Nicodemus came to Jesus *by n.* *John* 3:2; 19:39
the angel *by n.* opened. *Acts* 5:19
they took Paul *by n.* and let. 9:25
sent away Paul and Silas *by n.* 17:10
see **day**

in the **night**
his servants rose *in the n.* *Ex* 12:30
dew fell on the camp *in the n.* *Num* 11:9
child died *in the n.* *1 Ki* 3:19
king arose *in the n.* and. *2 Ki* 7:12
I arose *in the n.* *Neh* 2:12
I went up *in the n.* 15
in the n. they may be a guard. 4:22
yea, *in the n.* will they come. 6:10
noonday, as *in the n.* *Job* 5:14
in the n. the murderer. 24:14
stealeth him away *in the n.* 27:20
overturneth them *in the n.* 34:25
who giveth songs *in the n.*? 35:10
instruct me *in the n.* seasons. *Ps* 16:7

hast visited me *in the n.* *Ps* 17:3
I cry *in the n.* season, and. 22:2
and *in the n.* his song shall. 42:8
my sore ran *in the n.* and. 77:2
to remembrance my song *in the n.* 6
are but as a watch *in the n.* 90:4
fire to give light *in the n.* 105:39
thy name *in the n.* 119:55
taketh not rest *in the n.* *Eccl* 2:23
because of fear *in the n.* *S of S* 3:8
in the n. Ar and Kir of. *Isa* 15:1
have I desired thee *in the n.* 26:9
have a song as *in the n.* 30:29
at noonday as *in the n.* 59:10*
shall be cast out *in the n.* *Jer* 36:30
she weepeth sore *in the n.* *Lam* 1:2
cry out *in the n.* 2:19
fall with thee *in the n.* *Hos* 4:5
if a man walk *in the n.* *John* 11:10
a vision appeared to Paul *in the n.* *Acts* 16:9; 18:9
as a thief *in the n.* *1 Thes* 5:2; *2 Pet* 3:10
sleep *in the n.* are drunken *in the n.* *1 Thes* 5:7

nighthawk

owl and *n.* ye shall not eat. *Lev* 11:16; *Deut* 14:15

nights

rain forty days, forty *n.* *Gen* 7:4, 12
wearisome *n.* are appointed. *Job* 7:3
set in my ward whole *n.* *Isa* 21:8
see **days**

nightwatches

meditate on thee in the *n.* *Ps* 63:6
mine eyes prevent the *n.* 119:148

Nimrod

Cush begat *N.* *Gen* 10:8; *1 Chr* 1:10
as *N.* the mighty hunter. *Gen* 10:9
land of Assyria and *N.* *Mi* 5:6

Nimshi, *see* **Jehu**

nine

fifth day *n.* bullocks. *Num* 29:26
Lord commanded to give to the *n.* 34:13; *Josh* 13:7; 14:2
Og's bedstead was *n.* *Deut* 3:11
Joab came to Jerusalem at end of *n.* months. *2 Sam* 24:8
n. parts to dwell in other. *Neh* 11:1
but where are the *n.*? *Luke* 17:17
see **hundred**

nineteen

David's servants *n.* men. *2 Sam* 2:30

nineteenth

in the *n.* year of Nebuchadnezzar. *2 Ki* 25:8; *Jer* 52:12

ninety

Enos lived *n.* years, and. *Gen* 5:9
shall Sarah, that is *n.* years? 17:17
of the building *n.* cubits. *Ezek* 41:12

ninety-five

children of Gibbar *n.-five.* *Ezra* 2:20
children of Gibeon *n.-five.* *Neh* 7:25

ninety-six

Israel *n.-six* rams. *Ezra* 8:35
n.-six pomegranates. *Jer* 52:23

ninety-eight

Eli was *n.-eight* years. *1 Sam* 4:5
the children of Ater *n.-eight.* *Ezra* 2:16; *Neh* 7:21

ninety-nine

Abram was *n.-nine* years. *Gen* 17:1
was *n.-nine* years old when he. 24
doth he not leave the *n.* and *nine*? *Mat* 18:12, 13; *Luke* 15:4, 7

Nineveh

went and builded *N.* *Gen* 10:11
Sennacherib dwelt at *N.* *2 Ki* 19:36; *Isa* 37:37
go to *N.* *Jonah* 1:2; 3:2
now *N.* was an exceeding great. 3:3
should not I spare *N.*? 4:11
the burden of *N.* *Nah* 1:1
N. is like a pool. 2:8
N. is laid waste, who will? 3:7
N. a desolation, and. *Zeph* 2:13
N. shall rise in judgement and condemn. *Mat* 12:41; *Luke* 11:32

Ninevites

a sign unto the *N.* *Luke* 11:30

ninth

of old fruit till the *n.* year. *Lev* 25:22
in *n.* year of Hoshea Samaria taken. *2 Ki* 17:6; 18:10
in the *n.* year of Zedekiah. 25:1; *Jer* 39:1; 52:4; *Ezek* 24:1
Elzabad the *n.* captain. *1 Chr* 12:12
the *n.* lot came forth to. 24:11
n. captain for the *n.* month. 27:12
the sixth and *n.* hour. *Mat* 20:5
was darkness over all the land unto the *n.* hour. 27:45; *Mark* 15:33
n. hour Jesus gave up the ghost. *Mat* 27:46; *Mark* 15:34
prayer, being the *n.* hour. *Acts* 3:1
a vision about the *n.* hour. 10:3, 30
n. foundation was a. *Rev* 21:20
see **day, month**

Nisan

in the month *N.* *Neh* 2:1
first month *N.* *Esth* 3:7

Nisroch

worshipping in the house of *N.* his. *2 Ki* 19:37; *Isa* 37:38

nitre

as vinegar upon *n.* so is. *Pr* 25:20
wash thee with *n.* and. *Jer* 2:22*

no

let there be *no* strife. *Gen* 13:8
me thou hast given *no* seed. 15:3
that thou wilt do us *no* hurt. 26:29
shed *no* blood, and lay *no*. 37:22
there was *no* harlot in. 38:21, 22
no interpreter. 40:8
we are *no* spies. 42:11, 31, 34
have *no* pasture. 47:4; *Lam* 1:6
is *no* straw given to. *Ex* 5:16, 18
that *no* swarms of flies. 8:22
no work shall be done. 12:16; *Lev* 16:29; 23:3, 7, 21, 28, 31; *Num* 29:1; *Deut* 16:8
seven days *no* leaven shall be. *Ex* 12:19; 13:3, 7
were *no* graves in Egypt. 14:11
gathered little had *no* lack. 16:18
hurt a woman, and *no*. 21:12
there shall *no* blood be shed. 22:2
no gift; gift blindeth the wise. 23:8
thou shalt make *no* covenant. 32
ye shall offer *no* strange. 30:9
that there be *no* plague amongst. 12
for thou shalt worship *no*. 34:14
make thee *no* molten gods. 17
ye shall kindle *no* fire in your. 35:3
ye shall burn *no* leaven. *Lev* 2:11
put *no* oil upon it. 5:11
ye shall eat *no* fat. 7:23
ye shall eat *no* manner of blood. 26; 17:12, 14
touch *no* hallowed thing. 12:4
be *no* white hairs therein. 13:21, 26
no black hair. 31
there be *no* yellow hair. 32
do *no* unrighteousness. 19:15, 35
that there be *no* wickedness. 20:14
but there shall *no* stranger. 22:13
shall be *no* blemish therein. 21
houses which have *no* walls. 25:31
take thou *no* usury of him. 36
ye shall make you *no* idols. 26:1
no devoted thing shall. 27:28
if the man have *no*. *Num* 5:8
there be *no* witness against. 13
and shall drink *no* vinegar. 6:3
there shall *no* razor come upon. 5
he shall come at *no* dead body. 6
that *no* stranger come near. 16:40
Zelophehad had *no* sons. 26:33; 27:3, 4; *Josh* 17:3; *1 Chr* 23:22; 24:28
if a man die and *no* son. *Num* 27:8
and if he have *no* daughter. 9
be not as sheep that have *no* 17; *Ezek* 34:5; *Mat* 9:36
no satisfaction for the life of a murderer. *Num* 35:31, 32
saw *no* similitude. *Deut* 4:12, 15
thine eye shall have *no* pity. 7:16
Levi hath *no* part with. 10:9; 14:27, 29; 18:1; *Josh* 14:4; 18:7
there shall be *no* poor. *Deut* 15:4
if it will make *no* peace. 20:12
there shall be *no* might. *Deut* 28:32
nations thou shalt find *no* ease. 65
children in whom is *no* faith. 32:20
there was *no* day like. *Josh* 10:14
no part in the Lord. 22:25, 27
there was *no* king in Israel. *Judg* 17:6; 18:1; 21:25
there was *no* magistrate. 18:7
where there is *no* want. 10; 19:19
no deliverer. 18:28
for it is *no* good report. *1 Sam* 2:24
there was *no* open vision. 3:1
take it, for there is *no* other. 21:9
because he had *no* pity. *2 Sam* 12:6
no such thing ought to be. 13:12
if he say, I have *no* delight. 15:26
I have *no* son to keep my. 18:18
Sheba said, We have *no* part. 20:1
there is *no* God like. *1 Ki* 8:23
he would prophesy *no* good. 22:18
there is *no* God in Israel. *2 Ki* 1:16
because Ahaziah had *no* son. 17
Jehu took *no* heed to walk. 10:31
Sheshan had *no* sons. *1 Chr* 2:34
do my prophets *no* harm. 16:22; *Ps* 105:15
that have *no* shepherd. *2 Chr* 18:16; *Zech* 10:2
there is *no* iniquity with. *2 Chr* 19:7
we have *no* might against. 20:12
people made *no* burning for. 21:19
there was *no* passover like. 35:18
till there was *no* remedy. 36:16
that there should be *no*. *Ezra* 9:14
ye have *no* portion in. *Neh* 2:20
no king like Solomon. 13:26
he put *no* trust in his. *Job* 4:18
in seven there shall *no* evil. 5:19
see *no* good. 9:25
that *no* eye had seen me. 10:18
and there can be *no* opening. 12:14
wander where there is *no* way. 24
physicians of *no* value. 13:4
let my cry have *no* place. 16:18
he shall have *no* name in. 18:17
servant, he gave me *no*. 19:16
no eye shall see me. 24:15
have *no* helper. 30:13
there is *no* help for him. *Ps* 3:2
spirit there is *no* guile. 32:2
there is *no* want to them. 34:9
there is *no* fear of God. 36:1
in fear where *no* fear was. 53:5
they have *no* changes. 55:19
no good will he withhold. 84:11
there shall *no* evil befall thee. 91:10
there is *no* unrighteousness. 92:15
do *no* iniquity, they walk. 119:3
in whom there is *no* help. 146:3
shall *no* evil happen to. *Pr* 12:21
seeing he hath *no* heart to it. 17:16
there is *no* wisdom against. 21:30
they had *no* comforter. *Eccl* 4:1
is *no* work in the grave. 9:10
my love, there is *no*. *S of S* 4:7
sister, and she hath *no* breasts. 8:8
there is *no* soundness in it. *Isa* 1:6
field, till there be *no* place. 5:8
it is because there is *no* light. 8:20
government there shall be *no*. 9:7
no one of these shall fail. 34:16
to them that have *no* might. 40:29
beside me there is *no* saviour. 43:11
no peace to wicked. 48:22; 57:21
in darkness, and hath *no* light. 50:10
hath *no* form nor comeliness. 53:2
no weapon formed against. 54:17
and he that hath *no* money. 55:1
there is *no* hope. 57:10; *Jer* 2:25
there is *no* judgement. *Isa* 59:8
that there was *no* intercessor. 16
which are yet *no* gods. *Jer* 2:11
received *no* correction. 30
when there is *no* peace. 6:14; 8:11
cruel, and have *no* mercy. 6:23
looked for peace, but *no* good. 8:15; 14:19
and there is *no* breath in them. 10:14; 51:17
wherein is *no* pleasure. 22:28; 48:38
I will do you *no* hurt. 25:6
do him *no* harm. 39:12
shall see *no* war. 42:14
spoiler shall come, and *no*. 48:8

no sons ? hath he *no* heir ? *Jer* 49:1
she had *no* comforter. *Lam* 1:9
peace, and there was *no* peace. *Ezek* 13:10, 16
I have *no* pleasure in death of him. 18:32; 33:11
yet had he *no* wages, nor. 29:18
is *no* other god that can. *Dan* 3:29
because there is *no* truth. *Hos* 4:1
thou shalt be *no* priest to me. 6
shall say, We have *no* king. 10:3
I was *no* prophet. *Amos* 7:14
there is *no* answer of God. *Mi* 3:7
is there *no* king in thee ? 4:9
there is *no* healing of thy. *Nah* 3:19
things that have *no* ruler. *Hab* 1:14
unjust knoweth *no* shame. *Zeph* 3:5
love *no* false oath. *Zech* 8:17
no oppressor shall pass. 9:8
I have *no* pleasure in you. *Mal* 1:10
ye shall in *no* case enter. *Mat* 5:20
thou shalt by *no* means come. 26
take therefore *no* thought. 6:34
10:19; *Mark* 13:11; *Luke* 12:11, 22
there is *no* resurrection. *Mat* 22:23
Mark 12:18; *Acts* 23:8
1 Cor 15:12, 13
days, *no* flesh be saved. *Mark* 13:20
need *no* repentance. *Luke* 15:7
I find *no* fault in him. 23:4, 14
John 18:38; 19:4, 6
I have *no* husband. *John* 4:17
ye have *no* life. 6:53
of Galilee ariseth *no* prophet. 7:52
ye should have *no* sin. 9:41
there is *no* light in him. 11:10
if I wash thee not, thou hast *no*. 13:8
now they have *no* cloak for. 15:22
we have *no* king but Caesar. 19:15
no difference between. *Acts* 15:9
for I will be *no* judge of. 18:15
written they observe *no*. 21:25
Jews have I done *no* wrong. 25:10
the people shewed us *no* little. 28:2
for there is *no* difference. *Rom* 3:22
for where *no* law is, *no*. 4:15; 5:13
flesh dwelleth *no* good thing. 7:18
them that are *no* people. 10:19
love worketh *no* ill to his. 13:10
that *no* flesh glory. *1 Cor* 1:29
no certain dwelling place. 4:11
I will eat *no* flesh while the. 8:13
there hath *no* temptation. 10:13
we have *no* such custom. 11:16
I have *no* need of thee. 12:21
no charity. 13:2
if there be *no* interpreter. 14:28
for us, who knew *no* sin. *2 Cor* 5:21
giving *no* offence in any thing. 6:3
I pray to God that ye do *no* evil. 13:7
against such there is *no* law. *Gal* 5:23
have *no* fellowship. *Eph* 5:11
but made himself of *no*. *Phil* 2:7
and have *no* confidence in. 3:3
which have *no* hope. *1 Thes* 4:13
and have *no* company. *2 Thes* 3:14
shall proceed *no* further. *2 Tim* 3:9
could swear by *no* greater. *Heb* 6:13
no place have been sought. 8:7
without shedding of blood is *no*. 9:22
have *no* pleasure in him. 10:38
no chastening for the present. 12:11
found *no* place of repentance. 17
have we *no* continuing city. 13:14
whom is *no* variableness. *Jas* 1:17
and have *no* works, can faith ? 2:14
who did *no* sin, nor. *1 Pet* 2:22
no prophecy of private. *2 Pet* 1:20
in him is *no* darkness. *1 John* 1:5
if we say, we have *no* sin, we. 8
in him is *no* sin. 3:5
there is *no* fear in love. 4:18
I have *no* greater joy. *3 John* 4
mouth was found *no* guile. *Rev* 14:5
received *no* kingdom as yet. 17:12
no widow, and shall see *no*. 18:7
found *no* place for them. 20:11
no temple therein. 21:22
no need of the sun. 23
no night there, they need *no*. 25; 22:5
see **bread, child, children, inheritance, knowledge, man, more, power, water, wise, wrath**

no *rain*
that there be *no rain*. *Deut* 11:17
1 Ki 8:35; *2 Chr* 6:26; 7:13
there had been *no rain* in land.
1 Ki 17:7; *Jer* 14:4
they rain *no rain* upon it. *Isa* 5:6
hath been *no* latter *rain*. *Jer* 3:3
even upon them shall be *no rain*.
Zech 14:17
and if Egypt that have *no rain*. 18

no *rest*
but the dove found *no rest*. *Gen* 8:9
my sinews take *no rest*. *Job* 30:17
or laugh there is *no rest*. *Pr* 29:9
shalt thou have *no rest*. *Isa* 23:12
no rest till he establish. 62:7
sighing, and find *no rest*. *Jer* 45:3
heathen she findeth *no rest*. *Lam* 1:3
give thyself *no rest*. 2:18
we have *no rest*. 5:5
I had *no rest* in my spirit. *2 Cor* 2:13
our flesh had *no rest*. 7:5
they have *no rest* day. *Rev* 14:11

no *strength*
no strength in Saul. *1 Sam* 28:20
arm that hath *no strength*. *Job* 26:2
man that hath *no strength*. *Ps* 88:4
there remained *no strength* in me.
Dan 10:8, 17
I have retained *no strength*. 16
it is of *no strength* at all. *Heb* 9:17

no *where*
they were *no where*. *1 Sam* 10:14

no, *opposite of yes*
not let you go, *no* not by. *Ex* 3:19
whether walk in my law or *no*. 16:4
Deut 8:2
here, thou shalt say, *No*. *Judg* 4:20
no, but we will bind thee. 15:13
no, my lord, I am of. *1 Sam* 1:15
no, not when the Lord hath. 20:15
no, but he would put strength in me.
Job 23:6
no, not gold, nor the forces. 36:19
there is none that doeth good, *no*, not one. *Ps* 14:3; 53:3
curse not king, *no* not. *Eccl* 10:20
no, for we will flee. *Isa* 30:16
no, for I have loved. *Jer* 2:25
no, but we will go into the. 42:14
thee ? he shall say, *No*. *Amos* 6:10
answered and said, *No*. *Hag* 2:12
knowest what these be, I said, *No*.
Zech 4:5, 13
so great faith, *no* not in Israel.
Mat 8:10; *Luke* 7:9
to this time, *no*, nor ever. *Mat* 24:21
no not the angels, but my. 36
no room, *no* not so much. *Mark* 2:2
bind him, *no* not with chains. 5:3
tribute to Caesar, or *no* ? *Luke* 20:22
no nor yet Herod: for I sent. 23:15
that Prophet? he said, *No*. *John* 1:21
whether he be a sinner or *no*. 9:25
meat? they answered, *No*. 21:5
no not so much as to set. *Acts* 7:5
than they? *no*, in no wise. *Rom* 3:9
none righteous, *no* not one. 10, 12
with such an one, *no* not. *1 Cor* 5:11
no, not one that shall be able. 6:5
place by subjection, *no*. *Gal* 2:5

No
I will punish *N*. *Jer* 46:25
Ezek 30:14, 15, 16
better than populous *N*.? *Nah* 3:8

Noadiah
N. the son of Binnui. *Ezra* 8:33
think on the prophetess *N*. *Neh* 6:14

Noah, Noe
N. saying, This same. *Gen* 5:29
Lamech begat *N*. 30
N. found grace. 6:8
these are generations of *N*. 9; 10:1
32; *1 Chr* 1:4
N. only remained alive. *Gen* 7:23
God remembered *N*. and every. 8:1
N. opened the window of the ark. 6
N. builded an altar to the Lord. 20
N. awoke from his wine. 9:24
the days of *N*. 29
this is as the waters of *N*. *Isa* 54:9
these three, *N*. Daniel, Job.
Ezek 14:14, 20
as it was in the days of *N*.
Mat 24:37; *Luke* 17:26
was the son of *N*. *Luke* 3:36
by faith *N*. being warned. *Heb* 11:7
waited in the days of *N*. *1 Pet* 3:20
spared not the old world, but saved *N*. *2 Pet* 2:5

Noah
of Zelophehad were *N*. *Num* 26:33
27:1; 36:11; *Josh* 17:3

Nob
David came to *N*. *1 Sam* 21:1
son of Jesse coming to *N*. 22:9
to call the priests in *N*. 11
Doeg smote *N*. the city of. 19
of Benjamin dwelt at *N*. *Neh* 11:32
yet shall he remain at *N*. *Isa* 10:32

noble
whom the *n*. Asnapper. *Ezra* 4:10
king's most *n*. princes. *Esth* 6:9
planted thee a *n*. vine. *Jer* 2:21
Bereans more *n*. than. *Acts* 17:11
always, most *n*. Felix. 24:3; 26:25
how that not many *n*. *1 Cor* 1:26

nobleman
n. went into a far country. *Luke* 19:12
n. whose son was sick. *John* 4:46, 49

nobles
on the *n*. of Israel he. *Ex* 24:11
the *n*. of the people. *Num* 21:18
dominion over the *n*. *Judg* 5:13
letters to the *n*. in his city. *1 Ki* 21:8
Jehoiada took the *n*. *2 Chr* 23:20
as yet told it to the *n*. *Neh* 2:16
the *n*. put not their necks. 3:5
and I rebuked the *n*. and the. 5:7
the *n*. of Judah sent letters. 6:17
mine heart to gather the *n*. 7:5
their brethren, their *n*. 10:29
I contended with the *n*. of. 13:17
the *n*. held their peace. *Job* 29:10
make their *n*. like Oreb. *Ps* 83:11
bind their *n*. with fetters. 149:8
by me princes rule, and *n*. *Pr* 8:16
king is the son of *n*. *Eccl* 10:17
into the gates of the *n*. *Isa* 13:2
they shall call the *n*. to the. 34:12
brought down all their *n*. 43:14
n. sent their little ones to. *Jer* 14:3
carried captive *n*. of Judah. 27:20
and their *n*. shall be of. 30:21
king of Babylon slew all the *n*. of Judah. 39:6
of the king and his *n*. *Jonah* 3:7
Assyria, thy *n*. shall dwell. *Nah* 3:18

noise
the people heard the *n*. *Ex* 20:18*
he said, There is a *n*. of war. 32:17
but the *n*. of them that sing. 18
not shout nor make any *n*. *Josh* 6:10
delivered from the *n*. *Judg* 5:11
what meaneth the *n*. of this shout ?
1 Sam 4:6, 14
n. in the host of Philistines. 14:19*
wherefore is this *n*. of ? *1 Ki* 1:41
is the *n*. that ye have heard. 45
n. of chariots, and a *n*. of. *2 Ki* 7:6
Athaliah heard *n*. of guard. 11:13
2 Chr 23:12
a *n*. with psalteries. *1 Chr* 15:28
discern *n*. of joy, from *n*. *Ezra* 3:13
any understand the *n*. *Job* 36:29*
n. thereof sheweth concerning it. 33
attentively the *n*. of his voice. 37:2
skilfully with a loud *n*. *Ps* 33:3
deep calleth at the *n*. of thy. 42:7
my complaint, and make a *n*. 55:2*
they make a *n*. like a dog. 59:6, 14
stilleth the *n*. of the seas, *n*. 65:7*
make a joyful *n*. to God. 66:1; 81:1
95:1, 2; 98:4*, 6; 100:1
Lord is mightier than the *n*. 93:4*
battle is with confused *n*. *Isa* 9:5*
n. of a multitude in the mountains, a tumultuous *n*. of the. 13:4
the *n*. of thy viols is brought. 14:11
which make a *n*. like the *n*. 17:12*
n. of them that rejoice endeth. 24:8
he who fleeth from the *n*. of fear. 18
thou shalt bring down the *n*. 25:5
visited of the Lord with great *n*. 29:6

nor abase himself for the *n.* *Isa* 31:4
at the *n.* of the tumult the. 33:3
a voice of *n.* from the city. 66:6*
heart maketh a *n.* in me. *Jer* 4:19*
the city shall flee for the *n.* 29
behold, the *n.* of the bruit. 10:22*
with the *n.* of a great tumult. 11:16
a *n.* shall come to the ends. 25:31
king of Egypt is but a *n.* 46:17
at the *n.* of the stamping of. 47:3
at the *n.* of their fall, at the cry the *n.* was heard in the Red sea. 49:21
the *n.* of taking of Babylon. 50:46
a *n.* of their voice is uttered. 51:55
enemy made *n.* in house. *Lam* 2:7
I heard the *n.* of their wings, like the *n.* of great. *Ezek* 1:24; 43:2
the *n.* of the wheels, the *n.* of. 3:13
the land was desolate by the *n.* 19:7
thy walls shall shake at the *n.* 26:10
I will cause the *n.* of my songs. 13
as I prophesied, there was a *n.* 37:7
n. of chariots, like the *n.* of fire. *Joel* 2:5
take from me the *n.* of. *Amos* 5:23
they shall make a great *n.* *Mi* 2:12
the *n.* of a whip, *n.* of. *Nah* 3:2
the *n.* of a cry from the. *Zeph* 1:10
drink and make a *n.* *Zech* 9:15
people making a *n.* *Mat* 9:23*
pass away with great *n.* *2 Pet* 3:10
I heard as it were the *n.* *Rev* 6:1*

noised

Joshua, his fame was *n.* *Josh* 6:27
it was *n.* that he was. *Mark* 2:1
all these sayings were *n.* *Luke* 1:65
when this was *n.* abroad. *Acts* 2:6*

noisome

deliver thee from the *n.* pestilence. *Ps* 91:3
when I send the sword and *n.* beast. *Ezek* 14:21†
fell a *n.* and grievous. *Rev* 16:2

none

this is *n.* other but the. *Gen* 28:17
n. of you shall go out. *Ex* 12:22
put *n.* of these diseases. 15:26
7th day, in it there shall be *n.* 16:26
to gather, and they found *n.* 27
shalt have *n.* other gods before me. 20:3; *Deut* 5:7
n. shall appear before me empty. *Ex* 23:15; 34:20
n. shall approach to any. *Lev* 18:6
there shall *n.* be defiled. 21:1
shall leave *n.* of it until morrow. 22:30; *Num* 9:12
and if the man have *n.* *Lev* 25:26
shall lie down, and *n.* shall. 26:6
flee when *n.* pursueth. 17, 36, 37
sons of Kohath he gave *n.* *Num* 7:9
n. that came out of Egypt. 32:11
we destroyed, and left *n.* *Deut* 2:34
3:3; *Josh* 8:22; 10:28, 30, 33
11:8
will put *n.* of diseases of. *Deut* 7:15
be given, and *n.* to rescue. 28:31
thou shalt have *n.* assurance. 66
n. went out of Jericho, *n.* *Josh* 6:1
n. of you be freed from being. 9:23
n. moved his tongue against. 10:21
came *n.* to the camp. *Judg* 21:8
there is *n.* holy as. *1 Sam* 2:2
let *n.* of his words fall. 3:19
beware that *n.* touch. *2 Sam* 18:12
all vessels of pure gold; *n.* were of silver. *1 Ki* 10:21; *2 Chr* 9:20
proclamation, *n.* was exempted. *1 Ki* 15:22
blessing, I will receive *n.* *2 Ki* 5:16
n. but Elisha tells the king of. 6:12
shall be *n.* to bury Jezebel. 9:10
let *n.* go forth or escape. 15; 10:25
till Jehu left Ahab *n.* 10:11
the prophets of Baal, let *n.* be. 19
look there be *n.* of the servants. 23
n. ought to carry ark of. *1 Chr* 15:2
honour, such as *n.* of. *2 Chr* 1:12
he might let *n.* go out or. 16:1
so that *n.* is able to withstand. 20:6
they were dead bodies fallen, *n.* 24
n. which was unclean should. 23:19
found there *n.* of the sons. *Ezra* 8:15
n. of us put off our clothes. *Neh* 4:23
drinking according to law, *n.* did compel. *Esth* 1:8
n. might enter the king's gate. 4:2
sat down, and *n.* spake. *Job* 2:13
let it look for light but have *n.* 3:9
n. shall make him afraid. 11:19
Jer 30:10; 46:27
tabernacle, because it is *n.* *Job* 18:15
shall *n.* of his meat be left. 20:21
him that had *n.* to help him. 29:12
but *n.* saith, Where is God? 35:10
they cry, but *n.* giveth answer. 12
wickedness till thou find *n.* *Ps* 10:15
n. can keep alive his own. 22:29
let *n.* that wait on thee be. 25:3
n. that trust in him shall. 34:22
law in his heart, *n.* of his. 37:31
n. of them can redeem his. 49:7
and there be *n.* to deliver. 50:22
comforters, but found *n.* 69:20
and let *n.* dwell in their tents. 25
n. of the men of might found. 76:5
Israel would *n.* of me. 81:11
let there be *n.* to extend. 109:12
and ye would *n.* of my. *Pr* 1:25
they would *n.* of my counsel. 30
n. that go unto her return. 2:19
envy not, and choose *n.* of his. 3:31
bear twins, and *n.* is. *S of S* 4:2
they shall burn and *n.* *Isa* 1:31
n. shall be weary, *n.* shall. 5:27
carry it away safe, and *n.* shall. 29
persecuted, and *n.* hindereth. 14:6
n. shall be alone in his. 31
n. shall make them afraid. 17:2
Zeph 3:13
and *n.* shall shut, *n.* open. *Isa* 22:22
n. shall pass through it. 34:10
they shall call the nobles but *n.* 12
no one shall fail, *n.* shall want. 16
n. delivereth, and *n.* saith. 42:22
n. considereth in his heart. 44:19
I am, and *n.* else beside. 47:8, 10
n. seeth me. 10
n. shall save thee. 15
n. considering that righteous. 57:1
n. calleth for justice, nor. 59:4
I called, *n.* did answer. 66:4
that *n.* can quench it. *Jer* 4:4; 21:12
for the beasts, and *n.* shall. 7:33
burnt up, so that *n.* can pass. 9:10
a wilderness that *n.* passeth. 12
shall fall as dung, and *n.* shall. 22
cities shall be shut, and *n.* 13:19
shall have *n.* to bury them. 14:16
and *n.* doth return from. 23:14
that *n.* should serve himself. 34:9
n. should serve themselves. 10
to this day they drink *n.* but. 35:14
n. to sit on the throne of. 36:30
n. shall remain or escape. 42:17
n. shall return, but such as. 44:14
n. shall tread with shouting. 48:33
n. shall gather up him that. 49:5
land desolate, and *n.* shall. 50:3
arrows, *n.* shall return in vain. 9
and there shall be *n.* 20
camp against it, let *n.* thereof. 29
shall fall, and *n.* shall raise. 32
that *n.* shall remain in it. 51:62
Ezek 7:11
n. to comfort her. *Lam* 1:2, 17
n. come to the solemn feasts. 4
fell, and *n.* did help her. 7
there is *n.* to comfort me. 21
but *n.* goeth to the battle. *Ezek* 7:14
peace, and there shall be *n.* 25
n. of my words shall be. 12:28
n. followeth thee to commit. 16:34
hath spoiled *n.* by violence. 18:7
for a man, but found *n.* 22:30
n. of his sins shall be. 33:16
mountains desolate, that *n.* 28
and *n.* did search or seek. 34:6
dwell safely, and *n.* make afraid. 28
39:26; *Mi* 4:4; *Nah* 2:11
and have left *n.* of them. *Ezek* 39:28
n. found like Daniel. *Dan* 1:19
n. stay his hand, or say to him. 4:35
the vision, but *n.* understood it. 8:27
n. shall stand before him. 11:16
shall come to his end, and *n.* 45
n. of the wicked shall. 12:10
n. shall deliver her out of my hands. *Hos* 2:10; 5:14
they called, *n.* at all would. 11:7
Lord your God, and *n.* *Joel* 2:27
there be *n.* to quench it. *Amos* 5:6
n. that shall cast a cord by lot. *Mi* 2:5
will say, *n.* evil can come. 3:11
he teareth in pieces, and *n.* 5:8
they cry, Stand, but *n.* *Nah* 2:8
let *n.* of you imagine evil. *Zech* 7:10; 8:17
let *n.* deal treacherously. *Mal* 2:15
dry places, seeking rest and findeth *n.* *Mat* 12:43; *Luke* 11:24
witnesses came, yet found *n.* *Mat* 26:60; *Mark* 14:55
impart to him that hath *n.* *Luke* 3:11
to *n.* of them was Elias sent. 4:26
n. of them was cleansed save. 27
n. of them shall taste of. 14:24
n. is good, save one, that. 18:19
n. of you keepeth the law. *John* 7:19
if I had not done the works *n.* 15:24
n. is lost but the son of. 17:12
thou gavest me, I have lost *n.* 18:9
silver and gold have I *n.* *Acts* 3:6
he was fallen on *n.* of them. 8:16
Pray, that *n.* of these things. 24
the word to *n.* but Jews. 11:19
Gallio cared for none of. 18:17
n. of these things move me. 20:24
he should forbid *n.* of his. 24:23
if there be *n.* of these things. 25:11
n. other than the prophets. 26:22
not the Spirit, he is *n.* *Rom* 8:9
n. of us liveth, and *n.* dieth. 14:7
I thank God, I baptized *n.* *1 Cor* 1:14
whom *n.* of the princes of this. 2:8
wives be as though they had *n.* 7:29
but I have used *n.* of these. 9:15
give *n.* offence to the Jews. 10:32
and *n.* of them is without. 14:10
of the apostles saw I *n.* *Gal* 1:19
see that *n.* render evil. *1 Thes* 5:15
give *n.* occasion to. *1 Tim* 5:14
let *n.* of you suffer as a. *1 Pet* :15
fear *n.* of these things. *Rev* 2:10
see **effect, like**

***there is* none**

there is n. greater in. *Gen* 39:9
there is n. that can interpret. 41:15
there is n. so discreet and wise. 39
Lord is God, *there is n.* else. *Deut* 4:35, 39; *1 Ki* 8:60; *Isa* 45:5
6, 14, 18, 22; 46:9; *Mark* 12:32
for *there is n.* to redeem. *Ruth* 4:4
there is n. holy as the Lord; *there is n.* beside. *1 Sam* 2:2
there is n. that sheweth me, *there is n.* 22:8
a shadow, *there is n.* abiding. *1 Chr* 29:15
there is n. that can deliver. *Job* 10:7; *Ps* 7:2; 71:11
they are corrupt, *there is n.* that. *Ps* 14:1, 3; 53:1, 3; *Rom* 3:12
for *there is n.* to help. *Ps* 22:11
there is n. on earth I desire. 73:25
seek water, *there is n.* *Isa* 41:17
there is n. sheweth, *there is n.* 26
there is n. that can deliver. 43:13
and *there is n.* to guide. 51:18
judgement, but *there is n.* 59:11
and *there is n.* that calleth on. 64:7
there is n. to stretch. *Jer* 10:20
there is n. to plead. 30:13
there is n. that doth deliver us. *Lam* 5:8
there is n. that holdeth. *Dan* 10:21
there is n. of them that. *Hos* 7:7
is forsaken, *there is n.* *Amos* 5:2
there is n. upright among. *Mi* 7:2
that said in her heart, I am, and *there is n.* *Zeph* 2:15
but *there is n.* warm. *Hag* 1:6
there is n. good but one. *Mat* 19:17
Mark 10:18
there is n. other commandment. *Mark* 12:31
there is n. of thy kindred. *Luke* 1:61
there is n. other name. *Acts* 4:12
there is n. righteous, no. *Rom* 3:10

there is n. that understandeth, *there is n.* seeketh God. Rom 3:11
there is n. other God. 1 Cor 8:4

there was **none**

there was n. of men. Gen 39:11
there was n. that could interpret. 41:8
but *there was n.* that could. 24
until *there was n.* left. Num 21:35
and *there was n.* to save. Deut 22:27
there was n. to part them. 2 Sam 14:6
there was n. to be so much praised as Absalom. 25
they looked, but *there was n.* to save. 22:42; Ps 18:41
there was n. that followed the house. 1 Ki 12:20; 2 Ki 17:18
to have pity, but *there was n.* Ps 69:20
and *there was n.* to bury them. 79:3
and *there was n.* to help. 107:12
when as yet *there was n.* of. 139:16
there was n. moved the. Isa 10:14
there was n. to answer. 50:2
winepress alone, and of the people *there was n.* with me. 63:3
and I wondered that *there was n.* 5
there was n. that could deliver. Dan 8:7

noon

shall dine with me at *n.* Gen 43:16
against Joseph came at *n.* 25
tarried until after *n.* Judg 19:8
who lay on a bed at *n.* 2 Sam 4:5
on Baal even until *n.* 1 Ki 18:26
at *n.* Elijah mocked them, and. 27
and they went out at *n.* 20:16
he sat on her knees till *n.* 2 Ki 4:20
at *n.* will I pray, and. Ps 55:17
thy flock to rest at *n.* S of S 1:7
arise, let us go up at *n.* Jer 6:4
the sun to go down at *n.* Amos 8:9
about *n.* there shone. Acts 22:6

noonday

thou shalt grope at *n.* Deut 28:29
they grope in the *n.* as in. Job 5:14
be clearer than the *n.* 11:17
bring forth judgement as *n.* Ps 37:6
destruction that wasteth at *n.* 91:6
as the night, in midst of *n.* Isa 16:3
darkness shall be as the *n.* 58:10
we stumble at *n.* as in the. 59:10
have brought a spoiler at *n.* Jer 15:8
drive out Ashdod at *n.* Zeph 2:4

noontide

hear the shouting at *n.* Jer 20:16

Noph

the princes of *N.* are. Isa 19:13
the children of *N.* have. Jer 2:16
publish in *N.* 46:14
for *N.* shall be waste. 19
I will cause their images to cease out of *N.* Ezek 30:13
N. shall have distresses daily. 16

north

spread abroad to the *n.* Gen 28:14
three oxen looking toward the *n.* 1 Ki 7:25; 2 Chr 4:4
were toward the *n.* 1 Chr 9:24
he stretcheth out the *n.* Job 26:7
and cold cometh out of the *n.* 37:9
cometh out of the *n.*: with God is. 22
the sides of the *n.*, the city. Ps 48:2
n. and south, thou hast. 89:12
turneth about to the *n.* Eccl 1:6
if the tree fall toward the *n.* 11:3
sit in the sides of the *n.* Isa 14:13
I will say to the *n.* Give up. 43:6
pot's face is toward the *n.* Jer 1:13
out of *n.* an evil break forth. 14; 4:6 46:20
of the kingdoms of the *n.* 15
these words toward the *n.* 3:12
together out of the land of the *n.* 18
for evil appeareth out of the *n.* 6:1
led Israel out of the *n.* country. 23:8; 31:8
take all the families of the *n.* 25:9
all the kings of the *n.* far and. 26
stumble and fall toward the *n.* 46:6
sacrifice in the *n.* country. 10
delivered to people of *n.* Jer 46:24
waters rise up out of the *n.* 47:2
out of *n.* cometh up a nation. 50:3
whirlwind came out of *n.* Ezek 1:4
mine eyes the way toward the *n.* 8:5
toward the *n.* sat women weeping. 14
all faces from south to *n.* 20:47
all flesh from south to *n.* will. 21:4
princes of the *n.* all of them. 32:30
the prospect toward the *n.* 40:44, 46
door was toward the *n.* 41:11; 42:4
and building toward the *n.* 42:1
their doors *n.* 4
chambers toward the *n.* 11, 13
chambers looked toward the *n.* 46:19
this holy oblation toward *n.* 48:10
suburbs shall be toward the *n.* 17
come to the king of the *n.* Dan 11:6
more years than the king of the *n.* 8
fight with the king of the *n.* 11
the king of the *n.* shall return. 13
the king of the *n.* shall cast. 15, 40
but tidings out of the *n.* shall. 44
his hand against the *n.* Zeph 2:13
black horses go into the *n.* Zech 6:6
quieted my spirit in the *n.* 8
shall remove toward the *n.* 14:4
n. were three gates. Rev 21:13

from the **north**

gathered *from the n.* Ps 107:3
Isa 49:12; Jer 16:15; 23:8
from the n. a smoke. Isa 14:31
I raised up one *from the n.* 41:25
evil *from the n.* and great. Jer 4:6
6:22; 10:22; 50:9, 41; 51:48
a king of kings *from the n.* Ezek 26:7
to come up *from the n.* parts. 39:2
wander *from the n.* to the east. Amos 8:12
from the land of *the n.* Zech 2:6
from the n. and sit. Luke 13:29

north *border*

and this shall be your *n. border.* Num 34:7, 9

north *quarter*

Judah's border in *n. quarter.* Josh 15:5
Togarmah of *n. quarter.* Ezek 38:6

north *side*

tabernacle on the *n. side.* Ex 26:20
put the table on the *n. side.* 35
for *n. side* hangings of 100 cubits. 27:11; 38:11
Dan shall be on *n. side.* Num 2:25
pitched on *n. side* of Ai. Josh 8:11
on the *n. side* of them. Judg 7:1
feast on the *n. side* of Beth-el. 21:19
altar on *n. side* of altar. 2 Ki 16:14
the *n. side* 500 reeds. Ezek 42:17
of the city on the *n. side.* 48:30

northern

break the *n.* iron, and. Jer 15:12
remove from you the *n.* Joel 2:20

northward

lift up thine eyes *n.* and eastward. Gen 13:14; Deut 3:27
tabernacle *n.* without. Ex 40:22
the side of the altar *n.* Lev 1:11
mountain, turn you *n.* Deut 2:3
rock was situate *n.* 1 Sam 14:5
lot came out *n.* 1 Chr 26:14
n. were four Levites a day. 17
n. was this image of. Ezek 8:5
brought me out of the gate *n.* 47:2
three gates *n.*; one gate of. 48:31

nose

that hath a flat *n.* shall. Lev 21:18
put my hook in thy *n.* 2 Ki 19:28 Isa 37:29
his *n.* pierceth through. Job 40:24
canst thou put a hook into his *n.*? 41:2
the wringing of the *n.* Pr 30:33
thy *n.* is as the tower. S of S 7:4
smell of thy *n.* like apples. 8*
a smoke in my *n.*, a fire. Isa 65:5
the branch to their *n.* Ezek 8:17
they shall take away thy *n.* 23:25

nose jewels

take away their tinkling ornaments, the rings and *n. jewels.* Isa 3:21

noses

n. have they, but they. Ps 115:6
it shall stop the *n.* Ezek 39:11*

nostrils

God breathed into man's *n.* Gen 2:7
all in whose *n.* was breath of. 7:22
with blast of thy *n.* waters. Ex 15:8
it come out at your *n.* Num 11:20
went a smoke out of his *n.* 2 Sam 22:9; Ps 18:8
the blast of the breath of his *n.* 2 Sam 22:16; Ps 18:15
by breath of his *n.* they. Job 4:9*
Spirit of God is in my *n.* 27:3
glory of his *n.* is terrible. 39:20*
out of his *n.* goeth smoke. 41:20
whose breath is in his *n.* Isa 2:22
the breath of our *n.* Lam 4:20
stink of your camps to come into your *n.* Amos 4:10

not

I will afflict, but *n.* for. 1 Ki 11:39
upon me, and I am *n.* Job 7:8
he knoweth it *n.* 14:21; 35:15
n. unto us, O Lord, *n.* Ps 115:1
to thy testimonies, and *n.* 119:36
the wicked are *n.* Pr 12:7
buy the truth and sell it *n.* 23:23
riches are *n.* for ever, doth. 27:24
n. be an healer, make me *n.* Isa 3:7
n. as I have done to Samaria. 10:11
Moab, but his lies shall *n.* 16:6
but *n.* of me, *n.* of my spirit. 30:1
chosen thee, and *n.* cast. 41:9
thou shalt *n.* be forgotten. 44:21
let go my captives, *n.* for. 45:13
but *n.* in truth and. 48:1
they may forget, yet will I *n.* 49:15
peace, and thou fearest me *n.* 57:11
of them that sought me *n.* 65:1
a wind, *n.* to fan. Jer 4:11
and they are *n.* 10:20
I commanded, but they did them *n.* 11:8
leave us *n.* 14:9
I sent them *n.* neither have. 14, 15
23:32; 29:9, 31; Ezek 13:6
and *n.* for good. Jer 21:10; 39:16
and *n.* out of the mouth. 23:16
of peace, and *n.* of evil. 29:11
n. of peace. 30:5
because they were *n.* 31:15 Mat 2:18
darkness, but *n.* into light. Lam 3:2
have sinned, and are *n.* 5:7
things shall *n.* come. Ezek 16:16
but *n.* by thy covenant. 61
n. according to your wicked. 20:44
art a man, and *n.* God. 28:2
they will *n.* do them. 33:31, 32
I do *n.* this for your sakes. 36:22, 32
shall be mighty, but *n.* by. Dan 8:24
but *n.* for himself. 9:26
shall *n.* stand. 11:25
ye are *n.* my people, I will *n.* Hos 1:9
they return, but *n.* to the Most. 7:16
it shall *n.* be, saith. Amos 7:3, 6
shall speak, and *n.* lie. Hab 2:3
be ye *n.* as your fathers. Zech 1:4
n. by might nor power, but by. 4:6
I am the Lord, I change *n.* Mal 3:6
be *n.* like hypocrites. Mat 6:5, 8, 16
and it fell *n.* 7:25
and doeth them *n.* 26
n. as the scribes. 29; Mark 1:22
have mercy, and *n.* Mat 9:13; 12:7
shall *n.* be forgiven to men. 12:31, 32; Luke 12:10
saying, Lord, this shall *n.* Mat 16:22
but it shall *n.* be so among. 20:26
came *n.* to be ministered unto. 28
said, I go, sir, and went *n.* 21:30
but do *n.* ye after their works. 23:3
to have done, and *n.* to leave. 23
the end is *n.* yet. 24:6
let him *n.* come down. 17
clothed me *n.*, ye visited me *n.* 25:43
n. to one of these, did it *n.* to me. 45
n. on the feast day, lest there. 26:5
n. as I will, but as thou wilt. 39 Mark 14:36
see ye *n.*? hear ye *n.*? do ye *n.* remember? Mark 8:18

so it shall n. be among. Mark 10:43
but me ye have n. always. 14:7
he were the Christ or n. Luke 3:15
be healed, and n. on the. 13:14
I am n. as other men are. 18:11
woman, I know him n. 22:57
Peter said, Man, I am n. 58
I am n. the Christ. John 1:20; 3:28
n. because of thy saying. 4:42
ye will n. come to me, that ye. 5:40
I know ye have n. the love. 42
ye seek me n. because ye saw. 6:26
I came down, n. to do mine. 38
for I am n. alone, but I and the Father that sent me. 8:16; 16:32
I am n. of this world. 23
hireling, and n. the shepherd. 10:12
ye believe n., because ye are n. 26
said I n. unto thee, if thou? 11:40
this spake he, n. of himself, but. 51
and n. for that nation only. 52
this he said, n. that he cared. 12:6
I judge him n. for I came n. 47
Lord, n. my feet only, but. 13:9
ye are clean, but n. all. 10
if it were n. so. 14:2
Judas, n. Iscariot, . . . and n. unto? 22
n. as the world giveth, give I. 27
I call you n. servants, but. 15:15
n. away, the Comforter will n. 16:7
for he shall n. speak of himself. 13
saying, N. this man. 18:40
touch me n. 20:17
n. to speak at all in the. Acts 4:18
have n. kept it. 7:53
he opened n. his mouth. 8:32
and shewed him, n. to all. 10:41
it is the voice of a god, and n. 12:22
I am n. he. 13:25
he be n. far from every one. 17:27
hold n. thy peace. 18:9
n. knowing the things that. 20:22
wolves enter in, n. sparing. 29
for I am ready n. to be. 21:13
I wist n. that he was the. 23:5
n. the hearers of the law. Rom 2:13
these having n. the law, are a. 14
and n. in the letter. 29
but n. before God. 4:2
to him that worketh n. but. 5
n. in circumcision, but. 10
and n. as it was by one that. 5:16
n., what I would, that do I n. 7:15
but ye are n. in the flesh, but. 8:9
how shall he n. with him give? 32
n. of the Jews only, but of. 9:24
was said, Ye are n. my people. 26
have they n. heard? yes. 10:18
n. to think of himself more. 12:3
ought to bear, and n. to please. 15:1
to preach, n. where Christ was. 20
to whom n. only I give thanks. 16:4
things which are n. 1 Cor 1:28
eye hath n. seen, nor ear heard. 2:9
n. with meat. 3:2
ye n. carnal, and walk as men? 3, 4
n. to think of men above that. 4:6
and I will know, n. the speech. 19
n. with old leaven. 5:8
n. before the saints. 6:1
yet n. I, but the Lord. 7:10
to the rest speak I, n. the Lord. 12
am I n. an apostle? am I n. free? have I n. seen? 9:1
I therefore so run, n. as. 26
conscience, I say, n. thine. 10:29
have ye n. houses to eat in? 11:22
I am n. the eye, I am n. of. 12:16
yet n. I, but the grace of God. 15:10
n. as many which corrupt. 2 Cor 2:17
n. with ink, n. in tables of. 3:3
n. that we are sufficient of. 5
n. as Moses, which put a vail. 13
we faint n. 4:1, 16
may be of God, and n. of us. 7
n. forsaken, cast down, but n. 9
we have an house n. made. 5:1
we walk by faith, n. by sight. 7
in appearance and n. in heart. 12
God comforted us, n. by his. 7:7
I rejoice, n. that ye were made. 9
I did it n. for his cause that had. 12
and this they did, n. as we hoped. 8:5
and n. according to that he hath n. 12
dare n. make ourselves. 2 Cor 10:12
walked we n. in same spirit? 12:18
Paul an apostle, n. of men. Gal 1:1
I live, yet n. I. 2:20
and n. in another. 6:4
through faith, and that n. Eph 2:8
n. of works. 9
n. as fools, but as wise. 5:15
as to the Lord, and n. to men. 6:7
for we wrestle n. against flesh. 12
it is given to you, n. only. Phil 1:29
have obeyed, n. as in my. 2:12
and n. on him only, but on. 27
found in him, n. having mine. 3:9
n. as though I had already. 12
n. holding the head, from. Col 2:19
touch n. taste n. handle n. 21
on things above, n. on things. 3:2
to the Lord, and n. unto men. 23
that it was n. in vain. 1 Thes 2:1
ye received it n. as word of. 13
therefore let us n. sleep as do. 5:6
all men have n. faith. 2 Thes 3:2
n. because we have n. power. 9
n. given to wine, n. 1 Tim 3:3
n. according to our works. 2 Tim 1:9
Tit 3:5
and n. to me only, but. 2 Tim 4:8
please them, n. answering. Tit 2:9
n. now as a servant. Philem 16
n. without an oath, he. Heb 7:20
Lord pitched, and n. man. 8:2
n. without blood, which he. 9:7
n. made with hands, n. of this. 11
evidence of things n. seen. 11:1
died, n. having received the. 13
us should n. be made perfect. 40
then are ye bastards, n. sons. 12:8
n. with grief. 13:17
be a hearer, and n. a doer. Jas 1:23
n. by faith only. 2:24
offend n. in word. 3:2
yet ye have n., because ye ask n. 4:2
and doeth it n., to him it is sin. 17
n. a people, had n. 1 Pet 2:10
be subject, n. only to the good. 18
reviled n. again, he threatened n. 23
better for them n. to. 2 Pet 2:21
same hath n. the Father. 1 John 2:23
n. as Cain. 3:12
n. that we loved God. 4:10
hath n. the Son, hath n. life. 5:12
there is a sin n. unto death. 17
these be sensual, having n. Jude 19
are apostles, and are n. Rev 2:2, 9
see thou do it n. 19:10; 22:9
see **able, afraid, ashamed, answered, believe, confounded, departed, destroy, die, eat, enter, fear, few, find, forsaken, give, given, hear, hearken, hid, is, knew, know, no, obey, obeyed, passed, see, seek, so, will, would**

if not

I will go down, and if n. Gen 18:21
and if n. tell me, that I. 24:49
if n. blot me, I pray, out. Ex 32:32
if n. let fire come. Judg 9:15, 20
and if n. I will take it. 1 Sam 2:16
but if n. then we shall know. 6:9
if n. let Amnon go. 2 Sam 13:26
if n.; speak thou. 17:6
but if n. it shall not be. 2 Ki 2:10
if n. where, and who is he? Job 9:24
if n. hearken to me, hold. 33:33
and if n. forbear. Zech 11:12
if n. it shall turn to you. Luke 10:6
and if n. then thou shalt. 13:9

or not

journey prosperous or n. Gen 24:21
is Lord among us, or n.? Ex 17:7
word come to pass or n. Num 11:23
be wood therein or n. 13:20
fathers did keep it, or n. Judg 2:22

notable

(*Worthy of notice; remarkable*)
the goat had a n. horn. Dan 8:5
for it came up four n. ones. 8
had then a n. prisoner. Mat 27:16
before that n. day of the. Acts 2:20
a n. miracle hath been done. 4:16

note, -d

write it, and n. it in a. Isa 30:8*
that is n. in scripture. Dan 10:21*
n. that man, and have. 2 Thes 3:14

note

of n. among the apostles. Rom 16:7

nothing

now n. will be restrained. Gen 11:6
only unto these men do n. for. 19:8
as we have done to thee n. 26:29
here also have I done n. to. 40:15
n. die that is the children's. Ex 9:4
let n. of it remain until. 12:10
ye shall eat n. leavened in. 20
gathered much, had n. over. 16:18
2 Cor 8:15
if he have n. then he shall. Ex 23:3
there shall n. cast their young. 26
eat n. that is made of. Num 6:4
touch n. of theirs, lest ye be. 16:26
let n. hinder thee from. 22:16
lacked n. Deut 2:7; Neh 9:21
thou shalt save alive n. Deu 20:36
to the damsel thou shalt do n. 22:26
because he hath n. left him. 28:55
Joshua left n. undone. Josh 11:15
at the least such as before knew n. thereof. Judg 3:2
he rent him, and had n. in his. 14:6
Samuel told, and hid n. 1 Sam 3:18
my father will do n. but will. 20:2
servant knew n. of all this. 22:15
n. was missed of all. 25:21; 30:19
she told him n. less or more. 36
poor man had n. save. 2 Sam 12:3
that which doth cost me n. 24:24
victuals, they lacked n. 1 Ki 4:27
there was n. in the ark save. 8:9
silver was n. accounted of in. 10:21
he answered n. 11:22; Luke 23:9
tell me n. but that which is true.
1 Ki 22:16; 2 Chr 18:15
fall n. to earth of word. 2 Ki 10:10
n. in his house that he. 20:13
be carried into Babylon, n. shall be left. 17; Isa 39:2, 6
n. hid from Solomon. 2 Chr 9:2
ye have n. to do with us. Ezra 4:3
they found n. to answer. Neh 5:8
we will restore, and require n. 12
for whom n. is prepared. 8:10
so that they lacked n. 9:21
Esther required n. but. Esth 2:15
yet all this availeth me n. 5:13
let n. fail of all that thou. 6:10
they go to n. and perish. Job 6:18
for ye are n. 21
of yesterday, and know n. 8:9
make my speech n. worth. 24:25
he hangeth the earth upon n. 26:7
it profiteth a man n. that he should delight himself with. 34:9
tried me and shalt find n. Ps 17:3
and mine age is as n. before. 39:5
he shall carry n. away. 49:17
who love thy law, and n. 119:165
simple, and knoweth n. Pr 9:13
of wickedness profit n. 10:2
desireth, and hath n. 13:4; 20:4
maketh himself rich, yet hath n. 13:7
if thou hast n. to pay, why? 22:27
whatsoever God doeth, n. Eccl 3:14
and he shall take n. of his. 5:15
so that he wanteth n. for his. 6:2
man should find n. after him. 7:14
all her princes shall be n. Isa 34:12
are as n. they are counted to him less than n. and vanity. 40:17; 41:29
the princes to n. 40:23; 41:11, 12
lest thou bring me to n. Jer 10:24
done n. of all that thou. 32:23
thee a thing, hide n. from me. 38:14
left of the poor which had n. 39:10
I will keep n. back from you. 42:4
destroy her utterly, let n. 50:26
is it n. to you, all ye? Lam 1:12
prophets that have seen n. Ezek 13:3
earth reputed as n. Dan 4:35
a wilderness, yea, and n. Joel 2:3
will a young lion cry out if he have taken n.? Amos 3:4
take up a snare, and have taken n. 5
surely the Lord will do n. 7

in comparison of it as n.? Hag 2:3
they have n. to eat. Mat 15:32
Mark 6:36; 8:1, 2
n. shall be impossible to you.
Mat 17:20; Luke 1:37
he found n. thereon but leaves.
Mat 21:19; Mark 11:13
answerest thou n.? Mat 26:62
he answered n. 27:12; Mark 14:60
61; 15:3, 4, 5
n. to do with that just. Mat 27:19
saw that he could prevail n. 24
see thou say n. to any. Mark 1:44
and had spent all, and was n. 5:26
take n. for their journey. 6:8
Luke 9:3
forth by n. but by prayer. Mark 9:29
those days he did eat n. Luke 4:2
toiled all night and taken n. 5:5
John 21:3
they had n. to pay, he. Luke 7:42
and n. shall by any means. 10:19
I have n. to set before him. 11:6
and lo, n. worthy of death. 23:15
Acts 23:29; 25:25; 26:31
man hath done n. amiss. Luke 23:41
man can receive n. except. John 3:27
Son can do n. of himself. 5:19, 30
gather, that n. be lost. 6:12
I should lose n. 39
quickeneth, the flesh profiteth n. 63
and they say n. unto him. 7:26
I do n. of myself. 8:28
he could do n. 9:33
ye know n. at all. 11:49
how ye prevail n.? behold. 12:19
this world hath n. in me. 14:30
for without me ye can do n. 15:5
that day ye shall ask me n. 16:23
have ye asked n. in my name. 24
in secret have I said n. 18:20
could say n. against it. Acts 4:14
finding n. how they might. 21
and go with them, doubting n. 10:20
11:12
be quiet, and do n. rashly. 19:36
I kept back n. that was. 20:20
that those things are n. 21:24
we will eat n. until we have. 23:14
fasting, having taken n. 27:33
to n. the understanding. 1 Cor 1:19
I know n. by myself. 4:4
judge n. before the time. 5
he knoweth n. yet as he ought. 8:2
for though I preach, I have n. 9:16
not charity, I am n. 13:2; 2 Cor 12:11
charity, it profiteth me n. 1 Cor 13:3
having n. yet possessing. 2 Cor 6:10
for we can do n. against. 13:8
in confidence added n. Gal 2:6
heir when a child, differeth n. 4:1
Christ shall profit you n. 5:2
n. be done through strife. Phil 2:3
every creature is good, n. 1 Tim 4:4
doing n. by partiality. 5:21
proud, knowing n. 6:4
brought n. and we can carry n. out. 7
n. be wanting unto them. Tit 3:13
thy mind would I do n. Philem 14
he left n. that is not put. Heb 2:8
Moses spake n. concerning. 7:14
for the law made n. perfect. 19
and entire, wanting n. Jas 1:4
let him ask in faith, n. wavering. 6
they went forth taking n. 3 John 7

for nothing

shall go out free for n. Ex 21:2
that is profitable for n. Isa 44:10
was profitable for n. Jer 13:7, 10
salt have lost his savour, it is good
for n. Mat 5:13
lend, hoping for n. again. Luke 6:35
be careful for n. but by prayer.
Phil 4:6

in nothing

their time in n. else. Acts 17:21
receive damage by us in n. 2 Cor 7:9
in n. am I behind chiefest, though I
be n. 12:11
in n. I shall be ashamed. Phil 1:20
and in n. terrified by your. 28

is nothing

there is n. at all beside. Num 11:6
is n. else save the sword. Judg 7:14
there is n. better than. 1 Sam 27:1
and said, There is n. 1 Ki 18:43
there is n. among my treasures.
2 Ki 20:15; Isa 39:4
it is n. with thee to help. 2 Chr 14:11
this is n. else but sorrow. Neh 2:2
said, There is n. done. Esth 6:3
there is n. hid from the. Ps 19:6
there is n. froward or. Pr 8:8
there is n. better for a man.
Eccl 2:24; 3:22
begetteth a son, and there is n. 5:14
there is n. too hard. Jer 32:17
is n. covered that shall. Mat 10:26
Mark 4:22; Luke 12:2
swear by temple, it is n. Mat 23:16
swear by the altar, it is n. 18
there is n. from without a man that
can defile. Mark 7:15
myself, my honour is n. John 8:54
that there is n. unclean. Rom 14:14
is n., uncircumcision is n. 1 Cor 7:19
we know that an idol is n. in. 8:4
when he is n. he deceiveth. Gal 6:3
are defiled is n. pure. Tit 1:15

of nothing

of n. your work nought. Isa 41:24
ye may have lack of n. 1 Thes 4:12
increased, and have need of n.
Rev 3:17

notwithstanding

n. they hearkened not to. Ex 16:20
1 Sam 2:25; 2 Ki 17:14
n. if he continue a day. Ex 21:21
n. ye would not go up. Deut 1:26
n. in thy days I will. 1 Ki 11:12
n. I have spoken unto. Jer 35:14
n. being warned of God. Mat 2:22
n. he that is least in kingdom. 11:11
n. lest we should offend. 17:27
n. be sure of this that. Luke 10:11
n. in this rejoice, that spirits. 20
n. whether in pretence or. Phil 1:18
n. have well done, that ye. 4:14
n. she shall be saved in. 1 Tim 2:15
n. Lord stood with me. 2 Tim 4:17
n. ye give not those things. Jas 2:16
n. I have a few things. Rev 2:20

nought, see naught

nourish

[1] To feed or maintain, Gen 47:12. [2] To educate or bring up, Acts 7:21. [3] To instruct, 1 Tim 4:6. [4] To cherish and comfort, Ruth 4:15; Jas 5:5.

will I n. thee. Gen 45:11; 50:21
that man shall n. young. Isa 7:21†
nor do I n. up young men, nor. 23:4
an ash, the rain doth n. it. 44:14

nourished

Joseph n. his father. Gen 47:12
he brought and n. up. 2 Sam 12:3
I have n. and brought up. Isa 1:2
she n. her whelps among. Ezek 19:2
n. in his father's house. Acts 7:20
Pharaoh's daughter n. him. 21
their country was n. by the. 12:20*
n. up in words of faith. 1 Tim 4:6
have n. your hearts as in. Jas 5:5
n. for a time, times. Rev 12:14

nourisher

he shall be n. of thy old. Ruth 4:15

nourisheth

n. his flesh, as the Lord. Eph 5:29

nourishing

so n. them three years. Dan 1:5

nourishment

joints and bands having n. Col 2:19*

novice

not a n. lest being lifted. 1 Tim 3:6

now

Adam said, This is n. Gen 2:23
I will go down n. and see. 18:21
n. will we deal worse with. 19:9
n. I know that thou fearest. 22:12
thou art n. the blessed of the. 26:29
what shall I do n. to thee? 27:37
n. will I praise the Lord. 29:35
Laban, and stayed there till n. 32:4
if it be so n. do this. Gen 43:11
so n. it was not you that sent. 45:8
about cattle from youth till n. 46:34
not such hail been in Egypt even till
n. Ex 9:18
go n. ye that are men, and. 10:11
yet n. if thou wilt forgive. 32:32
heal her n. O God, I. Num 12:13
this people from Egypt till n. 14:19
I shall see him, but not n. 24:17
Lord's host am I n. come. Josh 5:14
tell me n. what thou hast done. 7:19
are ye come to me n.? Judg 11:7
n. I know that the Lord will. 17:13
thou shalt give it me n. 1 Sam 2:16
but n. the Lord saith, Be it far. 30
honour me n. I pray thee. 15:30
what have I n. done? 17:29
son, let us not all n. go. 2 Sam 13:25
I n. also be thy servant. 15:34
let us n. fall into the hand. 24:14
cut off, but what? even n. 1 Ki 14:14
it is enough, n. O Lord, take. 19:4
he said, Why are ye n. turned back?
2 Ki 1:5
was her's since she went till n. 8:6
know n. there shall fall to. 10:10
am I n. come up without the Lord.
18:25; Isa 36:10
n. have I brought it to pass.
2 Ki 19:35; Isa 37:26
remember n. how I have walked.
2 Ki 20:3; Isa 38:3
it n. known to the king. Ezra 4:13
even till n. hath it been building. 5:16
n. for a little space grace been. 9:8
n. there is hope in Israel. 10:2
put forth thy hand n. Job 1:11; 2:5
n. it is come upon thee. 4:5
for n. ye are nothing, ye see. 6:21
lay down n. 17:3
where is n. my hope? 15
and if it be not so n. 24:25
n. I am their son. 30:9
heard of thee, but n. my eye. 42:5
n. will I arise, saith the. Ps 12:5
n. know I that the Lord saveth. 20:6
n. Lord, what wait I for, my. 39:7
why heathen say, Where is n.? 115:2
save n. I beseech thee, O. 118:25
but n. have I kept thy word. 119:67
do this n. my son, and. Pr 6:3
n. she is without, n. in the. 7:12
go to n. Eccl 2:1
that which n. is shall all be. 16
what hath been is n. 3:15
I will rise n. and go. S of S 3:2
n. go to, I will tell you. Isa 5:5
but n. the Lord hath spoken. 16:14
let them tell thee n. 19:12
what aileth thee n. that thou? 22:1
n. will I rise, n. will I lift up. 33:10
but n. O Lord, thou art our. 64:8
n. what hast thou to do? Jer 2:18
n. will I give sentence against. 4:12
the word of the Lord let it n. 17:15
turn n. every one from his. 25:5
ask ye n. and see whether a. 30:6
ye were n. turned, and had. 34:15
return ye n. every man from. 35:15
woe is me n.! for the Lord hath. 45:3
Daniel, to thee am I n. Dan 10:11
it better with me than n. Hos 2:7
and n. they sin more and more. 13:2
turn ye n. from your evil. Zech 1:4
n. have I seen with mine eyes. 9:8
prove me n. herewith. Mal 3:10
n. all this was done. Mat 1:22
days of John the Baptist, till n. 11:12
Sleep on n. 26:45
thinkest that I cannot n. pray. 53
let him n. come down from. 27:42
let him deliver him n. 43
so that the ship was n. Mark 4:37
n. lettest thy servant. Luke 2:29
which n. of these three was? 10:36
all things are n. ready. 14:17
but n. he that hath a purse. 22:36
draw out n. and bear. John 2:8
hast kept the good wine until n. 10
he whom thou n. hast is not. 4:18
hour cometh, and n. is. 23; 5:25
blind, how then doth he n. see? 9:19
what I do thou knowest not n. 13:7

numbering
born until he left *n.* *Gen* 41:49
after the *n.* wherewith. *2 Chr* 2:17

numbers
these are the *n.* of the. *1 Chr* 12:23
are the *n.* of them. *2 Chr* 17:14
for I know not the *n.* *Ps* 71:15

Nun, *see* **Joshua**

nurse, *substantive*
Rebekah and her *n.* *Gen* 24:59
but Deborah, Rebekah's *n.* 35:8
call to thee a *n.* of Hebrew ? *Ex* 2:7
the child, and became *n.* *Ruth* 4:16
n. took him up and fled. *2 Sam* 4:4
they hid him and his *n.* *2 Ki* 11:2
2 Chr 22:11
were gentle, as a *n.* *1 Thes* 2:7

nurse
she may *n.* the child. *Ex* 2:7
child away, and *n.* it for me. 9

nursed
took the child, and *n.* it. *Ex* 2:9
thy daughters shall be *n.* *Isa* 60:4*

nursing
carry them in thy bosom, as a *n.*
Num 11:12
kings shall be thy *n.* fathers, queens thy *n.* mothers. *Isa* 49:23

nurture
bring them up in the *n.* of. *Eph* 6:4*

nuts
carry down a present, *n.* *Gen* 43:11
into the garden of *n.* *S of S* 6:11

Nymphas
salute *N.* and the church. *Col* 4:15

O

oak
hid the gods under the *o.* *Gen* 35:4
Deborah was buried under an *o.* 8
up there under an *o.* *Josh* 24:26
angel of the Lord sat under an *o.*
Judg 6:11
mule went under an *o.* *2 Sam* 18:9
Absalom hanged in an *o.* 10
alive in the *o.* 14
man of God under an *o.* *1 Ki* 13:14
their bones under *o.* in. *1 Chr* 10:12
as an *o.* whose leaf fadeth. *Isa* 1:30
teil tree, or *o.* whose substance. 6:13
he taketh the cypress and *o.* 44:14
idols under every thick *o.* *Ezek* 6:13

oaks
be ashamed of the *o.* *Isa* 1:29
day of the Lord on all the *o.* 2:13
of *o.* of Bashan have they. *Ezek* 27:6
burn incense upon the hills under *o.*
Hos 4:13
was strong as the *o.* *Amos* 2:9
fir tree, howl, O ye *o.* *Zech* 11:2

oar
all that handle the *o.* *Ezek* 27:29

oars
shall go no galley with *o.* *Isa* 33:21
Bashan they made thy *o.* *Ezek* 27:6

oath
(A solemn appeal to God to witness the truth of a declaration. It is also used of a solemn affirmation not invoking the Deity. The modern use of the word for profanity is not found in the Bible)
Oaths were forbidden to be taken by the Israelites. [1] *Idolatrously, in the name of any false gods, or in the name of inanimate things,* Josh 23:7; Jas 5:12. [2] *Deceitfully,* Jer 42:5, 20. [3] *Falsely,* Lev 6:3; 19:12. [4] *Rashly,* Lev 5:4; Mat 14:7.
clear from this my *o.* *Gen* 24:8, 41
o. which I sware to Abraham. 26:3
Deut 7:8; *Ps* 105:9; *Jer* 11:5
let there be now an *o.* betwixt us.
Gen 26:28
Joseph took an *o.* of children. 50:25
o. of the Lord shall be. *Ex* 22:11
shall pronounce with an *o.* *Lev* 5:4
shall charge her by an *o.* *Num* 5:19*
Lord make thee a curse and an *o.* 21
an *o.* to bind his soul. 30:2, 10
every binding *o.* to afflict soul. 13
his *o.* which the Lord maketh with.
Deut 29:12
you only do I make this *o.* 14
blameless of this thine *o.* *Josh* 2:17
be on us, because of the *o.* 9:20
Israel had made a great *o.* *Judg* 21:5
people feared the *o.* *1 Sam* 14:26
charged them with the *o.* 27, 28
king spared Mephibosheth, because of *o.* *2 Sam* 21:7
hast thou not kept the *o.*? *1 Ki* 2:43
o. be laid on him, and the *o.* come.
8:31; *2 Chr* 6:22
he took an *o.* of the. *1 Ki* 18:10
Jehoiada took an *o.* of. *2 Ki* 11:4
be mindful of his *o.* to. *1 Chr* 16:16
Judah rejoiced at the *o.* *2 Chr* 15:15
Nehemiah took an *o.* of. *Neh* 5:12
they entered into an *o.* to walk. 10:29
in regard of the *o.* of God. *Eccl* 8:2
as he that feareth an *o.* 9:2
which hast despised the *o.*
Ezek 16:59; 17:18, 19
hath taken an *o.* of him. 17:13
that made him king, whose *o.* 16
us, and *o.* written in law. *Dan* 9:11
love no false *o.* for this. *Zech* 8:17
he promised with an *o.* *Mat* 14:7
for the *o.*'s sake. 9; *Mark* 6:26
he denied with an *o.* *Mat* 26:72
the *o.* which he sware. *Luke* 1:73
sworn with an *o.* to him. *Acts* 2:30
bound themselves with an *o.* 23:21*
an *o.* for confirmation is. *Heb* 6:16
God confirmed it by an *o.* 17
an *o.* he was made priest. 7:20, 21
the *o.* which was since the law. 28
the earth, nor any other *o.* *Jas* 5:12

oaths
them that have sworn *o.* *Ezek* 21:23
naked, according to the *o.* *Hab* 3:9
to the Lord thine *o.* *Mat* 5:33

Obadiah
Ahab called *O.*, now *O.* *1 Ki* 18:3
O. took an hundred prophets. 4
as *O.* was in the way, behold. 7
so *O.* went to meet Ahab, and. 16
sons of *O.* *1 Chr* 3:21
son of Izrahiah, *O.* 7:3
O. son of Azel. 8:38; 9:44
O. the son of Shemaiah, the. 9:16
of Gadites men of might, *O.* 12:9
Ishmaiah son of *O.* 27:19
to his princes, to *O.* to. *2 Chr* 17:7
Jahath and *O.* the Levites. 34:12
O. son of Jehiel went up. *Ezra* 8:9
O. sealed. *Neh* 10:5
O. was a porter. 12:25
the vision of *O.* Thus saith. *Ob* 1

Obed
called his name *O.* *Ruth* 4:17
Boaz begat *O.* 21; *1 Chr* 2:12
Mat 1:5
Ephlal begat *O.* *1 Chr* 2:37
O. one of David's valiant. 11:47
Shemaiah begat *O.* 26:7
took Azariah son of *O.* *2 Chr* 23:1
which was the son of *O.* *Luke* 3:32

Obed-edom
the ark into the house of *O.*
2 Sam 6:10, 11; *1 Chr* 13:13, 14
Lord blessed the house of *O.*
2 Sam 6:11, 12; *1 Chr* 13:14
ark from house of *O.* into city of.
2 Sam 6:12; *1 Chr* 15:25
O. a porter. *1 Chr* 15:18, 24
O. with harp. 21
O.; and Jeiel with psalteries. 16:5
O. with their brethren, *O.* also. 38
sons of *O.* 26:4, 8
sons of *O.* fit for service. 8
the lot southward fell to *O.* 15
vessels found with *O.* *2 Chr* 25:24

obedience
(Subjection to the authority of another, whether to God or to a human being. In the Bible the word is used most often in the sense of subjection to the will of God, and to his commands. It is used in speaking of Jesus, who always did the will of God.
It is also used of hearts and inanimate things, which are subject to God's controlling power)
for *o.* to the faith among. *Rom* 1:5
by the *o.* of one shall many. 5:19
of sin to death, or of *o.* unto. 6:16
your *o.* is come abroad unto. 16:19
known to all nations for the *o.* 26
women are commanded to be under *o.* *1 Cor* 14:34*
he remembereth the *o.* *2 Cor* 7:15
bringing every thought to the *o.* 10:5
all disobedience, when your *o.* 6
confidence in thy *o.* *Philem* 21
learned he *o.* by the things. *Heb* 5:8
through sanctification of the Spirit to *o.* *1 Pet* 1:2

obedient
we will do, and be *o.* *Ex* 24:7
that Israel may be *o.* *Num* 27:20
shall be *o.* to his voice. *Deut* 4:30
because ye would not be *o.* 8:20*
strangers shall be *o.* *2 Sam* 22:45
reprover upon an *o.* ear. *Pr* 25:12
if *o.* ye shall eat the good. *Isa* 1:19
nor were they *o.* to his law. 42:24
priests were *o.* to the faith. *Acts* 6:7
to make Gentiles *o.* *Rom* 15:18*
know whether ye be *o.* *2 Cor* 2:9
servants, be *o.* to your masters.
Eph 6:5; *Tit* 2:9*
Christ became *o.* unto. *Phil* 2:8
wives, be *o.* *Tit* 2:5*
children, be *o.* *1 Pet* 1:14

obeisance
(A bodily movement in token of respect and submission)
your sheaves made *o.* *Gen* 37:7
eleven stars made *o.* to me. 9
bowed and made *o.* to Joseph. 43:28
Moses did *o.* to his. *Ex* 18:7
fell down and did *o.* to. *2 Sam* 1:2
the woman of Tekoah did *o.* 14:4
man came nigh to do him *o.* 15:5
Bath-sheba did *o.* to king. *1 Ki* 1:16
the princes of Judah made *o.* to the king. *2 Chr* 24:17

obey
(Revisions frequently substitute for this the word hearken*)*
therefore, my son, *o.* my voice.
Gen 27:8, 13, 43
Lord, that I should *o.* him ? *Ex* 5:2
now if ye will *o.* my voice. 19:5
o. his voice. 23:21
if thou shalt indeed *o.* his voice. 22
ye *o.* commands of Lord. *Deut* 11:27
o. his voice. 13:4; 27:10; 30:2, 8
1 Sam 12:14
thou mayest *o.* his voice. 30:20
Lord's voice will we *o.* *Josh* 24:24
to *o.* voice of Samuel. *1 Sam* 8:19
to *o.* is better than sacrifice. 15:22
and refused to *o.* neither. *Neh* 9:17
if they *o.* and serve him. *Job* 36:11
hear, they shall *o.* me. *Ps* 18:44
eye that despiseth to *o.* *Pr* 30:17
of Ammon shall *o.* them. *Isa* 11:14
o. my voice, and I will be your God.
Jer 7:23; 11:4, 7
o. the voice of the Lord your God.
26:13; 38:20; *Zech* 6:15
Rechabites *o.* their. *Jer* 35:14
o. the voice of Lord our God . . . well with us when we *o.* the. 42:6
dominions shall serve and *o.* him.
Dan 7:27
is this, that even winds and sea *o.*?
Mat 8:27; *Mark* 4:41; *Luke* 8:25
the unclean spirits *o.* *Mark* 1:27
plucked up, and it shall *o.* *Luke* 17:6
ought to *o.* God rather. *Acts* 5:29
hath given to them that *o.* him. 32
that *o.* unrighteousness. *Rom* 2:8
that ye should *o.* it in the. 6:12
yourselves servants to *o.*, his servants ye are to whom ye *o.* 16

children, *o.* your parents. *Eph* 6:1
Col 3:20
servants, *o.* in all things. *Col* 3:22
put them in mind to *o.* *Tit* 3:1
salvation to all that *o.* him. *Heb* 5:9
o. them that have the rule. 13:17
bits in horses' mouths, that they may *o.* *Jas* 3:3

not obey, obey not

if ye will *not o.* the commandments. *Deut* 11:28; 28:62; *1 Sam* 12:15
Job 36:12; *Jer* 12:17; 18:10
will *not o.* the voice. *Deut* 21:18, 20
didst thou *not o.*? *1 Sam* 15:19
will *not o.* the Lord. *Jer* 42:13
might *not o.* thy voice. *Dan* 9:11
our fathers would *not o.* *Acts* 7:39
and do *not o.* the truth. *Rom* 2:8
who hath bewitched you, that ye should *not o.*? *Gal* 3:1; 5:7
vengeance on them that *o. not* the gospel. *2 Thes* 1:8
if any man *o. not* our word. 3:14
if any *o. not* the word. *1 Pet* 3:1
be of them that *o. not* gospel ? 4:17

obeyed

all nations be blessed, because thou hast *o.* *Gen* 22:18; 26:5
that Jacob *o.* his father. 28:7
have *o.* my voice in all. *Josh* 22:2
Saul said, I have *o.* *1 Sam* 15:20
I feared the people, and *o.* 24
handmaid hath *o.* thy voice. 28:21
all Israel *o.* Solomon. *1 Chr* 29:23
they *o.* the words of. *2 Chr* 11:4
then they *o.* and let. *Jer* 34:10
thus have we *o.* the voice. 35:8, 10
because ye *o.* the commandment. 18
neither have we *o.* voice. *Dan* 9:10
the people *o.* the voice. *Hag* 1:12
many as *o.* Theudas. *Acts* 5:36, 37
have *o.* from heart that. *Rom* 6:17
ye have *o.*, not as in my presence only. *Phil* 2:12
by faith Abraham *o.* *Heb* 11:8
Sarah *o.* Abraham. *1 Pet* 3:6

***not* obeyed**

because they *o. not.* *Josh* 5:6
but ye have *not o.* my voice. *Judg* 2:2; 6:10
thou hast *not o.* the voice. *1 Ki* 20:36
because they *o. not* the. *2 Ki* 18:12
not o. the voice of my teachers. *Pr* 5:13
ye have *not o.* my voice. *Jer* 3:13
25; 42:21; 43:4, 7; 44:23
have *not o.* my voice. 9:13; 11:8
17:23; 32:23; 40:3; *Dan* 9:10, 14
she *o. not* the voice. *Zeph* 3:2
not all *o.* the gospel. *Rom* 10:16

obeyedst

because thou *o.* not the voice of. *1 Sam* 28:18
that thou *o.* not my voice. *Jer* 22:21

obeyeth

who that *o.* the voice ? *Isa* 50:10
this is a nation that *o.* *Jer* 7:28
cursed be the man that *o.* not. 11:3

obeying

their fathers *o.*, but they. *Judg* 2:17
in sacrifice, as in *o.* *1 Sam* 15:22
your souls in *o.* the truth. *1 Pet* 1:22

object

and *o.* if they had aught. *Acts* 24:19

oblation

(*An offering. From the Latin* oblatus, *offered*)
an *o.* of a meat offering baken. *Lev* 2:4, 5, 7, 13
as for *o.* of the firstfruits. 2:12
if his *o.* be a sacrifice of. 3:1
offer one out of the whole *o.* 7:14
he shall bring his *o.* to the Lord. 29
that will offer his *o.* for all. 22:18
every *o.* of theirs shall. *Num* 18:9
we have brought an *o.* for. 31:50
Egyptians shall do *o.* *Isa* 19:21
impoverished that he hath no *o.* 40:20
offereth an *o.* as if he offered. 66:3
they offer an *o.* I will. *Jer* 14:12†
o. shall be the priest's. *Ezek* 44:30
divide the land, offer an *o.* *Ezek* 45:1
this is the *o.* ye shall offer. 13; 48:9
20, 21
give this *o.* for the prince in. 45:16
they should offer an *o.* to. *Dan* 2:46
time of the evening *o.* 9:21
shall cause *o.* to cease. 27

oblations

Israel to offer their *o.* *Lev* 7:38
to distribute the *o.* of. *2 Chr* 31:14
bring no more vain *o.* unto. *Isa* 1:13
require the firstfruits of your *o.* *Ezek* 20:40
every sort of your *o.* shall be. 44:30

obscure

lamp shall be put out in *o.* darkness. *Pr* 20:20*

obscurity

blind shall see out of *o.* *Isa* 29:18
then shall thy light rise in *o.* 58:10*
we wait for light, but behold *o.* 59:9*

observation

God cometh not with *o.* *Luke* 17:20

observe

(*Frequently means to keep, or to celebrate, and is so rendered in the Revisions*)
ye shall *o.* the feast of unleavened. *Ex* 12:17, 24; *Deut* 16:1
o. the sabbath. *Ex* 31:16
o. thou that which I command thee. 34:11; *Deut* 12:28; 24:8
o. feast of weeks. *Ex* 34:22
nor shall ye use enchantments, *o.* times. *Lev* 19:26
ye shall *o.* all my statutes. 37
2 Chr 7:17; *Neh* 1:5; *Ps* 105:45
Ezek 37:24
sacrifice shall ye *o.* *Num* 28:2
o. the feast of tabernacles seven days. *Deut* 16:13
men did diligently *o.* *1 Ki* 20:33
whoso is wise, and will *o.* *Ps* 107:43
o. it with my whole heart. 119:34
and let thine eyes *o.* *Pr* 23:26*
crane and swallow *o.* time. *Jer* 8:7
neither *o.* their judgements nor. *Ezek* 20:18
as a leopard by the way will I *o.* them. *Hos* 13:7
that *o.* lying vanities. *Jonah* 2:8
teaching them to *o.* all. *Mat* 28:20
customs not lawful to *o.* *Acts* 16:21
Gentiles *o.* no such thing. 21:25
ye *o.* days, and months. *Gal* 4:10
then *o.* these things. *1 Tim* 5:21

see **do**

observed

father *o.* the saying. *Gen* 37:11*
it is a night to be much *o.* *Ex* 12:42
not *o.* commandments. *Num* 15:22
Levi *o.* thy word, kept. *Deut* 33:9
when Joab *o.* city, he. *2 Sam* 11:16
Manasseh *o.* times. *2 Ki* 21:6
2 Chr 33:6
I heard him, and *o.* him. *Hos* 14:8
feared John and *o.* him. *Mark* 6:20*
have I *o.* from my youth. 10:20

observer

not be found an *o.* of times. *Deut* 18:10*

observers

nations hearkened to *o.* of times. *Deut* 18:14*

observest

things, but thou *o.* not. *Isa* 42:20

observeth

he that *o.* the wind shall. *Eccl* 11:4

obstinate

God made his heart *o.* *Deut* 2:30
I knew that thou art *o.* *Isa* 48:4

obtain

I may *o.* children by. *Gen* 16:2
and shall *o.* favour of. *Pr* 8:35
they shall *o.* joy and gladness. *Isa* 35:10; 51:11
he shall *o.* the kingdom. *Dan* 11:21
accounted worthy to *o.* *Luke* 20:35*
they may *o.* mercy. *Rom* 11:31
so run that ye may *o.* *1 Cor* 9:24*
they do it to *o.* a corruptible. 25*
but to *o.* salvation by. *1 Thes* 5:9
may *o.* salvation which. *2 Tim* 2:10
that we may *o.* mercy. *Heb* 4:16*
that they might *o.* a better. 11:35
desire to have, and cannot *o.* *Jas* 4:2

obtained

after certain days I *o.* *Neh* 13:6*
Esther *o.* kindness. *Esth* 2:9
she *o.* grace. 17
her that had not *o.* mercy. *Hos* 2:23
o. part of this ministry. *Acts* 1:17*
with a great sum *o.* I this. 22:28
o. help of God I continue. 26:22
supposing that they had *o.* 27:13
Israel hath not *o.* that which he seeketh for . . . hath *o.* it. *Rom* 11:7
ye have now *o.* mercy through. 30
one that hath *o.* mercy. *1 Cor* 7:25
have *o.* an inheritance. *Eph* 1:11*
o. mercy, because I did it ignorantly. *1 Tim* 1:13, 16
o. a more excellent name. *Heb* 1:4
he had patiently endured, he *o.* 6:15
o. a more excellent ministry. 8:6
having *o.* eternal redemption. 9:12
elders *o.* a good report. 11:2*, 39*
Abel *o.* witness that he was. 4*
who *o.* promises, stopped. 11:33
not *o.* mercy, but now have *o.* *1 Pet* 2:10
have *o.* like precious. *2 Pet* 1:1

see **favour**

obtaining

to *o.* of the glory of. *2 Thes* 2:14

occasion

may seek *o.* against us. *Gen* 43:18
mayest do as thou shalt find *o.* *Judg* 9:33; *1 Sam* 10:7
Samson sought *o.* against. 14:4
great *o.* to enemies. *2 Sam* 12:14
which thou shalt have *o.* *Ezra* 7:20
o. who can turn her away ? *Jer* 2:24
not have *o.* any more. *Ezek* 18:3
sought to find *o.* and could find none *o.* *Dan* 6:4, 5
sin taking *o.* by the. *Rom* 7:8, 11
put not an *o.* to fall in his. 14:13
we give you *o.* to glory. *2 Cor* 5:12
by *o.* of the frowardness of. 8:8*
cut off *o.* from them which desire *o.* 11:12
use not liberty for an *o.* *Gal* 5:13
younger give none *o.* to. *1 Tim* 5:14
o. of stumbling in him. *1 John* 2:10

occasioned

I have *o.* the death of. *1 Sam* 22:22

occasions

and give *o.* of speech against her. *Deut* 22:14*, 17*
findeth *o.* against me. *Job* 33:10

occupation

shall say, What is your *o.*? *Gen* 46:33; 47:3; *Jonah* 1:8
for by *o.* they were tentmakers. *Acts* 18:3*
with the workmen of like *o.* 19:25

occupied

the gold that was *o.* *Ex* 38:24*
ropes that never were *o.* *Judg* 16:11*
Syria *o.* *Ezek* 27:16*
Dan and Javan *o.* 19*
Arabia *o.* 21*
Sheba *o.* in thy fairs. 22*
profited them that have *o.* *Heb* 13:9

occupiers

o. of thy merchandise. *Ezek* 27:27†

occupieth

he that *o.* the room of. *1 Cor* 14:16*

occupy

with mariners to *o.* thy. *Ezek* 27:9†
servants, *o.* till I come. *Luke* 19:13*

occurrent

adversary nor evil *o.* *1 Ki* 5:4

Ocran, *see* **Pagiel**

odd

the *o.* number is to be. *Num* 3:48

Oded

came on Azariah son of *O.* *2 Chr* 15:1
prophet of the Lord, called *O.* 28:9

odious
made themselves *o.* *1 Chr* 19:6
for an *o.* woman when. *Pr* 30:23

odour
house was filled with *o.* *John* 12:3
an *o.* of a sweet smell. *Phil* 4:18

odours
savour of your sweet *o.* *Lev* 26:31
in a bed of sweet *o.* *2 Chr* 16:14
oil of myrrh and sweet *o.* *Esth* 2:12
so shall they burn *o.* for thee. *Jer* 34:5*
offer sweet *o.* to Daniel. *Dan* 2:46
golden vials full of *o.* *Rev* 5:8
no man buyeth their *o.* 18:13

offence
[1] *Any thing that a man finds in his way, that may occasion him to stumble or fall, whether physically or morally. The Revisions often translate it* stumblingblock, *or* occasion of stumbling. [2] *A sin, or trespass.*
o. of heart to my lord. *1 Sam* 25:31
but a rock of *o.* to both. *Isa* 8:14
till they acknowledge their *o.* *Hos* 5:15
Satan, thou art *o.* to me. *Mat* 16:23
man by whom the *o.* cometh. 18:7
a conscience void of *o.* *Acts* 24:16
o. so also is the free gift, for if through the *o.* of. *Rom* 5:15, 18
by one man's *o.* death reigned. 17
the law entered that the *o.* 20
stumbling stone, and rock of *o.* 9:33
that man who eateth with *o.* 14:20
give none *o.* in any thing. *1 Cor* 10:32; *2 Cor* 6:3
an *o.* in abasing myself? *2 Cor* 11:7
then is the *o.* of the cross. *Gal* 5:11
may be without *o.* till. *Phil* 1:10
a rock of *o.* to them. *1 Pet* 2:8

offences
yielding pacifieth great *o.* *Eccl* 10:4
because of *o.*, for it must needs be that *o.* *Mat* 18:7; *Luke* 17:1
was delivered for our *o.* *Rom* 4:25
of many *o.* unto justification. 5:16
mark them which cause *o.* 16:17

offend
[1] *To commit any sin in thought, word, or deed,* Jas 3:2. [2] *To displease, thus the Pharisees were offended at Christ,* Mat 15:12. [3] *To be scandalized, or made to stumble by the example of another,* 1 Cor 8:13.
I will not *o.* any more. *Job* 34:31
I should *o.* against generation of. *Ps* 73:15
law, nothing shall *o.* them. 119:165
all that devour him shall *o.* *Jer* 2:3
adversaries said, We *o.* not. 50:7
harlot, let not Judah *o.* *Hos* 4:15
pass over and *o.* *Hab* 1:11
if thy right eye *o.* thee. *Mat* 5:29
if thy right hand *o.* thee. 30; 18:8, 9 *Mark* 9:43, 45, 47
gather all things that *o.* *Mat* 13:41
lest we should *o.* them, go. 17:27
whoso shall *o.* one of these little ones. 18:6; *Mark* 9:42; *Luke* 17:2
them, doth this *o.* you? *John* 6:61
my brother *o.*... lest he *o.* *1 Cor* 8:13
yet *o.* in one point, he. *Jas* 2:10
we *o.* all. If any man *o.* not. 3:2

offended
and what have I *o.* thee? *Gen* 20:9 *Jer* 37:18
the butler and baker had *o.* 40:1
saying, I have *o.*; return. *2 Ki* 18:14
we have *o.* against the. *2 Chr* 28:13
a brother *o.* is harder. *Pr* 18:19
Edom hath greatly *o.* *Ezek* 25:12
when Ephraim *o.* in Baal. *Hos* 13:1
blessed is he whosoever shall not be *o.* *Mat* 11:6; *Luke* 7:23
persecution ariseth . . . by and by he is *o.* *Mat* 13:21; *Mark* 4:17
and they were *o.* in him. *Mat* 13:57 *Mark* 6:3
the Pharisees were *o.* *Mat* 15:12
shall many be *o.* and betray. 24:10
all ye shall be *o.* because of. 26:31
all men shall be *o.* because of thee. *Mat* 26:33; *Mark* 14:29
that ye should not be *o.* *John* 16:1
against Caesar have I *o.* *Acts* 25:8
whereby thy brother is *o.* *Rom* 14:21
who is *o.* and I burn? *2 Cor* 11:29

offender
that make a man an *o.* *Isa* 29:21
if I be an *o.* or have. *Acts* 25:11

offenders
I and my son Solomon shall be counted *o.* *1 Ki* 1:21

offer
(*Revisions commonly use the word* sacrifice, *as having a more definite meaning*)
not delay to *o.* the first. *Ex* 22:29
not *o.* the blood. 23:18; 34:25
shalt *o.* every day a bullock. 29:36
thou shalt *o.* on altar two lambs. 38
one lamb thou shalt *o.* in the morning. 39, 41; *Num* 28:4, 8
shall *o.* no strange incense. *Ex* 30:9
every one that did *o.* silver. 35:24
o. a male without blemish. *Lev* 1:3; 3:6; 22:19, 20
will *o.* a meat offering to the Lord. 2:1, 14; 23:16; *Num* 6:17
offerings thou shalt *o.* salt. *Lev* 2:13
if he *o.* a peace offering, he shall *o.* 3:1, 6; 9:2; 19:5
if he *o.* a lamb for his. 3:7; 14:12
the goat he shall *o.* before. 3:12
o. a young bullock. 4:14; *Num* 15:24
o. that for sin offering. *Lev* 5:8; 9:7
the sons of Aaron shall *o.* 6:14, 22 14:19; 15:15 30; *Num* 6:11
o. of it all the fat. *Lev* 7:3
o. it for a thanksgiving. 12; 22:29
Israel to *o.* their oblations to. 38
o. their sacrifice to devils. 17:7
bringeth it not to the door to *o.* 9
eaten the same day ye *o.* it. 19:6
bread of their God they do *o.* 21:6
blemish shall not come nigh to *o.* 21
o. for a freewill offering. 22:23
they *o.* their offering. *Num* 7:11
shall *o.* the Levites. 8:11, 13, 15
kept back, that we may not *o.*? 9:7
shalt *o.* the third part of an. 15:7
if a stranger will *o.* an offering. 14
o. an heave offering. 19; 18:24 26, 28, 29
come near to *o.* incense. 16:40
shall ye observe to *o.* to me. 28:2
of your months ye shall *o.* 11
after this manner ye shall *o.* 24
shall choose, there *o.* *Deut* 12:14
priest's due from them that *o.* 18:3
o. sacrifices of righteousness. 33:19; *Ps* 4:5
he made an end to *o.* *Judg* 3:18
o. a great sacrifice to Dagon. 16:23
Elkanah went up to *o.* *1 Sam* 1:21
her husband to *o.* sacrifice. 2:19
did I choose him my priest to *o.*? 28
I *o.* thee three things. *2 Sam* 24:12 *1 Chr* 21:10
on thee shall he *o.* priests. *1 Ki* 13:2
should be able to *o.* so willingly. *1 Chr* 29:14, 17
vessels to *o.* withal. *2 Chr* 24:14
to *o.* sacrifices of sweet. *Ezra* 6:10
of blood will I not *o.* *Ps* 16:4
will I *o.* in his tabernacle. 27:6
o. to God thanksgiving, pay. 50:14
then shall they *o.* bullocks. 51:19
o. to thee burnt sacrifices. 66:15
Sheba and Seba shall *o.* gifts. 72:10
I will *o.* the sacrifice of. 116:17
wentest thou up to *o.* *Isa* 57:7
to whom they *o.* incense. *Jer* 11:12
when ye *o.* your gifts. *Ezek* 20:31
when ye *o.* my bread, the. 44:7
they shall *o.* to me the fat and. 15
ye shall *o.* an oblation to the Lord. 45:1, 13; 48:9
should *o.* an oblation. *Dan* 2:46
o. wine offerings to Lord. *Hos* 9:4
o. a sacrifice of. *Amos* 4:5
that which they *o.* there. *Hag* 2:14
ye *o.* polluted bread. *Mal* 1:7
if ye *o.* the blind, *o.* it now to. 8
o. to the Lord an offering in. 3:3
come and *o.* thy gift. *Mat* 5:24
o. gift Moses commanded. 8:4 *Mark* 1:44 *Luke* 5:14
smiteth on one cheek, *o.* *Luke* 6:29
if shall ask an egg, will he *o.*? 11:12
that he may *o.* both gifts. *Heb* 5:1
for himself to *o.* for sins. 3
needeth not to *o.* sacrifice, first. 7:27
to *o.*: it is of necessity that this man have somewhat also to *o.* 8:3
nor yet that he should *o.* 9:25
o. sacrifice of praise to God. 13:15
to *o.* spiritual sacrifices. *1 Pet* 2:5
he should *o.* it with prayers. *Rev* 8:3
see **burnt offerings**

offered
Jacob *o.* sacrifice on the mount. *Gen* 31:54; 46:1
every man *o.* an offering. *Ex* 35:22
he slew the goat, and *o.* *Lev* 9:15
Nadab and Abihu *o.* strange fire. 10:1; 16:1; *Num* 3:4; 26:61
the princes *o.* for the dedication. *Num* 7:2, 10
Aaron *o.* them as an offering. 8:21
250 men that *o.* incense. 16:35
Balak *o.* oxen and sheep. 22:40 23:2, 4, 14, 30
people willingly *o.* *Judg* 5:2, 9
Manoah took a kid and *o.* 13:19
was that Elkanah *o.* *1 Sam* 1:4
when any *o.* the priest's. 2:13
David *o.* peace. *2 Sam* 6:17; 24:25
and all Israel *o.* *1 Ki* 8:62, 63
Jeroboam *o.* in Beth-el. 12:32, 33
the people *o.* yet in the high. 22:43
meat offering was *o.* *2 Ki* 3:20
to the altar and *o.* 16:12
with the rulers *o.* *1 Chr* 29:6
rejoiced for that they *o.* willingly. 9
Asa *o.* to the Lord of. *2 Chr* 15:11
Amaziah willingly *o.* himself. 17:16
all that was willingly *o.* *Ezra* 1:6
some of fathers *o.* freely for. 2:68
o. at the dedication of this. 6:17
his counsellors freely *o.* to the. 7:15
Israel there present had *o.* 8:25
they *o.* a ram of the flock. 10:19
willingly *o.* themselves. *Neh* 11:2
day they *o.* great sacrifices. 12:43
hast *o.* a meat offering. *Isa* 57:6
as if he *o.* swine's blood. 66:3
o. incense unto Baal. *Jer* 32:29
o. there their sacrifices. *Ezek* 20:28
cause the reproach *o.* *Dan* 11:18
have ye *o.* to me sacrifices and offerings? *Amos* 5:25
o. a sacrifice to Lord. *Jonah* 1:16
every place incense be *o.* *Mal* 1:11
Simon *o.* them money. *Acts* 8:18
abstain from meats *o.* to idols. 15:29; 21:25
an offering should be *o.* for. 21:26
things *o.* unto idols. *1 Cor* 8:1, 4, 7 10; 10:19, 28
if I be *o.* on the service. *Phil* 2:17
am now ready to be *o.* *2 Tim* 4:6
he had *o.* up prayers. *Heb* 5:7
this he did once, when he *o.* 7:27
not without blood, which he *o.* 9:7
were *o.* gifts. 9
o. himself without spot to God. 14
Christ was once *o.* to bear the. 28
by faith Abel *o.* to God a more. 11:4
Abraham, when tried, *o.* up. 17
justified by works when he *o.* *Jas* 2:21

offereth
priest that *o.* it for sin. *Lev* 6:26
be imputed to him that *o.* it. 7:18
for he *o.* the bread of thy God 21:8
whoso *o.* praise glorifieth. *Ps* 50:23
he that *o.* oblation as if. *Isa* 66:3

offering
(*From earliest times in all known peoples and races, a sacrifice, generally by fire, was held to be pleasing to the God they worshipped, whether a heathen*

divinity or the true God. Sacrifices were, therefore, not originated by the Israelites, but regulated for them by the law. They were public, as the regular sacrifices of the tabernacle or temple, or were private, as expressive of thanks for some blessing or sorrow for some sin. As the laws of the sacrifices occupy practically the whole of Leviticus and are touched upon in other books also, the details are too long for a concordance, and should be studied in a Bible Dictionary)
Cain brought an *o.* unto. *Gen* 4:3
respect to Abel and to his *o.* 4
o. of every man, take my *o. Ex* 25:2
o. which ye shall take. 3; 35:5
an half shekel shall be the *o.* 30:13
an *o.* to the Lord to make. 15
ye shall bring your *o.* of. *Lev* 1:2
o. to Lord be of fowls. 14
o. of fine flour. 2:1
no meat *o.* shall be made. 11
his hand on the head of his *o.* 3:2, 8
lamb for his *o.* 7; *Num* 6:14
and if his *o.* be a goat. *Lev* 3:12
4:23, 28
o. of Aaron and of his sons. 6:20
o. be a vow, or a voluntary *o.* 7:16
an *o.* of jealousy, an *o. Num* 5:15
princes offered their *o.* before. 7:10
offer their *o.* each prince on his. 11
Levites before the Lord for an *o.*
8:11, 21
o. of the Lord in his appointed. 9:13
respect not thou their *o.* 16:15
kick ye at mine *o.*? *1 Sam* 2:29
purged with sacrifice nor *o.* 3:14
stirred thee up against me, let him accept an *o.* 26:19
o. of evening sacrifice. *1 Ki* 18:29
bring an *o.* and come. *1 Chr* 16:29
Ps 96:8
Israel shall bring the *o. Neh* 10:39
I have not caused thee to serve with an *o.* *Isa* 43:23
make his soul an *o.* for sin. 53:10
your brethren for an *o.* 66:20
provocation of their *o. Ezek* 20:28
my dispersed bring my *o. Zeph* 3:10
nor will I accept an *o. Mal* 1:10
an *o.*: should I accept this? 13
that he regardeth not the *o.* 2:13
offer to the Lord an *o.* in. 3:3
the *o.* up of Gentiles. *Rom* 15:16
o. and a sacrifice to God. *Eph* 5:2
o. thou wouldest not. *Heb* 10:5, 8
through the *o.* of the body of. 10
by one *o.* he hath perfected for. 14
there is no more *o.* for sin. 18
see **burnt** *offering*, **free** *offering*, **meat** *offerings*, **burnt, drink, fire, free, made, make**

offering, *verb*
as Samuel was *o.* the. *1 Sam* 7:10
David made an end of *o.*
2 Sam 6:18; *1 Chr* 16:2
Jehu had made an end of *o.*
2 Ki 10:25
o. according to commandment of Moses. *2 Chr* 8:13
made an end of *o.*, the king. 29:29
seven days, *o.* peace offerings. 30:22
of Aaron were busied in *o.* 35:14
priests *o.* willingly for the. *Ezra* 7:16
me to anger in *o.* to Baal. *Jer* 11:17
and *o.* him vinegar. *Luke* 23:36
every priest *o.* often the. *Heb* 10:11

heave **offering**
shoulder of the *heave o. Ex* 29:27
oblation for an *heave o. Lev* 7:14
offer up an *heave o. Num* 15:19, 20
of first of dough give an *heave o.* 21
they offer as an *heave o.* 18:24
Lord's *heave o.* to Aaron. 28
to Eleazar for an *heave o.* of. 31:29
which was the Lord's *heave o.* 41
see **burnt** *offering*

peace **offering**
sacrifice of *peace o. Lev* 3:1, 3, 6, 9

sin **offering**
shalt thou burn, it is a *sin o. Ex* 29:14
Lev 4:21, 24; 5:9, 11, 12
the blood of the *sin o. Ex* 30:10
bullock without blemish for a *sin o.*
Lev 4:3; 16:3, 27; *Num* 8:8
priest shall take of the blood of *sin o.*
Lev 4:25; 5:9
hand on the head of the *sin o.*, slay the *sin o.* in the place. 4:29, 33
a lamb for a *sin o.* 32; *Num* 6:14
a kid of goats for a *sin o. Lev* 5:6
9:3; 16:5, 15, 27; 23:19
which is for the *sin o.* first. 5:8
bring fine flour for a *sin o.* 11
is the law of the *sin o.* 6:25; 7:37
as the *sin o.* is, so is. 7:7; 14:13
thee a young calf for a *sin o.* 9:2
sought goat of the *sin o.* 10:16
why have ye not eaten *sin o.* in? 17
a turtle dove for a *sin o.* 12:6
fat of the *sin o.* shall be. 16:25
kid of the goats for a *sin o. Num* 7:16
22, 28; 15:24; 28:15; 29:5
sin o. should be made. *2 Chr* 29:24
he goats for a *sin o. Ezra* 8:35
sin o. hast thou not required. *Ps* 40:6
a bullock for a *sin o. Ezek* 43:19
day offer a kid for a *sin o.* 22
every day a goat for a *sin o.* 25
he shall offer his *sin o.* 44:27
meat offering and *sin o.* 29
where priest shall boil *sin o.* 46:20

trespass **offering**
shall bring his *trespass o. Lev* 5:6
without blemish for *trespass o.* 15
atonement with the ram of the *trespass o.* 16, 18; 6:6; 19:21, 22
in the day of his *trespass o.* 6:5
law of *trespass o.* 7:37
he lamb for *trespass o.* 14:12
21, 24, 25; *Num* 6:12
trespass o. is most holy. *Lev* 14:13
any wise return him a *trespass o.*
1 Sam 6:3
shall be the *trespass o.*? 4, 8, 17
two tables to slay the *trespass o.* on.
Ezek 40:39; 42:13
eat the *trespass o.* and every. 44:29
priests shall boil *trespass o.* 46:20

wave **offering**
wave them for a *wave o. Ex* 29:24
26; *Lev* 7:30; 8:27, 29; 9:21
10:15; 14:12, 24; 23:20
Num 6:20
the breast of the *wave o. Ex* 29:27
sheaf of the *wave o. Lev* 23:15

wood **offering**
cast lots for the *wood o. Neh* 10:34
wood o. at times appointed. 13:31

offerings
if his *o.* be of the flocks. *Lev* 1:10
o. thou shalt offer salt. 2:13
with chief of all the *o. 1 Sam* 2:29
no dew nor fields of *o. 2 Sam* 1:21
people brought in the *o. 2 Chr* 31:12
the priests for passover, *o.* 35:8, 9
other holy *o.* sod they in pots. 13
should bring the firstfruits of *o.*
Neh 10:37; 12:44
remember all thy *o. Ps* 20:3
with *o.* and incense. *Jer* 41:5
will I require your *o. Ezek* 20:40
sacrifice flesh for mine *o. Hos* 8:13
me *o.* forty years? *Amos* 5:25
o. of Judah and Jerusalem. *Mal* 3:4
robbed thee? in tithes and *o.* 8
cast in unto the *o. Luke* 21:4
bring alms to my nation and *o.*
Acts 24:17
see **burnt, drink, free**
made by **fire**

heave **offerings**
charge of mine *heave o. Num* 18:8
shall bring your *heave o. Deut* 12:6

offerings *of the Lord*
men abhorred the *o. of the Lord.*
1 Sam 2:17

peace **offerings**
shalt sacrifice thereon thy *peace o.*
Ex 20:24
sacrificed *peace o.* of oxen. 24:5
heave offering of *peace o. Ex* 29:28
people brought *peace o.* and. 32:6
from the bullock of *peace o. Lev* 4:10
as fat of *peace o.* 26, 31, 35; 6:12
law of sacrifice of *peace o.* 7:11
13, 37
and a ram for *peace o.* 9:4, 18
out of the sacrifice of *peace o.* 10:14
offer them for *peace o.* 17:5; 23:19
offer a sacrifice of *peace o.* 19:5
22:21
a lamb for *peace o. Num* 6:14
a ram for *peace o.* 17
peace o., two oxen, five lambs.
7:17, 23, 29, 35, 41; 29:39
sacrifice of your *peace o.* 10:10
Joshua sacrificed *peace o. Josh* 8:31
offer *peace o.*, let the Lord. 22:23
all Israel offered *peace o.*
Judg 20:26; 21:4
I will come and offer *peace o.*
1 Sam 10:8; 11:15
David offered *peace o. 2 Sam* 6:17
24:25; *1 Chr* 21:26
Solomon offered *peace o. 1 Ki* 3:15
8:63; 9:25
appointed priests for *peace o.*
2 Chr 31:2
Manasseh offered *peace o.* 33:16
I have *peace o.* with me. *Pr* 7:14
peace o. to make reconciliation.
Ezek 45:15, 17
priest prepare *peace o.* 46:2
prince his *peace o.* 12
not regard *peace o.* of. *Amos* 5:22

sin **offerings**
sin o. to make an. *Neh* 10:33

thank **offerings**
bring *thank o.* to house. *2 Chr* 29:31
sacrificed thereon *thank o.* 33:16

wave **offerings**
all the *wave o.* I have. *Num* 18:11

wine **offerings**
wine o. to be pleasing. *Hos* 9:4

office
me he restored to mine *o. Gen* 41:13
do the *o.* of a midwife. *Ex* 1:16
to the *o.* of Eleazar. *Num* 4:16*
they waited on their *o. 1 Chr* 6:32
ordain in their set *o.* 9:22
chief porters were in their set *o.* 26
brought to the king's *o. 2 Chr* 24:11
in their set *o.* they sanctified. 31:18
o. was to distribute to. *Neh* 13:13*
let another take his *o. Ps* 109:8
near to do *o.* of priest. *Ezek* 44:13
I magnify mine *o. Rom* 11:13*
have not the same *o.* 12:4
if a man desire the *o. 1 Tim* 3:1
the *o.* of a deacon. 10*, 13
who receive the *o.* of the. *Heb* 7:5

priest's **office**
minister to me in the *priest's o.*
Ex 28:1, 3, 4, 41; 29:1, 44; 30:30
35:19; 40:13, 15; *Lev* 7:35
16:32*; *Num* 3:3
priest's o. shall be theirs. *Ex* 29:9*
in the *priest's o.* 31:10; 39:41
ministered in *priest's o. Num* 3:4*
thy sons keep your *priest's o.* 18:7*
son ministered in the *priest's o.*
Deut 10:6
executed *priest's o.* in. *1 Chr* 6:10
cast them off from executing *priest's o.* *2 Chr* 11:14
while Zacharias executed the *priest's o.* *Luke* 1:8

officer
Potiphar an *o.* of Pharaoh.
Gen 37:36; 39:1
and Zebul his *o.*? *Judg* 9:28
Nathan, was the principal *o. 1 Ki* 4:5
Geber, son of Uri, was the only *o.* 19
Ahab called an *o.* and said. 22:9
king appointed an *o.* to. *2 Ki* 8:6
Nebuzaradan took an *o.* out. 25:19
judge deliver thee to the *o.* and the *o.* cast. *Mat* 5:25; *Luke* 12:58

officers
wroth with two of his *o. Gen* 40:2
Joseph asked Pharaoh's *o.* Why? 7
let Pharaoh appoint *o.* over. 41:34*

the o. of Israel cried to. Ex 5:15
the o. did see that they were in. 19
gather unto me the o. Num 11:16
Deut 31:28
I made them o. among. Deut 1:15
judges and o. shalt thou. 16:18
the o. shall speak to the. 20:5, 8
and give to his o. 1 Sam 8:15
Nathan, over the o. 1 Ki 4:5
Solomon had twelve o. over. 7
place where the o. were. 28
chief of Solomon's o. 5:16; 9:23
Jehoiada commanded o. 2 Ki 11:15*
appointed o. over the house. 18
2 Chr 23:18
went out with his o. 2 Ki 24:12
the o. and mighty men carried. 15
six thousand were o. 1 Chr 23:4
Chenaniah and his sons were for o.
26:29
Solomon's o. 250 that. 2 Chr 8:10
the Levites shall be o. before. 19:11
the o. of the king helped. Esth 9:3*
I will make thine o. peace. Isa 60:17
be o. in the house of. Jer 29:26
the chief priests sent o. John 7:32
the o. answered, Never man. 46
Judas having received o. 18:3
o. took Jesus. 12
one of the o. struck Jesus. 22
the o. found them not in. Acts 5:22

offices

into one of the priests' o. 1 Sam 2:36
priests according to o. 1 Chr 24:3*
waited on their o. 2 Chr 7:6
my good deeds for o. Neh 13:14*

offscouring

hast made us as the o. Lam 3:45
are the o. of all things. 1 Cor 4:13

offspring

thy o. as the grass of. Job 5:25
their o. is established before. 21:8
and his o. shall not be satisfied. 27:14
yea, let my o. be rooted out. 31:8*
hang on him the o. and. Isa 22:24
my blessing upon thine o. 44:3
the o. of thy bowels like the. 48:19
o. shall be known among the. 61:9
seed of the blessed, and o. 65:23
are also his o. Acts 17:28, 29
I am the Root and the O. Rev 22:16

oft

as o. as he passed by. 2 Ki 4:8
how o. cometh their destruction?
Job 21:17
how o. did they provoke him. Ps 78:40
the Pharisees fast o.? Mat 9:14
for o. times he falleth into the fire,
and o. into. 17:15; Mark 9:22
o. shall my brother sin? Mat 18:21
except they wash o. eat not. Mark 7:3
I punished them o. in. Acts 26:11
do ye as o. as ye drink. 1 Cor 11:25
in deaths o. 2 Cor 11:23
for he o. refreshed me. 2 Tim 1:16
up rain that cometh o. Heb 6:7

often

that being o. reproved. Pr 29:1
feared the Lord spake o. Mal 3:16
how o. would I have gathered thy.
Mat 23:37; Luke 13:34
o. bound with fetters. Mark 5:4
disciples of John fast o.? Luke 5:33
for as o. as ye eat this. 1 Cor 11:26
journeyings o., in perils. 2 Cor 11:26
watchings o., in fastings o. 27
of whom I have told you o. Phil 3:18
a little wine for thine o. infirmities.
1 Tim 5:23
should offer himself o. Heb 9:25
then he must o. have suffered. 26
to smite the earth as o. Rev 11:6

oftener

Felix sent for him o. Acts 24:26

oftentimes

worketh God o. with. Job 33:29
o. also thine own heart. Eccl 7:22
for o. it had caught him. Luke 8:29
for Jesus o. resorted. John 18:2
that o. I purposed to. Rom 1:13
have o. proved diligent. 2 Cor 8:22
and o. offering the same. Heb 10:11

Og

to them as he did to O. Deut 31:4
heard what you did to O. Josh 2:10
the cities of O. pertaining. 13:21
in the country of O. 1 Ki 4:19
see **Bashan**

oil

The most common oil in use was that made from the olive berry. This was used [1] *as food,* Ex 29:2. [2] *As a cosmetic, for anointing the body after a bath,* etc., Ps 104:15. [3] *Medicinal, as referred to in* Isa 1:6; Luke 10:34; Jas 5:14. [4] *For light,* Ex 27:20. [5] *Ritual, in the anointing of kings and priests,* Lev 8:12. [6] *In offerings.*

Jacob poured o. Gen 28:18; 35:14
take o. for the light. Ex 25:6
35:14; 39:37
tempered with o. 29:2, 40
shalt make it an o. of holy. 30:25
pour o. upon it. Lev 2:1, 6
flour mingled with o. 4, 5; 14:10
21; 23:13; Num 6:15; 7:13, 19
25, 31, 37, 43, 49, 55, 61, 67, 73, 79
8:8; 28:13; 29:3, 9, 14
thy meat offering put o. upon it.
Lev 2:15; 6:21
shall burn part of the o. 2:16
he shall put no o. on it. 5:11
Num 5:15
meat offering mingled with o.
Lev 7:10; 9:4; 14:10
shall offer cakes mingled with o.
7:12; Num 6:15
his right finger in the o. Lev 14:16
rest of the o. that is in. 17, 18, 29
all the o. vessels. Num 4:9
was as the taste of fresh o. 11:8
fourth part of an hin of o. 15:4
third part of an hin of o. 6
o. for one bullock, and o. 28:12
not anoint thyself with o. Deut 28:40
2 Sam 14:2; Mi 6:15
made him suck o. out of the flinty
rock. Deut 32:13
let Asher be acceptable, ... and dip
his foot in o. 33:24
Samuel took a vial of o. 1 Sam 10:1
horn with o. and go. 16:1, 13
priest took an horn of o. 1 Ki 1:39
Hiram twenty measures of o. 5:11
o. in a cruse. 17:12
nor cruse of o. fail. 14, 16
house save a pot of o. 2 Ki 4:2
the o. stayed. 6
go sell the o. and pay thy debt. 7
box of o. go to Ramoth-gilead. 9:1, 3
he poured the o. on his head. 6
over the cellars of o. 1 Chr 27:28
gave drink and o. to them. Ezra 3:7
with o. of myrrh. Esth 2:12
which make o. within. Job 24:11
poured me out rivers of o. 29:6
my head with o. Ps 23:5
words were softer than o. 55:21
and o. to make his face. 104:15
come like o. into his bones. 109:18
kindness, an excellent o. 141:5
is smoother than o. Pr 5:3
and o. in the dwelling of. 21:20
to give to them the o. of joy. Isa 61:3
we have treasures of o. Jer 41:8
flour, honey, and o. Ezek 16:13, 19
hast set mine o. and incense. 18
Judah traded in honey and o. 27:17
their rivers to run like o. 32:14
ordinance of o., bath of o. 45:14
ephah for a ram, an hin of o. 24
give me my bread and o. Hos 2:5
Assyrians, and o. is carried. 12:1
with 10,000 rivers of o.? Mi 6:7
empty the golden o. out. Zech 4:12
the foolish took no o. Mat 25:3
the wise took o. 4
give us of your o. 8
my head with o. thou. Luke 7:46
an hundred measures of o. 16:6
see **anointed, anointing, beaten, log**

wine with **oil**

best of the o. and w. Num 18:12
bless thy w. and thy o. Deut 7:13
gather thy w. and o. 11:14
tithe of thy w. and o. 12:17; 14:23
the firstfruits of w. and o. 18:4
2 Chr 31:5
not leave thee either w. or o.
Deut 28:51
oversee the w. and o. 1 Chr 9:29
nigh brought w. and o. 12:40
20,000 baths of w. and o.
2 Chr 2:10, 15
in strong holds o. and w. 11:11
storehouses for w. and o. 32:28
give w. and o. according. Ezra 6:9
of w. and 100 baths of o. 7:22
restore w. and o. that ye. Neh 5:11
firstfruits of w. and o. 10:37
offering of the corn, new w. and o. 39
tithes of corn, new w. and o. 13:5, 12
that loveth w. and o. shall not be
rich. Pr 21:17
to Lord for w. and o. Jer 31:12
w. and summer fruits and o. 40:10
drought on new w. and o. Hag 1:11
touch bread, w. or o. shall? 2:12
poured in o. and w. Luke 10:34
hurt not the w. and the o. Rev 6:6
no man buyeth their w. and o. 18:13

oiled

one cake of o. bread. Ex 29:23
Lev 8:26

oil olive

pure o. *olive* beaten for. Ex 27:20
unto thee of o. *olive* an hin. 30:24
unto thee pure o. *olive*. Lev 24:2
land of o. *olive*, and honey.
Deut 8:8; 2 Ki 18:32

oil tree

wilderness, the o. *tree*. Isa 41:19

ointment

(*This word often means oil and is so put in the Revisions*)

make oil of holy o. and o. Ex 30:25*
house of his precious things and
precious o. 2 Ki 20:13; Isa 39:2
the o. of the spices. 1 Chr 9:30*
sea to boil like pot of o. Job 41:31
it is like the precious o. Ps 133:2
o. and perfume rejoice. Pr 27:9
the o. of his right hand. 16
is better than precious o. Eccl 7:1
and let thy head lack no o. 9:8
dead flies cause the o. of. 10:1
thy name is as o. poured. S of S 1:3
nor mollified with o. Isa 1:6
thou wentest to the king with o. 57:9
a box of precious o. Mat 26:7
Mark 14:3; Luke 7:37
o. might have been sold for much.
Mat 26:9; John 12:5
hath poured out this o. Mat 26:12
waste of the o. made? Mark 14:4
his feet with o. Luke 7:38, 46
anointed the Lord with o. John 11:2
o. and anointed the feet of Jesus,
house ... odour of the o. 12:3

ointments

savour of thy good o. S of S 1:3
the smell of thine o. is better. 4:10
anoint themselves with the chief o.
Amos 6:6
prepared spices and o. Luke 23:56
their odours and o. Rev 18:13

old

Noah was 500 years o. Gen 5:32
Noah was 600 years o. when. 7:6
Shem was 100 years o. and. 11:10
Abraham 75 years o. when. 12:4
a ram of three years o. 15:9
Abram was fourscore and six years
o. when Hagar bare. 16:16
he that is eight days o. shall. 17:12
that is an hundred years o. 17
Abraham 99 years o. when. 24
Ishmael thirteen years o. when. 25
Abraham and Sarah were o. 18:11
waxed o. my lord being o. also. 12
of surety bear a child, who am o.? 13
compassed the house, o. and. 19:4
our father is o. 31
Isaac being eight days o. 21:4
Abraham 100 years o. 5

Sarah was 127 years o. Gen 23:1
Abraham was o. 24:1
Isaac 40 years o. when took. 25:20
Isaac was 60 years o. when she. 26
Esau forty years o. when he. 26:34
when Isaac was o., he called Esau. 27:1, 2; 35:29
Joseph being 17 years o. was. 37:2
Pharaoh said to Jacob, How o.? 47:8
couched as an o. lion, who. 49:9
Joseph died, being 110 years o. 50:26
Moses was eighty years o. and Aaron eighty-three years o. when. Ex 7:7
our young and our o. with sons. 10:9
are numbered from twenty years o. 30:14; 38:26; Num 1:3, 18; 14:29 1 Chr 23:27; 2 Chr 25:5; 31:17 Ezra 3:8
it is an o. leprosy in the. Lev 13:11
shall eat o. fruit. 25:22
shall eat o. store. 26:10
the male from 20 years o. even. 27:3
from five even to twenty years o. 5
month o. to five years o. 6
male, from a month o. Num 3:15 22, 28, 34, 39, 40, 43
from thirty years o. to fifty. 4:3 23:20; 1 Chr 23:3
Levites from 25 years o. Num 8:24
redeemed, from month o. 18:16
23,000 from month o. and. 26:62
Aaron was 123 years old. 33:39
thy raiment waxed not o. Deut 8:4 29:5; Neh 9:21
not regard the person of the o. Deut 28:50
I am 120 years o. this day. 31:2
Moses was an 120 years o. 34:7
eat of the o. corn. Josh 5:11, 12
men and women, young and o. 6:21
they took o. sacks. 9:4
o. shoes on their feet. 5, 13
Joshua was o. and. 13:1; 23:1, 2
forty years o. was I, when. 14:7
this day eighty-five years o. 10
Joshua died, being 110 years o. 24:29; Judg 2:8
too o. to have a husband. Ruth 1:12
now Eli was very o. 1 Sam 2:22
Eli was ninety and eight years o. 4:15
Samuel was o., he made. 8:1, 5; 12:2
Saul's son was forty years o. when. 2 Sam 2:10
lame, and five years o. 4:4
David thirty years o. when he. 5:4
now Barzillai was eighty years o. 19:32, 35
king David was o. 1 Ki 1:1, 15 1 Chr 23:1
Solomon was o. his wives. 1 Ki 11:4
dwelt an o. prophet in. 13:11
child, and her husband is o. 2 Ki 4:14
married when sixty years o. 1 Chr 2:21
males from three years o. and. 2 Chr 31:16
destroy all the Jews, young and o. Esth 3:13
wicked live, become o.? Job 21:7
am young, and ye are very o. 32:6
my bones waxed o. through. Ps 32:3
young, and now am o. 37:25
now when I am o. O God. 71:18
when o. he will not depart. Pr 22:6
remove not o. landmark. 23:10
thy mother when she is o. 22
wise child than an o. king. Eccl 4:13
pleasant fruits new and o. S of S 7:13
an heifer of three years o. Isa 15:5 Jer 48:34
young and o. naked. Isa 20:4
they shall wax o. as garment. 50:9
the o. waste places. 58:12; 61:4
child shall die 100 years o., but the sinner being 100 years o. 65:20
ask for the o. paths. Jer 6:16
thence o. clouts, o. rags. 38:11, 12
break in pieces young and o. 51:22
the young and o. lie on. Lam 2:21
my skin hath he made o. 3:4
slay utterly o. and young. Ezek 9:6
said to her that was o. in adulteries. 23:43
destroy it for o. hatred. Ezek 25:15
you after your o. estates. 36:11
kingdom, being 62 years o. Dan 5:31
with calves of year o. Mi 6:6
children from two years o. Mat 2:16
new cloth unto an o. garment. 9:16
new wine into o. bottles. 17 Mark 2:21, 22; Luke 5:36, 37
out of his treasure things new and o. Mat 13:52
Jesus twelve years o. Luke 2:42
for he saith, The o. is better. 5:39
one of the o. prophets is risen. 9:8
man be born when he is o.? John 3:4
thou art not yet fifty years o. 8:57
be o. another shall lead thee. 21:18
above forty years o. Acts 4:22
was full forty years o. 7:23
Mnason, an o. disciple. 21:16
went about 100 years o. Rom 4:19
purge out therefore the o. 1 Cor 5:7
the feast, not with o. leaven. 8
of the O. Testament. 2 Cor 3:14
o. things are passed away, all. 5:17
and o. wives' fables. 1 Tim 4:7
not taken under sixty years o. 5:9
he hath made the first o. That which decayeth and waxeth o. Heb 8:13
purged from his o. sins. 2 Pet 1:9
God spared not the o. world. 2:5
o. commandment is word. 1 John 2:7
o. serpent, called the devil. Rev 12:9
the dragon, that o. serpent. 20:2
see **wax**
days of **old**, *see of* **old**

old *age*

buried in a good o. age. Gen 15:15
Abraham a son of his o. age. 21:2, 7
Abraham died in a good o. age. 25:8
Joseph was the son of his o. age. 37:3; 44:20
Gideon died in a good o. age. Judg 8:32
nourisher in thine o. age. Ruth 4:15
Asa in o. age was. 1 Ki 15:23
David died in a good o. age, full of days and honour. 1 Chr 29:28
in whom o. age perished. Job 30:2
not off in the time of o. age. Ps 71:9
bring forth fruit in o. age. 92:14
to your o. age I am he. Isa 46:4
conceived a son in her o. age. Luke 1:36

old *gate, see* **gate**

old *man*

Abraham died an o. man. Gen 25:8
the o. man of whom ye spake? 43:27
we have a father, an o. man. 44:20
honour face of o. man. Lev 19:32
there came an o. man from his work. Judg 19:16
o. man said, Whither goest? 17, 20
spake to the o. man. 22
not be an o. man in thy house. 1 Sam 2:31, 32
Eli was an o. m. 4:18
Jesse was an o. m. 17:12
an o. man cometh up, and. 28:14
compassion on o. man. 2 Chr 36:17
nor o. man that hath not. Isa 65:20
I am an o. man, my wife. Luke 1:18
our o. man is crucified. Rom 6:6
put off the o. man which. Eph 4:22
ye have put off the o. man. Col 3:9

old *men*

Rehoboam consulted with the o. men. 1 Ki 12:6
forsook counsel of o. men. 8, 13 2 Chr 10:6, 8, 13
o. men and children. Ps 148:12
the crown of o. men. Pr 17:6
beauty of o. men is the grey. 20:29
dance, young men and o. Jer 31:13
hear this, ye o. men, and. Joel 1:2
o. men shall dream dreams. 2:28 Acts 2:17
o. men and women dwell. Zech 8:4

of **old**

of o., men of renown. Gen 6:4
those nations were of o. 1 Sam 27:8
Ham had dwelt there of o. 1 Chr 4:40
of o. there were chief. Neh 12:46
knowest thou not this of o.? Job 20:4
mercies have been ever of o. Ps 25:6
thou didst in the times of o. 44:1
even he that abideth of o. 55:19
heavens which were of o. 68:33
which hast purchased of o. 74:2
for God is my king of o. working. 12
I have considered the days of o. 77:5
remember thy wonders of o. 11
I will utter dark sayings of o. 78:2
thy throne is established of o. 93:2
of o. hast laid the foundation. 102:25
thy judgements of o. O Lord. 119:52
testimonies I have known of o. 152
I remember the days of o. 143:5 Isa 63:11
me before his works of o. Pr 8:22
counsels of o. are faithfulness and. Isa 25:1
for Tophet is ordained of o. 30:33
consider the things of o. 43:18
former things of o.: I am God. 46:9
awake, as in generations of o. 51:9
not I held my peace even of o.? 57:11
carried them all the days of o. 63:9
prophets before me and thee of o. Jer 28:8
Lord hath appeared of o. to. 31:3
be inhabited as in days of o. 46:26
she had in the days of o. Lam 1:7
he commanded in days of o. 2:17
as they that be dead of o. 3:6
Lord, renew our days as of o. 5:21
down with people of o. Ezek 26:20
build it as in days of o. Amos 9:11
forth have been from of o. Mi 5:2
in Bashan, as in the days of o. 7:14
to our fathers from the days of o. 20
Nineveh is of o. like a pool. Nah 2:8
pleasant to the Lord, as in the days of o. Mal 3:4
the heavens were of o. 2 Pet 3:5
who were of o. ordained to. Jude 4

old *time*

giants dwelt there in o. time. Deut 2:20
o. time set in thy inheritance. 19:14
fathers dwelt on other side in o. time. Josh 24:2
to speak in o. time. 2 Sam 20:18
moved sedition of o. time. Ezra 4:15
been already of o. time. Eccl 1:10
of o. time I have broken. Jer 2:20
bring thee down with people of o. time. Ezek 26:20
I have spoken in o. time. 38:17
said by them of o. time. Mat 5:21 27, 33
Moses of o. time hath. Acts 15:21
in o. time holy women. 1 Pet 3:5
prophecy came not in o. time by man. 2 Pet 1:21

old *way*

o. way which wicked men. Job 22:15

oldness

should not serve in o. of. Rom 7:6

olive

(Olives are one of the most common trees of Palestine, and the uses of the tree are many. The tree is often used as a figure for Israel)

in mouth was an o. leaf. Gen 8:11
for thine o. shall cast. Deut 28:40
the mount, and fetch o. Neh 8:15
off his flower as the o. Job 15:33
children like o. plants. Ps 128:3
the labour of the o. shall. Hab 3:17
be these two o. branches? Zech 4:12
can fig tree, my brethren, bear o. berries? Jas 3:12
see **oil**

olives

foxes burnt up the vineyards and o. Judg 15:5
shalt tread the o. but shalt. Mi 6:15
see **mount**

Olivet

by ascent to mount O. 2 Sam 15:30
returned from the mount called O. Acts 1:12

olive tree
beatest thine o. tree. Deut 24:20
o. tree, Reign over us. Judg 9:8
the o. tree said, Should I leave ? 9
two cherubims of o. tree. 1 Ki 6:23
he made doors of o. tree. 31, 32
posts of o. tree. 33
like a green o. tree in the. Ps 52:8
shaking of an o. tree. Isa 17:6; 24:13
thy name a green o. tree. Jer 11:16
shall be as the o. tree. Hos 14:6
as yet the o. tree hath not. Hag 2:19
of the fatness of o. tree. Rom 11:17
o. tree, graffed in a good o. tree. 24

wild **olive tree**
thou being wild o. tree. Rom 11:17

olive trees
o. trees which thou plantedst not. Deut 6:11
thou shalt have o. trees, but. 28:40
over the o. trees was Baal-hanan. 1 Chr 27:28
o. trees increased, palmer-. Amos 4:9
two o. trees by it on the. Zech 4:3
are the two o. trees. Rev 11:4

oliveyard
shalt thou do with thy o. Ex 23:11

oliveyards
and o. which ye planted not, do ye eat. Josh 24:13; Neh 9:25
king shall take your o. 1 Sam 8:14
to receive money and o.? 2 Ki 5:26
pray, to them their o. Neh 5:11

Olympas
salute Julia, O. and all. Rom 16:15

omitted
o. weightier matters. Mat 23:23*

omnipotent
Lord God o. reigneth. Rev 19:6*

Omri
all Israel made O. king. 1 Ki 16:16
half followed O. 21
but O. wrought evil. 25
Ahab son of O. did evil in the. 30
Athaliah daughter of O. 2 Ki 8:26
2 Chr 22:2
O. son of Becher. 1 Chr 7:8
O. son of Imri. 9:4
O. son of Michael. 27:18
for statutes of O. are kept. Mi 6:16

On
priest of O. Gen 41:45, 50; 46:20
O. the son of Peleth. Num 16:1

Onan
and called his name O. Gen 38:4
O. knew that the seed should. 9
sons of Judah, Er, O. 46:12
Num 26:19; 1 Chr 2:3
Er and O. died in the. Num 26:19

once
speak yet but this o. Gen 18:32
forgive my sin only this o. Ex 10:17
atonement . . . altar of incense o. a. 30:10; Lev 16:34; Heb 9:7, 12
let us go up at o. and. Num 13:30
not consume them at o. Deut 7:22
go round the city o. Josh 6:3, 11, 14
this o.: prove but this o. Judg 6:39
come up o. 16:18
strengthen me this o. 28
let me smite him to the earth at o. 1 Sam 26:8*
o. in three years came the navy of Tarshish. 1 Ki 10:22; 2 Chr 9:21
he saved himself not o. 2 Ki 6:10
o. in ten days all store of. Neh 5:18
merchants lodged o. or twice. 13:20
God speaks o., yea twice. Job 33:14
o. have I spoken, but I will. 40:5
God hath spoken o. Ps 62:11
down the carved work at o. 74:6
in sight when o. art angry ? 76:7
o. have I sworn by my. 89:35
perverse shall fall at o. Pr 28:18
destroy and devour at o. Isa 42:14
shall a nation be born at o.? 66:8
out the inhabitants at o. Jer 10:18*
be clean ? when shall it o. be ? 13:27
behold, I will o. cause. 16:21
yet o. it is a little while, and I will shake. Hag 2:6; Heb 12:26
when o. the master of. Luke 13:25
they cried all at o. saying. 23:18
died, he died unto sin o. Rom 6:10
I was alive without the law o. 7:9
above 500 brethren at o. 1 Cor 15:6
rods, o. was I stoned. 2 Cor 11:25
the faith he o. destroyed. Gal 1:23
let it not be o. named. Eph 5:3
ye sent o. and again to. Phil 4:16
have come to you o. 1 Thes 2:18
who were o. enlightened. Heb 6:4
this he did o. when he offered. 7:27*
but now o. in end of the world. 9:26*
it is appointed to men o. to die. 27
Christ was o. offered to bear sins. 28; 10:10
that the worshippers o. purged. 10:2
o. more signifieth the. 12:27
hath suffered o. for our. 1 Pet 3:18
o. longsuffering of God waited. 20
the faith o. delivered to. Jude 3*
though ye o. knew this. 5

one
[1] *One only, there being no other of that kind,* 1 Tim 2:5; Heb 10:14. [2] *The very same,* Gen 11:1; 40:5; 1 Sam 6:4. [3] *Some body, any one,* 2 Sam 23:15.

cleave to his wife, and they shall be o. flesh. Gen 2:24; Mat 19:5
Mark 10:8; 1 Cor 6:16
hast thou but o. blessing? Gen 27:38
not give our sister to o. that. 34:14
o. is not. 42:13, 32
o. went out from me. 44:28
yet will bring o. plague. Ex 11:1
in o. house shall it be eaten. 12:46
o. law shall be to him that is home-. 49; Lev 24:22; Num 15:16, 29
drive them out in o. year. Ex 23:29
every o. of the curtains shall have o. measure. 26:2; 36:9, 15
o. tabernacle. 26:6; 36:13
o. loaf of bread, o. cake, and o. 29:23
then he shall be guilty in o. of these. Lev 5:4, 5, 13
o. of your own country. 16:29; 17:15
bake your bread in o. oven. 26:26
if they blow but with o. Num 10:4
I have not taken o. ass. 16:15
o. rod shall be for the head. 17:3
of the tribe shall be wife to o. 36:8
I took twelve men, o. of. Deut 1:23
o. of these cities. 4:42; 19:5, 11
o. witness shall not rise up. 19:15
be free at home o. year. 24:5
should o. chase a thousand ? 32:30
Joshua took at o. time. Josh 10:42
Jericho o., the king of Ai o. 12:9
Jerusalem o., king of Hebron o. 10
but o. lot and o. portion ? 17:14
thou shalt not have o. lot only. 17
that o. reign over you ? Judg 9:2
what o. is there of the tribes ? 21:8
o. plague was on you all. 1 Sam 6:4
o., for Gaza o., for Askelon o. 17
and they came out with o. 11:7
son in law in o. of the twain. 18:21
what o. nation is like ? 2 Sam 7:23
with o. full line to keep alive. 8:2
there will not tarry o. with. 19:7
slew at o. time. 23:8; 1 Chr 11:11
O that o. would give me to drink. 2 Sam 23:15; 1 Chr 11:17
given me o. to sit on. 1 Ki 1:48
I ask o. petition of thee, deny. 2:16
were of o. measure, o. size. 6:25
there hath not failed o. word. 8:56
o. tribe to thy son. 11:13, 32, 36
prophets declare good to the king with o. mouth. 22:13; 2 Chr 18:12
carry thither o. of the. 2 Ki 17:27
o. of the priests came and. 28
will turn away face of o. captain. 18:24; Isa 36:9
for asking counsel of o. 1 Chr 10:13
o. of the least was over an. 12:14
worship before o. altar. 2 Chr 32:12
Hanani, o. of my brethren. Neh 1:2
bring o. of ten to dwell. 11:1
he cannot answer him o. Job 9:3
o. dieth in his full strength. 21:23
he is in o. mind, and who ? Job 23:13
if an interpreter o. among. 33:23
be not afraid when o. is. Ps 49:16
fall like o. of the princes. 82:7
I have laid help on o. that is. 89:19
sing us o. of the songs of Zion. 137:3
let us all have o. purse. Pr 1:14
is like o. that taketh a dog. 26:17
o. generation passeth away. Eccl 1:4
that o. event happeneth to. 2:14
yea, they have all o. breath. 3:19
all go unto o. place, all are. 20; 6:6
two better than o. 4:9
how can o. be warm ? 11
if o. prevail against him, two. 12
counting o. by o. to find out. 7:27
but o. sinner destroyeth much. 9:18
are given from o. shepherd. 12:11
with o. of thy eyes, with o. chain of thy neck. S of S 4:9
but o.; she is the only o. 6:9
vineyard shall yield o. bath. Isa 5:10
what shall o. answer messengers of nation ? 14:32
o. shall be called the city of. 19:18
to the days of o. king. 23:15
shall be gathered o. by o. 27:12
o. thousand shall flee at the rebuke of o. 30:17
no o. of these shall fail. 34:16
I have raised up o. from the. 41:25
I will give Jerusalem o. that. 27
o. shall say, I am the Lord's. 44:5
surely, shall o. say, in Lord. 45:24
o. saith, Destroy it not, a. 65:8
they four had o. likeness. Ezek 1:16
brought up o. of her whelps. 19:3
come forth out of o. land. 21:19
that they took both o. way. 23:13
that o. that had escaped. 33:21
Abraham was o.: we are many. 24
as a lovely song of o. 32
will set up o. shepherd. 34:23; 37:24
shall become o. in thy hand. 37:17
make them o. stick. 19
o. nation, o. king. 22
o. gate of Reuben. 48:31
o. gate of Joseph. 32
but o. decree for you. Dan 2:9
Daniel was astonied for o. hour. 4:19
o. like the Son of. 7:13; 10:16, 18
the covenant for o. week. 9:27
out of a branch shall o. stand. 11:7
o. shall certainly come and. 10
they shall speak lies at o. table. 27
Israel shall appoint themselves o. head. Hos 1:11
cities wandered to o. city. Amos 4:8
remain ten men in o. house. 6:9
the Lord with o. consent. Zeph 3:9
on o. stone shall be seven. Zech 3:9
three shepherds in o. month. 11:8
be o. Lord, and his name o. 14:9
did not he make o.? And wherefore o.? Mal 2:15
the voice of o. crying in. Mat 3:3
Mark 1:3; Luke 3:4; John 1:23
o. jot, or o. tittle shall not pass. Mat 5:18
whoso shall break o. of these. 19
that o. of thy members. 29, 30
canst not make o. hair white. 36
which of you can add o. cubit ? 6:27
was not arrayed like o. of these. 29
Luke 12:27
shall give to drink to o. Mat 10:42
you shall have o. sheep ? 12:11
Elias; and Jeremias, or o. of. 16:14
Mark 6:15; 8:28; Luke 9:8, 19
o. for thee, o. for Moses, and o. for. Mat 17:4; Mark 9:5; Luke 9:33
shall offend o. of these. Mat 18:6
Mark 9:42; Luke 17:2
heed ye despise not o. Mat 18:10
o. of these little ones should. 14
if not hear, then take with thee o. 16
none good but o. 19:17; Mark 10:18
Luke 18:19
last have wrought but o. hour. Mat 20:12
they beat o. and killed another. 21:35
went their ways, o. to his farm. 22:5
they will not move them with o. of their fingers. 23:4; Luke 11:46

for o. is your Master. Mat 23:8, 10
o. is your Father. 9
he gave to o. five talents, to. 25:15
he that had received the o. 18, 24
as ye have done it to o. 40
did it not to o. of the least. 45
o. of you shall betray me. 26:21
Mark 14:18; John 13:21
could ye not watch with me o. hour?
Mat 26:40; Mark 14:37
they more than o. loaf. Mark 8:14
whoever shall receive o. of. 9:37
o. casting out devils. 38; Luke 9:49
ask of you o. question. Mark 11:29
having yet o. son, he sent him. 12:6
to say, o. by o., Is it I? 14:19
at the feast he released o. 15:6
Luke 23:17
o. mightier than I. Luke 3:16
I say to o., Go, and he goeth. 7:8
he had o. only daughter, and. 8:42
there shall be five in o. house. 12:52
joy in heaven over o. 15:7, 10
to pass, than o. tittle of the. 16:17
if o. went from the dead. 30, 31
to see o. of the days of the 17:22
sell his garment, and buy o. 22:36
standeth o. among you. John 1:26
o. of you is a devil. 6:70
have done o. work. 7:21
went out o. by o. beginning at. 8:9
I am o. that bear witness of. 18
they said, We have o. Father 41
be o. fold, and o. shepherd. 10:16
I and my Father are o. 30
in o. the children of God 11:52
he hath o. that judgeth him. 12:48
that they may be o. 17:11, 21, 22
they may be made perfect in o. 23
thou not o. of this man's? 18:17, 25
o. be ordained to be. Acts 1:22
of o. heart and of o. soul. 4:32
go and enquire for o. Saul of. 9:11
there cometh o. after me. 13:25
there is another king, o. Jesus. 17:7
God hath made of o. blood all. 26
except it be for this o. voice. 24:21
had questions of o. Jesus. 25:19
Paul had spoken o. word. 28:25
for a righteous man will o. die.
Rom 5:7
for if through the offence of o. 15
by o. that sinned, for the judgement was by o. to condemnation. 16
death reigned by o.; . . . they shall reign in life by o., Jesus Christ. 17
by the offence of o.; . . . even so by the righteousness of o. 18
so by obedience of o. shall many. 19
Rebekah also had conceived by o.
9:10
o. saith, I am of Paul. 1 Cor 3:4
planteth and that watereth are o. 8
such fornication, that o. have. 5:1
there is none other God but o. 8:4
but o. God, and o. Lord Jesus. 6
all run, but o. receiveth the. 9:24
are o. bread and o. body. 10:17
o. is hungry. 11:21
to o. is given by the Spirit the. 12:8
o. Spirit are baptized into o. body. 13
o. that believeth not, or o. 14:24
let o. interpret. 27
for ye may all prophesy o. by o. 31
was seen of me as of o. born. 15:8
if o. died for all, then. 2 Cor 5:14
I have espoused you to o. 11:2
received I forty stripes save o. 24
of good comfort, be of o. mind.
13:11; Phil 2:2; 1 Pet 3:8
Rev 17:13
but as of o., And to thy seed, which is Christ. Gal 3:16
ye are all o. in Christ. 28
law is fulfilled in o. word. 5:14
gather together in o. all things.
Eph 1:10
who hath made both o. 2:14
o. new man. 15
both have access by o. Spirit. 18
as ye are called in o. hope of. 4:4
o. faith, o. Lord, o. baptism. 5
o. God and Father of all. 6
with o. spirit, with o. Phil 1:27

the husband of o. wife. 1 Tim 3:2
Tit 1:6
bishop, o. that ruleth well. 1 Tim 3:4
be the husbands of o. wife. 12
o. of themselves, even a. Tit 1:12
but o. in a certain place. Heb 2:6
that are sanctified are all of o. 11
ye have need that o. teach you. 5:12
but this man after he had offered o. sacrifice. 10:12
by o. offering he hath perfected. 14
sprang there even of o. so. 11:12
for o. morsel of meat sold. 12:16
no city, but we seek o. to. 13:14
yet offend in o. point, he is. Jas 2:10
if any err, and o. convert him. 5:19
these three are o. 1 John 5:7
these agree in o. 8
o. woe is past, there. Rev 9:12
o. of his heads as wounded. 13:3
on the cloud o. sat like unto. 14:14
power as kings o. hour. 17:12
in o. hour is thy judgement. 18:10
in o. hour so great riches come. 17
that great city, for in o. hour. 19
several gate was of o. pearl. 21:21
see **accord, another, day, every, God, heart, little, man, mighty, people**

as one

man is become *as* o. of us. Gen 3:22
seemed *as* o. that mocked. 19:14
Dan shall judge *as* o. of the. 49:16
shall be *as* o. that is born in the land.
Ex 12:48; Lev 19:34; 24:22
let her not be *as* o. dead. Num 12:12
Gibeon a great city, *as* o. Josh 10:2
young man was to him *as* o. of his.
Judg 17:11
this Philistine shall be *as* o. of them.
1 Sam 17:36
as when o. doth hunt a partridge.
26:20
uncovered *as* o. of the. 2 Sam 6:20
he shall eat at my table *as* o. 9:11
thou shalt be *as* o. of the fools. 13:13
the king speaketh this *as* o. 14:13
not be left so much *as* o. 17:12
as o. was felling a beam. 2 Ki 6:5
and singers were *as* o. 2 Chr 5:13
speakest *as* o. of the foolish women.
Job 2:10
I am *as* o. mocked of his. 12:4
he counteth me to him *as* o. of. 19:11
as o. that mourneth for. Ps 35:14
then the Lord awaked *as* o. 78:65
hast broken Rahab, *as* o. 89:10
I rejoice *as* o. that findeth. 119:162
thy poverty *as* o. that. Pr 6:11; 24:3
as the o. dieth, so dieth. Eccl 3:19
for why should I be *as* o.? S of S 1:7
then was I in his eyes *as* o. 8:10
as o. that gathereth eggs. Isa 10:14
thy voice *as* o. that hath a. 29:4
as o. whom his mother. 66:13
I will break *as* o. breaketh. Jer 19:11
mourn *as* o. in bitterness. Zech 12:10
as o. having authority. Mat 7:29
Mark 1:22
or *as* o. of the prophets. Mark 6:15
he was *as* o. dead. 9:26
as o. of thy hired servants. Luke 15:19
as o. that perverteth the people. 23:14
as o. that hath obtained. 1 Cor 7:25
so fight I, not *as* o. that. 9:26

is one

the people *is* o. Gen 11:6
the dream *is* o. 41:25, 26
this *is* o. of the Hebrew. Ex 2:6
the Lord our God *is* o. Lord.
Deut 6:4; Mark 12:29
Boaz *is* o. of our next. Ruth 2:20
in this place *is* o. greater. Mat 12:6
it *is* o. of the twelve. Mark 14:20
he is not a Jew that *is* o. Rom 2:28
a Jew who *is* o. inwardly. 29
seeing it *is* o. God who shall. 3:30
unto the Lord *is* o. spirit. 1 Cor 6:17
as body *is* o. and hath many. 12:12
glory of the celestial *is* o. and. 15:40
not a mediator of one, but God *is* o.
Gal 3:20
who *is* o. of you. Col 4:9, 12

not one

if they give *not* thee o. Gen 24:41
remained *not* o. Ex 8:31; 10:19
cattle of Israel died *not* o. 9:6, 7
where there was *not* o. dead. 12:30
shall *not* o. of these men. Deut 1:35
was *not* o. city too strong for. 2:36
is *not* o. of them left. 2 Sam 13:30
there be *not* o. small stone. 17:13
he left him *not* o. that. 1 Ki 16:11
out of an unclean, *not* o. Job 14:4
and did *not* o. fashion us in? 31:15
shall *not* o. be cast down at the? 41:9
there is none that doeth good, *not* o.
Ps 14:3; 53:3; Rom 3:12
was *not* o. feeble person. Ps 105:37
strong in power, *not* o. Isa 40:26
take heed ye despise *not* o. of these little ones. Mat 18:10
none righteous, no *not* o. Rom 3:10
no *not* o. that shall be able. 1 Cor 6:5
for the body is *not* o. member. 12:14

one in reference to *other*

o. was Adah, of *other* Zillah. Gen 4:19
the o. from the *other*. 13:11
o. end of Egypt to the *other*. 47:21
o. Shiphrah, of the *other*. Ex 1:15
o. came not near the *other*. 14:20
hands on o. side, and the *other*. 17:12
o. Gershom, of the *other*. 18:3
o. for a sin offering, the *other* for a.
Lev 5:7; 12:8; Num 6:11; 8:12
o. lot for the Lord, *other*. Lev 6:8
o. Eldad, the *other*. Num 11:26
o. lamb in morning, the *other* at. 28:4
o. side of heaven to *other*. Deut 4:32
o. end of earth to *other*. 13:7; 28:64
o. pillar and of the *other*. Judg 16:29
o. was Orpah, of *other*. Ruth 1:4
o. Hannah, the *other*. 1 Sam 1:2
o. Baanah, of the *other*. 2 Sam 4:2
men, o. rich, the *other* poor. 12:1
o. saith, This is my son: the *other* saith, Nay. 1 Ki 3:23
half to o. and half to the *other*. 25
pitched o. against the *other*. 20:29
o. hand wrought, with *other*. Neh 4:17
o. dieth, so dieth the *other*. Eccl 3:19
the o. over against the *other*. 7:14
Lord shall devour from o. end of the land to the *other*. Jer 12:12; 25:33
o. basket had good figs, *other*. 24:2
go thee o. way or *other*. Ezek 21:16
o. horn was higher than the *other*.
Dan 8:3
o. on this side of river, the *other*. 12:5
o. I called Beauty, the *other*.
Zech 11:7
o. and love the *other*, or hold to the o. and despise the *other*. Mat 6:24
Luke 16:13
the o. on thy right hand, and the *other* on. Mat 20:21; Mark 10:37
o. end of heaven to *other*. Mat 24:31
o. taken, the *other* left. 40, 41
Luke 17:34, 35, 36
thieves, the o. on his right hand, the *other*. Mark 15:27; Luke 23:33
o. cheek, offer the *other*. Luke 6:29
o. owed 500 pence, the *other*. 7:41
o. part, shineth to the *other*. 17:24
the o. a Pharisee, the *other*. 18:10
o. angel at the head, *other* at the.
John 20:12
departed asunder o. from *other*.
Acts 15:39
o. part Sadducees, the *other*. 23:6
defraud ye not o. the *other*. 1 Cor 7:5
to o. the savour of life, to *other* of.
2 Cor 2:16
o. by bondmaid, *other*. Gal 4:22
contrary, the o. to the *other*: 5:17
and o. is, the *other* is not yet come.
Rev 17:10

there is one

trespass offering, *there is* o. Lev 7:7
there is o. tribe cut off. Judg 21:6
there is o. law of his to put. Esth 4:11
there is o. alone, and there. Eccl 4:8
there is o. event to righteous. 9:2
this is an evil, that *there is* o. 3
if ye will not, *there is* o. Dan 2:9
there is o. come out of thee. Nah 1:11

there is o. God. Mark 12:32
1 Tim 2:5; Jas 2:19
there is o. that accuseth John 5:45
there is o. that seeketh and. 8:50
there is o. kind of flesh. 1 Cor 15:39
there is o. glory of sun, another. 41
there is o. lawgiver, who. Jas 4:12

one of them

as o. of them opened his sack.
Gen 42:27
not so much as o. of them. Ex 14:28
have I hurt o. of them. Num 16:15
if o. of them die, and. Deut 25:5
thou art o. of them that. Judg 11:35
shall be as o. of them. 1 Sam 17:36
lacked not o. of them. 2 Sam 17:22
I am o. of them that are. 20:19
three things, choose o. of them.
24:12; 1 Chr 21:10
Baal, let not o. of them escape.
1 Ki 18:40
life as the life of o. of them. 19:2
like the word of o. of them. 22:13
not o. of them is broken. Ps 34:20
every o. of them is gone back. 53:3
as a snail let every o. of them. 58:8
of every o. of them is deep. 64:6
o. of them in Zion appeareth. 84:7
there was not o. of them left. 106:11
be not thou o. of them that strike.
Pr 22:26
the labour of the foolish wearieth every o. of them. Eccl 10:15
yet every o. of them doth curse me.
Jer 15:10
things, every o. of them. Ezek 11:5
out of o. of them came forth. Dan 8:9
even thou wast as o. of them. Ob 11
o. of them sold for a farthing.
Mat 10:29; Luke 12:6
have 100 sheep, and o. of them be gone. Mat 18:12; Luke 15:4
surely thou art o. of them.
Mat 26:73; Mark 14:69, 70
o. of them when he saw. Luke 17:15
o. of them may take a little. John 6:7
Jesus by night, being o. of them. 7:50
Lazarus was o. of them that sat. 12:2
seeing o. of them suffer. Acts 7:24
and there stood up o. of them. 11:28

one thing

not o. thing hath failed. Josh 23:14
this is o. thing, therefore I said it.
Job 9:22
o. thing have I desired of the Lord.
Ps 27:4
o. thing befalleth them. Eccl 3:19
I will ask you o. thing. Mat 21:24
Luke 6:9; 20:3
o. thing thou lackest. Mark 10:21
Luke 18:22
but o. thing is needful. Luke 10:42
o. thing I know, that. John 9:25
some cried o. thing, some another.
Acts 19:32; 21:34
this o. thing I do, I press. Phil 3:13
ignorant of this o. thing. 2 Pet 3:8

wicked one

then cometh the wicked o. Mat 13:19
the children of the wicked o. 38
ye have overcome the wicked o.
1 John 2:13, 14
Cain, who was of that wicked o. 3:12
and that wicked o. toucheth. 5:18

ones

my sanctified o. I have also called my mighty o. for mine. Isa 13:3
came up four notable o. Dan 8:8
face to enter, and upright o. 11:17

Onesimus

O. a faithful and beloved. Col 4:9
beseech thee for my son O. Philem 10

Onesiphorus

mercy to the house of O. 2 Tim 1:16
and the household of O. 4:19

onions

we remember the o. and the garlick.
Num 11:5

only

thoughts of his heart are o. Gen 6:5
Noah o. remained alive, and. 7:23
o. to these men do nothing. 19:8
thy son, thine o. son Isaac. Gen 22:2
withheld thy son, thine o. son. 12, 16
o. bring not my son thither. 24:8
o. obey my voice, and go. 27:13
o. herein will the men. 34:22, 23
o. in the throne will I be. 41:40
o. the land of priests. 47:22, 26
remain in the river o. Ex 8:9, 11
I will let you go, o. ye shall not. 28
o. this once, that he may take away from me this death o. 10:17
o. let your flocks and your herds. 24
every man must eat, that o. 12:16
o. he shall pay for the loss. 21:19
to any, save to the Lord o. 22:20
for that is his covering, o. it is. 27
o. he shall not go in unto the vail.
Lev 21:23
o. the firstling of the beasts, it. 27:26
o. thou shalt not number. Num 1:49
hath the Lord indeed o. spoken? 12:2
rebel not ye against the Lord o. 14:9
o. they shall not come nigh. 18:3
I will o. go through on my feet.
20:19; Deut 2:28
o. the word that I shall. Num 22:35
o. the gold and the silver. 31:22
o. marry to the family of their. 36:6
o. take heed to thyself. Deut 4:9
saw no similitude, o. ye heard. 12
man doth not live by bread o. 8:3
o. the Lord had a delight in. 10:15
o. ye shall not eat the blood. 12:16
23; 15:23
the man o. that lay with her. 22:25
shalt be above o. not beneath. 28:13
thou shalt be o. oppressed. 29, 33
nor with you o. I make this. 29:14
o. be thou strong and very.
Josh 1:7, 18
o. Lord thy God be with thee. 17
o. that day compassed the city. 6:15
o. Rahab shall live. 17
burned Hazor o. 11:13
shalt not have one lot o. 17:17
might o. know to teach. Judg 3:2
if dew be on the fleece o. and. 6:37
let it not be dry o. upon the. 39, 40
deliver us o. we pray thee. 10:15
and she was his o. child. 11:34
I pray thee, o. this once. 16:28
the man said, O. lodge not. 19:20
Hannah o. moved her lips. 1 Sam 1:13
o. the Lord establish his word. 23
o. the stump of Dagon was left. 5:4
and serve him o. 7:3, 4; Mat 4:10
Luke 4:8
o. fear the Lord, and. 1 Sam 12:24
o. be thou valiant for me. 18:17
not o. while I live, shew. 20:14
o. Jonathan and David knew. 39
o. Amnon is dead. 2 Sam 13:32, 33
and I will smite the king o. 17:2
deliver him o. and I will. 20:21
returned after him o. to spoil. 23:10
o. the people sacrificed in. 1 Ki 3:2
Gebar was the o. officer who. 4:19
followed David, but Judah o. 12:20
David did that o. which was. 14:8
he o. of Jeroboam shall come. 13
save o. in the matter of Uriah. 15:5
I o. am left, and they. 19:10, 14
fight not, save o. with the. 22:31
worshippers of Baal o. 2 Ki 10:23
left but the tribe of Judah o. 17:18
art the Lord, even thou o. 19:19
Isa 37:20
o. the Lord give thee. 1 Chr 22:12
save o. to burn sacrifice. 2 Chr 2:6
thou o. knowest the hearts of. 6:30
yet to the Lord their God o. 33:17
not done wrong to king o. Esth 1:16
o. on himself put not forth. Job 1:12
I o. am escaped to tell. 15, 16, 17, 19
o. do not two things to me. 13:20
against a nation, or a man o. 34:29
thou, Lord, o. makest me. Ps 4:8
against thee o. have I sinned. 51:4
he o. is my rock and my. 62:2, 6
o. consult to cast him down. 4
my soul, wait thou o. upon God. 5
righteousness, even thine o. 71:16
God of Israel o. doth wondrous. 72:18
o. with thine eyes shalt thou. 91:8
tender and o. beloved in. Pr 4:3
let them be o. thine own, and. 5:17
the righteous is o. good. 11:23
o. by pride cometh contention. 13:10
the talk of the lips tendeth o. 14:23
evil man seeketh o. rebellion. 17:11
tend o. to plenteousness, o. to. 21:5
o. have I found, that God. Eccl 7:29
the o. one of her mother. S of S 6:9
o. let us be called by thy. Isa 4:1
we will o. make mention of. 26:13
it shall be a vexation o. to. 28:19
o. acknowledge thine. Jer 3:13
make mourning as for an o. son.
6:26; Amos 8:10
o. done evil, o. provoked. Jer 32:30
and evil, an o. evil. Ezek 7:5
they o. shall be delivered. 14:16, 18
they shall o. poll their heads. 44:20
you o. have I known of all families.
Amos 3:2
salute your brethren o. Mat 5:47
Lord, speak the word o. 8:8
give a cup of cold water o. 10:42
not lawful for him to eat, but o. 12:4
they might o. touch hem of. 14:36
they saw no man, save Jesus o. 17:8
Mark 9:8
nothing thereon but leaves o.
Mat 21:19
shall not o. do this which is done. 21
in heaven, but my Father o. 24:36
forgive sins, but God o.? Mark 2:7
Jesus saith, Be not afraid, o. believe.
5:36; Luke 8:50
for journey, save a staff o. Mark 6:8
was a dead man, o. son. Luke 7:12
one o. daughter. 8:42
he is my o. child. 9:38
art thou o. a stranger in. 24:18
not o. because he had broken sabbath.
John 5:18
honour that cometh from God o. 44
die, not for that nation o. 11:52
came not for Jesus' sake o. but. 12:9
Lord, not my feet o. but also. 13:9
know thee the o. true God. 17:3
o. they were baptized in. Acts 8:16
the word to none but Jews o. 11:19
Apollos taught, knowing o. 8:25
not o. our craft is in danger to. 19:27
ready not to be bound o. but to. 21:13
o. that they keep themselves from. 25
I would to God, that not o. 26:29
not o. do same, but have. Rom 1:32
is he God of Jews o.? is he? 3:29
this blessedness on circumcision o.?
4:9, 12
not to that o. which is of law. 16
not o. so, but we glory in. 5:3, 11
not o. they, but ourselves. 8:23
he called, not of Jews o. but. 9:24
ye must be subject, not o. for. 13:5
to whom not o. I give thanks. 16:4
to God o. wise be glory. 27
1 Tim 1:17; Jude 25
o. in the Lord. 1 Cor 7:39
I o. and Barnabas. 9:6
came word of God to you o.? 14:36
if in this life o. we have hope. 15:19
us, not by his coming o. 2 Cor 7:7
have begun not o. to do. 8:10
not that o. but was also chosen. 19
not o. in sight of Lord, but in. 21
heard o., he who persecuted. Gal 1:23
o. would that we should. 2:10
this o. would I learn of you. 3:2
not o. when I am present. 4:18
o. use not liberty for an occasion. 5:13
o. lest they should suffer. 6:12
every name named, not o. Eph 1:21
o. let your conversation be. Phil 1:27
is given not o. to believe on him. 29
obeyed, not as in my presence o. 2:12
God had mercy not on him o. 27
no church communicated with me, but ye o. 4:15
o. are my fellow-workers. Col 4:11
gospel came not in word o. 1 Thes 1:5
to you not gospel of God o. 2:8
o. he who now letteth. 2 Thes 2:7
not o. idle, but tattlers. 1 Tim 5:13
is the blessed and o. Potentate. 6:15
who o. hath immortality. 16

not to me *o.* *2 Tim* 4:8
o. Luke is with me. 11
which stood *o.* in meats. *Heb* 9:10
I shake not the earth *o.* 12:26
word, and not hearers *o.* *Jas* 1:22
by works, and not faith *o.* 2:24
not *o.* to good and gentle. *1 Pet* 2:18
not for our sins *o.* *1 John* 2:2
not by water *o.* 5:6
love in the truth, and not I *o.* *2 John* 1
denying the *o.* Lord God. *Jude* 4
but *o.* those which have. *Rev* 9:4
thee ? for thou *o.* art holy. 15:4
see **begotten**

onward
cloud was taken up, Israel went *o.* *Ex* 40:36

onycha
take thee spices, *o.* and. *Ex* 30:34

onyx
fourth row a beryl and an *o.* *Ex* 28:20; 39:13
wisdom cannot be valued with the *o.* *Job* 28:16
the topaz and the *o.* was. *Ezek* 28:13
see **stones**

open, *adjective*
and fowl that may fly in *o.* *Gen* 1:20
Tamar sat in an *o.* place by. 38:14*
every *o.* vessel not covered is unclean. *Num* 19:15
the man whose eyes are *o.* hath. 24:3, 4, 15
left Ai *o.* and pursued. *Josh* 8:17
was no *o.* vision. *1 Sam* 3:1†
carved with *o.* flowers. *1 Ki* 6:18
29:32, 35
eyes may be *o.* towards this house. 8:29, 52; *2 Chr* 6:20, 40; 7:15
eyes be *o.*, ear attentive. *Neh* 1:6
Sanballat with an *o.* letter sent. 6:5
as wicked men in the *o.* *Job* 34:26
their throat is an *o.* sepulchre. *Ps* 5:9; *Rom* 3:13
righteous, his ears are *o.* *Ps* 34:15
fool layeth *o.* his folly. *Pr* 13:16
o. rebuke is better than secret. 27:5
devour Israel with *o.* mouth. *Isa* 9:12
windows from on high are *o.* 24:18
gate shall be *o.* continually. 60:11
quiver is an *o.* sepulchre. *Jer* 5:16
both what was sealed and *o.* 32:11
eyes are *o.* on all the ways. 19
many bones in *o.* valley. *Ezek* 37:2
his windows being *o.* in chamber to Jerusalem. *Dan* 6:10
gates shall be set wide *o.* *Nah* 3:13
see heaven *o.*, angels. *John* 1:51
seeing prison doors *o.* *Acts* 16:27
the law is *o.* and there are. 19:38
we all with *o.* face beholding. *2 Cor* 3:18*
mouth is *o.* to you, our heart. 6:11
some men's sins are *o.* *1 Tim* 5:24*
put him to an *o.* shame. *Heb* 6:6
his ears are *o.* to their. *1 Pet* 3:12
I have set before thee an *o.* *Rev* 3:8
in his hand a little book *o.* 10:2, 8
see **field, fields**

open, *verb*
(*This word is frequently used in a figurative sense*)
if a man shall *o.* a pit. *Ex* 21:33
of such as *o.* every womb. *Num* 8:16
if earth *o.* her mouth, and. 16:30
thou shalt *o.* thy hand wide. *Deut* 15:8, 11
answer of peace, and *o.* to thee. 20:11
Lord shall *o.* to thee his good. 28:12
o. mouth of cave and. *Josh* 10:22
then *o.* door and flee. *2 Ki* 9:3
and he said, O. the window. 13:17
God would *o.* his lips. *Job* 11:5
I will *o.* my lips, and answer. 32:20
doth Job *o.* his mouth in vain. 35:16
who can *o.* the doors of his ? 41:14
I will *o.* my dark saying. *Ps* 49:4
I will *o.* my mouth in a parable. 78:2
o. thy mouth wide and I will. 81:10
o. to me the gates of. 118:19
o. thy mouth for the dumb. *Pr* 31:8
o. thy mouth, judge righteously. 9
o. to me, my sister, my. *S of S* 5:2
I rose up to *o.* to my beloved. 5
he shall *o.*, and none shall shut, shut and none shall *o.* *Isa* 22:22
o. the gates, that the righteous. 26:2
doth he *o.* and break clods ? 28:24
I will *o.* rivers in high places. 41:18
to *o.* blind eyes, to bring out. 42:7
o. before him the two leaved. 45:1
let the earth *o.*, let them bring. 8
be shut up, none shall *o.* *Jer* 13:19
o. her storehouses, cast her. 50:26
o. thy mouth and eat that. *Ezek* 2:8
I speak with thee, I will *o.* thy. 3:27
confounded and never *o.* 16:63
o. the mouth in the slaughter. 21:22
I will *o.* the side of Moab. 25:9
I will *o.* your graves, and cause. 37:12
one shall *o.* him the gate. 46:12
o. thy doors, O Lebanon. *Zech* 11:1
will not *o.* you windows. *Mal* 3:10
I will *o.* my mouth in. *Mat* 13:35
Lord, *o.* to us. 25:11; *Luke* 13:25
he knocketh, they may *o.* *Luke* 12:36
Paul was about to *o.* his. *Acts* 18:14
that I may *o.* my mouth. *Eph* 6:19
that God would *o.* to us door. *Col* 4:3
is worthy to *o.* the book ? *Rev* 5:2
no man was able to *o.* book. 3
no man was found worthy to *o.* and. 4
Root of David prevailed to *o.* book. 5
to take the book, and *o.* seals. 9
see **eyes**

opened
windows of heaven were *o.* *Gen* 7:11
Noah *o.* the window of the ark. 8:6
God *o.* Leah's womb. 29:31
he *o.* Rachel's. 30:22
Joseph *o.* all storehouses. 41:56
one of them *o.* his sack. 42:27
43:21; 44:11
when she had *o.* ark. *Ex* 2:6
earth *o.* her mouth, and swallowed. *Num* 16:32; *Ps* 106:17
o. not the doors, they *o.* *Judg* 3:25
she *o.* a bottle of milk and. 4:19
her lord *o.* doors, went out. 19:27
and Elisha *o.* the door. *2 Ki* 9:10
they *o.* not to him, therefore. 15:16
Hezekiah *o.* doors of. *2 Chr* 29:3
not gates of Jerusalem be *o.* *Neh* 7:3
Ezra *o.* book; when he *o.* it. 8:5
charged gates not to be *o.* till. 13:19
o. my doors to traveller. *Job* 31:32
the gates of death been *o.*? 38:17*
mine ears hast thou *o.* *Ps* 40:6
though he had *o.* the doors. 78:23
he *o.* the rock, and the. 105:41
I *o.* to my beloved. *S of S* 5:6
that *o.* not the house of. *Isa* 14:17*
time that thine ear was not *o.* 48:8
Lord God hath *o.* mine ear, not. 50:5
thee have I *o.* my cause. *Jer* 20:12*
Lord hath *o.* his armoury. 50:25
that the heavens were *o.* *Ezek* 1:1
Mat 3:16; *Mark* 1:10*; *Luke* 3:21
Acts 7:56
thou hast *o.* thy feet to. *Ezek* 16:25
when I have *o.* your graves. 37:13
gate shall not be *o.*, no man. 44:2
new moon it shall be *o.* 46:1
was set, the books were *o.* *Dan* 7:10
rivers shall be *o.*, palace. *Nah* 2:6
shall be a fountain *o.* to. *Zech* 13:1
when they had *o.* their. *Mat* 2:11
knock, and it shall be *o.* unto you. 7:7
Luke 11:9, 10
the graves were *o.* and many bodies arose. *Mat* 27:52
Ephphatha, that is, Be *o.* *Mark* 7:34
his ears were *o.* 35
when he *o.* book, he found. *Luke* 4:17
o. to us the scriptures. 24:32
then *o.* he their understanding. 45
the angel by night *o.* the. *Acts* 5:19
but when we had *o.* we found. 23
Peter saw heaven *o.* and a. 10:11
the iron gate which *o.* 12:10
o. not the gate, but ran in. 14
when they had *o.* the door. 16
he had *o.* the door of faith. 14:27
Lydia, whose heart the Lord *o.* 16:14
immediately all the doors were *o.* 26
door and effectual is *o.* unto me. *1 Cor* 16:9; *2 Cor* 2:12
are naked and *o.* to him. *Heb* 4:13
a door was *o.* in heaven. *Rev* 4:1
the Lamb *o.* one of the seals. 6:1
had *o.* the second. 3, 5, 7, 9, 12; 8:1
he *o.* the bottomless pit, and. 9:2
the temple of God was *o.* 11:19
of the testimony was *o.* 15:5
I saw heaven *o.* and behold. 19:11
were *o.*: the book of life was *o.* 20:12
see **days, mouth**

openest
thou *o.* thy hand, they are. *Ps* 104:28
o. thine hand and satisfiest. 145:16

openeth
whatsoever *o.* the womb. *Ex* 13:2
set apart all that *o.* 12, 15; 34:19
Num 3:12; 18:15; *Luke* 2:23
the rich man *o.* his eyes. *Job* 27:19
he *o.* ears of men, and sealeth. 33:16
he *o.* their ear to discipline. 36:10
he delivereth poor, *o.* their ears. 15
I as a dumb man that *o.* *Ps* 38:13
he that *o.* wide his lips. *Pr* 13:3
o. not his mouth in the gate. 24:7
she *o.* her mouth with wisdom. 31:26
brought as a lamb, so he *o.* *Isa* 53:7
the fire, all that *o.* womb. *Ezek* 20:26
the porter *o.*; sheep hear. *John* 10:3
he that *o.* and no man shutteth, and shutteth and no man *o.* *Rev* 3:7

opening
o. ears, but he heareth not. *Isa* 42:20
o. and alleging that Christ. *Acts* 17:3

opening, -s
o. of house of God. *1 Chr* 9:27
a man, there can be no *o.* *Job* 12:14
in the *o.* of the gates. *Pr* 1:21*
and the *o.* of my lips shall be. 8:6
proclaim the *o.* of the prison. *Isa* 61:1
I will give thee the *o.* of. *Ezek* 29:21

openly
harlot that was *o.* by the way side ? *Gen* 38:21*
hath he *o.* shewed. *Ps* 98:2
thy Father shall reward thee *o.* *Mat* 6:4, 6, 18
spake that saying *o.* *Mark* 8:32
seeketh to be known *o.* *John* 7:4
to the feast, not *o.* but in secret. 10
no man spake of him *o.* for fear. 13
Jesus walked no more *o.* 11:54
I spake *o.* to the world. 18:20
raised up, and shewed him *o.* *Acts* 10:40
they have beaten us *o.* 16:37
shew of them *o.* triumphing. *Col* 2:15

operation
they regard not the *o.* *Ps* 28:5
nor consider the *o.* of his. *Isa* 5:12
the faith of the *o.* of God. *Col* 2:12*

operations
there are diversity of *o.* *1 Cor* 12:6*

Ophel
much on the wall of O. *2 Chr* 27:3
Manasseh compassed about O. 33:14
Nethinims dwelt in O. *Neh* 3:26
11:21
repaired to the wall of O. 27

Ophir
Joktan begat O. *Gen* 10:29
1 Chr 1:23
they came to O. and fetched gold. *1 Ki* 9:28; *2 Chr* 8:18; 9:10
brought from O. great. *1 Ki* 10:11
made ships to go to O. for. 22:48
talents of gold of O. *1 Chr* 29:4
lay up the gold of O. *Job* 22:24
valued with the gold of O. 28:16
the queen in gold of O. *Ps* 45:9
precious than wedge of O. *Isa* 13:12

opinion
durst not shew you mine *o.* *Job* 32:6
I also will shew you mine *o.* 10, 17

opinions
halt ye between two *o.*? *1 Ki* 18:21

opportunity
he sought *o.* to betray him. *Mat* 26:16; *Luke* 22:6

as we have o. let us do good. Gal 6:10
careful, but ye lacked o. Phil 4:10
they might have had o. to. Heb 11:15

oppose

instructing those that o. 2 Tim 2:25

opposed

when they o. themselves. Acts 18:6

opposest

thy strong hand thou o. Job 30:21*

opposeth

o. and exalteth himself. 2 Thes 2:4

oppositions

avoiding o. of science. 1 Tim 6:20

oppress

the Egyptians o. them. Exod 3:9
vex nor o. a stranger. 22:21; 23:9
ye shall not o. one. Lev 25:14*, 17*
shalt not o. servant that. Deut 23:16
thou shalt not o. an hired. 24:14
Moabites did o. you. Judg 10:12
thee that thou shouldest o.? Job 10:3
earth may no more o. Ps 10:18
from the wicked that o. me. 17:9†
good, let not proud o. me. 119:122
nor o. the afflicted in. Pr 22:22
will feed them that o. thee. Isa 49:26
if ye o. not the stranger. Jer 7:6
I will punish all that o. them. 30:20
princes shall no more o. Ezek 45:8
merchant, he loveth to o. Hos 12:7
ye kine of Bashan which o. Amos 4:1
they o. a man and his house. Mi 2:2
o. not the widow nor the. Zech 7:10
witness against those that o. Mal 3:5
do not rich men o. you? Jas 2:6

oppressed

thou shalt be only o. Deut 28:29, 33
by reason of them that o. Judg 2:18
Jabin o. Israel. 4:3
out of the hand of the Egyptians, and of all that o. 6:9; 1 Sam 10:18
Philistines and Ammon o. Judg 10:8
whose ox have I taken? whom have I o.? 1 Sam 12:3
thou hast not defrauded, nor o. us. 4
Assyria o. them. 2 Ki 13:4
king of Syria o. Israel. 22
Asa o. some of the people the same time. 2 Chr 16:10
because he hath o. and. Job 20:19
they made the o. to cry. 35:9*
will be a refuge for the o. Ps 9:9
judge the fatherless and o. 10:18
103:6; 146:7
not the o. return ashamed. 74:21
enemies o. them, brought. 106:42
the tears of such as were o. Eccl 4:1
learn to do well, seek judgement, relieve o. Isa 1:17
the people shall be o. every. 3:5
O thou o. virgin, daughter. 23:12
O Lord, I am o., undertake. 38:14
Assyrian o. them without. 52:4
he was o. and afflicted, yet he. 53:7
fast? to let the o. go free. 58:6
Israel and Judah were o. Jer 50:33
hath not o. any, but. Ezek 18:7*, 16*
because he hath o. 12*
he cruelly o. 18
they have o. the stranger. 22:29
Ephraim is o. and broken. Hos 5:11
o. in the midst thereof. Amos 3:9
avenged him that was o. Acts 7:24
Jesus healed all that were o. 10:38

oppresseth

against him that o. you. Num 10:9
he fighting daily o. me. Ps 56:1
he that o. the poor. Pr 14:31; 22:16
a poor man that o. the poor. 28:3

oppressing

go from the o. sword. Jer 46:16
for fear of the o. sword. 50:16
woe to o. city, she obeyed. Zeph 3:1

oppression

I have seen o. wherewith. Ex 3:9
and looked on our o. Deut 26:7
the Lord saw the o. of. 2 Ki 13:4
openeth their ears in o. Job 36:15
for the o. of the poor. Ps 12:5*
o. of the enemy. 42:9; 43:2; 55:3
forgettest our o. 44:24
trust not in o. Ps 62:10
speak wickedly concerning o. 73:8
brought low through o. 107:39
me from the o. of man. 119:134
seest the o. of the poor. Eccl 5:8
o. maketh a wise man mad. 7:7*
but behold o. Isa 5:7
because ye trust in o. 30:12
thou shalt be far from o. 54:14
speaking o. and revolt. 59:13
she is wholly o. in the midst. Jer 6:6
eyes and heart are for o. 22:17
they dealt by o. with. Ezek 22:7
people of the land have used o. 29
not take inheritance by o. 46:18

oppressions

of the multitude of o. Job 35:9
I considered the o. done. Eccl 4:1
despiseth the gain of o. Isa 33:15

oppressor

not the voice of the o. Job 3:18*
of years is hidden to the o. 15:20
break in pieces the o. Ps 72:4
envy not o., choose none. Pr 3:31*
wanteth understanding is an o. 28:16
broken the rod of his o. Isa 9:4
how hath the o. ceased! 14:4
because of the fury of the o. 51:13
deliver him that is spoiled out of the hand of the o. Jer 21:12; 22:3
of the fierceness of the o. 25:38
no o. shall pass through. Zech 9:8
out of him came every o. 10:4*

oppressors

this is the heritage of o. Job 27:13
strangers risen and o. seek. Ps 54:3
leave me not to mine o. 119:121
on the side of their o. there. Eccl 4:1
children are their o., women. Isa 3:12
they shall rule over their o. 14:2
the o. are consumed out of. 16:4
cry to Lord because of the o. 19:20

oracle

[1] *A place of communication from God, as the Jewish Holy of Holies,* 1 Ki 6:16. [2] *The word of God, the Scriptures,* Acts 7:38. *The word, in the sense in which it is used in Greek history, is not found in the Bible, although there are instances where the thing itself seems referred to in other words.*

had enquired at the o. of God. 2 Sam 16:23
for it within, for the o. 1 Ki 6:16
the ark of Lord into the o. 8:6
should burn before the o. 2 Chr 4:20
my hands toward thy holy o. Ps 28:2

oracles

who received the lively o. Acts 7:38
committed the o. of God. Rom 3:2
principles of the o. of God. Heb 5:12
speak as the o. of God. 1 Pet 4:11

oration

Herod made an o. to them. Acts 12:21

orator

from Judah the eloquent o. Isa 3:3*
certain o. named Tertullus. Acts 24:1

orchard

an o. of pomegranates. S of S 4:13

orchards

I made me gardens and o. Eccl 2:5*

ordain

[1] *To command or enjoin,* 1 Cor 9:14. [2] *To appoint or design to a certain end or use,* Rom 7:10. [3] *To choose or set apart for an office or employment,* Mark 3:14.

David and Samuel did o. 1 Chr 9:22
I will o. a place for my people. 17:9*
Lord, thou wilt o. peace. Isa 26:12
so o. I in all churches. 1 Cor 7:17
thou shouldest o. elders. Tit 1:5*

ordained

an offering that was o. in. Num 28:6
Jeroboam o. a feast. 1 Ki 12:32, 33
idolatrous priests o. 2 Ki 23:5
Jeroboam o. priests for. 2 Chr 11:15*
offer the offerings as it was o. 23:18*
instruments o. by David. 2 Chr 29:27
o. the feast of Purim. Esth 9:27
mouth of babes hast thou o. Ps 8:2*
the stars which thou hast o. 3
this he o. in Joseph for a. 81:5*
I have o. a lamp for mine. 132:17
Tophet is o. of old, he. Isa 30:33*
I o. thee to be a prophet. Jer 1:5*
king had o. to destroy. Dan 2:24*
O Lord, thou hast o. them. Hab 1:12
Jesus o. twelve to be. Mark 3:14*
I have o. that ye should. John 15:16*
one o. to be witness with. Acts 1:22*
o. of God to be the judge of. 10:42
as many as were o. to eternal. 13:48
when they had o. them elders. 14:23*
decrees that were o. of apostles. 16:4
he will judge the world by that man whom he hath o. 17:31
which was o. to life. Rom 7:10
powers that be, are o. of God. 13:1
hidden wisdom which God o. 1 Cor 2:7*
the Lord hath o. that they. 9:14
the law was o. by angels. Gal 3:19
which God hath before o. Eph 2:10*
I am o. a preacher and. 1 Tim 2:7*
priest is o. for men. Heb 5:1*; 8:3*
things were thus o., the priests. 9:6*
who were of old o. to this. Jude 4*

ordaineth

he o. his arrows against. Ps 7:13*

order

priests of second o. 2 Ki 23:4
according to their o. 1 Chr 6:32
him not after the due o. 15:13*
the o. commanded to them. 23:31*
according to the o. of David. 25:2, 6
2 Chr 8:14*
darkness, without any o. Job 10:22
priest for ever, after the o. Ps 110:4
Heb 5:6, 10; 6:20; 7:11, 17, 21
given o. to churches of. 1 Cor 16:1
joying and beholding your o. Col 2:5
not be called after o. of. Heb 7:11

in order

Abraham laid wood in o. Gen 22:9
two tenons in o. Ex 26:17*
lamps set in o. 39:37
in o. the things that are to be set in o. 40:4; Lev 1:7, 8, 12; 6:12; 24:8
and he set bread in o. Ex 40:23
stalks of flax she had laid in o. upon the roof. Josh 2:6
put his house in o. 2 Sam 17:23
Elijah put wood in o. 1 Ki 18:33
set thine house in o. 2 Ki 20:1
Isa 38:1
shew bread also set they in o. 2 Chr 13:11
house of the Lord set in o. 29:35
set thy words in o. before. Job 33:5
reckoned up in o. to thee. Ps 40:5
I will set them in o. before. 50:21
the preacher set in o. Eccl 12:9
who declare it, and set it in o.? Isa 44:7
chambers were thirty in o. Ezek 41:6
in hand to set forth in o. Luke 1:1, 3
served before God in his o. 8
country of Phrygia in o. Acts 18:23
the rest will I set in o. 1 Cor 11:34
be done decently and in o. 14:40
shall rise in his o., Christ. 15:23
I left thee to set in o. Tit 1:5

order, ***verb***

Aaron and sons shall o. it. Ex 27:21
Lev 24:3, 4*
shall we o. the child? Judg 13:12
who shall o. the battle? 1 Ki 20:14*
o. my cause before him. Job 23:4
teach us, for we cannot o. 37:19
o. my steps in thy word. Ps 119:133
his kingdom to o. it. Isa 9:7*
o. ye the buckler and the. Jer 46:3*

ordered, -eth

to Lord in the o. place. Judg 6:26*
covenant o. and sure. 2 Sam 23:5
now, I have o. my cause. Job 13:18
steps of a good man are o. Ps 37:23*
to him who o. his conversation. 50:23

orderings

their *o.* under Aaron. *1 Chr* 24:19

orderly

walkest *o.* and keepest. *Acts* 21:24

ordinance

[1] *Any decree, statute, or law, made by civil governors,* 1 Pet 2:13.
[2] *A law, statute, or commandment of God,* Lev 18:4. *The Revisions frequently substitute the words* charge *or* statute.

Lord the feast of the passover, for an *o.* *Ex* 12:14, 24, 43; 13:10
for them a statute and an *o.* 15:25
according to *o.* of passover. *Num* 9:14
2 Chr 35:13
to you for an *o.* for ever. *Num* 10:8
o. shall be for you in your. 15:15
and to thy sons by an *o.* for ever. 18:8*; *2 Chr* 2:4
o. of law the Lord. *Num* 19:2; 31:21
and he set them an *o.* *Josh* 24:25
made it an *o.* for ever. *1 Sam* 30:25
and made them an *o.* *2 Chr* 35:25
after the *o.* of David. *Ezra* 3:10*
the law, changed the *o.* *Isa* 24:5
forsook not the *o.* of their God. 58:2
concerning the *o.* of oil. *Ezek* 45:14
an offering by a perpetual *o.* 46:14
that we have kept his *o.*? *Mal* 3:14
resisteth the *o.* of God. *Rom* 13:2
to every *o.* of man. *1 Pet* 2:13

ordinances

shalt teach them *o.* and. *Ex* 18:20
shall ye walk in their *o.* *Lev* 18:3
ye shall keep mine *o.* 4, 30; 22:9
2 Chr 33:8; *Ezek* 11:20; 43:11
1 Cor 11:2*
the *o.* of the passover. *Num* 9:12, 14
do they after their *o.* *2 Ki* 17:34
o. which he wrote for you. 37
made *o.* for us to charge. *Neh* 10:32
guide Arcturus? knowest thou the *o.*?
Job 38:33; *Jer* 31:35; 33:25
they kept the *o.* that he. *Ps* 99:7
according to thine *o.* 119:91
the *o.* of justice, delight. *Isa* 58:2
if those *o.* depart from. *Jer* 31:36
he said, These are the *o.* *Ezek* 43:18
o. of the house of the Lord. 44:5
are gone away from mine *o.* *Mal* 3:7
Zacharias and Elisabeth walking in all commandments and *o.* *Luke* 1:6
law of commandments contained in *o.* *Eph* 2:15
the handwriting of *o.* *Col* 2:14
in the world, are ye subject to *o.*? 20
the first covenant had *o.* of. *Heb* 9:1
stood in carnal *o.* imposed on. 10

ordinary

diminished thine *o.* food. *Ezek* 16:27

Oreb

slew princes of Midian, Zeeb, *O.*
Judg 7:25; 8:3
nobles like *O.* and Zeeb. *Ps* 83:11
Midian at the rock of *O.* *Isa* 10:26

organ, -s

(*Not the organ as we know it, but a perforated wind instrument, a pipe. It may be the ancient* pipes of Pan, *known to the Greeks. The Revisions translate it by the word* pipe)

father of such as handle *o.* *Gen* 4:21
rejoice at sound of the *o.* *Job* 21:12
o. turned into voice of them. 30:31
with the timbrel and *o.* *Ps* 150:4

Orion

who maketh *O.* and Pleiades.
Job 9:9; *Amos* 5:8
or canst thou loose the bands of *O.*?
Job 38:31

ornament

an *o.* of grace to thy head. *Pr* 1:9*
to thine head an *o.* of grace. 4:9*
an *o.* of fine gold, so is a wise. 25:12
ye shall defile *o.* of thy. *Isa* 30:22*
clothe thee with them all as with an *o.* 49:18
the beauty of his *o.* he set. *Ezek* 7:20
even the *o.* of a meek. *1 Pet* 3:4*

ornaments

no man did put on him his *o.* *Ex* 33:4
now put off thy *o.* from thee. 5, 6
Gideon took *o.* that. *Judg* 8:21*
rings that he requested, beside *o.* 26*
Saul, who put *o.* on your. *2 Sam* 1:24
shall take away tinkling *o.* *Isa* 3:18*
bonnets, and the *o.* of the legs. 20*
decketh himself with *o.* 61:10*
can maid forget her *o.* or ? *Jer* 2:32
deckest thee with *o.* of gold. 4:30
art come to excellent *o.* *Ezek* 16:7
decked thee with *o.*, put bracelets. 11
deckedst thyself with *o.* 23:40

Ornan

the threshingfloor of *O.*
1 Chr 21:15, 18, 28
and *O.* turned back, and saw. 20
David gave to *O.* for the place. 25

Orpah

the name of the one was *O.* *Ruth* 1:4
O. kissed Naomi, but Ruth. 14

orphans

we are *o.*, our mothers. *Lam* 5:3

Oshea, ***see*** **Joshua**

osprey, ossifrage

(*Revisions,* the gier eagle)
eagle, *osp.* and *ossif.* not eat.
Lev 11:13; *Deut* 14:12

ostrich

wings and feathers to *o.*? *Job* 39:13*

ostriches

become cruel, like *o.* in. *Lam* 4:3

other

Noah stayed yet *o.* *Gen* 8:10, 12
is none *o.* but the house. 28:17
me yet *o.* seven years. 29:27, 30
if thou take *o.* wives beside. 31:50
then the *o.* company that is left. 32:8
seven *o.* kine came up. 41:3, 19
send away your *o.* brother. 43:14
o. money have we brought down. 22
was turned again as his *o.* *Ex* 4:7
they asked each *o.* of their. 18:7
the *o.* lamb offer thou at even. 29:41
Num 28:8
ye shall not make any *o.* *Ex* 30:32
put off his garments, and put on *o.*
Lev 6:11; *Ezek* 42:14; 44:19
fat be used in any *o.* use. *Lev* 7:24
take *o.* stones and *o.* mortar. 14:42
take a wife beside the *o.* in. 18:18
separated you from *o.* 20:24, 26
and the *o.* did set up. *Num* 10:21
he went not as at *o.* times. 24:1
they gave *o.* names to the. 32:38
married to any of the *o.* tribes. 36:3
all *o.* cities they took. *Josh* 11:19
came to me the *o.* day. *Judg* 13:10
and be like any *o.* man. 16:17
I will go out as at *o.* times. 20
began to kill as at *o.* times. 20:31
Lord called as at *o.* times, Samuel.
1 Sam 3:10
with his hand as at *o.* times. 18:10
Saul sat on his seat as at *o.* 20:25
for there is no *o.* save. 21:9
evil is greater than *o.* *2 Sam* 13:16
to keep *o.* seven days. *2 Chr* 30:23
Hezekiah from hand of all *o.* 32:22
the *o.* half of them held. *Neh* 4:16
for *o.* men have our lands and. 5:5
flag withereth before any *o.* herb.
Job 8:12
out of the way, as all *o.* 24:24
in trouble as *o.* men, neither are they plagued like *o.* men. *Ps* 73:5
and peace kissed each *o.* 85:10
more rest than the *o.* *Eccl* 6:5
o. lords have had. *Isa* 26:13
after thou hast lost the *o.* 49:20
in thee from *o.* women. *Ezek* 16:34
none *o.* can shew it. *Dan* 2:11
not be left to *o.* people. 44
joy, O Israel, as *o.* people. *Hos* 9:1
where is any *o.* to save ? 13:10
he saw *o.* two brethren. *Mat* 4:21
cheek, turn to him the *o.* also. 5:39
restored whole as *o.* 12:13
Mark 3:5; *Luke* 6:10
then he taketh seven *o.* spirits.
Mat 12:45; *Luke* 11:26
o. fell into good ground. *Mat* 13:8
Mark 4:8; *Luke* 8:8
o. servants more. *Mat* 21:36; 22:4
he will let out his vineyard to *o.* 21:41
and not to leave *o.* undone. 23:23
Luke 11:42
came also the *o.* virgins. *Mat* 25:11
and made them *o.* five talents. 16
and the lusts of *o.* *Mark* 4:19
and many *o.* things there be. 7:4, 8
o. commandment is greater. 12:31
God, and there is none *o.* but. 32
preach kingdom of God to *o.* cities.
Luke 4:43
Lord appointed *o.* seventy also. 10:1
or else while the *o.* is yet a. 14:32
that I am not as *o.* men. 18:11
down justified rather than the *o.* 14
o. things blasphemously. 22:65
o. men laboured. *John* 4:38
o. sheep I have. 10:16
not done works none *o.* man. 15:24
went out that *o.* disciple. 18:16
there are many *o.* things. 21:25
to speak with *o.* tongues *Acts* 2:4
and with many *o.* words. 40
salvation in any *o.* none *o.* name under heaven whereby we must be. 4:12
of himself, or of some *o.* man.? 8:34
nor *o.* creature, shall be. *Rom* 8:39
any *o.* commandment, it is. 13:9
whether I baptized any *o.* *1 Cor* 1:16
o. foundation can no man lay. 3:11
lead about sister, as well as *o.* 9:5
every one taketh before *o.* 11:21
but the *o.* is not edified. 14:17
of *o.* tongues and *o.* lips I. 21
speak, and let the *o.* judge. 29
of wheat, or some *o.* grain. 15:37
for I mean not that *o.* *2 Cor* 8:13
not boasting of *o.* men's. 10:15
I robbed *o.* churches to do. 11:8
I write to them and to all *o.* 13:2
o. apostles saw I none. *Gal* 1:19
and the *o.* Jews dissembled. 2:13
which in *o.* ages was not. *Eph* 3:5
that ye walk not as *o.* Gentiles. 4:17
but the *o.* preach Christ. *Phil* 1:17
let each esteem *o.* better than. 2:3
if any *o.* thinketh that he might. 3:4
with Clement and with *o.* my. 4:3
charity toward each *o.* *2 Thes* 1:3
teach no *o.* doctrine. *1 Tim* 1:3
be any *o.* thing contrary to. 10
partaker of *o.* men's sins. 5:22
swear by any *o.* oath. *Jas* 5:12
as a busybody in *o.* *1 Pet* 4:15
they wrest, as they do *o.* *2 Pet* 3:16
on you none *o.* burden. *Rev* 2:24
by reason of the *o.* voices. 8:13

see **God, gods, one, side**

others

of the earth shall *o.* grow. *Job* 8:19
o. bow down upon her. 31:10
shall set *o.* in their stead. 34:24
them in the open sight of *o.* 26
leave their wealth to *o.* *Ps* 49:10
give thine honour to *o.* *Pr* 5:9
likewise hast cursed *o.* *Eccl* 7:22
yet will I gather *o.* to him. *Isa* 56:8
shall be turned to *o.* *Jer* 6:12
I will give their wives unto *o.* 8:10
and they have made *o.* *Ezek* 13:6
o. daubed it with untempered. 10
was diverse from all *o.* *Dan* 7:19
kingdom shall be plucked up for *o.* 11:4
do ye more than *o.*? *Mat* 5:47
o. say, that thou art Jeremias. 16:14
Mark 6:15; 8:28; *Luke* 9:8, 19
he saw *o.* standing idle. *Mat* 20:3
o. cut down branches from trees.
21:8; *Mark* 11:8
o. smote him with the palms of.
Mat 26:67
will give vineyard to *o.* *Mark* 12:9
Luke 20:16
He saved *o.*; himself he cannot save.
Mark 15:31; *Luke* 23:35
o. which ministered to. *Luke* 8:3
did *o.* tell it thee of me ? *John* 18:34
if I be not an apostle to *o.* *1 Cor* 9:2
if *o.* be partakers of this power. 12

I have preached to o. 1 Cor 9:27
not thine own, but of the o. 10:29
by my voice I might teach o 14:19
or need we, as some o., epistles of commendation? 2 Cor 3:1
of the forwardness of o. 8:8
children of wrath, even as o. Eph 2:3
also on the things of o. Phil 2:4
nor yet of o. sought we. 1 Thes 2:6
that ye sorrow not, as o. which. 4:13
let us not sleep as do o. but. 5:6
sin rebuke, that o. may. 1 Tim 5:20
be able to teach o. also. 2 Tim 2:2
every year with blood of o. Heb 9:25
o. were tortured, not. 11:35
o. had trial of cruel mockings. 36
o. save with fear, pulling. Jude 23

otherwise

o. I should have wrought falsehood against mine own. 2 Sam 18:13
o. it shall come to pass. 1 Ki 1:21
they eat passover o. 2 Chr 30:18
lest o. they should. Ps 38:16
o. have no reward of. Mat 6:1
o. grace is no more grace; then is it no more grace: o. Rom 11:6
toward thee goodness: o. thou. 22
if o. yet as a fool. 2 Cor 11:16
will be none o. minded. Gal 5:10
any thing you be o. minded. Phil 3:15
and they that are o. 1 Tim 5:25
if any man teach o. and consent. 6:3
o. it is of no strength at. Heb 9:17

Othniel

O. son of Kenaz took it. Josh 15:17
Judg 1:13
Lord raised a deliverer, O. Judg 3:9
O. died. 11
sons of Kenaz, O. Seraiah, sons of O. 1 Chr 4:13
captain was Heldai of O. 27:15

ouches

(*Ornaments set with jewels. American Revision changes to setting except in starred reference*)
set the stones in o. of gold.
Ex 28:11; 39:6, 13
shalt make o. of gold. 28:13
fasten wreathen chains to the o.
14; 39:18*
fasten in the two o. 28:25

ought, *see* owed

ought

that o. not to be done. Gen 20:9
34:7; Lev 4:2, 27
no such thing o. to be. 2 Sam 13:12
to know what Israel o. 1 Chr 12:32
none o. to carry the ark but. 15:2
o. ye not to know Lord. 2 Chr 13:5
o. ye not to walk in the? Neh 5:9
to him who o. to be feared. Ps 76:11
these o. ye to have done.
Mat 23:23; Luke 11:42
desolation standing where it o. not.
Mark 13:14
hour what ye o. to say. Luke 12:12
days in which men o. to work. 13:14
o. not this man to be loosed? 16
that men o. always to pray. 18:1
O fools, o. not Christ to? 24:26
the place where men o. John 4:20
o. to wash one another's feet. 13:14
and by our law he o. to die. 19:7
we o. to obey God. Acts 5:29
o. not to think the Godhead. 17:29
ye o. to be quiet, and to do. 19:36
how so labouring ye o. to. 20:35
that they o. not to circumcise. 21:21
who o. to have been here. 24:19
judgement seat, where I o. to. 25:10
crying, that he o. not to live. 24
that I o. to do many things. 26:9
what to pray for as we o. Rom 8:26
more highly than he o. 12:3
we o. to bear the infirmities of. 15:1
nothing as he o. to know. 1 Cor 8:2
o. not to cover his head. 11:7
the woman o. to have power. 10
of whom I o. to rejoice. 2 Cor 2:3
ye o. rather to forgive him. 7
I o. to have been commended. 12:11
the children o. not to lay up.
2 Cor 12:14
so o. men to love their. Eph 5:28
may speak boldly, as I o. to speak.
6:20; Col 4:4
know how ye o. to answer. Col 4:6
how ye o. to walk. 1 Thes 4:1
know how ye o. to follow. 2 Thes 3:7
speaking things which they o. not.
1 Tim 5:13
teaching things which they o. not.
Tit 1:11
we o. to give the more. Heb 2:1
he o. for people and for himself. 5:3
for when for the time ye o. 12
these things o. not so to be. Jas 3:10
for that ye o. to say, If the. 4:15
persons o. ye to be? 2 Pet 3:11
o. himself also to walk. 1 John 2:6
o. to lay down our lives for. 3:16
if God loved us, we o. also. 4:11
we therefore o. to receive. 3 John 8

ought, *substantive*

(*Practically everywhere the Revisions have changed this to* aught)
he knew not o. that he had. Gen 39:6
there is not o. left, but our bodies.
47:18
ye shall not diminish o. thereof.
Ex 5:8; 11:19
thou shalt not carry forth o. 12:46
if a man borrow o. of his. 22:14
o. of flesh of the consecrations. 29:34
beareth o. of carcase. Lev 11:25
if o. remain unto third day. 19:6
if thou sellest o. or buyest o. 25:14
redeem o. of his tithes. 27:31
if o. be committed by. Num 15:24
the soul that doeth o. 30
when she vowed, or uttered o. 30:6
add or diminish o. from it. Deut 4:2
lendeth o. to his neighbour. 15:2
neither have I taken away o. for any unclean use, nor given o. 26:14
there failed not o. of any. Josh 21:45
if o. but death part thee. Ruth 1:17
nor hast thou taken o. 1 Sam 12:4
that ye have not found o. in. 5
neither was there o. missing. 25:7
we will not give them o. 30:22
if I taste bread or o. 2 Sam 3:35
whoso saith o. to thee. 14:10
none can turn from o. my lord. 19
that thy brother hath o. Mat 5:23
if any man say o. to you, ye. 21:3
him no more to do o. Mark 7:12
and asked him if he saw o. 8:23
if ye have o. against any. 11:25
brought him o. to eat? John 4:33
neither said any that o. Acts 4:32
and object, if they had o. 24:19
that I had o. to accuse my. 28:19
if he oweth thee o. put to. Philem 18

oughtest

what thou o. to do to him. 1 Ki 2:9
thou o. to have put my. Mat 25:27
thee what thou o. to do. Acts 10:6
how thou o. to behave. 1 Tim 3:15

our, *see* brother, father, Lord

ours

saying, The water is o. Gen 26:20
from our father that is o. 31:16
every beast of theirs be o.? 34:23
side Jordan may be o. Num 32:32
Ramoth in Gilead is o. 1 Ki 22:3
ancient high places are o. Ezek 36:2
and inheritance shall be o.
Mark 12:7; Luke 20:14
Jesus, both theirs and o. 1 Cor 1:2
ye also are o. in the day. 2 Cor 1:14
let o. also learn to maintain. Tit 3:14

ourselves

and bow down o.? Gen 37:10
how shall we clear o.? 44:16
o. will go ready armed. Num 32:17
for a prey unto o. Deut 2:35; 3:7
we will discover o. 1 Sam 14:8
we o. together will build. Ezra 4:3
that we might afflict o. before. 8:21
among o. what is good. Job 34:4
let us take to o. houses. Ps 83:12
made us, and not we o. Ps 100:3
come, let us solace o. Pr 7:18
falsehood have we hid o. Isa 28:15
we will fill o. with strong. 56:12
come let us join o. to. Jer 50:5
we o. have heard. Luke 22:71
John 4:42
we will give o. to prayer. Acts 6:4
we have bound o. under a. 23:14
we o. groan within o. Rom 8:23
bear and not to please o. 15:1
if we would judge o. 1 Cor 11:31
wherewith we o. are. 2 Cor 1:4
that we should not trust in o. 9
again to commend o. to you? 3:1
not that we are sufficient of o. to think any thing as of o., but our. 5
commending o. to every man's. 4:2
for we preach not o. but Christ Jesus the Lord, and o. your servants. 5
for we commend not o. again. 5:12
whether we be beside o. it is. 13
in all things approving o. 6:4
let us cleanse o. from all. 7:1
or compare o. with some. 10:12
we stretch not o. beyond. 14
think ye we excuse o.? 12:19
we o. also are found. Gal 2:17
how holily we behaved o.
1 Thes 2:10
so that we o. glory in. 2 Thes 1:4
we behaved not o. disorderly. 3:7
make o. an ensample unto you. 9
for we o. were sometimes. Tit 3:3
the assembling of o. Heb 10:25
we deceive o., the truth. 1 John 1:8

out

o. of ground made Lord. Gen 2:9
she was taken o. of man. 23
for o. of it wast thou taken. 3:19
your sin will find you o. Num 32:23
as for the earth, o. of it. Job 28:5
o. of the mouth of babes. Ps 8:2
foundations of the earth are o. 82:5
thou teachest o. of thy law. 94:12
blessed you o. of house. 118:26
keep thy heart, for o. of it. Pr 4:23
candle goeth not o. by night. 31:18
sinners thereof o. of it. Isa 13:9
see o. of obscurity, o. of. 29:18
shall be saved o. of it. Jer 30:7
and o. of them shall proceed. 19
behold I will seek o. Ezek 34:11
that they bear them not o. into. 46:20
yet o. of thee shall he come forth to.
Mi 5:2; Mat 2:6
o. of him came forth. Zech 10:4
o. of the abundance of. Mat 12:34
o. of good treasure: . . . o. of evil. 35
o. of the heart proceed evil. 15:19
they were astonished o. Mark 10:26
nor enter to take any thing o. 13:15
o. of whom he had cast seven. 16:9
o. of thine own mouth. Luke 19:22
I have chosen you o. John 15:19
devout men, o. of every. Acts 2:5
both o. of the law, and o. 28:23
seen of me, as of one born o. of due time. 1 Cor 15:8
for o. of much affliction. 2 Cor 2:4
be a performance o. of that. 8:11
recover themselves o. of. 2 Tim 2:26
but o. of them all the Lord. 3:11
instant in season, o. of season. 4:2
o. of same mouth proceedeth blessing and cursing. Jas 3:10
see **camp, captivity, city, darkness, way, Zion**

outcast

they called thee an O. Jer 30:17

outcasts

he gathereth o. of Israel. Ps 147:2
Isa 56:8
he shall assemble the o. Isa 11:12
hide the o. 16:3
let my o. dwell with thee. 4
the o. in the land of Egypt. 27:13
whither the o. of Elam. Jer 49:36

outer

into the o. court. Ezek 46:21
way without to the o. gate. 47:2
be cast into o. darkness. Mat 8:12
22:13; 25:30

outgoings
the *o.* of it were at the sea. *Josh* 17:9; 19:39
o. of it shall be thine. 18
the *o.* of the border were. 18:19
o. thereof are in the valley. 19:14
the *o.* of their border were. 22, 33
thou makest the *o.* of the. *Ps* 65:8

outlandish
(*This word formerly meant strictly out-landish*; i.e. *anything which was from another country with other customs, hence* strange, *as the Revisions put it*)
even *o.* women caused Solomon to sin. *Neh* 13:26

outlived
elders that *o.* Joshua. *Judg* 2:7

outrageous
cruel and anger is *o.* *Pr* 27:4†

outrun
disciple did *o.* Peter. *John* 20:4

outside
Gideon went to *o.* of the. *Judg* 7:11
and when I come to the *o.* of. 17
came to the *o.* of the camp. 19
and so on *o.* toward the. *1 Ki* 7:9
behold a wall on the *o.* *Ezek* 40:5
make clean *o.* of the cup. *Mat* 23:25; *Luke* 11:39
o. of them may be clean also. 26

outstretched
out with an *o.* arm. *Deut* 26:8
against you with an *o.* hand. *Jer* 21:5
made the earth by my *o.* arm. 27:5

outward
for man looketh on the *o.* *1 Sam* 16:7
Chenaniah for the *o.* *1 Chr* 26:29
Levites for *o.* business. *Neh* 11:16
come into the *o.* court. *Esth* 6:4
me into the *o.* court. *Ezek* 40:17
which appear beautiful *o.* *Mat* 23:27
nor circumcision, which is *o.* *Rom* 2:28
though our *o.* man perish. *2 Cor* 4:16
on things after *o.* appearance? 10:7
not that *o.* adorning of. *1 Pet* 3:3

outwardly
ye *o.* appear righteous. *Mat* 23:28
for he is not a Jew which is one *o.* *Rom* 2:28

outwent
afoot thither, and *o.* *Mark* 6:33

oven
(*The word frequently means* furnace)
offering baken in the *o.* *Lev* 2:4; 7:9
be unclean, whether it be *o.* 11:35
bake your bread in one *o.* 26:26
make them as a fiery *o.* *Ps* 21:9
skin was black like an *o.* *Lam* 5:10
adulterers, as an *o.* heated. *Hos* 7:4
made ready their heart like an *o.* 6
are all hot as an *o.*, have devoured. 7
that shall burn as an *o.* *Mal* 4:1
grass, which to-morrow is cast into the *o.* *Mat* 6:30; *Luke* 12:28

ovens
frogs shall come into thine *o.* *Ex* 8:3

over
first red, all *o.* like an. *Gen* 25:25
lord *o.* thy brethren, let them. 27:29
Pharaoh said, Thou shalt be *o.* 41:40
gathered much had nothing *o.* *Ex* 16:18; *2 Cor* 8:15
what remaineth *o.* lay up. *Ex* 16:23
the mercy seat *o.* the testimony. 30:6; *Heb* 9:5
the cherubims covered *o.* the mercy seat. *Ex* 37:9
cloud was taken up from *o.* 40:36
one be killed *o.* running water. *Lev* 14:5; 6:50
shalt appoint Levites *o.* *Num* 1:50
o. and above them that were. 3:49
trumpets *o.* burnt offerings. 10:10
let the Lord set a man *o.* 27:16
dominion *o.* the nobles, *o.* *Judg* 5:13
and go to be promoted *o.* the trees. 9:9, 11, 13
o. Saul and Jonathan. *2 Sam* 1:17, 24
king *o.* Gilead, *o.* Ashurites, *o.* Jezreel, *o.* Ephraim and *o.* *2 Sam* 2:9
Edom made a king *o.* *2 Ki* 8:20
o. and above all I have. *1 Chr* 29:3
increased *o.* our heads. *Ezra* 9:6
not watch *o.* my sin? *Job* 14:16
he is a king *o.* the children. 41:34
my cup runneth *o.* *Ps* 23:5
deliver me not *o.* to the will. 27:12
but he hath not given me *o.* 118:18
his tender mercies are *o.* all. 145:9
neither make thyself *o.* wise. *Eccl* 7:16
past, rain is *o.* and gone. *S of S* 2:11
set thee *o.* nations and *o.* *Jer* 1:10
he setteth up *o.* it the basest of men. *Dan* 4:17
king thought to set him *o.* the. 6:3
people shall mourn *o.* it. *Hos* 10:5
shall be dark *o.* them. *Mi* 3:6
thee ruler *o.* many. *Mat* 25:21, 23
together, and running *o.* *Luke* 6:38
more joy *o.* one sinner. 15:7, 10
this man to reign *o.* us. 19:14
thou authority *o.* ten cities. 17
he beheld city, and wept *o.* it. 41
appoint *o.* this business. *Acts* 6:3
hath dominion *o.* a man. *Rom* 7:1
the potter power *o.* the clay? 9:21
given *o.* to lasciviousness. *Eph* 4:19
authority *o.* the man. *1 Tim* 2:12
eyes of the Lord are *o.* *1 Pet* 3:12
to him will I give power *o.* *Rev* 2:26
see **all, him, Jordan, Israel, me, thee, them, us, you**

over *against*
candlestick *o. against* table. *Ex* 26:35; 40:24
o. against candlestick. *Num* 8:2*, 3*
come on them *o. against* mulberry. *2 Sam* 5:23; *1 Chr* 14:14
pitched one *o. against.* *1 Ki* 20:29
one to be *o. against* house. *Neh* 7:3
set one *o. against* the. *Eccl* 7:14*
line shall yet go forth *o. against* it. *Jer* 31:39*
go into village *o. against.* *Mat* 21:2
Mark 11:2; *Luke* 19:30
and Mary sitting *o. against* the sepulchre. *Mat* 27:61

overcame
evil spirit was, *o.* them. *Acts* 19:16
even as I also *o.* and am. *Rev* 3:21
and they *o.* him by the blood. 12:11

overcharge
that I may not *o.* you all. *2 Cor* 2:5*

overcharged
lest your hearts be *o.* *Luke* 21:34

overcome
o. him, but he shall *o.* *Gen* 49:19*
that cry for being *o.* *Ex* 32:18
we are well able to *o.* it. *Num* 13:30
peradventure I be able to *o.* 22:11*
Ahaz, could not *o.* him. *2 Ki* 16:5
eyes, for they have *o.* me. *S of S* 6:5
head of them that are *o.* with wine. *Isa* 28:1
man whom wine hath *o.* *Jer* 23:9
a stronger shall *o.* him. *Luke* 11:22
I have *o.* the world. *John* 16:33
and mightest *o.* when. *Rom* 3:4*
be not *o.* of evil, but *o.* evil. 12:21
of whom a man is *o.*, of same is he brought. *2 Pet* 2:19
for if they are again entangled therein and *o.* 20
o. the wicked one. *1 John* 2:13, 14
ye are of God and have *o.* them. 4:4
beast shall *o.* witnesses. *Rev* 11:7
the saints, and to *o.* them. 13:7
and the Lamb shall *o.* them. 17:14

overcometh
of God, *o.* the world: this is victory that *o.* world, even. *1 John* 5:4
who is he that *o.* world, but he? 5
to him that *o.* will I give. *Rev* 2:7
he that *o.* shall not be hurt. 11
to him that *o.* will I give to eat. 17
to him that *o.* will I give power. 26
he that *o.* shall be clothed. 3:5
him that *o.* will I make pillar. 12
to him that *o.* will I grant. 21
he that *o.* shall inherit all. 21:7

overdrive
if men should *o.* them all. *Gen* 33:13

overflow
of Red sea to *o.* them. *Deut* 11:4
where the floods *o.* me. *Ps* 69:2
let not water flood *o.* me, nor. 15*
pass through Judah, *o.* *Isa* 8:8
consumption decreed shall *o.* 10:22
waters shall *o.* hiding place. 28:17
rivers they shall not *o.* thee. 43:2
north shall *o.* the land. *Jer* 47:2
one shall certainly come and *o.* *Dan* 11:10; 26:40
fats shall *o.* with wine and oil. *Joel* 2:24; 3:13

overflowed
rock, and streams *o.* *Ps* 78:20
world being *o.* with water. *2 Pet* 3:6

overfloweth
Jordan *o.* all his banks. *Josh* 3:15

overflowing
bindeth the floods from *o.* *Job* 28:11*
water course for *o.* of waters. 38:25
flood of mighty waters *o.* *Isa* 28:2
when the *o.* scourge shall. 15, 18
his breath as an *o.* stream. 30:28
north shall be an *o.* flood. *Jer* 47:2
be an *o.* shower. *Ezek* 13:11, 13
I will rain on him an *o.* rain. 38:22
o. of the water passed. *Hab* 3:10*

overflown
Jordan when it had *o.* *1 Chr* 12:15†
whose foundation was *o.* *Job* 22:16
flood shall they be *o.* *Dan* 11:22*

overlaid
shittim wood *o.* with gold. *Ex* 26:32
o. the staves of shittim wood. 38:6
died, because she *o.* it. *1 Ki* 3:19
he *o.* the doors of them. *2 Chr* 4:9
belly is as bright ivory *o.* *S of S* 5:14

overlay
shalt *o.* ark with pure gold. *Ex* 25:11, 24; 30:3
o. the horns of the altar with brass. 27:2; 38:2
see **gold**

overlaying
the *o.* of their chapiters. *Ex* 38:17
o. of their chapiters and fillets. 19

overlived
elders that *o.* Joshua. *Josh* 24:31*

overmuch
be not righteous *o.* *Eccl* 7:16
be not *o.* wicked. 17
be swallowed up with *o.* sorrow. *2 Cor* 2:7

overpass
they shine: they *o.* the deeds. *Jer* 5:28

overpast
until these calamities be *o.* *Ps* 57:1
until indignation be *o.* *Isa* 26:20

overplus
let him restore the *o.* *Lev* 25:27

overran
by plain and *o.* Cushi. *2 Sam* 18:23

overrunning
with an *o.* flood he will. *Nah* 1:8

oversee
some appointed to *o.* *1 Chr* 9:29*
and 3600 to *o.* them. *2 Chr* 2:2

overseer
he made him *o.* over. *Gen* 39:4, 5
Joel was their *o.* *Neh* 11:9
Zabdiel was *o.* 14
o. of Levites was Uzzi. 22
Jezrahiah was *o.* 12:42
the ant having no guide, *o.* *Pr* 6:7

overseers
let Pharaoh appoint *o.* *Gen* 41:34
Solomon set 3600 *o.* of the work. *2 Chr* 2:18
o. under hand of Cononiah. 31:13*
o. of all them that wrought. 34:12 13
money into hand of *o.* 17
H. G. hath made you *o.* *Acts* 20:28

overshadow
Highest shall *o.* thee. *Luke* 1:35
of Peter might *o.* them. *Acts* 5:15

overshadowed
a cloud *o.* them. *Mat* 17:5
Mark 9:7; *Luke* 9:34

oversight
peradventure it was an *o.* *Gen* 43:12
have the *o.* of them. *Num* 3:32
pertaineth the *o.* of all the. 4:16*
of them that had the *o.* *2 Ki* 12:11
22:5, 9; *2 Chr* 34:10
had the *o.* of the gates. *1 Chr* 9:23
o. of outward business. *Neh* 11:16
o. of the chamber of the house. 13:4*
taking *o.* not by constraint. *1 Pet* 5:2

overspread
was the whole earth *o.* *Gen* 9:19

overspreading
for the *o.* of abominations. *Dan* 9:27*

overtake
up, when thou dost *o.* *Gen* 44:4
I will pursue, I will *o.* *Ex* 15:9
lest avenger of blood *o.* *Deut* 19:6
shall come and *o.* thee. 28:2
these curses shall *o.* thee. 15, 45
them, for ye shall *o.* them. *Josh* 2:5
Shall I *o.* them? Pursue: for thou
shalt surely *o.* them. *1 Sam* 30:8
lest Absalom *o.* us. *2 Sam* 15:14
neither doth justice *o.* us *Isa* 59:9
ye feared shall *o.* you. *Jer* 42:16
she shall not *o.* her lovers. *Hos* 2:7
Gibeah did not *o.* them. 10:9
not *o.* nor prevent us. *Amos* 9:10
behold, the plowman shall *o.* 13
should *o.* you as a thief. *1 Thes* 5:4

overtaken
mine enemies and *o.* *Ps* 18:37
brethren, if a man be *o.* *Gal* 6:1

overtaketh
while sword *o.* thee. *1 Chr* 21:12

overthrew
God *o.* these cities. *Gen* 19:25, 29
Lord *o.* the Egyptians. *Ex* 14:27
Ps 136:15
Lord *o.* in his anger. *Deut* 29:23
as when God *o.* Sodom. *Isa* 13:19
Jer 50:40; *Amos* 4:11
be as the cities Lord *o.* *Jer* 20:16
Jesus *o.* tables of the. *Mat* 21:12
Mark 11:15; *John* 2:15

overthrow
I will not *o.* this city. *Gen* 19:21
thou shalt utterly *o.* them. *Ex* 23:24
ye shall *o.* their altars. *Deut* 12:3*
sent to spy it out and *o.* *2 Sam* 10:3
battle more strong, and *o.* it. 11:25
David hath sent to *o.* and. *1 Chr* 19:3
his hand to *o.* them in the. *Ps* 106:26
to *o.* their seed also among the. 27
who have purposed to *o.* 140:4*
the violent man to *o.* him. 11
not good to *o.* righteous. *Pr* 18:5*
I will *o.* the throne of kingdoms, I
will *o.* the chariots. *Hag* 2:22
of God, ye cannot *o.* it. *Acts* 5:39
and *o.* the faith of some. *2 Tim* 2:18

overthrow, *substantive*
out of the midst of the *o.* *Gen* 19:29
as in the *o.* of Sodom. *Deut* 29:23
Jer 49:18
the cities with an *o.* *2 Pet* 2:6

overthroweth
princes, and *o.* the mighty. *Job* 12:19
but wickedness *o.* the. *Pr* 13:6
God *o.* the wicked for. 21:12
he *o.* the words of the. 22:12
but he that receiveth gifts *o.* 29:4

overthrown
hast *o.* them that rose up. *Ex* 15:7
and many were *o.* *Judg* 9:40*
when some of them be *o.* at the first.
2 Sam 17:9*
Ethiopians were *o.* *2 Chr* 14:13*
that God hath *o.* me. *Job* 19:6
judges are *o.* in stony places.
Ps 141:6
city is *o.* by the mouth. *Pr* 11:11
the wicked are *o.*, and are not. 12:7
house of wicked shall be *o.* 14:11
your land is desolate, as *o.* *Isa* 1:7
but let them be *o.* before. *Jer* 18:23
sin of Sodom, that was *o.* *Lam* 4:6
countries shall be *o.* *Dan* 11:41
I have *o.* some of you. *Amos* 4:11
and Nineveh shall be *o.* *Jonah* 3:4
o. in the wilderness. *1 Cor* 10:5

overtook
they *o.* Jacob in the. *Gen* 31:23
Laban *o.* Jacob. 25
the steward *o.* them. 44:6
Egyptians *o.* them. *Ex* 14:9
Micah *o.* the children. *Judg* 18:22
but the battle *o.* the men. 20:42*
the army of Chaldees *o.* *2 Ki* 25:5
Jer 39:5; 52:8
all her persecutors *o.* her. *Lam* 2:3

overturn
waters, they *o.* earth. *Job* 12:15
I will *o.*, *o.*, *o.* it, until. *Ezek* 21:27

overturned
tent that it fell and *o.* it. *Judg* 7:13*

overturneth
which *o.* the mountains. *Job* 9:5
o. the mountains by the roots. 28:9
knoweth their works and *o.* 34:25

overwhelm
ye *o.* fatherless, dig a pit. *Job* 6:27*

overwhelmed
and horror hath *o.* me. *Ps* 55:5
when my heart is *o.* lead me. 61:2
and my spirit was *o.* 77:3; 142:3
143:4
but the sea *o.* their enemies. 78:53
then the waters had *o.* us. 124:4

owe
o. no man any thing. *Rom* 13:8

owed
o. him 10,000 talents. *Mat* 18:24
and found one which *o.* him an. 28
the one *o.* 500 pence. *Luke* 7:41

owest
pay me that thou *o.* *Mat* 18:28
how much *o.* thou unto my lord?
Luke 16:5, 7
thou *o.* to me even thine. *Philem* 19

oweth
hath wronged thee, or *o.* *Philem* 18

owl
(*While different sorts of owls are found in Palestine, the word so translated more often means some other bird or animal, usually the* ostrich)
o. and cuckow unclean. *Lev* 11:16*
Deut 14:15*, 16
the little *o.* and cormorant.
Lev 11:17; *Isa* 34:11, 15*
I am like an *o.* of desert. *Ps* 102:6

owls
(*Revisions in all cases,* ostriches)
companion to *o.*, a brother. *Job* 30:29
the wild beasts shall lie there, and *o.*
Isa 13:21; 34:13; *Jer* 50:39
the dragons and *o.* shall. 43:20
a mourning as the *o.* *Mi* 1:8

own
man in his *o.* image. *Gen* 1:27
begat a son in his *o.* likeness. 5:3
shall come of thine *o.* bowels. 15:4
I may go to mine *o.* place. 30:25
four parts shall be your *o.* 47:24
dead shall be his *o.* *Ex* 21:36
of the best of his *o.* field shall. 22:5
he shall offer it of his own. *Lev* 1:3
his *o.* hands shall bring the. 7:30
palm of his *o.* left hand. 14:15, 26
theirs is thine *o.* nakedness. 18:10
nor any of your *o.* nation, nor. 26
groweth of its *o.* accord. 25:5
and he shall return to his *o.* 41
his *o.* camp, by his *o.* *Num* 1:52
them of mine *o.* mind. 16:28; 24:13
sinners against their *o.* souls. 16:38
he called it after his *o.* name. 32:42
Deut 3:14
shall keep himself to his *o.* *Num* 36:9
eat grapes at thine *o.* *Deut* 23:24
sleep in his *o.* raiment. 24:13
every man shall be put to death for
o. sin. 16; *2 Ki* 14:6; *2 Chr* 25:4
fruit of thine *o.* body. *Deut* 28:53
nor knew he his *o.* children. 33:9
even among their *o.* stuff. *Josh* 7:11
from their *o.* doings. *Judg* 2:19
saying, Mine *o.* hand hath. 7:2
went to their *o.* home. *1 Sam* 2:20
ark go again to his *o.* place. 5:11
wast little in thine *o.* sight. 15:17
avenging with thine *o.* hand. 25:26
base in mine *o.* sight. *2 Sam* 6:22
dwell in a place of their *o.* 7:10
did eat of his *o.* meat, and. 12:3
to battle in thine *o.* person. 17:11
falsehood against mine *o.* life. 18:13
word against his *o.* life. *1 Ki* 2:23
blood on his *o.* head. 32, 37
carcase in his *o.* grave. 13:30
laid him upon his *o.* bed. 17:19
made gods of their *o.* *2 Ki* 17:29
and of thine *o.* have. *1 Chr* 29:14
store we prepared, is all thine *o.* 16
his way on his *o.* head. *2 Chr* 6:23
reproach on their *o.* head. *Neh* 4:4
should return on *o.* head. *Esth* 9:25
perish for ever like his *o.* *Job* 20:7
let them fall by their *o.* *Ps* 5:10
our lips are our *o.*: who is? 12:4
God, even our *o.* God, shall. 67:6
he gave them their *o.* desire. 78:29
up to their *o.* hearts' lust. 81:12
their *o.* iniquity, and shall cut them
off in their *o.* wickedness. 94:23
let them be only thy *o.* *Pr* 5:17
for mine *o.* sake. *Isa* 37:35; 43:25
48:11
o. pleasure, nor *o.* words. 58:13
my river is mine *o.* *Ezek* 29:3
to his *o.* righteousness. 33:13
now their *o.* doings have. *Hos* 7:2
forsake their *o.* mercy. *Jonah* 2:8
what I will with mine *o.*? *Mat* 20:15
hate not his *o.* life also. *Luke* 14:26
you that which is your *o.*? 16:12
o., his *o.* received him not. *John* 1:11
a lie, he speaketh of his *o.* 8:44
an hireling, whose *o.* the sheep. 10:12
having loved his *o.* that were in. 13:1
the world would love his *o.* 15:19
every man to his *o.* 16:32
as though by our *o.* power. *Acts* 3:12
thine *o.*? was it not in thine *o.*? 5:4
purchased with his *o.* blood. 20:28
he considered not his *o.* *Rom* 4:19
he that spared not his *o.* Son. 8:32
to his *o.* master he standeth. 14:4
ye are not your *o.* for ye. *1 Cor* 6:19
every man have his *o.* wife. 7:2
let no man seek his *o.* but. 10:24
conscience, I say, not thine *o.* 29
charity seeketh not her *o.* 13:5
for all seek their *o.* things. *Phil* 2:21
having mine *o.* righteousness. 3:9
provide not for his *o.*, his *o.* *1 Tim* 5:8
a prophet of their *o.* *Tit* 1:12
but by his *o.* blood he. *Heb* 9:12
our sins in his *o.* blood. *Rev* 1:5
see **counsel, country, eyes, heart, house, land, people, self, selves, soul, way, ways, will**

owner
but the *o.* of the ox. *Ex* 21:28
testified to his *o.*, his *o.* shall. 29
the *o.* of the pit shall make it. 34
and his *o.* hath not kept him in. 36
o. of it shall accept thereof. 22:11
make restitution to the *o.* 12
o. thereof not being with it. 14
but if *o.* thereof be with it, not. 15
after name of Shemer, *o.* *1 Ki* 16:24
ox knoweth his *o.*, the ass. *Isa* 1:3
centurion believed the *o.* *Acts* 27:11

owners
or have caused the *o.* to. *Job* 31:39
life of *o.* thereof. *Pr* 1:19
there to the *o.* thereof? *Eccl* 5:11
a sore evil, riches kept for *o.* 13
the *o.* said, Why loose? *Luke* 19:33

owneth
o. the house shall tell. *Lev* 14:35
bind man that *o.* this. *Acts* 21:11

ox
shalt not covet thy neighbour's *ox.*
Ex 20:17; *Deut* 5:21
if *ox* gore a man. *Ex* 21:28, 29, 32

if ox were wont to push. Ex 21:29, 36
if ox push a manservant or. 32
if an ox or ass shall fall into a pit. 33
if a man shall steal an ox. 22:1
whether it be ox or ass, he shall. 4
trespass for an ox. 9
deliver an ox to keep. 10
enemy's ox going astray. 23:4
that thine ox and thine ass. 12
every firstling of an ox or. 34:19
no manner of fat of ox or. Lev 7:23
what man soever killeth an ox. 17:3
each of princes an ox. Num 7:3
as the ox licketh up the grass. 22:4
thine ox shall do no work. Deut 5:14
the ox, the sheep, and goat. 14:4
whether it be ox or sheep. 18:3
thy brother's ox go astray. 22:1
thy brother's ox fall down. 4
shalt not plow with an ox and ass. 10
thou shalt not muzzle the ox. 25:4
1 Cor 9:9; 1 Tim 5:18
thine ox shall be slain. Deut 28:31
they destroyed ox and sheep.
Josh 6:21; 1 Sam 15:15
600 men with an ox goad. Judg 3:31
they left neither sheep nor ox. 6:4
Samuel said, Whose ox or ass have I taken? 1 Sam 12:3
every man his ox and sheep. 14:34
me daily one ox, six sheep. Neh 5:18
or loweth the ox over? Job 6:5
they take the widow's ox for. 24:3
eateth grass as an ox. 40:15
Lord better than an ox. Ps 69:31
glory into similitude of an ox. 106:20
goeth after her as an ox. Pr 7:22
is by strength of the ox. 14:4
better than a stalled ox, and. 15:17
the ox knoweth his owner. Isa 1:3
lion shall eat straw like the ox. 11:7
thither the feet of the ox. 32:20
that killeth an ox, as if he. 66:3
a lamb or an ox brought. Jer 11:19
had the face of an ox. Ezek 1:10
of you loose his ox on. Luke 13:15
shall have an ox or an ass. 14:5

wild ox

wild ox and chamois. Deut 14:5*

oxen

Abram had sheep, and o. Gen 12:16
gave Abraham sheep and o. 20:14
gave Abimelech sheep and o. 21:27
Jacob said thus, I have o. 32:5
Jacob took Shechem's o. 34:28*
hand of Lord is upon the o. Ex 9:3*
sacrifice thereon thine o. 20:24
shall restore five o. for one. 22:1
thou do with thine o. and sheep. 30
princes brought twelve o. Num 7:3
four o. he gave to the sons of. 7
and eight o. he gave to the sons. 8
Balak offered o. and sheep. 22:40
prepare me here seven o. 23:1*
money for o. or sheep. Deut 14:26
Joshua took Achan, his o. Josh 7:24
yoke of o. in pieces, and sent them . . . done to his o. 1 Sam 11:7
which yoke of o. might plow. 14:14*
the people took sheep and o. 32
Agag and the best of the o. 15:9
lowing of o. which I hear? 14
spared the best of the sheep and o. 15
Doeg smote the o. and sheep. 22:19
took away the sheep, and o. 27:9
Uzza took hold of it, for o. 2 Sam 6:6
David sacrificed o. and fatlings. 13
be o. for burnt sacrifice. 24:22
the threshingfloor and o. 24
Adonijah slew sheep and o.
1 Ki 1:9, 19, 25
provision, 10 fat o. 100 sheep. 4:23
one sea, 12 o. under it. 7:25, 44
2 Chr 4:4, 15
sacrificing sheep and o. 1 Ki 8:5
a sacrifice to the Lord of 22,000 o. and 120,000. 63; 2 Chr 7:5
plowing with twelve yoke of o.
1 Ki 19:19
Elisha left the o. and ran. 20
he took a yoke of o. and slew. 21
to receive sheep and o.? 2 Ki 5:26
bread on mules and on o. 1 Chr 12:40
of the spoil 700 o. 2 Chr 15:11
Ahab killed sheep and o. for. 18:2
consecrated things were 600 o. 29:33
they brought in the tithes of o. 31:6
passover three hundred o. 35:8
3000 camels, 500 yoke of o. Job 1:3
the o. were plowing, and the. 14
1000 yoke of o. 1000 asses. 42:12
to have dominion over o. Ps 8:7
that our o. may be strong. 144:14
where no o. are the crib. Pr 14:4
for the sending forth of o. Isa 7:25
joy and gladness, slaying o. 22:13
the o. and asses shall eat. 30:24
husbandman and his o. Jer 51:23
they shall make thee to eat grass as o.
Dan 4:25, 32, 33; 5:21
one plow there with o.? Amos 6:12
my o. and my fatlings. Mat 22:4
bought five yoke of o. Luke 14:19
temple those that sold o. John 2:14
out, the sheep and the o. 15
priest of Jupiter brought o. and.
Acts 14:13
God take care for o.? 1 Cor 9:9

Ozem

O., sixth son of Jesse. 1 Chr 2:15

Ozias

Joram begat O. Mat 1:8
O. begat Joatham. 9

P

Paarai

P. the Arbite, a mighty. 2 Sam 23:35

paces

when gone six p. he. 2 Sam 6:13

pacify, -ed, -eth

was king's wrath p. Esth 7:10
wise man will p. the wrath. Pr 16:14
a gift in secret p. anger. 21:14
p. great offences. Eccl 10:4*
when I am p. toward. Ezek 16:63*

Padan-aram

daughter of Bethuel of P. Gen 25:20
Isaac sent Jacob away to P. 28:6
Jacob was gone to P. 7
what he had gotten in P. 31:18
Jacob when he came from P. 35:9
sons born to him in P. 26; 46:15

paddle

shalt have a p. on thy. Deut 23:13

Pagiel

P. son of Ocran, prince of Asher.
Num 1:13; 7:72

paid

custom, was p. them. Ezra 4:20
this day have I p. vows. Pr 7:14
so he p. fare thereof. Jonah 1:3
not come out thence till thou hast p. uttermost. Mat 5:26; Luke 12:59
received tithes, p. tithes. Heb 7:9

pain

(*Used as now of great discomfort either of mind or body*)

flesh on him shall have p. Job 14:22
man travaileth with p. 15:20
he is chastened also with p. 33:19*
mine affliction and my p. Ps 25:18
p. as a woman in travail. 48:6
Isa 13:8; 26:17
my loins filled with p. Isa 21:3
child, we have been in p. 26:18
before her p. came, she was. 66:7
taken hold of us, and p. as of a woman in. Jer 6:24; 22:23
put themselves to p. but. 12:13
why is my p. perpetual? 15:18
it shall fall with p. on head. 30:23*
Babylon, take balm for her p. 51:8
great p. shall be in Ethiopia.
Ezek 30:4, 9
Sin shall have great p., No shall. 16
be in p. and labour to. Mi 4:10
p. is in all loins, faces. Nah 2:10
creation travaileth in p. Rom 8:22
their tongues for p. Rev 16:10
nor shall there be any more p. 21:4
see **pangs**

pained

my heart is sore p. within. Ps 55:4
p. at report of Tyre. Isa 23:5
I am p. at my very heart. Jer 4:19
people shall be much p. Joel 2:6
travailing in birth, and p. Rev 12:2

painful

it was too p. for me. Ps 73:16

painfulness

in weariness and p., in. 2 Cor 11:27

pains

she travailed, for her p. 1 Sam 4:19
and the p. of hell gat. Ps 116:3
having loosed p. of death. Acts 2:24
they blasphemed, because of their p.
Rev 16:11

painted

Jezebel p. her face, and. 2 Ki 9:30
cieled with cedar, and p. Jer 22:14

paintedst

thou p. thy eyes. Ezek 23:40

painting

rentest thy face with p. Jer 4:30*

pair

offer a p. of turtle doves. Luke 2:24
he had a pair of balances. Rev 6:5

palace

Revisions usually replace this by castle *or* court, *as the word generally suggests a fortified house. The word occasionally includes the entire city,* Esth 9:12; *again, it is restricted to a part of the royal apartments,* 1 Ki 16:18. *It is applied to the temple in Jerusalem in* 1 Chr 29:1.

Zimri burnt the king's p. 1 Ki 16:18
vineyard hard by the p. 21:1
Pekaiah in the p. 2 Ki 15:25
shall be eunuchs in p. of king. 20:18
p. is not for man, but. 1 Chr 29:1
a perfect heart to build the p. 19
terraces to the king's p. 2 Chr 9:11
maintenance from the p. Ezra 4:14
at Achmetha, in the p. a roll. 6:2
as I was in Shushan the p. Neh 1:1
beams for the gates of the p. 2:8
I gave Hanani, ruler of the p. 7:2
young virgins to the p. Esth 2:3
decree was given in Shushan, the p.
3:15; 8:14
500 men in Shushan the p. 9:12
enter into the king's p. Ps 45:15
after the similitude of a p. 144:12
build on her p. of silver. S of S 8:9
hast made a p. of strangers. Isa 25:2
flourishing in my p. Dan 4:4
king went to his p. and passed. 6:18
he shall plant his p. between. 11:45
ye shall cast them into p. Amos 4:3*
and p. shall be dissolved. Nah 2:6
Jesus afar off to the high priest's p.
Mat 26:58; Mark 14:54
strong man keepeth his p. Luke 11:21
bonds are manifest in all the p.
Phil 1:13*

palaces

and burnt all the p. 2 Chr 36:19
of myrrh, out of ivory p. Ps 45:8
God is known in her p. for. 48:3
bulwarks, consider her p. 13
his sanctuary like high p. 78:69*
prosperity within thy p. 122:7
spider is in king's p. Pr 30:28
cry in their pleasant p. Isa 13:22
p. shall be forsaken. 32:14
thorns come up in her p. 34:13
and let us destroy her p. Jer 6:5
come and is entered into our p. 9:21
devour the p. of Jerusalem. 17:27
consume the p. of Ben-hadad. 49:27
swallowed up all her p. Lam 2:5
knew their desolate p. Ezek 19:7
they shall set their p. in thee. 25:4*
in p. at Ashdod, in p. of Egypt.
Amos 3:9
violence and robbery in their p. 10
thy p. shall be spoiled. 11
I hate his p. 6:8
when he shall tread in our p. Mi 5:5
see **devour**

pale
his face now wax *p.* *Isa* 29:22
behold a *p.* horse: and his name was Death. *Rev* 6:8

paleness
all faces turned into *p.* *Jer* 30:6

Palestina
(*This word refers to the land of the Philistines and not to the whole of what we know as Palestine. Revisions change to* Philistia)
sorrow on men of *P.* *Ex* 15:14
rejoice not, thou whole *P.* *Isa* 14:29
thou whole *P.* art dissolved. 31

palm
pour it into *p.* of his. *Lev* 14:15, 26
struck Jesus with the *p.* *John* 18:22

palm branches
to mount and fetch *p. b.* *Neh* 8:15

palmerworm
(*The English word is one used for a variety of caterpillar. It is not however known to which variety the word refers*)
what the *p.* left, the locust. *Joel* 1:4
the years that *p.* hath eaten. 2:25
the *p.* devoured them. *Amos* 4:9

palms
both the *p.* of his hands. *1 Sam* 5:4
they found skull and *p.* *2 Ki* 9:35
I have graven thee on *p.* of my hands *Isa* 49:16
on the *p.* of my hands. *Dan* 10:10
smote him with the *p.* of their hands. *Mat* 26:67; *Mark* 14:65*
and *p.* in their hands. *Rev* 7:9

palm tree
(*The palm, especially the date-palm, is one of the most important trees in the East. The fruit is the daily food of millions; wine is made of the sap; the seeds are made into a food for camels; the fibres of the leaf-stems are woven into ropes and rigging; the tall trunk is a valuable timber; its leaves are made into many different articles.*)
The palm is also used as a symbol of victory, Rev 7:9.
under the *p.* of Deborah. *Judg* 4:5
shall flourish like the *p.* *Ps* 92:12
stature is like to a *p.* *S of S* 7:7
go up to the *p.*, I will take hold. 8
they are upright as the *p.* *Jer* 10:5
man was toward the *p.* *Ezek* 41:19
the *p.* and the apple tree. *Joel* 1:12

palm trees
where were seventy *p.* *Ex* 15:27
take you branches of *p.* *Lev* 23:40
city of *p.* unto Zoar. *Deut* 34:3
out of the city of *p.* *Judg* 1:16
and possessed city of *p.* 3:13
carved figures of *p.* *1 Ki* 6:29, 32, 35
7:36; *2 Chr* 3:5; *Ezek* 40:16
them to the city of *p.* *2 Chr* 28:15
took branches of *p.* *John* 12:13

palsies
many taken with *p.*, healed. *Acts* 8:7

palsy
(*An old word for the various sorts of paralysis*)
and those that had the *p.* *Mat* 4:24
9:2; *Mark* 2:3; *Luke* 5:18
lieth at home sick of the *p.* *Mat* 8:6
faith, said to the sick of the *p.*, Son. 9:2; *Mark* 2:5
Jesus saith to the sick of *p.*, Arise. *Mark* 2:10; *Luke* 5:24
Aeneas, who was sick of the *p.* *Acts* 9:33

Pamphylia
Paphos to Perga in *P.* *Acts* 13:13
John departed from *P.* 15:38
sailed over the sea of *P.* 27:5

pan
meat offering baken in a *p.* *Lev* 2:5
in a *p.* it shall be made with oil. 6:21
all that is dressed in *p.* shall be. 7:9
priest's servant stuck it into the *p.* *1 Sam* 2:14
Tamar took a *p.* and. *2 Sam* 13:9
take unto thee an iron *p.* *Ezek* 4:3

pangs
p. and sorrows shall take. *Isa* 13:8
p. have taken hold on me, as *p.* 21:3
woman crieth out in her *p.* 26:17
thou be when *p.* come. *Jer* 22:23
as the heart of a woman in her *p.* 48:41; 49:22
and *p.* as of a woman in travail. 50:43; *Mi* 4:9

pannag
traded in thy market, *p.* *Ezek* 27:17

pans
thou shalt make *p.* to. *Ex* 27:3
they baked manna in *p.* *Num* 11:8*
over the things made in the *p.* *1 Chr* 9:31; 23:29
offerings sod they in *p.* *2 Chr* 35:13

pant
that *p.* after the dust of. *Amos* 2:7

panted
I opened my mouth and *p.* *Ps* 119:131
my heart *p.*, fearfulness. *Isa* 21:4

panteth
my heart *p.*, my strength. *Ps* 38:10*
as hart *p.* so *p.* my soul after. 42:1

paper
(*The meaning in the Bible is either the papyrus, made into a sort of paper, or some preparation of skin*)
the *p.* reeds by the. *Isa* 19:7*
not write with *p.* and ink. *2 John* 12

Paphos
through the isle unto *P.* *Acts* 13:6, 13

paps
lewdness for the *p.* of. *Ezek* 23:21
blessed are *p.* which. *Luke* 11:27
blessed are the *p.* which never. 23:29
and girt about the *p.* with. *Rev* 1:13

parable
(*The word comes from the Greek* parabolé *which means a placing beside. It is therefore the placing of one subject by another as an illustration. Especially is it used for the illustration of spiritual things by familiar earthly objects or incidents. In the Bible the word is used more generally than elsewhere, being applied even to short proverbs*)
The prophets made use of Parables, to give a stronger impression to prince and people of the threatenings or of the promises they made to them. Nathan reproved David under the parable of a rich man that had taken away and killed the lamb of a poor man, 2 Sam 12:2, 3, etc. *Jotham, son of Gideon, proposed to the men of Shechem, the parable of the bramble, whom the trees had a mind to choose for their king*, Judg 9:7, 8, etc.
Our Saviour in the gospels often speaks to the people in parables, Mat 13:10, 13, etc. *He made use of them to veil the truth from those who were not willing to see it. Those who really desired to know would not rest till they had found out the meaning. This is given by Jesus as an illustration of* Isa 6:9, 10.
Baalam took up his *p.* and said. *Num* 23:7; 24:3, 15, 20, 21, 23
took up his *p.*, Rise up, Balak. 23:18
Job continued his *p.* *Job* 27:1; 29:1
incline mine ear to a *p.* *Ps* 49:4
my mouth, in a *p.*, I will utter. 78:2
so is a *p.* in the mouth. *Pr* 26:7, 9
speak a *p.* to the house. *Ezek* 17:2
utter a *p.* to the rebellious. 24:3
one shall take up a *p.* *Mi* 2:4
shall not all these take up a *p.* against him! *Hab* 2:6
the *p.* of the sower. *Mat* 13:18
another *p.* put he. 24, 31, 33; 21:33
without a *p.* spake. 13:34; *Mark* 4:34
the *p.* of the tares. *Mat* 13:36; 15:15
learn a *p.* of the fig tree. *Mat* 24:32
Mark 13:28; *Luke* 21:29
they asked him of *p.* *Mark* 4:10
7:17; *Luke* 8:9
know ye not this *p.*? *Mark* 4:13
he had spoken the *p.* against them. 12:12; *Luke* 20:19
he spoke a *p.* to them. *Luke* 5:36
6:39; 8:4; 12:16; 13:6; 14:7
15:3; 18:1, 9; 19:11; 20:9; 21:29
John 10:6
this *p.* to us, or to all? *Luke* 12:41

parables
doth he not speak *p.*? *Ezek* 20:49
spake many things to them in *p.* *Mat* 13:3, 13, 34; 22:1; *Mark* 3:23
4:2, 13, 33; 12:1
will ye know all *p.*? *Mark* 4:13
but others in *p.* that. *Luke* 8:10

paradise
thou be with me in *p.* *Luke* 23:43
was caught up into *p.* *2 Cor* 12:4
midst of the *p.* of God. *Rev* 2:7

paramours
she doted upon their *p.* *Ezek* 23:20

Paran
Ishmael dwelt in the wilderness of *P.* *Gen* 21:21
the wilderness of *P.* *Num* 10:12
12:16; 13:3, 26; *1 Sam* 25:1
shined from mount *P.* *Deut* 33:2
Holy One came from *P.* *Hab* 3:3

Parbar
the causeway, two at *P.* *1 Chr* 26:18

parcel
Jacob bought a *p.* of a field. *Gen* 33:19
Josh 24:32; *John* 4:5
Naomi selleth a *p.* of land. *Ruth* 4:3
p. of ground full. *1 Chr* 11:13*, 14*

parched
the *p.* ground shall. *Isa* 35:7*
but he shall inhabit the *p.* *Jer* 17:6
see **corn**

parchments
but especially the *p.* *2 Tim* 4:13

pardon
he will not *p.* your. *Ex* 23:21
p. our iniquity and our sin. 34:9
Num 14:19
I pray thee, *p.* my sin. *1 Sam* 15:25
in this thing the Lord *p.* *2 Ki* 5:18
which Lord would not *p.* 24:4
the good Lord *p.* *2 Chr* 30:18
thou art a God ready to *p.* *Neh* 9:17
why dost thou not *p.* my? *Job* 7:21
for thy name's sake *p.* *Ps* 25:11
for he will abundantly *p.* *Isa* 55:7
and I will *p.* it. *Jer* 5:1
how shall I *p.* thee for this? 7
I will *p.* all their iniquities. 33:8
for I will *p.* them whom. 50:20

pardoned
I have *p.* according to. *Num* 14:20
that her iniquity is *p.* *Isa* 40:2
rebelled, thou hast not *p.* *Lam* 3:42

pardoneth
to thee, that *p.* iniquity? *Mi* 7:18

pare
her head and *p.* her nails. *Deut* 21:12

parents
rise up against their *p.* and cause. *Mat* 10:21; *Mark* 13:12
when the *p.* brought in. *Luke* 2:27
her *p.* were astonished, but. 8:56
man that hath left *p.* or wife. 18:29
ye shall be betrayed both by *p.* 21:16
sin, this man or his *p.*? *John* 9:2
these words spake *p.* 22, 23
proud, disobedient to *p.* *Rom* 1:30
2 Tim 3:2
not to lay up for the *p.* *2 Cor* 12:14
children, obey your *p.* *Eph* 6:1
Col 3:20
learn to requite their *p.* *1 Tim* 5:4
three months of his *p.* *Heb* 11:23

parlour
sitting in a summer *p.* *Judg* 3:20*
Ehud shut the doors of the *p.* 23*
Samuel brought them into the *p.* *1 Sam* 9:22*

parlours
David gave Solomon a pattern of *p.* *1 Chr* 28:11*

Parmenas
Timon, *P.*, and Nicolas. *Acts* 6:5

part, *noun*
they stood at the nether *p.* *Ex* 19:17
the breast, it shall be thy *p.* 29:26
p. of the beaten corn, *p.* *Lev* 2:16
right shoulder for his *p.* 7:33
consecration was Moses' *p.* 8:29
if any *p.* of their carcase. 11:37, 38
his hair fallen off from the *p.* 13:41
nor have *p.* among them. *Num* 18:20
Deut 10:9; 12:12; 14:27, 29
18:1; *Josh* 14:4; 18:7
I am thy *p.* and thine. *Num* 18:20
might see utmost *p.* of the people.
Num 22:41; 23:13
he provided the first *p.* *Deut* 33:21
the *p.* of Judah was. *Josh* 19:9
have no *p.* in the Lord. 22:25, 27
her hap was to light on a *p.* *Ruth* 2:3
unto thee the *p.* of a kinsman. 3:13
tarried in the utmost *p.* *1 Sam* 14:2
our *p.* shall be to deliver. 23:20
as his *p.* is that goeth down to battle, so shall his *p.* be that. 30:24
we have no *p.* in David. *2 Sam* 20:1
come to uttermost *p.* *2 Ki* 7:5, 8
on thy *p.* to set riders. 18:23
Isa 36:8
greatest *p.* had kept. *1 Chr* 12:29
went into the inner *p.* *2 Chr* 29:16
cast out to the uttermost *p.* *Neh* 1:9
restore the hundredth *p.* of. 5:11
I will answer also my *p.* *Job* 32:17
their inward *p.* is very. *Ps* 5:9
in hidden *p.* shalt make me. 51:6
Lord taketh my *p.* with them. 118:7
nor highest *p.* of the dust. *Pr* 8:26
rejoicing in the habitable *p.* of. 31
shall have *p.* of inheritance. 17:2
fly that is in the utmost *p.* *Isa* 7:18
from utmost *p.* of earth. 24:16
he burneth *p.* thereof in the fire, with *p.* thereof he eateth. 44:16, 19
drink sixth *p.* of an hin. *Ezek* 4:11
leave but the sixth *p.* of thee. 39:2
sixth *p.* of an ephah of an. 45:13
it shall be the prince's *p.* to. 17
a meat offering the sixth *p.* 46:14
p. iron, and *p.* clay. *Dan* 2:33, 41, 42
the king saw *p.* of the hand. 5:5, 24
arms shall stand on his *p.* 11:31
great deep, did eat up a *p.* *Amos* 7:4
he was in the hinder *p.* of. *Mark* 4:38
is not against us, is on our *p.* 9:40
hath chosen that good *p.* *Luke* 10:42
inward *p.* is full of ravening. 11:39
as lightning that lighteneth out of one *p.* shining to other *p.* 17:24
hast no *p.* with me. *John* 13:8
four parts, every soldier a *p.* 19:23
and had obtained *p.* of. *Acts* 1:17
that he may take *p.* of this. 25
Ananias kept back *p.* of the price, and brought a certain *p.* 5:2, 3
thou hast neither *p.* nor lot in. 8:21
p. held with the Jews, *p.* with. 14:4
the chief city of that *p.* of. 16:12*
more *p.* knew not wherefore. 19:32
perceived that the one *p.* 23:6
the more *p.* advised to depart. 27:12
honour to that *p.* which. *1 Cor* 12:24
of whom the greater *p.* remain. 15:6
what was lacking on your *p.* 16:17
what *p.* he that believeth. *2 Cor* 6:15
the measure of every *p.* *Eph* 4:16
he of the contrary *p.* may. *Tit* 2:8
himself likewise took *p.* *Heb* 2:14*
on their *p.* he is evil spoken of, but on your *p.* he is. *1 Pet* 4:14
holy that hath *p.* in the. *Rev* 20:6
all liars shall have their *p.* 21:8
God shall take away his *p.* 22:19

part, *verb*
thou *p.* the meat offering. *Lev* 2:6
if aught but death *p.* *Ruth* 1:17
they shall *p.* alike. *1 Sam* 30:24
was none to *p.* them. *2 Sam* 14:6
shall they *p.* him among? *Job* 41:6
they *p.* my garments. *Ps* 22:18

in **part**
blindness *in p.* is happened.
Rom 11:25
we know *in p.* and we prophesy *in p.*
1 Cor 13:9
then that which is *in p.* shall be. 10
I know *in p.* but then shall I know. 12
acknowledged us *in p.* *2 Cor* 1:14
hath not grieved me but *in p.* 2:5

third **part**
flour mingled with the *third p.* of an.
Num 15:6; 28:14; *Ezek* 46:14
shalt offer the *third p.* of. *Num* 15:7
David sent a *third p.* *2 Sam* 18:2
a *third p.* that enter in. *2 Ki* 11:5
a *third p.* of you shall be porters.
2 Chr 23:4
with *third p.* of shekel. *Neh* 10:32
fire a *third p.*, a *third p.*, smite about it, a *third p.* *Ezek* 5:2, 12
third p. shall be left. *Zech* 13:8
the *third p.* through the fire. 9
third p. of the trees. *Rev* 8:7
and the *third p.* of the sea. 8
third p. of creatures died, *third p.* 9
it fell upon the *third p.* of. 10
third p. of the waters became. 11
third p. of the sun, moon, and stars, was smitten . . . for a *third p.* 12
for to slay the *third p.* of men. 9:15
was the *third p.* of men killed. 18
his tail drew *third p.* of the. 12:4

fourth **part**
flour mingled with the *fourth p.* of.
Ex 29:40; *Num* 15:4; 28:5
fourth p. of an hin of wine for a.
Lev 23:13; *Num* 15:5; 28:7, 14
have here the *fourth p.* of a shekel.
1 Sam 9:8
olive tree *fourth p.* of. *1 Ki* 6:33
the *fourth p.* of a cab. *2 Ki* 6:25
read one *fourth p.*; another *fourth p.*
Neh 9:3
over *fourth p.* of earth. *Rev* 6:8

fifth **part**
up *fifth p.* of the land. *Gen* 41:34
give *fifth p.* to Pharaoh. 47:24, 26
shall add the *fifth p.* *Lev* 5:16; 6:5
22:14; 27:13, 19, 27, 31; *Num* 5:7
posts were a *fifth p.* *1 Ki* 6:31

tenth **part**
an homer is the *tenth p.* *Ex* 16:36
offering the *tenth p.* of an ephah.
Lev 5:11; 6:20; *Num* 28:5
tenth p. of an ephah of. *Num* 5:15
shall offer even the *tenth p.* 18:26
may contain *tenth p.* *Ezek* 45:11
ye shall offer the *tenth p.* of a. 14
Abraham gave a *tenth p.* *Heb* 7:2
tenth p. of the city fell. *Rev* 11:13

partaker
and hast been *p.* with. *Ps* 50:18
should be *p.* of his hope. *1 Cor* 9:10
that I might be *p.* thereof. 23
if I by grace be *p.* why am I? 10:30
neither be *p.* of other. *1 Tim* 5:22
be thou *p.* of afflictions. *2 Tim* 1:8*
the husbandman must be first *p.* 2:6
who am also a *p.* of the glory.
1 Pet 5:1
is *p.* of his evil deeds. *2 John* 11

partakers
not been *p.* in blood. *Mat* 23:30
if Gentiles have been made *p.* of.
Rom 15:27
others be *p.* of this power. *1 Cor* 9:12
who wait at altar, are *p.* 13
for we are all *p.* of that one. 10:17
are not they which eat *p.* of? 18
be *p.* of the Lord's table, and. 21
are *p.* of the sufferings. *2 Cor* 1:7
and *p.* of his promise in. *Eph* 3:6
be not ye therefore *p.* with. 5:7
ye all are *p.* of my grace. *Phil* 1:7
meet to be *p.* of inheritance. *Col* 1:12
are *p.* of the benefit. *1 Tim* 6:2
as the children are *p.* of. *Heb* 2:14*
brethren, *p.* of the heavenly. 3:1
for we are made *p.* of Christ. 14
were made *p.* of the Holy Ghost. 6:4
chastisement, whereof all are *p.* 12:8
might be *p.* of his holiness. 10
as ye are *p.* of Christ's. *1 Pet* 4:13
p. of the divine nature. *2 Pet* 1:4
that ye be not *p.* of her. *Rev* 18:4

partakest
with them *p.* of root. *Rom* 11:17

parted
the river was *p.* into. *Gen* 2:10
a chariot *p.* them. *2 Ki* 2:11
the waters *p.* hither and. 14
what way is the light *p.*? *Job* 38:24
scattered, and *p.* my land. *Joel* 3:2
crucified him, and *p.* his garments.
Mat 27:35; *Mark* 15:24
Luke 23:34; *John* 19:24
blessed them, was *p.* *Luke* 24:51
p. them to all men, as. *Acts* 2:45

parteth
whatsoever *p.* the hoof. *Lev* 11:3
Deut 14:6
the lot *p.* between the. *Pr* 18:18

Parthians
P., we hear them speak in. *Acts* 2:9

partial
but have been *p.* in law. *Mal* 2:9*
are ye not then *p.* in? *Jas* 2:4*

partiality
observe these things, doing nothing by *p.* *1 Tim* 5:21
without *p.* and without. *Jas* 3:17*

particular
Christ, members in *p.* *1 Cor* 12:27*
every one of you in *p.* so. *Eph* 5:33*

particularly
Paul declared *p.* what. *Acts* 21:19*
we cannot now speak *p.* *Heb* 9:5*

parties
cause of both *p.* shall. *Ex* 22:9

parting
king of Babylon stood at the *p.* of the way. *Ezek* 21:21

partition
and he made a *p.* by. *1 Ki* 6:21*
broken down middle wall of *p.*
Eph 2:14

partly
be *p.* strong, *p.* broken. *Dan* 2:42
divisions, I *p.* believe it. *1 Cor* 11:18
p. whilst ye were made a . . . by afflictions, *p.* whilst ye. *Heb* 10:33

partner
whoso is *p.* with thief. *Pr* 29:24
Titus, he is my *p.* and. *2 Cor* 8:23
if count me a *p.* receive. *Philem* 17

partners
they beckoned to their *p.* *Luke* 5:7
James and John who were *p.* 10

partridge
one doth hunt a *p.* in. *1 Sam* 26:20
as the *p.* sitteth on eggs. *Jer* 17:11

parts
four *p.* shall be your. *Gen* 47:24
Aaron's sons shall lay the *p.* in.
Lev 1:8
any thing lacking in his *p.* 22:23
the prey into two *p.* *Num* 31:27
of the land into three *p.* *Deut* 19:3
if any be driven to utmost *p.* 30:4
they shall divide it into seven *p.*
Josh 18:5, 6, 9
emerods in their secret *p.* *1 Sam* 5:9*
ten *p.* in the king. *2 Sam* 19:43
divided into two *p.* *1 Ki* 16:21
two *p.* keep watch. *2 Ki* 11:7*
and nine *p.* to dwell in. *Neh* 11:1
lo, these are *p.* of his. *Job* 26:14
I will not conceal his *p.* nor. 41:12*
uttermost *p.* of earth for. *Ps* 2:8
shall go into lower *p.* of the. 63:9
that dwell in utmost *p.* 65:8
divided the Red sea into *p.* 136:13
uttermost *p.* of the sea. 139:9
into innermost *p.* *Pr* 18:8; 26:22
will discover their secret *p.* *Isa* 3:17
lower *p.* of the earth. 44:23
passed between the *p.* *Jer* 34:18, 19
in the low *p.* of earth. *Ezek* 26:20
delivered to the nether *p.* of earth.
31:14 18
in nether *p.* of earth. 16; 32:18 24

we are cut off for our p. Ezek 37:11*
out of the north p. 38:15; 39:2
length as one of the other p. 48:8
saith the Lord, two p. therein shall be cut off. Zech 13:8
turned aside into the p. Mat 2:22
came from uttermost p. 12:42 Luke 11:31
and made four p. John 19:23
he had gone over those p. Acts 20:2
more place in those p. Rom 15:23
uncomely p. have more. 1 Cor 12:23
for our comely p. have no need. 24
descended first into lower p. Eph 4:9
city was divided into three p. Rev 16:19
see back, hinder, inward

Pashur

P. the son of Malchijah. 1 Chr 9:12 Neh 11:12
the children of P. Ezra 2:38; 10:22 Neh 7:41
P. sealed. Neh 10:3
P. the son of Immer. Jer 20:1, 2
Lord called not thy name P. but. 3
P. go into captivity. 6
Zedekiah sent unto him P. 21:1
son of P. and P. the son of. 38:1

pass

after that ye shall p. on. Gen 18:5
shortly bring it to p. 41:32
will make my goodness p. Ex 33:19
father to p. to them. Num 27:7, 8
ye shall p. before your. Josh 1:14
he said to people, P. on. 6:7
bid the servants p. 1 Sam 9:27
Jesse made Abinadab p. 16:8
Jesse made seven of his sons p. 10
no place for the beast to p. Neh 2:14
brooks they p. away. Job 6:15
waters that p. away. 11:16
troubled, and p. away. 34:20
every one of them p. away. Ps 58:8
lips he bringeth evil to p. Pr 16:30
the simple p. on and are punished. 22:3; 27:12
grounded staff shall p. Isa 30:32
shall gallant ship p. thereby. 33:21
now have I brought it to p. 37:26
have given shall p. away. Jer 8:13
I will make thee to p. with. 15:14
the flocks shall p. again under. 33:13
nor doth any son of man p. 51:43
cause barber's razor to p. Ezek 5:1
cause you to p. under rod. 20:37
whom dost thou p. in beauty? 32:19
p. ye unto Calneh and. Amos 6:2
p. ye away, thou inhabitant. Mi 1:11
and their king shall p. before. 2:13
the day p. as the chaff. Zeph 2:2
thy iniquity to p. from. Zech 3:4
Till heaven and earth p., one tittle shall in no wise p. Mat 5:18
Father, let this cup p. from me. 26:39; Mark 14:35
would p. from hence to you cannot; nor can they p. to. Luke 16:26*
for he was to p. that way. 19:4
if she p. the flower of her. 1 Cor 7:36
grass he shall p. away. Jas 1:10
p. time of your sojourning here. 1 Pet 1:17
heavens shall p. away. 2 Pet 3:10
see came, come

pass by

my hand while I p. by. Ex 33:22
not let us p. by him. Deut 2:30
Shammah to p. by. 1 Sam 16:9
all they that p. by the. Ps 80:12
all that p. by the way spoil. 89:41
many nations shall p. by. Jer 22:8
all ye that p. by, behold. Lam 1:12
all that p. by clap their hands. 2:15
sight of all that p. by. Ezek 5:14
and caused me to p. by them. 37:2
caused me to p. by four. 46:21
I will not again p. by. Amos 7:8; 8:2
garments of them that p. by. Mi 2:8
that no man might p. by. Mat 8:28
hearing the multitude p. by. Luke 18:36
and to p. by you into. 2 Cor 1:16

not pass

we will not p. through. Num 20:17
thou shalt not p. by me. 18
his bounds he cannot p. Job 14:5
my way, that I cannot p. 19:8
decree, which shall not p. Ps 148:6
waters should not p. Pr 8:29
decree, that it cannot p. Jer 5:22
that shall not p. away. Dan 7:14
generation shall not p. Mat 24:34 Mark 13:30; Luke 21:32
my word shall not p. Mat 24:35 Mark 13:31; Luke 21:33

pass not

my lord, p. not away. Gen 13:3
beware that thou p. not. 2 Ki 6:9
avoid it, p. not by it. Pr 4:15
seek not Beth-el, p. not. Amos 5:5

pass over

wind to p. over the earth. Gen 8:1
will not p. over this heap. 31:52
p. over before me, and put. 32:16
let my lord p. over before. 33:14
blood, I will p. over you. Ex 12:13, 23
stone, till thy people p. over. 15:16
but thy servants will p. over. Num 32:27, 29, 32
if they will not p. over with. 30
thou art to p. over through Ar. Deut 2:18
p. over Arnon. 24
until I shall p. over Jordan. 29
ye shall p. over armed before. 3:18
thou art to p. over Jordan. 9:1; 11:31 27:2; Josh 1:11; 3:6, 14; 4:5
p. over into the land. Josh 22:19
not a man to p. over. Judg 3:28
we will p. over to Gibeah. 19:12
behold, we will p. over unto these men. 1 Sam 14:8
Ittai, Go and p. over. 2 Sam 15:22
plains, but speedily p. over. 17:16
they may not p. over. Ps 104:9
it is a glory to p. over. Pr 19:11
p. over to Tarshish. Isa 23:6
p. over to Chittim. 12
by morning shall p. over. 28:19
he shall p. over to his strong. 31:9
unclean shall not p. over. 35:8
uncover the thigh, p. over. 47:2
way for ransomed to p. over. 51:10
for p. over the isles of. Jer 2:10
yet can they not p. over it. 5:22
river that I could not p. over. Ezek 47:5
times p. over him. Dan 4:16, 25
the north shall p. over. 11:40
change, he shall p. over. Hab 1:11
and p. over judgement. Luke 11:42

pass through

I will p. through all thy. Gen 30:32
I will p. through land. Ex 12:12
the Lord will p. through to smite. 23
seed p. through the fire. Lev 18:21 Deut 18:10; 2 Ki 17:17
let us, I pray thee, p. through thy. Num 20:17
let me p. through thy land. 21:22 Deut 2:27
not suffer Israel to p. through. Num 21:23; Judg 11:20
ye are to p. through the coasts. Deut 2:4
only I will p. through on my feet. 28
p. through the host and. Josh 1:11
p. through brickkiln. 2 Sam 12:31
the land to p. through it. 1 Ki 18:6
to p. through the fire. 2 Ki 16:3 21:6; 23:10; 2 Chr 33:6 Jer 32:35; Ezek 20:26, 31
caused them to p. through the sea. Ps 78:13; 136:14
shall p. through Judah. Isa 8:8*
p. through it hardly bestead. 21
as whirlwinds in the south p. through, so it cometh. 21:1
p. through thy land as a river. 23:10
scourge shall p. through. 28:15, 18
none shall p. through it for. 34:10
that none can p. through. Jer 9:10
prayers should not p. through Lam 3:44
also shall p. through to thee. 4:21
pestilence and blood shall p. through thee. Ezek 5:17
beasts p. through land, no man may p. through. 14:15; 29:11; 33:28
passengers that p. through. 39:15
one shall come, p. through, and overflow. Dan 11:10
stranger shall p. through. Joel 3:17
I will p. through thee. Amos 5:17
when he shall p. through. Nah 1:12
no more p. through thee. 15
no oppressor shall p. through them. Zech 9:8
p. through Macedonia 1 Cor 16:5

passage

refused to give Israel p. Num 20:21
altar at the p. of Israel. Josh 22:11*
garrison of Philistines went out to p. 1 Sam 13:23
they are gone over the p. Isa 10:29

passages

slew him at the p. of Jordan Judg 12:6*
between the p. there. 1 Sam 14:4
and cry from the p. Jer 22:20*
to shew Babylon that the p. 51:32

passed

a lamp that p. between. Gen 15:17
have p. thy borders. Num 20:17
yet have not p. this way. Josh 3:4
the seven priests p. on before. 6:8
in all the way we went, among all people through whom we p. 24:17
Ehud escaped and p. Judg 3:26
Saul is gone about and p. on. 1 Sam 15:12
Philistines p. on by hundreds. 29:2
David's servants p. on. 2 Sam 15:18
it fell, that Elisha p. to. 2 Ki 4:8
Gehazi p. on before them, and. 31
Solomon p. all the kings. 2 Chr 9:22
then a spirit p. before. Job 4:15
my days are p. away as the. 9:26
and no stranger p. among. 15:19
his thick clouds p. Ps 18:12
yet he p. away, and lo. 37:36
all our days are p. away in. 90:9
was but a little that I p. S of S 3:4
come to Aiath, he is p. Isa 10:28
he pursued them, and p. 41:3
and the holy flesh is p. Jer 11:15
and p. between the parts. 34:18, 19
hath p. the time appointed. 46:17
nor smell of fire had p. Dan 3:27
the king went and p. the night. 6:18
hath not thy wickedness p.? Nah 3:19
now the time is far p. Mark 6:35
but is p. from death unto life. John 5:24; 1 John 3:14
so death p. on all men. Rom 5:12
high priest that is p. Heb 4:14
first earth were p. away. Rev 21:1
former things are p. away. 4

passed by

there p. by Midianites. Gen 37:28
Lord p. by before him. Ex 34:6
nations which ye p. by. Deut 29:16
behold, men p. by and. 1 Ki 13:25
the Lord p. by. 19:11
Elijah p. by Elisha. 19
as the king p. by he cried. 20:39
that as oft as he p. by. 2 Ki 4:8
the king p. by on the wall. 6:30
and there p. by a wild beast. 14:9 2 Chr 25:18
fierce lion, p. by it. Job 28:8
for lo, the kings p. by. Ps 48:4
when I p. by and saw. Ezek 16:6
on every one that p. by. 15, 25
in sight of all that p. by. 36:34
of the waters p. by. Hab 3:10
heard that Jesus p. by. Mat 20:30
they that p. by reviled him. 27:39
as he p. by he saw Levi. Mark 2:14
would have p. by them. 6:48
in the morning as they p. by. 11:20
Simon who p. by to bear. 15:21
he p. by on the other side. Luke 10:31, 32
through midst of them, and so p. by. John 8:59
as I p. by and beheld. Acts 17:23

passed *over*
and *p. over* the river. *Gen* 31:21
for with my staff I *p. over.* 32:10
who *p. over* houses of. *Ex* 12:27
when ye are *p. over* Jordan.
Num 33:51; *Deut* 27:3
they *p. over* right against. *Josh* 3:16
all the Israelites *p. over* on. 17
people were clean *p. over.* 4:1, 11
people hasted and *p. over.* 10
the ark *p. over.* 11
Reubenites and Gadites *p. over.* 12
Gideon *p. over* and 300. *Judg* 8:4
Ammon *p. over* Jordan. 10:9
Jephthah *p. over* to fight. 11:29, 32
the battle *p. over* to. *1 Sam* 14:23
David *p. over* with 600 men. 27:2
men *p. over* Jordan. *2 Sam* 2:29
Ittai *p. over.* 15:22
king and people *p. over.* 23
my judgement is *p. over. Isa* 40:27
could not be *p. over.* *Ezek* 47:5
but I *p. over* upon her. *Hos* 10:11
and waves *p. over* me. *Jonah* 2:3

passed *through*
Abram *p. through* the. *Gen* 12:6
land which we *p. through. Num* 14:7
p. through midst of the sea. 33:8
p. through mount Ephraim.*1 Sam* 9:4
posts *p. through* country of.
2 Chr 30:10
they *p. through* the gate. *Mi* 2:13
that no man *p. through.* *Zech* 7:14
he *p. through* the midst of Samaria.
Luke 17:11
as Peter *p. through* all quarters.
Acts 9:32
p. through one street. 12:10
all our fathers *p. through* the sea.
1 Cor 10:1
p. through the Red sea. *Heb* 11:29

passedst
why *p.* thou over to fight? *Judg* 12:1

passengers
she standeth to call *p.* *Pr* 9:15*
I will give Gog valley of *p.*: it shall
stop noses of the *p.* *Ezek* 39:11*
to bury with *p.* those that. 14*
when *p.* see a man's bone. 15*

passest
kingdoms whither thou *p. Deut* 3:21
on land whither thou *p.* over. 30:18
if thou *p.* on, thou shalt. *2 Sam* 15:33
day thou *p.* over the. *1 Ki* 2:37
when thou *p.* through waters.*Isa* 43:2

passeth
every one that *p.* *Ex* 30:13, 14
while my glory *p.* by. 33:22
whatsoever *p.* under the. *Lev* 27:32
even the Lord *p.* over. *Josh* 3:11
every one that *p.* by it shall be.
1 Ki 9:8; *2 Chr* 7:21
of God, which *p.* by us. *2 Ki* 4:9
money of every one that *p.* 12:4
he *p.* on also, but I. *Job* 9:11
against him, and he *p.* 14:20
and my welfare *p.* away. 30:15
but the wind *p.* and cleanseth. 37:21
whatever *p.* through seas. *Ps* 8:8
are a wind that *p.* away. 78:39
for the wind *p.* over it. 103:16
as a shadow that *p.* away. 144:4
as whirlwind *p.* so is. *Pr* 10:25
he that *p.* by and meddleth. 26:17
one generation *p.* away. *Eccl* 1:4
be as chaff that *p.* away. *Isa* 29:5
a land that no man *p. Jer* 2:6; 9:12
as stubble that *p.* away. 13:24
every one that *p.* shall be astonished.
18:16; 19:8
cut off from it him that *p. Ezek* 35:7
as early dew that *p.* away. *Hos* 13:3
God that *p.* by transgression.*Mi* 7:18
every one that *p.* by her. *Zeph* 2:15
streets waste, that none *p.* by. 3:6
because of him that *p.* by. *Zech* 9:8
told him that Jesus *p.* by. *Luke* 18:37
fashion of this world *p.* away.
1 Cor 7:31; *1 John* 2:17
love of Christ which *p.* *Eph* 3:19
the peace of God which *p.* understanding. *Phil* 4:7

passing
we are *p.* from Beth-lehem-judah.
Judg 19:18
thy love to me *p.* love. *2 Sam* 1:26
the people had done *p.* out. 15:24
as king of Israel was *p.* *2 Ki* 6:26
p. through valley of Baca. *Ps* 84:6
p. through the street near. *Pr* 7:8
and *p.* over he will preserve. *Isa* 31:5
p. through land to bury. *Ezek* 39:14
he *p.* through midst of. *Luke* 4:30
shadow of Peter *p.* by. *Acts* 5:15
Philip *p.* through, preached. 8:40
they *p.* by Mysia, came down. 16:8
and hardly *p.* Crete we came. 27:8

passion
(In the singular, the suffering and death of Christ. In the plural it means desires)
himself alive after his *p.* *Acts* 1:3

passions
men of like *p.* with you. *Acts* 14:15
man subject to like *p.* as. *Jas* 5:17

passover
This word comes from the Hebrew verb, pasach, *which signifies to pass, to leap, or skip over. They gave the name of* Passover *to the feast which was established in commemoration of the coming forth out of Egypt, because the night before their departure, the destroying angel, who slew the firstborn of the Egyptians, passed over the Israelites, who were marked with the blood of the lamb which was killed the evening before; and which for this reason was called the Paschal Lamb.*
The feast was kept for seven days, from the 14th to the 21st Nisan, corresponding to our March–April. As the beginning of the month was dependent on the moon there was nearly a month's difference between the possible times of beginning. This is the reason for the varying dates of our Easter, which must, as the commemoration of Christ's resurrection, be determined by the date of the Passover.
There were many rules as to the Passover Supper, some given in Exodus being for the first celebration only.
it is the Lord's *p.*, ye. *Ex* 12:11
27; *Lev* 23:5; *Num* 28:16
kill the *p.* *Ex* 12:21
this is ordinance of the *p.* 43
they kept the *p.* at even. *Num* 9:5
Josh 5:10
on the morrow of the *p.* *Num* 33:3
Josh 5:11
sacrifice the *p.* to Lord. *Deut* 16:2, 6
thou mayest not sacrifice *p.* 5
holden such a *p.* from days of judges,
nor in days of kings. *2 Ki* 23:22
wherein this *p.* was holden. 23
then they killed *p.* in second month.
2 Chr 30:15; 35:1, 11; *Ezra* 6:20
Mark 14:12; *Luke* 22:7
yet did they *eat p.* *2 Chr* 30:18
Josiah kept a *p.* unto the Lord. 35:1
17:19; *Ezra* 6:19
Josiah gave all for *p. 2 Chr* 35:7, 8, 9
they roasted *p.* with fire. 13
ye shall have *p.* a feast. *Ezek* 45:21
prepare for thee to eat *p.*? *Mat* 26:17
Mark 14:12; *Luke* 22:8, 11
and they made ready *p.* *Mat* 26:19
Mark 14:16; *Luke* 22:13
desired to eat this *p.* *Luke* 22:15
p. was at hand. *John* 2:13; 11:55
was in Jerusalem at the *p.* 2:23
Jerusalem before *p.* to purify. 11:55
six days before *p.* to Bethany. 12:1
that they might eat the *p.* 18:28
release to you one at the *p.* 39
preparation of the *p.* 19:14
Christ our *p.* is sacrificed. *1 Cor* 5:7
thro' faith he kept the *p.* *Heb* 11:28
see **feast, keep**

passovers
charge of killing of *p.* *2 Ch.* 30:17

past
days of mourning were *p. Gen* 50:4
2 Sam 11:27
with horn in time *p.* *Ex* 21:29, 36
go along, until we be *p. Num* 21:22
Emims dwelt therein in times *p.*
Deut 2:10
now of the days which are *p.* 4:32
hated him not in times *p.* 42; 19:4, 6
bitterness of death is *p. 1 Sam* 15:32
his presence as in times *p.* 19:7
for David in time *p.* to be king.
2 Sam 3:17
also in time *p.* when Saul was. 5:2
David was a little *p.* the top. 16:1
when midday was *p.* *1 Ki* 18:29
was ruler in time *p.* *1 Chr* 9:20
which doeth great things *p. Job* 9:10
secret, until thy wrath be *p.* 14:13
my days are *p.*, my purposes. 17:11
O that I were as in months *p.* 29:2
as yesterday when it is *p.* *Ps* 90:4
requireth that which is *p.* *Eccl* 3:15
for lo the winter is *p.* *S of S* 2:11
the harvest is *p.*, the. *Jer* 8:20
the time is now *p.*, send. *Mat* 14:15
sabbath was *p.*, Mary. *Mark* 16:1
the voice was *p.*, Jesus. *Luke* 9:36
when they were *p.* first. *Acts* 12:10
who in times *p.* suffered all. 14:16
fast was now already *p.*, Paul. 27:9
for remission of sins that are *p.*
Rom 3:25
for as ye in times *p.* have. 11:30
and his ways are *p.* finding out 33
old things *p.* away; all. *2 Cor* 5:17
my conversation in time *p. Gal* 1:13
persecuted us in times *p.* 23
I have also told you in time p. 5:21
in time *p.* ye walked. *Eph* 2:2
our conversation in times *p.* 3
who being *p.* feeling have. 4:19
that resurrection is *p.* *2 Tim* 2:18
who in time *p.* was to. *Philem* 11
who spake in time *p.* to. *Heb* 1:1
to conceive seed, when she was *p.*
11:11
p. were not a people. *1 Pet* 2:10
for the time *p.* of our life may. 4:3
darkness is *p.*, true. *1 John* 2:8
one woe is *p.* *Rev* 9:12
the second woe is *p.* 11:14

pastor
(The original meaning of this word was shepherd, and in this sense it is sometimes used in the Bible. The Eastern shepherd must both protect and feed his sheep—so there is a derived meaning of spiritual leader, minister, one given charge of a church of Christ, to care for spiritual interests of the people and feed their souls with spiritual food. This meaning also is found in the Bible)
hastened from being a *p. Jer* 17:16*

pastors
p. also transgressed. *Jer* 2:8*
I will give you *p.* according. 3:15*
for *p.* are become brutish. 10:21*
many *p.* have destroyed my. 12:10*
wind shall eat up all thy *p.* 22:22*
woe to the *p.* that destroy. 23:1*
thus saith Lord against *p.* that. 2*
and he gave some *p.* *Eph* 4:11

pasture
thy servants have no *p.* *Gen* 47:4
they went to seek *p.* *1 Chr* 4:39
they found fat *p.* 40
because there was *p.* 41
of the mountains is his *p. Job* 39:8
why doth thine anger smoke against
sheep of thy *p.*? *Ps* 74:1
so we sheep of thy *p.* will. 79:13
people of his *p.* 95:7; 100:3
wild asses, a *p.* of flocks. *Isa* 32:14
scatter sheep of my *p.* *Jer* 23:1
hath spoiled their *p.* 25:36
like harts that find no *p.* *Lam* 1:6
them in a good *p.*, a fat *p. Ezek* 34:14

small thing to have eaten good *p*. *Ezek* 34:18
ye my flock, the flock of my *p*., are. 31
according to their *p*. so. *Hos* 13:6
because they have no *p*. *Joel* 1:18
go in and out and find *p*. *John* 10:9

pastures
twenty oxen out of *p*. *1 Ki* 4:23
to lie down in green *p*. *Ps* 23:2
they drop upon the *p*. of. 65:12
p. are clothed with flocks. 13
cattle shall feed in large *p*. *Isa* 30:23
p. shall be in all high places. 49:9*
down residue of your *p*. *Ezek* 34:18
one lamb out of flock of fat *p*. 45:15
fire hath devoured *p*. *Joel* 1:19, 20
for the *p*. of the wilderness. 2:22

Patara
Rhodes we came unto *P*. *Acts* 21:1

pate
come down upon his own *p*. *Ps* 7:16

path
[1] *A beaten way by which men can walk*, Gen 49:17. [2] *The regular methods by which one lives, or shows his character. This is used of both God and man.*
Dan a serpent, an adder in *p*. that. *Gen* 49:17
the Lord stood in a *p*. *Num* 22:24*
there is a *p*. which no fowl. *Job* 28:7
mar my *p*. they set forward. 30:13
he maketh a *p*. to shine. 41:32
thou wilt shew me the *p*. *Ps* 16:11
thy way, lead me in a plain *p*. 27:11
thy way in sea, thy *p*. is. 77:19
make me to go in *p*. of thy. 119:35
lamp, and a light to my *p*. 105
thou compassest my *p*. and. 139:3
then thou knewest my *p*. 142:3
thy foot from their *p*. *Pr* 1:15
understand every good *p*. 2:9
enter not into the *p*. of the. 4:14
the *p*. of the just is as the. 18
ponder the *p*. of thy feet, and. 26
thou shouldest ponder the *p*. 5:6
thou dost weigh the *p*. of. *Isa* 26:7
the way, turn aside out of *p*. 30:11
and taught him in the *p*. 40:14
a *p*. in the mighty waters. 43:16
walk every one in his *p*. *Joel* 2:8

Pathros
of his people from *P*. *Isa* 11:11
return into the land of *P*. *Ezek* 29:14
will make *P*. desolate, I will. 30:14

paths
the *p*. of their way are. *Job* 6:18
so are the *p*. of all that forget. 8:13
narrowly to all my *p*. 13:27
he hath set darkness in my *p*. 19:8
neither abide they in the *p*. 24:13
in stocks, marketh all my *p*. 33:11
that thou shouldest keep the *p*. 38:20
through the *p*. of the seas. *Ps* 8:8
I have kept me from the *p*. 17:4
hold up my goings in thy *p*. that. 5
he leadeth me in the *p*. of. 23:3
O Lord, teach me thy *p*. 25:4
p. of the Lord are mercy. 10
and thy *p*. drop fatness. 65:11
he keepeth *p*. of judgement. *Pr* 2:8
leave *p*. of uprightness to walk. 13
they froward in their *p*. 15
her *p*. incline unto the dead. 18
nor take they hold of the *p*. of life. 19
thou mayest keep the *p*. of the. 20
he shall direct thy *p*. 3:6
all her *p*. are peace. 17
I have led thee in right *p*. 4:11
go not astray in her *p*. 7:25
in places of *p*. 8:2
I lead in the midst of the *p*. 20
and we will walk in his *p*. *Isa* 2:3
Mi 4:2
destroy the way of thy *p*. *Isa* 3:12
I will lead them in *p*. they. 42:16
he called, the restorer of *p*. 58:12
destruction are in their *p*. 59:7
have made them crooked *p*. 8
way, and ask for old *p*. *Jer* 6:16
from ancient *p*. to walk in *p*. 18:15
made my *p*. crooked. *Lam* 3:9
wall, she shall not find her *p*. *Hos* 2:6
make his *p*. straight. *Mat* 3:3
Mark 1:3; *Luke* 3:4
straight *p*. for your feet. *Heb* 12:13

pathway
in the *p*. thereof there is. *Pr* 12:28

patience
servant worshipped him, saying, Lord, have *p*. with. *Mat* 18:26, 29
bring forth fruit with *p*. *Luke* 8:15
in your *p*. possess ye your. 21:19
tribulation worketh *p*. *Rom* 5:3
and *p*. experience, and. 4
do we with *p*. wait for it. 8:25
we through *p*. and comfort. 15:4
the God of *p*. grant you to be. 5
as ministers of God in much *p*. *2 Cor* 6:4
wrought among you in all *p*. 12:12
with all might to all *p*. *Col* 1:11
remembering your *p*. of. *1 Thes* 1:3
glory in you for your *p*. *2 Thes* 1:4
and follow after love, *p*. *1 Tim* 6:11
hast fully known my *p*. *2 Tim* 3:10
be sound in faith, in *p*. *Tit* 2:2
who through faith and *p*. *Heb* 6:12
ye have need of *p*. that after. 10:36
let us run with *p*. the race set. 12:1
of your faith worketh *p*. *Jas* 1:3
but let *p*. have her perfect work. 4
husbandman hath long *p*. for it. 5:7
for an example of *p*. 10
have heard of *p*. of Job. 11
to temperance *p*.; to *p*. *2 Pet* 1:6
companion in *p*. of Jesus. *Rev* 1:9
I know thy *p*. 2:2, 19
and thou hast *p*. 3
hast kept word of my *p*. 3:10
the *p*. of the saints. 13:10; 14:12

patient
p. in spirit is better than. *Eccl* 7:8
who by *p*. continuance. *Rom* 2:7
rejoicing in hope, *p*. in. 12:12
be *p*. toward all men. *1 Thes* 5:14*
and unto the *p*. waiting. *2 Thes* 3:5
not greedy of lucre, but *p*. *1 Tim* 3:3*; *2 Tim* 2:24*
be *p*. brethren. *Jas* 5:7
be ye also *p*. 8

patiently
Lord, and wait *p*. for him. *Ps* 37:7
I waited *p*. for the Lord, and. 40:1
beseech thee to hear me *p*. *Acts* 26:3
after he had *p*. endured. *Heb* 6:15
buffeted for faults ye take it *p*. . . . suffer, ye take it *p*. *1 Pet* 2:20

Patmos
isle that is called *P*. *Rev* 1:9

patriarch
(*This name is given to the heads, or princes of the family, chiefly to those that lived before Moses. The name Patriarch comes from the Greek word*, Patriarchēs, *which signifies* Head of a family)
speak of the *p*. David. *Acts* 2:29
p. Abraham paid tithes. *Heb* 7:4

patriarchs
Jacob begat the twelve *p*. *Acts* 7:8
p. moved with envy sold Joseph. 9

patrimony
cometh from sale of his *p*. *Deut* 18:8

pattern
after the *p*. of all the. *Ex* 25:9
thou make them after their *p*. 40
candlestick was made after the *p*. *Num* 8:4
behold the *p*. of the altar. *Josh* 22:28
to Urijah the *p*. of altar. *2 Ki* 16:10
David gave Solomon *p*. *1 Chr* 28:11, 12, 18, 19
let them measure the *p*. *Ezek* 43:10
that in me first Jesus Christ might shew for a *p*. *1 Tim* 1:16*
thyself a *p*. of good works. *Tit* 2:7*
according to *p*. I shewed. *Heb* 8:5

patterns
necessary that the *p*. of. *Heb* 9:23*

Paul
Saul, called *P*. filled. *Acts* 13:9
religious proselytes follow *P*. 43
P. waxed bold. 46
raised persecution against *P*. 50
the same heard *P*. 14:9
P. Mercurius, was chief speaker. 12
having stoned *P*. drew him out. 19
P. thought not good to take. 15:38
P. chose Silas. 40
him would *P*. have to go. 16:3
a vision appeared to *P*. in the. 9
to the things spoken of *P*. 14
followed *P*. 17
but *P*. being grieved. 18
P. and Silas prayed, and sang. 25
but *P*. cried, saying, Do thyself. 28
P. as his manner was, went. 17:2
consorted with *P*. and Silas. 4
brethren sent *P*. away. 10, 14
while *P*. waited at Athens. 16
P. was pressed in spirit, and. 18:5
Lord spake to *P*. in the night. 9
miracles by the hands of *P*. 19:11
P. I know. 15
P. purposed in spirit to go to. 21
this *P*. hath persuaded and. 26
P. preached unto them, ready. 20:7
P. went down, and embracing. 10
wept sore, and fell on *P*.'s neck. 37
said to *P*. through the Spirit. 21:4
Agabus took *P*.'s girdle and. 11
the day following *P*. went in. 18
took *P*. and drew him out of. 30
saw soldiers, they left beating *P*. 32
P. stood on the stairs. 40
P. beholding. 23:1
lest *P*. should have been pulled. 10
be of good cheer, *P*. 11
not eat till they had killed *P*. 12, 14
P. prayed me to bring this. 18
soldiers brought *P*. to Antipatris. 31
informed governor against *P*. 24:1
that money should have been given him of *P*. 26
Felix left *P*. bound. 27
one Jesus, whom *P*. affirmed. 25:19
Festus said, *P*. thou art. 26:24
Julius courteously entreated *P*. 27:3
saying, Fear not, *P*. 24
P. besought them all to take meat. 33
the centurion, willing to save *P*. 43
but *P*. was suffered to dwell. 28:16
I am of *P*. *1 Cor* 1:12; 3:4
is Christ divided? was *P*.? 1:13
who then is *P*.? 3:5
whether *P*., or Apollos, or. 22
the salutation of me *P*. 16:21
Col 4:18; *2 Thes* 3:17
come to you, even I *P*. *1 Thes* 2:18
such an one as *P*. the aged. *Philem* 9
as our beloved brother *P*. *2 Pet* 3:15

Paulus
the deputy Sergius *P*. *Acts* 13:7

paved
as it were a *p*. work. *Ex* 24:10
midst thereof being *p*. *S of S* 3:10

pavement
he put the sea on a *p*. *2 Ki* 16:17
Israel bowed themselves upon the *p*. *2 Chr* 7:3
the beds were on a *p*. of. *Esth* 1:6
p. made for the court, thirty chambers were upon the *p*. *Ezek* 40:17
p. by the side of the gates, was the lower *p*. 18
over against the *p*. was gallery. 42:3
a place called the *p*. *John* 19:13

pavilion, -s
he made darkness his *p*. *2 Sam* 22:12; *Ps* 18:11
kings drinking in *p*. *1 Ki* 20:12
drinking himself drunk in *p*. 16
he shall hide me in his *p*. *Ps* 27:5
keep them secretly in a *p*. 31:20
spread his royal *p*. *Jer* 43:10

paw
delivered me out of *p*. *1 Sam* 17:37

paweth
the horse *p*. in the valley. *Job* 39:21

paws
whatsoever goeth on *p*. *Lev* 11:27

pay
only he shall *p.* for loss. *Ex* 21:19
and he shall *p.* as the judges. 22
he shall surely *p.* ox for ox. 36
found, let him *p.* double. 22:7, 9
p. according to the dowry. 17
water, I will *p.* for it. *Num* 20:19
vow, shall not slack to *p.* *Deut* 23:21
me go and *p.* my vow. *2 Sam* 15:7
p. a talent of silver. *1 Ki* 20:39
sell oil, and *p.* thy debt. *2 Ki* 4:7
did Solomon make to *p.* tribute. *2 Chr* 8:8
did children of Ammon *p.* to. 27:5
will they not *p.* toll and. *Ezra* 4:13
will *p.* 10,000 talents. *Esth* 3:9; 4:7
thou shalt *p.* thy vows. *Job* 22:27
I will *p.* my vows. *Ps* 22:25; 66:13 116:14, 18
and *p.* thy vows to the Most. 50:14
vow and *p.* to the Lord your. 76:11
given, will he *p.* again. *Pr* 19:17
if thou hast nothing to *p.* why? 22:27
defer not to *p.* it, *p.* that. *Eccl* 5:4
that thou shouldest vow and not *p.* 5
I will *p.* that which I have vowed. *Jonah* 2:9
doth not your master *p.*? *Mat* 17:24
as he had not to *p.*, his lord forgave him. 18:25, 27; *Luke* 7:42
I will *p.* thee all. *Mat* 18:26, 29
p. me that thou owest. 28
till he should *p.* debt. 30
till he should *p.* all that was due. 34
for ye *p.* tithe of mint, anise. 23:23
p. ye tribute also. *Rom* 13:6

payeth
borroweth and *p.* not. *Ps* 37:21

payment
all to be sold, and *p.* *Mat* 18:25

peace
(*This word is used in the Bible as we use it to-day. It was, however, much used as a salutation, with no stress on the meaning, although that meaning was most probably the origin of its use in that way*)
Pharaoh an answer of *p.* *Gen* 41:16
I will give *p.* in land. *Lev* 26:6
the Lord lift up his countenance and give thee *p.* *Num* 6:26
give to him my covenant of *p.* 25:12
Sihon with words of *p.* *Deut* 2:26
city, proclaim *p.* to it. 20:10
if it make thee answer of *p.* 11
if it will make no *p.* with thee. 12
thou shalt not seek their *p.* 23:6
I shall have *p.* though I walk. 29:19
was *p.* between Jabin. *Judg* 4:17
there was *p.* between Israel and. *1 Sam* 7:14
well, thy servant shall have *p.* 20:7
there is *p.* to thee, no hurt. 21
throne shall there be *p.* *1 Ki* 2:33
Solomon had *p.* on all sides. 4:24
there was *p.* between Hiram. 5:12
whether they come for *p.* 20:18
let him say, Is it *p.*? *2 Ki* 9:17, 18
what hast thou to do with *p.*? 19, 22
p. so long as her witchcrafts? 22
she said, Had Zimri *p.*, who slew? 31
is it not good, if *p.* be in my days? 20:19; *Isa* 39:8
I will give *p.* to Israel. *1 Chr* 22:9
there was no *p.* to him. *2 Chr* 15:5
beyond the river, *p.* *Ezra* 4:17
unto Darius the king, all *p.* 5:7
to Ezra perfect *p.* 7:12
nor seek their *p.* or their. 9:12
letters with words of *p.* *Esth* 9:30
Mordecai, speaking *p.* to all. 10:3
beasts of field shall be at *p.* *Job* 5:23
with him, and be at *p.* 22:21
maketh *p.* in his high places. 25:2
him that was at *p.* with. *Ps* 7:4
which speak *p.* to neighbours 28:3
bless his people with *p.* 29:11
do good, seek *p.* and pursue it. 34:14; *1 Pet* 3:11
they speak not *p.* but they devise. *Ps* 35:20
themselves in abundance of *p.* 37:11
end of the upright man is *p.* *Ps* 37:37
such as be at *p.* with him. 55:20
the mountains shall bring *p.* 72:3
in days abundance of *p.* so long. 7
he will speak *p.* to his people. 85:8
righteousness and *p.* have kissed. 10
great *p.* have they which. 119:165
dwelt with him that hateth *p.* 120:6
I am for *p.*, but when I speak they. 7
pray for *p.* of Jerusalem. 122:6
but *p.* shall be upon Israel. 125:5
shalt see *p.* upon Israel. 128:6
he maketh *p.* in thy borders. 147:14
pleasantness, her paths *p.* *Pr* 3:17
to the counsellors of *p.* is joy. 12:20
maketh his enemies to be at *p.* 16:7
of war, and a time of *p.* *Eccl* 3:8
The Prince of *P.* *Isa* 9:6
of the increase of his *p.* no end. 7
thou wilt ordain *p.* for us. 26:12
p. with me, and he shall make *p.* 27:5
righteousness shall be *p.* 32:17
the ambassadors of *p.* shall. 33:7
for *p.* I had great bitterness. 38:17
I make *p.* and create evil. 45:7
then had thy *p.* been as river. 48:18
no *p.* to the wicked. 22; 57:21
feet of him that publisheth *p.* 52:7 *Nah* 1:15
the chastisement of our *p.* *Isa* 53:5
nor shall covenant of my *p.* 54:10
shall be the *p.* of thy children. 13
with joy, led forth with *p.* 55:12
he shall enter into *p.* 57:2
fruit of the lips; *P. p.* to him. 19
the way of *p.* they know not. 59:8 *Rom* 3:17
I will make thine officers *p.* *Isa* 60:17
behold, I will extend *p.* to her. 66:12
ye shall have *p.* whereas. *Jer* 4:10
P. p. when there is no *p.* 6:14; 8:11
we looked for *p.* but no. 8:15; 14:19
if in land of *p.* they wearied. 12:5
sword devour, no flesh shall have *p.* 12
you assured *p.* in this place. 14:13
I have taken away my *p.* from. 16:5
prophet which prophesied of *p.* 28:9
seek *p.* of the city whither. 29:7
thoughts of *p.*, and not of evil. 11
a voice of fear, and not of *p.* 30:5
reveal to them abundance of *p.* 33:6
hast removed my soul far from *p.* *Lam* 3:17
they shall seek *p.* there. *Ezek* 7:25
P. and there was no *p.* 13:10, 16
them a covenant of *p.* 34:25; 37:26
by *p.* he shall destroy. *Dan* 8:25*
men at *p.* with thee have. *Ob* 7
with their teeth and cry *P.* *Mi* 3:5
this man shall be the *p.* when. 5:5
I will give *p.* saith the Lord. *Hag* 2:9
counsel of *p.* be between. *Zech* 6:13
nor was there any *p.* to him. 8:10
execute judgement of truth and *p.* 16
love *p.* 19
shall speak *p.* to the heathen. 9:10
with him of life and *p.* *Mal* 2:5
worthy, let your *p.* come upon it; if not, let your *p.* return. *Mat* 10:13
am come to send *p.* on earth. 34
he arose and said to the sea, *P.* be still. *Mark* 4:39
have *p.* one with another. 9:50
feet into the way of *p.* *Luke* 1:79
and on earth *p.*, good will. 2:14
if son of *p.* be there, your *p.* 10:6
to give *p.* on the earth? 12:51
desireth conditions of *p.* 14:32
p. in heaven, and glory in. 19:38
things which belong to thy *p.* 42
p. I leave with you, my *p.* *John* 14:27
that in me ye might have *p.* 16:33
preaching *p.* by Jesus Christ. *Acts* 10:36
Blastus their friend desired *p.* 12:20
p. from God the Father. *Rom* 1:7 *1 Cor* 1:3; *2 Cor* 1:2; *Gal* 1:3 *Eph* 1:2; *Phil* 1:2
but *p.* to every man that. *Rom* 2:10
justified, we have *p.* with God. 5:1
spiritually minded is life and *p.* 8:6
that preach the gospel of *p.* 10:15
kingdom of God is joy and *p.* 14:17
follow the things that make for *p.* 19
fill you with all joy and *p.* *Rom* 15:13
hath called us to *p.* *1 Cor* 7:15
but author of *p.* as in. 14:33
Spirit is love, joy, *p.* *Gal* 5:22
for he is our *p.* *Eph* 2:14
so making *p.* 15
Christ came and preached *p.* 17
the Spirit in the bond of *p.* 4:3
preparation of gospel of *p.* 6:15
p. of God, which passeth. *Phil* 4:7
grace and *p.* from God. *Col* 1:2, 20 *1 Thes* 1:1; *2 Thes* 1:2; *1 Tim* 1:2 *2 Tim* 1:2; *Tit* 1:4; *Philem* 3 *2 John* 3
let the *p.* of God rule in. *Col* 3:15
when they shall say, *P.* *1 Thes* 5:3
be at *p.* among themselves. 13
Lord of *p.* give you *p.* *2 Thes* 3:16
follow *p.* with all men. *2 Tim* 2:22 *Heb* 12:14
Salem, that is, king of *p.* *Heb* 7:2
and received spies in *p.* 11:31
p. of them that make *p.*? *Jas* 3:18
p. from him that is, was. *Rev* 1:4
was given to him to take *p.* 6:4
see **held, hold, made, offerings**

peace be
and he said, *P. be* to you. *Gen* 43:23
Lord, said, *P. be* to thee. *Judg* 6:23
and the old man said, *P. be.* 19:20
p. be to thee, *p. be* to house, *p. be.* *1 Sam* 25:6
p. be to thee, and *p. be.* *1 Chr* 12:18
p. be within thy walls. *Ps* 122:7
I will now say, *P. be* within thee. 8
p. be multiplied to you. *Dan* 4:1 6:25; *1 Pet* 1:2; *2 Pet* 1:2; *Jude* 2
p. be to thee, be strong. *Dan* 10:19
first say, *P. be* to this. *Luke* 10:5
he saith, *P. be* to you. 24:36 *John* 20:19, 21, 26
p. be on them, and mercy. *Gal* 6:16
p. be to brethren, and. *Eph* 6:23
p. be with you all that. *1 Pet* 5:14
p. be to thee, our friends. *3 John* 14

God of peace
the *God of p.* be with. *Rom* 15:33
the *God of p.* shall bruise. 16:20
God of p. shall be with you. *2 Cor* 13:11; *Phil* 4:9
very *God of p.* sanctify. *1 Thes* 5:23
now the *God of p.* make. *Heb* 13:20

in peace
sent thee away *in p.* *Gen* 26:29
departed from Isaac *in p.* 31
to my father's house *in p.* 28:21
as for you, get you up *in p.* 44:17
at Makkedah, *in p.* *Josh* 10:21
when I come again *in p.* *Judg* 8:9
when I return *in p.* whatever. 11:31
Abner went *in p.* *2 Sam* 3:21, 22
he is gone *in p.* 23
return to the city *in p.* and. 15:27
so all the people shall be *in p.* 17:3
until the day he came *in p.* 19:24
king is come again *in p.* 30
the blood of war *in p.* *1 Ki* 2:5
return every man *in p.* 22:17 *2 Chr* 18:16
in prison until I come *in p.* *1 Ki* 22:27; *2 Chr* 18:26
if thou return at all *in p.* *1 Ki* 22:28 *2 Chr* 18:27
shalt be gathered to thy grave *in p.* *2 Ki* 22:20; *2 Chr* 34:28
returned *in p.* *2 Chr* 19:1
tabernacle shall be *in p.* *Job* 5:24
I will lay me down *in p.* *Ps* 4:8
my soul *in p.* from the battle. 55:18
keep him *in* perfect *p.* *Isa* 26:3
in the *p.* thereof shall ye. *Jer* 29:7
but thou shalt die *in p.* 34:5
he walked with me *in p.* *Mal* 2:6
thy servant depart *in p.* *Luke* 2:29
palace his goods are *in p.* 11:21
conduct him forth *in p.* *1 Cor* 16:11
be of one mind, live *in p.* *2 Cor* 13:11
depart *in p.*, be ye. *Jas* 2:16
righteousness is sown *in p.* 3:18
found of him *in p.* *2 Pet* 3:14
see **go**

peaceable
these men are p. with. Gen 34:21
of them that are p. in 2 Sam 20:19
wide, quiet, and p. 1 Chr 4:40
my people dwell in a p. Isa 32:18
the p. habitations are. Jer 25:37
lead a quiet and p. life. 1 Tim 2:2*
it yieldeth the p. fruit. Heb 12:11
above is pure, p., gentle. Jas 3:17

peaceably
speak p. to him. Gen 37:4
restore those lands again p. Judg 11:13
send some to call p. to the. 21:13
comest thou p.? 1 Sam 16:4
he said, P. 5; 1 Ki 2:13
if ye be come p. to me. 1 Chr 12:17
one speaketh p. to his. Jer 9:8
he shall come in p. Dan 11:21*, 24*
live p. with all men. Rom 12:18

peacemakers
blessed are the p. for they. Mat 5:9

peacocks
navy came, bringing p. 1 Ki 10:22
2 Chr 9:21
the goodly wings to p.? Job 39:13*

pearl
(Pearls were considered by the ancients among the most precious of gems and were highly esteemed as ornaments. This is probably the reason the word is used metaphorically for anything of great value, and especially for wise sayings)
he found one p. of great. Mat 13:46
gate was of one p. Rev 21:21

pearls
be made of coral or p. Job 28:18*
neither cast ye your p. Mat 7:6
man seeking goodly p. 13:45
not with gold, or p. or. 1 Tim 2:9
decked with gold and p. Rev 17:4
the merchandise of p. 18:12, 16
twelve gates were twelve p. 21:21

peculiar
be a p. treasure to me. Ex 19:5†
to be a p. people. Deut 14:2†
26:18†; 1 Pet 2:9*
chosen Israel for his p. treasure. Ps 135:4†
I gathered the p. treasure. Eccl 2:8
purify to himself p. people. Tit 2:14*

pedigree
they declared their p. Num 1:18

peeled
nation scattered and p. Isa 18:2*, 7*
every shoulder was p. Ezek 29:18†

peep
to wizards that p. and. Isa 8:19*

peeped
opened the mouth or p. Isa 10:14*

Pekah
P. conspired against. 2 Ki 15:25
in days of P. came Tiglath-pileser. 29
a conspiracy against P. 15:30
against Judah came P. 37; 16:5
P. slew in Judah 120,000. 2 Chr 28:6
Rezin and P. went towards. Isa 7:1

Pekahiah
P. son of Manahem. 2 Ki 15:22, 23

Pelatiah
Hananiah, P. of Judah. 1 Chr 3:21
having for their captian P. 4:42
P. and Hanan sealed. Neh 10:22
P. the son of Benaiah. Ezek 11:13

pelican
swan and p unclean. Lev 11:18
Deut 14:17
I am like a p. of the. Ps 102:6

pen
they that handle the p. Judg 5:14*
graven with an iron p. Job 19:24
my tongue is the p. of a. Ps 45:1
write in it with a man's p. Isa 8:1
p. of the scribes is in vain. Jer 8:8
is written with a p. of iron. 17:1
I will not with ink and p. 3 John 13

pence
(The denarius, worth about 16 or 17 cents, or between 8d. and 9d., was the usual wage of an unskilled labourer for one day. American Revision changes to shillings)
owed him an hundred p. Mat 18:28
sold for more than 300 p.
Mark 14:5; John 12:5
the one owed 500 p. the. Luke 7:41
on morrow he took out two p. 10:35

Peniel
the name of the place P. Gen 32:30

penknife
Jehudi cut roll with a p. Jer 36:23

penny
with labourers for a p. Mat 20:2
they received every man a p. 9
not agree with me for a p.? 13
brought unto him a p. 22:19
he said, Bring me a p. Mark 12:15
Luke 20:24
of wheat for a p. and three measures of barley for a p. Rev 6:6

pennyworth
two hundred p. of bread. Mark 6:37
two hundred p. is not. John 6:7

Pentecost
This word is derived from the Greek word Pentecoste, fiftieth, *because the feast of Pentecost was celebrated the fiftieth day after the sixteenth of* Nisan, *which was the second day of the feast of the passover. The Hebrews call it* the Feast of Weeks, Ex 34:22, *because it was kept seven weeks after the passover.*
It was the Jewish harvest-home.
when the day of P. was. Acts 2:1
at Jerusalem the day of P. 20:16
tarry at Ephesus until P. 1 Cor 16:8

Penuel
as Jacob passed over P. Gen 32:31
Gideon went up thence to P. and. Judg 8:8
he beat down the tower of P. 17
then Jeroboam went and built P. 1 Ki 12:25
P. the father of Gedor. 1 Chr 4:4
Iphediah and P. the sons of. 8:25

penury
lips tendeth only to p. Pr 14:23
she of her p. hath cast. Luke 21:4*

people
(The Revisions often change the singular to the plural. In this case it has more distinctly the idea of nations or of people grouped together. In the New Testament the singular is more often changed to multitude)
let p. serve thee, and. Gen 27:29
he also shall become a p. 48:19
I will take you for a p. and be to you a God. Ex 6:7; Deut 4:20
2 Sam 7:24; Jer 13:11
thou art a stiffnecked p. Ex 33:3, 5
34:9; Deut 9:6
I separated you from other p. Lev 20:24, 26
thou art undone, O p. Num 21:29
a p. come out from Egypt. 22:5, 11
head over a p. in Midian. 25:15
did ever p. hear voice? Deut 4:33
chosen thee to be a special p. 7:6
chosen thee to be a peculiar p. 14:2
a p. more than thou, be not. 20:1
shall be given to another p. 28:32
may establish thee for a p. to. 29:13
with those that are not a p. 32:31
who is like to thee, O p.? 33:29
gone back to her p. Ruth 1:15
ye make the Lord's p. 1 Sam 2:24
to us, to slay us and our p. 5:10
let it slay us not, and our p. 11
went to redeem for a p. 2 Sam 7:23
afflicted p. thou wilt save. 22:28
Ps 18:27
a p. I knew not shall serve me.
2 Sam 22:44; Ps 18:43
hearken, O p. every one. 1 Ki 22:28
the p., that they should be the Lord's p. 2 Ki 11:17; 2 Chr 23:16
from one kingdom to another p.
1 Chr 16:20; Ps 105:13
valiantly for our p. 1 Chr 19:13
made me king over a p. 2 Chr 1:9
letters to every p. after. Esth 1:22
3:12; 8:9; Neh 13:24
Esther had not shewed her p. nor. Esth 2:10
there is a certain p. scattered. 3:8
request before him for her p. 4:8
when p. are cut off in. Job 36:20
ye p. pour out your hearts. Ps 62:8
O bless our God, ye p. 66:8
a p. that do err. 95:10
from a p. of a strange. 114:1
happy is that p. 144:15
a p. near to him. 148:14
a reproach to any p. Pr 14:34
wicked ruler over the poor p. 28:15
ants are a p. not strong. 30:25
a p. laden with iniquity. Isa 1:4
give ear to the law, ye p. of. 10
be broken, that it be not a p. 7:8
should not a p. seek unto? 8:19
is a p. of no understanding. 27:11
this is a rebellious p. 30:9; 65:2
I will give p. for thy life. 43:4
bring forth the blind p. that. 8
a p. that provoketh me to. 65:3
a rejoicing, and her p. a joy. 18
a p. cometh from the north.
Jer 6:22; 50:41
destroyed from being a p. 48:42
her p. fell into the hand. Lam 1:7
and there shall be, like p. Hos 4:9
O Israel, for joy as other p. 9:1
tell us, of what p. art? Jonah 1:8
it shall be exalted, and p. Mi 4:1
there shall come p. Zech 8:20
to make ready a p. Luke 1:17
to take out of them a p. Acts 15:14
by them that are no p. Rom 10:19
to himself a peculiar p. Tit 2:14
they shall be to me a p. Heb 8:10
but ye are a peculiar p. 1 Pet 2:9
p. of God, time past were not a p. 10
redeemed us out of every p. Rev 5:9

***all* people**
treasure above all p. Ex 19:5
Deut 7:6, 14; 10:15; Ps 99:2
the fewest of all p. Deut 7:7
scatter thee among all p. 28:64
came of all p. to hear. 1 Ki 4:34
all p. may know thy name. 8:43
2 Chr 6:33
byword among all p. 1 Ki 9:7
are diverse from all p. Esth 3:8
was published to all p. 14; 8:13
fear of them fell upon all p. 9:2
O clap your hands, all ye p. Ps 47:1
wonders among all p. 96:3
all ye nations, praise him, all ye p.
117:1; 148:11; Rom 15:11
to all p. a feast of fat. Isa 25:6
covering cast over all p. 7
called house of prayer for all p. 56:7
all her p. sigh, they. Lam 1:11
hear, I pray you, all p. 18; Mi 1:2
all p. and nations feared. Dan 5:19
all p. and nations should. 7:14
all p. will walk each in. Mi 4:5
heapeth unto him all p. Hab 2:5
a praise among all p. of earth. Zeph 3:20
a burdensome stone for all p. Zech 12:3*
tidings of joy, which shall be to all p. Luke 2:10
before the face of all p. 31

***all the* people**
all the p. of Sodom compassed. Gen 19:4
he and all the p. with him. 35:6
that sold to all the p. of. 42:6
get thee out, and all the p. Ex 11:8
all the p. stand by thee from. 18:14
out of all the p. able men. 21

all the p. answered. Ex 19:8; 24:3
come down in sight of all the p. 11
all the p. saw thunderings. 20:18
glory of the Lord appeared to all the
p. Lev 9:23
and before all the p. I will. 10:3
that all the Lord's p. were prophets.
Num 11:29
and all the p. we saw are. 13:32
all the p. were in ignorance. 15:26
afterwards the hand of all the p.
Deut 13:9; 17:7
all the p. shall hear and fear. 17:13
all the p. shall say, Amen. 27:15
16, 17, 18, 19, 20, 21
all the p. of the earth shall. 28:10
that all the p. of the earth. Josh 4:24
all the p. that came out were. 5:4, 5
all the p. shall shout. 6:5
let not all the p. go. 7:3
from before us all the p. 24:18
house fell upon all the p. Judg 16:30
and all the p. arose as one. 20:8
him among all the p. 1 Sam 10:24
all the p. wept. 11:4
all the p. feared greatly. 12:18
because the soul of all the p. 11:4
all the p. stood, and. 2 Sam 2:28
Abner's grave, all p. wept. 3:32, 34
and all the p. took notice of it. 36
bring back all the p. unto thee, so all
the p. shall be in peace. 17:3
and all the p. were at strife. 19:9
woman went to all the p. in. 20:22
separate them from all p. 1 Ki 8:53
that all the p. of the earth may. 60
handfuls for all the p. 20:10
all the p. stood to the covenant.
2 Ki 23:3
all the p. said, Amen. 1 Chr 16:36
all the p. will be wholly at. 28:21
king and all the p. offered. 2 Chr 7:4
may judge all the p. Ezra 7:25
in sight of all p. for he was above all
p. Neh 8:5
so the Levites stilled all the p. 11
O God, let all the p. Ps 67:3, 5
and all the p. see his glory. 97:6
blessed be the Lord God of Israel: let
all the p. say, Amen. 106:48
is no end of all the p. Eccl 4:16
to speak to all the p. Jer 26:8
all the p. were gathered against. 9
all the p. fought against. 34:1
a covenant with all the p. 8, 10
the hands of all the p. 38:4
all the p. obeyed the voice of. 43:4
all the p. are gone. Ezek 31:12
when all the p. heard the. Dan 3:7
covenant I made with all the p.
Zech 11:10
a cup of trembling to all the p. 12:2
the Lord will smite all the p. 14:12
base before all the p. Mal 2:9
unto him before all the p. Luke 8:47
all the p. rejoiced for the. 13:17
all the p. when they saw, gave. 18:43
all the p. were very attentive. 19:48
but if we say, Of men, all the p. 20:6
favour with all the p. Acts 2:47
reputation among all the p. 5:34
not to all the p. but unto witnesses.
10:41
of repentance to all the p. 13:24
stirred up all the p. and laid. 21:27
all the p., he sprinkled both book and
all the p. Heb 9:19

among the people

off from among the p. Lev 18:29
be a curse among the p. Num 5:27
yourselves among the p.1 Sam 14:34
ye brutish among the p. Ps 94:8
know thee among the p. Ezek 28:19
understand among the p. Dan 11:33
they say among the p. Joel 2:17
sow them among the p. Zech 10:9
all manner of disease among the p.
Mat 4:23; 9:35
be an uproar among the p. 26:5
murmuring among the p. John 7:12
was a division among the p. 43
be destroyed from among the p.
Acts 3:23
no further among the p. Acts 4:17
wrought among the p. 5:12; 6:8
Paul ran in among the p. 14:14
false prophets also among the p.
2 Pet 2:1
see **common, foolish, many, men**

people of God

assembly of the p. of God. Judg 20:2
thing against p. of God. 2 Sam 14:13
p. of the God of Abraham. Ps 47:9
a rest to the p. of God. Heb 4:9
affliction with p. of God. 11:25
but are now p. of God. 1 Pet 2:10
see **great**

his people

be cut off from his p. Gen 17:14
Ex 30:33, 38; 31:14; Lev 7:20, 21
25, 27; 17:4, 9; 19:8; 23:29
Num 9:13; 15:30
was gathered to his p. Gen 25:8
Ishmael was gathered to his p. 17
Isaac was gathered to his p. 35:29
Dan shall judge his p. as one of.
49:16, 33
depart from his p. Ex 8:29, 31
Amalek and his p. 17:13
Moses and for Israel his p. 18:1
blood, I will cut him off from among
his p. Lev 17:10; 20:3, 6; 23:30
for the dead among his p. 21:1
profane his seed among his p. 15
gathered to his p. Num 20:24, 26
delivered him into thy hand, and all
his p. 21:34, 35; Deut 2:33
Og and all his p. Deut 3:2, 3
thee to be his peculiar p. 26:18
for Lord's portion is his p. 32:9
shall judge his p. 36; Ps 135:14
with his p. he will be merciful to his
. . . his p. Deut 32:43; Rom 15:10
was gathered to his p. Deut 32:50
and bring Judah to his p. 33:7
Ai, the king and his p. Josh 8:1
Amorites before his p. Judg 11:23
Lord had visited his p. Ruth 1:6
forsake his p. for his great name's
. . . make you his p. 1 Sam 12:22
to be king over all his p. 15:1
make his p. Israel utterly to. 27:12
David executed justice to all his p.
2 Sam 8:15; 1 Chr 18:14
people shall go for his p. 1 Ki 20:42
The Lord make his p. a hundred
times so many more. 1 Chr 21:3
land is subdued before Lord and his
p. 22:18
God hath given rest to his p. 23:25
Lord hath loved his p. 2 Chr 2:11
Lord hath blessed his p. 31:10
that could deliver his p.? 32:14, 15
to Manasseh and his p. 33:10
had compassion on his p. 36:15
wrath of Lord arose against his p. 16
who among you of all his p. go up. 23
Ezra 1:3
seeking wealth of his p. Esth 10:3
nor nephew among his p. Job 18:19
captivity of his p. Ps 14:7; 53:6
give strength to his p.; the Lord will
bless his p. with. 29:11; 68:35
that he may judge his p. 50:4
therefore his p. return hither. 73:10
he provide flesh for his p.? 78:20
he gave his p. over also to. 62
him to feed Jacob his p. 71
will speak peace to his p. and. 85:8
will not cast off his p. 94:14
we are his p. 100:3
he increased his p. greatly. 105:24
turned their heart to hate his p. 25
he brought forth his p. 43
wrath of the Lord kindled against
his p. 106:40; Isa 5:25
shewed his p. the power. Ps 111:6
he sent redemption to his p.: holy. 9
with the princes of his p. 113:8
the presence of all his p. 116:14, 18
the Lord round about his p. 125:2
his p. through the wilderness. 136:16
exalteth the horn of his p. 148:14
Lord taketh pleasure in his p. 149:4
with the ancients of his p. Isa 3:14
and the heart of his p. Isa 7:2
remnant of his p. left. 11:11
highway for the remnant of his p. 16
the poor of his p. shall trust. 14:32
the rebuke of his p. shall he. 25:8
beauty to residue of his p. 28:5
bindeth up breach of his p. 30:26
hath comforted his p. 49:13; 52:9
pleadeth the cause of his p. 51:22
separated me from his p. 56:3
days of old, Moses and his p. 63:11
and serve him and his p. Jer 27:12
return every one to his p. 50:16
not good among his p. Ezek 18:18
he and his p. with him. 30:11
be jealous and pity his p. Joel 2:18
answer and say to his p. 19
Lord will be the hope of his p. 3:16
controversy with his p. Mi 6:2
them as a flock of his p. Zech 9:16
Jesus: he shall save his p. Mat 1:21
hath visited and redeemed his p.
Luke 1:68
knowledge of salvation to his p. 77
and that God hath visited his p. 7:16
hath God cast away his p.? Rom 11:1
God hath not cast away his p. 2
Lord shall judge his p. Heb 10:30
they shall be his p., and God. Rev 21:3
see **holy, Israel**

people of the land

himself to p. of the l. Gen 23:7, 12
that sold to all p. of the land. 42:6
p. of the l. are many, ye. Ex 5:5
p. of the l. shall stone him. Lev 20:2
if p. of the land do hide their. 4
neither fear ye p. of the l. Num 14:9
all p. of the l. rejoiced and blew with
trumpets. 2 Ki 11:14, 20
Jotham judged p. of the land. 15:5
2 Chr 26:21
p. of the l. slew all them that had
killed Amon, and p. of the l. made.
2 Ki 21:24; 2 Chr 33:25
p. of l. took Jehoahaz and anointed
him. 2 Ki 23:30; 2 Chr 36:1
was no bread for p. of the l.
2 Ki 25:3; Jer 52:6
mustered p. of the l. and sixty men of
p. of land. 2 Ki 25:19; Jer 52:25
gods of p. of the land. 1 Chr 5:25
p. of l. weakened hands. Ezra 4:4
wives of the p. of the land. 10:2
from the p. of the land. 11
daughters to p. of the l. Neh 10:30
if the p. of the l. bring ware. 31
many of the p. of the l. Esth 8:17
iron pillar against p. of l. Jer 1:18
all the p. of the land which. 34:19
hands of p. of the land. Ezek 7:27
p. of the l. have used oppression.
22:29
if p. of the land take man to. 33:2
and all the p. of the land shall. 39:13
p. of the land shall give this. 45:16
prince prepare for p. of the land. 22
p. of the l. shall worship at. 46:3
when p. of the land shall come. 9
spake to the p. of the land. Dan 9:6
be strong, all ye p. of the l. Hag 2:4
speak to all the p. of the land.
Zech 7:5

much people

Edom came out against him with
much p. Num 20:20
they went with much p. Josh 11:4
came much p. by way. 2 Sam 13:34
at Jerusalem much p. 2 Chr 30:13
there was gathered much p. 32:4
praise thee among much p. Ps 35:18
much p. gathered unto. Mark 5:21
Jesus went with him, and much p. 24
Jesus saw much p., was moved. 6:34
much p. of Jews knew. John 12:9
next day much p. took branches. 12
and drew away much p. Acts 5:37
and much p. was added unto. 11:24
for I have much p. in this city. 18:10
hath turned away much p. 19:26
I heard a voice of much p. Rev 19:1

my people

sons of my p. give I it. Gen 23:11
to thy word shall all my p. 41:10

to be gathered to my p. Gen 49:29
I have seen the affliction of my p.
Ex 3:7; Acts 7:34
mayest bring forth my p.Ex 3:10; 7:4
let my p. go. 5:1; 7:16; 8:1, 20
9:1, 13; 10:3
frogs from me and from my p. 8:8
wilt not let my p. go. 21; 10:4
land in which my p. dwell. 8:22, 23
thou thyself against my p. 9:17
I and my p. are wicked. 27
you forth from among my p. 12:31
money to any of my p. 22:25
I will be your God, ye shall by my p.
Lev 26:12 Jer 11:4; 30:22
behold I go unto my p. Num 24:14
my p. were at great strife. Judg 12:2
a woman among all my p.? 14:3
a riddle to children of my p. 16
people shall be my p. Ruth 1:16
for all the city of my p. doth. 3:11
captain over my p. that he may serve
my p. . . . on my p. 1 Sam 9:16
I will save my p. 2 Sam 3:18
I took thee to be ruler over my p. 7:8
2 Chr 6:5
art, my p. as thy people. 1 Ki 22:4
2 Ki 3:7; 2 Chr 18:3
the captain of my p. 2 Ki 20:5
I commanded to feed my p.
1 Chr 17:6
David said, Hear me, my p. 28:2
who am I, and what my p.? 29:14
thou mayest judge my p. 2 Chr 1:11
brought forth my p. out of Egypt. 6:5
pestilence among my p. 7:13
if my p. shall humble themselves. 14
let my p. be given me at. Esth 7:3
for we are sold, I and my p. to. 4
see evil shall come to my p. 8:6
who eat up my p. as. Ps 14:4; 53:4
hear, O my p. I will. 50:7; 81:8
slay them not, least my p. 59:11
I will bring my p. again. 68:22
give ear, O my p. to my law. 78:1
but my p. would not hearken. 81:11
O that my p. had hearkened. 13
my shield, who subdueth my p. 144:2
but Israel not know, my p. Isa 1:3
as for my p., children are their oppressors, O my p. they which. 3:12
what mean ye that ye beat my p.? 15
my p. are gone into captivity. 5:13
right from poor of my p. 10:2
O my p. that dwellest in Zion. 24
blessed be Egypt, my p. and. 19:25
come, my p. enter thou into. 26:20
my p. shall dwell in a. 32:18
comfort ye, comfort ye my p. 40:1
drink to my p. my chosen. 43:20
I was wroth with my p. 47:6
hearken unto me, my p. and. 51:4
say to Zion, Thou art my p. 16
my p. went down into Egypt. 52:4
saith Lord, that my p. is taken. 5
therefore my p. shall know my. 6
for transgression of my p. was. 53:8
out of the way of my p. 57:14
shew my p. their transgression. 58:1
surely they are my p., children. 63:8
Sharon a fold for my p. that. 65:10
Jerusalem, and joy in my p. 19
of a tree, are the days of my p. 22
but my p. have changed. Jer 2:11
for my p. have committed two. 13
why say my p., We are lords? 31
yet my p. have forgotten. 32; 18:15
for my p. is foolish, they have. 4:22
for among my p. are found. 5:26
and my p. love to have it so, 31
for a fortress among my p. 6:27
and ye shall be my p. 7:23
my p. know not the judgement. 8:7
that I might leave my p. and go. 9:2
diligently learn the ways of my p. as they taught my p. to. 12:16
I will destroy my p., since they. 15:7
the pastors that feed my p. 23:2
if they had caused my p. to hear. 22
cause my p. to forget my name. 27
cause my p. to err by their lies. 32
they shall be my p. 24:7; 31:1, 33
32:38; Ezek 11:20; 36:28; 37:23
27; Zech 8:8

behold good that I will do for my p.
Jer 29:32
my p. shall be satisfied with. 31:14
they have despised my p. 33:24
my p. hath been lost sheep. 50:6
my p. go ye out of midst of her.
51:45; Rev 18:4
derision to all my p. and. Lam 3:14
be in assembly of my p. Ezek 13:9
have seduced my p. 10
Will ye hunt the souls of my p.? 18
among my p. by lying to my p. 19
I will deliver my p. out of. 21, 23
off from the midst of my p. 14:8
but that they may be my p. and. 11
sword shall be upon my p. 21:12
even house of Israel are my p. 34:20
my p., I will open your. 37:12, 13
up against my p. Israel. 38:16
they shall teach my p. the. 44:23
shall no more oppress my p. 45:8
exactions from my p. saith Lord. 9
that my p. be not scattered. 46:18
God, are ye not my p.? Hos 1:9, 10
them which were not my p. 2:23
my p. are destroyed for lack. 4:6
they eat up the sin of my p. 8
my p. ask counsel at their stocks. 12
returned the captivity of my p. 6:11
my p. are bent to backsliding. 11:7
my p. shall never be. Joel 2:26, 27
with them there for my p. 3:2
they have cast lots for my p. 3
sinners of my p. shall die. Amos 9:10
into the gate of my p. Ob 13
come to the gate of my p. Mi 1:9
changed the portion of my p. 2:4
of late my p. is risen up as an. 8
the women of my p. have ye. 9
eat the flesh of my p. and flay. 3:3
prophets that make my p. err. 5
O my p. what have I done? 6:3, 5
bear the reproach of my p. 16
they reproached my p. Zeph 2:8
the residue of my p. shall spoil. 9*
nations shall be my p. Zech 2:11
I will save my p. from the east. 8:7
I will say, It is my p. and. 13:9
I will call them my p., which were not my p. Rom 9:25
it was said, Ye are not my p. 26
they shall be my p. 2 Cor 6:16
see **daughter**

of the **people**

two manner of p. shall. Gen 25:23
one of the p. might lightly. 26:10
the gathering of the p. be. 49:10
all the heads of the p. Num 25:4
take the sum of the p. from. 26:4
twelve men out of the p. Josh 4:2
he was higher than any of the p.
1 Sam 9:2; 10:23
for there is a sacrifice of the p. 9:12
none of the p. tasted any food. 14:24
then answered one of the p. 28
of the p. to destroy king. 26:15
nor did he leave of the p. 2 Ki 13:7
of the p. of those countries. Ezra 3:3
there was great cry of the p. Neh 5:1
and some of the p. dwelt in. 7:73
the tumult of the p. Ps 65:7
judge the poor of the p. 72:4
one chosen out of the p. 89:19
a present of a p. scattered. Isa 18:7
for a covenant of the p. 42:6
to rest for a light of the p. 51:4
and of the p. there was none. 63:3
prince not take of the p. Ezek 46:18
boil the sacrifice of the p. 24
and many of the p. John 7:31
because of the p. that stand. 11:42
punish, because of the p. Acts 4:21
himself, and errors of the p. Heb 9:7
they of the p. shall see their dead.
Rev 11:9
see **ears, elders**

one **people**

one p. shall be stronger. Gen 25:23
with you, and become one p. 34:16
dwell with us, to be one p. 22

own **people**

fault is in thine own p. Ex 5:16
virgin of his own p. Lev 21:14

went to redeem to be his own p.
1 Chr 17:21
deliver their own p. 2 Chr 25:15
forget also thine own p. Ps 45:10
made his own p. to go forth. 78:52
man turn to his own p. Isa 13:14
us go again to our own p. Jer 46:16

the **people**

behold the p. is one. Gen 11:6
why do ye let the p. from their work?
Ex 5:4
behold, the p. of the land now. 5
and the p. bowed the head. 12:27
God led the p. about. 13:18
was told that the p. fled. 14:5
the p. feared the Lord, and. 31
the p. shall hear and be afraid. 15:14
till the p. pass over which thou. 16
the p. murmured, saying, What? 24
the p. rested on the seventh. 16:30
there was no water for the p. 17:1
the p. did chide. 2; Num 20:3
there shall come water out of it, that the p. may drink. Ex 17:6
thou for the p. to God-ward. 18:19
the p. may hear when I speak. 19:9
Moses brought forth the p. out. 17
charge the p., lest they break. 21
let not the p. break through. 24
when the p. saw it, they. 20:18, 21
neither shall the p. go up. 24:2
blood and sprinkled it on the p. 8
atonement for thyself and the p.
Lev 9:7
offering for the p. 15, 18; 16:15
Moses and Aaron blessed the p. 9:23
the p. complained. Num 11:1
the p. cried to Moses. 2
and see the p. that dwelleth. 13:18
the p. be strong. 28
Caleb stilled the p. 30
the p. wept that night. 14:1
the p. mourned. 39
the p. spake against God and. 21:5
lo, the p. shall dwell alone. 23:9
behold, the p. shall rise up as. 24
gather me the p. together. Deut 4:10
priest's due from the p. 18:3
yea, he loved the p. 33:3
he shall push the p. 17
call the p. to the mountain. 19
the p. hasted and passed. Josh 4:10
so the p. shouted. 6:20
let the p. depart. 24:28
the p. that are with thee are too many. Judg 7:2, 4
up thou, and the p. that are. 9:32
custom with the p. was. 1 Sam 2:13
so the p. sent to Shiloh to. 4:4
did they not let the p. go? 6:6
the p. refused to obey the voice. 8:19
for the p. will not eat until. 9:13
the p. said to Saul, Shall Jonathan die? so the p. rescued. 14:45
for the p. spared the best. 15:15
the p. took of the spoil, sheep. 21
the p. answered after. 17:27, 30
David distressed, for the p. 30:6
that the p. are fled from. 2 Sam 1:4
the p. have made me afraid. 14:15
for the p. increased. 15:12
and the p. piped with pipes. 1 Ki 1:40
for the p. went to worship. 12:30
the p. that followed Omri . . . the p. that followed Tibni. 16:22
the p. answered him not. 18:21
pour out for the p. that. 2 Ki 4:41
he said, Give the p. that they. 43
the p. trode upon him in the. 7:17
between the king and the p. 11:17
as yet the p. did sacrifice. 12:3
14:4; 15:4, 35
the p. held their peace. 18:36
Lord for me and for the p. 22:13
the p. were without. 2 Chr 12:3
as yet the p. had not prepared.
20:33; 30:3
and the p. did yet corruptly. 27:2
Lord hearkened to Hezekiah and healed the p. 30:20
since the p. began to bring. 31:10
the p. rested on the words. 32:8
and the p. transgressed. 36:14

but the p. are many. Ezra 10:13
for the p. had a mind to. Neh 4:6
and the p. did according to. 5:13
city was large, but the p. were. 7:4
the p. stood in their place. 8:7
so the p. went and brought palm. 16
the p. blessed all that offered. 11:2
had shewed him the p. Esth 3:6
the p. also, to do with them as. 11
the p. of the king's provinces. 4:11
no doubt but ye are the p. Job 12:2
hypocrite reign not, lest the p. 34:30
why do the p. imagine? Ps 2:1
blessed are the p. whom he. 33:12
how thou didst afflict the p. 44:2
arrows, whereby the p. fall. 45:5
therefore shall the p. praise. 17
in thine anger cast down the p. 56:7
let the p. praise thee. 67:3, 5
blessed is the p. that know. 89:15
we are the p. of his pasture. 95:7
he shall judge the p. with his truth. 96:13
he shall judge the p. with equity. 98:9
the Lord reigneth, let the p. 99:1
his deeds among the p. 105:1
no counsel is, the p. fall. Pr 11:14
withholdeth corn, the p. 26; 24:24
the p. rejoiced, the p. mourn. 29:2
is no vision, the p. perish. 18
the p. shall be oppressed. Isa 3:5
the p. that walked in darkness. 9:2
the p. turneth not to him that. 13
and the p. shall be as the fuel. 19
against the p. of my wrath. 10:6
the p. shall take them and. 14:2
it shall be as with the p. so. 24:2
for the p. shall dwell in Zion. 30:19
the p. shall be forgiven their. 33:24
my sword shall come on the p. 34:5
the p. is grass. The grass. 40:7
the p. in whose heart is my. 51:7
I will tread down the p. in. 63:6
the p. of thy holiness have. 18
the p. that shall say, The burthen. Jer 23:34
the p. which were left of sword. 31:2
and went out among the p. 37:4
so he dwelt among the p. 39:14
dwell with him among the p. 40:5, 6
woe to thee, O Moab, the p. of. 48:46
the p. shall labour in vain. 51:58
gather you from the p. Ezek 11:17
I will bring you out from the p. 20:34
34:13
cut thee off from the p. 25:7
bring thee down with the p. 26:20
see sword come, and the p. 33:6
they come unto thee as the p. 31
these are the p. of the Lord. 36:20
thou shalt fall, and the p. that. 39:4
things which are for the p. 42:14
slay the sacrifice for the p. 44:11
shall not sanctify the p. with. 19
the p. of the prince. Dan 9:26
the p. that know their God. 11:32
the p. that doth not understand. Hos 4:14
for the p. thereof shall mourn. 10:5
and the p. shall be gathered. 10
the p. shall be much pained. Joel 2:6
the p. of Syria shall go. Amos 1:5
trumpet be blown, and the p.? 3:6
so the p. of Nineveh. Jonah 3:5
that the p. shall labour in the fire, and the p. shall weary. Hab 2:13
against the p. of Lord. Zeph 2:10
the p. did fear before. Hag 1:12
the p. against whom Lord hath indignation. Mal 1:4
the p. that sat in darkness. Mat 4:16
we fear the p. for all hold John as a prophet. 21:26; Mark 11:32
and the p. waited for. Luke 1:21
as the p. were in expectation. 3:15
the p. sought him. 4:42
the p. pressed upon him. 5:1
when returned, the p. gladly. 8:40
Whom say the p. that I am? 9:18
feared the p. 20:19; 22:2
he stirreth up the p. 23:5
one that perverteth the p. 14
the p. saw that Jesus. John 6:24
but he deceiveth the p. John 7:12
should die for the p. 11:50; 18:14
the p. magnified them. Acts 5:13
the p. with one accord gave. 8:6
the p. gave shout, saying, It. 12:22
the p. saw what Paul had. 14:11
scarce restrained they the p. 18
persuaded the p. and stoned. 19
delivering thee from the p. 26:17
nothing against the p. 28:17
as for the p. so also. Heb 5:3; 7:27
for under it the p. received. 7:11
that he might sanctify the p. 13:12
Lord having saved the p. Jude 5

this people

I will give this p. favour. Ex 3:21
so evil entreated this p.? 5:22
hath done evil to this p. 23
what shall I do to this p.? 17:4
thou wilt wear away, both thou and this p. 18:18
all this p. shall also go to their. 23
I have seen this p. 32:9
what did this p. unto thee? 21
this p. have sinned a great sin. 31
sayest to me, Bring up this p. 33:12
the burden of all this p. on me. Num 11:11
have I conceived all this p.? 12
flesh to give unto all this p. 13
able to bear all this p. alone. 14
long will this p. provoke me? 14:11
thou art among this p. 14
if thou shalt kill all this p. as. 15
was not able to bring this p. 16
this p., as thou hast forgiven this p. 19
indeed deliver this p. 21:2
I pray thee, curse this p. 22:6, 17
what this p. shall do to thy. 24:14
ye shall destroy all this p. 32:15
go over before this p. Deut 3:28
voice of the words of this p. 5:28
saying, I have seen this p. 9:13
stubbornness of this p. 27
thou must go with this p. 31:7
this p. will rise up and go. 16
to this p. thou shalt. Josh 1:6
because this p. have. Judg 2:20
would to God this p. were. 9:29
this the p. thou hast despised? 38
evil doings by this p. 1 Sam 2:23
Lord and this p., choose. 2 Sam 16:18
that I may answer this p. 1 Ki 12:6, 9; 2 Chr 10:6, 9
a servant to this p. this. 1 Ki 12:7
if this p. go up to do sacrifice . . . the heart of this p. shall turn. 27
I should be king over this p. 14:2
O Lord, that this p. may. 18:37
I pray thee, smite this p. 2 Ki 6:18
come in before this p. 2 Chr 1:10
was heavy on this p. Neh 5:18
that I have done for this p. 19
Go and tell this p., Hear. Isa 6:9
make the heart of this p. fat. 10; Mat 13:15; Acts 28:26, 27
this p. refuseth the waters. Isa 8:6
walk in the way of this p. 11
to whom this p. shall say. 12
the leaders of this p. cause. 9:16
this p. was not till Assyrian. 23:13
tongue will speak to this p. 28:11
men, that rule this p. 14
this p. draw near me with. 29:13
work among this p. 14
but this is a p. robbed and. 42:22
this p. have I formed for. 43:21
greatly deceived this p. Jer 4:10
words fire and this p. wood. 5:14
this p. hath a revolting heart. 23
I will bring evil on this p. 6:19
stumblingblocks before this p. 21
pray not thou for this p. 7:16
11:14; 14:11
carcases of this p. meat for. 7:33
why is this p. of Jerusalem? 8:5
I will feed even this p. with. 9:15
this evil p. who refuse to. 13:10
could not be toward this p. 15:1
away my peace from this p. 16:5
even so will I break this p. 19:11
they shall not profit this p. 23:32
and when this p. shall ask thee. 33
makest this p. to trust. Jer 28:15
a man to dwell among this p. 29:32
great evil upon this p. 32:42
considerest not what this p. 33:24
this p. have not hearkened. 35:16
pronounced against this p. 36:7
offended against this p.? 37:18
seeketh not welfare of this p. 38:4
the prophet of this p. Mi 2:11
this p. say, The time is. Hag 1:2
Haggai said, So is this p. 2:14
the remnant of this p. Zech 8:6
I will not be to this p. as in. 11
cause the remnant of this p. 12
this p. draweth nigh with. Mat 15:8
this p. honoureth me Mark 7:6
buy meat for this p. Luke 9:13
be wrath upon this p. 21:23
but this p. who knoweth. John 7:49
the God of this p. chose. Acts 13:17
lips I will speak to this p. 1 Cor 14:21

thy people

thou delivered thy p. Ex 5:23
frogs upon thy p. 8:3, 4
swarms of flies upon thy p. 21
all my plagues upon thy p. 9:14
that I smite thee and thy p. 15
till thy p. pass over, O Lord. 15:16
nor shalt curse the ruler of thy p. 22:28; Acts 23:5
the poor of thy p. may eat. Ex 23:11
that this nation is thy p. 33:13
I and thy p. have found grace. 16
covenant before all thy p. 34:10
talebearer among thy p. Lev 19:16
and an oath among thy p. Num 5:21
this people shall do to thy p. 24:14
shalt be gathered to thy p. 27:13
31:2; Deut 32:50
for thy p. have corrupted. Deut 9:12
destroy not thy p. 26
yet they are thy p. and inheritance. 29; Neh 1:10
return with thee to thy p. Ruth 1:10
thy p. shall be my people. 16
like thy p. . . . before thy p. which thou? 2 Sam 7:23; 1 Chr 17:21
in the midst of thy p. 1 Ki 3:8
heart to judge thy p. 9; 2 Chr 1:10
if thy p. go out to battle. 1 Ki 8:44
forgive thy p. that have sinned. 50
2 Chr 6:34, 39
they be thy p. 1 Ki 8:51
thy p. for his people. 20:42
I am as thou art, my people as thy p., my. 22:4; 2 Ki 3:7
thy hand be on thy p. 1 Chr 21:17
thoughts of heart of thy p. 29:18
with a plague will the Lord smite thy p., and thy children. 2 Chr 21:14
thy blessing is upon thy p. Ps 3:8
save thy p. and bless. 28:9; Jer 31:7
sellest thy p. for nought. Ps 44:12
shewed thy p. hard things. 60:3
wentest forth before thy p. 68:7
he shall judge thy p. with. 72:2
thine arm redeemed thy p. 77:15
thou leddest thy p. like a flock. 20
so we thy p. will give thee. 79:13
angry against prayer of thy p.? 80:4
crafty counsel against thy p. 83:3
forgiven the iniquity of thy p. 85:2
revive us, that thy p. may rejoice. 6
they break in pieces thy p. 94:5
thou bearest to thy p. 106:4
thy p. shall be willing in the. 110:3
thou hast forsaken thy p. Isa 2:6
bring on thee and thy p. days. 7:17
destroyed thy land and thy p. 14:20
thy p. shall be all righteous. 60:21
so didst thou lead thy p. 63:14
we are thy p. 64:9
hear, thou and thy p. Jer 22:2
will ye die, thou and thy p.? 27:13
get thee to thy p. and. Ezek 3:11
set thy face against the daughters of thy p. 13:17
he shall slay thy p. with. 26:11
speak to children of thy p. 33:2, 12
children of thy p. say, The way. 17
the children of thy p. still are. 30
when the children of thy p. 37:18
thy p. are become a. Dan 9:16

thy city and thy p. are. Dan 9:19
are determined upon thy p. 24
what shall befall thy p. 10:14
standeth for the children of thy p.
and at that time thy p. shall. 12:1
thy p. as they that strive. Hos 4:4
tumult arose among thy p. 10:14
spare thy p. Joel 2:17
feed thy p. Mi 7:14
thy p. in the midst of. Nah 3:13
thy p. is scattered on the. 18
forth for salvation of thy p. Hab 3:13

to or unto the people

be spokesman to the p. Ex 4:16
he said, What is this thing that thou doest to the p.? 18:14
go to the p. 19:10
thou shalt set bounds to the p. 12
down from mount to the p. 14, 25
priest shall speak to the p. Deut 20:2
officers shall speak to the p. 5, 8
loaves of bread to the p. Judg 8:5
shall come to a p. secure. 18:10, 27
and art come to a p. Ruth 2:11
all the words to the p. 1 Sam 8:10
Abishai came to the p. by. 26:7
David cried to the p. and to. 14
David came near to the p. 30:21
thy God add to the p. 2 Sam 24:3
hearkened not to the p. 1 Ki 12:15
Elijah came to the p. and. 18:21
Elisha gave to the p. and. 19:21
he said, Give to p. that. 2 Ki 4:42
Athaliah came to the p. 2 Chr 23:12
to carry tidings to the p. 1 Chr 10:9
Josiah gave to the p. 2 Chr 35:7*
princes gave willingly unto the p. 8
said I to the p. Lodge. Neh 4:22
were chargeable to the p. 5:15
minister judgement to the p. Ps 9:8
shall bring peace to the p. 72:3
breath to the p. upon it. Isa 42:5
set up my standard to the p. 49:22
for a witness to the p., a leader and commander to the p. 55:4
so I spake to the p. in. Ezek 24:18
kingdom be given to the p. Dan 7:27
shall sell them to the p. far. Joel 3:8
cometh up to the p. he. Hab 3:16
I will turn to the p. a. Zeph 3:9
Lord's message to the p. Hag 1:13
talked to the p., behold. Mat 12:46
was wont to release to the p. 27:15
began to speak to the p. Luke 7:24
as they spake to the p. Acts 4:1
speak in the temple to the p. 5:20
which gave alms to the p. and. 10:2
us to preach to the p. 42
bring Peter forth to the p. 12:4
who are his witnesses to the p. 13:31
to bring them out to the p. 17:5
have entered in to the p. 19:30
made his defence to the p. 33
suffer me to speak to the p. 21:39
beckoned with the hand to the p. 40
suffer, and shew light to the p. 26:23

peoples

prophesy before many p. Rev 10:11
waters thou sawest are p. 17:15

Peor

Balaam to top of P. Num 23:28
beguiled you in the matter of P. 25:18; 31:16
iniquity of P. too little? Josh 22:17

peradventure

(*Perhaps, supposing, possibly*)
p. there be fifty righteous. Gen 18:24
p. there shall lack five of the. 28
p. there be forty. 29, 30, 31
I will speak this once, p. ten. 32
p. the woman shall not. 24:5, 39
Jacob said, My father p. 27:12
p. thou wouldest take by. 31:31
I will see his face, p. he will. 32:20
for he said, Lest, p., mischief. 42:4
carry it again, p. it was an. 43:12
lest p. I see evil shall come. 44:34
Joseph will p. hate us, and. 50:15
lest p. the people repent. Ex 13:17
p. I shall make an atonement. 32:30
curse this people, p. I. Num 22:6, 11
p. the Lord will come to. Num 23:3
p. it will please God that thou. 27
men of Israel said, P. ye. Josh 9:7
p. he will lighten his hand. 1 Sam 6:5
p. he can shew us our way that. 9:6
p. we may find grass to. 1 Ki 18:5
or p. he sleepeth, and must be. 27
go out to the king, p. he will. 20:31
lest p. the Spirit of Lord. 2 Ki 2:16
watched for halting, p. Jer 20:10
p. for a good man some. Rom 5:7
p. God will give them. 2 Tim 2:25

perceive

given you a heart to p. Deut 29:4
this day we p. the Lord. Josh 22:31
that ye may p. your. 1 Sam 12:17
p. if Absalom had lived. 2 Sam 19:6
I p. that this is an holy. 2 Ki 4:9
but I p. him not. Job 9:11
I cannot p. him. 23:8
to p. the words of. Pr 1:2
I p. that there is nothing. Eccl 3:22
and see ye indeed, but p. Isa 6:9
speech than thou canst p. 33:19
shall see, and shall not p. Mat 13:14
Mark 4:12; Acts 28:26
do ye not p. that whatsoever entereth into the man? Mark 7:18
he said, p. ye not yet, neither? 8:17
I p. that virtue is gone. Luke 8:46
p. that thou art a prophet. John 4:19
p. ye how ye prevail nothing? 12:19
I p. thou art in the gall. Acts 8:23
I p. God is no respecter of. 10:34
I p. in all things ye are too. 17:22
p. the same epistle made. 2 Cor 7:8
hereby p. we the love. 1 John 3:16

perceived

he p. not when she lay down. Gen 19:33, 35
when Gideon p. he was. Judg 6:22
Eli p. that Lord had. 1 Sam 3:8
Saul p. that it was Samuel. 28:14
David p. that the Lord had. 2 Sam 5:12; 1 Chr 14:2
David p. that the child. 2 Sam 12:19
Joab p. the king's heart was. 14:1
captains of chariots p. that it was. 1 Ki 22:33; 2 Chr 18:32
lo, I p. that God had. Neh 6:12
they p. that this work was. 16
I p. portions of Levites had. 13:10
when Mordecai p. all. Esth 4:1
hast thou p. the breadth? Job 38:18
I p. that this also is vexation of. Eccl 1:17
I myself p. that one event. 2:14
nor p. by the ear what God. Isa 64:4
who hath p. and heard. Jer 23:18
for the matter was not p. 38:27
p. that he spake of them. Mat 21:45
Luke 20:19
Jesus p. their wickedness. Mat 22:18
Jesus p. in spirit that. Mark 2:8
they p. that he had seen. Luke 1:22
Jesus p. their thoughts. 5:22
was hid, that they p. it not. 9:45
but he p. their craftiness. 20:23
Jesus p. they would make him a king. John 6:15
they p. that they were unlearned. Acts 4:13
when Paul p. that one part. 23:6
when James p. the grace. Gal 2:9

perceivest

p. not in him lips of. Pr 14:7
but p. not beam that is. Luke 6:41

perceiveth

are brought low, but he p. Job 14:21
once, yet man p. it not. 33:14
p. that her merchandise. Pr 31:18

perceiving

p. that he had answered. Mark 12:28
Jesus p. the thought. Luke 9:47
and p. he had faith to. Acts 14:9

perdition

lost but the son of p. John 17:12
an evident token of p. Phil 1:28
sin be revealed, son of p. 2 Thes 2:3
men in destruction and p. 1 Tim 6:9
who draw back to p. Heb 10:39
and p. of ungodly men. 2 Pet 3:7*
the beast was, and is not, and shall go into p. Rev 17:8, 11

perfect

Noah was p. Gen 6:9
and be thou p. 17:1
offering shall be p. Lev 22:21
thou shalt be p. with. Deut 18:13
a p. weight, a p. measure. 25:15
Saul said, Give a p. lot. 1 Sam 14:41
he maketh my way p. 2 Sam 22:33
he maketh my way p. Ps 18:32
king, to Ezra, p. peace. Ezra 7:12
that man was p. and upright. Job 1:1, 8; 2:3
not cast away a p. man. 8:20
if I say, I am p. 9:20
though I were p. 21
he destroyeth the p. and the. 22
thou makest thy ways p.? 22:3
mark the p. man, his end. Ps 37:37
shoot in secret at the p. 64:4
myself wisely in a p. way. 101:2
he that walketh in a p. way shall. 6
Lord will p. what concerneth. 138:8
I hate them with p. hatred. 139:22
p. shall remain in it. Pr 2:21
shineth more and more unto p. 4:18
righteousness of the p. shall. 11:5
wilt keep him in p. peace. Isa 26:3
for it was p. through. Ezek 16:14
said, I am of p. beauty. 27:3
made thy beauty p. 11; 28:12
thou wast p. in thy ways. 28:15
p. even as your Father is p. Mat 5:48
if thou wilt be p. go and sell. 19:21
had p. understanding. Luke 1:3*
may be made p. in one. John 17:23
him this p. soundness. Acts 3:16
to the p. manner of law. 22:3*
having more p. knowledge of. 24:22*
is that p. will of God. Rom 12:2
among them that are p. 1 Cor 2:6†
my strength is made p. 2 Cor 12:9
be p., be of good comfort, be. 13:11
are ye made p. by flesh? Gal 3:3
till we come to p. man. Eph 4:13*
I were already p. Phil 3:12
let us, as many as be p. be. 15
every man p. in Christ. Col 1:28
may stand p. and complete in. 4:12
might p. that lacking in. 1 Thes 3:10
man of God may be p. 2 Tim 3:17
make Captain of their salvation p. Heb 2:10
being made p. he became Author. 5:9
for law made nothing p. but. 7:19
him that did the service p. 9:9
greater and more p. tabernacle. 11
make the comers thereunto p. 10:1
should not be made p. 11:40
spirits of just men made p. 12:23
God make you p. in every. 13:21
let patience have her p. work, that ye may be p. and. Jas 1:4
every good and p. gift is from. 17
whoso looketh into the p. law. 25
by works was faith made p. 2:22
in word, same is a p. man. 3:2
suffered, make you p. 1 Pet 5:10
is our love made p. 1 John 4:17
p. love casteth out fear, because fear hath torment . . . not made p. 18
see **heart**

***is* perfect**

He the Rock, his work is p. Deut 32:4
as for God, his way is p. 2 Sam 22:31; Ps 18:30
he that is p. in knowledge. Job 36:4; 37:16
law of the Lord is p. Ps 19:7
when the bud is p. Isa 18:5
who is blind as he that is p.? 42:19*
which is in heaven is p. Mat 5:48
every one that is p. shall. Luke 6:40
when that which is p. 1 Cor 13:10

perfected

house of God was p. 2 Chr 8:16
and work was p. by them. 24:13
thy builders have p. Ezek 27:4
babes thou hast p. praise. Mat 21:16
third day I shall be p. Luke 13:32
by one offering he hath p. Heb 10:14

is the love of God *p.* 1 John 2:5
another, his love is *p.* in us. 4:12

perfecting

p. holiness in the fear. 2 Cor 7:1
for *p.* of the saints, for. Eph 4:12

perfection

out the Almighty to *p.*? Job 11:7
nor prolong the *p.* thereof. 15:29*
he searcheth out all *p.* 28:3*
out of Zion, the *p.* of. Ps 50:2
I have seen an end of *p.* 119:96
upon thee in their *p.* Isa 47:9*
city that men call the *p.* of. Lam 2:15
and bring no fruit to *p.* Luke 8:14
we wish, even your *p.* 2 Cor 13:9
let us go on to *p.* Heb 6:1
if *p.* were by the Levitical. 7:11

perfectly

we shall consider it *p.* Jer 23:20
were made *p.* whole. Mat 14:36
way of God more *p.* Acts 18:26
something more *p.* 23:15*, 20*
he *p.* joined together in. 1 Cor 1:10
for yourselves know *p.* 1 Thes 5:2

perfectness

which is the bond of *p.* Col 3:14

perform

(Generally used with the idea of carrying out to completion something that had been promised, or what had been commanded)

I will *p.* the oath which I sware.
Gen 26:3; Deut 9:5; Luke 1:72
thou art not able to *p.* Ex 18:18
all that enter in to *p.* Num 4:23*
he commanded you to *p.* Deut 4:13
gone out of thy lips shalt *p.* 23:23
and *p.* duty of a husband's. 25:5
not *p.* duty of my husband's. 7
if he will *p.* the part of. Ruth 3:13
in that day I will *p.* against Eli.
1 Sam 3:12
that the king will *p.* 2 Sam 14:15
then I will *p.* my word. 1 Ki 6:12
that he might *p.* his saying. 12:15
2 Chr 10:15
to *p.* the words of this covenant.
2 Ki 23:3, 24; 2 Chr 34:31
if it please the king to *p.* Esth 5:8
their hands cannot *p.* Job 5:12
they are not able to *p.* Ps 21:11
that I may daily *p.* my vows. 61:8
I have sworn, and I will *p.* 119:106
I have inclined my heart to *p.* 112
Lord of hosts will *p.* this. Isa 9:7
vow to the Lord, and *p.* it. 19:21
Cyrus my shepherd shall *p.* 44:28
hasten my word to *p.* it. Jer 1:12
I may *p.* the oath which I. 11:5
Lord *p.* thy words thou hast. 28:6
I will *p.* my good word toward you.
29:10; 33:14
ye will *p.* your vows. 44:25
word, and will *p.* it. Ezek 12:25
thou wilt *p.* the truth. Mi 7:20
keep thy solemn feasts, *p.* Nah 1:15
thou shalt *p.* to the Lord. Mat 5:33
he was able also to *p.* Rom 4:21
how to *p.* that which is good. 7:18
now therefore *p.* the. 2 Cor 8:11
he will *p.* it until the day. Phil 1:6

performance

be a *p.* of those things. Luke 1:45
so may be a *p.* also out. 2 Cor 8:11*

performed

Saul hath not *p.* my. 1 Sam 15:11
I have *p.* the commandment. 13
they *p.* all that the king. 2 Sam 21:14
Lord hath *p.* his word. 1 Ki 8:20
2 Chr 6:10 Neh 9:8
Vashti hath not *p.* Esth 1:15
kingdom it shall be *p.* 5:6; 7:2
to thee shall the vow be *p.* Ps 65:1
when the Lord hath *p.* Isa 10:12
p. the thoughts. Jer 23:20; 30:24
who have not *p.* words. 34:18
words of Jonadab are *p.* 35:14, 16
purpose of the Lord shall be *p.* 51:29
have spoken and *p.* it. Ezek 37:14
these things shall be *p.* Luke 1:20
when they had *p.* all things by. 2:39
when I have *p.* this, I. Rom 15:28

performeth

every man that *p.* not. Neh 5:13
he *p.* the thing that is. Job 23:14
I will cry to God that *p.* Ps 57:2
that *p.* the counsel of his. Isa 44:26

performing

sacrifice in *p.* a vow. Num 15:3, 8

perfume, -s

thou shalt make it a *p.* Ex 30:35, 37
ointment and *p.* rejoice. Pr 27:9
thou didst increase thy *p.* Isa 57:9

perfumed

I have *p.* my bed with. Pr 7:17
cometh *p.* with myrrh? S of S 3:6

Perga

company came to *P.* Acts 13:13
preached the word in *P.* 14:25

Pergamos

send it to *P.* and Thyatira. Rev 1:11
to the angel of the church in *P.* 2:12

perhaps

if *p.* thy thought may. Acts 8:22
lest *p.* such a one be. 2 Cor 2:7*
p. he therefore departed. Philem 15

peril

bread with *p.* of our lives. Lam 5:9
shall famine, *p.*, or sword? Rom 8:35

perilous

in last days *p.* times. 2 Tim 3:1*

perils

in *p.* of waters, in *p.* of robbers, in *p.* by countrymen, in *p.* by heathen, in *p.* in city, in *p.* in wilderness, in *p.* in sea, in *p.* among false brethren. 2 Cor 11:26

perish

that the land *p.* not. Gen 41:36
and many of them *p.* Ex 19:21
eye of his maid, that it *p.* 21:26
die, we *p.*, we all *p.* Num 17:12
latter end shall be that he *p.* 24:20
lest ye *p.* quickly from. Deut 11:17
a Syrian ready to *p.* was. 26:5
until thou *p.* quickly. 28:20, 22
Josh 23:13
let all thine enemies *p.* Judg 5:31
shall descend into battle, and *p.*
1 Sam 26:10
and to cause to *p.* Esth 3:13; 7:4
and if I *p.*, I *p.* 4:16
to cause to *p.* all power. 8:11
nor the memorial of them *p.* 9:28
let the day *p.* wherein I. Job 3:3
by the blast of God they *p.* 4:9
they *p.* for ever, without any. 20
way go to nothing and *p.* 6:18
him that was ready to *p.* 29:13
any *p.* for want of clothing. 31:19
lest he be angry, and ye *p.* Ps 2:12
of the poor shall not *p.* 9:18
and the brutish person *p.* 49:10
like the beasts that *p.* 12, 20
so let the wicked *p.* 68:2; 83:17
they *p.* at the rebuke of thy. 80:16
in that day his thoughts *p.* 146:4
when the wicked *p.* Pr 11:10; 28:28
no vision, the people *p.* 29:18*
to him that is ready to *p.* 31:6
but those riches *p.* by. Eccl 5:14
all their memory to *p.* Isa 26:14
which were ready to *p.* 27:13
the law shall not *p.* Jer 18:18
you out, and ye should *p.* 27:10, 15
remnant in Judah should *p.* 40:15
I will cause thee to *p.* Ezek 25:7
and fellows should not *p.* Dan 2:18
on us that we *p.* not. Jonah 1:6; 3:9
O Lord, let us not *p.* for this. 14
members should *p.* Mat 5:29, 30
saying, Lord, save us, we *p.* 8:25
Luke 8:24
out, and the bottles *p.* Mat 9:17
little ones should *p.* 18:14
carest thou not that we *p.*? Mark 4:38
that a prophet *p.* out. Luke 13:33
have bread enough, and I *p.* 15:17
not an hair of your head *p.* 21:18
whoso believeth in him should not *p.*
John 3:15, 16
the whole nation *p.* not. 11:50
thy money *p.* with thee. Acts 8:20
despisers, and wonder, and *p.* 13:41
cross is to them that *p.* foolishness.
1 Cor 1:18
Christ in them that *p.* 2 Cor 2:15
but though our outward man *p.* 4:16
which all are to *p.* with. Col 2:22
unrighteousness in them that *p.*
2 Thes 2:10
that any should *p.* but. 2 Pet 3:9

shall perish

ye *shall p.* among the heathen.
Lev 26:38
also *shall p.* for ever. Num 24:24
ye *shall* soon utterly *p.* Deut 4:26
8:19, 20; 30:18; Josh 23:16
I *shall* one day *p.* by. 1 Sam 27:1
house of Ahab *shall p.* 2 Ki 9:8
hypocrite's hope *shall p.* Job 8:13
his remembrance *shall p.* 18:17
20:7; 36:12
all flesh *shall p.* together. 34:15
way of the ungodly *shall p.* Ps 1:6
wicked *shall p.* 37:20
are far from thee *shall p.* 73:27
thine enemies *shall p.* 92:9
shall p. but thou shalt endure. 102:26
desire of the wicked *shall p.* 112:10
expectation of wicked *shall p.*
Pr 10:28; 11:7
that speaketh lies *shall p.* 19:9
a false witness *shall p.* but. 21:28
their wise men *shall p.* Isa 29:14
strive with thee *shall p.* 41:11
not serve thee *shall p.* 60:12
heart of the king *shall p.* Jer 4:9
friend *shall p.* 6:21
gods *shall p.* 10:11, 15; 51:18
valley also *shall p.* and plain. 48:8
but the law *shall p.* from. Ezek 7:26
the Philistines *shall p.* Amos 1:8
flight *shall p.* from the swift. 2:14
and the houses of ivory *shall p.* 3:15
and the king *shall p.* Zech 9:5
take the sword *shall p.* Mat 26:52
and bottles *shall p.* Luke 5:37
ye *shall* all likewise *p.* 13:3, 5
sheep *shall* never *p.* nor. John 10:28
sinned without law, *shall p.* without.
Rom 2:12
shall weak brother *p.*? 1 Cor 8:11
they *shall p.* but thou. Heb 1:11
and *shall p.* in their. 2 Pet 2:12

perished

p. from the congregation. Num 16:33
Heshbon is *p.* even to Dibon. 21:30
that man *p.* not alone. Josh 22:20
weapons of war *p.*! 2 Sam 1:27
whoever *p.* being innocent. Job 4:7
in whom old age was *p.* 30:2
their memorial is *p.* Ps 9:6
the heathen are *p.* out of. 10:16
as Sisera and Jabin, which *p.* 83:10
I should have *p.* in mine. 119:92
their envy is *p.* Eccl 9:6
truth is *p.* Jer 7:28
riches that hath gotten are *p.* 48:36
is counsel *p.* from the prudent? 49:7
strength and hope is *p.* Lam 3:18
harvest of the field is *p.* Joel 1:11
which came up and *p.* Jonah 4:10
is thy counsellor *p.*? Mi 4:9
the good man is *p.* out of. 7:2
herd of swine ran and *p.* Mat 8:32
p. between the altar. Luke 11:51
he also *p.* and as many. Acts 5:37
asleep in Christ are *p.* 1 Cor 15:18
harlot Rahab *p.* not. Heb 11:31
overflowed with water *p.* 2 Pet 3:6
and *p.* in the gainsaying. Jude 11

perisheth

lion *p.* for lack of prey. Job 4:11
hope of unjust men *p.* Pr 11:7
there is a just man that *p.* Eccl 7:15
righteous *p.* and no man. Isa 57:1
for what the land *p.* and. Jer 9:12
people of Chemosh *p.* 48:46
for the meat which *p.* John 6:27
of the fashion of it *p.* Jas 1:11
more precious than gold *p.* 1 Pet 1:7

perishing

his life from *p.* by sword. Job 33:18

Perizzite
the *P.* dwelled then in. *Gen* 13:7
and I will drive out the *P.* *Ex* 33:2
34:11
when the *P.* and Hivite. *Josh* 9:1
Jabin sent to the *P.* and. 11:3

Perizzites
given to thy seed the land of the *P.* *Gen* 15:20; *Ex* 3:8, 17; 23:23
to stink among the *P.* *Gen* 34:30
wood in the land of the *P.* *Josh* 17:15
Lord delivered the *P.* to Judah. *Judg* 1:4, 5
Israel dwelt among the *P.* 3:5
Solomon made the *P.* *2 Chr* 8:7
abominations of *P.* *Ezra* 9:1

perjured
for liars and *p.* persons. *1 Tim* 1:10*

permission
I speak this by *p.* not by. *1 Cor* 7:6

permit
awhile, if the Lord *p.* *1 Cor* 16:7
will we do, if God *p.* *Heb* 6:3

permitted
Agrippa said, Thou art *p.* *Acts* 26:1
it is not *p.* to women. *1 Cor* 14:34

pernicious
follow their *p.* ways. *2 Pet* 2:2*

perpetual
[1] *Continual, or uninterrupted,* Ezek 35:5. [2] *Final,* Ps 9:6. [3] *Lasting to the end of the world,* Gen 9:12. [4] *During the continuance of the legal dispensation,* Ex 29:9; 30:8.

token of the covenant for *p.* *Gen* 9:12
priest's office be theirs for a *p.* statute. *Ex* 29:9
a *p.* incense before the Lord. 30:8
keep the sabbath for a *p.* 31:16
a *p.* statute not to eat fat. *Lev* 3:17
a *p.* meat offering for Aaron. 6:20
Aaron's by a *p.* statute. 24:9
not be sold, for it is their *p.* 25:34
a *p.* statute, that he. *Num* 19:21
destructions are come to a *p.* *Ps* 9:6*
lift up thy feet to the *p.* 74:3
he put them to a *p.* reproach. 78:66
by a *p.* decree, that it. *Jer* 5:22
people slidden back by a *p.*? 8:5
why is my pain *p.* and my? 15:18
land desolate and *p.* hissing. 18:16
bring upon you a *p.* shame. 23:40
make them *p.* desolations. 25:9, 12*
the cities thereof shall be *p.* 49:13
let us join to the Lord in a *p.* 50:5*
may sleep a *p.* sleep. 51:39, 57
hast had a *p.* hatred. *Ezek* 35:5
thee *p.* desolations. 9; *Zeph* 2:9
p. ordinance to the Lord. *Ezek* 46:14
he beheld, and the *p.* hills. *Hab* 3:6*

perpetually
my heart shall be there *p.* *1 Ki* 9:3; *2 Chr* 7:16
his anger did tear *p.* *Amos* 1:11

perplexed
city Shushan was *p.* *Esth* 3:15
the herds of cattle are *p.* *Joel* 1:18
Herod was *p.* *Luke* 9:7
as they were *p.* 24:4
p. but not in despair. *2 Cor* 4:8

perplexity
for it is a day of *p.* *Isa* 22:5
now shall be their *p.* *Mi* 7:4
on earth distress of nations, with *p* *Luke* 21:25

persecute
why do ye *p.* me as God? *Job* 19:22
why *p.* we him, seeing the root? 28
all them that *p.* me. *Ps* 7:1*
let the enemy *p.* my soul. 5*
wicked in his pride doth *p.* 10:2*
deliver me from them that *p.* 31:15
against them that *p.* me. 35:3*
angel of the Lord *p.* them. 6*
they *p.* him whom thou hast. 69:26
p. and take him, there is. 71:11*
so *p.* them with thy tempest. 83:15*
execute judgement on them that *p.* me. 119:84
they *p.* me wrongfully. *Ps* 119:86
be confounded that *p.* me. *Jer* 17:18
I will *p.* them with the sword. 29:18*
p. and destroy them in. *Lam* 3:66*
when men shall *p.* you. *Mat* 5:11
pray for them which *p.* you. 44
when they *p.* you in one city. 10:23
ye shall *p.* them from city. 23:34
they shall *p.* *Luke* 11:49; 21:12
did the Jews *p.* Jesus. *John* 5:16
me, they will also *p.* you. 15:20
bless them which *p.* you. *Rom* 12:14

persecuted
curses on them that *p.* *Deut* 30:7
because he *p.* the poor. *Ps* 109:16
princes have *p.* me without. 119:161
enemy hath *p.* my soul. 143:3
nations in anger is *p.* *Isa* 14:6
covered with anger, and *p.* us. *Lam* 3:43*
blessed which are *p.* for. *Mat* 5:10
so *p.* they the prophets before. 12
if they have *p.* me, they. *John* 15:20
have not your fathers *p.*? *Acts* 7:52
p. this way unto the death. 22:4
I *p.* them even to strange. 26:11
reviled, we bless; being *p.* we suffer it. *1 Cor* 4:12
because I *p.* the church of God. 15:9; *Gal* 1:13
are *p.* but not forsaken. *2 Cor* 4:9*
he which *p.* us in times. *Gal* 1:23
born after the flesh *p.* him. 4:29
have killed the Lord and *p.* us. *1 Thes* 2:15*
dragon *p.* woman that. *Rev* 12:13

persecutest
Saul, Saul, why *p.* thou me? *Acts* 9:4; 22:7; 26:14
I am Jesus, whom thou *p.* 9:5; 22:8
26:15

persecuting
zeal, *p.* the church. *Phil* 3:6

persecution
our necks are under *p.* *Lam* 5:5*
for when *p.* ariseth. *Mat* 13:21
Mark 4:17
at that time there was great *p.* *Acts* 8:1
scattered abroad upon the *p.* 11:19*
and raised *p.* against Paul and. 13:50
p. or sword, separate us? *Rom* 8:35
why do I yet suffer *p.*? *Gal* 5:11
suffer *p.* for cross of Christ. 6:12
live godly shall suffer *p.* *2 Tim* 3:12

persecutions
lands, with *p.* *Mark* 10:30
I take pleasure in *p.* for. *2 Cor* 12:10
your faith in all your *p.* *2 Thes* 1:4
my *p.* at Antioch, what *p.* *2 Tim* 3:11

persecutor
who was before a *p.* *1 Tim* 1:13

persecutors
their *p.* thou threwest. *Neh* 9:11*
his arrows against the *p.* *Ps* 7:13*
many are my *p.* 119:157
deliver me from my *p.* 142:6
and revenge me of my *p.* *Jer* 15:15
therefore my *p.* shall stumble. 20:11
all her *p.* overtook her. *Lam* 1:3
our *p.* are swifter than the. 4:19*

perseverance
thereunto with all *p.* *Eph* 6:18

Persia
the reign of the kingdom of *P.* *2 Chr* 36:20
a feast to the power of *P.* *Esth* 1:3
the seven princes of *P.* which. 14
the ladies of *P.* shall say to. 18
of *P.* and Lud were. *Ezek* 27:10
P. Ethiopia, and Libya with. 38:5
kings of Media and *P.* *Dan* 8:20
prince of *P.* withstood me; and I remained with the kings of *P.* 10:13
to fight with the prince of *P.* 20
stand up yet three kings in *P.* 11:2
see **king**

Persians, *see* Medes

Persis
salute *P.* which laboured. *Rom* 16:12

person
Joseph was a goodly *p.* *Gen* 39:6
no uncircumcised *p.* *Ex* 12:48
nor honour the *p.* *Lev* 19:15
any sin, that *p.* be guilty. *Num* 5:6
for an unclean *p.* shall take. 19:17
clean *p.* shall take hyssop and. 18
whatsoever unclean *p.* toucheth. 22
whosoever hath killed any *p.* 31:19
35:11, 15, 30; *Josh* 20:3 9
not testify against any *p.* *Num* 35:30
unclean and clean *p.* *Deut* 15:22
to slay an innocent *p.* 27:25
shall not regard the *p.* 28:60
a goodlier *p.* than he. *1 Sam* 9:2
David a comely *p.* 16:18
I have accepted thy *p.* 25:35
have slain a righteous *p.* *2 Sam* 4:11
nor doth God respect any *p.* 14:14
go to battle in thine own *p.* 17:11
shall save the humble *p.* *Job* 22:29
in whose eyes a vile *p.* *Ps* 15:4*
fool and the brutish *p.* perish. 49:10
will not know a wicked *p.* 101:4
not one feeble *p.* among. 105:37
naughty *p.* walketh with. *Pr* 6:12
shall be called mischievous *p.* 24:8
violence to the blood of any *p.* 28:17
the vile *p.* shall be no more. *Isa* 32:5†
vile *p.* will speak villany. 6†
Johanan took every *p.* *Jer* 43:6
that were near the king's *p.* 52:25
the loathing of thy *p.* *Ezek* 16:5
if sword come and take any *p.* 33:6
come at no dead *p.* 44:25
shall stand up a vile *p.* *Dan* 11:21
regardest not *p.* of men. *Mat* 22:16
Mark 12:14
of the blood of this just *p.* *Mat* 27:24
from you that wicked *p.* *1 Cor* 5:13
forgave I it in the *p.* *2 Cor* 2:10
p. hath inheritance in. *Eph* 5:5
express image of his *p.* *Heb* 1:3
or profane *p.* as Esau, who. 12:16
saved Noah, the eighth *p.* *2 Pet* 2:5

persons
give me *p.* and take the. *Gen* 14:21
to number of your *p.* *Ex* 16:16
p. shall be for the Lord. *Lev* 27:2
shall sprinkle it upon *p.* *Num* 19:18
both of the *p.*, beeves, asses. 31:28
thirty and two thousand *p.* in all. 35
which regardeth not *p.* *Deut* 10:17
into Egypt with seventy *p.* 22
Jerubbaal which were 70 *p.* *Judg* 9:2
Abimelech hired vain and light *p.* 4
slew threescore and ten *p.* 5, 18
to kill of Israel about 30 *p.* 20:39
which were about 30 *p.* *1 Sam* 9:22
Doeg slew on that day 85 *p.* 22:18
the death of all the *p.* 22
king's sons being 70 *p.* *2 Ki* 10:6
king's sons and slew 70 *p.* 7
I have not sat with vain *p.* *Ps* 26:4†
followeth vain *p.* *Pr* 12:11; 28:19
from Jerusalem 832 *p.* *Jer* 52:29
away captive of Jews 745 *p.* 30
forts to cut off many *p.* *Ezek* 17:17
they traded the *p.* of men. 27:13
more than 120,000 *p.* *Jonah* 4:11
are treacherous *p.* *Zeph* 3:4
over ninety-nine just *p.* *Luke* 15:7
with the devout *p.* *Acts* 17:17
us by means of many *p.* *2 Cor* 1:11
made for perjured *p.* *1 Tim* 1:10*
what manner of *p.* ought? *2 Pet* 3:11
having men's *p.* in admiration. *Jude* 16
see **respect**

persuade
who shall *p.* Ahab, to? *1 Ki* 22:20*
I will *p.* him. 21*
thou shalt *p.* him and prevail. 22*
doth not Hezekiah *p.*? *2 Chr* 32:11
beware, lest Hezekiah *p.* *Isa* 36:18
will *p.* him and secure. *Mat* 28:14
we *p.* men. *2 Cor* 5:11
do I now *p.* men? *Gal* 1:10†

persuaded
Ahab *p.* Jehoshaphat. *2 Chr* 18:2*
forbearing is a prince *p.* *Pr* 25:15
the chief priests *p.* the. *Mat* 27:20

will not be p. if one rose. Luke 16:31
for they be p. that John was. 20:6
p. them to continue in. Acts 13:43
who p. the people, and having. 14:19
Paul p. the Jews and the. 18:4
this Paul hath p. much people. 19:26
when he would not be p. 21:14
I am p. none of these things. 26:26
being p. that what he had promised. Rom 4:21
p. that nothing can separate us. 8:38
let every man be fully p. in. 14:5
I know and am p. there is. 14
I myself also am p. of you. 15:14
I am p. that in thee. 2 Tim 1:5
I am p. that he is able to keep. 12
are p. better things of you. Heb 6:9
seen them afar off, were p. of. 11:13

persuadest
almost thou p. me to. Acts 26:28*

persuadeth
when Hezekiah p. you. 2 Ki 18:32
Paul p. men to worship. Acts 18:13

persuading
p. things concerning. Acts 19:8
p. them concerning Jesus. 28:23

persuasion
this p. cometh not of him. Gal 5:8

pertain
peace offerings p. to Lord. Lev 7:20
and eat of the sacrifice which p. 21
if I leave all that p. 1 Sam 25:22
in those things which p. Rom 15:17
things p. to this life. 1 Cor 6:3
things that p. to life. 2 Pet 1:3

pertained
the half that p. to the. Num 31:43
buried in a hill that p. Josh 24:33
an oak that p. to Joash. Judg 6:11
of all that p. to Nabal. 1 Sam 25:21
which p. to Ish-bosheth. 2 Sam 2:15
all that p. to Obed-edom. 6:12
master's son all that p. to Saul. 9:9
all that p. to Mephibosheth. 16:4
vessels that p. to house. 1 Ki 7:48
all that p. to the king. 2 Ki 24:7
morning p. to them. 1 Chr 9:27
cities which p. to Judah. 2 Chr 12:4
abominations p. to Israel. 34:33

pertaineth
which p. to cleansing. Lev 14:32
to the office of Eleazar p. Num 4:16
not wear what p. to a man. Deut 22:5
Ziklag p. to the kings. 1 Sam 27:6
it p. not to thee, Uzziah. 2 Chr 26:18
to whom p. the adoption. Rom 9:4
he p. to another tribe. Heb 7:13

pertaining
half Gilead and cities p. Josh 13:31
every matter p. to God. 1 Chr 26:32
things p. to kingdom of God. Acts 1:3
of things p. to this life. 1 Cor 6:4
priest in things p. to God. Heb 2:17
for men in things p. to God. 5:1
not make him perfect, as p. to. 9:9

perverse
because thy way is p. Num 22:32
are a p. and crooked. Deut 32:5
thou son of the p. 1 Sam 20:30
cannot my taste discern p. things? Job 6:30*
shall also prove me p. 9:20
p. lips put far from thee. Pr 4:24
is nothing froward or p. in. 8:8
he that is of a p. heart shall. 12:8
p. in his ways despiseth him. 14:2
that hath p. tongue falleth. 17:20
than he that is p. in his lips. 19:1
thine heart shall utter p. 23:33*
than he that is p. in his ways. 28:6
he that is p. in his ways shall. 18
hath mingled a p. spirit. Isa 19:14
O p. generation. Mat 17:17
Luke 9:41
arise, speaking p. things. Acts 20:30
midst of a p. nation. Phil 2:15
p. disputings of men of. 1 Tim 6:5*

perversely
what servant did p. 2 Sam 19:19
and have done p. 1 Ki 8:47
they dealt p. with me. Ps 119:78*

perverseness
neither hath he seen p. Num 23:21
but p. of transgressors. Pr 11:3
but p. therein is a breach in. 15:4
ye trust in p. and stay. Isa 30:12
tongue hath muttered p. 59:3*
the land is full of blood, and the city full of p. Ezek 9:9*

pervert
a gift doth p. words of. Deut 16:19
shalt not p. the judgement. 24:17*
doth God p. judgement? Job 8:3
nor will the Almighty p. 34:12
to p. ways of judgement. Pr 17:23
and p. the judgement of any. 31:5
you, ye that p. equity. Mi 3:9
not cease to p. right? Acts 13:10
and would p. the gospel. Gal 1:7

perverted
took bribes, p. judgement. 1 Sam 8:3
I have p. what was right. Job 33:27
and knowledge, it hath p. Isa 47:10
they have p. their way. Jer 3:21
ye have p. the words of the. 23:36

perverteth
the gift p. the words of. Ex 23:8
cursed be he that p. Deut 27:19*
but he that p. his ways. Pr 10:9
the foolishness of a man p. 19:3*
this man as one that p. people. Luke 23:14

perverting
if thou seest the violent p. Eccl 5:8*
found this fellow p. the. Luke 23:2

pestilence
he fall on us with p. or. Ex 5:3
smite thee and thy people with p. 9:15
send the p. among you. Lev 26:25
smite them with the p. Num 14:12
the Lord shall make p. Deut 28:21
there be three days' p. 2 Sam 24:13
1 Chr 21:12
the Lord sent a p. on Israel. 2 Sam 24:15; 1 Chr 21:14
in the land of famine, p. 1 Ki 8:37
2 Chr 6:28; 7:13; 20:9
their life over to the p. Ps 78:50
thee from the noisome p. 91:3
nor for the p. that walketh in. 6
I will consume them by p. Jer 14:12
24:10; 27:8
of this city shall die by p. 21:6
Zedekiah from the p. 7
in city shall die by p. 9; 38:2
Why die by the sword and p.? 27:13
prophesied of war and of p. 28:8
will send upon them the p. 29:17
them with the famine and p. 18
the city is given because of the p. 32:24, 36
liberty for you to the p. 34:17
Egypt shall die by the p. 42:17, 22
punished Jerusalem by the p. 44:13
shall die with the p. Ezek 5:12
p. and blood shall pass through. 17
sword, famine, and the p. 6:11
that is far off shall die by the p. 12
a sword without, p. and. 7:15
few men of them from the p. 12:16
or if I send a p. into that land. 14:19
I send the p. to cut off man. 21
I will send to her p. and blood. 28:23
in caves shall die of the p. 33:27
plead against him with p. and. 38:22
sent among you the p. Amos 4:10
before him went the p. Hab 3:5

pestilences
and there shall be p. Mat 24:7
Luke 21:11

pestilent
this man a p. fellow. Acts 24:5

pestle
in a mortar with a p. Pr 27:22

Peter
P.'s wife's. Mat 8:14; Luke 4:38
P. was out of the ship. Mat 14:29
I say, That thou art P. 16:18
he said to P., Get thee behind me. 23
Mark 8:33
he taketh P. James and. Mat 17:1
26:37; Mark 5:37; 9:2; 14:33
Luke 8:51; 9:28
they that received tribute money came to P. Mat 17:24
P. followed him to the high. 26:58
P. remembered words of Jesus. 75
Mark 14:72
tell his disciples and P. Mark 16:7
and looked upon P. Luke 22:61
city of Andrew and P. John 1:44
whose ear P. cut off. 18:26
P. was grieved because he. 21:17
in those days P. stood. Acts 1:15
seeing P. and John about to go. 3:3
P. filled with the Holy Ghost. 4:8
when they saw the boldness of P. 13
at least the shadow of P. might 5:15
the apostles sent unto them P. 8:14
the disciples had heard that P. 9:38
P. put them all forth, and. 40
Rise, P. kill and eat. 10:13; 11:7
while P. spake these words. 10:44
as many as came with P. 45
further to take P. also. 12:3
P. was sleeping between two. 6
the angel of the Lord smote P. 7
as P. knocked at the door of. 13
what was become of P. 18
up to Jerusalem to see P. Gal 1:18
circumcision was committed to P. 2:7
wrought effectually in P. to the. 8
I said unto P. before them all. 14

Simon Peter
saw Simon called P. Mat 4:18
first Simon, who is called P. 10:2
Simon he surnamed P. Mark 3:16
Simon P. fell down at. Luke 5:8
Simon, whom he also named P. 6:14
cometh he to Simon P. John 13:6
and cometh to Simon P. 20:2
Jesus saith to Simon P., Simon. 21:15
one Simon, whose surname is P. Acts 10:5, 32; 11:13

petition
Israel grant thee thy p. 1 Sam 1:17
Lord hath given me my p. which. 27
now I ask one p. of thee. 1 Ki 2:16
I desire one small p. of thee, say. 20
the king said, What is thy p.? Esth 5:6; 7:2; 9:12
then Esther said, My p. and. 5:7
if it please the king to grant my p. 8
let my life be given me at my p. 7:3
ask a p. of any god. Dan 6:7, 12
his p. three times a day. 13

petitions
the Lord fulfil all thy p. Ps 20:5
we know we have the p. 1 John 5:15

Phalec
which was the son of P. Luke 3:35

Pharaoh
Sarai before P. Gen 12:15
plagued P. and his house. 17
Potiphar an officer of P. 39:1
P. was wroth against two. 40:2
shall P. lift up thine head. 13, 19
make mention of me to P. 14
P. dreamed. 41:1
so P. awoke. 4, 7
God shall give P. answer of. 16
let P. do this. 34
I am P. and without thee. 44
people cried to P. 55
by the life of P. 42:15, 16
thou art as P. 44:18
made me a father to P. 45:8
I will go up and shew P. 46:31
P. and went out from P. 47:10
and we will be P.'s servants. 25
of the priests became not P.'s. 26
in the ears of P. saying. 50:4
when P. heard, he sought. Ex 2:15
and I will send thee to P. 3:10
all those wonders before P. 4:21
P. said, Who is the Lord that? 5:2
officers came and cried unto P. 15
since I came to P. to speak. 23
see what I will do to P. 6:1
how then shall P. hear me? 12, 30
I have made thee a god to P. 7:1

I will harden *P.'s* heart. *Ex* 7:3
13, 14, 22; 8:19; 9:12
stand before *P.* 8:20; 9:13
P. sent for Moses. 9:27
bring one plague more upon *P.* 11:1
did all these wonders before *P.* 10
from the firstborn of *P.* 12:29
when *P.* had let people go. 13:17
will be honoured upon *P.* 14:4, 17
covered all the host of *P.* 28
made affinity with *P.* *1 Ki* 3:1
an house for *P.'s* daughter. 7:8
favour in the sight of *P.* 11:19
them from under *P.* *2 Ki* 17:7
so is *P.* to all that trust in him.
18:21; *Isa* 36:6
to commandment of *P.* *2 Ki* 23:35
signs and wonders on *P.* *Neh* 9:10
tokens and wonders on *P.* *Ps* 135:9
overthrew *P.* and his host. 136:15
of horses in *P.'s* chariots. *S of S* 1:9
how say ye to *P.* I am. *Isa* 19:11
themselves in strength of *P.* 30:2
the strength of *P.* shall be your. 3
P. and his servants. *Jer* 25:19
broken for fear of *P.'s* army. 37:11
did cry, *P.* king of Egypt. 46:17
word that came, before that *P.* 47:1
P. with his army not. *Ezek* 17:17
set thy face against *P.* king. 29:2
I am against thee, *P.* king. 3; 30:22
broken the arm of *P.* 30:21, 24, 25
this is *P.* and his multitude. 31:18
take up a lamentation for *P.* 32:2
kindred made known to *P.* *Acts* 7:13
P.'s daughter took him up and. 21
for scripture saith to *P.* *Rom* 9:17
the son of *P.'s* daughter. *Heb* 11:24

Pharaoh-hophra
will give *P.* into hand of. *Jer* 44:30

Pharaoh-nechoh
P. went against Assyria. *2 Ki* 23:29
P. put Jehoahaz in bands at. 33
P. make Eliakim king. 34
he taxed to give money to *P.* 35
word to Jeremiah against *P.* *Jer* 46:2

Pharez
name was called *P.* *Gen* 38:29
sons of Judah, *P.* and. 46:12
1 Chr 2:4; *Mat* 1:3; *Luke* 3:33
and the sons of *P.* were Hezron and
Hamul. *Gen* 46:12; *Num* 26:20, 21
Ruth 4:18; *1 Chr* 2:5; 9:4
be like the house of *P.* *Ruth* 4:12

Pharisee
The Pharisees were a religious party or school among the Jews at the time of Christ, so called from the Aramaic form of the Hebrew perûshim, *the separated ones. This name may have been given them by their enemies, as they usually called themselves* Haberim, *associates. They were formalists, very patriotic but bigoted in their patriotism as in their religion. Their political influence was great, though they were only about 6000 to 7000 in number.*
Jesus denounced the Pharisees for their hypocrisy, which was shown by their care for the minutest formalities imposed by the traditions of the elders, but not for the mind and heart which should correspond. They were ambitious, arrogant, and proudly self-righteous, all of which qualities were contrary to the teachings of Jesus. This explains in part their intense hostility to him. And their influence over the people, who had come to believe as they did, led to their demand for the crucifixion of Jesus.
thou blind *p.* cleanse. *Mat* 23:26
a certain *p.* besought. *Luke* 11:37
went to pray, one a *p.* the. 18:10
the *p.* stood and prayed thus. 11
one in the council, a *p.* *Acts* 5:34
I am a *p.* the son of a *p.* 23:6
after the most straitest sect of our
religion I lived a *p.* *Acts* 26:5
as touching the law, a *p.* *Phil* 3:5

Pharisees
righteousness of the *p.* *Mat* 5:20
why do we and the *p.* fast oft? 9:14
Mark 2:18
p. said, He casteth out devils.
Mat 9:34
knowest thou that the *p.*? 15:12
beware of the leaven of the *p.* 16:6
11; *Mark* 8:15; *Luke* 12:1
the *p.* also came to him. *Mat* 19:3
the scribes and *p.* sit in. 23:2
scribes and *p.* hypocrites. 13, 14, 15
23, 25, 27, 29; *Luke* 11:42, 43, 44
the scribes and *p.* *Luke* 5:30; 15:2
the scribes and *p.* watched. 6:7
but the *p.* rejected the counsel. 7:30
now do ye *p.* make clean. 11:39
p. who were covetous, heard. 16:14
sent were of the *p.* *John* 1:24
there was a man of the *p.* 3:1
p. and priests sent officers. 7:32
have any of the rulers or *p.*? 48
the *p.* gathered a council. 11:47
p. had given a commandment. 57
certain of sect of the *p.* *Acts* 15:5
arose a dissension between *p.* and
Sadducees. 23:7
there is no resurrection, but the *p.* 8

Pharpar, *see* **Abana**

Phebe
I commend unto you *P.* *Rom* 16:1

Phenice
travelled as far as *P.* *Acts* 11:19
Barnabas passed through *P.* 15:3
finding ship sailing over to *P.* 21:2
they might attain to *P.* 27:12

Philadelphia
write and send it unto *P.* *Rev* 1:11
to the angel of the church in *P.* 3:7

Philetus, *see* **Hymenaeus**

Philip
P. and Bartholomew. *Mat* 10:3
Mark 3:18; *Luke* 6:14; *Acts* 1:13
for Herodias' sake his brother *P.'s*
Mat 14:3; *Mark* 6:17; *Luke* 3:19
P. tetrarch of Iturea. *Luke* 3:1
Jesus findeth *P.* and. *John* 1:43
now *P.* was of Bethsaida, the. 44
P. findeth Nathanael, and saith. 45
the same came to *P.* and. 12:21
P. telleth Andrew; Andrew and *P.* 22
Hast thou not known me, *P.*? 14:9
P. the deacon. *Acts* 6:5
the Spirit said to *P.* 8:29
P. went down to Samaria. 5
to those things which *P.* spake. 6
believed *P.* preaching things. 12
Simon continued with *P.* and. 13
P. ran to him, and heard him read. 30
the Lord caught away *P.* 39
we entered into the house of *P.* 21:8

Philippi
from Neapolis we came to *P.* of
Macedonia. *Acts* 16:12
we sailed away from *P.* and. 20:6
we were shamefully entreated at *P.*
1 Thes 2:2

Philistia
P. triumph thou because. *Ps* 60:8
behold *P.* and Tyre, this man. 87:4
Moab my washpot, over *P.* 108:9

Philistim
out of whom came *P.* *Gen* 10:14
1 Chr 1:12

Philistine
am not I a *P.*? *1 Sam* 17:8
servant will fight with this *P.* 32
the *P.* cursed David. 43
David smote the *P.* in his. 49
sword of Goliath the *P.* 21:9; 22:10
Abishai smote the *P.* *2 Sam* 21:17

Philistines
sojourned in the *P.s'* land. *Gen* 21:34
Isaac had flocks, and the *P.* 26:14
P. stopped the wells. 15, 18
not through the land of *P.* *Ex* 13:17
the borders of *P.* not. *Josh* 13:2
Ekron five lords of *P.* 3; *Judg* 3:3
Shamgar slew of the *P.* *Judg* 3:31
served the gods of the *P.* 10:6
into the hands of the *P.* 7; 13:1
you from Egyptians and *P.* 11
an occasion against the *P* 14:4
be more blameless than the *P.* 15:3
the *P.* came up and burnt her. 6
that the *P.* are rulers over us? 11
Samson judged Israel in the days of
the *P.* 20
the *P.* be upon thee. 16:9, 12, 14, 20
the *P.* took Samson and put out. 21
at once avenged of the *P.* 28
Samson said, Let me die with *P.* 30
went out against the *P.* *1 Sam* 4:1
Lord smitten us before the *P.*? 3
yourselves like men, O ye *P.*! 9
the *P.* took the ark of God and. 5:1
the ark was in the land of *P.* 6:1
P. have brought again the ark. 21
us out of the hand of the *P.* 7:8
the *P.* drew near to battle. 10
the *P.* were subdued, and came. 13
the *P.* will come down upon. 13:12
Israelites went down to the *P.* 20
and let us go over to the *P.* 14:1
noise in the host of the *P.* went on. 19
was sore war against the *P.* all. 52
the *P.* saw their champion. 17:51
from chasing after the *P.* 53
hand of the *P.* be on him. 18:17, 21
then the princes of the *P.* went. 30
David fought with the *P.* 19:8
23:5; *2 Sam* 21:15
from following the *P.* *1 Sam* 24:1
escape into land of the *P.* 27:1
for the *P.* make war against. 28:15
displease not lords of the *P.* 29:7
P. followed hard upon Saul. 31:2
1 Chr 10:2
sent into land of the *P.* *1 Sam* 31:9
all the *P.* came up to. *2 Sam* 5:17
shall I go up to the *P.*? 19
David smote the *P.* 25; 8:1
gold got from *P.* 8:12
Eleazar smote the *P.* 23:10
Shammah slew *P.* 12
brake through the host of the *P.* 16
sojourned in land of the *P.* *2 Ki* 8:2
Jehoram the spirit of *P.* *2 Chr* 21:16
helped Uzziah against the *P.* 26:7
P. had invaded the cities of. 28:18
P. with the inhabitants. *Ps* 83:7
soothsayers like the *P.* *Isa* 2:6
Syrians before, and the *P.* 9:12
shall fly on shoulders of the *P.* 11:14
the kings of the *P.* shall. *Jer* 25:20
the Lord came against the *P.* 47:1
for the Lord will spoil the *P.* 4
to the daughters of *P.* *Ezek* 16:27
because the *P.* have dealt. 25:15
stretch mine hand upon the *P.* 16
the remnant of the *P.* *Amos* 1:8
go down to Gath of the *P.* 6:2
have not I brought the *P.*? 9:7
plain shall possess the *P.* *Ob* 19
O land of the *P.* I will. *Zeph* 2:5
cut off the pride of the *P.* *Zech* 9:6
see **daughters**

Philologus
salute *P.* Julia, and. *Rom* 16:15

philosophers
certain *p.* encountered. *Acts* 17:18

philosophy
man spoil you through *p.* *Col* 2:8

Phinehas
Eleazar's wife bare him *P.* *Ex* 6:25
P. hath turned my wrath from Israel.
Num 25:11
Moses sent them and *P.* to. 31:6
Israel sent *P.* to the. *Josh* 22:13
in a hill that pertained to *P.* 24:33
P. stood before the ark. *Judg* 20:28
Hophni and *P.* the priests. *1 Sam* 1:3
Hophni and *P.* shall both die. 2:34
thy two sons Hophni and *P.* 4:17
P.'s wife was with child, near. 19
son of *P.* the Lord's priest. 14:3
Eleazar begat *P.* *1 Chr* 6:4
P. begat Abishua. 50
P. son of Eleazar was ruler. 9:20

Abishua son of *P.* the son. *Ezra* 7:5
of the sons of *P.* Gershom went. 8:2
was Eleazar the son of *P.* 33
then stood up *P.* and. *Ps* 106:30

Phlegon
salute Asyncritus, *P.* *Rom* 16:14

Phrygia
had gone throughout *P.* *Acts* 16:6
over all the country of *P.* 18:23

Phurah
he went down with *P.* *Judg* 7:11

Phygellus, *see* **Hermogenes**

phylacteries
The same as frontlets. *They were strips of parchment on which were written four passages of Scripture,* Ex 13:2–10, 11–17; Deut 6:4–9, 13–23. *These were put in cases of black calfskin and bound on the forehead and the arm, in obedience to their understanding of* Ex 13:16. *The Pharisees affected to have the cases of their phylacteries broader than the other Jews wore, as a badge of distinction, and through ostentation, which is what our Saviour denounced.*
made broad their *p.* *Mat* 23:5

physician
(*These were not like our physicians, as the science had not progressed far. But they were* healers, *according to their ability. The word is also used of healers of the mind, comforters, and also of embalmers, as having to do with the human body*)
is there no balm in Gilead; is there no *p.* there? *Jer* 8:22
that be whole need not a *p.* but the. *Mat* 9:12; *Mark* 2:17; *Luke* 5:31
p. heal thyself. *Luke* 4:23
Luke the *p.* *Col* 4:14

physicians
his servants the *p.* to embalm his father; the *p.* *Gen* 50:2
to the Lord, but *p.* *2 Chr* 16:12
ye are all *p.* of no value. *Job* 13:4
had suffered many things of *p.* *Mark* 5:26; *Luke* 8:43

pick
the ravens shall *p.* it out. *Pr* 30:17

pictures
shall destroy all their *p.* *Num* 33:52*
of gold in *p.* of silver. *Pr* 25:11*
Lord on all pleasant *p.* *Isa* 2:16*

piece
he laid one *p.* against. *Gen* 15:10
beaten out of one *p.* *Ex* 37:7*
trumpets of a whole *p.* *Num* 10:2*
woman cast a *p.* of a millstone upon. *Judg* 9:53*; *2 Sam* 11:21
crouch to him for a *p.* of silver, that I may eat a *p.* of. *1 Sam* 2:36
they gave him a *p.* of a cake. 30:12
to every one a *p.* of flesh. *2 Sam* 6:19; *1 Chr* 16:3
was a *p.* of ground full of lentiles. *2 Sam* 23:11
mar every good *p.* *2 Ki* 3:19, 25
repaired the other *p.* *Neh* 3:11
next Ezer another *p.* 19, 20, 21, 24, 27, 30
as hard as a *p.* of the. *Job* 41:24*
every man also gave him a *p.* 42:11
brought to a *p.* of bread. *Pr* 6:26
for a *p.* of bread that man. 28:21
temples are a *p.* of pomegranate. *S of S* 4:3; 6:7
daily a *p.* of bread. *Jer* 37:21
every good *p.*, the thigh. *Ezek* 24:4
bring it out *p.* by *p.*, let no lot fall. 6
mouth of lion, a *p.* of ear. *Amos* 3:12
p. was rained on, and the *p.* 4:7
no man putteth a *p.* of new cloth to. *Mat* 9:16; *Mark* 2:21; *Luke* 5:36
find a *p.* of money. *Mat* 17:27*
I have bought a *p.* of. *Luke* 14:18
if she lose one *p.* she doth. 15:8
for I have found the *p.* that. 9
him a *p.* of a broiled fish. 24:42

pieces
passed between those *p.* *Gen* 15:17
thy brother 1000 *p.* of silver. 20:16
bought for 100 *p.* of money. 33:19; *Josh* 24:32
Joseph for twenty *p.* of silver. 37:28
Joseph is rent in *p.* 33; 44:28
to Benjamin thirty *p.* of silver. 45:22
if it be torn in *p.* let. *Ex* 22:13
have the two shoulder *p.* 28:7
on the shoulder *p.* 25; 39:4, 18
part the meat offering in *p.* *Lev* 2:6
Moses burnt the *p.* and fat. 8:20
burnt offering with the *p.* 9:13
Abimelech seventy *p.* of silver. *Judg* 9:4
give thee 1100 *p.* of silver. 16:5
concubine into twelve *p.* 19:29
a yoke of oxen in *p.* *1 Sam* 11:7
Samuel hewed Agag in *p.* 15:33
new garment in twelve *p.* *1 Ki* 11:30
to Jeroboam, Take thee ten *p.* 31
a strong wind brake in *p.* the. 19:11
Elisha rent his clothes in two *p.* *2 Ki* 2:12
with him 6000 *p.* of gold. 5:5
sold for eighty *p.* of silver. 6:25
images of Baal in *p.* 11:18; 23:14
brake in *p.* the brasen serpent. 18:4
of Baal, and brake the images in *p.* *2 Chr* 23:17; 31:1; 34:4; *Mi* 1:7
also shaken me in *p.* *Job* 16:12
his bones as strong *p.* of. 40:18*
rending in *p.* while none. *Ps* 7:2
lest I tear you in *p.* 50:22
submit with *p.* of silver. 68:30
heads of Leviathan in *p.* 74:14
the fruit bring 1000 *p.* *S of S* 8:11
ye beat my people to *p.*? *Isa* 3:15
that goeth out shall be torn in *p.*? *Jer* 5:6
breaketh the rock in *p.* 23:29
aside and pulled me in *p.* *Lam* 3:11
that which is torn in *p.* *Ezek* 4:14
pollute me for *p.* of bread? 13:19
gather the *p.* thereof into. 24:4
brake the image in *p.* *Dan* 2:34, 45
forasmuch as iron breaketh in *p.* 40
brake all their bones in *p.* 6:24
devoured and brake in *p.* 7:7, 19
to me for fifteen *p.* of silver. *Hos* 3:2
who chop my people in *p.* *Mi* 3:3
thou shalt beat in *p.* many. 4:13
as a lion teareth in *p.* and none. 5:8
lion did tear in *p.* enough. *Nah* 2:12
for my price thirty *p.* *Zech* 11:12
I took the thirty *p.* of silver. 13; *Mat* 27:6, 9
what woman having ten *p.* of silver? *Luke* 15:8
price 50,000 *p.* of silver. *Acts* 19:19
lest Paul be pulled in *p.* 23:10
broken *p.* of the ship. 27:44*
see **break, broken, cut, dash, dashed**

pierce
he shall *p.* them through. *Num* 24:8*
a man lean, it will go into his hand and *p.* it. *2 Ki* 18:21; *Isa* 36:6
a sword shall *p.* through. *Luke* 2:35

pierced
when she had *p.* through. *Judg* 5:26
my bones are *p.* in me. *Job* 30:17
they *p.* my hands and. *Ps* 22:16
look on me whom they have *p.* *Zech* 12:10; *John* 19:37
the soldiers *p.* his side. *John* 19:34
and *p.* themselves with. *1 Tim* 6:10
they also which *p.* him. *Rev* 1:7

pierceth
behemoth's nose *p.* *Job* 40:24

piercing
punish the *p.* serpent. *Isa* 27:1*
word of God is quick, *p.* *Heb* 4:12

piercings
that speaketh like the *p.* *Pr* 12:18

piety
let them learn to shew *p.* *1 Tim* 5:4

pigeon, *see* **young**

Pi-hahiroth, *see* **Baal-zephon**

Pilate
they delivered him to Pontius *P.* *Mat* 27:2; *Mark* 15:1
P. saw that he could. *Mat* 27:24
so that *P.* marvelled. *Mark* 15:5, 44
so *P.* willing to content the. 15
Pontius *P.* being governor. *Luke* 3:1
whose blood *P.* had mingled. 13:1
same day *P.* and Herod were. 23:12
this man went to *P.* and begged. 52
P. then went out to them. *John* 18:29
entered into the judgement hall. 33
when *P.* heard that, he was. 19:8
from thenceforth *P.* sought to. 12
P. wrote a title, and put it on. 19
Joseph besought *P.* and *P.* gave. 38
ye denied him in the presence of *P.* *Acts* 3:13
against Jesus, Herod and *P.* 4:27
yet desired they *P.* that he. 13:28
who before *P.* witnessed. *1 Tim* 6:13

pile
the *p.* of it is fire and. *Isa* 30:33
make the *p.* for fire. *Ezek* 24:9

pilgrimage
years of my *p.* are 130 years . . . the days of their *p.* *Gen* 47:9
them the land of their *p.* *Ex* 6:4*
in the house of my *p.* *Ps* 119:54

pilgrims
were strangers and *p.* *Heb* 11:13
I beseech you, as *p.* *1 Pet* 2:11

pillar
(*That which* supports, *either actually or metaphorically. The word is used of the cloud and fire which led the Israelites through the wilderness. It is also used in other places where the form is intended, not the idea of support*)
and became a *p.* of salt. *Gen* 19:26
Jacob set it up for a *p.* 28:18, 22; 35:14
thou anointedst the *p.* 31:13
behold this *p.* 51
and this *p.* be witness. 52
Jacob set a *p.* upon Rachel's grave, that is the *p.* 35:20
cloudy *p.* descended and. *Ex* 33:9
people saw the cloudy *p.* stand. 10
king, by the plain of the *p.* *Judg* 9:6
the flame arose with a *p.* 20:40
up a *p.*: he called the *p.* *2 Sam* 18:18
the right *p.*, the left *p.* *1 Ki* 7:21
king stood by *p.* *2 Ki* 11:14; 23:3; *2 Chr* 23:13
in day by a cloudy *p.* *Neh* 9:12
to them in the cloudy *p.* *Ps* 99:7
and a *p.* at the border. *Isa* 19:19
thee this day an iron *p.* *Jer* 1:18
the height of one *p.* was. 52:21
church, the *p.* and ground of the truth. *1 Tim* 3:15
that overcometh will I make a *p.* *Rev* 3:12
see **cloud, fire**

pillars
an altar and twelve *p.* *Ex* 24:4
hang the vail upon four *p.* 26:32
for the hanging five p. 37; 36:38
the 20 *p.*; hooks of the *p.* of silver. 27:10, 11; 38:10, 11, 12, 17
their *p.* ten. 27:12
their *p.* three. 14, 15; 38:14, 15
p. shall be four. 27:16
sockets for *p.* were of brass. 38:17
Samson between the *p.* *Judg* 16:25
the *p.* of the earth are. *1 Sam* 2:8
he cast two *p.* of brass. *1 Ki* 7:15
made of the almug trees *p.* 10:12
cut off gold from the *p.* *2 Ki* 18:16
brake in pieces the *p.* of brass and. 25:13, 16; *Jer* 52:17, 20
to rings and *p.* of marble. *Esth* 1:6
and the *p.* thereof tremble. *Job* 9:6; 26:11
dissolved, I bear up the *p.* *Ps* 75:3
hewn out her seven *p.* *Pr* 9:1
cometh like *p.* of smoke? *S of S* 3:6
he made the *p.* thereof of silver. 10
legs are as *p.* of marble set. 5:15
fire, and *p.* of smoke. *Joel* 2:30

Cephas who seemed to be *p.* *Gal* 2:9
his feet were as *p.* of fire. *Rev* 10:1

pilled

(*Revisions substitute the modern form* peeled)
Jacob *p.* white strakes. *Gen* 30:37
he set rods which he had *p.* 38

pillow, -s

put stones for his *p.* *Gen* 28:11
that he had put for his *p.* 18
a *p.* of goats' hair. *1 Sam* 19:13, 16
women that sew *p.* and. *Ezek* 13:18
I am against your *p.* 20
in the ship asleep on a *p.* *Mark* 4:38

pilots

O Tyrus, were thy *p.* *Ezek* 27:8
sound of the cry of thy *p.* 28

pin

with a *p.* . . . Samson awaked and went away with *p.* of. *Judg* 16:14
a *p.* of the vine tree? *Ezek* 15:3

pine

p. away, in iniquities of their fathers shall they *p.* away. *Lev* 26:39
fetch olive and *p.* *Neh* 8:15*
these *p.* away, stricken. *Lam* 4:9
ye shall *p.* away for. *Ezek* 24:23
if sins be upon us, and we *p.* 33:10

pineth

his teeth, and *p.* away. *Mark* 9:18

pine tree

p. and box tree together. *Isa* 41:19
the *p.* and box tree shall come. 60:13

pining

he will cut me off with *p.* *Isa* 38:12*

pinnacle

setteth him on a *p.* of temple.
Mat 4:5; *Luke* 4:9

pins

make all the *p.* of the tabernacle.
Ex 27:19; 35:18; 38:20, 31; 39:40
their sockets, their *p.* and their cords.
Num 3:37; 4:32

pipe, -s

of prophets with *p.* *1 Sam* 10:5
the people piped with *p.* *1 Ki* 1:40
the harp and *p.* are in. *Isa* 5:12
when one goeth with a *p.* 30:29
sound for Moab like *p.* *Jer* 48:36
workmanship of thy *p.* *Ezek* 28:13
and seven *p.* to the seven. *Zech* 4:2
through the golden *p.* empty. 12*
life, whether *p.* or harp. *1 Cor* 14:7

piped

people *p.* with pipes. *1 Ki* 1:40
saying, We have *p.* unto you.
Mat 11:17; *Luke* 7:32
be known what is *p.*? *1 Cor* 14:7

pipers

voice of *p.* shall be. *Rev* 18:22*

Pisgah

Balaam to the top of *P.* *Num* 23:14
get thee up into the top of *P.*
Deut 3:27; 34:1
plain, under the springs of *P.* 4:29

Pisidia

came to Antioch in *P.* *Acts* 13:14
had passed throughout *P.* 14:24

piss

drink own *p.* with you. *2 Ki* 18:27*
Isa 36:12*

pit, -s

(*This word is used metaphorically for deep trouble, and for the depths of hell*)
was full of slime *p.* *Gen* 14:10
us cast him into some *p.* 37:20*, 24
owner of the *p.* shall. *Ex* 21:34
a *p.* wherein is water. *Lev* 11:36
quick into the *p.* *Num* 16:30, 33
hid themselves in *p.* *1 Sam* 13:6
is now hid in some *p.* *2 Sam* 17:9
cast Absalom into a great *p.* 18:17
Benaiah slew a lion in a *p.* 23:20
1 Chr 11:22
Jehu slew them at the *p.* *2 Ki* 10:14
down to the bars of the *p.* *Job* 17:16
back his soul from the *p.* 33:18, 30
from going down into the *p.* 24, 28
sunk down into the *p.* *Ps* 9:15
them that go down into *p.* 28:1
not go down to the *p.* 30:3
blood, when I go down to the *p.*? 9
hid from me their net in a *p.* 35:7
up out of an horrible *p.* 40:2
to the *p.* of destruction. 55:23
let not the *p.* shut her mouth. 69:15
with them that go down into *p.* 88:4
hast laid me in the lowest *p.* 6
the proud have digged *p.* 119:85
let them be cast into deep *p.* 140:10
like unto them that go down into the *p.* 143:7 *Pr* 1:12
strange women is a deep *p.* *Pr* 22:14
woman is a narrow *p.* 23:27
fall himself into his own *p.* 28:10
a man shall flee to the *p.*; let no. 17
down to the sides of the *p.* *Isa* 14:15
to the stones of the *p.* 19
fear, and the *p.* and the snare. 24:17
Jer 48:43, 44
cometh out of the midst of *p.* *Isa* 24:18
prisoners are gathered in the *p.* 22
water withal out of the *p.* 30:14*
hast delivered it from the *p.* 38:17
they that go down into the *p.* 18
he should not die in the *p.* 51:14
led us through a land of *p.* *Jer* 2:6
they came to the *p.* and found. 14:3†
into the midst of the *p.* 41:7
the *p.* which Asa made for fear. 9
anointed taken in their *p.* *Lam* 4:20
was taken in their *p.* *Ezek* 19:4, 8
with them that descend into the *p.*
26:20; 28:8; 31:14, 16; 32:18, 24
25, 29, 30
are set in the sides of the *p.* 32:23
of nettles and salt *p.* *Zeph* 2:9
prisoners out of the *p.* *Zech* 9:11
if it fall into a *p.* on sabbath.
Mat 12:11; *Luke* 14:5*
see **bottomless, dig, digged**

pitch

p. it within and without with *p.*
Gen 6:14
with slime and with *p.* *Ex* 2:3
turned to *p.*, and the land thereof shall become burning *p.* *Isa* 34:9

pitch, *verb*

Israel shall *p.* every man. *Num* 1:52
the Levites shall *p.* round the. 53
man shall *p.* by his own standard. 2:2
camp of Judah *p.* 3
the Gershonites *p.* 3:23
sons of Kohath *p.* 29
Merari shall *p.* 35
you out a place to *p.* in. *Deut* 1:33
Joshua did *p.* twelve stones.
Josh 4:20
nor shall the Arabian *p.* *Isa* 13:20
shepherds shall *p.* their. *Jer* 6:3

pitched

(*American Revision changes this word, when used intransitively, to* encamped)
Abram *p.* his tent, and. *Gen* 12:8
Lot *p.* 13:12
Isaac *p.* in valley. 26:17, 25
Jacob *p.* in mount, Laban *p.* 31:25
Jacob *p.* his tent before. 33:18
from Sin, Israel *p.* in. *Ex* 17:1
come to desert, and had *p.* 19:2
Moses took tabernacle, *p.* it. 33:7
when tabernacle is *p.* *Num* 1:51
so they *p.* by their standards. 2:34
at commandment of the Lord they *p.* 9:18
the people *p.* in the wilderness. 12:16
Israel *p.* in Oboth. 21:10
p. in Ije-abarim. 11
Israel *p.* in Succoth. 33:5
they *p.* in Etham. 6
ambush *p.* on north side. *Josh* 8:11
set ark in tabernacle David had *p.*
2 Sam 6:17
Israel and Absalom *p.* in land. 17:26
Israel *p.* before them. *1 Ki* 20:27, 29
Nebuchadnezzar *p.* against it.
2 Ki 25:1; *Jer* 52:4
a place for the ark, and *p.* for it a tent. *1 Chr* 15:1; 16:1; *2 Chr* 1:4
tabernacle which Lord *p.* *Heb* 8:2

pitcher, -s

let down *p.* I pray thee. *Gen* 24:14
Rebekah came with her *p.* 15, 45
empty *p.* and lamps within the *p.*
Judg 7:16
they brake *p.* that were in. 19, 20
or the *p.* be broken at. *Eccl* 12:6
esteemed as earthen *p.*? *Lam* 4:2
man bearing a *p.* of water.
Mark 14:13; *Luke* 22:10

pitied

also to be *p.* of all. *Ps* 106:46
and the Lord hath not *p.* *Lam* 2:2
17, 21; 3:43
none eye *p.* thee, to do. *Ezek* 16:5

pitieth

like as a father *p.* his children, so the Lord *p.* them that. *Ps* 103:13
I will profane what your soul *p.*
Ezek 24:21

pitiful

hands of *p.* women have. *Lam* 4:10
that the Lord is very *p.* *Jas* 5:11
love as brethren, be *p.* *1 Pet* 3:8*

pity

thine eye shall have no *p.* *Deut* 7:16
because he had no *p.* *2 Sam* 12:6
to the afflicted, *p.* should. *Job* 6:14*
have *p.* on me, *p.* on me. 19:21
looked for some to take *p.* *Ps* 69:20
that hath *p.* on poor. *Pr* 19:17
they shall have no *p.* on. *Isa* 13:18
in his love and in his *p.* he. 63:9
for who shall have *p.* upon? *Jer* 15:5
nor have *p.* nor mercy. 21:7
nor will I have *p.* *Ezek* 5:11; 7:4, 9
8:18; 9:10
eye spare, neither have ye *p.* 9:5
but I had *p.* for mine holy. 36:21
Edom did cast off all *p.* *Amos* 1:11
had *p.* on the gourd. *Jonah* 4:10
as I had *p.* on thee. *Mat* 18:33*

pity, *verb*

nor shall thine eye *p.* him. *Deut* 13:8
19:13, 21
thine eye shall not *p.* 25:12
for him that will *p.* the poor. *Pr* 28:8
I will not *p.* nor spare. *Jer* 13:14
Lord will *p.* his people. *Joel* 2:18
their own shepherds *p.* *Zech* 11:5
for I will no more *p.* inhabitants. 6

place

Lord said, Look from *p.* *Gen* 13:14
destroy and not spare the *p.*? 18:24
spare the *p.* for their sakes. 26
thou shalt shew at every *p.* 20:13
third day Abraham saw the *p.* 22:4
I may go unto mine own *p.* 30:25
into prison, the *p.* where. 40:3
p. whereon thou standest is holy.
Ex 3:5; *Josh* 5:15
this people shall go to their *p.* in peace. *Ex* 18:23
to bring thee into the *p.* I. 23:20
he shall cast it by the *p.* *Lev* 1:16
first *p.* went standard. *Num* 10:14
ye shall eat it in every *p.* ye. 18:31
every *p.* whereon the soles of your.
Deut 11:24; *Josh* 1:3
p. the Lord God shall choose.
Deut 12:5, 14; 16:16
thy burnt offering in every *p.* 12:13
if the *p.* be too far. 21; 14:24
through thy land to my *p.* *Judg* 11:19
men of Israel gave *p.* to. 20:36
thou shalt mark the *p.* *Ruth* 3:4
and one of the same *p.* *1 Sam* 10:12
went to their own *p.* 14:46
and David's *p.* was empty. 20:25, 27
and died in the same *p.* *2 Sam* 2:23
in what *p.* my lord the king. 15:21
pit, or in some other *p.* 17:9
come upon him in some *p.* 12
to this day Absalom's *p.* 18:18*
eyes may be open toward *p.* *1 Ki* 8:29
strike his hand over the *p.* *2 Ki* 5:11
behold, *p.* where we dwell is. 6:1
grant me the *p.* of. *1 Chr* 21:22
to Ornan for the *p.* 600 shekels. 25
the priests stood in their *p.*
2 Chr 30:16; 35:10
sons of Asaph, were in their *p.* 35:15

p. of my father's sepulchre. Neh 2:3
there was no p. for beast under. 14
in what p. ye hear sound of. 4:20
and Levites in their p. 13:11
her maids to the best p. Esth 2:9
deliverance from another p. 4:14
consumed out of their p. Job 6:17
shake the earth out of her p. 9:6
let my cry have no p. 16:18
where is the p. of understanding ?
28:12, 20
and he knoweth the p. thereof. 23
people are cut off in their p. 36:20
for darkness, where is the p.? 38:19
the wicked in their p. 40:12*
the p. where thine honour. Ps 26:8
my foot standeth in an even p. 12
thou art my hiding p. 32:7; 119:114
from the p. of his habitation. 33:14
the p. thereof shall know it. 103:16
the p. of judgement, p. Eccl 3:16
all go unto one p.; all are of. 20; 6:6
to field, till there be no p. Isa 5:8
shall remove out of her p. 13:13
and bring them to their p. 14:2
so that there is no p. clean. 28:8
barley and rye in their p.? 25
in every p. where grounded. 30:32*
p. is too strait for me, give p. 49:20
enlarge the p. of thy tent. 54:2
I will make the p. of my feet. 60:13
where is the p. of my rest ? 66:1
go ye now unto my p. Jer 7:12
till there be no p. 32; 19:11
glorious throne is the p. of. 17:12
waters come from another p. 18:14*
p. where they did offer. Ezek 6:13
p. of my throne shall Israel. 43:7
he shall burn it in the appointed p. 21
that no p. was found. Dan 2:35
the p. of his sanctuary was. 8:11
go and return to my p. Hos 5:15
dead bodies in every p. Amos 8:3
their p. is not known. Nah 3:17
p. shall not be found. Zech 10:10
again in her own p. 12:6; 14:10
be offered in every p. Mal 1:11
come, see the p. where the Lord lay.
Mat 28:6; Mark 16:6
in what p. soever ye. Mark 6:10
p. where it was written. Luke 4:17
two and two unto every p. 10:1
a Levite, when he was at the p. 32
to thee, Give this man p. 14:9
Jerusalem is the p. of. John 4:20
because my word hath no p. 8:37*
two days still in the same p. 11:6
Romans shall take away our p. 48
betrayed him, knew the p. 18:2
with one accord in one p. Acts 2:1
when they had prayed, the p. 4:31
the p. whereon thou standest. 7:33
or what is the p. of my rest ? 49
the p. of scripture which he. 8:32
rather give p. unto wrath. Rom 12:19
but now having no more p. 15:23
with all that in every p. call on Jesus
Christ. 1 Cor 1:2
come together into one p. 11:20*
church be come into one p. 14:23*
his knowledge in every p. 2 Cor 2:14
to whom we gave p. . . . no. Gal 2:5
nor give p. to the devil. Eph 4:27
in every p. your faith God-ward.
1 Thes 1:8
in another p., Thou a priest. Heb 5:6
no p. should have been sought. 8:7
he found no p. of repentance. 12:17
the same p. sweet water. Jas 3:11*
nor was their p. found any. Rev 12:8
fly into wilderness to her p. 14
and there was found no p. 20:11
see **dwelling, holy,** *most* **holy**

a place
a p. where king's prisoners were.
Gen 39:20
appoint thee a p. to flee. Ex 21:13
behold, there is a p. by me. 33:21
place was a p. for cattle. Num 32:1
search you out a p. to pitch your.
Deut 1:33
a p. without the camp. 23:12
give him a p. in the city. Josh 20:4
where he could find a p. Judg 17:8
a p. where is no want of. 18:10
Saul set him up a p. 1 Sam 15:12*
my servants to such a p. 21:2
let them give me a p. in. 27:5
a p. for Israel, that they may dwell in
a p. 2 Sam 7:10; 1 Chr 17:9
assigned Uriah to a p. 2 Sam 11:16
I set there a p. for ark. 1 Ki 8:21
1 Chr 15:1
let us make us a p. 2 Ki 6:2
in such a p. shall be my camp. 8
beware thou pass not such a p. 9
I have built a p. for thy. 2 Chr 6:2
there is a p. for gold. Job 28:1
until I find out a p. for. Ps 132:5
have a p. of refuge. Pr 14:26
a p. of refuge from rain. Isa 4:6
Lord will be to us a p. of. 33:21
for herself a p. of rest. 34:14
and within my walls a p. 56:5*
Achor a p. for the herds. 65:10
a p. for the spreading. Ezek 26:5, 14
I will give to Gog a p. of. 39:11
she is become a p. for. Zeph 2:15
that is to say, a p. of a skull.
Mat 27:33 ; John 19:17
found colt in a p. where. Mark 11:4*
I go to prepare a p. John 14:2, 3
in a certain p. testified. Heb 2:6*
he spake in a certain p. of the. 4:4*
called to go out into a p. he. 11:8
hath a p. prepared of God. Rev 12:6
into a p. called Armageddon. 16:16
see **choose**

high place
went up to an high p. Num 23:3*
is a sacrifice to-day in high p.
1 Sam 9:12
prophets coming from high p. 10:5
an end, Saul came to high p. 13
that was great high p. 1 Ki 3:4
1 Chr 16:39
Solomon built an high p. 1 Ki 11:7
high p. that Jeroboam . . . the high
p., burnt the high p. 2 Ki 23:15
went to the high p. 2 Chr 1:3
journey to high p. at Gibeon. 13
is weary on the high p. Isa 16:12
made a high p. in every street.
Ezek 16:24, 25, 31
the high p. whereunto ye go ? 20:29

his place
and Abraham returned to his p.
Gen 18:33
rose up and returned to his p. 31:35
neither rose from his p. Ex 10:23
in his p., none go out of his p. 16:29
bright spot stay in his p. Lev 13:23
every man in his p. by. Num 2:17
Balaam rose up and returned to his
p. 24:25
to the gate of his p. Deut 21:19
be not cut off from his p. Ruth 4:10
laid down in his p. 1 Sam 3:2
went and lay down in his p. 9
set Dagon in his p. again. 5:3
ark go down to his own p. 11; 6:2
go and see his p. where. 23:22
and Saul returned to his p. 26:25
that he may go again to his p. 29:4
ark of the Lord in his p. 2 Sam 6:17
returned to his own p. 19:39
priests brought ark to his p.
1 Ki 8:6; 2 Chr 5:7
every man out of his p. 1 Ki 20:24
ark of the Lord to his p. 1 Chr 15:3
and gladness are in his p. 16:27
chest to his p. again. 2 Chr 24:11
king stood in his p. and made. 34:31
let men of his p. help. Ezra 1:4
for house of God to set it in his p.
2:68; 5:15; 6:7
every one from his own p. Job 2:11
neither shall his p. know him. 7:10
if he destroy him from his p. 8:18
is removed out of his p. 14:18
rock be removed out of his p.? 18:4
nor shall his p. any more. 20:9
hurleth him out of his p. 27:21
hands and hiss him out of his p. 23
is removed out of his p. 37:1
dayspring to know his p. 38:12
diligently consider his p. Ps 37:10
wandereth from his p. Pr 27:8
the sun hasteth to his p. Eccl 1:5
Lord cometh out of his p. Isa 26:21
his p. of defence shall be. 33:16
set him in his p.; from his p. shall he
not remove. 46:7
he is gone from his p. Jer 4:7
feed every one in his p. 6:3
glory of Lord from his p. Ezek 3:12
Lord cometh out of his p. Mi 1:3
worship every one from his p.
Zeph 2:11
grow up out of his p. Zech 6:12
thy sword into his p. Mat 26:52
might go to his own p. Acts 1:25
candlestick out of his p. Rev 2:5

in the place
not, am I in the p. of God ? Gen 50:19
plant them in the p. Ex 15:17
kill it in the p. where they kill.
Lev 4:24, 29, 33; 6:25; 7:2
in the p. of the boil there. 13:19
in the p. where the cloud. Num 9:17
inheritance be in the p. 33:54
twelve stones in the p. Josh 4:9
drunk water in the p. 1 Ki 13:22
in the p. where dogs licked. 21:19
in the p. that David. 2 Chr 3:1
sore broken us in the p. Ps 44:19
and stand not in the p. Pr 25:6
in the p. where the tree. Eccl 11:3
but he shall die in the p. Jer 22:12
38:9; 42:22
in the p. where the king dwelleth.
Ezek 17:16
judge thee in the p. where. 21:30
that in the p. where it was said.
Hos 1:10; Rom 9:26
not stay long in the p. of. Hos 13:13
in the p. where crucified. John 19:41

of the place
men of the p. asked him; lest men
of p. should kill. Gen 26:7
all the men of the p. 29:22
the name of the p. Peniel. 32:30
name of p. Succoth. 33:17
name of p. Beth el. 35:15
name of the p. Massah. Ex 17:7
name of the p. Taberah. Num 11:3
of the p. twelve stones. Josh 4:3
name of the p. Gilgal. 5:9
of p. called valley of Achor. 7:26
the men of the p. were. Judg 19:16
Naomi went forth out of the p.
Ruth 1:7
called name of the p. Perez-uzzah.
2 Sam 6:8
pattern of the p. of. 1 Chr 28:11
name of the p., valley. 2 Chr 20:26
breadth of the p. left. Ezek 41:11
raise them out of the p. Joel 3:7
end of the p. thereof. Nah 1:8

that place
called that p. Beer-sheba. Gen 21:31
that p. Jehovah-jireh. 22:14
called name of that p. Beth-el.28:19
name of that p. Mahanaim. 32:2
asked men of that p. 38:21
name of that p. Kibroth. Num 11:34
of them out of that p. Deut 12:3
the sentence they of that p. 17:10
name of that p. Bochim. Judg 2:5
that p. Ramath-lehi. 15:17
called that p. Selah-. 1 Sam 23:28
that p. was called Helkath-hazzurim.
2 Sam 2:16
called that p. Baal-perazim. 5:20
1 Chr 14:11
that p. is called Perez-. 1 Chr 13:11
men of that p. had. Mat 14:35
ye depart from that p. Mark 6:10
multitude being in that p. John 5:13
was in that p. where Martha. 11:30
both we and they of that p.
Acts 21:12

this place
bring them out of this p. Gen 19:12
we will destroy this p. 13
get out of this p. 14
fear of God is not in this p. 20:11
Lord is in this p. 28:16

dreadful is this p. Gen 28:17
no harlot in this p. 38:21, 22
God hath given me in this p. 48:9
brought you out from this p. Ex 13:3
us unto this evil p. Num 20:5
bare thee till ye came to this p.
Deut 1:31; 9:7; 11:5
he hath brought us into this p. 26:9
when ye came unto this p. 29:7
makest thou in this p.? Judg 18:3
prayer toward this p. 1 Ki 8:29, 30
35; 2 Chr 6:20, 21, 26, 40; 7:15
nor drink water in this p. 1 Ki 13:8, 16
come not against this p. 2 Ki 18:25
I will bring evil on this p. 22:16, 17
20; 2 Chr 34:24, 25, 28
and have chosen this p. 2 Chr 7:12
this the p. of him that. Job 18:21
innocent blood in this p. Jer 7:6
be poured out on this p. 20
you assured peace in this p. 14:13
sons nor daughters in this p. 16:2
cause to cease out of this p. the. 9
will bring evil upon this p. 19:3
they estranged this p., filled this p. 4
that this p. shall no more be. 6
thus will I do unto this p. 12; 40:2
went forth out of this p. 22:11; 24:5
restore them to this p. 27:22; 32:37
I will bring to this p. all. 28:3, 6
I will bring again to this p. 4
you to return to this p. 29:10
again be heard in this p. the. 33:10
ye shall see this p. no more. 42:18
punish you in this p. 44:29
hast spoken against this p. 51:62
this is the p. where the priests shall
boil the offering. Ezek 46:20
of Baal from this p. Zeph 1:4
in this p. will I give peace. Hag 2:9
in this p. one greater. Mat 12:6
into this p. of torment. Luke 16:28
from Galilee to this p. 23:5
shall destroy this p. Acts 6:14
forth and serve me in this p. 7:7
against the law and this p. 21:28
and in this p. again, if they. Heb 4:5

thy place

restore thee to thy p. Gen 40:13*
flee thou to thy p. Num 24:11
return to thy p. and. 2 Sam 15:19
rise against thee, leave not thy p.
Eccl 10:4
shalt remove from thy p. Ezek 12:3
38:15

to or unto the place

Abram went unto the p. Gen 13:3, 4
went unto the p. of which. 22:3, 9
to bring you unto the p. Ex 3:8
lead people unto the p. of. 32:34
journeying to the p. of. Num 10:29
go up to the p. which Lord. 14:40
carried stones to the p. Josh 4:8
come to the p. where. 1 Sam 20:19
as many as came to the p. stood.
2 Sam 2:23
sent to the p. which man. 2 Ki 6:10
bring ark to the p. that. 1 Chr 15:12
I will bring them to the p. Neh 1:9
they go to the p. that. Ps 104:8
present brought to the p. Isa 18:7
I will do to the p. which I. Jer 7:14
will bring you again to the p. 29:14
was entered into the p. Acts 25:23

place, verb

and p. such over them. Ex 18:21
in the p. which he shall choose to p.
Deut 14:23; 16:2, 6, 11; 26:2
and p. them in the house. Ezra 6:5
and I will p. salvation in. Isa 46:13
I shall p. you in your. Ezek 37:14, 26
shall p. the abomination. Dan 11:31
p. them in their houses. Hos 11:11*
bring them again to p. them. Zech 10:6

placed

God p. at east of the. Gen 3:24
Joseph p. his father and his. 47:11
Jeroboam p. in Beth-el. 1 Ki 12:32
and p. them in Halah. 2 Ki 17:6
and p. them in the cities of. 24, 26
he p. in the chariot cities. 2 Chr 1:14
he made tables, p. them in the. 4:8
he p. forces in all the. 2 Chr 17:2
of old, since man was p. Job 20:4
the tent which he had p. Ps 78:60
that they may be p. alone. Isa 5:8*
which p. sand for the. Jer 5:22
eagle p. it by the great. Ezek 17:5

places

will keep thee in all p. Gen 28:15
in all p. where I record. Ex 20:24
utterly destroy all the p. Deut 12:2
abode in their p. till. Josh 5:8
delivered in the p. of. Judg 5:11
to one of these p. to lodge. 19:13
Israel in all those p. 1 Sam 7:16
sent presents to all the p. 30:31
in all the p. wherein? 2 Sam 7:7
put down priests in p. 2 Ki 23:5
he filled their p. with the bones. 14
from all p. whence ye. Neh 4:12
in lower p. and on higher p. 13
Levites out of all their p. 12:27
where are the dwelling p.? Job 21:28*
dens and remain in their p. 37:8*
he sitteth in lurking p. of. Ps 10:8
fallen to me in pleasant p. 16:6
afraid out of their close p. 18:45
set them in slippery p. 73:18
the dark p. of the earth are. 74:20
all his works, in all p. 103:22
they ran in the dry p. like. 105:41
he shall fill the p. with the. 110:6
she standeth in the p. of. Pr 8:2*
that art in the secret p. S of S 2:14
dwell in quiet resting p. Isa 32:18
straight, and rough p. plain. 40:4
I will make the crooked p. 45:2
a wind from those p. shall. Jer 4:12
in all p. whither I have. 8:3; 29:14
from p. about Jerusalem. 17:26
to be a taunt and a curse in all p. 24:9
take witnesses in the p. 32:44
Jews returned out of all p. 40:12
give for a prey in all p. 45:5
he hath destroyed his p. Lam 2:6
deliver them out of all p. Ezek 34:12
I will make the p. round my hill. 26
he said, These are the p. of. 46:24*
but the miry p. thereof. 47:11
of bread in all your p. Amos 4:6
I will give thee p. to walk. Zech 3:7
he walketh through dry p.
Mat 12:43; Luke 11:24
some fell on stony p. Mat 13:5, 20
famines and earthquakes in divers p.
24:7; Mark 13:8; Luke 21:11
we accept it in all p. Acts 24:3
blessed us in heavenly p. Eph 1:3
at his own right hand in heavenly p. 20
together in heavenly p. in Christ. 2:6
to powers in heavenly p. might. 3:10
Christ are manifest in all p. Phil 1:13
island moved out of their p. Rev 6:14
see **desolate, holy**

high places

will destroy your high p. Lev 26:30
consumed lords of high p. of.
Num 21:28
up into the high p. of Baal. 22:41
pluck down all their high p. 33:52
made him ride on high p. Deut 32:13
tread upon their high p. 33:29
their lives in the high p. Judg 5:18
people hide themselves in high p.
1 Sam 13:6*
of Israel slain in high p. 2 Sam 1:19
thou wast slain in thy high p. 25
setteth me on my high p. 22:34
Ps 18:33
people sacrificed in high p. 1 Ki 3:2
2 Ki 17:32; 2 Chr 33:17
incense in high p. 1 Ki 3:3; 22:43
2 Ki 12:3; 15:4, 35; 16:4; 17:11
made an house of high p. 1 Ki 12:31
in Beth-el the priests of high p. 32
offer the priests of the high p. 13:2
all the houses of the high p. 32
the lowest of the people priests of
the high p. 33; 2 Ki 17:32
but the high p. were. 1 Ki 15:14
22:43; 2 Ki 12:3; 14:4; 15:4, 35
in houses of high p. 2 Ki 17:29
removed the high p. 18:4, 22
burn incense in the high p. 23:5
defiled the high p. ... and brake down
the high p. of gates. 2 Ki 23:8, 13
2 Chr 31:1; 32:12; Isa 36:7
priests of high p. came. 2 Ki 23:9
all the priests of the high p. 20
ordained priests for high p.
2 Chr 11:15
Asa took away the high p. 14:3, 5
the high p. were not taken away.
15:17; 20:33
took away the high p. 17:6
Jehoram made high p. 21:11
Ahaz made high p. 28:25
purge Jerusalem from high p. 34:3
peace in his high p. Job 25:2
provoked him with their high p.
Ps 78:58
on the top of the high p. Pr 8:2
seat in the high p. of the city. 9:14
is gone up to the high p. Isa 15:2
I will open rivers in high p. 41:18*
pastures shall be in all high p. 49:9*
cause thee to ride on high p. 58:14
thine eyes to the high p. Jer 3:2*
a voice was heard on the high p. 21*
a dry wind in the high p. of. 4:11*
a lamentation in the high p. 7:29
come up on all the high p. 12:12
did stand in the high p. 14:6*
I will give thy high p. for sin. 17:3
become as the high p. of the forest.
26:18; Mi 3:12
I will cause to cease in Moab him
that offereth in high p. Jer 48:35
I will destroy your high p. Ezek 6:3
deckedst thy high p. with. 16:16
break down thy high p. 39
the ancient high p. are ours. 36:2
the high p. of Aven. Hos 10:8
treadeth on high p. of earth.
Amos 4:13; Mi 1:3
the high p. of Isaac shall. Amos 7:9
what are the high p. of? Mi 1:5
to walk on mine high p. Hab 3:19
wickedness in high p. Eph 6:12
see **built**

waste places

waste p. of fat ones shall. Isa 5:17
comfort all her waste p. 51:3
sing together, ye waste p. 52:9
build the old waste p. 58:12

plague

and I will p. them that. Ps 89:23*

plague, substantive

yet I will bring one p. Ex 11:1
the p. shall not be on you to. 12:13
there be no p. among them. 30:12
when the hair in the p. Lev 13:3, 17
if the p. spread not in. 5, 6; 14:48
a p. then priest shall see the p.
13:30, 31, 32, 50, 51, 55; 14:37
he is a leprous man, his p. is. 13:44
and shut up it that hath the p. 50
or woof, it is a spreading p. 57*
if p. be departed from them. 58
there is as it were a p. in. 14:35
be no p. among Israel. Num 8:19
people with a very great p. 11:33
died by the p. before the Lord. 14:37
wrath is gone out, the p. 16:46, 47
the p. was stayed. 48, 50; 25:8
that died in the p. 16:49; 25:9
every p. which is not. Deut 28:61
not cleansed, although there was p.
Josh 22:17
one p. was on you all. 1 Sam 6:4
that p. may be stayed. 2 Sam 24:21
1 Chr 21:22
whatever p. or sickness. 1 Ki 8:37
shall know every man the p. of. 38
with a great p. will the. 2 Chr 21:14
nor any p. come nigh. Ps 91:10
p. brake in upon them. 106:29
judgement, so p. was stayed. 30
this shall be the p. Zech 14:12; 18
she was healed of that p. Mark 5:29
and be whole of thy p. 34
because of the p. of hail. Rev 16:21

plagued

the Lord p. Pharaoh. Gen 12:17
Lord p. the people for. Ex 32:35*
p. Egypt, and afterwards. Josh 24:5

that they should be p. *1 Chr* 21:17
nor are they p. like other. *Ps* 73:5
all the day have I been p. 14

plagues

Pharaoh with great p. *Gen* 12:17
this time send all my p. *Ex* 9:14
bring seven times more p. on you. *Lev* 26:21
make thy p. wonderful. *Deut* 28:59
when they see the p. of. 29:22
smote Egyptians with p. *1 Sam* 4:8
and hiss because of all the p. *Jer* 19:8
49:17; 50:13
O death, I will be thy p. *Hos* 13:14
to touch him, as many as had p. *Mark* 3:10
cured many of their p. *Luke* 7:21
were not killed by these p. *Rev* 9:20
to smite earth with p. 11:6
who hath power over these p. 16:9
that ye receive not of her p. 18:4
therefore shall her p. come in one. 8
God shall add to him the p. 22:18
see **seven**

plain, *adjective*

Jacob was a p. man. *Gen* 25:27
lead me in a p. path. *Ps* 27:11
they are p. to him that. *Pr* 8:9
of the righteous is made p. 15:19*
when he made p. the face. *Isa* 28:25
straight, and rough places p. 40:4
come on the p. country. *Jer* 48:21
write the vision, make it p. *Hab* 2:2
loosed, and he spake p. *Mark* 7:35

plain, *substantive*

they found a p. in the land. *Gen* 11:2
and Lot beheld all the p. of. 13:10
chose him all the p. of Jordan. 11
Lot dwelt in cities of the p. 12
Abram came and dwelt in the p. 18*
14:13*
neither stay thou in all the p. 19:17
those cities in all the p. 25
Joshua took the valley and the p. *Josh* 11:16*
made Abimelech king by p. of pillar. *Judg* 9:6*
the Ammonites to the p. 11:33*
come to the p. of Tabor. *1 Sam* 10:3*
his men were in the p. 23:24*
men walked through p. *2 Sam* 2:29*
Rechab gat them through the p. 4:7*
I will tarry in the p. till I hear. 15:28*
ran by the way of the p. 18:23
in p. of Jordan did king. *1 Ki* 7:46
against them in the p. 20:23, 25
king went towards the p. *2 Ki* 25:4*
Jer 52:7
repaired the priests of p. *Neh* 3:22
they shall come from p. bringing burnt offerings. *Jer* 17:26*
against thee, O rock of the p. 21:13
p. shall be destroyed, as Lord. 48:8
go forth in the p. *Ezek* 3:22, 23
vision that I saw in the p. 8:4

plainly

if the servant p. say, I. *Ex* 21:5
words of this law very p. *Deut* 27:8
did I p. appear unto the house of thy father? *1 Sam* 2:27*
he told us p. that the asses. 10:16
letter hath been p. read. *Ezra* 4:18
stammerers shall speak p. *Isa* 32:4
if the Christ, tell us p. *John* 10:24
to them p., Lazarus is dead. 11:14
shew you p. of the Father. 16:25
now speakest thou p. and. 29
such things declare p. *Heb* 11:14*

plainness

hope, we use great p. *2 Cor* 3:12*

plains

Lord appeared in the p. *Gen* 18:1*
Israel pitched in p. of Moab. *Num* 22:1; 33:48
who numbered Israel in the p. 26:63
spoil unto the camp in the p. 31:12
the Lord spake to Moses in the p. 33:50; 35:1
Lord commanded in the p. 36:13
Moses went up from the p. of Moab. *Deut* 34:1
Israel wept for Moses in the p. 8
lodge not in the p. of. *2 Sam* 17:16*
Chaldees overtook him in the p. *2 Ki* 25:5; *Jer* 39:5; 52:8
trees in the low p. *1 Chr* 27:28
sycamores in low p. *2 Chr* 9:27
had much cattle in the p. 26:10

plaister, *substantive*

lay it for a p. on boil. *Isa* 38:21†
wrote on the p. of the wall. *Dan* 5:5†

plaister, *verb*

take mortar and shall p. house. *Lev* 14:42†
and p. them with p. *Deut* 27:2†, 4

plaistered

if the plague come again after it is p. *Lev* 14:43†
spread after the house was p. 48†

plaiting

adorning let it not be p. *1 Pet* 3:3

planes

fitteth the image with p. *Isa* 44:13

planets

incense to sun, moon, p. *2 Ki* 23:5

planks

the floor with p. of fir. *1 Ki* 6:15*
were thick p. on face. *Ezek* 41:25*
chambers of house, and thick p. 26*

plant, *substantive*

Lord God made every p. *Gen* 2:5
bring forth boughs like p. *Job* 14:9
of Judah his pleasant p. *Isa* 5:7
thou shalt make thy p. grow. 17:11
before him as a tender p. 53:2
turned into degenerate p. *Jer* 2:21
for them a p. of renown. *Ezek* 34:29*
every p. my Father hath. *Mat* 15:13

plant, *verb*

p. them in mount of thy. *Ex* 15:17
shalt not p. a grove. *Deut* 16:21
thou shalt p. a vineyard. 28:30, 39
moreover, I will p. them. *2 Sam* 7:10; *1 Chr* 17:9
a sign unto thee, Ye shall p. vineyards, and eat the fruits. *2 Ki* 19:29
Isa 37:30; 65:21; *Ezek* 28:26
Amos 9:14
fields, and p. vineyards. *Ps* 107:37
shalt p. pleasant plants. *Isa* 17:10
I will p. in the wilderness. 41:19
that I may p. heavens, and lay. 51:16
shall not p. and another eat. 65:22
set thee to build and to p. *Jer* 1:10
kingdom to build and to p. 18:9
I will p. and not pluck. 24:6; 42:10
p. gardens, and eat the fruit. 29:5, 28
shall p. vines on the mountains. 31:5
over them to build and to p. 28
I will p. them in this land. 32:41
nor shall you sow seed, nor p. 35:7
I will p. it on a high. *Ezek* 17:22, 23
Lord build and p. that. 36:36
he shall p. tabernacles. *Dan* 11:45
I will p. them upon their. *Amos* 9:15
they shall p. vineyards, but not drink the wine thereof. *Zeph* 1:13

plantation

it by furrows of her p. *Ezek* 17:7

planted

the Lord God p. a garden. *Gen* 2:8
Noah p. a vineyard. 9:20
Abram p. a grove. 21:33
trees which Lord hath p. *Num* 24:6
that hath p. a vineyard? *Deut* 20:6
of oliveyards ye p. not. *Josh* 24:13
like a tree p. by the rivers. *Ps* 1:3; *Jer* 17:8
heathen, and p. the vine. *Ps* 80:8
which thy right hand hath p. 15
those that be p. in the house. 92:13
he that p. the ear, shall he? 94:9
Lebanon which he hath p. 104:16
I p. me vineyards. *Eccl* 2:4
I p. trees. 5
to pluck up that which is p. 3:2
p. it with the choicest vine. *Isa* 5:2
yea, they shall not be p. nor. 40:24
I had p. thee a noble vine. *Jer* 2:21
for the Lord of hosts that p. 11:17
thou hast p. them, they have. 12:2
what I have p. I will pluck up. 45:4
p. it in a fruitful field. *Ezek* 17:5, 8
yea, behold, being p. shall it? 10
p. by the waters: she was. 19:10
now she is p. in the wilderness. 13
Ephraim is p. in a. *Hos* 9:13
p. pleasant vineyards. *Amos* 5:11
every plant, which my heavenly Father hath not p. *Mat* 15:13
man p. a vineyard. 21:33
Mark 12:1; *Luke* 20:9
a fig tree p. in vineyard. *Luke* 13:6
and be thou p. in the sea. 17:6
they bought, they sold, they p. 28
if we have been p. together in his death. *Rom* 6:5*
I have p., Apollos. *1 Cor* 3:6

plantedst

which thou p. not. *Deut* 6:11
out heathen and p. them. *Ps* 44:2

planters

p. shall plant, and eat. *Jer* 31:5

planteth

her hands she p. vineyard. *Pr* 31:16
he p. an ash, and the. *Isa* 44:14
he that p. any thing. *1 Cor* 3:7
he that p. and he that watereth. 8
who p. a vineyard and eateth? 9:7

planting

branch of my p. work. *Isa* 60:21
they might be called the p. 61:3

plantings

I will make Samaria as p. of. *Mi* 1:6

plants

that dwell among p. *1 Chr* 4:23*
thy children like olive p. *Ps* 128:3
that our sons may be as p. 144:12
thy p. as an orchard of. *S of S* 4:13*
broken down principal p. *Isa* 16:8
shalt thou plant pleasant p. 17:10
thy p. are gone over sea. *Jer* 48:32*
rivers running round about his p. *Ezek* 31:4*

plat

in this p., now take and cast him into the p. of ground. *2 Ki* 9:26

plate

thou shalt make a p. *Ex* 28:36
made the p. of holy crown. 39:30
he put the golden p. *Lev* 8:9

plates

beat gold into thin p. *Ex* 39:3
of censers broad p. *Num* 16:38
were made broad p. for a. 39*
base had p. of brass. *1 Ki* 7:30*
silver spread into p. is. *Jer* 10:9

platted

had p. a crown of thorns. *Mat* 27:29*
Mark 15:17*; *John* 19:2*

platter

clean outside of the p. but within. *Mat* 23:25; *Luke* 11:39

play

the people rose up to p. *Ex* 32:6
1 Cor 10:7
to p. the whore in her. *Deut* 22:21
shall p. with his hand. *1 Sam* 16:16
now a man that can p. well. 17
this fellow to p. the madman. 21:15
let young men arise and p. before. *2 Sam* 2:14
will I p. before the Lord. 6:21
us p. the men for our people. 10:12
the beasts of the field p. *Job* 40:20
p. with him as with a bird? 41:5
p. skilfully with a loud. *Ps* 33:3
leviathan whom thou madest to p. therein. 104:26
sucking child shall p. on. *Isa* 11:8
and can p. well on an. *Ezek* 33:32

played

and his concubine p. *Judg* 19:2
David p. with his hand. *1 Sam* 16:23; 18:10; 19:9
women answered one another as they p. 18:7
I have p. the fool, and have. 26:21
David and all Israel p. *2 Sam* 6:5
1 Chr 13:8
pass when the minstrel p. *2 Ki* 3:15
hast p. the whore with. *Ezek* 16:28
see **harlot**

player
who is a cunning *p.* 1 Sam 16:16

players
the *p.* on instruments. Ps 68:25*
as well the singers as the *p.* 87:7*

playeth
as to a woman that *p.* Ezek 23:44

playing
seen a son of Jesse cunning in *p.*
1 Sam 16:18
David dancing and *p.* 1 Chr 15:29
were the damsels *p.* Ps 68:25
boys and girls *p.* in the. Zech 8:5

plea
too hard between *p.* and *p.* Deut 17:8

plead
ye *p.* for Baal ? he that will *p.* for.
Judg 6:31†
saying, Let Baal *p.* against him. 32†
set me a time to *p.*? Job 9:19*
who is he that will *p.* with? 13:19*
O that one might *p.* for a man. 16:21*
p. against me my reproach. 19:5
will he *p.* against me with his ? 23:6*
seek judgement, *p.* for the widow.
Isa 1:17
Lord standeth up to *p.* and. 3:13†
let us *p.* together, declare. 43:26
by fire will the Lord *p.* 66:16
p. with you, and with your children's children will I *p.* Jer 2:9†, 35*
wherefore will ye *p.* with me? 29
righteous art thou, O Lord, when I *p.* with thee. 12:1†
Lord will *p.* with all flesh. 25:31†
will *p.* with him there. Ezek 17:20†
I *p.* with you face to face. 20:35†
so will I *p.* with you, saith the. 36†
I will *p.* against him with. 38:22†
p. with your mother, *p.* Hos 2:2†
I will *p.* with them for my people.
Joel 3:2†
Lord will *p.* with Israel. Mi 6:2
see **cause**

pleaded
Lord that *p.* the cause. 1 Sam 25:39
hast *p.* causes of my soul. Lam 3:58
like as I *p.* with your fathers in the.
Ezek 20:36*

pleadeth
with God, as a man *p.* Job 16:21*
that *p.* cause of his people. Isa 51:22
justice, nor any *p.* for truth. 59:4

pleading
hearken to the *p.* of my lips. Job 13:6

pleasant
every tree grow that is *p.* Gen 2:9
was *p.* to the eyes, and a tree. 3:6*
saw the land that it was *p.* 49:15
Saul and Jonathan were *p.* in their lives. 2 Sam 1:23
Jonathan, very *p.* hast thou. 26
whatever is *p.* they. 1 Ki 20:6
situation of this city is *p.* 2 Ki 2:19
made treasuries for *p.* jewels.
2 Chr 32:27*
fallen to me in *p.* places. Ps 16:6
bring hither the *p.* harp with. 81:2
they despised the *p.* land. 106:24
how *p.* for brethren to dwell. 133:1
to his name, for it is *p.* 135:3
147:1
when knowledge is *p.* to. Pr 2:10
the loving hind and *p.* roe. 5:19
bread eaten in secret is *p.* 9:17
words of the pure are *p.* 15:26
p. words are as honeycomb. 16:24
for it is *p.* if thou keep them. 22:18
shall be filled with all *p.* riches. 24:4
p. it is for the eyes to behold the sun.
Eccl 11:7
my beloved, yea *p.* S of S 1:16
an orchard with *p.* fruits. 4:13*
come and eat his *p.* fruits. 16*
fair and *p.* art thou, O love. 7:6
are all manner of *p.* fruits. 13
Lord upon all *p.* pictures. Isa 2:16
men of Judah his *p.* plant. 5:7
shall cry in their *p.* palaces. 13:22
shalt thou plant *p.* plants. 17:10
they lament for *p.* fields. 32:12
thy borders of *p.* stones. Isa 54:12†
p. things are laid waste. 64:11
I give thee a *p.* land ? Jer 3:19
my *p.* portion a desolate. 12:10
p. places of the wilderness. 23:10
shall fall like a *p.* vessel. 25:34
dear son ? is he a *p.* child ? 31:20†
she remembered all her *p.* Lam 1:7
spread his hand on her *p.* things. 10
they have given their *p.* things. 11
slew all that were *p.* to the eye. 2:4
they shall destroy thy *p.* houses.
Ezek 26:12
song of one that hath *p.* voice. 33:32
great toward the *p.* land. Dan 8:9*
ate no *p.* bread, nor came flesh. 10:3
honour a god with *p.* things. 11:38
p. places nettles shall. Hos 9:6
Ephraim is planted in a *p.* place. 13
your temples my *p.* things. Joel 3:5†
ye planted *p.* vineyards. Amos 5:11
ye cast out from *p.* houses. Mi 2:9
glory out of all the *p.* Nah 2:9†
laid the *p.* land desolate. Zech 7:14
offering of Jerusalem be *p.* Mal 3:4

pleasantness
her ways are ways of *p.* Pr 3:17

please
if she *p.* not her master. Ex 21:8
peradventure it will *p.* God that thou mayest curse. Num 23:27
if it *p.* my father to. 1 Sam 20:13
let it *p.* thee to bless the house.
2 Sam 7:29; 1 Chr 17:27
if it *p.* I will give thee. 1 Ki 21:6
if thou *p.* they will be thy servants.
2 Chr 10:7
if it *p.* the king, and if thy servant have found. Neh 2:5, 7; Esth 1:19
3:9; 5:8; 7:3; 8:5; 9:13
it *p.* God to destroy me. Job 6:9
his children shall seek to *p.* 20:10
this also shall *p.* the Lord. Ps 69:31
man's ways *p.* the Lord. Pr 16:7
nor awake my love till he *p.*
S of S 2:7; 3:5; 8:4
p. themselves in children. Isa 2:6
accomplish that which I *p.* 55:11
choose the things that *p.* me. 56:4
those things that *p.* him. John 8:29
in the flesh cannot *p.* God. Rom 8:8
and not to *p.* ourselves. 15:1
let every one *p.* his neighbour. 2
careth how he may *p.* 1 Cor 7:32
p. his wife. 33
how she may *p.* her husband. 34
p. all men in all things. 10:33
do I seek to *p.* men ? Gal 1:10
p. not God are contrary. 1 Thes 2:15
ought to walk and to *p.* God. 4:1
may *p.* him who hath chosen him.
2 Tim 2:4
and to *p.* them well in all things.
Tit 2:9
but without faith it is impossible to *p.* him. Heb 11:6

pleased
Esau seeing daughters of Canaan *p.* not Isaac. Gen 28:8
and thou wast *p.* with me. 33:10
and their words *p.* Hamor. 34:18
it *p.* Pharaoh well and his. 45:16
Balaam saw it *p.* the Lord. Num 24:1
the saying *p.* me well. Deut 1:23
Israel . . . it *p.* them. Josh 22:30
if Lord were *p.* to kill us. Judg 13:23
he talked with her, and she *p.* 14:7
it *p.* Lord to make you his people.
1 Sam 12:22
it *p.* Saul that Michal loved. 18:20
it *p.* David to be the king's. 26
what the king did *p.* all. 2 Sam 3:36
saying *p.* Absalom well, and. 17:4
if all we had died, then it had *p.* 19:6
Solomon's speech *p.* the. 1 Ki 3:10
Solomon gave, *p.* not Hiram. 9:12
the thing *p.* the king. 2 Chr 30:4*
Neh 2:6; Esth 1:21; 2:4
the maiden *p.* the king. Esth 2:9
the thing *p.* Haman, he caused. 5:14
be *p.* O Lord, to deliver. Ps 40:13
be *p.* with sacrifices. 51:19
he hath done whatsoever he *p.*
Ps 115:3; 135:6; Jonah 1:14
yet it *p.* the Lord to bruise. Isa 53:10
it *p.* Darius to set over. Dan 6:1
will Lord be *p.* with thousands of rams ? Mi 6:7
offer it, will he be *p.*? Mal 1:8
daughter of Herodias danced before them, and *p.* Mat 14:6; Mark 6:22
saying *p.* whole multitude. Acts 6:5
because Herod saw it *p.* the. 12:3
for even Christ *p.* not. Rom 15:3
hath *p.* them of Macedonia. 26, 27
it *p.* God by foolishness. 1 Cor 1:21
and she be *p.* to dwell with him. 7:12
and if he be *p.* to dwell with her. 13
set members as it hath *p.* him. 12:18
a body as it hath *p.* him. 15:38
for if I yet *p.* men, I. Gal 1:10
when it *p.* God to reveal his Son. 15
it *p.* Father that in him all. Col 1:19
testimony, that he *p.* God. Heb 11:5

well pleased
Lord is *well* p. for his. Isa 42:21
beloved Son, in whom I am *well p.*
Mat 3:17; 12:18; 17:5; Mark 1:11
Luke 3:22; 2 Pet 1:17
them God was not *well p.* 1 Cor 10:5
sacrifices God is *well p.* Heb 13:16

men pleasers
not with eye service, as *men p.*
Eph 6:6; Col 3:22

pleaseth
do to her as it *p.* thee. Gen 16:6
dwell where it *p.* thee. 20:15
for she *p.* me well. Judg 14:3
maiden which *p.* the king. Esth 2:4
p. God shall escape. Eccl 7:26
he doeth whatsoever *p.* him. 8:3

pleasing
if I be *p.* in his eyes. Esth 8:5
shall they be *p.* to him. Hos 9:4
worthy of the Lord to all *p.* Col 1:10
so we speak, not as *p.* 1 Thes 2:4
those things that are *p.* 1 John 3:22

***well*-pleasing**
acceptable, *well-p.* to God. Phil 4:18
obey, for this is *well-p.* Col 3:20
working in you that which is *well-p.* in his sight. Heb 13:21

pleasure
after I am waxed old, shall I have *p.*? Gen 18:12
thy fill at thine own *p.* Deut 23:24
I know thou hast *p.* in. 1 Chr 29:17
king send his *p.* to us. Ezra 5:17
to Lord God, and do his *p.* 10:11
over our cattle at their *p.* Neh 9:37
according to every man's *p.* Esth 1:8
what *p.* hath he in his house after ?
Job 21:21
dieth, and never eateth with *p.* 25
is it any *p.* to Almighty that? 22:3
that hath *p.* in wickedness. Ps 5:4
hath *p.* in the prosperity. 35:27
good in thy good *p.* to Zion. 51:18
for thy servants take *p.* in. 102:14
bless Lord ye ministers of his, that do his *p.* 103:21
to bind his princes at his *p.* 105:22
all them that have *p.* therein. 111:2
he taketh not *p.* in the legs. 147:10
the Lord taketh *p.* in them that. 11
Lord taketh *p.* in his people. 149:4
he that loveth *p.* shall. Pr 21:17
therefore enjoy *p.* Eccl 2:1
he hath no *p.* in fools. 5:4
thou shalt say, I have no *p.* 12:1
the night of my *p.* he. Isa 21:4
shall perform all my *p.* 44:28
stand, I will do all my *p.* 46:10
he will do his *p.* on Babylon. 48:14
p. of the Lord shall prosper. 53:10
day of your fast ye find *p.* 58:3
p. on my holy day, and call the sabbath a delight . . . thine own *p.* 13
up the wind at her *p.* Jer 2:24
a vessel wherein is no *p.*? 22:28
at liberty at their *p.* to return. 34:16
like a vessel wherein is no *p.* 48:38
whom thou hast taken *p.* Ezek 16:37

have I any *p.* that the wicked die? *Ezek* 18:23, 32; 33:11
a vessel wherein is no *p.* *Hos* 8:8
and I will take *p.* in it. *Hag* 1:8
I have no *p.* in you. *Mal* 1:10
Father's good *p.* to give. *Luke* 12:32
Felix, willing to shew the Jews a *p.* left Paul. *Acts* 24:27*
willing to do the Jews a *p.* 25:9*
but have *p.* in them that. *Rom* 1:32
therefore I take *p.* in infirmities. *2 Cor* 12:10
good *p.* of his will. *Eph* 1:5, 9
and to do of his good *p.* *Phil* 2:13
fulfil the good *p.* of. *2 Thes* 1:11
believed not, but had *p.* in. 2:12
but she that liveth in *p.* *1 Tim* 5:6
in sacrifices thou hast no *p.* *Heb* 10:6, 8
my soul shall have no *p.* in him. 38
us after their own *p.* 12:10
ye have lived in *p.* on earth. *Jas* 5:5
that count it *p.* to riot. *2 Pet* 2:13
for thy *p.* they are and. *Rev* 4:11

pleasures
spend their years in *p.* *Job* 36:11
at thy right hand are *p.* *Ps* 16:11
drink of river of thy *p.* 36:8
thou that art given to *p.* *Isa* 47:8
are choked with the *p.* *Luke* 8:14
lovers of *p.* more than. *2 Tim* 3:4
serving divers lusts and *p.* *Tit* 3:3
than to enjoy the *p.* of sin. *Heb* 11:25

pledge
wilt thou give me a *p.*? *Gen* 38:17
what *p.* shall I give thee? 18
Judah sent to receive his *p.* 20
take thy neighbour's raiment to *p.* *Ex* 22:26
or upper millstone to *p.* for he taketh a man's life to *p.* *Deut* 24:6
into his house to fetch his *p.* 10, 11
shalt not sleep with his *p.* 12, 13
a widow's raiment to *p.* 17
how thy brethren fare, take their *p.* *1 Sam* 17:18
hast taken a *p.* from thy brother. *Job* 22:6
take the widow's ox for a *p.* 24:3
and they take a *p.* of the poor. 9
take *p.* for a strange woman. *Pr* 20:16; 27:13
to the debtor his *p.* *Ezek* 18:7, 16
hath not restored the *p.*, shall he? 12
if the wicked restore the *p.*, he. 33:15
on clothes laid to *p.* by. *Amos* 2:8

pledges
I pray thee, give *p.* to the king of Assyria. *2 Ki* 18:23; *Isa* 36:8

Pleiades
Arcturus, Orion, and *P.* *Job* 9:9
the sweet influences of *P.*? 38:31

plenteous
fifth part in the *p.* years. *Gen* 41:34
in the *p.* years the earth brought. 47
shall make thee *p.* *Deut* 28:11; 30:9
gold as *p.* as stones. *2 Chr* 1:15
art *p.* in mercy to all. *Ps* 86:5, 15
gracious, and *p.* in mercy. 103:8
with him is *p.* redemption. 130:7
bread shall be fat and *p.* *Isa* 30:23
fat, and their meat *p.* *Hab* 1:16
the harvest truly is *p.* *Mat* 9:37

plenteousness
the seven years of *p.* *Gen* 41:53*
of the diligent tend to *p.* *Pr* 21:5

plentiful
didst send a *p.* rain. *Ps* 68:9
out of the *p.* field. *Isa* 16:10*
and I brought you to a *p.* *Jer* 2:7
is taken from the *p.* field. 48:33*

plentifully
how hast thou *p.* declared! *Job* 26:3
and *p.* rewardeth. *Ps* 31:23
rich man brought forth *p.* *Luke* 12:16

plenty
God give thee *p.* of corn. *Gen* 27:28
seven years of great *p.* 41:29
all the *p.* shall be forgotten in. 30
and the *p.* shall not be known. 31
a pit, wherein there is *p.* *Lev* 11:36*
Ophir *p.* of almug trees. *1 Ki* 10:11
to eat, have left *p.* *2 Chr* 31:10
shalt have *p.* of silver. *Job* 22:25*
excellent in power and in *p.* 37:23
barns be filled with *p.* *Pr* 3:10
land shall have *p.* of bread. 28:19
had we *p.* of victuals. *Jer* 44:17
shall eat in *p.* and praise. *Joel* 2:26

plotteth
wicked *p.* against the just. *Ps* 37:12

plough
put his hand to the *p.* *Luke* 9:62

plow
shalt not *p.* with an ox. *Deut* 22:10
yoke of oxen might *p.* *1 Sam* 14:14*
they that *p.* iniquity. *Job* 4:8
sluggard will not *p.* *Pr* 20:4
doth the plowman *p.*? *Isa* 28:24
Judah shall *p.* Jacob. *Hos* 10:11
one *p.* there with oxen? *Amos* 6:12
plougheth should *p.* in hope. *1 Cor* 9:10

plowed, -ers
not *p.* with my heifer. *Judg* 14:18
the plowers *p.* on my. *Ps* 129:3
Zion shall be *p.* as a field. *Jer* 26:18 *Mi* 3:12
ye have *p.* wickedness. *Hos* 10:13

ploweth
that *p.* should plow in. *1 Cor* 9:10

plowing, *verb*
Elisha, who was *p.* *1 Ki* 19:19
the oxen were *p.* and the. *Job* 1:14
having a servant *p.* *Luke* 17:7

plowing
and the *p.* of the wicked. *Pr* 21:4*

plowman
doth the *p.* plow all day? *Isa* 28:24
the *p.* shall overtake the. *Amos* 9:13

plowmen
alien shall be your *p.* *Isa* 61:5
the *p.* were ashamed. *Jer* 14:4

plowshares
shall beat their swords into *p.* *Isa* 2:4; *Mi* 4:3
beat your *p.* into swords. *Joel* 3:10

pluck
shall *p.* away his crop. *Lev* 1:16
and quite *p.* down their. *Num* 33:52*
then thou mayest *p.* the ears with. *Deut* 23:25
then will I *p.* them up. *2 Chr* 7:20
p. the fatherless from. *Job* 24:9
he shall *p.* my feet out. *Ps* 25:15
p. thee out of thy dwelling. 52:5
thy right hand, *p.* it out of. 74:11
pass by the way do *p.* her. 80:12
to *p.* up what is planted. *Eccl* 3:2
p. out the house of Judah. *Jer* 12:14
I will utterly *p.* up and destroy. 17
a kingdom, to *p.* it up. 18:7
yet would I *p.* thee thence. 22:24
and not *p.* them up. 24:6; 42:10
watched over them to *p.* up. 31:28
I have planted I will *p.* up. 45:4
without many people to *p.* *Ezek* 17:9
p. off thine own breasts. 23:34
who *p.* off the skin from. *Mi* 3:2
I will *p.* up thy groves out of. 5:14
if thy right eye offend thee, *p.* it. *Mat* 5:29; 18:9; *Mark* 9:47
began to *p.* the ears of corn. *Mat* 12:1; *Mark* 2:23
nor shall any *p.* them. *John* 10:28
no man is able to *p.* them out. 29

plucked
was an olive leaf *p.* off. *Gen* 8:11
and he *p.* his hand out. *Ex* 4:7
ye shall be *p.* from off. *Deut* 28:63
a man *p.* off his shoe. *Ruth* 4:7
p. the spear out of Egyptian's hand. *2 Sam* 23:21; *1 Chr* 11:23
I *p.* off the hair of my. *Ezra* 9:3
I cursed them, and *p.* off. *Neh* 13:25
p. the spoil out of his. *Job* 29:17
my cheeks to them that *p.* *Isa* 50:6
wicked are not *p.* away. *Jer* 6:29
after I have *p.* them out. 12:15
it shall not be *p.* up, nor. 31:40
she was *p.* up in fury. *Ezek* 19:12
the wings thereof were *p.* *Dan* 7:4
three of the first horns *p.* up. 8
for his kingdom shall be *p.* 11:4
as a firebrand *p.* out of. *Amos* 4:11
is not this a brand *p.*? *Zech* 3:2
the chains had been *p.* *Mark* 5:4
his disciples *p.* ears of corn. *Luke* 6:1
be thou *p.* up by the root. 17:6
would have *p.* out your own eyes. *Gal* 4:15
twice dead, *p.* up by the roots. *Jude* 12

plucketh
the foolish *p.* it down. *Pr* 14:1

plumbline
behold the Lord stood upon a wall made by a *p.* with a *p.* *Amos* 7:7
and I said, A *p.* . . . Behold, I will set a *p.* in the midst of my people. 8

plummet
over Jerusalem the *p.* *2 Ki* 21:13
righteousness to the *p.* *Isa* 28:17
shall see the *p.* in hand. *Zech* 4:10

plunge
yet shalt thou *p.* me in the. *Job* 9:31

poets
of your own *p.* have said. *Acts* 17:28

point
p. out for you mount. *Num* 34:7*
p. out your border. 8*
p. out your east border. 10*

point, *substantive*
I am at the *p.* to die. *Gen* 25:32
is written with the *p.* of. *Jer* 17:1
my daughter lieth at the *p.* of death. *Mark* 5:23
was at the *p.* of death. *John* 4:47
offend in one *p.* is guilty. *Jas* 2:10

pointed
he spreadeth sharp *p.* *Job* 41:30*

points
in all *p.* as he came so. *Eccl* 5:16
but was in all *p.* tempted. *Heb* 4:15

poison
with the *p.* of serpents. *Deut* 32:24
their wine is *p.* of dragons. 33
the *p.* whereof drinketh. *Job* 6:4
he shall suck *p.* of asps. 20:16
their *p.* is like the *p.* of. *Ps* 58:4
like a serpent, adders' *p.* is. 140:3
the *p.* of asps is under. *Rom* 3:13
is an evil, full of deadly *p.* *Jas* 3:8

pole
set it upon a *p.* *Num* 21:8*
Moses put it on a *p.* 9*

policy
through his *p.* shall cause craft to. *Dan* 8:25

polished
p. after the similitude. *Ps* 144:12*
he hath made me a *p.* shaft. *Isa* 49:2
in colour to *p.* brass. *Dan* 10:6*

polishing
Nazarites purer, their *p.* *Lam* 4:7

poll, -s
of their names, every male by the *p.* *Num* 1:2; 18:20, 22; *1 Chr* 23:3 24
take five shekels a piece by the *p.* *Num* 3:47

poll
only *p.* their heads. *Ezek* 44:20†
make thee bald, and *p.* *Mi* 1:16†

polled
p. his head, at year's end he *p.* *2 Sam* 14:26†

pollute
neither shall ye *p.* the. *Num* 18:32*
so shall ye not *p.* the land. 35:33
called by name, to *p.* it. *Jer* 7:30
p. my secret place. *Ezek* 7:21*, 22*
will ye *p.* me among my? 13:19*
ye *p.* yourselves with idols. 20:31 23:30; 36:18
p. ye my holy name. 20:39*; 39:7*
in my sanctuary to *p.* it. 44:7*
shall *p.* the sanctuary. *Dan* 11:31*

polluted
upon it, thou hast *p.* it. *Ex* 20:25

Josiah p. the altar. 2 Ki 23:16
the priests p. the house. 2 Chr 36:14
therefore were they as p. Ezra 2:62; Neh 7:64
and the land was p. with. Ps 106:38
I was wroth, I have p. Isa 47:6*
how should my name be p.? 48:11*
thou say, I am not p.? Jer 2:23
that land be greatly p.? 3:1, 2
turned and p. my name. 34:16*
he hath p. the kingdom. Lam 2:2*
they have p. themselves with. 4:14
my soul hath not been p. Ezek 4:14
nor be p. with all their. 14:11
I saw thee p. in thine own blood. 16:6*, 22*
that it should not be p. 20:9*, 14, 22
they greatly p. 13*, 16*, 21*, 24*
I p. them in their own gifts. 26*
are ye p. after the manner of? 30
was p. with the Babylonians. 23:17
Gilead is a city that is p. Hos 6:8*
all that eat thereof shall be p. 9:4
shalt die in a p. land. Amos 7:17*
it is p., it shall destroy you. Mi 2:10
that is filthy and p. Zeph 3:1
her priests have p. sanctuary. 4*
p. bread upon mine altar, and say, Wherein have we p. thee? Mal 1:7
the table of the Lord is p. 12
p. this holy place. Acts 21:28

polluting

sabbath from p. it. Isa 56:2, 6

pollution

have they humbled her that was set apart for p. Ezek 22:10

pollutions

abstain from p. of idols. Acts 15:20
escaped p. of the world. 2 Pet 2:20

pollux, *see* **sign**

pomegranate

A kind of apple, covered without with a reddish rind, and red within, which opens lengthways, and shews red grains within, full of juice like wine, with little kernels. God gave orders to Moses *to put embroidered pomegranates, with golden bells between, at the bottom of the high priest's blue robe or ephod,* Ex 28:33, 34.

a golden bell and a p. upon the hem. Ex 28:34; 39:26
Saul tarried under a p. tree. 1 Sam 14:2
thy temples are like a piece of p. S of S 4:3; 6:7
to drink of juice of my p. 8:2
the p. tree and all trees. Joel 1:12
p. hath not brought forth. Hag 2:19

pomegranates

thou shalt make p. of blue. Ex 28:33; 39:24, 25
they brought of the p. Num 13:23
of seed, figs, vines, or p. 20:5
a land of p., oil olive. Deut 8:8
chapiters on top with p. 1 Ki 7:18*
2 Ki 25:17; 2 Chr 3:16; Jer 52:22
plants are an orchard of p. with. S of S 4:13
whether the p. budded. 6:11; 7:12

pommels

the pillars and p. of the. 2 Chr 4:12*

pomp

and their p. shall descend. Isa 5:14
thy p. is brought down to. 14:11
p. of the strong to cease. Ezek 7:24*
the p. of her strength shall cease. 30:18*; 33:28*
shall spoil the p. of Egypt. 32:12*
when Agrippa was come, and Bernice, with great p. Acts 25:23

ponder

p. the path of thy feet. Pr 4:26*
shouldest p. the path of life. 5:6*

pondered

Mary p. them in her heart. Luke 2:19

pondereth

ways of man, the Lord p. Pr 5:21*
Lord p. the heart. 21:2*
he that p. the heart. 24:12*

ponds

thy hand on their p. Ex 7:19*; 8:5
purposes, that make p. Isa 19:10*

Pontius, *see* **Pilate**

Pontus

dwellers in P. Acts 2:9; 18:2
1 Pet 1:1

pool

the one side of the p. 2 Sam 2:13
hanged them up over the p. 4:12
washed chariot in p. of. 1 Ki 22:38
stood by the conduit of the upper p. 2 Ki 18:17; Isa 7:3; 36:2
made a p. and conduit. 2 Ki 20:20
went on to the king's p. Neh 2:14
repaired the wall of the p. 3:15
the waters of the lower p. Isa 22:9
ditch for the water of the old p. 11
ground shall become a p. 35:7
the wilderness a p. of water. 41:18
Nineveh of old is like a p. of water. Nah 2:8
by the sheep market a p. John 5:2
an angel went down into the p. 4
no man to put me into the p. 7
wash in the p. of Siloam. 9:7, 11

pools

thy hand on all their p. Ex 7:19
rain also filleth the p. Ps 84:6
I made me p. of water. Eccl 2:6
make it for the p. of water. Isa 14:23
and I will dry up the p. and. 42:15

poor

(Used in the Bible both of those poor in this world's goods, and of those spiritually poor)

after them seven p. kine. Gen 41:19
that the p. of thy people. Ex 23:11
p. shall not give less than. 30:15
if he be p. and cannot. Lev 14:21
leave them for the p. and. 19:10
respect the person of the p. 15
if thy brother be waxen p. 25:25
35, 39, 47
there be no p. among you. Deut 15:4
for the p. shall never cease out. 11
not young men, p. or rich. Ruth 3:10
the Lord maketh p. and. 1 Sam 2:7
p. out of the dust. 8; Ps 113:7
rich, and the other p. 2 Sam 12:1
the guard left of the p. of. 2 Ki 25:12
Jer 39:10; 40:7; 52:15, 16
the p. from the sword. Job 5:15
so the p. hath hope, and. 16
seek to please the p. 20:10
oppressed and forsaken the p. 19
the p. of the earth hide. 24:4
and they take a pledge of the p. 9
the murderer killeth the p. 14
because I delivered the p. 29:12
soul grieved for the p.? 30:25
if I withheld the p. from. 31:16
seen any p. without covering. 19
the rich more than the p. 34:19
they cause the cry of the p. 28
he delivereth the p. in affliction. 36:15*; Ps 72:12
the expectation of the p. Ps 9:18
pride doth persecute the p. 10:2
are privily set against the p. 8
wait secretly to catch the p. 9
that the p. may fall by his. 10*
the p. committeth himself to. 14
for the oppression of the p. I. 12:5
the counsel of the p. 14:6
delivereth the p. from him. 35:10
their bow to cast down the p. 37:14
but I am p. 40:17; 69:29; 70:5
86:1; 109:22
he that considereth the p. 41:1
both low and high, rich and p. 49:2
of thy goodness for the p. 68:10
Lord heareth p. and despiseth. 69:33
he shall judge the p. of. 72:4
he shall spare the p. 13
let the p. and needy praise. 74:21
defend the p. 82:3
deliver the p. and needy. 4
yet setteth he p. on high. 107:41
at the right hand of the p. 109:31
will satisfy her p. with. 132:15
maintain the right of the p. 140:12
he becometh p. that dealeth. Pr 10:4
the destruction of the p. is. 15
that maketh himself p. 13:7
his riches, but the p. heareth. 8
in the tillage of the p. but. 23
the p. is hated even of his. 14:20
he that hath mercy on the p. 21
p. reproacheth his maker; he that honoureth him hath mercy on p. 31
whoso mocketh the p. 17:5
the p. useth entreaties, but. 18:23
the p. is separated from his. 19:4
all brethren of the p. do hate him. 7
his ears at the cry of the p. 21:13
the rich and p. meet together. 22:2
the rich ruleth over the p. and the. 7
oppresseth the p. to increase. 16
for him that will pity the p. 28:8
the p. that hath understanding. 11
ruler over the p. people. 15
the cause of the p. 29:7, 13
that faithfully judgeth the p. 14
lest I be p. and steal, and. 30:9
as swords, to devour the p. 14
and plead the cause of the p. 31:9
his kingdom, becometh p. Eccl 4:14
the oppression of the p. 5:8
what hath the p. that knoweth? 6:8
the spoil of the p. is in. Isa 3:14
that ye grind faces of the p.? 15
take away the right from the p. 10:2
cause it to be heard to Laish, O p. 30
shall he judge the p. 11:4
the firstborn of the p. shall. 14:30
and the p. of his people shall. 32*
even the feet of the p. shall. 26:6
p. among men shall rejoice. 29:19
to destroy the p. with lying. 32:7*
when the p. and needy seek. 41:17
bring the p. that are cast out. 58:7
blood of the p. innocents. Jer 2:34
these are p.; they are foolish. 5:4
delivered the soul of the p. 20:13
he judged the cause of the p. 22:16
strengthen hand of the p. Ezek 16:49
hath oppressed p. and needy. 18:12
taken off his hand from the p. 17
and they have vexed the p. 22:29
they sold the p. for a pair. Amos 2:6
the dust on the head of the p. 7
which oppress the p. and crush. 4:1
your treading is on the p. 5:11
turn aside the p. in the gate. 12
even to make the p. of the land. 8:4
that we may buy the p. for silver. 6
was to devour the p. Hab 3:14
the p. people shall trust. Zeph 3:12
and oppress not the widow nor p. Zech 7:10
I will feed even you, O p. 11:7
the p. of the flock that waited. 11
blessed are the p. in spirit. Mat 5:3
p. have the gospel preached. 11:5
for ye have the p. always with you. 26:11; Mark 14:7; John 12:8
a certain p. widow. Mark 12:42
p. widow hath cast. 43; Luke 21:3
blessed be ye p. for yours. Luke 6:20
call the p. the maimed. 14:13, 21
that he cared for the p. John 12:6
a contribution for the p. Rom 15:26
as p. yet making many. 2 Cor 6:10
yet for your sakes he became p. 8:9
should remember the p. Gal 2:10
hath not God chosen the p.? Jas 2:5
but ye have despised the p. 6
knowest not that thou art p. Rev 3:17
he causeth rich and p. to. 13:16

***is* poor**

of my people that *is* p. Ex 22:25
thou shalt not oppress hired servant that *is* p. Deut 24:14
for he *is* p. and setteth his heart. 15
behold, my family *is* p. Judg 6:15
better *is* the p. that walketh in his integrity, than he. Pr 19:1; 28:6
rob not poor because he *is* p. 22:22
better *is* a p. and wise child, than an old. Eccl 4:13
to him that *is* p. and of a. Isa 66:2

poor *man*

countenance a p. *man* in. Ex 23:3

if a *p. man*, harden not. *Deut* 15:7
if a *man* be *p.*, sleep not with. 24:12
seeing I am a *p. man*. *1 Sam* 18:23
p. man had nothing. *2 Sam* 12:3
but took the *p. man's* ewe lamb. 4
this *p. man* cried, and the. *Ps* 34:6
the *p.* and needy *man*. 109:16
and a *p. man* is better than a liar. *Pr* 19:22
pleasure shall be a *p. man*. 21:17
a *p. man* that oppresseth poor. 28:3
the *p.* and deceitful *man*. 29:13
a *p.* wise *man*, yet no man remembered that same *p. man*. *Eccl* 9:15
the *p. man's* wisdom is despised. 16
a *p. man* in vile raiment. *Jas* 2:2

to the poor

to the p. and stranger. *Lev* 23:22
of sending gifts *to the p.* *Esth* 9:22
I was a father *to the p.* *Job* 29:16
but he giveth right *to the p.* 36:6
he hath given *to the p.* *Ps* 112:9 *2 Cor* 9:9
of his bread *to the p.* *Pr* 22:9
giveth *to the p.* shall not lack. 28:27
out her hand *to the p.* 31:20
been a strength *to the p.* *Isa* 25:4
by shewing mercy *to the p.* *Dan* 4:27
sell all, and give *to the p.* *Mat* 19:21 *Mark* 10:21
sold for much, and given *to the p.* *Mat* 26:9; *Mark* 14:5; *John* 12:5
the gospel *to the p.* *Luke* 4:18; 7:22
and distribute *to the p.* 18:22
half of my goods I give *to the p.* 19:8
give something *to the p.* *John* 13:29
my goods to feed *the p.* *1 Cor* 13:3
say *to the p.*, Stand thou. *Jas* 2:3

thy poor

the judgement of *thy p.* *Ex* 23:6
hand from *thy p.* brother. *Deut* 15:7
be evil against *thy p.* brother. 9
thine hand wide to *thy p.* 11
he shall judge *thy p.* *Ps* 72:2
congregation of *thy p.* for ever. 74:19

poorer

if he be *p.* than thy. *Lev* 27:8

poorest

none remained, save *p.* *2 Ki* 24:14

poplar, -s

took rods of green *p.* *Gen* 30:37
incense under oaks and *p.* *Hos* 4:13

populous

great, mighty, and *p.* *Deut* 26:5
art thou better than *p.* No? *Nah* 3:8

porch

forth through the *p.* *Judg* 3:23
Solomon pattern of *p.* *1 Chr* 28:11
shut up doors of the *p.* *2 Chr* 29:7
month came they to the *p.* 17
between the *p.* and altar. *Ezek* 8:16
enter by way of *p.* of the gate. 44:3 46:2, 8
priests weep between *p.* *Joel* 2:17
gone out into the *p.* *Mat* 26:71
the *p.*; and cock crew. *Mark* 14:68
temple in Solomon's *p.* *John* 10:23
together in Solomon's *p.* *Acts* 3:11
one accord in Solomon's *p.* 5:12

porches

with the temple and *p.* *Ezek* 41:15
Bethesda, having five *p.* *John* 5:2

Porcius

P. Festus came into. *Acts* 24:27

porter

(*Revisions render* this door-keeper)

called to the *p.* and said. *2 Sam* 18:26
lepers called to the *p.* *2 Ki* 7:10
Zechariah was *p.* of door. *1 Chr* 9:21
and Kore the *p.* toward. *2 Chr* 31:14
and commanded the *p.* *Mark* 13:34
to him the *p.* openeth. *John* 10:3

porters

the *p.* were Shallum. *1 Chr* 9:17
and Jehiel the *p.* 15:18
and Hosah to be *p.* 16:38
the sons of Jeduthun were *p.* 42
four thousand were *p.* 23:5
the divisions of the *p.* 26:1, 12, 19
the *p.* by their courses. *2 Chr* 8:14
p. waited at every gate. 35:15
p. and Nethinims went up. *Ezra* 7:7
the Levites and *p.* dwelt. *Neh* 7:73

portion

let them take their *p.* *Gen* 14:24
any *p.* or inheritance for us? 31:14
priest had a *p.* assigned, and did eat their *p.* 47:22
I have given thee one *p.* above. 48:22
have given it them for *p.* *Lev* 6:17
this is the *p.* of the anointing. 7:35
of Israel's half take thou one *p.* *Num* 31:30, 36
Moses took one *p.* of fifty for the. 47
by giving him a double *p.* *Deut* 21:17
for Lord's *p.* is his people. 32:9
in a *p.* of the lawgiver was. 33:21
given me but one *p.*? *Josh* 17:14
but to Hannah he gave a worthy *p.* *1 Sam* 1:5
Samuel said, Bring the *p.* which. 9:23
what *p.* have we in David? *1 Ki* 12:16 *2 Chr* 10:16
let a double *p.* of thy. *2 Ki* 2:9
dogs shall eat Jezebel in *p.* of Jezreel. 9:10, 36, 37
Joram met him in *p.* of Naboth. 21
in the *p.* of Naboth's field. 25
Ahaz took a *p.* out of. *2 Chr* 28:11
Hezekiah appointed king's *p.* 31:3
to give the *p.* of the priests. 4, 16
no *p.* on this side the river. *Ezra* 4:16
p. nor right in Jerusalem. *Neh* 2:20
that a certain *p.* should be. 11:23
and porters, every day his *p.* 12:47
the *p.* of a wicked man. *Job* 20:29
p. is cursed in the earth. 24:18
little a *p.* is heard of? 26:14*; 27:13
for what *p.* of God is there? 31:2
shall be the *p.* of their cup. *Ps* 11:6
the Lord is the *p.* of mine. 16:5
from men who have their *p.* 17:14
shall be a *p.* for foxes. 63:10
God is my *p.* 73:26
art my *p.* O Lord. 119:57; 142:5
giveth a *p.* to her maidens. *Pr* 31:15*
was my *p.* of all my labour. *Eccl* 2:10
shall he leave it for his *p.* 21
should rejoice, for that is his *p.* 3:22 5:18; 9:9
him power to take his *p.* 5:19
nor have they any more *p.* for. 9:6
give a *p.* to seven, and also. 11:2
this is the *p.* of them. *Isa* 17:14
I will divide him a *p.* with. 53:12
among smooth stones of the stream is thy *p.* 57:6
they shall rejoice in their *p.* 61:7
the *p.* of Jacob is not like them. *Jer* 10:16; 51:19
my *p.* under foot, they have made my pleasant *p.* a desolate. 12:10
this is the *p.* of thy measures. 13:25
every day a *p.* until the day. 52:34
the Lord is my *p.* saith. *Lam* 3:24
shall offer an holy *p.* *Ezek* 45:1, 4
a *p.* shall be for prince on one. 7
to the coast of Hethlon, a *p.* 48:1
border of Dan a *p.* of Asher. 2
a *p.* for Naphtali. 3
a *p.* for Manasseh. 4
not defile himself with *p.* *Dan* 1:8
his *p.* be with the beasts. 4:15, 23
feed of the *p.* of his meat. 11:26
changed the *p.* of my people. *Mi* 2:4
by them their *p.* is fat. *Hab* 1:16
shall inherit Judah his *p.* *Zech* 2:12
shall appoint him his *p.* *Mat* 24:51
to give them their *p.* in. *Luke* 12:42
will appoint him his *p.* with. 46
give me the *p.* of goods that. 15:12

portions

they shall have like *p.* to eat. *Deut* 18:8
ten *p.* to Manasseh. *Josh* 17:5
sons and daughters *p.* *1 Sam* 1:4
to give *p.* to all the. *2 Chr* 31:19
eat the fat, and send *p.* *Neh* 8:10, 12
p. for the priests. 12:44
p. of the singers. 47
that the *p.* of the Levites had. 13:10
a day of sending *p.* to. *Esth* 9:19, 22
Joseph shall have two *p.* *Ezek* 47:13
against the *p.* for the prince. 48:21
devour them with their *p.* *Hos* 5:7

possess

thy seed shall *p.* the gate. *Gen* 22:17 24:60
let us go up at once and *p.* it, for we. *Num* 13:30; *Deut* 1:21
next kinsman shall *p.* it. *Num* 27:11
I give it, they shall *p.* it. *Deut* 1:39
begin to *p.* that thou mayest. 2:31
ye shall *p.* greater nations. 11:23† 12:2†, 29†; 18:14†; 31:3†
thou passest over Jordan to *p.* it. 30:18; 31:13†
Esau mount Seir to *p.* it. *Josh* 24:4
shouldest thou *p.* it? *Judg* 11:23
wilt not thou *p.* what Chemosh? 24
he is gone down to *p.* *1 Ki* 21:18
to *p.* months of vanity. *Job* 7:3
thou makest me *p.* iniquities. 13:26
and bittern shall *p.* it. *Isa* 34:11, 17
shall *p.* their houses. *Ezek* 7:24
shall be mine, we will *p.* 35:10
my people Israel to *p.* thee. 36:12
the saints shall *p.* the. *Dan* 7:18
for silver, nettles shall *p.* *Hos* 9:6
p. the remnant of Edom. *Amos* 9:12
shall *p.* their possessions. *Ob* 17
shall *p.* mount Esau, and Benjamin *p.* Gilead. 19
captivity of Israel shall *p.* that . . . and Jerusalem shall *p.* the. 20
the Chaldeans to *p.* the. *Hab* 1:6
my people shall *p.* them. *Zeph* 2:9
will cause remnant to *p.* *Zech* 8:12
give tithes of all that I *p.* *Luke* 18:12
in patience *p.* ye your souls. 21:19
know how to *p.* vessel. *1 Thes* 4:4

possess with *land*

I will give you their *land* to *p.* *Lev* 20:24; *Num* 33:53 *Deut* 3:18; 5:31; 17:14
shall *p.* it, I will bring into *land*. *Num* 14:24
go in and *p.* the *land*. *Deut* 1:8 4:1; 6:18; 8:1; 9:5, 23; 10:11 11:31; *Josh* 1:11
land whither ye go to *p.* it. *Deut* 4:5 14, 26; 5:33; 6:1; 7:1; 11:10, 11 29; 23:20
go over and *p.* that good *land*. 4:22
brought me to *p.* this *land*. 9:4
giveth not this *land* to *p.* for thy. 6
be strong and *p.* the *land*. 11:8
land which Lord God of thy fathers giveth thee to *p.* 12:1; 15:4 19:2, 14; 21:1; 25:19
consumed from off *land* thou goest to *p.* 28:21
plucked from off the *land* whither thou goest to *p.* it. 63
ye slack to *p.* the *land*? *Josh* 18:3
and ye shall *p.* their *land*. 23:5
that ye might *p.* their *land*. 24:8
every man to *p.* the *land*. *Judg* 2:6
to enter to *p.* the *land*. 18:9
may *p.* this good *land*. *1 Chr* 28:8
to *p.* is an unclean *land*. *Ezra* 9:11
they should *p.* the *land*. *Neh* 9:15
them in to *p.* the *land*. 23
p. them in the *land* of the Lord. *Isa* 14:2
do not rise nor *p.* the *land*. 21
trust in me shall *p.* the *land*. 57:13
land shall they *p.* the double. 61:7
return to *land* and *p.* it. *Jer* 30:3
shall ye *p.* the *land*? *Ezek* 33:25, 26
I brought you to *p.* *land*. *Amos* 2:10

possessed

Israel *p.* Sihon's land. *Num* 21:24
and people, and have *p.* the land. 35 *Deut* 3:12; 4:47; *Neh* 9:22
to land thy fathers *p.* *Deut* 30:5
brethren have *p.* the land. *Josh* 1:15
they *p.* their land on the other. 12:1
yet very much land to be *p.* 13:1
Dan took Leshem and *p.* it. 19:47
they *p.* it and dwelt. 21:43; 22:9
Eglon king of Moab *p.* *Judg* 3:13
Israel *p.* all the land of. 11:21, 22
men of Ava *p.* Samaria. *2 Ki* 17:24
for thou hast *p.* my reins. *Ps* 139:13

Lord *p.* me in the beginning. *Pr* 8:22
people hath *p.* it a little. *Isa* 63:18
vineyards shall be *p.* *Jer* 32:15*
they came in and *p.* it, but obeyed. 23
time came that saints *p.* *Dan* 7:22
told them by what means he that was *p.* was healed. *Luke* 8:36
none said that aught he *p.* *Acts* 4:32
a damsel *p.* with a spirit of. 16:16
as though they *p.* not. *1 Cor* 7:30
see **devils**

possessest
into land and *p.* it. *Deut* 26:1

possesseth
every daughter that *p.* *Num* 36:8
man's life consists not in things he *p.* *Luke* 12:15

possessing
as having nothing, yet *p.* *2 Cor* 6:10

possession
I will give all the land of Canaan for an everlasting *p.* *Gen* 17:8; 48:4
give me a *p.* of a buryingplace. 23:4, 9, 18, 20; 49:30; 50:13
Isaac had *p.* of flocks, of herds. 26:14
Edom in the land of their *p.* 36:43
and gave them a *p.* in the land. 47:11
Canaan, which I give to you for a *p.* *Lev* 14:34
ye shall return every man to his *p.* 25:10, 13, 27, 28, 41; *Deut* 3:20
sold away some of his *p.* *Lev* 25:25
the Levites' *p.* shall go out in. 33
strangers shall be your *p.* 45, 46
sanctify some part of his *p.* 27:16
p. thereof shall be the priest's. 21
return to whom the *p.* of the land. 24
be a *p.*, Seir also a *p.* *Num* 24:18
to the lot shall the *p.* be. 26:56*
give us a *p.* among brethren. 27:4
daughters of Zelophehad give a *p.* 7
given to thy servants for *p.* 32:5
this land shall be your *p.* before. 22
Levites of their *p.* cities. 35:2, 8
return to the land of his *p.* 28
given mount Seir to Esau for a *p.* *Deut* 2:5
given Ar to Lot for a *p.* 9, 19
in land of his *p.* Lord gave them. 12
swallowed up all in their *p.* 11:6
which I gave Israel for a *p.* 32:49
for a *p.* to Reubenites. *Josh* 12:6
get ye into the land of your *p.* 22:4
to Manasseh Moses had given a *p.* 7
returned to the land of their *p.* 9
if your *p.* be unclean, take *p.* 19
take *p.* of the vineyard. *1 Ki* 21:15
killed, and also taken *p.*? 19
cast out of thy *p.* *2 Chr* 20:11
dwelt every one in his *p.* *Neh* 11:3
parts of earth for thy *p.* *Ps* 2:8
got not the land in *p.* by their. 44:3
may dwell and have it in *p.* 69:35
take the houses of God in *p.* 83:12
the upright have good things in *p.* *Pr* 28:10*
I will make it a *p.* for. *Isa* 14:23
is this land given in *p.* *Ezek* 11:15
thee to men of the east for *p.* 25:4
high places are ours in *p.* 36:2
appointed my land into their *p.* 5
no *p.* in Israel, I am their *p.* 44:28
inheritance out of his own *p.* 46:18
with Sapphira sold a *p.* *Acts* 5:1
give it to him for a *p.* 7:5
with Jesus into *p.* of Gentiles. 45
redemption of the purchased *p.* *Eph* 1:14

possessions
and get you *p.* therein. *Gen* 34:10
Israel had *p.* therein and. 47:27
shall have *p.* among you. *Num* 32:30
you to the land of your *p.* *Josh* 22:4
whose *p.* were in Carmel. *1 Sam* 25:2
that dwelt in their *p.* *1 Chr* 9:2
the Levites left their *p.* *2 Chr* 11:14
provided *p.* of flocks and. 32:29
I had great *p.* of great. *Eccl* 2:7
Jacob shall possess their *p.* *Ob* 17
for he had great *p.* *Mat* 19:22; *Mark* 10:22
and sold their *p.* and. *Acts* 2:45
in the same quarters were *p.* 28:7*

possessor
most high God *p.* of. *Gen* 14:19, 22

possessors
whose *p.* slay them, and. *Zech* 11:5
as many as were *p.* of. *Acts* 4:34

possible
with God all things are *p.* *Mat* 19:26; *Mark* 10:27
if *p.*, shall deceive the very elect. *Mat* 24:24; *Mark* 13:22
if *p.* let this cup pass from me. *Mat* 26:39; *Mark* 14:35
all things are *p.* to him. *Mark* 9:23
all things are *p.* to thee. 14:36; *Luke* 18:27
was not *p.* he should be. *Acts* 2:24
if *p.* be at Jerusalem the day. 20:16
if it be *p.* live peaceably. *Rom* 12:18
p. ye would have plucked. *Gal* 4:15
not *p.* the blood of bulls. *Heb* 10:4

post, -s
(*The old meaning of* courier)
so the *p.* went with the letters from. *2 Chr* 30:6; *Esth* 3:13, 15; 8:10
p. rode on mules and. *Esth* 8:14
days are swifter than a *p.* *Job* 9:25
one *p.* shall run to meet. *Jer* 51:31

post
Eli sat on a seat by a *p.* *1 Sam* 1:9*
on each *p.* were palm. *Ezek* 40:16

posterity
to preserve you a *p.* in. *Gen* 45:7*
or if any of your *p.* be. *Num* 9:10
I will take away the *p.* *1 Ki* 16:3
take away the *p.* of Ahab. 21:21*
yet their *p.* approve. *Ps* 49:13*
his *p.* be cut off and blotted. 109:13
not be divided to his *p.* *Dan* 11:4
your *p.* with fishhooks. *Amos* 4:2

posts
on the *p.* of thy house. *Deut* 6:9*
Samson took the two *p.* *Judg* 16:3
all the doors and *p.* were. *1 Ki* 7:5
waiting at the *p.* of my doors. *Pr* 8:34
the *p.* of the door moved. *Isa* 6:4*
behind the *p.* thou set up thy. 57:8
the *p.* had one measure. *Ezek* 40:10
setting of their *p.* by my *p.* 43:8*
smite the lintel, that the *p.* may. *Amos* 9:1*
see **door**

side **posts**
strike the blood on the two *side p.* *Ex* 12:7, 22
seeth the blood on the *side p.* 23
lintel and *side p.* were a. *1 Ki* 6:31

pot
(*The English word is used to translate a number of Hebrew words, some of which have different meanings. These are substituted for pot in the Revisions*)
take a *p.* and put an. *Ex* 16:33
be sodden in a brazen *p.* *Lev* 6:28*
put the broth in a *p.* *Judg* 6:19
into the caldron or *p.* *1 Sam* 2:14
thing, save a *p.* of oil. *2 Ki* 4:2
set on great *p.* 38
there is death in the *p.* 40
meal into the *p.*, no harm in the *p.* 41
as out of a seething *p.* *Job* 41:20
the deep to boil like a *p.* 31*
the fining *p.* is. *Pr* 17:3; 27:21
I see a seething *p.* *Jer* 1:13*
saith Lord, Set on a *p.* *Ezek* 24:3*
woe to bloody city, to the *p.* whose. 6
in pieces, as for the *p.* *Mi* 3:3
every *p.* in Jerusalem. *Zech* 14:21
wherein was the golden *p.* *Heb* 9:4

water-**pot**
then left her *water-p.* *John* 4:28

potentate
the blessed and only *P.* *1 Tim* 6:15

Potiphar
the Midianites sold Joseph to *P.* *Gen* 37:36; 39:1

Poti-pherah
the daughter of *P.* *Gen* 41:45, 50

pots
made the *p.* and shovels. *Ex* 38:3
oven, or rangers for *p.* *Lev* 11:35
p. and shovels of brass. *1 Ki* 7:45; *2 Chr* 4:16
Huram made the *p.* *2 Chr* 4:11
holy offerings sod they in *p.* 35:13
before your *p.* can feel the. *Ps* 58:9
ye have lien among the *p.* 68:13*
were delivered from the *p.* 81:6*
Rechabites *p.* full of wine. *Jer* 35:5*
washing of cups and *p.* *Mark* 7:4, 8
see **flesh**

water-**pots**
set there six *water-p.* *John* 2:6
Jesus saith to them, Fill *water-p.* 7

potsherd, -s
(*A broken piece of earthenware*)
him a *p.* to scrape himself. *Job* 2:8
my strength is dried up like a *p.* *Ps* 22:15
are like a *p.* covered. *Pr* 26:23*
let the *p.* strive with *p.* of. *Isa* 45:9

pottage
Jacob sod *p.* and Esau. *Gen* 25:29
feed me with *p.* 30
Jacob gave Esau *p.* 34
seethe *p.* for sons of the. *2 Ki* 4:38
shred them into the pot of *p.* 39
as they were eating the *p.* they. 40
skirt do touch bread or *p.* *Hag* 2:12

potter
in pieces like a *p.*'s vessel. *Ps* 2:9
it as the breaking of the *p.*'s vessel. *Isa* 30:14; *Jer* 19:11; *Rev* 2:27
down to the *p.*'s house. *Jer* 18:2
go and get a *p.*'s earthen bottle. 19:1
of the hands of the *p.* *Lam* 4:2
said, Cast it unto the *p.* *Zech* 11:13
them for the *p.*'s field. *Mat* 27:10
see **clay**

potters
these were the *p.* and. *1 Chr* 4:23

pound, -s
three *p.* of gold went. *1 Ki* 10:17
treasure 5000 *p.* of silver. *Ezra* 2:69
treasure 2200 *p.* of silver. *Neh* 7:71
the rest gave 2000 *p.* of silver. 72
to his servants ten *p.* *Luke* 19:13
thy *p.* hath gained ten *p.* 16
hath gained five *p.* 18
behold, here is thy *p.* 20
take from him the *p.* 24
he hath ten *p.* 25
then Mary took a *p.* of. *John* 12:3
aloes about a 100 *p.* weight. 19:39

pour
shall take and *p.* water on. *Ex* 4:9
shall *p.* the anointing oil on. 29:7
thou shalt *p.* the blood of the bullock 12; *Lev* 4:7, 18, 25, 30, 34
nor *p.* drink offerings. *Ex* 30:9
he shall *p.* oil on the. *Lev* 2:1, 6
p. it into the palm of his. 14:15, 26
p. it on head of him that is to. 18
they shall *p.* out the dust that. 41
he shall *p.* out blood thereof. 17:13
he shall *p.* no oil upon. *Num* 5:15
he shall *p.* water out of his. 24:7*
p. blood out as water. *Deut* 12:16, 24; 15:23
take the flesh, and *p.* out. *Judg* 6:20
p. water on the burnt. *1 Ki* 18:33
p. out the oil into those. *2 Ki* 4:4
p. out for the people, that they. 41
and *p.* the oil on Jehu's head. 9:3
p. down rain according. *Job* 36:27*
I *p.* out my soul. *Ps* 42:4
ye people, *p.* out your heart. 62:8
p. out thine indignation on. 69:24
p. out thy wrath on the heathen 79:6
I will *p.* out my Spirit unto you. *Pr* 1:23; *Isa* 44:3; *Joel* 2:28, 29; *Acts* 2:17, 18
I will *p.* water on him. *Isa* 44:3
skies *p.* down righteousness. 45:8
I will *p.* it out on the children abroad. *Jer* 6:11
and to *p.* out drink offerings. 7:18
p. out thy fury on heathen. 10:25
I will *p.* their wickedness. 14:16
p. out their blood by force. 18:21*

to p. out drink offerings to the queen of heaven. Jer 44:17, 18, 19, 25
p. out thine heart like. Lam 2:19
now will I shortly p. out. Ezek 7:8
14:19; 20:8, 13, 21; 30:15
I will p. out mine indignation. 21:31
Zeph 3:8
set on the pot and p. Ezek 24:3
I will p. out my wrath. Hos 5:10
I will p. down the stones. Mi 1:6
p. on house of David. Zech 12:10
if I will not p. you out. Mal 3:10
p. out the vials of wrath of. Rev 16:1

poured

Jacob p. oil on the top. Gen 28:18
Jacob p. a drink offering. 35:14
the rain was not p. on Ex 9:33
upon flesh shall it not be p. 30:32
where ashes are p. he. Lev 4:12
Moses p. anointing oil on. 8:12
he p. the blood at the bottom. 15; 9:9
head the anointing oil was p. 21:10
to be p. to the Lord for a. Num 28:7
sacrifices shall be p. out. Deut 12:27
but I have p. out my soul. 1 Sam 1:15
drew water, and p. it out. 7:6
Samuel p. oil on Saul's head. 10:1
Tamar p. them out. 2 Sam 13:9
David would not drink thereof, but p. it out unto. 23:16; 1 Chr 11:18
rent, and ashes p. out. 1 Ki 13:3, 5
p. water on the hands. 2 Ki 3:11
vessels to her, and she p. out. 4:5
they p. out for the men to eat. 40
and Ahaz p. his drink offering. 16:13
my wrath not be p. out. 2 Chr 12:7
wrath that is p. out on us. 34:21
wrath shall be p. out on this place. 25
my roarings are p. out like. Job 3:24
not thou p. me out as milk? 10:10
rock p. me out rivers of oil. 29:6
my soul is p. out upon me. 30:16
I am p. out like water. Ps 22:14
grace is p. into thy lips. 45:2
clouds p. out water, skies. 77:17
I p. out my complaint before. 142:2
as ointment p. forth. S of S 1:3
they p. out a prayer. Isa 26:16
Lord hath p. on you the spirit. 29:10
till the spirit be p. on us from. 32:15
he hath p. on him the fury of. 42:25
hath p. out his soul to death. 53:12
hast p. out a drink offering. 57:6
my fury shall be p. out. Jer 7:20
they have p. out drink offerings. 19:13; 32:29
so shall it [fury] be p. out. 42:18
mine anger was p. forth. 44:6
when we p. drink offerings to. 19
he p. out his fury like fire. Lam 2:4; 4:11
my liver is p. upon earth. 11
their soul was p. out. 12
of the sanctuary are p. out. 4:1
filthiness was p. out. Ezek 16:36
p. out their drink offerings. 20:28
with fury p. out will I rule. 33, 34
that I the Lord have p. out. 22:22
therefore I p. out mine. 31
p. their whoredom upon her. 23:8
she p. it not on the ground to. 24:7
wherefore I p. out my fury. 36:18
p. out my spirit on the house. 39:29
therefore the curse is p. Dan 9:11
and that determined shall be p. 27
as waters that are p. down. Mi 1:4
fury is p. out like fire. Nah 1:6
their blood shall be p. out. Zeph 1:17
p. ointment on his head. Mat 26:7
12; Mark 14:3
he p. out the changers' money. John 2:15
on the Gentiles was p. Acts 10:45
wine of wrath of God p. Rev 14:10*
went and p. out his vial. 16:2, 3, 4
8, 10, 12, 17

pouredst

p. out thy fornications. Ezek 16:15

poureth

he p. contempt on princes. Job 12:21
Ps 107:40
he p. out my gall upon. Job 16:13
eye p. out tears unto God. 20
wine is red, and he p. Ps 75:8
but mouth of fools p. out. Pr 15:2
the mouth of the wicked p. out. 28
p. out waters on the. Amos 5:8; 9:6
he p. water into a bason. John 13:5

pouring

in p. thy fury on Jerusalem? Ezek 9:8
his wounds, p. in oil. Luke 10:34

pourtray

and p. upon it the city. Ezek 4:1

pourtrayed

all the idols of Israel p. Ezek 8:10
men p. on the wall, the images of the Chaldeans p. with. 23:14

poverty

all thou hast come to p. Gen 45:11
so thy p. come as an armed man. Pr 6:11; 24:34
destruction of poor is their p. 10:15
but it tendeth to p. 11:24*
p. be to him that refuseth. 13:18
sleep, lest thou come to p. 20:13
and glutton come to p. 23:21
persons, shall have p. enough. 28:19
considereth not that p. shall come. 22
give me neither p. nor riches. 30:8
let him drink and forget his p. 31:7
their deep p. abounded to. 2 Cor 8:2
became poor, that ye through his p. 9
I know thy works and p. Rev 2:9

powder

calf and ground it to p. Ex 32:20
the rain of thy land p. Deut 28:24
grove to p., cast the p. 2 Ki 23:6
the altar to p. 15; 2 Chr 34:7
it will grind him to p. Mat 21:44*
Luke 20:18*

powders

perfumed with all the p. S of S 3:6

power

(Generally for rule, or authority; frequently for might and strength)
hast thou p. with God. Gen 32:28*
dignity, excellency of p. 49:3
break the pride of your p. Lev 26:19
have I now any p. to say? Num 22:38
brought thee with his mighty p. Deut 4:37
it is he that giveth thee p. to. 8:18
seeth that their p. is gone. 32:36
is my strength and p. 2 Sam 22:33
the inhabitants were of small p. 2 Ki 19:26
Joab led forth the p. 1 Chr 20:1
thine is the p. and glory. 29:11
Mat 6:13
in thine hand is p. 1 Chr 29:12
2 Chr 20:6
God hath p. to help. 2 Chr 25:8
siege, and all his p. with him. 32:9
cease by force and p. Ezra 4:23
his p. and wrath against all. 8:22
nor is it in our p. to redeem them. Neh 5:5
he made a feast to p. of. Esth 1:3
perish the p. of the people. 8:11
the Jews hoped to have p. 9:1
redeem in war from the p. Job 5:20
also the mighty with his p. 24:22
helped him that is without p. 26:2
he divided the sea with his p. 12
the thunder of his p. who can? 14
God exalteth by his p. 36:22
conceal his parts nor his p. 41:12
my darling from the p. of. Ps 22:20
redeem my soul from the p. 49:15
p. belongeth unto God. 62:11
mountains girded with p. 65:6
he ruleth by his p. for ever. 66:7
he giveth strength and p. to. 68:35
by his p. he brought in the south wind. 78:26
who knoweth the p. of thine? 90:11
his mighty p. to be known. 106:8
he shewed his people the p. 111:6
in the firmament of his p. 150:1
oppressors there was p. Eccl 4:1
and hath given him p. to eat. 5:19
God giveth him not p. to eat. 6:2
word of a king is, there is p. 8:4
no man hath p. over the spirit. 8
their inhabitants were of small p. Isa 37:27
he giveth p. to the faint. Isa 40:29
bringeth forth the army and p. 43:17
from the p. of the flame. 47:14
the earth by his p. Jer 10:12; 51:15
were in thee to their p. Ezek 22:6
and the pride of her p. shall. 30:6
God hath given thee p. Dan 2:37
Daniel from the p. of lions. 6:27
ran in fury of his p. 8:6
but not in his p. 22
p. shall be mighty, but not by his p. 24
not retain the p. of the arm. 11:6
he shall stir up his p. and his. 25
but he shall have p. over the. 43
to scatter the p. of the holy. 12:7
he had p. with God. Hos 12:3
yea, he had p. over the angel. 4
I will ransom them from the p. 13:14
in the p. of their hand. Mi 2:1
I am full of p. by the Spirit of. 3:8
imputing this his p. unto. Hab 1:11
delivered from the p. of evil. 2:9
there was the hiding of his p. 3:4
not by might, nor by p. Zech 4:6
Lord will smite her p. in the sea. 9:4
Son of man hath p. on earth to. Mat 9:6; Mark 2:10; Luke 5:24
had given such p. to men. Mat 9:8
gave p. against unclean spirits. 10:1
Luke 9:1
coming in the clouds with p. Mat 24:30; Luke 21:27
sitting on right hand with p. Mat 26:64; Mark 14:62
all p. is given unto me in heaven and in earth. Mat 28:18
p. to heal sicknesses. Mark 3:15
kingdom of God come with p. 9:1
p. of the Highest shall. Luke 1:35
the devil said, All this p. will. 4:6
for his word was with p. 32
p. he commandeth unclean spirits. 36
the p. of the Lord was present. 5:17
I give you p. to tread on serpents, and over all the p. of the. 10:19
fear him that hath p. to cast. 12:5
they might deliver him to p. 20:20
and the p. of darkness. 22:53
until ye be endued with p. 24:49
to them gave he p. to become sons of God. John 1:12*
I have p. to lay it down, and p. 10:18
thou hast given him p. over. 17:2
I have p. to crucify thee, p. to. 19:10
the Father hath put in his own p. Acts 1:7*
shall receive p. after Holy Ghost. 8
as though by our own p. or. 3:12
they asked, By what p. have ye? 4:7
was it not in thine own p.? 5:4
faith and p., did great wonders. 6:8
saying, Give me also this p. 8:19
Jesus with Holy Ghost and p. 10:38
from the p. of Satan to God. 26:18
be the Son of God with p. Rom 1:4
his eternal p. and Godhead. 20
hath not the potter p. over? 9:21
willing to make his p. known. 22
resisteth the p., resisteth. 13:2
then not be afraid of the p.? 3
through p. of the Holy Ghost. 15:13
wonders, by the p. of the Spirit. 19
that is of p. to establish you. 16:25*
of the Spirit and p. 1 Cor 2:4
know, not the speech, but the p. 4:19
with the p. of our Lord Jesus. 5:4
brought under the p. of any. 6:12
will raise us up by his own p. 14
wife and husband have not p. of. 7:4
but hath p. over his own will. 37
we p. to eat and to drink? 9:4*
p. to lead about a sister, a wife? 5*
not p. to forbear working? 6
if others be partakers of this p. over you, we have not used this p. 12
the woman ought to have p. on. 11:10
put down all authority and p. 15:24
that the excellency of p. 2 Cor 4:7
p. yea, and beyond their p. 8:3
that the p. of Christ may rest. 12:9
according to the p. God hath. 13:10
his p. toward us, according to the working of his mighty p. Eph 1:19*
far above all principality, p. and. 21

prince of the *p.* of the air. *Eph* 2:2
by the effectual working of his *p.* 3:7
to the *p.* that worketh in us. 20
I may know the *p.* of his. *Phil* 3:10
according to his glorious *p.* *Col* 1:11*
us from the *p.* of darkness. 13
of all principality and *p.* 2:10
from the glory of his *p.* *2 Thes* 1:9
the work of faith with *p.* 11
working of Satan with all *p.* 2:9
not *p.* but to make ourselves. 3:9
whom be honour and *p.* *1 Tim* 6:16
God hath given us spirit of *p.*
2 Tim 1:7
of godliness, but denying the *p.* 3:5
things by word of his *p.* *Heb* 1:3
him that had *p.* of death. 2:14
after the *p.* of an endless life. 7:16
as his divine *p.* hath given. *2 Pet* 1:3
known the *p.* of our Lord. 16
to the only wise God our Saviour be
glory and *p.* *Jude* 25
I give *p.* over the nations. *Rev* 2:26
to receive honour and *p.* 4:11; 5:12
blessing, honour, glory, and *p.* 5:13
p. was given to him that sat on. 6:4
p. was given them over fourth. 8
honour, *p.*, and might be unto. 7:12
given *p.* as scorpions have *p.* 9:3
and their *p.* was to hurt men. 10
for their *p.* is in their mouth. 19
give *p.* to my two witnesses. 11:3
p. to shut heaven, *p.* over waters. 6
the *p.* of his Christ come. 12:10
gave him *p.* and his seat. 13:2, 4
p. was given to him to. 5, 7
he exerciseth all the *p.* of the. 12
had *p.* to give life. 15
had *p.* over fire. 14:18
filled with smoke from his *p.* 15:8
p. was given him to scorch. 16:8
blasphemed God who hath *p.* over. 9
receive *p.* as kings one hour. 17:12
shall give their *p.* and strength. 13
glory, honour, and *p.*, unto the. 19:1

see* great *power

power ***of God***

the scriptures, nor the *p. of God.*
Mat 22:29; *Mark* 12:24
all amazed at the mighty *p. of God.*
Luke 9:43*
the right hand of *p. of God.* 22:69
this man is the great *p. of God.*
Acts 8:10*
gospel is the *p. of God.* *Rom* 1:16
are saved, it is the *p. of God.*
1 Cor 1:18
Christ the *p. of God,* and. 24
stand but by the *p. of God.* 2:5
of truth, by the *p. of God.* *2 Cor* 6:7
liveth by *p. of God,* but we shall live
with him by *p. of God.* 13:4
of the afflictions of the gospel, according to the *p. of God.* *2 Tim* 1:8
kept by the *p. of God.* *1 Pet* 1:5

***in* power**

it is *in p.* of my hand. *Gen* 31:29
become glorious *in p.* *Ex* 15:6
the wicked mighty *in p.*? *Job* 21:7
he is excellent *in p.* and in. 37:23
when it is *in p.* of thy. *Pr* 3:27
death and life are *in* the *p.* 18:21
that he is strong *in p.* not. *Isa* 40:26
slow to anger, great *in p.* *Nah* 1:3
go before him *in* the *p.* of Elias.
Luke 1:17
in the *p.* of the Spirit. 4:14
kingdom of God not in word, but *in*
p. *1 Cor* 4:20
in weakness, it is raised *in p.* 15:43
be strong *in* the Lord and *in p.* *Eph* 6:10
came in word, and also *in p.*
1 Thes 1:5
greater *in p.* and might. *2 Pet* 2:11

***my* power**

all *my p.* I have served. *Gen* 31:6
to shew in thee *my p.* *Ex* 9:16
My p. hath gotten me. *Deut* 8:17
built by the might of *my p.* *Dan* 4:30
that I might shew *my p.* *Rom* 9:17
that I abuse not *my p.* in. *1 Cor* 9:18*

***no* power**

sell her he shall have *no p.* *Ex* 21:8
shall have *no p.* to stand. *Lev* 26:37
men of Ai had *no p.* to. *Josh* 8:20
people had *no p.* to weep. *1 Sam* 30:4
with them that have *no p.* *2 Chr* 14:11
house of Ahaziah had *no p.* to. 22:9
or have I *no p.* to deliver ? *Isa* 50:2
bodies the fire had *no p.* *Dan* 3:27
there was *no p.* in the ram to. 8:7
no p. against me, except. *John* 19:11
for there is *no p.* but. *Rom* 13:1
second death hath *no p.* *Rev* 20:6

***thy* power**

out by *thy* mighty *p.* *Deut* 9:29
all that he hath is in *thy p.* *Job* 1:12
sing, and praise *thy p.* *Ps* 21:13
scatter them by *thy p.* 59:11
will sing of *thy p.* 16
to see *thy p.* and thy glory. 63:2
through greatness of *thy p.* 66:3
and *thy p.* to every one that. 71:18
to the greatness of *thy p.* 79:11
be willing in day of *thy p.* 110:3
they shall talk of *thy p.* 145:11
fortify *thy p.* mightily. *Nah* 2:1

powerful

Lord is *p.* full of majesty. *Ps* 29:4
for his letters, say they, are *p.*
2 Cor 10:10*
word of God is quick, *p.* *Heb* 4:12*

powers

p. of heaven be shaken. *Mat* 24:29
Mark 13:25; *Luke* 21:26
when brought before *p.* *Luke* 12:11*
nor *p.* can separate from. *Rom* 8:38
the *p.* that be are ordained of. 13:1
p. in heavenly places. *Eph* 3:10
against principalities and *p.* 6:12
p. were created by him. *Col* 1:16
having spoiled *p.* he made a. 2:15
in mind to be subject to *p.* *Tit* 3:1*
tasted the *p.* of the world. *Heb* 6:5
on right hand of God, *p.* *1 Pet* 3:22

practices

heart exercised with covetous *p.*
2 Pet 2:14*

practise

not to *p.* wicked works. *Ps* 141:4*
person shall *p.* hypocrisy. *Isa* 32:6
destroy, prosper, and *p.* *Dan* 8:24*
morning is light, they *p.* it. *Mi* 2:1

practised

that Saul secretly *p.* mischief.
1 Sam 23:9*
the little horn *p.* and. *Dan* 8:12*

praise

(*Most frequently used with regard to praise rendered to God. The verb is frequently changed in the Revisions to* bless, *or* give thanks)

he is thy *p.* and he is. *Deut* 10:21
to make thee high in *p.* and. 26:19
I will sing *p.* to the Lord. *Judg* 5:3
Ps 7:17; 9:2; 57:7; 61:8; 104:33
we may glory in thy *p.* *1 Chr* 16:35
as taught to sing *p.* *2 Chr* 23:13
above all blessing and *p.* *Neh* 9:5
of David were songs of *p.* 12:46
shew forth all thy *p.* *Ps* 9:14
my *p.* shall be of thee in the. 22:25
that my glory may sing *p.* 30:12
p. is comely for the upright. 33:1
his *p.* shall be continually in. 34:1
tongue shall speak of thy *p.* 35:28
even *p.* to our God. 40:3
with voice of *p.* 42:4
so is thy *p.* to the ends of. 48:10
offereth *p.* glorifieth me. 50:23
mouth shall shew forth thy *p.* 51:15
p. waiteth for thee, O God. 65:1
honour, make his *p.* glorious. 66:2
and make the voice of his *p.* 8
my *p.* shall be continually of. 71:6
let my mouth be filled with thy *p.* 8
we will shew forth thy *p.* 79:13
rejoice and sing *p.* 98:4
enter into his courts with *p.* 100:4
declare his *p.* in Jerusalem. 102:21
who can shew forth all his *p.*? 106:2
then they sang his *p.* 12
triumph in thy *p.* 47
give *p.* even with my glory. *Ps* 108:1
O God of my *p.* 109:1
his *p.* endureth. 111:10
lips shall utter *p.* when. 119:171
before the gods will I sing *p.* 138:1
my mouth shall speak the *p.* 145:21
p. is comely. 147:1
sing *p.* on the harp. 7
the *p.* of all his saints. 148:14
sing his *p.* in the congregation. 149:1
so is a man to his *p.* *Pr* 27:21
I will not give my *p.* to. *Isa* 42:8
sing his *p.* from the end of the. 10
let them declare his *p.* in the. 12
they shall shew forth my *p.* 43:21
my *p.* will I refrain for thee. 48:9
thou shalt call thy gates *P.* 60:18
the garment of *p.* for the spirit. 61:3
will cause righteousness and *p.* 11
till he made Jerusalem a *p.* in. 62:7
might be to me for a *p.* *Jer* 13:11
O Lord, for thou art my *p.* 17:14
bringing sacrifices of *p.* 26; 33:11
it shall be to me a joy, a *p.* 33:9
there shall be no more *p.* of. 48:2
how is the city of *p.* not left ? 49:25
how is the *p.* of whole earth ? 51:41
earth was full of his *p.* *Hab* 3:3
will get them *p.* and fame. *Zeph* 3:19
make you a *p.* among all people. 20
thou hast perfected *p.* *Mat* 21:16
saw it, gave *p.* to God. *Luke* 18:43
unto him, Give God the *p.* *John* 9:24
p. of men more than *p.* of. 12:43
whose *p.* is not of men. *Rom* 2:29
thou shalt have *p.* of same. 13:3
every man have *p.* of God. *1 Cor* 4:5
whose *p.* is in the gospel. *2 Cor* 8:18
to *p.* of glory of his grace. *Eph* 1:6
to *p.* of glory who first. 12, 14
unto the *p.* of God. *Phil* 1:11
if there be any *p.* think on. 4:8
of the church will I sing *p.* *Heb* 2:12
him let us offer sacrifice of *p.* 13:15
faith might be found to *p.* *1 Pet* 1:7
and for the *p.* of them that do. 2:14
to whom be *p.* and dominion. 4:11

praise, ***verb***

whom thy brethren shall *p.* *Gen* 49:8
fruit holy to *p.* the Lord. *Lev* 19:24
instruments I made to *p.* *1 Chr* 23:5
and *p.* thy glorious name. 29:13
Levites to *p.* before the. *2 Chr* 8:14
that should *p.* the beauty. 20:21
began to sing and to *p.* 22
to *p.* in the gates of the tents. 31:2
so will we sing and *p.* *Ps* 21:13
ye that fear the Lord, *p.* him. 22:23
pit, shall the dust *p.* thee ? 30:9
hope in God, for I shall yet *p.* him.
42:5, 11; 43:5
God we boast, and *p.* thy name. 44:8
shall the people *p.* thee. 45:17
men will *p.* thee, when doest. 49:18
my lips shall *p.* thee. 63:3
mouth shall *p.* thee. 5
let the people *p.* thee. 67:3
let all the people *p.* thee. 5
heaven and the earth *p.* him. 69:34
I will yet *p.* thee more and. 71:14
let the poor and needy *p.* 74:21
wrath of man shall *p.* thee. 76:10
dead arise and *p.* thee ? 88:10
the heavens shall *p.* thy. 89:5
p. thy great and terrible name. 99:3
p. him in the assembly of. 107:32
p. him, O ye servants of the Lord.
113:1, 135:1
the dead *p.* not the Lord. 115:17
seven times a day do I *p.* 119:164
let my soul live and it shall *p.* 175
I will *p.* thy name for thy. 138:2
of the earth shall *p.* thee. 4
out of prison that I may *p.* 142:7
one generation shall *p.* thy. 145:4
all thy works shall *p.* thee. 10
p. the Lord, Jerusalem, *p.* 147:12
p. ye the Lord, *p.* him in the. 148:1
p. him, all his angels, *p.* him, ye. 2
p. him, sun and moon, *p.* him. 3
p. him, ye heavens of heavens. 4
p. his name in the dance. 149:3
p. God in his sanctuary, *p.* 150:1

p. him for his mighty acts, p. him. Ps 150:2
p. him with trumpet. 3
p. him with timbrel. 4
p. him upon the loud and. 5
let another man p. thee. Pr 27:2
they that forsake the law p. the. 28:4
let her own works p. her in. 31:31
the grave cannot p. thee. Isa 38:18
the living he shall p. thee, as. 19
publish, p. ye and say. Jer 31:7
I thank and p. thee, O. Dan 2:23
I p. extol, and honour the king. 4:37
p. the name of the Lord. Joel 2:26
disciples began to p. God with loud. Luke 19:37
now I p. you that ye. 1 Cor 11:2
I declare, I p. you not. 17, 22
saying, P. our God, all ye. Rev 19:5

I will, or *will I* **praise**

Leah said, Now *will I p.* Gen 29:35
I will p. Lord according. Ps 7:17
I will p. thee, O Lord, with my whole heart. 9:1; 111:1; 138:1
congregation *will I p.* thee. 22:22
with my song *will I p.* him. 28:7
I will give thee thanks, *I will p.* 35:18 57:9; 108:3; 109:30
on the harp *will I p.* thee. 43:4
I will p. thee for ever, because. 52:9
I will p. thy name, O Lord. 54:6
in God *I will p.* his word. 56:4, 10
I will p. the name of God. 69:30
I will also *p.* thee with the. 71:22
I will p. thee, O Lord my. 86:12
I will go into them, and will *p.* 118:19
I will p. thee, for thou hast heard. 21
thou art my God, and *I will p.* 28
I will p. thee with uprightness. 119:7
I will p. thee, for I am wonderfully made. 139:14
I will p. thy name for ever. 145:2
I will p. thee, though. Isa 12:1
I will p. thy name, thou hast. 25:1

praise *ye the Lord*, or **praise** *the Lord*

p. ye the Lord, for the avenging of Israel. Judg 5:2
Levites to *p. the Lord*. 1 Chr 16:4
morning to *p. the Lord*. 23:20
with a harp to *p. the Lord*. 25:3
stood up to *p. the Lord*. 2 Chr 20:19
p. the Lord, for his mercy. 21
cymbals to *p. the Lord*. Ezra 3:10
they shall *p. the Lord*. Ps 22:26
p. the Lord with harp, sing. 33:2
be created shall *p. the Lord*. 102:18
p. ye the Lord. 104:35; 106:1, 48 111:1; 112:1; 113:1, 9; 115:18 116:19; 117:2; 135:1; 146:1, 10 147:20; 148:1, 14; 149:1, 9 150:1, 6; Jer 20:13
Oh that men would *p. the Lord*. Ps 107:8, 15, 21, 31
I will greatly *p. the Lord*. 109:30
I will *p. the Lord*. 118:19
p. the Lord; for Lord is good. 135:3
while I live will I *p. the Lord*. 146:2
p. ye the Lord, for it is good. 147:1
p. the Lord, O Jerusalem, praise. 12
p. the Lord from the earth. 148:7
p. the Lord, call upon his. Isa 12:4
eat it, and *p. the Lord*. 62:9
p. the Lord of hosts, for. Jer 33:11
p. the Lord, all ye Gentiles. [illegible] 15:11

praised

the people p. their god. [illegible] 16:24
none p. as Absalom. 2 [illegible] 14:25
the Lord is worthy to be p. 22:4 Ps 18:3
Lord is great and greatly to be p. 1 Chr 16:25; Ps 48:1; 96:4; 145:3
the people p. the Lord. 1 Chr 16:36
and four thousand p. the Lord. 23:5; 2 Chr 7:3; Neh 5:13
of music p. the Lord. 2 Chr 5:13
David p. by the ministry. 7:6
Levites and priests p. the. 30:21
when they p. the Lord. Ezra 3:11
and daily shall he be p. Ps 72:15
of sun Lord's name is to be p. 113:3
feareth Lord shall be p. Pr 31:30
I p. the dead more than. Eccl 4:2
and concubines p. her. S of S 6:9
where our fathers p. thee. Isa 64:11
I p. and honoured him. Dan 4:34
they p. the gods of gold and. 5:4, 23
and Zacharias spake and p. God. Luke 1:64

praises

like thee, fearful in p.? Ex 15:11
sing p. to thy name. 2 Sam 22:50 Ps 18:49; 92:1; 135:3
Levites to sing p. to the Lord, and they sang p. with. 2 Chr 29:30
sing p. to the Lord that. Ps 9:11
thou that inhabitest p. of Israel. 22:3
yea, I will sing p. to God. 27:6 47:6; 68:32; 75:9; 108:3
God is king, sing ye p. with. 47:7
I will render p. unto. 56:12; 144:9
sing to God, sing p. to his. 68:4
generation to come p. of Lord. 78:4
I will sing p. to my God while. 146:2
for it is good to sing p. to. 147:1
let them sing p. to him. 149:3
let the high p. of God be in their. 6
shew forth the p. of Lord. Isa 60:6
mention of the p. of the Lord. 63:7
prayed and sang p. to. Acts 16:25
shew forth the p. of him. 1 Pet 2:9

praiseth

husband also, and he p. Pr 31:28

praising

one sound to be heard in p. the Lord. 2 Chr 5:13
Athaliah heard the people p. 23:12
they sang by course in p. Ezra 3:11
they will be still p. thee. Ps 84:4
heavenly host p. God. Luke 2:13
the shepherds returned, p. God. 20
in the temple p. God. 24:53
eat with gladness, p. God. Acts 2:47
and leaping, and p. God. 3:8, 9

prancing

the noise of the p. horses. Nah 3:2

prancings

broken by means of p. Judg 5:22

prating

but a p. fool shall fall. Pr 10:8, 10
p. against us with. 3 John 10

pray

(*Revisions frequently change to* beseech)

and shall p. for thee. Gen 20:7
Samuel said, I will p. 1 Sam 7:5
p. for thy servants to the. 12:19
that I should sin in ceasing to p. 23
found in his heart to p. this prayer. 2 Sam 7:27; 1 Chr 17:25
when they shall p. toward. 1 Ki 8:30 35, 42, 44, 48; 2 Chr 6:26, 34, 38
p. that my hand may be. 1 Ki 13:6
shall p. and make. 2 Chr 6:24, 32
and turn and p. in the land of. 37
if my people shall p. and. 7:14
and p. for the life of. Ezra 6:10
hear the prayer which I p. Neh 1:6
what profit should we have, if we p. unto him? Job 21:15
p. to God, and he will be. 33:26
my servant Job shall p. for. 42:8
God, for to thee will I p. Ps 5:2
and at noon will I p. 55:17*
p. for the peace of Jerusalem. 122:6
come to his sanctuary to p. Isa 16:12
p. to a god that cannot save. 45:20
p. not thou for this people. Jer 7:16 11:14; 14:11
seek peace of the city, p. to. 29:7
ye shall p. to me, and I will. 12
p. now to the Lord. 37:3; 42:2, 20
behold, I will p. to the Lord. 42:4
they sent men to p. Zech 7:2*
go speedily to p. before. 8:21*, 22*
and p. for them that despitefully. Mat 5:44; Luke 6:28
they love to p. standing. Mat 6:5
p. to thy Father which is in. 6
when ye p. use not vain. 7
after this manner p. ye, Our. 9
p. ye the Lord of the harvest. 9:38 Luke 10:2
he went . . . apart to p. Mat 14:23 Mark 6:46; Luke 6:12; 9:28
his hands on them and p. Mat 19:13
p. your flight be not in winter. 24:20; Mark 13:18
sit ye here while I go and p. yonder. Mat 26:36; Mark 14:32
watch and p. that ye enter not. Mat 26:41; Mark 13:33; 14:38 Luke 21:36; 22:40, 46
thinkest thou I cannot p.? Mat 26:53
to p. him to depart. Mark 5:17
things ye desire when ye p. 11:24
Lord, teach us to p. as. Luke 11:1
he said to them, When ye p. say. 2
that men ought always to p. 18:1
went up into the temple to p. 10
p. the Father. John 14:16; 16:26
I p. for them, I p. not for. 17:9
I p. not that thou take them. 15
neither p. I for these alone, but. 20
p. God, if perhaps the. Acts 8:22
Simon said, P. ye to the Lord. 24
up on the housetop to p. 10:9
not what we should p. for. Rom 8:26
a woman p. uncovered? 1 Cor 11:13
wherefore let him p. that he. 14:13
for if I p. in unknown tongue. 14
I will p. with spirit, p. with. 15
ambassadors for Christ, we p. you be reconciled. 2 Cor 5:20
now I p. to God, that ye do. 13:7
this I p. that your love. Phil 1:9
we do not cease to p. for. Col 1:9
p. without ceasing. 1 Thes 5:17
I p. God your whole spirit be. 23
brethren, p. for us. 25; 2 Thes 3:1 Heb 13:18
wherefore we p. always. 2 Thes 1:11
I will that men p. every. 1 Tim 2:8
I p. God it be not laid to. 2 Tim 4:16
is any afflicted? let him p. Jas 5:13
p. over him, anointing him. 14
confess your faults, and p. one. 16
I do not say that he shall p. for it. 1 John 5:16*

prayed

Abraham p. and God healed Abimelech. Gen 20:17
when Moses p. the fire. Num 11:2
and Moses p. for the people. 21:7 Deut 9:26
I p. for Aaron also the. Deut 9:20
Hannah p. to Lord. 1 Sam 1:10
for this child I p. 27
Samuel p. unto the Lord. 8:6
Elisha p. unto the Lord. 2 Ki 4:33 6:17, 18
Hezekiah p. 19:15; 20:2 2 Chr 30:18; 32:24
that which thou hast p. to me. 2 Ki 19:20; Isa 37:21
Isaiah p. 2 Chr 32:20
Manasseh p. 33:13
now when Ezra had p. Ezra 10:1 Neh 1:4; 2:4
the captivity when Job p. Job 42:10
Jeremiah p. Jer 32:16
Jonah p. Jonah 2:1; 4:2
Daniel p. three times. Dan 6:10; 9:4
p. let this cup pass from. Mat 26:39 42, 44; Mark 14:35, 39; Luke 22:41
a solitary place and p. Mark 1:35
he p. him that he might be. 5:18
Jesus p. him he would thrust out a. Luke 5:3
into the wilderness and p. 16
as he p. his countenance was. 9:29
the Pharisee stood and p. 18:11
but I have p. that thy faith. 22:32
being in an agony he p. more. 44
his disciples p. him. John 4:31
the disciples p. and said. Acts 1:24
when they p. they laid their. 4:31
Peter and John when come p. 8:15
Peter p. 9:40
Cornelius p. always. 10:2, 30
then they p. him to tarry. 48
they had fasted and p. 13:3; 14:23
man of Macedonia p. him. 16:9
at midnight Paul and Silas p. 25
Paul kneeled down and p. 20:36
kneeled down on shore and p. 21:5
while I p. in the temple, I. 22:17

Paul *p.* me to bring this young.
Acts 23:18
to whom Paul entered in and *p.* 28:8
Elias *p.* that it might. *Jas* 5:17
and he *p.* again, and the heaven. 18

prayer

heart to pray this *p.* *2 Sam* 7:27
have respect to the *p.* *1 Ki* 8:28
hearken to the *p.* 29; *2 Chr* 6:19, 20
p. shall be made by any man.
1 Ki 8:38; *2 Chr* 6:29
hear their *p.* *1 Ki* 8:45, 49
2 Chr 6:35, 39, 40
end of praying this *p.* *1 Ki* 8:54
lift up thy *p.* for remnant. *2 Ki* 19:4
Isa 37:4
be attent to the *p.* *2 Chr* 7:15
their *p.* came to his holy. 30:27
Manasseh's *p.* unto God. 33:18, 19
thou mayest hear the *p.* *Neh* 1:6
nevertheless we made our *p.* 4:9
yea thou restrainest *p.* *Job* 15:4
thou shalt make thy *p.* to him. 22:27
O thou that hearest *p.* *Ps* 65:2
p. shall be made for him. 72:15
how long be angry against *p.*? 80:4
he will regard the *p.* of the destitute,
and not despise their *p.* 102:17
but I give myself unto *p.* 109:4
and let his *p.* become sin. 7
the *p.* of the upright is. *Pr* 15:8
heareth the *p.* of the righteous. 29
his *p.* shall be abomination. 28:9
poured out a *p.* when. *Isa* 26:16
joyful in my house of *p.*: for mine
house shall be called an house of *p.*
56:7; *Mat* 21:13; *Mark* 11:17
Luke 19:46
cry nor *p.* for them. *Jer* 7:16; 11:14
that our *p.* should not pass. *Lam* 3:44
I set my face to the Lord, to seek by
p. *Dan* 9:3
yet made we not our *p.* before. 13
now, O our God, hear the *p.* of. 17
a *p.* of Habakkuk the. *Hab* 3:1
howbeit, this kind goeth not out but
by *p.* *Mat* 17:21; *Mark* 9:29
Zacharias, thy *p.* is. *Luke* 1:13
temple at the hour of *p.* *Acts* 3:1
ourselves continually to *p.* 6:4
Cornelius, thy *p.* is heard. 10:31
p. was made without ceasing. 12:5
we went out where *p.* was. 16:13*
as we went to *p.* a certain. 16
give yourselves to *p.* *1 Cor* 7:5
helping together by *p.* *2 Cor* 1:11
by their *p.* for you, which. 9:14
praying always with all *p.* *Eph* 6:18
always in every *p.* of mine. *Phil* 1:4
my salvation through your *p.* 19
in every thing by *p.* let requests. 4:6
by the word and *p.* *1 Tim* 4:5
the *p.* of faith shall save. *Jas* 5:15
the effectual *p.* of a righteous. 16*
sober, and watch unto *p.* *1 Pet* 4:7
see **heard**

***in* prayer**

the thanksgiving *in p.* *Neh* 11:17
speaking *in p.* Gabriel. *Dan* 9:21
whatever ye ask *in p.* *Mat* 21:22
all n ght *in p.* to God. *Luke* 6:12
with one accord *in p.* *Acts* 1:14
continuing instant *in p.* *Rom* 12:12
continue *in p.* and watch. *Col* 4:2

***my* prayer**

also *my p.* is pure. *Job* 16:17
have mercy upon me, and hear *my p.*
Ps 4:1; 17:1; 39:12; 54:2
in the morning will I direct *my p.* 5:3
the Lord will receive *my p.* 6:9
and *my p.* returned to mine. 35:13
and *my p.* to the God of my. 42:8
give ear unto *my p.* O God. 55:1
O God, attend to *my p.* 61:1; 64:1*
84:8; 86:6; 102:1; 143:1
attended to the voice of *my p.* 66:19
hath not turned away *my p.* 20
my p. is unto thee in an. 69:13
let *my p.* come before thee. 88:2
in the morning shall *my p.* 13
let *my p.* be set before thee. 141:2
for yet *my p.* shall be in their. 5
he shutteth out *my p.* *Lam* 3:8
my p. came in to thee. *Jonah* 2:7
brethren, *my p.* to God. *Rom* 10:1

prayers

p. of David, son of. *Ps* 72:20
when ye make many *p.* *Isa* 1:15
pretence make long *p.* *Mat* 23:14
Mark 12:40; *Luke* 20:47
Anna continued in *p.* *Luke* 2:37
disciples of John make *p.*? 5:33
breaking of bread and in *p.* *Acts* 2:42
thy *p.* and alms are come up. 10:4
make mention of you always in my *p.*
Rom 1:9; *Eph* 1:16; *1 Thes* 1:2
2 Tim 1:3; *Philem* 4
strive with me in your *p.* *Rom* 15:30
fervently for you in *p.* *Col* 4:12
I exhort that *p.* be made. *1 Tim* 2:1
continueth in *p.* night and day. 5:5
I trust through your *p.* I. *Philem* 22
when he had offered up *p.* *Heb* 5:7
heirs of life, that your *p.* *1 Pet* 3:7
his ears are open to their *p.* but. 12
full of odours, which are the *p.* of
saints. *Rev* 5:8
he should offer it with the *p.* 8:3
the smoke which came with the *p.* 4

prayest

when thou *p.* be not. *Mat* 6:5, 6

prayeth, -ing

as Hannah continued *p.* *1 Sam* 1:12
woman that stood *p.* by thee. 26
hearken to prayer which thy servant
p. *1 Ki* 8:28; *2 Chr* 6:19, 20
Solomon had made an end of *p.*
1 Ki 8:54; *2 Chr* 7:1
he worshippeth it and *p.* *Isa* 44:17
and found Daniel *p.* *Dan* 6:11
while I was speaking and *p.* 9:20
ye stand *p.*, forgive. *Mark* 11:25
people were *p.* without. *Luke* 1:10
and Jesus *p.*, the heaven. 3:21
he was alone *p.*, his disciples. 9:18
as he was *p.* in certain place. 11:1
behold he *p.* *Acts* 9:11
I was at Joppa *p.* 11:5
were gathered together *p.* 12:12
every man *p.* with his. *1 Cor* 11:4
every woman that *p.* uncovered. 5
spirit *p.* but my understanding. 14:14
p. us with much entreaty. *2 Cor* 8:4
p. always with all prayer. *Eph* 6:18
p. always for you. *Col* 1:3
p. also for us. 4:3
night and day *p.* exceedingly that we
might see your face. *1 Thes* 3:10
but ye, beloved, *p.* in the. *Jude* 20

preach

(*To proclaim or publish abroad*)
prophets to *p.* of thee. *Neh* 6:7
the Lord hath anointed me to *p.* good
tidings. *Isa* 61:1
p. to it the preaching. *Jonah* 3:2
time Jesus began to *p.* *Mat* 4:17
p. saying, The kingdom of God. 10:7
what ye hear, that *p.* ye upon. 27
he departed thence to *p.* in. 11:1
John did *p.* the baptism. *Mark* 1:4
that I may *p.* there. 38; *Luke* 4:43
he might send them forth to *p.*
Mark 3:14; *Luke* 9:2
to *p.* deliverance to. *Luke* 4:18, 19
go thou and *p.* the kingdom. 9:60
they ceased not to *p.* *Acts* 5:42
he commanded us to *p.* to. 10:42
and *p.* unto you that ye should. 14:15
in every city them that *p.* him. 15:21
forbidden by Holy Ghost to *p.* 16:6
Jesus whom I *p.* to you is. 17:3
word of faith which we *p.* *Rom* 10:8
and how shall they *p.* except? 15
we *p.* Christ crucified. *1 Cor* 1:23
though I *p.* gospel, I have nothing to
glory, woe is to me if I *p.* not. 9:16
I or they, so we *p.* and so. 15:11
we *p.* not ourselves, but. *2 Cor* 4:5
that I might *p.* him among. *Gal* 1:16
the gospel which I *p.* among the. 2:2
if I yet *p.* circumcision. 5:11
should *p.* among Gentiles. *Eph* 3:8
some indeed *p.* Christ of. *Phil* 1:15
the one *p.* Christ of contention. 16
whom we *p.*, warning. *Col* 1:28
p. the word, be instant. *2 Tim* 4:2

preached

I have *p.* righteousness in. *Ps* 40:9
poor have the gospel *p.* *Mat* 11:5
p. saying, There cometh. *Mark* 1:7
he *p.* in their synagogues. 39
many were gathered, he *p.* the. 2:2
went and *p.* that men should. 6:12
went forth and *p.* every where. 16:20
many other things *p.* he. *Luke* 3:18
he *p.* in the synagogues of. 4:44
time the kingdom of God is *p.* 16:16
remission of sins should be *p.* 24:27
who before was *p.* to you. *Acts* 3:20
p. through Jesus resurrection. 4:2
p. Christ to Samaria. 8:5
p. the word of the Lord, *p.* 25
p. Jesus to eunuch. 35
Philip *p.* in all cities till he came. 40
Saul *p.* Christ in synagogues. 9:20
Barnabas told how Saul had *p.* 27
the baptism which John *p.* 10:37
they *p.* the word of God in. 13:5
when John had first *p.* before. 24
through this man is *p.* to you. 38
these words might be *p.* the next. 42
had *p.* the word in Perga. 14:25
and visit where we have *p.* 15:36
word was *p.* of Paul at Berea. 17:13
because he *p.* Jesus and the. 18
Paul *p.*, ready to depart on. 20:7
lest when I have *p.* to. *1 Cor* 9:27
keep in memory what I *p.* 15:2
if Christ be *p.* that he rose from. 12
Jesus who was *p.* among you by us.
2 Cor 1:19
Jesus, whom we have not *p.* 11:4
than that we have *p.* to you. *Gal* 1:8
p. peace to you who were. *Eph* 2:17
Christ is *p.* and I therein. *Phil* 1:18
which was *p.* to every. *Col* 1:23
p. to Gentiles, believed. *1 Tim* 3:16
but the word *p.* did not. *Heb* 4:2
they to whom it was first *p.* 6
went and *p.* to the spirits. *1 Pet* 3:19
see **gospel**

preacher

the words of the *p.* the son. *Eccl* 1:1
I the *p.* was king over Israel. 12
of vanities, saith the *p.* all. 2; 12:8
have I found, saith the *p.* 7:27
because *p.* was wise, he still. 12:9
p. sought to find out acceptable. 10
how hear without a *p.*? *Rom* 10:14
whereunto I am ordained a *p.*
1 Tim 2:7; *2 Tim* 1:11
but saved Noah, a *p.* of. *2 Pet* 2:5

preachest, -eth, -ing

preach to it the *p.* that I. *Jonah* 3:2
in those days came John *p.* *Mat* 3:1
Luke 3:3
p. the gospel of the. *Mat* 4:23; 9:35
rise in judgement, because they repented at *p.* 12:41; *Luke* 11:32
Jesus came into Galilee *p.* the
gospel. *Mark* 1:14
p. and shewing glad. *Luke* 8:1
they went through the towns *p.* 9:6
went every where *p.* the. *Acts* 8:4
p. the things concerning the. 12
p. peace by Jesus Christ, he. 10:36
p. the word to none but to. 11:19
to the Greeks, *p.* the Lord. 20
continued in Antioch *p.* 15:35
by Jesus, whom Paul *p.* 19:13
Paul was long *p.*, Eutychus. 20:9
among whom I have gone *p.* 25
p. the kingdom of God. 28:31
p. a man should not steal. *Rom* 2:21
according to the *p.* of Jesus. 16:25
for the *p.* of the cross. *1 Cor* 1:18
by the foolishness of *p.* to save. 21
my *p.* was not with enticing. 2:4
not risen, then is our *p.* vain. 15:14
far as to you, *p.* gospel. *2 Cor* 10:14
that cometh *p.* another Jesus. 11:4
he *p.* the faith which. *Gal* 1:23
p. might be fully known. *2 Tim* 4:17
hath in due times manifested his
word through *p.* *Tit* 1:3

precept, -s

commandedst them *p.* *Neh* 9:14*
hast commanded us to keep thy *p.*
Ps 119:4

I will meditate in thy *p.* *Ps* 119:15, 78
understand the way of thy *p.* 27
I have longed after thy *p.* 40
for I seek thy *p.* 45
because I kept thy *p.* 56, 100, 168
them that keep thy *p.* 63, 69, 134
I forsook not thy *p.* 87
I will never forget thy *p.* 93
for I have sought thy *p.* 94
thro' thy *p.* I get understanding. 104
yet I erred not from thy *p.* 110
esteem all thy *p.* to be right. 128
yet do not I forget thy *p.* 141
consider how I love thy *p.* 159
for I have chosen thy *p.* 173
for *p.* must be upon *p.*, *p.* upon *p.* *Isa* 28:10, 13
taught by the *p.* of men. 29:13*
have kept all Jonadab's *p.* *Jer* 35:18
by departing from thy *p.* *Dan* 9:5
for the hardness of your heart he wrote you this *p.* *Mark* 10:5*
had spoken every *p.* *Heb* 9:19*

precious

to Rebekah's mother *p.* *Gen* 24:53
for the *p.* things of. *Deut* 33:13
p. fruits brought forth by sun. 14
p. things of the lasting hills. 15
for *p.* things of the earth, and. 16
word of the Lord was *p.* *1 Sam* 3:1
because my soul was *p.* in. 26:21
let my life be *p.* in. *2 Ki* 1:13, 14
shewed them *p.* things. 20:13 *Isa* 39:2
and *p.* jewels which. *2 Chr* 20:25
gave them gifts of *p.* things. 21:3
their hands with *p.* things. *Ezra* 1:6
two vessels of fine copper, *p.* 8:27
eye seeth every *p.* thing. *Job* 28:10
cannot be valued with the *p.* onyx. 16
of their soul is *p.* *Ps* 49:8*
and *p.* shall their blood be. 72:14
p. in the sight of Lord is the. 116:15
goeth forth bearing *p.* seed. 126:6*
it is like *p.* ointment on the. 133:2
how *p.* also are thy thoughts. 139:17
find all *p.* substance. *Pr* 1:13
wisdom is more *p.* than rubies. 3:15
adulteress will hunt for the *p.* 6:26
substance of a diligent man is *p.* 12:27
of knowledge are a *p.* jewel. 20:15
chambers filled with all *p.* and. 24:4
good name is better than *p.* *Eccl* 7:1
I will make a man *p.* *Isa* 13:12
I lay in Zion a *p.* corner stone. 28:16; *1 Pet* 2:6
thou wast *p.* in my sight. *Isa* 43:4
take the *p.* from the vile. *Jer* 15:19
I will deliver all the *p.* things. 20:5
the *p.* sons of Zion. *Lam* 4:2
treasure and *p.* things. *Ezek* 22:25
Dedan was thy merchant in *p.* 27:20
with their *p.* vessels of. *Dan* 11:8
power over all *p.* things of Egypt. 43
woman, having an alabaster box of very *p.* *Mat* 26:7; *Mark* 14:3
waiteth for the *p.* fruit. *Jas* 5:7
faith much more *p.* than gold. *1 Pet* 1:7
but with the *p.* blood of Christ. 19
stone, chosen of God, and *p.* 2:4
therefore which believe, he is *p.* 7
like *p.* faith with us. *2 Pet* 1:1
great and *p.* promises. 4
buyeth their *p.* vessels. *Rev* 18:12
was like unto a stone most *p.* 21:11

predestinate
(*Revisions*, foreordain)

did foreknow, he did *p.* *Rom* 8:29
and whom he did *p.* them. he 30

predestinated
(*Revisions*, foreordained)

p. us to the adoption of. *Eph* 1:5
being *p.* according to the purpose. 11

preeminence

a man hath no *p.* above. *Eccl* 3:19
things he might have the *p.* *Col* 1:18
loveth to have the *p.* *3 John* 9

prefer

if I *p.* not Jerusalem. *Ps* 137:6

preferred, -ing

p. her and her maidens. *Esth* 2:9*
Daniel was *p.* above the. *Dan* 6:3*
cometh after me is *p.* before me. *John* 1:15*, 27*
who is *p.* before me, for he was. 30*
in honour *p.* one. *Rom* 12:10
observe, without *p.* *1 Tim* 5:21*

premeditate

neither do ye *p.*: but whatsoever shall be given you. *Mark* 13:11

preparation

now make *p.* for it. *1 Chr* 22:5
torches in the day of *p.* *Nah* 2:3
followed the day of *p.* *Mat* 27:62 *Mark* 15:42; *Luke* 23:54 *John* 19:14, 31, 42
p. of the gospel of peace. *Eph* 6:15

preparations

p. of the heart in man. *Pr* 16:1

prepare

my God, and I will *p.* *Ex* 15:2*
on sixth day they shall *p.* that. 16:5
for a drink offering *p.* *Num* 15:5
or for a ram *p.* thou for a meat. 6
the number that ye shall *p.* 12
Balaam said, *P.* me seven oxen. 23:1
build me seven altars, and *p.* 29
thou shalt *p.* thee a way. *Deut* 19:3
p. you victuals to pass. *Josh* 1:11
we said, Let us now *p.* to. 22:26
p. your hearts to the Lord. *1 Sam* 7:3
say to Ahab, *P.* chariot. *1 Ki* 18:44
to *p.* shewbread every. *1 Chr* 9:32
O Lord God, *p.* their heart. 29:18
to *p.* me timber in. *2 Chr* 2:9
p. chambers in house of. 31:11
and *p.* yourselves. 35:4
sanctify yourselves, and *p.* 6
banquet that I shall *p.* *Esth* 5:8
p. thyself to the search. *Job* 8:8*
if thou *p.* thine heart toward. 11:13*
though he *p.* raiment as clay. 27:16
he may *p.* it. 17
thou wilt *p.* their heart. *Ps* 10:17
they *p.* themselves without. 59:4
O *p.* mercy and truth, which. 61:7
that they *p.* a city for. 107:36
p. thy work without. *Pr* 24:27
yet they *p.* their meat in. 30:25
p. slaughter for his. *Isa* 14:21
p. the table, watch in the. 21:5
of him that crieth, *P.* ye the way of the Lord. 40:3; *Mal* 3:1; *Mat* 3:3 *Mark* 1:2, 3; *Luke* 3:4; 7:27
workman to *p.* a graven. *Isa* 40:20
shall say, Cast ye up, *p.* the. 57:14
p. ye the way of the people. 62:10
p. a table for that troop. 65:11
p. ye war against her, arise. *Jer* 6:4
and *p.* them for the day of. 12:3
I will *p.* destroyers against. 22:7
say ye, Stand fast and *p.* thee. 46:14
set up watchmen, *p.* the. 51:12
blow the trumpet, *p.* nations. 27
thou shalt *p.* thy bread. *Ezek* 4:15
p. thee stuff for removing. 12:3
I will *p.* thee to blood, and blood. 35:6
p. for thyself, thou and all. 38:7
p. every day a goat, they shall also *p.* 43:25
shall *p.* the sin offering. 45:17
on that day shall prince *p.* 22; 46:12
p. a meat offering. 45:24; 46:7, 14
shall *p.* his burnt offering. 46:2, 13
they shall *p.* the lamb and. 15
p. war, wake up. *Joel* 3:9
p. to meet thy God. *Amos* 4:12
even *p.* war against him. *Mi* 3:5
messenger, who shall *p.* *Mat* 11:10
we *p.* for thee to eat the passover? 26:17; *Mark* 14:12; *Luke* 22:8, 9
to *p.* his ways. *Luke* 1:76
I go to *p.* a place for. *John* 14:2, 3
who shall *p.* himself to the battle? *1 Cor* 14:8
but withal *p.* me also a. *Philem* 22

prepared

I *p.* the house and room. *Gen* 24:31
neither had they *p.* any. *Ex* 12:39
into the place I have *p.* 23:30
Sihon be built and *p.* *Num* 21:27*
I have *p.* seven altars. *Num* 23:4
Absalom *p.* chariots. *2 Sam* 15:1
Adonijah *p.* *1 Ki* 1:5
they *p.* timber. 5:18
the oracle he *p.* in the house. 6:19
he *p.* provision and sent. *2 Ki* 6:23
brethren had *p.* for. *1 Chr* 12:39
David *p.* a place for ark of God. 15:1 3:12; *2 Chr* 1:4; 3:1
David *p.* iron in abundance for the nails. *1 Chr* 22:3
David *p.* abundantly before his. 5, 14; 29:2
work of Solomon was *p.* *2 Chr* 8:16
Rehoboam *p.* not his heart. 12:14
Jehoshaphat *p.* his heart to. 19:3
for as yet the people had not *p.* 20:33
Uzziah *p.* shields and spears. 26:14
Jotham *p.* his ways before the. 27:6
Ahaz cast away we have *p.* 29:19
that God had *p.* the people. 36
they *p.* chambers in the house. 31:11
the service was *p.*, the. 35:10, 16
when Josiah had *p.* the temple. 20
Ezra had *p.* his heart. *Ezra* 7:10
now that which was *p.* *Neh* 5:18
for whom nothing is *p.* 8:10
p. for him a great chamber. 13:5
to the banquet that I have *p.* *Esth* 5:4, 12; 6:14
on gallows Haman *p.* 6:4; 7:10
p. it, yea, and searched. *Job* 28:27
when I *p.* my seat in the. 29:7
he *p.* for him the instruments of. *Ps* 7:13
p. his throne for judgement. 9:7
p. a net for my steps. 57:6
p. of thy goodness for the. 68:10
thou hast *p.* the light and. 74:16
the Lord hath *p.* his throne. 103:19
when he *p.* the heavens. *Pr* 8:27
judgements are *p.* for scorners. 19:29
horse is *p.* against the day. 21:31
of old, for the king it is *p.* *Isa* 30:33
eye seen what he hath *p.* 64:4*
bed, and a table *p.* *Ezek* 23:41
of the pipes was *p.* in thee. 28:13
be thou *p.* and prepare for. 38:7
for ye have *p.* lying words. *Dan* 2:9
gold which they *p.* for Baal. *Hos* 2:8
his going forth is *p.* as the. 6:3
now the Lord had *p.* a. *Jonah* 1:17
God *p.* a gourd. 4:6
God *p.* a worm. 7
God *p.* a vehement east wind. 8
the defence shall be *p.* *Nah* 2:5
for the Lord hath *p.* a. *Zeph* 1:7
shall be given to them for whom it is *p.* *Mat* 20:23; *Mark* 10:40
I have *p.* my dinner. *Mat* 22:4
inherit the kingdom *p.* 25:34
into fire *p.* for devil. 41
a large upper room *p.* *Mark* 14:15
ready a people *p.* for. *Luke* 1:17
which thou hast *p.* before face. 2:31
his Lord's will, but *p.* not. 12:47
they *p.* spices, and rested the. 23:56; 24:1
he had afore *p.* to glory. *Rom* 9:23
things God hath *p.* for. *1 Cor* 2:9
vessel *p.* unto every. *2 Tim* 2:21
body hast thou *p.* me. *Heb* 10:5
Noah *p.* an ark to the saving. 11:7
their God, for he hath *p.* for. 16
and the seven angels *p.* *Rev* 8:6
the locusts were like to horses *p.* 9:7
which were *p.* for an hour, a day. 15
and the woman hath a place *p.* 12:6
kings of east may be *p.* 16:12
the holy city, *p.* as a bride for. 21:2

preparedst

thou *p.* room before it. *Ps* 80:9

preparest

when thou *p.* a bullock. *Num* 15:8
thou *p.* a table before me. *Ps* 23:5
earth, thou *p.* them corn. 65:9*

prepareth

that *p.* his heart to. *2 Chr* 30:19
their belly *p.* deceit. *Job* 15:35
who *p.* rain for earth. *Ps* 147:8

preparing

p. him a chamber in. *Neh* 13:7
while the ark was *p.* *1 Pet* 3:20

presbytery
laying on of hands of *p.* *1 Tim* 4:14

prescribed, -ing
salt without *p.* how. *Ezra* 7:22
grievousness which they have *p.*
Isa 10:1*

presence
hid themselves from *p.* *Gen* 3:8
Cain went out from the *p.* of. 4:16
gone from the *p.* of Isaac. 27:30
brethren were troubled at his *p.* 45:3
why should we die in thy *p.*? 47:15
out from Pharaoh's *p.* *Ex* 10:11
my *p.* shall go with thee. 33:14
if thy *p.* go not with me, carry. 15
Israel departed from the *p.* 35:20
shall be cut off from my *p.* *Lev* 22:3
Moses went from the *p.* *Num* 20:6
avoided out of his *p.* *1 Sam* 18:11
slipped away out of Saul's *p.* 19:10
to play the madman in my *p.* 21:15
as I served in thy father's *p.* so will
I be in thy *p.* *2 Sam* 16:19
from the *p.* of Solomon. *1 Ki* 12:2
I regard *p.* of Jehoshaphat. *2 Ki* 3:14
went out from his *p.* a leper. 5:27
neither cast them from his *p.* 13:23
cast them out from his *p.* 24:20
that were in the king's *p.* 25:19*
honour are in his *p.* *1 Chr* 16:27
trees sing at the *p.* of God. 33*
the king sought the *p.* of. *2 Chr* 9:23
before this house in thy *p.* 20:9
altars of Baalim in his *p.* 34:4
before sad in his *p.* *Neh* 2:1
Mordecai went from the *p.* *Esth* 8:15
Satan went from the *p.* *Job* 1:12; 2:7
I am troubled at his *p.* 23:15
fall and perish at thy *p.* *Ps* 9:3
in thy *p.* is fulness of joy. 16:11
come forth from thy *p.* 17:2
them in the secret of thy *p.* 31:20
cast me not away from thy *p.* 51:11
perish at the *p.* of God. 68:2
Sinai moved at the *p.* of God. 8
come before his *p.* with. 95:2
hills melted like wax at the *p.* 97:5
before his *p.* with singing. 100:2
tremble, thou earth, at the *p.* 114:7
shall I flee from thy *p.*? 139:7
upright shall dwell in thy *p.* 140:13
go from the *p.* of a foolish. *Pr* 14:7
devour your land in your *p.* *Isa* 1:7
Egypt shall be moved at his *p.* 19:1
angel of his *p.* saved them. 63:9
that mountains might flow (flowed)
down at thy *p.* 64:1, 3
nations may tremble at thy *p.* 2
the cities broken down at *p.* *Jer* 4:26
will ye not tremble at my *p.*? 5:22
cast you out of my *p.* 23:39; 52:3
men shall shake at my *p.* *Ezek* 38:20
Jonah rose to flee from the *p.* of.
Jonah 1:3
men knew he fled from the *p.* 10
earth is burnt at his *p.* *Nah* 1:5
hold thy peace at the *p.* *Zeph* 1:7
eaten and drunk in thy *p.* *Luke* 13:26
times of refreshing come from the *p.*
Acts 3:19
they departed from the *p.* of. 5:41
should glory in his *p.* *1 Cor* 1:29
who in *p.* am base. *2 Cor* 10:1
letters weighty, but his bodily *p.* 10
have obeyed, not as in my *p.* only.
Phil 2:12
being taken from you in *p.* not in
heart. *1 Thes* 2:17
destruction from the *p.* *2 Thes* 1:9
present you faultless before *p.* of his
glory. *Jude* 24

***in the* presence**
he shall dwell *in the p.* of. *Gen* 16:12
in the p. of my people I give. 23:11
in the p. of the children of Heth. 18
Ishmael died *in the p.* of all. 25:18
brother's wife come unto him *in the*
p. of the elders. *Deut* 25:9
should I not serve *in the p.* of his
son? *2 Sam* 16:19
Solomon stood *in the p.* *1 Ki* 8:22
against Naboth, *in the p.* of. 21:13
these cast lots *in the p.* *1 Chr* 24:31
in the *p.* of Ahasuerus. *Esth* 1:10
a table *in the p.* of mine. *Ps* 23:5
now *in the p.* of all his. 116:14, 18
become surety *in the p.* *Pr* 17:18
put not forth thyself *in the p.* 25:6
than be put lower *in the p.* of. 7
Hananiah spake *in the p.* *Jer* 28:1
in the p. of people. 11
in the p. of witnesses. 32:12
I am Gabriel, that stand *in the p.* of
God. *Luke* 1:19
worship *in the p.* of them. 14:10
joy *in the p.* of the angels. 15:10
signs did Jesus *in the p.* *John* 20:30
denied him *in the p.* of. *Acts* 3:13
soundness *in the p.* of you all. 16
he gave thanks to God *in the p.* 27:35
in the p. of our Lord. *1 Thes* 2:19
appear *in the p.* of God. *Heb* 9:24
in the p. of holy angels, *in the p.*
Rev 14:10

present, *substantive*
he took a *p.* for Esau. *Gen* 32:13, 18
I will appease him with the *p.* 20
so went the *p.* over before him. 21
if I have found grace in thy sight,
then receive my *p.* at. 33:10
carry down the man a *p.* 43:11
men took the *p.* 15
they made ready the *p.* 25
brought him the *p.* in their hand. 26
Israel sent a *p.* to Eglon. *Judg* 3:15
he brought the *p.* 17
made an end to offer the *p.* 18
come and bring forth my *p.* 6:18
not a *p.* for the man of. *1 Sam* 9:7
a *p.* of the spoil of the. 30:26
a *p.* to his daughter. *1 Ki* 9:16*
they brought every man his *p.* 10:25
2 Chr 9:24
sent thee a *p.* of silver. *1 Ki* 15:19
the king said, Take a *p.* *2 Ki* 8:8
so Hazael went . . . and took a *p.* 9
sent it for a *p.* to the king of. 16:8
brought no *p.* to the king. 17:4
make an agreement by a *p.* 18:31*
Isa 36:16*
sent letters and a *p.* to Hezekiah.
2 Ki 20:12; *Isa* 39:1
a *p.* brought to Lord of. *Isa* 18:7
a *p.* of ivory and ebony. *Ezek* 27:15
carried to Assyria for a *p.* *Hos* 10:6

present, *adjective*
the people *p.* with him. *1 Sam* 13:15
loaves, or what there is *p.* 21:3
and be thou here *p.* *2 Sam* 20:4
Israel were numbered, and were all
p. *1 Ki* 20:27*
people *p.* here to offer. *1 Chr* 29:17
priests *p.* were sanctified. *2 Chr* 5:11
Israel *p.* at Jerusalem. 30:21
all *p.* went out and brake the. 31:1
all that were *p.* to stand. 34:32*
and all Israel *p.* offered. *Ezra* 8:25
the Jews *p.* in Shushan. *Esth* 4:16
God is a very *p.* help in. *Ps* 46:1
power of the Lord was *p.* *Luke* 5:17
there were *p.* at that season. 13:1
manifold more in this *p.* life. 18:30
being yet *p.* with you. *John* 14:25
are we all *p.* before God. *Acts* 10:33
and all elders were *p.* 21:18
received us because of *p.* rain. 28:2
to will is *p.* with me, but. *Rom* 7:18
would do good, evil is *p.* with. 21
sufferings of this *p.* time. 8:18
nor things *p.* nor things to come. 38
1 Cor 3:22
even at this *p.* time there. *Rom* 11:5
even to this *p.* hour we both hunger.
1 Cor 4:11
but *p.* in spirit, have judged as
though I were *p.* 5:3
good for the *p.* distress. 7:26
greater part remain to this *p.* 15:6
willing rather to be *p.* *2 Cor* 5:8*
that whether *p.* or absent. 9*
that I may not be bold when *p.* 10:2
was *p.* with you and wanted. 11:9
I foretell, as if I were *p.* the. 13:2
I write, lest being *p.* I should. 10
might deliver us from this *p.* world.
Gal 1:4
not only when I am *p.* with. *Gal* 4:18
I desire to be *p.* with you. 20
loved this *p.* world. *2 Tim* 4:10
godly in this *p.* world. *Tit* 2:12
figure for the time then *p.* *Heb* 9:9
for the *p.* seemeth joyous. 12:11
be established in the *p.* truth.
2 Pet 1:12*

present, -ed, *verb*
Joseph *p.* himself to his. *Gen* 46:29
he *p.* five of his brethren to. 47:2
and *p.* thyself there to me. *Ex* 34:2
meat offering, when it is *p.* *Lev* 2:8
in the day when he *p.* them. 7:35
Aaron's sons *p.* to him the. 9:12, 18
and they *p.* the burnt offering. 13
the priest shall *p.* the man. 14:11*
the two goats, and *p.* them. 16:7*
the scapegoat shall be *p.* 10
p. himself before the priest. 27:8*
then he shall *p.* the beast. 11*
and *p.* the tribe of Levi. *Num* 3:6*
p. yourselves before the. *Deut* 31:14
p. themselves before God. *Josh* 24:1
it under oak, and *p.* it. *Judg* 6:19
the tribes of Israel *p.* 20:2
now *p.* yourselves. *1 Sam* 10:19
Goliath the Philistine *p.* 17:16
sons of God came to *p.* *Job* 1:6
Satan came to *p.* himself. 2:1
will *p.* their supplication. *Jer* 36:7
I *p.* my supplication before. 38:26
ye sent to *p.* your supplication. 42:9
they *p.* the provocation. *Ezek* 20:28
do not *p.* our supplications. *Dan* 9:18
they *p.* to him gifts, gold. *Mat* 2:11
they brought him to *p.* *Luke* 2:22
called the saints, *p.* her. *Acts* 9:41
they *p.* Paul also before. 23:33
that ye *p.* your bodies a. *Rom* 12:1
by Jesus and *p.* us with. *2 Cor* 4:14
that I may *p.* you as a chaste. 11:2
he might *p.* it to himself. *Eph* 5:27
to *p.* you holy and. *Col* 1:22
we may *p.* every man perfect. 28
is able to *p.* you faultless. *Jude* 24*

presenting
p. my supplication before. *Dan* 9:20

presently
let them not fail to burn the fat *p.*
1 Sam 2:16
a fool's wrath is *p.* known. *Pr* 12:16
and *p.* the fig tree. *Mat* 21:19*
he shall *p.* give me more. 26:53*
him I hope to send *p.* *Phil* 2:23*

presents
brought him no *p.* *1 Sam* 10:27
they brought *p.* and. *1 Ki* 4:21
gave Shalmanezer *p.* *2 Ki* 17:3
p. to Jehoshaphat. *2 Chr* 17:5, 11
p. to Hezekiah. 32:23*
kings shall bring *p.* unto. *Ps* 68:29
and the isles shall bring *p.* 72:10
let all bring *p.* to him that. 76:11
give *p.* to Moresheth-gath. *Mi* 1:14*

preserve
that we may *p.* seed. *Gen* 19:32, 34
send me before you to *p.* life. 45:5
God sent me to *p.* you a posterity. 7
that he might *p.* us alive. *Deut* 6:24
thou shalt *p.* them from. *Ps* 12:7
p. me, O God, for in thee do. 16:1
and uprightness *p.* me. 25:21
my hiding place, shalt *p.* me. 32:7
let thy truth continually *p.* me. 40:11
Lord will *p.* him and keep. 41:2
mercy and truth which may *p.* 61:7
p. my life from fear of enemy. 64:1
p. thou those that are. 79:11
p. my soul, for I am holy. 86:2
p. thee from all evil, he shall *p.* thy.
121:7*
p. thy going out and coming in. 8*
p. me from violent man. 140:1, 4
discretion shall *p.* thee. *Pr* 2:11*
and she shall *p.* thee. 4:6
lips of the wise shall *p.* them. 14:3
mercy and truth *p.* king. 20:28
eyes of Lord *p.* knowledge. 22:12
he will *p.* Jerusalem. *Isa* 31:5
I will *p.* thee, and give thee. 49:8
thy children, I will *p.* *Jer* 49:11

lose his life shall *p.* it. *Luke* 17:33
the Lord will *p.* me unto his heavenly kingdom. *2 Tim* 4:18*

preserved, -eth

God, and my life is *p.* *Gen* 32:30
and *p.* us in all the way. *Josh* 24:17
us, who hath *p.* us. *1 Sam* 30:23
Lord *p.* David whithersoever he. *2 Sam* 8:6*; *1 Chr* 18:6*, 13*
thy visitation hath *p.* my. *Job* 10:12
as in days when God *p.* me. 29:2*
he *p.* not the life of the wicked. 36:6
for the Lord *p.* the faithful. *Ps* 31:23
his saints; they are *p.* for. 37:28
he *p.* the souls of his saints. 97:10
the Lord *p.* the simple. 116:6
Lord *p.* all them that love. 145:20
the Lord *p.* the strangers. 146:9
p. the way of his saints. *Pr* 2:8
keepeth his way *p.* his soul. 16:17
to restore the *p.* of Israel. *Isa* 49:6
by a prophet was he *p.* *Hos* 12:13
new wine into new bottles, and both are *p.* *Mat* 9:17; *Luke* 5:38
soul and body *p.* blameless. *1 Thes* 5:23
and *p.* in Jesus Christ, and. *Jude* 1

preserver

thee, O thou *p.* of men ? *Job* 7:20*

preservest

thou Lord hast made . . . and thou *p.* *Neh* 9:6
thou *p.* man and beast. *Ps* 36:6

presidents

three *p.*; Daniel was first. *Dan* 6:2
this Daniel was preferred above *p.* 3
the *p.* sought to find occasion. 4
these *p.* and princes assembled. 6, 7

press

[1] *To squeeze*, Gen 40:11. [2] *To crowd*, Luke 8:45. [3] *To urge*, Gen 19:3. [4] *A crowd or throng*, Luke 19:3.

could not come nigh for the *p.* *Mark* 2:4; *Luke* 8:19
came in *p.* behind him. *Mark* 5:27
Jesus turned him about in the *p.* 30
not see Jesus for the *p.* *Luke* 19:3

press
(*Wine press*)

for the *p.* is full, the fats. *Joel* 3:13
fifty vessels out of the *p.* *Hag* 2:16
see **wine**

press, -ed, -eth

Lot *p.* on the two angels. *Gen* 19:3
they *p.* sore on Lot, and came near. 9
took the grapes and *p.* them. 40:11
Delilah *p.* him daily. *Judg* 16:16
Absalom *p.* him. *2 Sam* 13:25, 27
posts *p.* on by the king's. *Esth* 8:14
and thy hand *p.* me sore. *Ps* 38:2
were their breasts *p.* *Ezek* 23:3
I am *p.* under you as a cart is *p.* *Amos* 2:13
p. on him for to touch. *Mark* 3:10
people *p.* to hear the word. *Luke* 5:1
measure, *p.* down and shaken. 6:38
throng thee and *p.* thee. 8:45
every man *p.* into it. 16:16*
Paul was *p.* in spirit, and. *Acts* 18:5*
were *p.* above measure. *2 Cor* 1:8*
I *p.* toward the mark. *Phil* 3:14

presses

thy *p.* shall burst with. *Pr* 3:10
tread out no wine in their *p.* *Isa* 16:10

pressfat

when one came to the *p.* *Hag* 2:16*

presume

prophet who shall *p.* to. *Deut* 18:20*
he that durst *p.* in his. *Esth* 7:5

presumed

they *p.* to go up to hill. *Num* 14:44

presumptuous

servant also from *p.* sins. *Ps* 19:13
p. are they, selfwilled. *2 Pet* 2:10*

presumptuously

if a man come *p.* on his. *Ex* 21:14
the soul that doeth aught *p.* *Num* 15:30*; *Deut* 17:12

went *p.* up into the hill. *Deut* 1:43
shall hear, and do no more *p.* 17:13
prophet hath spoken it *p.* 18:22

pretence

for a *p.* make long prayers. *Mat* 23:14; *Mark* 12:40
every way, whether in *p.* or in truth, Christ is preached. *Phil* 1:18

prevail

upward did the waters *p.* *Gen* 7:20
peradventure I shall *p.* *Num* 22:6
by what means we may *p.* *Judg* 16:5
strength shall no man *p.* *1 Sam* 2:9
if I *p.* against him, then ye. 17:9
great things and shalt still *p.* 26:25
thou shalt persuade him, and *p.* *1 Ki* 22:22; *2 Chr* 18:21
O Lord, let not man *p.* *2 Chr* 14:11
thou shalt not *p.* against. *Esth* 6:13
they shall *p.* against him. *Job* 15:24
robber shall *p.* against him. 18:9*
arise, O Lord, let not man *p.* *Ps* 9:19
with our tongue will we *p.* 12:4
iniquities *p.* against me. 65:3
if one *p.* against him. *Eccl* 4:12
to war, but could not *p.* *Isa* 7:1
to pray, but he shall not *p.* 16:12
he shall *p.* against his enemies. 42:13*
if so be thou mayest *p.* 47:12
they shall not *p.* against thee, for. *Jer* 1:19; 15:20; 20:11
toss, yet can they not *p.* 5:22
will be enticed, and we shall *p.* 20:10
who shall deal against him and shall *p.* *Dan* 11:7
gates of hell shall not *p.* *Mat* 16:18
Pilate saw he could *p.* nothing. 27:24
perceive ye how ye *p.* nothing. *John* 12:19

prevailed

the waters *p.* and. *Gen* 7:18, 19
the waters *p.* on the earth. 24
with my sister and have *p.* 30:8
when he saw he *p.* not against. 32:25
as a prince hast thou power with God and men, and hast *p.* 28
the famine *p.* over them. 47:20
blessings of thy father have *p.* 49:26
Israel *p.*: when he let down his hand, Amalek *p.* *Ex* 17:11
of the house of Joseph *p.* *Judg* 1:35
Othniel's hand *p.* against. 3:10
Israel *p.* against Jabin. 4:24
Midian *p.* against Israel. 6:2
David *p.* over Goliath. *1 Sam* 17:50
the men *p.* against us. *2 Sam* 11:23
king's word *p.* against Joab. 24:4
that followed Omri *p.* *1 Ki* 16:22
the famine *p.* in the city. *2 Ki* 25:3
for Judah *p.* above his. *1 Chr* 5:2
p. against Hamath-zobah. *2 Chr* 8:3
Judah *p.* because they relied. 13:18
p. against the Ammonites. 27:5
lest mine enemy say, I have *p.* *Ps* 13:4
they have not *p.* against me. 129:2
thou art stronger than I, and hast *p.* *Jer* 20:7
friends have *p.* against thee. 38:22
I weep because the enemy *p.* *Lam* 1:16
the same horn *p.* against. *Dan* 7:21
power over angel and *p.* *Hos* 12:4
have deceived thee and *p.* *Ob* 7
of the chief priests *p.* *Luke* 23:23
in whom the evil spirit was, leaped on them and *p.* *Acts* 19:16
so grew word of God and *p.* 20
of David hath *p.* to open. *Rev* 5:5
dragon and his angels *p.* not. 12:8

prevailest

p. for ever against him. *Job* 14:20

prevaileth

into my bones, and it *p.* *Lam* 1:13

prevent

(*Usually used in its original sense of going before, either actually or symbolically*)

why did the knees *p.* me ? *Job* 3:12*
my mercy shall *p.* me. *Ps* 59:10†
mercies speedily *p.* us. 79:8†
morning shall my prayer *p.* 88:13*
eyes *p.* nightwatches. *Ps* 119:148*
The evil shall not *p.* us. *Amos* 9:10
we shall not *p.* them who are asleep. *1 Thes* 4:15*

prevented

the snares of death *p.* me. *2 Sam* 22:6*; *Ps* 18:5*
they *p.* me in the day of my calamities. 19*; *Ps* 18:18*
days of affliction *p.* me. *Job* 30:27*
who hath *p.* me that I ? 41:11*
I *p.* the dawning of. *Ps* 119:147†
they *p.* with their bread. *Isa* 21:14*
Jesus *p.* him, saying, Simon, of. *Mat* 17:25*

preventest

thou *p.* him with blessings. *Ps* 21:3†

prey

from the *p.* my son. *Gen* 49:9
he shall devour the *p.* 27
that our wives and children shall be a *p.*? *Num* 14:3, 31; *Deut* 1:39
lie down till he eat of *p.* *Num* 23:24
captives and *p.* to Moses. 31:12
take the sum of the *p.* that. 26
and divide the *p.* into two parts. 27
booty being the rest of the *p.* 32
only the cattle we took for a *p.* to. *Deut* 2:35; 3:7; *Josh* 8:2, 27; 11:14
divided the *p.*; to Sisera a *p.* of. *Judg* 5:30
give me the earrings of his *p.* 8:24
man the earrings of his *p.* 25
Judah shall become a *p.* *2 Ki* 21:14
a *p.* in the land of captivity. *Neh* 4:4
take the spoil of them for a *p.* *Esth* 3:13; 8:11
on the *p.* they laid not. 9:15, 16
perisheth for lack of *p.* *Job* 4:11
eagle that hasteth to the *p.* 9:26
as wild asses; rising betimes for a *p.* 24:5*
wilt thou hunt the *p.* for ? 38:39
thence she seeketh the *p.* 39:29
like a lion greedy of his *p.* *Ps* 17:12
than the mountains of *p.* 76:4
lions roar after their *p.* 104:21
not given us for a *p.* to their. 124:6
lieth in wait as for a *p.* *Pr* 23:28
roar and lay hold of the *p.* *Isa* 5:29
that widows may be their *p.* 10:2
the *p.* of an hypocritical nation. 6
young lion roaring on his *p.* 31:4
the *p.* of a great spoil divided. 33:23
for a *p.* and none delivereth. 42:22
p. be taken from the mighty ? 49:24
the *p.* of the terrible shall be. 25
he that departeth from evil a *p.* 59:15
his life shall be to him for a *p.* *Jer* 21:9; 38:2; 39:18; 45:5
p. on thee will I give for a *p.* 30:16
hands of strangers for *p.* *Ezek* 7:21
it learned to catch the *p.* 19:3
like wolves ravening the *p.* 22:27
make a *p.* of thy merchandise. 26:12
take her spoil, and take her *p.* 29:19
because my flock became a *p.* 34:8
flock shall no more be a *p.* 22, 28
to the cities that became a *p.* 36:4
minds, to cast it out for a *p.* 5
to take a spoil and a *p.* 38:12, 13
scatter among them the *p.* *Dan* 11:24
will lion roar when no *p.*? *Amos* 3:4
lion filled his holes with *p.* *Nah* 2:12
I will cut off thy *p.* from. 13
city, the *p.* departeth not. 3:1
that I rise up to the *p.* *Zeph* 3:8

price

[1] *The sum asked for a thing when selling it*, 2 Sam 24:24. [2] *The worth or value of a thing*, Job 28:18. [3] *Wages or hire*, Zech 11:12.

thou shalt increase the *p.* . . . thou shalt diminish the *p.* *Lev* 25:16, 50
shall give him again the *p.* of. 52
not bring *p.* of a dog. *Deut* 23:18*
I will buy it at a *p.* *2 Sam* 24:24; *1 Chr* 21:22, 24
merchants received the linen yarn at a *p.* *1 Ki* 10:28; *2 Chr* 1:16
man knoweth not the *p.* *Job* 28:13, 15
p. of wisdom is above rubies. 18

increase wealth by their p. Ps 44:12
a p. in hand of a fool? Pr 17:16
goats are the p. of the field. 27:26
virtuous woman, for her p. 31:10
go my captives not for p. Isa 45:13
buy wine and milk without p. 55:1
to the spoil without p. Jer 15:13
p. weighed for my p. Zech 11:12*
a goodly p. that I was prized at. 13
one pearl of great p. Mat 13:46
because it is the p. of blood. 27:6
took p. of him that was valued. 9
kept back part of the p. Acts 5:2, 3
they counted the p. of them. 19:19
for ye are bought with a p.
1 Cor 6:20; 7:23
in sight of God of great p. 1 Pet 3:4

prices

brought p. of the things. Acts 4:34

pricked

I was p. in my reins. Ps 73:21
they were p. in their heart. Acts 2:37

pricking

a p. briar to Israel. Ezek 28:24

pricks

those that remain be p. Num 33:55
it is hard to kick against the p.
Acts 9:5*; 26:14*

pride

I will break the p. of. Lev 26:19
I know thy p. and. 1 Sam 17:28
humbled himself for p. 2 Chr 32:26
that he may hide p. from man.
Job 33:17
they cry because of the p. 35:12
his scales are his p. shut up. 41:15
king over all children of p. 34
the wicked in his p. Ps 10:2
through p. of his countenance. 4
hide them from the p. of man. 31:20*
let not the foot of p. come. 36:11
let them be taken in their p. 59:12
p. compasseth them as chain. 73:6
p. . . . do I hate. Pr 8:13
when p. cometh. 11:2
by p. cometh contention. 13:10
the foolish is a rod of p. 14:3
p. goeth before destruction. 16:18
man's p. shall bring him low. 29:23
in the p. of their hearts. Isa 9:9
p. of Moab, even of his haughtiness
and his p. 16:6; Jer 48:29
stain the p. of all glory. Isa 23:9
shall bring down their p. 25:11
woe to the crown of p. 28:1, 3
I will mar the p. of Judah. Jer 13:9
my soul shall weep for your p. 17
the p. of thy heart hath. 49:16
blossomed, p. hath. Ezek 7:10
iniquity of thy sister Sodom, p. 16:49
not mentioned in the day of thy p. 56
and the p. of her power shall. 30:6
those that walk in p. he is. Dan 4:37
mind was hardened in p. 5:20
the p. of Israel doth testify.
Hos 5:5; 7:10
p. of thine heart hath deceived. Ob 3
they have for their p. Zeph 2:10
them away that rejoice in thy p. 3:11
the p. of the Philistines. Zech 9:6
the p. of Assyria shall be. 10:11
the p. of Jordan is spoiled. 11:3
the heart proceedeth p. Mark 7:22
lifted up p. he fall into. 1 Tim 3:6
the p. of life, is not of. 1 John 2:16

priest

There were priests in every nation, since the term is used of all who have charge of the religious life of a people. The Jewish priesthood as a definite body, dated from the appointment of Aaron and his sons as Priests of Jehovah at the time of the Exodus. At about the same time the entire tribe of Levi was set apart to do the non-priestly duties of the tabernacle, and the religious services. The priests were all descendants of Aaron, the legal head of the house of Aaron in each generation being High Priest. The priestly duties included the instruction of the people, sanitary and medicinal care for their welfare, and the services at the house of God.

Jesus Christ, as the fulfilment of the old dispensation, is called the High Priest of those who have accepted him.

p. of the most high God. Gen 14:18
Heb 7:1
p. of Midian had seven. Ex 2:16
that son that is p. in his stead.
29:30; Lev 16:32
the p. shall burn it all on the altar.
Lev 1:9, 13, 17; 2:2, 9, 16; 3:11
16; 4:10, 31, 35; 7:5, 31
the p. shall lay them in order. 1:12
when it is presented to the p. 2:8
if the p. that is anointed do sin. 4:3
the p. shall dip his finger. 6, 17
the p. shall make an atonement. 4:20
26; 5:6; 6:7; 12:8; 15:15, 30
16:30; 19:22
p. shall take of blood. 4:25; 30, 34
he shall bring them to the p. 5:8
the remnant shall be the p.'s. 13
p. shall put on his linen. 6:10
p. shall have to himself the skin. 7:8
it shall be the p.'s that offereth it. 9
14; 14:13
the p. shall look on the plague. 13:3
5, 6, 17, 20, 21, 25, 26, 27, 30, 31, 32
p. shall look on him and pronounce
unclean. 13:8, 11, 20, 22, 25, 30, 44
the p. shall shut him up. 4, 5, 31, 33
the p. shall pronounce him clean.
13:6, 17, 23, 28, 34
brought to the p. 13:9
come to the p. 16; 14:2
p. that maketh him clean. 14:11
the p. shall dip his right finger. 16
the house, shall come and tell p. 35
the p. shall pronounce the house. 48
if the daughter of a p. profane. 21:9
if the p. buy any soul with. 22:11
if p.'s daughter be married. 12, 13
a sheaf of firstfruits to the p. 23:10
the p. shall wave it before the. 11
p. shall value him, according. 27:8
possession thereof shall be p.'s. 21
trespass be recompensed to the p.
Num 5:8
man shall bring wife to the p. 15
the p. shall execute upon her. 30
this is holy for the p. with the. 6:20
p. shall wash and be unclean. 19:7
in land till death of high p. 35:32
will not hearken to p. Deut 17:12
the p.'s due from people. 18:3
are come nigh to battle, the p. 20:2
go to the p. in those days. 26:3
sons who became his p. Judg 17:5
and be unto me a father and a p. 10
seeing I have a Levite to my p. 13
Micah hired me, and I am his p. 18:4
a father and a p.: better a p. unto one
man, or a p. unto a tribe? 19
all that the p. took for. 1 Sam 2:14
give flesh to roast for the p. 15
choose him out of Israel to be my p.
28
I will raise me up a faithful p. 35
while Saul talked to the p. 14:19
said the p., Let us draw near to. 36
the p. answered, There is no. 21:4
p. gave them hallowed bread. 6
Abiathar from being p. 1 Ki 2:27
p. had said, Let her not be slain.
2 Ki 11:15
the same may be a p. of them that
are no gods. 2 Chr 13:9
Israel without a teaching p. 15:3
till there stood up a p. Ezra 2:63
Neh 7:65
a p. for ever after the order of.
Ps 110:4; Heb 5:6; 7:17, 21
Uriah the p. and Zechariah. Isa 8:2
as with people, so with the p. 24:2
p. and prophet have erred. 28:7
from prophet to the p. every one
dealeth falsely. Jer 6:13; 8:10
prophet and p. go to a land. 14:18
law shall not perish from p. 18:18
prophet and p. are profane. Jer 23:11
prophet and p. shall. 33, 34
thee p. instead of Jehoiada. 29:26
despised the king and the p. Lam 2:6
shall the p. and prophets be slain? 20
but the law shall perish from the p.
Ezek 7:26
near to do the office of a p. 44:13
nor shall any p. drink wine when. 21
a widow that had a p. before. 22
to the p. the first of your dough. 30
p. shall not eat of any thing. 31
that strive with the p. Hos 4:4
thou shalt be no p. to me. 6
shall be, like people, like p. 9
the p. of Beth-el sent to. Amos 7:10
and he shall be p. on. Zech 6:13
the p.'s lips should keep. Mal 2:7
go thy way, shew thyself to the p.
Mat 8:4; Mark 1:44; Luke 5:14
p. named Zacharias. Luke 1:5
there came down a certain p. 10:31
the p. of Jupiter brought oxen and
garlands. Acts 14:13
abideth a p. continually. Heb 7:3
what need another p. should rise? 11
Melchizedek ariseth another p. 15
not without oath he was made p. 20
on earth, he should not be a p. 8:4
every p. standeth daily. 10:11

see chief

high priest

high p. shalt not uncover. Lev 21:10
city of refuge till the death of the
high p. Num 35:25; Josh 20:6
much money in chest, the high p.
came. 2 Ki 12:10; 2 Chr 24:11
to Hilkiah the high p. 2 Ki 22:4
Eliashib the high p. rose up. Neh 3:1
Joshua the high p. standing.
Zech 3:1, 8; 6:11
to the palace of the high p.
Mat 26:3; Luke 22:54
struck servant of high p. Mat 26:51
Luke 22:50; John 18:10
led him to Caiaphas the high p.
Mat 26:57; John 18:24
the high p. rent his clothes.
Mat 26:65; Mark 14:63
days of Abiathar high p. Mark 2:26
Caiaphas being high p. John 11:49
51; 18:13
disciple was known to high p. 18:15
answerest thou the high p. so? 22
of the kindred of high p. Acts 4:6
said high p., Are these things? 7:1
Saul went to the high p. and. 9:1
high p. doth bear me witness. 22:5
revilest thou God's high p.? 23:4
might be a faithful high p. Heb 2:17
consider Apostle, High P. of. 3:1
great high p. that is passed. 4:14
not an high p. which cannot be. 15
every high p. is ordained. 5:1
Christ glorified not himself to be an
high p. 5
an high p. after the order. 10; 6:20
such an high p. became us. 7:26
we have such an high p. who. 8:1
high p. is ordained to offer gifts. 3
into second went high p. alone. 9:7
Christ being come an high p. of. 11
as high p. entereth holy place. 25
having an high p. over house. 10:21
into sanctuary by high p. 13:11

see office

priesthood

anointing shall be an everlasting p.
Ex 40:15; Num 25:13
and seek ye the p. also? Num 16:10
shall bear iniquity of your p. 18:1
for p. of the Lord is their. Josh 18:7
therefore were they, as polluted, put
from the p. Ezra 2:62; Neh 7:64
the p., the covenant of p. Neh 13:29
who receive the office of p. Heb 7:5
were by the Levitical p. 11
for the p. being changed, there. 12
spake nothing concerning the p. 14
this man hath an unchangeable p. 24
an holy p. 1 Pet 2:5
ye are a royal p. 9

priests

land of *p.* bought he not, for the *p.* had portion assigned. *Gen* 47:22
except land of *p.* only, not. 26
be to me a kingdom of *p.* *Ex* 19:6
the *p.* shall sprinkle. *Lev* 1:11; 3:2
males among the *p.* shall eat. 6:29
unto one of his sons the *p.* 13:2
make an atonement for the *p.* 16:33
holy to the Lord for the *p.* 23:20
shall stand before *p.* *Deut* 19:17
p. that bare the ark stood. *Josh* 3:17
where the *p.*' feet stood. 4:3, 9
the *p.* bare seven trumpets. 6:4, 13
p. took up the ark of the Lord. 12
were *p.* to tribe of Dan. *Judg* 18:30
Hophni and Phinehas *p.* *1 Sam* 1:3
nor the *p.* of Dagon tread on. 5:5
Philistines called for the *p.* 6:2
king said, Turn and slay the *p.* 22:17
Doeg, Turn thou and fall on the *p.* 18
that Saul had slain the Lord's *p.* 21
and the *p.* took up the ark. *1 Ki* 8:3
made *p.* of the lowest. 12:31; 13:33
on thee shall he offer the *p.* of. 13:2
Jehu slew Ahab's *p.*, he. *2 Ki* 10:11
call me all Baal's *p.*, let none. 19
p. had not repaired breaches. 12:6
carry thither one of the *p.* ye. 17:27
put down idolatrous *p.* of king. 23:5
slew all the *p.* of the high places. 20
sea was for *p.* to wash in. *2 Chr* 4:6
p. sounding with trumpets. 5:12
p. could not stand to minister. 14
let thy *p.* be clothed with. 6:41
appointed the courses of the *p.* 8:14
ordained *p.* for high places. 11:15
have ye not cast out the *p.*? 13:9
p. with trumpets to cry alarm. 12
into house of Lord save the *p.* 23:6
with him fourscore *p.* of the. 26:17
Uzziah was wroth with the *p.* 19
p. were too few, they could. 29:34
p. had not sanctified. 30:3
Josiah burnt bones of the *p.* 34:5
Josiah set *p.* in their charges. 35:2
to the *p.* for passover offerings. 8
set the *p.* in their divisions. *Ezra* 6:18
and killed the passover for *p.* 20
offering of the people and *p.* 7:16
and our *p.* been delivered into. 9:7
as yet told it to the *p.* *Neh* 2:16
repaired the *p.*, men of the plain. 3:22
hath come on us and our *p.* 9:32
we nor our *p.* kept thy law. 34
laid the offerings of the *p.* 13:5
their *p.* fell by the sword. *Ps* 78:64
Moses and Aaron among his *p.* 99:6
let thy *p.* be clothed with. 132:9
clothe her *p.* with salvation. 16
he sent elders of *p.* covered. *Isa* 37:2
but ye shall be named the *p.* of. 61:6
against the *p.* thereof. *Jer* 1:18
p. said not, Where is the Lord? 2:8
Israel ashamed; their kings, *p.* 26
p. shall be astonished. 4:9
p. bare rule by their means. 5:31
bones of the *p.* they shall bring. 8:1
fill the *p.* with drunkenness. 13:13
I will satiate the souls of the *p.* 31:14
me to anger, they and their *p.* 32:32
into captivity with his *p.* 48:7; 49:3
her *p.* sigh, her virgins. *Lam* 1:4
p. and elders gave up the ghost. 19
for the iniquities of her *p.* 4:13
respected not persons of *p.* 16
her *p.* violated my law. *Ezek* 22:26
said, This chamber is for *p.* 40:45
shall be for the *p.* 45:4; 48:10, 11
hear this, O *p.*; and hearken, ye house of Israel. *Hos* 5:1
p. murder in the way by. 6:9
p., the Lord's ministers, mourn. *Joel* 1:9, 13; 2:17
p. thereof teach for hire. *Mi* 3:11
I will cut off names of *p.* *Zeph* 1:4
her *p.* have polluted the. 3:4
ask *p.* concerning the law. *Hag* 2:11
O *p.* that despise my name. *Mal* 1:6
O ye *p.*, this commandment is. 2:1
only for the *p.* to eat. *Mat* 12:4
p. in temple profane the sabbath, and. 5; *Mark* 2:26; *Luke* 6:4
not lawful to eat but for *p.* *Mark* 2:26
shew yourselves to the *p.* *Luke* 17:14
the *p.* and captain came. *Acts* 4:1
company of *p.* were obedient. 6:7
sons of Sceva chief of the *p.* 19:14
those *p.* were made without an oath. *Heb* 7:21
they truly were many *p.* 23
seeing there are *p.* that offer. 8:4
p. went always into the first. 9:6
hath made us kings and *p.* to God. *Rev* 1:6; 5:10
be *p.* of God and of Christ. 20:6

see **chief, Levites, office**

high **priests**

and Caiaphas being *high p.* *Luke* 3:2
daily as those *high p.* to. *Heb* 7:27
for the law maketh men *high p.* 28

prince

This name is given, [1] *To God, who is the supreme Ruler and Governor*, Dan 8:11. [2] *To Christ, who is called the* Prince of Peace, Isa 9:6; the Prince of Life, Acts 3:15; the Prince of the kings of the earth, Rev 1:5. [3] *To the chief of the priests, called the* princes of *the sanctuary*, Isa 43:28. [4] *To men of princely excellency and worth*, Eccl 10:7. [5] *To the nobles, counsellors, and officers in a kingdom*, Isa 10:8. [6] *To the chief, or principal men of families, or tribes*, Num 17:6. [7] *To the devil, called* the prince of this world, *John* 12:31; *who boasts of having all the kingdoms of the earth at his disposal*, Mat 4:9.

thou art a mighty *p.* *Gen* 23:6
as a *p.* hast power with God. 32:28
when Shechem, *p.* of the. 34:2
who made thee a *p.* over? *Ex* 2:14
each *p.* shall offer on. *Num* 7:11
thyself altogether a *p.* over. 16:13
for each *p.* a rod, even twelve. 17:6
Cozbi the daughter of a *p.* 25:18
take one *p.* of every tribe to. 34:18
of each chief house a *p.* *Josh* 22:14
is a *p.* fallen in Israel? *2 Sam* 3:38
I will make him a *p.* all. *1 Ki* 11:34
a *p.* over my people. 14:7; 16:2
Sheshbazzar *p.* of Judah. *Ezra* 1:8
where is house of the *p.*? *Job* 21:28
as a *p.* would I go near unto. 31:37
but in want of people is destruction of *p.* *Pr* 14:28
much less do lying lips a *p.* 17:7
put lower in presence of the *p.* 25:7
by long forbearing is a *p.* 15*
p. that wanteth understanding. 28:16
how beautiful are thy feet, O *p.*'s daughter. *S of S* 7:1
the *P.* of Peace. *Isa* 9:6
Seraiah was a quiet *p.* *Jer* 51:59*
the *p.* shall be clothed. *Ezek* 7:27
this burden concerneth the *p.* 12:10
p. shall bear on his shoulder. 12
profane wicked *p.* of Israel. 21:25
son of man, say to *p.* of Tyrus. 28:2
be no more a *p.* of Egypt. 30:13
David a *p.* among them. 34:24
David shall be their *p.* for. 37:25
against Gog, the land of Magog, the chief *p.* of. 38:2, 3; 39:1
this gate is for the *p.*; the *p.* 44:3
and a portion shall be for the *p.* 45:7
it shall be the *p.*'s part to give. 17
shall the *p.* prepare a bullock. 22
p. shall enter by the porch. 46:2
the burnt offering that the *p.* shall. 4
and when the *p.* shall enter he. 8
and the *p.* in the midst of them. 10
p. prepares a voluntary burnt. 12
if the *p.* give a gift to any of his. 16
after, it shall return to the *p.* but. 17
p. shall not take of the people's. 18
residue shall be for the *p.* on. 48:21
to whom *p.* of the eunuchs. *Dan* 1:7
requested of *p.* of the eunuchs. 8
favour with the *p.* of the eunuchs. 9
magnified himself even to *p.* 8:11
up against the *p.* of princes. 25
unto the Messiah the *P.* 9:25
people of the *p.* that shall come. 26
p. of Persia withstood me. *Dan* 10:13
p. of Persia, *p.* of Grecia come. 20
with me, but Michael your *p.* 21
but a *p.* for his own behalf. 11:18
also the *p.* of the covenant. 22
Michael stand up, the great *p.* 12:1
Israel shall abide without *p.* *Hos* 3:4
the *p.* and the judge ask. *Mi* 7:3
casteth out devils by *p.* of devils. *Mat* 9:34; 12:24; *Mark* 3:22
p. of this world shall be. *John* 12:31
the *p.* of this world cometh. 14:30
the *p.* of this world is judged. 16:11
killed *P.* of life, whom. *Acts* 3:15
hath God exalted to be a *P.* 5:31
p. of the power of the air. *Eph* 2:2
Jesus Christ the *P.* of. *Rev* 1:5*

princes

the *p.* also of Pharaoh. *Gen* 12:15
twelve *p.* shall Ishmael beget. 17:20; 25:16
a wagon for two *p.* *Num* 7:3
the *p.* offered. 10
rose up 250 *p.* 16:2
the *p.* digged a well. 21:18
and the *p.* of Moab abode with. 22:8
Balak sent yet again *p.* more. 15
p. of the congregation. *Josh* 9:15
whom Moses smote with *p.* 13:21*
with Phinehas ten *p.* sent to. 22:14
kings, give ear, O ye *p.* *Judg* 5:3
and the *p.* of Issachar were with. 15
the two *p.* of the Midianites. 7:25
he described the *p.* of Succoth. 8:14
poor, to set them among *p.* *1 Sam* 2:8
p. of the Philistines were wroth. 29:4
young men of the *p.* *1 Ki* 20:14
p. in their families. *1 Chr* 4:38
p. and people will be at thy. 28:21*
left spoil before the *p.* *2 Chr* 28:14
do the commandment of *p.* 30:12
p. gave a thousand bullocks. 24
p. gave willingly to the people. 35:8
treasures of his *p.* brought. 36:18
all the king's mighty *p.* *Ezra* 7:28
hand of *p.* hath been chief. 9:2
according to the counsel of *p.* 10:8
our *p.* kept thy law. *Neh* 9:34
our *p.* Levites, and priests seal. 38
he made a feast to all his *p.* *Esth* 1:3; 2:18
advanced him above the *p.* 5:11
of one of the king's noble *p.* 6:9
with *p.* that had gold. *Job* 3:15
leadeth *p.* away spoiled. 12:19*
he poureth contempt on *p.* and. 21
the *p.* refrained talking, and. 29:9
is it fit to say to *p.*, Ye are? 34:18*
accepteth not the persons of *p.* 19
thou mayest make *p.* in all the earth. *Ps* 45:16
p. of the people are gathered. 47:9
the *p.* of Zebulun, the *p.* 68:27
p. shall come out of Egypt. 31
he shall cut off the spirit of *p.* 76:12
and fall like one of the *p.* 82:7
to bind his *p.* at his pleasure. 105:22
he poureth contempt upon *p.* 107:40
set him with *p.* even with the *p.* 113:8
than to put confidence in *p.* 118:9
p. also did sit and speak. 119:23
p. have persecuted me without. 161
put not your trust in *p.* nor in. 146:3
p. and all judges of the earth. 148:11
by me *p.* decree justice. *Pr* 8:15
p. rule. 16
it is not good to strike *p.* 17:26*
a servant to rule over *p.* 19:10
many are the *p.* thereof. 28:2
not for *p.* to drink strong drink. 31:4
p. walking as servants. *Eccl* 10:7
thy *p.* eat in the morning. 16
blessed art thou, when thy *p.* eat. 17
thy *p.* are rebellious. *Isa* 1:23
give children to be their *p.* 3:4
enter into judgement with the *p.* 14
are not my *p.* altogether kings? 10:8
p. of Zoan fools, *p.* of. 19:11, 13
ye *p.* and anoint the shield. 21:5
Tyre, whose merchants are *p.* 23:8
his *p.* were at Zoan, his. 30:4
his *p.* shall be afraid of the. 31:9
and *p.* shall rule in judgement. 32:1

all her p. shall be nothing. Isa 34:12
bringeth the p. to nothing. 40:23
come upon p. as on mortar. 41:25*
I have profaned the p. 43:28
p. also shall worship because. 49:7
brasen walls against the p. Jer 1:18
they, their kings and p. are. 2:26
the heart of the p. shall be. 4:9
bring out the bones of his p. 8:1
kings and p. sitting on throne. 17:25
the king of Judah and his p. 24:8
the p. said, This man is not worthy to die. 26:16
they and their kings and p. 32:32
his p. I will give to their. 34:21
p. were wroth with Jeremiah. 37:15
to the king of Babylon's p. 38:17
if p. hear that I have talked. 25
incense that ye and your p. 44:21
Chemosh and his p. go. 48:7; 49:3
will destroy from thence p. 49:38
a sword is on her p. and her. 50:35
I will make drunk her p. and. 51:57
p. are become like harts. Lam 1:6
polluted the kingdom and p. 2:2
p. are among the Gentiles. 9
p. are hanged up by hand. 5:12
p. like wolves ravening. Ezek 22:27
all of them p. to look to. 23:15
Edom and her p. with their. 32:29
there the p. of the north, all. 30
ye shall drink blood of the p. 39:18
my p. shall no more oppress. 45:8
to gather together the p. Dan 3:2*
set over the kingdom 120 p. 6:1*
Daniel preferred above the p. 3*
p. sought to find occasion against. 4*
stand up against prince of p. 8:25
who spake in thy name to our p. 9:6
confusion of face to our p. and. 8
Michael one of the chief p. 10:13
one of his p. shall be strong. 11:5
make p. glad with lies. Hos 7:3
p. have made him sick with wine. 5
their p. shall fall by the sword. 16
have made p. and I knew it not. 8:4
for the burthen of the king of p. 10
all their p. are revolters. 9:15
give me a king and p. 13:10
their king shall go into captivity, he and his p. Amos 1:15
hear, ye p. of Israel. Mi 3:1*, 9
the p. shall be a scorn. Hab 1:10
I will punish the p. and. Zeph 1:8
p. within her are roaring lions. 3:3
p. of Gentiles exercise. Mat 20:25*
wisdom of the p. of this. 1 Cor 2:6*
none of the p. of this world knew. 8*

all the **princes**

carried away all the p. 2 Ki 24:14
all the p. submitted. 1 Chr 29:24
and destroyed all the p. 2 Chr 24:23
done wrong to all the p. Esth 1:16
seat above all the p. that were. 3:1
all their p. as Zebah. Ps 83:11
Jeremiah spake to all the p. and. Jer 26:12
read it in ears of all the p. 36:21
all the p. of the sea. Ezek 26:16
will slay all the p. Amos 2:3
see **Israel**

princes *of Judah*

p. of Judah on wall. Neh 12:31
there is p. of Judah. Ps 68:27
slew all the p. of Judah. Jer 52:10
p. of Judah are like to. Hos 5:10
not least among p. of Judah. Mat 2:6

princess

p. among the provinces. Lam 1:1

princesses

Solomon had . . . wives, p. 1 Ki 11:3

principal

also unto thee p. spices. Ex 30:23*
even restore it in the p. Lev 6:5*
his trespass with the p. Num 5:7*
son of Nathan was p. 1 Ki 4:5*
the p. scribe of the host. 2 Ki 25:19*; Jer 52:25*
one p. household taken. 1 Chr 24:6*
priests, even p. fathers cast. 31*
Mattaniah p. to begin. Neh 11:17*
wisdom is the p. thing. 4:7
broken down p. plants. Isa 16:8*
cast in the p. wheat and. 28:25*
wallow in the ashes, ye p. Jer 25:34
no way to flee, nor the p. of flock. 35
against him eight p. men. Mi 5:5
p. men of the city entered with. Acts 25:23

principality, -ties

your p. shall come down. Jer 13:18*
angels, p. nor powers be able to. Rom 8:38
far above all p. and power. Eph 1:21
that now to p. might be known. 3:10
we wrestle against p. and. 6:12
p. were created by him. Col 1:16
the head of all p. and power. 2:10
having spoiled p. he made a shew. 15
in mind to be subject to p. Tit 3:1

principles

one teach you the first p. Heb 5:12
leaving the p. of the doctrine. 6:1

print

ye shall not p. any marks. Lev 19:28

print, *substantive*

thou settest a p. on heels. Job 13:27*
in his hands p. of nails, and put my finger into the p. of. John 20:25

printed

Oh that my words were p. Job 19:23*

Priscilla, *see* **Aquila**

prison

(*The prisons of Bible times were generally windowless dungeons, below ground; sometimes a cave or pit was used for the purpose. The prisoners were bound, or chained*)

Potiphar put Joseph in p. Gen 39:20
keeper of the p. committed to. 22
and baker in p. where Joseph. 40:3
bound in the house of your p. 42:19
put this fellow in p. 1 Ki 22:27; 2 Chr 18:26
bound Hoshea in p. 2 Ki 17:4
brought Jehoiachin out of p. 25:27
and changed his p. garments. 29; Jer 52:31, 33
Palal repaired by the court of the p. Neh 3:25*
my soul out of p. to praise. Ps 142:7
for out of p. he cometh. Eccl 4:14
shall be shut up in the p. Isa 24:22
bring out prisoners from the p. 42:7*
all of them hid in p. houses. 22
taken from p. and judgement. 53:8*
to proclaim opening of the p. 61:1
shouldest put him in p. Jer 29:26*
Jeremiah . . . in court of p. 32:2*
Jews that sat in court of the p. 12*
he was shut up in court of the p. 33:1*; 37:21*; 38:6*, 28*; 39:15*
they had not put him into p. 37:4
put him in p. in Jonathan's. 15
took Jeremiah out of the p. 39:14*
he put Zedekiah in p. till his. 52:11
John was cast into p. Mat 4:12*
and thou be cast into p. 5:25; Luke 12:58
John heard in p. the works. Mat 11:2
put him in p. for Herodias'. 14:3
he sent and beheaded John in p. 10; Mark 6:27
cast him into p. till he. Mat 18:30
in p. and ye came unto me. 25:36
thee in p. and came to thee? 39, 44
after John was put in p. Mark 1:14*
sent and bound John in p. 6:17
that he shut up John in p. Luke 3:20
thee both to p. and to death. 22:33
murder was cast into p. 23:19, 25
for John was not yet cast into p. John 3:24
put apostles in common p. Acts 5:18*
by night opened the p. doors. 19
sent to the p. 21*
found them not in the p. 22
committed them to p. 8:3
Peter was put in p. 12:4
he was kept in p. 5
light shined in the p. 7*
Lord brought him out of p. 17
Paul and Silas cast into p. 16:23
the inner p. Acts 16:24
seeing the p. doors open. 27*
saints did I shut up in p. 26:10
preached to spirits in p. 1 Pet 3:19
cast some of you into p. Rev 2:10
Satan be loosed out of his p. 20:7
see **gate**

prison *house*

grind in the p. house. Judg 16:21
for Samson out of the p. house. 25
Hanani in a p. house. 2 Chr 16:10
bring them that sit in darkness out of the p. house. Isa 42:7

prisoner

let sighing of the p. come. Ps 79:11
to hear groaning of the p. 102:20
release to the people a p. Mat 27:15
then a notable p. 16; Mark 15:6
Paul p. called me to him. Acts 23:18
unreasonable to send a p. 25:27
was I delivered p. to Romans. 28:17
Paul, the p. of Jesus. Eph 3:1; 4:1; Philem 1:9
not ashamed of me his p. 2 Tim 1:8
see **fellow**

prisoners

where king's p. were. Gen 39:20
committed to Joseph all the p. 22
took some of Israel p. Num 21:1*
there the p. rest together. Job 3:18
despiseth not his p. Ps 69:33
the Lord looseth the p. 146:7
bow down under the p. Isa 10:4
opened not the house of his p. 14:17
shall lead the Egyptians p. 20:4*
be gathered together as p. 24:22
to bring out the p. from the. 42:7
mayest say to the p., Go forth. 49:9*
crush under feet the p. Lam 3:34
forth thy p. out of the pit. Zech 9:11
strong hold, ye p. of hope. 12
and the p. heard them. Acts 16:25
supposing that the p. had fled. 27
Paul and certain other p. 27:1
soldiers' counsel was to kill the p. 42
delivered the p. to captain. 28:16

prisons

delivering you into p. Luke 21:12
delivering into p. men. Acts 22:4
in p. more frequent, in deaths oft. 2 Cor 11:23

private

no prophecy is of any p. 2 Pet 1:20

privately

disciples came p. saying. Mat 24:3
Jesus went into a ship p. Mark 6:32*; Luke 9:10*
Andrew ask him p. Mark 9:28; 13:3
his disciples and said p. Luke 10:23
with Paul's kinsman p. Acts 23:19
but p. to them that were. Gal 2:2

privily

he sent to Abimelech p. Josh 9:31*
cut off Saul's skirt p. 1 Sam 24:4
his eyes are p. set against the poor. Ps 10:8
that they may p. shoot at. 11:2*
pull me out of net laid p. for me. 31:4; 142:3
commune of laying snares p. 64:5
p. slandereth his neighbour. 101:5
let us lurk p. for the. Pr 1:11
lurk p. for their own lives. 18
to put her away p. Mat 1:19
Herod, when he had p. called. 2:7
do they thrust us out p.? Acts 16:37
who came in p. to spy out. Gal 2:4
who shall p. bring in. 2 Pet 2:1

privy

his p. member cut off. Deut 23:1
thy heart is p. to. 1 Ki 2:44
into their p. chambers. Ezek 21:14
his wife also being p. to it. Acts 5:2

prize

but one receiveth the p. 1 Cor 9:24
toward the mark for the p. Phil 3:14

prized

goodly price that I was p. Zech 11:13

proceed

the six branches that p. Ex 25:35
nor any word p. out of. Josh 6:10

none of my words be *p.* *Ezek* 12:28*
yet their lives were *p.* for. *Dan* 7:12

prolongeth

fear of the Lord *p.* days. *Pr* 10:27
wicked man that *p.* his life. *Eccl* 7:15

promise

The word in the New Testament is often taken for those promises that God made to Abraham *and the other patriarchs of sending the* Messiah. *It is in this sense that the apostle* Paul *commonly uses the word* promise, Rom 4:13, 14; Gal 3:16. *The Holy Spirit of promise,* Eph 1:13, *is the Holy Ghost, which God has promised to those that shall believe in him. The first commandment with promise is* Honour thy father and mother, Eph 6:2. *To which God has added this* promise, *that their days shall be long upon the earth,* Ex 20:12.

know my breach of *p.* *Num* 14:34*
failed one word of good *p.* *1 Ki* 8:56
let thy *p.* to David be. *2 Chr* 1:9
do according to this *p.* *Neh* 5:12
not this *p.* even thus be he shaken out. People did . . . to *p.* 13
doth his *p.* fail for? *Ps* 77:8
he remembered his holy *p.* 105:42*
I send *p.* of my Father. *Luke* 24:49
wait for the *p.* of Father. *Acts* 1:4
received *p.* of Holy Ghost. 2:33
p. is to you and to your children. 39
the time of the *p.* drew nigh. 7:17
to his *p.* hath raised a Saviour. 13:23
the *p.* made to fathers, God hath. 32
looking for a *p.* from thee. 23:21
for hope of the *p.* made of God. 26:6
to which *p.* our tribes, serving God. 7
p. that he shall be the heir. *Rom* 4:13
the *p.* is made of none effect. 14
p. might be sure to all the seed. 16
he staggered not at the *p.* 20
but children of the *p.* counted. 9:8
this is word of *p.* at this time. 9
that we might receive *p.* *Gal* 3:14
make the *p.* of none effect. 17
if of law, it is no more of *p.*: but God gave it to Abraham by *p.* 18
to whom the *p.* was made. 19
p. by faith of Jesus Christ might. 22
ye heirs according to the *p.* 29
we are the children of *p.* 4:28
with that Holy Spirit of *p.* *Eph* 1:13
strangers from covenants of *p.* 2:12
Gentiles be partakers of his *p.* 3:6
first commandment with *p.* 6:2
having the *p.* of the life. *1 Tim* 4:8
according to the *p.* of life. *2 Tim* 1:1
lest a *p.* left us of entering. *Heb* 4:1
for when God made *p.* to. 6:13
patiently endured, he obtained *p.* 15
to shew unto the heirs of *p.* 17
the *p.* of eternal life. 9:15; 10:36
sojourned in land of *p.* . . . heirs with him of the same *p.* 11:9
and these all received not the *p.* 39
saying, Where is the *p.* of? *2 Pet* 3:4
is not slack concerning his *p.* 9
according to his *p.* we look for. 13
p. that he hath promised. *1 John* 2:25

promise, *verb*

while they *p.* liberty. *2 Pet* 2:19

promised

according as he hath *p.* *Ex* 12:25
to the place the Lord *p.* *Num* 14:40
the Lord bless you as he hath *p.* *Deut* 1:11; 15:6
increase as the Lord *p.* thee. 6:3
bring them to the land he *p.* 9:28
is his inheritance, as he *p.* 10:9*
enlarge thy border, as he *p.* 12:20
give thee the land he *p.* to give. 19:8; 27:3
that which thou hast *p.* to God. 23:23
peculiar people, as he *p.* thee. 26:18
live, as the princes had *p.* *Josh* 9:21*
rest to your brethren, as he *p.* 22:4*
possess their land, as Lord *p.* 23:5*
for you, as he hath *p.* you. 10*
things are come the Lord *p.* you. 15*
hast *p.* this goodness to. *2 Sam* 7:28
me an house, as he *p.* *1 Ki* 2:24
Solomon wisdom, as he *p.* 5:12
throne of Israel as the Lord *p.* 8:20
rest to people, as he *p.* by Moses. 56
as I *p.* to David thy father. 9:5
as he *p.* to give a light. *2 Ki* 8:19 *2 Chr* 21:7
hast *p.* this goodness. *1 Chr* 17:26
the throne as Lord *p.* *2 Chr* 6:10
which thou hast *p.* David. 15, 16
thou hadst *p.* to fathers. *Neh* 9:23*
that Haman had *p.* to pay. *Esth* 4:7
will bring on them all the good I *p.* *Jer* 32:42; 33:14*
Herod *p.* with oath to. *Mat* 14:7
p. to give him money. *Mark* 14:11
mercy *p.* to our fathers. *Luke* 1:72*
he *p.* to betray him unto them. 22:6*
he *p.* to give it to him. *Acts* 7:5
which he had *p.* afore. *Rom* 1:2
that what he *p.* he was able to. 4:21
eternal life, *p.* before world. *Tit* 1:2
he is faithful that *p.* *Heb* 10:23
judged him faithful that had *p.* 11:11
he hath *p.* saying, Yet once. 12:26
Lord *p.* to them. *Jas* 1:12; 2:5
this is the promise that he hath *p.* us, even eternal. *1 John* 2:25

promisedst

David that thou *p.* him. *1 Ki* 8:24, 25
and *p.* that they should go into the land. *Neh* 9:15*

promises

to whom pertain the *p.* *Rom* 9:4
to confirm the *p.* made to the. 15:8
all *p.* of God in him are. *2 Cor* 1:20
having therefore these *p.* dearly. 7:1
to his seed were *p.* made. *Gal* 3:16
law against the *p.* of God? 21
and patience inherit *p.* *Heb* 6:12
blessed him that had the *p.* 7:6
was established upon better *p.* 8:6
died, not having received *p.* 11:13
had received the *p.*, offered up. 17
who through faith obtained *p.* 33
great and precious *p.* *2 Pet* 1:4

promising

wicked way, by *p.* life. *Ezek* 13:22*

promote

I will *p.* thee to great honour. *Num* 22:17; 24:11
am I not able indeed to *p.* thee? 37
and she shall *p.* thee. *Pr* 4:8

promoted

p. over the trees. *Judg* 9:9*, 11*, 13*
the king had *p.* him. *Esth* 5:11
then the king *p.* Shadrach. *Dan* 3:30

promotion

p. cometh neither from. *Ps* 75:6*
shame shall be the *p.* of. *Pr* 3:35

pronounce

man shall *p.* with an oath. *Lev* 5:4*
priest shall *p.* him unclean. 13:3, 6 8, 11, 15, 20, 22, 25, 27, 30, 44
shall *p.* him clean. 13:13, 17, 23, 28 34, 37; 14:7
law, to *p.* it clean or unclean. 13:59
priest shall *p.* the house clean. 14:48
could not frame to *p.* it. *Judg* 12:6

pronounced

but he *p.* this prophecy. *Neh* 6:12
the Lord hath *p.* evil. *Jer* 11:17
p. this great evil. 16:10; 19:15 35:17; 40:2
nation against whom I *p.*, turn. 18:8*
word which I have *p.* against. 25:13
Lord will repent of evil he *p.* 26:13
repented of the evil he had *p.* 19
for I have *p.* the word, saith. 34:5*
Lord hath *p.* against this people. 36:7
Jeremiah *p.* all these words. 18, 31

pronouncing

if a soul swear, *p.* to do. *Lev* 5:4*

proof

I might know the *p.* of you. *2 Cor* 2:9
shew ye to them the *p.* of your. 8:24
ye seek a *p.* of Christ speaking. 13:3
but ye know the *p.* of him. *Phil* 2:22
full *p.* of thy ministry. *2 Tim* 4:5†

proofs

alive by many infallible *p.* *Acts* 1:3

proper

(*Used with the old meaning of* one's own; *still retained in the French* propre)

mine own *p.* good. *1 Chr* 29:3*
called in their *p.* tongue. *Acts* 1:19*
hath his *p.* gift of God. *1 Cor* 7:7
saw he was a *p.* child. *Heb* 11:23*

prophecies

but whether *p.*, they. *1 Cor* 13:8
according to the *p.* that. *1 Tim* 1:18

prophecy

in the *p.* of Ahijah. *2 Chr* 9:29
when Asa heard *p.* of Obed. 15:8
he pronounced this *p.* *Neh* 6:12
p. man spake to Ithiel. *Pr* 30:1*
p. that his mother taught him. 31:1*
in them is fulfilled the *p.* of Esaias. *Mat* 13:14
p., by the same Spirit. *1 Cor* 12:10
though I have the gift of *p.* and. 13:2
the gift given thee by *p.* *1 Tim* 4:14
more sure word of *p.* *2 Pet* 1:19
no *p.* of scripture is of private. 20
p. came not in old time by the will. 21
hear the words of this *p.* *Rev* 1:3
rain not in the days of their *p.* 11:6
for the testimony of Jesus is the spirit of *p.* 19:10
keepeth the sayings of this *p.* 22:7
sayings of the *p.* of this book. 10
that heareth words of the *p.* of. 18
take from the words of this *p.* 19

prophesied

they *p.* and did not. *Num* 11:25
Eldad and Medad they *p.* in. 26
of God came upon Saul, and he *p.* *1 Sam* 10:10, 11; 18:10; 19:23, 24
messengers of Saul also *p.* 19:20, 21
they *p.* until the evening. *1 Ki* 18:29
prophets *p.* before them. 22:10, 12 *2 Chr* 18:9
sons of Asaph *p.* *1 Chr* 25:2
the sons of Jeduthun who *p.* 3
Eliezer *p.* against. *2 Chr* 20:37
Haggai and Zechariah *p.* *Ezra* 5:1
prophets *p.* by Baal. *Jer* 2:8
Pashur heard that Jeremiah *p.* 20:1
and all to whom thou *p.* lies. 6
the prophets of Samaria *p.* 23:13
not spoken to them, yet they *p.* 21
all that Jeremiah hath *p.* 25:13
why hast thou *p.* in the name of? 26:9
he hath *p.* against this city. 11, 20
Micah *p.* in days of Hezekiah. 18
Urijah *p.* 20
perform the words thou hast *p.* 28:6
p. against many countries. 8
Shemaiah hath *p.* to you. 29:31
prophets which *p.* to you? 37:19
when I *p.* Pelatiah died. *Ezek* 11:13
so I *p.* as I was commanded, and as I *p.* 37:7, 10
who *p.* I would bring thee. 38:17
be ashamed when they *p.* *Zech* 13:4
Lord, have we not *p.*? *Mat* 7:22
prophets and law *p.* until John. 11:13
well hath Esaias *p.* of you. *Mark* 7:6
Zachariah *p.* saying. *Luke* 1:67
Caiaphas *p.* that Jesus. *John* 11:51
spake with tongues and *p.* *Acts* 19:6
I would rather that ye *p.* *1 Cor* 14:5
Enoch also *p.* of these things. *Jude* 14

prophesieth

he never *p.* good to me. *2 Chr* 18:7
prophet which *p.* of peace. *Jer* 28:9
p. of times far off. *Ezek* 12:27
him through when he *p.* *Zech* 13:3
that *p.* with her head. *1 Cor* 11:5
he that *p.* speaketh unto men. 14:3
he that *p.* edifieth the church. 4
greater is he that *p.* than he. 5

prophesy *verb*

Eldad and Medad do *p.* *Num* 11:27
they shall *p.* *1 Sam* 10:5
thou shalt *p.* 6
doth not *p.* good of me. *1 Ki* 22:8
would not *p.* good. 18; *2 Chr* 18:17
who should *p.* with harps. *1 Chr* 25:1
p. not right things, *p.* *Isa* 30:10

the prophets p. falsely. Jer 5:31
p. not in the name of the Lord. 11:21
prophets p. lies, they p. false. 14:14
concerning the prophets that p. 15
people to whom they p. shall be. 16
Tophet, whither Lord sent to p. 19:14
not to the prophets that p. 23:16
that p. lies in my name. 25; 26:32
27:10, 14, 15, 16; 29:9, 21
p. against the inhabitants of. 25:30
Lord sent me to p. against. 26:12
why dost p. and say, I will? 32:3
shalt p. against Jerusalem. Ezek 4:7
p. against the mountains. 6:2; 36:1
p. against them, p. O son. 11:4
p. against prophets that p. 13:2, 17
p. against the forest of the. 20:46
p. against land of Israel. 21:2, 9
son of man, p. and smite thy. 14
p. and say concerning. 28; 25:2
p. against Zidon. 28:21
p. against Pharaoh. 29:2
p. against Egypt. 30:2
p. against the shepherds of. 34:2
p. against mount Seir. 35:2
p. concerning the land of. 36:6
p. upon these bones. 37:4
p to the wind. 9
p. against Gog. 38:2, 14; 39:1
your sons shall p. Joel 2:28
Acts 2:17, 18
commanded the prophets, saying, P. not. Amos 2:12; Mi 2:6
who can but p? Amos 3:8
eat bread and p. 7:12
p. not again at Beth-el. 13
Go p. to my people Israel. 15
p. not against Israel and the. 16
I will p. to thee of wine. Mi 2:11
that when any shall yet p. then his father. Zech 13:3
well did Esaias p. of you. Mat 15:7
p. thou Christ. 26:68; Mark 14:65
Luke 22:64
virgins, which did p. Acts 21:9
whether prophecy, let us p. Rom 12:6
know in part, and we p. 1 Cor 13:9
rather that ye may p. 14:1
if all p. 24
we may all p. one by one. 31
covet to p. 39
thou must p. again before. Rev 10:11
my two witnesses shall p. 11:3

prophesying

had made an end of p. 1 Sam 10:13
company of the prophets p. 19:20
prospered through p. of. Ezra 6:14
man p. having his head. 1 Cor 11:4
except by p. or by doctrine. 14:6
p. serveth not for them that. 22
despise not p., prove. 1 Thes 5:20

prophet

Ordinarily this word is understood as meaning one who foretells future events. It meant, at the time our English Bible was translated, also a preacher—and prophesying meant preaching. A meaning of the word less often recognized, but really as common, is one who tells —a forth-teller—who speaks for another, most usually for God. It is in this sense that many Bible characters are called prophets, as for example, Aaron, Moses, and Jesus Christ. Those prophets who wrote their prophecies, which are preserved to us in our Bible, are divided into two groups: four major prophets—Isaiah, Jeremiah, Ezekiel and Daniel—and 12 minor prophets, whose names are given to the last 12 books of the Old Testament. There are also a number of prophets named in the Old Testament who were important in their day, but who left no writings behind them. The most important of these are Elijah and Elisha, whose deeds are related in 1 Ki 17-21; 2 Ki 1-9, 13. *The periods of the prophecies preserved to us are in some cases a little uncertain. The following is, at least, approximately correct.*

1. Isaiah *began to prophesy near the time of the death of Uzziah, king of* Judah. *He continued to prophesy to the reign of* Manasseh, *who caused him to be put to death.*

2. Jeremiah *began in the thirteenth year of the reign of* Josiah *king of* Judah. *He continued to prophesy till the taking of Jerusalem by the Chaldeans; and it is thought he died two years after in* Egypt; Baruch *was his disciple and amanuensis.*

3. Ezekiel *was carried captive to Babylon, along with* Jeconiah *king of* Judah, *11 years before the destruction of Jerusalem. He preached during the captivity for about 22 years. We do not know when he died.*

4. Daniel *was taken into Chaldea in the third year of Jehoiakim king of Judah, and prophesied at Babylon to the end of the captivity.*

5. Hosea *prophesied under Jeroboam II. king of* Israel, *and his successors, perhaps to the destruction of* Samaria.

6. Joel *prophesied under Josiah about the same time as Jeremiah.*

7. Amos *began to prophesy the second year before the earthquake, which was in the reign of king Uzziah, about six years before the death of Jeroboam II. king of* Israel.

8. Obadiah *dwelt in Judea, probably after the taking of Jerusalem, and before the desolation of Idumea.*

9. Jonah *lived in the kingdom of* Israel *under the kings* Joash *and* Jeroboam II. *about the same time as* Hosea, Isaiah, *and* Amos.

10. Micah *lived under* Jotham, Ahaz, *and* Hezekiah, *kings of* Judah; *he was contemporary with* Isaiah, *but began later to prophesy.*

11. Nahum *appeared in* Judah *under the reign of Hezekiah, and after the expedition of* Sennacherib.

12. Habakkuk *lived in Judea during the reign of Jehoiakim, before the coming of Nebuchadnezzar into the country.*

13. Zephaniah *appeared at the beginning of the reign of* Josiah, *and before the twenty-eighth year of this prince.*

14. Haggai *was the great prophet of the Return to Jerusalem, and the rebuilding of the temple. He is supposed to have been an old man, as* Hag 2:3 *is taken to mean that he had seen the old temple before its destruction by Nebuchadnezzar.*

15. Zechariah *prophesied in Judea at the same time as Haggai, and continued to prophesy after him, being younger.*

16. Malachi, *the author of the last book in the Old Testament, lived about the time of Nehemiah's second visit to Jerusalem. Nothing whatever is known of him.*

Aaron shall be thy p. Ex 7:1
but the p. which shall presume.
Deut 18:20, 22
p. Gad said to David. 1 Sam 22:5
word of the Lord came to the p.
2 Sam 24:11
call me Nathan the p. 1 Ki 1:32
sent with him Nathan the p. 44
Ahijah the p. found Jeroboam. 11:29
an old p. in Beth-el. 13:11, 25
p. whom he had brought back. 23
p. took up the carcase of the man of God, and the old p. came to. 29
by p. Jehu came the word. 16:7, 12
Elijah p. came near and said. 18:36
p. came to king of Israel. 20:22
my lord were with the p. 2 Ki 5:3
p. had bid thee do some great. 13
Elisha the p. telleth what thou. 6:12
young man the p. went to. 9:4
Isaiah the p. cried to Lord. 20:11
with bones of p. that came out. 23:18
came Shemaiah the p. 2 Chr 12:5
in the story of the p. Iddo. 13:22
the prophecy of the p. Oded. 15:8
a writing from Elijah the p. 21:12
then the p. forbare, and said. 25:16
the p. Isaiah prayed and cried. 32:20
from the days of Samuel the p. 35:18
not himself before Jeremiah p. 36:12
Haggai the p. prophesied. Ezra 5:1
prophesying of Haggai the p. 6:14
there is no more any p. Ps 74:9
Lord doth take away the p. Isa 3:2
the p. that teacheth lies. 9:15
priest and p. have erred. 28:7
from the p. even unto the priest dealeth falsely. Jer 6:13; 8:10
nor shall word perish from p. 18:18
both p. and priests are profane. 23:11
p. that hath a dream let him. 28
the p. Jeremiah said, Amen. 28:6
p. which prophesieth of peace, when the word of the p. shall . . . p. 9
so Hananiah the p. died the. 17
Baruch and Jeremiah the p. 36:26
nor his servants hearken to p. 37:2
take up Jeremiah the p. out. 38:10
shall the p. be slain? Lam 2:20
they seek a vision of p. Ezek 7:26
and cometh to the p. I will. 14:4
if p. be deceived, I the Lord have deceived that p. 9
punishment of the p. shall be. 10
p. also shall fall with thee. Hos 4:5
the p. is a fool. 9:7
p. is a snare of a fowler. 8*
I was no p. nor p.'s son. Amos 7:14
he shall even be the p. Mi 2:11
prayer of Habakkuk the p. Hab 3:1
he shall say, I am no p. Zech 13:5
will send you Elijah the p. Mal 4:5
spoken by the p. Isaiah. Mat 1:22
2:15; 3:3; 4:14; 8:17; 21:4
Luke 3:4; John 1:23; 12:38
Acts 28:25
thus it is written by the p. Mat 2:5
spoken by Jeremy the p. 17; 27:9
but the sign of the p. Jonas. 12:39
Luke 11:29
spoken by the p. Mat 13:35
27:35
Jesus the p. of Nazareth of. 21:11
spoken of by Daniel the p. 24:15
Mark 13:14
child be called p. of the Highest.
Luke 1:76
to him book of the p. Esaias. 4:17
no p. is accepted in his own. 24
in the time of Eliseus the p. 27
not a greater p. than John. 7:28
of a truth this is the p. John 7:40
out of Galilee ariseth no p. 52
was spoken by the p. Joel. Acts 2:16
made with hands, as saith p. 7:48
he read Esaias the p. 8:28, 30
of whom speaketh the p. this? 34
judges until Samuel the p. 13:20
the ass forbad the madness of the p. 2 Pet 2:16

see **priest, Lord**

a prophet

restore man his wife, for he is a p.
Gen 20:7
if there be a p. among. Num 12:6
arise a p. or dreamer. Deut 13:1
I will raise up a p. from among.
18:15, 18; Acts 3:22; 7:37
when a p. speaketh in. Deut 18:22
arose not a p. in Israel like. 34:10
sent a p. to the children. Judg 6:8
established to be a p. 1 Sam 3:20
now called a p., was called. 9:9
he said, I am a p. also. 1 Ki 13:18
I, even I only remain a p. of. 18:22
anoint Elisha to be a p. 19:16
there came a p. unto Ahab. 20:13
is there not here a p. of the Lord?
22:7; 2 Ki 3:11; 2 Chr 18:6

there is *a p.* in Israel. *2 Ki* 5:8
sent *a p.* to Amaziah. *2 Chr* 25:15
a p. of Lord was there, Oded. 28:9
thee *a p.* to the nations. *Jer* 1:5
maketh himself *a p.* 29:26, 27
there hath been *a p.* *Ezek* 2:5; 33:33
cometh to *a p.* to enquire of. 14:7
by *a p.* the Lord brought Israel out of Egypt, and by *a p.* *Hos* 12:13
a p. in the name of *a p.* shall receive *a p.*'s reward. *Mat* 10:41
went ye out for to see ? *a p.*? 11:9
a p. is not without honour save. 13:57 *Mark* 6:4; *John* 4:44
they accounted him as *a p.* *Mat* 14:5 21:26; *Mark* 11:32; *Luke* 20:6
they took him for *a p.* *Mat* 21:46
others said, That it is *a p.* *Mark* 6:15
a great *p.* is risen. *Luke* 7:16
this man, if he were *a p.* would. 39
cannot be that *a p.* perish out. 13:33
Jesus, who was *a p.* mighty. 24:19
perceive that thou art *a p.* *John* 4:19
the blind man said, He is *a p.* 9:17
being *a p.* and knowing. *Acts* 2:30
a certain *p.* named Agabus. 21:10
think himself to be *a p.* *1 Cor* 14:37
a p. of their own land. *Tit* 1:12

false **prophet**
a *false p.*, a Jew named. *Acts* 13:6
out of mouth of *false p.* *Rev* 16:13
taken, with him the *false p.* 19:20
where beast and *false p.* are. 20:10

that **prophet**
to the words of *that p.* *Deut* 13:3
that p. or that dreamer. 5; 18:20
have deceived *that p.* *Ezek* 14:9
Art thou *that p.*? *John* 1:21, 25
this is of a truth *that p.* that. 6:14
will not hear *that p.* *Acts* 3:23

prophetess
Miriam *p.* took a timbrel. *Ex* 15:20
and Deborah a *p.* judged. *Judg* 4:4
went to Huldah the *p.* *2 Ki* 22:14 *2 Chr* 34:22
think on the *p.* Noadiah. *Neh* 6:14
p. and she conceived a son. *Isa* 8:3
there was one Anna a *p.* *Luke* 2:36
who called herself a *p.* *Rev* 2:20

prophets
Lord's people were *p.* *Num* 11:29
meet a company of *p.* *1 Sam* 10:5
company of *p.* met him. 10
prophesied among the *p.* 11
is Saul among the *p.*? 12; 19:24
answered him not by *p.* 28:6, 15
Obadiah hid 100 *p.* by 50. *1 Ki* 18:4
Jezebel slew the *p.* 13
gather *p.* of Baal 450. 19, 22
take the *p.* of Baal, let none. 40
have slain *p.* with the sword. 19:10 14; *Neh* 9:26
of Israel gathered the *p.* *1 Ki* 22:6
a lying spirit in *p.* 22; *2 Chr* 18:21
to *p.* of thy father, and *p.* *2 Ki* 3:13
Josiah went and *p.*, to house. 23:2
believe his *p.* so shall. *2 Chr* 20:20
Yet he sent *p.* to them. 24:19
they misused his *p.* 36:16
were the *p.* of God helping. *Ezra* 5:2
appointed *p.* to preach. *Neh* 6:7
by thy Spirit in thy *p.* 9:30
trouble that hath come on our *p.* 32
the *p.* and seers hath he. *Isa* 29:10
say to the *p.*, Prophesy not. 30:10 *Amos* 2:12
and *p.* prophesied by Baal. *Jer* 2:8
their priests and *p.* are ashamed. 26
sword hath devoured your *p.* 30
the *p.* shall wonder. 4:9
p. become wind. 5:13
p. prophesy falsely, and. 31
bring out the bones of the *p.* 8:1
will fill *p.* with drunkenness. 13:13
the *p.* say, Ye shall not see. 14:13
p. prophesy lies in my name. 14
sword and famine shall those *p.* 15
folly in the *p.* of Samaria. 23:13
seen in *p.* an horrible thing. 14
from *p.* is profaneness gone forth. 15
I have not sent these *p.*, yet. 21
I have heard what the *p.* *Jer* 23:25
p. of deceit of their own heart. 26
the *p.* that steal my word. 30, 31
priests and *p.* heard Jeremiah. 26:7
p. and people took Jeremiah. 8
the *p.*, This man is worthy to die. 11
hearken not to your *p.* 27:9, 16
ye and the *p.* might perish. 15
if they be *p.* and word of Lord. 18
p. that have been before me. 28:8
Jeremiah sent to the *p.* 29:1
saith the Lord, Let not your *p.* 8
Lord hath raised us up *p.* in. 15
they and their *p.* provoke me. 32:32
where are now your *p.*? 37:19
her *p.* also find no vision. *Lam* 2:9
thy *p.* have seen vain things. 14
for the sins of her *p.* that have. 4:13
prophesy against the *p.* *Ezek* 13:2
Woe unto the foolish *p.* 3
O Israel, thy *p.* are like foxes. 4
my hand shall be upon the *p.* that. 9
there is a conspiracy of her *p.* 22:25
p. daubed them with untempered. 28
I have hewed them by *p.* *Hos* 6:5
I have spoken by *p.* and. 12:10
raised up of your sons *p.* *Amos* 2:11
and commanded the *p.* saying. 12
sun shall go down over *p.* *Mi* 3:6
p. thereof divine for money. 11
her *p.* are light and. *Zeph* 3:4
to whom the former *p.* *Zech* 1:4
the *p.* do they live for ever ? 5
Lord hath cried by former *p.* 7:7
word Lord sent by former *p.* 12
I will cause the *p.* to pass out. 13:2
the *p.* shall be ashamed, each. 4
so persecuted they the *p.* *Mat* 5:12 *Luke* 6:23
not come to destroy the law and the *p.* *Mat* 5:17
for this is the law and the *p.* 7:12
many *p.* have desired to see. 13:17 *Luke* 10:24
on these hang all the law and the *p.* *Mat* 22:40
of them who killed the *p.* 23:31
I send unto you *p.* 34; *Luke* 11:49
thou that killest the *p.* *Mat* 23:37
written in *p.*, Behold I. *Mark* 1:2 *Luke* 18:31; 24:25; *John* 6:45
as he spake by his holy *p.* *Luke* 1:70; *2 Pet* 3:2
and *p.* were until John. *Luke* 16:16
They have Moses and *p.* 29, 31
slow to believe what the *p.* 24:25
found him of whom the *p.* *John* 1:45
Abraham is dead, and *p.* 8:52, 53
by the mouth of his *p.* *Acts* 3:18, 21
p. came from Jerusalem to. 11:27
in church at Antioch certain *p.* 13:1
after reading of law and the *p.* 15
which is spoken of in the *p.* 40
Judas and Silas being *p.* 15:32
things written in law and *p.* 24:14
none other things than *p.* did. 26:22
Agrippa, believest thou the *p.*? 27
promised afore by his *p.* *Rom* 1:2
witnessed by law and the *p.* 3:21
Lord, they have killed thy *p.* 11:3
apostles, secondarily *p.* *1 Cor* 12:28
are all *p.*? 29
let *p.* speak two or three. 14:29
on foundation of the *p.* *Eph* 2:20
as it is now revealed to his *p.* 3:5
and he gave some *p.* and. 4:11
killed Lord, and own *p.* *1 Thes* 2:15
spake to fathers by the *p.* *Heb* 1:1
take, my brethren, the *p.* *Jas* 5:10
which salvation the *p.* *1 Pet* 1:10
two *p.* tormented them. *Rev* 11:10
rejoice, ye holy apostles and *p.* 18:20
in her was found blood of *p.* and. 24
for I am of thy brethren the *p.* 22:9

all the **prophets**
he had slain *all the p.* *1 Ki* 19:1
throne, and *all the p.* prophesied. 22:10, 12; *2 Chr* 18:9, 11
call *all the p.* of Baal. *2 Ki* 10:19
against Israel by *all the p.* 17:13
all the p. prophesied until. *Mat* 11:13
that blood of *all the p.* *Luke* 11:50
see *all the p.* in kingdom. 13:28
all the p. he expounded. *Luke* 24:27
all the p. from Samuel. *Acts* 3:24
to him give *all the p.* witness. 10:43

false **prophets**
false p. in sheep's. *Mat* 7:15
many *false p.* shall rise. 24:11, 24 *Mark* 13:22
their fathers to *false p.* *Luke* 6:26
there were *false p.* also. *2 Pet* 2:1
because many *false p.* *1 John* 4:1

my **prophets**
mine anointed, and do *my p.* no. *1 Chr* 16:22; *Ps* 105:15

of the **prophets**
company *of the p.* met. *1 Sam* 10:10
saw the company *of the p.* 19:20
man of the sons *of the p.* *1 Ki* 20:35
that he was *of the p.* 41
words *of the p.* 22:13; *2 Chr* 18:12
sons *of the p.* at Beth-el. *2 Ki* 2:3
the sons *of the p.* at Jericho. 5
sons *of the p.* went to view afar. 7
sons *of the p.* said, The spirit. 15
woman of wives of sons *of the p.* 4:1
pottage for the sons *of the p.* 38
think of the rest *of the p.* *Neh* 6:14
because *of the p.* all my. *Jer* 23:9
to the words *of the p.* 16; 27:14
this be in the heart *of the p.*? 23:26
by ministry *of the p.* *Hos* 12:10
by the mouth *of the p.* *Zech* 8:9
Elias or one *of the p.* *Mat* 16:14 *Mark* 6:15; 8:28
ye build the tombs *of the p.* *Mat* 23:29; *Luke* 11:47
them in blood *of the p.* *Mat* 23:30
of the p. might be fulfilled 26:56
one *of the p.* was risen. *Luke* 9:8, 19
ye are children *of the p.* *Acts* 3:25
written in the book *of the p.* 7:42
of the p. have not your fathers ? 52
reading *of* the law and *the p.* 13:15
they knew not voice *of the p.* 27
to this agree words *of the p.* 15:15
concerning Jesus out *of the p.* 28:23
by scriptures *of the p.* *Rom* 16:26
spirits *of the p.* are subject to the prophets. *1 Cor* 14:32
on the foundation *of the p.* *Eph* 2:20
fail me to tell *of the p.* *Heb* 11:32
shed the blood *of the p.* *Rev* 16:6
Lord God *of the* holy *p.* sent. 22:6

servants the **prophets**
blood of my *serv. the p.* *2 Ki* 9:7
I sent by my *serv. the p.* 17:13
Lord said by all his *serv. the p.* 23
spake by his *serv. the p.* 21:10; 24:2
commanded by *serv. the p.* *Ezra* 9:11
sent you my *serv. the p.* *Jer* 7:25 25:4; 29:19; 35:15
to the words of my *serv. the p.* 26:5
spoken by my *serv. the p.* *Ezek* 38:17
hearkened to *serv. the p.* *Dan* 9:6
set before us by his *serv. the p.* 10
his secret to his *serv. the p.* *Amos* 3:7
which I commanded my *serv. the p.* *Zech* 1:6
declared to his *serv. the p.* *Rev* 10:7
give reward to *serv. the p.* 11:18

propitiation
hath set forth to be a *p.* *Rom* 3:25
and he is the *p.* *1 John* 2:2; 4:10

proportion
according to the *p.* *1 Ki* 7:36*
not conceal his comely *p.* *Job* 41:12†
according to *p.* of faith. *Rom* 12:6

proselyte
This term comes from the Greek *word,* Proselytos, *which signifies a* stranger, *one that comes from abroad, or from another place. The* Hebrew *word* Ger *or* Necher, *has the same signification. It means a convert to Judaism from among the Gentiles.*

The Talmud distinguishes between Proselytes of the Gate, *and* Proselytes of Righteousness. *The first are those who dwelt in the land of Israel and were not bound by circumcision. The term is derived*

from the expression the stranger that is within thy gates, Ex 20:10, etc.
The Proselytes of Righteousness *are those that were converted to Judaism, who received circumcision, and observed the whole law of Moses. They were therefore perfect Israelites.*

compass sea and land to make one p. Mat 23:15
Nicholas a p. of Antioch. Acts 6:5

proselytes

Jews and p., we do hear. Acts 2:10
Jews and religious p. followed Paul. 13:43

prospect

chambers whose p. was. Ezek 40:44
p. to the north. 46
p. to the east. 42:15; 43:4

prosper

his angel and p. thee. Gen 24:40
if now thou do p. my way. 42
that Joseph did to p. 39:3, 23
but it shall not p. Num 14:41
not p. in thy ways. Deut 28:29
that ye may p. 29:9; Josh 1:7*
1 Ki 2:3
Go up to Ramoth-gilead and p. 1 Ki 22:12, 15; 2 Chr 18:11, 14
son, the Lord p. thee. 1 Chr 22:11
shalt thou p. if thou takest heed. 13
fight ye not, for ye shall not p. 2 Chr 13:12
prophets, so shall ye p. 20:20
Why transgress ye, that ye cannot p.? 24:20
Lord God made Uzziah to p. 26:5
p. I pray thee, thy servant. Neh 1:11
God of heaven, he will p. us. 2:20
tabernacles of robbers p. Job 12:6
whatsoever he doeth shall p. Ps 1:3
ungodly who p. in the world. 73:12*
they shall p. that love thee. 122:6
his sins, shall not p. Pr 28:13
whether shall p. Eccl 11:6
pleasure of Lord shall p. Isa 53:10
formed against thee shall p. 54:17
shall p. in the thing whereunto. 55:11
thou shalt not p. in them. Jer 2:37
yet they p. 5:28
they shall not p. 10:21; 20:11
doth the way of wicked p.? 12:1
not p. in his days, for no man of his seed shall p. 22:30
a King shall reign and p. 23:5*
with Chaldeans ye shall not p. 32:5
are chief, her enemies p. Lam 1:5
thou didst p. Ezek 16:13
shall it p.? 17:9, 10
shall he p.? shall he escape? 17:15
destroy wonderfully and p. Dan 8:24
shall cause craft to p. in his hand. 25
lies, but it shall not p. 11:27, 36
all that thou mayest p. 3 John 2

prospered

seeing the Lord hath p. Gen 24:56
the hand of Israel p. Judg 4:24*
demanded how war p. 2 Sam 11:7
Hezekiah p. 2 Ki 18:7; 2 Chr 31:21 32:30
Solomon p. 1 Chr 29:23
Asa p. 2 Chr 14:7
Jews p. through the prophesying of Haggai. Ezra 6:14
against him and hath p.? Job 9:4
Daniel p. in the reign of. Dan 6:28
truth to the ground and it p. 8:12
lay by, as God hath p. 1 Cor 16:2

prospereth

work p. in their hands. Ezra 5:8
fret not because of him that p. Ps 37:7
a gift, whithersoever it turneth it p. Pr 17:8
health, even as thy soul p. 3 John 2

prosperity

thou shalt not seek their p. Deut 23:6
shall say to him that liveth in p. 1 Sam 25:6
and p. exceedeth fame. 1 Ki 10:7
in p., the destroyer shall. Job 15:21
shall spend their days in p. Job 36:11
in my p. I said, I shall. Ps 30:6
Lord hath pleasure in the p. of. 35:27
when I saw the p. of wicked. 73:3
I beseech thee, send now p. 118:25
peace be within thy walls, p. 122:7
the p. of fools shall. Pr 1:32
in the day of p. be joyful. Eccl 7:14
I spake to thee in thy p. Jer 22:21
all the p. that I procure to. 33:9*
far from peace, I forgat p. Lam 3:17
my cities through p. shall. Zech 1:17
when Jerusalem in p. 7:7

prosperous

Lord made his journey p. Gen 24:21
Joseph, he was a p. man. 39:2
thou make thy way p. Josh 1:8
way we go shall be p. Judg 18:5
would make the habitation of thy righteousness p. Job 8:6
he shall make his way p. Isa 48:15
for the seed shall be p. Zech 8:12*
I might have a p. journey. Rom 1:10

prosperously

Solomon p. effected all. 2 Chr 7:11
majesty ride p. because. Ps 45:4

prostitute

do not p. thy daughter. Lev 19:29*

protection

rise up and be your p. Deut 32:38

protest, -ed

the man did solemnly p. Gen 43:3
hearken, yet p. solemnly. 1 Sam 8:9
and I p. unto thee. 1 Ki 2:42
I earnestly p. to your. Jer 11:7
the angel of the Lord p. Zech 3:6
I p. by your rejoicing. 1 Cor 15:31

protesting

p. saying, Obey my voice. Jer 11:7

proud

p. helpers do stoop. Job 9:13*
he smiteth through the p. 26:12*
shall thy p. waves be stayed. 38:11
behold p. and abase him. 40:11
look on p., bring him low. 12
that speaketh p. things. Ps 12:3*
plentifully rewardeth the p. 31:23
man who respecteth not the p. 40:4
the p. are risen against me. 86:14
render a reward to the p. 94:2
him that hath a p. heart will I. 101:5
thou hast rebuked the p. 119:21
p. have had me greatly in derision. 51
p. have forged a lie against me. 69
let p. be ashamed, for they dealt. 78
the p. digged pits for me, not. 85
let not the p. oppress me. 122
filled with contempt of the p. 123:4
the p. waters had gone over. 124:5
the p. he knoweth afar off. 138:6
p. have hid a snare for me. 140:5
Lord hateth a p. look. Pr 6:17
destroy the house of the p. 15:25
one p. in heart is abomination. 16:5
to divide the spoil with the p. 19
an high look and p. heart is. 21:4
p. scorner ... deals in p. wrath. 24
p. heart stirreth up strife. 28:25*
patient better than the p. Eccl 7:8
Lord on every one that is p. Isa 2:12
arrogancy of the p. to cease. 13:11
the p. wrath of Moab. 16:6
be not p.: for the Lord. Jer 13:15
p. men answered Jeremiah. 43:2
Moab, he is exceeding p. 48:29
she hath been p. 50:29
O thou most p. 31
most p. shall stumble and fall. 32
he is a p. man, neither. Hab 2:5
we call the p. happy. Mal 3:15
p. as stubble. 4:1
he hath scattered the p. Luke 1:51
despiteful, p., boasters. Rom 1:30
he is p. knowing nothing. 1 Tim 6:4
covetous, boasters, p. 2 Tim 3:2
God resisteth the p. Jas 4:6
1 Pet 5:5

proudly

dealt p. he was above. Ex 18:11
no more so exceeding p. 1 Sam 2:3
thou knewest that they dealt p. Neh 9:10, 16, 29
their mouth they speak p. Ps 17:10
which speak grievous things p. 31:18
child shall behave p. Isa 3:5
shouldest thou have spoken p. Ob 12

prove

[1] *To try and examine,* 2 Cor 13:5. [2] *To show to be true by argument,* Acts 9:22; Rom 3:9. [3] *To find true,* Eccl 7:23.

that I may p. them. Ex 16:4
Deut 8:16
God is come to p. you. Ex 20:20
humble thee, and to p. Deut 8:2
whom thou didst p. at Massah. 33:8
that through them I may p. Israel. Judg 2:22; Isa 3:1, 4
let me p. thee but this once with fleece. Judg 6:39
she came to p. Solomon. 1 Ki 10:1
2 Chr 9:1
it shall p. me perverse. Job 9:20
O Lord, and p. me. Ps 26:2
I will p. thee with mirth. Eccl 2:1
p. thy servants, I beseech. Dan 1:12
bring the tithes, p. me now herewith. Mal 3:10
oxen, I go to p. them. Luke 14:19
this he said to p. him. John 6:6
neither can they p. the things. Acts 24:13; 25:7
p. what is that good will. Rom 12:2
to p. the sincerity of your. 2 Cor 8:8
p. your own selves, know ye? 13:5
let every man p. his own. Gal 6:4
p. all things; hold fast. 1 Thes 5:21

proved

hereby ye shall be p. Gen 42:15
that your words may be p. 16
and there he p. them. Ex 15:25
he had not p. his sword, David said, I have not p. them. 1 Sam 17:39
thou hast p. my heart. Ps 17:3
thou, O God, hast p. us. 66:10
p. thee at waters of Meribah. 81:7
fathers p. me and saw my. 95:9
this have I p. by wisdom. Eccl 7:23
and p. them ten days. Dan 1:14
we before p. both Jews. Rom 3:9
ye have often p. diligent. 2 Cor 8:22
these also be first p. 1 Tim 3:10
p. me, and saw my works. Heb 3:9

provender

we have both straw and p. Gen 24:25
the man gave straw and p. for. 32
opened sack to give his ass p. 42:27
the man gave their asses p. 43:24
there is both straw and p. Judg 19:19
him and gave p. to the asses. 21*
asses shall eat clean p. Isa 30:24

proverb

(This word has in the Bible, besides its ordinary modern use, that of a short parable, or a saying with a hidden meaning)

a p. and a byword. Deut 28:37
a p., Is Saul among? 1 Sam 10:12
as saith p. of the ancients. 24:13
Israel shall be a p. and. 1 Ki 9:7
will I make to be a p. 2 Chr 7:20
I became a p. to them. Ps 69:11
understand a p. and words. Pr 1:6
take up this p. against. Isa 14:4*
deliver them to be a p. Jer 24:9
what is that p. ye have? Ezek 12:22
I will make this p. cease ... no more use it as a p. in. 23; 18:2, 3
will make him a sign, and a p. 14:8
these take up a taunting p. Hab 2:6
surely say this p., Physician heal thyself. Luke 4:23†
thou plainly, and no p. John 16:29†
according to the p. 2 Pet 2:22

proverbs

that speak in p. say. Num 21:27
spake three thousand p. 1 Ki 4:32
the p. of Solomon. Pr 1:1; 10:1
25:1
preacher set in order many p. Eccl 12:9
every one that useth p. Ezek 16:44
I have spoken in p. . . . I shall no more speak in p. John 16:25†

proveth
for Lord your God *p.* you. *Deut* 13:3
provide
God will *p.* himself a lamb. *Gen* 22:8
when shall I *p.* for mine own ? 30:30
shalt *p.* out of the people able men. *Ex* 18:21
p. me a man that can play well. *1 Sam* 16:17
men whom David did *p.* *2 Chr* 2:7
can he *p.* flesh for his ? *Ps* 78:20
p. neither gold nor silver. *Mat* 10:9
p. yourselves bags. *Luke* 12:33
and *p.* them beasts to set. *Acts* 23:24
p. things honest in sight. *Rom* 12:17
but if any *p.* not for his. *1 Tim* 5:8
provided
he *p.* the first part. *Deut* 33:21
I have *p.* me a king. *1 Sam* 16:1
he had *p.* the king of. *2 Sam* 19:32
which *p.* victuals for. *1 Ki* 4:7, 27
Hezekiah *p.* possessions of flocks. *2 Chr* 32:29
corn, when thou hast *p.* *Ps* 65:9
whose shall those things be, which thou hast *p.*? *Luke* 12:20*
God having *p.* better. *Heb* 11:40
providence
to this nation by thy *p.* *Acts* 24:2
provideth
p. for the raven his food. *Job* 38:41
p. her meat in summer. *Pr* 6:8
providing
p. for honest things. *2 Cor* 8:21*
province, -s
by the princes of the *p.* *1 Ki* 20:14, 15, 17, 19
hurtful to kings and *p.* *Ezra* 4:15
found in the *p.* of the Medes. 6:2
gold thou canst find in the *p.* 7:16
are the children of the *p.* *Neh* 7:6
these are the chief of the *p.* 11:3
reigned over 127 *p.* *Esth* 1:1
wrong to people in all *p.* 16, 22
appoint officers in all the *p.* 2:3
king made a release to the *p.* 18
a people scattered in all *p.* of. 3:8
sent by posts to all the king's *p.* 13
all the people of the king's *p.* 4:11
127 *p.* and do every *p.* 8:9
in all *p.* of king Ahasuerus. 12
fame went through all the *p.* 9:4
they done in the rest of the *p.* 12
these days should be kept through every *p.* 28
the treasure of the *p.* *Eccl* 2:8
oppression in a *p.* marvel not. 5:8
princess among the *p.* *Lam* 1:1
against him from the *p.* *Ezek* 19:8
Daniel ruler over the *p.* *Dan* 2:48
image in the *p.* of Babylon. 3:1
promoted Shadrach in the *p.* of. 30
at Shushan in the *p.* of Elam. 8:2
on the fattest places of the *p.* 11:24
asked of what *p.* he was. *Acts* 23:34
Festus was come into the *p.* 25:1
proving
Saul *p.* that this is very. *Acts* 9:22
p. what is acceptable to. *Eph* 5:10
provision
give them *p.* for the way. *Gen* 42:25
gave them *p.* for the way. 45:21
all the bread of their *p.* *Josh* 9:5
bread we took hot for our *p.* 12
each man made *p.* *1 Ki* 4:7
Solomon's *p.* for one day was. 22
he prepared great *p.* *2 Ki* 6:23
for which I have made *p.* *1 Chr* 29:19
abundantly bless her *p.* *Ps* 132:15
appointed them a daily *p.* *Dan* 1:5*
make not *p.* for the flesh. *Rom* 13:14
provocation
Israel sin by his *p.* *1 Ki* 15:30
for the *p.* wherewith Ahab. 21:22
because of the *p.*, Manasseh. *2 Ki* 23:26
had wrought great *p* *Neh* 9:18, 26
eye continue in their *p.*? *Job* 17:2
harden not your hearts as in *p.* *Ps* 95:8*; *Heb* 3:8, 15
hath been to me as a *p.* *Jer* 32:31
presented *p.* of offering. *Ezek* 20:28

provoke
obey his voice, and *p.* *Ex* 23:21
will this people *p.* me ? *Num* 14:11*
if ye *p.* and break. *Deut* 31:20*
that *p.* God are secure. *Job* 12:6
how oft did they *p.* him ? *Ps* 78:40*
their doings are against Lord, to *p.* the eyes of his glory. *Isa* 3:8
do they *p.* me to anger ? *Jer* 7:19
in that ye *p.* me to wrath. 44:8
began to urge and *p.* *Luke* 11:53
I will *p.* you to jealousy by them that are no people. *Rom* 10:19
for to *p.* them to jealousy. 11:11, 14
do we *p.* the Lord to ? *1 Cor* 10:22
ye fathers, *p.* not your children to wrath. *Eph* 6:4
they had heard, did *p.* *Heb* 3:16
to *p.* to love and to good. 10:24
see **anger**
provoked
nor shall any of them that *p.* me see. *Num* 14:23*
these men have *p.* the Lord. 16:30*
in Horeb ye *p.* the Lord. *Deut* 9:8
at Taberah and Massah ye *p.* 22
her adversary also *p.* *1 Sam* 1:6
so she *p.* her, therefore she wept. 7
Judah *p.* him to jealousy. *1 Ki* 14:22
Manasseh had *p.* him. *2 Ki* 23:26
Satan *p.* David to number Israel. *1 Chr* 21:1*
our fathers had *p.* God. *Ezra* 5:12
tempted and *p.* the most high God. *Ps* 78:56*
but *p.* him at the sea. 106:7*
they *p.* him with their own. 29
because they *p.* the spirit. 33*, 43
when your fathers *p.* *Zech* 8:14
charity is not easily *p.* *1 Cor* 13:5
your zeal *p.* very many. *2 Cor* 9:2*
provokedst
forget not how thou *p.* *Deut* 9:7
provoketh
whoso *p.* him to anger. *Pr* 20:2
people that *p.* me to anger. *Isa* 65:3
where was image which *p.* *Ezek* 8:3
provoking
because of *p.* his sons. *Deut* 32:19
groves, *p.* Lord to anger. *1 Ki* 14:15
Baasha in *p.* the Lord. 16:7, 13
by *p.* the most High. *Ps* 78:17*
desirous of vain glory, *p.* *Gal* 5:26
prudence
son endued with *p.* *2 Chr* 2:12*
I wisdom dwell with *p.* *Pr* 8:12*
abounded in all wisdom and *p.* *Eph* 1:8
prudent
David *p.* in matters. *1 Sam* 16:18
p. man covereth shame. *Pr* 12:16
p. man concealeth knowledge. 23
every *p.* man dealeth with. 13:16
wisdom of the *p.* is to. 14:8
the *p.* man looketh well to his. 15
p. are crowned with knowledge. 18
he that regardeth reproof is *p.* 15:5
in heart shall be called *p.* 16:21
the heart of the *p.* getteth. 18:15
a *p.* wife is from the Lord. 19:14
p. man foreseeth evil. 22:3; 27:12
take away the *p.* and the. *Isa* 3:2*
woe to them that are *p.* in. 5:21
I have done it, for I am *p.* 10:13*
understanding of their *p.* men. 29:14
counsel perished from *p.*? *Jer* 49:7
who is *p.* and he shall ? *Hos* 14:9
the *p.* shall keep silence. *Amos* 5:13
hid these things from *p.* *Mat* 11:25*; *Luke* 10:21*
Sergius Paulus, a *p.* *Acts* 13:7*
understanding of the *p.* *1 Cor* 1:19
prudently
my servant shall deal *p.* *Isa* 52:13*
prune
six years shalt thou *p.* *Lev* 25:3
not sow thy field nor *p.* 4
pruned
waste, it shall not be *p.* *Isa* 5:6

pruning
beat spears into *p.* hooks. *Isa* 2:4; *Mi* 4:3
beat your *p.* hooks into. *Joel* 3:10
psalm
delivered first this *p.* *1 Chr* 16:7
take a *p.* *Ps* 81:2
with the voice of a *p.* 98:5
written in the second *p.* *Acts* 13:33
saith also in another *p.*, Thou. 35
how is it every one of you hath a *p.*? *1 Cor* 14:26
psalmist
David, sweet *p.* of Israel. *2 Sam* 23:1
psalms
sing *p.* to him. *1 Chr* 16:9*; *Ps* 105:2*
noise to him with *p.* *Ps* 95:2
David saith in book of *p.* *Luke* 20:42
written in *p.* concerning me. 24:44
written in the book of *p.* *Acts* 1:20
speaking to yourselves in *p.* and. *Eph* 5:19
admonishing one another in *p.* and. *Col* 3:16
any merry ? let him sing *p.* *Jas* 5:13*
psaltery
of prophets with a *p.* *1 Sam* 10:5
sing to him with the *p.* *Ps* 33:2; 144:9
awake *p.* and harp. 57:8; 108:2
praise thee with the *p.* 71:22; 92:3
pleasant harp with the *p.* 81:2
trumpet, the *p.* and harp. 150:3
when ye hear sound of the *p.* *Dan* 3:5, 7, 10, 15
public
to make her a *p.* example. *Mat* 1:19
publican, -s
A tax-gatherer. The taxes were farmed by the Roman Senate to the highest bidders. These delegated their duties to others, the one condition being that they should raise as much money as possible.
They were especially detested by the Jews, not so much on account of their frequent dishonesty, but because they were paid servants of the hated Romans. They were therefore considered as traitors and apostates.
the *p.* the same ? *Mat* 5:46, 47*
many *p.* sat with him. 9:10; *Mark* 2:15; *Luke* 5:29
eateth master with *p.* and sinners ? *Mat* 9:11; *Mark* 2:16; *Luke* 5:30
and Matthew the *p.* *Mat* 10:3
a friend of *p.* 11:19; *Luke* 7:34
as an heathen and a *p.* *Mat* 18:17
p. go into the kingdom of God. 21:31
p. and the harlots believed. 32
came *p.* to be baptized. *Luke* 3:12
saw a *p.* named Levi sitting. 5:27
p. justified God, being baptized. 7:29
then drew near to him the *p.* 15:1
one a Pharisee, and other a *p.* 18:10
thank thee, I am not as this *p.* 11
p. standing afar off, said, God. 13
Zacchaeus was chief among *p.* 19:2
publicly
p. convinced the Jews. *Acts* 18:28
have taught you *p.* 20:20
publish
I will *p.* name of Lord. *Deut* 32:3*
to *p.* it in the house. *1 Sam* 31:9*
p. it not in streets of. *2 Sam* 1:20
should *p.* that they bring. *Neh* 8:15
may *p.* with the voice. *Ps* 26:7*
p. in Jerusalem. *Jer* 4:5
p. against Jerusalem. 16
declare this, *p.* it in Judah. 5:20
p. ye and say, O Lord, save. 31:7
p. in Migdol, *p.* in Noph. 46:14
p. and conceal not, Babylon. 50:2
p. in palaces of Ashdod. *Amos* 3:9
proclaim and *p.* free offerings. 4:5
began to *p.* it much. *Mark* 1:45; 5:20
published
king's decree be *p.* through all. *Esth* 1:20, 22

Haman's decree was *p.* Esth 3:14; 8:13
company that *p.* it. Ps 68:11*
caused it to be *p.* through Nineveh. Jonah 3:7
a great deal they *p.* it. Mark 7:36
gospel must first be *p.* 13:10
he went and *p.* through. Luke 8:39
that word which was *p.* Acts 10:37
word of the Lord was *p.* 13:49*

publisheth

that *p.* peace, that *p.* Isa 52:7
voice *p.* affliction from. Jer 4:15
feet of him that *p.* peace. Nah 1:15

Publius

the father of *P.* lay sick. Acts 28:8

Pudens

greeteth thee and *P.* 2 Tim 4:21

puffed *up*

no one of you be *p. up.* 1 Cor 4:6
some are *p. up,* as though I. 18
speech of them that are *p. up.* 19
are *p. up,* and have not rather. 5:2
vaunteth not itself, is not *p. up.* 13:4
vainly *p. up* by his fleshly. Col 2:18

puffeth *at*

enemies, he *p. at* them. Ps 10:5
safety from him that *p. at* him. 12:5

puffeth *up*

knowledge *p. up,* charity. 1 Cor 8:1

Pul

P. king of Assyria came against Israel . . . gave *P.* 2 Ki 15:19
stirred up the spirit of *P.* 1 Chr 5:26
those that escape to *P.* Isa 66:19

pull, -ed

Noah *p.* the dove to him. Gen 8:9*
but the men *p.* Lot into the. 19:10*
Jeroboam could not *p.* 1 Ki 13:4
let timber be *p.* down. Ezra 6:11
p. me out of net they have. Ps 31:4*
from thy state shall *p.* Isa 22:19
set thee to *p.* down and destroy. Jer 1:10*; 18:7*
p. them out like sheep for. 12:3
them and not *p.* down. 24:6; 42:10
p. me in pieces, hath. Lam 3:11
shall he not *p.* up ? Ezek 17:9
shall no more be *p.* up. Amos 9:15*
ye *p.* off the robe with. Mi 2:8*
p. away the shoulder. Zech 7:11
Let me *p.* out the mote out of thine eye. Mat 7:4*; Luke 6:42*
I will *p.* down my barns. Luke 12:18
and will not *p.* out on the ? 14:5*
have been *p.* in pieces. Acts 23:10*

pulling

mighty to the *p.* down. 2 Cor 10:4*
others save with fear, *p.* Jude 23*

pulpit

stood upon *p.* of wood. Neh 8:4

pulse

beans and parched *p.* 2 Sam 17:28
let them give *p.* to eat. Dan 1:12, 16

punish

p. you seven times more for your sins. Lev 26:18, 24
to *p.* the just is not good. Pr 17:26
p. the stout heart of king. Isa 10:12
I will *p.* world for their evil. 13:11
Lord shall *p.* host of high ones. 24:21
Lord cometh to *p.* inhabitants. 26:21
sword shall *p.* leviathan. 27:1
I will *p.* all them that are circumcised. Jer 9:25
I will *p.* men of Anathoth. 11:22
say when he shall *p.* thee ? 13:21*
will *p.* you according to fruit. 21:14
I will even *p.* that man. 23:34
p. king of Babylon. 25:12; 50:18
will *p.* that nation. 27:8
I will *p.* Shemaiah. 29:32
p. all that oppress them. 30:20
p. Jehoiakim and his seed. 36:31
I will *p.* them in Egypt, as I *p.* 44:13
sign that I will *p.* you in this. 29
I will *p.* the multitude of No. 46:25
and I will *p.* Bel in Babylon. 51:44
will *p.* them for their ways. Hos 4:9
I will not *p.* your daughters. 14
p. Jacob according to his. Hos 12:2
I will *p.* you for your iniquities. Amos 3:2
day I will *p.* the princes. Zeph 1:8
I will *p.* all those that leap on. 9
I will *p.* men that are settled. 12
I thought to *p.* when your fathers. Zech 8:14*
how they might *p.* them. Acts 4:21

punished

he shall be surely *p.* Ex 21:20, 22
he shall not be *p.* for he is his. 21
thou hast *p.* less than. Ezra 9:13
it is an iniquity to be *p.* by judges. Job 31:11, 28
when scorner is *p.*, simple. Pr 21:11
but the simple pass on and are *p.* 22:3; 27:12
as I have *p.* Jerusalem. Jer 44:13
I have *p.* the king of Assyria. 50:18
howsoever I *p.* them. Zeph 3:7
shepherds, I *p.* the goats. Zech 10:3
to bring them bound to Jerusalem to be *p.* Acts 22:5
I *p.* them oft in every. 26:11
be *p.* with everlasting. 2 Thes 1:9
day of judgement to be *p.* 2 Pet 2:9

punishment

my *p.* is greater than. Gen 4:13
than accept the *p.* of their iniquity. Lev 26:41, 43
Saul sware, No *p.* shall. 1 Sam 28:10
and a strange *p.* to the workers of. Job 31:3*
great wrath shall suffer *p.* Pr 19:19
a man for *p.* of his sins. Lam 3:39
p. of my people is greater than the *p.* of Sodom. 4:6
the *p.* of thine iniquity is. 22
bear *p.* of their iniquity, *p.* of prophets as *p.* of. Ezek 14:10*
I will not turn away the *p.* Amos 1:3
6, 9, 11, 13; 2:1, 4, 6
the *p.* of Egypt. Zech 14:19
go into everlasting *p.* Mat 25:46
to such a man is this *p.* 2 Cor 2:6
of how much sorer *p.*? Heb 10:29
sent by him for the *p.* 1 Pet 2:14

punishments

wrath bringeth the *p.* Job 19:29
to execute *p.* upon the. Ps 149:7

pur

they cast *p.* that is, the lot. Esth 3:7
Haman had cast *p.* for to. 9:24
Purim, after the name of *p.* 26
see **Purim**

purchase, *substantive*

p. of field and cave. Gen 49:32
evidence of the *p.* Jer 32:11
I gave evidence of *p.* to. 12, 14, 16

purchase, -ed

field Abraham *p.* of. Gen 25:10
which thou hast *p.* Ex 15:16
if a man *p.* of the Levites. Lev 25:33*
Ruth have I *p.* to be my. Ruth 4:10
congregation thou hast *p.* Ps 74:2
his right hand had *p.* 78:54
this man *p.* a field with iniquity. Acts 1:18*
gift of God may be *p.* by. 8:20*
which he hath *p.* with his own. 20:28
redemption of the *p.* Eph 1:14*
office of deacon well, *p.* 1 Tim 3:13*

pure

that they bring the *p.* oil. Ex 27:20
Lev 24:2
take *p.* myrrh. Ex 30:23
with *p.* frankincense. 34
the *p.* candlestick. 31:8; 39:37
Lev 24:4
set cakes on the *p.* table. Lev 24:6
thou shalt put *p.* frankincense on. 7
didst drink the *p.* blood. Deut 32:14*
with the *p.* thou wilt shew thyself *p.* 2 Sam 22:27; Ps 18:26
measures of *p.* oil. 1 Ki 5:11
set on the *p.* table. 2 Chr 13:11
all were *p.* and killed. Ezra 6:20
shall a man be more *p.*? Job 4:17
if thou wert *p.* and upright. 8:6
hast said, My doctrine is *p.* 11:4
also my prayer is *p.* 16:17
stars are not *p.* in his sight. Job 25:5
words of the Lord are *p.* Ps 12:6
commandment of Lord is *p.* 19:8
word is very *p.*: therefore I. 119:140
the words of the *p.* are. Pr 15:26
say, I am *p.* from my sin ? 20:9
whether his work be *p.* 11
the *p.* his work is right. 21:8
every word of God is *p.* 30:5*
generation that are *p.* in their. 12
head like the *p.* wool. Dan 7:9
shall I count them *p.*? Mi 6:11
turn to the people a *p.* Zeph 3:9
in every place a *p.* offering. Mal 1:11
I am *p.* from the blood. Acts 20:26
all things indeed are *p.* Rom 14:20
whatsoever things are *p.* Phil 4:8
mystery of faith in a *p.* 1 Tim 3:9
of sins, keep thyself *p.* 5:22
with a *p.* conscience. 2 Tim 1:3
to the *p.* all things are *p.*, but to . . . nothing is *p.* Tit 1:15
our bodies washed with *p.* water. Heb 10:22
p. religion and undefiled. Jas 1:27
wisdom from above is first *p.* 3:17
I stir up your *p.* minds. 2 Pet 3:1
himself even as he is *p.* 1 John 3:3
angels clothed in *p.* linen. Rev 15:6
a *p.* river of water of life. 22:1
see **heart, gold**

purely

I will *p.* purge away. Isa 1:25

pureness

it is delivered by the *p.* Job 22:30
he that loveth *p.* of heart. Pr 22:11
approving ourselves, by *p.* 2 Cor 6:6

purer

Nazarites *p.* than snow. Lam 4:7
thou art of *p.* eyes than. Hab 1:13

purge

Josiah began to *p.* Judah. 2 Chr 34:3
p. me with hyssop. Ps 51:7
transgressions thou shalt *p.* 65:3†
and *p.* away our sins for thy. 79:9†
and purely *p.* away thy. Isa 1:25
I will *p.* from among. Ezek 20:38
shalt thou cleanse and *p.* it. 43:20*
seven days shall they *p.* altar. 26*
shall fall to *p.* them. Dan 11:35*
and *p.* them as gold. Mal 3:3*
he will throughly *p.* his floor, and. Mat 3:12*; Luke 3:17*
p. out therefore the old. 1 Cor 5:7
if a man therefore *p.* 2 Tim 2:21
p. your conscience from. Heb 9:14*

purged

Eli's house shall not be *p.* 1 Sam 3:14
when he had *p.* the land. 2 Chr 34:8
and truth, iniquity is *p.* Pr 16:6
shall have *p.* the blood of. Isa 4:4
taken away, and thy sin *p.* 6:7†
iniquity shall not be *p.* 22:14†
the iniquity of Jacob be *p.* 27:9†
have *p.* thee, and thou wast not *p.*, thou shalt not be *p.* Ezek 24:13†
when he had by himself *p.* our sins. Heb 1:3*
are by the law *p.* by blood. 9:22*
the worshippers once *p.* 10:2*
hath forgotten he was *p.* 2 Pet 1:9*

purgeth

beareth fruit, he *p.* it. John 15:2*

purging

draught, *p.* all meats. Mark 7:19*

purification, -s

it is a *p.* for sin. Num 19:9*
burnt heifer of *p.* for sin. 17*
according to *p.* of the. 2 Chr 30:19
the ward of their *p.* Neh 12:45
their things for *p.* be. Esth 2:3
so were the days of their *p.* 12
when days of her *p.* were. Luke 2:22
the accomplishment of the days of *p.* Acts 21:26

purified

and *p.* the altar, and. Lev 8:15
the Levites were *p.* Num 8:21
Ezra 6:20
shall be *p.* with water. Num 31:23
Bath-sheba was *p.* from. 2 Sam 11:4

are pure words, as silver *p.* *Ps* 12:6
many shall be *p.* and. *Dan* 12:10
from Asia found me *p.* *Acts* 24:18
things in the heavens be *p.* *Heb* 9:23
seeing ye have *p.* your. *1 Pet* 1:22

purifier

as refiner and *p.* of silver. *Mal* 3:3

purifieth

dead body and *p.* not. *Num* 19:13
that hath this hope *p.* *1 John* 3:3

purify

shall *p.* himself with. *Num* 19:12, 19
and shall not *p.* himself. 20
p. yourselves and your captives. 31:19
p. all your raiment, and all made. 20
by reason of breakings they *p.* *Job* 41:25
they *p.* themselves in. *Isa* 66:17
seven days shall they *p.* *Ezek* 43:26
and he shall *p.* the sons. *Mal* 3:3
went to Jerusalem to *p.* *John* 11:55
take and *p.* thyself. *Acts* 21:24
and *p.* to himself a people. *Tit* 2:14
p. your hearts, ye double. *Jas* 4:8

purifying

the blood of her *p.* *Lev* 12:4
when the days of her *p.* are. 6
sprinkle water of *p.* on. *Num* 8:7*
office was in *p.* all holy. *1 Chr* 23:28
with other things for *p.* of women. *Esth* 2:12
after the manner of the *p.* *John* 2:6
arose a question about *p.* 3:25
sanctifieth to the *p.* of. *Heb* 9:13

purifying, *verb*

p. their hearts by faith. *Acts* 15:9
and the next day *p.* himself. 21:26

Purim

(*Plural form of Hebrew* pur, *a lot. The annual festival instituted to commemorate the preservation of the Jews in Persia from the massacre designed by Haman. Haman, in his superstition, cast lots to determine the favourable day for the massacre*)
called these days *P.* *Esth* 9:26
that these days of *P.* should. 28
this sacred letter of *P.* 29, 31
Esther confirmed these *P.* 32

purity

example in faith, in *p.* *1 Tim* 4:12
younger as sisters, with all *p.* 5:2

purloining

not *p.* but shewing all good. *Tit* 2:10

purple

offering, blue, *p.* and scarlet. *Ex* 25:4
curtains of fine linen and *p.* 26:1
wires, to work in the *p.* 39:3
and spread a *p.* cloth. *Num* 4:13
p. raiment was on kings. *Judg* 8:26
cunning to work in *p.* *2 Chr* 2:7, 14
the vail of blue, and *p.* and. 3:14
cords of fine linen and *p.* *Esth* 1:6
with garment of linen and *p.* 8:15
clothing is silk and *p.* *Pr* 31:22
covering of it of *p.* *S of S* 3:10
hair of thine head like *p.* 7:5
and *p.* is their clothing. *Jer* 10:9
p. was that which covered thee. *Ezek* 27:7
in thy fairs with emeralds, *p.* 16
clothed him with *p.* *Mark* 15:17
they took off the *p.* from him. 20
rich man clothed in *p.* *Luke* 16:19
put on him a *p.* robe. *John* 19:2
forth wearing the *p.* robe. 5
Lydia, a seller of *p.* *Acts* 16:14
woman was arrayed in *p.* *Rev* 17:4
buyeth the merchandise or *p.* 18:12
that was clothed in *p.* and scarlet. 16

purpose

handfuls of *p.* for her. *Ruth* 2:16*
to frustrate their *p.* *Ezra* 4:5
they made for the *p.* *Neh* 8:4
withdraw man from his *p.* *Job* 33:17
every *p.* is established. *Pr* 20:18
and a time to every *p.* *Eccl* 3:1, 17; 8:6
to what *p.* is multitude ? *Isa* 1:11
this is the *p.* that is purposed. 14:26
shall help in vain, and to no *p.* 30:7
to what *p.* cometh to me incense ? *Jer* 6:20
Nebuchadnezzar conceived a *p.* 49:30
for every *p.* of the Lord shall stand. 51:29
that *p.* be not changed. *Dan* 6:17
To what *p.* is this waste ? *Mat* 26:8
with *p.* of heart, they. *Acts* 11:23
appeared to thee for this *p.* 26:16
that they had obtained their *p.* 27:13
centurion kept them from their *p.* 43
called according to his *p.* *Rom* 8:28
that the *p.* of God according to. 9:11
even for this same *p.* have I. 17
according to *p.* of him. *Eph* 1:11
according to the eternal *p.* in. 3:11
to you for the same *p.* 6:22; *Col* 4:8
according to his own *p.* *2 Tim* 1:9
thou hast fully known my *p.* 3:10
for this *p.* Son of God. *1 John* 3:8

purpose, -ed, *verb*

I *p.* to build an house. *1 Ki* 5:5
p. to keep under Judah. *2 Chr* 28:10
Sennacherib *p.* to fight against. 32:2
I am *p.* my mouth shall. *Ps* 17:3
who have *p.* to overthrow my. 140:4
as I have *p.*, so shall it. *Isa* 14:24
this is the purpose *p.* upon the. 26
the Lord hath *p.*, who shall ? 27
what the Lord hath *p.* upon. 19:12
Lord hath *p.* to stain the pride. 23:9
p. it, and I will also do it. 46:11
I have *p.* it, and will not. *Jer* 4:28
repent me of the evil which I *p.* 26:3
will hear all evil which I *p.* to. 36:3
purposes that he hath *p.* 49:20; 50:45
Lord hath *p.* to destroy. *Lam* 2:8
Daniel *p.* in his heart not. *Dan* 1:8
Paul *p.* in spirit to go to. *Acts* 19:21
Paul *p.* to return through. 20:3*
oftentimes I *p.* to come. *Rom* 1:13
things I *p.*, do I *p.* according to the flesh ? *2 Cor* 1:17
will which he hath *p.* in. *Eph* 1:9
eternal purpose which he *p.* in. 3:11

purposes

days are past, my *p.* are. *Job* 17:11
without counsel *p.* are. *Pr* 15:22
broken in the *p.* thereof. *Isa* 19:10
hear counsel of the Lord and *p.* *Jer* 49:20; 50:45

purposeth

every man as he *p.* in his. *2 Cor* 9:7

purposing

comfort himself, *p.* to kill. *Gen* 27:42

purse

lot, let us have one *p.* *Pr* 1:14
carry neither *p.* nor scrip. *Luke* 10:4
I sent you without *p.* and. 22:35
he that hath a *p.*, let him take it. 36

purses

nor brass in your *p.* *Mat* 10:9
take no money in their *p.* *Mark* 6:8

pursue

they did not *p.* after. *Gen* 35:5
enemy said, I will *p.*, I. *Ex* 15:9
lest the avenger of blood *p.* *Deut* 19:6; *Josh* 20:5
they shall *p.* thee until thou perish. *Deut* 28:22, 45
p. after them, ye shall. *Josh* 2:5
Ai were called together to *p.* 8:16
stay not, but *p.* after your. 10:19
whom dost thou *p.*? *1 Sam* 24:14
a man is risen to *p.* thee. 25:29
doth my lord thus *p.* me ? 26:18
shall I *p.* after this troop ? 30:8
arise and *p.* after David. *2 Sam* 17:1
servants, *p.* after Sheba. 20:6, 7
flee while enemies *p.* thee ? 24:13
p. the dry stubble ? *Job* 13:25
terrors *p.* my soul as the. 30:15*
seek peace and *p.* it. *Ps* 34:14
they that *p.* you be swift. *Isa* 30:16
the sword shall *p.* thee. *Jer* 48:2
blood shall *p.* thee. *Ezek* 35:6
enemy shall *p.* him. *Hos* 8:3
because Edom did *p.* his brother with the sword. *Amos* 1:11
darkness shall *p.* his. *Nah* 1:8

pursued

Abram *p.* them to Dan and Hobah. *Gen* 14:14, 15
brethren *p.* Jacob. 31:23, 36
the Egyptians *p.* after Israel. *Ex* 14:8; 9:23; *Deut* 11:4; *Josh* 24:6
***p.* the spies. *Josh* 2:7**
they of Ai *p.* 8:16, 17
***p.* after Adoni-bezek. *Judg* 1:6**
Barak *p.* after chariots. 4:16, 22
Gideon *p.* after. 7:23, 25; 8:12
Israel *p.* Benjamin unto. 20:45
Israel *p.* the Philistines. *1 Sam* 7:11; 17:52
Saul *p.* David. 23:25
David *p.* Amalekites. 30:10
Asahel *p.* after Abner. *2 Sam* 2:19
Joab *p.* Abner. 24
Joab *p.* Israel no more. 28
so Joab and Abishai *p.* 20:10
I have *p.* mine enemies. 22:38; *Ps* 18:37
fled, and Israel *p.* after. *1 Ki* 20:20
army of Chaldees *p.* the king. *2 Ki* 25:5; *Jer* 39:5; 52:8
Abijah *p.* after. *2 Chr* 13:19
Asa and people *p.* Ethiopians. 14:13
he *p.* them, and passed. *Isa* 41:3
they *p.* us upon the mountains, they laid wait for us. *Lam* 4:19*

pursuer, -s

lest *p.* meet you. *Josh* 2:16
until the *p.* returned, the *p.* 22
turned back upon the *p.* 8:20
without strength before *p.* *Lam* 1:6

pursueth, -ing

flee when none *p.* you. *Lev* 26:17
shall fall when none *p.* 36, 37
faint, yet *p.* them. *Judg* 8:4
I am *p.* Zebah and Zalmunna. 5
Saul returned from *p.* *1 Sam* 23:28
Joab came from *p.* a. *2 Sam* 3:22
returned from *p.* after Israel. 18:16
your god is *p.* or on a. *1 Ki* 18:27*
turned back from *p.* Jehoshaphat. 22:33; *2 Chr* 18:32
he that *p.* evil, *p.* it to. *Pr* 11:19
p. sinners, to the righteous. 13:21
he *p.* them with words, yet. 19:7
wicked flee when no man *p.* 28:1

purtenance

his head, legs, and *p.* *Ex* 12:9*

push

ox were wont to *p.* *Ex* 21:29*, 36*
if the ox *p.* a manservant or. 32*
with them he shall *p.* *Deut* 33:17
with these thou shalt *p.* Syrians. *1 Ki* 22:11; *2 Chr* 18:10
they *p.* away my feet. *Job* 30:12
through thee will we *p.* down our enemies. *Ps* 44:5
king of south *p.* at him. *Dan* 11:40*

pushed

p. all the diseased with. *Ezek* 34:21

pushing

I saw the ram *p.* westward. *Dan* 8:4

put

there God *p.* the man. *Gen* 2:8, 15
I will *p.* enmity between thee. 3:15
p. thy hand under my thigh. 24:2, 9; 47:29
and I *p.* the earring upon her. 24:47
p. them upon Jacob her. 27:15
she *p.* the skins of the kids. 16
Jacob *p.* the stones for his. 28:11
p. stone again on well's mouth. 29:3
p. own flocks by themselves. 30:40
when cattle were feeble, he *p.* not. 42
Rachel *p.* them in the camels'. 31:34
p. space betwixt drove and. 32:16
Tamar *p.* off her widow's. 38:14
all he had *p.* into Joseph's hand. 39:4
that they should *p.* me into. 40:15
he *p.* them altogether in ward. 42:17
Joseph shall *p.* his hand on. 46:4
p. thy right hand upon his. 48:18
p. off thy shoes from off thy feet. *Ex* 3:5; *Isa* 20:2; *Acts* 7:33

shall *p.* them on your sons. *Ex* 3:22
Lord said, *P.* now thy hand in. 4:6
speak to him, and *p.* words in. 15
to *p.* a sword in their hand. 5:21
I will *p.* a division between. 8:23
may know the Lord doth *p.* 11:7
will *p.* none of these diseases. 15:26
p. an homer full of manna. 16:33
p. his beast in another man's. 22:5
whether he have *p.* his hand. 8
an oath that he hath not *p.* his. 11
p. not thine hand with wicked. 23:1
thou shalt *p.* all in the hands of. 29:24
p. of the perfume before the. 30:36
p. every man his sword by his side. 32:27
now *p.* off thy ornaments. 33:5
p. thee in a cleft of the rock. 22
he *p.* all on Aaron's and. *Lev* 8:27
nor *p.* a stumblingblock. 19:14
p. the blasphemer in ward. 24:12
p. ten thousand to flight. 26:8
Deut 32:30
shall *p.* my name on the. *Num* 6:27
spirit which is on thee, and *p.* 11:17
the Lord would *p.* his Spirit. 29
serpent of brass, and *p.* it on a. 21:9
Lord *p.* word in Balaam's. 23:5, 16
thou shalt *p.* them in ark. *Deut* 10:2
p. the tables in the ark. 5:1
thou shalt *p.* the blessing on. 11:29
place he shall choose to *p.* 12:5, 21
ye shall rejoice in all ye *p.* 7
p. my words in his mouth. 18:18
thou shalt not *p.* any grapes. 23:24
p. it even among their. *Josh* 7:11
I *p.* my life in my hands. *Judg* 12:3
p. me into one of the priests' offices. *1 Sam* 2:36
he will *p.* your asses to work. 8:16
no man *p.* his hand to his. 14:26
and David *p.* them off him. 17:39
p. Goliath's armour in his tent. 54
did *p.* his life in his hand. 19:5
I have *p.* my life in my hand. 28:21
Lord *p.* them under the soles. *1 Ki* 5:3
to *p.* my name there. 9:3; 11:36
14:21
of the calves *p.* he in Dan. 12:29
on wood, and *p.* no fire under. 18:23
king, *P.* this fellow in prison. 22:27
he *p.* his mouth upon. *2 Ki* 4:34
king's son, they *p.* the crown. 11:12
p. thine hand upon bow, he *p.* 13:16
will *p.* hook in thy nose. 19:28
Isa 37:29
Jerusalem will I *p.* my name. 21:7
2 Chr 6:20; 12:13; 33:7
that have *p.* their lives. *1 Chr* 11:19
he *p.* his hand to the ark. 13:10
and the angel *p.* up his sword. 21:27
house have I *p.* the ark. *2 Chr* 6:11
the king of Egypt *p.* him down. 36:3
Cyrus *p.* the decree in writing. 22
Ezra 1:1
destroy kings that *p.* *Ezra* 6:12
p. such a thing in the king's heart. 7:27
what God had *p.* in. *Neh* 2:12
nobles *p.* not their necks to. 3:5
that every one *p.* them off. 4:23
Tobiah would have *p.* me in fear. 6:14, 19
decree drew near to be *p.* *Esth* 9:1
behold, he *p.* no trust in. *Job* 4:18
wherefore do I *p.* my life in ? 13:14
p. me in a surety with thee. 17:3
p. my brethren far from me. 19:13
but he would *p.* strength in me. 23:6
p. wisdom in inward parts. 38:36
canst thou *p.* an hook into his ? 41:2
thou hast *p.* gladness in. *Ps* 4:7
p. all things under his feet. 8:6
1 Cor 15:25, 27; *Eph* 1:22; *Heb* 2:8
p. in fear, O Lord, that. *Ps* 9:20
thou hast *p.* off my sackcloth. 30:11
let the lying lips be *p.* to. 31:18
he hath *p.* a new song in my. 40:3
p. to shame. 14; 44:7; 53:5
hast cast off and *p.* us to shame. 44:9
p. thou my tears into thy. 56:8
he *p.* them to a perpetual. 78:66
lover and friend hast thou *p.* 88:18

it is better to trust in the Lord than to *p.* confidence in man. *Ps* 118:8
than to *p.* confidence in princes. 9
O Lord, *p.* me not to shame. 119:31
p. a knife to thy throat. *Pr* 23:2
when thy neighbour hath *p.* 25:8
lest he that heareth it *p.* thee. 10
then must he *p.* to more. *Eccl* 10:10
I have *p.* off my coat, how shall I *p.*? *S of S* 5:3
my beloved *p.* in his hand by. 4
that *p.* darkness for light. *Isa* 5:20
p. down the inhabitants. 10:13
weaned child *p.* his hand on. 11:8
I have *p.* my Spirit upon him. 42:1
Mat 12:18
p. me in remembrance. *Isa* 43:26
thou shalt not be able to *p.* 47:11
I have *p.* my words in thy mouth and covered thee. 51:16; *Jer* 1:9
p. it into the hand of them. *Isa* 51:23
to bruise him, he hath *p.* 53:10
words I *p.* in thy mouth shall. 59:21
where is he that *p.* his Spirit ? 63:11
how shall I *p.* thee among ? *Jer* 3:19
our God hath *p.* us to silence. 8:14
have *p.* themselves to pain. 12:13
will *p.* my law in their inward. 31:33
p. my fear in their hearts. 32:40
O sword, *p.* up thyself into. 47:6
they *p.* the branch to. *Ezek* 8:17
I will *p.* a new spirit within. 11:19
36:26, 27; 37:14
comeliness I had *p.* upon thee. 16:14
priests have *p.* no difference. 22:26
I will *p.* hooks in thy jaws. 29:4; 38:4
I will *p.* a fear in Egypt. 30:13
and *p.* breath in you, and ye. 37:6
would, he *p.* down. *Dan* 5:19
p. in the sickle, for the. *Joel* 3:13
I will *p.* them together. *Mi* 2:12
trust not a friend, *p.* ye not. 7:5
where they have been *p.* *Zeph* 3:19
wages to *p.* it in a bag. *Hag* 1:6
light candle and *p.* it. *Mat* 5:15
nor do men *p.* new wine into. 9:17
let no man *p.* asunder. 19:6
Mark 10:9
p. the Sadducees to. *Mat* 22:34
p. my money to exchangers. 25:27
p. up again thy sword. 26:52
John 18:11
not lawful to *p.* them into. *Mat* 27:6
p. his hands on them. *Mark* 10:16
p. down mighty from. *Luke* 1:52
best robe, *p.* it on him, and *p.* 15:22
none to *p.* me into pool. *John* 5:7
he *p.* clay upon mine eyes. 9:15
p. it upon hyssop, and *p.* it to. 19:29
p. my finger into the print. 20:25
Father hath *p.* in his own. *Acts* 1:7
they *p.* the apostles in hold. 4:3
p. them in common prison. 5:18
the men whom ye *p.* in prison. 25
seeing ye *p.* the word of God. 13:46
and *p.* no difference between. 15:9
to *p.* a yoke upon the neck. 10
p. a stumblingblock. *Rom* 14:13
he shall have *p.* down. *1 Cor* 15:24
till he *p.* all his enemies under. 25
God, which *p.* the same earnest care. *2 Cor* 8:16
that ye *p.* off the old man. *Eph* 4:22
Col 3:9
ye also *p.* off all these. *Col* 3:8
if thou *p.* the brethren in remembrance. *1 Tim* 4:6; *2 Tim* 2:14
wherefore I *p.* thee in. *2 Tim* 1:6
p. them in mind to be subject. *Tit* 3:1
if he oweth, *p.* that on. *Philem* 18
to angels hath he not *p.* *Heb* 2:5
p. him to an open shame. 6:6
p. my laws into their mind. 8:10
p. my laws into their hearts. 10:16
we *p.* bits in the horses'. *Jas* 3:3
ye may *p.* to silence. *1 Pet* 2:15
to *p.* you always in. *2 Pet* 1:12
knowing that I must *p.* off this. 14
p. you also in remembrance. *Jude* 5
I will *p.* on you none. *Rev* 2:24
God hath *p.* in their hearts. 17:17

put *away*

p. away the strange gods. *Gen* 35:2
p. away the leaven out. *Ex* 12:15
nor take a woman *p. away*. *Lev* 21:7
p. away guilt of innocent blood. *Deut* 19:13; 21:9
he may not *p. away* all his days. 22:19, 29
p. away the strange gods. *Josh* 24:14
23; *Judg* 10:16; *1 Sam* 7:3
Eli said, *p. away* thy. *1 Sam* 1:14
Saul had *p. away*. 28:3
Saul whom I *p. away*. *2 Sam* 7:15
Lord hath *p. away* thy sin. 12:13
Jehoram *p. away* the. *2 Ki* 3:2
did Josiah *p. away*. 23:24
Asa *p. away* the abominable idols. *2 Chr* 15:8
covenant to *p. away* the wives. *Ezra* 10:3
they gave their hands to *p. away*. 19
in thine hand, *p.* it *away*. *Job* 11:14
p. away iniquity from thy. 22:23
I did not *p. away* his statutes from. *Ps* 18:22
p. not thy servant *away*. 27:9
p. away mine acquaintance. 88:8
p. away from thee a froward. *Pr* 4:24
have *p. away* ? for transgressions is your mother *p. away*. *Isa* 50:1
if a man *p. away* his wife. *Jer* 3:1
I had *p.* her *away* and given her. 8
if thou wilt *p. away* thine. 4:1
let them *p. away* their. *Ezek* 43:9
take her that is *p. away*. 44:22
let her *p. away* her whoredoms. *Hos* 2:2
p. far *away* the evil day. *Amos* 6:3
to *p.* her *away* privily. *Mat* 1:19
shall *p. away* his wife. 5:31, 32
19:9; *Mark* 10:11; *Luke* 16:18
man to *p. away* his wife ? *Mark* 10:2
if a woman shall *p. away* her. 12
p. away from you that wicked person. *1 Cor* 5:13
husband *p. away* his wife. 7:11, 12
I *p. away* childish things. 13:11
evil speaking be *p. away*. *Eph* 4:31
some having *p. away*. *1 Tim* 1:19
to *p. away* sin by the. *Heb* 9:26
see **death, evil**

put *forth*

lest he *p. forth* and take. *Gen* 3:22
Noah *p. forth* his hand and took. 8:9
men *p. forth* their hand and. 19:10
p. forth thine hand and. *Ex* 4:4
precious things *p. forth*. *Deut* 33:14
Ehud *p. forth* his left. *Judg* 3:21
angel *p. forth* the end of staff. 6:21
I will now *p. forth* a riddle. 14:12, 13
Samson *p. forth* and took. 15:15
Jonathan *p. forth* rod. *1 Sam* 14:27
servants not *p. forth* to slay. 22:17
not *p. forth* mine hand against. 24:10
Uzzah *p. forth* his hand to the ark of God. *2 Sam* 6:6; *1 Chr* 13:9
Absalom *p. forth* his hand. *2 Sam* 15:5
ye not *p. forth* my hand. 18:12
and his hand, which he *p. forth* against him, dried up. *1 Ki* 13:4
p. forth thine hand now and touch all that he hath. *Job* 1:11; 2:5
upon himself *p.* not *forth* thy. 12
p. forth his hands against. *Ps* 55:20
lest the righteous *p. forth*. 125:3
and understanding *p. forth* her voice? *Pr* 8:1
p. not *forth* thyself in presence. 25:6
Lord *p. forth* his hand and touched. *Jer* 1:9
p. forth form of an hand. *Ezek* 8:3
Son of man, *p. forth* a riddle. 17:2
Jesus *p. forth* his hand and. *Mat* 8:3
Mark 1:41; *Luke* 5:13
people were *p. forth*, he. *Mat* 9:25
parable *p.* he *forth*. 13:24, 31
Luke 14:7
to *p.* the apostles *forth*. *Acts* 5:34
but Peter *p.* them all *forth*. 9:40

put *on*

and raiment to *p. on*. *Gen* 28:20
Tamar *p. on* garments of her. 38:19
priest, shall *p.* them *on*. *Ex* 29:30
no man did *p. on* him his. 33:4

the priest shall p. on his. Lev 6:10
he shall p. on other garments. 11
p. on the holy linen coat. 16:4
he shall p. on his garments. 24
consecrated to p. on garment. 21:10
p. on incense, and go. Num 16:46
nor a man p. on a woman's. Deut 22:5
weep for Saul, who p. on. 2 Sam 1:24
I pray p. on now mourning. 14:2
Joab's garment he had p. on. 20:8
but p. thou on thy robes. 1 Ki 22:30; 2 Chr 18:29
able to p. on armour. 2 Ki 3:21
Mordecai p. on sackcloth. Esth 4:1
Esther p. on her royal apparel. 5:1
the just shall p. it on. Job 27:17
I p. on righteousness, and it. 29:14
how shall I p. it on? S of S 5:3
p. on strength. Isa 51:9; 52:1
p. on thy beautiful garments. 52:1
he p. on righteousness as a breastplate, he p. on garments. 59:17
and p. it on thy loins. Jer 13:1, 2
and p. on the brigandines. 46:4
p. on thy shoes upon thy. Ezek 24:17
p. on other garments. 42:14; 44:19
Nineveh p. on sackcloth. Jonah 3:5
nor what ye shall p. on. Mat 6:25; Luke 12:22
they p. on the ass and. Mat 21:7
and p. on him a scarlet robe. 27:28
platted a crown of thorns, they p. it on his head. 29; Jer 19:2
them p. a spunge on a reed. Mat 27:48; Mark 15:36
sandals, not p. on two coats. Mark 6:9
p. on him the best robe. Luke 15:22
a title and p. it on cross. John 19:19
p. on armour of light. Rom 13:12
but p. ye on the Lord Jesus. 14
corruptible must p. on. 1 Cor 15:53
shall have p. on immortality. 54
Christ, have p. on Christ. Gal 3:27
that ye p. on the new man. Eph 4:24; Col 3:10
p. on whole armour of. Eph 6:11
p. on therefore as elect. Col 3:12
p. on charity, which is the bond. 14

put out

one p. out his hand. Gen 38:28
p. out the remembrance. Ex 17:14
fire shall not be p. out. Lev 6:12
p. out of the camp every leper. Num 5:2, 4
and female shall ye p. out. 3
wilt thou p. out the eyes? 16:14
the Lord will p. out those. Deut 7:22
name be not p. out of Israel. 25:6
the Philistines p. out Samson's eyes. Judg 16:21
p. now this woman out. 2 Sam 13:17
he p. out his hand and. 2 Ki 6:7
p. out the eyes of Zedekiah and. 25:7; Jer 39:7; 52:11
have p. out the lamps. 2 Chr 29:7
wicked shall be p. out. Job 18:5
and his candle be p. out. 6; 21:17; Pr 13:9; 20:20; 24:20
hast p. out their name. Ps 9:5
when I p. thee out I will cover heaven. Ezek 32:7
when he had p. them all out. Mark 5:40; Luke 8:54
p. out of the stewardship. Luke 16:4
he should be p. out of the synagogue. John 9:22
lest they should be p. out of the synagogue. 12:42
p. you out of the synagogues. 16:2

put trust

come and p. your trust in my shadow. Judg 9:15
p. thy trust on Egypt. 2 Ki 18:24; Isa 36:9
p. their trust in him. 1 Chr 5:20
p. your trust in the Lord. Ps 4:5
p. their trust in thee rejoice. 5:11
my God, in thee do I p. my trust. 7:1; 16:1; 25:20; 71:1
thy name, will p. trust in thee. 9:10
in the Lord p. I my trust. Ps 11:1; 31:1; 71:1
savest them which p. their trust. 17:7
p. their trust under the shadow. 36:7
in God I have p. my trust, I. 56:4
I have p. my trust in the Lord. 73:28
p. not your trust in princes. 146:3
that p. their trust in him. Pr 30:5
hast p. thy trust in me. Jer 39:18
p. in trust with gospel. 1 Thes 2:4
I will p. my trust in him. Heb 2:13

put, participle

Joseph was p. in a coffin. Gen 50:26
the vessel, it must be p. Lev 11:32
but if any water be p. on seed. 38
shall be p. apart seven days. 15:19
as long as she is p. apart. 18:19
nor feet p. in fetters. 2 Sam 3:34
the kings having p. on their robes. 1 Ki 22:10
Judah was p. to the worse. 2 Ki 14:12; 2 Chr 25:22
the Syrians saw that they were p. to the worse. 1 Chr 19:16, 19
neither was the number p. in. 27:24
every device shall be p. 2 Chr 2:14
Israel be p. to the worse. 6:24
were p. from the priesthood. Ezra 2:62; Neh 7:64
be p. to shame that seek after my. Ps 35:4; 83:17
be p. to confusion, that desire. 70:2
let me never be p. to confusion. 71:1
shouldest be p. lower. Pr 25:7
nothing can be p. to it. Eccl 3:14
shalt not be p. to shame. Isa 54:4
ride, every one p. in array. Jer 50:42
have been p to shame. Zeph 3:19
is p. in to fill it up. Mat 9:16
John was p. in prison. Mark 1:14
new wine must be p. into new bottles. 2:22; Luke 5:38
no man having p. his hand to plough. Luke 9:62
Judas bare what was p. in. John 12:6
devil having now p. into the. 13:2
that is not p. under him, but now we see not yet all things p. Heb 2:8
bodies to be p. in graves. Rev 11:9

Puteoli

came the next day to P. Acts 28:13

putrifying

bruises, and p. sores. Isa 1:6*

puttest

p. thy nest in a rock. Num 24:21
bless all thou p. thine hands to. Deut 12:18; 15:10
thou p. on me will I bear. 2 Ki 18:14
thou p. my feet in stocks. Job 13:27
p. away the wicked like dross. Ps 119:119
that p. thy bottle to him. Hab 2:15*

putteth

who p. any on a stranger. Ex 30:33
word that God p. in my. Num 22:38
woman p. forth her hand. Deut 25:11
graven image, and p. it in a. 27:15
as he that p. off harness. 1 Ki 20:11
he p. no trust in his saints. Job 15:15
he p. forth his hand upon. 28:9
he p. my feet in the stocks. 33:11
p. not out his money to. Ps 15:5
God p. down one and setteth. 75:7
that p. his trust in Lord. Pr 28:25
who p. his trust in the Lord. 29:25
fig tree p. forth her. S of S 2:13*
p. his trust in me shall. Isa 57:13
as a shepherd p. on. Jer 43:12
he p. his mouth in dust. Lam 3:29
p. the stumblingblock. Ezek 14:4, 7
he that p. not into their. Mi 3:5
no man p. new cloth. Mat 9:16; Luke 5:36
tender and p. forth leaves ye know. Mat 24:32; Mark 13:28
no man p. new wine into old. Mark 2:22; Luke 5:37
immediately he p. in sickle. Mark 4:29
no man p. a candle under. Luke 8:16
no man, when he hath lighted a candle, p. it in a secret place. 11:33
whoso p. away his wife. Luke 16:18
when he p. forth his own. John 10:4

putting

p. it on Hagar's shoulder. Gen 21:14
p. them upon the head. Lev 16:21
p. their hand to their mouth and. Judg 7:6
p. forth of the finger. Isa 58:9
he hateth p. away. Mal 2:16
Ananias p. his hand. Acts 9:12, 17
they drew Alexander, Jews p. 19:33
as p. you in mind. Rom 15:15
p. away lying, speak truth. Eph 4:25
in p. off the body of the sins. Col 2:11
p. on the breastplate of. 1 Thes 5:8
p. me into the ministry. 1 Tim 1:12
by p. on of my hands. 2 Tim 1:6
not p. on of apparel, but. 1 Pet 3:3
not p. away the filth of the flesh. 21
to stir you up by p. you. 2 Pet 1:13

Q

quails

God gave quails *to the Israelites upon two occasions:* First, *in the wilderness of* Sin, *or* Zin, *a few days after they had passed over the Red Sea,* Ex 16:13. *The* second *time was at the encampment, called in* Hebrew, Kibroth-hataavah, *or* the graves of lust, Num 11:31, 32.

at even q. came up. Ex 16:13
the Lord brought q. Num 11:31
and they gathered the q. 32
and he brought q. Ps 105:40

quake

earth shall q. before. Joel 2:10
the mountains q. at him. Nah 1:5
earth did q. and rocks. Mat 27:51
I exceedingly fear and q. Heb 12:21

quaked

whole mount q. greatly. Ex 19:18
host trembled, and the earth q. 1 Sam 14:15

quaking

eat thy bread with q. Ezek 12:18
but a great q. fell on them. Dan 10:7

quantity

on him vessels of small q. Isa 22:24*

quarrel

a sword shall avenge q. Lev 26:25*
see how he seeketh a q. 2 Ki 5:7
Herodias had a q. against John. Mark 6:19*
if any man have a q. Col 3:13*

quarries

Ehud turned from the q. Judg 3:19
escaped and passed beyond q. 26

quarter

all people from every q. Gen 19:4
this was the west q. Josh 18:14
shall wander to his q. Isa 47:15
for his gain from his q. 56:11
to him from every q. Mark 1:45

see south

quarters

no leaven in thy q. Ex 13:7*
fringes on the four q. Deut 22:12*
in four q. were porters. 1 Chr 9:24*
winds from four q. of. Jer 49:36
as Peter passed through all q. Acts 9:32*
Jews which were in those q. 16:3*
in same q. were possessions. 28:7*
nations in four q. of earth. Rev 20:8*

Quartus

Q. a brother saluteth. Rom 16:23

quaternions

Peter to four q. of soldiers. Acts 12:4

queen

[1] *A sovereign princess, or chief ruler of a kingdom,* 1 Ki 10:1. [2] *The* queen of heaven, *a term applied to the moon by idolatrous moon-worshippers,* Jer 44:17, 25. *They set up altars to her upon the platforms or roofs of their houses*

or the corners of the streets, near their doors, and in groves. They offered cakes to her kneaded up with oil and honey, and made libations to her with wine and other liquors.
q. of Sheba heard of the fame of. *1 Ki* 10:1; *2 Chr* 9:1
q. had seen all Solomon's wisdom. *1 Ki* 10:4
no such spices as these the q. of Sheba gave. 10; *2 Chr* 9:9
king Solomon gave q. of Sheba all her desire. *1 Ki* 10:13; *2 Chr* 9:12
Hadad the sister of the q. *1 Ki* 11:19
Asa removed Maachah from being q. 15:13; *2 Chr* 15:16
salute children of the q. *2 Ki* 10:13
the q. sitting by him. *Neh* 2:6
Vashti the q. made a feast. *Esth* 1:9
to bring the q. 11
the q. refused to come. 12
shall we do to the q. Vashti? 15
q. hath not done wrong to the. 16
deed of q. shall come abroad. 17
have heard the deed of the q. 18
that pleaseth the king be q. 2:4
Esther q. instead of Vashti. 17
the q. exceedingly grieved. 4:4
what wilt thou, q. Esther? 5:3
q. let no man to the banquet. 12
what is thy petition, q. Esther? 7:2
was afraid before king and q. 6
request to the q. for his life. 7
will he force q. also before me? 8
house of Haman to Esther the q. 8:1
as Mordecai and Esther the q. 9:31
did stand the q. in gold. *Ps* 45:9
q. of heaven. *Jer* 7:18; 44:17, 25
say to the king and q., Humble yourselves. 13:18*
q. came into the banquet-. *Dan* 5:10
q. of the south shall rise up in the. *Mat* 12:42; *Luke* 11:31
Candace q. of Ethiopians. *Acts* 8:27
I sit a q. and am no widow. *Rev* 18:7

queens
there are threescore q. *S of S* 6:8, 9
q. thy nursing mothers. *Isa* 49:23

quench
shall q. my coal. *2 Sam* 14:7
that thou q. not the light of. 21:17
asses q. their thirst. *Ps* 104:11
waters cannot q. love. *S of S* 8:7
none shall q. them. *Isa* 1:31
flax shall he not q. 42:3; *Mat* 12:20
lest my fury come forth, and burn that none can q. it. *Jer* 4:4; 21:12
none to q. it in Beth-el. *Amos* 5:6
able to q. the fiery darts. *Eph* 6:16
q. not Spirit, despise. *1 Thes* 5:19

quenched
Moses prayed, fire was q. *Num* 11:2*; *2 Chr* 34:25
wrath shall not be q. *2 Ki* 22:17
they are q. as the fire. *Ps* 118:12
it shall not be q. night. *Isa* 34:10
they are q. as tow. 43:17
nor shall their fire be q. 66:24
my fury shall burn, and shall not be q. *Jer* 7:20; 17:27
flame shall not be q. *Ezek* 20:47, 48
that never shall be q. *Mark* 9:43, 45
where the fire is not q. 44, 46, 48
q. the violence of fire. *Heb* 11:34

question, *substantive*
lawyer asked him a q. *Mat* 22:35
I will ask you one q. *Mark* 11:29
no man after that durst ask him any q. 12:34; *Luke* 20:40
there arose a q. between. *John* 3:25
apostles about this q. *Acts* 15:2
q. of words and names. 18:15
in danger to be called in q. 19:40*
I am called in q. 23:6; 24:21
no q. for conscience. *1 Cor* 10:25, 27

question, *verb*
began to q. him. *Mark* 8:11
scribes, What q. ye with them? 9:16

questioned, -ing
Hezekiah q. priests. *2 Chr* 31:9
q. among themselves. *Mark* 1:27
q. what rising from the dead. 9:10
and scribes q. with them. *Mark* 9:14
Pilate q. with him in. *Luke* 23:9

questions
to prove him with q. *1 Ki* 10:1
told her all her q. 3; *2 Chr* 9:1, 2
durst any ask him more q. *Mat* 22:46
and asking them q. *Luke* 2:46
accused of q. of their law. *Acts* 23:29
had certain q. against him. 25:19
doubted of such manner of q. 20*
I know thee to be expert in q. 26:3
which minister q. rather. *1 Tim* 1:4
but doting about q. and strifes. 6:4
but unlearned q. avoid. *2 Tim* 2:23
Tit 3:9

quick
(*Very frequently used with the old meaning of* living)
there be q. raw flesh. *Lev* 13:10
the q. flesh that burneth have a. 24
down q. into the pit. *Num* 16:30*
go down q. into hell. *Ps* 55:15*
swallowed us up q. 124:3*
him of q. understanding. *Isa* 11:3*
judge of the q. and dead. *Acts* 10:42*
shall judge the q. and the dead. *2 Tim* 4:1; *1 Pet* 4:5
the word of God is q. *Heb* 4:12*

quicken
(*To bring back to life, either literally, as to restore life to the body, or figuratively, to stimulate the spirit which was deadened*)
thou shalt q. me again. *Ps* 71:20
q. us, and we will call on thy. 80:18
q. me according to thy word. 119:25, 107, 149, 154, 156
turn me from vanity, q. me in. 37
q. me in thy righteousness. 40
q. me after thy. 88, 159
q. me, O Lord, for thy. 143:11
shall also q. your mortal. *Rom* 8:11

quickened
thy word hath q. me. *Ps* 119:50
thy precepts thou hast q. me. 93
thou sowest, is not q. *1 Cor* 15:36
you hath he q., who were. *Eph* 2:1
hath q. us together with Christ. 5
Col 2:13
but q. by the Spirit. *1 Pet* 3:18

quickeneth
as the Father q. them; even so the Son q. whom. *John* 5:21
it is the Spirit that q. 6:63
even God who q. the dead. *Rom* 4:17
God, who q. all things. *1 Tim* 6:13

quickening
was made a q. spirit. *1 Cor* 15:45

quickly
ready q. three measures. *Gen* 18:6
hast found it so q. my son? 27:20
aside q. out of the way. *Ex* 32:8
Deut 9:12, 16; *Judg* 2:17
put on incense and go q. *Num* 16:46
shalt thou destroy them q. *Deut* 9:3
get thee down q. 12
lest ye perish q. 11:17
till thou perish q. because of. 28:20
pursue q. for ye shall. *Josh* 2:5
the ambush arose q. out of. 8:19
come up to us q. and save us. 10:6
shall perish q. from off the. 23:16
thou shalt go down q. *1 Sam* 20:19
send q. and tell David. *2 Sam* 17:16
went both of them away q. 18
David, Arise and pass q. over. 21
king said, Come down q. *2 Ki* 1:11
fetch q. Micaiah the. *2 Chr* 18:8
threefold cord is not q. *Eccl* 4:12
with thine adversary q. *Mat* 5:25
go q. and tell his disciples. 28:7
they departed q. with. 8; *Mark* 16:8
go q. into the streets. *Luke* 14:21
sit down q. and write fifty. 16:6
Mary arose q. and came. *John* 11:29
That thou doest, do q. 13:27
saying, Arise up q. *Acts* 12:7
get thee q. out of Jerusalem. 22:18
I will come to thee q. *Rev* 2:5, 16
behold, I come q. 3:11; 22:7, 12
behold third woe cometh q. 11:14
Surely I come q. Even so. 22:20

quicksands
should fall into the q. *Acts* 27:17*

quiet
laid wait and were q. *Judg* 16:2
Zidonians, q. and secure. 18:7
to a people that were at q. 27
rejoiced, and the city was in q. *2 Ki* 11:20; *2 Chr* 23:21
land was wide and q. *1 Chr* 4:40
land was q. ten years. *2 Chr* 14:1
the kingdom was q. before. 5; 20:30
should I have been q. *Job* 3:13
neither was I q., yet trouble. 26
being wholly at ease and q. 21:23
against them that are q. *Ps* 35:20
glad, because they be q. 107:30
hearkeneth to me shall be in q. *Pr* 1:33
wise men are heard in q. *Eccl* 9:17
Take heed and be q.; fear. *Isa* 7:4
earth is at rest, and is q. 14:7
shall dwell in q. resting places. 32:18
Jerusalem a q. habitation. 33:20
and be in rest and q. *Jer* 30:10
long will it be ere thou be q.? 47:6
how be q. seeing the Lord hath? 7
sorrow on sea, it cannot be q. 49:23
Seraiah was a q. prince. 51:59*
I will be q. and will be. *Ezek* 16:42
though they be q. they. *Nah* 1:12*
ye ought to be q. and do. *Acts* 19:36
that ye study to be q. *1 Thes* 4:11
lead a q. and peaceable. *1 Tim* 2:2
a meek and q. spirit. *1 Pet* 3:4

quieted
behaved and q. myself. *Ps* 131:2
these q. my spirit in the. *Zech* 6:8

quieteth
when he q. the earth. *Job* 37:17*

quietly
took Abner to speak q. *2 Sam* 3:27
q. wait for the salvation. *Lam* 3:26

quietness
was in q. forty years. *Judg* 8:28*
I will give q. to Israel. *1 Chr* 22:9
not feel q. in his belly. *Job* 20:20
when he giveth q. who can? 34:29
dry morsel and q. *Pr* 17:1
better is an handful with q. *Eccl* 4:6
in q. and confidence shall. *Isa* 30:15
effect of righteousness, q. 32:17
thee we enjoy great q. *Acts* 24:2*
we exhort that with q. *2 Thes* 3:12

quit
he that smote him be q. *Ex* 21:19
owner of the ox shall be q. 28
will be q. of thine oath. *Josh* 2:20*
q. yourselves like men. *1 Sam* 4:9
1 Cor 16:13

quite
q. devoured also our. *Gen* 31:15
thou shalt q. break down. *Ex* 23:24*
q. take away their murmurings. *Num* 17:10*
and q. pluck down all their. 33:52*
and he is q. gone. *2 Sam* 3:24
and is wisdom driven q.? *Job* 6:13
bow was made q. naked. *Hab* 3:9

quiver
therefore take thy q. and. *Gen* 27:3
q. rattleth against him. *Job* 39:23
man that hath his q. full. *Ps* 127:5
Elam bare the q. with. *Isa* 22:6
in his q. hath he hid me. 49:2
q. is as an open sepulchre. *Jer* 5:16
arrows of his q. to enter. *Lam* 3:13

quivered
when I heard, my lips q. *Hab* 3:16

R

Rabbah, *or* **Rabbath**
is it not in R. of the children of? *Deut* 3:11
Israel besieged R. *2 Sam* 11:1
Joab fought against R. and. 12:26
Shobi of R. brought beds. 17:27
Joab smote R. and. *1 Chr* 20:1

an alarm to be heard in *R. Jer* 49:2
cry, ye daughters of *R.*, gird with. 3
sword may come to *R.* *Ezek* 21:20
I will make *R.* a stable for. 25:5
a fire in the wall of *R.* *Amos* 1:14

Rabbi

(A title of respect meaning master, teacher, *given by the Jews to their teachers and spiritual leaders, and often addressed to our Lord. Another form of the title was* Rabboni. *The titles were used with different degrees of honour—the lowest being* rab, *master; second,* rabbi, *my master; and greatest of all,* rabboni, *my lord, master.*
The term rab *was also used in Babylonia and Assyria to mean* chief*—as* Rab-mag, *the chief of the magi, etc.)*

called of men, *r. r.* *Mat* 23:7
be not ye called *r.*, for one is. 8
R. where dwellest thou? *John* 1:38
R. thou art the Son of God. 49
R. we know thou art a teacher. 3:2
R. he that was with thee. 26
they said, *R.* when camest? 6:25

Rabboni

Mary saith, *R.* *John* 20:16
R., [R.V.] that I may receive my sight. *Mark* 10:51

Rab-shakeh

(Properly a title of a court officer)
the king of Assyria sent *R.* *2 Ki* 18:17; *Isa* 36:2
they told him the words of *R.* *2 Ki* 18:37; *Isa* 36:22
God will hear the words of *R.* *2 Ki* 19:4; *Isa* 37:4

raca

(A term of reproach and contempt meaning empty, *and hence* worthless. *It is a weaker word than* fool)
shall say to his brother, *R. Mat* 5:22

race

strong man to run a *r.* *Ps* 19:5*
the *r.* is not to the swift. *Eccl* 9:11
run in a *r.* run all. *1 Cor* 9:24
run with patience the *r.* *Heb* 12:1

Rachel

Jacob told *R.* that he. *Gen* 29:12
name of the younger was *R.* 16
R. was beautiful and well. 17
Jacob loved *R.* 18, 30
R. was barren. 31
seven years for *R.* 20, 25
Laban gave him *R.* his. 28
R. bare no children, *R.* envied. 30:1
kindled against *R.*: he said. 2
God remembered *R.* and opened. 22
R. had stolen her father's. 31:19, 34
then Laban went into *R.*'s tent. 33
Jacob put *R.* and Joseph. 33:2
R. died. 35:19; 48:7
sons of *R.* 35:24; 46:19, 22
make the woman like *R. Ruth* 4:11
find two men by *R.*'s. *1 Sam* 10:2
R. weeping. *Jer* 31:15; *Mat* 2:18

rafters

cedar, and our *r.* of fir. *S of S* 1:17

Ragau

was the son of *R.* *Luke* 3:35

rage, *substantive*

turned away in a *r.* *2 Ki* 5:12
I know thy *r.* against me. 19:27 *Isa* 37:28
Asa was in a *r.* with. *2 Chr* 16:10
and ye have slain them in a *r.* 28:9
swalloweth the ground with *r.* *Job* 39:24
cast abroad *r.* of thy wrath. 40:11*
thyself because of *r.* of. *Ps* 7:6
jealousy is *r.* of a man. *Pr* 6:34
Nebuchadnezzar commanded in his *r.* to bring. *Dan* 3:13
they shall fall for the *r.* *Hos* 7:16

rage, *verb*

why do the heathen *r.*? *Ps* 2:1 *Acts* 4:25
whether he *r.* or laugh. *Pr* 29:9
ye horses, *r.* ye chariots. *Jer* 46:9
chariots shall *r.* in streets. *Nah* 2:4

raged

heathen *r.*, the kingdoms. *Ps* 46:6

rageth

fool *r.* and is confident. *Pr* 14:16*

ragged

tops of the *r.* rocks. *Isa* 2:21

raging

thou rulest the *r.* of the sea. *Ps* 89:9
strong drink is *r.* *Pr* 20:1*
sea ceased from her *r.* *Jonah* 1:15
wind and *r.* of the water. *Luke* 8:24
r. waves of the sea foaming. *Jude* 13

rags

clothe a man with *r.* *Pr* 23:21
all our righteousnesses are as filthy *r.* *Isa* 64:6*
took old rotten *r.* *Jer* 38:11
put *r.* under thine arm holes. 12

Rahab, *person, place*

entered into house of *R.* *Josh* 2:1
only *R.* shall live. 6:17
Joshua saved *R.* 25
make mention of *R.* *Ps* 87:4
thou hast broken *R.* in pieces. 89:10
not it that hath cut *R.*? *Isa* 51:9
Salmon begat Booz of *R.* *Mat* 1:5
by faith the harlot *R.* *Heb* 11:31
was not *R.* also justified? *Jas* 2:25

rail

he wrote letters to *r.* *2 Chr* 32:17

railed

our master *r.* on them. *1 Sam* 25:14*
they that passed by *r.* *Mark* 15:29
one of malefactors *r.* on. *Luke* 23:39

railer

keep not company with *r. 1 Cor* 5:11*

railing, *adjective*

angels bring not *r.* *2 Pet* 2:11
Michael durst not bring against him a *r.* accusation. *Jude* 9

railing

cometh envy, strife, *r.* *1 Tim* 6:4
not rendering *r.* for *r.* *1 Pet* 3:9*

raiment

the servant gave *r.* to. *Gen* 24:53
Rebekah took goodly *r.* of. 27:15
Isaac smelled his *r.* and. 27
Lord will give me *r.* to put. 28:20
shaved, and changed his *r.* 41:14
gave to each man changes of *r.*, but to Benjamin five changes of *r.* 45:22
borrow of the Egyptians *r.* *Ex* 3:22 12:35
her food and *r.* shall he not. 21:10
trespass for sheep, for *r.* 22:9
thy neighbour's *r.* to pledge. 26, 27
unclean beast falls on *r.* *Lev* 11:32
purify all your *r.* all. *Num* 31:20
thy *r.* waxed not old. *Deut* 8:4
loveth stranger, giving him *r.* 10:18
she shall put *r.* of her captivity. 21:13
lost *r.* restore, and all lost. 22:3
that he may sleep in his *r.* 24:13
not take a widow's *r.* to pledge. 17
to your tents with much *r. Josh* 22:8
a dagger under his *r.* *Judg* 3:16
purple *r.* that was on kings. 8:26
and put thy *r.* upon thee. *Ruth* 3:3
himself and put on *r.* *1 Sam* 28:8
with him ten changes of *r. 2 Ki* 5:5
the lepers carried thence *r.* and. 7:8
Solomon, gold, and *r.* *2 Chr* 9:24
the queen sent *r.* to clothe. *Esth* 4:4
and though he prepare *r.* *Job* 27:16
to king in *r.* of needlework. *Ps* 45:14*
cast out as the *r.* of. *Isa* 14:19*
and I will stain all my *r.* 63:3
thy *r.* was of fine linen. *Ezek* 16:13
thee with change of *r.* *Zech* 3:4*
his *r.* of camels' hair. *Mat* 3:4
and the body more than *r.* 6:25 *Luke* 12:23
why take ye thought for *r.*? *Mat* 6:28
a man clothed in soft *r.* *Mat* 11:8; *Luke* 7:25
his *r.* white as light. *Mat* 17:2 *Mark* 9:3; *Luke* 9:29
put his own *r.* on him. *Mat* 27:31
his *r.* was white as snow. 28:3
who stripped him of *r.* *Luke* 10:30
they parted his *r.* and cast lots. 23:34; *John* 19:24
Paul shook his *r.* and. *Acts* 18:6
I kept the *r.* of them that. 22:20
having food and *r.* let us. *1 Tim* 6:8*
a poor man in vile *r.* *Jas* 2:2
be clothed in white *r.* *Rev* 3:5
buy white *r.* that thou mayest. 18
elders clothed in white *r.* 4:4

rain

Palestine has its rainy season and its dry season. During the latter the brooks dry up, and the first rains are very welcome. Early rain meant the autumn rain, Deut 11:14, *and latter rain that of the Spring,* Pr 16:15.

r. was upon the earth. *Gen* 7:12
r. from heaven was restrained. 8:2
the *r.* was not poured on. *Ex* 9:33
Pharaoh saw the *r.* ceased. 34
I will give you *r.* in due season. *Lev* 26:4; *Deut* 11:14; 28:12
land drinks water of *r.* *Deut* 11:11
heaven that there be no *r.* 17 *1 Ki* 8:35; *2 Chr* 6:26; 7:13
make *r.* of thy land. *Deut* 28:24
my doctrine shall drop as the *r.* 32:2
on the Lord to send *r.* *1 Sam* 12:17
sent thunder and *r.* that day. 18
no dew nor *r.* upon. *2 Sam* 1:21
by clear shining after *r.* 23:4
give *r.* upon thy land. *1 Ki* 8:36 *2 Chr* 6:27
shall not be dew nor *r.* *1 Ki* 17:1
because there had been no *r.* 7
till that day the Lord send *r.* 14
shew to Ahab, I will send *r.* 18:1
a sound of abundance of *r.* 41
that the *r.* stop thee not. 44
and there was a great *r.* 45
not see wind, nor see *r.* *2 Ki* 3:17
trembling for the great *r.* *Ezra* 10:9
and it is a time of much *r.* 13
giveth *r.* upon the earth. *Job* 5:10
he made a decree for *r.* and. 28:26
waited for me as for the *r.* 29:23
clouds pour down *r.* 36:27
to small *r.* and to great *r.* of. 37:6
hath *r.* a father? or who hath? 38:28
didst send a plentiful *r.* *Ps* 68:9
down like *r.* on mown grass. 72:6
the *r.* also filleth the pools. 84:6
he gave them hail for *r.* and. 105:32
he maketh lightnings for the *r.* 135:7
Lord, who prepareth *r.* for. 147:8
clouds and wind without *r.* *Pr* 25:14
the north wind driveth away *r.* 23
as snow in summer, and *r.* in. 26:1
poor, is like a sweeping *r.* 28:3
if clouds be full of *r.* *Eccl* 11:3
clouds return after the *r.* 12:2
winter is past, *r.* is over. *S of S* 2:11
a covert from storm and *r.* *Isa* 4:6
clouds they *r.* no *r.* on it. 5:6
then shall he give the *r.* of. 30:23
as ash, and *r.* doth nourish it. 44:14
as the *r.* cometh down. 55:10
the Lord that giveth *r.* *Jer* 5:24
lightnings with *r.* 10:13; 51:16
for there was no *r.* 14:4
vanities of Gentiles can cause *r.*? 22
bow in cloud in day of *r.* *Ezek* 1:28
I will *r.* an overflowing *r.* 38:22*
shall make us as the *r.* *Hos* 6:3
to come down for you *r.* *Joel* 2:23
withholden the *r.* from you. *Amos* 4:7
upon them shall be no *r.* *Zech* 14:17
go not up, that have no *r.* 18
he sendeth *r.* on just and. *Mat* 5:45
r. descended, and floods. 7:25, 27
did good, and gave us *r.* *Acts* 14:17
because of the present *r.* 28:2
which drinketh in the *r.* *Heb* 6:7
and the heaven gave *r.* *Jas* 5:18

see **latter**

rain, *verb*
Lord had not caused it to r. Gen 2:5
cause it to r. forty days. 7:4
I will cause it to r. Ex 9:18
I will r. bread from heaven. 16:4
God shall r. his fury. Job 20:23
cause it to r. on the earth. 38:26
wicked he shall r. snares. Ps 11:6
that they r. no rain on it. Isa 5:6
r. an overflowing rain. Ezek 38:22
r. righteousness on you. Hos 10:12
I caused it to r. on one city. Amos 4:7
earnestly it might not r. Jas 5:17
that it r. not in days of. Rev 11:6

rainbow
there was a r. round. Rev 4:3
I saw an angel, and a r. was. 10:1

rained
Lord r. upon Sodom. Gen 19:24
the Lord r. hail on land. Ex 9:23
had r. down manna. Ps 78:24, 27
the land not r. upon. Ezek 22:24
one piece was r. upon; and the piece whereupon it r. not. Amos 4:7
the same day it r. fire. Luke 17:29
it r. not for three years. Jas 5:17

rainy
dropping in a r. day. Pr 27:15

raise
marry her, and r. up seed. Gen 38:8
shalt not r. a false report. Ex 23:1
God will r. up a prophet. Deut 18:15
18; Acts 3:22; 7:37
refuseth to r. up to brother a name. Deut 25:7
r. thereon a great heap. Josh 8:29
to r. up the name of. Ruth 4:5, 10
I will r. me up a faithful priest. 1 Sam 2:35
I will r. up evil. 2 Sam 12:11
elders went to him to r. him. 17
Lord shall r. up a king. 1 Ki 14:14
I will r. up thy seed. 1 Chr 17:11
who are ready to r. up their mourning. Job 3:8
his troops r. up their way. 19:12
they r. up against me ways of. 30:12
merciful to me, and r. me. Ps 41:10
they shall r. up a cry of. Isa 15:5
I will r. forts against thee. 29:3
I will r. up decayed places. 44:26
my servant to r. up tribes. 49:6
r. up foundations of many. 58:12
they shall r. up the former. 61:4
r. to David a righteous. Jer 23:5
their king, whom I will r. up. 30:9
I will r. against Babylon. 50:9
none shall r. him up. 32
r. a destroying wind. 51:1
I will r. up thy lovers. Ezek 23:22
I will r. up for them a plant. 34:29
third day he will r. us up. Hos 6:2
I will r. them out of the. Joel 3:7
there is none to r. her up. Amos 5:2
I will r. a nation against you. 6:14
I will r. up the tabernacle of David, and I will r. up his ruins. 9:11
we shall r. against him. Mi 5:5
there are that r. up strife. Hab 1:3
I will r. up the Chaldeans. 6
I will r. up a shepherd. Zech 11:16
to r. up children to Abraham. Mat 3:9; Luke 3:8
cleanse lepers, r. dead. Mat 10:8
marry his wife, and r. up seed. 22:24; Mark 12:19; Luke 20:28
in three days I will r. it. John 2:19
will r. it up again. 6:39, 40, 44, 54
he would r. up Christ to. Acts 2:30
incredible that God should r.? 26:8
will also r. up us by his. 1 Cor 6:14
r. up us also by Jesus. 2 Cor 4:14
accounting God was able to r. him up. Heb 11:19
Lord shall r. him up. Jas 5:15

raised
I r. thee up to shew my power. Ex 9:16; Rom 9:17
children whom he r. up. Josh 5:7
they r. over him a great heap. 7:26
Lord r. up judges. Judg 2:16, 18
Lord r. up a deliverer. 3:9, 15
man who was r. up. 2 Sam 23:1
Solomon r. up a levy of Israel. 1 Ki 5:13; 9:15
and r. it up to the towers. 2 Chr 32:5; 33:14
whose spirit God r. to. Ezra 1:5
not awake, nor be r. out. Job 14:12
I r. thee up under. S of S 8:5
it r. up from their thrones. Isa 14:9
the Assyrian r. up the palaces. 23:13
who r. up the righteous man. 41:2
I have r. up one from north. 25
r. him up in righteousness. 45:13
a great nation shall be r. Jer 6:22
a great whirlwind shall be r. 25:32
Lord hath r. us up prophets. 29:15
many kings shall be r. from. 50:41
Lord r. up the spirit of kings. 51:11
a bear r. up itself on. Dan 7:5
I r. up of your sons for. Amos 2:11
is r. up out of his holy. Zech 2:13
when I have r. up thy sons. 9:13
Joseph being r. from sleep. Mat 1:24
the dead are r. up. 11:5; Luke 7:22
killed, and r. up again the third day. Mat 16:21; 17:23; Luke 9:22
hath r. up an horn of. Luke 1:69
now that the dead are r. 20:37
Lazarus whom he r. John 12:1, 9, 17
God hath r. up. Acts 2:24, 32; 3:15
26; 4:10; 5:30; 10:40; 13:30, 33
34; 17:31; Rom 10:9; 1 Cor 6:14
2 Cor 4:14; Gal 1:1; Eph 1:20
angel r. up Peter. Acts 12:7
he r. up David. 13:22
God r. to Israel a Saviour. 23
the Jews r. persecution against. 50
if we believe on him that r. Rom 4:24
r. again for our justification. 25
like as Christ was r. from dead. 6:4
Christ being r. from the dead. 9
him who is r. from the dead. 7:4
Spirit of him that r. up Jesus . . . he that r. up Christ. 8:11
r. up Christ; whom he r. 1 Cor 15:15
rise not, then is not Christ r. 16
if Christ be not r. your faith. 17
will say, How are the dead r.? 35
corruption, r. in incorruption. 42, 52
r. in glory, it is r. in power. 43
natural body, r. a spiritual body. 44
hath r. us up together in. Eph 2:6
operation of God who r. Col 2:12
his Son, whom he r. 1 Thes 1:10
remember Jesus was r. 2 Tim 2:8
their dead r. to life Heb 11:35
God that r. him up from the dead. 1 Pet 1:21

raiser
stand up a r. of taxes. Dan 11:20

raiseth
he r. poor out of the dust. 1 Sam 2:8; Ps 113:7
when he r. himself. Job 41:25
and r. stormy wind. Ps 107:25
he r. those that be bowed down. 145:14; 146:8
as Father r. up the dead. John 5:21
trust in God which r. 2 Cor 1:9

raising
baker who ceaseth from r. Hos 7:4
nor found they me r. up. Acts 24:12

raisins
hundred clusters of r. 1 Sam 25:18
Egyptians two clusters of r. 30:12
with 100 bunches of r. 2 Sam 16:1
brought bunches of r. 1 Chr 12:40

ram
take a r. of three years. Gen 15:9
a r. caught in a thicket. 22:13
take one r. Ex 29:15
thou shalt slay the r. 16
burn the whole r. 18; Lev 8:21
it is a r. of consecration. Ex 29:22
27, 31; Lev 8:22
eat the flesh of the r. Ex 29:32
take r. for burnt offering. Lev 9:2
r. for peace offering. 4
r. for trespass offering. 19:21
beside r. of atonement. Num 5:8
thus shall it be done for one r. 15:11
guilty, they offered a r. Ezra 10:19
shall offer a r. Ezek 43:23, 25
an ephah for a r. 45:24; 46:5, 7, 11
the prince shall offer a r. 46:4
new moon six lambs and a r. 6
I saw a r. which had two horns. Dan 8:3
I saw the r. pushing westward. 4
the goat ran to the r. that had. 6
come close to the r.: there was no power in the r.: none to deliver r. 7
the r. having two horns are. 20

Ram
Hezron begat R. and R. begat. Ruth 4:19; 1 Chr 2:9, 10
Jerahmeel, R. Bunah. 1 Chr 2:25
the sons of R. the firstborn. 27
Buzite of the kindred of R. Job 32:2

Ramah, Rama
R. a city of the tribe. Josh 18:25
Deborah dwelt between R. Judg 4:5
Elkanah came to his house in R. 1 Sam 1:19; 2:11
Samuel's return was to R. 7:17
15:34; 16:13
all the elders came unto R. 8:4
David fled, and came to R. 19:18
Saul went to R. 22, 23
Saul abode in R. 22:6
buried in his house at R. 25:1; 28:3
Baasha built R. 1 Ki 15:17
2 Chr 16:1
Baasha left off building of R. 1 Ki 15:21; 2 Chr 16:5
wounds the Syrians had given Joram at R. 2 Ki 8:29; 2 Chr 22:6
children of R. and Geba six hundred. Ezra 2:26; Neh 7:30
Benjamin dwelt at R. Neh 11:33
R. is afraid, Gibeah of. Isa 10:29
voice was heard in R. Jer 31:15
Mat 2:18
merchants of R. were. Ezek 27:22
blow ye the trumpet in R. Hos 5:8

Ramoth-gilead
R. i Gilead of the Gadites, a city. Deut 4:43; Josh 20:8; 21:38
Geber was officer in R. 1 Ki 4:13
know ye that R. is ours? 22:3
wilt thou go with me to battle to R.? 4; 2 Chr 18:3
shall I go against R.? 1 Ki 22:6
15; 2 Chr 18:14
saying, Go up to R. and prosper. 1 Ki 22:12; 2 Chr 18:11
Joram went against Hazael in R. 2 Ki 8:28; 2 Chr 22:5
take this box of oil, and go to R. 2 Ki 9:1
now Joram had kept R. 14
Gad to the Levites, R. 1 Chr 6:80

rampart
he made the r. and the wall. Lam 2:8
then populous No, whose r. Nah 3:8

rams
r. which leaped. Gen 31:10*, 12*
the r. of thy flock have I not. 38
Esau 200 ewes and 20 r. 32:14
r. of breed of Bashan. Deut 32:14
hearken than fat of r. 1 Sam 15:22
100,000 r. with wool. 2 Ki 3:4
to the Lord 1000 r. 1 Chr 29:21
Arabians brought 7700 r. 2 Chr 17:11
r. for offerings of the God. Ezra 6:9
dedication of the house 200 r. 17
with this money r., lambs. 7:17
offered ninety-six r. for a sin. 8:35
with the fat of r. Ps 66:15; Isa 34:6
mountains skipped like r. Ps 114:4, 6
the burnt offerings of r. Isa 1:11
is filled with fat of kidneys of r. 34:6
the r. of Nebaioth shall. 60:7
to the slaughter like r. Jer 51:40
occupied with thee in r. Ezek 27:21
I judge between the r. and. 34:17
ye shall drink the blood of r. 39:18
pleased with thousands of r. Mi 6:7
see **battering, seven**

rams' horns
bear before the ark seven trumpets of r. horns. Josh 6:4, 6, 8, 13
a long blast with the r. horns. 5

rams' skins
r. skins dyed red, and. *Ex* 25:5
26:14; 35:7; 36:19; 39:34

ran
Abraham *r.* to meet them. *Gen* 18:2
Abram *r.* to the herd. 7
servant *r.* to meet Rebekah. 24:17
Rebekah *r.* to the well to. 20
damsel *r.* and told her mother's. 28
r. out to the man to the well. 29
and Rachel *r.* and told her. 29:12
Laban *r.* to meet Jacob and. 13
Esau *r.* to meet him. 33:4
the fire *r.* along upon. *Ex* 9:23
r. a young man and. *Num* 11:27
Aaron *r.* into midst of the. 16:47
messenger *r.* to Aaron's. *Josh* 7:22
the ambush *r.* into Ai, and set. 8:19
all the host of Midian *r.* *Judg* 7:21
Jothan *r.* away, and fled. 9:21
Manoah's wife *r.* and shewed. 13:10
Samuel *r.* to Eli, and. *1 Sam* 3:5
a man of Benjamin *r.* out of the. 4:12
and they *r.* and fetched Saul. 10:23
David *r.* into the army and. 17:22
David *r.* and stood upon the. 51
as the lad *r.* he shot an arrow. 20:36
Cushi bowed himself to Joab and *r.*
2 Sam 18:21
Ahimaaz *r.* by the plain and. 23
servants of Shimei *r.* *1 Ki* 2:39
the water *r.* round about the. 18:35
Elijah *r.* before Ahab to Jezreel. 46
Elisha left the oxen and *r.* 19:20
the blood *r.* into the midst of. 22:35
my sore *r.* in the night. *Ps* 77:2*
waters *r.* in the dry places. 105:41
the ointment that *r.* down. 133:2
sent them, yet they *r.* *Jer* 23:21
the living creatures *r.* *Ezek* 1:14
r. out waters on the right side. 47:2
goat *r.* to the ram in fury. *Dan* 8:6
herd of swine *r.* violently. *Mat* 8:32*
Mark 5:13*; *Luke* 8:33*
one *r.* and filled a spunge.
Mat 27:48; *Mark* 15:36
many knew him, and *r.* *Mark* 6:33
r. through that whole region. 55
his father *r.* and fell on. *Luke* 15:20
Zacchaeus *r.* before and climbed. 19:4
then arose Peter and *r.* to the. 24:12
so they *r.* both together. *John* 20:4
the people *r.* together. *Acts* 3:11
they *r.* upon Stephen with. 7:57*
Philip *r.* to the chariot. 8:30
knew Peter's voice, she *r.* in. 12:14
Paul and Barnabas *r.* in. 14:14*
the people *r.* together and. 21:30
captain took soldiers and *r.* 32
they *r.* the ship aground and. 27:41
they *r.* greedily after the error of Balaam. *Jude* 11

rang
that the earth *r.* again. *1 Sam* 4:5
so that the city *r.* again. *1 Ki* 1:45

range
the *r.* of the mountains. *Job* 39:8

ranges
or *r.* for pots, they shall. *Lev* 11:35
that cometh within *r.* let. *2 Ki* 11:8*
have her forth without the *r.* 15*
2 Chr 23:14*

ranging
as a roaring lion, and a *r.* bear.
Pr 28:15

rank
ears came up upon one stalk, *r.* and good. *Gen* 41:5
devoured the seven *r.* ears. 7
forth in the second *r.* *Num* 2:16
go forward in the third *r.* 24
50,000 could keep *r.* *1 Chr* 12:33
men of war that could keep *r.* 38

ranks
against light in three *r.* *1 Ki* 7:4, 5
shall not break their *r.* *Joel* 2:7
they sat down in *r.* by. *Mark* 6:40

ransom, *substantive*
(*A price paid for freedom*)
give for the *r.* of his life. *Ex* 21:30*
every man a *r.* for his soul. 30:12
from pit, I have found a *r.* *Job* 33:24
a great *r.* cannot deliver. *Job* 36:18
give to God a *r.* for him. *Ps* 49:7
he will not regard any *r.* *Pr* 6:35
r. of a man's life are his riches. 13:8
the wicked shall be a *r.* for. 21:18
I gave Egypt for thy *r.* *Isa* 43:3
Son of man came to give his life a *r.*
Mat 20:28; *Mark* 10:45
who gave himself *r.* for all. *1 Tim* 2:6

ransom
r. them from power of. *Hos* 13:14

ransomed
r. of the Lord shall return. *Isa* 35:10
the sea a way for the *r.* to. 51:10*
redeemed Jacob and *r.* *Jer* 31:11

Rapha, and Raphu
Palti son of *Raphu.* *Num* 13:9
Rapha, father of Eleasah. *1 Chr* 8:37

rare
it is a *r.* thing that the king. *Dan* 2:11

rase
r. it, *r.* it, even to the. *Ps* 137:7

rash
be not *r.* with thy mouth. *Eccl* 5:2

rashly
quiet, and do nothing *r.* *Acts* 19:36

rate
gather certain *r.* every day. *Ex* 16:4
brought mules at a *r.* *1 Ki* 10:25
2 Chr 9:24
a daily *r.* for every. *2 Ki* 25:30
even after a certain *r.* *2 Chr* 8:13*

rather
if we have not *r.* done it. *Josh* 22:24
much *r.* when he saith to. *2 Ki* 5:13
chooseth death *r.* than life. *Job* 7:15
Jer 8:3
he justified himself *r.* *Job* 32:2
this hast thou chosen *r.* 36:21
and lying *r.* than to speak. *Ps* 52:3
r. be a doorkeeper in house. 84:10
receive knowledge *r.* than. *Pr* 8:10
to understanding *r.* than silver. 16:16
meet a man, *r.* than a fool. 17:12
a good name *r.* than great riches, loving favour *r.* than silver. 22:1
go *r.* to the lost sheep of. *Mat* 10:6
r. fear him that is able to. 28
r. than having two hands to. 18:8
r. than having two eyes to. 9
but go ye *r.* to them that sell. 25:9
but that *r.* tumult was made. 27:24
nothing bettered, but *r.* *Mark* 5:26
should *r.* release Barabbas. 15:11
r. rejoice, your names. *Luke* 10:20
r. blessed are they that hear. 11:28
but *r.* give alms of such things as. 41
but *r.* seek ye kingdom of God. 12:31
give peace? Nay *r.* division. 51
will not *r.* say unto him. 17:8
justified *r.* than the other. 18:14
men loved darkness *r.* than light.
John 3:19
obey God *r.* than men. *Acts* 5:29
not *r.* let us do evil, that. *Rom* 3:8
yea, *r.* that is risen again. 8:34
r. through their fall salvation. 11:11
avenge not, but *r.* give place. 12:19
another, but judge this *r.* 14:13
puffed up, and have not *r.* *1 Cor* 5:2
why do ye not *r.* take wrong? 6:7
if made free, use it *r.* 7:21
over you, are not we *r.*? 9:12
desire *r.* that ye may. 14:1, 5
had *r.* speak five words with my. 19
so that ye ought *r.* to forgive him.
2 Cor 2:7
ministration of the Spirit be *r.* 3:8
willing *r.* to be absent from. 5:8
therefore I will *r.* glory in. 12:9
God, or *r.* known of God. *Gal* 4:9
steal no more, but *r.* let. *Eph* 4:28
not named, but *r.* giving of. 5:4
with works of darkness, but *r.* 11
r. to the furtherance of. *Phil* 1:12
minister questions *r.* *1 Tim* 1:4
exercise thyself *r.* to godliness. 4:7
but *r.* do them service. 6:2
yet for love's sake I *r.* *Philem* 9
choosing *r.* to suffer. *Heb* 11:25
r. be in subjection to the. 12:9
but let it *r.* be healed. *Heb* 12:13
but I beseech you the *r.* to. 13:19
r. give diligence to. *2 Pet* 1:10

rattleth
quiver *r.* against him. *Job* 39:23

rattling
noise of the *r.* of wheels. *Nah* 3:2

raven, -s
Noah sent forth a *r.* *Gen* 8:7
every *r.* is unclean. *Lev* 11:15
Deut 14:14
I have commanded the *r.* *1 Ki* 17:4
and the *r.* brought Elijah bread. 6
who provideth for the *r.* his food?
Job 38:41; *Ps* 147:9
the *r.* of the valley. *Pr* 30:17
his locks bushy, and black as a *r.*
S of S 5:11
the owl and the *r.* shall. *Isa* 34:11
consider the *r.*: they. *Luke* 12:24

ravening
upon me as a *r.* lion. *Ps* 22:13
like a roaring lion *r.* *Ezek* 22:25
her princes are like wolves *r.*, the. 27
they are *r.* wolves. *Mat* 7:15
inward part is full of *r.* *Luke* 11:39*

ravenous
r. beast shall go up. *Isa* 35:9
calling a *r.* bird from the east. 46:11
give thee to the *r.* birds. *Ezek* 39:4

ravin
shall *r.* as a wolf. *Gen* 49:27
filled his dens with *r.* *Nah* 2:12

ravished
and be thou *r.* always. *Pr* 5:19
why wilt thou be *r.* with a strange? 20
thou hast *r.* my heart. *S of S* 4:9
the wives of Babylon shall be *r.*
Isa 13:16
r. the women in Zion. *Lam* 5:11
Jerusalem shall be *r.* *Zech* 14:2

raw
eat not of it *r.* nor sodden. *Ex* 12:9
if there be quick *r.* flesh. *Lev* 13:10
when the *r.* flesh appeareth. 14
priest see *r.* flesh, for *r.* flesh is. 15
have sodden flesh, but *r.* *1 Sam* 2:15

razor
shall no *r.* come upon his head.
Num 6:5; *Judg* 13:5; 16:17
1 Sam 1:11
thy tongue like a sharp *r.* *Ps* 52:2
shave with a *r.* hired. *Isa* 7:20
take thee a barber's *r.* *Ezek* 5:1

reach
a tower whose top may *r.* *Gen* 11:4
linen breeches shall *r.* *Ex* 28:42
your threshing shall *r.* to the vintage, and your vintage shall *r.* *Lev* 26:5
border shall *r.* to the sea. *Num* 34:11
head *r.* unto the clouds. *Job* 20:6
he shall *r.* even to the neck. *Isa* 8:8
breath shall *r.* to the midst. 30:28
thy plants *r.* to the sea. *Jer* 48:32
mountains shall *r.* to Azal. *Zech* 14:5
r. hither thy finger, and *r.* thy hand.
John 20:27
a measure to *r.* even. *2 Cor* 10:13

reached
the ladder's top *r.* to. *Gen* 28:12
he *r.* her parched corn. *Ruth* 2:14
the tree grew, and the height thereof *r.* to heaven. *Dan* 4:11, 20
as though we *r.* not to. *2 Cor* 10:14
Babylon's sins have *r.* *Rev* 18:5

reacheth
slain in a rage that *r.* up. *2 Chr* 28:9
thy faithfulness *r.* to the. *Ps* 36:5
thy truth *r.* to the clouds. 108:4
yea, she *r.* her hands to. *Pr* 31:20
sword *r.* unto the soul. *Jer* 4:10
because it *r.* to thine heart. 18
judgement *r.* to heaven. 51:9
greatness *r.* to heaven. *Dan* 4:22

reaching
r. forth to those things. *Phil* 3:13*

read
he *r.* in the audience. *Ex* 24:7
he *r.* all the words of the law.
Josh 8:34, 35

when king had *r.* letter. *2 Ki* 5:7
Hezekiah received and *r.* the. 19:14
Shaphan *r.* book of law. 22:8, 10
Josiah *r.* in their ears all the words. 23:2; *2 Chr* 34:30
curses in the book *r.* *2 Chr* 34:24
letter hath been plainly *r. Ezra* 4:18
king's letter was *r.* they made. 23
he *r.* the book of the law before the water gate. *Neh* 8:3, 8; 13:1
unto the last day he *r.* the law. 8:18
in their place and *r.* in the law. 9:3
book of the records was *r. Esth* 6:1
the letter, and *r.* it. *Isa* 37:14
Zephaniah the priest *r.* *Jer* 29:29
then *r.* Baruch the words of. 36:10
Jehudi *r.* it in ears of the king. 21
when he *r.* three or four leaves. 23
have ye not *r.*? *Mat* 12:3; 19:4
21:16; 22:31; *Mark* 2:25; 12:10
26; *Luke* 6:3
this title *r.* many of. *John* 19:20
the eunuch *r.* Esaias. *Acts* 8:28
place of scripture which he *r.* 32
prophets are *r.* every sabbath day. 13:27; 15:21
which when they had *r.* 15:31
when the governor had *r.* 23:34
our epistle, known and *r. 2 Cor* 3:2
when Moses is *r.* the vail is upon. 15
when this epistle is *r.* *Col* 4:16
that this epistle be *r.* *1 Thes* 5:27

read

the king shall *r.* therein. *Deut* 17:19
thou shalt *r.* this law before. 31:11
r. this, I pray thee. *Isa* 29:11, 12
book of the Lord and *r.* 34:16
go and *r.* in the roll thou. *Jer* 36:6
they said, Sit down now and *r.* 15
comest to Babylon and shalt *r.* 51:61
whosoever shall *r.* writing. *Dan* 5:7
king's wise men, they could not *r.* 8
gifts be to thyself, yet I will *r.* 17
did ye never *r.* in the ? *Mat* 21:42
and stood up for to *r.* *Luke* 4:16
heard him *r.* Esaias. *Acts* 8:30
write none other things than what ye *r.* *2 Cor* 1:13
ye *r.* ye may understand. *Eph* 3:4
likewise *r.* the epistle. *Col* 4:16
worthy to *r.* the book. *Rev* 5:4

readest

written in law, how *r.*? *Luke* 10:26
Philip said, Understandest thou what thou *r.*? *Acts* 8:30

readeth

he may run that *r.* it. *Hab* 2:2
abomination, whoso *r.* let him understand. *Mat* 24:15; *Mark* 13:14
blessed is he that *r.* and. *Rev* 1:3

readiness

received the word with *r. Acts* 17:11
there was a *r.* to will. *2 Cor* 8:11
having a *r.* to revenge all. 10:6

reading

them to understand the *r.* *Neh* 8:8
r. in book of words of the. *Jer* 36:8
hast made an end of *r.* this. 51:63
after the *r.* of the law. *Acts* 13:15
vail untaken away in *r.* *2 Cor* 3:14
give attendance to *r.* *1 Tim* 4:13

ready

be almost *r.* to stone me. *Ex* 17:4
be *r.* against the third. 19:11, 15
be *r.* in the morning, and. 34:2
we will go *r.* armed. *Num* 32:17
r. to go up into the hill. *Deut* 1:41
a Syrian *r.* to perish was my. 26:5
the city, but be ye all *r.* *Josh* 8:4
five sheep *r.* dressed. *1 Sam* 25:18
thy servants are *r.* to. *2 Sam* 15:15
thou hast no tidings *r.*? 18:22
Ezra was a *r.* scribe in. *Ezra* 7:6
art a God *r.* to pardon. *Neh* 9:17
r. against that day. *Esth* 3:14; 8:13
who are *r.* to raise up. *Job* 3:8
is *r.* to slip with his feet. 12:5
day of darkness is *r.* at hand. 15:23
prevail as a king *r.* to battle. 24
are *r.* to become heaps. 28
the graves are *r.* for me. 17:1
and destruction shall be *r.* 18:12
blessing of him *r.* to perish. *Job* 29:13
my belly is *r.* to burst like. 32:19
for I am *r.* to halt, and. *Ps* 38:17
tongue is pen of a *r.* writer. 45:1
art good, and *r.* to forgive. 86:5
I am afflicted, and *r.* to die. 88:15
to deliver those that are *r.* *Pr* 24:11
drink to him that is *r.* to. 31:6
be more *r.* to hear than. *Eccl* 5:1*
shall come who were *r.* to perish. *Isa* 27:13
shall be as a breach *r.* to fall. 30:13
stammerers be *r.* to speak. 32:4
Lord was *r.* to save me: we. 38:20
It is *r.* for the soldering. 41:7
as if he were *r.* to destroy. 51:13
now if ye be *r.* to fall. *Dan* 3:15
and all things are *r.* *Mat* 22:4
then saith he, The wedding is *r.* 8
Luke 14:17
therefore be ye also *r.* *Mat* 24:44
Luke 12:40
they that were *r.* went in. *Mat* 25:10
spirit is *r.* but the flesh. *Mark* 14:38*
servant sick, and *r.* to die. *Luke* 7:2*
Lord, I am *r.* to go with. 22:33
your time is alway *r.* *John* 7:6
to them, *r.* to depart. *Acts* 20:7*
I am *r.* not to be bound only. 21:13
come near, are *r.* to kill him. 23:15
are *r.*, looking for a promise. 21
r. to preach the gospel. *Rom* 1:15
of your *r.* mind. *2 Cor* 8:19
that Achaia was *r.* a year ago. 9:2
that, as I said, ye may be *r.* 3
same might be *r.* as a matter. 5
third time I am *r.* to come. 12:14
in good works, *r.* to. *1 Tim* 6:18
now *r.* to be offered. *2 Tim* 4:6*
put them in mind to be *r.* to. *Tit* 3:1
waxeth old, is *r.* to vanish. *Heb* 8:13*
r. to be revealed in. *1 Pet* 1:5
be *r.* always to give an answer. 3:15
account to him that is *r.* to. 4:5
not filthy lucre, but of a *r.* mind. 5:2
things that are *r.* to die. *Rev* 3:2
woman which was *r.* to be. 12:4*
see **made, make**

realm

the *r.* of Jehoshaphat. *2 Chr* 20:30
r. who are minded to go. *Ezra* 7:13
there be wrath against the *r.*? 23
better than all in his *r.* *Dan* 1:20
thought to set him over the *r.* 6:3
Darius, king over the *r.* of the. 9:1
he shall stir up all against *r.* 11:2

reap

and when ye *r.* . . . shall not wholly *r.* the. *Lev* 19:9; 23:10, 22
of itself thou shalt not *r.* 25:5
shall neither sow nor *r.* 11
eyes be on the field they *r.* *Ruth* 2:9
set your servants to *r.* *1 Sam* 8:12
in third year sow and *r.* *2 Ki* 19:29
Isa 37:30
wickedness *r.* the same. *Job* 4:8
they *r.* every one his corn. 24:6*
in tears shall *r.* in joy. *Ps* 126:5
iniquity, shall *r.* vanity. *Pr* 22:8
the clouds, shall not *r.* *Eccl* 11:4
wheat, but shall *r.* thorns. *Jer* 12:13
shall *r.* the whirlwind. *Hos* 8:7
righteousness, *r.* in mercy. 10:12
sow, but shalt not *r.* *Mi* 6:15
the fowls of the air *r.* not. *Mat* 6:26
Luke 12:24
thou knewest I *r.* where. *Mat* 25:26
r. whereon ye bestowed. *John* 4:38
if we shall *r.* your carnal. *1 Cor* 9:11
sparingly shall *r.* sparingly. . . bountifully shall *r.* bountifully. *2 Cor* 9:6
man soweth, that shall he *r.* *Gal* 6:7
of the flesh *r.* corruption . . . of the Spirit *r.* life everlasting. 8
in due season we shall *r.* if we. 9
in thy sickle, and *r.*: for the time is come for thee to *r.* *Rev* 14:15

reaped

wickedness, ye *r.* iniquity. *Hos* 10:13
labourers, which *r.* down . . . cries of them which *r.* are. *Jas* 5:4
sickle, the earth was *r.* *Rev* 14:16

reaper

the plowman shall overtake the *r.* *Amos* 9:13

reapers

Ruth gleaned after the *r.* *Ruth* 2:3
Boaz said to the *r.*, The Lord be. 4
let me glean after the *r.* 7
to his father to the *r.* *2 Ki* 4:18
to the *r.*, Gather the tares. *Mat* 13:30
enemy is devil, and *r.* are the. 39

reapest

riddance when thou *r.* *Lev* 23:22
r. that thou didst not. *Luke* 19:21

reapeth

harvestman *r.* the ears. *Isa* 17:5
r. receiveth wages, that both he that soweth and he that *r.* *John* 4:36
one soweth and another *r.* 37

reaping

of Beth-shemesh were *r. 1 Sam* 6:13
hard man, *r.* where thou hast not. *Mat* 25:24; *Luke* 19:22

reason

[1] *That faculty whereby we judge of things*, Dan 4:36. [2] *Proof, ground, or argument*, 1 Pet 3:15. [3] *To dispute, or argue*, Mat 16:8; Mark 8:16.

this is the *r.* of the levy. *1 Ki* 9:15
that can render a *r.* *Pr* 26:16
I applied to search the *r.* *Eccl* 7:25
same time my *r.* returned. *Dan* 4:36
It is not *r.* that we should leave the word of God. *Acts* 6:2
O ye Jews, *r.* would that I. 18:14
that asketh you a *r.* of. *1 Pet* 3:15

***by* reason**

plenty not known *by r.* *Gen* 41:31
land of Canaan fainted *by r.* 47:13
Israel sighed *by r.* of the. *Ex* 2:23
I heard their cry *by r.* of their. 3:7
corrupted *by r.* of the flies. 8:24
unclean *by r.* of a dead body. *Num* 9:10
hallowed things given *by r.* of. 18:8
shall bear no sin *by r.* of it. 32
afraid *by r.* of the fire. *Deut* 5:5
shoes are become old *by r. Josh* 9:13
for their groanings *by r.* *Judg* 2:18
Ahijah's eyes were set *by r.* of age. *1 Ki* 14:4
minister *by r.* of cloud. *2 Chr* 5:14
be not afraid *by r.* of this great. 20:15
by r. of the sickness. 21:15, 19
blackish, *by r.* of the ice. *Job* 6:16
is dim *by r.* of sorrow. 17:7
by r. of his highness I could. 31:23
by r. of oppressions . . . they cry out *by r.* of the arm. 35:9
we cannot order speech *by r.* 37:19
by r. of breakings they purify. 41:25
roared *by r.* of disquietness. *Ps* 38:8
blasphemeth *by r.* of enemy. 44:16
man that shouteth *by r.* of. 78:65
mourneth *by r.* of affliction. 88:9
if *by r.* of strength they be. 90:10
by r. of my groaning my. 102:5
not plow *by r.* of cold. *Pr* 20:4
by r. of the inhabitants. *Isa* 49:19
by r. of many waters. *Ezek* 19:10
terrors *by r.* of sword shall. 21:12*
by r. of the abundance of his. 26:10
Tyrus corrupted *by r.* of thy. 28:17
by r. of transgression. *Dan* 8:12
I cried *by r.* of my affliction. *Jonah* 2:2
noise *by r.* of multitude. *Mi* 2:12
sea arose *by r.* of a. *John* 6:18
by r. of him many believed. 12:11
by r. of him who subjected same. *Rom* 8:20
by r. of the glory that. *2 Cor* 3:10
by r. hereof he ought to. *Heb* 5:3
who *by r.* of use have senses. 14
to continue *by r.* of death. 7:23
by r. of whom the way of. *2 Pet* 2:2
by r. of the other voices. *Rev* 8:13
darkened *by r.* of the smoke. 9:2
rich *by r.* of the costliness. 18:19

reason, *verb*

that I may *r.* with you. *1 Sam* 12:7*
my words to *r.* with you. *Job* 9:14

and desire to r. with God. Job 13:3
he r. with unprofitable talk ? 15:3
and let us r. together. Isa 1:18
why r. ye among yourselves ?
Mat 16:8; Mark 2:8; 8:17
Pharisees began to r. Luke 5:21
Jesus said to them, What r. ye ? 22

reasonable

living sacrifice, which is your r. service. Rom 12:1†

reasoned

and they r. among. Mat 16:7; 21:15
Mark 8:16; 11:31; Luke 20:5
perceived that they so r. Mark 2:8
husbandmen r. among. Luke 20:14*
while they r. Jesus himself. 24:15
three sabbaths Paul r. Acts 17:2
he r. in the synagogue every. 18:4
Paul r. with Jews at Ephesus. 19
as he r. of righteousness and. 24:25

reasoning

hear my r. and hearken. Job 13:6
were certain scribes r. Mark 2:6
heard them r. together. 12:28
arose a r. among them. Luke 9:46
Jews departed, and had great r.
Acts 28:29

reasons

and gave ear to your r. Job 32:11
Bring forth your r., saith. Isa 41:21

Rebekah

Bethuel begat R. Gen 22:23
R. came out. 24:15
R. is before thee. 51
they sent away R. 59
they blessed R. 60
Isaac took R. 67; 25:20
R. loved Jacob. 25:28
lest men kill me for R. 26:7
a grief of mind to R. 35
words of Esau were told to R. 27:42
that he was R.'s son. 29:12
R.'s nurse died. 35:8
Isaac and R. his wife. 49:31
R. had conceived by. Rom 9:10

rebel

r. not against the Lord. Num 14:9
doth r. he shall die. Josh 1:18
an altar that ye might r. 22:16
seeing that ye r. to-day against. 18
r. not against the Lord, nor r. 19
God forbid that we should r. 29
and not r. against Lord. 1 Sam 12:14
not obey the Lord, but r. 15
will ye r. against the king ? Neh 2:19
thou and the Jews think to r. 6:6
that r. against the light. Job 24:13
if ye refuse and r. Isa 1:20
assemble for corn, and r. Hos 7:14

rebelled

thirteenth year they r. Gen 14:4
ye r. against my words. Num 20:24
27:14; Deut 1:26, 43; 9:23
so Israel r. against the house of.
1 Ki 12:19; 2 Chr 10:19
Moab r. against. 2 Ki 1:1, 3, 5, 7
Hezekiah r. against Assyria. 18:7
Jehoiakim r. against. 24:1
Zedekiah r. 20; 2 Chr 36:13
Jer 52:3
Jeroboam hath r. 2 Chr 13:6
were disobedient, and r. Neh 9:26
they have r. against thee. Ps 5:10
r. not against his word. 105:28
because they r. against the. 107:11
children, and they have r. Isa 1:2
r. and vexed his Holy Spirit. 63:10
I have r. Lam 1:18
I have grievously r. 20
r.: thou hast not pardoned. 3:42
to a nation that hath r. Ezek 2:3
r. in sending his ambassadors. 17:15
but they r. against me. 20:8, 13, 21
we have r. by departing. Dan 9:5
mercies, though we have r. against. 9
Samaria hath r. against. Hos 13:16

rebellest

On whom dost thou trust, that thou r.? 2 Ki 18:20; Isa 36:5

rebellion

know thy r. and thy stiff. Deut 31:27
shall know if it be in r. Josh 22:22
r. is as the sin of. 1 Sam 15:23
that r. hath been made. Ezra 4:19
and in their r. appointed. Neh 9:17
addeth r. unto his sin. Job 34:37
evil man seeketh only r. Pr 17:11
thou hast taught r. Jer 28:16; 29:32

rebellious

r. against Lord. Deut 9:7, 24; 31:27
a stubborn and r. son. 21:18
this our son is stubborn and r. 20
the perverse r. woman. 1 Sam 20:30
building the r. and. Ezra 4:12, 15
let not the r. exalt. Ps 66:7
r. dwell in a dry land. 68:6
yea, for the r. also. 18
and a r. generation. 78:8
thy princes are r. Isa 1:23
woe to the r. children, saith. 30:1
this is a r. people. 9
I was not r. 50:5
spread out my hands to a r. 65:2
hath been r. against me. Jer 4:17
hath a revolting and r. heart. 5:23
I send thee to a r. nation. Ezek 2:3
they are a r. house. 5, 6, 7; 3:9, 26
27; 12:2, 3
be not thou r. like that r. house. 2:8
in the midst of a r. house. 12:2
say now to the r. house. 17:12; 44:6
parable to the r. house. 24:3

rebels

for a token against the r. Num 17:10
said, Hear now, ye r. 20:10
from among you the r. Ezek 20:38

rebuke, *substantive*

shall send on thee r. Deut 28:20
this is a day of r. 2 Ki 19:3
Isa 37:3
at thy r., at the blast of. Ps 18:15
at thy r. both chariot and. 76:6
they perish at the r. of thy. 80:16
at thy r. they fled, they. 104:7
scorner heareth not r. Pr 13:1
but the poor heareth not r. 8*
r. is better than secret love. 27:5
better to hear r. of. Eccl 7:5
the r. of his people shall. Isa 25:8
thousand shall flee at r. of one, at r. of five shall ye flee. 30:17
behold, at my r. I dry up the. 50:2
full of the r. of thy God. 51:20
to render his r. with flames. 66:15
for thy sake I suffered r. Jer 15:15
be desolate in the day of r. Hos 5:9
without r. in midst of a. Phil 2:15

rebuke

any wise r. thy neighbour. Lev 19:17
glean them, and r. her not. Ruth 2:16
God look thereon, and r. 1 Chr 12:17
O Lord, r. me not. Ps 6:1; 38:1
r. the company of spearmen. 68:30
r. a wise man, and he. Pr 9:8
to them that r. him shall. 24:25
he shall r. many nations. Isa 2:4*
Mi 4:3*
but God shall r. them. Isa 17:13
not wroth with, nor r. thee. 54:9
Lord r. thee, even the Lord that hath chosen Jerusalem, r. Zech 3:2
I will r. the devourer. Mal 3:11
Peter began to r. him. Mat 16:22
Mark 8:32
brother trespass, r. him. Luke 17:3
said, Master, r. thy disciples. 19:39
r. not an elder, but. 1 Tim 5:1
them that sin, r. before all. 20*
r., exhort with all long. 2 Tim 4:2
r. them sharply. Tit 1:13; 2:15
said, The Lord r. thee. Jude 9
as many as I love, I r. Rev 3:19

rebuked

God hath seen and r. Gen 31:42
his father r. him, and said. 37:10
and I r. the nobles and. Neh 5:7*
hast r. the heathen, thou. Ps 9:5
he r. the Red sea also, and it. 106:9
thou hast r. the proud that. 119:21
he r. the wind. Mat 8:26
Mark 4:39; Luke 8:24
Jesus r. the devil; and. Mat 17:18
his disciples r. them. 19:13
Mark 10:13; Luke 18:15
multitude r. blind men. Mat 20:31
and Jesus r. him. Mark 1:25; 9:25
Luke 4:35; 9:42
Jesus r. Peter, saying. Mark 8:33
over her and r. the fever. Luke 4:39
turned, and r. James and John. 9:55
went before r. the blind man. 18:39
thief answering r. him. 23:40
when thou art r. of him. Heb 12:5
but Balaam was r. for. 2 Pet 2:16

rebuker

though I have been a r. of. Hos 5:2

rebukes

when thou with r. dost. Ps 39:11
execute judgements in furious r.
Ezek 5:15; 25:17

rebuketh

he that r. a wicked man. Pr 9:7
he that r. a man, shall find. 28:23
hate him that r. in gate. Amos 5:10
r. sea, and maketh it dry. Nah 1:4

rebuking

foundations of world discovered at the r. of the Lord. 2 Sam 22:16
r. them, suffered them. Luke 4:41

recall

this I r. to mind. Lam 3:21

receipt

Matthew sitting at the r. Mat 9:9*
Mark 2:14*; Luke 5:27*

receive

[1] *To take what is given, paid, or put into one's hands,* 2 Sam 18:12; 2 Ki 5:26. [2] *To entertain, lodge, or harbour,* Acts 28:2, 7. [3] *To bear with, or suffer,* 2 Cor 11:16. [4] *To hearken to,* Pr 2:1. [5] *To believe,* Mat 11:14; John 1:12. [6] *To admit one to be a member of the church,* Rom 14:1. [7] *To be endued with,* Acts 1:8.

thou shalt r. the wave. Ex 29:25
your tithes which you r. Num 18:28
shall r. of thy words. Deut 33:3
which thou shalt r. of. 1 Sam 10:4
though I should r. a thousand shekels. 2 Sam 18:12
thou shalt r. the cedar. 1 Ki 5:9
shall we r. good of God ? Job 2:10
shall r. of the Almighty. 27:13
Lord will r. my prayer. Ps 6:9
he shall r. the blessing from. 24:5
my soul, for he shall r. me. 49:15
afterward r. me to glory. 73:24
I shall r. the congregation. 75:2
if thou wilt r. my words. Pr 2:1
the wise in heart will r. 10:8
I r. comfort in these ? Isa 57:6*
thou shalt r. sisters. Ezek 16:61
ye shall r. of me gifts. Dan 2:6
Ephraim shall r. shame. Hos 10:6
r. of you his standing. Mi 1:11*
thou wilt r. instruction. Zeph 3:7
shall r. a prophet's reward . . . r. a righteous man's. Mat 10:41
blind r. their sight, lame walk. 11:5
if ye will r. it, this is Elias. 14
shall r. one such little child. 18:5
Mark 9:37; Luke 9:48
said, All men cannot r. Mat 19:11
r. an hundredfold. 29; Mark 10:30
is right, that shall ye r. Mat 20:7
ye ask, believing, ye shall r. 21:22
that they might r. fruits of it. 34
ye shall r. the greater damnation.
23:14; Mark 12:40; Luke 20:47
r. the word with gladness.
Mark 4:16; Luke 8:13
as hear the word and r. Mark 4:20
Lord, that I might r. my sight. 10:51
Luke 18:41
pray, believe that ye r. Mark 11:24
might r. from the husbandmen. 12:2
city ye enter, and they r. Luke 10:8
may r. me into their houses. 16:4
may r. you into everlasting. 9
for we r. the due reward of. 23:41
own name, him ye will r. John 5:43
can ye believe, which r. honour ? 44
on sabbath r. circumcision. 7:23
Spirit, which they that believe on him should r.: Holy Ghost was not. 39

I will come again, and r. John 14:3
r. of mine, and shew it to you. 16:14
ask and ye shall r. that your joy. 24
shall r. power after that. Acts 1:8
ye shall r. gift of Holy Ghost. 2:38
Jesus, whom heavens must r. 3:21
they might r. the Holy Ghost. 8:15
hands, may r. the Holy Ghost. 19
that he might r. his sight. 9:12
that thou mightest r. thy sight. 17
shall r. remission of sins. 10:43
that they may r. forgiveness. 26:18
r. abundance of grace. Rom 5:17
resist shall r. to themselves. 13:2
that ye r. her in the Lord, as. 16:2
shall r. his own reward. 1 Cor 3:8
if his work abide, he shall r. 14
if thou didst r. it, why dost thou ? 4:7
the church may r. edifying. 14:5
that every one may r. 2 Cor 5:10
touch not unclean thing, and I will r. 6:17
r. damage by us in nothing. 7:9
that we would r. the gift. 8:4
if ye r. another spirit ye have. 11:4
that we might r. promise. Gal 3:14
that we might r. the adoption. 4:5
the same shall he r. of. Eph 6:8
ye shall r. the reward of. Col 3:24
he shall r. for the wrong he. 25
shouldest r. him for ever. Philem 15
sons of Levi, who r. office. Heb 7:5
here men that die r. tithes. 8
which are called might r. promise. 9:15; 10:36
after r. for an inheritance. 11:8
think he shall r. any thing. Jas 1:7
he shall r. the crown of life. 12
shall r. greater condemnation. 3:1
until he r. early and latter rain. 5:7
ye shall r. a crown of glory. 1 Pet 5:4
shall r. the reward of. 2 Pet 2:13
we ask, we r. of him. 1 John 3:22
if we r. the witness of men. 5:9
that we r. a full reward. 2 John 8
if any man r. his mark in. Rev 14:9
but r. power as kings one hour. 17:12

receive, *imperatively*

then r. my present at. Gen 33:10
r. I pray thee, the law. Job 22:22
and r. my sayings. Pr 4:10
r. my instruction. 8:10; 19:20
let your ear r. the word. Jer 9:20
all my words r. in thine. Ezek 3:10
him, r. us graciously. Hos 14:2*
that is able, let him r. it. Mat 19:12
Jesus saith, R. thy sight. Luke 18:42
Acts 22:13
R. ye the Holy Ghost. John 20:22
Lord Jesus, r. my spirit. Acts 7:59
weak in the faith r. ye. Rom 14:1
r. ye one another, as Christ. 15:7
r. us, we have wronged. 2 Cor 7:2
yet as a fool r. me. 11:16
r. him in the Lord with. Phil 2:29
Marcus, if he come, r. him. Col 4:10
r. him that is mine own. Philem 12*
if thou count me a partner, r. him. 17
r. with meekness the. Jas 1:21

receive, *negatively*

said, I will r. none. 2 Ki 5:16
r. no more money of your. 12:7
shall we r. good, and shall we not r. evil ? Job 2:10
might not hear nor r. instruction. Jer 17:23
will ye not r. instruction to ? 35:13
r. no more reproach of. Ezek 36:30
not r. you nor hear. Mat 10:14
Mark 6:11; Luke 9:5
shall not r. the kingdom of God as a. Mark 10:15; Luke 18:17
not r. him, because his. Luke 9:53
and they r. you not, go into. 10:10
who shall not r. manifold. 18:30
and ye r. not our witness. John 3:11
a man can r. nothing, except it. 27
I r. not testimony from man. 5:34
I r. not honour from men. 41
in my Father's name, ye r. me not. 43
whom the world cannot r. 14:17
will not r. thy testimony. Acts 22:18
that thou didst not r.? 1 Cor 4:7
that ye r. not the grace. 2 Cor 6:1
against an elder r. not. 1 Tim 5:19
ye ask and r. not, because. Jas 4:3
r. him not into your house. 2 John 10
neither doth he himself r. 3 John 10
ye r. not of her plagues. Rev 18:4

to **receive**

to r. brother's blood. Gen 4:11
to r. his pledge from woman's. 38:20
his pans to r. his ashes. Ex 27:3
gone up to r. the tables. Deut 9:9
altar before the Lord was too little to r. 1 Ki 8:64; 2 Chr 7:7
is it a time to r. money, to r. garments ? 2 Ki 5:26
priest consented to r. no more. 12:8
to r. instruction of wisdom. Pr 1:3
refused to r. correction. Jer 5:3
not hearkened to r. instruction. 32:33
not room enough to r. it. Mal 3:10
to r. it, let him r. it. Mat 19:12
no room to r. them. Mark 2:2
of whom ye hope to r. Luke 6:34
nobleman went to r. for. 19:12
not lawful for us to r. Acts 16:21
the disciples to r. him. 18:27
blessed to give than to r. 20:35
therefore ought to r. such. 3 John 8
worthy, O Lord, to r. glory. Rev 4:11
worthy is Lamb to r. power. 5:12
causeth to r. a mark in their. 13:16

received

Isaac r. the same year an. Gen 26:12
and Aaron r. them at. Ex 32:4
and they r. of Moses all the. 36:3
Miriam be r. in again. Num 12:14
r. commandment to bless. 23:20
two tribes and half r. 34:14, 15
put to the inheritance of the tribe whereunto they are r. 36:3, 4
the Gadites have r. their. Josh 13:8
not r. their inheritance. 18:2
would not have r. burnt offering. Judg 13:23
have I r. any bribe ? 1 Sam 12:3*
David r. of Abigail that she. 23:35
merchants r. linen yarn at a price. 1 Ki 10:28; 2 Chr 1:16
Hezekiah r. the letter. 2 Ki 19:14
Isa 37:14
then David r. them. 1 Chr 12:18
Mordecai r. it not. Esth 4:4
mine ear r. a little thereof. Job 4:12
thou hast r. gifts for. Ps 68:18
it, and r. instruction. Pr 24:32
hath r. of the Lord's hand. Isa 40:2
your children, they r. no. Jer 2:30
not r. usury nor increase. Ezek 18:17
she r. not correction. Zeph 3:2
freely ye r., freely give. Mat 10:8
which r. seed by the way side. 13:19
r. seed into stony. 20, 22, 23
they that r. tribute money. 17:24
they r. every man a penny. 20:9, 10
and when they had r. it, they. 11
immediately their eyes r. sight. 34
r. five talents. 25:16
r. two talents. 17
had r. one talent. 18
should have r. mine own with. 27
things which they r. Mark 7:4
he r. his sight. 10:52; Luke 18:43
Acts 9:18
myrrh: but he r. it not. Mark 15:23
he was r. up into heaven. 16:19
Acts 1:9
woe to rich, for ye have r. Luke 6:24
the people gladly r. him. 8:40
r. them and spake to them. 9:11
come, that he should be r. up. 51
Martha r. him into her house. 10:38
because he hath r. him safe. 15:27
Zacchaeus came down and r. 19:6
returned, having r. kingdom. 15
own, his own r. him not. John 1:11
but as many as r. him. to them. 12
out of fulness have all we r. grace. 16
he that hath r. testimony, hath. 3:33
Galileans r. him, having seen. 4:45
willingly r. him into the ship. 6:21
washed, and I r. sight. 9:11
how he had r. his sight. 15
that he had r. his sight . . . him that had r. his sight. John 9:18
this commandment I r. of my. 10:18
he then having r. the sop. 13:30
words, and they have r. them. 17:8
Judas having r. band of men. 18:3
when Jesus had r. vinegar. 19:30
and a cloud r. him out. Acts 1:9
and having r. of the Father. 2:33
they that gladly r. his word. 41
feet and ancle bones r. 3:7
who r. the lively oracles to. 7:38
who have r. law by angels, and. 53
Samaria had r. the word of. 8:14
them, they r. the Holy Ghost. 17
r. meat, he was strengthened. 9:19
the vessel was r. again up. 10:16
which have r. the Holy Ghost. 47
that Gentiles had r. the word. 11:1
they were r. of the church. 15:4
having r. such charge, thrust. 16:24
hither also; whom Jason hath r. 17:7
Bereans r. the word with all. 11
have ye r. the Holy Ghost ? 19:2
ministry which I have r. of. 20:24
brethren r. us gladly. 21:17
from which I r. letters to. 22:5
having r. authority from the. 26:10
barbarians kindled a fire and r. 28:2
Publius r. us. 7
we neither r. letters out of Judaea. 21
Paul r. all that came. 30
by whom we have r. grace. Rom 1:5
r. the sign of circumcision. 4:11
by whom we have now r. the. 5:11
Spirit of bondage . . . but ye have r. Spirit of adoption. 8:15
for God hath r. him. 14:3
another, as Christ also r. us. 15:7
have r. not the spirit of. 1 Cor 2:12
as if thou hadst not r. it ? 4:7
I r. of the Lord, that which. 11:23
which also ye have r. 15:1
which I r. 3
as we have r. mercy. 2 Cor 4:1
and trembling ye r. him. 7:15
spirit, which ye have not r. 11:4
five times r. I forty stripes. 24
gospel than that ye have r. Gal 1:9
I r. it not of man, neither was. 12
r. ye the Spirit by works of the ? 3:2
but r. me as an angel of God. 4:14
things ye have r. and seen. Phil 4:9
as ye have r. Christ, so. Col 2:6
whom, ye r. commandments. 4:10
ministry thou hast r. in Lord. 17
having r. the word in. 1 Thes 1:6
r. word, ye r. it not as word. 2:13
as ye have r. of us how ye ought. 4:1
because they r. not the love of truth. 2 Thes 2:10
tradition which he r. of us. 3:6
in world, r. up into glory. 1 Tim 3:16
God hath created to be r. 4:3
creature is good, if it be r. with. 4
transgression r. just recompence of. Heb 2:2
r. tithes of Abraham and. 7:6*
under it the people r. the law. 11
sin wilfully after we have r. 10:26
faith Sarai r. strength to. 11:11
died, not having r. the promises. 13
he that r. promises offered up. 17
from whence also he r. him in. 19
had r. the spies. 31; Jas 2:25
women r. their dead. Heb 11:35
all having obtained a good report through faith, r. not the promise. 39
vain conversation r. by tradition. 1 Pet 1:18*
as every one hath r. the gift. 4:10
r. from God the Father. 2 Pet 1:17
anointing ye have r. 1 John 2:27
as we have r. a command. 2 John 4
even as I r. of my Father. Rev 2:27
how thou hast r. and heard. 3:3
who have r. no kingdom as yet. 17:12
had r. the mark of the beast. 19:20
had not r. the mark, reigned. 20:4

receivedst

thy lifetime r. thy good. Luke 16:25

receiver

scribe ? where is the r.? Isa 33:18*

receiveth

no man that r. me to. Judg 19:18
what r. he of thine hand? Job 35:7
wise is instructed, he r. knowledge. Pr 21:11
r. gifts, overthroweth it. 29:4*
that r. not correction. Jer 7:28
or r. offering with good. Mal 2:13
every one that asketh, r. Mat 7:8
Luke 11:10
he that r. you r. me, and he that r. me r. him that. Mat 10:40; John 13:20
he that r. a prophet . . . he that r. a righteous man. Mat 10:41
heareth word, and anon r. it. 13:20
little child in my name, r. me. 18:5
whoso shall receive me, r. not me, but him. Mark 9:37; Luke 9:48
this man r. sinners. Luke 15:2
no man r. his testimony. John 3:32
he that reapeth r. wages, and. 4:36
that rejecteth me, and r. not. 12:48
but one r. the prize. 1 Cor 9:24
for the earth r. blessing. Heb 6:7
tithes, but there he r. them. 7:8
Levi who r. tithes, payed tithes. 9
every son whom he r. 12:6
saving he that r. it. Rev 2:17
whosoever r. the mark of. 14:11

receiveth *not*

r. *not* the things of God. 1 Cor 2:14
Diotrephes r. us *not*. 3 John 9

receiving

spared Naaman, in not r. 2 Ki 5:20
and r. a commandment. Acts 17:15
r. in themselves that. Rom 1:27
shall r. of them be but life? 11:15
concerning giving and r. Phil 4:15
we r. a kingdom which. Heb 12:28
r. the end of your faith. 1 Pet 1:9

Rechab

R. the son of Rimmon. 2 Sam 4:2, 5
R. escaped. 6
on Jehonadab son of R. 2 Ki 10:15
son of R. went into the house of. 23
father of the house of R. 1 Chr 2:55
Malchiah son of R. Neh 3:14
Jonadab the son of R. Jer 35:6
see **Jonadab**

Rechabites

go to the house of the R. Jer 35:2

reckon

he shall r. with him that. Lev 25:50
shall r. to him the worth. 27:18, 23
by name ye shall r. the. Num 4:32*
r. to him seven days. Ezek 44:26
when he had begun to r. Mat 18:24
r. yourselves to be dead. Rom 6:11
I r. that the sufferings of this. 8:18

reckoned

your heave offering r. Num 18:27
people shall not be r. among. 23:9
for Beeroth also was r. to. 2 Sam 4:2
they r. not with the men. 2 Ki 12:15
genealogy is not to be r. by birthright. 1 Chr 5:1
genealogy of generations was r. 7
all these were r. by genealogies. 17
7:5, 7; 9:1, 22; 2 Chr 31:19
Ezra 2:62; 8:3; Neh 7:5, 64
to us cannot be r. up. Ps 40:5*
I r. till morning that. Isa 38:13*
he was r. amongst the. Luke 22:37
reward is not r. of grace. Rom 4:4
faith was r. to Abraham. 9
how was it then r.? 10

reckoneth

lord r. with them. Mat 25:19

reckoning

there was no r. made. 2 Ki 22:7
they were in one r. 1 Chr 23:11

recommended

whence they had been r. Acts 14:26*
being r. to the grace of God. 15:40*

recompence, *noun*

(*An equivalent given or received. Now spelled* recompense, *both noun and verb*)

vengeance and r. Deut 32:35
vanity shall be his r. Job 15:31
the r. of a man's hand. Pr 12:14
will come with a r. Isa 35:4
r. to his enemies, to the islands r. 59:18
Lord that rendereth r. to his. 66:6
he will render to her a r. Jer 51:6
render to them a r. Lam 3:64
days of r. are come. Hos 9:7
will ye render me a r.? Joel 3:4
I will return your r. on your own. 7
bid thee, and a r. be. Luke 14:12
that r. of their error. Rom 1:27
let their table be made a r. to. 11:9
now for a r. in the same. 2 Cor 6:13
transgression received a just r. of. Heb 2:2
hath great r. of reward. 10:35
respect to the r. of reward. 11:26

recompences

year of r. for controversy. Isa 34:8
Lord God of r. shall surely. Jer 51:56

recompense, *verb*

he shall r. his trespass. Num 5:7*
if he have no kinsman to r. the. 8*
the Lord r. thy work. Ruth 2:12
should the king r. me? 2 Sam 19:36
he will r. it, whether. Job 34:33
I will r. evil. Ps 20:22
I will r. into their bosom. Isa 65:6
first I will r. their iniquity. Jer 16:18
will r. according to their deeds. 25:14; Hos 12:2
r. work. Jer 50:29
r. abominations. Ezek 7:3, 8
r. thy ways. 4, 9; 9:10; 11:21; 16:43
oath and my covenant I will r. 17:19
they shall r. your lewdness. 23:49
if ye r. me, speedily will. Joel 3:4
for they cannot r. thee. Luke 14:14
r. to no man evil for evil. Rom 12:17
to r. tribulation to them. 2 Thes 1:6
that hath said, I will r. Heb 10:30

recompensed

let the trespass be r. to. Num 5:8
cleanness of my hands hath he r. me. 2 Sam 22:21, 25; Ps 18:20, 24
the righteous shall be r. Pr 11:31
shall evil be r. for good? Jer 18:20
their own way have I r. Ezek 22:31
be r. at the resurrection. Luke 14:14
and it shall be r. to him. Rom 11:35

recompensest

thou r. iniquity of fathers. Jer 32:18

recompensing

by r. his way upon his. 2 Chr 6:23

reconcile

brought to r. withal. Lev 6:30*
should he r. himself? 1 Sam 29:4
shall ye r. the house. Ezek 45:20*
r. both to God by cross. Eph 2:16
by him to r. all things. Col 1:20

reconciled

first be r. to thy brother. Mat 5:24
enemies we were r. to. Rom 5:10
be r. to her husband. 1 Cor 7:11
who hath r. us to himself. 2 Cor 5:18
we pray you be ye r. to God. 20
enemies, yet now hath he r. Col 1:21

reconciliation

to make a r. upon it. Lev 8:15*
they made r. with their blood. 2 Chr 29:24*
one lamb to make r. Ezek 45:15*, 17
to make r. for iniquity. Dan 9:24
to us the ministry of r. 2 Cor 5:18
committed unto us the word of r. 19
to make r. for the sins. Heb 2:17*

reconciling

an end of r. holy place. Lev 16:20*
if casting away be r. Rom 11:15
God was in Christ, r. 2 Cor 5:19

record

(Witness, *usually in Revisions*)

where I r. my name. Ex 20:24
I call heaven and earth to r. Deut 30:19; 31:28
appointed Levites to r. 1 Chr 16:4*
faithful witnesses to r. Isa 8:2
I take you to r. this day. Acts 20:26

record, *substantive*

and therein was a r. Ezra 6:2
behold, my r. is on high. Job 16:19*
this is the r. of John. John 1:19
John bare r. saying, I saw. 32, 34
r. of thyself, thy r. is not. 8:13
r. of myself, yet my r. is true. 14
people with him, bare r. 12:17
that saw bare r. and his r. is. 19:35
I bare them r. that. Rom 10:2
I call God for a r. 2 Cor 1:23
to their power I bear r., yea. 8:3
I bear you r., if it had. Gal 4:15
God is my r., how greatly. Phil 1:8
I bear him r. that he. Col 4:13
that bear r. in heaven. 1 John 5:7
believeth not r. God gave of his Son. 10
this is the r. that God hath. 11
we bare r. and our r. is. 3 John 12
who bare r. of the Word. Rev 1:2

recorded

Levites were r. chief of. Neh 12:22

recorder

Jehoshaphat was r. 2 Sam 8:16
20:24; 1 Ki 4:3; 1 Chr 18:15
Joah the son of Asaph the r. 2 Ki 18:18; Isa 36:3, 22
Joah son of Joahaz r. to repair. 2 Chr 34:8

records

search in the book of r. Ezra 4:15
to bring the book of r. Esth 6:1

recount

he shall r. his worthies. Nah 2:5*

recover

why did ye not r. them? Judg 11:26
without fail r. all. 1 Sam 30:8
went to r. his border. 2 Sam 8:3
whether I shall r. 2 Ki 1:2
the prophet would r. him of. 5:3
Naaman, that thou mayest r. 6
send to me to r. a man. 7
hand over place, and r. the leper. 11
enquire by him, shall I r.? 8:8, 9
thou mayest r. 10
that shouldest surely r. 14
nor did Jeroboam r. 2 Chr 13:20
that they could not r. 14:13
that I may r. strength. Ps 39:13
to r. the remnant of. Isa 11:11
so wilt thou r. me and. 38:16
plaister, and he shall r. 21
and I will r. my wool. Hos 2:9*
sick, and they shall r. Mark 16:18
that they may r. themselves out of the snare. 2 Tim 2:26

recovered

David r. all the. 1 Sam 30:18, 19
aught of spoil we have r. 22
Joash beat him, and r. 2 Ki 13:25
he warred, and r. Damascus. 14:28
Rezin king of Syria r. Elath. 16:6
laid it on the boil, and he r. 20:7
was sick, and was r. Isa 38:9; 39:1
the health of my people r.? Jer 8:22
took the people he had r. 41:16

recovering

to preach r. of sight to. Luke 4:18

red

first came out r. all over. Gen 25:25
Feed me with that same r. 30
his eyes shall be r. with. 49:12
rams' skins dyed r. Ex 25:5; 26:14
35:7; 36:19; 39:34
was found r. skins of rams. 35:23
bring thee a r. heifer. Num 19:2
saw the water r. as blood. 2 Ki 3:22
on a pavement of r., blue. Esth 1:6
in hand of Lord is cup and wine is r. 75:8
look not on the wine when it is r. Pr 23:31
though your sins be r. Isa 1:18
A vineyard of r. wine. 27:2
art thou r. in thine apparel? 63:2
shield of his mighty men is made r. Nah 2:3
a man riding on a r. horse and behind him were there r. Zech 1:8
in first chariot were r. horses. 6:2
will be fair weather, for sky is r. Mat 16:2, 3

another horse that was *r*. *Rev* 6:4
a great *r*. dragon, seven. 12:3

Red *sea*

locusts into the *R. sea*. *Ex* 10:19
by the way of the *R sea*. 13:18
drowned in the *R. sea*. 15:4
Israel from the *R. sea*. 22
bounds from the *R. sea*. 23:31
wilderness by the *R. sea*. *Num* 14:25
did he in the *R. sea*.? 21:14*
journey by the *R. sea*. *Deut* 1:40
made the *R. sea* to overflow. 11:4
Lord dried up the *R. sea*. *Josh* 2:10
your God did to the *R. sea*. 4:23
pursued after to the *R. sea*. 24:6
their cry by the *R. sea*. *Neh* 9:9
provoked him at the *R. sea*. *Ps* 106:7
he rebuked the *R. sea*, and it. 9
terrible things by the *R. sea*. 22
divided the *R. sea* in parts. 136:13
and his host in the *R. sea*. 15
was heard in the *R. sea*. *Jer* 49:21
wonders in the *R. sea*. *Acts* 7:36
they passed through the *R. sea*. *Heb* 11:29

reddish

a bright spot somewhat *r*. *Lev* 13:19
24:43
a white *r*. sore, it is a leprosy. 13:42
plague be *r*. in garment or. 49
with hollow strakes, *r*. 14:37

redeem

[1] *To buy again something that had been sold, by paying back the price to him that bought it*, Lev 25:25; 27:20. [2] *To deliver and bring out of bondage those who were kept prisoners by their enemies*, Deut 7:5; 32:6; Luke 1:68; 1 Tim 2:6; Tit 2:14.

To redeem time, *Eph* 5:16. *To embrace and improve every opportunity of doing good.*

I will *r*. you with a stretched. *Ex* 6:6
firstling of ass shall *r*. 13:13; 34:20
of my children I *r*. 15; 34:20
his kin come to *r*. it. *Lev* 25:25*
if he have none to *r*. it. 26
he may *r*. it. 29
the cities may the Levites *r*. 32
his brethren may *r*. him. 48
or any of kin may *r*. him. 49
but if he will at all *r*. it, then. 27:13
his house will *r*. it. 15, 19, 20, 31
of man shalt thou *r*. *Num* 18:15
from a month old shalt thou *r*. 16
goat thou shalt not *r*. 17
wilt *r*. it, if not, I will *r*. it. *Ruth* 4:4
cannot *r*. it for myself, *r*. thou it. 6
whom God went to *r*. to himself?
2 Sam 7:23; *1 Chr* 17:21
our power to *r*. them. *Neh* 5:5
in famine he shall *r*. thee. *Job* 5:20
to *r*. me from the hand of. 6:23
r. Israel, O God, out of all. *Ps* 25:22
r. me and be merciful unto. 26:11
r. us for thy mercies' sake. 44:26
none of them can *r*. his brother. 49:7
but God will *r*. my soul from. 15
draw nigh to my soul, and *r*. it. 69:18
r. their soul from deceit. 72:14
he shall *r*. Israel from all his. 130:8
shortened that it cannot *r*.? *Isa* 50:2
I will *r*. thee out of hand. *Jer* 15:21
will *r*. them from death. *Hos* 13:14
Lord shall *r*. thee from. *Mi* 4:10
to *r*. them that were under. *Gal* 4:5
that he might *r*. us from. *Tit* 2:14

redeemed

the angel which *r*. me. *Gen* 48:16
people whom thou hast *r*. *Ex* 15:13
then shall he let her be *r*. 21:8
with a bondmaid not *r*. *Lev* 19:20
if a house in a city be not *r*. 25:30
houses of villages may be *r*. 31
to a stranger may be *r*. again. 48
if he be not *r*. then go out in. 54
sold the field, it shall not be *r*. 27:20
an unclean beast not *r*. then. 27
no devoted thing shall be *r*. 28, 29
and the change shall not be *r*. 33
those be *r*. that are more. *Num* 3:46
those that are to be *r*. from. 18:16
the Lord hath *r*. you out of the.
Deut 7:8; 15:15; 24:18
thy people thou hast *r*. 9:26
Lord which *r*. you out of house. 13:5
Israel, whom thou hast *r*. 21:8
Lord hath *r*. my soul. *2 Sam* 4:9
1 Ki 1:29
whom thou hast *r*. out of Egypt.
1 Chr 17:21; *Neh* 1:10; *Ps* 77:15
ability have *r*. the Jews. *Neh* 5:8
thou hast *r*. me, O Lord. *Ps* 31:5
my soul which thou hast *r*. 71:23
thine inheritance thou hast *r*. 74:2
he *r*. them from the hand of. 106:10
let the *r*. of the Lord say so, whom he hath *r*. 107:2
hath *r*. us from our enemies. 136:24
Zion shall be *r*. with. *Isa* 1:27
the Lord, who *r*. Abraham. 29:22
no lion there, but the *r*. shall. 35:9
fear not, I have *r*. thee, thou. 43:1
for I have *r*. thee. 44:22
the Lord hath *r*. Jacob. 23; 48:20
Jer 31:11
the *r*. of the Lord shall. *Isa* 51:11
ye shall be *r*. without money. 52:3
r. Jerusalem. 9
holy people *r*. of Lord. 62:12
year of my *r*. is come. 63:4
in pity he *r*. them. 9
Lord, thou hast *r*. my life. *Lam* 3:58
though I *r*. them, yet they. *Hos* 7:13
I *r*. thee out of the house. *Mi* 6:4
for them, I have *r*. them. *Zech* 10:8
visited and *r*. his people. *Luke* 1:68
he who should have *r*. Israel. 24:21
Christ *r*. us from the curse. *Gal* 3:13
ye were not *r*. with. *1 Pet* 1:18
thou hast *r*. us to God. *Rev* 5:9
the 144,000 which were *r*. 14:3*
these were *r*. from among men. 4*

redeemedst

which thou *r*. to thee. *2 Sam* 7:23

Redeemer

I know that my *R*. liveth. *Job* 19:25
my strength and my *R*. *Ps* 19:14
the high God was their *R*. 78:35
their *R*. is mighty, he. *Pr* 23:11
thy *R*. the Holy One of Israel.
Isa 41:14; 54:5
thus saith the Lord your *R*. 43:14
thus saith the Lord, his *R*. the. 44:6
saith the Lord thy *R*. 24; 48:17
49:7; 54:8
as for our *R*., the Lord of. 47:4
I the Lord am thy *R*. 49:26; 60:16
R. shall come to Zion, to. 59:20
art our Father, our *R*. 63:16
their *R*. is strong, the. *Jer* 50:34

redeemeth

the Lord *r*. the souls. *Ps* 34:22
who *r*. life from destruction. 103:4

redeeming

the manner in Israel concerning *r*.
Ruth 4:7
r. time, because the days are evil.
Eph 5:16; *Col* 4:5

redemption

grant a *r*. for the land. *Lev* 25:24
give again the price of his *r*. 51, 52
Moses took the *r*. money. *Num* 3:49
r. of their soul is precious. *Ps* 49:8
he sent *r*. to his people. 111:9
with him there is plenteous *r*. 130:7
right of *r*. is thine. *Jer* 32:7, 8
to them that looked for *r*. *Luke* 2:38
look up, for your *r*. draweth. 21:28
the *r*. that is in Christ. *Rom* 3:24
to wit, the *r*. of our body. 8:23
to us sanctification and *r*. *1 Cor* 1:30
in whom we have *r*. through his blood. *Eph* 1:7; *Col* 1:14
until the *r*. of purchased. *Eph* 1:14
are sealed unto the day of *r*. 4:30
obtained eternal *r*. for us. *Heb* 9:12
for *r*. of the transgressions that. 15

redness

who hath *r*. of eyes? *Pr* 23:29

redound

that grace might *r*. to. *2 Cor* 4:15*

reed

[1] *A plant growing in fens and watery places*, Job 40:21. [2] *A staff or rod of a reed, which was put in our Saviour's hand at his passion, by way of derision, instead of a sceptre*, Mat 27:29. [3] *A* Jewish *measure of six cubits three inches, or three yards three inches*, Ezek 40:3.

smite Israel as a *r*. *1 Ki* 14:15
upon the staff of this bruised *r*.
2 Ki 18:21; *Isa* 36:6
a bruised *r*. shall he not break.
Isa 42:3; *Mat* 12:20
a staff of *r*. to Israel. *Ezek* 29:6
a man with a measuring *r*. 40:3
with measuring *r*. 42:16, 17, 18, 19
a *r*. shaken? *Mat* 11:7; *Luke* 7:24
put a *r*. in his right hand. *Mat* 27:29
smote him with a *r*. 30; *Mark* 15:19
put the spunge on a *r*. and gave.
Mat 27:48; *Mark* 15:36
given me a *r*. like a rod. *Rev* 11:1
had a golden *r*. to measure. 21:15
he measured with the *r*. 12,000. 16

reeds

he lieth in covert of the *r*. *Job* 40:21
the *r*. and flags shall. *Isa* 19:6, 7*
of dragons shall be *r*. 35:7
the *r*. they have burnt. *Jer* 51:32
he measured east side . . . five hundred *r*. *Ezek* 42:16, 17, 18, 19
the length 25,000 *r*. 45:1

reel

they *r*. to and fro. *Ps* 107:27
earth shall *r*. to and fro. *Isa* 24:20*

refine

I will *r*. them as silver. *Zech* 13:9

refined

for the altar *r*. gold. *1 Chr* 28:18
seven thousand talents of *r*. silver.
29:4
wines on the lees well *r*. *Isa* 25:6
behold, I have *r*. thee, but not. 48:10
refine them, as silver is *r*. *Zech* 13:9

refiner

he is like a *r*.'s fire, and. *Mal* 3:2
shall sit as a *r*. and purifier. 3

reformation

until the time of *r*. *Heb* 9:10

reformed

and if ye will not be *r*. *Lev* 26:23

refrain

then Joseph could not *r*. himself.
Gen 45:1
I will not *r*. my mouth. *Job* 7:11
my son, *r*. thy foot. *Pr* 1:15
there is a time to *r*. from. *Eccl* 3:5
I will *r*. for thee that I. *Isa* 48:9
wilt thou *r*. thyself for these? 64:12
r. voice from weeping. *Jer* 31:16
I say to you, *R*. from. *Acts* 5:38
let him *r*. his tongue. *1 Pet* 3:10

refrained

Joseph *r*. himself and. *Gen* 43:31
Haman *r*. himself. *Esth* 5:10
princes *r*. talking, and. *Job* 29:9
I have not *r*. my lips. *Ps* 40:9
I have *r*. my feet from. 119:101
still, and *r*. myself. *Isa* 42:14
they have not *r*. their feet. *Jer* 14:10

refraineth

that *r*. his lips is wise. *Pr* 10:19

refresh

with me and *r*. thyself. *1 Ki* 13:7
Julius suffered Paul to *r*. *Acts* 27:3
brother, *r*. my bowels. *Philem* 20

refreshed

stranger may be *r*. *Ex* 23:12
he rested and was *r*. 31:17
Saul was *r*. and well. *1 Sam* 16:23
r. themselves there. *2 Sam* 16:14
speak that I may be *r*. *Job* 32:20
I may with you be *r*. *Rom* 15:32
for they *r*. my spirit. *1 Cor* 16:18
spirit was *r*. by you. *2 Cor* 7:13
Onesiphorus oft *r*. me. *2 Tim* 1:16
of the saints are *r*. by. *Philem* 7

refresheth

for he *r.* the soul of. *Pr* 25:13

refreshing

this is *r.*, yet they would. *Isa* 28:12
times of *r.* shall come. *Acts* 3:19

refuge

Cities of refuge. *In order to provide for the security of those, who unawares and without any design should kill a man, the Lord commanded Moses to appoint six cities of refuge, that the manslayer might retire thither, and have time to prepare for justification before the judges, so that the kinsman of the deceased might not pursue him thither and kill him. Of these cities there were three on each side Jordan: those on the west of Jordan were* Kedesh *of* Naphtali, Hebron, *and* Shechem. *Those beyond Jordan were* Bezer, Golan, *and* Ramoth-gilead, *Josh* 20:7, 8. *These cities were to be easy of access, and to have smooth and good roads to them, and bridges where there should be occasion. When there were any cross-roads, they took care to set up posts with an inscription, directing the way to the* city of refuge. *This city was to be well supplied with water and all kind of provisions. The case then came before the judges, that if possible he might clear himself. If he was found innocent, he dwelt safely in the city to which he had retired; if otherwise, he was put to death, according to the severity of the law. Though he was found innocent, he was not therefore immediately set at liberty, but he was obliged to dwell in this city, without going out of it, till the death of the high priest: And if before this time he should any where go out of the city, the avenger of blood might safely kill him,* Num 35:25, 26, 27, etc.

shall ye have for *r.* *Num* 35:13, 15
eternal God is thy *r.* *Deut* 33:27*
your *r.* from avenger. *Josh* 20:3
high tower and my *r.* *2 Sam* 22:3
a *r.* for the oppressed, a *r.* *Ps* 9:9*
poor, because the Lord is his *r.* 14:6
God is our *r.* 46:1, 7, 11
God is known for a *r.* 48:3
thy wings I will make my *r.* 57:1
thou hast been my *r.* in the. 59:16
my *r.* is in God. 62:7
God is a *r.* for us. 8
thou art my strong *r.* 71:7; 142:5
he is my *r.* 91:2, 9
God is rock of my *r.* 94:22
high hills a *r.* for wild goats. 104:18
r. failed me. 142:4
thou art my *r.* and portion. 5
shall have a place of *r.* *Pr* 14:26
a place of *r.* *Isa* 4:6
to the needy a *r.* 25:4
we have made lies our *r.* 28:15
hail shall sweep away the *r.* 17
O Lord, my *r.* in the day. *Jer* 16:19
who have fled for *r.* to lay. *Heb* 6:18

refuse

that was vile and *r.* *1 Sam* 15:9
thou hast made us as *r.* *Lam* 3:45
sell the *r.* of wheat. *Amos* 8:6

refuse, *verb*

if thou *r.* to let them go. *Ex* 4:23
8:2; 9:2; 10:4
long wilt thou *r.* to humble? 10:3
r. ye to keep my? 16:28
if her father utterly *r.* to give. 22:17
whether thou *r.* or choose. *Job* 34:33
be wise, and *r.* it not. *Pr* 8:33
they *r.* to do judgement. 21:7
slothful, his hands *r.* to labour. 25
if ye *r.*, shall be devoured. *Isa* 1:20
may know to *r.* the evil. 7:15, 16
they *r.* to return. *Jer* 8:5
they *r.* to know me. 9:6
evil people which *r.* to. *Jer* 13:10
if they *r.* to take the cup. 25:28
if thou *r.* to go forth, this. 38:21
if I be an offender, I *r.* *Acts* 25:11
but *r.* profane and old. *1 Tim* 4:7
the younger widows *r.* 5:11
see that ye *r.* not him. *Heb* 12:25

refused

Jacob *r.* to be comforted. *Gen* 37:35
r. and said to master's wife. 39:8
Jacob *r.* to remove his hand. 48:19
Edom *r.* to give Israel. *Num* 20:21
people *r.* to obey the. *1 Sam* 8:19
look not on him for I have *r.* 16:7*
Saul *r.* and said, I will not. 28:23
Asahel *r.* to turn aside. *2 Sam* 2:23
but Amnon *r.* to eat. 13:9
man *r.* to smite him. *1 Ki* 20:35
vineyard he *r.* to give thee. 21:15
him to take it, but he *r.* *2 Ki* 5:16
and *r.* to obey. *Neh* 9:17
queen Vashti *r.* to come. *Esth* 1:12
that my soul *r.* to touch. *Job* 6:7
my soul *r.* to be comforted. *Ps* 77:2
they *r.* to walk in his law. 78:10
he *r.* tabernacle of Joseph. 67
stone which the builders *r.* 118:22*
I have called and ye *r.* *Pr* 1:24
when thou wast *r.* saith. *Isa* 54:6*
they *r.* to receive correction, they *r.* *Jer* 5:3
their fathers who *r.* to hear. 11:10
Rachel *r.* to be comforted. 31:15
all that took them *r.* to let. 50:33
for they have *r.* my. *Ezek* 5:6*
because they *r.* to return. *Hos* 11:5
but they *r.* to hearken. *Zech* 7:11
this Moses whom they *r.* *Acts* 7:35
nothing to be *r.* if it be. *1 Tim* 4:4
by faith Moses *r.* to be. *Heb* 11:24
r. him that spake on earth. 12:25

refusedst

thou *r.* to be ashamed. *Jer* 3:3

refuseth

r. to let the people go. *Ex* 7:14
Lord *r.* to give me leave. *Num* 22:13
Balaam *r.* to come with us. 14
brother *r.* to raise up name. *Deut* 25:7
but he that *r.* reproof. *Pr* 10:17*
shame shall be to him that *r.* 13:18
that *r.* instruction despiseth. 15:32
this people *r.* the waters. *Isa* 8:6
my wound which *r.* to be. *Jer* 15:18

regard, *noun*

in *r.* of the oath of God. *Eccl* 8:2
to him they had *r.* because he had. *Acts* 8:11*

regard, *verb*

[1] *To look upon with compassion,* Deut 28:50. [2] *To think of, consider, or lay to heart,* Isa 5:12. [3] *To have respect for,* 2 Ki 3:14. [4] *To hear and answer,* Ps 102:17. [5] *To observe,* Rom 14:6.

r. not your stuff. *Gen* 45:20
let them not *r.* vain. *Ex* 5:9
r. not them that have. *Lev* 19:31*
which shall not *r.* person. *Deut* 28:50
nor did she *r.* it. *1 Sam* 4:20
let not my lord *r.* this man. 25:25
r. not this, he is thy. *2 Sam* 13:20*
were it not that I *r.* *2 Ki* 3:14
that day, let not God *r.* it. *Job* 3:4
nor will the Almighty *r* it. 35:13
take heed, *r.* not iniquity. 36:21
they *r.* not the works of. *Ps* 28:5
I have hated them that *r.* 31:6
if I *r.* iniquity in my heart. 66:18
shall the God of Jacob *r.* it. 94:7*
he will *r.* the prayer of the. 102:17
thou mayest *r.* discretion. *Pr* 5:2*
will not *r.* any ransom, nor. 6:35
they *r.* not work of Lord. *Isa* 5:12
who will not *r.* silver. 13:17
will no more *r.* them. *Lam* 4:16
r. God of his fathers, nor *r.* any. *Dan* 11:37
r. the peace offering. *Amos* 5:22
behold, *r.* and wonder. *Hab* 1:5
will he *r.* your persons? *Mal* 1:9*
not God, nor *r.* man. *Luke* 18:4
to Lord he doth not *r.* it. *Rom* 14:6

regarded

he that *r.* not the word. *Ex* 9:21
voice, nor any that *r.* *1 Ki* 18:29
thou hast *r.* me as. *1 Chr* 17:17
he *r.* their affliction. *Ps* 106:44
my hand, and no man *r.* *Pr* 1:24
O king, have not *r.* thee. *Dan* 3:12
he *r.* the low estate of. *Luke* 1:48*
feared not God, neither *r.* man. 18:2
and I *r.* them not. *Heb* 8:9

regardest

thou *r.* not princes. *2 Sam* 19:6*
I stand up and thou *r.* *Job* 30:20
r. not the persons of men. *Mat* 22:16; *Mark* 12:14

regardeth

mighty and terrible, that *r.* not. *Deut* 10:17
nor *r.* the rich more. *Job* 34:19
r. the crying of the driver. 39:7*
a righteous man *r.* the life. *Pr* 12:10
he that *r.* reproof shall be. 13:18
but he that *r.* reproof is. 15:5
wicked *r.* not to know cause. 29:7*
higher than the highest *r.* *Eccl* 5:8
he that *r.* the clouds shall not. 11:4
cities, he *r.* no man. *Isa* 33:8
Daniel *r.* not thee, O king. *Dan* 6:13
he *r.* not the offering *Mal* 2:13
he that *r.* a day, *r.* it to. *Rom* 14:6

regarding

ever without any *r.* it. *Job* 4:20
nor *r.* his life to supply. *Phil* 2:30*

regeneration

Or the new birth, is the change and renovation of the soul by the Spirit and grace of God, John 3:5, 6.
in the *r.* when the Son of. *Mat* 19:28
us by the washing of *r.* *Tit* 3:5

region

all the *r.* of Argob. *Deut* 3:4, 13
in all *r.* of Dor. *1 Ki* 4:11*
dominion over all the *r.* 24
then went to him all the *r.* *Mat* 3:5
sat in *r.* and shadow of death. 4:16
throughout all the *r.* about Galilee. *Mark* 1:28; *Luke* 4:14; 7:17
whole *r.* round about. *Mark* 6:55
Philip tetrarch of the *r.* *Luke* 3:1
published throughout *r.* *Acts* 13:49
they fled to the *r.* that lieth. 14:6
gone throughout *r.* of Galatia. 16:6

regions

throughout the *r.* of Judaea. *Acts* 8:1
gospel in *r.* beyond you. *2 Cor* 10:16
stop me in the *r.* of Achaia. 11:10
came into the *r.* of Syria. *Gal* 1:21

register

these sought their *r.* *Ezra* 2:62
Neh 7:64
a *r.* of the genealogy. *Neh* 7:5*

rehearse

r. it in ears of Joshua. *Ex* 17:14
r. righteous acts of Lord. *Judg* 5:11

rehearsed

r. them in the ears of. *1 Sam* 8:21
they *r.* David's words. 17:31
Peter *r.* the matter from. *Acts* 11:4*
they *r.* all that God had done. 14:27

Rehoboam

R. the son of Solomon reigned. *1 Ki* 11:43; 14:21; *2 Chr* 9:31
R. consulted with the old men. *1 Ki* 12:6; *2 Chr* 10:6
R. reigned over them. *1 Ki* 12:17
2 Chr 10:17
to bring the kingdom again to *R.* *1 Ki* 12:21; *2 Chr* 11:1
their heart shall turn again to *R.* *1 Ki* 12:27
war between *R.* and. 14:30; 15:6
R. was Solomon's son. *1 Chr* 3:10
Mat 1:7
they made *R.* strong. *2 Chr* 11:17
R. loved Maachah daughter of. 21
R. made Abijah the son of. 22
against *R.* when *R.* was young. 13:7

Rehoboth

builded Nineveh and *R.* *Gen* 10:11
the name of the well *R.* 26:22
Saul of *R.* reigned. 36:37; *1 Chr* 1:48

Rehum

R. came with Zerubbabel. *Ezra* 2:2
Neh 12:3
R. the chancellor wrote. *Ezra* 4:8
the king sent an answer to *R.* and. 17
letter was read before *R.* 23
R. the son of Bani. *Neh* 3:17
R. of chief of the people. 10:25

reign

(*Used of temporal sovereigns; of God as spiritual ruler; and symbolically of sin or righteousness. Revisions frequently change to* rule)

Solomon's *r.* over Israel. *1 Ki* 6:1
in 8th year of his *r.* *2 Ki* 24:12
their cities to the *r.* *1 Chr* 4:31
David's acts with all his *r.* 29:30
till *r.* of the kingdom. *2 Chr* 36:20
priests recorded to *r.* *Neh* 12:22
king in 7th year of his *r.* *Esth* 2:16
year of the *r.* of Tiberius. *Luke* 3:1

reign, *verb*

thou indeed *r.* over us? *Gen* 37:8
Lord shall *r.* for ever. *Ex* 15:18
Ps 146:10
that hate you shall *r.* *Lev* 26:17
thou shalt *r.* over many nations, but they shall not *r.* *Deut* 15:6
70 *r.* over you, or one *r.*? *Judg* 9:2
trees said, *R.* thou. 8, 10, 12, 14
that I should not *r.* over. *1 Sam* 8:7
manner of king that shall *r.* 9, 11
Lord said, This same shall *r.* 9:17
shall Saul *r.* over us? 11:12
but a king shall *r.* over us. 12:12
thou mayest *r.* over all. *2 Sam* 3:21
that Adonijah doth *r.*? *1 Ki* 1:11
shall *r.* after me. 1:13, 17, 30
Adonijah shall *r.* after me? 1:24
faces on me, that I should *r.* 2:15
take thee, and thou shalt *r.* 11:37
Zimri did *r.* seven days in. 16:15
hast made to *r.* in his. *2 Chr* 1:8
Behold, the king's son shall *r.* 23:3
that the hypocrite *r.* not. *Job* 34:30
by me kings *r.* and princes. *Pr* 8:15
prison he cometh to *r.* *Eccl* 4:14
of hosts shall *r.* in Zion. *Isa* 24:23
behold, a king shall *r.* in. 32:1
shalt thou *r.* because? *Jer* 22:15
a king shall *r.* and prosper. 23:5
should not have a son to *r.* 33:21
the Lord shall *r.* over them. *Mi* 4:7
that Archelaus did *r.* *Mat* 2:22
shall *r.* over house of. *Luke* 1:33
will not have this man to *r.* 19:14
would not that I should *r.* over. 27
shall *r.* in life by one. *Rom* 5:17
even so might grace *r.* unto life. 21
let not sin *r.* in your mortal. 6:12
shall rise to *r.* over Gentiles. 15:12
would to God ye did *r.* that we might *r.* *1 Cor* 4:8
for he must *r.* till he put all. 15:25
if we suffer, we shall *r.* *2 Tim* 2:12
and we also shall *r.* *Rev* 5:10
and he shall *r.* for ever and. 11:15
they shall *r.* with him 1000 years. 20:6
they shall *r.* for ever and ever. 22:5

see **began**

reigned

r. in Edom before any king *r.* over. *Gen* 36:31; *1 Chr* 1:43
when Abimelech had *r.* *Judg* 9:22
Saul *r.* one year, and when he *r.* *1 Sam* 13:1
Saul's son *r.* two years. *2 Sam* 2:10
David *r.* forty years over. 5:4
David *r.* seven years in Hebron. 5
1 Ki 2:11; *1 Chr* 3:4; 29:27
David *r.* over Israel. *2 Sam* 8:15
1 Chr 18:14; 29:26
Hanun his son *r.* in his stead.
2 Sam 10:1; *1 Chr* 19:1
whose stead thou hast *r.* *2 Sam* 16:8
and Solomon *r.* *1 Ki* 4:21; 11:42
1 Chr 29:28; *2 Chr* 9:26, 30
Rezon *r.* in Damascus. *1 Ki* 11:24
r. over Syria. 25
Rehoboam *r.* 43; 12:17; *2 Chr* 9:31
10:17
Abijam his son *r.* *1 Ki* 14:31
2 Chr 12:16; 13:2
and Asa *r.* in his stead. *1 Ki* 15:8
9, 10; *2 Chr* 14:1
Jehoshaphat his son *r.* *1 Ki* 15:24
2 Chr 17:1; 20:31
Nadab *r.* *1 Ki* 15:25
Baasha *r.* 28, 29
Elah *r.* 16:6
Zimri *r.* in his stead. 10
Omri *r.* 22, 23
Omri died, and Ahab his son *r.* 28
Ahaziah, Ahab's son, *r.* 22:40, 51
2 Ki 8:24, 26; *2 Chr* 22:1, 2
Jehoshaphat *r.* 25 years. *1 Ki* 22:42
2 Chr 20:31
Jehoram *r.* *1 Ki* 22:50; *2 Ki* 3:1
8:17; *2 Chr* 21:5, 20
son that should have *r.* *2 Ki* 3:27
Hazael *r.* 8:15
Jehoahaz *r.* 10:35
Jehu *r.* 36
Jehoash *r.* forty years in. 12:1
Amaziah *r.* 21; 14:1
2 Chr 24:27; 25:1
Ben-hadad *r.* *2 Ki* 13:24
Jeroboam *r.* 14:16, 23
Zachariah *r.* 29
Azariah *r.* 15:2; *2 Chr* 26:3
and Jotham *r.* *2 Ki* 15:7, 33
2 Chr 26:23; 27:1, 8
Shallum *r.* *2 Ki* 15:10, 13
Menahem son of Gadi *r.* 14, 17
Pekahiah his son *r.* 22, 23
Pekah *r.* 25, 27
Hoshea *r.* 30
Ahaz *r.* 15:38; 16:2; *2 Chr* 28:1
Hezekiah *r.* *2 Ki* 16:20; 18:2
2 Chr 28:27; 29:1
Esarhaddon *r.* in his stead.
2 Ki 19:37; *Isa* 37:38
Manasseh *r.* *2 Ki* 20:21; 21:1
2 Chr 32:33; 33:1
Amon *r.* in his stead.
2 Ki 21:18, 19; *2 Chr* 33:20, 21
Josiah *r.* in his stead. *2 Ki* 21:26
22:1; *2 Chr* 34:1
Jehoahaz *r.* three months. *2 Ki* 23:31
2 Chr 36:2
Jehoiakim *r.* eleven years.
2 Ki 23:36; *2 Chr* 36:5
Jehoiachin his son *r.* *2 Ki* 24:6, 8
2 Chr 36:8, 9
Zedekiah *r.* *2 Ki* 24:18; *2 Chr* 36:11
Jer 37:1; 52:1
and Athaliah *r.* over. *2 Chr* 22:12
Ahasuerus *r.* from India. *Esth* 1:1
touching Shallum which *r.* *Jer* 22:11
death *r.* from Adam to. *Rom* 5:14
man's offence death *r.* by one. 17
r. unto death, so might grace reign. 21
ye have *r.* as kings. *1 Cor* 4:8
great power, and hast *r.* *Rev* 11:17
lived and *r.* with Christ. 20:4

reignest

thou *r.* over all, and in. *1 Chr* 29:12

reigneth

ye and the king that *r.* *1 Sam* 12:14
Absalom *r.* in Hebron. *2 Sam* 15:10
Adonijah *r.* *1 Ki* 1:18
the Lord *r.* *1 Chr* 16:31; *Ps* 96:10
97:1; 99:1
God *r.* over the heathen. *Ps* 47:8
Lord *r.*, he is clothed with. 93:1
for a servant when he *r.* *Pr* 30:22
unto Zion, Thy God *r.* *Isa* 52:7
which *r.* over the kings. *Rev* 17:18
Lord God omnipotent *r.* 19:6

reigning

I have rejected him from *r.* over.
1 Sam 16:1

reins

Kidneys *or* loins. *The Hebrews ascribe to the* reins *knowledge, joy, pain, pleasure: so in scripture it is often said, that God searcheth the hearts and the* reins, Ps 7:9; Jer 17:10; 20:12.

cleaveth my *r.* asunder. *Job* 16:13
though my *r.* be consumed. 19:27
God trieth the heart and *r.* *Ps* 7:9
my *r.* also instruct me in the. 16:7
examine me, O Lord, try my *r.* 26:2
thus I was pricked in my *r.* *Ps* 73:21
thou hast possessed my *r.* 139:13
yea, my *r.* shall rejoice. *Pr* 23:16
the girdle of his *r.* *Isa* 11:5
that triest the *r.* *Jer* 11:20
and far from their *r.* 12:2
I try the *r.* 17:10
that seest the *r.* 20:12
arrow to enter into my *r.* *Lam* 3:13
he who searcheth the *r.* *Rev* 2:23

reject

I will *r.* thee, that thou. *Hos* 4:6
he would not *r.* her. *Mark* 6:26
ye *r.* the commandment of. 7:9
and second admonition, *r.* *Tit* 3:13

rejected

not *r.* thee, but they *r.* *1 Sam* 8:7
ye have this day *r.* your God. 10:19
hast *r.* the word of the Lord, he hath *r.* thee from being king. 15:23, 26
I have *r.* him from being king. 16:1
they *r.* his statutes. *2 Ki* 17:15
Lord *r.* all the seed of Israel. 20
is despised and *r.* of men. *Isa* 53:3
for the Lord hath *r.* thy. *Jer* 2:37
r. my law. 6:19
because the Lord hath *r.* them. 30
Lord hath *r.* the generation of. 7:29
lo, they have *r.* the word of. 8:9
hast thou utterly *r.* Judah? 14:19
but thou hast utterly *r.* us. *Lam* 5:22
because thou hast *r.* *Hos* 4:6
stone which builders *r.* *Mat* 21:42
Mark 12:10; *Luke* 20:17
he shall be *r.* of the elders.
Mark 8:31; *Luke* 9:22
lawyers *r.* the counsel. *Luke* 7:30
but he must first be *r.* of. 17:25
ye despised not, nor *r.* *Gal* 4:14
thorns and briars is *r.* *Heb* 6:8
inherited blessing, was *r.* 12:17

rejecteth

that *r.* me, receiveth not. *John* 12:48

rejoice

ye shall *r.* in all. *Deut* 12:7; 14:26
thou shalt *r.* in thy feast. 16:14
bless thee, therefore thou shalt *r.* 15
thou shalt *r.* in every good. 26:11
Lord will *r.* over you. 28:63; 30:9
r. O ye nations, with his. 32:43
he said, *R.* Zebulun, in thy. 33:18
r. ye in Abimelech. *Judg* 9:19
Philistines gathered to *r.* 16:23
I *r.* in thy salvation. *1 Sam* 2:1
thou sawest it, and didst *r.* 19:5
let the heart of them *r.* that seek.
1 Chr 16:10; *Ps* 105:3
let the fields *r.* and all. *1 Chr* 16:32
and let thy saints *r.* *2 Chr* 6:41
made them to *r.* 20:27; *Neh* 12:43
and he shall not *r.* *Job* 20:18
they *r.* at the sound of the. 21:12
fear, *r.* with trembling. *Ps* 2:11
all that put their trust in thee *r.* 5:11
I will *r.* in thy salvation. 9:14
those that trouble me *r.* when. 13:4
my heart shall *r.* in thy salvation. 5
Jacob shall *r.* and Israel. 14:7
we will *r.* in thy salvation. 20:5*
how greatly shall he *r.*! 21:1
hast not made my foes to *r.* 30:1
for our heart shall *r.* in him. 33:21
my soul shall *r.* in his. 35:9
enemies wrongfully *r.* over me. 19
and let them not *r.* over me. 24
let them be ashamed that *r.* 26
lest they should *r.* over me. 38:16
let mount Zion *r.*; let Judah. 48:11
bones thou hast broken may *r.* 51:8
the righteous shall *r.* when. 58:10
in holiness, I will *r.* 60:6; 108:7
in shadow of thy wings will I *r.* 63:7
but the king shall *r.* in God. 11
morning and evening to *r.* 65:8
the little hills *r.* 12*
there did we *r.* 66:6
righteous *r.* yea, exceedingly *r.* 68:3
r. before him. 4
my lips shall greatly *r.* 71:23
revive us, that thy people may *r.* 85:6
r. the soul of thy servant. 86:4
Tabor and Hermon shall *r.* 89:12

in thy name shall they r. Ps 89:16
made all his enemies to r. 42
let the heavens r. 96:11
trees of the wood r. 12*
Lord reigneth, let the earth r. 97:1
make a loud noise, r. and sing. 98:4*
Lord shall r. in his works. 104:31
that I may r. in gladness of thy. 106:5
righteous shall see it and r. 107:42
ashamed, let thy servant r. 109:28
I r. at thy word, as one. 119:162
let Israel r. in him that. 149:2
who r. to do evil, and. Pr 2:14
r. with the wife of thy youth. 5:18
wise, mine heart shall r. 23:15
yea, my reins shall r. when. 16
righteous shall greatly r. 24
she that bare thee shall r. 25
r. not when thine enemy. 24:17
ointment and perfume r. the. 27:9
righteous men do r., there. 28:12*
are in authority, people r. 29:2
righteous doth sing and r. 6
shall r. in time to come. 31:25*
a man to r. and do good. Eccl 3:12
should r. in his works. 22; 5:19
come after, shall not r. in him. 4:16
live many years, and r. in them. 11:8
r. O young man, in thy youth. 9
and r. in Rezin and. Isa 8:6
as men r. when they divide. 9:3
them that r. in my highness. 13:3*
yea, the fir trees r. at thee. 14:8
r. not thou, whole Palestina. 29
Thou shalt no more r. O virgin. 23:12
the noise of them that r. 24:8
poor among men shall r. in. 29:19
the desert shall r. 35:1
shall blossom and r. 2
for confusion they shall r. in. 61:7
as a bridegroom, so shall God r. 62:5
my servants shall r., but ye. 65:13
I will r. in Jerusalem, and. 19
r. ye with Jerusalem, and. 66:10
see this, your heart shall r. 14
virgin r. in the dance, and I will make them r. from their. Jer 31:13
I will r. over them to do. 32:41
that they may r. and sleep. 51:39
thine enemy to r. over. Lam 2:17
let not the buyer r. nor. Ezek 7:12
r. at the inheritance of. 35:15
r. not, O Israel, for joy. Hos 9:1
ye which r. in a thing. Amos 6:13
r. not against me, O mine. Mi 7:8
take away them that r. Zeph 3:11
the Lord will r. over thee with. 17
r. O daughter of Zion. Zech 2:10
r. greatly, O daughter of Zion. 9:9
and their heart shall r. as. 10:7
and many shall r. at his. Luke 1:14
r. ye that day, and leap for. 6:23
in this r. not, rather r. because. 10:20
r. with me, for I have found. 15:6, 9
of the disciples began to r. 19:37
that reapeth may r. John 4:36
willing for a season to r. in. 5:35
if ye loved me, ye would r. 14:28
weep, but the world shall r. 16:20
you, and your heart shall r. 22
therefore did my heart r. Acts 2:26*
r. in hope of the glory. Rom 5:2
r. with them that do r. and. 12:15
he saith, R. ye Gentiles. 15:10
they that r. as though. 1 Cor 7:30
all the members r. with it. 12:26
of whom I ought to r. 2 Cor 2:3
now I r. not that ye were. 7:9
I r. that I have confidence in. 16
r. thou barren that. Gal 4:27
do r. yea, and will r. Phil 1:18
that I may r. in the day of. 2:16*
if I be offered, I joy and r. 17
same cause do ye joy and r. 18
see him again, ye may r. 28
we worship God, and r. in. 3:3*
now r. in my sufferings. Col 1:24
r. evermore. 1 Thes 5:16
let the brother of low degree r. Jas 1:9*
now ye r. in your boastings. 4:16
wherein ye greatly r. 1 Pet 1:6
r. with joy unspeakable and. 8
but r. in as much as ye are. 4:13
on earth shall r. over. Rev 11:10
therefore r. ye heavens, and. 12:12
r. over her, thou heaven. 18:20
see **glad**

rejoice *before the Lord*

shall r. before the Lord. Lev 23:40
Deut 12:12, 18; 16:11; 27:7

rejoice *in the Lord*

r. in the Lord, O ye righteous. Ps 33:1; 97:12
r. in the Lord, glory in. Isa 41:16
I will greatly r. in the Lord. 61:10
of Zion, r. in the Lord. Joel 2:23
yet I will r. in the Lord. Hab 3:18
heart shall r. in the Lord. Zech 10:7
brethren, r. in the Lord. Phil 3:1
r. in the Lord alway, and. 4:4

rejoiced

Jethro r. for all goodness. Ex 18:9
the Lord r. over you to. Deut 28:63
rejoice for good, as he r. over. 30:9
father of the damsel r. Judg 19:3
men of Beth-shemesh r. 1 Sam 6:13
the men of Israel r. greatly. 11:15
the people r. so that the. 1 Ki 1:40
Hiram r. greatly at Solomon's. 5:7
the people r. when Joash made king. 2 Ki 11:14, 20; 2 Chr 23:13, 21
people r. and David r. 1 Chr 29:9
all Judah r. at the oath. 2 Chr 15:15
princes and all the people r. 24:10
Hezekiah r. and all people. 29:36
of Israel and Judah r. 30:25
great sacrifices and r.: the wives also, and children r. Neh 12:43
for Judah r. for the priests. 44
the city of Shushan r. Esth 8:15*
if I r. because my wealth. Job 31:25
if I r. at the destruction of. 29
in mine adversity they r. Ps 35:15
the daughters of Judah r. 97:8
I have r. in the way of. 119:14
for my heart r. in all. Eccl 2:10
I r. not in the assembly. Jer 15:17
ye r. O destroyers of mine. 50:11
the Ammonites r. Ezek 25:6
the priests that r. on it. Hos 10:5
nor shouldest thou have r. Ob 12
the star, they r. with joy. Mat 2:10
my spirit hath r. in God. Luke 1:47
they r. with Elisabeth. 58
in that hour Jesus r. in spirit. 10:21
the people r. for the things. 13:17
your father Abraham r. to. John 8:56
r. in the works of their. Acts 7:41
which, when had read, they r. 15:31
the jailer r. believing in God. 16:34
as though they r. not. 1 Cor 7:30
so that I r. the more. 2 Cor 7:7
I r. in the Lord greatly. Phil 4:10
I r. greatly that I found. 2 John 4
3 John 3

rejoiceth

My heart r. in the Lord. 1 Sam 2:1
horse r. in his strength. Job 39:21
and my glory r. Ps 16:9
and r. as a strong man to. 19:5
therefore my heart greatly r. 28:7
well with righteous, city r. Pr 11:10
the light of the righteous r. 13:9
light of the eyes r. the heart. 15:30
whoso loveth wisdom r. his. 29:3
that r. shall descend into. Isa 5:14
as bridegroom r. over bride. 62:5
thou meetest him that r. and. 64:5
when the whole earth r. Ezek 35:14
I say to you, he r. more. Mat 18:13
bridegroom r. greatly. John 3:29
r. not in iniquity, but r. 1 Cor 13:6
and mercy r. against. Jas 2:13*

rejoicest

doest evil, then thou r. Jer 11:15

rejoicing

come up from thence r. 1 Ki 1:45
burnt offerings with r. 2 Chr 23:18
fill thy lips with r. Job 8:21*
his statutes are right, r. Ps 19:8
r. shall they be brought to. 45:15
declare his works with r. 107:22*
voice of r. is in tabernacle. 118:15
they are the r. of my heart. 119:111
doubtless come again with r. 126:6
I was his delight, r. always. Pr 8:30
r. in the habitable part of his. 31
I create Jerusalem a r. Isa 65:18
word was to me the r. Jer 15:16
their r. was to devour. Hab 3:14
this is the r. city that. Zeph 2:15
it on his shoulders r. Luke 15:5
r. that they were counted worthy. Acts 5:41
eunuch went on his way r. 8:39
r. in hope, patient in. Rom 12:12
I protest by your r. 1 Cor 15:31
our r. is this, testimony. 2 Cor 1:12*
that we are your r. even as ye. 14*
as sorrowful, yet always r. 6:10
then shall he have r. Gal 6:4
that your r. may be. Phil 1:26*
is our crown of r.? 1 Thes 2:19*
the r. of the hope firm. Heb 3:6
all such r. is evil. Jas 4:16*

release

seven years make a r. Deut 15:1
manner of the r.: it is the Lord's r. 2
the year of r. is at hand. 9
of the year of r. in feast. 31:10
he made a r. to provinces. Esth 2:18

release, *verb*

that lendeth shall r. it. Deut 15:2
with thy brother, hand shall r. 3
was wont to r. a prisoner. Mat 27:15
Luke 23:17; John 18:39
will ye that I r. unto you ? Mat 27:17
21; Mark 15:9; John 18:39
that he should rather r. Barabbas. Mark 15:11; Luke 23:18
chastise him, and r. him. Luke 23:16
willing to r. Jesus, spake again. 20
I have power to r. thee? John 19:10
Pilate sought to r. him. 12

released

then r. he Barabbas to. Mat 27:26
Mark 15:15; Luke 23:25
now at that feast he r. Mark 15:6

relied

because they r. on the. 2 Chr 13:18
r. on Syria, and hast not r. 16:7

relief

determined to send r. Acts 11:29

relieve

then thou shalt r. him. Lev 25:35*
r. the oppressed. Isa 1:17
things for meat to r. soul. Lam 1:11*
the comforter that should r. is 16*
while they sought meat to r. 19*
widows let them r. them; that it may r. them that are. 1 Tim 5:16

relieved

if she have r. afflicted. 1 Tim 5:10

relieveth

he r. the fatherless and. Ps 146:9*

religion

straitest sect of our r. Acts 26:5
conversation in Jews' r. Gal 1:13
profited in the Jews' r. above. 14
heart, this man's r. is vain. Jas 1:26
pure r. and undefiled before God. 27

religious

r. proselytes followed. Acts 13:43*
among you seem to be r. Jas 1:26

rely

because thou didst r. 2 Chr 16:8

remain

r. a widow at thy. Gen 38:11
that the frogs r. in. Ex 8:9, 11
let nothing of it r. until the. 12:10
nor fat of my sacrifice r. 23:18
if the flesh of consecrations r. 29:34
if aught r. till third day. Lev 19:6
that which is sold shall r. 25:28
to the years that r. 27:18
those which ye let r. Num 33:55
all, we left none to r. Deut 2:34
nor shall any of the flesh r. 16:4
those which r. shall hear and. 19:20
she shall r. in thine house. 21:13
his body shall not r. all night on. 23
and cattle shall r. Josh 1:14*
neither did there r. any more. 2:11
let none of them r. 8:22; 10:28, 30

by lot these nations that r. Josh 23:4
among these nations that r. 7
ye cleave to these nations that r. 12
why did Dan r. in ships ? Judg 5:17
wives for them that r. 21:7, 16
shalt r. by the stone. 1 Sam 20:19
six months did Joab r. 1 Ki 11:16
even I only, r. a prophet of. 18:22*
five of the horses that r. 2 Ki 7:13
for we r. yet escaped. Ezra 9:15*
shall he r. in the tomb. Job 21:32*
those that r. of him shall. 27:15
the beasts go to dens and r. 37:8
would I r. in wilderness. Ps 55:7*
perfect shall r. in the land. Pr 2:21
shall r. in congregation of. 21:16*
as yet shall he r. at Nob. Isa 10:32*
righteousness shall r. in the. 32:16*
which r. among the graves. 65:4*
earth shall r. before me, so shall your
seed and your name r. 66:22
residue of them that r. of. Jer 8:3
and this city shall r. for ever. 17:25
residue of Jerusalem that r. 24:8
those will I let r. still in. 27:11
concerning vessels that r. 19*, 21
the palace shall r. after the. 30:18
hands of men that r. 38:4
none shall r. 42:17; 44:14; 51:62
evil, to leave you none to r. 44:7
none of them shall r. Ezek 7:11
and they that r. shall be. 17:21
shall fowls of heaven r. 31:13*
I will cause the fowls to r. 32:4*
men to bury those that r. of. 39:14
r. ten men in one house. Amos 6:9
delivered those that did r. Ob 14
flying roll shall r. in. Zech 5:4*
all the families that r. shall. 12:14
in same house r. eating. Luke 10:7
the fragments that r. John 6:12
that my joy might r. in you. 15:11
that your fruit should r. 16*
that the bodies should not r. 19:31
let her r. unmarried. 1 Cor 7:11
of whom the greater part r. 15:6
we which are alive and r. till the
coming of the Lord. 1 Thes 4:15*
alive and r. shall be caught up. 17*
cannot be shaken may r. Heb 12:27
have heard r. in you. 1 John 2:24*
which r ready to die. Rev 3:2

remainder

thou shalt burn the r. Ex 29:34
the r. shall Aaron and. Lev 6:16
on the morrow also the r. shall. 7:16
but the r. on the third day shall. 17
neither name nor r. 2 Sam 14:7
the r. of wrath shalt. Ps 76:10

remained

Noah only r. alive, and. Gen 7:23*
and they that r. fled to the. 14:10
flies, there r. not one. Ex 8:31
there r. not any green thing. 10:15
there r. not one locust in all. 19
r. not so much as one chariot. 14:28
r. two of the men in. Num 11:26
because he should have r. 35:28
their inheritance r. in house. 36:12
Og, king of Bashan, r. Deut 3:11
when thou shalt have r. long. 4:25*
the rest who r. entered. Josh 10:20
in Gath there r. Anakims. 11:22
who r. of remnant of giants. 13:12
there r. of Israel seven tribes. 18:2
the Levites which r. of. 21:20, 26*
there r. with Gideon. Judg 7:3
they which r. were scattered so that
two not left. 1 Sam 11:11
David r. in a mountain. 23:14
David and his men r. in the. 24:3*
Tamar r. desolate in. 2 Sam 13:20
Sodomites which r. he. 1 Ki 22:46
Jehu slew all that r. 2 Ki 10:11, 17
and there r. the grove also. 13:6
that r., he set Gedaliah. 25:22*
the ark r. in Obed-edom. 1 Chr 13:14
my wisdom r. with me. Eccl 2:9
these defenced cities r. Jer 34:7
there r. but wounded men. 37:10
Jeremiah had r. many days in. 16
he r. in the court of the. 21; 38:13
people that r. in the city. 39:9; 52:15
away captive them that r. Jer 41:10
taste r. in him, his scent. 48:11
mighty men have r. in their. 51:30
Lord's anger none r. Lam 2:22
I r. there astonished. Ezek 3:15*
r. no strength in me. Dan 10:8, 17
and I r. there with the kings of. 13
in Sodom it would have r. Mat 11:23
fragments that r. twelve baskets.
14:20; Luke 9:17; John 6:13
beckoned, r. speechless. Luke 1:22
while it r. was it not ? Acts 5:4
forepart stuck fast, and r. 27:41

remainest

thou, O Lord, r. for ever.
Lam 5:19*; Heb 1:11*

remaineth

while earth r. seed time. Gen 8:22
which r. to you from. Ex 10:5
that which r. until morning. 12:10
that which r. over lay it up. 16:23
that r. of the flesh and. Lev 8:32
take the meat offering that r. 10:12
do for the tabernacle that r. 16:16*
destroy him that r. Num 24:19*
stones that r. to this day. Josh 8:29
there r. yet much land to be. 13:1
this is land that yet r.: all Geshuri. 2
he made him that r. Judg 5:13*
which stone r. unto. 1 Sam 6:18
Jesse said, There r. yet the. 16:11
ark r. under curtains. 1 Chr 17:1*
my error r. with myself. Job 19:4
answers there r. falsehood. 21:34
in his neck r. strength. 41:22*
he that r. in Jerusalem. Isa 4:3
he that r. in this city. Jer 38:2*
Tyrus every helper that r. 47:4
he that r. and is besieged. Ezek 6:12
so my Spirit r. among. Hag 2:5*
he that r. even he shall. Zech 9:7*
therefore your sin r. John 9:41
it r. that they that have wives be.
1 Cor 7:29*
that which r. is glorious. 2 Cor 3:11
until this day r. the same vail. 14
his righteousness r. for ever. 9:9*
seeing it r. that some. Heb 4:6
there r. therefore a rest to. 9
there r. no more sacrifice for. 10:26
for his seed r. in him. 1 John 3:9*

remaining

the cloud tarried, r. on. Num 9:22*
till none was left r. to Og. Deut 3:3
he left none r. Josh 10:33, 37, 39
40; 11:8
were r. of the families of the. 21:40
be destroyed from r. in the coasts of
Israel. 2 Sam 21:5
he left Ahab none r. 2 Ki 10:11
who r. in the chambers. 1 Chr 9:33*
nor shall have any r. Job 18:19
shall not be any r. of. Ob 18
shalt see the Spirit r. John 1:33*

Remaliah

fierce anger of son of R. Isa 7:4
the son of R. hath taken evil. 5
head of Samaria is R.'s son. 9
rejoice in Resin and R.'s son. 8:6

remedy

there was no r. 2 Chr 36:16
he be broken without r. Pr 6:15
be destroyed, and without r. 29:1

remember

did not butler r. Joseph. Gen 40:23
Moses said, R. this day. Ex 13:3
r. sabbath day to keep it holy. 20:8
r. Abraham, Isaac, and Israel. 32:13
Deut 9:27
we r. the fish which we. Num 11:5
r. all the commandments. 15:39
r. and do my commandments. 40
r. that thou wast a servant in the.
Deut 5:15; 15:15; 16:12; 24:18, 22
thou shalt r. what the Lord. 7:18
thou shalt r. all the way the. 8:2
r. the Lord giveth thee power. 18
r. how thou provokedst the. 9:7
r. that thou wast a bondman in.
15:15; 16:12; 24:18, 22
r. the day when thou camest. 16:3
r. what the Lord thy God did.
Deut 24:9
r. what Amalek did to thee. 25:17
r. the days of old, consider. 32:7
r. word which Moses. Josh 1:13
r. that I am your bone. Judg 9:2
Abigail said, Then r. 1 Sam 25:31
let the king r. the Lord. 2 Sam 14:11
neither do thou r. what thy. 19:19
r. when I and thou rode. 2 Ki 9:25
r. how I have walked before thee.
20:3; Isa 38:3
r. his marvellous works.
1 Chr 16:12; Ps 105:5
r. the mercies of David. 2 Chr 6:42
r. the word thou. Neh 1:8
r. the Lord, which is great. 4:14
r. them that have defiled. 13:29
r. who ever perished ? Job 4:7
O r. that my life is wind. 7:7
r. that thou hast made me. 10:9
r. it as waters that pass. 11:16
r. that thou magnify his work. 36:24
hand upon him, r. the battle. 41:8
r. all thy offerings and. Ps 20:3
will r. the name of the Lord. 7*
all ends of the world shall r. 22:27
r. thy mercies, they have. 25:6
r. not the sins of my youth, r. thou. 7
r. thy congregation which thou. 74:2
r. this, that the enemy hath. 18
r. how the foolish man. 22
O r. not against us former. 79:8
r. how short my time is. 89:47
r. Lord the reproach of thy. 50
and to those that r. his. 103:18
r. the word unto thy servant. 119:49
Lord, r. David, and all his. 132:1
r. O Lord, children of Edom. 137:7
let him drink, and r. his. Pr 31:7
not much r. the days. Eccl 5:20
let him r. days of darkness. 11:8
r. now thy Creator in the days. 12:1
we will r. thy love. S of S 1:4*
r. ye not the former things ?
Isa 43:18; 46:9
own sake I will not r. thy sins. 43:25
r. these, O Jacob and Israel. 44:21
r. this, and shew yourselves. 46:8
neither didst r. the latter end. 47:7
shalt not r. the reproach of. 54:4
meetest those that r. thee. 64:5
not wroth, neither r. iniquity. 9
neither shall they r. it. Jer 3:16
he will now r. their iniquity. 14:10
r., break not thy covenant with. 21
their children r. their altars. 17:2
r. that I stood before thee. 18:20
I do earnestly r. him still. 31:20
did not the Lord r. them ? 44:21
escaped, r. the Lord afar off. 51:50
r. O Lord, what is come. Lam 5:1
then shalt r. thy ways. Ezek 16:61
20:43; 36:31
mayest r. and be confounded. 16:63
shalt not r. Egypt any more. 23:27
will he r. their iniquity. Hos 8:13
therefore he will r. iniquity. 9:9
r. now what Balak. Mi 6:5
in wrath r. mercy. Hab 3:2
r. the law of Moses my. Mal 4:4
neither r. the five loaves. Mat 16:9
Mark 8:18
sir, we r. that deceiver. Mat 27:63
to r. his holy covenant. Luke 1:72
r. that thou in thy lifetime. 16:25
r. Lot's wife. 17:32
r. how he spake to you. 24:6
r. the word that I said. John 15:20
time shall come ye may r. 16:4
r. that by the space of. Acts 20:31
r. words of the Lord Jesus, how. 35
would that we should r. Gal 2:10
r. that ye being in time. Eph 2:11
r. my bonds. Grace be. Col 4:18
for ye r. brethren our. 1 Thes 2:9
r. ye not that I told ? 2 Thes 2:5
r. that Jesus Christ. 2 Tim 2:8
r. them that are in bonds. Heb 13:3
r. them which have the rule over. 7
r. the words spoken of. Jude 17
r. from whence thou art fallen.
Rev 2:5
r. how thou hast received. 3:3

I remember

saying, I do r. my faults. Gen 41:9
I r. that which Amalek. 1 Sam 15:2*
when I r. I am afraid. Job 21:6
when I r. these, I pour. Ps 42:4
when I r. thee upon my bed. 63:6
if I do not r. thee, let my. 137:6
I r. the days of old, I muse. 143:5
I r. thee, the kindness of. Jer 2:2
consider not that I r. all. Hos 7:2

I will remember

I will r. my covenant. Gen 9:15, 16
Lev 26:42; Ezek 16:60
I will for their sakes r. Lev 26:45
therefore will I r. thee. Ps 42:6
but I will r. the years of the. 77:10
I will r. the works, I will r. thy. 11*
I will r. their sin no more. Jer 31:34
Heb 8:12; 10:17
I will r. his deeds which. 3 John 10

remember me

r. me, that I may be. Judg 16:28
handmaid, and r. me. 1 Sam 1:11
r. me, O God. Neh 13:14, 22, 31
a set time, and r. me. Job 14:13
r me for thy goodness'. Ps 25:7
r. me with the favour that. 106:4
knowest, r. me, and visit. Jer 15:15
escape of you shall r. me. Ezek 6:9
r. me in far countries. Zech 10:9
Lord, r. me when thou comest into thy kingdom. Luke 23:42
that ye r. me in all. 1 Cor 11:2

remembered

God r. Noah. Gen 8:1
God r. Abraham. 19:29
God r. Rachel. 30:22
Joseph r. the dreams. 42:9
God r. his covenant. Ex 2:24; 6:5
shall be r. before the. Num 10:9
children of Israel r. not. Judg 8:34
the Lord r. Hannah. 1 Sam 1:19
thus Joash r. not the. 2 Chr 24:22
Ahasuerus r. Vashti. Esth 2:1
days of Purim should be r. 9:28
sinner shall be no more r. Job 24:20
thy name to be r. in all. Ps 45:17
I r. God and was troubled. 77:3
they r. that God was their. 78:35
for he r. that they were but flesh. 39
they r. not his hand, when he. 42
he r. his mercy toward the. 98:3
he hath r. his covenant for. 105:8
for he r. his holy promise. 42
they r. not the multitude of. 106:7
he r. for them his covenant, and. 45
iniquity of his fathers be r. 109:14
because that he r. not to shew. 16
wonderful works to be r. 111:4
I r. thy judgements of old. 119:52
I have r. thy name, O Lord. 55
who r. us in our low estate. 136:23
we wept, when we r. Zion. 137:1
yet no man r. that same. Eccl 9:15
that thou mayest be r. Isa 23:16
thou hast not r. me, nor laid. 57:11
then he r. the days of old. 63:11
heavens shall not be r. 65:17
name may be no more r. Jer 11:19
Jerusalem r. in the days. Lam 1:7
r. not his footstool in the day. 2:1
his righteousness shall not be r. Ezek 3:20; 33:13
thou hast not r. the days. 16:22, 43
your iniquity to be r. 21:24
thou shalt be no more r. 32
Ammonites may not be r. 25:10
they shall no more be r. Hos 2:17*
Zech 13:2
and r. not the brotherly. Amos 1:9
fainted, I r. the Lord. Jonah 2:7
Peter r. the words of Jesus. Mat 26:75; Luke 22:61
they r. his words, and. Luke 24:8
his disciples r. that it. John 2:17
risen, they r. that he had said. 22
was glorified, then they r. 12:16
then r. I the word of. Acts 11:16
hath r. her iniquities. Rev 18:5

rememberest

the slain whom thou r. no. Ps 88:5
there r. that thy brother. Mat 5:23

remembereth

maketh inquisition, he r. Ps 9:12
frame, he r. we are but dust. 103:14
she r. not her last end. Lam 1:9
she r. no more anguish. John 16:21
whilst he r. the obedience. 2 Cor 7:15

remembering

r. mine affliction and. Lam 3:19
r. without ceasing your. 1 Thes 1:3

remembrance

I will put out the r. Ex 17:14
bringing iniquity to r. Num 5:15
out the r. of Amalek. Deut 25:19
make the r. of them to cease. 32:26
keep my name in r. 2 Sam 18:18
to call my sin to r.? 1 Ki 17:18
his r. shall perish from. Job 18:17
in death is no r. of thee. Ps 6:5
give thanks at r. of his holiness. 30:4*; 97:12*
to cut off the r. of them from. 34:16
a psalm of David, to bring to r. 38:title; 70:title
call to r. my song in the night. 77:6
that Israel be no more in r. 83:4
thy r. unto all generations. 102:12*
righteous in everlasting r. 112:6
there is no r. of former. Eccl 1:11
no r. of wise more than fool. 2:16
our soul is to the r. of. Isa 26:8*
put me in r., let us plead. 43:26
hast thou set up thy r. 57:8*
soul hath them still in r. Lam 3:20
call to r. the iniquity. Ezek 21:23
I say that ye are come to r. 24
calling to r. the days of 23:19, 21
bringeth their iniquity to r. 29:16
a book of r. was written. Mal 3:16
Peter calling to r. saith. Mark 11:21
he hath holpen Israel in r. Luke 1:54
this do in r. of me. 22:19
1 Cor 11:24
bring all things to your r. John 14:26
thine alms are had in r. Acts 10:31
who shall bring you into r. 1 Cor 4:17
as oft as ye drink it, in r. of. 11:25
God upon every r. of you. Phil 1:3
good r. of us always. 1 Thes 3:6
put the brethren in r. 1 Tim 4:6*
that I have r. of thee. 2 Tim 1:3
when I call to r. the unfeigned. 5*
I put thee in r. that thou stir. 6
of these things put them in r. 2:14
there is a r. of sins. Heb 10:3
but call to r. the former days. 32
to put you always in r. 2 Pet 1:12
Jude 5
stir you up by putting you in r. 2 Pet 1:13
have these things always in r. 15
pure minds by way of r. 3:1
great Babylon came in r. Rev 16:19

remembrances

your r. are like to ashes. Job 13:12

remission

many, for the r. of sins. Mat 26:28
baptism of repentance for r. of sins. Mark 1:4; Luke 3:3
salvation by r. of sins. Luke 1:77
that r. should be preached in. 24:47
baptized for r. of sins. Acts 2:38
believeth shall receive r. of. 10:43
for the r. of sins that. Rom 3:25*
shedding of blood is no r. Heb 9:22
where r. is, there no more. 10:18

remit, -ed

sins ye r. they are r. John 20:23*

remnant

the r. of meat offering. Lev 2:3
r. shall be the priest's as. 5:13
the r. of the oil that is. 14:18
only Og remained of r. of giants. Deut 3:11; Josh 12:4; 13:12
his eye evil toward r. Deut 28:54
if ye cleave to the r. of. Josh 23:12
Gibeonites were of r. 2 Sam 21:2
speak to the r. of the. 1 Ki 12:23
I will take away the r. of. 14:10
r. of Sodomites, Jehoshaphat. 22:46
lift up thy prayer for the r. 2 Ki 19:4; Isa 37:4
the r. that is escaped shall yet take root. 2 Ki 19:30; Isa 37:31
shall go forth a r. 2 Ki 19:31
Isa 37:32
I will forsake the r. of. 2 Ki 21:14
the r. did Nebuzar-adan. 25:11
he will return to the r. 2 Chr 30:6
the r. of their brethren. Ezra 3:8
Lord to leave us a r. to escape. 9:8
so that there should be no r. 14
the r. that are left of the. Neh 1:3
the r. of them the fire. Job 22:20
had left us a very small r. Isa 1:9
set his hand, to recover the r. 11:11
an highway for the r. of his. 16
cut off from Babylon the r. 14:22
and he shall slay thy r. 30
I will bring lions on the r. of. 15:9
the r. shall be very small. 16:14
shall cease from r. of Syria. 17:3
hearken, all the r. of the house. 46:3
glean the r. of Israel. Jer 6:9
there shall be no r. of them. 11:23
it shall be well with thy r. 15:11
will gather the r. of my flock. 23:3
the r. of Ashdod did drink of. 25:20
O Lord, save thy people, the r. 31:7
Nebuzar-adan carried away r. 39:9
king of Babylon had left a r. 40:11
Jews be scattered, and r. of. 15
Johanan took the r. 41:16; 43:5
the Lord, even for all this r. 42:2
word of Lord, ye r. of Judah. 15
O ye r. of Judah, go ye not. 19
I will take the r. of Judah. 44:12
so that none of the r. of Judah. 14
the r. shall know whose words. 28
Lord will spoil r. of country of. 47:4
Ashkelon is cut off, with the r. 5
the whole r. of thee. Ezek 5:10
yet will I leave a r. that ye. 6:8
make an end of the r.? 11:13
therein shall be left a r. 14:22
and thy r. shall fall by the. 23:25
I will destroy the r. of the. 25:16
in the r. whom the Lord. Joel 2:32
the r. of the Philistines. Amos 1:8
God will be gracious to the r. 5:15
that they may possess the r. of. 9:12
I will surely gather the r. Mi 2:12
make her that halted, a r. 4:7
the r. of his brethren shall. 5:3
the r. of Jacob, in the midst. 7
the r. of Jacob shall be among. 8
the transgression of the r. 7:18
the r. of the people shall. Hab 2:8
and I will cut off the r. Zeph 1:4
for the r. of house of Judah. 2:7
the r. of my people shall possess. 9
the r. of Israel shall not do. 3:13
all the r. of the people. Hag 1:12
stirred up the spirit of the r. 14
marvellous in eyes of r. Zech 8:6
I will cause r. of this people. 12
the r. took his servants. Mat 22:6
Esaias also crieth, a r. Rom 9:27
at this time also there is a r. 11:5
the r. were affrighted. Rev 11:13
to make war with the r. 12:17
the r. were slain with the. 19:21

remove

father's hand to r. it. Gen 48:17
inheritance of Israel r. Num 36:7, 9
shalt not r. thy neighbour's land. Deut 19:14
then ye shall r. from. Josh 3:3
then would I r. Abimelech. Judg 9:29
so David would not r. 2 Sam 6:10
the Lord said, I will r. 2 Ki 23:27
came on Judah, to r. them. 24:3
I any more r. Israel. 2 Chr 33:8
some r. the landmarks. Job 24:2
I will not r. mine integrity. 27:5*
of the wicked r. me. Ps 36:11*
r. thy stroke away from me. 39:10
r. from me reproach. 119:22*
r. from me the way of lying, and. 29
turn not, r. thy foot from. Pr 4:27
r. thy way far from her, and. 5:8
r. not the ancient landmark. 22:28
23:10
r. from me vanity and lies. 30:8
therefore r. sorrow. Eccl 11:10

the earth shall r. out of. Isa 13:13*
from his place shall he not r. 46:7
then shalt thou not r. Jer 4:1
prophesy a lie, to r. you far. 27:10
that I should r. it from. 32:31
they shall r., they shall depart. 50:3*
r. out of the midst of Babylon. 8*
r. by day, thou shalt r. Ezek 12:3
saith the Lord, R. the diadem. 21:26
r. violence and spoil. 45:9
they were like them that r. Hos 5:10
but I will r. the northern. Joel 2:20
that ye might r. them from their. 3:6
ye shall not r. your necks. Mi 2:3
I will r. the iniquity of. Zech 3:9
half the mountain shall r. 14:4
r. hence, and it shall r. Mat 17:20
r. this cup from me. Luke 22:42
faith, so that I could r. 1 Cor 13:2
or else I will r. thy candlestick. Rev 2:5*

removed

(*In speaking of the journeying in the wilderness the Revisions have changed this word to* journeyed)

Noah r. the covering. Gen 8:13
Abram r. to Rehoboth. 12:8
Isaac r. from thence. 26:22
Jacob r. the he goats that. 30:35
and Joseph r. the people to. 47:21
the Lord r. the swarms. Ex 8:31
the angel of God r. and went. 14:19
the people saw it and r. and. 20:18*
people r. from Hazeroth. Num 12:16
they r. and pitched in the. 21:12, 13
Israel r. from Rameses. 33:5
they r. from Etham. 7, 9, 10
they r. from the Red sea. 11
r. from Alush. 14
r. from the desert of Sinai. 16
r. from Libnah. 21
r. from mount Shapher. 24
r. from Haradah. 25
r. from Makheloth. 26
r. from Tarah. 28
r. from Bene-jaakan. 32
r. from Jotbathah. 34
they r. from Ezion-gaber. 36
r. from Kadesh. 37
r. from Dibon-gad. 46
r. from Almon-diblathaim. 47
r. into all kingdoms. Deut 28:25*
they r. from Shittim. Josh 3:1
when the people r. to pass over. 14
hand is not r. from you. 1 Sam 6:3
Saul r. David from him. 18:13
he r. Amasa out of. 2 Sam 20:12*
Asa r. the idols. 1 Ki 15:12
Maachah his mother, he r. from being queen. 13; 2 Chr 15:16
the high places were not r. 1 Ki 15:14*; 2 Ki 15:4, 35
Ahaz r. the laver. 2 Ki 16:17
Lord r. Israel out of his sight. 17:18, 23; 23:27
nations which thou hast r. 17:26*
Hezekiah r. the high places. 18:4
r. the burnt offerings. 2 Chr 35:12
and the rock is r. out. Job 14:18
shall the rock be r. out? 18:4
and mine hope hath he r. 19:10*
so would he have r. thee. 36:16*
though the earth be r. Ps 46:2*
I r. his shoulder from. 81:6
so far hath he r. our. 103:12
it should not be r. for ever. 104:5*
Zion, which cannot be r. 125:1*
shall never be r. Pr 10:30
till the Lord have r. men. Isa 6:12
I have r. the bounds of. 10:13
Madmenah is r.: the inhabitants. 31*
in the sure place shall be r. 22:25*
the earth shall be r. like. 24:20*
thou hast r. it far to all ends. 26:15*
but have r. their heart far. 29:13
teachers be r. to a corner. 30:20*
of the stakes shall be r. 33:20*
mine age is r. from me as. 38:12*
the hills shall be r.: my kindness . . . shall not be r. saith. 54:10
I will cause them to be r. Jer 15:4*
I will deliver them to be r. 24:9* 29:18*; 34:17*
sinned, therefore she is r. Lam 1:8*
and thou hast r. my soul far. 3:17
their gold shall be r. Ezek 7:19*
I will give them to be r. and. 23:46*
uncleanness of a r. woman. 36:17*
banquet of them shall be r. Amos 6:7*
how hath he r. it from me! Mi 2:4
day shall the decree be far r. 7:11
if ye shall say, Be thou r. Mat 21:21*; Mark 11:23*
he r. Abraham into this land. Acts 7:4
when he had r. him, he raised. 13:22
are so soon r. from him. Gal 1:6

removeth

cursed be he that r. his neighbour's landmark. Deut 27:17
which r. the mountains. Job 9:5
he r. away the speech of the. 12:20
whoso r. stones shall be. Eccl 10:9*
seasons, he r. kings. Dan 2:21

removing

r. from thy flock all the. Gen 30:32
seeing I am a captive r. Isa 49:21*
prepare the stuff for r. Ezek 12:3, 4
signifieth the r. of those. Heb 12:27

Remphan

star of your god R. Acts 7:43

rend

that ephod should not r. Ex 39:23
neither r. your clothes. Lev 10:6
priest shall r. the plague out. 13:56
I will surely r. the kingdom. 1 Ki 11:11; 12:31
howbeit, I will not r. away. 1 Ki 11:13
I will r. the kingdom. 31; 14:8
didst r. thy clothes. 2 Chr 34:27
a time to r. and a time. Eccl 3:7
oh! that thou wouldest r. Isa 64:1
wind shall r. it. Ezek 13:11, 13
thou didst break and r. all. 29:7
and I will r. the caul. Hos 13:8
r. your heart, and not. Joel 2:13
turn again and r. you. Mat 7:6
let us not r. it, but cast. John 19:24

render

every offering they r. Num 18:9
I will r. vengeance to. Deut 32:41
he will r. vengeance to his. 43
evil of men of Shechem did God r. upon their heads. Judg 9:57*
Lord r. to every man. 1 Sam 26:23
r. to every man according to his. 2 Chr 6:30
for he will r. unto man. Job 33:26*
of a man shall he r. to him. 34:11
r. to them their desert. Ps 28:4
they that r. evil for good. 38:20
I will r. praises unto thee. 56:12
and r. to our neighbour. 79:12
lift up thyself, r. a reward. 94:2
what shall I r. to the Lord? 116:12
and shall not he r. to every man? Pr 24:12; Rom 2:6
say not, I will r. to man. Pr 24:29
than seven men that can r. 26:16
Lord will come, to r. his. Isa 66:15
he will r. to Babylon. Jer 51:6, 24
r. to them a recompence. Lam 3:64
so will we r. the calves. Hos 14:2
will ye r. me a recompence? Joel 3:4
I declare, that I will r. Zech 9:12
r. him the fruits in. Mat 21:41
r. unto Caesar. 22:21; Mark 12:17 Luke 20:25
r. therefore to all their. Rom 13:7
let husband r. to wife. 1 Cor 7:3
what thanks can we r.? 1 Thes 3:9
see that none r. evil for evil. 5:15

rendered

thus God r. wickedness. Judg 9:56*
the king of Moab r. to. 2 Ki 3:4
Hezekiah r. not. 2 Chr 32:25
man's hands be r. to him. Pr 12:14

renderest

r. to every man according. Ps 62:12

rendereth

a voice of the Lord that r. Isa 66:6

rendering

not r. evil for evil, or. 1 Pet 3:9

rendest

though thou r. thy face. Jer 4:30

rending

lest he tear my soul, r. Ps 7:2

renew

r. the kingdom there. 1 Sam 11:14
and r. a right spirit. Ps 51:10
that wait on Lord shall r. Isa 40:31
the people r. their strength. 41:1
O Lord, r. our days. Lam 5:21
if they fall away, to r. Heb 6:6

renewed

Asa r. the altar. 2 Chr 15:8
and my bow was r. Job 29:20
so that thy youth is r. Ps 103:5
inward man is r. day. 2 Cor 4:16
and be r. in the spirit. Eph 4:23
the new man, which is r. Col 3:10

renewest

thou r. thy witnesses. Job 10:17
and thou r. the face. Ps 104:30

renewing

be transformed by the r. Rom 12:2
he saved us by the r. Tit 3:5

renounced

have r. the hidden. 2 Cor 4:2

renown

giants of old, men of r. Gen 6:4
in congregation, men of r. Num 16:2
thy r. went forth among. Ezek 16:14
harlot because of thy r. 15
raise up for them a plant of r. 34:29
it shall be to them a r. 39:13
and hast gotten thee r. Dan 9:15

renowned

these were the r. of. Num 1:16*
evildoers shall never be r. Isa 14:20*
and great lords, and r. Ezek 23:23
the r. city which was strong. 26:17

rent, *substantive*

a girdle there shall be a r. Isa 3:24*
and the r. is made worse. Mat 9:16; Mark 2:21
the new maketh a r. Luke 5:36

rent, *verb*

Joseph is without doubt r. in pieces. Gen 37:33
ephod, that it be not r. Ex 28:32
bottles, old and r. Josh 9:4, 13
Samson r. the lion as he would have r. a kid, and he had. Judg 14:6
Saul r. the skirt of. 1 Sam 15:27
Lord hath r. the kingdom. 28; 28:17
Tamar r. her garment. 2 Sam 13:19
Hushai came with his coat r. 15:32
the earth r. with the. 1 Ki 1:40
Ahijah r. Jeroboam's new. 11:30
the altar shall be r. 13:3
altar was r. 5
and a strong wind r. the. 19:11
he r. Israel from the. 2 Ki 17:21
when I heard this, I r. Ezra 9:3
having r. my garment and my. 5
then Job arose, and r. Job 1:20
Job's friends r. every one. 2:12
and the cloud is not r. under. 26:8
were not afraid, nor r. Jer 36:24
and No shall be r. Ezek 30:16
veil of temple was r. in twain. Mat 27:51; Mark 15:38; Luke 23:45
spirit cried, and r. him. Mark 9:26
see **clothes**

repaid

righteous, good shall be r. Pr 13:21

repair

let the priests r. the breaches of the. 2 Ki 12:5; 22:5, 6; 2 Chr 24:4* 34:8, 10
r. ye not the breaches? 2 Ki 12:7
neither r. the breaches of the. 8
stone to r. the breaches. 12; 22:5, 6
money to r. the house. 2 Chr 24:5
hired carpenters to r. the house. 12*
reviving to r. the house. Ezra 9:9
shall r. the waste cities. Isa 61:4

repaired

Benjamin r. cities, and. Judg 21:23*
Solomon r. the breaches. 1 Ki 11:27

Elijah *r.* the altar of the. *1 Ki* 18:30
the priests had not *r.* *2 Ki* 12:6
and *r.* therewith the house of. 14
and Joab *r.* the rest of. *1 Chr* 11:8
Hezekiah *r.* the doors of. *2 Chr* 29:3
Hezekiah *r.* Millo in the. 32:5*
Manasseh *r.* the altar of. 33:16*
next to them *r.* *Neh* 3:4, 5, 7, 8
10, 12, 19
after him *r.* 6, 17, 18, 20, 22, 23, 24

repairer

thou shalt be called the *r.* *Isa* 58:12

repairing

concerning the *r.* of. *2 Chr* 24:27*

repay

he will *r.* him to his face. *Deut* 7:10
who shall *r.* him that? *Job* 21:31
that I should *r.* him? 41:11
deeds he will *r.* fury, and to the islands he will *r.* *Isa* 59:18
again, I will *r.* thee. *Luke* 10:35
vengeance is mine, I will *r.*, saith the Lord. *Rom* 12:19
written it, I will *r.* it. *Philem* 19

repayeth

and *r.* them that hate. *Deut* 7:10

repeateth

he that *r.* matter. *Pr* 17:9*

repent

(Repent *or* repentance *is used of regret and sorrow for having done some deed. It is not always used for godly repentance, which means such sorrow as shall cause a complete change of action. Judas repented of his betrayal of Jesus,* Mat 27:8, *but did not change his life. When the word is used in regard to God it is in a figure of speech, which speaks of him almost as if human; and since his actions are changed, attributes to him the feelings which, in a man, would cause such a change*)

lest the people *r.* *Ex* 13:17
turn from thy fierce wrath, and *r.* of this. 32:12
man, that he should *r.* *Num* 23:19
the Lord shall *r.* for his. *Deut* 32:36
will not *r.*: for he is not a man, that he should *r.* *1 Sam* 15:29
if they *r.* in captivity. *1 Ki* 8:47
I abhor myself, and *r.* *Job* 42:6
let it *r.* thee concerning. *Ps* 90:13
and will not *r.* 110:4; *Heb* 7:21
he will *r.* himself. *Ps* 135:14
and will not *r.* *Jer* 4:28
I will *r.* of the evil. 18:8; 26:13
if it do evil, then I will *r.* of. 18:10
that I may *r.* 26:3
for I *r.* of the evil. 42:10
r. and turn. *Ezek* 14:6; 18:30
spare, neither will I *r.* 24:14
knoweth if he will return and *r.*? *Joel* 2:14; *Jonah* 3:9
saying, *R.*, for the kingdom of heaven. *Mat* 3:2; 4:17
Jesus preaching, *r.* ye. *Mark* 1:15
preached that men should *r.* 6:12
except ye *r.* ye shall. *Luke* 13:3, 5
from the dead, they will *r.* 16:30
thy brother *r.* forgive him. 17:3, 4
r. and be baptized. *Acts* 2:38
r. ye therefore and be. 3:19
r. of this thy wickedness. 8:22
commandeth all men to *r.* 17:30
that they should *r.* and. 26:20
I do not *r.* though I did *r.* *2 Cor* 7:8
and *r.* . . . except thou *r.* *Rev* 2:5
r. or else I will come unto. 16
space to *r.* of her fornication. 21
except they *r.* of their deeds. 22
thou hast received, and *r.* 3:3
be zealous therefore and *r.* 19

repentance

r. shall be hid from mine. *Hos* 13:14
bring forth fruits meet for *r.* *Mat* 3:8; *Luke* 3:8
baptize with water unto *r.* *Mat* 3:11
to call sinners to *r.* 9:13; *Mark* 2:17
Luke 5:32
did preach baptism of *r.* *Mark* 1:4
Luke 3:3; *Acts* 13:24; 19:4
99 which need no *r.* *Luke* 15:7
that *r.* and remission of sins. 24:47
God exalted for to give *r.* *Acts* 5:31
Gentiles granted *r.* to life. 11:18
Greeks *r.* towards God. 20:21
and do works meet for *r.* 26:20
God leadeth thee to *r.* *Rom* 2:4
calling of God are without *r.* 11:29
that ye sorrowed to *r.* *2 Cor* 7:9
godly sorrow worketh *r.* to. 10
will give them *r.* *2 Tim* 2:25
the foundation of *r.* *Heb* 6:1
to renew them again to *r.* 6
found no place of *r.* though. 12:17
that all should come to *r.* *2 Pet* 3:9

repented

it *r.* the Lord, that he. *Gen* 6:6
the Lord *r.* of the evil. *Ex* 32:14
2 Sam 24:16; *1 Chr* 21:15
Jer 26:19
it *r.* the Lord because. *Judg* 2:18
Israel *r.* for Benjamin. 21:6, 15
the Lord *r.* that he made Saul king. *1 Sam* 15:35
the Lord *r.* according to. *Ps* 106:45
no man *r.* him of his. *Jer* 8:6
Lord overthrew, and *r.* not. 20:16
that I was turned, I *r.* 31:19
the Lord *r.* for this. *Amos* 7:3, 6
God *r.* of the evil that. *Jonah* 3:10
punish you, and I *r.* not. *Zech* 8:14
because they *r.* not. *Mat* 11:20
they would have *r.* long ago. 21; *Luke* 10:13
men of Nineveh shall rise because they *r.* *Mat* 12:41; *Luke* 11:32
not, but afterward he *r.* *Mat* 21:29
ye, when ye had seen it, *r.* not. 32
Judas *r.* himself, and brought. 27:3
not to be *r.* of. *2 Cor* 7:10
many that have not *r.* of the. 12:21
repent, and she *r.* not. *Rev* 2:21
these plagues, yet *r.* not. 9:20
neither *r.* of their murders. 21
blasphemed and *r.* not. 16:9, 11

repentest

art a gracious God, and *r.* thee of the evil. *Jonah* 4:2

repenteth

for it *r.* me that I have. *Gen* 6:7
it *r.* me that I have set. *1 Sam* 15:11
slow to anger, and *r.* *Joel* 2:13
over one sinner that *r.* *Luke* 15:7, 10

repenting

I am weary with *r.* *Jer* 15:6

repentings

my heart is turned, *r.* are. *Hos* 11:8

repetitions

use not vain *r.* as heathen. *Mat* 6:7

Rephaim

Philistines spread themselves in valley of *R.* *2 Sam* 5:18, 22; 23:13
1 Chr 11:15; 14:9
ears in the valley of *R.* *Isa* 17:5

Rephaims

smote the *R.* in Ashteroth. *Gen* 14:5
have I given the land of *R.* 15:20

Rephidim

Israel pitched in *R.* *Ex* 17:1
Num 33:4
fought with Israel in *R.* *Ex* 17:8
they were departed from *R.* 19:2; *Num* 33:15

replenish

and *r.* the earth. *Gen* 1:28; 9:1

replenished

be *r.* from the east. *Isa* 2:6*
of Zidon have *r.* Tyre. 23:2
r. every sorrowful soul. *Jer* 31:25
r., now she is laid waste. *Ezek* 26:2
thou wast *r.* and made very. 27:25

repliest

O man, who art thou that *r.* against God? *Rom* 9:20

report

(*Of good report,* of good reputation, Acts 6:3)

to his father their evil *r.* *Gen* 37:2
shalt not raise a false *r.* *Ex* 23:1
brought up an evil *r.* *Num* 13:32
did bring up the evil *r.* died. 14:37
who shall hear *r.* of thee. *Deut* 2:25
It is no good *r.* I hear. *1 Sam* 2:24
it was a true *r.* I heard. *1 Ki* 10:6
2 Chr 9:5
matter for an evil *r.* *Neh* 6:13
and a good *r.* maketh. *Pr* 15:30*
as at the *r.* concerning Egypt, so . . . at the *r.* of Tyre. *Isa* 23:5
vexation only to understand *r.* 28:19*
who hath believed our *r.*? 53:1†
John 12:38; *Rom* 10:16
Babylon hath heard the *r.* *Jer* 50:43*
seven men of honest *r.* *Acts* 6:3
Cornelius was of good *r.* 10:22*
Ananias, having a good *r.* of. 22:12
by evil *r.* and good *r.* as. *2 Cor* 6:8
things are of good *r.* *Phil* 4:8
must have a good *r.* of. *1 Tim* 3:7*
elders obtained a good *r.* *Heb* 11:2*
obtained a good *r.* through faith. 39*
Demetrius hath a good *r.* *3 John* 12*

report, *verb*

r. say they, and we will *r.* it. *Jer* 20:10
he will *r.* that God is. *1 Cor* 14:25

reported

it is *r.* among heathen. *Neh* 6:6
be *r.* to king according to these. 7
also they *r.* his good deeds. 19
despise their husbands, when it shall be *r.* *Esth* 1:17
which had the inkhorn, *r.* *Ezek* 9:11
this saying is commonly *r.* *Mat* 28:15
r. all that chief priests. *Acts* 4:23
Timotheus was well *r.* of. 16:2
as we be slanderously *r.* *Rom* 3:8
it is *r.* that there is. *1 Cor* 5:1
a widow, well *r.* of for. *1 Tim* 5:10
that are now *r.* to you. *1 Pet* 1:12

reproach

[1] *Scorn or derision,* Neh 2:17; 5:9. [2] *Shame or disgrace,* Pr 6:33. [3] *Censure or blame,* Isa 51:7. [4] *Injury, either in word or deed,* 2 Cor 12:10.

rolled away *r.* of Egypt. *Josh* 5:9
taketh away the *r.* *1 Sam* 17:26
in great affliction and *r.* *Neh* 1:3
and turn their *r.* upon their. 4:4
because of the *r.* of heathen. 5:9
make me not the *r.* of the. *Ps* 39:8
save me from *r.* of him. 57:3
for thy sake I have borne *r.* 69:7
r. hath broken my heart, I am. 20
let them be covered with *r.* 71:13
he put them to a perpetual *r.* 78:66
their *r.* wherewith they. 79:12
remember the *r.* of thy servants, how I bear in my bosom the *r.* 89:50
remove from me *r.* and. 119:22
r. shall not be wiped away. *Pr* 6:33
and with ignominy cometh *r.* 18:3
that causeth shame and *r.* 19:26
strife and *r.* shall cease. 22:10*
to take away our *r.* *Isa* 4:1
fear ye not the *r.* of men. 51:7
not remember the *r.* of thy. 54:4
an everlasting *r.* on you. *Jer* 23:40
because I did bear the *r.* of. 31:19
because we have heard *r.* 51:51
he is filled full with *r.* *Lam* 3:30
thou hast heard their *r.* O Lord. 61
consider and behold our *r.* 5:1
as at the time of thy *r.* *Ezek* 16:57
concerning *r.* of Ammonites. 21:28
nor shalt thou bear *r.* of the. 36:15
that ye receive no more *r.* 30
the *r.* offered by him to cease, without his own *r.* *Dan* 11:18
and his *r.* shall his Lord. *Hos* 12:14
not thine heritage to *r.* *Joel* 2:17
shall bear *r.* of my people. *Mi* 6:16
I have heard the *r.* of Moab. *Zeph* 2:8
r. of it was a burden. 3:18
I speak as concerning *r.* *2 Cor* 11:21*
good report lest fall into *r.* *1 Tim* 3:7
both labour and suffer *r.* 4:10*
esteeming the *r.* of Christ. *Heb* 11:26
without the camp, bearing his *r.* 13:13

reproach, *verb*
glean, and r. her not. Ruth 2:15
whom king of Assyria hath sent to r.
2 Ki 19:4*, 16; Isa 37:4*, 17*
that they might r. me. Neh 6:13
my heart shall not r. me. Job 27:6
mine enemies r. me. Ps 42:10
the adversary r. me? 74:10
mine enemies r. me all day. 102:8
when men shall r. you. Luke 6:22

a **reproach**
that were a r. to us. Gen 34:14
and lay it for a r. upon. 1 Sam 11:2
that we be no more a r. Neh 2:17
he that taketh not up a r. Ps 15:3
a r. of men, and despised. 22:6
I was a r. among all mine. 31:11
thou makest us a r. to our. 44:13
a r. to our neighbours. 79:4
he is a r. to his neighbours. 89:41
I became also a r. to them. 109:25
sin is a r. to any people. Pr 14:34
people that were a r. Isa 30:5
word of Lord is to them a r. Jer 6:10
word of Lord was made a r. 20:8
to be a r. and a proverb. 24:9; 29:18
42:18; 44:8, 12
Bozrah shall become a r. and. 49:13
I will make thee a r. Ezek 5:14
Jerusalem shall be a r. and a. 15
I have made thee a r. unto. 22:4
people are become a r. Dan 9:16
no more make you a r. Joel 2:19

my **reproach**
hath taken away my r. Gen 30:23
the cause of my r. 1 Sam 25:39
plead against me my r. Job 19:5
heard the check of my r. 20:3
when I wept, that was my r. Ps 69:10
known my r. and my shame. 19
turn away my r. which I. 119:39
to take away my r. Luke 1:25

reproached
whom hast thou r.? 2 Ki 19:22*
Isa 37:23*
by thy messengers thou hast r. the.
2 Ki 19:23* Isa 37:24
ten times have ye r. me. Job 19:3
not an enemy that r. me. Ps 55:12
that r. thee, are fallen upon me.
69:9; Rom 15:3
that the enemy hath r. Ps 74:18
have r. thee, O Lord. 79:12
thine enemies have r. O Lord, they
have r. the footsteps. 89:51
have r. my people. Zeph 2:8
r. and magnified themselves. 10
if ye be r. for Christ. 1 Pet 4:14

reproaches
r. of them that reproached thee.
Ps 69:9; Rom 15:3
I have given Israel to r. Isa 43:28*
I take pleasure in r. 2 Cor 12:10*
made a gazingstock by r. Heb 10:33

reproachest
Master, thou r. us also. Luke 11:45

reproacheth
aught presumptuously, r. the Lord.
Num 15:30*
voice of him that r. and. Ps 44:16
how the foolish man r. thee. 74:22
to answer him that r. me. 119:42
Pr 27:11
oppresseth poor r. his Maker.
Pr 14:31; 17:5

reproachfully
smitten me on the cheek r. Job 16:10
none occasion to speak r. Tim 5:14*

reprobate
r. silver shall men call. Jer 6:30*
over them to a r. mind. Rom 1:28
r. concerning the faith. 2 Tim 3:8
to every good work r. Tit 1:16

reprobates
you, except ye be r. 2 Cor 13:5
shall know that we are not r. 6
honest, though we be as r. 7

reproof
astonished at his r. Job 26:11*
turn you at my r. Pr 1:23
ye would none of my r. Pr 1:25
despised my r. 30
my heart depised r. 5:12
but he that refuseth r. erreth. 10:17
but he that hateth r. is brutish. 12:1
he that regardeth r. shall be. 13:18
that regardeth r. is prudent. 15:5
he that hateth r. shall die. 10
heareth the r. of life, abideth. 31
he that heareth r. getteth. 32
r. entereth more into a wise. 17:10*
the rod and r. give wisdom. 29:15
is profitable for r. 2 Tim 3:16

reproofs
in whose mouth are no r. Ps 38:14
r. of instruction are way. Pr 6:23

reprove
r. the words of Rab-shakeh.
2 Ki 19:4*; Isa 37:4*
doth your arguing r.? Job 6:25
do ye imagine to r. words? 26
he will surely r. you if ye. 13:10
will he r. thee for fear of? 22:4
I will not r. thee for burnt. Ps 50:8
I will r. thee, and set them. 21
let him r. me, it shall be an. 141:5
r. not a scorner, lest he. Pr 9:8
and r. one that hath. 19:25
lest he r. thee, and thou be. 30:6
neither r. after the hearing. Isa 11:3†
and r. with equity for the meek. 4†
backslidings shall r. thee. Jer 2:19
let no man strive nor r. Hos 4:4
he will r. the world of. John 16:8*
but rather r. them. Eph 5:11
r., rebuke, exhort with. 2 Tim 4:2

reproved
she was r. Gen 20:16*
Abraham r. Abimelech. 21:25
he r. kings for their sakes.
1 Chr 16:21; Ps 105:14
often r. hardeneth his neck. Pr 29:1
not r. Jeremiah? Jer 29:27*
answer when I am r. Hab 2:1*
Herod being r. by John. Luke 3:19
lest deeds should be r. John 3:20
all things that are r. are. Eph 5:13

reprover
wise r. upon an obedient. Pr 25:12
shalt not be to them a r. Ezek 3:26

reproveth
he that r. God, let him. Job 40:2*
he that r. a scorner. Pr 9:7
scorner loveth not one that r. 15:12
snare for him that r. Isa 29:21

reputation
that is in r. for wisdom. Eccl 10:1*
Gamaliel had in r. among. Acts 5:34*
which were of r. Gal 2:2*
but made himself of no r. Phil 2:7*
therefore, hold such in r. 29*

reputed
wherefore are we r. vile? Job 18:3*
all the inhabitants are r. Dan 4:35

request, -s
desire a r. of you. Judg 8:24
king shall perform the r. 2 Sam 14:15
fulfilled the r. of his servant 22
granted him all his r. Ezra 7:6
what dost thou make r.? Neh 2:4
to make r. before him. Esth 4:8
what is thy r.? 5:3,6; 7:2; 9:12
my people at my r. 7:3
Haman stood up to make r. 7
O that I might have my r.! Job 6:8
hast not withholden r. Ps 21:2
he gave them their r. but. 106:15
r. for a prosperous. Rom 1:10
every prayer making r. Phil 1:4
let your r. be made known. 4:6

requested
earrings that he r. Judg 8:26
Elijah r. that he might. 1 Ki 19:4
Jabez what he r. 1 Chr 4:10
he r. of the prince. Dan 1:8
Daniel r. of the king. 2:49

require
your blood will I r. . . . hand of man
will I r. the life of man. Gen 9:5
of my hand didst thou r. it. 31:39
of my hand shalt thou r. him. 43:9
what doth the Lord r.? Deut 10:12
Mi 6:8
I will r. it of him. Deut 18:19
Lord will surely r. it of thee. 23:21
let Lord himself r. it. Josh 22:23
1 Sam 20:16
but one thing I r. of. 2 Sam 3:13
shall not I r. his blood? 4:11
whatsoever thou shalt r. 19:38
as the matter shall r. 1 Ki 8:59
my Lord r. this thing? 1 Chr 21:3
look on it, and r. it. 2 Chr 24:22
Ezra shall r. of you. Ezra 7:21
to r. of the king a band. 8:22
and r. nothing of them. Neh 5:12
thou wilt not r. it. Ps 10:13
but his blood will I r. at thine hand.
Ezek 3:18, 20; 33:6, 8
and there will I r. your. 20:40
and I will r. my flock at. 34:10
the Jews r. a sign. 1 Cor 1:22*
if need so r., let him do what. 7:36

required
behold, his blood is r. Gen 42:22
such things as they r. Ex 12:36*
business r. haste. 1 Sam 21:8
when he r. they set. 2 Sam 12:20
every day's work r. 1 Chr 16:37
as duty of every day r. 2 Chr 8:14
Ezra 3:4
why hast thou not r. of the? 24:6
yet r. not I the bread. Neh 5:18
she r. nothing but what. Esth 2:15
and sin offering hast thou not r.
Ps 40:6
and they that wasted us, r. 137:3
two things I have r. of thee. Pr 30:7*
who hath r. this at your? Isa 1:12
r. of this generation. Luke 11:50, 51
this night thy soul shall be r. 12:20
of him shall be much r. 48
I might have r. mine own. 19:23
that it should be as they r. 23:24*
it is r. in stewards that. 1 Cor 4:2

requirest
will do all that thou r. Ruth 3:11*

requireth
God r. that which is past. Eccl 3:15*
rare thing that the king r. Dan 2:11

requiring
r. that he might be crucified.
Luke 23:23

requite
Joseph will certainly r. Gen 50:15
do ye thus r. Lord? Deut 32:6
and I will r. you this. 2 Sam 2:6
it may be the Lord will r. me. 16:12
I will r. thee in this. 2 Ki 9:26
beholdest to r. it with. Ps 10:14*
raise me up that I may r. 41:10
God shall surely r. Jer 51:56
let them learn to r. their. 1 Tim 5:4

requited
so God hath r. me. Judg 1:7
r. me evil for good. 1 Sam 25:21*

requiting
judge thy servants by r. 2 Chr 6:23

rereward
standard of Dan was r. Num 10:25
r. came after the ark. Josh 6:9, 13
David passed on in r. 1 Sam 29:2
God will be your r. Isa 52:12
glory of Lord shall be thy r. 58:8

rescue
have none to r. them. Deut 28:31
r. my soul from their. Ps 35:17
and none shall r. him. Hos 5:14

rescued
the people r. Jonathan. 1 Sam 14:45
David r. his two wives. 30:18
came I with an army, and r. him.
Acts 23:27

rescueth
he delivereth and r. and. Dan 6:27

resemblance
this is their r. through. Zech 5:6

resemble
I r. kingdom of God? Luke 13:18*

resembled
each one r. the children. Judg 8:18

reserve
will he r. his anger for ever ? Jer 3:5*
pardon them whom I r. 50:20*
to r. the unjust to the. 2 Pet 2:9*

reserved
thou not r. a blessing ? Gen 27:36
the most holy things r. Num 18:9
r. not to each his wife. Judg 21:22*
mother, that she had r. Ruth 2:18*
David r. horses for 100 chariots.
2 Sam 8:4; 1 Chr 18:4
wicked is r. to the day. Job 21:30
which I have r. against time. 38:23
but when Paul had appealed to be r.
Acts 25:21*
I have r. to myself 7000. Rom 11:4*
inheritance r. in heaven. 1 Pet 1:4
delivered them to be r. 2 Pet 2:4
mist of darkness is r. for ever. 17
the heavens and earth are r. 3:7
r. in everlasting chains. Jude 6*
to whom is r. the blackness. 13

reserveth
he r. to us the weeks of. Jer 5:24
r. wrath for his enemies. Nah 1:2

residue
locusts shall eat the r. Ex 10:5
r. of the sons of Kohath. 1 Chr 6:66
the r. of Israel were in. Neh 11:20
the r. of archers shall. Isa 21:17
Lord shall be a diadem to r. of. 28:5
I am deprived of the r. 38:10
r. thereof he maketh a god. 44:17
shall I make the r. thereof. 19
death chosen by all the r. Jer 8:3
r. of them will I deliver to. 15:9
and the r. of Jerusalem. 24:8
saith, concerning the r. of. 27:19
Jeremiah sent to r. of elders. 29:1
r. of the princes of Babylon. 39:3
Ishmael carried captive the r. 41:10
and the r. of the people that. 52:15
destroy all r. of Israel ? Ezek 9:8
thy r. shall be devoured. 23:25
tread the r. of your pastures. 34:18
possession unto r. of heathen. 36:3
a derision to the r. of the heathen. 4
I spoken against r. of heathen. 5
the r. in length over against. 48:18
the r. shall be for the prince. 21
and stamped the r. Dan 7:7, 19
r. of my people shall. Zeph 2:9
speak to Joshua and the r. Hag 2:2
I will not be to the r. Zech 8:11
r. of the people shall not be. 14:2
yet had he r. of spirit. Mal 2:15
and told it to the r. Mark 16:13
that the r. might seek. Acts 15:17

resist
Satan standing at his right hand to r.
Zech 3:1*
that ye r. not evil. Mat 5:39
shall not be able to r. Luke 21:15*
not able to r. the spirit. Acts 6:10*
always r. the Holy Ghost as. 7:51
they that r. shall receive. Rom 13:2*
these also r. the truth. 2 Tim 3:8*
r. the devil and he will. Jas 4:7
just, and he doth not r. you. 5:6
whom r. stedfast in the. 1 Pet 5:9*

resisted
who hath r. his will ? Rom 9:19*
have not yet r. unto blood. Heb 12:4

resisteth
whosoever r. the power, r. ordinance.
Rom 13:2*
God r. the proud. Jas 4:6; 1 Pet 5:5

resolved
I am r. what to do, when. Luke 16:4

resort
r. ye thither to us, God. Neh 4:20
I may continually r. Ps 71:3
the people r. to him. Mark 10:1*
whither Jews always r. John 18:20*

resorted
and Levites r. to him. 2 Chr 11:13
multitudes r. to him. Mark 2:13
and many r. to him. John 10:41*
Jesus ofttimes r. thither. 18:2
women who r. thither. Acts 16:13*

respect
(Respect of persons. *Favour or partiality toward the rich or powerful*)
the Lord had r. to Abel. Gen 4:4
to Cain, he had not r. 5
God looked, and had r. Ex 2:25*
for I will have r. unto. Lev 26:9
yet have thou r. unto the prayer.
1 Ki 8:28; 2 Chr 6:19
and the Lord had r. 2 Ki 13:23
is no iniquity nor r. of persons with
God. 2 Chr 19:7; Rom 2:11
Eph 6:9; Col 3:25
have r. unto covenant. Ps 74:20
when I have r. to all thy. 119:6
I will have r. unto thy ways. 15
I will have r. unto thy statutes. 117
yet hath he r. unto the lowly. 138:6
not good to have r. of persons in
judgement. Pr 24:23; 28:21
have r. to the Holy One. Isa 17:7
had r. to him that fashioned. 22:11
had no glory in this r. 2 Cor 3:10
not that I speak in r. of. Phil 4:11
let none judge you in r. of. Col 2:16
Moses had r. to. Heb 11:26*
faith with r. of persons. Jas 2:1
ye have r. to him that weareth. 3*
if ye have r. to persons, ye. 9
without r. of persons. 1 Pet 1:17

respect, *verb*
shalt not r. the person. Lev 19:15
Moses said, R. not thou. Num 16:15
ye shall not r. persons in judgement.
Deut 1:17; 16:19
neither doth God r. any person.
2 Sam 14:14*
nor shall r. that which. Isa 17:8

respected
they r. not the persons. Lam 4:16

respecter
God is no r. of persons. Acts 10:34

respecteth
he r. not any that are. Job 37:24*
blessed is man that r. not. Ps 40:4

respite
saw that there was r. Ex 8:15
Give us seven days' r. 1 Sam 11:3

rest
(*This word includes freedom from oppression by the enemy, and peace of spirit, as well as the ordinary meanings*)
Issachar saw that r. was. Gen 49:15
to-morrow the r. of holy. Ex 16:23
the seventh is the sabbath of r. 31:15
35:2; Lev 16:31; 23:3, 32; 25:4
thee, and I will give thee r. Ex 33:14
a year of r. to the land. Lev 25:5
until the Lord have given r.
Deut 3:20; Josh 1:13
not as yet come to the r. Deut 12:9
when he giveth you r. from. 10
thy God hath given thee r. 25:19
the sole of thy foot have r. 28:65
given your brethren r. Josh 1:15
the land had r. from war. 14:15
Judg 3:11; 5:31
the Lord gave them r. round about.
Josh 21:44; 2 Chr 15:15
God hath given r. Josh 22:4
Lord had given r. 23:1
land had r. eighty years. Judg 3:30
Lord grant you may find r. Ruth 1:9
shall I not seek r. for thee ? 3:1
for this man will not be in r. till. 18
Lord had given him r. 2 Sam 7:1
1 Ki 5:4; 8:56; 2 Chr 14:6, 7
after that the ark had r. 1 Chr 6:31
man of r. and I will give him r. 22:9
hath he not given you r.? 18
God of Israel hath given r. 23:25
to build a house of r. 28:2
for his God gave him r. 2 Chr 20:30
but after they had r. they. Neh 9:28
the Jews had r. from. Esth 9:16
slept, then had I been at r. Job 3:13
and there the weary be at r. 17
not in safety, neither had I r. 26*
shalt take thy r. in safety. 11:18
r. together is in the dust. Job 17:16
neither is there any r. in. Ps 38:3*
would I fly away and be at r. 55:6
that thou mayest give him r. 94:13
should not enter into my r. 95:11
return to thy r. O my soul. 116:7
arise, O Lord, into thy r., thou. 132:8
this is my r. for ever, here will. 14
son, he shall give thee r. Pr 29:17
his heart taketh not r. in. Eccl 2:23
this hath more r. than. 6:5
and his r. shall be glorious. Isa 11:10
give thee r. from thy sorrow. 14:3
whole earth is at r. 7; Zech 1:11
Lord said, I will take my r. Isa 18:4
this is r. wherewith ye cause. 28:12
in returning and r. shall ye. 30:15
find for herself a place of r. 34:14*
where is the place of my r.? 66:1
find r. for your souls. Jer 6:16
return and be in r. 30:10*; 46:27
that he may give r. to land. 50:34
go to them that are at r. Ezek 38:11*
Nebuchadnezzar was at r. Dan 4:4
for this is not your r. Mi 2:10
Damascus shall be the r. Zech 9:1
and I will give you r. Mat 11:28
ye shall find r. to your souls. 29
seeking r. and. 12:43; Luke 11:24
sleep on now, and take your r.
Mat 26:45; Mark 14:41
of taking r. in sleep. John 11:13
what is place of my r.? Acts 7:49
then had the churches r. 9:31*
who are troubled r. with. 2 Thes 1:7
not enter into my r. Heb 3:11, 18
being left us of entering into r. 4:1
have believed do enter into r. 3
if they shall enter into my r. 5
for if Jesus had given them r. 8
remaineth a r. to the people of. 9
he that is entered into his r. hath. 10
labour to enter into that r. 11
see **no**

rest
Jacob fed r. of Laban's. Gen 30:36
the names of the r. on. Ex 28:10
the r. of the blood shall. Lev 5:9
the r. of the oil that. 14:17, 29
beside the r. of them. Num 31:8
being the r. of the prey. 32*
the r. of Gilead gave I. Deut 3:13
r. entered into fenced. Josh 10:20
r. bowed down to drink. Judg 7:6
the r. have we utterly. 1 Sam 15:15
the r. of the people he delivered to.
2 Sam 10:10; 1 Chr 19:11
the r. fled to Aphek to. 1 Ki 20:30
and thy children of the r. 2 Ki 4:7
Joab repaired the r. of. 1 Chr 11:8
Jeduthun and the r. chosen. 16:41
the r. of the money. 2 Chr 24:14
nor told it to the r. that. Neh 2:16
r. of our enemies heard I had. 6:1
r. of the people also cast lots. 11:1
what have done in the r.? Esth 9:12
the r. to their babes. Ps 17:14
r. of trees of his forest. Isa 10:19
r. of the land shall give. Ezek 45:8
should not perish with r. Dan 2:18
let the r. eat the flesh of. Zech 11:9
r. said, Let us see if. Mat 27:49
ye thought for the r.? Luke 12:26
the eleven and to all the r. 24:9
said to Peter and the r. Acts 2:37
of r. durst no man join. 5:13
and the r., they escaped all. 27:44
election obtained it, and r. Rom 11:7
r. speak I, not the Lord. 1 Cor 7:12
r. will I set in order when I. 11:34
not live r. of his time to. 1 Pet 4:2
and to the r. in Thyatira. Rev 2:24
the r. that were not killed. 9:20
r. of the dead lived not again. 20:5
see **acts**

rest, *verb*
wash your feet, and r. Gen 18:4
ye make them r. from. Ex 5:5
year thou shalt let it r. 23:11
seventh day thou shalt r. 12; 34:21
and in harvest thou shalt r. 34:21
then shall the land r. Lev 26:34
did not r. in your sabbaths. 35

thy maidservant may *r.* *Deut* 5:14
feet of the priests shall *r.* *Josh* 3:13
let it *r.* on the head of. *2 Sam* 3:29
have caused thee to *r.* from. 7:11
neither the birds to *r.* on them. 21:10
the spirit of Elijah doth *r.* *2 Ki* 2:15
we *r.* on thee, in thy. *2 Chr* 14:11*
there the prisoners *r.* *Job* 3:18*
that he may *r.* till he shall. 14:6
my flesh shall *r.* in hope. *Ps* 16:9*
Acts 2:26*
r. in the Lord, and wait. *Ps* 37:7
rod of wicked shall not *r.* on. 125:3
nor will he *r.* content. *Pr* 6:35
thy flock to *r.* at noon. *S of S* 1:7
all of them shall *r.* in the. *Isa* 7:19
the Spirit of the Lord shall *r.* 11:2
shall the hand of the Lord *r.* 25:10
may cause the weary to *r.* 28:12
screech owl also shall *r.* 34:14
I will make my judgement to *r.* 51:4
enter into peace, they shall *r.* 57:2
troubled sea, when it cannot *r.* 20
Jerusalem's sake I will not *r.* 62:1
the Lord caused him to *r.* 63:14
went to cause him to *r.* *Jer* 31:2
put up into thy scabbard, *r.* 47:6
will cause my fury to *r.* *Ezek* 5:13
16:42; 21:17; 24:13
cause the blessing to *r.* 44:30
for thou shalt *r.* and. *Dan* 12:13
that I might *r.* in the day. *Hab* 3:16
he will *r.* in love, he will. *Zeph* 3:17
desert place, and *r.* a. *Mark* 6:31
there, your peace shall *r.* *Luke* 10:6
of Christ may *r.* on me. *2 Cor* 12:9
God did *r.* seventh day. *Heb* 4:4
they *r.* not day and night. *Rev* 4:8
that they should *r.* yet for a. 6:11
that they may *r.* from their. 14:13

rested
he *r.* on seventh day. *Gen* 2:2, 3
Ex 20:11; 31:17
the ark *r.* *Gen* 8:4
locusts *r.* in Egypt. *Ex* 10:14
the people *r.* on the seventh. 16:30
cloud abode, they *r.* *Num* 9:18*, 23*
cloud *r.* in the wilderness. 10:12*
when it *r.* he said, Return, O. 36
when spirit *r.* upon them. 11:25, 26
and the land *r.* from. *Josh* 11:23
the chambers *r.* on the. *1 Ki* 6:10
people *r.* on the words. *2 Chr* 32:8
day of the same *r.* *Esth* 9:17, 18
wherein the Jews *r.* from their. 22
bowels boiled and *r.* not. *Job* 30:27
they *r.* sabbath day. *Luke* 23:56

restest
thou art a Jew, and *r.* in. *Rom* 2:17

resteth
in safety, whereon he *r.* *Job* 24:23
wisdom *r.* in heart of him. *Pr* 14:33
for anger *r.* in the bosom. *Eccl* 7:9
Spirit of God *r.* upon. *1 Pet* 4:14

resting
to search out a *r.* place. *Num* 10:33
into thy *r.* place. *2 Chr* 6:41
spoil not his *r.* place. *Pr* 24:15
shall dwell in *r.* places *Isa* 32:18
forgotten their *r.* place. *Jer* 50:6

restitution
make full *r.* *Ex* 22:3, 5, 6, 12
his substance shall *r.* be. *Job* 20:18
until the times of the *r.* *Acts* 3:21*

restore
[1] *To give back again,* Gen 20:14; Judg 11:13. [2] *To bring back to the first state or condition,* Gen 40:13; Isa 1:26; Acts 1:6. [3] *To recover, or get again,* 2 Ki 14:25. [4] *To heal or cure,* Mat 12:13.
r. the man his wife, and if thou *r.* her. *Gen* 20:7
Pharaoh will *r.* thee to thy. 40:13
to *r.* every man's money. 42:25
he shall *r.* five oxen for. *Ex* 22:1*
found, he shall *r.* double. 4*
he shall *r.* that which he. *Lev* 6:4
he shall even *r.* it in the principal. 5
killeth a beast, he shall *r.* 24:21*
and *r.* the overplus to whom. 25:27
but if he be not able to *r.* it to. 28*
congregation shall *r.* *Num* 35:25
thou shalt *r.* again. *Deut* 22:2
therefore *r.* those lands. *Judg* 11:13
I will *r.* it. 17:3; *1 Sam* 12:3
1 Ki 20:34
I will *r.* thee all the land. *2 Sam* 9:7
he shall *r.* the lamb fourfold. 12:6
shall house of Israel *r.* me. 16:3
r. all that was hers. *2 Ki* 8:6
r. I pray you, to them. *Neh* 5:11
we will *r.* 12
and his hands shall *r.* *Job* 20:10
laboured for, shall he *r.* 18
r. to me the joy of thy. *Ps* 51:12
if he be found, he shall *r.* *Pr* 6:31
I will *r.* thy judges as. *Isa* 1:26
spoil, and none saith *r.* 42:22
to *r.* the preserved of Israel. 49:6
I will lead and *r.* comforts. 57:18
I will *r.* them to this. *Jer* 27:22
I will *r.* health to thee, and. 30:17
if the wicked *r.* pledge. *Ezek* 33:15
command to *r.* and to. *Dan* 9:25
I will *r.* to you the years. *Joel* 2:25
Elias shall come and *r.* *Mat* 17:11
have taken any thing, I *r.* *Luke* 19:8
Lord, wilt thou *r.* kingdom? *Acts* 1:6
r. such an one in the spirit. *Gal* 6:1

restored
Abimelech *r.* him Sarah. *Gen* 20:14
he *r.* the chief butler to his. 40:21
me he *r.* to mine office, him. 41:13
my money is *r.* and it is in. 42:28
shall not be *r.* to thee. *Deut* 28:31
r. 1100 shekels. *Judg* 17:3, 4
from Israel were *r.* *1 Sam* 7:14
that my hand may be *r.* to me: the king's hand was *r.* *1 Ki* 13:6
son he had *r.* to life. *2 Ki* 8:1, 5
he built and *r.* Elath to Judah.
14:22; *2 Chr* 26:2
r. coast of Israel from. *2 Ki* 14:25
the cities Huram had *r.* *2 Chr* 8:2*
brought to Babylon be *r.* *Ezra* 6:5
I *r.* that which I took not. *Ps* 69:4
but hath *r.* to the debtor. *Ezek* 18:7
violence, hath not *r.* pledge. 12
hand was *r.* whole like as the.
Mat 12:13; *Mark* 3:5; *Luke* 6:10
his sight was *r.* and he. *Mark* 8:25
that I may be *r.* to you. *Heb* 13:19

restorer
he shall be to thee a *r.* *Ruth* 4:15
shall be called *r.* of paths. *Isa* 58:12

restoreth
he *r.* my soul, he leadeth. *Ps* 23:3
Elias cometh first and *r.* *Mark* 9:12

restrain
dost thou *r.* wisdom? *Job* 15:8†
wrath shalt thou *r.* *Ps* 76:10*

restrained
rain from heaven was *r.* *Gen* 8:2
and now nothing will be *r.* 11:6*
Sarai said, Lord hath *r.* me. 16:2
were *r.* from bringing. *Ex* 36:6
sons vile, and he *r.* not. *1 Sam* 3:13
toward me, are they *r.*? *Isa* 63:15
I *r.* the floods thereof. *Ezek* 31:15
these sayings, scarce *r.* *Acts* 14:18

restrainest
thou *r.* prayer before God. *Job* 15:4

restraint
there is no *r.* to the Lord. *1 Sam* 14:6

rests
he made narrowed *r.* *1 Ki* 6:6*

resurrection
(*The rising from the dead and living again was a belief which was held by many Israelites, although it was not universal. It was a more important article of faith among the Christians, as Paul argued in* 1 Cor 15)
Sadducees, who say there is no *r.*
Mat 22:23; *Mark* 12:18
Acts 23:8; *1 Cor* 15:12
in the *r.* whose wife? *Mat* 22:28
Mark 12:23; *Luke* 20:33
in the *r.* they neither. *Mat* 22:30
as touching the *r.* have ye? 31
out of the graves after his *r.* 27:53
recompensed at the *r.* *Luke* 14:14
deny any *r.* 20:27
the children of the *r.* 36
good to the *r.* of life: evil, to the *r.* of damnation. *John* 5:29
brother shall rise in the *r.* 11:24
Jesus said, I am the *r.* and the. 25
witness with us of his *r.* *Acts* 1:22
David spake of *r.* of Christ. 2:31
preached through Jesus the *r.* 4:2
witness of the *r.* of the Lord. 33
he preached Jesus and the *r.* 17:18
heard of the *r.*, some mocked. 32
of the hope and *r.* I am called. 23:6
shall be a *r.* of the dead. 24:15
Touching *r.* of the dead. 21
declared by the *r.* from. *Rom* 1:4
in the likeness of his *r.* 6:5
but if there be no *r.* of. *1 Cor* 15:13
by man came the *r.* 21
so is the *r.* of the dead. 42
know the power of his *r.* *Phil* 3:10
if I might attain to the *r.* of. 11
that the *r.* is past. *2 Tim* 2:18
of *r.* from the dead, and. *Heb* 6:2
they might obtain a better *r.* 11:35
hope, by *r.* of Jesus. *1 Pet* 1:3
save us, by *r.* of Jesus Christ. 3:21
this is the first *r.* *Rev* 20:5
he that hath part in the first *r.* 6

retain
still *r.* thine integrity? *Job* 2:9*
he said, Let thine heart *r.* *Pr* 4:4
strong men *r.* riches. 11:16†
no man hath power to *r.* *Eccl* 8:8
she shall not *r.* the power. *Dan* 11:6
whose soever sins ye *r.* *John* 20:23
did not like to *r.* God. *Rom* 1:28*

retained
Gideon *r.* those 300. *Judg* 7:8
the damsel's father *r.* him. 19:4
and I *r.* no strength. *Dan* 10:8, 16
sins ye retain, they are *r.* *John* 20:23
whom I would have *r.* *Philem* 13

retaineth
every one that *r.* her. *Pr* 3:18
gracious woman *r.* honour. 11:16†
he *r.* not his anger for ever. *Mi* 7:18

retire
hottest battle, and *r.* *2 Sam* 11:15
toward Zion: *r.*, stay not. *Jer* 4:6*

retired
Israel *r.* in battle. *Judg* 20:39*
they *r.* from the city. *2 Sam* 20:22*

return, *substantive*
meet Abram after his *r.* *Gen* 14:17
Samuel's *r.* was to. *1 Sam* 7:17
at *r.* of year Syria. *1 Ki* 20:22, 26

return
(*Frequently means* turn again, *or* repent)
till thou *r.* to the ground: for dust thou art . . . thou *r.* *Gen* 3:19
r. to thy mistress and. 16:9
I will certainly *r.* to thee. 18:10, 14
r. to land of thy kindred. 31:3, 13
Lord, which saidst unto me, *R.* 32:9
let me *r.* to my brethren. *Ex* 4:18
Lord said unto Moses, Go *r.* 19
lest people repent, and *r.* to. 13:17
shall *r.* to his possession. *Lev* 25:10
13, 27, 28
r. unto his own family. 41
the field shall *r.* to him. 27:24
r. Lord, to the many thousands. *Num* 10:36
let us make a captain, and *r.* 14:4
the Lord said, *R.* unto Balak. 23:5
then afterward ye shall *r.* 32:22
slayer shall *r.* into the land of his.
35:28; *Josh* 20:6
r. every man to his possesssion.
Deut 3:20; *Josh* 1:15
cause people *r.* to Egypt. *Deut* 17:16
let him *r.* to his house. 20:5, 6, 7, 8
God will *r.* and gather thee. 30:3
thou shalt *r.* and obey the voice. 8
now *r.* ye, and get you. *Josh* 22:4
saying, *R.* with much riches. 8
and afraid, let him *r.* *Judg* 7:3
when I *r.* from the children of. 11:31

she might *r.* from Moab. *Ruth* 1:6
Naomi said, Go, *r.* to her mother's. 8
surely he will *r.* with thee to. 10
r. thou after thy sister in law. 15
r. him trespass offering. *1 Sam* 6:3
jewels of gold which ye *r.* him. 8
Saul said, Come, let us *r.* 9:5
said Saul, *R.* my son David. 26:21
said, Make this fellow *r.* 29:4, 7
ere thou bid people *r.*? *2 Sam* 2:26
said Abner to him, Go, *r.* 3:16
till beards be grown, then *r.* 10:5
1 Chr 19:5
goest thou also with us ? *r.*
2 Sam 15:19
I go whither I may, *r.* thou. 20
if thou *r.* to the city and say. 34
they said, *R.* thou and all thy. 19:14
see what answer I shall *r.* 24:13
shall *r.* his blood. *1 Ki* 2:32, 33
Lord shall *r.* thy wickedness. 44
so *r.* to thee with all their. 8:48
R. every man to his house. 12:24
kingdom *r.* to the house of David. 26
go, *r.* on thy way to the. 19:15
let them *r.* every man to his house.
22:17; *2 Chr* 11:4; 18:16
r. at all in peace. *1 Ki* 22:28
2 Chr 18:27
offended, *r.* from me. *2 Ki* 18:14
king of Assyria shall *r.* to his own land. 19:7, 33; *Isa* 37:7, 34
let the shadow *r.* *2 Ki* 20:10
shall *r.* and confess. *2 Chr* 6:24
if they *r.* to thee with all their. 38
that we may *r.* answer to. 10:9
fellow in the prison until I *r.* 18:26
he will *r.* to you. 30:6
if ye *r.* unto him. 9
said, When wilt thou *r.*? *Neh* 2:6
whence ye shall *r.* unto us. 4:12
r. Mordecai this answer. *Esth* 4:15
device *r.* upon his own head. 9:25
naked shall I *r.* thither. *Job* 1:21
r. yea, *r.* again, my. 6:29
he shall *r.* no more to his. 7:10
shall *r.* out of darkness. 15:22
as for you all, do ye *r.* and. 17:10
if thou *r.* to the Almighty. 22:23
he shall *r.* to the days of his. 33:25
commandeth that they *r.* from. 36:10
r. O Lord, deliver my soul. *Ps* 6:4
let mine enemies *r.* and be. 10
for their sakes therefore *r.* 7:7
his mischief shall *r.* upon his. 16
they *r.* at evening. 59:6
and let them *r.* 14
therefore his people *r.* hither. 73:10
let not oppressed *r.* ashamed. 74:21
r. we beseech thee, O God. 80:14
thou sayest, *R.* ye children. 90:3
r. O Lord, how long ? 13
judgement shall *r.* unto. 94:15
they die, and *r.* to their dust. 104:29
r. to thy rest, O my soul. 116:7
none that go unto her *r.* *Pr* 2:19
a stone, it will *r.* on him. 26:27
whence rivers come, thither they *r.*
Eccl 1:7
naked shall he *r.* to go as he. 5:15
nor the clouds *r.* after the rain. 12:2
dust shall *r.* to the earth, and spirit *r.* to God. 7
r. r. O Shulamite, *r. r.* *S of S* 6:13
yet in it a tenth shall *r.* *Isa* 6:13
remnant shall *r.* to God. 10:21, 22
watchman said . . . *R.*, come. 21:12
the ransomed of the Lord shall *r.*
35:10; 51:11
r. unto me, for I have. 44:22
r. for thy servant's sake. 63:17
r. to her again ? yet *r.* *Jer* 3:1
R. thou backsliding Israel. 12
r. ye backsliding children. 22
if thou wilt *r.*, *r.* unto me. 4:1
I will *r.* and have compassion. 12:15
if thou *r.* let them *r.* unto thee, but *r.* not thou unto them. 15:19
r. ye every one from. 18:11; 35:15
for he shall *r.* no more. 22:10
that none doth *r.* from his. 23:14
shall *r.* with their whole heart. 24:7
and Jacob shall *r.* 30:10; 46:27
great company shall *r.* thither. 31:8
that ye may *r.*, every man. *Jer* 36:3
it may be they will *r.* every. 7
Pharaoh's army shall *r.* to. 37:7
that they should *r.* into . . . for none shall *r.* but such. 44:14, 28
none shall *r.* in vain. 50:9
when Sodom and Samaria shall *r.* . . . daughters shall *r.* *Ezek* 16:55
wicked should *r.* from ways ? 18:23
after it shall *r.* to the prince. 46:17
I *r.* to fight with Persia. *Dan* 10:20
and shall *r.* into his own land. 11:9
10, 28
the king of the north shall *r.* 13
time appointed he shall *r.* and. 29
he shall be grieved and *r.* 30
I will go and *r.* to my first. *Hos* 2:7
I will *r.* and take away my corn. 9
the children of Israel *r.* 3:5
I will go and *r.* to my place. 5:15
r. but not to the most High. 7:16
visit their sins they shall *r.* 8:13; 9:3
his reproach shall his Lord *r.* 12:14
dwell under his shadow shall *r.* 14:7
who knoweth if he will *r.*? *Joel* 2:14
I *r.* recompence on your head. 3:4, 7
thy reward shall *r.* upon. *Ob* 15
they shall *r.* to the hire. *Mi* 1:7
remnant of his brethren shall *r.* 5:3
Edom saith, We will *r.* *Mal* 1:4
R. to me, and I will *r.* to you, saith Lord . . . Wherein shall we *r.*? 3:7
shall ye *r.* and discern between. 18
worthy, let your peace *r.* *Mat* 10:13
r. into my house. 12:44; *Luke* 11:24
is in the field, *r.* back. *Mat* 24:18
r. to thine own house. *Luke* 8:39
when he will *r.* from wedding. 12:36
after this I will *r.* and. *Acts* 15:16
I will again *r.* to you, if God. 18:21

to return

when thou goest *to r.* *Ex* 4:21
were it not better *to r.*? *Num* 14:3
nor cause the people *to r.* *Deut* 17:16
went *to r.* unto Judah. *Ruth* 1:7
not to leave thee, or *to r.* from. 16
David rose early *to r.* *1 Sam* 29:11
to r. answer to this. *2 Chr* 10:6, 9
appointed a captain *to r.* *Neh* 9:17
they have refused *to r.* *Jer* 5:3; 8:5
Hos 11:5
to the land where they desire *to r.*
Jer 22:27; 44:14
in causing you *to r.* 29:10; 30:3
32:44; 33:7, 11, 26; 34:22; 42:12
caused the servants *to r.* 34:11, 16
cause me not *to r.* 37:20; 38:26
shall I cause it *to r.*? *Ezek* 21:30
cause them *to r.* to Pathros. 29:14
caused me *to r.* to the brink. 47:6
because they refused *to r.* *Hos* 11:5
went to receive a kingdom and *to r.*
Luke 19:12
more *to r.* to corruption. *Acts* 13:34
to r. through Macedonia. 20:3

return *unto the Lord*

and shalt *r. unto the Lord.* *Deut* 30:2
if ye *r. unto the Lord.* *1 Sam* 7:3
r. unto the Lord, he shall. *Isa* 19:22
let him *r. unto the Lord,* he. 55:7
let us *r. unto the Lord,* for. *Hos* 6:1
they do not *r. unto the Lord.* 7:10
O Israel, *r. unto the Lord* thy. 14:1

not return

will *not r.* to our houses. *Num* 32:18
Samuel said, I will *not r.* with thee.
1 Sam 15:26
he shall *not r.* to me. *2 Sam* 12:23
I may *not r.* with thee. *1 Ki* 13:16
before I go whence I shall *not r.*
Job 10:21; 16:22
forth, and *r. not* unto them. 39:4
gone out, and shall *not r.* *Isa* 45:23
it shall *not r.* to me void, but. 55:11
turn away, and *not r.*? *Jer* 8:4
destroy, since they *r. not* from. 15:7
he shall *not r.* thither. 22:11, 27
the anger of the Lord shall *not r.*
23:20; 30:24
for seller shall *not r.* . . . multitude which shall *not r.* *Ezek* 7:13
that he should *not r.* from his. 13:22
my sword *not r.* any more. 21:5
thy cities shall *not r.* and. *Ezek* 35:9
he shall *not r.* by the way. 46:9
they do *not r.* to the Lord. *Hos* 7:10
he shall *not r.* into Egypt. 11:5
I will *not r.* to destroy Ephraim. 9
warned they should *not r.* *Mat* 2:12
let him likewise *not r.* *Luke* 17:31

returned

waters *r.* from off earth. *Gen* 8:3
the dove *r.* to him. 9
the dove *r.* not again. 12
Abraham *r.* unto his place. 18:33
Abraham *r.* to his young men. 22:19
Joseph *r.* again, communed. 42:24
we had *r.* this second time. 43:10
money that was *r.* in our sacks. 18
Moses *r.* to the Lord. *Ex* 5:22; 32:31
the sea *r.* to his strength. 14:27, 28
r. words of people to Lord. 19:8*
she is *r.* to her father's. *Lev* 22:13
Balaam rose up, and *r.* *Num* 24:25
till pursuers be *r.* *Josh* 2:16, 22
that waters of Jordan *r.* 4:18
of Reuben and Gad *r.* 22:9
the princes *r.* from Reuben. 32
judge was dead they *r.* *Judg* 2:19
yea, she *r.* answer to herself. 5:29
there *r.* of the people 22,000. 7:3
Gideon *r.* from battle before. 8:13
Gideon's daughter *r.* to her. 11:39
the Benjamites *r.* to their. 21:23
so Naomi and Ruth *r.* *Ruth* 1:22
they *r.* to Ekron same. *1 Sam* 6:16
David *r.* from slaughter of. 17:57
the Lord hath *r.* the. 25:39
the sword of Saul *r.* *2 Sam* 1:22
Go, return, and he *r.* 3:16
then David *r.* to bless his. 6:20
Lord *r.* on thee all the blood of. 16:8
thou seekest, is as if all *r.* 17:3
king *r.* and came to Jordan. 19:15
people *r.* after him only to. 23:10
r. not by way that he. *1 Ki* 13:10
Jeroboam *r.* not from his evil way. 33
Elisha *r.* and walked. *2 Ki* 4:35
he *r.* to man of God, he and. 5:15
r. home in great anger. *2 Chr* 25:10
Sennacherib *r.* with shame of. 32:31
thus they *r.* us answer. *Ezra* 5:11
we *r.* all of us to the wall. *Neh* 4:15
when they *r.* and cried unto. 9:28
my prayer *r.* into mine. *Ps* 35:13
they *r.* and enquired early. 78:34
so sun *r.* ten degrees. *Isa* 38:8
unto me. But she *r.* not. *Jer* 3:7
they *r.* with their vessels. 14:3
Jews *r.* out of all places. 40:12
creatures ran, and *r.* as. *Ezek* 1:14
they *r.* not when they went. 17
and have *r.* to provoke me to. 8:17
when I had *r.* behold, at the. 47:7
understanding *r.* unto me. *Dan* 4:34
at the same time my reason *r.* 36
when I *r.* the captivity of. *Hos* 6:11
yet have ye not *r.* to me. *Amos* 4:6
8, 9, 10, 11
they *r.* and said, Like as. *Zech* 1:6
thus saith the Lord; I am *r.* to. 16
no man passed through nor *r.* 7:14
I am *r.* to Zion, and will dwell. 8:3
morning as he *r.* into. *Mat* 21:18
when he *r.* he found. *Mark* 14:40
Mary *r.* to her own house. *Luke* 1:56
shepherds *r.* glorifying God. 2:20
Jesus full of the Holy Ghost *r.* 4:1
Jesus *r.* in power of the Spirit. 14
into the ship and *r.* back again. 8:37
when Jesus *r.*, the people gladly. 40
the apostles, when they were *r.* 9:10
the seventy *r.* again with joy. 10:17
that *r.* to give glory to God. 17:18
r. having received kingdom. 19:15
smote their breasts and *r.* 23:48
they *r.* and prepared spices. 56
r. from sepulchre and told. 24:9
they rose same hour, and *r.* to. 33
they worshipped him, and *r.* to. 52
then *r.* they to Jerusalem. *Acts* 1:12
found them not, they *r.* 5:22
the apostles *r.* to Jerusalem. 8:25
Barnabas and Saul *r.* from. 12:25
John *r.* to Jerusalem. 13:13
they *r.* again to Lystra and. 14:21

took ship, and they r. home. *Acts* 21:6
and r. to the castle. 23:32
I r. again unto Damascus. *Gal* 1:17
opportunity to have r. *Heb* 11:15
now r. to Shepherd of. *1 Pet* 2:25

returneth

his breath goeth, he r. *Ps* 146:4
r. to his vomit, so a fool r. *Pr* 26:11
the wind r. according to. *Eccl* 1:6
rain r. not thither, but. *Isa* 55:10
him that r. I will cut off. *Ezek* 35:7
because of him that r. *Zech* 9:8

returning

in r. and rest shall ye. *Isa* 30:15
r., found servant whole. *Luke* 7:10
r. and sitting in chariot. *Acts* 8:28
met Abraham r. from. *Heb* 7:1

Reuben

and called his name R. *Gen* 29:32
R. went in the days of wheat. 30:14
that R. went and lay with. 35:22
R., Jacob's firstborn. 23; 46:8
49:3; *Num* 26:5; *1 Chr* 5:1
R. said unto them, Shed. *Gen* 37:22
R. returned to the pit; Joseph. 29
the sons of R. 46:9; *Ex* 6:14
Num 16:1; 32:1, 37; *Deut* 11:6
Josh 4:12; *1 Chr* 5:3, 18
as R. and Simeon, they. *Gen* 48:5
standard of the camp of R.
Num 2:10; 10:18
numbered in the camp of R. 2:16
prince of the children of R. 7:30
Moses gave to children of R. 32:33
Josh 13:23
mount Ebal to curse; R. *Deut* 27:13
let R. live, and not die. 33:6
to the stone of Bohan the son of R.
Josh 15:6; 18:17
sent to the children of R. 22:13
for the divisions of R. *Judg* 5:15, 16
a portion for R. *Ezek* 48:6
one gate of R. 31

tribe of **Reuben**

of the *tribe of* R.; Elizur. *Num* 1:5
the *tribe of* R. were numbered. 21
of the *tribe of* R., Shammua. 13:4
the *tribe of* R. have received. 34:14
out of the *tribe of* R., Gad and.
Josh 20:8; 21:36; *1 Chr* 6:63, 78
of *tribe of* R. were sealed. *Rev* 7:5

Reubenites

the families of the R. *Num* 26:7
cities gave I to the R. *Deut* 3:12
16; 29:8; *Josh* 12:6; 13:8
spake to the R. *Josh* 1:12; 22:1
Hazael smote the R. *2 Ki* 10:33
the prince of the R. *1 Chr* 5:6
Tiglath-pilneser carried away R. 26
Adina a captain of the R. 11:42
his brethren over the R. 26:32
ruler of the R. was Eliezer. 27:16

reveal

shall r. his iniquity. *Job* 20:27
I will r. them abundance. *Jer* 33:6
couldest r. this secret. *Dan* 2:47
to whomsoever the Son will r. him.
Mat 11:27; *Luke* 10:22
grace, to r. his Son in me. *Gal* 1:16
God shall r. even this. *Phil* 3:15

revealed

but things r. to us. *Deut* 29:29
of the Lord r. to him. *1 Sam* 3:7
the Lord r. himself to Samuel. 21
hast r. to thy servant. *2 Sam* 7:27
it was r. in mine ears. *Isa* 22:14
from Chittim it is r. to them. 23:1
glory of the Lord shall be r. 40:5
to whom is the arm of the Lord r.?
53:1; *John* 12:38
righteousness is near to be r.
Isa 56:1
for unto thee have I r. *Jer* 11:20
then was the secret r. to. *Dan* 2:19
this secret is not r. to me for. 30
a thing was r. to Daniel, and. 10:1
nothing covered, that shall not be r.
Mat 10:26; *Luke* 12:2
and r. them to babes. *Mat* 11:25
Luke 10:21
and blood hath not r. it. *Mat* 16:17
it was r. to Simeon by. *Luke* 2:26
of many hearts may be r. *Luke* 2:35
when the Son of man is r. 17:30
righteousness of God r. *Rom* 1:17
the wrath of God is r. from. 18
glory which shall be r. in us. 8:18
God hath r. them to us. *1 Cor* 2:10
because it shall be r. by fire. 3:13
if any thing be r. to another. 14:30
should afterwards be r. *Gal* 3:23
as it is now r. to his holy. *Eph* 3:5
Lord Jesus shall be r. *2 Thes* 1:7
first, and that man of sin be r. 2:3
he might be r. in his time. 6
that wicked one be r., whom. 8
salvation, ready to be r. *1 Pet* 1:5
unto whom it was r. that not. 12
when his glory shall be r. 4:13
of the glory that shall be r. 5:1

revealer

your God is a God of gods, a r. of secrets. *Dan* 2:47

revealeth

a talebearer r. *Pr* 11:13; 20:19
he r. the deep and secret. *Dan* 2:22
God in heaven that r. secrets. 28
that r. secrets maketh known. 29
he r. his secrets to his. *Amos* 3:7

revelation

(A revealing; *in the Bible mainly the revealing by God of his character or deeds*)

and r. of the righteous. *Rom* 2:5
according to r. of mystery. 16:25
speak to you either by r. *1 Cor* 14:6
every one of you hath a r., hath. 26
by the r. of Jesus Christ. *Gal* 1:12
and I went up by r. and. 2:2
Spirit of wisdom and r. *Eph* 1:17
how that by r. he made. 3:3
grace brought at the r. *1 Pet* 1:13
the r. of Jesus Christ. *Rev* 1:1

revelations

come to visions and r. *2 Cor* 12:1
exalted through abundance of r. 7

revellings

works of the flesh are r. *Gal* 5:21
when ye walked in lusts, r. *1 Pet* 4:3

revenge

(*Most frequently found where* avenge *is used in modern English. Revisions make this change*)

O Lord, r. me of my. *Jer* 15:15
in a readiness to r. all. *2 Cor* 10:6

revenge, *substantive*

and we shall take our r. *Jer* 20:10
Philistines have dealt by r.
Ezek 25:15
r. it wrought in you. *2 Cor* 7:11

revenged

because Edom r. *Ezek* 25:12

revenger

the r. shall slay the. *Num* 35:19, 21
judge between slayer and r. 24
slayer out of the hand of the r. 25
if r. find him without, and r. kill. 27
minister of God, a r. *Rom* 13:4

revengers

thou wouldest not suffer the r.
2 Sam 14:11

revenges

from the beginning of r. *Deut* 32:42

revengeth

the Lord r. and is furious. *Nah* 1:2

revenging

by the r. of the blood of. *Ps* 79:10

revenue

endamage the r. of kings. *Ezra* 4:13*
my r. is better than. *Pr* 8:19
harvest of the river is her r. *Isa* 23:3

revenues

but in the r. of the wicked. *Pr* 15:6
than great r. without right. 16:8
be ashamed of your r. *Jer* 12:13*

reverence

(*Where this word is used in connection with men alone it is with the old meaning of* deference, *or of an act of homage, or merely* obeisance. *When used with reference to God it means* godly fear and awe)

r. my sanctuary. *Lev* 19:30; 26:2
servants in gate r. *Esth* 3:2
They will r. my son. *Mat* 21:37
Mark 12:6; *Luke* 20:13
the wife see that she r. *Eph* 5:33

reverence, *substantive*

Mephibosheth did r. to. *2 Sam* 9:6*
and did r. to king. *1 Ki* 1:31*
nor did him r. *Esth* 3:2, 5
to be had in r. of all. *Ps* 89:7*
we gave them r. *Heb* 12:9
serve God with r. 28

reverend

holy and r. is his name. *Ps* 111:9

reverse

hath blessed, and I cannot r. it. *Num* 23:20
let it be written, to r. *Esth* 8:5
with king's ring, may no man r. 8

revile

(*To use abusive language of any sort*)

thou shalt not r. the gods. *Ex* 22:28
ye when men shall r. you. *Mat* 5:11*

reviled

that passed by r. him. *Mat* 27:39
crucified with him r. *Mark* 15:32*
they r. him, and said. *John* 9:28
being r. we bless, being. *1 Cor* 4:12
when he was r., r. not. *1 Pet* 2:23

revilers

nor r. shall inherit. *1 Cor* 6:10

revilest

they said, R. thou God's? *Acts* 23:4

revilings

neither be afraid of their r. *Isa* 51:7
and the r. of Ammon. *Zeph* 2:8

revive

(*To make to live again, or to have new life*)

will they r. the stones? *Neh* 4:2
wilt thou not r. us again? *Ps* 85:6*
thou wilt r. me, thou shalt. 138:7
to r. spirit of the humble, and to r. the heart of the contrite. *Isa* 57:15
after two days will he r. us. *Hos* 6:2
they shall r. as corn, and grow. 14:7
Lord, r. thy work in. *Hab* 3:2

revived

spirit of Jacob r. *Gen* 45:27
came again, and he r. *Judg* 15:19
soul came, and he r. *1 Ki* 17:22
bones of Elisha, he r. *2 Ki* 13:21
commandment came, sin r. *Rom* 7:9
both died, rose, and r. 14:9*

reviving

to give us a little r. *Ezra* 9:8, 9

revolt

speaking oppression and r. *Isa* 59:13

revolt, *verb*

also did Libnah r. *2 Chr* 21:10
ye will r. more and more. *Isa* 1:5

revolted

in his days Edom r. *2 Ki* 8:20, 22
2 Chr 21:8, 10
Libnah r. at the same. *2 Ki* 8:22
Israel have deeply r. *Isa* 31:6
this people, they are r. *Jer* 5:23

revolters

are all grievous r. *Jer* 6:28
r. are profound to make. *Hos* 5:2
all their princes are r. 9:15

revolting

this people hath a r. and. *Jer* 5:23

reward

thy exceeding great r. *Gen* 15:1
for it is your r. for. *Num* 18:31
God, who taketh not r. *Deut* 10:17
cursed that taketh r. to slay. 27:25
a full r. be given thee. *Ruth* 2:12
have given him a r. *2 Sam* 4:10
it me with such a r. 19:36
I will give thee a r. *1 Ki* 13:7
Bring to me? or Give a r.? *Job* 6:22*
as an hireling looketh for r. 7:2*

nor taketh *r.* against. *Ps* 15:5
in keeping of them is *r.* 19:11
desolate for a *r.* of their. 40:15*
there is a *r.* for the righteous. 58:11
let them be turned back for *r.* 70:3*
see the *r.* of the wicked. 91:8
render a *r.* to the proud. 94:2*
let this be the *r.* of mine. 109:20
the fruit of the womb is his *r.* 127:3
righteousness, a sure *r.* *Pr* 11:18
a *r.* in the bosom strong wrath. 21:14*
then there shall be a *r.* 24:14
there shall be no *r.* to the evil. 20
they have a good *r.* for. *Eccl* 4:9
neither have they any more a *r.* 9:5
the *r.* of his hands shall. *Isa* 3:11
justify the wicked for *r.* 5:23
his *r.* is with him, and his work before him. 40:10; 62:11
let go my captives, not for *r.* 45:13
captain gave Jeremiah a *r.* *Jer* 40:5
thou givest *r.*, and no *r.* *Ezek* 16:34*
hast loved a *r.* upon every. *Hos* 9:1*
thy *r.* shall return upon thine. *Ob* 15*
heads thereof judge for *r.* *Mi* 3:11
and judge asketh for a *r.* 7:3
great is your *r.* in heaven. *Mat* 5:12
Luke 6:23
love you, what *r.* have ye? *Mat* 5:46
otherwise ye have no *r.* of your. 6:1
they have their *r.* 2, 5, 16
shall receive a prophet's *r.* . . . a righteous man's *r.* 10:41
he shall in no wise lose his *r.* 42
Mark 9:41
but do good, and your *r.* *Luke* 6:35
for we receive the due *r.* 23:41
field with *r.* of iniquity. *Acts* 1:18
r. not reckoned of grace. *Rom* 4:4
every man shall receive his own *r.*
1 Cor 3:8
work abide he shall receive a *r.* 14
thing willingly, I have a *r.* 9:17
what is my *r.* then? verily, that. 18
beguile you of your *r.* *Col* 2:18
ye shall receive the *r.* of the. 3:24
the labourer is worthy of his *r.*
1 Tim 5:18*
recompence of *r.* *Heb* 2:2
10:35; 11:26
r. of unrighteousness. *2 Pet* 2:13*
that we receive a full *r.* *2 John* 8
after error of Balaam for *r.* *Jude* 11*
thou shouldest give *r.* *Rev* 11:18
and my *r.* is with me. 22:12

reward, *verb*
I will *r.* them that hate. *Deut* 32:41
wherefore the Lord *r.* *1 Sam* 24:19
the Lord shall *r.* the. *2 Sam* 3:39
I say, how they *r.* us. *2 Chr* 20:11
he shall *r.* evil to mine. *Ps* 54:5
the Lord shall *r.* thee. *Pr* 25:22
will *r.* them their doings. *Hos* 4:9
Father himself shall *r.* thee openly.
Mat 6:4, 6, 18
shall *r.* every man according. 16:27
Lord *r.* him according. *2 Tim* 4:14*
r. her, even as she. *Rev* 18:6*

rewarded
have ye *r.* evil for good? *Gen* 44:4
thou hast *r.* me good . . . I have *r.* thee evil. *1 Sam* 24:17
Lord *r.* me according to my righteousness. *2 Sam* 22:21; *Ps* 18:20
your work shall be *r.* *2 Chr* 15:7
if I have *r.* evil to him. *Ps* 7:4
they *r.* me evil for good. 35:12
109:5
nor *r.* us according to our. 103:10
the commandment be *r.* *Pr* 13:13
for they have *r.* evil to. *Isa* 3:9
thy work shall be *r.*, saith. *Jer* 31:16
reward her even as she *r.* *Rev* 18:6*

rewarder
r. of them that diligently. *Heb* 11:6

rewardeth
he *r.* him and he shall. *Job* 21:19
plentifully *r.* proud doer. *Ps* 31:23
happy he that *r.* thee, as thou. 137:8
whoso *r.* evil for good. *Pr* 17:13
both *r.* the fool, and *r.* 26:10*

rewards
with the *r.* of divination. *Num* 22:7
followeth after *r.* *Isa* 1:23
of me gifts and *r.* honour. *Dan* 2:6
said, Give thy *r.* to another. 5:17
are my *r.* that my lovers. *Hos* 2:12*

Rezin
Lord began to send against Judah *R.* *2 Ki* 15:37; 16:5; *Isa* 7:1
that time *R.* recovered. *2 Ki* 16:6
took Damascus and slew *R.* 9
the children of *R.*, children of Nekoda and Gazzam. *Ezra* 2:48; *Neh* 7:50
fear not the fierce anger of *R.* *Isa* 7:4
and the head of Damascus is *R.* 8
as the people rejoice in *R.* 8:6
set up the adversaries of *R.* 9:11

Rhegium
compass and came to *R.* *Acts* 28:13

Rhesa
who was the son of *R.* *Luke* 3:27

Rhoda
a damsel named *R.* *Acts* 12:13

Rhodes
we came unto *R.* *Acts* 21:1

rib, -s
God took one of his *r.* *Gen* 2:21
the *r.* which God had taken. 22
Asahel under the fifth *r.* *2 Sam* 2:23*
Joab smote Abner and Amasa under the fifth *r.* 3:27*; 20:10*
smote Ish-bosheth under fifth *r.* 4:6*
beast had three *r.* in the. *Dan* 7:5

ribband
the borders a *r.* of blue. *Num* 15:38*

rich
Abram very *r.* in cattle. *Gen* 13:2
I have made Abram *r.* 14:23
r. shall not give more, nor. *Ex* 30:15
and if a stranger wax *r.* *Lev* 25:47
young men poor or *r.* *Ruth* 3:10
poor and maketh *r.* *1 Sam* 2:7
men in one city, one *r.* *2 Sam* 12:1
he shall not be *r.* neither. *Job* 15:29
nor regardeth the *r.* more. 34:19
the *r.* shall entreat. *Ps* 45:12
hear this, both *r.* and poor. 49:2
be not afraid when one is made *r.* 16
of the diligent maketh *r.* *Pr* 10:4
blessing of the Lord, maketh *r.* 22
there is that maketh himself *r.* 13:7
poor is hated, but the *r.* hath. 14:20
but the *r.* answereth roughly. 18:23
wine and oil shall not be *r.* 21:17
r. and poor meet together, Lord. 22:2
the *r.* ruleth over the poor, and. 7
he that giveth to the *r.* shall. 16
labour not to be *r.*: cease from. 23:4
perverse, though he be *r.* 28:6
he that maketh haste to be *r.* 20, 22
abundance of *r.* will not suffer.
Eccl 5:12
and the *r.* sit in low place. 10:6
curse not the *r.* in thy. 20
with the *r.* in his death. *Isa* 53:9
are great, and waxen *r.* *Jer* 5:27
in chests of *r.* apparel. *Ezek* 27:24
Yet I am become *r.* *Hos* 12:8
be the Lord, for I am *r.* *Zech* 11:5
were *r.*, cast in much. *Mark* 12:41
r. he hath sent empty. *Luke* 1:53
but woe unto you that are *r.* for. 6:24
is not *r.* toward God. 12:21
call not thy *r.* neighbours. 14:12
sorrowful, for he was very *r.* 18:23
Zacchaeus . . . and he was *r.* 19:2
same Lord is *r.* to all. *Rom* 10:12
full, now ye are *r.* *1 Cor* 4:8
yet making many *r.* *2 Cor* 6:10
though he was *r.* yet he became poor, that ye might be *r.* 8:9
God who is *r.* in mercy. *Eph* 2:4
they that will be *r.* fall. *1 Tim* 6:9
charge them that are *r.* in this. 17
that they do good, and be *r.* in. 18
let the *r.* rejoice in that. *Jas* 1:10
chosen the poor, *r.* in faith? 2:5
poverty, but thou art *r.* *Rev* 2:9
because thou sayest, I am *r.* 3:17
buy gold, that thou mayest be *r.* 18
he causeth the *r.* and poor to. 13:16
merchants of earth are waxed *r.*
Rev 18:3, 15, 19

rich *man* or *men*
r. man had exceeding. *2 Sam* 12:2
a traveller to the *r. man.* 4
r. man shall lie down. *Job* 27:19
the *r. man's* wealth is his strong.
Pr 10:15; 18:11
the *r. man* is wise in his. 28:11
let not the *r. man* glory. *Jer* 9:23
the *r. men* thereof are full. *Mi* 6:12
r. man shall hardly enter. *Mat* 19:23
than for a *r. man* to enter into. 24
Mark 10:25; *Luke* 18:25
came a *r. man* of Arimathaea.
Mat 27:57
the ground of a *r. man.* *Luke* 12:16
there was a certain *r. man.* 16:1
a *r. man* was clothed in purple. 19
fell from the *r. man's* table. 21
the *r. man* also died and was. 22
and saw the *r. men* casting. 21:1
so also shall the *r. man.* *Jas* 1:11
do not *r. men* oppress you? 2:6
go to now, ye *r. men,* weep. 5:1
great men, and *r. men.* *Rev* 6:15

richer
the fourth shall be far *r.* *Dan* 11:2

riches
the *r.* God hath taken. *Gen* 31:16
r. were more than they might. 36:7
return with much *r.* to. *Josh* 22:8
enrich with great *r.* *1 Sam* 17:25
neither hast asked *r.* *1 Ki* 3:11
2 Chr 1:11
given thee both *r.* and. *1 Ki* 3:13
Solomon exceeded all the kings of the earth for *r.* 10:23; *2 Chr* 9:22
both *r.* and honour. *1 Chr* 29:12
David died full of days, *r.* and. 28
Jehoshaphat had *r.* and honour.
2 Chr 17:5; 18:1
found *r.* with dead bodies. 20:25
Hezekiah had exceeding much *r.*
32:27
r. of his glorious kingdom. *Esth* 1:4
them of the glory of his *r.* 5:11
he swallowed down *r.* *Job* 20:15
will he esteem thy *r.*? no, not. 36:19
is better than the *r.* of. *Ps* 37:16
he heapeth up *r.* and knoweth. 39:6
boast themselves in their *r.* 49:6
trusted in the abundance of *r.* 52:7
if *r.* increase, set not your. 62:10
ungodly, they increase in *r.* 73:12
earth is full of thy *r.* 104:24
wealth and *r.* shall be in. 112:3
rejoiced as much as in all *r.* 119:14
and in her left hand *r.* *Pr* 3:16
r. and honour are with me. 8:18
r. profit not in the day of wrath. 11:4
and strong men retain *r.* 16
trusteth in his *r.* shall fall. 28
poor, yet hath great *r.* 13:7
of a man's life are his *r.* 8
crown of the wise is their *r.* 14:24
and *r.* are the inheritance of. 19:14
is rather to be chosen than *r.* 22:1
by the fear of the Lord are *r.* 4
the poor to increase his *r.* 16
r. certainly make themselves. 23:5
be filled with all pleasant *r.* 24:4
for *r.* are not for ever, and. 27:24
give me neither poverty nor *r.* 30:8
his eye satisfied with *r.* *Eccl* 4:8
even *r.* kept for the owners. 5:13
those *r.* perish by evil travail. 14
to whom God hath given *r.* 19; 6:2
r. to men of understanding. 9:11
the *r.* of Damascus shall. *Isa* 8:4
hand found as a nest the *r.* 10:14
they will carry their *r.* on. 30:6
I will give thee hidden *r.* of. 45:3
eat the *r.* of the Gentiles. 61:6
rich man glory in his *r.* *Jer* 9:23
so he that getteth *r.* and not. 17:11
because *r.* that he hath gotten. 48:36
make a spoil of thy *r.* *Ezek* 26:12
multitude of all kind of *r.* 27:12
18, 27, 33
thou hast gotten *r.* 28:4
increased thy *r.*, and thine heart is lifted up because of thy *r.* 5

through his r. shall stir up. *Dan* 11:2
north shall come with much r. 13
them the prey, spoil and r. 24
return into his land with great r. 28
deceitfulness of r. choke. *Mat* 13:22
Mark 4:19; *Luke* 8:14
hardly they that have r. *Mark* 10:23
how hard is it for them that trust in r. to enter! 24; *Luke* 18:24
your trust the true r.? *Luke* 16:11
or despisest thou the r. of? *Rom* 2:4
he might make known the r. 9:23
be the r. of the world, and the diminishing of them the r. of. 11:12
O the depth of the r. of the. 33
abounded to the r. of their. *2 Cor* 8:2
redemption according to r. *Eph* 1:7
what the r. of the glory of his. 18
that he might shew exceeding r. 2:7
preach unsearchable r. of Christ. 3:8
grant you according to the r. 16
according to his r. in glory. *Phil* 4:19
what the r. of the glory. *Col* 1:27
love, and unto all the r. of the. 2:2
nor trust in uncertain r. *1 Tim* 6:17
reproach of Christ greater r. than. *Heb* 11:26
your r. are corrupted. *Jas* 5:2
to receive power and r. *Rev* 5:12
in one hour so great r. are. 18:17

richly

of Christ dwell in you r. *Col* 3:16
living God, who giveth r. *1 Tim* 6:17

rid

that he might r. him out. *Gen* 37:22
I will r. you out of their. *Ex* 6:6
I will r. evil beasts out. *Lev* 26:6*
r. them out of the hand. *Ps* 82:4*
send thine hand, r. me. 144:7*, 11*

riddance

thou shalt not make clean r. of thy. *Lev* 23:22*
he shall make even speedy r. of. *Zeph* 1:18*

ridden

ass, which thou hast r.? *Num* 22:30

riddle

put forth a r. to you. *Judg* 14:12
13, 14, 15, 16, 17, 18, 19
Son of man, put orth a r. *Ezek* 17:2

ride

to r. in the second chariot. *Gen* 41:43
he made him r. on high. *Deut* 32:13
ye that r. on white asses. *Judg* 5:10
for king's household to r. *2 Sam* 16:2
saddle an ass that I may r. 19:26
cause Solomon to r. upon my mule. *1 Ki* 1:33, 38, 44
nim to r. in his chariot. *2 Ki* 10:16
to r. upon the wind. *Job* 30:22
and in thy majesty r. *Ps* 45:4
thou hast caused men to r. 66:12
but ye said, We will r. *Isa* 30:16
I will cause thee to r. on the. 58:14
tney r. on horses. *Jer* 6:23; 50:42
I will make Ephraim to r. *Hos* 10:11
we will not r. upon horses. 14:3
that thou didst r. upon. *Hab* 3:8
chariots, and those that r. *Hag* 2:22

rider

so that his r. shall fall. *Gen* 49:17
horse and r. thrown. *Ex* 15:1, 21
the horse and his r. *Job* 39:18
break in pieces horse and his r. . . . the chariot and his r. *Jer* 51:21
I will smite his r. with. *Zech* 12:4

riders

if thou be able to set r. on. *2 Ki* 18:23; *Isa* 36:8
letters by r. on mules. *Esth* 8:10
the horses and their r. *Hag* 2:22
the r. on horses shall be. *Zech* 10:5

rideth

what saddle he r. on shall. *Lev* 15:9
who r. upon the heaven. *Deut* 33:26
horse that king r. upon. *Esth* 6:8
that r. on the heavens. *Ps* 68:4, 33
Lord r. on a swift cloud. *Isa* 19:1
that r. the horse deliver. *Amos* 2:15

ridges

waterest the r. thereof. *Ps* 65:10*

riding

Balaam was r. on his ass. *Num* 22:22
slack not thy r. for me. *2 Ki* 4:24
kings shall enter r. in chariots. *Jer* 17:25; 22:4
young men, horsemen r. on horses. *Ezek* 23:6, 12
great lords, all of them r. 23
people with thee r. on horses. 38:15
a man r. on a red horse. *Zech* 1:8
thy king cometh: r. upon an ass. 9:9

rie, or rye

(*Properly* spelt, *a variety of wheat*)
wheat and r. not smitten. *Ex* 9:32
cast in wheat, barley and r. *Isa* 28:25

rifled

houses r. and the women. *Zech* 14:2

right, *substantive*

shall not the Judge of all the earth do r.? *Gen* 18:25
of Zelophehad speak r. *Num* 27:7
r. of firstborn is his. *Deut* 21:17
redeem thou my r. to. *Ruth* 4:6
what r. have I to cry? *2 Sam* 19:28
we have also more r. in David. 43
no portion nor r. in Jerusalem. *Neh* 2:20
thou hast done r., but we have. 9:33
should I lie against my r.? *Job* 34:6
he that hateth r. govern? 17
but he giveth r. to the poor. 36:6
maintained my r.: judging r. *Ps* 9:4*
hear the r. O Lord, attend to. 17:1
the Lord will maintain the r. 140:12
revenues without r. *Pr* 16:8
and they love him that speaketh r. 13
away the r. from poor. *Isa* 10:2
when the needy speaketh r. 32:7
the r. of the needy do. *Jer* 5:28
getteth riches, and not by r. 17:11
the r. of redemption is thine. 32:7, 8
to turn aside r. of a man. *Lam* 3:35
he come whose r. it is. *Ezek* 21:27
turn poor from their r. *Amos* 5:12
turn stranger from his r. *Mal* 3:5
they have no r. to eat. *Heb* 13:10
they may have r. to the tree of life. *Rev* 22:14

right, *adjective*

led me in the r. way. *Gen* 24:48
God of truth, just and r. *Deut* 32:4
do as seemeth good and r. *Josh* 9:25
frame to pronounce it r. *Judg* 12:6
the good and r. way. *1 Sam* 12:23
matters are good and r. *2 Sam* 15:3
is thy heart r. as my heart? *2 Ki* 10:15
things that were not r. 17:9
to seek of him a r. *Ezra* 8:21*
thou gavest them r. *Neh* 9:13
and the things seem r. *Esth* 8:5
how forcible are r. words! *Job* 6:25*
not lay on man more than r. 34:23
this to be r. that thou saidst? 35:2*
statutes of Lord are r. *Ps* 19:8
sceptre of thy kingdom is a r. 45:6*
O God, renew a r. spirit. 51:10
led them forth by the r. way. 107:7*
thy judgements are r. 119:75*
thy precepts are r. 128
I have led thee in r. paths. *Pr* 4:11*
my lips shall be r. things. 8:6
they are all r. to them that find. 9
thoughts of the righteous are r. 12:5*
way which seemeth r. 14:12; 16:25
work be pure, and whether r. 20:11
lips shall speak r. things. 23:16
his lips that giveth a r. answer. 24:26
considered every r. work. *Eccl* 4:4*
say, Prophesy not to us r. things. *Isa* 30:10
declare things that are r. 45:19
I had planted thee wholly a r. seed. *Jer* 2:21
evil, and their force is not r. 23:10
and had done r. in my sight. 34:15
ways of the Lord are r. *Hos* 14:19
for they know not to do r. *Amos* 3:10
clothed, and in his r. mind. *Mark* 5:15; *Luke* 8:35
hast answered r.: this. *Luke* 10:28
r. in sight of God. *Acts* 4:19
thy heart is not r. in the sight. 8:21
not cease to pervert the r. *Acts* 13:10
forsaken the r. way. *2 Pet* 2:15

right, *adv.*

people passed over r. *Josh* 3:16
see **foot, hand**

is **right**

and do that which *is* r. in his sight. *Ex* 15:26; *1 Ki* 11:38
thou shalt do that which *is* r. *Deut* 6:18; 12:25; 21:9
whatsoever *is* r. in own eyes. 12:8
doest that which *is* r. 28; 13:18
walked to do that *is* r. *1 Ki* 11:33
which *is* r. in my eyes. *2 Ki* 10:30
of me thing that *is* r. *Job* 42:7, 8
word of the Lord *is* r. *Ps* 33:4
the way of a fool *is* r. in. *Pr* 12:15
every way of man *is* r. in his. 21:2
as for the pure, his work *is* r. 8
man do that which *is* r. *Ezek* 18:5
done that which *is* lawful and r. 19
21:27; 33:14, 16, 19
whatsoever *is* r. I will. *Mat* 20:4
whatsoever *is* r. that shall ye. 7
judge ye not what *is* r.? *Luke* 12:57
in the Lord: this *is* r. *Eph* 6:1

was **right**

that which *was* r. in his own eyes. *Judg* 17:6; 21:25
David to do that only which *was* r. *1 Ki* 14:8; 15:5
Asa did that which *was* r. 15:11
2 Chr 14:2
Jehoshaphat doing that which *was* r. *1 Ki* 22:43; *2 Chr* 20:32
Jehoash did that which *was* r. *2 Ki* 12:2; *2 Chr* 24:2
Amaziah did that which *was* r. *2 Ki* 14:3; *2 Chr* 25:2
Azariah did that which *was* r. *2 Ki* 15:3; *2 Chr* 26:4
Jotham did that which *was* r. *2 Ki* 15:34; *2 Chr* 27:2
Ahaz did not that which *was* r. *2 Ki* 16:2
Hezekiah did that which *was* r. 18:3
2 Chr 29:2
Josiah did that which *was* r. *2 Ki* 22:2; *2 Chr* 34:2
the thing *was* r. in eyes. *1 Chr* 13:4
I have perverted that which *was* r. *Job* 33:27
their heart *was* not r. *Ps* 78:37
which came out of my lips *was* r. *Jer* 17:16*

right *cheek*

smite thee on the r. *cheek*. *Mat* 5:39

right *corner*

round from the r. *corner*. *2 Ki* 11:11

right *early*

God shall help her, and that r. *early*. *Ps* 46:5

right *forth*

driven every man r. *forth*. *Jer* 49:5

right on

let thine eyes look r. *on*. *Pr* 4:25
call passengers who go r. *on*. 9:15

right *pillar*

he set up the r. *pillar*. *1 Ki* 7:21

right *well*

my soul knoweth r. *well*. *Ps* 139:14

righteous

(*Frequently changed in the Revisions to* upright)
for thee have I seen r. *Gen* 7:1
wilt thou destroy the r. with? 18:23
if there be fifty r. wilt? 24, 26, 28
that be far from thee to slay r. 25
slay also a r. nation? 20:4
hath been more r. than I. 38:26
innocent and r. slay not. *Ex* 23:7
perverteth the words of the r. 8
Deut 16:19
the death of the r. *Num* 23:10
that hath judgements so r. *Deut* 4:8
they shall justify the r. 25:1
2 Chr 6:23
the r. acts of the Lord. *Judg* 5:11
1 Sam 12:7
art more r. than I. *1 Sam* 24:17
have slain a r. person. *2 Sam* 4:11

two men more r. than he. *1 Ki* 2:32
justifying the r. to give him. 8:32
Jehu said, Ye be r. *2 Ki* 10:9
Lord God of Israel, thou art r.
Ezra 9:15; *Neh* 9:8
where were the r. cut off? *Job* 4:7
whom, though I were r., yet. 9:15
if I be r. yet will I not lift. 10:15
that he should be r.? 15:14
r. also shall hold on his way. 17:9
to Almighty, that thou art r.? 22:3
the r. see it, and are glad. 19
Ps 107:42
there the r. might dispute. *Job* 23:7
was r. in his own eyes. 32:1
Job hath said, I am r. 34:5
if thou be r. 35:7
withdraweth not his eyes from the r.
36:7; *Ps* 34:15
that thou mayest be r. *Job* 40:8*
the congregation of the r. *Ps* 1:5
Lord knoweth way of the r. 6
for thou wilt bless the r. with. 5:12
for the r. God trieth the hearts. 7:9
God judgeth the r., God is angry. 11
what can the r. do? 11:3
Lord trieth the r. 5
God is in the generation of the r. 14:5
judgements of Lord are true and r.
19:9; 119:7, 62, 106, 160, 164
contemptuously against the r. 31:18
be glad . . . and rejoice, ye r. 32:11
rejoice in the Lord, O ye r. 33:1
97:12
the r. cry, and the Lord. 34:17
afflictions of r.: Lord delivereth. 19
they that hate the r. shall. 21
that favour my r. cause. 35:27
the Lord upholdeth the r. 37:17
but the r. sheweth mercy. 21
yet have I not seen r. forsaken. 25
the r. shall inherit the land. 29
the mouth of the r. speaketh. 30
the wicked watcheth the r. 32
but the salvation of the r. is of. 39
the r. also shall see, and fear. 52:6
he shall never suffer the r. to. 55:22
the r. shall rejoice when he. 58:10
verily there is a reward for the r. 11
r. shall be glad in the Lord. 64:10
but let the r. be glad, let them. 68:3
not be written with the r. 69:28
in his days shall r. flourish. 72:7
horns of r. shall be exalted. 75:10
the r. shall flourish like the. 92:12
gather against soul of the r. 94:21
light is sown for r. and. 97:11
of compassion and r. 112:4; 116:5
the r. shall be in everlasting. 6
the tabernacles of the r. 118:15
this gate, into which the r. shall. 20
sworn that I will keep thy r. 119:106
r. art thou, O Lord. 137; *Jer* 12:1
thy testimonies are r. *Ps* 119:138
not rest upon the lot of the r. lest the
r. put forth their hands. 125:3
the r. shall give thanks to. 140:13
let the r. smite me, it shall. 141:5
the r. shall compass me. 142:7
the Lord is r. in all his ways. 145:17
the Lord loveth the r., he. 146:8
sound wisdom for the r. *Pr* 2:7
mayest keep the paths of the r. 20
but his secret is with the r. 3:32
the Lord will not suffer the r. 10:3
labour of the r. tendeth to life. 16
the lips of the r. feed many. 21
but the desire of the r. shall. 24
but the r. is an everlasting. 25
hope of the r. shall be gladness. 28
the r. shall never be removed. 30
the lips of the r. know what is. 32
r. is delivered out of trouble. 11:8
when it goeth well with the r. 10
but the seed of the r. shall be. 21
the desire of the r. is only good. 23
r. shall flourish as a branch. 28
the fruit of the r. is a tree of life. 30
behold, r. shall be recompensed. 31
but the root of the r. shall not. 12:3
thoughts of the r. are right, but. 5
the house of the r. shall stand. 7
root of the r. yieldeth fruit. 12
the r. is more excellent than his. 26
the light of the r. rejoiceth. *Pr* 13:9
but to the r. good shall be. 21
the r. eateth to the satisfying of. 25
among the r. there is favour. 14:9
bow at the gates of the r. 19
r. hath hope in his death. 32
in the house of the r. is much. 15:6
way of the r. is made plain. 19
the heart of the r. studieth to. 28
heareth the prayer of the r. 29
r. lips are the delight of kings. 16:13
overthrow the r. in judgement. 18:5
the r. runneth into it, and is safe. 10
shall be a ransom for the r. 21:18
r. giveth, and spareth not. 26
father of the r. shall greatly. 23:24
against the dwelling of the r. 24:15
to the wicked, Thou art r. 24
r. are bold as a lion. 28:1
whoso causeth the r. to go astray. 10
wicked perish, the r. increase. 28
when the r. are in authority. 29:2
the r. doth sing and rejoice. 6
the r. considereth the cause of. 7
but the r. shall see their fall. 16
God shall judge the r. *Eccl* 3:17
be not r. over much, neither. 7:16
according to the work of the r. 8:14
the r. and the wise are in the. 9:1
there is one event to the r. and. 2
say ye to the r., that it shall. *Isa* 3:10
the righteousness of the r. 5:23
songs, even glory to the r. 24:16
open ye, that the r. nation. 26:2
that we may say, He is r. 41:26
my r. servant shall justify. 53:11
r. perisheth . . . none considering
that the r. is taken away from. 57:1
thy people also shall be all r. 60:21
r. art thou, O Lord, when. *Jer* 12:1
O Lord, that triest the r. 20:12
raise to David a r. branch. 23:5
have made the r. sad. *Ezek* 13:22
are more r. than thou. 16:52
righteousness of the r. shall. 18:20
but when the r. turneth. 24; 33:18
cut off r. and wicked. 21:3, 4
r. shall not deliver him, nor shall the
r. be able to live. 33:12
when I say to the r. he shall live. 13
they sold r. for silver. *Amos* 2:6
compass about the r. *Hab* 1:4
him that is more r. than he. 13
discern between the r. *Mal* 3:18
not come to call the r., but sinners.
Mat 9:13; *Mark* 2:17; *Luke* 5:32
then shall the r. shine. *Mat* 13:43
ye outwardly appear r. to. 23:28
garnish the sepulchres of r. 29
all r. blood shed on earth, from blood
of r. Abel to Zacharias. 35
r. answer, Lord, when saw? 25:37
r. shall go into life eternal. 46
and they were both r. *Luke* 1:6
who trusted they were r. and. 18:9
appearance, but judge r. *John* 7:24
O r. Father, the world hath. 17:25
and revelation of the r. *Rom* 2:5
it is written, There is none r. 3:10
of one, many be made r. 5:19
a manifest token of r. *2 Thes* 1:5
it is a r. thing with God to. 6
the Lord, the r. Judge. *2 Tim* 4:8
witness that he was r. *Heb* 11:4
of Lord are over the r. *1 Pet* 3:12
if r. scarcely be saved. 4:18
Lot vexed his r. soul. *2 Pet* 2:8
advocate, Jesus Christ the r.
1 John 2:1
if ye know that he is r., ye. 29
righteousness is r. as he is r. 3:7
were evil, and his brother's r. 12
Thou art r. O Lord. *Rev* 16:5
O Lord, true and r. are. 7; 19:2
he that is r. let him be r. 22:11

see **Lord is**

righteous *man*, or *men*
a little that a r. *man* hath. *Ps* 37:16
the mouth of a r. *man*. *Pr* 10:11
a r. *man* regardeth the life. 12:10
a r. *man* hateth lying, but. 13:5
a r. *man* wisely considereth. 21:12
a r. *man* falling down before. 25:26
when r. *men* do rejoice. *Pr* 28:12
who raised up the r. *man*. *Isa* 41:2
when a r. *man* doth turn. *Ezek* 3:20
18:26
if thou warn the r. *man*. 3:21
and the r. *men*, they shall. 23:45
r. *man* in the name of a r. *man* shall
receive a r. *man's*. *Mat* 10:41
many r. *men* have desired. 13:17
this was a r. *man*. *Luke* 23:47
for a r. *man* will one die. *Rom* 5:7
law not made for r. *man*. *1 Tim* 1:9
prayer of a r. *man* availeth. *Jas* 5:16
for that r. *man* dwelling. *2 Pet* 2:8

righteously
hear causes, and judge r.
Deut 1:16; *Pr* 31:9
judge the people r. *Ps* 67:4*; 96:10*
he that walketh r. shall. *Isa* 33:15
Lord, that judgest r. *Jer* 11:20
live soberly, r. and godly. *Tit* 2:12
to him that judgeth r. *1 Pet* 2:23

righteousness
(The quality of being right or just. This idea makes plain the difference indicated by Paul between the righteousness of the law and the righteousness of God and Christ)
and it shall be our r. if. *Deut* 6:25
it shall be r. to thee before. 24:13
shall offer sacrifices of r. 33:19
put on r., it clothed me. *Job* 29:14
ascribe r. to my Maker. 36:3
offer the sacrifices of r. *Ps* 4:5
Lord loveth r. 11:7; 33:5
he that worketh r. shall never. 15:2
he leadeth me in paths of r. 23:3
and r. from the God of his. 24:5
I have preached r. in the. 40:9
truth, and meekness, and r. 45:4
lovest r. and hatest. 7; *Heb* 1:9
hand, O God, is full of r. *Ps* 48:10
pleased with sacrifices of r. 51:19
lying, rather than to speak r. 52:3
speak r. O congregation? 58:1
judge thy people with r. 72:2
peace, and little hills by r. 3
r. and peace have kissed. 85:10
and r. shall look down from. 11
r. shall go before him, and set. 13
judgement shall return unto r. 94:15
judge the world with r. 96:13; 98:9
r. is the habitation of his. 97:2
executest r. in Jacob. 99:4; 103:6
blessed is he that doeth r. 106:3
open to me the gates of r., I. 118:19
the r. of thy testimonies is. 119:144
all thy commandments are r. 172
priests be clothed with r., thy. 132:9
understand r. and judgement. *Pr* 2:9
yea, durable riches and r. are. 8:18
I lead in the way of r. in midst. 20
but r. delivereth. 10:2; 11:4
the r. of the perfect shall. 11:5
r. of upright shall deliver. 6
to him that soweth r. shall be. 18
as r. tendeth to life, so he that. 19
truth, sheweth forth r. 12:17
in the way of r. is life, and. 28
r. keepeth him that is upright. 13:6
r. exalteth a nation. 14:34
that followeth after r. 15:9
better is a little with r. than. 16:8
throne is established by r. 12
if found in the way of r. 31
he that followeth after r. and mercy
findeth life, r. and honour. 21:21
and the place of r. that. *Eccl* 3:16
r. lodged in it, but now. *Isa* 1:21
the city of r. 26
and her converts with r. 27
which take away the r. of the. 5:23
decreed shall overflow with r. 10:22
with r. shall he judge the poor. 11:4
r. shall be the girdle of his loins. 5
judgement, and hasting r. 16:5
of the world will learn r. 26:9
yet will he not learn r. 10
r. will I lay to the plummet. 28:17
and r. shall remain in the. 32:16
the work of r. shall be peace, and
the effect of r. quietness and. 17
Zion with judgement and r. 33:5

and let skies pour down r. and let r.
spring up together. Isa 45:8
I the Lord speak r., I declare. 19
in the Lord have I r. 24*
ye that are far from r. 46:12
ye that follow after r. 51:1
ye that know r. 7
r. is of me, saith the Lord. 54:17
me as a nation that did r. 58:2
put on r. as a breastplate. 59:17
officers peace, thine exactors r. 60:17
might be called trees of r. 61:3
covered me with robe of r. 10
so Lord will cause r. and praise. 11
until the r. thereof go forth as. 62:1
that rejoiceth and worketh r. 64:5
the Lord which exercise r. Jer 9:24
execute ye judgement and r. 22:3
the Lord our r. 23:6; 33:16
the branch of r. to grow up to David,
and he shall execute r. 33:15
hath brought forth our r. 51:10
own souls by their r. Ezek 14:14, 20
the r. of the righteous shall be. 18:20
r. of the righteous shall not. 33:12
break off thy sins by r. Dan 4:27
O Lord, r. belongeth unto thee. 9:7
to bring in everlasting r. and. 24
they that turn many to r. shall. 12:3
till he come and rain r. Hos 10:12
and who leave off r. Amos 5:7
let r. run down as a mighty. 24
ye have turned the fruit of r. 6:12
that ye may know the r. Mi 6:5*
seek r., seek meekness. Zeph 2:3
shall the Sun of r. arise. Mal 4:2
becometh us to fulfil all r. Mat 3:15
that hunger and thirst after r. 5:6
except your r. exceed the r. 20
John came in the way of r. 21:32
in r. before him all days. Luke 1:75
reprove the world of sin and of r.
John 16:8
of r., because I go to my Father. 10
worketh r. is accepted. Acts 10:35
thou enemy of all r. wilt thou? 13:10
as he reasoned of r. and. 24:25
therein is the r. of God. Rom 1:17
if uncircumcision keep the r. 2:26*
commend the r. of God. 3:5
the r. of God without the law. 21
r. of God which is by faith of. 22
to whom God imputeth r. 4:6
a seal of r. of faith, that r. might. 11
promise was through the r. 13
which receive gift of r. shall. 5:17
so by r. of one the free gift came. 18
so might grace reign through r. 21
instruments of r. to God. 6:13
death, or of obedience unto r. 16
ye became the servants of r. 18
your members servants to r. 19
of sin, ye were free from r. 20
that the r. of the law might be. 8:4*
but the spirit is life because of r. 10
who followed not after r., have attained to r., even the r. 9:30
followed after the law of r., hath not
attained to the law of r. 31*
to establish their own r., have not
submitted to the r. of God. 10:3
Moses describeth the r. which is. 5
the r. which is of faith speaketh. 6
the heart man believeth unto r. 10
not meat and drink, but r. 14:17
Christ is made unto us r. 1 Cor 1:30
awake to r. and sin not, for. 15:34*
that we might be made the r. of God.
2 Cor 5:21
by the armour of r. on the right. 6:7
what fellowship hath r. with? 14
increase the fruits of your r. 9:10
as the ministers of r. 11:15
if r. come by law, Christ. Gal 2:21
verily, r should have been. 3:21
we wait for the hope of r. 5:5
fruit of the Spirit is in all r. Eph 5:9
having on the breastplate of r. 6:14
the fruits of r. by Jesus. Phil 1:11
touching r. which is in the law. 3:6
r. which is of God by faith. 9
and follow after r. 1 Tim 6:11
2 Tim 2:22
up for me a crown of r. 2 Tim 4:8

not by works of r. which. Tit 3:5
a sceptre of r. is sceptre. Heb 1:8*
is unskilful in the word of r. 5:13
by interpretation king of r. 7:2
and became heir of the r. which. 11:7
subdued kingdoms, wrought r. 33
peaceable fruit of r. 12:11
worketh not r. of God. Jas 1:20
the fruit of r. is sown in peace. 3:18
sin should live unto r. 1 Pet 2:24
faith through r. of God. 2 Pet 1:1
but saved Noah a preacher of r. 2:5
not to have known the way of r. 21
new earth, wherein dwelleth r. 3:13
every one that doeth r. 1 John 2:29
he that doeth r. is righteous. 3:7
whosoever doeth not r. is not of. 10
for the fine linen is the r. Rev 19:8*

for righteousness

counted it to him for r. Gen 15:6
Ps 106:31; Rom 4:3
for thy r.' sake bring. Ps 143:11
he looked for r. but behold. Isa 5:7
which are persecuted for r. Mat 5:10
his faith is counted for r. Rom 4:5
Gal 3:6
imputed to him for r. Rom 4:22
Jas 2:23
end of the law for r. Rom 10:4
if ye suffer for r.' sake. 1 Pet 3:14

his righteousness

Lord render to every man his r.
1 Sam 26:23
to give according to his r. 1 Ki 8:32
2 Chr 6:23
render unto man his r. Job 33:26
Lord according to his r. Ps 7:17
they shall declare his r. to a. 22:31
the heavens shall declare his r.
50:6; 97:6
his r. hath he openly shewed. 98:2
and his r. unto children's. 103:17
and his r. endureth for ever. 111:3
112:3, 9
that perisheth in his r. Eccl 7:15
pleased for his r. sake. Isa 42:21
brought salvation, and his r. 59:16
when a righteous man doth turn from
his r. Ezek 3:20; 18:24, 26
in his r. that he hath done. 18:22
not be able to live for his r. 33:12
if he trust to his own r. and commit
iniquity, his r. 13
and I shall behold his r. Mi 7:9
kingdom of God and his r. Mat 6:33
his r. for remission of sins.
Rom 3:25, 26
given to the poor, his r. 2 Cor 9:9

in righteousness

in r. shalt thou judge. Lev 19:15
before thee in truth and in r. 1 Ki 3:6
judge the world in r. Ps 9:8
I will behold thy face in r. 17:15
by terrible things in r. wilt thou. 65:5
words of my mouth are in r. Pr 8:8
throne shall be established in r. 25:5
shall be sanctified in r. Isa 5:16
a king shall reign in r. and. 32:1
Lord have called thee in r. 42:6
have raised him in r. and will. 45:13
gone out of my mouth in r. 23
God of Israel, but not in r. 48:1
in r. shalt thou be established. 54:14
that speak in r., mighty to. 63:1
the Lord liveth, in r. Jer 4:2
betroth thee unto me in r. Hos 2:19
sow to yourselves in r., reap. 10:12
God in truth and in r. Zech 8:8
offer an offering in r. Mal 3:3
judge the world in r. Acts 17:31
and cut it short in r. Rom 9:28
new man ... is created in r. Eph 4:24
for instruction in r. 2 Tim 3:16
and in r. he doth judge. Rev 19:11

my righteousness

so my r. answer for me. Gen 30:33
saying, For my r. Lord. Deut 9:4
Lord rewarded me according to my
r. 2 Sam 22:21, 25; Ps 18:20, 24
yea, return again, my r. Job 6:29
my r. I hold fast, and will. 27:6
saidst, my r. is more than. 35:2
I call, O God of my r. Ps 4:1

Lord, according to my Ps 7:8
the right hand of my r. Isa 41:10
I bring near my r. 46:13
my r. is near. 51:5
my r. shall not be abolished. 6
but my r. shall be for ever. 8
salvation is near to come, my r. 56:1
not having mine own r. Phil 3:9

our righteousnesses

all our r. are as filthy. Isa 64:6
not for our r. but for. Dan 9:18

thy righteousness

nor for thy r. or. Deut 9:5, 6
make the habitation of thy r. Job 8:6
and thy r. may profit the son. 35:8
lead me, O Lord, in thy r. Ps 5:8
deliver me in thy r. 31:1; 71:2
Lord, according to thy r. 35:24
shall speak of thy r. 28; 71:24
thy r. is like the great. 36:6
O continue thy r. to the upright. 10
he shall bring forth thy r. 37:6
I have not hid thy r. within. 40:10
shall sing aloud of thy r. 51:14
let them not come into thy r. 69:27
shew forth thy r. all day. 71:15
I will make mention of thy r. 16
thy r. O God, is very high. 19
and give thy r. unto the king's. 72:1
thy r. be known in land of. 88:12
and in thy r. shall they be. 89:16
quicken me in thy r. 119:40
for word of thy r. 123*
thy r. is an everlasting. 142
answer me, and in thy r. 143:1
for thy r.' sake, bring my soul. 11
and they shall sing of thy r. 145:7
had thy r. been as waves. Isa 48:18
I will declare thy r. and. 57:12
thy r. shall go before thee. 58:8
and the Gentiles shall see thy r. 62:2
according to all thy r. Dan 9:16

rightly

said, Is not he r. named? Gen 27:36
Thou hast r. judged. Luke 7:43
know that thou teachest r. 20:21
r. dividing the word of. 2 Tim 2:15*

rigour

Israel to serve with r. Ex 1:13, 14
thou shalt not rule with r. Lev 25:43
46, 53

Rimmon

Ain and R. cities of. Josh 15:32
fled towards the wilderness, to the
rock R. Judg 20:45, 47; 21:13
Baanah and Rechab sons of R.
2 Sam 4:2, 5, 9
goeth into the house of R. 2 Ki 5:18
of Simeon were Ain, R. 1 Chr 4:32
was given to Merari, R. 6:77
be turned as a plain to R. Zech 14:10

ring

(The signet ring of a monarch contained his seal, which was affixed to a document instead of a signature, as few people wrote in those days, and fewer still read. To give this ring to another was to give him the right to sign in place of the king. Rings of various sorts were also worn as ornaments, either by a monarch or others)

Pharaoh took off his r. Gen 41:42*
coupled unto one r. Ex 26:24; 36:29
king Ahasuerus took his r. Esth 3:10
with the king's r. 12; 8:8, 10
the king took off his r. 8:2
the father said, Put a r. Luke 15:22
a man with a gold r. Jas 2:2

ringleader

and a r. of the sect of. Acts 24:5

rings

four r. of gold for it. Ex 25:12
put staves into the r. 14, 15; 27:7
37:5; 38:7
their r. of gold. 26:29; 28:23, 26
27; 30:4; 36:34; 37:3, 13; 39:16
19, 20
upon net four brazen r. 27:4
the breastplate by the r. 28:28
jewels, bracelets, and r. Num 31:50*

fastened to silver r. pillars. Esth 1:6
his hands are as gold r. S of S 5:14
will take away the r. and. Isa 3:21
their r. so high that they were dreadful, their r. were full. Ezek 1:18

ringstraked
(*American Revision* ring-streaked)
he goats that were r. Gen 30:35
if he said, The r. shall be. 31:8
rams were r., speckled. 10, 12

rinsed
pot be both scoured and r. Lev 6:28
and hath not r. his hands. 15:11
every vessel of wood shall be r. 12

riot, *substantive*
children not accused of r. Tit 1:6
to the same excess of r. 1 Pet 4:4

riot
count it pleasure to r. 2 Pet 2:13*

rioting
walk not in r. and. Rom 13:13*

riotous
not amongst r. eaters. Pr 23:20*
he that is a companion of r. 28:7*
substance with r. living. Luke 15:13

rip
wilt r. up their women. 2 Ki 8:12

ripe
brought forth r. grapes. Gen 40:10
first of thy r. fruits. Ex 22:29
of the first r. grapes. Num 13:20
whatsoever is first r. in the. 18:13
even like the figs that are first r. Jer 24:2; Hos 9:10; Nah 3:12
sickle, for the harvest is r. Joel 3:13
desired the first r. fruit. Mi 7:1
for harvest of earth is r. Rev 14:15
for her grapes are fully r. 18

ripening
and the sour grape is r. Isa 18:5

ripped
all the women with child he r. up. 2 Ki 15:16
with child shall be r. up. Hos 13:16
because they have r. up. Amos 1:13

rise
if he r. again and walk. Ex 21:19
and a sceptre shall r. Num 24:17
r. that they r. not again. Deut 33:11
shall r. and go through. Josh 18:4
R. thou and fall upon us. Judg 8:21
thou shalt r. early, and set. 9:33
that he should r. to lie. 1 Sam 22:13
and suffered them not to r. 24:7
when child was dead, thou didst r. 2 Sam 12:21
all that r. against thee be. 18:32
upon my right hand r. Job 30:12
they were not able to r. Ps 18:38
though war should r. against. 27:3
down, shall not be able to r. 36:12
at midnight I will r. to give. 119:62
into deep pits, that they r. 140:10
calamity shall r. suddenly. Pr 24:22
when the wicked r. a man. 28:12, 28
I will r. now and go about the city. S of S 3:2
prepare slaughter, that they do not r. Isa 14:21
earth shall fall and not r. 24:20
deceased, they shall not r. 26:14
now will I r. saith the Lord. 33:10
down together, they shall not r. 43:17
every tongue that shall r. thou. 54:17
shall thy light r. in obscurity. 58:10
fall and r. no more. Jer 25:27
Babylon shall not r. from evil. 51:64
Israel shall no more r. Amos 5:2
I will r. against the house of. 7:9
he maketh sun to r. on. Mat 5:45
and third day he shall r. again. 20:19
Mark 9:31; 10:34; Luke 18:33; 24:7
for nation shall r. against. Mat 24:7
Mark 13:8; Luke 21:10
many false prophets shall r. Mat 24:11; Mark 13:22
r., let us be going. Mat 26:46
after three days I will r. again. Mat 27:63; Mark 8:31
and should sleep, and r. Mark 4:27
be of good comfort, r.; he. 10:49
when they shall r. 12:23, 25
the dead, that they r. 26
trouble me not, I cannot r. Luke 11:7
though he will not r. because he. 8
when ye see a cloud r. out of. 12:54
Why sleep ye? r. and pray. 22:46
to suffer and to r. from. 24:46
Jesus saith, R. take up thy. John 5:8
thy brother shall r. again. 11:23
I know he shall r. 24
that he must r. again. 20:9
r. Peter, kill and eat. Acts 10:13
r. and stand upon thy feet. 26:16
should be the first that should r. 23
he that shall r. to reign. Rom 15:12
if so be the dead r. not. 1 Cor 15:15, 16, 29, 32
in Christ shall r. first. 1 Thes 4:16
another priest should r. Heb 7:11
r. and measure the temple. Rev 11:1

rise up
ye shall r. up early and go. Gen 19:2
that I cannot r. up. 31:35
r. up and stand before Pharaoh. Ex 8:20; 9:13
r. up and get you forth from. 12:31
thou shalt r. up before. Lev 19:32
r. up, Lord, let enemies. Num 10:35
call thee up, r. up and go. 22:20
r. up, Balak, and hear, thou. 23:18
behold, the people shall r. up. 24
Now, r. up, said I, and. Deut 2:13
r. ye up, and pass over the. 24
if a man r. up against his. 19:11
one witness shall not r. up. 15
if a false witness r. up against. 16
thine enemies that r. up. 28:7
the generation that shall r. up. 29:22
this people will r. up, and. 31:16
their gods, let them r. up. 32:38
then ye shall r. up from. Josh 8:7
a great flame r. up. Judg 20:38, 40
wherefore r. up early. 1 Sam 29:10
they said, Let us r. up. Neh 2:18
and the earth shall r. up. Job 20:27
many are they that r. up. Ps 3:1
save them from those that r. up. 17:7
me above those that r. up. 18:48
false witnesses did r. up, they. 35:11
he shall r. up no more. 41:8
them under that r. up against. 44:5
them that r. up against me. 59:1
the tumult of those that r. up. 74:23
desire of the wicked that r. up. 92:11
who will r. up for me against? 94:16
it is vain for you to r. up. 127:2
grieved with those that r. up? 139:21
her children r. up, and call. Pr 31:28
the ruler r. up against. Eccl 10:4
he shall r. up at the voice. 12:4
unto me, R. up, my love. S of S 2:10
woe unto them that r. up. Isa 5:11
I will r. up against them. 14:22
Lord shall r. up as in mount. 28:21
r. up, ye women at ease. 32:9
should r. up every man. Jer 37:10
behold, waters r. up out of. 47:2
gather against her, and r. up. 49:14
against them that r. up against. 51:1
I am not able to r. up. Lam 1:14
it shall r. up wholly. Amos 8:8; 9:5
and never r. up again. 14
let us r. up against Edom. Ob 1
affliction shall not r. up. Nah 1:9
they not r. up suddenly? Hab 2:7
until the day that I r. up. Zeph 3:8
his hand r. up against. Zech 14:13
children shall r. up against their. Mat 10:21; Mark 13:12
the men of Nineveh shall r. up. Mat 12:41; Luke 11:32
queen of the south shall r. up. Mat 12:42; Luke 11:31
and if Satan r. up. Mark 3:26
r. up, lo, he that betrayeth me. 14:42
to say, R. up and walk. Luke 5:23
he said, R. up and stand forth. 6:8
in the name of Jesus r. up. Acts 3:6
I saw a beast r. up out. Rev 13:1

risen
the sun was r. when Lot. Gen 19:23
if sun be r. on him. Ex 22:3
ye are r. up in your. Num 32:14
ye are r. up against my. Judg 9:18
and when she was r. up. Ruth 2:15
a man is r. to pursue. 1 Sam 25:29
whole family is r. up. 2 Sam 14:7
I am r. up in room of David. 1 Ki 8:20; 2 Chr 6:10
of the man of God was r. 2 Ki 6:15
of Solomon is r. up. 2 Chr 13:6
when Jehoram was r. up to. 21:4
but we are r. and stand. Ps 20:8
for false witnesses are r. up. 27:12
for strangers are r. up against. 54:3
the proud are r. against. 86:14
glory of the Lord is r. Isa 60:1
violence is r. into a rod. Ezek 7:11
for the waters were r. waters. 47:5
even of late my people is r. Mi 2:8
hath not r. a greater. Mat 11:11
is John the Baptist, he is r. 14:2
Mark 6:14, 16; Luke 9:7
until the Son of man be r. again. Mat 17:9; Mark 9:9
after I am r. I will go before. Mat 26:32; Mark 14:28
disciples steal him away and say he is r. Mat 27:64
he is not here: for he is r. as he said. 28:6; Mark 16:6
when Jesus was r. early. Mark 16:9
which had seen him after he was r. 14; John 21:14
that a great prophet is r. Luke 7:16
one of old prophets was r. 9:8, 19
master of the house is r. up. 13:25
the Lord is r. indeed, and. 24:34
when therefore he was r. John 2:22
must needs have r. again. Acts 17:3
yea rather that is r. again. Rom 8:34
then Christ is not r. 1 Cor 15:13
if Christ be not r. 14
but now is Christ r. 20
in baptism ye are also r. Col 2:12
if ye be r. with Christ, seek. 3:1
sun is no sooner r. Jas 1:11

risest
shalt talk of them when thou r. Deut 6:7; 11:19

riseth
as when a man r. against. Deut 22:26
cursed that r. up and. Josh 6:26
light when the sun r. 2 Sam 23:4
the sun and it r. not. Job 9:7
man lieth down, and r. not. 14:12
he r. up, and no man is sure. 24:22
he that r. up against me, as. 27:7
shall I do when God r. up? 31:14
just man falleth, and r. Pr 24:16
r. also while it is yet night. 31:15
know from whence it r. Isa 47:11
Egypt r. up like a flood. Jer 46:8
the daughter r. up against. Mi 7:6
Jesus r. from supper, and. John 13:4

rising, *substantive*
if in skin of his flesh a r. Lev 13:2
see if the r. be white. 10; 19:43
if the spot stay, it is a r. of. 13:28
this is the law for a r. and. 14:56
held spears from the r. Neh 4:21
whom there is no r. Pr 30:31
to the brightness of thy r. Isa 60:3
what the r. from the dead should mean. Mark 9:10
for the fall and r. of. Luke 2:34

sun-rising
toward the r. of the *sun*. Num 2:3
before Moab, toward *sun-r*. 21:11
34:15; Deut 4:41, 47; Josh 12:1; 13:5; 19:12, 27, 34
from the r. of the *sun*. Ps 50:1
from r. of *sun*, Lord's name. 113:3
from r. of *sun* shall he call. Isa 41:25
know from the r. of the *sun*. 45:6
glory from the r. of the *sun*. 59:19
from r. of *sun* my name. Mal 1:11
sepulchre at r. of the *sun*. Mark 16:2

rising
messengers, r. betimes. 2 Chr 36:15
my leanness r. in me. Job 16:8
wild asses go forth, r. betimes. 24:5
murderer r. with the light killeth. 14

his friend, r. early. Pr 27:14
I spake unto you, r. up early.
Jer 7:13; 25:3; 35:14
the prophets to you r. up early. 7:25
25:4; 26:5; 29:19; 35:15; 44:4
r. early, and protesting. 11:7
though I taught them, r. up. 32:33
sitting down and r. up. Lam 3:63
in the morning, r. before. Mark 1:35

rites

according to all the r. Num 9:3*

river

(*Frequently this word is used where the Hebrew really means a valley; or where the stream is small and hardly deserves the name. When the river is referred to it usually means the* Nile. *Where the expression* river of Egypt *is used it may mean* [1] *the* Nile, *or* [2] *a small brook or desert stream which formed one of the boundaries of Egypt. The word is also used symbolically of a great abundance*)

and passed over the r. Gen 31:21
Saul of Rehoboth by the r. 36:37
1 Chr 1:48
behold, he stood by the r. Gen 41:1
ye shall cast into the r. Ex 1:22
of Pharaoh came to wash at r. 2:5
the water of the r. shall become. 4:9
the r. shall die, and r. stink. 7:18
the r. shall bring forth frogs. 8:3
may remain in the r. only. 8:9, 11
journey, pass over the r. Deut 2:24*
Gilead even to the r. Arnon. 3:16
the city that is in the midst of the r.
Josh 13:9*; 2 Sam 24:5*
draw to the r. Kishon. Judg 4:7
r. Kishon that ancient r. swept. 5:21
draw that city into the r. 2 Sam 17:13
reigned over from the r. 1 Ki 4:21
are on this side the r. Ezra 4:10
no portion on this side the r. 16
governor on this side the r. 5:3
to r. that runneth to Ahava. 8:15
behold he drinketh up a r. Job 40:23
make them drink of the r. Ps 36:8
a r. the streams shall make. 46:4
thou enrichest it with the r. 65:9
have dominion from the r. to. 72:8
her branches unto the r. 80:11
in the dry places like a r. 105:41
them the waters of the r. Isa 8:7
shake his hand over the r. 11:15
and the r. shall be wasted. 19:5
the harvest of the r. is her. 23:3*
pass through thy land as a r. 10*
off from channel of the r. 27:12
peace been as a r. O daughter. 48:18
extend peace to her like a r. 66:12
drink the waters of the r. Jer 2:18
out her roots by the r. 17:8
let tears run down like r. Lam 2:18
My r. is mine own. Ezek 29:3, 9
it was a r. that I could not. 47:5
live whither the r. cometh. 9
afflict you to the r. of. Amos 6:14*
from the fortress to the r. Mi 7:12
his dominion from the r. Zech 9:10
deeps of the r. shall dry up. 10:11*
were baptized in the r. Mark 1:5
we went by a r. side. Acts 16:13
pure r. of water of life. Rev 22:1
on either side of the r. was the. 2
see **bank, beyond, brink, Chebar, Euphrates**

rivers

stretch out thine hand on the r.
Ex 7:19*; 8:5*
whatsoever hath fins in r. Lev 11:9
all that have not fins in the r. 10
to Jotbath, a land of r. Deut 10:7*
r. of Damascus better? 2 Ki 5:12
I have dried up all the r. 19:24
Isa 37:25
not see the r. of honey. Job 20:17
he cutteth out the r. among. 28:10*
poureth me out r. of oil. 29:6†
planted by the r. of water. Ps 1:3*
thou driedst up mighty r. 74:15
waters to run down like r. 78:16
had turned their r. into blood. 44
set his right hand in the r. Ps 89:25
turneth r. into a wilderness. 107:33
r. of waters run down. 119:136
by the r. of Babylon there we. 137:1
and r. of waters in the. Pr 5:16†
in the hand of the Lord, as r. 21:1*
all r. run into the sea. Eccl 1:7
eyes of doves by the r. of waters.
S of S 5:12*
hiss for the fly in the r. Isa 7:18
a nation, whose land r. 18:2, 7
and they shall turn the r. far. 19:6
and on every high hill r. 30:25†
a man shall be as r. of water. 32:2†
be to us a place of broad r. 33:21
I will open r. in high places. 41:18
I will make the r. islands. 42:15
passest through the r. they. 43:2
and I will make r. in the. 19, 20
be dry, and will dry up thy r. 44:27
the thigh, pass over the r. 47:2
I make r. a wilderness, their. 50:2
them to walk by the r. Jer 31:9
are moved as the r. 46:7, 8
down with r. of waters. Lam 3:48†
Lord to the hills and r. Ezek 6:3*
that lieth in the midst of his r. 29:3
the fish of thy r. to stick to thy scales
. . . out of the midst of thy r. 4
and all the fish of thy r. 5
against thee, and against thy r. 10
I will make the r. dry, and. 30:12
him up on high with her r. 31:4
broken by the r. of the land. 12*
thou camest forth with thy r. 32:2
and the r. shall be full of thee. 6*
then will I cause their r. to run. 14
them on mountains by the r. 34:13*
in all thy r. shall they fall. 35:8*
say to the hills, to the r. and. 36:6*
whithersoever the r. shall. 47:9
for the r. of waters are. Joel 1:20*
all the r. of Judah shall flow. 3:18*
ten thousands of r. of oil. Mi 6:7
and drieth up the r. Nah 1:4
the gates of the r. shall be. 2:6
that was situate among the r. 3:8
displeased against the r.? Hab 3:8
didst cleave the earth with r. 9
flow r. of living water. John 7:38
on the third part of the r. Rev 8:10
poured out his vial on the r. 16:4

Rizpah

whose name was R. 2 Sam 3:7
two sons of R. to Gibeonites. 21:8
R. spread sackcloth for her on. 10

road

ye made a r. to-day. 1 Sam 27:10*

roar

let the sea r. 1 Chr 16:32; Ps 96:11
98:7
though waters thereof r. Ps 46:3
thine enemies r. in thy. 74:4
the young lions r. after their. 104:21
r. like young lions. Isa 5:29
in that day they shall r. against. 30
Lord shall r.; he shall prevail. 42:13*
we r. all like bears, and. 59:11
though they r. yet can. Jer 5:22
the Lord shall r. from on high. 25:30
when the waves thereof r. 31:35
their voice shall r. like the. 50:42
they shall r. together like lions. 51:38
when her waves do r. like great. 55
r. like a lion, when he shall r.
Hos 11:10
the Lord shall r. out of Zion.
Joel 3:16; Amos 1:2
will a lion r. if he hath? Amos 3:4

roared

lion r. against Samson. Judg 14:5
I have r. by reason of. Ps 38:8†
the sea, whose waves r. Isa 51:15
the young lions r. upon him. Jer 2:15
the lion hath r., who will? Amos 3:8

roareth

after it a voice r. he. Job 37:4
their voice r. like the sea. Jer 6:23
cried, as when a lion r. Rev 10:3

roaring, *substantive*

the r. of the lion. Job 4:10
from the words of my r.? Ps 22:1†
old through my r. all the. Ps 33:3†
king's wrath is as the r. Pr 19:12
the fear of a king is as the r. 20:2
their r. shall be like a lion. Isa 5:29
roar like the r. of the sea. 30
land was desolate by the noise of his
r. Ezek 19:7
a voice of the r. of young. Zech 11:3

roaring

upon me as a r. lion. Ps 22:13
as a r. lion, so is a wicked. Pr 28:15
as the young lion r. on. Isa 31:4*
conspiracy, like a r. lion. Ezek 22:25
within her are r. lions. Zeph 3:3
sea and the waves r. Luke 21:25
the devil, as a r. lion. 1 Pet 5:8

roarings

my r. are poured out. Job 3:24†

roast, -ed

flesh that night, r. with fire. Ex 12:8
but r. with fire. 9; Deut 16:7
flesh to r. for the priest. 1 Sam 2:15
they r. the passover. 2 Chr 35:13
he roasteth r., is satisfied. Isa 44:16
yea, also I have r. flesh, and. 19
king of Babylon r. in fire. Jer 29:22

roasteth

the slothful man r. not. Pr 12:27

rob

not r. thy neighbour. Lev 19:13
beasts, which shall r. you. 26:22
they r. the threshing. 1 Sam 23:1
r. not the poor, because. Pr 22:22
and that they may r. Isa 10:2*
the lot of them that r. us. 17:14
spoil, and r. those that. Ezek 39:10
will a man r. God? yet ye. Mal 3:8

robbed

and they r. all that came. Judg 9:25
in minds, as a bear r. 2 Sam 17:8
wicked have r. me. Ps 119:61*
let a bear r. of her whelps. Pr 17:12
I have r. their treasures. Isa 10:13
but this is a people r. and. 42:22
treasures, they shall be r. Jer 50:37
give again that he had r. Ezek 33:15
rob those that r. them. 39:10
r. me, wherein have we r.? Mal 3:8
with a curse, for ye have r. me. 9
I r. other churches. 2 Cor 11:8

robber

and the r. swalloweth up. Job 5:5*
and the r. shall prevail. 18:9*
beget a son that is a r. Ezek 18:10
is a thief and a r. John 10:1
Now Barabbas was a r. 18:40

robbers

tabernacles of r. prosper. Job 12:6
gave Israel to the r. Isa 42:24
house become a den of r.? Jer 7:11
the r. shall enter into it. Ezek 7:22
the r. of thy people. Dan 11:14*
troops of r. wait for a. Hos 6:9
and the troop of r. spoileth. 7:1
if r. by night, would they not? Ob 5
came before me are r. John 10:8
these men are not r. of. Acts 19:37
of waters, in perils of r. 2 Cor 11:26

robbery

and become not vain in r. Ps 62:10
the r. of the wicked shall. Pr 21:7*
I hate r. for burnt offering. Isa 61:8
have exercised r. and. Ezek 22:29
who store up r. in their. Amos 3:10
city is full of lies and r. Nah 3:1*
who thought it no r. to. Phil 2:6*

robbeth

whoso r. his father or. Pr 28:24

robe

make an ephod, and a r. Ex 28:4
shalt make the r. of the ephod. 31
on the hem of the r. 34; 39:25, 26
Aaron the coat and r. 29:5; Lev 8:7
stripped himself of his r. 1 Sam 18:4
off the skirt of Saul's r. 24:4
see the skirt of thy r. in my hand . . .
the skirt of thy r. and killed. 11
was clothed with a r. 1 Chr 15:27
judgement was as a r. Job 29:14
clothe him with thy r. Isa 22:21
hath covered me with r. of. 61:10

laid his *r.* from him. *Jonah* 3:6
ye pull off the *r.* with the garment. *Mi* 2:8
put on Jesus a scarlet *r.* *Mat* 27:28
after that, they took the *r.* off. 31
bring forth the best *r.* *Luke* 15:22
arrayed him in a gorgeous *r.* 23:11*
on Jesus a purple *r.* *John* 19:2*
wearing the purple *r.* 5*

robes

with such *r.* were virgins apparelled. *2 Sam* 13:18
having put on their *r.* *1 Ki* 22:10
put thou on thy *r.* 30; *2 Chr* 18:9, 29
shall lay away their *r.* *Ezek* 26:16
desire to walk in long *r.* *Luke* 20:46
and white *r.* were given. *Rev* 6:11
the Lamb, clothed with white *r.* 7:9
which are arrayed in white *r.*? 13
which have washed their *r.* 14

rock

before thee upon the *r.* *Ex* 17:6
thou shalt stand upon a *r.* 33:21
put thee in a cleft of the *r.* 22
speak to the *r.* before. *Num* 20:8
fetch you water out of this *r.*? 10
his rod smote the *r.* twice. 11
and thou puttest thy nest in a *r.* 24:21
thee water out of the *r.* *Deut* 8:15
he is the *R.*, his work is perfect. 32:4
suck honey and oil out of the *r.* 13
he lightly esteemed the *r.* of. 15
of the *R.* that begat thee thou. 18
except their *R.* had sold them. 30
for their *r.* is not as our *R.* 31
where is their *r.* in whom they? 37
and lay them upon this *r.* *Judg* 6:20
there rose up fire out of the *r.* 21
altar to the Lord on this *r.* 26*
they slew Oreb on the *r.* Oreb. 7:25
Manoah offered it on a *r.* to. 13:19
in the top of the *r.* Etam. 15:8
turned to the *r.* of Rimmon. 20:45
neither is there any *r.* *1 Sam* 2:2
a sharp *r.* on one side, sharp *r.* 14:4
David came down into a *r.* 23:25
sackcloth on the *r.* *2 Sam* 21:10
he said, Lord is my *r.* 22:2
Ps 18:2; 92:15
the God of my *r.* in him. *2 Sam* 22:3
and who is a *r.* save our God? 32
Ps 18:31
blessed be my *r.* . . . exalted be the God of *r.* *2 Sam* 22:47; *Ps* 18:46
God of Israel said, The *r.* *2 Sam* 23:3
captains went to the *r.* *1 Chr* 11:15
from the top of the *r.* *2 Chr* 25:12
water for them out of the *r.* for their. *Neh* 9:15; *Ps* 78:16; 105:41
the *r.* is removed out of. *Job* 14:18
and shall the *r.* be removed? 18:4
that they were graven in the *r.* 19:24
they embrace the *r.* for want of. 24:8
forth his hand upon the *r.* 28:9
and the *r.* poured out rivers. 29:6
time when wild goats of the *r.* 39:1
on the *r.* on the crag of the *r.* 28
set me up upon a *r.* *Ps* 27:5; 40:2
will I cry, O Lord, my *r.* 28:1
r. for an house of defence. 31:2
my *r.* and my fortress. 3; 71:3
I will say to God, My *r.* why? 42:9
lead me to the *r.* that is higher. 61:2
God only is my *r.* 62:2, 6
r. of my strength. 7
behold, he smote the *r.* 78:20
remembered that God was their *r.* 35
with honey out of the *r.* have. 81:16
r. of my salvation. 89:26
r. of my refuge. 94:22
make a joyful noise to the *r.* 95:1
which turned the *r.* into a. 114:8
way of a serpent upon a *r.* *Pr* 30:19
art in the clefts of the *r.* *S of S* 2:14
enter into the *r.* and hide. *Isa* 2:10
r. of offence to both houses. 8:14
slaughter of the *r.* of Oreb. 10:26
not mindful of the *r.* of thy. 17:10
an habitation for himself in a *r.* 22:16
as the shadow of a great *r.* 32:2
let inhabitants of the *r.* sing. 42:11*
caused waters to flow out of *r.* 48:21
look unto the *r.* whence ye. 51:1
faces harder than a *r.* *Jer* 5:3
girdle in a hole of the *r.* 13:4
which cometh from the *r.* 18:14
thee, O inhabitant of the *r.* 21:13
a hammer that breaketh the *r.* 23:29
cities, and dwell in the *r.* 48:28
dwellest in the clefts of the *r.* 49:16
it upon the top of a *r.* *Ezek* 24:7
blood upon the top of a *r.* 8
her like the top of a *r.* 26:4, 14
horses run upon the *r.*? *Amos* 6:12
in the clefts of the *r.* *Ob* 3
built his house upon a *r.* *Mat* 7:24
founded upon a *r.* 25; *Luke* 6:48*
upon this *r.* I will build. *Mat* 16:18
own new tomb, which he had hewn out in the *r.* 27:60; *Mark* 15:46
some fell upon a *r.* *Luke* 8:6
they on the *r.* 13
in Sion a stumbling stone, and *r.* of. *Rom* 9:33; *1 Pet* 2:8
spiritual *r.* that followed them, and that *r.* was Christ. *1 Cor* 10:4

rocks

for from the top of the *r.* *Num* 23:9
the people hid themselves in *r.* *1 Sam* 13:6
seek David upon the *r.* 24:2
brake in pieces the *r.* *1 Ki* 19:11
rivers among the *r.* *Job* 28:10
caves of the earth, and in *r.* 30:6
the *r.* in the wilderness. *Ps* 78:15
and the *r.* are a refuge for. 104:18
they their houses in the *r.* *Pr* 30:26
go into the holes of the *r.* *Isa* 2:19
the *r.* and tops of the ragged *r.* 21
rest in the holes of the *r.* 7:19
shall be the munitions of *r.* 33:16
under the clefts of the *r.* 57:5
city shall climb on the *r.* *Jer* 4:29
out of the holes of the *r.* 16:16
roll thee down from the *r.* 51:25
the *r.* are thrown down. *Nah* 1:6
quake, and the *r.* rent. *Mat* 27:51
have fallen upon the *r.* *Acts* 27:29*
in the dens and in the *r.* *Rev* 6:15
and said to the *r.*, Fall on us. 16

rod

(*This word is often used to mean the* shepherd's crook)

became a *r.* in his hand. *Ex* 4:4
thou shalt take this *r.* in thine. 17
Moses took the *r.* of God in. 20; 17:9
to Aaron, Take thy *r.* 7:9, 19
down every man his *r.* 12
he lifted up the *r.* and. 20; 14:16
smite a servant with a *r.* 21:20
passeth under the *r.* *Lev* 27:32
man's name on his *r.* *Num* 17:2
the *r.* of Aaron for the house of. 8
with his *r.* he smote the rock. 20:11
forth the end of the *r.* *1 Sam* 14:27
him with the *r.* of men. *2 Sam* 7:14
let him take his *r.* away. *Job* 9:34
neither is the *r.* of God upon. 21:9
break them with a *r.* of iron. *Ps* 2:9
thy *r.* and thy staff they. 23:4
remember the *r.* of thine. 74:2*
transgression with a *r.* 89:32
the Lord shall send the *r.* of. 110:2
r. of wicked shall not rest on. 125:3*
a *r.* for the back of. *Pr* 10:13; 26:3
he that spareth his *r.* hateth. 13:24
the foolish is a *r.* of pride. 14:3
r. of his anger shall fail. 22:8
the *r.* of correction shall drive. 15
beat him with the *r.* 23:13, 14
the *r.* and reproof give. 29:15
thou hast broken the *r.* of. *Isa* 9:4
O Assyrian, the *r.* of mine. 10:5
as if the *r.* should shake itself. 15
he shall smite with a *r.* and lift. 24
as his *r.* was on the sea, so. 26
shall come forth a *r.* out of. 11:1*
shall smite the earth with the *r.* 4
the *r.* of him that smote thee. 14:29
is beaten out with a *r.* 28:27
which smote with a *r.* 30:31
and said, I see a *r.* of an. *Jer* 1:11
Israel the *r.* of his inheritance. 10:16*; 51:19*
how is the beautiful *r.* broken! 48:17
by the *r.* of his wrath. *Lam* 3:1
the *r.* hath blossomed. *Ezek* 7:10
violence is risen up into a *r.* 11
out of a *r.* of her branches, so that she hath no strong *r.* to. 19:14
pass under the *r.* and bring. 20:37
the *r.* of my son. 21:10, 13
smite Judge of Israel with a *r.* *Mi* 5:1
hear ye the *r.* and who hath. 6:9
feed thy people with thy *r.* 7:14
you with a *r.* or in love? *1 Cor* 4:21
wherein was Aaron's *r.* *Heb* 9:4
with a *r.* of iron. *Rev* 2:27; 19:15
given me a reed like to a *r.* 11:1
all nations with a *r.* of iron. 12:5

rode

Rebekah and her damsels *r.* on. *Gen* 24:61
thirty sons that *r.* on. *Judg* 10:4
nephews that *r.* on ass colts. 12:14
Abigail *r.* on the ass. *1 Sam* 25:20, 42
four hundred which *r.* on camels. 30:17
Absalom *r.* upon a mule. *2 Sam* 18:9
he *r.* on a cherub, and did fly. 22:11
Ps 18:10
the old prophet *r.* on. *1 Ki* 13:13
and Ahab *r.* and went to. 18:45
Jehu *r.* in a chariot, and. *2 Ki* 9:16
remember when I and thou *r.* 25
save the beast that I *r.* *Neh* 2:12
the posts that *r.* on the. *Esth* 8:14

rods

Jacob took *r.* of green. *Gen* 30:37
might conceive among the *r.* 41
Aaron's rod swallowed up their *r.* *Ex* 7:12
gave him twelve *r.* *Num* 17:6
and Moses laid up the *r.* before. 7
she had strong *r.* for the. *Ezek* 19:11
her strong *r.* were broken and. 12
was I beaten with *r.* *2 Cor* 11:25

roe, -s

as swift as the *r.* on. *1 Chr* 12:8
as the hind and pleasant *r.* *Pr* 5:19*
deliver thyself as the *r.* from. 6:5
I charge you by the *r.* and hinds. *S of S* 2:7; 3:5
is like a *r.* or a young hart. 9
be thou like a *r.* or hart. 2:17; 8:14
it shall be as the chased *r.* *Isa* 13:14

see young

wild **roe**

Asahel was as light of foot as a *wild r.* *2 Sam* 2:18

roebuck, -s

ye may eat of the *r.* *Deut* 12:15*, 22*
14:5*; 15:22*
besides harts and *r.* *1 Ki* 4:23*

roll, *verb*

we cannot, till they *r.* *Gen* 29:8
and Joshua said, *R.* *Josh* 10:18
r. a great stone unto me this day. *1 Sam* 14:33
and I will *r.* thee down. *Jer* 51:25
in Aphrah, *r.* thyself. *Mi* 1:10
who shall *r.* us away? *Mark* 16:3

roll, *substantive*

found at Achmetha a *r.* *Ezra* 6:2
take thee a great *r.* and. *Isa* 8:1*
take thee a *r.* of a book. *Jer* 36:2
go and read in the *r.* 6
till after the *r.* was consumed. 23
take another *r.* 28
saith Lord, Thou hast burnt this *r.* 29
an hand was sent unto me, and lo, a *r.* *Ezek* 2:9
eat this *r.* 3:1
he caused me to eat that *r.* 2
fill thy bowels with this *r.* that. 3
and behold a flying *r.* *Zech* 5:1, 2

rolled

they *r.* the stone from. *Gen* 29:3
that Jacob went near, and *r.* 10
I have *r.* away reproach of. *Josh* 5:9
in desolation they *r.* *Job* 30:14
with noise, and garments *r.* *Isa* 9:5
the heavens shall be *r.* together. 34:4; *Rev* 6:14
his own new tomb, he *r.* a great stone to door. *Mat* 27:60; *Mark* 15:46

angel came and r. back. Mark 28:2
the stone was r. away. 16:4
found the stone r. away. Luke 24:2

roller

bound up, to put a r. to. Ezek 30:21

rolleth

he that r. a stone, it will. Pr 26:27

rolling

nations shall flee like a r. thing. Isa 17:13*

rolls

search was made in the house of the r. Ezra 6:1*

Roman

a man that is a R. Acts 22:25, 26
tell me, Art thou a R.? 27
that he was a R. 29; 23:27

Romans

the R. shall come and. John 11:48
us to observe, being R. Acts 16:21
beaten us, being R. 37
heard they were R. 38
prisoner into hands of the R. 28:17

Rome

strangers of R. we do. Acts 2:10
all Jews to depart from R. 18:2
I must see R. 19:21
bear witness also at R. 23:11
we came to R., Paul dwelt. 28:16
to all that be in R., beloved. Rom 1:7
preach gospel to you that are at R. 15
when he was in R. he. 2 Tim 1:17

roof

under the shadow of my r. Gen 19:8
a battlement for thy r. Deut 22:8
the r. and hid with flax which she had laid in order on r. Josh 2:6
on the r. were 3000. Judg 16:27
David walked on the r. . . . and from the r. he saw a woman. 2 Sam 11:2
watchman went up to the r. 18:24
booths on the r. of his. Neh 8:16
gate from the r. of one. Ezek 40:13
that thou shouldest come under my r. Mat 8:8; Luke 7:6
they uncovered the r. Mark 2:4

roof with *mouth*

tongue cleaved to r. of their mouth. Job 29:10
cleave to r. of my mouth. Ps 137:6
the r. of thy mouth like. S of S 7:9
cleaveth to r. of his mouth. Lam 4:4
tongue cleave to r. of thy mouth. Ezek 3:26

roofs

on whose r. they burnt incense. Jer 19:13; 32:29

room

is there r. in thy father's? Gen 24:23
we have r. to lodge in. 25
r. for the camels. 31
Lord hath made r. for us. 26:22
captain in the r. of Joab. 2 Sam 19:13
in Joab's r. and he put Zadok the priest in the r. of. 1 Ki 2:35
had anointed him king in the r. 5:1
thy son whom I will set in thy r. 5
I am risen in the r. of David. 8:20 2 Chr 6:10
thou anoint in thy r. 1 Ki 19:16
my feet in a large r. Ps 31:8*
thou preparedst r. before it. 80:9
a man's gift maketh r. Pr 18:16
shall not be r. enough. Mal 3:10
Archelaus reigned in the r. Mat 2:22
that there was no r. to. Mark 2:2
he will shew you a large upper r. 14:15; Luke 22:12
because there was no r. Luke 2:7
I have no r. to bestow my. 12:17
sit not down in the highest r. 14:8*
shame to take the lowest r. 9*
and sit down in the lowest r. 10*
it is done, and yet there is r. 22
went up to an upper r. Acts 1:13
Festus came into Felix' r. 24:27*
that occupieth the r. 1 Cor 14:16*

rooms

r. shalt thou make in the. Gen 6:14
captains in their r. 1 Ki 20:24
and dwelt in their r. 1 Chr 4:41*

uppermost r. at feasts. Mat 23:6* Mark 12:39*; Luke 20:46*
chose out the chief r. Luke 14:7*

root, *substantive*

a r. that beareth gall. Deut 29:18
out of Ephraim was a r. Judg 5:14
again take r. downward. 2 Ki 19:30
the foolish taking r. Job 5:3
though the r. thereof wax old. 14:8
seeing the r. of the matter is. 19:28
my r. was spread out by the. 29:19
the vine to take deep r. Ps 80:9
r. of the righteous shall. Pr 12:3
the r. of the righteous yieldeth. 12
so their r. shall be rottenness, and. Isa 5:24
there shall be a r. of Jesse. 11:10 Rom 15:12
for out of the serpent's r. Isa 14:29
I will kill thy r. with famine. 30
that come of Jacob to take r. 27:6 37:31
their stock shall not take r. 40:24
as a r. out of a dry ground. 53:2
have taken r.: they grow. Jer 12:2
r. was by great waters. Ezek 31:7
out of a branch of her r. Dan 11:7
smitten, their r. is dried. Hos 9:16
neither r. nor branch. Mal 4:1
axe is laid unto the r. of the trees. Mat 3:10; Luke 3:9
because they had not r. Mat 13:6 21; Mark 4:6, 17; Luke 8:13
thou plucked up by the r. Luke 17:6
if the r. be holy, so are. Rom 11:16
with them partakest of the r. 17
thou bearest not the r. but the r. 18
love of money is the r. 1 Tim 6:10
lest any r. of bitterness. Heb 12:15
r. of David hath prevailed. Rev 5:5
I am the r. and offspring of. 22:16

root

he shall r. up Israel. 1 Ki 14:15
and would r. out all. Job 31:12
and r. thee out of the land. Ps 52:5
have set thee to r. out. Jer 1:10*
lest ye r. up the wheat. Mat 13:29

rooted

the Lord r. them out. Deut 29:28
confidence shall be r. out. Job 18:14
let my offspring be r. out. 31:8
trangressors shall be r. out of it. Pr 2:22
Ekron shall be r. up. Zeph 2:4
not planted, shall be r. Mat 15:13
being r. and grounded. Eph 3:17
r. and built up in him. Col 2:7

roots

them up by the r. 2 Chr 7:20
his r. are wrapped about. Job 8:17
his r. shall be dried up. 18:16
the mountains by the r. 28:9
juniper r. for their meat. 30:4
shall grow out of his r. Isa 11:1
that spreadeth out her r. Jer 17:8
and the r. thereof were. Ezek 17:6
this vine did bend her r. toward. 7
not pull up the r. thereof? 9
the stump of his r. Dan 4:15, 23, 26
first horns plucked up by the r. 7:8
he shall cast forth his r. as. Hos 14:5
I destroyed his r. from. Amos 2:9
tree dried up from the r. Mark 11:20
dead, plucked up by the r. Jude 12

ropes

bind me with new r. Judg 16:11, 12
all Israel bring r. to. 2 Sam 17:13
let us put r. on our. 1 Ki 20:31, 32
the soldiers cut off the r. Acts 27:32

rose, *substantive*

I am the r. of Sharon, and. S of S 2:1
shall blossom as the r. Isa 35:1

rose, *verb*

Cain r. up against Abel. Gen 4:8
Lot r. up to meet them, and. 19:1
Abraham r. early, and went. 22:3
Esau did eat, and r. up, and. 25:34
the sun r. upon him as he. 32:31
his sons and daughters r. to. 37:35
nor r. any from his place. Ex 10:23
Pharaoh r. up in the night. 12:30

overthrown them that r. up. Ex 15:7
and all the people r. up and. 33:10
Phinehas r. up from. Num 25:7
the Lord r. up from Seir. Deut 33:2
the waters stood and r. Josh 3:16
there r. up fire out of. Judg 6:21
the men of Gibeah r. up. 20:5
she r. up before one. Ruth 3:14
them that r. up against me, hast thou. 2 Sam 22:40; Ps 18:39
and the king r. up to. 1 Ki 2:19
the lepers r. in the. 2 Ki 7:5
the leprosy r. up in his. 2 Chr 26:19
expressed by name r. up. 28:15
our side when men r. up. Ps 124:2
I r. up to open to my. S of S 5:5
then r. up certain of the. Jer 26:17
the lips of those that r. up. Lam 3:62
then Nebuchadnezzar r. Dan 3:24
I r. up and did the king's. 8:27
but Jonah r. up to flee. Jonah 1:3
they r. early and corrupted. Zech 3:7
r. up, and thrust him out. Luke 4:29
and he left all, r. up, and. 5:28
though one r. from the dead. 16:31
when he r. from prayer and. 22:45
they r. up the same hour, and. 24:33
Mary, that she r. up. John 11:31
then high priest r. up, and. Acts 5:17
these days r. up Theudas. 36
drink with him after he r. 10:41
king r. up, and the governor. 26:30
Christ both died and r. Rom 14:9*
the people did eat, and r. 1 Cor 10:7
he was buried and r. again. 15:4
preached that he r. from the dead. 12
who died and r. again. 2 Cor 5:15
Jesus died and r. again. 1 Thes 4:14
her smoke r. up for ever. Rev 19:3
see **morning**

rot

the Lord make thy thigh to r. Num 5:21*, 22*, 27*
name of the wicked shall r. Pr 10:7
a tree that will not r. Isa 40:20

rotten

and he, as a r. thing. Job 13:28
esteemeth brass as r. wood. 41:27
so Ebed-melech took old r. Jer 38:11
put now these r. rags under. 12
the seed is r. under their. Joel 1:17

rottenness

maketh ashamed, is as r. Pr 12:4
envy is the r. of the bones. 14:30
so their root shall be as r. Isa 5:24
to the house of Judah as r. Hos 5:12
when I heard r. entered. Hab 3:16

rough

heifer to a r. valley. Deut 21:4*
he stayeth his r. wind in. Isa 27:8
and the r. places shall be. 40:4
horses to come as r. Jer 51:27
the r. goat is the king. Dan 8:21
shall they wear a r. Zech 13:4*
and the r. ways shall be. Luke 3:5

roughly

Joseph spake r. Gen 42:7, 30
father answer thee r.? 1 Sam 20:10
answered the people r. and forsook. 1 Ki 12:13; 2 Chr 10:13
but the rich answereth r. Pr 18:23

round, *verb*

ye shall not r. the corners. Lev 19:27

round

compassed the house r. Gen 19:4
there lay a small r. thing. Ex 16:14
shall environ us r. Josh 7:9
the molten sea was r. 1 Ki 7:23
a r. compass. 35
top of the throne was r. 10:19
Bashan have beset me r. Ps 22:12
navel is like a r. goblet. S of S 7:2
take away their r. tires. Isa 3:18
shall compass thee r. Luke 19:43

round *about*

God was on cities r. about. Gen 35:5
digged r. about the river. Ex 7:24
morning dew lay r. about. 16:13
bounds to the people r. about. 19:12
house to be scraped r. about. Lev 14:41

Levites encamp r. about tabernacle. Num 1:50
Moses set the elders r. about. 11:24
all Israel, that were r. about. 16:34
up all that are r. about us. 22:4
people r. about you. Deut 6:14; 13:7
all your enemies r. about. 12:10
25:19; Josh 21:44; 2 Chr 15:15
measure the cities r. about him. Deut 21:2
and ye shall go r. about. Josh 6:3
house r. about. Judg 19:22; 20:5
Saul compassed David r. about. 1 Sam 23:26
sent into the land of Philistines r. about. 31:9; 1 Chr 10:9
he made darkness pavilions r. about him. 2 Sam 22:12; Ps 18:11
had peace on all sides r. about. 1 Ki 4:24
fame was in all nations r. about. 31
water ran r. about the altar. 18:35
of fire r. about Elisha. 2 Ki 6:17
they lodged r. about. 1 Chr 9:27
fashioned me r. about. Job 10:8
compass me r. about. 16:13
his troops encamp r. about. 19:12
snares are r. about thee. 22:10
it is turned r. about by his. 37:12
his teeth are terrible r. about. 41:14
against me r. about. Ps 3:6
above mine enemies r. about. 27:6
r. about them that fear him. 34:7
them that are r. about. 44:13; 79:4
Zion, and go r. about her. 48:12
go r. about the city. 59:6, 14
let all r. about him bring. 76:11
they came r. about me daily. 88:17
faithfulness r. about thee. 89:8
his enemies r. about him. 97:3
as the mountains are r. about. 125:2
olive plants r. about thy table. 128:3
I will camp against thee r. about. Isa 29:3
set him on fire r. about. 42:25
up thine eyes r. about. 49:18; 60:4
devour all things r. about. Jer 21:14
for fear was r. about, saith. 46:5*
against Babylon r. about. 50:29
shall be against her r. about. 51:2
full of eyes r. about. Ezek 10:12
will make places r. about. 34:26
gather yourselves together r. about. Joel 3:11
judge all the heathen r. about. 12
even r. about the land. Amos 3:11
me r. about, the weeds. Jonah 2:5
a wall of fire r. about. Zech 2:5
the vineyard r. about. Mat 21:33
all that dwelt r. about. Luke 1:65
the Lord shone r. about them. 2:9
shined r. about him a light. Acts 9:3
r. about to Illyricum, I. Rom 15:19
was a rainbow r. about. Rev 4:3
r. about the throne were four. 4
angels r. about the throne. 5:11
see **camp**

rouse
lion; who shall r. him up? Gen 49:9

rovers
they helped David against the r. 1 Chr 12:21

row, -s
four r. of stones. Ex 28:17; 39:10
the first r. 28:17; 39:10
the second r. 28:18; 39:11
the third r. 28:19; 39:12
the fourth r. 28:20; 39:13
cakes, six on a r. on the. Lev 24:6
pure frankincense on each r. 7
inner court with three r. 1 Ki 6:36
four r. of cedar pillars. 7:2
fifteen in a r. 3
there were windows in three r. 4
round about was with three r. 12
two r. with pomegranates. 18, 42
2 Chr 4:13
two r. of oxen cast. 2 Chr 4:3
a r. of new timber, three r. of. Ezra 6:4
thy cheeks comely with r. of jewels. S of S 1:10
boiling places under r. Ezek 46:23

rowed
men r. hard to bring it. Jonah 1:13
when they had r. 25 or. John 6:19

rowers
thy r. brought thee. Ezek 27:26

rowing
he saw them toiling in r. Mark 6:48

royal
shall yield r. dainties. Gen 49:20
as one of the r. cities. Josh 10:2
why dwell in the r. city? 1 Sam 27:5
and took the r. city. 2 Sam 12:26
her of his r. bounty. 1 Ki 10:13
mother of Ahaziah destroyed all the seed r. 2 Ki 11:1; 2 Chr 22:10
on Solomon r. majesty. 1 Chr 29:25
they gave them r. wine. Esth 1:7
the queen with the crown r. 11
give her r. estate to another that. 19
was taken into his house r. 2:16
so that he set the crown r. on. 17
Esther put on her r. apparel, and king sat on his r. throne in his r. 5:1
let r. apparel be brought, and the crown r. 6:8
Mordecai went in r. apparel. 8:15
a r. diadem in the hand. Isa 62:3
spread his r. pavilion. Jer 43:10
to establish a r. statute. Dan 6:7
Herod arrayed in r. Acts 12:21
if ye fulfil the r. law, ye. Jas 2:8
ye are a r. priesthood. 1 Pet 2:9

rubbing
and did eat, r. them in. Luke 6:1

rubbish
the stones out of the r. Neh 4:2
decayed and there is much r. 10

rubies
price of wisdom is above r. Job 28:18; Pr 8:11
is more precious than r. Pr 3:15
gold, and a multitude of r. 20:15
for her price is far above r. 31:10
were more ruddy than r. Lam 4:7

rudder bands
and loosed the r. bands. Acts 27:40

ruddy
David was r. and beautiful. 1 Sam 16:12; 17:42
my beloved is white and r. chiefest. S of S 5:10
Nazarites were more r. Lam 4:7

rude
though I be r. in speech. 2 Cor 11:6

rudiments
you after the r. of the. Col 2:8
if dead with Christ from the r. 20

rue
for ye tithe mint, and r. Luke 11:42

Rufus
Simon, father of Alexander and R. Mark 15:21
salute R. chosen in the. Rom 16:13

Ruhamah
say to your sisters, R. Hos 2:1

ruin
but they were the r. 2 Chr 28:23
brought his holds to r. Ps 89:40
who knoweth the r. of? Pr 24:22*
a flattering mouth worketh r. 26:28
and let this r. be under. Isa 3:6
land of the Chaldeans to r. 23:13
of a defenced city a r. 25:2
shall not be your r. Ezek 18:30
shall fall in the day of thy r. 27:27
upon his r. shall all the fowls. 31:13
it fell, the r. of that house. Luke 6:49

ruined
Jerusalem is r. and Judah. Isa 3:8
and the r. cities are. Ezek 36:35
I the Lord build the r. places. 36

ruinous
be to lay waste fenced cities into r. heaps. 2 Ki 19:25; Isa 37:26
it shall be a r. heap. Isa 17:1

ruins
that their r. may be. Ezek 21:15*
will I raise up his r. Amos 9:11
I will build again the r. Acts 15:16

rule, *substantive*
that had r. over Ahab's. 1 Ki 22:31
Jews had r. over them. Esth 9:1
shall have r. over a son. Pr 17:2
for a servant to have r. over. 19:10
he that hath no r. over his. 25:28*
yet shall he have r. over. Eccl 2:19
stretcheth out his r. Isa 44:13*
never barest r. over them. 63:19
have put down all r. 1 Cor 15:24
to the measure of the r. 2 Cor 10:13*
be enlarged according to our r. 15*
walk according to this r. Gal 6:16
let us walk by the same r. Phil 3:16
remember them that have r. over. Heb 13:7
obey them that have the r. over. 17
salute all them that have the r. 24
see **bare, bear**

rule
the greater light to r. the day, and lesser light to r. the. Gen 1:16
to r. over the day, and over. 18
and thy husband shall r. over. 3:16
desire, thou shalt r. over him. 4:7
not r. over him with rigour. Lev 25:43; 46:53
r. thou over us, thou. Judg 8:22
r. over you, nor shall my son r. 23
r. thou in the midst of thine enemies. Ps 110:2
sun to r. by day, for his mercy. 136:8
moon and stars to r. by night. 9
by me princes r. and. Pr 8:16
babes shall r. over them. Isa 3:4
as for my people, women r. 12
r. over their oppressors. 14:2
a fierce king shall r. over. 19:4
that r. this people that is in. 28:14
princes shall r. in judgement. 32:1
and his arm shall r. for him. 40:10
who made the righteous man r.? 41:2
they that r. over them make. 52:5
no strong rod to be a sceptre to r. Ezek 19:14
poured out, will I r. over you. 20:33
they shall no more r. over. 29:15
known that the heavens r. Dan 4:26
shall stand up, that shall r. 11:3
cause them to r. over many. 39
that the heathen should r. Joel 2:17
sit and r. on his throne. Zech 6:13
a governor that shall r. Mat 2:6*
who are accounted to r. Mark 10:42
let the peace of God r. Col 3:15
not how to r. his house. 1 Tim 3:5
elders that r. well, worthy of. 5:17
r. with a rod. Rev 2:27; 12:5; 19:15

ruled
his eldest servant that r. Gen 24:2
word shall all my people be r. 41:40
three thousand r. over. 1 Ki 5:16
have r. over all countries. Ezra 4:20
they that hated them r. Ps 106:41
he that r. nations in anger. Isa 14:6
servants have r. over us. Lam 5:8
with cruelty have ye r. Ezek 34:4
till he knew that God r. Dan 5:21

ruler
(*Revisions frequently translate this* prince, *or* governor)
Pharaoh made Joseph r. over all Gen 41:43; 45:8; Ps 105:21
Joseph said to the r. of. Gen 43:16*
thou shalt not curse r. of. Ex 22:28
when a r. hath sinned. Lev 4:22
every one a r. among. Num 13:2
appointed thee r. over. 1 Sam 25:30
2 Sam 6:21; 7:8; 1 Chr 11:2; 17:7
I took thee from following sheep to be r. 2 Sam 7:8; 1 Chr 17:7
appointed Solomon to be r. 1 Ki 1:35
of Judah came the chief r. 1 Chr 5:2
Azariah r. of house of God. 9:11
2 Chr 31:13
fail thee a man to be r. 2 Chr 7:18
he made Abijah r. among. 11:22
and Hananiah the r. of. Neh 7:2
Seraiah was r. of the house. 11:11
Benjamin with their r. Ps 68:27
even the r. of the people, let. 105:20
no guide, overseer, or r. Pr 6:7

sittest to eat with a r. Pr 23:1
so is a wicked r. over the. 28:15
if a r. hearken to lies, his. 29:12
many seek r.'s favour, but. 26
if the spirit of the r. rise. Eccl 10:4
which proceedeth from the r. 5
be thou our r. Isa 3:6
make me not a r. 7
send ye the lamb to the r. of. 16:1
in the land, r. against r. Jer 51:46
no king nor r. asked. Dan 2:10
and hath made thee r. over. 38, 48
shall be third r. in the. 5:7, 16, 29
he come that is to be r. Mi 5:2
things that have no r. Hab 1:14
there came a certain r. Mat 9:18
whom his Lord hath made r. 24:45 Luke 12:42
shall make him r. over all. Mat 24:47
I will make thee r. over. 25:21, 23
there came from the r. of the synagogue's. Mark 5:35; Luke 8:49
the r. of the synagogue. Luke 13:14
when the r. of the feast. John 2:9
a man named Nicodemus, a r. 3:1
who made thee a r.? Acts 7:27, 35
the same did God send to be r. 35
beat Sosthenes the chief r. 18:17
shalt not speak evil of the r. 23:5

rulers

then make them r. over. Gen 47:6
r. of thousands, r. Ex 18:21, 25
Moses called the r. of the. 34:31
the r. brought onyx stones to. 35:27
and I will make them r. Deut 1:13*
not the Philistines are r.? Judg 15:11
sons were chief r. 2 Sam 8:18*
were r. of his chariots. 1 Ki 9:22
Jehu wrote to the r. 2 Ki 10:1
Jehoiada set r. over. 11:4*, 19*
all there were r. of. 1 Chr 27:31
r. of the house of God. 2 Chr 35:8
the hand of the r. chief. Ezra 9:2
r. were behind the house. Neh 4:16
I rebuked the r. and said, Ye. 5:7
the r. of the people dwelt at. 11:1
and the half of the r. with me. 12:40
then contended I with the r. 13:11
the r. of the provinces. Esth 9:3
the r. take counsel against. Ps 2:2
hear word of the Lord, ye r. Isa 1:10
broken the sceptre of the r. 14:5
all thy r. are fled together. 22:3
and your r. the seers hath. 29:10*
to a servant of r. kings shall. 49:7
any of his seed to be r. Jer 33:26
in pieces captains and r. 51:23*
prepare against her r. 28*
made drunk her r. 57*
were captains and r. Ezek 23:6
raise up those r. against thee. 23
all the r. were gathered. Dan 3:3
her r. with shame do love. Hos 4:18
cometh one of the r. of. Mark 5:22
brought before r. 13:9*; Luke 21:12
called together the r. Luke 23:13
and r. also with the people. 35
how our priests and r. 24:20
do the r. know that? John 7:26
have any of r. believed on him? 48
many among the chief r. 12:42
ye did it, as also did r. Acts 3:17
the r. were gathered against. 4:26
the r. of the synagogue. 13:15
and their r. because they knew. 27
of the Jews, with their r. 14:5
masters drew them to the r. 16:19
they troubled the people and r. 17:8
r. not a terror to good. Rom 13:3
we wrestle against the r. Eph 6:12

rulest

and r. not thou over? 2 Chr 20:6
r. the raging of the sea. Ps 89:9

ruleth

he that r. over men. 2 Sam 23:3
let them know that God r. Ps 59:13
he r. by his power for ever. 66:7
and his kingdom r. over all. 103:19
that r. his spirit is better. Pr 16:32
rich r. over the poor, and. 22:7
wherein one man r. over. Eccl 8:9
more than cry of him that r. 9:17
the most High r. Dan 4:17, 25, 32
Judah yet r. with God. Hos 11:12
he that r. with diligence. Rom 12:8
r. well his own house. 1 Tim 3:4

ruling

must be just, r. in the. 2 Sam 23:3
sit on throne, and r. Jer 22:30
r. their children and. 1 Tim 3:12

rumbling

at r. of his wheels, fathers. Jer 47:3

rumour, -s

(*American Revision usually translates* tidings)
and he shall hear a r. 2 Ki 19:7 Isa 37:7
I have heard a r. from. Jer 49:14
r. in the land, a r. shall come one year, in another year a r. 51:46
on mischief, r. shall be upon r. Ezek 7:26
we have heard a r. from. Ob 1
of wars and r. of wars. Mat 24:6 Mark 13:7
r. of him went forth. Luke 7:17*

rump

(*Revisions*, the fat tail)
ram and the fat and the r. Ex 29:22 Lev 3:9; 7:3; 8:25; 9:19

run

whose branches r. over. Gen 49:22
whether his flesh r. with. Lev 15:3
if a woman's issue r. beyond. 25
lest angry fellows r. Judg 18:25*
some shall r. before his. 1 Sam 8:11
r. to the camp to thy brethren. 17:17*
asked me, that he might r. to. 20:6
r., find out now the arrows which. 36
horses, and fifty men to r. before. 2 Sam 15:1; 1 Ki 1:5
let me now r. and bear tidings. 2 Sam 18:19, 22, 23
I have r. through a troop. 22:30 Ps 18:29
that I may r. to the man. 2 Ki 4:22
r. now, I pray thee, to meet her. 26
as the Lord liveth, I will r. 5:20
eyes of Lord r. to and. 2 Chr 16:9
as strong man to r. a race. Ps 19:5
them melt as waters, which r. 58:7
they r. and prepare themselves. 59:4
he caused waters to r. down. 78:16
the springs, which r. among. 104:10
I will r. the way of thy. 119:32
rivers of waters r. down mine. 136
for their feet r. to evil. Pr 1:16 Isa 59:7
rivers r. into the sea. Eccl 1:7
draw me, we will r. S of S 1:4
of locusts shall he r. on. Isa 33:4*
they shall r. and not be weary. 40:31
knew not thee shall r. to thee. 55:5
r. ye to and fro through. Jer 5:1
that your eyes may r. down. 9:18
hast r. with the footmen. 12:5
mine eyes shall r. down with tears, because the Lord's. 13:17; 14:17
lament, and r. to and fro. 49:3
I will make him r. away. 19; 50:44
post shall r. to meet another. 51:31
let tears r. down like a. Lam 2:18
neither shall thy tears r. Ezek 24:16
cause their rivers to r. like oil. 32:14
many shall r. to and fro. Dan 12:4
horsemen, so shall they r. Joel 2:4
they shall r. like mighty men. 7
they shall r. in the city, shall r. on. 9*
judgement r. down as. Amos 5:24*
shall horses r. upon the rock? 6:12
shall r. to and fro to seek word. 8:12
r. like the lightnings. Nah 2:4
write vision, that he may r. Hab 2:2
and ye r. every man to his. Hag 1:9
R., speak to this young man. Zech 2:4
eyes of the Lord r. to and fro. 4:10
they did r. to bring his. Mat 28:8
r. in a race r. all, but one receiveth the prize, so r. that ye. 1 Cor 9:24
I therefore so r. not as. 26
I should r. or had r. in. Gal 2:2
ye did r. well, who did? 5:7
I have not r. in vain. Phil 2:16
let us r. with patience. Heb 12:1
that ye r. not to the same. 1 Pet 4:4

runnest

when thou r. thou shalt. Pr 4:12

runneth

he r. upon him, even on. Job 15:26
he breaketh me, he r. upon me. 16:14
thou anointest my head, my cup r. over. Ps 23:5
his word r. very swiftly. 147:15
the righteous r. into it. Pr 18:10
mine eyes r. down with water. Lam 1:16; 3:48
the bottles break, and the wine r. Mat 9:17*
then she r. and cometh. John 20:2
not of him that willeth, nor of him that r. Rom 9:16

running

one bird be killed over r. water. Lev 14:5, 6, 50
dip them in r. water, and sprinkle. 51
cleanse the house with the r. 52
any man hath a r. issue. 15:2; 22:4
shall bathe his flesh in r. water. 13
unclean person take r. Num 19:17
and behold, a man r. alone. 2 Sam 18:24, 26
the r. of the foremost is like r. 27
when Naaman saw him r. 2 Ki 5:21
Athaliah heard the people r. 2 Chr 23:12
and r. waters out of thine own well. Pr 5:15
feet that be swift in r. to. 6:18
the r. to and fro of locusts. Isa 33:4*
with her rivers r. about. Ezek 31:4
the people r. to him. Mark 9:15
when Jesus saw the people r. 25
there came one r. and. 10:17
good measure and r. over. Luke 6:38
and r. under a certain island. Acts 27:16
as the sound of chariots r. Rev 9:9

rush, *substantive*

r. grow without mire? Job 8:11
cut off branch and r. in one. Isa 9:14
any work which branch or r. 19:15

rush

nations shall r. like the rushing of many waters. Isa 17:13

rushed

Abimelech and company r. Judg 9:44
the liers in wait hasted and r. 20:37
they r. with one accord. Acts 19:29

rushes

where dragons lay shall be reeds and r. Isa 35:7

rusheth

every one turned, as horse r. Jer 8:6

rushing

and to the r. of nations, that make a r. like the r. of many. Isa 17:12
nations shall rush like the r. 13
at r. of chariots fathers. Jer 47:3
voice of a great r. Ezek 3:12, 13
as of a r. mighty wind. Acts 2:2

rust

where moth and r. Mat 6:19, 20
r. of them shall be a witness. Jas 5:3

Ruth

name of the other was R. Ruth 1:4
R. said. 1:14, 16, 22; 2:2, 21
then said Boaz unto R. 2:8
Naomi said unto R. 22
who art thou? I am R. 3:9
thou must buy it also of R. 4:5, 13
moreover, R. have I purchased. 10
Booz begat Obed of R. Mat 1:5

S

Sabaoth

A Hebrew word meaning Hosts *or* Armies. Jehovah Sabaoth, The Lord of hosts, Rom 9:29.

except the Lord of S. Rom 9:29
the ears of the Lord of s. Jas 5:4

sabbath

The Hebrew word means rest, *from the statement in* Gen 2:2, *that God rested and hallowed the seventh day. By the Jewish law given at Sinai the seventh day was to be a day of rest, in which no secular work was to be done, and which was to be kept holy to God. At a later period the simple Jewish law of early days was added to by the traditions of the elders, until the sabbath rules became burdensome, and, in some cases, foolish. It was against this, and not against God's law of the sabbath that Jesus set himself in his teaching and healing.*

The sabbath, *one day out of each week, was kept by the Jews on the day now called Saturday. How early this was taken to be the seventh day is not known. After the ascension of Jesus the disciples met on the first day of each week for prayer and praise. The Jewish Christians for a long time kept both the seventh and the first; but as Gentile Christians, having never kept any such day before, celebrated only the first day of the week as* the Lord's Day, *the celebration of the seventh by Christians was finally abandoned.*

Because of the rule that a long journey should not be made on the sabbath, the short distance permitted, about a mile, received the name of a sabbath day's journey.

The word sabbath *is often used in speaking of the rest of the fields from tillage, the rules for which are given in the Pentateuch.*

is rest of the holy *s.* *Ex* 16:23
eat that to-day, for to-day is a *s.* 25
Lord hath given you the *s.* 29
seventh day is the *s.* 20:10; 31:15
35:2; *Lev* 23:3; *Deut* 5:14
ye shall keep the *s.* *Ex* 31:14, 16
an atonement, it shall be a *s.* of rest.
Lev 16:31; 23:3, 32
s. priest shall wave it. 23:11
from the morrow after the *s.* 15
after the seventh *s.* shall ye. 16
1st of the month shall ye have a *s.* 24
shall ye celebrate your *s.* 32
shall be a *s.*, on the eighth a *s.* 39
every *s.* he shall set it in order. 24:8
shall the land keep a *s.* 25:2, 4, 6
burnt offering of every *s.* *Num* 28:10
neither new moon nor *s.* *2 Ki* 4:23
you that enter in on the *s.* 11:5
you that go forth on the *s.*, even they.
7, 9; *2 Chr* 23:8
covert for the *s.* turned. *2 Ki* 16:18
shewbread every *s.* *1 Chr* 9:32
desolate, she kept the *s.* *2 Chr* 36:21
known to them thy holy *s.* *Neh* 9:14
buy it of them on the *s.* 10:31
winepresses on the *s.* 13:15
brought ware, and sold on the *s.* 16
Israel, by profaning the *s.* 18
began to be dark before the *s.* 19
came they no more on the *s.* 21
man that keepeth the *s.* *Isa* 56:2, 6
the *s.*; call the *s.* a delight. 58:13
from one *s.* to another shall. 66:23
but on the *s.* it shall be. *Ezek* 46:1
saying, When will the *s.*? *Amos* 8:5
in the end of the *s.* came. *Mat* 28:1
s. was made for man, not man for
the *s.* *Mark* 2:27
is Lord of the *s.* 28; *Luke* 6:5
when the *s.* was past. *Mark* 16:1
on the second *s.* after. *Luke* 6:1
in the synagogue on the *s.* 13:10
doth not each on the *s.* loose? 15
and the *s.* drew on. 23:54
not only had broken the *s.* *John* 5:18
preached to them next *s.* *Acts* 13:42
on the *s.* we went out of city. 16:13
in the synagogue every *s.* 18:4
see **day, days**

sabbaths

saying, My *s.* ye shall keep.
Ex 31:13; *Lev* 19:3, 30; 26:2
seven *s.* shall be. *Lev* 23:15
beside the *s.* of the Lord. *Lev* 23:38
and thou shalt number seven *s.* 25:8
enjoy her *s.*, even then shall the land
. . . her *s.* 26:34, 43; *2 Chr* 36:21
did not rest in your *s.* *Lev* 26:35
burnt sacrifices in the *s.* *1 Chr* 23:31
2 Chr 2:4; 8:13; 31:3; *Neh* 10:33
new moons and *s.* I. *Isa* 1:13
to eunuchs that keep my *s.* 56:4
did mock at her *s.* *Lam* 1:7*
Lord caused *s.* to be forgotten. 2:6
also I gave them my *s.* *Ezek* 20:12
and my *s.* they greatly. 13, 16, 24
hast profaned my *s.* 22:8; 23:38
have hid their eyes from my *s.* 22:26
my laws and hallow my *s.* 44:24
part to give offerings for *s.* 45:17
worship at this gate in the *s.* 46:3
make to cease her *s.* *Hos* 2:11

Sabeans

the *S.* fell on the oxen. *Job* 1:15
merchandise of the *S.* *Isa* 45:14
with the men of the common sort
were brought *S.* *Ezek* 23:42*
shall sell them to the *S.* *Joel* 3:8

sack

to restore every man's money into
his *s.* *Gen* 42:25, 35; 43:21; 44:1
put my silver cup in *s.*'s mouth. 44:2
they took down every man his *s.* 11
cup was found in Benjamin's *s.* 12
or *s.* of unclean must be. *Lev* 11:32

sackbut

sound of the *s.* *Dan* 3:5, 7, 10, 15

sackcloth

(*A coarse cloth made of camel's and goat's hair. It was used for making the rough garments worn by mourners. It therefore became a symbol for sorrow and mourning*)

and Jacob put *s.* upon. *Gen* 37:34
said, Gird you with *s.* *2 Sam* 3:31
Rizpah took *s.* and spread it. 21:10
merciful kings, let us put *s.* on our
loins, and ropes. *1 Ki* 20:31, 32
s. on his flesh, and lay in *s.* 21:27
and he had *s.* within. *2 Ki* 6:30
Hezekiah covered himself with *s.*
19:1; *Isa* 37:1
elders of the priests covered with *s.*
2 Ki 19:2; *Isa* 37:2
David and elders were clothed with
s. *1 Chr* 21:16
clothes, and put on *s.* *Esth* 4:1
enter the gate clothed with *s.* 2
sewed *s.* upon my skin. *Job* 16:15
hast put off my *s.* and. *Ps* 30:11
sick, my clothing was *s.* 35:13
I made *s.* also my garment. 69:11
stomacher, a girding of *s.* *Isa* 3:24
gird themselves with *s.* 15:3
go, and loose the *s.* from off. 20:2
Lord call to girding with *s.* 22:12
make you bare, and gird *s.* 32:11
Jer 4:8; 6:26; 48:37; 49:3
I make *s.* the covering of the. 50:3
themselves with *s.*: virgins hang
down heads. *Lam* 2:10; *Ezek* 7:18
27:31
Lord with fasting and *s.* *Dan* 9:3
virgin girded with *s.* for. *Joel* 1:8
lie all night in *s.*, ye ministers. 13
and I will bring up *s.* *Amos* 8:10
of Nineveh put on *s.* *Jonah* 3:5
the king covered him with *s.* 6
man and beast he covered with *s.* 8
became black as *s.* of hair. *Rev* 6:12
prophesy, clothed in *s.* 11:3

sackclothes

Israel assembled with *s.* *Neh* 9:1

sacks

to fill their *s.* with corn. *Gen* 42:25*
44:1
brought again in your *s.* 43:12
who put our money in our *s.* 22
given you treasure in your *s.* 23
the Gibeonites took old *s.* *Josh* 9:4

sacrifice

An offering of any sort to a deity, with the idea of procuring favour or avoiding disaster. The idea of sacrifice is deeply rooted in the instincts of humanity; for it is found among every race at the earliest known period of its history as a well-established and thoroughly understood custom. The sacrifices were, in general, of two sorts: [1] *the offering of the first-fruits, or of incense, to show the dependence of man on his deity, and to thank him for his benefits;* [2] *the burnt offering, to appease an angry god when displeased and ready to bring distress upon him.*

Most probably the plan of sacrifices arranged by Moses was an adaptation of what had always been their customs, from the time of Abraham. One respect in which the Jews differed from the heathen nations around them was in the absence of human sacrifice.

The book of Hebrews shows how Jesus Christ, in becoming a sacrifice for man, made further sacrifices unnecessary.

The Jews ceased offering sacrifice when the Temple was destroyed, A.D. 70. The custom is now found only in savage tribes.

The word is also used symbolically, as the sacrifice of one's lips.

Revisions very often translate it offering.

then Jacob offered *s.* *Gen* 31:54
do *s.* to the Lord. *Ex* 5:17; 8:8
say, It is the *s.* of the Lord's. 12:27
not offer blood of *s.* 23:18*; 34:25
and thou eat of his *s.* 34:15
nor shall *s.* of passover be left. 25
then he shall offer with *s.* *Lev* 7:12
leavened bread with *s.* of. 13; 22:29
if *s.* be a vow, it shall be eaten. 16
offereth a *s.* and bringeth. 17:8
which they do not offer a *s.* 27:11
or make a *s.* in performing a vow.
Num 15:3, 8
it is for a sweet savour, a *s.* 28:6
8, 13, 19, 24; 29:6, 13, 36
from them that offer *s.* *Deut* 18:3
an altar, not for *s.* *Josh* 22:26
for to offer a great *s.* *Judg* 16:23
offer the yearly *s.* *1 Sam* 1:21; 2:19
wherefore kick ye at my *s.* 2:29
Eli's house not purged with *s.* 3:14
there is a *s.* of people to-day. 9:12
because he doth bless the *s.* 13
to obey is better than *s.* 15:22
call Jesse to the *s.* and I will. 16:3, 5
yearly *s.* for all the family. 20:6, 29
if this people do *s.* at. *1 Ki* 12:27
till time of the evening *s.* 18:29
at the time of evening *s.* Elijah. 36
not offer *s.* to other gods. *2 Ki* 5:17
for I have a great *s.* to do to. 10:19
and to him shall ye do *s.* 17:36
save only to burn *s.* before. *2 Chr* 2:6
king Solomon offered a *s.* of. 7:5
myself for an house of *s.* 12
astonied until the evening *s.* *Ezra* 9:4
at the evening *s.* I arose up from. 5
s. thou didst not desire. *Ps* 40:6
51:16
made a covenant with me by *s.* 50:5
I will offer to thee the *s.* 116:17
bind the *s.* with cords to. 118:27
of my hands as evening *s.* 141:2
s. of the wicked is an. *Pr* 15:8
more acceptable than *s.* 21:3
to hear than to give the *s.* *Eccl* 5:1
the Egyptians shall do *s.* *Isa* 19:21
for the Lord hath a *s.* in Bozrah. 34:6
wentest thou to offer *s.* 57:7
that bring the *s.* of praise. *Jer* 33:11
nor want a man to do *s.* 18
for God hath a *s.* in the north. 46:10
to my *s.*, even a great *s.* *Ezek* 39:17
till ye be drunken of my *s.* 19
they shall slay the *s.* for. 44:11
where ministers boil the *s.* 46:24
daily *s.* was taken away. *Dan* 8:11
9:27; 11:31
given him against the daily *s.* 8:12
be the vision of the daily *s.*? 13
from the time daily *s.* shall. 12:11

many days without a *s*. *Hos* 3:4
I desired mercy, and not *s*. 6:6
Mat 9:13; 12:7
offer a *s*. of thanksgiving. *Amos* 4:5
then the men offered a *s*. *Jonah* 1:16
for the Lord hath prepared a *s*.
Zeph 1:7, 8
if ye offer the blind for *s*. *Mal* 1:8
every *s*. shall be salted. *Mark* 9:49
and to offer a *s*. according. *Luke* 2:24
in those days they offered *s*. to.
Acts 7:41
and would have done *s*. with. 14:13
that they had not done *s*. unto. 18
your bodies a living *s*. *Rom* 12:1
in *s*. to idols. *1 Cor* 8:4; 10:19, 28
a *s*. to God for a sweet. *Eph* 5:2
if I be offered on the *s*. *Phil* 2:17
a *s*. acceptable, wellpleasing. 4:18
needeth not daily, as those high priests, to offer up *s*. *Heb* 7:27
to put away sin by the *s*. 9:26
he saith, S. and offering. 10:5, 8
had offered one *s*. for sins, for. 12
there remaineth no more *s*. for. 26
to God a more excellent *s*. 11:4
let us offer the *s*. of praise. 13:15
see **burnt, peace offering**

sacrifice, *verb*
let us go and *s*. to the Lord our God.
Ex 3:18; 5:3, 8; 8:27; 10:25
Go ye, *s*. 8:25
shall we *s*. the abomination of ? 26
in not letting the people go to *s*. 29
I *s*. to Lord all that openeth. 13:15
thou shalt *s*. thereon thy. 20:24
thou shalt not *s*. it. *Deut* 15:21; 17:1
thou shalt therefore *s*. 16:2, 6
not *s*. the passover within any. 5
yearly to *s*. to the Lord. *1 Sam* 1:3
the people spared the best to *s*. 15:15
should have been destroyed to *s*. 21
come to *s*. to the Lord. 16:2, 5
went to Gibeon to *s*. there. *1 Ki* 3:4
as yet the people did *s*. and.
2 Ki 14:4; *2 Chr* 33:17
nor shall *s*. to other gods. *2 Ki* 17:35
to Jerusalem to *s*. to. *2 Chr* 11:16
we seek your God, and do *s*. to.
Ezra 4:2
will they *s*.? will they ? *Neh* 4:2
I will freely *s*. to thee. *Ps* 54:6
let them *s*. sacrifices of. 107:22
gather to my *s*. that I do *s*. for you.
Ezek 39:17
they *s*. on the tops of. *Hos* 4:13
and they *s*. with harlots. 14
they *s*., but the Lord accepteth. 8:13
are vanity, they *s*. bullocks. 12:11
men that *s*. kiss the calves. 13:2
I will *s*. to thee with. *Jonah* 2:9
therefore they *s*. unto. *Hab* 1:16
they that *s*. shall seethe. *Zech* 14:21
things Gentiles *s*., they *s*. *1 Cor* 10:20

sacrificed
calf and *s*. thereunto. *Ex* 32:8
they *s*. unto devils, not. *Deut* 32:17
they *s*. thereon peace. *Josh* 8:31
and they *s*. there unto. *Judg* 2:5
said to the man that *s*. *1 Sam* 2:15
and *s*. sacrifices the same day. 6:15
went to Gilgal and *s*. 11:15
David *s*. oxen and. *2 Sam* 6:13
only the people *s*. in the high places.
1 Ki 3:2, 3; *2 Ki* 12:3; 15:4, 35
16:4; *2 Chr* 28:4
his strange wives, and *s*. *1 Ki* 11:8
lowest priests which *s*. *2 Ki* 17:32
then he *s*. there. *1 Chr* 21:28
assembled before ark *s*. *2 Chr* 5:6
Ahaz *s*. to the gods of. 28:23
Manasseh *s*. on the altar of. 33:16
for Amon *s*. to all the carved. 22
on graves of them that had *s*. 34:4
yea, they *s*. their sons. *Ps* 106:37
daughters, they *s*. to the idols. 38
these thou *s*. to them. *Ezek* 16:20
of my sacrifice which I have *s*. 39:19
s. to Baalim, and burnt. *Hos* 11:2
our Passover is *s*. for us. *1 Cor* 5:7
to eat things *s*. to idols. *Rev* 2:14, 20

sacrificedst
which thou *s*. the first day. *Deut* 16:4

sacrifices
Beer-sheba offered *s*. to. *Gen* 46:1
must give us also *s*. *Ex* 10:25
father in law, took *s*. for God. 18:12
of the *s*. of the Lord. *Lev* 10:13
the *s*. which they offer in the. 17:5
no more offer their *s*. to devils. 7
they called to the *s*. *Num* 25:2
my *s*. shall ye observe to offer. 28:2
bring your *s*. and tithes. *Deut* 12:6
which did eat the fat of their *s*. 32:38
there they shall offer the *s*. 33:19
s. of the Lord are their. *Josh* 13:14
the altar not for *s*.; but it. 22:28, 29
and sacrificed *s*. same. *1 Sam* 6:15
Lord as great delight in *s*.? 15:22
they sacrificed *s*. in. *1 Chr* 29:21
and consumed the *s*. *2 Chr* 7:1
bring *s*.: they brought in *s*. 29:31
where he offered *s*. be. *Ezra* 6:3
that they may offer *s*. to God. 10
day they offered great *s*. *Neh* 12:43
offer *s*. of righteousness. *Ps* 4:5
therefore I will offer *s*. of joy. 27:6
not reprove thee for thy *s*. 50:8
s. of God are a broken spirit. 51:17
then shalt thou be pleased with *s*. 19
Baal-peor, and eat *s*. of dead. 106:28
let them sacrifice the *s*. of. 107:22
than a house full of *s*. *Pr* 17:1
is the multitude of *s*.? *Isa* 1:11
year to year, let them kill *s*. 29:1
nor honoured me with thy *s*. 43:23
filled me with the fat of thy *s*. 24
their *s*. shall be accepted on. 56:7
nor are your *s*. sweet. *Jer* 6:20
burnt offerings to your *s*. 7:21
commanded them concerning *s*. 22
bringing *s*. of praise to house. 17:26
high hill and offered *s*. *Ezek* 20:28
be ashamed, because of their *s*.
Hos 4:19
their *s*. shall be as the bread. 9:4
and bring your *s*. every. *Amos* 4:4
have ye offered unto me *s*.? 5:25
Lord is more than all *s*. *Mark* 12:33
mingled with their *s*. *Luke* 13:1
have ye offered *s*. for ? *Acts* 7:42
that eat the *s*. partakers ? *1 Cor* 10:18
he may offer gifts and *s*. *Heb* 5:1
priest is ordained to offer *s*. 8:3
offered both gifts and *s*. 9:9
heavenly things with better *s*. 23
can never with those *s*. make. 10:1
but in those *s*. there is a. 3
in *s*. for sin thou hast had no. 6
offering oftentimes the same *s*. 11
for with such *s*. God is well. 13:16
to offer up spiritual *s*. *1 Pet* 2:5
see **burnt**

sacrificeth
he that *s*. to any god, save. *Ex* 22:20
s. and to him that *s*. not. *Eccl* 9:2
people that *s*. in gardens. *Isa* 65:3
he that *s*. a lamb as if he cut. 66:3
and *s*. a corrupt thing. *Mal* 1:14

sacrificing
him *s*. sheep and oxen. *1 Ki* 8:5
s. to the calves that he had. 12:32

sacrilege
dost thou commit *s*.? *Rom* 2:22*

sad
them, behold they were *s*. *Gen* 40:6
was no more *s*. *1 Sam* 1:18
why is thy spirit so *s*.? *1 Ki* 21:5
I had not been before *s*. *Neh* 2:1
Why is thy countenance *s*.? 2
should not my countenance be *s*.? 3
the heart of righteous *s*. whom I have not made *s*. *Ezek* 13:22
not as hypocrites, of a *s*. *Mat* 6:16
was *s*. at that saying. *Mark* 10:22*
as ye walk, and are *s*. *Luke* 24:17

saddle
what *s*. he rideth upon. *Lev* 15:9

saddle, *verb*
I will *s*. me an ass. *2 Sam* 19:26
s. me the ass. *1 Ki* 13:13, 27

saddled
early, and *s*. his ass. *Gen* 22:3
Balaam *s*. his ass. *Num* 22:21
the Levite two asses *s*. *Judg* 19:10
met David with a couple of asses *s*.
2 Sam 16:1
Ahithophel *s*. his ass, and gat. 17:23
Shimei *s*. and went after. *1 Ki* 2:40
so they *s*. him the ass. 13:13, 23, 27
she *s*. an ass. *2 Ki* 4:24

Sadducees
A religious party or sect among the Jews at the time of Christ. They were probably disciples of a Zadok—but authorities are uncertain who he was or when he lived. The sect was small but very wealthy, and included the higher priests. The chief distinction between these and the Pharisees was the insistence by the Sadducees that only the written law was obligatory.
The special doctrines of the Sadducees were [1] *the denial of a resurrection and a future life, with all that includes* ; [2] *the denial of the existence of angels or spirits.*

when he saw the S. come. *Mat* 3:7
the S. came tempting Jesus. 16:1
beware of the leaven of the S. 6, 11
beware of the doctrine of the S. 12
came to him the S. which say. 22:23
had heard that he had put the S. 34
the priests and the S. came. *Acts* 4:1
the S. laid their hands on. 5:17
the one part were S. 23:6
dissension between the Pharisees and S. 7
for the S. say, that there is no. 8

sadly
why look ye so *s*. to-day ? *Gen* 40:7

sadness
by *s*. of countenance the. *Eccl* 7:3

safe
and ye dwelled *s*. *1 Sam* 12:11*
man Absalom *s*.? *2 Sam* 18:29*, 32*
their houses are *s*. from. *Job* 21:9
up, and I shall be *s*. *Ps* 119:117
run into it, and are *s*. *Pr* 18:10
in the Lord shall be *s*. 29:25
carry the prey away *s*. *Isa* 5:29
they shall be *s*. in. *Ezek* 34:27*
had received him *s*. *Luke* 15:27
they may bring him *s*. *Acts* 23:24
they escaped all *s*. to land. 27:44
things, for you it is *s*. *Phil* 3:1

safeguard
me thou shalt be in *s*. *1 Sam* 22:23

safely
he led them on *s*. they. *Ps* 78:53
to me shall dwell *s*. *Pr* 1:33*
thou walk in thy way *s*. 3:23*
heart of her husband doth *s*. 31:11
them, and passed *s*. *Isa* 41:3
make them to lie down *s*. *Hos* 2:18
Jerusalem shall be *s*. *Zech* 14:11
and lead him away *s*. *Mark* 14:44
jailor to keep them *s*. *Acts* 16:23
see **dwell**

safety
I was not in *s*. nor had I. *Job* 3:26*
his children are far from *s*. and. 5:4
mourn may be exalted to *s*. 11
thou shalt take thy rest in *s*. 11:18
be given him to be in *s*. 24:23*
I will set him in *s*. from. *Ps* 12:5
an horse is a vain thing for *s*. 33:17
of counsellors is *s*. *Pr* 11:14; 24:6
horse is for battle, but *s*. is. 21:31*
shall lie down in *s*. *Isa* 14:30
found we shut with all *s*. *Acts* 5:23
shall say, Peace and *s*. *1 Thes* 5:3
see **dwell**

saffron
spikenard and *s*. *S of S* 4:14

said
Adam *s*. This is bone of. *Gen* 2:23
the serpent *s*. Hath God *s*. ye ? 3:1
Noah *s*. Blessed be the Lord. 9:26
Sarah hath *s*. hearken to her. 21:12
had *s*. It is my master. 24:65
began to come, as Joseph *s*. 41:54
returned to the Lord and *s*. *Ex* 5:22
serve the Lord as ye have *s*. 12:31
and herds, as ye have *s*. 32

Joshua did as Moses had s. Ex 17:10
out, as Moses had s. Lev 10:5
thou hast s. I will give. Num 11:21
ye s. should be a prey. 14:31
Deut 1:39
did as Balaam had s. Num 23:50
sons of Joseph hath s. well. 36:5
God of thy fathers hath s. Deut 1:21
Hebron to Caleb, as Moses s.
Judg 1:20
Israel, as thou hast s. 6:36, 37
thee, what Samuel s. 1 Sam 10:15
who is he that s. Shall Saul? 11:12
to you in all ye s. to me. 12:1
David s. I shall now perish. 27:1
Lord, do as thou hast s. 2 Sam 7:25
as thy servant s. so it is. 13:35
sweet psalmist of Israel s. 23:1
as my lord king hath s. 1 Ki 2:38
thou hast s. My name shall be there.
8:29; 2 Chr 6:20
Jeroboam s. Now shall. 1 Ki 12:26
s. to her, Go, do as thou hast s. 17:13
s. on this matter, another s. 22:20
the man of God had s. 2 Ki 7:17
Lord, do as thou hast s. 1 Chr 17:23
hast s. so must we do. Ezra 10:12
that s. We are many. Neh 5:2, 3
do as Esther hath s. Esth 5:5
to-morrow as the king hath s. 8
thou hast s., My doctrine. Job 11:4
if men of my tabernacle s. not. 31:31
when I s. Hitherto shalt thou. 38:11
who s. With our tongue. Ps 12:4
fool s. in his heart. 14:1; 53:1
my heart s. to thee, Thy face. 27:8
an impudent face, s. unto. Pr 7:13
thou hast s. I will ascend. Isa 14:13
s. We have made a covenant. 28:15
ye s. No, for we will flee. 30:16
thou hast s. None seeth me. 47:10
the priests s. not, Where? Jer 2:8
what the prophets s. 23:25
Jeremiah s. Amen. 28:6
because ye s. The Lord hath. 29:15
what thou hast s. to the king, also
what the king s. unto thee. 38:25
of whom we s. Under his. Lam 4:20
and I s. Ah, Lord God. Ezek 9:8
not the rebellious house s.? 12:9
Tyrus hath s. against. 26:2; 36:2
O Tyrus, thou hast s. I am. 27:3
hast s. I am a god, I sit. 28:2
which hath s. My river is mine. 29:3
Nebuchadnezzar s. Blessed be God.
Dan 3:28
another saint s. to that saint. 8:13
Jonah s. It is better for. Jonah 4:8
her who s. to me, Where? Mi 7:10
city that s. in her heart. Zeph 2:15
ye have s. it is vain to. Mal 3:14
behold, a voice which s. This is my
beloved Son. Mat 17:5; Luke 3:22
also s. all the disciples. Mat 26:35
saith unto him, Thou hast s. 64
that that deceiver s. 27:63
he s. to Levi, Follow me. Mark 2:14
the angel s. to him. Luke 1:13, 30
s., Master, thou hast well s. 20:39
had seen angels, who s. that. 24:23
even so as the women had s. 24
straight the way, as s. John 1:23
but s. also, that God was his. 5:18
as the scripture hath s. out. 7:38
these things s. Esaias, when. 12:41
even as the Father s. unto me. 50
then Peter s., Repent and. Acts 2:38
all the chief priests had s. 4:23
this is that Moses who s. 7:37
your own poets have s. 17:28
except law had s. Thou. Rom 7:7
as we s. before, so say. Gal 1:9
by him that s. to him. Heb 7:21
we know him that hath s. 10:30
the four beasts s. Amen. Rev 5:14
see **Jesus**

said, *participle*
wherefore it is s. even. Gen 10:9
as it is s. to this day, in. 22:14
after it was s. Ye shall. Ex 5:19
it was s. by the word. 1 Ki 13:17
perish, in which it was s. Job 3:3
surely it is meet to be s. to. 34:31
of Zion it shall be s. This. Ps 87:5
better it be s. to thee. Pr 25:7
thing whereof it may be s.? Eccl 1:10
it shall be s. in that day. Isa 25:9
it shall no more be s. The. Jer 16:14
shall it not be s. Where? Ezek 13:12
it was s. to them, Ye are. Hos 1:10
it was s. by them. Mat 5:21, 27, 33
heard it hath been s. 31, 38, 43
which is s. in law of Lord. Luke 2:24
having s. thus, he gave up. 23:46
it was s. The elder shall. Rom 9:12
that where it was s. Ye are not. 26
whilst it is s. To-day. Heb 3:15; 4:7
of whom it was s. In Isaac. 11:18
s. to them, They should. Rev 6:11

answered and **said**
all the people *answered and s.*
Ex 24:3
one of the same place *answered and*
s. 1 Sam 10:12
Satan *answered and s.* Skin for skin.
Job 2:4
Lord *answered* Job *and s.* 40:1
he *answered* one of them, *and s.*,
Friend, I do thee no. Mat 20:13
John *answered and s.* Luke 9:49
see **answered**

God **said**
yea, hath *God s.* ye.? Gen 3:1, 3
same day, as *God* had s. 17:23
whatsoever *God* hath s. 31:16
house of which *God s.* 2 Chr 33:7
and the nation will I judge, *s. God.*
Acts 7:7
living God, as *God* hath s. 2 Cor 6:16

he **said**
he s. Escape for thy life. Gen 19:17
s. he not unto me, She is my? 20:5
if *he s.*, The speckled shall. 31:8
he s. Lift up thine eyes and see. 12
he s. Let me go, for the day. 32:26
he s. What is thy name? and *he s.* 27
God, *s. he*, hath made me. 41:51
all that Jethro had s. Ex 18:24
stand before you, as *he* hath s.
Deut 11:25; 18:2; 29:13
Josh 13:14, 33
kept me alive, as *he s.* Josh 14:10
abated, when *he* had s. Judg 8:3
hide any thing *he s.* 1 Sam 3:17
not fail thee, *s. he*, a man. 1 Ki 2:4
do as *he* hath s., and fall upon him. 31
he s. by all his servants. 2 Ki 17:23
build the house, as *he s.* 1 Chr 22:11
he s. Lord, look on it. 2 Chr 24:22
to man *he s.* Behold. Job 28:28
he hath s. in his heart. Ps 10:6
11:13
he s. that he would destroy. 106:23
to whom *he s.* This is. Isa 28:12
the voice said, Cry, *he s.* What? 40:6
for *he s.* Surely they are my. 63:8
now the Lord hath done as *he* hath s.
Jer 40:3
to the others *he s.* in. Ezek 9:5
because *he* hath s. The river. 29:9
of the evil *he* had s. Jonah 3:10
for *he s.* I am the Son. Mat 27:43
he has risen, as *he s.* 28:6
came and found as *he s.*
Mark 14:16; Luke 22:13
there shall ye see him, as *he s.*
Mark 16:7
not knowing what *he s.* Luke 9:33
when *he s.* these things. 13:17
remembered that *he s.* John 2:22
this *he s.* to prove him, for. 6:6
what sayest thou? *he s.* He is. 9:17
this *he s.*, not that he cared. 12:6
this *he s.*, signifying what death. 33
as soon as *he s.* to them, I am. 18:6
he s. It is finished, and bowed. 19:30
when *he* had so s. he shewed. 20:20
when *he* had s. this, he breathed. 22
when *he* had s. this, he fell. Acts 7:60
he s. Who art thou, Lord? 9:5
how *he s.* It is more blessed. 20:35
when *he* had so s. there arose. 23:7
he s. My grace is sufficient for thee.
2 Cor 12:9
the angels s. *he* at any? Heb 1:5, 13
then *s. he*, Lo, I come to do. Heb 10:9
for *he* hath s. I will never. 13:5
he that s. Do not commit. Jas 2:11
he s. These things are. Rev 22:6

I **said**
I s. Lest I die for her. Gen 26:9
I have s. I will bring. Ex 3:17
in all things that *I* have s. 23:13
I s. I would scatter. Deut 32:26
that have I given, as *I s.* Josh 1:3
I s. unto you, I am the. Judg 6:10
I s. indeed, that thy. 1 Sam 2:30
portion, of which *I s.* Set it by. 9:23
I s. Thou and Ziba. 2 Sam 19:29
house of which *I s.* My. 2 Ki 23:27
thing, therefore *I s.* it. Job 9:22
I s. I shall die in my nest. 29:18
I s. Days should speak, and. 32:7
in prosperity *I s.* I shall. Ps 30:6
I s. I will take heed to my. 39:1
then *s. I*, Lo, I come. 40:7
Heb 10:7
I s. Lord, be merciful to. Ps 41:4
I have s. Ye are gods. 82:6
I s. My foot slippeth. 94:18
I s. O my God, take me not. 102:24
I s. Thou art my refuge and. 142:5
I s. in mine heart, Go to. Eccl 2:1, 15
3:17, 18
s. I, Lord, how long? Isa 6:11
I s. not, Seek ye me in vain. 45:19
I s. Behold me, to a nation. 65:1
I s. when thou wast in. Ezek 16:6
he of whom *I s.* After. John 1:30
marvel not that *I s.* Ye must be. 3:7
the same that *I s.* from the. 8:25
I s. I am the Son of God. 10:36
s. I not to thee, If thou. 11:40
I s. it, that they may believe. 42
ye have heard how *I s.* to you. 14:28
these things *I s.* not at the. 16:4
in secret have *I s.* nothing. 18:20
heard me, what *I* have s. 21
I s. Not so, Lord, for. Acts 11:8
I have s. that ye are in our hearts.
2 Cor 7:3
that as *I s.* ye may be ready. 9:3
see **Jesus**

she **said**
for God, *s. she*, hath appointed me.
Gen 4:25
she s. He is my brother. 20:5
this man? *she s.* I will. 24:58
then *she s.* A bloody. Ex 4:26
to say, and *she s.* Say on. 1 Ki 2:14
she s. Truth, Lord, yet. Mat 15:27
she s. No man, Lord. John 8:11
she had so s. she went her. 11:28
she had thus s. she turned. 20:14
she s. Yea, for so much. Acts 5:8

they **said**
and *they s.* All that the Lord. Ex 24:7
they have well s. all. Deut 5:28
s. they, He is the son of. 2 Chr 22:9
for *they s.* He is a leper. 26:23
they have s. Come, let us cut them.
Ps 83:4
neither *s. they*, Where is? Jer 2:6
believe ye? *they s.* unto him, Yea.
Mat 9:28
they all s. Let him be crucified. 27:22
for *they s.* He is beside. Mark 3:21
because *they s.* He hath an. 30
amazed, nor *s. they* any thing. 16:8
they s. The Lord hath. Luke 19:34
s. they, It is his angel. Acts 12:15

saidst
why s. thou, She is my? Gen 12:19
s. thou, She is my sister? 26:9
the Lord, which s. to me. 32:9
s. I will surely do thee good. 12
s. to them, I will multiply. Ex 32:13
mouth wherewith thou s. Judg 9:38
thou s. The word I have. 1 Ki 2:42
thou s. my righteousness. Job 35:2
s. Seek ye my face. Ps 27:8
thou s. I shall be a lady. Isa 47:7
and thou s. I will not. Jer 2:20
but thou s. There is no hope. 25
I spake, but thou s. I will. 22:21
I called: thou s. Fear not. Lam 3:57
because thou s., Aha. Ezek 25:3

whom thou *s.* Give me. *Hos* 13:10
in that *s.* thou truly. *John* 4:18

sail, *substantive*

could not spread the *s.* *Isa* 33:23
thou spreadest forth to be thy *s.* *Ezek* 27:7
they strake *s.* and so. *Acts* 27:17*
and hoised up the main *s.* to. 40

sail

as he was about to *s.* *Acts* 20:3
Paul had determined to *s.* 16
we should *s.* into Italy. 27:1
all them that *s.* with thee. 24

sailed

as they *s.* he fell asleep. *Luke* 8:23
when we launched, we *s.* *Acts* 27:4
and when we had *s.* slowly. 7

sailing

finding a ship *s.* over. *Acts* 21:2*
centurion found a ship *s.* 27:6
when *s.* was now dangerous. 9*

sailors

all the company in ships, and *s.* stood afar off. *Rev* 18:17*

saint

The Revisions translate this holy one, *and the plural* holy ones, *where marked, except in* Hos 11:12, *where it is* Holy One, *and* Rev 15:3, *where the word is* ages.

then I heard one *s.* speak, another *s.* said to that *s.* which. *Dan* 8:13*
salute every *s.* in Christ. *Phil* 4:21*

saints

with ten thousands of *s.* *Deut* 33:2*
he loved the people; all his *s.* are. 3
keep the feet of his *s.* *1 Sam* 2:9*
s. rejoice in goodness. *2 Chr* 6:41
and to which of the *s.*? *Job* 5:1*
putteth no trust in his *s.* 15:15*
but to the *s.* that are in. *Ps* 16:3
sing to the Lord, O ye *s.* of. 30:4
O love the Lord, all ye his *s.* 31:23
fear the Lord, ye his *s.* 34:9
Lord forsaketh not his *s.* 37:28
gather my *s.* together to me. 50:5
for it is good before thy *s.* 52:9
the flesh of thy *s.* to beasts. 79:2
in the congregation of the *s.* 89:5*
in the assembly of the *s.* 7*
preserveth the souls of his *s.* 97:10
precious . . . is death of his *s.* 116:15
and let thy *s.* shout for joy. 132:9
her *s.* shall shout aloud for joy. 16
all thy works praise, and *s.* 145:10
the praise of all his *s.* 148:14
praise in congregation of *s.* 149:1
let *s.* be joyful in glory, let them. 5
this honour have all his *s.* Praise. 9
the way of his *s.* *Pr* 2:8
but *s.* shall take. *Dan* 7:18, 22, 27
the horn made war with the *s.* 21
and shall wear out the *s.* of the. 25
is faithful with the *s.* *Hos* 11:12*
God shall come, and all the *s.* with thee. *Zech* 14:5*
many bodies of *s.* that. *Mat* 27:52
evil he hath done to thy *s.* *Acts* 9:13
Peter came down also to the *s.* 32
called the *s.* and widows. 41
s. did I shut up in prison. 26:10
of God, called to be *s.* *Rom* 1:7
maketh intercession for the *s.* 8:27
to the necessity of the *s.* 12:13
Jerusalem to minister to the *s.* 15:25
contribution for the poor *s.* 26
may be accepted of the *s.* 31
in the Lord as becometh the *s.* 16:2
salute all the *s.* 15; *Heb* 13:24
sanctified, called to be *s.* *1 Cor* 1:2
law, and not before the *s.*? 6:1
do ye not know that the *s.* shall? 2
as in all the churches of the *s.* 14:33
the collection for the *s.* 16:1
themselves to the ministry of *s.* 15
with all the *s.* which are. *2 Cor* 1:1
upon us the ministering to the *s.* 8:4
the ministering to the *s.* 9:1
supplieth the want of the *s.* 12
the *s.* salute you. 13:13; *Phil* 4:22
to the *s.* at Ephesus, and. *Eph* 1:1
of your love to all the *s.* *Eph* 1:15
glory of his inheritance in the *s.* 18
fellow citizens with the *s.* 2:19
less than the least of all *s.* 3:8
able to comprehend with all *s.* 18
of the *s.* for the ministry. 4:12
once named, as becometh *s.* 5:3
and supplication for all *s* 6:18
to all the *s.* in Christ. *Phil* 1:1
to all the *s.* and faithful. *Col* 1:2
of the love ye have to all the *s.* 4
inheritance of the *s.* in light. 12
now made manifest to his *s.* 26
our Lord with all his *s.* *1 Thes* 3:13
to be glorified in his *s.* *2 Thes* 1:10
washed the *s.*' feet. *1 Tim* 5:10
which thou hast to all *s.* *Philem* 5
the bowels of the *s.* are refreshed. 7
ministered to the *s.* *Heb* 6:10
once delivered to the *s.* *Jude* 3
with ten thousand of his *s.* 14*
prayers of the *s.* *Rev* 5:8; 8:3, 4
give reward to thy *s.* 11:18
to make war with the *s.* 13:7
patience and faith of the *s.* 10
here is the patience of the *s.* 14:12
thy ways, thou King of *s.* 15:3*
shed the blood of the *s.* 16:6
drunken with the blood of *s.* 17:6
found the blood of the *s.* 18:24
is the righteousness of the *s.* 19:8
the camp of the *s.* about. 20:9

saith

one *s.* This is my son that liveth, and the other *s.* Nay. *1 Ki* 3:23
thus *s.* Ben-hadad, Thy silver. 20:2
servant Ben-hadad *s.* I pray thee. 32
s. the king, Put this fellow in prison. 22:27; *2 Chr* 18:26
thus *s.* the king, Is it peace? *2 Ki* 9:18, 19
thus *s.* the great king, the. 18:19
s. king, Let not Hezekiah deceive. 29 31; *2 Chr* 32:10; *Isa* 36:14
thus *s.* Hezekiah, This day is a day of. *2 Ki* 19:3; *Isa* 37:3
thus *s.* Cyrus, king of Persia. *2 Chr* 36:23; *Ezra* 1:2
the depth *s.* and the sea *s.* *Job* 28:14
he *s.* Deliver him. 33:24
but none *s.* Where is God? 35:10
of the wicked *s.* *Ps* 36:1
understanding, she *s.* *Pr* 9:4, 16
naught, it is naught, *s.* the. 20:14
the slothful man *s.*, There is a lion. 22:13; 26:13
deceiveth, and *s.* Am not I? 26:19
who is he that *s.* and? *Lam* 3:37
not every one that *s.* to me. *Mat* 7:21
to him, Master *s.* My time. 26:18
Peter *s.* to him, Thou. *Mark* 8:29
fulfilled which *s.* 15:28; *Jas* 2:23
what the unjust judge *s.* *Luke* 18:6
who it is that *s.* Give. *John* 4:10
might be fulfilled, *s.* I thirst. 19:28
dwelleth not in temples made with hands, as *s.* *Acts* 7:48
thus *s.* the Holy Ghost, So. 21:11
the law *s.* it *s.* to them. *Rom* 3:19
for what *s.* the scripture? 4:3; 10:8
for scripture *s.* to Pharaoh. 9:17
for scripture *s.* Whosoever. 10:11
for Esaias *s.* 16, 20
first Moses *s.* 19
what the scripture *s.* of Elias? 11:2
but what *s.* the answer of God? 4
for while one *s.* I am of Paul. *1 Cor* 3:4
or *s.* not the law the same also? 9:8
be under obedience, as also *s.* 14:34
what *s.* the scripture? *Gal* 4:30 *1 Tim* 5:18
as the Holy Ghost *s.* If. *Heb* 3:7
do ye think the scriptures *s.* *Jas* 4:5
the Spirit *s.* to the churches. *Rev* 2:7 11, 17, 29; 3:6, 13, 22
s. the First and the Last. 2:8
s. the Son of God. 18
s. the Amen. 3:14
yea, *s.* the Spirit. 14:13
she *s.* I sit a queen, and am. 18:7
s. Surely I come quickly. 22:20

***God* saith**

what my *God s.* that. *2 Chr* 18:13
thus *s. God*, Why transgress? 24:20
to wicked *God s.* What? *Ps* 50:16
thus *s. God* the Lord. *Isa* 42:5
wast refused, *s.* thy *God*. 54:6
There is no peace, *s.* my *God*. 57:21
shut the womb, *s.* thy *God*. 66:9
come to pass in the last days *s. God*. *Acts* 2:17

***he* saith**

go to Joseph, what *he s.* *Gen* 41:55
all that *he s.* cometh. *1 Sam* 9:6
likewise what *he s.* *2 Sam* 17:5
when *he s.* to thee, Wash and be. *2 Ki* 5:13
for *he s.* to the snow, Be. *Job* 37:6
Eat and drink, *s. he* to. *Pr* 23:7
he that *s.* to wicked, Thou. 24:24
nor *s. he*, For whom do? *Eccl* 4:8
he s. to every one that he is. 10:3
he s. shall come to pass, he shall have whatsoever *he s.* *Mark* 11:23
whatsoever *he s.* to you. *John* 2:5
he s.? we cannot tell what *he s.* 16:18
knoweth that *he s.* true. 19:35
he s. to Peter, Feed my. 21:15, 16
which, *s. he*, ye have. *Acts* 1:4
more silence, and *he s.* 22:2
to Israel *he s.* *Rom* 10:21
again *he s.* 15:10
for two, *s. he*, shall be. *1 Cor* 6:16
or *s. he* it altogether for our? 9:10
he s. I have heard thee. *2 Cor* 6:2
he s. not, And to seeds. *Gal* 3:16
See, *s. he*, that thou. *Heb* 8:5
in that *he s.* A new covenant. 13

***see* Jesus, Lord**

sake

not curse the ground for man's *s.* *Gen* 8:21
Abram well for her *s.* 12:16
will not do it for forty's *s.* 18:29
not for twenty's *s* 31
not for ten's *s.* 32
slay me for my wife's *s.* 20:11
thy seed for Abraham's *s.* 26:24
Egyptian's house for Joseph's *s.* 39:5
done to Egypt for Israel's *s.* *Ex* 18:8
let him go free for eye's *s.* 21:26
for his tooth's *s.* 27
enviest thou for my *s.*? *Num* 11:29
he was zealous for my *s.* 25:11
day of the plague for Peor's *s.* 18
people for his name's *s.* *1 Sam* 12:22
destroy the city for my *s.* 23:10
kingdom for Israel's *s.* *2 Sam* 5:12
for thy word's *s.* hast done all. 7:21 *1 Chr* 17:19
kindness for Jonathan's *s.* *2 Sam* 9:1, 7
deal gently for my *s.* with. 18:5
out of a far country for thy name's *s.* *1 Ki* 8:41; *2 Chr* 6:32
David thy father's *s.* *1 Ki* 11:12 13, 32, 34; 15:4; *2 Ki* 8:19; 19:34 20:6; *Ps* 132:10
for Jerusalem's *s.* which I have. *1 Ki* 11:13
them for great mercies' *s.* *Neh* 9:31
entreated for children's *s.* *Job* 19:17
save me for thy mercies' *s.* *Ps* 6:4 31:16
for his name's *s.* 23:3; 31:3
me for thy goodness' *s.* 25:7
for thy name's *s.* pardon mine. 11
us for thy mercies' *s.* 44:26
not be confounded for my *s.* 69:6
our sins for thy name's *s.* 79:9
saved them for his name's *s.* 106:8
me, for thy name's *s.* 109:21
for thy mercy and truth's *s.* 115:1
for thy name's *s.*: for thy righteousness' *s.* bring my soul. 143:11
own *s.* and David's *s.* *Isa* 37:35
for his righteousness' *s.* 42:21
for your *s.* I have sent to. 43:14
transgressions for mine own *s.* 25
for Jacob's *s.* I have even. 45:4
for my name's *s.* will I defer. 48:9
even for mine own *s.* will I do it. 11
for Zion's *s.*. for Jerusalem's *s.* 62:1

return for thy servant's *s.* *Isa* 63:17
out for my name's *s.* said. 66:5
thou it for thy name's *s.* *Jer* 14:7
abhor us for thy name's *s.* 21
but I wrought for my name's *s.* that.
Ezek 20:9, 14, 22, 44; 36:22
sanctuary, for the Lord's *s.* *Dan* 9:17
defer not for thine own *s.* 19
for my *s.* this great. *Jonah* 1:12
shall Zion for your *s.* be. *Mi* 3:12
for righteousness' *s.* *Mat* 5:10
against you falsely for my *s.* 11
before governors and kings, for my *s.*
10:18; *Mark* 13:9; *Luke* 21:12
hated of all men, for my name's *s.*
Mat 10:22; 24:9; *Mark* 13:13
Luke 21:17
loseth his life for my *s.* *Mat* 10:39
16:25; *Mark* 8:35; *Luke* 9:24
Herod bound John for Herodias' *s.*
Mat 14:3; *Mark* 6:17
nevertheless, for the oath's *s.*
Mat 14:9; *Mark* 6:26
kingdom of heaven's *s.* *Mat* 19:12
left lands for my name's *s.* shall.
29; *Mark* 10:29; *Luke* 18:29
no flesh be saved, but for elect's *s.*
Mat 24:22; *Mark* 13:20
ariseth for the word's *s.* *Mark* 4:17
name for Son of man's *s.* *Luke* 6:22
not for Jesus' *s.* only. *John* 12:9
lay down thy life for my *s.*? 13:38
for the very works' *s.* 14:11
do to you for my name's *s.* 15:21
suffer for my name's *s.* *Acts* 9:16
for which hope's *s.* I am. 26:7
written for his *s.* alone. *Rom* 4:23
are enemies for your *s.* 11:28
be subject for conscience *s.* 13:5
for Lord's *s.* strive with. 15:30
for Christ's *s.* ye are wise. *1 Cor* 4:10
this I do for the gospel's *s.* 9:23
question for conscience *s.* 10:25, 27
eat not, for his *s.* that shewed it, and
for conscience *s.* 28
servants for Jesus' *s.* *2 Cor* 4:5
delivered to death for Jesus' *s.* 11
in distresses for Christ's *s.* 12:10
as God for Christ's *s.* *Eph* 4:32
also to suffer for his *s.* *Phil* 1:29
for his body's *s.* which. *Col* 1:24
for which thing's *s.* wrath of. 3:6
men we were for your *s.* *1 Thes* 1:5
highly for their work's *s.* 5:13
wine, for thy stomach's *s.* *1 Tim* 5:23
for filthy lucre's *s.* *Tit* 1:11
yet for love's *s.* I rather. *Philem* 9
ordinance for Lord's *s.* *1 Pet* 2:13
ye suffer for righteousness' *s.* 3:14
forgiven for name's *s.* *1 John* 2:12
for the truth's *s.* that. *2 John* 2
because for his name's *s.* *3 John* 7
and for my name's *s.* hast. *Rev* 2:3

thy sake

the ground for *thy s.* *Gen* 3:17
well with me for *thy s.* 12:13
hath blessed me for *thy s.* 30:27
for *thy s.* are we killed all day long.
Ps 44:22; *Rom* 8:36
because for *thy s.* I have borne.
Ps 69:7
against thee, shall fall for *thy s.*
Isa 54:15
know that for *thy s.* I have. *Jer* 15:15
down my life for *thy s.* *John* 13:37

sakes

the place for their *s.* *Gen* 18:26
I will for their *s.* remember the.
Lev 26:45
the Lord was angry with me for your
s. saying. *Deut* 1:37; 3:26; 4:21
to them for our *s.* *Judg* 21:22
me much for your *s.* *Ruth* 1:13
reproved kings for their *s.*
1 Chr 16:21; *Ps* 105:14
for their *s.* therefore. *Ps* 7:7
with Moses for their *s* 106:32
and companions' *s.* 122:8
for my servant's *s.* *Isa* 65:8
not this for your *s.* *Ezek* 36:22, 32
but for their *s.* that. *Dan* 2:30
and I will rebuke the devourer for
your *s.*, he shall not. *Mal* 3:11

for their *s.* which sat. *Mark* 6:26
I am glad for your *s.* I. *John* 11:15
not for me, but for your *s.* 12:30
and for their *s.* I sanctify. 17:19
for their fathers' *s.* *Rom* 11:28
transferred for your *s.* *1 Cor* 4:6
our *s.*? for our *s.* no doubt. 9:10
all things are for your *s.* *2 Cor* 4:15
though rich, yet for your *s.* 8:9
your *s.* before God. *1 Thes* 3:9
things for the elect's *s.* *2 Tim* 2:10

Salathiel

S. the son of Jechoniah. *1 Chr* 3:17
Mat 1:12
which was the son of *S.* *Luke* 3:27

sale

the years of the *s.* thereof. *Lev* 25:27
price of his *s.* shall be. 50
which cometh of the *s.* *Deut* 18:8

Salem

Melchizedek king of *S.* *Gen* 14:18
in *S.* also is his tabernacle. *Ps* 76:2
Melchizedek king of *S.* who blessed.
Heb 7:1
king of *S.* is king of peace. 2

Salmon

Nahshon begat *S.* *Ruth* 4:20
S. begat Boaz. 21; *1 Chr* 2:11
Mat 1:4, 5
white as snow in *S.* *Ps* 68:14
which was the son of *S.* *Luke* 3:32

Salmone

Crete, over against *S.* *Acts* 27:7

Salome

Mary, mother of *S.* *Mark* 15:40
16:1

salt

This was even more indispensable to the Hebrews than to us, as they used it as an antidote to the effects of the heat of the climate on animal food, and it also was used in the sacrifices. They had an inexhaustible and ready supply of it on the southern shores of the Salt Sea, now called the Dead Sea.

Salt symbolized hospitality, durability and purity. To eat the salt of the king was to owe him the utmost fidelity. To eat bread and salt together was to make an unbreakable league of friendship.

became a pillar of *s.* *Gen* 19:26
offerings thou shalt offer *s.* *Lev* 2:13
whole land thereof is *s.* *Deut* 29:23
Judah had the city of *s.* *Josh* 15:62
city, and sowed it with *s.* *Judg* 9:45
in the valley of *s.* *2 Sam* 8:13
cruse, put *s.* therein. *2 Ki* 2:20
and cast the *s.* in there. 21
Edom in the valley of *s.* 10,000.
14:7; *1 Chr* 18:12; *2 Chr* 25:11
need of, wheat, *s.*, wine. *Ezra* 6:9
and *s.* without prescribing. 7:22
be eaten without *s.*? *Job* 6:6
inhabit places in a *s.* land. *Jer* 17:6
the priest shall cast *s.* *Ezek* 43:24
thereof shall be given to *s.* 47:11
Moab shall be as *s.* pits. *Zeph* 2:9
s. of the earth, but if the *s.* *Mat* 5:13
shall be salted with *s.* *Mark* 9:49
s. have lost his saltness, wherewith
will ye season it ? have *s.* 50
s. is good, but if *s.* have. *Luke* 14:34
speech be seasoned with *s.* *Col* 4:6
no fountain can yield *s.* *Jas* 3:12
see **covenant of salt**

salt sea

(*Now called the Dead Sea*)
which is the *s. sea.* *Gen* 14:3
shall be at the *s. sea.* *Num* 34:12
coast even to the *s. sea.* *Deut* 3:17
came toward the *s. sea.* *Josh* 3:16
even to *s. sea.* 12:3; 15:2, 5; 18:19

salted

thou wast not *s.* at all. *Ezek* 16:4
wherewith shall it be *s.*? *Mat* 5:13
one shall be *s.* with fire and every
sacrifice shall be *s.* *Mark* 9:49

saltness

if salt have lost his *s.* *Mark* 9:50

salutation

what manner of *s.* this. *Luke* 1:29
at *s.* of Mary, babe leaped. 41, 44
you, the *s.* of me, Paul. *1 Cor* 16:21
Col 4:18; *2 Thes* 3:17

salutations

scribes who love *s.* in. *Mark* 12:38

salute

will *s.* thee and give. *1 Sam* 10:4
that he might *s.* Samuel. 13:10
David sent to *s.* our master 25:14
Joram his son to *s.* *2 Sam* 8:10
s. him not, if any *s.* thee. *2 Ki* 4:29
we go to *s.* the children of. 10:13
and if ye *s.* your brethren. *Mat* 5:47
come into an house, *s.* it. 10:12
and began to *s.* him. *Mark* 15:18
shoes, and *s.* no man. *Luke* 10:4
Bernice came to *s.* Festus. *Acts* 25:13
s. my wellbeloved. *Rom* 16:5
s. Andronicus. 7
s. Urbane our helper. 9
s. Apelles, *s.* them of Aristobulus'. 10
s. Herodian. 11
s. the beloved Persis. 12
s. Rufus chosen in the Lord. 13
s. with an holy kiss, churches *s.* 16
I Tertius, who wrote this, *s.* you. 22
the churches of Asia *s.* you. Aquila
and Priscilla *s.* you. *1 Cor* 16:19
all the saints *s.* you. *2 Cor* 13:13
Phil 4:22
s. every saint in Christ. *Phil* 4:21
s. the brethren in Laodicea. *Col* 4:15
s. the household of. *2 Tim* 4:19
all that are with me, *s.* thee. *Tit* 3:15
there *s.* thee Epaphras. *Philem* 23
s. them that have the rule over you;
they of Italy *s.* you. *Heb* 13:24
our friends *s.* thee, greet. *3 John* 14

saluted

the Danites came and *s.* *Judg* 18:15*
David came and *s.* *1 Sam* 17:22
to the people and *s.* them. 30:21
Jehu *s.* Jehonadab. *2 Ki* 10:15
running to Jesus, *s.* him. *Mark* 9:15
Mary entered, and *s.* *Luke* 1:40
Paul, when he had *s.* *Acts* 18:22
we came to Ptolemais, and *s.* 21:7
when Paul had *s.* James and. 19

saluteth

and Erastus *s.* you. *Rom* 16:23
my fellow-prisoner *s.* you. *Col* 4:10
servant of Christ, *s.* you. 12
is at Babylon *s.* you. *1 Pet* 5:13

salvation

[1] *Preservation from trouble or danger.* [2] *Deliverance from sin and its consequences.*

see the *s.* of the Lord. *Ex* 14:13
2 Chr 20:17
the rock of his *s.* *Deut* 32:15
the Lord wrought *s.* *1 Sam* 11:13*
hath wrought this great *s.* 14:45
the Lord wrought a great *s.* 19:5*
he is the tower of *s.* for his king.
2 Sam 22:51*
from day to day his *s.* *1 Chr* 16:23
save us, O God of our *s.* and. 35
be clothed with *s.* *2 Chr* 6:41
s. belongeth to the Lord. *Ps* 3:8
O that the *s.* of Israel. 14:7; 53:6
from the God of his *s.* 24:5
my soul shall rejoice in his *s.* 35:9
the *s.* of the righteous is of. 37:39
will I shew the *s.* of God. 50:23
answer us, O God of our *s.*? 65:5
Lord, even the God of our *s.* 68:19
our God, is the God of *s.* 20*
working *s.* in the midst of. 74:12
they trusted not in his *s.* 78:22
help us, O God of our *s.*, for. 79:9
turn us, O God of our *s.* 85:4
surely his *s.* is nigh them that. 9
joyful noise to the rock of our *s.* 95:1
forth his *s.* from day to day. 96:2
hath made known his *s.* 98:2
have seen the *s.* of our God. 3
I will take the cup of *s.* 116:13
the voice of *s.* is in. 118:15
s. is far from the wicked. 119:155
clothe her priests with *s.* 132:16

that giveth s. unto kings. Ps 144:10
beautify the meek with s. 149:4
water out of the wells of s. Isa 12:3
glad and rejoice in his s. 25:9
s. will God appoint for walls. 26:1
be thou our s. in the time of. 33:2
knowledge, and strength of s. 6
and let them bring forth s. 45:8
saved with an everlasting s. 17
I will place s. in Zion for. 46:13
in a day of s. have I helped. 49:8
him that publisheth s. 52:7
shall see the s. of our God. 10
we look for s. but it is far. 59:11
therefore his arm brought s. 16
he put on an helmet of s. upon. 17
but shalt call thy walls s. 60:18
me with the garments of s. 61:10
and the s. thereof as a lamp. 62:1
own arm brought s. to me. 63:5
is s. hoped for from the hills and mountains . . . s. of. Jer 3:23*
quietly wait for the s. Lam 3:26
S. is of the Lord. Jonah 2:9
ride on thy chariots of s. Hab 3:8
thou wentest forth for s. of thy people, even for s. with thine. 13
he is just, and having s. Zech 9:9
up an horn of s. for us. Luke 1:69
knowledge of s. to his people. 77
all flesh shall see the s. of. 3:6
Jesus said, This day is s. 19:9
we know what we worship, for s. is of the Jews. John 4:22
neither is there s. in any. Acts 4:12
the word of this s. sent. 13:26
thou shouldest be for s. unto the. 47
shew to us the way of s. 16:17
the s. of God is sent unto the. 28:28
the power of God unto s. Rom 1:16
confession is made unto s. 10:10
through their fall s. is come. 11:11
now is our s. nearer than. 13:11
comforted, it is for your s. 2 Cor 1:6
in the day of s. have I succoured thee; behold now is the day of s. 6:2
worketh repentance to s. 7:10
the gospel of your s. Eph 1:13
take the helmet of s. and. 6:17
an evident token of s. Phil 1:28
work out your own s. with. 2:12
an helmet the hope of s. 1 Thes 5:8
hath appointed us to obtain s. 9
chosen you to s. 2 Thes 2:13
obtain the s. in Christ. 2 Tim 2:10
able to make thee wise unto s. 3:15
God that bringeth s. Tit 2:11
shall be heirs of s. Heb 1:14
if we neglect so great s.? 2:3
the Captain of their s. perfect. 10
the Author of eternal s. 5:9
things that accompany s. 6:9
second time without sin unto s. 9:28
through faith unto s. 1 Pet 1:5
receiving the end of your faith, s. 9
of which s. the prophets have. 10
the longsuffering of the Lord is s. 2 Pet 3:15
to you of the common s. Jude 3
saying; S. to our God. Rev 7:10
s. and glory, unto the Lord. 19:1
now is come s. and strength. 12:10

my salvation

song, he is become my s. Ex 15:2
shield, the horn of my s. 2 Sam 22:3
the rock of my s. 47; Ps 18:46
for this is all my s. and. 2 Sam 23:5
he also shall be my s. Job 13:16
art the God of my s. Ps 25:5
the Lord is my light and my s. 27:1
62:6; Isa 12:2
O God of my s. Ps 27:9; 51:14; 88:1
O Lord my s. 38:22
God, from him cometh my s. 62:1
he only is my s. 2, 6
in God is my s. 7
my God, rock of my s. 89:26
him, and shew him my s. 91:16
become my s. 118:14, 21; Isa 12:2
Lord, strength of my s. Ps 140:7
my s. he is become my s. Isa 12:2
far off, my s. shall not tarry. 46:13
thou mayest be my s. to end. 49:6
my s. is gone forth. Isa 51:5
my s. shall be for ever. 6
and my s. from generation to. 8
my s. is near to come, and my. 56:1
the God of my s. my God. Mi 7:7
joy in the God of my s. Hab 3:18
that this shall turn to my s. Phil 1:19

thy salvation

I have waited for thy s. Gen 49:18
because I rejoice in thy s. 1 Sam 2:1
also given me the shield of thy s. 2 Sam 22:36; Ps 18:35
I will rejoice in thy s. Ps 9:14
my heart shall rejoice in thy s. 13:5
we will rejoice in thy s. 20:5
and in thy s. how greatly! 21:1
his glory is great in thy s. 5
say unto my soul, I am thy s. 35:3
thy faithfulness and thy s. 40:10
let such as love thy s. say, Lord. 16
me the joy of thy s. 51:12; 70:4
me in the truth of thy s. 69:13
I am poor, let thy s. set me up. 29
shall shew forth thy s. 71:15
O Lord, grant us thy s. 85:7
O visit me with thy s. 106:4
let thy s. come according. 119:41
my soul fainteth for thy s. 81
mine eyes fail for thy s. and. 123
Lord, I have hoped for thy s. 166
I have longed for thy s. O Lord. 174
forgotten the God of thy s. Isa 17:10
say to Zion, Behold, thy s. 62:11
eyes have seen thy s. Luke 2:30

Samaria

places which are in S. 1 Ki 13:32
Omri bought the hill S. of. 16:24
besieged S. 20:1; 2 Ki 6:24
if the dust of S. shall suffice. 1 Ki 20:10
there are men come out of S. 17
sat on their throne in the entrance of the gate of S. 22:10; 2 Chr 18:9
chariot in the pool of S. 1 Ki 22:38
were in the midst of S. 2 Ki 6:20
shekel in the gate of S. 7:1, 18
king of Assyria took S. 17:6; 18:10
have they delivered S. out of mine hand? 18:34; Isa 36:19
Jerusalem the line of S. 2 Ki 21:13
prophet that came out of S. 23:18
upon the cities; from S. 2 Chr 25:13
Asnapper set in the cities of S. Ezra 4:10
spake before army of S. Neh 4:2
Ephraim is S. and the head of S. is. Isa 7:9
and the spoil of S. shall be. 8:4
Ephraim and inhabitants of S. 9:9
is not Hamath as Arpad? S. 10:9
folly in the prophets of S. Jer 23:13
vines on the mountains of S. 31:5
certain from Shechem and S. 41:5
thine elder sister is S. Ezek 16:46
nor hath S. committed half. 51
S. is Aholah, and Jerusalem. 23:4
then the wickedness of S. Hos 7:1
thy calf, O S. hath cast thee. 8:5
but the calf of S. shall be broken. 6
inhabitants of S. shall fear. 10:5
as for S. her king is cut off as. 7
S. shall become desolate, she. 13:16
on mountains of S. Amos 3:9
Bashan, in mountain of S. 4:1
trust in the mountain of S. 6:1
swear by the sin of S. and. 8:14
possess the fields of S. Ob 19
which he saw concerning S. Mi 1:1
I will make S. as an heap of. 6
through the midst of S. Luke 17:11
must needs go through S. John 4:4
of me, who am a woman of S.? 9
through the regions of S. Acts 8:1
preached Christ to them of S. 5
the apostles heard that S. 14

in Samaria

Omri buried in S. 1 Ki 16:28
Ahab reigned in S. 29
was a sore famine in S. 18:2
as my father made in S. 20:34
king of Israel which is in S. 21:18
Ahab buried in S. 22:37
Ahaziah reigned in S. 51
Jehoram to reign in S. 2 Ki 3:1
were with the prophets in S. 5:3
was a great famine in S. 6:25
Jehu slew all that remained to Ahab in S. 10:17
Jehoahaz reigned in S. 13:1
remained the grove also in S. 6
Jehoahaz buried in S. 9
Jehoash to reign in S. 10
Joash, buried in S. 13; 14:16
Jeroboam reigned in S. 14:23
Zechariah reigned in S. 15:8, 13
Menahem to reign in S. 17
Pekah to reign in S. 27
Hoshea to reign in S. 17:1
for Ahaziah was hid in S. 2 Chr 22:9
so Israel that dwell in S. Amos 3:12
be witnesses to me in S. Acts 1:8
had the churches rest in S. 9:31

to or unto Samaria

displeased came to S. 1 Ki 20:43
so king was brought to S. 22:37
from Carmel to S. 2 Ki 2:25
but Elisha led them to S. 6:19
Jehu sent letters to S. 10:1
Jehu came to S. 12, 17
Jehoash took hostages, and returned to S. 14:14; 2 Chr 25:24
Menahem came to S. 2 Ki 15:14
king of Assyria went up to S. 17:5
Jehoshaphat went down to S. 2 Chr 18:2
brought the spoil of Judah to S. 28:8
as I have done unto S. Isa 10:11

Samaritan

but a certain S. came. Luke 10:33
gave thanks, and he was a S. 17:16
that thou art a S. and. John 8:48

Samaritans

places the S. had made. 2 Ki 17:29
into any city of the S. Mat 10:5
into a village of the S. Luke 9:52
no dealings with the S. John 4:9
many of the S. of that city. 39
the S. besought him to tarry. 40
many villages of the S. Acts 8:25

same

saying, This s. shall. Gen 5:29
the s. became mighty men. 6:4
Resen, the s. is a great city. 10:12
the s. is Zoar. 14:8
the s. is Hebron. 23:2, 19
let the s. be she that. 24:14, 44
appeared to Isaac the s. night. 26:24
spake them these s. words. 44:6
in the way of Ephrath, the s. 48:7
shall be of the s. Ex 25:31; 37:17
knops and branches shall be of the s. 25:36; 37:22
his horns shall be of the s. 27:2
37:25; 38:2
ephod shall be of the s. 28:8; 39:5
the s. goodness will we. Num 10:32
presumptuously, the s. 15:30
the Jebusite, the s. Josh 15:8
the s. shall go, the s. Judg 7:4
the s. shall reign over. 1 Sam 9:17
Zion, the s. is the city. 2 Sam 5:7
nor turn again by the s. way. 1 Ki 13:9
year ye shall eat that which springeth of the s. 2 Ki 19:29; Isa 37:30
Abram, the s. is. 1 Chr 1:27
hath confirmed the s. to Jacob. 16:17; Ps 105:10
the s. may be a priest. 2 Chr 13:9
s. is Micaiah the son of Imla. 18:7
hath not the s. Hezekiah? 32:12
Shimei, and Kelaiah, the s. is Kelita. Ezra 10:23
the thirteenth day of s. Esth 9:1
wickedness reap the s. Job 4:8
what ye know, the s. do I. 13:2
of thy dogs in the s. Ps 68:23*
he poureth out of the s. 75:8
but thou art the s., and thy years shall have no. 102:27; Heb 1:12
to the going down of the s. Ps 113:3; Mal 1:11
the s. is the companion. Pr 28:24
remembered that s. poor. Eccl 9:15
prophet died the s. year. Jer 28:17
s. wicked man shall die. Ezek 3:18
this shall not be the s.: exalt. 21:26

go out by the way of the *s.* *Ezek* 44:3
the *s.* horn made war. *Dan* 7:21
go in to the *s.* maid. *Amos* 2:7
s. shall be called great. *Mat* 5:19
even the publicans the *s.*? 46
the *s.* is my brother and sister.
12:50; *Mark* 3:35
s. is become the head of the corner.
Mat 21:42; *Luke* 20:17; *1 Pet* 2:7
shall endure, *s.* shall be saved.
Mat 24:13; *Mark* 13:13
he that dippeth his hand with me . . .
the *s.* shall betray me. *Mat* 26:23
that *s.* is he, hold. 48; *Mark* 14:44
thieves also cast the *s.* *Mat* 27:44
lose his life, the *s.* shall save it.
Mark 8:35; *Luke* 9:24
desire to be first, the *s.* *Mark* 9:35
sinners also do even the *s.* *Luke* 6:33
for with the *s.* measure that ye. 38
is forgiven, the *s.* loveth little. 7:47
the *s.* shall be great. 9:48
the *s.* was accused that he. 16:1
the *s.* shall receive greater. 20:47
the *s.* had not consented to. 23:51
the *s.* was in the beginning. *John* 1:2
the *s.* came for a witness of. 7
the *s.* is he which baptizeth with. 33
the *s.* is true. 7:18
the *s.* I said to you from the. 8:25
the *s.* is a thief. 10:1
he abode two days still in the *s.* 11:6
high priest that *s.* year. 49; 18:13
the *s.* shall judge him in the. 12:48
abideth in me, the *s.* bringeth. 15:5
this *s.* Jesus shall so. *Acts* 1:11
God made that *s.* Jesus both. 2:36
the *s.* dealt subtilly with our. 7:19
the *s.* did God send to be. 35
began at the *s.* scripture and. 8:35
God hath fulfilled the *s.* to. 13:33
the *s.* heard Paul speak. 14:9
the *s.* followed Paul and us. 16:17
or else let these *s.* here say. 24:20
not only do the *s.* *Rom* 1:32
which do such, and doest the *s.* 2:3
who hath subjected the *s.* 8:20
the *s.* Lord over all is rich to. 10:12
members have not the *s.* 12:4
be of the *s.* mind one toward. 16
1 Cor 1:10; *Phil* 4:2; *1 Pet* 4:1
have praise of the *s.* *Rom* 13:3
ye all speak the *s.* thing. *1 Cor* 1:10
or saith not the law the *s.* also ? 9:8
did all eat the *s.* spiritual meat. 10:3
the *s.* drink. 4
but the *s.* Spirit. 12:4; *2 Cor* 4:13
12:18
but the *s.* Lord. *1 Cor* 12:5
but it is the *s.* God. 6
all flesh is not the *s.* flesh. 15:39
but the *s.* which is made. *2 Cor* 2:2
I wrote this *s.* unto you, lest. 3
to the glory of the *s.* Lord. 8:19
s. might be ready as a matter. 9:5
the *s.* was mighty in me. *Gal* 2:8
the *s.* are the children of. 3:7
descended is the *s.* that. *Eph* 4:10
the *s.* shall he receive of Lord. 6:8
having the *s.* conflict. *Phil* 1:30
having *s.* love, being of one. 2:2
the *s.* rule, mind the *s.* things. 3:16
and watch in the *s.* with. *Col* 4:2
the *s.* commit thou to. *2 Tim* 2:2
likewise took part of the *s.* *Heb* 2:14
the heirs with him of the *s.* 11:9
Jesus Christ, the *s.* yesterday. 13:8
if any offend not, the *s.* is. *Jas* 3:2
even so minister the *s.* *1 Pet* 4:10
of the *s.* is he brought. *2 Pet* 2:19
by the *s.* word are kept in store. 3:7
denieth the Son, *s.* hath. *1 John* 2:23
as the *s.* anointing teacheth you. 27
overcometh, the *s.* shall. *Rev* 3:5
see **day, hour**

Samson

called his name *S.* *Judg* 13:24
S. went to Timnath. 14:1
she pleased *S.* well. 7
S. made there a feast. 10
S.'s wife wept before him. 16
S. caught foxes. 15:4
to bind *S.* are we come. 10
S. is come hither. *Judg* 16:2
S. lay till midnight. 3
be upon thee, *S.* 9, 12, 14, 20
our god hath delivered *S.* into. 23
they said, Call for *S.* 25
S. called unto the Lord. 28
S. took hold of the pillars. 29
S. said, Let me die with. 30
fail me to tell of *S.* *Heb* 11:32

Samuel

son, and called him *S.* *1 Sam* 1:20
S. ministered before the Lord. 2:18
child *S.* grew before the Lord. 21
the Lord called *S.*: and he answered,
Here am I. 3:4, 6, 8, 10
and *S.* feared to shew Eli the. 15
the Lord revealed himself to *S.* 21
and the word of *S.* came to all. 4:1
S. judged the children. 7:6, 15
S. cried to the Lord for Israel. 9
Philistines all the days of *S.* 13
displeased *S.* when they said. 8:6
refused to obey the voice of *S.* 19
and *S.* heard all the words of. 21
Lord told *S.* in his ear before. 9:15
so Saul did eat with *S.* that. 24
S. called Saul to the top of the. 26
S. took a vial of oil and. 10:1
we came to *S.* 14
tell me, I pray thee, what *S.* said. 15
then *S.* told the manner of the. 25
not forth after Saul and *S.* 11:7
the Lord sent *S.* 12:11
greatly feared the Lord and *S.* 18
he tarried the set time that *S.* 13:8
it grieved *S.* 15:11
S. turned about to go away, *S.*'s. 27
S. hewed Agag in pieces. 33
nevertheless, *S.* mourned for. 35
Jesse made seven of his sons to pass
before *S.* 16:10
S. took the horn of oil and. 13
David fled and came to *S.* 19:18
said, Where are *S.* and David ? 22
S. died. 25:1
Saul said, Bring me up *S.* 28:11
Saul perceived that it was *S.* 14
sons of *S.* *1 Chr* 6:28
whom David and *S.* the seer. 9:22
word of the Lord by *S.* 11:3
all that *S.* had dedicated. 26:28
like that from *S.* *2 Chr* 35:18
S. among them that call. *Ps* 99:6
Moses and *S.* stood. *Jer* 15:1
the prophets from *S.* *Acts* 3:24
judges 450 years till *S.* 13:20
would fail me to tell of *S.* *Heb* 11:32

Sanballat

when *S.* heard of it. *Neh* 2:10, 19
when *S.* heard we builded. 4:1, 7
S. sent to me. 6:2, 5
for Tobiah and *S.* had hired. 12
my God, think upon *S.* 14
Joiada was son in law to *S.* 13:28

sanctification

of God is made unto us *s.* *1 Cor* 1:30
of God, even your *s.* *1 Thes* 4:3
to possess his vessel in *s.* 4
through *s.* of the Spirit. *2 Thes* 2:13
1 Pet 1:2

sanctified

seventh day and *s.* it. *Gen* 2:3*
Moses *s.* the people. *Ex* 19:14
the tabernacle shall be *s.* for. 29:43
s. the tabernacle, and. *Lev* 8:10
s. the altar. 15
s. Aaron and his garments. 30
I will be *s.* in them that come. 10:3
if he that *s.* it will redeem. 27:15
and if he that *s.* the field will. 19
s. the tabernacle. *Num* 7:1
s. the firstborn of Israel. 8:17
because ye *s.* me not. *Deut* 32:51
s. Eleazar his son to. *1 Sam* 7:1
he *s.* Jesse and his sons to. 16:5
though it were *s.* this day in. 21:5
Levites *s.* themselves. *1 Chr* 15:14
priests present were *s.* *2 Chr* 5:11
I have chosen and *s.* 7:16*, 20*
and *s.* themselves. 29:15
they *s.* the house of the. 17
vessels have we prepared and *s.* 19
till other priests had *s.* *2 Chr* 29:34
the priests had not *s.* 30:3
sanctuary which he hath *s.* for ever. 8
were ashamed, and *s.* themselves. 15
congregation were not *s.* 17
a great number of the priests *s.* 24
in their set office they *s.* 31:18
and *s.* the sheep gate. *Neh* 3:1
they *s.* holy things to the Levites, and
the Levites *s.* them to the. 12:47
Job sent and *s.* his sons. *Job* 1:5
holy God shall be *s.* in. *Isa* 5:16
I have commanded my *s.* ones. 13:3
I *s.* thee, and ordained. *Jer* 1:5
I will be *s.* in you. *Ezek* 20:41
36:23
when I shall be *s.* in her. 28:22
I shall be *s.* in thee. 38:16
be *s.* in them in sight of. 25; 39:27
the priests that are *s.* 48:11
whom the Father *s.* *John* 10:36
that they also might be *s.* 17:19
an inheritance among them which
are *s.* *Acts* 20:32; 26:18
s. by the Holy Ghost. *Rom* 15:16
them that are *s.* in Christ. *1 Cor* 1:2
but now ye are *s.* in the name. 6:11
husband is *s.* . . . wife is *s.* 7:14
it is *s.* by the word of. *1 Tim* 4:5
shall be a vessel *s.* for. *2 Tim* 2:21
and they who are *s.* are. *Heb* 2:11
by the which will we are *s.* 10:10
perfected them that are *s.* 14
covenant wherewith he was *s.* 29
to them that are *s.* by God. *Jude* 1*

sanctifieth

temple that *s.* the gold ? *Mat* 23:17
the altar that *s.* the gift ? 19
both he that *s.* and they. *Heb* 2:11
if blood of bulls *s.* to the. 9:13

sanctify

[1] *To dedicate.* [2] *To set aside for holy uses.* [3] *To make holy.*

s. unto me all the firstborn. *Ex* 13:2
go and *s.* them to-day. 19:10
and let the priests also *s.* 22
about the mount, and *s.* it. 23
shalt anoint and *s.* 28:41; 29:33
40:13; *Lev* 8:12; 21:8
thou shalt *s.* the breast. *Ex* 29:27
shalt *s.* the altar. 36, 37; 40:10
I will *s.* the tabernacle and. 29:44
and thou shalt *s.* the. 30:29; 40:10
11; *Lev* 8:11
I am the Lord that doth *s.* *Ex* 31:13
Lev 20:8; 21:8; *Ezek* 20:12
ye shall *s.* yourselves. *Lev* 11:44
20:7; *Num* 11:18; *Josh* 3:5; 7:13
1 Sam 16:5
seed, I the Lord do *s.* *Lev* 21:15
I the Lord do *s.* them. 23; 22:9, 16
when a man shall *s.* his. 27:14
if a man shall *s.* his field. 16, 17
18, 22
firstling, no man shall *s.* 26
ye believed me not, to *s.* me.
Num 20:12; 27:14
keep the sabbath day to *s.* it.
Deut 5:12*; *Neh* 13:22
firstling males thou shalt *s.* 15:19
up, *s.* the people, *s.* *Josh* 7:13
s. yourselves. *1 Chr* 15:12
2 Chr 29:5; 35:6
he should *s.* the most. *1 Chr* 23:13
upright in heart to *s.* *2 Chr* 29:34
one that was not clean to *s.* 30:17
s. the Lord himself. *Isa* 8:13
they shall *s.* the Holy One. 29:23
they that *s.* themselves in. 66:17
I will *s.* my great name. *Ezek* 36:23
that I the Lord do *s.* Israel. 37:28
magnify myself, and *s.* myself. 38:23
shall not *s.* people with garments.
44:19; 46:20
s. ye a fast. *Joel* 1:14; 2:15
s. the congregation, assemble. 2:16
s. them through thy. *John* 17:17
and for their sakes I *s.* myself. 19
that he might *s.* and. *Eph* 5:26
very God of peace *s.* *1 Thes* 5:23
that he might *s.* people. *Heb* 13:12
but *s.* the Lord God in. *1 Pet* 3:15

sanctuaries
that he profane not my *s.* *Lev* 21:23
bring your *s.* to desolation. 26:31
strangers are come into *s.* *Jer* 51:51
hast defiled thy *s.* by. *Ezek* 28:18
the *s.* of Israel shall be. *Amos* 7:9

sanctuary
(*Generally a place set apart for the worship of God. Specifically the Temple at Jerusalem, most especially the Most Holy Place, or Holy of Holies. It is also used as meaning a refuge, or place of protection*)
plant them in the *s.* *Ex* 15:17
let them make me a *s.* 25:8
one after the shekel of the *s.* 30:13
shekels after the shekel of the *s.* 24
manner of work for the *s.* 36:1, 3, 4
more work for offering of the *s.* 6
the shekel of the *s.* 38:24, 25, 26
Lev 5:15; 27:3, 25; *Num* 3:47, 50
7:13, 19, 25, 31, 37; 18:16
cast the sockets of the *s.* *Ex* 28:27
before the vail of the *s.* *Lev* 4:6
brethren from before the *s.* 10:4
nor come into the *s.* till her. 12:4
atonement for the holy *s.* 16:33
shall reverence my *s.* 19:30; 26:2
go out of the *s.* nor profane the *s.* of his God. 21:12
keeping charge of the *s.* *Num* 3:28
Aaron keeping charge of the *s.* 38
they minister in the *s.* 4:12
an end of covering the *s.* 15
the service of *s.* belonging. 7:9
Israel come nigh to the *s.* 8:19
set forward, bearing the *s.* 10:21
bear the iniquity of the *s.* 18:1
not come nigh the vessels of the *s.* 3
shall keep the charge of the *s.* 5
because he hath defiled the *s.* 19:20
a great stone by the *s.* *Josh* 24:26
instruments of the *s.* *1 Chr* 9:29
arise, and build ye the *s.* of. 22:19
for the governors of the *s.* 24:5
build an house for the *s.* 28:10
built thee a *s.* therein. *2 Chr* 20:8
go out of the *s.* for thou. 26:18
for a sin offering for the *s.* and. 29:21
to Lord, and enter into his *s.* 30:8
to the purification of the *s.* 19
Babylon slew men in the *s.* 36:17
the vessels of the *s.* *Neh* 10:39
send thee help from the *s.* *Ps* 20:2
as I have seen thee in the *s.* 63:2
seen thy goings in the *s.* 68:24
till I went into the *s.* of God. 73:17
enemy hath done wickedly in *s.* 74:3
they have cast fire into thy *s.* 7
thy way, O God, is in the *s.* 77:13
to the border of his *s.* 78:54
built his *s.* like high palaces. 69
strength and beauty are in his *s.* 96:6
from the height of his *s.* 102:19
Judah was his *s.*, Israel his. 114:2
lift up your hands in the *s.* 134:2
Lord, praise God in his *s.* 150:1
hosts, he shall be for a *s.* *Isa* 8:14
that he shall come to his *s.* to. 16:12
profaned the princes of the *s.* 43:28
to beautify the place of my *s.* 60:13
trodden down thy *s.* 63:18
is the place of our *s.* *Jer* 17:12
entered into her *s.* *Lam* 1:10
the Lord hath abhorred his *s.* 2:7
prophet be slain in the *s.*? 20
stones of the *s.* are poured. 4:1
thou hast defiled my *s.* *Ezek* 5:11
will I be to them as a little *s.* 11:16
defiled my *s.* in the same day. 23:38
day into my *s.* to profane it. 39
between *s.* and the profane. 42:20*
with every going forth of the *s.* 44:5
day that he goeth into the *s.* 27
in it shall be the *s.* and most. 45:3
they issued out of the *s.* 47:12
s. shall be in the midst. 48:8, 10, 21
and the place of his *s.* *Dan* 8:11
to give the *s.* to be trodden. 13
he said to me, then shall the *s.* 14
face to shine upon thy *s.* 9:17
destroy the city and the *s.* 26
they shall pollute the *s.* 11:31
have polluted the *s.* *Zeph* 3:4
a minister of the *s.* and. *Heb* 8:2
covenant had a worldly *s.* 9:1
tabernacle which is called the *s.* 2*
blood is brought into the *s.* 13:11*

sand
(*The word is frequently used in the Bible as a symbol of uncounted multitudes, or a weight impossible to measure*)
seed as the *s.* *Gen* 22:17; 32:12
gathered corn as the *s.* of. 41:49
hid the Egyptian in the *s.* *Ex* 2:12
treasures hid in *s.* *Deut* 33:19
much people as the *s.* *Josh* 11:4
as the *s.* by the sea. *Judg* 7:12
gathered to fight as the *s.* *1 Sam* 13:5
all Israel be gathered as the *s.* *2 Sam* 17:11
are many, as the *s.* *1 Ki* 4:20
largeness of heart as the *s.* 29
be heavier than the *s.* *Job* 6:3
multiply my days as the *s.* 29:18
fowls like as the *s.* *Ps* 78:27
in number than the *s.* 139:18
a stone is heavy, and the *s.* *Pr* 27:3
Israel be as the *s.* *Isa* 10:22
thy seed also had been as *s.* 48:19
which placed the *s.* for. *Jer* 5:22
increased to me above the *s.* 15:8
as the *s.* of the sea, cannot. 33:22
shall be as the *s.* of the sea. *Hos* 1:10; *Rom* 9:27
the captivity as the *s.* *Hab* 1:9
built his house on *s.* *Mat* 7:26
of one, so many as the *s.* *Heb* 11:12
I stood upon the *s.* of the. *Rev* 13:1
the number of whom is as the *s.* 20:8

sandals
(*At first were only soles tied to the feet with strings or thongs; afterwards they were covered; and at last even shoes were called* Sandals)
but be shod with *s.* put. *Mark* 6:9
thyself, and bind thy *s.* *Acts* 12:8

sang
then *s.* Moses and Israel. *Ex* 15:1
Israel *s.* this song. *Num* 21:17
then *s.* Deborah and. *Judg* 5:1
David of whom they *s.*? *1 Sam* 29:5
the singers *s.* the. *2 Chr* 29:28
s. praises with gladness, and. 30
the singers *s.* aloud. *Neh* 12:42
when the morning stars *s.* *Job* 38:7
his word, *s.* his praise. *Ps* 106:12
Silas *s.* praises to God. *Acts* 16:25

sank
they *s.* into the bottom. *Ex* 15:5
they *s.* as lead in the mighty. 10

sap
the trees are full of *s.* *Ps* 104:16*

Saphir
thou inhabitant of *S.* *Mi* 1:11

Sapphira
Ananias, with *S.* his wife. *Acts* 5:1

sapphire
(*A precious stone of a bright blue colour. It is thought to mean lapis lazuli rather than our modern sapphire*)
paved work of *s.* stone. *Ex* 24:10
a *s.* a diamond. 28:18; 39:11
be valued with onyx or *s.* *Job* 28:16
their polishing was of *s.* *Lam* 4:7
as appearance of *s.* *Ezek* 1:26
over them as it were a *s.* 10:1
the *s.* and the emerald were. 28:13
of the wall was *s.* *Rev* 21:19

sapphires
of it are the place of *s.* *Job* 28:6
ivory overlaid with *s.* *S of S* 5:14
foundations with *s.* *Isa* 54:11

Sarah
not Sarai, but *S.* shall. *Gen* 17:15
S. thy wife shall bear. 19; 18:14
where is *S.* thy wife? 18:9
it ceased to be with *S.* after. 11
S. laughed. 12
wherefore did *S.* laugh? 13
Abraham said of *S.* She. *Gen* 20:2
Abimelech restored *S.* 14
because of *S.* 18
the Lord did unto *S.* as he. 21:1
S. should have given children. 7
in all that *S.* said to thee. 12
years of the life of *S.* 127. 23:1
S. died. 2
Abraham buried *S.* his wife. 19
into his mother *S.*'s tent. 24:67
Abraham buried, and *S.* 25:10; 49:31
daughter of Asher was *S.* *Num* 26:46
look to Abraham and to *S.* *Isa* 51:2
deadness of *S.*'s womb. *Rom* 4:19
at this time I will come, *S.* 9:9
through faith *S.* received strength. *Heb* 11:11
as *S.* obeyed Abraham. *1 Pet* 3:6

Sarai
Abraham's wife was *S.* *Gen* 11:29
but *S.* was barren, she. 30; 16:1
Pharaoh because of *S.* 12:17
when *S.* dealt hardly with. 16:6
from the face of my mistress *S.* 8
thou shalt not call her name *S.* 17:15

sardine or **sardius**
(*Probably carnelian*)
shall be a *s.* *Ex* 28:17; 39:10
the *s.* and diamond. *Ezek* 28:13
he that sat was to look upon like a *s.* stone. *Rev* 4:3
of the wall was a *s.* 21:20

Sardis
write and send it to *S.* and. *Rev* 1:11
of the church in *S.* write. 3:1
a few names in *S.* which have not. 4

sardonyx
(A Sardius *united to an* Onyx)
wall of the city was a *s.* *Rev* 21:20

Sarepta
save to *S.* a city of Sidon. *Luke* 4:26; *1 Ki* 17:9

Saron
and all that dwelt at *S.* *Acts* 9:35

Saruch
Nachor, the son of *S.* *Luke* 3:35

sat
Rachel had taken and *s.* *Gen* 31:34
Tamar, covered with a vail, *s.* 38:14
that *s.* on his throne. *Ex* 12:29
when we *s.* by the flesh pots. 16:3
on the morrow Moses *s.* 18:13
they wept and *s.* before. *Judg* 20:26
now Eli *s.* on a seat by. *1 Sam* 1:9
Eli *s.* on a seat by the wayside. 4:13
as soon as he *s.* on his. *1 Ki* 16:11
the children of Belial *s.* before. 21:13
the two kings *s.* each on his. 22:10
but Elisha *s.* in his house, and elders *s.* with him, and the. *2 Ki* 6:32
as David *s.* in his house. *1 Chr* 17:1
David *s.* before the Lord. 16
made booths, and *s.* *Neh* 8:17
their way, and *s.* chief. *Job* 29:25
I have not *s.* with vain. *Ps* 26:4
in the ways hast thou *s.* *Jer* 3:2
I *s.* not in the assembly of the mockers nor rejoiced; I *s.* 15:17
s. in the winterhouse. 36:22
I *s.* where they *s.* *Ezek* 3:15
as I *s.* in my house, the elders *s.* 8:1
s. women weeping for Tammuz. 14
enquire of the Lord, and *s.* 20:1
but Daniel *s.* in the gate. *Dan* 2:49
people who *s.* in darkness saw great light; to them that *s.* *Mat* 4:16
for them which *s.* with him. 14:9
Mark 6:26
I *s.* daily with you teaching in the. *Mat* 26:55
Peter *s.* with the servants, to see. 58
blind Bartimaeus *s.* by. *Mark* 10:46
Luke 18:35; *John* 9:8
and he *s.* on the right. *Mark* 16:19
he that was dead *s.* up. *Luke* 7:15
Mary *s.* at Jesus' feet, and. 10:39
a colt whereon never man *s.* 19:30
Mark 11:2
Jesus, wearied, *s.* thus. *John* 4:6
cloven tongues *s.* upon. *Acts* 2:3
he who *s.* for alms at the. 3:10

he that s. on the throne. Rev 4:3
on the cloud one s. like the. 14:14
he that s. upon him was called. 19:11
make war against him that s. 19

sat down

the people s. down to. Ex 32:6
and they s. down at thy. Deut 33:3
and s. down astonied. Ezra 9:3
they s. down to examine the. 10:16
I s. down and mourned. Neh 1:4
king and Haman s. down. Esth 3:15
Job s. down among ashes. Job 2:8
there we s. down, yea. Ps 137:1
s. down under his shadow. S of S 2:3
and s. down with him. Mat 9:10
he s. down with the twelve. 26:20
Luke 22:14
minister, and s. down. Luke 4:20
s. down and taught the people. 5:3
people came, he s. down. John 8:2
synagogue and s. down. Acts 13:14
we s. down and spake to the. 16:13
s. down on right. Heb 1:3; 10:12

Satan

A Hebrew *word, signifying an* adversary, *an* enemy, *an* accuser. *Most commonly* Satan *is taken for the* Devil, *or chief of the evil spirits. It is also used for those adversaries of Christianity who seemed filled with some malignant spirit in their persecution of the Church,* Mat 12:26; Rev 20:2.

S. provoked David to. 1 Chr 21:1
and S. came also. Job 1:6; 2:1
S., Whence comest thou? 1:7; 2:2
S., Hast thou considered? 1:8; 2:3
S. went out from the presence. 1:12
S., Behold, he is in thine. 2:6
so went S. forth from. 2:7
and let S. stand at his. Ps 109:6*
S. standing at his right. Zech 3:1
S., The Lord rebuke thee, O S. 2
him, Get thee hence, S. Mat 4:10
if S. cast out S. 12:26; Mark 3:23
26; Luke 11:18
get thee behind me, S. Mat 16:23
Mark 8:33; Luke 4:8
he was tempted of S. Mark 1:13
S. cometh and taketh. 4:15
I beheld S. as lightning. Luke 10:18
whom S. hath bound these. 13:16
entered S. into Judas Iscariot. 22:3
Simon, Simon, S. hath desired. 31
the sop, S. entered. John 13:27
why hath S. filled thine? Acts 5:3
from the power of S. to God. 26:18
God shall bruise S. under. Rom 16:20
one to S., that the spirit. 1 Cor 5:5
that S. tempt you not for your. 7:5
lest S. should get an. 2 Cor 2:11
S. himself is transformed. 11:14
given to me, the messenger of S. 12:7
come, but S. hindered. 1 Thes 2:18
after the working of S. 2 Thes 2:9
have delivered unto S. 1 Tim 1:20
already turned aside after S. 5:15
but the synagogue of S. Rev 2:9
where Satan's seat is: where S. 13
not known the depths of S. 24
of the synagogue of S. 3:9
dragon was cast out, called S. 12:9
on the dragon, which is S. 20:2
S. shall be loosed out of his. 7

satest

thou s. in the throne. Ps 9:4
s. upon a stately bed. Ezek 23:41

satiate

I will s. soul of the priests. Jer 31:14
the sword shall be s. with. 46:10

satiated

I have s. the weary soul. Jer 31:25

satisfaction

shall take no s. for life. Num 35:31*
take no s. for him that is fled. 32*

satisfy

to s. the desolate and. Job 38:27
O s. us early with thy. Ps 90:14
with long life will I s. him. 91:16
I will s. her poor with bread. 132:15
let her breasts s. thee at. Pr 5:19
if he steal to s. his soul when. 6:30
if thou s. the afflicted. Isa 58:10
Lord shall guide and s. thy soul. 11
they shall not s. their. Ezek 7:19
whence can a man s.? Mark 8:4

satisfied

shall be s. upon them. Ex 15:9
shall eat and not be s. Lev 26:26
shall eat and be s. Deut 14:29
O Naphtali, s. with favour. 33:23
and why are ye not s.? Job 19:22
his offspring shall not be s. 27:14
of his flesh! we cannot be s. 31:31
I shall be s., when I awake. Ps 17:15
the meek shall eat and be s. 22:26
they shall be s. with the. 36:8
famine they shall be s. 37:19
grudge if they be not s. 59:15
my soul shall be s. as with. 63:5
we shall be s. with the. 65:4
of rock should I have s. thee. 81:16
the earth is s. with the fruit. 104:13
he s. them with the bread. 105:40
his land shall be s. Pr 12:11*
a man shall be s. with good by. 14
and a good man shall be s. 14:14
a man's belly be s. with. 18:20*
he that hath it shall abide s. 19:23
eyes, and thou shalt be s. 20:13
things that are never s. 30:15
the eye is not s. with. Eccl 1:8
neither is his eye s. with riches. 4:8
that loveth silver, shall not be s. 5:10
eat and not be s. Isa 9:20; Mi 6:14
he roasteth roast and is s. Isa 44:16
of travail of his soul, and be s. 53:11
be s. with the breasts of her. 66:11
my people shall be s. Jer 31:14
spoil Chaldea shall be s. 50:10
his soul shall be s. on mount. 19
hand to Egyptians, to be s. Lam 5:6
couldest not be s. Ezek 16:28, 29
drink water, but were not s. Amos 4:8
death, and cannot be s. Hab 2:5

satisfiest

and thou s. the desire. Ps 145:16

satisfieth

who s. thy mouth with. Ps 103:5
for he s. the longing soul. 107:9
labour for that which s. not. Isa 55:2

satisfying

the righteous eateth to s. Pr 13:26
not in any honour to the s. Col 2:23*

satyr

and the s. shall cry to. Isa 34:14†

satyrs

dwell there, and s. dance. Isa 13:21†

Saul, *first king of Israel*

S. of Rehoboth reigned. Gen 36:37
S. died. 38
Kish had a son, whose name was S.
1 Sam 9:2; 14:51
Samuel a day before S. came. 9:15
when Samuel saw S. 17
S. drew near to Samuel. 18
set it before S., so S. did eat. 24
is S. also among the prophets?
10:11, 12; 19:24
S. was taken. 10:21
Spirit of God came upon S. 11:6
cometh not forth after S. and. 7
shall S. reign over us? 12
to Gilgal, there they made S. 15
S. blew the trumpet. 13:3
as for S. he was yet in Gilgal and. 7
S. went out to meet Samuel. 10
S. numbered the people. 15
for S. had adjured the people. 14:24
S. built an altar. 35
S. asked counsel of God. 37
S. went up from following the. 46
when S. saw any strong man, he. 52
me that I have set up S. 15:11
Samuel turned again after S. 31
Samuel came no more to see S. 35
long wilt thou mourn for S.? 16:1
if S. hear it. 2
Spirit of Lord departed from S. 14
the evil spirit from God was on S.
23; 18:10; 19:9
and you servants to S.? 17:8
for an old man in the days of S. 12
S. and all Israel were in the. 19
and S. armed David with his.
1 Sam 17:38
came out to meet king S. 18:6
S. eyed David from that day. 9
S. afraid; Lord departed from S. 12
when S. saw that he behaved. 15, 30
S. became David's enemy. 29
spake good of David to S. 19:4
Jonathan brought David to S. 7
S. sent messengers. 11, 14, 15, 20
Abner sat by S.'s side. 20:25
S. cast a javelin. 33
fled that day for fear of S. 21:10
saying, S. hath slain his. 11; 29:5
that he would surely tell S. 22:22
will S. come down as thy? 23:11
shall be king, and that S. my. 17
S. returned from pursuing after. 28
David cut off the skirt of S. 24:4
them not to rise against S. 7
David cried after S. 8
David sware to S. 22
David understood S. was. 26:4
beheld the place where S. lay. 5
behold, S. lay sleeping within. 7
S. knew David's voice. 17
S. returned. 25
one day by the hand of S. 27:1
behold, thou knowest what S. 28:9
S. sware to her by the Lord. 10
for thou art S. 12
S. fell straightway all along. 20
not this David servant of S.? 29:3
Philistines followed hard upon S.
31:2; 1 Chr 10:2
that S. and his sons were dead.
1 Sam 31:7; 1 Chr 10:7
what the Philistines had done to S.
1 Sam 31:11; 1 Chr 10:11
S. leaned on his spear. 2 Sam 1:6
the shield of S. 21
of Israel, weep over S. 24
be ye valiant, for your master S. 2:7
the house of S. waxed weaker. 3:1
to translate the kingdom from house of S. and to set. 10; 1 Chr 12:23
tidings saying, S is dead. 2 Sam 4:10
when S. was king. 5:2; 1 Chr 11:2
my mercy shall not depart, as I took it from S. 2 Sam 7:15
any left of the house of S.? 9:1, 3
all the land of S. thy father. 7
out of the hand of S. 12:7; 22:1
blood of the house of S. 16:8
for S. and for his bloody. 21:1
will have no silver nor gold of S. 4
David took the bones of S. 12
in the days of S. they. 1 Chr 5:10
S. died for his transgression. 10:13
himself close because of S. 12:1
enquired not at it in the days of S. 13:3
all that Samuel and S. had. 26:28
Gibeah of S. is fled. Isa 10:29
God gave unto them S. Acts 13:21

see **Jonathan**

Saul (Paul)

feet, whose name was S. Acts 7:58
and S. was consenting unto. 8:1
as for S. he made havoc of the. 3
S. S. why persecutest thou me?
9:4; 22:7; 26:14
enquire for one called S. of. 9:11
brother S. the Lord hath. 17; 22:13
but S. increased more in. 9:22
laying wait was known of S. 24
S. was come to Jerusalem. 26
went to Tarsus to seek S. 11:25
the hands of Barnabas and S. 30
prophets brought up with S. 13:1
separate me Barnabas and S. 2
called for Barnabas and S. 7
S. set his eyes on him, and said. 9

save

[1] *To preserve from danger.* [2] *To deliver from sin and its consequences.*

God sent me before you to s.
Gen 45:7
goeth with you to s. you. Deut 20:4
there was none to s. her. 22:27
and no man shall s. thee. 28:29
thou shalt s. Israel. Judg 6:14
O my Lord, wherewith shall I s.? 15

for Baal ? will ye s. him ? Judg 6:31
thou wilt s. Israel by mine. 36
know that thou wilt s. Israel. 37
that lapped will I s. you. 7:7
anoint him, that he may s. my. 1 Sam 9:16
people shouted and said, God s. the king. 10:24†; 2 Sam 16:16†
2 Ki 11:12†; 2 Chr 23:11
restraint, to s. by many. 1 Sam 14:6
if thou s. not thyself this. 19:11
David, go and s. Keilah. 23:2
of David I will s. Israel. 2 Sam 3:18
the afflicted people thou wilt s. 22:28; Ps 18:27
but there was none to s. them. 2 Sam 22:42; Ps 18:41
that thou mayest s. 1 Ki 1:12
behold they say, God s. king. 25†
God s. king Solomon. 34†, 39†
king, peradventure he will s. thy life. 20:31
for I will defend this city to s. it, for. 2 Ki 19:34; Isa 37:35
temple to s. his life. Neh 6:11
thine hand, but s. his life. Job 2:6
he shall not s. of that which. 20:20
and he shall s. the humble. 22:29
own right hand can s. thee. 40:14
s. Lord, let the king hear. Ps 20:9
s. thy people, feed them also. 28:9
Jer 31:7
he shall s. them, because. Ps 37:40
neither did their own arm s. 44:3
s. with thy right hand. 60:5; 108:6
for God will s. Zion, and. 69:35
he shall s. the children of the. 72:4
and he shall s. the souls of the. 13
when God arose to s. the meek. 76:9
O my God, s. thy servant that. 86:2
and s. the son of thine handmaid. 16
s. him from those that. 109:31
s. I beseech thee, O Lord. 118:25
hear their cry, and s. them. 145:19
and he shall s. thee. Pr 20:22
God will come and s. you. Isa 35:4
unto a god that cannot s. 45:20
he cannot answer, nor s. him. 46:7
astrologers stand up and s. 47:13
wander, none shall s. thee. 15
thus saith the Lord, I will s. 49:25
shortened, that it cannot s. 59:1
righteousness, mighty to s. 63:1
arise, if they can s. thee. Jer 2:28
but they shall not s. them at. 11:12
mighty man that cannot s. 14:9
for I am with thee to s. thee. 15:20
30:11; 42:11; 46:27
O Israel, I will s. thee from. 30:10
flee, s. your lives, be like the. 48:6
to warn the wicked, to s. Ezek 3:18
therefore will I s. my flock. 34:22
I will s. you. 36:29
I will s. them. 37:23
I will s. them by the Lord their God, and will not s. them by. Hos 1:7
any other that may s. thee? 13:10
of violence, and thou wilt not s. Hab 1:2
he will s., he will rejoice. Zeph 3:17
I will s. her that halteth, and. 19
I will s. my people from. Zech 8:7
Lord their God shall s. them. 9:16
will s. the house of Joseph. 10:6
the Lord also shall s. the tents. 12:7
Jesus, shall s. his people. Mat 1:21
for whosoever will s. his life. 16:25
Mark 8:35; Luke 9:24; 17:33
for the Son of man is come to s. Mat 18:11; Luke 19:10
the temple, and buildest it in three days, s. Mat 27:40; Mark 15:30
saved others, himself he cannot s. Mat 27:42; Mark 15:31
Elias will come to s. Mat 27:49
is it lawful to s. life or to kill ? Mark 3:4; Luke 6:9
Son of man is not come to destroy men's lives, but to s. Luke 9:56
s. himself, if he be Christ. 23:35
s. thyself. 37
if Christ, s. thyself and us. 39
but to s. the world. John 12:47
s. yourselves from this. Acts 2:40
willing to s. Paul. Acts 27:43
if I might s. some of them. Rom 11:14; 1 Cor 9:22
preaching to s. them. 1 Cor 1:21
s. thy husband, shalt s. thy. 7:16
the world to s. sinners. 1 Tim 1:15
in doing this thou shalt s. 4:16
to him that was able to s. Heb 5:7
he is able to s. them to the. 7:25
word, which is able to s. Jas 1:21
works, can faith s. him ? 2:14
one lawgiver, who is able to s. 4:12
the prayer of faith shall s. the. 5:15
shall s. a soul from death, and. 20
others s. with fear, pulling. Jude 23
see **alive**

save ***me***

s. me out of the hand. 2 Ki 16:7
arise, O Lord, s. me. Ps 3:7
s. me for thy mercies' sake. 6:4
31:16; 109:26
s. me from all them that. 7:1
s. me from the lion's mouth. 22:21
house of defence to s. me. 31:2
nor shall my sword s. me. 44:6
s. me, O God, by thy name. 54:1
and the Lord shall s. me. 55:16
from heaven and s. me. 57:3
deliver me, and s. me from. 59:2
s. me, for waters are come in. 69:1
thine ear unto me, and s. me. 71:2
commandment to s. me. 3
s. me, for I have sought. 119:94
I cried unto thee, s. me, and. 146
thy right hand shall s. me. 138:7
Lord was ready to s. me. Isa 38:20
O Lord, s. me, and I shall. Jer 17:14
saying, Lord s. me. Mat 14:30
Father, s. me from this. John 12:27

save ***us***

to us quickly, and s. us. Josh 10:6
if it be in rebellion, s us. not. 22:22
the ark may s. us from. 1 Sam 4:3
to the Lord, that he will s. us. 7:8
how shall this man s. us ? 10:27
if there be no man to s. us. 11:3
s. thou us out of his hand. 2 Ki 19:19; Isa 37:20
s. us, O God of our. 1 Chr 16:35
stir up thy strength, and come and s. us. Ps 80:2
s. us, O Lord our God. 106:47
for him, he will s. us. Isa 25:9
is our king, he will s. us. 33:22
trouble they will say, s. us. Jer 2:27
nation that could not s. us. Lam 4:17
Asher shall not s. us. Hos 14:3
saying, Lord s. us. Mat 8:25
doth also now s. us. 1 Pet 3:21

save, for ***except***

s. what the young men. Gen 14:24
he knew not aught, s. the. 39:6
s. that which every man. Ex 12:16
any god, s. to the Lord. 22:20
s. Caleb. Num 14:30; 26:65
32:12; Deut 1:36
s. when there shall be no poor. Deut 15:4
none, s. Hazor only. Josh 11:13
peace with Israel, s. the Hivite. 19
part to the Levites, s. cities. 14:4
there is nothing else, s. the sword of Gideon. Judg 7:14
there is none other, s. 1 Sam 21:9
there escaped none, s. 400. 30:17
s. to every man his wife and. 22
poor man had nothing, s. one little ewe lamb. 2 Sam 12:3
who is God, s. the Lord ? 22:32
Ps 18:31
in the house, s. we two. 1 Ki 3:18
in the ark s. the two tables. 8:9
s. in the matter of Uriah the. 15:5
fight not, s. with the king of. 22:31
anything, s. a pot of oil. 2 Ki 4:2
s. that the high places were. 15:4
s. only to burn sacrifice. 2 Chr 2:6
no son left, s. Jehoahaz the. 21:17
nor any with me, s. the. Neh 2:12
ask a petition, s. of thee, O king. Dan 6:7, 12
any the Father, s. Son. Mat 11:27
not without honour, s. in his. 13:57
they saw no man, s. Jesus only. Mat 17:8; Mark 9:8
cannot receive, s. they. Mat 19:11
no man to follow him, s. Peter, James. Mark 5:37; Luke 8:51
s. that he laid his hands. Mark 6:5
take nothing, s. a staff only. 8
sent, s. unto Sarepta, a. Luke 4:26
returned, s. this stranger. 17:18
good s one, that is God. 18:19
other boat, s. that one. John 6:22
hath seen the Father, s. he. 46
he needeth not, s. to. 13:10
s. that the Holy Ghost. Acts 20:23
s. to keep themselves from. 21:25
any thing, s. Jesus Christ. 1 Cor 2:2
s. the spirit of man which is in. 11
I forty stripes s. one. 2 Cor 11:24
I saw none, s. James. Gal 1:19
glory, s. in the cross. 6:14
buy or sell, s. he that. Rev 13:17

saved

they said, Thou hast s. Gen 47:25
midwives s. the men. Ex 1:17, 18
I had slain thee, and s. Num 22:33
Moses said, Have ye s. all? 31:15
Joshua s. Rahab the. Josh 6:25
mine own hand hath s. me. Judg 7:2
if he had s. them alive, I would. 8:19
wives which they had s. 21:14
David s. the inhabitants. 1 Sam 23:5
David s. neither man nor. 27:11
this day have s. thy life. 2 Sam 19:5
the king s. us, and now he is fled. 9
s. himself there, not. 2 Ki 6:10
saviours, who s. them. Neh 9:27
no king is s. by multitude. Ps 33:16
but thou hast s. us from our. 44:7
nevertheless, he s. them. 106:8
he s. them from him that hated. 10
I have declared, and have s. and. Isa 43:12
Look unto me, and be ye s. 45:22
that thou mayest be s. Jer 4:14
summer ended, and we are not s. 8:20
Who then can be s.? Mat 19:25
Mark 10:26; Luke 18:26
no flesh should be s. Mat 24:22
Mark 13:20
he s. others. Mat 27:42
Mark 15:31; Luke 23:35
that we should be s. Luke 1:71
Thy faith hath s. thee. 7:50; 18:42
should believe and be s. 8:12
Lord, are there few that be s.? 13:23
through him, might be s. John 3:17
I say, that ye might be s. 5:34
added such as should be s. Acts 2:47
name whereby we must be s. 4:12
circumcised, ye cannot be s. 15:1
what must I do to be s.? 16:30
all hope we should be s. 27:20
in the ship, ye cannot be s. 31
we are s. by hope. Rom 8:24
that they may be s. 10:1
to us who are s. it is the. 1 Cor 1:18
that the spirit may be s. in day. 5:5
many, that they may be s. 10:33
by which also ye are s. if ye. 15:2
savour in them that are s. 2 Cor 2:15
with Christ, by grace are s. Eph 2:5
for by grace are ye s. through. 8
that they might be s. 1 Thes 2:16
received not the love of the truth, that they might be s. 2 Thes 2:10
will have all men to be s. 1 Tim 2:4
to his mercy he s. us. Tit 3:5
wherein eight souls were s. by. 1 Pet 3:20
if the righteous scarcely be s. 4:18
s. Noah, the 8th person. 2 Pet 2:5
nations s. shall walk in. Rev 21:24

God **or** ***Lord*** **saved**

Lord s. Israel that day. Ex 14:30
1 Sam 14:23
O people, s. by Lord ? Deut 33:29
rejected your God, who s. you. 1 Sam 10:19
Lord s. them by hand. 2 Ki 14:27
Lord s. them by a great. 1 Chr 11:14
thus Lord s. Hezekiah. 2 Chr 32:22
Lord s. him out of all his. Ps 34:6
the Lord s. them out of their. 107:13

angel of his presence s. Isa 63:9
God who hath s. us and. 2 Tim 1:9
how that the Lord, having s. the. Jude 5

shall be saved

ye shall be s. from your enemies. Num 10:9
I shall be s. from mine enemies. 2 Sam 22:4; Ps 18:3
cause thy face to shine, we shall be s. Ps 80:3, 7, 19
uprightly shall be s. Pr 28:18
and rest shall ye be s. Isa 30:15
but Israel shall be s. in Lord. 45:17
continuance, and we shall be s. 64:5
save me, and I shall be s. Jer 17:14
Judah shall be s. 23:6; 33:16
Jacob's trouble; but he shall be s. 30:7
endureth to the end shall be s. Mat 10:22; 24:13; Mark 13:13
that believeth shall be s. Mark 16:16
man enter, he shall be s. John 10:9
call on name of the Lord, shall be s. Acts 2:21; Rom 10:13
thy house shall be s. Acts 11:14
through grace we shall be s. 15:11
Jesus, and thou shalt be s. 16:31
shall be s. from wrath. Rom 5:9
being reconciled, we shall be s. 10
sand, a remnant shall be s. 9:27
raised him, thou shalt be s. 10:9
so all Israel shall be s. as it is. 11:26
but he himself shall be s. 1 Cor 3:15
shall be s. in childbearing, if. 1 Tim 2:15

savest

my Saviour, thou s. 2 Sam 22:3
how s. thou the arm that? Job 26:2
O thou that s. by thy right. Ps 17:7

saveth

liveth, who s. Israel. 1 Sam 14:39
the Lord s. not with sword. 17:47
but he s. the poor from. Job 5:15
God, who s. the upright. Ps 7:10
now know I that the Lord s. 20:6
he s. such as be of a contrite. 34:18
they cry, he s. them out of. 107:19

saving

shewed me in s. my life. Gen 19:19
s. that every one put. Neh 4:23
with the s. strength of. Ps 20:6
he is the s. strength of his. 28:8
thy s. health among all nations. 67:2
s. the beholding of them. Eccl 5:11
s. that I will not utterly. Amos 9:8
s. for the cause of. Mat 5:32
cleansed, s. Naaman. Luke 4:27
believe to s. of the soul. Heb 10:39
Noah prepared an ark to the s. 11:7
no man knoweth, s. he. Rev 2:17

saviour

(In general used for any one who saves. In the New Testament especially it refers nearly always to our Lord and Saviour Jesus Christ)

my refuge, my s. 2 Sam 22:3
Lord gave Israel a s. 2 Ki 13:5
they forgat God their s. Ps 106:21
he shall send them a s. Isa 19:20
Holy One of Israel thy s. 43:3
beside me there is no s. 11
O God of Israel, the s. 45:15
a just God and a s.; there is. 21
know that I am thy s. 49:26
that I the Lord am thy s. 60:16
people, so he was their s. 63:8
the s. of Israel in time. Jer 14:8
for there is no s. beside. Hos 13:4
rejoiced in God my s. Luke 1:47
in the city of David a s. 2:11
this is Christ the s. of. John 4:42
to be a prince and s. Acts 5:31
raised unto Israel a s., Jesus. 13:23
and Christ is the s. of the. Eph 5:23
whence we look for the s. Phil 3:20
by the commandment of God our s. 1 Tim 1:1
in the sight of God our s. 2:3
God, who is the s. of all men. 4:10
the appearing of our s. 2 Tim 1:10
to the commandment of God our s. Tit 1:3
the Lord Jesus Christ our s. Tit 1:4
the doctrine of God our s. 2:10
glorious appearing of our s. 13
after the kindness of God our s. 3:4
abundantly through Christ our s. 6
of God and our s. 2 Pet 1:1
kingdom of our Lord and s. 11
knowledge of the Lord and s. 2:20
apostles of the Lord and s. 3:2
knowledge of our s. Christ. 18
sent the Son to be the s. 1 John 4:14
to the only wise God our s. Jude 25

saviours

thou gavest them s. who. Neh 9:27
and s. shall come up on. Ob 21

savour

(An odour or scent. Used frequently in a symbolic sense)

ye have made our s. Ex 5:21
will not smell s. of. Lev 26:31
send forth a stinking s. Eccl 10:1*
because of the s. of thy. S of S 1:3
his stink and his ill s. Joel 2:20
if the salt have lost his s. Mat 5:13
Luke 14:34
maketh manifest the s. 2 Cor 2:14
the s. of death unto death, s. of. 16

sweet savour

Lord smelled a sweet s. Gen 8:21
it is a sweet s. an offering. Ex 29:18
Lev 1:9, 13, 17; 2:9; 3:5; 8:21
Num 15:14; 18:17; 28:8
for a sweet s. an offering. Ex 29:25
41; Lev 2:12; 3:16; 4:31; 6:15
21; 8:28; 17:6; 23:13; Num 15:7
24; 28:2, 6, 13, 27; 29:2, 6, 8
Ezek 16:19
of sweet s. unto the Lord. Lev 23:18
Num 28:24; 29:13, 36
to make a sweet s. Num 15:3
a burnt offering of a sweet s. 28:13
did offer sweet s. to their idols. Ezek 6:13
they made their sweet s. 20:28
accept you with your sweet s. 41
for we are to God a sweet s. of. 2 Cor 2:15
for a sweet-smelling s. Eph 5:2*

savourest

thou s. not things of God. Mat 16:23*; Mark 8:33*

sweet savours

sacrifices of sweet s. Ezra 6:10

savoury

make me s. meat. Gen 27:4, 7, 14
Esau had made s. meat, and. 31

saw

the woman s. the tree was. Gen 3:6
sons of God s. the daughters. 6:2
Ham s. the nakedness of his. 9:22
they s. not their father's. 23
Abraham s. the place afar. 22:4
they said, We s. the Lord. 26:28
when he s. that he prevailed. 32:25
for she s. that Shelah was. 38:14
his master s. that the Lord. 39:3
in that we s. the anguish of. 42:21
when Joseph s. Benjamin. 43:16
when he s. the wagons which. 45:27
Issachar s. that rest was good. 49:15
his brethren s. that their. 50:15
Joseph s. Ephraim's children of. 23
when she s. that he was. Ex 2:2
when he s. that there was no. 12
they s. not one another for. 10:23
Israel s. that great work the. 14:31
they s. the God of Israel. 24:10, 11
all the people s. the cloudy. 33:10
we s. the children of. Num 13:28
ass s. the angel of Lord. 22:23, 27
and when Phinehas s. it he. 25:7
when they s. the land, they. 32:9
heard a voice, but s. no. Deut 4:12, 15
which thine eyes s. 7:19
all that s. it said, No. Judg 19:30
when she s. she was. Ruth 1:18
they s. the ark, and. 1 Sam 6:13
when we s. they were no where. 10:14
Israel, when they s. the man. 17:24
Saul s. that the Lord was. 18:28
David s. a woman. 2 Sam 11:2
s. that the wisdom of. 1 Ki 3:28
when Zimri s. that the city. 16:18
when Ahab s. Elijah, he said. 18:17
when he s. that, he arose and. 19:3
Elisha s. it, and he s. 2 Ki 2:12
s. the water on the other side. 3:22
man of God s. her afar off. 4:25
of the young man and he s. 6:17
he s. the oppression of Israel. 13:4
Ahaz s. an altar that was at. 16:10
they s. that the Lord. 2 Chr 15:9
and they s. one another in. 25:21
when princes s. heaps, they. 31:8
when s. these things they. Neh 6:16
the princes which s. the. Esth 1:14
he s. that there was evil. 7:7
they s. that his grief was. Job 2:13
as infants which never s. light. 3:16
eye which s. him, shall see. 20:9
the young men s. me, and. 29:8
when the eye s. me, it gave. 11
they s. it, and so they. Ps 48:5
waters s. thee, O God, the waters s. 77:16
your fathers proved me, and s. 95:9
the earth s. his lightnings and. 97:4
sea s. it and fled: Jordan. 114:3
s. ye him whom my soul loveth? S of S 3:3
isles s. it, and feared. Isa 41:5
sister Judah s. it. Jer 3:7
when Zedekiah s. them, and. 39:4
for then we were well, and s. 44:17
adversaries s. her and. Lam 1:7
I went in, and s. behold. Ezek 8:10
then they s. every high hill. 20:28
as soon as she s. them, she. 23:16
s. these men on whom. Dan 3:27
whereas the king s. a watcher. 4:23
the king s. part of the hand. 5:5
when Ephraim s. his sickness and Judah s. his wound. Hos 5:13
who among you s. this house? Hag 2:3
the star which they s. Mat 2:9
s. the Spirit of God descending. 3:16; Mark 1:10
dumb both spake and s. Mat 12:22
s. no man, save Jesus only. 17:8
husbandmen s. the son. 21:38
s. a man who had not on. 22:11
Lord, when s. we thee? 25:37, 44
when s. we thee a stranger? 38
when s. thee sick? 39
another maid s. him, and said. 26:71
Mark 14:69; Luke 22:58
Judas, when he s. that he. Mat 27:3
they s. him they worshipped. 28:17
when Jesus s. their faith. Mark 2:5
he asked him, if he s. aught. 8:23
saying, Master, we s. one casting out devils in thy. 9:38; Luke 9:49
when they s. what was. Luke 8:34
when the woman s. that she was. 47
when they were awake, they s. 9:32
his father s. him, and had. 15:20
one of them, when he s. he. 17:15
but him they s. not. 24:24
because ye s. miracles. John 6:26
Abraham s. my day, and was. 8:56
when he s. his glory. 12:41
he that s. it, bare record. 19:35
disciples were glad when they s. 20:20
when they s. the boldness. Acts 4:13
s. his face as it had been face. 6:15
Stephen s. the glory of God. 7:55
when Simon s. that Holy Ghost. 8:18
Philip, the eunuch s. him no more. 39
when his eyes were opened, he s. 9:8
all at Lydda s. him, and turned. 35
and when Tabitha s. Peter, she. 40
Cornelius s. a vision. 10:3
s. heaven opened. 11
and because he s. it pleased. 12:3
David s. corruption. 13:36
s. no corruption. 37
masters s. the hope of their. 16:19
he s. the city wholly given to. 17:16
they s. indeed the light and. 22:9
had looked, and s. no harm. 28:6
but when they s. that the gospel of the uncircumcision. Gal 2:7
conflict which ye s. Phil 1:30

your fathers s. my works. Heb 3:9
s. he was a proper child. 11:23
record of all things he s. Rev 1:2
great fear fell on them who s. 11:11
when the dragon s. that he. 12:13
cried, when they s. smoke of. 18:18

saw, substantive

shall the s. magnify? Isa 10:15

saw joined with Lord or God

and God s. the light that. Gen 1:4
God called the dry land earth, and
God s. 10, 12, 18, 21, 25, 31
God s. that the wickedness. 6:5
when the Lord s. that Leah. 29:31
when the Lord s. that he. Ex 3:4
when the Lord s. it, he. Deut 32:19
the Lord s. the affliction. 2 Ki 14:26
when the Lord s. they. 2 Chr 12:7
the Lord s. it, and it. Isa 59:15
Lord s. that there was no man. 16
God s. their works, that. Jonah 3:10
Lord s. her, he had compassion on.
Luke 7:13

I saw

such as I never s. in Egypt for.
Gen 41:19
one went out, and I s. him. 44:28
I s. among the spoils. Josh 7:21
I s. that he delivered. Judg 12:3
I s. the son of Jesse. 1 Sam 22:9
I s. gods ascending out of the. 28:13
I s. Absalom hanged. 2 Sam 18:10
I s. great tumult, but knew not. 29
I s. all Israel scattered. 1 Ki 22:17
I s. the Lord on his throne. 19
2 Chr 18:18
in those days s. I in Judah. Neh 13:15
I s. my help in the gate. Job 31:21
when I s. the prosperity. Ps 73:3
then I s. and considered. Pr 24:32
this also I s. from hand. Eccl 2:24
so I s. the wicked buried. 8:10
among whom I s. Jaazaniah son of.
Ezek 11:1
took them away as I s. good. 16:50
then I s. that she was defiled. 23:13
I s. your fathers as the. Hos 9:10
Ephraim, as I s. Tyrus, is. 13
I s. the Spirit descending. John 1:32
under the fig tree, I s. thee. 48
I s. in the way a light. Acts 26:13
the apostles s. I none. Gal 1:19
when I s. that they walked. 2:14
when I s. him, I fell at. Rev 1:17

sawed

costly stones s. with saws. 1 Ki 7:9

sawest

what s. thou, that thou? Gen 20:10
s. it and didst rejoice. 1 Sam 19:5
afraid, for what s. thou? 28:13
behold, thou s. him. 2 Sam 18:11
when thou s. a thief. Ps 50:18
king, s. a great image. Dan 2:31
thou s. till that a stone was. 34, 45
the tree thou s. which grew. 4:20
the ram which thou s. having. 8:20
seven stars thou s.; seven candlesticks thou s. Rev 1:20
the beast that thou s. was. 17:8
the ten horns which thou s. 12, 16
waters thou s. where the whore. 17:15
the woman which thou s. is that. 18

sawn

they were s. asunder. Heb 11:37

saws

he put Ammonites under s.
2 Sam 12:31; 1 Chr 20:3

say

lest thou shouldest s. Gen 14:23
what ye shall s. to me. 34:11, 12
for I heard them s. Let us. 37:17
we will s. Some evil beast hath. 20
I have heard s. that thou. 41:15
Judah said, What shall we s.? 44:16
so shall ye s. to Joseph, Forgive, I.
50:17
thou s. unto the children of Israel, I
AM hath. Ex 3:14,15; 19:3; 20:22
teach you what thou shalt s. 4:12
when your children shall s. 12:26
Pharaoh will s. of the children. 14:3
if the servant shall s. I love. 21:5
woman shall s. Amen. Num 5:22
that thou shouldest s. to me. 11:12
know what the Lord will s. 22:19
have I now any power at all to s.? 38
the Lord our God shall s. Deut 5:27
then thou shalt s. to thy son. 6:21
of whom thou hast heard s. 9:2
thou shalt s., and at even s. 28:67
so that they will s. in that. 31:17
lest they should s. Our hand. 32:27
your children may not s. Josh 22:27
when they should s. to us in time. 28
shalt hear what they s. Judg 7:11
canst thou s. I love thee? 16:15
is this ye s. to me, What? 18:24
in all they s. unto thee. 1 Sam 8:7
if they s. thus, Come up to us. 14:10
if he s. thus. 20:7
therefore thou shalt s. to my servant
David. 2 Sam 7:8; 1 Chr 7:21
he s. I have no delight. 2 Sam 15:26
what you shall s. that will I. 21:4
of my lord s. so too. 1 Ki 1:36
for he will not s. thee nay. 2:17
shall s. Why hath the Lord done thus
to this land? 9:8; 2 Chr 7:21
Lord did s. Eat no bread. 1 Ki 13:22
let not the king s. so.
2 Chr 18:7
if we s. We will enter. 2 Ki 7:4
so that they shall not s. this. 9:37
that thou s. nothing but truth to me.
2 Chr 18:15
they should s. to Iddo. Ezra 8:17
O our God, what shall we s.? 9:10
who will s. to him, What dost thou?
Job 9:12; Eccl 8:4
they s. unto God, Depart. Job 21:14
then shalt thou s. There is. 22:29
what he would s. to me. 23:5
destruction and death s. We. 28:22
searched out what to s. 32:11
if any s. I have sinned. 33:27
teach us what we shall s. 37:19
many s. of my soul, There. Ps 3:2
there be that s. Who will shew? 4:6
let them not s. We have. 35:25
so that a man shall s. There. 58:11
for who, s. they, doth hear? 59:7
yet they s. Lord shall not see. 94:7
nor do they who go by s. 129:8
if they s. Come, let us lay. Pr 1:11
s. I have made my heart? 20:9
when thou shalt s. I have. Eccl 12:1
people shall go and s. Isa 2:3
they s. Who seeth us? and. 29:15
shall the work s. of him that made
it? or the thing framed s. of? 16
who s. to the seers, See not. 30:10
the inhabitant shall not s. I. 33:24
one shall s. I am the Lord's. 44:5
surely shall one s. In the Lord. 45:24
lest thou shouldest s. My idol. 48:5
thou shouldest s. Behold, I knew. 7
Why have we fasted, s. they? 58:3
cry, and he shall s. Here I am. 9
in trouble they will s. Arise. Jer 2:27
understandest what they s. 5:15
shall ye s. to them, The gods. 10:11
Therefore thou shalt s. this. 14:17
Report, s. they, and we will. 20:10
shall no more s. The Lord. 23:7
they shall s. no more, Fathers. 31:29
do to him even as he shall s. 39:12
all that the Lord shall s. 42:20
ye s. The Lord saith it. Ezek 13:7
wilt thou yet s. before him that? 28:9
nor will we s. to the work. Hos 14:3
Ephraim shall s. What have I to? 8
prophesy ye not, s. they to. Mi 2:6
they will s. Is not the Lord? 3:11
see what he will s. to me. Hab 2:1
they that sell them s. I am. Zech 11:5
yet ye s., Wherein hast thou loved
us? Mal 1:2; 2:14, 17; 3:13
think not to s. within yourselves.
Mat 3:9; Luke 3:8
shall s. all manner of evil. Mat 5:11
will s. to me in that day. 7:22
have ye understood? they s. 13:51
Jesus said, Whom do men s.? 16:13
Mark 8:27; Luke 9:18
Whom s. ye that I am? Mat 16:15
Mark 8:29; Luke 9:20
s. aught to you, ye shall s. Mat 21:3
and s. to him, Hearest thou what
these s.? 16
if we should s. From heaven, he will
s. 25; Mark 11:31; Luke 20:5
if we shall s., Of men. Mat 21:26
Mark 11:32; Luke 20:6
do not their works, for they s.
Mat 23:3
and saith, See thou s. Mark 1:44
he wist not what to s. for they. 9:6
ye will surely s. this proverb,
Physician, heal thyself. Luke 4:23
Simon, I have somewhat to s. 7:40
no thought what ye shall s. 12:11
shall teach what ye ought to s. 12
ye s. That Jerusalem is. John 4:20
he speaketh, and they s. 7:26
I have many things to s. of you.
8:26; 16:12
S. we not well, that thou hast a? 8:48
ye s. that he is your God. 54
ye call me master, ye s. well. 13:13
hear in all things ye shall s. Acts 3:22
they could s. nothing against it. 4:14
we heard him s. that Jesus. 6:14
do therefore this that we s. 21:33
who hath something to s. 23:18
or else let these same here s. 24:20
things but what Moses did s. 26:22
what shall we s. Is God? Rom 3:5
as some affirm that we s. Let us. 8
what shall we then s.? 4:1; 6:1
7:7; 8:31; 9:14, 30
shall thing formed s. to him? 9:20
no man can s. that Jesus. 1 Cor 12:3
how shall he s. Amen at thy? 14:16
will they not s. that ye are mad? 23
how s. some that there is? 15:12
we, that we s. not. 2 Cor 9:4
for his letters, s. they, are. 10:10
this we s. to you by word of the.
1 Thes 4:15
neither what they s. 1 Tim 1:7
having no evil thing to s. Tit 2:8
albeit I do not s. how. Philem 19
have many things to s. Heb 5:11
as I may so s. Levi paid tithes. 7:9
that is to s. not of this building. 9:11
that is to s. his flesh. 10:20
they that s. such things. 11:14
we may boldly s. The Lord. 13:6
let no man s. when he is. Jas 1:13
go to now ye that s. To-day. 4:13
that ye ought to s. If the Lord. 15
we s. we have fellowship. 1 John 1:6
if we s. We have no sin, we. 8
if a man s. I love God, and. 4:20
I do not s. that he shall pray. 5:16
which s. they are apostles. Rev 2:2
which s. they are Jews. 9; 3:9
spirit and the bride s. Come. 22:17

see began

say, imperatively

s. I pray thee, thou art. Gen 12:13
at every place, s. of me, He. 20:13
s. unto them, Go not. Deut 1:42
s., The sword of the. Judg 7:18
they said to him, S. now. 12:6
he said to him, S. on. 1 Sam 15:16
2 Sam 14:12; 1 Ki 2:14, 16
Luke 7:40; Acts 13:15
s. not, Go and come again. Pr 3:28
s. not, I will do so to him as. 24:29
lest I deny thee, and s. Who? 30:9
s. not thou, What is the cause?
Eccl 7:10
s. ye to righteous, It. Isa 3:10
s. to them that are of fearful. 35:4
s. to cities of Judah, Behold. 40:9
hear, and s. It is truth. 43:9
neither let the eunuch s. I am. 56:3
s. ye to the daughter of Zion. 62:11
s. not, I am a child, for. Jer 1:7
s. ye, Stand fast, and prepare. 46:14
ask her that escapeth, and s. 48:19
s. Babylon is taken, Bel is. 50:2
thy foot, and s. Alas. Ezek 6:11
s. I am your sign, like as. 12:11
and s. What is thy mother? 19:2
s. A sword is sharpened. 21:9
s. The sword is drawn for the. 28
s. unto him, Take away all. Hos 14:2

let them *s.* Spare thy people.
Joel 2:17
let the weak *s.* I am strong. 3:10
s. unto them, Turn ye. *Zech* 1:3
s. The Lord hath need of them.
Mat 21:3; *Mark* 11:3
s. in a word, and my. *Luke* 7:7
streets of the same, and *s.* 10:10
s. not ye, There are yet. *John* 4:35
s. ye . . . Thou blasphemest ? 10:36
s. to Archippus, Take heed. *Col* 4:17

I say

his name, what shall *I s.*? *Ex* 3:13
I s. unto thee, Let my son. 4:23
speak all that *I s.* 6:29; *Ezek* 44:5
what shall *I s.* when Israel.*Josh* 7:8
of whom *I s.* This shall. *Judg* 7:4
if *I s.* expressly to the lad, Behold.
1 Sam 20:21
did not *I s.* Do not ? *2 Ki* 4:28
behold, *I s.* they are even as. 7:13
behold, *I s.* how they. *2 Chr* 20:11
did *I s.* Bring unto me ? *Job* 6:22
when *I s.* My bed shall. 7:13
if *I s.* I am perfect, it shall. 9:20
if *I s.* I will forget my complaint. 27
I will *s.* to God, Do not condemn.
10:2
good courage: wait, *I s.* *Ps* 27:14
if *I s.* I will speak thus, I. 73:15
I will *s.* He is my refuge. 91:2
I s. more than they that. 130:6
if *I s.* The darkness shall. 139:11
I s. an untimely birth is. *Eccl* 6:3
I s., sayest thou, but they. *Isa* 36:5
what shall *I s.*? he hath both. 38:15
I will *s.* to the north, Give up. 43:6
son of man, hear what *I s.* *Ezek* 2:8
I s. to the wicked. 3:18; 33:8, 14
I will *s.* the word, and will. 12:25
because *I s.* Ye are come to. 21:24
when *I s.* to the righteous. 33:13
I s. unto this man, Go. *Mat* 8:9
Luke 7:8
I s. not, Until seven. *Mat* 18:22
I s. to thee, Arise. *Mark* 2:11; 5:41
Luke 5:24; 7:14
the things which *I s.* *Luke* 6:46
these things *I s.* that ye. *John* 5:34
if *I s.* the truth, why do ye ? 8:46
if *I* should *s.* I know him not. 55
what shall *I s.*? Father, save. 12:27
commandment, what *I* should *s.* 49
to declare, *I s.*, his. *Rom* 3:26
I s. the truth in Christ, I lie not. 9:1
this *I s.* that every one. *1 Cor* 1:12
but this *I s.* brethren, the. 7:29
s. I these things as a man ? 9:8
I speak as to wise men, judge ye
what *I s.* *1 Cor* 10:15
what *s. I* then ? that the idol. 19
conscience, *I s.* not thy own. 29
what shall *I s.* to you ? 11:22
now this *I s.* brethren. 15:50
2 Cor 9:6; *Gal* 3:17; 5:16
Eph 4:17; *Col* 2:4
as we said before, so *s. I.* *Gal* 1:9
consider what *I s.* *2 Tim* 2:7
wilt do more than *I s.* *Philem* 21
what shall *I* more *s.*? *Heb* 11:32

I say unto you

when *I s. unto you,* Smite Amnon.
2 Sam 13:28
I not *s. unto you,* Go. *2 Ki* 2:18
I s. unto you, that Solomon in all.
Mat 6:29
I s. unto you, that publicans. 21:31
what *I s. unto you,* I. *Mark* 13:37
I s. not *unto you,* I. *John* 16:26
I Paul *s. unto you,* if ye. *Gal* 5:2
unto you I s. and to the rest in.
Rev 2:24

sayest

see, thou *s.* unto me, Bring. *Ex* 33:12
whatsoever thou *s.* *Num* 22:17
all that thou *s.* unto me. *Ruth* 3:5
and now thou *s.* Go. *1 Ki* 18:11, 14
thou *s.* I have counsel and strength.
2 Ki 18:20; *Isa* 36:5
thou *s.* Lo, thou hast. *2 Chr* 25:19
will we do as thou *s.* *Neh* 5:12
no such things as thou *s.* 6:8
and thou *s.* How doth ? *Job* 22:13
and *s.* Return, ye children of men.
Ps 90:3
if thou *s.* Behold, we. *Pr* 24:12
why *s.* thou, O Jacob. *Isa* 40:27
that *s.* in thine heart, I am. 47:8
s. Because I am innocent, I will plead
. . . because thou *s.* *Jer* 2:35
s. Prophesy not against. *Amos* 7:16
know not what thou *s.* *Mat* 26:70
Jews ? Jesus said unto him, Thou *s.*
27:11; *Mark* 15:2; *Luke* 23:3
John 18:37
neither understand I what thou *s.*
Mark 14:68; *Luke* 22:60
that thou *s.* rightly. *Luke* 20:21
Who art thou ? What *s.*? *John* 1:22
stoned, but what *s.* thou ? 8:5
s. thou, ye shall be made free ? 33
12:34; 14:9
man, What *s.* thou of him ? 9:17
s. thou this of thyself or ? 18:34
thou that *s.* a man should not steal.
Rom 2:22
not what thou *s.* *1 Cor* 14:16
because thou *s.* I am rich. *Rev* 3:17

saying, *substantive*

his father observed *s.* *Gen* 37:11
and the *s.* pleased me. *Deut* 1:23
the *s.* displeased Saul. *1 Sam* 18:8
s. pleased Absalom. *2 Sam* 17:4
shall we do after his *s.*? if not. 6
David, according to the *s.* of. 24:19
and Shimei said, The *s.* *1 Ki* 2:38
that he might perform his *s.* 12:15
when Jeroboam heard the *s.* 13:4
the *s.* which he cried by the. 32
s. of the Lord. 15:29; *2 Ki* 10:17
according to the *s.* of Elijah.
1 Ki 17:15; *2 Ki* 2:22
according to the *s.* of man of God.
2 Ki 5:14; 8:2
the *s.* pleased the king. *Esth* 1:21
I will open my dark *s.* *Ps* 49:4
was not this my *s.*? *Jonah* 4:2
after they heard this *s.* *Mat* 15:12
all men cannot receive this *s.* 19:11
young man heard this *s.* 22
this *s.* is commonly reported. 28:15
for this *s.* go thy way. *Mark* 7:29
and he spake that *s.* openly. 8:32
and they kept that *s.* with. 9:10
they understood not that *s.* 32
Luke 2:50; 9:45
he was sad at that *s.* *Mark* 10:22
she was troubled at his *s.* *Luke* 1:29
known abroad *s.* that was. 2:17
feared to ask him of that *s.* 9:45
this *s.* was hid from them. 18:34
herein is that *s.* true. *John* 4:37
many believed for the *s.* of the. 39
believe, not because of thy *s.* 42
this is an hard *s.*; who can ? 6:60
what manner of *s.* is this ? 7:36
they heard this *s.*, said. 40
if a man keep my *s.* 8:51, 52
but I know him and keep his *s.* 55
that the *s.* of Esaias might. 12:38
if they have kept my *s.* they. 15:20
that the *s.* of Jesus might. 18:9, 32
when Pilate heard that *s.* he. 19:8
then went this *s.* abroad. 21:23
the *s.* pleased the whole. *Acts* 6:5
then fled Moses at this *s.* 7:29
told this *s.* to Paul. 16:36
comprehended in this *s.* *Rom* 13:9
brought to pass the *s.* *1 Cor* 15:54
this is a faithful *s.* that Christ Jesus.
1 Tim 1:15; 4:9; *2 Tim* 2:11
Tit 3:8
this is a true *s.* if a man. *1 Tim* 3:1

saying

displeased in *s.* Why ? *1 Ki* 1:6
he prayed third time, *s.* *Mat* 26:44
s. I am Christ, and. *Mark* 13:6
Master, thus *s.* thou. *Luke* 11:45
a voice, *s.* Arise, Peter. *Acts* 11:7
s. none other things than those. 26:22

sayings

Moses told these *s.* to. *Num* 14:39
that when thy *s.* come. *Judg* 13:17
men told all those *s.* *1 Sam* 25:12
Abijah's *s.* are written. *2 Chr* 13:22
that are written among the *s.* 33:19
posterity approve their *s.* *Ps* 49:13
I will utter dark *s.* of old. 78:2
to understand the dark *s.* *Pr* 1:6
O my son, and receive my *s.* 4:10
incline thine ear to my *s.* 20
whoso heareth these *s.* *Mat* 7:24, 26
Luke 6:47
when Jesus had ended these *s.* the.
Mat 7:28; 19:1; 26:1; *Luke* 7:1
all these *s.* were noised. *Luke* 1:65
his mother kept all these *s.* 2:51
let these *s.* sink down into. 9:44
there was a division again for these
s. *John* 10:19
me not, keepeth not my *s.* 14:24
with these *s.* scarce. *Acts* 14:18
when they heard these *s.* they. 19:28
be justified in thy *s.* *Rom* 3:4
these are true *s.* of God. *Rev* 19:9
these *s.* are faithful and true. 22:6
blessed is he that keepeth the *s.* 7
and of them who keep the *s.* of. 9
seal not the *s.* of the prophecy of. 10

scab

in skin of his flesh a *s.* *Lev* 13:2
it is but a *s.* 6
if *s.* spread much in skin. 7, 8
this is the law for a *s.* 14:56
smite thee with a *s.* *Deut* 28:27*
Lord will smite with a *s.* *Isa* 3:17

scabbard

put up thyself into thy *s.* *Jer* 47:6

scabbed

he that is scurvy or *s.* *Lev* 21:20
or scurvy, or *s.* ye shall. 22:22

scaffold

had made a brasen *s.* *2 Chr* 6:13

scales

these that have *s.* eat ye. *Lev* 11:9
Deut 14:9
that have no *s.* ye shall not eat.
Lev 11:10, 12; *Deut* 14:10
his *s.* are his pride. *Job* 41:15
mountains in *s.* and hills. *Isa* 40:12
fish to stick to thy *s.* *Ezek* 29:4
his eyes as it had been *s.* *Acts* 9:18

scaleth

a wise man *s.* the city. *Pr* 21:22

scall

it is a dry *s.* even a. *Lev* 13:30
s. be not deeper than the skin, shall
shut up him that hath the *s.* 31, 33
if the *s.* spread not. 32, 34
he shall be shaven, but the *s.* 33
but if the *s.* spread much. 35, 36
if the *s.* be at a stay, the *s.* 37
all manner of leprosy and *s.* 14:54

scalp

wound the hairy *s.* of such. *Ps* 68:21

scant

and the *s.* measure that. *Mi* 6:10

scapegoat, *see* **goat**

scarce

Jacob was *s.* gone out. *Gen* 27:30
with these sayings *s.* *Acts* 14:18

scarcely

for *s.* for a righteous man. *Rom* 5:7
if the righteous *s.* be. *1 Pet* 4:18

scarceness

eat bread without *s.* *Deut* 8:9

scarest

then thou *s.* me with dreams.
Job 7:14

scarlet

bound a *s.* thread. *Gen* 38:28, 30
blue and purple, and *s.* *Ex* 25:4
26:1, 31, 36; 27:16; 28:5, 6, 8, 15
35:6, 23, 25; 38:18, 23
wires, to work it in *s.* 39:3
cedar wood, *s.* and hyssop. *Lev* 14:4
6, 49, 51, 52; *Num* 19:6
on them a cloth of *s.* *Num* 4:8
shalt bind this line of *s.* *Josh* 2:18
and she bound the *s.* line in the. 21
who clothed you in *s.* *2 Sam* 1:24
are clothed with *s.* *Pr* 31:21
like a thread of *s.* *S of S* 4:3
though your sins be as *s.* *Isa* 1:18
brought up in *s.* *Lam* 4:5

shall be clothed with *s.* *Dan* 5:7* 16*, 29*
valiant men are in *s.* *Nah* 2:3
put on Jesus a *s.* robe. *Mat* 27:28
took water, and *s.* wool. *Heb* 9:19
I saw a woman sit upon a *s.* coloured beast. *Rev* 17:3
arrayed in purple and *s.* 4
buyeth the merchandise of *s.* 18:12
was clothed with *s.* 16

scatter

Lord *s.* them on earth. *Gen* 11:9
in Jacob, *s.* them in Israel. 49:7
and I will *s.* you. *Lev* 26:33
censers, and *s.* the fire. *Num* 16:37
and the Lord shall *s.* *Deut* 4:27 28:64; *Jer* 9:16; *Ezek* 22:15
I said, I would *s.* them. *Deut* 32:26
he shall *s.* them beyond. *1 Ki* 14:15
if ye transgress, I will *s.* *Neh* 1:8
s. them by thy power. *Ps* 59:11
s. thou the people that delight. 68:30
lifted up his hand to *s.* 106:27
cast forth lightning, and *s.* 144:6
abroad fitches, and *s.* *Isa* 28:25
whirlwind shall *s.* them. 41:16
therefore I will *s.* them. *Jer* 13:24
I will *s.* them as with an. 18:17
woe to the pastors that *s.* 23:1
I will *s.* into all winds them that are. 49:32, 36; *Ezek* 5:10, 12
shalt *s.* in the wind. *Ezek* 5:2
I will *s.* your bones round. 6:5
fill thine hand, and *s.* the. 10:2
I will *s.* toward every wind. 12:14
when I shall *s.* them among. 15
that I would *s.* them among. 20:23
I will *s.* the Egyptians. 29:12 30:23, 26
hew down the tree, and *s.* *Dan* 4:14
he shall *s.* among them the. 11:24
to *s.* the power of the holy. 12:7*
as a whirlwind to *s.* me. *Hab* 3:14
horn over Judah to *s.* it. *Zech* 1:21

scattered

lest we be *s.* abroad. *Gen* 11:4
so the Lord *s.* them abroad from. 8
the people were *s.* to. *Ex* 5:12
let thine enemies be *s.* *Num* 10:35 *Ps* 68:1
thy God hath *s.* thee. *Deut* 30:3
that remained were *s.* *1 Sam* 11:11
people were *s.* from Saul. 13:8
because I saw the people were *s.* 11
the battle was *s.* over. *2 Sam* 18:8
he sent out arrows and *s.* them. 22:15; *Ps* 18:14
I saw all Israel *s.* *1 Ki* 22:17 *2 Chr* 18:16
army were *s.* from him. *2 Ki* 25:5 *Jer* 52:8
there is a certain people *s.* *Esth* 3:8
the stout lions' whelps are *s.* *Job* 4:11
brimstone shall be *s.* on his. 18:15
thou hast *s.* us among heathen. *Ps* 44:11; 60:1
God hath *s.* the bones of him. 53:5
Almighty *s.* kings in it. 68:14
thou hast *s.* thine enemies. 89:10
of iniquity shall be *s.* 92:9
our bones are *s.* at the grave's. 141:7
to a nation *s.* and peeled. *Isa* 18:2
be brought of a people *s.* 7
of thyself the nations were *s.* 33:3
and hast *s.* thy ways to. *Jer* 3:13
their flocks shall be *s.* 10:21
ye have *s.* my flock, and. 23:2
nations whither I have *s.* thee. 30:11
he that *s.* Israel will gather. 31:10
that all Jews should be *s.*? 40:15
Israel is a *s.* sheep: the lions. 50:17
when ye shall be *s.* through. *Ezek* 6:8
though I *s.* them, I will be. 11:16
you out of countries where ye have been *s.* 17; 20:34, 41; 28:25
they that remain shall be *s.* 17:21
whither they were *s.* 29:13
s. because there is no shepherd, they . . . when they were *s.* 34:5
my flock was *s.* on the face of. 6
among his sheep that are *s.* where they have been *s.* in the. 12
till ye have *s.* them. *Ezek* 34:21
s. them among the heathen. 36:19
that my people be not *s.* every. 46:18
people whom they have *s.* *Joel* 3:2
thy people is *s.* on the. *Nah* 3:18
mountains were *s.* *Hab* 3:6
horns which have *s.* *Zech* 1:19, 21
I *s.* them with whirlwind. 7:14
shepherd, and the sheep shall be *s.* 13:7; *Mat* 26:31; *Mark* 14:27
they were *s.* as sheep. *Mat* 9:36
he hath *s.* the proud. *Luke* 1:51
children that were *s.* *John* 11:52
now, that ye shall be *s.* 16:32
obeyed Theudas were *s.* *Acts* 5:36
were *s.* abroad through the. 8:1
were *s.* went every where. 4, 11, 19
tribes that are *s.* abroad. *Jas* 1:1
Peter to the strangers *s.* *1 Pet* 1:1*

scattereth

the thick cloud he *s.* his. *Job* 37:11
which *s.* the east wind upon. 38:24
he *s.* the hoarfrost like. *Ps* 147:16
there is that *s.* and yet. *Pr* 11:24
a king *s.* away all evil with. 20:8
a wise king *s.* the wicked. 26
the Lord *s.* the inhabitants. *Isa* 24:1
and he that gathereth not with me *s.* *Mat* 12:30; *Luke* 11:23
the wolf catcheth and *s.* *John* 10:12

scattering

shew his anger with *s.* *Isa* 30:30

scent

yet through the *s.* of water. *Job* 14:9
therefore his *s.* is not. *Jer* 48:11
the *s.* thereof be the wine. *Hos* 14:7

sceptre

(*The word originally meant a rod or a staff. Thence it came to mean a shepherd's crook, and then the wand or sceptre of a ruler. The references to it, save in Esther, are all metaphorical, expressing supreme power*)

the *s.* shall not depart. *Gen* 49:10
and a *s.* shall rise out. *Num* 24:17
hold out the golden *s.* *Esth* 4:11
to Esther the golden *s.* 5:2; 8:4
the *s.* of thy kingdom is a right *s.* *Ps* 45:6
Lord hath broken the *s.* *Isa* 14:5
rods for the *s.* of them. *Ezek* 19:11
no strong rod to be a *s.* to rule. 14
I will cut off him that holdeth the *s.* *Amos* 1:5, 8
and the *s.* of Egypt. *Zech* 10:11
the *s.* of righteousness is the *s.* of. *Heb* 1:8

Sceva

sons of one *S.* a Jew. *Acts* 19:14

schism

(*A division*)

should be no *s.* in the. *1 Cor* 12:25

scholar

they cast lots, the teacher as the *s.* *1 Chr* 25:8
cut off master and the *s.* *Mal* 2:12*

school

disputing in the *s.* of one. *Acts* 19:9

schoolmaster

(*The Roman* pedagogue, *who did not teach, but was the slave whose duty it was to take the child to the school*)

the law was our *s.* to. *Gal* 3:24*
are no longer under a *s.* 25

science

wisdom, understanding *s.* *Dan* 1:4
and oppositions of *s.* *1 Tim* 6:20*

scoff

they shall *s.* at the kings. *Hab* 1:10

scoffers

in last days *s.* walking. *2 Pet* 3:3

scorch

given him to *s.* men. *Rev* 16:8

scorched

when sun was up they were *s.* *Mat* 13:6; *Mark* 4:6
and men were *s.* with. *Rev* 16:9

scorn, *verb*

my friends *s.* me, mine. *Job* 16:20

scorn

he thought *s.* to lay hands. *Esth* 3:6
a reproach and *s.* *Ps* 44:13; 79:4
princes shall be a *s.* *Hab* 1:10*

***see* laughed**

scorner

(*A* Scorner, *as the word is used in Scripture, is one who makes a mock of sin, and of God's threatenings and judgements against sinners; one who derides all wholesome reproofs and counsels, and scoffs at religion. Usually the revisions change to* scoffer)

reproveth a *s.* getteth. *Pr* 9:7
reprove not a *s.*, lest he hate thee. 8
but a *s.* heareth not rebuke. 13:1
a *s.* seeketh wisdom, and. 14:6
a *s.* loveth not one that. 15:12
smite a *s.* 19:25
when the *s.* is punished. 21:11
s. is his name, who dealeth in. 24
cast out the *s.* 22:10
and the *s.* is an abomination. 24:9
the *s.* is consumed, and. *Isa* 29:20

scorners

how long will *s.* delight? *Pr* 1:12
surely he scorneth the *s.* but. 3:34
judgements are prepared for *s.* and. 19:29
stretched out his hand with *s.* *Hos* 7:5

scornest

if thou *s.* thou alone. *Pr* 9:12
in that thou *s.* hire. *Ezek* 16:31

scorneth

s. the multitude of the city. *Job* 39:7
the ostrich, she *s.* the horse. 18
surely he *s.* the scorners. *Pr* 3:34
witness *s.* judgement, and. 19:28

scornful

in the seat of the *s.* *Ps* 1:1
s. men bring a city into. *Pr* 29:8
of the Lord, ye *s.* men. *Isa* 28:14

scorning

drinketh up *s.* like water? *Job* 34:7
is filled with *s.* of those. *Ps* 123:4
scorners delight in their *s.* *Pr* 1:22

scorpion

A well-known venomous insect of hot climates, shaped much like a lobster, and closely akin to the spider. It is usually about 2 or 3 inches long, but in tropical climates grows much larger.

The word used in 1 Ki 12:11 *is metaphorical.*

will he offer him a *s.*? *Luke* 11:12
as the torment of a *s.* *Rev* 9:5

scorpions

wherein were *s.* *Deut* 8:15
I will chastise you with *s.* *1 Ki* 12:11, 14; *2 Chr* 10:11, 14
among *s.* be not afraid. *Ezek* 2:6
tread on serpents and *s.* *Luke* 10:19
power, as *s.* have power. *Rev* 9:3
they had tails like to *s.* and. 10

scoured

a brasen pot, it shall be *s.* *Lev* 6:28

scourge

A whip made of cords or leather thongs fastened into a handle. Usually there were three of these thongs in each scourge, and they were often reinforced with bits of metal which tore the skin and flesh. Notable scourgings mentioned in the Bible are those of Christ, in the Gospels, and of Paul, in 2 Cor 11:24. *The scourge of small cords used by Jesus in clearing the Temple, was merely a symbol of authority. Scourging differs from* beating, *which was done with rods.*

The word is also used as to-day, figuratively, for a cause of calamity of any sort.

hid from *s.* of the tongue. *Job* 5:21
if the *s.* slay suddenly, he. 9:23

shall stir up a *s.* for him. *Isa* 10:26
when the overflowing *s.* 28:15, 18
when he had made a *s.* *John* 2:15

scourge, *verb*

they will *s.* you in their. *Mat* 10:17
they shall *s.* him. 20:19
Mark 10:34; *Luke* 18:33
some of them ye shall *s.* *Mat* 23:34
for you to *s.* a Roman? *Acts* 22:25

scourged

maid, she shall be *s.* *Lev* 19:20
they had *s.* Jesus, he. *Mat* 27:26
Mark 15:15; *John* 19:1

scourges

s. in your sides, and. *Josh* 23:13

scourgeth

the Lord *s.* every son. *Heb* 12:6

scourging

should be examined by *s.* *Acts* 22:24

scourgings

others had trial of *s.*, yea. *Heb* 11:36

scrabbled

himself mad, and *s.* *1 Sam* 21:13

scrape

dust that they *s.* off. *Lev* 14:41
Job took a potsherd to *s.* *Job* 2:8
I will also *s.* her dust. *Ezek* 26:4

scraped

house to be *s.* within. *Lev* 14:41
after he hath *s.* the house. 43

screech owl

s. also shall rest there. *Isa* 34:14*

scribe

[1] *In the Old Testament any government clerk or secretary.* [2] *The* Sopherim (plur.) *who copied, taught, and explained the law. Ezra was one of the most noted of those in Old Testament times. Before the Exile this work was done by the Levites, but later it was gradually put into the hands of a specially trained body of laymen.*
Not only did they copy the written law, but they formulated and wrote down the detailed rules made by later authorities, which made up what was called the oral law, or the traditions of the elders. They had much opportunity for the exercise of that hypocrisy for which our Lord denounced them in company with the Pharisees.

Seraiah was the *s.* *2 Sam* 8:17
Sheva was *s.* 20:25
and Shebna the *s.* *2 Ki* 18:18, 37
19:2; *Isa* 36:3, 22; 37:2
Shaphan, the *s.* *2 Ki* 22:3, 8, 9, 10
12; *2 Chr* 34:15, 18, 20; *Jer* 36:10
he took the principal *s.* of the host.
2 Ki 25:19; *Jer* 52:25
and Shemaiah the *s.* *1 Chr* 24:6
a wise man and a *s.* 27:32
Shimshai the *s.* wrote a letter.
Ezra 4:8, 9, 17, 23
was a ready *s.* in the law. 7:6, 11
12; *Neh* 8:4, 9, 13; 12:26, 36
Ezra the *s.* stood upon. *Neh* 8:4
the priest, Zadok the *s.* 13:13
where is the *s.*? where? *Isa* 33:18
sat there, even Elishama the *s.*
Jer 36:12, 20, 21
Baruch the *s.* 26, 32
Jonathan the *s.* 37:15, 20
a *s.* said, Master, I will. *Mat* 8:19
s. instructed unto the. 13:52
the *s.* said unto him. *Mark* 12:32
where is the *s.*? where? *1 Cor* 1:20

scribes

Ahiah, sons of Shisha, *s.* *1 Ki* 4:3
the families of the *s.* *1 Chr* 2:55
of Levites there were *s.* *2 Chr* 34:13
then were the king's *s.* called.
Esth 3:12; 8:9
the pen of the *s.* is in. *Jer* 8:8
righteousness of the *s.* *Mat* 5:20
having authority, and not as the *s.*
7:29; *Mark* 1:22
many things of the *s.* *Mat* 16:21
why say *s.* Elias. 17:10; *Mark* 9:11
Son of man shall be betrayed unto the
chief priests and the *s.* *Mat* 20:18
Mark 10:33
when the *s.* saw, they. *Mat* 21:15
s. and Pharisees sit in. 23:2
woe to you *s.* 13, 14, 15, 23, 25, 27
29; *Luke* 11:44
priests and *s.* and elders. *Mat* 26:3
Mark 14:53; *Luke* 22:66
went certain *s.* *Mark* 2:6
when the *s.* saw him eat with. 16
the *s.* said, he hath Beelzebub. 3:22
be rejected of *s.* 8:31; *Luke* 9:22
the *s.* questioning with. *Mark* 9:14
the *s.* and chief priests heard it, and.
11:18; *Luke* 19:47
s. say, By what authority?
Mark 11:27
one of the *s.* asked, What is? 12:28
How say *s.* that Christ is the? 35
he said to them, Beware of *s.* 38
Luke 20:46
s. sought how to take. *Mark* 14:1
their *s.* and Pharisees murmured.
Luke 5:30; 15:2
s. watched him. 6:7
the *s.* began to urge him. 11:53
the *s.* came upon him. 20:1
priests and *s.* sought to lay. 19
the chief priests and *s.* sought. 22:2
s. stood and vehemently. 23:10
the *s.* brought a woman. *John* 8:3
the *s.* gathered against. *Acts* 4:5
the *s.* brought Stephen to. 6:12
the *s.* of the Pharisees' part. 23:9

scrip

(*Revisions,* wallet. *A sort of bag in which were carried a small amount of food and other necessary conveniences for a journey*)

smooth stones in a *s.* *1 Sam* 17:40
nor *s.* for your journey. *Mat* 10:10
Mark 6:8; *Luke* 9:3; 10:4
without *s.* lacked ye. *Luke* 22:35
take his purse and his *s.* 36

scripture

(*Literally from the Latin, a writing.*
The word as used in the Bible refers almost invariably to the sacred writings, which at that time consisted of the Old Testament only. It is also used of a part of it, especially when that part is quoted in a later passage)

noted in the *s.* of truth. *Dan* 10:21
read this *s.*, The stone? *Mark* 12:10
the *s.* was fulfilled, which. 15:28
said, This day is this *s.* *Luke* 4:21
they believed the *s.* and. *John* 2:22
on me, as the *s.* saith. 7:38
not the *s.* said, Christ cometh? 42
word came, and the *s.* cannot. 10:35
again another *s.* saith, They. 19:37
this *s.* must needs have. *Acts* 1:16
the place of the *s.* which. 8:32
Philip began at the same *s.* 35
what saith the *s.*? *Rom* 4:3; 11:2
Gal 4:30
for the *s.* saith. *Rom* 9:17; 10:11
1 Tim 5:18
the *s.* foreseeing that God. *Gal* 3:8
but the *s.* hath concluded all. 22
all *s.* is given by. *2 Tim* 3:16
do ye think the *s.* saith? *Jas* 4:5
the *s.*, Behold I lay in Sion. *1 Pet* 2:6
no prophecy of *s.* is of. *2 Pet* 1:20

scriptures

read in the *s.* the stone? *Mat* 21:42
ye do err, not knowing the *s.* 22:29
Mark 12:24
how then shall the *s.* be? *Mat* 26:54
but the *s.* must be. *Mark* 14:49
to them in all the *s.* *Luke* 24:27
while he opened to us the *s.*? 32
that they might understand the *s.* 45
search the *s.*; for in them. *John* 5:39
with them out of the *s.* *Acts* 17:2
and searched the *s.* daily. 11
Apollos, mighty in the *s.* 18:24
shewing by the *s.* that Jesus was. 28
prophets in the holy *s.* *Rom* 1:2
that we through comfort of *s.* 15:4
and by the *s.* made known. *Rom* 16:26
Christ died according to *s.* *1 Cor* 15:3
rose according to the *s.* 4
hast known the holy *s.* *2 Tim* 3:15
as they do also other *s.* *2 Pet* 3:16

scroll

rolled together as a *s.* *Isa* 34:4
departed as a *s.* rolled. *Rev* 6:14

scum

(*Revisions,* rust)

woe to the pot whose *s.* *Ezek* 24:6
s. of it may be consumed. 11
her great *s.* went not forth of her, her
s. shall be in the fire. 12

scurvy

none shall approach that is *s.* or.
Lev 21:20
the *s.* or scabbed ye shall not. 22:22

Scythian

neither barbarian, S. *Col* 3:11

sea

(*The molten sea made for the Temple*)

he made a molten *s.* *1 Ki* 7:23
2 Chr 4:2
were knops compassing *s.* *1 Ki* 7:24
the *s.* was set above upon oxen. 25
2 Chr 4:4
set the *s.* on right side of the. 39
took down the *s.* from. *2 Ki* 16:17
the *s.* did Chaldeans break. 25:13, 16
s. was for the priests. *2 Chr* 4:6
one *s.* and twelve oxen under. 15
concerning the pillars and *s.*
Jer 27:19

sea

The Hebrews knew little, and most of them nothing, about the ocean as we understand this word, though the ocean is probably referred to in Gen 1. [1] *The largest body of water really known to them was the* Mediterranean Sea, *which is probably referred to in* Deut 11:24, *and several other places.* [2] *The Red Sea was naturally a familiar name to them,* Ex 15:4. [3] *The Salt Sea, or* Dead Sea, *and other large inland waters are meant in such places as* Deut 3:17; Joel 2:20. [4] *Any great collections of waters, as the Nile,* Isa 19:5, *and the Euphrates,* Jer 51:36, *are in some places called Seas.*

hand over the *s.* *Ex* 14:16, 27
s. to go back, made the *s.* dry. 21
didst blow, the *s.* covered. 15:10
Lord made the *s.* and all. 20:11
Ps 95:5; *Jonah* 1:9; *Acts* 4:24
14:15
quails from the *s.* *Num* 11:31
beyond *s.* that thou shouldest say,
Who shall go over *s.*? *Deut* 30:13
you came unto the *s.* *Josh* 24:6
he brought the *s.* upon them. 7
at *s.* a navy of Tharshish. *1 Ki* 10:22
look toward the *s.* 18:43
coast to the *s.* of plain. *2 Ki* 14:25
let the *s.* roar. *1 Chr* 16:32
Ps 96:11; 98:7
against thee beyond *s.* *2 Chr* 20:2
divide the *s.*, went through the *s.*
Neh 9:11; *Job* 26:12; *Ps* 74:13
78:13; *Jer* 31:35
am I a *s.* or a whale? *Job* 7:12
is broader than the *s.* 11:9
as the waters fail from *s.* 14:11
s. saith, It is not with me. 28:14
or who shut up the *s.*? 38:8
he maketh the *s.* like a pot. 41:31
the *s.* into dry land. *Ps* 66:6
dominion from *s.* to *s.* 72:8
but the *s.* overwhelmed their. 78:53
she sent out her boughs to *s.* 80:11
so is this great and wide *s.* 104:25
down to the *s.* in ships. 107:23
the *s.* saw it and fled. 114:3
O thou *s.*, that thou? 5
gave to the *s.* his decree. *Pr* 8:29
as the waters cover the *s.* *Isa* 11:9
Hab 2:14

stretched and gone over s. Isa 16:8
the waters shall fail from the s. 19:5
Zidon that pass over s. 23:2
be ashamed, O Zion, for the s. 4
stretched his hand over the s. 11
shall cry aloud from the s. 24:14
ye that go down to the s. 42:10
my rebuke, I dry up the s. 50:2
which hath dried the s.? 51:10
are like the troubled s. 57:20
their voice roareth like the s. Jer 6:23
thy plants are gone over s. 48:32
voice shall roar like the s. 50:42
I will dry up her s. and make. 51:36
the s. is come up upon. 42
breach is great like the s. Lam 2:13
as the s. causeth his waves to. Ezek 26:3
came up from the s. Dan 7:3
wander from s. to s. Amos 8:12
shall we do, that the s.? Jonah 1:11
that day he shall come from s. to s. Mi 7:12
he rebuketh the s. and. Nah 1:4
whose rampart was the s. 3:8
was thy wrath against s.? Hab 3:8
thou didst walk through the s. 15
heavens, earth, and s. Hag 2:6
shall be from s. to s. Zech 9:10
through the s. with affliction. 10:11
and rebuked the s. Mat 8:26
even winds and s. obey him. 8:27; Mark 4:39, 41
go thou to the s. and cast an. Mat 17:27
for ye compass s. and land. 23:15
the s. and the waves. Luke 21:25
themselves to the s. Acts 27:40
he hath escaped the s. 28:4
passed through the s. 1 Cor 10:1
throne was a s. of glass. Rev 4:6
to hurt the earth and s. 7:2
Hurt not the earth nor the s. 3
who created the s. and the. 10:6
worship him that made the s. 14:7
I saw a s. of glass, mingled. 15:2
and the s. gave up the dead. 20:13
and there was no more s. 21:1
see **coast, great, red, salt**

by the sea

ye encamp by the s. Ex 14:2
encamping by the s. 9
be gathered as sand by the s. 2 Sam 17:11
Israel as sand by the s. 1 Ki 4:20
I will convey them by the s. 5:9
2 Chr 2:16
ambassadors by the s. Isa 18:2
as Carmel by the s. so. Jer 46:18
multitude was by the s. Mark 4:1
trade by the s. stood. Rev 18:17

in and into the sea

that came into the s. Ex 14:28
he thrown into the sea. 15:1, 21
host hath he cast into the s. 4
horsemen went into the s. 19
thy way is in the s. thy path. Ps 77:19
set his hand also in the s. 89:25
all rivers run into the s. Eccl 1:7
dragon that is in the s. Isa 27:1
maketh a way in the s. 43:16
was strong in the s. Ezek 26:17
the isles that are in the s. shall. 18
these waters go into the s. which being brought forth into the s. 47:8
tempest in the s. Jonah 1:4
forth the wares into the s. 5
cast me into the s. 12, 15
smite her power into the s. Zech 9:4
smite the waves into the s. 10:11
casting a net into the s. Mat 4:18
Mark 1:16
great tempest in the s. Mat 8:24
swine ran into the s. 32; Mark 5:13
like a net cast into the s. Mat 13:47
be thou cast into the s. 21:21
Mark 11:23
and he were cast into the s. Mark 9:42; Luke 17:2
be thou planted in the s. Luke 17:6
cast himself into the s. John 21:7
the wheat into the s. Acts 27:38
themselves first into the s. 43*
cloud, and in the s. 1 Cor 10:2
in perils in the s. 2 Cor 11:26
beast and things in the s. Jas 3:7
every creature in the s. Rev 5:13
burning was cast into the s. 8:8
living soul died in the s. 16:3
all that had ships in the s. 18:19
cast a millstone into the s. 21

of the sea

have dominion over fish of the s. Gen 1:26, 28; Ps 8:8
upon all fishes of the s. Gen 9:2
seed as the sand of the s. 32:12
corn as the sand of the s. 41:49
dwell at the haven of the s. 49:13
in the heart of the s. Ex 15:8
the waters of the s. upon them. 19
all the fish of the s. be? Num 11:22
the channels of the s. 2 Sam 22:16
a cloud out of the s. 1 Ki 18:44
than the sand of the s. Job 6:3
upon the waves of the s. 9:8
the fishes of the s. shall. 12:8
covered the bottom of the s. 36:30
into the springs of the s.? 38:16
waters of the s. together. Ps 33:7
people from depths of the s. 68:22
like as the sand of the s. 78:27
rulest the raging of the s. 89:9
than the mighty waves of the s. 93:4
uttermost parts of the s. 139:9
the roaring of the s. Isa 5:30
her by the way of the s. 9:1
as the sand of the s. yet a remnant shall. 10:22; Hos 1:10; Rom 9:27
even the strength of the s. Isa 23:4
as the waves of the s. 48:18
made the depths of the s. 51:10
abundance of the s. shall be. 60:5
them up out of the s. 63:11
for the bound of the s. Jer 5:22
neither the sand of the s. 33:22
the princes of the s. Ezek 26:16
situate at the entry of the s. 27:3
the ships of the s. were in thee. 9
all the pilots of the s. shall. 29
fishes of the s. shall shake. 38:20
the fishes of the s. shall be. Hos 4:3
calleth for the waters of the s. Amos 5:8; 9:6
in the bottom of the s. 9:3
sins into depths of the s. Mi 7:19
men as the fishes of the s. Hab 1:14
consume the fishes of the s. Zeph 1:3
by way of the s. beyond. Mat 4:15
drowned in the depth of the s. 18:6
is like a wave of the s. Jas 1:6
raging waves of the s. Jude 13
the third part of the s. Rev 8:8
of earth and of the s. 12:12
a beast rise up out of the s. 13:1
is as the sand of the s. 20:8
see **midst, sand**

on or upon the sea

afar off upon the s. Ps 65:5
there is sorrow on the s. Jer 49:23
walking on the s. Mat 14:25
Mark 6:48; John 6:19
disciples saw him walking on the s. Mat 14:26; Mark 6:49
should not blow on the s. Rev 7:1
his right foot upon the s. 10:2
which I saw stand upon the s. 5, 8
and I saw them stand on the s. 15:2
poured out his vial upon the s. 16:3

seafaring men

inhabited of s. men. Ezek 26:17

sea monsters

even the s. monsters draw out the. Lam 4:3*

sea shore

as sand which is upon the s. shore. Gen 22:17
saw the Egyptians dead upon s. shore. Ex 14:30
as sand upon s. shore. Josh 11:4
Asher continued on the s. shore. Judg 5:17
the Philistines as sand on the s. shore. 1 Sam 13:5
heart as sand on s. shore. 1 Ki 4:29
given it a charge against the s. shore Jer 47:7
sprang many, as sand by s. shore. Heb 11:12

sea side

the way of the s. side. Deut 1:7
as sand by the s. side. Judg 7:12
Eloth at the s. side. 2 Chr 8:17
sat by the s. side. Mat 13:1
forth again by the s. side. Mark 2:13
to teach by the s. side. 4:1
Simon, whose house is by the s. side. Acts 10:6, 32

seal

Because of the fact that few could read or write, the use of the seal was far more common in olden times than now. Each person had his own private seal which it was a capital crime to copy. This was affixed to every sort of a document, as we now sign our names.

The word is very frequently used symbolically, as in Rom 4:11; *circumcision is said to be a* seal *of the righteousness of faith.*

letters with Ahab's s. 1 Ki 21:8
as clay to the s. they. Job 38:14
shut up as with a close s. 41:15
s. on thy heart, as a s. on. S of S 8:6
hath set to his s. that God is true. John 3:33*
circumcision a s. of. Rom 4:11
the s. of mine apostleship are ye. 1 Cor 9:2
having this s. the Lord 2 Tim 2:19
he opened the second s. Rev 6:3
the third s. 5
the fourth s. 7
the fifth s. 9
the sixth s. 12
another angel, having the s. 7:2
opened the seventh s. 8:1
that have not the s. of God. 9:4
and shut him up, and set a s. 20:3

seal, verb

our princes and priests s. unto it. Neh 9:38; 10:1
s. the law among my. Isa 8:16
evidences, and s. them. Jer 32:44
seventy weeks to s. up. Dan 9:24
O Daniel, shut up the words, s. 12:4
s. those things the seven. Rev 10:4
s. not the sayings of the. 22:10

sealed

is not this s. up among? Deut 32:34
the letters were s. with. 1 Ki 21:8
written and s. with. Esth 3:12; 8:8
my transgression is s. Job 14:17
my spouse; a fountain s. S of S 4:12
the words of a book s. Isa 29:11
I subscribed and s. the. Jer 32:10
both that which was s. and. 11, 14
s. it with his own signet. Dan 6:17
and s. till the time. 12:9
God the Father s. John 6:27
when I have s. to them. Rom 15:28
who hath s. us and given. 2 Cor 1:22
ye were s. with that Holy. Eph 1:13
whereby ye are s. to-day. 4:30
book s. with seven seals. Rev 5:1
sea, till we have s. servants. 7:3
number of them which were s.; there were s. 144,000 of all the. 4
of Juda were s. 12,000; of Reuben; of Gad s. 5
of Nephthalim s.; of Manasses s. 6
of Levi; of Issachar were s. 7
of Joseph; of Benjamin were s. 8

sealest

thou s. up the sum full. Ezek 28:12

sealeth

commandeth the sun, and s. Job 9:7
he openeth their ears, and s. 33:16
he s. up hand of every man. 37:7

sealing

s. the stone and setting. Mat 27:66

seals

book sealed with seven s. Rev 5:1
who is worthy to loose the s.? 2
Juda prevailed to loose the s. 5
to take and open the s. 9
Lamb opened one of the s. 6:1

seam
was without s., woven. John 19:23

search
enquire and made s. Deut 13:14
that s. may be made in. Ezra 4:15
5:17
s. hath been made, and it. 4:19; 6:1
prepare thyself to the s. Job 8:8
hast thou walked in the s.? 38:16*
accomplish a diligent s. Ps 64:6
my spirit made diligent s. 77:6
not found it by secret s. Jer 2:34

search, verb
he shall not s. whether. Lev 27:33
to s. out a resting place. Num 10:33
that they may s. the land. 13:2
which we have gone to s. it. 32
passed through to s. it, is. 14:7
of the men that went to s. 38
men, and they shall s. Deut 1:22
before to s. you out a place. 33
men to s. the country. Josh 2:2, 3
the Danites sent men to s. Judg 18:2
land, I will s. him out. 1 Sam 23:23
servants unto thee to s. the city?
2 Sam 10:3; 1 Chr 19:3
servants, and they shall s. 1 Ki 20:6
s. that none of the servants.
2 Ki 10:23
is it good that he should s.? Job 13:9
shall not God s. this out? Ps 44:21
they s. and accomplish a. 64:6
s. me, O God, and know. 139:23
kings to s. out a matter. Pr 25:2
for men to s. their own glory. 27
I gave my heart to s. by wisdom.
Eccl 1:13; 7:25
I the Lord s. the heart. Jer 17:10
when ye shall s. for me. 29:13
let us s. our ways, and. Lam 3:40
and none did s. or seek. Ezek 34:6
neither did my shepherds s. for. 8
I will both s. my sheep, and. 11
of seven months shall they s. 39:14
I will s. and take them out. Amos 9:3
I will s. Jerusalem with. Zeph 1:12
and s. diligently for the. Mat 2:8
s. the scriptures; for in. John 5:39
s. for out of Galilee ariseth. 7:52

searched
Laban s. the tent. Gen 31:34, 35
whereas thou hast s. all my. 37
the steward s. for the cup. 44:12
so they went up, and s. Num 13:21
evil report of the land, and s. 32
Caleb s. the land. 14:6, 38
of days ye s. the land. 34
valley of Eshcol, and s. Deut 1:24
we have s. it, and know. Job 5:27
he prepared it, yea, and s. 28:27
which I knew not, I s. out. 29:16
whilst ye s. out what to say. 32:11
his years be s. out. 36:26
O Lord, thou hast s. me. Ps 139:1
foundations of the earth s. Jer 31:37
though it cannot be s. 46:23
things of Esau s. out. Ob 6
s. the scriptures daily. Acts 17:11
prophets s. diligently. 1 Pet 1:10

searchest
that thou s. after my sin. Job 10:6
if thou s. for her as for hid. Pr 2:4

searcheth
for the Lord s. all hearts. 1 Chr 28:9
and he s. out all perfection. Job 28:3
and he s. after every green. 39:8
cometh and s. him. Pr 18:17
understanding s. him out. 28:11
that s. hearts, knows. Rom 8:27*
Spirit s. all things. 1 Cor 2:10
that I am he which s. Rev 2:23

searching
they returned from s. Num 13:25
canst thou by s. find out God?
Job 11:7
s. all the inward parts. Pr 20:27
there is no s. of his. Isa 40:28
s. what time the Spirit. 1 Pet 1:11

searchings
of Reuben were great s. Judg 5:16

seared
having their conscience s. 1 Tim 4:2*

seas
gathering of the waters called he s.
Gen 1:10
and fill the waters in the s. 22
fins and scales in the s. eat. Lev 11:9
that have not fins in the s. be. 10
of abundance of the s. Deut 33:19
thou hast made the s. Neh 9:6
through paths of the s. Ps 8:8
founded it upon the s. 24:2
noise of the s., ... their waves. 65:7
let the s. praise him, and. 69:34
pleased, that did he in the s. 135:6
noise like noise of the s. Isa 17:12
increased above sand of s. Jer 15:8
thy borders in the midst of the s.
Ezek 27:4
glorious in midst of the s. 25
hath broken thee in the midst of s.
26, 27, 34
wares went forth out of the s. 33
seat of God, in midst of the s. 28:2
slain in the midst of the s. 8
art as a whale in the s. 32:2
palace between the s. Dan 11:45
me into midst of the s. Jonah 2:3
a place where two s. met. Acts 27:41

season
and they continued a s. Gen 40:4
this ordinance in his s. Ex 13:10
at the s. thou camest. Deut 16:6
unto thy land in his s. 28:12
the wilderness a long s. Josh 24:7*
about this s. thou shalt. 2 Ki 4:16
woman bare a son at that s. 17
altar was at that s. 1 Chr 21:29*
for long s. been without. 2 Chr 15:3
corn cometh in his s. Job 5:26
pierced in the night s. 30:17
Mazzaroth in his s. 38:32
bringeth forth fruit in his s. Ps 1:3
I cry in the night s. and am. 22:2
a word spoken in due s. Pr 15:23
to every thing there is a s. Eccl 3:1
to speak a word in s. Isa 50:4*
latter rain in his s. Jer 5:24
day and night in their s. 33:20
shower come down in s. Ezek 34:26
prolonged for a s. Dan 7:12
wine in the s. thereof. Hos 2:9
at the s. he sent to the. Mark 12:2
be fulfilled in their s. Luke 1:20
departed from him for a s. 4:13
were present at that s. some. 13:1
at the s. he sent a servant. 20:10
to see him of a long s. 23:8*
went down at a certain s. John 5:4
ye were willing for a s. to. 35
seeing the sun for a s. Acts 13:11
stayed in Asia for a s. 19:22*
when I have a convenient s. 24:25
though it were but for a s. 2 Cor 7:8
instant in s., out of s. 2 Tim 4:2
departed for a s. Philem 15
pleasures of sin for a s. Heb 11:25
though for a s. if need be. 1 Pet 1:6*
rest yet for a little s. Rev 6:11*
must be loosed a little s. 20:3*
see **appointed, due**

season, verb
shalt thou s. with salt. Lev 2:13
wherewith will ye s. it? Mark 9:50

seasoned
wherewith shall it be s.? Luke 14:34
be always with grace, s. Col 4:6

seasons
signs, and s. and days. Gen 1:14
the people at all s. Ex 18:22, 26
proclaim in their s. Lev 23:4
instruct me in the night s. Ps 16:7
he appointeth the moon for s. 104:19
the times and the s. Dan 2:21
the fruits in their s. Mat 21:41
know the times and the s. Acts 1:7
gave us rain and fruitful s. 14:17
been with you at all s. 20:18
of the s. ye have no. 1 Thes 5:1

seat
Eglon rose out of his s. Judg 3:20
Eli sat upon a s. by a post.
1 Sam 1:9; 4:13
he fell from off the s. 1 Sam 4:18
be missed, because thy s. 20:18
the king sat on his s. on a s. by. 25
the Tachmonite that sat in the s.
2 Sam 23:8*
caused a s. to be set. 1 Ki 2:19*
set Haman's s. above all. Esth 3:1
come even to his s.! Job 23:3
prepared my s. in the street. 29:7
nor sitteth in the s. of the. Ps 1:1
sitteth on a s. in the city. Pr 9:14
where was the s. of the. Ezek 8:3
I sit in the s. of God, in midst. 28:2
and cause the s. of violence to come.
Amos 6:3
Pharisees sit in Moses' s. Mat 23:2
where Satan's s. is. Rev 2:13*
see **judgement, mercy**

seated
the lawgiver was he s. Deut 33:21*

seats
moneychangers and the s. of them.
Mat 21:12; Mark 11:15
love chief s. in the synagogues.
Mat 23:6; Mark 12:39
the mighty from their s. Luke 1:52*
love the uppermost s. 11:43; 20:46
four-and-twenty s. upon. Rev 4:4*
sat before God on their s. 11:16*

Seba
the sons of Cush, S. Gen 10:7
the kings of Sheba and S. Ps 72:10
I gave Ethiopia and S. Isa 43:3

second
with s. and third stories. Gen 6:16
and so commanded he the s. 32:19
he made him to ride in the s. 41:43
the coupling of the s. Ex 26:4, 5
10; 36:11, 12, 17
the s. row shall be an. 28:18; 39:11
he shall offer the s. for. Lev 5:10
set forth in the s. rank. Num 2:16
the s. lot came forth to. Josh 19:1
the s. bullock of seven. Judg 6:25
take s. bullock and offer. 26
the s. was offered. 28
then he sent out a s. 2 Ki 9:19
brethren of s. degree. 1 Chr 15:18
him in the s. chariot. 2 Chr 35:24
silver basons of a s. sort. Ezra 1:10
to confirm this s. letter. Esth 9:29
alone, there is not a s. Eccl 4:8
with the s. child that shall. 15
the s. face was the. Ezek 10:14
behold, another beast, a s. like.
Dan 7:5
howling from the s. Zeph 1:10*
in the s. chariot were. Zech 6:2
he came to the s. and. Mat 21:30
likewise the s. had her, and. 22:26
Mark 12:21; Luke 20:30
s. commandment is like unto it.
Mat 22:39; Mark 12:31
and it came to pass on s. Luke 6:1
if he shall come in s. watch. 12:38
the s. came saying, Lord thy. 19:18
this is the s. miracle that. John 4:54
were past the s. ward. Acts 12:10
as it is written in the s. psalm. 13:33
the s. man is the Lord. 1 Cor 15:47
that ye might have a s. 2 Cor 1:15
after the first and s. Tit 3:10
have been sought for the s. Heb 8:7
and after the s. veil, the. 9:3
into the s. went the high priest. 7
that he may establish the s. 10:9
this s. epistle I now write. 2 Pet 3:1
hurt of the s. death. Rev 2:11; 20:6
the s. beast like a calf, the. 4:7
I heard the s. beast say, Come. 6:3
s. angel sounded, and as it. 8:8
the s. woe is past, the third. 11:14
the s. angel poured out his vial. 16:3
this is the s. death. 20:14; 21:8
the s. foundation of the wall. 21:19
see **day, month**

second time
called to Abraham the s. time.
Gen 22:15
and dreamed the s. time. 41:5
had returned this s. time. 43:10
be washed the s. time. Lev 13:58

an alarm the *s. time.* *Num* 10:6
circumcise Israel the *s. time.* *Josh* 5:2
smite him the *s. time.* *1 Sam* 26:8
sent to Joab the *s. time.* *2 Sam* 14:29
Solomon the *s. time.* *1 Ki* 9:2
s. time, they did it the *s. time.* 18:34
again to Elijah the *s. time.* 19:7
a letter the *s. time.* *2 Ki* 10:6
Solomon king *s. time.* *1 Chr* 29:22
gathered the *s. time.* *Esth* 2:19
his hand the *s. time.* *Isa* 11:11
came to me the *s. time* saying, What? *Jer* 1:13; 13:3; 33:1
came to Jonah the *s. time.* *Jonah* 3:1
not rise up the *s. time.* *Nah* 1:9
he went again the *s. time.* *Mat* 26:42
s. time the cock crew. *Mark* 14:72
can he enter the *s. time* ? *John* 3:4
Jesus saith to Peter the *s. time.* 21:16
at the *s. time* Joseph. *Acts* 7:13
to Peter again the *s. time.* 10:15
present the *s. time.* *2 Cor* 13:2
he shall appear the *s. time.* *Heb* 9:28

second *year*

they came the *s. year.* *Gen* 47:18
in the *s. year,* the first. *Ex* 40:17
in the *s. year* after. *Num* 1:1
in first month of *s. year.* 9:1
in the *s. year* the cloud was. 10:11
shall eat in the *s. year* that which. *2 Ki* 19:29; *Isa* 37:30
paid Jotham the *s. year.* *2 Chr* 27:5
in the *s. year* of their. *Ezra* 3:8
it ceased to the *s. year* of. 4:24
in the *s year* of reign. *Dan* 2:1
in *s. year* of Darius. *Hag* 1:1, 15
2:10; *Zech* 1:7

secondarily

God set *s.* prophets. *1 Cor* 12:28

secret

not thou into their *s.* *Gen* 49:6*
heard the *s.* of God ? *Job* 15:8
when the *s.* of God was upon. 29:4
and bind their faces in *s.* 40:13*
the *s.* of the Lord is with. *Ps* 25:14
in *s.* of his tabernacle. 27:5*; 31:20
that they may shoot in *s.* 64:4*
when I was made in *s.* 139:15
but his *s.* is with the. *Pr* 3:32
stolen waters, bread eaten in *s.* 9:17
a gift in *s.* pacifieth anger. 21:14
discover not a *s.* to another. 25:9
I have not spoken in *s.* *Isa* 45:19
48:16
no *s.* that they can hide. *Ezek* 28:3
God concerning this *s.* *Dan* 2:18
then was the *s.* revealed to. 19
the *s.* which the king hath. 27
this *s.* not revealed to me for. 30
thou couldest reveal this *s.* 47
because I know that no *s.* 4:9
he revealeth his *s.* to his. *Amos* 3:7
be in *s.*: and thy Father which seeth in *s.* shall reward. *Mat* 6:4, 6, 18
pray to thy Father which is in *s.* 6
to thy Father which is in *s.* 18
man doth any thing in *s.* *John* 7:4
feast as it were in *s.* 10
I speak openly, in *s.* have I. 18:20
are done of them in *s.* *Eph* 5:12

secret, *adjective*

idol in a *s.* place. *Deut* 27:15
s. things belong unto Lord. 29:29
I have a *s.* errand unto. *Judg* 3:19
my name, seeing it is *s.*? 13:18*
had emerods in their *s.* parts. *1 Sam* 5:9
take heed, abide in a *s.* place. 19:2
wouldest keep me *s.* *Job* 14:13
is there any *s.* with thee ? 15:11
shall be hid in his *s.* places. 20:26*
in *s.* places doth he. *Ps* 10:8*
lion lurking in *s.* places. 17:12
made darkness his *s.* place. 18:11*
cleanse thou me from *s.* faults. 19:12*
hide me from the *s.* counsel. 64:2
I answered thee in the *s.* 81:7
our *s.* sins in the light of thy. 90:8
that dwelleth in the *s.* place. *Ps* 91:1
Open rebuke is better than *s.* love. *Pr* 27:5*
bring into judgement every *s.* thing. *Eccl* 12:14*
art in the *s.* places. *S of S* 2:14*
discover their *s.* parts. *Isa* 3:17
hidden riches of *s.* places. 45:3
found it by *s.* search. *Jer* 2:34
my soul shall weep in *s.* 13:17
can any hide himself in *s.*? 23:24
have uncovered his *s.* places. 49:10
he was to me as a lion in *s.* places. *Lam* 3:10
pollute my *s.* place. *Ezek* 7:22
deep and *s.* things. *Dan* 2:22
I will utter things which have been kept *s.* *Mat* 13:35; *Rom* 16:25
he is in *s.* chambers, believe it not. *Mat* 24:26*
was anything kept *s.* *Mark* 4:22*
Luke 8:17
a candle in a *s.* place. *Luke* 11:33

secretly

thou flee away *s.*? *Gen* 31:27
if thy brother entice thee *s.* *Deut* 13:6
smiteth his neighbour *s.* 27:24
for want of all things *s.* 28:57
sent two men to spy *s.* *Josh* 2:1
commune with David *s.* and say. *1 Sam* 18:22
David knew that Saul *s.* 23:9
for thou didst it *s.* *2 Sam* 12:12
did *s.* those things that. *2 Ki* 17:9
now a thing was *s.* *Job* 4:12
will reprove you, if you *s.* 13:10
hath been *s.* enticed. 31:27
he lieth in wait *s.* as. *Ps* 10:9*
keep them *s.* in a pavilion. 31:20
Zedekiah asked *s.* Is ? *Jer* 37:17
Zedekiah the king sware *s.* 38:16
to Gedaliah in Mizpah *s.* 40:15
was to devour the poor *s.* *Hab* 3:14
went and called Mary her sister *s.* *John* 11:28
Joseph was a disciple, but *s.* 19:38

secrets

shew thee the *s.* of. *Job* 11:6
for he knoweth the *s.* of. *Ps* 44:21
a talebearer revealeth *s.* *Pr* 11:13
talebearer, revealeth *s.* 20:19
God that revealeth *s.* *Dan* 2:28
he that revealeth *s.* maketh. 29
God is the revealer of *s.* 47
God shall judge the *s.* *Rom* 2:16
thus are the *s.* of his. *1 Cor* 14:25

secrets

taketh him by the *s.* *Deut* 25:11

sect

This word is generally used to mean a party in religion, differing in belief from the main body. In our old version it is frequently translated heresy, *which the Revisions change to* sect. *There were several sects among the Jews in the time of Christ, the chief being:* [1] the Pharisees *or formalists;* [2] the Sadducees *or materialists; and* [3] the Essenes, *a sort of monastic body. Other divisions, as the Herodians and Zealots, were mainly political.*
The religion preached by Christ and his disciples was frequently called a sect, *for it was quite a number of years before it was extended to the Gentiles, and the Jews who embraced it were faithful to the major part of their ancestral faith.*

which is the *s.* of the. *Acts* 5:17
the *s.* of the Pharisees. 15:5
a ringleader of the *s.* of the. 24:5
straitest *s.* of our religion. 26:5
this *s.* is every where spoken. 28:22

secure

the host, for it was *s.* *Judg* 8:11
manner of the Zidonians, *s.* 18:7
shall come to a people *s.* 10, 27
thou shalt be *s.* because. *Job* 11:18
they that provoke God are *s.* 12:6
will persuade him, and *s.* you. *Mat* 28:14*

securely

seeing he dwelleth, *s.* by. *Pr* 3:29
them that pass by *s.* *Mi* 2:8

security

when they had taken *s.* *Acts* 17:9

sedition

that they moved *s.* *Ezra* 4:15, 19
for a certain *s.* cast into prison. *Luke* 23:19*, 25*
this man a mover of *s.* *Acts* 24:5*

seditions

works of the flesh are *s.* *Gal* 5:20*

seduce

signs and wonders to *s.* *Mark* 13:22
written concerning them that *s.* you. *1 John* 2:26*
sufferest Jezebel to *s.* *Rev* 2:20

seduced

Manasseh *s.* them to. *2 Ki* 21:9
they have also *s.* Egypt. *Isa* 19:13*
have also *s.* my people. *Ezek* 13:10

seducers

but *s.* shall wax worse. *2 Tim* 3:13*

seduceth

the wicked *s.* them. *Pr* 12:26*

seducing

faith, giving heed to *s.* *1 Tim* 4:1

see

unto Adam, to *s.* what he. *Gen* 2:19
he sent a dove to *s.* if the. 8:8
and the Lord came down to *s.* 11:5
he said unto him, *S.* I have. 19:21
s. the smell of my son is as. 27:27
he said, I *s.* your father's. 31:5
Dinah went out to *s.* the. 34:1
but to *s.* the nakedness. 42:9, 12
thou saidst, You shall *s.* 44:23
your eyes *s.* and the eyes of. 45:12
he said, *S.* that ye fall not out. 24
s. Joseph before I die. 28
I had not thought to *s.* thy. 48:11
when ye *s.* them upon the stools. *Ex* 1:16
I will turn aside and *s.* this. 3:3, 4
s. whether my brethren be. 4:18
s. that thou do those wonders. 21
the officers did *s.* they were. 5:19
now shalt thou *s.* what I will. 6:1
that one cannot be able to *s.* 10:5
take heed to thyself, *s.* my face. 28
I will *s.* thy face no more. 29
when I *s.* the blood, I will. 12:13
repent when they *s.* war. 13:17
stand still and *s.* the. 14:13
s. for the Lord hath given. 16:29
they may *s.* the bread. 32
for there shall no man *s.* 33:20
and thou shalt *s.* my back parts. 23
the people shall *s.* the work. 34:10
priest shall *s.* him. *Lev* 13:10, 17
s. her nakedness and she *s.* 20:17
shall not go in to *s.* *Num* 4:20
shalt *s.* whether my word. 11:23
s. the land, what it is. 13:18
that provoked me *s.* it. 14:23
that thence he might *s.* the. 22:41
top of the rocks I *s.* him. 23:9
come to another place, whence thou mayest *s.* them, thou shalt *s.* 13
I shall *s.* him, but not now. 24:17
and *s.* the land, which I. 27:12
from Kadesh to *s.* land. 32:8
men that came up out of Egypt shall *s.* the land. 32:11; *Deut* 1:35
save Caleb, he shall *s.* *Deut* 1:36
I pray thee, let me *s.* the. 3:25
the land which thou shalt *s.* 28
that he *s.* no unclean thing. 23:14
all people shall *s.* that thou. 28:10
eyes which thou shalt *s.* 34, 67
thou shalt *s.* it no more again. 68
not given you eyes to *s.* 29:4
when they *s.* the plagues of. 22
s. I have set before thee life. 30:15
he said, I will *s.* what their. 32:20
s. now, I, even I, am he, there. 39
yet thou shalt *s.* land before. 52

I have caused thee to s. Deut 34:4
there a great altar to s. Josh 22:10
Samson turned aside to s. Judg 14:8
s. wherein his great strength. 16:5
shall s. an enemy in. 1 Sam 2:32
ark, and rejoiced to s. it. 6:13
now s. this great thing. 12:16
ye may s. that your wickedness. 17
number now, and s. who. 14:17
and s. wherein this sin hath. 38
Samuel came no more to s. 15:35
thou mightest s. the battle. 17:28
and what I s. that I will tell. 19:3
messengers again to s. David. 15
me get away, I pray, and s. 20:29
Ye s. the man is mad. 21:14
know and s. his place, where. 23:22
my father s. yea, s. the skirt. 24:11
s. where king's spear is. 26:16
when thy father cometh to s. thee, let Tamar . . . may s. it. 2 Sam 13:5
now therefore, let me s. the. 14:32
S. thy matters are good and. 15:3
my lord the king may s. it. 24:3
s. what answer I shall return. 13
s. to thy house, David. 1 Ki 12:16
2 Chr 10:16
Elijah said, S. thy son liveth.
1 Ki 17:23
and s. how this man seeketh. 20:7
mark and s. what thou doest, 22
thou shalt s. in that day. 22:25
2 Chr 18:24
if thou s. when I am. 2 Ki 2:10
s. how he seeketh a. 5:7
open his eyes that he may s. 6:17
these men that they may s. 20
s. how this son of a murderer. 32
shalt s. it with thine eyes. 7:2, 19
let us send and s. 13
saying, Go and s. 14
went down to s. Joram. 8:29
9:16; 2 Chr 22:6
the watchman said, I s. a. 2 Ki 9:17
go s. now this cursed woman. 34
come with me, and s. my. 10:16
thine eyes, and s. 19:16; Isa 37:17
title is this that I s.? 2 Ki 23:17
he said, I did s. all Israel.
2 Chr 18:16
s. the salvation of the Lord. 20:17
go, and s. that ye hasten the. 24:5
come, let us s. one another. 25:17
was not meet to s. the. Ezra 4:14
didst s. affliction of our. Neh 9:9
to s. if Mordecai's. Esth 3:4
so long as I s. Mordecai the. 5:13
endure to s. the evil that shall come upon my people? to s. the. 8:6
neither let it s. the dawning. Job 3:9
mine eye shall no more s. 7:7
the eye that hath seen me shall s. 8
my days flee away, they s. no. 9:25
s. thou mine affliction. 10:15
as for my hope, who shall s.? 17:15
yet in my flesh shall I s. God. 19:26
whom I shall s. for myself. 27
the eye which saw him shall s. 20:9
eyes shall s. his destruction. 21:20
righteous s. it, and are glad. 22:19
know him not s. his days? 24:1
saith, No eye shall s. me. 15
did he s. it, and declare it. 28:27
doth not he s. my ways? 31:4
shall pray, and he will s. his. 33:26
his life shall s. the light. 28
look unto the heavens, and s. 35:5
every man may s. it. 36:25
God will never s. it. Ps 10:11
God looked to s. if any. 14:2; 53:2
Holy One to s. corruption. 16:10
Acts 2:27, 31; 13:35
all they that s. laughed me. Ps 22:7
believed to s. the goodness. 27:13
they that did s. me without. 31:11
O taste and s. that the Lord. 34:8
days, that he may s. good. 12
are cut off, thou shalt s. it. 37:34
many shall s. it and trust in. 40:3
if he come to s. me, he. 41:6
he shall go, they shall never s. 49:19
the righteous also shall s. and. 52:6
God shall let me s. my desire on my.
59:10; 92:11; 118:7

to s. thy power and glory. Ps 63:2
say, Who shall s. them? 64:5
all that s. them shall flee away. 8
come and s. the works of God. 66:5
the humble shall s. this, and. 69:32
which hate me may s. it. 86:17
thou shalt s. the reward of. 91:8
and all the people s. his glory. 97:6
that I may s. the good of. 106:5
these s. the works of the. 107:24
righteous shall s. it and rejoice. 42
till he s. his desire upon his. 112:8
the wicked shall s. it and be. 10
glad when they s. me. 119:74
thou shalt s. the good of. 128:5
thou shalt s. thy children's. 6
thy eyes did s. my substance. 139:16
search, s. if there be any. 24
lest the Lord s. and. Pr 24:18
but the righteous shall s. 29:16
whereof it may be said, S. Eccl 1:10
till I might s. what was good. 2:3
men might s. that themselves. 3:18
bring him to s. what shall be. 22
there is profit to them that s. 7:11
to s. the business that is done. 8:16
O my dove, let me s. S of S 2:14
I went into the garden of nuts to s. the fruits, and to s. 6:11; 7:12
his work, that we may s. Isa 5:19
lest they s. with their eyes. 6:10
that s. thee shall narrowly. 14:16
they shall s. and be ashamed. 26:11
eyes of the blind shall s. out. 29:18
eyes shall s. thy teachers. 30:20
the eyes of them that s. shall. 32:3
thine eyes shall s. the king. 33:17
thine eyes shall s. Jerusalem. 20
they shall s. the glory of the. 35:2
and all flesh shall s. it together. 40:5
that they may s. and know. 41:20
s. all this. 48:6
kings shall s. and arise. 49:7
for they shall s. eye to eye. 52:8
the earth shall s. salvation of our. 10
been told them shall they s. 15
when we shall s. him, there is. 53:2
he shall s. his seed, he shall. 10
he shall s. of travail of his soul. 11
then thou shalt s., and flow. 60:5
all that s. them shall. 61:9
the Gentiles shall s. thy. 62:2
behold, s. we beseech, we are. 64:9
and they shall come and s. 66:18
I s. a rod. Jer 1:11
s. a seething pot. 13
send to Kedar, s. if there be. 2:10
know and s. that it is an evil. 19
s. thy way in the valley, know. 23
and s. where thou hast not. 3:2
how long shall I s. the? 4:21
s. now and know, and seek. 5:1
stand ye in the ways and s. 6:16
go to my place, and s. what. 7:12
me s. thy vengeance. 11:20; 20:12
out of the womb to s. labour. 20:18
he shall die and s. this land. 22:12
s. whether man doth travail? why do I s. every man with his? 30:6
and shalt s. and shalt read. 51:61
s. O Lord, consider, for. Lam 1:11
s. if there be any sorrow like. 12
thou shalt s. greater abominations.
Ezek 8:6, 13, 15
that s. vanity. 13:9
s. visions of peace for her. 16
may s. all thy nakedness. 16:37
all flesh shall s. that I. 20:48
whiles they s. vanity unto. 21:29
Pharaoh shall s. them. 32:31
the watchman s. the sword. 33:6
all the heathen shall s. my. 39:21
why should he s. your? Dan 1:10
I s. four men loose, walking. 3:25
dream dreams, your young men shall s. visions. Joel 2:23; Acts 2:17
Calneh and s., go ye to. Amos 6:2
might s. what would. Jonah 4:5
the man of wisdom shall s. Mi 6:9
mine enemy shall s. it. 7:10
the nations shall s. and be. 16
I will watch to s. what he. Hab 2:1
to s. what is the breadth. Zech 2:2
shall s. the plummet in hand. 4:10

I s. a flying roll. Zech 5:2
lift your eyes, s. what is this that. 5
s. it, and fear, Geza shall s. it. 9:5
yea, their children shall s. it. 10:7
and your eyes shall s. Mal 1:5
for they shall s. God. Mat 5:8
they may s. your good works. 16
and then shalt thou s. clearly. 7:5
Luke 6:42
s. thou tell no man, shew Mat 8:4
9:30; Mark 1:44; Acts 23:22
things you hear and s. Mat 11:4
out into wilderness to s.? a reed shaken. 7, 8, 9, Luke 7:24, 25, 26
Master, we would s. a sign from.
Mat 12:38
seeing, ye shall s. 13:14; Mark 4:12
Acts 28:26
any time they should s. with their eyes. Mat 13:15; Acts 28:27
your eyes, for they s. Mat 13:16
to s. those things which ye s. 17
the blind to s. 15:31; Luke 7:22
they s. the Son of man. Mat 16:28
when the king came in to s. 22:11
shall hear of wars, s. that ye. 24:6
they shall s. the Son of man coming.
30; Mark 13:26; Luke 21:27
Peter sat with the servants, to s. the end. Mat 26:58
they said, S. thou to that. 27:4
s. ye to it. 24
let us s. whether Elias will. 49
come s. the place where the. 28:6
there shall they s. me. 10
they went out to s. what. Mark 5:14
he looked to s. her that had. 32
go and s. 6:38
I s. men as trees walking. 8:24
that we may s. and believe. 15:32
Bethlehem and s. this. Luke 2:15
flesh shall s. the salvation. 3:6
enter in may s. light. 8:16; 11:33
desiring to s. thee. 8:20
he desired to s. him. 9:9; 23:8
not taste of death till they s. 27
ground, I must go and s. it. 14:18
when ye shall desire to s. 17:22
s. here, or s. there, go not 23
Zacchaeus sought to s. Jesus. 19:3
sycamore tree to s. him. 4
him when they s. him. 20:13
myself, handle me and s. 24:39
on whom thou shalt s. the Spirit.
John 1:33
come and s. 39, 46; 11:34; Rev 6:1
3, 5, 7
shalt s. greater things. John 1:50
s. a man who told me all. 4:29
shall never s. death. 8:51
rejoiced to s. my day. 56
I washed, and do s. 9:15
how then doth he now s.? 19
I was blind, now I s. 25
that they who s. not might s. and that they who s. might be. 39
if believe, thou shouldest s. 11:40
but that they might s. Lazarus. 12:9
Sir, we would s. Jesus. 21
ye have sorrow, but I will s. 16:22
except I s. in his hands. 20:25
and s. how they do. Acts 15:36
I must also s. Rome. 19:21
ye all shall s. my face. 20:25, 38
know his will, and s. that. 22:14
I called you, to s. you. 28:20
for I long to s. you. Rom 1:11
I s. another law in my. 7:23
spoken of, they shall s. 15:21
to s. you in my journey. 24
if any man s. thee that. 1 Cor 8:10
s. that he may be with you. 16:10
s. that ye abound in. 2 Cor 8:7
Jerusalem to s. Peter. Gal 1:18
make all men s. what is. Eph 3:9
s. that ye walk circumspectly. 5:15
the wife s. that she reverence. 33
whether I come and s. Phil 1:27
so soon as I s. how it will go. 2:23
to s. your face with. 1 Thes 2:17
to s. us, as we also to s. you. 3:6
s. that none render evil for. 5:15
hath seen, nor can s. 1 Tim 6:16
greatly desiring to s. 2 Tim 1:4

s. thou make all according. Heb 8:5
no man s. the Lord. 12:14
s. that ye refuse not him that. 25
he come shortly, I will s. you. 13:23
s. that ye love one. 1 Pet 1:22
he that will s. good days. 3:10
if any man s. his brother sin a sin not unto death. 1 John 5:16
I shall shortly s. thee. 3 John 14
every eye shall s. him. Rev 1:7
to s. the voice that spake. 12
eyesalve, that thou mayst s. 3:18
and s. thou hurt not the oil. 6:6
shall s. their dead bodies. 11:9
lest he walk naked, and they s. 16:15
I sit a queen, shall s. no sorrow. 18:7
when they shall s. the smoke. 9
he said to me, S. thou. 19:10; 22:9
and they shall s. his face. 22:4

see not, or not see

let me not s. the death. Gen 21:16
old, that he could not s. 27:1
ye shall not s. my face. 43:3, 5
for we may not s. the man's. 44:26
were dim, he could not s. 48:10
thou canst not s. my face. Ex 33:20
let me not s. my wretchedness. Num 11:15
they shall not s. the land. 14:23
utmost part, and shall not s. 23:13
thou shalt not s. thy. Deut 22:1
shalt not s. thy brother's ass. 4
Eli, his eyes dim, he could not s. 1 Sam 3:2; 4:15
not s. my face, except. 2 Sam 3:13
let not Absalom s. my face. 14:24
Ahijah could not s. 1 Ki 14:4
not s. wind, nor shall ye s. 2 Ki 3:17
thine eyes shall not s. all evil. 22:20
by me, and I s. him not. Job 9:11
he shall not s. the rivers of. 20:17
that thou canst not s. 22:11
himself that I cannot s. him. 23:9
that which I s. not teach. 34:32
sayest, thou shalt not s. him. 35:14
men s. not the bright light. 37:21
should still live, and not s. Ps 49:9
pass away, that they may not s. the sun. 58:8
be darkened, that they s. not. 69:23
we s. not our signs, there. 74:9
and shall not s. death. 89:48
the Lord shall not s. 94:7
the eye, shall he not s.? 9
eyes have they, but they s. not. 115:5; 135:16; Jer 5:21
is lifted up, they will not s. Isa 26:11
say to the seers, S. not. 30:10
thou shalt not s. a fierce. 33:19
I shall not s. the Lord, even. 38:11
they s. not, that they may be. 44:9
eyes, that they cannot s. 18
they said, He shall not s. Jer 12:4
prophets say, Ye shall not s. 14:13
like heath, he shall not s. 17:6
he shall not s. when heat. 8
that I shall not s. him ? 23:24
cover thy face, that thou s. not the ground. Ezek 12:6, 12
yet shall he not s. it, though he. 13
gods of gold, which s. not. Dan 5:23
thou shalt not s. evil. Zeph 3:15
because they seeing s. not; and hearing they hear not. Mat 13:13
ye shall not s. me henceforth. 23:39 Luke 13:35
Jesus said, S. ye not all ? Mat 24:2
having eyes s. ye not ? Mark 8:18
not s. death, before. Luke 2:20
seeing, they might not s. 8:10
to s. and ye shall not s. it. 17:22
cannot s. the kingdom. John 3:3
shall not s. life, but wrath. 36
they who s. not might see. 9:39
that they should not s. with. 12:40
shall not s. me. 16:16, 17, 19
I not s. thee in the garden? 18:26
when I could not s. for. Acts 22:11
that they should not s. Rom 11:8
darkened that they may not s. 10
for I will not s. you. 1 Cor 16:7
but we s. not yet all things. Heb 2:8
he should not s. death. 11:5
now ye s. him not, yet. 1 Pet 1:8
he is blind, and cannot s. 2 Pet 1:9

we see

we shall s. what will. Gen 37:20
light shall we s. light. Ps 36:9
neither shall we s. sword. Jer 5:12
where we shall s. no war. 42:14
that we may s. and believe. Mark 15:32; John 6:30
now ye say, We s. your. John 9:41
for that we s. not. Rom 8:25
now we s. through a. 1 Cor 13:12
we might s. your face. 1 Thes 3:10
but we s. Jesus, who was. Heb 2:9
so we s. that they could not. 3:19
for we shall s. him as. 1 John 3:2

ye see, or see ye

ye shall s. them again. Ex 14:13
then ye shall s. the glory of. 16:7
when ye s. the ark of. Josh 3:3
s. ye him whom the ? 1 Sam 10:24
to hissing, as ye s. 2 Chr 29:8
to desolation, as ye s. 30:7
I said, Ye s. the distress. Neh 2:17
ye s. my casting down. Job 6:21
what will ye s. in the? S of S 6:13
and s. ye indeed, but. Isa 6:9
s. ye, when he lifteth up an. 18:3
ye blind, that ye may s. 42:18
when ye s. your hearts shall. 66:14
O generation, s. ye the word of the. Jer 2:31
ye shall s. this place no more. 42:18
therefore ye shall s. no. Ezek 13:23
ye shall s. their way and. 14:22
they shall comfort you when ye s. 23
because ye s. the thing. Dan 2:8
to s. those things which ye s. and. Mat 13:17; Luke 10:23
Jesus said S. ye not all? Mat 24:2
when ye shall s. all these. 33 Mark 13:29; Luke 21:31
hereafter shall ye s. the Son of. Mat 26:64; Mark 14:62
I am innocent, s. ye to it. Mat 27:24; Mark 15:36
into Galilee; there shall ye s. him Mat 28:7; Mark 16:7
when ye s. a cloud rise. Luke 12:54
and when ye s. the south wind. 55
when ye shall s. Abraham. 13:28
when ye shall s. Jerusalem. 21:20
ye s. and know of yourselves. 30
and bones, as ye s. me. 24:39
ye shall s. heaven open. John 1:51
except ye s. signs ye will not. 4:48
what if ye shall s. the Son of. 6:62
but ye s. me. 14:19
and ye s. me no more. 16:10
while ye shall s. me. 16, 17, 19
shed this which ye now s. Acts 2:33
whom ye s. and know. 3:16
ye s. and hear, that not alone. 19:26
ye s. this man, about whom. 25:24
for ye s. your calling. 1 Cor 1:26
ye s. how large a letter. Gal 6:11
when ye s. him again. Phil 2:28
much more, as ye s. day. Heb 10:25
ye s. how that by works. Jas 2:24
though now ye s. him not. 1 Pet 1:8

seed

[1] *The seed of plants.* [2] *The posterity of any particular man, as the* seed of Abraham, *referring to all his descendants.*

herbs yielding s. Gen 1:11, 12, 29
give us s. that we may live. 47:19
lo, here is s. for you. 23
shall be your own for s. 24
was like coriander s. Ex 16:31
fall on any sowing s. Lev 11:37
water be put upon the s. 38
sow thy field with mingled s. 19:19
shall sow your s. in vain. 26:16
according to the s. an homer of barley s. valued at 50. 27:16
s. of the land is the Lord's. 30
it is no place of s. or of figs. Num 20:5
where thou sowedst s. Deut 11:10
all the increase of thy s. 14:22
thy s. sown be defiled s. 22:9*
thou shalt carry much s. into. 28:38
the king will take the tenth of s. 1 Sam 8:15
two measures of s. 1 Ki 18:32
unicorn bring home thy s.? Job 39:12
forth bearing precious s. Ps 126:6
in the morning sow thy s. Eccl 11:6
the s. of an homer shall. Isa 5:10
in the morning make thy s. 17:11
great waters the s. of Sihor. 23:3
that it may give s. to the. 55:10
nor shall sow s. nor plant. Jer 35:7
have we vineyard, field, nor s. 9
he took also of the s. Ezek 17:5
the s. is rotten under. Joel 1:17
him that soweth s. Amos 9:13
is the s. yet in the barn ? Hag 2:19
s. shall be prosperous. Zech 8:12
I will corrupt your s. Mal 2:3
which receive s. by the. Mat 13:19
s. into stony places. 20
s. among the thorns. 22
but he that received s. into good. 23
a man which sowed good s. 24
didst not thou sow good s.? 27
he that soweth the good s. is. 37
the good s. are the children of. 38
if a man should cast s. Mark 4:26
and the s. should spring and. 27
to sow his s.: some fell by. Luke 8:5
parable is this; the s. is word. 11
every s. his own body. 1 Cor 15:38
that ministereth s. to. 2 Cor 9:10
not of corruptible s. 1 Pet 1:23
for his s. remaineth in. 1 John 3:9

seed for posterity

appointed me another s. Gen 4:25
to keep s. alive upon the face. 7:3
to me thou hast given no s. 15:3
preserve s. of our father. 19:32, 34
marry her, and raise up s. to. 38:8 Mat 22:24; Mark 12:19 Luke 20:28
Onan knew that the s. Gen 38:9
conceived s. and born. Lev 12:2
hath a blemish of the s. 21:21
what man of the s. of Aaron. 22:4
woman shall conceive s. Num 5:28
which is not of s. of Aaron. 16:40
their s. after them. Deut 1:8; 11:9
he chose their s. after them. 4:37 10:15
the mouths of their s. 31:21
s. the Lord shall give. Ruth 4:12
the Lord give thee s. 1 Sam 2:20
thou wilt not cut off my s. 24:21
king's s. in Edom. 1 Ki 11:14
will for this afflict the s. of David. 39
of Ahaziah, arose and destroyed all the s. 2 Ki 11:1; 2 Chr 22:10
the Lord rejected all the s. of. 2 Ki 17:20
Ishmael of the s. royal came. 25:25 Jer 41:1
O ye s. of Israel his. 1 Chr 16:13
they could not shew their s. Ezra 2:59; Neh 7:61
the holy s. have mingled. Ezra 9:2
the s. of Israel separated. Neh 9:2
if Mordecai be of the s. Esth 6:13
took upon them and their s. 9:27, 31
of them perish from their s. 28
their s. is established in. Job 21:8
their s. shalt thou destroy. Ps 21:10
ye the s. of Jacob, glorify him; and fear him, all ye the s. of. 22:23
a s. shall serve him, it shall be. 30
but the s. of the wicked shall. 37:28
the s. also of his servants. 69:36
their s. shall be established. 102:28
to overthrow their s. 106:27
the s. of righteous shall. Pr 11:21
ah, sinful nation, a s. of. Isa 1:4
the holy s. shall be the. 6:13
the s. of evildoers shall. 14:20
I said not unto s. of Jacob. 45:19
in the Lord shall all s. of Israel. 25
the s. of the adulterer and. 57:3
of transgression, a s. of falsehood. 4
their s. shall be known among the Gentiles; that they are s. 61:9
bring forth a s. out of Jacob. 65:9
they are the s. of the blessed. 23
thee wholly a right s. Jer 2:21

I will cast out the whole s. of. Jer 7:15
which led the s. of the house. 23:8
sow with s. of man and s. of. 31:27
then s. of Israel also shall cease. 36
off all the s. of Israel. 37; 33:26
so will I multiply the s. of. 33:22
taken of the king's s. Ezek 17:13
I lifted up my hand to the s. 20:5
that be of the s. of Zadok. 43:19
maidens of the s. of Israel. 44:22
children of the king's s. Dan 1:3
themselves with the s. of. 2:43
Darius of the s. of the Medes. 9:1
might seek a godly s. Mal 2:15
dying left no s. Mark 12:20, 21, 22
that Christ cometh of s. John 7:42
this man's s. hath God. Acts 13:23
was made of the s. of David.
Rom 1:3; 2 Tim 2:8
be sure to all his s. Rom 4:16
the promise counted for s. 9:8
of sabaoth had left us a s. 29
it was added, till the s. Gal 3:19
strength to conceive s. Heb 11:11
the remnant of her s. Rev 12:17

see **Abraham**

***his* seed**

with Isaac and his s. Gen 17:19
Jacob came, and all his s. 46:6, 7
and his s. shall become a. 48:19
a statute of his s. after him.
Ex 28:43; 30:21
giveth any of his s. to Molech.
Lev 20:2, 3, 4
nor shall ye profane his s. 21:15
servant Caleb and his s. Num 14:24
and his s. shall be in many. 24:7
he shall have it, and his s. 25:13
I multiplied his s. and. Josh 24:3
thee of Saul and his s. 2 Sam 4:8
to David and his s. for evermore.
2 Sam 22:51; Ps 18:50
on head of Joab and his s. for ever,
upon David and his s. 1 Ki 2:33
covenant to give it to his s. Neh 9:8
peace to all his s. Esth 10:3
his s. shall inherit the. Ps 25:13
nor have I seen his s. begging. 37:25
he is merciful, and his s. is. 26
his s. also will I make to endure.
89:29, 36
his s. shall be mighty. 112:2
he shall see his s. Isa 53:10
cast out, he and his s.? Jer 22:28
for no man of his s. shall prosper. 30
punish Shemaiah and his s. 29:32
I will not take any of his s. 33:26
Jehoiachim and his s. 36:31
Esau, his s. is spoiled. 49:10
him and his s. after him. Acts 7:5
that his s. should sojourn in a. 6

***thy* seed**

between thy s. and her s. Gen 3:15
to thy s. will I give this land. 12:7
13:15; 15:18; 17:8; 24:7; 26:3
28:4, 13; 35:12; 48:4; Ex 33:1
Deut 34:4
I will make thy s. as dust.
Gen 13:16; 16:10; 28:14
he said to him, So shall thy s. be.
15:5; Rom 4:18
that thy s. shall be a stranger in a.
Gen 15:13
between me and thy s. after thee;
. . . to thee and thy s. 17:7, 10
thou and thy s. after thee in. 9
a stranger not of thy s. shall. 12
in Isaac shall thy s. be called. 21:12
Heb 11:18
Ishmael a nation, because he is thy s.
Gen 21:13
thy s. possess the gate of enemies.
22:17; 24:60
in thy s. all the nations of the. 22:18
26:4; 28:14; Acts 3:25
and multiply thy s. for. Gen 26:24
will make thy s. as the sand. 32:12
shewed me also thy s. 48:11
not any of thy s. pass. Lev 18:21
whosoever of thy s. hath any. 21:17
I give thee and thy s. Num 18:19
sign on thy s. for ever. Deut 28:46
Lord will make plagues of thy s. 59
circumcise heart of thy s. Deut 30:6
choose life, that thou and thy s. 19
be between my s. and thy s.
1 Sam 20:42
I will set up thy s. 2 Sam 7:12
1 Chr 17:11
cleave to thee and thy s. 2 Ki 5:27
thy s. shall be great. Job 5:25
thy s. will I establish. Ps 89:4
I will bring thy s. from. Isa 43:5
I will pour my spirit upon thy s.
44:3
thy s. also had been as the. 48:19
and thy s. shall inherit the. 54:3
depart out of the mouth of thy s. nor
thy seed's s. 59:21
thy s. from the land of captivity.
Jer 30:10; 46:27
thy s. which is Christ. Gal 3:16

***your* seed**

will I give to your s. Ex 32:13
whosoever of your s. goeth. Lev 22:3
so shall your s. and your. Isa 66:22

seeds

vineyard with divers s. Deut 22:9
when he sowed, some s. Mat 13:4
which is the least of all s. 32
Mark 4:31
he saith not, and to s. as. Gal 3:16

seedtime

s. and harvest shall not. Gen 8:22

seeing, *substantive*

or who maketh the s.? Ex 4:11

seeing

driven away, no man s. Ex 22:10
s. him not, cast it upon him, that he
die. Num 35:23
mine eyes even s. it. 1 Ki 1:48
maketh the s. eye. Pr 20:12
eye is not satified with s. Eccl 1:8
dismayed at the s. of it. Isa 21:3
shutteth his eyes from s. evil. 33:15
s. many things, but thou. 42:20
s. vanity, and divining. Ezek 22:28
because they s. see not. Mat 13:13
s. ye shall see and shall not perceive. 14; Mark 4:12; Acts 28:26
washed and came s. John 9:7
he s. this, spake of the. Acts 2:31
s. Peter and John about to go. 3:3
s. one of them suffer wrong. 7:24
the people s. the miracles. 8:6
speechless, hearing a voice, but s. 9:7
be blind, not s. the sun for. 13:11
he endured as s. him. Heb 11:27
in s. and hearing, vexed. 2 Pet 2:8

seeing, *adverb*

what wilt thou give me, s. Gen 15:2
s. thou hast not withheld. 22:12
s. the Lord hath prospered. 24:56
come ye to me, s. ye hate me? 26:27
s. his life is bound up in. 44:30
s. all the congregation. Num 16:3
my name, s. it is secret. Judg 13:18
s. I have a Levite. 17:13
s. women are destroyed out. 21:16
s. the Lord hath testified. Ruth 1:21
s. I have rejected him. 1 Sam 16:1
s. the Lord is departed from. 28:16
s. there is no wrong in. 1 Chr 12:17
s. the root of the matter. Job 19:28
s. he judgeth those that are. 21:22
s. times are not hidden from. 24:1
s. thou hatest instruction. Ps 50:17
s. he dwelleth securely. Pr 3:29
s. I have lost my. Isa 49:21
s. the Lord hath given. Jer 47:7
s. thou couldest reveal. Dan 2:47
s. I know not a man. Luke 1:34
s. thou art in the same condemnation. 23:40
s. he is Lord of heaven. Acts 17:24
s. he giveth to all life and. 25
s. it is one God who shall. Rom 3:30
s. then that we have. 2 Cor 3:12
s. that ye have put off. Col 3:9
s. it remaineth some must. Heb 4:6
s. then that we have a great. 14
hard to be uttered, s. ye are dull.
5:11
s. they crucify the Son of God. 6:6
s. he ever liveth to make. 7:25
s. we are compassed about. Heb 12:1
s. ye have purified your. 1 Pet 1:22
s. ye look for such things, be diligent.
2 Pet 3:14
s. ye know these things before. 17

seek

I s. my brethren, tell. Gen 37:16
that he may s. occasion. 43:18
and s. ye the priesthood also?
Num 16:10
Balaam went not to s. for. 24:1
if thou s. him with all. Deut 4:29
to his habitation shall ye s. 12:5
till thy brother s. after it. 22:2
Saul his son, Go s. the asses.
1 Sam 9:3
ye? he said, To s. the asses. 10:14
to s. out a cunning player. 16:16
Saul come to s. his life. 23:15, 25
24:2; 26:2
they that s. evil to my Lord. 25:26
is risen to pursue and s. thy soul. 29
Israel is come out to s. a flea. 26:20
Saul shall despair to s. me. 27:1
s. me a woman that hath a. 28:7
came up to s. David. 2 Sam 5:17
Shimei went to s. his. 1 Ki 2:40
Lord hath not sent to s. the. 18:10
they s. my life to take. 19:10, 14
let them go and s. thy. 2 Ki 2:16
to the man whom ye s. 6:19
s. the commandments. 1 Chr 28:8
if thou s. him, he. 9; 2 Chr 15:2
thine heart to s. God. 2 Chr 19:3
that prepareth his heart to s. 30:19
to s. his God, he did it with. 31:21
Josiah began to s. after the. 34:3
build, for we s. your God. Ezra 4:2
prepared his heart to s. the. 7:10
to s. him a right way for us. 8:21
them for good that s. him. 22
to s the welfare of. Neh 2:10
I would s. unto God. Job 5:8
shalt s. me in morning, but. 7:21
if thou wouldest s. unto God. 8:5
his children shall s. to please. 20:10
will ye s. after leasing? Ps 4:2
forsaken them that s. thee. 9:10
s. out his wickedness till thou. 10:15
any that did s. God. 14:2; 53:2
of them that s. him. 24:6
that will I s. after. 27:4
s. ye my face, thy face, Lord, will I s.
8
s. peace, and pursue it. 34:14
1 Pet 3:11
let them be put to shame that s.
Ps 35:4
s. my life, they that s. 38:12
confounded that s. after my soul.
40:14; 70:2
oppressors s. after my soul. 54:3
God, early will I s. thee. 63:1
those that s. my soul go into the. 9
let not those that s. thee be. 69:6
heart shall live that s. God. 32
let all those that s. thee rejoice. 70:4
dishonour that s. my hurt. 71:13
unto shame that s. my hurt. 24
that they may s. thy name. 83:16
the young lions s. their meat. 104:21
his children s. their bread. 109:10
blessed, that s. him with. 119:2
I will walk at liberty, for I s. 45
as a sheep, s. thy servant. 176
I will s. thy good. 122:9
they shall s. me, but. Pr 1:28
and those that s. me early. 8:17
and fro of them that s. death. 21:6
sorrow? they that tarry long at
wine, they that go to s. 23:30
when I shall awake, I will s. it. 35
upright: the just s. his soul. 29:10
many s. the ruler's favour. 26
I gave my heart to s. Eccl 1:13
I applied mine heart to s. out. 7:25
though a man labour to s. it. 8:17
I will s. him whom my. S of S 3:2
thy beloved, that we may s. 6:1
learn to do well, s. Isa 1:17
s. unto them that have familiar
spirits; should not a people s.? 8:19
to it shall the Gentiles s. 11:10

they shall s. to the charmers. Isa 19:3
my spirit within me will I s. 26:9
s. ye out of book of the Lord. 34:16
thou shalt s. them, and not. 41:12
when the needy s. water, and. 17
I said not to Jacob, S. ye. 45:19
yet they s. me daily, and. 58:2
that s. her, in her month. Jer 2:24
thou thy way to s. love? 33
thee, they will s. thy life. 4:30
the men of Anathoth, that s. 11:21
to fall by them that s. 19:7; 21:7
they that s. their lives shall. 9
them that s. thy life. 22:25; 38:16
s. the peace of the city. 29:7
ye shall s. me, and find me. 13
them that s. their life. 34:20, 21
give Pharaoh into the hand of them that s. his life. 44:30
Egyptians to those that s. 46:26
them that s. their life. 49:37
all her people sigh, they s. Lam 1:11
they shall s. peace there. Ezek 7:25
then shall they s. a vision. 26
flock was scattered, none did s. 34:6
I will search my sheep, and s. 11
as a shepherd so will I s. out. 12
I will s. that which was lost. 16
I set my face unto God, to s. by prayer. Dan 9:3
he shall s. them, but not. Hos 2:7
saith the Lord, S. me. Amos 5:4
s. him that maketh the seven. 8
s. good and not evil, that ye. 14
to s. the word of the Lord. 8:12
shall I s. comforters for? Nah 3:7
thou shalt be hid, thou shalt s. 11
s. ye the Lord, ye meek. Zeph 2:3
a shepherd shall not s. Zech 11:16
in that day I will s. to destroy. 12:9
they should s. the law at. Mal 2:7
that he might s. a godly seed. 15
Herod will s. young child. Mat 2:13
things do the Gentiles s. 6:32
s. ye first the kingdom of God. 33
Luke 12:31
s. and ye shall find, knock.
Mat 7:7; Luke 11:9
for I know that ye s. Jesus.
Mat 28:5; Mark 16:6
they said to him, All men s.
Mark 1:37
thy mother and thy brethren s. 3:32
generation s. after a sign. 8:12; 11:29
do the nations s. after. Luke 12:30
many, I say unto you, will s. 13:24
doth she not s. diligently till? 15:8
whosoever shall s. to save. 17:33
the Son of man is come to s. 19:10
why s. ye the living among? 24:5
unto them, What s. ye? John 1:38
ye s. me, not because ye saw. 6:26
he whom they s. to kill? 7:25
ye shall s. me, and shall not. 34, 36
ye shall s. me, and shall die. 8:21
but ye s. to kill me. 37, 40
ye shall s. me, and whither I. 13:33
unto them, Whom s. ye? 18:4, 7
if ye s. me, let these go their way. 8
three men s. thee. Acts 10:19
I am he whom ye s. 21
to Tarsus, to s. Saul. 11:25
to them who s. for glory. Rom 2:7
and they s. my life. 11:3
and the Greeks s. 1 Cor 1:22
let no man s. his own, but. 10:24
s. that ye may excel to. 14:12
since ye s. a proof of. 2 Cor 13:3
do I persuade, or s. to? Gal 1:10
if, while we s. to be justified. 2:17
for all s. their own. Phil 2:21
if ye be risen, s. those things. Col 3:1
of them that s. him. Heb 11:6
they declare plainly that they s. 14
no city, but we s. one to come. 13:14
in those days shall men s. Rev 9:6
see **face, Lord**

not **seek**, or **seek** *not*

the priest shall not s. Lev 13:36
neither s. after wizards. 19:31
that ye s. not after. Num 15:39
thou shalt not s. their peace.
Deut 23:6; Ezra 9:12
daughter, shall I not s.? Ruth 3:1
the wicked will not s. Ps 10:4
they s. not thy statutes. 119:155
lovers, they s. thee not. Jer 30:14
great things? s. them not. 45:5
but s. not Beth-el. Amos 5:5
a shepherd shall not s. Zech 11:16
s. not what ye shall eat. Luke 12:29
because I s. not mine. John 5:30
s. not the honour that cometh. 44
I s. not mine own glory. 8:50
s. not to be loosed. Art thou loosed? s. not a wife. 1 Cor 7:27
for I s. not yours, but. 2 Cor 12:14

seekest

him, what s. thou? Gen 37:15
the man whom thou s. Judg 4:22
the man thou s. is as. 2 Sam 17:3
thou s. to destroy a mother. 20:19
that thou s. to go to. 1 Ki 11:22
if thou s. her as silver. Pr 2:4
s. thou great things? seek. Jer 45:5
yet no man said, What s.? John 4:27
woman, whom s. thou? 20:15

seeketh

Saul my father s. to. 1 Sam 19:2
that he s. my life? 20:1
that s. my life, s. thy life. 22:23
Saul s. to destroy the city. 23:10
saying, David s. thy hurt? 24:9
who came forth of my bowels s. my life. 2 Sam 16:11
and see how this man s. 1 Ki 20:7
see how he s. a quarrel. 2 Ki 5:7
thence she s. the prey. Job 39:29
watcheth righteous, and s. Ps 37:32
he that diligently s. good procureth favour, but he that s. Pr 11:27
a scorner s. wisdom and. 14:6
he that hath understanding s. 15:14
a transgression, s. love. 17:9
an evil man s. only rebellion. 11
he that exalteth his gate s. 19
having separated himself, s. 18:1
ear of the wise s. knowledge. 15
the virtuous woman s. wool. 31:13
which yet my soul s. but. Eccl 7:28
he s. unto him a cunning. Isa 40:20
any that s. the truth, I. Jer 5:1
Zion, whom no man s. after. 30:17
this man s. not the welfare. 38:4
the soul that s. him. Lam 3:25
him that s. unto him. Ezek 14:10
as a shepherd s. out his. 34:12
and he that s. findeth. Mat 7:8
Luke 11:10
an adulterous generation s. a sign.
Mat 12:39; 16:4
leaveth the 99, and s. that. 18:12
Father s. such to worship him.
John 4:23
doeth in secret, and s. to be. 7:4
s. his own glory; s. the glory. 18
is one that s. and judgeth. 8:50
there is none that s. Rom 3:11
not obtained that which he s. 11:7
charity s. not her own. 1 Cor 13:5

seeking

Mordecai s. the wealth. Esth 10:3
s. judgement, and hasting. Isa 16:5
s. rest, and findeth none.
Mat 12:43; Luke 11:24
like to a merchantman s. goodly.
Mat 13:45
s. of him a sign from. Mark 8:11
to Jerusalem, s. him. Luke 2:45
s. something out of his mouth. 11:54
come s. fruit, and find none. 13:7
and came to Capernaum, s. for Jesus. John 6:24
s. to turn away the deputy from.
Acts 13:8
went about s. some to lead him. 11
not s. mine own profit. 1 Cor 10:33
s. whom he may devour. 1 Pet 5:8

seem

s. to him a deceiver. Gen 27:12
not s. hard, when. Deut 15:18
then thy brother should s. vile. 25:3
if it s. evil unto you to. Josh 24:15
let not all the trouble s. Neh 9:32
if the thing s. right. Esth 8:5
the chariot shall s. like. Nah 2:4*
but if any man s. to. 1 Cor 11:16
those members which s. to be. 12:22
I may not s. as if I would terrify.
2 Cor 10:9
lest any of you should s. Heb 4:1
if any among you s. to be religious.
Jas 1:26*
see **good**

seemed

but he s. as one that. Gen 19:14
and they s. unto him but a. 29:20
this wisdom s. great unto. Eccl 9:13
given earth unto whom it s. meet.
Jer 27:5
their words s. to them. Luke 24:11*
but these who s. to be. Gal 2:6*
James, Cephas, and John, who s. 9*

seemeth

it s. there is a plague in. Lev 14:35
s. it but a small thing? Num 16:9
s. it light to be a king's son in law?
1 Sam 18:23
there is a way which s. right.
Pr 14:12; 16:25
in his own cause s. just. 18:17
s. it a small thing to? Ezek 34:18
taken what he s. to. Luke 8:18*
he s. a setter forth of. Acts 17:18
it s. unreasonable to send. 25:27
if any s. wise, let him. 1 Cor 3:18*
now no chastening s. to. Heb 12:11
see **good**

seemly

delight is not s. for a fool. Pr 19:10
honour is not s. for a fool. 26:1

seen

God hath s. mine affliction and.
Gen 31:42
fathers have not s. Ex 10:6
whether he hath s. or known.
Lev 5:1
those men which have s. Num 14:22
nor hath he s. perverseness. 23:21
thou hast s. it, thou shalt. 27:13
we have s. the sons of. Deut 1:28
thou hast s. how the Lord bare. 31
thine eyes have s. all the Lord. 3:21
s. what the Lord did because. 4:3
the things thine eyes have s. 9
we have s. that God doth talk. 5:24
things thine eyes have s. 10:21
have not s. the chastisement. 11:2
but your eyes have s. all the. 7
nor have our eyes s. it. 21:7
temptations thine eyes have s. 29:3
his mother, I have not s. him. 33:9
eyes have s. what I have. Josh 24:7
the elders who had s. the. Judg 2:7
because we have s. God. 13:22
we have s. the land, behold it is. 18:9
five lords had s. it. 1 Sam 6:16
see his place, and who hath s. 23:22
day thine eyes have s. how. 24:10
king what thou hast s. 2 Sam 18:21
queen of Sheba had s. 1 Ki 10:4
mine eyes had s. 7; 2 Chr 9:3, 6
had s. what way man. 1 Ki 13:12
hast thou s. all this great? 20:13
s.? Hezekiah said, All things in mine house . . . s. 2 Ki 20:15; Isa 39:4
when he had s. him. 2 Ki 23:29
many that had s. the first house.
Ezra 3:12
of that which they had s. Esth 9:26
eye that hath s. me shall. Job 7:8
say, I have not s. thee. 8:18
died, and no eye had s. me. 10:18
mine eye had s. all this, mine. 13:1
they that have s. him shall. 20:7
vulture's eye hath not s. 28:7
s. doors of the shadow? 38:17
or hast thou s. the treasures? 22
thou hast s. it, for. Ps 10:14
our eye hath s. 35:21
this thou hast s. 22
so have we s. in city of Lord. 48:8
mine eye hath s. his desire. 54:7
have s. thy goings, O God. 68:24
years wherein we have s. evil. 90:15
ends of earth have s. salvation. 98:3
whom thine eyes have s. Pr 25:7

who hath not s. the evil. Eccl 4:3
not s. the sun, nor known. 6:5
yea, though he live, yet hath he s. 6
eyes have s. the Lord. Isa 6:5
walked in darkness have s. 9:2
nor hath eye s. what he hath. 64:4
who hath heard, who hath s.? 66:8
isles afar off that have not s. 19
Lord, thou hast well s. Jer 1:12
hast thou s. what backsliding? 3:6
thou hast s. me, and tried my. 12:3
because they have s. her. Lam 1:8
she hath s. heathen entered. 10
thy prophets have s. vain and foolish
things for thee, they have s. 2:14
have found, we have s. it. 16
O Lord, thou hast s. my wrong. 3:59
thou hast s. all their vengeance. 60
thou hast s. what the. Ezek 8:12
then said he, Hast thou s. this? 15
17; 47:6
and have s. nothing. 13:3
they have s. vanity. 6
have ye not s. a vain vision? 7
Gabriel whom I had s. Dan 9:21
and the diviners have s. a lie.
Zech 10:2
s. his star in the east. Mat 2:2
to see those things which ye see, and
have not s. 13:17; Luke 10:24
and ye, when ye had s. Mat 21:32
they have s. the kingdom. Mark 9:1
what things they had s. 9
them which had s. him. 16:14
that he had s. a vision. Luke 1:22
for all things they had s. 2:20
not see death before he had s. 26
mine eyes have s. thy salvation. 30
saying, We have s. strange. 5:26
things which they had s. 9:36
works that they had s. 19:37
he hoped to have s. some. 23:8
saying, that they had s. a. 24:23
that they had s. a spirit. 37
no man hath s. God at any time, the.
John 1:18; 1 John 4:12
we testify that we have s. John 3:11
what he hath s. and heard. 32
the Galileans had s. all he did. 4:45
ye have not at any time s. 5:37
those men, when they had s. 6:14
not any man hath s. the Father. 46
hast thou s. Abraham? 8:57
which before had s. him. 9:8
that thou hast both s. and. 37
had s. what Jesus did. 11:45
he that hath s. me, hath s. 14:9
have s. and hated both me. 15:24
she had s. the Lord. 20:18
have s. the Lord. 25
because thou hast s. me. 29
speak things we have s. Acts 4:20
fashion that he had s. 7:44
he hath s. in a vision a man. 9:12
declared to them how he had s. 27
what this vision he had s. 10:17
how he had s. an angel. 11:13
when he had s. the grace of God. 23
after he had s. the vision. 16:10
they had s. the brethren, they. 40
they had s. before with him. 21:29
of what thou hast s. 22:15; 26:16
eye hath not s. nor ear. 1 Cor 2:9
s. Jesus Christ our Lord? 9:1
things ye have heard and s. Phil 4:9
as have not s. my face. Col 2:1
those things he hath not s. 18
whom no man hath s. 1 Tim 6:16
that which we have s. 1 John 1:1
and we have s. it. 2
that which we have s. declare. 3
whosoever sinneth hath not s. 3:6
we have s. and do testify. 4:14
not his brother whom he hath s., how
can he love God . . . not s.? 20
evil, hath not s. God. 3 John 11
things which thou hast s. Rev 1:19
when I had heard and s. I fell. 22:8

have I seen

thee have I s. righteous. Gen 7:1
now have I s. thy people to offer.
1 Chr 29:17
yet have I not s. righteous. Ps 37:25
all things have I s. in. Eccl 7:15
all this have I s. and applied. 8:9
this wisdom have I s. under. 9:13
wherefore have I s. them? Jer 46:5
for now have I s. with. Zech 9:3

I have seen

I have s. all that Laban. Gen 31:12
I have s. God face to face. 32:30
for therefore I have s. thy face.
33:10; 46:30
I have s. the affliction. Ex 3:7
I have also s. the oppression. 9, 16
I have s. this people. 32:9
Deut 9:13
alas, for because I have s. an angel.
Judg 6:22
I have s. a woman in Timnah. 14:2
I have s. a son of Jesse, cunning.
1 Sam 16:18
surely I have s. yesterday the blood
of Naboth. 2 Ki 9:26
I have s. thy tears. 20:5; Isa 38:5
as I have s., they that plow. Job 4:8
I have s. the foolish taking. 5:3
that which I have s. I declare. 15:17
if I have s. any perish for want. 31:19
I have s. the wicked in. Ps 37:35
I have s. violence and strife. 55:9
glory, so as I have s. thee in. 63:2
I have s. an end of all. 119:96
I have s. all the works. Eccl 1:14
I have s. the travail which. 3:10
is a sore evil which I have s. 5:13
I have s. it is good to eat. 18
evil which I have s. 6:1; 10:5
I have s. servants upon horses. 10:7
I am warm, I have s. Isa 44:16
I have s. his ways, and will. 57:18
behold, I have s. it, saith. Jer 7:11
I have s. thine adulteries. 13:27
I have s. folly in prophets. 23:13, 14
I have s. affliction by rod. Lam 3:1
known unto me the dream I have s.
Dan 2:26
dream that I have s. 4:9, 18
I have s. an horrible. Hos 6:10
I speak that I have s. John 8:38
I have s. the affliction. Acts 7:34

ye have seen

of all that ye have s. Gen 45:13
Egyptians whom ye have s. Ex 14:13
ye have s. what I did unto. 19:4
ye have s. that I have talked. 20:22
ye have s. all that the Lord did.
Deut 29:2; Josh 23:3
ye have s. their abominations.
Deut 29:17
what ye have s. me do. Judg 9:48
have ye s. this man? 1 Sam 17:25
ye yourselves have s. it. Job 27:12
ye have s. the breaches. Isa 22:9
ye have s. all the evil. Jer 44:2
ye have s. lies, therefore I am.
Ezek 13:8
what things ye have s. Luke 7:22
ye also have s. me, and. John 6:36
ye do that which ye have s. 8:38
ye know him, and have s. him. 14:7
as ye have s. him go. Acts 1:11
and ye have s. the end. Jas 5:11

seen, passive

tops of the mountains s. Gen 8:5
shall be s. in the cloud. 9:14
of the Lord it shall be s. 22:14
no leavened bread be s. Ex 13:7
Deut 16:4
but my face shall not be s. Ex 33:23
neither let any man be s. 34:3
Lord, art s. face to face. Num 14:14
a shield or spear s. Judg 5:8
no such deed done nor s. 19:30
they might not be s. 2 Sam 17:17
he was s. upon the wings. 22:11
there was no stone s. 1 Ki 6:18
ends of the staves were not s. 8:8
no such almug trees were s. 10:12
consumed, it cannot be s. Job 33:21
channels of water were s. Ps 18:15
s. that Moab is weary. Isa 16:12
thy shame shall be s. 47:3
and his glory shall be s. 60:2
and the Lord shall be s. Zech 9:14
alms to be s. of men. Mat 6:1, 5
saying, It was never so s. Mat 9:33
all their works they do to be s. 23:5
he had been s. of her. Mark 16:11
being s. of them forty days.
Acts 1:3; 13:31
things of him clearly s. Rom 1:20
but hope that is s. is not hope. 8:24
he was s. of Cephas. 1 Cor 15:5
after that he was s. of above 500. 6
s. of James. 7
last of all he was s. of me also. 8
we look not at things s., but at things
not s.: for things s. 2 Cor 4:18
in flesh, s. of angels. 1 Tim 3:16
evidence of things not s. Heb 11:1
so that things which are s. were. 3
warned of God of things not s. 7
having s. them afar off, were. 13
whom having not s. ye love. 1 Pet 1:8
there was s. in his temple the ark.
Rev 11:19

seer

(*Another word for Prophet. Seer one who sees, inferring that he sees visions*)

s. he that is a prophet was beforetime called a s. 1 Sam 9:9
is the s. here? 11
where the s.'s house is. 18
Saul, and said, I am the s. 19
art not thou a s.? 2 Sam 15:27
word came to Gad, David's s.
24:11; 1 Chr 21:9
Samuel the s. did ordain in their set
office. 1 Chr 9:22
Heman the king's s. in the. 25:5
all that Samuel the s. had. 26:28
in the book of Samuel the s. and in
the book of Gad the s. 29:29
visions of Iddo the s. 2 Chr 9:29
acts of . . . book of Iddo the s. 12:15
Hanani the s. came to Asa. 16:7
then Asa was wroth with the s. 10
Jehu son of Hanani the s. went. 19:2
of Gad the king's s. 29:25
David and Asaph the s. 30
Jeduthun the king's s. 35:15
said unto Amos, O thou s. flee.
Amos 7:12

seers

Israel and Judah by s. 2 Ki 17:13
words of the s. that spake.
2 Chr 33:18
among the sayings of the s. 19*
your rulers, the s. hath. Isa 29:10
who say to the s. see not, and. 30:10
shall the s. be ashamed. Mi 3:7

seest

the land thou s. to thee. Gen 13:15
that spake, Thou God s. me. 16:13
Laban said, All that thou s. is. 31:43
that day thou s. my face. Ex 10:28
lest when thou s. the sun. Deut 4:19
every place that thou s. 12:13
goest to battle and s. horses. 20:1
and s. among captives a. 21:11
thou s. the shadow of. Judg 9:36
s. thou how Ahab. 1 Ki 21:29
hast thou eyes, s. thou? Job 10:4
s. thou a man diligent? Pr 22:29
s. thou a man wise in his? 26:12
s. thou a man that is hasty? 29:20
if thou s. the oppression. Eccl 5:8
fasted, and thou s. not? Isa 58:3
when thou s. the naked, that. 7
to Jeremiah, What s. thou? Jer 1:11
13; 24:3; Amos 7:8; 8:2
Zech 4:2; 5:2
s. thou not what they do in cities?
Jer 7:17
O Lord, that s. the reins. 20:12
and behold, thou s. it. 32:24
son of man, s. thou? Ezek 8:6
declare all thou s. to the house. 40:4
and as thou s. deal. Dan 1:13
thou s. the multitude. Mark 5:31
Jesus said, S. thou these? 13:2
he said to Simon, S.? Luke 7:44
thou s. how many. Acts 21:20
s. thou how faith? Jas 2:22
what thou s. write in a book and.
Rev 1:11

seeth
after him that *s.* me? *Gen* 16:13
when he *s.* lad is not with us. 44:31
and when he *s.* thee he. *Ex* 4:14
and when he *s.* the blood. 12:23
priest *s.* the plague in. *Lev* 13:20
when he *s.* that their power is. *Deut* 32:36
Lord *s.* not as man *s.* *1 Sam* 16:7
pleasant, as my lord *s.* *2 Ki* 2:19
and *s.* the place of stones. *Job* 8:17
he *s.* wickedness also. 11:11
covering to him that he *s.* not. 22:14
and his eye *s.* every precious. 28:10
s. under the whole heaven. 24
his eyes are on man, he *s.* 34:21
but now mine eye *s.* thee. 42:5
for he *s.* that his day. *Ps* 37:13
he *s.* that wise men die. 49:10
shall rejoice, when he *s.* 58:10
neither day nor night *s.* *Eccl* 8:16
watchman declare what he *s.* *Isa* 21:6
looketh upon it, *s.* it. 28:4
and they say, Who *s.* us.? 29:15
none *s.* me. 47:10
Lord *s.* us not. *Ezek* 8:12; 9:9
the vision that he *s.* is for. 12:27
if he beget a son that *s.* 18:14
if when he *s.* the sword come. 33:3
when any *s.* a man's bone. 39:15
thy father who *s.* *Mat* 6:4, 6, 18
he *s.* tumult, and. *Mark* 5:38
he *s.* Abraham afar off. *Luke* 16:23
next day John *s.* Jesus. *John* 1:29
do nothing but what he *s.* 5:19
who *s.* the Son, and believeth. 6:40
by what means he now *s.* 9:21
but an hireling *s.* the wolf. 10:12
he stumbleth not, because he *s.* 11:9
s. me, *s.* him that sent me. 12:45
because it *s.* him not, nor. 14:17
a little while, and the world *s.* 19
s. the stone taken away. 20:1
Peter went in and *s.* the linen. 6
and *s.* two angels in white. 12
s. the disciple whom Jesus. 21:20
what a man *s.* why doth? *Rom* 8:24
what he *s.* me to be. *2 Cor* 12:6
s. brother have need. *1 John* 3:17

seethe
(*American Revision*, boil)
and *s.* that ye will *s.* *Ex* 16:23
thou shalt not *s.* a kid in his mother's milk. 23:19; 34:26; *Deut* 14:21
thou shalt *s.* his flesh. *Ex* 29:31
s. pottage for the sons. *2 Ki* 4:38
let them *s.* the bones. *Ezek* 24:5
come and *s.* therein. *Zech* 14:21

seething
came, while flesh was *s.* *1 Sam* 2:13
goeth smoke as out of a *s.* pot. *Job* 41:20
I said, I see a *s.* pot. *Jer* 1:13

Seir
to the land of *S.* the. *Gen* 32:3
till I come to my lord to *S.* 33:14
these are the sons of *S.* 36:20, 21
1 Chr 1:38
S. shall be a possession. *Num* 24:18
destroyed you in *S.* *Deut* 1:44
from Sinai and rose up from *S.* 33:2
thou wentest out of *S.* *Judg* 5:4
of the inhabitants of *S.* *2 Chr* 20:23
of children of *S.* 10,000. 25:11
gods of the children of *S.* 14
he calleth to me out of *S.* *Isa* 21:11
that Moab and S. do say. *Ezek* 25:8

***mount* Seir**
Horites in their *mount S.* *Gen* 14:6
dwelt Esau in *mount S.* 36:8, 9
we compassed *mount S.* *Deut* 2:1
have given *mount S.* to Esau. 5
Josh 24:4
sons of Simeon, 500 men went to *mount S.* *1 Chr* 4:42
mount S. whom thou wouldest not let Israel invade. *2 Chr* 20:10
ambushments against *mount S.* 22
Moab stood up against *mount S.* 23
face against *mount S.* *Ezek* 35:2
say to it, Behold, O *mount S.* 3
thus will I make *mount S.* 7, 15

seize
ye shall rise up and *s.* *Josh* 8:7
night, let darkness *s.* *Job* 3:6
let death *s.* upon them. *Ps* 55:15*
let us kill him, and *s.* *Mat* 21:38

seized
feeble, fear hath *s.* on. *Jer* 49:24

selah
This Hebrew word is found seventy one times in the book of Psalms, and three times in Habakkuk. It is very probably a musical or liturgical sign.
The older view was that it indicated a pause, but it is now believed to be derived from a word signifying Up! This may have been intended for the players, for the singers, or for the congregation, or for all of them.
help for him in God, *s.* *Ps* 3:2
heard me out of his holy hill, *s.* 4
blessing is upon thy people, *s.* 8
forgavest iniquity of my sin, *s.* 32:5
See Ps 4:2, 4; 7:5; 9:16, 20; 20:3
21:2; 24:6, 10; 32:4, 7; 39:5, 11
44:8; 46:3, 7, 11; 47:4; 48:8
49:13, 15; 50:6; 52:3, 5; 54:3
55:7, 19; 57:3, 6; 59:5, 13; 60:4
61:4; 62:4, 8; 66:4, 7, 15; 67:1
4; 68:7, 19, 32; 75:3; 76:3, 9
77:3, 9, 15; 81:7; 82:2; 83:8
84:4, 8; 85:2; 87:3, 6; 88:7, 10
89:4, 37, 45, 48; 140:3, 5, 8; 143:6
Hab 3:3, 9, 13

Seleucia
they departed unto *S.* *Acts* 13:4

***own* self**
swarest by thine *own s.* *Ex* 32:13
I can of mine *own s.* *John* 5:30
thou me with thine *own s.* 17:5
I judge not mine *own s.* *1 Cor* 4:3
even thine *own s.* *Philem* 19
who his *own s.* bare our. *1 Pet* 2:24

selfsame
healed the *s.* hour. *Mat* 8:13
that one and *s.* Spirit. *1 Cor* 12:11
wrought us for *s.* thing. *2 Cor* 5:5
this *s.* thing that ye. 7:11
see same **day**

selfwill
in their *s.*, they digged. *Gen* 49:6

selfwilled
bishop must not be *s.* *Tit* 1:7
presumptuous are they, *s.* *2 Pet* 2:10

sell
(*In case of extreme necessity the Hebrews were allowed to sell themselves and their children into temporary servitude. This was closely regulated, however, in the law*)
Jacob said, *S.* me this. *Gen* 25:31
come, let us *s.* him to the. 37:27
if a man *s.* his daughter. *Ex* 21:7
to *s.* her to strange nation, shall. 8
they shall *s.* the live ox and. 35
an ox, and kill it, or *s.* it. 22:1
if thou *s.* aught unto. *Lev* 25:14
if a man *s.* a dwelling house. 29
if thy brother *s.* himself unto. 47
thou shalt *s.* me meat. *Deut* 2:28
s. that which dieth of itself. 14:21
thou shalt not *s.* her at all. 21:14
s. Sisera into the hand. *Judg* 4:9
Ahab did *s.* himself to. *1 Ki* 21:25
go *s.* the oil, and pay. *2 Ki* 4:7
and will ye even *s.* your? *Neh* 5:8
on the sabbath day to *s.* 10:31
buy truth, and *s.* it not. *Pr* 23:23
s. land into the hand. *Ezek* 30:12
they shall not *s.* the firstfruits. 48:14
I will *s.* your sons and daughters into hand of Judah, they shall *s.* *Joel* 3:8
that we may *s.* corn. *Amos* 8:5
yea, and *s.* the refuse of the. 6
and they that *s.* them. *Zech* 11:5
go and *s.* that thou hast. *Mat* 19:21
Mark 10:21; *Luke* 12:33; 18:22
go ye rather to them that *s.* *Mat* 25:9
let him *s.* his garment. *Luke* 22:36
we will buy and *s.* and. *Jas* 4:13
no man might buy or *s.* *Rev* 13:17

seller
buyer, so with the *s.* *Isa* 24:2
rejoice, nor the *s.* mourn. *Ezek* 7:12
the *s.* shall not return to that. 13
woman named Lydia, a *s.* *Acts* 16:14

sellers
merchants and *s.* *Neh* 13:20

sellest
thou *s.* thy people for. *Ps* 44:12

selleth
a man and *s.* him, he shall surely. *Ex* 21:16; *Deut* 24:7
Naomi *s.* a part of land. *Deut* 4:3
head of him that *s.* corn. *Pr* 11:26
maketh fine linen and *s.* it. 31:24
that *s.* nations through. *Nah* 3:4
he *s.* all, and buyeth. *Mat* 13:44

selvedge
from the *s.* in the coupling. *Ex* 26:4; 36:11

selves
also of your own *s.* *Acts* 20:30
but first gave their own *s.* to the. *2 Cor* 8:5
own *s.* Know ye not your own *s.*? 13:5
lovers of their own *s.* *2 Tim* 3:2
deceiving your own *s.* *Jas* 1:22

Semei
which was the son of *S.* *Luke* 3:26

senate
they called all the *s.* *Acts* 5:21

senators
and teach his *s.* wisdom. *Ps* 105:22

send
God shall *s.* his angel. *Gen* 24:7, 40
I pray thee, *s.* me good speed. 12
he said, *S.* me away unto. 54, 56
a pledge, till thou *s.* it? 38:17
wilt *s.* our brother with us. 43:4
God did *s.* me before you, to. 45:5
s. by hand of him whom. *Ex* 4:13
that he *s.* children of Israel. 7:2*
s. therefore now, and gather. 9:19
that they might *s.* them out. 12:33
whom thou wilt *s.* with me. 33:12
s. him away by the hand. *Lev* 16:21
s. thou men to search land, of every tribe shall ye *s.* a man. *Num* 13:2
of every tribe *s.* a thousand. 31:4
we will *s.* men before us. *Deut* 1:22
thy God will *s.* the hornet. 7:20
the elders shall *s.* and fetch. 19:12
give her a bill of divorce, and *s.* 24:1
Lord shall *s.* upon thee. 28:20
Lord shall *s.* against thee. 48
thou didst *s.* come again. *Judg* 13:8
s. away the ark of God. *1 Sam* 5:11
6:8
tell us wherewith we shall *s.* it. 6:2
if ye *s.* away the ark of God, *s.* 3
saying, Up, that I may *s.* thee. 9:26
give us respite, that we may *s.* 11:3
the Lord shall *s.* thunder. 12:17
Samuel said to Jesse, *S.* 16:11
Saul sent, and said, *S.* me David. 19
young men thou didst *s.* 25:25
David sent saying, *S.* me. *2 Sam* 11:6
come hither, that I may *s.* 14:32
by them ye shall *s.* unto me. 15:36
now therefore *s.* quickly. 17:16
all thou didst *s.* for. *1 Ki* 20:9
ye shall not *s.* *2 Ki* 2:16
he said, *S.* 17
doth *s.* to me to recover a man. 5:7
that I may *s.* and fetch him. 6:13
let us *s.* and see. 7:13
s. to meet Jehu. 9:17
the Lord began to *s.* against. 15:37
let us *s.* abroad our. *1 Chr* 13:2
s. me therefore a man. *2 Chr* 2:7
s. me also cedar trees, fir trees. 8
then hear thou, and *s.* rain. 6:27
Ahaz did *s.* to king of Assyria. 28:16
Sennacherib did *s.* servants. 32:9
let king *s.* his pleasure. *Ezra* 5:17
that thou wouldest *s.* me. *Neh* 2:5
so it pleased the king to *s.* me. 6
eat, drink, and *s.* portions. 8:10, 12
s. forth their little ones *Job* 21:11

canst thou *s.* lightnings ? *Job* 38:35
s. thee help from sanctuary. *Ps* 20:2
O *s.* out thy light and truth. 43:3
he shall *s.* from heaven, and . . .
reproach; God shall *s.* forth. 57:3
God didst *s.* a plentiful rain. 68:9
he doth *s.* out his voice, a. 33*
shall *s.* rod of thy strength. 110:2
O Lord, I beseech thee, *s.* 118:25
s. thine hand from above, rid. 144:7*
sluggard to them that *s.* *Pr* 10:26
truth to them that *s.* to thee. 22:21
faithful messenger to them that *s.* him. 25:13
ointment to *s.* forth a. *Eccl* 10:1
whom shall I *s.*? I said, Here am I, *s.* *Isa* 6:8
Lord shall *s.* among his fat ones. 10:16
s. ye the lamb to the ruler of. 16:1
he shall *s.* them a Saviour. 19:20
that *s.* forth thither the feet. 32:20
didst *s.* thy messengers far off. 57:9
to all that I shall *s.* thee. *Jer* 1:7
s. unto Kedar. 2:10
s. for cunning women. 9:17
s. the yokes to king of Edom. 27:3
s. of them of the captivity. 29:31
for the which the Lord shall *s.* 42:5
the Lord, to whom we *s.* thee. 6
pray ye the Lord that he will *s.* forth labourers. *Mat* 9:38; *Luke* 10:2
that I am come to *s.* peace. 10:34
till he *s.* forth judgement. 12:20
Son of man shall *s.* forth his angels. 13:41; 24:31; *Mark* 13:27
s. her away, for she crieth. *Mat* 15:23
straightway he will *s.* them. 21:3 *Mark* 11:3
that he might *s.* them to preach. *Mark* 3:14; 6:7
would not *s.* them away out. 5:10
besought him, saying, *S.* us. 12
s. Lazarus. *Luke* 16:24
s. to my father's house. 27
whom the Father will *s.* *John* 14:26
believed that thou didst *s.* me. 17:8
shall *s.* Jesus Christ who. *Acts* 3:20
same did God *s.* to be ruler. 7:35
and now *s.* men to Joppa. 10:5, 32 11:13
disciples determined to *s.* 11:29
to *s.* chosen men of. 15:22, 25
that he would *s.* for him to. 25:3
it seemeth unreasonable to *s.* 27
Lord to *s.* Timotheus. *Phil* 2:19, 23
I supposed it necessary to *s.* 25
God shall *s.* delusion. *2 Thes* 2:11
when I shall *s.* Artemas. *Tit* 3:12
doth fountain *s.* sweet? *Jas* 3:11
write and *s.* it to seven. *Rev* 1:11
and they shall *s.* gifts one. 11:10

***I* send**

behold *I s.* an angel. *Ex* 23:20
did *I* not earnestly *s.*? *Num* 22:37
and *I s.* not to thee. *1 Sam* 20:12
business whereabout *I s.* thee. 21:2
if *I s.* pestilence. *2 Chr* 7:13 *Ezek* 14:19
say, Whom shall *I s.*? *Isa* 6:8
nations to whom *I s.* thee. *Jer* 25:15
I s. thee to the children of Israel. *Ezek* 2:3, 4
I s. my four sore judgements. 14:21
behold *I s.* you forth. *Mat* 10:16
behold *I s.* my messenger before. 11:10; *Mark* 1:2; *Luke* 7:27
behold *I s.* you prophets. *Mat* 23:34
if *I s.* them away fasting. *Mark* 8:3
I s. you forth as lambs. *Luke* 10:3
I s. the promise of my Father. 24:49
receiveth whom *I s.* *John* 13:20
sent me, even so *s. I* you. 20:21
to be kept till *I s.* him. *Acts* 25:21
unto whom now *I s.* thee. 26:17

***I will* send**

I will s. and fetch thee. *Gen* 27:45
come, and *I will s.* thee unto. 37:13
he said, *I will s.* thee a. 38:17
I will s. thee unto Pharaoh. *Ex* 3:10 *Acts* 7:34
I will s. swarms of flies. *Ex* 8:21
I will s. all my plagues upon. 9:14
I will s. my fear. 23:27
I will s. hornets. *Ex* 23:28
I will s. an angel before thee. 33:2
I will s. wild beasts. *Lev* 26:22
I will s. pestilence. 25
I will s. faintness. 36
I will s. grass in thy. *Deut* 11:15
I will s. the teeth of beasts. 32:24
I will s. thee a man. *1 Sam* 9:16
I will s. thee to Jesse the. 16:1
I will shew it thee, and *s.* thee. 20:13
and *I will s.* rain upon. *1 Ki* 18:1
yet *I will s.* my servants. 20:6
I will s. thee away with this. 34
I will s. a blast upon him. *2 Ki* 19:7 *Isa* 37:7
I will s. him against. *Isa* 10:6
I will s. those that escape. 66:19
behold *I will s.* serpents. *Jer* 8:17
I will s. a sword after them. 9:16
24:10; 25:16, 27; 29:17; 49:37
I will s. for many fishers. 16:16
I will s. and take the families. 25:9
I will s. Nebuchadnezzar my. 43:10
behold, *I will s.* unto him. 48:12
and *I will s.* unto Babylon. 51:2
I will s. famine. *Ezek* 5:16, 17
14:13; *Amos* 8:11
I will s. mine anger upon. *Ezek* 7:3
I will s. into her pestilence. 28:23
I will s. you corn, and. *Joel* 2:19
I will s. a curse. *Mal* 2:2
I will s. my messenger, and he. 3:1
I will s. Elijah. 4:5
I will not *s.* them away. *Mat* 15:32
I will s. them prophets. *Luke* 11:49
what shall I do? *I will s.* 20:13
the Comforter whom *I will s.* *John* 15:26; 16:7
I will s. thee far hence. *Acts* 22:21
approve, them *I will s.* *1 Cor* 16:3

see **fire**

sendest

when thou *s.* him. *Deut* 15:13*, 18*
whithersoever thou *s.* *Josh* 1:16
that thou *s.* to enquire. *2 Ki* 1:6
and *s.* him away. *Job* 14:20
thou *s.* thy Spirit, they. *Ps* 104:30

sendeth

latter husband *s.* her out. *Deut* 24:3
that the Lord *s.* rain. *1 Ki* 17:14
and who *s.* waters upon. *Job* 5:10
he *s.* them out, they overturn. 12:15
he *s.* the springs into. *Ps* 104:10
he *s.* forth his. 147:15, 18
that *s.* a message by the. *Pr* 26:6
my spikenard *s.* forth. *S of S* 1:12
that *s.* ambassadors by. *Isa* 18:2
and *s.* rain on the just. *Mat* 5:45
he *s.* forth two of his disciples. *Mark* 11:1; 14:13
s. and desireth conditions of peace. *Luke* 14:32
Claudius Lysias to Felix *s.* *Acts* 23:26

sending

evil in *s.* me away. *2 Sam* 13:16*
his *s.* messengers. *2 Chr* 36:15
Jer 7:25; 25:4; 26:5; 29:19 35:15; 44:4
and of *s.* portions. *Esth* 9:19, 22
by *s.* evil angels. *Ps* 78:49*
it shall be for the *s.* *Isa* 7:25
rebelled in *s.* ambassadors unto. *Ezek* 17:15
God *s.* his own Son in the likeness of sinful flesh. *Rom* 8:3

Sennacherib

S. came up against Judah. *2 Ki* 18:13; *Isa* 36:1
see and hear the words of *S.* *2 Ki* 19:16; *Isa* 37:17
thou hast prayed to me against *S.* *2 Ki* 19:20; *Isa* 37:21
S. departed and dwelt at Nineveh. *2 Ki* 19:36; *Isa* 37:37
the Lord saved Hezekiah from *S.* *2 Chr* 32:22

senses

have their *s.* exercised. *Heb* 5:14

sensual

is earthly, *s.*, devilish. *Jas* 3:15
be *s.* having not the Spirit. *Jude* 19

sent

s. coat of many colours. *Gen* 37:22
Judah *s.* the kid by hand. 38:20
Tamar *s.* to her father in law. 25
then Pharaoh *s.* and called. 41:14
but Benjamin, Jacob *s.* not. 42:4
it was not you that *s.* me. 45:8
s. messengers unto Joseph. 50:16
I AM hath *s.* me to you. *Ex* 3:14
why is it that thou hast *s.* me? 5:22
the names of the men Moses *s.* *Num* 13:16; 14:36
Balak king of Moab hath *s.* 22:10
Balak *s.* yet again princes more. 15
hid the messengers we *s.* *Josh* 6:17
old was I when Moses *s.* me. 14:7
I cut her in pieces and *s.* *Judg* 20:6
s. into the land of the. *1 Sam* 31:9
return to him that *s.* *2 Sam* 24:13
my lord hath not *s.* *1 Ki* 18:10
elders did as Jezebel had *s.* 21:11
return unto king that *s.* *2 Ki* 1:6
king of Israel *s.* to the place. 6:10
thistle *s.* to the cedar in. 14:9
according as Ahaz had *s.* 16:11
Rab-shakeh said to them, Hath my master *s.* me? 18:27; *Isa* 36:12
his master *s.* to reproach. *2 Ki* 19:4
Lord God of Israel, Tell the man that *s.* 22:15, 18; *2 Chr* 34:23
copy of the letter they *s.* *Ezra* 4:11
they *s.* unto me four times. *Neh* 6:4
king *s.* and loosed him. *Ps* 105:20
his Spirit hath *s.* me. *Isa* 48:16
their nobles have *s.* their. *Jer* 14:3
I have not *s.* these prophets. 23:21
because thou hast *s.* letters. 29:25
say unto the king that *s.* you. 37:7
whom ye *s.* to present. 42:9, 20
ye have *s.* for men. *Ezek* 23:40
who hath *s.* his angel. *Dan* 3:28
Ephraim went and *s.* *Hos* 5:13
when they had *s.* unto. *Zech* 7:2
receiveth him that *s.* me. *Mat* 10:40
Mark 9:37; *Luke* 9:48 *John* 13:20
s. Jesus two disciples. *Mat* 21:1
Pilate's wife *s.* unto him. 27:19
immediately the king *s.* *Mark* 6:27
John Baptist hath *s.* us. *Luke* 7:20
Jesus *s.* them two and two. 10:1
he *s.* his servant at supper. 14:17
they *s.* a message after him. 19:14
mocked him, and *s.* him. 23:11
to them that *s.* us. *John* 1:22
do the will of him that *s.* me. 4:34
the Father who hath *s.* me. 5:23
believeth on him that *s.* me. 24 12:44
but the will of the Father which hath *s.* me. 5:30; 6:38, 39, 40
ye *s.* unto John, and he. 5:33
bear witness that the Father hath *s.* 5:36, 37; 6:57; 8:16, 18
except the Father which *s.* me. 6:44
but his that *s.* me. 7:16
seeketh his glory that *s.* him. 18
Pharisees and priests *s.* officers. 32
the works of him that *s.* me. 9:4
whom the Father hath *s.* 10:36
believe thou hast *s.* me. 11:42
seeth him that *s.* me. 12:45
Father who *s.* me gave me a. 49
mine, but Father's who *s.* me. 14:24
know not him that *s.* me. 15:21
go my way to him that *s.* me. 16:5
know Jesus whom thou hast *s.* 17:3
s. me into the world, so have I *s.* 18
believe that thou hast *s.* me. 21
know thou hast *s.* me. 23
that thou hast *s.* me. 25
as my Father hath *s.* me. 20:21
s. to the prison to have. *Acts* 5:21
I ask for what intent ye have *s.* 10:29
s. it to elders by Barnabas. 11:30
the rulers of the synagogue *s.* 13:15
we have therefore *s.* Judas. 15:27
the magistrates have *s.* to. 16:36
Paul's friends *s.* unto him. 19:31
Christ *s.* me not to. *1 Cor* 1:17
we have *s.* with him. *2 Cor* 8:18
in Thessalonica ye *s.* once. *Phil* 4:16
testify that the Father *s.* the Son. *1 John* 4:14

sent *away*
Pharaoh **s.** *away* Abraham and his. *Gen* 12:20
s. Ishmael and Hagar *away.* 21:14
they **s.** *away* Rebekah their. 24:59
s. Keturah's children *away.* 25:6
me and have **s.** me *away.* 26:27
as we have **s.** thee *away* in peace. 29
Isaac **s.** *away* Jacob to. 28:5
blessed Jacob and **s.** him *away.* 6
I might have **s.** thee *away.* 31:27
surely thou hadst **s.** me *away.* 42
s. he his brethren *away.* 45:24
s. her *away,* may not. *Deut* 24:4
Rahab **s.** spies *away.* *Josh* 2:21
s. Reubenites and Gadites *away.* 22:6, 7
s. his daughter *away.* *Judg* 11:38
s. all the people *away.* *1 Sam* 10:25
thou **s.** *away* my enemy? 19:17
David **s.** Abner *away.* *2 Sam* 3:21
is it that thou hast **s.** him *away*? 24
cut garments, and **s.** them *away.* 10:4; *1 Chr* 19:4
lords of Philistines **s.** David *away.* *1 Chr* 12:19
s. widows *away* empty. *Job* 22:9
and beat him, and **s.** him *away.* *Mark* 12:3, 4; *Luke* 20:10, 11
he hath **s.** empty *away.* *Luke* 1:53
but Jesus **s.** him *away.* 8:38
them, they **s.** them *away.* *Acts* 13:3
s. *away* Paul and Silas. 17:10, 24

God **sent**
God **s.** me before you. *Gen* 45:7
God of your fathers hath **s.** me. *Ex* 3:13
the *God* of Jacob hath **s.** me. 15
God **s.** an evil spirit between Abimelech and. *Judg* 9:23
God **s.** an angel unto. *1 Chr* 21:15
that *God* had not **s.** him. *Neh* 6:12
Lord their *God* **s.** him. *Jer* 43:1
God hath not **s.** to thee to say. 2
God hath **s.** his angel. *Dan* 6:22
God **s.** not his Son to. *John* 3:17
he whom *God* hath **s.** speaketh. 34
raised up his Son Jesus, **s.** *Acts* 3:26
word of *God* **s.** unto the. 10:36
God **s.** forth his Son. *Gal* 4:4
God hath **s.** forth the Spirit of. 6
God **s.** his only begotten. *1 John* 4:9
God **s.** his Son to be a propitiation. 10
God **s.** his angel to shew. *Rev* 22:6

he **sent**
to his father *he* **s.** after. *Gen* 45:23
he **s.** Judah before him unto. 46:28
he had **s.** her back. *Ex* 18:2
hearkened not to words *he* **s.** *Judg* 11:28
and *he* **s.** for David. *1 Sam* 17:31
he **s.** of the spoil unto the. 30:26
he **s.** to meet them. *2 Sam* 10:5
1 Chr 19:5
when *he* **s.** again, he would. 14:29
he **s.** from above, he took me. 22:17; *Ps* 18:16
for *he* **s.** unto me for my. *1 Ki* 20:7
therefore *he* **s.** lions. *2 Ki* 17:26
yet *he* **s.** prophets. *2 Chr* 24:19
he **s.** unto Amaziah a prophet. 25:15
he **s.** and called for his. *Esth* 5:10
he **s.** them meat to the. *Ps* 78:25
he **s.** a man before them. 105:17
he **s.** Moses his servant and. 26
he **s.** darkness, and made it dark. 28
but *he* **s.** leanness into. 106:15
he **s.** his word and healed. 107:20
he **s.** redemption unto his. 111:9
he hath **s.** me to bind up the brokenhearted. *Isa* 61:1; *Luke* 4:18
he **s.** unto us in Babylon. *Jer* 29:28
for the which *he* hath **s.** me. 42:21
from above *he* **s.** fire. *Lam* 1:13
after the glory hath *he* **s.** *Zech* 2:8
he **s.** other servants. *Mat* 21:36
last of all *he* **s.** unto them his Son. 37; *Mark* 12:4
he **s.** forth his armies. *Mat* 22:7
he that **s.** me to baptize. *John* 1:33
for whom *he* hath **s.**, him. 5:38
on him whom *he* hath **s.** 6:29
he that **s.** me is true. *John* 7:28; 8:26
and *he* hath **s.** me. 7:29
and *he* that **s.** me is with me. 8:29
I of myself, but *he* **s.** me. 42
wherefore *he* **s.** for Paul. *Acts* 24:26
he **s.** and signified it by. *Rev* 1:1

I **sent**
I have **s.** to tell my lord. *Gen* 32:5
I **s.** this kid, and thou hast. 38:23
token that *I* have **s.** thee. *Ex* 3:12
fathers when *I* **s.** them. *Num* 32:8
I **s.** Moses also and Aaron. *Josh* 24:5; *Mi* 6:4
have not *I* **s.** thee? *Judg* 6:14
I have **s.** Naaman my. *2 Ki* 5:6
the law which *I* **s.** to you by. 17:13
my messenger that *I* **s.**? *Isa* 42:19
for your sake *I* have **s.** to Babylon. 43:14
in the thing whereto *I* **s.** it. 55:11
I **s.** unto you all my servants the. *Jer* 7:25; 26:5; 35:15; 44:4
I **s.** them not, nor commanded. 14:14, 15; 23:21, 32; 27:15; 29:9
I **s.** him not, he caused you. 29:31
surely had *I* **s.** thee. *Ezek* 3:6
to thee am *I* now **s.** *Dan* 10:11
my great army which *I* **s.** *Joel* 2:25
I have **s.** among you. *Amos* 4:10
I have **s.** forth thy prisoners out. *Zech* 9:11
know that *I* have **s.** this. *Mal* 2:4
for therefore am *I* **s.** *Luke* 4:43
when *I* **s.** you without. 22:35
so have *I* **s.** them into. *John* 17:18
for *I* have **s.** them. *Acts* 10:20
immediately therefore *I* **s.** to thee. 33
for this cause have *I* **s.** *1 Cor* 4:17
yet have *I* **s.** brethren. *2 Cor* 9:3
gain of you by any whom *I* **s.**? 12:17
desired Titus, and with him *I* **s.** 18
whom *I* have **s.** for the same purpose. *Eph* 6:22; *Col* 4:8
I **s.** him therefore. *Phil* 2:28
for this cause *I* **s.** to know. *1 Thes* 3:5
whom *I* have **s.** again. *Philem* 12

see **Lord**

sent *forth*
Noah **s.** *forth* a raven. *Gen* 8:7
s. *forth* a dove. 10
hath **s.** *forth* her maidens. *Pr* 9:3
Herod **s.** *forth* and slew. *Mat* 2:16
these twelve Jesus **s.** *forth.* 10:5
and **s.** *forth* his servants to. 22:3
Herod **s.** *forth* and laid. *Mark* 6:17
scribes **s.** *forth* spies. *Luke* 20:20
the brethren **s.** him *forth.* *Acts* 9:30
they **s.** *forth* Barnabas as far. 11:22

sent *out*
God **s.** Lot *out* of midst. *Gen* 19:29
David therefore **s.** *out.* *1 Sam* 26:4
and he **s.** *out* arrows. *2 Sam* 22:15
Ps 18:14
who hath **s.** *out* the wild? *Job* 39:5
poured out, skies **s.** *out.* *Ps* 77:17
she **s.** *out* her boughs to sea. 80:11
whom I have **s.** *out* of this place. *Jer* 24:5
she hath **s.** *out* her little. *Ezek* 31:4
Jacob **s.** *out* our fathers. *Acts* 7:12
Rahab had **s.** them *out.* *Jas* 2:25

sent, *passive*
it is a present **s.** to my. *Gen* 32:18
I am **s.** to thee with. *1 Ki* 14:6
forasmuch as thou art **s.** *Ezra* 7:14
shall be **s.** against him. *Pr* 17:11
an ambassador is **s.** unto. *Jer* 49:14
behold, a hand was **s.** *Ezek* 2:9
not **s.** to a people of a strange. 3:5
whom a messenger was **s.** 23:40
then was part of hand **s.** *Dan* 5:24
an ambassador is **s.** among. *Ob* 1
s. but unto lost sheep. *Mat* 15:24
and stonest them who are **s.** 23:37
Luke 13:34
I am Gabriel, and am **s.** *Luke* 1:19
angel Gabriel was **s.** from God. 26
of them was Elias **s.** save. 4:26
a man **s.** from God. *John* 1:6
John was **s.** to bear witness. 8*
they who were **s.** were of the. 24
I said, I am not Christ, but **s.** 3:28
which is by interpretation, **S.** *John* 9:7
is **s.** greater than he that **s.** 13:16
men that were **s.** had. *Acts* 10:17
to the men who were **s.** 21; 11:11
as soon as I was **s.** for. 10:29
so they being **s.** forth by. 13:4
word of this salvation **s.** 26
the salvation of God is **s.** 28:28
except they be **s.**? *Rom* 10:15
which were **s.** from you. *Phil* 4:18
spirits **s.** forth to minister for them. *Heb* 1:14
with the Holy Ghost **s.** *1 Pet* 1:12
as them that are **s.** by him. 2:14
the seven spirits **s.** forth. *Rev* 5:6

sentence
shall shew thee the **s.** *Deut* 17:9
do according to the **s.** 10*, 11*
let my **s.** come forth. *Ps* 17:2
a divine **s.** is in the lips. *Pr* 16:10
s. is not executed speedily. *Eccl* 8:11
now also will I give **s.** *Jer* 4:12*
Pilate gave **s.** that it. *Luke* 23:24
s. is that we trouble. *Acts* 15:19*
we had the **s.** of death. *2 Cor* 1:9

sentences
shewing of hard **s.** found. *Dan* 5:12
a king understanding dark **s.** 8:23

sentest
s. forth thy wrath which. *Ex* 15:7
land whither thou **s.** us. *Num* 13:27
the messengers thou **s.** us. 24:12
things thou **s.** to me for. *1 Ki* 5:8

separate, *verb*
[1] *To part or divide,* Gen 30:40. [2] *To consecrate and set apart for some special ministry or service,* Acts 13:2. [3] *To forsake the communion of the church,* Jude 19. [4] *To excommunicate,* Luke 6:22.
Abram said, S. thyself. *Gen* 13:9
Jacob did **s.** the lambs. 30:40
shall ye **s.** the children. *Lev* 15:31
and his sons that they **s.** 22:2
shall **s.** themselves to vow a vow, to **s.** themselves unto. *Num* 6:2
the Nazarite shall **s.** himself. 3
thus shalt thou **s.** the Levites. 8:14
s. yourselves from among. 16:21
shalt **s.** three cities. *Deut* 19:2, 7
Lord shall **s.** him unto evil. 29:21
didst **s.** them to be thine. *1 Ki* 8:53
s. yourselves from people of the. *Ezra* 10:11
Jeremiah went to **s.** himself thence. *Jer* 37:12*
he shall **s.** them, as a. *Mat* 25:32
when men shall **s.** you. *Luke* 6:22
s. me Barnabas and Saul. *Acts* 13:2
who shall **s.** us from the love of Christ? *Rom* 8:35
nor any other ... able to **s.** us from. 39
they who **s.** themselves. *Jude* 19

separate
head of Joseph and of him that was **s.** *Gen* 49:26; *Deut* 33:16
the **s.** cities of Ephraim. *Josh* 16:9
was before the **s.** place. *Ezek* 41:12
the house and the **s.** places. 13
the breadth of the **s.** place. 14
chamber over against the **s.** place. 42:1, 10, 13
come out from among them, and be ye **s.** *2 Cor* 6:17
undefiled, **s.** from sinners. *Heb* 7:26

separated
then Abram and Lot **s.** *Gen* 13:11
Lord said, after that Lot was **s.** 14
two manner of people be **s.** 35:23
so shall we be **s.** from. *Ex* 33:16
I am the Lord who have **s.** you. *Lev* 20:24
which I have **s.** from you as. 25
of Israel hath **s.** you. *Num* 16:9
the Lord **s.** the tribe of. *Deut* 10:8
when he **s.** sons of Adam. 32:8
there **s.** unto David. *1 Chr* 12:8
Aaron was **s.** that he should. 23:13
David **s.** to the service of sons. 25:1
then Amaziah **s.** them. *2 Chr* 25:10
all that had **s.** themselves. *Ezra* 6:21
then I **s.** twelve of the chief. 8:24

priests and Levites have not *s.* Ezra 9:1
who would not come, be *s.* 10:8
by their names were *s.* 16
we are *s.* upon the wall. Neh 4:19
Israel *s.* themselves from. 9:2
they that had *s.* clave to the. 10:28
they *s.* from Israel the mixed. 13:3
man having *s.* himself. Pr 18:1
but the poor is *s.* from his. 19:4
the Lord hath *s.* me from. Isa 56:3
iniquities have *s.* between. 59:2
for themselves are *s.* Hos 4:14
they went and *s.* themselves. 9:10
Paul departed and *s.* Acts 19:9
Paul an apostle, *s.* unto the. Rom 1:1
God who *s.* me from my. Gal 1:15
Peter withdrew and *s.* himself. 2:12

separateth

fulfilled in which he *s.* Num 6:5
the days he *s.* himself. 6
and a whisperer *s.* chief. Pr 16:28
he that repeateth a matter *s.* 17:9
of the stranger which *s.* Ezek 14:7

separation

the days of the *s.* for her. Lev 12:2
two weeks, as in her *s.* 5
out of the time of her *s.* 15:25
days of *s.* shall he eat. Num 6:4
all days of his *s.* no razor shall. 5
all the days of his *s.* he is holy. 8
to Lord the days of his *s.* and bring a lamb, because his *s.* was. 12
when the days of his *s.* are. 13
Nazarite shall shave the head of his *s.* and take the hair of his *s.* 18
after the hair of the Nazarite's *s.* 19
his *s.* after the law of *s.* 21
kept for a water of *s.* 19:9
the water of *s.* hath not. 13, 20
he that sprinkleth the water of *s.* . . . that toucheth water of *s.* 19:21
purified with the water of *s.* 31:23
wall round to make a *s.* Ezek 42:20

separating

weep in the fifth month, *s.* Zech 7:3

Sepharvaim

brought men from *S.* 2 Ki 17:24
where are the gods of *S.*? 18:34
Isa 36:19
where is the king of *S.*? 2 Ki 19:13
Isa 37:13

sepulchre

Or grave. The Hebrews have always taken great care about the burial of their dead. Most of their sepulchres were hollow places dug into rocks, as was that bought by Abraham, for the burying of Sarah, Gen 23:6, *those of the kings of Judah and Israel; and that wherein our Saviour was laid.*

Our Saviour in Mat 23:7, *compares the hypocritical Pharisees to* whited sepulchres *which appeared fine without, but inwardly were full of rottenness and corruption. It is said, that every year, on the fifteenth of February, the Jews took care to whiten their sepulchres anew.*

The Revisions usually change this to tomb.

withhold from thee his *s.* Gen 23:6
no man knoweth of his *s.* Deut 34:6
buried in his father's *s.* Judg 8:32
two men by Rachel's *s.* 1 Sam 10:2
Asahel in his father's *s.* 2 Sam 2:32
Ish-bosheth buried in Abner's *s.* 4:12
Ahithophel buried in the *s.* of. 17:23
bones of Saul in the *s.* of Kish. 21:14
shall not come to the *s.* 1 Ki 13:22
bury me in the *s.* wherein the man. 31
Ahaziah in the *s.* with. 2 Ki 9:28
they cast the man into the *s.* 13:21
Amon was buried in his *s.* in. 21:26
they told him. It is the *s.* of the. 23:17
Josiah buried in his own *s.* 30
2 Chr 35:24
their throat is an open *s.* Ps 5:9
Rom 3:13
hewed thee out a *s.* here as he that heweth out a *s.* on. Isa 22:16
stone to the door of *s.* Mat 27:60
Mary, sitting over against the *s.* 61
command that the *s.* be. 64, 66
Mary came to see the *s.* 28:1
depart quickly from the *s.* 8
and laid him in a *s.* . . . door of the *s.* Mark 15:46; Luke 23:53
Acts 13:29
the *s.* at rising of sun. Mark 16:2
the stone from the door of the *s.* 3
entering into the *s.* 5
they fled from the *s.* 8
women also beheld the *s.* Luke 23:55
morning they came to the *s.* 24:1
found the stone rolled from *s.* 2
John 20:1
returned from the *s.* Luke 24:9
Peter ran to the *s.* 12
which were early at the *s.* 22
with us went to the *s.* 24
in the garden there was a new *s.* John 19:41
for the *s.* was nigh at hand. 42
Mary when it was dark to the *s.* 20:1
taken away the Lord out of the *s.* 2
disciple came to the *s.* 3, 4, 8
Peter, and went into the *s.* 6
at the *s.* weeping . . . she stooped down and looked into the *s.* 11
and his *s.* is with us. Acts 2:29
Jacob laid in the *s.* that. 7:16

sepulchres

in the choice of our *s.* bury. Gen 23:6
Josiah spied the *s.* and took the bones out of the *s.* 2 Ki 23:16
Jehoram not buried in *s.* 2 Chr 21:20
Joash not buried in *s.* of. 24:25
Ahaz not in *s.* of kings. 28:27
buried in the chiefest of the *s.* 32:33
place of my fathers' *s.* Neh 2:3
me to the city of my fathers' *s.* 5
repaired to place over against *s.* 3:16
are like unto whited *s.* Mat 23:27
because ye garnish the *s.* of the. 29
ye build the *s.* of the prophets. Luke 11:47, 48

Seraiah

Zadok the priest, and *S.* 2 Sam 8:17
the captain of the guard took *S.* the chief. 2 Ki 25:18; Jer 52:24
to Gedaliah, *S.* 2 Ki 25:23
Jer 40:8
S. begat Joab. 1 Chr 4:14
Josibiah son of *S.* 35
Azariah begat *S.* and *S.* begat. 6:14
Ezra the son of *S.* Ezra 7:1
S. sealed. Neh 10:2
S. was ruler of the house. 11:11
S. the priest went up with. 12:1
the fathers: of *S.*, Meraiah. 12
king commanded *S.* to. Jer 36:26
Jeremiah commanded *S.* the son of Neriah, this *S.* was a. 51:59
Jeremiah said to *S.*, When thou. 61

seraphims

above it stood the *s.* each. Isa 6:2
then flew one of the *s.* having. 6

sergeants

sent the *s.* saying, Let. Acts 16:35
the *s.* told these words unto. 38

Sergius Paulus

S. Paulus a prudent man. Acts 13:7

serpent

There are several words in the Bible for various sorts of serpents. It is not always certain which of the many sorts is referred to. The Hebrew word nachash *is a general term for any sort of serpent. Satan is called a serpent partly because of various qualities of the serpent which seem similar to his; partly because he assumed the form of a serpent in Eden; and partly because the serpent was a common symbol for evil.*

In the wilderness the Israelites were plagued by fiery serpents. They were probably so called from the intense burning pain of their bite. The brazen serpent was made by Moses at the command of God to heal those who were so troubled This was preserved till the time of Hezekiah, when it was destroyed because it had become an object of worship.

the *s.* was more subtle. Gen 3:1
woman said, The *s.* beguiled me. 13
2 Cor 11:3
Dan shall be a *s.* by the. Gen 49:17
the rod became a *s.* Ex 4:3, 7, 9
10, 15
make thee a fiery *s.* Num 21:8
Moses made a *s.* of brass . . . if a *s.* had bitten any man . . . *s.* of. 9
in pieces the brasen *s.* 2 Ki 18:4
formed the crooked *s.* Job 26:13
like the poison of a *s.* Ps 58:4
their tongues like a *s.* 140:3
at the last it biteth like a *s.* Pr 23:32
the way of a *s.* upon a rock. 30:19
s. shall bite him. Eccl 10:8
surely the *s.* will bite without. 11
s.'s root shall come forth a cockatrice; his fruit . . . flying *s.* Isa 14:29
punish the *s.*, that crooked *s.* 27:1
viper and fiery flying *s.* 30:6
shall be the *s.*'s meat. 65:25
thereof shall go like a *s.* Jer 46:22
and a *s.* bit him. Amos 5:19
I will command the *s.* and. 9:3
lick the dust like a *s.* Mi 7:17
will he give him a *s.*? Mat 7:10
Luke 11:11
as Moses lifted up the *s.* John 3:14
that old *s.* called. Rev 12:9; 20:2
nourished, from face of the *s.* 12:14
the *s.* cast out of his mouth. 15

serpents

rods, they became *s.* Ex 7:12
the Lord sent fiery *s.* Num 21:6
take away the *s.* from us. 7
wherein were fiery *s.* Deut 8:15
also send the poison of *s.* 32:24*
I will send *s.* among you. Jer 8:17
be ye therefore wise as *s.* Mat 10:16
ye *s.* how can ye escape? 23:33
they shall take up *s.* Mark 16:18
power to tread on *s.* Luke 10:19
and were destroyed of *s.* 1 Cor 10:9
beasts and of *s.* is tamed. Jas 3:7
tails were like unto *s.* Rev 9:19

servant

This word in the Bible usually means bond-servant, *or* slave, *as there were rarely any others who acted as servants. See* **slave.** *It also means any one who serves another, as Joshua was the servant of Moses. Here the Revisions frequently change it to* minister.

Servant *is put for the subject of a prince. The servant of Pharaoh,* the servants *of* Saul *and those of* David, *are their subjects in general, and their domestics in particular,* 2 Sam 11:11; 12:19; 1 Chr 21:3. *In like manner also the* Philistines, *the* Syrians, *and several other nations, were* servants of David; *they obeyed him, they were his subjects, they paid him tribute,* 2 Sam 8:6.

Moses *is often called* the servant of the Lord, Deut 34:5, Josh 1:2.

Servant *is also taken* for a person *of a servile ignoble condition and spirit, who is altogether unfit for places of dignity,* Eccl 10:7.

Canaan, a *s.* of servants. Gen 9:25
I am Abraham's *s.* 24:34
became a *s.* to tribute. 49:15
if the *s.* plainly say. Ex 21:5
wast a *s.* in Egypt. Deut 5:15
thou shalt not deliver the *s.* 23:15
priest's *s.* came. 1 Sam 2:13, 15
Samuel said, Bid the *s.* pass. 9:27
let thy handmaid be a *s.* 25:41
is not this David the *s.* of? 29:3
I am a young man *s.* to an. 30:13
s. named Ziba. 2 Sam 9:2; 19:17

Ziba the s. of Mephibosheth. 2 Sam 16:1
king's s. and me thy s. 18:29
Jeroboam Solomon's s. 1 Ki 11:26
if thou wilt be a s. to this. 12:7
she said to her s., Drive. 2 Ki 4:24
when the s. of the man of. 6:15
Tobiah the s. the. Neh 2:10, 19
there; and the s. is free. Job 3:19
as a s. earnestly desireth the. 7:2
leviathan for a s. for ever? 41:4
who was sold for a s. Ps 105:17
the fool shall be s. to. Pr 11:29
is despised and hath a s. 12:9
favour is toward a wise s. 14:35
a wise s. shall have rule over. 17:2
much less for a s. to rule. 19:10
and the borrower is s. to the. 22:7
a s. will not be corrected. 29:19
accuse not s. to his master. 30:10
the earth cannot bear a s. when. 22
as with the s. so with. Isa 24:2
to a s. of rulers. 49:7
is Israel a s.? Jer 2:14
s. of the living God. Dan 6:20
can s. of my lord talk? 10:17
s. honoureth his master. Mal 1:6
nor the s. above his lord. Mat 10:24
it is enough for the s. to be. 25
s. fell down and worshipped. 18:26
the lord of that s. was moved. 27
O thou wicked s. I forgave. 32
chief among you, let him be your s. 20:27; 23:11; Mark 10:44
wise s. whom lord. Mat 24:45
blessed is that s. whom his lord. 46 Luke 12:43
but if that evil s. shall say. Mat 24:48; Luke 12:45
the lord of that s. shall come. Mat 24:50; Luke 12:46
good and faithful s. enter thou into joy. Mat 25:21, 23; Luke 19:17
thou wicked and slothful s. Mat 25:26; Luke 19:22
cast the unprofitable s. Mat 25:30
Peter struck a s. of the high priest, and smote off his ear. 26:51 Mark 14:47; John 18:10
and he sent to the husbandmen a s. Mark 12:2
that s. which knew his. Luke 12:47
so that s. came and shewed. 14:21
but which of you having a s. 17:7
he thank that s.? I trow not. 9
at the season he sent a s. 20:10, 11
sin, is the s. of sin. John 8:34
the s. abideth not in the house. 35
the s. is not greater than his lord. 13:16; 15:20
the s. knoweth not what. 15:15
Paul a s. of Jesus Christ. Rom 1:1
judgest another man's s.? 14:4
I commend to you Phebe, our s. 16:1
thou called being a s.? 1 Cor 7:21*
called, being a s. is the Lord's. 22*
yet I have made myself a s. 9:19*
I should not be the s. Gal 1:10
differeth nothing from a s. 4:1*
wherefore thou art no more a s. 7*
him the form of a s. Phil 2:7
Epaphras, a s. of Christ. Col 4:12
s. of Lord must not strive. 2 Tim 2:24
as a s. but above a s. a brother. Philem 16
in his house as a s. Heb 3:5
Simon Peter, a s. of. 2 Pet 1:1
Jude the s. of Jesus Christ. Jude 1

see **David, hired, maid**

servant, and **servants** *of God*

forgive the s. of the God of thy. Gen 50:17
as Moses the s. of God. 1 Chr 6:49
Moses the s. of God said. 2 Chr 24:9
law, which was given by Moses the s. of God to observe. Neh 10:29
he said, O Daniel, s. of the living God. Dan 6:20
law of Moses the s. of God. 9:11
a s. of God. Tit 1:1
James a s. of God. Jas 1:1
not using liberty, but as a s. of God. 1 Pet 2:16
sealed the s. of our God. Rev 7:3
song of Moses the s. of God. 15:3

his **servant**

and Canaan shall be his s. Gen 9:26 27
Lord and his s. Moses. Ex 14:31
if a man smite his s. and die. 21:20
if he smite the eye of his s. that. 26
but his s. Joshua departed. 33:11*
saith my Lord to his s.? Josh 5:14
God commanded his s. Moses. 9:24
down with Phurah his s. Judg 7:11
the Levite went, having his s. 19:3
rose to depart, he and his s. 9
king sin against his s. 1 Sam 19:4
impute any thing to his s. 22:15
the Lord hath kept his s. 25:39
thus pursue after his s.? 26:18
king hear the words of his s. 19
hath commanded his s. 2 Sam 9:11
fulfilled the request of his s. 14:22
my lord come to his s.? 24:21
he will not slay his s. 1 Ki 1:51
by the hand of Moses his s. 8:56
cause of his s. and Israel. 59
hand of his s. Ahijah. 14:18; 15:29
Elijah came and left his s. 19:3
he spake by his s. Elijah. 2 Ki 9:36
he spake by his s. Jonah. 14:25
Hoshea became his s. and. 17:3
and Jehoiakim became his s. 24:1
seed of Israel his s. 1 Chr 16:13
spake against his s. Hezekiah. 2 Chr 32:16
let every one with his s. Neh 4:22
in prosperity of his s. Ps 35:27
O ye seed of Abraham his s. 105:6
he sent Moses his s. and Aaron. 26
remembered Abraham his s. 42
heritage unto Israel his s. 136:22
that delicately bringeth up his s. Pr 29:21
that confirmeth the word of his s. Isa 44:26
redeemed his s. Jacob. 48:20
from the womb to be his s. 49:5
obeyeth the voice of his s. 50:10
caused every man his s. Jer 34:16
his s. was healed in the. Mat 8:13
he hath holpen his s. Luke 1:54
would come and heal his s. 7:3
and sent his s. at supper time. 14:17
his angel unto his s. John. Rev 1:1

see **Lord**

man-**servant**

shalt not do any work, thou, nor thy man-s. Ex 20:10; Deut 5:14
not covet thy neighbour's man-s. Ex 20:17; Deut 5:21
if he smite out his man-s.'s tooth. Ex 21:27
if the ox shall push a man-s. 32
eat them, thou, and thy man-s. Deut 12:18
Lord, thou and thy man-s. 16:11
feast, thou, and thy man-s. 14
the cause of my man-s. Job 31:13
should let his man-s. go free. Jer 34:9, 10

my **servant**

I will multiply thy seed for my s.'s sake. Gen 26:24
he with whom it is found shall be my s. 44:10*, 17*
my s. Moses is not so. Num 12:7
why were ye not afraid to speak against my s.? 8
but my s. Caleb had another. 14:24
Moses my s. is dead. Josh 1:2
that my son had stirred up my s. 1 Sam 22:8
therefore he shall be my s. 27:12
my lord, O king, my s. 2 Sam 19:26
sent Naaman my s. 2 Ki 5:6
according to the law my s. 21:8
considered my s. Job? Job 1:8; 2:3
I called my s. and he gave. 19:16
right, as my s. Job hath. 42:7
go to my s. Job, he shall pray. 8
like as my s. Isaiah. Isa 20:3
I will call my s. Eliakim. 22:20
Israel, art my s., fear not. Isa 41:8, 9
behold my s. whom I uphold. 42:1
blind but my s. that I sent? 19
ye are witnesses, and my s. 43:10
hear, O Jacob, my s. 44:1
fear not, O Jacob, my s. 2
for thou art my s. 21; 49:3
for Jacob my s.'s sake, and. 45:4
thou shouldest be my s. 49:6
behold, my s. shall deal. 52:13
so will I do for my s.'s sake. 65:8
Nebuchadnezzar my s. Jer 25:9 27:6; 43:10
fear thou not, O my s. Jacob. 30:10 46:27, 28
land I have given to my s. Jacob. Ezek 28:25; 37:25
thee, O Zerubbabel my s. Hag 2:23
bring forth my s. the BRANCH. Zech 3:8
the law of Moses my s. Mal 4:4
my s. lieth at home sick. Mat 8:6
speak, and my s. shall be healed. 8 Luke 7:7
and to my s., Do this, and he doeth it. Mat 8:9; Luke 7:8
behold, my s. whom I. Mat 12:18
there shall also my s. be. John 12:26

thy **servant**

I pray thee, from thy s. Gen 18:3
behold, thy s. hath found grace. 19:19; Neh 2:5
hast appointed for thy s. Gen 24:14
the mercies shewed to thy s. 32:10
shalt say, They be thy s. Jacob's. 18
which God hath given thy s. 33:5
grey hairs of thy s. our father. 44:31
thy s. became surety for the lad. 32
hast spoken unto thy s. Ex 4:10
for thee, and for thy s. Lev 25:6
thou afflicted thy s.? Num 11:11
hast begun to shew thy s. Deut 3:24
and he shall be thy s. for ever. 15:17
down with Phurah thy s. Judg 7:10
deliverance into hand of thy s. 15:18
speak, Lord, for thy s. heareth. 1 Sam 3:9, 10
thy s. slew both the lion. 17:36
if he say thus, thy s. shall. 20:7
for thy s. knew nothing of all. 22:15
I beseech thee, tell thy s. 23:11
know what thy s. can do. 28:2
hast spoken of thy s.'s house. 2 Sam 7:19
thou, Lord God, knowest thy s. 20
to bless the house of thy s. 29
answered, Behold thy s. 9:6
the king's sons came as thy s. 13:35
even there will thy s. be. 15:21
he hath slandered thy s. 19:27
away the iniquity of thy s. 24:10
but me, even me thy s. and Zadok the priest, and thy s. 1 Ki 1:26
king said, so will thy s. do. 2:38
and thy s. is in the midst of. 3:8
give thy s. understanding heart. 9
to the prayer of thy s. 8:28
but I thy s. fear the Lord. 18:12
this day that I am thy s. 36
thy s. Ben-hadad saith, I pray. 20:32
as thy s. was busy here and there. 40
thy s. my husband is dead, and thou knowest thy s. did fear. 2 Ki 4:1
pardon thy s. in this thing. 5:18
Gehazi said, Thy s. went no. 25
but what, is thy s. a dog? 8:13
I am thy s. 16:7
prosper, I pray thee, thy s. this day. Neh 1:11
by them is thy s. warned. Ps 19:11
thy s. from presumptuous sins. 13
put not thy s. away in anger. 27:9
shine upon thy s.: save me. 31:16
hide not thy face from thy s. 69:17
O my God, save thy s. that. 86:2
give thy strength unto thy s. 16
void the covenant of thy s. 89:39
truly I am thy s. 116:16; 119:125 143:12
lest thou hear thy s. Eccl 7:21
hear the prayer of thy s. Dan 9:17
now lettest thou thy s. Luke 2:29

servants

Canaan, a servant of *s.* *Gen* 9:25
have I given him for *s.* 27:37
children of Israel are *s.* *Lev* 25:55
and say, We are your *s.* *Josh* 9:11
that ye be not *s.* unto. *1 Sam* 4:9
Philistine, and you *s.* to Saul? 17:8
will we be your *s.*: but if I kill him,
then shall ye be our *s.* 9
but the *s.* of the king would. 22:17
many *s.* break away from. 25:10
to wash the feet of the *s.* of. 41
became David's *s.* *2 Sam* 8:2
Edom became David's *s.* 14
fifteen sons and twenty *s.* 9:10
all in the house of Ziba *s.* 12
Hanun took David's *s.* and shaved.
10:4; *1 Chr* 19:4
the *s.* of my Lord are. *2 Sam* 11:11
two of the *s.* of Shimei. *1 Ki* 2:39
the *s.* of Amon. *2 Ki* 21:23
not all my lord's *s.*? *1 Chr* 21:3
children of Israel Solomon made no
s. *2 Chr* 8:9
Babylon, where they were *s.* 36:20
we are the *s.* of the God. *Ezra* 5:11
their *s.* bare rule over. *Neh* 5:15
behold, we are *s.* this day, *s.* 9:36
they have slain the *s.* *Job* 1:15, 17
as the eyes of *s.* look. *Ps* 123:2
I got me *s.* and had *s.* born. *Eccl* 2:7
I have seen *s.* upon horses, and
princes walking as *s.* 10:7
shall possess them for *s.* *Isa* 14:2
s. whom they had let go free, to return ... subjection for *s.* *Jer* 34:11
s. have ruled over us. *Lam* 5:8
ye *s.* of the most high God. *Dan* 3:26
upon the *s.* will I pour. *Joel* 2:29
be a spoil to their *s.* *Zech* 2:9
then said the king to the *s.* *Mat* 22:13
the lord of those *s.* cometh. 25:19
the *s.* did strike Jesus. *Mark* 14:65*
blessed are those *s.* *Luke* 12:37, 38
say, We are unprofitable *s.* 17:10
I call you not *s.*, for. *John* 15:15
these men are *s.* of the. *Acts* 16:17
ye yield yourselves *s.* to obey.
Rom 6:16
that ye were the *s.* of sin. 17
made free, ye became the *s.* 18
your members *s.* to sin. 19
s. of sin, ye were free from. 20
and become *s.* to God. 22
be not ye the *s.* of men. *1 Cor* 7:23
and ourselves your *s.* *2 Cor* 4:5
s. be obedient to your. *Eph* 6:5
Col 3:22; *Tit* 2:9; *1 Pet* 2:18
eye service, but as the *s.* of. *Eph* 6:6
Paul and Timotheus the *s.* *Phil* 1:1
masters, give unto your *s.* *Col* 4:1
let as many *s.* as are. *1 Tim* 6:1
but as the *s.* of God. *1 Pet* 2:16
they themselves are the *s.* of.
2 Pet 2:19
till we have sealed the *s.* *Rev* 7:3
see **hired, Lord, maid, men, women**

his **servants**

feast unto all *his s.* *Gen* 40:20
Pharaoh made *his s.* *Ex* 9:20
in the night, he and *his s.* 12:30
his two *s.* with him. *Num* 22:22
repent himself for *his s.* *Deut* 32:36
the blood of *his s.* 43
and give to *his s.* *1 Sam* 8:14, 15
tenth, ye shall be *his s.* 17
Saul spake to all *his s.* to kill. 19:1
and all *his s.* were standing. 22:6
his s. came near. *2 Ki* 5:13; 10:19
are not *his s.* come to? *1 Chr* 19:3
they shall be *his s.* *2 Chr* 12:8
his s. spake yet more against. 32:16
therefore we *his s.* will. *Neh* 2:20
put no trust in *his s.* *Job* 4:18
the seed also of *his s.* *Ps* 69:36
to deal subtilly with *his s.* 105:25
himself concerning *his s.* 135:14
if hearken to lies, all *his s.* *Pr* 29:12
of the Lord, to be *his s.* *Isa* 56:6
the Lord shall call *his s.* by. 65:15
be known toward *his s.* 66:14
on horses, he and *his s.* *Jer* 22:4
punish him, his seed and *his s.* 36:31
prince give a gift to *his s.* *Ezek* 46:17
and delivered *his s.* that. *Dan* 3:28
take account of *his s.* *Mat* 18:23
he sent *his s.* to husbandmen. 21:34
he called *his* ten *s.* *Luke* 19:13
his s. ye are to whom. *Rom* 6:16
to shew *his s.* things. *Rev* 1:1; 22:6
hath avenged blood of *his s.* 19:2
praise God, all ye *his s.* and. 5
throne shall be in it, and *his s.* 22:3

my **servants**

they are *my s.* whom I brought.
Lev 25:42, 55
I have appointed *my s.* *1 Sam* 21:2
my s. shall be with thy servants.
1 Ki 5:6; *2 Chr* 2:8
yet I will send *my s.* *1 Ki* 20:6
let *my s.* go with thy servants. 22:49
the blood of *my s.* *2 Ki* 9:7
the half of *my s.* wrought. *Neh* 4:16
neither I nor *my s.* put off our. 23
I and *my s.* might exact of. 5:10
all *my s.* were gathered thither. 16
and some of *my s.* sat. 13:19
mine elect and *my s.* shall. *Isa* 65:9
my s. shall eat. 13
my s. shall sing for joy. 14
I have even sent to you all *my s.*
Jer 7:25; 44:4
world, then would *my s.* fight.
John 18:36
on *my s.* I will pour out. *Acts* 2:18
prophetess, to seduce *my s.* *Rev* 2:20
see **prophets**

thy **servants**

thy s. are no spies. *Gen* 42:11
out the iniquity of *thy s.* 44:16*
thy s. are shepherds, both we. 47:3
said, Behold, we be *thy s.* 50:18
wherefore dealest thou thus with *thy s.*? *Ex* 5:15
these *thy s.* shall bow down. 11:8
Abraham and Israel *thy s.* 32:13
Deut 9:27
thy s. will do as my lord.
Num 32:25, 31
to Joshua, We are *thy s.* *Josh* 9:8
slack not thy hand from *thy s.* 10:6
pray for *thy s.* to the. *1 Sam* 12:19
faithful among all *thy s.*? 22:14
comfortably to *thy s.* *2 Sam* 19:7
word, return thou and all *thy s.* 14
they told Shimei, *thy s.* *1 Ki* 2:39
my servants shall be with *thy s.* 5:6
2 Chr 2:8
and mercy with *thy s.* *1 Ki* 8:23
hear thou and judge *thy s.* 32
2 Chr 6:23
happy are these *thy s.* *1 Ki* 10:8
2 Chr 9:7
they will be *thy s.* for ever.
1 Ki 12:7; *2 Chr* 10:7
content, and go with *thy s.* *2 Ki* 6:3
now these are *thy s.* and. *Neh* 1:10
attentive to prayer of *thy s.* 11
the bodies of *thy s.* have. *Ps* 79:2
of the blood of *thy s.* shed. 10
Lord, the reproach of *thy s.* 89:50
repent thee concerning *thy s.* 90:13
let thy work appear unto *thy s.* 16
for *thy s.* take pleasure in. 102:14
children of *thy s.* shall continue. 28
this day, for all are *thy s.* 119:91
by *thy s.* hast thou. *Isa* 37:24
return, for *thy s.'* sake. 63:17
prove *thy s.* I beseech. *Dan* 1:12
as thou seest, deal with *thy s.* 13
grant unto *thy s.* that. *Acts* 4:29

serve

shall *s.* them 400 years. *Gen* 15:13
that nation whom they shall *s.* 14
elder shall *s.* the younger. 25:23
let people *s.* thee, nations. 27:29
by thy sword shalt thou live, and *s.* 40
therefore *s.* me for nought? 29:15
I will *s.* thee seven years for. 18
thou shalt *s.* with me seven. 27
they made Israel to *s.* *Ex* 1:13
ye shall *s.* God upon this mountain.
3:12
my son go, that he may *s.* me. 4:23
let my people go, that they may *s.*
7:16; 8:1, 20; 9:1, 13; 10:3
that we may *s.* Egyptians, for it had
been better for us to *s.* *Ex* 14:12
not bow down to them, nor *s.* them.
20:5; *Deut* 5:9
Hebrew servant, six years he shall *s.*
Ex 21:2
ear, and he shall *s.* him for ever. 6
him to *s.* as bondservant. *Lev* 25:39
s. thee unto the year of jubile. 40
the family of the Gershonites to *s.*
Num 4:24
made for them, so shall they *s.* 26
of fifty they shall *s.* no more. 8:25
Levi, for their service they *s.* 18:21
be driven to *s.* them. *Deut* 4:19
the Lord thy God, and *s.* him. 6:13
10:12, 20; 11:13; 13:4; *Josh* 22:5
24:14, 15; *1 Sam* 7:3; 12:14, 20
24
sold to thee, and *s.* six years.
Deut 15:12
to thee, and shall *s.* thee. 20:11
shalt thou *s.* thine enemies. 28:48
this day whom ye will *s.* *Josh* 24:15
should *s.* Shechem, should *s.* Hamor.
Judg 9:28
that we should *s.* him? 38
occasion shall *s.* thee. *1 Sam* 10:7
with us, and we will *s.* thee. 11:1
deliver us, and we will *s.* 12:10
be our servants, and *s.* us. 17:9
whom should I *s.*? should I not *s.*?
2 Sam 16:19
a people I knew not shall *s.* me.
22:44; *Ps* 18:43
heavy yoke lighter, and we will *s.*
1 Ki 12:4; *2 Chr* 10:4
Jehu shall *s.* Baal. *2 Ki* 10:18
the land, and *s.* the king of. 25:24
Jer 27:11, 12, 17; 28:14; 40:9
and *s.* him with a perfect heart.
1 Chr 28:9
chosen you to *s.* him. *2 Chr* 29:11*
Josiah made all present to *s.* 34:33
that we should *s.* him? *Job* 21:15
if they obey and *s.* him, they. 36:11
unicorn be willing to *s.* thee? 39:9
a seed shall *s.* him and. *Ps* 22:30
kings, all nations shall *s.* him. 72:11
all they that *s.* graven images. 97:7
perfect way, he shall *s.* me. 101:6*
wherein thou wast made to *s.* *Isa* 14:3
the Egyptians shall *s.* with. 19:23*
I have not caused thee to *s.* 43:23
but thou hast made me to *s.* 24†
themselves to the Lord, to *s.* 56:6*
the nation that will not *s.* thee. 60:12
so shall ye *s.* strangers. *Jer* 5:19
cause thee to *s.* thine enemies. 17:4
these nations shall *s.* the king. 25:11
many nations shall *s.* themselves.
14; 27:7
of field have I given to *s.* him. 27:6
the nation which will not *s.* the king. 8
that say, Ye shall not *s.* 9, 14
no more *s.* themselves of him. 30:8
that none should *s.* himself. 34:9, 10
fear not to *s.* the Chaldeans. 40:9
I will *s.* the Chaldeans. 10*
the countries to *s.* wood. *Ezek* 20:32
O house of Israel, go *s.* ye. 39
all of them in the land shall *s.* me. 40
his army *s.* a great service. 29:18
food to them that *s.* the city. 48:18*
that *s.* the city, shall *s.* it out of. 19*
God whom we *s.* is able. *Dan* 3:17
they might not *s.* any, except. 28
languages should *s.* him. 7:14
all dominions shall *s.* and obey. 27
s. him with one consent. *Zeph* 3:9
it is in vain to *s.* God. *Mal* 3:14
him only shalt thou *s.* *Mat* 4:10
Luke 4:8
no man can *s.* two masters; ye cannot *s.* God. *Mat* 6:24; *Luke* 16:13
delivered, might *s.* him. *Luke* 1:74
sister hath left me to *s.* alone. 10:40
he will come forth and *s.* them. 12:37
lo, these many years do I *s.* thee.
15:29
say, Gird thyself and *s.* me? 17:8
is chief, as he that doth *s.* 22:26
if any man *s.* me, let him follow.
John 12:26

word of God, and s. Acts 6:2
shall they come forth and s. 7:7
angel of God, whom I s. 27:23
whom I s. with my spirit in the gospel of his Son. Rom 1:9
we should not s. sin. 6:6
we should s. in newness of. 7:6
so then, with the mind I s. the. 25
it was said, the elder shall s. 9:12
they that are such s. not our. 16:18
but by love s. one another. Gal 5:13
for ye s. the Lord Christ. Col 3:24
turned from idols to s. 1 Thes 1:9
I thank God whom I s. 2 Tim 1:3
who s. unto the example and shadow of heavenly. Heb 8:5
purge from dead works to s.? 9:14
whereby ye may s. God. 12:28
no right to eat, which s. the. 13:10
they s. him day and night. Rev 7:15
and his servants shall s. him. 22:3
see Lord

serve joined with *gods*
thou shalt not s. their gods. Ex 23:24
Deut 6:14; 28:14; Josh 23:7
2 Ki 17:35; Jer 25:6; 35:15
if thou s. their gods it will. Ex 23:33
s. gods, the work of men's hands.
Deut 4:28; 28:36, 64; Jer 16:13
that they may s. other gods.
Deut 7:4; 31:20
s. other gods and worship. 8:19
11:16; 30:17; Josh 24:20
2 Chr 7:19
nations s. their gods? Deut 12:30
and s. other gods. 13:2, 6, 13
from God to s. other gods. 29:18
we should s. other gods. Josh 24:16
more than their fathers to s. other gods. Judg 2:19; Jer 11:10; 13:10
saying, Go s. other gods.
1 Sam 26:19
to anger, to s. other gods. Jer 44:3
they s. not thy gods. Dan 3:12
do ye not s. my gods? 14
we will not s. thy gods. 18

served
twelve years they s. Gen 14:4
Jacob s. seven years. 29:20, 30
children for whom I s. thee. 30:26
knowest how I have s. thee. 29
with all my power I have s. 31:6
I s. thee 14 years for thy two. 41
wherein the nations s. Deut 12:2
hath gone and s. other gods. 17:3
29:26; Josh 23:16
fathers s. other gods. Josh 24:2, 15
gods which your fathers s. 14
and Israel s. the Lord all the days of Joshua. 31; Judg 2:7
Israel s. Baalim. Judg 2:11, 13
3:7; 10:6, 10
to sons, and s. their gods. 3:6
Israel s. Chushan-rishathaim. 8
so Israel s. Eglon king of Moab. 14
Why hast thou s. us thus? 8:1
ye have forsaken me, and s. 10:13
they put away gods, s. 16; 1 Sam 7:4
peace and s. Israel. 2 Sam 10:19
s. in thy father's presence. 16:19
presents and s. Solomon. 1 Ki 4:21
because they s. other gods. 9:9
2 Chr 7:22
Ahab s. Baal. 1 Ki 16:31
Ahazian s. Baal. 22:53
Ahab s. Baal a little. 2 Ki 10:18
and s. their own gods. 17:33
Hezekiah s. not the king of. 18:7
Manasseh s. host. 21:3; 2 Chr 33:3
Amon s. the idols that his father s.
2 Ki 21:21; 2 Chr 33:22
Judah s. groves and. 2 Chr 24:18
they have not s. thee in. Neh 9:35
and they s. their idols. Ps 106:36
thee as thou hast s. us. 137:8
the king himself is s. Eccl 5:9
as ye have s. strange gods. Jer 5:19
and moon, whom they have s. 8:2
after other gods and s. them. 16:11
worshipped other gods and s. 22:9
he hath s. thee six years. 34:14
for the service which he had s.
Ezek 29:18, 20
the hands of those that s. Ezek 34:27
Israel s. for a wife, he. Hos 12:12
Anna s. God night and. Luke 2:37*
a supper and Martha s. John 12:2
after David had s. his. Acts 13:36
who worshipped and s. Rom 1:25
he hath s. with me in. Phil 2:22

servedst
thou s. not the Lord. Deut 28:47

servest
thy God whom thou s. Dan 6:16
is thy God whom thou s. able? 20

serveth
of Merari all that s. Num 3:36
his son that s. him. Mal 3:17
s. God, and him that s. not. 18
sitteth at meat or he that s.? but I am among . . . s. Luke 22:27
he that in these things s. Christ is.
Rom 14:18
prophecy s. not them. 1 Cor 14:22*
wherefore then s. the law? Gal 3:19

service
for the s. that thou. Gen 29:27
thou knowest the s. which. 30:26
s. in field; all their s. wherein they.
Ex 1:14
come to land, ye shall keep this s.
12:25; 13:5
say, What mean ye by this s.? 12:26
all vessels in all the s. 27:19
make the clothes of the s. 31:10
35:19
more than enough for the s. 36:5
tribe of Levi to do s. Num 3:7, 8
charge of Gershonites for the s. 26
s. of sanctuary the charge. 31; 4:4
shall appoint them to the s. 4:19
in to perform the s. to do work. 23
the s. of the Gershonites. 24, 27, 28
s. of the sons of Merari. 30, 33, 43
that they may do the s. of the. 7:5
Levites may execute the s. of. 8:11
they shall go in to wait upon s. 24
shall cease waiting on the s. 25
thing to bring you to the s. 16:9
joined to thee for all the s. 18:4
given as a gift to do the s. 6
tenth in Israel for their s. 21, 31
that we might do the s. Josh 22:27
thou the grievous s. lighter. 1 Ki 12:4
David set over the s. 1 Chr 6:31
very able men for the work of the s.
9:13; 26:8
distributed them in their s. 24:3
for all the work of the s. 28:13
be with thee for all the s. 21
to consecrate his s. to the Lord.? 29:5
and gave for the s. of house. 7
of the priests to their s. 2 Chr 8:14
they may know my s. and s. 12:8
money to such as did the s. 24:12
so the s. of the house was set. 29:35
every man according to his s. 31:2
work that he began in the s. 21
encouraged them to the s. of. 35:2
so the s. of the Lord was. 10, 16
in their courses, for the s. of God.
Ezra 6:18; 7:19
part of a shekel for s. Neh 10:32
to grow for the s. Ps 104:14
useth neighbour's s. without wages.
Jer 22:13
army to serve a great s. Ezek 29:18
charge of house for all the s. 44:14
who killeth you will think he doeth s. unto God. John 16:2
pertaineth the s. of God. Rom 9:4
which is your reasonable s. 12:1
that my s. may be accepted. 15:31*
administration of this s. 2 Cor 9:12
wages of them to do you s. 11:8*
did s. to them who by nature. Gal 4:8
with good will doing s. Eph 6:7
if I be offered upon the s. Phil 2:17
supply your lack of s. toward. 30
rather do s. because they. 1 Tim 6:2
had ordinances of divine s. Heb 9:1
the priests accomplishing the s. 6
make him that did the s. perfect. 9
works, and charity, and s. Rev 2:19*

bond-**service**
Solomon did levy a tribute of bond-s.
1 Ki 9:21

eye **service**
eye s. as men pleasers. Eph 6:6

servile
ye shall do no s. work. Lev 23:7
8, 21, 25, 35, 36; Num 28:18, 25
26; 29:1, 12, 35

serving
let Israel go from s. us. Ex 14:5
hired servant in s. thee. Deut 15:18
cumbered about much s. Luke 10:40
s. the Lord with all humility.
Acts 20:19
tribes instantly s. God day. 26:7
fervent in spirit, s. Lord. Rom 12:11
foolish, s. divers lusts. Tit 3:3

servitor
s. said, Should I set this? 2 Ki 4:43*

servitude
ease somewhat grievous s. of thy.
2 Chr 10:4*
gone because of great s. Lam 1:3

set
s. the stars in firmament. Gen 1:17
Lord s. a mark upon Cain. 4:15*
door of the ark shalt s. in the. 6:16
I do s. my bow in the cloud. 9:13
Abraham s. calf before them. 18:8
the angel s. Lot without the. 19:16
s. it before my brethren and. 31:37
Pharaoh s. him over the land. 41:33
I have s. thee over all the land. 41
if I bring him not, and s. him. 43:9
Jacob s. Ephraim before. 48:20
nor did he s. his heart. Ex 7:23*
s. apart to Lord all that open. 13:12
thou shalt s. bounds. 19:12, 23
which thou shalt s. before. 21:1
I will s. thy bounds from the. 23:31
thou shalt s. on table shew. 25:30
s. the table without. 26:35
s. in order things that are to be s. in.
40:4
thou shalt s. the altar of gold. 5
s. altar of burnt offering. 6
s. the laver between. 7
he s. the staves on the ark. 20
s. the bread in order. 23
sabbath he shall s. it in. Lev 24:8
I will s. my tabernacle among. 26:11
Judah, these shall first s. forth.
Num 2:9
as the camp is to s. forward. 4:15
the priest shall s. her before. 5:16
thou shalt s. the Levites. 8:13
s. forward bearing the. 10:17
Lord said, S. the fiery serpent. 21:8
let the Lord s. a man over. 27:16*
I have s. the land before you.
Deut 1:8, 21
as all this law which I s. 4:8, 44
Lord did not s. his love on. 7:7
I s. before you a blessing. 11:26
judgements which I s. before. 32
choose to s. his name there. 14:24
Neh 1:9
shalt say, I will s. a king. Deut 17:14
in any wise shalt s. him the. 15
which they of old time have s. 19:14
s. down the basket. 26:4, 10*
the Lord thy God will s. thee. 28:1
would not s. sole of her foot. 56
I have s. before you life. 30:15, 19
he s. bounds of the people by. 32:8
s. your hearts unto all the. 46
he s. them a statute in. Josh 24:25
till I bring and s. my. Judg 6:18
that lappeth, him shalt thou s. 7:5
but newly s. the watch. 19
Lord s. every man's sword. 22
out of the dust, to s. them among princes; he hath s. 1 Sam 2:8
the Philistines s. the ark of. 5:2
as for thine asses, s. not thy. 9:20
ye have said, Nay, but s. a. 10:19
the Lord hath s. a king over. 12:13
Israel s. the battle in array. 17:2, 8
2 Sam 10:17; 1 Ki 20:12
1 Chr 19:17

they s. the ark of God. *2 Sam* 6:3
s. Uriah in forefront of the. 11:15
yet didst thou s. thy servant. 19:28
that all Israel s. their. *1 Ki* 2:15
son, whom I will s. on throne. 5:5
he s. the one in Beth-el, the. 12:29
and s. Naboth on high among. 21:9
thou shalt s. aside that. *2 Ki* 4:4
let us s. for him there a bed. 10
s. on the great pot, and seethe. 38
what, should I s. this before an? 43
s. bread and water before. 6:22
s. thine house in order. 20:1
Isa 38:1
they s. the ark in midst. *1 Chr* 16:1
s. your heart to seek. 22:19
because I s. my affection to. 29:3
s. their hearts to seek. *2 Chr* 11:16
he feared, and s. himself to. 20:3
they s. the house of God. 24:13
Josiah s. the priests in their. 35:2
they s. the priests in. *Ezra* 6:18
pleased the king, and I s. *Neh* 2:6
we s. a watch against them. 4:9
increase to kings s. over us. 9:37
I gathered and s. them. 13:11
the terrors of God s. *Job* 6:4
thou shouldest s. thine heart. 7:17
why hast thou s. me as a mark? 20
shall s. me a time to plead? 9:19
and he hath s. darkness in. 19:8
have disdained to s. with. 30:1
they s. forward my calamity. 13
s. thy words in order before. 33:5
if he s. his heart upon man. 34:14
and s. others in their stead. 24
canst thou s. dominion? 38:33
the kings of the earth s. *Ps* 2:2
yet have I s. my king on my holy. 6
I will not be afraid if 10,000 s. 3:6
the Lord hath s. apart him that. 4:3
who hast s. thy glory above. 8:1
I will s. him in safety from. 12:5
I have s. the Lord always. 16:8
in them hath he s. a tabernacle. 19:4
thou hast s. my feet in a large room. 31:8
brought me up, and s. my feet. 40:2
I will s. them in order. 50:21
they have not s. God before. 54:3
if riches, s. not your heart. 62:10
surely thou didst s. them in. 73:18
thou hast s. all the borders of. 74:17
that they might s. their hope. 78:7
a generation that s. not their. 8
and shall s. us in the way. 85:13
violent men have not s. thee. 86:14
thou hast s. our iniquities. 90:8
s. his love upon me, therefore will I deliver him and s. 91:14
I will s. no wicked thing. 101:3
thou hast s. a bound that they. 104:9
s. thou a wicked man over. 109:6
that he may s. him with. 113:8
Lord answered, and s. me in. 118:5
fruit of thy body will I s. 132:11
proud have s. gins for me. 140:5
s. a watch, O Lord, before. 141:3
ye have s. at nought all. *Pr* 1:25
landmark which thy fathers have s. 22:28
wilt thou s. thine eyes on? 23:5
also he hath s. the world. *Eccl* 3:11
God hath s. the one against. 7:14
he sought out, and s. in order. 12:9
s. me as a seal upon thine heart. *S of S* 8:6
let us s. a king in midst of it. *Isa* 7:6
the Lord will s. them in their. 14:1
s. it with strange slips. 17:10
I will s. Egyptians against. 19:2
go s. a watchman, let him. 21:6
shall s. themselves in array. 22:7
who would s. briers and? 27:4
I will s. in the desert the fir. 41:19
till he have s. judgement. 42:4
who as I, shall s. it in order? 44:7
they carry him, and s. him. 46:7
mountain hast thou s. thy bed. 57:7
I have s. watchmen on thy walls. 62:6; *Jer* 6:17
I will s. a sign among. *Isa* 66:19
see, I have s. thee over. *Jer* 1:10
lay wait, they s. a trap. 5:26
I have s. thee for a tower. *Jer* 6:27
the place where I s. my. 7:12*
they s. their abominations in. 30
law which I s. before them. 9:13
I s. before you the way of life. 21:8
for I will s. mine eyes on. 24:6
to walk in my law, which I s. 26:4
his servant, whom he had s. 34:16
I s. pots of wine before sons. 35:5
my friends have s. thee on. 38:22
statutes which I s. before. 44:10
hath s. me in dark places. *Lam* 3:6
he hath s. me as a mark for. 12
I have s. it in the midst. *Ezek* 5:5
I s. it far from thee. 7:20
s. a mark on the foreheads. 9:4
for I have s. thee for a sign. 12:6
thou hast s. my oil before. 16:18, 19
off highest branch, I will s. it. 17:22
then nations s. against him on. 19:8
in thee have they s. light. 22:7
king of Babylon s. himself. 24:2
s. on a pot, s. it on, and also. 3
her blood, she s. it upon the. 7, 8
whereon they s. their minds. 25
I shall s. glory in the land. 26:20
they of Persia s. forth thy. 27:10
though thou s. thy heart. 28:2
cherub, and I have s. thee so. 14
they s. her a bed in the midst. 32:25
I will s. my sanctuary in. 37:26
I will s. my glory among. 39:21
s. thy heart upon all that I. 40:4
have s. keepers of my charge. 44:8
king thought to s. him. *Dan* 6:3
he s. his heart on Daniel to. 14
to walk in his laws which he s. 9:10
thou didst s. thine heart to. 10:12
lest I s. her as in the day. *Hos* 2:3
s. their heart on their iniquity. 4:8
Judah, he hath s. an harvest. 6:11
how shall I s. thee as Zeboim? 11:8
we may s. forth wheat. *Amos* 8:5
I will s. mine eyes upon them. 9:4
though thou s. thy nest. *Ob* 4
that he may s. his nest. *Hab* 2:9
I said, Let them s. a fair. *Zech* 3:5
it shall be s. there upon her. 5:11
make crowns, and s. them. 6:11
I s. all men, every one against. 8:10
I am come to s. a man. *Mat* 10:35
he shall s. the sheep on his. 25:33
and s. an hedge about it. *Mark* 12:1
to s. at liberty them. *Luke* 4:18
and s. him on his own beast. 10:34
I have nothing to s. before. 11:6
Herod with men of war s. 23:11
every man doth s. forth. *John* 2:10
he hath s. to his seal, that. 3:33
no, not so much as to s. *Acts* 7:5
then Paul s. his eyes on him. 13:9
I have s. thee to be a light to. 47
no man shall s. on thee to. 18:10
whom God s. forth to be. *Rom* 3:25
why dost thou s. at nought? 14:10
God hath s. forth us. *1 Cor* 4:9
s. them to judge who are least. 6:4
now God hath s. the members. 12:18
God hath s. some in the church. 28
when he s. him at his own. *Eph* 1:20
s. your affection on things. *Col* 3:2
thou didst s. him over work. *Heb* 2:7
I have s. before thee an open door. *Rev* 3:8
shut him up, and s. a seal. 20:3*

set up

stone and s. it *up* for a pillar, and. *Gen* 28:18, 22; 31:45; 35:14
shalt s. *up* the tabernacle. *Ex* 40:2
thou shalt s. *up* the court. 8, 18, 21
he s. *up* hanging at door of tabernacle. 28*, 33
nor shall ye s. *up* any. *Lev* 26:1*
when the tabernacle is pitched, the Levites shall s. it *up*. *Num* 1:51
that Moses had fully s. *up* the. 7:1
and other did s. it *up* against. 10:21
s. *up* these stones. *Deut* 27:2, 4
Joshua s. *up* twelve stones. *Josh* 4:9
shall he s. *up* gates of it. 6:26
1 Ki 16:34
children of Dan s. *up*. *Judg* 18:30
they s. them *up* Micah's graven. 31
it repenteth me I have s. *up* Saul. *1 Sam* 15:11
behold, Saul hath s. him *up* a. 12
to s. *up* throne of David. *2 Sam* 3:10
I will s. *up* thy seed after thee. 7:12
to s. *up* his son after. *1 Ki* 15:4
they s. them *up* images. *2 Ki* 17:10
s. them *up* an altar in. *1 Chr* 21:18*
Amaziah s. them *up* to. *2 Chr* 25:14
Manasseh s. *up* groves and. 33:19
offered freely to s. *up*. *Ezra* 2:68
Jews have s. *up* the walls thereof. 4:12, 13, 16
a great king of Israel, s. *up*. 5:11*
being s. *up*, let him be hanged. 6:11
to give us a reviving, to s. *up*. 9:9
they sanctified it, and s. *up*. *Neh* 3:1, 3, 6, 13, 14, 15; 7:1
time I had not s. *up* the doors. 6:1
to s. *up* on high those. *Job* 5:11
hath shaken me, and s. me *up*. 16:12
name of God we will s. *up*. *Ps* 20:5
he shall hide me, and s. me *up*. 27:5
O God, s. me *up* on high. 69:29
s. *up* their ensigns for signs. 74:4
thou hast s. *up* right hand of. 89:42*
I was s. *up* from everlasting, from. *Pr* 8:23
Lord shall s. *up* the. *Isa* 9:11
he shall s. *up* an ensign for. 11:12
they s. *up* towers thereof. 23:13
that s. *up* wood of their. 45:20*
I will s. *up* my standard. 49:22
s. *up* thy remembrance. 57:8
s. *up* the standard toward. *Jer* 4:6
none to s. *up* my curtains. 10:20
have ye s. *up* altars to that. 11:13
and I will s. *up* shepherds. 23:4
s. thee *up* way marks, make. 31:21
s. *up* a standard, publish. 50:2
51:12, 27
s. *up* the watchmen, prepare. 51:12
he hath s. *up* horn of thy. *Lam* 2:17*
these men have s. *up*. *Ezek* 14:3*
the deep s. him *up* on high. 31:4
I will s. *up* one shepherd. 34:23
God of heaven shall s. *up*. *Dan* 2:44
golden image I have s. *up*. 3:14
whom he would he s. *up* and. 5:19
that maketh desolate s. *up*. 12:11
they have s. *up* kings. *Hos* 8:4
work wickedness are s. *up*. *Mal* 3:15
and s. *up* over his head. *Mat* 27:37
and s. *up* false witnesses. *Acts* 6:13
again the ruins, and s. it *up*. 15:16

set, *passive*

there was s. meat before. *Gen* 24:33
because the sun was s. 28:11
a ladder was s. upon earth. 12
stones s. in ephod. *Ex* 25:7; 28:11
35:9, 27
two tenons s. in order. 26:17
they are s. on mischief. 32:22
the rings to be s. 37:3
the lamps s. in order. 39:37
name was much s. by. *1 Sam* 18:30
as thy life was much s. by. 26:24
crown was s. on David's head. *2 Sam* 12:30; *1 Chr* 20:2
a seat to be s. for the. *1 Ki* 2:19
could not see, for his eyes were s. 14:4
that every man is s. at. *2 Ki* 12:4*
appointed in their s. *1 Chr* 9:22
Joab saw that battle was s. 19:10
onyx stones and stones to be s. 29:2
I am s. on the throne. *2 Chr* 6:10
house of Lord was s. in. 29:35
in their s. office to give. 31:15
in their s. office they sanctified. 18
and what should be s. on. *Job* 36:16
eyes are privily s. against. *Ps* 10:8
s. thrones of judgement. 122:5
let my prayer be s. forth. 141:2
heart is fully s. in them. *Eccl* 8:11
folly s. in great dignity; rich. 10:6
are as the eyes of doves fitly s. *S of S* 5:12
his hands are as gold rings s. 14
s. upon sockets of fine gold. 15
thy belly as a heap of wheat s. 7:2
and instead of well s. hair. *Isa* 3:24
s. in my ward whole nights. 21:8

s. in array, as men for war. Jer 6:23; Joel 2:5
children's teeth are s. on edge. Jer 31:29; Ezek 18:2
teeth shall be s. on edge. Jer 31:30
her that was s. apart. Ezek 22:10
judgement was s., books. Dan 7:10
thy land shall be s. open. Nah 3:13
a city s. on a hill cannot. Mat 5:14
he was s. on judgement seat. 27:19
sun did s., they brought. Mark 1:32
a candle, and not to be s. on a. 4:21
things, and be s. at nought. 9:12
this child is s. for the. Luke 2:34
for I also am a man s. under. 7:8
eat such things as are s. 10:8
were s. six water pots. John 2:6
stone s. at nought of. Acts 4:11
in danger to be s. at nought. 19:27
this man might have been s. 26:32
whatsoever is s. before. 1 Cor 10:27
Christ had been evidently s. Gal 3:1
I am s. for the defence. Phil 1:17
to lay hold on the hope s. Heb 6:18
who is s. on the right hand of the throne. 8:1; 12:2
let us run the race that is s. 12:1
joy that was s. before him. 2
Timothy is s. at liberty. 13:23
cities are s. forth for an. Jude 7
s. down with my Father. Rev 3:21
a throne was s. in heaven, one. 4:2
see **face, faces, feasts**

set *day*
on a s. *day* Herod. Acts 12:21

set *time*
shall bear to thee at this s. *time*. Gen 17:21
at the s. *time* of which God. 21:2
appointed a s. *time*, saying. Ex 9:5
according to the s. *time* Samuel. 1 Sam 13:8
longer than the s. *time*. 2 Sam 20:5
appoint me a s. *time*. Job 14:13
s. *time* to favour her. Ps 102:13

Seth
after his image, and called him S. Gen 5:3
S. begat Enos. 6; 1 Chr 1:1
Luke 3:38

setter
s. forth of strange gods. Acts 17:18

settest
in all thou s. thy hand to. Deut 23:20*; 28:8*, 20*
am I a sea, that thou s. a watch? Job 7:12
thou s. a print upon the heels. 13:27†
thou s. a crown of gold. Ps 21:3
thou s. me before thy face. 41:12

setteth
when the tabernacle s. Num 1:51
when camp s. forward, Aaron. 4:5
poor, and s. his heart. Deut 24:15
cursed be he that s. light. 27:16
s. me on high places. 2 Sam 22:34
Ps 18:33
he s. an end to darkness. Job 28:3
he s. himself in a way. Ps 36:4
which by his strength s. fast. 65:6
God s. the solitary in families. 68:6
he putteth down one, and s. 75:7*
as a flame s. the mountains. 83:14
yet s. poor on high from. 107:41
wait as he that s. snares. Jer 5:26
Baruch s. thee on against us. 43:3
that s. up his idol in his heart. Ezek 14:4*, 7*
removeth kings and s. Dan 2:21
s. up over it the basest of men. 4:17
and s. him on a pinnacle. Mat 4:5
s. it on a candlestick. Luke 8:16*
tongue s. on fire the course. Jas 3:6

setting
in their s of their threshold by. Ezek 43:8
stone, and s. a watch. Mat 27:66*
when sun was s. they. Luke 4:40

settings
set in it s. of stones. Ex 28:17

settle
(*American Revision*, ledge)
ground even to lower s. Ezek 43:14
s. shall be fourteen cubits long. 17
blood on the four corners of the s. 20; 45:19

settle, *verb*
I will s. him in mine. 1 Chr 17:14
I will s. you after your. Ezek 36:11*
s. it in your hearts, not. Luke 21:14
God stablish, strengthen, s. you. 1 Pet 5:10

settled
built a s. place for thee. 1 Ki 8:13
he s. his countenance. 2 Ki 8:11
Lord, thy word is s. in. Ps 119:89
before mountains were s. Pr 8:25
he hath s. on his lees. Jer 48:11
punish men that are s. Zeph 1:12
in faith grounded and s. Col 1:23

settlest
thou s. the furrows thereof. Ps 65:10

seven
(A sacred number among the Jews, also indicating perfection or completion. It was used very often in a symbolic manner for the whole of a thing.
The number seven entered very largely into the religious life and observances of the Jews)
up s. well favoured kine. Gen 41:2
s. other kine came up. 3, 4, 18, 19, 20, 27
s. ears of corn, came up, rank. 5
s. thin ears, and blasted. 6, 7, 23, 24, 27
Bilhah, all the souls were s. 46:25
the priest of Midian had s. Ex 2:16
s. sabbaths shall be. Lev 23:15
number s. sabbaths of years. 25:8
build me here s. altars, and prepare s. oxen and s. Num 23:1, 29
I have prepared s. altars. 4, 14
s. nations greater and. Deut 7:1
s. weeks thou shalt number. 16:9
to flee before thee s. ways. 28:7
shalt flee s. ways before them. 25
s. priests bearing s. trumpets. Josh 6:4, 6, 8, 13
of Israel s. tribes not received. 18:2
shall divide it into s. parts. 5
by cities into s. parts in a book. 9
if they bind me with s. Judg 16:7
if thou weavest s. locks. 13
shave off s. locks. 19
barren hath borne s. 1 Sam 2:5
with the Philistines s. months. 6:1
Jesse made s. of his sons to. 16:10
they fell all s. together. 2 Sam 21:9
sons of Elioenai were s. 1 Chr 3:24
house of their fathers were s. 5:13
s. bullocks, s. rams. 2 Chr 29:21
sent of king and of his s. Ezra 7:14
s. chamberlains that. Esth 1:10
the s. princes which saw the. 14
he gave her s. maidens meet. 2:9
in s. troubles no evil shall. Job 5:19
yea, s. are an abomination. Pr 6:16
wisdom hath hewn out her s. 9:1
for there are s. abominations. 26:25
give a portion to s. also. Eccl 11:2
in that day s. women take. Isa 4:1
smite it in the s. streams. 11:15
hath borne s. languisheth. Jer 15:9
s. months shall they be. Ezek 39:12
after the end of s. months shall. 14
up unto it by s. steps. 40:22, 26
breadth of the door s. cubits. 41:3
Messiah, shall be s. weeks. Dan 9:25
we shall raise against him s. Mi 5:5
one stone shall be s. eyes. Zech 3:9
his s. lamps thereon, and s. pipes to s. lamps. 4:2
of Zerubbabel with those s. 10
they said, S. loaves. Mat 15:34, 36
Mark 8:5
they took up s. baskets full. Mat 15:37; Mark 8:8
nor the s. loaves. Mat 16:10
s. brethren, and the first deceased. 22:25; Mark 12:20; Luke 20:29
in the resurrection whose wife shall she be of the s.? Mat 22:28
and s. had her. Mark 12:22, 23
Luke 20:31, 33
out of whom he cast s. devils. Mark 16:9; Luke 8:2
when he destroyed s. Acts 13:19
who was one of the s. deacons. 21:8
s. churches in Asia. Rev 1:4
send it to the s. churches in Asia. 11
I saw s. golden candlesticks. 12
in midst of s. candlesticks one. 13
s. stars are angels of the churches. the s. candlesticks . . . are the s. 20
who walketh in midst of the s. 2:1
Lamb as slain, having s. horns, and s. eyes, which are the s. 5:6
I saw the s. angels which. 8:2
s. angels prepared themselves. 6
when he cried, s. thunders. 10:3
seal up what the s. thunders. 4
having s. heads, and s. crowns. 12:3; 13:1; 17:3, 7
I saw s. angels having the s. 15:1, 6
gave to s. angels s. golden vials. 7
to enter into the temple, till the s. plagues of the s. angels were. 8
voice, saying to the s. angels. 16:1
one of the s. angels which had the s. vials, and talked. 17:1; 21:9
the s. heads are s. mountains. 17:9
there are s. kings, five are fallen. 10
the beast is of s. and. Rev 17:11
see **days, hundred, lambs, lamps, seals, thousand**

seven *bullocks*
here s. *bullocks*, s. rams. Num 23:29
on the seventh day s. *bullocks*. 29:32
offered s. *bullocks*, s. rams. 1 Chr 15:26
brought s. *bullocks*, s. rams. 2 Chr 29:21
now, s. *bullocks*, s. rams. Job 42:8
prepare a burnt offering, s. *bullocks*. Ezek 45:23

seven *men*
let s. *men* of his sons. 2 Sam 21:6
s. *men* that can render. Pr 26:16
took s. *men* that were near the. Jer 52:25
look out s. *men* of honest report. Acts 6:3

seven *rams*, see **seven** *bullocks*

seven *sons*
daughter is better than s. *sons*. Ruth 4:15
were born unto him s. *sons*. Job 1:2
he had also s. *sons*, and. 42:13
there were s. *sons* of one Sceva. Acts 19:14

seven *spirits*
taketh with himself s. other *spirits*. Mat 12:45; Luke 11:26
from s. *spirits* before the. Rev 1:4
hath the s. *spirits* of God. 3:1
lamps, which are the s. *spirits*. 4:5
eyes, which are the s. *spirits*. 5:6

seven *stars*
that maketh the s. *stars*. Amos 5:8*
had in his right hand s. *stars*. Rev 1:16; 2:1; 3:1
mystery of s. *stars* . . . s. *stars* are the angels of the s. churches. 1:20

seven and *thirty*, *see* **thirty**

seven *times*
Jacob bowed before Esau s. *times*. Gen 33:3
priest shall sprinkle of the blood s. *times*. Lev 4:6, 17; 8:11; 14:7, 16:14, 19; Num 19:4
oil with his fingers s. *times*. Lev 14:16, 27
sprinkle the house s. *times*. 51
number s. *times* seven years. 25:8
punish you s. *times* more. 26:18, 21, 24, 28
compass city s. *times*. Josh 6:4, 15
and he said, Go again s. *times*. 1 Ki 18:43
child sneezed s. *times*. 2 Ki 4:35
wash in Jordan s. *times*. 5:10, 14

silver purified *s. times.* Ps 12:6
s. times a day do I praise. 119:164
falleth *s. times,* and riseth. *Pr* 24:16
heat the furnace one *s. times* more. *Dan* 3:19
let *s. times* pass over him. 4:16
23, 25, 32
shall I forgive ? till *s. times.* *Mat* 18:21
I say not, till *s. times,* but until seventy *times s.* 22
trespass against thee *s. times* a day, and *s. times* a day. *Luke* 17:4

seven *and twenty, see* **twenty**

seven *years*

I will serve thee *s. years.* *Gen* 29:18
served *s. years.* 20
serve *s.* other *years.* 27, 30
good kine are *s. years,* and the seven good ears are *s. years.* 41:26
kine are *s. years,* seven empty ears shall be *s. years* of famine. 27
come *s. years* of plenty. 29, 34, 47, 48
arise *s. years* of famine. 30, 36, 54
the *s. years* of plenteousness. 53
seven times *s. years.* *Lev* 25:8
was built *s. years* before Zoan. *Num* 13:22
end of every *s. years* a release. *Deut* 15:1; 31:10
Israel to Midian *s. years.* *Judg* 6:1
second bullock of *s. years* old. 25
Ibzan of Bethlehem judged Israel *s. years.* 12:9
David was king in Hebron *s. years.* *2 Sam* 2:11; 5:5; *1 Ki* 2:11
1 Chr 29:27
shall *s. years* of famine come ? *2 Sam* 24:13
Solomon was *s. years* in building. *1 Ki* 6:38
famine shall come upon land *s. years.* *2 Ki* 8:1
with the Philistines *s. years.* 2
s. years old was Jehoash when he. 11:21; *2 Chr* 24:1
at end of *s. years* let ye. *Jer* 34:14
burn weapons with fire *s. years.* *Ezek* 39:9
an husband *s. years.* *Luke* 2:36

sevenfold

shall be taken on him *s.* *Gen* 4:15
avenged *s.* Lamech 70 and *s.* 24
render *s.* into their bosom. *Ps* 79:12
found he shall restore *s.* *Pr* 6:31
of the sun shall be *s.* *Isa* 30:26

sevens

beast shalt thou take by *s.* *Gen* 7:2
air by *s.* the male and female. 3

seventeen

Joseph being *s.* years old. *Gen* 37:2
in the land of Egypt *s.* years. 47:28
reigned *s.* years in Jerusalem. *1 Ki* 14:21
son of Jehu reigned *s.* years. *2 Ki* 13:1
bought field, weighed *s.* *Jer* 32:9

seventeenth

on *s.* day the fountains. *Gen* 7:11
ark rested on the *s.* day in. 8:4
to reign the *s.* year. *1 Ki* 22:51
in *s.* year of Pekah son. *2 Ki* 16:1
the *s.* lot came to Hezir. *1 Chr* 24:15
s. lot came to Joshbekashah. 25:24

seventh

in *s.* he shall go out free. *Ex* 21:2
but in the *s.* is the sabbath. 31:15
after the *s.* sabbath. *Lev* 23:16
at the *s.* time when the. *Josh* 6:16
s. lot came out for the tribe. 19:40
at the *s.* time there arose a cloud. *1 Ki* 18:44
David was the *s.* son. *1 Chr* 2:15
s. lot came forth to Hakkoz. 24:10
Elioenai the *s.* son of. 26:3
Issachar was the *s.* son of. 5
s. captain for the *s.* month. 27:10
and the third, to the *s.* *Mat* 22:26
yesterday at *s.* hour the. *John* 4:52
Enoch the *s.* from Adam. *Jude* 14
he had opened the *s.* seal. *Rev* 8:1
of the voice of the *s.* angel. 10:7
the *s.* angel sounded, there. *Rev* 11:15
s. angel poured out his vial. 16:17
the *s.* foundation was a. 21:20

see **day**

seventh *month*

ark rested in *s. month* on. *Gen* 8:4
in *s. month* afflict your souls. *Lev* 16:29; 23:27; 25:9
in the *s. month* shall ye. 23:24
in *s. month* an holy. *Num* 29:1, 12
at feast of the *s. month.* *1 Ki* 8:2
in the *s. month* Ishmael smote Gedaliah. *2 Ki* 25:25; *Jer* 41:1
in *s. month* Solomon. *2 Chr* 7:10
the heaps in the *s. month.* 31:7
when *s. month* was come, and the. *Ezra* 3:1; *Neh* 7:73
the first day of *s. month.* *Ezra* 3:6
the *s. month* Ezra read. *Neh* 8:2
in feasts of *s. month* Israel. 14
died in the *s. month.* *Jer* 28:17
in the *s. month* shall he. *Ezek* 45:25
in the *s. month* the word. *Hag* 2:1
in fifth and *s. month.* *Zech* 7:5
the fast of the *s. month* shall. 8:19

seventh *year*

the *s. year* thou shalt let. *Ex* 23:11
in the *s. year* shall be a. *Lev* 25:4
shall we eat in the *s. year* ? 20
saying, The *s. year,* year of release. *Deut* 15:9
in the *s. year* thou shalt let. 12
in the *s. year* Jehoiada sent and. *2 Ki* 11:4; *2 Chr* 23:1
in *s. year* of Jehu. *2 Ki* 12:1
in *s. year* of Hoshea king of. 18:9
went up unto Jerusalem in the *s. year* of the king. *Ezra* 7:7, 8
leave *s. year,* and exaction. *Neh* 10:31
taken to king in *s. year.* *Esth* 2:16
away captive in *s. year.* *Jer* 52:28
the *s. year* elders came to enquire. *Ezek* 20:1

seventy

truly Lamech *s.* and sevenfold. *Gen* 4:24
and Cainan lived *s.* years. 5:12
Terah lived *s.* years and. 11:26
Abram was *s.*-five years old. 12:4
of Jacob were *s.* souls. *Ex* 1:5
and *s.* elders of Israel. 24:1, 9
the offering was *s.* talents. 38:29
was one silver bowl of *s.* shekels. *Num* 7:13, 19, 25, 31, 37, 43, 49
55, 61, 67, 73, 79
each bowl weighing *s.* shekels. 85
gather unto me *s.* men of. 11:16, 24
of the spirit unto the *s.* elders. 25
slaying his *s.* brethren. *Judg* 9:56
had *s.* sons in Samaria. *2 Ki* 10:1, 6
took king's sons, and slew *s.* 7
children of Hodaviah *s.*-four. *Ezra* 2:40; *Neh* 7:43
with Jeshaiah *s.* males. *Ezra* 8:7
Zabbud, with them *s.* males. 14
Tyre shall be forgotten *s.* years. *Isa* 23:15
after end of *s.* years, the Lord. 17
king of Babylon *s.* years. *Jer* 25:11
when *s.* years are accomplished. 12
29:10
there stood before them *s.* men. *Ezek* 8:11
accomplish *s.* years in. *Dan* 9:2
s. weeks are determined upon. 24
even those *s.* years, did. *Zech* 7:5
till seven times, but until *s.* times. *Mat* 18:22
Lord appointed other *s.* *Luke* 10:1
the *s.* returned again with joy. 17

sever

will *s.* in that day the land. *Ex* 8:22
Lord shall *s.* between cattle. 9:4
shall *s.* out men of continual employment. *Ezek* 39:14
and *s.* the wicked from. *Mat* 13:49

several

and a *s.* tenth deal of flour mingled. *Num* 28:13, 21, 29; 29:10, 15
Azariah ... his death, and dwelt in a *s.* house. *2 Ki* 15:5†; *2 Chr* 26:21†
in every *s.* city put. *2 Chr* 11:12
in every *s.* city of Judah. *2 Chr* 28:25
sons of Aaron in every *s.* city. 31:19
according to his *s.* ability. *Mat* 25:15
every *s.* gate was one of. *Rev* 21:21

severally

dividing to every man *s.* *1 Cor* 12:11

severed

I have *s.* you from other people. *Lev* 20:26*
Moses *s.* three cities. *Deut* 4:41*
Heber had *s.* himself. *Judg* 4:11

severity

the goodness and *s.* of God: on them which fell, *s.*; but. *Rom* 11:22

sew

time to rend and a time to *s.* *Eccl* 3:7
woe to the women that *s.* pillows to all armholes. *Ezek* 13:18

sewed

they *s.* fig leaves together. *Gen* 3:7
I have *s.* sackcloth upon. *Job* 16:15

sewest

in a bag, and thou *s.* up mine iniquity. *Job* 14:17*

seweth

no man *s.* a piece of new cloth on. *Mark* 2:21

shade

the Lord is thy *s.* upon. *Ps* 121:5

shadow

(*This word has often the rare meaning of a shelter. It also means at times, as in* Col 2:17, *a representation, a sample which gives an idea of what the real thing is to be. In many cases the American Revision changes to* shade)

they came under the *s.* of my roof. *Gen* 19:8
put your trust in my *s.* *Judg* 9:15
seest the *s.* of the mountains. 36
s. go forward ten degrees ? *2 Ki* 20:9
it is a light thing for the *s.* to go. 10
s. ten degrees backward. 11
our days on earth are as a *s.* *1 Chr* 29:15; *Job* 8:9
earnestly desireth the *s.* *Job* 7:2
he fleeth also as a *s.* and. 14:2
all my members are as a *s.* 17:7
trees cover him with their *s.* 40:22
hide me under the *s.* *Ps* 17:8
their trust under the *s.* 36:7; 57:1
in the *s.* of thy wings will. 63:7
covered with the *s.* of it. 80:10
shall abide under the *s.* of the. 91:1
my days are like a *s.* that. 102:11
I am gone like a *s.* when. 109:23
man is like to vanity: his days are as a *s.* 144:4; *Eccl* 8:13
he spendeth as a *s.* *Eccl* 6:12
I sat under his *s.* with. *S of S* 2:3
a tabernacle for a *s.* in daytime. *Isa* 4:6
make thy *s.* as the night in. 16:3
thou hast been a *s.* from the. 25:4
down the heat with *s.* of a cloud. 5
trust in the *s.* of Egypt. 30:2
and the trust in the *s.* of Egypt. 3
as the *s.* of a great rock in. 32:2
and gather under her *s.* 34:15
I will bring again the *s.* of the. 38:8
in *s.* of his hand hath he hid me. 49:2; 51:16
they stood under the *s.* *Jer* 48:45
under his *s.* we shall live. *Lam* 4:20
in the *s.* thereof shall. *Ezek* 17:23
and under his *s.* dwelt all. 31:6
are gone down from his *s.* 12
that dwelt under his *s.* in midst. 17
field had *s.* under it. *Dan* 4:12
under elms, because *s.* *Hos* 4:13
they that dwell under his *s.* 14:7
and sat under it in the *s.* *Jonah* 4:5
might be *s.* over his head. 6
lodge under the *s.* of it. *Mark* 4:32
that *s.* of Peter might. *Acts* 5:15
which are a *s.* of things. *Col* 2:17
who serve unto the *s.* of. *Heb* 8:5
the law having a *s.* of good. 10:1
with whom is no *s.* of. *Jas* 1:17

see **death**

shadowing
woe to the land *s.* with wings. *Isa* 18:1*
cedar with a *s.* shroud. *Ezek* 31:3
over cherubims of glory *s.* the. *Heb* 9:5*

shadows
until the day break, and the *s.* flee away. *S of S* 2:17; 4:6
for *s.* of the evening are. *Jer* 6:4

Shadrach, *see* **Abed-nego**

shady
he lieth under the *s.* trees.*Job* 40:21*
the *s.* trees cover him with. 22*

shaft
his *s.* and branches, his bowls and. *Ex* 25:31*; 31:17*; *Num* 8:4*
make me a polished *s.* *Isa* 49:2

shake
I will go out and *s.* myself.*Judg* 16:20
lap, and said, So God *s.* *Neh* 5:13
which made my bones to *s.* *Job* 4:14
he shall *s.* off his unripe grape. 15:33
could heap up words, and *s.* 16:4
out the lip, they *s.* head. *Ps* 22:7
though the mountains *s.* 46:3
their loins continually to *s.* 69:23
the fruit thereof shall *s.* like. 72:16
ariseth to *s.* the earth. *Isa* 2:19, 21
as if the rod should *s.* itself. 10:15†
he shall *s.* his hand against. 32
the Lord shall *s.* his hand. 11:15†
exalt the voice unto them, *s.* 13:2*
I will *s.* heavens. 13*; *Joel* 3:16 *Hag* 2:6, 21
foundations of the earth do *s.* *Isa* 24:18
Bashan and Carmel *s.* off. 33:9
s. thyself from the dust, O. 52:2
is broken, all my bones *s.* *Jer* 23:9
thy walls shall *s.* at noise of. *Ezek* 26:10
not the isles *s.* at the sound ? 15
the suburbs shall *s.* at the. 27:28
I made nations *s.* at the sound. 31:16
all men of the earth shall *s.* at. 38:20
s. off his leaves, and. *Dan* 4:14
lintel that the posts may *s.* *Amos* 9:1
I will *s.* all nations, desire. *Hag* 2:7
I will *s.* my hand on them. *Zech* 2:9
s. off the dust of your feet. *Mat* 10:14 *Mark* 6:11; *Luke* 9:5
fear of him the keepers did *s.* *Mat* 28:4*
house, and could not *s.* it. *Luke* 6:48
once more I *s.* not the earth only. *Heb* 12:26

shaked
they looked on me, they *s.* their. *Ps* 109:25

shaken
the sound of a *s.* leaf shall chase. *Lev* 26:36*
Israel as a reed is *s.* in water. *1 Ki* 14:15
the daughter of Jerusalem hath *s.* *2 Ki* 19:21; *Isa* 37:22
even thus be he *s.* out. *Neh* 5:13
taken me by my neck, *s.* *Job* 16:12*
that the wicked might be *s.* 38:13
of the hills were *s.* *Ps* 18:7
fir trees shall be terribly *s.* *Nah* 2:3
if *s.* they fall into the mouth. 3:12
a reed *s.* with the wind. *Mat* 11:7 *Luke* 7:24
and powers of heaven shall be *s.* *Mat* 24:29; *Mark* 13:25 *Luke* 21:26
good measure, pressed, *s.* together. *Luke* 6:38
prayed, the place was *s.* *Acts* 4:31
of the prison were *s.* 16:26
be not soon *s.* in mind. *2 Thes* 2:2
that are *s.*, that those things which cannot be *s.* may. *Heb* 12:27
as a fig tree when *s.* of. *Rev* 6:13

shaketh
which *s.* the earth out of. *Job* 9:6
the voice of the Lord *s.* *Ps* 29:8
breaches thereof, for it *s.* 60:2
magnify against him that *s.* it ? *Isa* 10:15†
the Lord which he *s.* over it. *Isa* 19:16
that *s.* hand from holding of. 33:15

shaking
laugheth at the *s.* of. *Job* 41:29*
the *s.* of the head among. *Ps* 44:14
as the *s.* of an olive tree. *Isa* 17:6 24:13
shall fear, because of the *s.* of. 19:16
battles of *s.* shall he fight. 30:32
s. and bones came. *Ezek* 37:7*
shall be a great *s.* in Israel. 38:19

Shalim
they passed through the land of *S.* *1 Sam* 9:4

Shalisha
through the land of *S.* *1 Sam* 9:4

Shallum
S. son of Jabesh killed. *2 Ki* 15:10
Menahem slew *S.* son of Jabesh. 14
to Huldah the prophetess, the wife of *S.* 22:14; *2 Chr* 34:22
of Judah, *S.* *1 Chr* 2:40
of Simeon, *S.* 4:25
of Levi, *S.* 6:12
S. the son of Naphtali. 7:13
S. a porter. 9:17, 19
S. the Korahite. 31
Jehizkiah the son of *S.* *2 Chr* 28:12
porters, the children of *S.* *Ezra* 2:42 10:24; *Neh* 7:45; *Jer* 35:4
S. the son of Zadok, the. *Ezra* 7:2
S. and Amariah had taken. 10:42
unto him repaired *S.* *Neh* 3:12, 15
thus saith the Lord touching *S.* son of. *Jer* 22:11
Hanameel the son of *S.* thine. 32:7

Shalmanezer
S. came up against Samaria. *2 Ki* 17:3; 18:9

shambles
sold in the *s.* that eat. *1 Cor* 10:25

shame
them naked unto their *s.* *Ex* 32:25
put them to *s.* in any. *Judg* 18:7
father had done him *s.* *1 Sam* 20:34
I cause my *s.* to go ? *2 Sam* 13:13
returned with *s.* of face. *2 Chr* 32:21
shall be clothed with *s.* *Job* 8:22
ye turn my glory into *s.*? *Ps* 4:2
put them to *s.* that seek after. 35:4*
let them be clothed with *s.* 26
let them be put to *s.* that wish me evil. 40:14*; 83:17
desolate for reward of their *s.* 40:15
to *s.* that hated us. 44:7; 53:5
hast cast off and put us to *s.* 44:9*
the *s.* of my face hath. 15; 69:7
known my reproach and *s.* 69:19
back for reward of their *s.* 70:3
let them be brought unto *s.* 71:24
fill their faces with *s.* O Lord. 83:16*
thou hast covered him with *s.* 89:45
mine adversaries be clothed with *s.* 109:29*
testimonies; O Lord, put me not to *s.* 119:31
enemies will I clothe with *s.* 132:18
but *s.* shall be the promotion of. *Pr* 3:35
a scorner, getteth *s.* 9:7†
is a son that causeth *s.* 10:5
pride cometh, then cometh *s.* 11:2
but a prudent man covereth *s.* 12:16
loathsome and cometh to *s.* 13:5
s. shall be to him that refuseth. 18
is against him that causeth *s.* 14:35
over a son that causeth *s.* 17:2
heareth, it is folly and *s.* to him.18:13
mother, is a son causeth *s.* 19:26
neighbour hath put thee to *s.* 25:8
heareth it put thee to *s.* 10
himself brings his mother to *s.* 29:15
uncovered, to *s.* of Egypt. *Isa* 20:4
chariots shall be the *s.* of. 22:18
Pharaoh shall be your *s.* 30:3, 5
be uncovered, yea, thy *s.* shall. 47:3
I hid not my face from *s.* 50:6
not be put to *s.* nor confounded, for thou shalt forget *s.* of. 54:4
for your *s.* ye shall have double. 61:7
s. devoured the labour. *Jer* 3:24*
we lie down in *s.* and our. 25
I will discover, that thy *s.* *Jer* 13:26
days may be consumed with *s.* 20:18
a perpetual *s.*, which shall. 23:40
nations have heard of thy *s.* 46:12
Moab turned back with *s.*! 48:39
s. hath covered our faces, for. 51:51*
s. shall be on all faces. *Ezek* 7:18
thine own *s.* for thy sins. 16:52, 54
thy mouth because of thy *s.* 63
have they borne their *s.* 32:24, 25
bear their *s.* with them that go. 30
nor bear the *s.* of the heathen. 34:29
because ye have borne the *s.* 36:6
they shall bear their *s.* 7; 44:13
nor cause to hear in thee the *s.* 36:15
they have borne their *s.* 39:26
shall awake, some to *s.* *Dan* 12:2
change their glory into *s.* *Hos* 4:7
her rulers with *s.* do love. 18
separated themselves unto that *s.* 9:10
Ephraim shall receive *s.* 10:6
for thy violence *s.* shall. *Ob* 10
pass ye away, having thy *s.* *Mi* 1:11
prophesy, they shall not take *s.* 2:6
s. shall cover her which said. 7:10
shew the kingdoms thy *s.* *Nah* 3:5
consulted *s.* to thy house. *Hab* 2:10
thou art filled with *s.* for glory. 16
the unjust knoweth no *s.* *Zeph* 3:5
where they have been put to *s.* 19
thou begin with *s.* to take. *Luke* 14:9
were counted worthy to suffer *s.* *Acts* 5:41*
these things to *s.* you. *1 Cor* 4:14
I speak to your *s.* 6:5; 15:34
a *s.* for a woman to be shorn. 11:6
if a man have long hair, it is a *s.* 14*
church of God, and *s.* them ? 22
it is a *s.* for a woman to speak. 14:35
a *s.* to speak of things. *Eph* 5:12
whose glory is in their *s.* *Phil* 3:19
and put him to an open *s.* *Heb* 6:6
the cross, despising the *s.* 12:2
foaming out their own *s.* *Jude* 13
that *s.* of thy nakedness. *Rev* 3:18
naked, and they see his *s.* 16:15

shamed
thou hast *s.* the faces. *2 Sam* 19:5
ye have *s.* the counsel. *Ps* 14:6

shamefacedness
adorn themselves with *s.* *1 Tim* 2:9*

shameful
up altars to that *s.* thing. *Jer* 11:13
and *s.* spewing be on thy glory. *Hab* 2:16*

shamefully
conceived them, hath done *s.* *Hos* 2:5
sent him away *s.* handled. *Mark* 12:4; *Luke* 20:11
and were *s.* entreated. *1 Thes* 2:2

shamelessly
vain fellows, *s.* uncovereth. *2 Sam* 6:20

shameth
of riotous men *s.* his father. *Pr* 28:7

Shamgar
after him was *S.* the son. *Judg* 3:31
the days of *S.* highways. 5:6

Shammah
the son of Reuel, *S.* *Gen* 36:13 17; *1 Chr* 1:37
S. the son of Jesse. *1 Sam* 16:9 17:13; *1 Chr* 2:13
after him was *S.* the Hararite. *2 Sam* 23:11, 33
S. the Harodite. 25
son of Zophah, *S.* *1 Chr* 7:37

Shammuah
to spy the land, *S.* son of Zacur. *Num* 13:4
S. the son of David. *2 Sam* 5:14 *1 Chr* 14:4
Abda son of *S.* dwelt at. *Neh* 11:17

shape
descended in bodily *s.* *Luke* 3:22*
his voice, nor seen his *s.* *John* 5:37*

shapen
I was *s.* in iniquity. *Ps* 51:5

shapes
s. of the locusts were like. *Rev* 9:7
Shaphan
Josiah sent *S.* the scribe to repair. *2 Ki* 22:3; *2 Chr* 34:8
Hilkiah gave the book to *S.* *2 Ki* 22:8; *2 Chr* 34:15
Ahikam the son of *S.* and *S.* the scribe. *2 Ki* 22:12
Ahikam the son of *S.* 25:22
Jer 39:14; 40:11
the hand of son of *S.* *Jer* 26:24
sent by Elasah son of *S.* 29:3
chamber of Gemariah son of *S.* 36:10
stood Jaazaniah son of *S.* *Ezek* 8:11
Shaphat
of the tribe of Simeon, *S.* *Num* 13:5
anoint Elisha son of *S.* *1 Ki* 19:16
if the head of Elisha the son of *S.* shall stand on him. *2 Ki* 6:31
Shemaiah, Neariah, *S.* *1 Chr* 3:22
of the Gadites, *S.* in Bashan. 5:12
in valleys was *S.* son of Adlai. 27:29
share
went down to sharpen every man his *s.* *1 Sam* 13:20
Sharezer
S. his son smote him. *2 Ki* 19:37
Isa 37:38
Sharon
in all the suburbs of *S.* *1 Chr* 5:16
over the herds that fed in *S.* 27:29
I am the rose of *S.* the. *S of S* 2:1
S. is like a wilderness. *Isa* 33:9
of Carmel and *S.* given thee. 35:2
S. shall be a fold of flocks. 65:10
sharp
Zipporah took a *s.* stone. *Ex* 4:25
make thee *s.* knives. *Josh* 5:2*
Joshua made *s.* knives and. 3*
between passages a *s.* *1 Sam* 14:4*
s. stones are under him, he spreadeth *s.* pointed things. *Job* 41:30*
arrows *s.* in the heart. *Ps* 45:5
thy tongue like a *s.* razor. 52:2
their tongue a *s.* sword. 57:4
s. arrows of mighty with. 120:4
her end is *s.* as a twoedged. *Pr* 5:4
bears false witness is *s.* arrow. 25:18
whose arrows are *s.* *Isa* 5:28
I will make thee a *s.* threshing. 41:15
my mouth like a *s.* sword. 49:2
take thee a *s.* knife. *Ezek* 5:1
the contention was so *s.* *Acts* 15:39
went a *s.* twoedged sword.
Rev 1:16; 19:15
he that hath the *s.* sword. 2:12
in his hand a *s.* sickle. 14:14, 17
to him that had the *s.* sickle. 18
sharpen
went down to *s.* every. *1 Sam* 13:20
a file for axes, and to *s.* 21*
sharpened
they *s.* their tongues. *Ps* 140:3
a sword is *s.* and furbished.
Ezek 21:9, 10, 11
sharpeneth
mine enemy *s.* his eyes. *Job* 16:9
iron *s.* iron, so a man *s.* *Pr* 27:17
sharper
the most upright is *s.* *Mi* 7:4*
the word of God is *s.* *Heb* 4:12
sharply
did chide with Gideon *s.* *Judg* 8:1
rebuke them *s.* that they. *Tit* 1:13
sharpness
present I should use *s.* *2 Cor* 13:10
Shaul
S. (sixth king of Edom). *1 Chr* 1:48
shave
but scall shall he not *s.* *Lev* 13:33
person shall *s.* off his hair. 14:8, 9
nor shall they *s.* the corner of. 21:5
shall *s.* his head in the day of his cleansing . . . shall he *s.* *Num* 6:9
Nazarite shall *s.* the head of his. 18
let them *s.* their flesh, and. 8:7*
captive shall *s.* her head. *Deut* 21:12
caused him to *s.* off seven locks.
Judg 16:19
Lord shall *s.* with a razor. *Isa* 7:20
neither shall they *s.* *Ezek* 44:20
be at charges, that they *s.* their.
Acts 21:24
shaved
Joseph *s.* and changed. *Gen* 41:14
s. off half their beards. *2 Sam* 10:4
1 Chr 19:4
Job rent his mantle and *s.* *Job* 1:20
shaven
be *s.* but the scall shall. *Lev* 13:33
hair of his separation is *s.* *Num* 6:19
if I be *s.* my strength. *Judg* 16:17
to grow again after he was *s.* 22
men having their beards *s.* *Jer* 41:5
all one as if she were *s.* *1 Cor* 11:5
if it be a shame to be *s.* let her. 6
sheaf
s. arose, and also stood upright . . . obeisance to my *s.* *Gen* 37:7
a *s.* of the firstfruits. *Lev* 23:10
wave the *s.* before the Lord. 11, 12
hast forgot a *s.* shalt not go to fetch it. *Deut* 24:19
they take away the *s.* *Job* 24:10
Judah like a torch in a *s.* *Zech* 12:6
Shealtiel, *see* **Zerubbabel**
shear
and Laban went to *s.* *Gen* 31:19
Judah goeth to Timnah to *s.* 38:13
nor shalt *s.* the firstling. *Deut* 15:19
Nabal did *s.* his sheep. *1 Sam* 25:4
shearer
a lamb dumb before his *s.* *Acts* 8:32
shearers
went up unto his sheep *s.* *Gen* 38:12
heard that thou hast *s.* *1 Sam* 25:7
my flesh I have killed for my *s.* 11
Absalom had *s.* in Baal-hazor.
2 Sam 13:23, 24
sheep before her *s.* is. *Isa* 53:7
shearing
and Nabal was *s.* sheep. *1 Sam* 25:2
shearing *house*
of Ahaziah at *s. house.* *2 Ki* 10:12
slew them at the pit of *s. house.* 14
Shear-jashub
meet Ahaz, thou and *S.* *Isa* 7:3
sheath
the sword out of his *s.* *1 Sam* 17:51
with a sword fastened in the *s.*
2 Sam 20:8
the angel put the sword into his *s.*
1 Chr 21:27
will draw his sword out of the *s.*
Ezek 21:3, 4, 5
cause it to return into his *s.*? will. 30
put up thy sword into *s.* *John* 18:11
sheaves
behold, we were binding *s.* *Gen* 37:7
let me glean and gather among the *s.*
Ruth 2:7, 15
sabbath bringing in *s.* *Neh* 13:15
he shall come bringing *s.* *Ps* 126:6
that bindeth *s.* his bosom. 129:7
a cart pressed full of *s.* *Amos* 2:13
shall gather them as the *s.* *Mi* 4:12
Sheba, Shebah
son of Raamah *S.* *Gen* 10:7
S. son of Joktan. 28
Jokshan begat *S.* and Dedan. 25:3
1 Chr 1:32
Isaac called the well *S.* *Gen* 26:33
in their inheritance *S.* *Josh* 19:2
queen of *S.* heard of the fame of.
1 Ki 10:1; *2 Chr* 9:1
the son of Raamah, *S.* *1 Chr* 1:9
son of Joktan, *S.* 22
children of Gad, *S.* and Jorai. 5:13
companies of *S.* waited. *Job* 6:19
kings of *S.* and Seba. *Ps* 72:10
to him shall be given of gold of *S.*
15; *Isa* 60:6
is incense from *S.*? *Jer* 6:20
merchants of *S.* thy merchants.
Ezek 27:22, 23
S. shall say, Art thou come? 38:13
see **Bichri**
Shebna
to the king, there came out to them *S.* *2 Ki* 18:18, 37; *Isa* 36:3
Hezekiah sent *S.* to Isaiah. *2 Ki* 19:2
Isa 37:2
thee to this treasurer, *S.* *Isa* 22:15
Shechem
to Salem a city of *S.* *Gen* 33:18
of Hamor, *S.'s* father. 19; *Acts* 7:16
S. lay with Dinah. *Gen* 34:2
they slew *S.* 26
under an oak that was by *S.* 35:4
their father's flock in *S.* 37:12
the vale of Hebron to *S.* 14
of *S.* the family of the. *Num* 26:31
lot for the children of *S.* *Josh* 17:2
S. in mount Ephraim a city of.
20:7; 21:21; *1 Chr* 6:67
the tribes of Israel to *S.* *Josh* 24:1
bones of Joseph buried they in *S.* 32
Gideon's concubine in *S.* *Judg* 8:31
son of Jerubbaal went to *S.* 9:1
hearken to me, ye men of *S.* 7
come out from the men of *S.* 20
who is *S.*? 28
Gaal and brethren come to *S.* 31
they should not dwell in *S.* 41
the evil of the men of *S.* did God. 57
Rehoboam went to *S.* *1 Ki* 12:1
2 Chr 10:1
Jeroboam built *S.* in mount Ephraim.
1 Ki 12:25
Shemida, Ahian and *S.* *1 Chr* 7:19
I will rejoice, I will divide *S.*
Ps 60:6; 108:7
came certain from *S.* *Jer* 41:5
shed
Joab *s.* Amasa's bowels to the.
2 Sam 20:10
is *s.* for many for the. *Mat* 26:28
promise of Holy Ghost, he hath *s.*
Acts 2:33*
love of God is *s.* abroad in. *Rom* 5:5
he *s.* on us abundantly. *Tit* 3:6*
see **blood**
shedder
beget a son that is a *s.* *Ezek* 18:10
sheddeth
whosoever *s.* man's blood, his.
Gen 9:6
the city *s.* blood in the. *Ezek* 22:3
shedding
and without *s.* of blood. *Heb* 9:22
sheep
Abel was a keeper of *s.* *Gen* 4:2
daughter cometh with the *s.* 29:6, 9
hand of Lord is upon the *s.* *Ex* 9:3*
ye shall take it out from the *s.* 12:5
sacrifice thereon thy *s.* and. 20:24
if a man steal a *s.* and kill it or sell.
22:1, 4, 9
to his neighbour a *s.* to keep. 10
with the firstling of *s.* 30; 34:19
if his offering be of the *s.* *Lev* 1:10
shall eat no manner of fat of *s.* 7:23
ye shall offer a male of the *s.* 22:19
sanctify the firstling of a *s.* 27:26
the firstling of *s.* *Num* 18:17
cities and folds for your *s.* 32:24, 36
bless the flocks of thy *s.* *Deut* 7:13*
thou shalt not sacrifice *s.* 17:1
from them that offer *s.* 18:3, 4
thy brother's *s.* go astray. 22:1
blessed shall be the flocks of thy *s.*
28:4
cursed shall be the flocks of thy *s.*
18; 31:51
butter of kine, milk of *s.* 32:14
at Jericho ox and *s.* *Josh* 6:21
Joshua took Achan's *s.* and. 7:24
left neither *s.* nor oxen. *Judg* 6:4
take tenth of your *s.* *1 Sam* 8:17*
upon the spoil and took *s.* 14:32
every man his ox and his *s.* 34
slay both ox and *s.* 15:3
Saul spread the *s.* 9
this bleating of *s.* in my ears? 14
the people took of the spoil, *s.* 21
behold, he keepeth the *s.* 16:11
my son, who is with the *s.* 19
returned to feed his father's *s.* 17:15
he rose early and left the *s.* with. 20

kept his father's s. 1 Sam 17:34
3000 s.: he was shearing his s. 25:2
Abigail hasted, and took five s. 18
David took away the s. 27:9
thee from following the s. 2 Sam 7:8
brought David butter and s. 17:29
Lo, I have sinned, but these s. what? 24:17; 1 Chr 21:17
Adonijah hath slain s. 1 Ki 1:19, 25
Solomon's provision for one day hundred s. 4:23
all the congregation sacrificing s. 8:5
Solomon offered s. 63; 2 Chr 5:6 7:5
is it a time to receive s.? 2 Ki 5:26
from Hagarites 250,000 s. 1 Chr 5:21
oxen and s. abundantly. 12:40
Asa carried from the Ethiopians s. 2 Chr 14:15
offered of the spoil 7000 s. 15:11
Ahab killed s. and oxen for. 18:2
consecrated things were 3000 s. 29:33
give 7000 s. and the princes gave to the congregation 10,000 s. 30:24
in the tithes of oxen and s. 31:6
daily one ox, six choice s. Neh 5:18
substance also was 7000 s., 3000 camels. Job 1:3
fallen, and hath burnt up the s. 16
warmed with fleece of my s. 31:20
for he had 14,000 s. and 6000. 42:12
given him all s. and oxen. Ps 8:7
thou hast given us like s. for. 44:11
like s. are laid in the grave. 49:14
anger smoke against thy s.? 74:1
own people go forth like s. 78:52
people and s. of thy pasture. 79:13
the s. of his hand. 95:7; 100:3
gone astray like a lost s. 119:176
that our s. may bring forth. 144:13
thy teeth are like a flock of s. S of S 4:2*; 6:6*
a man shall nourish two s. Isa 7:21
gladness, and killing of s. 22:13
all we like s. have gone astray. 53:6
pull them out like s. for. Jer 12:3
pastors that scatter the s. 23:1
my people hath been lost s. 50:6
Israel is a scattered s.; the lions. 17
my s. wander through. Ezek 34:6
I will search my s. and seek. 11, 12
and for a wife he kept s. Hos 12:12
the flocks of s. are made. Joel 1:18
as a young lion among the flocks of s. Mi 5:8
shepherd, and s. shall be scattered. Zech 13:7; Mat 26:31 Mark 14:27
false prophets in s.'s clothing. Mat 7:15
go rather to the lost s. of the. 10:6
if one s. fall into a pit on the. 12:11
is a man better than a s.? 12
unto the lost s. of Israel. 15:24
if a man have a 100 s. and. 18:12
he rejoiceth more of that s. 13 Luke 15:4, 6
as a shepherd divideth his s. Mat 25:32
he shall set s. on his right hand. 33
temple those that sold s. John 2:14
out of the temple, and the s. 15
by the door is shepherd of the s. 10:2
the s. hear his voice. 3, 27
the s. follow him. 4*
verily I am the door of the s. 7
were robbers, but the s. did not. 8
shepherd giveth his life for his s. 11
hireling leaveth the s. and fleeth. 12*
hireling careth not for the s. 13
good shepherd, I know my s. 14*
I lay down my life for the s. 15
other s. I have. 16
because ye are not of my s. 26
Peter, Feed my s. 21:16, 17
great Shepherd of s. Heb 13:20
none buyeth s., horses. Rev 18:13

as sheep

be not as s. which have. Num 27:17
Israel scattered on the hills as s. 1 Ki 22:17; 2 Chr 18:16
the day long; we are counted as s. Ps 44:22; Rom 8:36
it shall be as a s. that no. Isa 13:14
and as a s. before his shearers. 53:7
together as s. of Bozra. Mi 2:12
fainted and were scattered as s. Mat 9:36; Mark 6:34
I send you forth as s. Mat 10:16
led as s. to the slaughter. Acts 8:32
were as s. going astray. 1 Pet 2:25

sheepcote

took thee from the s. 2 Sam 7:8 1 Chr 17:7

sheepcotes

Saul came to the s. 1 Sam 24:3

sheepfold

he that entereth not the s. John 10:1

sheepfolds

build s. for our cattle. Num 32:16
thou among the s.? Judg 5:16
David, took him from the s. Ps 78:70

sheep gate

brethren built the s. gate. Neh 3:1
up of the corner to the s. gate. 32
they went on to the s. gate. 12:39

sheep market

Jerusalem by the s. market a pool. John 5:2

sheepmaster

Mesha king of Moab was a s. 2 Ki 3:4

see **shearers**

sheepskins

in the s. and goatskins. Heb 11:37

sheet

a vessel descending as a great s. Acts 10:11; 11:5

sheets

I will give you thirty s. Judg 14:12*
thirty s. and thirty change. 13*

shekel

(*The unit of weight and of money among the Jews. It weighed about ½ ounce, and as coined in silver was worth about two shillings and nine-pence, or 65 cents. In gold one or two pounds, or 4.85 to 9.69 dollars according to period*)

took an earring of half a s. Gen 24:22
a s. after the s. of the sanctuary, a s. Ex 30:13; Num 3:47; Ezek 45:12
give less than half a s. Ex 30:15
the fourth part of a s. 1 Sam 9:8
of fine flour for a s. 2 Ki 7:1, 16, 18
charged yearly with the third of a s. Neh 10:32
small, and the s. great. Amos 8:5

shekels

land is worth 400 s. Gen 23:15, 16
her hands of ten s. weight. 24:22
give her master thirty s. Ex 21:32
s. of sweet cinnamon 250 s., of sweet calamus 250 s. 30:23
the estimation by s. Lev 5:15 27:3, 4, 5, 6, 7, 16
one spoon of ten s. of gold, full of incense. Num 7:14, 20, 26, 32 38, 44, 50, 56, 62, 68, 74, 80
amerce him in 100 s. Deut 22:19
to the damsel's father fifty s. 29
saw in the spoils 200 s. Josh 7:21
earrings was 1700 s. Judg 8:26
the 1100 s. of silver were taken. 17:2
had restored the s. 3
I will give thee ten s. of silver. 10
Absalom weighed his hair, 200 s. 2 Sam 14:26
I would have given thee ten s. 18:11
David bought oxen for fifty s. 24:24
six hundred s. of gold to. 1 Ki 10:16
each man fifty s. of silver. 2 Ki 15:20
gave to Ornan 600 s. 1 Chr 21:25
governors had taken 40 s. by year. Neh 5:15
I bought the field for 17 s. Jer 32:9
by weight twenty s. a day. Ezek 4:10

see **sanctuary**

Shelah

Judah's son S. Gen 38:5
gave her not to S. my son. 26
Judah, Er, Onan and S. 46:12 Num 26:20; 1 Chr 2:3; 4:21
Arphaxad begat S. and S. Eber. 1 Chr 1:18, 24

Shelemiah

lot eastward fell to S. 1 Chr 26:14
S. and Nathan had taken strange. Ezra 10:39
I made S. the priest. Neh 13:13
S. son of Cushi. Jer 36:14
S. son of Abdeel. 26

shelter

the rock for want of a s. Job 24:8
for thou hast been s. for. Ps 61:3*

Shelumiel

the prince of Simeon, S. the son of. Num 1:6; 2:12; 7:36; 10:19

Shem

Noah begat S. Gen 5:32; 6:10 10:1; 1 Chr 1:4
S. took a garment and. Gen 9:23
blessed be the Lord God of S. 26
dwell in the tents of S. 27
the children of S. 10:21, 22, 31 11:10; 1 Chr 1:17
which was the son of S. Luke 3:36

Shemaiah

word of God came to S. the man. 1 Ki 12:22; 2 Chr 11:2; 12:7
Shimri the son of S. 1 Chr 4:37
of Reuben, S. the son of Joel. 5:4
of the Levites, S. 9:14, 16; 15:8 11; 24:6; 26:4, 6, 7; 2 Chr 17:8 29:14; 31:15; 35:9; Ezra 8:16 10:21, 31
S. (the son of Adonikam). Ezra 8:13
S. keeper of the east gate. Neh 3:29
I came to the house of S. son. 6:10
S. a priest sealed. 10:8
of the Levites, S. 11:15; 12:6, 18 35, 36
S. the priest. 12:34, 42
Urijah the son of S. Jer 26:20
say to S. the Nehelamite. 29:24 31, 32
and Delaiah the son of S. 36:12

Sheminith

with harps on the S. 1 Chr 15:21

Shenir

the Amorites call S. Deut 3:9
look from the top of S. S of S 4:8

Shephatiah

S. the fifth son of David. 2 Sam 3:4 1 Chr 3:3
Meshullam son of S. 1 Chr 9:8
S. the Haruphite came to David. 12:5
the ruler of the Simeonites was S. 27:16
the children of S., 372. Ezra 2:4, 57 Neh 7:9
S. heard the words of. Jer 38:1

shepherd

every s. is abomination. Gen 46:34
from thence is the s., the stone. 49:24
he put the stones into a s.'s bag. 1 Sam 17:40
the Lord is my s. I shall. Ps 23:1
give ear, O s. of Israel, thou. 80:1
words which are given from one s. Eccl 12:11
departed from me as a s. Isa 38:12
he shall feed his flock like a s. 40:11
saith of Cyrus, He is my s. 44:28
that brought them up with the s. 63:11
and keep him as a s. Jer 31:10
array himself as a s. putteth. 43:12
who is that s. that will stand? 49:19 50:44
I will also break in pieces s. 51:23
because there is no s. Ezek 34:5
prey, because there was no s. 8
as a s. seeketh out his flock. 12
s. over them, my servant David shall feed . . . be their s. 23; 37:24
s. taketh out of mouth. Amos 3:12
because there was no s. Zech 10:2
instruments of a foolish s. 11:15
raise up a s. in the land. 16
woe to the idle s. that leaveth. 17
O sword, against my s. and. 13:7
is an hireling, and not s. John 10:12
I am the good s., know my sheep. 14
shall be one fold and one s. 16

that great s. of the sheep. Heb 13:20
returned unto the s. 1 Pet 2:25
when the chief s. shall appear. 5:4
see **sheep**

shepherds
and the men are s. Gen 46:32
thy servants are s. 47:3
and the s. came and drove. Ex 2:17
delivered us out of the hand of s. 19
thy s. which were with. 1 Sam 25:7
kids beside the s.' tents. S of S 1:8
shall the s. make their. Isa 13:20
when multitude of s. is called. 31:4
and they are s. that cannot. 56:11
the s. with their flocks shall come. Jer 6:3
I will set up s. over them. 23:4
howl, ye s. and cry. 25:34
the s. have no way to flee. 35
a voice of the cry of the s. and. 36
shall be an habitation of s. 33:12
their s. have caused them to go. 56
the s. of Israel, woe to the s. of Israel ... should not s. feed? Ezek 34:2
nor did my s. search for my flock, but s. fed themselves and fed. 8
I am against the s. neither shall the s. feed themselves any more. 10
habitations of the s. shall. Amos 1:2
raise against him seven s. Mi 5:5
thy s. slumber, O king of Assyria. Nah 3:18
shall be cottages for s. Zeph 2:6
kindled against the s. Zech 10:3
voice of the howling of the s. 11:3
and their own s. pity them not. 5
three s. also I cut off in one. 8
same country s. in field. Luke 2:8
were told them by the s. 18
the s. returned, glorifying and. 20

sherd
shall not be found a s. Isa 30:14

sherds
thou shalt break the s. Ezek 23:34

sheriffs
sent to gather the s. Dan 3:2
then the s. and rulers were. 3

Sheshach
the king of S. shall drink. Jer 25:26
how is S. taken! how is the! 51:41

Sheshbazzar
he numbered them to S. Ezra 1:8
did S. bring up from Babylon. 11
delivered to S. whom he had. 5:14
S. laid the foundation of the. 16

shew, *substantive*
(In all places the American Revision uses the modern spelling show, when the word is retained)
walketh in a vain s. Ps 39:6
the s. of their countenance. Isa 3:9
and for a s. make long. Luke 20:47*
to make a fair s. in flesh. Gal 6:12
spoiled powers made a s. Col 2:15
which things have a s. of wisdom. 23

shew
speak, saying, S. a miracle. Ex 7:9
I raised up for to s. in thee. 9:16
that I might s. my signs. 10:1
and thou shalt s. thy son in. 13:8*
the salvation Lord will s. to. 14:13*
shalt s. way they must walk. 18:20
Deut 1:33
it according to all that I s. Ex 25:9
s. me now thy way. 33:13
s. me thy glory. 18
I stood to s. you the word of the. Deut 5:5
no covenant, nor s. mercy. 7:2
Lord may s. thee mercy. 13:17
they shall s. thee the sentence. 17:9
thou shalt do as they shall s. 10, 11
not regard old, nor s. favour. 28:50
ask thy father, and he will s. 32:7
he would not s. the land. Josh 5:6
s. us, we pray thee, the entrance into the city, and we will s. Judg 1:24
then s. me a sign that thou. 6:17
Samuel feared to s. Eli the vision. 1 Sam 3:15
s. them the manner of the. 8:9
man of God peradventure can s. 1 Sam 9:6*
stand, that I may s. thee the. 27*
I will come and s. thee what. 10:8
come up to us, and we will s. 14:12
do nothing, he will s. it me. 20:2*
not unto thee, and s. it thee. 12*
he fled, and did not s. it. 22:17*
men, and they will s. thee. 25:8*
he will s. me, both it. 2 Sam 15:25
if he will s. himself a. 1 Ki 1:52
therefore, and s. thyself a man. 2:2
to Elijah, Go s. thyself. 18:1, 2
will ye not s. me which? 2 Ki 6:11
to s. himself strong. 2 Chr 16:9
s. their father's house whether they. Ezra 2:59; Neh 7:61
the pillar of fire to s. Neh 9:19
to s. the people and. Esth 1:11
Mordecai charged her not to s. 2:10
of the writing to s. Esther. 4:8
s. me wherefore thou. Job 10:2
he would s. thee the secrets of. 11:6
I was afraid, durst not s. you. 32:6
if a messenger to s. to man. 33:23
many will say, Who will s.? Ps 4:6
may s. forth all thy praise. 9:14
wilt s. me the path of life. 16:11
s. me thy ways, O Lord, teach. 25:4
the Lord will s. them his. 14
mouth shall s. forth thy praise. 51:15
my mouth shall s. forth thy. 71:15*
we thy people will s. forth. 79:13
s. us mercy, O Lord, grant. 85:7
s. me a token of good, that. 86:17
wilt thou s. wonders to the? 88:10
to s. that Lord is upright, he. 92:15
O God, to whom vengeance belongeth, s. thyself. 94:1*
can s. forth all his praise? 106:2
a man must s. himself. Pr 18:24*
formed them will s. no. Isa 27:11
the Lord shall s. lightning. 30:30
them forth and s. us what shall happen, let them s. the. 41:22*
s. the things that are to come. 23*
who among them can s. us? 43:9
people have I formed, shall s. 21*
coming, let them s. to them. 44:7*
and s. yourselves men. 46:8
say to them in darkness, s. 49:9
s. my people their transgression. 58:1
they shall s. forth the praises. 60:6*
thou shalt s. them all. Jer 16:10
into a land, where I will not s. 13
thy God may s. us the way we. 42:3
to s. the king of Babylon. 51:31
thou shalt s. her all her. Ezek 22:2*
for with their mouth they s. 33:31
wilt thou not s. us what thou? 37:18
upon all that I shall s. thee. 40:4
son of man, s. the house to. 43:10
s. them the form of the house. 11*
the sorcerers for to s. king his. Dan 2:2*
will s. the interpretation. 4, 7
if ye s. the dream and interpretation, therefore s. the dream and. 6
not a man that can s. the king's. 10
s. the king the interpretation. 16
cannot the wise men s. to the. 27
I thought it good to s. the signs. 4:2
shall s. me the interpretation. 5:7
and I am come to s. thee. 9:23*
dost thou s. me iniquity? Hab 1:3
s. thyself to the priest. Mat 8:4
Mark 1:44; Luke 5:14; 17:14
go and s. John these. Mat 11:4*
he shall s. judgement to the. 12:18
therefore mighty works do s. forth. Mat 14:2*; Mark 6:14*
desired he would s. a sign. Mat 16:1
s. me the tribute money. 22:19
Luke 20:24
came to s. him the buildings of the. Mat 24:1
arise false Christs, and shall s. great. Mat 24:24; Mark 13:22
s. you a large upper room furnished. Mark 14:15; Luke 22:12
I am sent to s. thee these glad. Luke 1:19*
s. how great things God hath. 8:39*
he will s. him greater works. John 5:20
if thou do these things s. thyself. 7:4*
where he were, he should s. it. 11:57
s. us the Father and it. 14:8, 9
he will s. you things to come. 16:13*
he shall receive of mine, and s. it. 14*, 15*
but I shall s. you plainly of the. 25*
Lord s. whether of these. Acts 1:24
the land which I shall s. thee. 7:3
Go, s. these things to James. 12:17*
the men who s. to us the way. 16:17*
Felix willing to s. the Jews. 24:27
that he should s. light to. 26:23*
who s. work of the law. Rom 2:15
thee, that I might s. my power. 9:17
willing to s. his wrath, endured. 22
ye do s. the Lord's death till he come. 1 Cor 11:26*
yet s. I you a more excellent. 12:31
I s. you a mystery, we shall. 15:51*
s. ye to them the proof. 2 Cor 8:24
s. the exceeding riches. Eph 2:7
for they themselves s. 1 Thes 1:9*
that Christ might s. all. 1 Tim 1:16
let them learn first to s. piety. 5:4
which in his times he shall s. 6:15
study to s. thyself approved unto God. 2 Tim 2:15*
that every one of you s. Heb 6:11
God willing to s. to the heirs. 17
s. me thy faith without. Jas 2:18
let him s. his works out of. 3:13
ye should s. forth the praises of. 1 Pet 2:9
and s. unto you that eternal life. 1 John 1:2*
he sent his angel to s. his servants. Rev 1:1; 22:6

***I will* shew**
a land that *I will* s. thee. Gen 12:1
I will be gracious, *I will* s. mercy on whom *I will* s. mercy. Ex 33:19
I will s. thee the man. Judg 4:22
I will s. thee what thou. 1 Sam 16:3
evil, then *I will* s. it thee. 20:13*
I will surely s. myself. 1 Ki 18:15
I will s. you what Syrians. 2 Ki 7:12
I will s. thee that which. Job 15:17
I also *will* s. mine opinion. 32:10
17; 36:2
I will s. forth all thy marvellous. Ps 9:1
I will s. the salvation. 50:23; 91:16
I will s. them the back. Jer 18:17
I will s. thee great and mighty. 33:3
I will s. mercies unto you. 42:12*
I will s. the king the interpretation. Dan 2:24
I will s. thee what is noted. 10:21*
and now *I will* s. thee the truth. 11:2
I will s. wonders in heaven. Joel 2:30; Acts 2:19
I will s. to him marvellous things. Mi 7:15
I will s. the nations thy. Nah 3:5
angel said, *I will* s. thee. Zech 1:9
I will s. you to whom he. Luke 6:47
I will s. him how great things he. Acts 9:16
I will s. thee my faith by. Jas 2:18
I will s. thee things which. Rev 4:1
I will s. thee the judgement of. 17:1
I will s. thee the bride, the. 21:9
see **kindness**

shewbread
shall set upon a table s. Ex 25:30
make the table, and the s. 35:13
39:36
on table of s. shall. Num 4:7
was no bread but the s. 1 Sam 21:6
table of gold whereon the s. was. 1 Ki 7:48
Kohathites to prepare s. 1 Chr 9:32
service both for the s. and. 23:29
gave gold for the tables of s. 28:16
house for the continual s. 2 Chr 2:4
tables whereon the s. was set. 4:19
s. also they set in order. 13:11
have cleansed the s. table. 29:18
ourselves for the s. Neh 10:33

into the house of God, and did eat *s.* *Mat* 12:4; *Mark* 2:26; *Luke* 6:4
wherein was the *s.* *Heb* 9:2

shewed (showed)

a white spot, and it be *s.* to priest. *Lev* 13:19, 49
and *s.* them the fruit of the land. *Num* 13:26
which Moses *s.* in the sight of. *Deut* 34:12*
and when he *s.* them the entrance. *Judg* 1:25
s. Sisera, that Barak was gone up. 4:12*
haste, and *s.* her husband. 13:10*
come up, for he hath *s.* me. 16:18*
it hath been *s.* me all. *Ruth* 2:11
came and *s.* to the men. *1 Sam* 11:9
Jonathan *s.* him all those. 19:7
Abiathar *s.* David that Saul. 22:21*
Thou hast *s.* this day how. 24:18*
messenger *s.* David. *2 Sam* 11:22
thou hast not *s.* it to. *1 Ki* 1:27
his might that he *s.* 16:27; 22:45
where fell it? he *s.* him. *2 Ki* 6:6
took an oath, and *s.* them. 11:4
and *s.* them all the house of his. 20:13; *Isa* 39:2
there is nothing I have not *s.* *2 Ki* 20:15; *Isa* 39:4
s. riches of his glorious. *Esth* 1:4
Esther had not *s.* her. 2:10, 20
for they had *s.* him the people. 3:6
pity should be *s.* from. *Job* 6:14
s. thy strength to this. *Ps* 71:18*
they *s.* his signs among them. 105:27*; *Acts* 7:36*
my complaint, I *s.* before him my. *Ps* 142:2*
his wickedness shall be *s.* *Pr* 26:26
labour, wherein I have *s.* *Eccl* 2:19
who *s.* to him the way? *Isa* 40:14
they *s.* no difference. *Ezek* 22:26*
and *s.* to chief priests. *Mat* 28:11
devil *s.* him all kingdoms. *Luke* 4:5
the disciples of John *s.* him. 7:18
and he said, He that *s.* mercy. 10:37
that servant came and *s.* 14:21
are raised, Moses *s.* at bush. 20:37
good works have I *s.* you. *John* 10:32
he *s.* unto them his hands. 20:20
Jesus *s.* himself again. 21:1, 14* *Acts* 1:3
miracle of healing was *s.* *Acts* 4:22
Moses *s.* himself to them. 7:26*
had *s.* wonders and signs. 36
which *s.* before of the coming. 52
he *s.* how he had seen an. 11:13
confessed, *s.* their deeds. 19:18
but have *s.* and have taught. 20:20
I have *s.* you all things, how. 35*
tell no man thou hast *s.* 23:22
but first Paul *s.* to them of. 26:20
the barbarous people *s.* no. 28:2
none of brethren *s.* or spake. 21*
for his sake that *s.* it. *1 Cor* 10:28
love which ye have *s.* *Heb* 6:10
judgement, that hath *s.* no. *Jas* 2:13
angel *s.* me the city of. *Rev* 21:10
he *s.* me a pure river of water. 22:1
worship the angel who *s.* me. 8

God, or Lord* shewed, *expressly, or implicitly

thy mercy *s.* to me in. *Gen* 19:19
that thou hast *s.* kindness. 24:14
least of the mercies thou hast *s.* 32:10
the *Lord s.* Joseph mercy, and. 39:21
God s. Pharaoh what he is. 41:25*
forasmuch as *God* hath *s.* thee. 39
and lo, *God* hath *s.* me also. 48:11*
the *Lord s.* him a tree. *Ex* 15:25
make them after the pattern *s.* 25:40 26:30; 27:8; *Heb* 8:5
of the *Lord* might be *s.* *Lev* 24:12
the *Lord* had *s.* Moses. *Num* 8:4
all signs I have *s.* among them. 14:11*; *Deut* 6:22
and upon earth he *s.* *Deut* 4:36
behold, the *Lord* our *God s.* 5:24
the *Lord s.* him all the land. 34:1
nor would he have *s.* *Judg* 13:23
hast *s.* to thy servant David my. *1 Ki* 3:6; *2 Chr* 1:8
Lord hath *s.* me, he. *2 Ki* 8:10
the *Lord* hath *s.* me that thou. 13
the *Lord* had *s.* David. *2 Chr* 7:10
s. from *Lord* our *God.* *Ezra* 9:8
he hath *s.* me his marvellous. *Ps* 31:21
thou hast *s.* thy people hard. 60:3
thou hast *s.* me great and. 71:20
wonders he had *s.* them. 78:11
his righteousness hath *s.* in. 98:2
he *s.* his people the power of. 111:6
God is the *Lord* who hath *s.* 118:27*
let favour be *s.* to wicked. *Isa* 26:20
I have *s.* when there was no. 43:12
s. them; I did them suddenly. 48:3
before it came to pass I *s.* it thee. 5
Lord s. me two baskets. *Jer* 24:1
the word the *Lord* hath *s.* me. 38:21
the *Lord* hath *s.* me. *Ezek* 11:25
gave statutes and *s.* them. 20:11
thus hath the *Lord s.* me. *Amos* 7:1 4:7; 8:1
he hath *s.* thee, O man. *Mi* 6:8
and the *Lord s.* me four. *Zech* 1:20
s. me Joshua standing before the angel of the *Lord.* 3:1
he hath *s.* strength with. *Luke* 1:51
heard how *Lord* had *s.* great. 58*
which *God* before had *s.* *Acts* 3:18*
God s. I should not call any. 10:28
God raised him third day and *s.* 40*
God hath *s.* it to them. *Rom* 1:19*
Lord Jesus hath *s.* me. *2 Pet* 1:14*

shewedst

and *s.* signs and wonders. *Neh* 9:10
I know it; then thou *s.* *Jer* 11:18

shewest

s. thyself marvellous. *Job* 10:16
thou *s.* lovingkindness. *Jer* 32:18
Jews said, What sign *s.* thou to us? *John* 2:18; 6:30*

sheweth

to do, he *s.* to Pharaoh. *Gen* 41:28
whatsoever he *s.* me. *Num* 23:3
none *s.* me that my. *1 Sam* 22:8*
he *s.* mercy to his anointed, to. *2 Sam* 22:51; *Ps* 18:50
he *s.* them their work. *Job* 36:9
noise thereof *s.* concerning it. 33*
firmament *s.* his handywork. *Ps* 19:1
night unto night *s.* knowledge. 2
good man *s.* favour, and. 112:5*
he *s.* his word unto Jacob. 147:19
he that speaketh truth, *s.* *Pr* 12:17
the tender grass *s.* itself. 27:25
yea, there is none that *s.* *Isa* 41:26
and *s.* him all kingdoms. *Mat* 4:8
Father loveth, and *s.* the. *John* 5:20

shewing, *verb*

and *s.* mercy unto thousands. *Ex* 20:6; *Deut* 5:10
s. to generation to come. *Ps* 78:4*
my beloved *s.* himself. *S of S* 2:9
thine iniquities by *s.* *Dan* 4:27
s. of hard sentences found. 5:12
s. glad tidings of kingdom. *Luke* 8:1*
and *s.* the coats which. *Acts* 9:39
s. by scripture that Jesus. 18:28
of God, *s.* himself that. *2 Thes* 2:4*
in all things *s.* thyself. *Tit* 2:7
not purloining, but *s.* all good. 10
but be gentle, *s.* all meekness. 3:2

shewing

deserts till day of his *s.* to Israel. *Luke* 1:80

Shibboleth

say now *S.* and he said. *Judg* 12:6

shield

A piece of defensive armour, commonly of wood, covered with leather, plates of gold, or brass. Sometimes shields were made all of gold, or brass. Those that Solomon *made were of beaten gold,* 1 Ki 10:17. Shishak *king of* Egypt *took these away, and* Rehoboam *made others of brass to serve in their stead,* 1 Ki 14:26, 27.

In scripture God is often called the shield *of his people,* Gen 15:1, Ps 5:12. *Faith in scripture is likewise called a shield,* Eph 6:16.

Shields *were hung up upon towers for ornaments, or as trophies of victory. The tower of* David *was adorned with a thousand* shields, S of S 4:4.

I am thy *s.*, and thy exceeding great reward. *Gen* 15:1
saved by the Lord, the *s.* of thy. *Deut* 33:29
was there a *s.* or spear seen in Israel? *Judg* 5:8
one bearing a *s.* *1 Sam* 17:7, 41
me with a spear and a *s.* 45*
s. of the mighty is vilely cast away, *s.* *2 Sam* 1:21
he is my *s.* 22:3; *Ps* 3:3; 28:7 119:114; 144:2
given me the *s.* of thy salvation. *2 Sam* 22:36; *Ps* 18:35
of gold went to one *s.* *1 Ki* 10:17
come before it with a *s.* nor cast a. *2 Ki* 19:32; *Isa* 37:33
that could handle *s.* *1 Chr* 12:8
children of Judah that bare *s.* 24
of Naphtali with *s.* and spear. 34
could handle spear and *s.* *2 Chr* 25:5
spear and *s.* rattleth. *Job* 39:23*
compass him as with a *s.* *Ps* 5:12
the Lord is our *s.* 33:20; 59:11 84:9
take hold of the *s.* and buckler. 35:2
the arrows of bow, the *s.* 76:3
the Lord God is a sun and *s.* 84:11
be thy *s.* and buckler. 91:4
help and their *s.* 115:9, 10, 11
he is a *s.* to them that. *Pr* 30:5
princes, and anoint the *s.* *Isa* 21:5
quiver, Kir uncovered the *s.* 22:6
order buckler and *s.* *Jer* 46:3
Libyans, that handle the *s.* 9
the buckler and *s.* *Ezek* 23:24
hanged the *s.* and helmet. 27:10, 11
the *s.* of his mighty men. *Nah* 2:3
taking the *s.* of faith. *Eph* 6:16

shields

David took the *s.* of gold that were on. *2 Sam* 8:7; *1 Chr* 18:7
Solomon made 300 *s.* of beaten. *1 Ki* 10:17; *2 Chr* 9:16
all, even all *s.* of gold, which Solomon. *1 Ki* 14:26; *2 Chr* 12:9
Rehoboam made in their stead brazen *s.* *1 Ki* 14:27; *2 Chr* 12:10
priest gave king David *s.* *2 Ki* 11:10 *2 Chr* 23:9
every several city put *s.* *2 Chr* 11:12
out of Benjamin that bare *s.* 14:8 17:17
Uzziah prepared for them *s.* 26:14
darts and *s.* in abundance. 32:5, 27
half of them held spears and *s.* *Neh* 4:16
the *s.* of the earth belong. *Ps* 47:9
bucklers, all *s.* of mighty men. *S of S* 4:4
the arrows, gather the *s.* *Jer* 51:11
great company with bucklers and *s.* *Ezek* 38:4, 5
they shall burn the *s.* and. 39:9

Shiggaion

(*This word is found in the title of* Ps 7. *The meaning is not certainly known. It was perhaps a* wild, mournful ode)

Shiloah

refuseth the waters of *S.* *Isa* 8:6

Shiloh

(*It has long been supposed to refer directly to* Christ, *the* Messiah; *but as there is no reference to it in the* New Testament *many are now doubtful. Some consider it as referring to the city of Shiloh*)

the sceptre shall not depart from Judah, nor a lawgiver from between his feet, until S. come. *Gen* 49:10

Shiloh

assembled together at *S.* *Josh* 18:1
cast lots for you in *S.* 8, 10
departed from Israel out of *S.* 22:9
house of God was in *S.* *Judg* 18:31

the young virgins to *S.* *Judg* 21:12
feast of the Lord in *S.* yearly. 19
if the daughters of *S.* come out. 21
up to worship in *S.* *1 Sam* 1:3
to house of the Lord in *S.* 24
so did the priests in *S.* to all. 2:14
the Lord appeared again in *S.* 3:21
ark of the Lord out of *S.* 4:3
man came to *S.* with his clothes. 12
Ahitub the Lord's priest in *S.* 14:3
the house of Eli in *S.* *1 Ki* 2:27
get thee to *S.* to Ahijah the. 14:2
wife arose and went to *S.* 4
the tabernacle of *S.* *Ps* 78:60
my place which was in *S.* *Jer* 7:12
house as I have done to *S.* 14
I make this house like *S.* 26:6, 9
there came certain from *S.* 41:5

Shilonite, *see* **Ahijah**

Shimeah

friend, Jonadab son of *S.* *2 Sam* 13:3
32; 21:21; *1 Chr* 20:7
S. was born to David in. *1 Chr* 3:5
Berachiah, the son of *S.* 6:39

Shimei

S. son of Gera of Bahurim.
2 Sam 16:5; 19:16
S. went along on the hill's side. 16:13
thou hast with thee *S.* *1 Ki* 2:8
that two of the servants of *S.* 39
S. the son of Elah, officer in. 4:18
S. son of Pedaiah. *1 Chr* 3:19
S. son of Joel. 5:4
Mishma, Hamuel, Zaccur, *S.* 4:26
S. had sixteen sons and six. 27
S. son of Gershom. 6:17, 42, 23:7
S. son of Merari. 6:29
sons of *S.* 23:9, 10
the tenth lot to *S.* 25:17
over vineyards was *S.* 27:27
Heman, Jehiel and *S.* *2 Chr* 29:14
dedicated things was *S.* 31:12, 13
S. had taken a strange wife.
Ezra 10:23, 33, 38
of Jair, the son of *S.* *Esth* 2:5
the family of *S.* shall. *Zech* 12:13

Shimshai

S. the scribe wrote a. *Ezra* 4:8, 9
the king sent an answer to *S.* 17

Shinar

Calneh in the land of *S.* *Gen* 10:10
a plain in the land of *S.* 11:2
Amraphel king of *S.* 14:1
recover remnant from *S.* *Isa* 11:11
into the land of *S.* *Dan* 1:2
house in the land of *S.* *Zech* 5:11

shine

Lord make his face *s.* *Num* 6:25
neither let light *s.* on it. *Job* 3:4
s. on counsel of the wicked. 10:3
thou shalt *s.* forth, thou. 11:17*
spark of his fire shall not *s.* 18:5
and the light shall *s.* upon. 22:28
light he commandeth not to *s.* 36:32*
the light of his cloud to *s.* 37:15
light doth *s.* and his eyes. 41:18*
he maketh a path to *s.* after him. 32
make thy face to *s.* *Ps* 31:16
face to *s.* upon us. 67:1; 80:3, 7, 19
between cherubims, *s.* forth. 80:1
oil to make his face to *s.* 104:15
make thy face to *s.* upon. 119:135
maketh his face to *s.* *Eccl* 8:1
not cause her light to *s.* *Isa* 13:10
arise, *s.* for thy light is come. 60:1
are waxen fat, they *s.* *Jer* 5:28
cause thy face to *s.* *Dan* 9:17
wise shall *s.* as the brightness. 12:3
let your light so *s.* *Mat* 5:16
shall the righteous *s.* forth. 13:43
his face did *s.* as sun, and his. 17:2
gospel of Christ should *s.* *2 Cor* 4:4*
God who commanded light to *s.* 6
ye *s.* as lights in world. *Phil* 2:15
light of a candle shall *s.* *Rev* 18:23
sun nor moon to *s.* in it. 21:23

shined

the Lord *s.* forth from. *Deut* 33:2
when his candle *s.* upon. *Job* 29:3
if I beheld the sun when it *s.* 31:26
of beauty God hath *s.* *Ps* 50:2
upon them hath the light *s.* *Isa* 9:2
earth *s.* with his glory. *Ezek* 43:2
suddenly there *s.* about. *Acts* 9:3
the angel came, and a light *s.* 12:7
for God hath *s.* in our. *2 Cor* 4:6

shineth

moon, and it *s.* not. *Job* 25:5*
the night *s.* as the day. *Ps* 139:12
shining light that *s.* more. *Pr* 4:18
as lightning *s.* even to. *Mat* 24:27*
and *s.* to other part. *Luke* 17:24
the light *s.* in darkness. *John* 1:5
as to a light that *s.* in. *2 Pet* 1:19
the true light now *s.* *1 John* 2:8
was as the sun *s.* *Rev* 1:16

shining

by clear *s.* after rain. *2 Sam* 23:4
path of just is as the *s.* light. *Pr* 4:18
will create the *s.* of a. *Isa* 4:5
withdraw their *s.* *Joel* 2:10; 3:15
they went at the *s.* *Hab* 3:11
raiment became *s.* white. *Mark* 9:3
when the *s.* of a candle. *Luke* 11:36
two men stood by them in *s.* 24:4
a burning and a *s.* light. *John* 5:35
the brightness of sun *s.* *Acts* 26:13

ship

(*In the Gospels the Revisions change this word to* boat)

the way of a *s.* in the midst. *Pr* 30:19
no gallant *s.* shall pass. *Isa* 33:21
Jonah found a *s.* going. *Jonah* 1:3
a tempest, so that the *s.* was. 4
forth the wares into the *s.* 5
in a *s.* with Zebedee. *Mat* 4:21
and they left the *s.* and followed. 22
that the *s.* was covered with. 8:24
the *s.* was tossed with waves. 14:24
Mark 4:37
in the *s.* mending their. *Mark* 1:19
father Zebedee in the *s.* 20
hinder part of the *s.* asleep. 4:38
neither had they in the *s.* 8:14
immediately the *s.* was. *John* 6:21
net on right side of the *s.* 21:6
accompanied him to the *s.* *Acts* 20:38
finding a *s.* sailing over unto. 21:2
into a *s.* of Adramyttium. 27:2

ship *boards*

all thy *s.* *boards* of fir trees.
Ezek 27:5

shipmaster

s. said, What meanest? *Jonah* 1:6
every *s.* and sailors afar. *Rev* 18:17

shipmen

Hiram sent *s.* that had. *1 Ki* 9:27
the *s.* were about to flee out of.
Acts 27:30*

shipping

they took *s.* and came. *John* 6:24

ships

shall be an haven for *s.* *Gen* 49:13
and *s.* shall come from Chittim.
Num 24:24
thee into Egypt with *s.* *Deut* 28:68
did Dan remain in *s.*? *Judg* 5:17
king Solomon made a navy of *s.*
1 Ki 9:26
s. of Tarshish to go to Ophir, the *s.*
22:48; *2 Chr* 20:37
my servants go with thine in the *s.*
1 Ki 22:49
sent him *s.* and servants. *2 Chr* 8:18
king's *s.* went to Tarshish. 9:21
passed away as the swift *s.* *Job* 9:26
thou breakest the *s.* of. *Ps* 48:7
there go the *s.*: there is that. 104:26
down to the sea in *s.* that. 107:23
merchant *s.* she brings. *Pr* 31:14
Lord on the *s.* of Tarshish. *Isa* 2:16
howl, ye *s.* of Tarshish, no. 23:1, 14
whose cry is in the *s.* 43:14
the *s.* of Tarshish first, to. 60:9
all *s.* of the sea with. *Ezek* 27:9
s. of Tarshish did sing of thee. 25
come down from their *s.* 29
go forth from me in *s.* 30:9
for *s.* of Chittim shall. *Dan* 11:30
north shall come with many *s.* 40
they filled both the *s.* *Luke* 5:7
behold also the *s.* though. *Jas* 3:4
the third part of the *s.* *Rev* 8:9
the company in *s.* stood. *Rev* 18:17*
made rich all that had *s.* 19

shipwreck

stoned, thrice I suffered *s.*
2 Cor 11:25
faith have made *s.* *1 Tim* 1:19

Shishak

in fifth year of Rehoboam, *S.* king.
1 Ki 14:25; *2 Chr* 12:2
together because of *S.* I left you in the hand of *S.* *2 Chr* 12:5
be poured out on Jerusalem by *S.* 7
S. took away the treasures of. 9

shittah tree

in wilderness the *s. tree.* *Isa* 41:19

Shittim

Israel abode in *S.* *Num* 25:1
sent out of *S.* two men. *Josh* 2:1
they removed from *S.* and. 3:1
water the valley of *S.* *Joel* 3:18
him from *S.* to Gilgal. *Mi* 6:5

shittim wood

(Acacia, *as in Revisions*)

skins and *s. wood.* *Ex* 25:5; 35:7
shall make an ark of *s. wood.*
25:10; 37:1; *Deut* 10:3
make staves of *s. wood.* *Ex* 25:13
28; 27:6; 37:4, 15, 28; 38:6
thou shalt make a table of *s. wood.*
25:23; 37:10
make boards for tabernacle of *s. wood.* 26:15; 36:20
thou shalt make bars of *s. wood.*
26:26; 36:21
pillars of *s.* wood. 26:32, 37; 36:36
make an altar of *s. wood.* 27:1
30:1
with whom was found *s. wood.* 35:24

shivers

potter shall be broken to *s.* *Rev* 2:27

shock

like as a *s.* of corn cometh. *Job* 5:26

shocks

Samson burnt up the *s.* *Judg* 15:5

shod

captives and *s.* them. *2 Chr* 28:15
I *s.* thee with badgers'. *Ezek* 16:10
be *s.* with sandals, put not on.
Mark 6:9
s. with the preparation. *Eph* 6:15

shoe

To take off shoe was, [1] *A sign of reverence,* Ex 3:5; [2] *Of disgrace,* Deut 25:10; [3] *Of a contract,* Ruth 4:7; [4] *Of mourning,* Ezek 24:17.

wife shall loose his *s.* *Deut* 25:9
the house of him that hath his *s.* 10
thy *s.* is not waxen old upon. 29:5
thy *s.* from off thy foot. *Josh* 5:15
man plucked off his *s.* *Ruth* 4:7
it for thee, so he drew off his *s.* 8
over Edom will I cast out my *s.*
Ps 60:8; 108:9
and put off thy *s.* *Isa* 20:2

shoelatchet

take from thread to a *s.* *Gen* 14:23
whose *s.* I am not worthy. *John* 1:27

shoes

put off thy *s.* from thy feet.
Ex 3:5; *Acts* 7:33
with your *s.* on your feet. 12:11
s. shall be iron and. *Deut* 33:25*
old *s.* and clouted upon. *Josh* 9:5
our *s.* are become old with. 13
put the blood in his *s.* *1 Ki* 2:5
are thy feet with *s.*! *S of S* 7:1*
nor the latchet of their *s.* *Isa* 5:27
put on thy *s.* upon. *Ezek* 24:17, 23
they sold the poor for a pair of *s.*
Amos 2:6
buy the needy for a pair of *s.* 8:6
whose *s.* I am not worthy. *Mat* 3:11
carry neither *s.* nor staves. 10:10
Luke 10:4
s. I am not worthy to. *Mark* 1:7
Luke 3:16; *Acts* 13:25
ring on his hand, and *s.* *Luke* 15:22
you without purse and *s.* 22:35

shone
that the skin of his face *s.* *Ex* 34:29
the skin of his face *s.* they. 30, 35
rose up early, sun *s.* *2 Ki* 3:22
glory of the Lord *s.* round. *Luke* 2:9
suddenly there *s.* from. *Acts* 22:6
the day *s.* not for a third. *Rev* 8:12

shook
for oxen *s.* the ark. *2 Sam* 6:6*
the earth *s.* 22:8; *Ps* 18:7; 68:8* 77:18
I *s.* my lap, and said. *Neh* 5:13
out and *s.* the kingdoms. *Isa* 23:11
but they *s.* off the dust. *Acts* 13:51
he *s.* his raiment, and said. 18:6
he *s.* off the beast into the fire. 28:5
voice then *s.* the earth. *Heb* 12:26

shoot
middle bar to *s.* through. *Ex* 36:33*
I will *s.* three arrows. *1 Sam* 20:20
the arrows which I *s.* 36
not that they would *s.*? *2 Sam* 11:20
then Elisha said, *S.* *2 Ki* 13:17
he shall not *s.* an arrow there. 19:32; *Isa* 37:33
valiant men able to *s.* *1 Chr* 5:18
engines to *s.* arrows. *2 Chr* 26:15
they may privily *s.* at. *Ps* 11:2
they *s.* out the lip, they shake. 22:7
when he bendeth his bow to *s.* 58:7*
to *s.* their arrows, even bitter. 64:3
that they may *s.* in secret. 4
God shall *s.* at them with an. 7
s. out thine arrows, and. 144:6*
bend the bow, *s.* at her. *Jer* 50:14
neither *s.* up their top. *Ezek* 31:14*
ye shall *s.* forth your branches. 36:8
when they now *s.* forth. *Luke* 21:30

shooters
s. shot from off the. *2 Sam* 11:24

shooteth
and his branch *s.* forth. *Job* 8:16
measure when it *s.* forth. *Isa* 27:8*
mustard seed *s.* out. *Mark* 4:32*

shooting
right hand and left in *s.* *1 Chr* 12:2
in the *s.* up of the latter. *Amos* 7:1

shore
(*Revisions*, beach)
multitude stood on the *s.* *Mat* 13:2
it was full, they drew to *s.* 48
Jesus stood on the *s.* *John* 21:4
we kneeled down on the *s.* *Acts* 21:5
a certain creek with a *s.* 27:39
mainsail and made toward *s.* 40
see **sea**

shorn
like a flock of sheep that are even *s.* *S of S* 4:2
s. his head in Cenchrea. *Acts* 18:18
let her also be *s.*: but if it be a shame for a woman to be *s.* *1 Cor* 11:6

short
Lord's hand waxed *s.*? *Num* 11:23
the light is *s.* because. *Job* 17:12*
triumphing of the wicked is *s.* 20:5
how *s.* my time is. *Ps* 89:47
come *s.* of glory of God. *Rom* 3:23
because a *s.* work will Lord. 9:28*
brethren, the time is *s.* *1 Cor* 7:29*
from you for a *s.* time. *1 Thes* 2:17
he hath but a *s.* time. *Rev* 12:12
he must continue a *s.* space. 17:10*
see **come, cut**

shortened
days of his youth hast thou *s.* *Ps* 89:45
my strength, he *s.* my days. 102:23
years of wicked shall be *s.* *Pr* 10:27
is my hand *s.* at all, that? *Isa* 50:2
the Lord's hand is not *s.* 59:1
should be *s.* no flesh be saved, but for the elect's sake *s.* *Mat* 24:22 *Mark* 13:20

shorter
bed is *s.* than that a man. *Isa* 28:20

shortly
is established, and God will *s.* bring it to pass. *Gen* 41:32
vessels shall *s.* be brought again. *Jer* 27:16
now will I *s.* pour out. *Ezek* 7:8
would depart *s.* thither. *Acts* 25:4
bruise Satan under your feet *s.* *Rom* 16:20
I will come to you *s.* *1 Cor* 4:19
I trust to send Timotheus *s.* unto. *Phil* 2:19
I also myself shall come *s.* 24
hoping to come unto thee *s.* *1 Tim* 3:14
thy diligence to come *s.* *2 Tim* 4:9
come *s.* I will see you. *Heb* 13:23
s. I must put off this. *2 Pet* 1:14*
I trust I shall *s.* see. *3 John* 14
things that must *s.* come. *Rev* 1:1 22:6

shot, *verb*
her blossoms *s.* forth. *Gen* 40:10
the archers *s.* at him, and. 49:23
shall surely be stoned, or *s.* through. *Ex* 19:13
we have *s.* at them. *Num* 21:30
the arrow which Jonathan had *s.* *1 Sam* 20:37
the shooters *s.* from. *2 Sam* 11:24
said, Shoot, and he *s.* *2 Ki* 13:17
archers *s.* at king Josiah. *2 Chr* 35:23
s. out lightnings, and. *Ps* 18:14
tongue is an arrow *s.* out. *Jer* 9:8*
it became a vine, and *s.* *Ezek* 17:6
this vine *s.* forth her branches. 7
waters when he *s.* forth. 31:5
he hath *s.* up his top among. 10*

shot
down as it were a bow *s.* *Gen* 21:16

shoulder
bread on Hagar's *s.* *Gen* 21:14
her pitcher upon her *s.* 24:15, 45
Issachar bowed his *s.* to. 49:15
the ephod shall have two *s.* *Ex* 28:7
the chains on the *s.* pieces. 25
the *s.* of the heave offering. 29:27*
they made *s.* pieces for it to. 39:4
priest shall take sodden *s.* of the ram. *Num* 6:19; *Deut* 18:3
man a stone upon his *s.* *Josh* 4:5
laid a bow on his *s.* *Judg* 9:48
cook took up the *s.* *1 Sam* 9:24*
withdrew the *s.* and. *Neh* 9:29
I would take it upon my *s.* *Job* 31:36
I removed his *s.* from. *Ps* 81:6
broken the staff of his *s.* *Isa* 9:4
government shall be upon his *s.* 6
shall be taken from off thy *s.* 10:27
of David will I lay upon his *s.* 22:22
they bear him upon the *s.* 46:7
I bare it on my *s.* *Ezek* 12:7
prince shall bear upon his *s.* 12
even the thigh and *s.* 24:4
and rent all their *s.* 29:7, 18
thrust with side and with *s.* 34:21
and pulled away the *s.* *Zech* 7:11

shoulder *blade*
fall from my *s. blade.* *Job* 31:22

heave **shoulder**
the heave *s.* have I taken. *Lev* 7:34*; *Num* 6:20*
the heave *s.* shall ye eat. *Lev* 10:14*
the heave *s.* and wave breast. 15*

right **shoulder**
the ram the *right s.* *Ex* 29:22*
the *right s.* shall ye give. *Lev* 7:32*
offereth, shall have the *right s.* 33*
took the fat and the *right s.* 8:25*
fat, and upon the *right s.* 26*
the *right s.* waved is thine. 9:21* *Num* 18:18*

shoulders
laid the garment upon both their *s.* *Gen* 9:23
bound upon their *s.* *Ex* 12:34
two stones on *s.* of ephod. 28:12 39:7
of Kohath should bear on their *s.* *Num* 7:9
dwell between his *s.* *Deut* 33:12
took bar and all, and put them upon his *s.* *Judg* 16:3
from his *s.* and upward higher. *1 Sam* 9:2; 10:23
target of brass between his *s.* 17:6
bare the ark on their *s.* *1 Chr* 15:15
a burden upon your *s.* *2 Chr* 35:3
they shall fly on the *s.* of. *Isa* 11:14
burden depart from off their *s.* 14:25
will carry riches upon the *s.* 30:6
shall be carried upon their *s.* 49:22
shall bear it upon thy *s.* *Ezek* 12:6
lay them on men's *s.* *Mat* 23:4
it on his *s.* rejoicing. *Luke* 15:5

shout, *substantive*
and the *s.* of a king. *Num* 23:21
shouted with a great *s.* *Josh* 6:5, 20
with a great *s.* so that. *1 Sam* 4:5
the noise of this great *s.*? 6
men of Judah gave a *s.* *2 Chr* 13:15
with a great *s.* when they praised. *Ezra* 3:11
could not discern the *s.* of joy. 13
God is gone up with a *s.* *Ps* 47:5
Lord shall give a *s.* as. *Jer* 25:30
shall lift a *s.* against Babylon. 51:14
people gave a *s.* saying. *Acts* 12:22
shall descend from heaven with a *s.* *1 Thes* 4:16

shout
them that *s.* for mastery. *Ex* 32:18
trumpet, all people shall *s.* *Josh* 6:5
not *s.* till I bid you *s.*; then *s.* 10
s.; for the Lord hath given you. 16
s. unto God with the voice. *Ps* 47:1
s. thou inhabitants of Zion. *Isa* 12:6
let them *s.* from the top of. 42:11
s. ye lower parts of the earth. 44:23
sing and *s.* among chief. *Jer* 31:7
Babylon hath sinned. *S.* against. 50:14
when I *s.* he shutteth. *Lam* 3:8*
s. O Israel, be glad with. *Zeph* 3:14
s. O daughter of Jerusalem. *Zech* 9:9

shouted
as they *s.* he said, There. *Ex* 32:17
consumed, they *s.* and fell. *Lev* 9:24
so the people *s.* when. *Josh* 6:20
the Philistines *s.* against Samson. *Judg* 15:14
all Israel *s.* with a great. *1 Sam* 4:5
people *s.* and said, God save. 10:24
going forth and *s.* for battle. 17:20
the men of Israel and Judah *s.* 52
as Judah *s.* God smote. *2 Chr* 13:15
praised the Lord, they *s.* *Ezra* 3:11
people *s.* aloud for joy. 12, 13
see **joy**

shouteth
like a mighty man that *s.* because of wine. *Ps* 78:65

shouting
brought up ark with *s.* *2 Sam* 6:15 *1 Chr* 15:28
they sware to the Lord with *s.* *2 Chr* 15:14
he smelleth the battle and *s.* afar off. *Job* 39:25
wicked perish, there is *s.* *Pr* 11:10
the *s.* for summer fruits is fallen. *Isa* 16:9, 10*
let them hear the *s.* at. *Jer* 20:16
with *s.*; their *s.* shall be no *s.* 48:33
lift up the voice with *s.* *Ezek* 21:22
devour Rabbah with *s.* *Amos* 1:14
Moab shall die with tumult, *s.* 2:2

shoutings
forth the headstone with *s.* *Zech* 4:7

shovel
winnowed with the *s.* *Isa* 30:24

shovels
make his pans and his *s.* *Ex* 27:3
he made the pots, and the *s.* 38:3
on the purple cloth *s.* *Num* 4:14
lavers, the *s.* and the basons of brass. *1 Ki* 7:40, 45; *2 Chr* 4:11, 16
pots and *s.* he took away. *2 Ki* 25:14; *Jer* 52:18

for **show** *see* **shew**

shower
an overflowing *s.* *Ezek* 13:11, 13
I will cause *s.* to come down. 34:26
say, There cometh a *s.* *Luke* 12:54

showers
distil as *s.* on the grass. *Deut* 32:2
the poor are wet with *s.* *Job* 24:8
the earth soft with *s.* *Ps* 65:10

he shall come down as s. Ps 72:6
therefore the s. have been. Jer 3:3
can the heavens give s.? 14:22
shall be s. of blessing. Ezek 34:26
shall be as s. on grass. Mi 5:7
the Lord shall give them s. of rain. Zech 10:1

shrank
Israel eat not of sinew that s. Gen 32:32*

shred
came and s. wild gourds. 2 Ki 4:39

shrines
made silver s. for Diana. Acts 19:24

shroud
was a cedar with a shadowing s. Ezek 31:3

shrubs
child under one of the s. Gen 21:15

Shuah
Keturah bare Ishbak, S. Gen 25:2; 1 Chr 1:32
daughter of a Canaanite named S. Gen 38:2, 12; 1 Chr 2:3

Shual
turned to the land of S. 1 Sam 13:17

Shuhite, *see* **Bildad**

Shulamite
return, O S. What will ye see in the S.? S of S 6:13

shun
but s. profane and vain. 2 Tim 2:16

Shunammite
a fair damsel Abishag a S. 1 Ki 1:3
Abishag the S. to wife. 2:17
why dost thou ask Abishag the S.? 22
call this S. 2 Ki 4:12, 36
yonder is that S. 25

shunned
I have not s. the whole. Acts 20:27*

Shushan
to pass as I was in S. Neh 1:1
were gathered to S. Esth 2:8
but the city S. was perplexed. 3:15
gather all the Jews in S. and. 4:16
the city of S. rejoiced and. 8:15
number slain in S. was brought. 9:11
Jews slew in S. three hundred. 15
see **palace**

shut
the Lord s. him in. Gen 7:16
wilderness hath s. them in. Ex 14:3
let her be s. out from camp. Num 12:14
Miriam was s. out from the camp. 15
nor s. thy hand from. Deut 15:7
s. the gate of Jericho. Josh 2:7
they s. the tower to them. Judg 9:51
for he is s. in, by entering into. 1 Sam 23:7
gates to be s. till after. Neh 13:19
not the pit s. her mouth. Ps 69:15
s. their eyes, lest they. Isa 6:10
so he shall open and none shall s.; he shall s. and none shall. 22:22
for he hath s. their eyes. 44:18
and gates shall not be s. 45:1
kings shall s. their mouths. 52:15
thy gates shall not be s. day. 60:11
shall I s. the womb? saith. 66:9
Spirit said, Go s. thyself. Ezek 3:24
looked toward the east was s. 44:1
this gate shall be s., it shall not be opened, God . . . it shall be s. 2
the gate shall be s. the six. 46:1
the gate shall not be s. till the. 2
after his going forth, one shall s. 12
my God hath s. the lions'. Dan 6:22
prison truly found we s. Acts 5:23
power to s. heaven. Rev 11:6
gates shall not be s. by day. 21:25
see **door**

shut *up*
priest shall s. him up that hath. Lev 13:4, 5, 21, 26, 31, 33, 50, 54
the priest shall not s. him up. 11
priest shall s. up the house. 14:38
goeth in while the house is s. up. 46
the Lord's wrath be kindled, and he s. up the heaven. Deut 11:17
their rock the Lord had s. them up. Deut 32:30*
there is none s. up nor left. 36
Jericho was straitly s. up. Josh 6:1
Lord had s. up Hannah's womb. 1 Sam 1:5
because the Lord had s. up her. 6
hid them and s. up their calves. 6:10
concubines were s. up to day of. 2 Sam 20:3
when heaven is s. up. 1 Ki 8:35; 2 Chr 6:26; 7:13
from Jeroboam him that is s. up and. 1 Ki 14:10; 21:21; 2 Ki 9:8
was not any s. up. 2 Ki 14:26
king of Assyria s. him up. 17:4
Ahaz s. up doors of house. 2 Chr 28:24; 29:7
Shemaiah who was s. up. Neh 6:10
because it s. not up my. Job 3:10
if he cut off, and s. up, who? 11:10
or who hath s. up the sea? 38:8
his scales are s. up together. 41:15
hast not s. me up into. Ps 31:8
he in anger s. up his tender? 77:9
I am s. up, and I cannot come. 88:8
spring s. up, a fountain. S of S 4:12
every house is s. up, no. Isa 24:10
shall be s. up in the prison. 22
the south shall be s. up. Jer 13:19
as fire s. up in my bones. 20:9
the prophet was s. up by Zedekiah. 32:2, 3
word of Lord came, while he was s. up. 33:1; 39:15
I am s. up, I cannot go to the. 36:5
s. up the vision. Dan 8:26
s. up the words. 12:4
ye s. up kingdom of. Mat 23:13
he s. up John in prison. Luke 3:20
heaven was s. up three years. 4:25
many saints did I s. up. Acts 26:10
s. up unto the faith that. Gal 3:23
s. up the devil, and set. Rev 20:3

shutteth
he s. up a man, there. Job 12:14
he s. his eyes to devise. Pr 16:30
he that s. his lips is a man. 17:28
s. his eyes from seeing. Isa 33:15
also when I cry, he s. Lam 3:8
and s. up his bowels. 1 John 3:17
no man s.; and s., and no man openeth. Rev 3:7

shutting
about time of s. the gate. Josh 2:5

shuttle
swifter than a weaver's s. Job 7:6

sick
behold thy father is s. Gen 48:1
the law of her that is s. Lev 15:33
sent, she said, He is s. 1 Sam 19:14
three days ago I fell s. 30:13
the child, and it was s. 2 Sam 12:15
vexed, he fell s. for Tamar. 13:2
make thyself s. 5
Amnon made himself s. 6
son of Jeroboam fell s. 1 Ki 14:1
cometh to ask for son, for he is s. 5
son of the woman fell s. 17:17
down in Samaria, was s. 2 Ki 1:2
the king of Syria was s. 8:7
went to see Joram son of Ahab, because he was s. 29; 2 Chr 22:6
Elisha was fallen s. of. 2 Ki 13:14
was Hezekiah s. unto death. 20:1; 2 Chr 32:24; Isa 38:1
heard that Hezekiah had been s. 2 Ki 20:12; Isa 39:1
sad, seeing thou art not s.? Neh 2:2
when they were s., my clothing was sackcloth. Ps 35:13
maketh the heart s. Pr 13:12
stricken me, and I was not s. 23:35*
me with apples, I am s. of love. S of S 2:5
tell him that I am s. of love. 5:8
whole head is s. and the whole heart faint. Isa 1:5
shall not say, I am s. 33:24
when Hezekiah had been s. 38:9
behold them that are s. Jer 14:18
healed that which was s. Ezek 34:4
strengthen that which was s. 16
and was s. certain days. Dan 8:27
princes made him s. with. Hos 7:5
will I make thee s. in. Mi 6:13*
if ye offer the lame and s.? Mal 1:8
ye brought the lame, and the s. 13
brought to him all s. people. Mat 4:24
saw his wife's mother laid, and s. of a fever. 8:14; Mark 1:30
and healed all that were s. Mat 8:16; 14:14
not a physician, but they that are s. 9:12; Mark 2:17; Luke 5:31
heal the s., cleanse the lepers. Mat 10:8; Luke 9:2; 10:9
I was s. and ye visited. Mat 25:36
saw we thee s.? in prison? 39, 44
hands on a few s. folk. Mark 6:5
they laid the s. in the streets. 56; Acts 5:15
lay hands on the s. and. Mark 16:18
centurion's servant was s. Luke 7:2
whole that had been s. 10
nobleman's son was s. John 4:46
Lazarus of Bethany was s. 11:1, 2
he whom thou lovest is s. 3
he had heard he was s. he abode. 6
in those days Dorcas was s. and. Acts 9:37
unto the s. handkerchiefs. 19:12
father of Publius lay s. of a. 28:8
heard that he had been s. Phil 2:26
he was s. nigh unto death. 27
have I left at Miletum s. 2 Tim 4:20
is any s. let him call elders. Jas 5:14
prayer of faith shall save the s. 15
see **palsy**

sickle
as thou beginnest to put s. to. Deut 16:9
s. unto thy neighbour's corn. 23:25
cut off him that handleth s. Jer 50:16
put ye in the s. for the. Joel 3:13
he putteth in the s. Mark 4:29
and in his hand a sharp s. Rev 14:14
an angel crying, Thrust in thy s. 15
16, 18, 19
he also having a sharp s. 17

sickly
for this cause many are s. among. 1 Cor 11:30

sickness
I will take s. away from. Ex 23:25
man lie with a woman having her s. Lev 20:18
will take from thee all s. Deut 7:15
every s. that is not written. 28:61
whatsoever s. there be. 1 Ki 8:37; 2 Chr 6:28
his s. was so sore, there. 1 Ki 17:17
Elisha sick of the s. 2 Ki 13:14
great s. by disease of thy bowels, by reason of the s. 2 Chr 21:15
by reason of his s. so he died. 19
all his bed in his s. Ps 41:3
and wrath with his s. Eccl 5:17
was recovered of his s. Isa 38:9
will cut me off with pining s. 12
Ephraim saw his s., and Judah saw his wound. Hos 5:13
healing all manner of s. Mat 4:23
preaching and healing every s. 9:35
power to heal all manner of s. 10:1; Mark 3:15
this s. is not unto death. John 11:4

sicknesses
the sore s. and of long. Deut 28:59
when they see the s. Lord laid. 29:22
saying, Himself bare our s. Mat 8:17

side
shall set in the s. thereof. Gen 6:16
walked along by river s. Ex 2:5
blood on the two s. posts. 12:7, 22
blood on the lintel and s. posts. 23
Moses' hands, the one on the one s. and the other on the other s. 17:12
who is on Lord's s.? let him. 32:26
sword by his s. go in and out. 27*
he shall kill it on s. of. Lev 1:11
blood shall be wrung out at the s. 15
sin offering sprinkled on s. of. 5:9
s. and a wall on that s. Num 22:24

as gardens by the river's *s.* *Num* 24:6
inherit on yonder *s.* Jordan. 32:19
ask from one *s.* of heaven to the. *Deut* 4:32*
put the book of the law in the *s.* 31:26
a Levite sojourned on *s.* of Ephraim *Judg* 19:1, 18
fell backward by the *s.* *1 Sam* 4:18
put the mice in a coffer by the *s.* 6:8
I will shoot three arrows on the *s.* 20:20
and Abner sat by Saul's *s.* 25
sword into his fellow's *s.* *2 Sam* 2:16
came by way of the hill *s.* 13:34
on the hill *s.* over against. 16:13
Who is on my *s.*? who? *2 Ki* 9:32
David, and on thy *s.* *1 Chr* 12:18
Benjamin on his *s.* *2 Chr* 11:12*
his sword girded by his *s.* *Neh* 4:18
shall be ready at his *s.* *Job* 18:12
thousand shall fall at thy *s.* *Ps* 91:7
the Lord is on my *s.* I will. 118:6
the Lord who was on our *s.* 124:1, 2
the *s.* of their oppressors. *Eccl* 4:1
shall be nursed at thy *s.* *Isa* 60:4*
not turn from one *s.* to another. *Ezek* 4:8
days that thou shalt lie upon thy *s.* 9
writer's inkhorn by his *s.* 9:2, 3, 11
I will open the *s.* of Moab. 25:9
because ye have thrust with *s.* 34:21
it raised itself on one *s.* *Dan* 7:5
shall not stand on his *s.* 11:17
thieves, on either *s.* one. *John* 19:18
soldiers with a spear pierced his *s.* 34
them his hands and his *s.* 20:20
except I thrust my hand into his *s.* 25
and thrust it into my *s.* 27
the angel smote Peter on the *s.*, and raised him up. *Acts* 12:7
we went out by the river *s.* 16:13
on either *s.* of river was. *Rev* 22:2
see **chambers, left, sea, south, way, west**

every side

of Abiram on *every s.* *Num* 16:27
the trumpets on *every s.* *Judg* 7:18
delivered them from their enemies on *every s.* 8:34; *1 Sam* 12:11
enemies on *every s.* *1 Sam* 14:47
about him on *every s.* *1 Ki* 5:3
given me rest on *every s.* 4
hath he not given you rest on *every s.*? *1 Chr* 22:18
he hath given us rest on *every s.* *2 Chr* 14:7
Lord guided them on *every s.* 32:22
about all he hath on *every s.* *Job* 1:10
make him afraid on *every s.* 18:11
destroyed me on *every s.* I. 19:10
wicked walk on *every s.* *Ps* 12:8
fear was on *every s.* while. 31:13
little hills rejoice on *every s.* 65:12*
comfort me on *every s.* 71:21*
fear is on *every s.* *Jer* 6:25; 20:10 49:29
that they may come to thee on *every s.* *Ezek* 16:33
set against him on *every s.* 19:8
them against thee on *every s.* 23:22
sword upon her on *every s.* 28:23
swallowed you up on *every s.* 36:3
I will gather them on *every s.* 37:21
to my sacrifice on *every s.* 39:17
keep thee in on *every s.* *Luke* 19:43
we are troubled on *every s.* *2 Cor* 4:8; 7:5

farther side

farther s. of Jordan. *Mark* 10:1*

on this side

one cherub *on this s.*, other on that side. *Ex* 37:8
quails a day's journey *on this s.* *Num* 11:31
on this s. and on that side. 22:24
inheritance *on this s.* Jordan. 32:19 32*; 34:15*
refuge *on this s.* Jordan. 35:14*
some *on this s.* of Ai, and some on that side. *Josh* 8:22
Israel and judges stood *on this s.* 33
arrows are *on this s.* *1 Sam* 20:21
Saul went *on this s.* of the. 23:26
no portion *on this s.* the river. *Ezra* 4:16*
governor *on this s.* the river. 5:3* 6*, 6:13*; 8:36*
throne of the governor *on this s.* the river. *Neh* 3:7*
two wings, *on this s.* *Ezek* 1:23
two tables *on this s.* and two on that side. 40:39
on this s., four tables on that side. 41
on bank of river *on this s.* 47:12
stood other two, the one *on this s.* *Dan* 12:5
stealeth shall be cut off as *on this s.* ... sweareth on that side. *Zech* 5:3

on other side

your fathers dwelt *on* the *other s.* of the flood. *Josh* 24:2*
I and Jonathan will be *on* the *other s.* *1 Sam* 14:40
saw water *on other s.* *2 Ki* 3:22*
stood *on* one and *other s.* *2 Chr* 9:19
stoodest *on* the *other s.* *Ob* 11
found him *on* the *other s.* of the sea. *John* 6:25

right side

chamber was on *right s.* *1 Ki* 6:8
the *right s.* the house; set the sea on *right s.* 7:39; *2 Chr* 4:10
five candlesticks on the *right s.* *1 Ki* 7:49; *2 Chr* 4:8
of a lion on the *right s.* *Ezek* 1:10
lie again on thy *right s.* and shalt. 4:6
from under *right s.* of house. 47:1, 2
on *right s.* the bowl. *Zech* 4:3, 11
they saw a young man sitting on *right s.* of sepulchre. *Mark* 16:5
angel standing on *right s.* *Luke* 1:11
cast the net on the *right s.* *John* 21:6

sides

were written on both *s.* *Ex* 32:15
shall be thorns in your *s.* *Num* 33:55; *Judg* 2:3
be scourges in your *s.* *Josh* 23:13
needlework on both *s.* *Judg* 5:30
David and his men in *s.* of the cave. *1 Sam* 24:3*
peace on all *s.* round. *1 Ki* 4:24
beautiful is Zion on the *s.* *Ps* 48:2
wife as a fruitful vine by *s.* 128:3*
I will sit also in the *s.* *Isa* 14:13*
thou shalt be brought down to *s.* 15*
ye shall be borne upon her *s.* 66:12
nation raised from *s.* of the earth. *Jer* 6:22*
maketh her nest in the *s.* 48:28†
their calamity from all *s.* 49:32
upon their four *s.* *Ezek* 1:17; 10:11
whose graves are set in the *s.* 32:23*
these are his *s.* east and west. 48:1
say unto him that is by *s.* *Amos* 6:10*
Jonah was gone down into the *s.* of the ship. *Jonah* 1:5*

Sidon, called Zidon, *1 Chr* 1:13

Canaan begat *S.* his. *Gen* 10:15
Canaanites was from *S.* 19
Laish was far from *S.* *Judg* 18:28
done in Tyre and *S.* *Mat* 11:21
it shall be more tolerable for *S.* 22; *Luke* 10:13, 14
into the coasts of Tyre and *S.* behold, a woman. *Mat* 15:21; *Mark* 7:24
they about Tyre and *S.* came. *Mark* 3:8; *Luke* 6:17
the coasts of Tyre and *S.* *Mark* 7:31
sent, save to Sarepta a city of *S.* *Luke* 4:26
was displeased with them of *S.* *Acts* 12:20
next day we touched at *S.* 27:3

siege

cut to employ them in *s.* *Deut* 20:19
eat thy children in the *s.* 28:53
nothing left him in the *s.* 55, 57
whereon do ye trust, that ye abide in the *s.*? *2 Chr* 32:10
I will lay *s.* against thee. *Isa* 29:3
flesh of his friend in the *s.* *Jer* 19:9
lay *s.* against it and build a fort. *Ezek* 4:2, 3
days of the *s.* are fulfilled. 5:2
he hath laid *s.* against us. *Mi* 5:1
waters for the *s.*, fortify. *Nah* 3:14
trembling, when in the *s.* *Zech* 12:2

sieve

sift the nations with the *s.* of vanity. *Isa* 30:28
I will sift, like as corn is sifted in a *s.* *Amos* 9:9

sift

to *s.* the nations with. *Isa* 30:28
I will *s.* Israel as corn is. *Amos* 9:9
Satan hath desired to have you, that he may. *Luke* 22:31

sigh

all merry-hearted do *s.* *Isa* 24:7
her priests *s.* *Lam* 1:4
all her people *s.* 11
they have heard that I *s.* 21
foreheads of men that *s.* *Ezek* 9:4
breaking of thy loins, and with bitterness *s.* before their eyes. 21:6

sighed

Israel *s.* by reason of. *Ex* 2:23
up to heaven, he *s.* *Mark* 7:34
s. deeply in his spirit, and. 8:12

sighest

to thee, Wherefore *s.*? *Ezek* 21:7

sigheth

yea, she *s.* and turneth. *Lam* 1:8

sighing

my *s.* cometh before I eat. *Job* 3:24
for the *s.* of the needy. *Ps* 12:5
with grief, my years with *s.* 31:10
let the *s.* of the prisoner. 79:11
all the *s.* thereof have. *Isa* 21:2
sorrow and *s.* shall flee away. 35:10
I fainted in my *s.* and I. *Jer* 45:3

sighs

for my *s.* are many. *Lam* 1:22

sight

(*Revisions frequently change to* eyes)

that is pleasant to the *s.* *Gen* 2:9
turn and see this great *s.* *Ex* 3:3
s. of glory of Lord was like. 24:17*
the plague in *s.* be deeper. *Lev* 13:3*, 20*, 25*, 30*
in *s.* be not deeper. 4*, 31*, 32*, 34
if the plague in *s.* be lower. 14:37
in our own *s.* as grasshoppers, and so we were in their *s.* *Num* 13:33
give him charge in their *s.* 27:19
shalt be mad for *s.* *Deut* 28:34, 67
them from out of your *s.* *Josh* 23:5
did those great signs in our *s.* 24:17
reputed vile in your *s.*? *Job* 18:3
I am an alien in their *s.* 19:15
seed is established in their *s.* 21:8
them in the open *s.* of others. 34:26
be cast down at the *s.* of him? 41:9
the heathen in our *s.* *Ps* 79:10
better is the *s.* of the eyes. *Eccl* 6:9
prudent in their own *s.* *Isa* 5:21
he shall not judge after the *s.* 11:3
evil done in Zion in your *s.* *Jer* 51:24
shalt bake it with dung in their *s.* *Ezek* 4:12
remove by day in their *s.* 12:3
dig thou through the wall in their *s.* 5
in whose *s.* I made myself. 20:9
heathen in whose *s.* I brought. 14, 22
yourselves in your own *s.* 43; 36:31
a false divination in their *s.* 21:23
thereof, and write in their *s.* 43:11
s. thereof to end of. *Dan* 4:11, 20
whoredoms out of her *s.* *Hos* 2:2*
the blind receive their *s.*, the lame. *Mat* 11:5; 20:34; *Luke* 7:21
the recovering of *s.* to the blind. *Luke* 4:18
that came to that *s.* smote. 23:48
he vanished out of their *s.* 24:31
washed, and I received *s.* *John* 9:11
cloud received him out of their *s.* *Acts* 1:9
saw it, he wondered at the *s.* 7:31
was three days without *s.* 9:9
he received *s.* forthwith, arose. 18
walk by faith, not by *s.* *2 Cor* 5:7
so terrible was the *s.* *Heb* 12:21*

sight *of God*
good understanding in the *s. of God.* *Pr* 3:4
is abomination in the *s. of God.* *Luke* 16:15
right in the *s. of God* to. *Acts* 4:19
not right in the *s. of God.* 8:21
had in remembrance in the *s. of God.* 10:31
in the *s. of God* speak we. *2 Cor* 2:17
conscience in the *s. of God.* 4:2
our care for you in *s. of God.* 7:12
by the law in *s. of God.* *Gal* 3:11
remembering work of faith in *s. of God.* *1 Thes* 1:3
this is good and acceptable in the *s. of God.* *1 Tim* 2:3
thee charge in the *s. of God.* 6:13
which is in the *s. of God* of. *1 Pet* 3:4
see **Lord**

his **sight**
if thou wilt do that which is right in *his s.* *Ex* 15:26
if the plague in *his s.* be. *Lev* 13:5
scall be in *his s.* at a stay. 37
burn the heifer in *his s.* *Num* 19:5
he brought thee out in *his s.* *Deut* 4:37*
Lord departed out of *his s.* *Judg* 6:21
Lord, to do evil in *his s.*? *2 Sam* 12:9
went and made cakes in *his s.* 13:8
remove them out of *his s.* *2 Ki* 17:18, 20, 23; 24:3
do what is right in *his s.* *1 Chr* 19:13*
are not clean in *his s.* *Job* 15:15
stars are not pure in *his s.* 25:5
are far above out of *his s.* *Ps* 10:5
shall their blood be in *his s.* 72:14
to a man that is good in *his s.* *Eccl* 2:26
be not hasty to go out of *his s.* 8:3*
and we shall live in *his s.* *Hos* 6:2
immediately received *his s.* and. *Mark* 10:52; *Luke* 18:43
he had received *his s.* *John* 9:15, 18
he might receive *his s.* *Acts* 9:12
no flesh be justified in *his s.* *Rom* 3:20
present you holy in *his s.* *Col* 1:22
is manifest in *his s.* *Heb* 4:13
is well pleasing in *his s.* 13:21
things that are pleasing in *his s.* *1 John* 3:22

in the **sight**
grievous *in* Abraham's *s.* *Gen* 21:11
aught left *in the s.* of my lord. 47:18
signs *in the s.* of the people. *Ex* 4:30
he smote the waters *in the s.* 7:20
Moses sprinkled the ashes *in the s.* 9:8
great *in the s.* of Pharaoh's. 11:3
Moses did so *in the s.* of the. 17:6
come down *in the s.* of people. 19:11
fire by night *in the s.* of Israel. 40:38
shall be cut off *in the s.* *Lev* 20:17
out of Egypt *in the s.* of the. 26:45
ministered *in the s.* of Aaron. *Num* 3:4*
Eleazar went *in the s.* of. 20:27
woman *in the s.* of Moses. 25:6
went with high hand *in the s.* 33:3
is your wisdom *in the s.* of nations. *Deut* 4:6
Joshua *in the s.* of all Israel. 31:7
terror Moses shewed *in the s.* 34:12
to magnify thee *in the s.* of Israel. *Josh* 3:7; 4:14
he said, *In the s.* of Israel. 10:12
David accepted *in the s.* of the. *1 Sam* 18:5
lie with thy wives *in the s.* of this sun. *2 Sam* 12:11
in the s. of all Israel. *1 Chr* 28:8
Solomon *in the s.* of Israel. 29:25
Hezekiah magnified *in s.* of nations. *2 Chr* 32:23
in the s. of kings of Persia. *Ezra* 9:9
grant him mercy *in the s.* *Neh* 1:11
opened the book *in the s.* of all. 8:5
things did he *in the s.* of their fathers. *Ps* 78:12
he openly shewed *in the s.* of. 98:2
in vain net is spread *in the s.* *Pr* 1:17
beloved *in the s.* of my mother. *Pr* 4:3
walk *in the s.* of thine. *Eccl* 11:9
break the bottle *in the s.* *Jer* 19:10
I gave the evidence *in the s.* 32:12*
hid stones *in the s.* of the men. 43:9
execute judgements *in the s.* of the. *Ezek* 5:8
Jerusalem a reproach *in s.* of. 14
judgement on thee *in the s.* 16:41
name not polluted *in s.* of. 20:22
thee to ashes *in the s.* of all. 28:18
sanctified in them *in s.* of heathen. 25; 39:27
lay desolate *in the s.* of all. 36:34
I will discover lewdness *in s.* of. *Hos* 2:10
gave him wisdom *in the s.* *Acts* 7:10
provide things honest *in the s.* of all. *Rom* 12:17
come down *in s.* of men. *Rev* 13:13
miracles he had power to do *in s.* 14

my **sight**
bury my dead out of *my s.* *Gen* 23:4, 8
found grace in *my s.* *Ex* 33:12, 17
coming is good in *my s.* *1 Sam* 29:6
thou art good in *my s.* as an. 9
be base in *mine* own *s.* *2 Sam* 6:22
and dress the meat in *my s.* 13:5
me a couple of cakes in *my s.* 6
not fail thee a man in *my s.* *1 Ki* 8:25; *2 Chr* 6:16
hallowed for my name will I cast out of *my s.* *1 Ki* 9:7; *2 Chr* 7:20
do that is right in *my s.* *1 Ki* 11:38
which was evil in *my s.* *2 Ki* 21:15
Judah also out of *my s.* 23:27
shed much blood in *my s.* *1 Chr* 22:8
shall not tarry in *my s.* *Ps* 101:7
wast precious in *my s.* *Isa* 43:4
abominations out of *my s.* *Jer* 4:1
I will cast you of *my s.* as. 7:15
of Judah have done evil in *my s.* 30
cast them out of *my s.* and. 15:1
if it do evil in *my s.* that it. 18:10
and had done right in *my s.* 34:15
he went in *my s.* to fill. *Ezek* 10:2
up from the earth in *my s.* 19
be hid from *my s.* in the bottom. *Amos* 9:3
thee? Lord, that I might receive *my s.* *Mark* 10:51; *Luke* 18:41

thy **sight**
hath found grace in *thy s.* *Gen* 19:19
let it not be grievous in *thy s.* 21:12
If I have found grace in *thy s.* 33:10
47:29; *Ex* 33:13, 16; 34:9
Judg 6:17
rule with rigour in *thy s.* *Lev* 25:53
little in *thine* own *s.* *1 Sam* 15:17
cut off thine enemies out of *thy s.* *2 Sam* 7:9*
yet a small thing in *thy s.* 19
I have found grace in *thy s.* 14:22
let my life be precious in *thy s.* *2 Ki* 1:13, 14
I have done that which is good in *thy s.* 20:3; *Isa* 38:3
shall not stand in *thy s.* *Ps* 5:5
let heathen be judged in *thy s.* 9:19
heart be acceptable in *thy s.* 19:14
and done this evil in *thy s.* 51:4
who may stand in *thy s.*? 76:7
a thousand years in *thy s.* 90:4
for in *thy s.* shall no man. 143:2
been in *thy s.* O Lord. *Isa* 26:17
forgive not iniquity, neither blot out their sin from *thy s.* *Jer* 18:23
I am cast out of *thy s.* *Jonah* 2:4
so it seemed good in *thy s.* *Mat* 11:26; *Luke* 10:21
sinned against heaven and in *thy s.* *Luke* 15:21
unto him, Receive *thy s.* 18:42
that thou mightest receive *thy s.* *Acts* 9:17
Brother Saul, receive *thy s.* 22:13
see **favour, find**

sights
shall be fearful *s.* signs from. *Luke* 21:11*

sign
This word is used [1] *as we use the word sign or token,* Gen 9:12, 13. [2] *For a miracle,* Ex 4:17. [3] *The phenomena of the heavens,* Jer 10:2.

if they believe not nor hearken to voice of first *s.* they. *Ex* 4:8
to-morrow shall this *s.* be. 8:23
it shall be a *s.* to thee upon. 13:9
for it is a *s.* between me and you. 31:13, 17; *Ezek* 20:12, 20
and they shall be a *s.* *Num* 16:38
and they became a *s.* 26:10
bind them for a *s.* *Deut* 6:8; 11:18
a prophet, and giveth thee a *s.* 13:1
and *s.* come to pass whereof. 2
they shall be on thee for a *s.* 28:46
that this may be a *s.* *Josh* 4:6
shew me a *s.* that thou. *Judg* 6:17
appointed *s.* between Israel. 20:38
a *s.* to thee, in one day they shall. *1 Sam* 2:34; *2 Ki* 19:29
we will go up: and this shall be a *s.* *1 Sam* 14:10
gave a *s.* the same day, saying, This is the *s.* the Lord hath. *1 Ki* 13:3
according to the *s.* the man of. 5
shall be the *s.* that the? *2 Ki* 20:8
this *s.* shalt thou have of the Lord. 9
Isa 37:30; 38:7, 22
him, he gave him a *s.* *2 Chr* 32:24
ask thee a *s.* of the Lord. *Isa* 7:11
give you a *s.*; Behold a virgin shall. 14
be for a *s.* unto the Lord. 19:20
walked barefoot for a *s.* 20:3
a name, for an everlasting *s.* 55:13
I will set a *s.* among them. 66:19
set up a *s.* of fire in Beth-haccerem. *Jer* 6:1*
and this shall be a *s.* unto you. 44:29
Luke 2:12
this shall be a *s.* to the house of. *Ezek* 4:3
I have set thee for a *s.* to. 12:6, 11
I will make him a *s.* a proverb. 14:8
thus Ezekiel is a *s.* 24:24
thou shalt be a *s.* 27
then shall he set up a *s.* by it. 39:15
we would see a *s.* from. *Mat* 12:38
16:1; *Mark* 8:11; *Luke* 11:16
evil and adulterous generation seeketh after a *s.* *Mat* 12:39; 16:4
Mark 8:12; *Luke* 11:29
no *s.* be given to it, but the *s.* of the prophet Jonas. *Mat* 12:39
Mark 8:12; *Luke* 11:29, 30
be the *s.* of thy coming? *Mat* 24:3
shall appear the *s.* of the Son. 30
betrayed him gave them a *s.* 26:48
what *s.* when all these. *Mark* 13:4
for a *s.* which shall be. *Luke* 2:34
what *s.* shewest thou unto us? *John* 2:18; 6:30
a ship, whose *s.* was Castor and Pollux. *Acts* 28:11
s. of circumcision, a seal. *Rom* 4:11
for the Jews require a *s.*, and the Greeks seek. *1 Cor* 1:22
tongues are for a *s.*, not. 14:22
I saw another *s.* in heaven. *Rev* 15:1

sign, *verb*
decree, *s.* the writing. *Dan* 6:8

signed
king Darius *s.* the writing. *Dan* 6:9
knew that the writing was *s.* 10
hast thou not *s.* a decree? 12

signet
give me thy *s.* and. *Gen* 38:18, 25
engraver on stone, like engravings of a *s.* *Ex* 28:11, 21, 36; 39:14, 30
though Coniah were *s.* on. *Jer* 22:24
sealed it with his own *s.* *Dan* 6:17
and make thee as a *s.* *Hag* 2:23

signets
onyx stones graven as *s.* *Ex* 39:6

signification
none of them without *s.* *1 Cor* 14:10

signified
Agabus *s.* there should. *Acts* 11:28
s. it by his angel to his. *Rev* 1:1

signifieth
s. removing of those things shaken. Heb 12:27
signify
to s. the accomplishment of the. Acts 21:26*
s. thee to chief captain that. 23:15
and not to s. the crimes laid. 25:27
searching what the Spirit of Christ in them did s. 1 Pet 1:11
signifying
said, s. by what death he should die. John 12:33; 18:32; 21:19
the Holy Ghost this s. Heb 9:8
signs
for s. and for seasons. Gen 1:14
not believe these two s. Ex 4:9
in thy hand thou shalt do s. 17
all words of Lord and all s. which he. Ex 4:28, 30; Josh 24:17
I will multiply my s. in. Ex 7:3
mayest tell thy son my s. 10:2
for all the s. which I. Num 14:11
to take him a nation by s. Deut 4:34
26:8
Lord shewed s. on Egypt, on. 6:22
Neh 9:10; Ps 78:43
the great s. which thine. Deut 7:19; 29:3
in all s. which the Lord sent. 34:11
when these s. are come. 1 Sam 10:7
and all those s. came to pass. 9
set up their ensigns for s. Ps 74:4
we see not our s., there is no more. 9
shewed his s. among them. 105:27
I and the children are for s. Isa 8:18
be not dismayed at the s. Jer 10:2
which hast set s. and wonders. 32:20
Israel out of Egypt with s. 21
I thought it good to shew s. Dan 4:2
how great are his s.! how mighty! 3
he worketh s. in heaven and. 6:27
can ye not discern the s.? Mat 16:3
and false prophets, and shall shew great s. 24:24; Mark 13:22
these s. follow them. Mark 16:17
confirming the word with s. 20
made s. to his father. Luke 1:62
and great s. shall there be. 21:11
there shall be s. in the sun. 25
except ye see s. ye will. John 4:48
and many other s. truly did. 20:30
I will shew s. in the earth. Acts 2:19
a man approved of God by s. 22
many s. were done by the apostles. 43; 5:12
that s. may be done by the. 4:30
after he had shewed s. and. 7:36
beholding the s. done. 8:13
granted s. and wonders to be. 14:3
not wrought by me through mighty s. Rom 15:19; 2 Cor 12:12
working of Satan, with s. 2 Thes 2:9
bearing them witness with s. and. Heb 2:4
Sihon
S. would not suffer Israel to pass. Num 21:23; Judg 11:20
let the city of S. be. Num 21:27
gone out from the city of S. 28
do to him as thou didst to S. 34
Deut 3:2, 6
S. king of Heshbon would. Deut 2:30
behold, I have begun to give S. 31
S. came out against us. 32; 29:7
Judg 11:20
do to them as he did to S. Deut 31:4
all that he did to S. Josh 9:10
God delivered S. into. Judg 11:21
possessed the land of S. Neh 9:22
shall come from the midst of S. Jer 48:45
Sihon *king of the Amorites*
Israel sent messengers unto S. king of the Amorites. Num 21:21
Deut 2:26; Judg 11:19
Heshbon was a city of S. king of Amorites. Num 21:26; Josh 12:2
his daughters into captivity to S. king of Amorites. Num 21:29
as thou didst to S. king of Amorites. 34; Deut 3:2
slain S. king of the Amorites and. Deut 1:4; Ps 135:11; 136:19
cities of S. king of Amorites. Josh 13:10
kingdom of S. king of Amorites. 21
officer in country of S. king of Amorites. 1 Ki 4:19
Sihor
from S. which is before. Josh 13:3
to drink the waters of S. Jer 2:18
Silas
sent S. chief among the brethren. Acts 15:22, 27; 17:14
it pleased S. to abide there. 34
Paul chose S. 40
caught Paul and S. 16:19
at midnight Paul and S. prayed. 25
fell down before Paul and S. 29
consorted with Paul and S. 17:4
sent away S. by night. 10
receiving a commandment to S. 15
when S. was come. 18:5
silence
This word signifies not only the ordinary silence, or refraining from speaking; but also an entire ruin or destruction, a total subjection, Isa 15:1; Jer 8:14; *death and the grave,* Ps 94:17; 115:17.
before me, there was s. Job 4:16
men gave ear, and kept s. at. 29:21
lying lips be put to s. Ps 31:18*
I was dumb with s., I held. 39:2
my soul had almost dwelt in s. 94:17
any that go down into s. 115:17
to s.; Kir brought to s. Isa 15:1*
God hath put us to s. Jer 8:14
alone and keepeth s. Lam 3:28
cast them forth with s. Amos 8:3
had put Sadducees to s. Mat 22:34
was made a great s. he. Acts 21:40
in Hebrew, they kept more s. 22:2*
let woman learn in s. 1 Tim 2:11*
nor to usurp authority over the man, but to be in s. 12*
put to s. the ignorance. 1 Pet 2:15
there was s. in heaven. Rev 8:1
see keep, kept
silent
the wicked shall be s. 1 Sam 2:9
night season, and am not s. Ps 22:2
s. to me, lest if thou be s. 28:1*
sing praise to thee, not be s. 30:12
wicked be s. in the grave. 31:17
sit thou s. and get thee. Isa 47:5
cities, let us be s. there. Jer 8:14
be s. O all flesh, before. Zech 2:13
silk
her clothing is s. and. Pr 31:22
I covered thee with s. Ezek 16:10
thy raiment was of s. and. 13
their merchandise of s. Rev 18:12
silly
and envy slayeth the s. Job 5:2
Ephraim also is like a s. Hos 7:11
captive s. women laden. 2 Tim 3:6
Siloah, Siloam
the wall of pool of S. Neh 3:15
the tower of S. fell. Luke 13:4
wash in the pool of S. John 9:7, 11
Silvanus
among you by me and S. 2 Cor 1:19
Paul, S. 1 Thes 1:1; 2 Thes 1:1
by S. a faithful brother. 1 Pet 5:12
silver
is worth 400 shekels of s. Gen 23:15
weighed 400 shekels of s. 16
make gods of s. or gold. Ex 20:23
sockets of s. 26:19, 21, 25, 32
36:24, 26, 30, 36
hooks shall be of s. 27:17; 38:19
they did offer an offering of s. 35:24
s. of them that were numbered of. 38:25
estimation by shekels of s. Lev 5:15
of male 50 shekels of s. 27:3
female three shekels of s. 6
barley seed at fifty shekels of s. 16
was one s. charger, one s. bowl of 70 shekels. Num 7:13, 19, 25
31, 37, 43, 49, 55, 61, 67, 73, 79
chargers of s., twelve s. Num 7:84
each charger of s. weighing. 85
make thee two trumpets of s. 10:2
him in 100 shekels of s. Deut 22:19
damsel's father 50 shekels of s. 29
I saw 200 shekels of s. Josh 7:21
and the s. under it. 22, 24
1100 shekels of s. that were taken from thee, behold, s. Judg 17:2
when he had restored the s. 3
gave s. to the founder. 4
I will give thee ten shekels of s. 10
fourth part of a shekel of s. 1 Sam 9:8
given 10 shekels of s. 2 Sam 18:11
receive 1000 shekels of s. 12
oxen for 50 shekels of s. 24:24
none were of s. 1 Ki 10:21
2 Chr 9:20
s. to be in Jerusalem. 1 Ki 10:27
shalt pay a talent of s. 20:39
I pray thee, a talent of s. 2 Ki 5:22
each man fifty shekels of s. 15:20
Hezekiah gave him all the s. 18:15
that Hilkiah may sum the s. 22:4*
s. also for all instruments of s. 1 Chr 28:14; 29:2, 5
for candlesticks of s. 28:15
for every bason of s. 17
brought Jehoshaphat presents of s. 2 Chr 17:11
had taken 40 shekels of s. Neh 5:15
who filled houses with s. Job 3:15
thou shalt have plenty of s. 22:25
though he heap up s. as the. 27:16
innocent shall divide the s. 17
shall s. be weighed for price. 28:15
words are pure, as s. tried. Ps 12:6
O God, hast tried us, as s. 66:10
if thou seekest her as s. and. Pr 2:4
wisdom is better than . . . of s. 3:14
receive instruction, and not s. 8:10
and my revenue than choice s. 19
of the just is as choice s. 10:20
chosen rather than s. 16:16
fining pot is for s., and the. 17:3
away the dross from the s. 25:4
he that loveth s. shall not be satisfied with s. Eccl 5:10
on her a palace of s. S of S 8:9
thy s. is become dross. Isa 1:22
covering of thy images of s. 30:22
refined thee, but not with s. 48:10
for iron I will bring s. and for. 60:17
reprobate s. shall men. Jer 6:30
s. spread into plates is brought. 10:9
even seventeen shekels of s. 32:9
are even the dross of s. Ezek 22:18
as they gather s., brass, and iron. 20
as s. is melted in the midst. 22
with s. Tarshish traded in. 27:12
breast and arms were of s. Dan 2:32
pleasant places for s. Hos 9:6
molten images of their s. 13:2
sold the righteous for s. Amos 2:6
that we may buy poor for s. 8:6
howl, all they that bear s. Zeph 1:11
Tyrus heaped up s. as dust. Zech 9:3
refine them as s. is refined. 13:9
as a refiner and purifier of s. Mal 3:3
see fillets, gold, pieces
silver, *adjective*
put my s. cup in sack's mouth. Gen 44:2
covered with s. dross. Pr 26:23
or ever s. cord be loosed or the golden bowl be broken. Eccl 12:6
the goldsmith casteth s. Isa 40:19
chief priests took the s. Mat 27:6
Demetrius made s. shrines. Acts 19:24
talents of **silver**
for two talents of s. 1 Ki 16:24
with him ten talents of s. 2 Ki 5:5
and bound two talents of s. 23
gave Pul 1000 talents of s. 15:19
sent 1000 talents of s. 1 Chr 19:6
thousand thousand talents of s. 22:14
7000 talents of refined s. 29:4
mighty men for 100 talents of s. 2 Chr 25:6
gave Jotham 100 talents of s. 27:5
land in 100 talents of s. 36:3

decree it be done to 100 *talents of s.* *Ezra* 7:22
to their hand 650 *talents of s.* 8:26
ten thousand *talents of s.* *Esth* 3:9

vessels of **silver**

all the *s. vessels* weighed 2400 shekels. *Num* 7:85
with him *vessels of s.* *2 Sam* 8:10
his present, *vessels of s.* *1 Ki* 10:25
not made *vessels of s.* *2 Ki* 12:13
all manner of *vessels of s.*, gold and brass. *1 Chr* 18:10; *2 Chr* 24:14
hands with *vessels of s.* *Ezra* 1:6, 11
vessels of gold and *s.* of the. 5:14
let the golden and *s. vessels.* 6:5
I weighed *s. vessels.* 8:26
bring golden and *s. vessels.* *Dan* 5:2
precious *vessels of s.* and gold. 11:8
see **vessels**

silverlings

thousand vines at a thousand *s.* *Isa* 7:23

silversmith

Demetrius a *s.* made. *Acts* 19:24

Simeon

called his name *S.* *Gen* 29:33
S. and Levi took each man. 34:25
S. son of Leah. 35:23
Joseph took from them *S.* 42:24
S. is not. 36
and he brought *S.* out unto. 43:23
the sons of *S.* 46:10; *Ex* 6:15
Num 1:22; 26:12; *1 Chr* 4:24, 42
12:25
Reuben and *S.* they shall. *Gen* 48:5
S. and Levi are brethren. 49:5
S. son of Israel. *Ex* 1:2
prince of *S.* was Shelumiel. *Num* 1:6; 2:12; 7:36
S. Levi and Judah stand to bless. *Deut* 27:12
lot came forth to *S.* *Josh* 19:1
S. had their inheritance within. 9
S. went with Judah. *Judg* 1:3
Judah with *S.* 17
the strangers out of *S.* *2 Chr* 15:9
so did Josiah in the cities of *S.* 34:6
S. have a portion. *Ezek* 48:24
one gate of *S.* 33
whose name was *S.* *Luke* 2:25
S. blessed Joseph and Mary. 34
which was the son of *S.* 3:30
at Antioch, *S.* that was. *Acts* 13:1
S. hath declared how God. 15:14

tribe of **Simeon**

tribe of S. numbered. *Num* 1:23
the *tribe of S.* shall pitch. 2:12
over the host of the *tribe of S.* 10:19
of the *tribe of S.* Shaphat. 13:5
of *tribe of S.* Shemuel to. 34:20
second lot came out for the *tribe of S.* *Josh* 19:1
inheritance of the *tribe of S.* 8
Levites had out of *tribe of S.* 21:4
9; *1 Chr* 6:65
of the *tribe of S.* were. *Rev* 7:7

similitude

the *s.* of the Lord shall. *Num* 12:8*
heard voice of words, but saw no *s.* *Deut* 4:12* 15*
lest ye make the *s.* of any figure. 16*
under it was *s.* of oxen. *2 Chr* 4:3
glory into *s.* of an ox. *Ps* 106:20*
corner stones polished after *s.* 144:12
one like the *s.* of the. *Dan* 10:16
after the *s.* of Adam's. *Rom* 5:14*
after *s.* of Melchizedek ariseth. *Heb* 7:15*
made after the *s.* of God. *Jas* 3:9*

similitudes

I have used *s.* by ministry of. *Hos* 12:10

Simon

S. the Canaanite. *Mat* 10:4
Mark 3:18
his brethren James, Joses, and *S.* *Mat* 13:55; *Mark* 6:3
blessed art thou, *S.* Bar-jona. *Mat* 16:17
what thinkest thou, *S.* of? 17:25
in the house of *S.* the leper. *Mat* 26:6
Mark 14:3
man of Cyrene, *S.* by. *Mat* 27:32
Mark 15:21; *Luke* 23:26
they entered into the house of *S.* *Mark* 1:29; *Luke* 4:38
S. sleepest thou? *Mark* 14:37
the ships, which was *S.*'s. *Luke* 5:3
he said unto *S.* Launch out into. 4
John who were partners with *S.* 10
S. called Zelotes. 6:15; *Acts* 1:13
S. I have somewhat to. *Luke* 7:40
S. S. Satan hath desired to. 22:31
and hath appeared to *S.* 24:34
his own brother *S.* *John* 1:41
Jesus said, Thou art *S.* the son. 42
Judas Iscariot the son of *S.* 6:71
12:4; 13:2, 26
S. son of Jonas, lovest thou me? 21:15, 16, 17
a man, *S.* who before. *Acts* 8:9
then *S.* himself believed also. 13
Peter tarried many days at Joppa with one *S.* 9:43; 10:6, 17, 32
see **Peter**

simple

[1] *Undesigning, straightforward,* Rom 16:19. [2] *Ignorant, yet sincere and willing to be taught,* Prov 9:4. [3] *Silly, foolish, credulous, easily deceived with the smooth words and fair pretences of false and deceitful men,* Pr 14:15; 22:3.

law . . . making wise the *s.* *Ps* 19:7
Lord preserveth the *s.*: I was. 116:6
understanding to the *s.* 119:130
give subtilty to *s.*, to young. *Pr* 1:4
how long, ye *s.* ones, will ye? 22
the turning away of the *s.* shall. 32
among the *s.* ones a young. 7:7
O ye *s.* understand wisdom. 8:5
whoso is *s.* let him turn. 9:4, 16
a foolish woman is *s.* and. 13
s. believeth every word. 14:15
the *s.* inherit folly. 18
the *s.* will beware. 19:25
the scorner is punished, the *s.* 21:11
the *s.* pass on and are. 22:3; 27:12
do for him that is *s.* *Ezek* 45:20
deceive the hearts of *s.* *Rom* 16:18*
have you wise unto good, and *s.* 19

simplicity

they went in their *s.* *2 Sam* 15:11
simple ones, will ye love *s.*? *Pr* 1:22
let him do it with *s.* *Rom* 12:8*
in *s.* we had our. *2 Cor* 1:12*
be corrupted from the *s.* that. 11:3

sin

Any thought, word, action, omission, or desire, contrary to the law of God. Sin is taken both for the guilt and punishment of sin, Ps 32:1; Mat 9:2.

doest not well, *s.* lieth. *Gen* 4:7
forgiving iniquity, transgression, and *s.* *Ex* 34:7
if priest *s.* according to *s.* *Lev* 4:3
when *s.* is known, congregation. 14
offereth it for *s.* 6:26; 9:15
and not suffer *s.* upon thy. 19:17
the *s.* which he hath done shall. 22
or woman shall commit *s.* *Num* 5:6
thee lay not the *s.* upon us. 12:11
it is a purification for *s.* 19:9, 17
our father died in his own *s.* 27:3
he cry unto the Lord . . . and it be *s.* unto thee. *Deut* 15:9; 24:15
shall not rise up for any *s.* 19:15
committed *s.* worthy of death. 21:22
there is in damsel no *s.* 22:26
it, and it would be *s.* in thee. 23:21
to vow, it shall be no *s.* 22
be put to death for his own *s.* 24:16
2 Ki 14:6; *2 Chr* 25:4
for rebellion is as the *s.* *1 Sam* 15:23
forgive *s.* of thy people. *1 Ki* 8:34
forgive the *s.* of thy servants. 36
2 Chr 6:25, 27
this thing became a *s.* *1 Ki* 12:30; 13:34
the *s.* money was not. *2 Ki* 12:16
his bones are full of *s.* *Job* 20:11
blessed is he whose *s.* *Ps* 32:1
and in *s.* did my mother. *Ps* 51:5
s. of their mouth let them. 59:12
and let his prayer become *s.* 109:7
let not the *s.* of his mother. 14
the wicked tendeth to *s.* *Pr* 10:16
of words there wanteth not *s.* 19
fools make a mock at *s.* but. 14:9
s. is a reproach to any people. 34
plowing of the wicked is *s.* 21:4
thought of foolishness is *s.* 24:9
woe to them that draw *s.* *Isa* 5:18
that they may add *s.* to *s.* 30:1
your hands have made for *s.* 31:7
make his soul an offering for *s.* 53:10
he bare the *s.* of many, and. 12
s. of Judah written with. *Jer* 17:1
I will give thy high places for *s.* 3
their land was filled with *s.* 51:5
punishment of the *s.* of. *Lam* 4:6
eat up *s.* of my people. *Hos* 4:8
the *s.* of Israel shall be. 10:8
none iniquity in me that were *s.* 12:8
that swear by the *s.* of. *Amos* 8:14
she is the beginning of *s.* *Mi* 1:13
fruit of my body for *s.* of my. 6:7
a fountain opened for *s.* *Zech* 13:1
all manner of *s.* shall be. *Mat* 12:31
which taketh away the *s.* *John* 1:29
he that is without *s.* among. 8:7
committeth *s.* is the servant of *s.* 34
blind, he should have no *s.* 9:41
they had not had *s.* 15:22, 24
will reprove the world of *s.* 16:8
of *s.* because they believe not. 9
me unto thee hath greater *s.* 19:11
Lord, lay not this *s.* to. *Acts* 7:60
Gentiles are all under *s.* *Rom* 3:9
by the law is the knowledge of *s.* 20
blessed are they whose *s.* is. 4:7
the world, and death by *s.* 5:12
the law *s.* was in the world. 13
s. abounded, grace much more. 20
that as *s.* reigned unto death. 21
say? shall we continue in *s.*? 6:1
how shall we that are dead to *s.*? 2
the body of *s.* might be destroyed . . . we should not serve *s.* 6
that is dead is freed from *s.* 7
that he died, he died unto *s.* once. 10
to be dead indeed unto *s.* 11
let not *s.* therefore reign in your. 12
members as instruments to *s.* 13
for *s.* shall not have dominion. 14
servants ye are . . . whether of *s.* 16
ye were the servants of *s.* 17
being then made free from *s.* 18, 22
when ye were the servants of *s.* 20
for wages of *s.* is death, but the. 23
is the law *s.*? God forbid. Nay, I had not known *s.* 7:7
s. taking occasion wrought in me . . . for without the law *s.* was. 8
commandment came, *s.* revived. 9
for *s.* by the commandment. 11
s., that it might appear *s.*, that *s.* 13
but I am carnal, sold under *s.* 14
but *s.* that dwelleth in me. 17, 20
me into captivity to the law of *s.* 23
but with the flesh, the law of *s.* 25
and for *s.*, condemned *s.* in. 8:3
body is dead because of *s.* 10
is not of faith, is *s.* 14:23
every *s.* a man doth is. *1 Cor* 6:18
the sting of death is *s.* and the strength of *s.* is the law. 15:56
made him to be *s.* for us, who knew no *s.* *2 Cor* 5:21
Christ the minister of *s.*? *Gal* 2:17
hath concluded all under *s.* 3:22
man of *s.* be revealed. *2 Thes* 2:3
through the deceitfulness of *s.* *Heb* 3:13
like as we are, yet without *s.* 4:15
he appeared to put away *s.* 9:26
he shall appear without *s.* unto. 28
in sacrifices for *s.* thou hast. 10:6
offering for *s.* thou wouldest not. 8
is no more offering for *s.* 18
than to enjoy pleasures of *s.* 11:25
let us lay aside the *s.* that doth. 12:1
not yet resisted, striving against *s.* 4
those beasts, for *s.* are burned. 13:11
lust conceived, it bringeth forth *s.*: and *s.*, when finished. *Jas* 1:15

to persons, ye commit *s.* *Jas* 2:9
doeth not good, to him it is *s.* 4:17
did no *s.* neither was. *1 Pet* 2:22
flesh hath ceased from *s.* 4:1
cannot cease from *s.* *2 Pet* 2:14
the blood of Jesus Christ cleanseth us from all *s.* *1 John* 1:7
if we say we have no *s.* we. 8
committteth *s.* transgresseth also the law, for *s.* is the. 3:4
and in him is no *s.* 5
committeth *s.* is of the devil. 8
born of God doth not commit *s.* 9
his brother *s.* a *s.* which is not to death. There is a *s.* unto. 5:16
all unrighteousness is *s.* and there is a *s.* not unto death. 17
see **bear, offering**

sin, *verb*

how can I do this great wickedness and *s.* against God? *Gen* 39:9
Reuben said, Do not *s.* 42:22
before you, that ye *s.* not. *Ex* 20:20
make thee *s.* against me. 23:33
s. through ignorance against commandments. *Lev* 4:2
if the priest *s.* 3
if congregation *s.* 13
if any one of the common people *s.* 27
if a soul *s.* and hear the voice. 5:1
if a soul commit a trespass and *s.* 15, 17; *Num* 15:27
if a soul *s.* and lie unto. *Lev* 6:2
shall one man *s.* and wilt thou be? *Num* 16:22
so should you *s.* against Lord. *Deut* 20:18
shalt not cause the land to *s.* 24:4
s. against another; if a man *s.* against the Lord, who shall? *1 Sam* 2:25
God forbid I should *s.* in. 12:23
behold, the people *s.* against. 14:33
slay them, and *s.* not in eating. 34
let not the king *s.* against. 19:4
wherefore wilt thou *s.* against? 5
if they *s.* against thee. *1 Ki* 8:46
2 Chr 6:36
made Judah to *s.* with idols. *2 Ki* 21:11
if a man *s.* against his. *2 Chr* 6:22
afraid, and do so, and *s.* *Neh* 6:13
did not Solomon *s.* by these? 13:26
in all this did not Job *s.* *Job* 2:10
thy habitation and not *s.* 5:24
if I *s.*, then thou markest me. 10:14
I suffered my mouth to *s.* 31:30
stand in awe, and *s.* not. *Ps* 4:4
I will take heed, that I *s.* not. 39:1
I might not *s.* against thee. 119:11
not thy mouth to cause thy flesh to *s.* *Eccl* 5:6
to cause Judah to *s.* *Jer* 32:35
righteous *s.* not, and he doth not *s.* *Ezek* 3:21
made many altars to *s.*, altars shall be unto him to *s.* *Hos* 8:11
and now they *s.* more and. 13:2
oft shall my brother *s.*? *Mat* 18:21
s. no more, lest a worse. *John* 5:14
do I condemn thee, *s.* no. 8:11
who did *s.*, this man, or his? 9:2
shall we *s.* because we are not? *Rom* 6:15
s. so against the brethren and wound their conscience, ye *s.* *1 Cor* 8:12
righteousness, and *s.* not. 15:34
be ye angry, and *s.* not. *Eph* 4:26
them that *s.* rebuke. *1 Tim* 5:20
if we *s.* wilfully after. *Heb* 10:26
that ye *s.* not, and if any man *s.* we. *1 John* 2:1
cannot *s.* because he is born of. 3:9
if . . . *s.* not unto death, he shall give him life for them that *s.* 5:16
see **Israel**

great **sin**

and my kingdom *great s.* *Gen* 20:9
brought this *great s.* on them. *Ex* 32:21
said, Ye have sinned a *great s.* 30
this people have sinned a *great s.* 31
s. of the young men was very *great.* *1 Sam* 2:17
Jeroboam made them sin a *great s.* *2 Ki* 17:21

his **sin**

bring for *his s.* he sinned. *Lev* 4:3
or if *his s.* come to his knowledge. 23, 28
atonement for *his s.* and it shall be forgiven. 4:26, 35; 5:6, 10, 13
a kid of the goats for *his s.* 28
his trespass offering for *his s.* 5:6
Nadab walked in the way of *his s.* *1 Ki* 15:26
in the way of Jeroboam and *his s.* 34
Zimri in *his s.* which he did. 16:19
Omri walked in *his s.* 26
beside *his s.* wherewith. *2 Ki* 21:16
acts of Manasseh, and *his s.* 17
all *his s.* before he was humbled. *2 Chr* 33:19
addeth rebellion to *his s.* *Job* 34:37
fruit to take away *his s.* *Isa* 27:9
he shall die in *his s.* *Ezek* 3:20
18:24
if he turn from *his s.* and. 33:14
bound up; *his s.* is hid. *Hos* 13:12
to declare to Israel *his s.* *Mi* 3:8

my **sin**

what is *my s.* that thou hast? *Gen* 31:36
therefore forgive *my s.* *Ex* 10:17
I pray thee, pardon *my s.*, and turn again. *1 Sam* 15:25
what is *my s.* before thy father? 20:1
come to call *my s.* to? *1 Ki* 17:18
thou searchest after *my s.* *Job* 10:6
know transgression and *my s.* 13:23
thou not watch over *my s.*? 14:16
if I be cleansed from *my s.*? 35:3
my s. and iniquity to thee, and thou . . . iniquity of *my s.* *Ps* 32:5
in my bones because of *my s.* 38:3
for I will be sorry for *my s.* 18
cleanse me from *my s.* 51:2
my s. is ever before me. 3
not for *my s.* O Lord. 59:3
I am pure from *my s.*? *Pr* 20:9
I was confessing *my s.* *Dan* 9:20
see **offering**

our **sin**

our iniquity and *our s.* *Ex* 34:9
what is *our s.* we have? *Jer* 16:10

their **sin**

Lord said, Because *their s.* is very. *Gen* 18:20
forgive, I pray thee, *their s.* 50:17
2 Chr 7:14
if thou wilt forgive *their s.* *Ex* 32:32
when I visit, I will visit *their s.* 34
they shall confess *their s.* *Num* 5:7
look not unto the stubbornness, nor to *their s.* *Deut* 9:27
if they turn from *their s.* *1 Ki* 8:35
2 Chr 6:26
let not *their s.* be blotted. *Neh* 4:5
hast covered all *their s.* 85:2
declare *their s.* as Sodom. *Isa* 3:9
I will recompense *their s.* double. *Jer* 16:18
neither blot out *their s.* from. 18:23
and I will remember *their s.* 31:34
may forgive their iniquity and *their s.* 36:3
no cloke for *their s.* *John* 15:22

thy **sin**

hath put away *thy s.* *2 Sam* 12:13
is taken away, *thy s.* is purged. *Isa* 6:7

your **sin**

atonement for *your s.* *Ex* 32:30
be sure *your s.* will find you out. *Num* 32:23
I took *your s.*, the calf which ye. *Deut* 9:21
ye say, We see; therefore *your s.* remaineth. *John* 9:41
see **Israel**

Sin

into the wilderness of *S.* *Ex* 16:1
Israel journeyed from *S.* 17:1
Num 33:12
pour my fury upon *S.* *Ezek* 30:15
S. shall have great pain, No shall. 16

Sinai

Lord came from *S.* unto. *Deut* 33:2
melted, even that *S.* *Judg* 5:5
S. was moved at the. *Ps* 68:8
the Lord is among them as in *S.* 17
see **mount**

since

the Lord hath blessed thee *s.* my coming. *Gen* 30:30
and I saw him not *s.* 44:28
let me die, *s.* I have seen. 46:30
s. I came to Pharaoh. *Ex* 5:23
hail, such as not in Egypt *s.* the. 9:18
Egypt, *s.* it became a nation. 24
ridden ever *s.* I was thine. *Num* 22:30
arose not a prophet *s.* *Deut* 34:10
swear, *s.* I have shewed. *Josh* 2:12
Lord kept me alive, even *s.* 14:10
all that thou hast done . . . *s.* death of thy husband. *Ruth* 2:11
s. I said, I have invited. *1 Sam* 9:24
three days *s.* I came out. 21:5
I found no fault in him *s.* he. 29:3
s. the time that I brought. *2 Sam* 7:6
and *s.* I commanded judges. 11
1 Chr 17:10
s. the time of Solomon. *2 Chr* 30:26
s. the people began to bring. 31:10
s. the days of Esar-haddon king. *Ezra* 4:2
s. that time till now hath it. 5:16
s. days of our fathers have we. 9:7
s. man was placed upon. *Job* 20:4
commanded morning *s.* thy days? 38:12
s. thou art laid down. *Isa* 14:8
concerning Moab *s.* that time. 16:13
s. thou wast precious in my. 43:4
s. I appointed the ancient. 44:7
s. the beginning men have not. 64:4
s. they return not from. *Jer* 15:7
for *s.* I spake, I cried out, I. 20:8
but *s.* ye say, the burden of. 23:38
s. I spake against him, I. 31:20
s. we left off to burn incense. 44:18
s. thou speakest of him. 48:27
as never was *s.* there. *Dan* 12:1
s. those days were when one came. *Hag* 2:16
not *s.* the beginning. *Mat* 24:21
long is it ago *s.* this came to him? *Mark* 9:21
been *s.* the world began. *Luke* 1:70
John 9:32
s. the time I came in, she hath not. *Luke* 7:45
s. that time kingdom of God. 16:16
is the third day *s.* these things. 24:21
s. the world began. *Acts* 3:21
Rom 16:25
received the Holy Ghost *s.* ye believed? *Acts* 19:2
yet but twelve days *s.* I went. 24:11
for *s.* by man came death, by man. *1 Cor* 15:21
s. ye seek a proof of Christ in me. *2 Cor* 13:3
s. we heard of your faith. *Col* 1:4
word of oath which was *s.* the law. *Heb* 7:28
for *s.* the fathers fell asleep, all. *2 Pet* 3:4
as was not *s.* men were. *Rev* 16:18
see **day**

sincere

The Latin word, sincerus, *is derived from* sine *and* cera, *without wax, honey separated from the wax, or pure honey. In the scripture* sincere *signifies pure, or without mixture,* Phil 1:10; 1 Pet 2:1. Sincerity *is opposed to double-mindedness or deceit, when the sentiments of the heart are contrary to the language of the mouth,* 1 Cor 5:8.

ye may be *s.* till day. *Phil* 1:10
as babes, desire *s.* milk. *1 Pet* 2:2*

sincerely
now if ye have done truly and *s.* *Judg* 9:16*, 19*
one preach Christ, not *s.* *Phil* 1:16*

sincerity
serve the Lord in *s.* and. *Josh* 24:14
unleavened bread of *s.* *1 Cor* 5:8
in godly *s.* we have had. *2 Cor* 1:12
but as of *s.* in the sight of God. 2:17
to prove *s.* of your love. 8:8
them that love our Lord Jesus in *s.* *Eph* 6:24
doctrine shewing gravity, *s.* *Tit* 2:7

sinew
Israel eat not of the *s.* that shrank . . . Jacob in the *s.* *Gen* 32:32*
thy neck is an iron *s.* *Isa* 48:4

sinews
hast fenced me with bones and *s.* *Job* 10:11
pierced, and my *s.* take no. 30:17*
the *s.* of his stones are. 40:17
I will lay *s.* upon you. *Ezek* 37:6
the *s.* and the flesh came up. 8

sinful
an increase of *s.* men. *Num* 32:14
ah *s.* nation, a people. *Isa* 1:4
eyes of the Lord are on the *s.* kingdom. *Amos* 9:8
be ashamed in this *s.* generation. *Mark* 8:38
for I am a *s.* man, O Lord. *Luke* 5:8
into the hands of *s.* men. 24:7
that sin might become exceeding *s.* *Rom* 7:13
Son in the likeness of *s.* flesh. 8:3

sing
s. to the Lord. *Ex* 15:21
1 Chr 16:23; *Ps* 30:4; 95:1; 96:1
2; 98:1; 147:7; 149:1; *Isa* 12:5
noise of them that *s.* *Ex* 32:18
spring up, O well, *s.* ye. *Num* 21:17
did they not *s.* one? *1 Sam* 21:11
unto him, *s.* psalms. *1 Chr* 16:9
trees of the wood *s.* out. 33
when they began to *s.* *2 Chr* 20:22
commanded the Levites to *s.* 29:30
widow's heart to *s.* for. *Job* 29:13
so will we *s.* and praise. *Ps* 21:13
praise the Lord, *s.* unto him. 33:2
s. unto him a new song. 3; *Isa* 42:10
my tongue *s.* of thy righteousness. *Ps* 51:14; 145:7
shout for joy, they also *s.* 65:13
s. forth the honour of his name. 66:2
the earth *s.* to thee, they shall *s.* 4
nations be glad and *s.* for. 67:4
s. to God, ye kingdoms of. 68:32
to thee will I *s.* with the harp. 71:22
98:5
s. aloud unto God our strength. 81:1
the fowls which *s.* among the. 104:12
s. unto him, *s.* psalms unto. 105:2
saying, *S.* us one of the songs. 137:3
how shall we *s.* Lord's song in a? 4
yea, they shall *s.* in the ways. 138:5
let the saints *s.* aloud upon. 149:5
but the righteous doth *s.* *Pr* 29:6
seventy years shall Tyre *s.* *Isa* 23:15
they shall *s.* for the majesty. 24:14
awake and *s.* ye that dwell. 26:19
in that day *s.* ye unto her. 27:2
the tongue of the dumb *s.* 35:6
therefore we will *s.* my songs. 38:20
inhabitants of the rock *s.* 42:11
s. for Lord hath done it. 44:23
49:13
voice together shall they *s.* 52:8
s. to the Lord, ye waste places. 9
s. O barren, thou that didst. 54:1
my servants shall *s.* for joy. 65:14
s. with gladness for Jacob. *Jer* 31:7
they shall come and *s.* in the. 12
all that is therein shall *s.* 51:48
ships of Tarshish did *s.* *Ezek* 27:25
shall *s.* as in the days. *Hos* 2:15
their voice shall *s.* in. *Zeph* 2:14
s. O daughter. 3:14; *Zech* 2:10
merry? let him *s.* psalms. *Jas* 5:13
they *s.* the song of Moses. *Rev* 15:3

I will sing
I will s. to the Lord. *Ex* 15:1
Judg 5:3; *Ps* 13:6
my heart is fixed, *I will s.* *Ps* 57:7
I will s. unto thee among the. 9
I will s. of thy power, of. 59:16; 89:1
O my strength, *will I s.* for God. 17
I will s. of mercy and judgement. 101:1
I will s. unto the Lord as. 104:33
I will s. a new song unto. 144:9
will I s. to my wellbeloved a song. *Isa* 5:1
for this cause *will I s.* *Rom* 15:9
I will s. with the spirit, and *I will s.* with understanding. *1 Cor* 14:15
see **praise, praises**

singed
nor an hair of their head *s.* *Dan* 3:27

singer
Heman a *s.* the son. *1 Chr* 6:33
to chief *s.* on my stringed instruments. *Hab* 3:19*

singers
king made psalteries for *s.* *1 Ki* 10:12; *2 Chr* 9:11
these are the *s.*, chief of the Levites. *1 Chr* 9:33; 15:16
s. were appointed to sound. 15:19
and the *s.* had fine linen. 27
the trumpeters and *s.* *2 Chr* 5:13
Jehoshaphat appointed *s.* unto. 20:21
rejoiced and also the *s.* 23:13; 29:28
the *s.* the sons of Asaph. 35:15
the *s.* an hundred twenty. *Ezra* 2:41
s. dwelt in their. 70; *Neh* 7:73
some of the *s.* went up. *Ezra* 7:7
not lawful to impose toll upon *s.* 24
the *s.* gave their hands to. 10:24
the porters and the *s.* *Neh* 7:1
the *s.* clave to their brethren. 10:29
the *s.* were over the business. 11:22
a portion shall be for the *s.* 23
12:47; 13:5
sons of *s.* gathered themselves. 12:28
s. had builded them villages. 29
s. sang aloud. 42
s. kept ward of their God. 45
David, there were chief of *s.* 46
for the Levites and the *s.* 13:10
s. went before, players. *Ps* 68:25
as well the *s.* as the players. 87:7
the chambers of the *s.* *Ezek* 40:44

***men* singers, *women* singers**
I gat me *men s.* and *women s.* *Eccl* 2:8

singeth
so is he that *s.* songs to. *Pr* 25:20

singing
women came out of cities of Israel *s.* *1 Sam* 18:6
they ministered with *s.* *1 Chr* 6:32*
played before God with *s.* 13:8*
burnt offerings with *s.* *2 Chr* 23:18
s. with loud instruments unto. 30:21
dedication of the wall with *s.* *Neh* 12:27
his presence with *s.* *Ps* 100:2
our tongue filled with *s.* 126:2
time of the *s.* of birds. *S of S* 2:12
break forth into *s.* *Isa* 14:7
there shall be no *s.* 16:10
rejoice even with joy and *s.* 35:2
break forth into *s.* ye. 44:23
Chaldeans with a voice of *s.* 48:20
earth, and break forth into *s.* 49:13
shall come with *s.* to Zion. 51:11
break forth into *s.* O barren. 54:1
shall break forth into *s.* 55:12
will joy over thee with *s.* *Zeph* 3:17
s. in your heart to the Lord. *Eph* 5:19; *Col* 3:16

singing men, singing women
can I hear any more the voice of *s. men, s. women*? *2 Sam* 19:35
all the *s. men* spake. *2 Chr* 35:25
s. men, 200 *s. women*. *Ezra* 2:65
245 *s. men* and *s. women*. *Neh* 7:67

single
thine eye be *s.* thy whole body shall. *Mat* 6:22; *Luke* 11:34

singleness
with gladness and *s.* of heart. *Acts* 2:46
servants, be obedient, in *s.* of your heart. *Eph* 6:5; *Col* 3:22

singular
shall make a *s.* vow. *Lev* 27:2*

sink
I *s.* in deep mire where. *Ps* 69:2
out of the mire, and let me not *s.* 14
thus shall Babylon *s.* and. *Jer* 51:64
beginning to *s.* he cried. *Mat* 14:30
so that they began to *s.* *Luke* 5:7
let these sayings *s.* down. 9:44

sinned
Pharaoh *s.* yet more. *Ex* 9:34
Ye have *s.* a great sin. 32:30, 31
whosoever hath *s.* against me, him will I blot out of my book. 33
bring for the sin he hath *s.* *Lev* 4:3
sin the congregation have *s.* 14
when a ruler hath *s.* 22, 23
one of common people *s.* 28
he shall confess he hath *s.* 5:5
for sin which he hath *s.* shall. 6
atonement for the sin he hath *s.* and. 10, 11, 13; *Num* 6:11
he hath *s.*, he shall restore. *Lev* 6:4
lay not sin on us wherein we have *s.* *Num* 12:11
ye have *s.* against the Lord. 32:23
and, behold, ye had *s.* against the Lord. *Deut* 9:16
your sins which ye *s.* in doing. 18
Israel hath *s.* and transgressed. *Josh* 7:11
wherefore I have not *s.* *Judg* 11:27
because he hath not *s.* *1 Sam* 19:4
know that I have not *s.* 24:11
they have *s.* against thee, and shall. *1 Ki* 8:33, 35; *2 Chr* 6:24, 26
forgive thy people that *s.* *1 Ki* 8:50
2 Chr 6:39
sins of Jeroboam which he *s.* *1 Ki* 15:30; 16:13, 19
What have I *s.* that thou? 18:9
Israel had *s.* against. *2 Ki* 17:7
sin that Manasseh had *s.* 21:17
s. against thy judgements. *Neh* 9:29
may be that my sons have *s.* *Job* 1:5
in all this Job *s.* not, nor charged. 22
if children have *s.* against him. 8:4
the grave those which have *s.* 24:19
they *s.* yet more. *Ps* 78:17, 32
thy first father hath *s.* *Isa* 43:27
sayest, I have not *s.* *Jer* 2:35
they have *s.* against me. 33:8
because ye have *s.* and not obeyed. 40:3; 44:23
because they have *s.* against the. 50:7; *Zeph* 1:17
Babylon hath *s.* against. *Jer* 50:14
Jerusalem hath grievously *s.* *Lam* 1:8
our fathers have *s.* and are not. 5:7
in sin that he hath *s.*, in. *Ezek* 18:24
with violence, and thou hast *s.* 28:16
places wherein they *s.* 37:23
they increased so they *s.* *Hos* 4:7
O Israel, thou hast *s.* from. 10:9
hast *s.* against thy soul. *Hab* 2:10
neither this man *s.* nor. *John* 9:3
for as many as have *s.* without law; as have *s.* in the law. *Rom* 2:12
for all have *s.* and come short. 3:23; 5:12
over them that had not *s.* 5:14
not as it was by one that *s.* so. 16
marry, thou hast not *s.* and if a virgin . . . hath not *s.* *1 Cor* 7:28
bewail many that have *s.* *2 Cor* 12:21
which heretofore have *s.* 13:2
with them that had *s.*? *Heb* 3:17
spared not the angels that *s.* *2 Pet* 2:4
if we say we have not *s.* *1 John* 1:10

***I have* sinned**
Pharaoh said, *I have s.* this time. *Ex* 9:27; 10:16
Balaam said to angel of Lord, *I have s.* *Num* 22:34
indeed *I have s.* against the Lord God. *Josh* 7:20

Saul said, *I have s.* 1 Sam 15:24
30; 26:21
to Nathan, *I have s.* 2 Sam 12:13
24:10, 17; 1 Chr 21:8, 17
doth know that *I have s.* 2 Sam 19:20
I have s.; what shall I do? Job 7:20
if any say, *I have s.* 33:27
heal my soul; for *I have s.* Ps 41:4
against thee, thee only *have I s.* 51:4
I have s. against him. Mi 7:9
I have s. in betraying. Mat 27:4
Father, *I have s.* against heaven, and before thee. Luke 15:18, 21

we have sinned

not sin on us, wherein *we have s.* Num 12:11
we will go up, for *we have s.* 14:40
Deut 1:41
we have s., we have spoken. Num 21:7
we have s. because we have. Judg 10:10; 1 Sam 12:10
we have s.: do to us. Judg 10:15
that day, and said, *We have s.* 1 Sam 7:6
we have s. and have done perversely. 1 Ki 8:47
saying, *We have s.* 2 Chr 6:37
the sins which *we have s.* Neh 1:6
we have s. with our fathers. Ps 106:6
against whom *we have s.* Isa 42:24
art wroth, for *we have s.* 64:5
in our shame, for *we have s.* Jer 3:25
us water of gall, for *we have s.* 8:14
backslidings are many, *we have s.* 14:7
our wickedness, for *we have s.* 20
woe to us that *we have s.* Lam 5:16
we have s. and have committed. Dan 9:5
confusion, because *we have s.* 8
poured on us, because *we have s.* 11
O Lord, *we have s.* we have. 15

sinner

the wicked and the *s.* Pr 11:31
overthroweth the *s.* 13:6
the wealth of the *s.* is laid up. 22
to the *s.* he giveth travail. Eccl 2:26
but the *s.* shall be taken by her. 7:26
though *s.* do evil an hundred. 8:12
as is the good, so is the *s.* and. 9:2
but one *s.* destroyeth much good. 18
s. being 100 years old. Isa 65:20
in the city who was a *s.* Luke 7:37
what woman this is: for she is a *s.* 39
joy in heaven over one *s.* 15:7, 10
God be merciful to me a *s.* 18:13
guest with a man that is a *s.* 19:7
how can a man a *s.* do? John 9:16
we know this man is a *s.* 24
whether he be a *s.* I know not. 25
am I also judged as a *s.*? Rom 3:7
he that converteth a *s.* Jas 5:20
shall the ungodly and *s.* appear? 1 Pet 4:18

sinners

the men of Sodom were *s.* Gen 13:13
the censers of these *s.* Num 16:38
utterly destroy the *s.* 1 Sam 15:18
standeth not in the way of *s.* Ps 1:1
nor *s.* in the congregation of the. 5
therefore will he teach *s.* in. 25:8
gather not my soul with *s.* nor. 26:9
and *s.* shall be converted. 51:13
let the *s.* be consumed out. 104:35
if *s.* entice thee, consent not. Pr 1:10
evil pursueth *s.* but to the. 13:21
let not thine heart envy *s.* 23:17
the destruction of the *s.* Isa 1:28
he shall destroy the *s.* thereof. 13:9
the *s.* in Zion are afraid. 33:14
s. of my people shall die. Amos 9:10
many *s.* sat at meat with Jesus. Mat 9:10; Mark 2:15
why eateth your master with publicans and *s.*? Mat 9:11; Mark 2:16
Luke 5:30; 15:2
to call the righteous, but *s.* to. Mat 9:13; Mark 2:17; Luke 5:32
a friend of publicans and *s.* Mat 11:19; Luke 7:34
Son of man is betrayed into the hands of *s.* Mat 26:45; Mark 14:41
for *s.* also love those. Luke 6:32
what thank have ye? for *s.* also. 33
for *s.* also lend to *s.* to receive. 34
these were *s.* above all. 13:2, 4*
the publicans and *s.* for to. 15:1
that God heareth not *s.* John 9:31
while we were yet *s.*, Christ. Rom 5:8
disobedience many were made *s.* 19
we Jews by nature, not *s.* Gal 2:15
we ourselves also are found *s.* 17
the law is made for *s.* 1 Tim 1:9
that Christ Jesus came to save *s.* 15
holy, separate from *s.* Heb 7:26
endured such contradiction of *s.* 12:3
cleanse your hands, ye *s.*, purify. Jas 4:8
speeches which ungodly *s.* Jude 15

sinnest

if thou *s.* what doest? Job 35:6

sinneth

make atonement for soul that *s.* Num 15:28*
have one law for him that *s.* 29*
not rise, in any sin he *s.* Deut 19:15
if they sin against thee, for there is no man that *s.* not. 1 Ki 8:46
2 Chr 6:36; Eccl 7:20
he that *s.* against me. Pr 8:36
despiseth his neighbour *s.* 14:21
he that hasteth with his feet *s.* 19:2
whoso provoketh a king, *s.* 20:2
when the land *s.* then. Ezek 14:13
the soul that *s.* it shall die. 18:4, 20
righteousness in the day he *s.* 33:12
but fornicator *s.* against. 1 Cor 6:18
let him do what he will, he *s.* not. 7:36
he is subverted, and *s.* Tit 3:11
whosoever abideth in him *s.* not, whosoever *s.* hath. 1 John 3:6
is of the devil, for devil *s.* from. 8
whosoever is born of God *s.* not. 5:18

sinning

I withheld thee from *s.* Gen 20:6
that a man doth, *s.* therein. Lev 6:3

sins

He shall give Israel up, because of *s.* of Jeroboam. 1 Ki 14:16
Abijam walked in the *s.* of. 15:3
smote Nadab because of the *s.* 30
s. of Baasha, and the *s.* of. 16:13
for his *s.* which Zimri sinned. 19
a light thing to walk in the *s.* 31
Jehoram cleaved to the *s.* 2 Ki 3:3
from the *s.* of Jeroboam Jehu. 10:29
not from the *s.* of Jeroboam. 13:6, 11
departed not from the *s.* 14:24
departed from *s.* 15:9, 18, 24, 28
Israel walked in all the *s.* 17:22
Judah for the *s.* of Manasseh. 24:3
not even with you *s.*? 2 Chr 28:10
and confess the *s.* of the children. Neh 1:6
mine iniquities and *s.*? Job 13:23
from presumptuous *s.* Ps 19:13
remember not the *s.* of my. 25:7
holden with cords of his *s.* Pr 5:22
up strifes, love covereth all *s.* 10:12
he that covereth his *s.* shall. 28:13
double for all her *s.* Isa 40:2
made me to serve with thy *s.* 43:24
I will not remember thy *s.* 25
blotted out as a cloud thy *s.* 44:22
I give to spoil for all thy *s.* Jer 15:13
thy *s.* were increased. 30:14, 15
the *s.* of Judah sought for. 50:20
the punishment of his *s.* Lam 3:39
for the *s.* of her prophets and. 4:13
Edom, he will discover thy *s.* 22
neither hath Samaria committed half thy *s.* Ezek 16:51
thine own shame for thy *s.* 52
beget son that seeth all his father's *s.* 18:14
will turn from all his *s.* 21
and he shall bear the *s.* of. 23:49
none of his *s.* that he hath. 33:16
break off thy *s.* by. Dan 4:27
determined to make an end of *s.* 9:24
the *s.* of the house of Israel. Mi 1:5
desolate because of thy *s.* 6:13
for the remission of *s.* Mat 26:28
of repentance for the remission of *s.* Mark 1:4; Luke 3:3
that remission of *s.* should be. Luke 24:47
Thou wast altogether born in *s.* John 9:34
s. ye remit, whose soever *s.* ye. 20:23
baptized for remission of *s.* Acts 2:38
repentance and remission of *s.* 5:31
shall receive remission of *s.* 10:43
wash away thy *s.* calling on. 22:16
for the remission of *s.* Rom 3:25
the motions of *s.* did work in. 7:5
who were dead in *s.* Eph 2:1, 5
in putting off the body of *s.* Col 2:11
of other men's *s.* 1 Tim 5:22
some men's *s.* open beforehand. 24
silly women laden with *s.* 2 Tim 3:6
make reconciliation for *s.* Heb 2:17
offer gifts and sacrifices for *s.* 5:1
also for himself, to offer for *s.* 3
first for his own *s.* then for. 7:27
offered to bear *s.* of many. 9:28
no more conscience of *s.* 10:2
a remembrance again made of *s.* 3
blood of bulls not take away *s.* 4
can never take away *s.* 11
one sacrifice for *s.* for ever. 12
no more sacrifice for *s.* 26
shall hide multitude of *s.* Jas 5:20
we being dead to *s.* 1 Pet 2:24
hath once suffered for *s.* 3:18
cover the multitude of *s.* 4:8
purged from his old *s.* 2 Pet 1:9
but also for *s.* of the whole world. 1 John 2:2
be not partakers of her *s.* Rev 18:4
s. have reached unto heaven. 5

see **forgive, forgiven**

my sins

hide thy face from *my s.* Ps 51:9
O God, *my s.* are not hid. 69:5
thou hast cast *my s.* Isa 38:17

our sins

for we have added to all *our s.* this. 1 Sam 12:19
add more to *our s.* 2 Chr 28:13
kings set over us because of *our s.* Neh 9:37
purge away *our s.* for thy name's. Ps 79:9
our secret *s.* in the light of. 90:8
with us according to *our s.* 103:10
our s. testify against us. Isa 59:12
if *our s.* be upon us. Ezek 33:10
because of *our s.* thy people are. Dan 9:16
Christ died for *our s.* 1 Cor 15:3
who gave himself for *our s.* Gal 1:4
when he had by himself purged *our s.* Heb 1:3
who his own self bare *our s.* in his. 1 Pet 2:24
confess *our s.* he is faithful and just to forgive us *our s.* 1 John 1:9
propitiation for *our s.* 2:2; 4:10
manifested to take away *our s.* 3:5
washed us from *our s.* Rev 1:5

their sins

transgressions in *their s.* Lev 16:16
over the live goat all *their s.* 21
to make atonement for *their s.* 34
consumed in all *their s.* Num 16:26
they provoked him with *their s.* 1 Ki 14:22
me to anger with *their s.* 16:2
and confessed *their s.* Neh 9:2
house of Jacob *their s.* Isa 58:1
and visit *their s.* Jer 14:10
Hos 8:13; 9:9
cast all *their s.* into the. Mi 7:19
his people from *their s.* Mat 1:21
were baptized, confessing *their s.* 3:6; Mark 1:5
and *their s.* should be. Mark 4:12
the remission of *their s.* Luke 1:77
shall take away *their s.* Rom 11:27
to fill up *their s.* 1 Thes 2:16
will be merciful to *their s.* Heb 8:12
their s. and iniquities I will. 10:17

your sins

clean from all *your s.* Lev 16:30
seven times for *your s.* 26:18, 24, 28
plagues on you according to *your s.* 21

water, because of *your s.* *Deut* 9:18
will not forgive *your s.* *Josh* 24:19
though *your s.* be as scarlet, they shall be as white as snow. *Isa* 1:18
and *your s.* have hid his face. 59:2
your s. have withholden. *Jer* 5:25
in all your doings *your s.* appear. *Ezek* 21:24
know *your* transgressions and mighty *s.* *Amos* 5:12
and die in *your s.* *John* 8:21, 24
repent, that *your s.* may. *Acts* 3:19
not raised, ye are yet in *your s.* *1 Cor* 15:17
you being dead in *your s.* *Col* 2:13
your s. are forgiven. *1 John* 2:12

sir

s. we came at first time. *Gen* 43:20*
s. didst thou not sow? *Mat* 13:27
said, I go *s.* and went not. 21:30
s. we remember that that. 27:63
s. thou hast nothing to. *John* 4:11
s. give me this water that I. 15
s. I perceive that thou art a. 19
the nobleman saith, *S.* come ere. 49
s. I have no man to put me. 5:7
certain Greeks saying, *S.* we. 12:21
s. if thou have borne him. 20:15
I said unto him, *S.* thou. *Rev* 7:14*

Sirion

the Sidonians call *S.* *Deut* 3:9
Lebanon and *S.* like a. *Ps* 29:6

sirs

s. ye are brethren, why? *Acts* 7:26
crying out, *S.* why do ye? 14:15
he said, *S.* what must I do? 16:30
s. ye know that by this craft. 19:25
s. I perceive this voyage will. 27:10
Paul said, *S.* ye should have. 21
wherefore, *s.* be of good cheer. 25

Sisera

of Jabin's host was *S.* *Judg* 4:2
S. fled away on his feet. 17
S. lay dead. 22
the stars fought against *S.* 5:20
with the hammer she smote *S.* 26
the mother of *S.* looked out. 28
into the hand of *S.* *1 Sam* 12:9
children of *S.* went up. *Ezra* 2:53 *Neh* 7:55
do unto them, as to *S.* *Ps* 83:9

sister

This name has much the same latitude as that of brother. As Christian men were used to salute one another by the name of brothers or brethren, so they called Christian women, who professed the same faith in Christ, by the name of sisters, Jas 2:15, 16.

Rebekah their *s.* *Gen* 24:59
thou art our *s.*, be thou mother. 60
heard of Jacob his *s.'s* son. 29:13
Rachel envied her *s.* and said. 30:1
defiled Dinah their *s.* 34:13
we cannot give our *s.* to one. 14
should he deal with our *s.* 31
his *s.* stood afar off to wit. *Ex* 2:4
Jochebed his father's *s.* to wife. 6:20
Miriam *s.* of Aaron took a. 15:20
not uncover the nakedness of thy *s.* *Lev* 18:9
she is thy *s.* 11
not nakedness of father's *s.* 12
mother's *s.* 13
not take a wife to her *s.* 18
if a man take his *s.* and see. 20:17
of thy father's *s.*, mother's *s.* 19
for his *s.* a virgin; for her he. 21:3
not be defiled for his *s.* *Num* 6:7
he that lieth with his *s.* *Deut* 27:22
younger *s.* fairer than she? *Judg* 15:2
Absalom had a fair *s.* *2 Sam* 13:1
he fell sick for his *s.* Tamar. 2
I love my brother Absalom's *s.* 4
had forced his *s.* Tamar. 22, 32
Jehosheba *s.* of Ahaziah took Joash. *2 Ki* 11:2; *2 Chr* 22:11
a little *s.* and she hath no breasts . . . do for our *s.* in the? *S of S* 8:8
her treacherous *s.* Judah. *Jer* 3:7
her *s.* feared not. 8
her *s.* hath not turned. *Jer* 3:10
him, saying, Ah, my *s.* 22:18
thou art the *s.* of thy sisters who. *Ezek* 16:45
thy elder *s.* is Samaria, thy younger *s.* Sodom. 46
Sodom thy *s.* hath not done as. 48
this was the iniquity of thy *s.* 49
for thy *s.* Sodom was not. 56
in thee hath humbled his *s.* 22:11
elder, and Aholibah her *s.* 23:4
and when her *s.* Aholibah saw. 11
was alienated from her *s.* 18
walked in the way of thy *s.* 31
thy *s.'s* cup deep and large. 32, 33
for *s.* that hath no husband. 44:25
the same is my brother, *s.* *Mat* 12:50
she had a *s.* called Mary. *Luke* 10:39; *John* 11:1, 5
therefore his *s.* sent. *John* 11:3
by the cross his mother's *s.* 19:25
Paul's *s.'s* son heard of. *Acts* 23:16
commend to you Phœbe our *s.* a servant. *Rom* 16:1
a brother or a *s.* is not. *1 Cor* 7:15
power to lead about a *s.* a wife? 9:5*
Marcus *s.'s* son to Barnabas. *Col* 4:10*
if a brother or *s.* be naked. *Jas* 2:15
children of thy elect *s.* *2 John* 13

***my* sister**

pray thee, thou art *my s.* *Gen* 12:13
why saidst, She is *my s.*? 19; 20:2 5, 12; 26:7, 9
I have wrestled with *my s.* 30:8
Let *my s.* Tamar come. *2 Sam* 13:5, 6
Come lie with me, *my s.* 11
Hold now thy peace, *my s.* 20
said to the worm, Thou art *my s.* *Job* 17:14
Thou art *my s.*; and call. *Pr* 7:4
hast ravished my heart, *my s.* my. *S of S* 4:9
how fair is thy love, *my s.* my. 10
a garden inclosed is *my s.* my. 12
I am come into my garden, *my s.* 5:1
open to me, *my s.* my love, my. 2
same is my brother, *my s.* *Mark* 3:35
that *my s.* hath left me? *Luke* 10:40

sister in law

s. in law is gone back to her people . . . after thy *s. in law.* *Ruth* 1:15

sisters

will save alive my father, and *my s.* *Josh* 2:13
whose *s.* were Zeruiah. *1 Chr* 2:16
they called for their three *s.* *Job* 1:4
his brethren and all his *s.* 42:11
the sister of thy *s.* *Ezek* 16:45
thou hast justified thy *s.* in. 51, 52
when thy *s.* and daughters. 55
when thou shalt receive thy *s.* 61
unto your *s.* Ruhamah. *Hos* 2:1
are not his *s.* with us? *Mat* 13:56 *Mark* 6:3
s. or father, or mother. *Mat* 19:29 *Mark* 10:29; *Luke* 14:26
100 fold, houses, brethren, *s.* *Mark* 10:30
women, as *s.* with purity. *1 Tim* 5:2

sit

war, and shall ye *s.* here? *Num* 32:6
ye that *s.* in judgement. *Judg* 5:10
s. still, my daughter. *Ruth* 3:18
turn aside, *s.* down here. 4:1, 2
and make them *s.* in. *1 Sam* 9:22
we will not *s.* down till he. 16:11
I should not fail to *s.* with. 20:5
behold, the king doth *s.* *2 Sam* 19:8
Solomon shall *s.* *1 Ki* 1:13, 17
who hath given one to *s.* 48; 3:6
not fail thee a man to *s.* on the throne. 8:25; *2 Chr* 6:16; *Jer* 33:17
why *s.* we here? *2 Ki* 7:3, 4
thy sons shall *s.* on. 10:30; 15:12
men who *s.* on wall. 18:27; *Isa* 36:12
and will not *s.* with the. *Ps* 26:5
they that *s.* in the gate speak. 69:12
such as *s.* in darkness and. 107:10
said to my Lord, *S.* thou at. 110:1
princes also did *s.* and speak. 119:23
to rise early and *s.* up late. 127:2*
their children shall *s.* upon. 132:12
folly in dignity, and rich *s.* *Eccl* 10:6
being desolate, shall *s.* *Isa* 3:26
I will *s.* upon mount of the. 14:13
he shall *s.* upon the throne in. 16:5
their strength is to *s.* still. 30:7
bring them that *s.* in darkness. 42:7
s. in the dust, *s.* on. 47:1; 52:2
s. thou silent, get thee into. 47:5
thou that sayest, I shall not *s.* 8
nor a fire to *s.* before it. 14
why do we *s.* still? *Jer* 8:14
that *s.* on David's throne. 13:13
s. down now. 18; 36:15
he shall have none to *s.* 36:30
and *s.* in thirst. 48:18
how doth city *s.* solitary! *Lam* 1:1
elders of Zion *s.* on ground. 2:10
they shall *s.* upon the. *Ezek* 26:16
because thou hast said, I *s.* in. 28:2
and they *s.* before thee as. 33:31
prince shall *s.* in it to eat. 44:3
the ancient of days did *s.* *Dan* 7:9
but the judgement shall *s.* they. 26
there will I *s.* to judge. *Joel* 3:12
they shall *s.* every man. *Mi* 4:4
when I *s.* in darkness, Lord. 7:8
and thy fellows that *s.* *Zech* 3:8
he shall *s.* and rule upon. 6:13
s. as a refiner and purifier of silver. *Mal* 3:3
many shall *s.* down with. *Mat* 8:11
s. in the throne of his glory, ye also shall *s.* 19:28; 25:31; *Luke* 22:30
my two sons may *s.* on. *Mat* 20:21
but to *s.* on my right hand. 23 *Mark* 10:37, 40
s. thou on my right hand till I make. *Mat* 22:44; *Mark* 12:36 *Luke* 20:42; *Heb* 1:13
the scribes and Pharisees *s.* in. *Mat* 23:2
s. ye here while I pray yonder. 26:36; *Mark* 14:32
make them *s.* by fifties. *Luke* 9:14
make them to *s.* down, and. 12:37
shall *s.* down in the kingdom. 13:29
bidden, *s.* not down in highest. 14:8
take thy bill, *s.* down quickly. 16:6
will say to him, Go, and *s.* 17:7
Make the men *s.* down. *John* 6:10
would raise up Christ to *s.* on. *Acts* 2:30*
that he would come up and *s.* 8:31
to see thee *s.* at meat in. *1 Cor* 8:10
hath made us *s.* in heavenly. *Eph* 2:6
and say, *S.* thou here in a. *Jas* 2:3
will I grant to *s.* with me. *Rev* 3:21
a woman *s.* on a scarlet beast. 17:3
for she saith in her heart, I *s.* 18:7

sith

s. thou hast not hated blood, even. *Ezek* 35:6†

sittest

why *s.* thou thyself alone? *Ex* 18:14
talk of them when thou *s.* in thine house. *Deut* 6:7; 11:19
thou *s.* and speakest against thy. *Ps* 50:20
thou *s.* to eat with a ruler. *Pr* 23:1
hear, O king of Judah, that *s.* on. *Jer* 22:2
s. thou to judge me after? *Acts* 23:3

sitteth

from the firstborn that *s.* *Ex* 11:5
every thing whereon he *s.* *Lev* 15:4
whereon he or she *s.* be unclean. 6, 20, 23, 26
when he *s.* on the throne. *Deut* 17:18
Solomon *s.* on throne of. *1 Ki* 1:46
do so to Mordecai that *s.* *Esth* 6:10
nor *s.* in the seat of the. *Ps* 1:1
s. in the heavens shall laugh. 2:4
he *s.* in the lurking places. 10:8
s. on the flood; yea, the Lord *s.* king for ever, the Lord will. 29:10
God *s.* on the throne of his. 47:8
Lord reigneth, he *s.* between. 99:1
for she *s.* at the door of. *Pr* 9:14
a king that *s.* in the throne. 20:8
when he *s.* among the elders. 31:23
while king *s.* at his table. *S of S* 1:12
spirit of judgement to him that *s.* *Isa* 28:6

it is he that *s.* on the circle. *Isa* 40:22
partridge *s.* on eggs. *Jer* 17:11
saith of the king that *s.* upon. 29:16
he *s.* alone and keepeth. *Lam* 3:28
behold, all the earth *s.* *Zech* 1:11
a woman that *s.* in the midst. 5:7
sweareth by him that *s.* *Mat* 23:22
s. not down first and. *Luke* 14:28, 31
he that *s.* at meat or he that serveth ?
is not he that *s.* at meat ? 22:27
revealed to another that *s.* by.
1 Cor 14:30
where Christ *s.* on the right hand.
Col 3:1
he, as God, *s.* in the. *2 Thes* 2:4
power to him that *s.* *Rev* 5:13
from the face of him that *s.* 6:16
salvation to our God which *s.* 7:10
he that *s.* on throne shall dwell. 15
the whore that *s.* upon. 17:1, 15
mountains, on which the woman *s.* 9

sitting
dam *s.* on the young. *Deut* 22:6
s. in a summer parlour. *Judg* 3:20
seen the *s.* of his servants.
1 Ki 10:5; *2 Chr* 9:4
found the man of God *s.* *1 Ki* 13:14
I saw the Lord *s.* on his throne.
22:19; *2 Chr* 18:18; *Isa* 6:1
of the prophets were *s.* *2 Ki* 4:38
captains of the host were *s.* 9:5
the queen also *s.* by him. *Neh* 2:6
see Mordecai the Jew *s.* *Esth* 5:13
my down-*s.* and up-rising. *Ps* 139:2
kings and princes *s.* upon the throne
of David. *Jer* 17:25; 22:4, 30
the king then *s.* in the gate. 38:7
behold their *s.* down. *Lam* 3:63
s. at receipt of. *Mat* 9:9; *Mark* 2:14
Luke 5:27
like children *s.* in the markets.
Mat 11:16; *Luke* 7:32
behold, two blind men *s.* *Mat* 20:30
thy king cometh, *s.* on an ass.
21:5*; *John* 12:15
ye shall see the Son of man *s.* on the.
Mat 26:64; *Mark* 14:62
and *s.* down, they watched him there.
Mat 27:36
the other Mary *s.* over against. 61
that was possessed *s.* *Mark* 5:15
they saw a young man *s.* on. 16:5
found him *s.* in midst of. *Luke* 2:46
doctors of the law *s.* by. 5:17
found him *s.* clothed, and in. 8:35
s. in sackcloth and ashes. 10:13
changers of money *s.* *John* 2:14
two angels in white *s.* 20:12
house where they were *s.* *Acts* 2:2
eunuch was returning, and *s.* 8:28
saw twenty-four elders *s.* *Rev* 4:4

sitting place
each side of *s. place.* *2 Chr* 9:18*

situate
Tyrus, O thou that art *s.* at entry.
Ezek 27:3*
populous No that was *s.* *Nah* 3:8

situation
s. of the city is pleasant. *2 Ki* 2:19
beautiful for *s.*, the joy of. *Ps* 48:2*

Sivan
that is the month *S.* *Esth* 8:9

six
s. cakes on a row on the. *Lev* 24:6
s. covered waggons, and. *Num* 7:3
on every hand *s.* fingers, every foot *s.*
2 Sam 21:20; *1 Chr* 20:6
sixteen sons and *s.* *1 Chr* 4:27
eastward were *s.* Levites. 26:17
prince shall offer to Lord, shall be *s.*
lambs without blemish. *Ezek* 46:4
new moon shall be *s.* lambs. 6
see **branches, days, hundreds**

six *boards*
thou shalt make *s. boards.* *Ex* 26:22
tabernacle he made *s. boards.* 36:27

six *brethren*
moreover these *s. brethren.*
Acts 11:12

six *cities*
shall be *s. cities* for refuge.
Num 35:6, 13, 15

six *cubits*
Goliath's height was *s. cubits.*
1 Sam 17:4
chamber was *s. cubits.* *1 Ki* 6:6
reed of *s. cubits* long. *Ezek* 40:5
the little chambers were *s. cubits.* 12
he measured posts *s. cubits.* 41:1
doors *s. cubits.* 3
wall of the house *s. cubits.* 5
a full reed of *s.* great *cubits.* 8
of the image of gold *s. cubits.*
Dan 3:1

six *curtains*
couple *s. curtains* by themselves.
Ex 26:9; 36:16

six *measures*
gave Ruth of barley *s. measures.*
Ruth 3:15
she said, These *s. measures.* 17

six *men*
s. men came from the way. *Ezek* 9:2

six *months*
king . . . seven years, *s. months.*
2 Sam 2:11; 5:5; *1 Chr* 3:4
s. months Joab remained in Edom.
1 Ki 11:16
Zachariah reigned *s. months* over.
2 Ki 15:8
s. months with oil of myrrh and *s.*
months with sweet. *Esth* 2:12
heaven was shut up three years and
s. months. *Luke* 4:25; *Jas* 5:17
at Corinth a year and *s. months.*
Acts 18:11

six *names*
s. of their *names* on one stone, and
the other *s. names* of. *Ex* 28:10

six *paces*
when the Levites had gone *s. paces*
he. *2 Sam* 6:13

six *sheep*
for me daily *s.* choice *sheep.*
Neh 5:18

six *sons*
me, I have borne *s. sons.* *Gen* 30:20
sons of Shechaniah, *s.* *1 Chr* 3:22
and Azel had *s. sons,* whose names.
8:38; 9:44

six *steps*
the throne had *s. steps.* *1 Ki* 10:19
twelve lions on the *s. steps.* 20
2 Chr 9:18

six *things*
these *s. things* doth. *Pr* 6:16

six *times*
smitten five or *s. times.* *2 Ki* 13:19

six *troubles*
deliver thee in *s. troubles,* in seven.
Job 5:19

six *waterpots*
set there *s. waterpots* of stone.
John 2:6

six *wings*
each one had *s. wings.* *Isa* 6:2
beasts had each *s. wings.* *Rev* 4:8

six *years*
I served thee *s. years.* *Gen* 31:41
s. years he shall serve. *Ex* 21:2
Deut 15:12; *Jer* 34:14
s. years thou shalt sow. *Ex* 23:10
s. years thou shalt prune. *Lev* 25:3
hired servant in serving *s. years.*
Deut 15:18
judged Israel *s. years.* *Judg* 12:7
Omri reigned *s. years.* *1 Ki* 16:23
nurse in the house of the Lord *s.*
years. *2 Ki* 11:3; *2 Chr* 22:12

sixscore
Hiram sent Solomon *s.* *1 Ki* 9:14

sixth
bare Jacob the *s.* son. *Gen* 30:19
thou shall couple *s.* curtain. *Ex* 26:9
my blessing on you *s.* year. *Lev* 25:21
the *s.* lot came out for. *Josh* 19:32
Ithream, David's *s.* son. *2 Sam* 3:5
1 Chr 3:3
in *s.* year of Hezekiah. *2 Ki* 18:10
house was finished in *s.* *Ezra* 6:15
drink also water by measure, the *s.*
part of an hin. *Ezek* 4:11
in the *s.* year the hand of. 8:1
I will leave but the *s.* part of. 39:2
the oblation the *s.* part of an. 45:13
a meat offering the *s.* part. 46:14
went out about the *s.* *Mat* 20:5
all the land from the *s.* to ninth hour.
27:45; *Mark* 15:33; *Luke* 23:44
about the *s.* hour Jesus. *John* 4:6
it was about the *s.* hour. 19:14
pray about the *s.* hour. *Acts* 10:9
when he opened *s.* seal. *Rev* 6:12
s. angel sounded, and I heard. 9:13
saying to the *s.* angel, Loose. 14
s. angel poured out vial on. 16:12
the *s.* foundation of the wall. 21:20
see **day, month**

sixteen
Zilpah bare to Jacob *s.* *Gen* 46:18
sockets of silver, *s.* sockets.
Ex 26:25; 36:30
Jehoash reigned *s.* years. *2 Ki* 13:10
Azariah, when *s.* years old. 14:21
over Judah *s.* years in Jerusalem.
15:33; *2 Chr* 27:1, 8; 28:1
Shimei had *s.* sons. *1 Chr* 4:27
among sons of Eleazar were *s.* 24:4
sons and *s.* daughters. *2 Chr* 13:21

sixteenth
s. lot came forth to. *1 Chr* 24:14
the *s.* lot came forth to. 25:23

sixty
Mahalaleel lived *s.* years. *Gen* 5:15
Enoch lived *s.* five years and begat. 21
the male from twenty to *s.* *Lev* 27:3
if it be from *s.* years old above. 7
s. rams, *s.* he goats, *s.* lambs.
Num 7:88
brought forth *s.* fold. *Mat* 13:8, 23
Mark 4:8, 20

size
the curtains were all of one *s.*
Ex 36:9, 15
of one measure and *s.* *1 Ki* 6:25*
one measure, and of one *s.* 7:37*
for all manner of *s.* David left.
1 Chr 23:29

skies
of the *s.* his pavilions round about.
2 Sam 22:12; *Ps* 18:11
the *s.* sent out a sound. *Ps* 77:17
and let the *s.* pour down. *Isa* 45:8
is lifted up even to the *s.* *Jer* 51:9

skilful
Reuben and Gadites *s.* *1 Chr* 5:18
instructed, because he was *s.* 15:22
with thee every willing *s.* man. 28:21
deliver thee into the hand of men *s.*
to destroy. *Ezek* 21:31
children *s.* in all wisdom. *Dan* 1:4
such are *s.* of lamentation to.
Amos 5:16

skilfully
sing a new song, play *s.* *Ps* 33:3

skilfulness
and guided them by *s.* *Ps* 78:72

skill, *verb*
not any that can *s.* to hew timber.
1 Ki 5:6†; *2 Chr* 2:8
a man that can *s.* to grave. *2 Chr* 2:7†
that could *s.* of instruments. 34:12†

skill
nor yet favour to men of *s.* but.
Eccl 9:11
God gave them knowledge and *s.*
Dan 1:17
I am now come forth to give thee *s.*
9:22

skin
it is his raiment for *s.* *Ex* 22:27
flesh of the bullock, and his *s.* and
dung burn. 29:14; *Lev* 4:11
Moses wist not that the *s.* of his face.
Ex 34:29, 30, 35
offereth shall have the *s.* *Lev* 7:8
if dead fall on *s.* or sack it. 11:32
shall have in the *s.* a rising. 13:2
look on the plague in the *s.* of the
flesh, and if deeper than the *s.* 3
if bright spot be white in the *s.* 4

if the plague spread not in the *s.* *Lev* 13:5, 6, 22, 28
if scab spread abroad in the *s.* 7, 8, 27, 35, 36
if the rising be white in the *s.* 10
it is an old leprosy in the *s.* of. 11
rend it out of garment or *s.* 56
s. wherein is seed washed. 15:17
burn heifer, her *s.* and. *Num* 19:5
s. for *s.* all that a man hath. *Job* 2:4
my *s.* is broken, and become. 7:5
thou hast clothed me with *s.* 10:11
I sewed sackcloth on my *s.* 16:15
devour the strength of his *s.* 18:13*
to my *s.* and to my flesh, and I am escaped with the *s.* of my. 19:20
after my *s.* worms destroy. 26
my *s.* is black upon me. 30:30
canst thou fill his *s.* with barbed? 41:7
my bones cleave to my *s.* *Ps* 102:5*
Ethiopian change his *s.*? *Jer* 13:23
my flesh and *s.* hath he. *Lam* 3:4
their *s.* cleaveth to their bones. 4:8
our *s.* was black like an oven. 5:10
I will cover you with *s.*, and put breath in you. *Ezek* 37:6, 8
who pluck off their *s.* *Mi* 3:2
who eat flesh, and flay their *s.* 3
John had a girdle of *s.* *Mark* 1:6*

skins

Lord made coats of *s.* *Gen* 3:21
she put *s.* of kids of goats. 27:16
were found red *s.* of rams and badgers' *s.*, brought them. *Ex* 35:23
law of the plague of *s.* *Lev* 13:59
shall burn in fire their *s.* 16:27
raiment, all made of *s.* *Num* 31:20
in sheep *s.* and goat *s.* *Heb* 11:37

skip

maketh them also to *s.* *Ps* 29:6

skipped

mountains *s.* like rams. *Ps* 114:4, 6

skippedst

since thou spakest of him, thou *s.* for joy. *Jer* 48:27*

skipping

behold, he cometh *s.* upon. *S of S* 2:8

skirt

(*The lower part of the long mantle worn by the Jews*)
uncover his father's *s.* *Deut* 22:30
uncovereth his father's *s.* 27:20
spread therefore thy *s.* *Ruth* 3:9
he laid hold on the *s.* *1 Sam* 15:27
David cut off the *s.* of Saul's. 24:4
because he cut off Saul's *s.* 5
my father, see the *s.* of thy robe. 11
behold, I spread my *s.* *Ezek* 16:8
if one bear holy flesh in the *s.* and with his *s.* do touch. *Hag* 2:12
shall take hold of *s.* of. *Zech* 8:23

skirts

that went down to the *s.* of. *Ps* 133:2
in *s.* is found blood of poor. *Jer* 2:34
for thy iniquity are thy *s.* 13:22
will I discover thy *s.* 26; *Nah* 3:5
her filthiness is in her *s.* *Lam* 1:9
bind a few hairs in thy *s.* *Ezek* 5:3

skull

millstone to break his *s.* *Judg* 9:53
more of Jezebel than *s.* *2 Ki* 9:35
to say, the place of a *s.* *Mat* 27:33 *Mark* 15:22; *John* 19:17

sky

in his excellency on the *s.* *Deut* 33:26
him spread out the *s.*? *Job* 37:18
it will be fair weather: for the *s.* is red. *Mat* 16:2*, 3*
discern face of the *s.* *Luke* 12:56*
many as the stars of *s.* *Heb* 11:12*

slack

(*Sluggish, loosened, slowed down*)
he will not be *s.* to him. *Deut* 7:10
How long are ye *s.* to go? *Josh* 18:3
dealeth with a *s.* hand. *Pr* 10:4
said to Zion, Let not thine hands be *s.* *Zeph* 3:16
Lord is not *s.* concerning. *2 Pet* 3:9

slack, *verb*

vow a vow, thou shalt not *s.* to pay it. *Deut* 23:21
saying, *S.* not thy hand. *Josh* 10:6
s. not riding for me. *2 Ki* 4:24*

slacked

the law is *s.*, and judgement. *Hab* 1:4

slackness

slack, as some men count *s.* *2 Pet* 3:9

slain, *verb*

for I have *s.* a man to. *Gen* 4:23
therefore he hath *s.* them in. *Num* 14:16
surely now I had *s.* thee. 22:33
after he had *s.* Sihon. *Deut* 1:4*
be not known who hath *s.* him. 21:1
and have *s.* his sons. *Judg* 9:18
jaw bone of an ass have I *s.* 15:16*
thought to have *s.* me. 20:5
Saul hath *s.* his. *1 Sam* 18:7; 21:11
shewed David that Saul had *s.* 22:21
saying, I have *s.* the. *2 Sam* 1:16
Abner, because he had *s.* 3:30
men have *s.* a righteous person. 4:11
hast *s.* Uriah with the sword. 12:9
Absalom hath *s.* all king's sons. 13:30
they have not *s.* all, for Amnon. 32
when the Philistines had *s.* 21:12
Ishbi-benob thought to have *s.* 16
Adonijah hath *s.* oxen. *1 Ki* 1:19, 25
Pharaoh had gone up and *s.* 9:16
lion hath torn and *s.* him. 13:26
Zimri hath *s.* the king. 16:16*
Ahab told how he had *s.* all. 19:1
for Israel have *s.* thy. 10, 14
servants who had *s.* king. *2 Ki* 14:5
hast *s.* thy brethren. *2 Chr* 21:13
for the band of men had *s.* 22:1
when they had *s.* Ahaziah, they. 9
quiet after they had *s.* 23:21
s. them in rage that reacheth. 28:9
Jews have *s.* 500 men. *Esth* 9:12
the Sabeans have *s.* *Job* 1:15, 17
men have been *s.* by her. *Pr* 7:26
destroyed and *s.* people. *Isa* 14:20
bodies of men whom I have *s.* in my anger. *Jer* 33:5
he had *s.* Gedaliah. 41:4, 9, 16, 18
hast *s.* them in day. *Lam* 2:21; 3:43
hast *s.* my children. *Ezek* 16:21
s. their children to idols. 23:39
I have *s.* them by words. *Hos* 6:5
your young men have I *s.* *Amos* 4:10
by wicked hands have *s.* *Acts* 2:23
have *s.* them that shewed. 7:52
nothing till we have *s.* Paul. 23:14

slain

Jacob came upon the *s.* *Gen* 34:27
the blood of the *s.* bird. *Lev* 14:51
and ye shall be *s.* before. 26:17*
shall the flocks and the herds be *s.*? *Num* 11:22
toucheth any *s.* 19:16, 18; 31:19
drink the blood of the *s.* 23:24
name of the Israelite that was *s.* was Zimri. 25:14
woman that was *s.* was Cozbi. 15, 18
rest of them that were *s.* 31:8
if one be found *s.* in land giveth. *Deut* 21:1*
the city next to the *s.* man. 3
thine ox shall be *s.* before. 28:31
arrows drunk with blood of *s.* 32:42
will I deliver them up all *s.* *Josh* 11:6
among them that were *s.* 13:22
the woman that was *s.* *Judg* 20:4*
Hophni and Phinehas were *s.* *1 Sam* 4:11
as Lord liveth, he shall not be *s.* 19:6
to-morrow thou shalt be *s.* 11
shall he be *s.*? what hath? 20:32
Philistines, and fell down *s.* in mount Gilboa. 31:1; *1 Chr* 10:1
when the Philistines came to strip the *s.* *1 Sam* 31:8
beauty of Israel is *s.* *2 Sam* 1:19
from the blood of *s.* from fat. 22
O Jonathan, thou wast *s.* in. 25
Israel were *s.* before David's. 18:7*
was gone to bury the *s.* *1 Ki* 11:15
the kings are surely *s.* *2 Ki* 3:23*
from among them that were *s.* 11:2
within ranges let him be *s.* *2 Ki* 11:8
on her, and there was she *s.* 16
there fell down many *s.*, because the war was of God. *1 Chr* 5:22
fell *s.* of Israel 500,000. *2 Chr* 13:17
I and my people, to be *s.* *Esth* 7:4
number of the *s.* in Shushan. 9:11
and where the *s.* are. *Job* 39:30
ye shall be *s.* all of you. *Ps* 62:3
like the *s.* that lie in the grave. 88:5
Rahab in pieces as one *s.* 89:10
man saith, I shall be *s.* *Pr* 22:13
those that are ready to be *s.* 24:11
shall fall under the *s.* *Isa* 10:4
raiment of those that are *s.* 14:19
thy *s.* men were not *s.* with. 22:2
shall no more cover her *s.* 26:21
s. according to slaughter, or *s.* 27:7
their *s.* also shall be cast out. 34:3
and the *s.* of the Lord shall. 66:16
that I might weep for *s.* *Jer* 9:1
behold the *s.* with the sword. 14:18
men be *s.* by sword in battle. 18:21*
s. of the Lord be from one. 25:33
filled the pit with the *s.* 41:9
thus the *s.* shall fall in land. 51:4
her *s.* shall fall in the midst. 47
caused *s.* of Israel to fall, so at Babylon shall fall the *s.* of all. 49
priest and prophet be *s.* *Lam* 2:20
be *s.* with sword, are better than they that be *s.* with hunger. 4:9
and the *s.* shall fall in. *Ezek* 6:7
when the *s.* men shall be among. 13
and fill the courts with *s.* 9:7
your *s.* in the city, ye have filled the streets with the *s.* 11:6
your *s.*, they are the flesh, and this. 7
s. it is the sword of great men *s.* 21:14*
upon necks of them that are *s.* 29
daughters in field shall be *s.* 26:6
deaths of them that are *s.* 28:8
great pain when the *s.* shall. 30:4
shall fill the land with the *s.* 11
with him unto them that be *s.* 31:17
with them *s.* with sword. 18; 32:29
fall in the midst of the *s.* 32:20, 25
lie *s.* by the sword. 21, 22, 23, 24
circumcised, *s.* by sword. 25, 26, 30
all his army *s.* by sword. 31, 32
mountains with his *s.* men. 35:8
breathe upon these *s.* 37:9
wise men to be *s.*; they sought Daniel and his fellows to be *s.* *Dan* 2:13
was Belshazzar the king *s.* 5:30
I beheld, even till beast was *s.* 7:11
and many shall fall down *s.* 11:26
there is multitude of *s.* *Nah* 3:3
ye Ethiopians shall be *s.* *Zeph* 2:12
Son of man must be *s.* *Luke* 9:22
Theudas was *s.*; and all. *Acts* 5:36
ye offered to me *s.* beasts? 7:42
Pilate that he should be *s.* 13:28
by the cross, having *s.* *Eph* 2:16
they were stoned, were *s.* *Heb* 11:37
who was *s.* among you. *Rev* 2:13
stood a Lamb, as it had been *s.* 5:6
thou wast *s.* 9
the Lamb that was *s.* 12; 13:8
souls of them that were *s.* for. 6:9
in the earthquake were *s.* 11:13
the blood of all that were *s.* 18:24
remnant *s.* with sword of. 19:21

slander

bringing up a *s.* on land. *Num* 14:36*
for I have heard the *s.* *Ps* 31:13*
he that uttereth a *s.* *Pr* 10:18

slandered

he hath *s.* thy servant. *2 Sam* 19:27

slanderers

must be grave, not *s.* *1 Tim* 3:11

slanderest

s. thine own mother's son. *Ps* 50:20

slandereth

whoso *s.* his neighbour, him. *Ps* 101:5

slanderously

as we be *s.* reported. *Rom* 3:8

slanders

revolters walking with *s.* *Jer* 6:28
neighbour will walk with *s.* 9:4

slang
from his bag a stone and *s.* it. *1 Sam* 17:49

slaughter
that first *s.* which. *1 Sam* 14:14
not been now much greater *s.*? 30
as David returned from *s.* of Philistine. 17:57; 18:6; *2 Sam* 1:1
is *s.* among people who. *2 Sam* 17:9
was come from the *s.* *2 Chr* 25:14
as sheep for the *s.* *Ps* 44:22
after her, as an ox to the *s.* *Pr* 7:22
the *s.* of Midian at Oreb. *Isa* 10:26
prepare *s.* for his children. 14:21
according to *s.* of them that. 27:7
and delivered them to *s.* 34:2
he is brought as a lamb to the *s.* 53:7 *Jer* 11:19
shall all bow down to the *s.* *Isa* 65:12
Tophet, but valley of *s.* *Jer* 7:32 19:6
pull them out like sheep for *s.*, prepare them for day of *s.* 12:3
for the days of your *s.* are. 25:34
young men are gone down to *s.* 48:15
let them go down to the *s.* 50:27
them down like lambs to the *s.* 51:40
and every man a *s.* weapon in his. *Ezek* 9:2
is sharpened to make sore *s.* 21:10
it is wrapped up for the *s.* 15
to open the mouth in the *s.* 22
the sword is drawn: for the *s.* 28
when the *s.* is made in the. 26:15
are profound to make *s.* *Hos* 5:2
Esau may be cut off by *s.* *Ob* 9
Lord, Feed the flock of *s.* *Zech* 11:4
I will feed the flock of *s.* O poor. 7
he was led as a sheep to *s.* *Acts* 8:32
Saul yet breathing out *s.* against. 9:1
we are accounted as sheep for the *s.* *Rom* 8:36
Abraham returning from the *s.* of the kings. *Heb* 7:1
your hearts, as in day of *s.* *Jas* 5:5
see **great**

slave, -s
(*Slavery under the Hebrews was as mild as was possible in that age. No Hebrew could become permanently the slave of another Hebrew, but must be freed when he had paid the debt for which he was sold; in the seventh year of his service whether the debt was paid or not; and in the year of Jubilee, whatever the time he had served. Gentile slaves were mostly war captives, or purchased from regular slave-dealers. These could be freed at the will of the master, but there was no law requiring it*)
is he a homeborn *s.*? *Jer* 2:14
the merchandise of *s.* *Rev* 18:13

slay
that findeth me shall *s.* *Gen* 4:14
Lord, wilt thou *s.* also a ? 20:4
and they will *s.* me for my. 11
will I *s.* my brother Jacob. 27:41
gather together against me and *s.* 34:30*
therefore and let us *s.* him. 37:20
What profit is it if we *s.* brother ? 26
s. my two sons if I bring him. 42:37
bring these men home, *s.* 43:16
behold, I will *s.* thy son. *Ex* 4:23
the innocent and righteous *s.* 23:7
shalt *s.* ram and sprinkle. 29:16
bring them out to *s.* them. 32:12
s. every man his brother. 27
s. sin offering. *Lev* 4:29, 33
s. the lamb. 14:13
with a beast, ye shall *s.* beast. 20:15
one shall *s.* red heifer. *Num* 19:3
s. ye every one his men joined. 25:5
revenger of blood shall *s.* 35:19, 21
of blood pursue and *s.* *Deut* 19:6
Israel did *s.* Balaam. *Josh* 13:22
alive, would not *s.* you. *Judg* 8:19
his firstborn, Up and *s.* them. 20
s. me, that men say not. 9:54
Lord would *s.* them. *1 Sam* 2:25
ark of God that it *s.* us not. 5:11
any man his ox, and *s.* *1 Sam* 14:34
spare them not, but *s.* both. 15:3
up to me, that I may *s.* him. 19:15
if there be in me iniquity, *s.* 20:8
said, Turn and *s.* the priests. 22:17
me, stand upon me and *s.* *2 Sam* 1:9
let king swear to me he will not *s.* *1 Ki* 1:51
child, in no wise *s.* it. 3:26, 27
did Baasha *s.* and reigned. 15:28
find thee, he shall *s.* me. 18:12
shall Jehu *s.*: him that escapeth from sword of Jehu shall Elisha *s.* 19:17
art departed, a lion shall *s.* 20:36
young men wilt thou *s.* *2 Ki* 8:12
go in and *s.* them, let none. 10:25
sent lions, and they *s.* them. 17:26
s. her not in the house. *2 Chr* 23:14
priests too few to *s.* all the. 29:34
we will *s.* them and cause. *Neh* 4:11
if the scourge *s.* suddenly. *Job* 9:23
though he *s.* me, yet will I. 13:15
viper's tongue shall *s.* him. 20:16
evil shall *s.* wicked that. *Ps* 34:21
s. them not, lest my people. 59:11
they *s.* the widow and the. 94:6
that he might *s.* the broken. 109:16
thou wilt *s.* the wicked. 139:19
of the simple shall *s.* them. *Pr* 1:32
his lips shall he *s.* wicked. *Isa* 11:4
with famine, and he shall *s.* 14:30
Lord shall *s.* the dragon that. 27:1
for Lord God shall *s.* thee. 65:15
the forest shall *s.* them. *Jer* 5:6
Judah captive and *s.* them. 20:4
shall *s.* Ahab and Zedekiah. 29:21
I will *s.* Ishmael, son of Nathaniah; wherefore should he *s.*? 40:15
found that said, *S.* us not. 41:8
s. all her bullocks; woe unto. 50:27
s. utterly old and young. *Ezek* 9:6
they shall *s.* their sons and. 23:47
he shall *s.* with sword thy. 26:8
he shall *s.* thy people by. 11
they shall *s.* the burnt. 44:11
set her like a dry land and *s.* *Hos* 2:3
yet will I *s.* the fruit. 9:16
s. all princes thereof. *Amos* 2:3
I will *s.* the last of them with. 9:1
sword, and it shall *s.* them. 4
whose possessors *s.* them. *Zech* 11:5
some of them they shall *s.* and. *Luke* 11:49
bring hither, and *s.* them. 19:27

to **slay**
be far from thee *to s.* *Gen* 18:25
stretched his hand *to s.* his. 22:10
they conspired against him *to s.* him. 37:18
Pharaoh sought *to s.* Moses. *Ex* 2:15
sword in their hand *to s.* us. 5:21
man come on neighbour *to s.* 21:14
brought them out *to s.* *Deut* 9:28
cursed that taketh reward *to s.* 27:25
brought the ark *to s.* us. *1 Sam* 5:10
why then sin, *to s.* David ? 19:5
Saul went *to* watch him and *s.* 11
of his father *to s.* David. 20:33
the king *to s.* Abner. *2 Sam* 3:37
Saul sought *to s.* them in his. 21:2
thou come *to s.* my son ? *1 Ki* 17:18
the hand of Ahab *to s.* me. 18:9
utterly *to s.* and. *2 Chr* 20:23
to s. thee, in night *to s.* *Neh* 6:10
to s. the power that would assault. *Esth* 8:11
to s. such as be of upright. *Ps* 37:14
and seeketh *to s.* him. 32
sword *to s.* dogs, to tear. *Jer* 15:3
all their counsel *to s.* me. 18:23
sent Ishmael *to s.* thee ? 40:14
to s. the souls that. *Ezek* 13:19
two tables *to s.* thereon. 40:39
gone forth *to s.* wise men. *Dan* 2:14
continually *to s.* nations. *Hab* 1:17
Jesus, and sought *to s.* *John* 5:16
they took counsel *to s.* *Acts* 5:33
but they went about *to s.* him. 9:29
angels prepared *to s.* third. *Rev* 9:15

slayer
refuge that the *s.* may flee thither. *Num* 35:11; *Deut* 4:42; 19:3, 4 *Josh* 20:3
shall judge between *s.* *Num* 35:24
congregation shall deliver *s.* 25
if the *s.* shall at any time come. 26
of blood find and kill the *s.* 27
s. shall return into the land of his. 28 *Josh* 20:6
of blood pursue the *s.* *Deut* 19:6
not deliver the *s.* up. *Josh* 20:5
Hebron to be a city of refuge for *s.* 21:13
gave Shechem for the *s.* 21, 27, 32
to be a city of refuge for *s.* 38
sword is furbished to be given to *s.* *Ezek* 21:11

slayeth
to him, whosoever *s.* Cain. *Gen* 4:15
neighbour and *s.* him. *Deut* 22:26
wrath killeth and envy *s.* *Job* 5:2
that *s.* thee, I am God ? . . . man in hand of them that *s.* *Ezek* 28:9*

slaying
when Israel made an end of *s.* *Josh* 8:24; 10:20
rendered wickedness in *s.* *Judg* 9:56
on widow by *s.* her son. *1 Ki* 17:20
s. oxen, killing sheep. *Isa* 22:13
s. the children in the valleys. 57:5
while they were *s.* them. *Ezek* 9:8*

sleep
(Sleep *is used in the Bible for natural sleep; for the indolence and dullness of the soul; or figuratively for death*)
God caused a deep *s.* to. *Gen* 2:21
sun going down, a deep *s.* 15:12
Jacob awaked out of his *s.* 28:16
thus I was, my *s.* departed. 31:40
awaked out of his *s.* *Judg* 16:14, 20
a deep *s.* from God. *1 Sam* 26:12
when deep *s.* falleth on men. *Job* 4:13; 33:15
nor be raised out of their *s.* 14:12
lest I *s.* the *s.* of death. *Ps* 13:3
stouthearted slept their *s.* 76:5
horse are cast into a deep *s.* 6
awaked as one out of *s.* 78:65
them away, they are as a *s.* 90:5
for so he giveth his beloved *s.* 127:2
I will not give *s.* to mine eyes. 132:4
shalt lie down, and thy *s.* *Pr* 3:24
their *s.* is taken away, unless. 4:16
not *s.* to thine eyes, nor slumber. 6:4
wilt thou arise out of thy *s.*? 9
a little *s.* a little slumber. 10; 24:33
casteth into a deep *s.* 19:15
love not *s.* lest thou come. 20:13
the *s.* of a labouring man. *Eccl* 5:12
neither day nor night seeth *s.* 8:16
on you spirit of deep *s.* *Isa* 29:10
I awaked, and my *s.* *Jer* 31:26
sleep a perpetual *s.* 51:39, 57
spirit troubled, and his *s.* *Dan* 2:1
passed the night and his *s.* 6:18
I was in a deep *s.* on my. 8:18; 10:9
as a man that is wakened out of *s.* *Zech* 4:1
being raised from *s.* did. *Mat* 1:24
were heavy with *s.* *Luke* 9:32
may awake him out of *s.* *John* 11:11
spoken of taking of rest in *s.* 13
awaking out of his *s.* *Acts* 16:27
Eutychus being fallen into a deep *s.* 20:9
time to awake out of *s.* *Rom* 13:11

sleep, *verb*
down in that place to *s.* *Gen* 28:11
raiment, wherein shall he *s.*? *Ex* 22:27
thou shalt not *s.* with. *Deut* 24:12
he may *s.* in his own raiment. 13
thou shalt *s.* with thy fathers. 31:16 *2 Sam* 7:12
and she made him *s.* *Judg* 16:19
was laid down to *s.* *1 Sam* 3:3
my lord the king shall *s.* *1 Ki* 1:21
on that night could not the king *s.* *Esth* 6:1
shall I *s.* in the dust. *Job* 7:21
lay me down in peace and *s.* *Ps* 4:8
lighten mine eyes, lest I *s.* the. 13:3
shall neither slumber nor *s.* 121:4
s. not, except they have. *Pr* 4:16
how long wilt thou *s.* O ? 6:9
folding of the hands to *s.* 10; 24:33

the *s.* of a labouring man is sweet ... not suffer him to *s.* *Eccl* 5:12
I *s.* but my heart waketh. *S of S* 5:2
none shall slumber nor *s.* *Isa* 5:27
s. a perpetual sleep. *Jer* 51:39, 57
and they shall *s.* in. *Ezek* 34:25
many that *s.* in the dust. *Dan* 12:2
s. on now, and take your rest. *Mat* 26:45; *Mark* 14:41
and should *s.* and the seed should. *Mark* 4:27
he said, Why *s.* ye? *Luke* 22:46
Lord, if he *s.* he shall. *John* 11:12
many among you *s.* *1 Cor* 11:30
we shall not all *s.*, but we. 15:51
them who *s.* in Jesus. *1 Thes* 4:14
let us not *s.* as do others. 5:6
they that *s.* sleep in the night. 7
that whether we wake or *s.* 10

sleeper

what meanest thou, O *s.*? *Jonah* 1:6

sleepest

awake, why *s.* thou? *Ps* 44:23
when thou *s.* it shall. *Pr* 6:22
Simon, *s.* thou? *Mark* 14:37
awake, thou that *s.* and. *Eph* 5:14

sleepeth

Peradventure he *s.* *1 Ki* 18:27
he that *s.* in harvest is a son that causeth shame. *Pr* 10:5
their baker *s.* all night. *Hos* 7:6
place, for the maid is not dead but *s.* *Mat* 9:24; *Mark* 5:39; *Luke* 8:52
our friend Lazarus *s.* *John* 11:11

sleeping

behold, Saul lay *s.* *1 Sam* 26:7
watchmen blind: *s.* *Isa* 56:10*
suddenly he find you *s.* *Mark* 13:36
he cometh and findeth them *s.* 14:37
Peter was *s.* between. *Acts* 12:6

sleight

about by the *s.* of men. *Eph* 4:14

slept

Adam *s.* *Gen* 2:21
Pharaoh *s.* and dreamed. 41:5
Uriah *s.* at door of the. *2 Sam* 11:9
while thine handmaid *s.* *1 Ki* 3:20
as he lay and *s.* an angel. 19:5
I have been quiet and have *s.* *Job* 3:13
I laid me down and *s.* *Ps* 3:5
the stouthearted have *s.* 76:5
while men *s.* his enemy. *Mat* 13:25
tarried, they slumbered and *s.* 25:5
of saints which *s.* arose. 27:52
stole him away while we *s.* 28:13
the firstfruits of them that *s.* *1 Cor* 15:20

see fathers

slew

seed instead of Abel, whom Cain *s.* *Gen* 4:25
they *s.* all the males. 34:25
they *s.* Hamor. 26
for in their anger they *s.* a man. 49:6
Moses *s.* the Egyptian. *Ex* 2:12*
the Lord *s.* all the firstborn. 13:15
he *s.* the bullock and took the blood. *Lev* 8:15, 23
Aaron *s.* the calf of the. 9:8, 15
s. the burnt offering, presented. 12
they *s.* all the males. *Num* 31:7
s. kings of Midian, Balaam also they *s.* 8
and *s.* the men of Ai. *Josh* 8:21
Gibeonites, they *s.* them not. 9:26
Joshua *s.* the five kings and. 10:26
they *s.* of them in Bezek. *Judg* 1:4*
they *s.* Sheshai. 10*
they *s.* the Canaanites. 17*
they *s.* of Moab 10,000 men. 3:29*
Shamgar *s.* of the Philistines. 31*
they *s.* Oreb and Zeeb the. 7:25
he *s.* men of Penuel. 8:17
men were they whom ye *s.*? 18
s. Zebah, Zalmunna. 21
Abimelech *s.* his brethren. 9:5
Samson *s.* thirty men of. 14:19*
jawbone Samson *s.* 1000. 15:15*
delivered our enemy, which *s.* 16:24
the dead which he *s.* at his. 30
Hannah *s.* a bullock. *1 Sam* 1:25
the Philistines *s.* of Israel. *1 Sam* 4:2
Israel *s.* the Ammonites. 11:11*
and his armourbearer *s.* 14:13
the people *s.* oxen and calves. 32
every man brought his ox and *s.* 34
thy servant *s.* both the lion. 17:36*
put his life in his hand, and *s.* 19:5*
Doeg *s.* 85 persons that did. 22:18
sang, Saul *s.* his thousands. 29:5
the Amalekites *s.* not any. 30:2
the Philistines *s.* Jonathan. 31:2
Abishai his brother *s.* *2 Sam* 3:30
David *s.* them and cut off. 4:12
David *s.* of the Syrians. 8:5*
David *s.* the men of 700. 10:18
for Saul, because he *s.* 21:1
he *s.* two lion-like men of Moab, he *s.* lion in. 23:20; *1 Chr* 11:22
he *s.* an Egyptian, a goodly man. *2 Sam* 23:21; *1 Chr* 11:23
and Amasa, whom he *s.* *1 Ki* 2:5
Zimri on the throne *s.* all. 16:11*
what I did when Jezebel *s.* 18:13
they took them, and Elijah *s.* 40
Had Zimri peace, who *s.* his? *2 Ki* 9:31
behold, I *s.* him, but who *s.*? 10:9*
he *s.* all that remained to. 17*
people *s.* Mattan the priest. 11:18
they *s.* Athaliah. 20; *2 Chr* 23:15, 17
was confirmed Amaziah *s.* servants. *2 Ki* 14:5; *2 Chr* 25:3
but their children he *s.* not. *2 Ki* 14:6; *2 Chr* 25:4
he *s.* of Edom in valley of salt. *2 Ki* 14:7; *1 Chr* 18:12*
took Damascus and *s.* *2 Ki* 16:9
lions which *s.* some of them. 17:25
Amon conspired and *s.* him. 21:23
people of the land *s.* them. 24 *2 Chr* 33:25
Josiah *s.* all the priests. *2 Ki* 23:20
Nebuchadnezzar *s.* sons of Zedekiah. 25:7; *Jer* 39:6; 52:10
of Gath in that land *s.* *1 Chr* 7:21
Jehoram *s.* all his brethren with. *2 Chr* 21:4
Jehu found, and *s.* the princes. 22:8
Pekah *s.* in Judah in one day. 28:6
they *s.* thy prophets. *Neh* 9:26
the Jews *s.* of their. *Esth* 9:16
God *s.* the fattest of. *Ps* 78:31
when he *s.* them, then they. 34
waters into blood, and *s.* 105:29
who *s.* great kings. 135:10
s. famous kings. 136:18
killeth an ox is as if he *s.* *Isa* 66:3
because he *s.* me not. *Jer* 20:17
Ishmael *s.* all the Jews that. 41:3
he forbare, and *s.* them not. 8
s. all that were pleasant. *Lam* 2:4
fire *s.* the men that took. *Dan* 3:22
whom he would he *s.* 5:19
Herod sent, and *s.* all the children. *Mat* 2:16
took his servants and *s.* them. 22:6
ye *s.* between the temple. 23:35
tower in Siloam fell, and *s.* *Luke* 13:4
raised up Jesus, whom ye *s.* *Acts* 5:30
Jesus whom they *s.* and. 10:39
the commandment *s.* me. *Rom* 7:11
Cain who *s.* his brother. *1 John* 3:12

slew *him*

against Abel and *s. him.* *Gen* 4:8
wicked, and the Lord *s. him.* 38:7
displeased the Lord, and he *s. him.* 10
of me, A woman *s. him.* *Judg* 9:54
took and *s. him* at passages. 12:6
by beard and *s. him.* *1 Sam* 17:35
the Philistine and *s. him.* 50
so I stood upon him and *s. him.* *2 Sam* 1:10
Ish-bosheth and *s. him.* 4:7
I took hold of him, and *s. him.* 10
compassed Absalom and *s. him.* 18:15
the son of Shimeah *s. him.* 21:21
he went down and *s. him.* 23:21
upon Joab and *s. him.* *1 Ki* 2:34
a lion met him by the way and *s. him.* 13:24; 20:36
my master and *s. him.* *2 Ki* 10:9
they sent after him to Lachish, and *s. him.* *2 Ki* 14:19; *2 Chr* 25:27
against him and *s. him.* *2 Ki* 15:10
smote Shallum and *s. him.* 14
against Pekah and *s. him.* 30
Pharaoh-necho *s. him* at. 23:29
therefore he *s. him.* *1 Chr* 10:14
so that Athaliah *s. him* not. *2 Chr* 22:11
his own servants *s. him* on. 24:25
forth of his own bowels *s. him.* 32:21
his servants *s. him* in his. 33:24
Jehoiakim who *s. him.* *Jer* 26:23
Ishmael *s. him* whom the king. 41:2
cast him out of vineyard and *s. him.* *Mat* 21:39
raiment of them that *s. him.* *Acts* 22:20

slewest

Goliath whom thou *s.* *1 Sam* 21:9

slide

their foot shall *s.* in. *Deut* 32:35
in the Lord, I shall not *s.* *Ps* 26:1*
his heart, none of steps shall *s.* 37:31

slidden

this people of Jerusalem *s.* back? *Jer* 8:5

slideth

Israel *s.* back as a. *Hos* 4:16*

slightly

hurt of my people *s.* *Jer* 6:14; 8:11

slime

had brick for stone, *s.* *Gen* 11:3
she daubed the ark with *s.* *Ex* 2:3

slimepits

Siddim was full of *s.* *Gen* 14:10

sling, *verb*

every one could *s.* stones at an hair breadth. *Judg* 20:16
them shall he *s.* out. *1 Sam* 25:29
I will *s.* out inhabitants. *Jer* 10:18

sling

(A common weapon among the Jews, especially among the shepherds, who could sling a stone to a long distance with great accuracy, and thus drive away wild beasts when other weapons would be useless)

his *s.* in his hand. *1 Sam* 17:40
over the Philistine with a *s.* 50
as out of the middle of a *s.* 25:29
bindeth a stone in a *s.* so is. *Pr* 26:8

slingers

the *s.* went about it. *2 Ki* 3:25

slings

Uzziah prepared *s.* to. *2 Chr* 26:14*

slingstones

s. are turned with him. *Job* 41:28

slip

that my feet did not *s.* *2 Sam* 22:37 *Ps* 18:36
he that is ready to *s.* *Job* 12:5
that my footsteps *s.* not. *Ps* 17:5
we should let them *s.* *Heb* 2:1

slippery

their way be dark and *s.* *Ps* 35:6
didst set them in *s.* places. 73:18
be to them as *s.* ways. *Jer* 23:12

slippeth

and the head *s.* from. *Deut* 19:5
when my foot *s.* they. *Ps* 38:16
when I said, My foot *s.*; thy. 94:18

slips

shalt set it with strange *s.* *Isa* 17:10

slipt

David *s.* out of Saul's. *1 Sam* 19:10
my steps had well nigh *s.* *Ps* 73:2

slothful

be not *s.* to go to possess. *Judg* 18:9
the *s.* shall be under. *Pr* 12:24
s. roasteth not that he took in. 27
the way of the *s.* is a hedge. 15:19*
the *s.* is brother to him that. 18:9*
s. hideth his hand in. 19:24*; 26:15*
the desire of *s.* killeth him. 21:25
the *s.* man saith. 22:13*; 26:13*
I went by field of the *s.* 24:30

Thou wicked and s. servant. Mat 25:26
not s. in business, fervent in spirit. Rom 12:11
that ye be not s. but followers of. Heb 6:12

slothfulness

s. casteth into a deep. Pr 19:15
by much s. the building. Eccl 10:18

slow

s. of speech, and of a s. tongue. Ex 4:10
art a God s. to anger. Neh 9:17
is s. to wrath, is of great. Pr 14:29
O fools and s. of heart. Luke 24:25
the Cretians are liars, s. Tit 1:12*
every man be s. to speak, s. Jas 1:19
see anger

slowly

when we had sailed s. Acts 27:7

sluggard

go to the ant, thou s. Pr 6:6
how long wilt thou sleep, O s.? 9
eyes, so is the s. to them. 10:26
the soul of the s. desireth. 13:4
s. will not plow, therefore. 20:4*
s. is wiser in his own conceit. 26:16

sluices

that make s. and ponds. Isa 19:10*

slumber, *substantive*

I will not give s. to mine. Ps 132:4
give not sleep to thine eyes, nor s. Pr 6:4
yet a little sleep, a little s. 10; 24:33
given them the spirit of s. Rom 11:8*

slumber

keepeth thee will not s. Ps 121:3
Israel, shall neither s. nor sleep. 4
none shall s. nor sleep. Isa 5:27
lying down, loving to s. 56:10
thy shepherds s. O king. Nah 3:18

slumbered

while the bridegroom tarried they all s. Mat 25:5

slumbereth

their damnation s. not. 2 Pet 2:3

slumberings

God speaketh in s. upon. Job 33:15

small

it is a s. matter thou hast. Gen 30:15
it shall become s. dust in all. Ex 9:9
as round thing, as s. as the. 16:14
every s. matter they shall. 18:22, 26
beat some of it very s. 30:36
sweet incense beaten s. Lev 16:12
a s. thing that the God of? Num 16:9
is it a s. thing that thou hast? 13
Jair went and took the s. 32:41
calf s. even as s. as dust. Deut 9:21*
doctrine shall distil as s. rain. 32:2
a s. thing in thy sight, O Lord God. 2 Sam 7:19; 1 Chr 17:17
till there be not one s. stone found. 2 Sam 17:13
I beat them as s. as the dust. 22:43 Ps 18:42
I desire one s. petition. 1 Ki 2:20
after the fire, a still s. voice. 19:12
inhabitants were of s. power, they. 2 Ki 19:26; Isa 37:27
he brought out the grove and stamped it s. to powder. 2 Ki 23:6, 15
Syrians came with a s. 2 Chr 24:24
passover offerings 2600 s. 35:8
chief of Levites gave 500 s. cattle. 9
though thy beginning was s. Job 8:7
are the consolations of God s.? 15:11
for he maketh s. the drops. 36:27*
I am s. yet do not I. Ps 119:141
adversity, thy strength is s. Pr 24:10
had left to us a s. remnant. Isa 1:9
it a s. thing for you to weary? 7:13
the remnant shall be very s. 16:14
him all vessels of s. quantity. 22:24
strangers shall be like s. dust. 29:5
are counted as the s. dust. 40:15
mountains, and beat them s. 41:15
brought me the s. cattle. 43:23
for a s. moment have I. 54:7
a s. one shall become a strong. 60:22
and they shall not be s. Jer 30:19
yet a s. number shall return. 44:28
I will make thee s. among. Jer 49:15
whoredoms a s. matter? Ezek 16:20
seemeth it s. to have eaten? 34:18
strong with a s. people. Dan 11:23
Jacob arise? he is s. Amos 7:2, 5
I have made thee s. among. Ob 2
hath despised day of s. things? Zech 4:10
they had a few s. fishes. Mark 8:7
had made a scourge of s. cords. John 2:15
barley loaves and two s. fishes. 6:9
there was no s. stir. Acts 12:18
Paul and Barnabas had no s. 15:2
there arose no s. stir about. 19:23
Demetrius brought no s. gain. 24
and no s. tempest lay on us. 27:20
very s. thing that I should. 1 Cor 4:3
turned with a very s. helm. Jas 3:4
see great

smallest

Benjamite, of s. of tribes? 1 Sam 9:21
to judge the s. matters? 1 Cor 6:2

smart

for a stranger shall s. for it. Pr 11:15

smell

smelled the s. of his raiment, said, See, s. of my son is as s. Gen 27:27
spikenard sendeth forth the s. S of S 1:12*
tender grape give a good s. 2:13*
the s. of thy ointment better. 4:10
s. of thy garments is like the s. 11
s. of thy nose like apples. 7:8
mandrakes give a s. and at. 13*
instead of sweet s. there. Isa 3:24*
s. of the fire had passed. Dan 3:27
olive, his s. as Lebanon. Hos 14:6
sent an odour of sweet s. Phil 4:18

smell, *verb*

like unto that to s. thereto. Ex 30:38
I will not s. the savour. Lev 26:31
which neither see nor s. Deut 4:28
all thy garments s. of myrrh. Ps 45:8
noses have they, they s. not. 115:6
not s. in your solemn. Amos 5:21

smelled

Lord s. a sweet savour. Gen 8:21
Isaac s. smell of his raiment. 27:27

smelleth

he s. the battle afar off. Job 39:25

smelling

fingers with sweet s. myrrh on. S of S 5:5*
lilies dropping sweet s. myrrh. 13*
where were the s.? 1 Cor 12:17
sacrifice to God for sweet s. Eph 5:2

smite

The word smite *ordinarily meaning simply strike, is very often used in the Bible with the meaning of killing, or putting to death,* 1 Sam 17:49; 2 Sam 6:7. To smite with the tongue *is to utter such reproaches as shall hurt as do blows the physical body,* Jer 18:18.

to one company and s. it. Gen 32:8
lest he will come and s. me. 11
I will s. upon the waters. Ex 7:17
say to Aaron, S. the dust. 8:16
suffer the destroyer to s. you. 12:23
behold, thou shalt s. the rock. 17:6
together, and one s. another. 21:18
if a man s. his servant and he. 20
if a man s. the eye of his servant. 26
if he s. out his man servant's or. 27
that we may s. them. Num 22:6
sceptre out of Israel shall s. 24:17
vex the Midianites and s. 25:17
s. him with an instrument. 35:16
and if he s. him with throwing. 17
with a hand weapon of wood. 18
or in enmity s. him with his. 21
thou shalt s. Canaanites. Deut 7:2
shalt surely s. inhabitants. 13:15
if any s. his neighbour. 19:11
thou shalt s. every male. 20:13
or three thousand s. Ai. Josh 7:3
help me that we may s. Gibeon. 10:4
pursue after, and s. the. 19
did Moses and Israel s. 12:6; 13:12
thou shalt s. the Midianites as one. Judg 6:16
then Benjamin began to s. 20:31, 39
go and s. the inhabitants of. 21:10
go and s. Amalek, and. 1 Sam 15:3
I will s. thee, and take. 17:46
Saul said, I will s. David. 18:11
Saul sought to s. David to. 19:10
javelin at him to s. him. 20:33
shall I go and s. the Philistines? Go, s. Philistines. 23:2
let me s. him to the earth at once, I pray thee, and I will not s. the. 26:8
why should I s. thee? 2 Sam 2:22
I say, S. Amnon, then kill. 13:28
lest he s. city with the edge. 15:14
people shall flee, and I will s. 17:2
Joab said, Why didst thou not s. him there? 18:11
s. me, I pray thee, and the men refused to s. him. 1 Ki 20:35, 37
s. every fenced city. 2 Ki 3:19
I s. them? shall I s. them? 6:21
s. them, wouldest thou s. those? 22
shalt s. the house of Ahab. 9:7
Jehu, said, S. him also in. 27
shall s. Syrians, till thou. 13:17
he said to the king, S. upon. 18
now thou shalt s. Syria. 19
sun shall not s. thee. Ps 121:6
let righteous s. me, it shall. 141:5
s. a scorner, the simple. Pr 19:25
he shall s. thee with a rod. Isa 10:24
the heat nor sun s. them. 49:10
ye fast to s. with the fist of. 58:4
come, let us s. him with. Jer 18:18
king of Babylon shall s. Judah. 21:7
he shall s. the land of. 43:11; 46:13
Nebuchadrezzar shall s. 49:28
part of hair, and s. about it. Ezek 5:2
s. with thy hand, and stamp. 6:11
him through the city and s. 9:5
son of man, s. therefore. 21:12
prophesy, and s. thine hands. 14
he said, S. the lintel. Amos 9:1
shall s. judge of Israel. Mi 5:1
melteth, the knees s. Nah 2:10
and shall s. the waves. Zech 10:11
the men, and they shall s. 11:6
whoso shall s. thee on. Mat 5:39
to s. his fellow-servants. 24:49
Lord, shall we s. with? Luke 22:49
commanded to s. Paul. Acts 23:2
ye suffer, if a man s. 2 Cor 11:20
witnesses have power to s. the earth. Rev 11:6

smite, *referred to* God, *expressly or implicitly*

nor will I s. any more. Gen 8:21
out my hand and s. Egypt. Ex 3:20
behold, I will s. all thy borders. 8:2
that I may s. thee and thy. 9:15
I will s. all the firstborn in. 12:12
when I s. the land of Egypt. 13, 23
I will s. them with the. Num 14:12
Lord shall s. with consumption. Deut 28:22
Lord shall s. with the botch. 27
s. with madness. 28
Lord shall s. thee in the knees. 35
s. through the loins of them. 33:11
The Lord shall s. him. 1 Sam 26:10
for then shall the Lord go out to s. 2 Sam 5:24; 1 Chr 14:15
Lord shall s. Israel as a. 1 Ki 14:15
Elisha said, S. this people with. 2 Ki 6:18
plague will the Lord s. 2 Chr 21:14
s. with a scab daughters. Isa 3:17
he shall s. the earth with rod. 11:4
s. Egypt in the seven streams. 15 19:22
I will s. the inhabitants of this city. Jer 21:6
will also s. mine hands. Ezek 21:17
I shall s. them that dwell in. 32:15
I will s. thy bow out of thy. 39:3
will s. the winter house. Amos 3:15
Lord will s. the great house. 6:11
the Lord will s. her power. Zech 9:4
that day I will s. every horse. 12:4
awake, O sword, s. the shepherd. 13:7 Mat 26:31; Mark 14:27

her, that she may be a s. 1 Sam 18:21
wherefore then layest thou a s.? 28:9
a net, he walketh on a s. Job 18:8*
s. is laid for him in the ground. 10*
table become a s. unto them, and.
Ps 69:22; Rom 11:9
shall deliver thee from s. Ps 91:3
their idols: which were a s. 106:36
wicked have laid s. for me. 119:110
escaped as a bird out of the s. of the
fowlers; the s. is broken. 124:7
proud have hid a s. for me. 140:5
keep me from the s. which. 141:9
have they privily laid s. for. 142:3
as a bird hasteth to the s. Pr 7:23
a fool's lips are the s. of his. 18:7
s. to man who devoureth. 20:25
lest learn his ways, and get a s. 22:25
of an evil man is a s. 29:6
bring a city into s. but wise. 8*
the fear of man bringeth a s. 25
birds that are caught in s. Eccl 9:12
for a s. to the inhabitants. Isa 8:14
fear, and the pit, and the s. are upon.
24:17, 18; Jer 48:43, 44
that lay a s. for him. Isa 29:21
I have laid a s. for thee. Jer 50:24
s. is come upon us. Lam 3:47*
he shall be taken in my s.
Ezek 12:13; 17:20
because ye have been a s. Hos 5:1
prophet is a s. of a fowler. 9:8
a s. upon the earth where no gin is
for him? . . . up a s.? Amos 3:5
for as a s. shall it come. Luke 21:35*
not that I may cast a s. 1 Cor 7:35
lest he fall into the s. 1 Tim 3:7
will be rich, fall into a s. 6:9
may recover out of the s. 2 Tim 2:26

snared

silver, lest thou be s. Deut 7:25
take heed that thou be not s. 12:30
wicked is s. in the work of. Ps 9:16
art s. with the words. Pr 6:2; 12:13
so are the sons of men s. Eccl 9:12
stumble and fall and be s. Isa 8:15
might fall, and be s. and. 28:13
are all of them s. in holes. 42:22

snares

shall be s. and traps. Josh 23:13
s. of death. 2 Sam 22:6; Ps 18:5
therefore s. are round. Job 22:10
nose pierceth through s. 40:24
on wicked he shall rain s. Ps 11:6
after my life lay s. for me. 38:12
commune of laying s. privily. 64:5
to depart from the s. of death.
Pr 13:14; 14:27
thorns and s. are in the. 22:5
woman whose heart is s. Eccl 7:26
as he that setteth s. Jer 5:26*
they have digged and hid s. 18:22

snatch

he shall s. on right hand. Isa 9:20

sneezed

child s. seven times. 2 Ki 4:35

snorting

s. of his horses was heard. Jer 8:16

snout

jewel of gold in a swine's s. Pr 11:22

snow

hand was leprous as s. Ex 4:6*
leprous, white as s. Num 12:10
slew a lion in the midst of a pit, in the
time of s. 2 Sam 23:20
out a leper white as s. 2 Ki 5:27
and wherein the s. is hid. Job 6:16
if I wash myself in s. water. 9:30
heat consumeth s. waters. 24:19
he saith to the s., Be thou on. 37:6
into treasures of the s.? 38:22
I shall be whiter than s. Ps 51:7
it was white as s. in Salmon. 68:14*
he giveth s. like wool. 147:16
fire, hail s. and vapour. 148:8
as the cold of s. in time. Pr 25:13
as s. in summer, so honour. 26:1
she is not afraid of the s. for. 31:21
scarlet shall be white as s. Isa 1:18
as the s. from heaven. 55:10
will a man leave the s.? Jer 18:14
her Nazarites purer than s. Lam 4:7
garment was white as s. Dan 7:9
his raiment white as s. Mat 28:3
Mark 9:3*
his hairs as white as s. Rev 1:14

snowy

lion in a pit in a s. day. 1 Chr 11:22*

snuffed

wild asses s. up the wind. Jer 14:6*
ye have s. at it, saith the. Mal 1:13

snuffdishes

s. shall be of pure gold. Ex 25:38
37:23
cloth, and cover his s. Num 4:9

snuffers

s. of pure gold. Ex 37:23; 1 Ki 7:50
2 Chr 4:22
s. made of money that. 2 Ki 12:13
pots and s. took they away. 25:14
Jer 52:18

snuffeth

a wild ass that s. up the. Jer 2:24

so

so Abraham departed. Gen 12:4
as the stars, so. 15:5; Rom 4:18
Rebekah said, If it be so. Gen 25:22
done foolishly in so doing. 31:28
if it must be so now do this. 43:11
Moses spake so to the. Ex 6:9
let Lord be so with you, as. 10:10
even so shall ye make it. 25:9
as the Lord commanded, so. 39:43
as the sin offering, so is. Lev 7:7
so I am commanded. 8:35; 10:13
as he hath done, so shall. 24:19, 20
bear all that is made, so. Num 4:26
as ye are, so shall stranger. 15:15
so the plague was stayed. 25:8
Ps 106:30
so shall the Lord do to. Deut 7:19
as nations Lord destroyeth, so. 8:20
so thou shalt put the evil away. 17:7
19:19; 21:21; 22:21, 22, 24
as when man riseth, even so. 22:26
and as thy days, so shall. 33:25
as strength then, even so. Josh 14:11
as I have done, so God hath. Judg 1:7
so let all thine enemies perish. 5:31
As thou art, so were they. 8:18
man is, so is his strength. 21
as they did to me, so have I. 15:11
then speakest thou so to me?
1 Sam 9:21
so shall it be done unto his. 11:7
so shall thy mother be childless.
15:33
hast thou deceived me so? 19:17
as his name is, so is he. 25:25
so shall his part be that. 30:24
so shalt thou say to my. 2 Sam 7:8
as thy servant said, so it is. 13:35
so let him curse. Who shall then
. . . done so? 16:10; 1 Ki 1:6
so shall I be saved from mine.
2 Sam 22:4; Ps 18:3
so the Lord was entreated for.
2 Sam 24:25
even so will I certainly. 1 Ki 1:30
my lord the king say so too. 36
the king said, So shall thy. 20:40
not king say so. 22:8; 2 Chr 18:7
so it fell out to him. 2 Ki 7:20
so be established, so. 2 Chr 20:20
so kill the passover and. 35:6
so it ceased to the second year of.
Ezra 4:24
so I prayed. Neh 2:4
so God shake out. 5:13
not children of Israel done so. 8:17
so didst thou get thee a name. 9:10
and so will I go in unto. Esth 4:16
so it is, hear it. Job 5:27
I know it is so of truth: but? 9:2
and if it were so, why? 21:4
so should I be delivered for. 23:7
in so doing, my Maker. 32:22
so will we sing and. Ps 21:13
let them not say, So would. 35:25
do good, so shalt thou dwell. 37:3
so panteth my soul after thee. 42:1
so shall the King desire thy. 45:11
as we have heard, so have we. 48:8
so is thy praise to the ends. Ps 48:10
thy glory, so as I have seen. 63:2
so foolish was I, and ignorant. 73:22
so he fed them. 78:72
so we thy people. 79:13
so will we not go back from. 80:18
so I gave them up. 81:12
so is thy wrath. 90:11
so the Lord pitieth them. 103:13
so let it come, so let it be. 109:17
so is every one that. 115:8; 135:18
he hath not dealt so with. 147:20
so shalt thou find favour and. Pr 3:4
so shall they be life to thy soul 22
so shall thy poverty. 6:11; 24:34
whirlwind, so is the wicked. 10:25
in his heart, so is he. 23:7
as the one dieth, so dieth. Eccl 3:19
all points as he came, so shall. 5:16
as is the good, so is the sinner. 9:2
so shall it come to pass, so. Isa 14:24
for so Lord said to me, I will. 18:4
as with the people, so with. 24:2
so have we been in thy sight. 26:17
so is Pharaoh king of Egypt to. 36:6
hast laboured, if so be thou shalt be
able to profit; if so thou. 47:12
as a lamb, so he openeth not. 53:7
so shall thy sons; so shall God. 62:5
they are my people, so he was. 63:8
so will I comfort you, ye shall. 66:13
saith the Lord so shall your seed. 22
people love to have it so. Jer 5:31
that they may find it so. 10:18
so shall ye be my people, I your God.
11:4; Ezek 37:23
saith Lord, so will I break. Jer 19:11
Come, and let us go, so we. 35:11
obey the Lord, so shall it be. 38:20
so he dwelt among the people. 39:14
so shall be with all men that. 42:17
mouth in dust, if so be. Lam 3:29
as I have done, so shall. Ezek 12:11
saying, As is the mother, so is. 16:44
repent, so iniquity shall not. 18:30
covereth, I have set thee so. 28:14
so thou shalt do, so shall ye. 45:20
if it be so, our God is. Dan 3:17
shalt abide for me; so will. Hos 3:3
so were they filled. 13:6
so shall they run. Joel 2:4
so the Lord of hosts shall. Amos 5:14
so their dwelling should. Zeph 3:7
so my Spirit remaineth. Hag 2:5
so is this people, so is this. 14
to our doings, so hath. Zech 1:6
so will I save you, and ye. 8:13
so shall be plague of horse. 14:15
Suffer it to be so now. Mat 3:15
for so persecuted they. 5:12
let your light so shine. 16
shall teach men so. 19
if God so clothe the grass. 6:30
as thou hast believed, so be. 8:13
it was never so seen in. 9:33
even so, Father: for so it seemed
good in thy. 11:26; Luke 10:21
so shall the Son of man be. Mat 12:40
Luke 11:30; 17:24
if case of the man be so. Mat 19:10
when cometh shall find so doing..
24:46; Luke 12:43
are ye so without? Mark 7:18
so shall it not be among you. 10:43
watch, and find them so. Luke 12:38
and so it is. 54
found it so as the women said. 24:24
God so loved the world. John 3:16
Father said to me, so I speak. 12:50
ye say well, for so I am. 13:13
even so I do. 14:31
ye bear much fruit, so shall. 15:8
as the Father hath loved me, so. 9
so have I also sent them into world.
17:18; 20:21
thou the high priest so? 18:22
this Jesus shall so come. Acts 1:11
he hath so fulfilled. 3:18
are these things so? 7:1
as a lamb dumb, so opened he. 8:32
for so hath the Lord. 13:47
they so spake, that a great 14:1
so were the churches. 16:5
so mightily grew the word of. 19:20

for so had he appointed. Acts 20:13
so worship I the God. 24:14
so came to pass they escaped. 27:44
not as the offence, so also. Rom 5:15
so they that are in the flesh. 8:8
so then it is not of him that. 9:16
so all Israel shall be saved. 11:26
so doing shalt heap coals of. 12:20
so every one shall give. 14:12
saved, yet so as by fire. 1 Cor 3:15
let man so account of us. 4:1
concerning him that hath so. 5:3
is it so, that there is not a wise? 6:5
so let him walk, so ordain I. 7:17
good for a man so to be. 26
but she is happier if she so abide. 40
when ye sin so against the. 8:12
even so hath Lord ordained. 9:14
so run. 24, 26
so let him eat that bread. 11:28
one body, so also is Christ. 12:12
so we preach, and so ye. 15:11
as he is Christ's, so. 2 Cor 10:7
so will I keep myself from. 11:9
so am I; Israelites? so am I. 22
so, I did not burden you. 12:16
then persecuted, even so it is now. Gal 4:29
bear burdens, and so fulfil the. 6:2
new man, so making peace. Eph 2:15
mark them which walk so. Phil 3:17
my brethren, so stand fast in. 4:1
received Christ Jesus, so. Col 2:6
even so we speak, not. 1 Thes 2:4
and so shall we ever be with. 4:17
so I sware in my wrath. Heb 3:11
as I may so say, Levi paid. 7:9
so be ye holy. 1 Pet 1:15
so is the will of God. 2:15
if the will of God be so. 3:17
he ought himself so to walk. 1 John 2:6
God so loved us, we ought. 4:11
because as he is, so are we. 17
even so, amen. Rev 1:7
even so, come, Lord Jesus. 22:20
see **did, do, great, long, much**

so be it

said, According to your words, so be it. Josh 2:21
I answered and said, So be it, O. Jer 11:5

not so

do not so wickedly. Gen 19:7
oh not so, my Lord. 18
it must not be so done in. 29:26
not so, my father, this is. 48:18
not so, go ye that are. Ex 10:11
servant Moses is not so. Num 12:7
Lord, but they did not so. Judg 2:17
is it not so? 14:15
it is not so. 1 Sam 20:2
the matter is not so. 2 Sam 20:21
house be not so with God. 23:5
but it is not so with me. Job 9:35
if it be not so, who will? 24:25
but now because it is not so. 35:15
ungodly are not so, but are. Ps 1:4
the foolish doeth not so. Pr 15:7
not so, nor heart think so. Isa 10:7
but his lies shall not be so. 16:6
it shall not be so; his lies shall not so affect it. Jer 48:30
beginning it was not so. Mat 19:8
but it shall not be so among. 20:26
not so, lest there be not. 25:9
not so, but he shall be. Luke 1:60
over them, but shall not be so. 22:26
if it were not so, I would. John 14:2
Not so, Lord. Acts 10:14; 11:8
not only so, but we glory. Rom 5:3
not only so, but we also joy in. 11
ye have not so learned. Eph 4:20
things ought not so to be. Jas 3:10

so that

so that all that hear. Gen 21:6
so that I come again to my. 28:21
so that land of Egypt and. 47:13
so that he would not let Israel go. Ex 10:20; 11:10
smiteth a man, so that. 21:12
so that thou shalt be mad for. Deut 28:34
so that they could not. Judg 2:14
shouted, so that the. 1 Sam 4:5
so that his name was. 18:30
so that thy children take heed. 1 Ki 8:25; 2 Chr 6:16
his face, so that he died. 2 Ki 8:15
so that they shall not say. 9:37
so that after him was none. 18:5
so that there should be. Ezra 9:14
so that this man was. Job 1:3
set me as a mark, so that I am. 7:20
so that I am not able. Ps 40:12
so that a man shall say. 58:11
he led them safely, so that. 78:53
so that it went ill with. 106:32
so that he wanted nothing. Eccl 6:2
so that thou didst not lay. Isa 47:7
been forsaken, so that no. 60:15
so that I will not take. Jer 33:26
so that the Lord could no. 44:22
so that in all your doings your sins. Ezek 21:24
so that all the trees in Eden. 31:9
so that no beast might. Dan 8:4
so that no man did lift. Zech 1:21
answered not, so that. Mark 15:5
so that they which would pass to. Luke 16:26
so that they are without. Rom 1:20
so that from Jerusalem I. 15:19
so that contrariwise. 2 Cor 2:7
so that I rejoiced the more. 7:7
so that ye cannot do the. Gal 5:17
so that ye were ensamples to all. 1 Thes 1:7
so that we may boldly say, the Lord is my helper. Heb 13:6

was so, or so was

and it was so. Gen 1:7, 9, 11, 15 24, 30
interpreted to us, so it was. 41:13
so it was always, cloud. Num 9:16
so it was when cloud was on. 20
so it was when the cloud abode. 21
fleece only, and it was so. Judg 6:38
it was so that all who saw it. 19:30
men of Ashdod saw that it was so. 1 Sam 5:7
it was so that when he turned. 10:9
it was so from that day. 30:25
it was so when any came to the king. 2 Sam 15:2
it was so that when any man. 5
so was all the counsel of. 16:23
so was it charged me. 1 Ki 13:9
so it was that Israel. 2 Ki 17:7
so was Israel carried away to. 23
so was the commandment of the Lord. 2 Chr 29:25
and so it was that while. Luke 2:6
Jesus, who was so named of. 21
and so was also James and. 5:10
affirmed it was even so. Acts 12:15

So

he sent messengers to S. 2 Ki 17:4

soaked

their land shall be s. with. Isa 34:7*

sober

whether we be s. it is. 2 Cor 5:13*
but let us watch and be s. 1 Thes 5:6
are of the day be s., putting on. 8
a bishop then must be s. 1 Tim 3:2* Tit 1:8*
deacons' wives must be s. faithful. 1 Tim 3:11*
that aged men be s. grave. Tit 2:2*
teach the young women to be s. 4
loins of your mind, be s. 1 Pet 1:13
be ye therefore s. and watch. 4:7*
be s., be vigilant, because your. 5:8

soberly

but to think s. according. Rom 12:3
that we should live s. Tit 2:12

sober minded

exhort young men to be s. minded. Tit 2:6

soberness

the words of truth and s. Acts 26:25

sobriety

adorn themselves with s. 1 Tim 2:9
in faith and holiness with s. 15

socket

talents, a talent for a s. Ex 38:27

sockets

make forty s. of silver... two s. under one board for two tenons, two s. Ex 26:19, 21, 25; 36:24, 26
their s. of silver, sixteen s. 26:25 36; 30:36
thou shalt cast five s. of brass. 26:37 36:38
their twenty s. shall be of brass. 27:10; 38:10, 11
pillars ten, their s. ten. 27:12; 38:12
one side, their s. three. 27:14
side shall be three s. 15; 38:14, 15
be four, their s. four. 27:16
of silver and their s. brass. 17, 18
make bars, pillars, s. of. 35:11
court, pillars, and their s. 17
s. of the sanctuary, s. of the veil, hundred s. 38:27
brass of the offerings he made s. 30
s. of the court, and the s. of. 31
tabernacle and fastened his s. 40:18
charge of the sons of Merari shall be the s. Num 3:26, 37; 4:31, 32
marble set on s. of gold. S of S 5:15

sod

(American Revision, everywhere in the Old Testament, boiled)
Jacob s. pottage, Esau. Gen 25:29
offerings s. they in pots. 2 Chr 35:13

sodden

(American Revision, everywhere in the Old Testament, boiled)
eat not of it raw, nor s. Ex 12:9
wherein it is s. shall be broken, if it be s. in a brasen pot. Lev 6:28
priest shall take the s. Num 6:19
he will not have s. flesh. 1 Sam 2:15
the women have s. their. Lam 4:10

sodering

it is ready for s.; he fastened. Isa 41:7

Sodom

destroyed S. and Gomorrah. Gen 13:10
the men of S. were wicked. 13
goods of S. and Gomorrah. 14:11
they took Lot who dwelt in S. 12
king of S. went out to meet. 17
because the cry of S. is great. 18:20
if I find in S. fifty righteous. 26
Lord rained upon S. fire out. 19:24
like the overthrow of S. Deut 29:23 Isa 13:19; Jer 49:18; 50:40
vine is of the vine of S. Deut 32:32
we should have been as S. Isa 1:9
word of the Lord, ye rulers of S. 10
declare their sin as S. 3:9
of them unto me as S. Jer 23:14
punishment of the sin of S. Lam 4:6
thy younger sister is S. Ezek 16:46 48, 49, 55
again the captivity of S. 53
as God overthrew S. Amos 4:11
Moab shall be as S. Zeph 2:9
tolerable for land of S. Mat 10:15 11:24; Mark 6:11; Luke 10:12
Lot went out of S. Luke 17:29
seed, we had been as S. Rom 9:29
turning cities of S. and. 2 Pet 2:6
even as S. and Gomorrah. Jude 7
city spiritually called S. Rev 11:8

sodomite

there shall be no s. of. Deut 23:17

sodomites

there were also s. in. 1 Ki 14:24
Asa took away the s. 15:12
Jehoshaphat took the remnant of the s. 22:46
down the houses of the s. 2 Ki 23:7

soft

God maketh my heart s. Job 23:16*
speak s. words unto thee? 41:3
makest it s. with showers. Ps 65:10
a s. answer turneth. Pr 15:1
and a s. tongue breaketh. 25:15
s. raiment; they that wear s. clothing. Mat 11:8; Luke 7:25

softer

words were s. than oil. Ps 55:21

softly
I will lead on *s.*, as the children be able to endure. *Gen* 33:14
Jael went *s.* to him and. *Judg* 4:21
came *s.* and uncovered. *Ruth* 3:7
lay in sackcloth, went *s.* *1 Ki* 21:27
waters of Shiloah that go *s.* *Isa* 8:6
I shall go *s.* all my years in. 38:15
when south wind blew *s.* *Acts* 27:13

soil
it was planted in a good *s.* *Ezek* 17:8

sojourn
down into Egypt to *s.* *Gen* 12:10
This one fellow came in to *s.* 19:9
s. in this land, and I will be. 26:3
they said, For to *s.* in the land. 47:4
will *s.* with thee and keep. *Ex* 12:48
Lev 19:33; *Num* 9:14; 15:14
which *s.* that offereth sacrifice. *Lev* 17:8
of strangers that *s.* that eateth. 10
s. among you, that hunteth. 13
of strangers that *s.*, that giveth. 20:2
of strangers that *s.*, of them. 25:45
a Levite went to *s.* *Judg* 17:8
said to Micah, I go to *s.* where. 9
Elimelech went to *s.* *Ruth* 1:1
widow with whom I *s.* *1 Ki* 17:20
s. wheresoever thou canst *s.* *2 Ki* 8:1
woe is me, that I *s.* in Meshech. *Ps* 120:5
carry her afar off to *s.* *Isa* 23:7
went down into Egypt to *s.* 52:4
faces to enter into Egypt and go to *s.* *Jer* 42:15, 17; 44:12, 14, 28
place whither ye desire to *s.* 42:22
shall no more *s.* there. *Lam* 4:15
them from where they *s.* *Ezek* 20:38
and strangers who *s.* among. 47:22
that his seed should *s.* *Acts* 7:6

sojourned
from thence Abraham *s.* *Gen* 20:1
and *s.* in the Philistines' land. 21:34
I *s.* with Laban, and stayed. 32:4
Abraham and Isaac *s.* 35:27
come from where he *s.* *Deut* 18:6
s. in Egypt with a few, and. 26:5
s. in Bethlehem-judah. *Judg* 17:7
an old man of Ephraim *s.* in. 19:16
she *s.* in the land of the. *2 Ki* 8:2
Jacob *s.* in the land. *Ps* 105:23
by faith he *s.* in the land. *Heb* 11:9

sojourner
I am a *s.* with you, give. *Gen* 23:4
a *s.* of the priest shall not. *Lev* 22:10
relieve him: though he be a *s.* 25:35
shall be as a *s.* with thee. 40
s. wax rich by thee and brother sell himself to *s.* 47
six cities a refuge for Israel and *s.* *Num* 35:15
I am a stranger, a *s.*, as. *Ps* 39:12

sojourners
strangers and *s.* with me. *Lev* 25:23
the Beerothites were *s.* *2 Sam* 4:3
we are *s.* as were all. *1 Chr* 29:15

sojourneth
borrow of her that *s.* *Ex* 3:22
be to him that is homeborn, and to stranger that *s.* 12:49; *Lev* 16:29
stranger that *s.* eat blood. *Lev* 17:12
that *s.* among you shall keep. 18:26
meat for stranger that *s.* 25:6
be for you and for the stranger that *s.* *Num* 15:15; 16:29; 19:10
forgiven the stranger that *s.* 15:26
refuge for stranger that *s.* *Josh* 20:9
in any place where he *s.* *Ezra* 1:4
every one that *s.* in Israel. *Ezek* 14:7
in whatever tribe stranger *s.* 47:23

sojourning
the *s.* of Israel in Egypt. *Ex* 12:40
a certain Levite *s.* on. *Judg* 19:1
pass the time of your *s.* *1 Pet* 1:17

solace
come, let us *s.* ourselves. *Pr* 7:18

sold
Esau *s.* his birthright. *Gen* 25:33
father hath *s.* us, devoured. 31:15
s. Joseph to the Ishmaelites. 37:28
the Midianites *s.* him into. 36
Joseph *s.* corn unto the. *Gen* 41:56
was that *s.* to all the people. 42:6
Joseph your brother whom ye *s.* 45:4
angry with yourselves that ye *s.* 5
the Egyptians *s.* every man. 47:20
the priests *s.* not their lands. 22
nothing then shall be *s.* *Ex* 22:3
the land shall not be *s.* *Lev* 25:23
redeem that which his brother *s.* 25
house that was *s.* shall go out. 33
of the suburbs may not be *s.* 34
shall not be *s.* as bondmen. 42
no devoted thing shall be *s.* 27:28
and if thy brother be *s.* *Deut* 15:12
there shall ye be *s.* unto your. 28:68
except their Rock had *s.* them. 32:30
he *s.* them into the hands. *Judg* 2:14
s. them to Cushan-rishathaim. 3:8
s. to Jabin. 4:2
s. them into the hands of the. 10:7
s. them into the hand of Sisera. *1 Sam* 12:9
thou hast *s.* thyself to. *1 Ki* 21:20
ass's head was *s.* for 80. *2 Ki* 6:25
fine flour *s.* for a shekel. 7:1, 16
Israel *s.* themselves to do. 17:17
our brethren who were *s.* to the . . . they be *s.* unto us? *Neh* 5:8
in day wherein they *s.* victuals. 13:15
who brought ware and *s.* on. 16
are *s.* I and my people to be slain and perish; but . . . been *s.* *Esth* 7:4
Joseph who was *s.* for. *Ps* 105:17
creditors is it to whom I *s.* you? for your iniquities have ye *s.* *Isa* 50:1
ye have *s.* yourselves for. 52:3
brother who hath been *s.* *Jer* 34:14
our wood is *s.* unto us. *Lam* 5:4
return to that which is *s.* *Ezek* 7:13
and they have *s.* a girl. *Joel* 3:3
children of Judah have ye *s.* 6
out of place whither ye *s.* them. 7
s. the righteous for silver. *Amos* 2:6
are not two sparrows *s.*? *Mat* 10:29
went and *s.* all that he had. 13:46
commanded him to be *s.* 18:25
s. and bought, overthrew . . . that *s.* 21:12; *Mark* 11:15; *Luke* 19:45
might have been *s.* for much and. *Mat* 26:9; *Mark* 14:5; *John* 12:5
are not five sparrows *s.*? *Luke* 12:6
bought, they *s.* they planted. 17:28
the temple those that *s.* *John* 2:14
said to them that *s.* doves, Take. 16
and *s.* their possessions and goods. *Acts* 2:45; 4:34
Joses having land *s.* it and. 4:37
Ananias *s.* a possession. 5:1
after it was *s.* was it not in thine? 4
ye *s.* the land for so much? 8
I am carnal, *s.* under sin. *Rom* 7:14
is *s.* in shambles, that. *1 Cor* 10:25
one morsel of meat *s.* *Heb* 12:16

soldier
parts, to every *s.* a part. *John* 19:23
Cornelius called a devout *s.* that waited on. *Acts* 10:7
to dwell by himself, with a *s.* 28:16
hardness as a good *s.* *2 Tim* 2:3
who hath chosen him to be a *s.* 4

soldiers
the *s.* fell upon the. *2 Chr* 25:13*
to require of the king *s.* *Ezra* 8:22
the armed *s.* of Moab. *Isa* 15:4*
having *s.* under me. *Mat* 8:9 *Luke* 7:8
s. took Jesus, and gathered unto him the whole band of *s.* *Mat* 27:27
gave large money unto the *s.* 28:12
s. demanded, saying. *Luke* 3:14
the *s.* mocked him, offered. 23:36
s. platted a crown of. *John* 19:2
the *s.* took his garments, and. 23
these things the *s.* did. 24
s. brake the legs. 32
but one of the *s.* with a spear. 34
Peter to four quaternions of *s.* *Acts* 12:4
Peter was sleeping between two *s.* 6
no small stir among the *s.* 18
saw the chief captain and *s.* 21:32
that he was borne of the *s.* 35
make ready 200 *s.* to go to. 23:23
Paul said to the *s.* Except. *Acts* 27:31
then the *s.* cut off the ropes. 32
the *s.*' counsel was to kill. 42

sole
but the dove found no rest for the *s.* of her foot. *Gen* 8:9
a sore botch from the *s.* *Deut* 28:35
would not set the *s.* of her foot. 56
neither shall the *s.* of thy foot. 65
every place *s.* of your foot. *Josh* 1:3
from the *s.* of his foot to the crown of his head was no. *2 Sam* 14:25
Satan smote Job from *s.* *Job* 2:7
from *s.* of foot to head. *Isa* 1:6
s. of their feet like the *s.* *Ezek* 1:7
see **feet**

solemn
in your *s.* days ye. *Num* 10:10*
sing praise with a *s.* sound. *Ps* 92:3
it is iniquity, even the *s.* *Isa* 1:13
called as in a *s.* day. *Lam* 2:22
what will ye do in *s.* day? *Hos* 9:5
see **assembly, feast, feasts**

solemnities
Zion, the city of our *s.* *Isa* 33:20
offerings in *s.* of Israel. *Ezek* 45:17*
in the *s.* meat offering shall. 46:11

solemnity
in the *s.* of the year of. *Deut* 31:10*
shall have song as when a holy *s.* is. *Isa* 30:29*

solemnly
the man did *s.* protest. *Gen* 43:3
yet protest *s.* to them. *1 Sam* 8:9

solitarily
people which dwell *s.* in. *Mi* 7:14

solitary
that night be *s.*, let no. *Job* 3:7*
and famine they were *s.* 30:3*
setteth the *s.* in families. *Ps* 68:6
in the wilderness in a *s.* 107:4*
wilderness and *s.* place. *Isa* 35:1
how doth city sit *s.* that. *Lam* 1:1
Jesus departed into a *s.* *Mark* 1:35*

Solomon
born to David in Jerusalem, *S.* *2 Sam* 5:14; *1 Chr* 3:5; 14:4
he called his name *S.* *2 Sam* 12:24
S. his brother he called not. *1 Ki* 1:10, 19, 26
S. thy son shall reign after. 13, 17, 30
I and my son *S.* shall be. 1:21
God save king *S.* 34, 39
David even so be he with *S.* 37
hath made *S.* king. 43
God make the name of *S.* 47
let *S.* swear to me that he will. 51
David charged *S.* his son. 2:1
king *S.* sware. 23
established in the hand of *S.* 46
S. made affinity with Pharaoh. 3:1
S. loved the Lord. 3
the Lord appeared to *S.* 5; 9:2 *2 Chr* 1:7; 7:12
S. had asked this thing. *1 Ki* 3:10
S.'s provision for one day. 4:22
God gave *S.* wisdom. 29; 5:12
came to hear the wisdom of *S.* 4:34 *Mat* 12:42; *Luke* 11:31
Tyre sent his servants to *S.* *1 Ki* 5:1
king *S.* raised a levy out of. 13
so *S.* built the house and. 6:14 *2 Chr* 7:11; *Acts* 7:47
the work that *S.* made. *1 Ki* 7:51
S. assembled the elders of Israel. 8:1; *2 Chr* 5:2
S. spread forth his hands. *1 Ki* 8:22
when *S.* made an end of praying. 54; *2 Chr* 7:1
S. held a feast. *1 Ki* 8:65
S. made a navy of ships. 9:26
when the queen of Sheba heard of the fame of *S.* 10:1; *2 Chr* 9:1
all the earth sought to *S.* *1 Ki* 10:24 *2 Chr* 9:23
but king *S.* loved many. *1 Ki* 11:1
S. clave to these in love. 2
when *S.* was old. 4
S. went after Ashtoreth and. 5
S. did evil. 6
S. built for Chemosh and Molech. 7

the Lord was angry with S, 1 Ki 11:9
Edomite, an adversary to S. 14
S. built Millo. 27
S. made Jeroboam ruler over. 28
S. sought therefore to kill. 40
S. slept with his fathers. 43
fled from the presence of S. 12:2
shields of gold which S. made.
14:26; 2 Chr 12:9
of which the Lord said to David and
to S. 2 Ki 21:7; 2 Chr 33:7
S. my son is young. 1 Chr 22:5
for his name shall be S. 9
to help S. 17
S. thy son, he shall build. 28:6
thou S. my son, know the God. 9
David gave to S. the pattern. 11
S. my son, whom God alone. 29:1
give to S. my son a perfect. 19
S. sat on the throne of the. 23
Lord magnified S. exceedingly. 25
S. numbered all the. 2 Chr 2:17
are the things wherein S. 3:3
since time of S. not such joy. 30:26
children of S.'s servants. Ezra 2:55
58; Neh 7:57, 60; 11:3
the commandment of S. Neh 12:45
did not king S. sin by? 13:26
proverbs of S. Pr 1:1; 10:1; 25:1
of songs which is S.'s. S of S 1:1
but comely, as the curtains of S. 5
behold, his bed which is S.'s. 3:7
behold king S. 11
S. had a vineyard at. 8:11
S. must have a thousand. 12
the sea S. made was. Jer 52:20
David begat S. Mat 1:6
S. begat Roboam. 7
S. in all his glory. 6:29; Luke 12:27
a greater than S. is here.
Mat 12:42; Luke 11:31
Jesus walked in S.'s. John 10:23
people ran to them to S.'s. Acts 3:11
with one accord in S.'s porch. 5:12

some

Lot said, lest s. evil. Gen 19:19
let me now leave with thee s. 33:15
cast him into s. pit, and we will say,
S. evil beast hath. 37:20
took s. of his brethren and. 47:2
gathered s. more, s. less. Ex 16:17
but s. of them left of it till. 20
s. went out on seventh day. 27
shall put s. of the blood. Lev 4:7, 18
the priest shall dip his finger in s. 17
Arad took s. of them. Num 21:1
thou shalt put s. of thine. 27:20
because he hath found s. Deut 24:1
let fall s. of the handfuls. Ruth 2:16
s. bade me kill thee. 1 Sam 24:10
hid in s. pit, or in s. 2 Sam 17:9
in him there is found s. 1 Ki 14:13
s. mischief will come. 2 Ki 7:9
but I will grant s. deliverance.
2 Chr 12:7
Asa oppressed s. of the people. 16:10
s. had wives by whom. Ezra 10:44
s. said, We have mortgaged our.
Neh 5:3
saw I s. treading winepresses. 13:15
and s. of my servants set. 19
s. remove landmarks. Job 24:2
s. trust in chariots, s. Ps 20:7
I looked for s. to take pity. 69:20
unless they cause s. to fall. Pr 4:16
not leave s. gleaning? Jer 49:9
and it cast down s. of the. Dan 8:10
s. of them of understanding. 11:35
s. to everlasting life, and s. to. 12:2
overthrown s., as God. Amos 4:11
they not leave s. grapes? Ob 5
s. fell by the way side. Mat 13:4
Mark 4:4; Luke 8:5
s. fell on stony places, where they had
not much. Mat 13:5; Mark 4:5
and s. fell among thorns. Mat 13:7
Mark 4:7; Luke 8:7
S. say thou art John the Baptist, s.
Mat 16:14; Mark 8:28; Luke 9:19
be s. standing here, which shall not.
Mat 16:28; Mark 9:1; Luke 9:27
s. eunuchs which were so born, s.
made. Mat 19:12
s. ye shall kill and crucify, s.
Mat 23:34
they worshipped him, but s. 28:17
s. fell upon a rock, and. Luke 8:6
and s. of you shall cause to. 21:16
there are s. of you that. John 6:64
Peter overshadow s. of. Acts 5:15
giving out that himself was s. 8:9
how can I except s. man should? 31
seeking s. to lead him by. 13:11
s. of them believed. 17:4
hear s. new thing. 21
s. mocked. 32
s. cried one thing, s. 19:32; 21:34
I pray you take s. meat. 27:34
s. on boards, s. on broken. 44
s. believed and s. believed not. 28:24
that I may impart to you s.
Rom 1:11
that I might have s. fruit. 13
for what if s. did not believe? 3:3
as s. affirm that we say, Let us. 8
for a good man s. would even. 5:7
any means I might save s. of. 11:14
and if s. of the branches be. 17
now s. are puffed up. 1 Cor 4:18
such were s. of you, but ye. 6:11
for s. with conscience of the. 8:7
might by all means save s. 9:22
neither be idolaters as were s. 10:7
commit fornication, as s. of them. 8
as s. tempted Christ and were. 9
nor murmur ye as s. of them. 10
and God hath set s. in the. 12:28
greater part remain, but s. 15:6
how say s. that there is no? 12
for s. have not the knowledge. 34
I think to be bold against s. which
think of us as if. 2 Cor 10:2
not compare ourselves with s. 12
be s. that trouble you. Gal 1:7
s. prophets, s. evangelists. Eph 4:11
s. indeed preach Christ. Phil 1:15
there are s. among you. 2 Thes 3:11
charge s. that they teach. 1 Tim 1:3
from which s. having swerved. 6
s. having put away, have made. 19
in latter times s. shall depart. 4:1
s. are already turned aside. 5:15
s. men's sins open beforehand, s. 24
the good works of s. are. 25
which while s. coveted after. 6:10
overthrow the faith of s. 2 Tim 2:18
s. vessels to honour and s. 20
house is builded by s. man. Heb 3:4
for s. when they heard, did. 16
it remaineth, that s. must. 4:6
as the manner of s. is. 10:25
having provided s. better. 11:40
thereby s. entertained angels. 13:2
Lord is not slack, as s. 2 Pet 3:9
in which are s. things hard to be. 16
of s. have compassion. Jude 22
devil shall cast s. of you. Rev 2:10

somebody

Jesus said, S. hath touched me.
Luke 8:46*
boasting himself to be s. Acts 5:36

something

for he thought, s. hath. 1 Sam 20:26
that s. should be given. Mark 5:43
and seeking to catch s. Luke 11:54
should give s. to poor. John 13:29
to receive s. of them. Acts 3:5
as though ye would enquire s. 23:15*
man who hath s. to say to thee. 18
a man think himself to be s. Gal 6:3

sometime, -s

ye who were s. afar off. Eph 2:13*
for ye were s. darkness, but. 5:8*
you that were s. alienated. Col 1:21*
in which ye walked s. when. 3:7
also were s. foolish. Tit 3:3*
who s. were disobedient . . . in days
of Noah. 1 Pet 3:20*

somewhat

have done s. against commandments.
Lev 4:13*, 27*
ruler hath done s. through. 22*
if the plague be s. dark. 13:6, 21
26, 28, 56
bright spot, and s. reddish. 19, 24
he said, I have s. to say. 1 Ki 2:14
him, and take s. of him. 2 Ki 5:20
ease s. grievous servitude of.
2 Chr 10:4*
ease s. the yoke. 9*
make it s. lighter for us. 10
Simon, I have s. to say. Luke 7:40
as to enquire s. of him. Acts 23:20
that I might have s. to write. 25:26
if first I be s. filled with. Rom 15:24*
that you may have s. to. 2 Cor 5:12
though I should boast s. more. 10:8
those who seemed to be s. Gal 2:6
necessity this man have s. Heb 8:3
nevertheless, I have s. Rev 2:4

son

This word is used as now, and also for a grandson, 2 Sam 9:6, *and even for more remote descendants,* Isa 19:11. *The word is also used for a pupil, much as one uses it now, as a term of affection,* 1 Tim 1:2. *It is also used in such expressions as* son of Belial, 1 Sam 25:17.

I will give thee s. of Sarah.
Gen 17:16, 19; 18:10, 14
Sarah bare Abraham a s. 21:2, 7
cast this bondwoman and her s. 10
my master's wife bare a s. 24:36
appointed for my master's s. 44
let her be thy master's s.'s wife. 51
therefore given me this s. 29:33
heard me, and given me a s. 30:6
shall add to me another s. 24
shalt have this s. also. 35:17
because he was the s. of his. 37:3
if it be a s. then ye. Ex 1:16
every s. that is born ye shall. 22
grew, and he became her s. 2:10
cut off the foreskin of her s. 4:25
have gored a s. or a daughter. 21:31
the s. of thy handmaid may. 23:12
that s. that is priest in stead. 29:30
her purifying for a s. Lev 12:6
the s. of an Israelitish. 24:10
the Israelitish woman's s. 11
his uncle, or his uncle's s. may. 25:49
me, thou s. of Zippor. Num 23:18
because he hath no s. 27:4
if a man die and have no s. 8
if s. of thy mother entice. Deut 13:6
the s. of the beloved, firstborn, before the s. of the hated. 21:16, 17
a stubborn and rebellious s. 18
this our s. is stubborn and. 20
eye shall be evil towards her s. 28:56
in his youngest s. set up. Josh 6:26
border went by the valley of s. 15:8
arise, Barak, lead captivity captive,
thou s. of. Judg 5:12
have made thee the s. of his. 9:18
Is not he the s. of Jerubbaal? 28
the s. of a strange woman. 11:2
besides her he had neither s. 34
conceive and bear a s. 13:3, 5, 7
the woman bare a s. and called. 24
Ruth bare a s. Ruth 4:13
a s. born to Naomi. 17
Hannah gave her s. suck until.
1 Sam 1:23
Fear not, for thou hast born a s. 4:20
Kish had a s. whose name was. 9:2
that is come to s. of Kish? 10:11
I have seen a s. of Jesse. 16:18
whose s. is this? 17:55
whose s. art thou? 58
cometh not the s. of Jesse? 20:27
s. of the perverse rebellious. 30
as long as the s. of Jesse liveth. 31
will s. of Jesse give you fields. 22:7
Doeg said, I saw the s. of Jesse. 9
Hear now, thou s. of Ahitub. 12
who is the s. of Jesse? 25:10
he is such a s. of Belial. 17
am the s. of a stranger. 2 Sam 1:13
Jonathan hath yet a s. lame. 9:3
given thy master's s. all that. 9
master's s. may have food to eat;
Mephibosheth thy master's s. 10
I will shew kindness to the s. 10:2
where is thy master's s.? 16:3
my hand against the king's s. 18:12
I have no s. to keep my name in. 18
tidings, because king's s. is dead. 20

inheritance in the *s.* of Jesse. *2 Sam* 20:1
thou hast given him a *s.* *1 Ki* 3:6
bowels yearned upon her *s.* 26
David a wise *s.* over this. 5:7
Hiram was a widow's *s.* of. 7:14
neither inheritance in the *s.* of Jesse. 12:16; *2 Chr* 10:16
Abijah the *s.* of Jeroboam. *1 Ki* 14:1
to ask a thing of thee for her *s.* 5
the *s.* of the mistress of the. 17:17
on the widow, by slaying her *s.* 20
carry him back to Joash the king's *s.* 22:26; *2 Chr* 18:25
reigned, because he had no *s.* *2 Ki* 1:17
she said unto her *s.*, Bring me. 4:6
season thou shalt embrace a *s.* 16
and the woman bare a *s.* at. 17
did I desire a *s.* of my lord? 28
took up her *s.* 37
thy *s.* that we may eat him: and she hath hid her *s.* 6:29
see ye how this *s.* of a murderer. 32
the woman, whose *s.* he had. 8:1
her *s.* whom Elisha restored to. 5
Athaliah saw her *s.* was dead. 11:1
2 Chr 22:10
shewed them the king's *s.* *2 Ki* 11:4
he brought forth the king's *s.* and. 12
side, thou *s.* of Jesse. *1 Chr* 12:18
also was the *s.* of the giant. 20:6
behold, a *s.* shall be born to. 22:9
there was never a *s.* left him. *2 Chr* 21:17
buried him, because he is *s.* of. 22:9
he said, Behold, the king's *s.* 23:3
Zabdiel their overseer, *s.* *Neh* 11:14
he shall neither have *s.* *Job* 18:19
kiss the *S.* lest he be angry. *Ps* 2:12
thine own mother's *s.* 50:20
righteousness unto the king's *s.* 72:1
the *s.* of thine handmaid. 86:16
nor shall the *s.* of wickedness. 89:22
I am the *s.* of thine. 116:16
as a father the *s.* in whom he. *Pr* 3:12
I was my father's *s.*, only. 4:3
a wise *s.* maketh a glad father. 10:1
15:20
a wise *s.*: he that sleepeth in harvest is a *s.* causeth. 10:5; 17:2; 19:26
a wise *s.* heareth his father's. 13:1
foolish *s.* is a grief to his. 17:25
a foolish *s.* is the calamity. 19:13
keepeth the law, is a wise *s.* 28:7
what, the *s.* of my womb, *s.* of? 31:2
he begetteth a *s.*, nothing. *Eccl* 5:14
blessed land, when king is *s.* 10:17
not afraid of anger of the *s.* *Isa* 7:4
let us set a king in it, even the *s.* 6
Samaria is Remaliah's *s.* 9
virgin shall conceive and bear a *s.* 14
us a child is born, unto us a *s.* 9:6
fallen, O Lucifer, *s.* of. 14:12
I will cut off from Babylon *s.* 22
I am *s.* of the wise, the *s.* of. 19:11
not have compassion on the *s.* 49:15
the *s.* of the stranger speak. 56:3
mourning, as for an only *s.* *Jer* 6:26
should not have a *s.* to reign. 33:21
deliver neither *s.* nor daughter. *Ezek* 14:20
also the soul of the *s.* is mine. 18:4
if he beget *s.* that is a robber. 10
a *s.* that seeth his father's sins. 14
why, doth not *s.* bear iniquity of the father? when the *s.* hath done. 19
s. shall not bear the iniquity of the father, nor the father of the *s.* 20
for *s.* or daughter they may. 44:25
which bare him a *s.* *Hos* 1:3, 8
he is an unwise *s.* for he. 13:13
nor was I a prophet's *s.* *Amos* 7:14
as mourning of an only *s.* 8:10
for the *s.* dishonoureth. *Mi* 7:6
a *s.* honoureth his father. *Mal* 1:6
she shall bring forth a *s.* *Mat* 1:21
Luke 1:31
Jesus said, *S.* be of good cheer. *Mat* 9:2; *Mark* 2:5
he that loveth *s.* or. *Mat* 10:37
the *S.*, but the Father; nor any the Father, save the *S.*, and he to whom the *S.* 11:27; *Luke* 10:22
the carpenter's *s.* *Mat* 13:55
Mark 6:3; *Luke* 4:22
Christ the *s.* of the living. *Mat* 16:16
S. go work to-day in my. 21:28
but when husbandmen saw the *s.* 38
of Christ? whose *s.* is he? 22:42
having yet one *s.* his. *Mark* 12:6
and the father betray the *s.* 13:12
knoweth not the *s.*, but Father. 32
art thou the Christ, the *s.* of? 14:61
Elisabeth shall bear thee a *s.* *Luke* 1:13
be called the *S.* of the Highest. 32
Elisabeth conceived a *s.* 36
she brought forth a *s.* 57
mother said, *S.* why hast thou? 2:48
30 years, being, as was supposed, the *s.* of Joseph, who was *s.* 3:23
dead man carried out, only *s.* 7:12
if *s.* of peace be there, your. 10:6
if a *s.* shall ask bread of any. 11:11
shall be divided against the *s.* 12:53
the younger *s.* gathered all. 15:13
s. thou art ever with me, and all. 31
s. remember, that thou in. 16:25
forasmuch as he also is the *s.* 19:9
only begotten *s.* which is in the bosom of. *John* 1:18
Jesus of Nazareth, *s.* of Joseph. 45
the Father loveth the *s.*, and hath given all things. 3:35; 5:20
on the *s.*: he that believeth not *s.* 3:36
nobleman whose *s.* was sick. 4:46
s. can do nothing of himself, what things Father . . . the *s.* 5:19
even so the *s.* quickeneth whom. 21
committed all judgement to the *s.* 22
honour the *s.* He that honoureth not the *s.* honoureth not the Father. 23
so hath he given to the *s.* to have. 26
every one who seeth *s.* and. 6:40
said, Is not this Jesus the *s.*? 42
but the *S.* abideth ever. 8:35
if *s.* therefore shall make you free. 36
is this your *s.*? 9:19
We know that this is our *s.* 20
Father may be glorified in *s.* 14:13
none of them is lost, but the *s.* 17:12
Simon, *s.* of Jonas, lovest? 21:15
Barnabas, the *s.* of consolation, a Levite. *Acts* 4:36
and nourished for her own *s.* 7:21
David the *s.* of Jesse, a man. 13:22
Pharisee, the *s.* of a Pharisee. 23:6
Paul's sister's *s.* heard of their. 16
Sarah shall have a *s.* *Rom* 9:9
shall *s.* also himself. *1 Cor* 15:28
but *s.* and if *s.* then an heir. *Gal* 4:7
and her *s.*: for the *s.* of the bond-woman shall not be heir with *s.* 30
s. with father, he served. *Phil* 2:22
Marcus, sister's *s.* to. *Col* 4:10
man of sin, *s.* of perdition. *2 Thes* 2:3
I commit unto thee, *s.* Timothy. *1 Tim* 1:18
and he shall be to me a *s.* *Heb* 1:5
unto the *s.* he saith, Thy throne is. 8
but Christ as a *s.* over his. 3:6
though he were a *s.* yet learned. 5:8
of the oath maketh the *s.* 7:28
s. of Pharaoh's daughter. 11:24
and scourgeth every *s.* 12:6
for what *s.* is he whom father? 7
of Balaam, *s.* of Bosor. *2 Pet* 2:15
denieth Father and *s.* *1 John* 2:22
s. the same hath not the Father, but he that acknowledgeth the *s.* 23
ye also shall continue in the *s.* 24
sent the *s.* to be the Saviour. 4:14
he that hath the *s.* hath life, and he that hath not the *s.* of God. 5:12
from Lord Jesus Christ, *s.* *2 John* 3
hath both the Father and the *s.* 9
see **David**

son *of God*

fourth is like *s. of God.* *Dan* 3:25
if thou be the *s. of God*, command. *Mat* 4:3; 27:40; *Luke* 4:3, 9
do with thee, Jesus thou *s. of God*? *Mat* 8:29; *Luke* 8:28
truth thou art *s. of God.* *Mat* 14:33
thou be Christ the *s. of God.* 26:63
I am the *s. of God.* 27:43
truly this was the *s. of God.* *Mat* 27:54; *Mark* 15:39
Jesus Christ the *s. of God.* *Mark* 1:1
saying, Thou art the *s. of God.* 3:11; *John* 1:49
shall be called *s. of God.* *Luke* 1:35
son of Adam, which was the *s. of God.* 3:38
crying out, thou art Christ the *s. of God.* 4:41; *John* 6:69; 11:27
then the *s. of God*? *Luke* 22:70
this is the *s. of God.* *John* 1:34
the only begotten *s. of God.* 3:18
hear the voice of the *s. of God.* 5:25
thou believe on the *s. of God*? 9:35
I said, I am the *s. of God.* 10:36
s. of God might be glorified. 11:4
made himself the *s. of God.* 19:7
Jesus is Christ, the *s. of God.* 20:31
he said, I believe that Jesus Christ is the *s. of God.* *Acts* 8:37
that he is the *s. of God.* 9:20
declared to be the *s. of God* with. *Rom* 1:4
for the *s. of God* was not yea and nay. *2 Cor* 1:19
faith of the *s. of God.* *Gal* 2:20
of knowledge of *s. of God.* *Eph* 4:13
high priest, Jesus the *s. of God.* *Heb* 4:14
themselves the *s. of God* afresh. 6:6
like to the *s. of God* abideth. 7:3
trodden under foot *s. of God.* 10:29
for this purpose the *s. of God* was. *1 John* 3:8
confess Jesus is the *s. of God.* 4:15
believeth Jesus is the *s. of God.* 5:5
he that believeth on the *s. of God.* 10
believe on the name of *s. of God.* 13
we know that the *s. of God* is. 20
things saith the *s. of God.* *Rev* 2:18

his son

after name of *his s.* Enoch. *Gen* 4:17
what *his* younger *s.* had done. 9:24
grievous because of *his s.* 21:11
the knife to slay *his s.* 22:10
burnt offering instead of *his s.* 13
brother's daughter to *his s.* 24:48
sent from Isaac *his s.* while. 25:6
Abraham, God blessed *his s.* 11
Shechem *his s.* came to gate. 34:20
Hamor and Shechem *his s.* 26
Jacob mourned for *his s.* 37:34
betrothed her to *his s.* *Ex* 21:9
every man upon *his s.* 32:29
but for *his s.* he may. *Lev* 21:2
on Eleazar *his s.* *Num* 20:26, 28
as a man doth bear *his s.* *Deut* 1:31
thou shalt not give to *his s.* 7:3
as a man chasteneth *his s.* so the. 8:5
not any maketh *his s.* to pass. 18:10
mourned for *his s.* *2 Sam* 13:37
serve in presence of *his s.*? 16:19
king was grieved for *his s.* 19:2
out of *his s.*'s hand. *1 Ki* 11:35
and to *his s.* will I give one tribe. 36
give him a lamp, to set up *his s.* 15:4
for all the sins of Elah *his s.* 16:13
in *his s.*'s days will I bring. 21:29
took *his* eldest *s.*, offered. *2 Ki* 3:27
Ahaz made *his s.* to pass. 16:3
Manasseh made *his s.* pass. 21:6
said to David and to Solomon *his s.* 7; *2 Chr* 33:7
no man might make *his s.* pass. *2 Ki* 23:10
the king slew *his s.* *2 Chr* 24:22
his rod, hateth *his s.* *Pr* 13:24
shall have him become *his s.* 29:21
what is *his s.*'s name, if thou. 30:4
all nations shall serve *his s.* and *his* son's *s.* *Jer* 27:7
thou *his s.* O Belshazzar. *Dan* 5:22
as a man spareth *his s.* *Mal* 3:17
what man, whom if *his s.*? *Mat* 7:9
he sent unto them *his s.* 21:37
made a marriage for *his s.* 22:2
how is he then *his s.*? 45
Mark 12:37; *Luke* 20:44
gave *his* only begotten *s.* *John* 3:16
God sent not *his s.* to condemn. 17
Jacob gave to *his s.* Joseph. 4:5
come down and heal *his s.* 47

glorified his s. Jesus. Acts 3:13
God having raised up his s. 26
serve in the gospel of his s. Rom 1:9
reconciled to God by the death of his s. 5:10
God sending his own s. in. 8:3
to the image of his s. 29
he that spared not his own s. 32
fellowship of his s. Jesus. 1 Cor 1:9
God to reveal his s. in me. Gal 1:16
God sent forth his s. made. 4:4
God sent the spirit of his s. into. 6
into kingdom of his dear s. Col 1:13
and to wait for his s. 1 Thes 1:10
hath in these last days spoken unto us by his s. Heb 1:2
offered up his only begotten s. 11:17
offered Isaac his s. on altar. Jas 2:21
is with Father and his s. Jesus. 1 John 1:3
blood of Jesus Christ his s. 7
on the name of his s. Jesus. 3:23
God sent his only begotten s. 4:9
sent his s. to be the propitiation. 10
which he hath testified of his s. 5:9
hath made him a liar; he believeth not record God gave of his s. 10
this life is in his s. 11
we are in his s. Jesus. 20
see **beloved**

son *in law*

any besides ? s. in law. Gen 19:12
Samson the s. in law of. Judg 15:6
father said unto his s. in law. 19:5
s. in law to the king. 1 Sam 18:18, 23
shalt this day be my s. in law. 21
be the king's s. in law. 22
David well to be king's s. in law. 26
might be the king's s. in law. 27
faithful as the king's s. in law? 22:14
Jehoram was s. in law. 2 Ki 8:27
Tobiah was s. in law to. Neh 6:18
was s. in law to Sanballat the. 13:28

my **son**

not be heir with my s. Gen 21:10
wilt not deal falsely with my s. 23
he said, Here am I, my s. 22:7
my s. God will provide himself. 8
wife to my s. of Canaanites. 24:3, 37
and take a wife unto my s. 4, 7, 38
that thou bring not my s. 6, 8
my s. obey my voice. 27:8, 43
Upon me be thy curse, my s. 13
here am I; who art thou, my s.? 18
thou be my very s. Esau or not. 21, 24
see, the smell of my s. is as. 27
I do now unto thee, my s.? 37
the soul of my s. longeth for. 34:8
and said, It is my s.'s coat. 37:33
I will go into the grave to my s. 35
remain, till Shelah my s. 38:11
I gave her not to Shelah my s. 26
he said, My s. shall not go. 42:38
God be gracious to thee, my s. 43:29
it is enough, Joseph my s. 45:28
Jacob said, I know it, my s. 48:19
from the prey, my s. thou. 49:9
Israel is my s. even my. Ex 4:22
let my s. go, that he may serve. 23
my s. give glory to the. Josh 7:19
neither shall my s. rule. Judg 8:23
Blessed be thou of Lord, my s. 17:2
dedicated for my s. to make a. 3
I called not, my s.; lie. 1 Sam 3:6
What is there done, my s? 4:16
What shall I do for my s.? 10:2
though it be in Jonathan my s. 14:39
and Jonathan my s. will be. 40
between me and Jonathan my s. 42
that my s. hath made a league with the son of Jesse, or that my s. 22:8
is this thy voice, my s. David ? 24:16; 26:17
I have sinned, return, my s. 26:21
Blessed be thou, my s. David. 25
father, he shall be my s. 2 Sam 7:14
king said, Nay, my s. let us. 13:25
lest they destroy my s. 14:11
destroy me and my s. out of the. 16
behold my s. who came forth. 16:11
wherefore wilt thou run, my s.? 18:22
thus he said, My s. Absalom, my s. my s. Absalom. 33; 19:4
I and my s. be counted. 1 Ki 1:21
she arose and took my s. 3:20
behold, it was not my s. which. 21
Nay; but the living is my s. 22
thy son is the dead, and my s. 23
dress it for me and my s. 17:12
thou come to me to slay my s. 18
and we will eat my s. 2 Ki 6:28
my s. and did eat him: give thy s. 29
give thy daughter to my s. 14:9 2 Chr 25:18
shall be my s. 1 Chr 17:13; 22:10
now, my s. Lord will be with. 22:11
I have chosen him to be my s. 28:6
thou, Solomon my s. know God. 9
Solomon my s. whom God. 29:1
give to Solomon my s. a perfect. 19
Thou art my s.; this day. Ps 2:7 Acts 13:33; Heb 1:5; 5:5
my s. despise not the chastening of. Pr 3:11; Heb 12:5
do this now, my s. and. Pr 6:3
my s. give me thine heart. 23:26
my s. fear thou the Lord. 24:21
my s. be wise, and make. 27:11
what, my s.? and what, the s.? 31:2
further by these, my s. Eccl 12:12
is Ephraim my dear s.? Jer 31:20
it contemneth the rod of my s., as every tree. Ezek 21:10
I called my s. out of Egypt. Hos 11:1; Mat 2:15
This is my beloved s. Mat 3:17; 17:5
have mercy on my s.: for he. 17:15
they will reverence my s. 21:37 Mark 12:6
brought to thee my s. Mark 9:17
thee, look upon my s. Luke 9:38
for this my s. was dead and. 15:24
to Timothy my own s. 1 Tim 1:2
my s. be strong in grace. 2 Tim 2:1
to Titus mine own s. Tit 1:4
I beseech thee for my s. Philem 10
his God, he shall be my s. Rev 21:7

thy **son**

thy s. thine only s. Isaac. Gen 22:2
thou hast not withheld thy s. 12, 16
must I needs bring thy s.? 24:5
I am thy s. thy firstborn. 27:32
whether it be thy s.'s coat. 37:32
behold, thy s. Joseph cometh. 48:2
I will slay thy s. even. Ex 4:23
ears of thy s. and son's s. 10:2
thou shalt shew thy s. in that. 13:8
when thy s. asketh thee, what is this ? 14; Deut 6:20
not do any work, thou, nor thy s. Ex 20:10; Deut 5:14
shalt say unto thy s. Deut 6:21
shalt thou take unto thy s. 7:3
they will turn away thy s. from. 4
thou must eat them before the Lord, thou, and thy s. 12:18; 16:11, 14
if thy s. entice thee secretly. 13:6
bring out thy s. that. Judg 6:30
thou, thy s. and thy son's s. 8:22
send me David thy s. 1 Sam 16:19
servants, and to thy s. David. 25:8
one hair of thy s. fall. 2 Sam 14:11
and life of thy s. Solomon. 1 Ki 1:12
thy s. Solomon shall reign. 13, 17, 30
the dead is thy s. 3:22
and thy s. is the dead. 23
thy s. whom I will set upon. 5:5
out of the hand of thy s. 11:12
I will give one tribe to thy s. 13
for thee and for thy s. 17:13
give me thy s. 19
Elisha said, See, thy s. liveth. 23
he said, Take up thy s. 2 Ki 4:36
give thy s. that we may eat. 6:28, 29
I am thy servant, and thy s. 16:7
thy s. shall build my house . . . to be my s. 1 Chr 28:6; 2 Chr 6:9
chasten thy s. while. Pr 19:18
correct thy s. and he shall. 29:17
Jesus said, Bring thy s. Luke 9:41
worthy to be called thy s. 15:19, 21
as soon as this thy s. was come. 30
go thy way, thy s. liveth. John 4:50, 51, 53
glorify thy s. that thy s. also. 17:1
mother, Woman, behold thy s. 19:26

son *of man*

he said S. of man, stand. Ezek 2:1
s. of man, I send thee to the. 3
and thou, s. of man, be not. 6
thou s. of man, hear what I say. 8
s. of man, eat that thou findest. 3:1
s. of man, cause thy belly to eat. 3
s. of man, go get thee to the house. 4
s. of man, all the words that I. 10
s. of man, I have made thee a. 17
O s. of man, they shall put. 25
thou also s. of man, take thee. 4:1
s. of man, I will break staff of. 16
thou s. of man, take thee a. 5:1
s. of man, set thy face toward the mountains. 6:2
thou s. of man, thus saith the. 7:2
s. of man, lift up thine eyes. 8:5
he said, S. of man, seest thou? 6
S. of man, dig now in the wall. 8
s. of man, hast thou seen what? 12
thou seen this, O s. of man ? 15, 17
s. of man, these are the men. 11:2
prophesy, O s. of man. 4
s. of man, thy brethren are. 15
s. of man, thou dwellest in a. 12:2
thou s. of man, prepare thee. 3
s. of man, hath not the house of? 9
s. of man, eat thy bread with. 18
s. of man, what is that proverb? 22
s. of man, behold, they of house. 27
s. of man, prophesy against the prophets. 13:2
s. of man, set thy face against thy people. 17
s. of man, these men have set. 14:3
s. of man, when the land sinneth. 13
s. of man, What is the vine tree? 15:2
s. of man, cause Jerusalem. 16:2
s. of man, put forth a riddle. 17:2
s. of man, speak to the elders. 20:3
s. of man, wilt thou judge them ? 4
therefore s. of man, speak to. 27
s. of man, set thy face toward the south. 46
s. of man, set thy face toward Jerusalem. 21:2
sigh therefore, thou s. of man. 6
s. of man, prophesy and say, a. 9, 28
cry and howl s. of man, for it. 12
s. of man, prophesy and smite. 14
also thou s. of man, appoint. 19
s. of man, wilt thou judge ? 22:2
s. of man, house of Israel is to. 18
s. of man, say to her, Thou art. 24
s. of man, there were two women of. 23:2
s. of man, wilt thou judge Aholah? 36
s. of man, write thee the name. 24:2
s. of man, I take away the desire. 16
s. of man, shall it not be in day ? 25
s. of man, set thy face against the Ammonites. 25:2
s. of man, because that Tyrus. 26:2
s. of man, take up a lamentation. 27:2; 28:12
s. of man, say unto the prince. 28:2
s. of man, set thy face against Zidon. 21
s. of man, set thy face against Pharaoh. 29:2
s. of man, Nebuchadrezzar. 18
s. of man, prophesy, and say, Thus saith the Lord. 30:2
s. of man, I have broken the. 21
s. of man, speak to Pharaoh. 31:2
s. of man, take up a lamentation for Pharaoh. 32:2
s. of man, wail for the multitude. 18
s. of man, speak to children. 33:2
thou, O s. of man, I have set. 7
O s. of man, speak to the house. 10
s. of man, say to the children. 12
s. of man, they that inhabit. 24
s. of man, thy people still are. 30
s. of man, prophesy against the shepherds. 34:2
s. of man, set thy face against mount Seir. 35:2
thou s. of man, prophesy to. 36:1
s. of man, when the house of. 17
he said, S. of man, can these ? 37:3
prophesy, s. of man, and say. 9
s. of man, these bones are the. 11

s. of man, take thee one stick. Ezek 37:16
s. of man, set thy face against Gog. 38:2
s. of man, prophesy and say unto Gog. 14
s. of man, prophesy against Gog. 39:1
s. of man, thus saith the Lord. 17
43:18
s. of man, behold with thine. 40:4
he said, S. of man, the place. 43:7
s. of man, shew the house to. 10
s. of man, mark well, behold. 44:5
he said, S. of man, hast thou ? 47:6

see man

song

We find in Scripture several songs *composed upon important occasions; for example,* Moses *made one after the passage through the Red Sea, to thank God for the deliverance of his people,* Ex 15:1, 2, etc. *David composed a song in mourning for the death of Saul and Jonathan, and another for the death of Abner,* 2 Sam 1:18, 19; 3:33. *Jeremiah wrote his* Lamentations, *which are a* song, *wherein he deplores the calamities and ruin of* Jerusalem; *and he made another upon the death of Josiah king of Judah,* 2 Chr 35:25. *Deborah and Barak made a triumphant hymn after the defeat of Sisera,* Judg 5:1, 2, 3, etc. *The* Canticles, *or the* Song of Songs, *and the* 45th *Psalm, are songs to celebrate weddings, and are considered by many to be allegorical. Hannah the mother of Samuel, and king* Hezekiah, *returned thanks to God in* songs, *for the favours they had received,* 1 Sam 2:1, 2, etc.; Isa 38:10, 11, etc. *The* songs *of the Virgin* Mary, Zacharias *the father of* John *the* Baptist, *and old* Simeon *are of the same nature. They are thanksgivings to God for blessings received from him,* Luke 1:46, 68; 2:29, 30.

the children of Israel sang this s. unto. Ex 15:1; Num 21:17
the Lord is my strength and s. and. Ex 15:2; Ps 118:14; Isa 12:2
write this s.: that this s. Deut 31:19
this s. shall testify. 21
Moses wrote this s. 22
the words of this s. 30; 32:44
awake, Deborah, utter a s. Judg 5:12
to Lord words of this s. 2 Sam 22:1
whom David set over the service of s. 1 Chr 6:31
chief of Levites was for a s. 15:22, 27
under their father for s. in. 25:6
s. of the Lord began. 2 Chr 29:27
now I am their s., yea, I am. Job 30:9
and with my s. will I. Ps 28:7
unto him a new s. 33:3; Isa 42:10
and he hath put a new s. Ps 40:3
night his s. shall be with me. 42:8
the s. of the drunkards. 69:12
the name of God with a s. 30
remembrance my s. in night. 77:6
O sing a new s. 96:1; 98:1; 149:1
there they required of us a s. 137:3
how shall we sing the Lord's s. in? 4
I will sing a new s. unto. 144:9
man to hear the s. of fools. Eccl 7:5
the s. of songs which is. S of S 1:1
I sing a s. of my beloved. Isa 5:1
not drink wine with a s. 24:9
in that day shall this s. be sung. 26:1
shall have a s. as in the night. 30:29
a derision and their s. Lam 3:14
them as a very lovely s. Ezek 33:32
they sung a new s.. saying, Thou art worthy. Rev 5:9; 14:3
learn that s. but the 144,000. 14:3
s. of Moses and s. of the Lamb. 15:3

songs

sent thee away with s. Gen 31:27
his s. were a thousand. 1 Ki 4:32
were instructed in the s. 1 Chr 25:7*
of David there were s. Neh 12:46
maker who giveth s. in. Job 35:10
shall compass about with s. Ps 32:7
have been my s. in house. 119:54
Sing us one of the s. of Zion. 137:3
so is he that singeth s. Pr 25:20
the song of s. which is. S of S 1:1
sweet melody, sing s. Isa 23:16
part of earth have we heard s. 24:16
shall come to Zion with s. 35:10
will sing my s. to the stringed. 38:20
noise of thy s. to cease. Ezek 26:13
away from me the noise of thy s. Amos 5:23
s. of temple shall be howlings. 8:3
I will turn all your s. into. 10
in psalms and spiritual s. Eph 5:19
one another in hymns and spiritual s. Col 3:16

sons

(*In Revisions very frequently,* children)

the s. of Noah entered. Gen 7:13
the s. of Noah that went forth. 9:18
there are the three s. of Noah. 19
were s. born after the flood. 10:1
and spake to his s. in law. 19:14
in the presence of the s. of. 23:11
and let thy mother's s. bow. 27:29
s. of Jacob came upon slain. 34:27
lad was with the s. of Bilhah. 37:2
s. of Israel came to buy corn. 42:5
one man's s. we are no spies. 11, 32
the s. of Israel carried Jacob. 46:5
earrings in ears of your s. Ex 32:2
eat the flesh of your s. Lev 26:29
ye take too much upon you, ye s. of Levi. Num 16:7
of their tents, their wives and s. 27
in his own sin, and had no s. 27:3
if they be married to s. of. 36:3
a sodomite of the s. Deut 23:17
separated the s. of Adam. 32:8
Caleb drove three s. of Anak. Josh 15:14; Judg 1:20
they were even the s. Judg 8:19
Gideon had 70 s. 30
Jair had thirty s. 10:4
Abdon had forty s. and thirty. 12:14
s. of Belial beset house. 19:22
are there yet any more s.? Ruth 1:11
better to thee than ten s.? 1 Sam 1:8
s. of Eli were s. of Belial. 2:12
will take your s. and appoint. 8:11
there were three s. of. 2 Sam 2:18
these men s. of Zeruiah be too. 3:39
eat as one of the king's s. 9:11
invited all the king's s. 13:23
hath slain all the king's s. 30
what to do with you, ye s. of Zeruiah ? 16:10; 19:22
but s. of Belial shall be as. 23:6
all the king's s. 1 Ki 1:9, 19, 25
kindness to s. of Barzillai. 2:7
for he was wiser than the s. 4:31
a certain man of the s. of. 20:35
set two men, s. of Belial. 21:10
she shut the door upon her and upon her s. 2 Ki 4:5
meetest of your master's s. 10:3
the heads of the king's s. 8
stole him from the king's s. 11:2
2 Chr 22:11
they slew s. of Zedekiah before his. 2 Ki 25:7; Jer 39:6; 52:10
birthright was given to s. 1 Chr 5:1
Ornan and his four s. with. 21:20
Eleazar, who had no s. 24:28
among the s. of my fathers. 28:4
as the Lord said of the s. 2 Chr 23:3
for blood of the s. of Jehoiada. 24:25
one of the s. of Joiada. Neh 13:28
the ten s. of Haman. Esth 9:10
let Haman's ten s. be hanged. 13, 14
who among s. of mighty can? Ps 89:6
our s. may be as plants. 144:12
as apple tree so is my beloved among s. S of S 2:3
guide her among all the s. Isa 51:18
s. of the stranger that join. 56:6
draw near hither, ye s. of. 57:3
the s. of the stranger shall. 60:10
the s. of them that afflicted thee. 14
the s. of the alien shall be. 61:5
s. of the stranger shall not. Isa 62:8
the fathers and s. shall. Jer 6:21
even fathers and s. together. 13:14
high places to burn their s. 19:5
beget s., take wives for your s. 29:6
I set before s. of Rechabites. 35:5
no wine, ye, nor your s. for ever. 6
Israel no s.? hath he no heir ? 49:1
precious s. of Zion. Lam 4:2
fathers shall eat the s., s. Ezek 5:10
when ye make your s. pass. 20:31
they caused their s. to pass. 23:37
s. of the living God. Hos 1:10
I raised up of your s. Amos 2:11
he shall purify s. of Levi. Mal 3:3
therefore ye s. of Jacob are. 6
is, The s. of thunder. Mark 3:17
whom do your s. cast ? Luke 11:19
but as my beloved s. 1 Cor 4:14
receive the adoption of s. Gal 4:5
because ye are s., God hath sent. 6
bringing many s. to glory. Heb 2:10
blessed both s. of Joseph. 11:21
dealeth with you as with s. 12:7
then are ye bastards, and not s. 8

sons of God

the s. of God saw the. Gen 6:2
the s. of God came in to the. 4
s. of God came to present. Job 1:6
2:1
all the s. of God shouted for. 38:7
are s. of the living God. Hos 1:10
them power to become s. of God. John 1:12
led by the Spirit of God, they are the s. of God. Rom 8:14
the manifestation of s. of God. 19
be harmless, the s. of God. Phil 2:15
be called the s. of God. 1 John 3:1
beloved, now are we the s. of God. 2

his sons

Noah and his s. went into the ark. Gen 7:7
Noah went forth, and his s. 8:18
God blessed Noah and his s. 9:1
his s. Isaac and Ishmael buried. 25:9
them into the hands of his s. 30:35
his s. Esau and Jacob buried. 35:29
end of commanding his s. 49:33
his s. did unto him as he. 50:12
his s. carried him into the land. 13
Jethro came with his s. and. Ex 18:5
Aaron and his s. to minister. 28:1
put the garments on his s. 41; 29:8
tip of the right ear of his s. 29:20
sprinkle the blood upon his s. 21
sanctify that which is for his s. 27
Lev 8:30
priest of his s. that is anointed. Lev 6:22
smote Og and his s. Num 21:35
we smote Sihon, his s. Deut 2:33
Lord hath chosen him and his s. 18:5
when he maketh his s. to. 21:16
have slain his s. 70 persons on. Judg 9:18
Micah consecrated one of his s. 17:5
was to him as one of his s. 11
his s. were priests to tribe of. 18:30
now Eli heard all that his s. did. 1 Sam 2:22
his s. made themselves vile. 3:13
Samuel when old made his s. 8:1
his s. walked not in his ways. 3
me a king among his s. 16:1
grieved, every man for his s. 30:6
upon Saul and upon his s. and slew. 31:2; 1 Chr 10:2
let seven men of his s. 2 Sam 21:6
his s. came and told. 1 Ki 13:11
his s. had seen what way the. 12
blood of Naboth and his s. 2 Ki 9:26
his s. smote him with the sword. 19:37; Isa 37:38
Jeroboam and his s. 2 Chr 11:14
and his s. by a covenant of salt. 13:5
light to him, and to his s. for. 21:7
his s. save the youngest of his s. 17
were servants to him and his s. 36:20
life of the king and his s. Ezra 6:10
he and his s. be hanged. Esth 9:25
and his s. went and feasted. Job 1:4
his s. come to honour, he. 14:21

guide Arcturus with *his s.*? Job 38:32
Job saw *his s.* and *his s.'* sons. 42:16
Jonadab commanded *his s.* not to. Jer 35:14
give a gift to any of *his s.* Ezek 46:16
his s. shall be stirred up. Dan 11:10

my sons

his father, They are *my s.* Gen 48:9
nay, *my s.* for it is no good report I hear. 1 Sam 2:24
Samuel said, Behold, *my s.* 12:2
of all *my s.* he hath chosen. 1 Chr 28:5
Hezekiah said, *My s.* 2 Chr 29:11
Job said, It may be that *my s.* Job 1:5
to come concerning *my s.* Isa 45:11
but as *my* beloved *s.* I. 1 Cor 4:14
see **seven**

thy sons

into ark, thou and *thy s.* Gen 6:18
ark, thou, thy wife, and *thy s.* 8:16
ordinance to thee and *thy s.* Ex 12:24; Num 18:8
firstborn of *thy s.* shalt. Ex 22:29
make *thy s.* go a whoring. 34:16
all the firstborn of *thy s.* thou. 20
not drink wine, nor *thy s.* Lev 10:9
it is thy due, and *thy s.'* due. 14
thou and *thy s.* shall bear. Num 18:1
but thou and *thy s.* with thee. 2
thou and *thy s.* shall keep your. 7
holy for thee and for *thy s.* 9
given them to thee and to *thy s.* 11
teach them *thy s.* and *thy s.'* sons. Deut 4:9
and honourest *thy s.* 1 Sam 2:29
thou art old, and *thy s.* walk not. 8:5
to-morrow shalt thou and *thy s.* 28:19
and *thy s.* shall till. 2 Sam 9:10
door upon thee and *thy s.* 2 Ki 4:4
said to Jehu, *Thy s.* shall sit on. 15:12; 1 Chr 17:11
thy s. shall be eunuchs in Babylon. 2 Ki 20:18; Isa 39:7
bring *thy s.* in their arms. Isa 49:22
thy s. have fainted, they lie. 51:20
come to thee, *thy s.* shall. 60:4, 9
marrieth virgin, so shall *thy s.* 62:5
thy s. and daughters are. Jer 48:46
raised up *thy s.* O Zion, against *thy s.* Zech 9:13

two sons

to Eber were born *two s.* Gen 10:25; 1 Chr 1:19
two of the *s.* of Jacob. Gen 34:25
unto Joseph were born *two s.* 41:50
slay my *two s.* if I bring him. 42:37
that my wife bare me *two s.* 44:27
took with him his *two s.* 48:1, 5
Zipporah and her *two s.* Ex 18:3
the death of the *two s.* Lev 16:1
two s. Mahlon and. Ruth 1:1, 2
she was left and her *two s.* 3
left of her *two s.* 5
come upon thy *two s.* 1 Sam 2:34
the *two s.* of Eli were there. 4:4
thy *two s.* Hophni and Phinehas. 17
thy handmaid had *two s.* 2 Sam 14:6
there with them their *two s.* 15:36
but the king took the *two s.* 21:8
creditor to take *two s.* 2 Ki 4:1
grant that these my *two s.* may sit in thy kingdom. Mat 20:21
a certain man had *two s.* 21:28; Luke 15:11
took with him Peter and the *two s.* of Zebedee. Mat 26:37
Midian, where he begat *two s.* Acts 7:29
that Abraham had *two s.* Gal 4:22

soon

ye are come so *s.* to-day? Ex 2:18
ye shall *s.* utterly perish. Deut 4:26
my maker would *s.* take me. Job 32:22
they shall *s.* be cut down. Ps 37:2
shall *s.* stretch out her hands. 68:31
I should *s.* have subdued. 81:14
for it is *s.* cut off, and we. 90:10
they *s.* forgat his works. 106:13
that is *s.* angry dealeth. Pr 14:17
how *s.* is the fig tree! Mat 21:20
I marvel that ye are so *s.* Gal 1:6
ye be not *s.* shaken in. 2 Thes 2:2
not selfwilled, not *s.* angry. Tit 1:7

as soon as

as s. as he came nigh. Ex 32:19
ran *as s. as* he had stretched. Josh 8:19
as s. as they hear they shall be obedient to me. 2 Sam 22:45; Ps 18:44
they go astray *as s. as.* Ps 58:3
as s. as his ministration. Luke 1:23
as s. as I see how it will. Phil 2:23

sooner

be restored to you the *s.* Heb 13:19
sun is no *s.* risen, but it. Jas 1:11

soothsayer

Diviner *or* Magician. *These were very common among Eastern nations, magicians and soothsayers being referred to at various times, from the mention in* Ex 7:11 *of the magicians of Pharaoh, to the time of the Apostles, when the trade was still very lucrative,* Acts 8:9; 13:6; 19:19.

The law of Moses forbade the consultation of magicians and soothsayers, upon pain of death, Lev 20:6. Saul *did what he could to drive them out of the country of* Israel, 1 Sam 28:3. *But, for all this, many were still to be found; and the Israelites were always much addicted to these sorts of superstitions. And the same king who had been so eager in driving them out of his dominions, at last went to consult one himself,* 1 Sam 28:7, 8, *etc.*

see **divinations, exorcists**

Balaam the son of Beor the *s.*, did Israel slay. Josh 13:22

soothsayers

people, because they are *s.* Isa 2:6
the secret cannot the *s.* Dan 2:27
to bring Chaldeans and *s.* 5:7
king made master of the *s.* 11
shalt have no more *s.* Mi 5:12

soothsaying

masters much gain by *s.* Acts 16:16

sop

I shall give a *s.*, when he had dipped the *s.*, he gave it to. John 13:26
after the *s.* Satan entered. 27, 30

sope (soap)

wash and take thee much *s.* Jer 2:22
who may abide his coming? for he is like fuller's *s.* Mal 3:2

sorcerer

found a certain *s.* a false. Acts 13:6
Elymas the *s.* withstood them. 8

sorcerers

also called wise men and *s.* Ex 7:11
hearken not to your *s.* Jer 27:9
commanded to call *s.* Dan 2:2
swift witness against the *s.* Mal 3:5
s. shall have their part. Rev 21:8
for without are dogs and *s.* 22:15

sorceress

hither, ye sons of the *s.* Isa 57:3

sorceries

come on thee for thy *s.* Isa 47:9
with the multitude of thy *s.* 12
bewitched them with *s.* Acts 8:11
repented they of their *s.* Rev 9:21
for by thy *s.* were all nations. 18:23

sorcery

which beforetime used *s.* Acts 8:9

sore

they pressed *s.* upon the. Gen 19:9
because thou *s.* longest after. 31:30
day, when they were *s.* 34:25
the famine waxed *s.* in land. 41:56
s. in all lands. 57
s. in Canaan. 43:1; 47:4, 13
they mourned with a *s.* 50:10
Lord shewed signs great and *s.* on. Deut 6:22
smite thee with a *s.* botch. 28:35
s. sicknesses, and of long. Deut 28:59
so that Israel was *s.* Judg 10:9
because she lay *s.* upon him. 14:17
Samson was *s.* athirst, and. 15:18
against Gibeah, the battle was *s.* 20:34; 1 Sam 31:3*; 2 Sam 2:17; 2 Ki 3:26
lifted up their voices and wept *s.* Judg 21:2
also provoked her *s.* 1 Sam 1:6
prayed to the Lord, and wept *s.* 10
hand is *s.* on us, and on Dagon. 5:7
there was *s.* war against the. 14:52
I am *s.* distressed. 28:15, 21
his servants wept *s.* 2 Sam 13:36
sickness so *s.* no breath. 1 Ki 17:17
and there was a *s.* famine in. 18:2
Syria was *s.* troubled. 2 Ki 6:11
Hezekiah wept *s.* 20:3; Isa 38:3
know his own *s.* grief. 2 Chr 6:29*
so Jehoram died of *s.* 21:19
Ahaz transgressed *s.* against. 28:19
have me away, for I am *s.* 35:23
people wept very *s.* Ezra 10:1
it grieved me *s.* therefore. Neh 13:8
smote Job with *s.* boils. Job 2:7
he maketh *s.* and bindeth. 5:18
and vex in his *s.* displeasure. Ps 2:5
soul is *s.* vexed, but thou, O Lord. 6:3
enemies be ashamed, and *s.* 10
fast, thy hand presseth me *s.* 38:2
I am feeble and *s.* broken, I. 8
thou hast *s.* broken us in. 44:19
my heart is *s.* pained within. 55:4
shewed me great and *s.* 71:30
thou hast thrust *s.* at me. 118:13
chastened me *s.* but not given. 18
s. travail hath God. Eccl 1:13; 4:8
there is *s.* evil I have seen. 5:13, 16
with *s.* and great sword. Isa 27:1
we roar like bears, mourn *s.* 59:11
be not wroth very *s.* O Lord. 64:9
thy peace, afflict us very *s.*? 12
mine eye shall weep *s.* Jer 13:17
weep *s.* for him that goeth. 22:10
famine was *s.* in city, there. 52:6
she weepeth *s.* in the. Lam 1:2
mine enemies chased me *s.* 3:52
when I send my four *s.* Ezek 14:21
it is sharpened to make a *s.* 21:10
king was *s.* displeased. Dan 6:14
destroy you even with *s.* Mi 2:10
the Lord hath been *s.* Zech 1:2, 15
for he is lunatick, and *s.* vexed. Mat 17:15*
Hosanna, they were *s.* 21:15*
they were *s.* amazed in. Mark 6:51
spirit cried, rent him *s.* and. 9:26
Jesus began to be *s.* amazed. 14:33
wept *s.* and kissed Paul. Acts 20:37
see **afraid**

sore, *substantive*

if a white reddish *s.* it. Lev 13:42*
if rising of *s.* be white reddish. 43*
s. or sickness there be. 2 Chr 6:28*
stand aloof from my *s.* Ps 38:11*
my *s.* ran in the night and. 77:2*
there fell a grievous *s.* Rev 16:2

Sorek

a woman in valley of *S.* Judg 16:4

sorely

archers *s.* grieved him. Gen 49:23
so shall they be *s.* pained at. Isa 23:5

sorer

how much *s.* punishment. Heb 10:29

sores

bruises, and putrifying *s.* Isa 1:6
at his gate full of *s.* Luke 16:20, 21
blasphemed God because of their pains and *s.* Rev 16:11

sorrow

I will greatly multiply thy *s.* and conception, in *s.* thou shalt. Gen 3:16
in *s.* shalt thou eat of it all days. 17*
ye bring down my gray hairs with *s.* to the grave. 42:38; 44:29, 31
s. take hold of inhabitants. Ex 15:14*
terror shall cause *s.* of. Lev 26:16
shall give *s.* of mine. Deut 28:65*
I bare him with *s.* 1 Chr 4:9
this is nothing else but *s.* Neh 2:2

was turned from s. to joy. Esth 9:22
because it hid not s. from mine eyes. Job 3:10*
I would harden myself in s. 6:10*
mine eye is dim by reason of s. 17:7
and s. is turned into joy. 41:22
having s. in my heart. Ps 13:2
and my s. is continually. 38:17
I held my peace, and my s. 39:2
mischief also and s. are in. 55:10
their strength labour and s. 90:10
brought low through s. 107:39
I found trouble and s. 116:3
that winketh eye, causeth s. Pr 10:10
rich, he addeth no s. with it. 22
but by s. of heart the spirit. 15:13
a fool, doeth it to his s. 17:21
who hath woe? who hath s.? 23:29
he that increaseth knowledge. Eccl 1:18
he hath much s. and wrath. 5:17
s. is better than laughter, heart. 7:3
therefore remove s. from thy. 11:10
unto the land, behold s. Isa 5:30
shall give thee rest from thy s. 14:3
heap in the day of desperate s. 17:11
Ariel, and there shall be s. 29:2
s. and sighing shall flee away. 35:10
have, ye shall lie down in s. 50:11
and s. and mourning shall. 51:11
sing, but ye shall cry for s. 65:14
comfort myself against s. Jer 8:18
to see labour and s.? 20:18
why criest thou? thy s. is. 30:15
rejoice from their s. 31:13
hath added grief to my s. 45:3
there is s. on the sea, it cannot. 49:23
any s. like unto my s. Lam 1:12
behold my s. 18
give them s. of heart. 3:65
filled with drunkenness and s. Ezek 23:33
them sleeping for s. Luke 22:45
said these things, s. filled. John 16:6
sorrowful, but your s. shall be. 20
when she is in travail, hath s. 21
therefore have s. but I will see you again, and your heart shall. 22
that I have continual s. Rom 9:2
when I came, I should have s. 2 Cor 2:3
swallowed up with overmuch s. 7
godly s. worketh repentance to salvation, but the s. of the world. 7:10
also, lest I have s. upon s. Phil 2:27
s. give her: for she saith, I . . . shall see no s. Rev 18:7
no more death, neither s. 21:4

sorrow, verb

and they shall not s. any. Jer 31:12
land shall tremble and s. 51:29
they shall s. a little for. Hos 8:10
that ye s. not as others. 1 Thes 4:13

sorrowed

now I rejoice that ye s. to. 2 Cor 7:9
selfsame thing, that ye s. after a. 11

sorroweth

thy father s. for you. 1 Sam 10:2

sorrowful

a woman of a s. spirit. 1 Sam 1:15
things my soul refused to touch are as my s. meat. Job 6:7
poor and s.: let salvation. Ps 69:29
laughter the heart is s. Pr 14:13
replenished every s. soul. Jer 31:25
gather them that are s. Zeph 3:18
shall see it, and be very s. Zech 9:5
he went away s. Mat 19:22
Luke 18:23, 24
they were exceeding s. Mat 26:22
Mark 14:19
and he began to be s. Mat 26:37
my soul is exceeding s. even unto death. 38; Mark 14:34
ye shall be s. but sorrow. John 16:20
as s. yet always rejoicing. 2 Cor 6:10
and I may be the less s. Phil 2:28

sorrowing

father and I sought thee s. Luke 2:48
s. they should see his face no more. Acts 20:38

sorrows

their cry, for I know their s. Ex 3:7
s. of hell compassed me about. 2 Sam 22:6; Ps 18:4, 5; 116:3
I am afraid of all my s., . . . thou wilt not hold me innocent. Job 9:28
distributeth s. in his anger. 21:17
they cast out their s. 39:3
s. shall be multiplied that. Ps 16:4
many s. shall be to wicked. 32:10
rise up, to eat the bread of s. 127:2
for all his days are s. and. Eccl 2:23
pangs and s. shall take. Isa 13:8
a man of s. and acquainted. 53:3
borne our griefs and carried our s. 4
not s. take as a woman. Jer 13:21
s. have taken her as a woman. 49:24
by vision my s. are. Dan 10:16
s. of travailing woman. Hos 13:13
these are beginning of s. Mat 24:8
Mark 13:8
they pierced themselves through with many s. 1 Tim 6:10

sorry

of you that is s. for me. 1 Sam 22:8
holy to Lord, neither be ye s. Neh 8:10
I will be s. for my sin. Ps 38:18
who shall be s. for thee? Isa 51:19
and the king was s. Mat 14:9
Mark 6:26
they were exceeding s. Mat 17:23
if I make you s., . . . glad, but the same which is made s.? 2 Cor 2:2
you s., same epistle made you s. 7:8
ye were made s., for ye were s. 9

sort

two of every s. shalt bring into ark. Gen 6:19, 20
every bird of every s. into. 7:14
they divided one s. 1 Chr 24:5
be able to offer after this s. 29:14
silver basons of second s. Ezra 1:10
Artaxerxes king after this s. 4:8
four times after this s. Neh 6:4
men of the common s. Ezek 23:42
to ravenous birds of every s. 39:4
every oblation of every s. 44:30
than children of your s. Dan 1:10
no God can deliver after this s. 3:29
fellows of the baser s. Acts 17:5
more boldly in some s. Rom 15:15
work, of what s. it is. 1 Cor 3:13
sorrowed after a godly s. 2 Cor 7:11
of this s. are they who creep into. 2 Tim 3:6
journey after a godly s. 3 John 6

sorts

a garment of divers s. Deut 22:11
days store of all s. of wine. Neh 5:18
he sent divers s. of flies. Ps 78:45
105:31
instruments and that of all s. Eccl 2:8
merchants in all s. of things. Ezek 27:24
clothed with all s. of armour. 38:4

Sosipater

and S. my kinsmen. Rom 16:21

Sosthenes

the Greeks took S. and. Acts 18:17
Paul and S. to the church. 1 Cor 1:1

sottish

foolish, they are s. children. Jer 4:22

sought

he s. where to weep, entered his chamber. Gen 43:30
when Pharaoh heard, he s. Ex 2:15
men are dead which s. thy life. 4:19
that the Lord met him and s. 24
every one that s. the Lord went. 33:7
Moses diligently s. goat. Lev 10:16
was not his enemy, nor s. Num 35:23
because he s. to thrust. Deut 13:10
pursuers s. the spies. Josh 2:22
Samson s. occasion against. Judg 14:4
Danites s. them an inheritance 18:1
Saul s. to smite David. 1 Sam 19:10
Saul s. no more again for him. 27:4
ye s. for David in times past to be king. 2 Sam 3:17
head of thine enemy that s. thy life. 2 Sam 4:8
Saul s. to slay them in his zeal. 21:2
they s. for a fair damsel. 1 Ki 1:3
all the earth s. to Solomon. 10:24
Solomon s. therefore to kill. 11:40
s. three days for Elijah. 2 Ki 2:17
Hebronites were s. for. 1 Chr 26:31
have s. the Lord our God. 2 Chr 14:7
disease he s. not to the Lord. 16:12
Jehoshaphat s. not unto. 17:3
s. to the Lord God of his father. 4
he s. Ahaziah, and they caught him; because Jehoshaphat s. the. 22:9
s. after gods of Edom? 25:15, 20
he s. God in the days of Zechariah; as long as he s. the Lord. 26:5
these s. their register. Ezra 2:62
Neh 7:64
they s. the Levites out. Neh 12:27
s. to lay hand on. Esth 2:21; 6:2
wherefore Haman s. to destroy. 3:6
to lay hand on such as s. 9:2
I s. the Lord, and he heard me. Ps 34:4; 77:2
assemblies of violent men s. 86:14
s. out of all that have. 111:2
whole heart have I s. thee. 119:10
for I have s. thy precepts. 94
s. out many inventions. Eccl 7:29
preacher s. out and set in order. 12:9
the preacher s. to find. 10
shalt be called, s. out, city. Isa 62:12
s. of them that asked not for me; I am . . . s. not. 65:1; Rom 10:20
for my people that have s. me. Isa 65:10
moon, whom they have s. Jer 8:2
for the pastors have not s. 10:21
king s. to put him to death. 26:21
to Nebuchadrezzar that s. his. 44:30
iniquity of Israel shall be s. 50:20
they s. meat to relieve. Lam 1:19
and I s. for a man. Ezek 22:30
tho' s. for, yet shalt thou never. 26:21
neither have ye s. that which. 34:4
they s. Daniel and his. Dan 2:13
and my lords s. unto me. 4:36
s. occasion against Daniel. 6:4
even I, had s. for the meaning. 8:15
Esau's hidden things s. up. Ob 6
that have not s. the Lord. Zeph 1:6
bay went forth and s. to go. Zech 6:7
they are dead which s. Mat 2:20
s. to lay hands on him. 21:46
Mark 12:12; Luke 20:19
from that time he s. opportunity to betray him. Mat 26:16; Luke 22:6
they s. false witness against Jesus. Mat 26:59; Mark 14:55
s. how they might destroy him. Mark 11:18; 14:1; Luke 19:47
22:2
thy father and I s. thee. Luke 2:48
how is it that ye s. me? wist? 49
and they s. means to bring. 5:18
multitude s. to touch him. 6:19
others s. of him a sign from. 11:16
he s. fruit thereon, and. 13:6
Zacchaeus s. to see Jesus. 19:3
s. to slay him. John 5:16, 18; 7:1
then the Jews s. him. 7:11; 11:56
s. to take him. 7:30; 10:39
Master, the Jews of late s. 11:8
from thenceforth Pilate s. to. 19:12
and when Herod had s. Acts 12:19
they s. to bring them out to. 17:5
because s. it not by faith. Rom 9:32
nor of men s. we glory. 1 Thes 2:6
in Rome he s. me out. 2 Tim 1:17
no place should have been s. for. Heb 8:7
though he s. it carefully with. 12:17

sought him

he s. him he could not. 1 Sam 10:21
the Lord hath s. him a man. 13:14
Saul s. him every day, God. 23:14
we s. him not after the. 1 Chr 15:13
have s. him, he hath. 2 Chr 14:7
when they s. him, he was. 15:4
for they s. him with their whole. 15
I s. him, but he could not. Ps 37:36
slew them, then they s. him. 78:34

on my bed I s. him whom my soul loveth; I s. him. S of S 3:1, 2; 5:6
and they s. him among. Luke 2:44
people s. him, and came. 4:42

soul

(This word is used in the Bible in much the same variety of senses as it is used to-day. The Hebrews used the word rather more generally, and the renderings of Hebrew expressions given in the margins of many editions of the Bible frequently contain the word when it does not appear in the text, but some other word, as mind, life, or persons, is used. Frequently, where the word soul is used in the Authorised or " King James " Version the revisions have changed it to life)

man became a living s. Gen 2:7
the s. of my son longeth for. 34:8
as her s. was in departing. 35:18
if a s. shall sin through. Lev 4:2*
if a s. sin, and hear the voice. 5:1*
or if s. touch any unclean thing. 2*
if a s. swear. 4*
if a s. commit a trespass. 15
if a s. sin and commit any. 17*
if a s. lie. 6:2*
an atonement for the s. 17:11*
no s. of you shall eat blood. 12
if the priest buy any s. with. 22:11
whatsoever s. doth any work. 23:30
or if your s. abhor my. 26:15
because their s. abhorred my. 43
even the same s. shall. Num 9:13
the s. of the people was. 21:4
she hath bound her s. 30:4, 5, 6, 7, 8, 9, 10, 11, 12, 13
one s. of five hundred for. 31:28
serve him with all your s. Deut 11:13
lay up these my words in your s. 18
love the Lord God with all your s. 13:3; Josh 22:5; 1 Ki 2:4
s. of Jonathan was knit to s. of. 1 Sam 18:1
s. of my lord bound up in. 25:29
because the s. of all the people. 30:6
are hated of David's s. 2 Sam 5:8
the s. of David longed to go. 13:39
to thee with all their s. 1 Ki 8:48
let this child's s. come into. 17:21
let her alone for her s. is. 2 Ki 4:27
commandments with all their s. 23:3
your s. to seek the Lord. 1 Chr 22:19
to thee with all their s. 2 Chr 6:38
Lord God with all their s. 15:12
given to the bitter in s.? Job 3:20
in whose hand is the s. of. 12:10
if your s. were in my s.'s stead. 16:4
s. of the wounded crieth out. 24:12
is perfect, converting the s. Ps 19:7
to deliver their s. from death. 33:19
the Lord redeemeth the s. of. 34:22
the redemption of their s. is. 49:8†
redeem their s. from deceit. 72:14
O deliver not the s. of thy. 74:19
not their s. from death. 78:50
rejoice the s. of thy servant. 86:4
they gather against the s. of. 94:21
sent leanness into their s. 106:15
thirsty, their s. fainted in them. 107:5
longing s. and filleth hungry s. 9
s. abhorreth all manner of meat. 18
s. is melted because of trouble. 26
suffer the s. of righteous. Pr 10:3
liberal s. shall be made fat. 11:25
but the s. of transgressors. 13:2
the s. of the sluggard desireth. 4
accomplished is sweet to the s. 19
words are sweet to the s. 16:24
the s. be without knowledge. 19:2
and an idle s. shall suffer hunger. 15
s. of the wicked desireth evil. 21:10
Lord will spoil s. of those. 22:23*
he refresheth the s. of his masters. 25:13
as cold waters to a thirsty s. so is. 25
the full s. loatheth an honeycomb; but to the hungry s. every. 27:7
woe to their s.! they have. Isa 3:9
empty the s. of the hungry. 32:6
s. delight itself in fatness. Isa 55:2
hear, and your s. shall live. 3
thou satisfy the afflicted s. 58:10
their s. delighteth in their. 66:3
sword reacheth to the s. Jer 4:10†
delivered the s. of the poor. 20:13
their s. shall be as a watered. 31:12
satiate the s. of the priests. 14
satiated the weary s. and I have replenished every sorrowful s. 25
liveth, that made us this s. 38:16
meat to relieve the s. Lam 1:11
when their s. was poured out. 2:12
the Lord is good to the s. that. 3:25
as s. of father, so s. of son is mine, the s. that sinneth. Ezek 18:4, 20
what your s. pitieth shall. 24:21
their s. shall not come. Hos 9:4*
me about, even to the s. Jonah 2:5
able to kill the s.: fear him that can destroy both s. and. Mat 10:28
with all the heart and s. Mark 12:33
fear came upon every s.: and many wonders. Acts 2:43
every s. which will not hear. 3:23
believed of one heart and s. 4:32
anguish on every s. of man that. Rom 2:9
let every s. be subject to the. 13:1
that your s. and body. 1 Thes 5:23
piercing to dividing of s. Heb 4:12
we have as an anchor of the s. 6:19
believe to saving of the s. 10:39
shall save a s. from death. Jas 5:20
which war against the s. 1 Pet 2:11
Lot vexed his righteous s. 2 Pet 2:8
and every living s. died. Rev 16:3

see **afflicted, bitterness**

his soul

his s. clave to Dinah. Gen 34:3
we saw anguish of his s. 42:21
ransom for his s. to Lord. Ex 30:12
to bind his s. to Lord. Num 30:2
his s. was grieved for. Judg 10:16
she urged him, so that his s. 16:16
Josiah who turned to the Lord with all his s. 2 Ki 23:25; 2 Chr 34:31
and his s. within him. Job 14:22
in the bitterness of his s. 21:25
what his s. desireth, even. 23:13
when God taketh away his s. 27:8
by wishing a curse to his s. 31:30*
he keepeth back his s. from. 33:18
his s. abhorreth dainty meat. 20
yea, his s. draweth near unto. 22
he will deliver his s. from. 28, 30
loveth violence, his s. hateth. Ps 11:5
who hath not lifted up his s. 24:4
his s. shall dwell at ease. 25:13
he lived he blessed his s. 49:18
shall he deliver his s. from? 89:48
those that condemn his s. 109:31
if he steal to satisfy his s. Pr 6:30
eateth to satisfying of his s. 13:25
his way, preserveth his s. 16:17
lips are the snare of his s. 18:7
his mouth, keepeth his s. 21:23
that doth keep his s. shall be. 22:5
deliver his s. from hell. 23:14
but the just seek his s. 29:10*
that he should make his s. Eccl 2:24
wanteth nothing for his s. 6:2
and his s. be not filled with good. 3
his s. is empty; behold he is faint and his s. hath appetite. Isa 29:8
that he cannot deliver his s. 44:20
shalt make his s. an offering. 53:10
he shall see of the travail of his s. 11
because he poured out his s. 12
his s. shall be satisfied. Jer 50:19
deliver every man his s. 51:6*, 45
right, he shall save his s. Ezek 18:27
warning, shall deliver his s. 33:5
his s. that is lifted up, is not. Hab 2:4
lose his own s.? what can man . . . for s.? Mat 16:26*; Mark 8:37*
his s. was not left in hell. Acts 2:31*

my soul

and my s. shall live. Gen 12:13
thither, and my s. shall live. 19:20
that my s. may bless thee. 27:4, 25
O my s. come not thou into. 49:6
and my s. shall not. Lev 26:11, 30
O my s. thou hast trodden down. Judg 5:21
poured out my s. 1 Sam 1:15
yet thou huntest my s. to. 24:11†
because my s. was precious. 26:21*
who hath redeemed my s. 2 Sam 4:9; 1 Ki 1:29
the things my s. refused. Job 6:7
my s. chooseth strangling. 7:15
yet would I not know my s. 9:21*
my s. is weary of life, I will speak in bitterness of my s. 10:1
ye vex my s. with words? 19:2
who hath vexed my s. 27:2
pursue my s. as the wind. 30:15*
and now my s. is poured out. 16
my s. grieved for the poor? 25
which say of my s., There is. Ps 3:2
my s. is sore vexed. 6:3
deliver my s. 4; 17:13; 22:20; 116:4; 120:2
lest he tear my s. like a lion. 7:2
let the enemy persecute my s. 5
how say ye to my s. Flee as a? 11:1
I take counsel in my s.? 13:2
not leave my s. in hell. 16:10; Acts 2:27
he restoreth my s. Ps 23:3
to thee I lift my s. 25:1
O keep my s. and deliver me. 20
gather not my s. with sinners. 26:9
thou hast brought up my s. 30:3
thou hast known my s. in. 31:7
yea, my s. and my belly are. 9
my s. shall make her boast in. 34:2
my s. I am thy salvation. 35:3
put to shame that seek after my s. 4
they have digged a pit for my s. 7
and my s. shall be joyful in. 9
me to the spoiling of my s. 12
as for me, I humbled my s. 13
rescue my s. from their. 17
let them be confounded that seek after my s. 40:14
heal my s. for I have sinned. 41:4
as the hart, so panteth my s. 42:1
my s. thirsteth for the. 2; 143:6
I remember, I pour out my s. 42:4
cast down, O my s.? 5, 11; 43:5
O my God, my s. is cast down. 42:6
God will redeem my s. from. 49:15
oppressors seek after my s. 54:3
with them that uphold my s. 4
hath delivered my s. in peace. 55:18
steps, when they wait for my s. 56:6
for thou hast delivered my s. 13
be merciful, O God: for my s. 57:1
my s. is among lions. 4
my s. is bowed down. 6
for lo, they lie in wait for my s. 59:3
truly my s. waiteth upon God. 62:1
my s. wait thou only upon God. 5
O God, my s. thirsteth for. 63:1
my s. shall be satisfied as with. 5
my s. followeth hard after thee. 8
but those that seek my s. to. 9
what God hath done for my s. 66:16
waters are come in unto my s. 69:1
when I wept and chastened my s. 10
draw nigh to my s. and redeem it. 18
that seek after my s. 70:2; 71:13
my s. shall rejoice which. 71:23
my sore ran, my s. refused to. 77:2
my s. longeth for the courts. 84:2
preserve my s. 86:2
O Lord, do I lift up my s. 4; 143:8
thou hast delivered my s. 86:13
violent men sought after my s. 14
my s. is full of troubles, my life. 88:3
Lord, why castest thou off my s.? 14
my s. had almost dwelt in. 94:17
thy comforts delight my s. 19
bless the Lord, O my s. 103:1, 2, 22; 104:1, 35
that speak against my s. 109:20
return unto thy rest, O my s. 116:7
for thou hast delivered my s. 8
my s. breaketh for the. 119:20
my s. cleaveth to the dust. 25
my s. melteth for heaviness. 28
my s. fainteth for thy salvation. 81
my s. is continually in my hand. 109
therefore doth my s. keep them. 129
my s. hath kept thy testimonies. 167

let *my s.* live, and it. *Ps* 119:175
deliver *my s.* O Lord, from. 120:2
my s. hath dwelt with him that. 6
I wait for the Lord, *my s.* 130:5, 6
my s. is even as a weaned. 131:2
me with strength in *my s.* 138:3
my s. knoweth right well. 139:14
leave not *my s.* destitute. 141:8
no man cared for *my s.* 142:4
bring *my s.* out of prison, that I. 7
enemy hath persecuted *my s.* 143:3
O Lord, bring *my s.* out of. 11
praise the Lord, O *my s.* 146:1
I bereave *my s.* of good ? *Eccl* 4:8
which yet *my s.* seeketh, but. 7:28
O thou whom *my s.* loveth. *S of S* 1:7; 3:1, 2, 3, 4
my s. failed when he spake. 5:6
my s. made me like chariots. 6:12
and feasts *my s.* hateth. *Isa* 1:14
with *my s.* have I desired thee. 26:9
thou hast in love to *my s.* 38:17
mine elect, in whom *my s.* delighteth. 42:1
my s. shall be joyful in. 61:10
hast heard, O *my s.* *Jer* 4:19
my s. is wearied because of. 31
my s. be avenged ? 5:9, 29; 9:9
O Jerusalem, lest *my s.* depart. 6:8
beloved of *my s.* into the. 12:7
my s. shall weep in secret. 13:17
have digged a pit for *my s.* 18:20
over them with *my* whole *s.* 32:41
that should relieve *my s.* *Lam* 1:16
thou hast removed *my s.* far. 3:17
my s. hath them still in. 20
Lord is my portion, saith *my s.* 24
pleaded the causes of *my s.* 58
behold, *my s.* hath not. *Ezek* 4:14
my s. fainted within me. *Jonah* 2:7
my body for the sin of *my s.* *Mi* 6:7
my s. desired the first ripe fruit. 7:1
cut off, *my s.* loathed. *Zech* 11:8
beloved, in whom *my s.* *Mat* 12:18
my s. is exceeding sorrowful. 26:38 *Mark* 14:34
my s. doth magnify. *Luke* 1:46
I will say to *my s.*, Soul, eat. 12:19
my s. is troubled, and. *John* 12:27
for a record upon *my s.* *2 Cor* 1:23
my s. shall have no pleasure in. *Heb* 10:38

***our* soul**

our s. is dried away. *Num* 11:6
no bread, *our s.* loatheth this. 21:5
our s. waiteth for Lord. *Ps* 33:20
for *our s.* is bowed down. 44:25
who holdeth *our s.* in life. 66:9
our s. is exceedingly filled. 123:4
gone over *our s.* 124:4, 5
our s. is escaped as a bird out. 7
the desire of *our s.* is to. *Isa* 26:8

***own* soul**

if a friend is as thine *own s.* *Deut* 13:6
knit to David, and he loved him as his *own s.* *1 Sam* 18:1, 3; 20:17
keep alive his *own s.* *Ps* 22:29
destroyeth his *own s.* *Pr* 6:32
sinneth, wrongeth his *own s.* 8:36
doeth good to his *own s.* 11:17
he that refuseth instruction despiseth his *own s.* 15:32
wisdom, loveth his *own s.* 19:8
commandments keepeth his *own s.* 16
king, sinneth against his *own s.* 20:2
with thief, hateth his *own s.* 29:24
gain whole world and lose his *own s.*? *Mat* 16:26; *Mark* 8:36
pierce through thy *own s.* *Luke* 2:35

***that* soul**

that s. shall be cut off from his. *Gen* 17:14; *Ex* 31:14; *Lev* 7:20 21, 25, 27; 19:8; *Num* 15:30
that s. shall be cut off from Israel. *Ex* 12:15; *Num* 19:13
whoso eateth leavened bread, *that s.* shall be cut. *Ex* 12:19; *Num* 19:20
face against *that s.* *Lev* 17:10; 20:6
that s. shall be cut off. 22:3
that s. will I destroy from. 23:30
that s. shall utterly be. *Num* 15:31

***thy* soul**

eat, that *thy s.* may. *Gen* 27:19, 31
take heed, and keep *thy s.* *Deut* 4:9
if thou seek him with all *thy s.* 29
thy God with all *thy s.* 6:5; 30:6
Lord thy God with all *thy s.* 10:12
thy s. lusteth after. 12:15; 14:26
do them with all *thy s.* 26:16
with all thine heart and *thy s.* 30:2
unto the Lord with all *thy s.* 10
take as much as *thy s.* desireth. *1 Sam* 2:16
whatsoever *thy s.* desireth, I. 20:4
to all the desire of *thy s.* 23:20
risen to pursue and seek *thy s.* 25:29
reign according to all *thy s.* desireth. *1 Ki* 11:37
Lord shall preserve *thy s.* *Ps* 121:7
is pleasant to *thy s.* *Pr* 2:10
shall they be life to *thy s.* and. 3:22
and let not *thy s.* spare for. 19:18*
and get a snare to *thy s.* 22:25
he that keepeth *thy s.*, doth ? 24:12
knowledge of wisdom be to *thy s.* 14
give delight to *thy s.* 29:17
which have said to *thy s.* *Isa* 51:23
if thou draw out *thy s.* to. 58:10
the Lord shall satisfy *thy s.* 11
hath *thy s.* loathed Zion ? *Jer* 14:19
then *thy s.* shall live. 38:17, 20
hast delivered *thy s.* *Ezek* 3:19; 21 33:9
sinned against *thy s.* *Hab* 2:10
heart and with all *thy s.* *Mat* 22:37 *Mark* 12:30; *Luke* 10:27
this night *thy s.* shall be. *Luke* 12:20
prosper, even as *thy s.* prospereth. *3 John* 2
the fruits *thy s.* lusted. *Rev* 18:14
see **liveth**

souls

Abraham took *s.* they. *Gen* 12:5
the *s.* by Leah were thirty. 46:15
by Zilpah sixteen *s.* 18
by Rachel fourteen *s.* 22
all the *s.* Jacob had by Bilhah. 25
all the *s.* that came into Egypt. 26
Egypt, were two *s.*: all *s.* of house of Jacob were seventy *s.* 27; *Ex* 1:5
according to number of *s.* *Ex* 12:4
an atonement for your *s.* 30:15, 16 *Lev* 17:11; *Num* 31:50
even *s.* that commit. *Lev* 18:29
make your *s.* abominable. 20:25
against their own *s.* *Num* 16:38*
wherewith have bound their *s.* 30:9
destroyed them and all the *s.* that. *Josh* 10:28, 30, 32; 11:11
your hearts and in all your *s.* 23:14
s. of thine enemies. *1 Sam* 25:29
and shall save the *s.* of. *Ps* 72:13
preserveth the *s.* of his saints. 97:10
he that winneth *s.* is wise. *Pr* 11:30
a true witness delivereth *s.* 14:25
spirit should fail, and *s.* *Isa* 57:16
is found the blood of *s.* *Jer* 2:34
ye shall find rest for your *s.* 6:16 *Mat* 11:29
procure great evil against our *s.* *Jer* 26:19
great evil against your *s.*? 44:7
meat to relieve their *s.* *Lam* 1:19
not satisfy their *s.* *Ezek* 7:19
to hunt *s.* will ye hunt *s.* . . . will ye save the *s.* alive.? 13:18, 20
to slay the *s.* that should not die. 19
deliver but their own *s.* 14:14
all *s.* are mine. 18:4
they have devoured *s.* 22:25
are like wolves to destroy *s.* 27
patience possess your *s.* *Luke* 21:19
added to them 3000 *s.* *Acts* 2:41
Jacob and his kindred 75 *s.* 7:14
confirming *s.* of the disciples. 14:22
troubled you, subverting your *s.* 15:24
in all in the ship 276 *s.* 27:37
imparted our own *s.* *1 Thes* 2:8
for they watch for your *s.* *Heb* 13:17
is able to save your *s.* *Jas* 1:21
the salvation of your *s.* *1 Pet* 1:9
purified your *s.* in obeying truth. 22
to the Shepherd of your *s.* 2:25
wherein few, that is, eight *s.* 3:20
keeping of their *s.* to him. *1 Pet* 4:19
sin; beguiling unstable *s.* *2 Pet* 2:14
I saw under the altar the *s.* *Rev* 6:9
no man buyeth slaves and *s.* 18:13
I saw the *s.* of them that were. 20:4
see **afflict**

sound, *substantive*

his *s.* shall be heard. *Ex* 28:35
the *s.* of a shaken leaf. *Lev* 26:36
as soon as ye hear the *s.* of the trumpet. *Josh* 6:5, 20
hearest the *s.* of a going in the tops. *2 Sam* 5:24; *1 Chr* 14:15
ark with shouting and the *s.* of the. *2 Sam* 6:15; *1 Chr* 15:28
when ye hear the *s.* say. *2 Sam* 15:10
rent with the *s.* of them. *1 Ki* 1:40
when Joab heard the *s.* of the. 41
when Ahijah heard the *s.* of. 14:6
there is a *s.* of abundance of. 18:41
is not the *s.* of his master's feet behind him ? *2 Ki* 6:32
but Asaph made a *s.* *1 Chr* 16:5
those that should make a *s.* 42
as one, to make one *s.* *2 Chr* 5:13
in what place ye hear *s.* *Neh* 4:20
a dreadful *s.* in his ears. *Job* 15:21
at the *s.* of the organ. 21:12
hear the *s.* that goeth out. 37:2
nor believeth he it is the *s.* 39:24*
the Lord gone up with *s.* *Ps* 47:5
water, skies sent out a *s.* 77:17
people that know the joyful *s.* 89:15
the harp with a solemn *s.* 92:3
trumpets and *s.* of cornet. 98:6
praise him with the *s.* of. 150:3
s. of the grinding is low. *Eccl* 12:4
O my soul, the *s.* of. *Jer* 4:19
I hear the *s.* of the trumpet ? 21
Hearken to the *s.* of trumpet. 6:17
trembled at *s.* of the neighing. 8:16
I will take from them *s.* of. 25:10
where we shall hear no *s.* 42:14
s. of battle is in the land. 50:22
a *s.* of a cry cometh from. 51:54
s. of the cherubim's. *Ezek* 10:5
the *s.* of thy harps shall be. 26:13
shall not the isles shake at the *s.*? 15
suburbs shall shake at *s.* of. 27:28
I made nations to shake at *s.* 31:16
heareth the *s.* and taketh. 33:4
he heard *s.* of trumpet and took. 5
when ye hear the *s.* *Dan* 3:5, 7, 10, 15
Moab shall die with *s.* *Amos* 2:2
that chant to the *s.* of the viol. 6:5
his angels with a great *s.* *Mat* 24:31
hearest the *s.* but canst. *John* 3:8*
suddenly there came a *s.* *Acts* 2:2
verily their *s.* went into. *Rom* 10:18
without life giving *s.* *1 Cor* 14:7*
trumpet give an uncertain *s.* 8*
ye are not come to the *s.* *Heb* 12:19
s. of many waters. *Rev* 1:15*
s. of their wings was as the *s.* 9:9
the *s.* of a millstone shall be. 18:22*

sound, *adjective*

let my heart be *s.* in. *Ps* 119:80*
he layeth up *s.* wisdom. *Pr* 2:7
my son, keep *s.* wisdom and. 3:21
counsel is mine and *s.* wisdom. 8:14
s. heart is the life of the flesh. 14:30
received him safe and *s.* *Luke* 15:27
contrary to *s.* doctrine. *1 Tim* 1:10
but hath given us the spirit of a *s.* mind. *2 Tim* 1:7*
hold fast the form of *s.* words. 13
will not endure *s.* doctrine. 4:3
may be able by *s.* doctrine. *Tit* 1:9
rebuke them, that they may be *s.* 13
the things which become *s.* 2:1
that the aged men be *s.* in faith. 2
s. speech that cannot be. 8

sound, *verb*

of jubile to *s.* in day of atonement make the trumpet *s.* *Lev* 25:9*
ye shall not *s.* an alarm. *Num* 10:7
and Asaph were appointed to *s.* *1 Chr* 15:19
bowels shall *s.* for Moab. *Isa* 16:11
heart shall *s.* for Moab. *Jer* 48:36
and *s.* an alarm in my. *Joel* 2:1
therefore do not *s.* a. *Mat* 6:2
for the trumpet shall *s.* *1 Cor* 15:52

angels prepared themselves to *s.* *Rev* 8:6
three angels who are yet to *s.* 13
seventh angel shall begin to *s.* 10:7

sounded

the trumpet *s.* long. *Ex* 19:19
I have *s.* my father. *1 Sam* 20:12
priests *s.* trumpets. *2 Chr* 7:6, 13, 14
the people rejoiced, and *s.* 23:13
sang and the trumpeters *s.* 29:28
he that *s.* the trumpet. *Neh* 4:18
as soon as voice of salutation *s.* *Luke* 1:44
from you *s.* out the word. *1 Thes* 1:8
the first angel *s.* and there. *Rev* 8:7
the second *s.* 8, 10, 12
the fifth *s.* 9:1, 13
seventh *s.* 11:15

sounded (*of the sea*)

they *s.* and found it twenty fathoms; they *s.* again and. *Acts* 27:28

soundeth

when the trumpet *s.* long. *Ex* 19:13

sounding

instruments of music *s.* *1 Chr* 15:16
them 120 priests *s.* *2 Chr* 5:12
his priests with *s.* trumpets. 13:12*
upon the high *s.* cymbals. *Ps* 150:5
where is thy zeal, the *s.*? *Isa* 63:15*
the *s.* again of mountains. *Ezek* 7:7*
charity, I am as *s.* brass. *1 Cor* 13:1

soundness

there is no *s.* in my flesh. *Ps* 38:3, 7
no *s.* in it, but wounds. *Isa* 1:6
this perfect *s.* in presence. *Acts* 3:16

sounds

give a distinction in the *s.* *1 Cor* 14:7

sour

when the *s.* grape is. *Isa* 18:5*
fathers have eaten a *s.* grape, and. *Jer* 31:29; *Ezek* 18:2
man that eateth *s.* grape. *Jer* 31:30
their drink is *s.* they have. *Hos* 4:18

south

journeyed towards the *s.* *Gen* 12:9
Abram went up into the *s.* 13:1
spread abroad to north and *s.* 28:14
tabernacle toward the *s.* *Ex* 26:35
dwell in the land of the *s.* *Num* 13:29
possess thou west and *s.* *Deut* 33:23
smote country of the *s.* *Josh* 10:40
abide in their coast on the *s.* 18:5
the Canaanites in the *s.* *Judg* 1:9
out of a place toward *s.* *1 Sam* 20:41
against the *s.* of Judah, *s.* 27:10
had invaded the *s.* 30:1, 14
they went out to the *s.* *2 Sam* 24:7
three looking towards *s.* *1 Ki* 7:25
2 Chr 4:4
porters were toward *s.* *1 Chr* 9:24
Philistines invaded *s.* *2 Chr* 28:18
the chambers of the *s.* *Job* 9:9
out of *s.* cometh the whirlwind. 37:9
her wings toward the *s.* 39:26
neither from east nor *s.* *Ps* 75:6
the north and *s.* thou hast. 89:12
them from the north and *s.* 107:3
captivity as the streams in *s.* 126:4
goeth toward the *s.* *Eccl* 1:6
tree fall toward the *s.* or the. 11:3
as whirlwinds in the *s.* *Isa* 21:1
of the beasts of the *s.* 30:6
and I will say to the *s.*, Keep. 43:6
the cities of the *s.* shall. *Jer* 13:19
from the *s.* bringing burnt. 17:26
buy fields in the cities of the *s.* 32:44
in the cities of the *s.* shall the. 33:13
toward the *s.* and drop thy word toward *s.* . . . . *s.* field. *Ezek* 20:46
forest of *s.* . . . . faces from *s.* to. 47
against all flesh from *s.* to. 21:4
as the frame of a city on *s.* 40:2
he brought me toward the *s.* 24
prospect was toward the *s.* 44
another door was toward the *s.* 41:11
by way of the *s.* gate; and he that entereth by the way of *s.* go. 46:9
waxed great toward the *s.* *Dan* 8:9
and the king of the *s.* shall. 11:5
king's daughter of the *s.* shall. 6
king of the *s.* shall come into his. 9
king of the *s.* shall be moved. 11
arms of the *s.* shall not. *Dan* 11:15
and the king of the *s.* shall be. 25
return, and come toward the *s.* 29
the king of the *s.* shall push at. 40
they of *s.* shall possess. *Ob* 19
shall possess the cities of the *s.* 20
when men inhabited the *s.* *Zech* 7:7
go with whirlwinds of the *s.* 9:14
mountain remove toward the *s.* 14:4
queen of the *s.* shall rise. *Mat* 12:42
come from *s.* to sit down. *Luke* 13:29
and go toward the *s.* *Acts* 8:26
on the *s.* three gates, on. *Rev* 21:13

south *border*

s. border the outmost coast of the salt sea. *Num* 34:3
the *s. border* of Judah. *Josh* 15:2

south *country*

sojourned toward the *s. country.* *Gen* 20:1
dwelt in the *s. country.* 24:62
Joshua took all the *s. country.* *Josh* 11:16; 12:8
go forth toward *s. country.* *Zech* 6:6

south *field*

the forest of the *s. field.* *Ezek* 20:46

south *land*

thou hast given me a *s. land.* *Josh* 15:19; *Judg* 1:15

south *quarter*

s. quarter from Zin by. *Num* 34:3
s. quarter from end of. *Josh* 18:15

south *side*

twenty boards on the *s. side.* *Ex* 26:18; 36:23
on *s. side* shall be standard of. *Num* 2:10
camps which lie on the *s. side.* 10:6
he measured the *s. side.* *Ezek* 42:18
the waters came at the *s. side.* 47:1
and the *s. side* 4500. 48:16, 33

southward

to Abraham, Look *s.* *Gen* 13:14
pitch on side of tabernacle *s.* *Num* 3:29
Get ye up this way *s.* 13:17
I saw the ram pushing *s.* *Dan* 8:4

south *west*

lying towards the *s. west.* *Acts* 27:12

south *wind*

earth by the *s. wind.* *Job* 37:17
he brought in the *s. wind.* *Ps* 78:26
come, thou *s. wind.* *S of S* 4:16
when see *s. wind* blow. *Luke* 12:55
the *s. wind* blew softly. *Acts* 27:13

sow

the *s.* washed, to her. *2 Pet* 2:22

sow, *verb*

and ye shall *s.* the land. *Gen* 47:23
six years *s.* the land. *Ex* 23:10
Lev 25:3
shall not *s.* with mingled seed. *Lev* 19:19; *Deut* 22:9
7th year thou shalt not *s.* *Lev* 25:4, 11
we shall not *s.* nor gather. 20
ye shall *s.* the eighth year. 22
ye shall *s.* your seed in vain. 26:16
in the third year *s.* ye. *2 Ki* 19:29
Isa 37:30
they that *s.* wickedness. *Job* 4:8
then let me *s.* and let another. 31:8
s. fields, and plant. *Ps* 107:37
they that *s.* in tears shall. 126:5
he that observeth the wind shall not *s.* *Eccl* 11:4
in the morning *s.* thy seed, and. 6
plow all day to *s.*? *Isa* 28:24
give rain of seed, thou shalt *s.* 30:23
blessed are ye that *s.* beside. 32:20
break fallow ground, *s.* not. *Jer* 4:3
I will *s.* the house of Israel. 31:27
ye build house nor *s.* seed. 35:7
and I will *s.* her unto me. *Hos* 2:23
s. to yourselves in righteousness. 10:12
thou shalt *s.* but thou. *Mi* 6:15
I will *s.* them among. *Zech* 10:9
fowls of the air *s.* not. *Mat* 6:26
a sower went forth to *s.*; and when he. 13:3; *Mark* 4:3; *Luke* 8:5
didst not thou *s.* good seed? *Mat* 13:27
ravens: they neither *s.* *Luke* 12:24
that thou didst not *s.* 19:21, 22

sowed

Isaac *s.* in that land. *Gen* 26:12
Abimelech *s.* Shechem. *Judg* 9:45
when he *s.* some fell by the way. *Mat* 13:4; *Mark* 4:4; *Luke* 8:5
which *s.* good seed. *Mat* 13:24
the enemy *s.* tares. 25, 39

sowedst

Egypt, where thou *s.* *Deut* 11:10

sower

give seed to *s.* and bread. *Isa* 55:10
cut off *s.* from Babylon. *Jer* 50:16
behold, a *s.* went forth to sow. *Mat* 13:3; *Mark* 4:3; *Luke* 8:5
the parable of the *s.* *Mat* 13:18
s. soweth the word. *Mark* 4:14
ministereth seed to the *s.* *2 Cor* 9:10

sowest

that which thou *s.* is. *1 Cor* 15:36
thou *s.* not that body that shall. 37

soweth

he *s.* discord. *Pr* 6:14
he that *s.* discord. 19
to him that *s.* righteousness. 11:18
a froward man *s.* strife. 16:28*
he that *s.* iniquity shall. 22:8
overtake him that *s.* seed. *Amos* 9:13
he that *s.* good seed is. *Mat* 13:37
sower *s.* the word. *Mark* 4:14
both he that *s.* and reapeth. *John* 4:36
one *s.* and another reapeth. 37
s. sparingly; he who *s.* bountifully. *2 Cor* 9:6
for whatsoever a man *s.* *Gal* 6:7
that *s.* to his flesh, shall reap corruption; but he that *s.* to the. 8

sowing

fall upon any *s.* seed. *Lev* 11:37
shall reach to the *s.* time. 26:5

sown

fall on sowing seed to be *s.* *Lev* 11:37
valley neither eared nor *s.* *Deut* 21:4
lest the fruit of thy seed *s.* 22:9
that land is not *s.* nor beareth. 29:23
when Israel had *s.* the. *Judg* 6:3
light is *s.* for the righteous. *Ps* 97:11
every thing *s.* by the brooks. *Isa* 19:7
planted, yea, shall not be *s.* 40:24
garden causeth the things *s.* 61:11
after me in a land not *s.* *Jer* 2:2
they have *s.* wheat, but shall. 12:13
shall be tilled and *s.* *Ezek* 36:9
have *s.* the wind, shall. *Hos* 8:7
more of thy name be *s.* *Nah* 1:14
ye have *s.* much, and. *Hag* 1:6
catcheth away that which was *s.* *Mat* 13:19; *Mark* 4:15
reaping where thou hast not *s.* *Mat* 25:24
these are they which *s.* *Mark* 4:16
s. among thorns. 18
are *s.* in good ground. 20
which when it is *s.* is less than. 31
if we have *s.* to you. *1 Cor* 9:11
it is *s.* in corruption. 15:42
is *s.* in dishonour. 43
it is *s.* a natural body, it is raised. 44
multiply your seed *s.* and increase. *2 Cor* 9:10
righteousness is *s.* in peace. *Jas* 3:18

space

abode with him the *s.* of. *Gen* 29:14
and put a *s.* betwixt drove. 32:16
the *s.* of seven sabbaths. *Lev* 25:8*
if it be not redeemed in the *s.* of. 30
there shall be a *s.* between. *Josh* 3:4
s. between David's company and. *1 Sam* 26:13
for a little *s.* grace. *Ezra* 9:8*
s. of two full years. *Jer* 28:11
s. of one hour after. *Luke* 22:59
about *s.* of three hours. *Acts* 5:7
the apostles forth a little *s.* 34*
beasts by the *s.* of forty years. 7:42
gave judges about the *s.* 13:20
God gave them Saul for the *s.* 21
he spake boldly the *s.* of three. 19:8

continued by the s. of two years. Acts 19:10
all with one voice about s. of. 34
by the s. of three years I. 20:31
it rained not by the s. of. Jas 5:17*
I gave her s. to repent of her. Rev 2:21*
there was silence about the s. 8:1
blood came by the s. of 1600. 14:20*
he must continue a short s. 17:10*

Spain

take my journey into S. Rom 15:24
I will come by you into S. 28

spake

(*Revisions frequently change to* said)

Lot went out, and s. to. Gen 19:14
saying, Thus s. the man. 24:30
while he yet s. with them. 29:9
it came to pass as she s. to. 39:10
that is it that I s. unto you. 42:14
for he s. unto them by an. 23
old man of whom ye s. is. 43:27
younger brother of whom ye s.? 29
and Joseph wept when they s. 50:17
Miriam and Aaron s. Num 12:1
the people s. against God. 21:5
so I s. to you, and ye. Deut 1:43
bring thee by way whereof I s. 28:68
they s. to the master. Judg 19:22
kinsman of whom Boaz s. Ruth 4:1
now Hannah s. in her heart. 1 Sam 1:13
On this manner s. David. 18:24
nevertheless Saul s. not any. 20:26
for the people s. of stoning him. 30:6
was alive, we s. to him. 2 Sam 12:18
while he yet s., behold. 1 Ki 1:42
s. before king Solomon. 3:22
saying which Elisha s. 2 Ki 2:22
Thus and thus s. he to me. 9:12
went up at saying which Gad s. 1 Chr 21:19
one s. saying after. 2 Chr 18:19
Hezekiah s. comfortably to them. 30:22; 32:6
servant s. yet more against. 32:16
s. against the God of Jerusalem. 19
that s. to Manasseh in the. 33:18
children s. half in speech. Neh 13:24
to pass, when they s. Esth 3:4
they sat down, and none s. Job 2:13
and they s. against me. 19:18
after my words they s. not. 29:22
for they s. not, but stood still. 32:16
fire burned, then s. I with. Ps 39:3
yea, they s. against God. 78:19
so that he s. unadvisedly. 106:33
man s. to Ithiel and Ucal. Pr 30:1
my beloved s. and said. S of S 2:10
my soul failed when he s. 5:6
I hearkened and heard, they s. Jer 8:6
for since I s. I cried out, I cried. 20:8
so I s. to the people in. Ezek 24:18
words which the horn s. Dan 7:11
Ephraim s. trembling. Hos 13:1
that feared Lord s. often. Mal 3:16
while he s. these things. Mat 9:18
17:5; 26:47; Mark 5:35; 14:43
Luke 8:49; 22:47, 60
devil was cast out, dumb s.
Mat 9:33; 12:22; Luke 11:14
they perceived that he s. of them. Mat 21:45
as he s. to our fathers. Luke 1:55
not the saying which he s. 2:50
he s. unto them of the kingdom. 9:11
who s. of his decease which he. 31
other things blasphemously s. 22:65
remember how he s. to you. 24:6
as they s. Jesus stood in midst. 36
was he of whom I s. John 1:15
no man s. openly of him for. 7:13
Never man s. like this man. 46
not that he s. of the Father. 8:27
they were which he s. to them. 10:6
all things that John s. of this. 41
howbeit Jesus s. of his death. 11:13
this s. he not of himself. 51
others said, An angel s. to. 12:29
fulfilled which he s. 38; 18:9, 32
when he saw his glory, and s. 12:41
doubting of whom he s. John 13:22
who it should be of whom he s. 24
for what intent he s. this. 28
this s. he, signifying by what. 21:19
resist spirit by which he s. Acts 6:10
those things which Philip s. 8:6
while Peter yet s. these. 10:44
Jews s. against those things. 13:45
so s. that a great multitude. 14:1
but s. evil of that way before. 19:9
for the words which he s. 20:38
voice of him that s. to me. 22:9
as he thus s. for himself. 26:24
Well s. the Holy Ghost by. 28:25
child, I s. as child. 1 Cor 13:11
that ye all s. with tongues. 14:5
the blessedness ye s. of? Gal 4:15
of which tribe Moses s. Heb 7:14
him that s. on earth. 12:25
holy men of God s. as. 2 Pet 1:21
voice that s. with me. Rev 1:12
another beast s. as a dragon. 13:11

God spake

Jacob called the place where God s. Beth-el. Gen 35:15
God s. all these words. Ex 20:1
the Lord our God s. to us. Deut 1:6
not one thing failed of good things God s. Josh 23:14
how in the bush God s. Mark 12:26
we know that God s. John 9:29
and God s. on this wise. Acts 7:6
God who s. in time past. Heb 1:1

see **Lord**

Lord or God **spake,** *implicitly*

who s. to me, and sware. Gen 24:7
behold the man whom I s. to thee of. 1 Sam 9:17
Lord hath done to him as he s. 28:17
s. I a word with any of? 2 Sam 7:7
God said, The rock of Israel s. 23:3
word which I s. unto. 1 Ki 6:12
fulfilled that which he s. 2 Chr 6:4
he s. to him, and gave him. 32:24
he s. and it was done. Ps 33:9
he s. unto them in the cloudy. 99:7
he s. and there came flies. 105:31
he s. and the locusts came. 34
when I s. ye did not hear. Isa 65:12
66:4
I s. to you, rising up. Jer 7:13
I s. not to your fathers, I. 22
I sent them not, neither s. 14:14
commanded not, nor s. it. 19:5
I s. unto thee in thy prosperity. 22:21
for since I s. against him. 31:20
a voice of one that s. Ezek 1:28; 2:2
he s. unto the man clothed. 10:2
his words which he s. Dan 9:12
in Beth-el, there he s. with. Hos 12:4
as he s. by mouth of his. Luke 1:70
words which I s. to you. 24:44
he s. in a certain place. Heb 4:4

spakest

art thou the man that s.? Judg 13:11
the silver thou s. of also. 17:2
words which thou s. 1 Sam 28:21
thou s. also with thy mouth, and hast. 1 Ki 8:24; 2 Chr 6:15
be verified which thou s. 1 Ki 8:26
separate them, as thou s. by. 53
s. with them from heaven. Neh 9:13
then thou s. in vision to. Ps 89:19
since thou s. of him. Jer 48:27

span

a s. shall be the length, and a s. the. Ex 28:16; 39:9
height six cubits and a s. 1 Sam 17:4
out heaven with the s.? Isa 40:12
eat their children of a s. Lam 2:20*
of the altar shall be a s. Ezek 43:13

spanned

hath s. the heavens. Isa 48:13*

spare

not s. the place for the fifty righteous. Gen 18:24
then I will s. all the place. 26
thou shalt not s. nor. Deut 13:8
Lord will not s. him, but. 29:20*
Amalek, s. them not. 1 Sam 15:3
and s. me according to. Neh 13:22
let him not s.; I have not. Job 6:10
reins asunder, doth not s. Job 16:13
though he s. it and forsake. 20:13
cast upon him, and not s. 27:22
they s. not to spit in my face. 30:10
O s. me that I may. Ps 39:13
shall s. the poor and needy. 72:13*
he will not s. in the day. Pr 6:34
thy soul s. for his crying. 19:18*
no man shall s. his brother. Isa 9:19
eye shall not s. children. 13:18
break it, he shall not s. 30:14
s. not, lengthen cords. 54:2
cry aloud, s. not, lift up voice. 58:1
I will not s. them. Jer 13:14
Ezek 24:14
he shall not s. them. Jer 21:7
s. no arrows. 50:14
s. ye not her young men. 51:3
nor shall mine eye s. nor will I have.
Ezek 5:11; 7:4, 9; 8:18; 9:10
let not your eye s. neither. 9:5
let them say, S. thy people. Joel 2:17
should not I s. Nineveh? Jonah 4:11*
and not s. continually to. Hab 1:17
I will s. them as a man. Mal 3:17
have bread enough to s. Luke 15:17
lest he also s. not thee. Rom 11:21
trouble, but I s. you. 1 Cor 7:28
that to s. you I came not. 2 Cor 1:23
come again, I will not s. 13:2

spared

the people s. Agag. 1 Sam 15:9
for the people s. the best of the. 15
kill thee, but mine eye s. 24:10
s. to take of his own flock, and. 2 Sam 12:4
king s. Mephibosheth son of. 21:7
master hath s. Naaman. 2 Ki 5:20
he s. not their soul. Ps 78:50
mine eye s. them from. Ezek 20:17
he that s. not his own Son. Rom 8:32
if God s. not the natural. 11:21
if God s. not the angels. 2 Pet 2:4
and s. not the old world, but. 5

spareth

he that s. his rod. Pr 13:24
he that hath knowledge, s. 17:27
righteous giveth, and s. not. 21:26
them, as a man s. his son. Mal 3:17

sparing

enter in, not s. the flock. Acts 20:29

sparingly

who soweth s. shall reap s. 2 Cor 9:6

spark

and the s. of his fire shall. Job 18:5
maker of it shall be as a s. Isa 1:31

sparkled

s. like the colour of. Ezek 1:7

sparks

trouble, as s. fly upward. Job 5:7
go burning lamps, s. of fire. 41:19
yourselves about with s. Isa 50:11*

sparrow

s. hath found an house. Ps 84:3
I am as a s. alone upon the. 102:7

sparrows

are not two s. sold for? Mat 10:29
are of more value than many s. 31
Luke 12:7
are not five s. sold for? Luke 12:6

spat

spoken, he s. on ground. John 9:6

speak

(*Revisions frequently,* say *or* talk)

on me to s. to God. Gen 18:27, 31
we cannot s. unto thee bad. 24:50
take heed thou s. not to. 31:24
s. to my lord Esau. 32:4, 19
say? what shall we s.? 44:16
I know that he can s. well. Ex 4:14
since I came to s. to Pharaoh. 5:23
thou shalt s. all that I command. 7:2
shalt not s. in a cause to decline. 23:2
where I will meet you, to s. 29:42
wherefore should Egyptians s.? 32:12
until he went in to s. with. 34:35
were ye not afraid to s.? Num 12:8
the fame of thee will s. 14:15
why they that s. in proverbs. 21:27
as the Lord shall s. to me. 22:8
I s. to thee, that thou shalt s. 35

Balak, and thus thou shalt s. Num 23:5
must I not take heed to s. that? 12
of Zelophehad s. right. 27:7
words which he shall s. Deut 18:19
which shall presume to s. a word. 20
and thou shalt s. and say. 26:5
your children might s. to. Josh 22:24
that a man cannot s. to. 1 Sam 25:17
went also to s. to David. 2 Sam 3:19
Joab took him aside to s. with. 27
so did Nathan s. to David. 7:17
why s. ye not one word of? 19:10
near hither that I may s. with. 20:16
they were wont to s. in old time. 18
she went to s. to him. 1 Ki 2:19
wilt s. good words to them. 12:7
2 Chr 10:7
saying, Thus shalt thou s. 1 Ki 12:10
spirit from me to s. to thee. 22:24
2 Chr 18:23
sent me to thy master and to thee to s.? 2 Ki 18:27; Isa 36:12
what can David s.? 1 Chr 17:18
rail and s. against God. 2 Chr 32:17
could not s. in the Jews' language. Neh 13:24
to s. to the king to hang. Esth 6:4
wilt thou s. these things? Job 8:2
but, oh that God would s. 11:5
ye s. wickedly for God and? 13:7
and afterwards we will s. 18:2
my lips shall not s. wickedness. 27:4
I said, Days should s. and. 32:7
I have yet to s. on God's. 36:2
man s. he shall be swallowed. 37:20
will he s. soft words unto thee? 41:3
then shall he s. to them. Ps 2:5
destroy them that s. leasing. 5:6
they s. vanity, they s. with a. 12:2
their mouth they s. proudly. 17:10
which s. peace to their. 28:3
in his temple doth every one s. 29:9
s. grievous things proudly. 31:18
for they s. not peace, but. 35:20
my tongue shall s. of thy. 28
they s. mischievous things. 38:12
would declare and s. of them. 40:5
enemies s. evil of me, when? 41:5
my mouth shall s. of wisdom. 49:3
lovest lying rather than to s. 52:3
and lying which they s. 59:12
mouth of them that s. lies. 63:11
they that sit in the gate s. 69:12
for mine enemies s. against. 71:10
they s. wickedly, s. loftily. 73:8
what God the Lord will s.: for he will s. peace unto his people. 85:8
they utter and s. hard things? 94:4
reward of them that s. evil. 109:20
have mouths, but they s. not. 115:5
135:16
princes also did sit and s. 119:23
my tongue shall s. of thy word. 172
shall s. with the enemies. 127:5
for they s. against thee. 139:20
men shall s. of might of thy. 145:6
they shall s. of the glory of thy. 11
my mouth shall s. the praise. 21
my mouth shall s. truth. Pr 8:7
when lips s. right things. 23:16
silent, and a time to s. Eccl 3:7
those that are asleep to s. S of S 7:9
if they s. not according. Isa 8:20
shall s. and say unto thee. 14:10
five cities in Egypt shall s. 19:18
with another tongue shall he s. to this people. 28:11
shalt s. out of the ground. 29:4
stammerers shall s. plainly. 32:4
vile person will s. villany. 6
that I should know how to s. 50:4
that I am he that doth s. 52:6
trust in vanity, and s. lies. 59:4
whatsoever I command thee thou shalt s. Jer 1:7
because ye s. this word. 5:14
thou shalt s. all these words. 7:27
s. the truth, taught to s. lies. 9:5
as palm tree, but s. not. 10:5
believe not, though they s. fair. 12:6
shalt s. this word to them. 13:12
I shall s. about a nation. 18:7, 9
I stood before thee to s. good. 20
I said, I will not s. any more. Jer 20:9
s. a vision of their own heart. 23:16
s. all the words I commanded thee to s. 26:2, 8
the Lord hath sent me to s. 15
thus shalt thou also s. to. 29:24
and shall s. with him mouth. 32:4
he shall s. with thee mouth. 34:3
thou shalt s. my words. Ezek 2:7
words that I shall s. receive. 3:10
they say of me, Doth he not s.? 20:49
and thou shalt s. and be no. 24:27
mighty shall s. to him. 32:21
if dost not s. to warn wicked. 33:8
thus ye s. 10
and s. one to another. 30
children of thy people shall s. 37:18
prepared corrupt words to s. Dan 2:9
s. any thing amiss against the. 3:29
he shall s. great words. 7:25
shall s. lies at one table, but. 11:27
but at the end it shall s. Hab 2:3
how or what ye shall s. Mat 10:19
Mark 13:11
for it is not ye that s. Mat 10:20
Mark 13:11
how can ye being evil s.? Mat 12:34
every idle word that men shall s. 36
without, desiring to s. with. 46
why doth this man thus s.? Mark 2:7
do a miracle, that can lightly s. 9:39
not this man of whom ye s. 14:71
in my name they shall s. with. 16:17
I am sent to s. to thee. Luke 1:19
not able to s. till these shall. 20
when he came out he could not s. 22
suffered them not to s. 4:41
all men shall s. well of you. 6:26
and to provoke him to s. of. 11:53
s. a word against Son of man. 12:10
verily we s. that we do know, and. John 3:11
of age, ask him, he shall s. 9:21
s. of himself; that shall he s. 16:13
when I shall no more s. to you in. 25
are not all these which s.? Acts 2:7
we do hear them s. in tongues. 11
that they s. to no man in this. 4:17
not to s. at all in the name. 18; 5:40
we cannot but s. 4:20
boldness they may s. thy word. 29
him s. blasphemous words. 6:11
ceaseth not to s. blasphemous. 13
cometh shall s. unto thee. 10:32
as I began to s. 11:15
same heard Paul s. 14:9
I beseech thee suffer me to s. 21:39
thou shalt not s. evil of ruler. 23:5
permitted to s. for thyself. 26:1
I s. forth the words of truth and. 25
I will not dare to s. of. Rom 15:18
that ye all s. same thing. 1 Cor 1:10
things also we s., not man's. 2:13
not s. to you as to spiritual. 3:1
do all s. with tongues? 12:30
if all s. 14:23
for women to s. in church. 35
and forbid not to s. with tongues. 39
in the sight of God s. we. 2 Cor 2:17
we also believe and therefore s. 4:13
we s. before God in Christ. 12:19
it is a shame to s. of. Eph 5:12
manifest, as I ought to s. Col 4:4
so that we need not to s. 1 Thes 1:8
so we s. not as pleasing men. 2:4
forbidding us to s. to Gentiles. 16
put them in mind to s. evil. Tit 3:2
to come, whereof we s. Heb 2:5
though we thus s. 6:9
of which we cannot s. 9:5
let every man be slow to s. Jas 1:19
they s. against you as evil doers. 1 Pet 2:12
his lips that they s. no guile. 3:10
whereas they s. evil of you, as. 16
not afraid to s. evil of dignities. 2 Pet 2:10
s. evil of the things that they. 12
they s. great swelling words. 18
of world, therefore s. 1 John 4:5
these filthy dreamers s. evil. Jude 8
but these s. evil of those things. 10
depths of Satan, as they s. Rev 2:24
of the beast should both s. 13:15

speak, *imperatively*

s. thou with us, and we. Ex 20:19
s. ye to the rock before. Num 20:8
Lord said, S. no more to. Deut 3:26
s. thou unto us all that the Lord shall s. to thee. 5:27
s. ye that ride on white. Judg 5:10
consider, take advice, and s. 19:30
S. Lord, for thy. 1 Sam 3:9, 10
saying? if not; s. thou. 2 Sam 17:6
s. that which is good. 1 Ki 22:13
2 Chr 18:12
s. in Syrian language. 2 Ki 18:26
Isa 36:11
and to morrow s. thou. Esth 5:14
or s. to the earth, and it. Job 12:8
or let me s. and answer thou. 13:22
s. for I desire to justify thee. 33:32
s. what thou knowest. 34:33
lift not your horn: s. not. Ps 75:5
s. not in the ears of. Pr 23:9
s. word, it shall not stand. Isa 8:10
s. unto us smooth things. 30:10
s. ye comfortably to Jerusalem. 40:2
come near, then let them s. 41:1
son of a stranger s. saying. 56:3
s. to them all that I. Jer 1:17
hath my word, let him s. word. 23:28
I said, Let my lord s. Dan 10:19
s. every man the truth. Zech 8:16
Eph 4:25
s. word only, my servant. Mat 8:8
what I tell in darkness, that s. 10:27
shall be given you in that hour, s. ye. Mark 13:11
s. to my brother that he. Luke 12:13
let me freely s. to you of. Acts 2:29
go, stand and s. in the temple. 5:20
be not afraid, but s., hold not. 18:9
let him s. to himself. 1 Cor 14:28
let prophets s. two or three. 29
s. the things that become. Tit 2:1
these things s. and exhort. 15
so s. ye and do, as they. Jas 2:12
s. not evil one of another. 4:11
let him s. as the oracles. 1 Pet 4:11

I speak

people may hear when I s. Ex 19:9
shalt obey and do all that I s. 23:22
God putteth in my mouth that shall I s. Num 22:38
which I s. in your ears. Deut 5:1
I s. not with your children. 11:2
Lord saith, that will I s. 1 Ki 22:14
if I s. of strength, lo, he. Job 9:19
would I s. and not fear him. 35
I would s. to the Almighty. 13:3
let me alone, that I may s. 13
I also could s. as ye do, I. 16:4
though I s., my grief is not. 6
told him that I s.? if a man s. 37:20
I s. of things which I. Ps 45:1
troubled that I cannot s. 77:4
when I s. they are for war. 120:7
I the Lord s. righteousness. Isa 45:19
I that s. in righteousness. 63:1
ah, Lord God, I cannot s. for. Jer 1:6
to whom shall I s. and give? 6:10
hear this word that I s. in. 28:7
voice of the Lord which I s. 38:20
when I s. with thee, I. Ezek 3:27
O Daniel, understand words that I s. Dan 10:11
therefore s. I to them. Mat 13:13
Jesus saith, I that s. to. John 4:26
the words that I s. to you. 6:63
of God or whether I s. of myself. 7:17
I s. to the world those things. 8:26
as my Father hath taught me I s. 28
I s. that which I have seen with. 38
gave commandment what I should s. 12:49
whatsoever I s. therefore, as the Father said unto me, so I s. 50
I s. not of all, I know whom. 13:18
the words that I s. I s. not. 14:10
things I s. in the world. 17:13
may I s. unto thee? Acts 21:37
I also s. freely. 26:26
unrighteous? I s. as a man. Rom 3:5
I s. after the manner of men. 6:19
Gal 3:15
I s. to them that know the. Rom 7:1

I s. to you Gentiles, I am. Rom 11:13
I s. to your shame. 1 Cor 6:5; 15:34
I s. this by permission, not of. 7:6
but to the rest s. I, not the Lord. 12
and this I s. for your own profit. 35
I s. as to wise men, judge ye. 10:15
though I s. with tongues of men. 13:1
except I shall s. to you by. 14:6
I s. with tongues more than you. 18
I had rather s. five words with. 19
I s. as to my children. 2 Cor 6:13
I s. not this to condemn you. 7:3
that which I s., I s. it not after. 11:17
I s. as concerning reproach, I s. 21
are they ministers ? I s. as a fool. 23
but I s. concerning Christ. Eph 5:32
I may s. boldly, as I ought to s. 6:20
not that I s. in respect. Phil 4:11
I s. the truth in Christ, I. 1 Tim 2:7

I will speak, or will I speak

let not Lord be angry, and I will s. Gen 18:30, 32
and I will s. to him in a dream. Num 12:6
with him will I s. mouth to mouth. 8
what the Lord saith, that will I s. 24:13; 1 Ki 22:14; 2 Chr 18:13
O ye heavens, and I will s. Deut 32:1
Gideon said, I will s. but. Judg 6:39
I will s. to the king. 2 Sam 14:15
I will s. for thee to king. 1 Ki 2:18
I will s. in the anguish. Job 7:11
I will s. in the bitterness of. 10:1
I will s. that I may be. 32:20
hold thy peace, and I will s. 33:31
I beseech thee, and I will s. 42:4
O my people, and I will s. Ps 50:7
if I say, I will s. thus, I. 73:15
I will s. of thy testimonies. 119:46
I will s. of the honour. 145:5
hear, for I will s. of excellent things. Pr 8:6
me to great men, and I will s. Jer 5:5
feet, and I will s. to thee. Ezek 2:1
I will s. and the word I s. shall. 12:25
I will allure her, and s. Hos 2:14
with other lips will I s. 1 Cor 14:21

speaker

s. be established in earth. Ps 140:11
he was the chief s. Acts 14:12

speakest

wherefore then s. thou so to me ? 1 Sam 9:21
why s. thou any more ? 2 Sam 19:29
the words thou s. in thy. 2 Ki 6:12
thou s. as one of the foolish women. Job 2:10
thou sittest and s. against. Ps 50:20
be justified when thou s. 51:4
why s. thou, O Israel, My. Isa 40:27
thou s. falsely of Ishmael. Jer 40:16
thou s. falsely, the Lord hath. 43:2
him not warning, nor s. Ezek 3:18
for thou s. lies in the name of. Zech 13:3
why s. thou to them in ? Mat 13:10
Lord, s. thou this parable to us or to? Luke 12:41
now s. thou plainly, and s. no. John 16:29
Pilate saith to him, S. thou ? 19:10
this whereof thou s.? Acts 17:19

speaketh

mouth that s. to you. Gen 45:12
as a man s. unto his friend. Ex 33:11
all that the Lord s. Num 23:26
when a prophet s. in the. Deut 18:22
s. flattery to his friends. Job 17:5
for God s. once, yea, twice. 33:14
tongue that s. proud things. Ps 12:3
s. the truth in his heart. 15:2
the mouth of the righteous s. 37:30
to see me, he s. vanity. 41:6
whose mouth s. vanity. 144:8, 11
from the man that s. froward things. Pr 2:12
he s. with his feet, he teacheth. 6:13
a false witness that s. lies and. 19
the wicked s. frowardness. 10:32
he that s. truth, sheweth. 12:17
there is that s. like the piercings. 18
deceitful witness s. lies. 14:25
they love him that s. right. 16:13
that s. lies shall not escape. Pr 19:5
and he that s. lies shall perish. 9
the man that heareth s. constantly. 21:28
he s. fair, believe him not. 26:25
and every mouth s. folly. Isa 9:17
even when the needy s. right. 32:7
he that s. uprightly shall dwell. 33:15
their tongue s. deceit; one s. Jer 9:8
which the Lord s. to you. 10:1
thus s. the Lord the God of. 28:2
29:25; 30:2; Hag 1:2; Zech 6:12
7:9
voice of Almighty God when he s. Ezek 10:5
they abhor him that s. uprightly. Amos 5:10
Spirit of your Father who s. in you. Mat 10:20
whoso s. a word against the Son of man; but whosoever s. 12:32
for out of the abundance of the heart the mouth s. 34; Luke 6:45
he that is of the earth, s. John 3:31
he whom God sent, s. the words. 34
he that s. of himself, seeketh. 7:18
but lo, he s. boldly, they say. 26
s. a lie, he s. of his own. 8:44
who maketh himself a king, s. 19:12
pray, of whom s. the prophet this ? Acts 8:34
righteousness of faith s. Rom 10:6
s. in an unknown tongue; howbeit in the Spirit he s. 1 Cor 14:2
he that prophesieth, s. unto men. 3
s. in an unknown tongue edifieth. 4
prophesieth, than he that s. 5
unto him that s. a barbarian. 11
that s. in an unknown tongue. 13
now Spirit s. expressly. 1 Tim 4:1
he being dead yet s. Heb 11:4
exhortation which s. to you. 12:5
that s. better things than that. 24
refuse not him that s. . . . from him that s. from heaven. 25
he that s. evil of his brother and judgeth his brother, s. Jas 4:11
and their mouth s. great. Jude 16

speaking

done s., Rebekah came. Gen 24:15
before I had done s. in mine. 45
God s. out of the midst. Deut 5:26
s. of them when thou sittest. 11:19
then she left s. unto her. Ruth 1:18
s. peace to all his seed. Esth 10:3
yet s. another came. Job 1:16, 17, 18
can withhold himself from s.? 4:2
no more, they left off s. 32:15
thy lips from s. guile. Ps 34:13
as soon as they be born, s. lies. 58:3
away from thee s. vanity. Isa 58:9
nor s. thine own words. 13
in lying, and s. oppression. 59:13
they are yet s. I will hear. 65:24
rising up early and s. Jer 7:13
25:3; 35:14
he weakeneth the hands in s. 38:4
they left off s.; the matter was. 27
and a mouth s. great things. Dan 7:8; Rev 13:5
I heard one saint s. and. Dan 8:13
whiles I was s. praying. 9:20, 21
they abode, s. boldly. Acts 14:3
s. perverse things, to draw. 20:30
no man s. by the Spirit. 1 Cor 12:3
proof of Christ s. in me. 2 Cor 13:3
but s. the truth in love. Eph 4:15
s. to yourselves in psalms. 5:19
shall depart from faith, s. lies. 1 Tim 4:2
busybodies s. things which. 5:13
same excess of riot, s. evil of you. 1 Pet 4:4

see **end**

speaking, *substantive*

be heard for much s. Mat 6:7
let all evil s. be put away. Eph 4:31

speakings

all guile, envies, and evil s. 1 Pet 2:1

spear

Stretch out thy s. Josh 8:18*, 26*
was there a s. seen ? Judg 5:8
s. with any, but with. 1 Sam 13:22
s. was like a weaver's beam. 1 Sam 17:7; 2 Sam 21:19
1 Chr 20:5
a sword, and with a s. 1 Sam 17:45
saveth not with sword and s. 47
under thy hand s. or sword ? 21:8
and Saul's s. stuck in the. 26:7, 11
I pray thee, with the s. 8
now see where the king's s. is. 16
Saul leaned upon his s. 2 Sam 1:6
Abner with the end of the s. 2:23
with iron and staff of a s. 23:7
he lift up his s. against 800. 8
he lifted up his s. against 300 and slew them. 18; 1 Chr 11:11, 20
he slew Egyptian with his own s. 2 Sam 23:21; 1 Chr 11:23
quiver rattleth, glittering s. and. Job 39:23
s. of him that layeth at him. 41:26
laugheth at the shaking of a s. 29*
draw out also the s., stop. Ps 35:3
and cutteth s. in sunder. 46:9
lay hold on bow and s. Jer 6:23
lifteth up the sword and s. Nah 3:3
shining of the glittering s. Hab 3:11
soldier with a s. pierced. John 19:34

spearmen

rebuke the company of s. Ps 68:30*
ready two hundred s. Acts 23:23

spears

Hebrews make them swords or s. 1 Sam 13:19
to captains did priest give king David's s. 2 Ki 11:10; 2 Chr 23:9
city he put shields and s. 2 Chr 11:12
for them shields and s. 26:14
the people with their s. Neh 4:13
half of them held the s. 16, 21
whose teeth are s. and. Ps 57:4
shall beat s. into pruning hooks. Isa 2:4; Mi 4:3
furbish the s. and put on. Jer 46:4
they shall burn s. with. Ezek 39:9
pruning hooks into s. Joel 3:10

special

chosen thee to be a s. Deut 7:6*
God wrought s. miracles. Acts 19:11

see **especially**

speckled

from thence the s. cattle. Gen 30:32
the s. shall be thy wages; then the cattle bare s. 31:8
is to me as a s. bird. Jer 12:9
behind were red horses, s. Zech 1:8*

spectacle

made a s. to the world. 1 Cor 4:9

sped

have they not s.? have. Judg 5:30*

speech

hearken to my s. Gen 4:23
earth was of one s. 11:1
Lord, I am slow of s. Ex 4:10
and give occasion of s. Deut 22:14*
my s. shall distil as dew, as. 32:2
about this form of s. 2 Sam 14:20*
seeing the s. of all Israel. 19:11
s. pleased the Lord. 1 Ki 3:10
children spake half in s. of Ashdod. Neh 13:24
he removeth away the s. Job 12:20
hear diligently my s. and. 13:17
21:2; Ps 17:6; Isa 28:23; 32:9
my s. nothing worth ? Job 24:25
my s. dropped upon them. 29:22
order our s. by reason of. 37:19
day unto day uttereth s. Ps 19:2
there is no s. where their voice. 3
with her fair s. she caused. Pr 7:21
excellent s. becometh not a. 17:7
scarlet, thy s. is comely. S of S 4:3
thy s. shall be low out of the dust; thy s. shall whisper. Isa 29:4
of a deeper s. than thou canst. 33:19
shall use this s. in Judah. Jer 31:23
voice of s. as the noise. Ezek 1:24*
sent to a people of a strange s. 3:5, 6
O Lord, I have heard thy s. Hab 3:2*
art one of them, thy s. Mat 26:73
impediment in his s. Mark 7:32
art a Galilean, and thy s. 14:70
not understand my s.? John 8:43

saying in the *s.* of Lycaonia. *Acts* 14:11
continued his *s.* till midnight. 20:7
excellency of *s.* or wisdom. *1 Cor* 2:1
s. was not with enticing words. 4
and will know, not the *s.* but. 4:19
use great plainness of *s.* *2 Cor* 3:12
great is my boldness of *s.* 7:4
bodily presence weak, his *s.* 10:10
though I be rude in *s.* yet not in. 11:6
your *s.* be always with grace. *Col* 4:6
sound *s.* that cannot be. *Tit* 2:8

speeches

with him not in dark *s.* *Num* 12:8
and the *s.* of one that is. *Job* 6:26
or with *s.* wherewith he can ? 15:3
I answer him with your *s.* 32:14
by fair *s.* deceive the. *Rom* 16:18
them of all their hard *s.* *Jude* 15

speechless

garment, and he was *s.* *Mat* 22:12
beckoned unto them and remained *s.* *Luke* 1:22*
journeyed with him stood *s.* *Acts* 9:7

speed

Lord, I pray thee, send me good *s.* *Gen* 24:12
a decree, let it be done with *s.* *Ezra* 6:12*
shall come with *s.* swiftly. *Isa* 5:26
come to him with all *s.* *Acts* 17:15
nor bid him God *s.* *2 John* 10*
biddeth him God *s.* is partaker. 11*
see **make, made**

speedily

that I should *s.* escape. *1 Sam* 27:1
not in plains, but *s.* *2 Sam* 17:16*
offerings divided they *s.* *2 Chr* 35:13
the king had sent, so they did *s.* *Ezra* 6:13*
that thou mayest buy *s.* with. 7:17*
shall require, it be done *s.* 21*
let judgement be executed *s.* 26*
he *s.* gave her her things. *Esth* 2:9
deliver me *s.* *Ps* 31:2
hear me *s.* 69:17; 143:7
tender mercies *s.* prevent us. 79:8
when I call, answer me *s.* 102:2
sentence is not executed *s.* *Eccl* 8:11
shall spring forth *s.* *Isa* 58:8
and if ye recompense me, *s.* *Joel* 3:4
let us go *s.* and pray. *Zech* 8:21
he will avenge them *s.* *Luke* 18:8

speedy

make even a *s.* riddance. *Zeph* 1:18*

spend

I will *s.* mine arrows. *Deut* 32:23
they *s.* their days in wealth, and. *Job* 21:13
s. their days in prosperity. 36:11
we *s.* our years as a tale. *Ps* 90:9*
why *s.* money for that which is not ? *Isa* 55:2
because he would not *s.* *Acts* 20:16
I will very gladly *s.* *2 Cor* 12:15

spendest

whatsoever thou *s.* more, I will. *Luke* 10:35

spendeth

foolish man *s.* it up. *Pr* 21:20*
with harlots *s.* substance. 29:3*
which he *s.* as a shadow. *Eccl* 6:12

spent

and the water was *s.* in. *Gen* 21:15
not hide it how that our money is *s.* 47:18
strength shall be *s.* in vain. *Lev* 26:20
by Jebus, day was far *s.* *Judg* 19:11
for the bread is *s.* in. *1 Sam* 9:7
days are *s.* without hope. *Job* 7:6
for my life is *s.* with grief. *Ps* 31:10
s. my strength for naught. *Isa* 49:4
bread in the city was *s.* *Jer* 37:21
and had *s.* all that she had. *Mark* 5:26; *Luke* 8:43
when the day was now far *s.* *Mark* 6:35; *Luke* 24:29
the prodigal had *s.* all. *Luke* 15:14
s. their time to tell. *Acts* 17:21
the night is far *s.*, the day. *Rom* 13:12
spend and be *s.* for you. *2 Cor* 12:15

spewing

and shameful *s.* shall be on thy glory. *Hab* 2:16*

spice

rulers brought *s.* and oil. *Ex* 35:28
my myrrh with my *s.* *S of S* 5:1

spice

flesh and *s.* it well. *Ezek* 24:10

spice *merchants*

of the traffic of the *s. merchants.* *1 Ki* 10:15

spiced

thee to drink of *s.* wine. *S of S* 8:2

spicery

Ishmaelites bearing *s.* balm and. *Gen* 37:25

spices

a present, balm and *s.* *Gen* 43:11
s. for anointing oil. *Ex* 25:6; 35:8
thee principal *s.* of myrrh. 30:23, 34
the pure incense of sweet *s.* 37:29
camels that bare *s.* *1 Ki* 10:2, 10 *2 Chr* 9:1
they brought to Solomon *s.* *1 Ki* 10:25; *2 Chr* 9:24
shewed them *s.* ointment and all that was. *2 Ki* 20:13; *Isa* 39:2
appointed to oversee *s.* *1 Chr* 9:29
priests made the ointment of *s.* 30
Sheba gave Solomon *s.* *2 Chr* 9:9
divers *s.* prepared for the. 16:14
treasures for *s.* and gold. 32:27
thine ointments than all *s.* *S of S* 4:10
aloes, with all the chief *s.* 14
blow upon my garden, that *s.* 16
his cheeks are as a bed of *s.* 5:13
gone down to the beds of *s.* 6:2
hart upon the mountains of *s.* 8:14
fairs with chief of all *s.* *Ezek* 27:22
Mary had bought sweet *s.* *Mark* 16:1; *Luke* 24:1
returned and prepared *s.* *Luke* 23:56
it in linen with the *s.* *John* 19:40

spider

trust shall be a *s.'s* web. *Job* 8:14
the *s.* taketh hold with. *Pr* 30:28
eggs and weave *s.'s* web. *Isa* 59:5

spied

he *s.* an Egyptian smiting. *Ex* 2:11
s. the company of Jehu. *2 Ki* 9:17
they *s.* a band of men. 13:21
he *s.* sepulchres that were. 23:16
see **espy, espied**

spies

them, Ye are *s.* *Gen* 42:9, 14, 16
we are no *s.* 11, 31
the man took us for *s.* 30
then shall I know ye are no *s.* 34
by the way of the *s.* *Num* 21:1
men that were *s.* went in. *Josh* 6:23
the *s.* saw a man come. *Judg* 1:24
David therefore sent out *s.* and. *1 Sam* 26:4
Absalom sent *s.* throughout all the tribes of Israel. *2 Sam* 15:10
him and sent forth *s.* *Luke* 20:20
received *s.* with peace. *Heb* 11:31

spikenard

my *s.* sendeth forth. *S of S* 1:12
fruits, camphire with *s.* 4:13, 14
having an alabaster box of ointment of *s.* *Mark* 14:3; *John* 12:3

spilled

Onan *s.* it on the. *Gen* 38:9
bottles burst, and wine is *s.* *Mark* 2:22; *Luke* 5:37

spilt

we are as water *s.* on. *2 Sam* 14:14

spin

were wise hearted, did *s.* *Ex* 35:25
they toil not, neither do they *s.* *Mat* 6:28; *Luke* 12:27

spindle

her hands to the *s.* *Pr* 31:19*

spirit

In Hebrew, Ruach, *in* Greek, Pneuma, *wind, air. In scripture the word* Spirit *is taken,* [1] *For the Holy Ghost, the third person of the Trinity.* [2] *For the renewed nature, or spiritual part in man,* Mat 26:41. [3] *Signifies the soul, which continues in being even after the death of the body,* Acts 7:59. [4] *Good angels are called spirits,* Heb 1:14. [5] *The devils are often called unclean spirits, evil spirits,* Mark 5:13; *Luke* 7:21. *So in* 1 Sam 18:10. [6] *Spirit signifies an apparition or ghost,* Mat 14:26, Luke 24:37, 39. [7] *For the breath, the respiration, the animal life that is in beasts,* Eccl 3:21. [8] Spirit *is also taken for the wind,* Amos 4:13, He that createth the wind, *or* spirit. These are the four spirits of the heavens, *in* Hebrew, winds, Zech 6:5. *And in* John 3:8, The wind bloweth where it listeth, *in* Greek, pneuma, *the spirit.*

Pharaoh's *s.* was troubled. *Gen* 41:8
the *s.* of Jacob their father. 45:27
to Moses for anguish of *s.* *Ex* 6:9
every one whom his *s.* made. 35:21
I will take of the *s.* *Num* 11:17, 25
the *s.* rested upon them and. 26
that the Lord would put his *s.* 29
he had another *s.* with him. 14:24
a man in whom is the *s.* 27:18
thy God hardened his *s.* *Deut* 2:30
nor was there *s.* in them. *Josh* 5:1
when he had drunk, his *s.* *Judg* 15:19
when he had eaten, his *s.* came again to him. *1 Sam* 30:12
there was no *s.* in her. *1 Ki* 10:5 *2 Chr* 9:4
Why is thy *s.* so sad ? *1 Ki* 21:5
came forth a *s.* 22:21; *2 Chr* 18:20
portion of thy *s.* be on me. *2 Ki* 2:9
s. of Elijah doth rest on Elisha. 15
the Lord stirred up the *s.* *1 Chr* 5:26
the *s.* came upon Amasai. 12:18
all that he had by the *s.* 28:12
against Jehoram *s.* of. *2 Chr* 21:16
whose *s.* God raised to go up. *Ezra* 1:5
testifiedst by the *s.* in. *Neh* 9:30
s. passed before my face. *Job* 4:15
thou turnest thy *s.* against. 15:13
s. of my understanding causeth. 20:3
whose *s.* came from thee ? 26:4
by his *s.* he garnished the. 13
a *s.* in man, inspiration of. 32:8
s. within me constraineth me. 18
if he gather to himself his *s.* 34:14
in whose *s.* there is no guile. *Ps* 32:2
clean heart, renew a right *s.* 51:10
and uphold me with thy free *s.* 12
cut off the *s.* of princes. 76:12
and whose *s.* was not stedfast. 78:8
thou sendest forth thy *s.* 104:30
they provoked his *s.*, so. 106:33
whither shall I go from thy *s.*? 139:7
s. is good, lead me to land. 143:10
he that is hasty of *s.* *Pr* 14:29
therein is a breach in the *s.* 15:4
an haughty *s.* before a fall. 16:18
he that ruleth his *s.* than he that. 32
the *s.* of a man will sustain. 18:14
the *s.* of a man is the candle. 20:27
that hath no rule over his *s.* 25:28
the *s.* of man, *s.* of beast. *Eccl* 3:21
hasty in thy *s.* to be angry. 7:9
power over *s.* to retain the *s.* 8:8
s. of the ruler rise against. 10:4
not what is the way of the *s.* 11:5*
and the *s.* shall return to God. 12:7
the *s.* of Egypt shall fail. *Isa* 19:3
poured on you the *s.* of deep. 29:10
they that erred in *s.* shall come. 24
their horses flesh, and not *s.* 31:3
till the *s.* be poured upon us. 32:15
his *s.* it hath gathered them. 34:16
he that giveth *s.* to them that. 42:5
the Lord God and his *s.* hath. 48:16
forsaken and grieved in *s.* 54:6
the *s.* shall fail before me, and the souls. 57:15
the *s.* of the Lord God is upon me. 61:1; *Luke* 4:18
the garment of praise for the *s.* of. *Isa* 61:3
Lord raised the *s.* of king. *Jer* 51:11
whither *s.* was to go. *Ezek* 1:12, 20

s. was in wheels. *Ezek* 1:21; 10:17
s. entered into me when. 2:2; 3:24
then the s. took me up. 3:12; 11:24
so s. lifted me up, and took me away . . . heat of my s. 3:14; 8:3; 11:1
that follow their own s. 13:3
every s. shall faint, all knees. 21:7
Nebuchadnezzar's s. was. *Dan* 2:1
the s. of the holy gods: and before him I told. 4:8, 9, 18; 5:11, 14
excellent s. . . . were found. 5:12; 6:3
if a man walking in the s. *Mi* 2:11
Lord stirred up the s. of Zerubbabel. *Hag* 1:14
hath sent in his s. by. *Zech* 7:12
formeth s. of man within. 12:1
the residue of the s. Therefore take heed to your s. *Mal* 2:15, 16
Jesus was led up of the s. *Mat* 4:1 *Luke* 4:1
were troubled; saying, It is a s. *Mat* 14:26*; *Mark* 6:49*
how doth David in s. call? *Mat* 22:43
the s. indeed is willing. 26:41 *Mark* 14:38
s. descending on him. *Mark* 1:10 *John* 1:32
s. driveth him into the. *Mark* 1:12
and he sighed deeply in his s. 8:12
straightway the s. tare him. 9:20
the s. cried and rent him. 26*
go before him in the s. of Elias. *Luke* 1:17
child waxed strong in s. 80; 2:40
and he came by the s. into the. 2:27
in power of the s. into Galilee. 4:14
her s. came again, and she. 8:55
what manner of s. ye are of. 9:55
Jesus rejoiced in s. and said. 10:21
a woman who had a s. of. 13:11
that they had seen a s. 24:37
for a s. hath not flesh and. 39
shalt see s. descending. *John* 1:33
the s. by measure to him. 3:34
worship the Father in s. 4:23
s.: they must worship him in s. 24
it is the s. that quickeneth; words . . . they are s. and they. 6:63
this spake he of the s. 7:39
he groaned in s. 11:33
troubled in s. and testified. 13:21
spake as the s. gave them. *Acts* 2:4
were not able to resist the s. 6:10
then the s. said unto Philip. 8:29
the s. said unto Peter. 10:19; 11:12
Agabus signified by the s. 11:28
assayed, but the s. suffered. 16:7
his s. was stirred within him. 17:16
Paul was pressed in s. 18:5*
being fervent in s. 25
now I go bound in the s. to. 20:22
said to Saul through the s. 21:4
that there is no angel nor s. 23:8
if a s. or an angel hath spoken. 9
Son of God according to the s. *Rom* 1:4
is that of the heart, in the s. 2:29
not after the flesh, but after s. 8:1, 4
the law of the s. of life hath. 2
after the s. the things of the s. 5
in the flesh, but s. if so be that s. 9
but the s. is life because of. 10
s. of him that raised up Jesus from the dead . . . bodies by his s. 11
but if ye through the s. do mortify. 13
the s. itself beareth witness with our s. 16
who have firstfruits of the s. 23
s. also helpeth our infirmities; the s. itself maketh intercession. 26
what is the mind of the s. 27
fervent in s. 12:11
for the love of the s. 15:30
but in demonstration of s. *1 Cor* 2:4
revealed them to us by his s.: for s. searcheth all things, yea, the deep. 10
save the s. of a man which is. 11
not s. of the world, but the s. 12
absent in body, but present in s. 5:3
that s. may be saved in day of the. 5
joined to the Lord is one s. 6:17
God in your body and in your s. 20
holy both in body and s. 7:34
of gifts, but same s. 12:4, 8, 9, 11
is given by s. the word. *1 Cor* 12:8
s. are we all baptized into one body; and have been all . . . into one s. 13
in the s. he speaketh. 14:2
I will sing with the s. 15
shalt bless with the s. 16
was made a quickening s. 15:45
new testament, not of letter but of the s. . . . but the s. *2 Cor* 3:6
shall not ministration of the s.? 8
the Lord is that s.: where the s. 17
the same s. of faith, we. 4:13
all filthiness of the flesh and s. 7:1
because his s. was refreshed. 13
another s. which ye have not. 11:4
walked we not in the same s.? 12:18
received ye the s. by the? *Gal* 3:2
having begun in the s. 3
ministereth to you the s. 5
promise of the s. through faith. 14
sent forth the s. of his Son. 4:6
for we through s. wait for hope. 5:5
walk in the s. 16
lusteth against the s. and the s. 17
but if ye be led by the s. 18
the s., let us walk in the s. 25
soweth to s. shall of the s. reap. 6:8
grace of our Lord be with your s. 18 *Philem* 25
the s. that now worketh in. *Eph* 2:2
access by one s. unto the Father. 18
of God through the s. 22
to the apostles by the s. 3:5
might by his s. in inner man. 16
to keep unity of the s. in the. 4:3
there is one body, and one s. 4
and be renewed in the s. of. 23
with wine, but be filled with s. 5:18
take sword of the s. which is. 6:17
with all prayer in the s. 18
the supply of the s. of. *Phil* 1:19
that ye stand fast in one s. 27
if any fellowship of the s. 2:1
which worship God in the s. 3:3
to us your love in the s. *Col* 1:8
flesh, yet am I with you in s. 2:5
quench not s., despise. *1 Thes* 5:19
pray your s. soul, and body be. 23
neither by s. nor by word. *2 Thes* 2:2
Lord shall consume with the s. 8*
sanctification of the s. and belief. 13
justified in s. seen of angels. *1 Tim* 3:16
now the s. speaketh expressly. 4:1
an example in s., in faith. 12
Christ be with thy s. *2 Tim* 4:22
asunder of soul and s. *Heb* 4:12
who through the eternal s. 9:14
without the s. is dead. *Jas* 2:26
the s. that dwelleth in us. 4:5
through sanctification of the s. to. *1 Pet* 1:2
in obeying truth through the s. 22
of a meek and quiet s. 3:4
death in flesh, but quickened by s. 18
according to God in the s. 4:6
by the s. which he hath. *1 John* 3:24
beloved, believe not every s. 4:1
every s. that confesseth Jesus. 2
every s. that confesseth not that. 3
because he hath given us of his s. 13
s. that beareth witness, s. 5:6
witness in earth, the s. the water. 8
sensual, not having the s. *Jude* 19
in the s. on the Lord's. *Rev* 1:10
hear what the s. saith unto the churches. 2:7, 11, 17, 29; 3:6, 13, 22
and immediately I was in the s. 4:2
the s. of life from God. 11:11*
blessed dead: Yea, saith the s. 14:13
carried me away in the s. 17:3; 21:10
the s. and the bride say. 22:17
see **evil, holy, Lord, lying, vexation**

spirit *of adoption*
have received the s. *of adoption.* *Rom* 8:15

spirit *of antichrist*
this is that s. *of antichrist* ye heard. *1 John* 4:3

spirit *of bondage*
not received the s. *of bondage.* *Rom* 8:15

born of the **spirit**
except a man be *born of the s.* he. *John* 3:5
is *born of the s.* is spirit. 6
one that is *born of the s.* 8
that was *born* after *the s.* *Gal* 4:29

broken **spirit**
of God are a *broken s.* *Ps* 51:17
sorrow of the heart the s. is *broken.* *Pr* 15:13
a *broken s.* drieth the bones. 17:22
see **contrite**

spirit *of burning*
of Jerusalem by the s. *of burning.* *Isa* 4:4

spirit *of Christ*
have not the s. *of Christ.* *Rom* 8:9
what the s. *of Christ* in. *1 Pet* 1:11

spirit *of counsel*
the s. *of counsel* shall rest. *Isa* 11:2

spirit *of divination*
possessed with a s. *of divination.* *Acts* 16:16

dumb **spirit**
my son, who hath a *dumb s.* *Mark* 9:17
thou *dumb s.* I charge thee. 25

earnest of the **spirit**
hath given us the *earnest of the s.* *2 Cor* 1:22; 5:5

spirit *of error*
the s. *of* truth and *error.* *1 John* 4:6

faithful **spirit**
he that is of *faithful s.* *Pr* 11:13
see **familiar**

spirit *of fear*
given us the s. *of fear.* *2 Tim* 1:7

foul **spirit**
he rebuked the *foul s.* *Mark* 9:25
the hold of every *foul s.* *Rev* 18:2

fruit of the **spirit**
the *fruit of the s.* is love. *Gal* 5:22
for the *fruit of the s.* is in. *Eph* 5:9*

good **spirit**
thou gavest thy *good s.* *Neh* 9:20
thy s. is *good,* lead me. *Ps* 143:10

spirit *of God*
s. *of God* moved on the. *Gen* 1:2
man in whom the s. *of God.* 41:38
filled Bezaleel with the s. *of God.* *Ex* 31:3; 35:31
and the s. *of God* came. *Num* 24:2
the s. *of God* came on Saul, and. *1 Sam* 10:10; 11:6; 19:23
s. *of God* came on the messengers. 19:20
the s. *of God* came upon Azariah. *2 Chr* 15:1
s. *of God* is in my nostrils. *Job* 27:3
the s. *of God* hath made me. 33:4
in vision by the s. *of God* into Chaldea. *Ezek* 11:24
s. *of God* descending. *Mat* 3:16
out devils by the s. *of God.* 12:28
if so be that the s. *of God.* *Rom* 8:9
as are led by the s. *of God.* 14
by the power of the s. *of God.* 15:19
man, but the s. *of God.* *1 Cor* 2:11
the things of the s. *of God.* 14
s. *of God* dwelleth in you. 3:16
sanctified by the s. *of* our *God.* 6:11
also that I have the s. *of God.* 7:40
by the s. *of God,* calleth. 12:3
the s. *of* the living *God.* *2 Cor* 3:3
not the holy s. *of God.* *Eph* 4:30
s. *of God* resteth on. *1 Pet* 4:14
know ye the s. *of God.* *1 John* 4:2

spirit *of glory*
s. *of glory* resteth on. *1 Pet* 4:14

spirit *of grace*
I will pour upon the house of David the s. *of grace.* *Zech* 12:10
done despite to the s. *of grace.* *Heb* 10:29

humble **spirit**
is to be of an *humble s.* *Pr* 16:19
shall uphold the *humble* in s. 29:23
that is of an *humble s.* *Isa* 57:15

spirit *of jealousy*
and *s. of jealousy.* *Num* 5:14, 30

spirit *of judgement*
blood of Jerusalem by *s. of judgement.* *Isa* 4:4
be for a *s. of judgement* to him. 28:6

spirit *of knowledge*
s. of knowledge shall rest. *Isa* 11:2

spirit *of meekness*
come to you in the *s. of meekness* ? *1 Cor* 4:21
restore such a one in the *s. of meekness.* *Gal* 6:1

my **spirit**
my s. shall not always strive with. *Gen* 6:3
whereof drinketh up *my s.* *Job* 6:4
in the anguish of *my s.* 7:11
visitation hath preserved *my s.* 10:12
if so, why should not *my s.*? 21:4
thine hand I commit *my s.* *Ps* 31:5
I complained, and *my s.* was. 77:3
and *my s.* made diligent search. 6
my s. was overwhelmed in me. 142:3
is *my s.* overwhelmed in me. 143:4
hear me speedily, O Lord, *my s.* 7
pour out *my s.* unto you. *Pr* 1:23
yea, with *my s.* will I seek thee. *Isa* 26:9
a covering, but not of *my s.* 30:1
things is the life of *my s.* 38:16
I have put *my s.* upon him. 42:1
pour *my s.* upon thy seed. 44:3
my s. that is upon thee shall. 59:21
in the heat of *my s.* *Ezek* 3:14
and I will put *my s.* within you. 36:27; 37:14
for I have poured out *my s.* on. 39:29
my s. was troubled. *Dan* 2:3
grieved in *my s.* 7:15
I will pour out *my s.* upon all flesh. *Joel* 2:28, 29; *Acts* 2:17, 18
so *my s.* remaineth among you: fear. *Hag* 2:5
nor by power, but by *my s.* *Zech* 4:6
these have quieted *my s.* in the. 6:8
I will put *my s.* upon. *Mat* 12:18
my s. hath rejoiced in God my. *Luke* 1:47
hands I commend *my s.* 23:46
Lord Jesus, receive *my s.* *Acts* 7:59
whom I serve with *my s.* *Rom* 1:9
are gathered together and *my s.* *1 Cor* 5:4
my s. prayeth, but my. 14:14
they have refreshed *my s.* 16:18
I had no rest in *my s.* *2 Cor* 2:13

new **spirit**
I will put a *new s.* within you. *Ezek* 11:19; 36:26
a new heart and a *new s.* 18:31

newness of **spirit**
serve in *newness* of the *s.* *Rom* 7:6

patient **spirit**
patient in *s.* is better. *Eccl* 7:8

perverse **spirit**
mingled a *perverse s.* *Isa* 19:14

poor in **spirit**
blessed are the *poor in s.* *Mat* 5:3

spirit *of promise*
sealed with that holy *s. of promise.* *Eph* 1:13

spirit *of prophecy*
testimony of Jesus is the *s. of prophecy.* *Rev* 19:10

spirit *of slumber*
them the *s. of slumber.* *Rom* 11:8

sorrowful **spirit**
woman of a *sorrowful s.* *1 Sam* 1:15

spirit *of truth*
S. of truth whom world. *John* 14:17
even the *S. of truth* which. 15:26
when *S. of truth* is come. 16:13
we *s. of truth* and error. *1 John* 4:6

unclean **spirit**
I will cause *unclean s.* to pass out. *Zech* 13:2
when the *unclean s.* is gone out of a man. *Mat* 12:43; *Luke* 11:24
their synagogue a man with an *unclean s.* *Mark* 1:23
and when the *unclean s.* had. 26
said, He hath an *unclean s.* 3:30
him a man with an *unclean s.* 5:2
come out of the man, thou *unclean s.* 8; *Luke* 8:29
young daughter had an *unclean s.* *Mark* 7:25
Jesus rebuked *unclean s.* *Luke* 9:42

spirit *of understanding*
the *s. of understanding.* *Isa* 11:2

spirit *of whoredoms*
s. of whoredoms caused. *Hos* 4:12
for the *s. of whoredoms* is in. 5:4

spirit *of wisdom*
filled with *s. of wisdom.* *Ex* 28:3
full of the *s. of wisdom.* *Deut* 34:9
s. of wisdom shall rest. *Isa* 11:2
give to you *s. of wisdom.* *Eph* 1:17

wounded **spirit**
but a *wounded s.* who ? *Pr* 18:14

spirits
O God, the God of *s.* of all flesh. *Num* 16:22; 27:16
who maketh his angels *s.* *Ps* 104:4* *Heb* 1:7
the Lord weigheth the *s.* *Pr* 16:2
these are the four *s.* of. *Zech* 6:5
and he cast out the *s.* *Mat* 8:16
he gave them power against unclean *s.* 10:1; *Mark* 6:7
authority commandeth he the unclean *s.* *Mark* 1:27; *Luke* 4:36
unclean *s.* fell down. *Mark* 3:11
the unclean *s.* entered into. 5:13
rejoice not that *s.* are. *Luke* 10:20
were vexed with unclean *s.* *Acts* 5:16
for unclean *s.* crying, came. 8:7
another discerning of *s.* *1 Cor* 12:10
s. of the prophets are. 14:32
depart from faith, giving heed to seducing *s.* *1 Tim* 4:1
not all ministering *s.*? *Heb* 1:14
be in subjection to Father of *s.* 12:9
s. of just men made perfect. 23
and preached to the *s.* in prison. *1 Pet* 3:19
try the *s.* whether they. *1 John* 4:1
I saw three unclean *s.* *Rev* 16:13
s. of devils, working miracles. 14
see **evil, familiar, seven**

spiritual
the prophet is a fool, the *s.* *Hos* 9:7
impart to you some *s.* *Rom* 1:11
we know that the law is *s.* 7:14
partakers of their *s.* things. 15:27
speak, comparing *s.* things with *s.* *1 Cor* 2:13
but he that is *s.* judgeth all things. 15
not speak to you as unto *s.* 3:1
sown unto you *s.* things. 9:11
all eat the same *s.* meat. 10:3
s. drink, drank of that *s.* rock. 4
now concerning *s.* gifts. 12:1
desire *s.* gifts. 14:1
ye are zealous of *s.* gifts. 12
himself to be a prophet, or *s.* 37
s. body, there is a *s.* body. 15:44
which is *s.* but that which is natural; and afterwards that which is *s.* 46
ye which are *s.* restore. *Gal* 6:1
blessed us with all *s.* *Eph* 1:3
in psalms and *s.* songs. 5:19
wrestle against *s.* wickedness. 6:12
be filled with all *s.* understanding. *Col* 1:9
another in psalms and *s.* songs. 3:16
ye are built up a *s.* house, to offer up *s.* sacrifices. *1 Pet* 2:5

spiritually
but to be *s.* minded is. *Rom* 8:6
because are *s.* discerned. *1 Cor* 2:14
which *s.* is called Sodom. *Rev* 11:8

spit
that hath the issue, *s.* on. *Lev* 15:8
if her father had but *s.* *Num* 12:14
she shall *s.* in his face. *Deut* 25:9
and they spare not to *s.* *Job* 30:10
they did *s.* in his face. *Mat* 26:67
and they *s.* upon him and. 27:30
and he *s.* and touched. *Mark* 7:33
he had *s.* on his eyes. *Mark* 8:23
they shall *s.* upon him and. 10:34
began to *s.* on him. 14:65; 15:19

spite
for thou beholdest *s.* *Ps* 10:14

spitefully
they entreated them *s.* *Mat* 22:6*
shall be *s.* entreated. *Luke* 18:32*

spitted
spitefully entreated and *s.* on. *Luke* 18:32

spitting
face from shame and *s.* *Isa* 50:6

spittle
he let his *s.* fall down. *1 Sam* 21:13
till I swallow down my *s.* *Job* 7:19
he made clay of *s.* and. *John* 9:6

spoil, *substantive*
he shall divide the *s.* *Gen* 49:27
said, I will divide the *s.* *Ex* 15:9
Israel took the *s.* *Num* 31:9, 11
brought the prey and *s.* to Moses. 12
cattle we took for prey and the *s.* *Deut* 2:35; 3:7; *Josh* 8:27; 11:14
thou shalt gather all *s.* *Deut* 13:16
s. thou shalt take. 20:14; *Josh* 8:2
necks of them that take *s.* *Judg* 5:30
thirty men and took their *s.* 14:19
freely to-day of the *s.* *1 Sam* 14:30
the people flew upon the *s.* and. 32
but didst fly upon the *s.* and. 15:19
but the people took of the *s.* 21
because the great *s.* that. 30:16
neither *s.* nor any thing. 19
and said, This is David's *s.* 20
not give them aught of the *s.* 22
s. to the elders of Judah and his friends; behold, a . . . the *s.* 26
brought in a great *s.* *2 Sam* 3:22
he brought forth of the *s.* 12:30
Moab, to the *s.* *2 Ki* 3:23
they shall become a *s.* to. 21:14
be brought much *s.* *1 Chr* 20:2
they carried away *s.* *2 Chr* 14:13, 14
Lord at same time of the *s.* 15:11
take the *s.*: they were three days in gathering the *s.* it was. 20:25
the Syrians sent *s.* to the king. 24:23
of them, and took much *s.* 25:13
took much *s.* and brought *s.* 28:8
men left the captives and the *s.* 14
with the *s.* clothed all that were. 15
been delivered to a *s.* *Ezra* 9:7
to take the *s.* of them for a prey. *Esth* 3:13; 8:11
but on the *s.* laid they not. 9:10
I plucked the *s.* out of. *Job* 29:17
at home, divided the *s.* *Ps* 68:12
word, as one findeth great *s.* 119:162
fill our houses with *s.* *Pr* 1:13
than to divide the *s.* with. 16:19
he shall have no need of *s.* 31:11
the *s.* of the poor is in. *Isa* 3:14
the *s.* of Samaria shall be. 8:4
rejoice when they divide the *s.* 9:3
him a charge to take the *s.* 10:6
your *s.* shall be gathered, like. 33:4
prey of a great *s.* divided. 23
they are for a *s.* and none. 42:22
who gave Jacob for a *s.*? 24
he shall divide the *s.* with. 53:12
violence and *s.* is heard in. *Jer* 6:7
and treasures will I give to *s.* 15:13
substance and treasures to *s.* 17:3
I cried violence and *s.* 20:8
that *s.* thee shall be a *s.* 30:16
their cattle shall be a *s.* 49:32
and Chaldea shall be a *s.* 50:10
it to the wicked for a *s.* *Ezek* 7:21
Ammonites for a *s.* 25:7
Tyrus a *s.* 26:5, 12
Nebuchadrezzar shall take *s.* 29:19
I will go up to take a *s.* and. 38:12
art thou come to take a *s.*? 13
remove violence and *s.* 45:9
he shall scatter among them the *s.* *Dan* 11:24
they shall fall by *s.* many days. 33
s. of silver, take *s.* of gold. *Nah* 2:9
the *s.* of beasts shall. *Hab* 2:17
they shall be a *s.* to their. *Zech* 2:9
thy *s.* shall be divided in the. 14:1

spoil, *verb*
ye shall *s.* the Egyptians. *Ex* 3:22
s. them until morning. *1 Sam* 14:36
returned after him only to *s.*
2 Sam 23:10
they who hate us *s.* for. *Ps* 44:10
pass by the way *s.* him. 89:41
and let the stranger *s.* his labour.
109:11
will *s.* soul of those that. *Pr* 22:23
s. not his resting place. 24:15
take us the foxes that *s.* *S of S* 2:15
they shall *s.* them of the. *Isa* 11:14
portion of them that *s.* us. 17:14
when shalt cease to *s.* thou. 33:1
the evenings shall *s.* them. *Jer* 5:6
I will give Jerusalem to them that
shall *s.* it. 20:5
they that *s.* thee shall be a *s.* 30:16
the day that cometh to *s.* the. 47:4
go up to Kedar and *s.* the men. 49:28
that *s.* her shall be satisfied. 50:10
and they *s.* it, so that it. *Ezek* 14:15
and they shall *s.* the pomp. 32:12
s. those that spoiled them. 39:10
shall break their altars, shall *s.*
Hos 10:2
he shall *s.* the treasure of all. 13:15
of the people shall *s.* thee. *Hab* 2:8
my people shall *s.* them. *Zeph* 2:9
into a strong man's house, and *s.*?
Mat 12:29; *Mark* 3:27
beware lest any man *s.* *Col* 2:8

spoiled
sons of Jacob came and *s.* the city.
Gen 34:27
they *s.* all that was in Hamor's. 29
they *s.* the Egyptians. *Ex* 12:36
only oppressed and *s.* *Deut* 28:29
hand of spoilers that *s.* *Judg* 2:14
hand of those that *s.* them. 16
delivered Israel from them that *s.*
1 Sam 14:48
they *s.* the Philistines' tents. 17:53
Israel *s.* the tents of. *2 Ki* 7:16
Asa *s.* all the cities. *2 Chr* 14:14
he leadeth counsellors away *s.*
Job 12:17
away *s.*, overthroweth the mighty. 19
the stouthearted are *s.* *Ps* 76:5
soul of those that *s.* them. *Pr* 22:23
shall be *s.*, their wives. *Isa* 13:16
land the rivers have *s.* 18:2, 7
be utterly emptied and *s.* 24:3
spoilest, and wast not *s.* 33:1
is a people robbed and *s.* 42:22
servant? why is he *s.*? *Jer* 2:14
woe unto us, for we are *s.* 4:13
is *s.*: suddenly are my tents *s.* 20
and when thou art *s.* what wilt? 30
how are we *s.*! 9:19
my tabernacle is *s.* 10:20
deliver him that is *s.* 21:12; 22:3
for the Lord hath *s.* their. 25:36
Nebo is *s.* 48:1
Moab is *s.* and gone. 15, 20
howl, for Ai is *s.* 49:3
Esau, his seed is *s.* 10
the Lord hath *s.* Babylon. 51:55
and hath *s.* none by violence.
Ezek 18:7, 16
hath *s.* by violence. 12, 18
them to be removed and *s.* 23:46
spoil those that *s.* them. 39:10
fortresses shall be *s.* *Hos* 10:14
thy palaces shall be *s.* *Amos* 3:11
strengtheneth the *s.* against. 5:9
say, We be utterly *s.* *Mi* 2:4
hast *s.* many nations. *Hab* 2:8
the nations which *s.* you. *Zech* 2:8
howl, because the mighty are *s.* 11:2
is *s.*: for the pride of Jordan is *s.* 3
and having *s.* principalities. *Col* 2:15

spoiler
covert from face of *s.* the *s.* *Isa* 16:4
s. spoileth, go up, O Elam. 21:2
for the *s.* shall suddenly. *Jer* 6:26
I have brought upon them a *s.* 15:8
the *s.* shall come upon every. 48:8
the *s.* of Moab shall come upon. 18
s. is fallen upon thy summer. 32
because the *s.* is come upon. 51:56

spoilers
delivered them into the hand of *s.*
Judg 2:14; *2 Ki* 17:20
s. came out of camp. *1 Sam* 13:17
the garrison and the *s.* they. 14:15
the *s.* are come upon all. *Jer* 12:12
for the *s.* shall come to her. 51:48
yet from me shall *s.* come to her. 53

spoilest
woe to thee that *s.* and thou. *Isa* 33:1

spoileth
needy from him that *s.* *Ps* 35:10
the spoiler *s.* *Isa* 21:2
troop of robbers *s.* *Hos* 7:1
the cankerworm *s.* *Nah* 3:16

spoiling
me evil for good, to the *s.* *Ps* 35:12
of the *s.* of the daughter. *Isa* 22:4
a voice from Horonaim *s.* *Jer* 48:3
for *s.* and violence are. *Hab* 1:3
for ye took joyfully the *s.* *Heb* 10:34

spoils
I saw among the *s.* a goodly garment.
Josh 7:21
out of *s.* in battle did. *1 Chr* 26:27
their pride with the *s.* *Isa* 25:11
and divideth his *s.* *Luke* 11:22
gave the tenth of the *s.* *Heb* 7:4

spoken
what he hath *s.* of him. *Gen* 18:19
have *s.* in mine ears. *Num* 14:28
we have *s.* against the Lord. 21:7
hath he *s.* and shall he not? 23:19
words they have *s.* to thee, they have
well said . . . have *s.* *Deut* 5:28
because he hath *s.* to turn. 13:5
s. that which they have *s.* 18:17
done all he hath *s.* *1 Sam* 25:30
unless thou hadst *s.*, the people had
gone up. *2 Sam* 2:27
my lord the king hath *s.* 14:19
Ahithophel hath *s.* after this. 17:6
have not *s.* this word. *1 Ki* 2:23
answer this people who have *s.* to?
12:9; *2 Chr* 10:9
people said, It is well *s.* *1 Ki* 18:24
wouldest thou be *s.* for to? *2 Ki* 4:13
tongue hath *s.* in my. *Job* 33:2
Job hath *s.* without knowledge. 34:35
ye have not *s.* of me as. 42:7, 8
my mouth hath *s.* when. *Ps* 66:14
glorious things are *s.* of thee. 87:3
they have *s.* against me with. 109:2
a word *s.* in due season. *Pr* 15:23
a word fitly *s.* is like apples. 25:11
to all words that are *s.* *Eccl* 7:21
when she shall be *s.* for. *S of S* 8:8
for the sea hath *s.* *Isa* 23:4
he hath *s.* 38:15
defiled, your lips have *s.* lies. 59:3
hath *s.* to us in the name. *Jer* 26:16
and have *s.* lying words in. 29:23
not what this people have *s.*? 33:24
ye and your wives have *s.* 44:25
have ye not *s.* a lying? *Ezek* 13:7
because ye have *s.* vanity, and. 8
to thee it is *s.* *Dan* 4:31
yet they have *s.* lies. *Hos* 7:13
they have *s.* words, swearing. 10:4
with you, as ye have *s.* *Amos* 5:14
nor shouldest thou have *s.* *Ob* 12
thereof have *s.* lies. *Mi* 6:12
the idols have *s.* vanity. *Zech* 10:2
what have we *s.* so? *Mal* 3:13
he hath *s.* blasphemy. *Mat* 26:65
s. of for a memorial. *Mark* 14:9
things which were *s.* *Luke* 2:33
and for a sign which shall be *s.* 34
s. in darkness, what *s.* in ear. 12:3
they the things which were *s.* 18:34
if I had not come and *s.* *John* 15:22
as many as have *s.* *Acts* 3:24
none of these things ye have *s.* 8:24
lest that come upon you *s.* of. 13:40
the word first have been *s.* to you. 46
to the things that were *s.* 16:14
things cannot be *s.* against. 19:36
if a spirit or angel hath *s.* 23:9
things that were *s.* by Paul. 27:11
when he had thus *s.*, took bread. 35
every where it is *s.* against. 28:22
your faith is *s.* of through. *Rom* 1:8
according to that which was *s.*
Rom 4:18
your good be evil *s.* of. 14:16
to whom he was not *s.* of. 15:21
why am I evil *s.* of for? *1 Cor* 10:30
it be known what is *s.*? 14:9
hath in these last days *s.* *Heb* 1:2
if the word *s.* by angels was. 2:2
of those things to be *s.* after. 3:5
he would not afterward have *s.* 4:8
he of whom these things are *s.* 7:13
of things which we have *s.* 8:1
the word should not be *s.* any. 12:19
have *s.* unto you the word. 13:7
their part he is evil *s.* of. *1 Pet* 4:14
truth shall be evil *s.* of. *2 Pet* 2:2
of words which were *s.* before. 3:2
ungodly sinners have *s.* *Jude* 15
the words which were *s.* before. 17

spoken *with* God, *expressly*
of which God had *s.* to him. *Gen* 21:2
an holy people to thy God as he hath
s. *Deut* 26:19
God hath *s.* in his. *Ps* 60:6; 108:7
God hath *s.* once; twice. 62:11
was *s.* unto you by God. *Mat* 22:31
which God hath *s.* by. *Acts* 3:21
see **Lord**

I have, or *have I* **spoken**
which *I have s.* to thee. *Gen* 28:15
this is the thing *I have s.* 41:28
all this land *I have s.* *Ex* 32:13
the place of which *I have s.* 34
out of my grief *have I s.* *1 Sam* 1:16
Eli all things which *I have s.* 3:12
the matter which *I have s.* 20:23
and after that *I have s.* *Job* 21:3
once *have I s.* but I will not. 40:5
I believed, therefore *have I s.*
Ps 116:10; *2 Cor* 4:13
I have not *s.* in secret. *Isa* 45:19
48:16
I have s. it, I will also bring. 46:11
I, even I, *have s.*; yea, I have. 48:15
I have s. it, I have proposed it.
Jer 4:28
I have not *s.* to them yet. 23:21
I have s. unto you, rising early and.
25:3; 35:14
words *I have s.* to thee. 30:2; 36:2
because *I have s.* but they. 35:17
word which *I have s.* *Ezek* 12:28
saith it, albeit *I have* not *s.* 13:7
for *I have s.* it, saith the. 26:5; 28:10
fire of my jealousy *have I s.* 36:5, 6
art thou he of whom *I have s.*? 38:17
fire of my wrath *have I s.* 19
is the day whereof *I have s.* 39:8
I have also *s.* by the. *Hos* 12:10
the word that *I have s.* *John* 12:48
for *I have* not *s.* of myself but. 49
these things *have I s.* 14:25; 15:11
16:1, 25, 33
the word *I have s.* to you. 15:3
if *I have s.* evil, bear witness. 18:23

had **spoken**
the word Joseph *had s.* *Gen* 44:2
did as Balaam *had s.* *Num* 23:2
words he *had s.* to king. *1 Ki* 13:11
the Jezreelite *had s.* to him. 21:4
word which Elijah *had s.* *2 Ki* 1:17
as the man of God *had s.* 7:18
because we *had s.* unto. *Ezra* 8:22
king's words that he *had s.* *Neh* 2:18
Mordecai, who *had s.* good. *Esth* 7:9
had waited till Job *had s.* *Job* 32:4
wrote words the Lord *had s.* *Jer* 36:4
and when he *had s.* this. *Dan* 10:11
when he *had s.* such words. 15
when he *had s.* unto me, I was. 19
he *had s.*, the leprosy. *Mark* 1:42
they knew that he *had s.* the parable.
12:12; *Luke* 20:19
when he *had* thus *s.* *Luke* 19:28
24:40; *John* 9:6; 11:43; 18:22
Acts 19:41; 20:36; 26:30
the man believed the word that Jesus
had s. *John* 4:50
they thought he *had s.* of. 11:13
when he *had s.* this, he saith. 21:19
that he *had s.* unto him. *Acts* 9:27
departed, after Paul *had s.* 28:25
when Moses *had s.* every. *Heb* 9:19

spoken with *prophet*
but *prophet* hath *s.* it. *Deut* 18:22
if *prophet* be deceived when he hath *s.* *Ezek* 14:9
that which was *s.* by Jeremy the *prophet.* *Mat* 2:17; 27:9
might be fulfilled which was *s.* by the *prophet.* 2:23; 13:35; 27:35
s. of by the *prophet* Esaias. 3:3
which was *s.* by Esaias the *prophet.* 4:14; 8:17; 12:17; 21:4
of desolation *s.* of by Daniel the *prophet.* 24:15; *Mark* 13:14
believe all that the *prophets* have *s.* *Luke* 24:25
s. of by the *prophet* Joel. *Acts* 2:16
take *prophets,* who have *s.* *Jas* 5:10

thou hast **spoken**
this city for the which *thou hast s.* *Gen* 19:21
nor since *thou hast s.* to. *Ex* 4:10
Moses said, *Thou hast s.* well. 10:29
this thing that *thou hast s.* 33:17
be great, as *thou hast s.* *Num* 14:17
the thing which *thou hast s.* is good. *Deut* 1:14
thou hast s. friendly to. *Ruth* 2:13
maid servants which *thou hast s.* of. *2 Sam* 6:22
but *thou hast s.* also of thy servant's. 7:19, 25; *1 Chr* 17:17, 23
good is the word of the Lord which *thou hast s.* *2 Ki* 20:19; *Isa* 39:8
fail of all that *thou hast s.* *Esth* 6:10
surely *thou hast s.* in my. *Job* 33:8
behold, *thou hast s.* and done evil. *Jer* 3:5
and that which *thou hast s.* is. 32:24
the words which *thou hast s.* 44:16
O Lord, *thou hast s.* against. 51:62
I have heard all thy blasphemies which *thou hast s.* *Ezek* 35:12

spokes
their felloes and *s.* *1 Ki* 7:33

spokesman
thy *s.* unto the people. *Ex* 4:16

spoon
one *s.* of ten shekels of gold, full of. *Num* 7:14, 20, 26, 32, 38, 44, 50 56, 62

spoons
dishes thereof and *s.* *Ex* 25:29
he made his dishes and his *s.* 37:16
and put thereon the dishes and the *s.* *Num* 4:7
bowls, twelve *s.* of gold. 7:84, 86
the *s.* were of pure gold. *1 Ki* 7:50 *2 Chr* 4:22
the *s.* took he away. *2 Ki* 25:14 *Jer* 52:18, 19
of rest of the money *s.* *2 Chr* 24:14

sport
make *s.* And he made *s.* *Judg* 16:25
beheld while Samson made *s.* 27
it is a *s.* to a fool to do. *Pr* 10:23
and saith, Am not I in *s.*? 26:19

sport
against whom do ye *s.*? *Isa* 57:4

sporting
Isaac was *s.* with. *Gen* 26:8
s. themselves with their. *2 Pet* 2:13*

spot
a red heifer without *s.* *Num* 19:2
two lambs without *s.* 28:3* 9*, 11*; 29:17*, 26*
their *s.* is not the *s.* *Deut* 32:5
lift up thy face without *s.* *Job* 11:15
fair, there is no *s.* in thee. *S of S* 4:7
church, not having *s.* *Eph* 5:27
keep this commandment without *s.* *1 Tim* 6:14
who offered himself without *s.* to God. *Heb* 9:14*
as of a lamb without *s.* *1 Pet* 1:19
may be found without *s.* *2 Pet* 3:14
see **bright**

spots
can leopard change his *s.*? *Jer* 13:23
s. they are and blemishes, sporting themselves with their. *2 Pet* 2:13
these are *s.* in your feasts. *Jude* 12

spotted
thence all the *s.* cattle. *Gen* 30:32
every one that is not *s.* shall be. 33
forth cattle speckled and *s.* 39
the garment *s.* by the flesh. *Jude* 23

spouse
(*Revisions,* bride)
from Lebanon, my *s.* *S of S* 4:8
my heart, my sister, my *s.* 9
fair is thy love, my sister, my *s.* 10
thy lips, O my *s.* drop as the. 11
inclosed is my sister, my *s.* 12
into my garden, my sister, my *s.* 5:1

spouses
(*Revisions,* brides)
and your *s.* shall commit. *Hos* 4:13
I will not punish your *s.* when. 14

spouts, *see* **waterspouts**

sprang
and did yield fruit that *s.* up. *Mark* 4:8*; *Luke* 8:8*
for a light and *s.* in. *Acts* 16:29
it is evident our Lord *s.* *Heb* 7:14
s. of one so many as the stars. 11:12
see **sprung**

spread
field where Jacob had *s.* his tent. *Gen* 33:19; 35:21
and the plague *s.* *Lev* 13:5, 6, 23, 28
if the scall *s.* not. 32, 34
but if the scall *s.* much. 35, 36
if the plague be *s.* 51; 14:39, 44
and if the plague be not *s.* 55; 14:18
shall *s.* cloth of blue. *Num* 4:7, 11
they shall *s.* a scarlet cloth. 8
s. a purple cloth. 13
they shall *s.* on it a covering of. 14
s. the cloth before the. *Deut* 22:17
they *s.* a garment. *Judg* 8:25
Philistines *s.* themselves. 15:9
came and *s.* themselves in valley of. *2 Sam* 5:18, 22; *1 Chr* 14:9*, 13*
they *s.* Absalom a tent. *2 Sam* 16:22
woman *s.* a covering on the. 17:19
Rizpah *s.* sackcloth for her. 21:10
carvings of cherubims, and *s.* gold. *1 Ki* 6:32
he arose, with his hands *s.* 8:54
Hazael *s.* a thick cloth. *2 Ki* 8:15
s. the letter before the Lord. 19:14 *Isa* 37:14
he *s.* a cloud for a. *Ps* 105:39
they have *s.* a net by the way. 140:5
in vain net is *s.* in sight. *Pr* 1:17
worm is *s.* under thee. *Isa* 14:11
they that *s.* nets on the waters. 19:8
they could not *s.* the sail. 33:23
to *s.* sackcloth and ashes. 58:5
and they shall *s.* them. *Jer* 8:2
silver *s.* into plates is brought. 10:9
he hath *s.* net for my feet. *Lam* 1:13
s. the roll before me. *Ezek* 2:10
my net also will I *s.* 12:13; 17:20
thou shalt be a place to *s.* 26:14
because ye have been a net *s.* upon Tabor. *Hos* 5:1
when they shall go, I will *s.* 7:12
branches shall *s.*, his beauty. 14:6
as the morning *s.* upon. *Joel* 2:2
their horsemen shall *s.* *Hab* 1:8
behold, I will *s.* dung upon. *Mal* 2:3
s. their garments in the. *Mat* 21:8 *Mark* 11:8; *Luke* 19:36
but that it *s.* no further. *Acts* 4:17

spread *abroad*
families of the Canaanites were *s. abroad.* *Gen* 10:18
thou shalt *s. abroad* to west. 28:14
I will *s. abroad* my hands. *Ex* 9:29
Moses *s. abroad* his hands to. 33
he *s. abroad* the tent over. 40:19
but if the scab *s.* much *abroad.* *Lev* 13:7, 22, 27
they *s. abroad* the quails round the. *Num* 11:32
they were *s. abroad* on the earth. *1 Sam* 30:16
I did stamp and *s. abroad* mine enemies. *2 Sam* 22:43
the Philistines *s.* themselves *abroad.* *1 Chr* 14:13*
Uzziah's name *s. abroad.* *2 Chr* 26:8, 15
prosperity be *s. abroad.* *Zech* 1:17
I have *s.* you *abroad* as the. 2:6
departed, *s. abroad* his fame in all. *Mat* 9:31; *Mark* 1:28; 6:14
God-ward is *s. abroad.* *1 Thes* 1:8

spread *forth*
valleys are they *s. forth.* *Num* 24:6
the cherubims *s. forth.* *1 Ki* 8:7
Solomon *s. forth.* 22; *2 Chr* 6:12, 13
plague of his own heart, and *s. forth* his hands. *1 Ki* 8:38; *2 Chr* 6:29
when ye *s. forth* your hands. *Isa* 1:15
he shall *s. forth* hands, as he. 25:11
saith God, he that *s. forth* 42:5
a place to *s. forth* nets. *Ezek* 47:10

spread *over*
they shall *s. over* it a cloth. *Num* 4:6
s. therefore thy skirt *over.* *Ruth* 3:9
that is *s. over* all nations. *Isa* 25:7
s. his royal pavilion *over.* *Jer* 43:10
shall *s.* his wings *over* Moab. 48:40
s. his wings *over* Bozrah. 49:22
I *s.* my skirt *over* thee. *Ezek* 16:8
nations *s.* their net *over* him. 19:8

spread *out*
cherubims *s. out* wings. *Ex* 37:9 *1 Chr* 28:18
I *s. out* my hands to the. *Ezra* 9:5
my root was *s. out* by. *Job* 29:19
hast thou with him *s. out* the sky? 37:18
have *s. out* my hands. *Isa* 65:2
hath *s. out* his hand. *Lam* 1:10
I will therefore *s. out* my net over. *Ezek* 32:3

spreadest
fine linen which thou *s.* *Ezek* 27:7

spreadeth
if the priest see that scab *s.* *Lev* 13:8
as an eagle *s.* abroad. *Deut* 32:11
God who alone *s.* out. *Job* 9:8
and he *s.* his cloud upon it. 26:9
behold, he *s.* his light upon it. 36:30
he *s.* sharp pointed things. 41:30
flattereth his neighbour *s.* a net. *Pr* 29:5
as he that swimmeth *s.* *Isa* 25:11
and the goldsmith *s.* it over. 40:19
that *s.* the heavens as a tent. 22
I the Lord that *s.* abroad the. 44:24
the daughter of Zion *s.* *Jer* 4:31
a tree that *s.* out her roots. 17:8
Zion *s.* forth her hands. *Lam* 1:17

spreading
appears, it is a *s.* plague. *Lev* 13:57
the wicked *s.* himself. *Ps* 37:35
and became a *s.* vine. *Ezek* 17:6
place for the *s.* of nets. 26:5

spreadings
can any understand the *s.*? *Job* 36:29

sprigs
he shall cut off the *s.* with pruning hooks. *Isa* 18:5
a vine, and shot forth *s.* *Ezek* 17:6

spring, *substantive*
about *s.* of the day Samuel called. *1 Sam* 9:26
he went forth to the *s.* *2 Ki* 2:21
fountain and corrupt *s.* *Pr* 25:26
spouse, is a *s.* shut up. *S of S* 4:12
shalt be like *s.* of water. *Isa* 58:11
all the leaves of her *s.* *Ezek* 17:9*
his *s.* shall become dry. *Hos* 13:15
see **day** *spring*

spring
Israel sang, *S.* up, O. *Num* 21:17
depths that *s.* out of valleys and. *Deut* 8:7
day began to *s.* they. *Judg* 19:25
neither doth trouble *s.* *Job* 5:6
of the tender herb to *s.* forth. 38:27
truth shall *s.* out of the. *Ps* 85:11
wicked *s.* as the grass. 92:7
before they *s.* forth, I tell. *Isa* 42:9
new thing, now it shall *s.* 43:19
shall *s.* up as among the grass. 44:4
and let righteousness *s.* 45:8
and thine health shall *s.* forth. 58:8

causeth things that are sown to s.: Lord will cause praise to s. *Isa* 61:11
for the pastures do s. *Joel* 2:22
the seed should s., he. *Mark* 4:27

springeth
even to hyssop that s. *1 Ki* 4:33
the second year that which s. of. *2 Ki* 19:29; *Isa* 37:30
thus judgement s. up as. *Hos* 10:4

springing
there a well of s. water. *Gen* 26:19
as the tender grass s. *2 Sam* 23:4
thou blessedst the s. *Ps* 65:10
him a well of water s. up. *John* 4:14
any root of bitterness s. *Heb* 12:15

springs
to the plain under the s. of Pisgah. *Deut* 4:49*
all the country of the s. *Josh* 10:40*
in the plains and in the s. 12:8*
give me s. of water. And he gave her the upper s. 15:19; *Judg* 1:15
hast thou entered into the s. of the sea? *Job* 38:16
all my s. are in thee. *Ps* 87:7
s. into the valleys. 104:10
he turneth the water s. into. 107:33
dry ground into water s. 35
land become s. of water. *Isa* 35:7
I will make the dry land s. 41:18
even by the s. of water shall. 49:10
dry up her sea and make her s. dry. *Jer* 51:36

sprinkle
let Moses s. the ashes. *Ex* 9:8
he shall s. on him that. *Lev* 14:7
the priest shall s. of the oil. 16
priest shall s. of the oil with. 27
s. the house seven times. 51
shall s. on the mercy seat. 16:14, 15
s. water of purifying. *Num* 8:7
shall s. it upon the tent, and. 19:18
the clean person shall s. it on. 19
shall he s. many nations. *Isa* 52:15
will I s. clean water. *Ezek* 36:25

sprinkled
Moses s. the ashes up. *Ex* 9:10
was not s. on him. *Num* 19:13, 20
and s. dust on their heads. *Job* 2:12
he s. both the book and. *Heb* 9:19
having our hearts s. from an. 10:22
see **blood**

sprinkleth
priest's that s. the blood. *Lev* 7:14
he that s. the water. *Num* 19:21

sprinkling
the ashes of a heifer s. *Heb* 9:13
through faith he kept the s. 11:28
to Jesus, and to the blood of s. 12:24
and the s. of the blood. *1 Pet* 1:2

sprout
a tree that it will s. again. *Job* 14:7

sprung
seven thin ears s. up. *Gen* 41:6, 23
it is a leprosy s. up in. *Lev* 13:42
sat in shadow of death, light is s. up. *Mat* 4:16
forthwith they s. up. 13:5; *Mark* 4:5
the thorns s. up and choked them. *Mat* 13:7; *Luke* 8:7
but when blade was s. up. *Mat* 13:26
as soon as it was s. up. *Luke* 8:6

spue
that the land s. you not out also. *Lev* 18:28*; 20:22*
drink, s. and fall. *Jer* 25:27
so then I will s. thee out. *Rev* 3:16

spued
as it s. out nations. *Lev* 18:28*

spun
that which they had s. *Ex* 35:25
the women s. goats' hair. 26

spunge
(*Revisions*, sponge)
took a s. and filled it with vinegar. *Mat* 27:48; *Mark* 15:36; *John* 19:29

spy
men which Moses sent to s. land. *Num* 13:16, 17
Moses sent to s. out Jaazer. 21:32
Joshua sent two men to s. secretly. *Josh* 2:1; 6:23, 25
sent to s. the land. *Judg* 18:2, 14, 17
his servants to s. out the city. *2 Sam* 10:3; *1 Chr* 19:3
he said, Go and s. *2 Ki* 6:13
came in privily to s. out. *Gal* 2:4

square
all doors and posts were s. *1 Ki* 7:5
s. round about, and 50. *Ezek* 45:2
see **four-square**

squared
of the temple were s. *Ezek* 41:21

squares
in four s. thereof. *Ezek* 43:16*
fourteen broad in the four s. 17*

stability
knowledge shall be the s. *Isa* 33:6

stable, *substantive*
I will make Rabbah a s. *Ezek* 25:5

stable
world also shall be s. *1 Chr* 16:30

stablish, -ed, -eth, *see* **establish, -ed, -eth**

Stachys
salute Urbane, and S. *Rom* 16:9

stacks
so that the s. of corn. *Ex* 22:6*

stacte
(*This* Greek *word signifies the gum that distils from the myrrh trees.* Moses *speaks of* stacte *in the enumeration of the drugs that were to enter into the composition of the perfume, which was to be offered in the holy place upon the golden altar*)
take to thee sweet spices, s. and. *Ex* 30:34

staff
with my s. I passed. *Gen* 32:10
Thy signet and thy s. 38:18, 25
eat it, with your s. in. *Ex* 12:11
and walk abroad on his s. 21:19
bare one cluster of grapes between two upon a s. *Num* 13:23
smote the ass with a s. 22:27
put forth the end of his s. *Judg* 6:21
s. of his spear was like a weaver's. *1 Sam* 17:7; *2 Sam* 21:19
David took his s. in his hand, and. *1 Sam* 17:40
one that leaneth on a s. *2 Sam* 3:29
he must be fenced with the s. 23:7
to him with a s. 21; *1 Chr* 11:23
take my s.: lay my s. on. *2 Ki* 4:29
Gehazi laid the s. on the face. 31
on s. of this reed. 18:21; *Isa* 36:6
thy rod and thy s. *Ps* 23:4
take from Judah the s. *Isa* 3:1
for thou hast broken the s. 9:4
and the s. in their hand is. 10:5
or as if the s. should lift up. 15
and shall lift up his s. 10:24
the Lord hath broken the s. 14:5
are beaten out with a s. 28:27
where grounded s. shall pass. 30:32
say, How is the strong s.! *Jer* 48:17
have been a s. of reed. *Ezek* 29:6
and their s. declareth. *Hos* 4:12
every man with his s. in. *Zech* 8:4
and I took my s. even Beauty. 11:10
then I cut asunder my other s. 14
journey, save a s. only. *Mark* 6:8
leaning on the top of his s. *Heb* 11:21
see **bread**

stagger
to s. like a drunken man. *Job* 12:25; *Ps* 107:27
they s. but not with strong drink. *Isa* 29:9

staggered
he s. not at the promise of God. *Rom* 4:20*

staggereth
as a drunken man s. *Isa* 19:14

stain
the shadow of death s. it. *Job* 3:5*
Lord purposed to s. the pride of. *Isa* 23:9
their blood sprinkled, I will s. 63:3

stairs
up with winding s. *1 Ki* 6:8
him on the top of the s. *2 Ki* 9:13
stood on the s. Joshua. *Neh* 9:4
secret places of the s. *S of S* 2:14*
and his s. shall look. *Ezek* 43:17*
Paul stood on the s. *Acts* 21:40

stakes
not one of the s. shall. *Isa* 33:20
cords and strengthen thy s. 54:2

stalk
seven rank ears came up on one s. *Gen* 41:5, 22
it hath no s.: the bud. *Hos* 8:7*

stalks
and she hid them with the s. of flax. *Josh* 2:6

stall
eat the calves out of the midst of the s. *Amos* 6:4
grow up as calves of the s. *Mal* 4:2
loose his ox from the s. *Luke* 13:15

stalled
than a s. ox and hatred. *Pr* 15:17

stalls
Solomon had forty thousand s. of. *1 Ki* 4:26; *2 Chr* 9:25
Hezekiah had s. for all manner of beasts. *2 Chr* 32:28
shall be no herd in the s. *Hab* 3:17

stammerers
the tongue of the s. shall. *Isa* 32:4

stammering
s. lips and another tongue. *Isa* 28:11*
see a people of a s. tongue. 33:19*

stamp
I did s. them as the mire of the street. *2 Sam* 22:43
hand, s. with thy foot. *Ezek* 6:11

stamped
I s. the calf and ground. *Deut* 9:21
Josiah s. the grove. *2 Ki* 23:6
s. high places small to powder. 15
her idol and s. it. *2 Chr* 15:16*
hast s. with the feet. *Ezek* 25:6
fourth beast s. residue. *Dan* 7:7, 19
the he goat cast down and s. 8:7*
cast down some of stars, and s. 10*

stamping
at noise of s. of hoofs. *Jer* 47:3

stanched
her issue of blood s. *Luke* 8:44

stand
cloudy pillar s. at door. *Ex* 33:10
priest shall estimate it, so shall it s. *Lev* 27:14, 17
her vows shall s. *Num* 30:4, 5, 7, 11
her vows or her bond shall not s. 12
hath chosen him to s. *Deut* 18:5
if he s. to it and say, I like. 25:8
when he shall s. at entering gate. *Josh* 20:4
now s. and see this great thing. *1 Sam* 12:16
I will go out and s. before my. 19:3
the house, priests could s. to minister. *1 Ki* 8:11; *2 Chr* 5:14
as the Lord liveth, before whom I s. *1 Ki* 17:1; 18:15; *2 Ki* 3:14; 5:16
will come out and s. *2 Ki* 5:11
how then shall we s.? 10:4
the angel of the Lord s. *1 Chr* 21:16
to s. every morning to thank. 23:30
all present to s. to it. *2 Chr* 34:32
rulers of congregation s. *Ezra* 10:14*
see if Mordecai's matters would s. *Esth* 3:4
to gather themselves, and to s. 8:11
lean on his house, it shall not s. *Job* 8:15
he shall s. at the latter day. 19:25
and they s. as a garment. 38:14
and my kinsmen s. afar off. *Ps* 38:11
on right hand did s. queen. 45:9
and he made the waters to s. 78:13
Satan s. at his right hand. 109:6
he shall s. at the right hand. 31
our feet shall s. within thy. 122:2
if thou shouldest mark iniquities, O Lord, who shall s.? 130:3
house of righteous shall s. *Pr* 12:7

counsel of the Lord shall s. Pr 19:21
and s. not in the place of. 25:6
s. not in an evil thing. Eccl 8:3*
thus saith Lord God, It shall not s. Isa 7:7; 8:10
a root of Jesse, which shall s. 11:10
purposed, so it shall s. 14:24
my Lord, I s. continually on. 21:8
your agreement with hell shall not s. 28:18
liberal things shall he s. 32:8*
word of our God shall s. for. 40:8
counsel shall s. and I will do. 46:10
s. now with thine enchantments. 47:12
and strangers shall s. and feed. 61:5
s. ye in the ways and see. Jer 6:16
know whose word shall s. 44:28
did not s. because day was. 46:21
keeping of his covenant it might s. Ezek 17:14
their loins to be at a s. 29:7
and the kingdom shall s. Dan 2:44
king of the north shall not s. 11:6
king of the south shall not s. 25
nor shall he s. that handleth the. Amos 2:15
he shall s. and feed in. Mi 5:4
S., s., shall they cry. Nah 2:8
and who shall s. when he? Mal 3:2
kingdom divided against itself shall not s. Mat 12:25, 26; Mark 3:24
25; Luke 11:18
when ye s. praying. Mark 11:25
why s. ye gazing up? Acts 1:11
go, s. and speak in the temple. 5:20
Paul said, I s. at Caesar's. 25:10
I s. and am judged for hope. 26:6
this grace wherein we s. Rom 5:2
according to election might s. 9:11
God is able to make him s. 14:4
the gospel wherein ye s. 1 Cor 15:1
and why s. we in jeopardy? 30
joy, for by faith ye s. 2 Cor 1:24
having done all to s. Eph 6:13
s. having your loins girt about. 14
grace of God wherein ye s. 1 Pet 5:12
behold, I s. at the door. Rev 3:20
who shall be able to s.? 6:17
merchants s. afar off for fear. 18:15

stand *abroad*

s. abroad, man shall. Deut 24:11

stand *against*

neither shalt thou s. against the blood of thy neighbour. Lev 19:16
widow shall s. against. Num 30:9
that my words shall s. against you. Jer 44:29
to s. against wiles of devil. Eph 6:11

stand *aloof*

and my friends s. aloof. Ps 38:11

stand *back*

said, S. back. This fellow. Gen 19:9

stand *before*

rise up early, s. before Pharaoh. Ex 8:20; 9:13
could not s. before Moses. 9:11
I will s. before thee on the rock. 17:6
woman s. before a beast. Lev 18:23
no power to s. before your enemies. 26:37; Josh 7:12, 13; Judg 2:14
s. before the congregation to minister. Num 16:9
and he shall s. before Eleazar. 27:21
till he s. before congregation. 35:12
Josh 20:6
shall no man be able to s. before thee. Deut 7:24; 11:25; Josh 1:5
10:8; 23:9
can s. before the children? Deut 9:2
tribe of Levi to s. before the. 10:8
2 Chr 29:11; Ezek 44:11, 15
the men shall s. before. Deut 19:17
s. this day all of you before. 29:10
who is able to s. before? 1 Sam 6:20
I pray thee, s. before me. 16:22
virgin s. before the king. 1 Ki 1:2
happy are these thy servants who s. before thee. 10:8; 2 Chr 9:7
s. on the mount before. 1 Ki 19:11
we s. before this house. 2 Chr 20:9
we cannot s. before thee. Ezra 9:15
is able to s. before me? Job 41:10
can s. before his cold? Ps 147:17
in business? he shall s. before kings, he shall not s. before. Pr 22:29
who is able to s. before envy? 27:4
come and s. before me. Jer 7:10
thou shalt s. before me. 15:19
want a man to s. before me. 35:19
appoint? who is that shepherd that will s. before me? 49:19; 50:44
might s. before king. Dan 1:5
beasts might s. before him. 8:4
in the ram, to s. before him. 7
none shall s. before him, he. 11:16
s. before his indignation? Nah 1:6
s. before the Son of man. Luke 21:36
we shall all s. before judgement seat of Christ. Rom 14:10
I saw the dead, small and great, s. before God. Rev 20:12

stand *by*

behold I s. by the well. Gen 24:43
s. by the river's brink. Ex 7:15
and all the people s. by thee. 18:14
s. by the burnt offering. Num 23:3
while they s. by let them. Neh 7:3
who say, S. by thyself, I. Isa 65:5
s. by the way and ask. Jer 48:19
prince shall s. by the. Ezek 46:2
give places to walk among these that s. by. Zech 3:7
ones that s. by the Lord. 4:14
the people which s. by. John 11:42

stand *fast*

shall s. fast with him. Ps 89:28
all his commandments s. fast. 111:8*
say ye, S. fast, and. Jer 46:14
watch ye, s. fast in. 1 Cor 16:13
s. fast therefore in liberty. Gal 5:1
s. fast in one spirit. Phil 1:27
so s. fast in the Lord. 4:1
live, if ye s. fast in Lord. 1 Thes 3:8
s. fast and hold. 2 Thes 2:15

stand *forth*

get up, and s. forth with. Jer 46:4
he saith to the man, S. forth. Mark 3:3; Luke 6:8

stand *here*

s. here by well of water. Gen 24:13
he said, S. here by the burnt offering. Num 23:15
thee, s. thou here by me. Deut 5:31
turn aside, and s. here. 2 Sam 18:30
s. ye here all day idle? Mat 20:6
some s. here who shall not. Mark 9:1
even by him doth this man s. here whole. Acts 4:10

stand *in*

s. in the door of the tent. Judg 4:20
s. in holy place according. 2 Chr 35:5
the ungodly shall not s. in. Ps 1:5
s. in awe, sin not, commune. 4:4
foolish shall not s. in thy sight. 5:5
who shall s. in his holy place? 24:3
of the world s. in awe. 33:8
who may s. in thy sight when? 76:7
hast not made him to s. in. 89:43
s. in house of Lord. 134:1; 135:2
s. in gate of Lord's house. Jer 7:2
the wild asses did s. in the. 14:6
s. in the gate of the children. 17:19
s. in the court of the Lord's. 26:2
have not gone up to s. in the battle. Ezek 13:5
that should s. in gap before. 22:30
they shall s. in judgement. 44:24
had ability in them to s. in. Dan 1:4
s. in the glorious land. 11:16
shall s. in thy lot at the end. 12:13
feet s. in that day on. Zech 14:4
when ye see abomination s. in holy place. Mat 24:15
Gabriel, that s. in presence of God. Luke 1:19
not s. in wisdom of men. 1 Cor 2:5
to change my voice, for I s. in. Gal 4:20*

stand *on*

to-morrow I will s. on top. Ex 17:9
of Elisha shall s. on him. 2 Ki 6:31
shall not s. on his side. Dan 11:17
arms shall s. on his part, and they shall pollute. Dan 11:31
s. on sea of glass, having. Rev 15:2

stand *out*

eyes s. out with fatness. Ps 73:7

stand *perfect*

may s. perfect and complete in will. Col 4:12

stand *still*

Fear ye not, s. still and see the. Ex 14:13; 2 Chr 20:17
s. still, I will hear what. Num 9:8*
ye shall s. still in Jordan. Josh 3:8
sun s. still upon Gibeon, and. 10:12
s. thou still a while. 1 Sam 9:27
now s. still that I may reason. 12:7
we will s. still in our place. 14:9
s. still and consider the. Job 37:14
escaped sword s. not still. Jer 51:50
the chariot to s. still. Acts 8:38

stand *strong*

mountain to s. strong. Ps 30:7

stand *there*

that they may s. there. Num 11:16
as Levites who s. there. Deut 18:7
to the poor, S. thou there. Jas 2:3

stand *together*

let us s. together: who? Isa 50:8

stand *up*

s. up and bless the Lord. Neh 9:5
I s. up, and thou regardest me not. Job 30:20
in order before me, s. up. 33:5
take hold of shield, s. up. Ps 35:2
who will s. up for me against? 94:16
with child that shall s. up. Eccl 4:15
images shall not s. up. Isa 27:9*
let them s. up yet they shall. 44:11
prognosticators s. up. 47:13
them, they s. up together. 48:13
awake, s. up, O Jerusalem. 51:17
nor their trees s. up in. Ezek 31:14
four kingdoms shall s. up. Dan 8:22
of fierce countenance shall s. up. 23
he shall also s. up against prince. 25
there shall s. up three kings. 11:2
and a mighty king shall s. up. 3, 4
her roots shall one s. up. 7
many shall s. up against king. 14
s. up in his estate a raiser of taxes. 20
estate shall s. up a vile person. 21
time shall Michael s. up. 12:1
Peter said, S. up; I. Acts 10:26

stand *upon*

thou shalt s. upon a rock. Ex 33:21
s. upon mount Gerizim. Deut 27:12
these shall s. upon mount Ebal. 13
and they shall s. upon. Josh 3:13
Saul said, S. upon me. 2 Sam 1:9
s. upon the mount. 1 Ki 19:11
son of man, s. upon thy feet. Ezek 2:1; Acts 26:16
pilots of the sea shall s. upon the land. Ezek 27:29
ye s. upon sword, ye work. 33:26
fishes shall s. upon it from. 47:10
made s. upon the feet. Dan 7:4
I will s. upon my watch. Hab 2:1
while they s. upon feet. Zech 14:12
angel I saw s. upon sea. Rev 10:5

stand *upright*

risen and s. upright. Ps 20:8
understand words, s. upright. Dan 10:11
said, S. upright on thy feet. And he leaped and walked. Acts 14:10

stand *with*

men that shall s. with you. Num 1:5

stand *without*

not able to s. without. Ezra 10:13
s. without, desiring to speak. Mat 12:47; Luke 8:20
ye begin to s. without. Luke 13:25

standard

and every man by his own s. Num 1:52; 2:2, 17
east side shall the s. of Judah. 2:3
south side shall be the s. of. 10
west side shall be the s. of. 18
north side shall be the s. of Dan. 25
in the first place went the s. 10:14

I will set up my s. to the people. Isa 49:22*
Lord shall lift up a s. against. 59:19*
lift up a s. for the people. 62:10*
set up s. toward Zion. Jer 4:6
how long shall I see the s. and? 21
set ye up a s. in the land. 50:2
51:12, 27

standardbearer
they shall be as when a s. Isa 10:18

standards
hindmost with their s. Num 2:31
so they pitched by their s. and. 34

standest
come in; wherefore s. thou without? Gen 24:31
the place whereon thou s. is holy. Ex 3:5; Josh 5:15; Acts 7:33
why s. thou afar off? Ps 10:1
were broken off, thou s. by faith. Rom 11:20

standeth
and that thy cloud s. Num 14:14
son of Nun, which s. before thee. Deut 1:38
hearken to the priest that s. 17:12
but with him that s. with us. 29:15
to feel pillars whereon the house s. Judg 16:26*
Haman s. in the court. Esth 6:5
the gallows s. in the house of. 7:9
nor s. in the way of sinners. Ps 1:1
my foot s. in an even place. 26:12
the counsel of the Lord s. 33:11
God s. in the congregation. 82:1
but my heart s. in awe. 119:161
wisdom s. in the top of. Pr 8:2
behold, he s. behind. S of S 2:9
Lord s. up to plead, s. to. Isa 3:13
in his place, and he s. 46:7
justice s. afar off, truth is. 59:14
the great prince who s. for. Dan 12:1
feed that that s. still. Zech 11:16*
s. one among you, whom. John 1:26
the friend of the bridegroom s. 3:29
to his own master he s. Rom 14:4
that s. stedfast in heart. 1 Cor 7:37
no flesh while the world s. 8:13
thinketh he s. take heed. 10:12
the foundation of God s. 2 Tim 2:19
every priest s. daily. Heb 10:11
behold, the judge s. Jas 5:9
angel who s. on the sea. Rev 10:8

standing, *substantive*
mire where there is no s. Ps 69:2
receive of you his s. Mi 1:11*

standing
nor rear ye up a s. image. Lev 26:1*
angel of the Lord s. Num 22:23, 31
Samuel s. as appointed. 1 Sam 19:20
servants were s. about him. 22:6
and the lion s. by. 1 Ki 13:25, 28
host of heaven s. 22:19; 2 Chr 18:18
and two lions s. by. 2 Chr 9:18
Esther the queen s. in. Esth 5:2
turneth wilderness into a s. water. Ps 107:35*
the rock into a s. water. 114:8*
I saw the Lord s. upon. Amos 9:1
I will cut off thy s. images. Mi 5:13*
Satan s. at his right hand. Zech 3:1
which go forth from s. before. 6:5
they love to pray s. in. Mat 6:5
be some s. here. 16:28; Luke 9:27
s. idle in the market. Mat 20:3, 6
his mother s. without. Mark 3:31
the abomination s. where it. 13:14
an angel s. on the right. Luke 1:11
the publican s. afar off smote. 18:13
and woman s. in midst. John 8:9*
she turned and saw Jesus s. 20:14
but Peter s. up with. Acts 2:14
beholding the man healed s. 4:14
found the keepers s. without 5:23
the men are s. in the temple. 25
s. on the right hand of God. 7:55, 56
I was s. by and consenting. 22:20
first tabernacle was yet s. Heb 9:8
earth s. out of the water. 2 Pet 3:5*
four angels s. on four. Rev 7:1
two candlesticks s. before. 11:4
s. afar off for the fear of. Rev 18:10
I saw an angel s. in the sun. 19:17
see **corn**

stank
died, and the river s. Ex 7:21
frogs on heaps, and land s. 8:14
manna bred worms and s. 16:20
Ammon saw they s. 2 Sam 10:6*

star
This word included, for the Hebrew, all heavenly bodies except the sun and the moon. The stars and the grouping into constellations early attracted man's attention, and they are alluded to in the earliest-written of the books of the Bible. Among idolaters the stars soon became objects of worship. They were supposed to foretell events, and a whole science was built up around them.

Several stars spoken of especially in the New Testament have a figurative rather than a literal use.

[1] The day star *is given as a sign of Christ's coming, or as a symbol of the spirit's illumination of the heart of one who has accepted Christ,* 2 Pet 1:19.

[2] The morning star, *which precedes the coming of day, is given as a designation of Christ as bringing the day of gospel light,* Rev 2:28.

[3] The star of the wise men, *which is the subject of much discussion,* Mat 2:2.

The number of the stars was looked upon as infinite. When the scripture would express a very extraordinary increase and multiplication, it uses the symbol of the stars of heaven, or of the sand of the sea, Gen 15:5; 22:17; 26:4.

there shall come a s. out. Num 24:17
but ye have borne the s. Amos 5:26
for we have seen his s. Mat 2:2
of them what time s. appeared. 7
lo, the s. which they saw in east. 9
when they saw s. they rejoiced. 10
s. of your god Remphan. Acts 7:43
s. differeth from another s. in glory. 1 Cor 15:41
there fell a great s. Rev 8:10, 11
a s. fell from heaven unto. 9:1

day star
till the *day s.* arise in. 2 Pet 1:19

morning star
give him the *morning s.* Rev 2:28
the bright and *morning s.* 22:16

stare
may tell all my bones: they look and s. upon me. Ps 22:17

stargazers
let the s. stand up and. Isa 47:13

stars
lights, he made s. also. Gen 1:16
tell the s. if thou be able to. 15:5
sun, moon, and eleven s. made. 37:9
when thou seest s. should. Deut 4:19
the s. in their courses. Judg 5:20
the morning till the s. Neh 4:21
let the s. of the twilight. Job 3:9
sun, and sealeth up the s. 9:7
behold height of the s. how. 22:12
s. are not pure in his sight. 25:5
when the morning s. sang. 38:7
moon and s. which thou. Ps 8:3
moon and s. to rule by night. 136:9
he telleth number of the s. 147:4
sun, moon, all ye s. of light. 148:3
while the sun or s. be. Eccl 12:2
throne above s. of God. Isa 14:13
giveth the s. for a light. Jer 31:35
I will make the s. Ezek 32:7
it cast down some of the s. Dan 8:10
shall shine as the s. for ever. 12:3
s. shall withdraw. Joel 2:10; 3:15
set thy nest among the s. Ob 4
be signs in sun, moon, and s. Luke 21:25
when neither sun nor s. Acts 27:20
glory of s., for one star. 1 Cor 15:41
so many as s. of the sky. Heb 11:12
raging waves, wandering s. Jude 13
the third part of the s. Rev 8:12
head a crown of twelve s. 12:1
see **heaven, seven**

state
every man at his best s. is. Ps 39:5*
the last s. of that man is worse than. Mat 12:45; Luke 11:26
see **estate**

stately
satest upon a s. bed. Ezek 23:41

station
from thy s. and state. Isa 22:19*

stature
saw are men of great s. Num 13:32
on the height of his s. 1 Sam 16:7
s. with six fingers and with six toes. 2 Sam 21:20; 1 Chr 11:23; 20:6
this thy s. is like a palm tree and. S of S 7:7
the high ones of s. shall. Isa 10:33
men of s. shall come over. 45:14
upon head of every s. Ezek 13:18
a spreading vine of low s. 17:6
her s. was exalted among. 19:11
was a cedar of an high s. 31:3
not add one cubit to his s. Mat 6:27†; Luke 12:25
Jesus increased in wisdom and s. Luke 2:52
Zacchaeus little of s. climbed. 19:3
measure of the s. of fulness of Christ. Eph 4:13

statute
there he made a s. and. Ex 15:25
shall be theirs for perpetual s. 29:9
a perpetual s. Lev 3:17; 16:34
24:9; Num 19:21
it shall be for a s. of judgement. Num 27:11; 35:29
and he set them a s. Josh 24:25
David made it a s. for. 1 Sam 30:25
was a s. for Israel and. Ps 81:4
to establish a royal s. Dan 6:7
that no s. king establisheth may. 15

statutes
know the s. of God. Ex 18:16
teach Israel all the s. Lev 10:11
these are the s. the Lord. Num 30:16
shall hear all these s. Deut 4:6
Lord commanded us to do all these s. 6:24
shalt oberve and do these s. 16:12
to keep these s. to do them. 17:19
walking in the s. of David. 1 Ki 3:3
and walked in s. of the heathen. 2 Ki 17:8, 19
neither do they after their s. 34
the s. he wrote, ye shall. 37
take heed to do the s. 2 Chr 33:8
them s. and laws. Neh 9:14
s. of Lord are right. Ps 19:8
I gave them s. that. Ezek 20:25
walk in the s. of life. 33:15
for s. of Omri are kept. Mi 6:16
see statute for **ever**

his **statutes**
ear to his commandments and keep all *his s.* Ex 15:26; Deut 6:17
10:13; 11:1
shalt do *his s.* which I. Deut 27:10
not observe to do *his s.* 28:15
his s., I did not depart. 2 Sam 22:23
hearts be perfect to walk in *his s.* 1 Ki 8:61
they rejected *his s.* 2 Ki 17:15
made a covenant to keep *his s.* 23:3; 2 Chr 34:31
even a scribe of *his s.* Ezra 7:11
put away *his s.* from me. Ps 18:22
observe *his s.* and laws. 105:45
in his law, nor in *his s.* Jer 44:23
see **judgements**

my **statutes**
kept *my s.* and laws. Gen 26:5
ye shall therefore keep *my s.* Lev 18:5, 26; 19:19
ye shall do *my s.* 25:18
if ye walk in *my s.* 26:3
if ye despise *my s.* 15
they abhorred *my s.* 43

if thou wilt keep my s. 1 Ki 3:14
will not keep my s. 9:6
hast not kept my s. 11:11
he kept my s. 34
keep my s. 2 Ki 17:13
turn away, and forsake my s. 2 Chr 7:19
to do to declare my s.? Ps 50:16
if they break my s., keep not. 89:31
they walked in my s. Jer 44:10
hath changed my s. more. Ezek 5:6
ye have not walked in my s. 7
they may walk in my s. and. 11:20
son hath kept all my s 18:19
cause you to walk in my s. 36:27
my s. did take hold of. Zech 1:6

thy statutes

him a perfect heart to keep thy s. 1 Chr 29:19
O Lord, teach me thy s. Ps 119:12
26, 33, 64, 68, 124, 135
I will delight myself in thy s. 119:16
servant did meditate in thy s. 23
and I will meditate in thy s. 48
thy s. have been my songs in. 54
that I might learn thy s. 71
let my heart be sound in thy s. 80
bottle, yet do I not forget thy s. 83
heart to perform thy s. alway. 112
I will have respect to thy s. 117
them that err from thy s. 118
for the wicked seek not thy s. 155
when thou hast taught thy s. 171

staves

thou shalt make s. of shittim wood. Ex 25:13, 28; 27:6; 30:5; 37:4
put s. into rings. 25:14, 15; 27:7
37:5; 38:7
s. of shittim wood. 37:15, 28; 38:5
he set s. on the ark and put. 40:20
they shall put in s. thereof. Num 4:6, 8, 11, 14
people digged with their s. 21:18
am I a dog, that thou comest to me with s.? 1 Sam 17:43
carried the ark with s. 1 Chr 15:15
strike through with his s. Hab 3:14
I took unto me two s. I. Zech 11:7
nor take two coats nor s. Mat 10:10
Luke 9:3
great multitude with s. from chief priests. Mat 26:47; Mark 14:43
thief with sword and s.? Mat 26:55
Mark 14:48; Luke 22:52

stay, *substantive*

plague in his sight be at a s. Lev 13:5
scall in his sight be at a s. 37
but the Lord was my s. 2 Sam 22:19
Ps 18:18
away the s. and staff, the whole s. of bread, and the whole s. Isa 3:1
even they that are the s. 19:13*

stay

neither s. thou in all the. Gen 19:17
ye shall s. no longer. Ex 9:28
if bright spot s. Lev 13:23, 28
s. not, but pursue after. Josh 10:19
would ye s. for them from. Ruth 1:13
s. and I will tell thee. 1 Sam 15:16
make speed, haste, s. not. 20:38
s. now thine hand. 2 Sam 24:16
1 Chr 21:15
he will not s. them when. Job 37:4
or who can s. the bottles of? 38:37*
let no man s. him. Pr 28:17
s. me with flagons. S of S 2:5
shall no more s. on him. Isa 10:20†
s. yourselves and wonder, cry. 29:9
and s. on oppression. 30:12†
woe to them that s. on horses. 31:1†
for they s. themselves on the. 48:2
let him trust in Lord, and s. 50:10†
s. not, for I will bring evil. Jer 4:6
forbearing, I could not s. 20:9
none can s. his hand, or. Dan 4:35
not s. in the place of. Hos 13:13*

stayed

and Noah s. yet other seven days. Gen 8:10, 12
with Laban, and I have s. 32:4
flocks and herds be s. Ex 10:24
and Hur s. up Moses' hands. 17:12
dead and living, plague was s. Num 16:48, 50; 25:8; 2 Sam 24:25
Ps 106:30
I s. in mount forty days. Deut 10:10
still, and the moon s. Josh 10:13
hast s. three days. 1 Sam 20:19
David s. his servants with. 24:7*
that were left behind s. 30:9
now Jonathan s. by. 2 Sam 17:17
that the plague may be s. 24:21
1 Chr 21:22
king was s. up in his chariot, and died. 1 Ki 22:35; 2 Chr 18:34
a vessel more, and oil s. 2 Ki 4:6
and he smote thrice, and s. 13:18
the king of Assyria s. not in. 15:20
thy proud waves be s. Job 38:11
whose mind is s. on thee. Isa 26:3
no hands s. on her. Lam 4:6*
great waters were s. Ezek 31:15
heaven is s., the earth is s. Hag 1:10
came to him and s. him. Luke 4:42
but he himself s. in Asia. Acts 19:22

stayeth

he s. his rough wind in the day of. Isa 27:8*

stays

were s. on either side throne; two lions stood beside the s. 1 Ki 10:19; 2 Chr 9:18

stead

he closed up the flesh in s. Gen 2:21
me another seed in s. of Abel. 4:25
Abraham offered the ram in s. 22:13
am I in God's s. 30:2
abide in s. of the lad. 44:33
he shall be to thee in s. of a mouth, thou shalt be to him in s. Ex 4:16
to gather stubble in s. of straw. 5:12
that son that is priest in his s. 29:30
Lev 16:32
I have taken the Levites in s. of all firstborn. Num 3:12, 41, 45; 8:16
cattle of the Levites in s. 3:41, 45
in s. of thy husband. 5:19, 20, 29
mayest be to us in s. of eyes. 10:31
risen up in your father's s. 32:14
Esau dwelt in their s. Deut 2:12
dwelt in their s. 21, 22, 23
son ministered in his s. 10:6
whom he raised in their s. Josh 5:7
I pray, her sister in s. Judg 15:2
Saul, in whose s. thou. 2 Sam 16:8
he made Amasa captain in s. 17:25
sit on my throne in my s. 1 Ki 1:30
for he shall be king in my s. 35
made me king in s. of David. 3:7
Rehoboam made in their s. 14:27
placed in cities of Samaria in s. of Israel. 2 Ki 17:24
queen in s. of Vashti. Esth 2:4, 17
were in my soul's s. Job 16:4
let thistles grow in s. of wheat, and cockle in s. of barley. 31:40
to thy wish in God's s. 33:6*
shall set others in their s. 34:24
in s. of thy fathers shall. Ps 45:16
wicked cometh in his s. Pr 11:8
shall stand up in his s. Eccl 4:15
in s. of sweet smell there shall be stink, in s. of. Isa 3:24
in s. of the thorn shall come up fir tree, and in s. of the brier. 55:13
who taketh strangers in s. of her. Ezek 16:32
pray you in Christ's s. 2 Cor 5:20*
in thy s. might have. Philem 13*
see **reigned**

steads

they dwelt in their s. till. 1 Chr 5:22

steady

Moses' hands were s. Ex 17:12

steal

(*Theft was made the subject of one of the ten commandments. There was no penalty attached to theft of property but restitution, double or more, as the case might be. If restitution was not made it was treated as a case of debt, the property or even the person of the debt being sold to cover it. The man-stealer, who reduced his prey to slavery, was to be put to death*)

wherefore didst thou s.? Gen 31:27
how then should we s. silver? 44:8
thou shalt not s. Ex 20:15; Lev 19:11
Deut 5:19; Mat 19:18; Rom 13:9
if a man s. an ox, he shall. Ex 22:1
as people s. away. 2 Sam 19:3
if he s. to satisfy his soul. Pr 6:30
or lest I be poor and s. and. 30:9
will ye s., murder, and? Jer 7:9
prophets that s. my words. 23:30
and where thieves break through and s. Mat 6:19
do not break through nor s. 20
come and s. him away. 27:64
do not kill, do not s. Mark 10:19
Luke 18:20
cometh not, but for to s. John 10:10
preachest a man should not s., dost thou s.? Rom 2:21
him that stole s. no more. Eph 4:28

stealers

law was made for men-s. 1 Tim 1:10

stealeth

he that s. a man and. Ex 21:16
a tempest s. him away in. Job 27:20
that s. shall be cut off. Zech 5:3

stealing

if a man be found s. any. Deut 24:7
by swearing and s. they. Hos 4:2

stealth

the people gat them by s. 2 Sam 19:3

stedfast

yea, thou shalt be s. Job 11:15
whose spirit was not s. Ps 78:8
neither were they s. in his. 37*
living God, and s. for ever. Dan 6:26
he that standeth s. in his heart doeth well. 1 Cor 7:37
my beloved brethren, be ye s. 15:58
our hope of you is s. 2 Cor 1:7
for if the word spoken by angels was s. Heb 2:2
if we hold our confidence s. 3:14*
have as an anchor sure and s. 6:19
whom resist s. in faith. 1 Pet 5:9

stedfastly

that she was s. minded. Ruth 1:18
settled his countenance s. 2 Ki 8:11
he s. set his face to go. Luke 9:51
looked s., behold, two men. Acts 1:10
s. in the apostles' doctrine. 2:42
they all looking s. on him. 6:15*
up s. into heaven, saw glory. 7:55
who s. beholding him and. 14:9*
Israel could not s. behold. 2 Cor 3:7
could not s. look to the end of. 13

stedfastness

beholding the s. of your faith in Christ. Col 2:5
ye fall from your own s. 2 Pet 3:17

steel

(*Revisions*, brass)

a bow of s. is broken. 2 Sam 22:35
Ps 18:34
bow of s. shall strike. Job 20:24
iron break northern iron and s.? Jer 15:12

steep

the s. places shall fall. Ezek 38:20
are poured down a s. place. Mi 1:4
swine ran violently down a s. place. Mat 8:32; Mark 5:13; Luke 8:33

stem

a rod out of the s. of. Isa 11:1*

step

there is but a s. between. 1 Sam 20:3
if my s. hath turned out. Job 31:7

Stephanas

the household of S. 1 Cor 1:16
the house of S., the firstfruits. 16:15
I am glad of the coming of S. 17

Stephen

they chose S., a man. Acts 6:5, 8
they stoned S., calling upon God. 7:59
devout men carried S. to his. 8:2
on the persecution about S. 11:19
of thy martyr S. was shed. 22:20

stepped
whosoever first s. in was. John 5:4

steppeth
while I am coming, another s. down. John 5:7

steps
neither go up by s. to. Ex 20:26
thou hast enlarged my s. 2 Sam 22:37; Ps 18:36
the throne had six s. 1 Ki 10:19
2 Chr 9:18
twelve lions stood on the s. 1 Ki 10:20; 2 Chr 9:19
thou numberest my s. Job 14:16
the s. of his strength shall be. 18:7
my foot hath held his s. 23:11
I washed my s. with butter. 29:6
my ways and count my s. 31:4
to him the number of my s. 37
compassed us in our s. Ps 17:11
s. of a good man are ordered. 37:23*
the law in his heart, none of his s. 31
nor have our s. declined from. 44:18
mark my s. when they wait. 56:6
prepared a net for my s. 57:6
as for me, my s. had well. 73:2
set us in the way of his s. 85:13
order my s. in thy word. 119:133
when goest thy s. shall not. Pr 4:12
her s. take hold on hell. 5:5
but the Lord directeth his s. 16:9
the s. of the needy shall. Isa 26:6
it is not in man that walketh to direct his s. Jer 10:23
they hunt our s., we cannot. Lam 4:18
up to it by seven s. Ezek 40:22, 26
up to it had eight s. 31, 34, 37
he brought me by s. whereby. 49
the Ethiopians shall be at his s. Dan 11:43
but walk in s. of that faith. Rom 4:12
not in the same s.? 2 Cor 12:18
ye should follow his s. 1 Pet 2:21

stern
four anchors out of the s. Acts 27:29

steward
and the s. of my house. Gen 15:2*
near to the s. of Joseph's. 43:19
drinking himself drunk in the house of his s. 1 Ki 16:9
the lord saith unto his s. Mat 20:8
wife of Chuza, Herod's s. Luke 8:3
is that faithful and wise s. 12:42
certain rich man who had a s. 16:1
thou mayest be no longer s. 2
Lord commended the unjust s. 8
blameless, as the s. of God. Tit 1:7

stewards
and David assembled captains and s. 1 Chr 28:1*
as ministers and s. of. 1 Cor 4:1
it is required in s. that a man. 2
as good s. of manifold. 1 Pet 4:10

stewardship
give an account of thy s. Luke 16:2
taketh away from me the s. 3, 4

stick, *verb*
his bones, not seen, s. out. Job 33:21
his scales are joined, they s. 41:17
for thine arrows s. fast. Ps 38:2
I will cause the fish to s. Ezek 29:4

stick
cut down a s. and cast. 2 Ki 6:6
withered and become like a s. Lam 4:8
s. write upon it: then take another s. Ezek 37:16
one to another into one s. 17, 19

sticketh
there is a friend s. closer. Pr 18:24

sticks
a man that gathered s. Num 15:32
they found him gathering s. 33
woman was gathering s. 1 Ki 17:10
gathering two s. to go in. 12
and the s. whereon. Ezek 37:20
gathered a bundle of s. Acts 28:3

stiff
rebellion and thy s. neck. Deut 31:27
speak not with a s. neck. Ps 75:5
but made their neck s. Jer 17:23

stiffened
he s. his neck and. 2 Chr 36:13

stiffhearted
impudent children and s. Ezek 2:4

stiffnecked
people is a s. people. Ex 32:9
thou art a s. people. 33:3; Deut 9:6
Ye are a s. people. Ex 33:5
it is a s. people. 34:9; Deut 9:13
circumcise your heart, be no more s. Deut 10:16
be not s. as your fathers. 2 Chr 30:8
ye s. ye do always resist. Acts 7:51

still, *adjectve*
shall be as s. as a stone. Ex 15:16
good, and are ye s.? Judg 18:9
after fire a s. small voice. 1 Ki 19:12
Gilead is ours, and we be s. 22:3
and if we sit s. here. 2 Ki 7:4
for now should I have lain s. Job 3:13
your heart and be s. Ps 4:4
beside the s. waters. 23:2
be s. and know that I am. 46:10
the earth feared, and was s. 76:8
peace, and be not s. O God. 83:1
that waves thereof are s. 107:29
be s. ye inhabitants of. Isa 23:2
cried, their strength is to sit s. 30:7
I have been s. and refrained. 42:14
why do we sit s.? Jer 8:14
of the Lord, rest and be s. 47:6
feed that that standeth s. Zech 11:16
to the sea, Peace, be s. Mark 4:39

still, *adverb*
were s. ill favoured, as at. Gen 41:21
and wilt hold them s. Ex 9:2
and if it appear s. in. Lev 13:57
and Caleb lived s. Num 14:38
Balaam blessed you s. Josh 24:10
but if ye shall s. do. 1 Sam 12:25
Saul said, Thou also shalt s. 26:25
good to have been there s. 2 Sam 14:32
and cursed s. as he came. 16:5
the people sacrificed s. and burnt. 2 Ki 12:3; 15:4, 35; 2 Chr 33:17
had no power to keep s. 2 Chr 22:9
and s. he holdeth fast. Job 2:3
his wife said, Dost thou s. retain? 9
though he keep it s. within. 20:13
he should s. live for ever. Ps 49:9
such a one as goeth on s. 68:21
for all this they sinned s. 78:32
in thy house: they will be s. 84:4
they shall s. bring forth fruit. 92:14
when I awake, I am s. 139:18
he s. taught the people. Eccl 12:9
but his hand is stretched out s. Isa 5:25; 9:12, 17, 21; 10:4
they say s. unto them that. Jer 23:17
those will I let remain s. in. 27:11
I earnestly remember him s. 31:20
if ye will s. abide in this. 42:10
my soul hath them s. in. Lam 3:20
thy people s. are talking. Ezek 33:30
winding about s. upward. 41:7
when he had said these words, he abode s. in Galilee. John 7:9; 11:6
it pleased Silas to abide s. Acts 15:34; 17:14
s. in unbelief, be graffed. Rom 11:23
abide s. at Ephesus. 1 Tim 1:3
unjust s.: filthy s.: holy s. Rev 22:11

see **stand, stood**

still, *verb*
that thou mightest s. enemy. Ps 8:2

stilled
Caleb s. the people. Num 13:30
so the Levites s. all. Neh 8:11

stillest
waves arise thou s. them. Ps 89:9

stilleth
s. the noise of the seas. Ps 65:7

sting
O death, where is thy s.? 1 Cor 15:55
the s. of death is sin. 56

stingeth
it s. like an adder. Pr 23:32

stings
were s. in their tails. Rev 9:10

stink, *substantive*
smell, there shall be s. Isa 3:24*
their s. shall come out of. Isa 34:3†
s. shall come up, and ill. Joel 2:20†
made s. of your camps. Amos 4:10†

stink
ye have made me to s. Gen 34:30*
die, and the river shall s. Ex 7:18
that was laid up did not s. 16:24
my wounds s. and are. Ps 38:5

stinketh
their fish s. because there. Isa 50:2
Lord, by this time he s. John 11:39

stinking
to send forth a s. savour. Eccl 10:1†

stir, *verb*
he lay down as a lion, who shall s. him up? Num 24:9
innocent s. up himself. Job 17:8
is so fierce that dare s. him. 41:10
s. up thyself, and awake. Ps 35:23
and he did not s. up all his. 78:38
s. up thy strength, and come. 80:2
but grievous words s. Pr 15:1
that ye s. not up my love. S of S 2:7
3:5; 8:4
the Lord shall s. up a. Isa 10:26
behold, I will s. up the Medes. 13:17
he shall s. up jealousy like. 42:13
he shall s. up all against. Dan 11:2
shall s. up his power against. 25
that thou s. up the gift. 2 Tim 1:6
meet to s. you up. 2 Pet 1:13; 3:1

stir
was no small s. among the soldiers. Acts 12:18
small s. about that way. 19:23

stirred
whose heart s. him up. Ex 35:21
26; 36:2
that my son hath s. up. 1 Sam 22:8
if the Lord have s. thee up. 26:19
Lord s. up an adversary. 1 Ki 11:14
God s. him up another adversary. 23*
whom Jezebel his wife s. up. 21:25
God s. up the spirit. 1 Chr 5:26
Lord s. up against Jehoram the 2 Chr 21:16
Lord s. up the spirit of Cyrus. 36:22
Ezra 1:1
and my sorrow was s. Ps 39:2
but his sons shall be s. Dan 11:10*
king of the south shall be s. up. 25*
the Lord s. up the spirit. Hag 1:14
they s. up the people. Acts 6:12
17:13; 21:27
Jews s. up devout women. 13:50*
the unbelieving Jews s. up. 14:2
his spirit was s. in him. 17:16*

stirreth
an eagle s. up her nest. Deut 32:11
hatred s. up strifes, but. Pr 10:12
man s. up strife. 15:18; 29:22
that is of a proud heart s. 28:25
hell from beneath s. up. Isa 14:9
none s. up himself to take hold. 64:7
he s. up people teaching. Luke 23:5

stirs
full of s. a tumultuous city. Isa 22:2*

stock
or to the s. of the stranger's family. Lev 25:47
though the s. thereof die. Job 14:8
yea, their s. shall not take. Isa 40:24
down to the s. of a tree? 44:19
saying to a s., Thou art my father. Jer 2:27
are brutish, the s. is a doctrine. 10:8
of the s. of Abraham. Acts 13:26
of the s. of Israel, an. Phil 3:5

stocks
my feet also in the s. Job 13:27
he putteth my feet in s. 33:11
the correction of the s. Pr 7:22
adultery with stones and s. Jer 3:9
put Jeremiah in the s. 20:2, 3
put him in prison and s. 29:26*
ask counsel at their s. Hos 4:12
their feet fast in the s. Acts 16:24

Stoics
Were a school of Grecian philosophers, who took their name from the Greek word **stoa,** *meaning*

portico, *because* Zeno, *the head of the Stoics, taught in a portico in the city of Athens. They held, that a wise man ought to be free from all passions; never to be moved either with joy or grief, esteeming all things to be ordered by an inevitable necessity and fate. Josephus says, that the* Pharisees *approach very near to the sentiments of the Stoics. They affected the same stiffness, patience, apathy, austerity, and insensibility. The sect of the* Stoics *was still considerable at* Athens *when* St. Paul *visited that city,* Acts 17:18.

stole

Jacob *s.* away unawares. *Gen* 31:20
so Absalom *s.* the hearts of Israel. *2 Sam* 15:6
Jehosheba *s.* Joash from among king's. *2 Ki* 11:2; *2 Chr* 22:11
his disciples *s.* him. *Mat* 28:13
let him that *s.* steal no more, but. *Eph* 4:28

stolen

that shall be counted *s.* *Gen* 30:33
Rachel had *s.* her father's images. 31:19, 32
thou hast *s.* away unawares to. 26
hast thou *s.* my gods ? 30
whether *s.* by day, or *s.* by. 39
indeed I was *s.* away out. 40:15
if the stuff be *s.* out of. *Ex* 22:7
if it be *s.* from him, he shall. 12
s. and dissembled also. *Josh* 7:11
men of Judah *s.* thee? *2 Sam* 19:41
Jabesh had *s.* the bones of. 21:12
s. waters are sweet. *Pr* 9:17
would they not have *s* till? *Ob* 5

stomach

little wine for thy *s.*'s sake. *1 Tim* 5:23

stomacher

instead of a *s.* a girding. *Isa* 3:24*

stone

Precious stones *as named in the Bible are difficult to identify, as no sufficient description is given of them.*

The corner stone, *or the* head stone of the corner, Ps 118:22, *is that put as the angle of a building, whether at the foundation, or at the top of the wall, and is of fundamental importance. It is often used metaphorically. Jesus Christ is the* corner stone *rejected by the* Jews, *but become the corner stone of the church, and the stone that binds and unites the Jews and Gentiles in the union of the same faith,* Mat 21:42; Eph 2:20.

As Christ the Head is called the corner stone, so also his members, true believers, who are built upon, and derive spiritual life from the foundation, Christ, *are called* stones, 1 Pet 2:5. *As the law was engraven on two tables of stones, so believers have the law written in their hearts. They are* stones *for their constancy, strength, and unmovableness in all the storms of life.*

The white stone, Rev 2:17, *has been variously regarded. Some think it is an allusion to an ancient custom of delivering a* white stone *to those who were acquitted in judgement, or of giving a white stone as a reward to such as conquered in their games.*

Great heaps of stones, *raised up for a witness of any memorable event, and to preserve the remembrance of some matter of great importance are the most ancient monuments among the Hebrews. Jacob and Laban raised such a monument upon mount Gilead, in memory of their covenant,* Gen 31:46. Joshua *erected one at Gilgal made of stones taken out of the Jordan, to preserve the memorial of his miraculous passage over this river,* Josh 4:5, 6, 7. *The Israelites that dwelt beyond* Jordan, *also raised one upon the banks of the river, as a testimony that they constituted but one nation with their brethren on the other side,* Josh 22:10.

had brick for *s.* and slime. *Gen* 11:3
up a *s.* for a pillar. 28:18, 22; 31:45
they rolled *s.* from the well's mouth. 29:3, 8, 10
Jacob set up a pillar of *s.* 35:14
the shepherd, the *s.* of Israel. 49:24
Zipporah took a sharp *s.* *Ex* 4:25*
sank into the bottom as a *s.* 15:5
arm they shall be as still as *s.* 16
and they took a *s.* and put it. 17:12
wilt make an altar of *s.* 20:25
smite another with a *s.* 21:18
names on one *s.*, six on other *s.* 28:10
work of an engraver in *s.* 11
neither shall ye set up any image of *s.* in your land. *Lev* 26:1
with throwing a *s.* *Num* 35:17, 23
take you up every man of you a *s.* upon his shoulder. *Josh* 4:5
the border went up to the *s.* 15:6
descended to the *s.* of Bohan. 18:17
s. shall be a witness unto us. 24:27
slew seventy persons on one *s.* *Judg* 9:5, 18
which *s.* remaineth. *1 Sam* 6:18
Samuel set up a *s.* and called. 7:12
from his bag a *s.* and slang it, the *s.* sunk into the Philistine's. 17:49
over the Philistine with a *s.* 50
shalt remain by the *s.* Ezel. 20:19
died in him, he became as a *s.* 25:37
there be not one small *s.* *2 Sam* 17:13
house was built of *s.* *1 Ki* 6:7
cedar, there was no *s.* seen. 18
cast every man his *s.* *2 Ki* 3:25
with thee hewers of *s.* *1 Chr* 22:15
skilful to work in gold, silver, and *s.* *2 Chr* 2:14
thou threwest as a *s.* *Neh* 9:11
is molten out of the *s.* *Job* 28:2
waters are hid as with a *s.* 38:30
his heart is as firm as a *s.* 41:24
lest thou dash thy foot against a *s.* *Ps* 91:12; *Mat* 4:6; *Luke* 4:11
s. which builders refused . . . *s.* of. *Ps* 118:22; *Mat* 21:42; *Mark* 12:10
as he that bindeth a *s.* *Pr* 26:8
and he that rolleth a *s.* it will. 27
s. is heavy, a fool's wrath. 27:3
and to a *s.* thou hast. *Jer* 2:27
they shall not take of thee a *s.* for a corner, nor a *s.* for. 51:26
cast a *s.* upon me. *Lam* 3:53
a *s.* was cut out of the mountain. *Dan* 2:34, 45
s. was laid upon the mouth. 6:17
for the *s.* shall cry out. *Hab* 2:11
saith to the dumb *s.*, Arise. 19
s. was laid upon a *s.* in. *Hag* 2:15
s. that I have laid before Joshua, upon one *s.* shall be seven. *Zech* 3:9
shall bring forth the head *s.* 4:7
their hearts as an adamant *s.* 7:12
if his son ask bread, will he give him a *s.*? *Mat* 7:9; *Luke* 11:11
whosoever shall fall on this *s.* shall be broken. *Mat* 21:44; *Luke* 20:18
not left here one *s.* upon. *Mat* 24:2
Mark 13:2; *Luke* 19:44; 21:6
sealing the *s.* *Mat* 27:66
the angel rolled back the *s.* 28:2
saw that the *s.* was rolled away. *Mark* 16:4; *Luke* 24:2; *John* 20:1
command this *s.* that it be. *Luke* 4:3
s. which the builders rejected, 20:17; *Acts* 4:11; *1 Pet* 2:7
he was withdrawn from them about a *s.*'s cast. *Luke* 22:41
is by interpretation a *s.* *John* 1:42*
set there six waterpots of *s.* 2:6
let him first cast *s.* at her. 8:7
it was a cave, and a *s.* lay. 11:38
take ye away the *s.* 39
they took away the *s.* 41
is like to a *s.* graven. *Acts* 17:29
fell a great hail, every *s.* *Rev* 16:21
an angel took up a *s.* like a. 18:21
see **corner, great, hewed, stumbling, wall**

stone, *verb*

and will they not *s.* us ? *Ex* 8:26
they be almost ready to *s.* me. 17:4
people of land shall *s.* *Lev* 20:2
shall *s.* the wizards with stones. 27
let congregation *s.* him. 24:14, 16, 23
congregation bade *s.* *Num* 14:10
s. him with stones. 15:35, 36
shalt *s.* him with stones. *Deut* 13:10
shalt *s.* idolaters. 17:5
s. rebellious son. 21:21
they shall *s.* her that playeth. 22:21
ye shall *s.* adulterers with stones. 24
carry Naboth out, *s.* him. *1 Ki* 21:10
and they shall *s.* thee. *Ezek* 16:40
the company shall *s.* them. 23:47
men, the people will *s.* us. *Luke* 20:6
stones again to *s.* him. *John* 10:31
for which works do ye *s.* me ? 32
saying, For a good work we *s.* 33
Jews of late sought to *s.* thee. 11:8
assault made to *s.* them. *Acts* 14:5

burdensome **stone**

make Jerusalem a *burdensome s.* *Zech* 12:3

hewn **stone**

not build altar of *hewn s.* *Ex* 20:25
masons, to buy timber and *hewn s.* *2 Ki* 22:6; *2 Chr* 34:11
my ways with *hewn s.* *Lam* 3:9
tables were of *hewn s.* *Ezek* 40:42
built houses of *hewn s.* *Amos* 5:11
sepulchre *hewn* in *s.* *Luke* 23:53

living **stone**

to whom coming, as unto a *living s.* chosen of God. *1 Pet* 2:4

precious **stone**

a gift is a *precious s.* to him. *Pr* 17:8
I lay in Zion a *precious* corner *s.* *Isa* 28:16; *1 Pet* 2:6
every *precious s.* was. *Ezek* 28:13
decked with gold and *precious s.* *Rev* 17:4
like to a *s.* most *precious.* 21:11

tables of **stone**

I will give thee *tables of s.* *Ex* 24:12
31:18
Lord said, Hew thee two *tables of s.* 34:1; *Deut* 10:1
he hewed two *tables of s.* *Ex* 34:4
Deut 10:3
he wrote on the two *tables of s.* *Deut* 4:13; 5:22
up to receive the *tables of s.* 9:9
delivered to me two *tables of s.* 10
gave me the two *tables of s.* 11
in ark save two *tables of s.* *1 Ki* 8:9
not in *tables of s.* but in fleshly. *2 Cor* 3:3

tried **stone**

Zion a stone, a *tried s.* *Isa* 28:16

white **stone**

I will give him a *white s.* *Rev* 2:17

stone joined with *wood*

vessels of *wood* and *s.* *Ex* 7:19
gods the work of men's hands, *wood* and *s.* *Deut* 4:28; 28:36, 64
29:17; *2 Ki* 19:18; *Isa* 37:19
Ezek 20:32
praised the gods of gold, *wood*, and *s.* *Dan* 5:4, 23
not worship idols of *wood* and *s.* *Rev* 9:20

stone *of Zoheleth*

sheep by *s.* of *Zoheleth.* *1 Ki* 1:9

stoned

be *s.* or shot through. *Ex* 19:13
ox shall be surely *s.* 21:28, 29, 32
all Israel *s.* Achan. *Josh* 7:25
all Israel *s.* Adoram. *1 Ki* 12:18
2 Chr 10:18
they *s.* Naboth. *1 Ki* 21:13, 14, 15
they *s.* Zechariah in. *2 Chr* 24:21
beat one, *s.* another. *Mat* 21:35
that such should be *s.* *John* 8:5
they should have been *s.* *Acts* 5:26
they *s.* Stephen, calling. 7:58, 59
having *s.* Paul, drew him out. 14:19

beaten, once was I s. *2 Cor* 11:25
they were s. they were. *Heb* 11:37
the mount it shall be s. 12:20

stones

his brethren, gather s. *Gen* 31:46
engrave the two s. *Ex* 28:11, 12
settings of s., even four rows of s. 17
the s. shall be with the names of. 21
s. for a memorial to Israel. 39:7
they take away the s. *Lev* 14:40
other s. in the place of those s. 42
down the house, the s. of it. 45
or hath his s. broken. 21:20
a land whose s. are iron. *Deut* 8:9
that is wounded in the s. 23:1
these s. in mount Ebal. 27:4
build an altar of s. 5
write on the s. all the words. 8
you hence twelve s. *Josh* 4:3, 9
What mean ye by these s.? 6, 21
twelve s. out of the midst. 8
twelve s. did Joshua pitch. 20
on the s. a copy of the law. 8:32
every one could sling s. at an hair-breadth. *Judg* 20:16
him five smooth s. *1 Sam* 17:40
Shimei cast s. at David and. *2 Sam* 16:6, 13
prepared timber and s. *1 Ki* 5:18
s. of eight and s. of ten cubits. 7:10
silver to be in Jerusalem as s. and. 10:27; *2 Chr* 1:15; 9:27
took away the s. of Ramah. *1 Ki* 15:22; *2 Chr* 16:6
Elijah took twelve s. *1 Ki* 18:31
with the s. he built an altar. 32
good piece of land with s. *2 Ki* 3:19
Kir-haraseth left they the s. 25
it upon a pavement of s. 16:17
in hurling of s. and. *1 Chr* 12:2
Uzziah prepared slings to cast s. *2 Chr* 26:14
will they revive the s. out of the heaps? *Neh* 4:2
in league with s. of field. *Job* 5:23
strength the strength of s.? 6:12
and seeth the place of s. 8:17
the waters wear the s. 14:19
the gold of Ophir as the s. of. 22:24
the s. of it are the place of. 28:6
the sinews of his s. are. 40:17*
take pleasure in her s. *Ps* 102:14
thy little ones against the s. 137:9
away s., a time to gather s. *Eccl* 3:5
whoso removeth s. shall be. 10:9
and gathered out the s. *Isa* 5:2
down to the s. of the pit. 14:19
s. of the altar as chalk s. 27:9
behold, I will lay thy s. with. 54:11
thy borders of pleasant s. 12
smooth s. of the stream. 57:6
bring for s., iron. 60:17
gather out the s. 62:10
adultery with s. and stocks. *Jer* 3:9
set his throne on these s. 43:10
the s. of the sanctuary. *Lam* 4:1
lay thy s. in the water. *Ezek* 26:12
in the midst of the s. of fire. 28:14
from the midst of the s. of fire. 16
I will pour down the s. *Mi* 1:6
consume it with the s. *Zech* 5:4
as s. of a crown lifted up. 9:16
of these s. to raise up children. *Mat* 3:9; *Luke* 3:8
these s. be made bread. *Mat* 4:3
cutting himself with s. *Mark* 5:5
and at him they cast s. and. 12:4
Master, see what manner of s. 13:1
s. would immediately. *Luke* 19:40
took up s. to cast. *John* 8:59; 10:31
engraven in s. was glorious. *2 Cor* 3:7
ye as lively s. are built. *1 Pet* 2:5
see **costly, great, stone,** *verb*

corner **stones**

our daughters may be as *corner* s. *Ps* 144:12

stones *of darkness*

he searcheth out the s. *of darkness*. *Job* 28:3

stones *of emptiness*

stretch out upon it s. *of emptiness*. *Isa* 34:11

glistering **stones**

I have prepared *glistering* s. for house. *1 Chr* 29:2

gravel **stones**

hath broken my teeth with *gravel* s. *Lam* 3:16

heap of **stones**

raised a great *heap of* s. *Josh* 7:26
and raise a great *heap of* s. 8:29
they laid a *heap of* s. on Absalom. *2 Sam* 18:17

hewed **stones**

they brought *hewed* s. to. *1 Ki* 5:17*
the measures of *hewed* s. 7:9, 11

hewn **stones**

will build with *hewn* s. *Isa* 9:10

marble **stones**

I have prepared *marble* s. in. *1 Chr* 29:2

precious **stones**

gold with *precious* s. *2 Sam* 12:30
queen of Sheba came with *precious* s. *1 Ki* 10:2
navy of Hiram brought *precious* s. 11; *2 Chr* 9:10
I prepared all manner of *precious* s. *1 Chr* 29:2
whom *precious* s. were found. 8
the house with *precious* s. *2 Chr* 3:6
treasuries for *precious* s. 32:27
occupied in thy fairs with *precious* s. *Ezek* 27:22
honour with *precious* s. *Dan* 11:38
build on this foundation *precious* s. *1 Cor* 3:12
no man buyeth *precious* s. *Rev* 18:12
decked with gold and *precious* s. 16
garnished with *precious* s. 21:19

whole **stones**

shalt build the altar of *whole* s. *Deut* 27:6; *Josh* 8:31

wrought **stones**

masons to hew *wrought* s. *1 Chr* 22:2

stonesquarers

builders and s. did hew. *1 Ki* 5:18*

stonest

s. them that are sent to thee. *Mat* 23:37; *Luke* 13:34

stoning

people spake of s. David. *1 Sam* 30:6

stony

overthrown in s. places. *Ps* 141:6*
I will take the s. heart. *Ezek* 11:19; 36:26
some fell on s. places. *Mat* 13:5*, 20*; *Mark* 4:5*, 16*

stood

but Abraham s. yet. *Gen* 18:22
pillar of cloud s. behind. *Ex* 14:19
he s. between the dead. *Num* 16:48
ye came near and s. *Deut* 4:11
I s. between the Lord and you. 5:5
the waters s. and rose up. *Josh* 3:16
twelve stones where the priests' feet s. 4:3, 9
Joash said to all that s. *Judg* 6:31
pillars on which the house s. 16:29
Lord s. and called Samuel. *1 Sam* 3:10
when he s. among the people. 10:23
Goliath s. and cried to the. 17:8
servants that s. about him. 22:7
king said to footmen that s. 17
and all the congregation of Israel s. *1 Ki* 8:14; *2 Chr* 6:3; 7:6
Solomon s. and blessed. *1 Ki* 8:55
sons of prophets s. to view. *2 Ki* 2:7
the people s. to the covenant. 23:3
on scaffold Solomon s. *2 Chr* 6:13
they s. and confessed. *Neh* 9:2
the other Jews s. for. *Esth* 9:16
commanded and it s. fast. *Ps* 33:9
above it s. the seraphims. *Isa* 6:2
they s. not because Lord. *Jer* 46:15
they s. under the shadow. 48:45
those s., these s. *Ezek* 1:21; 10:17
when they s. they let down. 1:24
was a voice when they s. 25
came near where I s. *Dan* 8:17
when he had spoken this, I s. 10:11
s. to confirm and to strengthen. 11:1
I looked, and behold, there s. *Dan* 12:5
s. and measured the earth. *Hab* 3:6
he s. among the myrtle trees. *Zech* 1:8, 10, 11
brethren s. without. *Mat* 12:46
withered hand s. forth. *Luke* 6:8
the Pharisee s. and prayed. 18:11
Simon Peter s. and. *John* 18:25
but Mary s. without at. 20:11
the lame man leaping up s. *Acts* 3:8
the men that were with him s. 9:7
s. a man of Macedonia and. 16:9
Paul s. forth in the midst. 27:21
s. only in meats, and. *Heb* 9:10

stood *above*

Lord s. *above* the ladder. *Gen* 28:13
Zechariah s. *above* the people. *2 Chr* 24:20
the waters s. *above* the. *Ps* 104:6

stood *afar*

his sister s. *afar* off, to. *Ex* 2:4
removed and s. *afar* off. 20:18, 21
lepers who s. *afar* off. *Luke* 17:12
s. *afar* off beholding. 23:49
trade by sea s. *afar* off. *Rev* 18:17

stood *at*

they s. *at* nether part. *Ex* 19:17
they s. every man *at* his tent. 33:8
the cloudy pillar s. *at* door of. 9
Naaman s. *at* door of. *2 Ki* 5:9
singers s. *at* the east. *2 Chr* 5:12
the king s. *at* his pillar, at. 23:13
cherubims s. *at* door. *Ezek* 10:19
the king s. *at* the parting. 21:21
woman s. *at* his feet. *Luke* 7:38
but Peter s. *at* the door. *John* 18:16
another angel came and s. *at* the altar. *Rev* 8:3

stood *before*

to the place where he s. *before* the Lord. *Gen* 19:27
Egypt, and s. *before* Joseph. 43:15
ashes and s. *before* Pharaoh. *Ex* 9:10
the congregation s. *before*. *Lev* 9:5
Zelophehad s. *before* Moses. *Num* 27:2
s. *before* the congregation. *Josh* 20:9
Phinehas s. *before* ark. *Judg* 20:28
and s. *before* Saul. *1 Sam* 16:21
Bath-sheba s. *before*. *1 Ki* 1:28
Solomon s. *before* the ark. 3:15
were harlots s. *before* him. 16
Solomon s. *before* the altar. 8:22; *2 Chr* 6:12
old men that s. *before* Solomon. *1 Ki* 12:6; *2 Chr* 10:6
young men that s. *before* him. *1 Ki* 12:8; *2 Chr* 10:8
spirit s. *before* the Lord. *1 Ki* 22:21; *2 Chr* 18:20
the Shunammite s. *before* Elisha. *2 Ki* 4:12
returned and s. *before* Elisha. 5:15
Gehazi went in and s. *before*. 25
Hazael came and s. *before*. 8:9
two kings s. not *before* him. 10:4
arose, and s. *before* king. *Esth* 8:4
Moses his chosen s. *before* him. *Ps* 106:23
Samuel s. *before* me. *Jer* 15:1
I s. *before* thee to speak. 18:20
s. *before* them seventy. *Ezek* 8:11
therefore they s. *before* the king. *Dan* 1:19; 2:2
great image s. *before* thee. 2:31
they s. *before* the image. 3:3
times ten thousand s. *before*. 7:10
s. *before* the river a ram. 8:3
s. *before* me as the appearance. 15
Joshua s. *before* the angel. *Zech* 3:3
spake to those that s. *before* him. 4
and Jesus s. *before* the. *Mat* 27:11
three men s. *before* the. *Acts* 10:17
a man s. *before* me in bright. 30
Peter s. *before* the gate. 12:14
while I s. *before* the council. 24:20
multitude s. *before* throne. *Rev* 7:9
angels which s. *before* God. 8:2
dragon s. *before* the woman. 12:4

stood *beside*

Absalom s. *beside* the. *2 Sam* 15:2
lions s. *beside* the stays. *1 Ki* 10:19

which s. beside the king. Jer 36:21
the six men s. beside. Ezek 9:2
then he went in and s. beside. 10:6

stood *by*

lo, three men s. by him. Gen 18:2
behold, he s. by the camels. 24:30
and lo, he s. by the river. 41:1
not refrain himself before all that s. by him. 45:1
the people s. by Moses. Ex 18:13
Balak s. by his. Num 23:6, 17
all that s. by him went. Judg 3:19
the men s. by the entering of. 18:16
that s. by thee, praying. 1 Sam 1:26
servants s. by with. 2 Sam 13:31
and Jeroboam s. by the. 1 Ki 13:1
ass s. by it, the lion also s. by. 24
two s. by Jordan. 2 Ki 2:7, 13
king s. by a pillar. 11:14; 23:3
they came and s. by the conduit of the upper pool. 18:17; Isa 36:2
the angel s. by the. 1 Chr 21:15
the women that s. by. Jer 44:15
and the man s. by me. Ezek 43:6
to one of them that s. by. Dan 7:16
angel of the Lord s. by. Zech 3:5
one of them that s. by. Mark 14:47
some of them that s. by. 15:35
he s. by the lake of. Luke 5:1
he said to them that s. by. 19:24
two men s. by them in shining. 24:4
an officer that s. by. John 18:22
there s. by the cross of Jesus. 19:25
two men s. by them in. Acts 1:10
and all the widows s. by him. 9:39
to the centurion that s. by. 22:25
commanded them that s. by. 23:2
they that s. by said, Revilest? 4
night following the Lord s. by him. 11
there s. by me this night the. 27:23

stood *in*

Aaron, who s. in the way. Ex 5:20
then Moses s. in the gate. 32:26
Lord s. in the door of. Num 12:5
thereon, and s. in the door. 16:18
Dathan and Abiram s. in door. 27
the angel s. in the way. 22:22, 24
angel went further and s. in a. 26
the priests s. in midst of Jordan. Josh 3:17; 4:10
Jotham s. in the top of. Judg 9:7
Gaal s. in the entering of the. 35
Abimelech s. in the entering of. 44
the priests s. in the entering. 18:17
he s. in the midst of. 2 Sam 23:12
and he s. in the entering. 1 Ki 19:13
and s. in the border. 2 Ki 3:21
the Shunammite s. in the door. 4:15
and they s. in their place. 2 Chr 30:16; 35:10
king s. in his place, and. 34:31
and all the people s. in. Neh 8:7
Esther s. in the inner court. Esth 5:1
Jeremiah s. in court of. Jer 19:14
for who hath s. in counsel. 23:18
but if they had s. in my counsel. 22
Jaazaniah s. in the midst. Ezek 8:11
neither have s. in crossway. Ob 14
Jesus himself s. in the midst of them. Luke 24:36; John 20:19, 26
then Paul s. in the. Acts 17:22
in the midst of the elders s. Rev 5:6

stood *on*

Philistines s. on a mountain on the one side, Israel s. on. 1 Sam 17:3
then David s. on the top. 26:13
Benjamin s. on the top. 2 Sam 2:25
Asaph, who s. on his. 1 Chr 6:39
sons of Merari s. on the left. 44
the cherubims s. on. 2 Chr 3:13
cherubims s. on the. Ezek 10:3
whole multitude s. on. Mat 13:2
Jesus s. on the shore. John 21:4
Paul s. on the stairs. Acts 21:40
and lo, a lamb s. on the. Rev 14:1

stood *over*

pillar of cloud s. over. Deut 31:15
man s. over against him. Josh 5:13
glory of the Lord s. over the threshold of the house. Ezek 10:4
glory of the Lord s. over cherubims. 18

star s. over where young. Mat 2:9
s. over her and rebuked. Luke 4:39

stood *round*

sheaves s. round about. Gen 37:7
disciples s. round about. Acts 14:20
Jews s. round about Paul, and. 25:7
angels s. round about the. Rev 7:11

stood *still*

the sun s. still, and. Josh 10:13*
as for cities that s. still in. 11:13
came to the place s. still. 2 Sam 2:23
trumpet and all the people s. still. 28
saw that all people s. still. 20:12
and they s. still in the. Neh 12:39
it s. still, but I could not. Job 4:16
they spake not, but s. still. 32:16
sun and moon s. still in. Hab 3:11
and Jesus s. still and. Mat 20:32
Jesus s. still and commanded him. Mark 10:49
that bare him s. still. Luke 7:14

stood *there*

and s. with him there. Ex 34:5
the field and s. there. 1 Sam 6:14
twelve lions s. there. 1 Ki 10:20
2 Chr 9:19
glory of the Lord s. there. Ezek 3:23
from the days of Gibeah there they s. Hos 10:9
some of them that s. there. Mat 27:47; Mark 11:5
and officers s. there. John 18:18

stood *up*

Abraham s. up from. Gen 23:3
Abraham s. up and bowed. 7
but Moses s. up and. Ex 2:17
the people s. up all that. Num 11:32
Satan s. up against Israel. 1 Chr 21:1
then David the king s. up upon. 28:2
Abijah s. up and said. 2 Chr 13:4
the Levites s. up to praise. 20:19
Ammon and Moab s. up against. 23
s. up against them that came. 28:12
till there s. up a priest with Urim and. Ezra 2:63; Neh 7:65
when he opened the book the people s. up. Neh 8:5
they s. up in their place and. 9:3
then s. up upon the stairs, of. 4
that Mordecai s. not up. Esth 5:9
Haman s. up to make request. 7:7
the hair of my flesh s. up. Job 4:15
and the aged arose and s. up. 29:8
I s. up and cried in the. 30:28
then s. up Phinehas and. Ps 106:30
they lived, and s. up. Ezek 37:10
whereas four s. up for it. Dan 8:22
Jesus s. up to read in. Luke 4:16
a certain lawyer s. up and. 10:25
in those days Peter s. up. Acts 1:15
the kings of the earth s. up. 4:26
s. up one Gamaliel, a doctor. 5:34
Agabus s. up, and signified. 11:28
Paul s. up, and beckoning. 13:16
whom when the accusers s. up. 25:18

stood *upon*

behold I s. upon the bank. Gen 41:17
David ran and s. upon. 1 Sam 17:51
so I s. upon Saul and. 2 Sam 1:10
the sea s. upon twelve oxen. 1 Ki 7:25; 2 Chr 4:4
he revived and s. upon. 2 Ki 13:21
Ezra the scribe s. upon. Neh 8:4
glory of the Lord s. upon. Ezek 11:23
the Lord s. upon a wall. Amos 7:7
the two prophets s. upon. Rev 11:11
I s. upon the sand of the sea. 13:1

stood *with*

there s. with him no man. Gen 45:1
every man s. with his. 2 Ki 11:11
the Levites s. with. 2 Chr 29:26
then Joshua s. with his. Ezra 3:9
he s. with his right hand. Lam 2:4
two men that s. with him. Luke 9:32
Judas also s. with them. John 18:5
Peter s. with them and warmed. 18
no man s. with me. 2 Tim 4:16
Lord s. with me. 17

stoodest

that thou s. in the way. Num 22:34
day that thou s. before. Deut 4:10
in the day that thou s. on. Ob 11

stool

a bed, table, and a s. 2 Ki 4:10

stools

ye see them upon the s. Ex 1:16*

stoop

the proud helpers do s. Job 9:13
maketh the heart of man s. Pr 12:25
they s., they bow down. Isa 46:2
I am not worthy to s. Mark 1:7

stooped

Judah s. down, he couched. Gen 49:9
David s. to the earth. 1 Sam 24:8*
Saul s. to the ground. 28:14*
had no compassion on him that s. 2 Chr 36:17
Jesus s. down and wrote. John 8:6, 8
and as she wept, she s. down. 20:11

stoopeth

Bel boweth down, Nebo s. Isa 46:1

stooping

s. down saw the linen clothes. Luke 24:12; John 20:5

stop

that the rain s. thee not. 1 Ki 18:44
s. all wells of water. 2 Ki 3:19, 25
he took counsel to s. 2 Chr 32:3
s. the way against them. Ps 35:3
and all iniquity shall s. her. 107:42
it shall s. the noses of. Ezek 39:11
no man shall s. me of. 2 Cor 11:10

stopped

windows of heaven were s. Gen 8:2
Philistines had s. the wells. 26:15, 18
or his flesh be s. from. Lev 15:3
s. all the fountains and the brook. 2 Chr 32:4
Hezekiah s. the watercourse. 30
breaches began to be s. Neh 4:7
speaketh lies shall be s. Ps 63:11
that the passages are s. Jer 51:32*
refused, and s. their ears. Zech 7:11
they s. their ears and ran. Acts 7:57
every mouth may be s. Rom 3:19
whose mouths must be s. Tit 1:11
through faith s. the mouths of lions. Heb 11:33

stoppeth

the poor hath hope, and iniquity s. her mouth. Job 5:16
adder that s. her ear. Ps 58:4
whoso s. his ears at the. Pr 21:13
s. his ears from hearing. Isa 33:15

store

saith the Lord, who s. up violence and robbery in their. Amos 3:10

store, *substantive*

and great s. of servants. Gen 26:14*
that food shall be for s. to. 41:36
eat of the old s. Lev 25:22; 26:10
blessed shall be thy basket and thy s. Deut 28:5*, 17*
is not this laid up in s. with? 32:34
of spices very great s. 1 Ki 10:10
fathers have laid up in s. 2 Ki 20:17
all this s. cometh of. 1 Chr 29:16
he put s. of victuals. 2 Chr 11:11
is left is this great s. 31:10
s. of all sorts of wine. Neh 5:18
affording all manner of s. Ps 144:13
fathers have laid up in s. Isa 39:6
there is none end of the s. Nah 2:9
of you lay by him in s. 1 Cor 16:2
laying up in s. a good. 1 Tim 6:19
same word are kept in s. 2 Pet 3:7

store cities

cities of s. Solomon had. 1 Ki 9:19
2 Chr 8:6
and all the s. cities which he built. 2 Chr 8:4
all the s. cities of Naphtali. 16:4
Jehoshaphat built s. cities. 17:12

storehouse

the tithes into the s. Mal 3:10
neither have s. nor barn. Luke 12:24

storehouses

Joseph opened all the s. Gen 41:56
blessing on thee in thy s. Deut 28:8*
over the s. was Jehonathan. 1 Chr 27:25*
Hezekiah made s. also. 2 Chr 32:28

layeth up the depth in *s.* *Ps* 33:7
open her *s.*, cast her up. *Jer* 50:26

stories

with second and third *s.* *Gen* 6:16
galleries three *s.* over. *Ezek* 41:16
against gallery in three *s.* 42:3*, 6
he that buildeth his *s.* *Amos* 9:6*

stork

(*A bird of the heron family, white, with black wings and bright red beak, or entirely black. Both species were found in Palestine. They are migratory birds, and very regular in their coming and going. They feed upon offal, and were therefore not permitted to be used by the Israelites as food*)

the *s.* thou shalt not eat. *Lev* 11:19
Deut 14:18
as for the *s.*, the fir trees. *Ps* 104:17
s. knoweth her appointed. *Jer* 8:7
like the wings of a *s.* *Zech* 5:9

storm

and as chaff that the *s.* *Job* 21:18
and as *s.* hurleth him out of. 27:21
I would hasten my escape from the windy *s.* *Ps* 55:8
make them afraid with thy *s.* 83:15
he maketh the *s.* a calm. 107:29
and for a covert from *s.* *Isa* 4:6
hast been a refuge from the *s.* 25:4
which as destroying *s.* shall. 28:2
thou shalt be visited with *s.* 29:6*
ascend and come like a *s.* *Ezek* 38:9
in the whirlwind and *s.* *Nah* 1:3
there arose a great *s.* *Mark* 4:37
there came down a *s.* of wind. *Luke* 8:23

stormy

raiseth the *s.* wind. *Ps* 107:25
snow and vapour, *s.* wind. 148:8
s. wind shall rend. *Ezek* 13:11
I will rend it with a *s.* wind. 13

story

Abijah in the *s.* of Iddo. *2 Chr* 13:22*
written in the *s.* of the book. 24:27*

stout

the *s.* lion's whelps are. *Job* 4:11*
the fruit of the *s.* heart. *Isa* 10:12
whose look was more *s.* *Dan* 7:20
your words have been *s.* *Mal* 3:13

stouthearted

s. are spoiled, they slept. *Ps* 76:5
hearken unto me, ye *s.* *Isa* 46:12

stoutness

that say in the pride and *s.* *Isa* 9:9

straight

shall ascend every man *s.* *Josh* 6:5
the kine took *s.* the way. *1 Sam* 6:12
make thy way *s.* before. *Ps* 5:8
let thine eyelids look *s.* *Pr* 4:25
crooked cannot be made *s.* *Eccl* 1:15
make that *s.* he made crooked ? 7:13
make *s.* in desert a highway. *Isa* 40:3
the crooked shall be made *s.* 4
42:16; 45:2*; *Luke* 3:5
to walk in a *s.* way. *Jer* 31:9
and their feet were *s.* feet. *Ezek* 1:7
every one *s.* forward. 9, 12; 10:22
firmament were their wings *s.* 1:23
of Lord, make his paths *s.* *Mat* 3:3
Mark 1:3; *Luke* 3:4; *John* 1:23
made *s.* and glorified. *Luke* 13:13
street which is called *S.* *Acts* 9:11
and make *s.* paths for. *Heb* 12:13

straightway

shall *s.* find him before. *1 Sam* 9:13
then Saul fell *s.* all along. 28:20
he goeth after her *s.* as. *Pr* 7:22
s. there remained no. *Dan* 10:17
Jesus went up *s.* out of water.
Mat 3:16; *Mark* 1:10
and they *s.* left their nets.
Mat 4:20; *Mark* 1:18
Lord hath need of them, and *s.* he.
Mat 21:3; *Mark* 11:3
s. one of them ran and. *Mat* 27:48
s. the fountain of her. *Mark* 5:29
s. they knew him. 6:54
s. desireth new. *Luke* 5:39
will not *s.* pull him out ? 14:5

God shall *s.* glorify him. *John* 13:32
then fell she down *s.* at. *Acts* 5:10
and *s.* he preached Christ. 9:20
was baptized, he and all his, *s.* 16:33
then *s.* they departed from. 22:29
told me, I sent *s.* to thee. 23:30
s. forgetteth what manner. *Jas* 1:24

strain

guides *s.* at a gnat and. *Mat* 23:24

strait, *substantive*

saw that they were in a *s.* *1 Sam* 13:6
I am in a great *s.* *2 Sam* 24:14
1 Chr 21:13
would have removed thee out of the *s.* *Job* 36:16*
for I am in a *s.* betwixt. *Phil* 1:23

strait

we dwell is too *s.* for us. *2 Ki* 6:1
the place is too *s.* for. *Isa* 49:20
enter ye in at *s.* gate. *Mat* 7:13*
because *s.* is the gate and narrow is the way. 14*; *Luke* 13:24*

straiten

their lives, shall *s.* them. *Jer* 19:9†

straitened

his strength shall be *s.* *Job* 18:7
breadth of the waters is *s.* 37:10
thy steps shall not be *s.* *Pr* 4:12
therefore the building was *s.* more.
Ezek 42:6
is the spirit of the Lord *s.*? *Mi* 2:7
how am I *s.* till it be accomplished!
Luke 12:50
ye are not *s.* in us, but ye are *s.* in your. *2 Cor* 6:12

straiteneth

enlargeth nations and *s.* *Job* 12:23*

straitest

after the most *s.* sect. *Acts* 26:5

straitly

man asked us *s.* of our state and.
Gen 43:7
for Joseph had *s.* sworn. *Ex* 13:19
Jericho was *s.* shut up. *Josh* 6:1
thy father *s.* charged people with oath. *1 Sam* 14:28
he *s.* charged them, saying, See that,
Mat 9:30*; *Mark* 3:12*; 5:43*
Luke 9:21*
he *s.* charged him and. *Mark* 1:43*
but let us *s.* threaten them. *Acts* 4:17
did not we *s.* command you ? 5:28

straitness

shalt eat flesh of thy children in *s.*
Deut 28:53†, 55†, 57†
place where there is no *s.* *Job* 36:16
eat flesh of his friend in the *s.*
Jer 19:9†

straits

sufficiency he shall be in *s.* *Job* 20:22
overtook her between the *s.* *Lam* 1:3

strake

they fearing, *s.* sail. *Acts* 27:17*

see **struck**

strakes

Jacob piled white *s.* in. *Gen* 30:37†
the walls with hollow *s.* *Lev* 14:37†

strange

but Joseph made himself *s.* *Gen* 42:7
not ashamed that ye make yourselves *s.* to me. *Job* 19:3*
my breath is *s.* to my wife. 17
man is froward and *s.* *Pr* 21:8*
wherein they think it *s.* *1 Pet* 4:4
s. concerning trial, as though *s.* 12

see **children, god, gods**

strange *act*

pass his act, his *s.* *act.* *Isa* 28:21

strange *apparel*

clothed with *s.* *apparel.* *Zeph* 1:8*

strange *cities*

even to *s.* *cities.* *Acts* 26:11*

strange *country*

as in a *s.* *country.* *Heb* 11:9*

strange *doctrines*

be not carried about with *s.* *doctrines.*
Heb 13:9

strange *fire*

Abihu offered *s.* *fire* before the.
Lev 10:1; *Num* 3:4; 26:61

strange *flesh*

Gomorrah, going after *s.* *flesh.*
Jude 7

strange *incense*

shall offer no *s.* *incense.* *Ex* 30:9

strange *land*

have been a stranger in a *s.* *land.*
Ex 2:22; 18:3
shall we sing Lord's song in a *s.* *land?*
Ps 137:4
his seed should sojourn in a *s.* *land.*
Acts 7:6

strange *language*

a people of *s.* *language.* *Ps* 114:1

strange *lips*

shalt set it with *s.* *lips.* *Isa* 17:10

strange *nation*

to sell her to a *s.* *nation.* *Ex* 21:8

strange *punishment*

a *s.* *punishment* to the. *Job* 31:3*

strange *speech*

not sent to a people of *s.* *speech.*
Ezek 3:5, 6

strange *thing*

counted as a *s.* *thing.* *Hos* 8:12
as though some *s.* *thing.* *1 Pet* 4:12

strange *things*

seen *s.* *things* to-day. *Luke* 5:26
thou bringest certain *s.* *things* to.
Acts 17:20

strange *vanities*

me to anger with *s.* *vanities?* *Jer* 8:19

strange *vine*

plant of a *s.* *vine.* *Jer* 2:21

strange *waters*

and drunk *s.* *waters.* *2 Ki* 19:24

strange *wives*

he for all his *s.* *wives.* *1 Ki* 11:8
we have taken *s.* *wives.* *Ezra* 10:2
10, 14, 17, 44
yourselves from the *s.* *wives.* 11
were found to have taken *s.* *wives.* 18
in marrying *s.* *wives.* *Neh* 13:27

strange *woman*

the son of a *s.* *woman.* *Judg* 11:2
from the *s.* *woman.* *Pr* 2:16
the lips of a *s.* *woman* drop. 5:3
ravished with a *s.* *woman* ? 20
flattery of *s.* *woman.* 6:24*; 7:5
take a pledge of him for a *s.* *woman.*
20:16*; 27:13
and a *s.* *woman* is a narrow. 23:27

strange *women*

loved many *s.* *women.* *1 Ki* 11:1
the mouth of *s.* *women* is. *Pr* 22:14
eyes shall behold *s.* *women.* 23:33

strange *work*

do his work, his *s.* *work.* *Isa* 28:21

strangely

lest adversaries should behave themselves *s.* *Deut* 32:27

stranger

[1] *One that is in a strange land,* Gen 23:4. [2] *One that is not a Jew, but of some other nation,* Isa 14:1. [3] *One who is not of the king's stock and family,* Mat 17:25, 26. [4] *A woman that is not a man's own wife,* Pr 5:20. *The Revisions usually change this word to* alien, *or* foreigner; *occasionally to* sojourner.

thy seed shall be a *s.* in a land.
Gen 15:13
give land wherein thou art a *s.*
17:8; 28:4; 37:1
bought with money of any *s.* 17:12
bought with money of the *s.* 27
I am a *s.* with you. 23:4; *Ps* 39:12
119:19
I have been a *s.* in a. *Ex* 2:22
shall be cut off, whether a *s.* 12:19
Lev 16:29; 17:15; *Num* 15:30
no *s.* eat thereof. *Ex* 12:43; 29:33
when a *s.* will keep the passover.
12:48; *Num* 9:14
shall be to him that is homeborn and the *s.* *Ex* 12:49; *Lev* 24:22
Num 9:14; 15:15, 16, 29

nor s. that is within thy gates.
Ex 20:10; *Deut* 5:14
vex or oppress a *s.* *Ex* 22:21
ye know heart of a *s.* seeing. 23:9
shalt rest, that the *s.* may be. 12
putteth any of it upon a *s.* 30:33
neither shall any *s.* among. *Lev* 17:12
thou shalt leave them for *s.* 19:10
23:22; 25:6
if a *s.* sojourn in the land ye. 19:33
the *s.* be as one born among you.
34; *Num* 15:15
there shall no *s.* eat. *Lev* 22:10, 13
if she be married to a *s.* she. 12
neither from a *s.*'s hand shall ye. 25
as well *s.* when blasphemeth. 24:16
yea, though he be a *s.* thou. 25:35
if a *s.* wax rich by thee, and thy poor brother sell himself to the *s.* 47
Levites set up tabernacle, the *s.* that.
Num 1:51; 3:10, 38
and if a *s.* sojourn and will. 15:14
that no *s.* come near to offer. 16:40
and a *s.* shall not come nigh. 18:4
the *s.* that cometh nigh shall. 7
it shall be unto Israel and the *s.* 19:10
six cities of refuge for the *s.* 35:15
Josh 20:9
judge righteously between the *s.*
Deut 1:16
Lord loveth the *s.* in giving. 10:18
love the *s.*, for ye were strangers. 19
that dieth of itself: give to *s.* 14:21
not set a *s.* over thee who is. 17:15
thou wast a *s.* in his land. 23:7
unto a *s.* thou mayest lend. 20
not marry without to a *s.* 25:5
shalt rejoice, thou, and the *s.* 26:11
the *s.* shall get up above thee. 28:43
thy *s.* to enter into covenant. 29:11
s. that shall come from afar. 22
gather the people, and thy *s.* 31:12
as well the *s.* as he. *Josh* 8:33
aside to city of a *s.* *Judg* 19:12
grace, seeing I am a *s.*? *Ruth* 2:10
I am the son of a *s.* an Amalekite.
2 Sam 1:13
for thou art a *s.* and also an. 15:19
there was no *s.* with us. *1 Ki* 3:18
moreover concerning a *s.* 8:41
2 Chr 6:32
do according to all that the *s.* calleth.
1 Ki 8:43; *2 Chr* 6:33
and no *s.* passed among. *Job* 15:19
my maids count me for a *s.* 19:15
the *s.* did not lodge in street. 31:32
I am become a *s.* to my. *Ps* 69:8
they slay the widow and the *s.* 94:6
let the *s.* spoil his labour. 109:11
to deliver thee even from the *s.*
Pr 2:16
labours be in the house of a *s.* 5:10
embrace the bosom of a *s.*? 20
stricken thine hand with a *s.* 6:1
they may keep thee from the *s.* 7:5
he that is surety for a *s.* shall. 11:15
and a *s.* doth not intermeddle. 14:10
take his garment that is surety for a *s.* 20:16; 27:13
let a *s.* praise thee, and not. 27:2
eat thereof, but a *s.* eateth. *Eccl* 6:2
neither let the son of a *s.* *Isa* 56:3
the sons of the *s.* that join. 6
the sons of the *s.* shall not. 62:8
why shouldest thou be as a *s.* in ?
Jer 14:8
every *s.* that setteth up. *Ezek* 14:7
oppression with the *s.* 22:7, 29
no *s.* uncircumcised shall enter. 44:9
what tribe the *s.* sojourneth. 47:23
day that he became a *s.* *Ob* 12*
and that turn aside the *s.* *Mal* 3:5
I was a *s.* and ye. *Mat* 25:35, 43
when saw we thee a *s.*? 38, 44
returned, save this *s.* *Luke* 17:18
art thou only a *s.* in Jerusalem? 24:18
s. will they not follow, but. *John* 10:5
Moses was a *s.* in land. *Acts* 7:29
***see* fatherless, proselyte**

strangers

not counted of him *s.*? *Gen* 31:15
the land wherein they were *s.* 36:7
Ex 6:4
for ye were *s.* in the land of Egypt.
Ex 22:21; 23:9; *Lev* 19:34; 25:23
Deut 10:19
s. that offer an. *Lev* 17:8; 22:18
whatsoever of the *s.* that. 17:10
the *s.* that hunteth shall pour. 13
the *s.* that giveth of his seed. 20:2
children of the *s.* shall. 25:45
not oppress a servant though of *s.*
Deut 24:14
after gods of the *s.* of land. 31:16*
s. that were conversant. *Josh* 8:35
s. shall submit themselves unto me.
2 Sam 22:45
s. shall fade away and be afraid.
46; *Ps* 18:44, 45
when ye were *s.* in it. *1 Chr* 16:19
Ps 105:12
to gather the *s.* in Israel. *1 Chr* 22:2
for we are *s.* as were all. 29:15
numbered all the *s.* *2 Chr* 2:17
all Judah and the *s.* 15:9
the *s.* of Israel and all Judah. 30:25
seed of Israel separated themselves from all *s.* *Neh* 9:2
cleansed I them from all *s.* 13:30
for *s.* are risen up against me and.
Ps 54:3
the Lord preserveth the *s.* 146:9
lest *s.* be filled with thy. *Pr* 5:10
let them be only thine own, not *s.* 17
s. devour it in your presence, it is desolate as . . . by *s.* *Isa* 1:7
themselves in the children of *s.* 2:6
of the fat ones shall *s.* eat. 5:17*
and the *s.* shall be joined. 14:1
thou hast made a palace of *s.* 25:2
bring down the noise of *s.* 5
multitude of thy *s.* shall be. 29:5*
the sons of *s.* shall build up. 60:10
and *s.* shall stand and feed. 61:5
I have loved *s.* and after. *Jer* 2:25
scattered thy ways to the *s.* 3:13
so shall ye serve *s.* in a land. 5:19
s. shall no more serve. 30:8
live in the land where ye be *s.* 35:7
for *s.* are come into the. 51:51
our inheritance is turned to *s.*
Lam 5:2
give it into hand of *s.* *Ezek* 7:21
you into the hands of *s.* 11:9
a wife who taketh *s.* instead. 16:32
therefore I will bring *s.* upon. 28:7
the deaths by the hand of *s.* 10
land waste by the hand of *s.* 30:12
s. have cut him off. 31:12
brought into my sanctuary *s.* 44:7
inheritance to you and to the *s.* 47:22
s. have devoured his. *Hos* 7:9
if so be it yield, the *s.* shall. 8:7
there shall no *s.* pass. *Joel* 3:17
in the day that *s.* carried. *Ob* 11
take tribute ? of children or of *s.*?
Mat 17:25
Peter saith to him, Of *s.* 26
to bury *s.* in. 27:7
know not the voice of *s.* *John* 10:5
and *s.* of Rome, Jews. *Acts* 2:10
when they dwelt as *s.* in the. 13:17
s. from the covenants of. *Eph* 2:12
no more *s.* but fellow-citizens. 19
if she have lodged *s.*, if. *1 Tim* 5:10
confessed they were *s.* *Heb* 11:13
be not forgetful to entertain *s.* 13:2
so the *s.* scattered through Pontus.
1 Pet 1:1
I beseech you as *s.* and pilgrims. 2:11
whatsoever thou dost to *s.* *3 John* 5

strangled

the lion did tear and *s.* for. *Nah* 2:12
that they abstain from things *s.*
Acts 15:20, 29; 21:25

strangling

so that my soul chooseth *s.* *Job* 7:15

straw

we have both *s.* and. *Gen* 24:25
he gave *s.* and provender for. 32
ye shall no more give *s.* *Ex* 5:7
10, 16, 18
go ye, get you *s.* where you. 11
yet there is both *s.* and. *Judg* 19:19
brought barley also and *s* *1 Ki* 4:28
he esteemeth iron as *s.* *Job* 41:27
and the lion shall eat *s.* like the ox.
Isa 11:7; 65:25
be trodden down, even as *s.* 25:10

strawed

(*Revisions change to* strewed *or to* scattered)

he ground the calf, *s.* it. *Ex* 32:20
he *s.* upon the graves. *2 Chr* 34:4
cut down branches and *s.* them.
Mat 21:8; *Mark* 11:8
and gathering where thou hast not *s.*
Mat 25:24
and gather where I have not *s.* 26

stream

what he did at the *s.* *Num* 21:15*
and as the *s.* of brooks. *Job* 6:15*
then the *s.* had gone over. *Ps* 124:4
beat off to the *s.* of Egypt. *Isa* 27:12
breath as an overflowing *s.* 30:28
like a *s.* of brimstone, doth. 33
among smooth stones of the *s.* 57:6*
the Gentiles like a flowing *s.* 66:12
fiery *s.* issued and came. *Dan* 7:10
and righteousness as a mighty *s.*
Amos 5:24
s. beat vehemently. *Luke* 6:48, 49

streams

thine hand on their *s.* *Ex* 7:19; 8:5
s. whereof shall make glad. *Ps* 46:4
he brought *s.* also out of rock. 78:16
gushed out, the *s.* overflowed. 20
turn again our captivity as *s.* 126:4
well of living waters, *s.* *S of S* 4:15
smite it in the seven *s.* *Isa* 11:15
on every high hill shall be *s.* 30:25
place of broad rivers and *s.* 33:21
the *s.* thereof shall be turned. 34:9
break out, and *s.* in the desert. 35:6

street

we will abide in the *s.* *Gen* 19:2
shalt gather all the spoil into the midst of the *s.* *Deut* 13:16
of thy house into the *s.* *Josh* 2:19
he sat down in a *s.* of the city.
Judg 19:15, 17
only lodge not in the *s.* 20
had stolen from the *s.* *2 Sam* 21:12
them as the mire of the *s.* 22:43
and gathered them in the east *s.*
2 Chr 29:4*; 32:6*
in *s.* of house of God. *Ezra* 10:9*
people gathered as one man into the *s.* *Neh* 8:1*
he read therein before the *s.* 3*
so people made booths in the *s.* 16*
bring him on horseback through the *s.* *Esth* 6:9, 11
have no name in the *s.* *Job* 18:17
prepared my seat in the *s.* 29:7
stranger did not lodge in the *s.* 31:32
passing through the *s.* *Pr* 7:8
nor cause his voice to be heard in the *s.* *Isa* 42:2; *Mat* 12:19
laid thy body as the *s.* *Isa* 51:23
for truth is fallen in the *s.* 59:14
bread out of bakers' *s.* *Jer* 37:21
hunger in top of every *s.* *Lam* 2:19
out in the top of every *s.* 4:1
made thee an high place in every *s.*
Ezek 16:24, 31
the *s.* shall be built again. *Dan* 9:25
into the *s.* called Straight. *Acts* 9:11
and passed through one *s.* 12:10
shall lie in the *s.* of city. *Rev* 11:8
s. of the city was pure gold. 21:21
in the midst of the *s.* was. 22:2

streets

not in the *s.* of Askelon. *2 Sam* 1:20
make *s.* in Damascus. *1 Ki* 20:34
out as dirt in the *s.* *Ps* 18:42
guile depart not from her *s.* 55:11
sheep may bring forth ten thousands in our *s.* 144:13*
no complaining in our *s.* 14
uttereth her voice in the *s.* *Pr* 1:20*
and rivers of water in the *s.* 5:16
is she without, now in the *s.* 7:12*
a lion without, I shall be slain in the *s.* 22:13
man saith, A lion is in the *s.* 26:13
the doors shall be shut in the *s.*
Eccl 12:4*

mourners go about the s. Eccl 12:5
go about the city in s. S of S 3:2
carcases were torn in midst of s. Isa 5:25
down like the mire of the s. 10:6
in their s. they shall gird. 15:3*
a crying for wine in the s. 24:11
sons lie at the head of all the s. 51:20
run ye to and fro through s. Jer 5:1
seest thou not what they do in s.? 7:17
cease from the s. of Jerusalem. 34
cut off young men from the s. 9:21
proclaim these words in the s. 11:6
according to the number of the s. 13
people shall be cast out in s. 14:16
mirth shall be heard in s. of. 33:10
my anger was kindled in the s. 44:6
wickedness they have committed in s. of Jerusalem. 9
the incense that ye burn in s. 21
lamentations in the s. of Moab. 48:38
her young men shall fall in her s. 49:26; 50:30
are thrust through in her s. 51:4
sucklings swoon in the s. of the city. Lam 2:11, 12
the old lie on the ground in the s. 21
feed delicately, are desolate in s. 4:5
Nazarites are not known in the s. 8
wandered as blind men in the s. 14
steps, that we cannot go in our s. 18
cast their silver in the s. Ezek 7:19
ye have filled the s. thereof. 11:6
of his horses tread down thy s. 26:11
pestilence and blood into her s. 28:23
wailing be in all s. and. Amos 5:16*
down as mire of the s. Mi 7:10
rage in the s., shall justle. Nah 2:4
in pieces at the top of the s. 3:10
I made their s. waste. Zeph 3:6
old women shall dwell in s. Zech 8:4
s. of the city shall be full of boys. 5
up fine gold as mire in the s. 9:3
down their enemies in the s. 10:5
a trumpet before thee in s. Mat 6:2
to pray standing in corners of s. 5
they laid the sick in the s. Mark 6:56*; Acts 5:15
go out into the s. of. Luke 10:10
Thou hast taught in our s. 13:26
go out quickly into the s. and. 14:21

strength

not henceforth yield her s. Gen 4:12
by s. the Lord brought you out. Ex 13:3, 14, 16
he hath the s. of an unicorn. Num 23:22; 24:8
thou hast trodden down s. Judg 5:21
they are girded with s. 1 Sam 2:4
wicked be silent, for by s. shall. 9
he shall give s. unto his king. 10
the s. of Israel will not lie. 15:29
eat, that thou mayest have s. 28:22
girded me with s. to battle, hast. 2 Sam 22:40; Ps 18:32, 39
I have counsel and s. for war. 2 Ki 18:20; Isa 36:5
and there is not s. to bring forth. 2 Ki 19:3; Isa 37:3
s. and gladness are in. 1 Chr 16:27
give to the Lord glory and s. 28
Ps 29:1; 96:7
brethren, able men for s. 1 Chr 26:8
in thine hand it is to give s. 29:12
neither did Jeroboam recover s. 2 Chr 13:20
s. of the bearers of. Neh 4:10
if I speak of s. lo, he. Job 9:19
with him is wisdom and s. 12:13*, 16
weakened the s. of the mighty. 21*
devour the s. of his skin. 18:13*
no; but he would put s. in me. 23:6*
whereto might s. of their hands. 30:2
not esteem all the forces of s. 36:19
hast thou given the horse s.? 39:19*
in his neck remaineth s. 41:22
of babes hast ordained s. Ps 8:2
saving s. of his right hand. 20:6
the Lord is the s. of my life. 27:1
and he is the saving s. of his. 28:8*
the Lord will give s. to his. 29:11
not delivered by much s. 33:16
that I may recover s. 39:13
God is our refuge and s. Ps 46:1
81:1
Ephraim is the s. 60:7*; 108:8*
ascribe ye s. unto God, his s. 68:34
God of Israel is he that giveth s. 35
but God is the s. of my heart. 73:26
sing aloud unto God our s. 81:1
blessed is the man whose s. 84:5
they go from s. to s., every one. 7
and if by reason of s. they. 90:10
is clothed with majesty and s. 93:1
the s. of the hills is his also. 95:4*
s. and beauty are in his. 96:6
king's s. also loveth judgement. 99:4
thou strengthenedst me with s. 138:3
O God the Lord, the s. of my. 140:7
I have s. Pr 8:14*
the way of the Lord is s. 10:29*
increase is by the s. of ox. 14:4
casteth down the s. thereof. 21:22
of knowledge increaseth s. 24:5*
she girdeth her loins with s. 31:17
s. and honour are her clothing. 25
Wisdom is better than s. Eccl 9:16
then must he put to more s. 10:10
princes eat for s. and not for. 17
and men of s. to mingle. Isa 5:22
by the s. of my hand I have. 10:13
sea hath spoken, even the s. 23:4*
been a s. to the poor, a s. to. 25:4*
in Jehovah is everlasting s. 26:4*
for s. to them that turn the. 28:6
the s. of Pharaoh shall be. 30:3
shall be stability and s. of. 33:6*
lift up thy voice with s. 40:9
no might, he increaseth s. 29
he hath poured on him the s. 42:25
he worketh it with the s. 44:12*
have I righteousness and s. 45:24
awake, awake, put on thy s. 51:9
moreover I will deliver all the s. of this city. Jer 20:5*
fortify the height of her s. 51:53
they are gone without s. Lam 1:6
pour my fury on sin, s. Ezek 30:15*
the pomp of her s. shall. 18*; 33:28*
given thee power, s. glory. Dan 2:37
but there shall be in it of the s. 41
neither shall there be any s. 11:15
to enter with the s. of his whole. 17
pollute the sanctuary of s. 31*
the Lord the s. of the. Joel 3:16*
horns by our own s.? Amos 6:13
Ethiopia and Egypt were her s. Nah 3:9
thou also shalt seek s. because. 11*
destroy s. of kingdoms. Hag 2:22
he hath shewed s. with. Luke 1:51
ancle bones received s. Acts 3:7
without s., Christ died. Rom 5:6
the sting of death is sin; the s. of sin is the law. 1 Cor 15:56*
out of measure, above s. 2 Cor 1:8*
Sara herself received s. Heb 11:11
for thou hast a little s. Rev 3:8*
worthy is Lamb to receive s. 5:12*
Now is come salvation and s. 12:10*
their power and s. to beast. 17:13*
see no

***his* strength**

sea returned to his s. Ex 14:27
is the beginning of his s. Deut 21:17
as the man is, so is his s. Judg 8:21
see wherein his great s. lieth. 16:5
his s. was not known. 9
his s. went from him. 19
a bow with his full s. 2 Ki 9:24
seek the Lord and his s. 1 Chr 16:11
Ps 105:4
the steps of his s. shall. Job 18:7
his s. shall be hunger bitten. 12
of death shall devour his s. 13
one dieth in his full s. being. 21:23
to the great rain of his s. 37:6*
trust him because his s. is? 39:11
rejoiceth in his s. 21
his s. is in his loins. 40:16
deliver any by his great s. Ps 33:17*
that made not God his s. 52:7
because of his s. will I wait. 59:9
who by his s. setteth fast the. 65:6
ascribe s. to God, his s. is. 68:34
the generation to come his s. 78:4
delivered his s. into captivity. Ps 78:61
hungry, and his s. faileth. Isa 44:12
sworn by the arm of his s. 62:8
in the greatness of his s. 63:1
by his s. shall stir up all. Dan 11:2*
strangers devoured his s. Hos 7:9
and by his s. he had power. 12:3*
was as the sun in his s. Rev 1:16

***in* strength**

but his bow abode in s. Gen 49:24
went in the s. of that. 1 Ki 19:8
he is wise in heart, and mighty in s. Job 9:4; 36:5
I will go in the s. of the. Ps 71:16*
his angels that excel in s. 103:20
he delighteth not in the s. 147:10
themselves in s. of Pharaoh. Isa 30:2
and he shall feed in the s. Mi 5:4
increased the more in s. Acts 9:22

***my* strength**

the beginning of my s. Gen 49:3
Lord is my s. and song. Ex 15:2
2 Sam 22:33; Ps 18:2*; 28:7
118:14; Isa 12:2
as my s. was then, even so is my s. Josh 14:11
if I be shaven, my s. Judg 16:17
what is my s. that I should hope? Job 6:11
is my s. of stones? or is my? 12
love thee, O Lord, my s. Ps 18:1
O Lord, my s. 19:14*; 22:19*
my s. is dried up. 22:15
the net, for thou art my s. 31:4*
my s. fails because of mine iniquity. 10; 38:10; 71:9
art the God of my s. why go? 43:2
to thee, O my s. will I sing. 59:17
art rock of my s. 62:7
he weakened my s. 102:23
blessed be Lord my s. who. 144:1*
let him take hold of my s. Isa 27:5
I have spent my s. for nought. 49:4
my God shall be my s. 5
O Lord, my s. Jer 16:19
he made my s. to fall. Lam 1:14
I said, My s. and hope is. 3:18
the Lord God is my s. Hab 3:19
my s. in Lord of hosts. Zech 12:5
my s. is made perfect. 2 Cor 12:9*

***their* strength**

as for cities that stood still in their s. Josh 11:13*
he is their s. in the time. Ps 37:39*
their death, their s. is firm. 73:4
he smote the chief of their s. 78:51
105:36
art the glory of their s. 89:17
yet is their s. labour and. 90:10*
the glory of young men is their s. Pr 20:29
I have cried, their s. is. Isa 30:7*
on Lord shall renew their s. 40:31
let the people renew their s. 41:1
I will bring down their s. 63:6*
take from them their s. Ezek 24:25
and vine do yield their s. Joel 2:22

***thy* strength**

guided them in thy s. Ex 15:13
days, so shall thy s. be. Deut 33:25
wherein thy s. lieth. Judg 16:6, 15
thou, and the ark of thy s. 2 Chr 6:41
Ps 132:8
the king shall joy in thy s. Ps 21:1
O Lord, in thine own s. 13
thy name, judge me by thy s. 54:1
hath commanded thy s. 68:28
until I have shewed thy s. 71:18
divide the sea by thy s. 74:13
thou hast declared thy s. 77:14
stir up thy s. and come. 80:2*
O turn to me, give thy s. to. 86:16
Lord shall send rod of thy s. 110:2
if thou faint in day of adversity, thy s. Pr 24:10
give not thy s. unto women. 31:3
mindful of rock of thy s. Isa 17:10
awake, awake, put on thy s. 52:1
where is thy zeal and thy s.? 63:15
he shall bring down thy s. Amos 3:11

thy God with all thy heart and all *thy* s. *Mark* 12:30, 33; *Luke* 10:27

your strength
and *your s.* shall be spent in vain. *Lev* 26:20
joy of the Lord is *your s.* *Neh* 8:10
howl, ye ships, *your s.* *Isa* 23:14
in confidence will be *your s.* 30:15
excellency of *your s.* *Ezek* 24:21

strengthen
charge Joshua, and encourage him and *s.* him. *Deut* 3:28
s. me, I pray thee. *Judg* 16:28
go, *s.* thyself, and mark. *1 Ki* 20:22
to *s.* their hands in the. *Ezra* 6:22
now therefore, O God, *s.* *Neh* 6:9
but I would *s.* you with. *Job* 16:5
Lord send thee help, *s.* thee. *Ps* 20:2
wait on Lord, he shall *s.* thy heart. 27:14*; 31:24*
Lord will *s.* him upon the bed. 41:3*
s. that which thou hast. 68:28
mine arm also shall *s.* him. 89:21
s. thou me according to. 119:28
and I will *s.* him with. *Isa* 22:21
to *s.* themselves in the strength. 30:2
not well *s.* their mast. 33:23
s. ye the weak hands. 35:3
I will *s.* thee. 41:10
lengthen thy cords, and *s.* 54:2
s. also the hands of evil. *Jer* 23:14
nor shall any *s.* himself. *Ezek* 7:13
neither did she *s.* hand of poor. 16:49
I will *s.* arms of the king. 30:24, 25*
I will *s.* that which was sick. 34:16
to confirm and to *s.* him. *Dan* 11:1
strong shall not *s.* his. *Amos* 2:14
and I will *s.* the house. *Zech* 10:6
I will *s.* them in the Lord, they. 12
thou art converted, *s.* *Luke* 22:32*
you perfect, stablish, *s.* *1 Pet* 5:10
be watchful and *s.* things. *Rev* 3:2*

strengthened
Israel *s.* himself, and sat. *Gen* 48:2
the Lord *s.* Eglon against. *Judg* 3:12
shall thine hands be *s.* 7:11
and *s.* his hand in God. *1 Sam* 23:16
let your hands be *s.* *2 Sam* 2:7
who *s.* themselves. *1 Chr* 11:10
and Solomon was *s.* *2 Chr* 1:1
s. the kingdom of Judah. 11:17
when Rehoboam had *s.* himself. 12:1
have *s.* themselves against. 13:7
Jehoshaphat *s.* himself against. 17:1
Jehoram *s.* himself and slew. 21:4
Jehoiada *s.* himself and took. 23:1
house in his state, and *s.* it. 24:13
Amaziah *s.* himself, and led. 25:11*
Uzziah *s.* himself exceedingly. 26:8
and distressed Ahaz, but *s.* 28:20
Hezekiah *s.* himself, and built. 32:5*
all that were about them *s.* *Ezra* 1:6
I was *s.* as hand of my God. 7:28
they *s.* their hands for. *Neh* 2:18
hast *s.* the weak hands. *Job* 4:3
hast *s.* the feeble knees. 4*
and *s.* himself in his. *Ps* 52:7
for he hath *s.* the bars of. 147:13
when he *s.* the fountains of. *Pr* 8:28
ye have *s.* the hands of. *Ezek* 13:22
diseased have ye not *s.* nor. 34:4
one touched me, and *s.* me. *Dan* 10:18, 19
he that begat her and *s.* her. 11:6
many, but he shall not be *s.* by. 12*
though I have bound and *s.* *Hos* 7:15
Saul was *s.* *Acts* 9:19
to be *s.* with might by Spirit. *Eph* 3:16
s. with all might according. *Col* 1:11
stood with me and *s.* me. *2 Tim* 4:17

strengthenedst
s. me with strength in. *Ps* 138:3*

strengtheneth
he *s.* himself against. *Job* 15:25*
and bread which *s.* *Ps* 104:15
girdeth her loins, and *s.* *Pr* 31:17
wisdom *s.* the wise more. *Eccl* 7:19
the cypress and oak he *s.* *Isa* 44:14
s. the spoiled against. *Amos* 5:9*
I can do all things through Christ which *s.* me. *Phil* 4:13

strengthening
appeared an angel *s.* *Luke* 22:43
Paul went to Galatia, *s.* *Acts* 18:23*

stretch
s. out thy hand upon. *Ex* 7:19
s. forth thine hand over streams. 8:5
s. out thy rod and smite dust. 16
cherubims shall *s.* forth their. 25:20
s. out spear that is in. *Josh* 8:18
I will *s.* over Jerusalem. *2 Ki* 21:13
if thou *s.* thine hands. *Job* 11:13
doth the hawk *s.* her wings ? 39:26
shall soon *s.* out her hands. *Ps* 68:31
I *s.* my hands unto thee. 143:6
that a man can *s.* himself. *Isa* 28:20
s. forth the curtains of thy. 54:2
there is none to *s.* forth. *Jer* 10:20
king of Babylon shall *s.* *Ezek* 30:25
and *s.* themselves upon. *Amos* 6:4
man, *S.* forth thy hand. *Mat* 12:13
thou shalt *s.* forth thy. *John* 21:18
for we *s.* not ourselves. *2 Cor* 10:14

stretched
Abraham *s.* forth hand. *Gen* 22:10
Israel *s.* out right hand, laid. 48:14
Aaron *s.* out his hand. *Ex* 8:6, 17
Moses *s.* forth his rod. 9:23; 10:13
Moses *s.* forth his hand to heaven. 10:22; 14:21, 27
and Joshua *s.* out the spear. *Josh* 8:18, 26
they ran as soon as he had *s.* 19
the cherubims *s.* forth. *1 Ki* 6:27
he *s.* himself upon the child. 17:21
2 Ki 4:34, 35
angel with a sword *s.* *1 Chr* 21:16
who hath *s.* the line upon ? *Job* 38:5
or *s.* our hands to a. *Ps* 44:20
I have *s.* out my hands unto. 88:9
to him that *s.* out the earth. 136:6
because I have *s.* out. *Pr* 1:24
because they walk with *s.* *Isa* 3:16
s. forth his hand against them; his hand is *s.* 5:25; 9:12, 17, 21; 10:4
this is the hand that is *s.* out. 14:26
hand is *s.* out, and who shall ? 27
her branches are *s.* out. 16:8
he *s.* out his hand over sea. 23:11
that *s.* out the heavens. 42:5; 45:12
51:13
the shadows are *s.* out. *Jer* 6:4
he *s.* out the heavens. 10:12
he *s.* out heaven by his. 51:15
Lord hath *s.* out a line. *Lam* 2:8
and their wings were *s.* *Ezek* 1:11
one cherub *s.* forth his hand. 10:7
behold, I have *s.* out my hand. 16:27
he *s.* out his hand with. *Hos* 7:5
that *s.* themselves shall. *Amos* 6:7
a line shall be *s.* forth. *Zech* 1:16
and he *s.* forth his hand. *Mat* 12:13
Mark 3:5
ye *s.* forth no hands. *Luke* 22:53
Herod *s.* forth his hands. *Acts* 12:1
all day long I have *s.* *Rom* 10:21
see **arm**

stretchedst
thou *s.* out thy right hand. *Ex* 15:12

stretchest
who *s.* out the heavens. *Ps* 104:2

stretcheth
for he *s.* out his hand. *Job* 15:25
he *s.* out the north over the. 26:7
she *s.* out her hand to. *Pr* 31:20
that *s.* out the heavens. *Isa* 40:22
the carpenter *s.* out his rule. 44:13
that *s.* forth the heavens alone. 24
Zech 12:1

stretching
s. of his wings shall fill. *Isa* 8:8
by *s.* forth thy hand. *Acts* 4:30

stricken
Abram and Sarah well *s.* in age. *Gen* 18:11; 24:1
now Joshua was *s.* in years. *Josh* 13:1; 23:1, 2
when Jael had *s.* *Judg* 5:26
old and *s.* in years. *1 Ki* 1:1
if thou hast *s.* thy hand. *Pr* 6:1
they have *s.* me and I was. 23:35
why should ye be *s.* any more ? *Isa* 1:5
surely they are *s.* *Isa* 16:7
did esteem him *s.* 53:4
of my people was he *s.* 8
thou hast *s.* them, they. *Jer* 5:3
s. through for want of the. *Lam* 4:9
Elisabeth well *s.* in. *Luke* 1:7, 18

strife
there was a *s.* between. *Gen* 13:7
Abram said, Let there be no *s.* 8
ye rebelled in the *s.* of. *Num* 27:14
myself alone bear your *s.*? *Deut* 1:12
I and my people were at great *s.* with. *Judg* 12:2
all the people were at *s.* *2 Sam* 19:9
shalt keep them from *s.* *Ps* 31:20
for I have seen violence and *s.* 55:9
thou makest us a *s.* to our. 80:6
him at the waters of *s.* 106:32*
man stirreth up *s.* . . . slow to anger appeaseth *s.* *Pr* 15:18; 29:22
a froward man soweth *s.* 16:28
house full of sacrifices with *s.* 17:1
beginning of *s.* is as when one. 14
loveth transgression, that loveth *s.* 19
for a man to cease from *s.* 20:3
cast out the scorner, and *s.* 22:10
he that meddleth with *s.* 26:17
is no talebearer, the *s.* ceaseth. 20
so is a contentious man to kindle *s.* 21
a proud heart stirreth up *s.* 28:25
of wrath bringeth forth *s.* 30:33
behold, ye fast for *s.* and. *Isa* 58:4
hast borne me a man of *s* *Jer* 15:10
even to the waters of *s.* *Ezek* 47:19*; 48:28*
there are that raise up *s.* *Hab* 1:3
there was a *s.* among. *Luke* 22:24
walk honestly, not in *s.* *Rom* 13:13
there is among you *s.* *1 Cor* 3:3
of the flesh are wrath, *s.* *Gal* 5:20*
preach Christ even of *s.* *Phil* 1:15
let nothing be done through *s.* 2:3*
whereof cometh envy, *s.* *1 Tim* 6:4
to them an end of all *s.* *Heb* 6:16*
bitter envying and *s.* *Jas* 3:14*
where *s.* is, there is confusion. 16*

strifes
hatred stirreth up *s.*: love. *Pr* 10:12
envyings, wraths, *s.* *2 Cor* 12:20*
doting about questions and *s.* of words *1 Tim* 6:4*
that they do gender *s.* *2 Tim* 2:23

strike
and *s.* blood on the two side posts. *Ex* 12:7*, 22
shall *s.* off the heifer's. *Deut* 21:4
come and *s.* his hand. *2 Ki* 5:11*
who is he that will *s.* hands with ? *Job* 17:3
and the bow of steel shall *s.* 20:24
shall *s.* through kings in. *Ps* 110:5
till a dart *s.* through. *Pr* 7:23
it is not good to *s.* princes. 17:26
one of them that *s.* hands. 22:26
thou didst *s.* through. *Hab* 3:14
s. him with palms of. *Mark* 14:65*

striker
a bishop must be sober, no *s.* *1 Tim* 3:3; *Tit* 1:7

striketh
he *s.* them as wicked men. *Job* 34:26
of understanding *s.* hands. *Pr* 17:18
scorpion, when he *s.* a man. *Rev* 9:5

string
ready their arrow upon *s.* *Ps* 11:2
s. of his tongue was loosed, he. *Mark* 7:35*

stringed
him with *s.* instruments. *Ps* 150:4
will sing my songs to *s.* *Isa* 38:20
to chief singer on my *s.* *Hab* 3:19

strings
make ready their arrows upon *s.* *Ps* 21:12*
with the psaltery, and an instrument of ten *s.* 33:2; 92:3; 144:9

strip
and *s.* Aaron of his. *Num* 20:26
Philistines came to *s.* slain. *1 Sam* 31:8; *1 Chr* 10:8
s. ye, make ye bare, gird. *Isa* 32:11

they shall *s.* thee of thy clothes. *Ezek* 16:39; 23:26
lest I *s.* her naked, and. *Hos* 2:3

stripe

wound for wound, *s.* for *s. Ex* 21:25

stripes

(*Strokes given by a scourge or rod. The law forbade giving more than* 40 *and the Jews stopped at* 39 *for fear of wrong count*)

forty *s.* he may give him . . . above these with many *s.* *Deut* 25:3
and with *s.* of the children of men. *2 Sam* 7:14
visit their iniquity with *s.* *Ps* 89:32
than an hundred *s.* into. *Pr* 17:10
and *s.* prepared for the back. 19:29
so do *s.* the inward parts. 20:30
with his *s.* we are healed. *Isa* 53:5; *1 Pet* 2:24
be beaten with many *s.* *Luke* 12:47
not, shall be beaten with few *s.* 48
had laid many *s.* upon. *Acts* 16:23
same hour and washed their *s.* 33
in *s.*, in imprisonments. *2 Cor* 6:5
s. above measure, in prisons. 11:23
received I forty *s.* save one. 24

stripling

Inquire whose son the *s. 1 Sam* 17:56

stripped

that they *s.* Joseph out. *Gen* 37:23
Israel *s.* themselves of. *Ex* 33:6
Moses *s.* Aaron of his. *Num* 20:28
Jonathan *s.* himself of. *1 Sam* 18:4
Saul *s.* off his clothes also. 19:24
the Philistines *s.* Saul of his. 31:9
jewels which they *s.* off. *2 Chr* 20:25
he *s.* me of my glory. *Job* 19:9
for thou hast *s.* the naked of. 22:6
therefore I will go *s.* *Mi* 1:8
they *s.* Jesus, put on. *Mat* 27:28
thieves, which *s.* him. *Luke* 10:30

strive

spirit shall not always *s.* *Gen* 6:3
the herdmen of Gerar did *s.* 26:20
if men *s.* together, and. *Ex* 21:18
if man *s.* and hurt a woman with child, he shall. 22; *Deut* 25:11
with whom thou didst *s.* *Deut* 33:8
did he ever *s.* against Israel or? *Judg* 11:25
why dost thou *s.* against? *Job* 33:13
with them that *s.* with me. *Ps* 35:1
s. not with a man. *Pr* 3:30
go not forth hastily to *s.*, lest. 25:8
and they that *s.* with thee. *Isa* 41:11
potsherd *s.* with potsherds. 45:9*
let no man *s.*; thy people are as they that *s.* *Hos* 4:4
he shall not *s.*, nor cry. *Mat* 12:19
s. to enter in at the strait gate. *Luke* 13:24
s. with me in your prayers to. *Rom* 15:30
and if a man also *s.* *2 Tim* 2:5*
that they *s.* not about words. 14
of the Lord must not *s.* 24

strived

so have I *s.* to preach. *Rom* 15:20*

striven

because thou hast *s.* *Jer* 50:24

striveth

woe to him that *s.* with. *Isa* 45:9
every man that *s.* for mastery. *1 Cor* 9:25

striving

with one mind *s.* for faith. *Phil* 1:27
s. according to his working. *Col* 1:29
ye have not resisted to blood, *s.* against sin. *Heb* 12:4

strivings

delivered me from the *s.* of the people, and. *2 Sam* 22:44; *Ps* 18:43
avoid contentions and *s.* *Tit* 3:9*

stroke

hard between *s.* and *s.* *Deut* 17:8
and his hand fetcheth a *s.* 19:5
by their word shall every *s.* 21:5
their enemies with the *s.* *Esth* 9:5
my *s.* is heavier than. *Job* 23:2
take thee away with his *s.* 36:18
remove thy *s.* away from. *Ps* 39:10
people with a continual *s.* *Isa* 14:6
the Lord healeth the *s.* of. 30:26
of thine eyes with a *s.* *Ezek* 24:16

strokes

a fool's mouth calleth for *s. Pr* 18:6*

strong

Issachar is a *s.* ass. *Gen* 49:14
arms of his hands were made *s.* 24
with a *s.* hand shall he let them go. *Ex* 6:1; 13:9
the Lord turned a mighty *s.* 10:19
sea to go back by a *s.* east. 14:21
Edom came against him with a *s.* *Num* 20:20
children of Ammon was *s.* 21:24
Balaam said, *S.* is thy. 24:21
the *s.* wine to be poured out. 28:7
one city too *s.* for us. *Deut* 2:36*
as yet I am as *s.* this. *Josh* 14:11
were waxen *s.* 17:13; *Judg* 1:28
Lord hath driven out great nations and *s.* *Josh* 23:9
but there was a *s.* tower. *Judg* 9:51
out of the *s.* came forth. 14:14
that they were too *s.* for him. 18:26
Saul saw any *s.* man. *1 Sam* 14:52*
Abner made himself *s.* for the house of Saul. *2 Sam* 3:6
Syrians be too *s.* for me, if Ammon be too *s.* for. 10:11; *1 Chr* 19:12
make thy battle more *s. 2 Sam* 11:25
the conspiracy was *s.* 15:12
from my *s.* enemy; . . . for they were too *s.* for me. 22:18*; *Ps* 18:17
shall hear of thy name and *s.* hand. *1 Ki* 8:42
a great and *s.* wind rent the. 19:11
cities exceeding *s.* *2 Chr* 11:12
so they made Rehoboam *s.* 17
eyes run to shew himself *s.* 16:9
when Uzziah was *s.* he. 26:16
redeemed by thy *s.* hand. *Neh* 1:10
and they took *s.* cities and. 9:25*
mouth be like a *s.* wind. *Job* 8:2*
speak of strength, lo, he is *s.* 9:19*
with thy *s.* hand thou. 30:21*
spread out the sky, which is *s.*? 37:18
bones are as *s.* pieces of. 40:18*
and rejoiceth as a *s.* man. *Ps* 19:5
Lord *s.* and mighty, the Lord. 24:8
my mountain to stand *s.* 30:7
be thou my *s.* rock, and house. 31:2
me his kindness in a *s.* city. 21
poor from him that is too *s.* 35:10
are lively and they are *s.* 38:19
bring me into *s.* city? 60:9; 108:10
thou hast been a *s.* tower from. 61:3
be my *s.* habitation. 71:3*
thou art my *s.* refuge. 7
the branch thou madest *s.* 80:15, 17
O Lord, who is a *s.* Lord? 89:8*
s. is thy hand, and high is thy. 13
with a *s.* hand, and a stretched out arm. 136:12; *Jer* 32:21
yea, many *s.* men have. *Pr* 7:26*
rich man's wealth is his *s.* city. 10:15; 18:11
s. men retain riches. 11:16*
fear of the Lord is a *s.* tower. 14:26
name of the Lord is a *s.* tower. 18:10
is harder to be won than a *s.* city. 19
the bosom pacifieth *s.* wrath. 21:14
a wise man is *s.* 24:5
ants are a people not *s.* 30:25
the battle is not to the *s.* *Eccl* 9:11
and the *s.* men shall bow. 12:3
as a seal, for love is *s.* *S of S* 8:6
the *s.* shall be as tow. *Isa* 1:31
Lord bringeth on them waters, *s.* 8:7
spake thus to me with a *s.* 11
his *s.* cities shall be as a. 17:9
therefore shall the *s.* people. 25:3
be sung: We have a *s.* city. 26:1
with his *s.* sword shall punish. 27:1
Lord hath a mighty and *s.* one. 28:2
lest your bands be made *s.* 22
horsemen, because they are *s.* 31:1
will come with a *s.* hand. 40:10*
for that he is *s.* in power, not. 26
bring forth your *s.* reasons. 41:21
divide the spoil with the *s.* 53:12
a small one shall become a *s.* 60:22
against you with a *s.* arm. *Jer* 21:5
say ye, We are mighty, *s.*? 48:14*
How is the *s.* staff broken! 17
against habitation of the *s.* 49:19
Redeemer is *s.*; the Lord of. 50:34
up to the habitation of the *s.* 44
make the watch *s.*, set up. 51:12
thy face *s.* thy forehead *s. Ezek* 3:8*
but the hand of the Lord was *s.* 14
the pomp of the *s.* to cease. 7:24
had *s.* rods for sceptres of. 19:11
her *s.* rods were broken. 12
so she hath no *s.* rod to be a. 14
thy *s.* garrisons shall go. 26:11*
the renowned city which wast *s.* 17
bind it, to make it *s.* to hold. 30:21
and I will break the *s.* arms. 22
s. shall speak to him out of. 32:21
destroy the fat and the *s.* 34:16
tree grew, and was *s.* *Dan* 4:11, 20
O king, art grown and become *s.* 22
the fourth beast terrible, *s.* 7:7
when he was *s.* the great horn. 8:8
he shall become *s.* with a. 11:23
nation is come up on my land, *s.* *Joel* 1:6; 2:2
as the noise of a *s.* people set. 2:5
for he is *s.* that executeth his. 11
let the weak say, I am *s.* 3:10
the Amorite was *s.* as. *Amos* 2:9
and the *s.* shall not strengthen. 14
the spoiled against the *s.* 5:9
he shall rebuke *s.* nations. *Mi* 4:3
was cast far off, *s.* nation. 7
hear, ye *s.* foundations of the. 6:2*
make thy loins *s.*, fortify. *Nah* 2:1
s. nations shall come to. *Zech* 8:22
enter into a *s.* man's house . . . the *s.* man? *Mat* 12:29; *Mark* 3:27
grew and waxed *s. Luke* 1:80; 2:40
when a *s.* man armed keepeth. 11:21
through faith hath made this man *s.* *Acts* 3:16
was *s.* in faith, giving. *Rom* 4:20
we that are *s.* ought to bear. 15:1
weak, but ye are *s.* *1 Cor* 4:10
am weak, then am I *s.* *2 Cor* 12:10
we are weak, and ye are *s.* 13:9
God shall send them *s. 2 Thes* 2:11*
up prayers with *s.* crying. *Heb* 5:7
of milk, and not of *s.* meat. 12*
s. meat belongeth to them that. 14*
we might have a *s.* consolation. 6:18
weakness were made *s.* 11:34
ye are *s.*, word of God. *1 John* 2:14
I saw a *s.* angel proclaiming. *Rev* 5:2
a *s.* voice, Babylon is fallen. 18:2*
for *s.* is the Lord God who. 8

see **drink**

***be* strong**

see whether they *be s.* *Num* 13:18
the people *be s.* that dwell. 28
keep commandments, that ye may *be s.* *Deut* 11:8
drive out Canaanites, though they *be s.* *Josh* 17:18
be s. and quit yourselves. *1 Sam* 4:9
hands of all with thee shall *be s.* *2 Sam* 16:21
be thou *s.* and shew. *1 Ki* 2:2
be too *s.* for me, if Ammon *be* too *s.* for thee. *1 Chr* 19:12
Lord hath chosen thee, *be s.* 28:10
be s., your work shall. *2 Chr* 15:7
if thou wilt go, do it, *be s.* for. 25:8
that ye may *be s.* and eat. *Ezra* 9:12
that our oxen may *be s.* *Ps* 144:14*
fearful heart, *Be s.*, fear not. *Isa* 35:4
can thy hands be *s.*, in? *Ezek* 22:14
fourth kingdom shall *be s. Dan* 2:40
kingdom shall *be* partly *s.* 42
Peace be unto thee, *be s.*, yea, *be s.* 10:19
the south shall *be s.* and he shall *be s.* above him and have. 11:5
that know their God shall *be s.* 32
be s. O Zerubbabel, *be s.* O Joshua, *be s.* all ye people of. *Hag* 2:4
let your hands *be s.* ye that hear in these days. *Zech* 8:9
but let your hands *be s.* 13
quit you like men, *be s. 1 Cor* 16:13
finally, brethren, *be s.* in. *Eph* 6:10

my son, *be s.* in grace. *2 Tim* 2:1
see **courage**

strong *hold* and *holds*
tents or in *s. holds.* *Num* 13:19
them caves and *s. holds.* *Judg* 6:2
abode in wilderness in *s. holds.*
1 Sam 23:14
hide himself with us in *s. holds*? 19
and David dwelt in *s. holds.* 29
took the *s. hold* of Zion. *2 Sam* 5:7
and came to the *s. hold* of. 24:7
their *s. holds* wilt thou. *2 Ki* 8:12
fortified the *s. holds.* *2 Chr* 11:11
brought his *s. holds* to ruin. *Ps* 89:40
to destroy the *s. holds.* *Isa* 23:11
over to his *s. holds* for fear. 31:9
destroy thy *s. holds.* *Jer* 48:18
Kerioth is taken, the *s. holds.* 41
down *s. holds* of Judah. *Lam* 2:2
hath destroyed his *s. holds.* 5
forecast his devices against the *s.*
holds. *Dan* 11:24
he do in the most *s. holds.* 39*
the *s. hold* of the daughter. *Mi* 4:8*
Lord is a *s. hold* in the day. *Nah* 1:7
for siege, fortify thy *s. holds.* 3:14*
deride every *s. hold.* *Hab* 1:10
did build herself a *s. hold.* *Zech* 9:3
s. hold, ye prisoners of hope. 12
to pulling down of *s. holds.* *2 Cor* 10:4

strong *ones*
poor may fall by his *s. ones.* *Ps* 10:10
the neighing of his *s. ones.* *Jer* 8:16

stronger
one people shall be *s.* *Gen* 25:23
whensoever the *s.* cattle did. 30:41
were Laban's, and *s.* Jacob's. 42
be not able, they are *s.* *Num* 13:31
the men said, What is *s.*? *Judg* 14:18
Saul and Jonathan were *s.* than lions.
2 Sam 1:23
but David waxed *s.* and *s.* and. 3:1
but Ammon being *s.* than she. 13:14
gods of hills, therefore *s.*, surely we
shall be *s.* than. *1 Ki* 20:23, 25
hath clean hands shall be *s.* and *s.*
Job 17:9
he made them *s.* than. *Ps* 105:24
deliver me, for they are *s.* 142:6
thou art *s.* than I, and. *Jer* 20:7
him that was *s.* than he. 31:11
when a *s.* than he shall. *Luke* 11:22
weakness of God is *s.* *1 Cor* 1:25
provoke Lord ? are we *s.*? 10:22

strongest
a lion which is *s.* among. *Pr* 30:30*

strongly
foundation thereof be *s.* *Ezra* 6:3

strove
they *s.* with him. *Gen* 26:20, 21
well, and for that they *s.* not. 22
two men of the Hebrews *s.* *Ex* 2:13
and a man of Israel *s.* *Lev* 24:10
the children of Israel *s.* *Num* 20:13
Dathan, who *s.* against Moses. 26:9
they two *s.* together in. *2 Sam* 14:6
four winds *s.* upon the. *Dan* 7:2*
the Jews *s.* among. *John* 6:52
himself to them as they *s.* *Acts* 7:26
and *s.* saying, We find no evil. 23:9

struck
he *s.* it into the pan or. *1 Sam* 2:14
the Lord *s.* the child. *2 Sam* 12:15
Joab *s.* him not again, and. 20:10
the Lord *s.* Jeroboam. *2 Chr* 13:20
one of them *s.* a servant. *Mat* 26:51
s. Jesus on the face. *Luke* 22:64
John 18:22

struggled
children *s.* together. *Gen* 25:22

stubble
scattered to gather *s.* *Ex* 5:12
which consumed them as *s.* 15:7
thou pursue the dry *s.*? *Job* 13:25
they are as *s.* before the wind. 21:18
are turned with him into *s.* 41:28
darts are counted as *s.* 29
as *s.* before the wind. *Ps* 83:13
as fire devoureth the *s.* so. *Isa* 5:24
chaff and bring forth *s.* 33:11
take them away as *s.* 40:24
he gave them as driven *s.* 41:2
they shall be as *s.*, the fire. *Isa* 47:14
will I scatter them as *s.* *Jer* 13:24
flame, that devoureth the *s.* *Joel* 2:5
house of Esau shall be for *s.* *Ob* 18
devoured as *s.* fully dry. *Nah* 1:10
wickedly and proud be *s.* *Mal* 4:1
gold, wood, hay, *s.* *1 Cor* 3:12

stubborn
if a man have a *s.* *Deut* 21:18
say to elders, This our son is *s.* 20
not from their *s.* way. *Judg* 2:19
might not be as fathers, a *s.* *Ps* 78:8
she is loud and *s.*; her feet. *Pr* 7:11*

stubbornness
look not to *s.* of this. *Deut* 9:27
and *s.* is as iniquity. *1 Sam* 15:23

stuck
spear *s.* in the ground. *1 Sam* 26:7
I have *s.* unto thy. *Ps* 119:31
for part of the ship *s.* *Acts* 27:41*

studieth
heart of the righteous *s.* *Pr* 15:28
for their heart *s.* destruction. 24:2

studs
of gold with *s.* of silver. *S of S* 1:11

study
and much *s.* is a weariness of the.
Eccl 12:12
that ye *s.* to be quiet. *1 Thes* 4:11
s. to shew thyself approved unto.
2 Tim 2:15*

stuff
hast searched all my *s.* *Gen* 31:37
regard not your *s.*; the good of. 45:20
money or *s.* to keep. *Ex* 22:7
the *s.* they had was sufficient. 36:7
even among their own *s.* *Josh* 7:11
himself among the *s.* *1 Sam* 10:22†
two hundred abode by the *s.* 25:13†
part be that tarrieth by *s.* 30:24†
prepare thee *s.* for removing and.
Ezek 12:3
shalt thou bring forth thy *s.* 4, 7
and his *s.* in the house. *Luke* 17:31*

stumble
and thy foot not *s.* *Pr* 3:23; 4:12
know not at what they *s.* 4:19
none shall be weary, nor *s.* *Isa* 5:27
many among them shall *s.* 8:15
they err in vision, they *s.* 28:7
we grope, we *s.* at noon day. 59:10
that they should not *s.* 63:13
before your feet *s.* on dark mountains. *Jer* 13:16
they have caused them to *s.* 18:15
my persecutors shall *s.* 20:11
way wherein they shall not *s.* 31:9
they shall *s.* and fall toward. 46:6
and the most proud shall *s.* 50:32
he shall *s.* and fall. *Dan* 11:19
shall *s.* in their walk. *Nah* 2:5
multitude of slain, they *s.* upon. 3:3
caused many to *s.* at. *Mal* 2:8
offence to them that *s.* *1 Pet* 2:8

stumbled
and they that *s.* are girt. *1 Sam* 2:4
ark, for the oxen *s.* *1 Chr* 13:9
to eat up my flesh, they *s.* *Ps* 27:2
the mighty man hath *s.* *Jer* 46:12
for they *s.* at that stumblingstone.
Rom 9:32
I say then, Have they *s.* that? 11:11

stumbleth
let not thy heart be glad when he *s.*
Pr 24:17*
walk in the day, he *s.* not. *John* 11:9
walk in the night, he *s.* 10
any thing whereby thy brother *s.*
Rom 14:21

stumbling
there is none occasion of *s.* in him.
1 John 2:10

stumblingblock
a *s.* before the blind. *Lev* 19:14
take up the *s.* out of the way of my.
Isa 57:14
and I lay a *s.* before him. *Ezek* 3:20
it is the *s.* of their iniquity. 7:19
put the *s.* of their iniquity. 14:3, 4, 7
table be made a trap, a *s.* *Rom* 11:9
that no man put a *s.* in his. 14:13
Christ crucified, to Jews a *s.*
1 Cor 1:23
this liberty of yours become a *s.* 8:9
Balak to cast a *s.* before. *Rev* 2:14

stumblingblocks
behold, I will lay *s.* before. *Jer* 6:21
I will consume the *s.* *Zeph* 1:3

stumblingstone
shall be for a *stone* of *s.* *Isa* 8:14
stumbled at that *s.* *Rom* 9:32*
in Sion a *s.* and rock of offence. 33*
a *stone* of *s.* to them. *1 Pet* 2:8

stump
only the *s.* of Dagon. *1 Sam* 5:4
s. in the earth. *Dan* 4:15, 23, 26

subdue
God said, Replenish the earth and *s.*
it. *Gen* 1:28
s. all thine enemies. *1 Chr* 17:10
he shall *s.* the people. *Ps* 47:3
have holden, to *s.* nations. *Isa* 45:1
another rise, and he shall *s.* three.
Dan 7:24
turn again, he will *s.* *Mi* 7:19*
they shall devour and *s.* *Zech* 9:15*
able to *s.* all things. *Phil* 3:21

subdued
and the land be *s.* before. *Num* 32:22
land shall be *s.* before you. 29
bulwarks, until it be *s.* *Deut* 20:20*
and the land was *s.* *Josh* 18:1
so Moab was *s.* *Judg* 3:30
God *s.* Jabin. 4:23
thus Midian was *s.* 8:28
Ammon was *s.* 11:33
Philistines were *s.* *1 Sam* 7:13
2 Sam 8:1; *1 Chr* 18:1; 20:4
all nations which he *s.* *2 Sam* 8:11
them that rose up against me hast
thou *s.* under. 22:40; *Ps* 18:39
and the land is *s.* *1 Chr* 22:18
I should soon have *s.* *Ps* 81:14
things shall be *s.* unto. *1 Cor* 15:28*
who through faith *s.* *Heb* 11:33

subduedst
thou *s.* the inhabitants. *Neh* 9:24

subdueth
it is God that *s.* the people under me.
Ps 18:47; 144:2
iron breaks and *s.* all. *Dan* 2:40

subject
and was *s.* to them. *Luke* 2:51
even the devils are *s.* to us. 10:17
that the spirits are *s.* to you. 20
is not *s.* to the law of. *Rom* 8:7
creature was made *s.* to vanity. 20
let every soul be *s.* to the. 13:1
wherefore ye must needs be *s.* 5
spirits of prophets are *s.* *1 Cor* 14:32
Son also himself be *s.* to him. 15:28
church is *s.* to Christ. *Eph* 5:24
as though living in the world, are ye
s.? *Col* 2:20
put them in mind to be *s.* *Tit* 3:1
lifetime *s.* to bondage. *Heb* 2:15
Elias was *s.* to like. *Jas* 5:17
servants, be *s.* to your. *1 Pet* 2:18
and powers being made *s.* 3:22
all of you be *s.* one to another. 5:5*

subjected
of him who hath *s.* the. *Rom* 8:20

subjection
were brought into *s.* *Ps* 106:42
brought them into *s.* *Jer* 34:11, 16
bring my body into *s.* *1 Cor* 9:27*
they glorify God for your professed *s.*
2 Cor 9:13*
to whom we give place by *s.* *Gal* 2:5
learn in silence with all *s.* *1 Tim* 2:11
having his children in *s.* with. 3:4
put in *s.* the world to come. *Heb* 2:5
put all things in *s.* under his feet. 8
rather be in *s.* to the Father of. 12:9
wives, be in *s.* to your. *1 Pet* 3:1, 5

submit
return, and *s.* thyself. *Gen* 16:9
strangers shall *s.* themselves to me.
2 Sam 22:45; *Ps* 18:44
enemies shall *s.* themselves. *Ps* 66:3
till every one *s.* himself with. 68:30
that ye *s.* yourselves. *1 Cor* 16:16

wives, s. yourselves to your own husbands. Eph 5:22; Col 3:18
s. yourselves: for they. Heb 13:17
s. yourselves therefore to God. Jas 4:7
s. yourselves to every. 1 Pet 2:13
ye younger, s. yourselves to. 5:5

submitted

the sons of David s. 1 Chr 29:24
the Lord should have s. Ps 81:15
s. to the righteousness. Rom 10:3

submitting

s. yourselves one to another in fear. Eph 5:21

suborned

then they s. men who said. Acts 6:11

subscribe

another shall with his hand s. Isa 44:5
men shall s. evidences. Jer 32:44

subscribed

I s. the evidence, and. Jer 32:10
the witnesses that s. the book. 12

substance

destroy every living s. Gen 7:4*
every living s. was destroyed. 23*
Abram took all the s. they. 12:5
their s. was great, so that they. 13:6
shall come out with great s. 15:14
cattle and their s. be ours? 34:23
his cattle and all his s. 36:6*
how the earth swallowed them up, and all the s. Deut 11:6*
bless, Lord, his s. and accept. 33:11
Levites cities for their s. Josh 14:4
were the rulers of the s. 1 Chr 27:31
the stewards over all the s. of. 28:1
they carried away all s. 2 Chr 21:17
the king's portion of his s. 31:3
God had given Hezekiah s. 32:29
bullocks, these were of king's s. 35:7
a right way for our s. Ezra 8:21
not come, all his s. should. 10:8
Job's s. also was seven. Job 1:3
his s. is increased in the land. 10
robber swalloweth up their s. 5:5
give a reward for me of your s.? 6:22
rich, nor shall his s. continue. 15:29
according to his s. shall the. 20:18
our s. is not cut down, but. 22:20*
me up and dissolvest my s. 30:22*
their s. to their babes. Ps 17:14
Joseph ruler over all his s. 105:21
my s. was not hid from thee. 139:15*
eyes did see my s. yet being. 16
we shall find all precious s. Pr 1:13
honour the Lord with thy s. and. 3:9
he shall give all the s. of his. 6:31
those that love me inherit s. 8:21
but he casteth away the s. 10:3*
but the s. of a diligent man is. 12:27
by usury increaseth his s. 28:8
with harlots, spendeth his s. 29:3
give all his s. for love. S of S 8:7
as an oak, whose s. is in them, so the holy seed shall be s. Isa 6:13*
thy s. will I give to the spoil. Jer 15:13; 17:3
I am become rich, I have found me out s. Hos 12:8*
nor laid hands on their s. Ob 13
I will consecrate their s. Mi 4:13
to him of their s. Luke 8:3
wasted his s. with riotous. 15:13
knowing that ye have in heaven a better and enduring s. Heb 10:34*
now faith is the s. of things. 11:1*

subtil

the serpent was more s. Gen 3:1*
was a very s. man. 2 Sam 13:3*
an harlot, and s. of heart. Pr 7:10*

subtilly

that he dealeth very s. 1 Sam 23:22
to deal s. with his. Ps 105:25
the same dealt s. with. Acts 7:19

subtilty

thy brother came with s. Gen 27:35*
Jehu did it in s. that. 2 Ki 10:19
to give s. to the simple. Pr 1:4
might take Jesus by s. Mat 26:4
said, O full of all s. Acts 13:10*
beguiled Eve through s. 2 Cor 11:3

suburbs

but the field of the s. may. Lev 25:34
the s. of them shall be. Num 35:3
cities shall ye give with their s. 7
save cities with s. for their cattle. Josh 14:4; 21:2
horses by chamber in s. 2 Ki 23:11*
Levites left their s. and came to Judah. 2 Chr 11:14
the s. shall shake at the. Ezek 27:28
round about for the s. thereof. 45:2
place for dwelling and for s. 48:15
the s. of the city shall be. 17
see **cities**

subvert

to s. a man in his cause. Lam 3:36
who s. whole houses. Tit 1:11*

subverted

such is s. and sinneth. Tit 3:11*

subverting

with words, s. souls. Acts 15:24
words to no profit, but to s. of. 2 Tim 2:14

succeed

the firstborn shall s. his. Deut 25:6

succeeded

but the children of Esau s. them. Deut 2:12, 22
the Ammonites s. them, and. 21

succeedest

when thou s. them in their land. Deut 12:29*; 19:1

success

then thou shalt have good s. Josh 1:8

Succoth

to S. and made booths for his cattle, therefore it is called S. Gen 33:17
from Rameses to S. Ex 12:37
they took their journey from S. 13:20; Num 33:5, 6
Gad had in the valley, S. Josh 13:27
the men of S. give bread. Judg 8:5
answered as the men of S. 8
he taught the men of S. 16
king cast them in the clay-ground between S. 1 Ki 7:46; 2 Chr 4:17
I will mete out the valley of S. Ps 60:6; 108:7

Succoth-benoth

men of Babylon made S. 2 Ki 17:30

succour

when the Syrians came to s. Hadadezer. 2 Sam 8:5
it is better that thou s. us out. 18:3
he is able to s. them. Heb 2:18

succoured

Abishai s. him, and. 2 Sam 21:17
of salvation have I s. 2 Cor 6:2

succourer

she hath been a s. of. Rom 16:2

such

Jabal was the father of s. Gen 4:20
Jubal was the father of s. as. 21
savoury meat, s. as I love. 27:4, 9, 14
wife of daughters of Heth, s. as. 46
speckled and spotted, of s. 30:32
s. as I never saw in Egypt. 41:19
wot ye not that s. a man as? 44:15
s. hail as hath not. Ex 9:18, 24
no s. locusts as they, nor shall be s. 10:14
shall be a great cry, s. as there. 11:6
thou shalt provide able men, s. 18:21
s. as have not been done in all. 34:10
s. water cometh be unclean . . . be drunk in every s. Lev 11:34
two pigeons s. as he is. 14:22, 30, 31
the soul that turneth after s. 20:6
soul that hath touched any s. 22:6
giveth of s. to the Lord, shall. 27:9
instead of s. as open. Num 8:16
hath been any s. thing. Deut 4:32
O that there were s. an heart. 5:29
shalt do no more any s. 13:11; 19:20
s. abomination is wrought. 14; 17:4
s. time as thou beginnest. 16:9
at least s. as before knew. Judg 3:2
was no s. deed done or seen. 19:30
hath not been s. a thing. 1 Sam 4:7
he is s. a son of Belial. 1 Sam 25:17
look on s. a dead dog as I. 2 Sam 9:8
with s. robes were the virgins. 13:18
hast thou thought s. a thing? 14:13
s. as faint in wilderness. 16:2
recompense me with s.? 19:36
came no more s. abundance of spices. 1 Ki 10:10
no s. almug trees. 12; 2 Chr 9:11
thou pass not s. a place. 2 Ki 6:9
windows, might s. a thing be? 7:19
bringing s. evil on Jerusalem. 21:12
surely there was not holden s. 23:22
s. as went forth to. 1 Chr 12:33, 36
the Lord bestowed on him s. 29:25
s. as none of the kings. 2 Chr 1:12
nor was any s. spice as the. 9:9
s. as set their hearts to seek. 11:16
people rejoiced, and s. taught. 23:13
gave it to s. as did the work. 24:12
done it of a long time in s. sort. 30:5
and at s. a time. Ezra 4:10, 11, 17
7:12
all s. as had separated. 6:21
all s. as know the laws of. 7:25
which hath put s. a thing in. 27
and of s. as lay in wait by. 8:31
and hast given s. deliverance. 9:13
put away the wives, and s. are. 10:3
I said, Should s. a man? Neh 6:11
except s. to whom the king shall. Esth 4:11
the kingdom for s. a time. 14
to lay hand on s. as sought. 9:2
and upon all s. as joined 27
and lettest s. words go. Job 15:13
surely s. are the dwellings. 18:21
to s. as keep his covenant. Ps 25:10
103:18
and s. as breathe out cruelty. 27:12
to slay s. as be of upright. 37:14
s. as be blessed of him shall. 22
respecteth not proud nor s. 40:4
let s. as love thy salvation. 16; 70:4
his hands against s. as be at. 55:20
God is good to s. as are of. 73:1
s. as sit in darkness, and. 107:10
as for s. as turn aside to. 125:5
s. knowledge is too. 139:6
people that is in s. a case. 144:15
but s. as are upright. Pr 11:20
but s. as keep the law contend. 28:4
in cause of s. as are appointed. 31:8
behold, the tears of s. as. Eccl 4:1
dimness shall not be s. as. Isa 9:1
s. as are escaped of the. 10:20
behold, s. is our expectation. 20:6
eat this year s. as groweth. 37:30
is it s. a fast that I have? 58:5
s. a thing? who hath seen s.? 66:8
see if there be s. a thing. Jer 2:10
my soul be avenged on s. a nation. 5:9, 29; 9:9
s. as are for death, to death, s. as are for sword, s. as are for famine, s. as are for captivity. 15:2; 43:11
I will deliver s. as are left in. 21:7
in speaking s. words unto them. 38:4
for none shall return, but s. as. 44:14
s. as had ability in them. Dan 1:4
had spoken s. words to me. 10:15
s. as do wickedly shall be. 11:32
shall be a time of trouble, s. 12:1
shall call s. as are skilful. Amos 5:16
in anger and fury, s. they. Mi 5:15
s. as are clothed with. Zeph 1:8
glorified God who had given s. power to men. Mat 9:8
receive one s. little child in my name. 18:5; Mark 9:37
suffer little children to come unto me, for of s. Mat 19:14; Mark 10:14
Luke 18:16
then shall be great tribulation, s. as. Mat 24:21; Mark 13:19
in s. an hour as ye think. Mat 24:44
he said, Go into the city to s. a man. 26:18
sown among thorns, s. as. Mark 4:18
ground, are s. as hear the word. 20
with many s. parables spake he. 33
for the Father seeketh s. John 4:23
Moses commanded that s. 8:5
is a sinner do s. miracles? 9:16

the Lord added daily *s.* as should be saved. *Acts* 2:47
s. as I have give I thee, rise. 3:6
to whom we gave no *s.* 15:24
who having received *s.* a 16:24
will be no judge of *s.* matters. 18:15
that they observe no *s.* thing. 21:25
Away with *s.* a fellow from. 22:22
I doubted of *s.* manner of. 25:20
and altogether *s.* as I am. 26:29
that are *s.* serve not. *Rom* 16:18
s. fornication as is not. *1 Cor* 5:1
and *s.* were some of you, but. 6:11
is not under bondage in *s.* cases. 7:15
s. shall have trouble in the flesh. 28
no temptation, but *s.* as is. 10:13
we have no *s.* custom. 11:16
s. are they that are earthy, *s.* 15:48
that ye submit yourselves to *s.* 16:16
acknowledge ye them that are *s.* 18
sufficient to *s.* a man is. *2 Cor* 2:6
s. trust we have through Christ. 3:4
seeing then that we have *s.* hope. 12
let *s.* an one think, *s.* as we are in word by letters, *s.* will we. 10:11
for *s.* are false apostles. 11:13
not find you *s.* as I would; and that I shall be found to you *s.* as. 12:20
meekness, against *s.* *Gal* 5:23
spot or wrinkle, or any *s.* *Eph* 5:27
receive him, and hold *s.* *Phil* 2:29
is the avenger of all *s.* *1 Thes* 4:6
now them that are *s.* *2 Thes* 3:12
corrupt men, from *s.* *1 Tim* 6:5
traitors, heady, from *s.* *2 Tim* 3:5
he that is *s.* is subverted. *Tit* 3:11
ye are become *s.* as have. *Heb* 5:12
s. an high priest became us. 7:26
have *s.* an high priest, who is. 8:1
endured *s.* contradiction of. 12:3
for with *s.* sacrifices God is. 13:16
we will go into *s.* a city. *Jas* 4:13
all *s.* rejoicing is evil. 16
came *s.* a voice to him. *2 Pet* 1:17
we ought to receive *s.* *3 John* 8
s. as are in the sea. *Rev* 5:13
s. as was not since men were. 16:18
on *s.* the second death hath. 20:6

such *like*

and doeth not *s. like.* *Ezek* 18:14
revellings and *s. like.* *Gal* 5:21

such *a one*

find *s. a one* as this is. *Gen* 41:38
ho, *s. a one,* turn aside. *Ruth* 4:1
open thine eyes on *s. a one*? *Job* 14:3
I was *s. a one* as thyself. *Ps* 50:21
hairy scalp of *s. a one* as. 68:21
to deliver *s. an one.* *1 Cor* 5:5
if a drunkard, with *s. an one.* 11
s. a one be swallowed up. *2 Cor* 2:7
let *s. an one* think this, that. 10:11
s. an one caught up to the. 12:2
of *s. an one* will I glory, yet. 5
restore *s. an one* in the. *Gal* 6:1
I beseech thee, being *s. an one* as Paul. *Philem* 9

such *and* **such**

appointed my servants to *s. and s.* place. *1 Sam* 21:2
given *s. and s.* things. *2 Sam* 12:8
in *s. and s.* a place shall. *2 Ki* 6:8

such *things*

they lent *s. things* as. *Ex* 12:36
s. things have befallen. *Lev* 10:19
they that do *s. things.* *Deut* 25:16
nor have told us *s. things* as these. *Judg* 13:23
Why do ye *s. things*? *1 Sam* 2:23
shall eat *s. things* as. *2 Ki* 19:29
the captain took *s. things* as. 25:15
there are no *s. things* done as thou. *Neh* 6:8
with *s. things* as belonged. *Esth* 2:9
yea, who knoweth not *s. things* as? *Job* 12:3
I have heard many *s. things.* 16:2
and many *s. things* are with. 23:14
who hath heard *s. things.* *Jer* 18:13
shall he escape that doth *s. things*? *Ezek* 17:15
no king asked *s. things.* *Dan* 2:10
many other *s.* like *things* ye do. *Mark* 7:8, 13
troubled, *s. things* must. *Mark* 13:7
of whom I hear *s.* things? *Luke* 9:9
remain, eating *s. things* as. 10:7, 8
but give alms of *s. things.* 11:41
because they suffered *s. things.* 13:2
the people murmured *s. things.* *John* 7:32
no accusation of *s. things.* *Acts* 25:18
they laded us with *s. things* as. 28:10
who commit *s. things* are. *Rom* 1:32
them who commit *s. things.* 2:2
judgest them which do *s. things.* 3
that do *s. things* shall not inherit. *Gal* 5:21
they that say *s. things.* *Heb* 11:14
be content with *s. things* as. 13:5
that ye look for *s. things.* *2 Pet* 3:14

suck

made him to *s.* honey. *Deut* 32:13
shall *s.* of the abundance of. 33:19
breast that I should *s.*? *Job* 3:12
he shall *s.* the poison of asps. 20:16
young ones also *s.* up blood. 39:30
shalt *s.* the milk of the Gentiles, and shalt *s.* the breast of. *Isa* 60:16
that ye may *s.* and be satisfied. 66:11
then shall ye *s.*, ye shall be borne. 12
drink it and *s.* it out. *Ezek* 23:34*
and those that *s.* breasts. *Joel* 2:16

suck, *give*

that Sarah should have given children *s.* *Gen* 21:7
Hannah abode and gave her son *s.* *1 Sam* 1:23
to give my child *s.* *1 Ki* 3:21
the sea monsters give *s.* *Lam* 4:3
and to them that give *s.* *Mat* 24:19
Mark 13:17; *Luke* 21:23
paps that never gave *s.* *Luke* 23:29

sucked

that *s.* the breasts of. *S of S* 8:1
paps that thou hast *s.* *Luke* 11:27

sucking

nursing father beareth the *s.* child. *Num* 11:12
Samuel took a *s.* lamb. *1 Sam* 7:9
s. child shall play on the. *Isa* 11:8
woman forget her *s.* child? 49:15
tongue of the *s.* child. *Lam* 4:4

suckling

the *s.* also with the man. *Deut* 32:25
slay both man and woman, infant and *s.* *1 Sam* 15:3
off from you child and *s.* *Jer* 44:7

sucklings

children and *s.* of Nob. *1 Sam* 22:19
out of the mouth of babes and *s.* *Ps* 8:2; *Mat* 21:16
s. swoon in the streets. *Lam* 2:11

sudden

s. fear troubleth thee. *Job* 22:10
be not afraid of *s.* fear. *Pr* 3:25
s. destruction cometh. *1 Thes* 5:3

suddenly

man die very *s.* by him. *Num* 6:9
the Lord spake *s.* unto Moses. 12:4
but if he thrust him *s.* without. 35:22
Lord will destroy you *s.* *Deut* 7:4*
Joshua came unto them *s.* *Josh* 10:9; 11:7
lest he overtake us *s.* *2 Sam* 15:14*
the thing was done *s.* *2 Chr* 29:36
taking root, but *s.* I cursed. *Job* 5:3
scourge slay *s.* he will laugh. 9:23
return and be ashamed *s.* *Ps* 6:10
s. do they shoot at him and. 64:4
with an arrow *s.* shall they be. 7
therefore his calamity shall come *s.*; he shall be broken *s.* *Pr* 6:15
calamity shall rise *s.* 24:22
shall *s.* be destroyed, and. 29:1
it falleth *s.* upon them. *Eccl* 9:12
it shall be at an instant *s.* *Isa* 29:5
whose breaking cometh *s.* 30:13
shall come upon thee *s.* 47:11
I did them *s.* and they came. 48:3
s. are my tents spoiled. *Jer* 4:20
spoiler shall *s.* come upon us. 6:26
caused him to fall upon it *s.* 15:8
bring a troop *s.* on them. 18:22
s. make him run away. 49:19; 50:44
Babylon is *s.* fallen and. *Jer* 51:8
shall they not rise up *s.* *Hab* 2:7
the Lord shall *s.* come. *Mal* 3:1
s. saw no man any more. *Mark* 9:8
lest coming *s.* he find you. 13:36
s. there was with angel. *Luke* 2:13
a spirit taketh him, and he *s.* 9:39
and *s.* there came a sound. *Acts* 2:2
s. there shined a light. 9:3; 22:6
and *s.* there was a great. 16:26
should have fallen down dead *s.* 28:6
lay hands *s.* on no man. *1 Tim* 5:22*

sue

if any man will *s.* thee. *Mat* 5:40*

suffer

This word frequently means [1] bear, Pr 19:19; [2] bear with, Mat 17:17; [3] permit, 1 Tim 2:12.

s. the destroyer to come. *Ex* 12:23
thou shalt not *s.* a witch to. 22:18
nor shalt *s.* salt of the covenant to. *Lev* 2:13
shalt rebuke him, and not *s.* 19:17
or *s.* them to bear the iniquity. 22:16*
not *s.* Israel to pass. *Num* 21:23
s. them not to enter. *Josh* 10:19
not *s.* them to come down to the valley. *Judg* 1:34
would not *s.* him to go in. 15:1
Samson said, *S.* me that I. 16:26
not *s.* the revengers of blood any. *2 Sam* 14:11*
that he might not *s.* *1 Ki* 15:17
king's profit to *s.* them. *Esth* 3:8
he will not *s.* me to take. *Job* 9:18
s. me that I may speak, after. 21:3
winepresses, and *s.* thirst. 24:11
s. me a little, and I will shew. 32:2
trouble which I *s.* of them. *Ps* 9:13
neither *s.* thine Holy One to see corruption. 16:10; *Acts* 2:27; 13:35
young lions do lack and *s.* *Ps* 34:10
he will never *s.* the righteous. 55:22
while I *s.* thy terrors, I am. 88:15
nor *s.* my faithfulness to. 89:33
a proud heart will not I *s.* 101:5
he will not *s.* thy foot to be. 121:3
s. the soul of righteous to. *Pr* 10:3
an idle soul shall *s.* hunger. 19:15
man of wrath shall *s.* punishment. 19*
s. not thy mouth to cause. *Eccl* 5:6
rich not *s.* him to sleep. 12
nor *s.* their locks to. *Ezek* 44:20
S. it to be so now. *Mat* 3:15
s. me first to bury my father. 8:21
Luke 9:59
s. us to go away into the swine. *Mat* 8:31; *Luke* 8:32
that he must *s.* many things of the elders. *Mat* 16:21; 17:12
Mark 8:31; 9:12; *Luke* 9:22; 17:25
how long shall I *s.* you? *Mat* 17:17*
Mark 9:19*; *Luke* 9:41*
s. little children to come. *Mat* 19:14
Mark 10:14; *Luke* 18:16
neither *s.* ye them that. *Mat* 23:13
ye *s.* him no more to do. *Mark* 7:12
Jesus would not *s.* any man to. 11:16
desired to eat this passover before I *s.* *Luke* 22:15
s. ye thus far, and he touched his. 51
it behoved Christ to *s.* 24:46
Acts 3:18; 26:23
that Christ should *s.* *Acts* 3:18
counted worthy to *s.* shame. 5:41
seeing one of them *s.* wrong. 7:24
how great things he must *s.* for. 9:16
beseech thee, *s.* me to speak. 21:39*
if so be that we *s.* with. *Rom* 8:17
if any man's work be burnt, he shall *s.* loss. *1 Cor* 3:15
bless; being persecuted, we *s.* 4:12*
why not rather *s.* yourselves? 6:7
not used this power but *s.* 9:12*
will not *s.* you to be tempted. 10:13
one member *s.* all members *s.* 12:26
sufferings which we also *s.* *2 Cor* 1:6
for ye *s.* fools gladly, seeing. 11:19*
for ye *s.* if a man bring you. 20*
if I preach, why do I yet *s.*? *Gal* 5:11*
lest they should *s.* persecution. 6:12
to believe and to *s.* for. *Phil* 1:29
to abound and to *s.* need. 4:12*

before, that we should *s.* *1 Thes* 3:4
God for which ye also *s.* *2 Thes* 1:5
I *s.* not a woman to teach nor to. *1 Tim* 2:12*
we both labour and *s.* 4:10*
I also *s.* these things. *2 Tim* 1:12
wherein I *s.* trouble as an evil. 2:9
if we *s.* we shall also reign. 12*
all that live godly shall *s.* 3:12
rather to *s.* affliction. *Heb* 11:25*
remember them which *s.* 13:3*
s. the word of exhortation. 22*
ye do well, and *s.* for it. *1 Pet* 2:20
but if ye *s.* for righteousness. 3:14
it is better that ye *s.* for well. 17
none of you *s.* as a murderer. 4:15
yet if any man *s.* as a Christian. 16
let them that *s.* according to the. 19
those things thou shalt *s.* *Rev* 2:10
not *s.* dead bodies to be put. 11:9

suffered

s. I thee not to touch her. *Gen* 20:6
God *s.* him not to hurt me. 31:7
and hast not *s.* me to kiss my. 28
and *s.* thee to hunger. *Deut* 8:3
God hath not *s.* thee so to do. 18:14
s. not a man to pass over. *Judg* 3:28
David *s.* them not to rise. *1 Sam* 24:7
and *s.* not the birds. *2 Sam* 21:10
he *s.* no man to do them wrong. *1 Chr* 16:21; *Ps* 105:14
neither have I *s.* my. *Job* 31:30
for thy sake I *s.* rebuke. *Jer* 15:15
it to be so; then he *s.* him. *Mat* 3:15
Moses *s.* you to put away your. 19:8
nor *s.* his house to be broken. 24:43 *Luke* 12:39
I have *s.* many things. *Mat* 27:19
he *s.* not the devils to speak. *Mark* 1:34; *Luke* 4:41
howbeit, Jesus *s.* him not. *Mark* 5:19
s. many things of many. 26
and he *s.* no man to follow him. 37
Moses *s.* to write a bill of. 10:4
he *s.* them to enter. *Luke* 8:32*
he *s.* no man to go in, save. 51
were sinners, because they *s.* 13:2
Christ have *s.* these things? 24:26
about forty years *s.* he. *Acts* 13:18†
who *s.* all nations to walk in. 14:16
but the Spirit *s.* them not. 16:7
Christ must needs have *s.* 17:3
disciples *s.* him not to enter. 19:30
Paul was *s.* to dwell by. 28:16
his cause that *s.* wrong. *2 Cor* 7:12
thrice I *s.* shipwreck. 11:25
s. so many things in vain? *Gal* 3:4
for whom I have *s.* the loss. *Phil* 3:8
that we had *s.* before. *1 Thes* 2:2
ye have *s.* like things of your. 14
himself hath *s.* being tempted. *Heb* 2:18
obedience by things which he *s.* 5:8
they were not *s.* to continue. 7:23*
for then must he often have *s.* 9:26
Jesus also *s.* without the gate. 13:12
Christ *s.* for us, leaving. *1 Pet* 2:21
when he *s.* he threatened not. 23
for Christ hath once *s.* for sins. 3:18
as Christ hath *s.* for us in the flesh: he that hath *s.* in the flesh. 4:1
after ye have *s.* a while. 5:10

sufferest

s. that woman Jezebel. *Rev* 2:20

suffereth

bless God who *s.* not our. *Ps* 66:9
and *s.* not their cattle to. 107:38
of heaven *s.* violence. *Mat* 11:12
yet vengeance *s.* him. *Acts* 28:4
charity *s.* long and is kind, envieth not. *1 Cor* 13:4

suffering

wind not *s.* us, we sailed. *Acts* 27:7
s. of death, crowned. *Heb* 2:9
for an example of *s.* affliction, and of patience. *Jas* 5:10
if a man endure grief, *s.* *1 Pet* 2:19
an example, *s.* the vengeance. *Jude* 7

sufferings

I reckon that the *s.* of. *Rom* 8:18
for as the *s.* of Christ. *2 Cor* 1:5
enduring the same *s.* which we. 6
ye are partakers of the *s.* *2 Cor* 1:7
the fellowship of his *s.* *Phil* 3:10
who now rejoice in my *s.* *Col* 1:24
make the captain of their salvation perfect through *s.* *Heb* 2:10
the *s.* of Christ, and the. *1 Pet* 1:11
ye are partakers of Christ's *s.* 4:13
am a witness of the *s.* of Christ. 5:1

suffice

to *s.* them? or shall fish of the sea be gathered together to *s.*? *Num* 11:22
let it *s.* thee; speak no. *Deut* 3:26
if dust of Samaria shall *s.* for. *1 Ki* 20:10
let it *s.* you of all. *Ezek* 44:6; 45:9
may *s.* to have wrought. *1 Pet* 4:3

sufficed

yet so they *s.* them not. *Judg* 21:14
she did eat, and was *s.* *Ruth* 2:14
she had reserved, after she was *s.* 18

sufficeth

us the Father and it *s.* us. *John* 14:8

sufficiency

in fulness of his *s.* he shall. *Job* 20:22
sufficient, but our *s.* is of. *2 Cor* 3:5
s. in all things ye may abound. 9:8

sufficient

had was *s.* for work. *Ex* 36:7
thou shalt lend him *s.* *Deut* 15:8
let his hand be *s.* for him, thou. 33:7
honey as is *s.* for thee. *Pr* 25:16
Lebanon is not *s.* to burn, nor the beasts thereof *s.* for. *Isa* 40:16
s. unto the day is the evil. *Mat* 6:34
whether he have *s.* to. *Luke* 14:28
200 penny-worth of bread is not *s.* *John* 6:7
s. to such a man is this. *2 Cor* 2:6
who is *s.* for these things? 16
not that we are *s.* of ourselves. 3:5
he said to me, My grace is *s.* 12:9

sufficiently

sanctified themselves *s.* *2 Chr* 30:3
before the Lord to eat *s.* *Isa* 23:18

suit

give thee a *s.* of apparel. *Judg* 17:10
man who hath any *s.* *2 Sam* 15:4
yea, many shall make *s.* *Job* 11:19

suits

changeable *s.* of apparel. *Isa* 3:22*

sum

there be laid on him a *s.* *Ex* 21:30*
takest the *s.* of the children of. 30:12
this is the *s.* of the tabernacle. 38:21
take the *s.* of all the. *Num* 1:2; 26:2
not take the *s.* of the Levites. 49
s. of the sons of Kohath. 4:2
the *s.* of the sons of Gershon. 22
s. of people from twenty years. 26:4
take the *s.* of the prey that. 31:26
have taken the *s.* of the men. 49
Joab gave up the *s.* unto the king. *2 Sam* 24:9; *1 Chr* 21:5
may *s.* the silver brought. *2 Ki* 22:4
the *s.* of money that. *Esth* 4:7*
how great is the *s.* of! *Ps* 139:17
thou sealest up the *s.* full of wisdom. *Ezek* 28:12
Daniel told the *s.* of the. *Dan* 7:1
Abraham bought for a *s.* *Acts* 7:16*
with a great *s.* obtained I. 22:28
we have spoken this is the *s.* *Heb* 8:1

summer

s. and winter, day and. *Gen* 8:22
turned into drought of *s.* *Ps* 32:4
hast made *s.* and winter. 74:17
her meat in *s.* *Pr* 6:8; 30:25
he that gathereth in *s.* is a. 10:5
as snow in *s.* and as rain in. 26:1
the fowls shall *s.* upon. *Isa* 18:6
hasty fruit before the *s.* 28:4
the harvest is past, the *s.* *Jer* 8:20
as the chaff of the *s.* *Dan* 2:35
in *s.* and in winter shall. *Zech* 14:8
leaves, ye know that *s.* is. *Mat* 24:32 *Mark* 13:28; *Luke* 21:30

summer *chamber*

surely he covereth his feet in his *s.* *chamber.* *Judg* 3:24†

summer *fruit*

bread and *s. fruit* for. *2 Sam* 16:2
a basket of *s. fruit.* *Amos* 8:1, 2

summer *fruits*

Ziba brought 100 bunches of *s. fruits.* *2 Sam* 16:1
shouting for thy *s. fruits.* *Isa* 16:9
wine and *s. fruits.* *Jer* 40:10, 12
fallen on *s. fruits* and vintage. 48:32
have gathered *s. fruits.* *Mi* 7:1

summer *house*

I will smite winter house with *s. house.* *Amos* 3:15

summer *parlour*

sitting in a *s. parlour.* *Judg* 3:20†

sumptuously

fared *s.* every day. *Luke* 16:19

sun

(*The* sun *has been the object of worship and adoration to the greatest part of the people of the East. It is thought to be the sun that the Phenicians worshipped under the name of* Baal, *the Moabites under the name of Chemosh, the Ammonites by that of Moloch, and the Israelites by the name of Baal and by* the king of the host of heaven. *They did not separate his worship from that of the moon, whom they called* Astarte, *and the* queen of heaven)

when the *s.* went down. *Gen* 15:17
the *s.* was risen when Lot. 19:23
all night, because the *s.* was. 28:11
passed over Penuel, *s.* rose. 32:31
the *s.* moon, and stars made. 37:9
and when the *s.* waxed. *Ex* 16:21
if *s.* be risen, blood shall be. 22:3
and when the *s.* is down, he shall. *Lev* 22:7; *Deut* 23:11
before the Lord against the *s.* *Num* 25:4
seest the *s.* and moon. *Deut* 4:19
worshipped either the *s.* or. 17:3
shall the *s.* go down upon it. 24:15
fruits brought forth by *s.* 33:14
the going down of the *s.* *Josh* 1:4
as soon as the *s.* was down. 8:29
S. stand thou still upon. 10:12
and the *s.* stood still, and the. 13
as the *s.* when he goeth. *Judg* 5:31
Gideon returned before the *s.* 8:13*
as soon as the *s.* is up, thou. 9:33
they said to him before the *s.* 14:18
s. went down when they were. 19:14
by time the *s.* be hot. *1 Sam* 11:9
the *s.* went down, they. *2 Sam* 2:24
if taste bread or aught till the *s.* 3:35
thy wives in sight of this *s.* 12:11
this thing before Israel and the *s.* 12
morning when the *s.* riseth. 23:4
they rose, and *s.* shone. *2 Ki* 3:22
also that burn incense to *s.* 23:5
burnt the chariot of the *s.* with fire. 11
opened till the *s.* be hot. *Neh* 7:3
is green before the *s.* *Job* 8:16
which commandeth the *s.* 9:7
I went mourning without the *s.* 30:28
if I beheld *s.* when it shined. 31:26
he set a tabernacle for *s.* *Ps* 19:4
they may not see the *s.* 58:8
shall fear thee as long as *s.* 72:5
be continued as long as the *s.* 17
prepared the light and the *s.* 74:16
for the Lord God is a *s.* 84:11
throne shall endure as the *s.* 89:36
the *s.* ariseth, they gather. 104:22
s. shall not smite thee by day. 121:6
made the *s.* to rule by day. 136:8
praise ye him, *s.* and moon. 148:3
s. also ariseth, and the *s.* *Eccl* 1:5
he hath not seen the *s.* nor. 6:5
profit to them that see the *s.* 7:11
for the eyes to behold the *s.* 11:7
while the *s.* or the stars be. 12:2
s. hath looked upon me. *S of S* 1:6
fair as moon, clear as the *s.* 6:10
the *s.* shall be ashamed. *Isa* 24:23
moon shall be as the light of the *s.* and the light of the *s.* 30:26
gone down in *s.* dial, so the *s.* 38:8

nor shall the heat, nor s. Isa 49:10
s. shall be no more thy light. 60:19
s. shall no more go down, nor. 20
spread them before the s. Jer 8:2
her s. is gone down while it. 15:9
which giveth the s. for a light. 31:35
they worshipped the s. Ezek 8:16
cover the s. with a cloud. 32:7
s. and the moon shall be darkened.
Joel 2:10; 3:15; Mat 24:29
Mark 13:24; Luke 23:45
s. shall be turned into. Joel 2:31
I will cause the s. to go. Amos 8:9
s. did arise, and the s. beat on the head of Jonah. Jonah 4:8
the s. shall go down. Mi 3:6
but when the s. ariseth. Nah 3:17
s. and moon stood still. Hab 3:11
s. of righteousness arise. Mal 4:2
he maketh his s. to rise. Mat 5:45
when s. was up they were scorched.
13:6; Mark 4:6
righteous shine as the s. Mat 13:43
his face did shine as the s. 17:2
Rev 1:16; 10:1
when the s. did set they. Mark 1:32
when the s. was setting. Luke 4:40
shall be signs in the s. and. 21:25
the s. into darkness. Acts 2:20
blind, not seeing the s. for. 13:11
above the brightness of the s. 26:13
neither s. nor stars appeared. 27:20
is one glory of the s. 1 Cor 15:41
let not the s. go down. Eph 4:26
s. is no sooner risen. Jas 1:11
the s. became black as. Rev 6:12
nor shall the s. light on them. 7:16
third part of the s. was. 8:12
s. and the air were darkened. 9:2
a woman clothed with the s. 12:1
poured out his vial on the s. 16:8
angel standing in the s.; and he. 19:17
had no need of the s. 21:23; 22:5
see **goeth, going, rising**

under the **sun**

labour which he taketh under the s.?
Eccl 1:3; 2:18, 19, 20, 22; 5:18; 9:9
no new thing under the s. 1:9
all the works done under s.; all is vanity. 14; 2:17; 4:3; 8:17; 9:3
was no profit under the s. 2:11
I saw under the s. the place. 3:16
that are done under the s. 4:1
and I saw vanity under the s. 7
a sore evil I have seen under the s.
5:13; 6:1; 10:5
shall be after him under the s. 6:12
heart to every work under the s. 8:9
hath no better thing under the s. 15
in any thing under the s. 9:6
he hath given thee under the s. 9
I saw under the s. that race. 11
wisdom have I seen also under s. 13

sunder

cutteth the spear in s. Ps 46:9
he brake their bands in s. 107:14
cut the bars of iron in s. 16
stones that are beaten in s. Isa 27:9
I will cut in s. the bars of iron. 45:2
I will burst thy bonds in s. Nah 1:13
come and cut him in s. Luke 12:46

sundered

scales stick together, they cannot be s. Job 41:17

sundry

God who at s. times. Heb 1:1*

sung

they s. together by course. Ezra 3:11
day shall this song be s. Isa 26:1
when they had s. an hymn, they went.
Mat 26:30; Mark 14:26
they s. a new song, saying. Rev 5:9
they s. as it were a new song. 14:3

sunk

that the stone s. into. 1 Sam 17:49
and Jehoram s. down. 2 Ki 9:24
heathen are s. down in. Ps 9:15
no water, but mire: so Jeremiah s.
Jer 38:6
thy feet are s. in the mire, they. 22
her gates are s. into the. Lam 2:9
Eutychus s. down with. Acts 20:9*

sup

their faces shall s. up. Hab 1:9*
ready wherewith I may s. Luke 17:8
I will s. with him, and he. Rev 3:20

superfluity

lay apart all filthiness, s. Jas 1:21*

superfluous

man hath any thing s. Lev 21:18
lamb that hath any thing s. 22:23
the ministering, it is s. 2 Cor 9:1

superscription

(It was a custom among the Romans to write on a board the crime for which any man suffered death and to carry the board before him to execution)

is this image and s.? Mat 22:20
Mark 12:16; Luke 20:24
the s. of his accusation. Mark 15:26
Luke 23:38

superstition

questions against him of their own s.
Acts 25:19*

superstitious

in all things ye are too s. Acts 17:22*

supped

cup, when he had s. 1 Cor 11:25

supper

made a s. to his lords. Mark 6:21
makest a dinner or s. Luke 14:12
a certain man made a great s. 16
and sent his servant at s. time. 17
none bidden shall taste of my s. 24
likewise also the cup after s. 22:20
there they made Jesus a s.; Martha served. John 12:2
and s. being ended. 13:2
Jesus riseth from s. 4
leaned on his breast at s. 21:20
not to eat the Lord's s. 1 Cor 11:20
taketh before other his own s. 21
called to the marriage s. Rev 19:9
come to the s. of the great God. 17

supplant

brother will utterly s. Jer 9:4

supplanted

for he hath s. me these. Gen 27:36

supple

washed in water to s. Ezek 16:4*

suppliants

my s. shall bring mine. Zeph 3:10

supplication

and I have not made s. 1 Sam 13:12*
have respect to his s. 1 Ki 8:28
2 Chr 6:19
hearken thou to the s. 1 Ki 8:30
45:49; 2 Chr 6:35
and make s. to thee. 1 Ki 8:33, 47
2 Chr 6:24
eyes may be open to s. 1 Ki 8:52
praying all this prayer and s. 54
wherewith I have made s. 59
I have heard thy s. that thou. 9:3
what s. shall be made. 2 Chr 6:29
heard Manasseh's s. then. 33:13
and should make s. to. Esth 4:8
make thy s. to the Almighty. Job 8:5
make my s. to my judge. 9:15
heard my s.; receive my. Ps 6:9
Lord I made my s. 30:8; 142:1
hide not thyself from my s. 55:1
let my s. come before thee. 119:170
they shall make s. to thee. Isa 45:14
will present their s. to Lord. Jer 36:7
O king, let my s. be accepted. 37:20
I presented my s. before the. 38:26
let our s. be accepted before. 42:2
me to present your s. before. 9
and Daniel making s. Dan 6:11
while I was presenting my s. 9:20
he wept and made s. unto. Hos 12:4
accord in prayer and s. Acts 1:14*
with all prayer and s. in spirit for.
Eph 6:18
by prayer and s. let Phil 4:6

supplications

hearken to s. of thy. 2 Chr 6:21
their prayer and their s. 39
leviathan make many s.? Job 41:3
hear voice of my s. when I cry.
Ps 28:2; 140:6
because he hath heard the voice of my s. 28:6; 31:22; 116:1
attend to the voice of my s. 86:6
be attentive to my s. 130:2; 143:1
weeping and s. of Israel. Jer 3:21
come with weeping and with s. 31:9
to seek by prayer and s. Dan 9:3
prayer of thy servant and his s. 17
we do not present our s. for. 18
at the beginning of thy s. the. 23
the Spirit of grace and s. Zech 12:10
the first of all s. be made. 1 Tim 2:1
she continueth in s. and prayers. 5:5
offered up prayers and s. Heb 5:7

supplied

your part, they have s. 1 Cor 16:17
what was lacking to me, the brethren s. 2 Cor 11:9

supplieth

not only s. the want of. 2 Cor 9:12*
that which every joint s. Eph 4:16

supply, *substantive*

a s. for their want, that their abundance be a s. for your. 2 Cor 8:14
through prayer and the s. Phil 1:19

supply, *verb*

his life to s. lack of service. Phil 2:30
but my God shall s. all your. 4:19

support

ye ought to s. the weak. Acts 20:35*
1 Thes 5:14

suppose

let not my lord s. that. 2 Sam 13:32
I s. that he to whom. Luke 7:43
s. ye that I am come to give? 12:51
s. ye that these Galileans? 13:2
I s. the world could not. John 21:25
not drunken, as ye s. Acts 2:15
I s. that this is good. 1 Cor 7:26
I s. I was not behind. 2 Cor 11:5
sorer punishment s. ye? Heb 10:29
a faithful brother, as I s. 1 Pet 5:12

supposed

they s. they should have. Mat 20:10
s. it had been a spirit. Mark 6:49
Jesus being, as was s. Luke 3:23
terrified and s. that they. 24:37
for he s. his brethren. Acts 7:25
whom they s. that Paul had. 21:29
acusation of such things as I s. 25:18
I s. it necessary to send. Phil 2:25

supposing

they s. him to have been. Luke 2:44
she s. him to be the gardener, saith.
John 20:15
who drew Paul out, s. Acts 14:19
jailor s. that the prisoners. 16:27
s. that they had obtained. 27:13
s. to add affliction to my. Phil 1:16
men of corrupt minds, s. 1 Tim 6:5

supreme

it be to the king as s. 1 Pet 2:13

sure

cave, were made s. Gen 23:17, 20
I am s. the king will. Ex 3:19
and be s. your sin. Num 32:23
only be s. that thou eat. Deut 12:23
build him a s. house. 1 Sam 2:35
s. that evil is determined by. 20:7
will make my Lord a s. house. 25:28
because I was s. that. 2 Sam 1:10
ordered in all things and s. 23:5
build thee a s. house. 1 Ki 11:38
we make a s. covenant. Neh 9.38
no man is s. of life. Job 24:22
testimony of the Lord is s. Ps 19:7
thy testimonies are very s. 93:5
all his commandments are s. 111:7
and make s. thy friend. Pr 6:3
that hateth suretiship, is s. 11:15
righteousness shall be s. reward. 18
as a nail in a s. place. Isa 22:23, 25
I lay in Zion for a s. 28:16
my people shall dwell in s. 32:18
given him; waters shall be s. 33:16
even the s. mercies of David. 55:3
Acts 13:34
interpretation thereof is s. Dan 2:45
thy kingdom shall be s. unto. 4:26

sepulchre be made *s.* *Mat* 27:64, 66
your way, make it as *s.* as you. 65
be *s.* of this, that the kingdom of God
is come nigh. *Luke* 10:11
believe and are *s.* that. *John* 6:69
we are *s.* that thou knowest. 16:30
s. that the judgement of. *Rom* 2:2
to end the promise might be *s.* 4:16
I am *s.* that when I come. 15:29
of God standeth *s.* *2 Tim* 2:19
hope we have as anchor *s.* *Heb* 6:19
to make your calling *s.* *2 Pet* 1:10
we have also a more *s.* word. 19

surely

eatest thereof, thou shalt *s.* die. *Gen* 2:17
the woman, Ye shall not *s.* die. 3:4
and *s.* your blood of your lives. 9:5
Abraham shall *s.* become a. 18:18
her not, thou shalt *s.* die. 20:7
s. the fear of God is not in. 11
Jacob said, *S.* Lord is in this. 28:16
I will *s.* give the tenth unto. 22
Laban said, *S.* thou art my. 29:14
s. the Lord hath looked upon. 32
come in unto me, for *s.* I. 30:16
s. thou hadst sent me away. 31:42
and thou saidst, I will *s.* do. 32:12
s. ye are spies. 42:16
s. now we had returned this. 43:10
s. he is torn in pieces. 44:28
and I will also *s.* bring thee. 46:4
I die, God will *s.* visit you. 50:24
25; *Ex* 13:19
S. this thing is known. *Ex* 2:14
I have *s.* seen the affliction. 3:7, 16
she said, *S.* a bloody husband. 4:25
he shall *s.* thrust you out hence. 11:1
thou wilt *s.* wear away, thou. 18:18
but he shall *s.* be stoned. 19:13
he shall be *s.* punished. 21:20, 22
then the ox shall be *s.* stoned. 28
he shall *s.* pay ox for ox, dead. 36
he that kindleth fire shall *s.* 22:6
if it be hurt or die, he shall *s.* 14
if lie with her, he shall *s.* endow. 16
to me, I will *s.* hear their cry. 23
thou shalt *s.* bring it back to. 23:4
if thou see, thou shalt *s.* help. 5
if thou serve their gods, it will *s.* be a snare. 33; *1 Ki* 11:2
anointing shall *s.* be an. *Ex* 40:15
s. it floweth with milk. *Num* 13:27
s. they shall not see the land. 14:23
I will *s.* do it to all this evil. 35
of man shalt thou *s.* redeem. 18:15
s. now I had slain thee, and. 22:33
s. there is no enchantment. 23:23
had said, They shall *s.* die. 26:65
s. give them a possession of. 27:7
s. none from twenty years old and. 32:11; *Deut* 1:35
s. this great nation is. *Deut* 4:6
testify this day that ye shall *s.* perish. 8:19; 30:18
shalt *s.* kill the idolater. 13:9
shalt *s.* smite the inhabitants. 15
shalt *s.* lend him sufficient. 15:8
shalt *s.* give thy poor brother. 10
shalt *s.* rejoice in the feast. 16:15
shalt *s.* help him to lift them. 22:4
the Lord will *s.* require thy. 23:21
and I will *s.* hide my face. 31:18
s. the land shall be thine. *Josh* 14:9
they said, *S.* he covereth. *Judg* 3:24
and Deborah said, I will *s.* go. 4:9
the Lord said to Gideon, *S.* I. 6:16
forth to meet me, shall *s.* be. 11:31
we will bind, but *s.* we will. 15:13
s. they are smitten down. 20:39
he saith cometh *s.* to. *1 Sam* 9:6
Agag said, *S.* the bitterness. 15:32
they said, *S.* to defy Israel. 17:25
for Saul thought, *s.* he is. 20:26
I knew it that Doeg would *s.* 22:22
I know well that thou shalt *s.* 24:20
s. in vain have I kept all. 25:21
s. there had not been left to. 34
s. thou shalt know what thy. 28:2
s. as the Lord liveth, thou. 29:6
pursue, for thou shalt *s.* 30:8
s. the people had gone up. *2 Sam* 2:27
I will *s.* shew thee kindness for. 9:7
he said, *S.* the men prevailed. *2 Sam* 11:23
s. where the king shall be. 15:21
I will *s.* go forth with you. 18:2
she spake, They shall *s.* ask. 20:18
nay, but I will *s.* buy it of. 24:24
I have *s.* built thee house. *1 Ki* 8:13
I will *s.* rend the kingdom. 11:11
against the altar shall *s.* 13:32
I will *s.* shew myself unto. 18:15
s. we shall be stronger. 20:23, 25
they said, *S.* it is the king of. 22:32
s. were it not I regard. *2 Ki* 3:14
is blood, the kings are *s.* slain. 23
I thought, he will *s.* come out. 5:11
told me that thou shouldest *s.* 8:14
s. I have seen yesterday the. 9:26
the Lord will *s.* deliver us. 18:30
Isa 36:15
s. there was not holden. *2 Ki* 23:22
s. at command of the Lord. 24:3
not prevail, but shalt *s.* *Esth* 6:13
s. now he would awake for. *Job* 8:6
s. I would speak to the. 13:3
he will *s.* reprove you, if ye. 10
s. the mountain falling cometh. 14:18
s. such as are the dwellings. 18:21
s. he shall not feel quietness. 20:20
s. there is a vein for the silver. 28:1
s. take it upon my shoulder. 31:36
s. thou hast spoken in. 33:8
s. God will not do wickedly. 34:12
s. God will not hear vanity. 35:13
s. in the floods they. *Ps* 32:6
s. every man walketh in vain. 39:6
his beauty consumes, *s.* every. 11
s. thou didst set them in. 73:18
s. the wrath of man shall. 76:10
s. I will remember thy. 77:11
s. his salvation is nigh them. 85:9
s. he shall deliver thee from. 91:3
s. he shall not be moved. 112:6
s. I have behaved and quieted. 131:2
s. I will not come into my. 132:3
s. thou wilt slay the wicked. 139:19
s. the righteous shall give. 140:13
s. in vain the net is spread. *Pr* 1:17
s. he scorneth the scorners, but. 3:34
walketh uprightly, walketh *s.* 10:9
that giveth to the rich, shall *s.* 22:16
s. there is an end. 23:18
s. I am more brutish. 30:2
s. the churning of milk. 33
s. this also is vanity. *Eccl* 4:16
s. oppression maketh a wise. 7:7
s. it shall be well with them. 8:12
s. the serpent will bite. 10:11
will not believe, *s.* ye shall not be. *Isa* 7:9
s. as I have thought so shall. 14:24
shall mourn, *s.* are stricken. 16:7
s. the princes of Zoan are. 19:11
s. this iniquity shall not be. 22:14
behold, the Lord will *s.* cover. 17
he will *s.* violently turn and toss. 18
s. your turning of things. 29:16
grass withereth, *s.* the people. 40:7
s. God is in thee, and there. 45:14
s. in Lord have I righteousness. 24
yet *s.* my judgement is with. 49:4
s. he hath borne our griefs. 53:4
they shall *s.* gather together. 54:15
s. the isles shall wait for me. 60:9
s. I will no more give thy corn. 62:8
he said *S.* they are my people. 63:8
s. his anger shall turn from. *Jer* 2:35
s. as a wife treacherously. 3:20
s. thou hast greatly deceived. 4:10
s. they swear falsely. 5:2
I said, *S.* these are poor. 4
I will *s.* consume them, saith. 8:13
s. our fathers have inherited. 16:19
yet *s.* I will make thee a. 22:6
s. thou shalt be ashamed for. 22
s. thus saith the Lord, so will. 24:8
ye shall *s.* bring innocent. 26:15
have *s.* heard Ephraim. 31:18
s. after that I was turned. 19
therefore I will *s.* have mercy. 20
but thou shalt *s.* be taken. 34:3
we will *s.* tell the king of all. 36:16
the Chaldeans shall *s.* depart. 37:9
this city shall *s.* be given. 38:3
I will *s.* deliver thee, thou. 39:18
we will perform our vows. *Jer* 44:25
my words shall *s.* stand against. 29
s. as Carmel by the sea, so. 46:18
unpunished, but *s.* drink it. 49:12
s. the least of the flock shall draw. 20; 50:45
saying, *S.* I will fill thee. 51:14
of recompences shall *s.* requite. 56
he shall *s.* live, because. *Ezek* 3:21
18:9, 17, 19, 21, 28; 33:13, 15, 16
s. because thou hast defiled my. 5:11
s. in the place where the king. 17:16
s. with a mighty hand will I. 20:33
he shall *s.* deal with him. 31:11
s. they in the wastes shall fall. 33:27
as I live, *s.* because my flock. 34:8
s. in the fire of my jealousy. 36:5
s. the heathen, they shall bear. 7
s. in that day there shall be a. 38:19
known that which shall *s.* *Hos* 5:9
s. they are vanity, they. 12:11
s. the Lord will do nothing. *Amos* 3:7
Gilgal shall *s.* go into captivity. 5:5
Israel shall *s.* be led away. 7:11, 17
s. I will never forget any of. 8:7
I will *s.* assemble, O Jacob, all of thee, I will *s.* gather. *Mi* 2:12
because it will *s.* come. *Hab* 2:3
as I live, *s.* Moab shall. *Zeph* 2:9
s. thou wilt fear me, and. 3:7
s. thou also art one of them. *Mat* 26:73; *Mark* 14:70
things which are most *s.* *Luke* 1:1
ye will *s.* say unto me this. 4:23
known *s.* that I came. *John* 17:8
saying, *S.* blessing, I will. *Heb* 6:14
S. I come quickly, even. *Rev* 22:20
see **die**

surely *be put to death*

toucheth this man, shall *s. be put to d.* *Gen* 26:11
whosoever toucheth the mount, shall *be s. put to d.* *Ex* 19:12
killeth a man, shall *be s. put to d.* 21:12
smiteth his father, shall *be s. put to d.* 15
stealeth a man shall *s. be put to d.* 16
that curseth his father shall *s. be put to d.* 17; *Lev* 20:9
lieth with a beast, shall *s. be put to d.* *Ex* 22:19; *Lev* 20:15, 16
defileth the sabbath shall *s. be put to d.* *Ex* 31:14, 15
to Moloch, *s. be put to d.* *Lev* 20:2
adulteress shall *s. be put to d.* 10
wife, both shall *s. be put to d.* 11
daughter in law, both shall *s. be put to d.* 12
with mankind, both *s. be put to d.* 13
blasphemeth, shall *s. be put to d.* 24:16
killeth any man, shall *s. be put to d.* 17; *Num* 35:16, 17, 18, 21, 31
redeemed, but shall *s. be put to d.* *Lev* 27:29
came not up, shall *s. be put to d.* *Judg* 21:5
not *s. put* me to *d.*? *Jer* 38:15

sureties

them that are *s.* for debts. *Pr* 22:26

suretiship

he that hateth *s.* is sure. *Pr* 11:15

surety

One who undertakes to pay another man's debt, in case the principal debtor, either through unfaithfulness or poverty, should prove insolvent. It was an ancient custom in suretyship for the surety to give his hand to, or strike hands with the creditor, Job 17:3, Pr 6:1, 2.

I will be *s.* for him. *Gen* 43:9
for thy servant became *s.* for. 44:32
put me in a *s.* with thee. *Job* 17:3
be *s.* for thy servant. *Ps* 119:122
my son, if thou be *s.* for. *Pr* 6:1
he that is *s.* for a stranger. 11:15
and becometh *s.* in presence. 17:18
his garment that is *s.* for a stranger. 20:16; 27:13
Jesus made *s.* of a better. *Heb* 7:22

of a surety
know *of a s.* thy seed. *Gen* 15:13
shall I *of a s.* bear a child? 18:13
Abimelech said, Behold, *of a s.* 26:9
I know *of a s.* the Lord. *Acts* 12:11*

surfeiting
be overcharged with *s.* *Luke* 21:34

surmisings
cometh envy, strife, evil *s.* *1 Tim* 6:4

surname
and *s.* himself by the name of Israel. *Isa* 44:5
Lebbaeus, whose *s.* was. *Mat* 10:3
Simon, whose *s.* is Peter. *Acts* 10:5
32; 11:13
John, whose *s.* was Mark. 12:12
25; 15:37*

surnamed
I have *s.* thee, though. *Isa* 45:4
and Simon he *s.* Peter. *Mark* 3:16
Acts 10:18
he *s.* them Boanerges. *Mark* 3:17
Satan entered into Judas, *s.* Iscariot. *Luke* 22:3*
Barsabas, who was *s.* *Acts* 1:23
Joses, who by the apostles was *s.* Barnabas. 4:36
to send Judas, *s.* Barsabas. 15:22*

surprised
sinners afraid, fearfulness *s.* *Isa* 33:14†
the strong holds are *s.* *Jer* 48:41
praise of the whole earth *s.*! 51:41

Susanna
Joanna and *S.* ministered. *Luke* 8:3

sustain
widow woman to *s.* thee. *1 Ki* 17:9
years didst thou *s.* them. *Neh* 9:21
the Lord, he shall *s.* thee. *Ps* 55:22
the spirit of a man will *s.* *Pr* 18:14

sustained
and wine have I *s.* him. *Gen* 27:37
for the Lord *s.* me. *Ps* 3:5
righteousness, it *s.* him. *Isa* 59:16

sustenance
left no *s.* for Israel. *Judg* 6:4
provided the king of *s.* *2 Sam* 19:32
our fathers found no *s.* *Acts* 7:11

swaddled
those that I have *s.* hath. *Lam* 2:22*
salted at all nor *s.* at all. *Ezek* 16:4

swaddling
darkness a *s.* band for. *Job* 38:9
wrapped him in *s.* *Luke* 2:7, 12

swallow
(*The words* swallow *and* crane *are frequently interchanged in the old version of the Bible, so that the Revisions merely substitute the word* swallow *for* crane *and* crane *for* swallow *and the sense of the verse is not really changed.*
There are many varieties of this common bird found in Palestine)
the *s.* hath found a nest. *Ps* 84:3
as the *s.* by flying, so the. *Pr* 26:2
like a crane or a *s.* so. *Isa* 38:14
crane and *s.* observe. *Jer* 8:7

swallow, *verb*
earth open and *s.* them. *Num* 16:30
for they said, Lest the earth *s.* 34
why wilt thou *s.* up? *2 Sam* 20:19
far be it from me, that I should *s.* 20
let me alone till I *s.* down. *Job* 7:19
he shall restore, and not *s.* 20:18
the Lord shall *s.* them up. *Ps* 21:9
O God, man would *s.* me up. 56:1
would daily *s.* me up. 2
of him that would *s.* me up. 57:3
neither let the deep *s.* me up. 69:15
let us *s.* them up alive. *Pr* 1:12
lips of a fool will *s.* up. *Eccl* 10:12
will *s.* up death in victory. *Isa* 25:8
the strangers shall *s.* it up. *Hos* 8:7
hear this, O ye that *s.* up. *Amos* 8:4
drink, and they shall *s.* down. *Ob* 16
Lord prepared a fish to *s.* *Jonah* 1:17
at a gnat, and *s.* a camel. *Mat* 23:24

swallowed
but Aaron's rod *s.* up. *Ex* 7:12
right hand, the earth *s.* them. 15:12
earth opened and *s.* *Num* 16:32
26:10; *Deut* 11:6
lest the king be *s.* up. *2 Sam* 17:16
heavier than sand: therefore my words are *s.* up. *Job* 6:3*
he hath *s.* down riches, he. 20:15
surely he shall be *s.* up. 37:20
say, We have *s.* him up. *Ps* 35:25
the earth opened and *s.* up. 106:17
they had *s.* us up quick. 124:3
the priest and the prophet are *s.* up. *Isa* 28:7
they that *s.* thee up shall. 49:19
s. me up like a dragon. *Jer* 51:34
out of his mouth that which hath *s.* 44
hath *s.* up all the habitation of Jacob. *Lam* 2:2
he hath *s.* up Israel, he hath *s.* up. 5
they hiss and say, We have *s.* 16
because they have *s.* *Ezek* 36:3
Israel is *s.* up among the. *Hos* 8:8
death is *s.* up in victory. *1 Cor* 15:54
lest such one should be *s.* *2 Cor* 2:7
that mortality might be *s.* up. 5:4
the earth opened and *s.* *Rev* 12:16

swalloweth
and the robber *s.* up. *Job* 5:5*
he *s.* the ground with. 39:24*

swan
the *s.*, the pelican, unclean. *Lev* 11:18*; *Deut* 14:16*

sware
(*The old form of the past tense of* swear)
Beersheba, because they *s.* both of them. *Gen* 21:31
the Lord God of heaven that *s.* 24:7
the servant *s.* to him concerning. 9
Swear to me, and he *s.* to him. 25:33
perform the oath which I *s.* 26:3
Abimelech and Isaac *s.* to one. 31
and Jacob *s.* by the fear of his. 31:53
Joseph *s.* to Jacob his father. 47:31
to this land he *s.* to Abraham. 50:24
the land which the Lord *s.* *Ex* 13:5
11; 33:1; *Num* 14:16, 30; 32:11
Deut 1:8, 35; 6:10, 18, 23; 7:13
8:1; 11:9, 21; 26:3; 28:11; 30:20
31:21, 23; 34:4; *Josh* 1:6; 5:6
21:43
anger was kindled, and he *s.* saying. *Num* 32:10; *Deut* 1:34
were wasted, as Lord *s.* *Deut* 2:14
Lord *s.* that I should not go. 4:21
not forget the covenant which he *s.* 31
which he *s.* to thy salvation. 7:12
covenant which he *s.* 8:18; 9:5
bring out Rahab, as ye *s.* *Josh* 6:22
princes of congregation *s.* to. 9:15
because of the oath which we *s.* 20
Moses *s.* on that day, saying. 14:9
rest according to all that he *s.* 21:44
brought to land which I *s.* *Judg* 2:1
Saul *s.* that David shall. *1 Sam* 19:6
David *s.* moreover to Jonathan. 20:3
David *s.* to Saul; and Saul. 24:22
Saul *s.* to her by the Lord, . . . no punishment. 28:10
David *s.* he would not eat till sun. *2 Sam* 3:35
king David *s.* to Shimei. 19:23
1 Ki 2:8
king David *s.* to. *1 Ki* 1:29, 30
Solomon *s.* that Adonijah. 2:23
Gedaliah *s.* to them. *2 Ki* 25:24
Jer 40:9
they *s.* to the Lord with. *2 Chr* 15:14
they *s.* to put away. *Ezra* 10:5
to whom I *s.* in my wrath. *Ps* 95:11
Heb 3:11
how he *s.* to Lord and vowed. 132:2
so the king *s.* secretly. *Jer* 38:16
I *s.* and entered into. *Ezek* 16:8
s. by him that liveth for ever. *Dan* 12:7; *Rev* 10:6
Herod *s.* to the daughter. *Mark* 6:23
remember oath which he *s.* to Abraham. *Luke* 1:73
to whom *s.* he that they. *Heb* 3:18
swear by no greater, he *s.* *Heb* 6:13
that said, The Lord *s.* and will. 7:21
see their **fathers**

swarest
to whom thou *s.* by thine. *Ex* 32:13
land thou *s.* to fathers. *Num* 11:12
land given us, as thou *s.* *Deut* 26:15
thou *s.* that Solomon. *1 Ki* 1:17
kindnesses thou *s.* to. *Ps* 89:49

swarm
there came a grievous *s.* *Ex* 8:24
a *s.* of bees and honey in. *Judg* 14:8

swarms
s. of flies upon thee, houses of the . . . be full of *s.* of flies. *Ex* 8:21
no *s.* of flies shall be in Goshen. 22
that the *s.* of flies may depart. 29
he removed the *s.* of flies from. 31

swear
In the Bible this has either the meaning of profanity, which is forbidden, or of a solemn asseveration, *which is allowed,* Lev 19:12; Ex 20:7; Deut 6:13; Jer 4:2.
to Abraham, *S.* to me. *Gen* 21:23
and Abraham said, I will *s.* 24
and I will make thee *s.* by. 24:3
my master made me *s.* saying. 37
Jacob said, *S.* to me, and he. 25:33
Jacob said unto Joseph, *S.* 47:31
my father made me *s.*, saying 50:5
concerning which I did *s.* *Ex* 6:8*
if a soul *s.* *Lev* 5:4
and ye shall not *s.* by my. 19:12
if man *s.* an oath to bind. *Num* 30:2
and thou shalt *s.* by his name. *Deut* 6:13; 10:20
Rahab said to spies, *S.* to me. *Josh* 2:12
which thou hast made us *s.* 17, 20
nor cause to *s.* by their gods. 23:7
s. to me that ye will. *Judg* 15:12
Jonathan caused David to *s.* again. *1 Sam* 20:17
s. that thou wilt not cut off my. 24:21
s. by God that thou wilt. 30:15
I *s.* by the Lord. *2 Sam* 19:7
didst not thou *s.* unto thine? *1 Ki* 1:13
saying, Let king Solomon *s.* 51
did I not make thee to *s.*? 2:42
an oath be laid on him to cause him to *s.* 8:31; *2 Chr* 6:22
made him *s.* by God. *2 Chr* 36:13
then Ezra made Levites and all Israel to *s.* *Ezra* 10:5
I made them *s.* by God. *Neh* 13:25
in that day shall he *s.* I. *Isa* 3:7*
five cities in Egypt shall *s.* 19:18
to me every tongue shall *s.* 45:23
which *s.* by the Lord, but not. 48:1
that sweareth, shall *s.* by. 65:16
shalt *s.*, The Lord liveth. *Jer* 4:2
Lord liveth, they *s.* falsely. 5:2
will ye *s.* falsely? 7:9
ways of my people, to *s.* by my name, as they taught people to *s.* 12:16
I *s.* by myself, saith the Lord. 22:5
them this land thou didst *s.* 32:22
up to Beth-aven nor *s.* *Hos* 4:15
they that *s.* by the sin. *Amos* 8:14
that *s.* by the Lord, that *s.* *Zeph* 1:5
s. not at all. *Mat* 5:34
s. not by thy head. 36
shall *s.* by the temple; *s.* by. 23:16
whoso shall *s.* by the altar. 18
shall *s.* by the altar, sweareth. 20
shall *s.* by the temple. 21
shall *s.* by heaven. 22
then began he to curse and *s.* 26:74
Mark 14:71
could *s.* by no greater, he *s.* *Heb* 6:13
for men verily *s.* by the greater. 16
my brethren, *s.* not. *Jas* 5:12

swearers
be a swift witness against false *s.* *Mal* 3:5

sweareth
what was lost, and *s.* *Lev* 6:3*
that *s.* to his hurt, and. *Ps* 15:4
every one that *s.* by him shall. 63:11
s. as he that feareth an oath. *Eccl* 9:2
he that *s.* shall swear by. *Isa* 65:16

and every one that *s.* shall. *Zech* 5:3
enter into the house of him *s.* 4
whosoever *s.* by the gift. *Mat* 23:18
s. by the altar. 20
s. by temple, and by him. 21
s. by throne of God, and by him. 22

swearing
and hear the voice of *s.* *Lev* 5:1*
because of *s.* the land. *Jer* 23:10
s. and lying, and stealing. *Hos* 4:2
have spoken words, *s.* falsely. 10:4

sweat
in the *s.* of thy face. *Gen* 3:19
any thing that causeth *s.* *Ezek* 44:18
his *s.* was as it were great drops of blood. *Luke* 22:44

sweep
I will *s.* it with the besom. *Isa* 14:23
the hail shall *s.* away the. 28:17
doth not *s.* the house. *Luke* 15:8

sweeping
is like a *s.* rain which. *Pr* 28:3

sweet
waters were made *s.* *Ex* 15:25
take of myrrh and *s.* 30:23
David the *s.* psalmist. *2 Sam* 23:1
eat the fat, and drink the *s.* *Neh* 8:10
wickedness be *s.* in. *Job* 20:12
valley shall be *s.* to him. 21:33
thou bind the *s.* influences ? 38:31*
took *s.* counsel together and walked. *Ps* 55:14
meditation of him shall be *s.* 104:34
how *s.* are thy words unto! 119:103
my words, for they are *s.* 141:6
and thy sleep shall be *s.* *Pr* 3:24
stolen waters are *s.*, and bread. 9:17
the desire accomplished is *s.* 13:19
pleasant words are *s.* to the. 16:24
bread of deceit is *s.* to a man. 20:17
and lose thy *s.* words. 23:8
the honeycomb, which is *s.* 24:13
soul every bitter thing is *s.* 27:7
of a labouring man is *s.* *Eccl* 5:12
truly the light is *s.*, and. 11:7
his fruit was *s.* *S of S* 2:3
for *s.* is thy voice. 14
dropped with *s.* smelling myrrh. 5:5*
cheeks as a bed of spices, as *s.* flowers: his lips like lilies, dropping *s.* 13*
his mouth is most *s.* yea, he is. 16
instead of *s.* smell, there. *Isa* 3:24
put bitter for *s.* and *s.* for bitter. 5:20
make *s.* melody, sing songs to. 23:16
your sacrifices *s.* unto me. *Jer* 6:20*
awaked, and my sleep was *s.* 31:26
same place *s.* water. *Jas* 3:11
thy mouth *s.* as honey. *Rev* 10:9, 10
see **incense, odours, savour**

sweet *calamus*
take of *s. calamus* 250. *Ex* 30:23

sweet *cane*
hast brought me no *s. cane* with money. *Isa* 43:24
the *s. cane* came from a. *Jer* 6:20

sweet *spices*
take to thee *s. spices*. *Ex* 30:34
pure incense of *s. spices*. 37:29
bought *s. spices* that they. *Mark* 16:1

sweet *wine*
blood as with *s. wine*. *Isa* 49:26
mount shall drop *s. wine*. *Amos* 9:13
and *s. wine*, but shalt not. *Mi* 6:15*

sweeter
men of city said, What is *s.* than ? *Judg* 14:18
s. also than honey. *Ps* 19:10
thy words are *s.* than honey. 119:103

sweetly
worm shall feed *s.* on him. *Job* 24:20
wine, that goeth down *s.* *S of S* 7:9*

sweetness
should I forsake my *s.*? *Judg* 9:11
of the strong came forth *s.* 14:14
s. of the lips increaseth. *Pr* 16:21
so doth *s.* of a man's friend. 27:9
roll was in my mouth as honey for *s.* *Ezek* 3:3

swell
and thy belly to *s.* *Num* 5:21, 22
her belly shall *s.* and her thigh. 27
nor did thy foot *s.* these. *Deut* 8:4

swelled
40 years their feet *s.* not. *Neh* 9:21

swelling
shake with *s.* thereof. *Ps* 46:3
as a breach *s.* out in a. *Isa* 30:13
do in the *s.* of Jordan ? *Jer* 12:5*
from the *s.* of Jordan. 49:19*; 50:44*
speak great *s.* words. *2 Pet* 2:18
speaking great *s.* words. *Jude* 16

swellings
I fear lest there be *s.* *2 Cor* 12:20

swept
the river of Kishon *s.* *Judg* 5:21
valiant men *s.* away ? *Jer* 46:15
house, when come, he findeth it empty, *s.* *Mat* 12:44; *Luke* 11:25

swerved
which some having *s.* *1 Tim* 1:6

swift
shall bring a nation as *s.* *Deut* 28:49
were as *s.* as roes on. *1 Chr* 12:8
passed away as the *s.* ships. *Job* 9:26
he is *s.* as the waters, he. 24:18
feet that be *s.* in running. *Pr* 6:18
race is not to the *s.* *Eccl* 9:11
go, ye *s.* messengers. *Isa* 18:2
Lord rideth upon a *s.* cloud. 19:1
we will ride on the *s.*: therefore shall they that pursue you be *s.* 30:16
your brethren on *s.* beasts. 66:20
s. dromedary traversing her ways. *Jer* 2:23
let not *s.* flee away, nor mighty. 46:6
flight shall perish from *s.* *Amos* 2:14
he that is *s.* of foot shall not. 15
bind the chariot to *s.* beast. *Mi* 1:13
I will be a *s.* witness. *Mal* 3:5
their feet are *s.* to shed. *Rom* 3:15
let every man be *s.* to hear. *Jas* 1:19
themselves *s.* destruction. *2 Pet* 2:1

swifter
s. than eagles, stronger. *2 Sam* 1:23
s. than a weaver's shuttle. *Job* 7:6
now my days are *s.* than a post. 9:25
horses are *s.* than eagles. *Jer* 4:13
our persecutors are *s.* *Lam* 4:19
their horses are *s.* than. *Hab* 1:8

swiftly
his word runneth very *s.* *Ps* 147:15
shall come with speed *s.* *Isa* 5:26
Gabriel being caused to fly *s.* *Dan* 9:21
if ye recompense me *s.* *Joel* 3:4

swim
stick, and the iron did *s.* *2 Ki* 6:6
make I my bed to *s.* *Ps* 6:6
spreadeth forth hands to *s.* *Isa* 25:11
risen, waters to *s.* in. *Ezek* 47:5
lest any of them should *s.* out and. *Acts* 27:42
that they who could *s.* 43

swimmest
the land wherein thou *s.* *Ezek* 32:6

swimmeth
as he that *s.* spreadeth. *Isa* 25:11

swine
the *s.* is unclean to you. *Lev* 11:7
Deut 14:8
as a jewel of gold in a *s.'s*. *Pr* 11:22
eat *s.'s* flesh, and broth of. *Isa* 65:4
oblation, as if he offered *s.'s*. 66:3
eating *s.'s* flesh, and abomination. 17
cast ye your pearls before *s.* *Mat* 7:6
an herd of *s.* feeding. 8:30
Mark 5:11; *Luke* 8:32
suffer us to go into the herd of *s.* *Mat* 8:31; *Mark* 5:12
they went into the *s.* . . . the whole herd of *s.* ran. *Mat* 8:32
Mark 5:13; *Luke* 8:33
they that fed the *s.* fled. *Mark* 5:14
them also concerning the *s.* 16
into his field to feed *s.* *Luke* 15:15
belly with husks the *s.* did eat. 16

swollen
when he should have *s.* *Acts* 28:6

swoon
because the children *s.* *Lam* 2:11

swooned
they *s.* as the wounded. *Lam* 2:12

sword
The sword in scripture is often used for war, Gen 27:40; Lev 26:2. *By* sword *is understood the judgements which God inflicts upon sinners,* Deut 33:41, 42; *also the instrument which God uses to execute his judgements,* Ps 17:13. Sword *is figuratively put for power and authority,* Rom 13:4. *The word of God is called the* sword of the Spirit, Eph 6:17. *Moses calls God* the sword of Israel's excellency, Deut 33:29. *He is their strength, the author of all their past or approaching victories, by whose assistance they did excel, and gloriously conquer, and triumph over their enemies.*

cherubims, and flaming *s.* *Gen* 3:24
took each man his *s.* and. 34:25
put a *s.* in their hands. *Ex* 5:21
he said, Put every man his *s.* 32:27
nor shall the *s.* go through. *Lev* 26:6
bring a *s.* upon you. 25; *Ezek* 5:17
6:3; 14:17; 29:8, 33:2
I will draw out a *s.* after. *Lev* 26:33
fall as it were before a *s.* 37
the angel's *s.* drawn. *Num* 22:23, 31
I would there were a *s.* in mine. 29
s. without, and terror. *Deut* 32:25
and who is the *s.* of thy! 33:29
stood with his *s.* drawn. *Josh* 5:13
not with thy *s.* nor with thy. 24:12
this is nothing save the *s.* *Judg* 7:14
say, The *s.* of the Lord, and. 18, 20
and the Lord set every man's *s.* 7:22; *1 Sam* 14:20
120,000 men that drew *s.* *Judg* 8:10
the youth drew not his *s.* for. 20
he said unto him, Draw thy *s.* 9:54
400,000 that drew *s.* 20:2, 17
26,000 men that drew *s.* 15
all these drew the *s.* 25
25,100 men that drew the *s.* 35
25,000 that drew the *s.* 46
neither *s.* nor spear. *1 Sam* 13:22
as thy *s.* hath made women. 15:33
his *s.* on his armour. 17:39; 25:13
but there was no *s.* in the. 17:50
David ran and took his *s.* 51
even to his *s.* and to his bow. 18:4
under thy hand a spear or *s.* 21:8
the *s.* of Goliath is here wrapt. 9
and he gave him the *s.* of. 22:10
given him bread, and a *s.* 13
Gird ye on every man his *s.* and they girded on every man his *s.* 25:13
draw thy *s.* and thrust me through therewith. . . . Saul took a *s.* and fell upon it. 31:4; *1 Chr* 10:4
armourbearer fell likewise upon his *s.* and died with him. *1 Sam* 31:5
1 Chr 10:5
the *s.* of Saul returned. *2 Sam* 1:22
and thrust his *s.* through. 2:16
Abner said, Shall the *s.* devour ? 26
fail one that falleth on the *s.* 3:29
the *s.* devoureth one as well. 11:25
the *s.* shall never depart from. 12:10
wood devoured more than *s.* 18:8
Amasa took no heed to the *s.* 20:10
his hand clave unto the *s.* 23:10
800,000 men that drew the *s.* 24:9
a *s.* and they brought a *s.* *1 Ki* 3:24
him that escapeth the *s.* of. 19:17
to bear buckler and *s.* *1 Chr* 5:18
men that drew *s.* and Judah was 470,000 that drew *s.* 21:5
that the *s.* of thine enemies overtake, or else three days the *s.* 12
the angel having a *s.* drawn. 16
and he put up his *s.* again into. 27
he was afraid, because of the *s.* 30
s. of judgement cometh. *2 Chr* 20:9
our kings are delivered to the *s.* *Ezra* 9:7
one had his *s.* girded. *Neh* 4:18
their enemies with the *s.* *Esth* 9:5

in war to deliver from power of the s. Job 5:20
and he is waited for of the s. 15:22
s.: for wrath bringeth the punishments of the s. 19:29
the glittering s. cometh. 20:25*
multiplied, it is for the s. 27:14
make his s. to approach. 40:19
the s. of him that layeth at. 41:26
turn not, he will whet his s. Ps 7:12
the wicked, which is thy s. 17:13
wicked have drawn out the s. 37:14
their s. shall enter into their. 15
gird thy s. on thy thigh. 45:3
and their tongue a sharp s. 57:4
who whet their tongue like a s. 64:3
brake he the shield and the s. 76:3
his people over unto the s. 78:62
twoedged s. in their hand. 149:6
is sharp as a twoedged s. Pr 5:4
like the piercings of a s. 12:18
beareth false witness is a s. 25:18
every man hath his s. upon his thigh. S of S 3:8
nation shall not lift up s. Isa 2:4
s., not of a mean man, shall. 31:8
the s. of the Lord is filled. 34:6
them as the dust to his s. 41:2
my mouth like a sharp s. 49:2
the famine and the s. are. 51:19
will I number you to the s. 65:12
by his s. will the Lord plead. 66:16
your own s. devoured. Jer 2:30
whereas the s. reacheth unto. 4:10
neither shall we see s. 5:12; 14:13
for the s. of the enemy is. 6:25
will send a s. after them. 9:16; 24:10 25:27; 29:17; 49:37
for the s. of the Lord shall. 12:12
Ye shall not see the s. 14:13
say, S. and famine shall not be. 15
in the streets because of the s. 16
are for the s., to the s. 15:2; 43:11
I will appoint the s. to slay. 15:3
them will I deliver to the s. 9
blood by the force of the s. 18:21
be mad because of the s. 25:16
I will call for a s. 29; Ezek 38:21
that are wicked to the s. Jer 25:31
the people left of the s. found. 31:2
city is given because of the s. 32:24
a liberty for you, to the s. 34:17
the s. ye feared shall overtake. 42:16
number which escape the s. 44:28
the s. shall devour and. 46:10, 14
O thou s. of the Lord, how? 47:6
O madmen, the s. shall pursue. 48:2
cursed that keepeth back his s. 10
for fear of the oppressing s. 50:16
a s. is on the Chaldeans, saith. 35
a s. is on the liars, a s. is on. 36
a s. is on their horses, a s. on. 37
ye that have escaped the s. 51:50
by peril because of the s. Lam 5:9
I will draw out a s. Ezek 5:2, 12
I bring the s. upon thee. 17; 6:3
some that shall escape the s. 6:8
the s. is without, the pestilence. 7:15
the s. and I will bring a s. 11:8
if I bring a s. and say, S. go. 14:17
four sore judgements, the s. 21
prophesy and say, A s. a s. 21:9, 11
terrors, by reason of the s. on. 12
and what if the s. contemn? 13
s. be doubled, the s. of the great men slain, it is the s. of great men. 14
set the point of the s. against. 15
appoint two ways, that the s. 19
appoint a way, that s. may come. 20
the s. the s. is drawn for the. 28
s. shall come upon Egypt. 30:4
make it strong to hold the s. 21
I will cause the s. to fall out. 22
the s. of the king of Babylon. 32:11
if when he seeth the s. come. 33:3
if the s. come and take him. 4, 6
watchman see the s. come; if the s. come and take any person. 6
ye stand upon your s. and ye. 26
blood by the force of the s. 35:5
break the bow and the s. Hos 2:18
and the s. shall abide on. 11:6
will I command the s. Amos 9:4
nation shall not lift up s. Mi 4:3
will I give up to the s. Mi 6:14
the s. shall devour the. Nah 2:13
lifteth up both the bright s. 3:3
there the s. shall cut thee off. 15
made thee as the s. of. Zech 9:13
the s. shall be upon his arm. 11:17
O s. against my shepherd. 13:7
to send peace, but a s. Mat 10:34
one of them drew his s. and. 26:51 Mark 14:47; John 18:10
put up again thy s. Mat 26:52 John 18:11
a s. shall pierce through. Luke 2:35
he that hath no s. let him buy. 22:36
he drew his s. and. Acts 16:27
separate us? shall s.? Rom 8:35
for he beareth not the s. in. 13:4
s. of the Spirit, which is. Eph 6:17
than any twoedged s. Heb 4:12
went a twoedged s. Rev 1:16
which hath the sharp s. with. 2:12
given to him a great s. 6:4
mouth goeth a sharp s. 19:15, 21

by the sword

by the s. thou shalt live. Gen 27:40
shall fall before you by the s. Lev 26:7, 8
were fallen by the s. 2 Sam 1:12
have fallen by the s. 2 Chr 29:9
from perishing by the s. Job 33:18
they shall perish by the s. 36:12
got not the land by their s. Ps 44:3
their priests fell by the s. 78:64
Lord, Their young men shall die by the s. Jer 11:22; 18:21; Lam 2:21
consume them by the s. Jer 14:12
by s. and famine shall those. 15
shall be consumed by the s. 16:4 44:12, 18, 27
cause them to fall by the s. 19:7
abideth, shall die by the s. 21:9 38:2; 42:17, 22
why will ye die by the s.? 27:13
shall be delivered by the s. 32:36
are thrown down by the s. 33:4
thou shalt not die by the s. 34:4
punished Jerusalem by the s. 44:13
shall be slain by the s. Ezek 26:6
he shall slay thy people by the s. 11
be judged in her by the s. 28:23
them that be slain by the s. 31:18 32:20, 21, 22, 25, 30; 33:27
so they fell all by the s. 39:23
not save them by bow, nor by s. Hos 1:7
Jeroboam shall die by the s. Amos 7:11
people shall die by the s. 9:10
every one by the s. Hag 2:22
had the wound by a s. Rev 13:14

see edge, fall

from the sword

delivered me from the s. of. Ex 18:4
as fleeing from a s. Lev 26:36
him that escapeth from the s. of Jehu. 1 Ki 19:17
that escaped from the s. 2 Chr 36:20
saveth poor from the s. Job 5:15
turneth he back from the s. 39:22
deliver my soul from the s.; my darling from the power. Ps 22:20
David from the hurtful s. 144:10
fled from the drawn s. Isa 21:15
but he shall flee from the s. 31:8
such as are left from the s. Jer 21:7
let us go from the oppressing s. 46:16
few men of them from s. Ezek 12:16
is brought back from the s. 38:8

my sword

from Amorite with my s. Gen 48:22
I will draw my s. my. Ex 15:9
I whet my glittering s. Deut 32:41
and my s. shall devour flesh. 42
neither brought my s. 1 Sam 21:8
neither shall my s. save me. Ps 44:6
for my s. shall be bathed. Isa 34:5
I will draw my s. out. Ezek 21:3
therefore my s. shall go out of. 4
I the Lord have drawn my s. out. 5
I have put my s. in his. 30:24, 25
when I shall brandish my s. 32:10
shall be slain by my s. Zeph 2:12

with the sword

captives taken with the s. Gen 31:26
lest he fall on us with the s. Ex 5:3
I will kill you with the s. 22:24
toucheth one slain with the s. Num 19:16
out against thee with the s. 20:18
Balaam also they slew with the s. 31:8
the Lord shall smite thee with the s. Deut 28:22
whom Israel slew with the s. Josh 10:11; 13:22
king of Hazor with the s. 11:10
comest to me with a s. 1 Sam 17:45
the Lord saveth not with s. and. 47
killed Uriah with the s. 2 Sam 12:9
a girdle with a s. fastened. 20:8
being girded with a s. 21:16
will not slay his servant with the s. 1 Ki 1:51
not put thee to death with the s. 2:8
and slew them with the s. 32
slain all the prophets with the s. 19:1
slain thy prophets with the s. 10, 14
young men wilt thou slay with the s. 2 Ki 8:12
and him that followeth her, kill with the s. 11:15; 2 Chr 23:14
they slew Athaliah with the s. 2 Ki 11:20; 2 Chr 23:21
Sennacherib king of Assyria with the s. 2 Ki 19:37; 2 Chr 32:21 Isa 37:38
his brethren with the s. 2 Chr 21:4
their young men with the s. 36:17
as with a s. in my bones. Ps 42:10
be devoured with the s. Isa 1:20
slain, thrust through with a s. 14:19
men are not slain with the s. 22:2
the Lord with his strong s. 27:1
thy cities with the s. Jer 5:17
behold the slain with the s. 14:18
shall slay Judah with the s. 20:4
who slew Urijah with the s. 26:23
nation will I punish with the s. 27:8
persecute them with the s. 29:18
smote Gedaliah with the s. 41:2
that be slain with the s. Lam 4:9
shall die with the s. Ezek 7:15
slew her with the s. 23:10
daughters of Tyrus with the s. 26:8
with them that be slain with the s. 31:17; 32:28, 32; 35:8
his brother with the s. Amos 1:11
men have I slain with the s. 4:10
house of Jeroboam with the s. 7:9
slay the last of them with the s. 9:1
the land of Assyria with the s. Mi 5:6
s. shall perish with the s. Mat 26:52
we smite with the s.? Luke 22:49
killed James with the s. Acts 12:2
were tempted, were slain with the s. Heb 11:37
against them with the s. Rev 2:16
and power to kill with s. and. 6:8
with s. must be killed with s. 13:10
remnant were slain with the s. 19:21

swords

Hebrews make them s. 1 Sam 13:19
700 men that drew s. 2 Ki 3:26
the people with their s. Neh 4:13
his words were drawn s. Ps 55:21
behold, they belch out, s. are. 59:7
whose teeth are as s. Pr 30:14
they all hold, s., being. S of S 3:8
beat their s. into plowshares and their spears. Isa 2:4; Mi 4:3
they fled from the s. and. Isa 21:15
thrust thee through with their s. Ezek 16:40
dispatch them with their s. 23:47
strangers shall draw their s. 28:7
they shall draw their s. 30:11
by the s. of the mighty will. 32:12
they have laid their s. under. 27
your plowshares into s. Joel 3:10
a great multitude with s. from the chief. Mat 26:47; Mark 14:43
as against a thief with s. and staves to take me? Mat 26:55 Mark 14:48; Luke 22:52
behold, here are two s. Luke 22:38

sworn
by myself have I *s.* saith the Lord.
Gen 22:16; *Isa* 45:23; *Jer* 49:13
51:14; *Amos* 6:8
had straitly *s.* Israel. *Ex* 13:19
the Lord hath *s.* that he will. 17:16
about which he hath *s.* *Lev* 6:5
would keep the oath he had *s.*
Deut 7:8; *Jer* 11:5
multiply thee, as he hath *s.* to thy fathers. *Deut* 13:17
thy coast, as he hath *s.* 19:8
shall establish thee, as he hath *s.*
28:9; 29:13
to land Lord hath *s.* 31:7; *Neh* 9:15
because the princes had *s.* *Josh* 9:18
we have *s.* to them by the Lord. 19
2 Sam 21:2
for evil, as Lord had *s.* *Judg* 2:15
now the men of Israel had *s.* 21:1
we have *s.* not to give them. 7, 18
I have *s.* unto the house of Eli.
1 Sam 3:14
forasmuch as we have *s.* 20:42
Lord hath *s.* to David. *2 Sam* 3:9
children of Israel had *s.* to. 21:2
they had *s.* with all. *2 Chr* 15:15
many in Judah *s.* to. *Neh* 6:18
the land which thou hadst *s.* 9:15*
who hath not *s.* deceitfully. *Ps* 24:4
I have *s.* unto David my. 89:3
s. by my holiness that. 35; *Amos* 4:2
are mad against me, are *s.* *Ps* 102:8
the Lord hath *s.* and will. 110:4
I have *s.* and I will. 119:106
the Lord hath *s.* in truth to. 132:11
the Lord of hosts hath *s.* *Isa* 14:24
I have *s.* by myself, the word. 45:23
I have *s.* that waters of Noah no more go over the earth, so have I *s.* 54:9
Lord hath *s.* by his right hand. 62:8
they have *s.* by them. *Jer* 5:7
have *s.* by my great name. 44:26
them that have *s.* oaths. *Ezek* 21:23
hath *s.* by the excellency. *Amos* 8:7
the mercy thou hast *s.* *Mi* 7:20
knowing God hath *s.* by. *Acts* 2:30
drew nigh which God had *s.* 7:17*
I have *s.* in my wrath. *Heb* 4:3

sycamine
say to this *s.* tree, Be. *Luke* 17:6

sycamore, *see* **sycomore**

sycomore
This tree is not the sycamore *of England and America but an entirely different tree, the Egyptian fig tree, or* fig-mulberry. *It spreads its branches widely, making a delightful shade, for which reason it was often planted by the roadside,* Luke 19:4. *Its fruit was much like a fig, but to make it eatable it used to be thought necessary to puncture it three or four days before it was ripe,* Amos 7:14. *But this is not done now, the fruit ripening in the ordinary manner. The value of the tree was mainly in its timber.*

sycomore *fruit*
a gatherer of *s. fruit.* *Amos* 7:14

sycomore *tree*
climbed up into a *s. tree.* *Luke* 19:4

sycomore *trees*
Solomon made cedars to be as *s. trees.* *1 Ki* 10:27; *2 Chr* 1:15; 9:27
over the *s. trees* was Baal-hanan.
1 Chr 27:28
destroyed their *s. trees.* *Ps* 78:47

sycomores
the *s.* are cut down, but. *Isa* 9:10

synagogue
This word is found only once in the Old Testament in Ps 74:8, *and there is no indication that synagogues existed before the Exile, although there are some reasons to think that they were in existence centuries earlier. As to* Ps 74:8, They have burned up all the *synagogues* of God in the land; *the original is,* all the assemblies of God, *by which must be understood the places where the people assembled to worship God. But this does not infer that those places were what we now mean by synagogues. After the Maccabaean period there were synagogues in every settlement where there were enough Jews to erect one. It is said that there were in the city of Jerusalem alone no less than four hundred and sixty, or even four hundred and eighty; but this is most probably an exaggeration. Every trading fraternity had a* synagogue *of their own, and even strangers built some for those of their own nation. Hence it is, that in* Acts 6:9, *mention is made of* the synagogues of the Libertines, Cyrenians, Alexandrians, Cilicians, and Asiatics; *which were appointed for the use of such of the inhabitants of these cities, or of these nations, as should at any time be at Jerusalem. The synagogue worship became the regular worship of the people outside of Jerusalem, the temple being visited at one or more of the great feasts.*

In Palestine the synagogue was so built that the worshipper would face Jerusalem. At the upper end was the chest which contained the Book of the Law. Here were the chief seats *so desired by the Pharisees,* Mat 23:6; Jas 2:2, 3. *In later times the congregation was divided, men on one side and women on the other, with a lattice partition between.*

The word is used in the New Testament [1] *for the building,* Luke 7:5. [2] *For the* organization *which worshipped there,* Acts 6:9. *The* ruler of the synagogue *was the one who had the responsibility of maintaining order, deciding on the order of public worship, etc.,* Luke 8:41; Acts 18:8. *The* minister *had duties of a lower kind, more like those of a modern deacon, or of a sacristan.*

Worship was held in the synagogue every sabbath, and every feast day, the main part of the service being the reading of the law, with an exposition of what was read, Acts 15:21; 13:15.

The ordinary school for Jewish children was in the synagogue of each village. Every boy was supposed to attend, and the teaching was mostly in the Law and other Scriptures.

The organization of the synagogue, where possible, included a council of the elders; and in these cases they had a certain amount of judicial power, Mat 10:17.

The synagogue of the Libertines, or freedmen, Acts 6:9, *was, according to most interpreters, that of those Jews, who having been led away captive by Pompey and others, had afterwards recovered their liberty, and returned to Jerusalem, when Tiberias drove the Jews out of Italy.*

he went into their *s.* *Mat* 12:9
he taught them in their *s.* 13:54
Mark 6:2
and there was in their *s.* a man with.
Mark 1:23; *Luke* 4:33
when they were come out of the *s.*
Mark 1:29; *Luke* 4:38
one of the rulers of the *s.* besought.
Mark 5:22, 36, 38; *Luke* 8:41, 49
he went into the *s.* on the sabbath.
Luke 4:16
the eyes of all in the *s.* were. 20
nation and hath built us a *s.* 7:5
things said he in the *s.* *John* 6:59
he should be put out of the *s.*
John 9:22
they should be put out of *s.* 12:42
I ever taught in the *s.* and. 18:20
certain of the *s.* which is called the *s.* of the Libertines. *Acts* 6:9
the *s.* on the sabbath day. 13:14
the rulers of the *s.* sent to them. 15
the Jews were gone out of the *s.* 42
Barnabas went both into the *s.* 14:1
to Thessalonica where was a *s.* 17:1
therefore he disputed in the *s.* 17
and he reasoned in the *s.* 18:4
house joined hard to the *s.* 7
Crispus the chief ruler of the *s.* 8
Sosthenes chief ruler of the *s.* 17
to speak boldy in the *s.* 26
beat in every *s.* such. 22:19; 26:11
but are the *s.* of Satan. *Rev* 2:9
I will make them of the *s.* of. 3:9

synagogues
burned up all the *s.* of God. *Ps* 74:8
Jesus went teaching in their *s.* and.
Mat 4:23; 9:35; *Mark* 1:39
Luke 13:10
the hypocrites do in the *s.* *Mat* 6:2
love to pray standing in the *s.* 5
they will scourge you in their *s.*
10:17; 23:34
for they love the chief seats in the *s.*
23:6; *Mark* 12:39; *Luke* 11:43
20:46
and in the *s.* ye shall be. *Mark* 13:9
he taught in the *s.* being. *Luke* 4:15
and he preached in the *s.* of. 44
they bring you unto the *s.* 12:11
delivering you up to the *s.* 21:12
put you out of the *s.* *John* 16:2
of him letters to the *s.* *Acts* 9:2
he preached Christ in the *s.* 20
Barnabas preached in the *s.* 13:5
being read in the *s.* every. 15:21
up the people in the *s.* 24:12

Syria
served the gods of *S.* *Judg* 10:6
David put garrisons in *S.*
2 Sam 8:6; *1 Chr* 18:6
I abode at Geshur in *S.* *2 Sam* 15:8
for the kings of *S.* did. *1 Ki* 10:29
Rezon abhorred Israel and reigned over *S.* 11:25
anoint Hazael to be king of *S.* 19:15
2 Ki 13:3
war between *S.* and Israel. *1 Ki* 22:1
by Naaman deliverance given to *S.*
2 Ki 5:1
the bands of *S.* came no. 6:23
was no man in the camp of *S.* 7:5
that thou shalt be king of *S.* 8:13
the king of *S.* had destroyed. 13:7
arrow of deliverance from *S.* 17
but now thou shalt smite *S.* 19
S. recovered Elath to *S.* 16:6
thou shalt push *S.* *2 Chr* 18:10
the host of *S.* came up. 24:23
the gods of kings of *S.* help. 28:23
S. is confederate with. *Isa* 7:2
for head of *S.* is Damascus, and. 8
of the daughters of *S.* *Ezek* 16:57
S. was thy merchant for thy. 27:16
into the country of *S.* *Hos* 12:12
the people of *S.* shall go. *Amos* 1:5
went throughout all *S.* *Mat* 4:24
was governor of *S.* *Luke* 2:2
to the brethren in *S.* *Acts* 15:23
went through *S.* and Cilicia. 41
sailed thence into *S.* 18:18; 21:3
Gal 1:21
see **king**

Syriac
spake to the king in *S.* *Dan* 2:4

Syrian
daughter of Bethuel the *S.*, Laban the *S.* *Gen* 25:20; 28:5; 31:20, 24
a *S.* ready to perish. *Deut* 26:5
spared Naaman this *S.* *2 Ki* 5:20
speak in the *S.* language. 18:26
Isa 36:11
letter was written in the *S.* tongue and interpreted in the *S.* *Ezra* 4:7
saving Naaman the *S.* *Luke* 4:27

Syrians
S. of Damascus came to succour Hadadezer . . . of S. *2 Sam* 8:5
the S. became David's servants. 6
1 Chr 18:5, 6
from smiting of the S. *2 Sam* 8:13
sent and hired the S. 10:6
if the S. be too strong for me. 11
1 Chr 19:12
so the S. feared to help the children of. *2 Sam* 10:19; *1 Chr* 19:19
the S. fled and Israel. *1 Ki* 20:20
Israel's little flocks, but S. 27
Israel slew of the S. 100,000. 29
these shalt thou push the S. 22:11
the S. had taken a maid. *2 Ki* 5:2
beware, for thither the S. are. 6:9
fall into the host of the S. 7:4
the Lord made the host of the S. 6
we came to camp of the S. 10
S. wounded Joram. 8:28, 29; 9:15
2 Chr 22:5
from under the hand of S. *2 Ki* 13:5
for thou shalt smite the S. in. 17
the S. came to Elath and. 16:6
the S. before, and the. *Isa* 9:12
fear of the army of S. *Jer* 35:11
have not I brought the S.? *Amos* 9:7

Syrophenician
Greek, a S. by nation. *Mark* 7:26

T

Tabeal
midst of it, even the son of T. *Isa* 7:6

Taberah
name of the place T. *Num* 11:3
at T. he provoked the. *Deut* 9:22

tabering
the voice of doves t. *Nah* 2:7

tabernacle
This word literally means tent, *and is used of any sort of temporary tent or booth, as well as for the* tabernacle *erected for the worship of God. Where the word is plural, except in the expression* feast of tabernacles, *it has the meaning of* dwelling, *or* dwelling-place.
The Tabernacle *erected for worship in the wilderness was thirty cubits in length, and ten in breadth and in height. It was divided into two partitions: the first was called* The Holy Place, *which was twenty cubits long, and ten wide: here were placed the table of shewbread, the golden candlestick, and the golden altar of incense. The second was called* The most Holy Place, *whose length was ten cubits, and breadth ten cubits. Here the* ark of the covenant *was kept, which was a symbol of God's gracious presence with the Jewish church. The* most Holy *was divided from the* Holy Place *by a curtain, or veil of very rich cloth, which hung upon four pillars of shittim wood, that were covered with plates of gold,* Ex 26:1; Heb 9:2, 3. *St. Paul refers to our natural body as a tabernacle.* 2 Cor 5:1; 2 Pet 1:13.
The feast of tabernacles, *Lev* 23:34, *was so called, because the Israelites kept it under booths of branches in memory of their dwelling in tents in their passage through the wilderness. It was one of the three great yearly feasts, when all the males were obliged to present themselves before the Lord. It was celebrated after harvest, on the 15th day of the month Tisri, which answers to our month of October. The feast continued eight days; but the first day and the last were the most solemn.*
The Revised Versions most frequently use the word tent, *in place of* tabernacle.

the manner of the t. *Ex* 25:9
thou shalt make the t. with. 26:1
curtains, and it shall be one t.
6; 36:13
of goats' hair to be a covering upon the t. 26:7; 35:11; 36:14
for the t. of shittim wood. 26:15, 17
20, 26; 36:20, 22, 23, 28, 31, 32
make bars for the t. 26:26, 27
rear up the t. 30
vessels of t. of brass. 27:19; 39:40
the t. shall be sanctified. 29:43
all the furniture of the t. 31:7
Moses pitched the t. without. 33:7
departed not out of the t. 11
the pins of the t. 35:18; 38:20, 31
wrought the work of the t. 36:8
thus was the work of the t. 39:32
they brought the t. to Moses. 33
thou shalt set up the t. 40:2
anoint the t. 9
on the first day, the t. was reared up.
17, 18; *Num* 7:1
the tent over the t. *Ex* 40:19
he brought the ark into the t. 21
court round about the t. 33
glory of the Lord filled the t. 34, 35
cloud taken up from over the t. 36
Num 9:17; 10:11; 12:10
cloud was on the t. by day, and fire.
Ex 40:38; *Num* 9:18, 19, 22
Moses anointed the t. *Lev* 8:10
not when they defile my t. 15:31
not an offering before the t. 17:4
I will set my t. among you. 26:11
Levites over the t.; bear the t.; encamp round the t. *Num* 1:50, 53
the t. setteth forward, and when t. 51
keep the charge of the t. 53; 3:7
25; 18:3; 31:30, 47
t. to do the service of the t. 3:7
shall pitch behind the t. 23
pitch northward of the t. 35
those that encamp before the t. 38
oversight of the t. pertaineth. 4:16
bear the curtains of the t. 25
shall bear the boards of the t. 31
take of the dust of the t. 5:17
their offering before the t. 7:3
on the day that the t. was reared up, the cloud covered the t. 9:15
Kohathites did set up the t. 10:21
elders round about the t. 11:24
went not out unto the t. 26
small to do the service of the t. 16:9
get you up from about the t. 24, 27
whoso cometh near to the t. 17:13
Lord appeared in t. in. *Deut* 31:15
wherein the Lord's t. *Josh* 22:19
set the ark in the midst of the t.
2 Sam 6:17
walked in a tent and in a t. 7:6
Zadok took a horn of oil out of the t.
1 Ki 1:39
Joab fled to the t. of the Lord. 2:28
vessels in the t. were brought up.
8:4; *2 Chr* 5:5
the service of the t. *1 Chr* 6:48
keepers of the gates of the t. 9:19
oversight of the house of the t. 23
the priests, before t. of the. 16:39
but have gone from one t. 17:5
for the t. which Moses made. 21:29
no more carry the t. 23:26
brazen altar before the t. *2 Chr* 1:5
shalt know that thy t. *Job* 5:24
the light shall be dark in his t. 18:6
shall be rooted out of his t. 14
destruction shall dwell in his t. 15
encamp round about my t. 19:12
with him that is left in his t. 20:26
secret of God was upon my t. 29:4
if the men of my t. said not. 31:31
understand the noise of his t.?
36:29*
who shall abide in thy t.? *Ps* 15:1
in them hath he set a t. for. 19:4
in the secret of his t. shall. 27:5
I will offer in his t. sacrifices. 6
I will abide in thy t. for ever. 61:4
in Salem is his t., his dwelling. 76:2
so that he forsook the t. of. 78:60
moreover he refused the t. 67
I will not come into the t. 132:3, 7

the t. of the upright shall. *Pr* 14:11
there shall be a t. for a. *Isa* 4:6*
he shall sit upon it in the t. 16:5
a t. that shall not be taken. 33:20
my t. is spoiled, and all my. *Jer* 10:20
were pleasant in the t. *Lam* 2:4
violently taken away his t. 6
my t. also shall be. *Ezek* 37:27
was the breadth of the t. 41:1
but ye have borne the t. *Amos* 5:26*
day will I raise up the t. of. 9:11
took up the t. of Moloch. *Acts* 7:43
desired to find a t. for the God. 46
and will build again the t. 15:16
if our house of this t. *2 Cor* 5:1
we that are in this t. do groan. 4
true t. which the Lord. *Heb* 8:2
Moses was about to make the t. 5
there was a t. made, called. 9:2
t. which is called the holiest. 3
went always into the first t. 6
while as the first t. was yet. 8
by a greater and more perfect t. 11
he sprinkled with blood the t. 21
no right to eat which serve t. 13:10
as long as I am in this t. *2 Pet* 1:13
shortly I must put off my t. 14
to blaspheme his name and his t.
Rev 13:6
behold the temple of the t. 15:5
see **congregation, door**

tabernacle *of witness*
laid up the rods in the t. *of witness*.
Num 17:7
Moses went into the t. *of witness*. 8
before the t. *of witness*. 18:2
bring the collection for t. *of witness*.
2 Chr 24:6
fathers had the t. *of witness*.
Acts 7:44

tabernacles
how goodly are thy t. O. *Num* 24:5
wickedness dwell in thy t. *Job* 11:14
the t. of robbers prosper, and. 12:6
and fire shall consume the t. 15:34
away iniquity far from thy t. 22:23
bring me unto thy t. *Ps* 43:3
make glad the holy place of t. 46:4
their strength in t. of Ham. 78:51
t. of Edom have consulted. 83:6
how amiable are thy t. O Lord. 84:1
salvation is in the t. of the. 118:15
we will go into his t. and. 132:7
he shall plant the t. of. *Dan* 11:45
thorns shall be in their t. *Hos* 9:6
make thee to dwell in t. 12:9
cut off the man out of the t. *Mal* 2:12
let us make here three t. *Mat* 17:4
Mark 9:5; *Luke* 9:33
Abraham dwelling in t. *Heb* 11:9
see **feast**

Tabitha
a disciple named T. *Acts* 9:36
to the body, said, T. arise. 40

table
shalt also make a t. of. *Ex* 25:23
places of staves to bear the t. 27, 28
37:14
thou shalt set the t. without. 26:35
thou shalt anoint the t. and. 30:27
Bezaleel shall make the t. 31:8
he made the t. 37:10
the vessels on the t. 16
brought the t. unto Moses. 39:33
thou shalt bring in the t. and. 40:4
put the t. in the tent of the. 22
on a row on the pure t. *Lev* 24:6
charge shall be the t. *Num* 3:31
their meat under my t. *Judg* 1:7
not to the king's t. *1 Sam* 20:29
Jonathan arose from the t. in. 34
Mephibosheth shall eat bread at my t. *2 Sam* 9:7, 10, 11, 13; 19:28
those that eat at thy t. *1 Ki* 2:7
came to king Solomon's t. 4:27
when the queen of Sheba saw the meat of his t. 10:5; *2 Chr* 9:4
as they sat at t. word of. *1 Ki* 13:20
which eat at Jezebel's t. 18:19
let us set for him a t. *2 Ki* 4:10
at my t. 150 Jews. *Neh* 5:17
should be set on thy t. *Job* 36:16
thou preparest a t. *Ps* 23:5

let their *t.* become a snare. *Ps* 69:22
can God furnish a *t.* in the? 78:19
olive plants about thy *t.* 128:3
on the *t.* of thy heart. *Pr* 3:3; 7:3
hath also furnished her *t.* 9:2
the king sitteth at his *t.* *S of S* 1:12
prepare the *t.*, watch, eat. *Isa* 21:5
write it before them in a *t.* 30:8*
prepare a *t.* for that troop. 65:11
it is graven on the *t.* of. *Jer* 17:1
and a *t.* prepared before. *Ezek* 23:41
ye shall be filled at my *t.* 39:20
this is the *t.* that is before. 41:22
shall come near to my *t.* 44:16
speak lies at one *t.* *Dan* 11:27
the *t.* of the Lord is. *Mal* 1:7
ye say, The *t.* of the Lord is. 12
crumbs which fall from their master's *t.* *Mat* 15:27; *Mark* 7:28
fell from rich man's *t.* *Luke* 16:21
the hand of him that betrayeth me is with me on the *t.* 22:21
ye may eat and drink at my *t.* 30
one of them that sat at *t.* *John* 12:2*
no man at the *t.* knew for. 13:28
their *t.* be made a snare. *Rom* 11:9
devils, ye cannot be partakers of the Lord's *t.* and of the *t.* *1 Cor* 10:21
see **shewbread**

writing **table**
Zacharias asked for a *writing t.* *Luke* 1:63

tables
Frequently meaning tablets, Ex 32:15; Isa 30:8. To serve tables *was to oversee the caring for the poor*, Acts 6:2.
the *t.* were written on. *Ex* 32:15
t. were the work of God, graven on the *t.* 16
he cast the *t.* out of his hands. 19
on these *t.* the words in first *t.* 34:1
he wrote on the *t.* *Deut* 10:4
put the *t.* in the ark. 5; *Heb* 9:4
David gave gold for *t.* *1 Chr* 28:16
Solomon also made ten *t.* *2 Chr* 4:8
the *t.* whereon the shewbread. 19
all *t.* are full of vomit. *Isa* 28:8
eight *t.* whereupon they. *Ezek* 40:41
four *t.* were of hewn stone for. 42
and make it plain on *t.* *Hab* 2:2
he overthrew the *t.* of the money changers. *Mat* 21:12; *Mark* 11:15
cups, pots, and of *t.* *Mark* 7:4
and overthrew the *t.* *John* 2:15
leave the word of God, and serve *t.* *Acts* 6:2
t. of stone, but fleshly *t.* *2 Cor* 3:3
see **stone, two**

tablets
they brought *t.*, all jewels. *Ex* 35:22*
we brought *t.* to make. *Num* 31:50*
I will take away the *t.* *Isa* 3:20*

Tabor
and draw toward mount *T.* *Judg* 4:6
Barak was gone up to mount *T.* 12
they whom ye slew at *T.*? 8:18
come to the plain of *T.* *1 Sam* 10:3
T. and Hermon shall rejoice in thy name. *Ps* 89:12
surely, as *T.* is among. *Jer* 46:18
been a net spread upon *T.* *Hos* 5:1

tabret
away with *t.* and harp. *Gen* 31:27
high place with a *t.* *1 Sam* 10:5*
aforetime I was as a *t.* *Job* 17:6*
the *t.*, pipe, and wine are. *Isa* 5:12

tabrets
to meet Saul with *t.* *1 Sam* 18:6*
the mirth of *t.* ceaseth. *Isa* 24:8
shall be with *t.* and harps. 30:32
be adorned with thy *t.* *Jer* 31:4
workmanship of thy *t.* *Ezek* 28:13

taches
(*Revisions substitute the word* clasps)
thou shalt make fifty *t.* *Ex* 26:6
make fifty *t.* of brass. 11; 35:11
hang up the vail under the *t.* 26:33
he made fifty *t.* of gold. 36:13, 18
brought his *t.*, his boards. 39:33

tackling
we cast out the *t.* of. *Acts* 27:19

tacklings
thy *t.* are loosed, could. *Isa* 33:23

Tadmor
Solomon built *T.* in the. *2 Chr* 8:4

Tahapanes, *or* **Tehaphnehes**
children of *T.* have broken. *Jer* 2:26
thus came they even to *T.* 43:7
publish in Noph and *T.* 46:14
at *T.* also the day. *Ezek* 30:18

Tahpenes
sister of *T.* the queen. *1 Ki* 11:19

tail
hand, take it by the *t.* *Ex* 4:4
head, not the *t.* *Deut* 28:13, 44
foxes and turned *t.* to *t.* *Judg* 15:4
behemoth moveth his *t.* *Job* 40:17
off from Israel head and *t.* *Isa* 9:14
teacheth lies, he is the *t.* 15
the head or *t.* may do. 19:15
his *t.* drew the third. *Rev* 12:4

tails
firebrand between two *t.* *Judg* 15:4
two *t.* of these smoking firebrands. *Isa* 7:4
t. like to scorpions, stings in their *t.* *Rev* 9:10
power in their *t.*: their *t.* were. 19

take
wilt *t.* the left hand. *Gen* 13:9
the persons, *t.* the goods to. 14:21
arise, *t.* thy wife and thy. 19:15
t. now thy son, thine only son. 22:2
thou shalt not *t.* a wife to. 24:3, 37
to *t.* my master's brother's. 48
what is thine with me, *t.* it. 31:32
if thou *t.* other wives besides. 50
t. our daughters unto you. 34:9
will *t.* your daughters to us. 16
let her *t.* it to her, lest we be. 38:23
I will *t.* you to me for a. *Ex* 6:7
for thereof must we *t.* to. 10:26
and thy rod *t.* in thine hand. 17:5
shalt not *t.* the name of the Lord thy God. 20:7; *Deut* 5:11
t. him from mine altar. *Ex* 21:14
and thou shalt *t.* no gift. 23:8
Deut 16:19
pardon and *t.* us for. *Ex* 34:9
lest thou *t.* of their daughters. 16
Deut 7:3
neither *t.* her son's. *Lev* 18:17
neither shalt thou *t.* a wife to. 18
and if a man *t.* a wife, and. 20:14
not *t.* a wife that is a whore, nor *t.* a. 21:7; *Ezek* 44:22
t. a wife in her virginity. *Lev* 21:13
t. thou no usury of him, or. 25:36
ye shall *t.* them as an inheritance. 46
t. the Levites from among. *Num* 8:6
I will *t.* of the spirit that is on. 11:17
Korah said, Ye *t.* too much. 16:3, 7
ye shall *t.* no satisfaction. 35:31, 32
t. ye wise men and. *Deut* 1:13
and *t.* him a nation, from. 4:34
then thou shalt *t.* an awl and. 15:17
elders of that city shall *t.* 22:18
shall not *t.* his father's wife. 30
may not *t.* her again to be his. 24:4
no man shall *t.* a millstone to. 6
t. a widow's raiment to pledge. 17
if he say, I like not to *t.* her. 25:8
when ye *t.* of the accursed thing. *Josh* 6:18
family which the Lord shall *t.*; household which the Lord shall *t.* 7:14
they should *t.* his carcase. 8:29
their land did Joshua *t.* at. 10:42
they shall *t.* him into the city. 20:4
t. ye possession among us. 22:19
for the necks of them that *t.* spoil. *Judg* 5:30
that thou goest to *t.* a wife. 14:3
have ye called us to *t.* that? 15*
consider, *t.* advice, and speak. 19:30
t. knowledge of me. *Ruth* 2:10
t. as much as thy soul desireth, and if not I will *t.* it by. *1 Sam* 2:16
he will *t.* your sons for himself. 8:11
he will *t.* your daughters. 13
he will *t.* your fields. 14
t. the tenth of your seed. *1 Sam* 8:15
he will *t.* your menservants. 16
how thy brethren fare, and *t.* 17:18
and *t.* thine head from thee. 46
messengers to *t.* David. 19:14, 20
if thou wilt *t.* that, *t.* it, there. 21:9
huntest my soul to *t.* it. 24:11
shall I then *t.* my bread, and? 25:11
t. now the spear that is at his. 26:11
he spared to *t.* of his. *2 Sam* 12:4
I will *t.* thy wives before thine. 11
t. it, lest I *t.* the city, and it be. 28
t. the thing to his heart. 13:33; 19:19
me go over, and *t.* off his head. 16:9
said, Yea, let him *t.* all. 19:30
Jeroboam, *T.* ten pieces. *1 Ki* 11:31
will not *t.* the whole kingdom. 34
t. with thee ten loaves. 14:3
t. the prophets of Baal. 18:40
war or peace, *t.* them alive. 20:18
arise, *t.* possession of. 21:15, 16
t. Micaiah, carry him back. 22:26
2 Chr 18:25
creditor is come to *t.* *2 Ki* 4:1
t. my staff and go. 29
t. a blessing of thy servant. 5:15
urged him to *t.* it. 16
I will *t.* somewhat. 20
be content, *t.* two talents. 23
t. a present and go. 8:8
t. this box of oil in thine. 9:1, 3
t. ye the heads of your. 10:6
he said, *T.* them alive. 14
let the priests *t.* it. 12:5
said, *T.* bow and arrows. 13:15, 18
shall yet *t.* root downward. 19:30
Isa 37:31
I will not *t.* that which. *1 Chr* 21:24
those did Cyrus *t.* *Ezra* 5:14
t. these vessels. 15
not *t.* their daughters. 9:12
Neh 10:30; 13:25
t. the apparel, and do. *Esth* 6:10
knoweth the way that I *t.* *Job* 23:10
they *t.* the widow's ox for a. 24:3
and they *t.* a pledge of the poor. 9
and my sinews *t.* no rest. 30:17
surely I would *t.* it upon. 31:36
thou *t.* him for a servant for? 41:4
therefore *t.* to you now seven. 42:8
the rulers *t.* counsel. *Ps* 2:2
persecute my soul, and *t.* it. 7:5*
I will *t.* no bullock out of thy. 50:9
shouldest *t.* my covenant in. 16
and *t.* not thy Holy Spirit. 51:11
t. him, for there is none to. 71:11
t. a psalm, and bring. 81:2
t. the houses of God. 83:12
will I not utterly *t.* from him. 89:33
and let another *t.* his office. 109:8
t. the cup of salvation, and. 116:13
t. not the word of truth. 119:43
if I *t.* the wings of the. 139:9
and thine enemies *t.* thy name. 20
his own iniquities shall *t.* *Pr* 5:22
neither let her *t.* thee with her. 6:25
can a man *t.* fire in his bosom? 27
let us *t.* our fill of love until. 7:18
t. his garment that is surety for stranger, *t.* a pledge. 20:16; 27:13
and *t.* the name of my God. 30:9*
and shall *t.* nothing of. *Eccl* 5:15
and to *t.* his portion and rejoice. 19
t. us the foxes, the. *S of S* 2:15
them of Jacob to *t.* root. *Isa* 27:6
time it goeth, it shall *t.* you. 28:19
not a sherd to *t.* fire from. 30:14
is divided, the lame *t.* the. 33:23
their stock shall not *t.* root. 40:24
will *t.* thereof and warm. 44:15
t. the millstones, and grind. 47:2
I will *t.* vengeance, I will not. 3
vanity shall *t.* them, wind. 57:13*
t. delight in approaching to. 58:2
also *t.* of them for priests. 66:21
t. thee much sope [soap]. *Jer* 2:22
I will *t.* you one of a city. 3:14
t. the girdle that thou. 13:4, 6
shall not sorrows *t.* thee as a. 21
if thou *t.* forth the precious. 15:19
thou shalt not *t.* thee a wife. 16:2
have digged a pit to *t.* me. 18:22
t. of the ancients of the people. 19:1
we shall *t.* our revenge. 20:10

I will *t.* all the families. *Jer* 25:9
I will *t.* from them the voice. 10
if they refuse to *t.* the cup at. 28
t. ye wives, and beget sons. 29:6
come to the city to *t.* it. 32:24
money, and *t.* witnesses. 25, 44
king of Babylon shall *t.* it. 28
t. Jeremiah, and look well to. 39:12
Gilead, and *t.* balm. 46:11; 51:8
t. vengeance upon her; as she. 50:15
shall not *t.* of thee a stone. 51:26
behold I will *t.* vengeance for thee. 36
what thing shall I *t.* to witness ? *Lam* 2:13
t. thee a tile and lay it. *Ezek* 4:1
t. thou an iron pan. 3
t. unto thee wheat, barley, and. 9
t. a sharp knife, *t.* a razor, *t.* 5:1
t. fire from between the wheels. 10:6
I will *t.* the stony heart out. 11:19
that I may *t.* the house. 14:5
will men *t.* a pin of it to hang ? 15:3
remove the diadem, *t.* off the. 21:26
thou shalt *t.* thine inheritance. 22:16*
t. the choice of the flock, and. 24:5
fury to come up to *t.* vengeance. 8
I *t.* from them their strength. 25
t. a multitude, *t.* her spoil, *t.* 29:19
if people of the land *t.* a man. 33:2
I will *t.* you from among the. 36:24
t. thee one stick, *t.* another. 37:16
I will *t.* the stick of Joseph. 19
to *t.* a spoil, and to *t.* a prey. 38:12
art thou come to *t.* prey, to *t.* a ? 13
the prince not *t.* the people's. 46:18
but the saints shall *t.* the. *Dan* 7:18
the king shall *t.* the most. 11:15
to the isles, and shall *t.* many. 18
go *t.* unto thee a wife of. *Hos* 1:2
I was as they that *t.* off the. 11:4
t. with you words, and turn. 14:2
ye *t.* from him burdens. *Amos* 5:11
afflict the just, they *t.* a bribe. 12
shall mine hand *t.* them. 9:2, 3
t. I beseech thee, my life. *Jonah* 4:3
they covet fields and *t.* *Mi* 2:2
that they shall not *t.* shame. 6*
the Lord will *t.* vengeance. *Nah* 1:2
t. ye the spoil of silver, *t.* the. 2:9
heap dust and *t.* it. *Hab* 1:10
build the house; and I will *t.* *Hag* 1:8
I *t.* thee, O Zerubbabel my. 2:23
t. of them of the captivity. *Zech* 6:10
t. yet instruments of a foolish. 11:15
fear not to *t.* unto thee. *Mat* 1:20
and *t.* the young child and. 2:13
t. no thought for your life. 6:25* 28*, 31*, 34*; 10:19*; *Mark* 13:11* *Luke* 12:11*, 22* 26*
and the violent *t.* the. *Mat* 11:12
t. my yoke upon you, and learn. 29
It is not meet to *t.* the children's bread. 15:26; *Mark* 7:27
they had forgotten to *t.* bread. *Mat* 16:5; *Mark* 8:14
kings of earth *t.* custom. *Mat* 17:25
then *t.* with thee one or two. 18:16
t. that thine is and go thy. 20:14
on the house top not come down to *t.* any. 24:17; *Mark* 13:15
t. therefore the talent. *Mat* 25:28
that they might *t.* Jesus. 26:4 *Mark* 14:1, 44
took bread and said, *T.* *Mat* 26:26 *Mark* 14:22; *1 Cor* 11:24
sleep on now, and *t.* your rest. *Mat* 26:45; *Mark* 14:41
they that *t.* sword shall. *Mat* 26:52
with swords and staves to *t.* me. 55 *Mark* 14:48
t. nothing for their journey. *Mark* 6:8; *Luke* 9:3
his brother should *t.* his wife. *Mark* 12:19; *Luke* 20:28
casting lots what every man should *t.* *Mark* 15:24
whether Elias will come to *t.* 36
David did *t.* and eat the. *Luke* 6:4
forbid him not to *t.* thy coat. 29
said, *T.* care of him. 10:35
soul, *t.* thine ease. 12:19
then begin with shame to *t.* the. 14:9
t. thy bill and write. 16:6, 7
t. from him the pound. 19:24
t. this and divide it. *Luke* 22:17
hath a purse, let him *t.* it. 36
Jesus said to them, *T.* *John* 2:16
of them may *t.* a little. 6:7
that they would come and *t.* him. 15
they sought to *t.* him. 7:30, 32 10:39; 11:57
loveth me, because I lay down my life, that I might *t.* it. 10:17, 18
he shall *t.* of mine, and shew. 16:15
thou shouldest *t.* them out. 17:15
t. ye him, and judge him. 18:31
Pilate saith, *T.* ye him, and. 19:6
bishoprick let another *t.* *Acts* 1:20
further to *t.* Peter also. 12:3
to *t.* out of them a people. 15:14
Barnabas determined to *t.* with. 37
Paul thought not good to *t.* him. 38
there intending to *t.* in Paul. 20:13
I *t.* you to record this day. 26*
them *t.* and purify thyself. 21:24
besought them to *t.* meat. 27:33, 34
why not rather *t.* wrong ? *1 Cor* 6:7
shall I then *t.* the members of ? 15
doth God *t.* care for oxen ? 9:9
t. upon us the ministering. *2 Cor* 8:4
ye suffer, if a man *t.* of you. 11:20*
therefore I *t.* pleasure in. 12:10
t. to you the whole. *Eph* 6:13
and *t.* the helmet of salvation. 17
how shall he *t.* care of ? *1 Tim* 3:5
t. Mark, and bring him. *2 Tim* 4:11
a commandment to *t.* tithes. *Heb* 7:5
t. my brethren, the prophets, for an. *Jas* 5:10
if ye *t.* it patiently, it. *1 Pet* 2:20
hold fast, that no man *t.* *Rev* 3:11
thou art worthy to *t.* the book. 5:9
power given him to *t.* peace from. 6:4
t. the little book. 10:8
t. it and eat it. 9
let him *t.* the water of life. 22:17

***see* counsel**

take *away*

wouldest thou *t. away* my son's mandrakes ? *Gen* 30:15
ye will *t.* Benjamin *away*. 42:36
t. this child *away*, and. *Ex* 2:9
that he may *t. away* the frogs. 8:8
that he may *t. away* from me. 10:17
and I will *t.* sickness *away*. 23:25 *Deut* 7:15
I will *t. away* mine hand. *Ex* 33:23
it shall he *t. away*. *Lev* 3:4, 10, 15 4:9; 7:4
t. away all the fat thereof. 4:31, 35
that they *t. away* the stones. 14:40
shalt *t. away* the ashes. *Num* 4:13
thou shalt quite *t. away* their. 17:10
t. away the serpents from us. 21:7
until ye *t. a.* the accursed. *Josh* 7:13
shall I not *t.* you *away* ? *2 Sam* 4:11
except thou *t. away* the blind. 5:6
t. away the iniquity of thy. 24:10
mayest *t. away* the innocent blood. *1 Ki* 2:31
t. away the remnant of the. 14:10*
t. away the posterity. 16:3*; 21:21*
now, O Lord, *t. away* my life. 19:4
seek my life to *t.* it *away*. 10, 14
shall my servants *t. away*. 20:6
t. the kings *away* and put. 24
the Lord will *t. away*. *2 Ki* 2:3, 5
sent to *t. away* mine head. 6:32
till I come and *t.* you *away*. 18:32 *Isa* 36:17
I will not *t.* my mercy *away* from him. *1 Chr* 17:13
to *t. away* his sackcloth. *Esth* 4:4
why dost thou not *t. away* ? *Job* 7:21
t. his rod *away* from me. 9:34
they violently *t. away* flocks. 24:2
they *t. away* the sheaf from the. 10
my maker would soon *t.* me *a.* 32:22
lest he *t.* thee *away* with. 36:18*
devised to *t. away* my life. *Ps* 31:13
he shall *t.* thee *away* and. 52:5
he shall *t.* them *away* with. 58:9
t. me not *away* in the midst. 102:24
why should he *t. away* thy bed ? *Pr* 22:27
t. away the dross from the. 25:4
t. away the wicked from before. 5
I will *t. away* all thy tin. *Isa* 1:25
t. away the stay and staff. 3:1
t. away bravery. 18
to *t. away* our reproach. 4:1
I will *t. away* the hedge. 5:5
t. away the righteousness of. 23
to *t. away* the right from. 10:2
of his people shall he *t. away*. 25:8
all the fruit, to *t. away* his sin. 27:9
thy sons shall they *t. away*. 39:7
whirlwind shall *t.* them *away*. 40:24
if thou *t. away* from the midst. 58:9
t. away the foreskins of. *Jer* 4:4
destroy and *t. away* her. 5:10
t. me not *away* in thy long. 15:15
shall *t. away* the detestable things. *Ezek* 11:18
they shall *t. away* thy nose. 23:25
t. away thy fair jewels. 26
t. away thy labour. 29
behold, I *t. away* the desire. 24:16
come and *t.* him *away*. 33:4, 6
and I will *t. away* the stony. 36:26
t. away your exactions from. 45:9
and they shall *t. away*. *Dan* 7:26
they shall *t. away* the daily. 11:31
utterly *t.* them *away*. *Hos* 1:6
and *t. away* my corn in the. 2:9
for I will *t. away* the names. 17
and new wine *t. away* the heart. 4:11
I will *t. away* and none shall. 5:14
unto him, *T. away* all iniquity. 14:2
that he will *t.* you *away*. *Amos* 4:2
t. away from me the noise of. 5:23
they covet houses, and *t.* them *away*. *Mi* 2:2
I will *t. away* out of the midst of. *Zeph* 3:11
t. away the filthy garments. *Zech* 3:4
I will *t. away* his blood out. 9:7
one shall *t.* you *away*. *Mal* 2:3
and *t. away* thy coat, let. *Mat* 5:40
t. away and cast him into. 22:13
Father, *t. away* this cup. *Mark* 14:36
to *t. away* my reproach. *Luke* 1:25
not come down to *t.* it *away*. 17:31
said, *T. away* the stone. *John* 11:39
the Romans shall *t. away* our. 48
when I shall *t. away*. *Rom* 11:27
blood should *t. away* sins. *Heb* 10:4
manifested to *t. away*. *1 John* 3:5
t. away from the words of the book, God shall *t. away* his. *Rev* 22:19

take *heed*

t. heed that thou speak not to Jacob. *Gen* 31:24, 29
t. heed to thyself. *Ex* 10:28; 34:12 *Deut* 4:9; 12:13, 19, 30 *1 Sam* 19:2; *1 Tim* 4:16
t. heed to yourselves. *Ex* 19:12 *Deut* 2:4; 4:15, 23; 11:16 *Josh* 23:11; *Jer* 17:21
must I not *t. heed* to ? *Num* 23:12
t. heed in the plague of. *Deut* 24:8
t. heed and hearken, O. 27:9
t. diligent *heed* to do. *Josh* 22:5
if thy children *t. heed*. *1 Ki* 2:4 8:25; *2 Chr* 6:16
t. heed now; for the Lord. *1 Chr* 28:10
t. heed what ye do, for ye judge not for man. *2 Chr* 19:6
fear of the Lord be on you, *t. heed*. 7
so that they will *t. heed* to do. 33:8 *Ezra* 4:22
t. heed, regard not. *Job* 36:21
I said, I will *t. heed* to. *Ps* 39:1
t. no *heed* to all words. *Eccl* 7:21
T. heed and be quiet, for. *Isa* 7:4
t. heed every one of his. *Jer* 9:4
have left off to *t. heed* to. *Hos* 4:10
t. heed to your spirit. *Mal* 2:15, 16
t. heed that ye do not your alms before men. *Mat* 6:1
t. heed of the leaven of the Pharisees. 16:6; *Mark* 8:15
t. heed that ye despise. *Mat* 18:10
t. heed that no man deceive you. 24:4; *Mark* 13:5
he said to them, *T. heed*. *Mark* 4:24
t. heed to yourselves. 13:9 *Luke* 17:3; 21:34; *Acts* 5:35; 20:28
t. heed: behold, I have foretold you all things. *Mark* 13:23

t. ye *heed*, watch, pray. *Mark* 13:33
t. heed therefore how ye hear. *Luke* 8:18
t. heed that the light in thee. 11:35
t. heed and beware of. 12:15
he said, *T. heed* that ye be. 21:8
saying, *T. heed* what thou doest. *Acts* 22:26*
t. heed lest he also spare not thee. *Rom* 11:21*
let every man *t. heed*. *1 Cor* 3:10
t. heed lest this liberty of. 8:9
that standeth *t. heed* lest he. 10:12
t. heed that ye be not consumed one of another. *Gal* 5:15
t. heed to the ministry. *Col* 4:17
t. heed lest an evil heart. *Heb* 3:12
ye do well that ye *t. heed*. *2 Pet* 1:19

take *hold*

sorrow shall *t. hold* on. *Ex* 15:14
trembling shall *t. hold* upon. 15
that the loops *t. hold* one of. 26:5*
and if mine hand *t. hold*. *Deut* 32:41
terrors *t. hold* on him. *Job* 27:20
justice *t. hold* on thee. 36:17
it might *t. hold* on the ends. 38:13
t. hold of shield and. *Ps* 35:2
wrathful anger *t. hold* of. 69:24*
neither *t.* they *hold* of the paths of life. *Pr* 2:19*
t. fast *hold* of instruction, let. 4:13
her steps *t. hold* on hell. 5:5
it is good that thou *t. hold* of this. *Eccl* 7:18
will *t. hold* of the boughs. *S of S* 7:8
when a man shall *t. hold* of. *Isa* 3:6
seven women shall *t. hold* of. 4:1
sorrows shall *t. hold* of them. 13:8
let him *t. hold* of my strength. 27:5
to the eunuchs that *t. hold* of. 56:4
himself to *t. hold* of thee. 64:7
thou shalt *t. hold* but. *Mi* 6:14*
did they not *t. hold* of your fathers? *Zech* 1:6*
ten men shall *t. hold* of him. 8:23
that they might *t. hold*. *Luke* 20:20
could not *t. hold* of his words. 26

take *up*

t. up the fifth part of the. *Gen* 41:34
and the priest shall *t. up*. *Lev* 6:10
t. up the censers out of. *Num* 16:37
t. up the ark of the. *Josh* 3:6; 6:6
t. up every man a stone out. 4:5
the Lord would *t. up* Elijah. *2 Ki* 2:1
he said, *T. up* thy son. 4:36
t. up the iron. 6:7
t. up and cast him into the. 9:25
we *t. up* corn for them. *Neh* 5:2*
nor *t. up* their names. *Ps* 16:4
then the Lord will *t.* me *up*. 27:10
that thou shalt *t. up* this. *Isa* 14:4
t. up the stumblingblock out. 57:14
t. up a lamentation on the. *Jer* 7:29
for the mountains will I *t. up*. 9:10
t. up wailing for us. 18
t. up Jeremiah, before he die. 38:10
t. up a lamentation for the princes. *Ezek* 19:1
t. up a lamentation for Tyrus. 26:17; 27:2, 32
t. up a lamentation upon king of Tyrus. 28:12
t. up a lamentation for Pharaoh. 32:2
shall one *t. up* a snare. *Amos* 3:5*
hear his word which I *t. up*. 5:1
a man's uncle shall *t.* him *up*. 6:10
t. me *up* and cast me. *Jonah* 1:12
shall one *t. up* a parable. *Mi* 2:4
they *t. up* all of them. *Hab* 1:15
not all these *t. up* a parable? 2:6
Jesus saith, Arise, *t. up* thy bed. *Mat* 9:6; *Mark* 2:9, 11; *Luke* 5:24 *John* 5:8, 11, 12
let him *t. up* his cross and follow me. *Mat* 16:24; *Mark* 8:34; 10:21 *Luke* 9:23
and *t. up* the fish that. *Mat* 17:27
shall *t. up* serpents. *Mark* 16:18

taken

Lord God had *t.* from man. *Gen* 2:22
because she was *t.* out of man. 23
of the ground wast thou *t.* 3:19, 23
vengeance shall be *t.* on him. 4:15
the woman was *t.* into. *Gen* 12:15
so I might have *t.* her to me. 19
heard that his brother was *t.* 14:14
I have *t.* upon me to speak. 18:27
which thou hast *t.* is a wife. 20:3
is he that hath *t.* venison? 27:33
the riches God hath *t.* from. 31:16
now Rachel had *t.* the images. 34
staves shall not be *t.* *Ex* 25:15
shoulder have I *t.* of Israel. *Lev* 7:34
t. the Levites for the firstborn of. *Num* 3:12; 8:16, 18; 18:6
neither she be *t.* with the. 5:13
and the tabernacle was *t.* 10:17
I have not *t.* one ass from. 16:15
we have *t.* the sum of the. 31:49
their inheritance be *t.* from. 36:3
Lord hath *t.* you out of. *Deut* 4:20
wife, and hath not *t.* her. 20:7
when a man hath *t.* a wife. 24:1
t. a new wife, he shall be free at ... his wife which he hath *t.* 5
they have *t.* of the. *Josh* 7:11
he that is *t.* shall be burnt. 15
and the tribe of Judah was *t.* 16
and Zabdi was *t.* 17
and Achan was *t.* 18
Lord hath *t.* vengeance. *Judg* 11:36
he told not them that he had *t.* 14:9
because he had *t.* his wife. 15:6
the 1100 shekels that were *t.* 17:2
the ark of God was *t.* *1 Sam* 4:11 17, 19, 21, 22
which the Philistines had *t.* 7:14
and Saul was *t.* 10:21
whose ox have I *t.*? 12:3
nor hast thou *t.* aught of any. 4
Saul and Jonathan were *t.* 14:41
Cast lots, and Jonathan was *t.* 42
and David's two wives were *t.* 30:5
that they had *t.* to them. 19
hast *t.* his wife to. *2 Sam* 12:9, 10
and I have *t.* the city of waters. 27
thou art *t.* in thy mischief. 16:8
because they cannot be *t.* 23:6
saw that the city was *t.* *1 Ki* 16:18
killed and also *t.* possession? 21:19
when I am *t.* from thee. *2 Ki* 2:10
of Hosea, Samaria was *t.* 18:10
household being *t.* for Eleazar, and one *t.* for Ithamar. *1 Chr* 24:6
captives you have *t.* *2 Chr* 28:11
king had *t.* counsel to keep. 30:2
for they have *t.* of their. *Ezra* 9:2
and we have *t.* strange wives. 10:2* 14*, 17*, 18*
all these had *t.* strange wives. 44
had *t.* of them bread. *Neh* 5:15
who had *t.* Esther for his. *Esth* 2:15
so Esther was *t.* unto king. 16
king took off his ring he had *t.* 8:2
also *t.* me by my neck. *Job* 16:12
he hath *t.* the crown from. 19:9
thou hast *t.* a pledge from thy. 22:6
they are *t.* out of the way. 24:24
iron is *t.* out of the earth. 28:2
in net is their own foot *t.* *Ps* 9:15
let them be *t.* in the devices. 10:2
even be *t.* in their pride. 59:12
have *t.* crafty counsel against. 83:3
I *t.* as an heritage for ever. 119:111
thy foot from being *t.* *Pr* 3:26
thou art *t.* with the words of. 6:2
he hath *t.* a bag of money. 7:20
transgressors shall be *t.* in. 11:6
my labour which I had *t.* *Eccl* 2:18
nor any thing *t.* from it. 3:14
the sinner shall be *t.* by her. 7:26
as the fishes that are *t.* in. 9:12
t. evil counsel against thee. *Isa* 7:5
shall be broken, and snared, and *t.* 8:15
who hath *t.* this counsel? 23:8
shall be *t.* in the snare. 24:18 *Jer* 48:44
might be broken, snared, and *t.* *Isa* 28:13
that shall not be *t.* down. 33:20*
thou whom I have *t.* from ends. 41:9
shall the prey be *t.* from the? 49:24
I have *t.* the cup of trembling. 51:22
he was *t.* from prison and. 53:8
the wife shall be *t.* *Jer* 6:11
ashamed, dismayed, and *t.* 8:9
planted, they have *t.* root. *Jer* 12:2
shalt surely be *t.* 34:3; 38:23
day that Jerusalem was *t.* 38:28
when they had *t.* him, they. 39:5
he had *t.* him, being bound. 40:1
dwell in your cities, that ye have *t.* 10
Kiriathaim is *t.* 48:1
thy treasures, thou also shalt be *t.* 7
joy and gladness is *t.* from the. 33
Kirioth is *t.* 41
thy sons are *t.* captives. 46
hear the counsel he hath *t.* 49:20
sorrows have *t.* Damascus. 24
Nebuchadnezzar hath *t.* counsel. 30
publish and say, Babylon is *t.* 50:2 24; 51:31, 41
anointed of the Lord was *t.* *Lam* 4:20
the prince of Israel be *t.* *Ezek* 12:13
shall wood be *t.* thereof to do? 15:3
also *t.* thy fair jewels of gold. 16:17
thou hast *t.* thy sons and thy. 20
and hath *t.* the king thereof. 17:12
t. of the king's seed, hath *t.* 13
and he shall be *t.* in my snare. 20
neither hath *t.* any increase. 18:8
usury, and hath *t.* increase. 13
that hath *t.* off his hand from. 17*
he was *t.* in their pit. 19:4, 8
call to remembrance, that they may be *t.* 21:23
they *t.* gifts; thou hast *t.* usury. 22:12
have *t.* vengeance with a. 25:15
his father had *t.* out. *Dan* 5:2, 3
ye have *t.* my silver. *Joel* 3:5
if he have *t.* nothing? *Amos* 3:4, 5
so shall Israel be *t.* that dwell. 12*
have we not *t.* to us horns by? 6:13
the city shall be *t.* and. *Zech* 14:2
bridegroom shall be *t.* *Mat* 9:15
we have *t.* no bread. 16:7
the kingdom of God shall be *t.* 21:43
one shall be *t.* 24:40; *Luke* 17:34 35, 36
had *t.* counsel, they gave. *Mat* 28:12
from him *t.* even that. *Mark* 4:25
when he had *t.* the five loaves. 6:41
t. him in his arms, he said. 9:36
night, and have *t.* nothing. *Luke* 5:5
of fishes which they had *t.* 9
if I have *t.* any thing from. 19:8*
some would have *t.* him. *John* 7:44
a woman *t.* in adultery. 8:3, 4
ye have *t.* and by wicked. *Acts* 2:23
for his life is *t.* from the. 8:33
this man was *t.* of the Jews. 23:27*
fasting, having *t.* nothing. 27:33
not as though the word hath *t.* none effect. *Rom* 9:6*
no temptation *t.* you. *1 Cor* 10:13
being *t.* from you for. *1 Thes* 2:17*
will let, until he be *t.* *2 Thes* 2:7
let not a widow be *t.* *1 Tim* 5:9*
who are *t.* captive by him at his will. *2 Tim* 2:26
every high priest *t.* from. *Heb* 5:1
made to be *t.* and destroyed. *2 Pet* 2:12
when he had *t.* the book. *Rev* 5:8
hast *t.* to thee thy great. 11:17
beast was *t.* and with him. 19:20

taken *away*

servants had *t. away*. *Gen* 21:25
Jacob came and hath *t. away*. 27:35
he hath *t. away* my blessing. 36
God hath *t. away* my reproach. 30:23
Jacob hath *t. away* all that is. 31:1
thus God hath *t. away* the cattle. 9
hast thou *t.* us *away* to die? *Ex* 14:11
as the fat is *t. away* from the sacrifice. *Lev* 4:31, 35
trespass in a thing *t. away* by. 6:2
after that he hath *t. away* the. 14:43
nor *t. away* aught for. *Deut* 26:14
be violently *t. away* from. 28:31
have *t. away* my gods. *Judg* 18:24
day when it was *t. away*. *1 Sam* 21:6
the high places were not *t. away*. *1 Ki* 22:43; *2 Ki* 12:3; 14:4 *2 Chr* 15:17; 20:33
before I be *t. away* from thee. *2 Ki* 2:9
altars Hezekiah hath *t. away*. 18:22 *2 Chr* 32:12; *Isa* 36:7
t. away the groves. *2 Chr* 19:3

the Lord hath t. away. Job 1:21
hath violently t. away an. 20:19
God liveth, who hath t. away. 27:2
hath t. away my judgement. 34:5
and the mighty shall be t. away. 20
t. away all thy wrath. Ps 85:3
their sleep is t. away. Pr 4:16
thine iniquity is t. away. Isa 6:7
of Samaria shall be t. away. 8:4
the burden shall be t. away. 10:27
the gladness is t. away. 16:10
Damascus is t. away. 17:1
the mighty shall be t. away. 49:25
that my people is t. away for. 52:5
t. away, righteous is t. away. 57:1
like the wind have t. us away. 64:6
I have t. away my peace. Jer 16:5
hath violently t. away. Lam 2:6
t. away in his iniquity. Ezek 33:6
their dominion t. away. Dan 7:12
by him the daily sacrifice was t. away. 8:11; 12:11
fishes shall be t. away. Hos 4:3
and I have t. away your horses. Amos 4:10
t. away my glory for ever. Mi 2:9
the Lord hath t. away thy judgements. Zeph 3:15
from him shall be t. away. Mat 13:12
25:29; Luke 8:18; 19:26
the bridegroom shall be t. away. Mark 2:20; Luke 5:35
that good part which shall not be t. away. Luke 10:42
ye have t. away the key of. 11:52
they might be t. away. John 19:31
seeth the stone t. away from. 20:1
they have t. away the Lord. 2
they have t. away my Lord. 13
judgement was t. away. Acts 8:33
should be saved was t. away. 27:20
this, might be t. away. 1 Cor 5:2
vail shall be t. away. 2 Cor 3:16

taken *hold*

and have t. hold upon. 1 Ki 9:9
days of affliction have t. hold upon. Job 30:16
iniquities have t. hold. Ps 40:12*
anguish have t. hold on me. 119:143
pangs have t. hold on me. Isa 21:3
anguish hath t. hold on us. Jer 6:24

taken *up*

cloud was t. up from. Ex 40:36
not t. up, till the day it was t. up. 37
the cloud was t. up. Num 9:17, 21
but when it was t. up. 22; 10:11
Absalom was t. up. 2 Sam 18:9
they have t. up their. Isa 10:29
shall be t. up a curse. Jer 29:22
ye are t. up in the lips. Ezek 36:3
so Daniel was t. up out. Dan 6:23
there was t. up of the. Luke 9:17
day in which he was t. up. Acts 1:2
while they beheld, he was t. up. 9
this same Jesus which is t. up. 11*
day he was t. up from us. 22
and was t. up dead. 20:9
when they had t. up they. 27:17*
had t. up the anchors. 40*

takest

the water thou t. out of the. Ex 4:9
when thou t. the sum of. 30:12
journey thou t. not be. Judg 4:9
thou t. away their breath. Ps 104:29
what is man that thou t.? 144:3
and thou t. no knowledge. Isa 58:3
t. up that thou layedst. Luke 19:21

takest *heed*

if thou t. heed to fulfil. 1 Chr 22:13*

taketh

that t. his name in vain. Ex 20:7
Deut 5:11
persons nor t. reward. Deut 10:17
t. a man's life to pledge. 24:6
putteth her hand and t. him. 25:11
cursed be he that t. reward. 27:25
as an eagle t. them, beareth. 32:11
tribe which the Lord t. Josh 7:14
smiteth Kirjath-sepher and t. it. 15:16; Judg 1:12
and t. away reproach. 1 Sam 17:26
as a man t. away dung. 1 Ki 14:10*
t. it even out of the thorns. Job 5:5
he t. the wise in their craftiness. 13
1 Cor 3:19
he t. away, who can? Job 9:12*
and t. away the understanding. 12:20
he t. away the heart of the chief. 24
what is the hope, when God t.? 27:8
he t. it with his eyes, his nose. 40:24
nor t. up reproach against. Ps 15:3
nor t. reward against the innocent. 5
Lord t. my part with them. 118:7*
happy shall he be that t. 137:9
he t. not pleasure in the legs. 147:10
the Lord t. pleasure in them. 11
for the Lord t. pleasure in his. 149:4
which t. away the life. Pr 1:19
better than he that t. a city. 16:32
a wicked man t. a gift out of. 17:23
as he that t. away a garment. 25:20
is like one that t. a dog by. 26:17
of all his labour which he t. Eccl 1:3*
heart t. not rest in the night. 2:23
sheep that no man t. up. Isa 13:14
he t. up the isles as a very. 40:15
the carpenter t. the cypress. 44:14
nor is there any that t. her by. 51:18
who t. strangers instead. Ezek 16:32
and t. not warning. 33:4
but he that t. warning. 5
as the shepherd t. out of. Amos 3:12*
the devil t. him up into. Mat 4:5
t. him up into an exceeding high. 8
t. from garment, and rent is made worse. 9:16; Mark 2:21
and t. not his cross and. Mat 10:38
he goeth, t. seven other spirits. 12:45; Luke 11:26
Jesus t. Peter, James. Mat 17:1
Mark 9:2; 14:33
Satan cometh and t. away the word. Mark 4:15; Luke 8:12
he t. the father and. Mark 5:40
he t. him, he teareth him. 9:18
that t. away thy cloak. Luke 6:29
and of him that t. thy goods. 30
spirit t. him, and he suddenly. 9:39
a stronger t. from him all his. 11:22
my lord t. away from me the. 16:3
the Lamb of God which t. John 1:29
no man t. it from me, I lay it. 10:18
beareth not fruit, he t. away. 15:2
your joy no man t. from you. 16:22
Jesus then cometh, t. bread. 21:13
is God unrighteous, who t.? Rom 3:5*
in eating every one t. 1 Cor 11:21
no man t. this honour. Heb 5:4
he t. away the first that he may. 10:9

taketh *hold*

I am afraid, and trembling t. hold on my flesh. Job 21:6
the spider t. hold with. Pr 30:28
every one that t. hold of. Isa 56:6

taking

with God there is no t. of. 2 Chr 19:7
I have seen the foolish t. root. Job 5:3
by t. heed thereto. Ps 119:9
at noise of t. of Babylon. Jer 50:46
dealt against Judah by t. Ezek 25:12
I taught Ephraim also to go, t. them by their arms. Hos 11:3
which of you by t. thought? Mat 6:27*; Luke 12:25*
Son of man is as a man t. a far. Mark 13:34*
the devil, t. him up into. Luke 4:5
t. up that I laid not down. 19:22
he had spoken of t. rest. John 11:13
sin t. occasion by the. Rom 7:8, 11
t. my leave of them, I. 2 Cor 2:13
t. wages of them to do you. 11:8
above all t. the shield of. Eph 6:16
in flaming fire t. vengeance on them. 2 Thes 1:8*
t. the oversight thereof. 1 Pet 5:2*
they went forth t. nothing. 3 John 7

tale (*quantity*)

the t. of bricks which. Ex 5:8
he deliver the t. of bricks. 18
they gave the foreskins in full t. to the king. 1 Sam 18:27
bring vessels in and out by t. 1 Chr 9:28

tale

years as a t. that is told. Ps 90:9

talebearer

up and down as a t. Lev 19:16
a t. revealeth. Pr 11:13; 20:19
the words of a t. are. 18:8*; 26:22*
where there is no t., the strife. 26:20*

talent

[1] *A weight among the Jews, of 50 to 100 pounds, according to the standard in use at the time. The value of the gold talent would be as as much as 29,000 dollars, or nearly £6000, that of the silver talent up to 1940 dollars, or nearly £400. In the times of the New Testament the talent was reckoned only in silver, and was worth about 1150 dollars, or £240. These amounts are not intended to be absolutely exact, but give values in round numbers. There is great diversity in estimates given,* Ex 25:39; 38:25. [2] *The gifts of God bestowed on men,* Mat 25:15.

of a t. of pure gold make it. Ex 25:39; 37:24
sockets, a t. for a socket. 38:27
the weight of the crown was a t. 2 Sam 12:30
pay a t. of silver. 1 Ki 20:39
give them a t. of silver. 2 Ki 5:22
a tribute of a t. of gold. 23:33
2 Chr 36:3
lifted up a t. of lead. Zech 5:7
hid thy t. in the earth. Mat 25:25
take therefore the t. from him. 28
about the weight of a t. Rev 16:21

talents

of the offering, was 29 t. Ex 38:24
of 100 t. of silver were cast. 27
hill of Samaria for two t. 1 Ki 16:24
Naaman took ten t. 2 Ki 5:5
be content, take two t. 23
Menahem gave Pul 1000 t. 15:19
Hezekiah 300 t. and 30 of gold. 18:14
land to a tribute of 100 t. 23:33
2 Chr 36:3
Ammonites sent 1000 t. 1 Chr 19:6
David gave 3000 t. of gold. 29:4
gold, 5000 t. and of silver 10,000 t. 7
we do for the 100 t.? 2 Chr 25:9
of Ammon gave him 100 t. 27:5
owed him 10,000 t. Mat 18:24
gave five t., to another two. 25:15
see **gold, silver**

tales

men that carry t. to. Ezek 22:9*
their words seemed to them as idle t. Luke 24:11*

Talitha cumi

(*An Aramaic expression meaning Damsel, arise. Used by Jesus when raising Jairus's daughter*)

he said unto her, T., damsel, arise. Mark 5:41

talk

should a man full of t.? Job 11:2
reason with unprofitable t.? 15:3
the t. of the lips tendeth. Pr 14:23
end of his t. is mischievous. Eccl 10:13
entangle him in his t. Mat 22:15

talk, *verb*

I will come down and t. Num 11:17
God doth t. with man. Deut 5:24
t. of them when thou sittest. 6:7
t. no more so exceeding proudly. 1 Sam 2:3
t. not with us in the Jews' language. 2 Ki 18:26
sing psalms, t. ye of all his wondrous. 1 Chr 16:9; Ps 105:2
and will ye t. deceitfully? Job 13:7
they t. to the grief of. Ps 69:26
my tongue shall t. of thy. 71:24
meditate and t. of thy doings. 77:12
I t. of thy wondrous works. 119:27
kingdom and t. of thy power. 145:11
awakest it shall t. with thee. Pr 6:22
and their lips t. of mischief. 24:2
let me t. with thee of. Jer 12:1

arise and I will there *t.* *Ezek* 3:22
servant *t.* with my lord ? *Dan* 10:17
I will not *t.* much with. *John* 14:30

talked

brethren *t.* with him. *Gen* 45:15
ye have seen that I have *t.* with you. *Ex* 20:22; *Deut* 5:4
and the Lord *t.* with Moses. *Ex* 33:9
of his face shone while he *t.* 34:29
Saul *t.* unto the priest. *1 Sam* 14:19
to pass as he *t.* with him. *2 Chr* 25:16
princes hear that I have *t.* *Jer* 38:25
t. with him two men, Moses and. *Luke* 9:30
heart burn, while he *t.* with us? 24:32
marvelled that he *t.* with. *John* 4:27
Peter *t.* with Cornelius. *Acts* 10:27
and *t.* long, even till break of. 20:11
they *t.* between themselves. 26:31
he that *t.* with me had a. *Rev* 21:15

talkers

up in the lips of *t.* *Ezek* 36:3
unruly and vain *t.* *Tit* 1:10

talkest

sign that thou *t.* with me. *Judg* 6:17
yet *t.* with the king. *1 Ki* 1:14
no man said, Why *t.* thou with her? *John* 4:27

talketh

tongue *t.* of judgement. *Ps* 37:30
seen him, and it is he that *t.* with. *John* 9:37

talking

he left off *t.* with him. *Gen* 17:22
he is a god, he is *t.* or. *1 Ki* 18:27
they were *t.* with him. *Esth* 6:14
the princes refrained *t.* and. *Job* 29:9
thy people are still *t.* *Ezek* 33:30
Moses and Elias *t.* with him. *Mat* 17:3; *Mark* 9:4
neither filthiness, nor foolish *t.* *Eph* 5:4
a trumpet *t.* with me. *Rev* 4:1

tall

a people *t.* as the Anakims. *Deut* 2:10, 21; 9:2
cut down the *t.* cedar trees and the choice fir. *2 Ki* 19:23; *Isa* 37:24

taller

people is greater and *t.* *Deut* 1:28

Tamar

Er, whose name was *T.* *Gen* 38:6
was told Judah, *T.* hath played. 24
house of Pharez, whom *T.* bare to. *Ruth* 4:12; *1 Chr* 2:4; *Mat* 1:3
a fair sister, named *T.* *2 Sam* 13:1
Ammon fell sick for *T.* 2
he forced *T.* 22, 32
daughter, whose name was *T.* 14:27
side southward from *T.* *Ezek* 47:19

tame

nor could any man *t.* him. *Mark* 5:4
but the tongue can no man *t.*; it is an unruly evil. *Jas* 3:8

tamed

in sea, is *t.*, and hath been *t.* *Jas* 3:7

Tammuz

there sat women weeping for *T.* *Ezek* 8:14

tanner

Peter tarried with one Simon a *t.* *Acts* 9:43
lodged with one Simon a *t.* 10:6, 32

tapestry, *see* **coverings**

tare

the king arose and *t.* *2 Sam* 13:31*
two she bears *t.* forty. *2 Ki* 2:24
straightway the spirit *t.* him. *Mark* 9:20; *Luke* 9:42

tares

Darnel, *a weed of which some varieties are poisonous. It looks much like wheat until near harvest time, when the two can be readily distinguished,* Mat 13:29.

his enemy sowed *t.* *Mat* 13:25
up, then appeared the *t.* also. 26
from whence then hath it *t.*? 27
lest while ye gather up the *t.* 29
declare to us the parable of the *t.* 36

target

(*A large, heavy shield*)
Goliath had a *t.* of. *1 Sam* 17:6*
six hundred shekels of gold went to one *t.* *1 Ki* 10:16†; *2 Chr* 9:15†

targets

made two hundred *t.* *1 Ki* 10:16†
Asa had an army that bare *t.* and. *2 Chr* 14:8*

tarried

Abraham's servant *t.* all. *Gen* 24:54
Jacob *t.* there all night and. 28:11
Jacob and Laban *t.* all night in. 31:54
when the cloud *t.* *Num* 9:19, 22
t. till they were ashamed. *Judg* 3:25
Ehud escaped while they *t.* and. 26
they *t.* till afternoon and did. 19:8
save that she *t.* a little. *Ruth* 2:7
t. seven days according. *1 Sam* 13:8
but David *t.* still at. *2 Sam* 11:1
the king *t.* in a place that. 15:17
Zadok and Abiathar *t.* at. 29
but he *t.* longer than the set. 20:5
they came, for he *t.* at. *2 Ki* 2:18
and she that *t.* at home. *Ps* 68:12
while the bridegroom *t.* *Mat* 25:5
marvelled that he *t.* *Luke* 1:21
the child Jesus *t.* behind in. 2:43
then he *t.* with them. *John* 3:22
Peter *t.* many days in Joppa. *Acts* 9:43
Judas and Silas ... *t.* a space. 15:33
Paul *t.* a good while at Corinth and. 18:18
these going before *t.* for us at. 20:5
finding the disciples, we *t.* 21:4
as we *t.* many days at Caesarea. 10
Festus *t.* at Jerusalem more. 25:6
fourteenth day ye have *t.* fasting. 27:33
landing at Syracuse, we *t.* 28:12

tarriest

now why *t.* thou ? arise. *Acts* 22:16

tarrieth

shall his part be that *t.* *1 Sam* 30:24
that *t.* not for a man, nor. *Mi* 5:7

tarry

[1] *To remain,* Gen 27:41. [2] *To wait for,* Ex 24:14. [3] *To delay,* Gen 45:9.

and *t.* all night, and. *Gen* 19:2
and *t.* with Laban a few days. 27:44
found favour in thine eyes, *t.* 30:27
Come down to me, *t.* not. 45:9
thrust out, and could not *t.* *Ex* 12:39
t. ye here for us till we come. 24:14
leper shall *t.* out of his tent. *Lev* 14:8
I pray you *t.* here also. *Num* 22:19
why *t.* the wheels of ? *Judg* 5:28
he said, I will *t.* until thou. 6:18
and *t.* all night. 19:6, 9
the man would not *t.* 10
would ye *t.* for them till they were grown ? *Ruth* 1:13
t. this night, and it shall be. 3:13
t. until thou have weaned him. *1 Sam* 1:23
seven days shalt thou *t.* till I. 10:8
if they say, *T.* till we come. 14:9
t. at Jericho till your beards be. *2 Sam* 10:5; *1 Chr* 19:5
t. here to-day. *2 Sam* 11:12
I will *t.* in the plain. 15:28
Joab said, I may not *t.* thus. 18:14
will not *t.* one with thee. 19:7
t. here, I pray thee; for the Lord hath sent me. *2 Ki* 2:2, 4, 6
the lepers said, If we *t.* till the. 7:9
open door and flee, and *t.* not. 9:3
glory of this, and *t.* at home. 14:10
a liar shall not *t.* in my. *Ps* 101:7
that *t.* long at the wine. *Pr* 23:30
my salvation shall not *t.* *Isa* 46:13
that turneth aside to *t.* *Jer* 14:8
t., wait for it; for it will not *t.* *Hab* 2:3
t. ye here and watch. *Mat* 26:38
Mark 14:34
and he went in to *t.* *Luke* 24:29
but *t.* ye in the city of Jerusalem. 49
besought that he would *t.* *John* 4:40
if I will that he *t.* till. 21:22, 23
they prayed Peter to *t.* *Acts* 10:48

desired Paul to *t.* longer. *Acts* 18:20
were desired to *t.* with them. 28:14
wherefore *t.* one for. *1 Cor* 11:33
I trust to *t.* a while with you. 16:7
but I will *t.* at Ephesus until. 8
but if I *t.* long, that. *1 Tim* 3:15
he that shall come, will come and not *t.* *Heb* 10:37

tarrying

make no *t.* O my God. *Ps* 40:17
70:5

Tarshish

the sons of Javan; Elishah, and *T.* *Gen* 10:4; *1 Chr* 1:7
king had at sea a navy of *T.* with a. *1 Ki* 10:22; *2 Chr* 9:21
make ships to go to *T.* *2 Chr* 20:36
broken and not able to go to *T.* 37
thou breakest ships of *T.* *Ps* 48:7
the kings of *T.* shall bring. 72:10
Lord on all the ships of *T.* *Isa* 2:16
howl, ye ships of *T.* it is. 23:1, 14
over to *T.* howl, ye inhabitants. 6
thy land, O daughter of *T.* 10
the ships of *T.* shall wait for. 60:9
send those that escape to *T.* 66:19
silver is brought from *T.* *Jer* 10:9
T. was thy merchant. *Ezek* 27:12
the ships of *T.* did sing of thee. 25
the merchants of *T.* shall say. 38:13
rose up to flee unto *T.* *Jonah* 1:3
therefore I fled before unto *T.* 4:2

Tarsus

enquire for one Saul of *T.* *Acts* 9:11
brethren sent him forth to *T.* 30
Barnabas departed to *T.* to. 11:25
I am a man who am a Jew of *T.* 21:39; 22:3

Tartak

the Avites made *T.* *2 Ki* 17:31

task, -s

your works, your daily *t.* *Ex* 5:13
why not fulfilled your *t.* in ? 14
minish from your daily *t.* 19

taskmasters

set over them *t.* to afflict. *Ex* 1:11
cry by reason of their *t.* 3:7
and Pharaoh commanded *t.* 5:6
t. told them. 10
t. hasted them. 13
officers which the *t.* had set. 14

taste

the *t.* of manna was like. *Ex* 16:31
the *t.* of it was as the *t.* of fresh oil. *Num* 11:8
is there any *t.* in the white of an egg ? *Job* 6:6
cannot my *t.* discern perverse ? 30
are thy words to my *t.*! *Ps* 119:103
honeycomb is sweet to *t.* *Pr* 24:13
fruit was sweet to my *t.* *S of S* 2:3
his *t.* remained in him. *Jer* 48:11

taste, *verb*

[1] *To try the relish of any thing by the tongue,* Job 34:3. [2] *Figuratively, to prove,* Ps 34:8. [3] *To eat a little,* 1 Sam 14:29, 43.

did but *t.* a little honey. *1 Sam* 14:43
if I *t.* bread or aught else. *2 Sam* 3:35
can thy servant *t.* what I eat ? 19:35
the mouth *t.* his meat ? *Job* 12:11
O *t.* and see that the Lord. *Ps* 34:8
neither herd nor flock *t.* *Jonah* 3:7
standing here which shall not *t.* of. *Mat* 16:28; *Mark* 9:1; *Luke* 9:27
none bidden shall *t.* of. *Luke* 14:24
he shall never *t.* death. *John* 8:52
touch not, *t.* not, handle. *Col* 2:21
that he should *t.* death. *Heb* 2:9

tasted

so none *t.* any food. *1 Sam* 14:24
I *t.* a little of this honey. 29
Belshazzar, whiles he *t.* wine. *Dan* 5:2
when he had *t.* thereof. *Mat* 27:34
the ruler had *t.* the water. *John* 2:9
t. of the heavenly gift. *Heb* 6:4
have *t.* the good word of God. 5
have *t.* that the Lord. *1 Pet* 2:3

tasteth

words as the mouth *t*. *Job* 34:3

tattlers

not only idle but *t*. and. *1 Tim* 5:13

taught

I have *t*. you statutes. *Deut* 4:5
Moses *t*. the children of Israel. 31:22
with them he *t*. the men. *Judg* 8:16
and *t*. them how to fear. *2 Ki* 17:28
thou hast *t*. them the. *2 Chr* 6:27
Levites *t*. the people in Judah. 17:9
people rejoiced, such as *t*. 23:13
that *t*. the good knowledge of. 30:22*
said to the Levites that *t*. all. 35:3
that *t*. the people said. *Neh* 8:9
O God, thou hast *t*. me. *Ps* 71:17
119:102
when thou hast *t*. me. 119:171
he *t*. me also, and said. *Pr* 4:4
t. thee in the way of wisdom. 11
prophecy that his mother *t*. him. 31:1
he still *t*. the people. *Eccl* 12:9
their fear is *t*. by the. *Isa* 29:13
counsellor hath *t*. him. 40:13, 14
all thy children shall be *t*. 54:13
hast thou *t*. the wicked. *Jer* 2:33
t. their tongues to speak lies. 9:5
which their fathers *t*. them. 14
t. my people to swear by. 12:16
for thou hast *t*. them to be. 13:21
thou hast *t*. rebellion against. 28:16
he hath *t*. rebellion against. 29:32
though I have *t*. them, rising. 32:33
women *t*. not to do after. *Ezek* 23:48
as a heifer that is *t*. *Hos* 10:11
I *t*. Ephraim to go, taking them. 11:3
man *t*. me to keep cattle. *Zech* 13:5*
he *t*. them as one having authority.
Mat 7:29; *Mark* 1:22
and did as they were *t*. *Mat* 28:15
told him all things they had done and *t*. *Mark* 6:30
as he was wont he *t*. them. 10:1
while he *t*. in the temple. 12:35
Luke 19:47; 20:1; *John* 7:14, 28
teach us to pray, as John *t*. his.
Luke 11:1
thou hast *t*. in our streets. 13:26
shall be all *t*. of God. *John* 6:45
he sat down and *t*. them. 8:2
as my father hath *t*. me, I. 28
I ever *t*. in the synagogue and. 18:20
being grieved that they *t*. the people.
Acts 4:2
into the temple early and *t*. 5:21
Paul and Barnabas *t*. much people.
11:26; 14:21
certain men *t*. the brethren. 15:1
t. diligently the things of the. 18:25
I have shewed you, and *t*. 20:20
t. according to the perfect. 22:3
nor was I *t*. it but by. *Gal* 1:12
let him that is *t*. in the word. 6:6
been *t*. by him as truth. *Eph* 4:21
the faith, as ye have been *t*. *Col* 2:7
ye are *t*. of God to love. *1 Thes* 4:9
hold the traditions ye have been *t*.
2 Thes 2:15
the word, as he hath been *t*. *Tit* 1:9
anointing hath *t*. you. *1 John* 2:27
who *t*. Balak to cast a. *Rev* 2:14

taunt

will deliver them to be a *t*. *Jer* 24:9
a reproach and a *t*. *Ezek* 5:15

taunting

all these take up a *t*. proverb.
Hab 2:6

taverns

meet us as far as the three *t*.
Acts 28:15*

taxation

every one according to *t*. *2 Ki* 23:35

taxed

but Jehoiakim *t*. the. *2 Ki* 23:35
a decree that all the world should be *t*. *Luke* 2:1*
all went to be *t*. 3*
Joseph went to be *t*. 5*

taxes

stand up a raiser of *t*. *Dan* 11:20

taxing

and this *t*. was first made. *Luke* 2:2*
in the days of the *t*. *Acts* 5:37*

teach

and I will *t*. you what. *Ex* 4:15
in his heart that he may *t*. 35:34
that ye may *t*. Israel. *Lev* 10:11
to *t*. when it is unclean and 14:57
judgements which I *t*. you. *Deut* 4:1
and that they may *t*. their children. 10
Lord commanded me to *t*. 14; 6:1
t. you not to do after their. 20:18
priests the Levites shall *t*. you. 24:8
write and *t*. the children of. 31:19
shall *t*. Jacob thy judgements. 33:10
t. us what we shall do. *Judg* 13:8
I will *t*. you the good. *1 Sam* 12:23
bade them *t*. the use. *2 Sam* 1:18
to *t*. in the cities of. *2 Chr* 17:7
to *t*. in Israel statutes. *Ezra* 7:10
any *t*. God knowledge? *Job* 21:22
t. you by the hand of God. 27:11
of years should *t*. wisdom. 32:7
t. us what we shall say unto. 37:19
will *t*. sinners in the way. *Ps* 25:8
will he guide and *t*. his way. 9
him that feareth Lord shall he *t*. 12
t. you the fear of the Lord. 34:11
then will I *t*. trangressors. 51:13
so *t*. us to number our days. 90:12
and *t*. his senators wisdom. 105:22
t. a just man, and he will. *Pr* 9:9
and he will *t*. us of his ways. *Isa* 2:3
Mi 4:2
whom shall he *t*. knowledge? *Isa* 28:9
for his God doth instruct and *t*. 26
and *t*. your daughters. *Jer* 9:20
they shall *t*. no more every man his.
31:34; *Heb* 8:11
t. my people the difference between.
Ezek 44:23
whom they might *t*. learning of.
Dan 1:4
priests thereof *t*. for hire. *Mi* 3:11
stone, Arise, it shall *t*.! *Hab* 2:19
shall *t*. men so. *Mat* 5:19
t. all nations. 28:19
Lord, *t*. us to pray, as. *Luke* 11:1
Holy Ghost shall *t*. you what. 12:12
t. the Gentiles. *John* 7:35
dost thou *t*. us? 9:34
Holy Ghost shall *t*. you all. 14:26
Jesus began to do and *t*. *Acts* 1:1
speak nor *t*. in the name of Jesus.
4:18; 5:28
to *t*. and preach Jesus Christ. 5:42
t. customs which are not. 16:21
as I *t*. every where in. *1 Cor* 4:17
even nature itself *t*. you? 11:14
that by my voice I might *t*. 14:19
charge some they *t*. no. *1 Tim* 1:3
but I suffer not a woman to *t*. 2:12
bishop must be apt to *t*. 3:2
2 Tim 2:24
things command and *t*. *1 Tim* 4:11
these things *t*. and exhort. 6:2
if any man *t*. otherwise, he. 3
shall be able to *t*. others. *2 Tim* 2:2
that they *t*. young women. *Tit* 2:4
ye have need that one *t*. *Heb* 5:12
not that any man *t*. you. *1 John* 2:27
that woman Jezebel to *t*. *Rev* 2:20
see **began**

teach *me*

t. *me* and I will hold my. *Job* 6:24
I see not, *t*. thou *me*. 34:32
t. *me* thy paths. *Ps* 25:4
lead me and *t*. *me*. 5
t. *me* thy way, O Lord. 27:11; 86:11
t. *me* thy statutes. 119:12, 26, 33
64, 68, 124, 135
t. *me* good judgements. 119:66
t. *me* thy judgements. 108
t. *me* to do thy will, for. 143:10

teach *thee*

I will *t*. *thee* what thou. *Ex* 4:12
which they shall *t*. *thee*. *Deut* 17:11
shall not they *t*. *thee*? *Job* 8:10
beasts, and they shall *t*. *thee*. 12:7
earth, and it shall *t*. *thee*. 8
I shall *t*. *thee* wisdom. 33:33
I will *t*. *thee* in the way. *Ps* 32:8
thy right hand shall *t*. *thee*. 45:4

teach *them*

t. *them* ordinances and. *Ex* 18:20
that thou mayest *t*. *them*. 24:12
t. *them* thy sons, and. *Deut* 4:9
which thou shalt *t*. *them*. 5:31
t. *them* diligently to thy. 6:7; 11:19
know to *t*. *them* war. *Judg* 3:2
that thou *t*. *them* the good way.
1 Ki 8:36
t. *them* the manner of. *2 Ki* 17:27
t. ye *them* that know. *Ezra* 7:25
keep my testimony that I shall *t*. *them*. *Ps* 132:12
do and *t*. *them* shall be. *Mat* 5:19
he began to *t*. *them*. *Mark* 6:34
to *t*. *them* that the son of. 8:31

teacher

cast lots, as well the *t*. *1 Chr* 25:8
the image, a *t*. of lies. *Hab* 2:18
we know thou art a *t*. *John* 3:2
thou art a *t*. of babes. *Rom* 2:20
I am a *t*. *1 Tim* 2:7; *2 Tim* 1:11

teachers

more understanding than all my *t*.
Ps 119:99
obeyed the voice of my *t*. *Pr* 5:13
t. be removed into a corner any more . . . shall see thy *t*. *Isa* 30:20
thy *t*. have transgressed. 43:27*
certain prophets and *t*. *Acts* 13:1
hath set prophets, *t*. *1 Cor* 12:28
are all *t*.? 29
evangelists, pastors, and *t*. *Eph* 4:11
desiring to be *t*. of law. *1 Tim* 1:7
to themselves *t*. having. *2 Tim* 4:3
that the aged women be *t*. *Tit* 2:3
time ye ought to be *t*. *Heb* 5:12
as there shall be false *t*. *2 Pet* 2:1

teachest

the man whom thou *t*. *Ps* 94:12
thou art true, and *t*. the way of God.
Mat 22:16; *Mark* 12:14; *Luke* 20:21
thou *t*. the Jews to. *Acts* 21:21
thou that *t*. another, *t*.? *Rom* 2:21

teacheth

he *t*. my hands to war. *2 Sam* 22:35
Ps 18:34
t. us more than the beasts. *Job* 35:11
God exalteth, who *t*. like? 36:22
that *t*. man knowledge. *Ps* 94:10
which *t*. my hands to war. 144:1
a wicked man *t*. with. *Pr* 6:13*
of the wise *t*. his mouth. 16:23*
the prophet that *t*. lies. *Isa* 9:15
I am thy God which *t*. thee. 48:17
the man that *t*. all men. *Acts* 21:28
or he that *t*., on teaching. *Rom* 12:7
man's wisdom *t*. but which the Holy Ghost *t*. *1 Cor* 2:13
let him communicate to him that *t*.
Gal 6:6
as the same anointing *t*. *1 John* 2:27

teaching

been without a *t*. priest. *2 Chr* 15:3
rising up early and *t*. them.
Jer 32:33
Jesus went about Galilee, *t*. in their.
Mat 4:23; 9:35; *Luke* 13:10
worship me, *t*. for doctrines the.
Mat 15:9; *Mark* 7:7
unto him as he was *t*. *Mat* 21:23
I sat daily with you *t*. in. 26:55
t. them to observe all things. 28:20
t. throughout all Jewry. *Luke* 23:5
the apostles *t*. the people. *Acts* 5:25
Barnabas continued in Antioch, *t*. and preaching. 15:35
Paul *t*. the word of God at. 18:11
Paul *t*. at Rome with all. 28:31
or he that teacheth, on *t*. *Rom* 12:7
warning and *t*. every man. *Col* 1:28
t. and admonishing one another. 3:16
t. things which they. *Tit* 1:11
t. us, that denying ungodliness. 2:12

tear

then will I *t*. your flesh. *Judg* 8:7
lest he *t*. my soul like a lion. *Ps* 7:2
did *t*. me and ceased not. 35:15
lest I *t*. you in pieces. 50:22
over them the dogs to *t*. *Jer* 15:3
nor shall men *t*. themselves. 16:7*

pillows I will *t.* from. *Ezek* 13:20
kerchiefs will I *t.* and deliver. 21
I, even I, will *t.* and go. *Hos* 5:14
the wild beast shall *t.* them. 13:8
off pity, his anger did *t.* *Amos* 1:11
the lion did *t.* enough. *Nah* 2:12
the shepherd shall *t.* *Zech* 11:16

teareth

lion, and *t.* the arm. *Deut* 33:20
he *t.* me in his wrath. *Job* 16:9
he *t.* himself in his anger. 18:4
as a young lion *t.* in pieces. *Mi* 5:8
taketh him, he *t.* him and he foameth. *Mark* 9:18*; *Luke* 9:39

tears

I have seen thy *t.* *2 Ki* 20:5; *Isa* 38:5
but mine eye poureth out *t.* unto. *Job* 16:20
I water my couch with my *t.* *Ps* 6:6
hold not thy peace at my *t.* 39:12
my *t.* have been my meat day. 42:3
put thou my *t.* in thy bottle. 56:8
feedest them with the bread of *t.* and givest them *t.* to drink in. 80:5
delivered mine eyes from *t.* 116:8
that sow in *t.* shall reap in joy. 126:5
behold the *t.* of such as. *Eccl* 4:1
I will water thee with *t.* *Isa* 16:9
wipe away *t.* from all faces. 25:8
eyes were a fountain of *t.* *Jer* 9:1
our eyes may run down with *t.* 18
mine eyes shall run down with *t.* 13:17
let mine eyes run with *t.* 14:17
weeping, thine eyes from *t.* 31:16
she weepeth, and her *t.* are. *Lam* 1:2
mine eyes do fail with *t.* 2:11
let *t.* run down like a river. 18
neither shall thy *t.* *Ezek* 24:16
altar of the Lord with *t.* *Mal* 2:13
the father said with *t.* *Mark* 9:24
wash his feet with her *t.* *Luke* 7:38
she hath washed my feet with *t.* 44
serving the Lord with many *t.* *Acts* 20:19
to warn every one with *t.* 31
wrote to you with many *t.* *2 Cor* 2:4
being mindful of thy *t.* *2 Tim* 1:4
up supplications with *t.* *Heb* 5:7
sought it carefully with *t.* 12:17
shall wipe away all *t.* *Rev* 7:17; 21:4

teats

shall lament for the *t.* *Isa* 32:12*
they bruised the *t.* *Ezek* 23:3†, 21†

Tebeth

tenth month, which is *T.* *Esth* 2:16

tedious

that I be not further *t.* *Acts* 24:4

teeth

and his *t.* shall be white. *Gen* 49:12
flesh was yet between their *t.* *Num* 11:33
t. of beasts upon them. *Deut* 32:24
fleshhook of three *t.* *1 Sam* 2:13
the *t.* of the young lions. *Job* 4:10
I take my flesh in my *t.*? 13:14
with the skin of my *t.* 19:20
plucked the spoil out of his *t.* 29:17
Leviathan's *t.* are terrible. 41:14
thou hast broken the *t.* of. *Ps* 3:7
whose *t.* are spears and arrows. 57:4
break their *t.*, O God, in. 58:6
given us as a prey to their *t.* 124:6
as vinegar to the *t.* so. *Pr* 10:26
whose *t.* are swords, jaw-*t.* 30:14
thy *t.* are like a flock. *S of S* 4:2; 6:6
an instrument having *t.* *Isa* 41:15
children's *t.* are set on edge. *Jer* 31:29; *Ezek* 18:2
eateth sour grapes, his *t.* *Jer* 31:30
hath broken my *t.* with. *Lam* 3:16
ribs between the *t.* of it. *Dan* 7:5
beast had great iron *t.* 7, 19
hath the cheek *t.* of a lion. *Joel* 1:6
you cleanness of *t.* *Amos* 4:6
that bite with their *t.* *Mi* 3:5
from between his *t.* *Zech* 9:7
cast the same in his *t.* *Mat* 27:44*
t. were as the *t.* of lions. *Rev* 9:8
see **gnash**

tell *tree*

as a *t. tree* and as an oak. *Isa* 6:13

Tekel

written, Mene, Mene, *T.* *Dan* 5:25
T. thou art weighed in the. 27

Tekoah, *or* **Tekoa**

Joab sent to *T.* to fetch. *2 Sam* 14:2
when the woman of *T.* spake to. 4
Abiah bare Ashur the father of *T.* *1 Chr* 2:24
Ashur the father of *T.* had two. 4:5
built Etam and *T.* *2 Chr* 11:6
went into the wilderness of *T.* 20:20
blow the trumpet in *T.* *Jer* 6:1
was among herdmen of *T.* *Amos* 1:1

tell

[1] *To count, number, or reckon,* Gen 15:5. [2] *To declare or make known,* Gen 12:18; 21:26.

t. the stars if thou be. *Gen* 15:5
and I have sent to *t.* my Lord. 32:5
as to *t.* the man whether ye. 43:6
we cannot *t.* who put our money. 22
t. my father of all my glory. 45:13
mayest *t.* in the ears. *Ex* 10:2
t. the priest, saying, It. *Lev* 14:35
they will *t.* it to the. *Num* 14:14
t. us wherewith we shall *1 Sam* 6:2
give to the man of God, to *t.* 9:8
liveth, O king, I cannot *t.* 17:55
he would surely *t.* Saul. 22:22
I beseech thee *t.* thy servant. 23:11
should *t.* on us, saying, So. 27:11
t. it not in Gath. *2 Sam* 1:20
go *t.* my servant. 7:5; *1 Chr* 17:4
feared to *t.* him that. *2 Sam* 12:18
was alive, I said, Who can *t.*? 22
thou shalt *t.* to Zadok and. 15:35
go *t.* the king what thou hast. 18:21
that thou shouldest *t.* *1 Ki* 1:20
go, *t.* thy lord, Elijah is. 18:8, 11, 14
when I come and *t.* Ahab, he. 12
t. my lord the king, all thou. 20:9
t. him, let not him that girdeth. 11
that we may *t.* the king's. *2 Ki* 7:9
It is false; *t.* us now. 9:12
to go to *t.* it in Jezreel. 15
t. the man that sent you. 22:15; *2 Chr* 34:23
I may *t.* all my bones. *Ps* 22:17
publish and *t.* of all thy. 26:7
go round about her, *t.* the. 48:12
that ye may *t.* the generation. 13
son's name, if thou canst *t.* *Pr* 30:4
who can *t.* a man what shall be after? *Eccl* 6:12; 10:14
for who can *t.* him when it? 8:7
hath wings shall *t.* the matter. 10:20
t. him that I am sick of. *S of S* 5:8
go and *t.* this people. *Isa* 6:9
t. this. 48:20
t. such as are for death. *Jer* 15:2
dreams which they *t.* 23:27; 28:32
we will *t.* the king of all. 36:16
t. us now how thou didst write. 17
t. it in Arnon, that Moab is. 48:20
wilt thou not *t.* us what? *Ezek* 24:19
O king, *t.* thy servants the dream. *Dan* 2:4, 7, 9
t. the king the interpretation. 36
t. ye your children, and let your children *t.* their children. *Joel* 1:3
who can *t.* if God will? *Jonah* 3:9
see thou *t.* no man. *Mat* 8:4; *Mark* 8:26, 30; 9:9; *Luke* 5:14; 8:56; *Acts* 23:22
disciples that they should *t.* no man. *Mat* 16:20; *Mark* 7:36; *Luke* 9:21
t. the vision to no man. *Mat* 17:9
t. him his fault. 18:15
t. it unto the church. 17
t. ye the daughter of Sion. 21:5
t. us, when shall these things be? 24:3; *Mark* 13:4
that thou *t.* us, whether. *Mat* 26:63; *Luke* 22:67; *John* 10:24
go and *t.* his disciples that. *Mat* 28:7
as they went to *t.* his disciples. 9; *Mark* 16:7
anon they *t.* him of her. *Mark* 1:30
t. them how great things the. 5:19
said, We cannot *t.* 11:33; *Luke* 20:7
t. John what things ye. *Luke* 7:22
go ye, and *t.* that fox, I cast. 13:32
but canst not *t.* whence. *John* 3:8
when he is come, he will *t.* 4:25
but ye cannot *t.* whence I come. 8:14
we cannot *t.* what he saith. 16:18
or did other *t.* thee of me? 18:34
who shall *t.* you the. *Acts* 15:27
but either to *t.* or hear some. 17:21
certain thing to *t.* him. 23:17
the body I cannot *t.* *2 Cor* 12:2, 3
fail to *t.* of Gideon. *Heb* 11:32

tell *me*

why didst not *t. me* she? *Gen* 12:18
t. me nor heard I of it. 21:26
t. me whose daughter art? 24:23
t. me, and if not, *t. me* that I. 49
t. me what shall thy wages be? 29:15
from me, and didst not *t. me.* 31:27
t. me thy name. 32:29
t. me where they feed. 37:16
t. me now what thou hast done, hide. *Josh* 7:19
t. me wherein thy great. *Judg* 16:6
wilt not redeem it, *t. me.* *Ruth* 4:4
t. me where the seer's. *1 Sam* 9:18
t. me I pray thee what Samuel. 10:15
Saul said, *T. me* what thou. 14:43
Jonathan, who shall *t. me*? 20:10
how went the matter? *t. me,* I. *2 Sam* 1:4
lean, wilt thou not *t. me*? 13:4
that thou *t. me* nothing. *1 Ki* 22:16
shall I do for thee? *t. me.* *2 Ki* 4:2
t. me the great things that. 8:4
of understanding *t. me.* *Job* 34:34
t. me, O thou whom. *S of S* 1:7
which if ye *t. me.* *Mat* 21:24
t. me which of them. *Luke* 7:42
t. me where thou hast. *John* 20:15
t. me whether ye sold the. *Acts* 5:8
t. me, art thou a Roman? 22:27
is that thou hast to *t. me*? 23:19
t. me, ye that desire to. *Gal* 4:21

tell *thee*

one of the mountains I will *t. thee* of. *Gen* 22:2
land which I will *t. thee* of. 26:2
word we did *t. thee* in. *Ex* 14:12
sheweth me, I will *t. thee.* *Num* 23:3
the judgement which they shall *t. thee.* *Deut* 17:11
elders, and they will *t. thee.* 32:7
not told it and shall I *t.* it *thee*? *Judg* 14:16
he will *t. thee* what thou. *Ruth* 3:4
I will *t. thee* all that is. *1 Sam* 9:19
I will *t. thee* what the Lord. 15:16
I see, that I will *t. thee.* 19:3
then would not I *t.* it *thee*? 20:9
t. thee what shall become of the child. *1 Ki* 14:3
did I not *t. thee* that he would prophesy no good? 22:18; *2 Chr* 18:17
I *t. thee* that the Lord. *1 Chr* 17:10
I am escaped alone to *t. thee.* *Job* 1:15, 16, 17, 19
teach thee and *t. thee.* 8:10
the air, and they shall *t. thee.* 12:7
if I were hungry I would not *t. thee.* *Ps* 50:12
let thy wise men *t. thee.* *Isa* 19:12
words that I shall *t. thee.* *Jer* 19:2
I *t. thee* thou shalt not. *Luke* 12:59
t. thee, the cock shall not. 22:34
he shall *t. thee* what thou oughtest to do. *Acts* 10:6; 11:14
I will *t. thee* the mystery. *Rev* 17:7

I **tell** *you,* or **tell** *I you*

that *I* may *t. you* what. *Gen* 49:1
I will *t. you* what I will do. *Isa* 5:5
they spring forth, *I t. you.* 42:9
I t. you in darkness. *Mat* 10:27
neither *t. I you* by what authority. 21:27; *Mark* 11:33; *Luke* 20:8
I will *t. you* by what. *Mark* 11:29
but *I t. you* of a truth. *Luke* 4:25; 9:27
I t. you that many prophets. 10:24
I t. you nay, but rather. 12:51
I t. you nay, but except. 13:3, 5
I t. you I know not whence. 27
I t. you there shall be two. 17:34

I t. you that he will avenge. *Luke* 18:8
I t. you this man went to his. 14
I t. you that if these should. 19:40
he said, If *I t. you* ye will not. 22:67
shall ye believe if *I t. you*? *John* 3:12
because *I t. you* the truth. 8:45
Gal 4:16
I t. you before it come. *John* 13:19
I t. you the truth, it is. 16:7
of which *I t. you* before. *Gal* 5:21
of whom *I* now *t. you*. *Phil* 3:18

tellest
thou *t.* my wanderings. *Ps* 56:8

telleth
the Lord *t.* thee that he. *2 Sam* 7:11
Elisha *t.* the king of. *2 Ki* 6:12
goeth abroad he *t.* it. *Ps* 41:6
he that *t.* lies shall not tarry. 101:7
he *t.* the number of the stars. 147:4
under hands of him that *t. Jer* 33:13
Philip cometh and *t.* *John* 12:22

telling
when Gideon heard the *t. Judg* 7:15
hast made an end of *t. 2 Sam* 11:19
as he was *t.* the king how. *2 Ki* 8:5

Tema
sons of Ishmael, Hadar, *T.Gen* 25:15
1 Chr 1:30
the troops of *T.* looked. *Job* 6:19
the inhabitants of *T.* *Isa* 21:14
I made Dedan and *T.* *Jer* 25:23

Teman
Eliphaz were *T.* Omar. *Gen* 36:11
duke *T.*, duke Kenaz. 15, 42
1 Chr 1:53
Is wisdom no more in *T.*? *Jer* 49:7
Lord hath purposed against *T.* 20
make it desolate from *T. Ezek* 25:13
will send a fire upon *T.* *Amos* 1:12
thy mighty men, O *T.*, shall. *Ob* 9
God came from *T.* *Hab* 3:3

Temanite, *see* **Eliphaz**

temper
an hin of oil to *t.* with. *Ezek* 46:14*

temperance
as he reasoned of *t.* *Acts* 24:25
meekness, *t.*: against such. *Gal* 5:23
to knowledge *t.* and to *t.* *2 Pet* 1:6

temperate
for the mastery, is *t.* *1 Cor* 9:25
a bishop must be *t.* *Tit* 1:8
aged men *t.* 2:2

tempered
unleavened *t.* with oil. *Ex* 29:2*
a perfume *t.* together, pure. 30:35*
but God hath *t.* the body together.
1 Cor 12:24

tempest
[1] *A most violent commotion of the air, either with or without rain, hail, or snow,* Acts 27:18, 20. [2] *Grievous, and unexpected affliction,* Job 9:17.

breaketh me with a *t.* *Job* 9:17
a *t.* stealeth him away in. 27:20
on wicked shall he rain a *t. Ps* 11:6*
from the windy storm and *t.* 55:8
so persecute them with thy *t.* 83:15
one, which as a *t.* of hail. *Isa* 28:2
visited with storm and *t.* 29:6
shall be beaten with a *t.* 30:30
shall be a covert from the *t.* 32:2
afflicted, tossed with *t.* 54:11
with a *t.* in the day of the. *Amos* 1:14
there was a mighty *t.* in. *Jonah* 1:4
for my sake this great *t.* is come. 12
there arose a great *t.* *Mat* 8:24
tossed with a *t.* *Acts* 27:18*
no small *t.* lay on us, hope was. 20
come to darkness and *t.* *Heb* 12:18
are carried with a *t.* *2 Pet* 2:17*

tempestuous
it shall be very *t.* round. *Ps* 50:3
wrought and was *t.* *Jonah* 1:11, 13
against it a *t.* wind. *Acts* 27:14

temple
A house or dwelling of God, a building erected and set apart for the worship of the true God. The word is used in the Bible, [1] *Of the tabernacle,* 1 Sam 1:9. [2] *Of Solomon's temple, the wonder of the whole world. This is referred to in all parts of the Bible written before the captivity, when this temple was destroyed. It is also referred to at the time of the building of the second temple, after the Return.* [3] *The temple as rebuilt in the times of Ezra and Nehemiah. This was larger than that of Solomon, but not so rich and beautiful.* [4] *All references in the New Testament to the existing temple are to Herod's temple, built by Herod the Great to win the allegiance of the Jews.* [5] *Of Christ's body or human nature, in which the fulness of the Godhead dwelt,* John 2:19, 21; Col 2:9. [6] *Of the human body,* 1 Cor 3:16.

a seat by a post of the *t. 1 Sam* 1:9
he did hear my voice out of his *t.*, and my cry. *2 Sam* 22:7; *Ps* 18:6
the *t.* before it was 40. *1 Ki* 6:17
had prepared the *t.* *2 Chr* 35:20
and put the vessels in his *t.* 36:7
that they builded the *t.* *Ezra* 4:1
out of the *t.* brought to *t.* 5:14; 6:5
the *t.*, shut doors of the *t. Neh* 6:10
and to enquire in his *t.* *Ps* 27:4
in his *t.* doth every one speak. 29:9
thy lovingkindness, O God, in the midst of thy *t.* 48:9
because of thy *t.* at Jerusalem. 68:29
and his train filled the *t.* *Isa* 6:1
and to the *t.* thy foundation. 44:28
a voice from the *t.*, a voice. 66:6
declare the vengeance of his *t.*
Jer 50:28; 51:11
he brought me to the *t.* *Ezek* 41:1
vessels taken out of the *t. Dan* 5:2, 3
the songs of the *t.* shall. *Amos* 8:3
that the *t.* might be built. *Zech* 8:9
come suddenly to his *t.* *Mal* 3:1
set him on a pinnacle of the *t.*
Mat 4:5; *Luke* 4:9
is one greater than the *t.* *Mat* 12:6
Whosoever shall swear by the *t.* or by the gold of the *t.* 23:16, 17, 21
whom ye slew between the *t.* 35*
to shew him the buildings of the *t.*
24:1; *Luke* 21:5
I am able to destroy the *t. Mat* 26:61
thou that destroyest the *t.* 27:40
Mark 15:29
behold the vail of the *t.* *Mat* 27:51
Mark 15:38; *Luke* 23:45
any vessel through the *t. Mark* 11:16
I will destroy this *t.* made. 14:58
departed not from the *t.* *Luke* 2:37
drove them all out of the *t. John* 2:15
destroy this *t.* 19
forty and six years was this *t.* 20
he spake of *t.* of his body. 21
gate of the *t.* to ask alms of them that entered the *t.* *Acts* 3:2, 10
the *t.* of goddess Diana. 19:27
and drew him out of the *t.* 21:30
gone about to profane the *t.* 24:6
neither against the *t.* nor. 25:8
that ye are the *t.* of God? *1 Cor* 3:16
t. of God, him shall God destroy, for the *t.* of God is holy, which *t.* 17
your body is the *t.* of the Holy? 6:19
sit at meat in an idol's *t.* 8:10
live of the things of the *t.* 9:13
hath the *t.* of God with idols? for ye are the *t.* of the. *2 Cor* 6:16
day and night in his *t.* *Rev* 7:15
saying, Rise and measure the *t.* 11:1
t. of God was opened in heaven, and the . . . was seen in his *t.* 19
angel came out of the *t.* 14:15, 17
the *t.* of the tabernacle was. 15:5
seven angels came out of the *t.* 6
t. was filled with smoke from the. 8
a great voice out of the *t.* 16:1, 17
no *t.* therein, for the Lord God almighty and Lamb are *t.* 21:22

see **holy, Lord**

in, *or* **into the temple**
spears that were *in the t. 2 Ki* 11:10
priest's office *in the t.* *1 Chr* 6:10
head *in the t.* of Dagon. 10:10
candlesticks *in the t.* *2 Chr* 4:7, 8
these vessels *into the t.* *Ezra* 5:15
would go *into the t.* to save his life.
Neh 6:11
priests *in the t.* profane. *Mat* 12:5
into the t., cast out all them that sold and bought *in the t.* 21:12
Mark 11:15; *Luke* 19:45
blind and lame came to see him *in the t.* *Mat* 21:14
children crying *in the t.* and. 15
I sat daily teaching *in the t.* 26:55
Luke 21:37
pieces of silver *in the t. Mat* 27:5*
I was daily teaching *in the t.*
Mark 14:49; *Luke* 22:53
tarried so long *in the t.* *Luke* 1:21
he had seen a vision *in the t.* 22
by the spirit *into the t.* 2:27
they found him *in the t.* sitting. 46
two men went up *into the t.* 18:10
and were continually *in the t.* 24:53
one accord *in the t.* *Acts* 2:46
went up together *into the t.* 3:1
about to go *into the t.* 3
stand and speak *in the t.* 5:20
the men are standing *in the t.* 25
Paul entered *into the t.* 21:26
saw him *in the t.* 27
Greeks also *into the t.* 28, 29
even while I prayed *in the t.* 22:17
found me *in the t.* disputing. 24:12
found me purified *in the t.* 18
the Jews caught me *in the t.* 26:21
he as God sitteth *in the t.* of God.
2 Thes 2:4
will I make a pillar *in the t.* of my God. *Rev* 3:12
no man was able to enter *into t.* 15:8

temples
Maker, and buildeth *t.* *Hos* 8:14*
ye carried into your *t.* *Joel* 3:5
Most High dwelleth not in *t.* made with hands. *Acts* 7:48; 17:24

temples, *of the head*
Jael smote the nail into his *t.*
Judg 4:21, 22
she had stricken through his *t.* 5:26
thy *t.* like a piece of pomegranate.
S of S 4:3; 6:7

temporal
which are seen are *t.* *2 Cor* 4:18

tempt
[1] *When spoken of God it means to try or test, with the idea of proving man's faith and obedience, and the desire and certainty that man will not fail,* Gen 22:1. [2] *Man tempts God when he puts him to the proof simply to see if he will keep his promises,* Isa 7:12; Mat 4:7. [3] *The endeavour of the evil one or of evil men to cause a man to commit sin. It is nearly always in this sense that the word* temptation *is used.*

God did *t.* Abraham. *Gen* 22:1
do ye *t.* the Lord? *Ex* 17:2
ye shall not *t.* the Lord. *Deut* 6:16
I will not ask, nor will I *t.* *Isa* 7:12
yea, they that *t.* God are. *Mal* 3:15
is written again, Thou shalt not *t.* the. *Mat* 4:7; *Luke* 4:12
why *t.* ye me? *Mat* 22:18
Mark 12:15; *Luke* 20:23
together to *t.* the Spirit. *Acts* 5:9
now therefore why *t.* ye God? 15:10
that Satan *t.* you not for. *1 Cor* 7:5
neither let us *t.* Christ as. 10:9

temptation
harden not your hearts, as in the day of *t.* *Ps* 95:8*; *Heb* 3:8
and lead us not into *t.* *Mat* 6:13
Luke 11:4
that ye enter not into *t.* *Mat* 26:41
Mark 14:38; *Luke* 22:40, 46
devil had ended all his *t. Luke* 4:13
and in time of *t.* fall away. 8:13

hath no *t.* taken you; but will with the *t.* *1 Cor* 10:13
and my *t.* in my flesh ye. *Gal* 4:14
will be rich fall into *t.* *1 Tim* 6:9
man that endureth *t.* *Jas* 1:12
also from the hour of *t.* *Rev* 3:10

temptations

out of a nation by *t.* *Deut* 4:34
great *t.* thine eyes saw. 7:19; 29:3
with me in my *t.* *Luke* 22:28
with many tears and *t.* *Acts* 20:19
when ye fall into divers *t.* *Jas* 1:2
in heaviness through manifold *t.* *1 Pet* 1:6
deliver the godly out of *t.* *2 Pet* 2:9

tempted

and because they *t.* the. *Ex* 17:7
and have *t.* me now. *Num* 14:22
not tempt God as ye *t.* *Deut* 6:16
and they *t.* God in. *Ps* 78:18, 41
yet they *t.* and provoked the. 56
when your fathers *t.* me. 95:9
Heb 3:9
but lusted, and *t.* God in. *Ps* 106:14
to be *t.* of the devil. *Mat* 4:1
Mark 1:13; *Luke* 4:2
a lawyer *t.* him, saying. *Luke* 10:25
as some of them *t.* and. *1 Cor* 10:9
who will not suffer you to be *t.* 13
lest thou also be *t.* *Gal* 6:1
means the tempter *t.* you. *1 Thes* 3:5
he hath suffered being *t.* *Heb* 2:18
but was in all points *t.* like as. 4:15
were sawn asunder, were *t.* 11:37
when he is *t.*, I am *t.* of God; for God cannot be *t.* with evil. *Jas* 1:13
but every man is *t.* when he is. 14

tempter

when the *t.* came to him. *Mat* 4:3
lest by means the *t.* have. *1 Thes* 3:5

tempteth

cannot be tempted, neither *t.* he any. *Jas* 1:13

tempting

the Pharisees *t.* Christ. *Mat* 16:1
Mark 8:11; *Luke* 11:16
also came to him, *t.* him. *Mat* 19:3
him a question, *t.* him. 22:35
put away his wife, *t.* him. *Mark* 10:2
this they said *t.* him, that. *John* 8:6

ten

Abraham dwelt *t.* years. *Gen* 16:3
t. shall be found there: he said, I will not destroy it for *t.*'s sake. 18:32
the servant took *t.* camels of. 24:10
bracelets for her hands of *t.* 22
Jacob took *t.* bulls and *t.* 32:15
Joseph's *t.* brethren went to. 42:3
Joseph's sent *t.* asses and *t.* 45:23
tabernacle with *t.* curtains. *Ex* 26:1
pillars *t.* and their sockets *t.* 27:12
wrote *t.* commandments. 34:28
Deut 4:13; 10:4
t. women shall bake. *Lev* 26:26
for the female *t.* shekels. 27:5, 7
one spoon of *t.* shekels. *Num* 7:14
20, 26
least gathered *t.* homers. 11:32
the fourth day *t.* bullocks. 29:23
there fell *t.* portions to. *Josh* 17:5
lot out of Ephraim, Manasseh, and Dan, *t.* cities. 21:5; *1 Chr* 6:61
with Phinehas *t.* princes. *Josh* 22:14
Gideon took *t.* men of. *Judg* 6:27
judged Israel *t.* years. 12:11
I will give thee *t.* shekels of. 17:10
we will take *t.* men of an. 20:10
Moab about *t.* years. *Ruth* 1:4
Boaz took *t.* men of the elders. 4:2
am not I better to thee than *t.* sons? *1 Sam* 1:8
take these *t.* loaves and run. 17:17
carry these *t.* cheeses to the. 18
David sent out *t.* young men. 25:5
David left *t.* concubines to keep. *2 Sam* 15:16
have given thee *t.* shekels. 18:11
t. young men smote Absalom. 15
they said, We have *t.* parts. 19:43
the king took his *t.* concubines. 20:3
t. fat oxen in one day. *1 Ki* 4:23
t. knots in a cubit compassing. 7:24
made *t.* bases of brass. *1 Ki* 7:27, 37
he made *t.* lavers of brass. 38, 43
2 Chr 4:6
t. pieces; I will give *t.* *1 Ki* 11:31, 35
with thee *t.* loaves to Ahijah. 14:3
t. talents, *t.* changes. *2 Ki* 5:5
fifty horsemen and *t.* chariots. 13:7
Menahem reigned *t.* years. 15:17
Ishmael came and *t.* men with him. 25:25; *Jer* 41:1, 2
he made *t.* candlesticks. *2 Chr* 4:7
t. tables. 8
and *t.* brethren were. *Ezra* 8:24
bring one of *t.* to dwell. *Neh* 11:1
the *t.* sons of Haman. *Esth* 9:10, 12
and let Haman's *t.* sons be. 13, 14
instrument of *t.* strings. *Ps* 33:2
92:3; 144:9
more than *t.* mighty men. *Eccl* 7:19
t. acres of vineyard shall. *Isa* 5:10
an homer of *t.* baths, *t.* *Ezek* 45:14
the fourth beast had *t.* horns. *Dan* 7:7, 20, 24
shall leave *t.* to the house. *Amos* 5:3
if *t.* men remain in one house. 6:9
came to an heap of twenty measures, there were but *t.* *Hag* 2:16
of the roll is *t.* cubits. *Zech* 5:2
t. men shall take hold of him. 8:23
and when the *t.* heard it. *Mat* 20:24
Mark 10:41
be likened to *t.* virgins. *Mat* 25:1
to him that hath *t.* talents. 25:28
woman having *t.* pieces. *Luke* 15:8
there met him *t.* men that. 17:12
Were there not *t.* cleansed? 17
delivered them *t.* pounds. 19:13
thy pound hath gained *t.* pounds. 16
have thou authority over *t.* cities. 17
to him that hath *t.* pounds. 24
Lord, he hath *t.* pounds. 25
a dragon having *t.* horns. *Rev* 12:3
13:1; 17:3
of seven heads and *t.* horns. 17:7
t. horns thou sawest are the *t.* 12
the *t.* horns thou sawest shall. 16
see **cubits, days, degrees, thousand, thousands**

ten ***times***

and hath changed my wages *t. times.* *Gen* 31:7, 41
tempted me now these *t. times.* *Num* 14:22
they said unto us *t. times.* *Neh* 4:12
these *t. times* have ye. *Job* 19:3
he found them *t. times.* *Dan* 1:20

tend

thoughts of diligent *t.* to. *Pr* 21:5

tendeth

of the righteous *t.* to life. *Pr* 10:16
as righteousness *t.* to life, so. 11:19
is that withholdeth, but it *t.* to. 24
the talk of the lips *t.* only to. 14:23
the fear of the Lord *t.* to life. 19:23

tender

[1] *Weak and feeble,* Gen 33:13. [2] *Of a compassionate and forgiving temper,* Eph 4:32.

ran and fetched a calf *t.* and good. *Gen* 18:7
that the children are *t.* 33:13
so the man that is *t.* *Deut* 28:54
the *t.* and delicate woman. 56
the small rain on the *t.* herb. 32:2
as the *t.* grass springing. *2 Sam* 23:4
because thy heart was *t.* *2 Ki* 22:19
2 Chr 34:27
is young and *t.* *1 Chr* 22:5; 29:1
that the *t.* branch will not. *Job* 14:7
to cause the bud of the *t.* herb. 38:27
t. and beloved in sight. *Pr* 4:3
hay appears, and the *t.* grass. 27:25
the vines with *t.* grape. *S of S* 2:13
for our vines have *t.* grapes. 15*
see whether the *t.* grape. 7:12
thou shalt no more be called *t.* and. *Isa* 47:1
up before him as a *t.* plant. 53:2
I will crop off a *t.* one. *Ezek* 17:22
brought Daniel into *t.* love. *Dan* 1:9*
in earth, in the *t.* grass. 4:15, 23
when his branch is *t.* *Mat* 24:32
Mark 13:28
through the *t.* mercy. *Luke* 1:78
pitiful, and of *t.* mercy. *Jas* 5:11*
see **mercies**

tenderhearted

when Rehoboam was young and *t.* *2 Chr* 13:7
be kind and *t.* one to. *Eph* 4:32

tenderness

foot on the ground for *t.* *Deut* 28:56

tenons

two *t.* in one board. *Ex* 26:17, 19
36:22, 24

tenor

according to the *t.* of. *Gen* 43:7
after *t.* of these words. *Ex* 34:27

tens

such over them to be rulers of *t.* *Ex.* 18:21, 25
heads, captains over *t.* *Deut* 1:15

tent

(*This word is often used of the tabernacle. Tents were the only homes of the early patriarchs. Their use was common through all Bible times, as it is now among the desert tribes*)

was uncovered in his *t.* *Gen* 9:21
and pitched his *t.* 12:8; 13:3
Lot pitched his *t.* towards. 13:12
Abraham removed his *t.* and. 18
he sat in *t.* door. 18:1
he hastened into the *t.* 6
thy wife? he said, In the *t.* 9
her into his mother Sarah's *t.* 24:67
and Isaac pitched his *t.* in. 26:17
built an altar, and pitched his *t.* 25
Jacob had pitched his *t.* in. 31:25
Jacob's *t.*, Leah's *t.*, Rachel's *t.* 33
Jacob pitched his *t.* before. 33:18, 19
Israel spread his *t.* beyond. 35:21
Jethro came into the *t.* *Ex* 18:7
couple the *t.* together that it. 26:11
stood every man at his *t.* door. 33:8
every man in his *t.* door. 10
make the tabernacle, his *t.* 35:11
he made taches to couple the *t.* 36:18
he made a covering for the *t.* 19
brought the *t.* to Moses. 39:33
the *t.* over the tabernacle, and put the covering of the *t.* 40:19
leper shall tarry out of his *t.* seven. *Lev* 14:8
Gershon shall be the *t.* *Num* 3:25
the cloud covered the *t.* of. 9:15
weep every man in his *t.* 11:10
a man dieth in a *t.*: all that come into the *t.* and is in the *t.* 19:14
clean person shall sprinkle the *t.* 18
the man of Israel into the *t.* 25:8
earth in the midst of my *t.* *Josh* 7:21
the *t.*; and it was hid in his *t.* 22
out of the midst of the *t.* 23
all Israel burnt his *t.* and all. 24
Sisera fled on his feet to the *t.* of. *Judg* 4:17
stand in the door of the *t.* 20
Jael took a nail of the *t.* and. 21
be above women in the *t.* 5:24
of Israel every man to his *t.* 7:8
barley bread came unto a *t.* 13
will not any of us go to his *t.* 20:8
and they fled every man into his *t.* *1 Sam* 4:10; *2 Sam* 18:17; 19:8
sent every man to his *t.* *1 Sam* 13:2
Goliath's armour into his *t.* 17:54
but I have walked in a *t.* *2 Sam* 7:6
1 Chr 17:5
spread Absalom a *t.* on. *2 Sam* 16:22
retired every man to his *t.* 20:22
went into one *t.*, another *t.* *2 Ki* 7:8
David pitched a *t.* for. *1 Chr* 15:1
they set it in midst of the *t.* 16:1
2 Chr 1:4
fled every man to his *t.* *2 Chr* 25:22
the *t.* which he placed. *Ps* 78:60
nor Arabian pitch *t.* there. *Isa* 13:20
is removed as a shepherd's *t.* 38:12
spreadeth them out as a *t.* 40:22
enlarge the place of thy *t.* 54:2
to stretch forth my *t.* *Jer* 10:20
rise up every man in his *t.* 37:10

tenth
I will surely give the *t.* *Gen* 28:22
the *t.* shall be holy. *Lev* 27:32
children of Levi the *t.* *Num* 18:21*
enter to *t.* generation. *Deut* 23:2, 3
king will take the *t.* of. *1 Sam* 8:15
he will take the *t.* of your sheep. 17
t. captain of sons of. *1 Chr* 12:13
the *t.* lot came forth to. 24:11
t. lot came forth to Shimei. 25:17
the *t.* captain for the *t.* month. 27:13
but yet in it shall be a *t.* *Isa* 6:13
in the *t.* year of Zedekiah. *Jer* 32:1
it was about the *t.* hour. *John* 1:39
t. foundation a chrysoprasus. *Rev* 21:20
see **day, deal, month, part**

tentmakers
occupation they were *t.* *Acts* 18:3

tents
father of such as dwell in *t.* *Gen* 4:20
Japheth shall dwell in the *t.* 9:27
flocks, and herds, and *t.* 13:5
plain man, dwelling in *t.* 25:27
into the maid servants' *t.* 31:33
for them that are in *t.* *Ex* 16:16
Israel shall pitch their *t.* *Num* 1:52
cloud abode, they pitched *t.* 9:17
cloud abode, they rested in their *t.* 18, 20, 22, 23
whether they dwell in *t.* or. 13:19
depart from the *t.* of these. 16:26
stood in the door of their *t.* 27
Israel abiding in his *t.* 24:2
how goodly are thy *t.* O Jacob. 5
in your *t.* and said. *Deut* 1:27
a place to pitch your *t.* in. 33
Get ye into your *t.* again. 5:30
swallowed them up and their *t.* 11:6
turn and go unto thy *t.* 16:7
rejoice, Issachar, in thy *t.* 33:18
and get you into your *t.* *Josh* 22:4, 6
with much riches unto your *t.* 8
came with their *t.* *Judg* 6:5
of them that dwelt in *t.* 8:11
the Philistines' *t.* *1 Sam* 17:53
and Judah abide in *t.* *2 Sam* 11:11
every man to his *t.* 20:1
1 Ki 12:16; *2 Chr* 10:16
Israel went to their *t.* *1 Ki* 8:66
2 Chr 7:10
Syrians left their *t.* *2 Ki* 7:7, 10
Israel spoiled the *t.* of the. 16
people fled into their *t.* 8:21; 14:12
of Israel dwelt in their *t.* 13:5
smote the *t.* of Ham. *1 Chr* 4:41
dwelt in the Hagarites' *t.* 5:10
also the *t.* of cattle. *2 Chr* 14:15
to praise in the gates of the *t.* 31:2
at Ahava we abode in *t.* *Ezra* 8:15
none dwell in their *t.* *Ps* 69:25
Israel to dwell in their *t.* 78:55
than to dwell in the *t.* of. 84:10
murmured in their *t.* and. 106:25
woe is me, that I dwell in the *t.* 120:5
but comely, as the *t.* of Kedar. *S of S* 1:5
kids beside the shepherds' *t.* 8
suddenly are my *t.* spoiled. *Jer* 4:20
they shall pitch their *t.* against. 6:3
the captivity of Jacob's *t.* 30:18
days ye shall dwell in *t.* 35:7
but we have dwelt in *t.* and. 10
their *t.* and flocks shall they. 49:29
I saw the *t.* of Cushan in. *Hab* 3:7
the Lord shall save the *t.* *Zech* 12:7
plague shall be in these *t.* 14:15

Terah
Nahor begat *T.* *Gen* 11:24
1 Chr 1:26
T. begat Abram. *Gen* 11:26, 27
Josh 24:2
T. took Abram his son. *Gen* 11:31

teraphim
made an ephod and *t.* *Judg* 17:5
in these houses is *t.* 18:14
took the *t.* 20
abide many days without *t.* *Hos* 3:4

termed
be *t.* forsaken, neither shall thy land any more be *t.* desolate. *Isa* 62:4

terraces
made of algum trees *t.* *2 Chr* 9:11

terrestrial
there are bodies *t.*: the glory of the *t.* *1 Cor* 15:40

terrible
for it is a *t.* thing. *Ex* 34:10
went through that *t.* wilderness. *Deut* 1:19; 8:15
a mighty God and *t.* 7:21; 10:17
Neh 1:5; 4:14; 9:32
hath done for thee *t.* things. *Deut* 10:21; *2 Sam* 7:23
angel of God, very *t.* *Judg* 13:6
with God is *t.* majesty. *Job* 37:22
the glory of his nostrils is *t.* 39:20
his teeth are *t.* round about. 41:14
shall teach thee *t.* things. *Ps* 45:4
for the Lord Most High is *t.* 47:2
by *t.* things in righteousness. 65:5
say unto God, How *t.* art thou! 66:3
t. in his doing towards the children. 5
t. out of thy holy places. 68:35
t. to the kings of the earth. 76:12
praise thy great and *t.* name. 99:3
who had done *t.* things by. 106:22
of the might of thy *t.* acts. 145:6
thou art *t.* as an army. *S of S* 6:4*
lay low the haughtiness of the *t.* *Isa* 13:11
go to a people *t.* hitherto. 18:2
from a people *t.* hitherto. 7
from the desert, from a *t.* land. 21:1
the city of the *t.* nations shall. 25:3
when the blast of the *t.* ones is. 4
the branch of the *t.* ones shall be. 5
multitude of the *t.* ones shall. 29:5
for the *t.* one is brought to naught. 20
and the prey of the *t.* shall be. 49:25
when thou didst *t.* things. 64:3
out of the hand of the *t.* *Jer* 15:21
with me as a mighty *t.* one. 20:11
skin was black, because of *t.* famine. *Lam* 5:10*
colour of the *t.* crystal. *Ezek* 1:22
behold therefore I will bring the *t.* of. 28:7; 30:11; 31:12
I will cause to fall the *t.* of. 32:12
form of the image was *t.* *Dan* 2:31
fourth beast dreadful and *t.* 7:7*
day of Lord is very *t.* *Joel* 2:11
t. day of the Lord come. 31
the Chaldeans are *t.* and. *Hab* 1:7
the Lord will be *t.* unto. *Zeph* 2:11
so *t.* was the sight that. *Heb* 12:21

terribleness
Lord brought us out with great *t.* *Deut* 26:8
thee a name of greatness and *t.* *1 Chr* 17:21*
thy *t.* hath deceived thee. *Jer* 49:16

terribly
shake *t.* the earth. *Isa* 2:19*, 21*
fir trees shall be *t.* shaken. *Nah* 2:3

terrified
fear not nor be *t.* *Deut* 20:3
hear of wars, be not *t.* *Luke* 21:9
but they were *t.* and. 24:37
and in nothing *t.* by your. *Phil* 1:28

terrifiest
then thou *t.* me through. *Job* 7:14

terrify
blackness of the day *t.* it. *Job* 3:5
rod, and let not his fear *t.* 9:34
contempt of families *t.* me? 31:34
seem as if I would *t.* *2 Cor* 10:9

terror
and the *t.* of God was. *Gen* 35:5
even appoint over you *t.* *Lev* 26:16
the sword without and *t.* *Deut* 32:25
in all the great *t.* which Moses. 34:12
and that your *t.* is fallen. *Josh* 2:9
from God was a *t.* to me. *Job* 31:23
behold, my *t.* shall not make. 33:7
not be afraid for the *t.* *Ps* 91:5
lop the bough with *t.* *Isa* 10:33
land of Judah shall be a *t.* 19:17
thine heart shall meditate *t.* 33:18
thou shalt be far from *t.* 54:14
be not a *t.* to me. *Jer* 17:17
a *t.* to thyself. 20:4
forth Israel with great *t.* *Jer* 32:21
cause *t.* to be on all. *Ezek* 26:17
I will make thee a *t.* 21; 27:36
28:19
which caused *t.* in the land. 32:23
24, 25, 26, 27
with their *t.* they are ashamed. 30
I have caused my *t.* in the land. 32
for rulers are not a *t.* *Rom* 13:3
knowing therefore the *t.* *2 Cor* 5:11
be not afraid of their *t.* *1 Pet* 3:14

terrors
a nation by great *t.* *Deut* 4:34
t. of God do set themselves. *Job* 6:4
t. shall make him afraid on. 18:11
bring him to the king of *t.* 14
the sword cometh, *t.* are. 20:25
are in the *t.* of the shadow. 24:17
t. take hold on him as waters. 27:20
t. are turned upon me. 30:15
the *t.* of death are fallen. *Ps* 55:4
utterly consumed with *t.* 73:19
while I suffer thy *t.* I am. 88:15
wrath goeth over me, thy *t.* 16
I caused *t.* to fall upon. *Jer* 15:8
thou hast called my *t.* *Lam* 2:22
t. by reason of the sword shall be. *Ezek* 21:12

Tertius
I *T.* who wrote this epistle salute. *Rom* 16:22

Tertullus
certain orator named *T.* *Acts* 24:1
T. began to accuse Paul, saying. 2

testament
(*The usual meaning of this word, as in* Old Testament *and* New Testament, *is* covenant, *that is, the old and the new* Dispensation, *or relations between God and man. In a few cases it seems to mean the same as it does now in law, in the phrase* last will and testament, Heb 9:16, 17. *But the Revisions render the term in each case by the word* covenant)
this is my blood in new *t.* *Mat* 26:28; *Mark* 14:24
this cup is the new *t.* *Luke* 22:20
1 Cor 11:25
ministers of the new *t.* *2 Cor* 3:6
vail, in reading the old *t.* 14
a surety of a better *t.* *Heb* 7:22
of the new *t.* for the redemption of trangressions under first *t.* 9:15
where a *t.* is there must also. 16
for a *t.* is of force after men. 17
the blood of the *t.* which God. 20
the ark of his *t.* *Rev* 11:19

testator
be the death of the *t.* *Heb* 9:16*
no strength while the *t.* liveth. 17*

testified
and it hath been *t.* to his. *Ex* 21:29
hath *t.* falsely against. *Deut* 19:18
seeing the Lord hath *t.* *Ruth* 1:21
thy mouth hath *t.* *2 Sam* 1:16
yet the Lord *t.* against. *2 Ki* 17:13
his testimonies which he *t.* 15
prophets *t.* against them. *2 Chr* 24:19
Neh 9:26
I *t.* against them. *Neh* 13:15, 21
which the woman *t.* *John* 4:39
Jesus himself *t.* that a prophet. 44
13:21
when they had *t.* and. *Acts* 8:25
Paul *t.* to the Jews, that Jesus. 18:5
for as thou hast *t.* of me. 23:11
to whom he *t.* the kingdom. 28:23
are false, because we have *t.* of God. *1 Cor* 15:15
forewarned you and *t.* *1 Thes* 4:6
gave himself, to be *t.* *1 Tim* 2:6
in a certain place *t.* saying. *Heb* 2:6
when it *t.* beforehand. *1 Pet* 1:11
God hath *t.* of his Son. *1 John* 5:9
and *t.* of the truth that. *3 John* 3

testifiedst
and *t.* against them. *Neh* 9:29, 30

testifieth
the pride of Israel *t.* to. *Hos* 7:10
seen and heard, that he *t.* *John* 3:32

disciple which *t.* of these. *John* 21:24
t. thou art a priest for. *Heb* 7:17
he which *t.* these things. *Rev* 22:20

testify

one witness not *t.* against any. *Num* 35:30
I *t.* against you that ye. *Deut* 8:19
if a false witness *t.* against. 19:16
this song shall *t.* against. 31:21
hearts to the words which I *t.* 32:46
didst *t.* against them. *Neh* 9:34
yea, thine own lips *t.* *Job* 15:6
O Israel, I will *t.* against thee. *Ps* 50:7; 81:8
before thee, and our sins *t.* *Isa* 59:12
though our iniquities *t.* *Jer* 14:7
the pride of Israel doth *t.* *Hos* 5:5
t. in the house of Jacob. *Amos* 3:13
have I done ? *t.* against me. *Mi* 6:3
that he may *t.* to them. *Luke* 16:28
any should *t.* of man. *John* 2:25
and *t.* that we have seen. 3:11
they *t.* of me. 5:39
because I *t.* of it. 7:7
he shall *t.* of me. 15:26
other words did he *t.* *Acts* 2:40
t. that it is he who was ordained. 10:42
to *t.* the gospel of the grace. 20:24
life know they, if they would *t.* 26:5
I *t.* to every man that. *Gal* 5:3
t. in the Lord, that ye. *Eph* 4:17
seen, and do *t.*, that. *1 John* 4:14
have sent my angel to *t.* *Rev* 22:16
I *t.* to every man that heareth. 18

testifying

t. both to the Jews and. *Acts* 20:21
obtained witness, God *t.* *Heb* 11:4
t. that this is the true. *1 Pet* 5:12

testimonies

these are the *t.* which. *Deut* 4:45
ye shall diligently keep the *t.* 6:17
what mean the *t.* which God ? 20
keep his statutes and his *t.* *1 Ki* 2:3
2 Ki 23:3; *1 Chr* 29:19; *2 Chr* 34:31
rejected his *t.* and. *2 Ki* 17:15
kings hearkened to thy *t.* *Neh* 9:34
his covenant and his *t.* *Ps* 25:10
and keep not his *t.* 78:56
thy *t.* are sure. 93:5
kept his *t.* and the ordinance. 99:7
blessed are they that keep his *t.* and seek him. 119:2
rejoiced in the way of thy *t.* 14
for I have kept thy *t.* 22, 167, 168
thy *t.* are my delight. 24
I stuck to thy *t.* 31
incline my heart to thy *t.*, not to. 36
I will speak of thy *t.* also. 46
and I turned my feet to thy *t.* 59
let those that have known thy *t.* 79
but I will consider thy *t.* 95
for thy *t.* are my meditation. 99
t. have I taken as an heritage. 111
I love thy *t.* 119
that I may know thy *t.* 125
thy *t.* are wonderful, therefore. 129
thy *t.* are righteous and very. 138
the righteousness of thy *t.* is. 144
and I shall keep thy *t.* 146
concerning thy *t.*, I have known. 152
yet do I not decline from thy *t.* 157
not walked in his *t.* *Jer* 44:23

testimony

[1] *A witnessing evidence, or proof,* Acts 14:3. [2] *The whole scripture, or word of God, which declares what is to be believed and practised,* Ps 19:7. [3] *The two tables of stone, whereon the law, or ten commandments, were written, which were witnesses of that covenant made between God and his people,* Ex 25:16, 21; 31:18. [4] *The book of the law which testifies of God's will and man's duty,* 2 Ki 11:12. [5] *The ark in which the law was deposited,* Ex 16:34.

of manna before the *t.* *Ex* 16:34
put into the ark the *t.* 25:16, 21
vail which is before the *t.* 27:21
mercy seat that is over the *t.* *Ex* 30:6; *Lev* 16:13
and put it before the *t.* *Ex* 30:36
gave to Moses two tables of *t.* 31:18
the two tables of *t.* 32:15; 34:29
sum of the tabernacle of *t.* 38:21
over the tabernacle of *t.* *Num* 1:50
pitch about the tabernacle of *t.* 53
covered the tent of the *t.* 9:15
taken off the tabernacle of *t.* 10:11
up the rods before the *t.* 17:4
Aaron's rod again before the *t.* 10
shoe, and this was a *t.* in. *Ruth* 4:7
gave the king the *t.* *2 Ki* 11:12; *2 Chr* 23:11
for he established a *t.* *Ps* 78:5
ordained in Joseph for a *t.* 81:5
so shall I keep the *t.* of. 119:88
the tribes go up to the *t.* of. 122:4
children will keep my *t.* 132:12
bind up the *t.* *Isa* 8:16
to the law and to the *t.* 20
the gift Moses commanded for a *t.* *Mat* 8:4; *Mark* 1:44; *Luke* 5:14
for a *t.* against them. *Mat* 10:18; *Mark* 13:9
shake off the dust for a *t.* *Mark* 6:11; *Luke* 9:5
shall turn to you for a *t.* *Luke* 21:13
no man receiveth his *t.* *John* 3:32
he that receiveth his *t.* hath. 33
it is written, the *t.* of two men. 8:17
and we know that his *t.* is. 21:24
to whom also he gave *t.* *Acts* 13:22
who gave *t.* to the word of. 14:3
not receive thy *t.* of me. 22:18
as the *t.* of Christ was. *1 Cor* 1:6
unto you the *t.* of God. 2:1
the *t.* of our conscience. *2 Cor* 1:12
because our *t.* among. *2 Thes* 1:10
be not ashamed of the *t.* *2 Tim* 1:8
for a *t.* of those things. *Heb* 3:5
Enoch had this *t.* that he. 11:5
who bare record of the *t.* *Rev* 1:2
in the isle of Patmos for the *t.* 9
them that were slain for the *t.* 6:9
shall have finished their *t.* 11:7
by the word of their *t.* 12:11
them which have *t.* of Jesus. 17
tabernacle of the *t.* in heaven. 15:5
that have the *t.* of Jesus; for the *t.* of Jesus is the spirit of. 19:10
see **ark**

Tetrarch, *see* **Herod**

thank

that love you, what *t.* have you ? *Luke* 6:32, 33, 34

thank, *verb*

Levites to *t.* the Lord. *1 Chr* 16:4
David delivered this psalm to *t.* 7
to stand every morning to *t.* 23:30
we *t.* thee and praise thy. 29:13
I *t.* thee and praise thee. *Dan* 2:23
I *t.* thee, O Father, Lord of heaven and. *Mat* 11:25; *Luke* 10:21
doth he *t.* that servant ? *Luke* 17:9
God, I *t.* thee, that I am not. 18:11
Father, I *t.* thee, that. *John* 11:41
I *t.* my God through Jesus Christ. *Rom* 1:8; 7:25
I *t.* my God always on. *1 Cor* 1:4
I *t.* God that I baptized none. 14
I *t.* my God I speak with. 14:18
I *t.* my God on every remembrance of you. *Phil* 1:3
for this cause also *t.* *1 Thes* 2:13
we are bound to *t.* God. *2 Thes* 1:3
I *t.* Jesus Christ who hath enabled. *1 Tim* 1:12
I *t.* God, whom I serve with pure. *2 Tim* 1:3
I *t.* my God, making. *Philem* 4
see **offering**

thanked

bowed himself and *t.* *2 Sam* 14:22*
Paul *t.* God and took. *Acts* 28:15
but God be *t.* that ye were the servants. *Rom* 6:17

thankful

be *t.* to him, bless his name. *Ps* 100:4*; *Col* 3:15
him not, neither were *t.* *Rom* 1:21*

thankfulness

noble Felix, with all *t.* *Acts* 24:3

thanking

were as one in *t.* the Lord. *2 Chr* 5:13

thanks

companies that gave *t.* *Neh* 12:31
two companies that gave *t.* 40
he prayed and gave *t.* *Dan* 6:10
he took the cup and gave *t.* *Mat* 26:27; *Luke* 22:17
seven loaves and gave *t.* *Mark* 8:6
when he had given *t.* he gave. 14:23
Anna gave *t.* to the Lord. *Luke* 2:38
he took bread, and gave *t.* 22:19
when he had given *t.* *John* 6:11
after the Lord had given *t.* 23
and gave *t.* to God. *Acts* 27:35
Lord, for he giveth God *t.*; he eateth not, and giveth God *t.* *Rom* 14:6
when he had given *t.* *1 Cor* 11:24
for thou verily givest *t.* well. 14:17
t. be to God, who giveth us. 15:57
t. may be given to many. *2 Cor* 1:11
t. be to God who causeth us. 2:14
t. to God, who put the same. 8:16
t. be to God for his unspeakable gift. 9:15
giving *t.* always for all. *Eph* 5:20
what *t.* can we render ? *1 Thes* 3:9
of praise, giving *t.* *Heb* 13:15
give *t.* to him that sat. *Rev* 4:9
see **give, giving**

thanksgiving

[1] *An acknowledging and confessing with gladness, the benefits and mercies, which God bestows either upon ourselves or others,* Phil 4:6; 1 Tim 2:1. [2] *The sacrifice of* thanksgiving, Lev 7:12, 15. [3] *Psalms of* thanksgiving, Neh 12:8.

if he offer it for a *t.* *Lev* 7:12, 13, 15; 22:29
principal to begin the *t.* *Neh* 11:17
which was over the *t.*, he and. 12:8
of praise and *t.* to God. 46
publish with the voice of *t.* *Ps* 26:7
offer unto God *t.* and pay thy. 50:14
I will magnify him with *t.* 69:30
come before his face with *t.* 95:2
enter into his gates with *t.* 100:4
sacrifice sacrifices of *t.* 107:22
offer to thee sacrifices of *t.* 116:17
sing unto the Lord with *t.*; sing. 147:7
t. and melody shall be. *Isa* 51:3
of them shall proceed *t.* *Jer* 30:19
offer a sacrifice of *t.* *Amos* 4:5
to thee with the voice of *t.* *Jonah* 2:9
grace might through the *t.* *2 Cor* 4:15
which causeth through us *t.* 9:11
with *t.* let your requests. *Phil* 4:6
abounding therein with *t.* *Col* 2:7
watch in the same with *t.* 4:2
to be received with *t.* *1 Tim* 4:3
good, if it be received with *t.* 4
t. and honour be to our. *Rev* 7:12

thanksgivings

the dedication with *t.* *Neh* 12:27
abundant by many *t.* to. *2 Cor* 9:12

thankworthy

this is *t.* if a man. *1 Pet* 2:19*

that

t. is it which compasseth. *Gen* 2:11
what Adam called, *t.* was the. 19
t. be far from thee, to slay. 18:25
t. shalt be accounted stolen. 30:33
shall make like unto *t.* *Ex* 30:38
when Moses heard *t.* he. *Lev* 10:20
yet for all I will not cast. 26:44
besides *t. t.* his hand. *Num* 6:21
the word which I say, *t.* 22:20
t. will I speak. 24:13; *1 Ki* 22:14
anger was abated, when he had said *t.* *Judg* 8:3
do according to *t.* which. 11:36
behold, *t.* which is left. *1 Sam* 9:24
if thou wilt take *t.* take it. 21:9
for *t.* thou hast done to me. 24:19
with *t.* which the Lord hath. 30:23
if *t.* had been too little. *2 Sam* 12:8
in *t.* thou lovest thine enemies. 19:6
offer of *t.* which doth cost. 24:24

according to *t.* which was written. *2 Ki* 14:6; *2 Chr* 35:26
t. which thou hast prayed. *2 Ki* 19:20
t. which thou hast promised. *2 Chr* 6:15, 16
t. which they have need. *Ezra* 6:9
t. do after the will of your. 7:18
t. which I was afraid of is. *Job* 3:25
t. which I have seen I will. 15:17
he shall not save of *t.* which. 20:20
what his soul desireth even *t.* 23:13
t. which I see not, teach. 34:32
t. will I seek after, that. *Ps* 27:4
then I restored *t.* which I took. 69:4
when I wept, *t.* was to my. 10
the thing hath been, it is *t.* which shall be; *t.* which is done, is *t.* *Eccl* 1:9
t. which is wanting cannot be. 15
what was *t.* good for the sons of. 2:3
what profit in *t.* wherein he ? 3:9
and God requireth *t.* which is. 15
when thou vowest, pay *t.* thou. 5:4
knowest not whether this or *t.* 11:6
t. which I have heard. *Isa* 21:10
for *t.* which had not been told them shall they see, *t.* they had. 52:15
for *t.* which Manasseh. *Jer* 15:4
t. which I have built, *t.* which. 45:4
t. Daniel regardeth not thee, O king. *Dan* 6:13
for *t.* *t.* is determined shall. 11:36
t. *t.* dieth, let it die, *t.* *t.* *Zech* 11:9
for *t.* which is conceived. *Mat* 1:20
whole from *t.* hour. 9:22; 15:28
for Sodom than for *t.* city. 10:15 *Mark* 6:11
taken away *t.* he hath. *Mat* 13:12 25:29; *Mark* 4:25
t. shall ye receive. *Mat* 20:7
t. observe and do. 23:3
is *t.* to us ? see thou to *t.* 27:4
t. which cometh out, *t.* *Mark* 7:20
given in *t.* hour, *t.* speak. 13:11
all will I give, for *t.* is. *Luke* 4:6
even *t.* he seemeth to have. 8:18
he *t.* made *t.* which is without make *t.* which is within also ? 11:40
not faithful in *t.* which is. 16:12
t. which is highly esteemed. 15
we have done *t.* which was. 17:10
t. which was come to pass. 24:12
he was not *t.* light. *John* 1:8
t. was the light. 9
t. which is born of flesh, *t.* born. 3:6
we speak *t.* we know, testify *t.* 11
is not thy husband, in *t.* saidst. 4:18
is *t.* saying true, one soweth. 37
what man is *t.* which said to ? 5:12
labour for *t.* meat which. 6:27
Moses gave you not *t.* bread. 32
I am *t.* bread of life. 48
this is *t.* bread. 58
I speak *t.* I have seen with my Father; ye do *t.* which ye. 8:38
t. thou doest, do quickly. 13:27
t. will I do. 14:13
what he shall hear, *t.* shall. 16:13
what is *t.* to thee, follow. 21:22, 24
went abroad, that *t.* disciple. 23
this is *t.* which was spoken. *Acts* 2:16
all glorified God for *t.* which. 4:21
heard *t.* they lifted up. 24; 5:21, 33
this is *t.* Moses which said. 7:37
t. word you know, which. 10:37
because *t.* which may be. *Rom* 1:19
according to *t.* which was. 4:18
in *t.* he died, in *t.* he liveth. 6:10
t. being dead wherein we were held, *t.* we. 7:6
was then *t.* which is good made ? 13
t. I do, I allow not. 15
t. I would not, *t.* I do. 19
put away from you *t.* *1 Cor* 5:13
nay, you defraud, and *t.* your. 6:8
t. spiritual rock, and *t.* rock. 10:4
spoken of, for *t.* which I. 30
t. which also I delivered unto. 11:23
eat of *t.* bread, and drink of *t.* cup. 28
t. which is perfect, *t.* which. 13:10
and yet for all *t.* they will not. 14:21
and *t.* which thou sowest thou sowest not *t.* body that shall be. 15:37
t. was not first which is spiritual, but *t.* which. 46
if *t.* which is done away. *2 Cor* 3:11
it is accepted according to *t.* 8:12
what I do, *t.* I will do, *t.* I may. 11:2
what a man soweth, *t.* *Gal* 6:7
that I may apprehend *t.* *Phil* 3:12
might perfect *t.* which. *1 Thes* 3:10
all things; hold fast *t.* is good. 5:21
life *t.* now is, and of *t.* *1 Tim* 4:8
keep *t.* which is committed. 6:20
if he oweth, put *t.* on. *Philem* 18
and was heard in *t.* he. *Heb* 5:7
which entereth into *t.* within. 6:19
could not endure *t.* which. 12:20
for *t.* is unprofitable for you. 13:17
shall live, and do this or *t.* *Jas* 4:15
he *t.* will harm you, if ye be followers of *t.*? *1 Pet* 3:13; *3 John* 11
t. which was from the. *1 John* 1:1
t. which we have seen. 3; 2:24
let *t.* abide in you which ye. 2:24
t. which ye have, hold. *Rev* 2:25
see **after, day, man, place, so, soul, thing, time**

theatre

with one accord into the *t.* *Acts* 19:29
not adventure himself into the *t.* 31

Thebez

went Abimelech to *T.* and took *T.* *Judg* 9:50
that he died in *T.* *2 Sam* 11:21

thee

t. have I seen righteous. *Gen* 7:1
multiply *t.* exceedingly. 17:2
in blessing I will bless *t.* 22:17
I *t.*, and the cave I give it *t.* 23:11
back any thing from me but *t.* 39:9
the stranger shall get above *t.* *Deut* 28:43
have not rejected *t.* but. *1 Sam* 8:7
arrows are beyond *t.* 20:22, 37
the king charged *t.* *2 Sam* 18:12
they have not set *t.* *Ps* 86:14
enemy to entreat *t.* well. *Jer* 15:11
I will recompense *t.* *Ezek* 7:9
I will leave *t.* and all the fish. 29:5
when saw we *t.* an hungered, and fed *t.*? *Mat* 25:37
when saw we *t.* a stranger ? 38
when saw we *t.* sick ? 39
he that bade *t.* and him. *Luke* 14:9
but the root bearest *t.* *Rom* 11:18
lest he also spare not *t.* 21
see **teach, tell**

about **thee**

thou shalt dig *about t.* *Job* 11:18
shut thy doors *about t.* *Isa* 26:20
sword devour round *about t.* *Jer* 46:14; *Ezek* 5:12
all those that be *about t.* *Jer* 49:5
among nations that are round *about t.* *Ezek* 5:14
to the nations round *about t.* 15
cast a trench *about t.* *Luke* 19:43
cast thy garment *about t.* *Acts* 12:8

after **thee**

to thy seed *after t.* *Gen* 17:7, 8, 9 10; 35:12; 48:4
with thy children *after t.* *Deut* 4:40 12:25, 28
after t. Benjamin among. *Judg* 5:14
set up thy seed *after t.* *2 Sam* 7:12
will come in *after t.* and. *1 Ki* 1:14
nor *after t.* shall any arise like thee. 3:12; *2 Chr* 1:12
panteth my soul *after t.* *Ps* 42:1
my soul followeth hard *after t.* 63:8
my soul thirsteth *after t.* 143:6
we will run *after t.* *S of S* 1:4
they shall come *after t.* *Isa* 45:14
called a multitude *after t.* *Jer* 12:6
after t. shall rise another. *Dan* 2:39
cry at Beth-aven, *after t.* *Hos* 5:8

against **thee**

that rose *against t.* *Ex* 15:7
of the field multiply *against t.* 23:29
sinned, for we have spoken *against t.* *Num* 21:7
Lord be kindled *against t.* *Deut* 6:15
and he cry to the Lord *against t.* 15:9; 24:15
they hired Balaam *against t.* 23:4
against t. one way, and flee. 28:7
the Lord shall send *against t.* *Deut* 28:48, 49
there for a witness *against t.* 31:26
fortify the city *against t.* *Judg* 9:31
we have sinned *against t.* 10:10 *Neh* 1:6; *Jer* 14:7, 20
I have not sinned *against t.* *Judg* 11:27; *1 Sam* 24:11
he hath not sinned *against t.* *1 Sam* 19:4
hath testified *against t.* *2 Sam* 1:16
I will raise up evil *against t.* 12:11
that rose up *against t.* 18:31, 32
because they have sinned *against t.* *1 Ki* 8:33, 35; *2 Chr* 6:24, 26
if they sin *against t.* and repent. *1 Ki* 8:46; *2 Chr* 6:36
people that have sinned *against t.* and all their. *1 Ki* 8:50; *2 Chr* 6:39
king of Syria will come up *against t.* *1 Ki* 20:22
out to fight *against t.* *2 Ki* 19:9
man prevail *against t.* *2 Chr* 14:11
hath spoken evil *against t.* 18:22
a great multitude *against t.* 20:2
I come not *against t.* this day. 35:21
very corruptly *against t.* *Neh* 1:7
they rebelled *against t.* 9:26
why hast thou set me as a mark *against t.*? *Job* 7:20
would open his lips *against t.* 11:5
own lips testify *against t.* 15:6
my wrath is kindled *against t.* 42:7
have rebelled *against t.* *Ps* 5:10
they intended evil *against t.* 21:11
Lord, heal my soul, for I have sinned *against t.* 41:4
and I will testify *against t.* 50:7
against t. have I sinned, and done this evil. 51:4
that rise up *against t.* 74:23 139:21; *Eccl* 10:4
that I might not sin *against t.* *Ps* 119:11
for they speak *against t.* 139:20
evil counsel *against t.* *Isa* 7:5
shall lift up his staff *against t.* 10:24
fight *against t.* but they shall not prevail *against t.* *Jer* 1:19; 15:20
behold I am *against t.* 21:13; 50:31 51:25; *Ezek* 5:8; 21:3; 26:3 28:22; 29:3, 10; 35:3; 38:3 39:1; *Nah* 2:13; 3:5
thy enemies opened their mouth *against t.* *Lam* 2:16
still are talking *against t.* *Ezek* 33:30
hath conspired *against t.* *Amos* 7:10
spoken so much *against t.* *Mal* 3:13
that thy brother hath aught *against t.* *Mat* 5:23
if thy brother trespass *against t.* 18:15; *Luke* 17:3, 4
which these witness *against t.*? *Mat* 26:62; *Mark* 14:60; 15:4
I have somewhat *against t.* *Rev* 2:4
a few things *against t.* 14, 20

at **thee**

hath shaken her head *at t.* *2 Ki* 19:21 *Isa* 37:22
fir trees rejoice at *t.* *Isa* 14:8
as many were astonied *at t.* 52:14 *Ezek* 26:16; 27:35; 28:19
by clap their hands *at t.* *Lam* 2:15
shall hiss *at t.* *Ezek* 27:36
many people amazed *at t.* 32:10

before **thee**

is not whole land *before t.*? *Gen* 13:9
Ishmael might live *before t.* 17:18
behold my land is *before t.* 20:15 47:6
heaven shall send his angel *before t.* 24:7; *Ex* 23:20, 23; 32:34; 33:2
Rebekah is *before t.* *Gen* 24:51
I cannot rise up *before t.* 31:35
I will go *before t.* 33:12; *Isa* 45:2
set him *before t.* *Gen* 43:9
I will stand *before t.* there. *Ex* 17:6
I will send my fear *before t.* 23:27
before t. which shall drive out the Canaanites *before t.* 28, 29, 30, 31 34:11; *Deut* 4:38; 9:4, 5; 18:12
goodness pass *before t.* and I will proclaim . . . *before t.* *Ex* 33:19

I will cast out *before t.* *Ex* 34:24
Deut 6:19; 7:1; 9:4
hate thee flee *before t.* *Num* 10:35
no man able to stand *before t.*
Deut 7:24; *Josh* 1:5; 10:8
they shall flee *before t.* *Deut* 28:7
I have set *before t.* this day. 30:15
he shall go over *before t.* 31:3, 8
shalt see the land *before t.* 32:52
shall put incense *before t.* 33:10
Lord gone out *before t.*? *Judg* 4:14
bring forth, and set it *before t.* 6:18
1 Sam 9:24
let me set a morsel of bread *before t.* *1 Sam* 28:22
Lord go out *before t.* *2 Sam* 5:24
Saul, whom I put away *before t.* 7:15
be established for ever *before t.* 16, 26; *1 Chr* 17:24
as he walked *before t.* *1 Ki* 3:6
none like thee *before t.* 12
thy servants that walk *before t.* 8:23; *2 Chr* 6:14
which stand continually *before t.* *1 Ki* 10:8; *2 Chr* 9:7
done evil above all that were *before t.* *1 Ki* 14:9
how I have walked *before t.* *2 Ki* 20:3; *Isa* 38:3
for God is gone forth *before t.* *1 Chr* 14:15
from him that was *before t.* 17:13
before t. in our trespasses, we cannot stand *before t.* *Ezra* 9:15
sin be blotted out *before t.* *Neh* 4:5
his heart faithful *before t.* 9:8
trouble seem little *before t.* 32
Lord, all my desire is *before t.* and. *Ps* 38:9
age is as nothing *before t.* 39:5
adversaries are all *before t.* 69:19
I was as a beast *before t.* 73:22
the prisoner come *before t.* 79:11
let my prayer come *before t.*: incline thine ear unto my cry. 88:2; 141:2
hast set our iniquities *before t.* 90:8
my ways are *before t.* 119:168
let my cry come *before t.* 169
diligently what is *before t.* *Pr* 23:1
they joy *before t.* as men. *Isa* 9:3
righteousness shall go *before t.* 58:8
lips, was right *before t.* *Jer* 17:16
I stood *before t.* to turn. 18:20
the prophets that have been *before t.* of old. 28:8
all the land is *before t.*: go. 40:4
wickedness come *before t.* *Lam* 1:22
and they sit *before t.* *Ezek* 33:31
also *before t.* O king. *Dan* 6:22
I sent *before t.* Moses. *Mi* 6:4
fellows that sit *before t.* *Zech* 3:8
a trumpet *before t.* *Mat* 6:2
which shall prepare thy way *before t.* 11:10; *Mark* 1:2; *Luke* 7:27
I have sinned *before t.* *Luke* 15:18
to say *before t.* what. *Acts* 23:30
been here *before t.* to object. 24:19
before t. O king Agrippa. 25:26
set *before t.* an open door. *Rev* 3:8

behind **thee**

life, look not *behind t.* *Gen* 19:17
Amalek smote the feeble *behind t.* *Deut* 25:18
castest my words *behind t.* *Ps* 50:17
hear a word *behind t.* *Isa* 30:21

beside **thee**

to redeem it *beside t.* *Ruth* 4:4
there is none *beside t.* *1 Sam* 2:2
2 Sam 7:22; *1 Chr* 17:20
that I desire *beside t.* *Ps* 73:25
other lords *beside t.* have. *Isa* 26:13
eye seen, O God, *beside t.* 64:4

between **thee**

I will put enmity *between t.* *Gen* 3:15
my covenant *between* me and *t.* 17:2, 7
witness *between* me and *t.* 31:44
48:50
Lord watch *between* me and *t.* 49
the Lord be *between t.* and me for. *1 Sam* 20:23, 42
set it for a wall of iron *between t.* *Ezek* 4:3
been witness *between t.* *Mal* 2:14
fault *between t.* and. *Mat* 18:15

by **thee**

the people stand *by t.* *Ex* 18:14
woman that stood *by t.* *1 Sam* 1:26
I said to thee, Set it *by t.* 9:23
by t. I ran through a troop. *2 Sam* 22:30; *Ps* 18:29
by t. have I been holpen. *Ps* 71:6
when thou hast it *by t.* *Pr* 3:28
dwell securely *by t.* 29
but *by t.* only will we make mention of thy name. *Isa* 26:13
when I passed *by t.* *Ezek* 16:6, 8
seeing that *by t.* we enjoy quietness. *Acts* 24:2
saints are refreshed *by t.* *Philem* 7

concerning **thee**

Lord said *con. t.* and me. *Josh* 14:6
he hath spoken *con. t.* *1 Sam* 25:30
I will give charge *con. t.* *2 Sam* 14:8
spoken evil *con. t.* *1 Ki* 22:23
hath given commandment *con. t.* *Nah* 1:14
angels charge *con. t.* *Mat* 4:6
neither we letters *con. t.* *Acts* 28:21

for **thee**

food *for t.* and them. *Gen* 6:21
shall pray *for t.* 20:7
but as *for t.* and thy servants, I. *Ex* 9:30
sabbath shall be meat *for t.* and. *Lev* 25:6
shall be most holy *for t.* *Num* 18:9
as *for t.* stand by me. *Deut* 5:31
18:14; *2 Sam* 13:13
I will try them *for t.* *Judg* 7:4
have made ready a kid *for t.* 13:15
better *for t.* to be a priest to. 18:19
shall I not seek rest *for t.*? *Ruth* 3:1
buy it *for t.* 4:8
hath it been kept *for t.* *1 Sam* 9:24
soul desireth, I will do it *for t.* 20:4
I am distressed *for t.* *2 Sam* 1:26
be too strong *for t.*, help thee. 10:11
would God I had died *for t.* 18:33
requirest, that I will do *for t.* 19:38
I will speak *for t.* unto. *1 Ki* 2:18
and after make *for t.* and. 17:13
thou shalt make streets *for t.* 20:34
what I shall do *for t.* *2 Ki* 2:9
what is to be done *for t.*? 4:13
and as *for t.* *2 Chr* 7:17; *Dan* 2:29
Zech 9:11
surely now he would awake *for t.* *Job* 8:6
earth be forsaken *for t.*? 18:4
my soul thirsteth *for t.*, my. *Ps* 63:1
praise waiteth *for t.* O God. 65:1
it is time *for t.* O Lord. 119:126
fruits I have laid up *for t.* *S of S* 7:13
beneath is moved *for t.* *Isa* 14:9
have waited *for t.* 26:8; 33:2
Ethiopia and Seba *for t.* 43:3
therefore will I give men *for t.* 4
for my praise will I refrain *for t.* 48:9
who shall be sorry *for t.* 51:19
is nothing too hard *for t.* *Jer* 32:17
so shall they burn odours *for t.* 34:5
I will weep *for t.* 48:32
I laid a snare *for t.* 50:24
I take vengeance *for t.* 51:36
I take to witness *for t.* *Lam* 2:13
thy prophets have seen *for t.* 14
it watcheth *for t.*; behold. *Ezek* 7:6
be horribly afraid *for t.* 32:10
another, so will I be *for t.* *Hos* 3:3
he hath set a harvest *for t.* 6:11
I seek comfort *for t.* *Nah* 3:7
is profitable *for t.* *Mat* 5:29, 30
for Sodom than *for t.* 11:24
it is not lawful *for t.* to have her. 14:4; *Mark* 6:18
one *for t.*, and one for Moses. *Mat* 17:4; *Mark* 9:5; *Luke* 9:33
better *for t.* to enter into life. *Mat* 18:8, 9; *Mark* 9:43, 45
him, All men seek *for t.* *Mark* 1:37
thy brethren seek *for t.* 3:32
the Lord hath done *for t.* 5:19
but I have prayed *for t.* *Luke* 22:32
come, and calleth *for t.* *John* 11:28
hard *for t.* to kick against the pricks. *Acts* 9:5; 26:14
to send *for t.* into his house. 10:22
season, I will call *for t.* 24:25
grace is sufficient *for t.* *2 Cor* 12:9

from **thee**

be far *from t.* to slay. *Gen* 18:25
anger turn away *from t.* 27:45
hath withheld *from t.* the fruit. 30:2
behold, I go out *from t.* *Ex* 8:29
put off thy ornaments *from t.* 33:5
be too far *from t.* *Deut* 12:21; 14:24
him go free *from t.* 15:12, 13, 18
I will not go away *from t.* 16
cities far *from t.* 20:15
it is not hidden *from t.* neither. 30:11
shekels taken *from t.* *Judg* 17:2
Eli said unto her, Put away thy wine *from t.* *1 Sam* 1:14
hath rent the kingdom *from t.* 15:28
1 Ki 11:11
take thine head *from t.* *1 Sam* 17:46
far be it *from t.* 20:9; *Mat* 16:22
not withhold me *from t.* *2 Sam* 13:13
before I be taken *from t.* *2 Ki* 2:9
shall issue *from t.* 20:18; *Isa* 39:7
came up *from t.* to us. *Ezra* 4:12
be withholden *from t.* *Job* 42:2
groaning is not hid *from t.* *Ps* 38:9
sins are not hid *from t.* 69:5
they that are far *from t.* shall. 73:27
so will we not go back *from t.* 80:18
darkness hideth not *from t.* 139:12
my substance was not hid *from t.* 15
wrath I hid my face *from t.* *Isa* 54:8
shall not depart *from t.* 10
my soul depart *from t.* *Jer* 6:8
I will cut off *from t.* *Ezek* 21:3, 4
those that be far *from t.* shall. 22:5
I take away *from t.* the desire. 24:16
secret that they can hide *from t.* 28:3
gone into captivity *from t.* *Mi* 1:16
iniquity to pass *from t.* *Zech* 3:4
pluck it out and cast it *from t.* *Mat* 5:29, 30; 18:8, 9
I came out *from t.* *John* 17:8
for a promise *from t.* *Acts* 23:21

see **departed**

in **thee**

in t. shall all families be blessed. *Gen* 12:3; 28:14
in t. shall Israel bless. 48:20
to shew *in t.* my power. *Ex* 9:16
no unclean thing *in t.* *Deut* 23:14
it would be sin *in t.* 21
shall be no sin *in t.* 22
king hath delight *in t.* *1 Sam* 18:22
evil hath not been found *in t.* 25:28
29:6
I have no delight *in t.* *2 Sam* 15:26
good things found *in t.* *2 Chr* 19:3
put trust *in t.* . . . love thy name be joyful *in t.* *Ps* 5:11; 7:1; 9:10
16:1; 17:7; 25:2, 20; 31:1, 19
55:23
rejoice *in t.* 9:2; 40:16; 70:4; 85:6
S of S 1:4
our fathers trusted *in t.* *Ps* 22:4, 5
I trusted *in t.* 31:14
hope *in t.* 33:22; 38:15; 39:7
trust *in t.* 56:3; 57:1; 84:12; 86:2
141:8; 143:8
there shall no strange god be *in t.* 81:9
man whose strength is *in t.* 84:5
all my springs are *in t.* 87:7
there is no spot *in t.* *S of S* 4:7
because he trusteth *in t.* *Isa* 26:3
surely God is *in t.*; and there. 45:14
for the Lord delighteth *in t.* 62:4
that my fear is not *in t.* *Jer* 2:19
I will do *in t.* what I. *Ezek* 5:9
will execute judgements *in t.* 10, 15
the contrary is *in t.* from. 16:34
I will kindle a fire *in t.*, and it. 20:47
were *in t.* to their power to. 22:6
in t. have they set light by father. 7
in t. are men that carry tales. 9
in t. have they taken gifts. 12
set palaces *in t.*, dwellings *in t.* 25:4
O Tyrus, that were *in t.* 27:8, 9
till iniquity was found *in t.* 28:15
be sanctified *in t.* O Gog. 38:16

spirit of the holy gods is in t.
Dan 4:9, 18; 5:14
for in t. the fatherless. Hos 14:3
Israel were found in t. Mi 1:13
cry ? is there no king in t.? 4:9
if the light that is in t. Mat 6:23
which have been done in t. 11:23
my beloved Son; in t. I. Luke 3:22
the light which is in t. be not. 11:35
not leave in t. one stone. 19:44
art in me, and I in t. John 17:21
shew my power in t. Rom 9:17
in t. shall all nations. Gal 3:8
the gift that is in t. 1 Tim 4:14
faith that is in t. first in Lois and
Eunice, and . . . in t. 2 Tim 1:5
stir up the gift of God which is in t. 6
of the truth that is in t. 3 John 3
heard no more at all in t. Rev 18:22
shall shine no more at all in t. 23

into **thee**

no more into t. the. Isa 52:1

of **thee**

of t. a great nation. Gen 12:2
17:6; 35:11; 46:3; 48:4; Ex 32:10
and my soul shall live because of t.
Gen 12:13
I have heard say of t. that. 41:15
heard the fame of t. Num 14:15
I will put the dread of t. and the fear
of t. . . . because of t. Deut 2:25
Lord require of t. 10:12; Mi 6:8
take knowledge of t. Ruth 2:19
with my father of t. 1 Sam 19:3
and the Lord avenge me of t. 24:12
I will require of t. 2 Sam 3:13
but I will surely buy it of t. 24:24
one petition of t. 1 Ki 2:16, 20
as this is done of t. 11:11
house as he said of t. 1 Chr 22:11
and honour come of t. 29:12
all things come of t., and of thine. 14
God exacteth of t. less. Job 11:6
for I will demand of t. 38:3; 40:7
42:4
heard of t. by the hearing. 42:5
my praise shall be of t. Ps 22:25
71:6
glorious things are spoken of t. 87:3
lest he be weary of t. Pr 25:17
two things have I required of t. 30:7
they that shall be of t. Isa 58:12
up himself to take hold of t. 64:7
I will not make a full end of t.
Jer 30:11; 46:28
thus saith the Lord of t., Thou. 34:4
shall not take of t. a stone. 51:26
man and beast out of t. Ezek 29:8
rivers shall be full of t. 32:6
made known what we desired of t.
Dan 2:23
petition, save of t. O king. 6:7, 12
assemble all of t. Mi 2:12
yet out of t. shall come forth. 5:2
shall fear because of t. 7:17
come out of t. a wicked. Nah 1:11
who are of t. to whom. Zeph 3:18
for out of t. shall come. Mat 2:6
need to be baptized of t. 3:14
him that would borrow of t. 5:42
no man eat fruit of t. Mark 11:14
which shall be born of t. Luke 1:35
every man that asketh of t. 6:30
soul shall be required of t. 12:20
how is it that I hear this of t.? 16:2
hast given me are of t. John 17:7
and to hear words of t. Acts 10:22
nor spake any harm of t. 28:21
we desire to hear of t. what. 22
I have no need of t. 1 Cor 12:21
let me have joy of t. Philem 20

see, in the **midst**

off **thee**

head from off t. and birds shall eat
thy flesh from off t. Gen 40:19
break his yoke from off t. Nah 1:13

on or upon **thee**

my wrong be upon t. Gen 16:5
this breach be upon t. 38:29
of these diseases upon t. Ex 15:26
woollen come upon t. Lev 19:19
his face shine upon t. Num 6:25
up his countenance upon t. Num 6:26
of the spirit which is upon t. 11:17
all these things are come upon t.
Deut 4:30; 30:1
the Lord may have compassion upon
t. 13:17; 30:3
so blood be upon t. 19:10
blessings come on t. 28:2
all these curses shall come upon t.
28:15, 20, 45
the Philistines be upon t., Samson.
Judg 16:9, 12, 14, 20
is it not upon t. and thy. 1 Sam 9:20
hand shall not be upon t. 24:12, 13
all Israel are upon t. 1 Ki 1:20
upon t. shall he offer the priests, and
. . . shall be burnt upon t. 13:2
bring evil upon t. and take. 21:21
shalt shut door upon t. 2 Ki 4:4
Lord, for we rest upon t. 2 Chr 14:11
wrath upon t. from the Lord. 19:2
to do: but our eyes are upon t. 20:12
but now it is come upon t. Job 4:5
I have called upon t. Ps 17:6
31:17; 86:5, 7; 88:9; Lam 3:57
I was cast upon t. Ps 22:10
wait upon t. 25:3, 5, 21; 59:9
meditate on t. 63:6
these wait upon t. 104:27; 145:15
that we may look upon t. S of S 6:13
I will turn my hand upon t. Isa 1:25
pit, and the snare are upon t. 24:17
whose mind is stayed upon t. 26:3
they shall come upon t. in. 47:9
desolation shall come upon t. 11, 13
and bind them on t. as a. 49:18
will I have mercy on t. 54:8, 10
my spirit that is upon t. 59:21
glory of Lord is risen upon t. 60:1, 2
will wait upon t. for thou. Jer 14:22
for who shall have pity upon t.? 15:5
all that prey upon t. will I. 30:16
they shall put bands upon t.
Ezek 3:25; 4:8
and I will bring the sword upon t.
5:17; 29:8
when they leaned upon t. 29:7
as I had pity upon t. Mat 18:33
let no fruit grow on t. 21:19
the Holy Ghost shall come upon t.
Luke 1:35
days shall come upon t. that. 19:43
hand of Lord is upon t. Acts 13:11
no man shall set on t. to. 18:10
beat them that believed on t. 22:19
which went before on t. 1 Tim 1:18
on t. as a thief, and thou shalt not
know . . . come upon t. Rev 3:3

over **thee**

and he shall rule over t. Gen 3:16
shall not reign over t. Deut 15:6
him king over t.: thou mayest not set
a stranger over t. 17:15; 28:36
Lord will again rejoice over t. 30:9
give his angels charge over t.
Ps 91:11; Luke 4:10
God rejoice over t. Isa 62:5
them to be chief over t. Jer 13:21
enemy to rejoice over t. Lam 2:17
I spread my skirt over t. Ezek 16:8
spread out my net over t. 32:3
and seven times shall pass over t.
Dan 4:25, 32
shall clap the hands over t. Nah 3:19
will rejoice over t., he will joy over t.
Zeph 3:17

through **thee**

through t. will we push. Ps 44:5

to or unto **thee**

unto t. shall be his desire. Gen 4:7
to t. will I give it. 13:15, 17; 17:8
26:3; 28:4, 13; 35:12
certainly return unto t. 18:10, 14
to t. a covering of the eyes. 20:16
nations bow down to t. 27:29
which I have spoken to t. of. 28:15
give the tenth of all unto t. 22
better I give her to t. than to. 29:19
all that Laban doth unto t. 31:12
God hath said unto t. do. 16
thine with me, and take to t. 32
torn I brought not unto t. 39
not pass over this heap to t. 52
let me come in unto t. Gen 38:16
if I bring him not to t. 42:37; 43:9
44:32
money we brought again unto t. 44:8
for they did unto t. evil. 50:17
shall be a token unto t. Ex 3:12
to t. instead of a mouth. 4:16
be unto t. for a sign. 13:9
2 Ki 19:29; Isa 38:7
they shall bring unto t. Ex 18:22
take unto t. Aaron thy brother. 28:1
unto t. principal spices. 30:23
know what to do unto t. 33:5
shall be holy unto t. for. Lev 21:8
that they bring unto t. pure. 24:2
Lord be gracious unto t. Num 6:25
word shall come to pass unto t. 11:23
Levi may be joined unto t. 18:2, 4
it is a covenant of salt unto t. 19
Balak, lo, I am come unto t. 22:38
unto t. it was shewed. Deut 4:35
gold of their gods unto t. 7:25
and it be sin unto t. 15:9, 24:15
Lord will raise up unto t. 18:15
up a prophet like unto t. 18
and take the young to t. 22:7
from his master unto t. 23:15
who is like unto t., O people. 33:29
1 Sam 26:15; Ps 35:10; 71:19
will we hearken unto t. Josh 1:17
household home unto t. 2:18
of whom I say unto t. Judg 7:4
I will restore it unto t. 17:3
perform unto t. the part. Ruth 3:13
he shall be unto t. a restorer of thy
life: for thy daughter in law,
better to t. than seven sons. 4:15
am not I better to t. than ? 1 Sam 1:8
in all that they say unto t. 8:7
so do they unto t. 8
man I speak to t. of shall. 9:17
we will come out to t. 11:3
him whom I name unto t. 16:3
but I come to t. in the name. 17:45
for there is peace to t. 20:21
peace be to t. 25:6
whom I shall name unto t. 28:8
no punishment happen to t. 10
about all Israel unto t. 2 Sam 3:12
child that is born unto t. shall. 12:14
bring back all the people unto t. 17:3
that will be worse unto t. 19:7
his head shall be thrown to t. 20:21
I will give thanks unto t. 22:50
Ps 18:49; 30:12; 75:1; 119:62
that I may do it unto t. 2 Sam 24:12
any arise like unto t. 1 Ki 3:12
that they call for unto t. 8:52
will give ten tribes unto t. 11:31
and will give Israel unto t. 38
sent to t. with heavy tidings. 14:6
for what have I done to t.? 19:20
send my servants unto t. 20:6
inheritance of my fathers unto t. 21:3
from me to speak unto t.? 22:24
it shall be so unto t. 2 Ki 2:10
this letter is come unto t. 5:6
Naaman shall cleave unto t. 27
take it up to t. 6:7
what said Elisha to t.? 8:14
he said, I have an errand to t. 9:5
came this mad fellow to t.? 11
from whence came they unto t.?
20:14; Isa 39:3
peace be unto t. and. 1 Chr 12:18
unto t. will I give the land. 16:18
Ps 105:11
appertaineth not unto t. 2 Chr 26:18
matter belongeth unto t. Ezra 10:4
them to turn them to t. Neh 9:26
the silver is given to t. Esth 3:11
what shall I do unto t.? Job 7:20
for unto t. will I pray. Ps 5:2, 3
committeth himself unto t. 10:14
goodness extendeth not to t. 16:2
they cried unto t. and were. 22:5
unto t., O Lord, do I lift up my soul.
25:1; 86:4; 143:8
my heart said unto t., Thy face. 27:8
unto t. will I cry. 28:1, 2; 30:8
31:22; 56:9; 61:2; 86:3; 88:13
130:1; 141:1
may sing praise to t. 30:12; 56:12
59:17; 66:4; 71:22, 23

acknowledged my sin *unto t.* Ps 32:5
unto t. O Lord, belongeth. 62:12
and *unto t.* shall the vow be. 65:1
O thou that hearest prayer, *unto t.* 2
my prayer is *unto t.* in an. 69:13
gods there is none like *unto t.* 86:8
a strong Lord like *unto t.*? 89:8
unto t. O Lord, will I. 101:1; 108:3
138:1; 144:9; *Heb* 2:12
let my cry come *unto t.* *Ps* 102:1
what shall be given *unto t.*? 120:3
unto t. will I lift up. 123:1; 141:8
light are both alike *to t.* 139:12
made known *to t.* this day, even *to t.*
Pr 22:19
Eat and drink, saith he *to t.* 23:7
better it be said *unto t.* Come. 25:7
speak and say *unto t.* *Isa* 14:10
be very gracious *unto t.* 30:19
hath my master sent me *to t.*? 36:12
two things shall come *to t.* 47:9
thus shall they be *unto t.* with. 15
together and come *to t.* 49:18
two things are come *unto t.* 51:19
knew not thee shall run *unto t.* 55:5
moon give light *unto t.*: the Lord shall
be *unto t.* an everlasting. 60:19
come no more *unto t.* *Jer* 2:31
come *unto t.* for thou art our. 3:22
as there is none like *unto t.* 10:6
who would not fear, for *to t.* doth? 7
for *unto t.* have I revealed my.
11:20; 20:12
let them return *unto t.* but. 15:19
a man child is born *unto t.* 20:15
unto t. in thy prosperity. 22:21
done these things *unto t.* 30:15
I speak *unto t.*: so it shall be well
unto t. 38:20
I will look well *unto t.* 40:4
we will not hearken *unto t.* 44:16
but thy life will I give *unto t.* 45:5
Israel a derision *unto t.*? 48:27
I liken *to t.*, O Jerusalem? what shall
I equal *to t.*, that I? *Lam* 2:13
shall pass through *unto t.* 4:21
turn thou us *unto t.* and we. 5:21
hearkened *unto t.* *Ezek* 3:6
Israel will not hearken *unto t.* 7
to do any of these *unto t.* 16:5
I said *unto t.* when thou wast in. 6
no reward is given *unto t.* 34
establish *unto t.* an everlasting. 60
and I will give them *unto t.* for. 61
shall be sure *unto t.* *Dan* 4:26
to t. it is spoken, the kingdom is. 31
righteousness belongeth *unto t.* 9:7
what shall I do *unto t.*? *Hos* 6:4
to t. will I cry. *Joel* 1:19
the beasts cry *unto t.* 20
thus will I do *unto t.*: and because
I will do this *unto t.* *Amos* 4:12
shall we do *unto t.*? *Jonah* 1:11
my prayer came in *unto t.* 2:7
saying, I will prophesy *unto t.* of
wine. *Mi* 2:11
unto t. shall it come. 4:8
what have I done *unto t.*? 6:3
he shall come *to t.* even from. 7:12
I even cry out *unto t.* *Hab* 1:2
right hand be turned *unto t.* 2:16
Lord hath sent me *unto t.* *Zech* 2:11
behold, thy king cometh *unto t.* 9:9
Mat 21:5
hast believed, so be it done *unto t.*
Mat 8:13
hath not revealed it *unto t.* 16:17
and I say also *unto t.* that thou. 18
I will give *unto t.* the keys of. 19
this shall not be *unto t.* 22
him be *unto t.* as an heathen. 18:17
Jesus saith, I say not *unto t.* Until. 22
this last even as *unto t.* 20:14
thou stonest them sent *unto t.* 23:37
Luke 13:34
did not minister *unto t.*? *Mat* 25:44
I say *unto t.* Arise. *Mark* 5:41
Luke 5:24; 7:14
What wilt thou that I do *unto t.*?
Mark 10:51; *Luke* 18:41
I am sent to speak *unto t.* *Luke* 1:19
myself worthy to come *unto t.* 7:7
I have somewhat to say *unto t.* 40
God hath done *unto t.* 8:39

saith, I that speak *unto t.* am he.
John 4:26
a worse thing come *unto t.* 5:14
what did he *to t.*? 9:26
said I not *unto t.*? 11:40
world, and I am come *to t.* 17:11, 13
have delivered him *unto t.* 18:30
he that delivered me *unto t.* 19:11
what is that *to t.*? follow. 21:22, 23
appeared *unto t.* sent me. *Acts* 9:17
cometh, shall speak *unto t.* 10:32
therefore I sent *to t.* 33
captain, May I speak *unto t.*? 21:37
for I have appeared *unto t.* 26:16
will I confess *to t.* *Rom* 15:9
committed *unto t.* keep. *2 Tim* 1:14
but now profitable *to t.* *Philem* 11
but how much more *to t.*? 16
thou hast taken *to t.* thy. *Rev* 11:17

towards thee

his works have been very good *towards t.* *1 Sam* 19:4
I would not look *towards t.* nor.
2 Ki 3:14
mine heart *towards t.* *Jer* 12:3
so will I make my fury *towards t.* to
rest. *Ezek* 16:42
when I am pacified *towards t.* 63
but *towards t.* goodness. *Rom* 11:22

under thee

the earth that is *under t.* *Deut* 28:23
the people fall *under t.* *Ps* 45:5
take thy bed from *under t.*? *Pr* 22:27
worm is spread *under t.* *Isa* 14:11
laid a wound *under t.* *Ob* 7

with thee

with t. will I establish. *Gen* 6:18
my covenant is *with t.* 17:4
Ex 34:27; *Deut* 29:12
now will we deal worse *with t.* than.
Gen 19:9
saying, God is *with t.* in all. 21:22
will send his angel *with t.* 24:40
I will be *with t.* 26:3
I am *with t.* 24; 28:15; 31:3; 46:4
Ex 3:12; *Deut* 31:23; *Josh* 1:5
3:7; *1 Ki* 11:38; *Isa* 43:2
the Lord was *with t.* *Gen* 26:28
God shall be *with t.* *Ex* 18:19
I will meet *with t.* 25:22; 30:6, 36
my presence shall go *with t.* 33:14
Deut 31:6, 8; *Judg* 6:16
not abide *with t.* all night. *Lev* 19:13
if no man hath lien *with t.* be thou.
Num 5:19
some man hath lien *with t.* 20
What men are these *with t.*? 22:9
God hath been *with t.* *Deut* 2:7
go well *with t.* 4:40; 5:16; 6:3, 18
12:25, 28; 19:13; 22:7
go because he is well *with t.* 15:16
the Lord thy God is *with t.* 20:1
Josh 1:9; *Judg* 6:12; *2 Sam* 7:3
against the city that maketh war
with t. *Deut* 20:20
he shall dwell *with t.* even. 23:16
I will surely go *with t.* *Judg* 4:9
the people that are *with t.* 7:2
this shall go *with t.* 4
peace be *with t.* 19:20
that it may be well *with t.* *Ruth* 3:1
for God is *with t.* *1 Sam* 10:7
Luke 1:28
I am *with t.* according to. *1 Sam* 14:7
the Lord be *with t.* 17:37; 20:13
1 Chr 22:11, 16
and no man *with t.*? *1 Sam* 21:1
I will deliver Israel *with t.* 28:19
so long as I have been *with t.* 29:8
my hand shall be *with t.* *2 Sam* 3:12
I was *with t.* 7:9; *1 Chr* 17:8
Amnon been *with t.* *2 Sam* 13:20
Why should he go *with t.*? 26
Lord thy God will be *with t.* 14:17
1 Chr 28:20
and truth be *with t.* *2 Sam* 15:20
I may not tarry thus *with t.* 18:14
there will not tarry one *with t.* 19:7
thou hast *with t.* Shimei. *1 Ki* 2:8
uprightness of heart *with t.* 3:6
perform my word *with t.* 6:12
I will not go in *with t.* 13:8, 16

what have I to do *with t.*? *1 Ki* 17:18
2 Ki 3:13; *2 Chr* 35:21; *Mark* 5:7
Luke 8:28; *John* 2:4
is it well *with t.*? *2 Ki* 4:26
went not mine heart *with t.*? 5:26
even thou and Judah *with t.* 14:10
2 Chr 25:19
nothing *with t.* to help. *2 Chr* 14:11
we will be *with t.* 18:3; *Ezra* 10:4
let not the army of Israel go *with t.*
2 Chr 25:7
be at peace *with t.* *Job* 5:23
I know that this is *with t.* 10:13
me into judgement *with t.* 14:3
number of his months are *with t.* 5
of God small *with t.*? is there any
secret thing *with t.*? 15:11
perfect in knowledge *with t.* 36:4
behemoth, which I made *with t.*
40:15
nor shall evil dwell *with t.* *Ps* 5:4
with t. is the fountain of life. 36:9
I am a stranger *with t.* and. 39:12
I am continually *with t.* 73:23
have fellowship *with t.*? 94:20
dealt bountifully *with t.* 116:7
it shall be well *with t.* 128:2
but there is forgiveness *with t.* 130:4
awake, I am still *with t.* 139:18
my commandments *with t.* *Pr* 2:1
and not strangers *with t.* 5:17
it shall talk *with t.* 6:22
his heart is not *with t.* 23:7
may seek him *with t.* *S of S* 6:1
outcast dwell *with t.* Moab. *Isa* 16:4
I am *with t.* 41:10; 43:5; *Jer* 1:8
19; 15:20; 30:11; 46:28
Acts 18:10
they that strive *with t.* *Isa* 41:11, 12
that contendeth *with t.* 49:25
I would not be wroth *with t.* 54:9
I will plead *with t.* *Jer* 2:35
when I plead *with t.* 12:1
and he shall speak *with t.* 34:3
with t. will I break in pieces the
nations. 51:20
with t. will I break in pieces horse
and rider. 21
with t. will I break in pieces old and
young. 22
with t. will I break shepherd. 23
and thorns be *with t.* *Ezek* 2:6
I will there talk *with t.* 3:22
into a covenant *with t.* 16:8
I will even deal *with t.* as thou. 59
establish my covenant *with t.* 62
that I shall deal *with t.* 22:14
they occupied *with t.* in lambs. 27:21
beasts of the earth *with t.* 32:4
his bands and many people *with t.*
38:6, 9, 15; 39:4
the prophet shall fall *with t.* *Hos* 4:5
Is there yet any *with t.*? *Amos* 6:10
were at peace *with t.* *Ob* 7
all the saints *with t.* *Zech* 14:5
will he be pleased *with t.*? *Mal* 1:8
What have we to do *with t.*?
Mat 8:29; *Mark* 1:24; *Luke* 4:34
desiring to speak *with t.* *Mat* 12:47
then take *with t.* one or two. 18:16
Peter said, Though I should die *with
t.* 26:35; *Mark* 14:31
I am ready to go *with t.* *Luke* 22:33
he that was *with t.* *John* 3:26
is he that talketh *with t.* 9:37
glory which I had *with t.* 17:5
him, We also go *with t.* 21:3
Thy money perish *with t.* *Acts* 8:20
that it may be well *with t.*, and that
thou mayest live long. *Eph* 6:3
grace be *with t.* *1 Tim* 6:21
bring *with t.* *2 Tim* 4:11, 13

within thee

the stranger *within t.* *Deut* 28:43
say, Peace be *within t.* *Ps* 122:8
thy children *within t.* 147:13
if thou keep them *within t.* *Pr* 22:18
thoughts lodge *within t.* *Jer* 4:14
thy children *within t.* *Luke* 19:44

without thee

without t. shall no man lift up his.
Gen 41:44

theft, -s

be sold for his t. Ex 22:3
if the t. be certainly found in. 4
out of the heart proceed t.
Mat 15:19; Mark 7:22
repented they of their t. Rev 9:21

their's

be a stranger in a land that is not t.'s.
Gen 15:13
every beast of t.'s, be our's? 34:23
times as much as any of t.'s. 43:34
priests' office shall be t.'s. Ex 29:9
for t.'s is thine own nakedness.
Lev 18:10
and touch nothing of t.'s. Num 16:26
t.'s, every meat offering of t.'s. 18:9
for t.'s was the first lot. Josh 21:10
1 Chr 6:54
let thy word be like one of t.'s.
2 Chr 18:12
shall stand, mine, or t.'s. Jer 44:28
remain, nor any of t.'s. Ezek 7:11
thing in Israel shall be t.'s. 44:29
dwelling places that are not t.'s.
Hab 1:6
for t.'s is the kingdom. Mat 5:3, 10
call on our Lord, both t.'s. 1 Cor 1:2
manifest, as t's was. 2 Tim 3:9

them

male, female created he t. Gen 1:27
your little ones, t. will. Num 14:31
t. will the Lord bring. Deut 28:61
t. that honour me, I. 1 Sam 2:30
t. shall he sling out, as out. 25:29
t. they hold also to. 1 Ki 13:11
t. that burnt incense. 2 Ki 23:5
t. hath the Lord chosen. 1 Chr 15:2
t. did Solomon make to. 2 Chr 8:8
let t. shout for joy, let t. Ps 5:11
nor let t. wink with eye that. 35:19
let t. also that hate him flee. 68:1
even t. that contended. Isa 41:12
even t. will I bring to my. 56:7
they cast t. into the den. Dan 6:24
t. that worship the host. Zeph 1:5
take away t. that rejoice in thy. 3:11
shall gather out t. which. Mat 13:41
then let t. which be in Judea flee.
24:16; Mark 13:14; Luke 21:21
neither believed they t. Mark 16:13
to set at liberty t. that. Luke 4:18
and t. that were entering in. 11:52
cast out t. that sold and t. 19:45
and t. that were with t. 24:33
other sheep I have, t. John 10:16
that we trouble not t. Acts 15:19
t. take and purify thyself with t. 21:24
that I beat t. that believed. 22:19
t. he also called: t. he also justified:
and t. he also glorified. Rom 8:30
provoke to emulation t. which. 11:14
to judge t. also that. 1 Cor 5:12
but t. that are without God. 13
acknowledge ye t. that are. 16:18
even so t. also that. 1 Thes 4:14
now t. that are such, we. 2 Thes 3:12
shalt save thyself and t. 1 Tim 4:16
t. that sin rebuke before all. 5:20
hath perfected t. that. Heb 10:14
remember t. that are in bonds. 13:3
let t. that suffer according to will of
God. 1 Pet 4:19
horses and t. that sat on t. Rev 9:17
and measure t. that worship. 11:1
to blaspheme t. that dwell in. 13:6
beast was taken, and t. 19:20

see **teach**

above **them**

proudly, he was above t. Ex 18:11
were over and above t. Num 3:49
lifted above t. that rose against me.
2 Sam 22:49
images that were above t. he cut.
2 Chr 34:4

about **them**

cities round about t. Gen 35:5
city was moved about t. Ruth 1:19
the heathen that were about t.
2 Ki 17:15
make about t. walls. 2 Chr 14:7
all about t. strengthened. Ezra 1:6
eyes round about t. four. Ezek 1:18
despise them round about t. 28:26
great multitude about t. Mark 9:14
fear came on all that dwelt round
about t. Luke 1:65
of the Lord shone round about t. 2:9
and the cities about t. in. Jude 7

after **them**

seven other kine came up after t.
Gen 41:3, 19, 27
withered sprung up after t. 23
shall arise after t. seven years. 30
which thou begettest after t. 48:6
neither after t. shall be. Ex 10:14
he shall follow after t. and I. 14:4
go a whoring after t. Lev 20:6
and their seed after t. Deut 1:8
chose their seed after t. 4:37; 10:15
pursue after t. quickly. Josh 2:5
the men pursued after t. 7; 8:16
Judg 8:12; 20:45
generation after t. Judg 2:10
reap, go thou after t. Ruth 2:9
Philistines went after t. 1 Sam 6:12
they followed hard after t. in. 14:22
upon their children that were left
after t. 1 Ki 9:21; 2 Chr 8:8
went after t. to Jordan. 2 Ki 7:15
not from after t. to wit. 10:29
go not up after t. 1 Chr 14:14
and I after t. Neh 12:33
cried after t. as after. Job 30:5
strangers, and after t. Jer 2:25
send a sword after t. 9:16; 49:37
Ezek 5:2, 12; 12:14
Sheshach shall drink after t.
Jer 25:26
iniquity of the fathers into the bosom
of their children after t. 32:18
good of their children after t. 39
army pursued after t. 39:5
and utterly destroy after t. 50:21
shall look after t. Ezek 29:16
did search or seek after t. 34:6
king shall rise after t. Dan 7:24
horses go forth after t. Zech 6:6
land was desolate after t. 7:14
see here; or, see there: go not after
t. Luke 17:23; 21:8
away disciples after t. Acts 20:30

against **them**

against t. by night. Gen 14:15
my wrath may wax hot against t.
Ex 32:10; Num 12:9; Deut 2:15
31:17; Judg 2:15
congregation against t. Num 16:19
Bashan went out against t. 21:33
forcing an axe against t. Deut 20:19
go out one way against t. 28:25
song shall testify against t. 31:21
and earth to record against t. 28
and the other issued out of the city
against t. Josh 8:22
intend to go up against t. in. 22:33
strive or fight against t.? Judg 11:25
he moved David against t. to say.
2 Sam 24:1
he testified against t. 2 Ki 17:15
dwelt over against t. 1 Chr 5:11
they were helped against t. for. 20
ye down against t. 2 Chr 20:16, 17
prophets testified against t. 24:19
Neh 9:26, 29, 30, 34
stood up against t. that came. 28:12
hired counsellors against t. Ezra 4:5
but his wrath is against t. 8:22
we set a watch against t. Neh 4:9
set a great assembly against t. 5:7
dealt proudly against t. 9:10
brethren were over against t. 12:9
hired Balaam against t. 13:2
I testified against t. 15, 21
those that rise up against t. Ps 17:7
face of the Lord is against t. that do
evil. 34:16; 1 Pet 3:12
doth witness against t. Isa 3:9
forth his hand against t. 5:25
stir up the Medes against t. 13:17
I will rise up against t. 14:22
he fought against t. 63:10
I will utter my judgements against
t. Jer 1:16
I will give sentence against t. 4:12
I am against t. 23:32
prophesy against t. Jer 25:30
Ezek 6:2; 13:17; 25:2
evil he pronounced against t.
Jer 26:19; 35:17; 36:31
it prevaileth against t. Lam 1:13
set my face against t. Ezek 15:7
my anger against t. in Egypt. 20:8
out of thy hatred against t. 35:11
bring thee against t. 38:17
horn prevailed against t. Dan 7:21
is kindled against t. Hos 8:5
shall be gathered against t. 10:10
for a testimony against t. Mat 10:18
Mark 6:11; 13:9; Luke 9:5
spoken that parable against t.
Mark 12:12; Luke 20:19
off the dust of their feet against t.
Acts 13:51
rose up together against t. 16:22
spirit was prevailed against t. 19:16
I gave my voice against t. 26:10
being mad against t. 11
judgement of God is against t. that.
Rom 2:2
and be not bitter against t. Col 3:19
accusation against t. 2 Pet 2:11
shall make war against t. Rev 11:7

see **fight, over**

among or *amongst* **them**

men of activity among t. Gen 47:6
of Israel from among t. Ex 7:5
which I have done amongst t. 10:2
that I may dwell among t. 25:8
29:46; Ps 68:18
be no plague among t. Ex 30:12
defile my tabernacle that is among t.
Lev 15:31
not numbered among t. Num 1:47
fire of Lord burnt among t. 11:1, 3
the mixt multitude among t. 4
the Lord is among t. 16:3; Ps 68:17
Aaron shall have no part among t.
Num 18:20; Josh 14:3
shout of a king is among t.
Num 23:21
the hornet among t. Deut 7:20
that was born among t. Josh 8:33
were conversant among t. 35
that they dwelt among t. 9:16
that he may dwell among t. 20:4
that which I did amongst t. 24:5
the Canaanites dwelt among t.
Judg 1:30
strange gods from among t. 10:16
he wrought among t. 1 Sam 6:6
Neh 9:17
chiefest place among t. 1 Sam 9:22
and he prophesied among t. 10:10
thy servant among t. 2 Sam 19:28
the Lord sent lions among t.
2 Ki 17:25
Levi and Benjamin not counted
among t. 1 Chr 21:6
found mighty men among t. 26:31
found among t. abundance of spoil.
2 Chr 20:25
that were naked among t. 28:15
were among t. 200 singing men.
Ezra 2:65
midst among t. and slay. Neh 4:11
establish the Purim among t.
Esth 9:21
and Satan came also among t.
Job 1:6; 2:1
no stranger passed among t. 15:19
garments among t., and cast lots upon.
Ps 22:18; Mat 27:35; John 19:24
seize upon them; for wickedness is
among t. Ps 55:15
and I lie even among t. that. 57:4
among t. were damsels. 68:25
sorts of flies among t. 78:45
sending evil angels among t. 49
and Samuel among t. that call. 99:6
shewed his signs among t. 105:27
out Israel from among t. 136:11
barren among t. S of S 4:2; 6:6
weary or stumble among t. Isa 5:27
many among t. shall stumble. 8:15
there was no man among t. 41:28
who among t. can declare this? 43:9
which among t. hath declared. 48:14
I will set a sign among t. 66:19

they shall fall *among t.* that fall. *Jer* 6:15; 8:12
O congregation, what is *among t.* 18
house of Judah from *among t.* 12:14
and pestilence *among t.* 24:10
sword that I will send *among t.* 25:16
but wounded men *among t.* 37:10
ten men found *among t.* that. 41:8
as a menstruous woman *among t.* *Lam* 1:17
there hath been a prophet *among t.* *Ezek* 2:5; 33:33
and remained there *among t.* 3:15
shalt not go out *among t.* 25
one man *among t.* had a writer's. 9:2
Israel that are *among t.* 12:10
and the prince that is *among t.* 12
I am prophet *among t.* 22:26
I sought a man *among t.* 30
a prophet hath been *among t.* 33:33
David a prince *among t.* 34:24
myself known *among t.* 35:11
among t. was found none. *Dan* 1:19
came up *among t.* another. 7:8
shall scatter *among t.* the prey. 11:24
there is none *among t.* *Hos* 7:7
that is feeble *among t.* *Zech* 12:8
tumult shall be *among t.* 14:13
I say, *Among t.* that are born of. *Mat* 11:11
two fishes divided he *among t.* *Mark* 6:41
a reasoning *among t.* *Luke* 9:46
was also a strife *among t.* 22:24
Peter sat down *among t.* in. 55
was a division *among t.* *John* 9:16
if I had not done *among t.* 15:24
among t. that lacked. *Acts* 4:34
Paul departed from *among t.* 17:33
the word of God *among t.* 18:11
inheritance *among t.* that are. 20:32
26:18
were grafted in *among t.* *Rom* 11:17
we speak wisdom *among t.* that. *1 Cor* 2:6
come out from *among t.* *2 Cor* 6:17
man dwelling *amongst t.* *2 Pet* 2:8
preeminence *among t.* *3 John* 9
that are ungodly *among t.* *Jude* 15
on the throne shall dwell *among t.* *Rev* 7:15

at them

we have shot *at t.*: Heshbon is perished. *Num* 21:30
not be affrighted *at t.* *Deut* 7:21
his enemies, he puffeth *at t.* *Ps* 10:5
O Lord, shalt laugh *at t.* 59:8
but God shall shoot *at t.* 64:7
heathen are dismayed *at t.* *Jer* 10:2

before them

and set it *before t.* *Gen* 18:8
he passed over *before t.* 33:3
before t. there were no such locusts. *Ex* 10:14
the Lord went *before t.* by day. 13:21; *Num* 14:14
thou shalt set *before t.* *Ex* 21:1
ark of the Lord went *before t.* *Num* 10:33
to go out and in *before t.* 27:17
1 Sam 18:16
destroyed them from *before t.* *Deut* 2:12, 21, 22; *1 Chr* 5:25
Neh 9:24
shalt flee seven ways *before t.* *Deut* 28:25
armed men went *before t.* *Josh* 6:13
land was subdued *before t.* 18:1
man of their enemies *before t.* 21:44
Ehud *before t.* *Judg* 3:27
take *before t.* waters. 7:24
tabret, a pipe and harp, *before t.* *1 Sam* 10:5
and Shobach went *before t.* *2 Sam* 10:16; *1 Chr* 19:16
Amasa went *before t.* *2 Sam* 20:8
give them compassion *before t.* *1 Ki* 8:50; *2 Chr* 30:9
prophets prophesied *before t.* *1 Ki* 22:10; *2 Chr* 18:19
Moabites fled *before t.* *2 Ki* 3:24
Gehazi passed on *before t.* 4:31
so he set it *before t.* 44
bread and water *before t.* *2 Ki* 6:22
Lord carried away *before t.* 17:11
priest sounded trumpets *before t.* *2 Chr* 7:6
Ezra the scribe *before t.* *Neh* 12:36
will pay my vows *before t.* *Ps* 22:25
not set God *before t.* 54:3; 86:14
the heathen also *before t.* 78:55
he sent a man *before t.* 105:17
all that have been *before t.* *Eccl* 4:16
hatred by all that is *before t.* 9:1
now go write it *before t.* *Isa* 30:8
darkness light *before t.* 42:16
dividing the water *before t.* 63:12
lest I confound thee *before t.* *Jer* 1:17
my law which I set *before t.* 9:13
charged Baruch *before t.* 32:13
more be a nation *before t.* 33:24
to be dismayed *before t.* 49:37
before t. seventy men. *Ezek* 8:11
oil and incense *before t.* 16:18, 19
I will set judgement *before t.* 23:24
brandish my sword *before t.* 32:10
stand *before t.* to minister. 44:11
a fire devoureth *before t.* . . . garden of Eden *before t.* *Joel* 2:3
the earth shall quake *before t.* 10
the Amorite *before t.* *Amos* 2:9
breaker is come up *before t.* and their king . . . *before t.* *Mi* 2:13
angel of Lord *before t.* *Zech* 12:8
the star went *before t.* *Mat* 2:9
she danced *before t.* 14:6
and was transfigured *before t.* 17:2
Mark 9:2
but he denied *before t.* *Mat* 26:70
gave to his disciples to set *before t.* *Mark* 6:41; 8:6, 7
Jesus went *before t.* and they. 10:32
Judas went *before t.* *Luke* 22:47
he did eat *before t.* 24:43
shepherd goeth *before t.* *John* 10:4
so many miracles *before t.* 12:37
he set meat *before t.* *Acts* 16:34
set Paul *before t.* 22:30
I said to Peter *before t.* all. *Gal* 2:14

behind them

and stood *behind t.* *Ex* 14:19
of Ai looked *behind t.* *Josh* 8:20
the Benjamites looked *behind t.* *Judg* 20:40
a compass *behind t.* *2 Sam* 5:23
to come about *behind t.* *2 Chr* 13:13
behind t. a flame burneth, *behind t.* *Joel* 2:3

beside them

the asses were feeding *beside t.* *Job* 1:14
wheels turned not from *beside t.* *Ezek* 10:16, 19; 11:22
I have gained *beside t.* five talents. *Mat* 25:20, 22

between them

oath of the Lord shall be *between t.* *Ex* 22:11
and bells of gold *between t.* 28:33
valley *between t.* and Ai. *Josh* 8:11
a valley *between t.* and the Philistines. *1 Sam* 17:3
great space being *between t.* 26:13
Lord's oath *between t.* *2 Sam* 21:7
they divided the land *between t.* *1 Ki* 18:6
can come *between t.* *Job* 41:16
shall be *between t.* both. *Zech* 6:13
was so sharp *between t.* *Acts* 15:39

by them

neither seek after wizards, to be defiled *by t.* *Lev* 19:31
nor cause to swear *by t.* *Josh* 23:7
to prove Israel *by t.* *Judg* 3:1, 4
by t. ye shall send to. *2 Sam* 15:36
was perfected *by t.* *2 Chr* 24:13
for *by t.* judgeth he the. *Job* 36:31
by t. is thy servant. *Ps* 19:11
by t. beyond the river. *Isa* 7:20
and have sworn *by t.* that. *Jer* 5:7
the wheels went *by t.* *Ezek* 1:19
I be enquired of at all *by t.*? 14:3
by t. their portion is fat. *Hab* 1:16
that it was said *by t.* of old. *Mat* 5:21, 27, 33
would have passed *by t.* *Mark* 6:48
two men stood *by t.* in white. *Luke* 24:4; *Acts* 1:10
miracle has been done *by t.* *Acts* 4:16
God hath wrought *by t.* 15:12
things shall live *by t.* *Rom* 10:5
provoke you to jealousy *by t.* 19
by t. which are of the house of. *1 Cor* 1:11
thou *by t.* mightest war. *1 Tim* 1:18
confirmed to us *by t.* *Heb* 2:3
reported to you *by t.* *1 Pet* 1:12

concerning them

so *con. t.* Moses. *Num* 32:28
Samson said *con. t.*, Now I. *Judg* 15:3
commandment *con. t.* *Neh* 11:23
to be ignorant *con. t.* *1 Thes* 4:13
have I written *con. t.* *1 John* 2:26

for them

food for thee and *for t.* *Gen* 6:21
is large enough *for t.* 34:21
and they set on bread *for t.* 43:32
the Lord fighteth *for t.* *Ex* 14:25
make an atonement *for t.* *Lev* 4:20
9:7; 10:17; *Num* 8:21; 16:46
there is one law *for t.* the. *Lev* 7:7
a resting place *for t.* *Num* 10:33
for t., fishes gathered *for t.* 11:22
fail with longing *for t.* *Deut* 28:32
hand went a fiery law *for t.* 33:2
Joshua cast lots *for t.* *Josh* 18:10
Judah was too much *for t.* 19:9
Dan went out too little *for t.* 47
do for wives *for t.*? *Judg* 21:16
inheritance *for t.* escaped. 17
would ye tarry *for t.* till? *Ruth* 1:13
prayed *for t.* saying. *2 Chr* 30:18
of the Lord for me and *for t.* 34:21
God keepeth mercy *for t.* *Neh* 1:5
we take up corn *for t.* that we. 5:2
broughtest forth water *for t.* 9:15
banquet I shall prepare *for t.* *Esth* 5:8
of Sheba waited *for t.* *Job* 6:19
the Almighty do *for t.*? 22:17
wilderness yieldeth food *for t.* 24:5
laid up *for t.* that fear thee, *for t.* that trust in thee. *Ps* 31:19
thou hast founded *for t.* 104:8
and he remembered *for t.* 106:45
hath done great things *for t.* 126:2
Assyrian founded it *for t.* *Isa* 23:13
for her merchandise shall be *for t.* 18
he hath cast the lot *for t.*, and. 34:17
places shall be glad *for t.* 35:1
in the ways hast thou sat *for t.* as. *Jer* 3:2
lift up cry nor prayer *for t.* 7:16
nor shall men lament *for t.* 16:6
neither men tear themselves *for t.* 7
thee to speak good *for t.* 18:20
shalt make *for t.* yokes. 28:13
there be wailing *for t.* *Ezek* 7:11
but as *for t.* whose heart. 11:21
to pass through the fire *for t.* 16:21
a land I had espied *for t.* 20:6
flock may not be meat *for t.* 34:10
I will raise up *for t.* a plant. 29
enquired of to do *for t.* 36:37
make reconciliation *for t.* 45:15
his inheritance shall be his sons' *for t.* 46:17
for t. even for the priests. 48:10
no place was found *for t.* *Dan* 2:35
Rev 20:11
make a covenant *for t.* *Hos* 2:18
I will hiss *for t.* and. *Zech* 10:8
place shall not be found *for t.* 10
pray *for t.* which despitefully use. *Mat* 5:44; *Luke* 6:28
nor lawful *for t.* that. *Mat* 12:4
it shall be done *for t.* of my. 18:19
hard *for t.* that trust. *Mark* 10:24
there was no room *for t.* *Luke* 2:7
is not sufficient *for t.* *John* 6:7
I pray *for t.*: . . . but for them. 17:9, 20
and John prayed *for t.* *Acts* 8:15
Cornelius waited *for t.* and. 10:24
now while Paul waited *for t.* 17:16
God hath prepared *for t.* *1 Cor* 2:9
it is good *for t.* if they abide. 7:8

but prophesying serveth for t. 1 Cor 14:22
him which died for t. 2 Cor 5:15
what conflict I have for t. Col 2:1
hath a great zeal for t. that. 4:13
to minister for t. who shall? Heb 1:14
make intercession for t. 7:25
he hath prepared for t. a city. 11:16
it had been better for t. 2 Pet 2:21
give life for t. that sin. 1 John 5:16

from them

will be restrained from t. Gen 11:6
he took from t. Simeon and. 42:24
not taken one ass from t. Num 16:15
I have given you from t. 18:26
from t. that have many ye shall give many, but from t. that have. 35:8
and hide thyself from t. Deut 22:1, 4
hide my face from t. 31:17; 32:20 Ezek 7:22; Mi 3:4
their calves home from t. 1 Sam 6:7
them, turn away from t. 1 Chr 14:14
but they turned from t. 2 Chr 20:10
deliver me from t. that. Ps 31:15
defend me from t. that rise up. 59:1
will he withhold from t. 84:11
withhold not good from t. Pr 3:27
his soul shall be far from t. 22:5
desired I kept not from t. Eccl 2:10
little that I passed from t. S of S 3:4
given shall pass from t. Jer 8:13
leave my people and go from t. 9:2
turn away thy wrath from t. 18:20
I will take from t. the voice. 25:10
I will not turn away from t. 32:40
I have set it far from t. Ezek 7:20
mind was alienated from t. 23:17
the day when I take from t. 24:25
hid I my face from t. 39:23, 24
hide my face any more from t. 29
withdrawn himself from t. Hos 5:6
them, so they went from t. 11:2
with the garment from t. Mi 2:8
the bridegroom shall be taken from t. Mat 9:15; Mark 2:20; Luke 5:35
and fled from t. naked. Mark 14:52
understood not, it was hid from t. Luke 9:45; 18:34
parted from t. and carried. 24:51
did hide himself from t. John 12:36
but thrust him from t. Acts 7:39
delivered from t. that. Rom 15:31
sorrow from t. of whom. 2 Cor 2:3
I may cut off occasion from t. 11:12
is not counted from t. Heb 7:6
clean escaped from t. 2 Pet 2:18
death shall flee from t. Rev 9:6

see **depart, -ed**

in them

heaven and earth, the sea, and all that in t. is. Ex 20:11; Acts 4:24
and be consecrated in t. Ex 29:29
I will be sanctified in t. Lev 10:3
he shall live in t. 18:5; Neh 9:29 Ezek 20:11, 13, 21; Gal 3:12
was sanctified in t. Num 20:13
such an heart in t. Deut 5:29
any understanding in t. 32:28
nor was there spirit in t. Josh 5:1
built not, and ye dwell in t. 24:13
wash in t. and be clean? 2 Ki 5:12
how much less in t. that? Job 4:19
excellency in t. go away? 21
in t. hath he set a tabernacle. Ps 19:4
their soul fainteth in t. 107:5
so is every one that trusteth in t. 115:8; 135:18
pleasure in t. that fear. 147:11
froward or perverse in t. Pr 8:8
there is no good in t. Eccl 3:12
their heart is fully set in t. 8:11
I have no pleasure in t. 12:1
whose substance is in t. Isa 6:13
there is no light in t. 8:20
shalt not prosper in t. Jer 2:37
the word is not in t. 5:13
what wisdom is in t.? 8:9
cannot do evil nor is it in t. 10:5
there is no breath in t. 14; 51:17
houses, and dwell in t. 29:5, 28
have not walked in t. Ezek 5:6
accomplished my fury in t. 13
of the living creature was in t. 10:17
sin, in t. shall he die. Ezek 18:24, 26
be sanctified in t. in sight. 28:25
pine away in t. 33:10
was no breath in t. 37:8
concubines drank in t. Dan 5:3, 23
the just shall walk in t. Hos 14:9
ye shall not dwell in t. Amos 5:11
they shall kindle in t. and. Ob 18
evil, he delighteth in t. Mal 2:17
in t. is fulfilled the. Mat 13:14
in t. therefore come and. Luke 13:14
in t. ye think ye have. John 5:39
and I am glorified in t. 17:10
I in t., and thou in me. 23
may be in t. and I in t. 26
God, is manifest in t. Rom 1:19
but have pleasure in t. that do. 32
in t. that are saved, in t. 2 Cor 2:15
will dwell in t. and walk in t. 6:16
that we should walk in t. Eph 2:10
the ignorance that is in t. 4:18
walked, when ye lived in t. Col 3:7
all deceivableness in t. 2 Thes 2:10
continue in t.: for in. 1 Tim 4:16
with faith in t. that. Heb 4:2
Christ which was in t. 1 Pet 1:11
speaking in t. of these. 2 Pet 3:16
and all that are in t. Rev 5:13
and ye that dwell in t. 12:12
for in t. is filled up the. 15:1
dead which were in t. 20:13
in t. the names of the. 21:14

into them

the breath came into t. Ezek 37:10
into the swine, that we may enter into t. Mark 5:12; Luke 8:32
from God entered into t. Rev 11:11

of them

the eyes of t. both were. Gen 3:7
cry of t. is waxen great. 19:13
generation of t. that hate me. Ex 20:5; Deut 5:9
to thousands of t. that love me. Ex 20:6; Deut 5:10
of t. that do any work. Ex 35:35
do against any of t. Lev 4:2
of t. ye shall not eat. 11:4
of t. eat. 22; Deut 20:19
an offering by fire of t. Lev 22:22
of t. buy bondmen and. 25:44, 45
land also shall be left of t. 26:43
were numbered of t. Num 1:21 23, 25; 2:4, 13; 3:22, 34
took money of t. that. 3:49
take it of t. 7:5
were of t. that were written. 11:26
nor shall any of t. that. 14:23
fled at the cry of t. 16:34
not a man of t. 26:64
which ye let remain of t. 33:55
neither be afraid of t. Deut 1:29 7:18; 20:1, 3; Josh 11:6; Neh 4:14
buy meat of t., buy water of t. for. Deut 2:6
loins of t. that rise, and of t. 33:11
there shall not a man of t. Josh 10:8
and of t. shall I be had. 2 Sam 6:22
nor left he any of t. 2 Ki 10:14
he was intreated of t. 1 Chr 5:20
of t. were expressed by. Ezra 8:20
would not buy it of t. Neh 10:31
he perceiveth it not of t. Job 14:21
in keeping of t. there is. Ps 19:11
arrows against the face of t. 21:12
this is the generation of t. 24:6
delivered him out of t. all. 34:19
none of t. that trust in him shall. 22
if I would speak of t. they are. 40:5
and of t. that are afar off. 65:5
heart are the ways of t. 84:5
all of t. shall wax old like. 102:26
tossed to and fro of t. that. Pr 21:6
God shall come forth of t. Eccl 7:18
they that are led of t. Isa 9:16
portion of t. that spoil us. 17:14
he shall be intreated of t. 19:22
Hezekiah was glad of t. and. 39:2
that when I asked of t. 41:28
spring forth I tell you of t. 42:9
spoiled, they are all of t. snared. 22
image, are all of t. vanity. 44:9
of t. that asked not for me, I am found of t. 65:1; Rom 10:20
those that escape of t. Isa 66:19
I will take of t. for priests. 21
because of t. that dwell in. Jer 8:19
be not afraid of t. 10:5; Ezek 2:6 Luke 12:4
of t. unto me as Sodom. Jer 23:14
shall serve themselves of t. 25:14
and of t. shall be taken up. 29:22
and out of t. shall proceed. 30:19
should serve himself of t. 34:9, 10
and none of t. shall remain. 42:17 Ezek 7:11
all of t. mourning every. Ezek 7:16
all of t. in the land shall. 20:40
all of t. desirable young men. 23:6 12, 23
in dyed attire, all of t. princes. 15
of t. clothed with all sorts. 38:4
and gates all of t. dwelling. 11
they say of t. Let the men. Hos 13:2
all of t.; he that fleeth of t. Amos 9:1
off their skin from off t. Mi 3:2, 3
land desolate because of t. 7:13
a goodly price that I was prized at of t. Zech 11:13
whether of t. twain did. Mat 21:31
perceived that he spake of t. 45
whose wife shall she be of t.? Mark 12:23; Luke 20:33
of t. he chose twelve. Luke 6:13
tell me, which of t. will love? 7:42
which of t. should be greatest. 9:46; 22:24
which of t. it was that. 22:23
and said, Thou art also of t. 58
then enquired he of t. John 4:52
remember that I told you of t. 16:4
of t. which thou gavest me. 18:9
to take out of t. a people. Acts 15:14
there lie in wait of t. more. 23:21
if the fall of t. be the riches of world, and diminishing of t. Rom 11:12
if the casting away of t. be the. 15
out of t. all the Lord. 2 Tim 3:11
are not of t. who draw back, but of t. Heb 10:39
is sown in peace of t. Jas 3:18
of t. which keep sayings. Rev 22:9

see **both, one, some**

on or upon them

images and sat upon t. Gen 31:34
my name be named on t. 48:16
shall be satisfied upon t. Ex 15:9
Lord break forth upon t. 19:22, 24
so great a sin upon t. 32:21
will visit their sin upon t. 34
their blood shall be upon t. Lev 20:11, 12, 13, 16, 27
upon t. that are left will I. 26:36
of the spirit upon t. Num 11:17, 29
the earth closed upon t. and. 16:33
have no pity upon t. Deut 7:16
silver or gold that is on t. 25
on t. was written according. 9:10
not lift up any iron tool upon t. 27:5
I will heap mischiefs upon t. 32:23
shall come upon t. make haste. 35
down great stones upon t. Josh 10:11
upon t. came the curse. Judg 9:57
blood gushed out upon t. 1 Ki 18:28
if able to set riders upon t. 2 Ki 18:23; Isa 36:8
burnt men's bones upon t. 2 Ki 23:20
charge was upon t. 1 Chr 9:27
laid their hands on t. 2 Chr 29:23 Acts 6:6; 8:17; 13:3
Lord came not upon t. 2 Chr 32:26
Lord brought upon t. king. 33:11
he brought upon t. the king. 36:17
for fear was upon t. Ezra 3:3
of the Jews fell upon t. Esth 8:17
fear of Mordecai fell upon t. 9:3
Jews took upon t. to keep the. 27
nor is the rod of God upon t. Job 21:9
eye of the Lord is upon t. Ps 33:18
fear took hold upon t. there. 48:6
set not your heart upon t. 62:10
thine indignation upon t. 69:24
down manna upon t. to eat. 78:24
he rained flesh also upon t. as. 27
he cast upon t. the fierceness. 49
he shall bring upon t. their. 94:23

to everlasting *upon t.* *Ps* 103:17
plague brake in *upon t.* 106:29
I see my desire *upon t.* 118:7
upon t. hath the light. *Isa* 9:2
thy chastening was *upon t.* 26:16
will not have mercy *on t.* 27:11
he that hath mercy *on t.* shall. 49:10
evil shall come *upon t.* *Jer* 2:3
I will bring *upon t.* 11:8, 11; 23:12
36:31; 49:37
have compassion *on t.* 12:15
I will set mine eyes *upon t.* 24:6
32:42
I will have mercy *upon t.* 33:26
calamity was come *upon t.* 46:21
she doted *upon t.* *Ezek* 23:16
flesh came *upon t.* 37:8
no wool shall come *upon t.* 44:17
of fire had passed *on t.* *Dan* 3:27
pour out my wrath *upon t.* *Hos* 5:10
go, I will spread my net *upon t.* 7:12
mine eyes *upon t.* for evil. *Amos* 9:4
lookest thou *upon t.* that. *Hab* 1:13
I will bring them again: for I have mercy *upon t.* *Zech* 10:6
who will not come up *upon t.* 14:17
should put his hands *upon t.*
Mat 19:13; *Mark* 10:16
and his mercy is *on t.* *Luke* 1:50
angel of the Lord came *upon t.* 2:9
this, he breathed *on t.* *John* 20:22
Sadducees came *upon t.* *Acts* 4:1
they laid hands *on t.* 3
great grace was *upon t.* 33
fear came *on* all *t.* that heard. 5:5
the Holy Ghost fell *on t.* as on us.
11:15; 19:6
took *upon t.* to call over. 19:13
and the man leapt *on t.* and. 16
men which have a vow *on t.* 21:23
on t. which fell, severity. *Rom* 11:22
peace be *on t.* and mercy *Gal* 6:16
wrath is come *upon t.* *1 Thes* 2:16
destruction cometh *upon t.* 5:3
taking vengeance *on t.* *2 Thes* 1:8
and *on t.* that are out of. *Heb* 5:2
avenge our blood *on t.* *Rev* 6:10
nor shall the sun light *on t.* 7:16
and great fear fell *upon t.* 11:11
and *upon t.* which worshipped. 16:2

over **them**

set *over t.* taskmasters. *Ex* 1:11
taskmasters had set *over t.* 5:14
place such *over t.* to be rulers. 18:21
were *over t.* that were numbered.
Num 7:2
thy cloud standeth *over t.* 14:14
to anoint a king *over t.* *Judg* 9:8
Jephthah captain *over t.* 11:11
rejected me that I should not reign *over t.* *1 Sam* 8:7
the manner of the king that shall reign *over t.* 9
standing as appointed *over t.* 19:20
became a captain *over t.* 22:2
anointed me king *over t.* *2 Sam* 2:7
was the ruler *over t.* *1 Chr* 9:20
over t. that did the work was. 27:26
he that made thee king *over t.*
2 Chr 2:11; 9:8
had the dominion *over t.* *Neh* 9:28
the enemies of the Jews hoped to have power *over t.* *Esth* 9:1
have dominion *over t.* *Ps* 49:14
hated them ruled *over t.* 106:41
bringeth the wheel *over t.* *Pr* 20:26
babes shall rule *over t.* *Isa* 3:4
women rule *over t.* 12
a fierce king shall rule *over t.* 19:4
they that rule *over t.* make. 52:5
I will appoint *over t.* *Jer* 15:3
I will set shepherds *over t.* 23:4
watched *over t.*, to pluck up, so will I watch *over t.* to build. 31:28
yea, I will rejoice *over t.* to. 32:41
I will watch *over t.* for evil. 44:27
there appeared *over t.* as it were a sapphire stone. *Ezek* 10:1
of Israel was *over t.* 19; 11:22
set up one shepherd *over t.* 34:23
servant shall be king *over t.* 37:24
thee ruler *over t.* all. *Dan* 2:38
heathen should rule *over t.* *Joel* 2:17
shall be dark *over t.* *Mi* 3:6
the Lord shall reign *over t.* in. 4:7
that have no ruler *over t.* *Hab* 1:14
and the Lord shall be seen *over t.*
Zech 9:14
exercise dominion *over t.* *Mat* 20:25
Mark 10:42; *Luke* 22:25
men that walk *over t.* *Luke* 11:44
I should reign *over t.* 19:27
to call *over t.* that had. *Acts* 19:13
even *over t.* that had not sinned.
Rom 5:14
triumphing *over t.* in it. *Col* 2:15
they had a king *over t.* *Rev* 9:11
earth shall rejoice *over t.* 11:10

through **them**

that *through t.* I may prove Israel.
Judg 2:22
none can pass *through t.* *Jer* 9:10

to or *unto* **them**

will send thee *unto t.* *Gen* 37:13
unto t. and spake roughly *unto t.*
42:7
provision, thus did Joseph *unto t.* 25
spake kindly *unto t.* 50:21
and God had respect *unto t.*
Ex 2:25; *2 Ki* 13:23
what shall I say *unto t.*? *Ex* 3:13
darkness *to t.* 14:20
the waters were a wall *unto t.* 22
not bow down thyself *to t.* nor serve.
20:5; *Josh* 23:7; *2 Ki* 17:35
shall be a statute for ever *to t.*
Ex 30:21; *Lev* 17:7
I have given it *unto t.* *Lev* 6:17
but thus do *unto t.* *Num* 4:19
all that appertain *unto t.* 16:30
as I thought to do *unto t.* 33:56
and *to t.* ye shall add forty. 35:6
Lord sware to give *unto t.* *Deut* 1:8
31:23
hath God so nigh *unto t.*? 4:7
this we will do *unto t.* *Josh* 9:20
so did he *unto t.* 26
bowed themselves *unto t.* *Judg* 2:17
mayest do *to t.* as thou shalt. 9:33
unto me, so have I done *unto t.* 15:11
nothing lacking *to t.* *1 Sam* 30:19
sent spoil *to t.* 27, 28, 29, 30, 31
but went not in *unto t.* *2 Sam* 20:3
speak good words *to t.* *1 Ki* 12:7
messenger came *to t.* *2 Ki* 9:18, 20
let the priests take it *to t.* 12:5
thereof pertained *to t.* *1 Chr* 9:27
spake comfortably *to t.* *2 Chr* 32:6
custom was paid *unto t.* *Ezra* 4:20
separated themselves *unto t.* 6:21
restore *to t.* this day their. *Neh* 5:11
month was turned *unto t.* *Esth* 9:22
layeth not folly *to t.* *Job* 24:12
morning is *to t.* even as the. 17
give them, render *to t.* *Ps* 28:4
for there is no want *to t.* that. 34:9
thou hadst a favour *unto t.* 44:3
do *unto t.* as to the Midianites. 83:9
them are like *unto t.* 115:8; 135:18
do good *to t.* that are upright. 125:4
a buckler *to t.* that walk. *Pr* 2:7
a tree of life *to t.* that lay. 3:18
they are right *to t.* that find. 8:9
so is the sluggard *to t.* that. 10:26
mercy and truth be *to t.* that. 14:22
so is a faithful messenger *to t.* 25:13
a shield *unto t.* that put their. 30:5
wisdom giveth life *to t.* *Eccl* 7:12
to t. that have familiar. *Isa* 19:3
the word was *unto t.* precept. 28:13
to t. that have no might he. 40:29
hath given spirit *to t.* that walk. 42:5
these things will I do *unto t.* 16
to t. that are in darkness. 49:9
Mat 4:16; *Luke* 1:79
to t. will I give in mine. *Isa* 56:5
to t. hast thou poured a. 57:6
to t. that turn from transgression in Jacob. 59:20
everlasting joy shall be *unto t.* 61:7
thus shall it be done *unto t.* *Jer* 5:13
word of the Lord is *unto t.* 6:10
but return not thou *unto t.* 15:19
evil I thought to do *unto t.* 18:8
though I was husband *unto t.* 31:32
and do *unto t.* as thou. *Lam* 1:22
the Lord is good *unto t.* that.
Lam 3:25
of heart, thy curse *unto t.* 65
I do send thee *unto t.* *Ezek* 2:4
had I sent thee *unto t.* they. 3:6
and thou shalt not be *to t.* a. 26
yet will I be *to t.* as a little. 11:16
so shall it be done *unto t.* 12:11
I made myself known *unto t.* 20:9
lo, thou art *unto t.* as a very. 33:32
shall be *to t.* a renown. 39:13
because they ministered *unto t.* before idols. 44:12
oblation shall be *unto t.* 48:12
shall be for food *unto t.* 18
the dream be *to t.* that. *Dan* 4:19
might give account *unto t.* 6:2
and keeping mercy *to t.* that. 9:4
but many shall cleave *to t.* 11:34
staff declareth *unto t.* *Hos* 4:12
destruction *unto t.* because. 7:13
I was *to t.* as they that take off. 11:4
said, he would do *unto t.* *Jonah* 3:10
say they *to t.* that prophesy, they shall not prophesy *to t.* *Mi* 2:6
be ye not like *unto t.* *Mat* 6:8
do ye so *to t.* 7:12
he spake *unto t.* of John the. 17:13
servants, they did *unto t.* 21:36
but go ye rather *to t.* that sell. 25:9
but *to t.* that are without in parables.
Mark 4:11
shall be given *to t.* for whom. 10:40
and was subject *unto t.* *Luke* 2:51
do ye also *to t.* likewise. 6:31
if ye do good *to t.* that do good. 33
if ye lend *to t.* of whom ye hope. 34
give the Holy Spirit *to t.* that. 11:13
that he may testify *unto t.* 16:28
of the vineyard do *unto t.*? 20:15
Jesus turning *unto t.* said. 23:28
their words seemed *unto t.* as. 24:11
he expounded *unto t.* in all the. 27
to t. gave he power to become the sons of God, even *to t.* *John* 1:12
we may give an answer *to t.* that. 22
not commit himself *unto t.* 2:24
spake *to t.* of the Father. 8:27
they are remitted *unto t.* 20:23
who was guide *to t.* that. *Acts* 1:16
unto t. cloven tongues, as of. 2:3
added *unto t.* about 3000 souls. 41
durst no man join himself *to t.* 5:13
whom God hath given *to t.* that. 32
not done sacrifice *unto t.* 14:18
preach the gospel *unto t.* 16:10
my necessities, and *to t.* that. 20:34
no man may deliver me *unto t.* 25:11
God hath shewed it *unto t.* *Rom* 1:19
to t. who by patient continuance. 2:7
for good *to t.* that love God. 8:28
made manifest *unto t.* that. 10:20
unto t. that are sanctified. *1 Cor* 1:2
unto t. that are called, both. 24
my answer *to t.* that do examine. 9:3
not permitted *unto t.* to speak. 14:34
if gospel hid, it is hid *to t.* *2 Cor* 4:3
to t. which were apostles. *Gal* 1:17
unto t. who are of the household of faith. 6:10
preached peace *to t.* that. *Eph* 2:17
is *to t.* an evident token. *Phil* 1:28
tribulation *to t.* that trouble you.
2 Thes 1:6
meditate, give thyself wholly *to t.*
1 Tim 4:15
but *unto* all *t.* that love. *2 Tim* 4:8
nothing be wanting *unto t.* *Tit* 3:13
not enter, but *to t.* that believed not.
Heb 3:18
preached as well as *unto t.* 4:2
I will be *to t.* a God. 8:10
yieldeth *unto t.* that are. 12:11
word should not be spoken *to t.* 19
Lord promised *to t.* that love him.
Jas 1:12; 2:5
gospel preached also *to t.* *1 Pet* 4:6
to t. that obtained like. *2 Pet* 1:1
happened *unto t.* according to. 2:22
unto t. was given power, as. *Rev* 9:3
to t. it was given that they should. 5
they sat, and judgement was given *unto t.* 20:4

see **say, woe**

toward **them**

so great is his mercy *toward t.* that fear him. *Ps* 103:11
Jesus was moved with compassion *toward t.* *Mat* 14:14; *Mark* 6:34
walk in wisdom *toward t.* *Col* 4:5
honestly *toward t.* that. *1 Thes* 4:12

under **them**

clave asunder that was *under t.* *Num* 16:31
and the cloud is not *under t.* *Job* 26:8

with **them**

deal worse with thee than *with t.* *Gen* 19:9
Hamor communed *with t.* 34:8
Joseph saw Benjamin *with t.* 43:16
established my covenant *with t.* *Ex* 6:4
thou shalt make no covenant *with t.* 23:32; *Deut* 7:2
shall pine away *with t.* *Lev* 26:39
to break my covenant *with t.* 44
thou shalt not go *with t.* *Num* 22:12
arise, go *with t.* 20
we will not inherit *with t.* on. 32:19
meddle not *with t.* *Deut* 2:5, 19
that it might be well *with t.* 5:29
neither make marriages *with t.* 7:3 *Josh* 23:12
thus shall ye deal *with t.* *Deut* 7:5
who keepeth covenant *with t.* 9
and Joshua made peace *with t.* *Josh* 9:15, 16
and the Lord was *with t.* *Judg* 1:22
and do *with t.* what seemeth. 19:24
shalt prophesy *with t.* *1 Sam* 10:6
lest I destroy you *with t.* 15:6
nor did he eat *with t.* *2 Sam* 12:17
they have there *with t.* their. 15:36
and thou be angry *with t.* *1 Ki* 8:46 *2 Chr* 6:36
they that be *with t.* *2 Ki* 6:16
with t. that should go out on the sabbath and came. 11:9; *2 Chr* 23:8
no reckoning made *with t.* *2 Ki* 22:7
brethren were to come *with t.* *1 Chr* 9:25
and *with t.* 120 priests. *2 Chr* 5:12
with many, or *with t.* that. 14:11
with t. he sent Levites, and *with t.* 17:8
book of the law of the Lord *with t.* 9
and he was *with t.* hid in the. 22:12
with t. were the prophets. *Ezra* 5:2
thou spakest *with t.* *Neh* 9:13
that they might do *with t.* as. 24
and I contended *with t.* and. 13:25
to do *with t.* as it seemeth. *Esth* 3:11
seed is established in their sight *with t.* *Job* 21:8
is perished *with t.* *Ps* 9:6
secret of the Lord is *with t.* 25:14
plead my cause *with t.* that. 35:1
with t. to the house of God. 42:4
the Lord is *with t.* that. 54:4; 118:7
I am counted *with t.* that go. 88:4
for *with t.* thou hast. 119:93
not thou in the way *with t.* *Pr* 1:15
desire to be *with t.* 24:1
keep the law contend *with t.* 28:4
it shall be well *with t.* *Eccl* 8:12
shall be joined *with t.* *Isa* 14:1
thou shalt not be joined *with t.* 20
shall come down *with t.* 34:7
and made covenant *with t.* 57:8
this is my covenant *with t.* 59:21
silver and their gold *with t.* 60:9
everlasting covenant *with t.* 61:8
and their offspring *with t.* 65:23
deal thus *with t.* in time. *Jer* 18:23
word of the Lord be *with t.* 27:18
I will gather *with t.* the blind. 31:8
an everlasting covenant *with t.* 32:40
and didst commit whoredom *with t.* *Ezek* 16:17, 28; 23:7, 43
bring thee down *with t.* that. 26:20
with t. that go down to the pit. 31:14 32:18, 24, 25, 29
I will make *with t.* covenant of peace. 34:25; 37:26
I the Lord their God am *with t.* 34:30 *Zech* 10:5
my tabernacle also shall be *with t.* *Ezek* 37:27
also shall fall *with t.* *Hos* 5:5
as long as the bridegroom is *with t.*? *Mat* 9:15; *Mark* 2:19; *Luke* 5:34
also the wheat *with t.* *Mat* 13:29
have been partakers *with t.* 23:30
and took no oil *with t.* 25:3
the Lord working *with t.* *Mark* 16:20
he eateth *with t.* *Luke* 15:2
though he bear *with t.* 18:7
found the eleven and them that were *with t.* 24:33
while I was *with t.* in the world. *John* 17:12
betrayed him stood *with t.* 18:5
but Thomas was not *with t.* 20:24
he was *with t.* coming. *Acts* 9:28
made while she was *with t.* 39
arise, and go *with t.* 10:20
didst eat *with t.* 11:3
spirit bade me go *with t.* 12
hand of the Lord was *with t.* 21
they took *with t.* John. 12:25
all that God had done *with t.* 14:27 15:4
not good to take him *with t.* 15:38
down and prayed *with t.* all. 20:36
be at charges *with t.* that. 21:24
and *with t.* partakest of. *Rom* 11:17
rejoice *with t.* that do rejoice, and weep *with t.* that weep. 12:15
therefore partakers *with t.* *Eph* 5:7
grace be *with t.* that love our. 6:24
shall be caught up together *with t.* *1 Thes* 4:17
peace, *with t.* that call. *2 Tim* 2:22
was it not *with t.* that had sinned? *Heb* 3:17
for finding fault *with t.* he. 8:8
covenant I will make *with t.* 10:16
Rahab perished not *with t.* 11:31
in bonds, as bound *with t.* 13:3
ye husbands, dwell *with t.* *1 Pet* 3:7
that ye run not *with t.* to the. 4:4
latter end is worse *with t.* *2 Pet* 2:20
had heads, and *with t.* *Rev* 9:19
with men, he will dwell *with t.* 21:3

without **them**

while she lieth desolate *without t.* *Lev* 26:43

themselves

they wearied *t.* to find. *Gen* 19:11
t. for the Egyptians by *t.* 43:32
go and gather straw for *t.* *Ex* 5:7
prepared for *t.* victual. 12:39
people have corrupted *t.* 32:7 *Deut* 9:12; 32:5; *Judg* 2:19 *Hos* 9:9
wash, and so make *t.* *Num* 8:7
even our enemies *t.* *Deut* 32:31
sons made *t.* vile and. *1 Sam* 3:13
both of them discovered *t.* to. 14:11
if they shall bethink *t.* *1 Ki* 8:47 *2 Chr* 6:37
choose one bullock for *t.* *1 Ki* 18:23
Edom made a king over *t.* *2 Ki* 8:20; *2 Chr* 21:8
sold *t.* to do evil in the. *2 Ki* 17:17
made to *t.* of the lowest of them. 32
eat such things as grow of *t.* 19:29
had made *t.* odious to. *1 Chr* 19:6
people shall humble *t.* *2 Chr* 7:14
princes and king humbled *t.* 12:6, 7
which they stript off for *t.* 20:25
they made ready for *t.* and. 35:14
of their daughters for *t.* *Ezra* 9:2
decreed for *t.* and seed. *Esth* 9:31
they had marked for *t.* *Job* 24:16
they rolled *t.* upon me. 30:14
they are firm in *t.* 41:23
the kings of the earth set *t.* *Ps* 2:2
the nations may know *t.* to be. 9:20
which hate us spoil for *t.* 44:10
whereof they are fallen *t.* 57:6
they joined *t.* also to Baal. 106:28
desires, lest they exalt *t.* 140:8
riches make *t.* wings. *Pr* 23:5
might see that they *t.* *Eccl* 3:18
and they please *t.* in children. *Isa* 2:6
they have rewarded evil to *t.* 3:9
but *t.* are gone into captivity. 46:2
they shall not deliver *t.* from. 47:14
call *t.* of the holy city, and. 48:2
sons of the stranger that join *t.* 56:6
seek her will not weary *t.* *Jer* 2:24
and the nations shall bless *t.* 4:2
do they not provoke *t.* to the? 7:19
they weary *t.* 9:5
they had done against *t.* 11:17
have put *t.* to pain, but shall. 12:13
nor cut *t.* nor make *t.* bald for. 16:6
great kings shall serve *t.* of. 27:7
and their nobles shall be of *t.* 30:21
that none should serve *t.* of. 34:10
lifted up, these lift up *t.* *Ezek* 10:17
their appearance and *t.* 22
shall only be delivered *t.* 14:18
of Israel that do feed *t.* 32:2
nor shall the shepherds feed *t.* 10
Levites of the house have for *t.* 45:5
for *t.* are separated with. *Hos* 4:14
they assembled *t.* for corn. 7:14
but they separated *t.* to that. 9:10
shall proceed of *t.* *Hab* 1:7
the people shall weary *t.* for. 2:13
the golden oil out of *t.* *Zech* 4:12
who slay them, and hold *t.* 11:5
mighty works do shew forth *t.* in. *Mat* 14:2; *Mark* 6:14
reasoned among *t.* *Mat* 16:7 *Mark* 8:16; *Luke* 20:14
there be eunuchs, who made *t.* *Mat* 19:12
reasoned with *t.* 21:25; *Mark* 11:31 *Luke* 20:5
but they *t.* will not move. *Mat* 23:4
have no root in *t.* *Mark* 4:17
kept that saying with *t.* 9:10
counsel of God against *t.* *Luke* 7:30
certain which trusted in *t.* 18:9
spies which should feign *t.* 20:20
were at enmity between *t.* 23:12
my joy fulfilled in *t.* *John* 17:13
they *t.* went not into the. 18:28
Judas and Silas being prophets also *t.* *Acts* 15:32
but let them come *t.* and fetch. 16:37
and when they opposed *t.* and. 18:6
that they kept *t.* from things. 21:25
certain Jews bound *t.* 23:12, 21
hope toward God which they *t.* 24:15
they agreed not among *t.* 28:25
had great reasoning among *t.* 29
professing *t.* to be wise. *Rom* 1:22
their own bodies between *t.* 24
receiving in *t.* that recompence. 27
the law, are a law unto *t.* 2:14
have not submitted *t.* to 10:3
shall receive to *t.* damnation. 13:2
nor abusers of *t.* with. *1 Cor* 6:9
not henceforth live unto *t.* *2 Cor* 5:15
power they were willing of *t.* 8:3
measuring *t.* by *t.* comparing *t.* with *t.* 10:12
t. into the apostles of Christ. 11:13
neither do they *t.* keep. *Gal* 6:13
who have given *t.* over to. *Eph* 4:19
esteem other better than *t.* *Phil* 2:3
for they *t.* shew of us. *1 Thes* 1:9
them that defile *t.* with. *1 Tim* 1:10
t. in modest apparel. 2:9; *1 Pet* 3:5
purchased to *t.* a good. *1 Tim* 3:13
laying up in store for *t.* a good. 6:19
those that oppose *t.* *2 Tim* 2:25
may recover *t.* out of the snare. 26
heap to *t.* teachers, having. 4:3
one of *t.* even a prophet. *Tit* 1:12
seeing they crucify to *t.* *Heb* 6:6
that not to *t.* but us. *1 Pet* 1:12
bring upon *t.* swift. *2 Pet* 2:1
sporting *t.* with their own. 13
they *t.* are the servants of. 19
giving *t.* over to fornication. *Jude* 7
they corrupt *t.* 10
feeding *t.* without fear. 12
who separate *t.*, sensual, having. 19

see **gather, hide, spread**

then

t. began men to call. *Gen* 4:26
the Canaanite dwelt *t.* in. 13:7
t. shall thy seed also be. 16
t. will I slay my brother. 27:41
t. shall the Lord be my God. 28:21
if our brother be with us, *t.* we. 44:26
t. defiledst thou it; he went up. 49:4
if *t.* their hearts be humbled, and they *t.* accept of the. *Lev* 26:41

t. I will remember my covenant. *Lev* 26:42
as my strength was *t.* *Josh* 14:11
if the Lord be with me, *t.* I. 12
they choose new gods, *t.* *Judg* 5:8
what meaneth *t.* this bleating of the sheep? *1 Sam* 15:14
t. remember thine handmaid. 25:31
t. hear thou in heaven. *1 Ki* 8:32, 34 36, 39, 45, 49
there was *t.* no king in. 22:47
t. let fire come down. *2 Ki* 1:10
Jehoshaphat being *t.* king. 8:16
t. open the door and flee and. 9:3
and David was *t.* in. *1 Chr* 11:16
t. Manasseh knew the. *2 Chr* 33:13
t. the prophets prophesied. *Ezra* 5:1
t. rose up Zerubbabel to build the. 2
t. went Haman forth that. *Esth* 5:9
t. said Zeresh his wife, and his. 14
t. was the king's wrath. 7:10
I should have slept, *t.* *Job* 3:13
he seeth also, will he not *t.*? 11:11
t. shalt thou have delight in. 22:26
t. thou shalt say, There is lifting up. 29
because thou wast *t.* born. 38:21
t. the Lord will take me. *Ps* 27:10
t. will I teach transgressors. 51:13
was not an enemy, *t.* I could. 55:12
t. I restored that which I took not away. 69:4
t. believed they his words. 106:12
t. shall I not be ashamed. 119:6
t. shalt thou understand the fear of the Lord. *Pr* 2:5
t. shalt thou understand righteousness. 9
t. there shall be a reward. 24:14
t. judgement shall dwell. *Isa* 32:16
t. shall thy light break forth. 58:8
t. shalt thou call, and the Lord. 9
t. shalt thou not remove. *Jer* 4:1
when thou doest evil, *t.* thou. 11:15
t. thou shewedst me their doings. 18
t. they should have turned. 23:22
t. will I cast away the seed. 33:26
t. shall they know that. *Ezek* 39:28
t. was part of the hand. *Dan* 5:24
t. they that feared the Lord spake often. *Mal* 3:16
and *t.* come and offer. *Mat* 5:24
t. shall they fast. 9:15; *Mark* 2:20 *Luke* 5:35
t. will he spoil his house. *Mat* 12:29 *Mark* 3:27
and *t.* he shall reward. *Mat* 16:27
Jesus saith, *T.* are the. 17:26
saying, Who *t.* can be saved? 19:25 *Mark* 10:26; *Luke* 18:26
for a witness to all, *t.* *Mat* 24:14
for *t.* shall be great tribulation. 21
t. all the disciples forsook. 26:56
and whence is he *t.* his son? *Mark* 12:37
t. let them that be in Judaea flee to. 13:14; *Luke* 21:21
t. shalt thou see clearly. *Luke* 6:42
asked What *t.*? Art thou Elias? *John* 1:21
Why baptizest thou *t.*? 25
t. I go unto him that sent me. 7:33
t. shall ye know that I am he. 8:28
t. Peter said to them. *Acts* 2:38
t. they that gladly received his word. 41
t. hath God to the Gentiles granted. 11:18; 26:20
what fruit had ye *t.* in? *Rom* 6:21
what shall we say *t.*? Is the law sin? 7:7; 9:14
if children, *t.* heirs, heirs of. 8:17
so *t.* at this present time there. 11:5
t. shall every man have. *1 Cor* 4:5
what say I *t.*? that the idol is. 10:19
but *t.* face to face: now I know in part; *t.* shall I know even. 13:12
what is it *t.*? 14:15
t. am I strong. *2 Cor* 12:10
come by the law, *t.* Christ. *Gal* 2:21
if ye be Christ's, *t.* are ye. 3:29
but as *t.* he that was born. 4:29
t. shall he have rejoicing in. 6:4
t. sudden destruction. *1 Thes* 5:3
t. shall that Wicked be. *2 Thes* 2:8
first for his own sins, *t.* *Heb* 7:27
t. are ye bastards, and not. 12:8
t. have we confidence. *1 John* 3:21

thence

wife to my son from *t.* *Gen* 24:7
send and fetch thee from *t.* 27:45
from *t.* is the shepherd. 49:24
cut down from *t.* *Num* 13:23, 24
Curse me them from *t.* 23:13, 27
if from *t.* thou shalt seek. *Deut* 4:29
the Lord brought thee out *t.* 5:15 6:23; 24:18
send and fetch him *t.* 19:12
from *t.* will the Lord gather thee, and from *t.* 30:4; *Neh* 1:9
from *t.* am I. *Judg* 19:18
bring from *t.* the ark of. *1 Sam* 4:4 *2 Sam* 6:2; *1 Chr* 13:6
go not forth from *t.* *1 Ki* 2:36
shall not be from *t.* any more death. *2 Ki* 2:21
went up from *t.* to Beth-el. 23
from *t.* to Carmel, and from *t.* to. 25
the lepers carried *t.* silver and. 7:8
out Uzziah from *t.* *2 Chr* 26:20
therefore, be ye far from *t.* *Ezra* 6:6
depart, go ye out from *t.* *Isa* 52:11
no more *t.* an infant of days. 65:20
every one that goeth *t.* shall. *Jer* 5:6
signet, yet would I pluck thee *t.* 22:24
cause to cease from *t.* man. 36:29
forth, to separate himself *t.* 37:12
and he shall go forth from *t.* 43:12
I will bring thee down from *t.* 49:16
all abominations from *t.* *Ezek* 11:18
her vineyards from *t.* *Hos* 2:15
from *t.* go ye to Hamath. *Amos* 6:2
dig into hell, *t.* shall my hand. 9:2, 3
t. will I command the sword, it. 4
among stars, *t.* will I bring. *Ob* 4
by no means come out *t.* *Mat* 5:26
there abide, till ye go *t.* 10:11
when ye depart *t.* shake. *Mark* 6:11
that would come from *t.* *Luke* 16:26

thenceforth

t. it shall be accepted. *Lev* 22:27
was magnified from *t.* *2 Chr* 32:23
is *t.* good for nothing. *Mat* 5:13
from *t.* Pilate sought. *John* 19:12*

Theophilus

thee, most excellent *T.* *Luke* 1:3
treatise have I made, O *T.* *Acts* 1:1

there

t. he put the man whom. *Gen* 2:8
if I find forty-five *t.* I will. 18:28
he blessed him *t.* 32:29
t. God appeared. 35:7
t. they buried Abraham and Sarah, *t.* they buried Isaac and. 49:31
no swarms of flies shall be *t.* *Ex* 8:22
t. he made a statute, *t.* he. 15:25
behold, I will stand before thee *t.* 17:6
the mount, and be *t.* 24:12; 34:2
and he was *t.* with the Lord. 34:28
t. eat it. *Lev* 8:31
shall leave them *t.* 16:23
and talk with thee *t.* *Num* 11:17
we saw the children of Anak *t.* 13:28 33; *Deut* 1:28; *Josh* 14:12
died *t.* and was buried *t.* *Num* 20:1
Aaron shall die *t.* 26, 28; *Deut* 10:6
t. ye shall serve gods, work of. *Deut* 4:28; 28:36, 64; *Jer* 16:13
and *t.* they be unto this day. *Deut* 10:5; *Josh* 4:9
choose to put his name *t.* *Deut* 12:5 14:23; 16:2, 11; *1 Ki* 8:29; 9:3
it may be *t.* for a witness. *Deut* 31:26
where he bowed, *t.* he. *Judg* 5:27
I will try them for thee *t.* 7:4
inhabitants of Jabesh-gilead *t.* 21:9
where thou diest, *t.* will. *Ruth* 1:17
the priests of the Lord were *t.* *1 Sam* 1:3; 4:4
worshipped the Lord *t.* 1:28
and renew the kingdom *t.* 11:14
t. they made Saul king before the Lord, *t.* they sacrificed, and *t.* 15
of the servants of Saul *t.* 21:7
Doeg the Edomite was *t.* 22:22
Joab smote Abner *t.* *2 Sam* 3:27
God smote Uzzah *t.* and *t.* he died. *2 Sam* 6:7
even *t.* also will thy servant. 15:21
hast thou not *t.* Zadok and? 35
staves, and *t.* they are. *1 Ki* 8:8
chosen to put my name *t.* 11:36 *2 Ki* 23:27; *2 Chr* 6:5, 6; 7:16 *Neh* 1:9
the ravens to feed thee *t.* *1 Ki* 17:4
when they said, He is not *t.*; he. 18:10
and left his servant *t.* 19:3
and cast the salt in *t.* *2 Ki* 2:21
he came and lay *t.* 4:11
and we shall die *t.* 7:4
come, there was no man *t.* 5, 10
they left their gods, *t.* *1 Chr* 14:12
prophet of the Lord was *t.* *2 Chr* 28:9
they slew Sennacherib *t.* with. 32:21
God hath caused his name to dwell *t.* *Ezra* 6:12
t. the wicked cease from troubling, and *t.* the weary be at. *Job* 3:17
t. the prisoners rest together. 18
small and great are *t.*; the servant. 19
t. the righteous might dispute. 23:7
t. they cry, but none giveth. 35:12
and where the slain are, *t.* 39:30
t. were they in great fear. *Ps* 14:5 53:5
daughter of Tyre shall be *t.* 45:12
fear took hold upon them *t.* 48:6
went through flood, *t.* did we. 66:6
cities that they may dwell *t.* 69:35
Tyre, this man was born *t.* 87:4, 6
players on instruments shall be *t.* 7
t. go the ships, *t.* is that. 104:26
t. the Lord commanded the. 133:3
behold, thou art *t.* 139:8
t. shall thy hand lead me. 10
I was *t.*: when he set. *Pr* 8:27
that the dead are *t.* 9:18
where no wood is, *t.* the fire. 26:20
was *t.*, iniquity was *t.* *Eccl* 3:16
for *t.* is a time *t.* for every. 17
tree falleth, *t.* it shall be. 11:3
t. thy mother brought. *S of S* 8:5
nor shall shepherds make their fold *t.* *Isa* 13:20
beasts of the desert shall lie *t.* 21
t. shalt thou die, and *t.* the. 22:18
to Chittim, *t.* also shalt thou. 23:12
here a little, and *t.* a little. 28:10
t. glorious Lord will be a. 33:21
and an highway shall be *t.* 35:8
but the redeemed shall walk *t.* 9
from the beginning; *t.* am I. 48:16
my servant shall dwell *t.* 65:9
is *t.* no balm in Gilead, no physician *t.*? *Jer* 8:22
t. will I cause thee to hear. 18:2
t. thou shalt die, and shalt be buried *t.* 20:6
country: *t.* shall ye die. 22:26; 42:16
and *t.* shall they be till I. 27:22
he was *t.* when Jerusalem. 38:28
will go into Egypt, and *t.* will. 42:14
against Ashkelon, *t.* hath he. 47:7
go to the plain, I will *t.* *Ezek* 3:22
see it, though he shall die *t.* 12:13
I will plead with him *t.* for. 17:20
and they offered *t.* their sacrifices, *t.* they presented the. 20:28
and *t.* will I plead with you face. 35
t. will I accept them, *t.* 40
and I will leave you *t.* and. 22:20
t. were their breasts pressed, *t.* 23:3
and they shall be *t.* a base. 29:14
Ashur is *t.* and all her. 32:32
whereas the Lord was *t.* 35:10
name shall be, The Lord is *t.* 48:35
and she shall sing *t.* as. *Hos* 2:15
yea, grey hairs are here and *t.* 7:9
t. I hated them. 9:15
t. he spake with us. 12:4
I will plead with them *t.* *Joel* 3:2
one plow *t.* with oxen? *Amos* 6:12
t. eat bread and prophesy *t.* 7:12
t. be delivered, *t.* Lord shall. *Mi* 4:10
shall cry *t.* bitterly. *Zeph* 1:14
be thou *t.* till I bring. *Mat* 2:13
t. rememberest that thy brother. 5:23
leave *t.* thy gift before the altar. 24
where your treasure is, *t.* will. 6:21

t. shall be gnashing of teeth.
Mat 8:12; 22:13; 24:51
they enter in, and dwell t. 12:45
Luke 11:26
in my name, t. am I in. Mat 18:20
lo, here is Christ, or t. 24:23
Mark 13:21
I hid thy talent, t. thou. Mat 25:25
down, they watched him t. 27:36
in Galilee, t. shall ye see him. 28:7
Mark 16:7
I may preach t. also. Mark 1:38
and he could t. do no mighty. 6:5
and if the son of peace be t.
Luke 10:6
t. will I bestow all my fruits. 12:18
where I am, t. shall my. John 12:26
that where I am, t. ye may be. 14:3
that shall befall me t. Acts 20:22
t. it shall be told thee of all. 22:10
t. be called the children. Rom 9:26
for there shall be no night t.
Rev 21:25; 22:5
see **abode, is, none, one, stand, stood, was**

thereabout

were much perplexed t. Luke 24:4

thereat

their hands and feet t. Ex 30:19
40:31
there be which go in t. Mat 7:13*

thereby

t. shall I know thou hast. Gen 24:14
should be defiled t. Lev 11:43
with God, t. good will. Job 22:21
whoso is deceived t. is. Pr 20:1
shall be endangered t. Eccl 10:9
gallant ships pass t. Isa 33:21
passeth t. shall be astonished.
Jer 18:16; 19:8
any son of man pass t. 51:43
wall and carry on t. Ezek 12:5, 12
he shall not fall t. 33:12
he shall die t. 18*
do what is lawful, he shall live t. 19
also shall border t. Zech 9:2
God might be glorified t. John 11:4
having slain the enmity t. Eph 2:16
who are exercised t. Heb 12:11
root springing up, and t. many. 15
t. some have entertained. 13:2
word that ye may grow t. 1 Pet 2:2*

therefore

t. shall a man leave his. Gen 2:24
shall keep my covenant t. 17:9
guilty, t. is this distress. 42:21
t. God dealt well with. Ex 1:20
t. go. 4:12
they be idle, t. they cry. 5:8, 17
t. shall ye observe. 12:17; 13:10
t. he giveth you on the sixth. 16:29
ye shall keep the sabbath t. 31:14
ye shall t. sanctify yourselve, be holy;
for I am holy. Lev 11:44, 45; 21:6
t. I do visit the iniquity. 18:25
ye shall t. keep my statutes and. 26
t. keep my ordinances. 30; 19:37
20:22; 22:9
ye shall not t. oppress one. 25:17
t. the Levites shall be. Num 3:12
t. the Lord thy God commanded.
Deut 5:15; 15:11, 15; 24:18, 22
t. thou shalt serve thine. 28:48
t. we turn again to. Judg 11:8
t. also I have lent him. 1 Sam 1:28
t. hath the Lord done this. 28:18
t. Michal had no child. 2 Sam 6:23
be strong t. and shew. 1 Ki 2:2
t. thy life shall go for his life. 20:42
t. thou shalt not. 2 Ki 1:6, 16
t. they have destroyed them. 19:18
t. he slew Saul, and. 1 Chr 10:14
t. hath he brought all. 2 Chr 7:22
t. gave them up to desolation. 30:7
t. we his servants will arise and.
Neh 2:20
t. I chased him from me. 13:28
t. they say to God. Job 21:14
judgement is before him, t. 35:14
t. take unto you seven bullocks. 42:8
t. my heart is glad. Ps 16:9
t. lead me. 31:3
t. the children of men put. Ps 36:7
t. God hath blessed thee for. 45:2
t. God hath anointed thee with oil. 7
t. shall the people praise. 17
have no changes, t. they fear. 55:19*
t. in the shadow of thy wings. 63:7
t. his people return hither. 73:10
set his love upon me, t. will I. 91:14
t. he said that he would. 106:23
t. have I spoken. 116:10; 2 Cor 4:13
t. I hate every false way. Ps 119:104
are wonderful: t. doth my soul. 129
depart from me t. ye. 139:19
t. leave off contention. Pr 17:14
God is in heaven, t. let. Eccl 5:2
t. the misery of man is great. 8:6
t. the heart of men is set in them. 11
t. the Lord will smite. Isa 3:17
t. the Lord of hosts shall. 10:16
t. hath the curse devoured. 24:6
t. he hath poured the fury of. 42:25
t. his arm brought salvation. 59:16
t. they shall fall among. Jer 6:15
ye obeyed not, t. this thing is. 40:3
Lord is my portion, t. will. Lam 3:24
t. I fled before unto. Jonah 4:2
t. I am returned to Jerusalem with.
Zech 1:16
t. came a great wrath from. 7:12
t. ye sons of Jacob are. Mal 3:6
be ye t. perfect. Mat 5:48
fear ye not t. 10:31
what t. God hath joined. 19:6
what shall we have t.? 27
watch t. 24:42, 44; 25:13
Mark 13:35
go ye t. teach all nations. Mat 28:19
t. came I forth. Mark 1:38
do ye not t. err? 12:24
David t. himself calleth him Lord. 37
for t. am I sent. Luke 4:43
be ye t. merciful. 6:36
t. shall they be your judges. 11:19
t. also said the wisdom of God. 49
have married a wife, and t. I. 14:20
what t. shall the Lord of the vineyard do? 20:15; Mark 12:9
t. in the resurrection? Mat 20:33
this my joy t. is fulfilled. John 3:29
ye t. hear them not, because. 8:47
but ye say, We see; t. your sin. 9:41
t. doth my Father love me. 10:17
whatsoever I speak t., even as. 12:50
chosen you, t. the world. 15:19
repent ye t. and be converted.
Acts 3:19
t. it was imputed to. Rom 4:22
t. if thine enemy hunger. 12:20
t. glorify God in your body and.
1 Cor 6:20
not the hand, is it t. not of? 12:15, 16
t. be ye stedfast, unmoveable. 15:58
t. as ye abound in every. 2 Cor 8:7
be not ye t. partakers. Eph 5:7
t. as the church is subject to. 24
be not t. ashamed of the. 2 Tim 1:8
see **now**

therefrom

that ye turn not aside t. Josh 23:6
sins of Jeroboam, he departed not t.
2 Ki 3:3; 13:2

therein

multiply t. Gen 9:7
for fifty righteous t. 18:24
the cave that is t. I give. 23:11, 17, 20
you, dwell and trade t. 34:10, 21
was there any worm t. Ex 16:24
doeth any work t. be cut. 31:14; 35:2
shalt thou put t. the ark of. 40:3
tabernacle and all t. 9; Lev 8:10
sinning t. Lev 6:3
done in trespassing t. 7
no white hairs t. 13:21
black hairs t. 37
ordinances to walk t. 18:4
Judg 2:22; Isa 42:5
shall be no blemish t. Lev 22:21
ye shall do no work t.: it is. 23:3
Deut 16:8; Num 29:7; Jer 17:24
do no servile work t. Lev 23:7, 8, 21
25, 35, 36; Num 28:18; 29:35
eat your fill and dwell t. Lev 25:19
be wood t. or not. Num 13:20
put fire t. and put incense.
Num 16:7, 46
lest thou be snared t. Deut 7:25
destroy all that is t. 13:15
Josh 10:28, 39
if there be any blemish t. Deut 15:21
he shall read t. all the days. 17:19
people that is found t. shall. 20:11
nor any grass groweth t. 29:23
thou shalt meditate t. day. Josh 1:8
the city and all t. shall. 6:17, 24
my name might be t. 1 Ki 8:16
new cruse, and put salt t. 2 Ki 2:20
let the fields rejoice, and all that is t.
1 Chr 16:32; Ps 96:12
sedition been made t. Ezra 4:19
there was no breach left t. Neh 6:1
but the people were few t. 7:4
found it written t. 5, 13:1
he read t. 8:3
made the earth, the seas, and all that
is t. 9:6; Ps 24:1; 69:34; 98:7
let no joyful voice come t. Job 3:7
he shall not rejoice t. 20:18
shall dwell t. for ever. Ps 37:29
love his name shall dwell t. 69:36
for wickedness of them that dwell t.
107:34; Jer 12:4
that have pleasure t. Ps 111:2
thy commandments, t. do. 119:35
made the sea and all t. is. 146:6
Acts 14:15; 17:24; Rev 10:6
shall fall t. Pr 22:14; 26:27
Jer 23:12; Hos 14:9
make a breach t. for us. Isa 7:6
the people that dwell t. shall. 33:24
though fools, shall not err t. 35:8
gladness shall be found t. 51:3
they that dwell t. shall die in. 6
whosoever goeth t. shall not. 59:8
walk t.; we will not walk t. Jer 6:16
my voice, neither walked t. 9:13
and no man dwelleth t. 44:2
48:9; 50:3, 40
and all that is t. shall sing. 51:48
behold, t. shall be left. Ezek 14:22
city, to the pot whose scum is t. 24:6
mourn that dwelleth t. Hos 4:3
Amos 8:8; 9:5
t. shall be cut off and die, but the
third part shall be left t. Zech 13:8
he shall not enter t. Mark 10:15
Luke 18:17
and let no man dwell t. Acts 1:20
t. is the righteousness of God.
Rom 1:17
dead to sin, live any longer t.? 6:2
wherein he is called, t. 1 Cor 7:24
that t. I may speak boldly. Eph 6:20
and I t. do rejoice, and. Phil 1:18
taught, abounding t. with. Col 2:7
that some must enter t. Heb 4:6
not, nor hadst pleasure t. 10:8
of liberty, and continueth t. Jas 1:25
the earth and works t. 2 Pet 3:10
rise and measure them that worship
t. Rev 11:1
causeth them that dwell t. to. 13:12
and I saw no temple t. 21:22
see **dwelt**

thereinto

in the countries enter t. Luke 21:21

thereof

eatest t. surely die. Gen 2:17; 3:5
I will do in midst t. Ex 3:20
for t. must we take to serve. 10:26
no stranger shall eat t. 12:43
45:48; 2 Ki 7:2
then shall he eat t. Ex 12:44
I have not eaten t. in. Deut 26:14
shall eat and leave t. 2 Ki 4:43, 44
know not the ways t. Job 24:13
the humble shall hear t. Ps 34:2
the whole disposing t. Pr 16:33
not power to eat t. Eccl 6:2

thereon

shalt sacrifice t. the. Ex 20:24
cloud abode t. 40:35; Num 9:22
spread ground corn t. 2 Sam 17:19
an ass that I may ride t. 19:26
God of our fathers look t. 1 Chr 12:17
let him be hanged t. Ezra 6:11
said, Hang Haman t. Esth 7:9

perverseness, and stay t. Isa 30:12
it to hang a vessel t. Ezek 15:3
they set him t. Mat 21:7
Luke 19:35; John 12:14
and found nothing t. Mat 21:19
Mark 11:13; Luke 13:6
thought t. he wept. Mark 14:72
another buildeth t. 1 Cor 3:10
open the book or look t. Rev 5:3, 4
was given to him that sat t. 6:4
gates, and names written t. 21:12

thereout

he shall take t. his handful of flour. Lev 2:2
there came water t. Judg 15:19

thereto

unto that to smell t. Ex 30:38
add the fifth part t. Lev 5:16; 6:5
27:13, 31
before a beast to lie down t. 18:23
shall be put t. in a vessel. Num 19:17
thou shalt not add t. Deut 12:32
king of Edom would not hearken t. Judg 11:17
thou mayest add t. 1 Chr 22:14
heavy, but I will add t. 2 Chr 10:14
Jehoram compelled Judah t. 21:11*
by taking heed t. according to thy. Ps 119:9
and falleth down t. Isa 44:15
thy speech agreeth t. Mark 14:70
no man disannulleth or addeth t. Gal 3:15

thereunto

made a molten calf, and sacrificed t. Ex 32:8
all the places nigh t. Deut 1:7
and watching t. with all. Eph 6:18
that we are appointed t. 1 Thes 3:3
the comers t. perfect. Heb 10:1
ye are t. called, that ye. 1 Pet 3:9

thereupon

playedst the harlot t. Ezek 16:16
of Judah shall feed t. Zeph 2:7
heed how he buildeth t. 1 Cor 3:10
work abide which he hath built t. 14

therewith

to blind mine eyes t. 1 Sam 12:3
and cut off his head t. 17:51
and thrust me through t. 31:4
1 Chr 10:4
I have t. sent Naaman. 2 Ki 5:6
and repaired t. the house of. 12:14
treasure and trouble t. Pr 15:16
a stalled ox, and hatred t. 17
quietness t. 17:1
lest thou be filled t. and. 25:16
travail to be exercised t. Eccl 1:13
stones shall be hurt t. 10:9
prepare thy bread t. Ezek 4:15
oil, wine, ye shall be satisfied t. Joel 2:19
state, I have learned t. Phil 4:11
food and raiment, let us be t. content. 1 Tim 6:8
t. bless we God, and t Jas 3:9
and not content t. 3 John 10

these

by t. were the isles of. Gen 10:5, 32
Jacob take a wife of such as t. 27:46
t. daughters, t. children, t. 31:43
asketh, saying, Whose are t.? 32:17
Joseph said, Bring t. men home,
make ready, for t. men. 43:16
gave light by night to t. Ex 14:20
and if he do not t. three unto. 21:11
t. be thy gods, O Israel. 32:4, 8
hath sinned in one of t. Lev 5:13
t. shall ye not eat. 11:4
t. shall ye eat. 9, 21, 22; Deut 14:9
for t. ye shall be unclean. Lev 11:24
t. shall be unclean. 29
ye shall not offer t. to. 22:22, 25
unto t. the land shall. Num 26:53
but among t. there was not a. 64
t. stand on mount. Deut 27:12
and t. shall stand upon mount. 13
Lord hath not chosen t. 1 Sam 16:10
Saul, I cannot go with t. 17:39
meanest thou by t.? 2 Sam 16:2
as t. which the queen of. 1 Ki 10:10
Solomon clave to t. strange. 11:2
be dew nor rain t. years. 1 Ki 17:1
Lord, With t. shalt thou push the
Syrians. 22:11; 2 Chr 18:10
Lord said, T. have no master.
1 Ki 22:17; 2 Chr 18:16
Nebuzar-adan took t. 2 Ki 25:20
t. were of the king's. 2 Chr 35:7
t. sought their register. Ezra 2:62
t. went and could not shew. Neh 7:61
now t. that sealed the covenant. 10:1
who knoweth not such things as t.? Job 12:3
t. wait all upon thee, that. Ps 104:27
days were better than t. Eccl 7:10
further, by t. my son, be. 12:12
no one of t. shall fail. Isa 34:16
what said t. men? 39:3
remember t. O Jacob. 44:21
t. shall come from far, t. from north,
and from the west, and t. 49:12
begotten me t.? who that brought up
t.? I was left alone; t. where? 21
I receive comfort in t.? 57:6
but t. have altogether. Jer 5:5
t. men have done evil in all. 38:9
I give thee into hand of t. 16
pomegranates were like to t. 52:22
for t. pine away, stricken. Lam 4:9
when those went, t. went, and when
those stood, t. Ezek 1:21; 10:17
greater abominations than t. 8:15
t. men have set up their idols. 14:3
thee, to do any of t. to thee. 16:5
and t. hast thou sacrificed unto. 20
t. discovered her nakedness. 23:10
in t. were they thy merchants. 27:21
what thou meanest by t. 37:18
they brought t. men. Dan 3:13
t. men were bound. 21
princes saw t. men. 27
over t. Darius set three. 6:2
then t. men assembled, and. 11, 15
t. great beasts, which are four. 7:17
by a dead body touch t. Hag 2:13
I will shew thee what t. be.
Zech 1:9; 4:5, 13
I said to the angel, What be t.? 1:19
21; 4:12
what is more than t. cometh of evil. Mat 5:37
not arrayed like one of t. 6:29
Hearest thou what t. say? 21:16
on t. commandments hang. 22:40
t. ought ye to have done. 23:23
done it unto one of the least of t. 25:40
did it not to one of the least of t. 45
and t. shall go into everlasting. 46
what is it which t. witness? 26:62
Mark 14:60
no other commandment greater than
t. Mark 12:31
t. shall receive greater. 40
Seest thou t. great buildings? 13:2
am sent to shew thee t. Luke 1:19
God is able of t. stones to. 3:8
let t. sayings sink down into. 9:44
see greater things than t. John 1:50
in t. lay a great multitude of. 5:3
what he doeth, t. doeth the Son. 19
shew him greater works than t. 20
shall we buy bread that t.? 6:5
he do more miracles than t.? 7:31
neither pray I for t. alone. 17:20
and t. have known that thou. 25
seek me, let t. go their way. 18:8
lovest thou me more than t.? 21:15
of t. which companied. Acts 1:21
shew whether of t. two thou. 24
others said, T. men are full of. 2:13
likewise foretold of t. days. 3:24
What shall we do to t. men? 4:16
before t. days rose up. 5:36
refrain from t. men, and let. 38
can any forbid that t. should? 10:47
t. that have turned the world. 17:6
t. were more noble than those. 11
t. having not the law, are. Rom 2:14
more shall t. be graffed. 11:24
even so have t. also now not. 31
upon t. we bestow. 1 Cor 12:23
t. three, but the greatest of t. 13:13
having t. promises, let us cleanse.
2 Cor 7:1
but of t. who seemed to. Gal 2:6
t. only are my fellow-workers to.
Col 4:11
let t. also first be proved. 1 Tim 3:10
himself from t. he shall. 2 Tim 2:21
with t., but heavenly things with better sacrifices than t. Heb 9:23
now where remission of t. is. 10:18
by t. might be partakers. 2 Pet 1:4
but t. as brute beasts made. 2:12
Enoch also prophesied of t. Jude 14
t. be they who separate. 19
t. have power to shut heaven.
Rev 11:6
t. were redeemed. 14:4
t. have one mind. 17:13
he said, T. sayings are faithful. 22:6
see **abominations, things, words**

these *are*, or *are* **these**

by the man whose t. are. Gen 38:25
whose t. are. 48:8
t. are that Aaron and Moses. Ex 6:26
t. are the judgements. 21:1
Lev 26:46; Deut 6:1
t. are unclean. Lev 11:31
t. are my feasts. 23:2, 4
God said, What men are t. with
thee? Num 22:9
t. are tokens of her. Deut 22:17
what cities are t. thou? 1 Ki 9:13
happy are t. thy servants. 10:8
her sons are t. 1 Chr 2:18
t. are ancient things. 4:22
now t. are thy servants. Neh 1:10
t. are part of his ways. Job 26:14
behold, t. are the ungodly. Ps 73:12
who are t. that flee as a cloud, as?
Isa 60:8
t. are a smoke in my nose. 65:5
surely t. are poor, they. Jer 5:4
The temple of the Lord are t. 7:4
t. are the men that. Ezek 11:2
they said, T. are the people. 36:20
visions of thy head are t. Dan 2:28
spirit straitened? are t. his doings?
Mi 2:7
then said I, O my lord, what are t.?
Zech 1:9; 4:4; 6:4
and t. are they by the way side.
Mark 4:15, 16, 18, 20
famines, t. are the beginnings. 13:8
and brethren are t. which. Luke 8:21
t. are not the words of. John 10:21
but t. are in the world, and I. 17:11
but t. are written that ye. 20:31
t. are not drunken, as. Acts 2:15
t. are not the children of. Rom 9:8
t. are contrary the one to. Gal 5:17
flesh are manifest, which are t. 19
t. are wells without water. 2 Pet 2:17
t. are murmurers, walking. Jude 16
what are t. which are arrayed in?
Rev 7:13
t. are they which came out of. 14
t. are they which were not defiled with
women. T. are they which. 14:4
t. are the true sayings. 19:9; 22:6

Thessalonica

at T. was a synagogue. Acts 17:1
more noble than those of T. 11
one Aristarchus of T. being. 27:2
even in T. ye sent once. Phil 4:16
for Demas is departed into T.
2 Tim 4:10

Theudas

days rose up T. boasting. Acts 5:36

they

of thee a nation mightier than t.
Num 14:12
t. and all theirs went down. 16:33
not come nigh, that neither t. 18:3
more honourable than t. 22:15
be stronger than t. 1 Ki 20:23, 25
are more than t. that. 2 Ki 6:16
t. that hate me, t. would. Ps 69:4
there be higher than t. Eccl 5:8
and t. together shall be against.
Isa 9:21
but t. also have erred through. 28:7
therefore t. that pursue you. 30:16
t. are thy lot, to them thou. 57:6
t. that shall be of thee shall. 58:12
t., their kings and priests. Jer 2:26

whom neither *t.* nor their fathers. *Jer* 9:16; 19:4; 44:3
t. whose judgement was not. 49:12
t. and their fathers have. *Ezek* 2:3
wast corrupted more than *t.* in ways. 16:47
abominations more than *t.* 51, 52
know that *t.* are my people. 34:30
when an hungered, and *t.* that were. *Mat* 12:3; *Mark* 2:25; *Luke* 6:3
receive this, save *t.* to. *Mat* 19:11
t. that are great exercise. 20:25
t. that are whole have no need. *Mark* 2:17; *Luke* 5:31
and *t.* that had eaten were. *Mark* 8:9
hardly shall *t.* which have riches. 10:23
t. that went before and *t.* that. 11:9
and *t.* that were sent. *Luke* 7:10
t. on the rock are *t.* which. 8:13
t. which have continued. 22:28
for *t.* also went unto the feast. *John* 4:45
dead shall hear, and *t.* that. 5:25
t. that have done good, *t.* that. 29
scriptures: and *t.* are *t.* which. 39
what are *t.* amongst so many? 6:9
I am come, that *t.* which see not might see, and that *t.* which. 9:39
t. are not of the world, even. 17:16
that *t.* all may be one, as thou. 21
that *t.* may be made perfect. 23
Father, I will that *t.* whom thou hast given me be with me, that *t.* 24
t. went not in, lest *t.* 18:28
t. of circumcision contended with. *Acts* 11:2
now *t.* that were scattered. 19
t. that dwell at Jerusalem because *t.* 13:27
through grace we shall be saved even as *t.* 15:11
we and *t.* of that place. 21:12
are we better than *t.*? *Rom* 3:9
for if *t.* which are of the law. 4:14
t. that are in the flesh cannot. 8:8
not only *t.* but ourselves also. 23
t. which are the children of the. 9:8
t. also, if *t.* abide not still. 11:23
for *t.* that are such serve not. 16:18
t. that have wives, as though *t.* had none. *1 Cor* 7:29
t. that weep, *t.* that rejoice, *t.* 30
t. that use this world, as not. 31
that *t.* who run in a race run. 9:24
that *t.* which are approved. 11:19
whether it were I or *t.* so we. 15:11
then *t.* also which are fallen. 18
afterwards *t.* that are Christ's. 23
Gal 5:24
as is earthy, such are *t.* *1 Cor* 15:48
t. who seemed somewhat. *Gal* 2:6
t. gave the right hand of. 9
know ye, that *t.* which are. 3:7, 9
I would *t.* were cut off which. 5:12
t. who do such things shall not. 21
nor *t.* who are circumcised. 6:13
t. shew of us what entering in we had. *1 Thes* 1:9
for *t.* that sleep; *t.* that be. 5:7
t. that used the office. *1 Tim* 3:13
t. who labour in the word. 5:17
and *t.* that are otherwise cannot. 25
t. that will be rich fall into. 6:9
of this sort are *t.* which. *2 Tim* 3:6
that *t.* which have believed. *Tit* 3:8
more excellent name than *t.* *Heb* 1:4
seeing *t.* to whom it was first. 4:6
that *t.* without us should. 11:40
t. watch, as *t.* that must. 13:17
salute all the saints, *t.* of Italy. 24
as *t.* that shall be judged. *Jas* 2:12
t. went out that *t.* might be made manifest, that *t.* were. *1 John* 2:19
t. are of the world, *t.* speak. 4:5
these be *t.* who separate. *Jude* 19
t. who pierced him. *Rev* 1:7
for *t.* are worthy. 3:4; 16:6
whence came *t.*? 7:13
these are *t.* who came out of. 14
for *t.* are virgins. These are *t.* 14:4
here are *t.* that keep the. 12
but *t.* that are written in. 21:27

thick

art waxen fat, thou art grown *t.* *Deut* 32:15
the mule went under the *t.* boughs. *2 Sam* 18:9
he took a *t.* cloth and. *2 Ki* 8:15*
fetch branches of *t.* trees to make booths. *Neh* 8:15
runneth on the *t.* bosses. *Job* 15:26
axes on the *t.* trees. *Ps* 74:5*
be under every *t.* oak. *Ezek* 6:13
exalted among *t.* branches. 19:11
his top was among the *t.* boughs. 31:3, 10, 14
ladeth himself with *t.* clay. *Hab* 2:6
people were gathered *t.* together. *Luke* 11:29*

see **clouds, darkness**

thicker

little finger shall be *t.* than my father's loins. *1 Ki* 12:10; *2 Chr* 10:10

thicket

a ram caught in a *t.* by. *Gen* 22:13
the lion is come up from his *t.* *Jer* 4:7

thickets

themselves in *t.* in rocks. *1 Sam* 13:6
kindle in the *t.* of forest. *Isa* 9:18
he shall cut down the *t.* of. 10:34
shall flee and go into *t.* *Jer* 4:29

thickness

the *t.* of the sea was an. *2 Chr* 4:5
the *t.* of the pillars was. *Jer* 52:21
t. of the wall was five. *Ezek* 41:9
the chambers were in the *t.* 42:10

thief

(*The Revisions usually change* thief *and* thieves *to* robber *and* robbers, *as having a little more exactly the meaning*)

if a *t.* be found breaking. *Ex* 22:2, 7
if the *t.* be not found, then the. 8
then that *t.* shall die. *Deut* 24:7
in the night is as a *t.* *Job* 24:14
after them as after a *t.* 30:5
when thou sawest a *t.* *Ps* 50:18
men do not despise *t.* if. *Pr* 6:30
whoso is partner with a *t.* 29:24
as a *t.* is ashamed when. *Jer* 2:26
the *t.* cometh in, and. *Hos* 7:1
enter at windows like a *t.* *Joel* 2:9
into the house of the *t.* *Zech* 5:4
in what watch the *t.* would come. *Mat* 24:43; *Luke* 12:39
ye come as against a *t.*? *Mat* 26:55
Mark 14:48; *Luke* 22:52
in heaven, where no *t.* *Luke* 12:33
door, the same is a *t.* *John* 10:1
the *t.* cometh not but to steal. 10
but because he was a *t.* and. 12:6
day of the Lord cometh as a *t.* *1 Thes* 5:2; *2 Pet* 3:10
overtake you as a *t.* *1 Thes* 5:4
none of you suffer as a *t.* *1 Pet* 4:15
I will come on thee as a *t.* *Rev* 3:3
16:15

thieves

thy princes are companions of *t.* *Isa* 1:23
not Israel found among *t.*? *Jer* 48:27
if *t.* by night, they will. 49:9; *Ob* 5
and where *t.* break. *Mat* 6:19
and where *t.* do not break. 20
made it a den of *t.* 21:13
Mark 11:17; *Luke* 19:46
two *t.* crucified with him. *Mat* 27:38
Mark 15:27
t. also cast the same in. *Mat* 27:44
Jericho and fell among *t.* *Luke* 10:30
to him that fell among *t.*? 36
came before me are *t.* *John* 10:8
nor *t.*, shall inherit the kingdom of God. *1 Cor* 6:10

thigh

put thy hand under my *t.* *Gen* 24:2
9; 47:29
the hollow of Jacob's *t.* 32:25
he halted upon his *t.* 31
the Lord maketh thy *t.* to rot. *Num* 5:21, 22, 27
dagger on his right *t.* *Judg* 3:16
dagger from his right *t.* 21
smote them hip and *t.* 15:8
gird thy sword on thy *t.* *Ps* 45:3
hath his sword on his *t.* *S of S* 3:8
uncover the *t.*, pass over. *Isa* 47:2*
I smote upon my *t.* *Jer* 31:19
smite therefore upon *t.* *Ezek* 21:12
gather the *t.* and shoulder. 24:4
he hath on his *t.* a name. *Rev* 19:16

thighs

breeches shall reach from loins to the *t.* *Ex* 28:42
the joints of thy *t.* are. *S of S* 7:1
his belly and his *t.* were. *Dan* 2:32

thin

and behold seven *t.* ears. *Gen* 41:6
7, 23, 24
the seven *t.* kine are seven. 27
gold into *t.* plates. *Ex* 39:3
in it a yellow *t.* hair. *Lev* 13:30
additions made of *t.* work. *1 Ki* 7:29*
Jacob shall be made *t.* *Isa* 17:4

thine

any thing that is *t.* *Gen* 14:23
thou and all that are *t.* 20:7
discern what is *t.* with me. 31:32
issue after them shall be *t.* 48:6
it shall be *t.* and thy sons. *Lev* 10:15
Num 18:9, 11, 13, 14, 15, 18
ridden ever since I was *t.* *Num* 22:30
that which is *t.* with thy. *Deut* 15:3
if any of *t.* be driven into. 30:4
mountains shall be *t.* and the outgoings of it shall be *t.* *Josh* 17:18
the man of *t.* whom I. *1 Sam* 2:33
given it to a neighbour of *t.* 15:28
t. are all that pertained to Mephibosheth. *2 Sam* 16:4
mine nor *t.* but divide. *1 Ki* 3:26
O king, I am *t.* and all that. 20:4
shall lick thy blood, even *t.* 21:19
t. are we, David, and. *1 Chr* 12:18
not take that which is *t.* 21:24
t. O Lord, is the greatness, power, and glory: the earth is *t.*, *t.* is. 29:11
righteousness even *t.* *Ps* 71:16
day is *t.*, the night also is *t.* 74:16
are *t.*, the earth also is *t.* 89:11
I am *t.*, save me; I sought. 119:94
of Egypt shall be *t.* *Isa* 45:14
we are *t.*: thou never barest. 63:19
of inheritance is *t.* *Jer* 32:8
t. is the kingdom. *Mat* 6:13
take that is *t.* 20:14
there thou hast that is *t.* 25:25
worship me, all shall be *t.* *Luke* 4:7
but *t.* eat and drink? 5:33
all I have is *t.* 15:31
my will but *t.* be done. 22:42
t. they were. *John* 17:6
for they are *t.* 9
all mine are *t.* and *t.* are mine. 10

thing

the *t.* was very grievous. *Gen* 21:11
t. proceedeth from the Lord. 24:50
which *t.* ought not to be done. 34:7
2 Sam 13:12
young man deferred not to do the *t.* *Gen* 34:19
and the *t.* which he did displeased. 38:10; *2 Sam* 11:27
because the *t.* is established by. *Gen* 41:32
not any green *t.* in the. *Ex* 10:15
in the *t.* wherein they dealt. 18:11
Jethro said, The *t.* that thou. 17
for any manner of lost *t.* 22:9
if it be an hired *t.* it came for. 15
a terrible *t.* that I will do. 34:10
a *t.* most holy of your offerings. *Lev* 2:3, 10
and the *t.* be hid from the eyes. 4:13
trespass in a *t.* taken away. 6:2
t. deceitfully gotten, or the lost *t.* 4
she shall touch no hallowed *t.* 12:4
it is a wicked *t.*; they shall be. 20:17
but if the Lord make a new *t.*, and the earth. *Num* 16:30
the *t.* which thou hast spoken is. *Deut* 1:14
what *t.* soever I command. 12:32
and the *t.* certain. 13:14; 17:4
if the *t.* follow not, nor. 18:22
it is not a vain *t.* for you; it is. 32:47

from the accursed *t.* *Josh* 6:18
the *t.* pleased the children of. 22:33
which *t.* became a snare. *Judg* 8:27
do not so vile a *t.* 19:24
finished the *t.* to-day. *Ruth* 3:18
I will do a *t.* in Israel. *1 Sam* 3:11
what is the *t.* that the Lord hath? 17
there hath not been such a *t.* 4:7
the *t.* displeased Samuel, when. 8:6
and we will shew you a *t.* 14:12
Saul, and the *t.* pleased him. 18:20
not take the *t.* to heart. *2 Sam* 13:33
hast thou thought such a *t.*? 14:13
hide not the *t.* that I shall ask. 18
what *t.* thou shalt hear, tell. 15:35
she spread corn, and the *t.* 17:19
the wife of Jeroboam cometh to ask a *t.* of thee. *1 Ki* 14:5
Thou hast asked a hard *t.* *2 Ki* 2:10
in heaven, might such a *t.* be. 7:19
that the Lord will do the *t.* 20:9
t. was right in the eyes. *1 Chr* 13:4
let the *t.* thou hast spoken. 17:23
for the *t.* was done. *2 Chr* 29:36
the *t.* pleased the king and congregation. 30:4
hath put such a *t.* in. *Ezra* 7:27
the *t.* pleased the king and he did so. *Esth* 2:4
the *t.* was known to Mordecai. 22
the *t.* pleased Haman, and he. 5:14
and if the *t.* seem right before. 8:5
the *t.* I greatly feared is. *Job* 3:25
now a *t.* was secretly brought. 4:12
God would grant me the *t.* 6:8
he as a rotten *t.* consumeth. 13:28
who can bring a clean *t.* out? 14:4
thou shalt decree a *t.*, it shall. 22:28
he performeth the *t.* that is. 23:14
plentifully declared the *t.*? 26:3
of me the *t.* that is right. 42:7, 8
people imagine a vain *t.*? *Ps* 2:1
horse is a vain *t.* for safety. 33:17
because I follow the *t.* that. 38:20
nor alter the *t.* that is gone out. 89:34
I will set no wicked *t.* before. 101:3
wisdom is the principal *t.* *Pr* 4:7
for it is a pleasant *t.* if thou. 22:18
glory of God to conceal a *t.* 25:2
t. that hath been, it is that which shall be, and there is no new *t.* *Eccl* 1:9
better is the end of a *t.* than. 7:8
the interpretation of a *t.*? 8:1
a man hath no better *t.* than to. 15
pleasant *t.* it is for the eyes to. 11:7
is it a small *t.* for you to? *Isa* 7:13
there is no green *t.* 15:6
rolling *t.* before the whirlwind. 17:13
shall the *t.* framed say of him? 29:16
that turn aside the just for a *t.* 21
the isles as a very little *t.* 40:15
and they shall be as a *t.* of. 41:12
I will do a new *t.*; now it shall. 43:19
prosper in the *t.* whereto. 55:11
who hath heard such a *t.*? 66:8
see if there be such a *t.* *Jer* 2:10
a horrible *t.* is committed. 5:30
altars to that shameful *t.* 11:13
they prophesy unto you a *t.* 14:14
Israel hath done a horrible *t.* 18:13
in the prophets a horrible *t.* 23:14
Lord hath created a new *t.* in. 31:22
king said, I will ask thee a *t.* 38:14
that God may shew us the *t.* 42:3
that whatsoever *t.* the Lord. 4
we will do what *t.* goeth out. 44:17
what *t.* shall I take to witness for thee, what *t.* shall I? *Lam* 2:13
he hath spoken a *t.* *Ezek* 14:9
as if that were a very little *t.* 16:47
the king said, The *t.* is. *Dan* 2:5, 8
and it is a rare *t.* that the king. 11
Arioch made the *t.* known to. 15
Daniel made the *t.* known to. 17
the same hour was the *t.* 4:33
could not shew the interpretation of the *t.* 5:15
the interpretation of the *t.*: Mene. 26
t. is true, according to the law. 6:12
t. was revealed to Daniel; and *t.* was true: and he understood the *t.* 10:1
I have seen an horrible *t.* *Hos* 6:10
were counted as a strange *t.* 8:12
ye which rejoice in a *t.* *Amos* 6:13
to the Lord, a corrupt *t.* *Mal* 1:14
what *t.* is this? what? *Mark* 1:27
how or what *t.* ye shall. *Luke* 12:11
sin no more, lest a worse *t.* come. *John* 5:14
Herein is a marvellous *t.* 9:30
it is unlawful *t.* for man. *Acts* 10:28
tell or hear some new *t.* 17:21
they observe no such *t.* 21:25
for he hath a certain *t.* to tell. 23:17
of whom I have no certain *t.* 25:26
why should it be thought a *t.*? 26:8
which *t.* I also did in Jerusalem. 10
shall *t.* formed say to? *Rom* 9:20
I beseech you that ye all speak the same *t.* *1 Cor* 1:10
with me it is a very small *t.* 4:3
some eat it as a *t.* offered. 8:7
wrought us for the selfsame *t.* is God. *2 Cor* 5:5
this selfsame *t.* that ye. 7:11
let us mind the same *t.* *Phil* 3:16
seeing it is a righteous *t.* *2 Thes* 1:6
covenant an unholy *t.* *Heb* 10:29
a fearful *t.* to fall into the hands. 31
as though some strange *t.* *1 Pet* 4:12
which *t.* is true in him. *1 John* 2:8
doctrine of Nicolaitanes, which *t.* I hate. *Rev* 2:15
see **accursed, great, holy, light, one, small**

any thing

I will not take *any t.* that. *Gen* 14:23
is *any t.* too hard for the? 18:14
cannot do *any t.* till thou be. 19:22
neither do thou *any t.* unto. 22:12
Thou shalt not give me *any t.* 30:31
nor hath he kept back *any t.* 39:9
he looked not to *any t.* under. 23
unto thee any likeness of *any t.* *Ex* 20:4; *Deut* 4:18, 23, 25; 5:8
nor *any t.* that is thy neighbour's. *Ex* 20:17; *Deut* 5:21
forgiven him for *any t.* *Lev* 6:7
in *any t.* made of skin. 13:48, 49 52, 53, 57, 59
that sitteth on *any t.* 15:6, 23
who toucheth *any t.* that was. 10, 22
ye shall not eat *any t.* with. 19:26
or that hath *any t.* superfluous. 21:18, 22, 23
without doing *any t.* else. *Num* 20:19
any power at all to say *any t.*? 22:38
cast upon him *any t.* 35:22
hath been *any* such *t.* *Deut* 4:32
thou shalt not lack *any t.* in. 8:9
not eat *any* abominable *t.* 14:3
ye shall not eat *any t.* that dieth. 21
nor shall there *any t.* of the. 16:4
usury of *any t.* that is lent. 23:19
lend thy brother *any t.* 24:10
have not known *any t.* 31:13
failed not aught of *any t.* *Josh* 21:45
art thou *any t.* better? *Judg* 11:25
put them to shame in *any t.* 18:7
a place where there is no want of *any t.* 10; 19:19
thee, if thou hide *any t.* *1 Sam* 3:17
but Saul spake not *any t.* 20:26
but the lad knew not *any t.* 39
let no man know *any t.* of the. 21:2
let not the king impute *any t.* 22:15
neither missed we *any t.* 25:15
there was not lacking *any t.* 30:19
hard to do *any t.* to her. *2 Sam* 13:2
went in simplicity, they knew not *any t.* 15:11
there was not *any t.* hid. *1 Ki* 10:3
turned not aside from *any t.* 15:5
whether *any t.* would come. 20:33
hath not *any t.* save a. *2 Ki* 4:2
hath dedicated *any t.* *1 Chr* 26:28
silver was not *any t.* *2 Chr* 9:20
that none unclean in *any t.* 23:19
is there *any* secret *t.*? *Job* 15:11
if thou hast *any t.* to say. 33:32
shall not want *any* good *t.* *Ps* 34:10
my heart to *any* evil *t.* 141:4
any t. whereof it may be said. *Eccl* 1:10
nothing be put to it, nor *any t.* 3:14
heart not be hasty to utter *any t.* 5:2
dead know not *any t.* nor have. 9:5
is there *any t.* too hard? *Jer* 32:27
is not he that can do *any t.* 38:5
nor *any t.* for which he hath. 42:21
which speak *any t.* amiss. *Dan* 3:29
man nor beast taste *any t.* *Jonah* 3:7
agree touching *any t.* *Mat* 18:19
to take *any t.* out of his house. 24:17; *Mark* 13:15
nor was *any t.* kept secret. *Mark* 4:22; *Luke* 8:17
thou canst do *any t.* have. *Mark* 9:22
if haply he might find *any t.* 11:13
neither said they *any t.* to. 16:8
if I have taken *any t.* *Luke* 19:8
lacked ye *any t.*? and they. 22:35
was not *any t.* made. *John* 1:3
can there *any* good *t.* come? 46
no man that doeth *any t.* in. 7:4
if ye ask *any t.* in my name. 14:14
I have never eaten *any t.* *Acts* 10:14
as though he needed *any t.* 17:25
Caesar, have I offended *any t.* 25:8
committed *any t.* worthy of. 11
lay *any t.* to the charge? *Rom* 8:33
owe no man *any t.* but to love. 13:8
any t. whereby thy brother. 14:21
nor to know *any t.* save. *1 Cor* 2:2
neither is he that planteth *any t.* 3:7
think that he knoweth *any t.* 8:2
that the idol is *any t.* 10:19
if they will learn *any t.* let. 14:35
to whom ye forgive *any t.* I forgive, for if I forgive *any t.* *2 Cor* 2:10
not sufficient to think *any t.* as. 3:5
giving no offence in *any t.* that. 6:3
for if I have boasted *any t.* to. 7:14
neither circumcision availeth *any t.* *Gal* 5:6
wrinkle, or *any* such *t.* *Eph* 5:27
if in *any t.* ye be. *Phil* 3:15
need not to speak *any t.* *1 Thes* 1:8
if there be *any* other *t.* *1 Tim* 1:10
that he shall receive *any t.* *Jas* 1:7
if we ask *any t.* according to his will. *1 John* 5:14
not hurt *any* green *t.* *Rev* 9:4
in no wise enter *any t.* that. 21:27

every thing

every t. that is in the. *Gen* 6:17
Noah and *every* living *t.* 8:1
every moving *t.* that liveth. 9:3
every t. whereon he sitteth, unclean. *Lev* 15:4
every t. she sitteth on shall. 20
ye shall offer *every t.* upon. 23:37
every devoted *t.* is most holy. 27:28
every t. devoted in Israel shall be. *Num* 18:14; *Ezek* 44:29
every t. that openeth the matrix be. *Num* 18:15
every t. that may abide fire. 31:23
from *every* wicked *t.* *Deut* 23:9
the priests stood till *every t.* was. *Josh* 4:10
every t. that was vile. *1 Sam* 15:9
send unto me *every t.* *2 Sam* 15:36
told *every t.* that had. *Esth* 6:13
eye seeth *every* precious *t.* *Job* 28:10
searcheth after *every* green *t.* 39:8
that thou canst do *every t.* 42:2
let *every t.* that hath breath praise. *Ps* 150:6
every bitter *t.* is sweet. *Pr* 27:7
to *every t.* there is a season. *Eccl* 3:1
hath made *every t.* beautiful in. 11
judgement with *every* secret *t.* 12:14
every t. sown by the brooks. *Isa* 19:7
every t. shall live where. *Ezek* 47:9
told *every t.* and what was befallen. *Mat* 8:33
in *every t.* ye are enriched. *1 Cor* 1:5 *2 Cor* 9:11
as ye are bound in *every t.* in faith. *2 Cor* 8:7
and *every* high *t.* that exalteth. 10:5
their husbands in *every t.* *Eph* 5:24
in *every t.* by prayer and. *Phil* 4:6
in *every t.* give thanks. *1 Thes* 5:18
see **creepeth, creeping, evil, good, living**

that thing

hide from Abraham *that t.* *Gen* 18:17
and the Lord did *that t.* *Ex* 9:6

he hath sinned in that t. Lev 5:5
committed that wicked t. Deut 17:5
to tell no man that t. Luke 9:21
if ye be not able to do that t. 12:26
not himself in that t. Rom 14:22

this **thing**

thee concerning this t. Gen 19:21
thou hast done this t. 20:10
hath done this t.; neither. 21:26
done this t. and not withheld. 22:16
if wilt do this t. I will again. 30:31
we cannot do this t. to give. 34:14
this is the t. I have spoken. 41:28
should do according to this t. 44:7
why have ye done this t.? Ex 1:18
Moses said, Surely this t. 2:14
Pharaoh heard this t., he sought. 15
Lord shall do this t. in land. 9:5
observe this t. for an. 12:24
this is the t. which the Lord. 16:16
32; 35:4; Lev 8:5; 9:6; 17:2
Num 30:1; 36:6; Deut 15:15
24:18, 22
what is this t. thou doest? Ex 18:14
this t. is too heavy for thee. 18
if thou shalt do this t. and God. 23
this is the t. that thou shalt. 29:1
I will do this t. that thou. 33:17
if ye will do this t., if ye. Num 32:20
this t. Lord doth command. 36:6
yet in this t. ye did not. Deut 1:32
for this t. the Lord thy God. 15:10
if this t. be true, and tokens. 22:20
through this t. ye shall prolong. 32:47
and have done this t. Josh 9:24
done it for fear of this t. 22:24
Who hath done this t.? Gideon hath
done this t. Judg 6:29
let this t. be done for me, let. 11:37
this shall be the t. which we. 20:9
and this is the t. that ye. 21:11
my father hide this t. from me?
1 Sam 20:2
that I should do this t. 24:6
this t. is not good that. 26:16
happen to thee for this t. 28:10
Lord hath done this t. unto thee. 18
ye have done this t. 2 Sam 2:6
liveth, I will not do this t. 11:11
say to Joab, Let not this t. 25
man that hath done this t. 12:5
because he did this t. and had. 6
but I will do this t. before all. 12
brother; regard not this t. 13:20
the king doth speak this t. as. 14:13
I am come to speak of this t. 15
thy servant Joab hath done this t. 20
why doth my lord the king delight in
this t.? 24:3
is this t. done by my? 1 Ki 1:27
Solomon had asked this t. 3:10, 11
him concerning this t. 11:10
return every man, for this t. 12:24
made two calves, and this t. 30
after this t. Jeroboam. 13:33
this t. became sin to the house. 34
tell my lord the king this t. 20:9
do this t., take the kings away. 24
the Lord pardon in this t. 2 Ki 5:18
Syria was troubled for this t. 6:11
windows, might this t. be. 7:2
this is the t. that ye shall do. 11:5
2 Chr 23:4
Ye shall not do this t. 2 Ki 17:12
God forbid that I should do this t.
1 Chr 11:19
my lord require this t.? 21:3
was displeased with this t. 7
because I have done this t. 8
return every man, this t. 2 Chr 11:4
with him, because of this t. 16:10
when I heard this t. I rent. Ezra 9:3
Israel concerning this t. 10:2
have transgressed in this t. 13
what is this t. that ye do? Neh 2:19
Lord will do this t. that. Isa 38:7
but this is the t. that I command.
Jer 7:23
if ye do this t. indeed, then. 22:4
therefore this t. is come upon. 40:3
Thou shalt not do this t. 16
oh do not this abominable t. 44:4
her that had done this t. Mark 5:32
and see this t. which is. Luke 2:15
it was that should do this t. 22:23
sayest thou this t. of? John 18:34
why hast thou conceived this t. in
thine heart? Acts 5:4
for this t. was not done in a. 26:26
continually upon this very t.
Rom 13:6
if I do this t. willingly, I. 1 Cor 9:17
for this t. I besought. 2 Cor 12:8
being confident in this very t. that.
Phil 1:6
but this one t. I do, I press. 3:13

unclean **thing**

if a soul touch any unclean t.
Lev 5:2; 7:21
flesh that toucheth unclean t. 7:19
wife, it is an unclean t. 20:21
no unclean t. in thee. Deut 23:14
and eat not any unclean t. Judg 13:4
7, 14
touch no unclean t. Isa 52:11
2 Cor 6:17
we are all as an unclean t. Isa 64:6
any t. that is unclean. Acts 10:14

things

with the good t. of Egypt. Gen 45:23
if a soul sin through ignorance concerning t. Lev 4:2, 13, 22, 27
lest thou forget t. thine. Deut 4:9
with all lost t. of thy brother's. 22:3
the secret t. belong unto the. 29:29
t. that shall come on them. 32:35
for the chief t. of the ancient. 33:15
took the t. which Micah. Judg 18:27
ye go after vain t. 1 Sam 12:21
people took the chief of the t. 15:21
I offer thee three t. 2 Sam 24:12
1 Chr 21:10
Solomon brought in the t. 1 Ki 7:51
Asa brought in the t. 15:15
2 Chr 15:18
wicked t. to provoke 2 Ki 17:11
and these are ancient t. 1 Chr 4:22
the office over t. that were. 9:31
t. of gold, silver for t. of silver, brass
for t. of brass, iron for t. 29:2
and also in Judah t. 2 Chr 12:12
let t. for purification. Esth 2:3, 12
who doth marvellous t. Job 5:9
the t. that my soul refuseth. 6:7
my taste discern perverse t.? 30
he discovereth deep t. out of. 12:22
only do not two t. to me: then. 13:20
writest bitter t. against me. 26
he beholdeth all high t. 41:34
I have uttered t. too wonderful. 42:3
that speaketh proud t. Ps 12:3
thine eyes behold the t. 17:2
speak grievous t. proudly. 31:18
they laid to my charge t. I. 35:11
hurt, speak mischievous t. 38:12
I speak of the t. which I. 45:1
hand shall teach thee terrible t. 4
shewed thy people hard t. 60:3
by terrible t. wilt thou answer. 65:5
who only doeth wondrous t. 72:18
marvellous t. did he in. 78:12; 98:1
and dost wondrous t. 86:10
glorious t. are spoken of thee. 87:3
utter and speak hard t.? 94:4
terrible t. by the Red sea. 106:22
himself to behold the t. that. 113:6
I may behold wondrous t. 119:18
great matters, or in t. too high. 131:1
that speaketh froward t. Pr 2:12
of excellent t. . . . shall be right t. 8:6
eyes to devise froward t. 16:30
written to thee excellent t. 22:20
when thy lips speak right t. 23:16
heart shall utter perverse t. 33
two t. have I required of thee. 30:7
there are three t. that are never. 15
there be three t. that be too. 18
for three t. the earth is. 21
four t. which are little on the. 24
there be three t. which go well. 29
any remembrance of t. Eccl 1:11
wisdom, and the reason of t. 7:25
he hath done excellent t. Isa 12:5
thou hast done wonderful t. 25:1
unto all people a feast of fat t. 6
surely your turning of t. 29:16
prophesy not to us right t. Isa 30:10
liberal deviseth liberal t. and by
liberal t. shall he stand. 32:8
shew the t. that are to come. 41:23
t. come to pass, and new t. 42:9
I will make crooked t. straight. 16
the t. that are coming and. 44:7
of t. to come concerning my. 45:11
I the Lord speak, I declare t. 19
thee new t., even hidden t. 48:6
the eunuchs that choose the t. 56:4
when thou didst terrible t. 64:3
and all our pleasant t. are laid. 11
broth of abominable t. is in. 65:4
walked after t. that do not profit.
Jer 2:8; 16:19
the t. I have given them shall. 8:13
shall eat them as common t. 31:5
Jerusalem remembered her pleasant
t. Lam 1:7
they have given her pleasant t. 11
prophets have seen foolish t. 2:14
I know the t. that come. Ezek 11:5
like t. shall not come, neither. 16:16
at the same time shall t. 38:10
the deep and secret t. Dan 2:22
shall speak marvellous t. 11:36
your temples my goodly t. Joel 3:5
t. of Esau searched out! how are
his hidden t. sought up! Ob 6
unto him marvellous t. Mi 7:15
who hath despised the day of small
t.? Zech 4:10
thought for t. of itself. Mat 6:34
bringeth out of his treasure t. 13:52
savourest not t. that be of God.
16:23; Mark 8:33
to Caesar the t. that are Caesar's, and
to God the t. that are God's.
Mat 22:21; Mark 12:17; Luke 20:25
lusts of other t. Mark 4:19
but the t. which come out of. 7:15
seen strange t. to-day. Luke 5:26
call me Lord, and do not the t. 6:46
the eyes which see the t. 10:23
in the abundance of the t. he. 12:15
and did commit t. worthy of. 48
the t. which are impossible. 18:27
hadst known the t. which. 19:42
for the t. concerning me. 22:37
all people beholding the t. 23:48
hast not known the t. which. 24:18
he expounded the t. concerning. 27
thou shalt see greater t. John 1:50
told you earthly t., heavenly t.? 3:12
the Spirit will shew you t. 16:13
speaking of t. pertaining. Acts 1:3
we cannot but speak the t. 4:20
the people imagine vain t.? 25
that aught of the t. he possessed. 32
preaching the t. concerning. 8:12
abstain from t. strangled. 15:20, 29
she attended to the t. spoken. 16:14
Apollos taught diligently the t. 18:25
persuading the t. concerning the. 19:8
not knowing the t. that shall. 20:22
arise, speaking perverse t. to. 30
that they keep from t. offered. 21:25
neither can they prove the t. 24:13
saying none other t. than the. 26:22
some believed the t. that were. 28:24
invisible t. of him are clearly seen,
being understood by t. Rom 1:20
judgest, doest the same t. 2:1
Gentiles do by nature t. contained. 14
and approvest the t. that are. 18
mind the t. of the flesh, mind t. 8:5
nor t. present, nor t. to come. 38
1 Cor 3:22
mind not high t. Rom 12:16
provide t. honest. 17
follow after t. that make for. 14:19
whatsoever t. were written. 15:4
partakers of spiritual t., their duty is
to minister to them in carnal t. 27
foolish t. of the world, weak t. to confound t. which are. 1 Cor 1:27
base t. and t. despised hath. 28
the t. which God hath prepared. 2:9
the Spirit searcheth the deep t. 10
knoweth the t. of a man, even so the
t. of God knoweth no man. 11
we might know the t. that are. 12
t. we speak, comparing spiritual t. 13

man receiveth not the t. of. 1 Cor 2:14
will bring to light the hidden t. 4:5
much more t. shall pertain to. 6:3, 4
careth for the t. of the Lord. 7:32, 34
married careth for the t. that are. 33
as touching t. offered to idols. 8:1
sown spiritual t. if reap carnal t. 9:11
the t. which the Gentiles. 10:20
a man, I put away childish t. 13:11
and even t. without life giving. 14:7
acknowledge that the t. that. 37
let all your t. be done with. 16:14
write none other t. unto. 2 Cor 1:13
or the t. that I purpose, do I. 17
but have renounced the hidden t. 4:2
the t. which are seen, t. seen are temporal, t. not seen are. 18
every one may receive the t. 5:10
old t. are passed away, all t. are. 17
providing for honest t., not only. 8:21
do ye look on t. after the? 10:7
we will not boast of t. without. 13, 15
boast in another man's line of t. 16
I will glory of the t. which. 11:30
if I build again the t. Gal 2:18
which t. are an allegory, for. 4:24
so that ye cannot do the t. 5:17
and, ye masters, do the same t. unto. Eph 6:9
that ye may approve t. that. Phil 1:10
the t. which happened unto me. 12
look not on his own t., but every man also on the t. of others. 2:4
of t. in heaven, t. in earth, t. 10
not the t. which are Jesus Christ's. 21
to write the same t. 3:1
who mind earthly t. 19
whatsoever t. are true, honest. 4:8
having received the t. sent from. 18
t. in earth, or t. in heaven. Col 1:20
which are a shadow of t. to come. 2:17; Heb 10:1
t. have indeed a shew of. Col 2:23
affection on t. above, not on t. 3:2
for which t.'s sake the wrath of. 6
suffered like t. of your. 1 Thes 2:14
and will do the t. which. 2 Thes 3:4
speaking t. which they. 1 Tim 5:13
the t. which thou hast. 2 Tim 2:2
continue in t. which thou. 3:14
set in order the t. wanting. Tit 1:5
teaching t. they ought not for. 11
speak thou the t. which become. 2:1
give heed to the t. which. Heb 2:1
be faithful high priest in t. pertaining to God. 17; 5:1
learned he obedience by the t. 5:8
persuaded better t. of you, and t. that accompany salvation. 6:9
that by two immutable t., in which. 18
of the t. we have spoken this. 8:1
shadow of heavenly t. 5
patterns of t. in the heavens be purified, but heavenly t. with. 9:23
now faith is the substance of t. hoped for, the evidence of t. not. 11:1
t. seen were not made of t. which. 3
Noah being warned of God of t. 7
Esau concerning t. to come. 20
that speaketh better t. than. 12:24
and t. in the sea are tamed. Jas 3:7
minister t. which are now reported; which t. the angels. 1 Pet 1:12
redeemed with corruptible t. 18
speak evil of t. they. 2 Pet 2:12
neither the t. that are. 1 John 2:15
Jesus Christ to shew to his servants t. which must shortly. Rev 1:1; 22:6
t. which thou hast seen, the t. which are, and t. which shall be. 1:19
a few t. against thee, ... to eat t. sacrificed unto idols. 2:14, 20
strengthen the t. which remain. 3:2
I will shew thee t. which must. 4:1
who created heaven, earth, sea, and all t. that therein are. 10:6
former t. are passed away. 21:4
take his part from t. written. 22:19
see **creeping, dedicate, detestable, evil, former, holy, many, precious, such**

all **things**

herb have I given you all t. Gen 9:3
blessed Abraham in all t. Gen 24:1
the servant told Isaac all t. that. 66
in all t. I have said. Ex 23:13
do according to all t. which I. 29:35
Aaron and his sons did all t. Lev 8:36
the Levites over all t. Num 1:50
and purify all t. made of. 31:20
I commanded you all t. Deut 1:18
as the Lord our God is in all t. 4:7
ye shall not do after all t. that. 12:8
for the abundance of all t. 28:47
thine enemies in want of all t. 48
want of all t. secretly in siege. 57
we hearkened to Moses in all t. Josh 1:17
the spies told him all t. that. 2:23
manner, to confirm all t. Ruth 4:7
perform all t. concerning. 1 Sam 3:12
if thou hide any of all t. he said. 17
shewed David all those t. 19:7
told David all the t. 2 Sam 11:18
to know all t. that are in. 14:20
covenant ordered in all t. 23:5
he did all t. as did the. 1 Ki 21:26
captains did according to all t. that Jehoiada. 2 Ki 11:9; 2 Chr 23:8
Amaziah, according to all t. that. 2 Ki 14:3
they have seen all t. that are. 20:15
all t. come of thee. 1 Chr 29:14
Solomon brought all t. 2 Chr 5:1
tithe of all t. brought they in. 31:5
the Lord made all t. Neh 9:6
Acts 14:15; 17:24, 25; Col 1:16
Rev 4:11
he beholdeth all high t. Job 41:34
thou hast put all t. under his feet. Ps 8:6; 1 Cor 15:27; Eph 1:22
that performeth all t. for me. Ps 57:2
precepts concerning all t. to. 119:128
precious than all t. Pr 3:15; 8:11
the Lord hath made all t. for. 16:4
great God that formed all t. 26:10
seek the Lord understand all t. 28:5
all t. are full of labour. Eccl 1:8
all t. have I seen in days. 7:15
all t. come alike to all, there. 9:2
this is an evil among all t. done. 3
but money answereth all t. 10:19
I am the Lord that maketh all t. Isa 44:24; 66:2
for he is the former of all t. Jer 10:16; 51:19
heart is deceitful above all t. 17:9
do not even according to all t. 42:5
we wanted all t. and have. 44:18
I spake all t. the Lord. Ezek 11:25
all creeping t. shall shake. 38:20
the first of all t. shall be. 44:30
as iron subdueth all t. Dan 2:40
I will consume all t. Zeph 1:2
all t. ye would that men. Mat 7:12
all t. are delivered unto me of my Father. 11:27; Luke 10:22
they shall gather all t. Mat 13:41
Elias shall restore all t. 17:11
Mark 9:12
is impossible, but with God all t. are. Mat 19:26; Mark 10:27; 14:36
all t. whatsoever ye shall. Mat 21:22
behold all t. are ready, come unto the marriage. Mat 22:4; Luke 14:17
sweareth by it, and by all t. thereon. Mat 23:20
teaching them to observe all t. 28:20
he expounded all t. to. Mark 4:34
told him all t., both what they. 6:30
He hath done all t. well. 7:37
all t. are possible to him. 9:23
I have foretold you all t. 13:23
praising God for all t. Luke 2:20
performed all t. according to. 39
they wondered at all t. which. 9:43
and behold, all t. are clean. 11:41
all t. written concerning Son. 18:31
21:22; 24:44; John 19:28
all t. were made by him. John 1:3
and hath given all t. 3:35; 13:3
is come, he will tell us all t. 4:25
see a man who told me all t. 29
Father sheweth the Son all t. 5:20
all t. that John spake of him. 10:41
Holy Ghost, he shall teach you all t., and bring all t. to your. 14:26
all t. I have heard, I have. John 15:15
all t. that the Father hath. 16:15
sure that thou knowest all t. 30
that all t. thou hast given me. 17:7
Jesus therefore knowing all t. 18:4; 19:28
Lord, thou knowest all t. 21:17
had all t. common. Acts 2:44; 4:32
of restitution of all t. 3:21
him shall ye hear in all t. he shall. 22
to hear all t. commanded. 10:33
we are witnesses of all t. 39
are justified from all t. 13:39
heaven, earth, sea, and all t. 14:15
you all t. how ye ought. 20:35
it shall be told thee of all t. 22:10
believing all t. which are. 24:14
touching all the t. whereof. 26:2
and we know that all t. Rom 8:28
also freely give us all t.? 32
him, and to him, are all t. 11:36
that he may eat all t. 14:2
all t. indeed are pure, but it is. 20
Spirit searcheth all t. 1 Cor 2:10
he that is spiritual judgeth all t. 15
no man glory in men, for all t. 3:21
are the offscouring of all t. 4:13
all t. are lawful unto me, but all t. are ... all t. are lawful. 6:12; 10:23
of whom are all t.; and one Lord Jesus Christ, by whom are all t. 8:6
suffer all t. 9:12
I am made all t. to all men. 22
that striveth is temperate in all t. 25
as I please all men in all t. 10:33
that ye remember me in all t. 11:2
but all t. are of God. 12; 2 Cor 5:18
charity beareth all t., believeth all t., hopeth all t., endureth all t. 1 Cor 13:7
let all t. be done unto edifying. 14:26
let all t. be done decently. 40
all t. shall be subdued, then shall the Son be subject ... all t. 15:28
ye be obedient in all t. 2 Cor 2:9
for all t. are for your sakes. 4:15
old things are passed away; behold all t. are. 5:17
in all t. approving ourselves. 6:4
nothing, yet possessing all t. 10
in all t. ye have approved. 7:11
but as we speak all t. to you. 14
confidence in you in all t. 16
all sufficiency in all t. 9:8
made manifest to you in all t. 11:6
in all t. I kept myself from being. 9
but we do all t. for your. 12:19
continueth not in all t. Gal 3:10
in one all t. in Christ. Eph 1:10
worketh all t. after the counsel. 11
gave him to be head over all t. 22
in God, who created all t. by. 3:9
up, that he might fill all t. 4:10
grow up into him in all t. which. 15
all t. that are reproved are. 5:13
giving thanks always for all t. 20
shall make known to you all t. 6:21
Col 4:9
do all t. without murmurings. Phil 2:14
I count all t. but loss for knowledge of Christ ... loss of all t. 3:8
he is able even to subdue all t. to. 21
and in all t. I am instructed. 4:12
I can do all t. through Christ. 13
is before all t., by him all t. Col 1:17
in all t. he might have the. 18
and by him to reconcile all t. 20
obey your parents in all t. 3:20
obey in all t. your masters. 22
prove all t.; hold fast. 1 Thes 5:21
must be faithful in all t. 1 Tim 3:11
is profitable unto all t. 4:8
of God who quickeneth all t. 6:13
who giveth us richly all t. to enjoy. 17
understanding in all t. 2 Tim 2:7
endure all t. for the elect's sake. 10
but watch thou in all t., endure. 4:5
unto pure all t. are pure. Tit 1:15
all t. shewing thyself a pattern. 2:7
and please them well in all t. 9
the doctrine of God in all t. 10
appointed heir of all t. Heb 1:2
upholding all t. by the word of. 3

put all t. in subjection under his feet;
but now we see not yet all t. Heb 2:8
are all t. and by whom are all t. 10
in all t. it behoved him to be like. 17
he that built all t. is God. 3:4
all t. are naked and opened. 4:13
make all t. according to the. 8:5
almost all t. are by the law. 9:22
in all t. willing to live. 13:18
above all t. my brethren. Jas 5:12
the end of all t. is at hand. 1 Pet 4:7
above all t. have fervent charity. 8
God in all t. may be glorified. 11
hath given us all t. that. 2 Pet 1:3
all t. continue as they were. 3:4
ye have an unction, and ye know all t.
1 John 2:20
anointing teacheth you all t. 27
heart, and knoweth all t. 3:20
I wish above all t. that. 3 John 2
who bare record of all t. Rev 1:2
thou hast created all t. and. 4:11
I make all t. new. 21:5
he shall inherit all t. 7

these things

them of her mother's house these t.
Gen 24:28
Jacob said, All these t. are. 42:36
he shall be guilty in one of these t.
Lev 5:5, 17
yourselves in any of these t. 18:24
committed all these t. 20:23
not be reformed by these t. 26:23
these t. are the burden of sons of.
Num 4:15
of the country shall do these t. 15:13
these t. ye shall do to Lord. 29:39
these t. shall be for a statute. 35:29
when all these t. are. Deut 4:30
all that do these t. are an. 18:12
when all these t. are come. 30:1
as we heard these t., our. Josh 2:11
have shewed us these t. Judg 13:23
had told him these t. 1 Sam 25:37
these t. did these three mighty.
2 Sam 23:17; 1 Chr 11:19
these t. did Benaiah. 2 Sam 23:22
1 Chr 11:24
these t. did Araunah. 2 Sam 24:23
I have done all these t. 1 Ki 18:36
proclaimed these t. 2 Ki 23:17
in these t. was Solomon. 2 Chr 3:3
Solomon sin by these t.? Neh 13:26
wilt thou speak these t.? Job 8:2
these t. hast thou hid in. 10:13
lo, all these t. worketh God. 33:29
he that doeth these t. Ps 15:5
I remember these t., I pour. 42:4
these t. hast thou done and. 50:21
these six t. doth the Lord. Pr 6:16
these t. also belong to wise. 24:23
for these t. God will bring. Eccl 11:9
O Lord, by these t. men live, and in
all these t. is the life. Isa 38:16
who hath created these t.? 40:26
these t. will I do, and not. 42:16
I the Lord do all these t. 45:7
not lay these t. to heart. 47:7
these two t. shall come to thee. 9
save thee from these t. 13
them hath declared these t. 48:14
these two t. are come unto. 51:19
refrain thyself for these t.? 64:12
she had done all these t. Jer 3:7
procured these t. unto thee. 4:18
shall I not visit for these t.? 5:9
29; 9:9
have turned away these t. 5:25
for in these t. do I delight. 9:24
come these t. on me? 13:22
thou hast made all these t. 14:22
thy sins I have done these t. 30:15
for these t. I weep, mine. Lam 1:16
our heart is faint; for these t. 5:17
seeing thou doest all these t.
Ezek 16:30; 17:18
hast fretted me in all these t. 16:43
know ye not what these t.? 17:12
like to any one of these t. 18:10
I will do these t. unto thee. 23:30
thou not tell what these t.? 24:19
none that holdeth with me in these t.
Dan 10:21
all these t. shall be finished. Dan 12:7
what shall be the end of these t.? 8
shall understand these t. Hos 14:9
these are the t. which ye shall do.
Zech 8:16
for all these are t. that I hate. 17
he thought on these t. Mat 1:20
when Herod heard these t. 2:3
these t. do the Gentiles seek . . . all
these t. 6:32; Luke 12:30
all these t. shall be added unto you.
Mat 6:33; Luke 12:31
hast hid these t. from the wise.
Mat 11:25; Luke 10:21
ye understood these t.? Mat 13:51
hath this man these t.? 56; Mark 6:2
these are the t. which defile a man.
Mat 15:20
all these t. have I kept from. 19:20
by what authority doest thou these t.?
21:23; Mark 11:28; Luke 20:2
authority I do these t. Mat 21:24
27; Mark 11:29, 33; Luke 20:8
all these t. shall come on. Mat 23:36
See ye not all these t.? 24:2
when shall these t. be? 3
Mark 13:4; Luke 21:7
all these t. must come to pass.
Mat 24:6; Luke 21:9, 28
ye shall see all these t. Mat 24:33
Mark 13:29; Luke 21:31
till all these t. be fulfilled.
Mat 24:34; Mark 13:30
till the day that these t. Luke 1:20
but Mary kept all these t. and. 2:19
not answer him to these t. 14:6
asked what these t. meant. 15:26
understood none of these t. 18:34
to escape all these t. that. 21:36
do these t. in a green tree. 23:31
is third day since these t. 24:21
Christ to have suffered these t.? 26
and ye are witnesses of these t. 48
Take these t. hence. John 2:16
seeing that thou doest these t. 18
to him, How can these t. be? 3:9
Israel, and knowest not these t.? 10
he had done these t. on the. 5:16
if thou do these t. shew thyself. 7:4
these t. understood not his disciples,
they . . . these t. were. 12:16
these t. said Esaias, when he. 41
if ye know these t. happy. 13:17
all these t. will they do. 15:21; 16:3
these t. therefore the soldiers. 19:24
these t. were done, that the. 36
his witnesses of these t. Acts 5:32
are these t. so? 7:1
my hand made all these t.? 50
when they heard these t. they. 54
pray for me, that none of these t.
8:24
sirs, why do ye these t.? 14:15
Lord, who doeth all these t. 15:17
know what these t. mean. 17:20
seeing these t. cannot be. 19:36
none of these t. move me. 20:24
saying that these t. were so. 24:9
and there be judged of these t. 25:9
thee a witness of these t. 26:16
the king knoweth of these t. 26
then say to these t.? Rom 8:31
for he that in these t. serveth. 14:18
say I these t. as a man. 1 Cor 9:8
I used none of these t. nor have. 15
these t. were our examples. 10:6
sufficient for these t.? 2 Cor 2:16
because of these t. cometh. Eph 5:6
praise, think on these t. Phil 4:8
and above all these t. put. Col 3:14
in remembrance of these t. 1 Tim 4:6
these t. command. 11
meditate on these t. 15
these t. give in charge. 5:7
observe these t. 21
these t. exhort. 6:2; Tit 2:15
flee these t. 1 Tim 6:11
of these t. put them. 2 Tim 2:14
these t. I will that thou affirm constantly.
These t. are good. Tit 3:8
for he of whom these t. are spoken.
Heb 7:13
brethren, these t. ought not. Jas 3:10
for if these t. be in you. 2 Pet 1:8
he that lacketh these t. is. 2 Pet 1:9
for if ye do these t. ye shall. 10
in remembrance of these t. 12
to have these t. always in. 15
seeing all these t. shall be. 3:11
speaking in them of these t. 16
seeing ye know these t. before. 17
angel who shewed me these t.
Rev 22:8
to testify to you these t. in the. 16
he which testifieth these t. 20

those things

eat those t. wherewith. Ex 29:33
in those t. which they. Lev 22:2
those t. which are revealed.
Deut 29:29
did secretly those t. 2 Ki 17:9
will observe those t. Ps 107:43
for all those t. hath mine hand made,
and all those t. have. Isa 66:2
approach to those t. Ezek 42:14
those t. which ye see, and hear those
t. Mat 13:17; Luke 10:24
offer those t. which Moses commanded.
Mark 1:44
a performance of those t. Luke 1:45
wondered at those t. told them. 2:18
then whose shall those t. be, which
thou hast provided? 12:20
I do always those t. John 8:29
but those t. he hath so fulfilled.
Acts 3:18
gave heed to those t. which. 8:6
spake against those t. which. 13:45
searched whether those t. 17:11
cared for none of those t. 18:17
of those t. in which I will appear.
26:16
those t. spoken by Paul. 27:11
to do those t. which are. Rom 1:28
calleth those t. which be not. 4:17
in those t. whereof ye are now
ashamed, for end of those t. 6:21
the man that doeth those t. 10:5
I may glory in those t. which. 15:17
to speak of any of those t. 18
eating of those t. 1 Cor 8:4, 10
besides those t. which. 2 Cor 11:28
even to speak of those t. Eph 5:12
forgetting those t. which are behind,
and reaching to those t. Phil 3:13
those t. which ye have learned. 4:9
intruding into those t. he. Col 2:18
seek those t. which are above. 3:1
for a testimony of those t. Heb 3:5
the removing of those t. which are
shaken, that those t. which. 12:27
ye give not those t. which. Jas 2:16
do those t. that are pleasing in his.
1 John 3:22
we lose not those t. we. 2 John 8
but speak evil of those t. Jude 10
they that keep those t. Rev 1:3
fear none of those t. which. 2:10
those t. the seven thunders. 10:4
were judged out of those t. 20:12

unclean things

and they shall eat unclean t. Hos 9:3

what things

tell thy son what t. I have. Ex 10:2
Father knoweth what t. ye. Mat 6:8
should tell no man what t. Mark 9:9
began to tell them what t. 10:32
what t. soever ye desire. 11:24
go, tell John what t. ye. Luke 7:22
what t. they said to him. 24:19
and they told what t. were done. 35
what t. soever he doeth. John 5:19
they understood not what t. 10:6
some told them what t. Jesus. 11:46
what t. God wrought. Acts 21:19
what t. were gain to me. Phil 3:7

think

but t. on me, when it be. Gen 40:14
let them marry to whom they t. best.
Num 36:6
to t. that all the king's. 2 Sam 13:33
ye t. to withstand kingdom of Lord.
2 Chr 13:8
t. on me, my God, for. Neh 5:19
thou and the Jews t. to rebel. 6:6
my God, t. thou on Tobiah and. 14
t. not thou shalt escape. Esth 4:13

why then should I t. upon? Job 31:1
t. the deep to be hoary. 41:32
wise man t. to know it. Eccl 8:17
nor doth his heart t. so. Isa 10:7
t. to cause my people. Jer 23:27
I know the thoughts that I t. 29:11
and thou shalt t. an evil. Ezek 38:10
he shall t. to change times. Dan 7:25
if so be that God will t. Jonah 1:6
if ye t. good, give me. Zech 11:12
and t. not to say within. Mat 3:9
t. not that I am come to destroy. 5:17
t. they shall be heard for much. 6:7
why t. ye evil in your hearts? 9:4
t. not I am come to send. 10:34
how t. ye? if a man have. 18:12
what t. ye? a certain man had. 21:28
what t. ye of Christ? 22:42
what t. ye? 26:66; Mark 14:64
in such an hour as ye t. not. Mat 24:44; Luke 12:40
t. ye that they were sinners above. Luke 13:4
them ye t. ye have eternal. John 5:39
do not t. I will accuse you to. 45
what t. ye, that he will not? 11:56
killeth you will t. that he doeth. 16:2
whom t. ye that I am? Acts 13:25
not to t. that the Godhead. 17:29
t. myself happy, king Agrippa. 26:2
not to t. of himself more highly than he ought to t., but to t. Rom 12:3
in us not to t. of men. 1 Cor 4:6
I t. that God hath set forth us. 9
if any man t. that he behaveth. 7:36
I t. also that I have the Spirit. 40
if any man t. that he knoweth. 8:2
of body, which we t. to be less. 12:23
if any man t. himself to be a. 14:37
ourselves to t. any thing. 2 Cor 3:5
I t. to be bold against some, which t. of us as if we walked. 10:2
that he is Christ, let him t. 7, 11
I say again, Let no man t. me. 11:16
lest any t. of me above what. 12:6
if a man t. himself to be. Gal 6:3
above all that we ask or t. Eph 3:20
if there be any praise, t. Phil 4:8
let not that man t. he shall. Jas 1:7
do ye t. that the scripture? 4:5
wherein they t. strange. 1 Pet 4:4
t. it not strange concerning the. 12
I t. it meet as long as I am in this. 2 Pet 1:13

thinkest

t. thou that David doth honour thy? 2 Sam 10:3; 1 Chr 19:3
t. thou this right, that? Job 35:2
Jesus said, What t. thou? Mat 17:25
tell us what t. thou? 22:17
t. thou that I cannot pray? 26:53
which t. thou was neighbour to? Luke 10:36
hear of thee what thou t. Acts 28:22
t. thou this, O man, that? Rom 2:3

thinketh

me t. the running of the. 2 Sam 18:27
yet the Lord t. on me. Ps 40:17
for as he t. in his heart. Pr 23:7
let him that t. he standeth, take heed. 1 Cor 10:12
seeketh not her own, t. no evil. 13:5
man t. he hath whereof. Phil 3:4

thinking

t. to have brought good. 2 Sam 4:10
t., David cannot come in hither. 5:6

third

he the second and the t. Gen 32:19
saw Ephraim's children of t. 50:23
to t. and fourth generation. Ex 20:5
34:7; Num 14:18; Deut 5:9
and the t. row a ligure, an agate. Ex 28:19; 39:12
Ephraim in the t. rank. Num 2:24
Edomite shall enter in t. Deut 23:8
the t. lot came up for. Josh 19:10
a captain of the t. fifty. 2 Ki 1:13
the t. lot came forth to. 1 Chr 24:8
t. lot came forth for Zaccur. 25:10
t. captain of the host for the t. 27:5
shall Israel be the t. with. Isa 19:24
t. was the face of a lion. Ezek 10:14
and another t. kingdom. Dan 2:39
t. ruler in kingdom. Dan 5:7; 16:29
t. chariot white horses. Zech 6:3
out about the t. hour. Mat 20:3
likewise the second also, and the t. 22:26; Mark 12:21; Luke 20:31
it was t. hour, and they. Mark 15:25
come in the t. watch. Luke 12:38
he sent a t. and they. 20:12
it is but the t. hour of the. Acts 2:15
fell down from the t. loft. 20:9
be ready at the t. hour of. 23:23
up to the t. heaven. 2 Cor 12:2
the t. beast had a face as a. Rev 4:7
the t. seal, I heard the t. beast. 6:5
the t. angel sounded, there fell. 8:10
and behold, the t. woe cometh. 11:14
and the t. angel followed them. 14:9
the t. angel poured out his vial. 16:4
the t. foundation was a. 21:19
see **day, month, part**

third *time*

Samuel the t. time. 1 Sam 3:8
messengers again the t. time. 19:21
do it the t. time. And they did it the t. time. 1 Ki 18:34
be doubled the t. time. Ezek 21:14
and he prayed the t. time. Mat 26:44; Mark 14:41
t. time Jesus shewed. John 21:14
t. time, Lovest thou me? Peter was grieved . . . to him t. time. 17
the t. time I am ready to come. 2 Cor 12:14; 13:1

third *year*

t. year, which is the year. Deut 26:12
in t. year of Asa, did Baasha slay. 1 Ki 15:28, 33
Lord came to Elijah in t. year. 18:1
in t. year, Jehoshaphat came to. 22:2
in the t. year of Hoshea. 2 Ki 18:1
in the t. year sow ye and reap. 19:29; Isa 37:30
in t. year of Jehoshaphat's reign. 2 Chr 17:7
paid the second and t. year. 27:5
t. year of the reign of Ahasuerus. Esth 1:3
t. year of the reign of Jehoiakim. Dan 1:1
t. year of the reign of Belshazzar. 8:1
t. year of Cyrus king of Persia. 10:1

thirdly

t. teachers, after that. 1 Cor 12:28

thirst, *substantive*

our children with t. Ex 17:3
serve thine enemies in t. Deut 28:48
to add drunkenness to t. 29:19*
shall die for t. and fall. Judg 15:18
you to die by t. 2 Chr 32:11
water for their t. Neh 9:15, 20
winepresses and suffer t. Job 24:11
in my t. they gave me. Ps 69:21
wild asses quench their t. 104:11
multitude dried up with t. Isa 5:13
their tongue faileth for t. 41:17
fish stinketh, and dieth for t. 50:2
thy throat from t. Jer 2:25
from thy glory, and sit in t. 48:18
roof of his mouth for t. Lam 4:4
naked, and slay her with t. Hos 2:3
not a t. for water, but of. Amos 8:11
young men shall faint for t. 13
in hunger and t. 2 Cor 11:27

thirst, *verb*

they shall not hunger nor t. Isa 49:10
which hunger and t. after. Mat 5:6
this water, shall t. again. John 4:13
drinketh, shall never t. 14; 6:35
this water, that I t. not. 15
if any man t. let him come unto. 7:37
after this Jesus saith, I t. 19:28
if thine enemy t. give. Rom 12:20
this present hour we t. 1 Cor 4:11
and they shall not t. Rev 7:16

thirsted

people t. there for water. Ex 17:3
they t. not when he led. Isa 48:21

thirsteth

my soul t. for God. Ps 42:2; 63:1* 143:6*
ho, every one that t., come. Isa 55:1

thirsty

little water, for I am t. Judg 4:19
the people is t. in the. 2 Sam 17:29
my flesh longeth in a t. land. Ps 63:1; 143:6
hungry and t., their soul. 107:5
if thine enemy be t. give. Pr 25:21
as cold water to a t. soul, so is. 25
water to him that was t. Isa 21:14
it shall be as when a t. man. 29:8
the drink of the t. to fail. 32:6
t. land shall become springs. 35:7
pour water upon him that is t. 44:3
shall drink, but ye shall be t. 65:13
in a dry and t. ground. Ezek 19:13
for I was t. and ye gave. Mat 25:35
when saw we thee t. and gave? 37
for I was t. and ye gave me no. 42

thirteen

Ishmael his son was t. Gen 17:25
ye shall offer t. young bullocks. Num 29:13, 14
his own house t. years. 1 Ki 7:1
brethren of Hosah t. 1 Chr 26:11
of the gate t. cubits. Ezek 40:11

thirteenth

t. year they rebelled. Gen 14:4
the t. lot came forth. 1 Chr 24:13
t. lot came forth to Shubael. 25:20
in the t. year of the reign. Jer 1:2
from the t. year of Josiah the. 25:3
see **day**

thirtieth

Shallum to reign in nine and t. year. 2 Ki 15:13
in the nine and t. year of king. 17
seven and t. year of the captivity of. 25:27; Jer 52:31
five and t. year of Asa. 2 Chr 15:19
in the six and t. year of the. 16:1
the two and t. year of Artaxerxes. Nah 5:14; 13:6

thirty

height of the ark was t. Gen 6:15
Salah lived t. years, and. 11:14
Peleg lived t. years, and. 18
Serug lived t. years, and. 22
shall be t. found, he said, I will not do it if I find t. there. 18:30
t. milch camels with their. 32:15
Joseph was t. years old. 41:46
their master t. shekels. Ex 21:32
the length of one curtain t. cubits. 26:8; 36:15
thy estimation shall be t. Lev 27:4
from t. years old and upwards. Num 4:3, 23, 30, 35, 39, 43, 47
1 Chr 23:3
Jair had t. sons, and they had t. Judg 10:4
t. sons and t. daughters he sent abroad, took in t. daughters. 12:9
forty sons and t. nephews. 14
they brought t. companions. 14:11
give you t. sheets, t. change. 12
ye shall give t. sheets, t. change. 13
Samson slew t. men, and took. 19
to smite about t. men of. 20:31, 39
them, about t. persons. 1 Sam 9:22
David was t. years old. 2 Sam 5:4
and three of the t. chief. 23:13
Benaiah was more honourable than the t. 23; 1 Chr 11:15, 25; 27:6
Asahel, brother of Joab, was one of the t. 2 Sam 23:24
provision for one day was t. 1 Ki 4:22
house of the Lord was t. cubits. 6:2
house of the forest was t. cubits. 7:2
of the porch was t. cubits. 6
a line of t. cubits did compass. 23
to Hezekiah t. talents. 2 Ki 18:14
captain, and t. with him. 1 Chr 11:42
of them was t. chargers. Ezra 1:9
t. basons of gold, silver basons. 10
take from hence t. men. Jer 38:10
t. chambers were on. Ezek 40:17
and the side chambers were t. 41:6
there were courts joined of t. 46:22
for my price t. pieces. Zech 11:12
and I took the t. pieces of silver. 13
Mat 27:9

brought some t. fold. Mat 13:8, 23
Mark 4:8, 20
with him for t. pieces. Mat 26:15
again the t. pieces of silver. 27:3
Jesus began to be about t. Luke 3:23
about 25 or t. furlongs. John 6:19
see **days, thousand**

thirty *one*
the kings Joshua subdued t. and one. Josh 12:24
in the t. and first year. 1 Ki 16:23
Josiah eight years old, and reigned t. and one. 2 Ki 22:1; 2 Chr 34:1

thirty *two*
Reu lived t. two years. Gen 11:20
Lord's tribute was t. two persons. Num 31:40
t. two kings were with Ben-hadad. 1 Ki 20:1, 16
king commanded his t. two captains. 22:31
Jehoram was t. two years. 2 Ki 8:17
2 Chr 21:5, 20

thirty *three*
all the souls of sons and daughters t. three. Gen 46:15
purifying t. three days. Lev 12:4
in Jerusalem t. and three. 2 Sam 5:5
1 Ki 2:11; 1 Chr 3:4; 29:27

thirty *four*
Eber lived t. four years. Gen 11:16

thirty *five*
lived five and t. years. Gen 11:12
Jehoshaphat was t. five years old. 1 Ki 22:42; 2 Chr 20:31
made two pillars t. five. 2 Chr 3:15

thirty *six*
Ai smote t. six men. Josh 7:5

thirty *seven*
Hittite, t. seven in all. 2 Sam 23:39
in the t. and seventh. 2 Ki 13:10

thirty *eight*
brook Zered, t. eight years. Deut 2:14
in the t. and eighth year of Asa. 1 Ki 16:29
the t. and eighth year of Azariah. 2 Ki 15:8
an infirmity t. eight years. John 5:5

thirty *nine*
Asa in the t. and ninth. 2 Chr 16:12

this
t. same shall comfort us. Gen 5:29
T. shall not be thine heir. 15:4
and I will speak but t. once. 18:32
they said, T. one fellow came. 19:9
we will give thee t. also for. 29:27
but in t. will we consent. 34:15
sent the coat, and said, T. 37:32
bound a thread, saying, T. 38:28
is not t. it in which my lord? 44:5
if ye take t. from me, and mischief. 29
t. shall be a token that I. Ex 3:12
in t. thou shalt know that I. 7:17
neither did he set his heart to t. 23
t. they shall give, each half. 30:13
t. shall be thine of the most holy. Num 18:9; Deut 18:3
live when God doth t.? Num 24:23
O that they were wise, that they understood t. Deut 32:29
is not t. laid up in store with me? 34
t. shall go with thee, t. Judg 7:4
come up t. once, for he hath. 16:18
the Lord chosen t. 1 Sam 16:8, 9
Let not Jonathan know t. 20:3
that t. be no grief unto thee. 25:31
t. was a small thing in. 2 Sam 7:19
Shimei be put to death for t.? 19:21
is not t. the blood of the men? 23:17
to judge t. thy so great. 1 Ki 3:9
and t. was the cause that he. 11:27
I will for t. afflict the seed of. 39
by t. I know that thou art a. 17:24
should I set t. before an. 2 Ki 4:43
glory of t. and tarry at home. 14:10
commandment of Lord came t. 24:3
because t. was in thine heart, not. 2 Chr 1:11
able to give thee more than t. 25:9
his pleasure concerning t. Ezra 5:17
be made a dunghill for t. Ezra 6:11
put such a thing as t. in the. 7:27
besought our God for t. 8:23
given us such deliverance as t. 9:13
stand before thee because of t. 15
remember me concerning t. Neh 13:14, 22
to kingdom for such a time as t. Esth 4:14
lo, t. we have searched it. Job 5:27
of the Lord hath wrought t. 12:9
men shall be astonied at t. 17:8
for t. I make haste. 20:2
knowest thou not t. of old? 4
hear and let t. be your. 21:2
in t. thou art not just, I will. 33:12
thinkest thou t. to be right? 35:2
t. shall be the portion. Ps 11:6
though war rise, in t. will I. 27:3
for t. shall every one that is. 32:6
t. thou hast seen, keep not. 35:22
by t. I know that thou. 41:11
shall not God search t. out? 44:21
for t. God is our God for ever. 48:14
t. their way is their folly. 49:13
now consider t. ye that forget. 50:22
shall turn back, t. I know. for. 56:9
twice have I heard t. that. 62:11
t. also shall please the Lord. 69:31
the humble shall see t. and be. 32
when I thought to know t. it. 73:16
the Lord heard t. and was. 78:21, 59
for t. was a statute for Israel. 81:4
t. he ordained in Joseph for a. 5
neither doth a fool understand t. 92:6
let t. be the reward of mine. 109:20
t. I had, because I kept. 119:56
t. honour have all his saints. 149:9
for t. a man is envied of. Eccl 4:4
t. hath more rest than the other. 6:5
enquire wisely concerning t. 7:10
thou shouldest take hold of t.; yea also from t. withdraw not. 18
t. have I found. 27
lo, t. only have I found. 29
whether shall prosper, either t. 11:6
who hath required t.? Isa 1:12
and he said, Lo t. hath touched. 6:7
Lord of hosts will perform t. 9:7
surely t. iniquity shall not be. 22:14
by t. shall the iniquity of Jacob. 27:9
t. also cometh forth from. 28:29
Read t. I pray thee. 29:11, 12
have I cried concerning t. 30:7
them can declare t.? 43:9; 45:21
remember t. 46:8
hear now t. 47:8; 48:1, 16; 51:21
declare ye, tell t. 48:20
t. shall ye have of mine hand. 50:11
blessed is the man that doeth t. 56:2
wilt thou call t. a fast? 58:5
is not t. the fast that I have? 6
when ye see t. your hearts. 66:14
O ye heavens, at t. Jer 2:12
procured t. unto thyself? 17
for t. gird you with sackcloth. 4:8
for t. shall the earth mourn. 28
shall I pardon thee for t.? 5:7
shall not my soul be avenged on such a nation as t.? 9, 29; 9:9
that glorieth, glory in t. 9:24
I will t. once cause them to. 16:21
was not t. to know me? saith. 22:16
t. hath been thy manner from thy. 21
long shall t. be in the heart? 23:26
t. shall be the covenant that I. 31:33
I knew that t. was the word. 32:8
t. I call to mind, therefore I hope. Lam 3:21
for t. our heart is faint; our. 5:17
he said, Hast thou seen t.? Ezek 8:15, 17; 47:6
t. was the iniquity of thy. 16:49
in t. your fathers have. 20:27
saith the Lord, t. shall not be. 21:26
her sister Aholibah saw t. 23:11
t. cometh, ye shall know. 24:24
33:33
I will yet for t. be enquired. 36:37
t. gate shall be shut, no man. 44:2
not find occasion against t. Daniel. Dan 6:5, 28
t. shall be their derision. Hos 7:16
t. liketh you, O children. Amos 4:5
the Lord repented for t. Amos 7:3, 6
the land tremble for t.? 8:8
saith the Lord that doeth t. 9:12
was not t. my saying? Jonah 4:2
t. shall they have for their pride. Zeph 2:10
t. shall come to pass if ye will obey Lord. Zech 6:15
t. shall be the plague. 14:12, 15
t. shall be the punishment of. 19
t. hath been by your means. Mal 1:9
should I accept t. of your hands? 13
will cut off the man that doeth t. 2:12
known what t. meaneth. Mat 12:7
is not t. the carpenter's son? 13:55
Mark 6:3; Luke 4:22; John 6:42
saying, Lord, t. shall not. Mat 16:22
know t. that if the good man of the house. 24:43; Luke 12:39
shall also t. that t. woman. Mat 26:13
saying, Truly t. was the Son. 27:54
if t. come to the governor's. 28:14
the second is like, namely, t. Mark 12:31
I know t.? for I am old. Luke 1:18
how shall t. be, seeing I know? 34
manner of child shall t. be? 66
added yet t. above all, that. 3:20
have ye not read so much as t.? 6:3
be sure of t. 10:11
in t. rejoice not. 20
t. my son was dead and is. 15:24
take t. and divide it among. 22:17
t. must yet be accomplished. 37
certainly T. was a righteous. 23:47
saying, T. was he of. John 1:15
remembered he had said t. 2:22
on t. came his disciples. 4:27
is not t. the Christ? 29
marvel not at t. 5:28
he said t. to prove him, for. 6:6
is not t. he whom they seek? 7:25
t. did not Abraham. 8:40
believest thou t.? 11:26
t. spake he not of himself. 51
t. he said, not that he cared. 12:6
for what intent he spake t. 13:28
by t. shall all men know ye are. 35
love hath no man than t. 15:13
by t. we believe that thou. 16:30
t. Jesus shall so come in. Acts 1:11
what meaneth t.? 2:12
he seeing t. before. 31
t. Jesus hath God raised up. 32
he hath shed forth t. which ye. 33
when they heard t. they were. 37
Israel, why marvel ye at t? 3:12
whereunto t. would grow. 5:24
that t. Jesus of Nazareth shall destroy t. place. 6:14
t. Moses whom they refused. 7:35
as for t. Moses, we wot not. 40
repent therefore of t. thy. 8:22
scripture which he read was t. 32
is not t. he that destroyed? 9:21
when the Gentiles heard t. 13:48
to t. agree the words of the. 15:15
t. did she many days, but. 16:18
when they heard t. they were. 19:5
but t. I confess to thee, that. 24:14
thinkest thou t. O man. Rom 2:3
knowing t. that our old man is. 6:6
not only t. but when Rebecca. 9:10
therefore I have performed t. 15:28
t. I say, every one saith. 1 Cor 1:12
to them that examine me is t. 9:3
in t. that I declare to you. 11:17
shall I praise you in t.? 22
not knowledge, I speak t. to. 15:34
in t. we groan, earnestly. 2 Cor 5:2
I speak not t. to condemn you. 7:3
t. they did, not as we hoped. 8:5
of himself think t. again. 10:7, 11
and t. also we wish, even your. 13:9
t. would I learn of you. Gal 3:2
fulfilled in one word, even in t. 5:14
t. I say therefore, and. Eph 4:17
for t. ye know, that no whoremonger. 5:5
t. I pray, that your love. Phil 1:9
I know that t. shall turn to my. 19
when with you, t. we. 2 Thes 3:10
knowing t. 1 Tim 1:9; Jas 1:3
2 Pet 1:20; 3:3

doing t. thou shalt both. 1 Tim 4:16
but t. with an oath. Heb 7:21
t. did he once. 27
t. the children of God. 1 John 3:10
in t. was manifested the love. 4:9
by t. we know that we love. 5:2
remembrance, though ye once knew t. Jude 5
t. thou hast, that thou hatest. Rev 2:6
see **after, all, book, cause, child, city, day, do, doctrine, done, evil, house, land, law, life, man, month, people, thing, word, world**

is this

the woman, What is t. that thou ?
Gen 3:13; 12:18; 26:10; 29:25
what man is t. that walketh in the ? 24:65
what is t. that God hath ? 42:28
is t. your younger brother ? 43:29
what deed is t. that ye have ? 44:15
saying, What is t.? Ex 13:14
Judg 18:24
is t. that thou hast brought ? Ex 17:3
what trespass is t. ye ? Josh 22:16
what is t. thou hast done ?
Judg 15:11; 2 Sam 12:21
what wickedness is t.? Judg 20:12
what is t. come to the son of Kish ?
1 Sam 10:11
Saul said, Is t. thy voice ? 24:16
is t. the manner of man ? 2 Sam 7:19
is t. thy kindness to thy friend ? 16:17
what confidence is t.? 2 Ki 18:19
is t. a work of one day. Ezra 10:13
who is t. that darkeneth ? Job 38:2
who is t. cometh out of ? S of S 3:6
who is t. that cometh up from ? 8:5
is t. your joyous city ? Isa 23:7
who is t. that cometh from ? 63:1
who is t. that engaged ? Jer 30:21
who is t. that cometh up as ? 46:7
is t. of thy whoredoms a small matter ? Ezek 16:20
is not t. a brand plucked ? Zech 3:2
see what is t. that goeth forth. 5:5
manner of man is t. that the winds ?
Mat 8:27; Mark 4:41; Luke 8:25
said, Is not t. the son ? Mat 12:23
who is t.? 21:10
what thing is t.? Mark 1:27
whence is t. to me, that ? Luke 1:43
a word is t.! with authority he. 4:36
who is t. which speaketh ? 5:21
who is t. that forgiveth sins ? 7:49
but who is t. of whom I hear ? 9:9
he said, What is t. then that ? 20:17
of saying is t. he said ? John 7:36
is t. your son, who ye say was ? 9:19
what is t. that he saith ? 16:17, 18
for our rejoicing is t. 2 Cor 1:12
unto me is t. grace given, that I should preach. Eph 3:8
religion and undefiled is t. Jas 1:27

this is

Adam said, T. is now bone. Gen 2:23
t. is thy kindness which thou. 20:13
T. is none other but the house of God, and t. is the gate of. 28:17
Jacob saw them, he said, T. is. 32:2
Can we find such a one as t. is ? 41:38
for t. is the firstborn. 48:18
t. is my name for ever. Ex 3:15
the magicians said, T. is the. 8:19
t. is that which the Lord. 16:23
t. is that the Lord spake. Lev 10:3
t. is it that belongeth. Num 8:24
and t. is thine, the heave. 18:11
such wickedness as t. is. Deut 13:11
and t. is the manner of the. 15:2
anoint him, for t. is he. 1 Sam 16:12
t. is done of thee. 1 Ki 11:11
t. is the sign which the Lord. 13:3
t. is but a light thing in. 2 Ki 3:18
t. is not the way, neither is. 6:19
t. is the woman, and t. is her. 8:5
so that they shall not say, T. is. 9:37
t. is that king Ahaz. 2 Chr 28:22
t. is nothing but sorrow. Neh 2:2
t. is thy God that brought thee. 9:18
behold, t. is the joy of. Job 8:19

I know that t. is with thee. Job 10:13
t. is the place of him that. 18:21
t. is the portion of a wicked man.
20:29; 27:13
t. is the generation of. Ps 24:6
t. is the hill God desireth to. 68:16
t. is my infirmity, but I will. 77:10
know that t. is thy hand. 109:27
t. is the Lord's. 118:23; Mat 21:42
t. is my comfort in mine. Ps 119:50
t. is my rest for ever, here. 132:14
may be said, See, t. is new. Eccl 1:10
to rejoice in labour, t. is the. 5:19
t. is the whole duty of man. 12:13
t. is my beloved, and t. is. S of S 5:16
sing to the Lord; t. is known. Isa 12:5
lo, t. is our God, we have. 25:9
t. is all the fruit, to take away. 27:9
t. is the rest, and t. is the. 28:12
saying, T. is the way, walk. 30:21
for t. is as the waters of Noah. 54:9
t. is the heritage of the servants. 17
as for me, t. is my covenant. 59:21
t. is thy wickedness, it. Jer 4:18
t. is a nation that obeyeth not. 7:28
t. is a grief. 10:19
t. is thy lot. 13:25
t. is the name whereby . . . The Lord our Righteousness. 23:6; 33:16
t. is Zion, whom no man. 30:17
t. is Jerusalem, I set it. Ezek 5:5
t. is a lamentation, and shall. 19:14
t. is Pharaoh and all his. 31:18
t. is the writing that. Dan 5:25
arise, depart, for t. is not. Mi 2:10
t. is the rejoicing city. Zeph 2:15
t. is the curse that. Zech 5:3
he said, T. is an ephah that. 6
t. is wickedness. 8
for t. is he that was spoken. Mat 3:3
t. is my beloved Son. 17; 17:5
Mark 9:7; Luke 9:35
for t. is the law and. Mat 7:12
t. is he of whom it is written. 10:11
Luke 7:27
t. is Elias which was for. Mat 11:14
t. is he which received seed. 13:19
Jesus said, With men t. is. 19:26
t. is the heir. 21:38; Mark 12:7
Luke 20:14
t. is the first commandment.
Mat 22:38; Mark 12:30
Take, eat, t. is my body. Mat 26:26
t. is my blood. 28; Mark 14:22, 24
Luke 22:19, 20; 1 Cor 11:24, 25
t. is one of them, and. Mark 14:69
manner of woman t. is. Luke 7:39
t. is your hour and the power. 22:53
t. is the record of John. John 1:19
t. is he of whom I said, After. 30
I bare record that t. is the Son. 34
t. is the condemnation, that. 3:19
that t. is indeed the Christ. 4:42
7:26, 41
t. is the work of God, that. 6:29
t. is the Father's will. 39, 40
t. is the bread which cometh. 50
t. is that bread which came. 58
t. is an hard saying, who can ? 60
some said, T. is he. 9:9
we know t. is our son. 20
t. is my commandment, that. 15:12
t. is life eternal, that they. 17:3
t. is that which was spoken by the prophet Joel. Acts 2:16
t. is that Moses which said. 7:37
t. is he that was in the church. 38
Saul increased, proving that t. is very Christ. 9:22
t. is my covenant. Rom 11:27
Heb 8:10; 10:16
t. is not to eat the. 1 Cor 11:20
obey your parents, for t. is. Eph 6:1
if I live, t. is the fruit. Phil 1:22
for t. is well pleasing. Col 3:20
for t. is the will of God. 1 Thes 4:3
5:18
t. is a faithful saying. 1 Tim 1:15
3:1; 4:9; Tit 3:8
for t. is acceptable in the. 1 Tim 2:3
for t. is thankworthy, if. 1 Pet 2:19
take it patiently, t. is acceptable. 20
t. is the message. 1 John 1:5; 3:11
and t. is the promise, even. 2:25

t. is his commandment that we.
1 John 3:23
t. is that spirit of antichrist. 4:3
t. is the love of God, that we. 5:3
and t. is the victory, even our. 4
t. is he that came by water. 6
t. is the witness of God which. 9
t. is the record, that God hath. 11
t. is the confidence that we have. 14
t. is the true God, and eternal. 20
t. is love, that we walk. 2 John 6
t. is a deceiver and an antichrist. 7
years were finished, t. is. Rev 20:5
into lake of fire, t. is the second. 14

thistle

t. that was in Lebanon, a wild . . . the t. 2 Ki 14:9; 2 Chr 25:18
thorn and t. shall come. Hos 10:8

thistles

thorns and t. shall it. Gen 3:18
let t. grow instead of. Job 31:40
do men gather figs of t.? Mat 7:16

thither

near, oh let me escape t. Gen 19:20
escape t. till thou be come t. 22
bring not my son t. 24:6, 8
bring in t. the ark. Ex 26:33
that the slayer may flee t. Num 35:6
11, 15; Deut 4:42; 19:3, 4
Josh 20:3, 9
saying, Thou shalt not go in t.
Deut 1:37, 38, 39
unto his habitation, t. thou. 12:5
t. ye shall bring your burnt. 6, 11
Israel went t. a whoring. Judg 8:27
and t. fled all the men and. 9:51
to Israelites that came t. 1 Sam 2:14
the ark of God about t. 5:8
if the man should come t. 10:22
before it was brought t. 1 Ki 6:7
waters were divided hither and t.
2 Ki 2:8, 14
turned in t. to eat bread. 4:8, 11
t. the Syrians are come down. 6:9
saying, Carry t. one of the. 17:27
resort ye t. to us: our God. Neh 4:20
t. brought I again the vessels. 13:9
they came t. and were. Job 6:20
the rain returneth not t. Isa 55:10
he shall not return t. Jer 22:11
but to the land, t. shall they not. 27
t. was their spirit to go. Ezek 1:20
Israel shall come t. and shall. 11:18
these waters shall come t. 47:9
t. cause thy mighty ones. Joel 3:11
he was afraid to go t. Mat 2:22
t. will the eagles be. Luke 17:37
where I am, t. ye. John 7:34, 36
and goest thou t. again ? 11:8
Jesus ofttimes resorted t. 18:2
Judas cometh t. with lanterns. 3
Philip ran t. to him, and. Acts 8:30
women which resorted t. 16:13

thitherward

t. and came to Micah's. Judg 18:15
Zion, with their faces t. Jer 50:5

Thomas

T. and Matthew the. Mat 10:3
Mark 3:18; Luke 6:15; Acts 1:13
T. said, Let us go and. John 11:16
T. was not with them when. 20:24
T. was with them. 26
T. Reach hither thy finger. 27
Simon Peter and T. 21:2

thongs

as they bound him with t. Acts 22:25

thorn

(There are some 18 or 20 Hebrew words which point to different kinds of prickly shrubs, which are variously rendered in the Authorized Version. Probably there is no other country where so many plants of this sort exist. There are at least 200 different species of thorny plants found there)

bore his jaw through with a t.?
Job 41:2*
as a t. goeth into the hand. Pr 26:9
instead of the t. shall. Isa 55:13
no more any grieving t. Ezek 28:24
the t. shall come up on. Hos 10:8

is sharper than a t. hedge. Mi 7:4
there was given me a t. 2 Cor 12:7

thorns

t. and thistles shall it. Gen 3:18
break out and catch in t. Ex 22:6
they shall be t. in your sides.
Num 33:55; Judg 2:3
but they shall be t. in your eyes.
Josh 23:13
of Belial shall be as t. 2 Sam 23:6
Manasseh among the t. 2 Chr 33:11*
pots can feel the t., he shall. Ps 58:9
quenched as the fire of t. 118:12
man is an hedge of t. Pr 15:19
t. and snares are in the way. 22:5
was all grown over with t. 24:31
as the crackling of t. under. Eccl 7:6
as the lily among t. so is. S of S 2:2
they shall rest upon all t. Isa 7:19
as t. cut up shall they be. 33:12
and t. shall come up in her. 34:13
and sow not among t. Jer 4:3
sown wheat, but shall reap t. 12:13
hedge up thy way with t. Hos 2:6
t. shall be in their tabernacles. 9:6
be folden together as t. Nah 1:10
do men gather grapes of t.?
Mat 7:16; Luke 6:44
fell among t. Mat 13:7, 22
Mark 4:7, 18; Luke 8:7, 14
platted a crown of t. Mat 27:29
Mark 15:17; John 19:2
see **briers**

those

Esau said, Who are t.? Gen 33:5
let them be of t. that. 1 Ki 2:7
upon t. did Solomon levy a. 9:21
t. did Cyrus king of Persia. Ezra 1:8
did what they would to t. Esth 9:5
to set up on high t. Job 5:11
seeing he judgeth t. that. 21:22
are of t. that rebel. 24:13
so doth the grave t. which. 19
t. that remain of him shall. 27:15
t. that wait on the Lord. Ps 37:9
t. that have made a covenant. 50:5
t. planted in house of Lord. 92:13
t. that fear thee turn unto me, and t.
that have known thy. 119:79
to do to t. that love thy name. 132
am not I grieved with t. that? 139:21
t. that seek me early shall. Pr 8:17
with t. that shall come. Eccl 1:11
but it shall be for t. Isa 35:8
t. that remember thee in thy ways,
in those is continuance. 64:5
t. will I let remain in. Jer 27:11
t. that walk in pride he. Dan 4:37
t. that have not sought. Zeph 1:6
thou savourest t. things. Mat 16:23
among t. that are born. Luke 7:28
but t. mine enemies bring. 19:27
woman, where are t.? John 8:10
keep through thy name t. thou. 17:11
t. that thou gavest me I have. 12
from Samuel and t. that. Acts 3:24
there come in t. that. 1 Cor 14:23
what things were gain, t. I. Phil 3:7
Saviour, especially of t. 1 Tim 4:10
belongeth to t. who by. Heb 5:14
an ensample to t. that. 2 Pet 2:6
allure t. that were clean escaped. 18
see **days, things**

thou

the woman whom t. gavest. Gen 3:12
know thou, that t. shalt surely die, t.
20:7; 1 Sam 22:16
t. art our sister, be t. Gen 24:60
t. art now the blessed of the. 26:29
discreet and wise as t. art. 41:39
throne will I be greater than t. 40
t. shalt be near to me, t. and. 45:10
t. art he whom thy brethren. 49:8
t. shalt come up, t. and. Ex 19:24
t. and all the company. Num 16:11
be t. and they, and Aaron before. 16
may rest as well as t. Deut 5:14
nations mightier than t. 7:1; 20:1
t. hast not known, t. nor. 13:6; 28:64
that both t. and thy seed. 30:19
that is better than t. 1 Sam 15:28
T. are more righteous than I. 24:17
blessed be t. that kept me. 25:33

Nathan said to David T. 2 Sam 12:7
said, Of what city art t.? 15:2
T. and Ziba divide the land. 19:29
t. even t. knowest the. 1 Ki 8:39
t. and thy father's house. 18:18
order the battle? he said T. 20:14
that when I and t. rode. 2 Ki 9:25
that t. shouldest fall, even t. and.
14:10; 2 Chr 25:19
t. art the God, even t. 2 Ki 19:15
19; Neh 9:6; Isa 37:20
but t. art a God, ready to. Neh 9:17
t. and thy father's house shall be
. . . whether t. art. Esth 4:14
which are higher than t. Job 35:5
I will fear no evil, for t. Ps 23:4
it was t., a man mine equal. 55:13
t. art he that took me out of. 71:6
t. even t. art to be feared, and who
may stand . . . once t. art? 76:7
t. whose name is Jehovah. 83:18
t. art the same, thy years. 102:27
they may know, that t. Lord. 109:27
t. art my God, and I will. 118:28
t. art my hiding place. 119:114
arise into thy rest, t. and ark. 132:8
up into heaven, t. art there. 139:8
tell me, O t. whom my. S of S 1:7
t. art my servant, I have. Isa 41:9
and saith, Deliver me, for t. 44:17
verily t. art a God that hidest. 45:15
who art t., that t. shouldest be? 51:12
t. art our father t. O Lord. 63:16
to me, I am holier than t. 65:5
t. shalt continue from. Jer 17:4
there t. shalt die, t. and all thy. 20:6
will ye die, t. and thy people? 27:13
t. O Lord, remainest for. Lam 5:19
O t. that dwellest in the. Ezek 7:7
more righteous than t. 16:52
it is t. O king, that art. Dan 4:22
t. his son hast not humbled. 5:32
whence comest t.? of what people art
t.? Jonah 1:8
O t. that art named the. Mi 2:7
t. O tower of the flock, to thee. 4:8
art t. not from everlasting? Hab 1:12
art t. O great mountain? Zech 4:7
but t. when t. prayest. Mat 6:6
but t. when t. fastest, anoint. 17
t. art the Christ, the Son of the. 16:16
Mark 8:29; Luke 4:41; John 11:27
not as I will, but as t. wilt. Mat 26:39
saying, T. also wast with Jesus. 69
Mark 14:67
hail, t. that art highly. Luke 1:28
saying, Art t. he that? 7:19, 20
lest a more honourable than t. 14:8
owest t. unto my lord? 16:5, 7
t. in thy lifetime receivedst thy
good things . . . and t. art. 25
if thou hadst known, even t. 19:42
to ask him, Who art t.? John 1:19
22; 8:25; 21:12
they asked, art t. Elias? art t.? 1:21
t. art Simon thou shalt be called. 42
art t. a master in Israel? 3:10
that t. being a Jew, askest. 4:9
to him, Art t. also of Galilee? 7:52
but what sayest t.? 8:5
t. art his disciple. 9:28
t. hast seen him, and he. 37
I in them, and t. in me, that. 17:23
art not t. one of this man's? 18:17
t. Lord, who knowest. Acts 1:24
t. art in the gall of bitterness. 8:23
whereby t. and thy house. 11:14
t. child of the devil, t. enemy, wilt t.
not cease to pervert the? 13:10
t. art my son, this day have I. 33
art not t. that Egyptian which? 21:38
tell me, art t. a Roman? he. 22:27
I would, that not only t. but. 26:29
t. therefore which teachest another.
Rom 2:21
but be t. an example. 1 Tim 4:12
t. O man of God, flee these. 6:11
be not t. ashamed of the. 2 Tim 1:8
t. therefore, my son, be strong. 2:1
t. therefore receive him. Philem 12
t., Lord, hast laid the foundation of
the earth. Heb 1:10
they shall be changed, but t. art. 12
who art t. that judgest? Jas 4:12

t. art worthy, O Lord, to. Rev 4:11
t. art worthy to take the book. 5:9
see **alone**

though

vine was as t. it budded. Gen 40:10
t. he wist it not, yet is. Lev 5:17
thou shalt relieve him, t. he be. 25:35
t. I walk in the imagination of.
Deut 29:19
drive out Canaanites, t. they have
iron chariots and t. Josh 17:18
t. thou detain me, I will. Judg 13:16
t. ye have done this, yet will. 15:7
t. I be not like one of thy hand-
maidens. Ruth 2:13
t. it be in Jonathan. 1 Sam 14:39
I will shoot arrows, as t. I. 20:20
t. it were sanctified this day. 21:5
I am this day weak, t. 2 Sam 3:39
t. I should receive a thousand. 18:12
t. there were of you cast. Neh 1:9
t. he slay me, yet will I. Job 13:15
t. wickedness be sweet in. 20:12
what the hypocrite's hope, t. 27:8
t. he heap up silver as the dust. 16
as t. he had been my friend or.
Ps 35:14
t. he fall, he shall not utterly. 37:24
t. the Lord be high, yet hath. 138:6
t. hand join in hand. Pr 11:21; 16:5
than he that is perverse, t. 28:6
t. he understand, he will not. 29:19
the wayfaring men t. fools. Isa 35:8
surnamed thee, t. thou hast not.
45:4, 5
he cause grief, yet will he. Lam 3:32
t. briers and thorns be with thee, t.
Ezek 2:6; 3:9; 12:3
t. these three men. 14:14, 16, 18, 20
t. thou be sought for, yet. 26:21
not humbled, t. thou. Dan 5:22
t. thou be little among. Mi 5:2
t. they be quiet, and. Nah 1:12
ye will not believe, t. it. Hab 1:5
t. it tarry, wait for it, it will. 2:3
t. I should die with thee. Mat 26:35
face was as t. he would. Luke 9:53
avenge his elect, t. he bear. 18:7
he made as t. he would have. 24:28
wrote on the ground, as t. John 8:6
t. ye believe not me, believe. 10:38
t. he were dead, yet shall. 11:25
as t. by our own power we. Acts 3:12
ye shall not believe, t. a man. 13:41
as t. he needed any thing. 17:25
t. he be not far from every one. 27
as t. ye would enquire. 23:15, 20
t. he hath escaped the sea. 28:4
things which be not, as t. Rom 4:17
no adulteress, t. she be married. 7:3
that have wives, be as t. 1 Cor 7:29
as t. they wept not, as t. they. 30
but t. our outward man. 2 Cor 4:16
t. he was rich, yet for our sakes. 8:9
for t. we walk in the flesh, we. 10:3
in nothing am I behind, t. I. 12:11
do what is honest, t. we be. 13:7
t. we or an angel preach. Gal 1:8
heir differeth nothing t. he be. 4:1
t. I might also have confidence in.
Phil 3:4
not as t. I had attained or were. 12
t. I be absent in the flesh. Col 2:5
why, as t. living, are ye subject. 20
t. he were a son, yet learned.
Heb 5:8
better things, t. we thus speak. 6:9
t. he sought it carefully with. 12:17
t. a man say he hath faith. Jas 2:14
as t. some strange thing. 1 Pet 4:12
put you in remembrance, t. ye know.
2 Pet 1:12
put you in remembrance, t. ye once
knew this. Jude 5

thought

I t. the fear of God is not. Gen 20:11
Judah saw her, he t. her to. 38:15
Israel said, I had not t. to. 48:11
but as for you, ye t. evil. 50:20*
of the evil he t. to do. Ex 32:14*
I t. to promote thee to. Num 24:11
I shall do unto you, as I t. 33:56
ye do to him, as ye t. Deut 19:19

I verily *t.* that thou hadst hated her. *Judg* 15:2
the men of Gibeah *t.* to have. 20:5
therefore Eli *t.* she had. *1 Sam* 1:13
Saul *t.* to make David fall. 18:25
who *t.* that I would have given him a reward. *2 Sam* 4:10*
Amnon *t.* it hard to do any. 13:2
Ishbi-benob *t.* to have slain. 21:16
I *t.* he will surely come. *2 Ki* 5:11
Rehoboam *t.* to make. *2 Chr* 11:22*
Sennacherib *t.* to win them. 32:1
t. to do me mischief. *Neh* 6:2
he *t.* scorn to lay hands. *Esth* 3:6
Haman *t.* in his heart, to. 6:6*
we have *t.* of thy loving. *Ps* 48:9
when I *t.* to know this, it was 73:16
I *t.* on my ways, and turned. 119:59
if thou hast *t.* evil, lay. *Pr* 30:32
as I have *t.* so shall it. *Isa* 14:24
of the evil I *t.* to do. *Jer* 18:8
Lord of hosts *t.* to do to us. *Zech* 1:6
as I *t.* to punish you. 8:14
I *t.* to do well. 15
a book for them that *t.* *Mal* 3:16
but while he *t.* on these. *Mat* 1:20
and when he *t.* thereon. *Mark* 14:72
nor *t.* I myself worthy. *Luke* 7:7
he *t.* within himself, what. 12:17*
they *t.* the kingdom of God. 19:11*
they *t.* he had spoken. *John* 11:13
t. the gift of God may. *Acts* 8:20
while Peter *t.* on the vision. 10:19
wist not it was true, but *t.* he. 12:9
Paul *t.* not good to take him. 15:38
why should it be *t.* a thing? 26:8*
I *t.* that I ought to do many things. 9
when I was a child, I *t.* *1 Cor* 13:11
t. it not robbery to be. *Phil* 2:6*
punishment he be *t.* *Heb* 10:29*

thought, *substantive*

that there be not a *t.* in. *Deut* 15:9
my father take *t.* for us. *1 Sam* 9:5†
is despised in the *t.* of him. *Job* 12:5
that no *t.* can be withholden. 42:2*
their *t.* is, their houses. *Ps* 49:11
the inward *t.* of every one of. 64:6
thou understandest my *t.* 139:2
t. of foolishness is sin. *Pr* 24:9
king, no not in thy *t.* *Eccl* 10:20
shalt think an evil *t.* *Ezek* 38:10*
to man what is his *t.* *Amos* 4:13
I say to you, Take no *t.* *Mat* 6:25* 31, 34*; 10:19*; *Mark* 13:11* *Luke* 12:11*, 22*
which of you by taking *t.* can add one cubit? *Mat* 6:27*; *Luke* 12:25*
why take *ye t.* for raiment? *Mat* 6:28*; *Luke* 12:26*
if the *t.* of thy heart. *Acts* 8:22
bringing into captivity every *t.* to the obedience of Christ. *2 Cor* 10:5

thoughtest

thou *t.* I was such a one. *Ps* 50:21

thoughts

imagination of the *t.* of his. *Gen* 6:5
for Reuben there were great *t.* of heart. *Judg* 5:15*
understandeth the *t.* *1 Chr* 28:9
the imagination of the *t.* 29:18
in *t.* from the visions. *Job* 4:13
are broken off, even my *t.* 17:11
therefore do my *t.* cause me. 20:2
I know your *t.* and devices. 21:27
God is not in all his *t.* *Ps* 10:4
and the *t.* of his heart to all. 33:11
thy *t.* cannot be reckoned. 40:5
all their *t.* are against me. 56:5
thy works! thy *t.* are very deep. 92:5
Lord knoweth the *t.* of man. 94:11
in the multitude of my *t.* 19
I hate vain *t.* but thy law. 119:113*
how precious are thy *t.* 139:17
O God, try me, and know my *t.* 23
in that very day his *t.* perish. 146:4
the *t.* of the righteous. *Pr* 12:5
the *t.* of the wicked are an. 15:26*
and thy *t.* shall be established. 16:3
the *t.* of the diligent tend to. 21:5
man forsake his *t.* *Isa* 55:7
for my *t.* are not your *t.* saith. 8
so are my *t.* higher than your *t.* 9
evil their *t.* are *t.* of iniquity. 59:7
walketh after their own *t.* *Isa* 65:2
their works and their *t.* 66:18
vain *t.* lodge in thee? *Jer* 4:14
even the fruit of their *t.* 6:19
till he have performed the *t.* 23:20*
I know the *t.* that I think towards you, *t.* of peace and not. 29:11
mightest know the *t.* of. *Dan* 2:30
Nebuchadnezzar's *t.* upon bed. 4:5
Daniel was astonished, and his *t.* 19
Belshazzar's *t.* troubled him. 5:6
Let not thy *t.* trouble thine. 10
but they know not the *t.* *Mi* 4:12
Jesus, knowing their *t.* said. *Mat* 9:4 12:25; *Luke* 5:22*; 6:8; 9:47 11:17
out of the heart proceed evil *t.* *Mat* 15:19; *Mark* 7:21
the *t.* of many hearts. *Luke* 2:35
and why do *t.* arise in your? 24:38*
their *t.* accusing, or else. *Rom* 2:15
the Lord knoweth the *t.* *1 Cor* 3:20*
God is a discerner of the *t.* *Heb* 4:12
become judges of evil *t.* *Jas* 2:4

thousand

thy brother a *t.* pieces. *Gen* 20:16
of every tribe a *t.* shall ye send to the war. *Num* 31:4, 5, 6
suburbs of cities are *t.* cubits. 35:4
you a *t.* times so many. *Deut* 1:11
covenant to a *t.* generations. 7:9
how should one chase a *t.*? 32:30 *Josh* 23:10
died, about a *t.* men. *Judg* 9:49
Samson slew a *t.* men. 15:15, 16
an hundred of a *t.*, a *t.* out of. 20:10
the captain of their *t.* *1 Sam* 17:18
David his captain over a *t.* 18:13
three *t.* sheep and a *t.* goats. 25:2
from him a *t.* chariots and seven. *2 Sam* 8:4; *1 Chr* 18:4
though I should receive a *t.* 18:12
t. men of Benjamin with him. 19:17
a *t.* burnt offerings did Solomon. *1 Ki* 3:4; *2 Chr* 1:6
gave Pul a *t.* talents. *2 Ki* 15:19
craftsmen and smiths a *t.* 24:16
greatest was over a *t.* *1 Chr* 12:14
of Naphtali a *t.* captains, and. 34
word he commanded to a *t.* 16:15
Ammon sent a *t.* talents. 19:6
sacrifices unto the Lord a *t.* bullocks, a *t.* rams, and a *t.* lambs. 29:21
did give a *t.* bullocks. *2 Chr* 30:24
bring forth a *t.* chargers. *Ezra* 1:9
gold, and other vessels a *t.* 10
answer him one of a *t.* *Job* 9:3
interpreter, one of a *t.* 33:23
t. yoke of oxen, a *t.* she asses. 42:12
cattle on a *t.* hills are. *Ps* 50:10
day in courts is better than a *t.* 84:10
a *t.* years in thy sight are but. 90:4
a *t.* shall fall at thy side, and. 91:7
yea, though he live a *t.* *Eccl* 6:6
one man among a *t.* have I. 7:28
whereon there hang a *t.* *S of S* 4:4
fruit was to bring a *t.* pieces. 8:11
thou, O Solomon, must have a *t.* 12
a *t.* vines, at a *t.* silverlings. *Isa* 7:23
one *t.* shall flee at the rebuke. 30:17
a little one shall become a *t.* 60:22
measured a *t.* cubits. *Ezek* 47:3
again he measured a *t.* and. 4, 5
feast to a *t.* of his lords, and drank wine before the *t.* *Dan* 5:1
out by a *t.* shall leave. *Amos* 5:3
day is with the Lord as a *t.* years, and a *t.* years as one day. *2 Pet* 3:8
bound Satan a *t.* years. *Rev* 20:2
deceive nations no more, till *t.* 3
reigned with Christ a *t.* years. 4
and when the *t.* years are expired. 7

one **thousand** *two hundred sixty*

prophesy *one t.* 260 days. *Rev* 11:3
feed her *one t.* 260 days. 12:6

one **thousand** *two hundred ninety*

be *one t.* 290 days. *Dan* 12:11

one **thousand** *three hundred thirty-five*

to the *t.* 335 days. *Dan* 12:12

one **thousand** *six hundred*

of *one t.* 600 furlongs. *Rev* 14:20

two **thousand**

two t. cubits, on the west side *two t.*, south side *two t.* *Num* 35:5
you and the ark *two t.* *Josh* 3:4
sea contained *two t.* baths. *1 Ki* 7:26
deliver thee *two t.* horses if thou be able. *2 Ki* 18:23; *Isa* 36:8
gave *two t.* pounds of. *Neh* 7:72
about *two t.* swine were. *Mark* 5:13

two **thousand** *two hundred*

two t. 200 pounds of silver. *Neh* 7:71

two **thousand** *three hundred*

two t. 300 days, sanctuary. *Dan* 8:14

two hundred **thousand**

captive of brethren 200 *t.* *2 Chr* 28:8

two hundred eighty **thousand**

out of Benjamin *two hundred eighty t.* *2 Chr* 14:8

two hundred **thousand thousand**

of horsemen were *two hundred thousand thousand.* *Rev* 9:16*

three **thousand**

of the people *three t.* *Ex* 32:28
to Ai about *three t.* men. *Josh* 7:4
three t. went to bind. *Judg* 15:11
upon the roof *three t.* men. 16:27
Saul chose *three t.* men. *2 Sam* 13:2
took *three t.* chosen men. 24:2; 26:2
three t. sheep and a *t.* goats. 25:2
spake *three t.* proverbs. *1 Ki* 4:32
sea held *three t.* baths. *2 Chr* 4:5
his substance was *three t.* *Job* 1:3
captive *three t.* Jews. *Jer* 52:28
to them *three t.* souls. *Acts* 2:41

four **thousand**

Israel about *four t.* men. *1 Sam* 4:2
four t. porters, *four t.* *1 Chr* 23:5
Solomon had *four t.* stalls for horses. *2 Chr* 9:25
they that did eat were *four t.* *Mat* 15:38; *Mark* 8:9
seven loaves among *four t.* *Mat* 16:10; *Mark* 8:20
wilderness *four t.* men. *Acts* 21:38

four **thousand** *five hundred*

of the city *four t.* 500 measures, east side . . . *four t.* 500 measures. *Ezek* 48:16, 30, 32, 33, 34

five **thousand**

about *five t.* men. *Josh* 8:12
of them *five t.* men. *Judg* 20:45
of gold *five t.* talents. *1 Chr* 29:7
for offerings *five t.* *2 Chr* 35:9
they gave *five t.* pounds. *Ezra* 2:69
eaten were about *five t.* *Mat* 14:21
neither remember the five loaves of the *five t.* 16:9; *Mark* 6:44; 8:19 *Luke* 9:14; *John* 6:10
number that believed were about *five t.* *Acts* 4:4

five **thousand** *four hundred*

and silver *five t.* 400. *Ezra* 1:11

six **thousand**

with *six t.* horsemen. *1 Sam* 13:5
six t. pieces of gold. *2 Ki* 5:5
and *six t.* were officers. *1 Chr* 23:4
for Job had *six t.* camels. *Job* 42:12

six **thousand** *seven hunderd and twenty*

asses, *six t. seven hundred and twenty.* *Ezra* 2:67; *Neh* 7:69

seven **thousand**

seven t. in Israel who have not. *1 Ki* 19:18; *Rom* 11:4
Israel, being *seven t.* *1 Ki* 20:15
men of might, *seven t.* *2 Ki* 24:16
mighty men, *seven t.* *1 Chr* 12:25
from him *seven t.* horsemen. 18:4
the Syrians *seven t.* men. 19:18
I prepared *seven t.* talents of. 29:4
they offered *seven t.* *2 Chr* 15:11
congregation *seven t.* sheep. 30:24
also was *seven t.* sheep. *Job* 1:3
were slain *seven t.* men. *Rev* 11:13

seven **thousand** *seven hundred*

brought Jehoshaphat *seven t.* 700 rams, *seven t.* 700. *2 Chr* 17:11

ten **thousand**

an hundred shall put *ten t.* *Lev* 26:8
two put *ten t.* to flight? *Deut* 32:30

them in Bezek *ten t.* men. *Judg* 1:4
they slew of Moab *ten t.* men. 3:29
Barak, go, and take *ten t.* men. 4:6
he went up with *ten t.* men. 10, 14
remained to Gideon *ten t.* 7:3
against Gibeah *ten t.* men. 20:34
art worth *ten t.* of us. *2 Sam* 18:3
Lebanon, *ten t.* a month. *1 Ki* 5:14
Jehoahaz *ten t.* footmen. *2 Ki* 13:7
Edom in the valley *ten t.* 14:7
away even *ten t.* captives. 24:14
children of Seir *ten t.* *2 Chr* 25:11
other *ten t.* left alive, did Judah. 12
gave Jotham the same year *ten t.* . . . *ten t.* of barley. 27:5
congregation *ten t.* sheep 30:24
I will pay *ten t.* talents. *Esth* 3:9
ten t. shall fall at thy. *Ps* 91:7
chiefest among *ten t.* *S of S* 5:10
the breadth of the land shall be *ten t.* *Ezek* 45:1, 3, 5; 48:9, 10, 13, 18
ten t. times *ten t.* stood. *Dan* 7:10
him *ten t.* talents. *Mat* 18:24
able with *ten t.* to meet. *Luke* 14:31
though ye have *ten t.* *1 Cor* 4:15
than *ten t.* words in an. 14:19
was *ten t.* times *ten t.* *Rev* 5:11

twelve **thousand**

fell of Ai were *twelve t.* *Josh* 8:25
sent *twelve t.* men to. *Judg* 21:10
Solomon had *twelve t.* *1 Ki* 4:26
10:26; *2 Chr* 1:14; 9:25
of tribe of Juda, Reuben, Gad, sealed *twelve t.* *Rev* 7:5
of Aser, Naphthalim, Manasses, sealed *twelve t.* 6
of Simeon, Levi, Issachar, were sealed *twelve t.* 7
of Zabulon, Joseph, Benjamin, sealed *twelve t.* 8
city *twelve t.* furlongs. 21:16

fourteen **thousand**

Job had *fourteen t.* sheep. *Job* 42:12

fourteen **thousand** *seven hundred*

plague *fourteen t.* 700. *Num* 16:49

sixteen **thousand**

were *sixteen t.* *Num* 31:40, 46

sixteen **thousand** *seven hundred fifty*

gold of offering *sixteen t. seven hundred* and *fifty.* *Num* 31:52

seventeen **thousand** *two hundred*

sons of Jediael *seven t. two hundred.* *1 Chr* 7:11

eighteen **thousand**

Israel *eighteen t.* men. *Judg* 20:25
of Benjamin *eighteen t.* men. 44
Manasseh *eighteen t.* *1 Chr* 12:31
of the Edomites *eighteen t.* 18:12
they gave of brass *eighteen t.* 29:7

twenty **thousand**

Hadadezer king of Zobah, *twenty t.* *2 Sam* 8:4; *1 Chr* 18:4
of Ammon hired Syrians, *twenty t.* *2 Sam* 10:6
Absalom's company *twenty t.* 18:7
Hiram *twenty t.* measures of wheat. *1 Ki* 5:11; *2 Chr* 2:10
work *twenty t.* drams. *Neh* 7:71, 72
chariots of God *twenty t.* *Ps* 68:17
cometh, with *twenty t.* *Luke* 14:31

twenty two **thousand**

Levites *twenty two t.* *Num* 3:39
males were *twenty two t.* 43
Simeonites *twenty two t.* 26:14
returned of Gideon's army *twenty two t.* *Judg* 7:3
of Israel *twenty two t.* 20:21
David slew of the Syrians *twenty two t.* *2 Sam* 8:5; *1 Chr* 18:5
Solomon offered *twenty two t.* oxen. *1 Ki* 8:63; *2 Chr* 7:5
of Tola *twenty two t.* *1 Chr* 7:2
of Bela *twenty two t.* 7

twenty three **thousand**

Levites *twenty three t.* *Num* 26:62
day *three* and *twenty t.* *1 Cor* 10:8

twenty four **thousand**

plague *twenty four t.* *Num* 25:9
twenty four t. Levites to forward. *1 Chr* 23:4
served were *twenty four t.* 27:1

twenty five **thousand**

destroyed of Benjamites *twenty five t.* *Judg* 20:35, 46
of land *twenty five t.* *Ezek* 45:1
3, 5, 6; 48:8, 9, 10, 13

twenty six **thousand**

numbered *twenty six t.* *Judg* 20:15
apt to war, *twenty six t.* *1 Chr* 7:40

twenty seven **thousand**

twenty seven t. men. *1 Ki* 20:30

twenty eight **thousand**

expert in war, *twenty eight t.* *1 Chr* 12:35

thirty **thousand**

and the asses were *thirty t.* *Num* 31:39, 45
Joshua chose *thirty t.* *Josh* 8:3
Israel *thirty t.* footmen. *1 Sam* 4:10
men of Judah were *thirty t.* 11:8
Philistines gathered *thirty t.* 13:5
David gathered *thirty t.* *2 Sam* 6:1
levy was *thirty t.* men. *1 Ki* 5:13

thirty two **thousand**

thirty two t. women. *Num* 31:35
Ammon hired *thirty two t.* chariots. *1 Chr* 19:7

thirty two **thousand** *two hundred*

number of Manasseh *thirty two t. two hundred.* *Num* 1:35; 2:21

thirty two **thousand** *five hundred*

of Ephraim were numbered *thirty two t. five hundred.* *Num* 26:37

thirty three **thousand**

gave *thirty three t.* *2 Chr* 35:7

thirty five **thousand**

of Benjamin were *thirty five t.* *Num* 1:37

thirty six **thousand**

were *thirty* and *six t.* *Num* 31:38
congregation *thirty six t.* beeves. 44
soldiers were *thirty six t.* *1 Chr* 7:4

thirty seven **thousand**

Naphtali *thirty* and *seven t.* *1 Chr* 12:34

thirty eight **thousand**

Levites from thirty years, *thirty eight t.* *1 Chr* 23:3

forty **thousand**

about *forty t.* prepared. *Josh* 4:13
was there a shield seen among *forty t.*? *Judg* 5:8
David slew *forty t.* *2 Sam* 10:18
Solomon had *forty t.* *1 Ki* 4:26
expert in war, *forty t.* *1 Chr* 12:36
slew of Assyrians *forty t.* 19:18

forty **thousand** *five hundred*

of Ephraim were *forty t. five hundred.* *Num* 1:33; 2:19
Gad were numbered *forty t.* and *five hundred.* 26:18

forty one **thousand** *five hundred*

of Asher numbered *forty one t. five hundred.* *Num* 1:41; 2:28

forty two **thousand**

Ephraimites *forty two t.* *Judg* 12:6
whole congregation *forty two t.* *Ezra* 2:64; *Neh* 7:66

forty three **thousand** *seven hundred thirty*

of Reubenites *forty three t. seven hundred thirty.* *Num* 26:7

forty four **thousand** *seven hundred sixty*

of Reubenites to war *forty four t. seven hundred sixty.* *1 Chr* 5:18

forty five **thousand** *four hundred*

of Naphtali were *forty five t. four hundred.* *Num* 26:50

forty five **thousand** *six hundred*

of Benjamin *forty five t. six hundred.* *Num* 26:41

forty five **thousand** *six hundred fifty*

numbered of Gad *forty five t. six hundred fifty.* *Num* 1:25; 2:15

forty six **thousand** *five hundred*

of Reuben *forty six t.* and *five hundred.* *Num* 1:21, 2:11

fifty **thousand**

the Lord smote *fifty t.* *1 Sam* 6:19
Hagarites' sheep *fifty t.* *1 Chr* 5:21
of Zebulun *fifty t.* could keep. 12:33
the book *fifty t.* pieces. *Acts* 19:19

fifty two **thousand** *seven hundred*

of Manasseh *fifty two t.* and *seven hundred.* *Num* 26:34

fifty three **thousand** *four hundred*

of Naphtali *fifty three t. four hundred.* *Num* 1:43; 2:30

fifty four **thousand** *four hundred*

of Issachar *fifty four t. four hundred.* *Num* 1:29; 2:6

fifty seven **thousand** *four hundred*

of Zebulun *fifty seven t. four hundred.* *Num* 1:31; 2:8

fifty nine **thousand** *three hundred*

of Simeon *fifty nine t. three hundred.* *Num* 1:23; 2:13

sixty **thousand**

sixty t. horsemen. *2 Chr* 12:3

sixty **thousand** *five hundred*

of Zebulunites, *sixty t.* and *five hundred.* *Num* 26:27

sixty one **thousand**

was *sixty one t.* asses. *Num* 31:34
they gave *sixty one t.* *Ezra* 2:69

sixty two **thousand** *seven hundred*

of tribe of Dan *sixty two t. seven hundred.* *Num* 1:39; 2:26

sixty four **thousand** *three hundred*

of Issachar *sixty four t.* and *three hundred.* *Num* 26:25

sixty four **thousand** *four hundred*

of the Shuhamites *sixty four t. four hundred.* *Num* 26:43

seventy **thousand**

the people *seventy t.* *2 Sam* 24:15
Solomon had *seventy t.* that bare. *1 Ki* 5:15; *2 Chr* 2:2, 18
fell of Israel *seventy t.* *1 Chr* 21:14

seventy two **thousand**

booty of beeves was *seventy two t.* *Num* 31:33

seventy four **thousand** *six hundred*

number of Judah *seventy four t.* and *six hundred.* *Num* 1:27; 2:4

seventy five **thousand**

seventy five t. sheep. *Num* 31:32
their foes *seventy five t.* *Esth* 9:16

seventy six **thousand** *five hundred*

numbered of Judah *seventy six t. five hundred.* *Num* 26:22

eighty **thousand**

Solomon had *eighty t.* hewers in the. *1 Ki* 5:15; *2 Chr* 2:2, 18

eighty seven **thousand**

of Issachar, reckoned *eighty seven t.* *1 Chr* 7:5

thousand thousand

of Israel were *a t. t.* *1 Chr* 21:5
have prepared a *t. t.* talents. 22:14
came with a host of *a t. t.* *2 Chr* 14:9

two hundred **thousand thousand**

army of horsemen *two hundred t. t.* *Rev* 9:16

thousands

be thou the mother of *t.* *Gen* 24:60
over them rulers of *t.* *Ex* 18:21, 25
shewing mercy to *t.* of them. 20:6
Deut 5:10
keeping mercy for *t.* *Ex* 34:7
heads of *t.* in Israel. *Num* 1:16
10:4; *Josh* 22:14, 21, 30
to the many *t.* of Israel. *Num* 10:36
were delivered out of the *t.* 31:5
them captains over *t.* *Deut* 1:15
the Lord came with ten *t.* of saints. 33:2; *Jude* 14
are the *t.* of Manasseh. *Deut* 33:17
him captains over *t.* *1 Sam* 8:12
yourselves by your *t.* 10:19
they have ascribed but *t.* 18:8
make you all captains of *t.*? 22:7
search him out throughout *t.* 23:23
Philistines passed on by *t.* 29:2

people came out by *t.* *2 Sam* 18:4
thy law is better than *t.* *Ps* 119:72
lovingkindness unto *t.* *Jer* 32:18
thousand *t.* ministered. *Dan* 7:10
thou be little among the *t.* *Mi* 5:2
Lord be pleased with *t.* of rams ? 6:7
how many *t.* of Jews. *Acts* 21:20
number of them was *t.* of *t.* *Rev* 5:11
see **captains**

ten **thousands**

the *ten t.* of Ephraim. *Deut* 33:17
David slain his *ten t.* *1 Sam* 18:7 8; 21:11; 29:5
I will not be afraid of *ten t.* *Ps* 3:6
sheep may bring forth *ten t.* 144:13
cast down many *ten t.* *Dan* 11:12
ten t. of rivers of oil. *Mi* 6:7

thread

take from a *t.* to a latchet. *Gen* 14:23
his hand a scarlet *t.* 38:28, 30
shalt bind this scarlet *t.* *Josh* 2:18
withs as a *t.* of tow. *Judg* 16:9*
ropes from his arms as a *t.* 12
thy lips are like a *t.* of. *S of S* 4:3

threaten, -ed

but let us straitly *t.* them not to. *Acts* 4:17, 21
when he suffered he *t.* not. *1 Pet* 2:23

threatening, -s

Lord, behold their *t.* and. *Acts* 4:29
Saul yet breathing out *t.* and. 9:1
same things unto them, forbearing *t.* *Eph* 6:9

three

he looked, and lo, *t.* men. *Gen* 18:2
not these *t.* unto her. *Ex* 21:11
t. branches of the candlestick. 25:32; 37:18
t. bowls made like unto. 33; 37:19
altar shall be *t.* cubits. 27:1; 38:1
pillars *t.*, their sockets *t.* 14, 15 38:14, 15
t. tenth deals of fine flour for a meat. *Lev* 14:10; *Num* 15:9; 28:12
for the female estimation *t.* *Lev* 27:6
come out ye *t.* And they *t.* came out. *Num* 12:4
t. tenth deals for a bullock. 28:20 28; 29:3, 9, 14
ye shall give *t.* cities on this. 35:14
Moses severed *t.* cities. *Deut* 4:41 19:2, 3, 7, 9
at the mouth of *t.* 17:6; 19:15
and Caleb drove thence the *t.* sons. *Josh* 15:14; *Judg* 1:20
t. men for each tribe. *Josh* 18:4
the *t.* companies blew. *Judg* 7:20
he divided the people into *t.* 9:43
Hannah took with her *t.* *1 Sam* 1:24
with fleshhook of *t.* teeth. 2:13
Hannah bare *t.* sons and two. 21
t. men, one carrying *t.* kids, another carrying *t.* loaves of bread. 10:3
people in *t.* companies. 11:11
the *t.* eldest of Jesse's. 17:13, 14
I will shoot *t.* arrows on the. 20:20
Saul died, and his *t.* sons. 31:6 *1 Chr* 10:6
Saul and his *t.* sons. *1 Sam* 31:8
there were born *t.* sons. *2 Sam* 14:27
Joab thrust *t.* darts through. 18:14
Eleazar, one of the *t.* mighty. 23:9 *1 Chr* 11:12
t. of the thirty chief. *2 Sam* 23:13
t. mighty brake through. 16, 17
Abishai brother of Joab chief among *t.* 23:18, 19
attained not to the first *t.* 19, 23
Benaiah had the name among *t.* 22
I offer thee *t.* things. 24:12 *1 Chr* 21:10
inner court with *t.* rows. *1 Ki* 6:36
were windows in *t.* rows. 7:4
t. oxen looking toward the north *t.* to the west, *t.* to the south, *t.* to. 25
t. pound of gold went to one. 10:17
Alas ! that the Lord hath called these *t.* kings. *2 Ki* 3:10, 13
sons of Zeruiah were *t.* *1 Chr* 2:16
sons of Neariah *t.* 3:23
sons of Mushi *t.* 23:23
fourteen sons and *t.* daughters. 25:5
be laid with *t.* rows. *Ezra* 6:4
to Job *t.* daughters. *Job* 1:2; 42:13
the Chaldeans made out *t.* 1:17
Job's *t.* friends heard of all. 2:11
t. things which are never. *Pr* 30:15
there be *t.* things too wonderful. 18
t. things the earth is disquieted. 21
there be *t.* things which go well. 29
two or *t.* berries in the top. *Isa* 17:6
though these *t.* men were in it. *Ezek* 14:14, 16, 18
the little chambers were *t.* 40:10, 21
the side chambers were *t.* 41:6
t. gates, after names of tribes. 48:31 32, 33, 34
did not we cast *t.* men ? *Dan* 3:24
set over these *t.* presidents. 6:2
it had *t.* ribs in the mouth. 7:5
were *t.* of the first horns. 8, 20, 24
mourning *t.* full weeks. 10:2, 3
there shall stand up *t.* kings. 11:2
for *t.* transgressions. *Amos* 1:3, 6, 9 11, 13
t. transgressions of. 2:1, 4, 6
so two or *t.* cities wandered. 4:8
t. shepherds I cut off. *Zech* 11:8
hid in *t.* measures of meal. *Mat* 13:33; *Luke* 13:21
let us make here *t.* tabernacles. *Mat* 17:4; *Mark* 9:5; *Luke* 9:33
in the mouth of two or *t.* witnesses. *Mat* 18:16; *2 Cor* 13:1
where two or *t.* are gathered together in my name. *Mat* 18:20
t. was neighbour to ? *Luke* 10:36
Friend, lend me *t.* loaves. 11:5
divided, *t.* against two, and two against *t.* 12:52
t. hours after, when his. *Acts* 5:7
t. men seek thee. 10:19; 11:11
us as far as The *t.* taverns. 28:15
faith, hope, charity . . . *t.* *1 Cor* 13:13
by two, or at most by *t.* and. 14:27
let the prophets speak two or *t.* 29
but before two or *t.* *1 Tim* 5:19
two or *t.* witnesses. *Heb* 10:28
there are *t.* that bear record in heaven: these *t.* are one. *1 John* 5:7
t. bear witness in earth, and these *t.* 8
and *t.* measures of barley. *Rev* 6:6
trumpet of *t.* angels who are. 8:13
by these *t.* was the third part. 9:18
I saw *t.* unclean spirits like. 16:13
city was divided into *t.* parts. 19
on the east *t.* gates, on the north *t.* gates, on south *t.* . . . west *t.* 21:13
see **days, hundred**

three *months*

about *t. months* after. *Gen* 38:24
she hid him *t. months.* *Ex* 2:2
in house of Obed-edom, *t. months.* *2 Sam* 6:11; *1 Chr* 13:14
wilt thou flee *t. months* before ? *2 Sam* 24:13; *1 Chr* 21:12
son of Josiah reigned *t. months.* *2 Ki* 23:31; *2 Chr* 36:2
Jehoiachin reigned *t. months.* *2 Ki* 24:8; *2 Chr* 36:9
there were yet *t. months.* *Amos* 4:7
nourished up *t. months.* *Acts* 7:20
boldly the space of *t. months.* 19:8
Paul abode in Greece *t. months.* 23
Moses was hid *t. months.* *Heb* 11:23

three *times*

t. times thou shalt keep. *Ex* 23:14
t. times in the year all thy males. 17 *Deut* 16:16
thou hast smitten me these *t. times.* *Num* 22:28, 32
turned from me these *t. times.* 33
blessed them these *t. times.* 24:10
hast mocked me these *t. times.* *Judg* 16:15
and bowed *t. times.* *1 Sam* 20:41
offered *t. times* a year. *1 Ki* 9:25
himself on the child *t. times.* 17:21
t. times did Joash beat. *2 Ki* 13:25
offering *t. times* in the. *2 Chr* 8:13
his knees *t. times* a day. *Dan* 6:10
his petition *t. times* a day. 13
this was done *t. times.* *Acts* 11:10

three *years*

heifer of *t. years* old, a she goat *t. years* old . . . *t. years.* *Gen* 15:9
uncircumcised *t. years.* *Lev* 19:23
bring forth fruit for *t. years.* 25:21
at the end of *t. years.* *Deut* 14:28
had reigned *t. years.* *Judg* 9:22
in Geshur *t. years.* *2 Sam* 13:38
in the days of David *t. years.* 21:1
at end of *t. years* Shimei's servant. *1 Ki* 2:39
once in *t. years* came the navy. 10:22; *2 Chr* 9:21
Abijam reigned *t. years* in Jerusalem. *1 Ki* 15:2; *2 Chr* 13:2
they continued *t. years.* *1 Ki* 22:1
besieged Samaria *t. years.* *2 Ki* 17:5
and at the end of *t. years.* 18:10
became his servant *t. years.* 24:1
either *t. years'* famine, or three months to be. *1 Chr* 21:12
strong *t. years, t. years* they walked in way of David. *2 Chr* 11:17
Abijah reigned *t. years.* 13:2
males, from *t. years* old. 31:16
an heifer of *t. years* old. *Isa* 15:5* *Jer* 48:34*
within *t. years*, as years of. *Isa* 16:14
walked barefoot *t. years.* 20:3
nourishing them *t. years.* *Dan* 1:5
your tithes after *t. years.* *Amos* 4:4
heaven shut up *t. years.* *Luke* 4:25 *Jas* 5:17
t. years I come seeking. *Luke* 13:7
t. years I ceased not to. *Acts* 20:31
after *t. years* I went up. *Gal* 1:18

threefold

t. cord is not quickly. *Eccl* 4:12

threescore

Isaac *t.* years old when. *Gen* 25:26
took from them *t.* cities. *Deut* 3:4 *Josh* 13:30
so that three hundred and *t.* died. *2 Sam* 2:31
pertained *t.* great cities. *1 Ki* 4:13
his provision was *t.* measures. 22
The house . . . built for the Lord, the length thereof was *t.* cubits. 6:2; *2 Chr* 3:3
and he took *t.* men. *2 Ki* 25:19
married when *t.* years. *1 Chr* 2:21
Rehoboam took *t.* *2 Chr* 11:21
temple *t.* cubits, breadth *t.* *Ezra* 6:3
t. valiant men are. *S of S* 3:7
there are *t.* queens, fourscore. 6:8
put to death *t.* men of the. *Jer* 52:25
whose height was *t.* cubits. *Dan* 3:1
from Jerusalem about *t.* *Luke* 24:13
widow be taken under *t.* *1 Tim* 5:9
see **sixty**

threescore *and one*

Lord's tribute of asses, *t. and one.* *Num* 31:39

threescore *and two*

able men *t. and two.* *1 Chr* 26:8
t. and two years old. *Dan* 5:31
in *t. and two* weeks the street. 9:25
after *t. and two* weeks Messiah. 26

threescore *and five*

within *t. and five* years. *Isa* 7:8

threescore *and six*

souls which came with Jacob *t. and six.* *Gen* 46:26
of her purifying *t. and six* days. *Lev* 12:5

threescore *and seven*

t. and seven priests'. *Neh* 7:72

threescore *and eight*

brethren *t. and eight.* *1 Chr* 16:38

threescore *and ten*

which came into Egypt, were *t. and ten.* *Gen* 46:27; *Deut* 10:22
for Israel *t. and ten* days. *Gen* 50:3
twelve wells of water, and *t. and ten* palm trees. *Ex* 15:27; *Num* 33:9
t. and ten kings, their. *Judg* 1:7
had *t. and ten* sons. 8:30; 9:2
they gave him *t. and ten* pieces. 9:4
he slew *t. and ten* persons. 5, 18, 24
rode on *t. and ten* ass colts. 12:14
brought *t. and ten* bullocks. *2 Chr* 29:32
sabbath, to fulfil *t. and ten.* 36:21
of our years are *t. and ten.* *Ps* 90:10

thou hast had indignation these *t. and ten* years? *Zech* 1:12
t. and ten horsemen. *Acts* 23:23
see **seventy**

threescore *and twelve*
t. and twelve beeves. *Num* 31:38

threescore *and fifteen*
kindred *t. and fifteen.* *Acts* 7:14

threescore *and seventeen*
Succoth *t. and seventeen. Judg* 8:14

thresh
thou shalt *t.* the mountains. *Isa* 41:15
it is time to *t.* her. *Jer* 51:33*
arise, and *t.* O daughter. *Mi* 4:13
thou didst *t.* the heathen. *Hab* 3:12

threshed
Gideon *t.* wheat by the. *Judg* 6:11*
fitches not *t.* with a threshing. *Isa* 28:27
because they *t.* Gilead. *Amos* 1:3

thresheth
t. in hope, be partaker. *1 Cor* 9:10

threshing
your *t.* shall reach unto. *Lev* 26:5
here be *t.* instruments. *2 Sam* 24:22
1 Chr 21:23
like the dust by *t.* *2 Ki* 13:7
Ornan was *t.* wheat. *1 Chr* 21:20
O my *t.* and the corn of my floor. *Isa* 21:10
he will not ever be *t.* it. 28:28
will make thee a new sharp *t.* 41:15
see **floor, floors**

threshold
hands were upon the *t.* *Judg* 19:27
hands cut off upon the *t. 1 Sam* 5:4
tread not on the *t.* of Dagon. 5
to *t.* the child died. *1 Ki* 14:17
the glory of God was gone up to the *t.* of the house. *Ezek* 9:3; 10:4
God departed from the *t.* 10:18
in their setting of their *t.* by. 43:8
prince shall worship at the *t.* 46:2
out from under the *t.* eastward. 47:1
all that leap on the *t.* *Zeph* 1:9

thresholds
keeping ward at the *t.* *Neh* 12:25*
of their threshold by my *t. Ezek* 43:8
desolation shall be in the *t.* *Zeph* 2:14

threw
Shimei *t.* stones at David and cast dust. *2 Sam* 16:13
they *t.* Jezebel down. *2 Ki* 9:33
and they *t.* down the. *2 Chr* 31:1*
a certain poor widow and she *t.* in two mites, which. *Mark* 12:42
the devil *t.* him down. *Luke* 9:42
as they cried, and *t.* *Acts* 22:23

threwest
their persecutors thou *t.* *Neh* 9:11

thrice
t. in the year shall. *Ex* 34:23, 24
and Joash smote *t.* *2 Ki* 13:18
thou shalt smite Syria but *t.* 19
thou shalt deny me *t.* *Mat* 26:34
75; *Mark* 14:30, 72; *Luke* 22:34
61; *John* 13:38
this was done *t.* *Acts* 10:16
t. was I beaten with rods, once was I stoned, *t.* I suffered. *2 Cor* 11:25
I besought the Lord *t.* 12:8

throat
their *t.* is an open sepulchre. *Ps* 5:9; *Rom* 3:13
crying, my *t.* is dried. *Ps* 69:3
nor speak they through their *t.* 115:7
put a knife to thy *t.* if. *Pr* 23:2
and withhold thy *t.* from. *Jer* 2:25
servant took him by the *t. Mat* 18:28

throne
The seat in which a king sits on ceremonial occasions. The scripture describes the throne *of Solomon as the finest and richest* throne *in the world,* 1 Ki 10:20. *It was all of ivory, and plated with pure gold. The ascent was six steps; the back was round, and two arms supported the seat. Twelve golden lions, one on each side of every step, made a principal part of its ornament.*

Throne *is also used as a symbol of sovereign power and dignity; thus Pharaoh tells Joseph,* Gen 41:40, Only in the *throne* will I be greater than thou.

Heaven is the throne *of God,* Isa 66:1. Justice and judgement are the habitation of the *throne* of the Lord, Ps 89:14. Christ Jesus is set down at the right hand of the *throne* of God, Heb 12:2.

only in the *t.* will I be. *Gen* 41:40
when he sitteth on *t.* of. *Deut* 17:18
make them inherit the *t.* *1 Sam* 2:8
to set up the *t.* of David. *2 Sam* 3:10
stablish *t.* of his kingdom. 7:13, 16
Solomon shall sit on my *t.* *1 Ki* 1:13, 17, 24, 30, 35
given one to sit on my *t.* this day. 48
not fail thee a man on the *t.* 2:4; 8:25
9:5; *2 Chr* 6:16; *Jer* 33:17
Solomon sat on *t.* of. *1 Ki* 2:12, 24
8:20; 10:9; *1 Chr* 29:23
2 Chr 6:10
the king made a great *t. 1 Ki* 10:18
2 Chr 9:17
set him on his father's *t.* *2 Ki* 10:3
fourth generation shall sit on the *t.* 30; 15:12
Joash sat on *t.* 11:19; *2 Chr* 23:20
repaired unto the *t.* of the. *Neh* 3:7
kings are they on the *t.* *Job* 36:7
thou satest in the *t.* *Ps* 9:4
the Lord's *t.* is in heaven, his. 11:4
thy *t.* O God, is for ever. 45:6
Lam 5:19; *Heb* 1:8
God sitteth on the *t.* of. *Ps* 47:8
I will build thy *t.* to all. 89:4
judgement are habitation of thy *t.* 14
t. of iniquity have fellowship? 94:20
thy body will I set on thy *t.* 132:11
children shall sit on thy *t.* 12
a king that sitteth in the *t.* *Pr* 20:8
the Lord sitting upon a *t.* *Isa* 6:1
on *t.* of David and his kingdom. 9:7
I will exalt my *t.* above the. 14:13
shall be for a glorious *t.* 22:23
there is no *t.* O daughter. 47:1
the heaven is my *t.* and earth. 66:1
Acts 7:49
shall call Jerusalem the *t.* *Jer* 3:17
kings that sit on David's *t.* 13:13
disgrace the *t.* of thy glory. 14:21
a glorious high *t.* from the. 17:12
kings sitting on the *t.* 25; 22:4, 30
O king, that sittest upon the *t.* 22:2
29:16
none to sit on the *t.* of David. 36:30
I will set my *t.* in Elam. 49:38
was the likeness of a *t.* *Ezek* 1:26
10:1
the place of my *t.* shall Israel. 43:7
I will overthrow the *t.* of. *Hag* 2:22
by heaven, for it is God's *t.* *Mat* 5:34; 23:22
the Son of man shall sit in the *t.* 19:28; 25:31
give him the *t.* of David. *Luke* 1:32
let us come boldly to the *t. Heb* 4:16
right hand the *t.* of God. 8:1; 12:2
I grant to sit in my *t.* *Rev* 3:21
a *t.* was set in heaven, and one. 4:2
a rainbow round about the *t.* 3
about the *t.* were four and. 4
t. proceeded lightnings and thunderings ... seven lamps before *t.* 5
before the *t.* there was a sea of glass, in *t.* and round about the *t.* were. 6
thanks to him that sat on the *t.* 9
fall down before him that sat on the *t.* 10; 7:11
him that sat on the *t.* a book. 5:1
midst of the *t.* stood a Lamb. 6
right hand of him that sat on the *t.* 7
many angels about the *t.* 11
be unto him that sitteth upon the *t.* 13
6:16
multitude stood before the *t.* 7:9
our God which sitteth on the *t.* 10
are they before the *t.* of God and serve him: he that sitteth on *t.* 15
the Lamb in midst of the *t.* shall. *Rev* 7:17
altar which was before the *t.* 8:3
a new song before the *t.* 14:3
without fault before the *t.* of God. 5
a voice from the *t.* 16:17; 19:5
God that sat on the *t.* 19:4
I saw a great white *t.* and. 20:11
he that sat on *t.* said, Behold. 21:5
river, proceeding out of the *t.* 22:1
the *t.* of God and of the Lamb. 3

his **throne**
from firstborn of Pharaoh that sitteth on *his t.* *Ex* 11:5; 12:29
and the king and *his t.* *2 Sam* 14:9
the Lord make *his t.* greater. *1 Ki* 1:37, 47
and sat down on *his t.* 2:19
upon his seed, and on *his t.* shall. 33
Zimri sat on his *t.*, he slew. 16:11
and Jehoshaphat king of Judah, sat each on *his t.* 22:10; *2 Chr* 18:9
I saw the Lord sitting on *his t.* *1 Ki* 22:19; *2 Chr* 18:18
and Jeroboam sat upon *his t.* *2 Ki* 13:13
set *his t.* above *t.* 25:28; *Jer* 52:32
back the face of *his t.* *Job* 26:9
he hath prepared *his t.* *Ps* 9:7
his t. to endure as the days. 89:29
shall endure, and *his t.* as the sun. 36
thou hast cast *his t.* down to. 44
the habitation of *his t.* 97:2
the Lord hath prepared *his t.* 103:19
and *his t.* is upholden. *Pr* 20:28
set each *his t.* at the gates. *Jer* 1:15
should not have a son on *his t.* 33:21
and I will set *his t.* upon these. 43:10
deposed from *his* kingly *t.* *Dan* 5:20
his t. was like the fiery flame. 7:9
Nineveh rose from *his t.* *Jonah* 3:6
rule upon *his t.* and he shall be a priest on *his t.* and. *Zech* 6:13
Christ to sit on *his t.* *Acts* 2:30
from seven spirits which are before *his t.* *Rev* 1:4
sit down with my Father in *his t.* 3:21
caught up to God, to *his t.* 12:5
see **establish, established**

thrones
for there are set *t.* of. *Ps* 122:5
raised up from their *t.* *Isa* 14:9
come down from their *t. Ezek* 26:16
till the *t.* were cast down. *Dan* 7:9
upon twelve *t.* judging the twelve. *Mat* 19:28; *Luke* 22:30
him, whether they be *t.* *Col* 1:16
I saw *t.* and they sat upon. *Rev* 20:4

throng
lest they should *t.* him. *Mark* 3:9
the multitude *t.* thee. *Luke* 8:45*

thronged
and much people *t.* him. *Mark* 5:24
Luke 8:42

thronging
thou seest the multitude *t.* thee. *Mark* 5:31

through
thrust both of them *t.* *Num* 25:8
Ahaziah fell *t.* a lattice. *2 Ki* 1:2
yet *t.* the scent of water. *Job* 14:9
their tongue walketh *t.* *Ps* 73:9
t. idleness the house droppeth *t.* *Eccl* 10:18
shewing himself *t.* the. *S of S* 2:9
I would go *t.* them, I would burn. *Isa* 27:4
thou passest *t.* the waters, and *t.* 43:2
go *t.* go *t.* the gates, prepare. 62:10
after he brought me *t.* *Ezek* 46:19
and brought me *t.* the waters. 47:4
the third part *t.* fire. *Zech* 13:9
he walketh *t.* dry places. *Mat* 12:4
they let him down *t.* the. *Luke* 5:19
ye are clean *t.* the word I. *John* 15:3
keep *t.* thine own name those. 17:11
sanctify them *t.* thy truth, thy. 17
believing ye might have life *t.* 20:31
peace with God *t.* our Lord Jesus. *Rom* 5:1
is eternal life *t.* Jesus Christ. 6:23
if ye *t.* the spirit do mortify the. 8:13

of him, *t.* him, to him, are. *Rom* 11:36
to God be glory *t.* Jesus Christ. 16:27
t. the thanksgiving of. *2 Cor* 4:15
for I *t.* the law am dead to. *Gal* 2:19
kindness towards us *t.* Christ Jesus. *Eph* 2:7
habitation of God *t.* the Spirit. 22
is above all, and *t.* all, in you all. 4:6
t. the ignorance that is in them. 18
pierced themselves *t.* *1 Tim* 6:10
who *t.* the eternal Spirit. *Heb* 9:14
t. the vail, that is to say. 10:20
t. the blood of the everlasting. 13:20

throughly
(*American Revision changes to* thoroughly)
cause him to be *t.* healed. *Ex* 21:19
his images brake they in pieces *t.* *2 Ki* 11:18
my grief were *t.* weighed. *Job* 6:2*
wash me *t.* from mine. *Ps* 51:2
shall *t.* glean the remnant. *Jer* 6:9
if ye *t.* amend your ways and your doings, if ye *t.* execute. 7:5
he shall *t.* plead their cause. 50:34
I *t.* washed away thy. *Ezek* 16:9
he will *t.* purge his floor. *Mat* 3:12
Luke 3:17
been *t.* made manifest. *2 Cor* 11:6
man of God *t.* furnished unto all. *2 Tim* 3:17*

throughout
I led Abraham *t.* the land. *Josh* 24:3
search him *t.* thousands of Judah. *1 Sam* 23:23
Hezekiah *t.* all Judah. *2 Chr* 31:20
be preached *t.* the world. *Mark* 14:9
woven from the top *t.* *John* 19:23
is spoken of *t.* the world. *Rom* 1:8
see **generations**

throw
ye shall *t.* down their altars. *Judg* 2:2*
t. down the altar of Baal thy. 6:25
t. her down. So they. *2 Ki* 9:33
the nations to *t.* down. *Jer* 1:10
as I have watched over them, to *t.* down. 31:28
they shall *t.* down thine. *Ezek* 16:39
I will *t.* down all thy strong. *Mi* 5:11
build, but I will *t.* down. *Mal* 1:4

throwing
him with *t.* a stone. *Num* 35:17*

thrown
the horse and his rider hath he *t.* *Ex* 15:1, 21
because he hath *t.* down. *Judg* 6:32
his head be *t.* to thee. *2 Sam* 20:21
Israel have *t.* down thine altars. *1 Ki* 19:10, 14
it shall not be *t.* down. *Jer* 31:40
her walls are *t.* down. 50:15
the Lord hath *t.* down. *Lam* 2:2
he hath *t.* down, and hath not. 17
I will leave thee *t.* into. *Ezek* 29:5
mountains shall be *t.* down. 38:20
and the rocks are *t.* down. *Nah* 1:6
upon another, that shall not be *t.* *Mat* 24:2; *Mark* 13:2; *Luke* 21:6
when the devil had *t.* him. *Luke* 4:35
Babylon shall be *t.* down. *Rev* 18:21

thrust
he shall surely *t.* you. *Ex* 11:1
because they were *t.* out of. 12:39
Balaam's ass *t.* herself. *Num* 22:25
Phinehas *t.* both of them. 25:8
but if he *t.* him of hatred. 35:20
but if he *t.* him suddenly without. 22
hath spoken . . . to *t.* thee. *Deut* 13:5
because he sought to *t.* thee from. 10
t. the awl through his ear. 15:17
he shall *t.* out the enemy. 33:27
Ehud *t.* the dagger into. *Judg* 3:21
he *t.* the fleece together, and. 6:38
and Zebul *t.* out Gaal and. 9:41
his young men *t.* Abimelech. 54
wives' sons grew up, and they *t.* 11:2
t. out all your right eyes. *1 Sam* 11:2
T. me through therewith . . . come and *t.* me. 31:4; *1 Chr* 10:4
and *t.* his sword in his. *2 Sam* 2:16
Joab *t.* 3 darts through heart. 18:14
shall be as thorns *t.* away. *2 Sam* 23:6
Solomon *t.* out Abiathar. *1 Ki* 2:27
came near to *t.* her away. *2 Ki* 4:27
they *t.* Uzziah out. *2 Chr* 26:20
thou hast *t.* at me, that. *Ps* 118:13
found shall be *t.* through. *Isa* 13:15
of those that are *t.* through. 14:19
they that are *t.* through. *Jer* 51:4
shall *t.* thee through with swords. *Ezek* 16:40
t. with side and shoulder. 34:21
to *t.* them out of their. 46:18
neither one *t.* another. *Joel* 2:8
shall *t.* him through. *Zech* 13:3
they rose and *t.* him. *Luke* 4:29
and prayed him he would *t.* out. 5:3
shalt be *t.* down to hell. 10:15
and you yourselves *t.* out. 13:28
and *t.* my hand into his side. *John* 20:25, 27
he that did the wrong *t.* *Acts* 7:27
but our fathers *t.* him from them. 39
t. them into the inner prison. 16:24
and now do they *t.* us out privily? 37
if it were possible, to *t.* in. 27:39
stoned or *t.* through with. *Heb* 12:20
t. in thy sickle, for the. *Rev* 14:15
he sat on the cloud, *t.* in his sickle. 16
t. in thy sharp sickle and gather. 18
the angel *t.* in his sickle into. 19

thrusteth
God *t.* him down, not man. *Job* 32:13

thumb
thou put it on the *t.* of their right hand. *Ex* 29:20; *Lev* 8:23, 24
14:14, 17, 25, 28

thumbs
him and cut off his *t.* *Judg* 1:6
their *t.* and toes cut off. 7

Thummim
Urim *and* Thummim; *According to the Hebrew,* Ex 28:30, *the literal signification of these two words is,* lights *and* perfections, *or* the shining *and* the perfect. *According to St. Jerome,* doctrine *and* judgement. *According to the LXX,* declaration *or* manifestation, *and* truth. *They were worn in or attached to the breastplate of the high priest when inquiring of God.*
breastplate of judgement, the Urim and the *T.* *Ex* 28:30; *Lev* 8:8
let thy *T.* and Urim be with thy Holy One. *Deut* 33:8
stood up priest with Urim and *T.* *Ezra* 2:63; *Neh* 7:65

thunder
the Lord sent *t.* and hail. *Ex* 9:23
the *t.* shall cease, nor shall. 29
thundered with great *t.* *1 Sam* 7:10
he shall send *t.* 12:17
the Lord sent *t.* 18
the *t.* of his power who? *Job* 26:14
a way for the lightning of the *t.* 28:26; 38:25
clothed his neck with *t.*? 39:19*
smelleth the *t.* of the captains. 25
the voice of thy *t.* was in. *Ps* 77:18
in the secret place of *t.* 81:7
at the voice of thy *t.* they. 104:7
visited of the Lord with *t.* *Isa* 29:6
which is, The sons of *t.* *Mark* 3:17
as it were the noise of *t.* *Rev* 6:1
as the voice of a great *t.* 14:2

thunder, *verb*
shall he *t.* upon them. *1 Sam* 2:10
or canst thou *t.* with a voice? *Job* 40:9

thunderbolts
their flocks to hot *t.* *Ps* 78:48

thundered
the Lord *t.* with a great. *1 Sam* 7:10
the Lord *t.* from heaven. *2 Sam* 22:14; *Ps* 18:13
heard it, said that it *t.* *John* 12:29

thundereth
he *t.* with the voice of his. *Job* 37:4
God *t.* marvellously with his. 5
the God of glory *t.* *Ps* 29:3

thunderings
be no more mighty *t.* *Ex* 9:28
and all the people saw the *t.* 20:18
out of the throne proceeded *t.* *Rev* 4:5; 19:6
there were voices and *t.* 8:5; 11:19

thunders
the *t.* and hail ceased. *Ex* 9:33, 34
there were *t.* and lightnings. 19:16
Rev 16:18
see **seven**

thus
t. did Noah, according as God. *Gen* 6:22
t. she was reproved. 20:16
why am I *t.*? 25:22
dealest thou *t.* with us? *Ex* 5:15
t. shall ye eat it, with your. 12:11
hast thou dealt *t.* with us? 14:11
t. separate the children. *Lev* 15:31
t. shall Aaron come into the. 16:3
t. shalt thou separate the. *Num* 8:14
deal *t.* with me, kill me. 11:15
hath the Lord done *t.*? *Deut* 29:24
wherefore liest thou *t.* on? *Josh* 7:10
hast thou served us *t.*? *Judg* 8:1
why askest thou *t.* after my? 13:18
if they say *t.* to us, Tarry. *1 Sam* 14:9
but if they say *t.*, Come up to us. 10
if he say *t.*, It is well. 20:7
2 Sam 15:26
be more vile than *t.* *2 Sam* 6:22
I may not tarry *t.* with thee. 18:14
t. he said, O my son Absalom. 33
t. they spake before. *1 Ki* 3:22
t. the Lord saved Hezekiah. *2 Chr* 32:22
and *t.* they returned. *Ezra* 5:11
and therein was a record *t.* 6:2
even *t.* be he shaken out. *Neh* 5:13
t. shall it be done to. *Esth* 6:9, 11
why then are ye *t.*? *Job* 27:12
if I say I will speak *t.* *Ps* 73:15
t. my heart was grieved, and. 21
t. shall the man be blessed. 128:4
when *t.* it shall be in the. *Isa* 24:13
t. shall they be unto thee with. 47:15
for *t.* hath the Lord. *Jer* 4:27; 6:6
t. shall it be done unto them. 5:13
deal *t.* with them in time of. 18:23
why hath the Lord done *t.* to? 22:8
t. might we procure evil. 26:19
to whom art thou *t.* like? *Ezek* 31:18
is it not even *t.* O children of Israel? *Amos* 2:11
t. ye brought an offering. *Mal* 1:13
t. it is written of the prophet. *Mat* 2:5; *Luke* 24:46
t. it becomes us to fulfil. *Mat* 3:15
scriptures be fulfilled, that *t.* 26:54
t. hath Lord dealt with. *Luke* 1:25
hast thou *t.* dealt with us? 2:48
master, *t.* saying, thou reproachest. 11:45
t. shall it be when Son of man. 17:30
Pharisee prayed *t.*, God, I. 18:11
said, Suffer ye *t.* far. 22:51
having said *t.* he gave up. 23:46
t. spake, Jesus himself stood in. 24:36
when he had *t.* spoken, he. 40
it is written, *t.* it behoved Christ. 46
journey, sat *t.* on well. *John* 4:6
when he *t.* had spoken, he cried. 11:43
if we let him *t.* alone, all will. 48
he said, *T.* saith the Holy. *Acts* 21:11
Why hast made me *t.*? *Rom* 9:20
t. are the secrets of his heart made manifest. *1 Cor* 14:25
love of Christ constraineth us, because we *t.* judge, that if. *2 Cor* 5:14
be perfect, be *t.* minded. *Phil* 3:15
though we *t.* speak. *Heb* 6:9
t. I saw horses in vision. *Rev* 9:17
because thou hast judged *t.* 16:5
see **did, do, Lord**

thus *and* **thus**
Achan said *t. and t.* *Josh* 7:20
t. and t. dealeth Micah. *Judg* 18:4
t. and t. did Ahithophel counsel Absalom, and *t. and t.* have I. *2 Sam* 17:15
t. and t. shalt thou say to. *1 Ki* 14:5

T. and t. said the maid. *2 Ki* 5:4
he said, *T. and t.* spake he to. 9:12

Thyatira

Lydia, of the city of *T.* *Acts* 16:14
send it to *T.* *Rev* 1:11
of the church in *T.* write. 2:18
unto you and unto the rest in *T.* 24

thyine

merchandise of *t.* wood. *Rev* 18:12

thyself

separate *t.* I pray thee. *Gen* 13:9
persons, and take goods to *t.* 14:21
return, and submit *t.* under. 16:9
that thou hast unto *t.* 33:9
as yet exaltest *t.* *Ex* 9:17
wilt thou refuse to humble *t.*? 10:3
take heed to *t.*, see my face.28; 34:12
Deut 4:9; 12:13, 19, 30
1 Sam 19:2
why sittest thou *t.* alone ? *Ex* 18:14
so shall it be easier for *t.* and. 22
come and present *t.* there. 34:2
an atonement for *t.* *Lev* 9:7
neighbour's wife to defile *t.* 18:20
lie with any beast to defile *t.* 23
love thy neighbour as *t.* 19:18
Mat 19:19; 22:39; *Mark* 12:31
thou shalt love him as *t.* *Lev* 19:34
bear it not *t.* alone. *Num* 11:17
except thou make *t.* a prince. 16:13
nations greater than *t.* *Deut* 9:1
spoil shalt thou take to *t.* 20:14
wherewith thou coverest *t.* 22:12
redeem thou my right to *t.* *Ruth* 4:6
if iniquity be in me, slay me *t.*
1 Sam 20:8
thee from avenging *t.* 25:26
thou shalt bestir *t.* *2 Sam* 5:24
has confirmed to *t.* thy people. 7:24
thy bed and make *t.* sick. 13:5
feign *t.* a mourner and put. 14:2
t. wouldest have set *t.* against. 18:13
thou wilt shew *t.* merciful. 22:26
Ps 18:25
with the pure thou wilt shew *t.* pure.
2 Sam 22:27; *Ps* 18:26
and shew *t.* a man. *1 Ki* 2:2
thou hast not asked for *t.* long life.
3:11; *2 Chr* 1:11
with me and refresh *t.* *1 Ki* 13:7
pray thee, and disguise *t.* 14:2
why feignest thou *t.* to be ? 6
go shew *t.* to Ahab, and I. 18:1
strengthen *t.* and see what. 20:22
so shall thy judgement be, *t.* hast. 40
because thou hast sold *t.* to. 21:20
hast humbled *t.* *2 Ki* 22:19
2 Chr 34:27
advise with *t.* what. *1 Chr* 21:12
thou hast joined *t.* with Ahaziah.
2 Chr 20:37
thy brethren, better than *t.* 21:13
think not with *t.* that thou. *Esth* 4:13
dost restrain wisdom to *t.*? *Job* 15:8
acquaint *t.* with him, and. 22:21
thou opposest *t.* against me. 30:21
thine anger, lift up *t.* *Ps* 7:6
why hidest thou *t.* in times ? 10:1
stir up *t.* and awake to my. 35:23
delight *t.* also in the Lord. 37:4
when thou doest well to *t.* 49:18
altogether such an one as *t.* 50:21
boastest thou *t.* in mischief ? 52:1
displeased, O turn *t.* to us. 60:1
madest strong for *t.* 80:15, 17
shew *t.* 94:1
lift up *t.* thou judge. 2
do this, my son, and deliver *t.*
Pr 6:3, 5
thou shalt be wise for *t.* 9:12
fret not *t.* because of evil men. 24:19
and make it fit for *t.* in the. 27
put not forth *t.* in presence of. 25:6
boast not *t.* of to-morrow. 27:1
foolishly in lifting up *t.* 30:32
make *t.* over wise; why shouldest
thou destroy *t* ? *Eccl* 7:16
that thou *t.* also hast cursed. 22
hide *t.* as for a little. *Isa* 26:20
lifting up *t.* the nations were. 33:3
art a God that hidest *t.* 45:15
shake *t.* from the dust, loose *t.* 52:2
thou hast discovered *t.* to. 57:8
thou didst debase *t.* even. *Isa* 57:9
thou delight *t.* in the Lord. 58:14
make *t.* a glorious name. 63:14
wilt thou refrain *t.* for these? 64:12
which say, Stand by *t.*, come. 65:5
procured this unto *t.* *Jer* 2:17
clothest *t.* with crimson, in vain shalt
thou make *t.* fair; thy lovers. 4:30
sackcloth, wallow *t.* in ashes. 6:26
t. shall discontinue from. 17:4
I will make thee a terror to *t.* 20:4
because thou clothest *t.* in. 22:15
redemption is thine, buy it for *t.* 32:8
seekest thou great things for *t.* 45:5
furnish *t.* to go into captivity. 46:19
how long wilt thou cut *t.*? 47:5
O sword, put up *t.* into thy. 6
give *t.* no rest, let not. *Lam* 2:18
thou hast covered *t.* with. 3:44
be drunken, make *t.* naked. 4:21
go shut *t.* within thine. *Ezek* 3:24
thou madest to *t.* images. 16:17
and thou hast defiled *t.* in. 22:4
for whom thou didst wash *t.* 23:40
hast lifted up *t.* in height. 31:10
prepare for *t.* and all thy. 38:7
said, Let thy gifts be to *t.* *Dan* 5:17
but hast lifted up *t.* against. 23
and to chasten *t.* before thy. 10:12
thou hast destroyed *t.* *Hos* 13:9
though thou exalt *t.* as the. *Ob* 4
Aphrah roll *t.* in dust. *Mi* 1:10
now gather *t.* in troops, O. 5:1
make *t.* many as the. *Nah* 3:15
deliver *t.* O Zion, that. *Zech* 2:7
If thou be the Son of God, cast *t.*
down. *Mat* 4:6; *Luke* 4:9
shalt not forswear *t.* *Mat* 5:33
shew *t.* to priest. 8:4; *Mark* 1:44
Luke 5:14
save *t.* *Mat* 27:40; *Mark* 15:30
Luke 23:39
Physician, heal *t.* *Luke* 4:23
when thou *t.* beholdest not. 6:42
Lord, trouble not *t.* for I am. 7:6
love thy neighbour as *t.* 10:27
Rom 13:9; *Gal* 5:14; *Jas* 2:8
will not rather say, Make ready and
gird *t.* *Luke* 17:8
what sayest thou of *t.*? *John* 1:22
if thou do these things, shew *t.* 7:4
thou bearest record of *t.* it. 8:13
whom makest thou *t.*? 53
a man, makest *t.* God. 10:33
thou wilt manifest *t.* unto us? 14:22
sayest thou this of *t.*? or did? 18:34
young, thou girdest *t.* 21:18
join *t.* to this chariot. *Acts* 8:29
gird *t.* 12:8
do *t.* no harm. 16:28
purify *t.* with them, that all may
know that thou *t.* walkest. 21:24
t. mayest take knowledge. 24:8
permitted to speak for *t.* . . . Festus
said, Paul, thou art beside *t.* 26:1
thou condemnest *t.* *Rom* 2:1
that thou *t.* art guide of the blind. 19
teachest thou not *t.*? 21
hast thou faith ? have it to *t.* 14:22
considering *t.* lest thou. *Gal* 6:1
oughtest to behave *t.* *1 Tim* 3:15
and exercise *t.* rather unto. 4:7
these things, give *t.* wholly to. 15
take heed to *t.* and to the doctrine;
in doing this thou shalt save *t.* 16
other men's sins: keep *t.* pure. 5:22
minds, from such withdraw *t.* 6:5
to shew *t.* approved. *2 Tim* 2:15
shewing *t.* a pattern of. *Tit* 2:7

Tiberias

which is the sea of *T.* *John* 6:1
there came other boats from *T.* 23

Tibni

half of the people followed *T.*
1 Ki 16:21
against those that followed *T.* 22

tidings

heard these evil *t.* *Ex* 33:4
wife heard the *t.* *1 Sam* 4:19
they told the *t.* of the men of Jabesh.
11:4*, 5*
alive to bring *t.* to Gath. 27:11*
when *t.* came of Saul. *2 Sam* 4:
t. came, saying, Absalom. 13:3
run and bear the king *t.* 18:19
shalt not bear *t.* this day. 20
thou hast no *t.* ready. 22
Cushi came, Cushi said, *T.* my. 31
then *t.* came to Joab. *1 Ki* 2:28
sent to thee with heavy *t.* 14:6
and sent to carry *t.* to. *1 Chr* 10:9
not be afraid of evil *t.* *Ps* 112:7
man that brought *t.* *Jer* 20:15
for they have heard evil *t.* 49:23
shalt answer for the *t.* *Ezek* 21:7
t. out of the east shall. *Dan* 11:44
I am sent to shew thee these glad *t.*
Luke 1:19; 2:10
shewing the glad *t.* of the. 8:1
t. of these things came. *Acts* 11:22*
we declare unto you glad *t.* 13:32
t. came to the chief captain. 21:31
that bring glad *t.* of good. *Rom* 10:15
see **good**

tie

and *t.* the kine. *1 Sam* 6:7, 10
bind on thy heart and *t.* *Pr* 6:21

tied

they *t.* to it a lace of blue. *Ex* 39:31
but horses *t.*, and asses *t.* *2 Ki* 7:10
ye shall find as ass *t.* *Mat* 21:2
Mark 11:2, 4; *Luke* 19:30

Tiglath-pileser

T. came and took Ijon. *2 Ki* 15:29
Ahaz sent messengers to *T.* 16:7
T. carried away Beerah. *1 Chr* 5:6
stirred up the spirit of *T.* 26
T. came and distressed Ahaz.
2 Chr 28:20

tile

son of man, take thee a *t.* *Ezek* 4:1

tiling

they let him down through the *t.*
Luke 5:19*

till

do any thing *t.* thou be. *Gen* 19:22
t. I know what God will. *1 Sam* 22:3
if I taste bread *t.* the. *2 Sam* 3:35
he was helped *t.* he. *2 Chr* 26:15
t. the wrath arose, *t.* there. 36:16
t. there stood up a priest. *Ezra* 2:63
Neh 7:65
be angry with us *t.* thou. *Ezra* 9:14
all the days will I wait *t.* *Job* 14:14
t. I die. 27:5
not purged, *t.* ye die. *Isa* 22:14
wickedness *t.* thou find. *Ps* 10:15
a wise man keepeth it in *t.* *Pr* 29:11*
t. I might see what was. *Eccl* 2:3
stir not up my love *t.* he please.
S of S 2:7; 3:5
that lay field to field, *t.* *Isa* 5:8
no rest, *t.* he establish, and *t.* he
make Jerusalem a praise. 62:7
destroy *t.* they. *Jer* 49:9; *Ob* 5
t. he had cast them out. *Jer* 52:3
t. the Lord look down. *Lam* 3:50
wast perfect, *t.* iniquity. *Ezek* 28:15
t. seven times pass over. *Dan* 4:23
but go thou thy way *t.* the. 12:13
t. they acknowledge their. *Hos* 5:15
t. he rain righteousness upon. 10:12
t. she had brought forth. *Mat* 1:25
t. heaven and earth pass, one. 5:18
I am straitened *t.* it be. *Luke* 12:50
doth not seek diligently *t.* she. 15:8
he said unto them, Occupy *t.* 19:13
if I will that he tarry *t.* I come.
John 21:22, 23
t. another king arose. *Acts* 7:18
not eat, *t.* they had killed Paul.
23:12, 14, 21
t. we all come in the. *Eph* 4:13
without offence, *t.* the day. *Phil* 1:10
t. I come, give attendance to reading. *1 Tim* 4:13
which ye have, hold fast *t.* I come.
Rev 2:25
t. we have sealed the servants. 7:3
t. the seven plagues were. 15:8
t. the thousand years should. 20:3
see **consumed, morning, until**

till, *verb*

was not a man to *t.* the ground.
Gen 2:5; 3:23

thy servants shall t. 2 Sam 9:10
they shall t. it, and dwell therein.
Jer 27:11

tillage

was over them that were for t.
1 Chr 27:26
have the tithes of t. Neh 10:37
much food is in the t. Pr 13:23

tilled

ye shall be t. and sown. Ezek 36:9
the desolate land shall be t. 34

tiller

but Cain was a t. of. Gen 4:2

tillest

when thou t. ground, it. Gen 4:12

tilleth

he that t. land shall. Pr 12:11
he that t. his land shall have. 28:19

timber

break down the t. thereof. Lev 14:45
prepared t. and stones to build.
1 Ki 5:18; 1 Chr 22:14; 2 Chr 2:9
away the t. of Ramah. 1 Ki 15:22
t. is laid in the walls. Ezra 5:8
let t. be pulled down from. 6:11*
that he may give me t. Neh 2:8
they shall lay thy t. in. Ezek 26:12
the beam out of the t. Hab 2:11
consume it with the t. Zech 5:4

timbrel

and Miriam took a t. in. Ex 15:20
they take the t. and harp. Job 21:12
bring hither the t. Ps 81:2
praises to him with the t. 149:3
praise him with the t. and. 150:4

timbrels

went out after her with t. Ex 15:20
his daughter came out with t.
Judg 11:34
of Israel played before the Lord on t.
2 Sam 6:5; 1 Chr 13:8
damsels playing with t. Ps 68:25

time

(*This word is frequently used with the meaning of* season)

return according to the t. of life.
Gen 18:10, 14
the t. that women go out to. 24:11
from the t. he had made him. 39:5
the t. drew nigh that Israel. 47:29
pay for loss of his t. Ex 21:19
if beyond the t. of her. Lev 15:25
a wife besides the other in her life t.
18:18
the t. was the t. of first. Num 13:20
what t. the fire devoured. 26:10
t. thou put the sickle. Deut 16:9
at the t. of the going down of the sun.
Josh 10:27; 2 Chr 18:34
did Joshua take at one t. Josh 10:42
all the t. the house of. Judg 18:31
the t. I commanded. 2 Sam 7:11
at the t. when kings go forth. 11:1
eight hundred he slew at one t. 23:8
is it t. to receive money? 2 Ki 5:26
were to come from t. to t. 1 Chr 9:25
on this side the river, and at such a t.
Ezra 4:10, 17; 7:12
and it is a t. of rain. 10:13
return? and I set him a t. Neh 2:6
what t. they wax warm. Job 6:17
who shall set me a t. to plead? 9:19
accomplished before his t. 15:32
which were cut down out of t. 22:16
which I reserved against the t. 38:23
knowest thou the t. they bring forth?
39:1, 2
in a t. when thou mayest. Ps 32:6
not be ashamed in the evil t. 37:19
the Lord will deliver him in t. 41:1
what t. I am afraid, I will. 56:3
to thee in an acceptable t. 69:13
their t. should have endured. 81:15
remember how short my t. is. 89:47
until the t. that his word. 105:19
there is a t. to every purpose.
Eccl 3:1, 17; 8:6
a t. to be born, and a t. to die; a t.
3:2
thou die before thy t.? 7:17
a wise man's heart discerneth t. 8:5
but t. and chance happeneth. 9:11
of men snared in an evil t. Eccl 9:12
that draweth near the t. Isa 26:17
from the t. it goeth forth it. 28:19
declared this from ancient t.? 45:21*
from the t. that it was. 48:16
in an acceptable t. have I heard thee.
49:8; 2 Cor 6:2
Lord will hasten it in his t. Isa 60:22
at the t. I visit, they shall. Jer 6:15
crane and swallow observe the t. 8:7
looked for a t. of health, and. 15
the Saviour thereof in t. 14:8
and for the t. of healing, and. 19
it is even the t. of Jacob's. 30:7
and the t. of their visitation. 46:21
50:27
the t. that I will visit him. 49:8
50:31
will appoint me the t.? 49:19; 50:44
floor, it is t. to thresh her. 51:33
from t. to t. shalt thou. Ezek 4:10
thy t. was the t. of love, I. 16:8
as at the t. of thy reproach of. 57
day is near, it shall be the t. 30:3
ye would gain the t. Dan 2:8
to speak before me, till the t. 9
that he would give him t. 16
at what t. ye hear the sound of cornet. 3:5, 15
were prolonged for a t. 7:12
t. came that the saints possessed. 22
t. and the dividing of t. 25; 12:7
at the t. of the end shall be. 8:17
about the t. of evening. 9:21
forecast his devices for a t. 11:24
to make them white, even to the t. 35
at the t. of the end shall the king. 40
shall be a t. of trouble. 12:1
even to the t. of the end. 4, 9
from the t. the daily sacrifice. 11
it is t. to seek the Lord. Hos 10:12
till the t. that she which travaileth.
Mi 5:3
is it t. to dwell in your? Hag 1:4
that at evening t. it. Zech 14:7
her fruit before the t. Mal 3:11
the t. they were carried. Mat 1:11
Herod enquired what t. the star. 2:7
to torment us before the t.? 8:29
and when the t. of the fruit. 21:34
master saith, My t. is. 26:18
the t. is fulfilled, repent. Mark 1:15
and so endure but for a t. 4:17
this is a desert, and now the t. 6:35
for the t. of figs was not yet. 11:13
ye know not when the t. is. 13:33
Elisabeth's full t. came. Luke 1:57
all kingdoms in a moment of t. 4:5
but this woman, since the t. 7:45
which in t. of temptation fall. 8:13
ye shall not see me, till the t. 13:35
thou knewest not the t. of thy. 19:44
t. is not come, your t. John 7:6
the t. cometh that whosoever. 16:2
the t. cometh when I shall no. 25
all the t. the Lord went. Acts 1:21
but when the t. of the promise. 7:17
in which t. Moses was born. 20
spent their t. in nothing else. 17:21
it is high t. to awake. Rom 13:11
judge nothing before the t. 1 Cor 4:5
except with consent for a t. 7:5
but this I say, brethren, the t. 29
redeeming the t. Eph 5:16
Col 4:5
from you for a short t. 1 Thes 2:17
that he might be revealed in his t.
2 Thes 2:6
t. come, when they will. 2 Tim 4:3
and the t. of my departure is. 6
grace to help in t. of need.
Heb 4:16
when for the t. ye ought to. 5:12
which was a figure for the t. 9:9
imposed on them till the t. 10
the t. would fail me to tell of. 11:32
appeareth a little t. Jas 4:14
what manner of t. the. 1 Pet 1:11
pass the t. of your sojourning. 17
should live the rest of his t. 4:2
for the t. is at hand. Rev 1:3; 22:10
sware, that there should be t. 10:6
t. of the dead, that they. 11:18
that he hath but a short t. 12:12
she is nourished for a t. and times, and half a t. Rev 12:14
see **appointed, before, come, day, due, last, long, many, old, past, process, second, set, third**

any **time**

may redeem at any t. Lev 25:32
if the slayer at any t. Num 35:26
sounded my father to-morrow at any t. 1 Sam 20:12
displeased him at any t. 1 Ki 1:6
bear thee up, lest at any t. thou dash.
Mat 4:6; Luke 4:11
lest at any t. the adversary deliver.
Mat 5:25
lest at any t. they should see. 13:15
Mark 4:12
transgressed I at any t. Luke 15:29
lest at any t. your hearts be. 21:34
hath seen God at any t. John 1:18
ye heard his voice at any t. 5:37
unclean hath at any t. entered.
Acts 11:8
who goeth a warfare any t. at his own charges? 1 Cor 9:7
nor at any t. used we. 1 Thes 2:5
to which of the angels said he at any t.? Heb 1:5, 13
lest at any t. we should let. 2:1
hath seen God at any t. 1 John 4:12

in the **time**

came to pass in the t. of. Gen 38:27
commanded in the t. of. Ex 34:18
them deliver in the t. Judg 10:14
in the t. of wheat harvest. 15:1
in the t. of old age he. 1 Ki 15:23
in the t. of distress. 2 Chr 28:22
in the t. of their trouble. Neh 9:27
more than in the t. when corn. Ps 4:7
as a fiery oven in the t. of. 21:9
in the t. of trouble he shall. 27:5
he is their strength in the t. 37:39
cast me not off in the t. of. 71:9
as the cold of snow in the t. of harvest. Pr 25:13
unfaithful man in the t. of. 19
salvation in the t. of trouble. Isa 33:2
in the t. of trouble they. Jer 2:27
if they can save thee in the t. 28
in the t. of visitation they shall be cast down. 8:12
in the t. of visitation they shall perish.
10:15; 51:18
shall not save them at all in the t. of trouble. 11:12
I will not hear them in the t. that. 14
enemy to entreat thee well in the t. of evil, and in the t. of. 15:11
deal thus with them in the t. 18:23
handleth the sickle in the t. 50:16
in the t. when thou shalt. Ezek 27:34
a perpetual hatred, in the t. of their calamity, in the t. that their. 35:5
I will take away my corn in the t. thereof. Hos 2:9
ask rain in the t. of the. Zech 10:1
in the t. of harvest I. Mat 13:30
many lepers in the t. of. Luke 4:27

same **time**

Lord's anger was kindled the same t.
Num 32:10
for Aaron also the same t. Deut 9:20
then Libnah revolted at the same t.
2 Ki 8:22; 2 Chr 21:10
the same t. 700 oxen. 2 Chr 15:11
the people at the same t. 16:10
at the same t. came to. Ezra 5:3
vineyards at the same t. Jer 39:10
at the same t. shalt thou think evil.
Ezek 38:10
at the same t. my reason. Dan 4:36
as never was to that same t. 12:1
the same t. there arose. Acts 19:23

that **time**

not recover in that t.? Judg 11:26
to-morrow by that t. the sun be hot.
1 Sam 11:9
since that t. hath it been. Ezra 5:16
to pass from that t. forth.
Neh 4:16; 13:21
spoken concerning Moab since that t.
Isa 16:13

in *that t.* shall the present be. *Isa* 18:7
I not told thee from *that t.*? 44:8
hath told it from *that t.*? 45:21
from *that t.* that thine ear. 48:8
that t. Israel shall come. *Jer* 50:4
in *that t.* the iniquity of Israel. 20
keep silence in *that t.* *Amos* 5:13
from *that t.* Jesus began. *Mat* 4:17
from *that t.* began to shew. 16:21
from *that t.* Judas sought. 26:16
since *that t.* the kingdom of God is preached. *Luke* 16:16
that t. many disciples. *John* 6:66
about *that t.* Herod. *Acts* 12:1

at that **time**

king of Moab *at that t.* *Num* 22:4
and I spake to you *at that t.* saying. *Deut* 1:9
judges *at that t.* saying. 16
I commanded you *at that t.* 18; 3:18
Joshua *at that t.* saying. 3:21
I besought the Lord *at that t.* 23
the Lord and you *at that t.* 5:5
the Lord hearkened to me *at that t.* 9:19; 10:10
the ark was *at that t.* *1 Sam* 14:18
Israel brought under *at that t.* *2 Chr* 13:18
not keep the passover *at that t.* 30:3
kept the passover *at that t.* 35:17
at that t. they shall call. *Jer* 3:17
at that t. shall they bring out. 8:1
at that t. cause the branch of. 33:15
at that t. shall Michael. *Dan* 12:1
face from them *at that t.* *Mi* 3:4
at that t. I will search. *Zeph* 1:12
at that t. I will undo all that. 3:19
at that t. will I bring you again. 20
at Jerusalem *at that t.* *Luke* 23:7
at that t. there was a great. *Acts* 8:1
at that t. ye were without Christ. *Eph* 2:12

this **time**

this t. will my husband. *Gen* 29:34
Pharaoh hardened his heart at *this t.* *Ex* 8:32
I will at *this t.* send all my. 9:14
to-morrow about *this t.* I will. 18
said, I have sinned *this t.* 27
according to *this t.* it. *Num* 23:23
nor would as at *this t.* *Judg* 13:23
not give unto them at *this t.* 21:22
for about *this t.* ye shall find him. *1 Sam* 9:13
the counsel is not good at *this t.* *2 Sam* 17:7
I will not at *this t.* put. *1 Ki* 2:26
by to-morrow about *this t.* 19:2; 20:6
2 Ki 7:1, 18; 10:6
in all *this t.* was not I at. *Neh* 13:6
thy peace at *this t.*: art come to the kingdom . . . *t.* as *this*? *Esth* 4:14
blessed be the Lord from *this t.* forth. *Ps* 113:2
bless the Lord from *this t.* forth. 115:18
will preserve thee from *this t.* 121:8
new things from *this t.* *Isa* 48:6
wilt thou not from *this t.*? *Jer* 3:4
this is the *t.* of the Lord's. 51:6
haughtily; for *this t.* is evil. *Mi* 2:3
since the beginning of the world to *this t.* *Mat* 24:21; *Mark* 13:19
receive an hundred-fold now in *this t.* *Mark* 10:30; *Luke* 18:30
do not discern *this t.*? *Luke* 12:56
by *this t.* he stinketh. *John* 11:39
wilt thou at *this t.* restore? *Acts* 1:6
go thy way for *this t.* 24:25
to declare at *this t.* *Rom* 3:26
sufferings of *this* present *t.* 8:18
at *this t.* will I come, and Sarah. 9:9
so at *this* present *t.* there is. 11:5
not to come at *this t.* *1 Cor* 16:12
that now at *this t.* your. *2 Cor* 8:14

times

he hath supplanted me these two *t.* *Gen* 27:36
ye shall not observe *t.* *Lev* 19:26*
Deut 18:10*, 14*
hated him not in *t.* past. *Deut* 4:42
the Spirit of the Lord began to move him at *t.* *Judg* 13:25
as at other *t.* and shake. *Judg* 16:20
in array as at other *t.* 20:30
began to kill as at other *t.* 31
as at other *t.*, Samuel. *1 Sam* 3:10
with his hand as at other *t.* 18:10*
on his seat as at other *t.* 20:25
not heard of ancient *t.* that I have formed it? *2 Ki* 19:25; *Isa* 37:26
Manasseh observed *t.* *2 Ki* 21:6*
2 Chr 33:6*
understanding of the *t.* *1 Chr* 12:32
the *t.* that went over him and. 29:30
in those *t.* there was no. *2 Chr* 15:5
men which knew the *t.* *Esth* 1:13
t. are not hidden from. *Job* 24:1
Lord will be a refuge in *t.* *Ps* 9:9
thyself in *t.* of trouble? 10:1
my *t.* are in thy hand, deliver. 31:15
thou didst in the *t.* of old. 44:1
the years of ancient *t.* 77:5
be the stability of thy *t.* *Isa* 33:6
from ancient *t.* things not. 46:10
of the *t.* far off. *Ezek* 12:27
he changeth the *t.* and. *Dan* 2:21
he shall think to change *t.* 7:25
shall be built in troublous *t.* 9:25
in those *t.* there shall many. 11:14
t. and an half. 12:7; *Rev* 12:14
not discern the signs of the *t.*? *Mat* 16:3
the *t.* of the Gentiles. *Luke* 21:24
for you to know the *t.* *Acts* 1:7
when the *t.* of refreshing. 3:19
till the *t.* of restitution of all. 21
who in *t.* past suffered all. 14:16*
hath determined the *t.* 17:26*
the *t.* of this ignorance God. 30
as ye in *t.* past have not. *Rom* 11:30
of Jews five *t.* received I forty stripes. *2 Cor* 11:24
persecuted us in *t.* past. *Gal* 1:23
and months, *t.* and years. 4:10
of the fulness of *t.* *Eph* 1:10
the *t.* ye have no need. *1 Thes* 5:1
in latter *t.* some shall. *1 Tim* 4:1
in his *t.* he shall shew, who is. 6:15
perilous *t.* shall come. *2 Tim* 3:1
hath in due *t.* manifested. *Tit* 1:3
God who at sundry *t.* spake to the. *Heb* 1:1*
see **appointed, many, seven, ten, three**

all **times**

that he come not at *all t.* *Lev* 16:2
of his people at *all t.* *1 Ki* 8:59
I will bless the Lord at *all t.*: his praise. *Ps* 34:1
trust in him at *all t.* ye people. 62:8
doeth righteousness at *all t.* 106:3
to thy judgements at *all t.* 119:20
satisfy thee at *all t.* *Pr* 5:19
a friend loveth at *all t.* 17:17

Timnath

to his shearers in *T.* *Gen* 38:12
Samson went down to *T.* *Judg* 14:1

Timotheus

a certain disciple named *T.* *Acts* 16:1
T. my workfellow saluteth you. *Rom* 16:21
if *T.* come. *1 Cor* 16:10
T. our brother. *2 Cor* 1:1
was preached even by me and *T.* 19
Lord to send *T.* to you. *Phil* 2:19
we sent *T.* to establish. *1 Thes* 3:2
to *T.* my own son. *1 Tim* 1:2, 18
2 Tim 1:2
T. is set at liberty. *Heb* 13:23

tin

t. that may abide fire. *Num* 31:22
take away all thy *t.* *Isa* 1:25
brass, and *t.* and iron. *Ezek* 22:18
lead and *t.* into the furnace. 20
thy merchant in *t.* and lead. 27:12

tingle

ears of every one that heareth it shall *t.* *1 Sam* 3:11; *2 Ki* 21:12
Jer 19:3

tinkling

mincing and making a *t.* *Isa* 3:16
bravery of their *t.* ornaments. 18*
as a *t.* cymbal. *1 Cor* 13:1*

tip

may dip the *t.* of his finger in water. *Luke* 16:24
see right **ear**

tire

bind the *t.* of thy head. *Ezek* 24:17

tired

Jezebel *t.* her head. *2 Ki* 9:30

tires

Lord will take away their *t.* *Isa* 3:18*
and your *t.* shall be on. *Ezek* 24:23

Tirshatha

(*This word is not strictly a proper name, but the title of the Governor of Judaea, under the Persians. In some places it is rendered* governor)
T. said that they should not eat of the holy things. *Ezra* 2:63; *Neh* 7:65
the *T.* gave gold to the. *Neh* 7:70
sealed were Nehemiah the *T.* 10:1

Tirzah

Hoglah, Milcah, and *T.* *Num* 26:33
27:1; 36:11; *Josh* 17:3
smote the king of *T.* *Josh* 12:24
wife came to *T.* *1 Ki* 14:17
dwelt and reigned in *T.* 15:21, 33
Elah reigned in *T.* 16:8
Zimri reigned in *T.* 15
Omri besieged *T.* 17
Omri reigned in *T.* 23
smote coasts from *T.* *2 Ki* 15:16
O my love, as *T.* *S of S* 6:4

Tishbite, *see* **Elijah**

tithe

The practice of paying tithes *is very ancient; for we find,* Gen 14:20, *that Abraham gave* tithes *to Melchizedek, king of Salem, at his return from his expedition against Chedorlaomer, and the four kings in confederacy with him. Abraham gave him the* tithe *of all the booty taken from the enemy. Jacob imitated this piety of his grandfather when he vowed to the Lord the* tithe *of all the substance he might acquire in Mesopotamia,* Gen 28:22. *Under the law, Moses ordained,* Lev 27:30, 31, 32, All the *tithe* of the land, whether of the seed of the land, or of the fruit of the tree, is the Lord's; it is holy unto the Lord, etc.
There were three sorts of tithes *to be paid from the people (besides those from the Levites to the priests),* Num 28:26, 27, etc. (1) *To the Levites, for their maintenance,* Num 18:21, 24. (2) *For the Lord's feasts and sacrifices, to be eaten* in the place which the Lord should choose to put his name there; *to wit, where the ark should be, the tabernacle or temple. This tenth part was either sent to Jerusalem in kind, or, if it was too far, they sent the value in money, which was to be laid out for oxen, sheep, wine, or what else they pleased,* Deut 14:22, 23, 24, etc. (3) *Besides these two, there was to be, every third year, a tithe for the poor, to be eaten in their own dwellings,* Deut 14:28, 29.
In the New Testament, *neither our Saviour, nor his apostles have commanded any thing in this affair of* tithes.

all the *t.* of the land is. *Lev* 27:30
concerning the *t.* of the herd. 32
a tenth part of the *t.* *Num* 18:26
thy gates the *t.* of corn. *Deut* 12:17
eat *t.* in the place the Lord. 14:23
three years bring forth the *t.* 28
firstfruits of corn and the *t.* of all. *2 Chr* 31:5, 6, 12; *Neh* 13:12
shall bring up *t.* of tithes. *Neh* 10:38
ye pay *t.* of mint, anise. *Mat* 23:23

tithe, *verb*

t. increase of thy seed. *Deut* 14:22
for ye *t.* mint, and rue. *Luke* 11:42

tithes
Melchizedek t. of all. Gen 14:20
redeem aught of his t. Lev 27:31
the t. I have given to. Num 18:24
take of the children of Israel t. 26
unto the Lord of all your t. 28
shall bring your t. Deut 12:6, 11
made an end of tithing the t. 26:12
Levites might have the t. Neh 10:37
were appointed for the t. 12:44
they laid the t. of corn. 13:5
bring your t. after three years.
Amos 4:4; Mal 3:10
ye have robbed me. In t. Mal 3:8
I give t. of all that I. Luke 18:12
priesthood have commandment to take t. Heb 7:5
he received t. of Abraham, and. 6
and here men that die receive t. 8
Levi who receiveth t. payed t. in. 9

tithing
hast made an end of t., third year which is the year of t. Deut 26:12

title
he said, What t. is that? 2 Ki 23:17*
Pilate wrote a t. and put it on the cross. John 19:19
t. then read many of the Jews. 20

titles
give flattering t. to man. Job 32:21
for I know not to give flattering t. 22

tittle
one t. shall in no wise pass. Mat 5:18
than for one t. of the law. Luke 16:17

Titus
because I found not T. 2 Cor 2:13
us by the coming of T. 7:6
joyed we for the joy of T. 13
boasting which I made before T. 14
we desired T. 8:6
care into the heart of T. 16
whether any enquire of T. he is. 23
I desired T. Did T. make a? 12:18
I took T. with me. Gal 2:1
neither T. was compelled to. 3
T. is departed to. 2 Tim 4:10

to and fro, see fro

Tobiah
children of T. not shew. Ezra 2:60
Sanballat and T. heard. Neh 2:10
19; 4:7; 6:1
T. had hired him. 6:12
my God, think thou upon T. 14
and T. sent letters to put me. 19
Eliashib was allied to T. 13:4
all the household stuff of T. 8

to-day, see day

toe
great t. of their right foot. Ex 29:20
Lev 8:23, 24; 14:14, 17, 25, 28

toes
thumbs and his great t. Judg 1:6
having thumbs and t. cut off. 7
fingers and t. were. 1 Chr 20:6, 24
the t. part of iron. Dan 2:41, 42

Togarmah
sons of Gomer, Riphath, T.
Gen 10:3; 1 Chr 1:6
they of the house of T. Ezek 27:14

together
plow with ox and ass t. Deut 22:10
he divided her, t. with. Judg 19:29
died that same day t. 1 Sam 31:6
we were t., there was no. 1 Ki 3:18
women, t. with the daughter. 11:1
when I and thou rode t. 2 Ki 9:25
we ourselves t. will build. Ezra 4:3
let us take counsel t. Neh 6:7
let us meet t. 10
there the prisoners rest t. Job 3:18
have fashioned me t. round. 10:8
go down, when our rest t. is. 17:16
the poor hide themselves t. 24:4
all flesh shall perish t. 34:15
counsel t. against the Lord. Ps 2:2
all t. become filthy. 14:3; Rom 3:12
and let us exalt his name t. Ps 34:3
the transgressors be destroyed t.
37:38; Isa 1:28
the rich and poor meet t. Pr 22:2
and the deceitful man meet t. 29:13
if two lie t. then they. Eccl 4:11
t. shall be against Judah. Isa 9:21
t. with my dead body shall. 26:19
that we may behold it t. 41:23
with the voice t. shall they. 52:8, 9
and the lamb shall feed t. 65:25
the bones came t., bone. Ezek 37:7
he and his princes t. Amos 1:15
can two walk t. except they? 3:3
or three are gathered t. Mat 18:20
what God hath joined t.
Mark 10:9
he calleth t. his friends. Luke 15:6
that believed were t. Acts 2:44
ye have agreed t. to tempt. 5:9
all things work t. for good. Rom 8:28
hath quickened us t. Eph 2:5
hath raised us t. 6
building fitly framed t. 21, 22
striving t. for the faith. Phil 1:27
brethren, be followers t. of me. 3:17
being knit t. in love. Col 2:2, 19
dead in sins, hath he quickened t. 13
shall be caught up t. 1 Thes 4:17
we should live t. with him. 5:10
you by our gathering t. 2 Thes 2:1
as being heirs t. of the. 1 Pet 3:7
see dwell

toil
concerning our work and t. Gen 5:29
hath made me forget my t. 41:51

toil, verb
they t. not, neither do they spin.
Mat 6:28; Luke 12:27

toiled
Master, we have t. all. Luke 5:5

toiling
and he saw them t. Mark 6:48*

token
this is the t. of the covenant.
Gen 9:12, 13, 17
and it shall be a t. of the. 17:11
this shall be a t. that I. Ex 3:12
the blood shall be for a t. on. 12:13
it shall be for a t. upon. 13:16*
to be kept for a t. Num 17:10
and give me a true t. Josh 2:12
shew me a t. for good. Ps 86:17
given them a t. saying. Mark 14:44
is to them an evident t. Phil 1:28
a manifest t. of righteous. 2 Thes 1:5
of Paul, which is the t. in. 3:17

tokens
being t. of damsel's virginity.
Deut 22:15, 17, 20
and do ye not know their t.? Job 21:29
they are afraid at thy t. Ps 65:8
who sent t. in the midst of. 135:9*
that frustrateth the t. of. Isa 44:25

Tola
T. the son of Issachar. Gen 46:13
1 Chr 7:1
T. son of Puah arose to. Judg 10:1

told
who t. thee that thou wast naked?
Gen 3:11
and Ham t. his two brethren. 9:22
till I have t. mine errand. 24:33
Joseph t. his brethren. 37:5, 9
he t. it to his father and his. 10
T. not I thee, All that? Num 23:26
it be t. thee, and behold. Deut 17:4
which our fathers t. of. Judg 6:13
was a man that t. a dream. 7:13
I asked not, neither t. he me. 13:6
nor would as at this time have t. 23
he came up, and t. his father. 14:2
but he t. not his father. 6, 9, 16
1 Sam 14:1
day he t. her, she t. the riddle.
Judg 14:17
she urged him, he t. her. 16:17, 18
he t. us that the asses were found.
1 Sam 10:16
Abigail t. not her husband. 25:19
and the woman sent and t. David.
2 Sam 11:5
and t. them, they t. David. 17:17
t. her all her questions, not any . . .
he t. not. 1 Ki 10:3; 2 Chr 9:2
the words they t. also to. 1 Ki 13:11
came and t. it in the city where. 25
hast t. thou wilt build. 1 Chr 17:25
I t. them what they should say to.
Ezra 8:17
Haman t. of the glory of. Esth 5:11
for Esther had t. what he was. 8:1
which wise men have t. Job 15:18
fathers have t. us. Ps 44:1; 78:3
have not I t. thee from? Isa 44:8
who hath t. it from that time? 45:21
what had not been t. them. 52:15
because he had t. them. Jonah 1:10
the city and t. every thing. Mat 8:33
body, and went and t. Jesus. 14:12
they went and t. it to. Mark 16:13
the man t. the Jews it. John 5:15
it shall be t. thee what thou must do.
Acts 9:6; 22:10
into the castle and t. Paul. 23:16
he t. us your earnest. 2 Cor 7:7

told, participle
it was certainly t. thy. Josh 9:24
oxen could not be t. 1 Ki 8:5
was it not t. my lord what? 18:13
gave money, being t. 2 Ki 12:11
years as a tale that is t. Ps 90:9
it was t. the house of David. Isa 7:2
and the vision which is t. Dan 8:26
there shall this be t. for. Mat 26:13
a performance of things which were t.
Luke 1:45
those things t. by shepherds. 2:18

told him
which God had t. him. Gen 22:3, 9
I have t. him, I will judge his.
1 Sam 3:13
Samuel t. him every whit and. 18
the kingdom he t. him not. 10:16
she t. him nothing till morning. 25:36
the man of God t. him. 2 Ki 6:10
be t. him that I speak. Job 37:20
but the woman t. him. Mark 5:33

told me
thou hast mocked me and t. me lies.
Judg 16:10, 13
hast not t. me wherein thy. 15
for it is t. me that he dealeth very subtilly. 1 Sam 23:22
when one t. me, saying, Saul is dead.
2 Sam 4:10
the half was not t. me. 1 Ki 10:7
2 Chr 9:6
t. me I should be king. 1 Ki 14:2
me and hath not t. me. 2 Ki 4:27
he t. me that thou shouldest. 8:14
see a man which t. me all things.
John 4:29, 39
even as it was t. me. Acts 27:25

told you
hath it not been t. you? Isa 40:21
believe, though it be t. you. Hab 1:5
I have t. you before. Mat 24:25
see him, lo, I have t. you. 28:7
if I have t. you earthly. John 3:12
a man that hath t. you truth. 8:40
he said, I have t. you already. 9:27
10:25
I would have t. you. 14:2
now I have t. you before it. 29
have I t. you, that when time shall come . . . t. you of them. 16:4
Jesus said, I have t. you that. 18:8
I t. you before, and. 2 Cor 13:2
as I have also t. you in. Gal 5:21
of whom I have t. you. Phil 3:18
we t. you that we should suffer.
1 Thes 3:4
when with you, I t. you. 2 Thes 2:5
they t. you there should. Jude 18

tolerable
it shall be more t. for Sodom and.
Mat 10:15; 11:24; Mark 6:11
Luke 10:12
more t. for Tyre and Sidon
Mat 11:22; Luke 10:14

toll
then will they not pay t. Ezra 4:13*
t., tribute, and custom, was paid. 20*
lawful to impose t. on them. 7:24*

tomb
shall remain in the t. Job 21:32
Joseph laid the body in his own new t.
Mat 27:60

disciples laid John's corpse in a *t.* *Mark* 6:29

tombs

met him two possessed with devils, coming out of the *t.* *Mat* 8:28
Mark 5:2, 3, 5; *Luke* 8:27
because ye build the *t.* *Mat* 23:29*

to-morrow, *see* **morrow**

tongs

(*American Revision changes this word to* snuffers)
shalt make thee *t.* thereof. *Ex* 25:38
they shall cover his *t.* *Num* 4:9
lamps and *t.* of gold. *1 Ki* 7:49
2 Chr 4:21
a coal which he had taken with the *t.* *Isa* 6:6
smith with the *t.* worketh. 44:12*

tongue

This word is taken in three different senses. (1) *For the material* tongue, *or organ of speech,* Jas 3:5. (2) *For the* tongue *or language that is spoken in any country,* Deut 28:49. (3) *For good or bad discourse,* Pr 12:18; 17:20.

To gnaw one's *tongue, is a token of fury, despair, and torment. The men that worship the beast are said* to gnaw their *tongues* for pain, Rev 16:10. The scourge of the *tongue,* Job 5:21, *is malicious scandal, calumny, insulting, and offensive speeches.*

The gift of *tongues, which God granted to the Apostles and disciples assembled at Jerusalem, on the day of Pentecost,* Acts 2:3, 4, etc., *is not fully understood. St. Paul speaks of it as still existing,* 1 Cor 12:10; 14:2.

not a dog move his *t.* *Ex* 11:7
none moved his *t.* against. *Josh* 10:21
the water with his *t.* *Judg* 7:5
from the scourge of the *t.* *Job* 5:21
and thou choosest the *t.* of. 15:5
hide wickedness under his *t.* 20:12
poison of asps, the viper's *t.* shall. 16
their *t.* cleaved to roof of. 29:10
they flatter with their *t.* *Ps* 5:9
under his *t.* is mischief and. 10:7
shall cut off the *t.* that speaketh. 12:3
who have said, With our *t.* will. 4
that backbiteth not with his *t.* 15:3
keep thy *t.* from evil. 34:13
1 Pet 3:10
and his *t.* talketh of. *Ps* 37:30
and thy *t.* frameth deceit. 50:19
thy *t.* deviseth mischiefs like. 52:2
and their *t.* is a sharp sword. 57:4
who whet their *t.* like a sword. 64:3
shall make their *t.* to fall on. 8
t. of thy dogs shall be dipped. 68:23
and their *t.* walketh through. 73:9
against me with a lying *t.* 109:2
done to thee, thou false *t.*? 120:3
our *t.* filled with singing. 126:2
a proud look, a lying *t.* *Pr* 6:17
from the flattery of the *t.* of a. 24
the *t.* of the just is as choice. 10:20
the froward *t.* shall be cut out. 31
t. of the wise is health. 12:18
but a lying *t.* is but for a. 19
t. of the wise useth knowledge. 15:2
a wholesome *t.* is a tree of life. 4
and the answer of the *t.* is. 16:1
giveth heed to a naughty *t.* 17:4
he that hath a perverse *t.* falleth. 20
life are in the power of the *t.* 18:21
treasures by a lying *t.* is vanity. 21:6
whoso keepeth his *t.* keepeth. 23
soft *t.* breaketh the bone. 25:15
angry countenance a backbiting *t.* 23
lying *t.* hateth those afflicted. 26:28
that flattereth with the *t.* 28:23
and in her *t.* is the law of. 31:26
milk are under thy *t.* *S of S* 4:11
because their *t.* is against. *Isa* 3:8
Lord shall destroy the *t.* 11:15
t. is as a devouring fire. 30:27
the *t.* of the stammerers shall. 32:4
a people of a stammering *t.* 33:19
hall the *t.* of the dumb sing. 35:6
and when their *t.* faileth for. *Isa* 41:17
that unto me every *t.* shall. 45:23
the Lord hath given me the *t.* 50:4
t. that shall rise against thee. 54:17
whom draw ye out the *t.*? 57:4
t. hath muttered perverseness. 59:3
their *t.* like their bow. *Jer* 9:3
taught their *t.* to speak lies. 5
their *t.* is as an arrow shot out. 8
let us smite him with the *t.* 18:18
the *t.* of the sucking child cleaveth. *Lam* 4:4
I will make thy *t.* cleave. *Ezek* 3:26
princes shall fall for the rage of their *t.* *Hos* 7:16
holdest thy *t.* when the wicked devoureth. *Hab* 1:13*
their *t.* shall consume. *Zech* 14:12
spit, and touched his *t.* *Mark* 7:33
and straightway his *t.* was loosed. 35; *Luke* 1:64
and bridleth not his *t.* *Jas* 1:26
so the *t.* is a little member. 3:5
the *t.* is a fire. 6
the *t.* can no man tame. 8
nor let us love in *t.* but. *1 John* 3:18
see **deceitful, hold**

my **tongue**

his word was in *my t.* *2 Sam* 23:2
sold, I had held *my t.* *Esth* 7:4
is there iniquity in *my t.*? *Job* 6:30
nor shall *my t.* utter deceit. 27:4
my t. hath spoken in my mouth. 33:2
and *my t.* cleaveth to my. *Ps* 22:15
my t. shall speak of thy righteousness. 35:28; 51:14; 71:24
that I sin not with *my t.* 39:1
was hot, then spake I with *my t.* 3
my t. is the pen of a ready. 45:1
God was extolled with *my t.* 66:17
my t. shall speak of thy. 119:172
let *my t.* cleave to the roof. 137:6
not a word in *my t.* but thou. 139:4
finger, and cool *my t.* *Luke* 16:24
rejoice, *my t.* was glad. *Acts* 2:26

tongue for *language, speech*

isles were divided every one after his *t.* *Gen* 10:5
of speech, and of a slow *t.* *Ex* 4:10
a nation whose *t.* shall. *Deut* 28:49
letter was written in the Syrian *t.* and interpreted in Syrian *t.* *Ezra* 4:7*
for with another *t.* will. *Isa* 28:11
they might teach the *t.* of. *Dan* 1:4
called in the Hebrew *t.* Bethesda. *John* 5:2
field called in their proper *t.* Aceldama. *Acts* 1:19*
every man in our own *t.*? 2:8*
in the Hebrew *t.* Saul, Saul. 26:14*
every *t.* shall confess. *Rom* 14:11
he that speaketh in an unknown *t.* *1 Cor* 14:2, 4, 13, 14, 19, 27
except ye utter by the *t.* words. 9
hath a psalm, hath a *t.* 26
that every *t.* confess that. *Phil* 2:11
hast redeemed us out of every *t.* *Rev* 5:9
in the Hebrew *t.* is Abaddon. 9:11
the gospel to preach to every *t.* 14:6
the Hebrew *t.* Armageddon. 16:16

tongued

be grave, not double-*t.* *1 Tim* 3:8

tongues

of Ham, after their *t.* *Gen* 10:20
sons of Shem, after their *t.* 31
them from the strife of *t.* *Ps* 31:20
O Lord, and divide their *t.* 55:9
lied to him with their *t.* 78:36
they sharpened their *t.* like. 140:3
gather all nations and *t.* *Isa* 66:18
that use their *t.* and say. *Jer* 23:31
shall speak with new *t.* *Mark* 16:17
there appeared to them cloven *t.* *Acts* 2:3
began to speak with other *t.* 4
we hear in our *t.* the wonderful. 11
heard them speak with *t.* 10:46
and they spake with *t.* and. 19:6
with their *t.* they have used deceit. *Rom* 3:13
to another divers kinds of *t.* *1 Cor* 12:10, 28
do all speak with *t.*? do all? 30
though I speak with the *t.* of. 13:1
there be *t.*, they shall cease. 8
I would ye all spake with *t.* 14:5
if I come to you speaking with *t.* 6
I thank God, I speak with *t.* 18
with men of other *t.* will I speak. 21
t. are for a sign. 22
if all speak with *t.* 23
forbid not to speak with *t.* 39
people and *t.* stood before. *Rev* 7:9
again before nations and *t.* 10:11
t. and nations shall see their. 11:9
power was given him over all *t.* 13:7
and they gnawed their *t.* for. 16:10
sawest are nations and *t.* 17:15

took

Enoch was not, for God *t.* him. *Gen* 5:24
his mother *t.* him a wife out. 21:21
God, which *t.* me from my. 24:7
the lord of the land *t.* us for. 42:30
Moses *t.* the redemption money. *Num* 3:49, 50
the Lord *t.* of the Spirit that. 11:25
king Arad *t.* some of them. 21:1
I *t.* thee to curse mine. 23:11
so I *t.* the chief of your. *Deut* 1:15
only the cattle we *t.* for a prey. 2:35
there was not a city we *t.* not. 3:4
I *t.* your sin, the calf which. 9:21
I *t.* this woman and found. 22:14
I coveted them, and *t.* *Josh* 7:21
the men *t.* of their victuals. 9:14
I *t.* your father Abraham. 24:3
Philistines *t.* Samson. *Judg* 16:21
silver is with me, I *t.* it. 17:2
no man *t.* them into his house. 19:15
the man *t.* his concubine, and. 25
I *t.* my concubine, and cut. 20:6
brought up, the priest *t.* *1 Sam* 2:14
Philistines *t.* the ark of God. 5:1, 2
Samuel *t.* a vial of oil and. 10:1
so Saul *t.* the kingdom over. 14:47
people *t.* of the spoil, sheep. 15:21
Samuel *t.* horn of oil and. 16:13
Saul *t.* him, would not let him. 18:2
David *t.* the spear from. 26:12
I *t.* the crown and. *2 Sam* 1:10
Uzzah *t.* hold of it for the. 6:6
I *t.* thee from the sheepcote. 7:8
not depart, as I *t.* it from Saul. 15
but *t.* the poor man's lamb. 12:4
Zadok the priest *t.* an. *1 Ki* 1:39
she arose and *t.* my son from. 3:20
the cities my father *t.* I will. 20:34
but Jehu *t.* no heed to. *2 Ki* 10:31
yet David *t.* the castle. *1 Chr* 11:5
which *t.* Manasseh among thorns. *2 Chr* 33:11
vessels which Nebuchadnezzar *t.* *Ezra* 5:14; 6:5
whom Mordecai *t.* for his. *Esth* 2:7
then *t.* Haman the apparel and. 6:11
t. upon them, that they would. 9:27
he that *t.* me out of the womb. *Ps* 22:9; 71:6
fear *t.* hold upon them there. 48:6
we *t.* sweet counsel together. 55:14
he chose David, and *t.* from. 78:70
I *t.* me faithful witnesses. *Isa* 8:2
with whom *t.* he counsel? 40:14
then *t.* I the cup at the. *Jer* 25:17
in the day I *t.* them by the hand. 31:32; *Heb* 8:9
even they *t.* Jeremiah out. *Jer* 39:14
and he *t.* me by a lock. *Ezek* 8:3
he *t.* fire from between the. 10:7
he heard the trumpet, and *t.* 33:5
the Lord *t.* me as I followed the. *Amos* 7:15
I *t.* me two staves, Beauty and Bands. *Zech* 11:7
I *t.* the thirty pieces and cast. 13
himself *t.* our infirmities. *Mat* 8:17
like leaven which a woman *t.* 13:33
Luke 13:21
the foolish virgins *t.* no oil. *Mat* 25:3
ye *t.* me in. 35
I was a stranger and ye *t.* me not. 43
the first *t.* a wife, and. *Mark* 12:20

second t. her and died. Mark 12:21
Luke 20:29, 30
in the temple teaching, and ye t. me not. Mark 14:49
that disciple t. her to his. John 19:27
to them who t. Jesus. Acts 1:16
but Barnabas t. him, and. 9:27
t. with them John whose. 12:25
t. on them to call over them. 19:13
whom we t. and would have judged according to our law. 24:6
Paul thanked God and t. 28:15
I went up, and t. Titus. Gal 2:1
and t. upon him the form. Phil 2:7
t. it out of the way. Col 2:14
he also himself t. part. Heb 2:14
ye t. joyfully the spoiling of. 10:34
he t. the book. Rev 5:7
angel t. the censer. 8:5
I t. the little book out of the. 10:10

took *away*

he t. *away* my birthright. Gen 27:36
a west wind t. *away* the. Ex 10:19
he t. not *away* the pillar of. 13:22
shall restore that which he t. *away*. Lev 6:4
Gideon t. *away* their. Judg 8:21
Israel t. *away* my land when. 11:13
Israel t. not *away* the land. 15
David t. *away* the. 1 Sam 27:9
Shishak t. *away* the treasures. 1 Ki 14:26
Asa t. *away* the sodomites. 15:12
and they t. *away* the stones of. 22
Josiah t. *away* the horses. 2 Ki 23:11
all the vessels wherewith they ministered the Chaldeans t. *away*. 25:14, 15; Jer 52:18, 19
Asa t. *away* the altars. 2 Chr 14:3, 5
Jehoshaphat t. *away* the high. 17:6
Hezekiah t. *away* the altars. 30:14
Manasseh t. *away* the strange. 33:15
I restored that which I t. not *away*. Ps 69:4
keepers t. *away* my vail. S of S 5:7
I t. them *away* as I saw good. Ezek 16:50
and I t. the king *away* in my wrath. Hos 13:11
flood came and t. them all *away*. Mat 24:39
then they t. *away* the stone from. John 11:41

he **took**

Shechem saw her, *he* t. Gen 34:2
when *he* t. it out, his hand. Ex 4:6
he t. the book of the covenant. 24:7
and *he* t. the calf which they. 32:20
he t. the vail off, until he. 34:34
he t. all the fat on the inwards. Lev 8:16, 25
he t. the elders of the city. Judg 8:16
he t. men of the elders. Ruth 4:2
he t. a yoke of oxen. 1 Sam 11:7
when Saul saw any valiant man, *he* t. him unto him. 14:52
he t. Agag king of the. 15:8
he t. his staff in his hand. 17:40
he t. hold of her, and. 2 Sam 13:11
he t. three darts, and thrust. 18:14
above, *he* t. me. 22:17; Ps 18:16
he t. her son out of. 1 Ki 17:19
he t. the mantle of. 2 Ki 2:14
he t. his eldest son and. 3:27
he t. them from their hand. 5:24
he t. a thick cloth and dipped. 8:15
and *he* t. unto him bow and. 13:15
he t. him a potsherd to. Job 2:8
slothful roasteth not that which *he* t. Pr 12:27
he t. his brother by the. Hos 12:3
he t. the seven loaves. Mat 15:36
Mark 8:6
he t. the cup. Mat 26:27
Luke 22:17; 1 Cor 11:25
he t. with him Peter, James, John. Mat 26:37; Luke 9:28
he t. water and washed. Mat 27:24
and *he* t. the blind man. Mark 8:23
he t. a child and set him in. 9:36
he t. the five loaves. Luke 9:16
he t. out two pence and gave. 10:35
he t. bread. 22:19; 24:30 Acts 27:35
he t. them the same hour. Acts 16:33
he t. Paul's girdle and bound. 21:11
he t. not on him the. Heb 2:16
he t. the blood of calves. 9:19

they **took**

they t. them wives. Gen 6:2
and *they* t. all the goods of. 14:11
they t. Lot, Abram's brother's son. 12
and *they* t. every man. Num 16:18
and *they* t. of the fruit. Deut 1:25
people went up and *they* t. the city. Josh 6:20
the king of Ai *they* t. alive. 8:23
save Hivites, all other *they* t. 11:19
they t. their daughters. Judg 3:6
they t. them alive and. 2 Ki 10:14
they t. the young men. Lam 5:13
I saw that *they* t. both. Ezek 23:13
and *they* t. his glory. Dan 5:20
because *they* t. him for a prophet. Mat 21:46
so *they* t. the money, and did. 28:15
they t. him, and killed him, and cast. Mark 12:8
they t. him and led him. Luke 22:54
John 19:16
and *they* t. knowledge. Acts 4:13
they t. him down from the tree and laid. 13:29
they t. him, and expounded. 18:26

took *up*

Balaam t. *up* his parable. Num 23:7
18; 24:3, 15, 20, 21, 23
the priests t. *up* the ark. Josh 3:6
6:12; 1 Ki 8:3
then the man t. *up* his. Judg 19:28
cook t. *up* the shoulder. 1 Sam 9:24
they t. *up* Asahel and. 2 Sam 2:32
Mephibosheth's nurse t. him *up*. 4:4
prophet t. *up* the carcase. 1 Ki 13:29
he t. *up* also the mantle. 2 Ki 2:13
the Shunammite t. *up* her son. 4:37
and he t. him *up* to him into. 10:15
I t. *up* the wine and gave. Neh 2:1
they t. Jeremiah *up* out of. Jer 38:13
then the Spirit t. me *up*. Ezek 3:12
11:24; 43:5
flame slew men that t. *up* Shadrach, Meshach and Abed-nego. Dan 3:22
so they t. *up* Jonah. Jonah 1:15
they t. *up* the body of John. Mat 14:12; Mark 6:29
t. *up* of the fragments. Mat 14:20
15:37; Mark 6:43; 8:8, 20
many baskets ye t. *up*. Mat 16:9, 10
and he t. *up* the bed and. Mark 2:12
he t. them *up* in his arms. 10:16
t. him *up* in his arms. Luke 2:28
t. *up* stones to cast at him. John 8:59; 10:31
daughter t. Moses *up*. Acts 7:21
yea, ye t. *up* the tabernacle of. 43
but Peter t. him *up*, saying. 10:26
we t. *up* our carriages and. 21:15
angel t. *up* a stone. Rev 18:21

tookest

though thou t. vengeance. Ps 99:8
and t. thy broidered. Ezek 16:18

tool

if thou lift up thy t. upon it. Ex 20:25
fashioned it with a graving t. 32:4
lift up any iron t. on them. Deut 27:5
nor *any* t. of iron heard. 1 Ki 6:7

tooth

give t. for t. Ex 21:24; Lev 24:20
Deut 19:21; Mat 5:38
or his maidservant's t. he shall let him go free for his t.'s. Ex 21:27
is like a broken t., a foot. Pr 25:19

top

tower whose t. may reach. Gen 11:4
the t. of the ladder reached to. 28:12
Jacob poured oil on the t. of. 18
on the t. of the mount: and called Moses to the t. Ex 19:20; 34:2
like devouring fire on the t. 24:17
be an hole in the t. of it. 28:32*
the t. with pure gold. 30:3; 37:26
they gat up into the t. . Num 14:40
Aaron died there in the t. of. 20:28
for from the t of the rocks. 23:9
the t. of Pisgah. Deut 3:27; 34:1
from sole of foot to the t. Deut 28:35*
on t. of the head of him that. 33:16*
build an altar on the t. Judg 6:26
the people gat up to the t. of. 9:51*
Samson dwelt in the t. of the. 15:8*
communed on the t. of the house. 1 Sam 9:25, 26
spread a tent on the t. of the house. 2 Sam 16:22
the t. of the throne. 1 Ki 10:19
him on the t. of the stairs. 2 Ki 9:13
from the t. of the rock. 2 Chr 25:12
the t. of the sceptre. Esth 5:2
of corn on t. of mountains. Ps 72:16
a sparrow alone on the house-t. 102:7
she standeth in the t. of. Pr 8:2
It is better to dwell in a corner of the house-t. 21:9; 25:24
lieth on the t. of a mast. 23:34
t. of Amana, from the t. S of S 4:8
Lord's house shall be established in the t. Isa 2:2; Mi 4:1
two or three berries in the t. Isa 17:6
beacon on the t. of a mountain. 30:17
let them shout from the t. of. 42:11
faint for hunger in t. of every street. Lam 2:19†
poured out in t. of every street. 4:1†
he cropped off the t. of. Ezek 17:4*
from the t. of his young twigs. 22*
she set it on the t. of a rock. 24:7*
blood on the t. of a rock. 8*
her like the t. of a rock. 26:4*, 14*
his t. was among the thick boughs. 31:3, 10, 14
law of the house: on the t. of. 43:12
her children were dashed at the t. of all the streets. Nah 3:10†
on the house-t. not come. Mat 24:17
Mark 13:15; Luke 17:31
vail rent from t. to the bottom. Mat 27:51; Mark 15:38
house-t. and let down. Luke 5:19
was woven from the t. John 19:23
leaning on t. of his staff. Heb 11:21
see **Carmel, hill**

topaz

(*A green gem of golden hue, one of the stones in the high priest's breastplate*)
the first row a sardius, a t. Ex 28:17
39:10
the t. of Ethiopia shall. Job 28:19
the sardius, the t. Ezek 28:13
beryl, the ninth a t. Rev 21:20

Tophet

Tophet, "place of burning," *was at Jerusalem, lying to the south of the city, in the valley of the children of Hinnom. There they burned the carcases and other filthiness from the city. It was in the same place that they cast away the ashes and remains of the images of false gods, when they demolished their altars, and broke down their statues. Isaiah seems to allude to this custom of burning dead carcases* in Tophet, *when speaking of the defeat of the army of Sennacherib,* Isa 30:33.
Josiah defiled T. in the. 2 Ki 23:10
for T. is ordained of old. Isa 30:33
built the high places of T. Jer 7:31
no more be called T. 32; 19:6
they shall bury in T., till. 7:32; 19:11
and even make this city as T. 19:12
Jerusalem shall be defiled as T. 13
then came Jeremiah from T. 14

tops

the t. of the mountains. Gen 8:5
sound of a going in the t. of the. 2 Sam 5:24; 1 Chr 14:15
as the grass upon the house-t. 2 Ki 19:26; Ps 129:6; Isa 37:27
and cut off as the t. of. Job 24:24
t. of the ragged rocks. Isa 2:21*
on the t. of houses every one. 15:3
wholly gone up to the house-t. 22:1
be lamentation on all house-t. Jer 48:38

their slain men shall be in all the *t.* of the mountains. *Ezek* 6:13
they sacrifice on the *t.* of. *Hos* 4:13
worship the host of heaven on house-*t.* *Zeph* 1:5
that preach ye upon the house-*t.* *Mat* 10:27
proclaimed on the house-*t.* *Luke* 12:3

torch

make the governors of Judah like a *t.* *Zech* 12:6

torches

shall be with flaming *t.* *Nah* 2:3*
the chariots shall seem like *t.* 4
with lanterns and *t.* *John* 18:3

torment

into this place of *t.* *Luke* 16:28
because fear hath *t.* *1 John* 4:18*
their *t.* was as the *t.* of. *Rev* 9:5
smoke of their *t.* ascendeth. 14:11
so much *t.* and sorrow give her. 18:7
afar off for the fear of her *t.* 10, 15

torment, *verb*

art thou come to *t.* us? *Mat* 8:29
that thou *t.* me not. *Mark* 5:7
Luke 8:28

tormented

lieth grievously *t.* *Mat* 8:6
send Lazarus, for I am *t.* in this flame. *Luke* 16:24*
comforted, and thou art *t.* 25*
destitute, afflicted, *t.* *Heb* 11:37*
but that they should be *t.* *Rev* 9:5
two prophets *t.* them that. 11:10
he shall be *t.* with fire and. 14:10
and shall be *t.* day and night. 20:10

tormentors

delivered him to the *t.* *Mat* 18:34

torments

taken with divers diseases and *t.* *Mat* 4:24
in hell he lift up his eyes, being in *t.* *Luke* 16:23

torn

that which was *t.* of beasts I brought not. *Gen* 31:39
Surely he is *t.* in pieces. 44:28
if *t.* in pieces, let him bring it for witness . . . what was *t.* *Ex* 22:13
shall eat any flesh *t.* of beasts. 31
fat of that which is *t.* may. *Lev* 7:24
if any eat that which was *t.* 17:15
dieth of itself, or *t.* of beasts. 22:8
lion, which hath *t.* him. *1 Ki* 13:26
not eaten carcase nor *t.* the ass. 28
carcases *t.* in the midst of. *Isa* 5:25*
goeth out shall be *t.* *Jer* 5:6
not eaten of that which is *t.* *Ezek* 4:14
not eat any thing that is *t.* 44:31
for he hath *t.* and he will. *Hos* 6:1
brought that which was *t.* *Mal* 1:13*
when the unclean spirit hath *t.* him. *Mark* 1:26

tortoise

This is probably a sort of lizard. It is numbered among the unclean animals, Lev 11:29.

the *t.* shall be unclean. *Lev* 11:29*

tortured

others were *t.* not accepting deliverance. *Heb* 11:35

toss

he will turn and *t.* thee. *Isa* 22:18
though the waves thereof *t.* *Jer* 5:22

tossed

I am *t.* up and down. *Ps* 109:23
is a vanity, *t.* to and fro. *Pr* 21:6
O thou afflicted, *t.* with. *Isa* 54:11
was now *t.* with waves. *Mat* 14:24*
t. with a tempest. *Acts* 27:18*
children, *t.* to and fro. *Eph* 4:14
wavereth is like a wave *t.* *Jas* 1:6

tossings

I am full of *t.* to and fro. *Job* 7:4

tottering

all of you as a *t.* fence. *Ps* 62:3

touch

not eat of it, nor shall ye *t.* *Gen* 3:3
suffered I thee not to *t.* her. 20:6
that ye *t.* not the border. *Ex* 19:12
there shall not an hand *t.* it. *Ex* 19:13
if a soul *t.* any unclean. *Lev* 5:2
or if he *t.* the uncleanness of man. 5:3; 7:21
whatsoever shall *t.* the flesh. 6:27
their carcase ye shall not *t.* 11:8
Deut 14:8
whosoever doth *t.* them when dead. *Lev* 11:31
he shall *t.* no hallowed thing. 12:4
they shall not *t.* any holy. *Num* 4:15
depart and *t.* nothing of theirs. 16:26
we may not *t.* them. *Josh* 9:19
they should not *t.* thee. *Ruth* 2:9
and he shall not *t.* thee any more. *2 Sam* 14:10
t. the young man Absalom. 18:12
the man that shall *t.* them. 23:7
t. not mine anointed. *1 Chr* 16:22
Ps 105:15
but *t.* all he hath and he will curse. *Job* 1:11
t. his bone and his flesh, he will. 2:5
there shall no evil *t.* thee. 5:19
that my soul refused to *t.* 6:7
t. the mountains and they. *Ps* 144:5
t. no unclean thing. *Isa* 52:11
2 Cor 6:17
that *t.* the inheritance of. *Jer* 12:14
so that men could not *t.* *Lam* 4:14
it is unclean, depart, *t.* not. 15
if one with his skirt do *t.* *Hag* 2:12
if one that is unclean *t.* any of. 13
if I may but *t.* his garment. *Mat* 9:21; *Mark* 5:28
they might *t.* the hem. *Mat* 14:36
Mark 5:28; 6:56; 8:22
they pressed on him to *t.* him. *Mark* 3:10; *Luke* 6:19
they besought him to *t.* the blind. *Mark* 8:22
ye yourselves *t.* not the. *Luke* 11:46
that he would *t.* them. 18:15
unto her, *T.* me not. *John* 20:17
a man not to *t.* a woman. *1 Cor* 7:1
t. not, taste not, handle not. *Col* 2:21
firstborn, should *t.* them. *Heb* 11:28
if so much as a beast *t.* the. 12:20

touched

as we have not *t.* thee. *Gen* 26:29
t. the hollow of Jacob's. 32:25, 32
the soul which hath *t.* *Lev* 22:6
and whosoever hath *t.* *Num* 31:19
the angel of the Lord *t.* *Judg* 6:21
hearts God had *t.* *1 Sam* 10:26
the wings of cherubims *t.* *1 Ki* 6:27
an angel *t.* him and said. 19:5, 7
when the man *t.* the bones of Elisha. *2 Ki* 13:21
so Esther *t.* the top of. *Esth* 5:2
the hand of God hath *t.* *Job* 19:21
lo, this hath *t.* thy lips. *Isa* 6:7
Lord *t.* my mouth. *Jer* 1:9
and the he goat *t.* not. *Dan* 8:5
but he *t.* me. 18; 9:21; 10:10, 16, 18
and Jesus *t.* him. *Mat* 8:3
Mark 1:41; *Luke* 5:13
t. her hand, and the fever. *Mat* 8:15
with an issue of blood *t.* the hem. 9:20; *Mark* 5:27; *Luke* 8:44
then *t.* he their eyes, saying. *Mat* 9:29; 20:34
as many as *t.* him were made perfectly whole. 14:36; *Mark* 6:56
who *t.* my clothes? *Mark* 5:30, 31
Luke 8:45, 47
into his ears, and he spit, and *t.* his tongue. *Mark* 7:33
he came and *t.* the bier. *Luke* 7:14
what cause she had *t.* him. 8:47
and Jesus *t.* his ear and. 22:51
next day we *t.* at Sidon. *Acts* 27:3
priest which cannot be *t.* *Heb* 4:15
mount that might be *t.* 12:18

toucheth

he that *t.* this man shall. *Gen* 26:11
whosoever *t.* the mount. *Ex* 19:12
whatsoever *t.* the altar shall. 29:37
that *t.* them, shall be holy. 30:29
Lev 6:18
the flesh that *t.* any. *Lev* 7:19
whosoever *t.* their carcase. 11:24
27, 36, 39
every one that *t.* them shall. *Lev* 11:26
whoso *t.* his bed, shall wash. 15:5
t. his flesh. 7
t. any thing under him. 10
whomsoever he *t.* that hath the. 11
the vessel of earth that he *t.* shall. 12
whoso *t.* her. 19
whosoever *t.* her bed. 21
whosoever *t.* any thing that she. 22
if on her bed, when he *t.* it, he shall. 15:23, 27; 22:4, 5; *Num* 19:22
he that *t.* the dead body. *Num* 19:11
13, 16
t. a bone. 18
t. the water of separation. 21
broken when it *t.* fire. *Judg* 16:9
it *t.* thee and thou art. *Job* 4:5
he *t.* the hills and they. *Ps* 104:32
whosoever *t.* her, shall not. *Pr* 6:29
when the east wind *t.* it. *Ezek* 17:10
out, and blood *t.* blood. *Hos* 4:2
Lord is he that *t.* the land. *Amos* 9:5
he that *t.* you, *t.* the apple. *Zech* 2:8
what woman this is that *t.* him. *Luke* 7:39
and that wicked one *t.* *1 John* 5:18

touching

Esau, as *t.* thee, doth. *Gen* 27:42
for him, as *t.* his sin that. *Lev* 5:13
thus do to the Levites *t.* *Num* 8:26
t. matter thou and I. *1 Sam* 20:23
t. the words which thou. *2 Ki* 22:18
t. the Almighty, we cannot find him. *Job* 37:23
I have made *t.* the king. *Ps* 45:1
a song of my beloved, *t.* *Isa* 5:1
utter judgements *t.* all. *Jer* 1:16
t. the house of the king of. 21:11
thus saith the Lord *t.* Shallum. 22:11
the vision is *t.* the whole. *Ezek* 7:13
as *t.* any thing that they. *Mat* 18:19
as *t.* the resurrection of the. 22:31
Mark 12:26; *Acts* 24:21
t. those things whereof. *Luke* 23:14
to do as *t.* these men. *Acts* 5:35
as *t.* the Gentiles who believe. 21:25
as *t.* the election, they. *Rom* 11:28
now as *t.* things offered. *1 Cor* 8:1
t. our brother Apollos. 16:12
as *t.* the ministering to. *2 Cor* 9:1
of the Hebrews, as *t.* the. *Phil* 3:5
t. the righteousness in the law. 6
t. whom ye received. *Col* 4:10
t. brotherly love, ye. *1 Thes* 4:9
in the Lord *t.* you. *2 Thes* 3:4

tow

a thread of *t.* is broken. *Judg* 16:9
and the strong shall be as *t.* *Isa* 1:31
they are quenched as *t.* 43:17*

toward, *or* **towards**

Ephraim *t.* Israel's left hand, Manasseh *t.* Israel's right. *Gen* 48:13
face *t.* the wilderness. *Num* 24:1
his eye shall be evil *t.* *Deut* 28:54
shall be evil *t.* her husband. 56
heart is *t.* the governors. *Judg* 5:9
behold, if there be good *t.* David. *1 Sam* 20:12
prayer thy servant shall make *t.* *1 Ki* 8:29, 30, 35; *2 Chr* 6:21
done good in Israel, both *t.* God, and *t.* his house. *2 Chr* 24:16
endureth for ever *t.* Israel. *Ezra* 3:11
I will worship *t.* thy holy temple. *Ps* 5:7; 138:2
eyes are ever *t.* the Lord. 25:15
hands *t.* thy holy oracle. 28:2
favour is *t.* a wise servant. *Pr* 14:35
the great goodness *t.* house. *Isa* 63:7
my mind could not be *t.* *Jer* 15:1
being open *t.* Jerusalem. *Dan* 6:10
horn waxed great *t.* the south. 8:9
look *t.* thy holy temple. *Jonah* 2:4
as it began to dawn *t.* the first day. *Mat* 28:1
peace, good will *t.* men. *Luke* 2:14
treasure, and not rich *t.* God. 12:21
with us, for it is *t.* evening. 24:29
Greeks, repentance *t.* God, and faith *t.* our Lord Jesus. *Acts* 20:21
of offence *t.* God and *t.* men. 24:16

faith which thou hast *t.* the Lord Jesus Christ, and *t.* all. *Philem* 5
see **heaven, him, me, thee, them, us, you**

towel

he riseth, and took a *t.* *John* 13:4
wipe their feet with the *t.* 5

tower

[1] Watch-towers *or fortified posts in frontier or exposed places are mentioned in Scripture, as the tower of Edar, etc.,* Gen 35:21; Isa 21:5, 8, 11; Mi 4:8.
[2] *Besides these military towers we read of towers built in vineyards as an almost necessary addition to them, Isa* 5:2; Mat 21:33.
[3] *God is often alluded to as a tower, with the idea of protection,* Ps 61:3; Pr 18:10.

let us build us a city and *t.* *Gen* 11:4
came down to see the city and *t.* 5
tent beyond the *t.* of Edar. 35:21
I will break down this *t.* *Judg* 8:9
he beat down the *t.* of Penuel. 17
men of the *t.* of Shechem. 9:46
but there was a strong *t.* within. 51
is the *t.* of salvation. *2 Sam* 22:51*
when he came to the *t.* he. *2 Ki* 5:24*
hast been a strong *t.* *Ps* 61:3
the Lord is a strong *t.* *Pr* 18:10
like the *t.* of David. *S of S* 4:4
neck is as a *t.* of ivory, thy nose is as the *t.* of Lebanon, looking. 7:4
he built a *t.* in the midst. *Isa* 5:2
I have set thee for a *t.* *Jer* 6:27†
city shall be built from *t.* of. 31:38
Egypt desolate, from the *t.* of Syene. *Ezek* 29:10
from the *t.* of Syene shall they fall in it. 30:6
O *t.* of the flock, to thee. *Mi* 4:8
set me upon the *t.* and. *Hab* 2:1
be inhabited from *t.* of. *Zech* 14:10
built a *t.* and let it out to husbandmen. *Mat* 21:33; *Mark* 12:1
those 18 on whom the *t.* *Luke* 13:4
you intending to build a *t.* 14:28

high **tower**

God is my *high t.* *2 Sam* 22:3
Ps 18:2; 144:2
day of Lord on every *high t. Isa* 2:15

towers

build cities and make *t.* *2 Chr* 14:7
moreover Uzziah built *t.* in. 26:9
he built *t.* in the desert and. 10
Jotham built castles and *t.* 27:4
raised up the wall to the *t.* 32:5
Zion and tell her *t.* *Ps* 48:12
and my breasts like *t.* *S of S* 8:10
the Assyrian set up the *t.* *Isa* 23:13
hill rivers, when the *t.* fall. 30:25
the forts and *t.* shall be for. 32:14
he that counted the *t.*? 33:18
they shall break down her *t.* *Ezek* 26:4, 9
Gammadims were in thy *t.* 27:11
their *t.* are desolate. *Zeph* 3:6

to wit

to wit whether the Lord had made his journey. *Gen* 24:21
to wit what would be done. *Ex* 2:4
to wit, that God was in Christ reconciling. *2 Cor* 5:19
you *to wit* of the grace of God. 8:1

town

(*The Revised Versions frequently change this reading either to* city *or to* village *according as either is appropriate*)

house was on the *t.* wall. *Josh* 2:15
and the elders of *t.* *1 Sam* 16:4
shut in, by entering into a *t.* 23:7
give me a place in some *t.* 27:5
woe to him that builds a *t. Hab* 2:12
t. ye shall enter. *Mat* 10:11
blind man out of the *t.* *Mark* 8:23
nor go into the *t.* nor tell it to. 26
Christ cometh out of the *t.* of. *John* 7:42
the *t.* of Mary and her sister. 11:1
Jesus was not yet come into the *t.* 30

townclerk

the *t.* had appeased the. *Acts* 19:35

towns

dwelt in unwalled *t.* *Esth* 9:19
on all her *t.* the evil. *Jer* 19:15
Jerusalem be inhabited as *t.* without walls. *Zech* 2:4
went through the *t.* *Luke* 9:6
that they may go into the *t.* 12

trade

their *t.* hath been about cattle. *Gen* 46:32*, 34*

trade, *verb*

dwell and *t.* ye. *Gen* 34:10, 21
as many as *t.* by sea. *Rev* 18:17*

traded

Tarshish *t.* in thy fairs. *Ezek* 27:12
Javan, Tubal, Meshech, *t.* the. 13
Togarmah *t.* with horses. 14
Judah and Israel *t.* in thy market. 17
five talents, went and *t.* *Mat* 25:16

trading

how much every man had gained by *t.* *Luke* 19:15

tradition

(*Usually this word means laws and regulations handed down orally from one generation to another, and forming the Oral Law of the Jews, which Jesus frequently denounced when it was against the real law of God*)

why do thy disciples transgress the *t.* of? *Mat* 15:2; *Mark* 7:5
transgress the commandment of God by your *t.*? *Mat* 15:3; *Mark* 7:9
commandment of God of none effect by your *t.* *Mat* 15:6; *Mark* 7:13
t. of the elders. *Mark* 7:3, 8, 9
after the *t.* of men. *Col* 2:8
not after the *t.* which he. *2 Thes* 3:6
received by *t.* from. *1 Pet* 1:18*

traditions

being zealous of the *t.* *Gal* 1:14
hold the *t.* ye have. *2 Thes* 2:15

traffick

ye shall *t.* in the land. *Gen* 42:34

traffick, *substantive*

of *t.* of merchants. *1 Ki* 10:15
it into a land of *t.* *Ezek* 17:4
by thy *t.* hast thou increased. 28:5
sanctuaries by iniquity of *t.* 18

traffickers

whose *t.* are the honourable. *Isa* 23:8

train

Jerusalem with a great *t.* *1 Ki* 10:2
his *t.* filled the temple. *Isa* 6:1

train, *verb*

t. up a child in the way. *Pr* 22:6

trained

his *t.* servants, 318. *Gen* 14:14

traitor

Iscariot, which was the *t. Luke* 6:16

traitors

men shall be *t.*, heady. *2 Tim* 3:4

trample

the dragon shalt thou *t.* *Ps* 91:13
will *t.* them in my fury. *Isa* 63:3
pearls, lest they *t.* them. *Mat* 7:6

trance

vision falling into a *t. Num* 24:4*, 16*
he fell into a *t.* and saw. *Acts* 10:10
and in a *t.* I saw a vision. 11:5
in the temple, I was in a *t.* 22:17

tranquillity

lengthening of thy *t.* *Dan* 4:27

transferred

have in figure *t.* to myself. *1 Cor* 4:6

transfigured

(*The history of Christ's* transfiguration *is recorded in each of the first three Gospels. All three agree that this* transfiguration *was celebrated upon a mountain, which modern commentators think was Mount Hermon*)

and he was *t.* before them. *Mat* 17:2; *Mark* 9:2

transformed

but be ye *t.* by renewing. *Rom* 12:2
for Satan is *t.* into an. *2 Cor* 11:14*
if his ministers also be *t.* 15*

transforming

t. themselves into. *2 Cor* 11:13*

transgress

wherefore now do ye *t.* the commandment? *Num* 14:41; *2 Chr* 24:20
the Lord's people to *t.* *1 Sam* 2:24
if ye *t.* I will scatter you. *Neh* 1:8
shall we hearken to you to *t.*? 13:27
my mouth shall not *t.* *Ps* 17:3
let them be ashamed who *t.* 25:3
bread that man will *t.* *Pr* 28:21
thou saidst, I will not *t.* *Jer* 2:20
purge out them that *t.* *Ezek* 20:38
come to Beth-el and *t.* *Amos* 4:4
why do thy disciples *t.*? *Mat* 15:2
t. the commandment of God? 3
who by circumcision dost *t.* the law. *Rom* 2:27

transgressed

I have not *t.* thy commandments. *Deut* 26:13
Israel hath sinned, and they have also *t.* my covenant. *Josh* 7:11, 15
t. covenant of Lord your God. 23:16
he said, Ye have *t.* *1 Sam* 14:33
I have *t.* the commandment. 15:24
wherein they have *t.* *1 Ki* 8:50
Achar, who *t.* in the. *1 Chr* 2:7*
they *t.* against the God of. 5:25*
because they *t.* against. *2 Chr* 12:2*
Uzziah *t.* against the Lord, 26:16*
and Ahaz *t.* sore against. 28:19*
the priests and the people *t.* 36:14*
ye have *t.* and taken. *Ezra* 10:10*
we are many that have *t.* in. 13
they have *t.* the laws. *Isa* 24:5
teachers have *t.* against me. 43:27
carcases of men that have *t.* 66:24
the pastors *t.* against me. *Jer* 2:8
why will ye plead? ye all have *t.* 29
acknowledge that thou hast *t.* 3:13
iniquities whereby they *t.* 33:8
I will give the men that *t.* 34:18
we have *t.* and have rebelled. *Lam* 3:42
they and their fathers have *t.* *Ezek* 2:3
transgressions whereby ye *t.* 18:31
yea, all Israel have *t.* *Dan* 9:11
because they have *t.* *Hos* 7:13
not ashamed for doings wherein thou *t.* *Zeph* 3:11
nor *t.* I at any time thy. *Luke* 15:29
see **covenants**

transgressest

why *t.* thou the king's? *Esth* 3:3

transgresseth

his mouth *t.* not in judgement. *Pr* 16:10
because he *t.* by wine. *Hab* 2:5*
committeth sin, *t.* law. *1 John* 3:4*
whoso *t.* and abideth not. *2 John* 9*

transgressing

wrought wickedness in *t. Deut* 17:2
in *t.* and lying against. *Isa* 59:13

transgression

forgiving *t.* and sin. *Ex* 34:7
Num 14:18
or if it be in *t.* against. *Josh* 22:22*
that there is no *t.* in. *1 Sam* 24:11
carried to Babylon for their *t.* *1 Chr* 9:1
so Saul died for his *t.* which. 10:13*
Ahaz cast away in *t.* *2 Chr* 29:19*
because of *t.* of those carried away. *Ezra* 9:4*
mourned because of their *t.* 10:6*
thou not pardon my *t.*? *Job* 7:21
cast them away for their *t.* 8:4
make me to know my *t.* and. 13:23
my *t.* is sealed up in a bag. 14:17
I am clean without *t.* 33:9
is incurable without *t.* 34:6
innocent from the great *t.* *Ps* 19:13
is he whose *t.* is forgiven. 32:1
the *t.* of the wicked saith. 36:1
against me; not for my *t.* 59:3
visit their *t.* with a rod. 89:32

fools because of their t. are. Ps 107:17
the wicked is snared by t. Pr 12:13
covereth a t. seeketh love. 17:9
he loveth t. that loveth strife. 19
glory to pass over a t. 19:11
for the t. of a land many are. 28:2
and saith, It is no t. 24
in the t. of an evil man there. 29:6
when the wicked are multiplied, t. 16
and a furious man aboundeth in t. 22
the t. thereof shall be. Isa 24:20
for the t. of my people was he. 53:8
ye not children of t., a seed of ? 57:4
shew my people their t. 58:1
and to them that turn from t. 59:20
him in the day of his t. Ezek 33:12
against the daily sacrifice by reason of t. Dan 8:12
concerning sacrifice, and the t. 13
determined to finish the t. 9:24
at Gilgal multiply t., bring. Amos 4:4
t. of Jacob is all this, and for the sins . . . what is the t.? Mi 1:5
power to declare to Jacob his t. 3:8
firstborn for my t.? 6:7
that passeth by the t. of the. 7:18
which Judas by t. fell. Acts 1:25*
no law is, there is no t. Rom 4:15
after similitude of Adam's t. 5:14
the woman being deceived was in the t. 1 Tim 2:14
every t. received just recompence of. Heb 2:2
for sin is the t. of the. 1 John 3:4*

transgressions

pardon your t. for my. Ex 23:21
atonement because of their t. Lev 16:16
confess over the goat all their t. 21
will not forgive your t. Josh 24:19
thy people all their t. 1 Ki 8:50
if I covered my t. as Adam, by hiding. Job 31:33
if thy t. be multiplied, what ? 35:6
them their work and t. 36:9
in the multitude of their t. Ps 5:10
sins of my youth, nor my t. 25:7
I said I will confess my t. 32:5
deliver me from all my t. and. 39:8
blot out all my t. 51:1
for I acknowledge my t.: my sin. 3
as for our t. thou shalt purge. 65:3
so far hath he removed our t. 103:12
he that blotteth out thy t. Isa 43:25
out as a thick cloud thy t. 44:22
for your t. is your mother put. 50:1
but he was wounded for our t. 53:5
t. are multiplied before thee, and our sins testify . . . for our t. 59:12
because their t. are many. Jer 5:6
for the multitude of her t. Lam 1:5
the yoke of my t. is bound by. 14
as hast done to me for all my t. 22
any more with their t. Ezek 14:11
all his t. shall not be. 18:22
turneth away from all his t. 28
turn yourselves from your t. 30
cast away all your t. whereby. 31
in that your t. are discovered. 21:24
if our t. be upon us and we pine. 33:10
themselves any more with t. 37:23
according to their t. have I. 39:24
for three t. of Damascus. Amos 1:3
for three t. of Gaza. 6
for three t. of Ammon. 13
I will visit the t. of Israel. 3:14
I know your manifold t. and. 5:12
for the t. of Israel were. Mi 1:13
the law was added because of t., till the seed. Gal 3:19
for the redemption of the t. Heb 9:15

transgressor

the t. shall be a ransom. Pr 21:18*
the words of the t. 22:12*
thou wast called a t. Isa 48:8
I make myself a t. Gal 2:18
kill, thou art become a t. Jas 2:11

transgressors

the t. shall be destroyed. Ps 37:38
then will I teach t. thy ways. 51:13
be not merciful to any wicked t. 59:5
t. shall be rooted out. Pr 2:22*
the perverseness of t. shall. 11:3*
t. shall be taken in their own naughtiness. 6*
but the soul of the t. shall eat. 13:2*
but the way of t. is hard. 15*
and she increaseth the t. 23:28*
rewardeth the fool and the t. 26:10*
the destruction of t. shall. Isa 1:28
bring it again to mind, O ye t. 46:8
numbered with the t. and bare the sin of many, . . . for the t. 53:12
when the t. are come to. Dan 8:23
but the t. shall fall therein. Hos 14:9
he was numbered with t. Mark 15:28
Luke 22:37
convinced of the law as t. Jas 2:9

translate

to t. the kingdom from. 2 Sam 3:10

translated

t. us into the kingdom of. Col 1:13
Enoch was t. that he should not see death. Heb 11:5

translation

before his t. he had this. Heb 11:5

transparent

was as it were t. glass. Rev 21:21

trap, -s

but they shall be t. Josh 23:13
and a t. is laid for him. Job 18:10
let it become a t. Ps 69:22
they lay wait, set a t. Jer 5:26
be made a snare, a t. Rom 11:9

travail

time of her t. behold. Gen 38:27
Moses told Jethro, all the t. Ex 18:8
them as of a woman in t. Ps 48:6
Jer 6:24; 13:21; 22:23; 49:24
50:43; Mi 4:9, 10
this sore t. hath God. Eccl 1:13
are sorrows, his t. is grief. 2:23
but to the sinner he giveth t. 26
I have seen the t. God hath. 3:10
again I considered all t. and. 4:4
than both the hands full with t. 6
vanity, yea it is a sore t. 8
riches perish by evil t. 5:14
I t. not. Isa 23:4
see of the t. of his soul. 53:11
sing, thou that didst not t. 54:1
voice as of a woman in t. Jer 4:31
whether a man doth t.? . . . as a woman in t.? 30:6
compassed me with gall and t. Lam 3:5
a woman when she is in t. hath sorrow. John 16:21
my children, of whom I t. in birth. Gal 4:19
for ye remember our labour and t. 1 Thes 2:9
destruction cometh, as t. 5:3
but wrought with t. night and day. 2 Thes 3:8

travailed

Rachel t. Gen 35:16
Tamar t. 38:28
Phinehas' wife bowed herself, and t. 1 Sam 4:19
she t. she brought forth. Isa 66:7
as soon as Zion t. she brought. 8

travailest

cry, thou that t. not. Gal 4:27

travaileth

behold, he t. with iniquity. Ps 7:14
they shall be in pain as a woman that t. Isa 13:8
as the pangs of a woman that t. 21:3
and with them her that t. Jer 31:8
till she who t. hath brought. Mi 5:3
the whole creation t. in pain until now. Rom 8:22

travailing

I cry like a t. woman. Isa 42:14
sorrows of a t. woman. Hos 13:13
a woman cried, t. in birth. Rev 12:2

travel

thou knowest the t. that. Num 20:14
Paul's companion in t. Acts 19:29
chosen of the churches to t. with us. 2 Cor 8:19

travelled

t. as far as Phenice and. Acts 11:19

traveller

there came a t. to the. 2 Sam 12:4
opened my doors to the t. Job 31:32

travellers

the t. walked through. Judg 5:6

travelleth

wicked man t. with pain. Josh 15:20
poverty come as one that t. Pr 6:11*; 24:34*

travelling

in Arabia lodge, O ye t. Isa 21:13†
who is this t. in the greatness ? 63:1
heaven is as a man t. Mat 25:14

traversing

thou art a swift dromedary t. her ways. Jer 2:23

treacherous

t. dealer dealeth treacherously. Isa 21:2; 24:16
turned not, and her t. sister Judah. Jer 3:7
her t. sister Judah feared not. 8
her t. sister Judah hath not. 10
Israel hath justified herself more than t. Judah. 11
be an assembly of t. men. 9:2
are light and t. persons. Zeph 3:4

treacherously

men of Shechem dealt t. Judg 9:23
and dealest t., and they dealt not t. with thee. Isa 33:1
thou wouldest deal very t. 48:8
as a wife t. departeth. Jer 3:20
the house of Judah hath dealt t. 5:11; Mal 2:11
happy that deal very t.? Jer 12:1
even they have dealt t. with thee. 6
all her friends have dealt t. Lam 1:2
they have dealt t. against. Hos 5:7
there have they dealt t. against. 6:7
why do we deal t. every ? Mal 2:10
against whom thou hast dealt t. 14
let none deal t. against the wife. 15
your spirit, that ye deal not t. 16

treachery

Joram said, There is t. 2 Ki 9:23

tread

soles of your feet t. Deut 11:24
you on all the land that ye t. 25
thou shalt t. upon their high. 33:29
none t. on the threshold. 1 Sam 5:5
t. their winepresses, and. Job 24:11
and t. down the wicked in. 40:12
let him t. down my life. Ps 7:5
name will we t. them under. 44:5
t. down our enemies. 60:12; 108:13
thou shalt t. upon the lion. 91:13
who hath required this at your hand, to t. my courts ? Isa 1:12*
to t. them down, like the mire. 10:6
upon my mountains t. him. 14:25
treaders shall t. out no wine. 16:10
the foot shall t. it down. 26:6
t. them in mine anger. 63:3, 6
a shout, as they that t. Jer 25:30
wine to fail, none shall t. 48:33
with his hoofs shall he t. Ezek 26:11
but ye must t. the residue. 34:18
fourth beast shall t. it. Dan 7:23
Ephraim loveth to t. Hos 10:11
the Lord will t. on the. Mi 1:3
when the Assyrian shall t. 5:5
thou shalt t. the olives, but. 6:15
t. the mortar, make. Nah 3:14
as mighty men which t. Zech 10:5
and ye shall t. down the. Mal 4:3
I will give you power to t. on scorpions. Luke 10:19
holy city shall they t. Rev 11:2

treader, -s

t. shall tread out no wine. Isa 16:10
the t. of grapes shall overtake the sower. Amos 9:13

treadeth

not muzzle ox when he t. Deut 25:4
1 Cor 9:9; 1 Tim 5:18
which t. upon the waves. Job 9:8
come as the potter t. clay. Isa 41:25
thy garments like him that t. 63:2

he that t. on the high places of the earth. Amos 4:13
and when he t. within. Mi 5:6
if he go through, he both t. down. 8
he t. the winepress of. Rev 19:15

treading

in those days saw I some t. winepresses on the sabbath. Neh 13:15
it shall be for the t. of. Isa 7:25
of trouble and of t. down. 22:5
forasmuch as your t. Amos 5:11*

treason

acts of Zimri and his t. 1 Ki 16:20
Athaliah cried, T. T. 2 Ki 11:14
2 Chr 23:13

treasure

The word treasure, *among the Hebrews, signifies anything collected together; provisions, stores. So they say, a* treasure *of corn, of wine, of oil, of honey,* Jer 41:8. *So also* treasures *of gold, silver, brass,* Ezek 28:4; Dan 11:43. *Snow, winds, hail, rain, waters, are in the* treasuries *of God,* Job 38:22; Ps 135:7. *The wise men opened their* treasures, *that is, their boxes or bundles, to offer presents to our Saviour,* Mat 2:11.

God hath given you t. Gen 43:23
ye shall be a peculiar t. to me.
Ex 19:5†; Ps 135:4
open to thee his good t. Deut 28:12
gave them to the t. of. 1 Chr 29:8
after their ability to t. of work.
Ezra 2:69*
the Tirshatha gave to t. Neh 7:70*
the fathers gave to the t. of. 71*
thou fillest with hid t. Ps 17:14
Israel for his peculiar t. 135:4†
of the righteous is much t. Pr 15:6
a little, than great t. and trouble. 16
there is a t. to be desired. 21:20
I gathered the peculiar t. Eccl 2:8
fear of the Lord is his t. Isa 33:6
have taken the t. and. Ezek 22:25
he shall spoil t. of all. Hos 13:15
for where your t. is, there. Mat 6:21
Luke 12:34
t. of his heart, an evil man out of the evil t. Mat 12:35; Luke 6:45
heaven is like to a t. hid. Mat 13:44
who bringeth out of his t. things. 52
shalt have t. in heaven. 19:21
Mark 10:21; Luke 18:22
so is he that layeth up t. Luke 12:21
provide a t. in the heavens. 33
had charge of all her t. Acts 8:27
we have this t. in earthen. 2 Cor 4:7
ye have heaped t. for the. Jas 5:3

treasure *cities*

for Pharaoh t. cities. Ex 1:11

treasure *house*

let search be made in the king's t. house. Ezra 5:17
out of the king's t. house. 7:20
Levites shall bring up the tithe into the t. house. Neh 10:38
brought vessels into t. house of his god. Dan 1:2

treasured

Tyre, it shall not be t. Isa 23:18

treasurer

forth the vessels by the t. Ezra 1:8
get thee unto this t., even. Isa 22:15

treasurers

make a decree to all t. Ezra 7:21
and I made t. over the. Neh 13:13
gathered the t. Dan 3:2, 3

treasures

sealed up among my t. Deut 32:34
suck of t. hid in the sand. 33:19
he put dedicated things among the t.
1 Ki 7:51*
Shishak took away the t. of. 14:26
Asa took gold left in the t. 15:18
2 Chr 16:2
Jehoash took gold found in t.
2 Ki 12:18; 14:14
gold that was found in the t. 16:8
gave him silver found in the t. 18:15
and gold and all that was found in his t. 2 Ki 20:13, 15; Isa 39:2, 4
thence all the t. of the house of the Lord, and the t. of the king's.
2 Ki 24:13; 2 Chr 36:18
Ahijah was over t. of. 1 Chr 26:20*
Shebuel was ruler of the t. 24*
his brethren were over the t. 26
and over the king's t. was. 27:25*
concerning the t. 2 Chr 8:15
appointed for the t. Neh 12:44
it more than for hid t. Job 3:21
into the t. of the snow ? or hast thou seen the t. of the hail ? 38:22*
if thou searchest for her as for hid t.
Pr 2:4
I will fill the t. of those that. 8:21*
t. of wickedness profit. 10:2
the getting of t. by a lying. 21:6
neither any end of their t. Isa 2:7
I have robbed their t. 10:13
their t. on bunches of camels. 30:6
and I will give thee the t. 45:3
he bringeth wind out of his t.
Jer 10:13*; 51:16*
thy t. I will give to the spoil. 15:13
17:3; 20:5
slay us not: for we have t. 41:8*
thou hast trusted in thy t. 48:7
daughter, that trusted in her t. 49:4
a sword is on her t.; they shall. 50:37
many waters, abundant in t. 51:13
silver and gold into thy t. Ezek 28:4
power over the t. of gold. Dan 11:43
are there yet the t. of wickedness in the house of ? Mi 6:10
they had opened their t. Mat 2:11
lay not up for yourselves t. 6:19
but lay up for yourselves t. 20
in whom are hid all the t. Col 2:3
than the t. in Egypt. Heb 11:26

treasurest

t. up wrath against the. Rom 2:5

treasuries

Levites were over the t. 1 Chr 9:26
Solomon pattern of the t. 28:11, 12
Hezekiah made t. for. 2 Chr 32:27
the tithe unto the t. Neh 13:12
I made treasurers over the t. 13
to bring it into the king's t. Esth 3:9
promised to pay to the king's t. 4:7
the wind out of his t. Ps 135:7

treasury

they shall come into the t. of the Lord.
Josh 6:19, 24
the house under the t. Jer 38:11
it is not lawful to put them into the t.
Mat 27:6
the t., and beheld how the people cast money into the t. Mark 12:41
rich men casting their gifts into the t.
Luke 21:1
spake Jesus in the t. John 8:20

treatise

former t. have I made. Acts 1:1

tree

you every t. for meat. Gen 1:29
God made every t. to grow, the t. of life also, and the t. of. 2:9
of every t. of the garden thou. 16
but of the t. of knowledge. 17; 3:3
when the woman saw that the t. 3:6
hast thou eaten of the t.? 11, 17
the woman gave me of the t. 12
lest he take also of the t. of life. 22
keep the way of the t. of life. 24
rest yourselves under the t. 18:4
he stood by them under the t. 8
Pharaoh shall hang thee on a t. 40:19
the hail brake every t. Ex 9:25
the locusts shall eat every t. 10:5
and the Lord shewed him a t. 15:25
seed or fruit of t. is Lord's. Lev 27:30
a stroke to cut down the t. Deut 19:5
t. of the field is man's life. 20:19
and if thou hang him on a t. 21:22
not remain all night on the t. 23
bird's nest in the way in any t. 22:6
take the king of Ai down from the t.
Josh 8:29
now Saul abode under a t. in Ramah.
1 Sam 22:6*
buried them under a t. at Jabesh.
1 Sam 31:13*
shall fell every good t. 2 Ki 3:19
were both hanged on a t. Esth 2:23
there is hope of a t. if it. Job 14:7
hath he removed like a t. 19:10
shall be broken as a t. 24:20
like a t. planted by the rivers. Ps 1:3
she is a t. of life to them. Pr 3:18
the fruit of the righteous is a t. 11:30
desire cometh, it is a t. of life. 13:12
tongue is a t. of life. 15:4
if the t. fall toward the south or the north; where the t. Eccl 11:3
a t. that will not rot. Isa 40:20
down to the stock of a t.? 44:19
eunuch say, I am a dry t. 56:3
as days of a t. are the days. 65:22
themselves behind one t. 66:17
for one cutteth a t. out. Jer 10:3
destroy the t. with the fruit. 11:19
he shall be as a t. planted by. 17:8
vine t. more than any t.? Ezek 15:2
the high t., exalted the low t., dried up the green t., made dry t. to. 17:24
rod of my son, as every t. 21:10
nor any t. in the garden of. 31:8
the t. of the field shall yield. 34:27
multiply the fruit of the t. 36:30
and behold a t. Dan 4:10
the t. grew. 11, 20
said thus, Hew down the t. 4:14, 23
fear not for the t. beareth. Joel 2:22
every t. that bringeth not forth good fruit. Mat 3:10; 7:19; Luke 3:9
good t. bringeth forth good fruit, but a corrupt t. Mat 7:17; Luke 6:43
good t. cannot bring forth. Mat 7:18
the t. good and his fruit good; for the t. is known. 12:33; Luke 6:44
mustard seed becometh a t.
Mat 13:32; Luke 13:19
say to the sycamine t. Luke 17:6
ye slew and hanged on a t. Acts 5:30
they slew, and hanged on a t. 10:39
took him down from the t. 13:29
one that hangeth on a t. Gal 3:13
in his own body on the t. 1 Pet 2:24
I give to eat of the t. of life. Rev 2:7
should not blow on any t. 7:1
hurt any green thing, nor t. 9:4
was there the t. of life. 22:2
have right to the t. of life. 14
see **green**

trees

amongst the t. of garden. Gen 3:8
all the t. were made sure. 23:17
did eat the fruit of the t. Ex 10:15
planted all manner of t. Lev 19:23
the boughs of goodly t. 23:40
and the t. of the field shall. 26:4
neither shall the t. of the land. 20
as t. of lign aloes which the Lord . . . as cedar t. beside. Num 24:6
not plant a grove of any t. Deut 16:21
not destroy t. thereof by axe. 20:19
t. thou knowest not to be t. for. 20
all thy t. and fruit shall the. 28:42
hanged them on five t. Josh 10:26
took them down off the t. 27
the t. went forth to anoint. Judg 9:8
be promoted over the t. 9, 11, 13
the t. said to the fig tree, reign. 10
t. said to the vine. 12
t. said to the bramble. 14
cut down a bough from the t. 48
spake of t. from cedar. 1 Ki 4:33
felled all the good t. 2 Ki 3:25
then shall the t. of the wood sing.
1 Chr 16:33; Ps 96:12
firstfruits of all t. Neh 10:35, 37
under the shady t. Job 40:21, 22
lifted up axes on thick t. Ps 74:5
their sycamore t. with frost. 78:47
the t. of the Lord are full of. 104:16
and brake the t. of their. 105:33
fruitful t. and cedars praise. 148:9
I planted t. of all kinds. Eccl 2:5
apple tree among the t. S of S 2:3
with all t. of frankincense. 4:14
heart was moved as the t. Isa 7:2
the rest of the t. of his forest. 10:19
strengtheneth among the t. 44:14

t. of fields shall clap their. *Isa* 55:12
called *t.* of righteousness. 61:3
Lord said, Hew down *t.* *Jer* 6:6
be poured out upon the *t.* 7:20
all the *t.* of the field. *Ezek* 17:24
they saw all the thick *t.* 20:28
was exalted above all the *t.* 31:5
so that all the *t.* of Eden. 9
many *t.* on the one side and. 47:7
by the rivers shall grow all *t.* 12
all the *t.* of the field are. *Joel* 1:12
the flame hath burnt all the *t.* 19
the axe is laid unto the root of the *t.* *Mat* 3:10; *Luke* 3:9
others cut down branches from the *t.* *Mat* 21:8; *Mark* 11:8*
I see men as *t.* walking. *Mark* 8:24
fig tree and all the *t.* *Luke* 21:29
t. whose fruit withereth. *Jude* 12
hurt not the *t.* till we have. *Rev* 7:3
and the third part of the *t.* 8:7
see **palm**

tremble

nations shall *t.* because. *Deut* 2:25
fear not and do not *t.* 20:3
of those that *t.* at the. *Ezra* 10:3
earth, the pillars thereof *t.* *Job* 9:6
the pillars of heaven *t.* and. 26:11
hast made the earth to *t.* *Ps* 60:2
Lord reigneth, let the people *t.* 99:1
t. thou earth at the presence. 114:7
of the house shall *t.* *Eccl* 12:3
hills did *t.*, their carcases. *Isa* 5:25
man that made the earth to *t.* 14:16
t. ye women that are at ease. 32:11
that the nations may *t.* at thy. 64:2
hear word of Lord, ye that *t.* 66:5
will ye not *t.* at my presence? *Jer* 5:22
at his wrath the earth shall *t.* 10:10
and they shall *t.* for all the. 33:9
the land of Babylon shall *t.* 51:29
they shall *t.* at every moment. *Ezek* 26:16; 32:10
now shall isles *t.* in the day. 26:18
men *t.* before the God. *Dan* 6:26
then the children shall *t.* *Hos* 11:10
t. as a bird out of Egypt. 11
inhabitants of the land *t.* *Joel* 2:1
quake, the heavens shall *t.* 10
shall not the land *t.* for. *Amos* 8:8
the land of Midian did *t.* *Hab* 3:7
devils also believe and *t.* *Jas* 2:19*

trembled

Isaac *t.* very exceedingly. *Gen* 27:33
that was in the camp *t.* *Ex* 19:16
earth *t.* and the heavens. *Judg* 5:4
2 Sam 22:8; *Ps* 18:7; 77:18; 97:4
Eli's heart *t.* for the. *1 Sam* 4:13
the spoilers *t.* 14:15
the elders of the town *t.* 16:4
and his heart greatly *t.* 28:5
to me every one that *t.* *Ezra* 9:4
and lo the mountains *t.* *Jer* 4:24
Hab 3:10*
whole land *t.* at neighing. *Jer* 8:16
all people and nations *t.* *Dan* 5:19
when I heard, my belly *t.* and I *t.* in. *Hab* 3:16
sepulchre, for they *t.* *Mark* 16:8
then Moses *t.* *Acts* 7:32
Felix *t.* 24:25*

trembleth

at this also my heart *t.* *Job* 37:1
looketh on earth and it *t.* *Ps* 104:32
my flesh *t.* for fear of thee. 119:120
I will look, to him that *t.* *Isa* 66:2

trembling

t. take hold on the mighty. *Ex* 15:15
shall give thee a *t.* heart. *Deut* 28:65
people followed him *t.* *1 Sam* 13:7
there was a very great *t.* 14:15
all people sat *t.* because. *Ezra* 10:9
fear came upon me and *t.* *Job* 4:14
I am afraid and *t.* taketh. 21:6*
fear and rejoice with *t.* *Ps* 2:11
fearfulness and *t.* are come. 55:5
the dregs of the cup of *t.* *Isa* 51:17*
out of thy hand the cup of *t.* 22*
have heard a voice of *t.* *Jer* 30:5
drink thy water with *t.* *Ezek* 12:18
clothe themselves with *t.* 26:16
spoken this, I stood *t.* *Dan* 10:11
when Ephraim spake *t.* *Hos* 13:1
Jerusalem a cup of *t.* *Zech* 12:2*
the woman fearing and *t.* *Mark* 5:33
Luke 8:47
Saul *t.* said, Lord, what wilt thou have me to do? *Acts* 9:6
gaoler came *t.* and fell down. 16:29
you in fear and much *t.* *1 Cor* 2:3
how with fear and *t.* ye. *2 Cor* 7:15
obedient with fear and *t.* *Eph* 6:5
salvation with fear and *t.* *Phil* 2:12

trench

David came to the *t.* *1 Sam* 17:20*
lay sleeping within the *t.* 26:5*, 7*
Elijah made a *t.* about. *1 Ki* 18:32
and he filled the *t.* also. 35, 38
enemies shall cast a *t.* *Luke* 19:43*

trespass

(*American Revision usually, and English sometimes, substitutes the word* guilt *for this word*)

what is my *t.* that thou? *Gen* 31:36
we pray thee, forgive the *t.* 50:17*
of *t.* whether for ox. *Ex* 22:9
he shall bring for his *t.* *Lev* 5:15
if they shall confess their *t.* 26:40
when any do a *t.* against. *Num* 5:6
he shall recompense his *t.* with. 7
no kinsman to recompense the *t.* 8
if she have done *t.* against her. 27
forgive the *t.* of thine. *1 Sam* 25:28
why will he be a cause of *t.* to? *1 Chr* 21:3
on Judah for their *t.* *2 Chr* 24:18
add more to our sins and *t.* 28:13
Manasseh's prayer and *t.* are. 33:19
have been chief in this *t.* *Ezra* 9:2
and our *t.* is grown up unto the. 6
we have been in a great *t.* 7, 13
wives, to increase *t.* of Israel. 10:10
a ram of the flock for their *t.* 19
with him there for his *t.* *Ezek* 17:20
in his *t.* he hath trespassed. 18:24
because of their *t.* they. *Dan* 9:7
see **commit, committed, offering**

trespass, *verb*

if any man *t.* against his. *1 Ki* 8:31
warn that they *t.* not. *2 Chr* 19:10
Ahaz did *t.* yet more against. 28:22
if brother *t.*, tell him his. *Mat* 18:15
if thy brother *t.* against. *Luke* 17:3*
if he *t.* against thee seven times. 4

trespass *money*

the *t.* *money* was not. *2 Ki* 12:16

trespassed

he hath certainly *t.* against. *Lev* 5:19
their trespass which they *t.* 26:40
him against whom he *t.* *Num* 5:7
because ye *t.* against me. *Deut* 32:51
go out of sanctuary, for thou hast *t.* *2 Chr* 26:18
for our fathers have *t.* and. 29:6
be not like your fathers who *t.* 30:7
but Amon *t.* more and more. 33:23
who have *t.* against our God. *Ezra* 10:2
his trespass that he *t.* *Ezek* 17:20
they *t.* against me. 39:23, 26
their trespass that they *t.* *Dan* 9:7
because they have *t.* *Hos* 8:1

trespasses

are before thee in our *t.* *Ezra* 9:15
as goeth on still in his *t.* *Ps* 68:21
they have borne their shame and *t.* *Ezek* 39:26
if ye forgive men their *t.* *Mat* 6:14
not men their *t.* neither will your Father forgive your *t.* 15; 18:35
may forgive you your *t.* *Mark* 11:25
your Father forgive your *t.* 26
not imputing their *t.* *2 Cor* 5:19
were dead in *t.* and sins. *Eph* 2:1
having forgiven you all *t.* *Col* 2:13

trespassing

that he hath done in *t.* *Lev* 6:7
sinneth against me by *t.* *Ezek* 14:13

trial

he will laugh at the *t.* of. *Job* 9:23
because it is a *t.* *Ezek* 21:13
how that in a great *t.* *2 Cor* 8:2
others had *t.* of cruel. *Heb* 11:36
that the *t.* of your faith. *1 Pet* 1:7*
strange concerning the fiery *t.* 4:12

tribe

Jacob had twelve sons, who were the heads of so many great families, which altogether formed a great nation; every one of these families was called a tribe. *But Jacob on his death bed adopted Ephraim and Manasseh, the sons of Joseph, as two* tribes *of Israel,* Gen 48:5. *Instead of twelve* tribes, *there were now thirteen, that of Joseph being divided into two. However, in the distribution of lands to the people made by Joshua, by the command of God, they counted but twelve* tribes, *and made but twelve lots. For the* tribe *of Levi, which was appointed to the service of the tabernacle of the Lord, had no share in the distribution of the land, but only some cities to dwell in, and the firstfruits, tithes and oblations of the people,* Num 35:2; Josh 13:7, 8, 14, 33.

The twelve tribes, *while they were in the desert, encamped round about the tabernacle of the covenant, every one according to its order. The Levites were distributed around the tabernacle, nearer the holy place than the other* tribes, Num 2:2, 3, *etc.*

In the marches of the army of Israel, the twelve tribes *were divided into four great bodies, as bodies of troops, each composed of three* tribes. *Between the second and third there came the Levites and priests, with the ark of the Lord, the curtain, the planks, the pillars, and all the other furniture of the tabernacle.*

The twelve tribes *continued united under one head, making but one state, one people, and one monarchy, till after the death of Solomon. Then ten of the* tribes *of Israel revolted from the house of David, and received for their king Jeroboam, the son of Nebat; and only the* tribes *of Judah and Benjamin continued under the government of Rehoboam,* 1 Ki 12:16, 20. *After a separate existence of a little over 200 years, Shalmaneser, king of Assyria, took the city of Samaria, destroyed it, took away the rest of the inhabitants of Israel, carried them beyond the Euphrates, and sent other inhabitants into the country to cultivate and possess it,* 2 Ki 17:6, 24; 18:10, 11. *This ended the kingdom of the ten* tribes *of Israel.*

As to the tribes *of Judah and Benjamin, who remained under the government of the kings of the family of David, they continued a much longer time in their own country. But at last Nebuchadnezzar took the city of Jerusalem, entirely ruined it, and burnt the temple, and took away all the inhabitants of Judah and Benjamin to Babylon, and to the other provinces of his empire. This captivity continued for seventy years, as the prophet had foretold them,* Jer 25:11, 12; 29:10.

Then came the Return under Ezra and Nehemiah, the rebuilding of Jerusalem and the temple. But the people never entirely regained their independence. There has been much discussion of the identity of the ten tribes after the destruction of their kingdom, on the understanding that they were destroyed as a race as well as a nation. But the Jews are always

spoken of in the New Testament as the twelve tribes, never as the two, and Ezra 6:17 certainly indicates that they were thus considered at the time of the Return.
shall be a man of every *t.* head of house of. *Num* 1:4; 13:2; 34:18
cut ye not off the *t.* of the. 4:18
the *t.* of thy father bring thou. 18:2
of every *t.* a thousand. 31:4, 5, 6
the *t.* of the sons of Joseph. 36:5
they shall marry only to the family of the *t.* 6, 8
neither shall the inheritance remove from one *t.* to another *t.*; but. 9
I took one of a *t.* *Deut* 1:23
Josh 3:12; 4:2, 4
family or *t.* whose heart. *Deut* 29:18
t. which the Lord taketh. *Josh* 7:14
from you three men for each *t.* 18:4
thou be a priest to a *t.* *Judg* 18:19
should be one *t.* lacking. 21:3, 6
but will give one *t.* to thy son. *1 Ki* 11:13, 32, 36
of the family of that *t.* *1 Chr* 6:61
in what *t.* the stranger. *Ezek* 47:23
pertaineth to another *t.* *Heb* 7:13
of Judah; of which *t.* Moses. 14
see **Reuben, Simeon** *and the rest*

tribes
according to the twelve *t.* *Ex* 28:21
39:14
tents according to their *t.* *Num* 24:2
according to *t.* of your fathers. 33:54
to give to the nine *t.* 34:13
Josh 13:7; 14:2
the two *t.* and the half have received. *Num* 34:15; *Josh* 14:3
wise men, known among your *t.* *Deut* 1:13
the place which the Lord shall choose out of all your *t.* to. 12:5, 14
chosen him out of all thy *t.* 18:5
ye shall be brought according to your *t.* *Josh* 7:14
before Lord by your *t.* *1 Sam* 10:19
and I will give ten *t.* *1 Ki* 11:31
according to number of the *t.* 18:31
feeble among their *t.* *Ps* 105:37
whither the *t.* go up, the *t.* 122:4
that are the stay of *t.* *Isa* 19:13
be my servant to raise up the *t.* 49:6
return for the *t.* of thine. 63:17
according to their *t.* *Ezek* 45:8
to the oaths of the *t.* *Hab* 3:9
then shall all the *t.* of the earth. *Mat* 24:30
which promise our 12 *t.* *Acts* 26:7
to the twelve *t.* which are. *Jas* 1:1
144,000 of all the *t.* *Rev* 7:4
see **Israel**

tribulation
when thou art in *t.* if thou. *Deut* 4:30
let them deliver you in the time of *t.* *Judg* 10:14*
deliver me out of all *t.* *1 Sam* 26:24
when *t.* ariseth, he is. *Mat* 13:21
then shall be great *t.*, such. 24:21
immediately after the *t.* 29
Mark 13:24
ye shall have *t.*: but be. *John* 16:33
we must through much *t.* enter the kingdom. *Acts* 14:22
t. and anguish on every soul. *Rom* 2:9
knowing that *t.* worketh. 5:3
shall *t.* separate us from the? 8:35
rejoicing in hope, patient in *t.* 12:12
comforteth us in all our *t.* *2 Cor* 1:4*
exceeding joyful in all our *t.* 7:4*
we told you, that we should suffer *t.* *1 Thes* 3:4*
recompense *t.* to them. *2 Thes* 1:6*
am your companion in *t.* *Rev* 1:9
I know thy works, and *t.* and. 2:9
ye shall have *t.* ten days. 10
I will cast them into great *t.* 22
which came out of great *t.* 7:14

tribulations
you out of all your *t.* *1 Sam* 10:19*
but we glory in *t.* also. *Rom* 5:3
ye faint not at my *t.* *Eph* 3:13
for your faith in all *t.* *2 Thes* 1:4*

tributaries
found therein shall be *t.* *Deut* 20:11
the Canaanites became *t.* *Judg* 1:30
33, 35

tributary
how is she become *t.*! *Lam* 1:1

tribute
[1] *Tribute was exacted at all times from conquered nations. The Jews paid it when dependent and received it when powerful.* [2] *The tribute money mentioned in* Mat 17:24, 25 *was the half shekel paid by every Israelite toward the general expenses of the temple.* [3] *The tribute named in* Mat 22:17 *was the tax paid to Rome.*
became a servant to *t.* *Gen* 49:15*
levy a *t.* to the Lord. *Num* 31:28
the Lord's *t.* of the sheep was. 37
beeves, the Lord's *t.* was 72. 38
asses, the Lord's *t.* was 61. 39
16,000, the Lord's *t.* 32 persons. 40
with a *t.* of a freewill. *Deut* 16:10
Canaanites serve under *t.* *Josh* 16:10*; 17:13*
was over the *t.* *2 Sam* 20:24
1 Ki 4:6*; 12:18*; *2 Chr* 10:18*
did Solomon levy a *t.* *1 Ki* 9:21*
put the land to a *t.* *2 Ki* 23:33
Solomon make to pay *t.* *2 Chr* 8:8*
Philistines brought *t.* silver. 17:11
then will they not pay *t.* *Ezra* 4:13
and toll, *t.* and custom was. 20
of the *t.* expences be given 6:8
not lawful to impose *t.* on. 7:24
money for king's *t.* *Neh* 5:4
slothful shall be under *t.* *Pr* 12:24*
t. money came to Peter and said, Doth not . . . pay *t.*? *Mat* 17:24*
kings of the earth take *t.*? 25
is it lawful to give *t.* to? 22:17
Mark 12:14; *Luke* 20:22
shew me the *t.* money. *Mat* 22:19
to give *t.* to Caesar. *Luke* 23:2
cause pay ye *t.* also. *Rom* 13:6
therefore *t.* to whom *t.* is due. 7

trickleth
mine eye *t.* down. *Lam* 3:49*

tried
shall every stroke be *t.* *Deut* 21:5
the word of the Lord is *t.* *2 Sam* 22:31; *Ps* 18:30
when he hath *t.* me, I. *Job* 23:10
desire is that Job may be *t.* 34:36
silver is *t.* in a furnace. *Ps* 12:6
thou hast *t.* me and shalt find. 17:3
hast *t.* us, as silver is *t.* 66:10
the word of the Lord *t.* him. 105:19
I lay in Zion a *t.* stone. *Isa* 28:16
thou hast *t.* mine heart. *Jer* 12:3
shall be purified and *t.* *Dan* 12:10*
try them as gold is *t.* *Zech* 13:9
Abraham when he was *t.* *Heb* 11:17
when *t.* he shall receive. *Jas* 1:12*
gold, though it be *t.* *1 Pet* 1:7*
hast *t.* them which say. *Rev* 2:2
into prison, that ye may be *t.* 10
thee to buy of me gold *t.* 3:18*

triest
I know that thou *t.* *1 Chr* 29:17
O Lord, that *t.* the reins. *Jer* 11:20
but, O Lord of hosts, that *t.* 20:12

trieth
ear *t.* words, as the mouth. *Job* 34:3
the righteous God *t.* the. *Ps* 7:9
the Lord *t.* the righteous. 11:5
but the Lord *t.* the hearts. *Pr* 17:3
God who *t.* our hearts. *1 Thes* 2:4*

trimmed
Mephibosheth had not *t.* his beard. *2 Sam* 19:24
all those virgins arose and *t.* their lamps. *Mat* 25:7

trimmest
why *t.* thou thy way to? *Jer* 2:33

triumph, *verb*
of the uncircumcised *t.* *2 Sam* 1:20
let not mine enemies *t.* *Ps* 25:2
enemy doth not *t.* over me. 41:11
Philistia, *t.* thou because of. *Ps* 60:8*
t. in the works of thy hands. 92:4
how long shall the wicked *t.*? 94:3
us to give thanks and *t.* 106:47
over Philistia will I *t.* 108:9*
causeth us to *t.* in Christ. *2 Cor* 2:14

triumph
with the voice of *t.* *Ps* 47:1

triumphed
hath *t.* gloriously. *Ex* 15:1, 21

triumphing
that the *t.* of the wicked. *Job* 20:5
made a show of them, *t.* *Col* 2:15

Troas
by Mysia they came to *T.* *Acts* 16:8
loosing from *T.* 11
tarried for us at *T.* 20:5
when I came to *T.* to. *2 Cor* 2:12
the cloke I left at *T.* *2 Tim* 4:13

trodden
I give the land that he hath *t.* upon. *Deut* 1:36; *Josh* 14:9
O my soul, thou hast *t.* *Judg* 5:21*
which wicked men have *t.* *Job* 22:15
the lion's whelps have not *t.* it. 28:8
thou hast *t.* down all. *Ps* 119:118*
vineyard shall be *t.* down. *Isa* 5:5
art cast out, as carcase *t.* 14:19
meted out and *t.* down. 18:2, 7
t. under him as straw is *t.* 25:10
Ephraim shall be *t.* under. 28:3
then ye shall be *t.* down. 18
I have *t.* the winepress alone. 63:3
our adversaries have *t.* down. 18
they have *t.* my portion. *Jer* 12:10
the Lord hath *t.* under foot the mighty men, he hath *t.* *Lam* 1:15*
my flock eat what ye have *t.* under feet. *Ezek* 34:19
sanctuary and host to be *t.* *Dan* 8:13
now shall she be *t.* as mire. *Mi* 7:10
salt unsavoury to be *t.* *Mat* 5:13
way side and was *t.* down. *Luke* 8:5
Jerusalem shall be *t.* down of. 21:24
who hath *t.* under foot. *Heb* 10:29
the winepress was *t.* *Rev* 14:20

trode
t. the grapes and cursed. *Judg* 9:27
Israel *t.* the Benjamites. 20:43
the people *t.* upon him in the gate. *2 Ki* 7:17, 20
Jehu *t.* Jezebel under foot. 9:33
a beast *t.* down the thistle. 14:9
2 Chr 25:18
insomuch that they *t.* *Luke* 12:1

troop
a *t.* cometh. *Gen* 30:11
Gad, a *t.* shall overcome him. 49:19
I pursue after this *t.*? *1 Sam* 30:8
Benjamin became one *t.* *2 Sam* 2:25*
Joab came from pursuing a *t.* 3:22
by thee have I run through a *t.* 22:30; *Ps* 18:29
Philistines were gathered into a *t.* *2 Sam* 23:11
the *t.* pitched in the valley of. 13
ye are they that prepare a table for that *t.* *Isa* 65:11*
when thou shalt bring a *t.* *Jer* 18:22
the *t.* of robbers spoileth. *Hos* 7:1
he hath founded his *t.* *Amos* 9:6*

troops
t. of Tema looked. *Job* 6:19*
his *t.* come together and raise. 19:12
they assembled by *t.* in *Jer* 5:7
and as *t.* of robbers wait. *Hos* 6:9
in *t.* O daughter of *t.* *Mi* 5:1
invade them with his *t.* *Hab* 3:16

trouble
in my *t.* I prepared for. *1 Chr* 22:14*
when they in their *t.* did turn unto the Lord. *2 Chr* 15:4*; *Neh* 9:27
let not all the *t.* seem. *Neh* 9:32*
I quiet, yet *t.* came. *Job* 3:26
neither doth *t.* spring out of. 5:6
yet man is born to *t.* as the sparks. 7
few days and full of *t.* 14:1
t. and anguish shall make. 15:24*
will God hear his cry when *t.*? 27:9
weep for him that was in *t.*? 30:25
quietness, who can make *t.*? 34:29*

reserved against time of t. Job 38:23
be a refuge in times of t. Ps 9:9
O Lord, consider my t. which. 13*
thou thyself in times of t.? 10:1
be not far from me, for t. is. 22:11
for in time of t. he shall hide. 27:5
thou hast considered my t. 31:7*
upon me, O Lord, for I am in t. 9*
thou shalt preserve me from t. 32:7
strength in the time of t. 37:39
deliver him in time of t. 41:1*
refuge, a present help in t. 46:1
hath delivered me out of t. 54:7
give us help from t.: for vain. 60:11*
spoken when I was in t. 66:14*
face from me, for I am in t. 69:17*
not in t. as other men. 73:5
years did he consume in t. 78:33*
upon them indignation and t. 49
thou calledst in t. and I. 81:7
I will be with him in t.; I will. 91:15
face from me when I am in t. 102:2*
they cried unto the Lord in their t. 107:6, 13, 19
their soul is melted because of t. 26
cry unto the Lord in their t. 28
hell gat hold on me, I found t. 116:3
t. and anguish have taken. 119:143
though I walk in the midst of t. 138:7
out my complaint before him, I shewed before him my t. 142:2
bring my soul out of t. 143:11
righteous is delivered out of t. Pr 11:8; 12:13
revenues of the wicked is t. 15:6
little, than great treasure and t. 16
unfaithful man in t. is like. 25:19
they are a t. to me. Isa 1:14
look to the earth and behold t. 8:22*
and behold, at eveningtide t. 17:14
Lord, in t. have they visited. 26:16
into the land of t. they will. 30:6
salvation also in time of t. 33:2
not save him out of his t. 46:7
nor bring forth for t. 65:23*
in time of t. they will say. Jer 2:27
save thee in the time of thy t. 28
for health, and behold t. 8:15*
save them at all in time of t. 11:12
they cry to me for their t. 14
Saviour of Israel in time of t. 14:8
time of healing, and behold t. 19*
it is the time of Jacob's t. 30:7
have heard of my t. Lam 1:21
be a time of t. such as. Dan 12:1
have t. in the flesh. 1 Cor 7:28*
be able to comfort them which are in t. 2 Cor 1:4*
not have you ignorant of our t. 8*
wherein I suffer t. as. 2 Tim 2:9*
see **day**

trouble, *verb*

lest ye t. the camp. Josh 6:18
Joshua said, The Lord shall t. 7:25
one of them that t. me. Judg 11:35
they cried in the Jews' speech unto the people to t. them. 2 Chr 32:18
increased that t. me! Ps 3:1*
those that t. me, rejoice when. 13:4*
the foot of man t. them any more, nor the hoofs of beasts t. Ezek 32:13
the interpretation t. thee. Dan 4:19
let not thy thoughts t. thee. 5:10
out of the north shall t. him. 11:44
why t. ye the woman? Mat 26:10
Mark 14:6
Lord, t. not thyself, for. Luke 7:6
he shall say, T. me not, the. 11:7
that we t. not Gentiles. Acts 15:19
these men do exceedingly t. 16:20
t. not yourselves, for his life. 20:10*
but there be some that t. Gal 1:7
were cut off who t. you. 5:12*
henceforth let no man t. me. 6:17
tribulation to them that t. you. 2 Thes 1:6*
lest any root of bitterness t. you. Heb 12:15

troubled

ye have t. me, to make. Gen 34:30
Pharaoh's spirit was t. 41:8
his brethren were t. at his. 45:3
the Lord t. the host of. Ex 14:24*
Why hast thou t. us? Josh 7:25
Jonathan said, My father hath t. the land. 1 Sam 14:29
evil spirit from the Lord t. him. 16:14
saw that Saul was sore t. 28:21
all the Israelites were t. 2 Sam 4:1
I have not t. Israel. 1 Ki 18:18
Syria was sore t. for this. 2 Ki 6:11
then the people t. them in. Ezra 4:4
thee and thou art t. Job 4:5
why should not my spirit be t.? 21:4*
am I t. at his presence. 23:15
shall be t. at midnight. 34:20*
hide thy face and I was t. Ps 30:7
I am t. 38:6*
waters thereof roar and be t. 46:3
the kings were t., and hasted. 48:5*
I remembered God, and was t. 77:3*
I am so t. that I cannot speak. 4
afraid, the depths also were t. 16*
let them be confounded and t. 83:17*
by thy wrath are we t. 90:7
hidest thy face, they are t. 104:29
is as a t. fountain and. Pr 25:26
and years shall ye be t. Isa 32:10
tremble, ye women, be t. ye. 11
wicked are like the t. sea. 57:20
my bowels are t. for him. Jer 31:20†
I am in distress, my bowels are t. Lam 1:20; 2:11
of the people shall be t. Ezek 7:27
are in the sea shall be t. 26:18*
their kings shall be t. in. 27:35
Nebuchadnezzar's spirit was t. Dan 2:1, 3
and the visions of my head t. me. 4:5; 7:15
Daniel astonied, his thoughts t. 4:19
Belshazzar's thoughts t. him. 5:6, 9
my cogitations much t. me. 7:28
were t. because there. Zech 10:2*
Herod was t. and all Jerusalem. Mat 2:3
saw him on sea, they were t. 14:26
Mark 6:50
see that ye be not t. for all. Mat 24:6
Mark 13:7; John 14:1, 27
Zacharias was t. Luke 1:12
Mary was t. 29
Martha, thou art t. about. 10:41
why are ye t. and why do? 24:38
down and t. the water. John 5:4
I have no man when water is t. 7
Jesus groaned and was t. 11:33
12:27; 13:21
from us have t. you. Acts 15:24
and they t. the people and. 17:8
we are t. on every side. 2 Cor 4:8*
7:5*
and to you that are t. 2 Thes 1:7*
ye be not t. neither by spirit. 2:2
of their terror, nor be t. 1 Pet 3:14

troubledst

and thou t. the waters. Ezek 32:2

troubler

Achar, the t. of Israel. 1 Chr 2:7

troubles

many evils and t. Deut 31:17, 21
he shall deliver thee in six t.: yea. Job 5:19
the t. of mine heart. Ps 25:17
O God, out of all his t. 22
saved him out of all his t. 34:6
thou hast shewed me sore t. 71:20
for my soul is full of t. 88:3
keepeth his soul from t. Pr 21:23
former t. are forgotten. Isa 65:16
shall be famine and t. Mark 13:8

troublest

why t. thou the Master? Mark 5:35

troubleth

spirit from God t. 1 Sam 16:15
Art thou he that t. Israel? 1 Ki 18:17
sudden fear t. thee. Job 22:10
my heart soft, Almighty t. me. 23:16
he that is cruel t. his. Pr 11:17
he that t. his own house shall. 29
he that is greedy of gain t. 15:27
I know that no secret t. Dan 4:9
because this widow t. me. Luke 18:5
he that t. you shall bear. Gal 5:10

troubling

there the wicked cease from t. and there the weary. Job 3:17
stepped in first after the t. John 5:4

troublous

be built again in t. times. Dan 9:25

trough, -s

her pitcher into the t. Gen 24:20
rods in the watering t. 30:38
filled the t. to water. Ex 2:16
see **kneedingtroughs**

trow

that servant? I t. not. Luke 17:9

trucebreakers

last days men shall be t. 2 Tim 3:3*

true

see comment on **truth**
we are t. men. Gen 42:11, 31
if ye be t. men. 19
I know that ye are t. men. 33, 34
if ye be t. and thing certain. Deut 17:4; 22:20
and give me a t. token. Josh 2:12
it is t. that I am thy. Ruth 3:12
God, and thy words be t. 2 Sam 7:28
it was a t. report I heard. 1 Ki 10:6
2 Chr 9:5
but that which is t. 1 Ki 22:16
thou gavest them t. laws. Neh 9:13
of the Lord are t. Ps 19:9
thy word is t. from the. 119:160
a t. witness delivereth. Pr 14:25
the Lord be a t. witness. Jer 42:5
he that hath executed t. Ezek 18:8
is it t. O Shadrach, do? Dan 3:14*
t. O king. 24
king said, The thing is t. 6:12
vision which is told is t. 8:26
revealed and the thing was t. 10:1
execute t. judgement and. Zech 7:9
we know that thou art t. Mat 22:16
Mark 12:14
your trust the t. riches. Luke 16:11
that was the t. light. John 1:9
when the t. worshippers shall. 4:23
is that saying t., One soweth. 37
myself, my witness is not t. 5:31
he witnesseth of me is t. 32
giveth you the t. bread. 6:32
the same is t. 7:18
he that sent me is t. 28; 8:26
thy record is not t. 8:13
yet my record is t. 14
my judgement is t. 16
the testimony of two men is t. 17
John spake of this man were t. 10:41
I am the t. vine, my Father. 15:1
and his record is t. 19:35; 21:24
wist not that it was t. Acts 12:9
but as God is t., our. 2 Cor 1:18*
as deceivers, and yet t. 6:8
after God is created in t. holiness. Eph 4:24
also, t. yokefellow, help. Phil 4:3
things are t., think on these. 8
this is a t. saying, If. 1 Tim 3:1*
this witness is t. Wherefore. Tit 1:13
t. tabernacle which the Lord pitched. Heb 8:2
which are the figures of the t. 9:24
let us draw near with a t. 10:22
t. grace of God wherein. 1 Pet 5:12
according to the t. proverb, The dog is. 2 Pet 2:22
which thing is t. in him and in you: because . . . t. light. 1 John 2:8
that we may know him that is t. and we are in him that is t., even. 5:20
that our record is t. 3 John 12
that is holy, he that is t. Rev 3:7
the faithful and t. witness. 14
How long, O Lord, holy and t.? 6:10
just and t. are thy ways, thou. 15:3
t. and righteous are. 16:7; 19:2
the t. sayings of God. 19:9; 22:6
was called Faithful and T. 19:11
write, for these words are t. 21:5

true *God*

without the t. God. 2 Chr 15:3
the Lord is the t. God. Jer 10:10
to know the only t. God. John 17:3

idols to serve the *t. God. 1 Thes* 1:9
this is the *t. God* and. *1 John* 5:20

truly

and now if ye will deal *t.*
Gen 24:49; 47:29
t. his younger brother shall. 48:19
as *t.* as I live, saith. *Num* 14:21, 28
thou shalt *t.* tithe the. *Deut* 14:22
that we will deal *t.* and. *Josh* 2:14
t. the Lord hath delivered all. 24
if ye have done *t.* *Judg* 9:16, 19
t. there is but a step between me and death. *1 Sam* 20:3
for *t.* my words shall not. *Job* 36:4
t. my soul waiteth upon. *Ps* 62:1
t. God is good to Israel, even. 73:1
t. I am thy servant, I am. 116:16
they that deal *t.* are his. *Pr* 12:22
t. the light is sweet. *Eccl* 11:7
t. in vain is salvation hoped for from hills, *t.* in the Lord. *Jer* 3:23
t. this is a grief and I. 10:19
known that the Lord hath *t.* 28:9
judgements to deal *t.* *Ezek* 18:9
but *t.* I am full of power. *Mi* 3:8
the harvest *t.* is plenteous.
Mat 9:37; *Luke* 10:2
Elias *t.* shall first come. *Mat* 17:11
saying, *T.* this was the Son. 27:54
the spirit *t.* is ready. *Mark* 14:38
the way of God *t.* *Luke* 20:21
t. Son of man goeth, as it. 22:22
I have no husband: in that saidst thou *t.* *John* 4:18
for John *t.* baptized with. *Acts* 1:5
Moses *t.* said to the fathers. 3:22
the prison *t.* found we shut. 5:23
t. signs of an apostle. *2 Cor* 12:12
and they *t.* were many. *Heb* 7:23
t. if they had been mindful. 11:15
t. our fellowship is with. *1 John* 1:3

trump

at the last *t.*: the dead. *1 Cor* 15:52
descend with the *t.* of God.
1 Thes 4:16

trumpet

the voice of the *t.* exceeding loud.
Ex 19:16
heard the noise of the *t.* 20:18
blow but with one *t.* *Num* 10:4
and he put a *t.* in every. *Judg* 7:16
when I blow with a *t.* then. 18
blow up the *t.* in the. *Ps* 81:3
and when he bloweth a *t.* *Isa* 18:3
great *t.* shall be blown and. 27:13
lift up thy voice like a *t.* 58:1
blow ye the *t.* in the land. *Jer* 4:5
blow the *t.* in Tekoah and set. 6:1
blow the *t.* among the. 51:27
they have blown the *t.* *Ezek* 7:14
if he blow the *t.* and warn. 33:3
watchman blow not the *t.* 6
blow ye the *t.* in Ramah. *Hos* 5:8
set the *t.* to thy mouth. 8:1
blow the *t.* in Zion. *Joel* 2:1, 15
shall a *t.* be blown? *Amos* 3:6
a day of the *t.* against. *Zeph* 1:16
God shall blow the *t.* *Zech* 9:14
I heard a great voice, as of a *t.*
Rev 1:10; 4:1
the other voices of the *t.* 8:13
sixth angel which had the *t.* 9:14
see **blew, sound,** *subst. verb*

trumpeters

princes and *t.* stood. *2 Ki* 11:14
as the *t.* and singers. *2 Chr* 5:13
the singers sang, and the *t.* 29:28
the voice of *t.* shall be. *Rev* 18:22

trumpets

a memorial of blowing *t.* *Lev* 23:24
Num 29:1
make two *t.* of silver of. *Num* 10:2
sons of Aaron shall blow with the *t.* 8
blow an alarm with the *t.* 9
shall blow with *t.* over your. 10
and with the *t.* to blow in his. 31:6
shall blow with the *t.* *Josh* 6:4
priests bearing the seven *t.* of. 8
that blew with the *t.* 9, 13, 16, 20
the two hundred men took *t.*
Judg 7:8, 16
when I blow, then blow ye the *t.* 18
they blew the *t.*, brake the.
Judg 7:19, 20, 22
they blew with *t.* saying. *2 Ki* 9:13
and trumpeters blew with *t.* 11:14
made for house of the Lord *t.* 12:13
cymbals and with *t.* *1 Chr* 13:8
priests did blow with *t.* 15:24
16:6, 42; *2 Chr* 5:12; 7:6
13:12, 14
all Israel brought up the ark with *t.*
1 Chr 15:28
lift up their voice with *t.* *2 Chr* 5:13
the song began with the *t.* 29:27
saith among the *t.* Ha, ha. *Job* 39:25
with *t.* make a joyful noise. *Ps* 98:6
see **feast, seven**

trust

and whose *t.* shall be a. *Job* 8:14
putteth no *t.* in his saints. 15:15
that maketh the Lord his *t.* *Ps* 40:4
O Lord God, thou art my *t.* 71:5
in thee is my *t.*; leave not. 141:8
that thy *t.* may be in. *Pr* 22:19
that putteth his *t.* in the Lord. 28:25
who putteth his *t.* in the Lord. 29:25
the *t.* in Egypt shall be. *Isa* 30:3
that putteth *t.* in me shall. 57:13†
commit to your *t.* the. *Luke* 16:11
such *t.* have we through Christ to.
2 Cor 3:4
was committed to my *t.* *1 Tim* 1:11
which is committed to thy *t.* 6:20*
see **put**

trust, *verb*

wings thou art come to *t.* *Ruth* 2:12
in him will I *t.* *2 Sam* 22:3†
Ps 18:2; 91:2
a buckler to all that *t.* in him.
2 Sam 22:31; *Ps* 18:30
now on whom dost thou *t.*? *2 Ki* 18:20
2 Chr 32:10; *Isa* 36:5
so is Pharaoh to all that *t.* in him.
2 Ki 18:21; *Isa* 36:6
if ye say, We *t.* in the Lord our God.
2 Ki 18:22; *Isa* 36:7
make you *t.* in the Lord, saying, The Lord. *2 Ki* 18:30; *Isa* 36:15
yet will I *t.* in him. *Job* 13:15†
that is deceived *t.* in vanity. 15:31
judgement is before him, therefore *t.* in him. 35:14*
wilt thou *t.* him because he? 39:11
some *t.* in chariots, and. *Ps* 20:7
I *t.* in thee. 25:2; 31:6; 55:23
56:3; 143:8
for them that *t.* in thee. 31:19†
none that *t.* in him shall be. 34:22†
t. in the Lord. 37:3, 5; 40:3; 62:8
115:9, 10, 11; *Pr* 3:5; *Isa* 26:4
because they *t.* in him. *Ps* 37:40*
I will not *t.* in my bow, nor. 44:6
they that *t.* in their wealth. 49:6
I *t.* in the mercy of God for. 52:8
I will *t.* in the covert of. 61:4*
t. not in oppression, become. 62:10
be glad, and *t.* in him. 64:10†
under his wings shalt thou *t.* 91:4*
better to *t.* in the Lord. 118:8, 9
I shall have to answer, for I *t.* 119:42
that *t.* in the Lord shall be as. 125:1
shield, and he in whom I *t.* 144:2†
her husband doth *t.* in her. *Pr* 31:11
God my salvation, I will *t.* *Isa* 12:2
poor of his people shall *t.* in it. 14:32*
and to *t.* in the shadow of. 30:2
because ye *t.* in oppression and. 12
and *t.* in chariots, because. 31:1
be ashamed that *t.* in graven. 42:17
let him *t.* in the name of the. 50:10
and on mine arm shall they *t.* 51:5
they *t.* in vanity and speak lies. 59:4
t. ye not in lying words. *Jer* 7:4
ye *t.* in lying words that cannot. 8
by my name, wherein ye *t.* 14
take ye heed, and *t.* ye not in. 9:4
makest this people to *t.* in a lie.
28:15; 29:31
Pharaoh and all that *t.* in him. 46:25
and let thy widows *t.* in me. 49:11
but thou didst *t.* in thy beauty.
Ezek 16:15
t. to his own righteousness. 33:13
because thou didst *t.* in. *Hos* 10:13
them that *t.* in the mountain of.
Amos 6:1*
t. ye not in a friend, put. *Mi* 7:5
them that *t.* in him. *Nah* 1:7†
they shall *t.* in the name of the Lord.
Zeph 3:12†
and in his name shall the Gentiles *t.*
Mat 12:21*; *Rom* 15:12*
them that *t.* in riches. *Mark* 10:24
Moses, in whom ye *t.* *John* 5:45
for I *t.* to see you in. *Rom* 15:24*
but I *t.* to tarry a while. *1 Cor* 16:7
that we should not *t.* in. *2 Cor* 1:9
in whom we *t.* that he will yet. 10*
I *t.* ye shall acknowledge even. 13*
I *t.* are made manifest in. 5:11*
if any man *t.* to himself, that he. 10:7
I *t.* ye shall know we are not. 13:6*
thinketh he hath whereof to *t.*
Phil 3:4*
because we *t.* in the living God.
1 Tim 4:10*
that they *t.* not in uncertain. 6:17*
for we *t.* we have a good. *Heb* 13:18*
but I *t.* to come unto you. *2 John* 12*
but I *t.* I shall shortly see. *3 John* 14

trusted

rock in whom they *t.*? *Deut* 32:37†
Sihon *t.* not Israel to. *Judg* 11:20
because they *t.* to the liers. 20:36
he *t.* in the Lord God of. *2 Ki* 18:5
but I have *t.* in thy mercy. *Ps* 13:5
fathers *t.* in thee; they have *t.* 22:4, 5
he *t.* on the Lord that he would. 8*
I have *t.* also in the Lord. 26:1
28:7; 31:14
have *t.* in his holy name. 33:21
familiar friend in whom I *t.* 41:9
but *t.* in the abundance of his. 52:7
they *t.* not in his salvation. 78:22
t. in thy wickedness. *Isa* 47:10
thou hast *t.* in falsehood. *Jer* 13:25
thou hast *t.* in thy works. 48:7
daughter that *t.* in her treasures.
49:4
servants that *t.* in him. *Dan* 3:28
she *t.* not in the Lord. *Zeph* 3:2
he *t.* in God, let him. *Mat* 27:43
armour wherein he *t.* *Luke* 11:22
he spake to certain which *t.* 18:9
we *t.* it had been he which should have redeemed Israel. 24:21*
who first *t.* in Christ. *Eph* 1:12*
in whom ye also *t.* after ye heard. 13
women who *t.* in God. *1 Pet* 3:5*

trustedst

down wherein thou *t.* *Deut* 28:52
shall impoverish thy fenced cities wherein thou *t.* *Jer* 5:17
land of peace wherein thou *t.* 12:5*

trustest

what confidence is this wherein thou *t.*? *2 Ki* 18:19; *Isa* 36:4
thou *t.* on staff of this bruised reed.
2 Ki 18:21; *Isa* 36:6
let not thy God in whom thou *t.*
2 Ki 19:10; *Isa* 37:10

trusteth

he *t.* that he can draw up. *Job* 40:23*
for the king *t.* in the Lord. *Ps* 21:7
t. in the Lord, mercy shall. 32:10
the man that *t.* in him. 34:8†; 84:12
Pr 16:20; *Jer* 17:7
for my soul *t.* in thee. *Ps* 57:1*
save thy servant that *t.* 86:2
so is every one that *t.* in them.
115:8; 135:18
he that *t.* in his riches. *Pr* 11:28
he that *t.* in his own heart. 28:26
thou wilt keep him in perfect peace, because he *t.* in thee. *Isa* 26:3
cursed be the man that *t.* *Jer* 17:5
the maker of his work *t.* *Hab* 2:18
widow indeed, *t.* in God. *1 Tim* 5:5*

trusting

his heart is fixed, *t.* in. *Ps* 112:7

trusty

removeth away the speech of the *t.*
Job 12:20

truth

[1] *What is opposed to a falsehood, lie, or deceit,* Pr 12:17. [2]

Fidelity, sincerity, and punctuality in keeping promises. Generally to truth, *taken in this sense, if referred to God, is joined* mercy *or* kindness, *as in* Gen 24:27. [3] Truth *is put for the true doctrine of the gospel,* Gal 3:1. [4] Truth *is opposed to hypocrisy, dissimulation or formality,* Heb 10:22.
not left destitute of his *t.* Gen 24:27
of the least of all the *t.* 32:10
whether there be any *t.* in. 42:16
men of *t.* Ex 18:21
Lord abundant in *t.* 34:6
behold, if it be *t.* Deut 13:14
a God of *t.* 32:4
kindness and *t.* to you. 2 Sam 2:6
return thou, mercy and *t.* be. 15:20
of Lord in thy mouth is *t.* 1 Ki 17:24
if peace and *t.* be in my days. 2 Ki 20:19; Isa 39:8
say nothing but the *t.* 2 Chr 18:15
wrought that which was *t.* 31:20*
with words of peace and *t.* Esth 9:30
he that speaketh the *t.* in. Ps 15:2
of the Lord are mercy and *t.* 25:10
redeemed me, O Lord God of *t.* 31:5
prosperously, because of *t.* 45:4
desirest *t.* in the inward parts. 51:6
send forth his mercy and his *t.* 57:3
be displayed because of the *t.* 60:4
O prepare mercy and *t.*, which. 61:7
mercy and *t.* are met together. 85:10
t. shall spring out of the earth. 11
plenteous in mercy and *t.* 86:15
mercy and *t.* shall go before. 89:14
his *t.* shall be thy shield and. 91:4
judge the people with his *t.* 96:13
remembered his mercy and his *t.* 98:3*
his *t.* endureth to all. 100:5*; 117:2
I have chosen the way of *t.* 119:30*
and thy law is the *t.* 142, 151
God who keepeth *t.* for ever. 146:6
let not mercy and *t.* Pr 3:3
for my mouth shall speak *t.* 8:7
he that speaketh *t.* sheweth. 12:17
lip of *t.* shall be established. 19
mercy and *t.* be to them that. 14:22
mercy and *t.* iniquity is purged. 16:6
mercy and *t.* preserve the. 20:28
of the words of *t.*; thou mightest answer the words of *t.* 22:21
buy the *t.* and sell it not. 23:23
written were words of *t.* Eccl 12:10
are faithfulness and *t.* Isa 25:1
the nation which keepeth *t.* 26:2†
forth judgement unto *t.* 42:3
them hear, and say, It is *t.* 43:9
nor any pleadeth for *t.*: they. 59:4
for *t.* is fallen in the street and. 14
yea *t.* faileth, and he that. 15
any that seeketh the *t.* Jer 5:1
are not thine eyes upon the *t.*? 3
is perished and cut off from. 7:28
they are not valiant for the *t.* 9:3
and will not speak the *t.* 5
abundance of peace and *t.* 33:6
the king of heaven, all whose works are *t.* Dan 4:37
I asked him the *t.* of all. 7:16, 19
and it cast down the *t.* to the. 8:12
noted in the scripture of *t.* 10:21
now will I shew thee the *t.* 11:2
there is no *t.* nor mercy. Hos 4:1
thou wilt perform the *t.* Mi 7:20
be called a city of *t.* Zech 8:3
speak ye every man the *t.* 16
Eph 4:25
execute the judgement of *t.* and peace. Zech 8:16
love the *t.* and peace. 19
the law of *t.* was in his. Mal 2:6
she said, *T.* Lord, yet dogs eat the. Mat 15:27*
fearing told him all the *t.* Mark 5:33
Master, thou hast said the *t.* 12:32*
full of grace and *t.* John 1:14
but grace and *t.* came by Jesus. 17
he bare witness unto the *t.* 5:33
ye shall know the *t.*, the *t.* shall. 8:32
a man that told you the *t.* 40
t. because there is no *t.* in him. 44
because I tell you the *t.* ye. 45
if I say the *t.* why do ye? John 8:46
I am the way, and the *t.* and. 14:6
I tell you the *t.*; It is expedient. 16:7
of *t.* will guide you into all *t.* 13
sanctified through the *t.* 17:19
should bear witness to the *t.* Every one that is of the *t.* heareth. 18:37
Pilate saith unto him What is *t.*? 38
forth the words of *t.* Acts 26:25
who hold the *t.* in. Rom 1:18
who changed the *t.* of God into. 25
of God is according to *t.* 2:2
that do not obey the *t.* 8
which hast the form of the *t.* in. 20
for if the *t.* of God hath more. 3:7
I say the *t.* in Christ, I lie not. 9:1
circumcision for *t.* of God. 15:8
unleavened bread of *t.* 1 Cor 5:8
but by manifestation of the *t.* 2 Cor 4:2
boasting, I made, is found a *t.* 7:14
as the *t.* of Christ is in me. 11:10
a fool, for I will say the *t.* 12:6
nothing against *t.*, but for the *t.* 13:8
the *t.* of the gospel might. Gal 2:5
they walked not according to *t.* 14
that ye should not obey the *t.* 3:1
5:7
because I tell you the *t.*? 4:16
but speaking the *t.* in love. Eph 4:15
have been taught by him as the *t.* 21
fruit of the Spirit is in all *t.* 5:9
your loins girt about with *t.* 6:14
not the love of the *t.* 2 Thes 2:10
damned who believed not the *t.* 12
salvation, through belief of the *t.* 13
knowledge of the *t.* 1 Tim 2:4
I speak the *t.* in Christ and. 7
pillar and ground of the *t.* 3:15
of them which know the *t.* 4:3
and destitute of the *t.* 6:5
who concerning the *t.* 2 Tim 2:18
to acknowledging of the *t.* 25
to the knowledge of the *t.* 3:7
so do these resist the *t.* 8
turn away their ears from the *t.* 4:4
the acknowledging of *t.* Tit 1:1
of men that turn from the *t.* 14
after we received knowledge of the *t.* Heb 10:26
and lie not against the *t.* Jas 3:14
if any of you err from the *t.* 5:19
your souls in obeying *t.* 1 Pet 1:22
the way of *t.* shall be evil. 2 Pet 2:2
we lie and do not the *t.* 1 John 1:6
we deceive ourselves, the *t.* is. 8
the *t.* is not in him. 2:4
ye know not the *t.*, but because ye know it, and no lie is of the *t.* 21
is *t.* and is no lie. 27
know that we are of the *t.* 3:19
because the Spirit is *t.* 5:6
that have known the *t.* 2 John 1
for the *t.*'s sake which dwelleth in. 2
came and testified of the *t.* 3 John 3
be fellow-helpers to the *t.* 8
of all men and of the *t.* 12
see **spirit**

in **truth**

serve him *in t.* Josh 24:14
1 Sam 12:24
if *in t.* ye anoint me king. Judg 9:15
walk *in t.* 1 Ki 2:4
as he walked *in t.* 3:6
I have walked *in t.* 2 Ki 20:3
all his works are done *in t.* Ps 33:4*; 111:8
the Lord hath sworn *in t.* 132:11
to all that call upon him *in t.* 145:18
the Holy One of Israel *in t.* Isa 10:20
he shall sit upon it *in t.* judging. 16:5
God of Israel, but not *in t.* 48:1
I will direct their work *in t.* and. 61:8
the Lord liveth *in t.* Jer 4:2
I will be their God *in t.* Zech 8:8
teachest the way of God *in t.* Mat 22:16; Mark 12:14
shall worship the Father in spirit and *in t.* John 4:23, 24
all things to you *in t.* 2 Cor 7:14
in pretence or *in t.* Christ is. Phil 1:18
the grace of God *in t.* Col 1:6
but as it is *in t.* the word of God. 1 Thes 2:13
love in tongue, but *in t.* 1 John 3:18
the Son of the Father, *in t.* 2 John 3
rejoiced that I found of thy children walking *in t.* 4; 3 John 4

in the **truth**

hear me *in the t.* of. Ps 69:13
he was a murderer and abode not *in the t.* John 8:44
charity rejoiceth not in iniquity, but *in the t.* 1 Cor 13:6
established *in the* present *t.* 2 Pet 1:12
elect lady, whom I love *in the t.* 2 John 1; 3 John 1
thou walkest *in the t.* 3 John 3

of a **truth**

of a t. women have been. 1 Sam 21:5
of a t. Lord, the kings of Assyria. 2 Ki 19:17; Isa 37:18
I know it is so *of a t.* Job 9:2
of a t. many houses shall. Isa 5:9
for *of a t.* the Lord hath. Jer 26:15
of a t. it is, your God. Dan 2:47
of a t. thou art the Son. Mat 14:33
I tell you *of a t.* Luke 4:25; 9:27
of a t. I say unto you. 12:44; 21:3
of a t. this fellow also was. 22:59
this is *of a t.* that prophet. John 6:14; 7:40
of a t. against thy holy. Acts 4:27
of a t. I perceive that God is. 10:34
God is in you *of a t.* 1 Cor 14:25

thy **truth**

lead me in *thy t.* and. Ps 25:5
and I have walked in *thy t.* 26:3
praise and declare *thy t.*? 30:9
and *thy t.* from the great. 40:10
let *thy t.* continually preserve. 11
send out thy light and *thy t.* 43:3
cut them off in *thy t.* 54:5
thy t. unto the clouds. 57:10; 108:4
I will praise *thy t.* 71:22
will walk in *thy t.* 86:11
swarest to David in *thy t.* 89:49*
glory for *thy t.*'s sake. 115:1; 138:2
that go into the pit cannot hope for *thy t.* Isa 38:18
children shall make known *thy t.* 19
might understand *thy t.* Dan 9:13
thy t.: thy word is truth. John 17:17

word of **truth**

take not *word of t.* out. Ps 119:43
approving ourselves by the *word of t.* 2 Cor 6:7
ye heard the *word of t.* Eph 1:13
whereof ye heard before in the *word of t.* Col 1:5
dividing the *word of t.* 2 Tim 2:15
begat he us by *word of t.* Jas 1:18

try

and I will *t.* them for thee. Judg 7:4
God left him to *t.* him. 2 Chr 32:31
that thou shouldest *t.* Job 7:18
doth not the ear *t.* words? 12:11
his eyelids *t.* the. Ps 11:4
t. my reins and my heart. 26:2
t. me. 139:23
thou mayest know and *t.* Jer 6:27
I will melt them and *t.* them. 9:7
Zech 13:9
I *t.* the reins. Jer 17:10
search and *t.* our ways. Lam 3:40
shall fall to *t.* them. Dan 11:35*
the fire shall *t.* every. 1 Cor 3:13*
fiery trial which is to *t.* you. 1 Pet 4:12*
t. the spirits whether. 1 John 4:1*
hour of temptation to *t.* Rev 3:10

trying

the *t.* of your faith worketh. Jas 1:3

Tryphena, Tryphosa

salute *T.* and *T.* Rom 16:12

Tubal

sons of Japheth, Javan, *T.* Gen 10:2
1 Chr 1:5
those that escape to *T.* Isa 66:19
Javan, *T.* they were. Ezek 27:13
there is Meshech, *T.* and her. 32:26
the chief prince of Meshech and *T.* 38:2, 3; 39:1

tumbled
a cake of barley bread t. Judg 7:13

tumult
the noise of this t.? 1 Sam 4:14
I saw a t. but knew not. 2 Sam 18:29
rage against me and thy t. is come.
2 Ki 19:28*; Isa 37:29*
which stilleth the t. of. Ps 65:7
the t. of those that rise up. 74:23
thine enemies make a t. 83:2
at the noise of the t. the. Isa 33:3
with noise of a great t. Jer 11:16
t. rise among thy people. Hos 10:14
and Moab shall die with t. Amos 2:2
a great t. from the Lord. Zech 14:13
but rather a t. was made. Mat 27:24
he seeth the t. and them. Mark 5:38
know the certainty for t. Acts 21:34*
multitude, nor with t. 24:18

tumults
behold the great t. in the. Amos 3:9
as ministers in t. 2 Cor 6:5
whisperings, swellings, t. 12:20

tumultuous
a t. noise of the kingdoms gathered.
Isa 13:4
thou that art a t. city. 22:2
the head of the t. ones. Jer 48:45

turn
when every maid's t. was come to.
Esth 2:12
now when the t. of Esther was. 15

turn, *verb*
that I may t. to the right. Gen 24:49
make thine enemies t. Ex 23:27
t. from thy fierce wrath and. 32:12
t. ye not unto idols, nor. Lev 19:4
to-morrow t. you, get. Num 14:25
we will not t. to the right. 20:17
we will not t. into the fields. 21:22
he smote the ass to t. her. 22:23
was no way to t. to the right or. 26
t. you, and go to the mount. Deut 1:7
and t. ye, take your journey. 40
that the Lord may t. from. 13:17
then shall t. it into money. 14:25
then the Lord will t. 30:3
then will they t. to other gods. 31:20
t. not from it to the right. Josh 1:7
an altar to t. from following. 22:23, 29
then he will t. and do you hurt. 24:20
nor will any of us t. Judg 20:8
t. thee, behold, I am. 1 Sam 14:7
t. and slay the priests of. 22:17, 18
none can t. to the right. 2 Sam 14:19
the king said, Let him t. to his. 24
Lord, t. Ahithophel's counsel. 15:31
t. from their sin. 1 Ki 8:35
2 Chr 6:26, 37; 7:14
if ye shall at all t. from. 1 Ki 9:6
get hence, t. thee eastward. 17:3
he said, T. thine hand. 22:34
2 Chr 18:33
and Jehu said, T. thee behind me.
2 Ki 9:18, 19
t. ye from your evil ways. 17:13
Jer 18:8; 26:3; Zech 1:3, 4
to t. the kingdom of. 1 Chr 12:23
but Josiah would not t. his face.
2 Chr 35:22
if ye t. and keep my. Neh 1:9
Ezek 3:20; 18:21; 33:11, 14, 19
and t. their reproach on. Neh 4:4
prophets which testified to t. 9:26
of the saints wilt thou t.? Job 5:1
t. from him that he may rest. 14:6
mind, and who can t. him? 23:13
t. the needy out of the way. 24:4
how long will ye t. my glory? Ps 4:2
if he t. not, he will whet his. 7:12
thou shalt make them t. their. 21:12
t. thee unto me. 25:16; 69:16
86:16
t. us, O God of our salvation. 85:4
let those that fear thee t. 119:79
to David, he will not t. 132:11
t. you at my reproof, I. Pr 1:23
pass not by it, t. from it. 4:15
t. not to the right hand nor to. 27
all are of dust, and all t. Eccl 3:20
t. my beloved, and be. S of S 2:17
I will t. my hand on thee. Isa 1:25
they shall every man t. to his. 13:14
and they shall t. the rivers. 19:6
he will violently t. and toss. 22:18
she shall t. to her hire, and. 23:17
for strength to them that t. 28:6
when ye t. to the right hand. 30:21
t. ye to him from whom Israel. 31:6
t. from transgression. 59:20
surely his anger shall t. Jer 2:35
and I said, T. unto me. 3:7, 14
t. it into the shadow of death. 13:16
for I will t. their mourning. 31:13
t. thou me, and I shall be turned. 18
hearkened not to t. from. 44:5
they shall t. every one to. 50:16
t. us unto thee, O Lord. Lam 5:21
he t. not from his wickedness.
Ezek 3:19; 33:9
shall not t. thee from one side. 4:8
my face will I t. also from. 7:22
repent and t. yourselves from your
idols. 14:6; 18:30, 32; 33:9, 11
Hos 12:6; Joel 2:12
I will t. unto you, and ye. Ezek 36:9
to t. thine hand upon the. 38:12
that we might t. from. Dan 9:13
t. his face unto the isles, and take
many; shall cause . . . t. 11:18
then he shall t. his face toward. 19
and they that t. many to. 12:3
not frame their doings to t. Hos 5:4
therefore t. thou to thy God. 12:6
and I will t. mine hand. Amos 1:8
ye who t. judgement. 5:7
and I will t. your feasts. 8:10
let them t. every one from his evil
way. Jonah 3:8
then will I t. to people. Zeph 3:9
t. ye to the strong hold, ye. Zech 9:12
I will t. mine hand upon the. 13:7
t. the heart of fathers. Mal 4:6
on thy right cheek, t. Mat 5:39
to t. the hearts of the fathers to.
Luke 1:17
and it shall t. to you for a. 21:13
of life, lo we t. to. Acts 13:46
that ye should t. from these. 14:15
and to t. them from darkness. 26:18
that they should repent and t. 20
I know this shall t. to. Phil 1:19
commandments of men that t.
Tit 1:14
and we t. about their. Jas 3:3
to t. from the holy. 2 Pet 2:21
and have power to t. Rev 11:6

turn *again*
if the raw flesh t. again. Lev 13:16
therefore we t. again. Judg 11:8
she said, T. again, my daughters.
Ruth 1:11, 12
I pray thee, t. again with me.
1 Sam 15:25, 30
shall t. again to thee. 1 Ki 8:33
heart of this people t. again. 12:27
eat not, nor t. again by the. 13:9, 17
go t. again to the king. 2 Ki 1:6
t. again and tell Hezekiah. 20:5
t. again to the Lord. 2 Chr 30:6
if ye t. again. 9
and man shall t. again. Job 34:15
nor did I t. again till. Ps 18:37
O t. thyself to us again. 60:1
t. us again, O Lord God. 80:3, 7, 19
them not t. again to folly. 85:8
they t. not again to cover. 104:9
t. again our captivity, as. 126:4
t. ye again every one from. Jer 25:5
t. again, O virgin of Israel, t. again.
31:21
try our ways and t. again to the
Lord. Lam 3:40
t. again and thou shalt see.
Ezek 8:6, 13, 15
he will t. again, he will. Mi 7:19
children and t. again. Zech 10:9
lest they t. again and rend. Mat 7:6
shall t. to you again. Luke 10:6
times in a day t. again to thee. 17:4
how t. ye again to the weak elements? Gal 4:9

turn *aside*
I will now t. aside and. Ex 3:3
shall not t. aside to the. Deut 5:32
and ye t. aside and serve. 11:16, 28
that he t. not aside from. 17:20
my death ye will t. aside. 31:29
that ye t. not aside therefrom to the.
Josh 23:6; 1 Sam 12:20, 21
ho, such a one, t. aside. Ruth 4:1
Asahel, t. aside and. 2 Sam 2:21
howbeit he refused to t. aside. 23
the king said, T. aside and. 18:30
such as t. aside to lies. Ps 40:4
of them that t. aside. 101:3
as for such as t. aside to. 125:5
to t. aside the needy from. Isa 10:2
t. aside the just for a thing. 29:21
get out of the way, t. aside. 30:11
to t. aside the right of a. Lam 3:35
and that t. aside the way. Amos 2:7
and they t. aside the poor in. 5:12
that t. aside the stranger. Mal 3:5

turn *away*
brother's fury t. away. Gen 27:44
till thy brother's anger t. away. 45
for if ye t. away from after him.
Num 32:15; Deut 30:17
Josh 22:16; 2 Chr 7:19
they will t. away thy son. Deut 7:4
he hath spoken to t. you away. 13:5
that his heart t. not away. 17:17
no unclean thing and t. away. 23:14
surely they will t. away your heart.
1 Ki 11:2
how wilt thou t. away the face of one
captain? 2 Ki 18:24; Isa 36:9
go not up; t. away. 1 Chr 14:14
O Lord God, t. not away the face of.
2 Chr 6:42; Ps 132:10
Amaziah did t. away from following.
2 Chr 25:27
that his wrath may t. away. 29:10
30:8; Ps 106:23; Pr 24:18
Lord will not t. away his face.
2 Chr 30:9
t. away mine eyes from. Ps 119:37
t. away my reproach which I fear. 39
infamy t. not away. Pr 25:10
but wise men t. away wrath. 29:8
t. away thine eyes from. S of S 6:5
thou t. away thy foot from. Isa 58:13
who can t. her away? Jer 2:24
and thou shalt not t. away. 3:19
saith Lord, Shall he t. away? 8:4
I stood to t. away thy wrath. 18:20
I will t. away your captivity. 29:14
Zeph 2:7
I will not t. away from. Jer 32:40
to t. away captivity. Lam 2:14
t. away your faces from. Ezek 14:6
and for four I will not t. away the.
Amos 1:3, 6, 9, 11, 13; 2:1, 4, 6
God will t. away from. Jonah 3:9
and did t. many away from iniquity.
Mal 2:6
of thee, t. not thou away. Mat 5:42
seeking to t. away the. Acts 13:8
t. away ungodliness. Rom 11:26
heady, from such t. away. 2 Tim 3:5
they shall t. away their ears. 4:4
how escape, if we t. away from him?
Heb 12:25

turn *back*
t. back and cover that. Deut 23:13
a hook in thy nose and t. thee back.
2 Ki 19:28; Isa 37:29
makest us to t. back. Ps 44:10
shall mine enemies t. back. 56:9
who shall t. it back? Isa 14:27
neither will I t. back. Jer 4:28
t. back thine hand as a. 6:9
behold, I will t. back the. 21:4
flee ye, t. back, dwell deep. 49:8
I will t. thee back. Ezek 38:4; 39:2
when I t. back your. Zeph 3:20
not t. back to take up. Mark 13:16

turn *in*
now, my lords, t. in, I. Gen 19:2
t. in, my lord, t. in to. Judg 4:18
let us t. in to this city of. 19:11
of God shall t. in thither. 2 Ki 4:10
let him t. in hither. Pr 9:4, 16

turn *to the Lord*
if thou t. to the Lord thy God.
Deut 4:30; 30:10

trouble did *t. to the Lord.* 2 *Chr* 15:4
world shall *t. to the Lord.* *Ps* 22:27
let us try our ways and *t. to the Lord.* *Lam* 3:40
take with you words and *t. to the Lord.* *Hos* 14:2
heart and *t. to the Lord.* *Joel* 2:13
many of Israel shall he *t. to the Lord.* *Luke* 1:16
nevertheless, when it shall *t. to the Lord.* 2 *Cor* 3:16

turned

sword which *t.* every way. *Gen* 3:24
Joseph *t.* about from them. 42:24
the rod which was *t.* *Ex* 7:15
in the river shall be *t.* to blood. 17, 20 *Ps* 78:44; 105:29
heart of Pharaoh was *t.* *Ex* 14:5
when the hair is *t.* white. *Lev* 13:3 10, 17, 20, 25
they *t.* and went by way. *Num* 21:33
ass saw me and *t.* from me. 22:33
t. the curse into a blessing. *Deut* 23:5; *Neh* 13:2
in that they are *t.* unto. *Deut* 31:18
so the Lord *t.* from the fierceness of his anger. *Josh* 7:26
they *t.* quickly out of. *Judg* 2:17
Samson took firebrands and *t.* 15:4
therefore they *t.* their backs. 20:42
and thou shalt be *t.* into another man. 1 *Sam* 10:6
even they also *t.* to be with. 14:21
whithersoever he *t.* himself he. 47
as Samuel *t.* about to go. 15:27
David *t.* from him towards. 17:30
Asahel *t.* not from. 2 *Sam* 2:19
the victory that day was *t.* 19:2
the kingdom is *t.* about. 1 *Ki* 2:15
Joab *t.* after Adonijah, though. 28
the king *t.* his face about. 8:14
because his heart was *t.* from. 11:9
so Naaman *t.* and went. 2 *Ki* 5:12
Ahaz *t.* the covert from the. 16:18
t. his face to the wall, and prayed. 20:2; *Isa* 38:2
Josiah *t.* himself he spied. 2 *Ki* 23:16
was no king that *t.* to the Lord. 25
Lord *t.* not from the fierceness. 26
he *t.* the kingdom unto. 1 *Chr* 10:14
the wrath of the Lord *t.* 2 *Chr* 12:12
t. from them and destroyed. 20:10
for our fathers have *t.* their. 29:6
t. the heart of the king of. *Ezra* 6:22
wrath of our God be *t.* from. 10:14
neither *t.* they from their. *Neh* 9:35
though it was *t.* to the contrary. *Esth* 9:1
the mouth which was *t.* to them. 22
God *t.* me into the hands. *Job* 16:11
and they whom I loved are *t.* 19:19
yet his meat in his bowels is *t.* 20:14
under it is *t.* up as it were fire. 28:5
terrors are *t.* upon me. 30:15
my harp is *t.* to mourning, and. 31
if my step hath *t.* out of the. 31:7
it is *t.* as clay to the seal. 38:14
and sorrow is *t.* into joy. 41:22
and the Lord *t.* the captivity. 42:10
the wicked shall be *t.* *Ps* 9:17
thou hast *t.* my mourning. 30:11
he *t.* the sea into dry land. 66:6
and *t.* my hand against their. 81:14
he *t.* their heart to hate. 105:25
which *t.* the rock into a. 114:8
I *t.* my feet unto thy. 119:59
and I *t.* myself to behold. *Eccl* 2:12
night of my pleasure he *t.* *Isa* 21:4
Lebanon shall be *t.* into a. 29:17
the streams thereof shall be *t.* 34:9
we have *t.* every one to his. 53:6
therefore he was *t.* to be their. 63:10
how then art thou *t.* into a degenerate plant? *Jer* 2:21
they have *t.* their back to me. 27
Judah hath not *t.* to me with. 3:10
their houses shall be *t.* unto. 6:12
no man repented, every one *t.* 8:6
should have *t.* them from. 23:22
and I shall be *t.* 31:18
after that I was *t.* 19
they *t.* unto me the back. 32:33
now *t.* and had done right. 34:15
but ye *t.* and polluted my. 16
how hath Moab *t.* the? *Jer* 48:39
Lord, mine heart is *t.* *Lam* 1:20
surely against me is he *t.* 3:3
our inheritance is *t.* to strangers. 5:2
our dance is *t.* into mourning. 15
O Lord, and we shall be *t.* 21
they *t.* not when they went. *Ezek* 1:9, 12; 10:11
a vine, whose branches *t.* 17:6
she is *t.* unto me, I shall be. 26:2
my comeliness was *t.* *Dan* 10:8
vision my sorrows are *t.* upon me. 16
Ephraim is a cake not *t.* *Hos* 7:8
Ephraim, mine heart is *t.* 11:8
sun shall be *t.* into darkness. *Joel* 2:31; *Acts* 2:20
ye have *t.* judgement. *Amos* 6:12
they *t.* from their evil. *Jonah* 3:10
cup shall be *t.* unto thee. *Hab* 2:16
all the land shall be *t.* *Zech* 14:10
Jesus *t.* about in press. *Mark* 5:30
the Lord *t.* and looked. *Luke* 22:61
but your sorrow shall be *t.* into joy. *John* 16:20
God *t.* and gave them up. *Acts* 7:42
all at Lydda saw him and *t.* 9:35
believed and *t.* to the Lord. 11:21
Gentiles are *t.* to God. 15:19
t. the world upside down. 17:6
shew how ye *t.* to God. 1 *Thes* 1:9
and they shall be *t.* unto. 2 *Tim* 4:4
t. to flight the armies. *Heb* 11:34
lest that which is lame be *t.* 12:13
t. with a very small helm. *Jas* 3:4
let your laughter be *t.* to. 4:9
the dog is *t.* to his own. 2 *Pet* 2:22

turned *again*

behold it was *t. again* as. *Ex* 4:7
Ehud *t. again* from the. *Judg* 3:19
Israel *t. again*, went a whoring. 8:33
t. again, Benjamites amazed. 20:41
Samuel *t. again* after. 1 *Sam* 15:31
I *t.* not *again* till I. 2 *Sam* 22:38
when the man *t. again* from his chariot. 2 *Ki* 5:26
Lord *t. again* the captivity. *Ps* 126:1

turned *aside*

that he *t. aside* to see. *Ex* 3:4
they have *t. aside* quickly. 32:8 *Deut* 9:12, 16
he *t. aside* to see the. *Judg* 14:8
the kine *t.* not *aside*. 1 *Sam* 6:12
but *t. aside* after lucre, and. 8:3
David *t.* not *aside* from. 1 *Ki* 15:5
a man *t. aside* and brought. 20:39
Josiah *t.* not *aside* to. 2 *Ki* 22:2
of their way are *t. aside*. *Job* 6:18
they were *t. aside* like. *Ps* 78:57
is thy beloved *t. aside*? *S of S* 6:1
heart hath *t.* him *aside*. *Isa* 44:20
he hath *t. aside* my ways. *Lam* 3:11
have *t. aside* unto vain. 1 *Tim* 1:6
for some are already *t. aside*. 5:15

turned *away*

because ye are *t. away*. *Num* 14:43
wherefore Israel *t. away*. 20:21
of the Lord may be *t. away*. 25:4
t. my wrath *away* from Israel. 11
wives *t. away* his heart. 1 *Ki* 11:3, 4
Ahab *t. away* and would eat. 21:4
our fathers *t. away* their. 2 *Chr* 29:6
which hath not *t. away*. *Ps* 66:20
time *t.* he his anger *away*. 78:38
his anger is not *t. away*, but his hand. *Isa* 5:25; 9:12, 17, 21; 10:4
thy anger is *t. away*. 12:1
nor *t.* I *away*. 50:5
and judgement is *t. away*. 59:14
your iniquities have *t. away* these. *Jer* 5:25
sunk, they are *t. away* back. 38:22
have seen them *t. away* back? 46:5
shepherds have *t.* them *away*. 50:6
let thy fury be *t. away*. *Dan* 9:16
for mine anger is *t. away*. *Hos* 14:4
the Lord hath *t. away* excellency of Jacob. *Nah* 2:2
this Paul hath *t. away*. *Acts* 19:26
Asia be *t. away* from me. 2 *Tim* 1:15

turned *back*

the people *t. back* upon. *Josh* 8:20
Joshua at that time *t. back*. 11:10
Saul is *t. back* from. 1 *Sam* 15:11
of Jonathan *t.* not *back*. 2 *Sam* 1:22
t. their heart *back*. 1 *Ki* 18:37
not king of Israel, they *t. back*. 22:33
when the messengers *t. back*, Why are ye now *t. back*? 2 *Ki* 1:5
he *t. back* and looked on them. 2:24
so the king of Assyria *t. back*. 15:20
Ornan *t. back*, and. 1 *Chr* 21:20
because they *t. back*. *Job* 34:27
enemies are *t. back*. *Ps* 9:3
let them be *t. back* that devise. 35:4; 70:2, 3
our heart is *t. back* from. 44:18
children of Ephraim *t. back* in. 78:9
yea, they *t. back* and tempted. 41, 57
and let them be *t. back* that. 129:5
they shall be *t. back* that. *Isa* 42:17
the anger of the Lord is not *t. back*. *Jer* 4:8
they are *t. back* to iniquities. 11:10
they also are *t. back*, and. 46:21
he hath *t.* me *back*, and. *Lam* 1:13
them that are *t. back* from the Lord. *Zeph* 1:6
t. back again to Jerusalem seeking. *Luke* 2:45
out of the lepers *t. back*, and. 17:15
she *t.* herself *back* and. *John* 20:14
in their hearts *t. back*. *Acts* 7:39

turned *in*

the two angels *t. in*. *Gen* 19:3
Judah *t. in* to Hirah the. 38:1
when Sisera had *t. in*. *Judg* 4:18
the Danites *t. in* thither and. 18:3
Elisha *t. in* thither to. 2 *Ki* 4:8
he *t. into* the chamber and lay. 11

turnest

whithersoever thou *t.* 1 *Ki* 2:3
that thou *t.* thy spirit. *Job* 15:13
thou *t.* man to destruction. *Ps* 90:3

turneth

soul that *t.* after wizards. *Lev* 20:6
whose heart *t.* away this. *Deut* 29:18
shall I say, when Israel *t.*? *Josh* 7:8
the horse *t.* not back. *Job* 39:22
he *t.* rivers into a. *Ps* 107:33
he *t.* the wilderness into a. 35
the way of the wicked he *t.* 146:9
a soft answer *t.* away. *Pr* 15:1
a gift, whithersoever it *t.* 17:8
he *t.* the king's heart. 21:1
as the door *t.* upon his hinges. 26:14
that *t.* away his ear from. 28:9
a lion that *t.* not away for. 30:30
the wind *t.* about unto. *Eccl* 1:6
be as one that *t.* aside? *S of S* 1:7
the people *t.* not to him. *Isa* 9:13
the Lord *t.* the earth upside. 24:1
that *t.* wise men backward. 44:25
that *t.* aside to tarry. *Jer* 14:8
Damascus is feeble, and *t.* 49:24
yea, she sigheth and *t.* *Lam* 1:8
he *t.* his hand against me all. 3:3
when righteous *t.* away. *Ezek* 18:24 26; 33:18
when the wicked man *t.* away. 18:27, 28; 33:12
t. the shadow of death. *Amos* 5:8

turning

Jerusalem as a dish, *t.* it. 2 *Ki* 21:13
he hardened his heart from *t.* unto the Lord. 2 *Chr* 36:13
the *t.* away of the simple. *Pr* 1:32
your *t.* of things upside. *Isa* 29:16
t. away he hath divided. *Mi* 2:4
to bless you in *t.* you. *Acts* 3:26
whom is no shadow of *t.* *Jas* 1:17
t. Sodom and Gomorrah. 2 *Pet* 2:6
t. the grace of God into. *Jude* 4

turtle, -s, turtledove, -s
(*Turtle means* turtledove)

take a *t.* and a young pigeon. *Gen* 15:9
his offering of *t.* *Lev* 1:14
for his trespass two *t.* or two pigeons. 5:7; 12:8; 14:22, 30; 15:14, 29
be not able to bring two *t.* 5:11
she shall bring a *t.* for. 12:6
day he shall bring two *t.* *Num* 6:10
O deliver not the soul of thy *t.* unto the wicked. *Ps* 74:19

the voice of the *t.* is. *S of S* 2:12
t. and crane observe the. *Jer* 8:7
to offer a sacrifice, A pair of *t.* or two young pigeons. *Luke* 2:24

tutors

the heir while a child is under *t.* and governors. *Gal* 4:2*

twain

thou shalt be my son in law in the one of the *t.* *1 Sam* 18:21*
shut the door on them *t.* and prayed. *2 Ki* 4:33
with *t.* he covered his face, with *t.* he covered his feet, with *t.* *Isa* 6:2
they cut the calf in *t.* *Jer* 34:18
both *t.* shall come out. *Ezek* 21:19
go a mile, go with him *t.* *Mat* 5:41
cleave to his wife, and they *t.* 19:5
wherefore they are no more *t.* 6
Mark 10:8
whether of *t.* did the ? *Mat* 21:31
whether of the *t.* will ye ? 27:21
the vail of the temple was rent in *t.* 51
Mark 15:38
to make in himself of *t.* *Eph* 2:15

twelfth

oxen, he with the *t.* *1 Ki* 19:19
the *t.* lot came forth to Jakim. *1 Chr* 24:12
the *t.* lot came forth to Hashabiah. 25:19
t. captain for the *t.* month. 27:15
in the *t.* year of Josiah's reign. *2 Chr* 34:3
in the *t.* year of king. *Esth* 3:7
in the *t.* year, in the *t.* *Ezek* 32:1
in the *t.* year and fifteenth day. 17
in the *t.* year of our captivity. 33:21
the *t.* foundation was an. *Rev* 21:20
see **day, month**

twelve

t. years they served. *Gen* 14:4
t. princes shall Ishmael beget. 17:20; 25:16
now the sons of Jacob were *t.* 35:22
they said, Thy servants are *t.* brethren. 42:13, 32
all these are the *t.* tribes. 49:28
they came to Elim, where were *t.* wells. *Ex* 15:27
t. pillars according to the *t.* 24:4
t. precious stones. 28:21; 39:14
thou shalt bake *t.* cakes. *Lev* 24:5
t. princes. *Num* 1:44
they brought *t.* oxen. 7:3
t. chargers, *t.* silver bowls, *t.* 84
t. bullocks, rams *t.*, lambs of the first year *t.* 87
t. rods, according to house. 17:2, 6
on second day offer *t.* young. 29:17
I took *t.* men of you. *Deut* 1:23
take ye *t.* men out of the tribes. *Josh* 3:12; 4:2
take ye *t.* stones out of Jordan. 4:3, 8, 9, 20
went over by number *t.* of Benjamin, and *t.* of the servants. *2 Sam* 2:15
Solomon had *t.* officers. *1 Ki* 4:7
the sea stood on *t.* oxen. 7:25, 44
2 Chr 4:15
t. lions on the one side. *1 Ki* 10:20
2 Chr 9:19
Jeroboam's garment in *t.* pieces. *1 Ki* 11:30
Elijah took *t.* stones and built. 18:31
found Elisha plowing with *t.* 19:19
with brethren and sons *t.* *So to the end.* *1 Chr* 25:9
for a sin offering *t.* he goats. *Ezra* 6:17; 8:35
I separated *t.* of the chief. 8:24
t. years not eaten bread. *Neh* 5:14
t. brazen bulls, Nebuzar-adan took. *Jer* 52:20
the altar shall be *t.* cubits long, *t.* broad. *Ezek* 43:16
land according to the *t.* tribes. 47:13
at end of *t.* months he. *Dan* 4:29
diseased with an issue of blood *t.* *Mat* 9:20; *Mark* 5:25; *Luke* 8:43
the names of the *t.* apostles. *Mat* 10:2; *Luke* 6:13
they took up of fragments *t.* baskets. *Mat* 14:20; *Mark* 6:43; 8:19
Luke 9:17; *John* 6:13
sit upon *t.* thrones, judging the *t.* tribes. *Mat* 19:28; *Luke* 22:30
he sat down with the *t.* *Mat* 26:20
Mark 14:17; *Luke* 22:14
yet spake, Judas one of the *t.* came. *Mat* 26:47; *Mark* 14:10, 43
Luke 22:47; *John* 6:71
than *t.* legions of angels. *Mat* 26:53
she was of the age of *t.* years. *Mark* 5:42; *Luke* 8:42
of the *t.*, that dippeth. *Mark* 14:20
and when Jesus was *t.* *Luke* 2:42
have I not chosen you *t.*? *John* 6:70
not *t.* hours in the day ? 11:9
Thomas one of the *t.* was. 20:24
and Jacob begat the *t.* *Acts* 7:8
all the men were about *t.* 19:7
but *t.* days since I went up. 24:11
to which promise our *t.* tribes. 26:7
of Cephas, then of the *t.* *1 Cor* 15:5
to the *t.* tribes which are. *Jas* 1:1
head a crown of *t.* stars. *Rev* 12:1
t. gates, at the gates *t.* angels. 21:12
city had *t.* foundations, and in them the names of the *t.* apostles. 14
the *t.* gates were *t.* pearls. 21
tree of life bare *t.* manner of. 22:2
see **hundred, thousand**

twenty

shall be *t.* found there. He said, I will not destroy it for *t.*'s. *Gen* 18:31
this *t.* years have I been. 31:38, 41
for Esau, *t.* he goats, *t.* rams. 32:14
and ten bulls, *t.* she asses. 15
they sold Joseph for *t.* pieces. 37:28
a shekel is *t.* gerahs. *Ex* 30:13
Lev 27:25; *Num* 3:47; 18:16
Ezek 45:12
t. years old and above. *Ex* 30:14
38:26; *Num* 1:3, 18, 20; 14:29
26:2; 32:11; *1 Chr* 23:24, 27
2 Chr 25:5; 31:17; *Ezra* 3:8
of the male from *t.* years. *Lev* 27:3
5 years old to *t.* years, *t.* shekels. 5
shall not eat neither ten days, nor *t.* days. *Num* 11:19
the shekel is *t.* gerahs. 18:16
oppressed Israel *t.* years. *Judg* 4:3
from Aroer even *t.* cities. 11:33
judged Israel *t.* years. 15:20; 16:31
in Kirjath-jearim *t.* years. *1 Sam* 7:2
armourbearer slew *t.* men. 14:14
to David with *t.* men. *2 Sam* 3:20
Ziba had fifteen sons and *t.* servants. 9:10; 19:17
provision daily, *t.* oxen. *1 Ki* 4:23
at the end of *t.* years, when Solomon. 9:10; *2 Chr* 8:1
Solomon gave Hiram *t.* *1 Ki* 9:11
man of God *t.* loaves. *2 Ki* 4:42
I even weighed *t.* basons. *Ezra* 8:27
weight, *t.* shekels a day. *Ezek* 4:10
of the porch was *t.* cubits. 40:49
the breadth of the door was *t.* 41:2
heap of *t.* measures, to draw out fifty vessels . . . but *t.* *Hag* 2:16
the flying roll *t.* cubits. *Zech* 5:2
and found it *t.* fathoms. *Acts* 27:28

twenty *two*

judged Israel *t. two* years. *Judg* 10:3
Jeroboam reigned *t. two* years. *1 Ki* 14:20
Ahab reigned over Israel *t. two* years. 16:29
t. and *two* years old was Ahaziah. *2 Ki* 8:26
Amon *t. two* years old when. 21:19
of his father's house *t. two* captains. *1 Chr* 12:28
but Abijah begat *t.* and *two* sons. *2 Chr* 13:21

twenty *three*

Tola judged Israel *t. three* years. *Judg* 10:2
Jehoahaz was *t. three* years old. *2 Ki* 23:31
Jair had *t. three* cities. *1 Chr* 2:22
of Josiah to *t. third* year. *Jer* 25:3
in the *t. third* year of. 52:30

twenty *four*

were *t.* and *four* bullocks. *Num* 7:88
fingers and toes *t. four.* *2 Sam* 21:20
reigned *t.* and *four* years. *1 Ki* 15:33
consider from *t. fourth* day and. *Hag* 2:18
the throne were *t. four* seats, and on the seats I saw *t. four.* *Rev* 4:4
the *t. four* elders fell down. 5:8
11:16; 19:4

twenty *five*

from *t. five* years old. *Num* 8:24
reigned *t.* and *five* years in Jerusalem. *1 Ki* 22:42; *2 Chr* 20:31
t. five years old when he began to. *2 Ki* 14:2; *2 Chr* 25:1
Jotham *t. five* years old. *2 Ki* 15:33
2 Chr 27:1, 8
Hezekiah *t. five* years old. *2 Ki* 18:2
2 Chr 29:1
Jehoiakim *t. five* years. *2 Ki* 23:36
2 Chr 36:5
the wall finished in *t. fifth* day. *Neh* 6:15
t. fifth day Evil-merodach lifted. *Jer* 52:31

twenty *six*

in the *t. sixth* year of Asa. *1 Ki* 16:8

twenty *seven*

t. seventh day of second month. *Gen* 8:14
27th year of Asa. *1 Ki* 16:10, 15
on *t. seventh* day of twelfth month. *2 Ki* 25:27

twenty *eight*

length of curtain *t. eight* cubits. *Ex* 26:2; 36:9
reigned *t.* and *eight* years. *2 Ki* 10:36
Rehoboam begat *t. eight* sons. *2 Chr* 11:21

twenty *nine*

Nahor lived *t. nine* years. *Gen* 11:24
Amaziah reigned *t. nine* years. *2 Ki* 14:2
Hezekiah reigned *t. nine* years. 18:2
2 Chr 25:1; 29:1
see **thousand**

twice

dream was doubled *t.* *Gen* 41:32
shall be *t.* as much. *Ex* 16:5, 22
rod he smote the rock *t.* *Num* 20:11
out of his presence *t.* *1 Sam* 18:11
appeared unto him *t.* *1 Ki* 11:9
there, not once nor *t.* *2 Ki* 6:10
Jerusalem once or *t.* *Neh* 13:20
speaketh once, yea *t.* *Job* 33:14
yea *t.*; but I will proceed no. 40:5
Lord gave Job *t.* as much as. 42:10
t. have I heard, power. *Ps* 62:11
a thousand years *t.* told. *Eccl* 6:6
before cock crow *t.* thou shalt deny me. *Mark* 14:30, 72
I fast *t.* in the week. *Luke* 18:12
t. dead, plucked up by. *Jude* 12

twigs

the top of his young *t.* *Ezek* 17:4
off from the top of his young *t.* 22

twilight

smote them from the *t.* *1 Sam* 30:17
the lepers rose in the *t.* to go to the. *2 Ki* 7:5
they arose and fled in the *t.* 7
let the stars of the *t.* thereof be dark. *Job* 3:9
adulterer waiteth for the *t.* 24:15
way to her house in the *t.* *Pr* 7:9
shalt carry it forth in the *t.* *Ezek* 12:6*
and brought it forth in the *t.* 7*
the prince shall bear it in the *t.* 12*

twined, *see* **fine**

twinkling

all be changed, in the *t.* *1 Cor* 15:52

twins

Rebekah had *t.* *Gen* 25:24
Tamar had *t.* 38:27
every one bear *t.* *S of S* 4:2; 6:6
like two roes that are *t.* 4:5; 7:3

two

took unto him *t.* wives. *Gen* 4:19
t. of every sort shalt thou bring. 6:19

of beasts that are not clean by t. Gen 7:2; 9:15
t. nations are in thy womb, and t. manner of people shall be. 25:23
he hath supplanted me these t. 27:36
and now I am become t. bands. 32:10
Issachar is an ass couching between t. burdens. 49:14
they gathered t. omers. Ex 16:22
if he continue a day or t. 21:21
t. turtledoves or t. pigeons. Lev 5:7 12:8; 14:22; 15:14, 29; Num 6:10
not able to bring t. turtledoves. Lev 5:11
she shall be unclean t. weeks. 12:5
Aaron shall take t. goats. 16:7
cast lots upon t. 8
shalt set the cakes in t. rows. 24:6
brought a waggon for t. Num 7:3
t. oxen. 17, 23, 29, 35, 41, 47, 53 59, 65, 71
make thee t. trumpets of silver. 10:2
his ass, Balaam's t. servants. 22:22
t. rams. 29:14, 17, 20, 23, 26, 29, 32
and divide the prey into t. 31:27
t. kings. Deut 3:8, 21; 4:47 Josh 2:10; 9:10
at the mouth of t. or three witnesses, be put to death. Deut 17:6; 19:15 Mat 18:16; 2 Cor 13:1
if a man have t. wives. Deut 21:15
should t. put ten thousand to? 32:30
t. tribes. Josh 14:3, 4; 21:16
t. cities. 21:25
man a damsel or t. Judg 5:30
let me alone t. months, that. 11:37
be avenged for my t. eyes. 16:28
t. went till they came to. Ruth 1:19
which t. did build the house. 4:11
t. wives. 1 Sam 1:2; 27:3; 30:5 18; 2 Sam 2:2
with t. lines measured. 2 Sam 8:2
he did to the t. captains. 1 Ki 2:5
there was none save we t. in. 3:18
Hiram and Solomon, t. made. 5:12
t. months they were at. home. 14
and they t. were alone in. 11:29
Jeroboam made t. calves. 12:28 2 Ki 17:16
I am gathering t. sticks. 1 Ki 17:12
how long halt ye between t.? 18:21
Israel pitched like t. little. 20:27
fire burnt up the t. 2 Ki 1:14
they t. went on. 2:6
came forth t. she bears. 24
give, I pray thee, t. changes. 5:22
be content, take t. talents, and. 23
t. measures of barley for. 7:1, 16, 18
behold, t. kings stood not. 10:4
of Tekoah, had t. wives. 1 Chr 4:5
more honourable than the t. 11:21
Jehoiada took for Joash t. wives. 2 Chr 24:3
only do not t. things unto. Job 13:20
kindled against thy t. friends. 42:7
t. things have I required. Pr 30:7
t. are better than one. Eccl 4:9
if t. lie together. 11
t. shall withstand him. 12
thy t. breasts are like t. young roes. S of S 4:5; 7:3
it were company of t. armies. 6:13
t. or three berries in top of. Isa 17:6
but these t. things shall come. 47:9
these t. things are come unto. 51:19
have committed t. evils. Jer 2:13
I will take one of a city, and t. 3:14
son of man, appoint thee t. ways. Ezek 21:19
were t. women, daughters of. 23:2
hast said, These t. nations. 35:10
shall be no more t. nations. 37:22
Joseph shall have t. portions. 47:13
behold, there stood other t. Dan 12:5
can t. walk together? Amos 3:3
so t. or three cities wandered. 4:8
t. olive trees by it. Zech 4:3, 11, 12
these are the t. anointed ones. 4:14
there came out t. women who. 5:9
four chariots from between t. 6:1
I took unto me t. staves and. 11:7
t. parts therein shall be cut off. 13:8
no man can serve t. masters. Mat 6:24; Luke 16:13
than having t. hands or t. feet. Mat 18:8; Mark 9:43
rather than having t. eyes. Mat 18:9; Mark 9:47
with thee one or t. more. Mat 18:16
that if t. of you shall agree on. 19
where t. or three are gathered. 20
on these t. hang all the law. 22:40
then shall t. be in the field. 24:40
received t. he gained other t. 25:17
send them forth by t. and t. Mark 6:7
he sendeth t. disciples. 11:1; 14:13 Luke 19:29
she threw in t. mites. Mark 12:42
after that Jesus appeared to t. 16:12
he that hath t. coats, let. Luke 3:11
certain creditor which had t. 7:41
neither take money, nor have t. 9:3
took out t. pence and gave. 10:35
shew whether of these t. Acts 1:24
for t. shall be one flesh. 1 Cor 6:16 Eph 5:31
let it be by t. or at the. 1 Cor 14:27
let the prophets speak t. or three. 29
these are the t. covenants. Gal 4:24
a strait betwixt t., a desire. Phil 1:23
but before t. or three. 1 Tim 5:19
that by t. immutable things . . . we. Heb 6:18
died without mercy under t. 10:28
there come t. woes more. Rev 9:12
I will give power to my t. 11:3
these are t. olive trees and t. 4
because these t. prophets. 10
woman were given t. wings. 12:14
he had t. horns like a lamb. 13:11
see **daughters, days, fifty, forty, hundred, kidneys, lambs, sons, thirty, thousand, twenty**

two *men*

t. men of the Hebrews. Ex 2:13
there remained t. men. Num 11:26
out t. men to spy secretly. Josh 2:1
Rahab hid the t. men. 4
the t. men returned. 23
find t. men by Rachel's. 1 Sam 10:2
there were t. men in one city, one rich. 2 Sam 12:1
fell on t. men more. 1 Ki 2:32
set t. men, sons of Belial. 21:10, 13
t. blind men followed. Mat 9:27
talked with him t. men. Luke 9:30
t. men in one bed. 17:34
t. men in the field. 36
t. men went up to the temple. 18:10
perplexed, behold, t. men stood. Luke 24:4; Acts 1:10
testimony of t. men is true. John 8:17
they sent t. men to Peter. Acts 9:38

two *tables*

gave to Moses t. tables. Ex 31:18
the t. tables were in his hands. 32:15; 34:29
hew thee t. tables of stone. 34:1 Deut 10:1
he hewed t. tables of stone. Ex 34:4; Deut 10:3
he wrote upon t. tables. Deut 4:13 5:22
the Lord delivered unto me t. tables. 9:10, 11
nothing in the ark save the t. tables. 1 Ki 8:9; 2 Chr 5:10
t. tables on this side. Ezek 40:39
t. tables on that. 40

two *years*

begat Arphaxad t. years. Gen 11:10
these t. years hath the famine. 45:6
when Saul had reigned t. years. 1 Sam 13:1
Ish-bosheth Saul's son reigned t. years. 2 Sam 2:10
after t. years, Absalom had. 13:23
Absalom dwelt t. years in. 14:28
Nadab reigned over Israel t. years. 1 Ki 15:25
Elah reigned t. years. 16:8
Ahaziah reigned t. years. 22:51 2 Ki 15:23; 21:19
after t. years his bowels. 2 Chr 21:19
within t. full years will I bring again the vessels. Jer 28:3, 11
words of Amos, t. years. Amos 1:1
slew children from t. years. Mat 2:16
t. years they in Asia. Acts 19:10
Paul dwelt t. years in his. 28:30

twofold

ye make him t. more the child of hell. Mat 23:15

Tychicus

T. of Asia accompanied. Acts 20:4
T. shall make known to. Eph 6:21
all my state shall T. Col 4:7
and T. have I sent to. 2 Tim 4:12
when I shall send T. Tit 3:12

Tyrannus

disputing in the school of one T. Acts 19:9

Tyre

coast turneth to the strong city T. Josh 19:29
the strong hold of T. 2 Sam 24:7
fetched Hiram out of T. 1 Ki 7:13
his father was a man of T. 14 2 Chr 2:14
Hiram came out from T. to. 1 Ki 9:12
and drink to them of T. Ezra 3:7
there dwelt men of T. Neh 13:16
the daughter of T. shall. Ps 45:12
with the inhabitants of T. 83:7
Philistia and T. 87:4
the burden of T. Isa 23:1
pained at the report of T. 5
this counsel against T.? 8
T. shall be forgotten. 15
Lord will visit T. 17
what have ye to do with me, O T.? Joel 3:4
if the mighty works had been done in T. Mat 11:21; Luke 10:13
Herod was displeased with them of T. Acts 12:20
see **king, Sidon**

Tyrus

made all the kings of T. Jer 25:22
send yokes to the kings of T. 27:3
to cut off from T. and Zidon. 47:4
because T. said against. Ezek 26:2
behold, I am against thee, O T. 3
take up a lamentation for T. 27:2
what city is like T., like the? 32
say to the prince of T. 28:2
lamentation on the king of T. 12
great service against T. 29:18
Ephraim, as I saw T. Hos 9:13
transgressions of T. Amos 1:9
a fire on the wall of T. 10
T. and Zidon, though it. Zech 9:2
T. build herself a strong hold. 3

U

Ucal

spake to Ithiel and U. Pr 30:1

unaccustomed

Ephraim, as a bullock u. Jer 31:18

unadvisedly

so that he spake u. with. Ps 106:33

unawares

Jacob stole away u. to Laban. Gen 31:20, 26
slayer may flee thither, who killeth any person u. Num 35:11*, 15* Deut 4:42; Josh 20:3*, 9*
let destruction come on him at u. Ps 35:8
day come upon you u. Luke 21:34*
because of false brethren u. Gal 2:4*
have entertained angels u. Heb 13:2
certain men crept in u. Jude 4*

unbelief

did not many mighty works there because of their u. Mat 13:58
could not cast him out, because of your u. 17:20*
because of their u. Mark 6:6
help thou mine u. 9:24
upbraided them with their u. 16:14
shall their u. make faith? Rom 3:3*
not at the promise through u. 4:20

because of *u.* they were. *Rom* 11:20
if they abide not still in *u.* shall. 23
obtained mercy through their *u.* 30*
concluded them all in *u.* 32*
did it ignorantly in *u.* *1 Tim* 1:13
you an evil heart of *u.* *Heb* 3:12
not enter in because of *u.* 19; 4:6*
lest any fall after the same example of *u.* 4:11*

unbelievers

him his portion with *u.* *Luke* 12:46*
goeth to law before *u.* *1 Cor* 6:6
come in those that are *u.* 14:23
unequally yoked with *u.* *2 Cor* 6:14

unbelieving

the *u.* Jews stirred up. *Acts* 14:2
for the *u.* husband is sanctified by the wife, the *u.* wife is. *1 Cor* 7:14
u. depart, let him depart. 15
unto them that are *u.* *Tit* 1:15
the *u.* shall have their part. *Rev* 21:8

unblameable

to present you holy, *u.* *Col* 1:22*
stablish your hearts *u.* *1 Thes* 3:13

unblameably

how *u.* we have behaved ourselves. *1 Thes* 2:10

uncertain

trumpet give an *u.* *1 Cor* 14:8
nor trust in *u.* riches. *1 Tim* 6:17

uncertainly

I therefore so run, not as *u.*; so fight I. *1 Cor* 9:26

unchangeable

but this man hath an *u.* *Heb* 7:24

uncircumcised

the *u.* man child shall. *Gen* 17:14
sister to one that is *u.* 34:14
then shall Pharaoh hear me, who am of *u.* lips? *Ex* 6:12, 30
for no *u.* person shall eat of. 12:48
shall count the fruit *u.* *Lev* 19:23
if then their *u.* hearts be. 26:41
for they were *u.* *Josh* 5:7
to take a wife of the *u.* *Judg* 14:3
fall into the hands of these *u.* 15:18
let us go over unto the garrison of these *u.* *1 Sam* 14:6
who is this *u.* Philistine? 17:26, 36
lest these *u.* come and abuse me. 31:4; *1 Chr* 10:4
the daughters of the *u.* *2 Sam* 1:20
come into thee the *u.* *Isa* 52:1
their ear is *u.*, they cannot. *Jer* 6:10
the circumcised with the *u.* 9:25
are *u.*, all house of Israel are *u.* 26
die the death of the *u.* *Ezek* 28:10
thou shalt lie in the midst of the *u.* 31:18; 32:19, 21, 24, 25, 26, 27, 28, 29, 30, 32
ye have brought strangers *u.* in heart and *u.* in flesh into my. 44:7, 9
stiffnecked and *u.* in heart and ears. *Acts* 7:51
thou wentest in to men *u.* and. 11:3
faith which he had yet being *u.* *Rom* 4:11, 12
let him not become *u.* *1 Cor* 7:18

uncircumcision

thy circumcision is made *u.* *Rom* 2:25
u. keep the righteousness of the law, shall not his *u.* be counted? 26
shall not *u.* which is by nature? 27
justify the *u.* through faith. 3:30
cometh this blessedness then upon the circumcision or the *u.*? 4:9
when he was in circumcision or in *u.*? not in circumcision but *u.* 10
is any man called in *u.*? *1 Cor* 7:18
circumcision is nothing, and *u.* 19
gospel of *u.* was committed. *Gal* 2:7
neither circumcision availeth nor *u.* 5:6; 6:15
who are called *u.* by that. *Eph* 2:11
you being dead in the *u.* *Col* 2:13
neither circumcision nor *u.* but. 3:11

uncle

Uzziel, the *u.* of Aaron. *Lev* 10:4
if a man lie with his *u.'s* wife, he hath uncovered his *u.'s*. 20:20
either his *u.* or *u.'s* son. *Lev* 25:49
and Saul's *u.* said. *1 Sam* 10:14, 15
Abner, son of Ner, Saul's *u.* 14:50
Jonathan David's *u.* a. *1 Chr* 27:32
Mordecai brought up Hadassah his *u.'s* daughter. *Esth* 2:7, 15
son of Shallum thine *u.* *Jer* 32:7
Hanameel my *u.'s* son came. 8, 9, 12
and a man's *u.* shall. *Amos* 6:10

unclean

any *u.* thing, the carcase of *u.* cattle or *u.* things . . . be *u.* *Lev* 5:2; 11:26
put difference between *u.* and clean. 10:10; 11:47
it is *u.* to you. 11:4, 5, 6, 7, 29; *Deut* 14:19
they are *u.* unto you. *Lev* 11:8; 26, 27, 28, 31; *Deut* 14:7
ye shall be *u.*; *u.* until the evening. *Lev* 11:24, 25, 28, 31, 32, 33, 39, 40; 14:46; 15:5, 6, 7, 8, 10, 11, 16, 17, 18, 19, 21, 22, 23, 27; 17:15; 22:6; *Num* 19:7, 8, 10, 21, 22
it shall be *u* *Lev* 11:32, 33, 34, 35, 36, 38; 15:4, 9, 20, 24, 26
then she shall be *u.* seven days. 12:2, 5; 15:25
priest shall look on him and pronounce him *u.* 13:3, 8, 11, 15, 20, 22, 25, 27, 30, 44, 59
he is *u.* 13:11, 14, 36, 44, 46; 15:2, 24
plague is, shall cry, *U. u.* 13:45
cast them into an *u.* place. 14:40, 41, 45
to teach when it is *u.* and. 57
whereby he may be made *u.* 22:5
not make himself *u.* for. *Num* 6:7
u. and clean eat thereof. *Deut* 12:15, 22; 15:22
of your possession be *u.* *Josh* 22:19
to possess is an *u.* land. *Ezra* 9:11
hypocrites is among the *u.* *Job* 36:14
event to the clean and *u.* *Eccl* 9:2
man of *u.* lips, I dwell in the midst of a people of *u.* lips. *Isa* 6:5
the *u.* shall not pass over it. 35:8
no more come into thee the *u.* 52:1
depart ye, it is *u.*; depart. *Lam* 4:15
put no difference between clean and *u.* *Ezek* 22:26
discern between the clean and *u.* 44:23
they shall eat *u.* things in. *Hos* 9:3
one that is *u.* touch any of these, shall it be *u.*? *Hag* 2:13
they offer there is *u.* 14
had a spirit of an *u.* devil. *Luke* 4:33
not call any man common or *u.* *Acts* 10:28; 11:8
u. of itself . . . any thing to be *u.*, to him it is *u.* *Rom* 14:14
else were your children *u.* *1 Cor* 7:14
touch not the *u.* thing. *2 Cor* 6:17
that no *u.* person hath any. *Eph* 5:5
of heifer sprinkling the *u.* *Heb* 9:13
Babylon is become a cage of every *u.* bird. *Rev* 18:2

see **beast, spirit, thing**

unclean *spirits*

he gave power against *u. spirits.* *Mat* 10:1; *Mark* 6:7
he commandeth *u. spirits.* *Mark* 1:27; *Luke* 4:36
u. spirits, when they saw. *Mark* 3:11
u. spirits went out and entered. 5:13
were vexed with *u. spirits.* *Acts* 5:16
for *u. spirits* came out of many. 8:7
I saw three *u. spirits.* *Rev* 16:13

uncleanness

if he touch the *u.* of man, whatsoever *u.* it be. *Lev* 5:3; 7:21; 22:5
having his *u.* on him. 7:20; 22:3
is to be cleansed from his *u.* 14:19
separate Israel from their *u.* 15:31
she is put apart for her *u.* 18:19
not gone aside to *u.* *Num* 5:19
he shall be unclean, his *u.* is. 19:13
by reason of *u.* that. *Deut* 23:10
he hath found some *u.* in her. 24:1*
was purified from her *u.* *2 Sam* 11:4
brought out all the *u.* *2 Chr* 29:16
have filled the land with their *u.* *Ezra* 9:11
as the *u.* of a removed. *Ezek* 36:17
according to their *u.* have I. 39:24
shall be a fountain opened for sin and *u.* *Zech* 13:1
full of bones, and all *u.* *Mat* 23:27
also gave them up to *u.* *Rom* 1:24
your members servants to *u.* 6:19
not repented of the *u.* *2 Cor* 12:21
flesh are these, *u.*, strife. *Gal* 5:19
to work all *u.* with. *Eph* 4:19
all *u.*, let it not be once named. 5:3
fornication, *u.* and covetousness. *Col* 3:5
for our exhortation was not of *u.* *1 Thes* 2:3
God hath not called us to *u.* 4:7
walk in the lust of *u.* *2 Pet* 2:10*

uncleannesses

I will save you from all your *u.* *Ezek* 36:29

unclothed

not for that we would be *u.* *2 Cor* 5:4

uncomely

he behaveth *u.* toward. *1 Cor* 7:36*
u. parts have more abundant. 12:23

uncondemned

they have beaten us openly *u.*, being Romans. *Acts* 16:37
a man that is a Roman and *u.* 22:25

uncorruptness

doctrine shewing *u.*, gravity. *Tit* 2:7

uncover

u. not your heads neither. *Lev* 10:6
not *u.* nakedness of one that. 18:6
thy father shalt thou not *u.* 7
of thy father's wife shalt not *u.* 8
son's daughter shalt not *u.* 10
nakedness of thy father's . . . not *u.* 11
not *u* . . . of father's sister. 12, 13
u. the nakedness of thy father's. 14
not *u.* . . . of thy daughter in law. 15
not *u.* the nakedness of a woman. 17
not *u.* the nakedness of thy wife's. 18
not *u.* nakedness of a woman put apart. 19; 20:18
the high priest shall not *u.* 21:10
the priest shall *u.* the. *Num* 5:18
go in and *u.* his feet. *Ruth* 3:4
u. thy locks, *u.* the thigh. *Isa* 47:2*

uncovered

and Noah was *u.* within. *Gen* 9:21
he hath *u.* his father's. *Lev* 20:11
u. his sister's nakedness. 17
she hath *u.* the fountain of her. 18
u. his uncle's nakedness. 20
she came softly and *u.* *Ruth* 3:7
who *u.* himself as the. *2 Sam* 6:20
with their buttocks *u.* *Isa* 20:4
quiver, and Kir *u.* the shield. 22:6
thy nakedness shall be *u.*, thy. 47:3
but I have *u.* his secret. *Jer* 49:10
and thine arm shall be *u.* *Ezek* 4:7
let thy foreskin be *u.* *Hab* 2:16*
they *u.* the roof where. *Mark* 2:4
with her head *u.* *1 Cor* 11:5*
a woman pray unto God *u.*? 13*

uncovereth

for he *u.* his near kin. *Lev* 20:19
he *u.* his father's skirt. *Deut* 27:20
vain fellows *u.* himself. *2 Sam* 6:20

unction

but ye have an *u.* from. *1 John* 2:20*

undefiled

blessed are the *u.* in. *Ps* 119:1*
my love, my dove, my *u.* *S of S* 5:2
my dove, my *u.* is one; she is. 6:9
who is holy, harmless, *u.* *Heb* 7:26
in all, and the bed *u.* 13:4
pure religion and *u.* *Jas* 1:27
to an inheritance incorruptible, *u.* *1 Pet* 1:4

under

the deep that lieth *u.* *Gen* 49:25
I will bring you out from *u.* *Ex* 6:6
of my tent, and silver *u.* it. *Josh* 7:21
u. whose wings thou art. *Ruth* 2:12
what is *u.* thy hand give. *1 Sam* 21:3
and put no fire *u.* *1 Ki* 18:23
revolted from *u.* the hand. *2 Ki* 8:20
Israel went out from *u.* the. 13:5

purpose to keep *u.* Judah for. *2 Chr* 28:10
name will we tread them *u.* *Ps* 44:5
should be *u.* my head. *S of S* 8:3
with idols *u.* every green tree. *Isa* 57:5; *Jer* 2:20
perish from the earth, and from *u.* *Jer* 10:11; *Lam* 3:66
get away from *u.* it. *Dan* 4:14
u. the whole heaven hath not. 9:12
gone a whoring from *u.* *Hos* 4:12
from two years old and *u.* *Mat* 2:16
u. authority, having soldiers *u.* 8:9
enter *u.* my roof. *Luke* 7:6
when thou wast *u.* the fig tree. *John* 1:48
have proved that they are all *u.* sin. *Rom* 3:9
not *u.* the law, but *u.* grace. 6:15
but I am carnal, sold *u.* sin. 7:14
brought *u.* power of any. *1 Cor* 6:12
u. the law, as *u.* the law. 9:20
I keep *u.* my body and bring it. 27
our fathers were *u.* the cloud. 10:1
u. the curse. *Gal* 3:10
hath concluded all *u.* sin. 22
we were kept *u.* the law. 23
faith is come, we are no longer *u.* 25
and things *u.* the earth. *Phil* 2:10
as are *u.* the yoke. *1 Tim* 6:1
for *u.* it the people. *Heb* 7:11
in chains *u.* darkness. *Jude* 6
see **feet, him, law, me, sun, thee, them, us**

undergirding
used helps, *u.* the ship. *Acts* 27:17

underneath
u. are the everlasting. *Deut* 33:27

undersetters
the four corners thereof had *u.* *1 Ki* 7:30, 34

understand
they may not *u.* one. *Gen* 11:7
thou canst *u.* a dream. 41:15
ye shall *u.* that these. *Num* 16:30
tongue thou shalt not *u.* *Deut* 28:49
servants in the Syrian language, for we *u.* it. *2 Ki* 18:26; *Isa* 36:11
the Lord made me *u.* *1 Chr* 28:19
before those that could *u.* *Neh* 8:3
the people to *u.* the law. 7, 8, 13
cause me to *u.* wherein. *Job* 6:24
I would *u.* what he would say. 23:5
of his power who can *u.*? 26:14
nor do the aged *u.* judgement. 32:9
can any *u.* the spreadings ? 36:29
if there were any that did *u.* *Ps* 14:2; 53:2
who can *u.* his errors? cleanse. 19:12
know not, neither will they *u.* 82:5
neither doth a fool *u.* this. 92:6
u. ye brutish among the people. 94:8
u. the lovingkindness of. 107:43
make me to *u.* the way of. 119:27
I *u.* more than the ancients. 100
then shalt thou *u.* the fear. *Pr* 2:5
then shalt thou *u.* righteousness. 9
u. wisdom, and, ye fools, be of. 8:5
prudent is to *u.* his way. 14:8
reprove one, and he will *u.* 19:25
how can a man then *u.* his ? 20:24
evil men *u.* not judgement, but they that seek the Lord *u.* all. 28:5
for though he *u.* he will not. 29:19
Hear ye indeed, but *u.* not. *Isa* 6:9
lest they *u.* with their heart. 10 *John* 12:40
whom shall he make to *u.*? *Isa* 28:9
it shall be a vexation only to *u.* 19
the heart of the rash shall *u.* 32:4
tongue that thou canst not *u.* 33:19
u. together that the Lord. 41:20
that ye may know and *u.* 43:10
hearts, that they cannot *u.* 44:18
shepherds that cannot *u.* 56:11
who is the wise man that may *u.* this ? *Jer* 9:12
words thou canst not *u.* *Ezek* 3:6
make this man to *u.* the. *Dan* 8:16
but he said unto me, *U.* O son. 17
and *u.* thy truth. 9:13
u. the matter. 23, 25
didst set thy heart to *u.* 10:12
I am come to make thee *u.* *Dan* 10:14
and they that *u.* shall instruct. 11:33
none . . . *u.*, but the wise shall *u.* 12:10
people that doth not *u.* *Hos* 4:14
and he shall *u.* these things ? 14:9
neither *u.* they the counsel. *Mi* 4:12
neither do they *u.* *Mat* 13:13
hear and not *u.* 14
hear and *u.* 15:10; *Mark* 7:14
do not ye yet *u.*? *Mat* 15:17; 16:9, 11 *Mark* 8:17, 21
whoso readeth, let him *u.* *Mat* 24:15 *Mark* 13:14
and not perceive, that hearing they may hear and not *u.* *Mark* 4:12 *Luke* 8:10; *Acts* 28:26
I know not nor *u.* I what. *Mark* 14:68
that they might *u.* the. *Luke* 24:45
ye not *u.* my speech? *John* 8:43
have not heard shall *u.* *Rom* 15:21
and though I *u.* all mysteries . . . I am nothing. *1 Cor* 13:2
through faith we *u.* worlds. *Heb* 11:3
evil of things they *u.* not. *2 Pet* 2:12*

understandest
what *u.* thou, which is not ? *Job* 15:9
thou *u.* my thoughts. *Ps* 139:2
neither *u.* thou what they. *Jer* 5:15
Philip said, *U.* thou what ? *Acts* 8:30

understandeth
Lord *u.* the imaginations. *1 Chr* 28:9
God *u.* the way thereof. *Job* 28:23
is in honour and *u.* not. *Ps* 49:20
all plain to him that *u.* *Pr* 8:9
easy unto him that *u.* 14:6
in this, that he *u.* me. *Jer* 9:24
the word and *u.* it not. *Mat* 13:19
heareth the word and *u.* it. 23
there is none that *u.* *Rom* 3:11
men, for no man *u.* *1 Cor* 14:2
say Amen, seeing he *u.* not what ? 16

understanding
Bezaleel with wisdom and *u.* and in. *Ex* 31:3; 35:31; 36:1
wisdom and your *u.* *Deut* 4:6
neither is there any *u.* in. 32:28
hast asked for thyself *u.* *1 Ki* 3:11
Solomon wisdom and *u.* 4:29
was filled with wisdom and *u.* 7:14
were men that had *u.* *1 Chr* 12:32
give thee wisdom and *u.* 22:12
a wise son endued with *u.* *2 Chr* 2:12
Zechariah had *u.* in the visions. 26:5
for Elnathan, men of *u.* *Ezra* 8:16*
could hear with *u.* *Neh* 8:2
knowledge and having *u.* 10:28
but I have *u.* as well as you. *Job* 12:3
in length of days is *u.* 12
he hath *u.* 13
away the *u.* of the aged. 20
hid their heart from *u.* 17:4
the spirit of my *u.* causeth me. 20:3
and by his *u.* he smiteth. 26:12
where is the place of *u.*? 28:12, 20
to depart from evil is *u.* 28
Almighty giveth them *u.* 32:8
hearken to me, ye men of *u.* 34:10
if now thou hast *u.* hear this. 16
let men of *u.* tell me, let a wise. 34
declare, if thou hast *u.* 38:4
who hath given *u.* to the heart? 36
he imparted to her *u.* 39:17
mule that hath no *u.* *Ps* 32:9
sing ye praises with *u.* 47:7
of my heart shall be of *u.* 49:3
give me *u.* 119:34, 73, 125, 144, 169
I have more *u.* 99
through thy precepts I get *u.* 104
thy word giveth *u.* 130
our Lord, his *u.* is infinite. 147:5
to perceive words of *u.* *Pr* 1:2
that thou apply thine heart to *u.* 2:2
liftest up thy voice for *u.* 3
cometh knowledge and *u.* 6
thee, *u.* shall keep thee. 11
and lean not unto thine own *u.* 3:5
happy is the man that getteth *u.* 13
by *u.* hath he established the. 19
ye children, attend to know *u.* 4:1
get *u.* 5, 7
my son, bow thine ear to my *u.* 5:1
committeth adultery, lacketh *u.* 6:32
and call *u.* thy kinswoman. 7:4
not *u.* put forth her voice ? *Pr* 8:1
I am *u.* 14
as for him that wanteth *u.* 9:4, 16
and go in the way of *u.* 6
knowledge of the holy is *u.* 10
that hath *u.* wisdom is found. 10:13
slow to wrath is of great *u.* 14:29
in the heart of him that hath *u.* 33
hath *u.* seeketh knowledge. 15:14
heareth reproof getteth *u.* 32
to get *u.* rather to be chosen. 16:16
u. is a wellspring of life to him. 22
before him that hath *u.* 17:24
a fool hath no delight in *u.* but. 18:2
he that keepeth *u.* shall find. 19:8
reprove one that hath *u.* he will. 25
wandereth out of the way of *u.* 21:16
there is no *u.* nor counsel against. 30
and instruction, and *u.* 23:23
by *u.* an house is established. 24:3
poor that hath *u.* searcheth. 28:11
the prince that wanteth *u.* is an. 16
and have not the *u.* of a man. 30:2
yet riches to men of *u.* *Eccl* 9:11
the spirit of *u.* shall rest. *Isa* 11:2
make him of quick *u.* in the fear. 3*
for it is a people of no *u.* 27:11
the *u.* of their prudent men. 29:14
framed it, He had no *u.*? 16
erred in spirit shall come to *u.* 24
shewed to him the way of *u.*? 40:14
there is no searching of his *u* 28
is there knowledge nor *u.* 44:19
which shall feed you with *u.* *Jer* 3:15
is foolish, they have no *u.* 4:22
people and without *u.* 5:21
out the heaven by his *u.* 51:15
with thy *u.* thou hast got. *Ezek* 28:4
u. science. *Dan* 1:4
Daniel had *u.* in visions. 17
in all matters of *u.* he found. 20
knowledge to them that know *u.* 2:21
u. returned to me, I blessed. 4:34
light and *u.* was found. 5:11, 12, 14
u. dark sentences. 8:23
came forth to give thee *u.* 9:22
had *u.* of the vision. 10:1
some of them of *u.* shall fall. 11:35
according to their own *u.* *Hos* 13:2
there is no *u.* in him. *Ob* 7
shall I not destroy *u.* out of the ? 8
are ye also yet without *u.*? *Mat* 15:16; *Mark* 7:18
and to love him with all the *u.* *Mark* 12:33
to me, having had perfect *u.* of. *Luke* 1:3*
were astonished at his *u.* 2:47
then opened he their *u.* that. 24:45
without *u.*, unmerciful. *Rom* 1:31
bring to nothing the *u.* of. *1 Cor* 1:19
my spirit prayeth, but my *u.* is. 14:14
pray with the *u.*, sing with the *u.* 15
speak five words with my *u.* 19
be not children in *u.*, but in *u.* 20
the eyes of your *u.* being. *Eph* 1:18
having the *u.* darkened, being. 4:18
but *u.* what the will of the Lord. 5:17
God which passeth all *u.* *Phil* 4:7
filled with all spiritual *u.* *Col* 1:9
the full assurance of *u.* 2:2
u. neither what they say. *1 Tim* 1:7
the Lord give thee *u.* in. *2 Tim* 2:7
Son hath given us an *u.* *1 John* 5:20
him that hath *u.* count. *Rev* 13:18
see **good**

understanding, *adjective*
take ye wise men and *u.* *Deut* 1:13
great nation is an *u.* people. 4:6
give thy servant an *u.* *1 Ki* 3:9
thee a wise and an *u.* heart. 12
be ye of an *u.* heart. *Pr* 8:5

man of **understanding**
brought us a *man of u.* *Ezra* 8:18
a *man of u.* shall attain. *Pr* 1:5
but a *man of u.* hath wisdom. 10:23
man of u. holdeth his peace. 11:12
man of u. walketh uprightly. 15:21
a *man of u.* is of an excellent. 17:27
lips, is esteemed a *man of u.* 28*
but a *man of u.* will draw out. 20:5
but by a *man of u.* and. 28:2

void of **understanding**
young man *void of u.* *Pr* 7:7
a rod for back of him that is *void of u.* 10:13
vain persons is *void of u.* 12:11
a man *void of u.* striketh. 17:18
vineyard of the man *void of u.* 24:30

understood
not that Joseph *u.* them. *Gen* 42:23
were wise, that they *u.* *Deut* 32:29
they *u.* that ark of Lord. *1 Sam* 4:6
David *u.* that Saul was come. 26:4
people *u.* it was not of David to. *2 Sam* 3:37
they had *u.* the words. *Neh* 8:12
I *u.* of the evil Eliashib did. 13:7
ear hath heard and *u.* it. *Job* 13:1
have I uttered that I *u.* not. 42:3
went to sanctuary, then *u.* *Ps* 73:17*
a language that I *u.* not. 81:5
fathers *u.* not thy wonders. 106:7
u. from foundations of. *Isa* 40:21
not known nor *u.*: for he shut. 44:18
at the vision, but none *u.* *Dan* 8:27
I Daniel *u.* by books. 9:2
he *u.* the vision. 10:1
I heard, but I *u.* not: then. 12:8
have ye *u.* all these things? *Mat* 13:51
u. they how he bade them. 16:12
u. that he spake of John. 17:13
they *u.* not that saying. *Mark* 9:32
Luke 2:50; 9:45; *John* 8:27; 10:6
and they *u.* none of. *Luke* 18:34
these things *u.* not his. *John* 12:16
have *u.* that God by his hand would . . . but they *u.* not. *Acts* 7:25
I rescued him, having *u.* he. 23:27
I *u.* that he was of Cilicia. 34
being *u.* by the things that. *Rom* 1:20
child, I *u.* as a child. *1 Cor* 13:11
by tongue words easy to be *u.* 14:9
some things hard to be *u.* *2 Pet* 3:16

undertake
oppressed, *u.* for me. *Isa* 38:14*

undertook
Jews *u.* to do as they. *Esth* 9:23

undo
to *u.* heavy burdens. *Isa* 58:6
at that time I will *u.* all. *Zeph* 3:19*

undone
thou art *u.* O people. *Num* 21:29
Joshua left nothing *u.* *Josh* 11:15
woe is me, for I am *u.* *Isa* 6:5
not to leave the other *u.* *Mat* 23:23
Luke 11:42

undressed
grapes of thy vine *u.* *Lev* 25:5, 11

unequal
are not your ways *u.*? *Ezek* 18:25, 29

unequally
be ye not *u.* yoked with. *2 Cor* 6:14

unfaithful
confidence in an *u.* man. *Pr* 25:19

unfaithfully
they dealt *u.* like their. *Ps* 78:57*

unfeigned
Holy Ghost, by love *u.* *2 Cor* 6:6
a pure heart and faith *u.* *1 Tim* 1:5
remembrance the *u.* faith. *2 Tim* 1:5
through the Spirit unto *u.* love of the brethren. *1 Pet* 1:22

unfruitful
riches, choke word, and he becometh *u.* *Mat* 13:22; *Mark* 4:19
my understanding is *u.* *1 Cor* 14:14
no fellowship with the *u.* works. *Eph* 5:11
works, that they be not *u.* *Tit* 3:14
be barren nor *u.* in the. *2 Pet* 1:8

ungirded
the man *u.* the camels. *Gen* 24:32

ungodliness
the wrath of God revealed against all *u.* *Rom* 1:18
and he shall turn away *u.* 11:26
increase unto more *u.* *2 Tim* 2:16
that, denying *u.* and worldly. *Tit* 2:12

ungodly
death compassed me, the floods of *u.* men. *2 Sam* 22:5; *Ps* 18:4
Shouldest thou help *u.*? *2 Chr* 19:2*
delivered me to the *u.* *Job* 16:11
say to princes, Ye are *u.*? 34:18*
in the counsel of the *u.* *Ps* 1:1*
the *u.* are not so. 4*
u. not stand in judgement. 5*
but the way of the *u.* shall perish. 6*
broken the teeth of the *u.* 3:7*
cause against an *u.* nation. 43:1
these are the *u.* who prosper. 73:12*
an *u.* man diggeth up evil. *Pr* 16:27*
an *u.* witness scorneth. 19:28*
that justifieth the *u.* *Rom* 4:5
Christ died for the *u.* 5:6
the law is for the *u.* and. *1 Tim* 1:9
where shall the *u.* and sinner? *1 Pet* 4:18
flood on world of the *u.* *2 Pet* 2:5
those who after should live *u.* 6
and perdition of *u.* men. 3:7
u. men turning the grace. *Jude* 4
that are *u.* of their *u.* deeds. 15
walk after their own *u.* lusts. 18

unholy
may put difference between holy and *u.* *Lev* 10:10*
law was made for the *u.* *1 Tim* 1:9
shall be unthankful, *u.* *2 Tim* 3:2
of covenant an *u.* thing. *Heb* 10:29

unicorn
(*This animal is mythical. The word as used in the Bible probably means the wild ox, as the Revised Versions render it*)
as it were the strength of an *u.* *Num* 23:22; 24:8
will the *u.* be willing to? *Job* 39:9
canst thou bind the *u.* in the? 10
Sirion like a young *u.* *Ps* 29:6
exalt like the horn of an *u.* 92:10

unicorns
like the horns of *u.* *Deut* 33:17
from the horns of the *u.* *Ps* 22:21
and the *u.* shall come. *Isa* 34:7

unite
u. my heart to fear thy. *Ps* 86:11

united
mine honour, be not thou *u.* *Gen* 49:6

unity
to dwell together in *u.* *Ps* 133:1
endeavouring to keep the *u.* *Eph* 4:3
till we come in the *u.* of the faith. 13

unjust
deliver me from the *u.* *Ps* 43:1
and the hope of *u.* men. *Pr* 11:7*
who by *u.* gain increaseth his. 28:8
an *u.* man is an abomination. 29:27
u. knoweth no shame. *Zeph* 3:5
rain on the just and *u.* *Mat* 5:45
the Lord commended the *u.* steward. *Luke* 16:8*
he that is *u.* in the least, is *u.* 10*
hear what the *u.* judge saith. 18:6*
I am not as other men are, *u.* 11
both of the just and *u.* *Acts* 24:15
go to law before the *u.*? *1 Cor* 6:1*
the just for the *u.* *1 Pet* 3:18*
reserve the *u.* to the day of judgement. *2 Pet* 2:9*
he that is *u.* let him be *u.* still. *Rev* 22:11*

unjustly
how long will ye judge *u.*? *Ps* 82:2
in land of uprightness will he deal *u.* *Isa* 26:10*

unknown
To the *u.* God. *Acts* 17:23
that speaketh in an *u.* tongue. *1 Cor* 14:2, 4, 13, 27
if I pray in an *u.* tongue, my. 14
than ten thousand words in an *u.* 19
as *u.* and yet well known. *2 Cor* 6:9
I was *u.* by face unto the churches of Judaea which were. *Gal* 1:22

unlade
there the ship was to *u.* *Acts* 21:3

unlawful
an *u.* thing for a man. *Acts* 10:28
with their *u.* deeds. *2 Pet* 2:8*

unlearned
that they were *u.* *Acts* 4:13
occupieth the room of the *u.* *1 Cor* 14:16
come in those that are *u.* 23, 24
but foolish and *u.* questions avoid. *2 Tim* 2:23*
which they that are *u.* *2 Pet* 3:16

unleavened
they baked *u.* cakes of. *Ex* 12:39
it shall be an *u.* cake of fine flour mingled with oil, or *u.* *Lev* 2:4, 5
he shall offer *u.* cakes mingled. 7:12
and Moses took one *u.* cake. 8:26
priest shall take one *u.* cake, one *u.* wafer, and put them. *Num* 6:19
old corn of the land *u.* *Josh* 5:11
ready a kid and *u.* cakes. *Judg* 6:19
take the flesh and the *u.* cakes. 20
and *u.* cakes; fire out of the rock consumed the flesh and *u.* 21
for flour and *u.* cakes. *1 Chr* 23:29
a new lump, as ye are *u.* *1 Cor* 5:7
see **bread**

unless
unclean *u.* he wash his. *Lev* 22:6
u. she had turned from me, I had. *Num* 22:33
u. thou hadst spoken. *2 Sam* 2:27
I had fainted, *u.* I had. *Ps* 27:13
u. the Lord had been my help. 94:17
u. thy law had been my. 119:92
sleep not, *u.* they cause. *Pr* 4:16
ye are saved, *u.* ye have. *1 Cor* 15:2

unloose
not worthy to stoop down and *u.* *Mark* 1:7; *Luke* 3:16; *John* 1:27

unmarried
I say to the *u.* *1 Cor* 7:8
let her remain *u.* 11
he that is *u.* 32
the *u.* woman careth for. 34

unmerciful
implacable, *u.* *Rom* 1:31

unmindful
begat thee thou art *u.* *Deut* 32:18

unmoveable
of the ship remained *u.* *Acts* 27:41
be ye stedfast, *u.* *1 Cor* 15:58

unoccupied
Shamgar, highways were *u.* *Judg* 5:6

unperfect
substance, yet being *u.* *Ps* 139:16

unprepared
with me, and find you *u.* *2 Cor* 9:4

unprofitable
reason with *u.* talk? *Job* 15:3
cast the *u.* servant into. *Mat* 25:30
We are *u.* servants. *Luke* 17:10
altogether become *u.* *Rom* 3:12
genealogies, for they are *u.* *Tit* 3:9
time past was to thee *u.* *Philem* 11
for that is *u.* for you. *Heb* 13:17

unprofitableness
weakness and *u.* thereof. *Heb* 7:18

unpunished
wicked shall not be *u.* *Pr* 11:21
the proud shall not be *u.* 16:5
at calamities, shall not be *u.* 17:5
false witness shall not be *u.* 19:5, 9
utterly *u.*? ye shall not be *u.* *Jer* 25:29
not leave thee altogether *u.* 30:11
not leave thee wholly *u.* 46:28
go *u.*? thou shalt not go *u.* 49:12

unquenchable
garner, but burn up the chaff with *u.* fire. *Mat* 3:12; *Luke* 3:17

unreasonable
it seemeth to me *u.* to send a. *Acts* 25:27
delivered from *u.* men. *2 Thes* 3:2

unrebukeable
this commandment *u.* *1 Tim* 6:14*

unreproveable
to present you holy, *u.* in. *Col* 1:22

unrighteous
hand to be an *u.* witness. *Ex* 23:1
against me, be as the *u.* *Job* 27:7
out of the hand of the *u.* *Ps* 71:4
woe unto them that decree *u.* *Isa* 10:1
let the *u.* man forsake his. 55:7
not been faithful in the *u.* *Luke* 16:11
is God *u.* who taketh ? *Rom* 3:5
the *u.* shall not inherit. *1 Cor* 6:9
for God is not *u.* to forget. *Heb* 6:10

unrighteously
all that do *u.* are an. *Deut* 25:16

unrighteousness
ye shall do no *u.* in judgement. *Lev* 19:15, 35
there is no *u.* in him. *Ps* 92:15
buildeth his house by *u.* *Jer* 22:13
the mammon of *u.* *Luke* 16:9
and no *u.* is in him. *John* 7:18
all *u.* of men who hold the truth in *u.* *Rom* 1:18
filled with all *u.*, fornication. 29
them that obey *u.*, indignation. 2:8
if our *u.* commend the. 3:5
members as instruments of *u.* 6:13
is there *u.* with God ? 9:14
righteousness with *u.*? *2 Cor* 6:14
deceiveableness of *u.* *2 Thes* 2:10
not, but had pleasure in *u.* 12
be merciful to their *u.* *Heb* 8:12*
receive the reward of *u.* *2 Pet* 2:13*
who loved the wages of *u.* 15*
to cleanse us from all *u.* *1 John* 1:9
all *u.* is sin: there is a sin not. 5:17

unripe
shake off his *u.* grape. *Job* 15:33

unruly
warn them that are *u.* *1 Thes* 5:14
not accused of riot, or *u.* *Tit* 1:6
for there are many *u.* and vain. 10
the tongue is an *u.* evil. *Jas* 3:8*

unsatiable
because thou wast *u.* *Ezek* 16:28

unsavoury
can what is *u.* be eaten ? *Job* 6:6

unsearchable
great things and *u.* *Job* 5:9
Lord, his greatness is *u.* *Ps* 145:3
heart of kings is *u.* *Pr* 25:3
how *u.* are his judgements, and his ways! *Rom* 11:33
the *u.* riches of Christ. *Eph* 3:8

unseemly
working that which is *u.* *Rom* 1:27
not behave itself *u.* *1 Cor* 13:5

unshod
thy foot from being *u.* *Jer* 2:25

unskilful
babe is *u.* in the word. *Heb* 5:13*

unspeakable
be to God for his *u.* gift. *2 Cor* 9:15
paradise and heard *u.* words. 12:4
in whom ye rejoice with joy *u.* and full of glory. *1 Pet* 1:8

unspotted
to keep himself *u.* from. *Jas* 1:27

unstable
u. as water, thou shalt. *Gen* 49:4†
a double minded man is *u.* in all. *Jas* 1:8
from sin, beguiling *u.* *2 Pet* 2:14
are unlearned and *u.* wrest. 3:16

unstopped
ears of the deaf shall be *u.* *Isa* 35:5

untaken
the same vail *u.* away. *2 Cor* 3:14

untempered
and lo others daubed it with *u.* *Ezek* 13:10, 11, 14, 15; 22:28

unthankful
for he is kind to the *u.* *Luke* 6:35
blasphemers, *u.*, unholy. *2 Tim* 3:2

until
u. I have done that I. *Gen* 28:15
and stayed there *u.* now. 32:4
our youth, even *u.* now. 46:34
nor a lawgiver depart, *u.* 49:10
this people *u.* now. *Num* 14:19
to Dan *u.* the captivity. *Judg* 18:30
will not eat *u.* he come. *1 Sam* 9:13
to see Saul *u.* his death. 15:35
from thy youth *u.* now. *2 Sam* 19:7
nor trimmed, *u.* the day he. 24
with bread and water of affliction, *u.* I come. *1 Ki* 22:27; *2 Chr* 18:26
she left the land, *u.* now. *2 Ki* 8:6
city be not built, *u.* *Ezra* 4:21
since then *u.* now hath it. 5:16
u. the fierce wrath of God. 10:14
keep me secret *u.* thy. *Job* 14:13
u. his iniquity be found. *Ps* 36:2
u. I went into the sanctuary. 73:17
u. I find a place for the Lord. 132:5
u. the day break. *S of S* 2:17; 4:6
u. the spirit be poured. *Isa* 32:15
u. I come and take you away. 36:17
u. the righteousness thereof. 62:1
and there shall he be *u.* *Jer* 32:5
be consumed *u.* there be an. 44:27
overturn, *u.* he come. *Ezek* 21:27
bear indignation, *u.* he. *Mi* 7:9
be thou there *u.* I bring. *Mat* 2:13
the prophets and the law prophesied *u.* John. 11:13; *Luke* 16:16
trodden down *u.* the times of the Gentiles. *Luke* 21:24; *Rom* 11:25
u. ye be endued with power from on high. *Luke* 24:49
u. the day in which he. *Acts* 1:2
for *u.* the law, sin was. *Rom* 5:13
judge nothing *u.* the. *1 Cor* 4:5
will perform it *u.* the day of Jesus Christ. *Phil* 1:6
will let, *u.* he be taken out. *2 Thes* 2:7
u. the appearing of our Lord Jesus. *1 Tim* 6:14
u. the words of God. *Rev* 17:17
lived not *u.* the 1000 years. 20:5

untimely
or as an hidden *u.* birth. *Job* 3:16
pass away like the *u.* birth. *Ps* 58:8
I say that an *u.* birth is. *Eccl* 6:3
fig tree casteth her *u.* figs. *Rev* 6:13

untoward
save yourselves from this *u.* *Acts* 2:40*

unwalled
took sixty cities, beside *u.* towns. *Deut* 3:5
dwelt in the *u.* towns. *Esth* 9:19
land of *u.* villages. *Ezek* 38:11

unwashen
but to eat with *u.* hands defileth not. *Mat* 15:20; *Mark* 7:2, 5*

unweighed
left all the vessels *u.* *1 Ki* 7:47

unwise
do you thus requite the Lord, O *u.* people ? *Deut* 32:6
he is an *u.* son, he should not stay. *Hos* 13:13
to the wise and to the *u.* *Rom* 1:14*
not *u.* but understanding. *Eph* 5:17*

unwittingly
if a man eat of the holy thing *u.* *Lev* 22:14
killeth any person *u.* *Josh* 20:3*, 5*

unworthily
this cup of the Lord *u.* *1 Cor* 11:27
and drinketh *u.* eateth. 29

unworthy
ourselves *u.* of life. *Acts* 13:46
are ye *u.* to judge the ? *1 Cor* 6:2

up ! *exclamation*
Lot said, *U.*, get you out. *Gen* 19:14
Joseph said, *U.* follow after. 44:4
u. make us gods that. *Ex* 32:1
u. sanctify the people. *Josh* 7:13
u. for this is the day in. *Judg* 4:14
he said to his firstborn, *U.*, slay. 8:20
u. thou and the people that. 9:32
u. and let us be going, but. 19:28
saying, *U.* that I may. *1 Sam* 9:26

up
rose *u.* early and gat them *u.* saying, We . . . will go *u.* *Num* 14:40
go not *u.* for the Lord is not. 42
they presumed to go *u.* unto. 44
from battle before sun *u.* *Judg* 8:13
as soon as sun is *u.* thou. *Judg* 9:33
as soon as ye be *u.* early, depart. *1 Sam* 29:10
when David was *u.* *2 Sam* 24:11
to die from my youth *u.* *Ps* 88:15
from the ground *u.* to. *Ezek* 41:16
when the sun was *u.* they were. *Mat* 13:6; *Mark* 4:6
kept from my youth *u.* *Mat* 19:20
Luke 18:21
and they filled them *u.* *John* 2:7
see **down**

upbraid
with whom ye did *u.* me. *Judg* 8:15*
then began he to *u.* the. *Mat* 11:20

upbraided
he *u.* them with their. *Mark* 16:14

upbraideth
all men liberally and *u.* not. *Jas* 1:5

Upharsin
MENE, MENE, TEKEL, *U.* *Dan* 5:25

Uphaz
gold is brought from *U.* *Jer* 10:9
girded with gold of *U.* *Dan* 10:5

upheld
salvation and my fury it *u.* me. *Isa* 63:5

uphold
and *u.* me with thy free. *Ps* 51:12
the Lord is with them that *u.* 54:4
u. me according to thy word. 119:116
honour shall *u.* the humble in spirit. *Pr* 29:23*
I will *u.* thee with the right hand. *Isa* 41:10
behold my servant whom I *u.* 42:1
that there was none to *u.* 63:5
they also that *u.* Egypt. *Ezek* 30:6

upholden
thy words have *u.* him. *Job* 4:4
the king's throne is *u.* *Pr* 20:28

upholdest
as for me, thou *u.* me in mine. *Ps* 41:12

upholdeth
but the Lord *u.* the. *Ps* 37:17
for the Lord *u.* him with his. 24
thy right hand *u.* me. 63:8
the Lord *u.* all that fall. 145:14

upholding
u. all things by the word. *Heb* 1:3

upper
shall strike blood on the *u.* *Ex* 12:7*
covering on his *u.* lip. *Lev* 13:45
no man take the *u.* millstone to. *Deut* 24:6
he gave her the *u.* springs. *Josh* 15:19; *Judg* 1:15
they stood by the conduit of the *u.* pool. *2 Ki* 18:17; *Isa* 7:3; 36:2
shall lodge in *u.* lintels. *Zeph* 2:14*
he will shew you a large *u.* room. *Mark* 14:15; *Luke* 22:12
up into an *u.* room. *Acts* 1:13
passed through the *u.* coasts. 19:1
see **chamber**

uppermost
in the *u.* basket were all. *Gen* 40:17
in the top of the *u.* bough. *Isa* 17:6
cities shall be as an *u.* branch. 9
they love the *u.* rooms at. *Mat* 23:6* *Mark* 12:39*; *Luke* 11:43*

upright
my sheaf arose and also stood *u.* *Gen* 37:7
yoke and made you go *u.* *Lev* 26:13
Surely as Lord liveth, thou hast been *u.* *1 Sam* 29:6; *2 Chr* 29:34
I was also *u.* before him. *2 Sam* 22:24*; *Ps* 18:23*
with the *u.* man thou wilt shew thyself *u.* *2 Sam* 22:26*; *Ps* 18:25*
were more *u.* in heart. *2 Chr* 29:34
Job was a perfect and *u.* man. *Job* 1:1, 8; 2:3
if thou wert *u.* he would awake. 8:6
the just *u.* man is laughed. 12:4*
u. men shall be astonished. 17:8

doth behold the u. Ps 11:7
then shall I be u., I shall be. 19:13
the Lord is good and u. 25:8; 92:15
praise is comely for the u. 33:1
to slay such as be of u. 37:14
knoweth the days of the u. 18
perfect man and behold the u. 37
the u. shall have dominion. 49:14
Lord in the assembly of the u. 111:1
the generation of the u. 112:2
unto the u. there ariseth light. 4
righteous art thou, and u. are. 119:137
do good to them that are u. 125:4
the u. shall dwell in thy. 140:13
for the u. shall dwell in. Pr 2:21
of Lord is strength to the u. 10:29
integrity of the u. shall guide. 11:3
the righteousness of the u. shall. 6
by the blessings of the u. the city. 11
such as are u. in their way are. 20*
mouth of the u. shall deliver. 12:6
righteousness keepeth the u. 13:6
the tabernacle of the u. shall. 14:11
but the prayer of the u. is his. 15:8
highway of the u. is to depart. 16:17
shall be a ransom for the u. 21:18
but as for the u. he directeth. 29
the u. shall have good things. 28:10*
the bloodthirsty hate the u. 29:10*
he that is u. is an abomination to. 27
God hath made man u. Eccl 7:29
was written was u. words. 12:10*
remember thy love, the u. love. S of S 1:4*
thou most u. dost weigh. Isa 26:7
they are u. as palm tree. Jer 10:5
touched me and set me u. Dan 8:18
enter and u. ones with him. 11:17
is none u. among men. Mi 7:2
the most u. is sharper than a. 4
soul lifted up is not u. Hab 2:4
see **heart, stand, stood**

uprightly

walketh u. shall abide in. Ps 15:2
do ye judge u.? 58:1
I will judge u. 75:2
from them that walk u. 84:11
buckler to them that walk u. Pr 2:7*
he that walketh u. walketh. 10:9
of understanding walketh u. 15:21
walketh u. shall be saved. 28:18
he that speaketh u. shall. Isa 33:15
him that speaketh u. Amos 5:10
my words do good to him that walketh u. Mi 2:7
that they walked not u. Gal 2:14

uprightness

before thee in u. of heart. 1 Ki 3:6
thou hast pleasure in u. 1 Chr 29:17
is not this thy hope and the u. of thy ways? Job 4:6*
to shew unto man his u. 33:23*
minister judgement to the people in u. Ps 9:8
let integrity and u. preserve. 25:21
for ever and are done in u. 111:8
lead me into the land of u. 143:10
paths of u. to walk. Pr 2:13
he that walketh in u. feareth. 14:2
poor that walketh in his u. 28:6*
the way of the just is u. Isa 26:7
in the land of u. will he deal. 10
each one walking in his u. 57:2
see **heart**

uprising

my downsitting and u. Ps 139:2

uproar

city being in an u. 1 Ki 1:41
lest there be an u. Mat 26:5; Mark 14:2
all the city on an u. Acts 17:5
in question for this day's u. 19:40*
after the u. was ceased, Paul. 20:1
that all Jerusalem was in an u. 21:31
Egyptian who madest an u.? 38

upside *down*

Jerusalem as a man wipeth a dish, turning it u. down. 2 Ki 21:13
wicked he turneth u. down. Ps 146:9
turneth the earth u. down. Isa 24:1
turning of things u. down. 29:16
have turned the world u. down. Acts 17:6

upward

twenty years old and u. Ex 38:26
Num 1:3, 20, 22, 24, 26, 28; 14:29
1 Chr 23:24; 2 Chr 31:17; Ezra 3:8
shalt number every male from a month old and u. Num 3:15, 22
28, 34, 39, 40, 43; 26:62
u. even to fifty. 4:3, 23, 30, 35
39, 43, 47; 1 Chr 23:3
five years old and u. Num 8:24
Saul was higher from shoulders u. 1 Sam 9:2; 10:23
remnant shall bear fruit u. 2 Ki 19:30; Isa 37:31
males from three years old and u. 2 Chr 31:16
to trouble as sparks fly u. Job 5:7
spirit of man that goeth u. Eccl 3:21
king and God, and look u. Isa 8:21
mine eyes fail with looking u. 38:14
from appearance of his loins u. Ezek 1:27; 8:2
was a winding about still u. 41:7*
from this day and u. Hag 2:15, 18

Ur

before his father in U. Gen 11:28
brought thee out of U. of the Chaldees. 15:7; Neh 9:7
Eliphal the son of U. 1 Chr 11:35

Urbane

Salute U., our helper. Rom 16:9

urge

pharisees began to u. Luke 11:53*

urged

Jacob u. Esau, and he. Gen 33:11
Delilah u. Samson. Judg 16:16
his father in law u. him. 19:7
when they u. him till. 2 Ki 2:17
Naaman u. Elisha to take it. 5:16
he u. Gehazi. 23

urgent

the Egyptians were u. Ex 12:33
commandment was u. Dan 3:22

Uri

Bezaleel the son of U. Ex 31:2
35:30; 38:22; 1 Chr 2:20
2 Chr 1:5
Geber the son of U. 1 Ki 4:19
Shallum, Telem, and U. Ezra 10:24

Uriah, *called* **Urijah**

is not this Bath-sheba the wife of U.? 2 Sam 11:3
send me U. 6
sent it by U. 14
U. is dead. 21
thou hast killed U. the Hittite. 12:9
U. one of David's worthies. 23:39
1 Chr 11:41
in the matter of U. 1 Ki 15:5
by Meremoth son of U. Ezra 8:33
next repaired Meremoth the son of U. Neh 3:4, 21
Ezra and beside him stood U. 8:4
I took faithful witnesses, U. Isa 8:2
Solomon of the wife of U. Mat 1:6

Urijah

Ahaz sent U. the fashion. 2 Ki 16:10
thus did U. as king Ahaz. 16
U. prophesied. Jer 26:20
U. fled into Egypt. 21

Urim

breastplate of judgement, the U. Ex 28:30; Lev 8:8
counsel after the judgement of U. Num 27:21
let thy U. be with thy. Deut 33:8
neither by dreams, by U. 1 Sam 28:6
stood up a priest with U. and. Ezra 2:63; Neh 7:65
see **Thummim**

us

with u. even u. who are all of u. Deut 5:3
save thyself and u. Luke 23:39
even u. whom he hath. Rom 9:24
God hath set forth u. 1 Cor 4:9
and will also raise up u. by. 6:14
acknowledged u. in part. 2 Cor 1:14
he which establisheth u. with. 21
who hath reconciled u. to. 5:18
brethren, as ye have u. Phil 3:17
let u. who are of the. 1 Thes 5:8
for God hath not appointed u. 1 Thes 5:9
of his own will begat he u. Jas 1:18

about **us**

lick up all that are round about u. Num 22:4
heathen that are about u. Neh 5:17
the heathen about u. saw. 6:16
a reproach to all about u. Dan 9:16

after **us**

will come out after u. Josh 8:6
to our generations after u. 22:27
away, for she crieth after u. Mat 15:23

against **us**

seek occasion against u. Gen 43:18
enemies and fight against u. Ex 1:10
that ye murmur against u.? 16:7
are not against u. but God. 8
Sihon came out against u. Deut 2:32; 29:7
Og came out against u. 3:1
of Ai came out against u. Josh 8:5
Amorites gathered against u. 10:6
rebel not against the Lord, nor against u. 22:19
ye come up against u.? Judg 15:10
delivered company that came against u. 1 Sam 30:23
surely the men prevailed against u. 2 Sam 11:23
man that devised against u. 21:5
wrath of Lord against u. 2 Ki 22:13
great company that cometh against u. 2 Chr 20:12
under that rise against u. Ps 44:5
remember not against u. 79:8
when men rose up against u. 124:2
wrath was kindled against u. 3
feller is come up against u. Isa 14:8
and our sins testify against u. 59:12; Jer 14:7
all this evil against u. Jer 16:10
maketh war against u. 21:2
shall come down against u.? 13
setteth thee on against u. 43:3
their mouth against u. Lam 3:46
art very wroth against u. 5:22
words he spake against u. Dan 9:12
Forbid him not. For he that is not against u. Mark 9:40; Luke 9:50
who can be against u.? Rom 8:31
blotting out the handwriting that was against u. Col 2:14
prating against u. with. 3 John 10

among or *amongst* **us**

mighty prince among u. Gen 23:6
the Lord among u. or not? Ex 17:7
I pray thee, go among u. 34:9
God is not among u. Deut 31:17
ye dwell among u. Josh 9:7, 22
take possession among u. 22:19
perceive the Lord is among u. 31
voice be heard among u. Judg 18:25
among u. it may save us. 1 Sam 4:3
not among u. any that can skill to hew. 1 Ki 5:6
his hands amongst u. Job 34:37
not among u. any that knoweth. Ps 74:9
cast in thy lot among u. Pr 1:14
who among u. shall dwell with the devouring fire? Isa 33:14
Is not the Lord among u.? Mi 3:11
a great prophet is risen up among u. Luke 7:16
Word was made flesh and dwelt among u. John 1:14
Lord Jesus went in and out among u. Acts 1:21
God made choice among u. 15:7

at **us**

if it first begin at u. 1 Pet 4:17

before **us**

make us gods which shall go before u. Ex 32:23; Acts 7:40
will send men before u. Deut 1:22
God delivered him before u. 2:33
dried up from before u. Josh 4:23
they flee before u. 8:6
drave out before u. 24:18
the Lord shall drive out before u. Judg 11:24

down *before u.* as. *Judg* 20:32, 39
king may judge us and go out *before u.* *1 Sam* 8:20
thy servant pass on *before u.* 9:27
land is yet *before u.* *2 Chr* 14:7
cause the Holy One of Israel to cease from *before u.* *Isa* 30:11
laws which he set *before u.* *Dan* 9:10
to lay hold on the hope set *before u.* *Heb* 6:18
the race that is set *before u.* 12:1

behind **us**

also he is *behind u.* *Gen* 32:18, 20

between or *betwixt* **us**

now an oath *betwixt u.* *Gen* 26:28
may judge *betwixt u.* both. 31:27
God of Abraham judge *betwixt u.* 53
Jordan a border *between u.* *Josh* 22:25
be a witness *between u.* 27, 28, 34
the Lord be witness *between u.* *Judg* 11:10; *Jer* 42:5
neither is there any daysman *betwixt u.* *Job* 9:33
between u. and you. *Luke* 16:26
put no difference *between u.* and. *Acts* 15:9
the middle wall of partition *between u.* *Eph* 2:14

by **us**

hath not the Lord spoken also *by u.*? *Num* 12:2
man of God passeth *by u.* *2 Ki* 4:9
Jesus was preached among you *by u.* *2 Cor* 1:19
to the glory of God *by u.* 20
savour of his knowledge *by u.* 2:14
of Christ, ministered *by u.* 3:3
God did beseech you *by u.* 5:20
ye might receive damage *by u.* 7:9
which is administered *by u.* 8:19, 20

concerning **us**

do according to all which is written *concerning u.* *2 Ki* 22:13

for **us**

hath made room *for u.* *Gen* 26:22
yet any inheritance *for u.*? 31:14
better *for u.* to serve. *Ex* 14:12
tarry ye here *for u.* until. 24:14
better *for u.* to return. *Num* 14:3
people, for they are bread *for u.* 9
one city too strong *for u.* *Deut* 2:36
say, Who shall go up *for u.*? 30:12
Who shall go over the sea *for u.*? 13
art thou *for u.* or for our? *Josh* 5:13
of Peor too little *for u.*? 22:17
who go up *for u.* against? *Judg* 1:1
cry unto the Lord *for u.* *1 Sam* 7:8
lest father take thought *for u.* 9:5
the Lord will work *for u.* 14:6
they will not care *for u.* *2 Sam* 18:3
neither *for u.* shalt thou kill. 21:4
hast been careful *for u.* *2 Ki* 4:13
we dwell is too strait *for u.* 6:1
as *for u.* the Lord is. *2 Chr* 13:10
him a right way *for u.* *Ezra* 8:21
our God shall fight *for u.* *Neh* 4:20
he shall choose our inheritance *for u.* *Ps* 47:4
God is a refuge *for u.* 62:8
that thou hast wrought *for u.* 68:28
hath done great things *for u.* 126:3
send, and who will go *for u.*? *Isa* 6:8
thou wilt ordain peace *for u.* 26:12
take up a wailing *for u.* *Jer* 9:18
there is no healing *for u.* 14:19
I pray thee, of the Lord *for u.* 21:2
pray to the Lord our God *for u.* 37:3
42:2, 20
as *for u.* our eyes as. *Lam* 4:17
Lord, it is good *for u.* to be here. *Mat* 17:4; *Mark* 9:5; *Luke* 9:33
there be not enough *for u.* *Mat* 25:9
there make ready *for u.* *Mark* 14:15
hast raised up an horn of salvation *for u.* *Luke* 1:69
is not against us is *for u.* 9:50
for u. to whom it shall. *Rom* 4:24
sinners, Christ died *for u.* 5:8
maketh intercession *for u.* 8:26
if God be *for u.* who can be? 31
but delivered him up *for u.* all. 32
maketh intercession *for u.* 34
Christ is sacrificed *for u.* *1 Cor* 5:7
together by prayer *for u.* *2 Cor* 1:11
light affliction worketh *for u.* 4:17
made him to be sin *for u.* 5:21
us, made a curse *for u.* *Gal* 3:13
us, and given himself *for u.* *Eph* 5:2
praying *for u.* that God. *Col* 4:3
who died *for u.*, that we should live. *1 Thes* 5:10; *1 John* 3:16
pray *for u.* *1 Thes* 5:25; *2 Thes* 3:1 *Heb* 13:18
who gave himself *for u.* *Tit* 2:14
the forerunner is *for u.* entered. *Heb* 6:20
eternal redemption *for u.* 9:12
in the presence of God *for u.* 24
he hath consecrated *for u.* 10:20
provided some better thing *for u.* 11:40
because Christ hath suffered *for u.* *1 Pet* 2:21; 4:1

from **us**

said to Isaac, Go *from u.* *Gen* 26:16
shall he go up *from u.*? *1 Sam* 6:20
and see who is gone *from u.* 14:17
his wrath turn *from u.* *2 Chr* 29:10 *Ezra* 10:14
away their cords *from u.* *Ps* 2:3
our transgressions *from u.* 103:12
judgement far *from u.* *Isa* 59:9
salvation, but it is far off *from u.* 11
hast hid thy face *from u.* 64:7
the anger of the Lord is not turned *from u.* *Jer* 4:8
Nebuchadrezzar may go up *from u.* 21:2
hide it not *from u.*, we will not. 38:25
he was taken up *from u.* *Acts* 1:22
certain who went out *from u.* 15:24
nor by letter as *from u.* *2 Thes* 2:2
they went out *from u.*, but they were not of us. *1 John* 2:19

see **depart**

in **us**

if the Lord delight *in u.* *Num* 14:8
thou, which is not *in u.* *Job* 15:9
thou hast wrought all our works *in u.* *Isa* 26:12
also may be one *in u.* *John* 17:21
law might be fulfilled *in u.* *Rom* 8:4
which shall be revealed *in u.* 18
ye might learn *in u.* not. *1 Cor* 4:6
of Christ abound *in u.* *2 Cor* 1:5
so death worketh *in u.* but. 4:12
ye are not straitened *in u.* but. 6:12
power that worketh *in u.* *Eph* 3:20
by Holy Ghost which dwelleth *in u.* *2 Tim* 1:14
that dwelleth *in u.* lusteth. *Jas* 4:5
truth is not *in u.* *1 John* 1:8
his word is not *in u.* 10
we know that he abideth *in u.* 3:24
God dwelleth *in u.* 4:12, 13
for the truth's sake which dwelleth *in u.* *2 John* 2

of **us**

the man is become as one *of u.* *Gen* 3:22
lacketh not a man *of u.* *Num* 31:49
faint because *of u.* *Josh* 2:24
which slew many *of u.* *Judg* 16:24
which *of u.* shall go up first? 20:18
which *of u.* is for the king of Israel? *2 Ki* 6:11
he was entreated *of u.* *Ezra* 8:23
hath been mindful *of u.* *Ps* 115:12
laid on him the iniquity *of u.* all. *Isa* 53:6
Abraham be ignorant *of u.* 63:16
hath taken hold *of u.* *Jer* 6:24
O Lord, art in the midst *of u.* 14:9
he be not far from every one *of u.* *Acts* 17:27
who is the father *of u.* all. *Rom* 4:16
account *of u.* as ministers. *1 Cor* 4:1
advantage *of u.* for we. *2 Cor* 2:11
be of God and not *of u.* 4:7
some who think *of u.* as if we. 10:2
is the mother *of u.* all. *Gal* 4:26
but to every one *of u.* is. *Eph* 4:7
became followers *of u.* *1 Thes* 1:6
they themselves shew *of u.* what. 9
the word which ye heard *of u.* 2:13
remembrance *of u.* always. *1 Thes* 3:6
that as ye have received *of u.* 4:1
tradition he received *of u.* *2 Thes* 3:6
the commandment *of u.* *2 Pet* 3:2
of u., for if they had been *of u.* they might shew . . . *of u.* *1 John* 2:19

on **us**, or *upon* **us**

brought guiltiness *upon u.* *Gen* 26:10
this distress come *upon u.* 42:21
fall *upon u.* and take us for. 43:18
upon u. with pestilence. *Ex* 5:3
lay not the sin *upon u.* *Num* 12:11
evils come *upon u.*? *Deut* 31:17
lest wrath be *upon u.* *Josh* 9:20
Rise thou and fall *upon u.* *Judg* 8:21
his hand is sore *upon u.* *1 Sam* 5:7
heavy yoke which he put *upon u.* *1 Ki* 12:4, 9; *2 Chr* 10:4, 9
some mischief will come *upon u.* *2 Ki* 7:9
made a breach *upon u.* *1 Chr* 15:13
cometh *upon u.* as sword. *2 Chr* 20:9
the wrath poured *upon u.* 34:21
by the good hand of our God *upon u.* *Ezra* 8:18, 31
after all that is come *upon u.* 9:13
let not all the trouble seem little that hath come *upon u.* *Neh* 9:32
all that is brought *upon u.* 33
bring all this evil *upon u.*? 13:18
his hand *upon u.* both. *Job* 9:33
thy countenance *upon u.* *Ps* 4:6
mercy, O Lord, be *upon u.* 33:22
all this is come *upon u.*; yet. 44:17
cause his face to shine *upon u.* 67:1
beauty of the Lord be *upon u.* 90:17
till he have mercy *upon u.* 123:2
upon u. O Lord, have mercy *upon u.* 3 *Mat* 9:27; 20:30, 31; *Luke* 17:13
Spirit be poured *upon u.* *Isa* 32:15
snare is come *upon u.* *Lam* 3:47
O Lord, what is come *upon u.* 5:1
and sins be *upon u.* *Ezek* 33:10
curse is poured *upon u.* *Dan* 9:11
by bringing *upon u.* a great evil. 12, 13, 14
and to the hills, Fall *on u.* *Hos* 10:8 *Luke* 23:30; *Rev* 6:16
cause this evil is *on u.* *Jonah* 1:7, 8
None evil can come *upon u.* *Mi* 3:11
have compassion *upon u.* 7:19
his blood be *on u.* and. *Mat* 27:25
Peter, said, Look *on u.* *Acts* 3:4
so earnestly *on u.* as though? 12
bring this man's blood *upon u.* 5:28
Holy Ghost on them, as *on u.* 11:15
Mary, who bestowed much labour *on u.* *Rom* 16:6
shed *on u.* abundantly. *Tit* 3:6
love the Father hath bestowed *on u.* *1 John* 3:1

over **us**

indeed reign *over u.*? *Gen* 37:8
who made thee a prince and a judge *over u.*? *Ex* 2:14; *Acts* 7:27
thyself a prince *over u.* *Num* 16:13
Gideon, Rule *over u.* *Judg* 8:22
to the olive tree, Reign *over u.* 9:8 10, 12, 14
but we will have a king *over u.* *1 Sam* 8:19; 10:19
Shall Saul reign *over u.*? 11:12
Saul was king *over u.* *2 Sam* 5:2
whom we anointed *over u.* 19:10
thou hast set *over u.* *Neh* 9:37
own: who is lord *over u.*? *Ps* 12:4
had dominion *over u.* *Isa* 26:13
servants have ruled *over u.*: there is none. *Lam* 5:8
this man to reign *over u.* *Luke* 19:14

through **us**

through u. thanksgiving to God. *2 Cor* 9:11

to or *unto* **us**

a man to come in *unto u.* *Gen* 19:31
hast thou done *unto u.*? 20:9; 26:10
their daughters *to u.* for wives. 34:21
Hebrew *unto u.* to mock us. 39:14
What is this that God hath done *unto u.*? 42:28; *Jer* 5:19
thou mayest be *to u.* *Num* 10:31
Lord shall do *unto u.*, the same. 32
speak thou *unto u.* and. *Deut* 5:27

revealed belong unto u. Deut 29:29
heaven and bring it unto u. 30:12
the sea and bring it unto u. 13
seemeth good and right to thee to do
unto u. Josh 9:25; Judg 10:15
of God come again unto u. Judg 13:8
to him, as he hath done to u. 15:10
with us, and be to u. a father. 18:19
woe unto u. 1 Sam 4:8; Jer 4:13
6:4; Lam 5:16
if they say thus unto u. 1 Sam 14:9
were very good unto u. 25:15
they were a wall unto u. by. 16
the ark of God to u. 1 Chr 13:3
came from thee to u. Ezra 4:12
brethren be sold unto u.? Neh 5:8
let us choose to u. judgement.
Job 34:4
O turn thyself to u. again. Ps 60:1
not unto u. O Lord, not unto u. 115:1
except had left unto u. a. Isa 1:9
unto u. a child is born, unto u. 9:6
Art thou become like unto u.? 14:10
shall not come unto u. 28:15
prophesy not unto u. right things,
speak unto u. smooth. 30:10
Lord will be unto u. a place. 33:21
speak not to u. in the Jews'. 36:11
to u. the appointed weeks. Jer 5:24
hath spoken to u. in the name. 26:16
the Lord shall send thee to u. 42:5
thou hast spoken unto u. 44:16
our wood is sold unto u. Lam 5:4
unto u. is this land given. Ezek 11:15
what these things are to u.? 24:19
but unto u. confusion. Dan 9:7, 8
he shall come unto u. Hos 6:3
what should a king do to u.? 10:3
may be calm unto u. Jonah 1:11
Lord thought to do unto u. Zech 1:6
made them equal unto u. Mat 20:12
saying, Lord, Lord, open to u. 25:11
Luke 13:25
what is that to u.? see. Mat 27:4
delivered them unto u. Luke 1:2
hath made known unto u. 2:15
devils are subject unto u. 10:17
this parable unto u.? 12:41
neither can they pass to u. 16:26
shewest thou unto u.? John 2:18
manifest thyself unto u.? 14:22
that he sayeth unto u.? 16:17
oracles to give unto u. Acts 7:38
to u. who did eat and drink. 10:41
the like gift as unto u. 11:17
fulfilled the same unto u. 13:33
Holy Ghost which is given unto u.
Rom 5:5
but unto u. it is the power. 1 Cor 1:18
of God is made unto u. wisdom. 30
God revealed them unto u. 2:10
but to u. there is but one God. 8:6
committed to u. word of. 2 Cor 5:19
gave themselves unto u. by. 8:5
as ye abound in your love to u. 7
who declared unto u. Col 1:8
that God would open unto u. 4:3
for unto u. was the gospel. Heb 4:2
unto u. they did minister. 1 Pet 1:12

toward **us**

thine anger toward u. to cease.
Ps 85:4
kindness is great toward u. 117:2
his love toward u. Rom 5:8
hath abounded toward u. Eph 1:8
in his kindness toward u. 2:7
love of God toward u. 1 John 4:9

under **us**

subdue the people under u. Ps 47:3

with **us**

no man is with u. Gen 31:50
make ye marriages with u. 34:9
ye shall dwell with u. 10
they dwell with u. 23
send our brother with u. 43:4; 44:26
lad is not with u. 44:30, 31
the God of the Hebrews met with u.
Ex 3:18; 5:3
hast thou dealt thus with u.? 14:11
speak thou with u.: but let not God
speak with u. 20:19
not in that thou goest with u.? 33:16
come thou with u., we. Num 10:29
it shall be, if thou go with u.
Num 10:32
was well with u. in Egypt. 11:18
and the Lord is with u. 14:9
refuseth to come with u. 22:14
made a covenant with u. Deut 5:2, 3
standeth here with u., also with him
that is not here with u. 29:15
make a league with u. Josh 9:6, 11
if the Lord be with u. Judg 6:13
thou mayest go with u. 11:8
Hold thy peace and go with u. 18:19
the ark of God shall not abide with
u. 1 Sam 5:7
Amnon go with u. 2 Sam 13:26
no more out with u. to battle. 21:17
stranger with u. in house. 1 Ki 3:18
the Lord our God be with u. 8:57
be with u. are more than they that.
2 Ki 6:16; 2 Chr 32:7
God is with u. 2 Chr 13:12; 32:8
you have nothing to do with u. to
build. Ezra 4:3
be angry with u. till thou? 9:14
with u. are the gray-headed and.
Job 15:10
Lord of hosts is with us. Ps 46:7, 11
wilt thou be angry with u. for? 85:5
he hath not dealt with u. 103:10
come with u. Pr 1:11
God is with u. Isa 8:10
transgressions are with u. 59:12
law of the Lord is with u. Jer 8:8
break not thy covenant with u. 14:21
that it may be well with u. 42:6
Bethel, there he spake with u.
Hos 12:4
so hath he dealt with u. Zech 1:6
interpreted, is, God with u. Mat 1:23
his sisters are all with u. 13:56
Mark 6:3
there were with u. seven. Mat 22:25
thou thus dealt with u.? Luke 2:48
he followeth not with u. 9:49
abide with u. 24:29
while he talked with u. 32
numbered with u. and had. Acts 1:17
his sepulchre is with u. unto. 2:29
one that helpeth with u. 1 Cor 16:16
chosen to travel with u. 2 Cor 8:19
are troubled, rest with u. 2 Thes 1:7
like precious faith with u. 2 Pet 1:1
have fellowship with u. 1 John 1:3
have continued with u. 2:19
the truth shall be with u. 2 John 2

within **us**

our hearts burn within u. while he
opened to us the? Luke 24:32

without **us**

reigned as kings without u. 1 Cor 4:8
that they without u. should not be
made perfect. Heb 11:40

use

be used in any other u. Lev 7:24
aught for any unclean u. Deut 26:14
teach Judah the u. of bow. 2 Sam 1:18
according to the u. of. 1 Chr 28:15
did change the natural u. Rom 1:26
the men leaving the natural u. 27
which is good to the u. Eph 4:29
shall be a vessel meet for the
master's u. 2 Tim 2:21
by u. have their senses. Heb 5:14

use, *verb*

ye u. enchantment. Lev 19:26
u. trumpets for calling. Num 10:2
after which ye u. to go a. 15:39
could u. both right. 1 Chr 12:2
that u. their tongues, and. Jer 23:31
as yet they shall u. this speech. 31:23
in vain shalt thou u. many. 46:11
they shall no more u. it as a proverb.
Ezek 12:23
shall u. this proverb against. 16:44
what mean ye, that ye u.? 18:2
ye shall not have occasion to u. 3
Babylon stood to u. divination. 21:21
you, pray for them that despitefully
u. you. Mat 5:44; Luke 6:28
when ye pray, u. not vain. Mat 6:7
an assault made, to u. them despitefully. Acts 14:5
be made free, u. it rather. 1 Cor 7:21
they that u. this world as. 1 Cor 7:31
did I u. lightness? 2 Cor 1:17
we u. great plainness. 3:12
lest being present, I should u. 13:10
u. not liberty for an occasion to the.
Gal 5:13
the law is good if a man u. 1 Tim 1:8
then let them u. the office of. 3:10
u. a little wine for thy. 5:23
u. hospitality one to another.
1 Pet 4:9

used

if the ox hath u. to push. Ex 21:36*
the fat may be u. in any. Lev 7:24
for so u. the young. Judg 14:10
whom Samson had u. as his. 20
u. enchantments. 2 Ki 17:17; 21:6
2 Chr 33:6*
a wild ass u. to the. Jer 2:24
people of land have u. Ezek 22:29
thy envy which thou hast u. 35:11
and u. similitudes by. Hos 12:10
the disciples of John u. Mark 2:18*
man, called Simon, which beforetime
u. Acts 8:9
them which u. curious arts. 19:19*
tongues they u. deceit. Rom 3:13
not u. this power. 1 Cor 9:12
u. none of these things. 15
nor at any time u. we. 1 Thes 2:5
they that have u. the office of a.
1 Tim 3:13
of them that were so u. Heb 10:33

uses

to maintain good works for necessary
u. Tit 3:14

usest

as thou u. to those that. Ps 119:132

useth

any that u. divination. Deut 18:10
apparel which the king u. Esth 6:8
the tongue of the wise u. Pr 15:2*
the poor u. entreaties, but rich. 18:23
u. his neighbour's service. Jer 22:13
u. proverbs, shall use. Ezek 16:44
every one that u. milk. Heb 5:13*

using

to perish with the u. Col 2:22
and not u. your liberty. 1 Pet 2:16

usurer

not be to him as an u. Ex 22:25*

usurp

woman to u. authority. 1 Tim 2:12*

usury

By usury *is generally understood in the Bible any interest on a loan, whether in money or in wheat or other commodities. Modern usage has confined the meaning of the word to an unlawful interest.*

The law of God prohibits rigorous imposing of interest or exacting it, or a return of a loan without regard to the condition of the borrower; whether poverty occasioned his borrowing, or a visible prospect of gain by employing the borrowed goods.

The Hebrews were plainly commanded in Ex 22:25, *etc., not to receive interest for money from any that borrowed for necessity, as in the case in* Neh 5:5, 7.

thou lay upon him u. Ex 22:25
take thou no u. of him. Lev 25:36, 37
shalt not lend on u. Deut 23:19
thou mayest lend upon u. 20
ye exact u. Neh 5:7
let us leave off this u. 10
not his money to u. Ps 15:5
he that by u. increaseth. Pr 28:8
as with the taker of u., so with the
giver of u. Isa 24:2
I have neither lent on u. nor men
have lent to me on u. Jer 15:10
not given forth on u. Ezek 18:8, 17
given forth on u. 13
thou hast taken u. 22:12
received mine own with u.
Mat 25:27*; Luke 19:23

us-ward

thy thoughts which are to u. Ps 40:5

the greatness of his power to *u.* *Eph* 1:19
but his longsuffering to *u.* *2 Pet* 3:9

utmost, outmost

to the *u.* bound of the. *Gen* 49:26
might see the *u.* of the people. *Num* 22:41; 23:13
be driven out to *o.* parts. *Deut* 30:4
Edom and all that are in the *u.* corners. *Jer* 9:26*; 25:23*; 49:32*
she came from *u.* parts. *Luke* 11:31

utter

if he do not *u.* it, then he. *Lev* 5:1
our life if ye *u.* it not this. *Josh* 2:14
if thou *u.* it, we will quit. 20
awake, Deborah, *u.* song. *Judg* 5:12
shall not they *u.* words? *Job* 8:10
should a wise man *u.* vain? 15:2*
nor shall my tongue *u.* deceit. 27:4
lips shall *u.* knowledge. 33:3*
I will *u.* dark sayings. *Ps* 78:2
how long shall they *u.* hard? 94:4*
who can *u.* the mighty acts? 106:2
my lips shall *u.* praise. 119:171
they shall *u.* the memory. 145:7
false witness will *u.* lies. *Pr* 14:5
thine heart shall *u.* use. 23:33
of labour, man cannot *u.* it. *Eccl* 1:8
let not thine heart be hasty to *u.* 5:2
a vile person will *u.* error. *Isa* 32:6
tell this, *u.* it even to the end. 48:20
I will *u.* my judgements. *Jer* 1:16
u. his voice from his holy. 25:30
u. a parable unto the. *Ezek* 24:3
the Lord shall *u.* his voice. *Joel* 2:11
u. his voice from Jerusalem. 3:16 *Amos* 1:2
I will *u.* things kept. *Mat* 13:35
except *u.* words easy to. *1 Cor* 14:9
not lawful for a man to *u.* *2 Cor* 12:4

utter, outer

a man I appointed to *u.* *1 Ki* 20:42
heard to the *o.* court. *Ezek* 10:5
me forth into the *u.* court. 42:1*
he will make an *u.* end of. *Nah* 1:8*
there shall be no more *u.* destruction. *Zech* 14:11*

utterance

as the Spirit gave them *u.* *Acts* 2:4
enriched by him in all *u.* *1 Cor* 1:5
in *u.* and knowledge. *2 Cor* 8:7
that *u.* may be given. *Eph* 6:19
open to us a door of *u.* *Col* 4:3*

uttered

if she had a husband when she *u.* *Num* 30:6*, 8*
Jephthah *u.* all his words before the Lord. *Judg* 11:11*
the most High *u.* his voice. *2 Sam* 22:14; *Ps* 46:6
whom hast thou *u.* words? *Job* 26:4
therefore have I *u.* that I. 42:3
which my lips *u.* when. *Ps* 66:14
deep *u.* his voice and. *Hab* 3:10
groanings which cannot be *u.* *Rom* 8:26
to say, and hard to be *u.* *Heb* 5:11*
had cried, seven thunders *u.* their voices. *Rev* 10:3
when the seven thunders had *u.* 4

uttereth

for thy mouth *u.* thine. *Job* 15:5*
day unto day *u.* speech. *Ps* 19:2
wisdom *u.* her voice in. *Pr* 1:20
in the city she *u.* her words. 21
and he that *u.* a slander is. 10:18
a fool *u.* all his mind, but a. 29:11
when he *u.* his voice. *Jer* 10:13 51:16
the great man *u.* his. *Mi* 7:3

uttering

u. from the heart words. *Isa* 59:13

utterly

u. put out remembrance. *Ex* 17:14
if her father *u.* refuse to give. 22:17
thou shalt *u.* overthrow their. 23:24
pronounce him *u.* unclean. *Lev* 13:44*
enemies I will not destroy *u.* 26:44
that soul shall *u.* be cast. *Num* 15:31
I will *u.* destroy their cities. 21:2
if her husband hath *u.* made. 30:12
u. destroying men, women. *Deut* 3:6
yourselves, ye shall *u.* perish. 4:26
thou shalt *u.* destroy the Canaanites. 7:2; 20:17
shalt *u.* detest the silver and. 7:26
ye shall *u.* destroy the. 12:2
destroying *u.* city of idolaters. 13:15
after my death ye will *u.* 31:29
that he might *u.* destroy. *Josh* 11:20
put Canaanites to tribute, but did not *u.* drive. 17:13; *Judg* 1:28
I thought thou hadst *u.* *Judg* 15:2
shall *u.* destroy every male. 21:11
smite, *u.* destroy. *1 Sam* 15:3, 18
he hath made Israel *u.* to. 27:12
valiant shall *u.* melt. *2 Sam* 17:10
the sons of Belial . . . shall be *u.* burned with fire. 23:7
Israel could not *u.* destroy. *1 Ki* 9:21
lands, by destroying them *u.* *2 Ki* 19:11; *Isa* 37:11
u. to slay them of. *2 Chr* 20:23
thou didst not *u.* consume. *Neh* 9:31
though he fall shall not *u.* *Ps* 37:24
the wicked are *u.* consumed. 73:19
my lovingkindness not *u.* 89:33
statutes, O forsake me not *u.* 119:8
take not the word of truth *u.* out. 43
substance for love, it would *u.* be. *S of S* 8:7
and the idols he shall *u.* *Isa* 2:18
answered, until the land be *u.* 6:11
Lord *u.* destroy the tongue of. 11:15
land be *u.* emptied. 24:3
earth is *u.* broken. 19
done by destroying them *u.* 37:11
young men shall *u.* fall. 40:30
Lord hath *u.* separated me. 56:3
nations shall be *u.* wasted. 60:12
for every brother will *u.* *Jer* 9:4
if they will not obey, I will *u.* 12:17
hast thou *u.* rejected Judah? 14:19
behold, I, even I will *u.* 23:39
I will *u.* destroy them. 25:9; 50:21 26; 51:3, 58
should ye be *u.* unpunished? 25:29
but thou hast *u.* rejected. *Lam* 5:22
slay *u.* old and young. *Ezek* 9:6
being planted, shall it not *u.*? 17:10
make themselves *u.* bald. 27:31
the land of Egypt *u.* waste. 29:10
shall go forth *u.* to make. *Dan* 11:44
but I will *u.* take them. *Hos* 1:6
the king of Israel be *u.* cut off. 10:15
I will *u.* destroy the house. *Amos* 9:8
one say, We be *u.* spoiled. *Mi* 2:4
for the wicked: . . . he is *u.* *Nah* 1:15
I will *u.* consume all. *Zeph* 1:2
right eye shall be *u.* *Zech* 11:17
now there is *u.* a fault. *1 Cor* 6:7
shall *u.* perish in their. *2 Pet* 2:12
Babylon shall be *u.* burnt. *Rev* 18:8
see **destroyed**

uttermost

when lepers came to *u.* part of camp. *2 Ki* 7:5*, 8*
you cast out to *u.* part. *Neh* 1:9
I shall give thee *u.* parts for. *Ps* 2:8
till thou hast paid the *u.* *Mat* 5:26*
she came from the *u.* parts to. 12:42*
elect from the *u.* part. *Mark* 13:27
I will know the *u.* of. *Acts* 24:22
wrath is come upon them to the *u.* *1 Thes* 2:16
able to save them to the *u.* *Heb* 7:25
see **utmost**

Uz

children of Aram; *U.*, Hul. *Gen* 10:23
children of Dishan; *U.*, Aran. 36:28 *1 Chr* 1:42
Shem; Lud, Aram, and *U.* *1 Chr* 1:17
a man in the land of *U.* *Job* 1:1
I made the king of *U.* *Jer* 25:20
daughter of Edom, in *U.* *Lam* 4:21

Uzza, Uzzah

U. and Ahio drave the cart. *2 Sam* 6:3; *1 Chr* 13:7
U. put forth his hand to the ark. *2 Sam* 6:6; *1 Chr* 13:9
because the Lord had made a breach upon *U.* *2 Sam* 6:8
buried in the garden of *U.* *2 Ki* 21:18
Amon buried in the garden of *U.* 26
sons of Merari, Mahli, *U.* *1 Chr* 6:29
removed them, and begat *U.* 8:7
the children of *U.* *Ezra* 2:49 *Neh* 7:51

Uzziah, *called* **Azariah, Ozias**

A. made king. *2 Ki* 14:21; *2 Chr* 26:1
to reign in 39th year of *U.* *2 Ki* 15:13
Jotham did all that his father *U.* 34
a son of Kohath, *U.* *1 Chr* 6:24
U. the Ashterathite, a valiant. 11:44
storehouses, was the son of *U.* 27:25
the Ammonites gave gifts to *U.* *2 Chr* 26:8
U. prepared shields and slings. 14
it pertaineth not unto thee, *U.* to. 18
U. the king was a leper to the day. 21
U. son of Harim had taken a strange wife. *Ezra* 10:21
dwelt Athaiah son of *U.* *Neh* 11:4
vision in the days of *U.* *Isa* 1:1 *Hos* 1:1; *Amos* 1:1
in the year *U.* died, I saw. *Isa* 6:1
earthquake in days of *U.* *Zech* 14:5
Joram begat *Ozias.* *Mat* 1:8
Ozias begat Joatham. 9

Uzziel

Kohath, Amram, Izhar, *U.* *Ex* 6:18 *Num* 3:19; *1 Chr* 6:2, 18; 23:12
sons of *U.* *Ex* 6:22; *Lev* 10:4 *Num* 3:30; *1 Chr* 15:10; 23:20 24:24
of Simeon had *U.* for. *1 Chr* 4:42
U. son of Bela. 7:7
U. the son of Heman. 25:4
Jeduthun; Shemaiah, *U.* *2 Chr* 29:14
U. of the goldsmiths. *Neh* 3:8

V

vagabond

a fugitive and *v.* shalt. *Gen* 4:12*
I shall be a fugitive and *v.* 14*
then certain *v.* Jews. *Acts* 19:13*

vagabonds

let his children be *v.* *Ps* 109:10

vail, or **veil**

The use of the vail in the East was not so general in ancient as in modern times, as much of the present custom dates from the time of Mohammed only. The vail was worn only as an article of ornamental dress; by betrothed maidens in the presence of their future husbands and at the wedding; or by loose women for purposes of concealment.

The vail of the temple *was that separating the Holy Place from the Holy of Holies. This signified separation, since none but the high priest could pass beyond into the most sacred place, and he only on the Day of Atonement. It was rent at the time of the crucifixion to show that now all men could freely come to God.*

The Apostle speaks of the vail of ignorance, blindness, and hardness of heart, which kept the Jews from understanding the scriptures of the Old Testament, the spiritual sense and meaning of the law, and from seeing that Christ is the end of the law for righteousness, John 9:39; 2 Cor 3:14, 15.

Rebekah took a *v.* and. *Gen* 24:65
covered herself with a *v.* 38:14
shalt make a *v.* of blue. *Ex* 26:31
Moses put a *v.* on his face. 34:33, 35
made a *v.* of blue. 36:35; *2 Chr* 3:14
cover the ark with the *v.* *Ex* 40:3
holy place within the *v.* *Lev* 16:2
bring his blood within the *v.* 15
not go unto the *v.* nor come. 21:23
without the *v.* shall Aaron. 24:3
v. that thou hast upon. *Ruth* 3:15*
keepers took away my *v.* *S of S* 5:7*
destroy the *v.* spread. *Isa* 25:7

v. of the temple was rent. *Mat* 27:51
Mark 15:38; *Luke* 23:45
Moses, which put a *v.* *2 Cor* 3:13
for until this day remaineth the same *v.* untaken away; which *v.* is. 14
even to this day the *v.* is upon. 15
v. shall be taken away. 16
into that within the *v.* *Heb* 6:19
the second *v.*, the tabernacle. 9:3
through the *v.*, that is to say. 10:20

vails

Lord will take away the *v.* *Isa* 3:23

vain

(Vain *and* vanity *are used in the Bible entirely with the idea of emptiness, fruitlessness, or worthlessness, not in the sense of conceited or conceit.* Vain *is often used of an idol, as an empty worthless substitute for God*)

not regard *v.* words. *Ex* 5:9*
for it is not a *v.* thing. *Deut* 32:47
Abimelech hired *v.* persons. *Judg* 9:4
there were gathered *v.* men. 11:3
after *v.* things, which cannot profit nor deliver . . . are *v.* *1 Sam* 12:21
as one of the *v.* fellows. *2 Sam* 6:20
became *v.* and went after heathen. *2 Ki* 17:15
but they are but *v.* words. 18:20
Isa 36:5
to Jeroboam *v.* men. *2 Chr* 13:7†
he knoweth *v.* men, he. *Job* 11:11
for *v.* man would be wise, though. 12
wise man utter *v.* knowledge? 15:2
Job said, Shall *v.* words? 16:3
are ye thus altogether *v.*? 27:12
the people imagine a *v.* thing?
Ps 2:1; *Acts* 4:25
I have not sat with *v.* *Ps* 26:4†
an horse is a *v.* thing for. 33:17
man walketh in a *v.* shew. 39:6
for *v.* is the help of man. 60:11
108:12
become not *v.* in robbery. 62:10
I hate *v.* thoughts, but. 119:113*
it is *v.* for you to rise up. 127:2
followeth *v.* persons is. *Pr* 12:11
that followeth *v.* persons shall. 28:19
deceitful and beauty is *v.* 31:30
all days of his *v.* life which. *Eccl* 6:12
bring no more *v.* oblations; incense is an abomination. *Isa* 1:13
they are but *v.* words, I have. 36:5
vanity, and are become *v.* *Jer* 2:5
how long thy *v.* thoughts? 4:14*
customs of the people are *v.* 10:3
the prophets make you *v.* 23:16
have seen *v.* things. *Lam* 2:14
our eyes failed for our *v.* help. 4:17
no more any *v.* vision. *Ezek* 12:24
have ye not seen a *v.* vision? 13:7
ye have said, It is *v.* *Mal* 3:14
when ye pray, use not *v.* *Mat* 6:7
but became *v.* in their. *Rom* 1:21
thoughts of wise are *v.* *1 Cor* 3:20
then is our preaching *v.* and your faith is also *v.* 15:14, 17
let no man deceive you with *v.* words. *Eph* 5:6*
lest any spoil you through philosophy and *v.* deceit. *Col* 2:8
have turned aside to *v.* *1 Tim* 1:6
avoiding profane and *v.* babblings.
6:20; *2 Tim* 2:16
unruly and *v.* talkers. *Tit* 1:10
for they are unprofitable and *v.* 3:9
this man's religion is *v.* *Jas* 1:26
wilt thou know, O *v.* man? 2:20
your *v.* conversation. *1 Pet* 1:18

in **vain**

not take the name of the Lord *in v.*
Ex 20:7; *Deut* 5:11
sow your seed *in v.* *Lev* 26:16
strength shall be spent *in v.* 20
in v. have I kept all. *1 Sam* 25:21
why then labour I *in v.*? *Job* 9:29
comfort ye me *in v.* seeing? 21:34
Job open his mouth *in v.* 35:16
her labour is *in v.* without. 39:16
the hope of him is *in v.* 41:9
they are disquieted *in v.* *Ps* 39:6
cleansed my heart *in v.* 73:13
thou made all men *in v.*? *Ps* 89:47
in v.: watchman waketh *in v.* 127:1
enemies take thy name *in v.* 139:20
surely *in v.* the net is. *Pr* 1:17
the name of my God *in v.* 30:9*
Egyptians shall help *in v.* *Isa* 30:7
it not *in v.*, he formed it. 45:18*
seed of Jacob, Seek ye me *in v.* 19
have laboured *in v.*, I have spent my strength for nought and *in v.* 49:4
they shall not labour *in v.* 65:23
in v. have I smitten your. *Jer* 2:30
in v. is salvation hoped for. 3:23
in v. shalt thou make thyself. 4:30
the founder melteth *in v.* 6:29
lo, certainly *in v.* made he it, the pen of the scribes is *in v.* 8:8*
in v. shalt thou use many. 46:11
arrows, none shall return *in v.* 50:9
people shall labour *in v.* 51:58
that I have not said *in v.* *Ezek* 6:10
diviners comfort *in v.* *Zech* 10:2
but *in v.* they do worship me.
Mat 15:9; *Mark* 7:7
for he beareth not the sword *in v.*
Rom 13:4
ye have believed *in v.* *1 Cor* 15:2
his grace bestowed upon me was not *in v.* 10
your labour is not *in v.* in the Lord. 58
the grace of God *in v.* *2 Cor* 6:1
boasting of you should be *in v.* 9:3*
means I should run *in v.* *Gal* 2:2
law, then Christ is dead *in v.* 21
have ye suffered so many things *in v.*? if it be yet *in v.* 3:4
bestowed on you labour *in v.* 4:11
that I may rejoice that I have not run *in v.* nor laboured *in v.* *Phil* 2:16
that it was not *in v.* *1 Thes* 2:1
and our labour be *in v.* 3:5
the scripture saith *in v.*? *Jas* 4:5

vainglory

not be desirous of *v.* *Gal* 5:26
nothing be done through *v.* *Phil* 2:3

vainly

v. puffed up by his fleshly. *Col* 2:18

vale

kings were joined in the *v.* of Siddim.
Gen 14:3, 8
the *v.* of Siddim was full of. 10
out of the *v.* of Hebron. 37:14
in the hills and in the *v.* *Deut* 1:7*
the country of the *v.* *Josh* 10:40*
and cedars as sycamore trees in the *v.* *1 Ki* 10:27*; *2 Chr* 1:15*
in the cities of the *v.* *Jer* 33:13*

valiant

when Saul saw any *v.* *1 Sam* 14:52
son of Jesse, a mighty *v.* man. 16:18
be *v.* for me, and fight the. 18:17
Art not thou a *v.* man? 26:15
all the *v.* men took the body. 31:12
ye be *v.* *2 Sam* 2:7; 13:28
he knew that *v.* men were. 11:16
he that is *v.* 17:10
of Jehoiada, the son of a *v.* man of Kabzeel. 23:20; *1 Chr* 11:22
for thou art a *v.* man. *1 Ki* 1:42*
of Tola were *v.* men. *1 Chr* 7:2
the *v.* men of the armies. 11:26*
eighty priests, *v.* men. *2 Chr* 26:17
Solomon's; threescore *v.* men are about it, of the *v.* of. *S of S* 3:7*
inhabitants like a *v.* man. *Isa* 10:13
v. ones shall cry without. 33:7
are not *v.* for the truth. *Jer* 9:3*
are thy *v.* men swept away? 46:15*
the *v.* men are in scarlet. *Nah* 2:3
waxed *v.* in fight. *Heb* 11:34*

valiantest

12,000 men of the *v.* *Judg* 21:10

valiantly

Edom a possession, Israel shall do *v.*
Num 24:18
behave ourselves *v.* *1 Chr* 19:13*
through God we shall do *v.*
Ps 60:12; 108:13
the right hand of the Lord doeth *v.*
118:15, 16

valley

Sometimes meaning gorge *or* ravine.

The valleys most referred to in Scripture, or best known in Jewish history, are:

[1] The vale of Siddim, *or the slime pits, in which were the cities of Sodom and Gomorrah,* Gen 14:3.

[2] The valley of Eshcol, *where were famous vineyards,* Num 32:9.

[3] The valley of Achor, *where Achan was punished,* Josh 7:24.

[4] The valley of Elah, *where David killed Goliath,* 1 Sam 17:2, 19.

[5] The valley of Jezreel, *the city where Ahab's palace was built, and where Naboth's vineyard was,* Josh 19:18; 1 Ki 21:1, 23.

[6] The valley of Jehoshaphat, *which Joel prophesied should be the place of final judgement,* Joel 3:2. *It is not certain where this was, as the name was applied to the ravine between Jerusalem and the Mt. of Olives only in the middle of the fourth century.*

[7] The valley of Hinnom, *or Gehenna, near Jerusalem. See* **Tophet.**

of Sodom met him at *v.* *Gen* 14:17
they went up to *v.* of. *Num* 32:9
they came to *v.* of Eshcol. *Deut* 1:24
heifer to a rough *v.* and strike off the heifer's neck in the *v.* 21:4
the plain of *v.* of Jericho, a. 34:3
he buried Moses in a *v.* in the. 6
brought them to the *v.* of. *Josh* 7:24
moon, in the *v.* of Ajalon. 10:12
which is at the end of the *v.* 15:8
out inhabitants of the *v.* *Judg* 1:19
was sent on foot into the *v.* 5:15
Midian was beneath in the *v.* 7:8, 12
a woman in the *v.* of Sorek. 16:4
wheat harvest in the *v.* *1 Sam* 6:13
slewest in the *v.* of Elah. 21:9
spread themselves in the *v.* of Rephaim. *2 Sam* 5:18, 22; 23:13
the Syrians in the *v.* of salt. 8:13
cast him into some *v.* *2 Ki* 2:16
make this *v.* full of ditches. 3:16
he slew of Edom in the *v.* of salt ten thousand. 14:7; *1 Chr* 18:12
in *v.* of Berachah. *2 Chr* 20:26
in the *v.* of Hinnom. 28:3
to fight in *v.* of Megiddo. 35:22
the clods of the *v.* shall. *Job* 21:33
he paweth in the *v.* and. 39:21
through the *v.* of death. *Ps* 23:4
out the *v.* of Succoth. 60:6; 108:7
who passing through *v.* of Baca. 84:6
the ravens of the *v.* shall. *Pr* 30:17
see the fruits of the *v.* *S of S* 6:11
ears in the *v.* of Rephaim. *Isa* 17:5
the burden of the *v.* of vision. 22:1
trouble in the *v.* of vision. 5
is on the head of the fat *v.* 28:4
wroth as in the *v.* of Gibeon. 21
every *v.* shall be exalted. 40:4
v. of Achor a place for herds. 65:10
see thy way in the *v.* *Jer* 2:23
v. of Hinnom, but *v.* 7:32; 19:6
thee, O inhabitant of the *v.* 21:13
the *v.* also shall perish, and. 48:8
thou in thy flowing *v.*? 49:4
in the *v.* which was full. *Ezek* 37:1
break the bow of Israel in the *v.* of.
Hos 1:5
give the *v.* of Achor for a. 2:15
bring them into the *v.* of. *Joel* 3:2
multitudes, multitudes in the *v.* 14
shall water the *v.* of Shittim. 18
as the mourning in the *v.* *Zech* 12:11
and there shall be a great *v.* 14:4
flee to the *v.* of the mountains. 5
every *v.* be filled every. *Luke* 3:5
see **gate**

valleys

as the *v.* are they spread. *Num* 24:6
depths that spring out of the *v.* and.
Deut 8:7
land is a land of hills and *v.* 11:11

but he is not God of the *v.* *1 Ki* 20:28
clifts of *v.* in caves of earth. *Job* 30:6
or will he harrow the *v.* after? 39:10
the *v.* are covered over. *Ps* 65:13
they go down by the *v.* unto. 104:8
he sendeth the springs into the *v.* 10
the lily of the *v.* *S of S* 2:1
thy choicest *v.* shall be full. *Isa* 22:7
are on the head of the fat *v.* 28:1
fountains in midst of the *v.* 41:18
slaying the children in the *v.* 57:5
gloriest thou in the *v.*? *Jer* 49:4
Lord to the *v.* *Ezek* 6:3; 36:4, 6
mountains like doves of the *v.* 7:16

valour

Moab 10,000 men of *v.* *Judg* 3:29
thou mighty man of *v.* 6:12
Gileadite, a mighty man of *v.* 11:1
was a mighty man of *v.* *1 Ki* 11:28
Naaman, a mighty man in *v.* *2 Ki* 5:1
Zadok, man of *v.* *1 Chr* 12:28
a mighty man of *v.* *2 Chr* 17:17
see mighty **men**

value

lies, ye are all physicians of no *v.* *Job* 13:4
ye are of more *v.* than many sparrows. *Mat* 10:31; *Luke* 12:7

value, *verb*

the priest shall *v.* him. *Lev* 27:8
priest shall *v.* it, whether it be. 12
children of Israel did *v.* *Mat* 27:9*

valued

of barley seed *v.* at 50. *Lev* 27:16
wisdom cannot be *v.* with. *Job* 28:16
neither shall it be *v.* with pure. 19
price of him that was *v.* *Mat* 27:9*

valuest

as thou *v.* it who art the priest, so shall it be. *Lev* 27:12

vanish

wax warm, they *v.* *Job* 6:17
the heavens shall *v.* away. *Isa* 51:6
knowledge, it shall *v.* *1 Cor* 13:8*
old, is ready to *v.* away. *Heb* 8:13

vanished

hosts; is their wisdom *v.*? *Jer* 49:7
he *v.* out of their sight. *Luke* 24:31

vanisheth

consumed and *v.* away. *Job* 7:9
a vapour that *v.* away. *Jas* 4:14

vanities

me to anger with their *v.* *Deut* 32:21
1 Ki 16:13, 26; *Jer* 8:19
them that regard lying *v.* *Ps* 31:6
vanity of *v.* saith the preacher. *Eccl* 1:2; 12:8
of dreams there are also *v.* 5:7
the stock is a doctrine of *v.* *Jer* 10:8*
are there any among the *v.* of the Gentiles that can cause rain? 14:22
they that observe lying *v.* *Jonah* 2:8
turn from these *v.* *Acts* 14:15*

vanity

see meaning of **vain**

they followed *v.* and. *2 Ki* 17:15
so am I made to possess months of *v.* *Job* 7:3
let me alone, for my days are *v.* 16
let not him that is deceived trust in *v.*, for *v.* shall be his. 15:31
mischief and bring forth *v.* 35*
if I have walked with *v.* or. 31:5
surely God will not hear *v.* 35:13
how long will ye love *v.*? *Ps* 4:2
his tongue is mischief and *v.* 10:7*
they speak *v.* every one to his. 12:2†
not lifted up his soul unto *v.* 24:4
his best estate is altogether *v.* 39:5
every man is *v.* 11
come to see me, he speaketh *v.* 41:6†; 144:8†, 11†
low degree are *v.*, lighter than *v.* 62:9
days did he consume in *v.* 78:33
thoughts of man, they are *v.* 94:11
mine eyes from beholding *v.* 119:37
man is like to *v.*: his days are. 144:4
wealth gotten by *v.* shall. *Pr* 13:11
by a lying tongue is *v.* 21:6
soweth iniquity shall reap *v.* 22:8*
remove from me *v.* and lies. 30:8
v. of vanities, saith the preacher, all is *v.* *Eccl* 1:2, 14; 3:19; 11:8 12:8
this is also *v.* 2:1, 15, 19, 21, 23 4:8, 16; 5:10; 6:2, 9; 7:6; 8:10, 14
behold, all was *v.* and vexation. 2:11, 17, 26; 4:4
I saw *v.* 4:7
for he cometh in with *v.* 6:4
many things that increase *v.* 11
I seen in the days of my *v.* 7:15
there is a *v.* that is done on. 8:14
with wife all the days of thy *v.* 9:9
childhood and youth are *v.* 11:10
that draw iniquity with cords of *v.* *Isa* 5:18
nations with the sieve of *v.* 30:28
to him are counted *v.* 40:17
the judges of the earth as *v.* 23
behold, they are all *v.* 41:29; 44:9
v. shall take them: but he that. 57:13
if thou take away, speaking *v.* 58:9
they trust in *v.* 59:4
they have walked after *v.* *Jer* 2:5
they are *v.* and the work of errors. 10:15; 51:18
fathers have inherited *v.* 16:19
have burnt incense to *v.* 18:15
they have seen *v.* and divination. *Ezek* 13:6; 22:28
because ye have spoken *v.* 13:8
prophets see *v.* 9; 21:29
shall see no more *v.* 13:23
surely they are *v.* *Hos* 12:11
people shall weary themselves for very *v.* *Hab* 2:13
the idols have spoken *v.* *Zech* 10:2
was made subject to *v.* *Rom* 8:20
not as Gentiles walk in *v.* *Eph* 4:17
they speak great swelling words of *v.* *2 Pet* 2:18

vapour

pour down rain according to the *v.* *Job* 36:27
cattle also concerning the *v.* 33
and *v.* fulfilling his word. *Ps* 148:8
shew signs in the earth, *v.* of smoke. *Acts* 2:19
your life? it is even a *v.* *Jas* 4:14

vapours

v. to ascend from the ends of the. *Ps* 135:7; *Jer* 10:13; 51:16

variableness

lights, with whom is no *v.* *Jas* 1:17

variance

set a man at *v.* against. *Mat* 10:35
of the flesh are hatred, *v.* *Gal* 5:20*

Vashti

V. the queen made a feast. *Esth* 1:9
queen *V.* refused to come at. 12
that *V.* come no more before. 19
Esther queen instead of *V.* 2:17

vaunt

lest Israel *v.* themselves. *Judg* 7:2

vaunteth

charity *v.* not itself. *1 Cor* 13:4

vehement

fire that hath a *v.* flame. *S of S* 8:6*
prepared a *v.* east wind. *Jonah* 4:8*
what *v.* desire it wrought in you! *2 Cor* 7:11

vehemently

he spake the more *v.* *Mark* 14:31
the stream beat *v.* on that house. *Luke* 6:48*, 49*
began to urge him *v.* 11:53
stood and *v.* accused him. 23:10

veil, *see* **vail**

vein

there is a *v.* for the silver. *Job* 28:1*

vengeance

v. shall be taken on him. *Gen* 4:15
to me belongeth *v.* and recompence. *Deut* 32:35; *Ps* 94:1; *Heb* 10:30
I will render *v.* to mine enemies. *Deut* 32:41
for he will render *v.* to his. 43
the Lord hath taken *v.* *Judg* 11:36
when he seeth the *v.* *Ps* 58:10
tookest *v.* of their inventions. 99:8
to execute *v.* upon the heathen. 149:7
not spare in the day of *v.* *Pr* 6:34
it is the day of the Lord's *v.* and. *Isa* 34:8; 61:2; *Jer* 51:6
God will come with *v.* *Isa* 35:4
I will take *v.* 47:3; *Jer* 51:36
garments of *v.* for clothing. *Isa* 59:17
day of *v.* is in mine heart. 63:4
let me see thy *v.* on them. *Jer* 11:20 20:12
a day of *v.* 46:10
the *v.* of the Lord, take *v.* 50:15, 28
the *v.* of Lord, the *v.* of his temple. 28; 51:11
thou hast seen all their *v.* *Lam* 3:60
fury come up to take *v.* *Ezek* 24:8
Edom by taking *v.* hath. 25:12
I will lay my *v.* on Edom. 14
Philistines have taken *v.* 15
when I shall lay my *v.* on the. 17
I will execute great *v.* *Ezek* 25:17 *Mi* 5:15
Lord will take *v.* on his. *Nah* 1:2
these be the days of *v.* *Luke* 21:22
whom *v.* suffereth not to live. *Acts* 28:4*
unrighteous who taketh *v.*? *Rom* 3:5
v. is mine, I will repay, saith. 12:19
flaming fire, taking *v.* *2 Thes* 1:8
an example, suffering the *v.* *Jude* 7*

venison

because he did eat of his *v.* *Gen* 25:28
field and take me some *v.* 27:3, 7
thee, and eat of my *v.* 19, 31
I will eat of my son's *v.* 25
where is he that hath taken *v.*? 35

venom

is the cruel *v.* of asps. *Deut* 32:33

venomous

saw the *v.* beast hang. *Acts* 28:4

vent

wine which hath no *v.* *Job* 32:19

venture

drew a bow at a *v.* and smote the king. *1 Ki* 22:34; *2 Chr* 18:33

verified

so shall your words be *v.* *Gen* 42:20
let thy word be *v.* *1 Ki* 8:26 *2 Chr* 6:17

verily

are *v.* guilty concerning. *Gen* 42:21
saying, *V.* my sabbaths. *Ex* 31:13
I *v.* thought thou hadst hated her. *Judg* 15:2
v. our Lord hath made. *1 Ki* 1:43
v. she hath no child, her. *2 Ki* 4:14
I will *v.* buy it for the. *1 Chr* 21:24
my acquaintance are *v.* *Job* 19:13
do good, and *v.* thou. *Ps* 37:3
v. every man at his best state. 39:5
v. there is a reward for the righteous, *v.* he is a God that. 58:11
but *v.* God hath heard me. 66:19
v. I have cleansed my heart. 73:13
v. thou art a God that hidest thyself. *Isa* 45:15
v. it shall be well with thy remnant, *v.* I will cause the. *Jer* 15:11
v. I say unto you. *Mat* 5:18; 6:2, 5 16; 8:10; 10:15, 23, 42; 11:11 13:17; 16:28; 17:20; 18:3, 13, 18 19:23, 28; 21:21, 31; 23:36; 24:2 34, 47; 25:12, 40, 45; 26:13 *Mark* 3:28; 6:11; 8:12; 9:1, 41 10:15, 29; 11:23; 12:43; 13:30 14:9, 18, 25; *Luke* 4:24; 11:51 12:37; 13:35; 18:17, 29; 21:32
v. I say unto thee. *Mat* 5:26; 26:34 *Mark* 14:30; *Luke* 23:43
Elias *v.* cometh first. *Mark* 9:12
nay *v.* let them come. *Acts* 16:37
John *v.* baptized with baptism. 19:4
am *v.* a man which am a Jew. 22:3
I *v.* thought I ought to do. 26:9
for circumcision *v.* profiteth if thou. *Rom* 2:25
v. their sound went into all. 10:18
pleased them *v.*; debtors they. 15:27
I *v.* as absent in body. *1 Cor* 5:3
v. righteousness had been. *Gal* 3:21
for *v.* he took not on him the nature of angels. *Heb* 2:16
for men *v.* swear by the greater. 6:16

for they v. for a few days. Heb 12:10
who v. was foreordained. 1 Pet 1:20
in him v. is the love of. 1 John 2:5

verily, verily

v. v. I say unto you. John 1:51
5:19, 24, 25; 6:26, 32, 47, 53
8:34, 51, 58; 10:1, 7; 12:24
13:16, 20, 21; 14:12; 16:20, 23
v. v. I say unto thee. 3:3; 5:11
13:38; 21:18

verity

works of his hands are v. Ps 111:7*
Gentiles in faith and v. 1 Tim 2:7*

vermilion

cedar and painted with v. Jer 22:14
pourtrayed with v. Ezek 23:14

very

thou be my v. son Esau. Gen 27:21
in v. deed for this I. Ex 9:16
Moses was v. meek. Num 12:3
but the word is v. nigh. Deut 30:14
in v. deed except thou. 1 Sam 25:34
Saul was come in v. deed. 26:4
have done v. foolishly. 2 Sam 24:10
king Ahaziah did v. 2 Chr 20:35
we have dealt v. corruptly. Neh 1:7
inward part is v. wickedness. Ps 5:9
into that v. destruction let. 35:8
also, O God, is v. high. 71:19
establish in the v. heavens. 89:2
thy thoughts are v. deep. 92:5
thy testimonies are v. sure. 93:5
testimonies are v. faithful. 119:138
thy word is v. pure, therefore. 140
in that v. day his thoughts. 146:4
word runneth v. swiftly. 147:15
he separateth v. friends. Pr 17:9
for yet a v. little while. Isa 10:25
29:17
the land that is v. far off. 33:17
he taketh up the isles as a v. 40:15
be ye v. desolate, saith. Jer 2:12
I am pained at my v. heart. 4:19
transgressed to this v. day. Ezek 2:3
that were a v. little thing. 16:47
labour in the v. fire, and the people weary themselves for v. Hab 2:13
the v. hairs of your head. Mat 10:30
shall deceive the v. elect. 24:24
that this is the v. Christ. John 7:26
Acts 9:22
taken in adultery, in v. act. John 8:4
me for the v. works' sake. 14:11
the v. God of peace. 1 Thes 5:23
and not the v. image of. Heb 10:1
the Lord is v. pitiful, of. Jas 5:11
see **great, much**

vessel

not put any in thy v. Deut 23:24
though sanctified this day in the v.
1 Sam 21:5
a little water in a v. 1 Ki 17:10
v. There is not a v. more. 2 Ki 4:6
pieces like a potter's v. Ps 2:9
I am like a broken v. 31:12
forth a v. for the finer. Pr 25:4
an offering in a clean v. Isa 66:20
the v. was marred in the hand of the potter. Jer 18:4
v. wherein is no pleasure ? 22:28
shall fall like a pleasant v. 25:34
been emptied from v. to v. 48:11
have broken Moab like a v. 38
hath made me an empty v. 51:34
put them in one v. and. Ezek 4:9
a pin of it to hang any v.? 15:3
shall be as a v. wherein is. Hos 8:8
carry any v. through the temple.
Mark 11:16
no man covereth a candle with a v.
Luke 8:16
for he is a chosen v. Acts 9:15
Peter saw a certain v. 10:11; 11:5
hath power to make one v. Rom 9:21
know to possess his v. in. 1 Thes 4:4
he shall be a v. to honour. 2 Tim 2:21
giving honour unto the wife as unto the weaker v. 1 Pet 3:7

vessels

best fruits in your v. Gen 43:11
anoint the altar and v. Ex 40:10
Lev 8:11
Levites not come nigh v. Num 18:3
bread is spent in our v. 1 Sam 9:7
and the v. of the young men. 21:5
borrow thee v. abroad of all thy neighbours, even empty v. 2 Ki 4:3
the v. king Ahaz did. 2 Chr 29:19
king brought forth the v. Ezra 1:7
take these v. 5:15
v. are given to thee. 7:19
he weighed the silver and the v.
8:25, 33
thither brought I again the v. of the house of God. Neh 13:9
even in v. of bulrushes. Isa 18:2
v. of small quantity, the v. 22:24
be ye clean that bear the v. 52:11
abominable things is in their v. 65:4
returned with their v. Jer 14:3
v. of the Lord's house. 27:16; 28:3
they have brought the v. Dan 5:23
he shall spoil treasure of all pleasant v. Hos 13:15
to draw out fifty v. out. Hag 2:16
gathered the good into v. Mat 13:48
the wise took oil in their v. 25:4
the v. of wrath. Rom 9:22
the v. of mercy. 23
as v. of a potter shall. Rev 2:27
see **brass, earthen, gold, silver**

vestments

bring forth v. for the. 2 Ki 10:22

vestry

him that was over the v. 2 Ki 10:22

vesture, -s

Joseph in v. of fine linen. Gen 41:42
the quarters of thy v. Deut 22:12
they cast lots upon my v. Ps 22:18
Mat 27:35; John 19:24
as a v. shalt thou change. Ps 102:26
and as a v. shalt thou fold. Heb 1:12*
he was clothed with a v. dipped in blood. Rev 19:13*
his v. and on his thigh a name. 16*

vex

thou shalt not v. a stranger.
Ex 22:21*; Lev 19:33*
not take a wife to her sister to v.
Lev 18:18*
v. the Midianites and. Num 25:17
for they v. you with their wiles. 18
ye let remain shall v. you. 33:55
how will he v. himself ? 2 Sam 12:18
God did v. them with. 2 Chr 15:6
how long will ye v. my soul ?
Job 19:2
and v. them in his sore. Ps 2:5
let us go up against Judah and v. it.
Isa 7:6
Judah shall not v. Ephraim. 11:13
I will v. the hearts of. Ezek 32:9
shall they not awake that shall v. thee ? Hab 2:7
Herod did v. certain of. Acts 12:1*

vexation

(Where this word occurs in Ecclesiastes the Revised Versions change it to striving)

shall send on thee v. Deut 28:20*
is vanity and v. of spirit. Eccl 1:14
2:11, 17
this also is v. of spirit. 1:17; 2:26
4:4, 16; 6:9
man of the v. of his heart ? 2:22
both the hands full with v. 4:6
such as was in her v. Isa 9:1*
be a v. only to understand. 28:19*
shall howl for v. of spirit. 65:14

vexations

great v. were on all the. 2 Chr 15:5

vexed

the Egyptians v. us. Num 20:15*
reason of them that v. Judg 2:18
the Ammonites v. Israel. 10:8
so that his soul was v. unto. 16:16
Saul v. his enemies on. 1 Sam 14:47†
Amnon was so v. that. 2 Sam 13:2
alone, for her soul is v. 2 Ki 4:27
to enemies who v. them. Neh 9:27*
the Almighty, who hath v. Job 27:2
my bones are v. Ps 6:2
my soul is sore v. 3
be ashamed and sore v. 10
they rebelled and v. his. Isa 63:10*
infamous and much v. Ezek 22:5*
in thee they v. the fatherless. 7*
v. the poor. 29
my daughter is grievously v. with a devil. Mat 15:22
he is lunatic and sore v. 17:15*
they that were v. with unclean spirits.
Luke 6:18*; Acts 5:16
delivered just Lot, v. 2 Pet 2:7*
v. his righteous soul from day. 8

vial

(Where this word or the plural occurs in Revelation the Revised Versions change it to bowl)

Samuel took a v. of oil. 1 Sam 10:1
first angel poured his v. Rev 16:2
second v. upon the sea. 3
third v. upon the rivers. 4
fourth v. upon the sun. 8
fifth v. upon the seat of the beast. 10
sixth v. upon the Euphrates. 12
seventh v. into the air. 17

vials

golden v. full of odours. Rev 5:8
seven angels seven golden v. 15:7
pour out the v. of the wrath. 16:1
angels which had seven v. 17:1; 21:9

victory

v. that day was turned. 2 Sam 19:2
the Lord wrought a great v. that day.
23:10, 12
thine, O Lord, is the v. 1 Chr 29:11
hath gotten him the v. Ps 98:1*
swallow up death in v. and wipe away tears. Isa 25:8*; 1 Cor 15:54
forth judgement unto v. Mat 12:20
O grave, where is thy v.? 1 Cor 15:55
to God, who giveth us the v. 57
and this is the v., even. 1 John 5:4
the v. over the beast. Rev 15:2

victual, -s

goods of Sodom, and v. Gen 14:11
they prepared any v. Ex 12:39
him thy v. for increase. Lev 25:37
usury of v. of any thing. Deut 23:19
prepare v. Josh 1:11
take v. with you. 9:11*
the men took of their v. and. 14*
suit of apparel and v. Judg 17:10
he gave him v. and sword of Goliath.
1 Sam 22:10
which provided v. for the king.
1 Ki 4:7, 27
Pharaoh appointed him v. 11:18
if the people bring v. Neh 10:31
in the day they sold v. 13:15
so captain gave Jeremiah v. Jer 40:5
for then had we plenty of v. 44:17
went into villages to buy v.
Mat 14:15*; Luke 9:12†

view

go v. the land. Josh 2:1
v. the country. 7:2*
of prophets stood to v. 2 Ki 2:7*, 15

viewed

the men v. Ai. Josh 7:2
I v. the people. Ezra 8:15
and I v. the walls of. Neh 2:13, 15

vigilant

a bishop must be v. 1 Tim 3:2*
be sober, be v. because. 1 Pet 5:8

vile

lest thy brother should seem v. to thee. Deut 25:3
man do not so v. a thing. Judg 19:24*
because his sons made themselves v. 1 Sam 3:13*
every thing that was v. they destroyed. 15:9
yet be more v. than. 2 Sam 6:22
why are we reputed v. in ? Job 18:3*
I am v.; what shall I answer ? 40:4*
in whose eyes a v. person. Ps 15:4*
the v. person be no more. Isa 32:5†
for the v. person will speak. 6†
the precious from the v. Jer 15:19
make them like v. figs. 29:17
Lord, for I am become v. Lam 1:11
in his estate shall stand up a v. person. Dan 11:21

image, and will make thy grave, for thou art v. Nah 1:14
filth on thee and make thee v. 3:6
God gave them up to v. Rom 1:26
change our v. body. Phil 3:21*
come in a poor man in v. raiment. Jas 2:2

vilely

mighty is v. cast away. 2 Sam 1:21

viler

of base men, they were v. Job 30:8*

vilest

wicked when the v. men. Ps 12:8

village

go into the v. over against. Mat 21:2
Mark 11:2; Luke 19:30
two of them went that same day to a v. Luke 24:13
they drew nigh unto the v. 28

villages

frogs died out of the v. Ex 8:13*
houses of the v. counted. Lev 25:31
the inhabitants of the v. Judg 5:7*
together in one of the v. Neh 6:2
Jews of v. made the 14th day of. Esth 9:19
let us lodge in the v. S of S 7:11
I will go up to the land of unwalled v. Ezek 38:11
strike the head of his v. Hab 3:14*
they may go into the v. and buy.
Mat 14:15; Mark 6:36
see **cities**

villany

vile person will speak v. Isa 32:6*
they have committed v. Jer 29:23*

vine

God compares his people to a vine, *which he had brought out of Egypt, and planted in Palestine, as a good soil, but which, instead of bringing forth good fruit, brought forth only bitter fruit, and wild grapes,* Ps 80:8; Isa 5:1, *etc. In* John 15:1, *Christ says,* I am the true vine, and my Father is the husbandman.

The *vine* of Sodom, Deut 32:32, *is probably what is known as the* apples of Sodom, *which appear as edible fruit, but on being plucked turn at once to dust, like a puff-ball. The phrase is perhaps figurative, no real fruit being intended.*

Noah planted the vine after the deluge, and was the first that cultivated it, Gen 9:20. *Many are of opinion, that wine was not unknown before the deluge, and that this Patriarch only continued to cultivate the vine after this great catastrophe, as he had done before. But others think that he knew not the force of wine, having never used it before, nor having ever seen any one use it. He is supposed to be the first that pressed out the juice of the grape, and to have reduced it to a liquor. Before him, men only ate the grapes, like other fruit.*

in my dream, behold, a v. Gen 40:9
v. were three branches. 10
binding his foal to the v. and his ass's colt to the choice v. 49:11
nor gather grapes of thy v. undressed. Lev 25:5, 11
nothing made of the v. tree. Num 6:4
for their v. is of the v. Deut 32:32
said to v., Reign over us. Judg 9:12
thing that cometh of the v. 13:14
every man under his v. 1 Ki 4:25
found a wild v. and. 2 Ki 4:39
eat ye every man of his own v.
18:31; Isa 36:16
his unripe grape as the v. Job 15:33
thou hast brought a v. Ps 80:8
behold, and visit this v. 14
thy wife shall be as a fruitful v. 128:3
to see whether the v. flourished.
S of S 6:11; 7:12
shall be as clusters of the v. 7:8
it with the choicest v. Isa 5:2
for the v. of Sibmah. 16:8
I will bewail the v. of Sibmah. 9
Jer 48:32
the v. languisheth. Isa 24:7
lament for the fruitful v. 32:12
falleth off from the v. as a fig. 34:4
a noble v.: how then turned into degenerate plant of . . . v.? Jer 2:21
the remnant of Israel as a v. 6:9
grapes on the v. nor figs. 8:13
what is the v. tree more? Ezek 15:2
as the v. tree which I have given. 6
spreading v. of low stature. 17:6
this v. did bend her roots. 7
thy mother is like a v. in. 19:10
Israel is an empty v. Hos 10:1
revive as corn, grow as the v. 14:7
he laid my v. waste. Joel 1:7
the v. is dried up, the fig tree. 12
the fig tree and the v. yield. 2:22
every man under his v. Mi 4:4
as yet the v. hath not brought forth. Hag 2:19
every man under the v. Zech 3:10
the v. shall give her fruit. 8:12
neither shall your v. cast. Mal 3:11
v., until in my Father's. Mat 26:29
Mark 14:25; Luke 22:18
true v., my Father is. John 15:1, 5
bear fruit, except it abide in v. 4
can a v. bear figs? Jas 3:12
gather clusters of the v. Rev 14:18
the angel gathered the v. of. 19*

vinedressers

captain of guard left the poor of the land to be v. 2 Ki 25:12; Jer 52:16
had husbandmen and v. 2 Chr 26:10
of alien shall be your v. Isa 61:5
howl, O ye v. Joel 1:11

vinegar

(*The Hebrew word translated* vinegar *was applied to a beverage turned sour, or made artificially so. It was not pleasant to take but was used by labourers. The vinegar of the Romans was much the same, and was probably that given to Jesus while on the cross*)

shall drink no v. of wine. Num 6:3
dip thy morsel in the v. Ruth 2:14
gall for my meat, in my thirst they gave me v. Ps 69:21; Mat 27:34*
as v. to the teeth, so is. Pr 10:26
as v. upon nitre, so is he. 25:20
they took a spunge and filled it with v. Mat 27:48; Mark 15:36
Luke 23:36; John 19:29, 30

vines

of v. or pomegranates. Num 20:5
a land of wheat, and barley, and v. Deut 8:8
their v. with hail. Ps 78:47
their v. also and fig trees. 105:33
v. give a good smell. S of S 2:13
little foxes, that spoil the v.; for our v. have tender grapes. 15*
were a thousand v. Isa 7:23
they shall eat up thy v. Jer 5:17
thou shalt yet plant v. on. 31:5*
I will destroy her v. and. Hos 2:12
nor shall fruit be in the v. Hab 3:17

vineyard

Noah planted a v. and. Gen 9:20
if a man shall cause a v. Ex 22:5
thou shalt deal with thy v. 23:11
shalt not glean thy v. Lev 19:10
thou shalt prune thy v. 25:3
thy field, nor prune thy v. 4
he that hath planted a v.? Deut 20:6
not sow thy v. with divers seeds, lest the fruit of thy seed and v. 22:9
into thy neighbour's v. 23:24
gatherest the grapes of thy v. 24:21
thou shalt plant a v. and not. 28:30
Naboth had a v. hard by. 1 Ki 21:1
v., I will give thee a better v. 2, 6
eat bread, I will give thee the v. 7
the v. thy right hand. Ps 80:15*
I went by the v. of the man void of. Pr 24:30
of her hand she planted a v. 31:16
mine own v. have I not. S of S 1:6
Solomon had a v.; he let the v. 8:11
my v. which is mine. 12
daughter of Zion is left as a cottage in a v. Isa 1:8
for ye have eaten up the v. 3:14
my beloved touching his v. 5:1
for the v. of the Lord of hosts is. 7
yea, ten acres of v. shall yield. 10
sing ye to her, A v. of red wine. 27:2
have destroyed my v. Jer 12:10
Rechabites shall not plant v. 35:7, 9
I will make Samaria as plantings of a v. Mi 1:6
hire labourers into his v. Mat 20:1
them, Go ye also into the v. 4, 7
go work to-day in my v. 21:28
a certain householder planted a v.
33; Mark 12:1; Luke 20:9
fig tree planted in his v. Luke 13:6
to the dresser of the v., Behold. 7
who planteth a v. and? 1 Cor 9:7

vineyards

given us inheritance of v. Num 16:14
not pass through the v. 20:17; 21:22
Lord stood in a path of the v. 22:24
give thee v. and olive trees which thou plantedst not. Deut 6:11
Josh 24:13; Neh 9:25
thou shalt plant v. and. Deut 28:39
burnt up the corn, with v. Judg 15:5
Go and lie in wait in the v. 21:20
your fields and your v. 1 Sam 8:14
give every one of you v.? 22:7
to receive v. and sheep? 2 Ki 5:26
to a land of bread and v. 18:32
in the third year . . . plant v. 19:29
over the v. was Shimei, over the increase of the v. for. 1 Chr 27:27
we have mortgaged our v. Neh 5:3
restore to them their v. and. 11
not the way of the v. Job 24:18
and plant v. to yield. Ps 107:37
houses, I planted me v. Eccl 2:4
me the keeper of the v. S of S 1:6
as a cluster of camphire in the v. 14
let us get up early to the v. 7:12
in the v. there shall be no singing. Isa 16:10
houses and inhabit; shall plant v. and eat the fruit. 65:21; Amos 9:14
houses and v. shall be. Jer 32:15
gave the poor v. and fields. 39:10
build houses and plant v. Ezek 28:26
I will give her her v. Hos 2:15
worm devoured your v. Amos 4:9
ye have planted v. but ye shall. 5:11
and in all v. shall be wailing. 17
they shall plant v. but not. Zeph 1:13

vintage

shall reach to the v. and the v. shall reach to the. Lev 26:5
than the v. of Abiezer? Judg 8:2
the v. of the wicked. Job 24:6
I have made their v. shouting to cease. Isa 16:10
grapes when v. is done. 24:13
the v. shall fail, gathering. 32:10
the spoiler is fallen upon thy v. Jer 48:32
grapegleanings of the v. Mi 7:1
the forest of the v. is. Zech 11:2*

viol

harp and v. and wine. Isa 5:12*
that chant to the sound of the v. Amos 6:5

violated

her priests have v. my. Ezek 22:26

violence

earth was filled with v. Gen 6:11, 12
thing taken away by v. Lev 6:2*
thou savest me from v. 2 Sam 22:3
him that loveth v. his. Ps 11:5
v. and strife in the city. 55:9
weigh the v. of your hands. 58:2
redeem their soul from v. 72:14
therefore v. covereth them as. 73:6
they drink the wine of v. Pr 4:17
v. covereth the mouth of. 10:6, 11
transgressors shall eat v. 13:2
a man that doeth v. to the. 28:17*
done no v. nor was deceit. Isa 53:9
and the act of v. is in their. 59:6

v. shall no more be heard. Isa 60:18
v. and spoil is heard in. Jer 6:7
I cried v. and spoil. 20:8
do no v. to the stranger. 22:3
thine eyes, thine heart are for v. 17
v. done to me and my flesh. 51:35
a rumour, v. in the land. 46
v. is risen up into a rod. Ezek 7:11
for the city is full of v. 23
filled the land with v. 8:17; 28:16
because of the v. of them. 12:19
hath spoiled none by v. 18:7, 16
spoiled and oppressed by v. 12, 18
O princes of Israel, remove v. 45:9
be a wilderness, for the v. Joel 3:19
who store up v. in their. Amos 3:10
ye that cause the seat of v. to. 6:3
for thy v. shame shall. Ob 10
every one from the v. Jonah 3:8
fields, and take them by v. Mi 2:2*
rich men thereof are full of v. 6:12
how long shall I cry unto thee of v.! Hab 1:2
v. is before me. 3
they shall come all for v. 9
and for the v. of the land. 2:8
v. of Lebanon cover thee, v. of. 17
houses with v. and deceit. Zeph 1:9
have done v. to the law. 3:4
for one covereth v. with. Mal 2:16
of heaven suffereth v. Mat 11:12
do v. to no man, nor accuse any. Luke 3:14
captain brought them without v. Acts 5:26
Paul borne of soldiers for v. 21:35
hinder part was broken with v. 27:41
quenched the v. of fire. Heb 11:34*
with v. shall Babylon. Rev 18:21*

violent

thou hast delivered me from the v. man. 2 Sam 22:49; Ps 18:48
his v. dealing come on his. Ps 7:16
the assemblies of v. men. 86:14
preserve me from the v. 140:1, 4
evil shall hunt the v. man to. 11
a v. man enticeth his. Pr 16:29
if thou seest v. perverting. Eccl 5:8
the v. take it by force. Mat 11:12

violently

servants had v. taken. Gen 21:25
shall restore that which he took v. Lev 6:4*
thine ass shall be v. Deut 28:31
he hath v. taken away. Job 20:19
they v. take away flocks, and. 24:2
he will surely v. turn. Isa 22:18
he hath v. taken away. Lam 2:6
swine ran v. into the sea. Mat 8:32* Mark 5:13*; Luke 8:33*

viols

the noise of thy v. is. Isa 14:11
hear the melody of thy v. Amos 5:23

viper

(The viper is one of the most poisonous serpents, but the word is used in the New Testament for any poisonous serpent)

of asps, the v.'s tongue. Job 20:16
from whence come the v. Isa 30:6
crushed breaketh out into a v. 59:5
came a v. and fastened. Acts 28:3

vipers

O generation of v. Mat 3:7; 12:34 23:33; Luke 3:7

virgin

In Greek, parthenos; *in Hebrew,* almah. *These words properly signify an unmarried young woman, who has preserved the purity of her body. But sometimes* virgin *is made use of to express a young woman whether she has kept her virginity or no,* Joel 1:8.

fair to look upon, a v. Gen 24:16
when the v. cometh forth to. 43
for his sister, a v. he. Lev 21:3
take a v. of his own people. 14
an evil name upon a v. Deut 22:19
a v. betrothed. 23
a v. not betrothed. 28
the young man and the v. 32:25
fell sick for Tamar; for she was a v. 2 Sam 13:2
sought for king a young v. 1 Ki 1:2
the v. daughter of Zion hath despised thee. 2 Ki 19:21; Isa 37:22
behold a v. shall conceive. Isa 7:14 Mat 1:23
O thou oppressed v. Isa 23:12
in the dust, O v. of Babylon. 47:1
marrieth a v. so thy sons. 62:5
the v. daughter of my. Jer 14:17
v. of Israel hath done a. 18:13
be built, O v. of Israel. 31:4
the v. rejoice in the dance. 13
turn again, O v. of Israel, to. 21
take balm, O v. the daughter. 46:11
trodden the v. daughter of. Lam 1:15
thee, O v. daughter of Zion. 2:13
lament like a v. girded. Joel 1:8
the v. of Israel is fallen. Amos 5:2
sent from God to a v. Luke 1:27
if a v. marry, she hath. 1 Cor 7:28
between a wife and a v. 34
decreed that he will keep his v. 37
I may present you as a chaste v. 2 Cor 11:2

virginity

take a wife in her v. Lev 21:13
tokens of her v. Deut 22:15, 17, 20
bewail my v. Judg 11:37, 38
the teats of their v. Ezek 23:3, 8
Anna lived seven years from her v. Luke 2:36

virgins

pay according to the dowry of v. Ex 22:17
daughters that were v. 2 Sam 13:18
favour above all the v. Esth 2:17
the v. her companions. Ps 45:14
as ointment, therefore do the v. love thee. S of S 1:3
threescore queens and v. 6:8
nor do I bring up v. Isa 23:4
her priests sigh, her v. Lam 1:4
my v. and young men are gone. 18
the v. of Jerusalem hang. 2:10
v. and young men are fallen. 21
shall the fair v. faint. Amos 8:13
heaven be likened to ten v. Mat 25:1
Philip had four daughters, v. Acts 21:9
concerning v. I have no. 1 Cor 7:25
not defiled, for they are v. Rev 14:4

young **virgins**

Jabesh-gilead were four hundred *young* v. Judg 21:12
there be fair *young* v. sought for king. Esth 2:2
together all the fair *young* v. 3

virtue

v. had gone out of him. Mark 5:30 Luke 6:19*; 8:46*
if there be any v. think. Phil 4:8
hath called us to glory and v. 2 Pet 1:3
add to your faith v. and to v. 5

virtuous

thou art a v. woman. Ruth 3:11†
a v. woman is a crown. Pr 12:4†
who can find a v. woman? 31:10†

virtuously

have done v. but thou. Pr 31:29†

visage

his v. was marred more. Isa 52:14
their v. is blacker than. Lam 4:8
and the form of his v. Dan 3:19

visible

were all things created, v. and invisible. Col 1:16

vision

the v. of the Almighty. Num 24:4, 16
there was no open v. 1 Sam 3:1
feared to shew Eli the v. 15
according to all these words and this v. 2 Sam 7:17; 1 Chr 17:15
they are written in the v. 2 Chr 32:32
as a v. of the night. Job 20:8
thou spakest in v. to thy. Ps 89:19
no v. the people perish. Pr 29:18
the v. of Isaiah. Isa 1:1
a grievous v. is declared. 21:2
burden of the valley of v. Isa 22:1, 5
they err in v., they stumble. 28:7
as a dream of a night v. 29:7
the v. is become as a book. 11
unto you a false v. Jer 14:14
they speak a v. of their own. 23:16
prophets find no v. from. Lam 2:9
v. is touching the whole. Ezek 7:13
then shall they seek a v. of. 26
according to the v. that I saw. 8:4 11:24; 43:3
prolonged and every v. 12:22
say to them, the effect of every v. 23
no more any vain v. nor. 24
the v. that he seeth is for many. 27
have ye not seen a vain v.? 13:7
to Daniel in a night v. Dan 2:19
I saw in my v. by night, the. 7:2
a v. appeared unto me, even. 8:1
how long shall be the v. concerning sacrifice? 13
man to understand the v. 16
time of the end shall be the v. 17
shut up the v. 26
I was astonished at the v. 27
whom I had seen in the v. at. 9:21
consider the v. 23
and to seal up the v. 24
had understanding of the v. 10:1
the v.: men with me saw not v. 7, 8
for yet the v. is for many days. 14
by v. my sorrows are turned. 16
themselves to establish the v. 11:14
v. of Obadiah. Ob 1
that ye shall not have a v. Mi 3:6
the book of the v. of. Nah 1:1
write the v. and make it. Hab 2:2
for the v. is yet for an appointed. 3
the prophets shall be ashamed every one of his v. Zech 13:4
charged, saying, Tell the v. to no man. Mat 17:9
that he had seen a v. Luke 1:22
they had seen a v. of angels. 24:23
doubted of the v. Acts 10:17, 19
in a trance I saw a v., A vessel. 11:5
true, but thought he saw a v. 12:9
a v. appeared to Paul. 16:9; 18:9
disobedient to the heavenly v. 26:19
I saw the horses in the v. Rev 9:17
see **oracle, prophet, Thummim**

in a **vision**

came to Abram *in a* v. Gen 15:1
make myself known to him *in a* v. Num 12:6
brought me *in a* v. by. Ezek 11:24
I saw *in a* v. and I was. Dan 8:2
said the Lord *in a* v. Acts 9:10
Saul hath seen *in a* v. a man. 12
Cornelius saw *in a* v. an angel. 10:3

visions

God spake to Israel in v. Gen 46:2
written in the v. of Iddo. 2 Chr 9:29
understanding in v. of God. 26:5
in thoughts from the v. Job 4:13
terrifiest me through v. 7:14
and I saw the v. of God. Ezek 1:1
he brought me in the v. of God. 8:3
see v. of peace for her. 13:16
in v. he brought me to the land. 40:2
understanding in all v. Dan 1:17
the v. of thy head on thy bed. 2:28
and the v. of my head troubled. 4:5
Daniel had v. of his head. 7:1
I saw in the night v. and. 7, 13
v. of my head troubled me. 15
I have multiplied v. Hos 12:10
your young men shall see v. Joel 2:28; Acts 2:17
I will come to v. and. 2 Cor 12:1

visit

(To come with a special purpose, either of blessing or punishment)

God will surely v. you. Gen 50:24 25; Ex 13:19
when I v. I will v. their. Ex 32:34
I do v. the iniquity. Lev 18:25
thou shalt v. thy habitation and not sin. Job 5:24
v. him every morning. 7:18
O Lord, awake to v. all. Ps 59:5
from heaven and v. this vine. 80:14
I v. their transgression with. 89:32

remember me, O v. me with. Ps 106:4
the Lord will v. Tyre. Isa 23:17
neither shall they v. the ark of the. Jer 3:16
v. for these things? 5:9, 29; 9:9
at time I v. them, they shall. 6:15
will remember iniquity and v. 14:10
knowest, remember and v. 15:15
I will v. on you the evil of. 23:2
shall they be till I v. them. 27:22
I will v. you and perform. 29:10
there shall he be till I v. him. 32:5
the time I will v. Esau. 49:8
v. Babylon. 50:31
he will v. thine iniquity. Lam 4:22
I will v. on her the days. Hos 2:13
now will he v. their sins. 8:13; 9:9
I will also v. the altars. Amos 3:14
Lord shall v. and turn. Zeph 2:7
which shall not v. those. Zech 11:16
it came into his heart to v. Acts 7:23
hath declared how God did v. 15:14
go again and v. our brethren in. 36
is this, to v. the fatherless. Jas 1:27

visitation

after the v. of all men. Num 16:29
thy v. hath preserved. Job 10:12
ye do in the day of v.? Isa 10:3
in the time of their v. shall. Jer 8:12
in the time of v. they shall perish. 10:15; 51:18
of Anathoth, even in the year of their v. 11:23; 23:12; 48:44
the time of their v. 46:21; 50:27
the days of v. are come. Hos 9:7
thy v. cometh, now shall be. Mi 7:4
not the time of thy v. Luke 19:44
they may glorify God in the day of v. 1 Pet 2:12

visited

and the Lord v. Sarah as. Gen 21:1
I have surely v. you. Ex 3:16
that the Lord had v. Israel. 4:31
if they be v. after visitation of all men. Num 16:29
that Samson v. his wife. Judg 15:1
she heard how the Lord had v. his. Ruth 1:6
the Lord v. Hannah. 1 Sam 2:21
now it is not so, he hath v. in his anger. Job 35:15
thou hast v. me, thou. Ps 17:3
he shall not be v. with evil. Pr 19:23
days shall they be v. Isa 24:22
therefore hast thou v. and. 26:14
Lord, in trouble have they v. 26
thou shalt be v. of the Lord. 29:6
Jerusalem is the city to be v. Jer 6:6
flock and have not v. them. 23:2
days thou shalt be v. Ezek 38:8
the Lord of hosts hath v. Zech 10:3
I was sick, and ye v. me. Mat 25:36
ye v. me not. 43
he hath v. and redeemed. Luke 1:68
dayspring from on high hath v. us. 78
saying, That God hath v. his. 7:16

visitest

and the son of man, that thou v. him? Ps 8:4; Heb 2:6
thou v. the earth and waterest it. Ps 65:9

visiteth

when he v. what shall I? Job 31:14

visiting

v. the iniquity of the fathers. Ex 20:5
34:7; Num 14:18; Deut 5:9

vocation

ye walk worthy of the v. Eph 4:1*

voice

By this word is not only understood the voice *of a man or beast, but all other sorts of sounds, noises, or cries. And even thunder is also called the* voice *of God. To hear or to hearken to any one's voice is to obey him,* Ex 15:26.

the v. of thy brother's. Gen 4:10
v. is Jacob's v. but the hands. 27:22
and Jacob lifted up his v. and. 29:11
heard that I lifted up my v. 39:15
believe the v. of latter sign. Ex 4:8
God answered him by a v. 19:19
beware of him, obey his v. Ex 23:21
people answered with one v. 24:3
it is not the v. of them that. 32:18
if a soul hear the v. of. Lev 5:1
the congregation lifted up their v. Num 14:1
be obedient to his v. Deut 4:30
not be obedient to his v. 8:20
any noise with your v. Josh 6:10
they knew the v. of the. Judg 18:3
is this thy v. my son David? 1 Sam 24:16; 26:17
and the most High uttered his v. 2 Sam 22:14
was no v. nor any that answered. 1 Ki 18:26, 29
after the fire a still small v. 19:12
there was neither v. nor. 2 Ki 4:31
there was no v. of man, but. 7:10
hast thou exalted thy v. and lifted up thine eyes? 19:22; Isa 37:23
by lifting up the v. with. 1 Chr 15:16
Job's friends lifted up their v. and. Job 2:12
to be solitary, let no joyful v. 3:7
my organ into the v. of them. 30:31
a v. roareth, he thundereth with the v. 37:4
marvellously with his v. 5
thunder with a v. like him? 40:9
the Highest gave his v. Ps 18:13
I may publish with the v. of. 26:7
thou heardest the v. of my. 31:22
house of God with the v. of. 42:4
for the v. of him that. 44:16
he uttered his v., the earth. 46:6
shout unto God with the v. 47:1
he hath attended to the v. of. 66:19
his v. and that a mighty v. 68:33
forget not the v. of thine. 74:23
I cried unto the Lord with my v. 77:1; 142:1
the v. of thy thunder was in. 77:18
attend to the v. of my. 86:6
floods have lifted up their v. 93:3
sing unto the Lord with the v. 98:5
by reason of the v. of my. 102:5
hearkening to the v. of his. 103:20
at v. of thy thunder they. 104:7
v. of rejoicing in tabernacles. 118:15
give ear to my v. when I cry. 141:1
her v. in the streets. Pr 1:20
if thou liftest up thy v. 2:3
I have not obeyed the v. of. 5:13
understanding put forth her v.? 8:1
to you, O men, I call, my v. is. 4
a fool's v. is known by. Eccl 5:3
God be angry at thy v.? 6
bird of the air shall carry the v. 10:20
he shall rise up at the v. of. 12:4
the v. of my beloved. S of S 2:8
the v. of the turtle is heard in. 12
it is the v. of my beloved. 5:2
posts moved at the v. of. Isa 6:4
exalt the v. unto them, shake. 13:2
thy v. be as one that hath a. 29:4
be gracious to thee at the v. 30:19
will not be afraid of their v. 31:4
the v. of him that crieth in. 40:3
Mat 3:3; Mark 1:3; Luke 3:4
v. said, Cry. Isa 40:6
with the v. of singing. 48:20
that obeyeth the v. of his. 50:10
joy, thanksgiving, and the v. 51:3
with the v. together shall they. 52:8
v. of weeping shall be no more heard in her, nor v. of crying. 65:19
a v. of noise, a v. from temple, a v. 66:6
a v. declareth from Dan. Jer 4:15
give out their v. against the cities. 16
their v. roareth like the sea. 6:23
50:42
v. of mirth, v. of gladness, v. of the bridegroom, v. of bride. 7:34
16:9; 25:10; 33:11
v. of the cry of the daughter. 8:19
uttereth his v., there is a multitude of waters. 10:13; 51:16
a v. of the cry of shepherds. 25:36
and the v. of them that make. 30:19
a v. was heard in Ramah. 31:15
saith the Lord, refrain thy v. 16
the v. thereof shall go like. 46:22*
a v. of crying shall be from. Jer 48:3*
the v. of them that flee. 50:28
hath destroyed out of her the great v. 51:55
I heard as the v. of the Almighty. Ezek 1:24*
as the v. of the Almighty God. 10:5
and a v. of a multitude. 23:42
of one that hath a pleasant v. 33:32
his v. was like a noise of many waters. 43:2; Rev 1:15; 19:6
fell a v. from heaven. Dan 4:31
lamentable v. to Daniel. 6:20
v. of his words like the v. of. 10:6
Lord shall utter his v. Joel 2:11
shall utter his v. from Jerusalem. 3:16; Amos 1:2
I will sacrifice with v. Jonah 2:9
as with the v. of doves. Nah 2:7
a v. from heaven, This is my beloved Son, in. Mat 3:17; Mark 1:11
Luke 3:22
a v. out of the cloud, This is. Mat 17:5; Mark 9:7; Luke 9:35, 36
as soon as the v. of thy. Luke 1:44
the v. of one crying in. John 1:23
of the bridegroom's v. 3:29
him, for they know his v. 10:4
for they know not the v. of. 5
a v. saying, I have glorified it. 12:28
this v. came not because of me. 30
is of the truth heareth my v. 18:37
hearing a v., but seeing no. Acts 9:7
came a v. saying, Rise, Peter. 10:13
and the v. spake unto him. 15; 11:9
when she knew Peter's v. she. 12:14
it is the v. of a god, and not. 22
all with one v. cried, Great is. 19:34
except it be for this one v. 24:21
I gave my v. against them. 26:10*
the meaning of the v. 1 Cor 14:11
that by my v. I might teach. 19
now to change my v. Gal 4:20
with v. of the archangel. 1 Thes 4:16
v. then shook the earth. Heb 12:26
came a v. from the excellent glory. 2 Pet 1:17
ass speaking with man's v. 2:16
I turned to see the v. Rev 1:12
there came a great v. saying. 16:17

voice joined with *hear*

hear my v. ye wives of. Gen 4:23
did ever people *hear* v.? Deut 4:33
he made thee to *hear* his v. 36
if we *hear* the v. of God. 5:25
he said, *Hear*, Lord, the v. 33:7
can I *hear* the v. of? 2 Sam 19:35
and he did *hear* my v. out of. 22:7
they *hear* not the v. of the. Job 3:18
hear attentively the noise of his v. 37:2
my v. shalt thou *hear* in. Ps 5:3
hear, O Lord, when I cry with my v. 27:7; 28:2; 64:1; 119:149; 130:2
140:6
hear me, because of the v. of. 55:3
aloud and he shall *hear* my v. 17
to-day if ye will *hear* his v., harden not. 95:7; Heb 3:7, 15; 4:7
hear thy v., for sweet is thy v. S of S 2:14
hear my v. ye careless. Isa 32:9
nor can men *hear* the v. Jer 9:10
any man *hear* his v. Mat 12:19
the dead shall *hear* the v. of the Son of God. John 5:25, 28
and sheep *hear* his v. 10:3, 16, 27
and shouldest *hear* the v. Acts 22:14
if any man *hear* my v. Rev 3:20
see **heard, lift, Lord, loud, obey, obeyed**

voice with *hearken, hearkened*

because thou hast *hearkened* unto the v. of thy wife. Gen 3:17
Abram *hearkened* to the v. 16:2
hath said *hearken* to her v. 21:12
shall *hearken* to thy v. Ex 3:18
will not *hearken* unto my v. 4:1
nor *hearken* to the v. of the first. 8
neither *hearken* unto thy v. 9
if diligently *hearken* to the v. 15:26
hearken unto my v., I will give. 18:19
hearkened to the v. of Jethro. 24

and not *hearkened* to my *v.*
Num 14:22; *Deut* 9:23; 28:45
Lord *hearkened* to the *v. Num* 21:3
the Lord would not *hearken* to your *v.* *Deut* 1:45
hearken to the *v.* of the Lord. 13:18
only if thou carefully *hearken* to the *v.* 15:5; 26:17; 28:1, 2; 30:10
not *hearken* to the *v.* of Lord. 28:15
hearkened to the *v.* of a man. *Josh* 10:14
this people have not *hearkened* to my *v.* *Judg* 2:20
and God *hearkened* to the *v.* 13:9
not *hearken* to the *v.* of Israel. 20:13
they *hearkened* not unto the *v.* of their father. *1 Sam* 2:25
hearken to the *v.* of the people. 8:7
9:22
I have *hearkened* to your *v.* 12:1
Saul *hearkened* to the *v.* 19:6
I have *hearkened* to thy *v.* 25:35
hearken thou to the *v.* of thy. 28:22
he would not *hearken* to our *v.* *2 Sam* 12:18
not *hearken* to her *v.* 13:14
Ben-hadad *hearkened* to their *v.* *1 Ki* 20:25
will *hearken* to my *v.* *2 Ki* 10:6
not believe he had *hearkened* to my *v.* *Job* 9:16
hearken to *v.* of my words. 34:16
hearken to the *v.* of my cry. *Ps* 5:2
will not *hearken* to the *v.* of. 58:5
would not *hearken* to my *v.* 81:11
the companions *hearken* to thy *v.* *S of S* 8:13
hearken to the *v.* of them. *Jer* 18:19

voices
lepers lifted up their *v. Luke* 17:13
instant with loud *v.* that he might be crucified, the *v.* of them. 23:23
knew him not nor the *v. Acts* 13:27
they lift up their *v.* and said. 22:22
so many *v.* in the world. *1 Cor* 14:10
out of the throne proceeded *v.* *Rev* 4:5; 16:18
into the earth: and there were *v.* 8:5
woe, by reason of the other *v.* 13
thunders uttered their *v.* 10:3, 4
there were great *v.* in heaven. 11:15
was opened, and there were *v.* 19

void
the earth was without form and *v.* *Gen* 1:2; *Jer* 4:23
but if her husband made them *v.* *Num* 30:12, 15
they are a people *v.* of. *Deut* 32:28
kings sat in a *v.* place. *1 Ki* 22:10*
2 Chr 18:9*
made *v.* the covenant of. *Ps* 89:39*
have made *v.* thy law. 119:126
v. of wisdom despiseth. *Pr* 11:12
my word shall not return to me *v.* *Isa* 55:11
I will make *v.* the counsel. *Jer* 19:7
Nineveh is empty, *v.* *Nah* 2:10
conscience *v.* of offence. *Acts* 24:16
then make *v.* the law ? *Rom* 3:31*
law be heirs, faith is made *v.* 4:14
make my glorying *v.* *1 Cor* 9:15
see **understanding**

volume
Lo, I come: in the *v.* of the book it is written. *Ps* 40:7*; *Heb* 10:7*

voluntarily
prepare offerings *v.* to. *Ezek* 46:12*

voluntary
it of his own *v.* will. *Lev* 1:3*
a *v.* offering shall be eaten. 7:16*
princes shall prepare a *v.* burnt. *Ezek* 46:12*
in a *v.* humility and. *Col* 2:18

vomit
riches and shall *v.* them. *Job* 20:15
eaten shalt thou *v.* up. *Pr* 23:8
filled with honey and *v.* it. 25:16

vomit, *substantive*
dog returneth to his *v.* *Pr* 26:11
man staggereth in his *v.* *Isa* 19:14
for all tables are full of *v.* 28:8
shall wallow in his *v.* *Jer* 48:26
turned to his own *v.* *2 Pet* 2:22

vomited
the fish *v.* out Jonah on dry land. *Jonah* 2:10

vomiteth
the land *v.* out her inhabitants. *Lev* 18:25

vow
Is a promise made to God, of doing some good thing hereafter. The use of vows *was common in Bible times. When Jacob went into Mesopotamia he vowed to God the tenth of his estate, and promised to offer it at Beth-el to the honour and service of God,* Gen 28:20, 22. *There are several laws for the regulation and due execution of* vows. *A man might devote himself, or his children, to the Lord. Samuel was vowed and consecrated to the service of the Lord, and was offered to him, to serve in the tabernacle,* 1 Sam 1:22, 28. *If a man or woman vowed themselves, or their children to the Lord, they were obliged to adhere strictly to his service, according to the conditions of the vow; if not, they were to be redeemed. The price for redeeming persons of such and such an age is particularly limited,* Lev 27:2, 3, *etc. Only if the person was poor, and could not procure the sum limited, the priest imposed a ransom upon him according to his abilities.*

If any one had vowed an animal that was clean, he had not the liberty of redeeming it, or of exchanging it, but was obliged to sacrifice it to the Lord, or give it to the priest, according to the manner of his vow. *If it was an unclean animal, and such as was not allowed to be sacrificed, the priest made valuation of it; and if the proprietor would redeem it, he added a fifth part to the value, by way of forfeit. The same was done in proportion, when the thing vowed was a house or a field.* See Lev 27:9, 10, *etc. They could not devote the firstlings of beasts, because they belonged to the Lord,* Lev 27:26. *Whatsoever was solemnly devoted to the Lord could not be redeemed, of whatever nature or quality it was,* Lev 27:28. *Concerning the* vows *of the* Nazarites, *see* **Nazarite.**

The vows and promises of children were void, except they were ratified, either by the express or tacit consent of their parents. And it was the same with the vows *of married women; they were of no validity, unless they were confirmed by the express or tacit consent of their husbands,* Num 30:1, 2, 3, *etc.*

Under the New Testament, a vow *is either general to all Christians, as that which is made at baptism; or particular and special, as when we bind ourselves to a greater endeavour, to leave some sin, or perform some duty. A* vow, *as one observes, must be made deliberately and devoutly, for a sudden passion makes not a* vow; *and we ought to* vow *nothing but what is in our power to perform. Some* vows *are of evil things to an evil end; such* vows *ought neither to be made nor kept; of this kind was the* vow *or* curse *which the Jews bound themselves under, who conspired to murder Paul,* Acts 23:12.

The performance of solemn vows *is strictly enjoined upon us in scripture,* Eccl 5:4.

Jacob vowed a *v. Gen* 28:20; 31:13
if the sacrifice be a *v.* *Lev* 7:16
22:18, 21
but for a *v.* it shall not. 22:23
shall make a singular *v.* 27:2
vow a *v.* of a Nazarite. *Num* 6:2
the days of the *v.* 5
according to the *v.* 21
sacrifice in performing a *v.* 15:3, 8
Israel vowed a *v.* to the Lord. 21:2
if a man vow a *v.* 30:2
if a woman vow a *v.* 3
and her father hear her *v.* and. 4
every *v.* of a widow shall stand. 9
every *v.* her husband may. 13
price of a dog for a *v.* *Deut* 23:18
when thou shalt vow a *v.* unto. 21
Jephthah vowed a *v.* *Judg* 11:30
with her according to his *v.* 39
Hannah vowed a *v.* and. *1 Sam* 1:11
up to offer to the Lord his *v.* 21
let me go and pay my *v. 2 Sam* 15:7
servant vowed a *v.* at Geshur. 8
to thee shall the *v.* be. *Ps* 65:1
when thou vowest a *v.* *Eccl* 5:4
they shall vow a *v.* unto. *Isa* 19:21
head, for he had a *v.* *Acts* 18:18
men which have a *v.* on them. 21:23

vow, *verb*
themselves to *v.* a vow. *Num* 6:2
if forbear to *v.*, it shall. *Deut* 23:22
and *v.* and pay to the Lord your God. *Ps* 76:11
that thou shouldest not *v.* *Eccl* 5:5

vowed
Jacob *v.* a vow. *Gen* 28:20; 31:13
ability that *v.* shall priest. *Lev* 27:8
Nazarites who hath *v.* *Num* 6:21
Israel *v.* a vow to the Lord. 21:2
if all an husband when she *v.* 30:6
and if she *v.* in her husband's. 10
shalt keep according as thou hast *v.* *Deut* 23:23
Jephthah *v.* a vow unto. *Judg* 11:30
and *v.* to the mighty God. *Ps* 132:2
pay that which thou hast *v. Eccl* 5:4
pay that that I have *v.* *Jonah* 2:9

vowest
when thou *v.* a vow, defer. *Eccl* 5:4

voweth
who *v.* to the Lord a. *Mal* 1:14

vows
his oblation for all his *v. Lev* 22:18
gifts and beside all your *v.* 23:38
shall do beside your *v.* *Num* 29:39
then all her *v.* shall stand. 30:4
7, 9, 11
not any of her *v.* or bonds. 5, 8, 12
then he established all her *v.* 14
thither bring your *v.* *Deut* 12:6, 11
17, 26
thou shalt pay thy *v.* *Job* 22:27
I will pay my *v.* unto the Lord. *Ps* 22:25; 66:13; 116:14, 18
pay thy *v.* 50:14
thy *v.* are upon me, O God. 56:12
O God, hast heard my *v.* 61:5
I may daily perform my *v.* 8
this day have I paid my *v.* *Pr* 7:14
it is a snare after *v.* to make. 20:25
and what, the son of my *v.*? 31:2
surely perform our *v.* *Jer* 44:25
feared the Lord and made *v.* *Jonah* 1:16
O Judah, keep thy solemn feasts, perform thy *v.* *Nah* 1:15

voyage
I perceive this *v.* will be. *Acts* 27:10

vulture
(*A bird of prey, which was declared unclean,* Lev 11:14. *Probably the word means the* kite *as the Revised Versions give it usually, or the* falcon *as in Job*)
v. and the kite after his kind shall. *Lev* 11:14; *Deut* 14:13
a path which the *v.* eye. *Job* 28:7*
there shall the *v.* also be. *Isa* 34:15

W

wafer
one *w*. out of the basket of the unleavened. *Ex* 29:23; *Lev* 8:26
one cake, one *w*. on. *Num* 6:19

wafers
taste of it was like *w*. *Ex* 16:31
and *w*. unleavened anointed. 29:2
w. anointed with oil. *Lev* 2:4; 7:12
Num 6:15

wag
passeth by shall *w*. his. *Jer* 18:16*
w. their heads at daughter. *Lam* 2:15
passeth shall *w*. his hand. *Zeph* 2:15

wages
what shall thy *w*. be ? *Gen* 29:15
appoint me thy *w*. and I will. 30:28
changed my *w*. ten times. 31:7, 41
the speckled shall be thy *w*. 8
this child, I will give thee *w*. *Ex* 2:9
w. of hired not abide. *Lev* 19:13
service without *w*. *Jer* 22:13
yet had he no *w*. nor. *Ezek* 29:18
her spoil shall be the *w*. for. 19
earneth *w*. to put into a. *Hag* 1:6
the hireling in his *w*. *Mal* 3:5
be content with your *w*. *Luke* 3:14
reapeth receiveth *w*. *John* 4:36
for the *w*. of sin is death. *Rom* 6:23
taking *w*. of them to do. *2 Cor* 11:8
Balaam loved the *w*. *2 Pet* 2:15

wagging
passed by reviled him, *w*. their heads. *Mat* 27:39; *Mark* 15:29

waggon
brought a *w*. for two of the princes.
Num 7:3

waggons
w. out of Egypt. *Gen* 45:19, 21
when Jacob saw the *w*. Joseph. 27
two *w*., four oxen to sons. *Num* 7:7
four *w*. and eight oxen to the. 8
against thee with *w*. *Ezek* 23:34

wail
w. for the multitude of. *Ezek* 32:18
I will *w*. and howl. *Mi* 1:8
earth shall *w*. for him. *Rev* 1:7*

wailed
them that wept and *w*. greatly.
Mark 5:38

wailing
decree came there was *w*. *Esth* 4:3
for the mountains will I take up *w*.
Jer 9:10
let them take up a *w*. for us. 18
for a voice of *w*. is heard out of. 19
teach your daughters *w*. 20
neither shall there be *w*. *Ezek* 7:11
weep for thee with bitter *w*. 27:31*
w. shall be in all streets and they shall say . . . to *w*. *Amos* 5:16
and in all vineyards shall be *w*. 17
I will make a *w*. like the. *Mi* 1:8
there shall be *w*. and gnashing of teeth. *Mat* 13:42*, 50*
the merchants stand afar off, *w*.
Rev 18:15*, 19*

wait
him by laying of *w*. *Num* 35:20
any thing without laying *w*. 22
in his heart he layeth his *w*. *Jer* 9:8*
see **laid, lay**

wait
Aaron and sons shall *w*. on their priest's office. *Num* 3:10; 8:24
1 Chr 23:28; *2 Chr* 5:11; 13:10
should I *w*. for the Lord ? *2 Ki* 6:33
of my time I will *w*. till. *Job* 14:14
if I *w*. the grave is my house. 17:13
let none that *w*. on thee be ashamed.
Ps 25:3; 69:6
God of salvation, on thee do I *w*. 25:5
preserve me, for I *w*. on thee. 21
w. on the Lord. 27:14; 37:34
Pr 20:22
w. patiently for him. *Ps* 37:7
that *w*. on the Lord shall inherit. 9
Lord, what *w*. I for ? 39:7
I will *w*. on thy name. 52:9
mark my steps when they *w*. *Ps* 56:6
because of his strength will I *w*. 59:9
w. only on God. 62:5
mine eyes fail while I *w*. for. 69:3
these all *w*. upon thee. 104:27
145:15
so our eyes *w*. on the Lord. 123:2
I *w*. for the Lord, my soul doth *w*.
130:5
I will *w*. upon the Lord. *Isa* 8:17
Lord *w*. to be gracious to you, blessed are all they that *w*. 30:18
but they that *w*. on the Lord shall renew their strength. 40:31
the isles shall *w*. for his law. 42:4
shall not be ashamed that *w*. 49:23
isles shall *w*. upon me. 51:5
we *w*. for light, but behold. 59:9
the isles shall *w*. for me. 60:9
we will *w*. upon thee. *Jer* 14:22
Lord is good to them that *w*. for him.
Lam 3:25
a man hope and quietly *w*. 26
as troops of robbers *w*. *Hos* 6:9
keep mercy and *w*. on thy God. 12:6
I will *w*. for the God of. *Mi* 7:7
though vision tarry, *w*. for. *Hab* 2:3
therefore *w*. ye upon me. *Zeph* 3:8
ship should *w*. on him. *Mark* 3:9
like unto men that *w*. *Luke* 12:36
but *w*. for the promise. *Acts* 1:4
with patience *w*. for it. *Rom* 8:25
or ministry, let us *w*. on. 12:7*
which *w*. at the altar. *1 Cor* 9:13
we through the Spirit *w*. *Gal* 5:5
and to *w*. for his Son. *1 Thes* 1:10
see **liars**

waited
w. for thy salvation. *Gen* 49:18
the prophet *w*. for king. *1 Ki* 20:38
w. on Naaman's wife. *2 Ki* 5:2
and then they *w*. on their office.
1 Chr 6:32, 33
porters that *w*. in king's gate. 9:18
2 Chr 35:15
and the priests *w*. on. *2 Chr* 7:6
and Levites that *w*. *Neh* 12:44
the companies of Sheba *w*. *Job* 6:19
he is *w*. for of the sword. 15:22
to me men gave ear, *w*. and. 29:21
w. for me as for the rain. 23
when I *w*. for light, there came. 30:26
now Elihu had *w*. till Job had. 32:4
I *w*. patiently for the Lord. *Ps* 40:1
they *w*. not for counsel. 106:13
wicked have *w*. for me to. 119:95
God, we have *w*. for him. *Isa* 25:9
judgements have we *w*. for. 26:8
us, we have *w*. for thee. 33:2
she saw that she had *w*. *Ezek* 19:5
of Maroth *w*. carefully. *Mi* 1:12
flock that *w*. upon me. *Zech* 11:11
Joseph of Arimathaea, who also *w*.
Mark 15:43; *Luke* 23:51
the people *w*. for Zacharias.
Luke 1:21
a soldier that *w*. on him. *Acts* 10:7
Cornelius *w*. for Peter and. 24
Paul *w*. for them, his spirit. 17:16
longsuffering of God *w*. in days of Noah. *1 Pet* 3:20

waiteth
eye of the adulterer *w*. *Job* 24:15
our soul *w*. for the Lord. *Ps* 33:20
truly my soul *w*. upon. 62:1; 130:6
praise *w*. for thee, O God. 65:1
he that *w*. on his master. *Pr* 27:18
prepared for him that *w*. *Isa* 64:4
blessed is he that *w*. and cometh to the 1335 days. *Dan* 12:12
as showers that *w*. not. *Mi* 5:7
w. for the manifestation of. *Rom* 8:19
the husbandman *w*. for. *Jas* 5:7

waiting
from the age of 50 years they shall cease *w*. upon the. *Num* 8:25
w. at the posts of my doors. *Pr* 8:34
Simeon *w*. for the consolation of.
Luke 2:25
folk *w*. for the moving. *John* 5:3
groan, *w*. for the adoption. *Rom* 8:23
w. for the coming of our Lord Jesus Christ. *1 Cor* 1:7
into the patient *w*. for Christ.
2 Thes 3:5

wake, awake
when I *a*., I am still with. *Ps* 139:18
perpetual sleep and not *w*. *Jer* 51:39
prepare war, *w*. up the mighty men.
Joel 3:9*
whether we *w*. or sleep. *1 Thes* 5:10

waked
angel came again and *w*. *Zech* 4:1

wakened
let heathen be *w*. and. *Joel* 3:12*
as a man that is *w*. out. *Zech* 4:1

wakeneth
he *w*. morning by morning, he *w*. mine ear. *Isa* 50:4

waketh
city, watchman *w*. in vain. *Ps* 127:1
I sleep but my heart *w*. *S of S* 5:2

waking
thou holdest mine eyes *w*. *Ps* 77:4

walk
the Lord, before whom I *w*. *Gen* 24:40
my fathers did *w*. bless. 48:15
whether they will *w*. in. *Exod* 16:4
way wherein they must *w*. 18:20
if he *w*. abroad, he that smote. 21:19
neither shall ye *w*. in their ordinances. *Lev* 18:3; 20:23
if ye *w*. in my statutes and. 26:3
1 Ki 6:12; *Ezek* 33:15; *Zech* 3:7
I will *w*. among you. *Lev* 26:12
if ye *w*. contrary to me. 21, 23, 27
then will I *w*. contrary to you. 24, 28
shall *w*. in all the ways. *Deut* 5:33
13:4; 28:9; *Ezek* 37:24
if ye *w*. after other gods. *Deut* 8:19
though I *w*. in the imagination. 29:19
take diligent heed to *w*. *Josh* 22:5
speak, ye that *w*. by the. *Judg* 5:10
thy house should *w*. before me for ever. *1 Sam* 2:30
he shall *w*. before mine anointed. 35
thou art old, thy sons *w*. not in. 8:5
w. to keep my commandments as . . . David did *w*. *1 Ki* 3:14; 8:25
9:4; 11:38; *2 Chr* 7:17
with thy servants that *w*. before thee with all. *1 Ki* 8:23; *2 Chr* 6:14
the good way wherein they should *w*.
1 Ki 8:36; *2 Chr* 6:27
the wicked *w*. on every. *Ps* 12:8
though I *w*. through the valley. 23:4
but as for me, I will *w*. in mine. 26:11
that I may *w*. before God in. 56:13
they know not; they *w*. on in. 82:5
from them that *w*. uprightly. 84:11
teach me, O Lord, I will *w*. 86:11
shall *w*. in the light of thy. 89:15
if his children *w*. not in my. 30
I will *w*. in my house with a. 101:2
have they, but they *w*. not. 115:7
I will *w*. before the Lord in. 116:9
they do no iniquity, they *w*. 119:3
I will *w*. at liberty, for I seek. 45
I *w*. in the midst of trouble. 138:7
way wherein I should *w*. 143:8
he is a buckler to them that *w*. uprightly. *Pr* 2:7
that thou mayest *w*. in the way. 20
then shalt thou *w*. in thy way. 3:23
we will *w*. in his paths. *Isa* 2:3
Mi 4:2
Jacob, let us *w*. in the light. *Isa* 2:5
they *w*. with stretched forth. 3:16
that I should not *w*. in the way. 8:11
redeemed shall *w*. there. 35:9
they that wait on Lord shall *w*. 40:31
spirit to them that *w*. therein. 42:5
for they would not *w*. in his ways. 24
wait for brightness, but we *w*. 59:9
nor *w*. after imagination. *Jer* 3:17
the house of Judah shall *w*. with. 18
but they said, We will not *w*. 6:16
if ye *w*. not after other gods to. 7:6
will ye *w*. after other gods whom? 9
every neighbour will *w*. with. 9:4
w. in imagination of their heart, and *w*. after. 13:10; 16:12; 18:12
adultery, and *w*. in lies. 23:14
way wherein we may *w*. 42:3

the foxes *w.* upon it. *Lam* 5:18
w. in my statutes. *Ezek* 11:20
shall *w.* in my judgements. 37:24
those that *w.* in pride. *Dan* 4:37
they shall *w.* after the Lord: he shall roar like a. *Hos* 11:10
the just shall *w.* in them. 14:9
they shall *w.* every one. *Joel* 2:8
two *w.* together except? *Amos* 3:3
w. every one in name of his god, and we will *w.* in the name. *Mi* 4:5
and ye *w.* in the counsels of. 6:16
thou didst *w.* through the sea. *Hab* 3:15*
that they shall *w.* like blind men. *Zeph* 1:17
they might *w.* to and fro through the earth. *Zech* 6:7
they shall *w.* up and down. 10:12
the lame *w.*, the lepers are cleansed. *Mat* 11:5; *Luke* 7:22
why *w.* not thy disciples? *Mark* 7:5
men that *w.* over them. *Luke* 11:44
I must *w.* to-day and. 13:33
communications as ye *w.*? 24:17
for Jesus would not *w.* *John* 7:1
shall not *w.* in darkness but. 8:12
if any man *w.* in the day. 11:9
if a man *w.* in the night, he. 10
who also *w.* in the steps of that faith of. *Rom* 4:12
so we should *w.* in newness of. 6:4
who *w.* not after flesh, but. 8:1, 4
for we *w.* by faith, not. *2 Cor* 5:7
I will dwell in them and *w.* 6:16
we *w.* in the flesh, not war. 10:3
as many as *w.* according. *Gal* 6:16
ordained we should *w.* *Eph* 2:10
ye *w.* worthy of the vocation. 4:1
that ye *w.* not as other Gentiles. 17
then that ye *w.* circumspectly. 5:15
mark them which *w.* so. *Phil* 3:17
many *w.* of whom I told you. 18
that ye might *w.* worthy of the Lord. *Col* 1:10; *1 Thes* 2:12
ye may *w.* honestly. *1 Thes* 4:12
some which *w.* among you disorderly. *2 Thes* 3:11
but chiefly them that *w.* *2 Pet* 2:10
have fellowship, and *w.* in darkness. *1 John* 1:6
but if we *w.* in the light as he. 7
w. after his commandments, as ye . . . ye should *w.* *2 John* 6
to hear that my children *w.* *3 John* 4
mockers should *w.* after. *Jude* 18
shall *w.* with me in white. *Rev* 3:4
see, nor hear, nor *w.* 9:20
watcheth, lest he *w.* naked. 16:15
the nations shall *w.* in the light. 21:24

walk, *imperatively*

arise, *w.* through the land. *Gen* 13:17; *Josh* 18:8
Almighty God, *w.* before me. *Gen* 17:1
w. about Zion and go. *Ps* 48:12
my son, *w.* not in the way. *Pr* 1:15
w. in the ways of thy heart and eyes. *Eccl* 11:9
O Jacob, let us *w.* in the. *Isa* 2:5
This is the way, *w.* ye in it. 30:21
w. in the light of your fire and. 50:11
the good way, *w.* therein. *Jer* 6:16
go not forth into fields, nor *w.* 25
w. ye in all the ways I. 7:23
w. ye not in statutes. *Ezek* 20:18
they might *w.* to and fro. *Zech* 6:7
or to say, Arise and *w.* *Mat* 9:5 *Mark* 2:9; *Luke* 5:23; *John* 5:8 11, 12; *Acts* 3:6
w. while ye have the light, lest darkness. *John* 12:35
let us *w.* honestly as in the day. *Rom* 13:13
as the Lord hath called every one, so let him *w.* *1 Cor* 7:17
w. in the Spirit, and not fulfil the lusts. *Gal* 5:16, 25
w. in love. *Eph* 5:2
w. as children of light. 8
let us *w.* by the same rule. *Phil* 3:16
Christ, so *w.* ye in him. *Col* 2:6
w. in wisdom toward them. 4:5

to **walk**

to w. in my ordinances. *Lev* 18:4
to w. in his ways, and fear him. *Deut* 8:6; 10:12; 11:22; 13:5 19:9; 26:17; 30:16; *Josh* 22:5 *Judg* 2:22; *1 Ki* 2:3; 8:58 *2 Chr* 6:31
take heed *to w.* before. *1 Ki* 2:4
heart perfect, *to w.* in his statutes. 8:61; *Ezek* 36:27
a light thing *to w.* in sins. *1 Ki* 16:31
Jehu took no heed *to w.* *2 Ki* 10:31
Josiah made a covenant *to w.* after. 23:3; *2 Chr* 34:31
take heed *to w.* in my law. *2 Chr* 6:16
ought ye not *to w.* in the fear of God? *Neh* 5:9
they entered into an oath *to w.* 10:29
they refused *to w.* in his. *Ps* 78:10
leave right *to w.* in ways. *Pr* 2:13
poor that knoweth *to w.* *Eccl* 6:8
to w. in paths, in a way. *Jer* 18:15
if ye will not hearken *to w.* 26:4
I will cause them *to w.* in a. 31:9
I will cause men *to w.* *Ezek* 36:12
nor have we obeyed *to w.* *Dan* 9:10
to w. humbly with thy God. *Mi* 6:8
he will make me *to w.* *Hab* 3:19
whom Lord hath sent *to w.* *Zech* 1:10
will give places *to w.* among. 3:7
they saw the lame *to w.* *Mat* 15:31
the scribes desire *to w.* *Luke* 20:46
had made this man *to w.* *Acts* 3:12
suffered all nations *to w.* 14:16
to circumcise, nor *to w.* after. 21:21
how ye ought *to w.* and. *1 Thes* 4:1
ought himself so *to w.* *1 John* 2:6

walked

Enoch *w.* with God. *Gen* 5:22, 24
Noah was a just man, and *w.* 6:9
Israel *w.* upon the dry. *Ex* 14:29
that also they have *w.* *Lev* 26:40
Israel *w.* forty years in. *Josh* 5:6
of the way their fathers *w.* in. *Judg* 2:17
travellers *w.* through byways. 5:6
when Israel *w.* through the. 11:16
Samuel's sons *w.* not. *1 Sam* 8:3
Abner and his men *w.* *2 Sam* 2:29
David *w.* on the roof of the. 11:2
that they walk before me as thou hast *w.* *1 Ki* 8:25
as David thy father *w.* 9:4 *2 Chr* 6:16; 7:17
have not *w.* in my ways. *1 Ki* 11:33 *Ezek* 5:6, 7; 11:12; 20:13, 16, 21
he *w.* in the way of his father. *1 Ki* 15:26; 22:52
in the sight of the Lord and *w.* in. 15:34; 16:2; *2 Ki* 13:6; 17:22
returned, and *w.* in house. *2 Ki* 4:35
Hoshea *w.* in the statutes of. 17:8
Judah kept not commandments of the Lord, but *w.* in. 19; *2 Chr* 21:13
forsook the Lord, and *w.* not in the way of the Lord. *2 Ki* 21:22 *Jer* 9:13; 32:23; 44:10, 23
Josiah *w.* in the ways of David. *2 Ki* 22:2; *2 Chr* 34:2
for three years they *w.* in the way of David. *2 Chr* 11:17
Jehoshaphat *w.* in God's. 17:4
hast not *w.* in the ways of. 21:12
when by his light I *w.* *Job* 29:3
if mine heart *w.* after mine. 31:7
we *w.* to the house of. *Ps* 55:14
to hearts' lust: they *w.* in. 81:12
O that Israel had *w.* in my ways! 13
in the way I *w.* have they. 142:3
people that *w.* in darkness. *Isa* 9:2
as my servant Isaiah hath *w.* 20:3
that they have *w.* after vanity. *Jer* 2:5, 8
but *w.* in counsels of their evil heart. 7:24; 11:8
after whom they have *w.* 8:2; 9:14 16:11
yet hast not thou *w.* *Ezek* 16:47
hath *w.* in my statutes and. 18:9, 17
thou hast *w.* in the way of. 23:31
hast *w.* in the midst of the. 28:14
way which their fathers *w.* *Amos* 2:4
even the old lion, *w.* *Nah* 2:11

we have *w.* to and fro through the earth. *Zech* 1:11; 6:7
what profit that we have *w.* mournfully? *Mal* 3:14
damsel arose and *w.* *Mark* 5:42
to two of them as they *w.* 16:12
many disciples *w.* no more with him. *John* 6:66
Jesus *w.* no more openly. 11:54
and he leaping up, stood and *w.* *Acts* 3:8; 14:10
a cripple, who never had *w.* 14:8
who think as if we *w.* *2 Cor* 10:2
gain of you? *w.* we not in the same spirit? *w.* we not in? 12:18
but when I saw they *w.* not. *Gal* 2:14
wherein in time past ye *w.* *Eph* 2:2 *Col* 3:7
w. in lasciviousness. *1 Pet* 4:3

he **walked**

to David, as *he w.* before. *1 Ki* 3:6
Abijam *w.* in all the sins of his father. 15:3; *2 Ki* 21:21
for *he w.* in all the ways. *1 Ki* 16:26
he w. in all the ways of Asa. 22:43 *2 Chr* 20:32
and *he w.* in the way of the kings of. *2 Ki* 8:18, 27; 16:3; *2 Chr* 21:6 22:3, 5; 28:2
he w. in the first ways. *2 Chr* 17:3
Nebuchadnezzar *w.* in the palace of. *Dan* 4:29
he willingly *w.* after the. *Hos* 5:11
he w. with me in peace. *Mal* 2:6
Peter *w.* on the water. *Mat* 14:29
to walk even as *he w.* *1 John* 2:6

I have **walked**

and that *I have w.* *Lev* 26:41
I have w. before you from childhood. *1 Sam* 12:2
I have w. in a tent and tabernacle. *2 Sam* 7:6
in all places wherein *I have w.* 7
remember how *I have w.* *2 Ki* 20:3
if *I have w.* with vanity. *Job* 31:5
judge me, for *I have w.* *Ps* 26:1
I have w. in thy truth. 3; *Isa* 38:3

walkedst

when young, *w.* whither. *John* 21:18

walkest

shalt talk of them when thou *w.* *Deut* 6:7; 11:19
day thou *w.* abroad. *1 Ki* 2:42
thou *w.* through the fire. *Isa* 43:2
thou thyself *w.* orderly. *Acts* 21:24
brother grieved, now *w.* *Rom* 14:15
truth in thee even as thou *w.* *3 John* 3

walketh

what man is this that *w.*? *Gen* 24:65
thy God *w.* in midst of. *Deut* 23:14
behold, the king *w.* *1 Sam* 12:2
he is cast into a net, and he *w.* *Job* 18:8
he *w.* in the circuit of heaven. 22:14
goeth in company, and *w.* with. 34:8
blessed the man that *w.* not in. *Ps* 1:1
he that *w.* uprightly shall dwell. 15:2
man *w.* in a vain shew. 39:6
and their tongue *w.* through. 73:9
nor for the pestilence that *w.* 91:6
he that *w.* in a perfect way. 101:6
who *w.* upon the wings of. 104:3
blessed is every one that *w.* 128:1
a wicked man *w.* with a. *Pr* 6:12
w. uprightly *w.* surely. 10:9; 28:18
he that *w.* with wise men. 13:20
he that *w.* in uprightness. 14:2
a man of understanding *w.* 15:21*
better is the poor that *w.* 19:1; 28:6
just man *w.* in his integrity. 20:7
whoso *w.* wisely, he shall. 28:26
the fool *w.* in darkness. *Eccl* 2:14
when he that is a fool *w.* by. 10:3
he that *w.* righteously. *Isa* 33:15
that *w.* in darkness and hath. 50:10
which *w.* in a way that was. 65:2
it is not in man that *w.* *Jer* 10:23
that *w.* after the imagination. 23:17
whose heart *w.* after the heart of their detestable things. *Ezek* 11:21
my words do good to him that *w.* uprightly. *Mi* 2:7

spirit is gone out, he *w.* through dry. *Mat* 12:43; *Luke* 11:24
he that *w.* in darkness. *John* 12:35
from brother that *w.* *2 Thes* 3:6
devil *w.* about seeking. *1 Pet* 5:8
hateth his brother, *w.* *1 John* 2:11
w. in midst of the seven. *Rev* 2:1

walking

voice of Lord *w.* in garden. *Gen* 3:8
Lord knoweth thy *w.* through this great wilderness. *Deut* 2:7
Solomon, *w.* as David. *1 Ki* 3:3
Zimri *w.* in the way of. 16:19
from *w.* up and down in the earth. *Job* 1:7; 2:2
or beheld the moon *w.* in. 31:26
I have seen princes *w.* *Eccl* 10:7
haughty, *w.* and mincing. *Isa* 3:16
and he did so, *w.* naked. 20:2
each one *w.* in his uprightness. 57:2
all grievous revolters, *w.* *Jer* 6:28
I see four men loose, *w.* *Dan* 3:25
if a man *w.* in the spirit and. *Mi* 2:11
Jesus went to them *w.* *Mat* 14:25
saw him *w.* on the sea, they were troubled. 26; *Mark* 6:48
I see men as trees *w.* *Mark* 8:24
w. in all the commandments blameless. *Luke* 1:6
lame man *w.* and leaping. *Acts* 3:8, 9
were edified, *w.* in the fear. 9:31
not *w.* in craftiness, nor. *2 Cor* 4:2
scoffers, *w.* after their own lusts. *2 Pet* 3:3; *Jude* 16
thy children *w.* in truth. *2 John* 4

wall

in their selfwill they digged down a *w.* *Gen* 49:6*
branches run over the *w.* 22
waters were a *w.* to them. *Ex* 14:22
sight lower than the *w.* *Lev* 14:37
a *w.* being on this side, a *w.* on. *Num* 22:24*
Balaam's foot against the *w.* 25
house upon the town *w.* *Josh* 2:15
the *w.* of the city shall fall down flat. 6:5, 20
I will smite David to the *w.* *1 Sam* 18:11; 19:10
sat upon his seat by the *w.* 20:25
they were a *w.* to us both. 25:16
morning light any that pisseth against the *w.* 22*; 34*; *1 Ki* 14:10* 16:11*; 21:21*; *2 Ki* 9:8*
they fastened Saul's body to the *w.* *1 Sam* 31:10
knew ye not that they would shoot from the *w.*? *2 Sam* 11:20
the *w.*, why went ye nigh the *w.*? 21
the people battered the *w.* 20:15
head shall be thrown over the *w.* 21
by my God have I leaped over a *w.* 22:30; *Ps* 18:29
that springs out of the *w.* *1 Ki* 4:33
a *w.* fell upon 27,000 of the. 20:30
dogs shall eat Jezebel by *w.* 21:23*
a burnt offering upon the *w.* *2 Ki* 3:27
a little chamber on the *w.* 4:10
king was passing by upon the *w.* 6:26
was sprinkled on the *w.* 9:33
language in the ears of the people that are on the *w.* 18:26; *Isa* 36:11
then Hezekiah turned his face to the *w.* *2 Ki* 20:2; *Isa* 38:2
Joash brake down the *w.* of Jerusalem. *2 Chr* 25:23
Nebuchadnezzar brake down the *w.* 36:19
who hath commanded you to make this *w.*? *Ezra* 5:3
to give us a *w.* in Judah. 9:9
the *w.* of Jerusalem is. *Neh* 1:3
I viewed the *w.* 2:15
let us build the *w.* 17
break down their stone *w.* 4:3
so built we the *w.*; all the *w.* was. 6
all of us to the *w.*, every one. 15
thou buildest the *w.*, that thou. 6:6
so the *w.* was finished in the. 15
at the dedication of the *w.* of. 12:27
Why lodge ye about the *w.*? 13:21
as a bowing *w.* shall ye be. *Ps* 62:3
as an high *w.* in his. *Pr* 18:11
the stone *w.* thereof was. *Pr* 24:31
standeth behind our *w.* *S of S* 2:9
if she be a *w.*, we will build. 8:9
I am a *w.* 10
of Lord on every fenced *w.* *Isa* 2:15
I will break down the *w.* of. 5:5*
is as a storm against the *w.* 25:4
swelling out in an high *w.* 30:13
we grope for the *w.* like the. 59:10
thee a fenced brasen *w.* *Jer* 15:20
I will kindle a fire in the *w.* of. 49:27
yea, the *w.* of Babylon shall. 51:44
to destroy the *w.* of the. *Lam* 2:8
their heart cried, O *w.* of the. 18
for a *w.* of iron between. *Ezek* 4:3
a hole in the *w.* 8:7
dig in the *w.* 8; 12:5
Israel pourtrayed upon the *w.* 8:10
lo, when the *w.* is fallen. 13:12, 15
accomplish my wrath upon the *w.* 15
every *w.* shall fall. 38:20
after he measured the *w.* of. 41:5
in setting the *w.* between me. 43:8
on the plaster of the *w.* *Dan* 5:5
street shall be built, and the *w.* 9:25*
I will make a *w.* that she shall not find. *Hos* 2:6*
they shall climb the *w.* *Joel* 2:7
they shall run upon the *w.* and. 9
a fire on the *w.* of Gaza. *Amos* 1:7
on the *w.* of Tyrus. 10
in the *w.* of Rabbah. 14
hand on the *w.*, a serpent bit. 5:19
behold, the Lord stood upon a *w.* 7:7
haste to the *w.* thereof. *Nah* 2:5
shall cry out of the *w.* *Hab* 2:11
disciples by night let him down by the *w.* *Acts* 9:25; *2 Cor* 11:33
smite thee, thou whited *w.* *Acts* 23:3
broken down the middle *w.* *Eph* 2:14
the *w.* of the city had twelve foundations. *Rev* 21:14
the building of the *w.* of it was. 18
***see* built**

walled

if a man sell a dwelling house in a *w.* city. *Lev* 25:29
the house in the *w.* city shall. 30
the cities *w.* and very great. *Num* 13:28*; *Deut* 1:28*

wallow

gird thee with sackcloth, *w.* *Jer* 6:26
cry, *w.* yourselves in ashes. 25:34
Moab shall *w.* in his vomit. 48:26
they shall *w.* themselves. *Ezek* 27:30

wallowed

Amasa *w.* in blood in. *2 Sam* 20:12
fell on the ground and *w.* *Mark* 9:20

wallowing

and the sow washed to *w.* *2 Pet* 2:22

walls

if plague be in the *w.* *Lev* 14:37, 39
having no *w.* counted as fields. 25:31
were fenced with high *w.* *Deut* 3:5
till thy high fenced *w.* come. 28:52
men fled between two *w.* *2 Ki* 25:4
Chaldees brake down the *w.* of Jerusalem round. 10; *Jer* 39:8
if this city be built and *w.* set up. *Ezra* 4:13, 16
timber is laid in the *w.* 5:8
heard that the *w.* of Jerusalem. *Neh* 4:7
oil within their *w.* *Job* 24:11
build thou the *w.* of. *Ps* 51:18
they go about it on *w.* thereof. 55:10
peace be within thy *w.* 122:7
broken down, without *w.* *Pr* 25:28
keepers of the *w.* took. *S of S* 5:7
of breaking down the *w.* *Isa* 22:5
the fortress of thy *w.* shall. 25:12
salvation will God appoint for *w.* and bulwarks. 26:1
w. are continually before me. 49:16
w. a place and a name better. 56:5
strangers shall build up thy *w.* 60:10
thou shalt call thy *w.* salvation. 18
I have set watchmen on thy *w.* 62:6
against the *w.* of Jerusalem. *Jer* 1:15
go ye up upon her *w.* and. 5:10
Babylon's *w.* are. 50:15; 51:58
they shall destroy the *w.* of Tyrus. *Ezek* 26:4, 12
of Arvad were upon thy *w.* 27:11
talking against thee by the *w.* 33:30
dwelling without *w.* or gates. 38:11
in the day that thy *w.* *Mi* 7:11
as towns without *w.* *Zech* 2:4
by faith the *w.* of Jericho fell down. *Heb* 11:30

wander

caused me to *w.* from. *Gen* 20:13
children shall *w.* in the wilderness. *Num* 14:33; 32:13; *Ps* 107:40
that causeth blind to *w.* *Deut* 27:18
he causeth them to *w.* in. *Job* 12:24
when his young ravens *w.* for. 38:41
then would I *w.* far off. *Ps* 55:7
let them *w.* up and down. 59:15
O let me not *w.* from thy. 119:10
they shall *w.* every one. *Isa* 47:15
Thus have they loved to *w.* *Jer* 14:10
that shall cause him to *w.* 48:12
shall *w.* from sea to sea. *Amos* 8:12

wandered

Hagar *w.* in the wilderness of Beer-sheba. *Gen* 21:14
they *w.* in the wilderness. *Ps* 107:4 *Isa* 16:8
have *w.* as blind men. *Lam* 4:14
my sheep *w.* through. *Ezek* 34:6
two or three cities *w.* to. *Amos* 4:8
w. about in sheepskins. *Heb* 11:37
they *w.* in deserts, in mountains. 38

wanderers

I will send to him *w.* *Jer* 48:12
they shall be *w.* among. *Hos* 9:17

wanderest

every green tree thou *w.* *Jer* 2:20

wandereth

he *w.* abroad for bread. *Job* 15:23
that *w.* out of the way. *Pr* 21:16
as a bird that *w.* from her nest, so is a man that *w.* from his. 27:8
bewray not him that *w.* *Isa* 16:3
none shall gather up him that *w.* *Jer* 49:5

wandering

was *w.* in the field. *Gen* 37:15
bird by *w.*, as the swallow. *Pr* 26:2
sight of the eyes than the *w.* *Eccl* 6:9
it shall be as a *w.* bird. *Isa* 16:2
to be idle, *w.* about. *1 Tim* 5:13
w. stars to whom is reserved darkness. *Jude* 13

wanderings

thou tellest my *w.* *Ps* 56:8

want

serve thy enemies in *w.* *Deut* 28:48
she shall eat them for *w.* of all. 57
a place where is no *w.* *Judg* 18:10 19:19
they embrace the rock for *w.* of. *Job* 24:8
for *w.* and famine they were. 30:3
if I have seen any perish for *w.* 31:19
there is no *w.* to them. *Ps* 34:9
and thy *w.* as an armed man. *Pr* 6:11; 24:34
fools die for *w.* of wisdom. 10:21*
there is that is destroyed for *w.* of judgement. 13:23*
in *w.* of people is destruction. 14:28
that is hasty only to *w.* 21:5
to rich shall surely come to *w.* 22:16
stricken through for *w.* of. *Lam* 4:9
I have given you *w.* of bread in. *Amos* 4:6
she of her *w.* cast in. *Mark* 12:44
he began to be in *w.* *Luke* 15:14
be a supply for their *w.* *2 Cor* 8:14
not only supplieth the *w.* of. 9:12
not speak in respect of *w.* *Phil* 4:11

want, *verb*

my shepherd, I shall not *w.* *Ps* 23:1
Lord shall not *w.* any good. 34:10
of the wicked shall *w.* *Pr* 13:25
none shall *w.* her mate. *Isa* 34:16
David not *w.* a man to sit. *Jer* 33:17
Levites not *w.* a man. 1
Jonadab shall not *w.* a man. 35·
that they may *w.* bread. *Ezek*

wanted
we have w. all things. Jer 44:18
when they w. wine. John 2:3*
I w. I was chargeable. 2 Cor 11:9

wanteth
shall lend him for his need in that he w. Deut 15:8
that w. understanding. Pr 9:4, 16
in multitude of words there w. 10:19
prince that w. understanding. 28:16
so that he w. nothing for his soul. Eccl 6:2
goblet that w. not liquor. S of S 7:2

wanting
and all his priests, let none be w.: whoso be w. shall not. 2 Ki 10:19
words, yet they are w. to. Pr 19:7*
that which is w. cannot. Eccl 1:15
thou art weighed in the balances, and art found w. Dan 5:27
the things that are w. Tit 1:5
that nothing be w. unto them. 3:13
ye may be perfect and entire, w. nothing. Jas 1:4*

wanton
Zion walk with w. eyes. Isa 3:16
to wax w. against Christ. 1 Tim 5:11
ye have lived in pleasure and been w. Jas 5:5*

wantonness
walk honestly, not in chambering and w. Rom 13:13
they allure through lusts and much w. 2 Pet 2:18*

wants
let all thy w. lie on me. Judg 19:20
that ministered to my w. Phil 2:25*

war
We may distinguish two kinds of wars among the Hebrews. Some were of obligation as being expressly commanded by the Lord; but others were free and voluntary. The first were such as God commanded them to undertake. For example, against the Amalekites and the Canaanites, which were nations devoted to destruction for their sins. The others were undertaken by the captains of the people, to revenge some injuries offered to the nation, to punish some insults or offences. Such was that which the Hebrews made against the city of Gibeah, and against the tribe of Benjamin, which would uphold them in their fault, Judg 20:8. *And such was that which David made against the Ammonites, whose king had affronted his ambassadors,* 2 Sam 10:1-14. *Or to maintain and defend their allies; as that of Joshua against the kings of the Canaanites, to protect the Gibeonites,* Josh 10:6-11.

The common meaning of war, in scripture, is a state of hostility between nations, states, provinces, or parties, as in 1 Ki 14:30; Luke 14:31, *and many other places: but it is taken in a spiritual sense in* 2 Cor 10:3, *where the apostle says,* We do not *war* after the flesh.

when there is w. they join. Ex 1:10
repent when they see w. 13:17
will have w. with Amalek. 17:16
a noise of w. in the camp. 32:17
all that are able to go forth to w. Num 1:3; 20:22; 26:2; Deut 3:18
ye go to w. ye shall blow. Num 10:9
Arm some of yourselves to w. 31:3
1000 shall ye send to w. 4
shall your brethren go to w.? 32:6
armed before the Lord to w. 20, 27
hath God assayed to take him a nation by w.? Deut 4:34
but will make w. against thee. 20:12, 19, 20
when thou goest forth to w. 21:10*
taken a wife, he shall not go to w. 24:5
and the land rested from w. Josh 11:23; 14:15
so is my strength now, for w. 14:11
that Israel might know to teach them w. Judg 3:2
chose new gods, then was w. in. 5:8
not to each his wife in the w. 21:22
was sore w. against Philistines. 1 Sam 14:52; 19:8
for the Philistines make w. 28:15
long w. between the house of Saul and the house of David. 2 Sam 3:1
David demanded how the w. 11:7
shed the blood of w. in peace, and put the blood of w. 1 Ki 2:5
w. between Rehoboam and Jeroboam. 14:30; 15:6
there was w. between Abijam. 15:7
there was w. between Asa and. 16, 32
or be come out for w., take. 20:18
three years without w. 22:1
counsel and strength for w. 2 Ki 18:20
they made w. with the Hagarites. 1 Chr 5:10, 19
many slain, because the w. was. 22
if thy people go to w. 2 Chr 6:34*
no w. to the 35th year. 15:19
house wherewith I have w. 35:21
redeem in w. from power. Job 5:20
changes and w. are against. 10:17*
reserved against the day of w. 38:23
though w. should rise. Ps 27:3
words smooth, but w. was in. 55:21
the people that delight in w. 68:30
I speak, they are for w. 120:7
are gathered together for w. 140:2
good advice make w. Pr 20:18
counsel thou shalt make thy w. 24:6
a time of w., and a time. Eccl 3:8
there is no discharge in that w. 8:8
nor shall they learn w. any more. Isa 2:4; Mi 4:3
thy mighty shall fall in w. Isa 3:25
from the grievousness of w. 21:15
counsel and strength for w. 36:5
hast heard the alarm of w. Jer 4:19
prepare ye w. against her, arise. 6:4
in array as men for w. against. 23*
Nebuchadnezzar maketh w. 21:2
where we shall see no w. 42:14
We are mighty men for w.? 48:14
an alarm of w. to be heard in. 49:2
nor Pharaoh make for him in w. Ezek 17:17
the same horn made w. Dan 7:21
to the end of the w. are. 9:26
prepare w., wake up the. Joel 3:9
as men averse from w. Mi 2:8
they even prepare w. against. 3:5
king going to make w.? Luke 14:31
the beast shall make w. Rev 11:7
there was w. in heaven against. 12:7
to make w. with the remnant of. 17
who is able to make w. with? 13:4
to make w. with saints. 7; 17:14
righteousness doth he make w. 19:11
kings gathered to make w. 19
see **expert, man, men**

war, *verb*
doest me wrong to w. Judg 11:27
he teacheth my hands to w. 2 Sam 22:35; Ps 18:34; 144:1
Rezin and Pekah came up to Jerusalem to w. 2 Ki 16:5; Isa 7:1
they that w. against thee. Isa 41:12
walk in flesh, we do not w. 2 Cor 10:3
that thou mightest w. a. 1 Tim 1:18
of your lusts that w. in. Jas 4:1
ye fight and w. yet ye have not. 2
from lusts which w. 1 Pet 2:11

weapons of **war**
girded on *weapons of w.* Deut 1:41
six hundred with *weapons of w.* Judg 18:11, 16, 17
how are the *weapons of w.* perished! 2 Sam 1:27
better than *weapons of w.* Eccl 9:18
back the *weapons of w.* Jer 21:4
battle axe and *weapons of w.* 51:20
hell with *weapons of w.* Ezek 32:27

ward
put them in w. Gen 40:3, 4, 7
wroth and put me in w. 41:10
Joseph put his brethren in w. 42:17
the blasphemer in w. Lev 24:12
gatherer of sticks in w. Num 15:34
ten concubines in w. 2 Sam 20:3
had kept the w. of the house of Saul. 1 Chr 12:29*
they cast lots, w. against w. 25:8*
lot came by causeway of going up, w. against w. 26:16
to give thanks w. over against w. Neh 12:24
were porters keeping the w. at. 25
kept w. of their God and w. of. 45
set in my w. whole nights. Isa 21:8
Irijah a captain of the w. Jer 37:13
they put Zedekiah in w. Ezek 19:9*
they were past first and second w. Acts 12:10

wardrobe
the wife of Shallum, the keeper of the w. 2 Ki 22:14; 2 Chr 34:22

wards
of the tabernacle by w. 1 Chr 9:23
having w. one against another to minister. 26:12*
I appointed the w. of. Neh 13:30

ware
w. no clothes nor abode. Luke 8:27

ware
Lord shall come in an hour he is not w. of. Mat 24:50
they were w. of it and fled to Lystra. Acts 14:6
coppersmith be thou w. 2 Tim 4:15

ware, *substantive*
if people bring w. on. Neh 10:31
brought all manner of w. 13:16
sellers of all kind of w. lodged. 20

wares
gather up thy w. out of. Jer 10:17
by reason of the multitude of w. Ezek 27:16*, 18*, 33
the mariners cast forth w. Jonah 1:5

warfare
gathered armies for w. 1 Sam 28:1
cry to her that her w. is. Isa 40:2
goeth a w. any time at? 1 Cor 9:7*
the weapons of our w. 2 Cor 10:4
mightest war a good w. 1 Tim 1:18

warm
and the flesh of the child waxed w. 2 Ki 4:34
what time they wax w. Job 6:17
how thy garments are w. 37:17
how can one be w. alone? Eccl 4:11
he will take thereof and w. Isa 44:15
and saith, Aha, I am w. 16
not be a coal to w. at nor fire. 47:14
ye clothe you, but there is none w. Hag 1:6

warmed
he were not w. with fleece. Job 31:20
Peter w. himself. Mark 14:54; John 18:18, 25
depart in peace, be ye w. Jas 2:16

warmeth
ostrich that w. her eggs. Job 39:14
w. himself and saith, Aha. Isa 44:16

warming
when she saw Peter w. Mark 14:67

warn
shall w. them that they trespass not. 2 Chr 19:10
nor speakest to w. Ezek 3:18; 33:8
yet if thou w. wicked. 3:19; 33:9
if thou w. the righteous. 3:21
w. the people 33:3, 7
I ceased not to w. every. Acts 20:31
beloved sons I w. you. 1 Cor 4:14
w. them that are unruly. 1 Thes 5:14

warned
place man of God w. him. 2 Ki 6:10
by them is thy servant w. Ps 19:11
live, because he is w. Ezek 3:21
see and the people be not w. 33:6
Joseph being w. of God departed. Mat 2:12, 22
of vipers, who hath w. you to flee from the wrath? 3:7; Luke 3:7
Cornelius w. from God. Acts 10:22
by faith Noah being w. Heb 11:7

warning
I speak and give w.? Jer 6:10
word and give them w. Ezek 3:17
thou givest him not w. nor. 18, 20
taketh not w. 33:4
he heard and took not w. 5
w. every man, and teaching. Col 1:28

warp
plague in the w. or woof. Lev 13:48
49, 51, 57, 59
burn w. 52
rend w. 56
wash the w. 58

warred
and they w. against the Midianites.
Num 31:7
Balak king of Moab w. Josh 24:9*
Jeroboam, how he w. 1 Ki 14:19
acts of Jehoshaphat, how he w. 22:45
the king of Syria w. 2 Ki 6:8
Uzziah w. against the. 2 Chr 26:6

warreth
no man that w. entangleth. 2 Tim 2:4*

warring
found the king of Assyria w. against.
2 Ki 19:8; Isa 37:8
law in my members w. Rom 7:23

warrior, -s
chosen men who were w. 1 Ki 12:21
2 Chr 11:1
battle of the w. is with. Isa 9:5*

wars
it is said in the book of the w. of the.
Num 21:14
had not known all the w. of Canaan.
Judg 3:1
David, for Hadadezer had w. with
Toi. 2 Sam 8:10; 1 Chr 18:10
hast made great w. 1 Chr 22:8
thou shalt have w. 2 Chr 16:9
he maketh w. to cease. Ps 46:9
ye shall hear of w. and rumours of w.
Mat 24:6; Mark 13:7; Luke 21:9
from whence come w.? Jas 4:1

was
with God and w. not. Gen 5:24
God w. with the lad, he grew. 21:20
that the Lord w. with thee. 26:28
Jacob told Rachel, he w. her. 29:12
thus I w. in the day, drought. 31:40
and behold, Joseph w. not. 37:29
Lord w. with Joseph, he. 39:2, 22
drew near where God w. Ex 20:21
w. not in the company. Num 27:3
as I w. with Moses, so I. Josh 1:5
God be with thee as he w. 17
the Lord w. with Joshua, and. 6:27
as yet I am as strong as I w. 14:11
how w. this wickedness? Judg 20:3
they went where the man of God w.
1 Sam 9:10
the ewe lamb w. unto. 2 Sam 12:3
the counsel of Ahithophel w. 16:23
whose the living child w. 1 Ki 3:26
God be with us as he w. with. 8:57
the Lord w. not in the wind, the Lord
w. not in the earthquake. 19:11
w. not in the fire. 12
king discerned him that he w. 20:41
to Ahab all that w. in my. 2 Ki 10:30
told what he w. to her. Esth 8:1
I w. not in safety, neither. Job 3:26
as I w. in the days of my youth. 29:4
away and lo he w. not. Ps 37:36
I w. as a man that heareth not. 38:14
fear, where no fear w. 53:5
not be such as w. in her. Isa 9:1
people w. not till Assyrian. 23:13
w. not Israel a derision unto thee?
w. he found among? Jer 48:27
I w. no prophet, neither w. I a
prophet's son, but I w. Amos 7:14
I pray thee, Lord, w. not? Jonah 4:2
w. not Esau Jacob's brother? Mal 1:2
such as w. not since the beginning of.
Mat 24:21; Mark 13:19
the roof where he w. Mark 2:4
always night and day he w. 5:5
baptism of John, w. it from heaven,
or of men? 11:30; Luke 20:4
and the Word w. with God, and
the Word w. God. John 1:1
w. the true light, that lighteth. 9
saying, He w. before me. 15, 30
he that w. with thee beyond. 3:26
ascend up where he w. before. 6:62
before Abraham w., I am. 8:58
I am glad for your sakes I w. 11:15
I said, because I w. with you. 16:4
with thee before the world w. 17:5
one of twelve w. not with them. 20:24
full of fishes, yet w. not the. 21:11
after sold, w. it not in thy? Acts 5:4
sold Joseph, but God w. with him. 7:9
what w. I that I could withstand
God? 11:17
near, demanded who he w. 21:33
our word w. not yea. 2 Cor 1:18, 19
I w. not a whit behind chiefest. 11:5
our entrance unto you w. 1 Thes 2:1
our exhortation w. not in deceit. 3
manifest as theirs also w. 2 Tim 3:9
how great this man w. Heb 7:4
the world w. not worthy. 11:38
what manner of man he w. Jas 1:24
from him which is and which w.
Rev 1:4, 8; 4:8
the beast thou sawest w. 17:8, 11
see **so**

it **was**
came to pass as he interpreted, so it
w. Gen 41:13
he it w. sold to all the people. 42:6
now it w. not you that sent me. 45:8
they wist not what it w. Ex 16:15
it w. of the Lord to harden their
hearts. Josh 11:20
I brought Moses word as it w. 14:7
so it w. when Israel had sown.
Judg 6:3
it w. not of the king to. 2 Sam 3:37
but I knew not what it w. 18:29
is my brother's: for it w. 1 Ki 2:15
his hand became as it w. 13:6
perceived that it w. not the. 22:33
left the camp as it w. 2 Ki 7:7
command to Mordecai to know what
it w. and why it w. Esth 4:5
return to earth as it w. Eccl 12:7
it w. but a little that I. S of S 3:4
as it w. to Israel in the. Isa 11:16
from the time that it w. 48:16
his it w. Ezek 16:15
thus it w. saith the Lord. 19
went to see what it w. Mark 5:14
not tell whence it w. Luke 20:7
enquire which of them it w. 22:23
knew not whence it w. John 2:9
was healed wist not who it w. 5:13
and knew not that it w. Jesus. 20:14
21:4
knowing that it w. the Lord. 21:12
not as it w. by one that. Rom 5:16

behold it **was**
God saw every thing, behold it w.
Gen 1:31
looked on earth, behold it w. 6:12
morning, behold, it w. Leah. 29:25
behold it w. not toward Jacob. 31:2
Pharaoh awoke and behold it w. 41:7
for behold it w. in the sack's. 42:27
and behold it w. burnt. Lev 10:16
1 Sam 30:3
behold it w. dead, behold it w. my.
1 Ki 3:21

there **was**
light, and there w. light. Gen 1:3
and there w. not a man to till. 2:5
there w. not found an help meet. 20
there w. a great cry in Egypt, for
there w. not ... there w. Ex 12:30
there w. not a man. Num 26:64
there w. not one city too strong.
Deut 2:36; 3:4
there w. no strange god with. 32:12
there w. not a man left. Josh 8:17
there w. not a word Joshua read. 35
there w. not any left to. 11:11
there w. not a city that made. 19
host of Sisera fell; there w. not a
man left. Judg 4:16
for there w. his house, there he
judged. 1 Sam 7:17
there w. not a man that came not.
2 Ki 10:21
and there w. she slain. 11:16
there w. not one of them left.
Ps 106:11
and there w. the hiding. Hab 3:4
there w. a readiness. 2 Cor 8:11
see **none**

behold there **was**
behold there w. not one of cattle.
Ex 9:7
behold there w. a man told a dream.
Judg 7:13
behold there w. a swarm of. 14:8
behold there w. an image in the bed.
1 Sam 19:16
behold there w. a cake. 1 Ki 19:6
behold there w. no man there.
2 Ki 7:5, 10
behold there w. lifted up a talent of.
Zech 5:7
behold there w. a great earthquake.
Mat 28:2

wash
Since the common foot-coverings of the East were sandals, and the roads were hot and dusty during the dry season and muddy during the rains, it was a necessary custom to see that the feet were washed on entering a house. The common utensils made it hard to wash one's own feet, and as a rule it was the task of a menial, but when one wished to honour his visitor extremely, or to indicate his own humility, he would himself perform the service.

At the Lord's Supper the feet of the Apostles had to be washed; no disciple would acknowledge himself the lowest among them; and it was our Saviour himself who, to give them an example of humility, washed their feet, John 13:5.

Ceremonial washing, *as distinct from washing for cleanliness, was one of the traditions of the Jews,* Heb 9:10. To wash one's feet in butter, *etc.,* Job 29:6; Ps 58:10, *was a figurative expression to indicate a great quantity of these things.* To wash one's hands *was a sign of innocence,* Mat 27:4.

I pray you w. your feet. Gen 18:4
19:2; 24:32
Pharaoh came to w. Ex 2:5
sons thou shalt bring and w. them.
29:4; 30:19, 20, 21; 40:12
shalt w. that whereon it. Lev 6:27
w. the thing wherein the plague is.
13:54
of skin it be, which thou shalt w. 58
shave and w. himself in water. 14:8
Deut 23:11
w. his flesh in water. Lev 14:9; 15:16
16:4, 24; 22:6
if he w. not, he shall bear. 17:16
shall w. their hands. Deut 21:6
w. thyself therefore and anoint.
Ruth 3:3
let thy handmaid be a servant to w.
feet. 1 Sam 25:41
Go down and w. thy feet. 2 Sam 11:8
Elisha said, Go w. in Jordan seven.
2 Ki 5:10
may I not w. in them and be? 12
when he saith to thee, W. and? 13
lavers to w. in, sea for priests to w.
in. 2 Chr 4:6
if I w. myself with snow water.
Job 9:30
I will w. my hands in. Ps 26:6
w. me throughly from mine. 51:2
w. me and I shall be whiter. 7
shall w. his feet in the blood. 58:10
w. you, make you clean. Isa 1:16
w. thee with nitre and. Jer 2:22
O Jerusalem, w. thy heart. 4:14
for whom thou didst w. Ezek 23:40
but when thou fastest, w. Mat 6:17
they w. not their hands when. 15:2

except they *w.* oft they. *Mark* 7:3, 4
a woman began to *w.* his feet with tears. *Luke* 7:38
Jesus said, Go *w.* in the. *John* 9:7, 11
began to *w.* the disciples' feet. 13:5
Lord, dost thou *w.* my feet ? 6
never *w.* my feet. If I *w.* thee not. 8
ye also ought to *w.* one another's. 14
be baptized, and *w.* away thy sins *Acts* 22:16
see **clothes, feet**

washed
gave them water, they *w. Gen* 43:24
Joseph *w.* his face and went out. 31
Judah *w.* his garments in. 49:11
w. as the Lord commanded Moses. *Ex* 40:32
on plague after it is *w. Lev* 13:55
be *w.* the second time and. 58
concubine *w.* their feet. *Judg* 19:21
arose and *w.* himself. *2 Sam* 12:20
w. the chariot in pool. *1 Ki* 22:38
I *w.* my steps with butter. *Job* 29:6
I have *w.* my hands in. *Ps* 73:13
a generation not *w. Pr* 30:12
I have *w.* my feet, how? *S of S* 5:3
his eyes are *w.* with milk and. 12
w. away the filth of the. *Isa* 4:4
nor wast *w.* in water to. *Ezek* 16:4
I throughly *w.* away thy blood. 9
Pilate took water and *w. Mat* 27:24
she hath *w.* my feet. *Luke* 7:44*
marvelled he had not first *w.* 11:38
he went and *w.* and came seeing. *John* 9:7, 11, 15
is *w.* needeth not save to. 13:10
Lord and Master have *w.* 14
whom when they had *w. Acts* 9:37
took them, *w.* their stripes. 16:33
but ye are *w.*, but ye are sanctified. *1 Cor* 6:11
have *w.* the saints' feet. *1 Tim* 5:10
having our bodies *w. Heb* 10:22
sow that was *w.* to her wallowing. *2 Pet* 2:22
that *w.* us from our sins. *Rev* 1:5*
have *w.* their robes and made. 7:14
see **clothes**

washest
thou *w.* away the things. *Job* 14:19

washing
David saw a woman *w. 2 Sam* 11:2
but the fisherman were *w. Luke* 5:2

washing, -s
somewhat dark after *w. Lev* 13:56
that every one put them off for *w. Neh* 4:23*
like sheep which came up from the *w. S of S* 4:2; 6:6
as the *w.* of cups, pots. *Mark* 7:4, 8
cleanse it with *w.* of water. *Eph* 5:26
he saved us, by the *w.* of. *Tit* 3:5
in meats and divers *w. Heb* 9:10

washpot
Moab is my *w. Ps* 60:8; 108:9

wast
thou *w.* a servant in land. *Deut* 5:15
thou *w.* a bondman in the land of Egypt. 15:15; 16:12; 24:18, 22
because thou *w.* a stranger. 23:7
thou *w.* he that leddest. *2 Sam* 5:2
where *w.* thou when I laid the foundations of the earth ? *Job* 38:4
thou art taken and *w.* not. *Jer* 50:24
I said to thee, when thou *w.* in thy blood. *Ezek* 16:6
even thou *w.* as one of them. *Ob* 11
Peter, saying, Thou also *w.* with Jesus. *Mat* 26:69; *Mark* 14:67
when thou *w.* under the fig tree, I saw thee. *John* 1:48
which art, and *w.* and art to come. *Rev* 11:17; 16:5

waste, *adjective*
the desolate *w.* ground and. *Job* 38:27
young lions yelled and made his land *w. Jer* 2:15
for Noph shall be *w.* and. 46:19*
Bozrah shall become a *w.* 49:13
will make Jerusalem *w. Ezek* 5:14*
the land of Egypt shall be *w.* 29 : 9
10 ; 30 : 12
which have been always *w. Ezek* 38:8
empty, and void and *w. Nah* 2:10
have made their streets *w. Zeph* 3:6
mine house that is *w. Hag* 1:9
see **cities, lay, laid, places**

waste, *substantive*
he found him in the *w. Deut* 32:10
solitary, fleeing into the *w. Job* 30:3
Lord maketh the earth *w. Isa* 24:1
I will make *w.* mountains. 42:15
they that made the *w.* shall. 49:17
to what purpose is this *w.*? *Mat* 26:8; *Mark* 14:4

waste, *verb*
meal shall not *w. 1 Ki* 17:14
of wickedness *w.* them. *1 Chr* 17:9
of the wood doth *w.* it. *Ps* 80:13*
w. inhabitants of Pekod. *Jer* 50:21*
shall *w.* the land of Assyria. *Mi* 5:6

wasted
till your carcases be *w. Num* 14:33*
the Kenite shall be *w.* 24:22
of men of war were *w. Deut* 2:14*
barrel of meal *w.* not. *1 Ki* 17:16
Joab *w.* the country of. *1 Chr* 20:1
that *w.* us required of us. *Ps* 137:3
till the cities be *w. Isa* 6:11
and the river shall be *w.* and. 19:5
nations shall be utterly *w.* 60:12
are *w.* and desolate as. *Jer* 44:6
field is *w.*, the corn is *w. Joel* 1:10
the younger son *w.* his. *Luke* 15:13
was accused that he had *w.* his. 16:1
the church and *w.* it. *Gal* 1:13*

wasteness
a day of *w.*, desolation. *Zeph* 1:15

waster
him that is a great *w. Pr* 18:9*
I have created the *w. Isa* 54:16

wastes
they shall build the old *w. Isa* 61:4
cities shall be perpetual *w. Jer* 49:13
that inhabit those *w.* of. *Ezek* 33:24
surely they in the *w.* shall fall. 27
the Lord to the desolate *w.* 36:4
and the *w.* shall be builded. 10, 33

wasteth
man dieth and *w.* away. *Job* 14:10†
nor for destruction that *w. Ps* 91:6
he that *w.* father and. *Pr* 19:26*

wasting
w. and destruction are in. *Isa* 59:7
not heard *w.* nor destruction. 60:18*

watch
Watch *is used in three senses:* [1] *to watch in order to guard,* [2] *to watch, meaning to look for,* [3] *a watch in the night. The night was divided, not into hours, but into* watches. *In the Old Testament, three are named: the* First Watch, *till midnight; the* Middle Watch, *till 3 a.m.; and the* Morning Watch, *till* 6 *a.m. In the New Testament there were four watches of three hours each, from 6 p.m. to 6 a.m. See* **watches.**
morning *w.* Lord looked. *Ex* 14:24
middle *w.*; and they had but newly set the *w. Judg* 7:19
Saul came in the morning *w. 1 Sam* 11:11
so shall ye keep the *w.* of the house. *2 Ki* 11:6, 7; *2 Chr* 23:6
prayed to God and set a *w. Neh* 4:9
one in his *w.* and over against. 7:3
that thou settest a *w.*? *Job* 7:12
a thousand years as a *w. Ps* 90:4
set a *w.* O Lord, before my. 141:3
the *w.* strong, set up. *Jer* 51:12
I will stand upon my *w. Hab* 2:1
in the fourth *w.* of the night Jesus. *Mat* 14:25; *Mark* 6:48
had known what *w.* the thief would. *Mat* 24:43
ye have a *w.* 27:65
sealing the stone, setting a *w.* 66
behold, some of the *w.* came. 28:11
the shepherds keeping *w. Luke* 2:8
in the second *w.* or third. 12:38

watch, *verb*
the Lord *w.* between me. *Gen* 31:49
Saul sent to *w.* David. *1 Sam* 19:11
w. ye, keep the vessels. *Ezra* 8:29
thou not *w.* over my sin ? *Job* 14:16
I *w.* and am as a sparrow. *Ps* 102:7
more than they that *w.* for. 130:6
w. in the watchtower. *Isa* 21:5
and all that *w.* for iniquity. 29:20
a leopard shall *w.* over. *Jer* 5:6
will I *w.* over them to build. 31:28
I will *w.* over them for evil. 44:27
the munition, *w.* the way. *Nah* 2:1
I will *w.* to see what he. *Hab* 2:1
w. therefore, ye know not the hour. *Mat* 24:42; 25:13; *Mark* 13:35
Luke 21:36; *Acts* 20:31
Jesus said, Tarry ye here, and *w.* with me. *Mat* 26:38
could ye not *w.* with me ? 40
Mark 14:34, 37
w. and pray. *Mat* 26:41
Mark 13:33; 14:38; *Col* 4:2
who commanded the porter to *w. Mark* 13:34
unto you, I say unto all, *W.* 37
w. ye, stand fast in faith. *1 Cor* 16:13
let us *w.* and be sober. *1 Thes* 5:6
1 Pet 4:7
w. thou in all things. *2 Tim* 4:5
obey them, for they *w. Heb* 13:17

watched
all my familiars *w.* for. *Jer* 20:10
like as I have *w.* over them. 31:28
w. for a nation that could. *Lam* 4:17
Lord *w.* upon evil, and. *Dan* 9:14
good man would have *w. Mat* 24:43
Luke 12:39
and sitting down they *w. Mat* 27:36
they *w.* him whether he would heal. *Mark* 3:2; *Luke* 6:7; 14:1
they *w.* him and sent forth spies. *Luke* 20:20
w. the gates day and. *Acts* 9:24

watcher, -s
published that *w.* come. *Jer* 4:16
a *w.* and an holy one. *Dan* 4:13
by decree of the *w.* 17
the king saw a *w.* 23

watches
brethren over against them in *w. Neh* 12:9
on thee in the night *w. Ps* 63:6
eyes prevent the night *w.* 119:148
in beginning of the *w.* pour. *Lam* 2:19

watcheth
wicked *w.* the righteous. *Ps* 37:32
end is come, it *w.* for thee. *Ezek* 7:6
blessed is he that *w.* and. *Rev* 16:15

watchful
be *w.*, strengthen the things. *Rev* 3:2

watching
Eli sat on a seat by the wayside *w. 1 Sam* 4:13
blessed heareth me, *w.* daily. *Pr* 8:34
our *w.* we have watched. *Lam* 4:17
centurion *w.* Jesus, saw. *Mat* 27:54
the lord when he cometh shall find *w. Luke* 12:37
praying and *w.* with all. *Eph* 6:18

watchings
in tumults, in labours, in *w.* in fastings. *2 Cor* 6:5
in *w.* often, in hunger, thirst. 11:27

watchman
the *w.* cried and told. *2 Sam* 18:25
the *w.* saw another man running. 26
the *w.* told, he cometh not again. *2 Ki* 9:18, 20
keepeth city, *w.* waketh. *Ps* 127:1
go set a *w. Isa* 21:6
w., what of the night ? 11
set up the *w.*, prepare the ambushes. *Jer* 51:12
Son of man, I have made thee a *w. Ezek* 3:17; 33:7
set him up for their *w.* 33:2
the *w.* of Ephraim was. *Hos* 9:8

watchmen
w. that go about the city found me. *S of S* 3:3; 5:7
w. shall lift up the voice. *Isa* 52:8

his w. are blind, they are. Isa 56:10
I have set w. on thy walls. 62:6
also I set w. over you. Jer 6:17
w. on mount Ephraim shall. 31:6
the day of thy w. and. Mi 7:4

watch tower

when Judah came toward the w. tower. 2 Chr 20:24
watch in the w. tower. Isa 21:5
I stand continually on the w. tower. 8

water

Hagar by a fountain of w. Gen 16:7
let a little w. I pray you, be. 18:4
Abraham took a bottle of w. 21:14
Laban gave the man w. to. 24:32
I pray thee, a little w. to drink. 43
the w. is ours. 26:20
we have found w. 32
Joseph's house gave them w. 43:24
unstable as w., thou shalt not. 49:4
raw, nor sodden with w. Ex 12:9
shall come w. out of the rock. 17:6
any likeness that is in the w. 20:4
bless thy bread and thy w. 23:25
sons shall wash them with w. 29:4
30:20; 40:12; Lev 8:6; 16:4, 24
strawed it on the w. Ex 32:20
shall be scoured and rinsed in w. Lev 6:28; 15:12
vessel, it must be put into w. 11:32
but if any w. be upon the seed. 38
w. that causeth the curse. Num 5:22
sprinkle w. of purification upon. 8:7
for a w. of separation. 19:9, 13, 20
21; 31:23
thou shalt bring forth to them w. out of the rock. 20:8, 10, 11; Neh 9:15
Ps 114:8
this is the w. of Meribah. Num 20:13
24; 27:14
nor is there any w. 21:5
people, and I will give them w. 16
he shall pour the w. out of. 24:7
shall make go through the w. 31:23
to a land of brooks of w. Deut 8:7
the land drinketh w. of rain. 11:11
shalt pour it on earth as w. 12:16
24; 15:23
met you not with w. in way. 23:4
Neh 13:2
melted and became as w. Josh 7:5
he asked w. and she gave. Judg 5:25
bring them down to the w. 7:4, 5
w. came out of the jaw and. 15:19
to Mizpeh and drew w. 1 Sam 7:6
take my bread and my w.? 25:11
take now the cruse of w. 26:11
nor drunk any w. three days. 30:12
we are as w. spilt on. 2 Sam 14:14
pass quickly over the w. 17:21
till w. dropped on them out. 21:10
bread and drank w. 1 Ki 13:19
hast eaten bread and drunk w. 22
as a reed is shaken in the w. 14:15
I pray thee, a little w. 17:10
them with bread and w. 18:4, 13
w. ran about the altar, filled trench with w. 35
fire of the Lord . . . licked up the w. 38
feed him with bread and w. of affliction till I. 22:27; 2 Chr 18:26
the w. is naught, and. 2 Ki 2:19
Elisha, who poured w. on. 3:11
valley shall be filled with w. 17
and the sun shone on the w. 22
the axe head fell into the w. 6:5
set bread and w. before them. 22
he dipped a thick cloth in w.,and.8:15
made a conduit, brought w. 20:20
of Assyria find much w. 2 Chr 32:4
can flag grow without w.? Job 8:11
the scent of w. it will bud. 14:9
drinketh iniquity like w. 15:16
thou hast not given w. to the. 22:7
who drinketh scorning like w. 34:7
I am poured out like w. Ps 22:14
river of God that is full of w. 65:9
through fire and through w. 66:12
have they shed like w. 79:3
round about me daily like w. 88:17
into his bowels like w. 109:18
as when one letteth out w. Pr 17:14
heart of man is like deep w. 20:5
in w. face answereth to face. Pr 27:19
earth that is not filled with w. 30:16
thy wine mixed with w. Isa 1:22
take away the whole stay of w. 3:1
land of Tema brought w. to him that was thirsty. 21:14
not found a sherd to take w. 30:14
though the Lord gave you the w. 20
when the poor seek w. and. 41:17
I will pour w. on him that is. 44:3
dividing the w. before them. 63:12
girdle and put it not in w. Jer 13:1
them drink the w. of gall. 23:15
mine eyes run down with w. Lam 1:16; 3:48
pour out thy heart like w. 2:19
we have drunken our w. for. 5:4
may want bread and w. Ezek 4:17
all knees shall be weak as w. 7:17
21:7
nor wast thou washed in w. to. 16:4
then washed I thee with w. and. 9
then will I sprinkle clean w. 36:25
lovers that give me my w. Hos 2:5
my wrath upon them like w. 5:10
king is cut off as foam upon w. 10:7
of bread nor thirst for w. Amos 8:11
but Nineveh is of old like a pool of w. Nah 2:8
the overflowing of the w. Hab 3:10
with w. unto repentance. Mat 3:11
Mark 1:8; Luke 3:16; John 1:26
Jesus went up out of the w. Mat 3:16; Mark 1:10
whoso giveth a cup of cold w. Mat 10:42; Mark 9:41
bid me come unto thee on the w. Mat 14:28
oft into the fire and w. 17:15
Pilate took w. and washed. 27:24
a man bearing a pitcher of w.: follow. Mark 14:13; Luke 22:10
ship was filled with w. Luke 8:23
rebuked the w. 24
the w. obeyed him. 25
dip the tip of his finger in w. 16:24
Fill the waterpots with w. John 2:7
except a man be born of w. and. 3:5
because there was much w. there. 23
given thee living w. 4:10, 11
give me this w. 15
again where he made w. wine. 46
waiting for the moving of the w. 5:3
down and troubled the w. 4
of his belly shall flow living w. 7:38
after that he poureth w. into a. 13:5
came thereout blood and w. 19:34
for John truly baptized with w. Acts 1:5; 11:16
here is w. 8:36
they went down both into the w. 38
can any forbid w., these be ? 10:47
it with the washing of w. Eph 5:26
blood of calves with w. Heb 9:19
bodies washed with pure w. 10:22
yield salt w. and fresh. Jas 3:12
eight souls were saved by w. 1 Pet 3:20
are wells without w. 2 Pet 2:17
overflowed with w., perished. 3:6
he that came by w. and. 1 John 5:6
witness, Spirit, w. and blood. 8
clouds they are without w. Jude 12
cast out of his mouth w. Rev 12:15
Euphrates, and w. dried up. 16:12
of the fountain of the w. of life. 21:6
me a pure river of w. of life. 22:1
let him take the w. of life freely. 17
see **bathe, bitter, draw, drew, drink, well**

water, verb

a river went out of Eden to w. the garden. Gen 2:10
w. ye the sheep and go and. 29:7, 8
I w. my couch with my. Ps 6:6
come down as showers that w. 72:6
pools of water to w. the. Eccl 2:6
w. thee with my tears. Isa 16:9
I will w. it every moment, lest. 27:3
he might w. it by furrows. Ezek 17:7
I will w. with my blood the land. 32:6
a fountain shall w. the valley of Shittim. Joel 3:18

no water

there was no w. in it. Gen 37:24
they went three days and found no w. Ex 15:22; 17:1; Num 20:2
33:14; Deut 8:15
Lord said, Eat no bread and drink no w. 1 Ki 13:22
was no w. for the host, and. 2 Ki 3:9
thirsty land where no w. is. Ps 63:1
as a garden that hath no w. Isa 1:30
the smith drinketh no w. 44:12
fish stinketh because there is no w. 50:2
cisterns that can hold no w. Jer 2:13
to the pits and found no w. 14:3
there was no w. but mire. 38:6
sent prisoners out of pit wherein is no w. Zech 9:11
thou gavest me no w. for my feet. Luke 7:44

waterbrooks

the hart panteth after the w. Ps 42:1

watercourse

stopped the upper w. 2 Chr 32:30
who hath divided a w.? Job 38:25

watercourses

they shall spring as willows by the w. Isa 44:4

watered

a mist that w. the face. Gen 2:6
Jordan, that it was well w. 13:10
of that well they w. flocks. 29:2, 3
Jacob w. the flock of Laban. 10
Moses helped and w. their flocks. Ex 2:17, 19
he that watereth shall be w. himself. Pr 11:25
shalt be like a w. garden. Isa 58:11
shall be as a w. garden. Jer 31:12
I have planted, Apollos w. 1 Cor 3:6

wateredst

w. it with thy foot as a. Deut 11:10

waterest

the earth and w. it. Ps 65:9
thou w. the ridges thereof. 10

watereth

he w. the hills from his. Ps 104:13
that w. shall be watered. Pr 11:25
rain returneth not, but w. Isa 55:10
neither he that planteth any thing, nor he that w. 1 Cor 3:7, 8

waterflood

let not the w. overflow me. Ps 69:15

watering

rods in the w. troughs. Gen 30:38
by w. he wearieth the thick cloud. Job 37:11*
doth not each of you lead his ass to w.? Luke 13:15

waterpot, -s

set there six w. of stone. John 2:6
Jesus saith, Fill the w. with water. 7
the woman then left her w. 4:28

waters

God moved upon face of w. Gen 1:2
divide the w. from the w. 6, 7
let the w. be gathered. 9
w. bring forth. 20
do bring a flood of w. on earth. 6:17
w. increased. 7:17
w. prevailed. 18, 19, 20, 24
w. decreased. 8:1, 3, 5
w. were dried up. 13
not be cut off any more by w. 9:11
behold, I will smite the w. Ex 7:17
w. were turned to blood. 20
out his hand over the w. 8:6
by a strong east wind the w. 14:21
w. were a wall. 22, 29
w. returned. 28; 15:19
the w. were gathered together. 15:8
they could not drink of the w. of. 23
they encamped there by the w. 27
as cedar trees beside w. Num 24:6
to Jotbath, land of rivers of w. Deut 10:7
ye trespassed at the w. of. 32:51
strive at the w. of Meribah. 33:8
the w. which came down. Josh 3:16
the w. of Jordan were cut off. 4:7
dried up the w. of Jordan. 23; 5:1
pitched at the w. of Merom. 11:5

Canaan by *w.* of Megiddo. *Judg* 5:19
and take the *w.* before them. 7:24
Lord hath broken forth as a breach of *w.* *2 Sam* 5:20; *1 Chr* 14:11
Joab said, I have taken the city of *w.* *2 Sam* 12:27
Elijah smote the *w.* *2 Ki* 2:8, 14
the spring of the *w.*, thus saith the Lord, I have healed these *w.* 21
are not . . . rivers of Damascus, better than all the *w.* of Israel? 5:12
counsel to stop the *w.* *2 Chr* 32:3
are poured out like the *w.* *Job* 3:24
sendeth *w.* upon the fields. 5:10
remember thy misery as *w.* 11:16
he withholdeth the *w.* and. 12:15
as the *w.* fail from the sea. 14:11
the *w.* wear the stones: thou. 19
and abundance of *w.* cover thee. 22:11; 38:34
he is swift as the *w.*; their. 24:18
formed from under the *w.* 26:5
he bindeth up the *w.* in his thick. 8
he hath compassed the *w.* with. 10
terrors take hold on him as *w.* 27:20
the *w.* forgotten of the foot. 28:4
weighed the *w.* by measure. 25
was spread out by the *w.* 29:19
as a wide breaking in of *w.* 30:14
and the breadth of the *w.* is. 37:10
the *w.* are hid as with a stone. 38:30
he leadeth me beside the still *w.* *Ps* 23:2
gathered the *w.* of the seas. 33:7
though the *w.* thereof roar. 46:3
let them melt away as *w.* 58:7
for the *w.* are come in unto. 69:1
w. of a full cup are wrung. 73:10
w. saw thee, O God, the *w.* 77:16
he made the *w.* to stand as. 78:13
and caused *w.* to run down like. 16
he smote the rock, that the *w.* gushed out. 20; 105:41; 114:8; *Isa* 48:21
I proved thee at the *w.* of Meribah. *Ps* 81:7; 106:32
w. stood above the mountains. 104:6
turned their *w.* into blood. 105:29
the *w.* covered their enemies. 106:11
rivers of *w.* run down. 119:136
the *w.* had overwhelmed us. 124:4
then the proud *w.* had gone. 5
him that stretched the earth above the *w.* 136:6
wind to blow and *w.* flow. 147:18
ye *w.* above the heavens. 148:4
drink *w.* out of thine own. *Pr* 5:15
let rivers of *w.* be dispersed. 16
that the *w.* should not pass. 8:29
stolen *w.* are sweet, and bread. 9:17
as cold *w.* to a thirsty soul. 25:25
who hath bound the *w.* in a? 30:4
cast thy bread upon the *w.* *Eccl* 11:1
a well of living *w.* and. *S of S* 4:15
people refuseth the *w.* of. *Isa* 8:6
the Lord bringeth on them *w.* 7
as the *w.* cover the seas. 11:9 *Hab* 2:14
for the *w.* of Nimrim. *Isa* 15:6
for the *w.* of Dimon shall be. 9
like the rushing of mighty *w.* 17:12
and the *w.* shall fail from. 19:5
and ye gathered the *w.* of the. 22:9
w. shall overflow the hiding. 28:17
ye that sow beside all *w.* 32:20
bread be given him, his *w.* 33:16
for in the wilderness shall *w.* 35:6
who hath measured the *w.* in. 40:12
when thou passest through *w.* I. 43:2
a path in the mighty *w.* 16
I give *w.* in the wilderness and. 20
forth out of the *w.* of Judah. 48:1
he caused the *w.* to flow out. 21
which hath dried the *w.* of. 51:10
is as *w.* of Noah unto me, *w.* 54:9
thirsteth, come ye to the *w.* 55:1
like the sea, whose *w.* cast up. 57:20
of water, whose *w.* fail not. 58:11
me the fountain of living *w.* *Jer* 2:13
to drink the *w.* of Sihor? 18
as a fountain casteth out her *w.* 6:7
God hath given us *w.* of gall. 8:14
O that my head were *w.* and. 9:1
eyelids gush out with *w* 18
is a multitude of *w.* in the heavens. *Jer* 10:13; 51:16
nobles sent little ones to the *w.* 14:3
as a liar, and as *w.* that fail? 15:18
as a tree planted by the *w.* 17:8
the Lord, fountain of living *w.* 13
shall the cold flowing *w.* be? 18:14
whose *w.* are moved as the rivers. 46:7, 8
behold, *w.* rise up out of the. 47:2
for the *w.* of Nimrim shall. 48:34
a drought is upon her *w.* and. 50:38
w. flowed over mine head. *Lam* 3:54
is like a vine by the *w.* *Ezek* 19:10
w. made him great, the deep. 31:4
that none of the trees by *w.* exalt. 14
and troublest the *w.* with thy. 32:2
behold, *w.* issued from under. 47:1
brought me through *w.*; the *w.* 3, 4
for the *w.* were risen, *w.* to. 5
these *w.* issue out toward the. 8, 12
even to the *w.* of strife. 19; 48:28
to the man upon the *w.* *Dan* 12:6, 7
calleth for *w.* of sea. *Amos* 5:8; 9:6
let judgement run down as *w.* 5:24
w. compassed me about. *Jonah* 2:5
as *w.* that are poured down. *Mi* 1:4
No, that had the *w.* round? *Nah* 3:8
draw the *w.* for the siege. 14
living *w.* shall go from. *Zech* 14:8
in perils of *w.*, in perils of. *2 Cor* 11:26
lead them unto living fountains of *w.* *Rev* 7:17
the *w.* became wormwood, and many died of the *w.* because. 8:11
have power over *w.* to turn. 11:6
made the fountain of *w.* 14:7
angel poured his vial on the *w.* 16:4
I heard the angel of the *w.* say. 5
the *w.* where the whore sits. 17:15

see **deep, great**

in, or *into* waters

as lead *in* the mighty *w.* *Ex* 15:10
a tree, which when cast *into* the *w.* 25
ye eat of all that are *in* the *w.*: whatsoever hath fins and scales *in* the *w.* *Lev* 11:9; 10:46; *Deut* 14:9
hath no fins nor scales *in* the *w.* unclean. *Lev* 11:12
the likeness of any fish *in* the *w.* *Deut* 4:18; 5:8
of priests rest *in* the *w.* *Josh* 3:13
stone *into* the mighty *w.* *Neh* 9:11
heads of dragons *in w.* *Ps* 74:13
beams of his chambers *in w.* 104:3
and perished *in* the *w.* *Mat* 8:32
him into fire and *into w.* *Mark* 9:22

many waters

seed shall be in *many w.* *Num* 24:7
he drew me out of *many w.* *2 Sam* 22:17; *Ps* 18:16
the Lord is upon *many w.* *Ps* 29:3
than the noise of *many w.* 93:4
many w. cannot quench love, neither can floods. *S of S* 8:7
the rushing of *many w.* *Isa* 17:13
dwellest upon *many w.* *Jer* 51:13
by reason of *many w.* *Ezek* 19:10
like a noise of *many w.*: and the earth shined. 43:2; *Rev* 1:15; 14:2; 19:6
that sitteth on *many w.* *Rev* 17:1

waterspouts

deep at noise of thy *w.* *Ps* 42:7

watersprings

he turneth the *w.* into. *Ps* 107:33
turneth dry ground into *w.* 35

wave

is like a *w.* of the sea. *Jas* 1:6*

wave, *verb*

shalt *w.* them for a wave offering. *Ex* 29:24; *Lev* 23:20; *Num* 6:20
thou shalt *w.* the breast. *Ex* 29:26
w. the shoulder. 27; *Lev* 7:30 8:29; 9:21; 10:15
he shall *w.* the sheaf. *Lev* 23:11, 12
the priest shall *w.* the. *Num* 5:25

waved

w. them for a wave. *Lev* 8:27, 29
take one lamb to be *w.* 14:21

see **breast, loaves, offering**

wavereth

he that *w.* is like a wave. *Jas* 1:6*

wavering

hold fast profession of faith without *w.* *Heb* 10:23
ask in faith, nothing *w.* *Jas* 1:6*

waves

all thy *w.* are gone over me. *Ps* 42:7; *Jonah* 2:3
stilleth the noise of their *w.* *Ps* 65:7 89:9; 107:29
afflicted me with all thy *w.* 88:7
voice, floods lift up their *w.* 93:3
is mightier than mighty *w.* 4*
wind which lifteth up the *w.* 107:25
righteousness as the *w.* *Isa* 48:18
I am the Lord, that divided the sea, whose *w.* roared. 51:15; *Jer* 31:35
though the *w.* toss, yet can. *Jer* 5:22
with the multitude of the *w.* 51:42
when her *w.* do roar like great. 55
as the sea causeth his *w.* *Ezek* 26:3
and shall smite the *w.* *Zech* 10:11
was covered with the *w.* *Mat* 8:24
but the ship was tossed with *w.* 14:24; *Mark* 4:37
signs, the sea and *w.* *Luke* 21:25*
was broken with the *w.* *Acts* 27:41
raging *w.* of sea, foaming. *Jude* 13

wax, *substantive*

my heart is like *w.* *Ps* 22:14
as *w.* melteth, so the wicked. 68:2
the hills melted like *w.* at the. 97:5
the valleys cleft as *w.* *Mi* 1:4

wax

my wrath shall *w.* hot. *Ex* 22:24 32:10
Lord, why doth thy wrath *w.*? 32:11
the anger of my lord *w.* hot. 22
or a stranger *w.* rich by thee, and thy brother by him *w.* *Lev* 25:47
his eyes began to *w.* dim. *1 Sam* 3:2
what time they *w.* warm. *Job* 6:17
though the root thereof *w.* old. 14:8
all of them shall *w.* old. *Ps* 102:26 *Isa* 50:9; 51:6; *Heb* 1:11
his flesh shall *w.* lean. *Isa* 17:4
shall his face now *w.* pale. 29:22
our hands *w.* feeble, anguish hath. *Jer* 6:24
the love of many shall *w.* cold. *Mat* 24:12
provide bags which *w.* *Luke* 12:33
began to *w.* wanton. *1 Tim* 5:11
seducers shall *w.* worse. *2 Tim* 3:13

waxed

(*grew, increased*)

Isaac *w.* great. *Gen* 26:13
famine *w.* sore. 41:56
Israel *w.* exceeding. *Ex* 1:7, 20
and when the sun *w.* hot. 16:21
when the trumpet *w.* louder. 19:19
Moses' anger *w.* hot, and he. 32:19
is the Lord's hand *w.*? *Num* 11:23
raiment *w.* not old. *Deut* 8:4; 29:5 *Neh* 9:21
w. fat, and kicked. *Deut* 32:15
that Joshua *w.* old and. *Josh* 23:1
she that hath many children is *w.* feeble. *1 Sam* 2:5
but David *w.* stronger. *2 Sam* 3:1 *1 Chr* 11:9
and David went down, fought, and *w.* faint. *2 Sam* 21:15
of the child *w.* warm. *2 Ki* 4:34
Abijah *w.* mighty and. *2 Chr* 13:21
Jehoshaphat *w.* great. 17:12
Jehoiada *w.* old. 24:15
Mordecai *w.* greater. *Esth* 9:4
silence, my bones *w.* old. *Ps* 32:3
Damascus is *w.* feeble. *Jer* 49:24
Babylon's hands *w.* feeble. 50:43
the he goat *w.* great. *Dan* 8:8, 9, 10
this people's heart is *w.* gross. *Mat* 13:15; *Acts* 28:27
the child *w.* strong in spirit. *Luke* 1:80; 2:40
a grain of mustard seed *w.* 13:19*
Paul and Barnabas *w.* *Acts* 13:46
w. valiant in fight. *Heb* 11:34
of the earth are *w.* rich. *Rev* 18:3

waxen, waxed

after I am *w.* old shall? *Gen* 18:12
cry of Sodom was *w.* great. 19:13
brother be *w.* poor. *Lev* 25:25, 35, 39

w. fat, then will they turn to other gods. Deut 31:20
of Israel were w. strong. Josh 17:13
become great and w. rich. Jer 5:27
they are w. fat, they shine, they. 28
increased and w. great. Ezek 16:7

waxeth

mine eye w. old because. Ps 6:7
what w. old, is ready. Heb 8:13

waxing

brethren w. confident by. Phil 1:14

way

Is taken in a moral sense, [1] *For* conduct, Ps 1:6. [2] Ways *are put for the laws of the Lord,* Gen 18:19; Ps 18:21. [3] Way *is put for custom, manners, and* way *of life,* Gen 6:12; Jer 10:2. [4] The *method of salvation, or doctrine of the gospel,* Acts 19:9.

To go the *way* of all the earth, *means* dying *and the* grave, Josh 23:14.

Jesus Christ is called the way, John 14:6, *because it is by him alone that believers obtain eternal life.*

if thou do prosper my w. Gen 24:42
to give them provision for the w. 42:25; 45:21
led not through the w. of. Ex 13:17
led the people through the w. 18
of cloud to lead them the w. 21
shew them the w. 18:20; Neh 9:19
Ps 107:4
discouraged because of w. Num 21:4
there was no w. to turn to. 22:26
by what w. we must go. Deut 1:22
Josh 3:4
remember the w. which. Deut 8:2
if the w. be too long for thee. 14:24
return no more that w. 17:16
thou shalt prepare thee a w. 19:3
the w. is long. 6
thou shalt go out one w. 28:25
ye will turn aside from the w. 31:29
behold I am going w. of. Josh 23:14
Lord preserved us in all the w. 24:17
from their stubborn w. Judg 2:19
all that came along that w. 9:25
whether our w. which we go. 18:5
before the Lord is your w. 6
get you early on your w. 19:9
kine took straight w. 1 Sam 6:12
can shew us our w. to go. 9:6*
the man of God to tell us our w. 8
the good and the right w. 12:23
I have gone the w. the Lord. 15:20
thy servant will go a little w. over Jordan. 2 Sam 19:36
I go the w. of all the earth. 1 Ki 2:2
them the good w. to walk. 8:36
nor turn again by the same w. 13:9
he went another w. 10
what w. went he? 12
one w., Obadiah another w. 18:6
which w. went the Spirit of the Lord from me? 22:24; 2 Chr 18:23
which w. shall we go? w. 2 Ki 3:8
departed from him a little w. 5:19
all the w. full of garments. 7:15
taught them the good w. 2 Chr 6:27
to seek of him a right w. Ezra 8:21
to a man whose w. is hid. Job 3:23
to wander where there is no w. 12:24; Ps 107:40
I shall go the w. whence. Job 16:22
hast thou marked the old w.? 22:15
but he knoweth the w. 23:10
God understandeth the w. 28:23
where is the w. where light? 38:19
Lord knoweth the w. of. Ps 1:6
lest ye perish from the w. 2:12
he setteth himself in a w. 36:4
he made a w. to his anger. 78:50
wisely in a perfect w. 101:2, 6
make me understand the w. 119:27
remove from me the w. of lying. 29
I have chosen the w. of truth. 30
I will run the w. of thy. 32
teach me, O Lord, the w. 33; 143:8
I hate every false w. 119:104, 128
be any wicked w. in me. Ps 139:24
the w. of the wicked he turneth. 146:9
he preserveth the w. of. Pr 2:8
to deliver thee from the w. 12
the w. of the wicked is as. 4:19
reproofs of instruction are the w. of life. 6:23; 15:24; Jer 21:8
her corner, he went the w. Pr 7:8
her house is the w. to hell, going. 27
the w. of a fool is right in. 12:15
the w. of the wicked seduceth. 26
but the w. of transgressors. 13:15
there is a w. which seemeth right. 14:12; 16:25
the w. of the wicked is an. 15:9
to him that forsaketh the w. 10
the w. of the slothful man is as an hedge of thorns, but the w. 19
leadeth him into the w. that. 16:29
the w. of man is froward and. 21:8
w. of an eagle, of a serpent. 30:19
such is the w. of an adulterous. 20
knowest not what is the w. of the Spirit. Eccl 11:5
to err and destroy the w. Isa 3:12
w. of the just is uprightness. 26:7
an highway and a w., called w. 35:8
who shewed him the w. of? 40:14
maketh a w. in the sea. 43:16; 51:10
I will even make a w. in the. 43:19
all my mountains a w. 49:11
prepare a w. 57:14
the w. of peace they know not. 59:8; Rom 3:17
cast up the high w. Isa 62:10
where is the good w. Jer 6:16
learn not the w. of heathen. 10:2
I know that the w. of man is not. 23
wherefore doth the w. of the? 12:1
to walk in paths, in a w. not. 18:15
them one heart and one w. 32:39
thy God may shew us the w. 42:3
they shall ask the w. to Zion. 50:5
appoint a w. that the sword may come. Ezek 21:20
saw that they took both one w. 23:13
glory of God came from the w. 43:2
and turn aside the w. Amos 2:7
munition, watch the w. Nah 2:1
he shall prepare the w. Mal 3:1
broad is the w. that leadeth. Mat 7:13
narrow is the w. which leadeth. 14
no man might pass by that w. 8:28
not into the w. of the Gentiles. 10:5
art true, and teachest the w. of God. 22:16; Mark 12:14; Luke 20:21
by what w. they might. Luke 5:19
a certain priest that w. 10:31
he was yet a great w. off. 15:20
for he was to pass that w. 19:4
some other w. is a thief. John 10:1
the w. ye know. 14:4
Lord, how can we know the w.? 5
I am the w., the truth, and the life. 6
which shew to us the w. Acts 16:17
expounded to him w. of God. 18:26
but spake evil of that w. 19:9
no small stir about that w. 23
after the w. which they call. 24:14
to fall in brother's w. Rom 14:13
with the temptation also make a w. to escape. 1 Cor 10:13
unto you a more excellent w. 12:31
our Lord Jesus direct our w. unto. 1 Thes 3:11
the w. into the holiest not. Heb 9:8
by a living w. which he hath. 10:20
she had sent them out another w. Jas 2:25
the w. of truth shall be. 2 Pet 2:2
forsaken the right w. and are gone astray, following the w. of. 15
known the w. of righteousness. 21
that the w. of kings of the. Rev 16:12

by the **way**

befall him by the w. ye go. Gen 42:38
Joseph said, See that ye fall not out by the w. 45:24
a serpent by the w., an adder. 49:17
by the w. in the inn, the. Ex 4:24
you into the wilderness, by the w. of the Red sea. Num 14:25; 21:4
Deut 1:2, 40; 2:1
talk of them, when thou walkest by the w. Deut 6:7; 11:19
Amalek did to thee by the w. 25:17
met thee by the w. 18; 1 Sam 15:2
bring thee by the w. I spake. 28:68
men of war died by the w. Josh 5:4
not circumcised them by the w. 7
nor turn again by the same w. that thou camest. 1 Ki 13:9, 17
a lion met him by the w. and. 24
waited for the king by the w. 20:38
water by the w. of Edom. 2 Ki 3:20
bridle in lips, I will turn thee back by the w. 19:28; Isa 37:29, 34
as lay in wait by the w. Ezra 8:31
have ye not asked them that go by the w.? Job 21:29
pass by the w. plucked her. Ps 80:12
all that pass by the w. spoil. 89:41
when fools walk by the w. Eccl 10:3
bring blind by the w. they. Isa 42:16
that leadeth thee by the w. 48:17
forsaken God when he led thee by the w. Jer 2:17
walk not by the w. for the sword of the enemy. 6:25
came by the w. of gate. Ezek 43:4
prince shall enter by the w. of porch. 44:3; 46:2, 8
he that entereth by the w. 46:9
as a leopard by the w. Hos 13:7
if I send them away fasting, they will faint by the w. Mark 8:3
by the w. he asked his disciples. 27
ye disputed by the w.? 9:33, 34
salute no man by the w. Luke 10:4
he talked with us by the w. 24:32
for I will not see you now by the w. 1 Cor 16:7

every **way**

a flaming sword which turned every w. Gen 3:24
refrained my feet from every evil w. Ps 119:101
I hate every false w. 104, 128
every w. of man right in. Pr 21:2
buildest thine eminent place in the head of every w. Ezek 16:31
much every w. because to. Rom 3:2
every w., whether in. Phil 1:18
see **evil**

his **way**

all flesh had corrupted his w. on earth. Gen 6:12
as for God, his w. is perfect. 2 Sam 22:31; Ps 18:30
condemning the wicked, to bring his w. 1 Ki 8:32; 2 Chr 6:23
this is the joy of his w. Job 8:19
also shall hold on his w. 17:9
who shall declare his w. to? 21:31
his w. have I kept and not. 23:11
hath enjoined him his w.? 36:23
meek will he teach his w. Ps 25:9
who prospereth in his w. 37:7
and he delighteth in his w. 23
wait on the Lord and keep his w. 34
a young man cleanse his w.? 119:9
me in beginning of his w. Pr 8:22
righteousness of the perfect direct his w. 11:5
prudent is to understand his w. 14:8
a man's heart deviseth his w. 16:9
he that keepeth his w. preserveth. 17
of man perverteth his w. 19:3
when he is gone his w., then. 20:14
upright, he directeth his w. 21:29
make his w. prosperous. Isa 48:15
let the wicked forsake his w. 55:7
the destroyer of the Gentiles is on his w. Jer 4:7
to warn the wicked from his wicked w. Ezek 3:18
and he turn not from his wicked w. 3:19; 33:8, 9
not return from his wicked w. 13:22
the Lord hath his w. in. Nah 1:3
himself and goeth his w. Jas 1:24
sinner from the error of his w. 5:20
see **went**

in the **way**

I being in the w. the Lord. Gen 24:27
Lord who led me in the right w. 48

Lord was with me *in the w.* *Gen* 35:3
Rachel buried *in the w.* 19; 48:7
Aaron stood *in the w.* *Ex* 5:20
send angel before thee to keep thee *in the w.* 23:20
who went *in the w.* *Deut* 1:33
you not with bread *in the w.* 23:4
Jeroboam *in the w.* *1 Ki* 11:29
his carcase was cast *in the w.* 13:24
25, 28
he walked *in the w.* of his father. 15:26; 22:52
and walked *in the w.* of Jeroboam. 15:34; 16:2, 19, 26; 22:52
as Obadiah was *in the w.* 18:7
he walked *in the w.* of the kings of. *2 Ki* 8:18; 16:3; *2 Chr* 21:6, 13
he walked *in the w.* of the house of Ahab. *2 Ki* 8:27
and walked not *in the w.* 21:22
three years they walked *in the w.* of David. *2 Chr* 11:17
he walked *in the w.* of Asa. 20:32
help us against the enemy *in the w.* *Ezra* 8:22
to give them light *in the w.* *Neh* 9:12
by day to lead *in the w.* 19
a trap for him *in the w.* *Job* 18:10
nor standeth *in the w.* *Ps* 1:1
will he teach sinners *in the w.* 25:8
shall he teach *in the w.* 12; 32:8
and shalt set us *in the w.* 85:13
my strength *in the w.* 102:23
drink of the brook *in the w.* 110:7
the undefiled *in the w.* 119:1
I have rejoiced *in the w.* 14
and lead me *in the w.* 139:24
in the w. have they privily. 142:3
walk not thou *in the w.* *Pr* 1:15
that thou mayest walk *in the w.* 2:20
I have taught thee *in the w.* 4:11
go not *in the w.* of evil men. 14
lead *in the w.* of righteousness. 8:20
go *in the w.* of understanding. 9:6
he is *in the w.* of life that. 10:17
in the w. of righteousness is. 12:28
him that is upright *in the w.* 13:6
if it be found *in the w.* of righteousness. 16:31
thorns and snares are *in the w.* 22:5
train up a child *in the w.* he. 6
guide thy heart *in the w.* 23:19
saith, There is a lion *in the w.* 26:13
upright *in the w.* is. 29:27
fears shall be *in the w.* *Eccl* 12:5
should not walk *in the w.* *Isa* 8:11
in the w. of thy judgements. 26:8
went on frowardly *in the w.* 57:17
which walked *in the w.* that. 65:2
to do *in the w.* of Egypt ? or what hast thou to do *in the w.*? *Jer* 2:18
in the w. of thy sister. *Ezek* 23:31
so priests murder *in the w.* *Hos* 6:9
agree quickly whiles thou art *in the w.* *Mat* 5:25
garments *in the w.*; **others** strewed branches *in the w.* 21:8
Mark 11:8; *Luke* 19:36
John came *in the w.* of. *Mat* 21:32
to guide our feet *into the w.* of peace. *Luke* 1:79
as thou art *in the w.* give. 12:58
appeared to thee *in the w.* *Acts* 9:17
he had seen the Lord *in the w.* 27
they have gone *in the w.* *Jude* 11
see Lord

my **way**
the Lord hath prospered *my w.* *Gen* 24:56
he maketh *my w.* perfect. *2 Sam* 22:33; *Ps* 18:32
fenced up *my w.* that I. *Job* 19:8
why sayest thou, *My w.*? *Isa* 40:27
hear, O Israel, is not *my w.* equal ? *Ezek* 18:25
I go *my w.* *John* 8:21
brought on *my w.* *Rom* 15:24
to be brought on *my w.* *2 Cor* 1:16*

out of the **way**
turned aside quickly *out of the w.* I commanded them. *Ex* 32:8
Deut 9:12, 16; *Judg* 2:17
the ass turned aside *out of the w.* *Num* 22:23
turn aside *out of the w.* *Deut* 11:28
thrust thee *out of the w.* 13:5
blind to wander *out of the w.* 27:18
the needy *out of the w.* *Job* 24:4
they are taken *out of the w.* 24
step hath turned *out of the w.* 31:7
wandereth *out of the w.* *Pr* 21:16
and through strong drink are *out of the w.* *Isa* 28:7*
get you *out of the w.* 30:11
stumblingblock *out of the w.* 57:14
are departed *out of the w.* *Mal* 2:8
are all gone *out of the w.* *Rom* 3:12
he took the handwriting *out of the w.* *Col* 2:14
he be taken *out of the w.* *2 Thes* 2:7
compassion on them that are *out of the w.* *Heb* 5:2*
is lame be turned *out of the w.* 12:13

own **way**
the fruit of their *own w.* *Pr* 1:31
a man understand his *own w.*? 20:24
every one to his *own w.* *Isa* 53:6
they all look to their *own w.* 56:11
their *own w.* have I. *Ezek* 22:31
they defiled Israel by their *own w.* 36:17

their **way**
take heed to *their w.* to walk before. *1 Ki* 2:4; 8:25; *2 Chr* 6:16
the paths of *their w.* are. *Job* 6:18
his troops raise up *their w.* 19:12
I chose out *their w.*, sat chief. 29:25
let *their w.* be dark. *Ps* 35:6
this *their w.* is their folly. 49:13
perverted *their w.* and. *Jer* 3:21
know and try *their w.* 6:27
their w. shall be to them as. 23:12
do to them after *their w.* and judge. *Ezek* 7:27; 9:10; 11:21
ye shall see *their w.* and. 14:22
as for them *their w.* is not. 33:17
their w. was before me as. 36:17
according to *their w.* and doings. 19
being brought on *their w.* *Acts* 15:3
see went

this **way**
me in *this w.* that I go. *Gen* 28:20
Moses looked *this w.* and. *Ex* 2:12
to flee *this w.* or that. *Josh* 8:20
Elisha said, *This* is not the *w.*; follow me. *2 Ki* 6:19
saying, *This* is the *w.*, walk ye in it. *Isa* 30:21
if he found any of *this w.* *Acts* 9:2
I persecuted *this w.* unto the. 22:4

thy **way**
Lord will prosper *thy w.* *Gen* 24:40
I pray, shew me *thy w.* *Ex* 33:13
thy w. is perverse. *Num* 22:32
make *thy w.* prosperous. *Josh* 1:8
return on *thy w.* to the wilderness. *1 Ki* 19:15
make *thy w.* straight. *Ps* 5:8
teach me *thy w.* O Lord, lead me. 27:11; 86:11
commit *thy w.* unto the Lord. 37:5
our steps declined from *thy w.* 44:18
that *thy w.* may be known. 67:2
thy w. O God, is in the. 77:13
thy w. is in the sea, thy path in. 19
quicken thou me in *thy w.* 119:37
thou walk in *thy w.* safely. *Pr* 3:23
remove *thy w.* far from her. 5:8
in the greatness of *thy w.* *Isa* 57:10
see *thy w.* in the valley. *Jer* 2:23
why trimmest thou *thy w.* to ? 33
thou about to change *thy w.*? 36
thy w. have procured these. 4:18
will recompense *thy w.* *Ezek* 16:43
I will hedge up *thy w.* *Hos* 2:6
thou didst trust in *thy w.* 10:13
messenger, who shall prepare *thy w.* *Mat* 11:10; *Mark* 1:2; *Luke* 7:27

wayfaring
he saw a *w.* man in the. *Judg* 19:17
his own flock, to dress for the *w.* man. *2 Sam* 12:4
highways lie waste, the *w.* *Isa* 33:8
w. men, though fools, shall. 35:8
a lodging place of *w.* men. *Jer* 9:2
thou be as a *w.* man ? 14:8

waymarks
set thee up *w.*, make thee. *Jer* 31:21

ways
shall rise early and go on your *w.* *Gen* 19:2
walk in all the *w.* Lord. *Deut* 5:33
walked in the *w.* of Asa. *1 Ki* 22:43
he walked in all the *w.* of Manasseh. *2 Ki* 21:21
he walked in all the *w.* of David. 22:2
2 Chr 17:3; 34:2
not walked in the *w.* of. *2 Chr* 21:12
walked in the *w.* of the house. 22:3
he walked in the *w.* of the kings. 28:2
they know not the *w.* of. *Job* 24:13
they raise up the *w.* of their. 30:12
eyes are upon the *w.* of men. 34:21
the chief of the *w.* of God. 40:19
heart are the *w.* of them. *Ps* 84:5
so are the *w.* of every one greedy. *Pr* 1:19
to walk in the *w.* of darkness. 2:13
whose *w.* are crooked, and they. 15
wisdom's *w.* are *w.* of. 3:17
paths . . . her *w.* are moveable. 5:6
w. of man are before the eyes. 21
go to the ant, consider her *w.* 6:6
heart decline to her *w.* 7:25
the end thereof are the *w.* of death. 14:12; 16:25
the *w.* of man are clean in his. 16:2
when a man's *w.* please the Lord. 7
taketh a gift to pervert the *w.* 17:23
she looketh well to the *w.* of. 31:27
O young man, walk in the *w.* of thy heart. *Eccl* 11:9
they shall feed in the *w.* *Isa* 49:9
traversing her *w.* *Jer* 2:23
in the *w.* hast thou sat for. 3:2
stand in the *w.* and see, ask. 6:16
amend your *w.* and your doings. 7:3, 5; 26:13
walk in all the *w.* I have. 7:23
if they diligently learn the *w.* 12:16
make your *w.* and your doings. 18:11
thine eyes are open on the *w.* of. 32:19
the *w.* of Zion do mourn. *Lam* 1:4
let us search and try our *w.* 3:40
are not your *w.* unequal ? *Ezek* 18:25, 29
shall ye remember your *w.* 20:43
your wicked *w.* or doings. 44
son of man, appoint thee two *w.*, that the sword may. 21:19
stood at head of the two *w.* to use. 21
consider your *w.* *Hag* 1:5, 7
do to us according to our *w.* and. *Zech* 1:6
and the rough *w.* shall. *Luke* 3:5
known to me the *w.* of life. *Acts* 2:28
see by-ways, evil, high, seven

any **ways**
do *any w.* hide their eyes. *Lev* 20:4
if ye shall *any w.* make. *Num* 30:15
any w. able to deliver. *2 Chr* 32:13

his **ways**
of Lord, to walk in *his w.* and fear him. *Deut* 8:6; 26:17; 28:9
30:16; *1 Ki* 2:3
to walk in all *his w.* *Deut* 10:12
11:22; *Josh* 22:5; *1 Ki* 8:58
and walk ever in *his w.* *Deut* 19:9
all *his w.* are judgement. 32:4
Dan 4:37
walked not in *his w.* *1 Sam* 8:3
David behaved wisely in *his w.* 18:14
and give to every man according to *his w.* *1 Ki* 8:39; *2 Chr* 6:30
and *his w.* are written. *2 Chr* 13:22
Jotham prepared *his w.* before. 27:6
his w. are written in book. 7; 28:26
these are parts of *his w.* *Job* 26:14
man find according to *his w.* 34:11
not consider any of *his w.* 27
his w. are always grievous. *Ps* 10:5
he made known *his w.* unto Moses. 103:7
iniquity, they walk in *his w.* 119:3
one that walketh in *his w.* 128:1
is righteous in all *his w.* 145:17

choose none of *his w.* *Pr* 3:31
he that perverteth *his w.* 10:9
he that is perverse in *his w.* 14:2
he that despiseth *his w.* shall. 19:16
lest thou learn *his w.* and. 22:25
that is perverse in *his w.* 28:6
he that is perverse in *his w.* shall. 18
he will teach us of *his w.* *Isa* 2:3
Mi 4:2
they would not walk in *his w.* *Isa* 42:24
I will direct all *his w.* saith. 45:13
seen *his w.* and will heal. 57:18
give every man according to *his w.*
Jer 17:10; 32:19
that he should return from *his w.*
Ezek 18:23
I will judge Israel according to *his w.* 30; 33:20
of a fowler in all *his w.* *Hos* 9:8
punish Jacob according to *his w.* 12:2
march on every one in *his w.* *Joel* 2:7
the hills did bow, *his w.* *Hab* 3:6
thou shalt go before the Lord to prepare *his w.* *Luke* 1:76
his w. are past finding. *Rom* 11:33
man is unstable in all *his w.* *Jas* 1:8
rich man fade away in *his w.* 11
see **Lord**

my **ways**

if thou wilt walk in *my w.* as thy father. *1 Ki* 3:14; 11:38; *Zech* 3:7
and not walked in *my w.* *1 Ki* 11:33
doth not he see *my w.*? *Job* 31:4
I will take heed to *my w.* *Ps* 39:1
Israel had walked in *my w.* 81:13
they have not known *my w.* 95:10
Heb 3:10
O that *my w.* were directed. *Ps* 119:5
I have declared *my w.* and thou. 26
I thought on *my w.* and turned. 59
all *my w.* are before thee. 168
acquainted with all *my w.* 139:3
blessed are they that keep *my w.*
Pr 8:32
let thine eyes observe *my w.* 23:26
neither are your ways *my w.* *Isa* 55:8
so are *my w.* higher than your. 9
and delight to know *my w.* 58:2
he hath inclosed *my w.* *Lam* 3:9
he turned aside *my w.* and. 11
my w. equal, your *w.*? *Ezek* 18:29
if thou wilt walk in *my w.* *Zech* 3:7
ye have not kept *my w.* *Mal* 2:9
remembrance of *my w.* *1 Cor* 4:17

own **ways**

I will maintain my *own w.* *Job* 13:15
be filled with his *own w.* *Pr* 14:14
not doing thine *own w.* *Isa* 58:13
have chosen their *own w.* 66:3
then remember your *own* evil *w.*
Ezek 36:31
be ashamed for your *own w.* 32
nations to walk in *own w.* *Acts* 14:16

their **ways**

pray and turn from *their* wicked *w.*
2 Chr 7:14
eyes are upon *their w.* *Job* 24:23
turn to *their* crooked *w.* *Ps* 125:5
who go right on *their w.* *Pr* 9:15
return not from *their w.* *Jer* 15:7
mine eyes are upon all *their w.* 16:17
them to stumble in *their w.* 18:15
comfort you when ye see *their w.*
Ezek 14:23
not walked after *their w.* 16:47
punish them for *their w.* *Hos* 4:9
misery are in *their w.* *Rom* 3:16
follow *their* pernicious *w.* *2 Pet* 2:2

thy **ways**

not prosper in *thy w.* *Deut* 28:29
sons walk not in *thy w.* *1 Sam* 8:5
may fear thee to walk in *thy w.*
2 Chr 6:31
uprightness of *thy w.* *Job* 4:6
the knowledge of *thy w.* 21:14
thou makest *thy w.* perfect? 22:3
light shall shine upon *thy w.* 28
shew me *thy w.* O Lord. *Ps* 25:4
I teach transgressors *thy w.* 51:13
to keep thee in all *thy w.* 91:11
have respect unto *thy w.* 119:15
in all *thy w.* acknowledge him. *Pr* 3:6
let *thy w.* be established. *Pr* 4:26
nor *thy w.* to that which destroyeth kings. 31:3
made us err from *thy w.* *Isa* 63:17
remember thee in *thy w.* 64:5
taught the wicked *thy w.* *Jer* 2:33
thou hast scattered *thy w.* 3:13
judge thee according to *thy w.*
Ezek 7:3, 4, 8, 9
corrupted more than they in all *thy w.* 16:47
then remember *thy w.* and be. 61
according to *thy w.* shall they. 24:14
thou wast perfect in *thy w.* 28:15
whose hand are all *thy w.* *Dan* 5:23
just and true are *thy w.* *Rev* 15:3

way *side*

where is harlot that was by the *w. side*? *Gen* 38:21
Eli sat on a seat by the *w. side* watching. *1 Sam* 4:13
the proud have spread a net by the *w. side.* *Ps* 140:5
seeds fell by the *w. side.* *Mat* 13:4
19; *Mark* 4:4, 15; *Luke* 8:5, 12
two blind men sitting by the *w. side.*
Mat 20:30
blind Bartimaeus sat by the high *w. side.* *Mark* 10:46; *Luke* 18:35

we

been about cattle, *w.* and. *Gen* 46:34
the men said, We be not able; for they are stronger than *w.* *Num* 13:31
greater and taller than *w.* *Deut* 1:28
that *w.* may be like all. *1 Sam* 8:20
w. will be with thee, be. *Ezra* 10:4
w. his servants will arise. *Neh* 2:20
w., our sons and our daughters. 5:2
w. after our ability have. 8
w. are but of yesterday. *Job* 8:9
w. are his people, sheep. *Ps* 100:3
become weak as *w.* are? *Isa* 14:10
w. are thine. 63:19
for *w.* are many. *Mark* 5:9
why could not *w.* cast him out? 9:28
that *w.* being delivered. *Luke* 1:74
w. be Abraham's seed. *John* 8:33
thou art his disciple, *w.* are. 9:28
are *w.* blind also? 40
they may be one as *w.* 17:11, 22
and *w.* are his witnesses. *Acts* 5:32
10:39
the Holy Ghost as well as *w.* 10:47
w. are men of like passions. 14:15
w., or ever he come, are ready. 23:15
w., being many, are one body in Christ. *Rom* 12:5
w. that are strong ought to bear. 15:1
w. are labourers together. *1 Cor* 3:9
w. are fools, but ye are wise, *w.* 4:10
w. bless, persecuted, *w.* suffer it. 12
w. in him; one Lord and *w.* by. 8:6
are not *w.* rather? 9:12
w. being many are one bread. 10:17
do *w.* provoke Lord, are *w.*? 22
w. are your rejoicing. *2 Cor* 1:14
w., that *w.* say not, ye, should. 9:4
Christ's, so are *w.* Christ's. 10:7
they may be found even as *w.* 11:12
though *w.* or an angel. *Gal* 1:8
so *w.*, when *w.* were children. 4:3
now *w.*, as Isaac, are the children. 28
w. are his workmanship. *Eph* 2:10
w. which are alive shall be caught in . . . so shall *w.* ever. *1 Thes* 4:17
w. are not of the night nor of. 5:5
whose house are *w.* if *w.* hold fast.
Heb 3:6
w. are not of them who draw. 10:39
w. are of God. Hereby *w.* *1 John* 4:6
w. know that *w.* are of God. 5:19

weak

they be strong or *w.* *Num* 13:18
then shall I be *w.* as other men.
Judg 16:7, 11, 17
I am this day *w.* though. *2 Sam* 3:39
let not your hands be *w.* *2 Chr* 15:7*
strengthened the *w.* hands. *Job* 4:3
I am *w.* *Ps* 6:2*
my knees are *w.* 109:24
also become *w.* as we? *Isa* 14:10
strengthen ye the *w.* hands. 35:3
shall be *w.* as water. *Ezek* 7:17; 21:7
how *w.* is thy heart? *Ezek* 16:30
the *w.* say, I am strong. *Joel* 3:10
but the flesh is *w.* *Mat* 26:41
Mark 14:38
ought to support the *w.* *Acts* 20:35
being not *w.* in faith, he. *Rom* 4:19
for the law was *w.* through the. 8:3
him that is *w.* in the faith. 14:1
another who is *w.* eateth herbs. 2
brother stumbleth or is made *w.* 21
bear the infirmities of the *w.* 15:1
w. things to confound the. *1 Cor* 1:27
we are *w.* 4:10
conscience being *w.* 8:7, 10
wound their *w.* conscience. 12
to the *w.* became I as *w.*, that I might gain the *w.*: I am made. 9:22
for this cause many are *w.* 11:30
bodily presence is *w.* *2 Cor* 10:10
I speak as though we had been *w.*
11:21
who is *w.* and I am not *w.*? 29
for when I am *w.* then am I. 12:10
which to you-ward is not *w.* but. 13:3
for we are *w.* in him, but shall live. 4
are glad when we are *w.* 9
how turn ye again to the *w.*? *Gal* 4:9
support the *w.*, be patient toward all. *1 Thes* 5:14

weaken

which didst *w.* nations. *Isa* 14:12*

weakened

of the land *w.* Judah. *Ezra* 4:4
their hands shall be *w.* *Neh* 6:9
he *w.* my strength in. *Ps* 102:23

weakeneth

he *w.* the strength of. *Job* 12:21*
he *w.* the hands of the men of war.
Jer 38:4

weaker

Saul's house *w.* and *w.* *2 Sam* 3:1
to the wife as the *w.* vessel. *1 Pet* 3:7

weak handed

while he is *w. handed.* *2 Sam* 17:2

weakness

the *w.* of God is stronger. *1 Cor* 1:25
I was with you in *w.* and. 2:3
it is sown in *w.*; it is raised. 15:43
made perfect in *w.* *2 Cor* 12:9
though crucified through *w.* 13:4
going before for the *w.* *Heb* 7:18
out of *w.* were made strong. 11:34

wealth

of Jacob took all their *w.* *Gen* 34:29
my hand got me this *w.* *Deut* 8:17
giveth thee power to get *w.* 18
kinsman, a man of *w.* *Ruth* 2:1
thou shalt see an enemy in all the *w.*
1 Sam 2:32
Menahem exacted money of men of *w.* *2 Ki* 15:20
thou hast not asked *w.* *2 Chr* 1:11
I will give thee riches, and *w.* 12
nor seek their peace or *w.* for ever.
Ezra 9:12*
Mordecai seeking the *w.* *Esth* 10:3*
spend their days in *w.* *Job* 21:13*
if I rejoiced because my *w.* was great. 31:25
and dost not increase *w.* *Ps* 44:12
they that trust in *w.* and boast. 49:6
die and leave their *w.* to others. 10
w. and riches shall be in his. 112:3
lest strangers be filled with thy *w.*
Pr 5:10*
rich man's *w.* is his. 10:15; 18:11
w. gotten by vanity shall be. 13:11
the *w.* of the sinner is laid up. 22
w. maketh many friends, the. 19:4
God hath given *w.* *Eccl* 5:19; 6:2
w. of all the heathen shall be.
Zech 14:14
this craft we have *w.* *Acts* 19:25
but seek every man another's *w.*
1 Cor 10:24*

common **wealth**

being aliens from the *common w.* of Israel. *Eph* 2:12

wealthy

us out into a *w.* place. *Ps* 66:12
up into the *w.* nation. *Jer* 49:31*

weaned
Isaac grew and was *w.* *Gen* 21:8
not go till the child be *w.* *1 Sam* 1:22
whom Tahpenes *w.* in. *1 Ki* 11:20
as a child that is *w.* of his mother, my soul is as a *w.* child. *Ps* 131:2
the *w.* child put his hand. *Isa* 11:8
that are *w.* from the milk. 28:9
when she *w.* Lo-ruhama. *Hos* 1:8

weapon
a paddle upon thy *w.* *Deut* 23:13
other hand held a *w.* *Neh* 4:17
flee from the iron *w.* *Job* 20:24
no *w.* formed against thee. *Isa* 54:17
with his destroying *w.* *Ezek* 9:1, 2

weapons
take, I pray thee, thy *w.* *Gen* 27:3
neither my sword nor *w.* *1 Sam* 21:8
round about, every man with his *w.* in. *2 Ki* 11:8, 11; *2 Chr* 23:7, 10
even the Lord and the *w.* of his indignation. *Isa* 13:5; *Jer* 50:25
every one with his *w.* *Jer* 22:7
on fire and burn *w.* *Ezek* 39:9, 10
with lanterns and *w.* *John* 18:3
the *w.* of our warfare. *2 Cor* 10:4
see **war**

wear
thou wilt surely *w.* away. *Ex* 18:18
woman not *w.* what. *Deut* 22:5
thou shalt not *w.* garment of. 11
to burn incense, to *w.* an. *1 Sam* 2:28
85 persons that did *w.* an. 22:18
royal apparel the king useth to *w.* *Esth* 6:8
the waters *w.* the stones. *Job* 14:19
we eat our own bread and *w* *Isa* 4:1
shall *w.* out the saints of. *Dan* 7:25
nor shall they *w.* a rough garment. *Zech* 13:4
that *w.* soft clothing are. *Mat* 11:8
day began to *w.* away. *Luke* 9:12

weareth
ye respect him that *w.* the. *Jas* 2:3

wearied
they *w.* themselves to. *Gen* 19:11
nor have I *w.* thee with. *Isa* 43:23
thou hast *w.* me with thine. 24
thou art *w.* in the multitude of. 47:13
thou art *w.* in the greatness of. 57:10
my soul is *w.* because of. *Jer* 4:31*
w. thee? If in land of peace, wherein thou trustedst, they *w.* thee. 12:5
she hath *w.* herself with lies. *Ezek* 24:12
wherein have I *w.* thee? *Mi* 6:3
w. the Lord. Yet ye say, Wherein have we *w.* him? *Mal* 2:17
Jesus being *w.* sat thus. *John* 4:6
lest ye be *w.* and faint in. *Heb* 12:3

wearieth
by watering he *w.* the. *Job* 37:11*
labour of the foolish *w.* *Eccl* 10:15

weariness
much study is a *w.* of. *Eccl* 12:12
be said, What a *w.* is it! *Mal* 1:13
in *w.* and painfulness. *2 Cor* 11:27*

wearing
in Shiloh *w.* an ephod. *1 Sam* 14:3
Jesus came forth *w.* the. *John* 19:5
let it not be *w.* of gold. *1 Pet* 3:3

wearisome
and *w.* nights are appointed. *Job* 7:3

weary
Rebekah said, I am *w.* *Gen* 27:46
Amalek smote thee, when thou wast *w.* *Deut* 25:18
Sisera was fast asleep and *w.* *Judg* 4:21*
bread unto thy men that are *w.*? 8:15
all the people came *w.* *2 Sam* 16:14
upon him while he is *w.* 17:2
Philistines till his hand was *w.* 23:10
wicked cease, and the *w.* *Job* 3:17
my soul is *w.* of my life, leave. 10:1
now he hath made me *w.* 16:7
not given water to *w.* to drink. 22:7
I am *w.* with my groaning, I. *Ps* 6:6
confirm thy inheritance when *w.* 68:9
w. of my crying my throat. 69:3
my son, be not *w.* of Lord's. *Pr* 3:11
lest he be *w.* of thee, and so. 25:17
feasts are trouble, I am *w.* *Isa* 1:14
none shall be *w.* nor stumble. 5:27
to *w.* men, but will ye *w.*? 7:13
it is seen that Moab is *w.* in. 16:12
ye may cause the *w.* to rest. 28:12
of a great rock in a *w.* land. 32:2
fainteth not, neither is *w.* 40:28
the youths shall faint and be *w.* 30
they shall run, and not be *w.* 31
but thou hast been *w.* of me. 43:22
a burden to the *w.* beast. 46:1
in season to him that is *w.* 50:4
all that seek her will not *w.* *Jer* 2:24
I am *w.* with holding in, I will. 6:11
they *w.* themselves to commit. 9:5
will destroy thee, I am *w.* 15:6
I was *w.* with forbearing, I. 20:9
I have satiated the *w.* soul. 31:25
labour in the fire and be *w.* 51:58
Babylon sink: and they shall be *w.* 64
w. themselves for vanity. *Hab* 2:13
lest by her continual coming she *w.* me. *Luke* 18:5*
let us not be *w.* in well doing. *Gal* 6:9; *2 Thes* 3:13

weasel
the *w.* and the mouse. *Lev* 11:29

weather
fair *w.* cometh out of. *Job* 37:22*
a garment in cold *w.* *Pr* 25:20
it will be fair *w.*: for the. *Mat* 16:2
it will be foul *w.* to day. 3

weave
they that *w.* networks. *Isa* 19:9
cockatrice' eggs and *w.* spider's. 59:5

weaver
to work the work of *w.* *Ex* 35:35
Goliath's spear was like a *w.*'s beam. *1 Sam* 17:7; *2 Sam* 21:19
1 Chr 11:23; 20:5
swifter than a *w.*'s shuttle. *Job* 7:6
I have cut off like a *w.* *Isa* 38:12

weavest
if thou *w.* seven locks. *Judg* 16:13

web
seven locks with the *w.* *Judg* 16:13
with pin of beam and the *w.* 14
trust shall be a spider's *w.* *Job* 8:14
weave the spider's *w.* *Isa* 59:5

webs
their *w.* shall not become. *Isa* 59:6

wedding
that were bidden to *w.* *Mat* 22:3*
the *w.* is ready. 8
the *w.* is furnished. 10
that had not on a *w.* garment. 11
will return from the *w.* *Luke* 12:36*
bidden of any man to a *w.* 14:8*

wedge
Achan saw a *w.* of gold. *Josh* 7:21
Joshua took Achan and the *w.* 24
precious than golden *w.* *Isa* 13:12*

wedlock
as women that break *w.* *Ezek* 16:38

weeds
the *w.* were wrapped. *Jonah* 2:5

week
The Hebrews had three sorts of weeks. [1] Weeks *of days, which were reckoned from one sabbath to another.* [2] Weeks *of years, which were reckoned from one sabbatical year to another, and which consisted of seven years.* [3] Weeks *of seven times seven years, or* of *forty nine years, which are reckoned from* one *jubilee to another.*
fulfil her *w.* *Gen* 29:27
and fulfilled her *w.* 28
covenant with many for one *w.*: and in the midst of the *w.* *Dan* 9:27
to dawn toward the first day of the *w.* *Mat* 28:1; *Mark* 16:2, 9
Luke 24:1; *John* 20:1, 19
I fast twice in the *w.* *Luke* 18:12
the first day of the *w.* Paul preached. *Acts* 20:7
on the first day of the *w.* *1 Cor* 16:2

weeks
shall be unclean two *w.* *Lev* 12:5
bring a meat offering after your *w.* *Num* 28:26
appointed *w.* of harvest. *Jer* 5:24
seventy *w.* are determined on thy people. *Dan* 9:24
threescore and two *w.* 25, 26
mourning three full *w.* 10:2
till three *w.* were fulfilled. 3
see **feast, seven**

weep
(*Weeping and other open expressions of emotion, whether of joy or sorrow, were common among the people of the East, contrary to the repression common in the West. The louder the wail the greater the grief. For that reason men and women were hired to weep and wail at funerals*)
mourn and *w.* for Sarah. *Gen* 23:2
did yearn, sought where to *w.* 43:30
Moses heard the people *w.* throughout their families. *Num* 11:10
they *w.* unto me, saying, Give. 13
what aileth the people that they *w.*? *1 Sam* 11:5
they had no more power to *w.* 34
Israel, *w.* over Saul. *2 Sam* 1:24
thou didst *w.* for the child. 12:21
and didst rend thy clothes, and *w.* *2 Chr* 34:27
mourn not, nor *w.* *Neh* 8:9
widows shall not *w.* *Job* 27:15*
did not I *w.* for him that? 30:25
into the voice of them that *w.* 31
a time to *w.* and a time. *Eccl* 3:4
to the high places to *w.* *Isa* 15:2
I will *w.* bitterly, labour not to. 22:4
thou shalt *w.* no more, he will. 30:19
of peace shall *w.* bitterly. 33:7
that I might *w.* day and. *Jer* 9:1
not hear it, my soul shall *w.* in secret places . . . shall *w.* sore. 13:17
w. ye not for the dead, nor bemoan him: but *w.* sore for him that. 22:10
Sibmah, I will *w.* for thee. 48:32
for these things I *w.* *Lam* 1:16
nor shalt thou mourn nor *w.* *Ezek* 24:16, 23
w. for thee with bitterness. 27:31
awake, ye drunkards, *w.* *Joel* 1:5
let the priests *w.* between the. 2:17
declare it not in Gath, *w.* *Mi* 1:10
should I *w.* in fifth month. *Zech* 7:3
ye this ado, and *w.*? *Mark* 5:39
blessed are ye that *w.* *Luke* 6:21
to you that laugh now, ye shall *w.* 25
Lord saw her and said, *W.* not. 7:13; 8:52; *Rev* 5:5
w. not for me, but *w.* for. *Luke* 23:28
the grave to *w.* there. *John* 11:31
ye shall *w.* and lament, but. 16:20
what mean ye to *w.* and break my heart? *Acts* 21:13
w. with them that *w.* *Rom* 12:15
they that *w.* as though they wept not. *1 Cor* 7:30
and mourn, and *w.* *Jas* 4:9
go to now, ye rich men, *w.* and. 5:1
merchants of earth shall *w.* and. *Rev* 18:11

weepest
Hannah, why *w.* thou? *1 Sam* 1:8
and they say unto her, Woman, why *w.* thou? *John* 20:13, 15

weepeth
Joab, behold the king *w.* *2 Sam* 19:1
Hazael said, Why *w.*? *2 Ki* 8:12
he that goeth forth and *w.* *Ps* 126:6
she *w.* sore in night, her. *Lam* 1:2

weeping
w. before the door of. *Num* 25:6
days of *w.* for Moses. *Deut* 34:8
her husband went along with her *w.* *2 Sam* 3:16
they went up, *w.* as they. 15:30
noise of joy from *w.* *Ezra* 3:13

prayed and confessed, *w.* *Ezra* 10:1
province was fasting and *w.* *Esth* 4:3
my face is foul with *w.* *Job* 16:16
heard the voice of my *w.* *Ps* 6:8
w. may endure for a night. 30:5
mingled my drink with *w.* 102:9
in their streets howl, *w.* *Isa* 15:3
bewail with the *w.* of Jazer the vine of Sibmah. 16:9; *Jer* 48:32
Lord of hosts call to *w.* *Isa* 22:12
the voice of *w.* shall be no. 65:19
the *w.* of Israel heard. *Jer* 3:21
mountains will I take up a *w.* 9:10
they shall come with *w.* and. 31:9
lamentation and bitter *w.*; Rachel *w.* for her children. 15; *Mat* 2:18
restrain thy voice from *w.* *Jer* 31:16
went forth to meet them *w.* 41:6
continual *w.* shall go up, a cry. 48:5
Judah going and *w.* to seek. 50:4
there sat women *w.* for. *Ezek* 8:14
with fasting and with *w.* *Joel* 2:12
altar of the Lord with *w.* *Mal* 2:13
there shall be *w.* and. *Mat* 8:12
22:13; 24:51; 25:30; *Luke* 13:28
at his feet behind him *w.* *Luke* 7:38
when Jesus saw her *w.* and the Jews also *w.* which came. *John* 11:33
without at the sepulchre, *w.* 20:11
widows stood by him *w.* *Acts* 9:39
often, now tell you even *w.* *Phil* 3:18
shall stand afar off *w.* *Rev* 18:15
shipmaster and sailors cried, *w.* 19

weigh

crown to *w.* a talent. *1 Chr* 20:2
keep them until ye *w.* *Ezra* 8:29
ye *w.* the violence of your. *Ps* 58:2
thou dost *w.* the path of. *Isa* 26:7

weighed

Abraham *w.* to Ephraim. *Gen* 23:16
by the Lord actions are *w.* *1 Sam* 2:3
his spear's head *w.* 600 shekels. 17:7; *2 Sam* 21:16
Absalom *w.* the hair of. *2 Sam* 14:26
priests *w.* to them the silver and gold. *Ezra* 8:25
w. into their hands the silver. 26, 33
my grief were throughly *w.*! *Job* 6:2
nor shall silver be *w.* for the. 28:15
let me be *w.* in an even balance. 31:6
hath *w.* the mountains. *Isa* 40:12
Jeremiah *w.* him the money. *Jer* 32:9
Tekel, thou art *w.* in. *Dan* 5:27
so they *w.* for my price. *Zech* 11:12

weigheth

and he *w.* the waters. *Job* 28:25
but the Lord *w.* the spirits. *Pr* 16:2

weighing

each charger *w.* *Num* 7:85
golden spoons *w.* 86

weight

As the Hebrews had not the use of coined money, which was of a certain determined weight, *they* weighed *all the gold and silver they used in trade. The shekel, the half shekel, and the talents, are not only denominations of money of a certain value, of gold and silver, but also of a certain* weight. *When Moses named the drugs which were to compose the perfume to be burnt upon the golden altar, he says, that they were to take* five hundred shekels of myrrh, *etc.*, Ex 30:23. *And in* 2 Sam 14:26, *it is said, that* Absalom's hair *weighed* two hundred shekels.
The shekel of the sanctuary, *according to several interpreters, was double the common shekel; but others think it was the same as the common shekel, and the words* of the sanctuary, *are added, to express a just and exact* weight, *according to the standards that were kept in the temple, or tabernacle.*

mouth of sack, in full *w.* *Gen* 43:21
shall there be a like *w.* *Ex* 30:34
unrighteousness in *w.* *Lev* 19:35
you your bread by *w.* 26:26
a perfect and just *w.* *Deut* 25:15
w. of golden earrings. *Judg* 8:26
w. of king's crown a. *2 Sam* 12:30
neither was the *w.* of the brass found out. *1 Ki* 7:47; *2 Ki* 25:16
gave gold by *w.* for things of gold, silver also by *w.* *1 Chr* 28:14
the *w.* for the winds. *Job* 28:25
just *w.* is his delight. *Pr* 11:1
a just *w.* and balance are. 16:11
thy meat shall be by *w.* *Ezek* 4:10
and they shall eat bread by *w.* 16
he cast the *w.* of lead. *Zech* 5:8
us a more exceeding *w.* *2 Cor* 4:17
let us lay aside every *w.* *Heb* 12:1
every stone of hail the *w.* of a talent. *Rev* 16:21

weightier

ye have omitted the *w.* *Mat* 23:23

weights

just *w.* shall ye have. *Lev* 19:36
in thy bag divers *w.* *Deut* 25:13
all the *w.* of the bag. *Pr* 16:11
divers *w.* and measures. 20:10, 23
the bag of deceitful *w.* *Mi* 6:11

weighty

heavy and the sand *w.* *Pr* 27:3
for his letters, say they, are *w.* *2 Cor* 10:10

welfare

of their *w.* and said. *Gen* 43:27
each other of their *w.* *Ex* 18:7
Tou sent to David to enquire of his *w.* *1 Chr* 18:10
was come a man to seek the *w.* of *Neh* 2:10
and my *w.* passeth away. *Job* 30:15
have been for their *w.* *Ps* 69:22
this man seeketh not the *w.* of his people. *Jer* 38:4

well, *substantive*

she saw a *w.* of water. *Gen* 21:19
witness I have digged this *w.* 30
here by *w.* of water. 24:13, 43
a fruitful bough by a *w.* 49:22
is the *w.* whereof the. *Num* 21:16
spring up, O *w.* 17
princes digged the *w.* 18
man that had a *w.* in. *2 Sam* 17:18
drink of the water of the *w.* of Bethlehem. 23:15; *1 Chr* 11:17, 18
who passing . . . make it a *w.* *Ps* 84:6
drink waters out of thine own *w.* *Pr* 5:15
righteous man is a *w.* of life. 10:11
a *w.* of living waters. *S of S* 4:15
w. was there. Jesus being wearied . . . sat thus on the *w.* *John* 4:6
the *w.* is deep. 11
Jacob gave us the *w.* 12
shall be in him a *w.* of water. 14

well, *adverb*

if thou doest not *w.*, sin. *Gen* 4:7
that it may be *w.* with me. 12:13
he entreated Abram *w.* for her. 16
Jordan was *w.* watered. 13:10
Abraham and Sarah *w.* stricken in age. 18:11; 24:1
Jacob said, Is he *w.*? and they said, He is *w.* 29:6
when it shall be *w.* with thee. 40:14
father *w.*? is he yet alive? 43:27
dealt *w.* with the midwives. *Ex* 1:20
I know that he can speak *w.* 4:14
for it was *w.* with us. *Num* 11:18
Caleb said, We are *w.* able. 13:30
of sons of Joseph hath said *w.* 36:5
saying pleased me *w.* *Deut* 1:23
brethren, as *w.* as you. 3:20
that it may go *w.* with thee. 4:40
5:16; 6:3, 18; 12:25, 28; 19:13
22:7; *Ruth* 3:1; *Eph* 6:3
may rest as *w.* as thou. *Deut* 5:14
I heard the words of this people: they have *w.* said. 28; 18:17
that it might be *w.* with them. 5:29
that it may be *w.* with you. 33
Jer 7:23
but shalt *w.* remember. *Deut* 7:18
because he is *w.* with thee. 15:16
if thou hast dealt *w.* with. *Judg* 9:16
me, for she pleaseth me *w.* 14:3, 7
as *w.* men of every city. *Judg* 20:48
w. let him do the kinsman's part. *Ruth* 3:13
he shall play and thou shalt be *w.* *1 Sam* 16:16
if he say thus, It is *w.* 20:7
I know *w.* thou shalt surely. 24:20
he dealt bread as *w.* *2 Sam* 6:19
called, and said, All is *w.* 18:28
David, Thou didst *w.* that it was in thine heart to. *1 Ki* 8:18; *2 Chr* 6:8
answered, It is *w.* spoken. *1 Ki* 18:24
Is it *w.* with thee? is it *w.* with thy husband? is it *w.* with the child? It is *w.* *2 Ki* 4:26
Is all *w.*? 5:21; 9:11
we do not *w.* 7:9
of Babylon; and it shall be *w.* with. 25:24; *Ps* 128:2; *Jer* 40:9
Judah things went *w.* *2 Chr* 12:12
thou doest *w.* to thyself. *Ps* 49:18
thou hast dealt *w.* with thy. 119:65
when it goeth *w.* with. *Pr* 11:10
the prudent man looketh *w.* 14:15
I saw and considered it *w.* 24:32
things which go *w.*, yea, four. 30:29
she looketh *w.* to the ways of. 31:27
it shall be *w.* with them. *Eccl* 8:12
but it shall not be *w.* with the. 13
it shall be *w.* with him. *Isa* 3:10
me, Thou hast *w.* seen. *Jer* 1:12
Lord said, It shall be *w.* with. 15:11
It was *w.* with him, he. 22:15, 16
take him, look *w.* to him, do. 39:12
come, and I will look *w.* to. 40:4
that it may be *w.* with us. 42:6
for then we were *w.* and. 44:17
make it boil *w.* and seethe. *Ezek* 24:5
spice it *w.* 10
mark *w.*, behold, and hear. 44:5
of one that can play *w.* on. 33:32
said the Lord, Doest thou *w.* to be angry? *Jonah* 4:4
I do *w.* to be angry, even unto. 9
hypocrites, *w.* did Esaias prophesy. *Mat* 15:7; *Mark* 7:6; *Acts* 28:25
w. done, thou good and faithful servant. *Mat* 25:21, 23; *Luke* 19:17
he hath done all things *w.* *Mark* 7:37
he had answered them *w.* 12:28
Zacharias and Elisabeth *w.* *Luke* 1:7
when all men speak *w.* of you. 6:26
if it bear fruit, *w.*; and if not. 13:9
Master, thou hast *w.* said. 20:39
John 4:17
say we not *w.* thou hast a devil. *John* 8:48
ye call me Lord, ye say *w.* 13:13
if *w.* why smitest thou me? 18:23
keep his virgin, doeth *w.* *1 Cor* 7:37
giveth her in marriage, doeth *w.* 38
affect you, but not *w.* *Gal* 4:17
run *w.*; who did hinder you? 5:7
ye have *w.* done, ye did. *Phil* 4:14
one that ruleth *w.* his. *1 Tim* 3:4
let the elders that rule *w.* be. 5:17
and to please them *w.* *Tit* 2:9
is one God; thou doest *w.* *Jas* 2:19
see **as, do, doing, favoured, pleased**

very **well**

as thou *very w.* knowest. *Acts* 25:10
he ministered to me, thou knowest *very w.* *2 Tim* 1:18

wellbeloved

myrrh is my *w.* unto. *S of S* 1:13
now will I sing to my *w.* *Isa* 5:1
he sent his *w.* son. *Mark* 12:6
salute *w.* Epenetus. *Rom* 16:5
the elder to the *w.* Gaius. *3 John* 1

well *nigh*

as for me, my steps had *w. nigh* slipped. *Ps* 73:2

wells

w. Abraham's servants. *Gen* 26:15
and Isaac digged again the *w.* 18
where were twelve *w.* *Ex* 15:27
drink of the water of *w.* *Num* 20:17
and *w.* digged which thou. *Deut* 6:11
and ye shall stop all the *w.* *2 Ki* 3:19
they stopped all the *w.* of water. 25
towers and digged *w.* *2 Chr* 26:10
shall draw water out of *w.* *Isa* 12:3

these are *w.* without water, clouds that are. *2 Pet* 2:17

wellspring

understanding is a *w.* of. *Pr* 16:22
the *w.* of wisdom as a. 18:4

wen

maimed, or having a *w.* *Lev* 22:22

wench

a *w.* told Jonathan. *2 Sam* 17:17*

went

with me in the way I *w.* *Gen* 35:3
in the first place *w.* standard of Judah. *Num* 10:14
into the land whereto he *w.* 14:24
kindled because Balaam *w.* 22:22
Balaam *w.* not to seek for. 24:1
Phinehas *w.* after the man. 25:8
in all the way ye *w.* *Deut* 1:31
he preserved us in all the way we *w.* *Josh* 24:17
so Simeon *w.* with Judah. *Judg* 1:3
and Judah *w.* with Simeon. 17
strength *w.* from him. 16:19
said, Whither *w.* ye? *1 Sam* 10:14
there *w.* with Saul a band. 26
the man *w.* for an old man. 17:12
but David *w.* to feed his father's. 15
David and his men *w.* wherever they could go. 23:13
because they *w.* not with us. 30:22
how *w.* the matter? *2 Sam* 1:4
as he *w.* to recover his border. 8:3; *1 Chr* 18:3
Lord preserved David whithersoever he *w.* *2 Sam* 8:6, 14; *1 Chr* 18:6, 13
w. in their simplicity. *2 Sam* 15:11
as he *w.*, thus he said, O my. 18:33
Solomon *w.* not fully. *1 Ki* 11:6
said, What way *w.* he? 13:12
he *w.* after the man of God. 14
he said, Which way *w.* the Spirit of the Lord? 22:24; *2 Chr* 18:23
but they *w.* not. *1 Ki* 22:48
they two *w.* on. *2 Ki* 2:6
he said, *W.* not my heart with thee? 5:26
for he *w.* with them, and they. 6:4
when he *w.* in to his wife. *1 Chr* 7:23
when they *w.* from nation to nation. 16:20; *Ps* 105:13
so all Israel *w.* to their. *2 Chr* 10:16
in Judah things *w.* well. 12:12
people *w.* to house of Baal. 23:17
knew not whither I *w.* *Neh* 2:16
in the evening she *w.*, and on the morrow returned. *Esth* 2:14
I *w.* with them to the house of God. *Ps* 42:4
it *w.* ill with Moses for their. 106:32
a young man *w.* the way to. *Pr* 7:8
he *w.* on frowardly in the way of his heart. *Isa* 57:17
they *w.* every one straight forward. *Ezek* 1:9
turned not when they *w.* 12; 10:11
they *w.* on their four sides. 1:17
when those *w.*, these *w.* 21
for their heart *w.* after their. 20:16
she *w.* after her lovers. *Hos* 2:13
then *w.* Ephraim to the. 5:13
they *w.* to Baal-peor and. 9:10
as they called them, so they *w.* 11:2
before him *w.* the pestilence, burning coals. *Hab* 3:5
of thine arrows, they *w.* 11
he repented and *w.* *Mat* 21:29
said, I go, sir, but *w.* not. 30
while they *w.* to buy, the. 25:10
they left their father and *w.* after. *Mark* 1:20
all *w.* to be taxed, every. *Luke* 2:3
one *w.* to them from the dead. 16:30
as they *w.* they were cleansed. 17:14
Joseph *w.* to Pilate and. 23:52
the Galileans also *w.* to. *John* 4:45
every man *w.* to his own house. 7:53
I *w.* and washed and I. 9:11
from God and *w.* to God. 13:3
they *w.* backward and fell to. 18:6
then *w.* this saying abroad. 21:23
they *w.* every where preaching the. *Acts* 8:4
Saul .. threatenings *w.* unto the. 9:1
as they *w.* on their journey, Peter *w.* to pray. *Acts* 10:9
they *w.* both into synagogue. 14:1
w. not with them to the work. 15:38
as we *w.* to prayer, a damsel. 16:16
as I *w.* to Damascus with. 26:12
he *w.* and preached to. *1 Pet* 3:19

see **along**

went *about*

the people *w. about.* *Num* 11:8
the slingers *w. about* it. *2 Ki* 3:25
they *w. about* and taught. *2 Chr* 17:9
I *w. about* to cause my. *Eccl* 2:20
the watchmen that *w. about* found me. *S of S* 5:7
Jesus *w. about* teaching. *Mat* 4:23
9:35; *Mark* 6:6
they *w. about* to slay him. *Acts* 9:29; 21:31; 26:21
Jesus *w. about* doing good. 10:38
he *w. about* seeking some to. 13:11

see **arose**

went *aside*

Jesus took them and *w. aside* privately. *Luke* 9:10
chief captain *w. aside.* *Acts* 23:19

went *astray*

afflicted I *w. astray.* *Ps* 119:67
when Israel *w. astray* after idols. *Ezek* 44:10, 15
priests which *w.* not *astray* when Israel *w. astray* as Levites *w. astray.* 48:11
than of the ninety and nine which *w.* not *astray.* *Mat* 18:13

went *away*

Samson *w. away* with doors of the gates. *Judg* 16:3
and *w. away* with the pin of. 14
and his concubine *w. away.* 19:2
the mule that was under him *w. away.* *2 Sam* 18:9
was wroth, and *w. away.* *2 Ki* 5:11
queen of Sheba *w. away.* *2 Chr* 9:12
he *w. away* sorrowful. *Mat* 19:22
Mark 10:22
he *w. away* second time. *Mat* 26:42
he *w. away* the third time. 44
Mark 14:39
of him many *w. away.* *John* 12:11
the disciples *w. away* to their. 20:10
morrow Peter *w. away.* *Acts* 10:23

went *back*

so he *w. back* and did. *1 Ki* 13:19
king Joram *w. back* to. *2 Ki* 8:29
many disciples *w. back.* *John* 6:66

went *before*

the Lord *w. before.* *Ex* 13:21
the angel of God which *w. before* the camp. 14:19
the ark of the covenant *w. before* them. *Num* 10:33; *Josh* 3:6
the armed men *w. before* the priests. *Josh* 6:9, 13
one bearing a shield *w. before* him. *1 Sam* 17:7, 41
Ahio *w. before* the ark. *2 Sam* 6:4
and Shobach *w. before* them. 10:16
1 Chr 19:16
Amasa *w. before* them. *2 Sam* 20:8
they that *w. before* were affrighted. *Job* 18:20
the singers *w. before.* *Ps* 68:25
they saw *w. before* them. *Mat* 2:9
multitudes that *w. before* them cried. 21:9; *Mark* 11:9
they which *w. before* rebuked him. *Luke* 18:39
he *w. before,* to Jerusalem. 19:28
Judas *w. before,* drew near. 22:47
prophecies which *w. before.* *1 Tim* 1:18

went *behind*

the angel removed and *w. behind.* *Ex* 14:19

went *down*

Abram *w. down* into Egypt to sojourn. *Gen* 12:10
sun *w. down,* a smoking furnace and. 15:17; *Judg* 19:14; *2 Sam* 2:24
Joseph's brethren *w. down.* *Gen* 42:3
Benjamin *w. down.* 43:15
Moses *w. down* from the mount to the people. *Ex* 19:14, 25; 32:15
w. down alive into pit. *Num* 16:33
how our fathers *w. down* into. 20:15
Deut 10:22; 26:5; *Josh* 24:4
Israel *w. down* after. *Judg* 3:27, 28
Barak *w. down* from mount. 4:14
Gideon *w. down* with Phurah. 7:11
Samson *w. down* to Timnath and saw a woman. 14:1, 5, 7
him before the sun *w. down.* 18
Samson *w. down* to Ashkelon. 19
Ruth *w. down* unto the. *Ruth* 3:6
the Israelites *w. down.* *1 Sam* 13:20
his father's house *w. down* to him. 22:1
David heard, and *w. down* to the hold. *2 Sam* 5:17
but Uriah *w.* not *down.* 11:9, 10, 13
court, whither they *w. down.* 17:18
David *w. down* against the. 21:15
three of the thirty chief *w. down* and. 23:13; *1 Chr* 11:15
Benaiah *w. down* and slew a lion in. *2 Sam* 23:20
Benaiah *w. down* to the Egyptian, and slew. 21; *1 Chr* 11:22, 23
Elijah *w. down* with him. *2 Ki* 1:15
Elijah and Elisha *w. down.* 2:2
Naaman *w. down* and dipped. 5:14
Ahaziah *w. down* to see Joram. 8:29; *2 Chr* 22:6
Jehoshaphat *w. down.* *2 Chr* 18:2
ointment that *w. down.* *Ps* 133:2
w. down into the garden. *S of S* 6:11
people *w. down* aforetime. *Isa* 52:4
I *w. down* to the potter's. *Jer* 18:3
in the day when he *w. down* to the grave. *Ezek* 31:15
they also *w. down* to hell. 17
Jonah *w. down* to Joppa. *Jonah* 1:3
I *w. down* to the bottoms of. 2:6
man *w. down* justified. *Luke* 18:14
angel *w. down* and troubled the water. *John* 5:4
Jacob *w. down* into. *Acts* 7:15
Philip *w. down* to Samaria. 8:5
and they both *w. down* into the. 38
then Peter *w. down* to the. 10:21
Herod *w. down* from Judaea. 12:19
Paul *w. down* and embracing. 20:10

went *forth*

a raven *w. forth.* *Gen* 8:7
w. forth from Ur. 11:31
Noah *w. forth,* his sons and. 18, 19
out of that land *w. forth.* 10:11
they *w. forth* to go into land. 12:5
there *w. forth* a wind. *Num* 11:31
the princes *w. forth* to. 31:13; 33:1
trees *w. forth* to anoint. *Judg* 9:8
as he *w. forth* it fell out. *2 Sam* 20:8
Elisha *w. forth* unto the spring of the waters. *2 Ki* 2:21
whithersoever he *w. forth.* 18:7
then *w.* Haman *forth.* *Esth* 5:9
Satan *w. forth* from. *Job* 1:12; 2:7
angel of the Lord *w. forth.* *Isa* 37:36
the former things *w. forth,* I. 48:3
Shallum who *w. forth.* *Jer* 22:11
thy renown *w. forth* among the heathen. *Ezek* 16:14
her great scum *w.* not *forth.* 24:12
that which *w. forth* by an. *Amos* 5:3
burning coals *w. forth.* *Hab* 3:5
behold, a sower *w. forth.* *Mat* 13:3
ten virgins *w. forth* to meet. 25:1
took up bed and *w. forth.* *Mark* 2:12
name's sake they *w. forth.* *3 John* 7
he *w. forth* conquering. *Rev* 6:2

went *her way*

woman *w. her way.* *1 Sam* 1:18
the woman *w. her way.* *John* 4:28
so said, she *w. her way.* 11:28

went *his way*

and the Lord *w. his way.* *Gen* 18:33
Rebekah and *w. his way.* 24:61
and drink and *w. his way.* 25:34
Jethro *w. his way* into. *Ex* 18:27
Saul *w. his way.* *1 Sam* 24:7
David *w.* on *his way.* 26:25
of Adonijah *w. his way.* *1 Ki* 1:49
so Mordecai *w. his way.* *Esth* 4:17
Jeremiah *w. his way.* *Jer* 28:11

his enemy sowed tares and w. his way. Mat 13:25
he passing through midst of them, w. his way. Luke 4:30
he w. his way and published. 8:39
Judas w. his way and communed with priests. 22:4
man believed, and w. his way. John 4:50
eunuch w. on his way. Acts 8:39
Ananias w. his way and. 9:17
see **Jesus, went**

went in, or into
Noah w. into the ark and. Gen 7:7
w. in two and two. 9
w. in male and female. 16
Joseph w. into the house to. 39:11
Moses and Aaron w. in to Pharaoh. Ex 5:1; 7:10
Israel w. into the midst of the. 14:22
the Egyptians w. in. 23; 15:19
until Moses w. in to speak. 34:35
when Aaron w. into the. Lev 16:23
that were spies w. in. Josh 6:23
the haft also w. in after. Judg 3:22
so the Levite w. in and dwelt. 17:10
when the Levite w. in to lodge. 19:15
Saul w. in to cover. 1 Sam 24:3
then w. David in before. 2 Sam 7:18
Bath-sheba w. in unto. 1 Ki 1:15
disguised w. into the battle. 22:30
Elisha w. in, shut the. 2 Ki 4:33
then she w. in, fell at his feet. 37
and one w. in and told his lord. 5:4
Gehazi w. in and stood before. 25
when they w. in to offer. 10:24
Uzziah w. into the temple of the Lord. 2 Chr 26:16
Azariah the priest w. in after. 17
so the children w. in. Neh 9:24
the king w. into the palace garden. Esth 7:7
until I w. into the sanctuary of God. Ps 73:17
Urijah fled and w. into. Jer 26:21
so I w. in. Ezek 8:10
six men w. in. 9:2
clothed with linen w. in. 10:2, 3, 6
when they w. into captivity. 25:3
Israel w. into captivity for. 39:23
Daniel w. in and desired of the king. Dan 2:16
w. in unto Arioch. 24
he w. into his house to pray. 6:10
the devils w. into the herd of swine. Mat 8:32
certain householder w. into. 21:33
Mark 12:1; Luke 19:12; 20:9
they that were ready w. in to the marriage. Mat 25:10
w. into the holy city, and. 27:53
how David w. into the house of God. Mark 2:26; Luke 6:4
Joseph w. in boldly to Pilate. Mark 15:43
burn incense when he w. in. Luke 1:9
Mary w. into the hill country. 39
and he w. in to tarry with. 24:29
that disciple w. in with. John 18:15
clothes lying, yet w. he not in. 20:5
then w. in also that other disciple. 8
all the time the Lord w. in. Acts 1:21
as Peter talked he w. in and. 10:27
he departed and w. into. 12:17
they w. into the synagogue on. 13:14
Paul w. into the synagogue. 17:2
10; 19:8
their sound w. into all. Rom 10:18

went in, as to a woman
Abram w. in unto Hagar. Gen 16:4
the firstborn w. in and lay. 19:33
Leah; and he w. in unto her. 29:23
he w. in also unto Rachel. 30
Jacob w. in unto Bilhah. 30:4
saw Shuah and w. in to her. 38:2
Onan w. in to his brother's wife. 9
harlot and w. in unto her. Judg 16:1
Boaz w. in unto Ruth. Ruth 4:13
David comforted Bath-sheba his wife, and w. in. 2 Sam 12:24
Absalom w. in to his father's. 16:22
Ithra w. in to Abigail the daughter of Nahash. 17:25
David w. not in to them. 2 Sam 20:3
Hezron w. in to. 1 Chr 2:21
when Ephraim w. in to his wife. 7:23
yet they w. in unto her. Ezek 23:44

went over
there arose and w. over. 2 Sam 2:15
and they w. over Jordan. 19:17
Barzillai w. over Jordan with. 31
so they two w. over on. 2 Ki 2:8
smote the waters and w. over. 14
these w. over Jordan. 1 Chr 12:15
and times that w. over him. 29:30
other company w. over. Neh 12:38
street, to them that w. over. Isa 51:23

went out
Cain w. out from the presence of the Lord. Gen 4:16
Isaac w. out to meditate in. 24:63
Dinah w. out to see the daughters of the land. 34:1
washed his face and w. out. 43:31
and the one w. out from me. 44:28
Moses w. out to his brethren. Ex 2:11, 13
Aaron w. out from Pharaoh. 8:12, 30
9:33
hosts of the Lord w. out. 12:41; 14:8
all the women w. out after. 15:20
there w. out some people on. 16:27
Moses w. out to meet his. 18:7
every one w. out unto the. 33:7
there w. out fire from. Lev 10:2
them when they w. out. Num 10:34
two men w. out into the. 11:26
Sihon w. out against Israel. 21:23
Og, the king of Bashan, w. out. 33
behold, I w. out to withstand. 22:32
none w. out, and none. Josh 6:1
the men of Ai w. out. 8:14, 17
the Canaanite w. out and all. 11:4
they w. out, the Lord was. Judg 2:15
all that stood by him w. out. 3:19
master of the house w. out. 19:23
I w. out full, and came. Ruth 1:21
ere the lamp of God w. out in the temple. 1 Sam 3:3
I w. out after the bear, and. 17:35
David w. out where Saul sent him. 18:5, 13, 16; 19:8
even he w. out to lie on. 2 Sam 11:13
they w. out every man from. 13:9
the day the king w. out of. 19:19
they w. out at noon. 1 Ki 20:16
w. out first. 17
the king of Israel w. out and. 21
the child w. out to his father to the reapers. 2 Ki 4:18
took up her son, and w. out. 37
Gehazi w. out from his presence a leper. 5:27
they w. out each in his chariot. 9:21
arrow w. out of Jehoram's. 24
David w. out to meet. 1 Chr 12:17
David heard of it, and w. out. 14:8
Azariah w. out to meet. 2 Chr 15:2
was no peace to him that w. out. 5
Jehu w. out to meet. 19:2
to praise as they w. out. 20:21
Josiah w. out against Pharaoh-necho. 35:20
as the word w. out of the king's mouth. Esth 7:8
when I w. out to the gate through the city. Job 29:7
that I w. not out of the door? 31:34
when he w. out through the land of Egypt. Ps 81:5
Jeremiah came in and w. out among people. Jer 37:4
the cherub and w. out. Ezek 10:7
the city that w. out by. Amos 5:3
neither any peace to him that w. out. Zech 8:10
Jesus said, What w. ye out into the? Mat 11:7, 8, 9; Luke 7:24, 25, 26
a man who w. out early to. Mat 20:1
he w. out about third hour. 3, 5, 6
those servants w. out into. 22:10
his friends w. out to lay hold on him: He is beside himself. Mark 3:21
unclean spirits w. out and entered. 5:13; Luke 8:33; Acts 19:12
they w. out to see what it was that was done. Mark 5:14; Luke 8:35
for there w. virtue out. Luke 6:19
Peter w. out and wept. 22:62
they which heard it, w. out. John 8:9
Jesus hid himself and w. out. 59
rose up hastily, and w. out. 11:31
received the sop w. out. 13:30
w. out that other disciple. 18:16
the Lord w. in and out. Acts 1:21
certain w. out from us have. 15:24
Abraham w. out, not. Heb 11:8
they w. out from us, but were not of us, they w. out. 1 John 2:19

went their way
of Dan w. their way. Judg 18:26
Amalekites burnt Ziklag and w. their way. 1 Sam 30:2
all the people w. their way to eat. Neh 8:12
w. their way as a flock. Zech 10:2
that kept swine fled and w. their way. Mat 8:33
whatsoever is right I will give you. And they w. their way. 20:4
light of it and w. their ways. 22:5
these words, they w. their way. 22
w. their way and found the colt. Mark 11:4; Luke 19:32
but some w. their ways. John 11:46
as they w. on their way. Acts 8:36

went through
thou didst divide the sea, they w. through. Neh 9:11; Ps 66:6
we w. through fire and. Ps 66:12
forsaken, so that no man w. through thee. Isa 60:15
he w. through the corn fields on the. Mark 2:23; Luke 6:1

went up
God w. up from Abraham. Gen 17:22
God w. up from Jacob in. 35:13
w. up to father's bed, he w. up. 49:4
Moses, Aaron and Hur w. up. Ex 17:10
Moses w. up unto God. 19:3, 20
24:13, 15; 34:4; Deut 10:3
w. up, and searched the. Num 13:21
but the men that w. up with. 31
they w. up into mount Hor. 20:27
33:38
w. presumptuously up. Deut 1:43
so that the people w. up. Josh 6:20
brethren that w. up with me. 14:8
Judah w. up and the Lord. Judg 1:4
the house of Joseph also w. up. 22
Barak and Deborah w. up with. 4:10
Gideon w. up thence to. 8:8, 11
Elkanah w. up out of his city. 1 Sam 1:3, 7, 21
Hannah w. not up; until child. 22
the cry of the city w. up to. 5:12
as he w. up barefoot. 2 Sam 15:30
David, according to the saying of Gad, w. up. 24:19; 1 Chr 21:19
Elijah w. up by a whirlwind to heaven. 2 Ki 2:11
Elisha w. up and lay upon. 4:34, 35
Hezekiah w. up. 19:14; Isa 37:14
Josiah w. up into the house of the Lord. 2 Ki 23:2; 2 Chr 34:30
Joab w. up first and was. 1 Chr 11:6
children of the province that w. up. Ezra 2:1, 59; Neh 7:6, 61
they w. up in haste to Jerusalem to the Jews. Ezra 4:23
Ezra w. up. 7:6
genealogy of them that w. up. 8:1
the priest that w. up. Neh 12:1
it w. up and down among. Ezek 1:13
cloud of incense w. up. 8:11
the glory of the Lord w. up. 10:4
11:23, 24
he w. up and down among the lions. 19:6
Jesus w. up straightway. Mat 3:16
and seeing the multitudes he w. up. 5:1; 14:23; 15:29; Luke 9:28
two men w. up into the. Luke 18:10
then w. he also up unto. John 7:10
as he w. up, two men. Acts 1:10
Peter and John w. up into the. 3:1
Peter w. up upon the housetop. 10:9

Paul *w. up* to Jerusalem. *Acts* 24:11
Gal 1:18; 2:1, 2
w. I *up* to Jerusalem. *Gal* 1:17
they *w. up* on the breadth. *Rev* 20:9

went *a whoring*

Israel *w. a whoring* after other gods.
Judg 2:17; 8:33
w. a whoring with her. *Ps* 106:39

wentest

Reuben, thou *w.* up to. *Gen* 49:4
Lord, when thou *w.* out of. *Judg* 5:4
whithersoever thou *w.* *2 Sam* 7:9
w. thou not with thy friend? 16:17
w. thou not with me? 19:25
O God, when thou *w.* *Ps* 68:7
even thither *w.* thou up. *Isa* 57:7
thou *w.* to the king with ointment. 9
when thou *w.* after me in. *Jer* 2:2
heart toward the way thou *w.* 31:21
thou *w.* forth for salvation. *Hab* 3:13
thou *w.* in to men uncircumcised.
Acts 11:3

wept

Hagar sat and *w.* *Gen* 21:16
Esau *w.* 27:38
Jacob *w.* 29:11; 33:4; 37:35
Hos 12:4
from his brethren and *w.* *Gen* 42:24
43:30; 45:2, 14, 15; 46:29; 50:1, 17
and, behold, the babe *w.* *Ex* 2:6
and the children of Israel also *w.*
Num 11:4, 18, 20; 14:1; *Deut* 1:45
34:8; *Judg* 2:4; 20:23, 26; 21:2
Samson's wife *w.* before. *Judg* 14:16
daughters and *w.* *Ruth* 1:9, 14
Hannah *w.* and did. *1 Sam* 1:7, 10
all people *w.* 11:4; *2 Sam* 3:32, 34
Jonathan and David *w.* *1 Sam* 20:41
Saul *w.* 24:16
David *w.* 30:4; *2 Sam* 1:12
David *w.* at the grave. *2 Sam* 3:32
was yet alive I fasted and *w.* 12:22
the king and servants *w.* sore. 13:36
all the country *w.* 15:23
w. as he went. 30
king was much moved and *w.* 18:33
the man of God *w.* *2 Ki* 8:11
Joash *w.* over Elisha and. 13:14
remember how I have walked.
Hezekiah *w.* sore. 20:3; *Isa* 38:3
king of Judah hath *w.* *2 Ki* 22:19
seen the first house *w.* *Ezra* 3:12
people *w.* very sore. 10:1; *Neh* 8:9
I heard these words, I *w.* *Neh* 1:4
lifted up their voice and *w.* *Job* 2:12
when I *w.* and chastened. *Ps* 69:10
Babylon, we sat down and *w.* 137:1
Peter *w.* *Mat* 26:75; *Mark* 14:72
Luke 22:62
he seeth them that *w.* *Mark* 5:38
Luke 8:52
as they mourned and *w.* *Mark* 16:10
you, and ye have not *w.* *Luke* 7:32
he beheld the city and *w.* 19:41
Jesus *w.* *John* 11:35
at the sepulchre: as she *w.* 20:11
they *w.* sore and fell on. *Acts* 20:37
as though they *w.* not. *1 Cor* 7:30
I *w.* because no man. *Rev* 5:4

were

cannot do this, for that *w.* *Gen* 34:14
third day when they *w.* sore. 25
Jacob said to all that *w.* with. 35:2
gave all the strange gods that *w.* 4
Israel saw they *w.* in evil. *Ex* 5:19
since day they *w.* upon earth. 10:6
w. ye not afraid to speak? *Num* 12:8
we *w.* in our own sight as grasshoppers, and so we *w.* in. 13:33
w. it not better for us to? 14:3
O that there *w.* such an. *Deut* 5:29
for ye *w.* strangers in the. 10:19
whereas ye *w.* as the stars. 28:62
w. it not that I feared the. 32:27
O that they *w.* wise, that they. 29
I wist not whence they *w.* *Josh* 2:4
thou seest mountains as if they *w.*
men. *Judg* 9:36
and there they *w.* not. *1 Sam* 9:4
that valiant men *w.* *2 Sam* 11:16
we *w.* together; there. *1 Ki* 3:18
place where the officers *w.* 4:28
did evil above all that *w.* 16:30, 33
w. it not that I regard. *2 Ki* 3:14
and the tents as they *w.* 7:10
as many as *w.* of a free heart.
2 Chr 29:31
though there *w.* of you cast. *Neh* 1:9
for there *w.* that said, We. 5:2, 3, 4
seed, whether they *w.* *Job* 7:61
Oh that I *w.* as in months. 29:2
a sojourner, as all my fathers *w.*
Ps 39:12
whose captives they *w.* *Isa* 14:2
they *w.* no gods, but work of. 37:19
because they *w.* not. *Jer* 31:15
though Noah, Daniel, and Job *w.* in.
Ezek 14:14, 16, 18, 20
heathen among whom they *w.* 20:9
there *w.* but ten, there *w.* *Hag* 2:16
persecuted prophets which *w.* before.
Mat 5:12
David did and they that *w.*? 12:3, 4
Mark 2:25, 26; *Luke* 6:3, 4
whether he *w.* the Christ. *Luke* 3:15
this man, if he *w.* a prophet. 7:39
w. not ten cleansed? where? 17:17
if this man *w.* not of God. *John* 9:33
if any man knew where he *w.* 11:57
if ye *w.* of the world, world. 15:19
thine they *w.*, and thou gavest. 17:6
they said, If he *w.* not a. 18:30
w. not a little comforted. *Acts* 20:12
saying that these things *w.* so. 24:9
calleth things that be not as though
they *w.* *Rom* 4:17
them my people that *w.* not. 9:25
if whole body *w.* an eye, where *w.*
hearing? if whole *w.* hearing, where
w. smelling? *1 Cor* 12:17
whatsoever they *w.* maketh. *Gal* 2:6
w. by nature children of. *Eph* 2:3
for even when we *w.* *2 Thes* 3:10
things continue as they *w.* *2 Pet* 3:4
until their brethren, be killed as they
w., should be fulfilled. *Rev* 6:11

as it **were**

it seemeth, there is *as it w.* a plague.
Lev 14:35
as *it w.* the company. *S of S* 6:13
that draw sin *as it w.* *Isa* 5:18
as if staff lift up itself *as it w.* 10:15
hide thyself *as it w.* for a. 26:20
and we hid *as it w.* our faces. 53:3
his sweat *as it w.* great. *Luke* 22:44
up not openly, but *as it w.* *John* 7:10
sought it *as it w.* by works. *Rom* 9:32
apostles, *as it w.* to death. *1 Cor* 4:9
and his face was *as it w.* *Rev* 10:1
I saw one of his heads *as it w.* 13:3
they sung *as it w.* a new song. 14:3
I saw *as it w.* a sea of glass. 15:2

if it **were**

if it w. so, why should not my spirit
be troubled? *Job* 21:4
if it w. possible to deceive the very
elect. *Mat* 24:24
they might touch *if it w.* the border.
Mark 6:56
if it w. not so, I would. *John* 14:2
if it w. a matter of wrong. *Acts* 18:14

wert

O that thou *w.* as my. *S of S* 8:1
I would thou *w.* cold or. *Rev* 3:15

west

spread abroad to the *w.* *Gen* 28:14
the *w.* and the south. *Deut* 33:23
looking toward the *w.* *1 Ki* 7:25
on quarters were porters, toward the
east, *w.* *1 Chr* 9:24; *2 Chr* 4:4
they put to flight them toward east
and *w.* *1 Chr* 12:15
cometh not from the *w.* *Ps* 75:6
as east is from the *w.*, so far. 103:12
them from the east and *w.* 107:3
Philistines toward the *w.* *Isa* 11:14
and gather thee from the *w.* 43:5
they may know from the *w.* 45:6
come from the north and *w.* 49:12
fear the Lord from the *w.* 59:19
are his sides east and *w.* *Ezek* 48:1
he goat came from the *w.* *Dan* 8:5
tremble from the *w.* *Hos* 11:10
I will save my people from the *w.*
Zech 8:7
of Olives shall cleave toward *w.* 14:4
from east and *w.* and sit down with.
Mat 8:11; *Luke* 13:29
east and shineth to *w.* *Mat* 24:27
cloud rise out of the *w.* *Luke* 12:54
on south three gates, and *w.* three
gates. *Rev* 21:13

west *border*

great sea for border, this shall be
w. border. *Num* 34:6
w. border was to the great sea.
Josh 15:12
w. border a portion. *Ezek* 45:7

west *quarter*

this was the *w. quarter.* *Josh* 18:14

west *side*

on *w. side* hanging 50 cubits.
Ex 27:12; 38:12
the *w. side* the standard. *Num* 2:18
measure on the *w. side* of the. 35:5
even to the *w. side* a portion.
Ezek 48:3, 4, 5, 6, 7, 8, 23, 24

western

as for the *w.* border. *Num* 34:6

westward

looked eastward and *w.* *Gen* 13:14
behind the tabernacle *w.* *Num* 3:23
lift up thine eyes *w.* *Deut* 3:27
shall be 10,000 *w.* *Ezek* 48:18
I saw the ram pushing *w.* *Dan* 8:4

west *wind*

a strong *w. wind* took. *Ex* 10:19

wet

they are *w.* with showers. *Job* 24:8
let it be *w.* with the dew of heaven.
Dan 4:15, 23, 25, 33; 5:21

whale

(*The word sometimes translated* whale *in the Old Testament is at other times translated* dragon, serpent, *or* sea-monster. *The* whale of Jonah *is called in that book merely* a great fish. *In the New Testament the word used in the original may mean almost any large sea-animal, whale, seal, shark, or tunny*)

am I a sea, or a *w.* that? *Job* 7:12*
Pharaoh, thou art as a *w.* in the.
Ezek 32:2*
days in the *w.'s* belly. *Mat* 12:40

whales

God created great *w.* *Gen* 1:21*

what

w. shall I do now to? *Gen* 27:37
my master wotteth not *w.* is. 39:8
w. shall we say to my lord? *w.* shall
we speak? 44:16
know not with *w.* we. *Ex* 10:26
when son asketh, *W.* is this? 13:14
w. are we? 16:7
for they wist not *w.* it was. 15
say, *W.* shall we eat? *Lev* 25:20
and see the land *w.* it. *Num* 13:18
w. the land is, and *w.* cities. 19, 20
it was not declared *w.* 15:34
w. is Aaron? 16:11
w. hath the Lord spoken? 23:17
but *w.* the Lord saith, that. 24:13
1 Ki 22:14; *2 Chr* 18:13
w. the Lord did because. *Deut* 4:3
w. Lord did to Pharaoh. 7:18; 11:6
Israel, *w.* doth the Lord require of
thee? 10:12; *Mi* 6:8
w. man is there? *Deut* 20:5, 6, 7, 8
O Lord, *w.* shall I say? *Josh* 7:8
and Caleb said to her, *W.*? 15:18
Judg 1:14; *1 Ki* 1:16; *Mat* 20:21
w. have ye to do with the Lord God
of Israel? *Josh* 22:24
thou shalt hear *w.* they. *Judg* 7:11
w. hast thou to do with me? 11:12
w. say ye? 18:8
the priest said, *W.* do ye? 18
w. have I more? *w.* is this? *w.* aileth
thee? 24
and he will tell thee *w.* thou shalt.
Ruth 3:4; *1 Sam* 10:8
w. is the thing the Lord? *1 Sam* 3:17
and he said, *W.* is there done? 4:16
w. have I to do with you?
2 Sam 16:10; 19:22
let us hear likewise *w.* he saith. 17:5

a tumult, but I knew not *w.* *2 Sam* 18:29
their father said, *W.*? *1 Ki* 13:12
cut off house of Jeroboam *w.*? 14:14
w. have I to do with thee? 17:18
2 Ki 3:13; *2 Chr* 35:21; *John* 2:4
said, Ask *w.* I shall do for thee? *2 Ki* 2:9; 4:2
Jehu said, *W.* hast thou? 9:18, 19
w. said these men, and from whence? 20:14; *Isa* 39:3
w. have they seen in thine house? *2 Ki* 20:15; *Isa* 39:4
Jehoshaphat said, Take heed *w.* ye do. *2 Chr* 19:6
nor know *w.* to do, but our. 20:12
w. shall we do for the hundred? 25:9
w. shall we say after this? *Ezra* 9:10; *Job* 37:19
king said, For *w.* dost? *Neh* 2:4
W. thing is this ye do? 19; 13:17
to know *w.* it was, and why. *Esth* 4:5
w. wilt thou, queen Esther? *w.* is thy request? 5:3, 6; 7:2; 9:12
w. is man, that thou? *Job* 7:17
15:14; *Ps* 8:4; 144:3; *Heb* 2:6
w. shall I do unto thee? *Job* 7:20
who will say unto him, *W.*? 9:12
Eccl 8:4; *Ezek* 12:9; *Dan* 4:35
let come on me *w.* will. *Job* 13:13
w. then shall I do? *w.* shall? 31:14
Luke 10:25; 12:17; 16:3
let us know *w.* is good. *Job* 34:4 *Mi* 6:8
w. doest thou against him? *w.* doest to him? *Job* 35:6
if thou be righteous, *w.* givest? 7
w. man is he that feareth the Lord? *Ps* 25:12; 34:12; 89:48
I will hear *w.* God the Lord. 85:8
w. shall be given unto thee? *w.*? 120:3
consider diligently *w.* is. *Pr* 23:1
lest thou know not *w.* to do. 25:8
w. is his name? *w.* is his? 30:4
w. my son? and *w.* the son? 31:2
I said of mirth, *W.* doeth? *Eccl* 2:2
Watchman, *w.* of the night? *Isa* 21:11
w. hast thou here? 22:16
w. shall I say? 38:15; *John* 12:27
therefore *w.* have I here? *Isa* 52:5
w. wilt thou do? *Jer* 4:30
saying, *W.* have I done? 8:6
w. wilt thou say? 13:21
and say, *W.* is done? 48:19
O Ephraim, *w.* shall I? *Hos* 6:4
give them, O Lord; *w.* wilt.? 9:14
w. have I do any more with idols? 14:8
yea, and *w.* have ye to do with me? *Joel* 3:4
and declare unto man *w.* *Amos* 4:13
O my Lord, *w.* are these? *Zech* 1:9
4:4; 6:4
I said, *W.* be these? 1:19; 4:5, 13
w. is it? 5:6
w. do ye more than? *Mat* 5:47
no thought *w.* ye shall eat, or *w.* 6:25, 31; *Luke* 12:22, 29
w. have we to do with thee, Jesus? *Mat* 8:29; *Mark* 1:24; 5:7
Luke 4:34; 8:28
have ye not read *w.* David did? *Mat* 12:3; *Mark* 2:25; *Luke* 6:3
have forsaken all; *w.*? *Mat* 19:27
they said, *W.* is that to us? 27:4
told *w.* they had done, and *w.* they. *Mark* 6:30
for he wist not *w.* to say. 9:6
this cup, not *w.* I will, but *w.* 14:36
people asked, *W.* shall we do then? *Luke* 3:10; 12:17
the Lord said, to *w.* are they? 7:31
w. will I, if it be already? 12:49
they know not *w.* they do. 23:34
w. then? *John* 1:21
w. did he to thee? 9:26
w. I should say, and *w.* I. 12:49
w. is this that he saith? 16:18
w. is that to thee? follow. 21:22, 23
w. shall we do? *Acts* 2:37; 4:16
Lord, *W.* wilt thou have me to do? 9:6; 22:10
w. is it, Lord? 10:4
w. was I, that I could? *Acts* 11:17
w. must I do? 16:30
Unto *w.* then were ye baptized? 19:3
w. is it therefore? 21:22
w. shall we say? *Rom* 3:5; 4:1
6:1; 7:7
w. then? 3:9; 6:15; 8:31; 9:14, 30
11:7; *1 Cor* 10:19; 14:15
Phil 1:18
w. I would that do I not, but *w.* I hate, that do I. *Rom* 7:15
w. will ye? shall I come? *1 Cor* 4:21
w. I do, that I will do. *2 Cor* 11:12
yet *w.* I shall choose I. *Phil* 1:22
understanding neither *w.* *1 Tim* 1:7
consider *w.* I say; and the Lord give thee. *2 Tim* 2:7
w. shall I more say? *Heb* 11:32
ye know not *w.* shall be on the morrow. For *w.* is your life? *Jas* 4:14
searching *w.* or *w.* manner. *1 Pet* 1:11
it doth not yet appear *w.* *1 John* 3:2
see **things**

whatsoever

now *w.* God hath said. *Gen* 31:16
even of *w.* passeth under. *Lev* 27:32
I will do *w.* thou sayest. *Num* 22:17
nor *w.* the Lord our God. *Deut* 2:37
w. I command you, observe. 12:32
do thou to us *w.* *Judg* 10:15
1 Sam 14:36
w. plague, *w.* sickness. *1 Ki* 8:37
w. supplication be made. 38
2 Chr 6:28
w. is under the whole. *Job* 41:11
leaf not wither; *w.* he doeth. *Ps* 1:3
w. passeth through the paths. 8:8
God is in the heavens, he hath done *w.* he. 115:3, 135:6; *Eccl* 8:3
w. God doeth, it shall. *Eccl* 3:14
w. I command thee, thou. *Jer* 1:7
we will do *w.* goeth out of. 44:17
w. is more than these. *Mat* 5:37
w. ye would that men should. 7:12
Herod promised with an oath to give her *w.* she. 14:7; *Mark* 6:22
have done unto him *w.* they listed. *Mat* 17:12; *Mark* 9:13
and *w.* is right I will give you. *Mat* 20:4, 7
all things *w.* ye shall ask in prayer, believing, ye shall. 21:22
Mark 11:23, 24; *John* 14:13
w. they bid you observe. *Mat* 23:3
observe all things *w.* I have. 28:20
his mother saith, *W.* he saith to you. *John* 2:5
ye are my friends, if ye do *w.* 15:14
w. ye shall ask in my name. 16
16:23
him hear in all things *w.* *Acts* 3:22
for *w.* is not of faith. *Rom* 14:23
w. is sold in the shambles, that eat. *1 Cor* 10:25
w. is set before you, eat. 27
or *w.* ye do, do all to the glory. 31
w. they were, it maketh. *Gal* 2:6
w. a man soweth, that shall. 6:7
w. things are true, *w.* *Phil* 4:8
I have learned in *w.* state I am. 11
w. ye do in word . . . do all in the name of the Lord Jesus. *Col* 3:17
w. ye do, do it heartily as to. 23
w. we ask we receive of him. *1 John* 3:22; 5:15
thou doest faithfully *w.* *3 John* 5

wheat

Reuben found mandrakes in *w.* *Gen* 30:14
but the *w.* and rye were. *Ex* 9:32
the firstfruits of *w.* harvest. 34:22
Num 18:12
goats, with the fat of kidneys of *w.* *Deut* 32:14
and Gideon threshed *w.* *Judg* 6:11
time of *w.* harvest, Samson. 15:1
to glean unto the end of *w.* harvest. *Ruth* 2:23
they of Beth-shemesh reaping *w.* *1 Sam* 6:13
is it not *w.* harvest day? 12:17
would have fetched *w.* *2 Sam* 4:6
Solomon gave Hiram *w.* *1 Ki* 5:11
I give the *w.* for the meat offering. *1 Chr* 21:23
have need of, *w.* salt, wine. *Ezra* 6:9
to an hundred measures of *w.* 7:22
let thistles grow instead of *w.* *Job* 31:40
fed them with finest of *w.* *Ps* 81:16
thee with the finest of *w.* 147:14
fool in a mortar among *w.* *Pr* 27:22
thy belly is like a heap of *w.* set. *S of S* 7:2
they have sown *w.* but. *Jer* 12:13
what is the chaff to the *w.*? 23:28
flow together, for *w.*, for wine. 31:12
Judah traded in *w.* of. *Ezek* 27:17
floors shall be full of *w.* *Joel* 2:24
from him burdens of *w.* *Amos* 5:11
that we may set forth *w.* 8:5
poor, and sell refuse of *w.* 6
gather his *w.* into the garner. *Mat* 3:12; *Luke* 3:17
sowed tares among the *w.* *Mat* 13:25
lest ye root up also the *w.* 29
to burn them, but gather the *w.* 30
said 100 measures of *w.* *Luke* 16:7
that he may sift you as *w.* 22:31
except a corn of *w.* fall. *John* 12:24
and cast out the *w.* *Acts* 27:38
it may chance of *w.* or. *1 Cor* 15:37
I heard a voice, a measure of *w.* *Rev* 6:6
merchandise of *w.* is departed. 18:13
see **barley**

wheaten

cakes and wafers; of *w.* flour shalt thou make them. *Ex* 29:2*

wheel

make them like a *w.* *Ps* 83:13
a wise king bringeth the *w.* *Pr* 20:26*
w. broken at the cistern. *Eccl* 12:6
nor break it with the *w.* *Isa* 28:28
one *w.* upon the earth. *Ezek* 1:15
w. in the midst of a *w.* 16; 10:10
wheels, in my hearing, O *w.* 10:13

wheels

took off their chariot *w.* *Ex* 14:25
why tarry the *w.* of his? *Judg* 5:28
their *w.* like a whirlwind. *Isa* 5:28
a work on the *w.* *Jer* 18:3
the rumbling of his *w.* 47:3
the appearance of the *w.* *Ezek* 1:16
of *w.* over against them. 3:13
the *w.* also were beside them. 10:19; 11:22
come against thee with *w.* 23:24
at the noise of the *w.* 26:10
and his *w.* a burning fire. *Dan* 7:9
of the rattling of the *w.* *Nah* 3:2

whelp, -s

a bear robbed of her *w.* *2 Sam* 17:8
let a bear robbed of her *w.* *Pr* 17:12
she nourished her *w.* *Ezek* 19:2
one of her *w.* . . . a young lion. 3
she took another of her *w.* and. 5
bear bereaved of her *w.* *Hos* 13:8
the lion did tear enough for his *w.* *Nah* 2:12

see **lions**

when

w. it is unclean and *w.* *Lev* 14:57
w. thou sittest and *w.* thou walkest, *w.* thou liest down, and *w.* thou risest up. *Deut* 6:7; 11:19
w. I begin, I will also. *1 Sam* 3:12
hear thou in heaven thy dwelling place: *w.* thou hearest. *1 Ki* 8:30
the king said, *W.* wilt? *Neh* 2:6
ye fools, *w.* will ye be wise? *Ps* 94:8
for who can tell him *w.*? *Eccl* 8:7
clean? *w.* shall it once be? *Jer* 13:27
w. ye fasted. *Zech* 7:5
w. ye did eat, and *w.* ye did drink. 6
w. shall these things be? and what? *Mat* 24:3; *Mark* 13:4; *Luke* 21:7
w. he is come, he will tell us all things. *John* 4:25; 16:8
w. he had so said, he shewed. 20:20
w. they heard this, they. *Acts* 2:37
w. we were with you. *2 Thes* 3:10
w. he shall appear, we. *1 John* 2:28

whence
the angel said, Hagar, w. camest thou? Gen 16:8
Joseph said to them, W. come ye? 42:7; Josh 9:8
is not like Egypt, from w. ye came out. Deut 11:10
I wist not w. they were. Josh 2:4
I asked him not w. he. Judg 13:6
Micah said, W. comest thou? 17:9
19:17; 2 Sam 1:3; 2 Ki 5:25
Job 1:7; 2:2; Jonah 1:8
men? from w. came these men unto thee? 2 Ki 20:14; Isa 39:3
before I go w. I shall not return. Job 10:21; 16:22
not know from w. it riseth. Isa 47:11
look to the rock w. ye are. 51:1
I will return to my house, w. I came. Mat 12:44; Luke 11:24
w. hath this man this wisdom? Mat 13:54
w. hath this man all these things? 56; Mark 6:2
calleth him Lord, w. is? Mark 12:37
w. is this to me, that the mother of my Lord? Luke 1:43
I know you not w. ye are. 13:25, 27
W. knowest thou me? John 1:48
and ye know w. I am. 7:28
ye cannot tell w. I come. 8:14
we know not from w. he is. 9:29, 30
from w. we look for the. Phil 3:20
from w. he received him. Heb 11:19
w. come wars and fightings? Jas 4:1
remember from w. thou. Rev 2:5
in white robes? w. came they? 7:13

whensoever
w. ye will ye may do. Mark 14:7

where
w. art thou? Gen 3:9
w. is he? Ex 2:20; 2 Sam 9:4
Job 14:10
in all places w. I record. Ex 20:24
w. I will meet you to speak. 29:42
30:6, 36
shall say, W. are their gods? Deut 32:37
if not, w. and who is he? Job 9:24
W. is God my maker who? 35:10
w. wast thou? 38:4
to me, W. is thy God? Ps 42:3, 10
wherefore should heathen say, W. is their God? 79:10; 115:2; Joel 2:17
these, w. had they been? Isa 49:21
said they, W. is the Lord? Jer 2:6, 8
let no man know w. ye be. 36:19
w. it was said to them. Hos 1:10
fathers, w. are they? Zech 1:5
they said, W. Lord? Luke 17:37
Jews said, W. is he? John 7:11
9:12
w. I am. 7:34; 12:26; 14:3; 17:24

whereabout
know w. I send thee. 1 Sam 21:2

whereas
w. I rewarded thee evil. 1 Sam 24:17
w. it was in thine heart. 1 Ki 8:18
w. ye say, The Lord. Ezek 13:7
will possess it, w. the Lord. 35:10
w. ye know not what will. Jas 4:14

whereby
iniquity w. they have sinned. Jer 33:8
transgressions w. ye have transgressed. Ezek 18:31
trespasses w. they have trespassed. 39:26
w. shall I know this? Luke 1:18
no other name w. we must. Acts 4:12
the Spirit, w. we cry. Rom 8:15
w. ye are sealed to the day. Eph 4:30

wherefore
w. should I fast? can I bring him? 2 Sam 12:23
who shall then say, W. hast? 16:10
w. one? That he might seek a godly seed. Mal 2:15
O thou of little faith, w.? Mat 14:31
Jesus said, Friend, w. art? 26:50
what is the cause w. ye? Acts 10:21

whereto
in the thing w. I sent it. Isa 55:11
w. we have already attained, let us walk. Phil 3:16

wherewith
O my Lord, w. shall I? Judg 6:15
the Lord said to him, W.? 1 Ki 22:22; 2 Chr 18:20
but against the house w. I have war. 2 Chr 35:21
so shall I have w. to. Ps 119:42
w. shall I come before? Mi 6:6
if salt lose its savour, w. shall it be? Mat 5:13; Mark 9:5; Luke 14:34
the love w. thou hast. John 17:26
for this great love w. he. Eph 2:4

wherewithal
what shall we eat? or w.? Mat 6:31

whet
if I w. my glittering sword I will reward. Deut 32:41
if he turn not, he will w. Ps 7:12
who w. their tongue like a. 64:3
iron blunt and he do not w. Eccl 10:10

whether
w. they be for peace, or w. 1 Ki 20:18
w. they were of Israel. Ezra 2:59
Neh 7:61
w. they will hear or forbear. Ezek 2:5, 7; 3:11
w. of them twain did the will of his father? Mat 21:31
w. is greater, the gold or? 23:17
doctrine, w. it be of God. John 7:17
w. we live or die, we are. Rom 14:8
w. it were I or they, so. 1 Cor 15:11
w. in the body, or w. out of the body. 2 Cor 12:2, 3
but try the spirits w. 1 John 4:1

which
of the tree w. I commanded thee, saying. Gen 3:17
in w. there shall be neither. 45:6
a heifer upon w. never. Num 19:2
in w. there shall not be. Luke 21:6
w. of you convinceth me? John 8:46
for w. of those works do ye? 10:32
in the w. I will appear. Acts 26:16
in the w. ye also walked. Col 3:7
a better hope; by w. we. Heb 7:19
of w. we cannot now speak. 9:5
follow peace with all men, and holiness, without w. no man. 12:14
that worthy name, by w. Jas 2:7
by w. he preached to. 1 Pet 3:19

while, whiles
w. I am yet alive with. Deut 31:27
thou shalt not only w. yet I live shew me the kindness. 1 Sam 20:14
w. the child was yet alive. 2 Sam 12:18, 21, 22
Lord is with you w. ye. 2 Chr 15:2
w. Josiah was yet young, he. 34:3
God shall rain it on him w. Job 20:23
tear my soul, w. there is none. Ps 7:2
though w. he lived he blessed. 49:18
thus will I bless thee w. I live. 63:4; 146:2
will praise God w. I have my being. 104:33; 146:2
w. he may be found. Isa 55:6
her sun is gone down w. it was yet day. Jer 15:9
w. he was not yet gone back. 40:5
agree w. thou art in the. Mat 5:25
that deceiver said, w. he. 27:63
of bride-chamber fast w. the bridegroom? Mark 2:19; Luke 5:34
I spake w. I was yet. Luke 24:44
do work of him that sent me w. it is day. John 9:4
that liveth in pleasure is dead w. she liveth. 1 Tim 5:6
w. it is said, To-day if. Heb 3:15
see **little**

a **while**
Joseph wept on his neck a good w. Gen 46:29
Samuel said to Saul, Stand thou still a w. 1 Sam 9:27
spoken for a great w. 2 Sam 7:19
root, but dureth for a w. Mat 13:21
which for a w. believe, and in time of temptation fall away. Luke 8:13
he would not for a w.: but. Luke 18:4
after have suffered a w. 1 Pet 5:10

all the **while**
all the w. David was in. 1 Sam 22:4
none missing all the w. they were in Carmel. 25:7, 16
will be his manner all the w. 27:11
all the w. my breath is in me and Spirit of God. Job 27:3

long **while**
had talked a long w. even till break of day. Acts 20:11

whip
a w. for the horse, a rod. Pr 26:3
the noise of a w., the noise. Nah 3:2

whips
father chastised you with w., I will. 1 Ki 12:11, 14; 2 Chr 10:11, 14

whirleth
wind w. continually and. Eccl 1:6*

whirlwind
Lord would take up Elijah by a w. 2 Ki 2:1, 11
cometh the w. and cold. Job 37:9*
the Lord answered Job out of the w. 38:1; 40:6
as with a w., both living and. Ps 58:9
Pr 10:25; Hos 13:3
destruction cometh as a w. Pr 1:27
counted it like flint and their wheels like a w. Isa 5:28
a rolling thing before the w. 17:13*
the w. shall take them away. 40:24
shalt fan them, the w. shall. 41:16
Lord come with chariots like a w. 66:15; Jer 4:13
a w. of the Lord is gone. Jer 23:19*
a great w. shall be raised up. 25:32*
a continuing w. shall fall on. 30:23*
behold, a w. came out of. Ezek 1:4*
king shall come against him like a w. Dan 11:40
they shall reap the w. Hos 8:7
devour palaces in the day of the w. Amos 1:14
the Lord hath his way in the w. Nah 1:3
out as a w. to scatter. Hab 3:14
but I scattered them with a w. Zech 7:14

whirlwinds
as w. in the south pass. Isa 21:1
Lord shall go forth with w. Zech 9:14

whisper
all that hate me w. together. Ps 41:7
thy speech shall w. out. Isa 29:4

whispered
when David saw that his servants w. 2 Sam 12:19

whisperer
a w. separateth chief. Pr 16:28

whisperers
envy, murder, deceit, w. Rom 1:29

whisperings
be w. swellings, tumults. 2 Cor 12:20

whit
shalt burn every w. Deut 13:16
Samuel told Eli every w. 1 Sam 3:18
a man every w. whole. John 7:23
feet, but is clean every w. 13:10
I was not a w. behind. 2 Cor 11:5

white
Jacob made the w. appear in the rods. Gen 30:37
and his teeth shall be w. 49:12
like coriander seed, w. Ex 16:31
if the hair be turned w. Lev 13:3
4, 20, 25
if the bright spot be w. 4, 19, 24*
rising be w. in the skin. 10, 19, 43*
be no w. hairs therein. 21, 26
Miriam became leprous, w. as snow. Num 12:10
ye that ride on w. asses. Judg 5:10
Gehazi went out a leper w. as snow. 2 Ki 5:27
the Levites being arrayed in w. linen. 2 Chr 5:12*
Mordecai went out in w. apparel. Esth 8:15
taste in the w. of an egg? Job 6:6

w. as snow in Salmon. Ps 68:14*
garments be always w. Eccl 9:8
my beloved is w. and ruddy, the. S of S 5:10
be as scarlet, they shall be as w. as snow. Isa 1:18
Damascus traded in w. wool. Ezek 27:18
garment was w. as snow. Dan 7:9
shall fall to make them w. 11:35
be purified and made w. 12:10
thereof are made w. Joel 1:7
horses, speckled and w. Zech 1:8
not make one hair w. or black. Mat 5:36
his raiment was w. as the light. 17:2; Luke 9:29
the angel's raiment was w. Mat 28:3; Acts 1:10
a man clothed in a long w. garment. Mark 16:5
fields are w. already. John 4:35
and his hairs were w. Rev 1:14
will give him a w. stone and. 2:17
they shall walk with me in w. 3:4
shall be clothed in w. raiment. 5
4:4; 7:9, 13; 15:6; 19:8, 14
buy w. raiment, that thou. 3:18
behold a w. horse. 6:2; 19:11
made them w. in the blood. 7:14
a w. cloud. 14:14
I saw a w. throne. 20:11

white, *verb*

no fuller on earth can w. Mark 9:3

whited

like to w. sepulchres. Mat 23:27
smite thee, thou w. wall. Acts 23:3

whiter

I shall be w. than snow. Ps 51:7
her Nazarites are w. than milk. Lam 4:7

whither

maid, w. wilt thou go? Gen 16:8
keep thee in all places w. 28:15
Saul's uncle said, W. went ye? 1 Sam 10:14
Thy servant went no w. 2 Ki 5:25
w. is thy beloved gone? S of S 6:1
I said, W. do these bear the ephah? Zech 5:10
went, not knowing w. Heb 11:8
see **go, goest, goeth**

whithersoever

the Lord preserved David w. he. 2 Sam 8:6, 14; 2 Ki 18:7
1 Chr 18:6, 13
w. it turneth it prospereth. Pr 17:8
he turneth the king's heart w. 21:1
I will follow thee w. thou goest. Mat 8:19; Luke 9:57
these follow the Lamb w. Rev 14:4

who

w. art thou, my son? Gen 27:18, 32
Ruth 3:9, 16; John 1:19, 22
8:25; 21:12
Esau said, W. are those? Gen 33:5
48:8
w. am I? Ex 3:11; 1 Sam 18:18
2 Sam 7:18
w. is the Lord? Ex 5:2; Pr 30:9
John 9:36
w. is like thee, O Lord, among the gods? Ex 15:11; Deut 33:29
1 Sam 26:15; Ps 35:10
Moses stood and said, W.? Ex 32:26
w. is David? and w. is? 1 Sam 25:10
w. is on my side, w.? 2 Ki 9:32
but w. slew all these? 10:9
Jehu said, W. are ye? 13
w. would go into the temple to save his life? Neh 6:11
w. is he? and where is he?
Esth 7:5; Job 17:3; 42:3; Jer 9:12
W. will shew us any good? Ps 4:6
for w., say they, doth hear? 59:7
w. hath woe? w. hath sorrow? w. hath . . . ? w. hath? Pr. 23:29
w. will go for us? Isa 6:8
W. seeth us? 29:15
w. shall come down? Jer 21:13
saying, W. shall come unto? 49:4
w. is like me? w. will? 19; 50:44
of Zion: w. can heal thee? Lam 2:13
w. is he that saith, and it? 3:37
saying, W. is this? Mat 21:10
Luke 5:21; 7:49; 9:9
W. is he that smote thee? Mat 26:68
to see Jesus w. he was. Luke 19:3
healed, wist not w. it. John 5:13
Lord, w. is it? 13:25
he said, W. art thou, Lord? Acts 9:5; 22:8; 26:15
but w. are ye? 19:15
captain demanded w. he was. 21:33
w. then is Paul? and w.? 1 Cor 3:5
and w. is sufficient? 2 Cor 2:16
w. is weak? w. is offended? 11:29
w. art thou that judgest? Jas 4:12
w. is a liar, but he that? 1 John 2:22
w. shall be able to stand? Rev 6:17
saying, W. is like unto the beast? w. is able to? 13:4
w. shall not fear thee, O Lord? 15:4

whole

shalt burn w. ram on altar. Ex 29:18; Lev 8:21
even the w. bullock shall. Lev 4:12
w. house of Israel bewail. 10:6
Joshua took the w. land. Josh 11:23
because my life is yet w. 2 Sam 1:9
him with their w. desire. 2 Chr 15:15
shalt be pleased with w. Ps 51:19
them up alive, and w. Pr 1:12
the w. disposing thereof is. 16:33
for this is the w. duty. Eccl 12:13
thy Redeemer, the Holy One, the God of w. earth shall he be called. Isa 54:5; Mi 4:13; Zech 4:14
a vessel that cannot be made w. Jer 19:11
pluck up, even this w. land. 45:4
when w. it was meet. Ezek 15:5
ye have robbed me, even this w. nation. Mal 3:9
not that thy w. body. Mat 5:29, 30
the w. herd of swine ran. 8:32
till the w. was leavened. 13:33
Luke 13:21
profited if he shall gain the w. world and lose his own soul? Mat 16:26
Mark 8:36; Luke 9:25
w. multitude of them arose and led him. Luke 23:1
and himself believed, and his w. house. John 4:53
expedient that the w. nation. 11:50
came almost the w. city. Acts 13:44
if w. body were an eye. 1 Cor 12:17
I pray your w. spirit. 1 Thes 5:23
shall keep the w. law. Jas 2:10
end of the w. world. 1 John 2:2
and the w. world lieth in. 5:19
see **congregation, heart**

whole for *sound*

they abode in the camp till they were w. Josh 5:8
and his hands make w. Job 5:18
w. need not a physician. Mat 9:12
Mark 2:17; Luke 5:31
touch his garment, I shall be w. Mat 9:21; Mark 5:28
woman was made w. Mat 9:22
his hand was made w. 12:13
Mark 3:5; Luke 6:10
daughter was made w. Mat 15:28
saw the maimed to be w. 31
thee w.; go in peace and be w. of. Mark 5:34; Luke 8:48; 17:19
found the servant w. Luke 7:10
Wilt thou be made w.? John 5:6
thou art made w.: sin no more. 14
made a man every whit w. 7:23
what means he is made w. Acts 4:9
Jesus Christ maketh thee w. 9:34

wholesome

a w. tongue is a tree of. Pr 15:4
consent not to w. words. 1 Tim 6:3*

wholly

it shall be w. burnt. Lev 6:22, 23
thou shalt not w. reap corners. 19:9
for they are w. given to. Num 3:9
a cloth w. of blue. 4:6
are w. given me. 8:16
because they have not w. 32:11
give the land, because he hath w. Deut 1:36; Josh 14:8, 9, 14
I had w. dedicated the. Judg 17:3
a sucking lamb w. 1 Sam 7:9
all the people w. at thy. 1 Chr 28:21
one dieth, being w. at ease. Job 21:23
thou art w. gone up to the. Isa 22:1
planted thee w. a right seed. Jer 2:21
she is w. oppression in the. 6:6
Judah shall be w. carried. 13:19
if ye w. set your faces to. 42:15
yet will I not leave thee w. 46:28
Babylon not be inhabited, but w. desolate. 50:13
of Israel w., are they. Ezek 11:15
and it shall rise up w. as a flood. Amos 8:8; 9:5
he saw the city w. given. Acts 17:16
of peace sanctify you w. 1 Thes 5:23
give thyself w. to them. 1 Tim 4:15

whom

take thy only son Isaac w. Gen 22:2
wives, for w. I served thee. 30:26
the old man of w. ye spake, is he alive? 43:27, 29
will be gracious to w. I. Ex 33:19
after w. they have gone. Lev 17:7
people, amongst w. I am. Num 11:21
they are children in w. Deut 32:20
where their gods? their rock in w. 37
choose you this day w. Josh 24:15
that of w. I say, this shall. Judg 7:4
and to w. shall he go up from us? 1 Sam 6:20
and on w. is all the desire of? 9:20
David, of w. they sang one. 29:5
David said unto him, To w.? 30:13
and again, w. should I serve? 2 Sam 16:19
Ahab said, By w.? 1 Ki 20:14; 22:8
Ezra 10:44; Rom 1:5; 5:2, 11
Gal 6:14
thy God in w. thou trustest. 2 Ki 19:10; Isa 37:10
but to the saints, in w. Ps 16:3
my God, my strength, in w. I. 18:2
w. have I in heaven but thee? 73:25
not trust in son of man, in w. 146:3
as a father the son, in w. Pr 3:12
good from them to w. it is due. 27
a king against w. there is no. 30:31
he, For w. do I labour? Eccl 4:8
w. my soul loveth. S of S 3:1, 2, 3
I heard a voice saying, W. shall I send? Isa 6:8
in day of visitation? to w. will? 10:3
what hast thou here? w.? 22:16
turn to him from w. Israel. 31:6
to w. then will ye liken God? 40:18, 25; 46:5
behold mine elect, in w. my. 42:1
art my servant, O Israel, in w. 49:3
famine and sword; by w. shall? 51:19
against w. do ye sport? 57:4
of w. hast thou been afraid? 11
w. they have loved, w. they have served, after w. they have walked, and w. they sought. Jer 8:2
from w. I am not able to rise up. Lam 1:14
w. we said, Under his shadow. 4:20
Son of man, speak unto Pharaoh, . . . W. art thou like? Ezek 31:2
to w. art thou like in glory? 18
w. he would he slew, w. he . . . and w. he would he. Dan 5:19
O Lord, by w. shall Jacob arise? Amos 7:2, 5
on w. hath not thy wickedness passed? Nah 3:19
in w. I am well pleased. Mat 3:17
17:5; Mark 1:11; 2 Pet 2:17
this is he of w. it is written. Mat 11:10; John 1:15, 30
w. say ye that I am? Mat 16:15
Mark 8:29; Luke 9:20
quickeneth w. he will. John 5:21
Moses, in w. ye trust. 45
Lord, to w. shall we go? 6:68
w. thou hast sent. 17:3
of w. speaketh the? Acts 8:34
whose I am, and w. I serve. 27:23
to w. he was not spoken. Rom 15:21

God is faithful, by w. ye. 1 Cor 1:9
but ministers by w. ye believed ? 3:5
liberty to be married to w. 7:39
one God, of w. are all things. 8:6
Heb 2:10
in w. we trust that he. 2 Cor 1:10
in w. we have redemption through.
Eph 1:7; Col 1:14
in w. also we have obtained.
Eph 1:11
in w. ye also trusted: in w. also. 13
among w. also we all had our. 2:3
in w. the building groweth to a. 21
in w. ye also are builded. 22
in w. ye have boldness and. 3:12
among w. ye shine as. Phil 2:15
for w. I have suffered the loss. 3:8
w. we preach. Col 1:28
in w. are hid all the treasures. 2:3
in w. ye are circumcised. 11
that wicked, w. the Lord. 2 Thes 2:8
to save sinners, of w. I. 1 Tim 1:15
of w. is Hymenaeus and Alexander.
20; 2 Tim 2:17
of w. are Phygellus. 2 Tim 1:15
the coppersmith, of w. be. 4:15
to w. be glory for ever. 18
Gal 1:5; Heb 13:21; 1 Pet 4:11
with w. was he grieved ? Heb 3:17
to w. sware he they should not ? 18
to the eyes of him with w. 4:13
to w. Abraham gave the tenth. 7:2
of w. the world was not. 11:38
father of lights, with w. Jas 1:17
unto w. it was revealed. 1 Pet 1:12
to w. coming, as unto a living. 2:4
to w. darkness is reserved.
2 Pet 2:17; Jude 13
for of w. a man is overcome, . . .
brought in bondage. 2 Pet 2:19
to w. it was given to hurt. Rev 7:2
with w. kings of earth. 17:2
see before

whomsoever

w. thou findest thy gods. Gen 31:32
w. the Lord our God. Judg 11:24
he giveth it to w. he will. Dan 4:17
25:32; 5:21
he to w. the Son will. Mat 11:27
but on w. it shall fall. 21:44
Luke 20:18
the devil said, To w. I. Luke 4:6
to w. much is given, much. 12:48
on w. I lay hands, may. Acts 8:19
w. ye shall approve by. 1 Cor 16:3

whore

(Revised Versions change this to harlot, and often make same change in its derivatives)
do not cause her to be a w. lest the land. Lev 19:29
not take a wife that is a w. 21:7
profane herself by playing the w. 9
to play the w. in her. Deut 22:21
no w. of the daughters of. 23:17
bring the hire of a w. or price. 18
his concubine played the w. Judg 19:2
a w. is a deep ditch. Pr 23:27
adulterer and the w. Isa 57:3
thou hadst a w.'s forehead. Jer 3:3
thou hast played the w. Ezek 16:28
judgement of the great w. Rev 17:1
19:2
waters where the w. sitteth. 17:15
these shall hate the w. and make. 16

whoredom

she is with child by w. Gen 38:24
lest the land fall to w. Lev 19:29
the lightness of her w. she. Jer 3:9
the lewdness of thy w. 13:27
come to thee for thy w. Ezek 16:33
they poured their w. upon her. 23:8
defiled her with their w. 17
defile my holy name by their w. 43:7
let them put away their w. far. 9
w. and wine take away. Hos 4:11
O Ephraim, thou committest w. 5:3
is the w. of Ephraim, Israel. 6:10

whoredoms

shall wander and bear w. Num 14:33
w. of thy mother Jezebel. 2 Ki 9:22
like to the w. of the house of Ahab.
2 Chr 21:13
thou hast polluted the land with thy w. Jer 3:2
is this of thy w. a small ? Ezek 16:20
all thy w. hast not remembered. 22
hast multiplied thy w. 25
hast increased thy w. 26
from other women in thy w. 34
also thy lewdness and thy w. 23:35
a wife and children of w. Hos 1:2
let her put away her w. out of. 2:2
for they be the children of w. 4
the spirit of w. hath. 4:12; 5:4
of w., that selleth nations through her w. and families. Nah 3:4
see commit

whoremonger

no w. hath any inheritance in the kingdom of Christ. Eph 5:5

whoremongers

(Revised Versions change this to fornicators)
the law made for w. 1 Tim 1:10*
but w. and adulterers God. Heb 13:4
w. shall have their part. Rev 21:8
for without are w. and. 22:15

whores

they give gifts to all w. Ezek 16:33
are separated with w. Hos 4:14

whoring, see **go, gone, went**

whorish

by means of a w. woman. Pr 6:26
broken with their w. heart. Ezek 6:9
an imperious w. woman. 16:30

whose

w. art thou ? w. are ? Gen 32:17
w. ox, or w. ass have ? 1 Sam 12:3
w. is the land ? make. 2 Sam 3:12
a remnant shall know w. Jer 44:28
w. name is the Lord. 48:15; 51:57
the God in w. hands thy. Dan 5:23
saith Lord, w. name is. Amos 5:27
he saith to them, W. is ? Mat 22:20
Mark 12:16; Luke 20:24
w. son is he ? Mat 22:42
then w. shall those ? Luke 12:20
w. it shall be. John 19:24
angel of God, w. I am. Acts 27:23
Christ over his house, w. Heb 3:6
see heart

who-, whosesoever

w. would, he consecrated. 1 Ki 13:33
blessed w. shall not be. Mat 11:6
w. hath, to him shall be given: w. hath not, from. 13:12; Luke 8:18
w. sins ye remit, w. John 20:23
O man, w. thou art that. Rom 2:1
w. shall eat this bread 1 Cor 11:27
his judgement, w. he be. Gal 5:10
w. will, let him take of. Rev 22:17

why

it be so, w. am I thus ? Gen 25:22
w. are ye come to me ? Judg 11:7
Judah said, W. are ye come ? 15:10
turn again, w. will ye ? Ruth 1:11
Eli said, W. do ye such things ?
1 Sam 2:23
w. art thou alone, and no man ? 21:1
king said, W. should he go with thee?
2 Sam 13:26
in saying, W. hast thou done so ?
1 Ki 1:6
forbear, w. shouldest thou be smitten ? 2 Chr 25:16
what it was and w. it was. Esth 4:5
w. sayest thou, O Jacob, My way is hid ? Isa 40:27
w. do ye sit still ? assemble yourselves. Jer 8:14
w. will ye die ? 27:13; Ezek 18:31
33:11
us, W. did ye not then ? Mat 21:25
Mark 11:31; Luke 20:5
he saith, W. make ye this ado, and weep ? Mark 5:39
w. hast thou thus dealt ? Luke 2:48
they said, W. have ye ? John 7:45
He is mad, w. hear ye him ? 10:20
and heard a voice, Saul, Saul, w. persecutest thou me ? Acts 9:4
22:7; 26:14
Sirs, w. do ye these things ?
Acts 14:15
W. doth he yet find fault? Rom 9:19
thing formed say, W. hast thou ? 20
w. am I evil spoken of ? 1 Cor 10:30

wicked

wilt thou also destroy the righteous with the w.? Gen 18:23, 25
Er was w. 38:7
I and my people are w. Ex 9:27
for I will not justify the w. 23:7
it is a w. thing, they. Lev 20:17*
thought in thy w. heart. Deut 15:9
committed that w. thing. 17:5
keep thee from every w. thing. 23:9
condemn the w. 25:1; 1 Ki 8:32
the w. shall be silent. 1 Sam 2:9
proceedeth from the w. 24:13
Israel wrought w. things. 2 Ki 17:11
servants, by requiting w. 2 Chr 6:23
themselves and turn from their w.
7:14; Ezek 18:21; 33:11, 19
Athaliah that w. woman. 2 Chr 24:7
nor turned they from their w. ways.
Neh 9:35; Ezek 3:19; 13:22
the adversary is this w. Esth 7:6
Haman's w. device shall return. 9:25
there the w. cease from. Job 3:17
the perfect and the w. 9:22
if I be w. why then labour I in vain ?
29; 10:15
thou knowest that I am not w. 10:7
wherefore do the w. live ? 21:7
the w. is reserved to the day. 30
let mine enemy be as the w. 27:7
say to a king, Thou art w.? 34:18
that the w. might be shaken. 38:13
from the w. their light is. 15
and tread down the w. in. 40:12
God is angry with the w. Ps 7:11
thou hast destroyed the w. for. 9:5
the w. is snared in the work of his. 16
w. shall be turned into hell. 17
the w. in pride doth persecute. 10:2
the w. boasteth. 3
the w. will not seek God. 4
wherefore doth the w. contemn ? 13
lo, the w. bend their bow. 11:2
but the w. and him that. 5
upon the w. he shall rain snares. 6
the w. walk on every side. 12:8
keep me from the w. that. 17:9
deliver my soul from the w. 13
and I will not sit with the w. 26:5
when the w. came upon me. 27:2
draw me not away with the w. 28:3
let the w. be ashamed and silent in the grave. 31:17
evil shall slay the w.: and they. 34:21
man who bringeth w. devices. 37:7
yet a little, the w. shall not be. 10
Pr 10:25
the w. plotteth. Ps 37:12
the w. have drawn out the sword. 14
the riches of many w. 16
the w. shall perish. 20
the w. borroweth, and payeth not. 21
the w. watcheth the righteous. 32
when the w. are cut off, thou. 34
I have seen the w. in great power. 35
deliver them from the w. 40
keep my mouth, while the w. 39:1
the w. are estranged from the. 58:3
be not merciful to any w. 59:5
so let the w. perish at the. 68:2
the w. of the earth shall wring. 75:8
when the w. spring as the grass. 92:7
Lord, how long shall the w.? 94:3
the pit be digged for the w. 13
I will set no w. thing before. 101:3
I will not know a w. person. 4
I will early destroy all the w. 8
consumed and let the w. be. 104:35
the flame burnt up the w. 106:18
the w. shall see it and be. 112:10
the w. have waited for me. 119:95
the w. laid a snare for me, yet. 110
thou puttest away all the w. 119
salvation is far from the w. 155
surely thou wilt slay the w. 139:19
if there be any w. way in me. 24
further not his w. device lest. 140:8
to practise w. works with. 141:4

w. fall into their own nets. *Ps* 141:10
all the *w.* will he destroy. 145:20
he casteth the *w.* down to. 147:6
the *w.* shall be cut off. *Pr* 2:22
iniquities shall take the *w.* 5:22
a heart that deviseth *w.* 6:18
but the *w.* shall not inhabit. 10:30
the *w.* shall fall by his own. 11:5
when a *w.* man dieth, his. 7
righteous delivered, the *w.* cometh. 8
and when the *w.* perish there. 10
w. worketh a deceitful work. 18
w. shall not be unpunished. 21, 31
but a man of *w.* devices. 12:2
the *w.* are overthrown. 7; 21:12
the *w.* desireth the net of evil. 12:12
w. is snared by the transgression. 13
but the *w.* shall be filled with. 21
a *w.* messenger falleth into. 13:17
and a man of *w.* devices is. 14:17
the *w.* bow at the gates of the. 19
the *w.* is driven away in his. 32
the Lord is far from the *w.* 15:29
yea, even the *w.* for the day. 16:4
a *w.* doer giveth heed to. 17:4
he that justifieth the *w.* and he. 15
when the *w.* cometh, then. 18:3
a wise king scattereth the *w.* 20:26
the *w.* shall be ransom for. 21:18
when he bringeth it with a *w.* mind. 27
but the *w.* shall fall into. 24:16
neither be thou envious at the *w.* 19
take away the *w.* from before. 25:5
man falling down before the *w.* 26
a *w.* heart is like a potsherd. 26:23
the *w.* flee when no man. 28:1
forsake the law praise the *w.* 4
when the *w.* rise. 12, 28
so is a *w.* ruler. 15
when the *w.* beareth rule. 29:2
w. regardeth not to know it. 7
his servants are *w.* 12
the *w.* are multiplied. 16
judge the righteous and *w.* *Eccl* 3:17
be not overmuch *w.* neither. 7:17
I saw the *w.* buried, they. 8:10
not be well with the *w.* 13
which justify the *w.* for. *Isa* 5:23
of his lips shall he slay the *w.* 11:4
I will punish the *w.* for. 13:11
he deviseth *w.* devices to. 32:7
he made his grave with the *w.* 53:9
let the *w.* forsake his way. 55:7
w. are like the troubled sea. 57:20
thou hast taught the *w.* *Jer* 2:33
for the *w.* are not plucked. 6:29
deceitful and desperately *w.* 17:9*
he will give the *w.* to the. 25:31
to warn the *w.* *Ezek* 3:18, 19; 33:8, 9
behold the *w.* abominations. 8:9
these men give *w.* counsel in. 11:2
I any pleasure that the *w.*? 18:23
not according to your *w.* 20:44
the righteous and the *w.* 21:3, 4
profane *w.* prince of Israel whose. 25
if the *w.* restore the pledge. 33:15
but the *w.* shall do. *Dan* 12:10
pure with *w.* balances? *Mi* 6:11
not at all acquit the *w.* *Nah* 1:3
out of thee a *w.* counsellor. 11
for the *w.* shall no more pass. 15
w. doth compass about the righteous. *Hab* 1:4
the *w.* devoureth the man. 13
stumblingblocks with the *w.* *Zeph* 1:3
between righteous and *w.* *Mal* 3:18
and ye shall tread down the *w.* 4:3
w. than himself. Even so shall it be to this *w.* *Mat* 12:45; *Luke* 11:26
angels shall sever the *w.* *Mat* 13:49
a *w.* generation seeketh after. 16:4
thou *w.* servant. 18:32; 25:26 *Luke* 19:22
and by *w.* hands have. *Acts* 2:23*
were a matter of *w.* lewdness. 18:14
put away that *w.* person. *1 Cor* 5:13
in your mind by *w.* works. *Col* 1:21
and then shall that *w.* be. *2 Thes* 2:8*

see **man, men**

of the **wicked**

the place *of the w.* shall come to naught. *Job* 8:22
given into the hand *of the w.* 9:24
shine upon the counsel *of w.* *Job* 10:3
but the eye *of the w.* shall. 11:20
me into the hands *of the w.* 16:11
the light *of the w.* shall be. 18:5
are the dwellings *of the w.* 21
the triumphing *of the w.* 20:5
every hand *of the w.* shall. 22*
the counsel *of the w.* is far from me. 21:16; 22:18
how oft is candle *of the w.* put out? 21:17; *Pr* 13:9; 24:20
dwelling places *of the w.*? *Job* 21:28
gathered the vintage *of the w.* 24:6
and I brake the jaws *of the w.* 29:17
preserveth not the life *of the w.* 36:6
fulfilled the judgement *of the w.* 17
let the wickedness *of the w.* *Ps* 7:9
the arm *of the w.* man. 10:15
the assembly *of the w.* have. 22:16
the transgression *of the w.* 36:1
let not the hand *of the w.* 11
the arms *of the w.* shall be. 37:17
but the seed *of the w.* shall be. 28
end *of the w.* shall be cut off. 38
of the oppression *of the w.* 55:3
his feet in the blood *of the w.* 58:10
me from the counsel *of the w.* 64:2
deliver me out of the hand *of the w.* 71:4; 74:19; 82:4; 97:10
saw the prosperity *of the w.* 73:3
all the horns *of the w.* also. 75:10
ye accept the persons *of the w.*? 82:2
and see the reward *of the w.* 91:8
shall hear my desire *of the w.* 92:11
the mouth *of the w.* is opened. 109:2
desire *of the w.* shall perish. 112:10 *Pr* 10:28
because *of the w.* that forsake thy law. *Ps* 119:53
the hands *of the w.* have robbed. 61
the rod *of the w.* shall not. 125:3
asunder the cords *of the w.* 129:4
Lord, from the hands *of the w.* 140:4
O Lord, the desires *of the w.* 8
the way *of the w.* he turneth. 146:9
in frowardness *of the w.* *Pr* 2:14
of the desolation *of the w.* 3:25
curse is in the house *of the w.* 33
not into the path *of the w.* 4:14
the way *of the w.* is as darkness. 19
away the substance *of the w.* 10:3
covereth the mouth *of the w.* 6, 11
but the name *of the w.* 10:7
fruit *of the w.* tendeth to sin. 16
heart *of the w.* is little worth. 20
the fear *of the w.* it shall come. 24
but the years *of the w.* shall be. 27
the mouth *of the w.* speaketh. 32
overthrown by mouth *of the w.* 11:11
expectation *of the w.* is wrath. 23
but the counsels *of the w.* 12:5
the words *of the w.* are to lie in. 6
but the tender mercies *of the w.* 10
but the way *of the w.* seduceth. 26
belly *of the w.* shall want. 13:25
the house *of the w.* shall be. 14:11
but in the revenues *of the w.* 15:6
sacrifice *of the w.* is an abomination. 8; 21:27
the way *of the w.* is an abomination to the Lord. 15:9
the thoughts *of the w.* are an. 26
the mouth *of the w.* poureth out. 28
to accept the person *of the w.* 18:5
mouth *of the w.* devoureth. 19:28
plowing *of the w.* is sin. 21:4
robbery *of the w.* shall destroy. 7
the soul *of the w.* desireth evil. 10
considereth the house *of the w.* 12
broken the staff *of the w.* *Isa* 14:5
the deeds *of the w.* *Jer* 5:28
the way *of the w.* prosper? 12:1
thee out of the hand *of the w.* 15:21
whirlwind shall fall upon the head *of the w.* 23:19; 30:23
have strengthened the hands *of the w.* *Ezek* 13:22
wickedness *of the w.* shall. 18:20
upon the necks *of the w.* 21:29
land into the hand *of the w.* 30:12
I have no pleasure in the death *of the w.* 33:11
as for the wickedness *of the w.* 12
none *of the w.* shall. *Dan* 12:10
treasures of wickedness in house *of the w.* *Mi* 6:10
woundedst the head out of the house *of the w.* *Hab* 3:13
able to quench all the fiery darts *of the w.* *Eph* 6:16
conversation *of the w.* *2 Pet* 2:7
away with the error *of the w.* 3:17

see **one**

to or *unto the* **wicked**

destruction *to the w.*? *Job* 31:3
shall be *to the w.* *Ps* 32:10
unto the w. God saith, What? 50:16
he that saith *unto the w.* *Pr* 24:24
is abomination *to the w.* 29:27
the righteous and *to the w.* *Eccl* 9:2
woe *unto the w.*! it shall be. *Isa* 3:11
let favour be shewed *to w.* 26:10
no peace, saith the Lord, *unto the w.* 48:22; 57:21
when I say *unto the w.* *Ezek* 3:18 33:8, 14
give it *to the w.* of the earth. 7:21

wickedly

Lot said, Do not so *w.* *Gen* 19:7 *Judg* 19:23
ye sinned in doing *w.* *Deut* 9:18
but if ye shall still do *w.* *1 Sam* 12:25
kept the ways of the Lord and have not *w.* *2 Sam* 22:22; *Ps* 18:21
I have sinned and have done *w.* *2 Sam* 24:17*
Manasseh hath done *w.* *2 Ki* 21:11
have done amiss, dealt *w.* *2 Chr* 6:37 *Neh* 9:33; *Ps* 106:6; *Dan* 9:5, 15
of Israel, did very *w.* *2 Chr* 20:35
his counsellor to do *w.* 22:3
you speak *w.* for God? *Job* 13:7
surely God will not do *w.* 34:12
they speak *w.* concerning. *Ps* 73:8
the enemy hath done *w.* in. 74:3
they speak against thee *w.* 139:20
such as do *w.* against. *Dan* 11:32
but the wicked shall do *w.* 12:10
all that do *w.* shall be. *Mal* 4:1

wickedness

God saw that the *w.* of. *Gen* 6:5
how can I do this great *w.*? 39:9
it is *w.* *Lev* 18:17; 20:14
land full of *w.* 19:29
be no *w.* among you. 20:14
w. of these nations. *Deut* 9:4, 5
shall do no more any such *w.* 13:11
be any that hath wrought *w.* 17:2
of the *w.* of thy doings. 28:20
thus God rendered the *w.* *Judg* 9:56
Tell us, how was this *w.*? 20:3
what *w.* is this that is done? 12
you may see that your *w.* is great. *1 Sam* 12:17
ye have done all this *w.*: yet. 20
w. proceedeth from the. 24:13
returned the *w.* of Nabal on. 25:39
evil according to his *w.* *2 Sam* 3:39
neither shall the children of *w.* afflict them any. 7:10; *Ps* 89:22
but if *w.* be found in. *1 Ki* 1:52
knowest all the *w.* thy heart. 2:44
We have committed *w.* 8:47
Ahab sold himself to work *w.* 21:25
Manasseh wrought much *w.* *2 Ki* 21:6
nor the children of *w.* *1 Chr* 17:9
sow *w.*, reap the same. *Job* 4:8*
he seeth *w.* 11:11
not *w.* dwell in thy tabernacles. 14
w. be sweet in his mouth. 20:12
w. shall be broken. 24:20
my lips shall not speak *w.* 27:4
God that he should do *w.* 34:10
not God hath pleasure in *w.* *Ps* 5:4
their inward part is very *w.* 9
let the *w.* of the wicked come. 7:9
seek out his *w.* 10:15
according to the *w.* of their. 28:4
thou hatest *w.* 45:7
strengthened himself in his *w.* 52:7
w. is in the midst thereof. 55:11
w. is in their dwellings and. 15
ye work *w.*; ye weigh violence. 58:2
dwell in the tents of *w.* 84:10
fruitful land into barrenness for the *w.* of them. 107:34; *Jer* 12:4
eat the bread of *w.* *Pr* 4:17

and w. is an abomination to. Pr 8:7
treasures of w. profit nothing. 10:2
wicked shall fall by his own w. 11:5
not be established by w. 12:3
w. overthroweth the sinner. 13:6
driven away in his w. 14:32
to kings to commit w. 16:12
the wicked for their w. 21:12
his w. shall be shewed before. 26:26
saith, I have done no w. 30:20
place of judgement, that w. Eccl 3:16
prolongeth his life in w. 7:15
heart to know the w. of folly. 25
nor shall w. deliver those that. 8:8
for w. burneth as the fire. Isa 9:18
ye smite with the fist of w. 58:4
chosen, to loose the bands of w. 6
thine own w. shall correct. Jer 2:19
wash thine heart from w. 4:14
so she casteth out her w. 6:7
see what I did for the w. of. 7:12
no man repented of his w. 8:6
we acknowledge, O Lord, our w. and iniquity. 14:20
doth return from his w. 23:14
city whose w. I hid my face. 33:5
w. of your kings, their wives, your own w. and the w. of? 44:9
if he turn not from his w. Ezek 3:19
changed my judgement into w. 5:6
is risen up into a rod of w. 7:11
the w. of the wicked shall. 18:20
turneth from the w. he hath. 27
driven him out for his w. 31:11
he turneth from his w. 33:12, 19
the w. of Samaria was. Hos 7:1
for the w. of their doings I. 9:15
ye have plowed w. and. 10:13
do to you because of your w. 15
fats overflow; for their w. is great. Joel 3:13
are there treasures of w. in the house of the wicked? Mi 6:10
and he said, This is w. And he cast it into the. Zech 5:8
them the border of w. Mal 1:4
yea, they that work w. are. 3:15
out of the heart proceedeth w., deceit. Mark 7:22
inward part is full of w. Luke 11:39
this man, if any w. in him. Acts 25:5
being filled with all w. Rom 1:29
leaven of malice and w. 1 Cor 5:8
against spiritual w. in. Eph 6:12
whole world lieth in w. 1 John 5:19

their wickedness

look not to their w. Deut 9:27
them off in their own w. Ps 94:23
the wicked for their w. Pr 21:12
touching all their w. Jer 1:16
for I will pour their w. upon. 14:16
house have I found their w. 23:11
desolation, because of their w. 44:3
their ear to turn from their w. 5
let all their w. come before. Lam 1:22
consider not that I remember all their w. Hos 7:2
they make king glad with their w. 3
all their w. is in Gilgal, there. 9:15
Nineveh, for their w. is come up. Jonah 1:2
but Jesus perceived their w. and said. Mat 22:18

thy wickedness

Lord shall return thy w. 1 Ki 2:44
is not thy w. great? Job 22:5
thy w. may hurt a man as. 35:8
hast trusted in thy w. Isa 47:10
polluted the land with thy w. Jer 3:2
this is thy w. for it is bitter. 4:18
confounded for all thy w. 22:22
to pass after all thy w. Ezek 16:23
before thy w. was discovered. 57
upon whom hath not thy w.? Nah 3:19
therefore of this thy w. Acts 8:22

wide

but thou shalt open thy hand w. Deut 15:8*; 11*
the land was w. 1 Chr 4:40
opened their mouth w. as for rain. Job 29:23
came on me as a w. breaking. 30:14
opened their mouth w. against me. Ps 35:21
open thy mouth w. and I. 81:10
so is this great and w. sea. 104:25
he that openeth w. his lips shall have destruction. Pr 13:3
than to dwell with a brawling woman in a w. house. 21:9; 25:24
make ye a w. mouth? Isa 57:4
will build me a w. house. Jer 22:14
thy gates be set w. open. Nah 3:13
w. is the gate that leadeth. Mat 7:13

wideness

between chambers the w. of 20 cubits. Ezek 41:10*

widow

Among the Hebrews, even before the law, a widow who had no children by her husband, was allowed to marry the brother of her deceased husband, in order to raise up children who might enjoy his inheritance, and perpetuate his name and family, Gen 38:6, 8, 9, 11. *The law that appoints these marriages is delivered in* Deut 25:5, 6, *etc.*

It was looked upon as a great unhappiness for a man to die without an heir, and to see his inheritance pass into another family. This law was not confined to brothers in law only, but was extended to more distant relatives of the same line, as may be seen in the example of Ruth, who married Boaz, after she had been refused by a nearer kinsman. Widowhood, as well as barrenness, was a kind of shame and reproach in Israel, Isa 54:4. *It was presumed, that a woman of merit and reputation might have found a husband, either in the family of her deceased husband, if he died without children or in some other family, if he had left children.*

God frequently recommends to his people to be very careful in affording relief to the widow *and orphan,* Ex 22:22; Deut 10:18. *St. Paul would have us honour widows that are widows indeed, and desolate, that is, destitute of such as ought to help and relieve them, such as their husbands and children,* 1 Tim 5:3, 4, 5. *There were* widows *in the Christian church, who, because of their poverty, were maintained at the charge of the faithful, and who were to attend upon the poor and sick.*

remain a w. in thy. Gen 38:11
she put her w.'s garments off. 14
ye shall not afflict any w. Ex 22:22
a w. or an harlot shall. Lev 21:14
if the priest's daughter be a w. 22:13
every vow of a w. shall. Num 30:9
execute the judgement of a w. Deut 10:18
the stranger, fatherless, and w. 14:29; 16:11, 14; 26:12
a w.'s raiment to pledge. 24:17
shall be for the stranger, for the fatherless and w. 19, 20, 21; 26:13
the judgement of the w. 27:19
I am a w. woman. 2 Sam 14:5
he was a w.'s son of tribe. 1 Ki 7:14
Zeruah was a w. woman. 11:26
I have commanded a w. to. 17:9
they take the w.'s ox for. Job 24:3
and doeth not good to the w. 21
I caused the w.'s heart to sing. 29:13
caused the eyes of the w. to. 31:16
they slay the w. and the. Ps 94:6
be fatherless, his wife a w. 109:9
the fatherless and the w. 146:9
the border of the w. Pr 15:25
plead for the w. Isa 1:17
neither doth the cause of the w. 23
I shall not sit as a w. nor. 47:8
if ye oppress not the w. Jer 7:6
22:3; Zech 7:10
how is she become as a w.! Lam 1:1
they vexed the w. Ezek 22:7
but take a w. that had a. 44:22
those that oppress the w. Mal 3:5
certain poor w. threw. Mark 12:42
w. cast in more than all. 43
Luke 21:3
Anna was a w. about. Luke 2:37
his mother, and she was a w. 7:12
there was a w. in that city. 18:3
because this w. troubleth me, I. 5
if any w. have children. 1 Tim 5:4
she that is a w. indeed trusteth. 5
let not a w. be taken into the. 9
as queen, and am no w. Rev 18:7

widowhood

the garments of her w. Gen 38:19
David's concubines shut up, living in w. 2 Sam 20:3
loss of children, and w. Isa 47:9
the reproach of thy w. 54:4

widows

wives shall be w. Ex 22:24
thou hast sent w. away. Job 22:9
be buried in death, and w. 27:15
and a judge of the w., is God. Ps 68:5
w. made no lamentation. 78:64
he have mercy on their w. Isa 9:17
w. may be their prey, that. 10:2
their w. are increased. Jer 15:8
let their wives be w. and. 18:21
leave thy children, let thy w. 49:11
our mothers are as w. Lam 5:3
have made her many w. Ezek 22:25
ye devour w.' houses, for pretence make long prayers. Mat 23:14
Mark 12:40; Luke 20:47
were many w. in Israel. Luke 4:25
murmuring because their w. were neglected. Acts 6:1
all the w. stood by him. 9:39
called the saints and w. 41
I said to the w., It is good. 1 Cor 7:8
honour w. that are w. 1 Tim 5:3
but the younger w. refuse, they. 11
if any have w., let them relieve. 16
pure religion is to visit the fatherless and w. in affliction. Jas 1:27

wife

Abraham's w. was Sarai. Gen 11:29
31; 12:17, 20; 20:18; 24:36
hast taken is a man's w. 20:3
Hagar took a w. for Ishmael. 21:21
a w. to my son Isaac. 24:4, 38
Abraham took a w., her name. 25:1
Jacob take a w. of the daughters of Heth, what good? 27:46; 28:1, 6
Judah took a w. for Er his. 38:6
go in unto thy brother's w. and. 8
his master's w. cast her eyes. 39:7
covet thy neighbour's w. nor any thing. Ex 20:17; Deut 5:21
if his master have given him a w. Ex 21:4
if he take him another w. her food. 10
nakedness of thy father's w. shalt. Lev 18:8; 20:11; Deut 27:20
of thy son's w. Lev 18:15
thy brother's w. 16, 20, 21
neither shalt thou take a w. 18
lie with thy neighbour's w. 20; 20:10
if a man take a w. and her. 20:14
if a man lie with his uncle's w. 20
priests shall not take a w. 21:7*
the high priest shall take a w. 13
if any man's w. go aside. Num 5:12
29
be a w. to one of the family. 36:8
or if the w. of thy bosom. Deut 13:6
what man hath betrothed a w.? 20:7
if any man take a w. and. 22:13
humbleth his neighbour's w. 24
not take his father's w. 30
a man hath taken a w. and. 24:1
and be another man's w. 2
hath taken a new w. he shall not. 5
w. of the dead shall not marry. 25:5
like not to take his brother's w. 7
then shall his brother's w. come. 9
the w. of the one draweth near. 11
betroth a w. and another lie. 28:30
his eye be evil toward the w. 54
Deborah, w. of Lapidoth. Judg 4:4

Jael the *w.* of Heber the Kenite.
Judg 4:17, 21; 5:24
thou goest to take a *w.* of the. 14:3
Samson's *w.* wept before him. 16
but his *w.* was given to his. 20
cursed be he that giveth a *w.* 21:18
buy it of Ruth, the *w.* of. *Ruth* 4:5
thou hast taken the *w.* *2 Sam* 12:10
be not known to be the *w.* *1 Ki* 14:2
Ahijah said, Come in, thou *w.* 6
waited on Naaman's *w.* *2 Ki* 5:2
w. of Jehoiada hid him. *2 Chr* 22:11
with the *w.* of thy youth. *Pr* 5:18
in to his neighbour's *w.* 6:29
whoso findeth a *w.* findeth. 18:22
contentions of a *w.* a. 19:13
and a prudent *w.* is from the. 14
live joyfully with the *w.* *Eccl* 9:9
children of the married *w.* *Isa* 54:1
hath called thee as a *w.* of youth. 6
surely as a *w.* treacherously departeth. *Jer* 3:20
neighed after his neighbour's *w.* 5:8
the husband and the *w.* shall. 6:11
shalt not take thee a *w.* in. 16:2
as a *w.* that committeth. *Ezek* 16:32
nor hath defiled his neighbour's *w.* 18:6, 15
and defiled his neighbour's *w.* 11
22:11; 33:26
take unto thee a *w.* of. *Hos* 1:2
Israel served for a *w.* and. 12:12
between thee and the *w.* of thy youth, the *w.* of thy. *Mal* 2:14
treacherously against his *w.* 15
of her that had been the *w.* *Mat* 1:6
for sake of Philip's *w.* 14:3
hath forsaken *w.* or children for my.
19:29; *Mark* 10:29; *Luke* 18:29
the first, when he had married a *w.*, deceased. *Mat* 22:25
Mark 12:20; *Luke* 20:29
I have married a *w.* *Luke* 14:20
remember Lot's *w.* 17:32
should have his father's *w.* *1 Cor* 5:1
render to the *w.* due benevolence, and likewise also the *w.* 7:3
the *w.* hath not power over her. 4
let not the *w.* depart from her. 10
if any brother hath a *w.* that. 12
unbelieving *w.* is sanctified by. 14
what knowest thou, O *w.*? 16
loosed from a *w.*? seek not a *w.* 27
between a *w.* and a virgin. 34
the *w.* is bound as long as her. 39
is the head of the *w.* *Eph* 5:23
his *w.* even as himself, and the *w.* see that she reverence her. 33
the husband of one *w.* *1 Tim* 3:2
12; *Tit* 1:6
a widow, having been the *w.* of one man. *1 Tim* 5:9
giving honour to *w.* as. *1 Pet* 3:7*
the bride, the Lamb's *w.* *Rev* 21:9

his wife

mother, and shall cleave unto *his w.*
Gen 2:24; *Mat* 19:5; *Mark* 10:7
naked, the man and *his w.* *Gen* 2:25
they shall say, This is *his w.* 12:12
hold on the hand of *his w.* 19:16
but *his w.* looked back from. 26
restore the man *his w.* 20:7
became *his w.* 24:67; *1 Sam* 25:42
the Lord for *his w.* *Gen* 25:21
place asked him of *his w.* 26:7
toucheth this man or *his w.* shall. 11
because thou art *his w.* 39:9
then *his w.* shall go out. *Ex* 21:3
endow her to be *his w.* 22:16
not approach to *his w.* *Lev* 18:14
he be jealous of *his w.* *Num* 5:14, 30
the man shall bring *his w.* 15
between a man and *his w.* 30:16
she shall be *his w.* *Deut* 22:19, 29
he shall cheer up *his w.* that. 24:5
Manoah arose and went after *his w.*
Judg 13:11
Samson visited *his w.* with. 15:1
catch you every man *his w.* 21:21
save to every man *his w.* and children. *1 Sam* 30:22
thou hast taken *his w.* *2 Sam* 12:9
whom Jezebel *his w.* *1 Ki* 21:25
of Ahab was *his w.* *2 Ki* 8:18
called his friends and *his w.*
Esth 5:10
and let *his w.* be a widow. *Ps* 109:9
if a man put away *his w.* *Jer* 3:1
Mat 5:31, 32; 19:9; *Mark* 10:11
Luke 16:18
he saw *his w.'s* mother sick of a fever. *Mat* 8:14
Is it lawful for a man to put away *his w.*? 19:3; *Mark* 10:2
of a man be so with *his w.* *Mat* 19:10
seven brethren, the first deceased, and left *his w.* to. 22:25
Mark 12:19; *Luke* 20:28
and hate not *his w.* *Luke* 14:26
his w. also being privy to it. *Acts* 5:2
his w. not knowing what was. 7
Paul found Aquila with *his w.* 18:2
came with *his w.* Drusilla. 24:24
man have *his* own *w.* *1 Cor* 7:2
the husband put away *his w.* 11
how he may please *his w.* 33
he that loveth *his w.* *Eph* 5:28
shall be joined to *his w.* 31
so love *his w.* 33
and *his w.* hath made. *Rev* 19:7

***my* wife**

slay me for *my w.'s* sake. *Gen* 20:11
she became *my w.* 12
she is *my w.* 26:7
give me *my w.* 29:21
I love *my w.* *Ex* 21:5
I will go in to *my w.* *Judg* 15:1
saying, Deliver me *my w.* Michal.
2 Sam 3:14
my house to lie with *my w.*? 11:11
is strange to *my w.* *Job* 19:17
then let *my w.* grind unto. 31:10
so I spake, and at even *my w.* died.
Ezek 24:18
she is not *my w.* nor. *Hos* 2:2
my w. is well stricken. *Luke* 1:18

***thy* wife**

to the voice of *thy w.* *Gen* 3:17
not tell me she was *thy w.* 12:18
behold *thy w.*, take her, and go. 19
Sarah, *thy w.* shall bear thee a son.
17:19; 18:10
arise, take *thy w.* and thy. 19:15
Of a surety she is *thy w.* 26:9
might lightly have lien with *thy w.* 10
unto thee, and *thy w.* *Ex* 18:6
wouldest have her to *thy w.*
Deut 21:11
to her, and she shall be *thy w.* 13
taken the wife of Uriah to be *thy w.*
2 Sam 12:10
thy w. shall be as a. *Ps* 128:3
thy w. shall be an harlot. *Amos* 7:17
thou shalt save *thy w.* *1 Cor* 7:16

***to* wife**

taken her to me *to w.* *Gen* 12:19
Get me this damsel *to w.* 34:4
give him her *to w.* 8, 12
not given to Shelah *to w.* 38:14
gave Joseph *to w.* Asenath. 41:45
of his own people *to w.* *Lev* 21:14
I gave my daughter to this man *to w.* *Deut* 22:16
will I give Achsah my daughter *to w.*
Josh 15:16, 17; *Judg* 1:12, 13
get her for me *to w.* *Judg* 14:2
Merab, her will I give thee *to w.*
1 Sam 18:17
the Shunammite, *to w.* *1 Ki* 2:17
cedar, give thy daughter to my son *to w.* *2 Ki* 14:9; *2 Chr* 25:18
daughter of Ahab *to w.* *2 Chr* 21:6
the seven had her *to w.* *Mark* 12:23
Luke 20:33
the second took her *to w.* and died.
Luke 20:30

wild

Ishmael will be a *w.* man. *Gen* 16:12*
which is *w.* by nature. *Rom* 11:24

see **ass, beast, beasts**

wilderness

A wilderness, *or* desert place, *in the Bible means simply a place that is not inhabited and usually not cultivated. Much could be used as pasture.*

The desert of Arabia, wherein the Israelites sojourned forty years after the Exodus, is called* wilderness, Neh 9:19, 21; Ps 78:40, 52, 107:4; Jer 2:2.

The *wilderness of* Shur *lies towards the Red Sea. This was the place of Hagar's wandering,* Gen 16:7; *and the Israelites passed through it after the Exodus,* Ex 15:22.

The *wilderness of* Paran *was in Arabia Petrea. Ishmael, the son of Abraham, dwelt in the borders of this* wilderness, Gen 21:21. *It was from hence that Moses sent out spies to bring intelligence concerning the land of promise,* Num 13:3.

The *wilderness of* Sin, *between Elim and Sinai,* Ex 16:1.

The desert of Sinai, *is that which lies about, and is adjacent to, mount* Sinai. *The people encamped there a long time, and received the greater part of those laws which are written in the books of Moses,* Ex 19:2.

are entangled, the *w.* *Ex* 14:3
we had died in this *w.* *Num* 14:2
shall fall in this *w.* 29, 32, 35
went through all that terrible *w.*
Deut 1:19; 8:15
in the waste howling *w.* 32:10
way to *w.* of Damascus. *1 Ki* 19:15
the *w.* yieldeth food for. *Job* 24:5
through the depths as through the *w.*
Ps 106:9; 136:16; *Amos* 2:10
he turneth the *w.* into. *Ps* 107:35
cometh out of *w.*? *S of S* 3:6; 8:5
that made world as a *w.*? *Isa* 14:17
w. and solitary place shall be. 35:1
I will make the *w.* a pool. 41:18
let the *w.* and cities lift up. 42:11
I make the rivers a *w.* 50:2
and he will make her *w.* like. 51:3
cities are a *w.*, Zion is a *w.* 64:10
a *w.* unto Israel? *Jer* 2:31
lo, the fruitful place was a *w.* 4:26
pleasant portion a desolate *w.* 12:10
will make thee a *w.* 22:6; *Hos* 2:3
more desolate than the *w.*
Ezek 6:14
behind them a desolate *w.* *Joel* 2:3
shall be a desolate *w.* 3:19
Nineveh dry like a *w.* *Zeph* 2:13

***in the* wilderness**

which I did *in the w.* *Num* 14:22
leave them *in the w.* and ye shall.
32:15; *Ezek* 29:5
Lord led thee forty years *in the w.*
Deut 8:2; 29:5; *Josh* 5:6; 14:10
who fed thee *in the w.* *Deut* 8:16
thou sustain them *in w.* *Neh* 9:21
of temptation *in the w.* *Ps* 95:8
better dwell *in the w.* *Pr* 21:19
shall dwell *in the w.* *Isa* 32:16
for *in the w.* shall waters. 35:6
the voice of him that crieth *in the w.*
40:3; *Mat* 3:3; *Mark* 1:3
Luke 3:4; *John* 1:23
I will plant *in the w.* the. *Isa* 41:19
make a way *in the w.* 43:19
wentest after me *in the w.* *Jer* 2:2
in the w. a lodging place. 9:2
left found grace *in the w.* 31:2
like the heath *in the w.* 48:6
laid wait for us *in the w.* *Lam* 4:19
she is planted *in the w.* *Ezek* 19:13
Israel rebelled against me *in the w.*
20:13
hand to them *in the w.* 15, 23
shall dwell safely *in the w.* 34:25
like grapes *in the w.* *Hos* 9:10
in the w. in the dry land. 13:5
John came preaching *in the w.* of Judaea. *Mat* 3:1
we have so much bread *in the w.*, as to fill? *Mat* 15:33; *Mark* 8:4
ninety and nine *in the w.* *Luke* 15:4
an angel appeared to him *in the w.*
Acts 7:30, 38
in perils *in the w.* *2 Cor* 11:26

into the wilderness

send goat into the w. Lev 16:21, 22
bring you into the w. Ezek 20:10, 35
and bring her into the w. Hos 2:14
Jesus was led into the w. Mat 4:1, Mark 1:12; Luke 4:1
what went ye out into the w. to see? a reed? Mat 11:7; Luke 7:24
of the devil into the w. Luke 8:29
which leddest into the w. Acts 21:38
woman fled into the w. Rev 12:6, 14
me in the spirit into the w. 17:3

wiles

vex you with their w. Num 25:18
against the w. of the devil. Eph 6:11

wilfully

if we sin w. after we have. Heb 10:26

wilily

work w. and took old sacks. Josh 9:4

will

for good w. of him that. Deut 33:16
deliver me not to w. of. Ps 27:12
wilt not deliver him to w. of. 41:2
delivered thee to w. of. Ezek 16:27
or receiveth it with good w. at your hand. Mal 2:13
that doeth the w. of my Father. Mat 7:21; 12:50
it is not the w. of your Father. 18:14
whether of them did the w. of? 21:31
on earth peace, good w. Luke 2:14
delivered Jesus to their w. 23:25
were born, not of the w. John 1:13
meat is to do the w. of him that. 4:34
I seek the w. of my Father. 5:30
and this is the Father's w. 6:39, 40
saying, The w. of the Lord be done. Acts 21:14
understanding what the w. Eph 5:17
with good w. doing service, as. 6:7
some also preach Christ of good w. Phil 1:15
by the which w. we are. Heb 10:10
have wrought the w. of. 1 Pet 4:3
came not by the w. of. 2 Pet 1:21

see self

will

(The word will as a verb is sometimes the future auxiliary, but it often means to wish, to exercise will, to be willing)

her go whither she w. Deut 21:14
let come on me what w. Job 13:13
king's heart whither he w. Pr 21:1
and giveth it to whomsoever he w. Dan 4:17, 25, 32; 5:21
I w., be thou clean. Mat 8:3; Mark 1:41; Luke 5:13
what I w. with mine? Mat 20:15
what w. ye that I shall do? 32
not as I w. but as thou wilt. 26:39; Mark 14:36
whom w. ye that I? Mat 27:17, 21; Mark 15:9; John 18:39
I w. that thou give me. Mark 6:25
whensoever ye w. ye may do. 14:7
what w. ye then that I should? 15:12
to whomsoever I w. I. Luke 4:6
and what w. I, if it be? 12:49
even so the Son quickeneth whom he w. John 5:21
wherefore hear it again? w. ye? 9:27
what ye w. it shall be done. 15:7
I w. that they be with me. 17:24
if I w. that he tarry till. 21:22, 23
I w. return again to you. Acts 18:21
to w. is present with me. Rom 7:18
hath he mercy on whom he w. have mercy, and whom he w. he. 9:18
shortly, if the Lord w. 1 Cor 4:19
what w. ye? shall I come to you? 21
let him do what he w. 7:36
be married to whom she w. 39
every man severally as he w. 12:11
was a readiness to w. 2 Cor 8:11
worketh in you, both to w. Phil 2:13
I w. that men pray. 1 Tim 2:8
I w. that the younger women. 5:14
these things I w. that thou. Tit 3:8
if the Lord w. we shall do. Jas 4:15
as often as they w. Rev 11:6
whosoever w. let him take. 22:17

his will

doeth according to his w. Dan 4:35
he did according to his w. 8:4
do his w. 11:3, 16, 36
neither did according to his w. Luke 12:47
if any man will do his w. John 7:17
shouldest know his w. Acts 22:14
knowest his w. Rom 2:18
who hath resisted his w.? 9:19
power over his own w. 1 Cor 7:37
his w. was not at all to come. 16:12
good pleasure of his w. Eph 1:5
known to us the mystery of his w. 9
with knowledge of his w. Col 1:9
captive by him at his w. 2 Tim 2:26
good work to do his w. Heb 13:21
according to his w. he hears. 1 John 5:14
hearts to fulfil his w. Rev 17:17

my will

nevertheless, not my w. Luke 22:42
who shall fulfil all my w. Acts 13:22
this thing against my w. 1 Cor 9:17

will not

so w. not we go back. Ps 80:18
I w. not be enquired. Ezek 20:3
I w. not again pass by them any more. Amos 7:8; 8:2
and said, I w. not. Mat 21:29
yet w. I not deny thee. 26:35
though all shall be offended, yet w. not I. Mark 14:29
ye w. not come to me that ye may have life. John 5:40

will of God

after the w. of your God. Ezra 7:18
who shall do the w. of God is my brother. Mark 3:35
w. of man, but of God. John 1:13
generation by w. of God. Acts 13:36
journey by w. of God. Rom 1:10
maketh intercession according to the w. of God. 8:27
and perfect w. of God. 12:2
with joy, by the w. of God. 15:32
an apostle of Jesus Christ by the w. of God. 1 Cor 1:1; 2 Cor 1:1; Eph 1:1; Col 1:1; 2 Tim 1:1
to us by the w. of God. 2 Cor 8:5
according to the w. of God. Gal 1:4
doing the w. of God from. Eph 6:6
may stand complete in all the w. of God. Col 4:12
for this is the w. of God. 1 Thes 4:3; 5:18
done the w. of God. Heb 10:36
so is the w. of God that. 1 Pet 2:15
if the w. of God be so. 3:17
lusts of men, but to w. of God. 4:2
suffer according to the w. of God. 19
he that doeth the w. of God abideth. 1 John 2:17

own will

it of his own voluntary w. Lev 1:3
ye shall offer it as your own w. 19:5; 22:19, 29
according to his own w. Dan 11:16
I seek not mine own w. John 5:30
not to do mine own w. 6:38
after counsel of his own w. Eph 1:11
gifts of Holy Ghost, according to his own w. Heb 2:4
of his own w. begat he us. Jas 1:18

thy will

I delight to do thy w. Ps 40:8
teach me to do thy w.; thou. 143:10
thy w. be done in earth. Mat 6:10; Luke 11:2
not pass, thy w. be done. Mat 26:42
lo, I come to do thy w. Heb 10:7, 9

willeth

so then it is not of him that w. nor of him that runneth. Rom 9:16

willing

the woman will not be w. Gen 24:5
if the woman will not be w. 8
whosoever is of a w. heart. Ex 35:5; 21, 22, 29*
God with a w. mind. 1 Chr 28:9
who is w. to consecrate his? 29:5
will the unicorn be w.? Job 39:9*
thy people shall be w. in. Ps 110:3
if ye be w. ye shall eat good. Isa 1:19
not w. to make her public. Mat 1:19
the spirit is w. but the flesh. 26:41
Pilate w. to content. Mark 15:15*
but he, w. to justify. Luke 10:29*
if thou be w. remove this. 22:42
Pilate therefore w. to. 23:20*
ye were w. for a season. John 5:35
Felix w. to shew the Jews a pleasure. Acts 24:27*
but Festus w. to do the Jews. 25:9*
but the centurion, w. to save. 27:43*
what if God, w. to shew? Rom 9:22
w. rather to be absent. 2 Cor 5:8
they were w. of themselves. 8:3*
if there be first a w. mind. 12*
w. to have imparted. 1 Thes 2:8*
ready to distribute, w. 1 Tim 6:18
God, w. to shew to the heirs of. Heb 6:17*
w. to live honestly in all. 13:18*
not w. that any should perish, but. 2 Pet 3:9*

willingly

every man that giveth w. Ex 25:2
the people w. offered. Judg 5:2, 9
we will w. give the earrings. 8:25
and rulers offered w. 1 Chr 29:6, 9, 14, 17; 2 Chr 35:8; Ezra 1:6; 3:5
Amasiah w. offered. 2 Chr 17:16
blessed the men that w. Neh 11:2
she worketh w. with. Pr 31:13
he doth not afflict w. Lam 3:33
Ephraim w. walked. Hos 5:11
they w. received him. John 6:21
the creature made subject to vanity not w. Rom 8:20
if I do this thing w. 1 Cor 9:17
not as of necessity, but w. Philem 14; 1 Pet 5:2
for this they w. are. 2 Pet 3:5

willows

ye shall take w. of the. Lev 23:40
the w. of the brook compass him. Job 40:22
our harps upon the w. Ps 137:2
away to the brook of w. Isa 15:7
they shall spring up as w. by. 44:4

willow tree

he set it as a w. tree. Ezek 17:5

will worship

of wisdom in w. worship. Col 2:23

wilt

Caleb said to her, What w. thou? Judg 1:14; Esth 5:3; Mat 20:21; Mark 10:51; Luke 18:41
if thou w. look on thine. 1 Sam 1:11
w. not thou, O God? Ps 60:10; 108:11
w. thou be angry with us? 85:5
w. thou not revive us again to? 6
why w. thou, my son, be ravished? Pr 5:20
w. thou not from this time cry unto me? Jer 3:4
O Jerusalem, w. thou not be? 13:27
w. thou judge them, son of man? Ezek 20:4; 22:2
w. thou not tell us what? 24:19
w. thou yet say before him? 28:9
Lord, if thou w. thou canst make. Mat 8:2; Mark 1:40; Luke 5:12
w. thou then that we go and gather them up? Mat 13:28
unto thee even as thou w. 15:28
if thou w. let us make three. 17:4
the disciples said, Where w. thou? 26:17; Mark 14:12; Luke 22:9
not as I will, but as thou w. Mat 26:39; Mark 14:36
king said, Ask of me whatsoever thou w. Mark 6:22
w. thou that we command fire to? Luke 9:54
Jesus said, W. thou be made whole? John 5:6
w. thou at this time restore the kingdom? Acts 1:6

wimples

away mantles and w. Isa 3:22*

win

he thought to w. them. 2 Chr 32:1
that I may w. Christ. Phil 3:8

wind

The powerful operations of God's Spirit, quickening or reviving the heart toward God, are compared to the blowing of the wind, John 3:8. *For as with the* wind, *man perceives, by the effects of it, that there is such a thing, and that it does blow, yet his power cannot restrain it, neither can his reason reach to know whence it rises, or from how far it comes, or how far it reaches; so is the spiritual change wrought in the soul, freely, where, in whom, when, and in what measure the Spirit pleases; and also powerfully, so as to make an evident sensible change, though the manner thereof be incomprehensible.*

God made a w. to pass. Gen 8:1
blow with thy w. Ex 15:10
the w. brought quails. Num 11:31
he was seen upon the wings of the w. 2 Sam 22:11; Ps 18:10; 104:3
black with cloud and w. 1 Ki 18:45
strong w. rent the mountains, but the Lord was not in the w. 19:11
ye shall not see w. nor. 2 Ki 3:17
there came a w. from. Job 1:19
speeches which are as w. 6:26
O remember that my life is w. 7:7†
mouth be like a strong w. 8:2
as stubble before the w. 21:18
pursue my soul as the w. 30:15
thou liftest me up to the w. 22
not light in the clouds, but the w. 37:21; Ps 103:16
like chaff which the w. Ps 1:4
w. that passeth away and. 78:39
he bringeth the w. out of. 135:7
he causeth his w. to blow. 147:18
he shall inherit the w. Pr 11:29
clouds and w. without rain. 25:14
north w. driveth away rain. 23
hideth her, hideth the w. 27:16
gathered the w. in his fists. 30:4
w. goeth toward the south, and turneth . . . and the w. Eccl 1:6
he that hath laboured for the w.? 5:16
he that observeth the w. 11:4
awake, O north w. come. S of S 4:16
trees are moved with the w. Isa 7:2
with his w. shake his hand. 11:15
as it were brought forth w. 26:18
rough w. in day of his east w. 27:8*
as a hiding place from the w. 32:2
the w. shall carry them away. 41:16 57:13
their molten images are w. 41:29
our iniquities, like the w. have. 64:6
a full w. from those places. Jer 4:12
prophets shall become w. 5:13
brings the w. out of his treasuries. 10:13; 51:16
the w. shall eat up all thy. 22:22
thou shalt scatter in the w. Ezek 5:2
I will scatter toward every w. 12:14
w. son of man, say to the w. 37:9
and the w. carried them. Dan 2:35
the w. hath bound her up. Hos 4:19
they have sown w. and shall reap. 8:7
on w. and followeth the east w. 12:1
he that createth the w. Amos 4:13
Lord sent out a great w. Jonah 1:4
and the w. was in their. Zech 5:9
a reed shaken with the w.? Mat 11:7 Luke 7:24
w. was contrary. Mat 14:24 Mark 6:48; Acts 27:4
the w. ceased. Mat 14:32 Mark 4:39; 6:51
w. bloweth where it. John 3:8
sound as of a mighty w. Acts 2:2
carried about with every w. Eph 4:14
like a wave driven with the w. and. Jas 1:6
shaken of a mighty w. Rev 6:13
that the w. should not blow. 7:1

window

a w. shalt thou make. Gen 6:16*
Noah opened the w. of the ark. 8:6
Gerar looked out at a w. 26:8
spies down through a w. Josh 2:15
bound the scarlet line in the w. 21
Sisera's mother looked out at a w. Judg 5:28
Michal looked through a w., and saw David. 2 Sam 6:16
Jezebel painted her face, and looked out at a w. 2 Ki 9:30
Open the w. eastward. 13:17
at the w. of my house. Pr 7:6
there sat in a w. a certain young man. Acts 20:9
through a w. was I let. 2 Cor 11:33

windows

and the w. of heaven. Gen 7:11
w. of heaven were stopped. 8:2
if the Lord make w. in heaven. 2 Ki 7:2, 19
those that look out of the w. be darkened. Eccl 12:3
looked forth at the w. S of S 2:9
w. from on high are. Isa 24:18
I will make thy w. of agates. 54:12*
flee as the doves to their w. 60:8
come up into our w. Jer 9:21
that cutteth him out w. 22:14
his w. being open in his. Dan 6:10
they shall enter in at the w. like a thief. Joel 2:9
shall sing in the w. Zeph 2:14
if I will not open the w. Mal 3:10

winds

weight for the w. Job 28:25
come from the four w. Ezek 37:9
the w. blew, and beat. Mat 7:25, 27
rebuked the w. 8:26; Luke 8:24
even the w. and the sea obey him? Mat 8:27; Mark 4:41; Luke 8:25
are driven of fierce w. Jas 3:4
clouds carried about of w. Jude 12
see **east, four, scatter, stormy**

windy

hasten from the w. storm. Ps 55:8

wine

There were many excellent vineyards in Palestine, and wine was made for common use. Water was scanty, especially at some seasons, and likely to be infected. Wine and milk were therefore the common beverages. The use of wine *was forbidden to the priests during all the time they were in the tabernacle, and employed in the service of the altar,* Lev 10:9. *This liquor was also forbidden to the Nazarites* Num 6:3.

In Gen 27:28, 37, corn and wine *denote all sorts of temporal good things. In the style of the sacred writers, the* wine, *or the* cup, *often represents the anger of God,* Ps 60:3; Jer 25:15. *There were certain charitable women at Jerusalem, as they tell us, who used to mix certain drugs with wine, to make it stronger, and more capable of easing pain. Some think it was such a mixture that was offered to our Saviour to drink, before he was fastened to the cross,* Mark 15:23.

Noah awoke from his w. Gen 9:24
brought forth bread and w. 14:18
garments in w. and clothes in. 49:11
his eyes were red with w. 12
part of an hin of w. for a drink. Ex 29:40; Lev 23:13; Num 15:5
separate himself from w. Num 6:3
half an hin of w. 15:10; 28:14
shalt cause the strong w. 28:7*
their w. is the poison. Deut 32:33
leave w. which cheereth. Judg 9:13
there is also bread and w. for. 19:19
away thy w. from thee. 1 Sam 1:14
when the w. was gone out of. 25:37
piece of flesh, and a flagon of w. 2 Sam 6:19*; 1 Chr 16:3*
when Amnon's heart is merry with w. 2 Sam 13:28
the w. that such as be faint. 16:2
w. was before him, I took up the w. Neh 2:1
had taken bread and w. 5:15
ten days store of all sorts of w. 18
lading asses with w. and. 13:15
they gave them royal w. Esth 1:7
king was merry with w. 10
Esther at the banquet of w. 5:6; 7:2
from the banquet of w. 7:7
drinking w. in eldest brother's house. Job 1:13, 18
behold, my belly is as w. that. 32:19
the w. is red, it is full of. Ps 75:8
shouteth by reason of w. 78:65
w. that maketh glad the. 104:15
she hath mingled her w. Pr 9:2
w. is a mocker, strong drink. 20:1
sorrow? they that tarry long at the w.; they that go to seek mixt w. 23:30
look not thou upon the w. when. 31
give w. to those that be of. 31:6
heart to give myself to w. Eccl 2:3
w. maketh merry, but money. 10:19
for thy love is better than w. S of S 1:2; 4:10
I have drunk my w. with my. 5:1
of thy mouth like the best w. 7:9
thy silver dross, thy w. Isa 1:22
that continue till night, till w. 5:11
pipe and w. are in their feasts. 12
eating flesh and drinking w. 22:13
there is a crying for w. in the. 24:11
a vineyard of red w. 27:2
that are overcome with w.! 28:1
w., and through strong drink are out of the way; they are . . . of w. 7
drunken, but not with w. 29:9; 51:21
yea, come, buy w. and milk. 55:1
say they, I will fetch w. 56:12
whom w. hath overcome. Jer 23:9
take the w. cup of this fury. 25:15
pots full of w. 35:5
Jews gathered w. 40:12
I have caused w. to fail from. 48:33
drunken of her w. are mad. 51:7
Damascus merchant in w. Ezek 27:18
the king gave of the w. Dan 1:5
not to defile himself with the w. 8
Belshazzar drank w. before. 5:1, 4
whiles he tasted w. 2
concubines drunk w. 23
neither came w. nor flesh. 10:3
take away my w. in the. Hos 2:9
gods and love flagons of w. 3:1*
the scent shall be as the w. 14:7
all ye drinkers of w. Joel 1:5
prophesy to thee of w. Mi 2:11
he transgresseth by w. Hab 2:5
make a noise, as through w. Zech 9:15
shall rejoice, as through w. 10:7
neither drinking w. Luke 7:33
wanted w., the mother of Jesus saith unto him, They have no w. John 2:3
water that was made w. 9; 4:46
doth set forth good w., but thou hast kept good w. till now. 2:10
be not drunk with w. Eph 5:18
not given to w. 1 Tim 3:3*, 8 Tit 1:7*; 2:3
use a little w. for thy stomach's sake. 1 Tim 5:23
walked in excess of w. 1 Pet 4:3*
give her the cup of the w. Rev 16:19
made drunk with the w. of her fornication. 17:2; 18:3
see **bottle, corn, drink, new, offerings, oil, sweet**

winebibber, -s

be not among w. Pr 23:20
behold a man gluttonous, and a w. Mat 11:19; Luke 7:34

wine *bottles*

Gibeonites took w. *bottles* old and rent. Josh 9:4*
bottles of w. which we filled. 13*

wine *cellars*

over the w. *cellars* was. 1 Chr 27:27

winefat

him that treadeth in the w.? Isa 63:2†
a place for the w. Mark 12:1*

winepress
fulness of the *w*. *Num* 18:27, 30
furnish him out of thy *w*. *Deut* 15:14
wheat by the *w*. *Judg* 6:11
slew at the *w*. of Zeeb. 7:25
help thee out of the *w*.? *2 Ki* 6:27
he also made a *w*. therein. *Isa* 5:2
I have trodden the *w*. alone. 63:3
of Judah as in a *w*. *Lam* 1:15
the floor and *w*. shall not. *Hos* 9:2
digged a *w*. in it, and. *Mat* 21:33
the angel cast it into the great *w*. *Rev* 14:19
the *w*. was trodden without the city, blood came out of the *w*. 20
he treadeth the *w*. of the wrath. 19:15

winepresses
treading *w*. on sabbath. *Neh* 13:15
tread their *w*. and. *Job* 24:11
wine to fail from the *w*. *Jer* 48:33
upon the king's *w*. *Zech* 14:10

wines
a feast, of *w*. on the lees. *Isa* 25:6

wing
w. of the cherub, five cubits the other *w*. *1 Ki* 6:24, 27; *2 Chr* 3:11, 12
none that moved the *w*. *Isa* 10:14
dwell fowl of every *w*. *Ezek* 17:23

winged
God created every *w*. *Gen* 1:21
likeness of any *w*. fowl. *Deut* 4:17
eagle with great wings, long-*w*. of divers colours, full of. *Ezek* 17:3

wings
I bare you on eagles' *w*. *Ex* 19:4
w. covering the mercy seat with their *w*. 25:20; 37:9; *1 Ki* 8:7
cleave it with *w*. thereof. *Lev* 1:17
abroad her *w*., taketh them, beareth them on her *w*. *Deut* 32:11*
under whose *w*. thou art. *Ruth* 2:12
was seen upon the *w*. *2 Sam* 22:11
goodly *w*. to the peacock? or *w*. and feathers to the ostrich? *Job* 39:13*
the shadow of thy *w*. *Ps* 17:8
fly on the *w*. of the wind. 18:10
104:3
their trust under the shadow of thy *w*. 36:7; 57:1; 61:4; 91:4
Oh that I had *w*. like a dove! 55:6
in the shadow of thy *w*. will. 63:7
yet shall ye be as the *w*. 68:13
take the *w*. of the morning. 139:9
riches make themselves *w*. *Pr* 23:5
that which hath *w*. shall. *Eccl* 10:20
stood the seraphims: each one had six *w*. *Isa* 6:2
the stretching out of his *w*. 8:8
the land shadowing with *w*. 18:1
mount up with *w*. as eagles. 40:31
give *w*. to Moab, it may fly. *Jer* 48:9
spread his *w*. over Moab. 40
spread his *w*. over Bozrah. 49:22
four faces and four *w*. *Ezek* 1:6
their *w*. were joined. 9
I heard the noise of their *w*. . . . let down their *w*. 24, 25; 3:13; 10:5
w. full of eyes. 10:12
a great eagle with great *w*. 17:3
another great eagle with great *w*. 7
lion and had eagle's *w*.: I beheld till the *w*. thereof were. *Dan* 7:4
upon the back of it four *w*. of a fowl. 6
bound her up in her *w*. *Hos* 4:19
the wind was in their *w*. *Zech* 5:9
arise with healing in his *w*. *Mal* 4:2
as a hen gathereth her chickens under her *w*. *Mat* 23:37; *Luke* 13:34
the sound of their *w*. as of. *Rev* 9:9
to the woman were given two *w*. 12:14

wink
what do thy eyes *w*. at? *Job* 15:12†
nor let them *w*. with the eye. *Ps* 35:19

winked
this ignorance God *w*. at. *Acts* 17:30*

winketh
a wicked man *w*. with. *Pr* 6:13
he that *w*. with the eye. 10:10

winneth
he that *w*. souls is wise. *Pr* 11:30

winnowed
which hath been *w*. with. *Isa* 30:24

winnoweth
behold, Boaz *w*. barley. *Ruth* 3:2

winter
summer and *w*. shall not. *Gen* 8:22
made summer and *w*. *Ps* 74:17
for lo, the *w*. is past, the. *S of S* 2:11
in summer and in *w*. *Zech* 14:8
flight be not in the *w*. nor on the. *Mat* 24:20; *Mark* 13:18
dedication was in *w*. *John* 10:22
do thy diligence to come before *w*. *2 Tim* 4:21

winter, *verb*
beasts shall *w*. on them. *Isa* 18:6
haven was not commodious to *w*. in, the more . . . to *w*. *Acts* 27:12
abide and *w*. with you. *1 Cor* 16:6
determined there to *w*. *Tit* 3:12

wintered
in a ship which had *w*. *Acts* 28:11

winterhouse
king sat in the *w*. *Jer* 36:22
I will smite the *w*. with the summer house. *Amos* 3:15

wipe
I will *w*. Jerusalem as. *2 Ki* 21:13
w. not out my good deeds I have done. *Neh* 13:14
swallow up death in victory; Lord will *w*. *Isa* 25:8; *Rev* 7:17; 21:4
a woman did *w*. them with hairs of. *Luke* 7:38, 44; *John* 11:2; 12:3
he began to *w*. them. *John* 13:5

wiped
shall not be *w*. away. *Pr* 6:33

wipeth
as a man *w*. a dish. *2 Ki* 21:13
she eateth, *w*. her mouth. *Pr* 30:20

wiping
w. it, and turning it. *2 Ki* 21:13

wires
they cut gold plates into *w*. to work it. *Ex* 39:3

wisdom
(*This word is used in the Scriptures not only for learning, but for skill in the arts; the instinct of birds or beasts; discretion; and spiritual insight*)
filled him with the Spirit of God in *w*. *Ex* 31:3, 6; 35:31, 35
whose heart stirred them up in *w*. 35:26; 36:1, 2
for this is your *w*. and. *Deut* 4:6
according to the *w*. of an angel of God. *2 Sam* 14:20
to all the people in her *w*. 20:22
saw that the *w*. of God. *1 Ki* 3:28
God gave Solomon *w*. 4:29; 5:12
2 Chr 1:12
Solomon's *w*. excelled *w*. of Egypt. *1 Ki* 4:30, 34; 7:14; 10:4, 23, 24
2 Chr 9:3, 22, 23
only Lord give thee *w*. *1 Chr* 22:12*
give me *w*. *2 Chr* 1:10
but hast asked *w*. 11
thou Ezra, after the *w*. *Ezra* 7:25
they die, even without *w*. *Job* 4:21
the people, *w*. shall die with you. 12:2
and it should be your *w*. 13:5
dost thou restrain *w*. to thyself? 15:8
counselled him that hath no *w*.? 26:3
but where shall *w*. be found? 28:12
cometh *w*. and where place? 20
of years should teach *w*. 32:7
say, We have found out *w*. 13
me and I shall teach thee *w*. 33:33
Job's words were without *w*. 34:35
mighty in strength and *w*. 36:5*
number the clouds in *w*.? 38:37
hath deprived her of *w*. 39:17
of the righteous speaketh *w*. *Ps* 37:30
shalt make me to know *w*. 51:6
apply our hearts unto *w*. 90:12
in *w*. hast thou made all. 104:24
and teach his senators *w*. 105:22
to him that by *w*. made. 136:5*
to know *w*. *Pr* 1:2
fools despise *w*. and instruction. 7
w. crieth. *Pr* 1:20; 8:1
incline thine ear unto *w*. 2:2
the Lord giveth *w*. 6
he layeth up sound *w*. for the. 7
w. entereth into thine heart. 10
happy is the man that findeth *w*. 3:13
the Lord by *w*. hath founded. 19
keep sound *w*. 21
get *w*. 4:5, 7
my son, attend unto my *w*. 5:1
say to *w*., Thou art my sister. 7:4
understand *w*. 8:5*
I *w*. dwell with prudence, and. 12
counsel is mine, and sound *w*. 14
w. builded her house. 9:1
man of understanding hath *w*. 10:23
the just bringeth forth *w*. 31
commended according to his *w*. 12:8
a scorner seeketh *w*. and. 14:6
the *w*. of the prudent is to. 8
w. resteth in heart of him that. 33
better is it to get *w*. than gold! 16:16
in hand of a fool to get *w*.? 17:16
man intermeddleth with all *w*. 18:1
he that getteth *w*. loveth. 19:8
is no *w*. against the Lord. 21:30
cease from thine own *w*. 23:4
for a fool will despise the *w*. 9
buy *w*. 23
through *w*. is an house built. 24:3
whoso loveth *w*. rejoiceth his. 29:3
the rod and reproof give *w*. 15
I neither learned *w*. nor have. 30:3
openeth her mouth with *w*. 31:26
heart to search out by *w*. *Eccl* 1:13
I have gotten more *w*. than all. 16
I gave my heart to know *w*. and. 17
for in much *w*. is much grief. 18
acquainting mine heart with *w*. 2:3
so I was great, and my *w*. 9
I turned myself to behold *w*. 12
w. excelleth folly. 13
whose labour is in *w*. 21
God giveth to a man *w*. 26
w. giveth life. 7:12
w. strengtheneth the wise. 19
all this have I proved by *w*. 23
heart to know and seek out *w*. 25
a man's *w*. maketh his face. 8:1
applied my heart to know *w*. 16
there is no *w*. in the grave. 9:10
this *w*. have I seen also under. 13
a poor man by his *w*. delivered. 15
that is in reputation for *w*. 10:1
his *w*. faileth him, and he saith he. 3*
by my *w*. I have done it. *Isa* 10:13
for the *w*. of their wise men. 29:14
w. shall be the stability of. 33:6
wise man glory in his *w*. *Jer* 9:23
the world by his *w*. 10:12; 51:15
were skilful in all *w*. *Dan* 1:4, 17
with counsel and *w*. 2:14*
for *w*. and might are his. 20
he giveth *w*. to the wise, and. 21
O God, who hast given me *w*. 23
not revealed for any *w*. I have. 30
w. like the *w*. of the gods was. 5:11
came from utmost parts to hear the *w*. of. *Mat* 12:42; *Luke* 11:31
hath this man this *w*.? *Mat* 13:54
turn the disobedient to the *w*. of. *Luke* 1:17
Jesus filled with *w*. 2:40
increased in *w*. 52
said the *w*. of God, I will send. 11:49
give you a mouth and *w*. 21:15
look out seven men full of the Holy Ghost and *w*. *Acts* 6:3
were not able to resist the *w*. 10
gave Joseph *w*. in the sight of. 7:10
was learned in all the *w*. of the. 22
to preach the gospel: not with *w*. of words. *1 Cor* 1:17
I will destroy the *w*. of the wise. 19
foolish the *w*. of this world. 20
after that in the *w*. of God the world by *w*. knew not God. 21
sign, and Greeks seek after *w*. 22
power of God and the *w*. of. 24
who of God is made unto us *w*. 30
not with words of man's *w*. 2:4
not stand in the *w*. of men. 5
we speak *w*. 6
but we speak the *w*. of God. 7

which man's w. teacheth. 1 Cor 2:13
w. of this world is foolishness. 3:19
not with fleshly w. 2 Cor 1:12
toward us in all w. Eph 1:8
known the manifold w. of God. 3:10
might be filled with all w. Col 1:9
teaching every man in all w. 28
words dwell in you in all w. 3:16
walk in w. toward them that are. 4:5
if any lack w. let him ask. Jas 1:5
this w. descendeth not from. 3:15
according to the w. given. 2 Pet 3:15
the Lamb to receive w. Rev 5:12
blessing, and glory, and w. 7:12
the mind which hath w. 17:9

wisdom, joined with *is*

and is w. driven quite? Job 6:13
with the ancient is w. 12:12, 13, 16
the price of w. is above rubies. 28:18; Pr 8:11
fear of the Lord that is w. Job 28:28
w. is the principal thing, get w. Pr 4:7
understanding w. is found. 10:13
but with the lowly is w. 11:2
but with the well advised is w. 13:10
w. of prudent is to understand. 14:8
w. is before him that hath. 17:24
w. is too high for a fool, he. 24:7
for in much w. is much grief. Eccl 1:18
w. is good with an inheritance. 7:11
for w. is a defence, and money. 12
w. is better than strength; nevertheless, the poor man's w. is. 9:16
w. is better than weapons of. 18
but w. is profitable to direct. 10:10
word what w. is in them? Jer 8:9
Is w. no more in Teman? is their w. vanished? 49:7
that excellent w. is found. Dan 5:14
sinners, but w. is justified of her children. Mat 11:19; Luke 7:35
what w. is this which is given to him? Mark 6:2
the w. that is from above. Jas 3:17
here is w. Let him that. Rev 13:18

***of* wisdom**

shew thee the secrets of w. Job 11:6
price of w. is above rubies. 28:18
my mouth shall speak of w. Ps 49:3
the fear of the Lord is the beginning of w. 111:10; Pr 9:10
to receive the instruction of w. Pr 1:3
taught thee in the way of w. 4:11
but fools die for want of w. 10:21*
that is void of w. despiseth. 11:12
to him that is destitute of w. 15:21
of the Lord is the instruction of w. 33
the wellspring of w. as a. 18:4
so shall the knowledge of w. 24:14
great experience of w. Eccl 1:16
thou sealest up the sum, full of w. Ezek 28:12
in all matters of w. he found them better. Dan 1:20
the man of w. shall see. Mi 6:9
O the depth of the w. of God! Rom 11:33
of speech or of w. 1 Cor 2:1
by the Spirit the word of w. 12:8
hid all the treasures of w. Col 2:3
have indeed a shew of w. 23
works with meekness of w. Jas 3:13
see **spirit**

***thy* wisdom**

according to thy w. 1 Ki 2:6
report that I heard of thy w. 10:6
thy w. and prosperity exceedeth. 7
that stand before thee continually and hear thy w. 8; 2 Chr 9:5, 7
the half of thy w. was. 2 Chr 9:6
the hawk fly by thy w.? Job 39:26
thy w., it hath perverted. Isa 47:10
with thy w. hast gotten. Ezek 28:4, 5
thou hast corrupted thy w. by. 17

wise

be desired to make one w. Gen 3:6
is none so discreet and w. 41:39
the gift blindeth the w. Ex 23:8
Deut 16:19
great nation is a w. people. Deut 4:6
O that they were w., that they. 32:29
her w. ladies answered. Judg 5:29
my lord is w. according. 2 Sam 14:20
I have given thee a w. 1 Ki 3:12
given David a w. son over this great people. 5:7; 2 Chr 2:12
for Zachariah his son, a w. counsellor. 1 Chr 26:14*
he taketh the w. in their own craftiness. Job 5:13
he is w. in heart and mighty. 9:4
for vain man would be w. 11:12*
he that is w. may be profitable. 22:2
great men are not always w. 32:9
not any that are w. of heart. 37:24
be w. now, O ye kings. Ps 2:10
is sure, making w. the simple. 19:7
he hath left off to be w. and. 36:3
fools, when will ye be w.? 94:8
whoso is w. and will observe. 107:43
a w. man shall attain to w. Pr 1:5*
to understand the words of the w. 6
be not w. in thine own eyes. 3:7
the w. shall inherit glory: but. 35
be w. 6:6; 8:33; 23:19; 27:11
if thou be w. thou shalt be w. 9:12
a w. son maketh a glad father. 10:1
15:20
gathereth in summer is a w. son. 10:5
the w. in heart will receive. 8
he that refraineth his lips is w. 19
servant to the w. in heart. 11:29
he that winneth souls is w. 30
hearkeneth to counsel is w. 12:15
tongue of the w. is health. 18
a w. son heareth his father's. 13:1
the law of the w. is a fountain. 14
with w. men shall be w. 20
but the lips of the w. shall. 14:3
crown of the w. is their riches. 24
is toward a wise servant. 35
tongue of w. useth knowledge. 15:2
the lips of the w. disperse. 7
a scorner will not go to the w. 12
the way of life is above to the w. 24
reproof abideth among the w. 31
the w. in heart shall be called prudent. 16:21
the heart of the w. teacheth his. 23
a w. servant shall have rule. 17:2
holdeth his peace is counted w. 28
the ear of the w. seeketh. 18:15
that thou mayest be w. in thy latter end. 19:20
is deceived thereby, is not w. 20:1
a w. king scattereth the wicked. 26
simple is made w.: when the w. is instructed he receiveth. 21:11
oil in the dwelling of the w. 20
ear, hear the words of the w. 22:17
thy heart be w. my heart shall. 23:15
he that begetteth a w. son shall. 24
for by w. counsel thou shalt. 24:6
also belong to the w. 23
so is a w. reprover upon an. 25:12
answer a fool lest he be w. 26:5
seest thou a man w. in his own 12
keepeth the law is a w. son. 28:7
rich man is w. in his own conceit. 11
four things that are exceeding w. 30:24
and why was I more w.? Eccl 2:15
no remembrance of the w. 16
I have shewed myself w. 19
better is a w. child than a. 4:13
for what hath the w. more than? 6:8
heart of the w. is in the house. 7:4
hear the rebuke of the w. 5
neither make thyself over w. 16
wisdom strengtheneth w. more. 19
I said, I will be w. but it was. 23
the w. and their works are in the. 9:1
I saw that bread is not to the w. 11
preacher was w., he taught. 12:9
the words of the w. are as goads. 11
woe to them that are w. Isa 5:21
I am the son of the w.? 19:11
is w. and will bring evil. 31:2
they are w. to do evil. Jer 4:22
We are w., and the law of. 8:8
counsel perish from the w. 18:18
God giveth wisdom to w. Dan 2:21
they that be w. shall shine as. 12:3
none of the wicked; but the w. 10
the w. shall understand. Hos 14:9
and Zidon be very w. Zech 9:2
therefore w. as serpents. Mat 10:16
hast hid these things from w. and prudent, and. 11:25; Luke 10:21
then is a faithful and w.? Mat 24:45
five virgins were w. and. 25:2
the w. took oil in their vessels. 4
faithful and w. steward? Luke 12:42
I am debtor to the w. Rom 1:14
professing themselves w., they. 22
lest ye should be w. in your. 11:25
be not w. in your own. 12:16
I would have you w. to. 16:19
to God only w., be glory. 27
1 Tim 1:17; Jude 25
I will destroy the wisdom of the w. 1 Cor 1:19
where is the w.? 20
to confound the w. 27
as a w. masterbuilder, I. 3:10
to be w. in this world, let him become a fool, that he may be w. 18
he taketh the w. in their own. 19
knoweth the thoughts of the w. 20
but ye are w. in Christ. 4:10
themselves, are not w. 2 Cor 10:12*
seeing ye yourselves are w. 11:19
not as fools, but as w. Eph 5:15
are able to make thee w. 2 Tim 3:15
see **man, men**

***any* wise**

afflict them in any w. Ex 22:23
shall in any w. rebuke. Lev 19:17*
if he will in any w. redeem. 27:19*
in any w. set him king. Deut 17:15†
thou shalt in any w. bury. 21:23*
shalt in any w. let the dam. 22:7†
in any w. keep from the. Josh 6:18
if ye do in any w. go back. 23:12
in any w. send a trespass. 1 Sam 6:3
let me go in any w. 1 Ki 11:22
fret not thyself in any w. Ps 37:8*
not deny thee in any w. Mark 14:31

***in no* wise**

the fat of beasts torn, in no w. eat of it. Lev 7:24
give the child, and in no w. slay it. 1 Ki 3:26, 27
one tittle shall in no w. pass from the law. Mat 5:18
he shall in no w. lose his. 10:42
a woman could in no w. Luke 13:11
shall in no w. enter therein. 18:17
Rev 21:27
I will in no w. cast out. John 6:37
ye shall in no w. believe. Acts 13:41
than they? no, in no w. Rom 3:9

***on this* wise**

on this w. ye shall bless. Num 6:23
the birth of Jesus Christ was on this w. Mat 1:18
and on this w. shewed. John 21:1
God spake on this w. Acts 7:6
he said on this w., I will give. 13:34
speaketh on this w. Rom 10:6
the seventh day on this w. Heb 4:4

wise *hearted*

to all that are w. hearted. Ex 28:3
I have put wisdom in all that are w. hearted. 31:6
every w. hearted among you. 35:10
that were w. hearted did spin. 25
wrought every w. hearted man. 36:1
Aholiab and every w. hearted man. 2
every w. hearted man made ten. 8

wise *men*

all the magicians of Egypt, and all the w. men. Gen 41:8; Ex 7:11

wise *woman*

and Joab fetched thence a w. woman. 2 Sam 14:2
then cried a w. woman out. 20:16
every w. woman buildeth. Pr 14:1

wisely

come on, let us deal w. Ex 1:10
David behaved himself w. 1 Sam 18:5, 14, 15, 30
Rehoboam dealt w. 2 Chr 11:23
charming never so w. Ps 58:5
for they shall w. consider of. 64:9
I will behave myself w. in a. 101:2
handleth a matter w. Pr 16:20
w. considereth the house. 21:12

whoso walketh *w.* shall be. *Pr* 28:26
thou dost not enquire *w.* *Eccl* 7:10
because he had done *w.* *Luke* 16:8

wiser

for Solomon was *w.* *1 Ki* 4:31
who maketh us *w.* than the fowls of heaven? *Job* 35:11
thou hast made me *w.* *Ps* 119:98
and he will be yet *w.* *Pr* 9:9
the sluggard is *w.* in his own. 26:16
behold, thou art *w.* than. *Ezek* 28:3
are in their generation *w.* *Luke* 16:8
foolishness of God is *w.* *1 Cor* 1:25

wish

I am according to thy *w.* *Job* 33:6*
put to shame that *w.* evil. *Ps* 40:14*
more than heart could *w.* 73:7
I could *w.* myself accursed. *Rom* 9:3
this also we *w.*, even. *2 Cor* 13:9*
I *w.* above all things. *3 John* 2*

wished

Jonah fainted, and *w.* *Jonah* 4:8*
they cast anchor, and *w.* *Acts* 27:29

wishing

my mouth to sin, by *w.* *Job* 31:30*

wist

(*American Revision substitutes the more modern word* knew)
it is manna: for they *w.* not. *Ex* 16:15
Moses *w.* not that his face. 34:29
though he *w.* not, yet is he guilty. *Lev* 5:17, 18
but I *w.* not whence. *Josh* 2:4
w. not that there were liers. 8:14
he *w.* not that the Lord. *Judg* 16:20
he *w.* not what to say. *Mark* 9:6
neither *w.* they what to. 14:40
w. ye not I must be about? *Luke* 2:49
he that was healed *w.* not. *John* 5:13
w. not that it was true. *Acts* 12:9
said Paul, I *w.* not he was. 23:5

witch

not suffer a *w.* to live. *Ex* 22:18*
not be among you a *w.* *Deut* 18:10*

witchcraft

is as the sin of *w.* *1 Sam* 15:23
Manasseh used *w.* and. *2 Chr* 33:6*
the works of the flesh are idolatry, *w.* *Gal* 5:20*

witchcrafts

so long as Jezebel's *w.* *2 Ki* 9:22
I will cut off *w.* out of. *Mi* 5:12
w. that selleth nations through her . . . through her *w.* *Nah* 3:4

withal

w. how Elijah had slain. *1 Ki* 19:1
whilst that I *w.* escape. *Ps* 141:10
and not *w.* to signify. *Acts* 25:27

withdraw

priest, *W.* thine hand. *1 Sam* 14:19
will not *w.* his anger. *Job* 9:13
w. thine hand far from me: let. 13:21
that he may *w.* man from. 33:17
w. thy foot from thy neighbour's house. *Pr* 25:17*
from this *w.* not thine hand. *Eccl* 7:18
shall thy moon *w.* itself. *Isa* 60:20
the stars shall *w.* their shining. *Joel* 2:10; 3:15
w. yourselves from every brother. *2 Thes* 3:6
corrupt minds *w.* thyself. *1 Tim* 6:5

withdrawest

why *w.* thou thy right? *Ps* 74:11*

withdraweth

he *w.* not his eyes from. *Job* 36:7

withdrawn

have *w.* the inhabitants. *Deut* 13:13
but my beloved had *w.* *S of S* 5:6
he hath not *w.* his hand. *Lam* 2:8
that hath *w.* his hand. *Ezek* 18:8
the Lord hath *w.* himself. *Hos* 5:6
w. from them about a. *Luke* 22:41*

withdrew

they *w.* the shoulder and. *Neh* 9:29
I *w.* mine hand. *Ezek* 20:22
knew it, he *w.* himself. *Mat* 12:15
Jesus *w.* himself from thence. *Mark* 3:7; *Luke* 5:16

but when they were come, he *w.* *Gal* 2:12*

wither

his leaf also shall not *w.* *Ps* 1:3
and they shall *w.* as the green. 37:2
reeds and flags shall *w.* *Isa* 19:6
by the brooks shall *w.* 7*
upon them, and they shall *w.* 40:24
the herbs of the field *w.*? *Jer* 12:4
cut off the fruit thereof that it *w.*? it shall *w.* in all the. *Ezek* 17:9
utterly *w.*? it shall *w.* in furrows. 10
top of Carmel shall *w.* *Amos* 1:2

withered

behold seven ears *w.* thin. *Gen* 41:23
my heart is smitten and *w.* *Ps* 102:4
I am *w.* 11
hay is *w.* away, the grass. *Isa* 15:6
thereof are *w.*, be broken off. 27:11
the Nazarite's skin is *w.* *Lam* 4:8
her strong rods were *w.* *Ezek* 19:12
of the field are *w.*: joy is *w.* *Joel* 1:12
broken down, for the corn is *w.* 17
whereupon it rained not *w.* *Amos* 4:7
the gourd that it *w.* *Jonah* 4:7
and behold there was a man which had his hand *w.* *Mat* 12:10
Mark 3:1, 3; *Luke* 6:6, 8
were scorched, because having no root, they *w.* *Mat* 13:6; *Mark* 4:6
presently the fig tree *w.* *Mat* 21:19
20; *Mark* 11:21
it *w.* away because it. *Luke* 8:6
of *w.* folk, waiting for. *John* 5:3
forth as a branch and is *w.* 15:6

withereth

the flag *w.* before any. *Job* 8:12
it is cut down and *w.* *Ps* 90:6
as the grass which *w.* before it. 129:6
the grass *w.*, the flower fadeth. *Isa* 40:7, 8; *1 Pet* 1:24
risen, but it *w.* the grass. *Jas* 1:11
trees whose fruit *w.* without fruit. *Jude* 12*

withheld

for I *w* thee from sinning. *Gen* 20:6
seeing thou hast not *w.* thy. 22:12
who *w.* from thee the fruit? 30:2
if I have *w.* the poor. *Job* 31:16
I *w.* not my heart from. *Eccl* 2:10

withheldest

w. not thy manna from. *Neh* 9:20

withhold

none of us shall *w.* from. *Gen* 23:6
for he will not *w.* me. *2 Sam* 13:13
but who can *w.* himself? *Job* 4:2
w. not thy tender mercies. *Ps* 40:11
no good thing will he *w.* from. 84:11
w. not good from them to. *Pr* 3:27
w. not correction from the. 23:13
in the evening *w.* not thy. *Eccl* 11:6
w. thy foot from being unshod. *Jer* 2:25

withholden

Lord hath *w.* thee from. *1 Sam* 25:26
thou hast *w.* bread from. *Job* 22:7
from the wicked their light is *w.* 38:15
that no thought can be *w.* 42:2*
hast not *w.* the request. *Ps* 21:2
showers have been *w.* *Jer* 3:3
your sins have *w.* good things. 5:25
hath not *w.* the pledge. *Ezek* 18:16*
the drink offering is *w.* *Joel* 1:13
also I have *w.* the rain. *Amos* 4:7

withholdeth

behold, he *w.* the waters. *Job* 12:15
there is that *w.* more. *Pr* 11:24
he that *w.* corn, the people. 26
and now ye know what *w.* that he might be revealed. *2 Thes* 2:6*

within

none of men was *w.* *Gen* 39:11
w. a full year he may. *Lev* 25:29*
of Simeon was *w.* Judah. *Josh* 19:1*
why not recover them *w.* that time? *Judg* 11:26
thou camest not *w* the. *1 Sam* 13:11
w. the oracle he made. *1 Ki* 6:23
to the king's house *w.* *2 Ki* 7:11
whoso would not come *w.* *Ezra* 10:8
daughter is all glorious *w.* *Ps* 45:13*
will walk *w.* my house with a. 101:2

little city, few men *w.* it. *Eccl* 9:14
shut thyself *w.* thy house. *Ezek* 3:24
any vain vision *w.* Israel. 12:24
minister in the gates and *w.* 44:17
her princes *w.* are roaring. *Zeph* 3:3*
think not to say *w.* yourselves. *Mat* 3:9; *Luke* 3:8
w. herself, If I but touch. *Mat* 9:21
w. they are full of extortion. 23:25
cleanse first what is *w.* the cup. 26
are *w.* full of dead men's bones. 27
w. ye are full of hypocrisy. 28
for from *w.* proceed. *Mark* 7:21
all these evil things come from *w.* 23
from *w.* shall answer. *Luke* 11:7
he thought *w.* himself. 12:17 16:3
18:4
his disciples were *w.* *John* 20:26
we found no man *w.* *Acts* 5:23
judge them that are *w.*? *1 Cor* 5:12
fightings, *w.* were fears. *2 Cor* 7:5
full of eyes *w.*: rest not. *Rev* 4:8*
a book written *w.* and on the back. 5:1
see **gates, him, me, thee, them us, without, you**

without

wherefore standest thou *w.*? *Gen* 24:31
the wife of the dead shall not marry *w.* unto a stranger. *Deut* 25:5
appointed eighty men *w.* *2 Ki* 10:24
Have her forth *w.* the ranges. 11:15*
I now come up *w.* the Lord against this place? 18:25; *Isa* 36:10
Israel hath been long *w.* *2 Chr* 15:3
Jehoram departed *w.* 21:20
they that did see me *w.* *Ps* 31:11
wisdom crieth *w.*; she. *Pr* 1:20*
now she is *w.* 7:12*
there is a lion *w.* 22:13
prepare thy work *w.*, and. 24:27
valiant ones shall cry *w.* *Isa* 33:7
be redeemed *w.* money. 52:3
milk *w.* money and *w.* price. 55:1
cut off the children from *w.* *Jer* 9:21
w. man, *w.* beast, and *w.* 33:10, 12
w. a king, *w.* a prince, *w.* a sacrifice, *w.* an image, *w.* an ephod, and *w.* a teraphim. *Hos* 3:4
not fall *w.* your father. *Mat* 10:29
to them that are *w.* all. *Mark* 4:11
whatsoever from *w.* entereth. 7:18
whole multitude were praying *w.* *Luke* 1:10
to judge them that are *w.* *1 Cor* 5:12
them that are *w.* God judgeth. 13
having no hope, and *w.* *Eph* 2:12
walk in wisdom toward them that are *w.* *Col* 4:5
walk honestly toward them that are *w.* *1 Thes* 4:12
report of them that are *w.* *1 Tim* 3:7
w. father, *w.* mother, *w.* *Heb* 7:3
also suffered *w.* the gate. 13:12
that they also may *w.* *1 Pet* 3:1
w. are dogs and sorcerers. *Rev* 22:15

without, joined with *within*

pitch the ark *within* and *w.* *Gen* 6:14
overlay the ark *within and w.* *Ex* 25:11; 37:2
be bare *within* or *w.* *Lev* 13:55
the sword *w.* and terror *within.* *Deut* 32:25
written *within* and *w.* *Ezek* 2:10
is *w.* and famine *within.* 7:15
made that which is *w.* make that which is *within* also? *Luke* 11:40
w. were fightings, *within.* *2 Cor* 7:5
see **blemish, camp, cause, city, fail, fear, him, knowledge, law, me, stand, stood, us, you**

withs

(*withes*)
if they bind me with seven green *w.* *Judg* 16:7
the lords brought *w.* 8
he brake the *w.* 9

withstand

went out to *w.* Balaam. *Num* 22:32*
young, could not *w.* them. *2 Chr* 13:7
now ye think to *w.* the kingdom. 8
none is able to *w.* thee. 20:6
no man could *w.* the Jews. *Esth* 9:2

prevail, two shall *w.* him. *Eccl* 4:12
arms of the south shall not *w.*, neither any strength to *w.* *Dan* 11:15
I that I could *w.* God ? *Acts* 11:17
able to *w.* in the evil day. *Eph* 6:13

withstood

they *w.* Uzziah the king. *2 Chr* 26:18
prince of Persia *w.* me. *Dan* 10:13
Elymas the sorcerer *w.* *Acts* 13:8
at Antioch I *w.* Peter. *Gal* 2:11*
and Jambres *w.* Moses. *2 Tim* 3:8
hath greatly *w.* our words. 4:15

witness

Since there was little writing among most of the people in olden times the evidence of a transaction was most often given by some tangible memorial, as in Gen 21:30; Josh 22:10, *or some significant ceremony.*

Witness *in Greek is* Martūs, *or* Martūr, *and signifies one that gives testimony to the truth at the expense of his life. It is in this sense that the word is mainly used in the New Testament, and our word* martyr *has come from this also.*

The law appoints, that in case of a capital charge one witness *only was not sufficient,* Deut 17:6. *When any one was condemned to die the* witnesses *were the first that began the execution. They threw the first stone, for example, if the party was to be stoned,* Deut 17:7. *The law condemned a false* witness *to the same punishment that he would have subjected his neighbour to,* Deut 19:16, 17, 18, 19. *On the whole the law was very careful to provide evidence in all cases, and to punish both false swearing and one who kept back a part of the truth.*

The disciples who had been with Jesus, were to be witnesses for him, Luke 24:48, *and when they chose another apostle in place of Judas, they thought fit to appoint one who had been a* witness *of the resurrection along with them,* Acts 1:22.

The apostle Paul, in Rom 8:16 *says, that* the Spirit itself beareth *witness* with our spirit, that we are the children of God.

they may be a *w.* that I digged this well. *Gen* 21:30
let this covenant be a *w.* 31:44
this heap is a *w.*; this pillar. 48, 52
God is *w.* between me and thee. 50
1 Thes 2:5
let him bring it for a *w.* *Ex* 22:13
hand to be an unrighteous *w.* 23:1
if a soul sin, and is a *w.* *Lev* 5:1
be no *w.* against her. *Num* 5:13
one *w.* shall not testify against. 35:30
Deut 17:6; 19:15
that this song may be a *w.* for me against. *Deut* 31:19, 21, 26
the altar is a *w.* between us.
Josh 22:27, 28, 34
this stone shall be a *w.* to us. 24:27
Lord be *w.* between us. *Judg* 11:10
Jer 42:5
the Lord is *w.* against you this day.
1 Sam 12:5
wrinkles, which is a *w.* *Job* 16:8
behold, my *w.* is in heaven, my. 19
when the eye saw me, it gave *w.* to me. 29:11
established as a faithful *w.* *Ps* 89:37
a faithful *w.* will not lie, but a false *w.*
Pr 14:5
a true *w.* delivereth souls, but a deceitful *w.* 25*
an ungodly *w.* scorneth. 19:28
not *w.* against thy neighbour. 24:28
it shall be for a *w.* to the Lord of hosts. *Isa* 19:20
I have given him for a *w.* to. 55:4
I know, and am a *w.* *Jer* 29:23
Lord be a true and faithful *w.* 42:5
let the Lord God be *w.* *Mi* 1:2
Lord be *w.* between thee. *Mal* 2:14
I will be a swift *w.* against the. 3:5
be preached for a *w.* to. *Mat* 24:14*
the council sought for *w.* *Mark* 14:55
w. agreed not together. 56, 59
need we further *w.*? *Luke* 22:71
for a *w.* to bear *w.* *John* 1:7
and ye receive not our *w.* 3:11
to whom thou bearest *w.* 26
if I bear *w.* of myself, my *w.* 5:31
I know the *w.* he witnesseth of. 32
but I have greater *w.* than. 36
sent me hath borne *w.* of me. 37
ordained to be a *w.* with us. *Acts* 1:22
gave *w.* of the resurrection. 4:33
to him give all the prophets *w.* 10:43
he left not himself without *w.* 14:17
for thou shalt be his *w.* to all. 22:15
a minister and a *w.* of these. 26:16
God is my *w.* whom I serve. *Rom* 1:9
conscience also bearing *w.* 2:15; 9:1
this *w.* is true. Rebuke. *Tit* 1:13*
God also bearing them *w.* *Heb* 2:4
the Holy Ghost is a *w.* to us. 10:15
by which Abel obtained *w.* 11:4
shall be *w.* against you. *Jas* 5:3*
Peter a *w.* of the sufferings of Christ.
1 Pet 5:1
w. of men, the *w.* of God is greater, for this is the *w.* of. *1 John* 5:9
he that believeth hath the *w.* 10
borne *w.* of thy charity. *3 John* 6
who is the faithful *w.* *Rev* 1:5
these things saith the true *w.* 3:14
were beheaded for the *w.* 20:4*
see **bare, bear, beareth, false, tabernacle**

witness, *verb*

I call heaven and earth to *w.* against.
Deut 4:26
behold, here I am, *w.* *1 Sam* 12:3
their countenance doth *w.* *Isa* 3:9
I take to *w.* for thee ? *Lam* 2:13*
what is it which these *w.* against ?
Mat 26:62; *Mark* 14:60
thou not how many things they *w.* against ? *Mat* 27:13; *Mark* 15:4*

witnessed

the men of Belial *w.* against Naboth.
1 Ki 21:13
being *w.* by the law and. *Rom* 3:21
who before Pontius Pilate *w.* a good confession. *1 Tim* 6:13
it is *w.* that he liveth. *Heb* 7:8

witnesses

to death by mouth of *w.* *Num* 35:30
at the mouth of two or three *w.*
Deut 17:6; 19:15; *2 Cor* 13:1
the hands of the *w.* shall be first upon him. *Deut* 17:7
are *w.* against yourselves that ye . . . We are *w.* *Josh* 24:22
ye are *w.* that I have bought.
Ruth 4:9, 10
and the elders said, We are *w.* 11
thou renewest thy *w.* *Job* 10:17
I took to me faithful *w.* *Isa* 8:2
nations bring forth their *w.* 43:9
ye are my *w.* saith the Lord. 10, 12
44:8
they are their own *w.*; they see. 44:9
evidence and took *w.* *Jer* 32:10, 12
field for money, and take *w.* 25, 44
mouth of two or three *w.* *Mat* 18:16
be *w.* to yourselves that ye. 23:31
what further need of *w.*? 26:65
Mark 14:63
and ye are *w.* of these. *Luke* 24:48
ye shall be *w.* to me in. *Acts* 1:8
this Jesus hath God raised up, whereof we all are *w.* 2:32; 3:15
we are his *w.* of these things. 5:32
10:39
w. laid down their clothes at. 7:58
but unto *w.* chosen before of. 10:41
his *w.* unto the people. 13:31
ye are *w.* and God also. *1 Thes* 2:10
receive no accusation but before two or three *w.* *1 Tim* 5:19
good profession before many *w.* 6:12
things heard of me among many *w.*
2 Tim 2:2
died without mercy under two or three *w.* *Heb* 10:28
with so great a cloud of *w.* 12:1
give power to my two *w.* *Rev* 11:3
see **false**

witnesseth

the witness that he *w.* *John* 5:32
save that Holy Ghost *w.* *Acts* 20:23*

witnessing

w. both to small and. *Acts* 26:22*

wits'

and are at their *w.* end. *Ps* 107:27

wittingly

guided his hands *w.* for. *Gen* 48:14

witty

I find out knowledge of *w.* inventions.
Pr 8:12*

wives

took unto him two *w.* *Gen* 4:19
they took them *w.* of all which. 6:2
give me my *w.* and children. 30:26
if thou take other *w.* besides. 31:50
that our *w.* and children. *Num* 14:3
nor shall he multiply *w.* *Deut* 17:17
if a man have two *w.*, one. 21:15
sons: for he had many *w.* *Judg* 8:30
how shall we do for *w.*? 21:7, 16
we may not give them *w.* of. 18
Elkanah. He had two *w.*; Hannah and Peninnah. *1 Sam* 1:2
also both of them David's *w.* 25:43
David took more *w.* out. *2 Sam* 5:13
I gave thee thy master's *w.* 12:8
Solomon had 700 *w.* *1 Ki* 11:3
his *w.* turned away his heart. 4
he sent unto me for my *w.* 20:7
Ashur had two *w.* *1 Chr* 4:5
the sons of Uzzi had many *w.* 7:4
Shaharaim had two *w.* 8:8
Rehoboam loved Maachah above all his *w.* *2 Chr* 11:21
and he desired many *w.* 23
Jehoiada took for him two *w.* 24:3
and our *w.* are in captivity for. 29:9
to put away all the *w.* *Ezra* 10:3, 44
the *w.* also and children. *Neh* 12:43*
I saw Jews that had married *w.* 13:23
the *w.* shall give to husbands honour.
Esth 1:20
take ye *w.*, and take *w.* *Jer* 29:6
wine, we, nor our *w.* nor sons. 35:8
his *w.* and concubines. *Dan* 5:2, 3
drank, they married *w.* *Luke* 17:27
us on our way, with *w.* *Acts* 21:5
they that have *w.* be as though they had none. *1 Cor* 7:29
w. submit yourselves to. *Eph* 5:22
Col 3:18; *1 Pet* 3:1
so let the *w.* be to their. *Eph* 5:24
refuse profane and old *w.*' *1 Tim* 4:7
by the conversation of *w.* *1 Pet* 3:1
see **strange**

their **wives**

little ones, and *their w.* took they.
Gen 34:29; *1 Sam* 30:3
they took their daughters to be *their w.* *Judg* 3:6
all Judah with *their w.* *2 Chr* 20:13
would put away *their w.* *Ezra* 10:19
a great cry of the people and of *their w.* *Neh* 5:1
their w. and daughters entered into an oath. 10:28
and *their w.* ravished. *Isa* 13:16
houses shall be turned to others, with *their* fields and *w.* *Jer* 6:12; 8:10
have none to bury *their w.* 14:16
let *their w.* be bereaved of. 18:21
the wickedness of *their w.* 44:9
men who knew *their w.* had. 15
nor take for *their w.* a. *Ezek* 44:22
cast them and *their w.* *Dan* 6:24
their w. shall mourn apart.
Zech 12:12, 13, 14
to love *their w.* as their. *Eph* 5:28
even so must *their w.* be grave, sober. *1 Tim* 3:11*

thy **wives**

I will take *thy w.* before thine eyes, . . . lie with *thy w.* *2 Sam* 12:11

saved the lives of *thy w.* *2 Sam* 19:5
gold is mine, and *thy w.* *1 Ki* 20:3
deliver me *thy w.* and children. 5
Lord will smite thy people and *thy w.* *2 Chr* 21:14
bring *thy w.* and children. *Jer* 38:23
thy w. and concubines. *Dan* 5:23

your **wives**

take waggons for *your w.* *Gen* 45:19
come not at *your w.* *Ex* 19:15*
your w. shall be widows. 22:24
golden earrings of *your w.* 32:2
your w. and your little ones and your cattle. *Deut* 3:19; *Josh* 1:14
your w.: shouldest enter into covenant with the Lord. *Deut* 29:11
fight for *your w.* and. *Neh* 4:14
wickedness of *your w.* *Jer* 44:9
Lord, saying; Ye and *your w.* 25
you to put away *your w.* *Mat* 19:8
husbands, love *your w.* *Eph* 5:25
Col 3:19

wizard

a *w.* shall surely be put. *Lev* 20:27
be found among you a *w.* *Deut* 18:11

wizards

nor seek after *w.* to be. *Lev* 19:31
the soul that turneth after *w.* 20:6
Saul had put *w.* out of the land. *1 Sam* 28:3, 9
Manasseh dealt with *w.* *2 Ki* 21:6
2 Chr 33:6
Josiah put the *w.* and. *2 Ki* 23:24
Seek unto *w.* that peep. *Isa* 8:19
shall seek to idols and *w.* 19:3

woe

w. to thee, Moab! *Num* 21:29
Jer 48:46
w. unto us, for there hath. *1 Sam* 4:7
8; *Jer* 4:13; 6:4; *Lam* 5:16
who hath *w.*? who hath? *Pr* 23:29
w. to him that is alone. *Eccl* 4:10
w. to thee, O land, when. 10:16
w. to their soul, for they. *Isa* 3:9
w. unto the wicked! it shall be. 11
w. to the multitude of. 17:12
w. to the land shadowing. 18:1
w. to the crown of pride, to. 28:1
w. to Ariel. 29:1
w. to the rebellious children. 30:1
w. to thee that spoilest. 33:1
w. to him that striveth with. 45:9
w. to him that saith to fatherless. 10
w. unto thee, O Jerusalem. *Jer* 13:27
w. to him that buildeth by. 22:13
w. to the pastors that destroy. 23:1
w. to Nebo. 48:1
written, mourning and *w.* *Ezek* 2:10
w. to foolish prophets, that. 13:3
w. to women that sew pillows. 18
w. *w.* to thee. 16:23
w. to bloody city. 24:6, 9; *Nah* 3:1
Howl, *W.* worth the day! *Ezek* 30:2
w. be to the shepherds that. 34:2
w. to you that desire the. *Amos* 5:18
w. to him that increaseth. *Hab* 2:6
w. to him that coveteth an evil. 9
w. to him that buildeth a town. 12
w. to him that giveth his. 15
w. to him that saith to the wood. 19
w. to the inhabitants of. *Zeph* 2:5
w. to her that is filthy. 3:1
w. to the idol shepherd. *Zech* 11:17
w. unto thee, Chorazin! *w.* unto thee. *Mat* 11:21; *Luke* 10:13
w. unto the world because of offences, *w.* *Mat* 18:7; *Luke* 17:1
w. unto you scribes and. *Mat* 23:13
14, 15, 23, 25, 27, 29; *Luke* 11:44
w. unto you, ye blind guides, which say. *Mat* 23:16
but *w.* unto that man by. 26:24
Mark 14:21; *Luke* 22:22
w. unto you that are rich. *Luke* 6:24
w. to you that are full, *w.* to you. 25
w. unto you when all men speak. 26
but *w.* unto you Pharisees. 11:42, 43
he said, *W.* to you also. 46, 47. 52
I heard an angel flying, saying, *W. w. w.* *Rev* 8:13; 12:12
one *w.* is past. 9:12
the second *w.* is past. 11:14

woe *is me*

w. is me, that I sojourn. *Ps* 120:5
w. is me! for I am undone. *Isa* 6:5
w. is me now, for my soul. *Jer* 4:31
w. is me for my hurt. 10:19
w. is me, my mother. 15:10
w. is me, for the Lord hath. 45:3
w. is me! for I am as when. *Mi* 7:1

woe *unto me*

if I be wicked, *w. unto me*. *Job* 10:15
My leanness, *w. unto me*. *Isa* 24:16
w. unto me if I preach. *1 Cor* 9:16

woe *to them*

w. to them that join house to house. *Isa* 5:8
w. to them that rise up early in. 11
w. to them that draw iniquity. 18
w. to them that call evil good. 20
w. to them that are wise in their. 21
w. to them that are mighty to. 22
w. to them that decree. 10:1
w. to them that seek deep to. 29:15
w. to them that go down into. 31:1
w. to them, for their day. *Jer* 50:27
w. to them, for they have. *Hos* 7:13
w. to them when I depart from. 9:12
w. to them that are at. *Amos* 6:1
w. to them that devise. *Mi* 2:1
w. to them which are with child, and to them that give. *Mat* 24:19
Mark 13:17; *Luke* 21:23
w. unto them! for they have gone in the way of Cain. *Jude* 11

woeful

neither I desired the *w.* day. *Jer* 17:16

woes

behold, there come two *w.* *Rev* 9:12

wolf

In a country where a large part of wealth consisted of flocks of sheep the habits of wolves became thoroughly well known, and were often used as symbols of such habits and actions of mankind as might bear a resemblance to them, as Gen 49:27.

Isaiah describing the tranquillity of the reign of the Messiah, *says,* The *wolf* shall dwell with the lamb, and the leopard shall lie down with the kid, *etc.*, Isa 11:6. *Persecutors are elsewhere compared to wolves,* Mat 10:16, Behold, I send you forth as sheep in the midst of *wolves*.

shall ravin as a *w.* *Gen* 49:27
the *w.* shall dwell with. *Isa* 11:6
the *w.* and the lamb shall. 65:25
a *w.* of the evenings shall. *Jer* 5:6
but he that is an hireling, seeth the *w.* coming: and the *w.* *John* 10:12

wolves

her princes are like *w.* *Ezek* 22:27
fiercer than evening *w.* *Hab* 1:8
her judges evening *w.* *Zeph* 3:3
they are ravening *w.* *Mat* 7:15
as sheep in the midst of *w.* 10:16
as lambs among *w.* *Luke* 10:3
grievous *w.* shall enter in. *Acts* 20:29

woman

Woman *was created to be a companion and helper to man. She was equal to him in that authority and jurisdiction that God gave them over all other animals. But after the fall, God made her subject to the government of man,* Gen 3:16.

Weak and ineffectual men are sometimes spoken of as women, Isa 3:12; 19:16.

and the rib, taken from man, made he a *w.* *Gen* 2:22
she shall be called *W.*, she was. 23
between thee and the *w.* 3:15
the *w.* will not come. 24:5, 39
let the same be the *w.* the Lord. 44
and hurt a *w.* with child. *Ex* 21:22
nor shall a *w.* stand. *Lev* 18:23
with mankind as with a *w.* 20:13*
he shall set the *w.* *Num* 5:18, 30
the *w.* shall be a curse among. 27
brought a Midianitish *w.* in. 25:6
Phinehas thrust the *w.* through. 8
if a *w.* vow a vow unto the Lord. 30:3
now kill every *w.* that hath. 31:17
I took this *w.* and found. *Deut* 22:14
the *w.* took the two men. *Josh* 2:4
bring out thence the *w.* 6:22
Sisera into the hand of a *w.* *Judg* 4:9
a certain *w.* cast a piece of a millstone. 9:53; *2 Sam* 11:21
men say not of me, a *w.* *Judg* 9:54
man that spakest to the *w.*? 13:11
is there never a *w.* among? 14:3
Samson loved a *w.* in the. 16:4
the *w.* in the dawning of the. 19:26
the *w.* was left of her sons. *Ruth* 1:5
know thou art a virtuous *w.* 3:11
w. like Rachel and Leah. 4:11
Hannah said, I am a *w.* of a sorrowful spirit. *1 Sam* 1:15
I am the *w.* that stood by thee. 26
Lord give thee seed of this *w.* 2:20
seek me a *w.* that hath a. 28:7
me concerning this *w.* *2 Sam* 3:8
from the roof David saw a *w.* 11:2
put now this *w.* out from me. 13:17
the *w.* spread a covering over. 17:19
then *w.* went unto all people. 20:22
I and this *w.* dwell in. *1 Ki* 3:17
herself to be another *w.* 14:5
the son of the *w.* fell sick. 17:17
where was a great *w.* *2 Ki* 4:8
there cried a *w.* saying, Help. 6:26
this is the *w.* 8:5
see this cursed *w.* 9:34
Athaliah that wicked *w.* *2 Chr* 24:7
if my heart have been deceived by a *w.* *Job* 31:9
pain as of a *w.* in travail. *Ps* 48:6
Isa 13:8; 21:3; 26:17; *Jer* 4:31
6:24; 13:21; 22:23; 30:6; 31:8
48:41; 49:22, 24; 50:43
thee from the evil *w.* *Pr* 6:24
met him a *w.* subtle of heart. 7:10
a foolish *w.* is clamorous. 9:13
a virtuous *w.* is a crown. 12:4; 31:10
every wise *w.* buildeth her. 14:1
than with a brawling *w.* in. 21:9, 19
who can find a virtuous *w.*? 31:10
a *w.* that feareth the Lord shall. 30
the *w.* whose heart is snares and nets. *Eccl* 7:26
but a *w.* among all those have I. 28
cry like a travailing *w.* *Isa* 42:14
or to the *w.*, What hast thou? 45:10
can a *w.* forget her sucking? 49:15
Lord hath called thee as a *w.* 54:6*
of Zion to a delicate *w.* *Jer* 6:2
created a new thing, a *w.* 31:22
Jerusalem is a menstruous *w.* *Lam* 1:17
imperious whorish *w.* *Ezek* 16:30†
unto her, as they go in to a *w.* 23:44
uncleanness of a removed *w.* 36:17
go yet, love a *w.* beloved. *Hos* 3:1
the sorrows of a travailing *w.* shall come upon. 13:13; *Mi* 4:9, 10
this is a *w.* that sitteth in. *Zech* 5:7
whoso looketh on a *w.* to lust after her. *Mat* 5:28
a *w.* which was diseased with an issue. 9:20; *Mark* 5:25; *Luke* 8:43
leaven, which a *w.* took. *Mat* 13:33
O *w.*, great is thy faith, be it. 15:28
and last of all the *w.* died also. 22:27
Mark 12:22; *Luke* 20:32
Why trouble ye the *w.*? *Mat* 26:10
this that this *w.* hath done shall. 13
if a *w.* shall put away. *Mark* 10:12
manner of *w.* this is? *Luke* 7:39
Simon, Seest thou this *w.*? 44
ought not this *w.*, being a daughter of Abraham? 13:16
w. what have I to do with thee? *John* 2:4
askest drink of me who am a *w.*? 4:9
on him for the saying of the *w.* 39
brought to him a *w.* taken in. 8:3, 4
when Jesus saw none but the *w.* 10
he saith to his mother, *W.* 19:26
Dorcas: this *w.* was full. *Acts* 9:36
and a *w.* named Damaris. 17:34

the natural use of the *w.* *Rom* 1:27
the *w.* which hath an husband is. 7:2
for a man not to touch a *w.* *1 Cor* 7:1
every *w.* have her own husband. 2
but every *w.* that prayeth. 11:5
if the *w.* be not covered, let her. 6
the *w.* is the glory of the man. 7
man is not of the *w.*; but the *w.* 8
neither man for the *w.*; but the *w.* 9
the *w.* ought to have power on. 10
nevertheless, neither is the man without the *w.*, nor the *w.* 11
as the *w.* is of the man, even so is the man also by the *w.* 12
comely that a *w.* pray uncovered? 13
if a *w.* have long hair, it is a glory. 15
forth his Son, made of a *w.* *Gal* 4:4
then destruction cometh as travail on a *w.* *1 Thes* 5:3
I suffer not a *w.* to teach. *1 Tim* 2:12
the *w.* being deceived, was in the. 14
sufferest that *w.* Jezebel. *Rev* 2:20
there appeared *w.* clothed with. 12:1
the *w.* fled. 6
the earth helped the *w.* 16
dragon was wroth with the *w.* 17
I saw a *w.* sit on a scarlet. 17:3
a *w.* drunken. 6
I will tell the mystery of the *w.* 7
see **born, man, strange**

***young* woman**
the seed which Lord shall give thee of this *young w.* *Ruth* 4:12

womankind
with mankind as with *w.* *Lev* 18:22

womb
two nations are in thy *w.* *Gen* 25:23
there were twins in her *w.* 24; 38:27
Lord opened Leah's *w.* 29:31
God opened Rachel's *w.* 30:22
of breasts, and of *w.* 49:25
openeth the *w.* is mine. *Ex* 13:2
are given me, instead of such as open every *w.*, even. *Num* 8:16
Nazarite from the *w.* *Judg* 13:5, 7
any more sons in my *w.*? *Ruth* 1:11
had shut up her *w.* *1 Sam* 1:5, 6
why died I not from the *w.*? *Job* 3:11
brought me forth of the *w.*? 10:18
the *w.* shall forget him, he. 24:20
that made me in the *w.* make him? fashion us in the *w.*? 31:15
if it had issued out of the *w.* 38:8
out of whose *w.* came the ice? 29
who took me out of the *w.* *Ps* 22:9
I was cast upon thee from the *w.* 10
are estranged from the *w.* 58:3
I been holden up from the *w.* 71:6
from the *w.* of the morning. 110:3
the barren *w.* saith not, It. *Pr* 30:16
what, the son of my *w.*? 31:2
nor how bones grow in *w.* *Eccl* 11:5
Lord formed thee from the *w.* *Isa* 44:2, 24; 49:5
which are carried from the *w.* 46:3
a transgressor from the *w.* 48:8
called me from the *w.* 49:1
compassion on the son of her *w.*? 15
bring forth, and shut the *w.*? 66:9
camest forth out of the *w.* *Jer* 1:5
because he slew me not from the *w.*; or my mother's *w.* to be. 20:17
why came I forth of the *w.*? 18
pass through the fire all that openeth the *w.* *Ezek* 20:26
their glory shall fly away from the birth and *w.* *Hos* 9:11*
give them a miscarrying *w.* 14
brother by the heel in the *w.* 12:3
shalt conceive in thy *w.* *Luke* 1:31
leaped in her *w.* for joy. 41, 44
he was conceived in the *w.* 2:21
every male that openeth the *w.* 23
see **fruit, mother**

wombs
fast closed up all the *w.* *Gen* 20:18
blessed are the *w.* that. *Luke* 23:29

women
the time that *w.* go out to. *Gen* 24:11
all the *w.* went out after. *Ex* 15:20
w. that were wise hearted. 35:25
all the *w.* whose heart stirred. 26
ten *w.* shall bake your bread in one oven. *Lev* 26:26
Moses said, Have ye saved all the *w.* alive? *Num* 31:15
the *w.* and little ones. *Deut* 20:14
the law before the *w.* *Josh* 8:35
blessed above *w.* shall Jael wife of. *Judg* 5:24
they saved alive of the *w.* of. 21:14
they lay with the *w.* *1 Sam* 2:22
as thy sword hath made *w.* 15:33
the *w.* came out of the cities. 18:6
the *w.* answered one another as. 7
kept themselves from *w.* 21:4
of a truth *w.* have been kept. 5
Amalekites had taken the *w.* 30:2
passing the love of *w.* *2 Sam* 1:26
the king left ten *w.* to keep. 15:16
then came two *w.* that. *1 Ki* 3:16
and rip up their *w.* with child. *2 Ki* 8:12, 15, 16
where the *w.* wove hangings. 23:7
even him did outlandish *w.* cause to sin. *Neh* 13:26
made a feast for the *w.* *Esth* 1:9
loved Esther above all the *w.* 2:17
little children and *w.* 3:13; 8:11
no *w.* found so fair as. *Job* 42:15
among thy honourable *w.* *Ps* 45:9
give not thy strength to *w.* *Pr* 31:3
O thou fairest among *w.* *S of S* 1:8 5:9; 6:1
as for my people, *w.* rule. *Isa* 3:12
in that day seven *w.* shall take. 4:1
day Egypt shall be like to *w.* 19:16
the *w.* come, and set them. 27:11
rise up, ye *w.* that are at ease. 32:9
careless *w.* 10
tremble, ye *w.* that are at ease. 11
the *w.* knead their dough. *Jer* 7:18
mourning and cunning *w.* 9:17
word of the Lord, O ye *w.* 20
w. left, shall be brought to. 38:22
Jeremiah said to all the *w.* 44:24
they shall become as *w.* and. 50:37
men of Babylon became as *w.* 51:30
shall the *w.* eat children? *Lam* 2:20
the pitiful *w.* have sodden. 4:10
they ravished *w.* in Zion, and. 5:11
there sat *w.* weeping. *Ezek* 8:14
maids, little children, and *w.* 9:6
woe to *w.* that sew pillows to. 13:18
is in thee from other *w.* 16:34
I will judge thee as *w.* that. 38
there were two *w.*, daughters. 23:2
judge after the manner of *w.* 45
w. may be taught not to do after. 48
he shall give him the daughter of *w.* *Dan* 11:17
nor shall regard the desire of *w.* 37
their *w.* with child shall. *Hos* 13:16
because they have ripped up *w.* with child. *Amos* 1:13
the *w.* of my people have. *Mi* 2:9
in the midst of thee are *w.* *Nah* 3:13
two *w.* and had wings. *Zech* 5:9
old *w.* shall dwell in the streets. 8:4
the houses rifled, the *w.* shall. 14:2
that are born of *w.* there hath not risen a greater. *Mat* 11:11; *Luke* 7:28
they that had eaten were 5000 men, besides *w.* *Mat* 14:21; 15:38
two *w.* grinding at the mill. 24:41 *Luke* 17:35
and many *w.* were then. *Mat* 27:55
blessed art thou among *w.* *Luke* 1:28, 42
certain *w.* also made us. 24:22
and found it even so as the *w.* 24
in prayer with the *w.* *Acts* 1:14
stirred up the devout *w.* 13:50
we spake to the *w.* which. 16:13
of the chief *w.* not a few. 17:4, 12
their *w.* did change the. *Rom* 1:26
let your *w.* keep silence. *1 Cor* 14:34
shame for *w.* to speak in churches. 35
help those *w.* which laboured with me. *Phil* 4:3
w. adorn themselves in. *1 Tim* 2:9
which becometh *w.* professing. 10
let the *w.* learn in silence with. 11
intreat the elder *w.* as mothers. 5:2
that the younger *w.* marry. 14*
captive silly *w.* laden. *2 Tim* 3:6
aged *w.* behave as becometh. *Tit* 2:3
they may teach the younger *w.* 4
w. received their dead. *Heb* 11:35
the holy *w.* adorned. *1 Pet* 3:5
they had hair as hair of *w.* *Rev* 9:8
that are not defiled with *w.* 14:4
see **children, men, singing, strange**

womenservants
gave *w.* to Abraham. *Gen* 20:14
had menservants and *w.* 32:5*

won
out of the spoils *w.* in. *1 Chr* 26:27
a brother offended is harder to be *w.* *Pr* 18:19
w. by the conversation. *1 Pet* 3:1*

wonder
give thee a sign or a *w.* *Deut* 13:1
and the sign or the *w.* come. 2
upon thee for a sign and a *w.* 28:46
him to enquire of the *w.* *2 Chr* 32:31
I am as a *w.* to many. *Ps* 71:7
walked barefoot for a *w.* *Isa* 20:3
marvellous work and a *w.* 29:14
they were filled with *w.* *Acts* 3:10
a great *w.* in heaven. *Rev* 12:1*, 3*

wonder, *verb*
stay yourselves, and *w.*; cry. *Isa* 29:9
the prophets shall *w.* *Jer* 4:9
behold ye, regard and *w.* *Hab* 1:5
behold, ye despisers, *w.* *Acts* 13:41
dwell on the earth shall *w.* *Rev* 17:8

wondered
he *w.* there was no. *Isa* 59:16
I *w.* that there was none. 63:5
for they are men *w.* at. *Zech* 3:8*
all they that heard it *w.* *Luke* 2:18
they all *w.* at the gracious. 4:22
believed not for joy, and *w.* 24:41
Moses *w.* *Acts* 7:31
Simon [Magus] *w.* 8:13*
all the world *w.* after. *Rev* 13:3
I saw her, I *w.* with great. 17:6

wonderful
make thy plagues *w.* *Deut* 28:59
thy love to me was *w.* *2 Sam* 1:26
house . . . shall be *w.* great. *2 Chr* 2:9
things too *w.* for me. *Job* 42:3
thy testimonies are *w.* *Ps* 119:129
knowledge is too *w.* for me. 139:6
there be three things that are too *w.* *Pr* 30:18
his name shall be called *W.* *Isa* 9:6
for thou hast done *w.* things. 25:1
of hosts who is *w.* in counsel. 28:29
a *w.* thing is committed. *Jer* 5:30
when they saw the *w.* *Mat* 21:15
see **works**

wonderfully
when he had wrought *w.* *1 Sam* 6:6
thee for I am *w.* made. *Ps* 139:14
Jerusalem came down *w.* *Lam* 1:9
he shall destroy *w.* and. *Dan* 8:24

wondering
the man *w.* at her, held. *Gen* 24:21*
Peter *w.* at that which was come to pass. *Luke* 24:12
ran together greatly *w.* *Acts* 3:11

wonderously, wondrously
angel did *w.*: Manoah. *Judg* 13:19*
the Lord hath dealt *w.* *Joel* 2:26

wonders
my hand and smite Egypt with all my *w.* *Ex* 3:20; 7:3; 11:9 *Deut* 6:22; 7:19; 26:8; 34:11
see thou do those *w.* *Ex* 4:21
did these *w.* 11:10
fearful in praises, doing *w.*? 15:11
hath God assayed to go and take a nation by *w.*? *Deut* 4:34
to-morrow the Lord will do *w.* among you. *Josh* 3:5
remember his *w.* *1 Chr* 16:12 *Ps* 105:5
thou shewedst *w.* upon. *Neh* 9:10
nor were mindful of thy *w.* 17 *Ps* 78:11, 43
doeth *w.* without number. *Job* 9:10
remember thy *w.* of old. *Ps* 77:11
thou art the God that doest *w.* 14
shew *w.* to the dead? 88:10

shall thy *w.* be known in the? *Ps* 88:12
shall praise thy *w.* O Lord. 89:5
his *w.* among all people. 96:3*
they shewed his *w.* in the. 105:27
our fathers understood not thy *w.* in Egypt. 106:7
see his works and his *w.* 107:24
who sent *w.* into the midst of. 135:9
who alone doeth great *w.* 136:4
I and the children are for *w.* in Israel. *Isa* 8:18
who hath set signs and *w.* *Jer* 32:20
brought forth thy people with *w.* 21
to shew the signs and *w.* *Dan* 4:2
signs! how mighty his *w.*! 3
he worketh *w.* in heaven. 6:27
it be to the end of these *w.*? 12:6
I will shew *w.* in heaven. *Joel* 2:30
Acts 2:19
false prophets, and shall shew great *w.* *Mat* 24:24; *Mark* 13:22
Except ye see signs and *w.* *John* 4:48
approved of God by *w.* *Acts* 2:22
fear on every soul, many signs and *w.* were. 43; 5:12; 14:3; 15:12
that *w.* may be done by the. 4:30
Stephen did great *w.* among. 6:8
after he had shewed *w.* in the land of Egypt. 7:36
obedient through *w.* *Rom* 15:19
an apostle wrought in *w.* *2 Cor* 12:12
is with signs and lying *w.* *2 Thes* 2:9
witness with signs and *w.* *Heb* 2:4
he doeth great *w.*, so that he maketh fire come down. *Rev* 13:13*

wondrous

sing psalms, talk ye of all his *w.* *1 Chr* 16:9; *Ps* 26:7; 105:2
119:27; 145:5
consider the *w.* works. *Job* 37:14
dost thou know the *w.* works? 16
I declared thy *w.* works. *Ps* 71:17
the God of Israel, who only doeth *w.* things. 72:18; 86:10
that thy name is near, thy *w.* 75:1
they believed not for his *w.* 78:32
who had done *w.* works in. 106:22
that I may behold *w.* things. 119:18
according to his *w.* works. *Jer* 21:2

wont

if the ox were *w.* to push. *Ex* 21:29
was I ever *w.* to do so to thee? *Num* 22:30
where David and his men were *w.* to haunt. *1 Sam* 30:31
were *w.* to speak in. *2 Sam* 20:18
seven times more than *w.* *Dan* 3:19
the governor was *w.* to. *Mat* 27:15
as he was *w.*, he taught. *Mark* 10:1
he went as he was *w.* to. *Luke* 22:39*
where prayer was *w.* to. *Acts* 16:13

wood

Abraham took *w.* and put. *Gen* 22:6
Behold the fire and the *w.* 7
whether there be *w.* *Num* 13:20
things that are made of *w.* 31:20
make thee an ark of *w.* *Deut* 10:1
goeth into a *w.* to hew *w.* 19:5*
from the hewer of thy *w.* 29:11
Josh 9:21, 23, 27; *Jer* 46:22
the mountain is a *w.* *Josh* 17:18*
and they clave the *w.* *1 Sam* 6:14
they of the land came to a *w.* 14:25
went to David into the *w.* 23:16
the *w.* devoured more. *2 Sam* 18:8*
lay the bullock on *w.* *1 Ki* 18:23
she bears out of the *w.* *2 Ki* 2:24
I have prepared *w.* for things of *w.* *1 Chr* 29:2
the boar out of the *w.* *Ps* 80:13
it in the fields of the *w.* 132:6
as when one cleaveth *w.* 141:7
where no *w.* is, there the. *Pr* 26:20
as *w.* to fire, so is a contentious 21
he that cleaveth *w.* shall. *Eccl* 10:9
itself as if it were no *w.* *Isa* 10:15
thereof is fire and much *w.* 30:33
they that set up the *w.* of. 45:20
will bring silver, for *w.* brass. 60:17
I will make my words fire, this people *w.* *Jer* 5:14
the children gather *w.*, the. 7:18
the yokes of *w.* but shalt. 28:13
shall *w.* be taken thereof to do any work? *Ezek* 15:3
heap on *w.* 24:10
no *w.* out of the field. 39:10
dwell solitary in the *w.* *Mi* 7:14*
that saith to the *w.* Awake. *Hab* 2:19
go up, bring *w.* and build. *Hag* 1:8
hearth of fire among the *w.* *Zech* 12:6
on this foundation, *w.*, hay. *1 Cor* 3:12
but also vessels of *w.* *2 Tim* 2:20
see **offering, stone**

woods

sleep safely in the *w.* *Ezek* 34:25

woof

be in the warp or *w.* *Lev* 13:48
be spread in the warp or the *w.* 51
whether warp or *w.* 52
be not spread, wash the *w.* 53, 58
rend it out of the warp or *w.* 56
of leprosy in the warp or *w.* 59

wool

I will put a fleece of *w.* *Judg* 6:37
100,000 rams with *w.* *2 Ki* 3:4
giveth snow like *w.* *Ps* 147:16
she seeketh *w.* and flax. *Pr* 31:13
like crimson, shall be as *w.* *Isa* 1:18
like *w.*: but my righteousness. 51:8
was thy merchant in *w.* *Ezek* 27:18
ye clothe you with the *w.* 34:3
and no *w.* shall come upon. 44:17
the hair of his head like *w.* *Dan* 7:9
Rev 1:14
lovers that give me my *w.* *Hos* 2:5
I will recover my *w.* and my flax. 9

woollen

whether *w.* or linen. *Lev* 13:47, 59
the warp or woof of *w.* 48, 52
mingled of linen and *w.* come upon thee. 19:19*; *Deut* 22:11

word

(Word, *the Greek* logos, *is sometimes used of Jesus Christ,* John 1. The word of God *is a name often given to the scriptures, and the law of God*)

go and bring me *w.* again. *Gen* 37:14
Mat 2:8
O my lord, let me speak a *w.* *Gen* 44:18; *2 Sam* 14:12
according to *w.* of Moses. *Ex* 8:13
Israel did according to the *w.* 12:35
Levi did according to the *w.* 32:28
Lev 10:7
they brought back *w.* *Num* 13:26
lodge here, I will bring you *w.* 22:8
Deut 1:22
yet the *w.* I shall say to. *Num* 22:20
the *w.* I shall speak. 35
the *w.* God putteth. 38
the Lord put a *w.* in Balaam's. 23:5
they brought us *w.* again. *Deut* 1:25
ye shall not add unto the *w.* I. 4:2
but by every *w.* that proceedeth out. 8:3*; *Mat* 4:4
presume to speak a *w.* *Deut* 18:20
how shall we know the *w.*? 21
Jer 28:9
by their *w.* shall every controversy be tried. *Deut* 21:5
the *w.* is nigh thee. 30:14; *Rom* 10:8
remember the *w.* Moses. *Josh* 1:13
not a *w.* which Joshua read not. 8:35
I brought him *w.* 14:7
brought them *w.* 22:32
the *w.* of Samuel came. *1 Sam* 4:1
not answer Abner a *w.* *2 Sam* 3:11
in all places spake I a *w.* 7:7
1 Chr 17:6
the *w.* thou hast spoken concerning thy servant. *2 Sam* 7:25
till there come *w.* from you. 15:28
speak ye not a *w.* of bringing. 19:10
the king's *w.* prevailed. 24:4
1 Chr 21:4
brought the king *w.* again. *1 Ki* 2:30
2 Ki 22:9, 20; *2 Chr* 34:16, 28
w. that I have heard is good. *1 Ki* 2:42*
hath not failed one *w.* of all. 8:56
the people answered not a *w.* 18:21
Isa 36:21
he smote according to the *w.* of Elisha. *2 Ki* 6:18
hear the *w.* of the great king. 18:28
mindful of the *w.* which he commanded. *1 Chr* 16:15; *Ps* 105:8
advise what *w.* I shall. *1 Chr* 21:12*
remember, the *w.* that thou. *Neh* 1:8
he did according to the *w.* *Esth* 1:21
as the *w.* went out of the king's. 7:8
none spake a *w.* to Job. *Job* 2:13
by the *w.* of thy lips, I have. *Ps* 17:4
the Lord gave the *w.* 68:11
remember the *w.* unto thy. 119:49
mine eyes fail for the *w.* of thy. 123
not a *w.* in my tongue. 139:4
a good *w.* maketh the. *Pr* 12:25
whoso despiseth the *w.* shall. 13:13
simple believe the *w.* but. 14:15
w. spoken in due season, how! 15:23
a *w.* fitly spoken is like apples. 25:11
where the *w.* of a king is. *Eccl* 8:4
despised *w.* of the Holy. *Isa* 5:24
speak *w.* and it shall not stand. 8:10
the Lord sent a *w.* to Jacob, it. 9:8
man an offender for a *w.* 29:21
thine ears shall hear a *w.* 30:21
counsellor could answer a *w.* 41:28
that confirmeth the *w.* of. 44:26
w. is gone out of my mouth. 45:23
should know how to speak a *w.* 50:4
become wind, and the *w.* *Jer* 5:13
let your ear receive *w.* 9:20; 10:1
nor shall the *w.* perish from. 18:18
for every man's *w.* shall be. 23:36
them, diminish not a *w.* 26:2
for I have pronounced the *w.* 34:5
king said, Is there any *w.*? 37:17
for the *w.* thou hast spoken. 44:16
therefore hear the *w.* at my mouth. *Ezek* 3:17; 33:7
the *w.* that I shall speak. 12:25
the *w.* that I have spoken shall. 28
would confirm the *w.* 13:6
hear what is *w.* that cometh. 33:30
changed the king's *w.* *Dan* 3:28
the demand is by the *w.* of. 4:17
while the *w.* was in the king's. 31
for *w.* came to the king. *Jonah* 3:6
to the *w.* I covenanted. *Hag* 2:5
speak the *w.* only, he shall. *Mat* 8:8
whoso speaketh a *w.* against the Son of man. 12:32; *Luke* 12:10
every idle *w.* men. *Mat* 12:36
when any one heareth the *w.* of the kingdom. 13:19, 20, 22, 23
Mark 4:16, 18, 20; *Luke* 8:15
or persecution ariseth because of the *w.*, he. *Mat* 13:21; *Mark* 4:17
he answered her not a *w.* *Mat* 15:23
that every *w.* may be established. 18:16; *2 Cor* 13:1
able to answer him a *w.* *Mat* 22:46
he answered him to never a *w.* 27:14
to bring his disciples *w.* 28:8
sower soweth the *w.* *Mark* 4:14
Peter called to mind the *w.* 14:72
the Lord confirming the *w.* 16:20
saying, What a *w.* is this! *Luke* 4:36
say in a *w.* and my servant shall. 7:7
Jesus, a prophet mighty in *w.* 24:19
the *W.* and the *W.* was with God, and the *W.* was God. *John* 1:1
the *W.* was made flesh, and. 14
they believed the *w.* that Jesus said. 2:22; 4:50
w. I have spoken shall judge. 12:48
w. which ye hear is not mine. 14:24
ye are clean through the *w.* I. 15:3
remember the *w.* that I said. 20
that *w.* might be fulfilled, written. 25
believe on me through their *w.* 17:20
the *w.* which God sent to. *Acts* 10:36
if ye have any *w.* of exhortation, say on. 13:15
to you is the *w.* of this salvation. 26
by my mouth, should hear *w.* 15:7
they received the *w.* with all. 17:11
I commend you to the *w.* of. 20:32
Paul had spoken one *w.* 28:25
that is, the *w.* of faith. *Rom* 10:8
make Gentiles obedient by *w.* 15:18
kingdom of God is not in *w.* *1 Cor* 4:20

w. of wisdom, to another the w. of knowledge. 1 Cor 12:8
w. toward you was not. 2 Cor 1:18
God committed to us the w. of. 5:19
such as we are in w. by letters. 10:11
law is fulfilled in one w. Gal 5:14
let him that is taught in the w. 6:6
washing of water by the w. Eph 5:26
are bold to speak the w. Phil 1:14
holding forth the w. of life to. 2:16
heard in the w. of the truth. Col 1:5
let the w. of Christ dwell in. 3:16
whatsoever ye do in w. or deed. 17
our gospel came not to you in w. only. 1 Thes 1:5
having received the w. in much. 6
w. . . , ye receive it not as w. of men, but as it is in truth, w. of God. 2:13
not by Spirit, nor by w. 2 Thes 2:2
have been taught, whether by w. 15
and stablish you in every good w. 17
if any man obey not our w. by. 3:14
be thou an example of believers in w. 1 Tim 4:12
they who labour in the w. 5:17
their w. will eat as doth. 2 Tim 2:17
preach w.; be instant in season. 4:2
holding fast the faithful w. Tit 1:9
upholding all things by the w. of his power. Heb 1:3
if the w. spoken by angels was. 2:2
but the w. preached did not. 4:2
is unskilful in the w. of. 5:13
but the w. of the oath, which. 7:28
intreated w. should not be. 12:19
brethren, suffer the w. of. 13:22
meekness the ingrafted w. Jas 1:21
be ye doers of the w. and not. 22
if any be a hearer of the w. and. 23
if any man offend not in w., the. 3:2
the sincere milk of the w. 1 Pet 2:2
who stumble at the w. being. 8
not the w., may without the w. 3:1
we have a more sure w. of prophecy. 2 Pet 1:19
the heavens by the same w. are. 3:7
handled, of the w. of life. 1 John 1:1
let us not love in w. but in. 3:18
the Father, the W. and. 5:7
because thou hast kept w. Rev 3:10
they overcame by the w. of. 12:11

word of God

that I may shew thee the w. of God. 1 Sam 9:27
the w. of God came to Shemaiah, 1 Ki 12:22
the w. of God came to Nathan. 1 Chr 17:3
every w. of God is pure. Pr 30:5
the w. of our God shall. Isa 40:8
making the w. of God. Mark 7:13
w. of God came unto John. Luke 3:2
alone, but by every w. of God. 4:4
on him to hear the w. of God. 5:1
the seed is the w. of God. 8:11
these that hear the w. of God. 21
they that hear the w. of God. 11:28
gods to whom w. of God. John 10:35
they spake the w. of God. Acts 4:31
should leave the w. of God. 6:2
the w. of God increased. 7; 12:24
Samaria had received the w. of God. 8:14
Gentiles had received the w. of God. 11:1
desired to hear the w. of God. 13:7
city came to hear the w. of God. 44
w. of God should have been first. 46
mightily grew the w. of God. 19:20
not as though the w. of God hath taken none effect. Rom 9:6
hearing by the w. of God. 10:17
came the w. of God out from you? 1 Cor 14:36
corrupt the w. of God. 2 Cor 2:17
not handling the w. of God. 4:2
and the sword of the Spirit, which is the w. of God. Eph 6:17
which is given me to fulfil the w. of God. Col 1:25
received the w. of God. 1 Thes 2:13
it is sanctified by the w. of God and prayer. 1 Tim 4:5
but the w. of God is not bound. 2 Tim 2:9
the w. of God be not blasphemed. Tit 2:5
the w. of God is quick. Heb 4:12
tasted the good w. of God. 6:5
framed by the w. of God. 11:3
spoken to you the w. of God. 13:7
being born again by the w. of God. 1 Pet 1:23
by the w. of God the heavens were of old. 2 Pet 3:5
are strong, and the w. of God abideth in you. 1 John 2:14
record of the w. of God. Rev 1:2
isle of Patmos, for the w. of God. 9
that were slain for w. of God. 6:9
name is called the w. of God. 19:13
beheaded for the w. of God. 20:4

see **heard**

his word

at his w. shall they go out, and at his w. they shall come. Num 27:21
he shall not break his w. 30:2
the Lord stablish his w. 1 Sam 1:23
his w. was in my tongue. 2 Sam 23:2
may continue his w. 1 Ki 2:4
the Lord hath performed his w. that he spake. 8:20; 2 Chr 6:10
to enquire of his w. 2 Ki 1:16
might perform his w. 2 Chr 10:15
in God I will praise his w., in God I have put my trust. Ps 56:4, 10
unto the voice of his w. 103:20
the time that his w. came. 105:19
rebelled not against his w. 28
they believed not his w. but. 106:24
he sent his w. and healed. 107:20
I wait for the Lord and in his w. do I hope. 130:5
his w. runneth very swiftly. 147:15
sendeth out his w. and melteth. 18
he sheweth his w. unto Jacob. 19
wind fulfilling his w. 148:8
that tremble at his w. Isa 66:5
but his w. was in my heart as a fire. Jer 20:9
he hath fulfilled his w. Lam 2:17
that executeth his w. Joel 2:11
out the spirits with his w. Mat 8:16
for his w. was with power. Luke 4:32
many believed because of his own w. John 4:41
ye have not his w. abiding. 5:38
gladly received his w. Acts 2:41
but hath in due times manifested his w. Tit 1:3
whoso keepeth his w. 1 John 2:5

see **Lord**

my word

whether my w. shall come to pass. Num 11:23
ye rebelled against my w. 20:24
will I perform my w. 1 Ki 6:12
rain, but according to my w. 17:1
so shall my w. be that goeth forth out of my mouth. Isa 55:11
him that trembleth at my w. 66:2
hasten my w. to perform. Jer 1:12
my w., let him speak my w. 23:28
is not my w. like as a fire? 29
the prophets that steal my w. 30
I will perform my good w. 29:10
but my w. shall not pass. Mat 24:35
he that heareth my w. John 5:24
continue in my w., then are ye. 8:31
kill me because my w. hath. 37
ye cannot hear my w. 43
thou hast kept my w., and hast not denied my name. Rev 3:8

this word

is not this the w. that? Ex 14:12
since the Lord spake this w. to Moses. Josh 14:10
they sent this w. to the king. 2 Sam 19:14*
hast not spoken this w. 1 Ki 2:23
this is the w. that the Lord hath spoken of him. 2 Ki 19:21
Isa 16:13; 24:3; 37:22
shall alter this w. Ezra 6:11
should do according to this w. 10:5
not according to this w. Isa 8:20
because ye despise this w. Isa 30:12
ye speak this w. Jer 5:14; 23:38
proclaim there this w. and say. 7:2
speak unto them this w. 13:12
thou say this w. to them. 14:17
down, and speak there this w. 22:1
in the reign of Jehoiakim this w. came. 26:1; 27:1; 34:8; 36:1
hear now this w. 28:7; Amos 3:1; 4:1; 5:1
spoken this w. to me. Dan 10:11
this is the w. of the Lord. Zech 4:6
him audience to this w. Acts 22:22
for this is w. of promise. Rom 9:9
this w., Yet once more. Heb 12:27
this is the w. which is. 1 Pet 1:25

thy word

be according to thy w. Gen 30:34
according to thy w. shall my. 41:40
Be it according to thy w. Ex 8:10
I have pardoned, according to thy w. Num 14:20
have observed thy w. Deut 33:9
done according to thy w. 1 Ki 3:12
let thy w. I pray thee, be. 8:26
done all these things at thy w. 18:36
let thy w. I pray thee, be like the word of one of. 22:13; 2 Chr 18:12
heed according to thy w. Ps 119:9
thy w. have I hid in mine heart. 11
statutes, I will not forget thy w. 16
live, and keep thy w. 17, 101
quicken me according to thy w. 25, 107, 154
strengthen thou me according to thy w. 28, 116
stablish thy w. 38
salvation according to thy w. 41
I trust in thy w. 42
comfort in affliction, for thy w. 50
be merciful to me according to thy w. 58, 65, 76
but now have I kept thy w. 67
I have hoped in thy w. 74, 147
I hope in thy w. 81, 114
mine eyes fail for thy w. 82
ever, O Lord, thy w. is settled. 89
thy w. is a lamp. 105
order my steps in thy w., let not. 133
thy w. is pure. 140
that I might meditate in thy w. 148
because they kept not thy w. 158
thy w. is true. 160
standeth in awe of thy w. 161
I rejoice at thy w. 162
give me understanding according to thy w. 169
deliver me according to thy w. 170
my tongue shall speak of thy w. 172
thou hast magnified thy w. 138:2
thy w. was to me the joy. Jer 15:16
drop thy w. toward the south. Ezek 20:46
drop thy w. toward the holy. 21:2
drop not thy w. against. Amos 7:16
made naked, even thy w. Hab 3:9
according to thy w. Luke 1:38
in peace, according to thy w. 2:29
nevertheless at thy w. I will let. 5:5
and they have kept thy w. John 17:6
I have given them thy w. 14
thy w. is truth. 17
with all boldness they may speak thy w. Acts 4:29

see **truth**

words

shalt put w. in his mouth. Ex 4:15
let them not regard vain w. 5:9
returned the w. of the people. 19:8
the gift perverteth the w. of the righteous. 23:8; Deut 16:19
the w. which were in the first tables. Ex 34:1
Moses wrote the w. of the covenant. 28; Deut 10:2
I sent to Sihon with w. Deut 2:26
go aside from any of the w. 28:14
keep the w. of his covenant. 29:9
2 Ki 23:3, 24; 2 Chr 34:31
hear, O earth, the w. of. Deut 32:1
Ps 54:2; 78:1; Pr 7:24
Saul was afraid of the w. of Samuel. 1 Sam 28:20

the *w.* of men of Judah were fiercer. *2 Sam* 19:43
w. of prophets declare good to the king. *1 Ki* 22:13; *2 Chr* 18:12
Elisha telleth the *w.* *2 Ki* 6:12
but they are but vain *w.* 18:20
Isa 36:5
sing praises with the *w. 2 Chr* 29:30
the people rested on the *w.* 32:8
he sent letters with *w.* of peace and truth. *Esth* 9:30
ye imagine to reprove *w.*? *Job* 6:26
shall *w.* of thy mouth be like ? 8:2
not the ear try *w.*? 12:11; 34:3
thou lettest such *w.* go out. 15:13
shall vain *w.* have an end ? 16:3
I could heap up *w.* against you. 4
ere ye make an end of *w.*? 18:2
ye break me in pieces with *w.*? 19:2
I would know the *w.* he would. 23:5
I have esteemed the *w.* of his. 12
he multiplieth *w.* without. 35:16
darkeneth counsel by *w.*? 38:2
let the *w.* of my mouth. *Ps* 19:14
why so far from the *w.* of ? 22:1
the *w.* of his mouth are iniquity. 36:3
thou lovest all devouring *w.* 52:4
w. of his mouth were smoother than butter. 55:21
for *w.* of their lips, let them. 59:12
to understand the *w.* of. *Pr* 1:6
decline not from the *w.* 4:5; 5:7
thou art snared with the *w.* of. 6:2
in multitude of *w.* there wanteth not sin. 10:19
w. of the wicked are to lie in wait for blood. 12:6
w. of the pure are pleasant *w.* 15:26
the *w.* of a man's mouth are as. 18:4
w. of a talebearer are as wounds. 8; 26:22
he pursueth them with *w.* 19:7
he causeth thee to err from *w.* 27
he overthroweth the *w.* of the. 22:12
bow down thine ear, hear the *w.* 17
certainty of the *w.* of truth; that thou mightest answer the *w.* of. 21
thou shalt lose thy sweet *w.* 23:8
will not be corrected by *w.* 29:19
a fool's voice is known by multitude of *w.* *Eccl* 5:3; 10:14
the *w.* of a wise man's mouth. 10:12
find out acceptable *w.*: that which was written, even *w.* of truth. 12:10
the *w.* of the wise are as goads. 11
become as the *w.* of a book sealed. *Isa* 29:11
it may be God will hear the *w.* 37:4
uttering from the heart *w.* of. 59:13
w. of this covenant. *Jer* 11:2, 6
because of the Lord, and the *w.* 23:9
w. of Jonadab son of Rechab. 35:14
remnant shall know whose *w.* 44:28
whose *w.* thou canst not. *Ezek* 3:6
shall speak great *w.* against most High. *Dan* 7:25
shut up the *w.* 12:4
the *w.* are closed up. 9
I have slain them by the *w.* of my mouth. *Hos* 6:5
take with you *w.* and turn to. 14:2
good and comfortable *w.* *Zech* 1:13
should ye not hear the *w.*? 7:7
saying the same *w.* *Mat* 26:44
Mark 14:39
wondered at gracious *w.* *Luke* 4:22
the *w.* that I speak unto you, they are spirit. *John* 6:63
to whom we go ? thou hast the *w.* 68
I have given to them the *w.* 17:8
with many other *w.* did. *Acts* 2:40
Moses was mighty in *w.* and. 7:22
was warned to hear *w.* of thee. 10:22
Peter, who shall tell thee *w.* 11:14
to this agree the *w.* of the prophets. 15:15
have troubled you with *w.* 24
but if it be a question of *w.* 18:15
to remember the *w.* of the. 20:35
most of all for the *w.* he spake. 38
but I speak forth *w.* of truth. 26:25
by good *w.* deceive hearts of the simple. *Rom* 16:18*

not with wisdom of *w.* *1 Cor* 1:17
2:4, 13
except ye utter *w.* easy to. 14:9*
I had rather speak five *w.* with. 19
deceive you with vain *w.* *Eph* 5:6
nourished up in *w.* of faith and doctrine. *1 Tim* 4:6
that they strive not about *w.* to no profit. *2 Tim* 2:14
greatly withstood our *w.* 4:15
be mindful of the *w.* spoken by prophets. *2 Pet* 3:2
hear the *w.* of this prophecy. *Rev* 1:3; 22:18
take away from the *w.* of this. 22:19

all the words

all the w. of Joseph. *Gen* 45:27
Moses told Aaron *all the w.* of the Lord. *Ex* 4:28
Moses told the people *all the w.* 24:3; *Num* 11:24
Moses wrote *all the w.* of the Lord. *Ex* 24:4
on the tables were written *all the w.* *Deut* 9:10
keep *all the w.* 17:19
write on stones *all the w.* 27:3, 8
that confirmeth not *all the w.* 26
not observe to do *all the w.* 28:58
may do *all the w.* of this law. 29:29
and observe to do *all the w.* 31:12
Moses spake *all the w.* of. 32:44
set your hearts to *all the w.* 46
he read *all the w.* of the law, the blessings and. *Josh* 8:34
Samuel told *all the w.* of the Lord. *1 Sam* 8:10
Lord will hear *all the w.* of Rabshakeh. *2 Ki* 19:4; *Isa* 37:17
Josiah read *all the w.* of the covenant. *2 Ki* 23:2; *2 Chr* 34:30
all the w. of my mouth. *Pr* 8:8
unto *all the w.* spoken. *Eccl* 7:21
bring on them *all the w.* *Jer* 11:8
speak *all the w.* that I command thee. 26:2
to *all the w.* of Jeremiah. 20
write *all the w.* I have spoken. 30:2; 36:2
Baruch wrote *all the w.* of the Lord. 36:4, 32
had ended *all the w.* of Lord. 43:1
speak to the people *all the w.* of this life. *Acts* 5:20

words of God

hath said, which heard the *w. of God.* *Num* 24:4, 16
Heman the king's seer in the *w. of God.* *1 Chr* 25:5
every one that trembleth at the *w. of God.* *Ezra* 9:4
they rebelled against the *w. of God.* *Ps* 107:11
he whom God sent, speaketh *w. of God.* *John* 3:34
of God, heareth the *w. of God.* 8:47
until the *w. of God* be fulfilled. *Rev* 17:17

see **heard**

his words

they hated him yet the more for *his w.* *Gen* 37:8
thou heardest *his w.* out of the fire. *Deut* 4:36
Jephthah uttered all *his w.* before the Lord. *Judg* 11:11
he let none of *his w.* fall to the ground. *1 Sam* 3:19
but they despised *his w. 2 Chr* 36:16
and lay up *his w.* in thine. *Job* 22:22
he hath not directed *his w.* 32:14
his w. were without wisdom. 34:35
for he multiplieth *his w.* against. 37
his w. softer than oil. *Ps* 55:21
then believed they *his w.* 106:12
knowledge spareth *his w.* *Pr* 17:27
seest thou a man that is hasty in *his w.*? 29:20
add thou not unto *his w.*, lest. 30:6
will not call back *his w.* *Isa* 31:2
heed to any of *his w.* *Jer* 18:18
he hath confirmed *his w.* *Dan* 9:12

the land is not able to bear all *his w.* *Amos* 7:10
the disciples were astonished at *his w.* *Mark* 10:24
to catch him in *his w.* 12:13
Luke 20:20
not take hold of *his w. Luke* 20:26*
they remembered *his w.* 24:8

see **lord**

my words

he said, Hear now *my w. Num* 12:6
Job 34:2
make them hear *my w.* *Deut* 4:10
therefore lay up *my w.* in. 11:18
and I will put *my w.* in his. 18:18
whosoever will not hearken to *my* 19; *Jer* 29:19; 35:13
and they uttered *my w.* *Neh* 6:19
therefore *my w.* are swallowed up. *Job* 6:3
Oh that *my w.* were now written! 19:23
after *my w.* they spake not. 29:22
hearken to all *my w.* 33:1; 34:16
Acts 2:14
my w. shall be of the uprightness of my heart. *Job* 33:3; 36:4
give ear to *my w.* O Lord. *Ps* 5:1
seeing thou castest *my w.* 50:17
every day they wrest *my w.* 56:5
they shall hear *my w.*: for they.141:6
known *my w.* unto you. *Pr* 1:23
if thou wilt receive *my w.* 2:1
let thine heart retain *my w.* 4:4
attend to *my w.* 4:20
keep *my w.* 7:1
I have put *my w.* in thy mouth, and say unto Zion. *Isa* 51:16; *Jer* 1:9
my w. which I have put. *Isa* 59:21
I will make *my w.* in thy mouth fire. *Jer* 5:14
have not hearkened to *my w.* 6:19
refused to hear *my w.* 11:10; 13:10
will cause thee to hear *my w.* 18:2
they might not hear *my w.* 19:15
my people to hear *my w.* 23:22
ye have not heard *my w.* 25:8
bring upon that land all *my w.* 13
I will bring *my w.* on this city. 39:16
you may know *my w.* shall. 44:29
thou shalt speak *my w.* unto them *Ezek* 2:7; 3:4, 10
there shall none of *my w.* 12:28
do not *my w.* do good to ? *Mi* 2:7
my w. did they not take hold of your fathers ? *Zech* 1:6
whosoever shall be ashamed of me and *my w. Mark* 8:38; *Luke* 9:26
but *my w.* shall not pass away. *Mark* 13:31; *Luke* 21:33
thou believest not *my w.* *Luke* 1:20
shall ye believe *my w.*? *John* 5:47
if any man hear *my w.* and. 12:47
he that receiveth not *my w.* 48
will keep *my w.* 14:23
my w. abide in you. 15:7

their words

their w. pleased Hamor. *Gen* 34:18
I believed not *their w.* *2 Chr* 9:6
through all the earth, *their w.* to end of the world. *Ps* 19:4; *Rom* 10:18
be not afraid of *their w.* *Ezek* 2:6
their w. seemed to them as idle tales. *Luke* 24:11

these words

according to *these w.* *Gen* 39:17
to the tenor of *these w.* 43:7
these are the *w.* thou shalt speak. *Ex* 19:6, 7
God spake all *these w.* 20:1
Deut 5:22
Lord said, Write thou *these w.* *Ex* 34:27; *Jer* 36:17
these are the *w.* which the Lord. *Ex* 35:1; *Deut* 6:6; 29:1
as he had made an end of speaking all *these w.* *Num* 16:31
Deut 32:45; *1 Sam* 24:16
observe, hear all *these w.* *Deut* 12:28; *Zech* 8:9
David laid up *these w. 1 Sam* 21:12
his servants with *these w.* 24:7

to all *these w.*, and this vision, so did. *2 Sam* 7:17; *1 Chr* 17:15
thy master and to thee to speak *these w.*? *2 Ki* 18:27; *Isa* 36:12
the man of God proclaimed *these w.* *2 Ki* 23:16
go proclaim *these w.* *Jer* 3:12
speak all *these w.* unto. 7:27; 26:15
all *these w.* 16:10
ye will not hear *these w.* 22:5
prophesy thou all *these w.* 25:30
Let no man know of *these w.* 38:24
when he had written *these w.* 45:1
51:60
thou shalt read all *these w.* 51:61
these are the *w.* I spake. *Luke* 24:44
these w. spake his parents, because they feared Jews. *John* 9:22
these are not *w.* of him that. 10:21*
hear *these w.*; Jesus of. *Acts* 2:22
while Peter yet spake *these w.* 10:44
besought *these w.* might be preached to them. 13:42
when he had said *these w.* 28:29
comfort one another with *these w.* *1 Thes* 4:18
for *these w.* are true. *Rev* 21:5

***thy* words**

shall receive of *thy w.* *Deut* 33:3
will not hearken to *thy w. Josh* 1:18
do not according to *thy w. Judg* 11:10
Manoah said, Now let *thy w.* 13:12
transgressed *thy w.* *1 Sam* 15:24
hearkened to *thy w.* 28:21
thy w.' sake hast thou done all these great things. *2 Sam* 7:21
that God, and *thy w.* be true. 28
in and confirm *thy w.* *1 Ki* 1:14
hast performed *thy w.* *Neh* 9:8
thy w. upheld him that was falling. *Job* 4:4
said I would keep *thy w. Ps* 119:57
how sweet are *thy w.* to my! 103
entrance of *thy w.* giveth light. 130
enemies have forgotten *thy w.* 139
shalt lose *thy* sweet *w.* *Pr* 23:8
despise the wisdom of *thy w.* 9
therefore let *thy w.* be few. *Eccl* 5:2
thy w. were found, and I did eat them. *Jer* 15:16
hear *thy w.* but do them not. *Ezek* 33:31, 32
the first day *thy w.* were heard, and I am come for *thy w.* *Dan* 10:12
for by *thy w.* thou shalt be justified, and by *thy w.* thou. *Mat* 12:37

***your* words**

that *your w.* be proved. *Gen* 42:16
bring Benjamin, so shall *your w.* 20
let it be according unto *your w.* 44:10; *Josh* 2:21
the voice of *your w. Deut* 1:34; 5:28
I waited for *your w.*; I gave ear. *Job* 32:11
that heareth *your w.* *Isa* 41:26
to God according to *your w.Jer* 42:4
multiplied *your w.* against me. *Ezek* 35:13
ye have wearied the Lord with *your w.* *Mal* 2:17
your w. have been stout. 3:13
you nor hear *your w.* *Mat* 10:14

work

Is taken, [1] *For such business as is proper to every man's calling, which may be done in six days.* Ex 20:9, Six days shalt thou labour and do all thy *work.* [2] *For any thought, word, or outward action, whether good or evil,* Eccl 12:14, God shall bring every *work* into judgement. [3] Work *is put for miracle,* John 7:21.

The *works* of God, denote, [1] *His* work *of creation.* [2] *His* works *of providence in preserving and governing the world.* [3] *His* work *of redemption, and particularly the faith of true believers is called* the work of God.

By good works *are to be understood all manner of duties inward and outward, thoughts as well as words and actions, toward God or man, which are commanded in the law of God, and proceed from a pure heart and faith unfeigned.*

let there more *w.* be laid on the men. *Ex* 5:9
no manner of *w.* shall be done. 12:16; 20:10; *Lev* 16:29; 23:3, 28 31; *Num* 29:7
shew them *w.* that they. *Ex* 18:20
whoso doeth any *w.* therein shall be cut off. 31:14, 15; *Lev* 23:30
six days shall *w.* be. *Ex* 35:2; 20:9
sufficient for all the *w.* and. 36:7
convocation, ye shall do no servile *w.* *Lev* 23:7, 8, 21, 25, 35, 36 *Num* 28:18, 25, 26; 29:1, 12, 35
the *w.* of men's hands. *Deut* 4:28 27:15; *2 Ki* 19:18; *2 Chr* 32:19 *Ps* 115:4; 135:15
in it thou shalt not do any *w.* *Deut* 5:14; 16:8; *Jer* 17:22, 24
that the Lord may bless thee in all *w.* *Deut* 14:29; 24:19; 28:12; 30:9
do no *w.* with the firstling of. 15:19
anger through the *w.* of your hands. 31:29; *1 Ki* 16:7; *Jer* 32:30
bless the Lord and accept *w.* 33:11
officers which were over the *w.* *1 Ki* 5:16; 9:23; *1 Chr* 29:6 *2 Chr* 2:18
another court of the like *w. 1 Ki* 7:8
into the hands of them that did the *w.* *2 Ki* 12:11; 22:5*, 9
employed in that *w.* day. *1 Chr* 9:33
to minister as every day's *w.* 16:37
Solomon young, and the *w.* is great. 29:1; *Neh* 4:19
every *w.* that he began. *2 Chr* 31:21
the men did the *w.* faithfully. 34:12
then ceased the *w.* of. *Ezra* 4:24
this *w.* goeth fast on, prospereth. 5:8
let the *w.* of this house of God. 6:7
hands in the *w.* of house of God. 22
neither is it a *w.* of one day. 10:13
put not their necks to *w.* *Neh* 3:5
slay them, and cause the *w.* 4:11
why should the *w.* cease whilst? 6:3
they perceived this *w.* was. 16
fathers gave to the *w.* 7:70
thou hast blessed the *w.* *Job* 1:10
thou shouldest despise the *w.* 10:3
thou wilt have a desire to *w.* 14:15
go they forth to their *w.* 24:5
for the *w.* of a man shall he render unto him. 34:11; *1 Pet* 1:17
are all the *w.* of his hands. *Job* 34:19
he sheweth them their *w.* and. 36:9
when I consider the *w.* of thy fingers. *Ps* 8:3, 6
the wicked is snared in the *w.* 9:16
firmament sheweth his handy *w.* 19:1
after the *w.* of their hands. 28:4
we heard what *w.* thou didst. 44:1
establish thou the *w.* of our. 90:17
proved me and saw my *w.* 95:9
I hate the *w.* of them that. 101:3
the heavens are the *w.* of thy. 102:25
on the *w.* of thy hands. 143:5
worketh a deceitful *w.* *Pr* 11:18
time there for every *w.* *Eccl* 3:17
why should God destroy the *w.*? 5:6
I applied my heart to every *w.* 8:9
according to *w.* of the wicked, according to the *w.* of the. 14
there is no *w.* in the grave. 9:10
God will bring every *w.* into. 12:14
w. of the hands of a cunning workman. *S of S* 7:1
they worship the *w.* of their own hands. *Isa* 2:8; 37:19; *Jer* 1:16 10:3, 9, 15; 51:18
he shall not look to the *w.* *Isa* 17:8
neither shall there be any *w.* 19:15
blessed be Assyria the *w.* of. 25
do his *w.*, his strange *w.* 28:21
shall the *w.* say of him that? 29:16*
he seeth his children, and the *w.* 23
the *w.* of righteousness shall. 32:17
concerning the *w.* of my hands command me. 45:11
my *w.* is with my God. 49:4*
they shall inherit the *w* of my 60:21
will direct their *w.* in truth. 61:8*
all are the *w.* of thy hands. *Isa* 64:8
mine elect shall long enjoy *w.* 65:22
great in counsel and mighty in *w.* *Jer* 32:19
recompense her according to her *w.* 50:29; *Lam* 3:64
be taken to do any *w.*? *Ezek* 15:3
is it meet for any *w.*? 4
it was meet for no *w.* 5
w. of an imperious whorish. 16:30
w. of the craftsman. *Hos* 13:2
we will say no more to the *w.* 14:3
shalt no more worship *w.* *Mi* 5:13
for I will work a *w.* in. *Hab* 1:5
and so is every *w.* of. *Hag* 2:14
there do no mighty *w.* *Mark* 6:5
I have done one *w.* and. *John* 7:21
finished the *w.* thou gavest me. 17:4
if this *w.* be of men it will. *Acts* 5:38
for the *w.* whereunto I have. 13:2
wonder, for I work a *w.* in your days, a *w.* which ye will not believe. 41
the *w.* which they fulfilled. 14:26
not with them to the *w.* 15:38
which shew *w.* of the law. *Rom* 2:15
a short *w.* will the Lord make. 9:28
otherwise *w.* is no more *w.* 11:6*
every man's *w.* shall be. *1 Cor* 3:13
if any man's *w.* abide. 14
if *w.* be burnt. 15
are not ye my *w.* in the Lord? 9:1
he gave some for the *w.* *Eph* 4:12
for the *w.* of Christ he. *Phil* 2:30
that God may fulfil the *w.* of faith. *2 Thes* 1:11
every good word and *w.* 2:17
do the *w.* of an evangelist. *2 Tim* 4:5
patience have her perfect *w. Jas* 1:4
but a doer of the *w.* shall be. 25

see **evil, needle**

work, *verb*

go and *w.* *Ex* 5:18
six days thou shalt *w.* 34:21
whoso doeth *w.* therein shall. 35:2
they did *w.* wilily and went. *Josh* 9:4
the Lord will *w.* for us. *1 Sam* 14:6
sold thyself to *w.* evil. *1 Ki* 21:20, 25
people had a mind to *w.* *Neh* 4:6
left hand, where he doth *w. Job* 23:9
in heart ye *w.* wickedness. *Ps* 58:2
time for thee, Lord, to *w.* 119:126
w. a deceitful work. *Pr* 11:18
they that *w.* in flax, shall. *Isa* 19:9
I will *w.* and who shall let it? 43:13
ye *w.* abomination and. *Ezek* 33:26
he shall *w.* deceitfully. *Dan* 11:23
woe to them that *w.* evil. *Mi* 2:1
I will *w.* a work in your days, which. *Hab* 1:5; *Acts* 13:41
w. for I am with you. *Hag* 2:4
they that *w.* wickedness. *Mal* 3:15
son, go *w.* to-day in. *Mat* 21:28
six days in which men ought to *w.* *Luke* 13:14
my Father worketh hitherto, and I *w.* *John* 5:17
that we might *w.* the works. 6:28
What dost thou *w.*? 30
w. the works of him that sent me . . . cometh when no man can *w.* 9:4
sin by the law did *w.* in. *Rom* 7:5
we know that all things *w.* 8:28
to *w.* all uncleanness. *Eph* 4:19
w. out your own salvation. *Phil* 2:12
study to *w.* with your own hands. *1 Thes* 4:11
of iniquity doth *w.* *2 Thes* 2:7
if any would not *w.*, neither. 3:10
that with quietness they *w.* 12

see **iniquity**

work *of God,* **works** *of God*

tables were the *w. of God. Ex* 32:16
wondrous *w. of God.* *Job* 37:14
declare the *w. of God.* *Ps* 64:9
come and see the *w. of God.* 66:5
not forget the *w. of God.* 78:7
consider the *w. of God.* *Eccl* 7:13
beheld all the *w. of God.* 8:17
knowest not the *w. of God.* 11:5
work the *w. of God.* *John* 6:28
this is the *w. of God* that ye. 29
the *w. of God* should be made manifest in him. 9:3

speak the *w. of God.* *Acts* 2:11
destroy not *w. of God.* *Rom* 14:20
see **good, great**

his **work**

God ended *his w.* **Gen 2:2**
rested from *his w.* 3
every man from *his w.* *Ex* 36:4
he is the rock, *his w.* *Deut* 32:4
an old man came from *his w.* at even. *Judg* 19:16
asses and put to *his w.* *1 Sam* 8:16
and wrought all *his w.* *1 Ki* 7:14
with the king for *his w.* *1 Chr* 4:23
of Israel he made no servants for *his w.* *2 Chr* 8:9
Baasha let *his w.* cease, he. 16:5
every man to *his w.* *Neh* 4:15
for the reward of *his w.* *Job* 7:2*
that thou magnify *his w.* 36:24
that all men may know *his w.* 37:7
renderest to every man according to *his w.* *Ps* 62:12; *Pr* 24:29
man goeth forth to *his w.* *Ps* 104:23
his w. is honourable and. 111:3
all the weights of the bag are *his w.* *Pr* 16:11
whether *his w.* be pure or. 20:11
but as for the pure *his w.* is. 21:8
let him hasten *his w.* that. *Isa* 5:19
performed *his* whole *w.* 10:12
may do *his w.*, *his* strange *w.* 28:21
behold, *his w.* is before him. 40:10* 62:11*
an instrument for *his w.* 54:16
giveth him not for *his w.* *Jer* 22:13*
the maker of *his w.* *Hab* 2:18
to every man *his w.* *Mark* 13:34
my meat is to finish *his w.* *John* 4:34
every man prove *his* own *w.* *Gal* 6:4
give every man as *his w.* *Rev* 22:12
see **Lord**

our **work**

this shall comfort us concerning *our w.* *Gen* 5:29

thy **work**

six days do all *thy w.* *Ex* 20:9 23:12; *Deut* 5:13
Lord recompense *thy w.* *Ruth* 2:12
meditate also of all *thy w.* *Ps* 77:12
let *thy w.* appear unto thy. 90:16
made me glad through *thy w.* 92:4
prepare *thy w.* without. *Pr* 24:27
or *thy w.*, He hath no hands? *Isa* 45:9
for *thy w.* shall be rewarded, saith the Lord. *Jer* 31:16
revive *thy w.* in the midst. *Hab* 3:2

your **work**

not aught of *your w.* *Ex* 5:11
for *your w.* shall be rewarded. *2 Chr* 15:7
ye are of nothing, *your w.* is of nought. *Isa* 41:24
remembering *your w.* of faith, and labour of love. *1 Thes* 1:3
God is not unrighteous to forget *your w.* *Heb* 6:10

worker

was a *w.* in brass. *1 Ki* 7:14

workers

w. with familiar spirits. *2 Ki* 23:24
we then as *w.* together. *2 Cor* 6:1
false apostles, deceitful *w.* 11:13
beware of evil *w.* *Phil* 3:2
see **iniquity**

worketh

lo, all these things *w.* God. *Job* 33:29
he that walketh uprightly, and *w.* righteousness. *Ps* 15:2
he that *w.* deceit shall not. 101:7
w. a deceitful work. *Pr* 11:18*
a flattering mouth *w.* ruin. 26:28
w. willingly with her hands. 31:13
what profit hath he that *w.*? *Eccl* 3:9
the smith with his tongs *w.* in the coals, and he *w.* it. *Isa* 44:12
thou meetest him that *w.* 64:5
he *w.* signs and wonders. *Dan* 6:27
my Father *w.* hitherto. *John* 5:17
he that *w.* righteousness. *Acts* 10:35
glory and peace to every one that *w.* good. *Rom* 2:10
to him that *w.* is the reward. *Rom* 4:4
to him that *w.* not, but believeth. 5
because the law *w.* wrath, for. 15
knowing that tribulation *w.* 5:3
love *w.* no ill to his neighbour. 13:10
God that *w.* all in all. *1 Cor* 12:6
all these *w.* that one and the. 11
for he *w.* the work of the. 16:10
so then death *w.* in us. *2 Cor* 4:12
w. for us a more exceeding. 17
w. repentance to salvation, but the sorrow of the world *w.* death. 7:10
w. miracles among you. *Gal* 3:5
but faith, which *w.* by love. 5:6
who *w.* all things after. *Eph* 1:11
the spirit that now *w.* in the. 2:2
the power that *w.* in us. 3:20
for it is God that *w.* in you. *Phil* 2:13
his working, which *w.* in. *Col* 1:29
effectually *w.* in you. *1 Thes* 2:13
of your faith *w.* patience. *Jas* 1:3
the wrath of man *w.* not. 20
nor whatsoever *w.* abomination. *Rev* 21:27

workfellow

Timothy my *w.* saluteth. *Rom* 16:21*

working

like a sharp razor, *w.* *Ps* 52:2
w. salvation in the midst of. 74:12
who is excellent in *w.* *Isa* 28:29*
be shut the six *w.* days. *Ezek* 46:1
the Lord *w.* with them. *Mark* 16:20
men with men *w.* that. *Rom* 1:27
sin *w.* death in me by that. 7:13
and labour, *w.* with our. *1 Cor* 4:12
not we power to forbear *w.*? 9:6
to another the *w.* of miracles. 12:10
according to the *w.* of. *Eph* 1:19
given me by the effectual *w.* 3:7
according to the effectual *w.* 4:16
w. with his hands the. 28
according to the *w.* whereby he is able. *Phil* 3:21
his *w.* which worketh in. *Col* 1:29
is after the *w.* of Satan. *2 Thes* 2:9
w. not at all, but are. 3:11
w. in you that which is. *Heb* 13:21
spirits of devils *w.* miracles. *Rev* 16:14

workman

wisdom to work all manner of work of the cunning *w.* *Ex* 35:35; 38:23
the work of a cunning *w.* *S of S* 7:1
the *w.* melteth a graven. *Isa* 40:19
he seeketh to him a cunning *w.* 20
work of the *w.* with the axe. *Jer* 10:3
the *w.* made it therefore. *Hos* 8:6
w. is worthy of his meat. *Mat* 10:10*
a *w.* that needeth not be. *2 Tim* 2:15

workmanship

and in all manner of *w.* *Ex* 31:3, 5 35:31
to all the *w.* thereof. *2 Ki* 16:10
the *w.* of tabrets was. *Ezek* 28:13
for we are his *w.* created in Christ Jesus. *Eph* 2:10

workmen

they gave that to the *w.* to repair. *2 Ki* 12:14, 15; *2 Chr* 34:10, 17
there are *w.* with thee. *1 Chr* 22:15
number of *w.* 25:1
w. wrought. *2 Chr* 24:13
to set forward the *w.* in. *Ezra* 3:9
the *w.*, they are of men. *Isa* 44:11
called with the *w.* of like occupation. *Acts* 19:25

works

fulfil your *w.* and your. *Ex* 5:13
the Lord hath sent me to do all these *w.* *Num* 16:28
the Lord blessed thee in all the *w.* *Deut* 2:7; 16:15
which knew not the *w.* *Judg* 2:10
according to all the *w.* they have done. *1 Sam* 8:8
w. the man of God did. *1 Ki* 13:11
me to anger with all the *w.* of their hands. *2 Ki* 22:17; *2 Chr* 34:25
from their wicked *w.* *Neh* 9:35
have done abominable *w.* *Ps* 14:1
concerning the *w.* of men, by the word of thy lips. 17:4
I will triumph in the *w.* of. 92:4
the *w.* of the Lord are great. *Ps* 111:2
the *w.* of his hands are verity. 7
forsake not the *w.* of. 138:8
to practise wicked *w.* with. 141:4
let her own *w.* praise her. *Pr* 31:31
I have seen the *w.* *Eccl* 1:14; 2:11
wrought all our *w.* in us. *Isa* 26:12
have done all these *w.* *Jer* 7:13
to anger with the *w.* of your hands to. 25:6, 7; 44:8
according to their deeds and the *w.* 25:14; *Rev* 2:23
w. may be abolished. *Ezek* 6:6
honour him whose *w.* *Dan* 4:37
the *w.* of the house of. *Mi* 6:16
John heard in prison the *w.* *Mat* 11:2
shew him greater *w.* *John* 5:20
the *w.* which the Father hath given me, the same *w.* that I do. 36
thy disciples may see the *w.* 7:3
because I testify that the *w.* 7
if children, ye would do the *w.* 8:39
I must work the *w.* of him. 9:4
w. that I do in my Father's. 10:25
of these *w.* do ye stone me? 32
if I do not the *w.* 37
believe the *w.* 38
he doeth the *w.* 14:10
believe me for the very *w.*' 11
the *w.* that I do, shall he do; . . . *w.* 12
not done among them the *w.* 15:24
they rejoiced in the *w.* *Acts* 7:41
Gentiles should do *w.* meet. 26:20
by what law? of *w.*? *Rom* 3:27
if Abraham were justified by *w.* 4:2
imputeth righteousness without *w.* 6
not of *w.* but of him that. 9:11
but as it were by the *w.* of. 32
is it no more of *w.*: . . . but if it be of *w.*, is it no more of grace. 11:6
let us therefore cast off the *w.* 13:12
is not justified by the *w.* of the law, for by the *w.* of the law. *Gal* 2:16
Spirit by the *w.* of the law? 3:2
doeth he it by the *w.* of the law? 5
as many as are of *w.* of the law. 10
the *w.* of the flesh are manifest. 5:19
not of *w.* lest any man. *Eph* 2:9
unfruitful *w.* of darkness. 5:11
in your mind by wicked *w.* *Col* 1:21
to esteem them in love for their *w.*'s sake. *1 Thes* 5:13
saved us, not according to our *w.* *2 Tim* 1:9; *Tit* 3:5
but in *w.* they deny God. *Tit* 1:16
the heavens are the *w.* *Heb* 1:10
thou didst set him over the *w.* 2:7
your fathers . . . saw my *w.* forty. 3:9
although the *w.* were finished. 4:3
of repentance from dead *w.* 6:1
purge conscience from dead *w.* 9:14
if he have not *w.* can? *Jas* 2:14
faith without *w.* is dead. 17, 20, 26
w.: shew me thy faith without *w.* 18
Abraham justified by *w.*? 2:21
by *w.* was faith made perfect. 22
ye see then that by *w.* a man. 24
was not the harlot justified by *w.*? 25
the earth and the *w.* *2 Pet* 3:10
that he might destroy *w.* *1 John* 3:8
keepeth my *w.* to the end. *Rev* 2:26
yet repented not of the *w.* of. 9:20
double according to her *w.* 18:6
see **evil, good, work** *of God*

his **works**

his w. have been to thee very good. *1 Sam* 19:4
Hezekiah prospered in all *his w.* *2 Chr* 32:30
and all *his w.* are done. *Ps* 33:4
forgat *his w.* and his wonders. 78:11; 106:13
bless the Lord, all *his w.* 103:22
Lord shall rejoice in *his w.* 104:31
let them declare *his w.* with. 107:22
people the power of *his w.* 111:6
mercies are over all *his w.* 145:9
the Lord is holy in all *his w.* 17
possessed me before *his w.* *Pr* 8:22
to every man according to *his w.*? 24:12; *Mat* 16:27; *2 Tim* 4:14
rejoice in *his* own *w.* *Eccl* 3:22
righteous in all *his w.* *Dan* 9:14

to God are all *his w.* **Acts 15:18**
seventh day from all **his w. Heb** 4:4
ceased from *his* own *w.*? 10
faith wrought with *his w.*? *Jas* 2:22
of a good conversation *his w.* 3:13
see **Lord, marvellous, mighty**

their **works**

let the people from *their w.*? *Ex* 5:4
shalt not do after *their w.* 23:24
according to these *their w. Neh* 6:14
he knoweth *their w.* *Job* 34:25
considereth all *their w.* *Ps* 33:15
and they learned *their w.* 106:35
defiled with *their* own *w.* 39
and *their w.* are in the hand of God. *Eccl* 9:1
their w. are in the dark. *Isa* 29:15
they are vanity, *their w.* 41:29
nor shall they cover themselves with *their w.*: *their w.* are works. 59:6
their w. and their thoughts. 66:18
forget any of *their w.* *Amos* 8:7
God saw *their w.* that. *Jonah* 3:10
not ye after *their w.* *Mat* 23:3
all *their w.* they do to be seen. 5
be according to *their w. 2 Cor* 11:15
and *their w.* do follow. *Rev* 14:13
the dead judged according to *their w.* 20:12, 13

thy **works**

according to *thy w.*? *Deut* 3:24
bless thee in all *thy w.* 15:10
Lord hath broken *thy w. 2 Chr* 20:37
tell of all *thy* wondrous *w.* *Ps* 26:7
145:4
How terrible art thou in *thy w.*! 66:3
that I may declare all *thy w.* 73:28
nor any works like unto *thy w.* 86:8
O Lord, how great are *thy w.*! 92:5
satisfied with fruit of *thy w.* 104:13
how manifold are *thy w.*! 24
I meditate on all *thy w.* 143:5
all *thy w.* shall praise thee. 145:10
commit *thy w.* unto the. *Pr* 16:3
now God accepteth *thy w.* *Eccl* 9:7
I will declare *thy w.* *Isa* 57:12
hast trusted in *thy w.* *Jer* 48:7
faith without *thy w.* *Jas* 2:18
I know *thy w.* *Rev* 2:2, 9, 13, 19
3:1, 8, 15
I have not found *thy w.* perfect. 3:2

wonderful **works**

Lord, are thy *wonderful w.* *Ps* 40:5
his *wonderful w.* that he. 78:4
Lord for his *wonderful w.* to the children of men! 107:8, 15, 21, 31
made his *wonderful w.* to be. 111:4
in thy name have done many *wonderful w.* *Mat* 7:22
do hear them speak in our tongues the *wonderful w.* of. *Acts* 2:11
see **wondrous**

world

To the Eastern people of earliest times the world *was very small, including little except Mesopotamia, Canaan, Arabia, and parts of Egypt. During Old Testament times it remained much the same, extending a little to the East, as the nations there grew to power; and other parts of Asia and Africa became somewhat known to the adventurous. Few knew more than rumours of Italy and even Greece. In the time of Christ* the world *really meant the Roman Empire, with parts of Asia and Africa which were more or less under its sway. All outside of this was vague. In Bible language* world *is frequently used for the inhabitants of the world, and, in the New Testament, of mortal existence in distinction from spiritual life.*

The Revised Versions often substitute the word earth.

he hath set the *w.* *1 Sam* 2:8
the foundations of the *w.* were discovered. *2 Sam* 22:16; *Ps* 18:15
the *w.* also shall not. *1 Chr* 16:30
chased out of the *w.* *Job* 18:18
disposed the whole *w.*? *Job* 34:13
do on the face of the *w.* 37:12
he shall judge the *w.* in righteousness. *Ps* 9:8; 96:13; 98:9
soul from the men of the *w.* 17:14
their words to end of the *w.* 19:4
Rom 10:18
all the ends of the *w.* *Ps* 22:27
the earth and the *w.* is the Lord's.
24:1; 98:7; *Nah* 1:5
let the inhabitants of the *w. Ps* 33:8
all ye inhabitants of the *w.* 49:1
for the *w.* is mine. 50:12
the lightnings lightened the *w.* 77:18
97:4
thou hast founded the *w.* 89:11
formed the earth and the *w.* 90:2
the *w.* also is established, it. 93:1
w. also shall be established. 96:10
not made the dust of the *w. Pr* 8:26
also he hath set the *w.* *Eccl* 3:11†
I will punish the *w.* for. *Isa* 13:11
is this he that made the *w.*? 14:17
the face of the *w.* with cities. 21
w. languisheth and fadeth. 24:4
the face of the *w.* with fruit. 27:6
let the *w.* hear, and all that. 34:1
ye shall not be confounded, *w.* 45:17
the devil sheweth him all the kingdoms of *w.* *Mat* 4:8; *Luke* 4:5
ye are the light of the *w.* *Mat* 5:14
the field is the *w.*; good seed. 13:38
it be in the end of this *w.* 40, 49
gain the whole *w.* and lose his own? 16:26; *Mark* 8:36; *Luke* 9:25
woe to the *w.* because of. *Mat* 18:7
gospel of kingdom shall be preached in all the *w.* 24:14; *Mark* 14:9
which have been since the *w.* began.
Luke 1:70†; *Acts* 3:21†
a decree that all the *w.* *Luke* 2:1
worthy to obtain that *w.* 20:35
in the *w.*, the *w.* was made by him, and *w.* *John* 1:10; *Acts* 17:24
taketh away the sin of *w. John* 1:29
God so loved the *w.* that he. 3:16
that the *w.* through him might. 17
Christ, the Saviour of the *w.*
4:42; *1 John* 4:14
that giveth life unto the *w. John* 6:33
I give for the life of the *w.* 51
things, shew thyself to the *w.* 7:4
the *w.* cannot hate you, but me. 7
I am the light of the *w.* 8:12; 9:5
the *w.* is gone after him. 12:19
not to judge, but to save the *w.* 47
the Spirit, whom the *w.* 14:17
a little while and the *w.* seeth. 19
thou wilt manifest thyself unto us and not unto the *w.*? 22
I give, not as the *w.* giveth. 27
that the *w.* may know I love. 14:31
if *w.* hate you. 15:18; *1 John* 3:13
if ye were of the *w.*, the *w. John* 15:19
but the *w.* shall rejoice. 16:20
the *w.* and go to the Father. 28
I have overcome the *w.* 33
with thee before the *w.* was. 17:5
men thou gavest me out of the *w.* 6
I pray not for the *w.* but for them. 9
w. hated them, because they are not of the *w.* 14
not take them out of the *w.* 15
the *w.*, even as I am not of *w.* 16
that the *w.* may believe thou. 21, 23
O Father, the *w.* hath not known. 25
I spake openly to the *w.* 18:20
suppose *w.* could not contain. 21:25
turned the *w.* upside down. *Acts* 17:6
Diana, whom Asia and the *w.* worshippeth. 19:27
a mover of sedition among all the Jews throughout the *w.* 24:5
your faith is spoken of through the whole *w.* *Rom* 1:8
how shall God judge the *w.*? 3:6
that all the *w.* may become guilty. 19
should be heir of the *w.* 4:13
of them be the riches of the *w.* 11:12
of them be the reconciling of *w.* 15
the *w.* by wisdom knew. *1 Cor* 1:21
God ordained before the *w.* 2:7
received not the spirit of the *w.* 12
or the *w.*, or life, or death. 3:22
are made a spectacle to *w. 1 Cor* 4:9
we are made as the filth of *w.* 13
must ye needs go out of the *w.* 5:10
saints shall judge the *w.*? 6:2
things that are in the *w.* 7:33, 34
I will eat no flesh while the *w.* 8:13*
not be condemned with the *w.* 11:32
God reconciling the *w.* *2 Cor* 5:19
Jesus, by whom the *w.* is crucified to me, and I to the *w.* *Gal* 6:14
in Christ before the *w.* began.
2 Tim 1:9*; *Tit* 1:2*
subjection the *w.* to come. *Heb* 2:5
have tasted the powers of the *w.* 6:5*
the *w.* was not worthy. 11:38
unspotted from the *w.* *Jas* 1:27
the tongue is a fire, a *w.* of. 3:6
the friendship of the *w.* is enmity with God? A friend of the *w.* is. 4:4
spared not the old *w.*, bringing in the flood upon the *w.* *2 Pet* 2:5
whereby the *w.* that then was. 3:6
propitiation for sins of *w. 1 John* 2:2
love not the *w.* 15
but is of the *w.* 16
the *w.* passeth away, and the. 17
the *w.* knoweth us not, because. 3:1
w.: therefore speak they of the *w.* 4:5
of God, overcometh the *w.* 5:4, 5
we are of God, and whole *w.* lieth. 19
shall come upon all the *w. Rev* 3:10
deceiveth the whole *w.* 12:9
and all the *w.* wondered after. 13:3
see **foundation**

in, or *into the* **world**

who prosper *in the w.* *Ps* 73:12*
preached *in the* whole *w. Mat* 26:13
hundred-fold, and *in the w.* to come eternal. *Mark* 10:30; *Luke* 18:30
lighteth every man that cometh *into the w.* *John* 1:9
he was *in the w.* and the world. 10
God sent not his Son *into the w.* to condemn the world. 3:17
light is come *into the w.* and men. 19
prophet that should come *into the w.*
6:14; 11:27
in the w., I am the light of world. 9:5
I am come a light *into the w.* 12:46
in w. ye shall have tribulation. 16:33
I am no more *in the w.*, but these are *in the w.* 17:11
while I was with them *in the w.* 12
cause came I *into the w.* 18:37
as by one man sin entered *into the w.*
Rom 5:12
until the law, sin was *in the w.* 13
an idol is nothing *in the w. 1 Cor* 8:4
having no hope, without God *in the w.* *Eph* 2:12
gospel is come to you as it is *in* all *the w.* *Col* 1:6
Christ Jesus came *into the w.* to save sinners. *1 Tim* 1:15
and believed on *in the w.* 3:16
he cometh *into the w.* *Heb* 10:5
afflictions that are *in the w. 1 Pet* 5:9
things that are *in the w. 1 John* 2:15
false prophets are gone out *into the w.* 4:1
even now already is it *in the w.* 3
greater than he that is *in the w.* 4
Son *into the w.* that we might live. 9
many deceivers are entered *into the w.* *2 John* 7

this **world**

forgiven him in *this w.* *Mat* 12:32
the care of *this w.* choke the word.
13:22; *Mark* 4:19
for the children of *this w.* are wiser than. *Luke* 16:8
The children of *this w.* marry. 20:34
ye are of *this w.*; I am not of *this w.*
John 8:23
I am come into *this w.* 9:39
he that hateth life in *this w.* 12:25
is the judgement of *this w.*; now shall the prince of *this w.* be cast. 31
he should depart out of *this w* 13:1
for prince of *this w.* cometh. 14:30
because the prince of *this w.* 16:11
My kingdom is not of *this w.*: if my kingdom were of *this w.* 18:36

be not conformed to *this w.*: but be ye. *Rom* 12:2
of *this w.*? hath not God made foolish the wisdom of *this w.*? *1 Cor* 1:20
not the wisdom of *this w.* 2:6
seemeth to be wise in *this w.* 3:18
wisdom of *this w.* is foolishness. 19
the fornicators of *this w.* 5:10
they that use *this w.* as not. 7:31
the god of *this w.* hath blinded the minds. *2 Cor* 4:4
he might deliver us from *this* present evil *w.* *Gal* 1:4
not only in *this w.*, but in. *Eph* 1:21
to the course of *this w.* 2:2
the rulers of the darkness of *this w.* 6:12
nothing into *this w.* *1 Tim* 6:7
that are rich in *this w.* 17
loved *this* present *w.* *2 Tim* 4:10
godly in *this* present *w.* *Tit* 2:12
chosen the poor of *this w.* *Jas* 2:5
but whoso hath *this w.'s.* *1 John* 3:17
is, so are we in *this w.* 4:17

worldly

denying ungodliness and *w.* *Tit* 2:12
the first covenant had a *w.* *Heb* 9:1

worlds

by whom also he made the *w.* *Heb* 1:2
the *w.* were framed by the. 11:3

worm

was there any *w.* therein. *Ex* 16:24
I have said to the *w.*, Thou. *Job* 17:14
the *w.* shall feed sweetly on. 24:20
much less man that is a *w.* 25:6
but I am a *w.* and no man. *Ps* 22:6
the *w.* is spread under. *Isa* 14:11
fear not, thou *w.* Jacob, and. 41:14
w. shall eat them like wool. 51:8
for their *w.* shall not die, nor their fire. 66:24; *Mark* 9:44, 46, 48
God prepared a *w.*, it smote the gourd. *Jonah* 4:7

worms

their manna bred *w.* *Ex* 16:20
grapes, for the *w.* shall. *Deut* 28:39
my flesh is clothed with *w.* *Job* 7:5
though *w.* destroy this body. 19:26
they shall lie down, and *w.* 21:26
worm under thee, and the *w.* cover. *Isa* 14:11
out of their holes like *w.* *Mi* 7:17
Herod was eaten of *w.* *Acts* 12:23

wormwood

a root that beareth *w.* *Deut* 29:18
her end is bitter as *w.*, sharp as a sword. *Pr* 5:4
I will feed them with *w.* *Jer* 9:15 23:15
made me drunken with *w.* *Lam* 3:15
remembering my misery, the *w.* 19
who turn judgement to *w.* *Amos* 5:7
star is called *w.* and the third part of the waters became *w.* *Rev* 8:11

worse

we will deal *w.* with thee. *Gen* 19:9
be *w.* than all that befell. *2 Sam* 19:7
Omri did *w.* than all. *1 Ki* 16:25*
Judah was put to the *w.* before. *2 Ki* 14:12; *2 Chr* 25:22
the Syrians were put to the *w.* *1 Chr* 19:16, 19
people be put to the *w.* *2 Chr* 6:24*
Manasseh made Jerusalem do *w.* 33:9*
they did *w.* than their fathers. *Jer* 7:26; 16:12
see your faces *w.* liking ? *Dan* 1:10
the rent is made *w.* *Mat* 9:16 *Mark* 2:21
the last state of that man is *w.* than first. *Mat* 12:45; *Luke* 11:26
last error shall be *w.* *Mat* 27:64
bettered, but grew *w.* *Mark* 5:26
then that which is *w.* *John* 2:10
sin no more, lest a *w.* thing. 5:14
eat not, are we the *w.* *1 Cor* 8:8
for the better, but for the *w.* 11:17
denied the faith, and is *w.* *1 Tim* 5:8
shall wax *w.* and *w.* *2 Tim* 3:13
the latter end is *w.* *2 Pet* 2:20

worship

lad will go yonder and *w.* *Gen* 22:5
to Lord, and *w.* ye afar off. *Ex* 24:1
for thou shalt *w.* no other god. 34:14
be driven to *w.* them. *Deut* 4:19
if thou *w.* other gods. 8:19; 11:16 30:17
before Lord, and *w.* before the Lord. 26:10; *Ps* 22:27, 29; 86:9
man went up early to *w.* *1 Sam* 1:3
turn again, that I may *w.* 15:25, 30
the people went to *w.* *1 Ki* 12:30
to *w.* in house of Rimmon. *2 Ki* 5:18
ye fear, and him shall ye *w.* 17:36*
hath said to Judah, Ye shall *w.* 18:22 *2 Chr* 32:12; *Isa* 36:7
w. the Lord in the beauty of holiness. *1 Chr* 16:29; *Ps* 29:2; 66:4; 96:9 *Mat* 4:10; *Luke* 4:8
I will *w.* toward thy holy temple. *Ps* 5:7; 138:2
he is thy Lord, and *w.* thou. 45:11
neither shalt thou *w.* any. 81:9
O come let us *w.* and bow. 95:6
w. him, all ye gods. 97:7
w. at his footstool, for. 99:5; 132:7
exalt the Lord, and *w.* at his. 99:9
they *w.* the work of their hands. *Isa* 2:8, 20; 46:6
w. the Lord in the holy mount. 27:13
princes also shall *w.* because. 49:7
all flesh shall come to *w.* 66:23
that enter in at these gates to *w.* *Jer* 7:2; 26:2
they that *w.* other gods, be. 13:10
go not after other gods to *w.* 25:6
we *w.* her without our men ? 44:19
he shall *w.* at threshold. *Ezek* 46:2
the people of the land shall *w.* 3
he that entereth to *w.* by the. 9
w. the golden image. *Dan* 3:5, 10, 15
not *w.* the image. 12, 18, 28
do not ye *w.* the golden image ? 3:14
if ye *w.* 15
no more *w.* the work of. *Mi* 5:13
them that *w.* the host. *Zeph* 1:5
men shall *w.* him, every one. 2:11
to *w.* the King the Lord of hosts. *Zech* 14:16, 17
star, and come to *w.* him. *Mat* 2:2
that I may come and *w.* him also. 8
if thou wilt fall down and *w.* me. 4:9; *Luke* 4:7
in vain do they *w.* me. *Mat* 15:9 *Mark* 7:7
Jerusalem is the place where men ought to *w.* *John* 4:20
ye *w.* ye know not what: we know what we *w.*: for salvation. 4:22
they shall *w.* the Father in. 23, 24
certain Greeks came up to *w.* 12:20
God gave up to *w.* *Acts* 7:42*, 43
came to Jerusalem to *w.* 8:27
whom ye ignorantly *w.* 17:23
persuaded men to *w.* God. 18:13
to Jerusalem to *w.* God. 24:11
they call heresy, so *w.* I the. 14*
down, he will *w.* God. *1 Cor* 14:25
which *w.* God in spirit. *Phil* 3:3
the angels of God *w.* him. *Heb* 1:6
make them come and *w.* *Rev* 3:9
and *w.* him that liveth for ever. 4:10
that they should not *w.* devils. 9:20
of God, and them *w.* therein. 11:1
all on the earth shall *w.* 13:8, 12
they that would not *w.* the image. 15
w. him that made heaven, earth. 14:7
if any man *w.* the beast and. 9
who *w.* the beast, have no rest. 11
all nations shall come and *w.* 15:4
I fell at his feet to *w.* 19:10; 22:8
w. God. 22:9

worshipped

Abraham bowed and *w.* the Lord. *Gen* 24:26, 48
Abraham's servant *w.* the Lord. 52
Israel bowed and *w.* *Ex* 4:31 12:27; 33:10
a calf, and *w.* it. 32:8; *Ps* 106:19
Moses *w.* *Ex* 34:8
other gods, and *w.* *Deut* 17:3; 29:26 *1 Ki* 9:9; *2 Ki* 21:21; *2 Chr* 7:22 *Jer* 1:16; 8:2; 16:11; 22:9
Gideon *w.* *Judg* 7:15
Hannah *w.* before Lord. *1 Sam* 1:19
Samuel *w.* 28
Saul *w.* the Lord. 15:31
then David arose and *w.* *2 Sam* 12:20; 15:32
and *w.* Ashtaroth. *1 Ki* 11:33
Baal and *w.* him. 16:31; 22:53
w. all the host of heaven and served. *2 Ki* 17:16; 21:3; *2 Chr* 33:3
congregation bowed down and *w.* the Lord. *1 Chr* 29:20; *2 Chr* 7:3 29:28, 29, 30
all people *w.* the Lord. *Neh* 8:6; 9:3
Job *w.* *Job* 1:20
w. the sun. *Ezek* 8:16
king *w.* Daniel. *Dan* 2:46
w. the golden image. 3:7
fell down and *w.* Christ. *Mat* 2:11
a leper came and *w.* him. 8:2
a certain ruler *w.* him. 9:18
were in the ship *w.* him. 14:33
woman came and *w.* him. 15:25
fell down and *w.* his lord. 18:26
by the feet and *w.* him. 28:9
his disciples *w.* him. 17; *Luke* 24:52
out of the tombs and *w.* *Mark* 5:6
and bowing knees, *w.* him. 15:19
our fathers *w.* in this. *John* 4:20
blind man believed, and *w.* him. 9:38
fell down and *w.* Peter. *Acts* 10:25
Lydia *w.* God. 16:14
neither is *w.* with men's. 17:25*
Justus *w.* God. 18:7
w. the creature more. *Rom* 1:25
above all that is *w.* *2 Thes* 2:4
Jacob *w.* *Heb* 11:21
the twenty-four elders *w.* *Rev* 5:14 11:16; 19:4
the angels *w.* God. 7:11
they *w.* the dragon, they *w.* 13:4
a sore fell on them which *w.* 16:2
them that *w.* his image. 19:20
souls that had not *w.* the beast. 20:4

worshipper

if any man be a *w.* of God. *John* 9:31
the city of Ephesus is a *w.* of Diana. *Acts* 19:35*

worshippers

destroy the *w.* of Baal. *2 Ki* 10:19
all the *w.* of Baal came. 21
that there be none but the *w.* 23
then the true *w.* shall. *John* 4:23
the *w.* once purged. *Heb* 10:2

worshippeth

host of heaven *w.* thee. *Neh* 9:6
yea, he maketh a god, and *w.* it. *Isa* 44:15, 17
falleth not down and *w.* *Dan* 3:6, 11
Asia and the world *w.* *Acts* 19:27

worshipping

as he was *w.* in the house of Nisroch. *2 Ki* 19:37; *Isa* 37:38
fell before the Lord, *w.* *2 Chr* 20:18
mother of Zebedee's children came *w.* *Mat* 20:20
beguile you in *w.* of angels. *Col* 2:18

worst

I will bring the *w.* of the. *Ezek* 7:24

worth

as much money as it is *w.* *Gen* 23:9
the land is *w.* four hundred. 15
priest shall reckon the *w.* *Lev* 27:23
hath been *w.* a double. *Deut* 15:18
but thou art *w.* ten thousand of us. *2 Sam* 18:3
give the *w.* of thy vineyard. *1 Ki* 21:2
thy speech nothing *w.* *Job* 24:25
heart of wicked is little *w.* *Pr* 10:20
howl ye, Woe *w.* the day! *Ezek* 30:2

worthies

he shall recount his *w.* *Nah* 2:5

worthily

do thou *w.* in Ephratah. *Ruth* 4:11

worthy

I am not *w.* of the least. *Gen* 32:10
if the wicked man be *w.* *Deut* 25:2
he gave a *w.* portion. *1 Sam* 1:5*
Lord liveth, ye are *w.* to die. 26:16
who is *w.* to be praised. *2 Sam* 22:4 *Ps* 18:3

shew himself a *w.* man. *1 Ki* 1:52
this man is *w.* to die. *Jer* 26:11
he is not *w.* 16
whose shoes I am not *w.* *Mat* 3:11
Lord, I am not *w.* that thou shouldest come under. 8:8; *Luke* 7:6
for the workman is *w.* of his meat. *Mat* 10:10
enquire who in it is *w.* and. 11
be *w.* . . . but if it be not *w.* 13
me, he is not *w.* of me. 37, 38
which were bidden were not *w.* 22:8
I am not *w.* to unloose. *Mark* 1:7
Luke 3:16; *John* 1:27; *Acts* 13:25
bring forth fruits *w.* of. *Luke* 3:8
that he was *w.* for whom. 7:4
nor thought I myself *w.* to come. 7
for the labourer is *w.* of his. 10:7
commit things *w.* of stripes. 12:48
I am no more *w.* to be. 15:19, 21
shall be accounted *w.* to. 20:35
be accounted *w.* to escape. 21:36*
very *w.* deeds are done. *Acts* 24:2
are not *w.* to be compared with the glory. *Rom* 8:18
that ye walk *w.* of the. *Eph* 4:1
that ye might walk *w.* of. *Col* 1:10
would walk *w.* of God. *1 Thes* 2:12
w. of all acceptation. *1 Tim* 1:15; 4:9
the labourer is *w.* of his reward. 5:18
sorer punishment, suppose ye, shall he be thought *w.*? *Heb* 10:29
of whom the world was not *w.* 11:38
blaspheme that *w.* name? *Jas* 2:7*
in white, for they are *w.* *Rev* 3:4
thou art *w.* to receive glory. 4:11
5:12
Who is *w.* to open the book? 5:2
found *w.* to open the book. 4
thou art *w.* to take the book and. 9
to drink, for they are *w.* 16:6
***see* count, counted, death**

wot, -teth

(*The American Revision everywhere, and the English Revision usually, put here the modern word* know, *which has the same meaning*)
I *w.* not who hath done. *Gen* 21:26
my master *w.* not what is with. 39:8
w. ye not that such a man? 44:15
as for this Moses, we *w.* *Ex* 32:1
23; *Acts* 7:40
I *w.* he whom thou blessest is blessed. *Num* 22:6
the men went I *w.* not. *Josh* 2:5
I *w.* that through ignorance ye did it. *Acts* 3:17
w. ye not what the scripture saith? *Rom* 11:2
I shall choose I *w.* not. *Phil* 1:22

would

I *w.* it might be according. *Gen* 30:34
I *w.* there were a sword. *Num* 22:29
whosoever *w.*, he consecrated him *1 Ki* 13:33
do with them as they *w.* *Neh* 9:24
Jews did what they *w.* to. *Esth* 9:5
not hearken, and Israel *w.* *Ps* 81:11
but ye *w.* none of my. *Pr* 1:25
they *w.* none of my counsel. 30
whom he *w.* he slew, and whom he *w.* he kept alive, and whom he *w.* he set up, and *w.* *Dan* 5:19
whatsoever ye *w.* that men should. *Mat* 7:12; *Luke* 6:31
to release a prisoner whom they *w.* *Mat* 27:15
calleth to him whom he *w.*, and they came unto him. *Mark* 3:13
we *w.* thou shouldest do for us. 10:35
what *w.* ye that I should do? 36
fishes as much as they *w.* *John* 6:11
reason *w.* that I should. *Acts* 18:14
what I *w.* that I do not. *Rom* 7:15
for the good that I *w.* I do not. 19
I *w.* that all men were. *1 Cor* 7:7
I *w.* that ye all spake with. 14:5
not find you such as I *w.* *2 Cor* 12:20
w. that we should remember. *Gal* 2:10
I *w.* they were cut off which. 5:12
do the things that ye *w.* 17
I *w.* ye knew what great. *Col* 2:1
forbiddeth them that *w.* *3 John* 10
I know thy works, I *w.* *Rev* 3:15

would *God*

w. God we had died in Egypt, when. *Ex* 16:3; *Num* 14:2
w. God that all the Lord's people were prophets! *Num* 11:29
w. God we had died when our. 20:3
w. God it were even, *w. God* it were morning! *Deut* 28:67
w. to *God* we had dwelt on the other side Jordan! *Josh* 7:7
w. God this people were. *Judg* 9:29
w. God I had died for. *2 Sam* 18:33
w. God my lord were. *2 Ki* 5:3
w. God that all were such as I am. *Acts* 26:29
I *w.* to *God* ye did reign. *1 Cor* 4:8
w. to *God* ye could bear with me. *2 Cor* 11:1

would *not*

if I knew, then *w. not* I tell it thee? *1 Sam* 20:9
his armourbearer *w. not.* 31:4
1 Chr 10:4
he *w. not,* nor did he eat with them. *2 Sam* 12:17
but Amnon *w. not* hearken. 13:16
howbeit David *w. not* go, but. 25
but Joab *w. not* come to. 14:29
but Jehoshaphat *w. not.* *1 Ki* 22:49
which Lord *w. not* pardon. *2 Ki* 24:4
yet *w.* they *not* give ear. *Neh* 9:30
yet *w.* I *not* believe he. *Job* 9:16
and ye *w. not.* *Isa* 30:15
Mat 23:37; *Luke* 13:34
besought him to have patience, he *w. not.* *Mat* 18:30
were bidden: they *w. not* come. 22:3
we *w. not* have been partakers with them. 23:30
w. not have suffered his house. 24:43
tasted, he *w. not* drink. 27:34
he *w. not* that any man. *Mark* 9:30
angry, and *w. not* go in. *Luke* 15:28
he *w. not* for a while, but. 18:4
he *w. not* lift so much as his. 13
who *w. not* that I should reign. 19:27
he *w. not* walk in Jewry. *John* 7:1
that he *w. not* delay to. *Acts* 9:38
when he *w. not* be persuaded. 21:14
I do that which I *w. not.* *Rom* 7:16
I *w. not,* brethren, that ye should be. 11:25; *1 Cor* 10:1
I *w. not* ye should have fellowship. *1 Cor* 10:20
you, such as ye *w. not.* *2 Cor* 12:20
because we *w. not* be chargeable to you. *1 Thes* 2:9
then *w.* he *not* afterward. *Heb* 4:8

wouldest

Caleb said, What *w.* thou? *Josh* 15:18; *1 Ki* 1:16
walkedst whither thou *w.* *John* 21:18

wouldest *not*

whither thou *w. not.* *John* 21:18
offering thou *w. not.* *Heb* 10:5, 8

wound, *substantive*

give *w.* for *w.*, stripe for. *Ex* 21:25
blood ran out of the *w.* *1 Ki* 22:35
my *w.* is incurable without transgression. *Job* 34:6
a *w.* and dishonour. *Pr* 6:33
the blueness of a *w.* cleanseth. 20:30
the stroke of their *w.* *Isa* 30:26
woe is me, for my *w.* is. *Jer* 10:19
and why is my *w.* incurable? 15:18
w. is grievous. 30:12; *Nah* 3:19
thee with *w.* of an enemy. *Jer* 30:14
Judah saw his *w.* . . . yet could he not cure your *w.* *Hos* 5:13
they that eat have laid a *w.* *Ob* 7*
her *w.* is incurable, it is. *Mi* 1:9
and his deadly *w.* was healed. *Rev* 13:3*, 12*, 14*

wound

alive; I *w.* and I heal. *Deut* 32:39
God shall *w.* the head. *Ps* 68:21*
he shall *w.* the heads over. 110:6*
when ye *w.* their weak. *1 Cor* 8:12

wound, *verb*

they *w.* body of Jesus. *John* 19:40*
young men *w.* up Ananias. *Acts* 5:6*

wounded

is *w.* in the stones. *Deut* 23:1
w. of the Philistines. *1 Sam* 17:52
Saul was *w.* of the archers. 31:3*
1 Chr 10:3*
I have *w.* mine enemies. *2 Sam* 22:39*; *Ps* 18:38*
in smiting he *w.* him. *1 Ki* 20:37
carry me out, for I am *w.* 22:34
2 Chr 18:33
the Syrians *w.* Joram. *2 Ki* 8:28
for I am sore *w.* *2 Chr* 35:23
soul of the *w.* crieth out. *Job* 24:12
suddenly shall they be *w.* *Ps* 64:7
of those whom thou hast *w.* 69:26
my heart is *w.* within me. 109:22
cast down many *w.* *Pr* 7:26
a *w.* spirit who can bear? 18:14*
found me, they *w.* me. *S of S* 5:7
art thou not it that *w.*? *Isa* 51:9*
but he was *w.* for our. 53:5
I *w.* thee with the wound. *Jer* 30:14
but *w.* men among them. 37:10
through all the land the *w.* 51:52
when they swooned as *w.* *Lam* 2:12
when the *w.* cry, shall? *Ezek* 26:15
the *w.* shall be judged in the. 28:23
groanings of a deadly *w.* 30:24
when they fall on the sword, shall not be *w.* *Joel* 2:8*
I was *w.* in the house. *Zech* 13:6
cast stones and they *w.* him in the head. *Mark* 12:4; *Luke* 20:12
thieves, which *w.* him. *Luke* 10:30
they fled out of that house naked and *w.* *Acts* 19:16
heads, as it were *w.* *Rev* 13:3*

woundedst

thou *w.* the head out of. *Hab* 3:13

woundeth

he *w.*, and his hands make. *Job* 5:18

wounding

slain a man to my *w.* *Gen* 4:23

wounds, *substantive*

went back to be healed of the *w.* *2 Ki* 8:29; 9:15; *2 Chr* 22:6
he multiplied my *w.* *Job* 9:17
my *w.* stink, are corrupt. *Ps* 38:5
and bindeth up their *w.* 147:3
words of a talebearer are as *w.* *Pr* 18:8*; 26:22*
who hath woe? who hath *w.*? 23:29
faithful are *w.* of friend, but. 27:6
in it, but *w.*, bruises, and. *Isa* 1:6
continually is grief and *w.* *Jer* 6:7
I will heal thee of thy *w.* saith. 30:17
what are these *w.* in thy hands? *Zech* 13:6
bound up his *w.* *Luke* 10:34

wove

the women *w.* hangings. *2 Ki* 23:7

woven

ephod have binding of *w.* work. *Ex* 28:32; 39:22
made coats of fine linen *w.* 39:27
the coat was without seam, *w.* *John* 19:23

wrap

he can *w.* himself in it. *Isa* 28:20
a reward; so they *w.* it up. *Mi* 7:3*

wrapped

Tamar *w.* herself and sat. *Gen* 38:14
Goliath's sword is *w.* *1 Sam* 21:9
Elijah *w.* his face in. *1 Ki* 19:13
mantle and *w.* it together. *2 Ki* 2:8
roots are *w.* about the heap. *Job* 8:17
sinews of his stones are *w.* 40:17*
the sword is *w.* up for. *Ezek* 21:15*
the weeds were *w.* about. *Jonah* 2:5
Joseph *w.* the body in a clean linen cloth. *Mat* 27:59; *Mark* 15:46*
Luke 23:53
Mary *w.* him in swaddling clothes. *Luke* 2:7
babe *w.* in swaddling clothes. 12
napkin *w.* together in a. *John* 20:7*

wrath

(Generally the Revised Versions use the more modern terms anger, vexation, indignation, fury)

cursed be their w. for it. Gen 49:7
lest w. come upon all. Lev 10:6
that no w. be on the congregation. Num 1:53; 18:5
for there is w. gone out from. 16:46
remember, how thou provokedst the Lord thy God to w. Deut 9:7, 22
the Lord rooted them out in anger and w. 29:28
were it not I feared the w. 32:27
let them live, lest w. Josh 9:20
and w. fell on all the. 22:20
if the king's w. arise. 2 Sam 11:20
turned not from great w. 2 Ki 23:26
because there fell w. 1 Chr 27:24
therefore is w. upon thee. 2 Chr 19:2
they trespass not, and so w. 10
w. came upon Judah for. 24:18
and there is fierce w. 28:13
that his fierce w. may turn. 29:10
therefore there was w. upon. 32:25
provoked God to w. Ezra 5:12
should there be w. against? 7:23
yet ye bring more w. Neh 13:18
shall arise too much w. Esth 1:18
when the w. of the king was. 2:1
not, then Haman full of w. 3:5
was the king's w. pacified. 7:10
for w. killeth the foolish man. Job 5:2
w. bringeth the punishments. 19:29
he shall drink of the w. of. 21:20
hypocrites in heart heap up w. 36:13
because there is w., beware. 18
forsake w. Ps 37:8
in w. they hate me. 55:3
surely the w. of man shall praise thee, the remainder of w. 76:10
stretch thy hand against w. of. 138:7
of the wicked is w. Pr 11:23
a fool's w. presently known. 12:16
that is slow to w. is of great. 14:29
a soft answer turneth away w. 15:1
w. of a king is as messengers. 16:14
king's w. is as the roaring. 19:12
a man of great w. shall suffer. 19
bosom pacifieth strong w. 21:14
who dealeth in proud w. 24
but a fool's w. is heavier. 27:3
w. is cruel, and anger is. 4
but wise men turn away w. 29:8
forcing of w. bringeth forth. 30:33
much w. with his sickness. Eccl 5:17
day of Lord cometh with w. Isa 13:9
he who smote the people in w. 14:6
in a little w. I hid my face. 54:8
fight against you in w. Jer 21:5
driven them in great w. 32:37
in that ye provoke me to w. 44:8
w. is on all the multitude. Ezek 7:12
and he reserveth w. for. Nah 1:2
O Lord, in w. remember. Hab 3:2
not deliver in day of w. Zeph 1:18
therefore came a great w. Zech 7:12
fathers provoked me to w. 8:14
to flee from w. to come. Mat 3:7 Luke 3:7
they were filled with w. Luke 4:28 Acts 19:28
be w. on this people. Luke 21:23
but treasurest up w. against the day of w. Rom 2:5
that obey unrighteousness, w. 8
because the law worketh w. 4:15
we shall be saved from w. 5:9
endured the vessels of w. fitted. 9:22
but rather give place unto w. 12:19
minister of God to execute w. 13:4
be subject, not only for w. 5
works of flesh are w., strife. Gal 5:20
by nature the children of w. Eph 2:3
not sun go down upon your w. 4:26
let all w., anger, and clamour. 31
provoke not your children to w. 6:4
put off all these; w., malice. Col 3:8
who delivered us from the w. to come. 1 Thes 1:10
for w. is come on them to. 2:16
hath not appointed us to w. 5:9
holy hands, without w. 1 Tim 2:8
Moses not fearing the w. of the king. Heb 11:27
slow to speak, slow to w. Jas 1:19
w. of man worketh not. 20
and hide us from the w. Rev 6:16
come down, having great w. 12:12
she made all nations drink wine of w. 14:3; 18:3

day of **wrath**

his goods flow away in the day of his w. Job 20:28
the wicked brought forth to the day of w. 21:30
Lord strike through kings in day of his w. Ps 110:5
profit not in the day of w. Pr 11:4
that day is a day of w. Zeph 1:15
w. against the day of w. Rom 2:5
the great day of his w. is. Rev 6:17

wrath *of God*

the fierce w. of God is. 2 Chr 28:11
till the w. of God be turned from us. Ezra 10:14
the w. of God came. Ps 78:31
but the w. of God abideth. John 3:36
the w. of God is revealed. Rom 1:18
things, w. of God cometh on the children. Eph 5:6; Col 3:6
shall drink of the wine of the w. of God. Rev 14:10
into winepress of the w. of God. 19
is filled up the w. of God. 15:1
golden vials full of the w. of God. 7
vials of the w. of God on earth. 16:1
winepress of the w. of God. 19:15

his **wrath**

Lord overthrew in his w. Deut 29:23
nor executedst his w. 1 Sam 28:18
turned not from his w. 2 Ki 23:26
his fierce w. may turn away. 2 Chr 29:10; 30:8
his w. is against them. Ezra 8:22
from the banquet in his w. Esth 7:7
he teareth me in his w. Job 16:9
the fury of his w. on him. 20:23
he speak to them in his w. Ps 2:5
swallow them up in his w. 21:9
take them away in his w. 58:9
did not stir up all his w. 78:38
the fierceness of his w. 49
stood to turn away his w. 106:23
his w. against him that. Pr 14:35
turn away his w. from him. 24:18
Moab's pride and his w. Isa 16:6
the Lord hath forsaken the generation of his w. Jer 7:29
at his w. the earth shall. 10:10
I know his w., saith the Lord. 48:30
hath thrown down in his w. Lam 2:2
affliction by the rod of his w. 3:1
because he kept his w. Amos 1:11
God willing to shew his w. Rom 9:22
of fierceness of his w. Rev 16:19
see **kindled,** *wrath of the* **Lord**

my **wrath**

my w. shall wax hot. Ex 22:24
let me alone, that my w. 32:10
hath turned my w. away. Num 25:11
my w. shall not be poured out on Jerusalem. 2 Chr 12:7
to whom I sware in my w. Ps 95:11
against the people of my w. Isa 10:6
for in my w. I smote thee. 60:10
for my w. is on all the multitude. Ezek 7:14
thus will I accomplish my w. 13:15
thee in fire of my w. 21:31; 22:21
them with the fire of my w. 22:31
of my w. have I spoken. 38:19
I will pour out my w. on. Hos 5:10
I took him away in my w. 13:11
so sware in my w. they. Heb 3:11
as I have sworn in my w., if they. 4:3

thy **wrath**

thou sentest thy w. which. Ex 15:7
doth thy w. wax hot against? 32:11
turn from thy fierce w. and. 12
keep me secret until thy w. be past. Job 14:13
cast abroad the rage of thy w. 40:11
rebuke me not in thy w. Ps 38:1
pour out thy w. on the heathen. 79:6
taken away all thy w. Ps 85:3
thy w. lieth hard on me. 88:7
thy fierce w. goeth over me. 16
how long shall thy w. burn? 89:46
and by thy w. are we troubled. 90:7
days are passed away in thy w. 9
according to thy fear, so is thy w. 11
thine indignation and thy w. 102:10
I stood to turn away thy w. Jer 18:20
was thy w. against the sea. Hab 3:8
thy w. is come, and time. Rev 11:18

wrathful

let thy w. anger take. Ps 69:24
a w. man stirreth up. Pr 15:18

wraths

be envyings, w., strifes. 2 Cor 12:20

wreath

two rows of pomegranates on each w. 2 Chr 4:13*

wreathed

my transgressions are w. Lam 1:14*

wreathen

two chains at the ends, of w. work. Ex 28:14, 22, 24, 25; 39:15, 17, 18
pillar of w. work he carried away. 2 Ki 25:17*

wreaths

w. of chain work for. 1 Ki 7:17
two w. to cover the. 2 Chr 4:12*
pomegranates on the two w. 13*

wrest

many, to w. judgement. Ex 23:2
thou shalt not w. the judgement of thy poor. 6
thou shalt not w. judgement; neither take a gift. Deut 16:19
day they w. my words. Ps 56:5
they that are unstable w. 2 Pet 3:16

wrestle

we w. not against flesh. Eph 6:12

wrestled

wrestlings have I w. with. Gen 30:8
there w. a man with him. 32:24
thigh was out of joint as he w. 25

wrestlings

with great w. have I wrestled with my sister. Gen 30:8

wretched

O w. man that I am! Rom 7:24
knowest not thou art w. Rev 3:17

wretchedness

let me not see my w. Num 11:15

wring

the priest shall w. off his head. Lev 1:15; 5:8
all the wicked shall w. Ps 75:8†

wringed

Gideon w. the dew out. Judg 6:38

wringing

the w. of the nose bringeth forth blood. Pr 30:33

wrinkle

a glorious church not having spot or w. Eph 5:27

wrinkles

hast filled me with w. Job 16:8*

write

I will w. on these tables. Ex 34:1 Deut 10:2
W. thou these words. Ex 34:27
w. thou every man's. Num 17:2
thou shalt w. Aaron's name on. 3
w. them on posts. Deut 6:9; 11:20
then let him w. her a bill of divorcement, and. 24:1, 3; Mark 10:4
w. on the stones the. Deut 27:3, 8
now therefore w. ye this. 31:19
Uzziah did Isaiah w. 2 Chr 26:22
we might w. the names. Ezra 5:10
sure covenant and w. it. Neh 9:38
w. ye also for the Jews. Esth 8:8
w. them on the table. Pr 3:3; 7:3
w. in the great roll with. Isa 8:1
that w. grievousness which. 10:1
few, that a child may w. them. 19
now go, w. it before them. 30:8
saith the Lord, W. ye. Jer 22:30
w. the words I have spoken. 30:2 36:2, 17, 28

I will *w.* it in their hearts. *Jer* 31:33
Heb 8:10
son of man, *w.* the name. *Ezek* 24:2
w. upon the sticks for. 37:16
w. it in their sight, that they. 43:11
w. the vision and make it. *Hab* 2:2
it seemed good to me to *w.* to thee in order. *Luke* 1:3
take thy bill and *w.* fifty. 16:6
w. fourscore. 7
and the prophets did *w.* *John* 1:45
w. not, King of the Jews, but. 19:21
that we *w.* to them that. *Acts* 15:20
thing to *w.* unto my lord, that I might have somewhat to *w.* 25:26
I *w.* not these things to. *1 Cor* 4:14
things I *w.* are the. 14:37
for we *w.* none other things to you.
2 Cor 1:13
to this end also did I *w.*, that. 2:9
it is superfluous for me to *w.* to. 9:1
I *w.* to them which heretofore. 13:2
therefore I *w.* these things, being. 10
now the things I *w.* unto. *Gal* 1:20
to *w.* the same things. *Phil* 3:1
not that I *w.* to you. *1 Thes* 4:9; 5:1
so I *w.* *2 Thes* 3:17
these things I *w.* *1 Tim* 3:14
minds will I *w.* them. *Heb* 10:16
I now *w.* unto you. *2 Pet* 3:1
1 John 2:1
these things *w.* we to. *1 John* 1:4
brethren, I *w.* no new. 2:7
again, a new commandment I *w.* 8
I *w.* to you, little children. 12, 13
I *w.* to you, fathers, I *w.* to you. 13
having many things to *w.* *2 John* 12
ink and pen *w.* to you. *3 John* 13
diligence to *w.* of common salvation, it was needful for me to *w.* *Jude* 3
what thou seest, *w.* *Rev* 1:11, 19
unto the angel of the church of . . . *w.*
2:1, 8, 12, 18; 3:1, 7, 14
I will *w.* on him the name of my God . . . I will *w.* upon him my new. 3:12
to *w.*: a voice saying, *w.* not. 10:4
W., Blessed are the dead which. 14:13
W., Blessed are they which. 19:9
w.: for these words are true. 21:5
see **book**

writer

handle the pen of the *w.* *Judg* 5:14*
the pen of a ready *w.* *Ps* 45:1
a man with a *w.'s* inkhorn by his side. *Ezek* 9:2, 3

writest

for thou *w.* bitter things. *Job* 13:26
sticks whereon thou *w.* *Ezek* 37:20

writeth

count, when he *w.* up. *Ps* 87:6

writing

and the *w.* was the *w.* of. *Ex* 32:16
plate of the holy crown a *w.* 39:30
according to the first *w.* *Deut* 10:4
made an end of *w.* the law. 31:24
the Lord made me understand in *w.*
1 Chr 28:19
Huram answered in *w.* *2 Chr* 2:11
came a *w.* from Jehoram. 21:12
prepare according to the *w.* of. 35:4
Cyrus put the proclamation in *w.*
36:22; *Ezra* 1:1
the *w.* of the letter was in. *Ezra* 4:7
unto all provinces according to the *w.*
Esth 1:22; 3:12; 8:9; 9:27
copy of the *w.* was published. 3:14
to Hatach a copy of the *w.* 4:8
the *w.* in the king's name may. 8:8
the *w.* of Hezekiah, when. *Isa* 38:9
not written in the *w.* of. *Ezek* 13:9
whosoever shall read this *w.* *Dan* 5:7
could not read the *w.* 8
should read this *w.* 15
if thou canst read the *w.* thou. 16
yet I will read the *w.* to the king. 17
this is the *w.* that was. 24, 25
sign the *w.* 6:8
king Darius signed the *w.* 9
when Daniel knew that the *w.* 10
give her a *w.* of divorcement.
Mat 5:31; 19:7
the *w.* was, Jesus of. *John* 19:19

***hand*-writing**

blotting out the *hand-w.* *Col* 2:14

writings

if ye believe not his *w.* *John* 5:47

writing table

asked for a *w. table.* *Luke* 1:63

written

w. with the finger of God. *Ex* 31:18
Deut 9:10
elders did as it was *w.* *1 Ki* 21:11
these *w.* by name smote. *1 Chr* 4:41
the passover as it was *w.* *2 Chr* 30:5
a letter wherein was *w.* *Ezra* 5:7
therein was a record thus *w.* 6:2
weight of the vessels was *w.* 8:34
sent an open letter, wherein was *w.*
Neh 6:6
they found *w.* in the law. 8:14
and therein was found *w.* 13:1
it be *w.* among the laws. *Esth* 1:19
let it be *w.* that they may be. 3:9
of king Ahasuerus was it *w.* 12
found *w.* that Mordecai told of. 6:2
let it be *w.* to reverse Haman's. 8:5
let them not be *w.* with. *Ps* 69:28
be *w.* for the generation to. 102:18
on them the judgement *w.* 149:9
have not I *w.* to thee excellent things? *Pr* 22:20
that which was *w.* was. *Eccl* 12:10
shall be *w.* in the earth. *Jer* 17:13
hast *w.*, saying, The king? 36:29
the roll was *w.* within. *Ezek* 2:10
nor *w.* in the writing of house. 13:9
writing that was *w.* *Dan* 5:24, 25
set up his accusation *w.* *Mat* 27:37
is it not *w.*, My house? *Mark* 11:17
of his accusation was *w.* 15:26
Luke 23:38; *John* 19:20
place where it was *w.* *Luke* 4:17
rejoice that your names are *w.* 10:20
all things *w.* shall be accomplished.
18:31; 21:22
disciples remembered that it was *w.*
John 2:17
Is it not *w.* in your law, I said? 10:34
but these are *w.* that ye might. 20:31
w. every one, the world could not contain the books . . . be *w.* 21:25
fulfilled all that was *w.* *Acts* 13:29
the Gentiles, we have *w.* 21:25
the work of the law *w.* *Rom* 2:15
now it was not *w.* for his sake. 4:23
they are *w.* for our admonition.
1 Cor 10:11
ye are our epistle *w.* in our. *2 Cor* 3:2
w. not with ink, but with the. 3
if the ministration of death *w.* in. 7
I Paul have *w.* with. *Philem* 19
firstborn *w.* in heaven. *Heb* 12:23*
things which are *w.* therein. *Rev* 1:3
and in the stone a new name *w.* 2:17
not *w.* in the book of life. 13:8
having his Father's name *w.* 14:1
upon her head was a name *w.* 17:5
name *w.* on his thigh. 19:12, 16
names of the twelve tribes *w.* 21:12

***is* written**

observe to do all that *is w.* *Josh* 1:8
that which *is w.* concerning us.
2 Ki 22:13
for writing which *is w.* in. *Esth* 8:8
every one that *is w.* among. *Isa* 4:3
sin of Judah *is w.* with. *Jer* 17:1
oath that *is w.* in the law. *Dan* 9:11
what *is w.* in the law? *Luke* 10:26
What is this then that *is w.*? 20:17
this that *is w.* must be. 22:37
be fulfilled that *is w.* *John* 15:25
to think of men above that which *is w.* *1 Cor* 4:6
for our sakes, no doubt, this *is w.* 9:10
the saying that *is w.*, Death. 15:54

***it is* written**

as *it is w.* in the law of. *Josh* 8:31
1 Ki 2:3; *2 Chr* 23:18; 25:4; 31:3
35:12; *Ezra* 3:2, 4; 6:18
Neh 8:15; 10:34, 36; *Dan* 9:13
it is w. of me. *Ps* 40:7; *Heb* 10:7
it is w. before me. *Isa* 65:6
thus *it is w.* by the prophet.
Mat 2:5; *Luke* 24:46
this is he of whom *it is w.*
Mat 11:10; *Luke* 7:27
as *it is w.* of him. *Mat* 26:24
Mark 9:13; 14:21
it is w. *Mat* 26:31; *Mark* 14:27
Luke 4:8; *Acts* 23:5
and how *it is w.* of the. *Mark* 9:12
as *it is w.* in the law. *Luke* 2:23
according as *it is w.* *Rom* 11:8
1 Cor 1:31; *2 Cor* 4:13
for *it is w.* *Rom* 12:19; 14:11
Gal 3:10
not himself, but as *it is w.* *Rom* 15:3
so *it is w.*, The first man. *1 Cor* 15:45
because *it is w.*, Be ye holy; for I am holy. *1 Pet* 1:16

***I have,* or *have I* written**

commandment, *I have w.* *Ex* 24:12
I have w. to him great. *Hos* 8:12
Pilate said, What *I have w. I have w.* *John* 19:22
I have w. to you fathers. *1 John* 2:14
these things *have I w.* 26; 5:13

***were* written**

of them that *were w.* *Num* 11:26
words *were* now *w.* *Job* 19:23
fulfilled which *were w.* *Luke* 24:44
things *were w.* of him. *John* 12:16
were w. aforetime *were w.* for our learning. *Rom* 15:4
see **book, chronicle**

wrong

Sarai said, My *w.* be. *Gen* 16:5
to him that did the *w.* *Ex* 2:13
against him what is *w.* *Deut* 19:16
thou doest me *w.* to war. *Judg* 11:27
seeing there is no *w.* in. *1 Chr* 12:17
no man to do them *w.*: yea, he reproved kings for. 16:21; *Ps* 105:14
not done *w.* to the king. *Esth* 1:16
behold, I cry out of *w.* *Job* 19:7
do no *w.*, do no violence. *Jer* 22:3
buildeth his chambers by *w.* 13*
seen my *w.*: judge thou. *Lam* 3:59
therefore *w.* judgement. *Hab* 1:4*
Friend, I do thee no *w.* *Mat* 20:13
one of them suffer *w.* *Acts* 7:24
why do ye *w.* one to another? 26
neighbour *w.* thrust him away. 27
if it were a matter of *w.* 18:14
the Jews have I done no *w.* 25:10
do ye not rather take *w.*? *1 Cor* 6:7
nay, ye do *w.* and defraud your. 8
that had done the *w.* nor for his cause that suffered *w.* *2 Cor* 7:12
I was not burdensome to you? forgive me this *w.* 12:13
w. shall receive for the *w.* *Col* 3:25

wronged

receive us, we have *w.* *2 Cor* 7:2
if he hath *w.* thee, or. *Philem* 18

wrongeth

he that sinneth against me *w.* his own soul. *Pr* 8:36

wrongfully

the devices ye *w.* *Job* 21:27
let not mine enemies *w.* *Ps* 35:19
they that hate me *w.* are. 38:19
being mine enemies *w.* 69:4
me *w.*, help thou me. 119:86
they have oppressed the stranger *w.*
Ezek 22:29
endure grief, suffering *w.* *1 Pet* 2:19

wrote

Moses *w.* all the words of the Lord and rose. *Ex* 24:4; *Deut* 31:9
Lord *w.* upon the tables words of.
Ex 34:28; *Deut* 4:13; 5:22; 10:4
and Moses *w.* their. *Num* 33:2
Moses *w.* this song the. *Deut* 31:22
Joshua *w.* upon the. *Josh* 8:32
Samuel *w.* the manner of the kingdom. *1 Sam* 10:25
David *w.* a letter to Joab.
2 Sam 11:14, 15
Jezebel *w.* letters in. *1 Ki* 21:8, 9
Jehu *w.* *2 Ki* 10:1, 6
Shemaiah *w.* *1 Chr* 24:6
Hezekiah *w.* letters to. *2 Chr* 30:1
Sennacherib *w.* to rail on the. 32:17
they *w.* an accusation. *Ezra* 4:6
Rehum *w.* **8, 9**

letters which Haman *w*. *Esth* 8:5
Mordecai *w*. letters. 10; 9:20, 29
Baruch *w*. from Jeremiah. *Jer* 36:4
18, 27, 32
so Jeremiah *w*. in a book. 51:60
fingers of a man's hand *w*. *Dan* 5:5
then king Darius *w*. unto all. 6:25
Daniel had a dream; then he *w*. 7:1
your hardness Moses *w*. *Mark* 10:5
Master, Moses *w*. to us. 12:19
Luke 20:28
Zacharias *w*. saying. *Luke* 1:63
for Moses *w*. of me. *John* 5:46
Jesus with his finger *w*. 8:6, 8
Pilate *w*. a title and put. 19:19
John *w*. and testified of. 21:24
the apostles *w*. letters. *Acts* 15:23
the brethren *w*. exhorting. 18:27
Lysias *w*. a letter after. 23:25
who *w*. this epistle. *Rom* 16:22
I *w*. unto you. *1 Cor* 5:9; *2 Cor* 2:3, 4
7:12; *Eph* 3:3; *Philem* 21
things whereof ye *w*. to me. *1 Cor* 7:1
not as though I *w*. a new. *2 John* 5
I *w*. to the church. *3 John* 9

wroth

Cain was very *w*. *Gen* 4:5
why art thou *w*.? 6
Jacob was *w*. 31:36
Jacob's sons were *w*. 34:7
w. with two officers. 40:2; 41:10
Moses was *w*. *Ex* 16:20
Num 16:15; 31:14
wilt thou be *w*. with all? *Num* 16:22
your words and was *w*. *Deut* 1:34
3:26; 9:19; *2 Sam* 22:8; *2 Chr* 28:9
Ps 18:7; 78:21, 59, 62
Saul was very *w*. *1 Sam* 18:8; 20:7
Philistines were *w*. with him. 29:4
Abner was *w*. *2 Sam* 3:8
David was *w*. 13:21
but Naaman was *w*. *2 Ki* 5:11
and the man of God was *w*. 13:19
Asa was *w*. *2 Chr* 16:10
Uzziah was *w*. 26:19
Sanballat was *w*. *Neh* 4:1, 7
Ahasuerus was very *w*. *Esth* 1:12
Bigthan and Teresh were *w*. 2:21
thou hast been *w*. with. *Ps* 89:38
shall be *w*. as in the. *Isa* 28:21
I was *w*. with my people. 47:6
I would not be *w*. with thee. 54:9
nor will I be always *w*. 57:16
of his covetousness was I *w*. and
smote him: I hid me . . . was *w*. 17
behold, thou art *w*.; for we. 64:5
be not *w*. very sore, O Lord; we. 9
princes were *w*. *Jer* 37:15
rejected us, thou art very *w*. against
us. *Lam* 5:22
Herod was *w*. *Mat* 2:16
his lord was *w*., and. 18:34
king was *w*. 22:7
dragon was *w*. *Rev* 12:17

wrought

Shechem had *w*. folly in. *Gen* 34:7
what things I have *w*. in. *Ex* 10:2
then *w*. Bezaleel and Aholiab. 36:1
all the wise men *w*. the. 4, 8; 39:6
they have *w*. confusion. *Lev* 20:12
What hath God *w*.? *Num* 23:23
of them all *w*. jewels. 31:51
that such abomination is *w*.
Deut 13:14; 17:4
that hath *w*. wickedness. 17:2
heifer which hath not been *w*. 21:3
w. folly in Israel. 22:21; *Josh* 7:15
Judg 20:10
for the evils which they shall have *w*.
Deut 31:18
she had *w*., The man's name with
whom I *w*. to-day. *Ruth* 2:19
Lord had *w*. wonderfully. *1 Sam* 6:6
w. salvation in Israel. 11:13; 19:5
for Jonathan hath *w* with. 14:45
otherwise I should have *w*. falsehood. *2 Sam* 18:13
the Lord *w*. a great victory. 23:10, 12
who ruled over the people that *w*.
1 Ki 5:16; 9:23
of the sea was *w*. like. 7:26
and the treason he *w*. 16:20
but Omri *w*. evil in the eyes. 25
Jehoram *w*. evil. *2 Ki* 3:2; *2 Chr* 21:6
Israel *w*. wicked things. *2 Ki* 17:11
Neh 9:18
Manasseh *w*. much wickedness.
2 Ki 21:6; *2 Chr* 33:6
families that *w*. fine. *1 Chr* 4:21
masons to hew *w*. stones. 22:2
and he *w*. cherubims. *2 Chr* 3:14
they hired such as *w*. iron. 24:12
so the workman *w*. 13; 34:10, 13
half of my servants *w*. *Neh* 4:16
every one with one of his hands *w*. 17
this work was *w*. of our. 6:16
the Lord hath *w*. this. *Job* 12:9
thou hast *w*. iniquity? 36:23
hast *w*. for them that trust. *Ps* 31:19
clothing is of *w*. gold. 45:13
which thou hast *w*. for us. 68:28
how he had *w*. his signs in. 78:43
made in secret, curiously *w*. 139:15
all works my hands had *w*. *Eccl* 2:11
works *w*. under the sun. 17
for thou hast *w*. all our works in us.
Isa 26:12
we have not *w*. any deliverance. 18
who hath *w*. and done it? 41:4
she hath *w*. lewdness. *Jer* 11:15
and behold, he *w*. a work. 18:3
I *w*. for my name's sake. *Ezek* 20:9
14, 22, 44
because they *w*. for me. 29:20
wonders that God hath *w*. *Dan* 4:2
the sea *w*. and was. *Jonah* 1:11, 13
meek of earth who have *w*. *Zeph* 2:3
these last have *w*. but. *Mat* 20:12*
she hath *w*. a good work on me.
26:10; *Mark* 14:6
that they are *w*. of God. *John* 3:21
wonders were *w*. among. *Acts* 5:12
God hath *w*. 15:12; 21:19
abode with Aquila and *w*. 18:3
God *w*. special miracles by. 19:11
w. in me all manner of. *Rom* 7:8
Christ hath not *w*. by me. 15:18
he that hath *w*. us for. *2 Cor* 5:5
what carefulness it *w*. in you? 7:11
the signs of an apostle were *w*.
12:12
for he that *w*. effectually. *Gal* 2:8
which he *w*. in Christ. *Eph* 1:20
but we *w*. with labour. *2 Thes* 3:8
who, through faith, *w*. *Heb* 11:33
seest thou how faith *w*.? *Jas* 2:22
to have *w*. the will of. *1 Pet* 4:3
lose not those things which we have
w. *2 John* 8
the false prophet that *w*. *Rev* 19:20

wroughtest

to her, Where *w*. thou? *Ruth* 2:19

wrung

the blood shall be *w*. out. *Lev* 1:15*
5:9*
waters are *w*. to them. *Ps* 73:10†
thou hast *w*. out of the dregs of the
cup. *Isa* 51:17*

Y

yarn

y. out of Egypt, the king's merchants
. . . *y*. *1 Ki* 10:28*; *2 Chr* 1:16*

ye

ye shall be as gods. *Gen* 3:5
but *ye* have no portion in. *Neh* 2:20
ye are they which justify. *Luke* 16:15
but *ye* are washed, *ye* are sanctified,
ye are justified in. *1 Cor* 6:11
ye are bought with a price. 20
ye also helping by prayer. *2 Cor* 1:11
ye are our epistle, written. 3:2
ye are not straitened in us. 6:12
not that other men be eased, *ye*. 8:13
as I am, for I am as *ye* are. *Gal* 4:12
ye which are spiritual, restore. 6:1
ye who sometimes were. *Eph* 2:13
in whom *ye* also are builded. 22
joy, are not even *ye*? *1 Thes* 2:19
ye are our glory. 20
if *ye* stand fast in the Lord. 3:8
but *ye*, brethren, are not in. 5:4
ye are all children of light and. 5
but *ye*, brethren, be. *2 Thes* 3:13
but *ye* are a chosen. *1 Pet* 2:9

yea

y., hath God said, Ye. *Gen* 3:1
but let your communication be *Y*., *y*.;
Nay, nay. *Mat* 5:37; *Jas* 5:12
said unto him, *Y*. *Mat* 9:28; 13:51
Sapphira said, *Y*. for so. *Acts* 5:8
thou a Roman? he said, *Y*. 22:27
y. *y*. and nay, nay. *2 Cor* 1:17
toward you was not *y*. and nay. 18
Son of God was not *y*. and nay. 19
God in him are *y*. and amen. 20
I do rejoice, *y*. and will. *Phil* 1:18
y. and I count all things but loss. 3:8
y. and all that live godly. *2 Tim* 3:12
y. brother, let me have. *Philem* 20

year

shall bear the next *y*. *Gen* 17:21
Isaac received the same *y*. 26:12
with bread that *y*. 47:17
first month of the *y*. *Ex* 12:2
keep it a feast unto the Lord in the
y. 23:14; *Lev* 23:41
three times in the *y*. all thy males.
Ex 23:17; 34:23, 24; *Deut* 16:16
out from thee in one *y*. *Ex* 23:29
ingathering at the *y*.'s end. 34:22
atonement once a *y*. *Lev* 16:34
it is a *y*. of rest. 25:5
redeem it within a *y*. 29
if it were a *y*. that the. *Num* 9:22
each day for a *y*. shall ye. 14:34
saying, The *y*. of release. *Deut* 15:9
the third *y*., which is the *y*. of. 26:12
fruit of Canaan that *y*. *Josh* 5:12
that *y*. the Ammonites. *Judg* 10:8
to lament four days in a *y*. 11:40
thee ten shekels by the *y*. 17:10
David dwelt a *y*. and. *1 Sam* 27:7
that after the *y*. was. *2 Sam* 11:1
it was at every *y*.'s end that. 14:26
three times in a *y*. did. *1 Ki* 9:25
gold that came to Solomon in one *y*.
10:14; *2 Chr* 9:13
this *y*. such things as grow of themselves in second and third *y*.
2 Ki 19:29; *Isa* 37:30
gave him the same *y*. *2 Chr* 27:5
keep two days every *y*. *Esth* 9:27
thou crownest the *y*. with. *Ps* 65:11
in the *y*. that king Uzziah. *Isa* 6:1
in the *y*. that king Ahaz died. 14:28
in a *y*. all the glory of Kedar. 21:16
to proclaim the acceptable *y*. of the
Lord, and the. 61:2; *Luke* 4:19
and the *y*. of my redeemed. *Isa* 63:4
bring evil on the men of Anathoth,
even the *y*. *Jer* 11:23; 23:12; 48:44
shall not be careful in the *y*. 17:8
thus saith the Lord; this *y*. 28:16
prophet died the same *y*. 17
shall both come in one *y*. 51:46
each day for a *y*. *Ezek* 4:6
it shall be his to the *y*. of. 46:17
with calves of a *y*. old? *Mi* 6:6
his parents went to Jerusalem every
y. *Luke* 2:41
let it alone this *y*. also. 13:8
high priest that same *y*., said, Ye
know. *John* 11:49, 51; 18:13
whole *y*. they assembled. *Acts* 11:26
Paul continued a *y*. at Corinth. 18:11
to be forward a *y*. ago. *2 Cor* 8:10
was ready a *y*. ago; your zeal. 9:2
went in once a *y*. *Heb* 9:7, 25
made of sins every *y*. 10:3
continue there a *y*. and buy. *Jas* 4:13
who were prepared for a month and
a *y*. *Rev* 9:15
see **first, second, third, fifth, seventh**

year *after* year

there was a famine three years *y*.
after *y*. *2 Sam* 21:1

year *by* year

increase of thy seed that the field
bringeth forth *y*. *by* *y*. *Deut* 14:22
eat it before the Lord *y*. *by* *y*. 15:20
as he did so *y*. *by* *y*., so. *1 Sam* 1:7
gave to Hiram *y*. *by* *y*. *1 Ki* 5:11

they brought a rate *y.* by *y.* *1 Ki* 10:25; *2 Chr* 9:24
as he had done *y.* by *y.* *2 Ki* 17:4
wood offering *y.* by *y.* *Neh* 10:34
firstfruits of all trees *y.* by *y.* 35
which they offered *y.* by *y.* *Heb* 10:1

year *to* year

ordinance from *y. to y.* *Ex* 13:10
coat to him from *y. to y.* *1 Sam* 2:19
Samuel went from *y. to y.* in. 7:16
your God from *y. to y.* *2 Chr* 24:5
add ye *y. to y.*; let them. *Isa* 29:1
from *y. to y.* to worship. *Zech* 14:16

yearly

as a *y.* hired servant. *Lev* 25:53
daughters of Israel went *y.* to lament. *Judg* 11:40
of the Lord in Shiloh *y.* 21:19
Elkanah went up *y.* to. *1 Sam* 1:3
to offer the *y.* sacrifice. 21; 2:19
there is a *y.* sacrifice there. 20:6
keep 14th day of month Adar, and fifteenth of same *y.* *Esth* 9:21

yearn

for his bowels did *y.* *Gen* 43:30

yearned

for her bowels *y.* upon. *1 Ki* 3:26

years

for seasons, days, and *y.* *Gen* 1:14
these are the days of the *y.* 25:7
an old man and full of *y.* 8
an hundred thirty seven *y.* 17
few and evil have the *y.* of. 47:9
according to the number of *y.* *Lev* 25:15, 16, 50, 52
the money according to the *y.* 27:18
consider the *y.* of many. *Deut* 32:7
Joshua was old and stricken in *y.* *Josh* 13:1
been with me these *y.* *1 Sam* 29:3
David was old and stricken in *y.* *1 Ki* 1:1
not be dew nor rain these *y.* 17:1
Asa had no war in those *y.* *2 Chr* 14:6
after certain *y.* he went down. 18:2
are thy *y.* as man's days? *Job* 10:5
the number of *y.* is hidden to. 15:20
when a few *y.* are come, I. 16:22
and multitude of *y.* should. 32:7
they shall spend their *y.* in. 36:11
nor can number of his *y.* be. 26
and my *y.* are spent. *Ps* 31:10
wilt prolong his *y.* as many. 61:6
I considered the *y.* of ancient. 77:5
I will remember the *y.* of the. 10
their *y.* did he consume in. 78:33
for a thousand *y.* in thy sight are but. 90:4; *2 Pet* 3:8
we spend our *y.* as a tale. *Ps* 90:9
our *y.* are threescore *y.* and ten. 10
according to the *y.* wherein we. 15
thy *y.* are throughout all. 102:24
thou art the same, thy *y.* shall. 27
the *y.* of thy life shall be many. *Pr* 4:10; 9:11
lest thou give thy *y.* unto. 5:9
the *y.* of the wicked shall be. 10:27
evil days come not, nor *y.* *Eccl* 12:1
the *y.* of an hireling. *Isa* 21:16
of the residue of my *y.* 38:10
I shall go softly all my *y.* 15
I have laid on thee the *y.* *Ezek* 4:5
art come even unto thy *y.* 22:4
in latter *y.* thou shalt come. 38:8
by books the number of the *y.* *Dan* 9:2
in the end of *y.* they shall join. 11:6
continue more *y.* than the king. 8
shall come after certain *y.* 13
even to the *y.* of many. *Joel* 2:2
I will restore the *y.* the locusts. 25
in the midst of the *y.* *Hab* 3:2
the offering be pleasant as in the former *y.* *Mal* 3:4
well stricken in *y.* *Luke* 1:7, 18
days and months, and *y.* *Gal* 4:10
thy *y.* shall not fail. *Heb* 1:12
by faith Moses, when he was come to *y.*, refused. 11:24
bound Satan a thousand *y.* *Rev* 20:2
till the thousand *y.* should be. 3
reigned with Christ a thousand *y.* 4
when the thousand *y.* are expired. 7
see numeral words in their places, as **hundred, two, three.** *Also* **many, old, sin**

yell

like lions, they shall *y.* *Jer* 51:38*

yelled

roared and *y.* on him. *Jer* 2:15

yellow

behold, if there be in it a *y.* thin hair. *Lev* 13:30
if there be in it no *y.* hair. 32
priests shall not seek for *y.* hair. 36
covered with *y.* gold. *Ps* 68:13

yesterday

fulfilled your task *y.*? *Ex* 5:14
why came not the son of Jesse to meat *y.*? *1 Sam* 20:27
thou camest but *y.* *2 Sam* 15:20
I have seen *y.* the blood. *2 Ki* 9:26
we are but of *y.* and know. *Job* 8:9
a thousand years in thy sight are but as *y.* *Ps* 90:4
y. at the seventh hour. *John* 4:52
didst the Egyptian *y.*? *Acts* 7:28
Jesus Christ, the same *y.* *Heb* 13:8

yesternight

behold, I lay *y.* with my. *Gen* 19:34
your fathers spake to me *y.* 31:29
affliction, and rebuked thee *y.* 42

yet

y. did not the butler. *Gen* 40:23
as *y.* exaltest thyself. *Ex* 9:17
knowest thou not *y.* that Egypt? 10:7
if ye will not *y.* hearken. *Lev* 26:18
y. for all that, when they be. 44
y. in this thing ye did. *Deut* 1:32
y. they are thy people and. 9:29
ye are not as *y.* come to the. 12:9
y. the Lord hath not given you. 29:4
as *y.* I am as strong. *Josh* 14:11
Lord said, The people are *y.* too many. *Judg* 7:4
y. ye have forsaken me and. 10:13
y. honour me now before the elders. *1 Sam* 15:30
y. he hath made with me an everlasting covenant. *2 Sam* 23:5
y. hast not been as my. *1 Ki* 14:8
y. I have left me 7000. 19:18
there is *y.* one by whom we. 22:8
as *y.* the people did sacrifice. 43
2 Ki 14:4
y. the Lord would not destroy Judah. *2 Ki* 8:19
them from his presence as *y.* 13:23
as *y.* the people had not prepared. *2 Chr* 20:33
people did *y.* corruptly. 27:2
not cleansed, *y.* did they eat. 30:18
temple was not *y.* laid. *Ezra* 3:6
y. our God hath not forsaken us. 9:9; *Neh* 9:19
y. required not I bread. *Neh* 5:18
y. ye bring more wrath upon. 13:18
y. all this availeth me. *Esth* 5:13
while he was *y.* *Job* 1:16, 17, 18
then should I *y.* have comfort. 6:10
though he slay me, *y.* will I. 13:15
y. he shall perish for ever. 20:7
when the Almighty was *y.* 29:5
y. he knoweth it not in great. 35:15
y. have I set my king on my. *Ps* 2:6
y. have I not seen the righteous forsaken. 37:25
I shall *y.* praise him. 42:5, 11
43:5; 71:14
this is come, *y.* have we. 44:17
y. have I not declined. 119:51, 157
y. do I not forget thy statutes. 83
109, 141
y. will not his foolishness. *Pr* 27:22
y. is not washed from their. 30:12
better is he which hath not *y.* been. *Eccl* 4:3
kiss thee, *y.* I should. *S of S* 8:1
y. a remnant of them. *Isa* 10:22
for the Lord will *y.* choose. 14:1
y. gleaning grapes shall be. 17:6
while it is *y.* in his hand, he. 28:4
this is the rest, *y.* they would. 12
y. he also is wise, and will. 31:2
Israel be not gathered, *y.* shall. 49:5
they may forget, *y.* will I not. *Isa* 49:15
he was oppressed, *y.* he. 53:7
I will *y.* plead with you. *Jer* 2:9
y. return to me. 3:1
y. they prosper. 5:28
y. my mind could not be. 15:1
prophets, *y.* they ran: *y.* they. 23:21
y. they were not afraid, nor. 36:24
though they cry, *y.* will. *Ezek* 8:18
y. will I be to them as a little. 11:16
said, I am a god, *y.* thou art a. 28:2
I will *y.* for this be enquired. 36:37
y. made we not our prayer before God. *Dan* 9:13
because it is *y.* for a time. 11:35
y. he shall come to his end. 45
grey hairs are upon him, *y.* *Hos* 7:9
y. I am the Lord thy God from. 13:4
given you want of bread, *y.* have ye not returned to me. *Amos* 4:6
8, 9, 10, 11; *Hag* 2:17
he shall say, Is there *y.*? *Amos* 6:10
y. I will look toward thy. *Jonah* 2:4
y. forty days and Nineveh. 3:4
was my saying, when I was *y.* 4:2
are there *y.* the treasures? *Mi* 6:10
y. was she carried away. *Nah* 3:10
y. I will rejoice in the Lord, I will joy. *Hab* 3:18
y. is she thy companion. *Mal* 2:14
do not ye *y.* understand, that? *Mat* 15:17; 16:9; *Mark* 8:17
I kept, what lack I *y.*? *Mat* 19:20
but the end is not *y.* 24:6
Mark 13:7
time of figs was not *y.* *Mark* 11:13
words I spake while *y.* *Luke* 24:44
unto her, Mine hour is not *y.* come. *John* 2:4; 7:6, 30; 8:20
for the Holy Ghost was not *y.* 7:39
though he were dead *y.* shall. 11:25
for as *y.* they knew not the. 20:9
as *y.* the Holy Ghost was fallen upon none of them. *Acts* 8:16
he had *y.* being uncircumcised. *Rom* 4:11, 12
we were *y.* without strength. 5:6
while we were *y.* sinners. 8
why doth he *y.* hope for? 8:24
Why doth he *y.* find fault? 9:19
ye are *y.* carnal. *1 Cor* 3:3
y. so as by fire. 15
to the married I command, *y.* not I, but the Lord. 7:10
y. for all that will they not. 14:21
y. not I, but the grace of God. 15:10
your faith is vain, ye are *y.* 17
that he will *y.* deliver. *2 Cor* 1:10
to spare you I came not as *y.* 23
y. true, as unknown, *y.* known. 6:8
y. not I, but Christ. *Gal* 2:20
in vain? if it be *y.* in vain. 3:4
I, brethren, if I *y.* preach. 5:11
when I was *y.* with you. *2 Thes* 2:5
y. is he not crowned. *2 Tim* 2:5
we see not *y.* all things. *Heb* 2:8
like as we are, *y.* without sin. 4:15
for he was *y.* in the loins of. 7:10
and by it he being dead *y.* 11:4
warned of things not seen as *y.* 7
keep the whole law, *y.* *Jas* 2:10
y. if thou kill. 11
y. ye have not. 4:2
it doth not *y.* appear. *1 John* 3:2
and is not, and *y.* is. *Rev* 17:8
and the other is not *y.* come. 10
received no kingdom as *y.* 12
see **alive**

yield

the ground, it shall not henceforth *y.* her strength. *Gen* 4:12
fat, shall *y.* royal dainties. 49:20
that it may *y.* to you the increase. *Lev* 19:25
y. her increase, trees *y.* fruit. 26:4
for your land shall not *y.* her. 20
but *y.* yourselves to the Lord. *2 Chr* 30:8
the land shall *y.* her increase. *Ps* 67:6; 85:12
plant vineyards, which may *y.* 107:37
speech she caused him to *y.* *Pr* 7:21

vineyard shall y. one bath, and the seed of an homer shall y. *Isa* 5:10
the bud shall y. no meal: if so be it y. the stranger shall. *Hos* 8:7
the fig tree and vine y. *Joel* 2:22
fields shall y. no meat. *Hab* 3:17
but do not thou y. unto. *Acts* 23:21
nor y. ye your members as instruments of . . . sin, y. *Rom* 6:13*
that to whom ye y. yourselves servants. 16*
y. your members servants to. 19*
no fountain y. salt water. *Jas* 3:12

yielded

his sons, y. up the ghost. *Gen* 49:33
rod of Aaron y. almonds. *Num* 17:8
y. their bodies that they. *Dan* 3:28
Jesus cried again, and y. *Mat* 27:50
then Sapphira y. up the. *Acts* 5:10
ye have y. your members. *Rom* 6:19

yieldeth

it y. much increase. *Neh* 9:37
wilderness y. food for. *Job* 24:5
y. the peaceable fruit of. *Heb* 12:11

yielding

bring forth herb y. seed, tree y. fruit. *Gen* 1:11, 12
given you every tree y. seed. 29
for y. pacifieth great. *Eccl* 10:4
see **fruit**

yoke

This term is used both literally and figuratively in the Bible. Figuratively it is used [1] *Of the yoke of bondage, or slavery,* Lev 26:13; *Deut* 28:48. [2] *Of the yoke of afflictions and crosses,* Lam 3:27. [3] *Of the yoke of punishment for sin,* Lam 1:14. [4] *Of the yoke of Christ's service,* Mat 11:29, 30.

that thou shalt break his y. *Gen* 27:40; *Jer* 30:8
I have broken the bands of your y. *Lev* 26:13; *Ezek* 34:27
a red heifer without blemish, on which never came y. *Num* 19:2
Deut 21:3; *1 Sam* 6:7
he shall put a y. of iron upon thy neck. *Deut* 28:48; *Jer* 28:14
Saul took a y. of oxen. *1 Sam* 11:7
an half acre, which a y. of. 14:14
y. grievous, make his heavy y. *1 Ki* 12:4, 10, 11, 14; *2 Chr* 10:4
with twelve y. of oxen. *1 Ki* 19:19
he took a y. of oxen, and slew. 21
Job had five hundred y. *Job* 1:3
he had a thousand y. of oxen. 42:12
thou hast broken the y. of his burden. *Isa* 9:4; 10:27; 14:25
hast very heavily laid thy y. 47:6
and that ye break every y. 58:6
I have broken thy y. *Jer* 2:20
altogether broken the y. 5:5
not put their neck under the y. 27:8
bring their neck under the y. 11, 12
broken the y. of the king. 28:2; 4, 11
Hananiah had broken the y. 12*
unaccustomed to the y. 31:18
husbandman and his y. 51:23
the y. of my transgressions. *Lam* 1:14
good for a man to bear the y. 3:27
they that take off the y. *Hos* 11:4
now will I break his y. *Nah* 1:13
take my y. upon you. *Mat* 11:29
my y. is easy. 30
bought five y. of oxen. *Luke* 14:19
to put a y. on the disciples' neck. *Acts* 15:10
be not entangled with the y. *Gal* 5:1
as are under the y. *1 Tim* 6:1

yoked

be not unequally y. with. *2 Cor* 6:14

yokefellow

I intreat thee also, true y. *Phil* 4:3

yokes

make thee bonds and y. *Jer* 27:2*
y. of wood; but make y. of iron. 28:13
break the y. of Egypt. *Ezek* 30:18

yonder

I and the lad will go y. *Gen* 22:5
scatter thou the fire y. *Num* 16:37
while I meet the Lord y. 23:15
y. is that Shunammite. *2 Ki* 4:25
Remove hence to y. place. *Mat* 17:20
here, while I go and pray y. 26:36

you

a space between y. and ark. *Josh* 3:4
and shake my head at y. *Job* 16:4
your iniquities have separated between y. and your God. *Isa* 59:2
and I will put a new spirit within y. *Ezek* 11:19; 36:26, 27
are about y., bear shame. 36:7, 36
I am pressed under y. *Amos* 2:13
y. only have I known of all. 3:2
he that heareth y. heareth me; and he that despiseth y. *Luke* 10:16
and y. yourselves thrust out. 13:28
the name of God is blasphemed through y. *Rom* 2:24
lest they come and find y. unprepared. *2 Cor* 9:4
gospel in the regions beyond y. 10:16
for I seek not yours but y. 12:14
y. hath he quickened. *Eph* 2:1
y. that were sometime alienated and enemies. *Col* 1:21
y., being dead in your sins, hath he quickened. 2:13
see **tell**

after **you**

with you, and seed *after* y. *Gen* 9:9
inheritance for your children *after* y. *Lev* 25:46; *1 Chr* 28:8
draw out a sword *after* y. *Lev* 26:33
as they pursued *after* y. *Deut* 11:4
that shall rise up *after* y. 29:22
behold, I come *after* y. *1 Sam* 25:19
shall follow close *after* y. *Jer* 42:16
which long *after* y. *2 Cor* 9:14
Phil 1:8
longed *after* y. *Phil* 2:26

against **you**

I have sinned *against* y. *Ex* 10:16
I will set my face *against* y. *Lev* 26:17; *Jer* 44:11
they murmur *against* y. *Num* 17:5
came out *against* y. *Deut* 1:44
earth to witness *against* y. this day, that ye shall soon. 4:26; 30:19
I testify *against* y. that ye. 8:19
the Lord was wroth *against* y. 9:19
11:17; *Josh* 23:16
Jericho fought *against* y. *Josh* 24:11
the Lord is witness *against* y. *1 Sam* 12:5; *Mi* 1:2
Ammonites came *against* y. *1 Sam* 12:12
hand of Lord shall be *against* y. 15
counselled *against* y. *2 Sam* 17:21
to cry alarm *against* y. *2 Chr* 13:12
heap up words *against* y. *Job* 16:4
I devise a device *against* y. *Jer* 18:11
will fight *against* y. in anger. 21:5
of evil pronounced *against* y. 26:13
Chaldeans that fight *against* y. 37:10
the king of Babylon shall not come *against* y. 19
cannot do any thing *against* y. 38:5
words shall stand *against* y. 44:29
conceived a purpose *against* y. 49:30
I am *against* y. *Ezek* 13:8
enemy said *against* y. 36:2
Lord hath spoken *against* y. *Amos* 3:1; 5:1; *Zeph* 2:5
I will raise up *against* y. a nation. *Amos* 6:14
take up a parable *against* y. *Mi* 2:4
manner of evil *against* y. *Mat* 5:11
go into the village over *against* y. 21:2; *Mark* 11:2; *Luke* 19:30
the very dust of your city we do wipe off *against* y. *Luke* 10:11
be a witness *against* y. *Jas* 5:3
whereas they speak *against* y. as evil doers. *1 Pet* 2:12

among or *amongst* **you**

strange gods that are *among* y. *Gen* 35:2; *Josh* 24:23; *1 Sam* 7:3
tabernacle *amongst* y. *Lev* 26:11
I will walk *among* y. and will. 12
I will send wild beasts *among* y. 22
I will send pestilence *among* y. 25
despised the Lord who is *among* y. *Num* 11:20; 14:42; *Deut* 6:15
7:21; *Josh* 3:10
who is there *among* y.? *2 Chr* 36:23
Ezra 1:3
who *among* y. will give? *Isa* 42:23
who is *among* y. that feareth? 50:10
purge out from *among* y. *Ezek* 20:38
who is left *among* y. that? *Hag* 2:3
who is there *among* y.? *Mal* 1:10
it shall not be so *among* y. *Mat* 20:26; *Mark* 10:43
among y. let him be your servant. *Mat* 20:27; 23:11; *Luke* 22:26
he that is least *among* y. *Luke* 9:48
but I am *among* y. as he. 22:27
standeth one *among* y. *John* 1:26
he that is without sin *among* y. 8:7
brethren, look ye out *among* y. seven men. *Acts* 6:3
and whosoever *among* y. 13:26
let them who *among* y. are. 25:5
some fruit *among* y. *Rom* 1:13
every man that is *among* y. 12:3
no divisions *among* y. *1 Cor* 1:10
contentions *among* y. 11; 11:18
to know any thing *among* y. 2:2
is *among* y. envying, strife. 3:3
if any man *among* y. seemeth. 18
there is fornication *among* y. 5:1
taken away from *among* y. 2
how say some *among* y. that? 15:12
Christ who was preached *among* y. *2 Cor* 1:19
in presence am base *among* y. 10:1
will humble me *among* y. 12:21
not be once named *among* y. *Eph* 5:3
what manner of men were *among* y. *1 Thes* 1:5
if any man *among* y. *Jas* 1:26
is any *among* y. afflicted? 5:13
is any sick *among* y.? 14
feed the flock of God which is *among* y. *1 Pet* 5:2
false teachers *among* y. *2 Pet* 2:1
who was slain *among* y. *Rev* 2:13
see **sojourneth**

before **you**

the land shall be *before* y. *Gen* 34:10
God did send me *before* y. 45:5, 7
for evil is *before* y. *Ex* 10:10
these the nations are defiled which I cast out *before* y. *Lev* 18:24
20:23; *Num* 33:52, 55; *Deut* 11:23
Josh 3:10; 9:24; 23:5, 9; 24:8
12; *Judg* 6:9
men of the land done which were *before* y. *Lev* 18:27, 28, 30
shall fall *before* y. 26:7, 8
are there *before* y. *Num* 14:43
shall be subdued *before* y. 32:29
set the land *before* y. *Deut* 1:8
Lord who goeth *before* y. shall. 30
set *before* y. this day. 4:8; 11:32
I set *before* y. a blessing and a curse. 11:26; 30:19
dried up Jordan *before* y. *Josh* 4:23
I sent the hornet *before* y. 24:12
behold, he is *before* y. *1 Sam* 9:12
the king walketh *before* y. 12:2
my statutes which I have set *before* y. *2 Chr* 7:19; *Jer* 26:4; 44:10
Lord will go *before* y. *Isa* 52:12
behold, I set *before* y. the. *Jer* 21:8
so persecuted they the prophets which were *before* y. *Mat* 5:12
kingdom of God *before* y. 21:31
risen again, I will go *before* y. 26:32
28:7; *Mark* 14:28; 16:7
eat such things as are set *before* y. *Luke* 10:8; *1 Cor* 10:27
doth this man stand here *before* y. whole. *Acts* 4:10

by **you**

I will not be enquired of *by* y. *Ezek* 20:3, 31
I trust to be brought on my way *by* y. *Rom* 15:24
if the world shall be judged *by* y. *1 Cor* 6:2

was refreshed *by y.* all. *2 Cor* 7:13
shall be enlarged *by y.* 10:15

concerning **you**

what Lord will command *concerning y.* *Num* 9:8
which the Lord spake *concerning y.* *Josh* 23:14
hath said *concerning y.* *Jer* 42:19
this is the will of God *concerning y.* *1 Thes* 5:18

for **you**

as *for y.* *Gen* 44:17; 50:20
Num 14:32; *Deut* 1:40; *Josh* 23:9
Job 17:10
one ordinance shall be *for y.* *Num* 15:15, 16
all that he did *for y.* *Deut* 1:30
4:34; *1 Sam* 12:24
as *for y.* O house of Israel. *Ezek* 20:39; 34:17
behold I am *for y.* and I will. 36:9
but one decree *for y.* *Dan* 2:9
to what end is it *for y.*? *Amos* 5:18
is it not *for y.* to know judgement? *Mi* 3:1
is it time *for y.*, to dwell? *Hag* 1:4
commandment is *for y.* *Mal* 2:1
more tolerable for Tyre and Sidon, than *for y.* *Mat* 11:22; *Luke* 10:14
kingdom prepared *for y.* *Mat* 25:34
that I should do *for y.* *Mark* 10:36
this is my body which is given *for y.* *Luke* 22:19
blood shed *for y.* 20; *1 Cor* 11:24
prepare a place *for y.* *John* 14:2, 3
I will pray the Father *for y.* 16:26
is not *for y.* to know the times or the seasons. *Acts* 1:7
therefore have I called *for y.* 28:20
God through Christ *for y.* *Rom* 1:8
was Paul crucified *for y.*? *1 Cor* 1:13
care *for y.* appear. *2 Cor* 7:12; 8:16
by their prayer *for y.* 9:14; *Phil* 1:4
Col 1:3, 9; 4:12; *2 Thes* 1:11
and be spent *for y.* *2 Cor* 12:15
I cease not to give thanks *for y.*
Eph 1:16; *1 Thes* 1:2; 3:9
2 Thes 1:3; 2:13
at my tribulations *for y.* *Eph* 3:13
Col 1:24
is not grievous, but *for y.* *Phil* 3:1
which is laid up *for y.* *Col* 1:5
which is given to me *for y.* 25
great conflict I have *for y.* 2:1
that he hath a great zeal *for y.* 4:13
is unprofitable *for y.* *Heb* 13:17
reserved in heaven *for y.* *1 Pet* 1:4
on him, for he careth *for y.* 5:7

from **you**

sent me away *from y.* *Gen* 26:27
we are very far *from y.* *Josh* 9:22
not removed *from y.* *1 Sam* 6:3
come word *from y.* *2 Sam* 15:28
wrath turn away *from y.* *2 Chr* 30:8
turn away his face *from y.* 9
will hide mine eyes *from y.* *Isa* 1:15
have hid his face *from y.* 59:2
good things *from y.* *Jer* 5:25
which are gone *from y.* 34:21
keep nothing back *from y.* 42:4
cast away *from y.* your. *Ezek* 18:31
remove far *from y.* the. *Joel* 2:20
I have withholden the rain *from y.* *Amos* 4:7
kingdom of God shall be taken *from y.* *Mat* 21:43
no man taketh *from y.* *John* 16:22
who is taken up *from y.* *Acts* 1:11
but seeing ye put it *from y.* 13:46
word of God out *from y.* *1 Cor* 14:36
of commendation *from y.* *2 Cor* 3:1
let evil speaking be put away *from y.* *Eph* 4:31
for *from y.* sounded out. *1 Thes* 1:8
but we being taken *from y.* 2:17
and he will flee *from y.* *Jas* 4:7

in **you**

be any truth *in y.* *Gen* 42:16
let him also rejoice *in y.* *Judg* 9:19
sanctified *in y.* *Ezek* 20:41; 36:23
will put breath *in y.* 37:6, 14
I have no pleasure *in y.* saith the Lord. *Mal* 1:10
but the Spirit which speaketh *in y.* *Mat* 10:20
works which were done *in y.* 11:21
not his word abiding *in y.* *John* 5:38
not the love of God *in y.* 42
the flesh, ye have no life *in y.* 6:53
he shall be *in y.* 14:17
and I *in y.* 20; 15:4
if my words abide *in y.* 15:7
1 John 2:14, 24
the Spirit dwelleth *in y.* *Rom* 8:9
1 John 2:27
and if Christ be *in y.* *Rom* 8:10
as much as lieth *in y.*, live. 12:18
Christ is confirmed *in y.* *1 Cor* 1:6
Holy Ghost which is *in y.* 6:19
God is *in y.* of a truth. 14:25
having confidence *in y.* all. *2 Cor* 2:3
7:16; 8:22; *Gal* 5:10
but life *in y.* *2 Cor* 4:12
he was comforted *in y.* 7:7
he would finish *in y.* the same. 8:6
exceeding grace of God *in y.* 9:14
is not weak, but mighty *in y.* 13:3
that Jesus Christ is *in y.*? 5
I travail, till Christ be formed *in y.* *Gal* 4:19
one God . . . who is above all, and through all, and *in y.* all. *Eph* 4:6
let this mind be *in y.* which. *Phil* 2:5
it is God which worketh *in y.* 13
which bringeth forth fruit, as it doth also *in y.* *Col* 1:6
which is Christ *in y.*, the hope. 27
Christ dwell *in y.* richly. 3:16
worketh *in y.* *1 Thes* 2:13
so that we glory *in y.* *2 Thes* 1:4
Christ may be glorified *in y.* 12
every good thing *in y.* *Philem* 6
working *in y.* that which is well-pleasing. *Heb* 13:21
the hope that is *in y.* *1 Pet* 3:15
if these things be *in y.* *2 Pet* 1:8
which thing is true in him and *in y.* *1 John* 2:8
greater is he that is *in y.* than. 4:4

of **you**

why should I be deprived *of y.* both? *Gen* 27:45
may be done *of y.* *Ex* 12:16
unto me every one *of y.* *Deut* 1:22
faint because *of y.* *Josh* 2:9
to these nations because *of y.* 23:3
that all *of y.* have conspired against me. *1 Sam* 22:8
O people, every one *of y.* *1 Ki* 22:28
what Ezra requires *of y.* *Ezra* 7:21
though there were *of y.* cast out unto uttermost part of heaven. *Neh* 1:9
ye shall be slain all *of y.* *Ps* 62:3
that escape *of y.* shall. *Ezek* 6:9
he shall receive *of y.* *Mi* 1:11
which *of y.* by taking thought can add one cubit? *Mat* 6:27; *Luke* 12:25
doth not each one *of y.*? *Luke* 13:15
of y. convinceth me of? *John* 8:46
I speak not *of y.* all, I know. 13:18
which God did by him in the midst *of y.* *Acts* 2:22
in turning every one *of y.* 3:26
which was set at nought *of y.* 4:11
faith both *of y.* and me. *Rom* 1:12
declared to me *of y.* *1 Cor* 1:11
such were some *of y.* but ye. 6:11
the feet, I have no need *of y.* 12:21
every one *of y.* hath a psalm. 14:26
let every one *of y.* lay by him. 16:2
and our hope *of y.* is. *2 Cor* 1:7
boasted any thing to him *of y.* 7:14
suffer, if a man take *of y.* 11:20
did I make a gain *of y.*? 12:17
Did Titus make a gain *of y.*? 18
this only would I learn *of y.* *Gal* 3:2
for as many *of y.* as have been. 27
voice, for I stand in doubt *of y.* 4:20
brother, who is one *of y.* *Col* 4:9, 12
neither *of y.* sought we. *1 Thes* 2:6
every one *of y.* should know. 4:4
no evil thing to say *of y.* *Tit* 2:8
the hire which is *of y.* kept. *Jas* 5:4
they speak evil *of y.* *1 Pet* 3:16; 4:4

on, or *upon* **you**

plague shall not be *upon y.* *Ex* 12:13
bestow *upon y.* a blessing. *Ex* 32:29
oil of the Lord is *upon y.* *Lev* 10:7
they said, Ye take too much *upon y.* *Num* 16:3, 7
not set his love *upon y.* *Deut* 7:7
things are come *upon y.* *Josh* 23:15
they will be *upon y.* *Neh* 4:12
of the Lord be *upon y.* *Ps* 129:8
upon y. the spirit of sleep. *Isa* 29:10
he may have mercy *upon y.* 30:18
Jer 42:12
I will visit *upon y.* the. *Jer* 23:2
this thing is come *upon y.* 40:3
I will blow *upon y.* in. *Ezek* 22:21
days shall come *upon y.* *Amos* 4:2
before the fierce anger of the Lord come *upon y.* *Zeph* 2:2
upon y. may come the. *Mat* 23:35
of God is come *upon y.* *Luke* 11:20
and so that day come *upon y.* 21:34
I send the promise of my Father *upon y.* 24:49
darkness come *upon y.* *John* 12:35
Holy Ghost is come *upon y.* *Acts* 1:8
not cast a snare *upon y.* *1 Cor* 7:35
upon y. labour in vain. *Gal* 4:11
howl for your miseries that shall come *upon y.* *Jas* 5:1
of God resteth *upon y.* *1 Pet* 4:14
I will put *upon y.* none. *Rev* 2:24

over **you**

I will even appoint *over y.* *Lev* 26:16
hate you shall reign *over y.* 17
rejoiced *over y.* to do you good, he will rejoice *over y.* *Deut* 28:63
rule *over y.* nor my son rule *over y.*: Lord shall rule *over y.* *Judg* 8:23
seventy reign *over y.* or one? 9:2
ye anoint me king *over y.* 15
that shall reign *over y.* *1 Sam* 8:11
I have made a king *over y.* 12:1
the Lord hath set a king *over y.* 13
David to be king *over y.* *2 Sam* 3:17
chief priest is *over y.* *2 Chr* 19:11
watchmen *over y.* saying. *Jer* 6:17
fury poured out will I rule *over y.* *Ezek* 20:33
heaven *over y.* is stayed. *Hag* 1:10
me a divider *over y.*? *Luke* 12:14
not have dominion *over y.* *Rom* 6:14
of this power *over y.* *1 Cor* 9:12
over y. with godly zeal. *2 Cor* 11:2
we were comforted *over y.* in affliction. *1 Thes* 3:7
know them which are *over y.* 5:12
remember them which have the rule *over y.* *Heb* 13:7
obey them that have the rule *over y.* 17
salute them that have the rule *over y.* 24

to or *unto* **you**

every herb *to y.* it shall. *Gen* 1:29
and take our daughters *unto y.* 34:9
and will be *to y.* a God. *Ex* 6:7
children shall say *unto y.* 12:26
not make *unto y.* gods of gold. 20:23
it shall be *unto y.* most holy. 30:36
I will also do this *unto y.* *Lev* 26:16
they shall be *to y.* for an. *Num* 10:8
be *to y.* a memorial. 10
unto y. for a fringe. 15:39
I shall do *unto y.* as I thought. 33:56
to them, and they *to y.* *Josh* 23:12
as they have been *to y.* *1 Sam* 4:9
unto y. O men, I call. *Pr* 8:4
this iniquity shall be *to y.* *Isa* 30:13
to y. it is commanded. *Dan* 3:4
unto y. that fear my name. *Mal* 4:2
that men should do *to y.* *Mat* 7:12
Luke 6:31
to your faith be it *unto y.* *Mat* 9:29
because it is given *unto y.* to know.
13:11; *Mark* 4:11; *Luke* 8:10
unto y. that hear shall. *Mark* 4:24
unto y. is born this day a Saviour. *Luke* 2:11
to them which do good *to y.* 6:33
I appoint *unto y.* a kingdom. 22:29
for the promise is *unto y.* *Acts* 2:39
unto y. first, God having raised. 3:26
therefore came I *unto y.* 10:29
to y. is the word of this. 13:26

doubtless I am *to y.* *1 Cor* 9:2
word of God *unto y.* only ? 14:36
to reach even *unto y.* *2 Cor* 10:13
we are come as far as *to y.* 14
but *to y.* of salvation. *Phil* 1:28
unto y. it is given not only to. 29
our gospel came not *unto y.* in word.
1 Thes 1:5
to y. who are troubled. *2 Thes* 1:7
unto y. that believe. *1 Pet* 2:7
but *unto y.* I say, and. *Rev* 2:24
see **say, told**

toward **you**

good work *toward y.* *Jer* 29:10
thoughts I think *toward y.* 11
judgement is *toward y.* *Hos* 5:1
our word *toward y.* was. *2 Cor* 1:18
is more abundant *toward y.* 7:15
all grace abound *toward y.* 9:8
being absent am bold *toward y.* 10:1
by the power of God *toward y.* 13:4
abound in love one toward another, as we do *toward y.* *1 Thes* 3:12

with **you**

then we will dwell *with y.* *Gen* 34:16
but God shall be *with y.* 48:21
my bones hence *with y.* *Ex* 13:19
that I have talked *with y.* 20:22
Aaron and Hur are *with y.* 24:14
with y. shall be a man. *Num* 1:4
where I will meet *with y.* 17:4
it may be well *with y.* *Deut* 5:33
no part *with y.* 12:12
God goeth *with y.* 20:4
nor *with y.* only do I make. 29:14
neither will I be *with y.* *Josh* 7:12
said, The Lord be *with y.* *Ruth* 2:4
and mother be *with y.* *1 Sam* 22:3
me, and I will go *with y.* 23:23
what have I to do *with y.*?
2 Sam 16:10; 19:22
go forth *with y.* myself. 18:2
master's sons are *with y.* *2 Ki* 10:2
see there be *with y.* none of. 23
and it shall be well *with y.* 25:24
Jer 40:9
Lord your God *with y.*? *1 Chr* 22:18
there are *with y.* golden calves.
2 Chr 13:8
the Lord is *with y.* while ye. 15:2
for the Lord, who is *with y.* in. 19:6
the Lord will be *with y.* 20:17
with y., even *with y.*, sins ? 28:10
let us build *with y.*: for we. *Ezra* 4:2
lest I deal *with y.* after. *Job* 42:8
do *with y.* as this potter ? *Jer* 18:6
I am *with y.* 42:11; *Hag* 1:13; 2:4
will I plead *with y.* *Ezek* 20:35, 36
when I have wrought *with y.* 44
the Lord shall be *with y.* *Amos* 5:14
with y., for God is *with y.* *Zech* 8:23
how long shall I be *with y.*? *Mat* 17:17
Mark 9:19; *Luke* 9:41
the poor always *with y.*, but me ye.
Mat 26:11; *John* 12:8
I drink it new *with y.* in. *Mat* 26:29
I am *with y.* alway, unto the. 28:20
you, while I was *with y.* *Luke* 24:44
yet a little while am I *with y.*, then I go to. *John* 7:33; 12:35; 13:33
Have I been so long *with y.*? 14:9
that he may abide *with y.* 16
he dwelleth *with y.* 17
being present *with y.* 25
peace I leave *with y.* 27
because I was *with y.* 16:4
I should bear *with y.* *Acts* 18:14
I have been *with y.* at all. 20:18
comforted together *with y.* *Rom* 1:12
I may *with y.* be refreshed. 15:32
now the God of peace be *with y.* all.
33; *2 Cor* 13:11; *Phil* 4:9
the grace of our Lord Jesus Christ be *with y.* *Rom* 16:20, 24
1 Cor 16:23; *Phil* 4:23; *Col* 4:18
1 Thes 5:28; *2 Thes* 3:18
2 Tim 1:2; 4:22; *Tit* 3:15
Heb 13:25; *2 John* 3; *Rev* 22:21
was *with y.* in weakness. *1 Cor* 2:3
that we also might reign *with y.* 4:8
see that he may be *with y.* 16:10
my love be *with y.* all in Christ. 24
establisheth us *with y.* *2 Cor* 1:21
and present us *with y.* *2 Cor* 4:14
hearts to die and live *with y.* 7:3
when I was present *with y.* 11:9
Gal 4:18, 20
I joy and rejoice *with y.* *Phil* 2:17
am I *with y.* in the spirit. *Col* 2:5
glorified, as it is *with y.* *2 Thes* 3:1
the Lord be *with y.* all. 16
God dealeth *with y.* as. *Heb* 12:7
peace be *with y.* all. *1 Pet* 5:14
spots and blemishes, while they feast *with y.* *2 Pet* 2:13

young

have not cast their *y.* *Gen* 31:38
the flocks and herds with *y.* 33:13
nothing cast their *y.* *Ex* 23:26
not kill it and her *y.* *Lev* 22:28
take the dam with the *y.* *Deut* 22:6
let the dam go and take the *y.* 7
shew favour to the *y.* 28:50
eagle fluttereth over her *y.* 32:11
had a *y.* son Micha. *2 Sam* 9:12
my son is *y.* *1 Chr* 22:5; 29:1
when Rehoboam was *y.* *2 Chr* 13:7
Josiah, while he was yet *y.* 34:3
ewes great with *y.* *Ps* 78:71
where she may lay her *y.* 84:3
those that are with *y.* *Isa* 40:11
for the *y.* of the flock. *Jer* 31:12
cropped off the top of his *y.* twigs.
Ezek 17:4, 22
whose *y.* daughter had. *Mark* 7:25*
when *y.* thou girdedst. *John* 21:18
see **child, children, man, men, old**

young *ass*, or *asses*

the shoulders of *y. asses.* *Isa* 30:6
the *y. asses* shall eat clean. 24
he found a *y. ass*, sat. *John* 12:14
see **bullock**

young *bullocks*

shall offer two *y. bullocks.*
Num 28:11, 19, 27
need, both *y. bullocks.* *Ezra* 6:9

young *calf*

take thee a *y. calf* for. *Lev* 9:2*

young *cow*

man shall nourish a *y. cow.* *Isa* 7:21

young *dromedaries*

he sent letters by riders on *y. dromedaries.* *Esth* 8:10*

young *eagles*

y. eagles shall eat it. *Pr* 30:17

young *hart*

my beloved is like a *y. hart.*
S of S 2:9, 17; 8:14
see **lion, lions**

young *one*

her eye shall be evil toward her *y. one.* *Deut* 28:57
neither shall seek the *y. one*, nor heal. *Zech* 11:16*

young *ones*

whether they be *y. ones.* *Deut* 22:6
when his *y. ones* cry to. *Job* 38:41
bring forth their *y. ones.* 39:3
their *y. ones* are in good liking. 4
is hardened against her *y. ones.* 16
the eagles' *y. ones* also suck. 30
their *y. ones* shall lie. *Isa* 11:7
give suck to their *y. ones.* *Lam* 4:3

young *pigeon*

dove, and a *y. pigeon.* *Gen* 15:9
bring a *y. pigeon* for a. *Lev* 12:6

young *pigeons*

offering of *y. pigeons.* *Lev* 1:14
a lamb, he shall bring two *y. pigeons.*
5:7; 12:8; 14:22, 30; 15:14, 29
Num 6:10; *Luke* 2:24
if he be not able to bring two *y. pigeons.* *Lev* 5:11

young *ravens*

food to *y. ravens* which cry. *Ps* 147:9

young *roes*

thy breasts are like two *y. roes.*
S of S 4:5; 7:3

young *unicorn*

Sirion like a *y. unicorn.* *Ps* 29:6

young *virgin*

for my lord a *y. virgin.* *1 Ki* 1:2

young *virgins*

found 400 *y. virgins.* *Judg* 21:12
let fair *y. virgins* be sought. *Esth* 2:2
together all the *y. virgins.* 3

young *woman*

thee of this *y. woman.* *Ruth* 4:12

young *women*

they may teach *y. women.* *Tit* 2:4

younger

Noah knew what his *y.* son. *Gen* 9:24*
firstborn said to the *y.* 19:31, 34
and the *y.* she also bare a son. 38
the elder shall serve the *y.* 25:23
Rom 9:12
on Jacob her *y.* son. *Gen* 27:15
called Jacob her *y.* son. 42
the name of the *y.* daughter. 29:16
seven years for the *y.* 18
to give the *y.* before firstborn. 26
is this your *y.* brother ? 43:29*
his right hand on the *y.* 48:14
his *y.* brother shall be greater. 19
Caleb's *y.* brother. *Judg* 1:13; 3:9
is not her *y.* sister fairer ? 15:2
Saul's *y.* daughter. *1 Sam* 14:49
cast lots over against their *y.* brethren. *1 Chr* 24:31
that are *y.* than I, have me in derision. *Job* 30:1
y. sister is Sodom. *Ezek* 16:46
sisters, thine elder and *y.* 61
y. said, Father, give me. *Luke* 15:12
the *y.* son gathered all, and took. 13
let him be as the *y.* 22:26
intreat the *y.* men as. *1 Tim* 5:1
the *y.* women as sisters, with all. 2
the *y.* widows refuse, for when. 11
that the *y.* women marry. 14
likewise, ye *y.* submit. *1 Pet* 5:5

youngest

the *y.* is this day with our father.
Gen 42:13, 32
except your *y.* brother come. 15, 20
34; 44:23, 26
they sat, the *y.* according. 43:33
in the sack's mouth of the *y.* 44:2
eldest, and left off at the *y.* 12
in his *y.* son shall he set up gates of it. *Josh* 6:26; *1 Ki* 16:34
yet Jotham the *y.* son. *Judg* 9:5
remaineth yet the *y.* *1 Sam* 16:11
David was the *y.*: the eldest. 17:14
save Jehoahaz the *y.* *2 Chr* 21:17
his *y.* son king in his stead. 22:1

yours

the land of Egypt is *y.* *Gen* 45:20
feet tread shall be *y.* *Deut* 11:24
answered, Our life for *y.* *Josh* 2:14
the battle is not *y.* but. *2 Chr* 20:15
in land that is not *y.* *Jer* 5:19
y. is the kingdom of God. *Luke* 6:20
they will keep *y.* also. *John* 15:20
for all things are *y.* *1 Cor* 3:21, 22
lest this liberty of *y.* become. 8:9
refreshed my spirit and *y.* 16:18
for I seek not *y.* but you. *2 Cor* 12:14

yourselves

wash, and rest *y.* under. *Gen* 18:4
be not angry with *y.* that ye. 45:5
gather *y.* together. 49:1, 2; *Jer* 6:1
Ezek 39:17; *Joel* 3:11; *Zeph* 2:1
Rev 19:17
take heed unto *y.* *Ex* 19:12
Deut 2:4; 4:15, 23; 11:16
Josh 23:11; *Jer* 17:21
as for the perfume, ye shall not make to *y.* *Ex* 30:37
consecrate *y.* to-day to the. 32:29
ye shall not make *y.* abominable, neither shall ye make *y.* *Lev* 11:43
sanctify *y.* 11:44; 20:7; *Num* 11:18
Josh 3:5; 7:13; *1 Sam* 16:5
1 Chr 15:12; *2 Chr* 29:5; 35:6
ye defile *y.* *Lev* 11:44; 18:24, 30
nor make to *y.* molten gods. 19:4
lift you up *y.*? *Num* 16:3
separate *y.* from this. 21
Moses saying, Arm some of *y.* 31:3
women-children keep for *y.* 18
purify both *y.* and your. 19

lest ye corrupt *y.* *Deut* 4:16, 25
mightier nations than *y.* 11:23
not cut *y.* for the dead. 14:1
present *y.* in the tabernacle. 31:14
ye will utterly corrupt *y.* 29
hide *y.* there three days. *Josh* 2:16
keep *y.* from the accursed thing, lest
ye make *y.* accursed. 6:18
take for a prey unto *y.* 8:2
nor serve them, nor bow *y.* unto. 23:7
and bowed *y.* to them. 16
ye are witnesses against *y.* that ye
have chosen. 24:22
not fall upon me *y.* *Judg* 15:12
quit *y.* like men, O ye. *1 Sam* 4:9
present *y.* before the Lord. 10:19
Saul said, Disperse *y.* 14:34
you one bullock for *y.* *1 Ki* 18:25
set *y.* in array, and they set. 20:12
2 Chr 20:17; *Jer* 50:14
have consecrated *y.* *2 Chr* 29:31
but yield *y.* unto the Lord. 30:8
to give over *y.* to die by. 32:11
prepare *y.* by the houses of. 35:4
separate *y.* from the. *Ezra* 10:11
their daughters for *y.* *Neh* 13:25
that ye make *y.* strange. *Job* 19:3
if ye will indeed magnify *y.* 5
all ye *y.* have seen it. 27:12
and offer up for *y.* a burnt. 42:8
associate *y.*, O ye people: gird *y.*
Isa 8:9; *Joel* 1:13
stay *y.* *Isa* 29:9
shew *y.* men. 46:8
are in darkness, shew *y.* 49:9
for iniquities have ye sold *y.* 50:1
that compass *y.* about with. 11
ye have sold *y.* for nought. 52:3
against whom do ye sport *y.* 57:4
by inflaming *y.* with idols under. 5
in their glory shall ye boast *y.* 61:6
circumcise *y.* to the Lord. *Jer* 4:4
humble *y.* 13:18; *Jas* 4:10; *1 Pet* 5:6
wallow *y.* in ashes, ye. *Jer* 25:34
innocent blood upon *y.* 26:15
saith the Lord, deceive not *y.* 37:9
that ye might cut *y.* off and. 44:8
repent and turn *y.* *Ezek* 14:6
18:30, 32
defile not *y.* with the idols. 20:7, 18
ye pollute *y.* with all your idols. 31
then shall ye lothe *y.* 43; 36:31
keepers of my charge for *y.* 44:8
to *y.* in righteousness. *Hos* 10:12
your God ye made to *y.* *Amos* 5:26
eat for *y.* and drink for *y.* *Zech* 7:6
think not to say within *y.* *Mat* 3:9
Luke 3:8
lay not up for *y.* *Mat* 6:19
lay up for *y.* 20
Why reason ye among *y.*? 16:8
neither go in *y.* 23:13; *Luke* 11:52
child of hell than *y.* *Mat* 23:15
ye be witnesses unto *y.* 31
go ye rather, and buy for *y.* 25:9
come ye *y.* apart into. *Mark* 6:31
that ye disputed among *y.*? 9:33
have salt in *y.* and peace one. 50
but take heed to *y.*: they shall deliver
you up. 13:9; *Luke* 17:3; 21:34
Acts 5:35; 20:28
ye *y.* touch not the. *Luke* 11:46
provide *y.* bags which wax. 12:33
ye *y.* like unto men that wait for. 36
why even of *y.* judge ye not? 57
kingdom, ye *y.* thrust out. 13:28
make to *y.* friends of the. 16:9
ye are they which justify *y.* 15
he said, Go shew *y.* unto the. 17:14
know of *y.* that summer is. 21:30
and divide it among *y.* 22:17
but weep for *y.* and for. 23:28
ye *y.* bear me witness. *John* 3:28
said, Murmur not among *y.* 6:43
do ye enquire among *y.* of? 16:19
signs God did, as you *y.* *Acts* 2:22
save *y.* from this untoward. 40
seeing ye judge *y.* unworthy. 13:46
from which if ye keep *y.* ye. 15:29
trouble not *y.* for his life. 20:10
you *y.* know, that these hands. 34
reckon ye also *y.* to be. *Rom* 6:11
but yield *y.* unto God, as those. 13
whom ye yield *y.* servants to. 16
dearly beloved, avenge not *y.*, but
rather give place. *Rom* 12:19
put from *y.* that wicked. *1 Cor* 5:13
ye not rather suffer *y.* to be? 6:7
ye may give *y.* to fasting and. 7:5
judge in *y.*: is it comely that? 11:13
I beseech, that ye submit *y.* 16:16
yea, what clearing of *y.*, in all things
ye have approved *y.* *2 Cor* 7:11
seeing ye *y.* are wise. 11:19
examine *y.* whether ye be in. 13:5
faith, and that not of *y.* *Eph* 2:8
speaking to *y.* in psalms. 5:19
submitting *y.* one to another. 21
wives, submit *y.* unto your. *Col* 3:18
y., brethren, know our entrance in
unto you. *1 Thes* 2:1
y. know that we are appointed. 3:3
ye *y.* are taught of God, to. 4:9
y. know that the day of the Lord. 5:2
wherefore comfort *y.* together. 11
and be at peace among *y.* 13, 15
that ye withdraw *y.* *2 Thes* 3:6
y. know how ye ought to follow us. 7
knowing in *y.* ye have. *Heb* 10:34
remember, as being *y.* also. 13:3
and submit *y.*: for they watch for. 17
ye not then partial in *y.*? *Jas* 2:4
submit *y.* to God. 4:7
not fashioning *y.* to. *1 Pet* 1:14
submit *y.* to every ordinance. 2:13
arm *y.* likewise with the same. 4:1
fervent charity among *y.* 8
ye younger, submit *y.* unto. 5:5
keep *y.* from idols. *1 John* 5:21
look to *y.* that we lose not. *2 John* 8
building up *y.* on your most. *Jude* 20
keep *y.* in the love of God, looking. 21

youth

is evil from his *y.* *Gen* 8:21
youngest according to his *y.* 43:33
about cattle, from our *y.* 46:34
father's house, as in her *y.* *Lev* 22:13
being in her father's house in her *y.*
Num 30:3, 16
the *y.* drew not a sword, because yet
a *y.* *Judg* 8:20
thou art but a *y.*, and he a man of
war from his *y.* *1 Sam* 17:33
for he was but a *y.* 42
whose son is this *y.*? 55
befell thee from thy *y.* *2 Sam* 19:7
fear the Lord from my *y.* *1 Ki* 18:12
the iniquities of my *y.* *Job* 13:26
are full of the sin of his *y.* 20:11
as I was in the days of my *y.* 29:4*
on my right hand rise the *y.* 30:12*
from my *y.* he was brought up. 31:18
return to the days of his *y.* 33:25
hypocrites die in *y.* and. 36:14
not the sins of my *y.* *Ps* 25:7
thou art my trust from my *y.* 71:5
hast taught me from my *y.* 17
and ready to die from my *y.* 88:15
the days of his *y.* hast thou. 89:45
so that thy *y.* is renewed. 103:5
thou hast the dew of thy *y.* 110:3
so are the children of thy *y.* 127:4
afflicted me from my *y.* 129:1
as plants grown up in *y.* 144:12
the guide of her *y.* *Pr* 2:17
with the wife of thy *y.* 5:18
O young man, in thy *y.* *Eccl* 11:9
for childhood and *y.* are vanity. 10*
Creator in the days of thy *y.* 12:1
hast laboured from thy *y.* *Isa* 47:12
thy merchants from thy *y.* 15
forget the shame of thy *y.* 54:4
hath called thee as a wife of *y.* 6
the kindness of thy *y.* *Jer* 2:2
thou art the guide of my *y.* 3:4
of our fathers from our *y.* 24
we and our fathers from our *y.* 25
been thy manner from thy *y.* 22:21
bear the reproach of my *y.* 31:19
evil before me from their *y.* 32:30
been at ease from his *y.* 48:11
bear the yoke in his *y.* *Lam* 3:27
been polluted from my *y.* *Ezek* 4:14
remembered days of thy *y.* 16:22, 43
my covenant in days of thy *y.* 60
whoredoms in their *y.* 23:3
her *y.* they lay with her and. 8
the days of her *y.* *Ezek* 23:19, 21
as in the days of her *y.* *Hos* 2:15
for the husband of her *y.* *Joel* 1:8
to keep cattle from my *y.* *Zech* 13:5
and the wife of thy *y.* *Mal* 2:14
let none deal treacherously against
the wife of his *y.* 15
all these have I kept from my *y.*
up; what lack I yet? *Mat* 19:20
Mark 10:20; *Luke* 18:21
life from my *y.* know all. *Acts* 26:4
let no man despise thy *y.* *1 Tim* 4:12

youthful

flee also *y.* lusts, but. *2 Tim* 2:22

youths

I discerned among the *y.* *Pr* 7:7
even the *y.* shall faint. *Isa* 40:30

you-ward

which to *y.-ward* is not. *2 Cor* 13:3
grace given me to *y.-ward.* *Eph* 3:2

Z

Zacchaeus

Z. make haste and. *Luke* 19:5

Zachariah, Zechariah

Z. son of Jeroboam reigned.
2 Ki 14:29; 15:8, 11
Abi daughter of *Z.* 18:2; *2 Chr* 29:1
chief of the Reubenites; Jeiel, *Z.*
1 Chr 5:7
Z. porter of the door. 9:21; 15:18
20, 24; 26:2
Geder, Ahio, *Z.* and Mickloth. 9:37
next to Asaph, *Z.* 16:5
Z. son of Isshiah. 24:25
Z. the fourth son of Hosah. 26:11
Z. the son of Shelemiah, a wise. 14
was Iddo the son of *Z.* 27:21
Jehoshaphat sent to *Z.* *2 Chr* 17:7
on Jahaziel son of *Z.* 20:14
Jehiel and *Z.* the sons of. 21:2
Spirit of God came upon *Z.* 24:20
sought God in the days of *Z.* 26:5
of the sons of Asaph, *Z.* 29:13
Z. of the Kohathites was. 34:12
Hilkiah, *Z.* rulers of the house. 35:8
Z. the son of Iddo prophesied to.
Ezra 5:1; 6:14; *Neh* 12:16
sons of Pharosh, *Z.* *Ezra* 8:3
Z. the son of Bebai. 11
Elam, *Z.* 10:26
on Ezra's left hand stood *Z.* *Neh* 8:4
Z. the son of Amariah. 11:4
Z. the son of Shiloni. 5
Z., the son of Pashur. 12
Z. the son of Jonathan. 12:35
Z. with trumpets. 41
Z. the son of Jeberechiah. *Isa* 8:2
Z. the son of Barachiah. *Zech* 1:1
7:1; *Mat* 23:35; *Luke* 11:51
see also Zacharias, p. **783**

Zadok

Z. and Abimelech. *2 Sam* 8:17
Z. and Abiathar carried the. 15:29
hast thou not with thee *Z.* and? 35
Z. and Abiathar were priests. 20:25
1 Ki 4:4
but *Z.* was not with Adonijah.
1 Ki 1:8, 26
Z. and Nathan have anointed. 45
and *Z.* the priest. 2:35; *1 Chr* 29:22
Azariah the son of *Z.* *1 Ki* 4:2
Jerusha the daughter of *Z.* was.
2 Ki 15:33; *2 Chr* 27:1
Ahitub begat *Z.* *1 Chr* 6:8; 12:53
9:11; 18:16
Z. a young man, mighty man. 12:28
both *Z.* of the sons of Eleazar. 24:3
of the Aaronites, *Z.* was. 27:17
priest of the house of *Z.* *2 Chr* 31:10
Shallum, the son of *Z.* *Ezra* 7:2
Z. repaired. *Neh* 3:4, 29
Z. sealed. 10:21
of the priests, the son of *Z.* 11:11
made *Z.* the scribe treasurer. 13:13

these are the sons of *Z. Ezek* 40:46
43:19; 44:15
priests sanctified of sons of *Z.* 48:11

Zalmunna

after Zebah and *Z.* *Judg* 8:5
Zebah and *Z.* in thy hand. 6, 15
arose and slew Zebah and *Z.* 21
princes as Zebah and *Z.* *Ps* 83:11

Zarah, *see also* **Zerah**

Judah's son was called *Z.*
Gen 38:30; 46:12
Tamar bare Pharez and *Z.*
1 Chr 2:4; *Mat* 1:3
the sons of *Z.*, Zimri, and. *1 Chr* 2:6

Zarephath

get thee to *Z.* *1 Ki* 17:9
he went to *Z.* 10
Israel shall possess to *Z.* *Ob* 20

zeal

to slay them in his *z.* *2 Sam* 21:2
come and see my *z.* for. *2 Ki* 10:16
the *z.* of the Lord shall do this. 19:31
Isa 37:32
the *z.* of thy house hath eaten me up
and. *Ps* 69:9; *John* 2:17
my *z.* hath consumed. *Ps* 119:139
the *z.* of the Lord will. *Isa* 9:7
and he was clad with *z.* as. 59:17
where is thy *z.* and thy? 63:15
have spoken it in my *z.* *Ezek* 5:13
that they have *z.* of God. *Rom* 10:2
yea, what *z.*! *2 Cor* 7:11
your *z.* provoked many. 9:2
concerning *z.*, persecuting. *Phil* 3:6
hath a great *z.* for you. *Col* 4:13*

zealous

was *z.* for my sake. *Num* 25:11*
he was *z.* for his God and made. 13*
are all *z.* of the law. *Acts* 21:20
Paul was *z.* towards God. 22:3
Gal 1:14
are *z.* of spiritual gifts. *1 Cor* 14:2
purify a peculiar people, *z. Tit* 2:14
I rebuke and chasten: be *z. Rev* 3:19

zealously

they *z.* affect you, but. *Gal* 4:17
it is good to be *z.* affected in a. 18

Zebah, *see* **Zalmunna**

Zebedee

ship with *Z.* their father. *Mat* 4:21
apostles, James and John the sons of
Z. 10:2; 26:37; *Mark* 1:19; 3:17
10:35; *Luke* 5:10; *John* 21:2
mother of *Z.*'s children. *Mat* 20:20
27:56
they left their father *Z.* *Mark* 1:20

Zeboim

king of *Z.* *Gen* 14:2
overthrow of *Z.* *Deut* 29:23
the valley of *Z.* to the. *1 Sam* 13:18
Benjamin dwelt at *Z.* *Neh* 11:34
how shall I set thee at *Z.*? *Hos* 11:8

Zebul

the son of Jerubbaal, and *Z.* his
officer. *Judg* 9:28
Z. thrust out Gaal and his. 41

Zebulun

Leah called his name *Z.* *Gen* 30:20
Reuben, Simeon, Judah, *Z.* 35:23
the sons of *Z.* 46:14; *Num* 1:30
26:26
Z. shall dwell at the. *Gen* 49:13
of *Z.*: Eliab the son of Helon.
Num 1:9; 2:7; 7:24; 10:16
mount Ebal to curse; Reuben, Gad,
Asher, *Z.* *Deut* 27:13
of *Z.* he said, Rejoice, *Z.* in. 33:18
third lot came up for *Z.* *Josh* 19:10
nor did *Z.* drive out the. *Judg* 1:30
Barak called *Z.* and Naphtali. 4:10
out of *Z.* they that handle. 5:14
Z. and Naphtali were a people that
jeoparded their lives. 18
he sent messengers to *Z.* 6:35
buried in the country of *Z.* 12:12
of *Z.* Ishmaiah was the. *1 Chr* 27:19
divers of *Z.* humbled. *2 Chr* 30:11
the princes of *Z.* and. *Ps* 68:27
afflicted the land of *Z.* *Isa* 9:1
Z. a portion. *Ezek* 48:26
one gate of *Z.* 33

in the borders of *Z.* *Mat* 4:13
the land of *Z.* and Nephthalim. 15

tribe of **Zebulun**

the *tribe* of *Z.* 57,400. *Num* 1:31
then the *tribe of Z.*: Eliab.2:7; 10:16
tribe of Z., Gaddiel to spy. 13:10
prince of the *tribe of Z.* to. 34:25
out of the *tribe of Z.* twelve cities.
Josh 21:7, 34; *1 Chr* 6:63, 77
of the *tribe of Z.* were sealed 12,000.
Rev 7:8

Zedekiah

Z. made horns of iron. *1 Ki* 22:11
2 Chr 18:10
Z. smote Micaiah on the cheek.
1 Ki 22:24; *2 Chr* 18:23
changed his name to *Z.* *2 Ki* 24:17
sons of *Z.* and put out the eyes of *Z.*
25:7; *Jer* 39:6, 7; 52:10, 11
son of Josiah, *Z.* *1 Chr* 3:15
sons of Jehoiakim: *Z.* 16
Z. his brother king. *2 Chr* 36:10
I will deliver *Z.* and his. *Jer* 21:7
Lord make thee like *Z.* and. 29:22
Z. shall not escape from the. 32:4
he shall lead *Z.* to Babylon. 5
the army overtook *Z.* 39:5; 52:8

Zeeb, *see* **Oreb**

Zelophehad

Z. had no sons, but daughters.
Num 26:33; *Josh* 17:3
the daughters of *Z.* speak. *Num* 27:7
daughters of *Z.* were married. 36:11

Zelotes, *see* **Simon**

Zelzah

Rachel's sepulchre at *Z.* *1 Sam* 10:2

Zenas

bring *Z.* the lawyer and. *Tit* 3:13

Zephaniah

the captain took *Z.* second priest.
2 Ki 25:18; *Jer* 52:24
Z. of the sons of the. *1 Chr* 6:36
Zedekiah sent *Z.* to. *Jer* 21:1
letters in thy name to *Z.* 29:25
Z. read this letter in the ears. 29
Z. the son of Maaseiah. 37:3
the word came to *Z.* *Zeph* 1:1
house of Josiah son of *Z. Zech* 6:10
be to Hen the son of *Z.* 14

Zerah, *see also* **Zarah**

the son of Reuel, *Z.* *Gen* 36:13, 17
1 Chr 1:37
Jobab the son of *Z.* reigned.
Gen 36:33; *1 Chr* 1:44
of *Z.* the family. *Num* 26:13, 20
of Zabdi, the son of *Z.* *Josh* 7:1
did not Achan the son of *Z.*? 22:20
sons of Simeon were *Z.* *1 Chr* 4:24
Z. son of Iddo. 6:21
Ethni the son of *Z.* 41
of the sons of *Z.* Jeuel dwelt in. 9:6
Z. the Ethiopian came. *2 Chr* 14:9
of the children of *Z.* *Neh* 11:24

Zeresh

Haman called for *Z.* his. *Esth* 5:10

Zerubbabel

of Pedaiah, *Z.*, sons of *Z. 1 Chr* 3:19
which came up with *Z.* *Ezra* 2:2
Neh 12:1
Z. the son of. *Ezra* 3:2, 8; 5:2
Israel in the days of *Z.* *Neh* 12:47
Lord by Haggai to *Z.* *Hag* 1:1
then *Z.* obeyed the voice of. 12
stirred up the spirit of *Z.* 14
yet now be strong, O *Z.* 2:4
speak to *Z.* of Judah. 21
word of the Lord unto *Z.* *Zech* 4:6
before *Z.* thou shalt become. 7
the hands of *Z.* have laid. 9

Zeruiah

three sons of *Z.* there. *2 Sam* 2:18
the sons of *Z.* be too hard. 3:39
Joab son of *Z.* 8:16; *1 Chr* 18:15
What have I do with you, ye sons of
Z.? *2 Sam* 16:10; 19:22
whose sisters were *Z.* *1 Chr* 2:16

Ziba

art thou *Z.*? *2 Sam* 9:2
Z. had fifteen sons. 10
the king said to *Z.*, Thine are. 16:4
I said, Thou and *Z.* divide. 19:29

Zibeon

Anah the daughter of *Z.* the Hivite.
Gen 36:2, 14
these are the children of *Z.* 24
1 Chr 1:40
duke *Z.* *Gen* 36:29

Zidon

border shall be to *Z.* *Gen* 49:13
chased them to great *Z.* *Josh* 11:8
Kanah, even unto great *Z.* 19:28
and served the gods of *Z. Judg* 10:6
because it was far from *Z.* 18:28
which belongeth to *Z.* *1 Ki* 17:9
drink unto them of *Z.* *Ezra* 3:7
whom the merchants of *Z. Isa* 23:2
be thou ashamed, O *Z.*: the sea. 4
O thou virgin, daughter of *Z.* 12
all the kings of *Z.* *Jer* 25:22
yokes to the king of *Z.* 27:3
to cut off from Tyre and *Z.* 47:4
the inhabitants of *Z.* *Ezek* 27:8
set thy face against *Z.* and. 28:21
I am against thee, O *Z.* 22
what have ye to do with me, O Tyre,
and *Z.*? *Joel* 3:4
Z. though it be very wise. *Zech* 9:2

Zidonians

Z. and Amalekites did. *Judg* 10:12
after the manner of the *Z.* 18:7
but king Solomon loved women of *Z.*
1 Ki 11:1
Ashtoreth, goddess of the *Z.* 33
Z. that are gone down. *Ezek* 32:30

Zif

the month of *Z.* which is. *1 Ki* 6:1
was laid in the month *Z.* 37

Ziklag

Achish gave *Z.* to. *1 Sam* 27:6
we burnt *Z.* 30:14
abode two days in *Z.* *2 Sam* 1:1
I slew them in *Z.* 4:10
they dwelt at *Z.* *1 Chr* 4:30
Neh 11:28
came to David to *Z.* 12:1, 20

Zilpah

Laban gave to Leah, *Z.* *Gen* 29:24
Leah gave *Z.* her maid. 30:9
Z. Leah's maid bare Jacob. 10, 12
the sons of *Z.*, Gad. 35:26; 46:18
was with the sons of *Z.* 37:2

Zimri

that was slain was *Z.* *Num* 25:14
Z. conspired against. *1 Ki* 16:9, 16
Z. reigned seven days in Tirzah. 15
had *Z.* peace, who slew? *2 Ki* 9:31
the sons of Zorah, *Z.* *1 Chr* 2:6
Z. the son of Jehoadah. 8:36
Jarah begat *Z.* 9:42
I made all the kings of *Z.* *Jer* 25:25

Zin

from wilderness of *Z.* *Num* 13:21
to the desert of *Z.* 20:1; 33:36
ye rebelled in the desert of *Z.*
27:14; *Deut* 32:51

Zion, Sion

David took strong hold of *Z.* the.
2 Sam 5:7; *1 Chr* 11:5
the city of David, which is *Z.*
1 Ki 8:1; *2 Chr* 5:2
king on my holy hill of *Z.* *Ps* 2:6
walk about *Z.* and go round. 48:12
thy good pleasure unto *Z.* 51:18
for God will save *Z.* and. 69:35
the Lord loveth the gates of *Z.* 87:2
he said of *Z.*, This and that man. 5
Z. heard and was glad. 97:8
arise and have mercy on *Z.* 102:13
Lord shall build up *Z.* 16
turned the captivity of *Z.* 126:1
turned back that hate *Z.* 129:5
the Lord hath chosen *Z.* 132:13
dew on the mountains of *Z.* 133:3
when we remembered *Z.* 137:1
Sing us one of the songs of *Z.* 3
reign, even thy God, O *Z.* 146:10
praise the Lord, O Jerusalem, praise
thy God, O *Z.* 147:12
let the children of *Z.* be. 149:2
Z. shall be redeemed. *Isa* 1:27
shout, thou inhabitant of *Z.* 12:6
that the Lord hath founded *Z.* 14:32
the Lord hath filled *Z.* with. 33:5

look on *Z*. *Isa* 33:20
for controversy of *Z*. 34:8
come to *Z*. with songs. 35:10
O *Z*. that bringest good tidings. 40:9
the first shall say to *Z*. 41:27
but *Z*. said, The Lord hath. 49:14
for the Lord shall comfort *Z*. 51:3
come with singing unto *Z*. 11
and say unto *Z*., Thou art my. 16
put on thy strength, O *Z*. 52:1
saith unto *Z*., Thy God reigneth ! 7
Lord shall bring again *Z*. 8
Redeemer shall come to *Z*. 59:20
call thee the *Z*. of the holy. 60:14
for *Z*.'s sake will I not hold. 62:1
Z. is a wilderness, Jerusalem. 64:10
as soon as *Z*. travailed, she. 66:8
I will bring you to *Z*. *Jer* 3:14
set up the standard toward *Z*. 4:6
Judah ? thy soul lothed *Z*. 14:19
Z. shall be plowed like a field.
26:18; *Mi* 3:12
this is *Z*. whom no man. *Jer* 30:17
arise ye, and let us go up to *Z*. 31:6
and sing in the height of *Z*. 12
they shall ask the way to *Z*. 50:5
shall the inhabitant of *Z*. say. 51:35
the ways of *Z*. do mourn. *Lam* 1:4
Z. spreadeth forth her hands, and. 17
the precious sons of *Z*. 4:2
because the mountain of *Z*. 5:18
be glad, ye children of *Z*. *Joel* 2:23
Lord will roar from *Z*. *Amos* 1:2
they build up *Z*. with. *Mi* 3:10
for the law shall go forth of *Z*. 4:2
say, Let our eye look upon *Z*. 11
I am jealous for *Z*. *Zech* 1:14
The Lord shall yet comfort *Z*. 17
deliver thyself, O *Z*. 2:7
jealous for *Z*. 8:2
Lord, I am returned to *Z*. 3
raised up thy sons, O *Z*. 9:13
see **daughter, daughters**

in **Zion**

praises to the Lord, who dwelleth *in*
Z. *Ps* 9:11; 76:2; *Joel* 3:21
praise waiteth for thee, O God, *in*
Z. *Ps* 65:1
every one *in Z*. appeareth. 84:7
Lord is great *in Z*.; he is high. 99:2
name of the Lord *in Z*. 102:21
that is left *in Z*. shall be. *Isa* 4:3
my people that dwellest *in Z*. 10:24
I lay *in Z*. for a foundation a stone,
a tried stone. 28:16; *1 Pet* 2:6
people shall dwell *in Z*. *Isa* 30:19
the Lord, whose fire is *in Z*. 31:9
the sinners *in Z*. are afraid. 33:14
I will place salvation *in Z*. 46:13
unto them that mourn *in Z*. 61:3
is not Lord *in Z*.? is not ? *Jer* 8:19
declare *in Z*. the vengeance. 50:28
let us declare *in Z*. the work. 51:10
that they have done *in Z*. 24
sabbaths be forgotten *in Z*. *Lam* 2:6
hath kindled a fire *in Z*. 4:11
they ravished the women *in Z*. 5:11
blow ye the trumpet *in Z*. and sound.
Joel 2:1, 15
your God dwelling *in Z*. 3:17
that are at ease *in Z*. *Amos* 6:1
behold, I lay *in Z*. a. *Rom* 9:33

mount **Zion**

a remnant, they that escape out of
mount Z. *2 Ki* 19:31; *Isa* 37:32
joy of whole earth *mount Z*. *Ps* 48:2
let *mount Z*. rejoice. 11
this *mount Z*. wherein thou. 74:2
the *mount Z*. which he loved. 78:68
as *mount Z*. which cannot be. 125:1
of *mount Z*. a cloud. *Isa* 4:5
dwelleth in *mount Z*. 8:18; 18:7
his work upon *mount Z*. 10:12
shall reign in *mount Z*. 24:23
fight against *mount Z*. 29:8
fight for *mount Z*. 31:4
in *mount Z*. shall be deliverance.
Joel 2:32; *Ob* 17
come up on *mount Z*. *Ob* 21
reign over them in *mount Z*. *Mi* 4:7
are come unto *mount Z*. *Heb* 12:22
lo, a Lamb stood on the *mount Z*.
Rev 14:1

out of **Zion**

Oh that the salvation of Israel were
come *out of Z*.! *Ps* 14:7; 53:6
the Lord strengthen thee *out of Z*.
20:2; 110:2
bless thee *out of Z*. 128:5; 134:3
blessed be the Lord *out of Z*. 135:21
for *out of Z*. shall go. *Isa* 2:3
wailing is heard *out of Z*. *Jer* 9:19
shall roar *out of Z*. *Joel* 3:16
shall come *out of Z*. *Rom* 11:26

Zippor, *see* **Balak**

Zipporah

Jethro gave Moses *Z*. *Ex* 2:21
Z. took a sharp stone. 4:25
Jethro took *Z*. 18:2

Zoan

seven years before *Z*. *Num* 13:22
things did he in *Z*. *Ps* 78:12, 43
princes of *Z*. are fools. *Isa* 19:11, 13
for his princes were at *Z*. 30:4
I will set fire in *Z*. and. *Ezek* 30:14

Zoar

of Bela, which is *Z*. *Gen* 14:2, 8
the city was called *Z*. 19:22
city of palm trees to *Z*. *Deut* 34:3
fugitives shall flee unto *Z*. *Isa* 15:5
their voice from *Z*. *Jer* 48:34

Zobah

against the kings of *Z*. *1 Sam* 14:47
Hadadezer the king of *Z*. *2 Sam* 8:3
1 Ki 11:24; *1 Chr* 18:3, 9
Igal son of Nathan of *Z*. *2 Sam* 23:36
fled from the king of *Z*. *1 Ki* 11:23

Zophar

Z. the Naamathite. *Job* 2:11; 11:1
20:1; 42:9

Zorah

coast of inheritance of Dan, was *Z*.
Josh 19:41
man of *Z*. named Manoah. *Judg* 13:2
Spirit moved Samson between *Z*. 25
buried Samson between *Z*. 16:31
the Danites sent from *Z*. 18:2
unto their brethren to *Z*. 8
Rehoboam built *Z*. and. *2 Chr* 11:10

Zorobabel

Salathiel begat *Z*. *Mat* 1:12
Z. begat Abiud. 13
Rhesa the son of *Z*. *Luke* 3:27

Zuar, *see* **Nethaneel**

Zur

Cozbi the daughter of *Z*. *Num* 25:15
Z. a prince of Midian slain. 31:8
Josh 13:21
Z. the son of. *1 Chr* 8:30; 9:36

Zurishaddai, *see* **Shelumiel**

Zuzims

the kings smote the *Z*. *Gen* 14:5

APPENDIX

A List of Proper Names, seldom mentioned in Scripture, and not included in the body of the Concordance

ABDIEL. *1 Chr* 5:15
Abelshittim. *Num* 33:49
Abez. *Josh* 19:20
Abi. *2 Ki* 18:2
Abiasaph. *Ex* 6:24
Abida. *Gen* 25:4; *1 Chr* 1:33
Abiel. (1) *1 Sam* 9:1; 14:51. (2) *1 Chr* 11:32
Abihud. *1 Chr* 8:3
Abilene. *Luke* 3:1
Abimael. *Gen* 10:26-28; *1 Chr* 1:20-22
Abishalom. *1 Ki* 15:2, 10
Abishua. (1) *1 Chr* 6:4, 5, 50; *Ezra* 7:5. (2) *1 Chr* 8:4
Abishur. *1 Chr* 2:28, 29
Abital. *2 Sam* 3:4; *1 Chr* 3:3
Abitub. *1 Chr* 8:11
Accad. *Gen* 10:10
Achaz (Ahaz). *Mat* 1:9
Achbor. (1) *Gen* 36:38, 39; *1 Chr* 1:49. (2) *2 Ki* 22:12, 14. (3) *Jer* 26:22; 36:12
Adadah. *Josh* 15:21, 22
Adah. (1) *Gen* 4:19, 20, 23. (2) *Gen* 36:2, 4, 10, 12, 16
Adaiah. (1) *2 Ki* 22:1. (2) *1 Chr* 6:41. (3) *1 Chr* 8:12-21. (4) *1 Chr* 9:10-12; *Neh* 11:12. (5) *2 Chr* 23:1. (6) *Ezra* 10:29. (7) *Ezra* 10:34-39. (8) *Neh* 11:5
Adalia. *Esth* 9:8
Adamah. *Josh* 19:35, 36
Adami. *Josh* 19:33
Adbeel. *Gen* 25:13; *1 Chr* 1:29
Addan (Addon). *Ezra* 2:59; *Neh* 7:61
Addar. (1) *Josh* 15:3. (2) *1 Chr* 8:3
Ader. *1 Chr* 8:15
Adiel. (1) *1 Chr* 4:36. (2) *1 Chr* 9:12. (3) *1 Chr* 27:25
Adin. (1) *Ezra* 2:15; *Neh* 7:20. (2) *Ezra* 8:6. (3) *Neh* 10:14-16
Adina. *1 Chr* 11:42
Adino. *2 Sam* 23:8
Adithaim. *Josh* 15:33-36
Adlai. *1 Chr* 27:29
Admatha. *Esth* 1:14
Adna. (1) *Ezra* 10:30. (2) *Neh* 12:12-15
Adnah. (1) *1 Chr* 12:20. (2) *2 Chr* 17:14
Adoniram. *1 Ki* 4:6; 5:14
Adonizedek. *Josh* 10:1. 3
Adoraim. *2 Chr* 11:5-9
Adoram. *2 Sam* 20:24. *1 Ki* 12:18
Adummin. *Josh* 15:7; 18:17
Aeneas. *Acts* 9:33, 34
Aenon. *John* 3:23
Aharah. *1 Chr* 8:1
Aharhel. *1 Chr* 4:8
Ahasai. *Neh* 11:13
Ahasbai. *2 Sam* 23:34
Ahban. *1 Chr* 2:29
Aher. *1 Chr* 7:12
Ahi. (1) *1 Chr* 5:15. (2) *1 Chr* 7:34
Ahiam. *2 Sam* 23:33; *1 Chr* 11:35
Ahian. *1 Chr* 7:19
Ahiezer. (1) *Num* 1:12; 2:25; 7:66, 71; 10:25. (2) *1 Chr* 12:3
Ahihud. (1) *Num* 34:27. (2) *1 Chr* 8:7
Ahilud. *2 Sam* 8:16; 20:24; *1 Ki* 4:3, 12; *1 Chr* 18:15
Ahimoth. *1 Chr* 6:25
Ahinadab. *1 Ki* 4:14
Ahira. *Num* 1:15; 2:29; 7:78, 83; 10:27
Ahiram. *Num* 26:38
Ahishahar. *1 Chr* 7:10
Ahishar. *1 Ki* 4:6
Ahlab. *Judg* 1:31
Ahlai. (1) *1 Chr* 2:31. (2) *1 Chr* 11:41
Ahoah. *1 Chr* 8:4
Ahumai. *1 Chr* 4:2
Ahuzam. *1 Chr* 4:6
Ahuzzath. *Gen* 26:26
Aiah, Ajah. (1) *Gen* 36:24; *1 Chr* 1:40. (2) *2 Sam* 3:7; 21:8, 10, 11
Aija. *Neh* 11:31
Aijalon, Ajalon. (1) *Josh* 19:42; 21:24; *Judg* 1:35. (2) *Judg* 12:12. (3) *1 Sam* 14:31; *1 Chr* 8:13; *2 Chr* 11:10; 28:18. (4) *1 Chr* 6:69
Aijeleth Shahar. *Ps* 22 title
Akan (Jakan). *Gen* 36:27; *1 Chr* 1:42
Akkub. (1) *1 Chr* 3:24. (2) *1 Chr* 9:17; *Neh* 11:19; 12:25. (3) *Ezra* 2:42; *Neh* 7:45. (4) *Ezra* 2:45. (5) *Neh* 8:7
Akrabbim. *Num* 34:4; *Josh* 15:3
Alameth. *1 Chr* 7:8
Alammelech. *Josh* 19:26
Alamoth. *1 Chr* 15:20; *Ps* 46 title
Alemeth. (1) *1 Chr* 6:60. (2) *1 Chr* 8:36; 9:42
Aliah (Alva). *Gen* 36:40; *1 Chr* 1:51
Alian (Alvan). *Gen* 36:23; *1 Chr* 1:40
Allon. (1) *Josh* 19:33. (2) *1 Chr* 4:37
Allon Bachuth. *Gen* 35:8
Almodad. *Gen* 10:26; *1 Chr* 1:20
Almon. *Josh* 21:18
Almon-Diblathaim. *Num* 33:46, 47
Aloth. *1 Ki* 4:16
Altaschith. *Ps* 57 title; 58 title; 59 title; 75 title.
Alvan. *See* Alian
Amad. *Josh* 19:26
Amal. *1 Chr* 7:35
Amam. *Josh* 15:26
Amariah. (1) *1 Chr* 6:7, 52; *Ezra* 7:3. (2) *1 Chr* 6:11. (3) *1 Chr* 23:19; 24:23. (4) *2 Chr* 19:11. (5) *2 Chr* 31:15. (6) *Ezra* 10:42 (7) *Neh* 10:3; 12:2, 13. (8) *Neh* 11:4. (9) *Zeph* 1:1
Amasai. (1) *1 Chr* 6:25, 35; *2 Chr* 29:12. (2) *1 Chr* 12:18. (3) *1 Chr* 15:24
Amashai. *Neh* 11:13
Amasiah. *2 Chr* 17:16
Ami. *Ezra* 2:57
Amittai. *2 Ki* 14:25; *Jonah* 1:1
Ammiel. (1) *Num* 13:12. (2) *2 Sam* 9:4, 5; 17:27. (3) *1 Chr* 3:5. (4) *1 Chr* 26:5
Ammihud. (1) *Num* 1:10; 2:18; 7:48, 53; 10:22; *1 Chr* 7:26. (2) *Num* 34:20. (3) *Num* 34:28. (4) *2 Sam* 13:37. (5) *1 Chr* 9:4
Ammihur. *2 Sam* 13:37
Ammishaddai. *Num* 1:12; 2:25; 7:66, 71; 10:25
Ammizabad. *1 Chr* 27:6
Amok. *Neh* 12:7, 20
Amraphel. *Gen* 14:1, 9
Amzi. (1) *1 Chr* 6:46. (2) *Neh* 11:12
Anab. *Josh* 11:21; 15:50
Anaharath. *Josh* 19:19
Anaiah. (1) *Neh* 8:4. (2) *Neh* 10:22
Anamim. *Gen* 10:13; *1 Chr* 1:11
Anan. *Neh* 10:26
Anani. *1 Chr* 3:24
Ananiah. *Neh* 3:23
Anath. *Judg* 3:31; 5:6
Anem. *1 Chr* 6:73
Aniam. *1 Chr* 7:19
Anim. *Josh* 15:50
Antothijah. *1 Chr* 8:24
Anub. *1 Chr* 4:8
Aphekah. *Josh* 15:53
Aphiah. *1 Sam* 9:1
Aphik. *Josh* 13:4; 19:30; *Judg* 1:31
Aphrah. *Mi* 1:10
Aphses. *1 Chr* 24:15
Appaim. *1 Chr* 2:30, 31
Apphia. *Philem* 2
Ara. *1 Chr* 7:38
Arabah. *Josh* 18:18
Arad. (1) *Num* 21:1; 33:40. (2) *1 Chr* 8:15. (3) *Josh* 12:14. *Judg* 1:16
Arah. (1) *1 Chr* 7:39. (2) *Ezra* 2:5; *Neh* 7:10. (3) *Neh* 6:18
Aramnaharaim. *Ps* 60 title
Aramzobah. *Ps* 60 title
Aran. *Gen* 36:28; *1 Chr* 1:42
Archi. *Josh* 16:2
Ard. (1) *Gen* 46:21. (2) *Num* 26:40
Ardon. *1 Chr* 2:18
Areli. *Gen* 46:16; *Num* 26:17
Aridai. *Esth* 9:9
Aridatha. *Esth* 9:8
Arieh. *2 Ki* 15:25
Arisai. *Esth* 9:9
Armoni. *2 Sam* 21:8
Arnan. *1 Chr* 3:21
Arod. *Num* 26:17
Arodi. *Gen* 46:16
Aruboth. *1 Ki* 4:10
Arumah. *Judg* 9:41
Arvad. *Ezek* 27:8, 11
Arza. *1 Ki* 16:9
Asareel. *1 Chr* 4:16
Asarelah. *1 Chr* 25:2
Aser. *Luke* 2:36; *Rev* 7:6

Ashan. Josh 15:42; 19:7; 1 Chr 4:32; 6:59
Ashbea. 1 Chr 4:21
Ashbel. Gen 46:21; Num 26:38; 1 Chr 8:1
Ashdoth Pisgah. Deut 3:17; 4:49; Josh 12:3; 13:20
Ashima. 2 Ki 17:30
Ashkenaz. (1) Gen 10:3; 1 Chr 1:6. (2) Jer 51:27
Ashnah. (1) Josh 15:33. (2) Josh 15:43
Ashpenaz. Dan 1:3
Ashteroth Karnaim. Gen 14:5
Ashvath. 1 Chr 7:33
Asiel. 1 Chr 4:35
Asnah. Ezra 2:50
Aspatha. Esth 9:7
Asriel. (1) Num 26:31; Josh 17:2. (2) 1 Chr 7:14
Asshurim. Gen 25:3
Assir. (1) Ex 6:24; 1 Chr 6:22. (2) 1 Chr 6:23, 37. (3) 1 Chr 3:17
Assos. Acts 20:13, 14
Asuppim. 1 Chr 26:15, 17
Atarah. 1 Chr 2:26
Ataroth. (1) Num 32:3, 34. (2) Josh 16:5. (3) Josh 16:2, 7. (4) 1 Chr 2:54. (5) Num 32:35
Ater. (1) Ezra 2:16; Neh 7:21. (2) Ezra 2:42; Neh 7:45. (3) Neh 10:17
Athaiah. Neh 11:4
Athlai. Ezra 10:28
Attai. (1) 1 Chr 2:35, 36. (2) 1 Chr 12:11. (3) 2 Chr 11:20
Ava. 2 Ki 17:24
Avim. (1) Deut 2:23; Josh 13:3. (2) Josh 18:23
Avith. Gen 36:35; 1 Chr 1:46
Azal. Zech 14:5
Azaliah. 2 Ki 22:3; 2 Chr 34:8
Azaniah. Neh 10:9
Azareel. (1) 1 Chr 12:6. (2) 1 Chr 25:18. (3) 1 Chr 27:22. (4) Ezra 10:41. (5) Neh 11:13; 12:36
Azaz. 1 Chr 5:8
Azaziah. (1) 1 Chr 15:21. (2) 1 Chr 27:20. (3) 2 Chr 31:13
Azbuk. Neh 3:16
Azel. 1 Chr 8:37, 38; 9:43, 44
Azem. Josh 15:29; 19:3; 1 Chr 4:29
Azgad. (1) Ezra 2:12; Neh 7:17. (2) Ezra 8:12. (3) Neh 10:15
Aziel. 1 Chr 15:20
Aziza. Ezra 10:27
Azmaveth. (1) 2 Sam 23:31; 1 Chr 11:33. (2) 1 Chr 8:36; 9:42. (3) 1 Chr 12:3. (4) Ezra 2:24; Neh 12:29. (5) 1 Chr 27:25
Azmon. Num 34:4, 5; Josh 15:4
Aznoth Tabor. Josh 19:34
Azor. Mat 1:13, 14
Azotus. Acts 8:40
Azriel. (1) 1 Chr 5:24. (2) 1 Chr 27:19. (3) Jer 36:26
Azrikam. (1) 1 Chr 3:23. (2) 1 Chr 8:38; 9:44. (3) 1 Chr 9:14; Neh 11:15. (4) 2 Chr 28:7
Azubah. (1) 1 Ki 22:42; 2 Chr 20:31. (2) 1 Chr 2:18, 19
Azur (Azzur). (1) Neh 10:17. (2) Jer 28:1. (3) Ezek 11:1
Azzah. Deut 2:23; 1 Ki 4:24; Jer 25:20
Azzan. Num 34:26

BAALAH. Josh 15:9
Baalath. Josh 19:44; 1 Ki 9:18; 2 Chr 8:6
Baalath-beer. Josh 19:8
Baale. 2 Sam 6:2
Baal-gad. Josh 11:17; 12:7; 13:5
Baal-hanan. (1) Gen 36:38, 39; 1 Chr 1:49, 50. (2) 1 Chr 27:28
Baal-hazor. 2 Sam 13:23
Baal-hermon. Judg 3:3; 1 Chr 5:23
Baara. 1 Chr 8:8
Baaseiah. 1 Chr 6:40
Bakbakkar. 1 Chr 9:15
Bakbuk. Ezra 2:51; Neh 7:53
Bakbukiah. Neh 11:17; 12:9, 25
Bamoth. Num 21:19, 20
Bamoth-baal. Josh 13:17
Bani. (1) 2 Sam 23:36. (2) 1 Chr 6:46. (3) 1 Chr 9:4. (4) Ezra 2:10; 10:29. (5) Ezra 10:34. (6) Ezra 10:38. (7) Neh 3:17; 8:7; 9:4, 5. (8) Neh 9:4; 10:13. (9) Neh 10:14. (10) Neh 11:22
Barachiah. Zech 1:1, 7
Bariah. 1 Chr 3:22
Barkos. Ezra 2:53; Neh 7:55
Bashan-havoth-jair. Deut 3:14
Basmath. 1 Ki 4:15
Bath-rabbim. S of S 7:4
Bathshua. 1 Chr 3:5
Bavai. Neh 3:18
Bazlith. Ezra 2:52; Neh 7:54
Bealiah. 1 Chr 12:5
Bealoth. Josh 15:24
Bebai. (1) Ezra 2:11; Neh 7:16. (2) Ezra 8:11; 10:28. (3) Neh 10:15
Bechorath. 1 Sam 9:1
Bedad. Gen 36:35; 1 Chr 1:46
Bedeiah. Ezra 10:35
Beeliada. 1 Chr 14:7
Beer. (1) Num 21:16. (2) Judg 9:21
Beera. 1 Chr 7:37
Beerah. 1 Chr 5:6
Beer-elim. Isa 15:8
Beeri. (1) Gen 26:34. (2) Hos 1:1
Beer-lahai-roi. Gen 16:14; 24:62; 25:11
Beeroth. (1) Deut 10:6. (2) Josh 9:17; 18:25; 2 Sam 4:2; Ezra 2:25; Neh 7:29
Beeshterah. Josh 21:27
Bela. (1) Gen 14:2, 8. (2) Gen 36:32, 33; 1 Chr 1:43, 44. (3) Gen 46:21; Num 26:38, 40; 1 Chr 7:6, 7; 8:1, 3. (4) 1 Chr 5:8
Ben. 1 Chr 15:18
Beneberak. Josh 19:45
Benejaakan. Num 33:31, 32
Benhail. 2 Chr 17:7
Benhanan. 1 Chr 4:20
Beninu. Neh 10:13
Beno. 1 Chr 24:26, 27
Benzoheth. 1 Chr 4:20
Beon. Num 32:3
Bera. Gen 14:2
Beraiah. 1 Chr 8:21
Berechiah. (1) 1 Chr 3:20. (2) 1 Chr 6:39; 15:17. (3) 1 Chr 9:16. (4) 1 Chr 15:23. (5) 2 Chr 28:12. (6) Neh 3:4, 30; 6:18
Bered. (1) Gen 16:14. (2) 1 Chr 7:20
Beri. 1 Chr 7:36
Beriah. (1) Gen 46:17; Num 26:44, 45; 1 Chr 7:30, 31. (2) 1 Chr 7:23. (3) 1 Chr 8:13, 16. (4) 1 Chr 23:10, 11
Berodach-baladan. See Merodach-baladan
Berothah. Ezek 47:16
Besai. Ezra 2:49; Neh 7:52
Besodeiah. Neh 3:6
Betah. 2 Sam 8:8
Beten. Josh 19:25
Bethanath. Josh 19:38; Judg 1:33
Bethanoth. Josh 15:59
Betharabah. Josh 15:6, 61; 18:22
Betharam. Josh 13:27
Betharbel. Hos 10:14
Bethazmaveth. Neh 7:28
Bethbaalmeon. Josh 13:17
Bethbarah. Judg 7:24
Bethbirei. 1 Chr 4:31
Bethcar. 1 Sam 7:11
Bethdagon. (1) Josh 15:41. (2) Josh 19:27
Bethemek. Josh 19:27
Bethgader. 1 Chr 2:51
Bethharan. Num 32:36
Bethhoglah. Josh 15:6; 18:19, 21
Bethjeshimoth. Num 33:49; Josh 12:3; 13:20; Ezek 25:9
Bethlebaoth. Josh 19:6
Bethmaachah. 2 Sam 20:14, 15, 18; 2 Ki 15:29
Bethmarcaboth. Josh 19:5; 1 Chr 4:31
Bethmeon. Jer 48:23
Bethnimrah. Num 32:36; Josh 13:27
Bethpalet. Josh 15:27; Neh 11:26
Bethpazzez. Josh 19:21
Bethrapha. 1 Chr 4:12
Bethrehob. Judg 18:28; 2 Sam 10:6
Bethshean. Josh 17:11, 16; Judg 1:27; 1 Ki 4:12; 1 Chr 7:29
Bethshittah. Judg 7:22
Bethtappuah. Josh 15:53
Bethul. Josh 19:4
Bethzur. (1) Josh 15:58; 2 Chr 11:7; Neh 3:16. (2) 1 Chr 2:45
Betonim. Josh 13:26
Bezai. (1) Ezra 2:17; Neh 7:23. (2) Neh 10:18
Bezer. (1) Deut 4:43; Josh 20:8; 21:36; 1 Chr 6:78. (2) 1 Chr 7:37
Bigtha. Esth 1:10
Bigvai. (1) Ezra 2:2; Neh 7:7. (2) Ezra 2:14; Neh 7:19. (3) Ezra 8:14. (4) Neh 10:16
Bileam. 1 Chr 6:70
Bilgah. (1) 1 Chr 24:14. (2) Neh 12:5, 18
Bilgai. Neh 10:8
Bilhan. (1) Gen 36:27; 1 Chr 1:42. (2) 1 Chr 7:10
Bilshan. Ezra 2:2; Neh 7:7
Bimhal. 1 Chr 7:33
Binea. 1 Chr 8:37; 9:43
Binnui. (1) Ezra 8:33. (2) Ezra 10:30. (3) Ezra 10:38. (4) Neh 3:24; 10:9. (5) Neh 7:15. (6) Neh 12:8
Birsha. Gen 14:2
Birzavith. 1 Chr 7:31
Bishlam. Ezra 4:7
Bithiah. 1 Chr 4:18
Bithron. 2 Sam 2:29
Bizjothjah. Josh 15:28
Biztha. Esth 1:10
Bocheru. 1 Chr 8:38; 9:44
Bohan. Josh 15:6; 18:17
Bozez. 1 Sam 14:4
Bozkath. Josh 15:39; 2 Ki 22:1
Bunah. 1 Chr 2:25
Bunni. (1) Neh 9:4. (2) Neh 11:15. (3) Neh 10:15

CALAH. Gen 10:11, 12
Calcol. 1 Chr 2:6
Canneh. Ezek 27:23
Caphtorim. Gen 10:14; Deut 2:23; 1 Chr 1:12
Carcas. Esth 1:10
Careah. 2 Ki 25:23
Carshena. Esth 1:14
Casluhim. Gen 10:14; 1 Chr 1:12
Chanaan (see Canaan). Acts 7:11; 13:19
Chedorlaomer. Gen 14:1, 4, 5, 9, 17
Chelal. Ezra 10:30
Chellub. (1) 1 Chr 4:11. (2) 1 Chr 27:26
Chelluh. Ezra 10:35
Chelubai. 1 Chr 2:9
Chenaanah. (1) 1 Ki 22:11, 24; 2 Chr. 18:10, 23. (2) 1 Chr 7:10
Chenani. Neh 9:4
Chephar-haammonia. Josh 18:24
Chephirah. Josh 9:17; 18:26; Ezra 2:25; Neh 7:29
Cheran. Gen 36:26; 1 Chr 1:41
Chesalon. Josh 15:10
Chesed. Gen 22:22
Chesil. Josh 15:30
Chesulloth. Josh 19:18
Chezib. Gen 38:5
Chidon. 1 Chr 13:9
Chinnereth. Num 34:11; Deut 3:17; Josh 11:2; 12:3; 13:27; 19:35; 1 Ki 15:20
Chislon. Num 34:21
Chisloth-tabor. Josh 19:12
Chorashan. 1 Sam 30:30
Chozeba. 1 Chr 4:22
Chub. Ezek 30:5
Chun. 1 Chr 18:8

Cinneroth. 1 Ki 15:20
Clauda. Acts 27:16
Claudia. 2 Tim 4:21
Claudius. (1) Acts 11:28; 18:2. (2) Acts 23:26
Clement. Phil 4:3
Cnidus. Acts 27:7
Colhozeh. (1) Neh 3:15. (2) Neh 11:5
Conaniah (Cononiah). (1) 2 Chr 31:12; 31:13. (2) 2 Chr 35:9
Coos. Acts 21:1
Core. Jude 11
Cosam. Luke 3:28
Coz. 1 Chr 4:8
Cuthah or Cuth. 2 Ki 17:24, 30

DABAREH. Josh 21:28
Dalaiah. 1 Chr 3:24
Dalphon. Esth 9:7
Danjaan. 2 Sam 24:6
Dannah. Josh 15:49
Dara. 1 Chr 2:6
Darda. 1 Ki 4:31
Debir. (1) Josh 10:3. (2) Josh 10:38, 39; 11:21; 12:13; 15:7, 15, 49; 21:15; Judg 1:11; 1 Chr 6:58. (3) Josh 13:26
Dekar. 1 Ki 4:9
Delaiah. (1) 1 Chr 24:18. (2) Ezra 2:60; Neh 7:62. (3) Neh 6:10. (4) Jer 36:12, 25
Derbe. Acts 14:6, 20; 16:1; 20:4
Deuel. Num 1:14; 2:14; 7:42, 47; Deut 10:20
Diblaim. Hos 1:3
Diblath. Ezek 6:14
Dibri. Lev 24:11
Diklah. Gen 10:27; 1 Chr 1:21
Dilean. Josh 15:38
Dimnah. Josh 21:35
Dimonah. Josh 15:22
Dinhabah. Gen 36:32; 1 Chr 1:43
Dishan. Gen 36:21, 28, 30; 1 Chr 1:38, 42
Dishon. (1) Gen 36:21, 26, 30; 1 Chr 1:38. (2) Gen 36:25; 1 Chr 1:38, 41
Dizahab. Deut 1:1
Dodai. 1 Chr 27:4
Dodanim. Gen 10:4; 1 Chr 1:7
Dodavah. 2 Chr 20:37
Dodo. (1) Judg 10:1. (2) 2 Sam 23:9; 1 Chr 11:12. (3) 2 Sam 23:24; 1 Chr 11:26
Dophkah. Num 33:12, 13

EBIASAPH. 1 Chr 6:23, 37; 9:19
Ebronah. Num 33:34
Eder. (1) Gen 35:21. (2) Josh 15:21. (3) 1 Chr 23:23; 24:30
Edrei. (1) Num 21:33; Deut 1:4; 3:1, 10; Josh 12:4; 13:12, 31. (2) Josh 19:37
Ehi. Gen 46:21
Eker. 1 Chr 2:27
Eladah. 1 Chr 7:20
Elasah. (1) Ezra 10:22. (2) Jer 29:3
Eldaah. Gen 25:4; 1 Chr 1:33
Elead. 1 Chr 7:21
Eleph. Josh 18:28
Eliadah. 1 Ki 11:23
Eliah. (1) 1 Chr 8:27. (2) Ezra 10:26
Eliahba. 2 Sam 23:32; 1 Chr 11:33
Eliasaph. (1) Num 1:14; 2:14; 7:42, 47; 10:20. (2) Num 3:24
Eliathah. 1 Chr 25:4, 27
Elidad. Num 34:21
Eliel. (1) 1 Chr 6:34. (2) 1 Chr 5:24. (3) 1 Chr 8:20. (4) 1 Chr 8:22. (5) 1 Chr 11:46. (6) 1 Chr 11:47. (7) 1 Chr 12:11. (8) 1 Chr 15:9. (9) 1 Chr 15:11. (10) 2 Chr 31:13
Elienai. 1 Chr 8:20
Elika. 2 Sam 23:25
Elioenai. (1) 1 Chr 3:23, 24. (2) 1 Chr 4:36. (3) 1 Chr 7:8. (4) Ezra 10:22. (5) Ezra 10:27. (6) Neh 12:41. (7) 1 Chr 26:3 (8) Ezra 8:4
Eliphal. 1 Chr 11:35
Elipheleh. 1 Chr 15:18, 21
Elishaphat. 2 Chr 23:1
Elizaphan. (1) Num 3:30; 1 Chr 15:8. (2) Num 34:25 (3) 2 Chr 29:13
Elizur. Num 1:5; 2:10; 7:30, 35; 10:18
Ellasar. Gen 14:1, 9
Elnaam. 1 Chr 11:46
Eloi. Mark 15:34
Elon-beth-hanan. 1 Ki 4:9
Eloth. 1 Ki 9:26; 2 Chr 8:17; 26:2
Elpaal. 1 Chr 8:11, 12, 18
Elpalet. 1 Chr 14:5
Elparan. Gen 14:6
Eltekeh. Josh 19:44; 21:23
Eltekon. Josh 15:59
Eltolad. Josh 15:30; 19:4
Eluzai. 1 Chr 12:5
Elzabad. (1) 1 Chr 12:12. (2) 1 Chr 26:7
Elzaphan. (1) Ex 6:22; Lev 10:4. (2) Num 34:25
Enam. Josh 15:34
Enan. Num 1:15; 2:29; 7:78, 83; 10:27
Engannim. (1) Josh 15:34. (2) Josh 19:21; 21:29
Enhaddah. Josh 19:21
Enhakkore. Judg 15:19
Enhazor. Josh 19:37
Enmishpat. Gen 14:7
Enrimmon. Neh 11:29
Enshemesh. Josh 15:7; 18:17
Entappuah. Josh 17:7
Ephal. Jer 40:8
Epher. (1) Gen 25:4; 1 Chr 1:33. (2) 1 Chr 4:17. (3) 1 Chr 5:24
Ephlal. 1 Chr 2:37
Ephod. Num 34:23
Eran. Num 26:36
Erech. Gen 10:10
Eri. Gen 46:16; Num 26:16
Eshbaal. 1 Chr 8:33; 9:39
Eshban. Gen 36:26; 1 Chr 1:41
Eshean. Josh 15:52
Eshek. 1 Chr 8:39
Eshtaol. Josh 15:33; 19:41; Judg 13:25; 16:31; 18:2, 8, 11
Eshtemoa. (1) Josh 15:50; 21:14; 1 Sam 30:28; 1 Chr 6:57. (2) 1 Chr 4:17, 19
Eshton. 1 Chr 4:11, 12
Ethbaal. 1 Ki 16:31
Ether. Josh 15:42; 19:7
Ethnan. 1 Chr 4:7
Ethni. 1 Chr 6:41
Evi. Num 31:8; Josh 13:21
Ezar. 1 Chr 1:38
Ezbai. 1 Chr 11:37
Ezbon. (1) Gen 46:16. (2) 1 Chr 7:7
Ezekias. Mat 1:9, 10
Ezem. 1 Chr 4:29
Ezer. (1) 1 Chr 7:21. (2) Neh 12:42. (3) 1 Chr 4:4. (4) 1 Chr 12:9. (5) Neh 3:19. (6) Gen 36:21, 27, 30; 1 Chr 1:38, 42
Ezion-gaber (Ezion-geber). Num 33:35, 36; Deut 2:8; 1 Ki 9:26; 22:48; 2 Chr 8:17; 20:36
Ezri. 1 Chr 27:26

GAASH. Josh 24:30; Judg 2:9; 2 Sam 23:30; 1 Chr 11:32
Gaba. Josh 18:24; Ezra 2:26; Neh 7:30
Gabbai. Neh 11:8
Gaddi. Num 13:11
Gaddiel. Num 13:10
Gadi. 2 Ki 15:14, 17
Gaham. Gen 22:24
Gahar. Ezra 2:47; Neh 7:49
Galal. (1) 1 Chr 9:15. (2) 1 Chr 9:16; Neh 11:17
Gamul. 1 Chr 24:17
Gareb. (1) 2 Sam 23:38; 1 Chr 11:40. (2) Jer 31:39.
Gashmu. Neh 6:6
Gatam. Gen 36:11, 16; 1 Chr 1:36
Gath-hepher. 2 Ki 14:25
Gath-rimmon. (1) Josh 19:45. (2) Josh 21:25; 1 Chr 6:69
Gazez. (1) 1 Chr 2:46. (2) 1 Chr 2:46
Gazzam. Ezra 2:48; Neh 7:51
Geber. (1) 1 Ki 4:13. (2) 1 Ki 4:19
Geder. Josh 12:13
Gederah. Josh 15:36
Gederoth. Josh 15:41; 2 Chr 28:18
Gederothaim. Josh 15:36
Gedor. (1) Josh 15:58. (2) 1 Chr 12:7. (3) 1 Chr 8:31; 9:37. (4) 1 Chr 4:4, 18. (5) 1 Chr 4:39
Geliloth. Josh 18:17
Gemalli. Num 13:12
Genubath. 1 Ki 11:20
Gesham. 1 Chr 2:47
Geshem. Neh 2:19; 6:1, 2
Gether. Gen 10:23; 1 Chr 1:17
Geuel. Num 13:15
Gezer. Josh 10:33; 12:12; 16:3, 10; 21:21; Judg 1:29; 1 Ki 9:15, 16, 17; 1 Chr 6:67; 7:28; 20:4
Gibbar. Ezra 2:20
Gibethon. Josh 19:44; 21:23; 1 Ki 15:27; 16:15, 17
Gibea. 1 Chr 2:49
Giddalti. 1 Chr 25:4, 29
Giddel. (1) Ezra 2:47; Neh 7:49. (2) Ezra 2:56; Neh 7:58.
Gidom. Judg 20:45
Gilalia. Neh 12:36
Giloh. Josh 15:51; 2 Sam 15:12
Gimzo. 2 Chr 28:18
Ginath. 1 Ki 16:21, 22
Ginnethon. Neh 10:6; 12:4, 16
Gispa. Neh 11:21
Gittah-hepher. Josh 19:13
Gittaim. (1) 2 Sam 4:3. (2) Neh 11:33
Goath. Jer 31:39
Gudgodah. Deut 10:7
Guni. (1) Gen 46:24; Num 26:48; 1 Chr 7:13. (2) 1 Chr 5:15
Gurbaal. 2 Chr 26:7

HAAHASHTARI. 1 Chr 4:6
Habaiah. Ezra 2:61; Neh 7:63
Habakkuk. Hab 1:1; 3:1
Habaziniah. Jer 35:3
Habor. 2 Ki 17:6; 18:11; 1 Chr 5:26
Hachaliah. Neh 1:1; 10:1
Hachmoni. 1 Chr 27:32
Hadad. (1) Gen 36:35, 36; 1 Chr 1:46, 47. (2) 1 Ki 11:14, 17, 19, 21, 25. (3) 1 Chr 1:30 (4) 1 Chr 1:50, 51
Hadar. (1) Gen 25:15. (2) Gen 36:39
Hadashah. Josh 15:37
Hadattah. Josh 15:25
Hadid. Ezra 2:33; Neh 7:37; 11:34
Hadlai. 2 Chr 28:12
Hagab. Ezra 2:46
Hagabah. Ezra 2:45; Neh 7:48
Haggeri. 1 Chr 11:38
Haggi. Gen 46:16; Num 26:15
Haggiah. 1 Chr 6:30
Hai. Gen 12:8; 13:3
Hakkatan. Ezra 8:12
Hakkoz. 1 Chr 24:10
Hakupha. Ezra 2:51; Neh 7:53
Halah. 2 Ki 17:6; 18:11; 1 Chr 5:26
Halak. Josh 11:17; 12:7
Halhul. Josh 15:58
Hali. Josh 19:25
Halohesh. (1) Neh 3:12. (2) Neh 10:24
Hamath-zobah. 2 Chr 8:3
Hammath. Josh 19:35
Hammelech. Jer 36:26; 38:6
Hammoleketh. 1 Chr 7:18
Hammon. (1) Josh 19:28. (2) 1 Chr 6:76
Hammoth-dor. Josh 21:32
Hamonah. Ezek 39:16
Hamuel. 1 Chr 4:26
Hamul. Gen 46:12; Num 26:21; 1 Chr 2:5
Hamutal. 2 Ki 23:31; 24:18; Jer 52:1

Dalmanutha. Mark 8:10

Hanan. (1) *1 Chr* 8:23. (2) *1 Chr* 8:38; 9:44. (3) *1 Chr* 11:43. (4) *Ezra* 2:46; *Neh* 7:49. (5) *Neh* 8:7. (6) *Neh* 10:10; 13:13. (7) *Neh* 10:22. (8) *Neh* 10:26. (9) *Jer* 35:4
Hanes. *Isa* 30:4
Hannathon. *Josh* 19:14
Hanniel. (1) *Num* 34:23. (2) *1 Chr* 7:39
Haphraim. *Josh* 19:19
Haradah. *Num* 33:24, 25
Hareph. *1 Chr* 2:51
Hareth. *1 Sam* 22:5
Harhaiah. *Neh* 3:8
Harhas. *2 Ki* 22:14
Harhur. *Ezra* 2:51; *Neh* 7:53
Harim. (1) *1 Chr* 24:8; *Ezra* 2:39; 10:21; *Neh* 3:11; 7:42. (2) *Ezra* 2:32; *Neh* 7:35. (3) *Ezra* 10:31. (4) *Neh* 10:5. (5) *Neh* 10:27. (6) *Neh* 12:15
Hariph. (1) *Neh* 7:24. (2) *Neh* 10:19
Harnepher. *1 Chr* 7:36
Haroeh. *1 Chr* 2:52
Harsha. *Ezra* 2:52; *Neh* 7:54
Harum. *1 Chr* 4:8
Harumaph. *Neh* 3:10
Haruz. *2 Ki* 21:19
Hasadiah. *1 Chr* 3:20
Hasenuah. *1 Chr* 9:7
Hashabiah. (1) *1 Chr* 6:45. (2) *1 Chr* 9:14. (3) *1 Chr* 25:3. (4) *1 Chr* 26:30. (5) *1 Chr* 27:17. (6) *2 Chr* 35:9. (7) *Ezra* 8:19. (8) *Ezra* 8:24. (9) *Neh* 3:17. (10) *Neh* 10:11. (11) *Neh* 11:15. (12) *Neh* 11:22. (13) *Neh* 12:21. (14) *Neh* 12:24
Hashbadana. *Neh* 8:4
Hashem. *1 Chr* 11:34
Hashmonah. *Num* 33:29, 30
Hashub. (1) *1 Chr* 9:14; *Neh* 11:15. (2) *Neh* 3:11. (3) *Neh* 3:23. (4) *Neh* 10:23
Hashubah. *1 Chr* 3:20
Hashum. (1) *Ezra* 2:19; 10:33; *Neh* 7:22. (2) *Neh* 8:4. (3) *Neh* 10:18
Hasrah. *2 Chr* 34:22
Hassenaah. *Neh* 3:3
Hasupha. *Ezra* 2:43; *Neh* 7:46
Hatach. *Esth* 4:5, 6, 9, 10
Hathath. *1 Chr* 4:13
Hatipha. *Ezra* 2:54; *Neh* 7:56
Hatita. *Ezra* 2:42; *Neh* 7:45
Hattil. *Ezra* 2:57; *Neh* 7:59
Hattush. (1) *1 Chr* 3:22. (2) *Ezra* 8:2; *Neh* 3:10; 10:4. (3) *Neh* 12:2
Hauran. *Ezek* 47:16, 18
Havilah. (1) *Gen* 10:7; *1 Chr* 1:9. (2) *Gen* 10:29; *1 Chr* 1:23. (3) *Gen* 2:11. (4) *Gen* 25:18; *1 Sam* 15:7
Havoth-jair. *Num* 32:41; *Deut* 3:14; *Judg* 10:4
Hazaiah. *Neh* 11:5
Hazar-addar. *Num* 34:4
Hazar-enan. *Num* 34:9, 10; *Ezek* 47:17; 48:1
Hazar-gaddah. *Josh* 15:27
Hazar-hatticon. *Ezek* 47:16
Hazarmaveth. *Gen* 10:26; *1 Chr* 1:20
Hazarshual. *Josh* 15:28; 19:3; *1 Chr* 4:28; *Neh* 11:27
Hazarsusah. *Josh* 19:5
Hazerim. *Deut* 2:23
Hazezon-tamar. *Gen* 14:7; *2 Chr* 20:2
Haziel. *1 Chr* 23:9
Hazo. *Gen* 22:22
Heber. (1) *1 Chr* 4:18. (2) *1 Chr* 5:13. (3) *1 Chr* 8:17. (4) *1 Chr* 8:22. (*See also* p. 296)
Helah. *1 Chr* 4:5, 7
Helbah. *Judg* 1:31
Heleb. *2 Sam* 23:29
Heled. *1 Chr* 11:30
Helek. *Num* 26:30; *Josh* 17:2
Helem. (1) *1 Chr* 7:35. (2) *Zech* 6:14
Heleph. *Josh* 19:33
Helez. (1) *2 Sam* 23:26; *1 Chr* 11:27; 27:10. (2) *1 Chr* 2:39
Helkai. *Neh* 12:15
Helkath. *Josh* 19:25; 21:31
Helon. *Num* 1:9; 2:7; 7:24, 29; 10:16
Hemam (Homam). *Gen* 36:22; *1 Chr* 1:39
Hemath. (1) *Amos* 6:14. (2) *1 Chr* 2:55
Hemdan. *Gen* 36:26
Hena. *2 Ki* 18:34; 19:13; *Isa* 37:13
Henadad. *Ezra* 3:9; *Neh* 3:18, 24; 10:9
Hepher. (1) *Num* 26:32; 27:1; *Josh* 17:2, 3. (2) *1 Chr* 4:6. (3) *1 Chr* 11:36. (4) *Josh* 12:17; *1 Ki* 4:10
Heres. *Judg* 1:35
Heresh. *1 Chr* 9:15
Hesed. *1 Ki* 4:10
Heshmon. *Josh* 15:27
Hethion. *Ezek* 47:15; 48:1
Hezeki. *1 Chr* 8:17
Hezion. *1 Ki* 15:18
Hezir. (1) *1 Chr* 24:15. (2) *Neh* 10:20
Hezrai. *2 Sam* 23:35
Hezro. *1 Chr* 11:37
Hiddai. *2 Sam* 23:30
Hierapolis. *Col.* 4:13
Hilen. *1 Chr* 6:58
Hillel. *Judg* 12:13, 15
Hirah. *Gen* 38:1, 12
Hizkiah. *Zeph* 1:1
Hizkijah. *Neh* 10:17
Hobah. *Gen* 14:15
Hod. *1 Chr* 7:37
Hodaiah. *1 Chr* 3:24
Hodaviah. (1) *1 Chr* 5:24. (2) *1 Chr* 9:7. (3) *Ezra* 2:40
Hodesh. *1 Chr* 8:9
Hodevah. *Neh* 7:43
Hodiah. (1) *1 Chr* 4:19. (2) *Neh* 8:7; 9:5; 10:10, 13. (3) *Neh* 10:18
Hoglah. *Num* 26:33; 27:1; 36:11; *Josh* 17:3
Hoham. *Josh* 10:3
Holon. (1) *Josh* 15:51; 21:15 (2) *Jer* 48:21
Homam. *1 Chr* 1:39
Horam. *Josh* 10:33
Horem. *Josh* 19:38
Hori. (1) *Gen* 36:22, 30; *1 Chr* 1:39. (2) *Num* 13:5
Horim. *Gen* 14:6; 36:20, 21, 29; *Deut* 2:12, 22
Hosah. (1) *Josh* 19:29. (2) *1 Chr* 16:38; 26:10, 11, 16
Hoshaiah. (1) *Neh* 12:32. (2) *Jer* 42:1; 43:2
Hoshama. *1 Chr* 3:18
Hotham. (1) *1 Chr* 7:32. (2) *1 Chr* 11:44
Hothir. *1 Chr* 25:4, 28
Hukkok. *Josh* 19:34
Hukok. *1 Chr* 6:75
Hul. *Gen* 10:23; *1 Chr* 1:17
Huldah. *2 Ki* 22:14; *2 Chr* 34:22
Humtah. *Josh* 15:54
Hupham. *Num* 26:39
Huppah. *1 Chr* 24:13
Huppim. *Gen* 46:21; *1 Chr* 7:12, 15
Huram. (1) *1 Chr* 8:5. (2) *2 Chr* 2:3, 11, 12. (3) *2 Chr* 4:11, 16
Hushah. *1 Chr* 4:4
Husham. *Gen* 36:34, 35; *1 Chr* 1:45, 46
Hushim. (1) *Gen* 46:23. (2) *1 Chr* 7:12. (3) *1 Chr* 8:8, 11
Huz. *Gen* 22:21

IBLEAM. *Josh* 17:11; *Judg* 1:27; *2 Ki* 9:27
Ibneiah. *1 Chr* 9:8
Ibnijah. *1 Chr* 9:8
Ibri. *1 Chr* 24:27
Ibzan. *Judg* 12:8, 10
Idalah. *Josh* 19:15
Idbash. *1 Chr* 4:3
Igal. (1) *Num* 13:7. (2) *2 Sam* 23:36
Igeal. *1 Chr* 3:22
Iim. (1) *Num* 33:45. (2) *Josh* 15:29
Ijeabarim. *Num* 21:11; 33:44
Ijon. *1 Ki* 15:20; *2 Ki* 15:29; *2 Chr* 16:4
Ikkesh. *2 Sam* 23:26; *1 Chr* 11:28; 27:9
Ilai. *1 Chr* 11:29
Imla. *1 Ki* 22:8, 9; *2 Chr* 18:7, 8
Immer. (1) *1 Chr* 9:12; *Ezra* 2:37; 10:20; *Neh* 7:40; 11:13. (2) *1 Chr* 24:14. (3) *Ezra* 2:59; *Neh* 7:61. (4) *Neh* 3:29. (5) *Jer* 20:1
Imna. *1 Chr* 7:35
Imnah. (1) *1 Chr* 7:30. (2) *2 Chr* 31:14
Imrah. *1 Chr* 7:36
Imri. (1) *1 Chr* 9:4. (2) *Neh* 3:2
Ir. *1 Chr* 7:12
Iram. *Gen* 36:43; *1 Chr* 1:54
Iri. *1 Chr* 7:7
Irnahash. *1 Chr* 4:12
Irpeel. *Josh* 18:27
Irshemesh. *Josh* 19:41
Iru. *1 Chr* 4:15
Iscah. *Gen* 11:29
Ishbah. *1 Chr* 4:17
Ishbak. *Gen* 25:2; *1 Chr* 1:32
Ishbibenob. *2 Sam* 21:16
Ishi. (1) *1 Chr* 2:31. (2) *1 Chr* 4:20. (3) *1 Chr* 4:42. (4) *1 Chr* 5:24. (5) *Hos* 2:16
Ishiah. (1) *1 Chr* 7:3. (2) *1 Chr* 24:21. (3) *1 Chr* 24:25. (4) *Ezra* 10:31
Ishma. *1 Chr* 4:3
Ishmaiah. *1 Chr* 27:19
Ishmerai. *1 Chr* 8:18
Ishod. *1 Chr* 7:18
Ishpan. *1 Chr* 8:22
Ishtob. *2 Sam* 10:6, 8
Ishuah. *Gen* 46:17; *1 Chr* 7:30
Ishui. (1) *Gen* 46:17; *Num* 26:44; *1 Chr* 7:30. (2) *1 Sam* 14:49
Ismachiah. *2 Chr* 31:13
Ismaiah. *1 Chr* 12:4
Ispah. *1 Chr* 8:16
Ithai. *1 Chr* 11:31
Ithmah. *1 Chr* 11:46
Ithnan. *Josh* 15:23
Ithra. *2 Sam* 17:25
Ithran. (1) *Gen* 36:26; *1 Chr* 1:41. (2) *1 Chr* 7:37
Ithream. *2 Sam* 3:5; *1 Chr* 3:3
Ittah-kazin. *Josh* 19:13
Ittai. *2 Sam* 15:19, 21, 22; 18:2, 5, 12
Izhar. *Ex* 6:18, 21; *Num* 3:19; 16:1; *1 Chr* 6:2, 18, 38; 23:12, 18
Izrahiah. *1 Chr* 7:3
Izri. *1 Chr* 25:11

JAAKAN. *Deut* 10:6; *1 Chr* 1:42
Jaakobah. *1 Chr* 4:36
Jaala. *Ezra* 2:56; *Neh* 7:58
Jaanai. *1 Chr* 5:12
Jaareoregim. *2 Sam* 21:19
Jaasau. *Ezra* 10:37
Jaasiel. (1) *1 Chr* 11:47. (2) *1 Chr* 27:21
Jaazer. *Num* 21:32; 32:35; *Josh* 13:25; 21:39; *2 Sam* 24:5; *1 Chr* 6:81; 26:31; *Jer* 48:32
Jaaziah. *1 Chr* 24:26, 27
Jaaziel. *1 Chr* 15:18
Jabneel. (1) *Josh* 15:11. (2) *Josh* 19:33
Jabneh. *2 Chr* 26:6
Jachan. *1 Chr* 5:13
Jada. *1 Chr* 2:28, 32
Jadau. *Ezra* 10:43
Jaddua. (1) *Neh* 10:21. (2) *Neh* 12:11, 22
Jadon. *Neh* 3:7
Jagur. *Josh* 15:21
Jahath. (1) *1 Chr* 4:2. (2) *1 Chr* 6:20, 43. (3) *1 Chr* 23:10, 11. (4) *1 Chr* 24:22. (5) *2 Chr* 32:12
Jahaziah. *Ezra* 10:15
Jahaziel. (1) *1 Chr* 12:4. (2) *1 Chr* 16:6. (3) *1 Chr* 23:19; 24:23. (4) *2 Chr* 20:14. (5) *Ezra* 8:5
Jahdai. *1 Chr* 2:47

Jahdiel. *1 Chr* 5:24
Jahdo. *1 Chr* 5:14
Jahleel. *Gen* 46:14; *Num* 26:26
Jahmai. *1 Chr* 7:2
Jahzah. *1 Chr* 6:78
Jahzeel. *Gen* 46:24; *Num* 26:48; *1 Chr* 7:13
Jahzerah. *1 Chr* 9:12
Jakim. (1) *1 Chr* 8:19. (2) *1 Chr* 24:12
Jalon. *1 Chr* 4:17
Jamin. (1) *Gen* 46:10; *Ex* 6:15; *Num* 26:12; *1 Chr* 4:24. (2) *1 Chr* 2:27. (3) *Neh* 8:7
Jamlech. *1 Chr* 4:34
Janoah. *2 Ki* 15:29
Janohah. *Josh* 16:6, 7
Janum. *Josh* 15:53
Japhia. (1) *Josh* 10:3. (2) *Josh* 19:12. (3) *2 Sam* 5:15; *1 Chr* 3:7; 14:6
Japhlet. *1 Chr* 7:32, 33
Japhleti. *Josh* 16:3
Japho. *Josh* 19:46
Jarah. *1 Chr* 9:42
Jaresiah. *1 Chr* 8:27
Jarha. *1 Chr* 2:34, 35
Jarib. (1) *1 Chr* 4:24. (2) *Ezra* 8:16. (3) *Ezra* 10:18
Jarmuth. (1) *Josh* 10:3, 5, 23; 12:11; 15:35; *Neh* 11:29. (2) *Josh* 21:29
Jaroah. *1 Chr* 5:14
Jashen. *2 Sam* 23:32
Jashobeam. (1) *1 Chr* 11:11; 27:2. (2) *1 Chr* 12:6
Jashub. (1) *Num* 26:24; *1 Chr* 7:1. (2) *Ezra* 10:29
Jashubilehem. *1 Chr* 4:22
Jathniel. *1 Chr* 26:2
Jattir. *Josh* 15:48; 21:14; *1 Sam* 30:27; *1 Chr* 6:57
Jaziz. *1 Chr* 27:31
Jearim. *Josh* 15:10
Jeaterai. *1 Chr* 6:21
Jeberechiah. *Isa* 8:2
Jebus. *Josh* 18:16, 28; *Judg* 19:10, 11; *1 Chr* 11:4, 5
Jecamiah. *1 Chr* 3:18
Jecholiah. *2 Ki* 15:2; *2 Chr* 26:3
Jechonias. *Mat* 1:11, 12
Jedaiah. (1) *1 Chr* 4:37. (2) *Neh* 3:10
Jedaiah. (1) *1 Chr* 9:10; 24:7; *Ezra* 2:36; *Neh* 7:39. (2) *Neh* 11:10; 12:6, 19; *Zech* 6:10, 14. (3) *Neh* 12:7, 21
Jediael. (1) *1 Chr* 7:6, 10, 11. (2) *1 Chr* 11:45. (3) *1 Chr* 12:20. (4) *1 Chr* 26:2
Jedidah. *2 Ki* 22:1
Jeezer. *Num* 26:30
Jehaleleel. (1) *1 Chr* 4:16. (2) *2 Chr* 29:12
Jehdeiah. (1) *1 Chr* 24:20. (2) *1 Chr* 27:30
Jehezekel. *1 Chr* 24:16
Jehiah. *1 Chr* 15:24
Jehiel. (1) *1 Chr* 15:18, 20; 16:5. (2) *1 Chr* 23:8; 29:8. (3) *1 Chr* 27:32. (4) *2 Chr* 21:2. (5) *2 Chr* 29:14. (6) *2 Chr* 31:13. (7) *2 Chr* 35:8. (8) *Ezra* 8:9. (9) *Ezra* 10:2. (10) *Ezra* 10:21. (11) *Ezra* 10:26
Jehieli. *1 Chr* 26:21, 22
Jehizkiah. *2 Chr* 28:12
Jehoadah. *1 Chr* 8:36
Jehoaddan. *2 Ki* 14:2; *2 Chr* 25:1
Jehohanan. (1) *1 Chr* 26:3. (2) *2 Chr* 17:15. (3) *2 Chr* 23:1. (4) *Ezra* 10:28. (5) *Neh* 12:13. (6) *Neh* 12:42.
Jehoiarib. (1) *1 Chr* 9:10. (2) *1 Chr* 24:7
Jehonathan. (1) *1 Chr* 27:25. (2) *2 Chr* 17:8. (3) *Neh* 12:18
Jehoshabeath. *2 Chr* 22:11
Jehosheba. *2 Ki* 11:2
Jehozabad. (1) *2 Ki* 12:21; *2 Chr* 24:26. (2) *1 Chr* 26:4. (3) *2 Chr* 17:18
Jehozadak. *1 Chr* 6:14, 15
Jehubbah. *1 Chr* 7:34
Jehucal. *Jer* 37:3; 38:1
Jehud. *Josh* 19:45
Jehudi. *Jer* 36:14, 21, 23
Jehudijah. *1 Chr* 4:18
Jehush. *1 Chr* 8:39
Jeiel. (1) *1 Chr* 5:7. (2) *1 Chr* 9:35. (3) *1 Chr* 11:44. (4) *1 Chr* 15:18, 21; 16:5. (5) *2 Chr* 20:14. (6) *2 Chr* 26:11. (7) *2 Chr* 29:13. (8) *2 Chr* 35:9. (9) *Ezra* 8:13. (10) *Ezra* 10:43
Jekabzeel. *Neh* 11:25
Jekameam. *1 Chr* 23:19; 24:23
Jekamiah. *1 Chr* 2:41
Jekuthiel. *1 Chr* 4:18
Jemima. *Job* 42:14
Jemuel. *Gen* 46:10; *Ex* 6:15
Jerah. *Gen* 10:26; *1 Chr* 1:20
Jered. *1 Chr* 4:18
Jeremai. *Ezra* 10:33
Jeremoth. (1) *1 Chr* 8:14. (2) *Ezra* 10:26. (3) *Ezra* 10:27. (4) *1 Chr* 23:23. (5) *1 Chr* 25:22
Jeriah. *1 Chr* 23:19; 24:23; 26:31
Jeribai. *1 Chr* 11:46
Jeriel. *1 Chr* 7:2
Jerioth. *1 Chr* 2:18
Jeroham. (1) *1 Sam* 1:1; *1 Chr* 6:27, 34. (2) *1 Chr* 8:27. (3) *1 Chr* 9:8. (4) *1 Chr* 9:12; *Neh* 11:12. (5) *1 Chr* 12:7. (6) *1 Chr* 27:22. (7) *2 Chr* 23:1
Jeruel. *2 Chr* 20:16
Jerusha. *2 Ki* 15:33; *2 Chr* 27:1
Jesaiah. (1) *1 Chr* 3:21. (2) *1 Chr* 25:3, 15. (3) *1 Chr* 26:25. (4) *Ezra* 8:7. (5) *Ezra* 8:19. (6) *Neh* 11:7
Jeshanah. *2 Chr* 13:19
Jesharelah. *1 Chr* 25:14
Jeshebeah. *1 Chr* 24:13
Jesher. *1 Chr* 2:18
Jeshimon. (1) *Num* 21:20; 23:28. (2) *1 Sam* 23:24; 26:1
Jeshishai. *1 Chr* 5:14
Jeshohaiah. *1 Chr* 4:36
Jesiah. (1) *1 Chr* 12:6. (2) *1 Chr* 23:20
Jesimiel. *1 Chr* 4:36
Jesui. *Num* 26:44
Jether. (1) *Judg* 8:20. (2) *1 Ki* 2:5, 32; *1 Chr* 2:17. (3) *1 Chr* 2:32. (4) *1 Chr* 4:17. (5) *1 Chr* 7:38
Jetheth. *Gen* 36:40; *1 Chr* 1:51
Jethlah. *Josh* 19:42
Jetur. (1) *Gen* 25:15; *1 Chr* 1:31. (2) *1 Chr* 5:19
Jeuel. *1 Chr* 9:6
Jeush. (1) *Gen* 36:5, 14, 18; *1 Chr* 1:35. (2) *1 Chr* 7:10. (3) *1 Chr* 23:10, 11. (4) *2 Chr* 11:19
Jeuz. *1 Chr* 8:10
Jezaniah. *Jer* 40:8; 42:1
Jezer. *Gen* 46:24; *Num* 26:49; *1 Chr* 7:13
Jeziah. *Ezra* 10:25
Jeziel. *1 Chr* 12:3
Jezliah. *1 Chr* 8:18
Jezoar. *1 Chr* 4:7
Jezrahiah. *Neh* 12:42
Jibsam. *1 Chr* 7:2
Jidlaph. *Gen* 22:22
Jimnah. *Gen* 46:17; *Num* 26:44
Jiphtah. *Josh* 15:43
Jiphthahel. *Josh* 19:14, 27
Joahaz. *2 Chr* 34:8
Joatham. *Mat* 1:9
Jobab. (1) *Gen* 10:29; *1 Chr* 1:23. (2) *Gen* 36:33, 34; *1 Chr* 1:44, 45. (3) *Josh* 11:1. (4) *1 Chr* 8:9. (5) *1 Chr* 8:18
Jochebed. *Ex* 6:20; *Num* 26:59
Joed. *Neh* 11:7
Joelah. *1 Chr* 12:7
Joezer. *1 Chr* 12:6
Jogbehah. *Num* 32:35; *Judg* 8:11
Jogli. *Num* 34:22
Joha. (1) *1 Chr* 8:16. (2) *1 Chr* 11:45
Joiada. *Neh* 12:10, 11, 22; 13:28
Joiakim. *Neh* 12:10, 12, 26
Joiarib. (1) *Ezra* 8:16. (2) *Neh* 11:5. (3) *Neh* 11:10; 12:6, 19
Jokdeam. *Josh* 15:56
Jokim. *1 Chr* 4:22
Jokmeam. *1 Chr* 6:68
Jokneam. (1) *Josh* 12:22; 19:11; 21:34. (2) *1 Ki* 4:12
Jokshan. *Gen* 25:2, 3; *1 Chr* 1:32
Joktan. *Gen* 10:25, 26, 29; *1 Chr* 1:19, 20, 23
Joktheel. (1) *Josh* 15:38. (2) *2 Ki* 14:7
Jonan. *Luke* 3:30
Jonath-elem-rechokim. *Ps* 56 title
Jorah. *Ezra* 2:18
Jorai. *1 Chr* 5:13
Jorkoam. *1 Chr* 2:44
Josaphat. *Mat* 1:8
Joshah. *1 Chr* 4:34
Joshaphat. *1 Chr* 11:43
Joshaviah. *1 Chr* 11:46
Joshbekashah. *1 Chr* 25:4, 24
Josibiah. *1 Chr* 4:35
Josiphiah. *Ezra* 8:10
Jotbah. *2 Ki* 21:19
Jotbathah. *Num* 33:33, 34; *Deut* 10:7
Jozabad. (1) *1 Chr* 12:4. (2) *1 Chr* 12:20. (3) *2 Chr* 31:13. (4) *2 Chr* 35:9. (5) *Ezra* 8:33. (6) *Ezra* 10:22. (7) *Ezra* 10:23. (8) *Neh* 8:7. (9) *Neh* 11:16
Jozachar. *2 Ki* 12:21
Jozadak. *Ezra* 3:2, 8; 5:2; 10:18; *Neh* 12:26
Jubal. *Gen* 4:21
Jucal. *Jer* 38:1
Judith. *Gen* 26:34
Julia. *Rom* 16:15
Julius *Acts* 27:1, 3
Junia. *Rom* 16:7
Jushab-hesed. *1 Chr* 3:20

KABZEEL. *Josh* 15:21; *2 Sam* 23:20; *1 Chr* 11:22
Kadmiel. (1) *Ezra* 2:40; *Neh* 7:43. (2) *Ezra* 3:9. (3) *Neh* 9:4, 5; 10:9; 12:8, 24
Kallai. *Neh* 12:20
Kanah. (1) *Josh* 16:8; 17:9. (2) *Josh* 19:28
Karkaa. *Josh* 15:3
Karkor. *Judg* 8:10
Kartah. *Josh* 21:34
Kartan. *Josh* 21:32
Kattath. *Josh* 19:15
Kedemah. *Gen* 25:15; *1 Chr* 1:31.
Kedemoth. (1) *Deut* 2:26. (2) *Josh* 13:18; 21:37; *1 Chr* 6:79
Kedesh. (1) *Josh* 12:22; 19:37. (2) *Josh* 20:7; 21:32; *Judg* 4:6; 9:10, 11; *2 Ki* 15:29; *1 Chr* 6:76. (3) *1 Chr* 6:72. (4) *Josh* 15:23
Kehelathah. *Num* 33:22, 23
Kelaiah. *Ezra* 10:23
Kelita. (1) *Ezra* 10:23. (2) *Neh* 8:7. (3) *Neh* 10:10
Kemuel. (1) *Gen* 22:21. (2) *Num* 34:24. (3) *1 Chr* 27:17
Kenan. *1 Chr* 1:2
Kenath. *Num* 32:42; *1 Chr* 2:23
Keren-happuch. *Job* 42:14
Keros. *Ezra* 2:44; *Neh* 7:47
Kezia. *Job* 42:14
Keziz. *Josh* 18:21
Kibroth-hattaavah. *Num* 11:34, 35; 33:16, 17; *Deut* 9:22
Kibzaim. *Josh* 21:22
Kinah. *Josh* 15:22
Kirjath. *Josh* 18:28
Kirjath-arim. *Ezra* 2:25
Kirjath-baal. *Josh* 15:60; 18:14
Kirjath-huzoth. *Num* 22:39
Kirjath-sannah. *Josh* 15:49
Kirjath-sepher. *Josh* 15:15, 16; *Judg* 1:11, 12
Kishi. *1 Chr* 6:44
Kishion. *Josh* 19:20; 21:28
Kishon. *Judg* 4:7, 13; 5:21; *1 Ki* 18:40; *Ps* 83:9
Kithlish. *Josh* 15:40
Kitron. *Judg* 1:30
Koa. *Ezek* 23:23
Kolaiah. (1) *Neh* 11:7. (2) *Jer* 29:21
Kore. (1) *1 Chr* 9:19; 26:1, 19. (2) *2 Chr* 31:14
Koz. *Ezra* 2:61; *Neh* 7:63
Kushaiah. *1 Chr* 15:17

Jasiel. *1 Chr* 11:47

LAADAH. 1 Chr 4:21
Laadan. (1) 1 Chr 7:26. (2) 1 Chr 23:7, 8, 9; 26:21
Lael. Num 3:24
Lahad. 1 Chr 4:2
Lahairoi. Gen 24:62; 25:11
Lahmam. Josh 15:40
Lahmi. 1 Chr 20:5
Lakum. Josh 19:33
Lapidoth. Judg 4:4
Lasea. Acts 27:8
Lasha. Gen 10:19
Lasharon. Josh 12:18
Lebanah. Ezra 2:45; Neh 7:48
Lebaoth. Josh 15:32
Lebonah. Judg 21:19
Lecah. 1 Chr 4:21
Lehabim. Gen 10:13; 1 Chr 1:11
Lehi. Judg 15:9, 14, 19
Leshem. Josh 19:47
Letushim. Gen 25:3
Leummim. Gen 25:3
Libni. (1) Ex 6:17; Num 3:18; 1 Chr 6:17, 20. (2) 1 Chr 6:29.
Likhi. 1 Chr 7:19
Linus. 2 Tim 4:21
Lod. 1 Chr 8:12; Ezra 2:33; Neh 7:37; 11:35
Lodebar. 2 Sam 9:4, 5; 17:27
Lotan. Gen 36:20, 22, 29; 1 Chr 1:38, 39
Lubims. 2 Chr 12:3; 16:8; Nah 3:9
Lud. (1) Gen 10:22; 1 Chr 1:17. (2) Isa 66:19; Ezek 27:10
Ludim. Gen 10:13; 1 Chr 1:11
Luhith. Isa 15:5; Jer 48:5
Lycia, Acts 27:5

MAADAI. Ezra 10:34
Maadiah. Neh 12:5
Maai. Neh 12:36
Maaleh-acrabbim. Josh 15:3
Maarath. Josh 15:59
Maasiai. 1 Chr 9:12
Maaz. 1 Chr 2:27
Maaziah. (1) 1 Chr 24:18. (2) Neh 10:8
Machbanai. 1 Chr 12:13
Machbenah. 1 Chr 2:49
Machi. Num 13:15
Machnadebai. Ezra 10:40
Madai. Gen 10:2; 1 Chr 1:5
Madmannah. (1) Josh 15:31. (2) 1 Chr 2:49
Madmenah. Isa 10:31
Madon. Josh 11:1; 12:19
Magbish. Ezra 2:30
Magdalene. Mat 27:56, 61; 28:1; Mark 15:40, 47; 16:1, 9; Luke 8:2; 24:10; John 19:25; 20:1, 18
Magdiel. Gen 36:43; 1 Chr 1:54
Magor-missabib. Jer 20:3
Magpiash. Neh 10:20
Mahalah. 1 Chr 7:18
Mahalath. (1) Gen 28:9. (2) 2 Chr 11:8. (3) Ps 53 title; Ps 88 title
Mahanehdan. Judg 18:12
Maharai. 2 Sam 23:28; 1 Chr 11:30; 27:13
Mahath. (1) 1 Chr 6:35; 2 Chr 29:12. (2) 2 Chr 31:13
Mahazioth. 1 Chr 25:4, 30
Mahlah. Num 26:33; 27:1; 36:11; Josh 17:3
Mahli. (1) Ex 6:19; Num 3:20; 1 Chr 6:19, 29; 23:21; 24:26, 28; Ezra 8:18. (2) 1 Chr 6:47; 23:23; 24:30
Mahol. 1 Ki 4:31
Makaz. 1 Ki 4:9
Makheloth. Num 33:25, 26
Makkedah. Josh 10:10, 16, 17, 21, 28, 29; 12:16; 15:41
Maktesh. Zeph 1:11
Malachi. Mal 1:1
Malchiah. (1) 1 Chr 6:40. (2) 1 Chr 9:12; Neh 11:12. (3) 1 Chr 24:9. (4) Ezra 10:25. (5) Ezra 10:25. (6) Ezra 10:31. (7) Neh 3:11. (8) Neh 3:14. (9) Neh 3:31. (10) Neh 8:4. (11) Neh 10:3; 12:42. (12) Jer 21:1; 38:1
Malchiel. Gen 46:17; Num 26:45; 1 Chr 7:31
Malchiram. 1 Chr 3:18
Maleleel. Luke 3:37
Malothi. 1 Chr 25:4, 26
Malluch. (1) 1 Chr 6:44. (2) Ezra 10:29. (3) Ezra 10:32. (4) Neh 10:4; 12:2. (5) Neh 10:27
Manahath. (1) Gen 36:23; 1 Chr 1:40. (2) 1 Chr 8:6
Maoch. 1 Sam 27:2
Maon. (1) Josh 15:55; 1 Sam 25:2. (2) 1 Chr 2:45
Maralah. Josh 19:11
Mareshah. (1) Josh 15:44; 2 Chr 11:8; 14:9, 10; 20:37; Mi 1:15. (2) 1 Chr 2:42. (3) 1 Chr 4:21
Maroth. Mi 1:12
Marsena. Esth 1:14
Maschil. Ps 32 title, and 42, 44, 45, 52, 53, 54, 55, 74, 78, 88, 89, 142
Mash. Gen 10:23
Mashal. 1 Chr 6:74
Masrekah. Gen 36:36; 1 Chr 1:47
Massa. Gen 25:14; 1 Chr 1:30
Matred. Gen 36:39; 1 Chr 1:50
Matri. 1 Sam 10:21
Mattanah. Num 21:18, 19
Mattaniah. (1) 2 Ki 24:17. (2) 1 Chr 9:15; 2 Chr 20:14; Neh 11:17, 22; 12:8, 25, 35. (3) 1 Chr 25:4, 16. (4) 2 Chr 29:13. (5) Ezra 10:26. (6) Ezra 10:27. (7) Ezra 10:30. (8) Ezra 10:37. (9) Neh 13:13
Mattatha. Luke 3:31
Mattathah. Ezra 10:33
Mattenai. (1) Ezra 10:33. (2) Ezra 10:37. (3) Neh 12:19
Matthan. Mat 1:15.
Matthat. (1) Luke 3:24. (2) Luke 3:29
Mattithiah. (1) 1 Chr 9:31. (2) 1 Chr 15:18, 21; 16:5. (3) 1 Chr 25:3, 21. (4) Ezra 10:43. (5) Neh 8:4
Meah. Neh 3:1; 12:39
Mearah. Josh 13:4
Mebunnai. 2 Sam 23:27
Medan. Gen 25:2; 1 Chr 1:32
Medeba. Num 21:30; Josh 13:9, 16; 1 Chr 19:7; Isa 15:2
Mehetabel. (1) Gen 36:39; 1 Chr 1:50. (2) Neh 6:10
Mehida. Ezra 2:52; Neh 7:54
Mehir. 1 Chr 4:11
Mehujael. Gen 4:18
Mehuman. Esth 1:10
Mehunim. Ezra 2:50; Neh 7:52
Mejarkon. Josh 19:46
Mekonah. Neh 11:28
Melatiah. Neh 3:7
Melchishua. 1 Sam 14:49; 31:2; 1 Chr 8:33; 9:39; 10:2
Melea. Luke 3:31
Melech. 1 Chr 8:35; 9:41
Melicu. Neh 12:14
Melita. Acts 28:1
Melzar. Dan 1:11, 16
Menan. Luke 3:31
Meonenim. Judg 9:37
Meonothai. 1 Chr 4:14
Mephaath. Josh 13:18; 21:37; 1 Chr 6:79; Jer 48:21
Meraiah. Neh 12:12
Meraioth. (1) 1 Chr 6:6, 7, 52; Ezra 7:3. (2) 1 Chr 9:11; Neh 11:11. (3) Neh 12:15
Merathaim. Jer 50:21
Mered. 1 Chr 4:17, 18
Meremoth. (1) Ezra 8:33; Neh 3:4, 21. (2) Ezra 10:36. (3) Neh 10:5; 12:3
Meres. Esth 1:14
Meribbaal. 1 Chr 8:34; 9:40
Merodath-baladan. 2 Ki 20:12; Isa 39:1
Mesha. (1) Gen 10:30. (2) 2 Ki 3:4. (3) 1 Chr 2:42. (4) 1 Chr 8:9
Meshelemiah. 1 Chr 9:21; 26:1, 2, 9
Meshezabeel. (1) Neh 3:4. (2) Neh 10:21; 11:24
Meshillemith. 1 Chr 9:12
Meshillemoth. (1) 2 Chr 28:12. (2) Neh 11:13
Meshobab. 1 Chr 4:34
Meshullam. (1) 2 Ki 22:3. (2) 1 Chr 3:19. (3) 1 Chr 5:13. (4) 1 Chr 8:17. (5) 1 Chr 9:7. (6) 1 Chr 9:8. (7) 1 Chr 9:11; Neh 11:11. (8) 1 Chr 9:12. (9) 2 Chr 34:12. (10) Ezra 8:16. (11) Ezra 10:15. (12) Ezra 10:29. (13) Neh 3:4, 30; 6:18. (14) Neh 3:6. (15) Neh 8:4. (16) Neh 10:7. (17) Neh 10:20. (18) Neh 11:7. (19) Neh 12:13, 33. (20) Neh 12:16. (21) Neh 12:25
Meshullemeth. 2 Ki 21:19
Mezahab. Gen 36:39; 1 Chr 1:50
Miamin. (1) Ezra 10:25. (2) Neh 12:5
Mibhar. 1 Chr 11:38
Mibsam. (1) Gen 25:13; 1 Chr 1:29. (2) 1 Chr 4:25
Mibzar. Gen 36:42; 1 Chr 1:53
Micha. (1) 2 Sam 9:12. (2) Neh 10:11. (3) Neh 11:17, 22
Michmas. Ezra 2:27; Neh 7:31
Michmash. 1 Sam 13:2, 5, 11, 16, 23; 14:5, 31; Neh 11:31; Isa 10:28
Michmethah. Josh 16:6; 17:7
Michri. 1 Chr 9:8
Michtam. Ps 16 title, and 56, 57, 58, 59, 60
Middin. Josh 15:61
Migdalel. Josh 19:38
Migdalgad. Josh 15:37
Migdol. (1) Ex 14:2; Num 33:7. (2) Jer 44:1; 46:14
Migron. 1 Sam 14:2; Isa 10:28
Mijamin. (1) 1 Chr 24:9. (2) Neh 10:7
Mikloth. (1) 1 Chr 8:32; 9:37, 38. (2) 1 Chr 27:4
Mikneiah. 1 Chr 15:18, 21
Milalai. Neh 12:36
Miniamin. (1) 2 Chr 31:15. (2) Neh 12:17, 41
Minni. Jer 51:27
Minnith. Judg 11:33; Ezek 27:17
Miphkad. Neh 3:31
Mirma. 1 Chr 8:10
Misgab. Jer 48:1
Misham. 1 Chr 8:12
Misheal. Josh 19:26; 21:30
Mishma. Gen 25:14; 1 Chr 1:30; 4:25, 26
Mishmannah. 1 Chr 12:10
Mispereth. Neh 7:7
Misrephothmaim. Josh 11:8; 13:6
Mithcah. Num 33:28, 29
Mithredath. (1) Ezra 1:8. (2) Ezra 4:7
Mitylene. Acts 20:14
Mizpar. Ezra 2:2
Mizraim. Gen 10:6, 13; 1 Chr 1:8, 11
Mizzah. Gen 36:13, 17; 1 Chr 1:37
Moadiah. Neh 12:17
Moladah. Josh 15:26; 19:2; 1 Chr 4:28; Neh 11:26
Molid. 1 Chr 2:29
Moreh. (1) Gen 12:6; Deut 11:30. (2) Judg 7:1
Moreshethgath. Mi 1:14
Mosera. Deut 10:6
Moseroth. Num 33:30, 31
Moza. (1) 1 Chr 2:46. (2) 1 Chr 8:36, 37; 9:42, 43
Mozah. Josh 18:26
Muppim. Gen 46:21
Mushi. Ex 6:19; Num 3:20; 1 Chr 6:19, 47; 23:21, 23; 24:26, 30
Muthlabben. Ps 9 title

NAAM. 1 Chr 4:15
Naamah. (1) Gen 4:22. (2) 1 Ki 14:21, 31; 2 Chr 12:13. (3) Josh 15:41
Naarah. 1 Chr 4:5, 6
Naarai. 1 Chr 11:37
Naaran. 1 Chr 7:28
Naarath. Josh 16:7
Nachon. 2 Sam 6:6
Nachor. Luke 3:34
Nahaliel. Num 21:19
Nahallal. Josh 19:15; 21:35; Judg 1:30

Naham. 1 Chr 4:19
Nahamani. Neh 7:7
Naharai. 2 Sam 23:37; 1 Chr 11:39
Nahath. (1) Gen 36:13, 17; 1 Chr 1:37. (2) 1 Chr 6:26. (3) 2 Chr 31:13
Nahbi. Num 13:14
Nahshon, see Naashon, p. 447
Nahum. Nah 1:1
Naphish. (1) Gen 25:15; 1 Chr 1:31. (2) 1 Chr 5:19
Naphtuhim. Gen 10:13; 1 Chr 1:11
Narcissus. Rom 16:11
Nathan-melech. 2 Ki 23:11
Neah. Josh 19:13
Neariah. (1) 1 Chr 3:22, 23. (2) 1 Chr 4:42
Nebajoth. (1) Gen 25:13; 28:9; 36:3; 1 Chr 1:29. (2) Isa 60:7
Neballat. Neh 11:34
Nebushasban. Jer 39:13
Necho. 2 Chr 35:20, 22; 36:4
Nedabiah. 1 Chr 3:18
Neginah. Ps 4 title
Nehiloth. Ps 5 title
Nehum. Neh 7:7
Nehushta. 2 Ki 24:8
Neiel. Josh 19:27
Nekeb. Josh 19:33
Nekoda. (1) Ezra 2:48; Neh 7:50. (2) Ezra 2:60; Neh 7:62
Nemuel. (1) Num 26:9. (2) Num 26:12; 1 Chr 4:24
Nepheg. (1) Ex 6:21. (2) 2 Sam 5:15; 1 Chr 3:7; 14:6
Nephishesim. Neh 7:52
Nephthalim. Mat 4:13, 15; Rev 7:6
Nephtoah. Josh 15:9; 18:15
Nephusim. Ezra 2:50
Nergal-sharezer. Jer 39:3, 13
Neri. Luke 3:27
Netophah. Ezra 2:22; Neh 7:26
Netophathi. Neh 12:28
Neziah. Ezra 2:54; Neh 7:56
Nezib. Josh 15:43
Nibhaz. 2 Ki 17:31
Nibshan. Josh 15:62
Nicolas. Acts 6:5
Nimrah. Num 32:3
Nimrim. Isa 15:6; Jer 48:34
Nobah. (1) Num 32:42. (2. Name of place) Num 32:42; Judg 8:1
Nod. Gen 4:16
Nodab. 1 Chr 5:19
Nogah. 1 Chr 3:7; 14:6
Nohah. 1 Chr 8:2
Non. 1 Chr 7:27
Nophah. Num 21:30

OBAL. Gen 10:28
Oboth. Num 21:10, 11; 33:43, 44
Ohad. Gen 46:10; Ex 6:15
Ohel. 1 Chr 3:20
Omar. Gen 36:11, 15; 1 Chr 1:36
Omega. Rev 1:8, 11; 21:6; 22:13
Omer. Ex 16:16, 18, 22, 32, 33, 36
Onam. (1) Gen 36:23; 1 Chr 1:40. (2) 1 Chr 2:26, 28
Ono. (1) 1 Chr 8:12; Ezra 2:33; Neh 7:37; 11:35. (2) Neh 6:2
Ophni. Josh 18:24
Ophrah. (1) Josh 18:23; 1 Sam 13:17. (2) Judg 6:11, 24; 8:27, 32; 9:5. (3) 1 Chr 4:14
Oren. 1 Chr 2:25
Osee (Hosea). Rom 9:25
Othni. 1 Chr 26:7
Ozni. Num 26:16

PADAN. Gen 48:7
Padon. Ezra 2:44; Neh 7:47
Pahath-moab. (1) Ezra 2:6; 10:30; Neh 3:11; 7:11. (2) Ezra 8:4. (3) Neh 10:14
Pai. 1 Chr 1:50. (Pau. Gen 36:39)
Palal. Neh 3:25
Pallu. Gen 46:9; Ex 6:14; Num 26:5, 8; 1 Chr 5:3
Palti. Num 13:9
Paltiel. (1) Num 34:26; (2) 2 Sam 3:15
Parah. Josh 18:23
Parmashta. Esth 9:9
Parnach. Num 34:25
Parosh. (1) Ezra 2:3; Neh 7:8. (2) Ezra 8:3. (3) Ezra 10:25. (4) Neh 3:25. (5) Neh 10:14
Parshandatha. Esth 9:7
Paruah. 1 Ki 4:17
Parvaim. 2 Chr 3:6
Pasach. 1 Chr 7:33
Pasdammim. 1 Chr 11:13
Paseah. (1) 1 Chr 4:12. (2) Ezra 2:49; Neh 7:51. (3) Neh 3:6
Pathrusim. Gen 10:14; 1 Chr 1:12
Patrobas. Rom 16:14
Pedahel. Num 34:28
Pedahzur. Num 1:10; 2:20; 7:54, 59; 10:23
Pedaiah. (1) 2 Ki 23:36. (2) 1 Chr 3:18, 19. (3) 1 Chr 27:20. (4) Neh 3:25. (5) Neh 8:4; 13:13. (6) Neh 11:7
Pekod. Jer 50:21; Ezek 23:23
Pelaiah. (1) 1 Chr 3:24. (2) Neh 8:7. (3) Neh 10:10
Pelaliah. Neh 11:12
Peleg. Gen 10:25; 11:16, 17, 18, 19; 1 Chr 1:19, 25
Pelet. (1) 1 Chr 2:47. (2) 1 Chr 12:3
Peleth. (1) Num 16:1. (2) 1 Chr 2:33
Peninnah. 1 Sam 1:2, 4
Peresh. 1 Chr 7:16
Perezuzzah. 2 Sam 6:8; 1 Chr 13:11
Perida. Neh 7:57
Peruda. Ezra 2:55
Pethahiah. (1) 1 Chr 24:16. (2) Ezra 10:23. (3) Neh 9:5. (4) Neh 11:24
Pethor. Num 22:5; Deut 23:4
Pethuel. Joel 1:1
Peulthai. 1 Chr 26:5
Phalti. 1 Sam 25:44
Phanuel. Luke 2:35
Phibeseth. Ezek 30:17
Phichol. Gen 21:22, 32; 26:26
Philemon. Philem 1
Phut. (1) Gen 10:6; 1 Chr 1:8. (2) Ezek 27:10. (3) Nah 3:9
Phuvah. (1) Gen 46:13; Num 26:23; 1 Chr 7:1. (2) Judg 10:1
Pildash. Gen 22:22
Pileha. Neh 10:24
Piltai. Neh 12:17
Pinon. Gen 36:41; 1 Chr 1:52
Piram. Josh 10:3
Pirathon. Judg 12:15
Pison. Gen 2:11
Pithom. Ex 1:11
Pithon. 1 Chr 8:35; 9:41
Pochereth. Ezra 2:57; Neh 7:59
Poratha. Esth 9:8
Prisca. See Priscilla
Prochorus. Acts 6:5
Ptolemais. Acts 21:7
Punon. Num 33:42, 43
Putiel. Ex 6:25

RAAMAH. (1) Gen 10:7; 1 Chr 1:9. (2) Ezek 27:22
Raamiah. Neh 7:7
Raamses. Ex 1:11
Rabbith. Josh 19:20
Rabmag. Jer 39:3, 13
Rabsaris. (1) Jer 39:3, 13. (2) 2 Ki 18:17
Rachal. 1 Sam 30:29
Raddai. 1 Chr 2:14
Raguel. Num 10:29
Raham. 1 Chr 2:44
Rakem. 1 Chr 7:16
Rakkath. Josh 19:35
Rakkon. Josh 19:46
Ramath. Josh 19:8
Ramathaim-zophim. 1 Sam 1:1
Ramathlehi. Judg 15:17
Ramathmizpeh. Josh 13:26
Rameses. Gen 47:11; Ex 12:37; Num 33:3, 5
Ramiah. Ezra 10:25
Reaiah. (1) 1 Chr 4:2. (2) 1 Chr 5:5. (3) Ezra 2:47; Neh 7:50
Reba. Num 31:8; Josh 13:21
Rechah. 1 Chr 4:12
Reelaiah. Ezra 2:2
Regem. 1 Chr 2:47
Regemmelech. Zech 7:2
Rehabiah. 1 Chr 23:17; 24:21; 26:25
Rehob. (1) Num 13:21; Josh 19:28, 30; 21:31; Judg 1:31; 2 Sam 10:8; 1 Chr 6:75. (2) 2 Sam 8:3, 12. (3) Neh 10:11
Rei. 1 Ki 1:8
Rekem. (1) Num 31:8; Josh 13:21 (2) 1 Chr 2:43, 44. (3) Josh 18:27
Remeth. Josh 19:21
Remmon. Josh 19:7
Remmon-methoar. Josh 19:13
Rephael. 1 Chr 26:7
Rephah. 1 Chr 7:25
Rephaiah. (1) 1 Chr 3:21. (2) 1 Chr 4:42. (3) 1 Chr 7:2. (4) 1 Chr 9:43. (5) Neh 3:9
Resen. Gen 10:12
Resheph. 1 Chr 7:25
Reu. Gen 11:18, 19, 20, 21; 1 Chr 1:25
Reuel. (1) Gen 36:4, 10, 13, 17; 1 Chr 1:35, 37. (2) Ex 2:18. (3) Num 2:14. (4) 1 Chr 9:8
Reumah. Gen 22:24
Rezeph. 2 Ki 19:12; Isa 37:12
Rezia. 1 Chr 7:39
Rezon. 1 Ki 11:23
Ribai. 2 Sam 23:29; 1 Chr 11:31
Riblah. Num 34:11; 2 Ki 23:33; 25:6, 21; Jer 39:5, 6; 52:9, 10, 26, 27
Rimmon-parez. Num 33:19, 20
Rinnah. 1 Chr 4:20
Riphath. Gen 10:3; 1 Chr 1:6
Rissah. Num 33:21, 22
Rithmah. Num 33:18, 19
Rogelim. 2 Sam 17:27; 19:31
Rohgah. 1 Chr 7:34
Romanti-ezer. 1 Chr 25:4, 31
Rumah. 2 Ki 23:36

SABTAH. Gen 10:7; 1 Chr 1:9
Sabtecha. Gen 10:7; 1 Chr 1:9
Sacar. (1) 1 Chr 11:35. (2) 1 Chr 26:4
Sadoc. Mat 1:14
Sala, Salah. Gen 10:24; 11:12, 13, 14, 15; Luke 3:35
Salamis. Acts 13:5
Salchah. Deut 3:10; Josh 12:5; 13:11; 1 Chr 5:11
Salim. John 3:23
Sallai. (1) Neh 11:8. (2) Neh 12:20
Sallu. (1) Neh 12:7. (2) 1 Chr 9:7; Neh 11:7
Salma. 1 Chr 2:51, 54
Samgar-nebo. Jer 39:3
Samlah. Gen 36:36, 37; 1 Chr 1:47, 48
Samos. Acts 20:15
Samothracia. Acts 16:11
Sansannah. Josh 15:31
Saph. 2 Sam 21:8
Saraph. 1 Chr 4:22
Sargon. Isa 20:1
Sarid. Josh 19:10, 12
Sarsechim. Jer 39:3
Sebat. Zech 1:7
Secacah. Josh 15:61
Sechu. 1 Sam 19:22
Secundus. Acts 20:4
Segub. (1) 1 Ki 16:34. (2) 1 Chr 2:21, 22
Seirath. Judg 3:26
Sela. 2 Ki 14:7; Isa 16:1
Sela-hammahlekoth. 1 Sam 23:28
Seled. 1 Chr 2:30
Sem. Luke 3:36
Semachiah. 1 Chr 26:7
Senaah. Ezra 2:35; Neh 7:38
Seneh. 1 Sam 14:4
Senir. 1 Chr 5:23; Ezek 27:5
Senuah. Neh 11:9
Seorim. 1 Chr 24:8
Sephar. Gen 10:30
Sepharad. Ob 20
Serah (Sarah). Gen 46:17; Num 26:46; 1 Chr 7:30
Sered. Gen 46:14; Num 26:26

Serug. *Gen* 11:20, 21, 22, 23; *1 Chr* 1:26
Sethur. *Num* 13:13
Shaalabbin. *Josh* 19:42
Shaalbim. *Judg* 1:35; *1 Ki* 4:9
Shaaph. (1) *1 Chr* 2:47. (2) *1 Chr* 2:49
Shaaraim. *Josh* 15:36; *1 Sam* 17:52; *1 Chr* 4:31
Shaashgaz. *Esth* 2:14
Shabbethai. (1) *Ezra* 10:15. (2) *Neh* 8:7. (3) *Neh* 11:16
Shachia. *1 Chr* 8:10
Shaharaim. *1 Chr* 8:8
Shahazimah. *Josh* 19:22
Shalem. *Gen* 33:18
Shallecheth. *1 Chr* 26:16
Shalmai. *Ezra* 2:46; *Neh* 7:48
Shalman. *Hos* 10:14
Shama. *1 Chr* 11:44
Shamer. (1) *1 Chr* 6:46. (2) *1 Chr* 7:32, 34
Shamhuth. *1 Chr* 27:8
Shamir. (1) *Josh* 15:48. (2) *Judg* 10:1, 2. (3) *1 Chr* 24:24
Shammai. *1 Chr* 2:28, 32. (2) *1 Chr* 2:44, 45. (3) *1 Chr* 4:17
Shammoth. *1 Chr* 11:27
Shamsherai. *1 Chr* 8:26
Shapham. *1 Chr* 5:12
Shapher. *Num* 33:23, 24
Sharai. *Ezra* 10:40
Sharar. *2 Sam* 23:33
Sharuhen. *Josh* 19:6
Shashai. *Ezra* 10:40
Shashak. *1 Chr* 8:14, 25
Shaul. (1) *Gen* 46:10; *Ex* 6:15; *Num* 26:13; *1 Chr* 4:24. (2) *1 Chr* 6:24
Shaveh. *Gen* 14:17
Shavehkiriathaim. *Gen* 14:5
Shavsha. *1 Chr* 18:16
Sheal. *Ezra* 10:29
Sheariah. *1 Chr* 8:38; 9:44
Shebam. *Num* 32:3
Shebaniah. (1) *1 Chr* 15:24. (2) *Neh* 9:4, 5; 10:10. (3) *Neh* 10:4; 12:14. (4) *Neh* 10:12
Shebarim. *Josh* 7:5
Sheber. *1 Chr* 2:48
Shebna. (1) *2 Ki* 18:18, 26, 37; 19:2; *Isa* 36:3, 11, 22; 37:2. (2) *Isa* 22:15
Shebuel. (1) *1 Chr* 23:16; 26:24. (2) *1 Chr* 25:4
Shecaniah. (1) *1 Chr* 24:11. (2) *2 Chr* 31:15
Shechaniah. (1) *1 Chr* 3:21, 22. (2) *Ezra* 8:3. (3) *Ezra* 8:5. (4) *Ezra* 10:2. (5) *Neh* 3:29. (6) *Neh* 6:18. (7) *Neh* 12:3
Shedeur. *Num* 1:5; 2:10; 7:30, 35; 10:18
Shehariah. *1 Chr* 8:26
Sheleph. *Gen* 10:26; *1 Chr* 1:20
Shelesh. *1 Chr* 7:35
Shelomi. *Num* 34:27
Shelomith. (1) *Lev* 24:11. (2) *1 Chr* 3:19. (3) *1 Chr* 23:9. (4) *1 Chr* 23:18. (5) *1 Chr* 26:25, 26, 28. (6) *2 Chr* 11:20. (7) *Ezra* 8:10
Shelomoth *1 Chr* 24:22
Shema. (1) *Josh* 15:26. (2) *1 Chr* 2:43, 44. (3) *1 Chr* 5:8. (4) *1 Chr* 8:13. (5) *Neh* 8:4
Shemaah. *1 Chr* 12:3
Shemariah. (1) *1 Chr* 12:5. (2) *2 Chr* 11:19. (3) *Ezra* 10:32. (4) *Ezra* 10:41
Shemeber. *Gen* 14:2
Shemer. *1 Ki* 16:24
Shemidah. *Num* 26:32; *Josh* 17:2; *1 Chr* 7:19
Shemiramoth. (1) *1 Chr* 15:18, 20; 16:5. (2) *2 Chr* 17:8
Shemuel. (1) *Num* 34:20. (2) *1 Chr* 6:33. (3) *1 Chr* 7:2
Shen. *1 Sam* 7:12
Shenazar. *1 Chr* 3:18
Shepham. *Num* 34:10, 11
Shepho. *Gen* 36:23; *1 Chr* 1:40
Shephuphan. *1 Chr* 8:5
Sherah. *1 Chr* 7:24
Sherebiah. (1) *Ezra* 8:18, 24; *Neh* 8:7; 9:4, 5. (2) *Neh* 10:12; 12:8, 24
Sheresh. *1 Chr* 7:16
Sheshai. *Num* 13:22; *Josh* 15:14; *Judg* 1:10
Sheshan. *1 Chr* 2:31, 34, 35
Sheth. *Num* 24:17
Shethar. *Esth* 1:14
Shethar-boznai. *Ezra* 5:3, 6; 6:6, 13
Sheva. (1) *2 Sam* 20:25. (2) *1 Chr* 2:49
Shibmah. *Num* 32:38
Shicron. *Josh* 15:11
Shihon. *Josh* 19:19
Shihorlibnath. *Josh* 19:26
Shilhi. *1 Ki* 22:42; *2 Chr* 20:31
Shilhim. *Josh* 15:32
Shillem. *Gen* 46:24; *Num* 26:49
Shiloni (Shilonite). *Neh* 11:5
Shilshah. *1 Chr* 7:37
Shimea. (1) *1 Chr* 20:7. (2) *1 Chr* 3:5. (3) *1 Chr* 6:30. (4) *1 Chr* 6:39
Shimeam. *1 Chr* 9:38
Shimeath. *2 Ki* 12:21; *2 Chr* 24:26
Shimeon. *Ezra* 10:31
Shimma. *1 Chr* 2:13
Shimon. *1 Chr* 4:20
Shimrath. *1 Chr* 8:21
Shimri. (1) *1 Chr* 4:37. (2) *1 Chr* 11:45. (3) *1 Chr* 26:10. (4) *2 Chr* 29:13
Shimrith. *2 Chr* 24:26
Shimron. (1) *Gen* 46:13; *Num* 26:24; *1 Chr* 7:1. (2) *Josh* 11:1; 19:15
Shimron-meron. *Josh* 12:20
Shinab. *Gen* 14:2
Shiphi. *1 Chr* 4:37
Shiphrah. *Ex* 1:15
Shiphtan. *Num* 34:24
Shisha. *1 Ki* 4:3
Shitrai. *1 Chr* 27:29
Shiza. *1 Chr* 11:42
Shoa. *Ezek* 23:23
Shobab. (1) *2 Sam* 5:14; *1 Chr* 3:5; 14:4. (2) *1 Chr* 2:18
Shobach. *2 Sam* 10:16 18
Shobai. *Ezra* 2:42; *Neh* 7:45
Shobal. (1) *Gen* 36:20, 23, 29; *1 Chr* 1:38, 40. (2) *1 Chr* 2:50, 52. (3) *1 Chr* 4:1, 2
Shobek. *Neh* 10:24
Shobi. *2 Sam* 17:27
Shoham. *1 Chr* 24:27
Shomer. (1) *2 Ki* 12:21. (2) *1 Chr* 7:32
Shophach. *1 Chr* 19:16, 18
Shophan. *Num* 32:35
Shoshannim. *Ps* 45 title; 69 title; 80 title
Shua. *1 Chr* 7:32
Shual. *1 Chr* 7:36
Shubael. (1) *1 Chr* 24:20. (2) *1 Chr* 25:20
Shuham. *Num* 26:42
Shunem. *Josh* 19:18; *1 Sam* 28:4; *2 Ki* 4:8
Shuni. *Gen* 46:16; *Num* 26:15
Shupham. *Num* 26:39
Shuppim. (1) *1 Chr* 7:12, 15. (2) *1 Chr* 26:16
Shur. *Gen* 16:7; 20:1; 25:18; *Ex* 15:22; *1 Sam* 15:7; 27:8
Shushaneduth. *Ps* 60 title
Shuthelah. (1) *Num* 26:35 36; *1 Chr* 7:20. (2) *1 Chr* 7:21
Siaha. *Ezra* 2:44; *Neh* 7:47
Sibbechai. *2 Sam* 21:18; *1 Chr* 11:29; 20:4; 27:11
Sibmah. *Josh* 13:19; *Isa* 16:8, 9; *Jer* 48:32
Sibraim. *Ezek* 47:16
Sichem (Shechem). *Gen* 12:6
Siddim. *Gen* 14:3, 8, 10
Silla. *2 Ki* 12:20
Sinim. *Isa* 49:12
Siphmoth. *1 Sam* 30:28
Sippai. *1 Chr* 20:4
Sirah. *2 Sam* 3:26
Sisamai. *1 Chr* 2:40
Sitnah. *Gen* 26:21
Socho. (1) *1 Chr* 4:18. (2) *2 Chr* 11:7; 28:18
Socoh. (1) *Josh* 15:35; *1 Sam* 17:1; *1 Ki* 4:10. (2) *Josh* 15:48
Sodi. *Num* 13:10
Sopater. *Acts* 20:4
Sophereth. *Ezra* 2:55; *Neh* 7:57
Sotai. *Ezra* 2:55; *Neh* 7:57
Suah. *1 Chr* 7:36
Sur. *2 Ki* 11:6
Susi. *Num* 13:11
Sychar. *John* 4:5
Sychem. *See* Shechem
Syene. *Ezek* 29:10; 30:6
Syntyche. *Phil* 4:2
Syracuse. *Acts* 28:12

TAANACH. *Josh* 12:21; 17:11; 21:25; *Judg* 1:27; 5:19; *1 Ki* 4:12; *1 Chr* 7:29
Taanath. *Josh* 16:6
Tabbaoth. *Ezra* 2:43; *Neh* 7:46
Tabbath. *Judg* 7:22
Tabeel. *Ezra* 4:7
Tabrimon. *1 Ki* 15:18
Tahan. (1) *Num* 26:35. (2) *1 Chr* 7:25
Tahath. (1) *Num* 33:26, 27. (2) *1 Chr* 6:24, 37. (3) *1 Chr* 7:20. (4) *1 Chr* 7:20
Tahrea. *1 Chr* 9:41
Tahtimhodshi. *2 Sam* 24:6
Talmai. (1) *Num* 13:22; *Josh* 15:14; *Judg* 1:10. (2) *2 Sam* 3:3; 13:37; *1 Chr* 3:2
Talmon. *1 Chr* 9:17; *Ezra* 2:42; *Neh* 7:45; 11:19; 12:25
Tanhumeth. *2 Ki* 25:23; *Jer* 40:8
Taphath. *1 Ki* 4:11
Tappuah. (1) *Josh* 12:17; 15:34. (2) *Josh* 16:8; 17:8. (3) *1 Chr* 2:43
Tarah. *Num* 33:27, 28
Taralah. *Josh* 18:27
Tarea. *1 Chr* 8:35
Tartan. *2 Ki* 18:17; *Isa* 20:1
Tatnai. *Ezra* 5:3, 6; 6:6, 13
Tebah. *Gen* 22:24
Tebaliah. *1 Chr* 26:11
Tehaphnehes. *Ezek* 30:18
Tehinnah. *1 Chr* 4:12
Tel-abib. *Ezek* 3:15
Telah. *1 Chr* 7:25
Telaim. *1 Sam* 15:4
Telem. (1) *Josh* 15:24. (2) *Ezra* 10:24
Tel-melah. *Ezra* 2:59; *Neh* 7:61
Temeni. *1 Chr* 4:6
Teresh. *Esth* 2:21; 6:2
Thaddaeus. *Mat* 10:3; *Mark* 3:18
Thahash. *Gen* 22:24
Thamah. *Ezra* 2:53; *Neh* 7:55
Thamar. *Mat* 1:3
Thara. *Luke* 3:34
Thelasar. *2 Ki* 19:12; *Isa* 37:12
Tiberius Caesar. *Luke* 3:1
Tibhath. *1 Chr* 18:8
Tidal. *Gen* 14:1, 9
Tikvah. (1) *2 Ki* 22:14; *2 Chr* 34:22. (2) *Ezra* 10:15
Tilon. *1 Chr* 4:20
Timaeus. *Mark* 10:46
Timna. (1) *Gen* 36:12. (2) *Gen* 36:22; *1 Chr* 1:39. (3) *1 Chr* 1:36
Timnah, Thimnathah. (1) *Gen* 36:40; *1 Chr* 1:51. (2) *Josh* 15:10, 57; 19:43; *2 Chr* 28:18
Timnath-heres. *Judg* 2:9
Timnath-serah. *Josh* 19:50; 24:30
Timon. *Acts* 6:5
Tiphsah. (1) *1 Ki* 4:24. (2) *1 Ki* 15:16
Tiras. *Gen* 10:2; *1 Chr* 1:5
Tirhakah. *2 Ki* 19:9; *Isa* 37:9
Tirhanah. *1 Chr* 2:48
Tiria. *1 Chr* 4:16
Toah. *1 Chr* 6:34
Tob. *Judg* 11:3, 5
Tobadonijah. *2 Chr* 17:8
Tochen. *1 Chr* 4:32
Tohu. *1 Sam* 1:1
Toi. *2 Sam* 8:9, 10; *1 Chr* 18:9, 10
Tolad. *1 Chr* 4:29

Tophel. *Deut* 1:1
Trachonitis. *Luke* 3:1
Trogyllium. *Acts* 20:15
Trophimus. *Acts* 20:4; 21:29; *2 Tim* 4:20
Tubal-cain. *Gen* 4:22

UEL. *Ezra* 10:34
Ulai. *Dan* 8:2, 16
Ulam. (1) *1 Chr* 7:16, 17. (2) *1 Chr* 8:39, 40
Ulla. *1 Chr* 7:39
Ummah. *Josh* 19:30
Unni. (1) *1 Chr* 15:18, 20. (2) *Neh* 12:9
Uriel. (1) *1 Chr* 6:24; 15:5, 11. (2) *2 Chr* 13:2
Uthai. (1) *1 Chr* 9:4. (2) *Ezra* 8:14
Uzai. *Neh* 3:25
Uzal. *Gen* 10:27; *1 Chr* 1:21
Uzzensherah. *1 Chr* 7:24
Uzzi. (1) *1 Chr* 6:5, 6, 51; *Ezra* 7:4. (2) *1 Chr* 7:2, 3. (3) *1 Chr* 7:7. (4) *1 Chr* 9:8. (5) *Neh* 11:22. (6) *Neh* 12:19, 42

VAJEZATHA. *Esth* 9:9
Vaniah. *Ezra* 10:36
Vashni. *1 Chr* 6:28
Vophsi. *Num* 13:14

ZAANAIM. *Judg* 4:11
Zaanan. *Mi* 1:11
Zaanannim. *Josh* 19:33
Zaavan. *Gen* 36:27; *1 Chr* 1:42
Zabad. (1) *1 Chr* 2:36, 37. (2) *1 Chr* 7:21. (3) *1 Chr* 11:41. (4) *2 Chr* 24:26. (5) *Ezra* 10:27. (6) *Ezra* 10:33. (7) *Ezra* 10:43
Zabbai. (1) *Ezra* 10:28. (2) *Neh* 3:20
Zabbud. *Ezra* 8:14
Zabdi. (1) *Josh* 7:1, 17, 18. (2) *1 Chr* 8:19. (3) *1 Chr* 27:27. (4) *Neh* 11:17
Zabdiel. (1) *1 Chr* 27:2. (2) *Neh* 11:14
Zabud. *1 Ki* 4:5
Zaccai. *Ezra* 2:9; *Neh* 7:14
Zaccur. (1) *Num* 13:4. (2) *1 Chr* 4:26. (3) *1 Chr* 24:27. (4) *1 Chr* 25:2, 10; *Neh* 12:35. (5) *Neh* 3:2. (6) *Neh* 10:12. (7) *Neh* 13:13
Zacharias. *Luke* 1:5, 12, 13, 18, 21, 40, 67; 3:2
Zacher. *1 Chr* 8:31
Zaham. *2 Chr* 11:19
Zair. *2 Ki* 8:21
Zalaph. *Neh* 3:30
Zalmon. (1) *Judg* 9:48; *Ps* 68:14. (2) *2 Sam* 23:28
Zalmonah. *Num* 33:41, 42
Zamzummim. *Deut* 2:20
Zanoah. (1) *Josh* 15:34; *Neh* 3:13; 11:30. (2) *Josh* 15:56. (3) *1 Chr* 4:18
Zaphnath-paaneah. *Gen* 41:45
Zareah. *Neh* 11:29
Zared. *Num* 21:12; *Deut* 2:13, 14
Zaretan. *Josh* 3:16; *1 Ki* 4:12; 7:46
Zareth-shahar. *Josh* 13:19
Zattu. (1) *Ezra* 2:8; 10:27; *Neh* 7:13. (2) *Neh* 10:14
Zaza. *1 Chr* 2:33
Zebadiah. (1) *1 Chr* 8:15. (2) *1 Chr* 8:17. (3) *1 Chr* 12:7. (4) *1 Chr* 26:2. (5) *1 Chr* 27:7. (6) *2 Chr* 17:8. (7) *2 Chr* 19:11. (8) *Ezra* 8:8. (9) *Ezra* 10:20
Zebaim. *Ezra* 2:57; *Neh* 7:59
Zebina. *Ezra* 10:43
Zebudah. *2 Ki* 23:36
Zedad. *Num* 34:8; *Ezek* 47:15
Zelah. *Josh* 18:28; *2 Sam* 21:14
Zelek. *2 Sam* 23:37; *1 Chr* 11:39
Zemaraim. (1) *Josh* 18:22. (2) *2 Chr* 13:4
Zemira. *1 Chr* 7:8
Zenan. *Josh* 15:37
Zephath. *Judg* 1:17
Zephathah. *2 Chr* 14:10
Zepho. *Gen* 36:11, 15; *1 Chr* 1:36
Zephon. *Num* 26:15
Zerahiah. (1) *1 Chr* 6:6, 51; *Ezra* 7:4. (2) *Ezra* 8:4
Zereda. *1 Ki* 11:26
Zeredathah. *2 Chr* 4:17
Zererath. *Judg* 7:22
Zereth. *1 Chr* 4:7
Zeri. *1 Chr* 25:3
Zeror. *1 Sam* 9:1
Zeruah. *1 Ki* 11:26
Zetham. *1 Chr* 23:8; 26:22
Zethan. *1 Chr* 7:10
Zethar. *Esth* 1:10
Zia. *1 Chr* 5:13
Zibia. *1 Chr* 8:9
Zibiah. *2 Ki* 12:1; *2 Chr* 24:1
Zichri. (1) *Ex* 6:21. (2) *1 Chr* 8:19. (3) *1 Chr* 8:23. (4) *1 Chr* 8:27. (5) *1 Chr* 9:15. (6) *1 Chr* 26:25. (7) *1 Chr* 27:16. (8) *2 Chr* 17:16. (9) *2 Chr* 23:1. (10) *2 Chr* 28:7. (11) *Neh* 11:9. (12) *Neh* 12:17
Ziddim. *Josh* 19:35
Zidkijah. *Neh* 10:1
Ziha. (1) *Ezra* 2:43; *Neh* 7:46. (2) *Neh* 11:21
Zillah. *Gen* 4:19, 22, 23
Zilthai. (1) *1 Chr* 8:20. (2) *1 Chr* 12:20
Zimmah. (1) *1 Chr* 6:20. (2) *1 Chr* 6:42. (3) *2 Chr* 29:12
Zimran. *Gen* 25:2; *1 Chr* 1:32
Zina. *1 Chr* 23:10
Zior. *Josh* 15:54
Ziph. (1) *Josh* 15:24; *1 Sam* 23:14, 15, 24; 26:2; *2 Chr* 11:8. (2) *Josh* 15:55. (3) *1 Chr* 2:42. (4) *1 Chr* 4:16
Ziphah. *1 Chr* 4:16
Ziphion. *Gen* 46:16
Ziphron. *Num* 34:9
Zithri. *Ex* 6:22
Ziz. *2 Chr* 20:16
Ziza. (1) *1 Chr* 4:37. (2) *1 Chr* 23:11. (3) *2 Chr* 11:20
Zobebah. *1 Chr* 4:8
Zoheleth. *1 Ki* 1:9
Zoheth. *1 Chr* 4:20
Zophah. *1 Chr* 7:35, 36
Zophai. *1 Chr* 6:26
Zophim. (1) *Num* 23:14. (2) *1 Sam* 1:1
Zuph. (1) *1 Sam* 1:1; *1 Chr* 6:35 (2) *1 Sam* 9:5
Zuriel. *Num* 3:35